The following pages are damaged in the original:

63-64, 183-184,
601-602

CASSELL'S

LATIN DICTIONARY

(Latin-English and English-Latin)

REVISED BY

J. R. V. MARCHANT, M.A.

FORMERLY SCHOLAR OF ... COLLEGE, OXFORD

AND

JOSEPH F. CHARLES, B.A.

[illegible]-MASTER AT THE CITY OF LONDON SCHOOL, FORMERLY [illegible] COLLEGE, OXFORD

CASSELL AND COMPANY, LIMITED
LONDON, PARIS, NEW YORK & MELBOURNE. MCMIV

PREFACE.

IN preparing a Revised Edition of the Latin-English part of this Dictionary, the aim has been so to adapt the work that it may be suited for the middle forms of public schools. It is above all intended to be a Dictionary of Classical Latin, and thus a large number of archaic, or post-Augustan words, have been omitted, while nearly all the important articles have been entirely re-written, chiefly with the view of introducing a greater number of quotations to illustrate constructions and usage. The historical and geographical notices have been largely increased in nu
and lessened in size. Etymologies have been added.
those of an unambitious kind. It is hoped that tl
changes that have been made in type and classificati
the work more intelligible, and so more useful. T
closely follows and in many points is based on the
Dictionary of Professor Georges.*

* Ausführliches Lateinisch-Deutsches Handwörterbuch von Karl Ernst Georges. Siebente Auflage. Leipzig. 1879.

EXPLANATION OF SIGNS AND ABBREVIATIONS USED IN THIS WORK.

ablat. ablative.
absol. absolute, absolutely, i.e. without dependent case or adjunct.
abstr. abstract.
accus. accusative.
act. active.
adj. adjective.
adv. adverb.
al. l. alia lectio or alii legunt (a different reading).
ap. followed by a proper noun, e.g., ap. Cic. = in the works of.
appellat. appellative (when a proper noun is used as a common noun, e.g. when Achilles = a brave, handsome man).
attrib. attribute or attributive.
a. Aug. ante-Augustan.
Aug. Augustan.
c. common.
conj. conjunction.
collect. collective.
compar. comparative.
concr. concrete.
conn. connected.
correl. correlative.
constr. construction.
contr. contraction or contracted.
cp. compare.
dat. dative.
decl. declension.
defect. defective.
demonstr. demonstrative.
dep. deponent.
desider. desiderative.
diff. different.
dim. diminutive.
dissyll. dissyllable.
distrib. distributive.
dub. doubtful.
eccl. ecclesiastical
ed. edition.
e.g. exempli gratiā (for example).
ellipt. elliptical, elliptically.
enclit. enclitic.
Eng. English.
esp. especially.
etc. et cetera.
eth. dat. ethic dative.
etym. etymology.
euphem. euphemism or euphemistical.
euphon. euphonic, euphonically.
ex. exs. example, examples.
f. feminine.
fig. figurative or figure.
fin. or *ad fin.* at the end.
foll. followed by.
follg. following.
fr. from.
Fr. French.
freq. frequently or frequentative.
fut. future.
gen. general or generally.
genit. genitive.
geogr. geographical.
Germ. German.
Gr. Greek.
gram. grammatical.
heterocl. heteroclite.
heterog. heterogeneous.
ib. ibidem.
id. idem.
i.e. id est (that is).
imper. imperative.
imperf. imperfect.
impers. impersonal.
inanim. inanimate.
inchoat. inchoative, inceptive.
indecl. indeclinable.
indef. indefinite.
indic. indicative.
infin. infinitive.
init., in, or *ad init.* at the beginning.
intens. intensive.
interrog. interrogative.

SIGNS AND ABBREVIATIONS (*continued*).

intr intransitive.
i q idem quod
irreg irregular
It Italian
Lat Latin
lit literal
l lectio (reading)
local casus locativus
m masculine
mathem mathematical
med medical or medically.
met metaphorically
meton by metonymy
mid middle
milit military
Ms. manuscript
MSS manuscripts
n neuter.
naut nautical
neg negative
neut neuter
nom. nominative
num numeral.
object objective or objectively
onomatop onomatopoeia or onomatopoeic
opp. opposite to
ord ordinal
orig original or originally
p page
p adj participial adjective
p Aug post Augustan
partic participle.
partit partitive.
pass passive
perf perfect
pers person, personal, or personally
philosoph philosophical or philosophy
pleonast pleonastical or pleonastically
plur. plural
plupeif pluperfect
poet poetical or poetically
polit political or politically
posit positive
preced preceding
prep preposition
pres present
prob probably
pron pronoun
prop properly
prov proverb or proverbially
q v quod or quae vide (which see)
refl reflective or reflectively
reg regular or regularly
rel relative
relig religious
rhet rhetoric, rhetorical, or rhetorically
Rom Roman
Sansc Sanscrit
sc scilicet (that is to say, namely)
script scriptor (writer)
sing singular
sq sequens (and the following)
subj subjunctive
subject subjective or subjectively
subst substantive
suff suffix
sup supine
superl superlative
s v sub voce
syl syllable
syncop syncope or syncopated
synonym synonymous
t t technical term
transf transferred
transl translation or translated
trisyll trisyllable
v verb, vide, or vox.
voc vocative

LATIN ABBREVIATIONS.

A. Aulus, Augustus, absolvo, antiquo, annus.
a.d. Ante diem (in dates).
A.U.C. Anno urbis conditae, ab urbe condita.

B. Bonus or bene.
B.D. Bona Dea, bonum datum.
B.L. Bona lex.
B.O. Bono omine, bona omina.
B.P. Bono publico, bona possessio.
B.M. Bene merenti.
B.V.V. Bene vale, vale!

C. Cajus, conjux, condemno.
C. As num. sign = centum.
Cal. Calendae.
Cn. Cnaeus.
Corn. Cornelius.

D. Decimus, Divus, deus, dominus, decurio, dies, dabam.
D.D. Dono dedit.
D.D.D. Dat donat dedicat.
D.M Diis manibus.
D.O.M. Deo optimo maximo.
D.P.S. De pecunia sua.
D.S. De suo.
D.N. Dominus noster.

E. Emeritus, evocatus.
E.M.V. Egregiae memoriae vir.
E.P. Equo publico.
E.Q.R. Eques Romanus.

F. Filius, fecit, fidelis, felix.
F.C. Faciendum curavit.
F.I. Fieri jussit.
Fl. Flavius
Fl. P. Flamen perpetuus.

G. Gajus, Gallica, Gemina.
G.I. Germania Inferior.

H. Hic, etc., habet, hastata (cohors), heres, honos.
Har. Haruspex.
H.C. Hispania citerior.
Hor. Horatiā tribu.
H.S. Hic situs est.
H.S. (Mistake for IIS.), sestertius, sestertium.
H.S.S. Hic siti sunt.

I. In, infra, ipse.
I.D. Idus.
I.H.F.C. Ipsius heres faciendum curavit.
Im. Immunis.
Imp. imperium, imperator.

K. Kaeso.
Kal. Kalendae.

L. Lucius, libra.
L. As num. sign = 50.

M. Marcus.
M'. Manius.
M. As num. sign = mille.

N. Numerius.
Non. Nonae.

O. Optimus, omnis.

P. Publius.
P.C. Patres conscripti.
P.M. Pontifex Maximus.
P.R. Populus Romanus.
P. VIII. Pedum octo.
Prid. Pridie.

Q. Quintus, que.

R. Rufus, Romanus, recte, regnum, resci-

LATIN ABBREVIATIONS (*continued*)

R P. Respublica
R R Rationes relatae

S Sextus, Senatus, semissis
S or Sp Spurius
S C Senatus consultum
S P Q R Senatus populusque Romanus

T Titus, tribunus

Ti Tiberius
Tr pl Tribunus plebis

U Urbs (Roma)

V Valeo, vir, vivus, vivens, veteran

X = 10, and also in coins denarius
X V Decemviri
XV V Quindecimviri

ABBREVIATIONS OF THE NAMES OF LATIN AUTHORS REFERRED TO IN THIS WORK.

App. Lucius Appuleius, philosopher, born about 130 B.C.
Auct. b. Afr. Auctor belli Africani.
Auct. b. Alex. Auctor belli Alexandrini.
Auct. b. Hisp. Auctor belli Hispani.

Caes. Caius Julius Caesar, historian, died 44 B.C.
Cat. C. Valerius Catullus, poet, born 87 B.C.
Cato. M. Porcius Cato, orator and historian, died 147 B.C.
Cic. M. Tullius Cicero, orator and philosopher, died 43 B.C.
Col. L. Jun. Moderatus Columella, writer on husbandry, of the 1st cent. A.D.

Enn. Q. Ennius, poet, died 169 B.C.
Eutr. Flavius Eutropius, historian of the 4th cent. A.D.

Hirt. Aulus Hirtius, historian, died 43 B.C.
Hor. Q. Horatius Flaccus, poet, died 8 B.C.

Juv. D. Junius Juvenalis, poet of the 1st cent. A.D.

Liv. T. Livius Patavinus, historian, died 16 B.C.
Lucan. M. Annaeus Lucanus, poet, died 65 A.D.
Lucr. T. Lucretius Carus, poet, died about 50 B.C.

Mart. M. Valerius Martialis, poet of the 1st cent. A.D.

Nep. Cornelius Nepos, writer of biographies of the 1st cent. A.D.

Ov. P. Ovidius Naso, poet, died 16 A.D.

Pers. A. Persius Flaccus, satirist, died 62 A.D.
Petr. T. Petronius Arbiter, satirist, died 67 A.D.
Phaedr. Phaedrus, fabulist of the 1st cent. A.D.
Plaut. M. Accius (or T. Maccius) Plautus, died 184 B.C.
Plin. C. Plinius Secundus (major), naturalist, died 79 A.D. C. Plinius Caecilius Secundus (minor), died about 100 A.D.
Prop. Sex. Aurelius Propertius, poet, died 15 B.C.

Q. Cic. Quintus Cicero, brother of M. Tullius.
Quint. M. Fabius Quintilianus, rhetorician of the 1st cent. A.D.

Sall. C. Crispius Sallustius, died 34 B.C.
Sen. L. Annaeus Seneca, philosopher, died 65 A.D.
Stat. P. Papinius Statius, poet of the 1st cent. A.D.
Suet. C. Suetonius Tranquillus, writer of biographies of the 1st and 2nd cent. A.D.

Tac. C. Cornelius Tacitus, historian, born between 50 and 60 A.D.
Ter. P. Terentius Afer, writer of comedies of the 2nd cent. B.C.
Tib. Albius Tibullus, poet, died 18 B.C.

Varr. M. Terentius Varro, writer on husbandry, etc., born 82 B.C.
Vell. P. Velleius Paterculus, historian of the 1st cent. A.D.
Verg. P. Vergilius Maro, poet, died about 19 B.C.
Vitr. Vitruvius Pollio, writer on architecture, died about 14 B.C.

TABLE OF THE ROMAN CALENDAR.

Days of the Month.	January, August, December—31 days.	March, May, July, October—31 days.	April, June, Sept., November—30 days.	February—28 days, in leap year, 29.
1	Kal. Jan. Aug. Dec.	Kal. Mart. Mai. Jul. Oct.	Kal. Apr. Jun. Sept. Nov.	Kal. Febr.
2	a.d. (ante diem) IV. Non. (Jan., Aug., Dec.)	a.d. VI. Non. Mart. Mai. Jul. Oct.	a.d. IV. Non. Apr. Jun. Sept. Nov.	a.d. IV. Non. Febr.
3	a.d. III. ,, ,,	a.d. V. ,, ,,	a.d. III. ,, ,,	a.d. III. ,, ,,
4	Pridie ,, ,,	a.d. IV. ,, ,,	Pridie ,, ,,	Pridie ,, ,,
5	Non. Jan. Aug. Dec.	a.d. III. ,, ,,	Non. Apr. Jun. Sept. Nov.	Non. Febr.
6	a.d. VIII. Id. Jan. Aug. Dec.	Pridie ,, ,,	a.d. VIII. Id. Apr. Jun. Sept. Nov.	a.d. VIII. Id. Febr.
7	a.d. VII. ,, ,,	Non. Mart. Mai. Jul. Oct.	a.d. VII. ,, ,,	ad. VII. ,, ,,
8	a.d. VI. ,, ,,	a.d. VIII. Id. Mart. Mai. Jul. Oct.	a.d. VI. ,, ,,	a.d. VI. ,, ,,
9	a.d. V. ,, ,,	a.d. VII. ,, ,,	a.d. V. ,, ,,	a.d. V. ,, ,,
10	a.d. IV. ,, ,,	a.d. VI. ,, ,,	a.d. IV. ,, ,,	a.d. IV. ,, ,,
11	a.d. III. ,, ,,	a.d. V. ,, ,,	a.d. III. ,, ,,	a.d. III. ,, ,,
12	Pridie ,, ,,	a.d. IV. ,, ,,	Pridie ,, ,,	Pridie ,, ,,
13	Id. Jan. Aug. Dec.	a.d. III. ,, ,,	Id. Apr. Jun. Sept. Nov.	Id. Febr.
14	a.d. XIX. Kal. Febr. Sept. Jan. ,,	Pridie ,, ,,	a.d. XVIII. Kal. Mai. Jul. Oct. Dec.	a.d. XVI. Kal. Mart.
15	a.d. XVIII. ,, ,,	Id. Mart. Mai. Jul. Oct.	a.d. XVII. ,, ,,	a.d. XV. ,, ,,
16	a.d. XVII. ,, ,,	a.d. XVII. Kal. Apr. Jun. Aug. Nov.	a.d. XVI. ,, ,,	a.d. XIV. ,, ,,
17	a.d. XVI. ,, ,,	a.d. XVI. ,, ,,	a.d. XV. ,, ,,	a.d. XIII. ,, ,,
18	a.d. XV. ,, ,,	a.d. XV. ,, ,,	a.d. XIV. ,, ,,	a.d. XII. ,, ,,
19	a.d. XIV. ,, ,,	a.d. XIV. ,, ,,	a.d. XIII. ,, ,,	a.d. XI. ,, ,,
20	a.d. XIII. ,, ,,	a.d. XIII. ,, ,,	a.d. XII. ,, ,,	a.d. X. ,, ,,
21	a.d. XII. ,, ,,	a.d. XII. ,, ,,	a.d. XI. ,, ,,	a.d. IX. ,, ,,
22	a.d. XI. ,, ,,	a.d. XI. ,, ,,	a.d. X. ,, ,,	a.d. VIII. ,, ,,
23	a.d. X. ,, ,,	a.d. X. ,, ,,	a.d. IX. ,, ,,	a.d. VII. ,, ,,
24	a.d. IX. ,, ,,	a.d. IX. ,, ,,	a.d. VIII. ,, ,,	a.d. VI. ,, ,,
25	a.d. VIII. ,, ,,	a.d. VIII. ,, ,,	a.d. VII. ,, ,,	a.d. V. ,, ,,
26	a.d. VII. ,, ,,	a.d. VII. ,, ,,	a.d. VI. ,, ,,	a.d. IV. ,, ,,
27	a.d. VI. ,, ,,	a.d. VI. ,, ,,	a.d. V. ,, ,,	a.d. III. ,, ,,
28	a.d. V. ,, ,,	a.d. V. ,, ,,	a.d. IV. ,, ,,	*Pridie* ,, ,,
29	a.d. IV. ,, ,,	a.d. IV. ,, ,,	a.d. III. ,, ,,	
30	a.d. III. ,, ,,	a.d. III. ,, ,,	Pridie ,, ,,	
31	Pridie ,, ,,	Pridie ,, ,,		

SIGNS AND ABBREVIATIONS PECULIAR TO THE ENGLISH-LATIN SECTION.

I.—(a) Brackets ( ) enclosing the first syllable of a compound verb, denote that both the simple and compound forms of the verb are in use, as *(de)currĕre*. Lack of space, as a rule, has prevented the explanation of the difference in shades of meaning between the two forms. Where the student finds this a difficulty, a reference to the Latin-English section will at once relieve him. An English-Latin Dictionary serves its best purpose when it encourages the beginner to consult quotations from Roman authors in a good Latin Dictionary.

(b) Brackets enclosing a single letter denote that the word was written sometimes with and sometimes without that letter. Thus, *ex(s)pectare* shows that the two forms *exspectare* and *expectare* were both in use. The table at the beginning of Messrs. Lewis and Short's Latin Dictionary has frequently been consulted in respect to the spelling of doubtful words.

(c) Brackets enclosing a whole word denote that the word may be inserted or omitted according to the context. Thus for "tide," *aestus (maritimus)* implies that *aestus maritimus* is the full phrase, for which *aestus* alone may sometimes serve.

II.—Space has not allowed the insertion of much help in the way of declensions and conjugations, but the genitive of nouns in the fourth declension is given to distinguish them from those of the first. Where such a genitive occurs in a phrase, it is given thus, *aestus, -ūs, maritimus*. In a few other instances of doubtful words, genitives are also given.

III.—* prefixed to a word denotes that it is of modern or very late Latin origin. † appended to a word denotes that it is only used, in the Classical period, by poets.

IV.—

alqs	= *aliquis*	*alqm*	= *aliquem*
alqd	= *aliquid*	*alqam*	= *aliquam*
alcjs	= *alicujus*	*alqo*	= *aliquo*
alci	= *alicui*	*alqâ*	= *aliquâ*

Ante and Post Aug = used by writers before and after the time of Augustus

Circumloc = circumlocution

Class = Classical, i e belonging to the best period of Latin literature

Com = used by the comic poets

Comb = in combination

Eccl = used by the ecclesiastical writers The asterisk (*) is sometimes used to prevent a repetition of Eccl after each of the derivatives in a single paragraph

Gram = used by the Latin grammarians

Inscrip = found in inscriptions.

Jct = used by the Jurisconsults, or lawyers

Late, very late = used by authors after the Classical period.

Med Lat = Latin of the Middle Ages

Opp = in opposition to

V — Abbreviations of the names of authors peculiar to the English-Latin section of the Dictionary

Ammian Ammianus Marcellinus, historian 4th cent A D

Cels A Cornelius Celsus, writer on medicine, 1st cent A D

Curt Q Curtius Rufus historian, probably 1st cent A D

Linn Karl von Linné, or Linnaeus, modern botanist 18th cent

Prisc. Priscianus grammarian 5th cent A D

Veget Flavius Renatus Vegetius military writer 4th cent A D

Val. Max. Valerius Maximus, compiler of anecdotes, 1st cent A D.

LATIN-ENGLISH.

LATIN-ENGLISH DICTIONARY.

A a, the first letter of the Latin Alphabet. **a** as an abbreviation, see the Table.

a, ah, interj. *Ah!* Verg.

ā, ăb, abs, prep. with abl. (ā stands before consonants except h; ab before vowels, h, and consonants; abs only before c, q, t). Ab denotes motion in any direction from a fixed point (opp. ad). **I.** Lit., in space, **A.** Of motion, **1,** *away from;* fuga ab urbe, Cic.; **2, a,** *from . . . to;* ad carceres a calce revocari, Cic.; ab aliquo (esp. a me, a te, a se, a nobis, a vobis), *from the house of,* Cic. With verbs of taking, hearing, etc., such as accipio, emo, audio, cognosco, comperio; a me, *from my purse,* Cic.; of dependents or disciples, Zeno et qui ab eo sunt, *Zeno and his school,* Cic.; **b,** *down from;* suspendere columbam a malo, Verg.; **c,** usque ab, *right away from;* plausus usque ab capitolio excitatus, Cic. **B.** 1, of direction, *from;* a supero mari Flaminia (via), ab infero Aurelia, Cic.; **2,** *on the side of;* a septentrionibus, *on the north,* Caes.; a fronte, a tergo, a latere, a dextro cornu, Cic.; ab novissimis, *in the rear,* Caes. **C.** Of distance, *from;* **1,** Lit., *from* a point, with such verbs as abesse, distare, and with procul, longe, prope; ab millibus passuum, *a thousand paces distant,* Caes.; **2,** Transf., to express difference, with such verbs as differre, discrepare; quantum mutatus ab illo, Verg.; **3,** of number or position, *after;* quartus ab Arcesila, Cic. **II.** Transf., **A.** Of time, **1,** with reference to duration, *from;* ab hora tertia bibebatur, Cic.; a pueris, *from boyhood,* Cic.; **2,** with reference to distance of time, *from;* cuius a morte hic tertius et tricesimus annus, Cic. **B.** Of various relations implying the notion of starting from a point; **1,** of agency, with pass. and intrans. verbs, *by;* reprehendi ab aliquo, Cic.; interire ab aliquo, Cic.; **2,** of origin, *from, of;* **a,** id facinus natum a cupiditate, Cic.; **b,** of naming, puero ab inopia Egerio inditum nomen, Liv.; **3,** *in relation to;* imparati quum a militibus tum a pecunia, Cic.; **4,** *from, out of* (of part of a number); nonnulli ab novissimis, Caes.; **5,** in relation to the part of the body with which a person serves; servus a pedibus, *footman,* Cic.; a manu servus, *amanuensis,* Suet.

ăbactus -a -um, partic. of abigo.

ăbăcus -i, m. (ἄβαξ). **1,** *a counting-board,* Pers.; **2,** *a gaming-board divided into compartments,* Suet.; **3,** *a sideboard,* Cic.; **4,** in architecture, **a,** *mosaic panelling;* **b,** *the square slab on the top of a column.*

ăbălĭēnātĭo -ōnis, f. *alienation of property,* Cic.

ăbălĭēno, 1. *to separate.* **A.** Lit., **1,** *to separate,* Plaut.; **2,** *to alienate* (property); agros populi, Cic. **B.** Transf., **1,** *to deprive;* abalienati jure civium, Liv.; **2,** *to estrange;* aliquem ab aliquo, Cic.

Ăbās -antis, m. *king of Argos, father of Acrisius;* hence, **a,** adj., **Ăbantēus** -a -um; **b, Ăbantĭădes** -ae, m. *a descendant of Abas, Acrisius (son of Abas), Perseus (great-grandson of Abas).*

ăbăvus -i, m. *a great-great-grandfather,* Cic.; and in general, *forefather,* Cic.

Abdēra -orum, n. plur. (Ἄβδηρα, τά). **I.** *a town in Thrace* (now *Polystilo* or *Asperosa*), *birthplace of Protagoras and Democritus, noted for the stupidity of its inhabitants;* hic Abdera, *here reigns stupidity,* Cic.; also **Abdēra** -ae, f. Ov. **II.** *a town in Spain* (now *Adra*). **Abdērītēs** -ae (abl. -a), m. *an inhabitant of Abdera,* Cic.

abdĭcātĭo -ōnis, f. **1,** *disowning of a son,* Plin.; **2,** *renouncing of an office;* dictaturae, Liv.

1. **abdĭco,** 1. **1,** *to renounce, disown;* aliquem patrem, Liv.; **2,** *to abdicate* (a magistracy by a formal declaration), se non modo consulatu sed etiam libertate, Cic.; in Sall. and Liv. with simple accusative, magistratum, Sall.; dictaturam, Liv.; absol., ut abdicarent consules, Cic.

2. **abdīco** -dixi -dictum, 3. t. t. of augury, *to refuse assent to, disapprove of* (opp. addico); quum tres partes (vineae) aves abdixissent, Cic.

abdĭtē, adv. *secretly,* Cic.

abdĭtīvus -a -um, *removed, separated,* Plaut.

abdĭtus -a -um, p. adj. (of abdo), *concealed, secret.* **I.** Lit., vis abdita quaedam, Lucr. **II.** Transf., res abditae et obscurae, Cic.; neut. plur., abdita rerum, *deep thoughts,* Hor.

abdo -dĭdi -dĭtum, 3. **A.** Gen., *to put away, withdraw, remove;* copias ab eo loco abditas, Caes.; hence, **1,** of a weapon, *to drive in;* lateri capulo tenus ensem, Verg.; **2,** reflex., abdere se in aliquem locum; *to withdraw oneself, to retire;* in intimam Macedoniam, Cic.; in bibliothecam; in litteras (or litteris), Cic. **B.** *to secrete, to hide;* ferrum veste, Liv.; se in scalarum tenebras, Cic.

abdōmĕn -inis, n. *the belly,* Plaut.; especially as seat of the appetite, *gluttony;* manebat insaturabile abdomen, Cic.; natus abdomini suo, *whose god is his belly,* Cic.; abdominis voluptates, *pleasures of appetite,* Cic.

abdūco -duxi -ductum, 3. *to lead* or *take away.* **I. A.** Lit., **1,** aliquem e foro, Cic.; **2,** *to take away* for punishment; collegam vi de foro, Liv.; in lautumias, Cic.; **3,** *to elope with;* filiam mimi Isidori, Cic.; **4,** *to steal;* mancipia, Cic.; armenta, Ov. **B.** Transf., *to seduce* a person from his allegiance; equitatum Dolabellae ad se, Cic. **II.** In a wider sense, **A.** *to relieve;* animum a sollicitudine, Cic. **B.** *to bring down, to lower;* artem ad mercedem atque quaestum, Cic.

Ăbella -ae, f. *town in Campania* (now *Avella Vecchia*). Adj., **Ăbellānus** -a -um.

ăbĕo -ii -itum -īre, *to go away* I. A. Lit., 1, Gen., ex agris atque urbibus, Cic.; ab urbe, Liv.; de Sicilia, Cic.; comitio, Liv.; si abis periturus, *if you go to death*, Verg.; imper., abi, a, *good, very well*, non es avarus, abi, Hor.; b, *be off with you*, so abin (for abisne), abi in malam rem, *go to the devil*, Plaut.; abi hinc cum tribunatibus ac rogationibus tuis, Liv. Of things, abeuntia vela, Ov.; sol abit, Plaut.; cornus sub altum pectus abit, Verg. 2, Esp., a, *to come off* (e.g. from a battle), Romani semper victores certamine abire, Liv.; nemo non donatus abibit, Verg.; absol., abiturum eum non esse, si accessisset, *he could not have got off unpunished*, Cic.; b, *to retire* from a public office, consulatu, Cic.; c, of the dying, *to depart*, ad deos, Cic.; ad plures, *to "the great majority,"* Petr.; e vita, Cic.; d, in auctions, *not to be knocked down to*, si res abiret a mancipe, Cic. B. Transf., 1, Gen., non longe abieris, *you have not far to go* (for an example), Cic.; quorsum abeant, *on which side will they range themselves?* Hor.; 2, Esp., of a discussion, *to digress*; illuc, unde abii, redeo, Hor.; quid ad istas ineptias abis? Cic.; etiam tu hinc abis, *will you also go away?* Cic. II. With notion of disappearing, 1, of time, *to pass away*; abiit ille annus, Cic.; 2, of diseases, jam abiit pestilentia, Cic.; 3, of other things, *to disappear, vanish*; sensus abiit, Cic.; timor, fides abiit, Liv.; 4, of the consequences of an action, non posse istaec sic abire, *be without consequences*, Cic. III. With notion of transference from one person or thing to another, 1, *to go over*, a, to a person, ad sanos abeat tutela propinquos, Hor.; b, to a thing, vigor ingenii velocis in alas et pedes abiit, Ov.; 2, *to change into*, sic deus in flammas abiit, Ov.

ăbĕquĭto, 1 *to ride off*, Liv.

ăberrātĭo, -ōnis, f. *an escape or relief from anything irksome*, Cic.

ăberro, 1 *to wander, lose one's way* I. Lit., pecore, Liv.; aberrantes ex agmine naves, Liv. II. Transf., 1, *to deviate from*, a proposito, Cic.; 2, *to free oneself from something irksome*, a miseria quasi aberrare, Cic.

ăbhinc, adv. *from hence* I. Of space, aufer abhinc lacrimas, Lucr. II. Of time, reckoned from the present moment backward, annos tres, triennium, annis tribus abhinc, *three years ago*, Cic.

ăbhorrĕo, 2 I. Lit., *to shrink back from, to be disinclined to*, a pace, Caes.; a ducenda uxore, Cic.; with abl. alone, spectaculorum oblectamentis, Tac.; absol., omnes aspernabantur, omnes abhorrebant, Cic. II. Transf., *to be inconsistent with or opposed to*, oratio abhorret a persona hominis gravissimi, Cic.; a fide, *to be incredible*, Liv.; spes ab effectu haud abhorrens, *hope capable of being realised*, Liv.; orationes abhorrent inter se, *are inconsistent with one another*, Liv.; with simple abl., neque abhorret vero, Tac.; with dat., huic tam pacatae profectioni abhorrens mos, Liv. Pres. part., as an adjective, *unseasonable, inappropriate*, absurdae atque abhorrentes lacrimae, Liv.

ăbiegnus -a -um (abies), *made of fir wood or deal*, Cic.

ăbĭēs -ĕtis, f. I. *the fir tree* (Pinus picea, Linn.), Liv. II. Meton., *anything made of deal; a letter*, because formerly written on wood, Plaut.; *a ship*, Verg.; *a spear*, Verg. (Abiĕtis, abiĕtĕ, trisyll., Verg.)

ăbĭgo -ēgi -actum, 3 (ab and ago) I. Lit., A. Gen., *to drive away*, volucres et feras, Cic. B. Esp., 1, pecus, *to steal cattle*, Cic.; 2, partum medicamentis, *to procure abortion*, Cic.; 3, uxorem, *to divorce*, Suet. II. Fig., *to banish, get rid of*, pauperem epulis regum, Hor. Abacti oculi, *deep sunk eyes*, Stat.

ăbĭtĭo -ōnis, f. = abitus (q. v.)

ābīto, 3 *to go away*, Plaut.

ăbĭtus -ūs, m. (abeo), 1, *a going away, departure*, post abitum hujus, Cic.; 2, *place of egress* (opp. aditus), Verg.

abjectē, adv. *abjectly, in a spiritless and cowardly manner*, Cic.; *meanly*, Tac.

abjectĭo -ōnis, f. I. Lit., *a throwing away, rejection* II. Transf., animi, *despondency, despair*, Cic.

abjectus -a -um, p. adj. with compar. and superl. (abjicio), 1, of position, *low, common*, familia abjecta atque obscura, Cic.; 2, of character, *cowardly, mean-spirited*, animus, Cic.; 3, *despicable*, contemptus atque abjectus, Cic.; 4, *without force, prosaic*, versus, Cic.; oratio humilis et abjecta, Cic.

abjĭcĭo -jēci -jectum, 3 (ab and jacio), *to throw down, or away* I. Lit., 1, scutum, arma, Cic.; se ad pedes alicujus, Cic.; 2, *to throw down violently*, aliquem ad tribunal, ad pedes tuos, ad terram virgis et verberibus, Cic.; so in battle, *to strike to the ground* Verg. II. Transf., 1, *to pronounce carelessly, to break off abruptly*, versum, Cic.; ambitus non est abjiciendus, *the period must not be broken off abruptly*, Cic.; 2, *to get rid of, to dispose of*, pecuniam, Cic.; 3, *to give up, to let go*, memoriam beneficiorum, Cic.; *to abandon*, Scaurum, Cic.; 4, *to dash to the ground, to deprive of all power*, senatus auctoritatem, Cic.; with reference to character, *to dishearten*, se perculsum atque abjectum esse sentit, Cic.; abjecta metu filia, *desponding*, Cic.; 5, Fig., *to throw away*, cogitationes in rem tam humilem, Cic.; se abjicere, *to degrade oneself*, Cic.

abjūdĭco, 1 (opp. adjudico), as a judge *to give sentence against any one, to take away by judgment*, aliquid ab aliquo, Cic.; sibi libertatem, Cic.

abjungo -junxi -junctum, 3 I. *to unharness*, juvencum, Verg. II. Transf., *to estrange, detach*, abjuncto Labieno, Caes.; se ab hoc dicendi genere, *to keep from*, Cic.

abjūro, 1 *to abjure, deny on oath*, pecuniam, Cic.; creditum, Sall.

ablātīvus -a -um, *ablative* Subst., **ablātīvus** -i, m. (sc. casus), *the ablative, the sixth case of the Latin noun*, Quint.

ablēgātĭo -ōnis, f. I. Gen., *a sending away*, juventutis ad bellum, Liv. II. Esp., *banishment*, = relegatio, Plin.

ablēgo, 1 I. Lit., *to send away, remove to a distance*, honestos homines, Cic.; pueros venatum, Liv.; aliquem a penatibus suis, Liv. II. Fig., 1, haec (legatio) a fratris adventu me ablegat, *prevents me from being present on my brother's arrival*, Cic.; 2, milit. t. t., *to dislodge*, aliquem, Liv.

ablĭgūrĭo, 4 *to consume in luxury*, patria bona, Ter.

ablŏco, 1 *to let on lease*, Suet.

ablūdo, 3 Lit. *to be out of tune with*, hence *to be unlike*, haec a te non multum abludit imago, Hor.

ablŭo -lŭi -lūtum, 3 *to wash* I. In the sense of cleansing, pedes alicujus, Cic.; pass., ablui, *to be washed clean*, Cic. II. In the sense of removing, *to wash away* A. Lit., maculas e veste, Plin.; lacrimas, Tac.; poet., sitis de corpore abluitur, *is quenched*, Lucr. B. Transf., omnis perturbatio animi placatione abluatur, Cic.

ablūtĭo -ōnis, f. *a washing away, ablution*, Plin.

abnĕgo, 1. *to deny, refuse;* alicui conjugium et dotes, Verg.; nec comitem se abnegat, Hor.; absol., abnegat, Verg.

abnĕpos -ōtis, m. *great-great-grandson,* Suet.

abneptis -is, f. *a great-great-granddaughter,* Suet.

Abnŏba -ae, m. *a range of mountains in Germany, where the Danube rises.*

abnocto, 1. *to stay out all night,* Sen.

abnormis -e (ab and norma), *irregular, unconventional;* abnormis sapiens, *one of Nature's philosophers,* Hor.

abnŭo -nŭi -nŭitūrus, 3. *to refuse by a motion of the head or eye, deny;* manu abnuit quidquam opis in se esse, *gave a sign with his hand that he could not help,* Liv.; regi pacem, Sall.; nemo abnuit a se commissum esse facinus, Cic.; spes abnuit, *it does not admit of hope,* Tib.; of soldiers, *to refuse to fight,* Liv.

abnūto, 1. *to deny* (by a nod) *repeatedly,* Plaut.

ăbŏlĕo -ēvi -ĭtum, 2. *to destroy.* **I.** Lit., Poppaeae corpus non igni abolitum, Tac.; viscera undis, *to cleanse,* Verg. **II.** Fig., *to do away with;* magistratum, Liv.; dedecus armis, Verg.; ritus, sacrificandi disciplinam, Liv.

ăbŏlesco -ēvi, no sup., 3. *to perish;* non abolescet gratia facti, Verg.; nomen vetustate abolevit, Liv.

ăbŏlĭtĭo -ōnis, f. *a removing, abrogating, annulling, abolition;* legis, *repeal,* Suet.; tributorum, Tac.; facti, *amnesty,* Suet.

ăbolla -ae, f. *cloak of thick woollen cloth,* worn by soldiers; prov., facinus majoris abollae, *a crime on a larger scale,* Juv.

ăbōmĭno = abominor (q.v.).

ăbōmĭnor -atus sum, 1. dep. (ab and omen), **1,** *to deprecate an unfavourable omen;* aliquid, Liv.; quod abominor, *God forbid,* Ov.; **2,** *to hate, detest, abominate* (opp. optare), Liv.; abominandus, *detestable,* Liv.; abominatus, *detested,* Hor.

Ăbŏrīgĭnes -um, m. (Ἀβοριγῖνες), *the Aborigines,* an Italian tribe from whom the Latins were said to be descended; hence *original inhabitants of a country* (= αὐτόχθονες), Plin.

ăbŏrĭor -ortus sum, 4. dep. (opp. exorior), **1,** of the heavenly bodies, *to set, to disappear,* Varr.; **2,** *to perish by untimely birth,* Plin.; **3,** poet., of the voice, *to fail,* Lucr.

ăbŏriscor = aborior (q.v.).

ăbortĭo -ōnis, f. *an untimely birth, miscarriage,* Cic.

ăbortīvus -a -um, *prematurely born;* Sisyphus, Hor.; ovum, *addled,* Mart. Subst., **ăbortīvum** -i, n. (sc. medicamentum), *drug for procuring abortion,* Juv.

ăbortus -ūs, m. *a miscarriage,* Cic.

abrādo -rasi -rasum, 3. **I.** Lit., *to scrape off, shave;* supercilia, Cic. **II.** Transf., *to squeeze money out of a person, to extort;* nihil se ab A. Caecina posse litium terrore abradere, Cic.

abrĭpio -rĭpŭi -reptum, 3. (ab and rapio), *to snatch away, tear off, drag off.* **I. A.** Lit., abripi vi fluminis, Caes. **B.** Transf., Romulum si natura ad humanum exitum abripuit, Cic. **II. A.** *to rob;* non dona tantum sed simulacra numinum, Tac. **B. 1,** *to drag away;* Cappadocem de grege venalium, Cic.; **2,** *to drag away to punishment;* aliquem de convivio in vincula, Cic.; **3,** *to take away by force;* filios e complexu parentum, Cic.

abrōdo -si -sum, 3. *to gnaw off, away,* Pers.

abrŏgātĭo -ōnis, f. *an annulling or repealing;* legis, Cic.

abrŏgo, 1. **A. 1,** *to repeal a law wholly, to annul;* legem, Cic.; huic legi nec abrogari fas est, neque derogari ex hac aliquid licet neque tota abrogari potest, Cic.; **2,** *to deprive* (a magistrate of his office); si tibi magistratum abrogasset, Cic. **B.** Transf., *to take away;* fidem, *to take away a man's credit,* Cic.

abrŏtŏnum -i, n. and **abrŏtŏnus** -i, f. (ἀβρότονον), *southern-wood, an aromatic herb,* Lucr., Hor.

abrumpo -rūpi -ruptum, 3. **I.** *to break off, loosen, separate.* **A.** Lit., ramos, Ov.; vincula, Liv. **B.** Transf., se latrocinio Antonii, *to break away from,* Cic. **II.** *to tear off, to separate forcibly, to sever.* **A.** Lit., pontem, Tac. **B.** Transf., **1,** *to violate;* fas, Verg.; **2,** *to break off prematurely, to destroy;* vitam, Verg.; medium sermonem, *to break off in the middle of a speech,* Verg.

abruptĭo -ōnis, f. (abrumpo). **I.** *a tearing away;* corrigiae, *of a shoe-latchet,* Cic. **II.** Transf., *divorce,* Cic.

abruptus -a -um, p. adj. with compar. and superl. (abrumpo), *torn off;* hence, **I.** *steep, precipitous.* Subst., **abruptum** -i, n. *a steep ascent or descent;* sorbet in abruptum fluctus, Verg. **II.** Transf., **A.** Gen. only subst., abruptum -i, n. *a precipice, the precipice of danger, the road to ruin;* in abruptum tractus, Tac. **B.** Of character, *rough;* contumacia, Tac.

abscēdo -cessi -cessum, 3. *to go away, depart.* **I.** Lit., **A.** Of persons, a curia, e foro, Liv.; as milit. t. t., *to withdraw, retire;* a Capua, Liv.; impers., Regio abscessum est, Liv. **B.** Of things, *to retire;* quantum mare abscedebat, Liv. **II.** Transf., **A.** of persons, **1,** *to retire from* an office or employment; non militaribus modo sed civilibus quoque muneribus, Liv.; **2,** *to desert* one; Pallada abscessisse mihi, Ov. **B.** Of things, **1,** *to go away;* somnus ut abscessit, Ov.; **2,** *to desert;* cives earum urbium quae regno abscedunt, Liv.

abscessĭo -ōnis, f. (abscedo), *a going away, a separation,* Cic.

abscessus -ūs, m. (abscedo), *a going away;* **1,** of persons, *going away* (especially in battle), *withdrawal;* Rutulum, Verg.; continuus abscessus, Tac.; **2,** of inanimate objects, solis, Cic.

abscīdo -cīdi -cīsum. 3. (abs and caedo), *to cut off.* **I.** Lit., funes, Caes.; aquam, Liv.; caput, Liv. **II. A.** Transf., *to separate;* intersaeptis munimentis hostis pars parti abscisa erat, Liv.; abscisus in duas partes exercitus, Caes. **B.** *to take away;* regibus spem auxilii sui, Liv.

abscindo -scĭdi -scissum, 3. *to tear off, wrench away.* **I.** Lit., tunicam a pectore, Cic.; vestem humeris, Verg.; venas, *to open the veins,* Tac.; poet., abscissa comas, *with her hair torn,* Verg. **II.** Transf., **A.** *to divide;* terras Oceano, Hor. **B.** *to separate;* inane soldo, Hor. **C.** *to take away;* reditus dulces, Hor.

abscīsus -a -um, p. adj. (from abscido), *cut off,* hence *precipitous;* rupes, Liv.

abscondĭtē, adv. *obscurely, abstrusely,* Cic.

abscondo -condi (-condĭdi) -condĭtum (-consum), 3. **I.** *to conceal;* gladios, Cic. **II. A.** *to obscure;* galea frontem abscondit, Juv.; hence pass. of stars, *to set,* Verg. **B.** *to lose sight of;* Phaeacum arces, Verg. **C.** *to keep out of sight;* quod quo studiosius ab istis opprimitur et absconditur eo magis eminet et apparet, Cic.

absens -entis (absum), p. adj. *absent,* Cic.

absentia -ae, f (absum), *absence*, Cic

absilio, 4 (ab and salio), *to spring forth*, or *away*, Lucr

absimilis e, *unlike*, non absimili forma, Caes.

absinthium i, n (ἀψίνθιον), *wormwood*, Lucr

absisto -stiti, -stitum, 3 1, *to go away*, followed by ab or the abl alone, limine, Verg, ab signis, Caes, absol, tandem abstiterunt, Liv, of things, ab ore scintillae absistunt, Verg, 2, *to desist from*, with abl, obsidione, spe, Liv, with infin, absiste moveri, *cease to be moved*, Verg, with gerund, sequendo, *from following*, Liv, accusator abstitit, *the accuser withdrew* (i e from his accusation), Tac

absŏlūtē, adv *perfectly, completely*, vivere feliciter, absolute, Cic.

absŏlūtio ōnis, f (absolvo), 1, *acquittal*, majestatis, *on the charge of treason*, Cic, 2, *perfection*, virtus quae rationis absolutio definitur, Cic

absŏlūtōrius -a -um, *relating to acquittal*, tabella, *the voting tablet that acquits*, Suet Subst, **absŏlūtōrium** -ii, n (sc remedium), *means of escape from*, Plin

absŏlūtus a -um, p adj with compar and superl (absolvo) **I.** *perfect, complete* vita, Cic. **II.** *unfettered, unconditional, absolute*, causa, Cic

absolvo -solvi -solutum, 3 **A.** Lit, *to loosen* **B.** Transf, **1**, **a**, *to free*, se a Fannio judicio, Cic, aliquem regni suspicione, Liv, **b**, *to acquit*, improbitatis, Cic, capitis, Nep; reos culpa, Ov, de praevaricatione, Cic, 2 *to dispose of in narration, to relate*, de Catilinae conjuratione paucis absolvam, Sall, 3, *to complete, to finish*, tectum, Cic, opera, Caes, absolve beneficium tuum, Liv

absŏnus -a um **I.** Lit, *inharmonious*, vox, Cic **II.** Transf, *disagreeing with, not correspondent with*, absoni a voce motus, Liv, with dat., nihil absonum fidei divinae originis fuit, Liv

absorbĕo ui, 2 *to swallow, to gulp down* **I.** Lit, placentas, Hor, Oceanus vix videtur tot res absorbere potuisse, Cic **II.** Transf, hunc absorbuit aestus gloriae, *carried him off*, Cic, tribunatus absorbet meam orationem, *absorbs, engrosses*, Cic

absque, prep with abl *without*; absque argumento, Cic

abstēmius -a um (abs and temum = temetum), *one who abstains from intoxicating liquors, temperate, abstemious, moderate*, Ov, Hor

abstergĕo -tersi -tersum, 2 *to wipe off, to dry by wiping* **I** Lit, cruorem, Liv **II.** Transf, *to remove something disagreeable*, omnes senectutis molestias, Cic

absterrĕo -terrui territum, 2. *to frighten away, to drive away by fear* **I** Lit, hostes saxis, Liv, neminem a congressu meo, Cic **II.** Transf *to frighten from, keep off from*, eos a tam detestabili consilio, Liv; animos vitiis, *from vices*, Hor, aliquem bello, Tac

abstinens -entis, p adj with compar. and superl. (abstineo), *abstinent, continent, temperate*, Cic, with genit., pecuniae, Hor.

abstinentĕr, adv *abstinently, continently*, Cic.

abstinentia -ae, f **I.** *abstinence, continence, self-denial, temperance*, absol, *fasting*, abstinentia vitam finire, Tac **II.** *uprightness*, Cic, *freedom from avarice*, Cic

abstĭnĕo -tinui -tentum, 2 (abs and teneo), *to hold back, to keep away from* **I.** Transf, manus, Liv, gen with a and the abl or with the abl alone, militem a praeda, Liv manus a se, *to abstain from suicide*, Cic **II.** Reflex, abstinere se, or simply abstinere, **a**, with the abl or with ab and the abl, se scelere, Cic, a legatis violandis Liv, publico, *not to go out*, Tac, **b**, with genit, irarum, Hor; **c**, with acc, liberas urbes, Liv, **d**, with acc of thing and dat of person, Aeneae Antenorique omne jus belli, **e**, with ne and the subj, Liv, **f**, absol, non tamen abstinuit, Verg

absto, 1 *to stand at a distance, stand aloof*, Hor

abstrăho -traxi, -tractum, 3 **I.** Lit, *to drag away*, aliquem de matris complexu, Cic, naves e portu, Liv, aliquem a penetralibus, Liv, liberos in servitutem, Caes **II** Transf, **A.** aliquem ex tanto comitatu clarissimorum virum, *to exclude*, Cic, animus a corpore abstractus, Cic, a bono in pravum, Sall **B. 1**, *to estrange*, copias a Lepido, Cic, **2**, *to restrain* ingressos in castra ab direptione abstrahere non poterat, Liv, a rebus gerendis senectus abstrahit, **3**, *to draw away from*, a bonis, Cic, se a sollicitudine, Cic

abstrūdo -trūsi -trūsum, 3 *to push away from any place, to hide* **I.** Lit, se in silvam densam, Cic, semina flammae abstrusa in venis silicis, Verg **II.** Transf, penitus abstrusus animi dolor, *deep-seated grief*, Cic

abstrūsus -a -um, p adj with compar (from abstrudo). **A.** Lit, *concealed, secret*, Plin, **B.** Transf, **1**, *abstruse*, disputatio abstrusior, Cic, **2**, of character, *reserved*, Tac

absum (abfŭi, abesse, āfŭi, āfŭtūrus, āfŏrem, āfŏre, etc, also occur) **I.** With regard to motion, *to be away, to be absent* **A.** Gen, ab urbe or ex urbe, Cic **B.** Esp, **1**, *to take no part in*, ab hoc concilio, Caes, ab his studiis, Cic, toto bello, Caes, **2**, *not to help*, quo plus intererat, eo plus aberas a me, *the more I needed you, the less you helped me*, Cic, longe iis paternum nomen populi Romani afuturum, *would be of no avail*, Caes, **3**, *to be wanting*, studium semper sit, cunctatio absit, Cic, semper aves quod abest, Lucr, neque corpus neque animus a vobis aberit, Sall, abest historia nostris litteris, Cic **II.** As regards position, **A.** Lit, *to be distant*, ab urbe milia passuum ducenta, Cic, quatridui iter Laodicea, Cic **B.** Transf, **1**, *to be far from*, longe a spe, Cic, so the impers phrase, tantum abest ut — ut, e g tantum abest ab eo ut malum sit mors ut verear, *so far is death from being an evil that I fear*, etc, Cic, so haud multum, or procul abest, or paulum abest, or minimum abest quin, etc, haud multum afuit quin interficeretur, *he was nearly killed*, Liv, **2**, *to be free from* (a fault), a culpa, Cic, a cupiditate pecuniae, Nep **3**, *to be far removed* (especially in phrases expressing a wish), procul absit gloria vulgi, Tib, nomen ipsum crucis absit non modo a corpore civium Romanorum, etc, Cic; **4**, *to be firmly opposed to*, a consilio fugiendi, Cic, **5**, *to be inconsistent with*, quod certe abest a tua virtute et fide, Cic

absūmēdo -inis, f *consumption*, Plaut.

absūmo sumpsi -sumptum 3 *to take away* **I. A.** *to lessen, destroy, consume*, res maternas atque paternas, Hor.; absumptis frugum alimentis, Liv **B.** Of time, *to waste*, tempus dicendo, Cic **II.** *to destroy utterly*. **A.** Of things, incendium domos absumpsit, Liv **B.** Of living beings, *to kill*, multos pestilentia absumpsit, Liv.

absurdē, adv 1, *harshly, discordantly*;

canere, Cic.; **2,** *in bad taste;* absurde et aspere respondere verbis vultuque, Cic.

absurdus -a -um. **I.** Lit., *that which offends the ear, unmelodious, harsh;* vox, Cic. **II.** Transf., *foolish, unreasonable.* **A.** Of things, vestrae istae absurdae atque abhorrentes lacrimae, Liv.; haud absurdum est, *it is not out of place,* Sall. **B.** Of persons, *incapable;* homo, Cic.; ingenium haud absurdum, Sall.; absurdus ingenio, Tac.

Absyrtus -i, m. (Ἄψυρτος), *brother of Medea, killed by his sister on her flight from Colchis.*

ăbundans -antis, p. adj. with compar. and superl. (abundo). **I.** Lit., of rivers, *overflowing;* amnis abundantissimus, Cic. **II.** Transf., **A.** *abundant, rich;* with abl., locus fontibus abundans, Cic.; with genit., lactis, Verg. **B. 1,** *abounding in* (thoughts, devices, etc.); abundantior consilio, Cic.; **2,** in a bad sense, *overloaded;* non erat abundans, non inops tamen oratio, Cic. **C.** *numerous;* abundante multitudine freti, Liv.; abundantes voluptates, Liv.

ăbundantĕr, adv. **1,** *abundantly;* abundantius occurrere, Cic.; **2,** of discourse, *copiously;* loqui, Cic.

ăbundantĭa -ae, f. **1,** *abundance, richness, plenty;* omnium rerum quas natura desiderat, Cic.; voluptatum, Cic.; **2,** *riches, wealth,* Tac.

ăbundē, adv. *copiously, excessively, extravagantly;* promittere, Lucr.; satisfacere, Cic.; with adj., abunde magnus, Sall.; tibi abunde est, *you are more than satisfied,* Plin.; abunde libertatem ratus, *thinking liberty more than enough,* Sall. Subst. with genit., terrorum ac fraudis abunde est, Verg.

ăbundo, 1. *to overflow.* **I.** Lit., flumina, Lucr.; abundat aqua, Liv. **II.** Transf., **A.** *to grow in abundance;* de terris abundant herbarum genera, Lucr. **B.** *to abound;* porco, Cic.; ingenio et doctrina, Cic.; absol., *to be rich;* quum ex reliquis vel abundare debeam, cogor mutuari, Cic.

ăbūsĭo -ōnis, f. (abutor), in rhetoric, *a false use of words,* Cic.

ăbusquĕ, prep. with abl. = usque ab, *from;* **1,** as regards position, Oceano abusque, Tac.; **2,** as regards time, Tiberio abusque, Tac.

ăbūsus -ūs, m. (abutor), *using up, wasting,* Cic.

ăbūtor -ūsus sum, 3. dep., with abl. **I.** *to use;* nisi omni tempore, quod mihi lege concessum est, abusus ero, Cic. **II.** *to make full use of, to use fully.* **A.** In a good sense, sagacitate canum ad utilitatem nostram, Cic. **B.** In a bad sense, *to waste;* militum sanguine, Cic.; insolenter et immodice indulgentia populi Romani, Liv. **C.** *to use a word wrongly;* verbo, Cic.

Ăbȳdus (Abydos) -i, f. and **Ăbȳdum** -i, n. (Ἄβυδος). **I.** *a town in Asia Minor, on the Hellespont* (modern *Aïdos* or *Avido*). **II.** *a town in Egypt.* Adj., **Abydēnus** -a -um; juvenis or absol., *Leander,* Ov.; plur., **Abydēni** -orum, *the inhabitants of Abydos,* Liv.

Ăbȳla -ae, f. (Ἀβύλη), *a mountain on the African side of the Straits of Gibraltar, forming one of the so-called Pillars of Hercules* (now *Sierra Zimiera*).

ac, v. atque.

Ăcădēmĭa -ae, f. (Ἀκαδήμεια), *the Academy,* a grove near Athens where Plato taught; hence, meton., *the Academic school of philosophy,* Cic.; hence, too, *a gymnasium on Cicero's estate at Tusculum,* called after the Athenian Academy.

Ăcădēmĭcus -a -um (Ἀκαδημικός). **I.** *belonging to the Academy at Athens;* philosophi, Cic.; hence plur. subst., **Ăcădēmĭci** -ōrum, m. *the Academic philosophers.* **II.** *belonging to Cicero's gymnasium, called the Academy;* hence plur. subst., **Ăcădēmĭca** -ōrum, n. *a treatise of Cicero on the Academic philosophy.*

Ăcădēmus -i, m. (Ἀκάδημος), *a Greek hero,* after whom the Academia was named.

ăcălanthis -ĭdis, f. (ἀκαλανθίς) = acanthis, q.v.

Ăcămās -antis, m. (Ἀκάμας), **1,** *son of Theseus and Phaedra,* Verg.; **2,** *promontory in Cyprus,* Plin.

ăcanthis -ĭdis, f. (ἀκανθίς), *a small dark green bird, the thistle-finch,* Plin.

1. **ăcanthus** -i, m. (ἄκανθος), **1,** *bear's foot, a plant,* Verg.; **2,** *a thorny evergreen Egyptian tree,* Verg.

2. **Ăcanthus** -i, f. (Ἄκανθος), *a town in the Macedonian peninsula—Chalcidice.*

ăcapnŏs -ŏn (ἄκαπνος), *without smoke;* ligna, *burning without smoke,* Mart.

Ăcarnānes -um, m. (Ἀκαρνᾶνες), *Acarnanians;* Acarnanum amnis, *the Achelous,* Ov.; sing., **Acarnān** -anis, *an Acarnanian,* Verg.; hence **Acarnānĭa** -ae, *Acarnania, a country on the west of Greece, between Epirus and Aetolia.* Adj., **Acarnānĭcus** -a -um.

Ăcastus -i, m. (Ἄκαστος). **I.** *son of the Thessalian king Pelias, father of Laodamia, brother of Alcestis.* **II.** *a slave of Cicero.*

Acca Lārentia, *a Roman goddess of the fields,* according to the legend, the wife of the herdsman Faustulus, and the nurse of Romulus and Remus. **Lārentalia** or **Accālia** -ium, n. *her festival at Rome in December.*

accēdo -cessi -cessum, 3. (ad and cedo), *to approach, to come near.* **I.** Lit., **A.** Gen., **1,** of persons, with the accusative and ad; ad urbem, Cic.; alicui ad aurem et dicere, *to approach any one to whisper,* Cic.; with in, in aedes, Cic.; in funus, *to join the funeral procession,* Cic.; with simple accusative, scopulos, Verg.; Jugurtham, Sall.; absol., *to approach,* Cic.; **2,** of lifeless subjects, febris accedit, Cic. **B.** Esp., **1,** *to come as a suppliant;* senatus supplex accedit ad Caesarem, Cic.; quo accedam aut quos appellem, Sall.; **2,** *to come as an enemy;* usque ad castra, Caes.; with simple acc., loca hostiliter, Sall.; **3,** *to come to an auction to bid;* ad illud scelus sectionis, Cic.; ad hastam, Liv.; **4,** *to approach the city (Rome) as a candidate for a triumph;* ad urbem, Cic. **II.** Transf., **A.** Gen., **1,** of persons, ad amicitiam Philippi, Nep.; sed propius accedam, de his nostris testibus dicam, Cic.; **2,** of lifeless subjects, accedit manus extrema operibus, Cic.; fervor accedit capiti, *the wine mounts to his head,* Hor. **B.** Esp., **1,** of time, *to approach;* quo propius ad mortem accedam, Cic.; **2,** *to enter upon some work;* ad rem publicam, *to begin public life,* Cic.; ad vectigalia, *to engage in the collection of the taxes,* Cic.; **3,** *to assent to;* ad conditiones, Cic.; **4,** *to be added, to increase;* ad eas (naves) captivae Massiliensium accesserunt sex, Caes.; quo plus aetatis ei accederet, *the older he became,* Cic.; iis tantum fiduciae accessit ut, etc., Caes.; hence the phrases, huc accedit, eo accedit, huc accedit summus timor, Cic.; often followed by ut and quod, with the meaning of simply *moreover;* **5,** *to fall to one's share, to come to one;* num tibi stultitia accessit, Plaut.; alicui animus accedit, Cic.; **6,** *to approach, to become like;* propius ad deos, Cic.

accĕlĕro, 1. **I.** Trans., *to quicken, to accelerate;* iter, Caes.; consulatum alicui, Tac. **II.**

Intrans, *to hasten*, si accelerare volent, Cic.; accelera, signifer, Liv.

accendo -cendi -censum 3 (ad and * cando, causat. of candeo), *to kindle, to set on fire.* **I.** A Lit, faces, Cic, tus, Liv **B.** Met, *to lighten up*, luna radiis solis accensa, Cic **II.** Transf, **A.** Gen, *to kindle as a light*, virtutum quasi scintillulae e quibus accendi philosophi ratio debet, Cic **B** Esp, **1,** *to inflame;* plebis animum, Sall, animos bello, *to excite to war*, Verg, ira accensus, Liv, **2,** *to provoke*, spem invidiam, Liv, studia Numidarum in Jugurtham accensa, *the enthusiasm of the N. for J.*, Sall, **3,** *to increase*, quum eo magis vis venti accensa esset, Liv

accenseo -censum, 2 *to reckon in addition*, accenseor illi, *I am his comrade*, Ov

1 **accensus** -a -um, part of accenseo **I** Generally used in plural, **accensi** -orum, lit *those numbered with*, originally, *the fifth class of Roman citizens*, who in battle stood in the last ranks, and were also employed in constructing public roads, hence *the supernumeraries*, Liv **II. accensus** -i, m *a subordinate public officer* (in the service of the decemviri, consuls, and praetors), Cic

2 **accensus** -a um, partic of accendo

acceptio -ōnis, f *a reception, acceptance*, Cic, frumenti, *receipt*, Sall

accepto, 1 (intens of accipio), *to receive*, Plaut.

acceptŏr -ōris, m *one who approves*, Plaut

acceptrix -īcis, f *she who receives*, Plaut

acceptus -a -um, p adj with compar and superl (from accipio), *welcome, pleasant, agreeable*, 1, of persons, with the dat, qui maxime plebi acceptus erat, Caes, 2, of things, nihil est deo acceptius quam, etc, Cic

accerso = arcesso (q v)

accessio ōnis, f (accedo), *a going or coming to* **I.** Lit, suis accessionibus, *by the audiences which he gave*, Cic **II.** Transf, **A.** *increase*, dignitatis, Cic; pecuniae, Nep **B** *addition, appendage*, accessionem adjunxit aedibus, Cic, minima accessio semper Epirus regno Macedoniae fuit, Liv **C.** *addition to a tax*, decumae, Cic

accessus -ūs, m (accedo) *an approach to* **I.** Lit, **A.** ad urbem nocturnus, Cic, accessus stellarum et recessus, Cic, accessus et recessus aestuum, *ebb and flow*, Cic **B.** *admittance* to a person, dare alicui accessum, Ov **C.** *means of approach, entrance*, omnem accessum lustrare, Verg **II.** Transf, ad res salutares, *inclination to*, Cic, ad causam, *leading up to a subject*, Cic

1 **accīdo** -cidi -cisum, 3 (ad and caedo), **1,** Lit, *to hew or hack at*, aut ab radicibus subruere aut accidere arbores, Caes **2,** Transf, *to weaken, ruin*, Latinorum etsi pariter accisae copiae sint, Liv, res accisae, Cic

2 **accĭdo** -cidi, no sup 3 (ad and cado), *to fall down, to fall to.* **I.** Lit, **A.** Gen, ad terram, Plaut **B** Esp, **1,** of missiles, tela ab omni parte accidebant, Liv, **2,** *to fall at the feet of, to ask assistance*, ad pedes omnium, Cic, **3,** *to come to the ears or notice of*, vox accidit ad hostes, Liv **II.** Transf, **A.** *to happen* (generally of misfortunes, opposed to evenio), si quid adversi accidisset, Caes, impers, **1,** accidit, followed by ut, casu accidit ut id primus nuntiaret, Cic, by quod, accidit perincommode quod eum nusquam vidisti, Cic, by infinitive, nec accidernt mihi opus esse, Cic, **2,** si quid alicui acciderit, *if anything happens*, i e *if he dies*, Cic. **B.** *to fall out*, ut omnia contra opinionem acciderent, Caes.

accĭeo, 2. obs form of accio (q v)

accingo -cinxi -cinctum 3 **I.** Lit., *to gird to or on*, ensem lateri, Verg; miles non accinctus, *unarmed*, Tac. **II.** Transf, *to equip, to arm*, reflex, se accingere, and pass accingi, **a,** *to arm one's self*, studio popularium accinctus, Tac; magicas accingier artes, Verg., **b,** *to make one's self ready*, accingi ad consulatum, *to strive for the consulship*, Liv; accingunt operi = se accingunt, Verg (Infin pass, accingier, Verg)

accio ivi (-ii) itum, 4 *to call to, summon, fetch*, haruspices ex Etruria Cic, aliquem in adoptionem, Tac, with double acc, aliquem doctorem filio, Cic

accĭpio -cēpi ceptum, 3. (ad and capio) **I.** *to take, receive* **A** Gen, **1,** accipere pecuniam, Cic., **2,** of business transactions, aliquid (alicui) acceptum referre, *to enter on the credit side of an account book*, Cic, hence subst, **acceptum** i, *what is received*, codex accepti et expensi, *an account book*, Cic, **3,** where the thing received is a person, cujus abavi manibus esset accepta (Mater Idaea), Cic, **4,** *to receive* in or on a part of the body, alvus omne quod accepit cogit atque confundit, Cic, aliquem gremio, Verg, **5,** *to receive in a friendly manner*, **a,** Romanos in arcem, Liv, in amicitiam, Cic, in deditionem, Caes, **b,** of places, pavidos Samnites castra sua accepere, Liv, **c,** *to receive as a guest*, hospitio, Cic; **6,** *to treat*, **a,** *in a friendly way*, aliquem leniter clementerque, Cic, **b,** *in a hostile way*, aliquem verberibus ad necem, Cic, **7,** with reference to the senses, *to hear*, orationem, Cic, pronis auribus accipi, *to be willingly listened to*, Tac; of the understanding, *to grasp*, quae parum accepi, Cic, of the judgment, *to take*, aliquid in bonum partem, *to take in good part*, Cic, verisimilia pro veris, Liv, with double acc, beneficium contumeliam, *to take a kindness for an insult*, Cic **B.** *to accept, not to reject*, pacem, Liv; omen, Cic, legem, Cic **II.** In a wider sense, *to get, receive, obtain*, **1,** lucrum, Cic, adulterinos nummos pro bonis, Cic, **2,** *to feel*, dolorem, Cic, **3,** *to hear*, multa auribus accepisse, multa vidisse, Cic; ut accepi a senibus, Cic, **4,** *to learn*, primas artes ab iisdem magistris, Ov, usum ac disciplinam ab aliquo, Caes

accĭpĭter -tris, m **I.** Lit, *a hawk*, Cic **II.** Transf, pecuniae, *an avaricious person*, Plaut

accītus ūs, m *a summons*, Cic.

Accius -a -um, *name of a Roman gens, the most famous member of which was Accius, a celebrated dramatic poet* (born A C 170) Adj, **Acciānus** a -um, *of Accius*, versus, Cic

acclāmātĭo -ōnis, f *a loud cry;* 1, *an outcry against;* non modo ut acclamatione sed ut convicio et maledictis impediretur, Cic, 2, *a cry of approbation*, Liv, Cic

acclāmo, 1 (ad and clamo), **1,** *to cry out at* (in derision or disapproval), alicui, Cic, populus cum risu acclamavit ipsa esse, Cic, **2,** *to cry out* in approval, omnes acclamarunt gratias se inter cetera etiam ob hoc agere, quod, etc, Liv, **3,** with acc of person, *to name by acclamation*, aliquem servatorem liberatoremque, Liv; si nocentem acclamaverant, Tac

acclāro, 1 *to make clear, to reveal* (of omens), Liv, uti tu signa nobis certa acclarassis (for acclaraveris), Liv

acclīnis -e **I.** Lit, *leaning on anything*, trunco arboris, Verg **II.** Transf, *inclined to*, acclinis falsis animus, Hor

acclīno, 1 (ad and * clino) **I.** Lit, *to lean on anything*, se in illum, Ov; castra tumuli sunt acclinata, Liv **II.** Transf, *to incline to*, haud gravate se acclinaturos ad causam senatus, Liv.

acclīvis -e (ad and clivus), *gently inclined upwards;* pars viae, Cic.; collis leniter ab infimo acclivis, Caes.

acclīvĭtas -ātis, f. *acclivity, gentle inclination upwards,* Caes.

acclīvus -a -um, v. acclivis.

accŏla -ae, m. (ad and colo), *one who lives near, a neighbour;* Oceani, Liv.; Cereris, *near the temple of Ceres,* Cic.; as adj., pastor accola ejus loci, *dwelling near that place,* Liv.; accolae fluvii, *neighbouring rivers,* Tac.

accŏlo -cŏlŭi -cultum, 3. *to live near;* locum, Cic.; gentes quae Macedoniam accolunt, Liv.

accommŏdātē, adv. *agreeably to;* ad veritatem, Cic.

accommŏdātĭo -ōnis, f. **1**, *a proportion* or *adjusting of one thing to another;* verborum et sententiarum ad inventionem acc., Cic.; **2**, *courteousness, complaisance;* ex liberalitate atque accommodatione magistratuum, Cic.

accommŏdātus -a -um, p. adj. with compar. and superl. (from accommodo), *adapted, suitable to;* **1**, of things, with ad and the acc., puppes ad magnitudinem fluctuum tempestatemque accommodatae, Caes.; with dat., oratio hominum sensibus ac mentibus accommodata, Cic.; **2**, of persons, with ad and the acc., homo ad Verris flagitia libidinesque accommodatus, Cic.; with dat., servus vilissimus nec cuiquam serio ministerio accommodatus, Tac.

accommŏdo, 1. (ad and commodo), *to fit, put on.* **I.** Lit., insignia, Caes.; coronam sibi ad caput, Cic.; lateri ensem, Verg. **II.** Transf., *to make suitable, to adjust;* testes ad crimen, Cic.; orationem auribus auditorum, Cic.; in omnem eventum consilia, Liv.; se accommodare or accommodari, *to adapt oneself;* ad voluntatem alicuius et arbitrium et nutum totum se fingere et accommodare, Cic.

accommŏdus -a -um, *fit, adapted to,* Verg.

accrēdo -didi -ditum, 3. (ad and credo), *to believe, give credence to;* alicui, Hor.; absol., vix accredens, Cic.

accresco -crēvi -crētum, 3. (ad and cresco), *to grow, to increase.* **I.** Lit., flumen subito accrevit, Cic. **II.** Transf., quum dictis factisque omnibus ad fallendum instructis varia accresceret fides, Liv.; trimetris accrescere jussit nomen iambeis, *ordered to be joined to,* Hor.

accrētĭo -ōnis, f. (accresco), *increase;* luminis, Cic.

accŭbĭtĭo (accŭbātĭo) -ōnis, f. *the act of reclining at table,* Cic.

accŭbĭtus -ūs, m. = accubitio (q.v.).

accŭbo, 1. (ad and cubo), *to lie by the side of.* **I.** Gen., humi, Liv.; of wine, Sulpiciis horreis, Hor. **II.** Esp., *to recline at table;* in convivio, Cic.; cum aliquo, *next to,* Plaut.; apud aliquem, *at the house of* (as a guest), Cic.; accuba, *take your place,* Plaut.

accūdo, 3. *to hammer together,* Plaut.

accumbo -cŭbui -cŭbĭtum, 3. (ad and cumbo), *to lie down;* **1**, in via, Plaut.; **2**, especially used of the Romans at the dinner table, where each person lay upon a sofa, supported on his left elbow; in sinu alicujus, *to sit next to any one at table,* Liv.; cum aliquo, *next to,* Mart.; apud aliquem, *at the house of* (as a guest), Cic.

accŭmŭlātē, adv. *abundantly, copiously,* Cic.

accŭmŭlātor -ōris, m. *one who heaps together;* opum, Tac.

accŭmŭlo, 1. (ad and cumulo), *to heap up, to accumulate.* **I.** Lit., auget, addit, accumulat, Cic. **II.** Transf., **1**, *to heap on a person, give in abundance;* alienas res, Liv.; alicui summum honorem, Ov.; **2**, *to overwhelm;* animam nepotis his donis, Verg.; **3**, *to increase;* caedem caede, Lucr.; curas, Ov.

accūrātē, adv. *carefully, exactly, accurately;* aliquid studiose accurateque facere, Cic.; perscribere, Cic.; aedificare, Caes.

accūrātĭo -ōnis, f. *accuracy, carefulness,* Cic.

accūrātus -a -um, p. adj. with compar. and superl. (from accuro), *careful, exact, accurate;* oratio, Cic.; accuratiorem delectum habere, Liv.; accuratissima diligentia, Cic.

accūro, 1. (ad and curo), *to take care of, to prepare with care;* victum et cultum, Cic.

accurro -curri and -cucurri -cursum, 3. (ad and curro), *to run to, to run up, to hasten up;* ad praetorem, Cic.; equo admisso ad aliquem, Caes.; of things, *to occur;* istae imagines ita nobis dicto audientes sunt, ut, simulatque velimus, accurrant, Cic.

accursus -ūs, m. *a running to, concourse,* Tac.

accūsābĭlis -e, *blameworthy,* Cic.

accūsātĭo -ōnis, f. **I.** *an accusation;* accusationem factitare, Cic.; comparare atque constituere, *to prepare with evidence,* Cic.; plur., acres accusationes, Cic. **II.** Met., *the indictment;* accusationis quinque libri, *of the orations against Verres,* Cic.

accūsātor -ōris, m. **1**, *an accuser* (strictly only in regard to state offences, while petitor is a plaintiff in a private suit); petitoris personam cupere, accusatoris deponere, Cic.; **2**, *an informer,* Juv.

accūsātōrĭē, adv. *after the manner of an accuser;* loqui, Cic.

accūsātōrĭus -a -um, *pertaining to an accuser;* lex, Cic.

accūsātrix -icis, f. *a female accuser,* Plaut.

accūsĭto, 1. (freq. of accuso), *to accuse frequently,* Plaut.

accūso, 1. (ad and causa), *to accuse* (generally in public cases); **1**, aliquem ad populum (of the tribunes), Liv.; **a**, with genit., of the offence, aliquem ambitus, Cic.; **b**, with abl., de veneficiis, Cic.; **c**, with propter, propter injurias, Cic.; **d**, with inter, inter sicarios, *of assassination,* Cic.; **e**, with genit., of the punishment, capitis, *on a capital charge,* Cic.; **2**, *to blame, find fault with;* aliquem aspere et acerbe in senatu, Cic.; followed by quod and the subj., and by cur with the subj., Cic.

1. **ăcer** -ĕris, n. *the maple tree,* Ov.

2. **ācer** -cris -cre (from root AC, as acuo, acies, etc.), *sharp, cutting.* **I.** Lit., of sharp tools, hastas acri ferro, Tac. **II.** Transf., **A.** Of the senses; **1**, of taste, *biting;* rapula, Hor.; **2**, of touch, *sharp;* dolor corporis cujus morsus est acerrimus, Cic.; **3**, of hearing, *shrill;* vox, Lucr.; flammae sonitus, *crackling,* Verg.; **4**, of smell, *penetrating;* unguenta summa et acerrima suavitate condita, Cic.; **5**, of sight, *keen;* acerrimus sensus videndi, Cic. **B.** Relating to the feelings; **1**, of emotions, *painful;* cura, Lucr.; **2**, of the understanding, *vigorous;* judicium acrius et certius, Cic.; **3**, of the character, **a**, *energetic;* homo ad perdiscendum acerrimus, Cic.; in ferro, *brave in fight,* Cic.; **b**, *passionate;* acerrima uxor, Plaut.; so of the passions themselves, amor gloriae, Cic.; **c**, hence of abstractions, supplicium, Cic. Subst., **ācre** -is, n. *acrimony, severity* (opp. to ridiculum), Hor.

ăcerbē, adv **I.** *bitterly, harshly*, accusare, Cic, acerbius invehi in aliquem, Cic, acerbissime dicere, Caes **II.** *with difficulty* or *pain*, aliquid ferre, Cic

ăcerbĭtas -ātis, f **I.** Lit, *bitterness of taste*, Cic **II.** Transf, 1, *harshness*, morum, Cic, 2, *painfulness;* temporis Sullani, Cic, in plur, *calamities*, Cic

ăcerbo, 1. *to make bitter, to aggravate* or *heighten*, crimen, Verg

ăcerbus -a -um **I. A.** Lit, 1, *bitter in taste, sour*, used especially of unripe fruit, hence = *raw, unripe, immature*, uva, Phaedr, partus, *premature*, Ov **B.** Transf, 1, of the voice, *harsh*, stridor, Plin; acerba sonans, Verg, 2, of the touch, *rough;* frigus, Hor, 3, of the look, *dark, gloomy*, vultus acerbi, Ov, acerba tuens, *with angry look*, Verg **II.** Fig, **A.** Of persons, *morose*, acerbos e Zenonis schola exire (of the Stoics), Cic **B.** Of things, 1, *painful, severe, harsh*, acerbissima tributa, Cic, 2, of speech or writing, *bitter*, minaces et acerbae litterae, Cic, 3, of events, *painful*, incendium, Cic

ăcernus -a -um (1 acer), *made of maple wood*, Verg, Hor

ăcerra ae, f *a casket for keeping incense*, Cic

Ăcerrae -ārum, f *town in Campania, on the river Clanius* (now *Acerra*)

ăcersĕcŏmēs -ae, m (ἀκερσεκόμης), *having unshorn hair*, Juv.

ăcervālis -e, *that which is heaped up* = σωρείτης, *an argument by accumulation*, Cic

ăcervātim, adv **I.** Lit, *in heaps*, Lucr **II.** Transf, dicere, *to sum up, to speak comprehensively*, Cic, multa acervatim frequentans, *crowding together a number of thoughts*, Cic

ăcervo, 1 *to heap up*, promiscue acervati cumuli hominum, Liv

ăcervus i, m (connected with ἀγείρω), *a heap.* **I.** Lit, tritici, Cic; insepulti acervi civium, Cic **II.** Transf, **A.** *a multitude*, facinorum, Cic **B.** Logical term, *argument by accumulation*, Cic

ăcesco ăcŭi, 3 (aceo), *to grow sour*, Hor

Ăcesta ae, f (Ἄκεστη), *an old town in the north of Sicily*, also called Egesta and Segesta (now *Castel a Mare di Golfo*), hence **Acestenses** ium, *inhabitants of Acesta.*

Ăcestes -ae, m *king in Sicily, of Trojan descent*

ăcētum -i, n (aceo) **I.** Lit, *vinegar*, Cic **II.** Transf, *acuteness, wit*, Italo perfusus aceto, Hor

Ăchaei ōrum, m (Ἀχαιοί) **I.** *the Achaeans, inhabitants of the Greek country of Achaia*, Liv, also, **a**, *the Greeks in general*, Plin, **b**, *the inhabitants of the Roman province of Achaia*, Cic, **c**, *inhabitants of a Greek colony on the Euxine*, Ov **II.** Hence, 1, **Achaeus** -a um, **a**, *belonging to the Greek country of Achaia*, Lucr, **b**, *Greek, belonging to the Roman province of Achaia*, Cic, 2, **Achāia** ae, f (Ἀχαΐα), or **Achāja** ae, f **a**, *the Greek country of Achaia*, in the north of the Peloponnese, Ov, **b**, after 146 B C, *the Roman province of Achaia* (including the whole of Greece except Thessaly), Cic, 3, **Achāias** ădis, f *a Greek woman*, Ov., 4, **Achāicus** a-um, *Greek*, Cic, 5, **Achāis** -ĭdos, *an Achaean woman*, Ov, poet = *Greece*, Ov, 6, **Achāius** a -um, *Greek*, Verg, 7, **Achivi** -orum, m *the Homeric Greeks* (genit plur, Achivom and Achivum) Adj, **Achivus** -a -um, *Greek*, Ov

Ăchaemĕnēs -is, m (Ἀχαιμένης), *grandfather of Cyrus, and founder of the Persian line of the Achaemenidae* Hence adj, **Achaemĕnius** a -um, *Persian*, Ov

Ăcharnae -ōrum, f (Ἀχαρναί), *a town in Attica* Hence adj, **Acharnānus** -a -um, *born at Acharnae*

Ăchātes -ae, m (Ἀχάτης), 1, *river in Sicily*, 2, *friend of Aeneas*

Ăchĕlōus -i, m (Ἀχελῷος) *a river between Acarnania and Aetolia*, hence, **A. Achĕlōĭas** ădis, f *daughter of the river-god Achelous, Parthenope*, Ov **B. Achelōĭus** -a um, *belonging to the river god Achelous*, Ov **C. Achelōides** um, f *the Sirens*, Ov

Ăchĕron -ontis, m (Ἀχέρων), 1, *a river in Thesprotia*, flowing through the swamp Acherusia (now *Gurla*, or *river of Suli*), 2, *a river in Bruttii* (now *Mucone* or *Lese*), 3, Mythol, *river in the lower world*, hence *the lower world itself*, Acheronta movebo, Verg, fugere Acheronta, *to become immortal*, Hor

Ăchĕrontĭa ae, f *a small town in Apulia*, Hor

Ăchĕruns untis, m and f Latin form of Acheron, *the lower world* Hence adj, **Ăchĕrūsius** -a -um Subst, **Acherusia** -ae, f **a**, *a swamp in Thesprotia*, **b**, *a lake in Campania*, **c**, *a cavern in Bithynia*

Ăchilles -is, m (Ἀχιλλεύς), and **Ăchillēus** ĕi, m *a Greek hero, son of Peleus and Thetis*, appell, *a brave handsome man, a hero*, Verg, hence, 1, **Achillēus** a -um, *relating to Achilles*, 2, **Achillides** -ae, m (Ἀχιλλείδης), *a descendant of Achilles*

Achīvus -a um = Achaeus (q v)

Achradīna -ae, f (Ἀχραδινή), *the most important part of the city of Syracuse*, Cic

Ăcīdălĭa -ae, f (Ἀκιδαλία), *a surname of Venus*, from the fountain Acidalia in Boeotia, where the Graces, daughters of Venus, bathed Adj, **Acīdălius** -a -um, *belonging to Venus;* nodus, *the girdle of Venus*, Mart

ăcĭdus -a -um (aceo), *sharp* **I.** Lit, *sour in taste, acid*, Hor **II.** Transf, *disagreeable, unpleasant*, Hor

ăcĭēs -ēi, f (AC, root of acuo), *keenness, edge* **I.** Lit, of a sharp instrument, securis, Cic, fig, patimur hebescere aciem horum auctoritatis, Cic **II.** Transf, **A.** Of the eye, 1, *piercing look*, ne vultum quidem atque aciem oculorum ferre potuisse, Caes, 2, *vision*, bonum incolumis acies, malum caecitas, Cic., poet, *the twinkling of the stars*, Verg, 3, *the pupil of the eye*, Cic, met, *the eye itself*, Verg, hence, 4, of the mind, *insight, keenness*, animi, ingenii, mentis, Cic **B.** Milit t t, 1, *an army drawn up in line of battle*, **a**, *a single line*, prima, Caes; novissima, Liv, and **b**, *the whole army*, aciem instruere, Cic, 2, *battle*, Pharsalica, Cic., in acie vincere, Caes, poet, Vulcania, *mass of fire*, Verg Transf, *a battle in words*, Cic

Ăcīlius a -um, *name of a Roman gens*, the most famous members of which were 1, *Man Acil Glabrio, Consul* A C 192, *conqueror of Antiochus and the Aetolians*, 2, *C Acil Glabrio, author of a Roman history in Greek*

Ăcilla, and **Ăcylla**, and **Ăcholla** -ae, f *town of the Carthaginians in Byzacium* (near modern Elalia)

ăcīnăcēs -is, m (ἀκινάκης), *a short Persian sabre*, Hor

ăcĭnus -i, m and **ăcĭnum** -i, n *a berry* (esp *grape*), Cic

ăcĭpenser -ĕris (ăcipensis -is), m *a fish, highly prized by the Romans, the sturgeon* according to Cuvier, Cic

Ăcis -idis, m. (Ἄκις), 1, *a river in Sicily*, near Aetna, famous for its cold water (now *Fiume di Jaci*), Ov.; 2, Mythol., *a beautiful shepherd, lover of Galatea*, Ov.

ăclys -ȳdis, f. (perhaps shortened from ἀγκυλίς), *a small javelin*, Verg.

Acmŏnĭa -ae, f. *a town of Phrygia*, on the road from Dorylaeum to Philadelphia (now *Ahatkoi*); hence **Acmŏnensis** -e, *relating to Acmonia*.

Acmŏnĭdes -ae, m. (Ἀκμονίδης), *one of the workmen of Vulcan*.

ăcŏnītum -i, n. (ἀκόνιτον), *a poisonous herb, monk's hood, aconite*, Plin.; poet. = poison, Verg.

acquĭesco -quiēvi -quiētum, 3. (ad and quiesco), *to rest, repose*; 1, physically, a, of persons, tres horas, Cic.; euphem., *to die*; anno acquievit sexagesimo, Nep.; b, of things, aures in eo acquiescant, Cic.; rem familiarem acquiescere, *not to be seized*, Liv.; 2, mentally, a, mentis agitatio quae numquam acquiescit, Cic.; b, *to find rest* or *comfort in*; in his (litteris tuis) acquiesco, Cic.; c, *to be satisfied* or *pleased with*; in adolescentium caritate, Cic.; Clodii morte, Cic.

acquīro -quīsivi -quīsitum, 3. (ad and quaero). I. *to add to, acquire*, as an increase to what is already possessed; dignitatem, Cic.; vires acquirit eundo, Verg. II. A. Gen., *to acquire, get*; triumphos de populis, Tac. B. Absol., *to amass money*; acquirendi insatiabile votum, Juv.

acra -ae, f. (ἄκρα), *a summit, height, promontory*, Plin.

Acraeus -a -um (ἀκραῖος), *that which is upon a height, surname of Jupiter and Juno*, Liv.

ăcrātŏphŏron -i, n. (ἀκρατοφόρον), *a vessel for holding unmixed wine*, Cic.

ăcrēdŭla -ae, f. *a bird* (variously explained as *the thrush, the owl*, or *the nightingale*), Cic.

ăcrĭcŭlus -a -um (2. acer), *somewhat sharp, violent*; ille acriculus, Cic.

ăcrĭmōnĭa -ae, f. 1, *sharpness of taste* or *pungency of smell*, Plin.; 2, *energy of speech and demeanour*, Cic.

Ăcrĭsĭus -ii, m. (Ἀκρίσιος), *a king of Argos, father of Danaë*. Hence, 1, **Acrĭsĭōne** -es, f. *Danaë*; 2, **Ăcrĭsĭōnĭădes** -ae, m. *Perseus, son of Danaë*; 3, adj., **Acrĭsĭōnēus** -a -um, arces, *Argos*, Ov.

ăcrĭtĕr, adv. (2. acer), *sharply, violently, strongly*; 1, of the senses; a, of the sight, acriter intueri solem, *steadfastly, without being dazzled*, Cic.; b, of touch, *painfully*; caedunt acerrime virgis, Cic.; c, of hearing, *penetratingly*, Plin.; 2, of the mind, etc.; a, of the understanding, *with sharp insight*; videre vitia, Cic.; b, of action, *courageously*; se morti offerre, Cic.; c, of the passions, *passionately*; acerrime exspectare, *longingly*, Cic.; in speech, *violently*; vituperare, Cic.

ăcrŏāmă -ătis, n. (ἀκρόαμα), *that which is heard with pleasure*; Esp., 1, *an entertainment at table of reading* or *music*, Cic.; 2, Meton., *the person who conducts such an entertainment, a reader, actor*, or *singer*, Cic.

ăcrŏāsis -is, f. (ἀκρόασις), *an assembly of persons to listen to reading aloud*, Cic.

Ăcrŏcĕraunĭa -orum, n. 1, *part of the Ceraunian mountains*, v. Ceraunius; 2, appell., *a dangerous place*; haec Acroceraunia vita, Ov.

Ăcrŏcŏrinthus -i, f. (Ἀκροκόρινθος), *the citadel of Corinth*, Liv.

1. **acta** -ae, f. (ἀκτή), *the sea-shore, the beach*, especially as a place of recreation, Cic.; hence, meton., *the pleasures of life at the seaside*, Cic.

2. **acta** -ōrum, n. (part. of ago), 1, *actions*; Caesaris non modo acta verum etiam cogitata, Cic.; 2, *public acts, ordinances*; servare, Cic.; especially *the register* of these acts; a, of the senate, Tac.; b, of the people, Cic.; c, of courts of justice, Cic.; acta diurna, *a kind of official gazette published daily in Rome*, Tac.

Actaeōn -ŏnis, m. (Ἀκταίων), *son of Aristaeus, a hunter, who for seeing Diana while bathing was turned into a stag, and torn to pieces by his dogs*.

Actē -ēs, f. (Ἀκτή), *coast land, an old name of Attica*; hence, a, **Actaeus** -a -um, *belonging to Attica* or *Athens*; subst., **Actaei** -orum, *the people of Attica*; b, **Actiăs** -ădis, f. *Attic*, Verg.

Actĭăcus -a -um, v. under Actium.

actĭo -ōnis, f. (ago). I. *motion*, hence *the action of the body*; 1, of an orator, *gesture*, Cic.; 2, of an actor, *action*, Cic. II. A. Gen., *doing, action*; gratiarum, *giving of thanks*, Cic.; primas eius actiones horreo, Cic. B. Esp., *public action*; 1, *the action of any magistrate, proposal*; consularis, Cic.; actio de pace sublata est, Liv.; 2, *action in a court of justice*; a, *the bringing of an action*; inquieta urbs actionibus, Tac.; b, *the action itself*; actionem instituere, constituere, intendere, Cic.; and so, c, *the formula used in bringing an action*; actiones componere, *to draw statements of claim*, Cic.; and gen., *a legal formula*; actiones Hostilianae, Cic.; d, *the speech on an indictment*; actiones Verrinae, Cic.; e, *the permission* or *right to bring an action*; actionem habere, postulare, dare, accipere, restituere, Cic.; f, *the hearing of an action*; altera, tertia, Cic.

actĭto, 1. (freq. of ago), *to be busy in pleading* or *acting*, used of the theatres and courts of law; causas multas, Cic.; tragoedias, Cic.

Actĭum -ii, n. (Ἄκτιον). I. *a promontory in Acarnania*, on which stood a temple of Apollo; hard by was fought the naval battle (A.C. 31) in which Augustus conquered Antony and Cleopatra. II. *a roadstead near Corcyra*. Hence adj., 1, **Actĭăcus** -a -um; frondes, *the leaves of the bay tree*, sacred to Apollo, Ov.; legiones, *those that fought at Actium*, Tac.; 2, **Actĭus** -a -um; bella, *the battle of Actium*, Verg.

actor -ōris, m. (ago), 1, *a driver*; pecoris, Ov.; 2, *an actor*; secundarum et tertiarum partium, Cic.; 3, a, *one who accomplishes anything*; rerum, Cic.; b, *a public speaker*, Cic.; c, *the plaintiff in an action*, Cic.; d, *the manager of property* or *finances*; actor publicus, *one who manages public property*, Tac.

Actŏrĭdēs -ae, m. (Ἀκτορίδης), *a descendant of Actor, e.g., Menoetius* (son of Actor), or *Patroclus* (grandson of Actor), Ov.

actŭārĭŏla -ae, f. (dim. of actuaria), *a small skiff*, Cic.

actŭārĭus -a -um (ago), *easily moved, swift*; actuaria navis, *a swift-sailing vessel*, Caes.; navigium actuarium, Caes. Subst., **actŭārĭa** -ae, f. Cic.

actŭōsē, adv. *actively, with energy*, Cic.

actŭōsus -a -um, *active*; virtus, Cic.; of a speech, *effective*, Cic.

actus -ūs, m. (ago). I. *motion*; fertur magno mons improbus actu, Verg. II. *putting in motion*. A. 1, *driving of cattle*; levi admonitu, non actu, inflectit illam feram, Cic.; 2, Meton., *right of way for driving cattle, carts, etc.*, Cic. B. *movement of the body*; of an actor or orator, *gesture*, Liv. C. 1, esp., *presentation of a piece on the stage*; fabellarum, Liv.; 2, *division of a piece, an act*; in extremo actu corruere, Cic.; 3, Transf., extremus actus aetatis, Cic.

actūtum, adv *immediately, directly,* Liv

ăcŭlĕātus a -um (aculeus) I Lit, of plants and animals, *provided with prickles or stings,* Plin II. Transf, *sharp pointed, stinging,* litterae, Cic, sophisma, *hair-splitting, subtle,* Cic

ăcŭlĕus -i, m (dim of acus), *sting* I. A. Of animals, apis, Cic B. Of missiles, *point,* sagittae, Liv II. Transf, especially in plur, A. *sarcasm,* aculei in C Caesarem, Cic B. *sting,* sollicitudinum, Cic C. *deep impression* (of a speech), orator cum delectatione aculeos relinquit in animis, Cic

ăcūmen -inis, n (acuo), *the sharp point of anything.* I. Lit., stili, Cic II. Transf, A. *point* (of something witty), etiam interpretatio nominis habet acumen, Cic B. *sharpness of understanding,* ubi est acumen tuum? Cic C. *cunning, trickery,* argutiae et acumen ejus, Cic

ăcŭo -ŭi -ūtum, 3. (AC, root of acus and acies), *to sharpen to a point* I. Lit, *to whet* (a cutting instrument), gladios, Liv II. Transf, *to sharpen, practise.* A. linguam exercitatione dicendi, *to make more fluent,* Cic, ingenia adolescentium, Cic B. *to inflame,* iram hostis ad vindicandas injurias, Liv C. *to encourage, incite,* juventutem ad dicendum, Cic

ăcus ūs, f (AC, root of acuo and acies), *a needle, a bodkin,* vulnus, quod acu punctum videtur, Cic, acu pingere, *to embroider,* Verg, acu rem tetigisti, *you have hit the right nail on the head,* Plaut.

ăcūtē, adv (acutus), *keenly* I. Of the senses, cernere, Lucr, of the voice, *shrilly,* sonare, Cic II. Of the understanding, *keenly,* acute arguteque respondere, Cic

ăcūtŭlus a -um (dim of acutus), *somewhat subtle,* Cic

ăcūtus -a -um, p adj with compar and superl (from acuo), *sharpened, pointed, acute* I. Lit, sagitta, Ov, of anything pointed, cornua lunae, Cic. II. Transf, A. Of physical sensations, 1, referring to particular senses, a, of hearing, *shrill,* vox, Cic; acc neut as adv, resonare triste et acutum, Hor, b, of touch, *piercing,* gelu, Hor, 2, of the whole body, *painful;* morbus, Hor poet, acuta belli, *the hardships of war,* Hor B. Of mental perceptions, 1, *sharp, keen,* populi Romani oculos esse acres atque acutos, Cic, acc neut as adv, cernis acutum, *you have keen sight* (for the failings of others), Hor., 2, of persons, *keen-sighted, vigorous,* homo acutus magis quam eruditus, Cic, of orators, *effective,* orator, Cic

ad, prep with acc, expressing direction, *towards, to* I Of space, A. Lit, 1, of motion, *towards,* concurrere ad curiam, Cic, ad Dianae venire, *to the temple of Diana* (sc aedem), Ter, ad me, ad te, etc, *to my house,* Cic, so of extension, ab imis unguibus usque ad verticem summum, Cic, 2, of rest, *in the direction of, near,* sedere ad latus ejus, Cic, esse ad portas (of Roman generals waiting outside Rome for a triumph), Cic, esse ad aliquem, *to be on a visit to a person,* Cic; ad judicem, *before a judge,* Cic, ad tibiam, *to the sound of the flute,* Cic B. Transf, 1, to express direction or extent, a, of direction (α) esp with verbs implying motion, as movere, ducere, etc, (β) of striving after an object, with such nouns as cupiditas, aviditas, etc, and such adjectives, as acer, propensus, etc, (γ) of aim or purpose, *to, for,* adjutorem ad injuriam, Cic, so with adj like natus, aptus, etc, and verbs as adjuvare, etc, ad id, *for that object,* Liv, quid ad rem? *what is the object of this?* Cic, quid ad me, *what has this to do with me?* Cic, so (αα) of medicines, *for, against,* radicum genera ad (*to cure*) morsus bestiarum, Cic, (ββ) of occupation, *to, for,* servos ad remum dare, Liv, (δ) *in relation to* impiger ad labores belli, Cic, (ε) *in comparison with,* scuta ad amplitudinem corporum parum lata, Liv, b, of extent, *to, up to,* (α) virgis ad necem caedi, Cic, ad extremum, ultimum, *entirely,* homo non ad extremum perditus, Liv, ad summam, *on the whole,* Cic, (β) of numbers, *to the amount of,* etc, ad unum omnes, *all to a man,* Cic, ad assem perdere, *to lose your last farthing,* Hor, (γ) *near to, about,* (fuimus) omnino ad ducentos, Cic, 2, a, *in addition to,* ad cetera hanc quoque plagam infligere, Cic, ad hoc, *besides,* Sall, b, *in consequence of,* ad famam belli novas legiones scribere, Liv, c, *according to* (some standard), ad istorum normam Cic, ad verbum, *literally,* Cic II. Of time, 1, a, of extent, *up to,* ab hora octava ad vesperum, Cic, ad hoc tempus, *till now,* Cic, quem ad finem? *how long?* Cic, b, of duration, ad paucos dies, *for a few days,* 2, of point of time, a, *at, towards,* nos te hic ad mensem Januarium exspectamus, Cic, ad lucem, *in the morning,* Cic, ad tempus, *in due time,* Cic, b, *within,* ad annum tribunum plebis fore, Cic

ădactĭo -ōnis, f (adigo), *a driving to, compulsion,* jurisjurandi (*obligation*), Liv

ădactus -ūs, m (adigo), *a bringing to,* dentis, *a bite,* Lucr

ădaequē, adv *in like manner,* Liv

ădaequo, 1 A. Lit, *to make equal with,* moles moenibus, Caes B. Transf, 1, *to equalise,* a, with cum and the abl, cum virtute fortunam, Cic, b, with dat, se virtute nostris, Cic, so *to compare,* formam, aetatem, genus mortis magni Alexandri fatis, Tac, 2, *to come near to,* altitudinem muri, Caes, deorum vitam, Cic

ădămantēus -a -um, *hard as steel,* Ov

ădămantĭnus a -um (ἀδαμάντινος), *made of hard steel, adamantine,* Hor

ădămas -antis, m (ἀδάμας), 1, *the hardest steel, adamant,* nexae adamante catenae, Ov, poet *anything that is firm unyielding, and durable,* in pectore ferrum aut adamanta gerit, Ov, voce sua adamanta movere, *a heart of steel,* Mart, 2, *the diamond,* Plin

ădambŭlo, 1 *to walk by or near anything,* Plaut

ădămo, 1 I. *to fall in love with;* aliquem, Liv II. *to find pleasure in,* equos, Cic, gloriam, Cic

ădamussim, v amussis

ădăpĕrĭo -pĕrŭi pertum, 4 *to open fully;* adapertae fores portae, Liv

ădăpertĭlis e, *that which is capable of being opened,* latus tauri, Ov

ădapto, 1 *to fit to, adapt,* Suet

ădăquo, 1 *to supply with water, to give to drink,* Plin

ădăquor, 1 dep *to fetch water,* of soldiers, Caes

ădauctus ūs, m (adaugeo), *an increase,* Lucr

ădaugĕo auxi -auctum, 2 1, *to increase, to augment,* bonum, Cic, 2, of sacrifices, *to devote,* Plaut

ădaugesco, 3 *to begin to increase,* Cic poet

ădbĭbo -bĭbi -bĭbĭtum, 3 1, Lit, *to drink, drink in,* Ter, 2, Transf, of the ears, verba puro pectore, Hor.

adbīto, 3 *to go near,* Plaut

addĕcet, v impers *it becomes, suits,* Plaut

addensĕo, 2. and **addenso**, 1. *to make thick, or compact;* extremi addensent acies, Verg.

addīco -dixi -dictum, 3. *to assent to;* **1**, t.t. in augury, *to promise favourably* (of the omens of birds), Liv.; **2**, *to award;* **a**, of a judge, especially the praetor (whose formula was do, dico, addico); alicui bona, Cic.; liberum corpus in servitutem, Liv.; esp., *to award a debtor as a slave to his creditor;* ob creditam pecuniam addici, Liv.; addictus, *a debtor thus adjudged a slave,* Liv.; **b**, of an auctioneer, *to knock down to a bidder;* fundum alicui, Cic.; alicui aliquid nummo sestertio, or simply nummo, *to give* (by a fictitious sale), Cic., Hor.; *to put up for sale* (of the vendor); aedes, Cic.; transf., regna pecunia, Cic.; **3**, *to give up* or *over,* alicuius bona in publicum, *to confiscate,* Cic.; aliquem perpetuae servituti, Caes.; so addictus, *bound, pledged;* nullius addictus jurare in verba ministri, Hor.; se alicui, in a bad sense, *to give oneself up to slavishly;* se senatui, Cic.

addictĭo -ōnis, f. (addico), *the judge's award;* bonorum possessionumque, Cic.

addictus -a -um, v. addico.

addisco -didĭci, no sup. 3. *to learn in addition;* artem, Cic.

addĭtāmentum -i, n. *an addition;* Ligus, additamentum inimicorum meorum, Cic.

addo -didi -dĭtum, 3. **I.** *to give to, to give, to place.* **A.** Lit., epistolas in fasciculum, Cic.; soleam pedi, Ov.; of persons, alicui comitem, Verg. **B.** Transf., *to inspire, to cause, produce;* alicui alacritatem scribendi, Cic. **II.** *to add, increase,* Liv. **A.** Lit., **1**, unum granum, Cic.; gradum, *to hasten,* Liv.; **2**, of writing, *to add;* in orationem quaedam, *to make some additions,* Cic.; **3**, of reckoning, *to add;* addendo deducendoque, *by addition and subtraction;* videre quae reliqui summa fiat, Cic. **B.** Transf., **1**, hunc laborem ad quotidiana opera, Caes.; sceleri scelus, Liv.; **2**, *to give as a respite* (of time); paucos dies ad rem publicam gerendam, Cic.; **3**, *to add to something said, to say in addition;* addunt etiam de Sabini morte, Caes.; with acc. and infin., addit etiam illud, equos non optimos fuisse, Cic.; adde, or adde huc, or eo, with acc. subst. or quod, *add to this;* adde eo exsilia, luctus, Cic.

addŏcĕo, 2. *to teach in addition, to teach,* Hor.

addŭbĭto, 1. *to incline to doubt, to begin to doubt;* followed by de, in, num, an, utrum, quid; res addubitata, *a question undecided,* Cic.

addūco -duxi -ductum, 3. **I.** *to draw to oneself.* **A.** Gen., parvis colla lacertis (of children embracing their mother), Ov. **B.** Esp., **1**, *to draw tight to oneself;* balistae et reliqua tormenta contenta atque adducta vehementius, Cic.; **2**, *to draw together, to wrinkle;* adducit cutem macies, Ov. **II.** *to bring* (as a guide), or *lead* a thing or a person. **A.** Lit., **1**, of persons, aliquem in conspectum populi, Liv.; aliquem in jus or judicium, or simply aliquem, *to bring to justice,* Cic.; **2**, of things, aurum secum, Liv.; esp. of bringing water (by an aqueduct, etc.), aquam, Cic. **B.** Transf., **1**, *to bring to a certain condition;* aliquem in vituperationem, invidiam, Cic.; eo adduxit eos ut, etc., Cic.; se suumque regnum in ultimum discrimen, Liv.; **2**, *to bring a person to a certain state of mind;* in fletum, in metum, Cic.; adduci ad suspicandum, Cic.; followed by ut and the subj., adducis me ut tibi assentiar, Cic.; with infin., in spem adducti, hunc ipsum annum salutarem civitati fore, Cic.; with genit., in spem adductus conficiendi belli, Sall.; so adductus, *influenced;* spe mercedis, Cic.; absol., adducor igitur et prope modum assentior, Cic.

adductĭus, adv. compar. (adductus), *more severely,* Tac.

adductus -a -um, p. adj. (from adduco), of persons, *severe,* Tac.

ădĕdo -ēdi -ēsum, 3. *to nibble, to gnaw.* **I. A.** Lit., adesi favi, Liv. **B.** Transf., scopulus adesus aquis, Ov. **II.** *to consume, waste away;* non adesa jam sed abundanti etiam pecunia, Cic.

ădemptĭo -ōnis, f. (adimo), *a taking away;* civitatis, Cic.

1. **ădĕō**, adv. (ad and eoi, old dat. of is), *to that point, so far.* **I.** Lit., **A.** Of space, *so far,* Ter. **B.** Of time, *so long,* used with usque and followed by dum, donec, quoad, Cic. **II.** Transf., of degree, **a**, *so much, so,* followed by ut, Cic.; **b**, *even, what is more;* ducem hostium intra moenia atque adeo in senatu videmus, Cic.; **c**, used enclitically with pron., *just;* id adeo, Cic.; with conj., si, nisi, sive, aut, vel, Cic.; **d**, *to such an extent, so;* adeo prope omnis senatus Hannibalis fuit, Liv.; **e**, with non, *much less,* Tac.

2. **ădĕo** -ĭi -ĭtum, 4. *to go or come to, approach.* **I.** Lit., **A.** Gen., ad istum fundum, Cic.; curiam, Liv. **B.** Esp., **1**, adire in praetorem in jus; or simply in jus, *to go to law,* Cic.; **2**, *to travel to, to visit;* casas aratorum, Cic.; **3**, *to go to some one* for counsel or help; praetorem, Cic.; or for consulting about the future; magos, Cic.; or for prayer for help; aras, Cic.; **4**, *to approach as an enemy;* ad quemvis numerum ephippiatorum equitum adire audere, Cic. **II.** Transf., **1**, *to undertake some business;* ad causas privatas et publicas, Cic.; ad rempublicam, *to enter public life,* Cic.; **2**, *to come to some condition, to undergo, incur;* periculum capitis, Cic.; **3**, legal t. t., adire hereditatem, *to enter on an inheritance,* Cic.

ădeps -ĭpis, c. (connected with ἀλείφω), *the soft fat of animals;* meton., Cassii adipem, *the corpulent Cassius,* Cic.

ădeptĭo -ōnis, f. (adipiscor), *attainment, obtaining;* filii; commodi, Cic.

ădĕquĭto, 1. *to ride to;* with dat., ipsis portis, Liv.; with ad, ad nostros, Caes.; absol., Liv.

ădesdum, or ades dum, *come hither,* Ter.

ădēsŭrĭo, 4. *to hunger after anything,* Plaut.

adf, v. under aff . . .

adg, v. under agg . . .

ădhaerĕo -haesi -haesum, 2. *to hang to, stick to, adhere.* **A.** Lit., manus oneri adhaerentes, *frozen to,* Tac.; saxis, Liv. **B.** Transf., **1**, *to border on, to be near;* modica silva adhaerebat, Tac.; **2**, *to keep close to a person, to be always at the side of;* lateri adhaerere gravem dominum, *to sit on the neck of,* Liv.; so nulli fortunae adhaerebat animus, *depended upon,* Liv.; of things, cui canis cognomen adhaeret, *the nickname clings to him,* Hor.; of an appendage, summusque in margine versus adhaesit, *was written on the edge for want of room,* Ov.; so, of persons, te vix extremum adhaesisse, Cic.

ădhaeresco -haesi -haesum, 3. *to hang to, to adhere.* **A.** Lit., gravis lateri craterae limus adhaesit, Hor.; of burning missiles, ad turrim, Caes.; fig., in me uno consulares faces . . . in me omnia conjurationis tela adhaeserunt; of shipwrecks, ad saxa sironum, Cic.; fig., ad quamcumque sunt disciplinam quasi tempestate delati, ad eam tam quam ad saxum adhaerescunt, Cic. **B.** Transf., **1**, *to cling to, to remain;* in his locis adhaerescere, Cic.; justitiae honestatique, *not to swerve from,* Cic.; ad omnium vestrum studium, *sympathise with,* Cic.; **2**, of an orator, *to stick fast, stop,* Cic.

ădhaesĭo -ōnis, f (adhaereo), *clinging to*, atomorum, Cic

ădhaesus -ūs, m (adhaereo), *an adhering*, Lucr

ădhĭbĕo -ŭi -ĭtum, 2 (ad and habeo), *to bring one thing to another, to apply to* **I.** Gen, manus genibus, Ov, manus vectigalibus, *to lay hands on, to seize*, Cic., adhibete animos et mentes vestras, non solum aures, Cic **II.** Esp, **A** *to join, associate, add*, studio adhibito atque usu, Cic **B.** 1, *to apply* something to some particular end or object, orationem ad vulgus, Cic, aliem vim, Cic, morbis remedia, Cic, iambum in fabulis, Cic, fidem, Cic. 2, *to employ* or *call* a person to help or advise, etc, aliquem in consilium, Cic, aliquem in convivium, *to invite*, Cic, medicum, Cic, with double acc, aliquem patronum, Cic, Siciliam testem, Cic, with adv, *to treat*, aliquem liberaliter, Cic

ădhinnio, 4 *to neigh after* **I.** Lit, Ov **II** Transf, sic ad illius orationem adhinnivit, *neighed with joy at*, Cic

ădhortātĭo -ōnis, f *an exhortation*, Cic

ădhortātor -ōris, m *one who exhorts*; operis, Liv

ădhortor, 1 dep *to exhort, encourage* (especially of soldiers), omnes cohortes ordinesque, Caes, in bellum, Tac, ad defendendam rem publicam, Cic

ădhūc, adv (ad and huc, shortened to huc), *thus far, hitherto*, properly of place, but generally used of time, *hitherto*, 1, *up to the present time, till now*, a, of the actual present, usque adhuc, adhuc semper, adhuc dum, Cic, used with unus, non, neque, nihil, nullus, Cic, b, of the historic present, fluctuans adhuc animo, Liv, 2, of something which is continuing *still*; adhuc de consuetudine exercitationis loquor, nondum de ratione et sapientia, Cic, followed by ut or qui with the subj = *so far that*, Cic

Ădĭăbēnē -ēs, f (Ἀδιαβηνή), *a province of Assyria* (now *Kurdistan*) Adj, **Adĭăbēnus** -a um, *Adiabenian*

ădĭcĭo = adjicio (q v)

ădĭgo ēgi actum, 3 (ad and ago), *to drive to* **A.** Lit, 1, of cattle, pecus e vicis longinquioribus, Caes, 2, of men, aliquem fulmine ad umbras, Verg, so legal t t, arbitrum (old Lat for ad arbitrium), adigere aliquem, *to summon before an arbiter*, Cic; 3, of things, triremes per aestuaria Tac, quodam loco turri adacta, Caes **B.** Transf, 1, *to drive to, to compel to*, ad mortem, Tac, absol, adigit ita Postumia et Servius filius, Cic; legal and milit t t, aliquem ad jusjurandum, Caes, or jusjurandum, Cic, or jurejurando, or sacramento, Liv, *to put a man on his oath, to swear in*, 2, *to fashion*, in faciem prorae pinus adacta novae, Prop

ădĭmo ēmi emptum, 3 (ad and emo), *to take away*, 1, something painful, vincula canibus, Ov, dolores, Hor, 2, *to take away* (property), alicui pecuniam, vitam, Cic, with a and the abl, Cic, 3, *to take away* (a person), aliquem alicui, Cic.; esp of death, hence ademptus, poet *dead*, Hor

ădĭpātus -a um (adeps) **I.** Lit, *fatty, greasy* Subst, **ădĭpāta** -orum n *pastry made with grease*, Juv **II.** Transf, of style, *bombastic*, adipatae dictionis genus, Cic.

ădĭpiscor -eptus, 3 dep (ad and apiscor) **I.** *to come up to, to overtake*, fugientem, Liv **II.** Transf, *to obtain*, laudem, Cic, gloriam ex aliqua re, Nep, quod adeptus est per scelus, Cic, with genit, rerum adeptus, Tac, part, adeptus, used passively, eandem accusant adeptam, *when reached*, Cic., De Sen ii. 4.

ădĭtĭo -ōnis, f *a going to, an approach*, Plaut

ădĭtus -ūs, m (2 adeo), *a going to, an approach, access* **I. A.** Lit, 1, difficiles aditus habere ad pastum, Cic, 2, *right or possibility of entrance to*, aditus in id sacrarium non est viris, Cic, of audience of a person, homo rari aditus, *difficult of access*, Liv, faciles aditus ad eum privatorum, Cic, aditus ad aliquem intercludere, Cic, petentibus non dare, Nep, ad aliquem postulare, Tac **B.** Meton, *entrance to a place, approach*, aditus insulae muniti, Cic, aditus templi, Cic, ad castra, Caes, in Siciliam, Cic, omnes aditus claudere, or intercludere, Cic **II.** Transf, *opportunity of obtaining*, ad honorem, Cic, laudis, Cic

adjăcĕo, 2 *to lie by the side of, to be adjacent*, ad ostium Rhodani, Caes, with acc alone, Etruriam, Liv, with dat, agro Romano, Liv, absol, adjacente Tibri, Tac Subst, **adjăcentĭa** -ium, n *the neighbourhood*, Tac

adjectĭo -ōnis, f (adjicio) *an adding to*, adjectione populi Albani, Liv, illiberali adjectione, *a paltry advance*, Liv, Hispaniensibus familiarum adjectiones dedit, *incorporated new families*, Tac

adjectus -ūs, m (adjicio), *an adding to*, Lucr

adjĭcĭo jēci -jectum, 3 (ad and jacio), *to throw to* **I. A.** Lit, telum, Caes **B.** Transf 1, *to cast* a longing look upon, oculum hereditati, Cic, 2, *to direct* the thoughts to, dictis mentem, Ov **II. A.** *to apply*, stimulos frementi, Ov **B.** *to add*, 1, Lit, aggerem ad munitiones, Caes, 2, Transf, a, ad belli laudem doctrinae et ingenii gloriam, Cic, b, *to add* to what has been said, Liv, 3, *to outbid* at an auction, supra adjecit Aeschrio, Cic

adjūdĭco, 1 *to award as a judge, adjudicate, to decide as a judge* **I.** Lit, causam alicui, in favour of any one, Cic, regnum Ptolemaeo, *to assign* the kingdom to Ptolemy, Cic **II.** Transf, Italis adjudicat armis, *assigns to the Roman power*, Hor, alicui salutem imperii hujus atque orbis terrarum, Cic

adjūmentum, -i, n (adjuvo), *help, assistance*, alicuius rei, ad aliquid, alicui rei, in aliqua re, Cic

adjunctĭo -ōnis, f (adjungo), *a joining to* **I.** *addition to, union*, a, naturae ad hominem, Cic, b, a rhet figure = συνεζευγμένον, where the predicate stands either at the beginning or the end of a clause **II.** *a joining to, adding to, connexion, union*, a, verborum, Cic, b, in rhet, *a limitation, restriction*, Cic

adjunctor -ōris, m (adjungo), *one who joins, connects*, ille Galliae ulterioris adjunctor (i e, Pompeius, who caused Gallia Ulterior to be added to Caesar's province), Cic

adjunctus a -um, p adj (from adjungo), *bound to, belonging to*, propiora hujus causae et adjunctiora, Cic Subst, **adjuncta** -ōrum, n *things closely connected with*, or *suitable to*, anything, Cic

adjungo -junxi -junctum, 3 *to join to, bind to* **I.** Lit, 1, of animals, plostello mures, Hor, 2, of vines, ulmis vites, Verg **II.** Transf, *to join, add* **A.** 1, of space, a, of things, parietem ad parietem communem, Cic, adjunctus fundus, *neighbouring*, Cic, b, of persons, belluis adjuncto humano corpori, Cic, juris scientiam eloquentiae tamquam ancillulam pedisequamque, Cic, 2, of time, pass, *to be near in age*, ei proxime adjunctus Drusus frater fuit, Cic **B.** to express any connection or relation, 1, of things, a, in speaking, *to join*, verba ad nomen adjuncta, *epithets*, Cic., similitudines adjungens,

Cic. ; **b,** in argument, *to connect;* rebus praesentibus adjungere atque annectere futuras, Cic. ; **c,** of territory, *to add;* Ciliciam ad imperium populi Romani, Cic. ; agros populo, Cic. ; **d,** *to connect* in any kind of relation, *to give, to attribute;* fidem visis, Cic. ; sibi auxilium, Cic. ; insolentiam honestati, Cic. ; animum ad aliquod studium, Ter. ; **2,** of persons, **a,** *to bring in as a participator;* aliquem ad suos sermones, Cic. ; **b,** *to bind, unite;* urbem ad amicitiam, Liv. ; aliquem sibi socium, or simply socium, Cic. ; with double acc., se comitem fugae, Cic.

adjūro, 1. **1,** *to swear in addition,* Liv. ; **2,** *to swear, to promise on oath;* qui omnia adjurant, Cic. ; **a,** with acc. and infin., adjuras id te invito me non esse facturum, Cic. ; **b,** with per and the acc., per Jovem, Plaut. ; **c,** with the simple acc., adjuro Stygii caput implacabile fontis, Verg.

adjūtābĭlis -e, *full of help, serviceable,* Plaut.

adjūto, 1. *to be serviceable, to help,* Plaut., Ter.

adjūtor -ōris, m. (adjuvo), *a helper;* **1,** victoriae populi Romani, Cic. ; **a,** with in and the abl., in re gerenda, Cic. ; **b,** with ad and the acc., adjutores ad injuriam, Cic. ; **c,** with contra and the acc., his adjutor contra patriam inventus est nemo, Cic. ; **2,** *a regular assistant; one who played secondary parts on the stage,* Hor. ; esp., *the assistant of a public officer, deputy:* P. Manlius in Hispaniam citeriorem adjutor consuli datus, Liv.

adjūtrix -īcis, f. (adjutor), **1,** of persons, *she that helps, a female assistant, a helper;* Minerva adjutrix consiliorum meorum, Cic. ; **2,** of things, *aid;* quae res Plancio in petitione fuisset adjutrix, Cic. ; **3,** *name of reserve legions under the empire,* Tac.

adjŭvo -jūvi -jūtum, 1. *to help, assist, support.* **I.** aliquem in aliqua re, Cic. ; ad bellum, Liv. ; followed by ut with the subj., Cic. ; maerorem nationis lacrimis suis, Cic. **II.** *to be of service, to avail;* jam nihil te Neronis judicium adjuvat, Cic. ; philos. t. t., causae adjuvantes, *mediate,* Cic. ; impers., followed by the infin., nihil igitur adjuvat procedere et progredi in virtute, Cic.

adl, v. under all . . .

admātūro, 1. *to hasten;* admaturari defectionem, Caes.

admētĭor -mensus, 4. dep. *to measure out to;* frumentum alicui, Cic.

Admētus -i, m. (Ἄδμητος), **1,** *ruler of Pherae, in Thessaly, husband of Alcestis, who died for him;* **2,** *king of the Molossi, friend of Themistocles.*

admigro, 1. *to wander to, to come to,* Plaut.

admĭnĭcŭlo, 1. *to support, prop;* vitem, Cic.

admĭnĭcŭlum -i, n. (ad and *mineo). **I.** Lit., *a prop, a support, the pole on which a vine is trained,* Cic. **II.** Transf., *aid, help;* ad aliquod tamquam adminiculum anniti, Cic. ; egere adminiculis, Tac.

admĭnister -stri, m. *an attendant, an assistant;* Jovi se consiliarium atque administrum datum, Cic. ; in a bad sense, audaciae satelles atque administer tuae, Cic.

admĭnistra -ae, f. (administer), *she that helps;* artes hujus administrae comitesque virtutis, Cic.

admĭnistrātĭo -ōnis, f. **1,** *the giving of help;* sine hominum administratione, Cic. ; **2,** *direction, government;* navis, Caes. ; belli, Cic. ; mundi, rerum, reipublicae, Cic.

admĭnistrātor -ōris, m. *an administrator, manager;* quidam belli gerendi, Cic.

admĭnistro, 1. **1,** *to help, assist,* Plaut. ; **2,** *to manage, direct, administer;* rempublicam, Cic. ; navem, *to steer,* Caes. ; of war, bellum cum Cimbris, Cic. ; exercitum, Cic. ; of other things, provinciam, Cic. ; leges et judicia, Cic. ; omnem mundum, Cic.

admīrābĭlis -e, *worthy of admiration, admirable;* **1,** admirabilis et singularis sapientia, Cic. ; **2,** *astonishing, strange* (to translate παράδοξα), Cic.

admīrābĭlĭtas -ātis, f. *admirableness,* Cic. ; haec animi despicientia magnam admirabilitatem facit, *excites wonder,* Cic.

admīrābĭlĭter, adv. **1,** *admirably, wonderfully;* laudari, Cic. ; **2,** *strangely* (Gr. παραδόξως), Cic.

admīrandus -a -um (admiror) = admirabilis, *worthy of admiration;* homo, Cic.

admīrātĭo -ōnis, f. **1,** *admiration;* summam hominum admirationem excitare, Cic. ; habere, Cic. ; in magna admiratione esse, Cic. ; plur., admirationes, *outbursts of admiration;* clamores et admirationes efficere, Cic. ; **2,** *wonder, astonishment;* tam atrocis rei, *at so cruel a deed,* Cic. ; admiratio consulem incessit quod, Liv. ; admiratio orta est, followed by acc. with infin., Liv. ; fit clamor et admiratio populi, followed by acc. with infin., Cic.

admīror, 1. dep. **1,** *to admire;* res gestas, Cic. ; **2,** *to be astonished at;* with adv., leviter, vehementer, magnopere, etc., aliquid, Cic. ; nihil, Cic. ; in aliqua re, de aliquo, Cic. ; with acc. and infin., Cic. ; with quod, cur, quo pacto, unde, Cic.

admiscĕo -miscŭi -mixtum (-mistum), 2. **I.** *to mix with, to add to by mixing.* **A.** Lit., aquae admixtus calor, Cic. **B.** Transf., *to join;* admiscerenturne plebeii, Liv. ; ad id consilium admiscear, Cic. **II.** *to mix with something.* **A.** Lit., aër multo calore admixtus, Cic. **B.** Transf., urbes maritimae admiscentur novis sermonibus ac disciplinis, *become familiar with,* Cic.

admissārĭus, -i, m. (admitto), *a stallion;* fig., *a lascivious man,* Cic.

admissĭo -ōnis, f. *an audience,* esp. of a royal person, Plin.

admissum -i, m. *a crime,* Cic.

admitto -mīsi -missum, 3. *to send to.* **I.** *to let go.* **A.** Lit., **1,** *to let a horse go at full speed, to urge on, to put to a gallop;* equo admisso, Cic. ; **2,** *to hurry;* admisso passu, *with hurried step,* Ov. **B.** Transf., *to let go;* quod semel admissum coerceri reprimique non potest, Cic. **II.** *to let in, to give access to.* **A.** Lit., **1,** aliquem ad capsas, Cic. ; **2,** *to give audience to;* aliquem, Cic. ; **3,** *to admit a person to share* in an undertaking, etc. ; aliquem ad consilium, Cic. **B.** Transf., **1,** of words, entreaties, etc., *to allow to reach;* eas conditiones vix auribus, Liv. ; **2,** of an act, *to allow;* litem, Cic. ; of omens, admittunt aves, *the auguries allow it,* Liv. ; **3,** *to commit a crime;* in te tantum facinus, Cic.

admixtĭo -ōnis, f. (admisceo), *a mingling, an admixture;* corporis, Cic.

admŏdĕrātē, adv. *appropriately,* Lucr.

admŏdĕror, 1. dep. *to moderate,* Plaut.

admŏdum adv. (ad and modum), *up to the measure, up to the mark;* hence, **I.** With numbers, *about;* turres admodum CXX., Caes. **II.** Of degree, *completely, quite;* **A.** Gen., **1,** with adjectives or adverbs, forma admodum impolita et plane rudis, Cic. ; admodum raro, Cic. ; with nihil and nullus, litterarum admodum nihil sciebat, *entirely ignorant of,* Cic. ; of age, puer admodum, *a mere boy,* Liv. ; non admodum grandis natu, Cic. ; **2,** with verbs, me admodum diligunt, Cic. **B.** In affirmative answer, *certainly,* Ter.

admoenio, 4 *to besiege*, Plaut

admōlior, 4 dep *to move to*, Plaut.

admŏnĕo -ŭi -ĭtum, 2 *to admonish, remind, call the attention to*, 1, aliquem alicuius rei, or de aliqua re, Cic, aliquem haec, eam rem, multa, Cic, followed by acc and infin, Liv, or rel sentence with quantus, qui, Cic, 2, in business language, *to remind of a debt*, aliquem aeris alieni, Cic, 3, a, *to advise to do something*, followed by ut or ne and the subj, or by the simple subj, by ad or in and the acc, or by the infin, Cic, ad thesaurum reperiendum admoneri, Cic, b, *to urge or incite*, telo bijugos, Verg

admŏnĭtĭo -ōnis, f *a reminding*, 1, Gen, Cic, 2, *friendly admonition*, admonitio in consilio dando familiaris, Cic, in plur, nec precibus nec admonitionibus nostris reliquit locum, Cic

admŏnĭtor -ōris, m *one who reminds*, Cic

admŏnĭtum -i, n *an admonition, a calling to mind*, Cic

admŏnĭtus -ūs, m *a reminding*, 1, locarum admonitu, Cic, 2, *admonishing, warning*, amici tali admonitu, Cic, mortis, Ov

admordĕo morsum, 2 1, *to bite at, to gnaw*, Prop, 2, *to fleece*, Plaut

admōtĭo ōnis, f *a moving to*, digitorum, *playing on the harp*, Cic

admŏvĕo -mōvi -mōtum, 2 *to move, bring to* A. Gen, 1, fasciculum ad nares, Cic, alicui stimulos, Cic, manum operi, *to engage in a work*, Ov, manus nocentibus, *to lay hands on the guilty*, Liv, so manus vectigalibus, Cic; aspidem ad corpus, Cic, angues curribus, *to yoke*, Ov, with acc alone, ignem, Cic, aurem, Cic, 2, *to direct, devote*, mentes suas, non solum aures ad haruspicum vocem, Cic, 3, milit t t, *to bring up* war machines, opus ad turrim hostium, Caes, *to bring up* soldiers, armatos muris, Liv, 4, of sacrifices, *to bring to the altar*, fibram victimam aris, Liv, 5, *to bring near, place near*, urbem ad mare, Cic B 1, *to apply*, curationem ad aliquem, Cic orationem ad sensus animorum atque motus inflammandos, Cic; 2, of time, in the pass, *to draw near*, admotus supremis, *drawing near to death*, Tac, se admovere, *to draw near*, se applicare et propius admovere, Cic

admūgĭo, 4 *to bellow after*, Ov

admurmŭrātĭo -ōnis, f *a murmuring* (either of approbation or disapprobation), Cic

admurmŭro, 1 *to murmur at* (in approval or disapproval), Cic

admŭtĭlo, 1 *to shear, shave*, hence, transf, *to fleece*, Plaut

adn, v agn or ann

ădŏlĕo -ŭi, 2 1, Intrans, *to smell*, Plaut, 2, Trans, *to make to smell, to set on fire, to burn* (of sacrifices), viscera tauri flammis, Ov; honores Junoni, *to honour by burning sacrifices to*, Verg, so of the altar itself, *to light up* with sacrificial fire altaria flammis, Lucr, flammis Penates (= focos), Verg, cruore captivo aras, *to feed the altars with*, etc, Tac

ădŏlescens (ădŭlescens) -entis (part of adolesco) A. Adj (with compar), *young*, admodum adolescens, Cic, adolescentior academia, Cic B. Subst, 1, masc, *a young man* (with out reference to any particular age), puer sive jam adolescens Cic, adolescens vel puer potius Cic, used (like junior in English) to distinguish a person from some one of the same name, but older, P Crassus adol, Caes, 2, fem, *a girl*, gen as an attribute, filia adol, Cic

ădŏlescentĭa ae, f *youth*, citius adolescentiae senectus quam pueritiae adolescentia obrepit, Cic, ineunte adolescentia, Cic, ab adolescentia, a prima adol, ab ineunte adol, *from youth upward*, Cic, meton, *the young*, Cic.

ădŏlescentŭla -ae, f *a very young girl*, used as a term of endearment, Plaut

ădŏlescentŭlus -i, m *a very young man* applied by Cic to himself in his 27th year, and by Sallust to Caesar when Caesar was about 33 or 35, ab adolescentulo, *from youth upward*, Cic

1 **ădŏlesco** -ŏlēvi -ultum, 3 *to grow, to grow up to maturity* A. Lit, 1, of men, is qui adolevert, Cic, 2, of plants, viriditas herbescens quae sensim adolescit, Cic B Transf, *to grow, increase*, of time, *to advance*, cum matura adoleverit aetas, Verg, ver donec adolesceret, Tac, of the mind, *to be developed, to come to maturity*, ratio quum adolevit atque perfecta est, Cic, ea cupiditas adolescit una cum aetatibus, Cic

2 **ădŏlesco** -ĕre (adoleo), *to blaze*, adolescunt ignibus arae, Verg

Ădōneus -ĕi, m = Adonis (q v)

Ădōnis -idis (Ἄδωνις), and **Adōn** -ōnis, m (Ἄδων), *a beautiful youth, son of Cinyras, king of Cyprus, beloved of Venus, slain by a wild boar but changed after death by Venus into a flower* (adonium)

ădŏpĕrĭo -pĕrŭi pertum, 4 1, *to cover*, capite adoperto, Liv, humus floribus adoperta, Ov, 2, *to close*, adoperta lumina somno, Ov

ădŏpīnor, 1 dep *to guess*, Lucr

ădoptātīcius -a -um, *adopted as a child*, Plaut

ădoptātĭo ōnis, f = adoptio (q v)

ădoptĭo -ōnis, f *the adoption of a child*, emancipare filium alicui in adoptionem, *to give in adoption*, Cic, asciscere aliquem in or per adoptionem, *to adopt*, Tac

ădoptīvus -a -um I. *relating to adoption*, filius, pater, frater, soror, *adopted son*, etc Suet sacra, *the rites of the family into which the person was adopted*, Cic, nobilitas, Ov II. Transf, of plants, *grafted*, Ov

ădopto, 1 I. Gen *to choose for one's self*, sibi aliquem patronum, Cic, of things, Etruscas opes, *to take to one's aid*, Ov II. Esp, A. Lit, *to adopt* as child or grandchild (per aes et libram, *by a fictitious sale*, or testamento, *by will*), sibi filium, Cic, aliquem ab aliquo, *from the natural father*, Cic, in regnum, Sall B. Transf, 1, in jest, C Stalenus qui ipse se adoptaverat et de Staleno Aelium fecerat, *had changed his name by adopting himself*, Cic, frater, pater adde, ut cuique est aetas, ita quemque facetus adopta, *adopt him by calling him brother, father*, etc, Hor, nomen or cognomen adoptare, Mart, 2, of plants, *to graft*, fac ramus ramum adoptet, Ov

ădor -ōris, n *a species of grain, spelt* (Triticum spelta, Linn), Hor

ădōrātĭo -ōnis, f. *a praying to, adoration*, Plin

ădōrĕa (ădōria) -ae, f (adoro), *reward of valour, glory*, ille dies, qui primus alma risit adorea, Hor

ădōrĕus a -um (ador), *relating to spelt*, liba, Verg

ădŏrĭor -ortus, 4. dep *to rise up* I. *to attack*, a, aliquem fustibus, gladiis Cic a tergo, Cic, pagum, Caes, b, *to besiege with entreaties*, threats, etc, aliquem minis, Tac, aliquem tumultuosissime, Cic II. *to attempt, undertake*, hoc ipsum, Cic, majus nefas, Verg followed by infin, convellere ea, etc, Cic,

ădorno, 1. *to prepare, furnish, provide.* **I.** Gen., naves onerarias, Caes.; Italiae duo maria maximis classibus firmissimisque praesidiis, Cic.; accusationem, Cic. **II.** *to adorn.* **A.** Lit., forum magno ornatu, Cic.; aliquem insigni veste, Liv. **B.** Transf., justi honores aliquem adornant, Liv.

ădōro, 1. **A.** Gen., *to speak to.* **B.** Esp., **1**, *to address* a deity, *to entreat, to ask for,* **a**, with acc. of person and acc. of thing; pacem deum, Liv.; **b**, followed by ut and the subj., Liv.; **2**, *to honour;* Phoebum, Ov.

adp, v. under app.

adq, v. under acq.

adr, v. under arr.

adrādo -rāsi -rāsum, 3. *to scrape, shave;* adrasum quendam, Hor.

Adrămyttēum -i, n. (Ἀδραμύττειον), *town on the coast of Mysia, not far from the foot of Mount Ida* (now *Adramiti* or *Edremit*). Hence **Adramyttēnus** -i, m. *a native of Adramyttеum.*

Adrastus -i, m. (Ἄδραστος), *king of Argos, father-in-law of Polynices and Tydeus, one of the Seven against Thebes, and the only one who escaped, afterwards one of those who destroyed Thebes in the war of the Epigoni.* Adj., **Adrastēus** -a -um.

Adria = Hadria (q.v.).

Adrūmētum (Hadrūmētum) -i, n. *town on the coast of the Roman province of Africa.*

ads, v. under ass.

adsc, v. under asc.

adsp, v. under asp.

adst, v. under ast.

adt, v. under att.

Adŭātŭci -ōrum, m. *people in Gallia Belgica,* in modern South Brabant, Caes.

ădŭlātĭo -ōnis, f. **I.** *fawning* (of dogs), Cic. **II.** *cringing, flattery,* Cic., Liv.; so of oriental prostration, humi jacentium adulationes, Liv.; used with adversus or in and the acc.; adversus superiores, Tac.; patrum in Augustum, Tac.

ădŭlātor -ōris, m. *a base flatterer,* Suet.

ădŭlātōrĭus -a -um, *flattering;* dedecus, Tac.

ădŭlescens, etc., v. adolescens.

ădŭlo, 1. *to fawn;* pinnata cauda nostrum adulat sanguinem, *wipes off our blood fawningly* (of a dog), Lucr.

ădŭlor, 1. dep. **A.** Lit., *to fawn* (of dogs and other animals); ferae adulantes, Ov. **B.** Transf., **1**, *to greet with servile prostrations;* more adulantium procumbere, Liv.; **2**, *to flatter, to cringe before;* **a**, with acc., omnes, Cic.; plebem, Liv.; fortunam alterius, Cic.; **b**, with dat., plebi, Liv.; **c**, absol., aperte adulans, Cic.

ădulter -ĕri, m., **ădultĕra** -ae, f. *an adulterer, adulteress.* **I.** Subst., sororis, Cic.; in nepti Augusti, Tac.; Dardanius adulter, *Paris,* Verg.; Lacaena adultera, *Helen,* Hor.; poet., *a gallant,* Hor. **II.** Adj., *adulterous;* virgo, Ov.; crines, *the locks of an adulterer,* Hor.; mens, Ov.; clavis, Ov.

ădultĕrīnus -a -um (adulter), **1**, *adulterous,* Plin.; **2**, *not genuine, forged;* nummus, Cic.; signum, *a forged seal,* Cic.; clavis, *a double key,* Sall.

ădultĕrĭum -ii, n. *adultery;* in adulterio deprehendi, Cic.; Mutiliae, *adultery with,* Tac.

ădultĕro, 1. **I.** Intrans., *to commit adultery,* Cic. **II.** Trans., **A.** Of animals, adulteretur et columba miluo, *let the kite wed the dove,* Hor.; adulteratus nidus (of a nest where the cuckoo has laid its eggs), Plin. **B.** Transf., *to falsify, corrupt;* jus civile pecuniā, Cic.; faciem arte (of Proteus), *changes his form,* Ov.

ădultus -a -um, p. adj. with compar. (adolesco). **I.** *grown up, adult;* virgo, Cic. Plur. subst., **ădulti**, *adults,* Cic. **II.** Transf., **A.** Of time, puer aetate adulta, *near manhood,* Cic.; aestas, *midsummer,* Sall., Tac. **B.** Fig., of growth; **1**, in power, Athenae, Cic.; pestis (of Catilina), Cic.; Parthi nondum adulti, Tac.; **2**, of mental development, populus, Cic.

ădumbrātim, adv. *in outline,* Lucr.

ădumbrātĭo -ōnis, f. *a sketch,* Cic.

ădumbrātus -a -um, p. adj. (adumbro), **1**, *sketched, imperfect;* imago gloriae, Cic.; adumbratae intelligentiae rerum, *imperfect, confused notions,* Cic.; **2**, *shadowy, unreal;* opimo, Cic.; laetitia, Tac.

ădumbro, 1. *to shade,* esp. *to sketch, to sketch in words;* fictos luctus dicendo, Cic.

ădunçĭtas -ātis, f. *a bending inwards;* rostrorum, Cic.

ăduncus -a -um, *bent inwards, crooked;* unguis, Cic.; nasus, *an aquiline nose,* Ter.

ădurgĕo, 2. *to press to,* or *against;* poet., *to pursue closely;* aliquem remis, Hor.

ădūro -ussi -ustum, 3. *to set fire to, to kindle, consume by burning;* sine gemitu aduruntur, Cic.; candente carbone sibi capillum, *to singe,* Cic.; panis adustus, *burnt bread,* Hor.; of frost or wind, *to nip,* Verg.; fig., of love, Venus non erubescendis adurit ignibus, Hor.

ădusquĕ = usque ad; **1**, prep. with acc. *as far as,* Verg.; **2**, adv. = usque, *thoroughly, entirely,* Ov.

ădustus -a -um, p. adj. with compar. (from aduro), *burnt by the sun, brown;* hominum color, Liv.

advectīcĭus -a -um, *that which is brought from a distance, foreign;* vinum, Sall.

advecto, 1. (intens. from adveho), *to convey often;* rei frumentariae copiam, Tac.

advectus -ūs, m. *a conveying, carrying,* Tac.

advĕho -vexi -vectum, 3. 1. *to carry, bring, convey to a place.* **I.** Act., frumentum ex agris Romam, Cic.; ultrices unda advehit rates, Ov.; frumentum Romam, Cic. **II.** Pass., advehi, *to be borne to* a place (on horseback, in a chariot, on a ship, etc.); advecta classis, Verg.; e Pompeiano navi in Luculli hospitium, Cic.; citato equo in eam partem, Liv.; Corcyram insulam advehitur, *reaches,* Tac.; with dat. of person, quum tibi tota cognatio serraco advehatur, Cic.; with acc. of person, Dardanos, Verg.; so ut quosque advectus erat, Tac.

advēlo, 1. *to draw a veil over;* poet., *to crown;* tempora lauro, Verg.

advĕna -ae, c. (advenio), **1**, of men, *a stranger, foreigner* (opp. indigena), Cic.; indigenae advenaeque, Tac.; dei advenae, *foreign gods,* Cic.; **2**, of birds, *a bird of passage;* grus, Hor.; **3**, of things, Tibris, Ov.; amor, *love for a foreigner,* Ov.

advĕnĭo -vēni -ventum, 4. *to come to.* **A.** Lit., **1**, of men, advenis modo? Cic.; ex Hyperboreis Delphos, Cic.; in provinciam belli gerendi causa, Cic.; with acc. only, Tyriam urbem, Verg.; with dat., Tac.; **2**, of things, esp. of ships, a quibus adveniat navis Miletida sospes ad urbem, Ov. **B.** Transf., **1**, of time, *to come;* interea dies advenit, Cic.; **2**, of events, *to happen, to come near, to break out;* urbi periculum advenit, Sall.; morbi advenientes, Cic.; **3.** of acquisitions, *to come to*, res sua sponte mox ad eum advenit, Liv

adventīcius -a -um (advenio), *coming from without* **A.** Gen, *outward*, externus et adventicius tepor, Cic **B.** Esp, **1**, *coming from a foreign country, foreign*, auxilia, Cic, doctrina transmarina atque adventicia, Cic, **2**, *casual, extraordinary, accidental*, pecunia, *money not inherited*, Cic

advento, 1 (intens of advenio), *to approach, arrive at*, gen with notion of haste, ad Italiam, Cic, with dat of person, Parthis, Tac, in subsidium, Tac, of things and abstractions, quod fere jam tempus adventat, Cic

adventor -ōris, m (advenio), *one who arrives, a visitor*, Plaut

adventus -ūs, m (advenio) **I.** *an arrival*, nocturnus ad urbem, Cic, in plur, invitationes adventusque nostrorum hominum, Cic, of things, veris, Hor, in animos et introitus imaginum, Cic **II.** Transf, malorum, Cic

adversārius -a -um (adversus), *turned towards* **I.** Subst, **adversāria** -orum, n (*that which is always open, or lying in front of one*), *a day book, journal, memorandum*, adversaria negligenter scribere, Cic **II.** Adj, *opposed, contrary*, with dat, Cic, factio, Nep Subst, **adversārius** -ii, m *adversary, rival antagonist*, Cic, plur, *enemies*, Cic, **adversāria** orum, n *the assertions of an opponent*, adversaria evertere, Cic

adversor, 1, dep (adversus), *to oppose, resist*, absol, of persons, non adversante collega, Cic, of things, adversante fortuna, Cic, with dat, alicui infestius, Cic, legi, Cic, Liv, cum duae causae perspicuis et evidentibus rebus adversentur, Cic

1 **adversus** -a -um, p adj (adverto), *turned towards* **A.** Lit, *fronting, opposite*, dentes, *the front teeth*, Cic, adversa vulnera, *wounds in the front*, Cic, solem adversum intueri, *to look straight at the sun*, Cic, adversos concitare equos, *to ride towards*, Liv, adversis hostibus occurrere, *to meet the enemy*, Caes, adverso colle, *on the front of the hill*, Caes; adverso flumine, *against the stream*, Caes, venti adversi, *contrary winds*, Liv, with prep, in adversum, *against*, Verg, Liv, ex adverso, *over against*, Liv. **B.** Transf, **1**, of persons, *opposed*, adversus alicui Cic, adverso Marte, Verg, adverso senatu, *against the will of the senate*, Liv, **2**, of things, **a**, *unfavourable, unpropitious*, adversis auribus, Liv, valetudo, *ill health*, Liv, bellum, *cruel*, Hor, proelium, *unsuccessful*, Caes, res adversae, Cic, fortuna adversa, Verg, *misfortune*, with dat, res plebi adversa, Liv, **b**, *hated*, quis omnia regna adversa sunt, Sall Subst, **adversum** -i, n *misfortune*, si quid adversi acciderit, Cic

2 **adversus**, **adversum** (adverto), *opposed to* **I.** Adv, *against*, nemo adversus ibat, Liv, adversus arma ferre, Nep **II.** Prep with acc **A.** Of direction, **1**, as regards place, *towards*, adversus clivum, Caes, **2**, of action, etc, *against*, adversus quem ibatur, Liv, adversus rempublicam facere, Caes, respondere adversus ea, *to answer to*, Liv, adversus legem, Cic, adversus quod convenisset, *against the agreement*, Liv, adversus blanditias incorruptus, Tac, munitus adversum aliquem or aliquid, Sall **B.** Of position, **1**, as regards place, *over against*, adversus aedes publicas, Liv, **2**, of comparison, quid autem esse duo prospera in tot saeclis bella Samnitium adversus tot decora populi Romani, *compared with*, Liv., **3**, of behaviour, *in the presence of*, quonam modo me gererem adversus Caesarem, Cic, so of respect to, *towards*, reverentia adversus homines, Cic

adverto (advorto) -verti (-vorti) -versum (-vorsum), 3 *to turn towards* **A.** agmen urbi, Verg, esp used of ships, *to steer*, classem in portum, Liv, pass, notae advertuntur arenae, *they steer to*, Verg, Scythicas advertitur oras, Ov **B.** Of the senses and thoughts, etc, *to direct*, **1**, of the senses, especially the eyes, lumina in quamcumque aedis partem, Ov; of the gods, malis advertite numen, *direct your powers to*, Verg, aures ad vocem, Ov, **2**, of the mind, animum, and (sometimes) mentem advertere, **a**, *to direct one's attention to*, animos ad religionem, Lucr, with dat, animos monitis, Ov, followed by ne and the subj animum animadvertant, ne quos offendant, *take care not to*, etc, Cic, absol, Cic, **b**, *to perceive*, aliquem in contione stantem, Cic, followed by acc and infin, Cic, or relative clause, Cic, with animo or animis, animis advertite vestris, Verg, **c**, *to punish*, in aliquem, Tac, **d**, *to draw the attention of some one else*, gemitus et planctus etiam militum aures oraque advertere, *roused the attention of*, Tac

advespĕrascit -āvit, 3 (impers and inchoat), *evening approaches*, Cic

advĭgĭlo, 1 *to watch by, to guard* **I.** Lit, parvo nepoti, Tib, ad custodiam ignis, Cic. **II.** Fig, *to be vigilant*, Plaut

advŏcātĭo -ōnis, f *calling to one's aid* **I.** *summoning persons to advise*, maximarum rerum, *on the most important points*, Cic, frequentissimae advocationes, Cic **II.** Esp, **1**, *legal advice*, advocationem postulare, petere, dare, consequi, Cic, **2**, concr, *the bar*, Cic

advŏcātus -i, m *one who is called in to help in a legal process, whether as advocate or as witness*, Cic

advŏco, 1 *to summon, to call* **I.** Gen, contionem populi, Cic, aliquem in consilium, Cic, advocari ad obsignandum, Cic, with dat, advocari aegro, Ov, gaudiis, Hor, non desiderat fortitudo iracundiam advocatam, *called to its aid*, Cic **II.** Esp, **A.** Legal t t, of a judge, *to ask the opinion of a jurist*, Cic, of the parties to an action, *to consult an advocate*, aliquem contra aliquem, Cic, with dat, aliquem sibi, Plaut; absol, aderat frequens, advocabat, Cic. **B.** Of the gods, *to ask for help*, deum sibi, Cat, deos, Liv

advŏlātus, abl -ū, m *a flying to*, Cic poet

advŏlo, 1 *to fly to* **I.** Lit, of birds and insects, ad eas aves quae, etc, Cic **II.** Transf, *to hasten towards, to fly to*, **1**, of persons, absol, advolone an maneo, Cic ad urbem, Cic, rostra, Cic, **2**, of things, fama mali tanti advolat Aeneae, *flies to the ears of*, Verg

advolvo -volvi -vŏlūtum, 3 *to roll to*, robora focis, *to the hearth*, Verg, ornos montibus, *from the mountains*, Verg, hence advolvi, or se advolvere, *to throw oneself at the feet of*, genibus alicuius, Liv, genua alicuius, Sall

advorsum, advorsus, advorto = adversum, adversus, adverto (q v)

ădȳtum, -i, n (ἄδυτον = not to be entered) **I.** Lit, gen in plur, *the inmost and holiest portion of a temple, the shrine*, Verg, Hor, adytis ab imis, *from the bottom of a grave*, Verg **II.** Transf, ex adyto tamquam cordis, *from the bottom of the heart*, Lucr

Aeăcus -i, m (Αἰακος), *a mythical king of Aegina, father of Peleus and Telamon, grandfather of Ajax and Achilles, after his death judge in the infernal regions*, hence **Aeăcĭdes** ae, m *a descendant of Aeacus, one of his sons*, as *Peleus* or *Phocus*, Ov, *his grandson, Achilles*, Verg, *his great-grandson, Pyrrhus (Neoptolemus)*, Verg; *one of his remote descendants, Pyrrhus (king of Epirus)*, Enn;

Perseus, king of Macedonia, Verg. **B. Aeăcĭdēĭŭs** -a -um; regna (Aegina), Ov. **C. Aeăcĭdinus** -a -um.

Aeaeē -ēs, f. (Αἰαίη νῆσος), *the island of the sorceress Circe, or of Calypso*; hence **Aeaeus** -a -um; **a**, surname of Circe, Verg.; Aeaeae artes, Aeaea carmina, *sorceries*, Ov.; Aeaeus Telegonus, *son of Circe*, Prop.; **b**, surname of *Calypso*; puella, Prop.

Aeās -antis, m. (Αἴας), *a river in Greece, flowing by Apollonia*.

Aebura -ae, f. *a town in Hispania Tarraconensis*, now *Cuerva*, Liv.

Aeculānum -i, n. *town of the Hirpini in Samnium*, Cic.

aedēs (aedis) -is, f.; originally, *a building*. **I.** Sing., **A.** *a room*, Plaut. **B.** *a temple*; gen., where the context is not clear, with the name of some god, or with sacra; aedes sacra, Cic.; aedes Minervae, Cic.; *in plur.*, complures aedes sacrae, Cic.; aedes alone, *the temple of the Palatine Apollo*, Hor. **II.** Plur., **A.** Lit., *a house*, Cic.; aedes liberae, *empty*, Liv. **B.** Meton., **1**, *the family*, Plaut.; **2**, Transf., **a**, *the cells of bees*, Verg.; **b**, *the chambers of the ears, the ears*, Plaut.

aedĭcŭla -ae, f. (dim. of aedes), *a small building*; **1**, *a small temple*; Victoriae, Liv.; also *a niche*, or *shrine* for the image of a god, Cic.; **2**, in plur., *a little house*, Cic.

aedĭfĭcātĭo -ōnis, f. (aedifico), *building*; **1**, Abstr., *the act of building*; consilium aedificationis, Cic.; aedificationem deponere or abjicere, *to give up building*, Cic.; **2**, Concr., *the building itself*; domus tua et aedificatio omnis, Cic.

aedĭfĭcātĭuncŭla -ae, f. (dim. of aedificatio), *a small building*, Cic.

aedĭfĭcātor -ōris, m. (aedifico), **1**, *a builder, architect*; fig., mundi, Cic.; **2**, *one who has a passion for building*, Juv.

aedĭfĭcĭum -i, n. (aedifico), *a building*; aedificia publica privata, sacra profana, Cic.; opposed to inhabited houses, aedes aedificiaque, Liv.; opposed to a number of houses together, vicis aedificiisque incensis, Caes.; opposed to the site, cujus (domus) amoenitas non aedificio sed silva constabat, Nep.; opposed to a palace, plebis aedificiis obseratis, patentibus atriis principum, Liv.

aedĭfĭco, 1. (aedes and facio). **I.** Lit., *to build, erect, establish*; villam, porticum, domum, urbem, navem, hortos, Cic. **II.** Fig., aedificare mundum, *to create*, Cic.; rempublicam, *to frame*, Cic.

aedīlīcĭus -a -um (aedilis), *relating to the aediles*; munus, Cic.; vectigal, *tax paid by the provinces for the shows of the aediles*, Cic. Subst., **aedīlīcĭus** -i, m. *one who has been aedile*, Cic.

aedīlis -is, m. (aedes), *an aedile, a public officer at Rome who had the superintendence of the buildings of the city, the roads, markets, theatres, dramatic performances, and police*; under the Republic there were four, two aediles curules (originally patricians, but afterwards patricians and plebeians), and two aediles plebis, or plebei, or plebeii.

aedīlĭtas -ātis, f. (aedilis), *the aedileship*; aedilitate fungi, Cic.

aedĭtĭmus (aeditumus) -i, m. an old form of aedituus (q.v.).

aedĭtŭens -entis, m. = aedituus (q.v.).

aedĭtŭus -i, m. (aedes), *the keeper* or *guardian of a temple*, Cic.

Aedŭi (Haedŭi) -ōrum, *a Gallic people between the Arar* (Saone) *and the Liger* (Loire), whose chief town was Bibracte.

Aeēta -ae, m., and **Aeētēs** -ae, m. (Αἰήτης), *king of Colchis, father of Medea*; hence, **A. Aeētias** -ădis, f. *Medea*, Ov. **B. Aeētīnē** -ēs, f. *Medea*, Ov. **C. Aeētaeus** -a -um, *belonging to Colchis*; fines, *Colchis*, Cat.

Aefŭla -ae, f., and **Aefŭlum** -i, n. *town in Latium, north of Praeneste*; hence **Aefŭlānus** -a -um, *belonging to Aefula*.

Aegae (Aegaeae, Aegēae, Aegiae) -ārum, f. (Αἰγαί, Αἰγεαί) **1**, *town in Macedonia*; **2**, *town in Aeolis*; **3**, *town in Cilicia*, now *Castle of Ajas Kala*.

Aegaeōn -ōnis, m. (Αἰγαίων), *another name for Briareus*, Verg.; *a sea-god*, Ov.

Aegaeus -a -um (Αἰγαῖος), *Aegean*; mare, *the Aegean Sea, the Archipelago*, Cic. Subst., **Aegaeum** -i, n. *the Aegean Sea*, Hor.

Aegātes -ium, f., and **Aegātae** -ārum, f. (with or without insulae), *a group of three islands on the west coast of Sicily*, near which the decisive battle of the first Punic war was fought (241 B.C.).

aeger -gra -grum, *sick, ill*. **A.** Of physical illness; **1**, of persons; **a**, of persons themselves, homines aegri gravi morbo, Cic.; ex vulnere, Cic.; pedibus, Sall.; oculis, Liv.; manum, Tac. Subst., **aeger** -gri, m. *an invalid*, Cic.; **b**, of bodies or parts of the body, corpus, Cic.; dens, Mart.; so of states regarded as bodies; pars reipublicae, Cic.; civitas, Liv.; **c**, of bodily conditions, valetudo, Cic.; anhelitus, Verg.; **2**, of plants, seges, Verg.; **3**, of things, quid in toto terrarum orbe validum, quid aegrum, *unsound*, Tac. **B.** Of ailments of the mind, *ill* from any cause, love, hope, fear, sorrow, etc.; **1**, of persons, mortales aegri, Verg.; aegra amans, Verg.; aegra municipia, *mutinous*, Tac.; animo magis quam corpore aeger, Liv.; amore, Liv.; animi, *in mind*, Liv.; consilii, Sall.; **2**, of conditions, or relations, or abstractions, *painful*; amor, mors, Verg.; aegris oculis, *with envious eyes*, Tac.

Aegeus -ĕi, m. (Αἰγεύς), *king of Athens, father of Theseus*; hence **Aegīdēs** -ae, m. *Theseus*, or *any one of the descendants of Aegeus*.

Aegimūrus -i, f., and **Aegimŏrŏs** -i, f. (Αἰγίμουρος and Αἰγίμορος), *an island near Carthage*, now *Al Djamur* or *Zimbra*.

Aegīna -ae, f. (Αἴγινα), *an island near Athens*; hence **Aegīnensis** -e, *belonging to Aegina*; **Aegīnenses** -ium, m. **Aegīnētae** -ārum, m. *natives of Aegina*.

Aegīnĭum -ii, n. (Αἰγίνιον), *town in Macedonia, on the borders of Epirus*, now *Erkinia*; hence **Aegīnienses** -ium, m. *the inhabitants of Aeginium*.

Aegĭon (Aegĭum) -ii, n. (Αἴγιον), *one of the twelve Achaean towns on the Corinthian Gulf*, now *Vostiza*.

aegis -ĭdis, f. (αἰγίς). **A.** *the aegis, or shield*; **1**, *of Jupiter*, Verg.; **2**, *of Minerva with the Medusa's head*, Ov. **B.** Transf., *a protection, bulwark*, Ov.

Aegīsos -i, f. (Αἴγισσος), *an old town in Moesia, on the banks of the Danube*, now *Isaccze*.

Aegisthus -i, m. (Αἴγισθος), *son of Thyestes, murderer of Agamemnon, afterwards husband of Clytemnestra, himself murdered by Orestes*, Cic.

Aegĭum = Aegion (q.v.).

Aeglē, -ēs, f. (Αἴγλη), *name of one of the Naiads*.

Aegŏcĕrōs -ōtis, m. (αἰγοκέρως), *a sign of the zodiac, Capricorn*, Lucr.

aegrē, adv. with compar. and superl. (aeger). **I.** *painfully*; aegre est mihi or meo animo, *I am grieved*, Plaut.; aegre ferre, *to be distressed*. **II.** **1**, *with difficulty*; aegre divelli, aegrius depelli, Cic.; **2**, *hardly, scarcely* (by itself and with vix);

se tenere, Cic , 3, *unwillingly*, ferro aliquid, Cic , aegre ferre, foll by acc and infin , *to take it ill that*, etc , Cic

aegrĕo, 2 (aeger), *to be sick*, Lucr.

aegresco, 3, (aegreo), *to fall ill* **I.** Lit , Lucr **II.** Transf , **A** *to become worse, more violent*, violentia Turni aegrescit medendo, Verg. **B** *to be disturbed in mind, to trouble one's self*, longiore sollicitudine, Tac

aegrīmōnia ae, f (aeger), *grief, trouble of mind*, Cic

aegrĭtūdo inis, f (aeger), *sickness* **I.** Of body, Plaut , Tac **II.** Of mind, *grief*, se totum aegritudini dedere, Cic , aegritudine emori, Cic in aegritudinem incidere, Cic , aegritudinem levare lenire, sedare, adimere alicui, depellere, efficere, Cic , plur , aegritudines leniores facere, Cic

aegror -ōris, m (aeger), *sickness*, Lucr

aegrōtātĭo ōnis, f (aegroto), *sickness* **I.** Of body, Cic **II** Of the mind, Cic

aegrōto, 1 (aegrotus), *to be sick or ill* **I** Lit , **A.** Of the body, graviter, vehementer diuque, leviter, periculose, Cic , of cattle, Hor , of plants, Plin **B.** Of the mind, ea res ex qua animus aegrotat, Cic **II.** Of abstractions, aegrotat fama vacillans, Lucr

aegrōtus -a um (aeger), *sick, ill*, **1**, in body, Cic , **2**, in mind, Ter ; of abstract things, respublica, Cic

Aegyptus -i (Αἴγυπτος) **A.** Mythol , m *son of Belus, brother of Danaus* **B.** Geogr , f *Egypt* Adj , **1**, **Aegyptĭăcus** a -um, **2**, **Aegyptĭus** -a -um, *Egyptian*, Cic Subst , **Aegyptĭus** -i, m *an Egyptian*, Cic

aelĭnos i, m (αἴλινος), *a dirge*, Ov

Aemĭliānus -a -um, *relating to the gens Aemilia, a surname of Scipio Africanus minor, the son of L. Aemilius Paulus*, adopted by the elder Scipio Africanus

Aemĭlĭus -a um, gens, *name of one of the oldest and most distinguished patrician families of Rome*, Aemilia via, and simply Aemilia, *a road made by the consul M Aem Lepidus*, leading from Ariminum to Placentia, pons, *a bridge near the pons sublicius*, Juv , ratis, *the ship in which the spoils of Perseus were brought home by Aem Paulus*, Prop , ludus, *a gladiatorial school founded by P Aemilius Lepidus*, Hor

Aemŏnia, etc , v Haemŏnia

aemŭlātĭo -ōnis, f (aemulor), *a striving after or up to, emulation* **I.** In a good sense, laudis, Nep , gloriae, Liv **II.** In a bad sense, *jealousy, envy, ill natured rivalry*, Cic , plur , *rivalries*, Cic

aemŭlātor -ōris, m (aemulor), *a rival*, Catonis aemulator, *an imitator*, Cic

aemŭlātus -ūs, m (aemulor) = aemulatio (q v)

aemŭlor, 1 dep (aemulus), *to rival, emulate, strive to attain to* **I.** In a good sense, aliquem, Nep , eius instituta, Cic , Albanum vinum, *to come near to*, Plin **II.** In a bad sense, *to envy*, with dat , alicui, Cic , cum aliquo, Liv , inter se, Tac

aemŭlus a um, *emulous, vying with, rivalling* **I.** In a good sense **A.** Lit , gen with genitive, mearum laudium, Cic , with dat , dictator Caesar summis oratoribus aemulus, Tac Subst , **aemulus** i m , aliquius, Cic , esp , *a zealous follower of a philosophical system*, cuius (Zenonis) inventorum aemuli Stoici nominantur, Cic **B.** Transf , *coming near to, approaching to* (in excellence, etc), tibia tubae aemula, Hor **II.** In a bad sense, *zealous, rivalling*, Carthago aemula imperii Romani, Sall aemula senectus, *jealous*, Verg Subst , **aemŭlus** i, m and **aemŭla** ae, f *a rival in love*, Cic. and Ov

Aemus = Haemus (q v)

Aenārĭa -ae, f *a volcanic island on the west coast of Italy, opposite Campania* (now *Ischia*)

Aenēa ae, f (Αἴνεια), *a town in Chalcidice*, hence, **Aenēātes** um, m (Αἰνεᾶται), *inhabitants of Aenea*

Aenēas ae, m (Αἰνείας), *son of Venus and Anchises, hero of Vergil's Aeneid, myth ancestor of the Romans*, Aeneae mater, *Venus*, Ov , Aeneae urbs, *Rome*, Ov , hence **A. Aenĕădes** ae, m *a descendant of Aeneas*, **a**, *his son Ascanius*, Verg , **b**, *Augustus*, Ov , plur , Aeneadae arum, m , **a**, *the companions of Aeneas*, Verg , or *the Trojans*, Verg , **b**, *the Romans*, Verg , Ov **B Aenēĭs** idos, f *Vergil's Aeneid* **C. Aenēĭus** -a um, *relating to Aeneas* **D. Aenīdēs** = Aeneades

ăēnĕātor ōris, m (aeneus), *a trumpeter*, Suet

ăēnĕus and **ăhēnĕus** a -um (aenum, ahenum) **I.** Lit , **1**, *made of brass, copper, or bronze*, Cic **2**, *of a bronze colour*, Suet. **II.** Transf , **1**, *hard as metal*, murus, Hor , **2**, aenea proles, *the brazen age*, Ov

Aenĭānes -um, m (Αἰνιᾶνες), *a Greek race in the south of Thessaly*

aenigma -ătis, n (αἴνιγμα), *a riddle* **I.** Quint **II.** Transf , *what is obscure, mystery*; somniorum, Cic

ăēnĭpes (ăhēnĭpes) pĕdis (ăēnĕus and pes), *brazen footed*, Ov

1 **ăēnus** (ăhēnus)-a um (aes), **1**, *made of brass, copper, or bronze*, Verg Subst , **ăēnum** -i, n *a brazen vessel*, Verg , **2**, *firm, inexorable*, manus, Hor

2 **Aenus** i **I** Aenos (Αἶνος) i, f (Αἶνος), *a town in Thrace, at the mouth of the Hebrus*, now *Enos*; hence **Aenii** -orum, m *its inhabitants* **II Aenus** -i, m *a river between Vindelicia and Noricum* (now *the Inn*)

Aeŏles -um, m *the Aeolians, one of the chief races of the Greeks*, the most important settlements of whom were in Boeotia and Lesbos, hence, **a**, **Aeŏlĭcus** -a -um, and **b**, **Aeŏlĭus** -a -um, *Aeolic*, with especial reference to Sappho, the Lesbian poetess

Aeŏlĭa -ae, f (Αἰολία), **1**, *the north part of the coast of Asia Minor, opposite to Greece*, Cic , **2**, plur , **Aeŏlĭae insulae**, *a group of volcanic islands on the north coast of Sicily (the Lipari isles)*, *myth seat of Aeolus and Vulcan.*

Aeŏlis idis, f (Αἰολίς), *a part of Mysia, in Asia Minor, north of the Hermus*, Liv

Aeŏlus (Aeŏlŏs) -i, m (Αἴολος) **I.** *son of Hellen, myth founder of the Aeolian race* **II.** *son or grandson of Hippotes, ruler of the Aeolian islands and of the winds* **III.** *a Trojan*, Verg , hence, **A. Aeŏlĭdes** ae, m *a descendant of Aeolus*, **1**, *his sons, Sisyphus*, Ov ; *Athamas*, Ov , *Salmoneus*, Ov , *his grandsons, Cephalus*, Ov *Ulysses*, Verg **B. Aeŏlis** idos, f *female descendant of Aeolus*, **1**, *his daughters, Canace* Ov , *Alcyone*, Ov **C. Aeŏlĭus** a -um, *belonging to Aeolus*, **1**, *belonging to Aeolus* (**I.**), postes (*of Athamas*), Ov , pecus, *the golden fleece*, Mart , **2**, *belonging to Aeolus* (**II.**), virgo, *his daughter Arne*, Ov tyrannus, *Aeolus*, Ov , antra, *the caves where the winds were kept*, Ov procellae, Verg

aequābĭlis -e (aequo), *like, similar, equal*, **1**, praedae partitio, Cic , **2**, *that which is equal to itself uniform, equable*, amnis, Cic , **3**, *fair, just*, nihil ea iurisdictione aequabilius, Cic , of persons, cunctis vitae officiis aequabilis, Tac, in suos, *affable*, Tac.

aequābĭlĭtas ātis, f (aequabilis), *uniformity, equability*, motus, Cic ; hence, **a,** juris, *impartiality*, Cic , b, *equality of political rights*, Cic ; **c,** *equanimity*, Cic

aequābĭlĭtĕr, adv. with compar (aequabilis), *equably, uniformly, fairly*, praedam dispertire, Cic , aequabilius provinciae regentur, Tac

aequaevus -a -um (aequus and aevum), *of equal age*, Verg

aequālis -e (aequo), *equal* **I.** *level*, loca, Sall **II.** *equal in height, size*, etc , **1,** *corresponding to*, with dat., pars pedis aequalis alteri parti, Cic. ; with inter, virtutes sunt inter se aequales et pares, Cic , **2,** *of the same age with*, with dat , exercitus aequalis stipendiis suis, *that had served as many campaigns as he himself*, Liv , with genit , calo quidam aeq Hieronymi, Liv , of things, aequali corpore nymphae, *of the same age and growth*, Verg , with genit , sacrificium aequale hujus urbis, *contemporary with*, Cic , with dat., cui (Ennio) si aequalis fuerit Livius, Liv ; with genit , Philistus aequalis temporum illorum, Cic , memoria aequa illius aetatis, Cic Subst., **aequālis** -is, c *a comrade, person of the same age*, P Orbius meus fere aequalis, Cic , **3,** *uniform*; imber lentior aequaliorque accidens auribus, Liv , nihil aequale homini fuit illi, Hor

aequālĭtas -ātis, f (aequalis), **1,** *evenness, smoothness*, Plin ; **2,** *equality*, similitudo aequalitasque verborum (of a pun), Cic. , paterna, *complete harmony in thought*, etc , Cic , *equality of age*, Cic , **3,** *equality of political privileges*, Tac

aequālĭtĕr, adv (aequalis), **1,** *evenly*, collis ab summo aequaliter declivis, *gently sloping*, Caes , **2,** *equally*, distribuere, Cic , **3,** *uniformly*, oratio aequaliter constanterque ingrediens, *symmetrically*, Cic

aequănĭmĭtas -ātis, f (aequanimus, from aequus and animus), **1,** *impartiality*, Ter , **2,** *calmness*, Plin

aequātĭo -ōnis, f (aequo), *a making equal;* bonorum, *communism*, Cic , juris, Liv

aequē, adv (aequus), *in like manner, equally* **I. 1,** duae trabes aeque longae, Caes , aeque dolere, Cic , with adv , aeque lubenter, Cic , **2,** *in comparison, just as, equally with*, **a,** foll by et, atque, ac si, quam, quam ut, etc , eosdem labores non esse aeque graves imperatori et militi, Cic , hi coluntur aeque atque illi, Cic , with cum and the abl , ut aeque mecum haec scias, Plaut , with abl alone, Plaut , with compar , homo me miserior nullus est aeque, Plaut , b, when the object of the comparison is to be understood, pauci quibuscum essem aeque libenter (sc ac tecum), Cic **II.** *fairly, justly*, societatem conditionis humanae munifice et aeque tuens, Cic

Aequi (Aequĭcŭli, Aequĭcŏli, Aequĭcŭlāni) -ōrum, m *a people in Latium*, with whom the Romans waged frequent wars , hence, a, **Aequĭcus** -a -um, *Aequian*, b, **Aequĭcŭlus** -a -um, *Aequian*

aequĭlībrĭtas -ātis, f *the equal distribution of natural forces* = ἰσονομία, Cic.

Aequĭmaelĭum ii, n *an open space in Rome, on the west side of the Capitol, where the cattle for the sacrifices were kept*, Cic

aequĭnoctĭālis -e (aequinoctium), *equinoctial, relating to the equinox*, Cat

aequĭnoctĭum ii, n (aequus and nox), *the equinox*, Cic

aequĭpăro (aequĭpĕro), 1 (aequus and paro), **1,** *to compare*, with ad and the acc., suas virtutes ad tuas, Plaut , with dat , mari tranquillo quod ventis concitatum multitudinem Aetolorum, Liv , **2,** *to equal*, aliquem, Liv ; nec calamis solum sed voce magistrum, Verg

aequĭtas -ātis, f. (aequus), **1,** *uniformity, symmetry*, membrorum, Suet , **2,** *equanimity* (with or without animi), Cic , **3,** *impartiality, equity, fairness, justice*, causae, Cic , conditionum, Caes , servare aequitatem, Cic

aequo, 1 (aequus) **I.** *to make level*, locum, Caes , aequata agri planities, Cic , aequare frontem, milit t t , *to form a line*, Liv **II.** *to make equal with something else* **A. 1,** *to distribute equally;* sortes, *to shake up the lots*, Cic , pecunias, Cic ; aequato omnium periculo, Cic , **2,** *to make things of different kind equal* , a, of height, solo, *to level with the ground*, Suet , fig , solo aequandae sunt dictaturae consulatusque, *must be abolished*, Liv. , machina aequata caelo, *as high as the heavens*, Verg , fig , aliquem caelo laudibus, *to extol to the heavens*, Verg , **b,** of number, qui (libri) se jam illis aequarunt, Cic , per somnum vinumque dies noctibus, *to turn day into night by sleeping and drinking*, Liv , nocti ludum, *to spend the whole night in play*, Verg , **c,** of rights, *to make equal*, inventum est temperamentum quo tenuiores cum principibus aequari se putarent, Cic , **d,** *to compare*, Hannibali Philippum, Liv **B.** *to equal, to come up to* , Appii odium, Liv , sagitta aequans ventos, Verg , aliquem passibus, Verg ; aliquem equestri gloria, Liv

aequor -ŏris, n (aequus), *a flat surface* **I.** Gen , speculorum, Lucr **II.** Esp , **1,** *the flat surface of a plain* (with campi), camporum patentium aequor, Cic ; poet (without campi), immensum aequor, *of a desert*, Verg , **2,** poet , *the flat surface of the sea, the sea* , with ponti or maris, vastum maris aequor, Verg , oftener without maris, etc , Ionium, Lucr , vastum, Verg , plur , saeva aequora, Verg , meton , *the sea-water in a ship*, aequor refundere in aequor, Ov ; rarely, *the surface of a river*, as the Tiber, Verg

aequŏrĕus -a -um (aequor), *belonging to the sea*, genus, *fishes*, Verg ; rex, *Neptune*, Ov , Britanni, *sea-girt*, Ov. , Achilles, *a son of Thetis*, Lucan.

aequus a -um, adj. with compar and superl *equal.* **I.** *equal in itself* **A.** Lit , **1,** of the surface of the ground, *level*, aequus et planus locus, Cic ; ex aequo loco loqui, *to speak in the senate* (opp to ex inferiore loco, *in the presence of the judges*, and ex superiore loco, *in the presence of the people*), Cic , ex superiore et ex aequo loco sermones habitos, *public and private conversations*, Cic Neut. subst , **aequum** -i, n *level ground*, facile in aequo campi victoriam fore, Liv. , **2,** of other things, *level*, aequa frons, milit t t , *a straight line*, Liv **B.** Transf , **1,** of places, *favourable, advantageous*, locum se aequum ad dimicandum dedisse, Caes , et tempore et loco aequo instructos, Liv , **2,** of character, *quiet, contented*, concedo et quod animus aequus est et quia necesse est, Cic , aequam rebus in arduis servare mentem, Hor , esp in the phrase aequo animo, *patiently, with resignation*, pati or ferre with acc , and acc with infin , Cic , tolerare, Sall. , accipere, Sall , spectare Cic , animo aequissimo mori, Cic , in plur , animis lubentibus aut aequis aliquid remittere, Cic **II.** *equal to something else* **A.** Lit , *equal*, in breadth, height, etc , aequo fere spatio abesse, Caes , sequitur patrem non passibus aequis, *with shorter steps*, Verg , urbs nubibus aequa, *as high as the clouds*, Ov , aequis portionibus or pensionibus (*equal payments*), dare, solvere, etc , Liv , foll by atque quam, cum, aequo et pari cum civibus jure vivere, Cic , quum aequam partem tibi sumpseris atque populo Romano miseris, Cic. **B.** Transf , **1,** in aequa laude ponere, Cic , aequa pugna, *an indecisive battle*, Liv. ; so aequo proelio or marte discedere, *to fight an indecisive battle*, Caes, so aequa manu, or aequis manibus, Tac and Liv, adv, ex aequo, *equally*, sol ex aequo medii distabat utrique, *was equally distant*, Ov, 2, of behaviour etc, *equal, impartial*, a, of persons, *fair*, se alicui aequum praebere, Cic praetor, judex, testis, Cic, b, of things, judicium, Cic lex, Cic, aequum est, *it is just*, with the acc and infin, aequum esse eum et officio meo consulere et tempori, Cic subst, **aequum** i, n *fairness*, quid in jure (*strict law*) aut in aequo (*equity*) verum aut esset aut non esset, Cic, per aequa per iniqua, *by fair means or foul*, Liv, gravius aequo, *than is right*, Sall, aequum et bonum, *what is right, fit*, reus magis ex bono aequoque quam ex jure gentium Bomilcar, Sall, as a legal formula, quod or quantum aequius melius, *as is more equitable*, Cic, so aequi bonique facere aliquid, *not to find fault with*, Cic, 3, *favourable to others, propitious*, nobilitate inimica, non aequo senatu, Cic, non aequa Pallas, Verg, minus aequis animis auditus est Scipio, Liv, meis aequissimis utuntur auribus, *I hear them with the greatest pleasure*, Cic, with dat aequa Venus Teucris, Ov, ipsis est aer avibus non aequus, *harmful to*, Verg Plur subst, **aequi**, *friends* in the phrase aequi iniquique, *friends and enemies*, Cic

ăēr, āĕris, m (ἀήρ), *the lower air, the atmosphere around us*, crassus, Cic, purus et tenuis, Cic, temperatus, Cic, aer summus arboris, *the airy summit of a tree*, Verg, aere septus obscuro, *surrounded by a cloud*, Verg

aera ae, f (αἶρα), *a [weed] growing among grain, darnel, tares*, Plin

aerāmentum -i, n *bronze* or *copper ware*, Plin

aerārĭa -ae, f, v aerarius, I B 2

aerārĭum -ii, n, v aerarius, II B 2

aerārĭus ii, m (aes) **I.** *belonging to brass* or *copper* **A.** Adj, lapis, *copper*, Plin, structurae, *copper mines*, Caes **B.** Subst, **1, aerārius** ii, m *a worker in brass*, Plin, **2, aerārĭa** ae, f *smelting-works*, Plin **II.** *belonging to money* **A.** Adj, ratio, *standard of the copper coinage*, Cic, milites, *mercenaries*, Varr, illa vetus aeraria fabula, *the old tale about the copper coin that Vettius gave to Clodia*, Cic **B.** Subst, **1, aerārius** -ii, m gen in plur, aerarii, *the citizens of the lowest class in Rome, who had no votes, but had to pay a certain sum for the expenses of the state*, a class to which citizens of the higher ranks might be degraded by the censors for punishment, aliquem aerarium facere, *to degrade*, Liv; aliquem in aerarios referri jubere, Cic, **2, aerārium** -ii, n a, *the exchequer, treasury*, at Rome, under or behind the temple of Saturn, where the treasures and archives of the state were kept, pecuniam in aerarium referre, inferre, deferre, redigere, Cic, decreta patrum ad aerarium deferre, Tac, meton, *the money in the treasury*, Cic, **b,** *any public treasury*, Cic

aerātus a um (aes), **I. 1,** *covered or fitted with brass* or *bronze*, navis, Caes, lecti, *with bronze feet*, Cic, poet, acies, *an armed line of troops*, Verg, **2,** *provided with money, rich*, tribuni non tam aerati, quam ut appellantur aerarii (with a play on the words, vide aerarius II B 1), Cic **II.** *made of brass or bronze*, securis, Verg, transf, *as firm as brass* nodi, Prop

aerĕus -a um (aes), **1,** *made of brass* or *copper*, signa aerea et marmorea, Liv, **2,** *covered with brass*, puppis, Verg

aerĭfĕr -fĕra fĕrum (aes and fero), *bearing brazen cymbals*, Ov.

aerĭfĭcē, adv (aes and facio), *skilfully* (of work in brass). Varr,

aerĭnus -a um (αἴρινος), *made of darnel* or *tares*, Plin

aerĭpes pĕdis (aes and pes), *brazen-footed*, Verg, Ov

ăĕrĭus (ăĕrĕus) a -um (aer), **1,** *belonging to the air, airy*, alterum (animantium genus), pennigerum et aerium, *living in the air*, Cic, domus, *the heavens*, Hor, aerias vias carpere, *to fly through the air*, Ov, mel (from the belief that honey fell in dew from the sky), Verg, **2,** *high in the air, lofty*, Alpes, Verg

aero ōnis, *a wicker basket*, Plin

Āĕrŏpē -ēs, f and **Āĕrŏpa** ae, f (Ἀερόπη), *mother of Agamemnon and Menelaus*

aerōsus -a -um (aes), *rich in copper*, aurum, *mixed with copper*, Plin

aerūgĭnōsus a -um (aerugo), *covered with verdigris or copper-rust*, Sen

aerūgo -ĭnis, f (aes) **I. A.** *the rust of copper, verdigris*, Cic **B.** Meton = *rusty money*, Juv **II.** Transf, **1,** *envy*, Hor, **2,** *avarice*, Hor

aerumna -ae, f *hard labour, toil, hardship*, Herculis perpeti aerumnas, Cic

aerumnābĭlis -e (aerumna), *calamitous, pitiable*, Lucr

aerumnōsus a -um (aerumna), *full of hardship and calamity*, Regulus, Cic

aes, aeris, n *copper* **I.** Lit, *copper ore*, and *the alloy of copper, brass*, or *bronze*, pedestris ex aere statua, Cic, poet, of the brazen age, ut inquinavit aere tempus aureum, Hor **II.** Meton, *something made of bronze*, etc **A.** Gen (esp in poets), *a vessel, statue*, etc, made of bronze, etc, aes cavum, *kettle*, Ov, aera aere repulsa, *cymbals*, Ov, Corybantia, *cymbals used in the service of Cybele*, Verg, eius aera refigere, *the brazen tablets on which the laws were engraved*, Cic, aes publicum, *public inscriptions*, Tac, aere ciere viros, *with the trumpet*, Verg, dempto aere, *the helmet*, Ov **B.** Esp *money*, **1,** *copper* or *brass money*, aes grave, *the as* (of a pound weight), which was weighed instead of counted, denis millibus aeris gravis reos condemnavit, Liv, quinquaginta millia aeris (for assium), Liv, argentum aere solutum est, *three-fourths of the debts were remitted by payment of a (copper) as for a (silver) sesterce*, Sall *small change* (cf Engl, *coppers*), aera dabant olim, Ov, **2,** *money generally*, gravis aere dextra, Verg, pueri qui nondum aere lavantur (= *boys under four years, who use the baths without paying*) Juv, esp, **a,** aes meum, *my property*, est aliquis in meo aere, *he is bound to me*, Cic. aes alienum, *debt*, facere, contrahere, in aes alienum incidere, esse in aere alieno, Cic, solvere, Cic, so aes mutuum, Sall, **b,** *pay*, Juv, esp *soldiers' pay*, aera militibus constituere, dare, Liv, **c,** aes circumforaneum, *money borrowed from the money changers, who had their booths round the forum*, Cic. **3,** plur, aera, *counters*, Cic

Aesăcŏs and **Aesăcus** i, m (Αἴσακος), *son of Priam, husband of Asterope or Hesperia*

Aesăr -ăris, n *a river in Bruttii, now Esaro*, hence adj, **Aesărĕus** -a um, *belonging to the river Aesar*

Aeschĭnes is and i, m (Αἰσχίνης) **I.** *an Athenian philosopher, disciple of Socrates* **II.** *a Neapolitan philosopher, pupil of Carneades* **III.** *the celebrated Athenian orator, opponent of Demosthenes* **IV.** *an orator of Miletus, contemporary with Cicero*

Aeschўlus -i, m (Αἰσχύλος) **I.** *an Athenian tragic poet* (born about B c 525), hence **Aeschylēus** -a um, *belonging to Aeschylus*, cothurnus, Prop **II.** *a rhetorician of Cnidos, contemporary with Cicero*

Aescŭlāpĭum -ĭi, n. *a temple of Aesculapius.*

Aescŭlāpĭus -ĭi, m. (Ἀσκληπιός), *the god of medicine, son of Apollo and Coronis, worshipped at Epidaurus.*

aescŭlētum -i, n. (aesculus), *an oak forest*, Hor.

aescŭlĕus -a -um (aesculus), *relating to the winter oak*, Ov.

aescŭlus -i, f. *the winter* or *Italian oak*, Verg.

Aesernĭa -ae, f. *town in Samnium*, now *Isernia*; hence **Aesernīnus** -a -um, *belonging to Aesernia; surname of M. Marcellus, who was taken prisoner at Aesernia; name of a celebrated gladiator*, Cic.

Aesĭs -is, m. *river in Picenum*, now *Esino* or *Fiumesino*; hence adj., **Aesīnās** -ātis.

Aeson -ŏnis, m. (Αἴσων), *a Thessalian prince, father of Jason*; hence, **a**, **Aesŏnĭdes** -ae, m. *a descendant of Aeson (Jason)*, Prop.; **b**, **Aesŏnĭus** -a -um, *relating to Aeson*; heros, *Jason*, Ov.

Aesōpus -i, m. (Αἴσωπος). **I.** *a celebrated Greek fabulist of Phrygia, supposed to have lived in the 6th cent.* B.C. **II.** Claudius (Clodius) Aesopus, *a tragic actor in Rome, contemporary and friend of Cicero.*

aestas -ātis, f. (connected with αἴθω = to burn, and aestus), *summer*. **I.** Lit., ineunte, Cic.; novā, *at the beginning of summer*, Verg.; mediā, Cic.; adultā, Tac.; summā, Cic.; exactā, *at the end of*, Sall.; esp. used of the summer as *the time for military operations*; unis litteris totius aestatis (*summer campaign*) res gestas ad senatum perscribere, Cic.; so quae duabus aestatibus gesta, Tac. **II.** Meton., *clear summer weather*, Verg.; *summer heat*, Hor.

aestĭfĕr -fĕra -fĕrum (aestus and fero), *heat-bringing*, Verg.; ignis, Lucr.

aestĭmābĭlis -e (aestimo), *valuable*, Cic.

aestĭmātĭo -ōnis, f. (aestimo). **I.** Lit., *an appraising according to value in money*; aequam aestimationem facere, Caes.; census, *the valuation of the census*, Cic.; frumenti, *valuation of the corn allowance* for the governor of a province, or the amount to be paid by the aratores of the province instead of this allowance, Cic.; litis, *assessment of damages*, Cic.; so, multae, Liv.; possessionis, *valuation of property*, Cic.; praedia in aestimatione ab aliquo accipere, *to take estates at the higher valuation that prevailed before the civil war*, Cic. **II.** Transf., **1**, *the valuation* of a thing, a person, *according to its true value*; honoris, Liv.; **2**, as a philosoph. t. t. (Gr. ἀξία), propria aestimatio virtutis, *the absolute worth of virtue*, Cic.

aestĭmātor -ōris, m. (aestimo), **1**, *one who estimates, an appraiser*; frumenti, Cic.; **2**, *one who values a thing according to its worth*; fidei, Liv.

aestĭmātus -ūs, m. = aestimatio (q.v.).

aestĭmo (aestŭmo), 1. (aes), *to appraise, estimate the value of anything*. **I.** *to estimate pecuniary value*; frumentum (vid. aestimatio frumenti), Cic.; with abl. or gen., of value; aliquid ternis denariis, Cic.; ut liceat, quanti quisque velit, tanti aestimet, Cic.; with adv., tenuissime, *at a very low rate*, Cic.; with ex and abl., aliquid ex artificio, *according to the standard of workmanship*, Cic.; litem alicui or alicuius, legal t. t., *to assess the damages in a law-suit*, Cic.; pugnatum est ut lis haec capitis aestimaretur, *should be held a capital charge*, Cic. **II.** In a wider sense, **1**, *to value according to any standard*; with abl. or gen., magno, Cic.; magni, Cic.; with adv., carius, Cic.; levius tempestatis quam classis periculum, Caes.; with ex and abl., vulgus ex veritate pauca, ex opinione multa aestimat, Cic.; virtutem annis, Hor.; satis aestimare, *to estimate at full value*, with acc. and infin., Tac.; **2**, *to judge*, sicuti ego aestimo, Sall.

aestīva -ōrum, n., v. aestivus.

aestīvē, adv. (aestivus), *as in summer*, Plaut.

aestīvo, 1. (aestivus), *to pass the summer*, Plin.

aestīvus -a -um (aestus), *relating to summer*; tempora, Cic.; aura, Hor.; saltus, *summer pasturage of cattle*, Liv.; aurum, *the gold ring of the military tribunes, worn for six months*, Juv.; aestivum tonat, *it thunders as in summer*, Juv. Plur. subst., **aestīva** -orum, n.; **a**, (sc. castra), *a summer camp*, Cic.; meton. (because the ancients generally waged war only in the summer), *a campaign*, Cic.; **b**, *summer pastures for cattle*, Varr.; meton., *the cattle in summer pastures*, Verg.

aestŭārium -ii, n. (aestus). **1**, *low ground covered by the sea at high water, morass*; itinera aestuariis concisa, Caes.; **2**, *a firth, creek*, or *part of the river up which the tide flows*; in aestuario Tamesae, Tac.

aestŭo, 1. (aestus), *to boil, to be hot*. **I.** Of fire, aestuat ignis, Verg.; or the results of fire; ventis pulsa aestuat arbor, *is heated*, Lucr.; si dixeris "aestuo" (*I am warm*) sudat, Juv. **II. A.** Lit., of liquids, *to boil*, or (of the sea) *to rage*; gurges aestuat, Verg. **B.** Fig., of the passions, *to be inflamed* or *excited*; ut desiderio te nostri aestuare putarem, Cic.; nobilitas invidia aestuabat, Sall.; so of love, rex in illa aestuat, *burns with love for*, Ov.; aestuabat dubitatione, Cic.

aestuōsē, adv. with compar. (aestuosus), *hotly*, Hor.

aestuōsus -a -um, adj. with superl. (aestus), **1**, *hot*; via, Cic.; **2**, *agitated*; freta, Hor.

aestus -ūs, m. (αἴθω). **I.** *heat*; **1**, of fire, propiusque aestus incendia volvunt, Verg.; **2**, of the sun, meridiei aestus, Liv.; plur., *hot days*, Verg.; **3**, of fever, aestu febrique jactari, Cic. **II. 1**, *seething and raging*, of the sea; ferventes aestibus undae, Ov.; minuente aestu, *the storm lessening*, Caes.; **2**, Transf., **a**, *rage*; civilis belli, Hor.; of love, pectoris, Ov.; **b**, *fervour*; ne aestus nos consuetudinis absorbeat, Cic.; **c**, *unrest, anxiety*; qui tibi aestus, qui error, quae tenebrae erant, Cic.; magno curarum fluctuat aestu, Verg.

aetas -ātis, f. (contr. from aevitas, from aevum), *age*. **I. A.** *lifetime*; **a**, breve tempus aetatis, Cic.; aetatem agere, degere, conterere, consumere, Cic.; aetas mea, tua = *I, you*, Plaut.; **b**, *a generation* (gen., 30 years; sometimes, in poets, 100); tertiam jam aetatem hominum vivebat, Cic. **B.** *the age of a man*; **1**, Lit., **a**, filius id aetatis, *of that age*, Cic.; sometimes, *youth*; qui aliquid formae aetatis artificiique habebant, Cic.; carus eris Romae donec te deseret aetas, Hor.; sometimes, *old age*; nusquam tantum tribuitur aetati, nusquam senectus est honoratior, Cic.; sometimes, *manhood*; in aetatem pervenire, Liv.; **b**, with narrower meaning, iniens aetas, *youth*, Cic.; so flos aetatis, bona aetas, Cic.; ad petendum (magistratum) legitima aetas, Cic.; aetas militaris, *the seventeenth year*, Sall.; quaestoria, *the twenty-fifth*, Quint.; senatoria, *the twenty-fifth*, Tac.; consularis, *the forty-third*, Cic.; adulta, Cic.; ingravescens, Cic.; aestate jam affecta, *far advanced in years*, Cic.; **2**, Meton., *the persons of a particular age*; vestra, Cic.; puerilis, *boys*, Cic.; senilis, *old men*, Cic. **II.** *the time at which a person lives*; clarissimus imperator suae aetatis, Liv.; **1**, nostra aetas, *the men of our time*, Liv.; verborum vetus aetas, *obsolete words*, Hor.; **2**, used gen. for time; aurea, *the golden age*, Ov.; omnia fert aetas, Verg.

aetātŭla -ae, f. (dim of aetas), *youthful age*, prima illa aetatula sua, Cic.

aeternĭtas -ātis, f (aeternus) **I.** *eternity;* ex omni aeternitate verum esse, Cic **II. a,** *immortality*, animorum, Cic , alicui aeternitatem immortalitatemque donare, Cic , **b,** in imperial times, *a title of the Emperor*, similar to majestas, divinitas, etc , Plin

aeterno, 1 (aeternus), *to make eternal, to immortalize*, Hor

aeternus a -um, adj with compar (contr from aeviternus), *eternal, immortal* **I.** deus, Cic **II.** *everlasting, lasting, undying*, bellum, Cic , urbs, *Rome*, Tib , amore aeterno Cic , in aeternum, *for ever*, Liv , so aeternum, Verg , aeterno, *everlastingly*, Plin., neut. plur subst , aeterna moliri, *to do deathless deeds*, Cic

aether ĕris, acc ĕra, m (αἰθήρ) **I. A.** *the upper air*, Cic , poet , *heaven*, Juppiter aethere summo despiciens, Verg , meton , *the gods*, oneravit aethera votis, Verg **B.** Poet (= aer), *the lower air*, verberare aethera pennis, Verg , *the upper world* (opposed to the infernal regions), aethere in alto, Verg **II.** Proper name, **Aether,** *son of Erebus and Night, identified with Jupiter*

aethĕrius (aethĕrĕus) a -um (αἰθέριος) **I.** *ethereal, relating to the ether*, natura, Cic , esp , *relating to the heavens as the abode of the gods, heavenly*, domus, *heaven*, Hor , ignes, *heavenly inspiration*, Ov , equi, *the horses of the sun*, Ov **II. 1,** *belonging to the air*, aqua, *rain*, Ov , **2,** *belonging to the upper world* (as opposed to the lower world), vesci aura aetheria, *to live*, Verg

Aethĭŏpes um, acc. as, m (Αἰθίοπες), *the inhabitants of Aethiopia*, Cic , sing , **Aethiops** -ŏpis, m *a black man*, Juv , cum stipite Aethiope, *stupid*, Cic , hence, **1, Aethiopia** ae, f in wider sense, *all the land to the south of the world as known to the ancients*, in narrow sense, *the country south of Egypt*, **2, Aethĭŏpicus** a -um, *Aethiopian* **3, Aethĭŏpis** -idis, f *a plant, a kind of sage*, Plin

1 **Aethra** -ae, f (Αἴθρα) **I.** *daughter of king Pittheus of Troezen, mother of Theseus by Aegeus* **II.** *daughter of Oceanus, mother of the Hyades and of Hyas*

2 **aethra** -ae, f (αἴθρα), *the upper air, the clear sky*, Verg

Aetna -ae, f (Αἴτνη) **I** *Aetna, a volcano in Sicily*, according to one legend, the mountain that Jupiter cast on the giant Typhoeus (or Typhon), or Enceladus , so proverb, onus Aetna gravius, Cic , according to another legend, the interior was the workshop of Vulcan and the Cyclopes, who there forged Jupiter's thunderbolts, hence **Aetnaeus** a um, *belonging to Aetna*, fratres, *the Cyclopes*, Verg , pastor, *the Cyclops Polyphemus*, Ov , meton , tellus, *Sicily*, Ov **II** *a town at the foot of Mount Aetna*, also called *Inessa*, hence **Aetnensis** -e, *belonging to the town of Aetna*

Aetōli ōrum, m (Αἰτωλοί), *the Aetolians, the inhabitants of Aetolia* Adj **Aetōlus** -a -um, *Aetolian*, plagae (alluding to Meleager and the hunt of the Calydonian boar), Hor , arma, cuspis (of the Aetolian Diomedes), Verg , urbs or Arpi, a town in Apulia, said to have been founded by Diomedes, Verg , hence, **1, Aetōlia** ae, f *Aetolia, a country in the west of Greece, between Ozolian Locris and Acarnania*. **2, Aetōlicus** -a -um, *Aetolian*, bellum, Liv , **3, Aetōlis** idis, f *an Aetolian woman*, Deianira, *daughter of Oeneus king of Aetolia*, Ov ; **4, Aetōlius** -a -um, heros, *Diomedes*, Ov

aevĭtas -ātis, f old form of aetas

aevum i, n (αἰών) **I.** *eternity;* in aevum, *for ever*, Hor. **II.** *time* **A 1,** *time of life*, degere, Cic , per brevis aevi Carthaginem esse, Liv ; **2,** *a generation* (thirty years); ter aevo functus, Hor , **3,** *age*, **a,** flos aevi, *youth*, Lucr , integer aevi, *in the bloom of youth*, Verg primo exstingui in aevo, *in early youth*, Ov , **b,** esp , of old age, aevo macieque senescunt, Lucr , aevi maturus, *far advanced in years*, Verg **B. 1,** *time at which a person is living*, omnis aevi clari viri, *of every age*, Liv , **2,** *time in gen* , veteris non inscius aevi, Ov

Āfer, v Afri.

affābĭlis -e, adj with compar (affor), *easy to be spoken to, affable*, in omni sermone affabilem et jucundum esse velle, Cic

affābĭlĭtas ātis, f (affabilis), *affability;* comitas affabilitasque sermonis, Cic

affăbrē, adv. (ad and faber), *in a workmanlike way, skilfully*, factus, Cic

affătim, adv (ad and fatim), *sufficiently, enough*, satisfacere alicui, Cic Subst with genit , copiarum affatim esse, Liv

affātus -ūs, m (affor), *an address, speech, accosting*, Verg

affectātĭo -ōnis, f (affecto), *a violent desire and striving*, quietis, Tac , Germanicae originis, *eagerness to pass for Germans*, Tac

affectātor ōris, m (affecto), *one who strives after anything*, Quint

affectātus -a -um, p adj (affecto), in rhet , *elaborate, studied*, Quint

affectĭo -ōnis, f (afficio) **I.** Active, *influence*, praesentis mali sapientis affectio nulla est, *the wise man is not affected by evil*, Cic **II** Passive, *condition* , **1,** *relation* , quaedam ad res aliquas affectio, Cic , **2,** *state*, caeli, Cic , **3,** *condition*, **a,** of the body, firma corporis affectio, *good health*, Cic , **b,** of the mind, with or without animi, *favourable disposition of the mind*, Cic , nulla affectione animi, *without predilection*, Tac

affecto (adfecto), 1 (afficio) **I.** *to grasp*, ubi nulla datur dextra affectare (navem) potestas, Verg , viam, *to aim after*, Plaut , eam rem, *to meddle with*, Liv , regnum, *to obtain*, Liv. **II.** *to strive after*, **1,** munditiam, non affluentiam, Nep , spes potiendae Africae, *to entertain hopes*, Liv , bellum Hernicum, *to try to get the command of the war*, etc , Liv , imperium, Liv , **2,** *to affect*, in verbis effusiorem cultum, Quint

1 **affectus** ūs, m (afficio), *a condition, disposition*, of the mind, **1,** animi, Cic ; absol , *feeling*, veri affectus, Tac , **2,** *emotions, passions*, amoris, avaritiae, metus, Quint , *desire*, Tac , **3,** *affection*, Plin

2 **affectus** a um, p adj with superl (afficio) **A.** *provided, furnished with*, virgis, Plaut , virtutibus, vitiis, Cic **B.** *disposed in any way* as to mind or body , **1,** of the body, **a,** cum manus recte affecta est quum in tumore est, Cic , transf , quomodo affecto caelo compositisque sideribus quodque animal oriatur, *under what disposition of the stars*, Cic , **b,** *indisposed, disordered*, Caesarem graviter affectum jam viderim, Cic , valetudine affectus, Caes , transf , civitas aegra et affecta, Cic , **c,** *near completion*, bellum affectum videmus et, ut vere dicam, paene confectum, Cic , **2,** of the mind, *disposed*, eodem modo erit sapiens affectus erga amicum, quo in se ipsum, Cic

affĕro, attŭli, allātum, afferre (ad and fero), *to carry*, or *bring to* **I.** Lit , **A.** Of persons, aliquid domum, Cic , epistolam, litteras, *to* *bring a letter*, Cic. ; is qui litteras attulit, *the bearer of this letter*, Cic. **B.** Of things, si tantum notas odor attulit auras, Verg. **II.** Transf., **A.** Gen., *to bring;* animum vacuum ad res difficiles scribendas, Cic. ; manus afferre alicui or alicui rei, *to seize*, Cic. ; manus sibi, *to commit suicide*, ap. Cic. ; manus suis vulneribus, *to tear open*, Cic. ; alicui vim, *to offer violence to*, Cic. **B.** Esp., **1,** *to bring news;* alicui non jucundissimum nuntium, Cic. ; eo de Hortensii morte mihi est allatum, *news was brought me*, Cic. ; foll. by acc. and infin., Caelium ad illum attulisse se quaerere, etc., Cic. ; **2,** *to bring as an excuse* or *reason;* rationes, cur hoc ita sit, Cic. ; aetatem, *to allege in excuse*, Cic. ; **3,** *to produce, cause;* alicui mortem, Cic. ; **4,** *to bring as a help;* ad bene vivendum aliquid, Cic. ; **5,** *to bring as an addition;* quis attulerit, *who added the clause to the bill*, Cic.

afficio -fēci -fectum, 3. (ad and facio). **I.** *to do something to;* in rhet., *to connect;* eae res quae quodammodo affectae sunt ad id de quo quaeritur, Cic. **II.** *to influence.* **A.** aliquem aliqua re, *to affect in any way;* aliquem maxima laetitia, Cic. ; quanta me molestia affecerit, Cic. ; cives Romani morte, cruciatu, cruce, Cic. ; aliquem sepultura, *to bury*, Cic. ; aliquem capitali poena, *to punish*, Liv. ; so in passive, morbo gravi et mortifero affectum esse, Cic. ; magna difficultate affici, *to be placed in a difficult position*, Caes. ; beneficio affici, *to be benefited*, Cic. ; pio dolore affectum, Cic. **B.** aliquem, *to affect the body* or *mind ;* **1,** the body, exercendum corpus et ita afficiendum est ut, etc., Cic. ; aestus, labor, fames, sitis afficiunt corpora, *weaken*, Liv. ; **2,** of the mind, litterae tuae sic me affecerunt ut, etc., Cic.

affictio -ōnis, f. *an adding to*, Phaedr.

affigo -fixi -fixum, 3. (ad and figo), *to fasten to, affix.* **I.** Lit., litteram illam (K) ita vehementer ad caput, ut, etc., *to brand*, Cic. ; Prometheum Caucaso, Cic. ; cruci, Liv. ; of trophies of war, signa affixa delubris, Hor. **II.** Transf., **a,** Ithaca illa in asperrimis saxis tamquam nidulus affixa, Cic. ; alicui affixum esse tamquam magistro, *not to leave the side of*, Cic. ; **b,** of the mind, *to imprint*, ea maxime affigi animis nostris, Cic.

affingo -finxi -fictum, 3. (ad and fingo), *to form, feign, invent in addition, to add to.* **I.** Lit., of artists, partem corporis, Cic. **II.** Transf., *to invent;* qui nihil opinione affingat assumatque ad aegritudinem, Cic. ; multa rumore affingebantur, Caes.

affinis -e (ad and finis). **I.** Lit., *neighbouring;* gens affinis Mauris, Liv. **II.** Transf., **1,** *related by marriage;* alter mihi affinis erat, Cic. Subst., **affinis** -is, m. *brother-, sister-, father-, mother-in-law;* cognati et affines, *blood relations and connections by marriage*, Cic. ; **2,** *connected with, privy to;* hujus suspicionis, Cic. ; huic facinori, Cic.

affinitas -ātis, f. (affinis). **I.** *neighbourhood*, Varr. **II. A.** *relationship by marriage;* affinitate sese devincire cum aliquo, Cic. ; in affinitatem alicuius pervenire, Cic. ; plur., conjunctio hominum inter homines serpit sensim foras, cognationibus primum, deinde affinitatibus, deinde amicitiis, Cic. ; meton., *relations by marriage*, Plaut. **B.** *union* of any kind ; litterarum, Quint.

affirmātē, adv. with superl. (affirmatus), *certainly, positively*, promittere aliquid, Cic.

affirmātio -ōnis, f. *asseveration, positive assertion*, Cic.

affirmo, 1. (ad and firmo). **I.** *to strengthen;* societas jurejurando affirmatur, Liv. **II. a,** *to support a statement, to prove ;* quod breviter dictum est rationibus affirmatum, Cic. ; **b,** *to assert as true;* quis rem tam veterem pro certo affirmet, Liv. ; omni asseveratione tibi affirmo (followed by acc. and infin.), Cic. ; with de and the abl., quid opus est de Dionysio tam valde affirmare.

affixus -a -um (p. adj. from affigo), *fixed to, closely joined to, affixed ;* Pyrenaeo, *closely adjacent to*, Plin.

afflātus -ūs, m. (afflo). **I.** *a blowing* or *a breathing on ;* maris, *sea breeze*, Plin. ; denegat afflatus ventus et aura suos, Ov. ; used of the breath of men and animals, Ov. **II.** *inspiration ;* sine aliquo afflatu divino, Cic.

afflĕo -flēvi -flētum, 2. (ad and fleo), *to weep at*, Plaut.

afflictātio -ōnis, f. (afflicto), *bodily pain, torture*, Cic.

afflicto, 1. (intens. of affligo). **I.** *to strike* or *beat.* **A.** Lit., afflictare se, *to beat one's breast in grief*, Sall. **B.** Transf., afflictare se, or afflictari, *to be troubled;* de quibus vehementer afflictor, Cic. **II.** *to damage by striking.* **A.** Lit., onerarias (naves) tempestas afflictabat, Caes. **B.** Transf., *to harass, to torment;* gravius vehementiusque afflictari (morbo), Cic.

afflictor -ōris, m. (affligo), *a destroyer;* dignitatis et auctoritatis, Cic.

afflictus -a -um, p. adj. (affligo), **1,** *damaged, shattered ;* fortuna, amicitia, Cic. ; **2,** *broken down, spiritless, desponding;* aegritudine afflictus, debilitatus, jacens, Cic. ; **3,** *vile, contemptible;* homo afflictus et perditus, Cic.

affligo -flixi -flictum, 3. **I. A.** *to strike, dash against;* vasa parietibus, Liv. **B.** *to dash to the ground;* statuam, Cic. ; equi virique afflicti, *struck down in battle*, Sall. **II.** *to ill-treat, damage.* **A.** fusti caput alicuius, Tac. ; naves quae gravissime afflictae erant, Caes. **B.** Transf., *to weaken, discourage, injure;* non vitium nostrum sed virtus nostra nos afflixit, Cic. ; non plane me enervavit nec afflixit senectus, Cic. ; causam susceptam, *to drop a law suit*, Cic. ; vectigalia bellis affliguntur, *suffer through war*, Cic. ; animos affligere et debilitare metu, Cic.

afflo (ad-flo), 1. **I.** *to blow on.* **A.** Lit., afflabat acrior frigoris vis, Liv. ; odores qui afflarentur e floribus, Cic. **B.** Transf., **1,** Intrans., *to blow propitiously;* felix cui placidus leniter afflat amor, Tib. ; **2,** Trans., *to bring;* rumoris nescio quid afflaverat commissione Graecorum frequentiam non fuisse, Cic. ; **3,** *to breathe, to communicate secretly;* laetos oculis afflarat honores, Verg. **II. A.** *to breathe on;* velut illis Canidia afflasset, Hor. ; nosque, ubi primus equis Oriens afflavit anhelis, Verg. ; of fire and heat, saucii afflatique incendio, *scorched*, Liv. **B.** *to inspire;* afflata est numine quando jam propiore dei, Verg.

afflŭens -entis (p. adj. of affluo), *rich, affluent, abundant, plentifully provided with, full of;* opibus et copiis, Cic. ; omni scelere, Cic. ; ex affluenti, *in abundance*, Tac.

afflŭentĕr, adv. with compar. (affluens), *richly, abundantly*, voluptate affluentius haurire, Cic.

afflŭentia -ae, f. (affluens), *overflow, abundance;* omnium rerum, Cic.

afflŭo (ad-fluo) -fluxi -fluxum, 3. *to flow to.* **A.** Lit., **1,** of rivers, Aufidus amnis utrisque castris affluens, Liv. ; **2, a,** of the concourse of atoms in the Epicurean philosophy, Lucr. ; **b,** of men, *to flock together;* affluente quotidie multitudine ad famam belli spemque praedae, Liv. **B.** Transf., **1,** *to come;* nihil ex istis locis non modo litterarum, sed ne rumoris quidem affluxit, Cic. ; **2,** *to abound;* quum domi otium et divitiae affluerent, Sall. ; unguentis affluens, *dripping with unguents*, Cic. ; voluptatibus, Cic.

affor (ad-for), 1 dep, *to accost, address*, versibus aliquem, Cic.; esp., *to say farewell* to the dead, aliam extremum, Verg.; *to pray to*, deos, Verg. (1st pers. of pres. indic. not found; only used in the other persons of the pres. indic., the 1st pers. imperf. indic., the 2nd pers. imper., the infin., and partic.)

affōrmīdo, 1 *to be in fear*, Plaut.

affrīco -fricui -fricatum, 1 *to rub*, Plin.

affrictus -ūs, m. (affrico), *a rubbing on*, Plin.

affulgĕo -fulsi, 2 *to shine, glitter*. **A.** Lit., Venus (*the planet*), affulsit, Ov. **B.** Transf., 1, of a deity, *to look favourably upon*, vultus ubi tuus affulsit, Hor.; 2, of hope, *to appear*, consuli rei majoris spes affulsit, Liv.

affundo -fūdi -fūsum, 3 *to pour into*. **I.** Lit., venenum vulneri, Tac.; colonia amne affusa, *washed by a river*, Plin. **II.** 1, of men, *to add*, ut equitum tria millia cornibus affunderentur, Tac.; 2, affundere se or affundi, *to prostrate oneself on the ground*, affusaque poscere vitam, Ov.

Āfrānius a -um, *name of a Roman plebeian gens*, the most famous of which were **I.** L. Afranius, *a Roman comic poet* (born probably about 130 A.C.), *contemporary of Terence*. **II.** L. Afranius, *dependent and legate of Cn. Pompeius, killed after the battle of Thapsus*.

Āfri -ōrum, m. *the dwellers in Africa*, especially in the narrow sense of the district round Carthage; sing., dirus Afer, *Hannibal*, Hor. Adj., **Āfĕr** -fra -frum; aqua, *sea between Sicily and Africa*, Ov.; avis, *guinea fowl*, Hor.; sorores, *the Hesperides*, Juv. Hence **A. Āfrĭca** -ae, f. 1, in wider sense, *the continent of Africa*, Sall.; 2, in narrower sense, Africa propria or Africa provincia, *the country around and formerly belonging to Carthage*, and in a narrower sense still, *the district of Zeugis with its capital Carthage*. **B. Āfrĭcānus** -a -um, *belonging to Africa*, bellum, *Caesar's war against the Pompeians in Africa*, Cic.; gallinae, *guinea fowl*, Varr. Subst., **Africanae** -ārum, f. (sc. bestiae) *African wild beasts, lions, etc.*, used in the circus at Rome, Liv. As a surname, Africanus, see Cornelius. **C. Āfrĭcus** -a -um, *African*, bellum, *the second Punic war*, Liv.; *Caesar's war against the Pompeians*, Caes.; mare, *south-west part of the Mediterranean sea*, Sall.; ventus Africus or Africus alone, *the S.W. stormy rain-wind*, praeceps, Hor.

Agămemnōn -ŏnis, m. (Ἀγαμέμνων), *a king of Mycenae, leader of the Greek expedition to Troy*; hence, 1, **Agamemnŏnĭdes** -ae, m., *a son or descendant of Agamemnon, Orestes*, Juv.; 2, **Agamemnŏnĭus** a -um, *relating to Agamemnon*, puella, *Iphigenia*, Prop.

Ăgănippē -ēs, f. (Ἀγανίππη), *a fountain in Boeotia, sacred to the Muses*, Verg.; hence, 1, **Agănippis** -ĭdis, f. *Aganippean*, Ov.; 2, **Agănippēus** -a -um, *relating to Aganippe, sacred to the Muses*, lyra, Prop.

ăgāso -ōnis, m. (ago), *a horse boy, groom*, Liv.; *donkey-driver*, Liv.; *awkward servant*, Hor.

Ăgăthoclēs -is and -i, m. (Ἀγαθοκλῆς), 1, *a tyrant of Syracuse, born 361 A.C.*; 2, *a Greek philosopher and writer on husbandry*; 3, *a Greek historian*.

Ăgăthyrna -ae, f. (Ἀγάθυρνα), or **Ăgăthyrnum** -i, n. (Ἀγάθυρνον), *a town on the N. coast of Sicily, now S. Agatha*.

Ăgăthyrsi -ōrum, m. (Ἀγάθυρσοι), *a Scythian people living on the Maris, in modern Hungary, who tattooed themselves blue*, picti, Verg.

Ăgāvē -ēs, f. (Ἀγαύη), *daughter of Cadmus, mother of Pentheus, whom she killed in a Bacchic frenzy*.

Ăgendĭcum -i, n. *capital of the Senones, in Gallia Lugdunensis, now Sens*.

Ăgĕlastus -i, m. (ἀγέλαστος, never laughing), *surname of M. Crassus, grandfather of the triumvir, said to have laughed only once in his life*.

ăgellus -i, m. (dim. of ager), *a little field*, Cic.

ăgēma -ătis, n. (ἄγημα), *a corps in the Macedonian army*, Liv.

Ăgēnor -ŏris, m. (Ἀγήνωρ), *a king of Phoenicia, father of Cadmus and Europa*; urbs Agenoris, *Carthage*, Verg.; Agenore natus, *Cadmus*, Ov.; hence, 1, **Ăgēnŏrĭdes** -ae, m. *a son or descendant of Agenor, Cadmus*, Ov.; *Perseus, as descendant of Danaus, nephew of Agenor*, Ov.; 2, **Ăgēnŏrĕus** -a -um, *relating to Agenor*, domus, *house of Cadmus*, Ov.; bos, *the bull that bore away Europa*, Ov.; aenum, *the kettle used for the Phoenician purple dye*, Mart.

ăgens -entis (partic. of ago), *lively, active*, acer orator, incensus et agens, Cic.

ăger, agri, m. (ἀγρός). **I.** 1, *land in cultivation, a field, piece of land*; colere, Cic.; homo ab agro remotissimus, *knowing nothing of agriculture*, Cic.; 2, *open country in opposition to the town*, vastati agri sunt, urbs assiduis exhausta funeribus, Liv.; 3, *the land opposed to the sea*, arx Crotonis una parte imminens mari, altera parte vergente in agrum, Liv.; 4, in agrum, *in depth* (opp. in frontem, *in length*), Hor. **II.** *the territory of a state*, Tusculanus, Cic.

Ăgēsĭlāus -i, m. (Ἀγησίλαος), *a king of Sparta who conquered the Persians on the Pactolus in Asia Minor* (A.C. 395), *and the Boeotians, Athenians, and other Greeks at Coronea in Boeotia*.

Ăgēsimbrŏtus -i, m. (Ἀγησίμβροτος), *commander of the Rhodian fleet against Philip of Macedon*.

Ăgēsĭpŏlis -pŏlĭdis, m. (Ἀγησίπολις), *son of Cleombrotos and king of Sparta about 195 A.C.*

aggĕmo (ad-gemo), 3 *to groan at, to weep at*, Ov.

agger -ĕris, m. (2 aggero). **I.** *material brought together to form a heap or mound*, aggerem comportare, petere, Caes.; paludem aggere explere, Caes.; poet., moliri aggere tecta, *to build and fortify with a mound*, Verg. **II.** 1, *a mound, rampart*, apparare, jacere, facere, instruere, Caes.; agger Tarquinii, or simply agger, *a rampart said to have been built by Tarquinius Superbus to protect Rome*; 2, *a rampart to protect a harbour*, Verg.; *the bank of a river*, gramineus ripae agger, Verg.; *the causeway of a road*, agger viae, Verg.; 3, poet., *any kind of elevation*, tumuli ex aggere, Verg.; aggeres Alpini, Verg.; arenae, Verg.; *a funeral pile*, Ov.

1\. **aggĕro**, 1 (agger), *to form a mound, to heap up*. **I.** Lit., Tac.; cadavera, Verg. **II.** Fig., *to increase*, dictis iras, Verg.

2\. **aggĕro** (ad-gero) -gessi -gestum, 3 (ad and gero). **I.** Lit., *to carry to, bring to*; luta et limum, Cic.; with dat., aggeritur tumulo tellus, Verg. **II.** Fig., *to load, heap on*, probra, Tac.

aggestus -ūs, m. (2 aggero), *a carrying to, accumulation*, pabulae, materiae, lignorum, Tac.

agglŏmĕro (ad-glomero), 1 Lit. *to wind on a ball*, *to add*; addunt se socios et lateri agglomerant nostro, *throng to our side*, Verg.

agglūtĭno (ad-glutino), 1 *to glue to, to fasten to*, Cic.

aggrăvesco (ad-gravesco), 3. *to become severe, to grow worse* (of sickness), Ter.

aggrăvo (ad-gravo), 1. **I.** Lit., *to make heavier*, Plin. **II.** Transf., *to make worse;* inopiam sociorum, Liv.; *to heighten;* summam invidiae ejus, Liv.

aggrĕdĭo, 3. active form of aggredior (q.v.).

aggrĕdior -gressus sum, 3. dep. (ad and gradior). **A.** 1, *to go to, approach;* ad aliquem, Plaut.; non repellitur quo aggredi cupiet, Cic.; **2,** *to approach a person;* **a,** in a friendly manner, quem ego Romae aggrediar, Cic.; aliquem pecunia, Sall.; Venerem dictis, *to address*, Verg.; **b,** in a hostile manner, *to attack;* eos impeditos et inopinantes, Caes.; murum, Sall. **B.** Transf., *to begin, to undertake, to attempt;* ancipitem causam, Cic.; facinus, *to begin*, Liv.; with ad and the acc., ad causam, ad crimen, ad disputationem, ad historiam, Cic.; with ad and the gerund, ad dicendum, Cic.; followed by the infin., oppidum altissimis moenibus oppugnare, Caes.

aggrĕgo (ad-grego), 1. *to add to, join with;* **a,** with adv., eodem ceteros undique collectos naufragos, Cic.; **b,** with in and the acc., ego te in nostrum numerum aggregare soleo, Cic.; **c,** with ad and the acc., se ad eorum amicitiam, Caes.; **d,** with dat., se Romanis, Liv.; **e,** absol., alius alia ex navi, quibuscumque signis occurrerat, se aggregabat, Caes.

aggressĭo -ōnis, f. (aggredior), *the introduction to a speech;* prima aggressione animos occupare, Cic.

ăgĭlis -e (ago). **A.** Of things, **1,** *easily moved, light;* classis, Liv.; **2,** *quick;* rivus agilior, Plin. **B.** Of persons, **1,** *light, nimble;* dea, *Diana*, Ov.; Cyllenius, *Mercury*, Ov.; **2,** *active;* oderunt agilem gnavumque remissi, Hor.; nunc agilis fio, *busy*, Hor.

ăgĭlĭtas -ātis, f. (agilis), *the power of being easily moved, quickness, agility, lightness;* navium, Liv.; naturae, Cic.

Āgis -idis, m. (Ἆγις), *name of three kings of Sparta.*

ăgĭtābĭlis -e (agito), *easily moved, light;* aer, Ov.

ăgĭtātĭo -ōnis, f. (agito). **I.** Act., **A.** Lit., *motion;* anceps telorum armorumque, Liv. **B.** *management;* rerum magnarum agitatio atque administratio, Cic. **II.** Pass., *state of motion.* **A.** Lit., agitatio et motus linguae, Cic.; tantas agitationes fluctuum, Cic. **B.** Transf., *activity;* numquam animus agitatione et motu esse vacuus potest, Cic.

ăgĭtātor -ōris, m. (agito), **1,** *one who sets in motion, a driver;* aselli, Verg.; **2,** *a charioteer, who contended for the prize in the circus*, Cic.

ăgĭtātus -ūs, m. = agitatio (q.v.).

ăgĭto, 1. (intens. of ago), *to put in constant motion, to drive about.* **I.** Lit., **1,** of animals, *to drive;* spumantem equum, Verg.; or *to hunt;* aquila insectans alias aves et agitans, Cic.; **2,** of the wind on the sea, *to agitate, toss up and down;* mare ventorum vi agitari atque turbari, Cic.; **3,** *to stir up* in any way, *to move hastily;* quod pulsu agitatur externo, Cic.; corpora huc illuc, Sall. **II.** Transf., **1,** *to vex, agitate, harass;* ut eos agitent insectenturque furiae, Cic.; Tyrrhenam fidem aut gentes agitare quietas, *to trouble*, Verg.; seditionibus tribuniciis atrociter res publica agitabatur, Sall.; *to ridicule*, quas personas agitare solemus, non sustinere, Cic.; **2,** in speech, *to handle, treat of, argue, discuss;* agraria lex vehementer agitabatur, Cic.; **3,** in thought, *to think about, consider* (with or without in corde, in mente, in animo, or simply animo or mente); in animo bellum, Liv.; rem mente, Cic.; **a,** with infin., aliquid invadere magnum mens agitat mihi, Verg.; **b,** with de, de inferendo bello, Liv.; **c,** with rel. sent., id plebes agitabat quonam modo, etc., Liv.; **4,** *to practise, exercise;* quibus agitatus et exercitatus animus, Cic.; **5,** of festivals, *to keep;* dies festos, Cic.; **6,** *to manage, observe, keep;* imperium, Sall.; gaudium atque laetitiam, *to express*, Sall.; praecepta parentis mei, *to observe* or *practise*, Sall.; **7,** of time, *to live;* sub legibus aevum, Verg.; **8,** (sc. se), *to pass time, stay;* laeti neque procul Germani agitant, Tac.; Libyes propius mare agitant, Sall.; **9,** *to act* (on the stage), Plaut.

Āglăĭē -ēs, f. (Ἀγλαΐα and Ἀγλαΐη), *the oldest of the graces*, Verg.

aglaspis -idis, m. (ἀγλαὴ ἀσπίς, *a bright shield*), *soldiers with bright shields, name of a division in the Macedonian army*, Liv.

agmĕn -inis, n. (ago), *something driven* or *moved, a mass in movement.* **I.** Gen., **A.** Of things with life, **1,** of men, *a band, a throng;* stipatus agmine patriciorum, Liv.; Eumenidum agmina, Verg.; **2,** of animals, agmen ferarum, Ov.; aligerum agmen, *swans*, Verg.; graniferum agmen, *ants*, Ov. **B.** Of things without life, **1,** *a large stream* of water, leni fluit agmine flumen, Verg.; so of rain, immensum agmen aquarum, Verg.; **2,** of the atoms, Lucr.; **3,** of the clouds, Lucr.; **4,** of the movement of oars, Verg.; **5,** of the gliding of snakes, extremae agmina caudae, Verg. **II.** As milit. t. t., *an army.* **A.** Abstr., *the march of an army;* citato agmine, Liv.; rudis agminum, Hor. **B.** Concr., **1,** *the army on march;* **a,** of infantry, phalanx agmen magis quam acies (acies = *the army in line of battle*), Liv.; agmine ingredi, ire, Liv.; agmine instructo, *ready for march*, Liv.; agmine facto, *in close marching order*, Verg.; tripartito agmine, *a march in three columns*, Tac.; agmen pilatum, Verg., or justum, *an army in close marching order*, Tac.; quadratum, *a march in a hollow square*, Sall.; primum, *the vanguard*, Caes.; medium, *the centre*, Caes.; extremum or novissimum, *the rear*, Cic.; ducere, *to lead*, Cic.; cogere, *to act as rearguard*, Caes.; so fig., ut nec duces simus nec agmen cogamus, Cic.; **b,** of cavalry, equitum, Liv.; **2,** of a fleet, Liv.; **3,** of the baggage of an army, impedimentorum, Tac.; rerum captarum, Liv.; **4,** Transf., of animals marching in order, decedens agmine magno corvorum exercitus, Verg.; and so of things personified, venti velut agmine facto, qua data porta, ruunt, Verg.; stellae quarum agmina cogit Lucifer, Ov.

agna -ae, f. (agnus), *a female lamb*, Hor.

Agnālĭa -ium = Agonalia (q.v.).

agnascor (ad-gnascor) -nātus, 3. *to be born in addition to*, legal t. t. of children born after their father's will, either in his lifetime or after his death, Cic.

agnātĭo -ōnis, f. (agnascor), *relationship reckoned through males only*, Cic.

agnātus -i, m. (agnascor), **1,** *a relation descended from a common ancestor in the male line*, Cic.; **2,** *a child born into a family where a regular heir already exists*, Tac.

agnellus -i, m. (dim. of agnus), *a little lamb*, Plaut.

agnīnus -a -um (agnus), *relating to a lamb*, Plaut. Subst., **agnīna** -ae, f. (sc. caro), *lamb's flesh*, Hor.

agnĭtĭo -ōnis, f. (agnosco). **1,** *recognition;* cadaveris, Plin.; **2,** *knowledge;* animi, *of the nature of the mind*, Cic.

agnōmen (ad nomen) -inis, n. *surname, name given to a man for some service,* e.g. Africanus, Asiaticus.

agnosco (ad gnosco) -nōvi -nitum, 3 (ad and gnosco = nosco). **I.** *to perceive* (in its true character), *to recognise,* deum ex operibus suis, Cic.; veterem Anchisen agnoscit amicum, Verg.; parvam Trojam, Verg. **II.** *to recognise as true or genuine, to acknowledge,* filium quem ille natum non agnorat, eundem moriens suum dixerat, Nep.; aliquem non ducem, Liv.; of things, crimen, Cic.; quod meum quodammodo agnosco, Cic.; with acc. and infin., et ego ipse me non esse verborum admodum inopem agnosco, Cic.

agnus -i, m. *a lamb*, collect., abundare agno, Cic.; prov., agnum lupo eripere velle, *to wish for the impossible,* Plaut.

ăgo, ēgi, actum (ἄγω), 3. *to set in motion.* **I.** Lit., **A.** *to drive,* **1,** cattle, etc., boves Romam, Liv.; **2,** *to lead or drive* men, agmen agere, *to set an army in motion,* Liv.; se agere, *to go,* Plaut.; **3,** *to ride* a horse or *drive* a carriage, *to set a ship in motion,* equum, Tac.; carpentum, Liv.; naves, Liv.; **4,** of things, *to put in motion, drive,* vineas turresque, Caes.; nubes ventus agens, Lucr. **B. 1,** *to drive with force or violence;* turba fugientium, actus, Liv.; animam agere, *to give up the ghost,* Cic.; glebis aut fustibus aliquem de fundo, Cic.; **2,** Esp., *to plunder, to drive away cattle,* often with ferre or portare, res quae ferri agique possunt, Liv.; **3,** *to construct, build, lay,* fundamenta, Cic.; **4,** of plants, *to strike root,* Plin.; fig., vera gloria radices agit, Cic. **II.** Transf., **A.** Gen., as regards actions, *to drive, incite,* in arma, Liv.; aliquem in fraudem, Verg.; se agere or agere absol., *to live,* multo et familiariter cum aliquo, Sall. **B. 1,** of time, *to pass,* quartum annum ago et octogesimum, *I am in my eighty-fourth year,* Cic.; aetatem in litteris, Cic.; **2,** *to act, to do,* quid vos agitis? Cic.; quid agam? Ter.; absol., industria in agendo, Cic.; male, bene, praeclare agere cum aliquo, *to treat a person well or badly,* Cic.; nihil agere, Cic.; id agere ut or ne, *to give attention to, to do one's best,* id agunt ut viri boni esse videantur, Cic.; **3,** of outward expression, **a,** of orators, *to declaim,* agere cum dignitate ac venustate, Cic.; **b,** of actors, *to play, represent, deliver,* nunquam agit Roscius hunc versum eo gestu quo potest, Cic.; fabulam, *to play in a piece* (comedy), Cic.; primas partes, *to play leading parts,* Ter.; agere aliquem, *to represent some character,* ministrum imperatoris, Tac.; **c,** *to express* gratitude, grates, Cic.; **4, a,** of a festival, *to keep,* festos dies anniversarios, Cic.; **b,** *to keep, observe,* pacem, Sall.; **c,** *to keep* watch, Sall.; vigilias, Cic.; **d,** *to hold* a meeting, *to execute* some function, *to transact,* forum or conventum, *to hold the assizes,* Cic., Caes.; esp., agere bellum, *to have the conduct of a war,* Liv.; **5, a,** *to treat with,* ut agerem cum Lucceio de vestra vetere gratia reconcilianda agente Servilia, *through the agency of Servilia,* Cic.; **b,** in politics, *to bring questions before the senate or people for decision,* in senatu de aliqua re, Ov.; cum populo, Cic.; nihil omnino actum est de nobis, Cic.; agere causam alicuius, *to take the side of some politician,* Cic.; **c,** in law, agere causam, *to plead some one's cause,* Cic.; absol., agere, *to bring an action, to sue,* ex syngrapha, Cic.; non enim gladiis tecum sed litibus agetur, Cic.; used esp. with jure and lege, agere lege in hereditatem, Cic.; with genit. of accusation, furti, *to indict for theft,* Cic.; qua de re agitur, *the point at dispute,* Cic.; in quo agitur populi Romani gloria, *is at stake,* Cic.; acta res est or actum est, *the transaction is finished,* so followed by de, *it is all over with,* acta ne agamus, *act when it is too late,* Cic. Imperat., age, agite, used with dum, as an interjection, *come! well! good!* Cic.

ăgōn -ōnis, m. (ἀγών), *a contest in the public games,* Plin., Suet.

Ăgōnālia -ium and -ōrum, n. *the festival of Janus*; hence adj., **Ăgōnālis** -e, *relating to the Agonalia,* Agonalis lux, *the day of the Agonalia,* Ov.

Ăgōnĭa -ōrum, n. **1,** *the animals for sacrifice;* **2,** = Agonalia, Ov.

ăgŏrānŏmus -i, m. (ἀγορανόμος), *a market inspector in Greece,* Plaut.

ăgrārius -a -um (ager), *relating to land,* lex, *law relating to the division of the public land,* Cic.; res, *the division of public lands,* Cic.; triumvir, *the officer who presided over the division,* Liv. Subst., **ăgrārii** -ōrum, m. *the agrarian party,* who proposed to distribute the public land among the people, Cic.; **ăgrāria** -ae, f. (sc. lex), *an agrarian law,* Cic.

agrestis -e (ager), *relating to the fields or country.* **A. 1,** *wild,* taurus, Liv.; **2,** *savage,* vultus, Ov. **B. 1,** *belonging to the country, rustic;* hospitium, Cic.; homo, Cic. Subst., **agrestis** -is, m. *a countryman,* Cic.; **2,** *rough, boorish, clownish,* servi agrestes et barbari, Cic.; rustica vox et agrestis, Cic.; agrestiores Musae, *the muses of the coarser, practical arts,* e.g. *eloquence,* opposed to mansuetiores Musae, e.g. *philosophy,* Cic.

1. **agrĭcŏla** -ae, m. (ager and colo) *a tiller of the fields, farmer,* agricola et pecuarius, Cic.; deus agricola, *Silvanus,* Tib.; caelites agricolae, *the gods of the country,* Tib.

2. **Agrĭcŏla** -ae, m. *Gnaeus Julius* (40–93 A.D.), *father-in-law of Tacitus, governor of Britain.*

agricultio ōnis, f. = agricultura (q.v.).

agricultor ōris, m. = agricola (q.v.).

agricultura ae, f. *agriculture,* Cic.

Agrigentum -i, n. (Gr. Ἀκράγας and Lat. Acragas), *a flourishing Greek town on the south coast of Sicily.* Adj., **Agrigentīnus** -a -um, and **Acrăgantīnus** -a -um, *Agrigentine.*

agrĭpĕta -ae, m. (ager and peto), *a landgrabber,* Cic.; *a settler or squatter,* Cic.

Agrippa -ae, m. **I.** *Roman family name.* **A.** Menenius Agrippa, the author of the fable of the belly and the members, by which he was said to have reconciled the plebeians and patricians, Liv. ii. 32. **B. 1,** M. Vipsanius Agrippa, (63–12 B.C.), the friend and adviser of Augustus, whose niece, Marcella, and daughter, Julia, he successively married, a celebrated general and statesman, who adorned Rome with many large buildings. **2,** Agrippa Postumus, son of the above, banished to Planasia by Augustus, said to have been murdered there at the beginning of Tiberius's reign. **II.** *Name of two Kings of the Herod family in Judaea,* Herodes Agrippa I. and Herodes Agrippa II.

Agrippīna -ae, f. *the name of several Roman women.* **I. A.** daughter of M. Vipsanius Agrippa by his first wife, wife of Tiberius. **B.** daughter of Agrippa by Julia, and wife of Germanicus, banished to Pandataria after her husband's death. **II.** The granddaughter of Agrippa, daughter of Germanicus and Agrippina (I. B.), gen. known as Younger Agrippina, wife of her uncle the Emperor Claudius, murdered by order of her son, the Emperor Nero; hence **Colonia Agrippinensis,** *a town of Germany* (now *Cologne*), named in honour of Agrippina (II.).

Ăgyieus -ĕi or -ĕos, m. (Ἀγυιεύς), *surname of Apollo, as protector of streets,* Hor.

Ăgylla -ae, f. (Ἄγυλλα), *Greek name of the*

Etruscan town Caere Adj., a, **Agyllīnus** a -um, *relating to Agylla*, urbs = Agylla, Verg., b, **Agyllēus** ĕos, m *epithet of Apollo, who had a temple at Agylla*, Hor

Ăgȳrĭum ii, n ('Αγύριον), *a town in Sicily, birth-place of the historian Diodorus*, now *S. Filippo d'Argiro*, hence **Agȳrĭnensis** -e, *relating to Agyrium.*

ah, interj., *ah! oh!*

Ahāla -ae, m., C Servilius, *the master of the horse under the dictator Cincinnatus*, B.C. 439, *who slew Sp Maelius*

Aharna -ae, f. *a town in Etruria*, now *Bargiano*

Ahenobarbus, v Domitius.

ai (aï), *ah!* an interjection of grief, Ov

Āiax -ācis, m (Αἴας), *the name of two Homeric heroes* 1, Aiax Telamonius, *son of Telamon, king of Salamis*, who committed suicide because he failed in the contest with Ulysses for the arms of Achilles, 2, Aiax Oileus, *king of the Locri*

āiens -entis (partic of aio), *affirmative*, Cic

āio, defective verb I. *to say yes, to affirm* (opp nego), Plaut II. *to say, to assert, to state*, Cic., ut aiunt, *as the people say*, Cic., quid ais? *what is your opinion?* Ter., ain', ais ne, *do you really mean it? is it possible?* Cic

Āius Lŏquens or **Āius Locūtĭus**, m (aio and loquor), *the speaker saying*, i.e. *the voice which is said to have warned the Romans of the coming of the Gauls, afterwards honoured as a god in a temple erected to it*, Cic.

āla -ae, f (for ag-la, from ago). I. *a wing*, of birds, galli plausu premunt alas, Cic., of gods, hic paribus nitens Cyllenius alis constitit, Verg., poet., of the oars of a ship, classis centenis remiget alis, Prop.; or the sails, velorum pandimus alas, Verg., and to express anything swift, fulminis ocior alis, Verg., used of death, Hor., of sleep, Tib II. Transf., A. *the shoulders and armpits of a man*, sub ala fasciculum portare librorum, Hor B. Milit. t. t., *the cavalry* (originally disposed on both sides of the legions like wings), *a squadron* (generally composed of allied troops), Cic

Ălăbanda ae, f., and -orum, n (ἡ and τὰ 'Αλάβανδα), *a town in Caria, near the Maeander*, famous for its wealth and luxury, founded by Alabandus, son of Euippus and Callirrhoe, hence, 1, **Ălăbandensis** -e, *belonging to Alabanda*; 2, **Ălăbandēus** -ĕos, m *born at Alabanda* Plur Gr nom., **Alabandis** ('Αλαβανδεῖς), *the inhabitants of Alabanda*, Cic.

Alăbarches (Arabarches) -ae, m ('Αλαβάρχης), *a magistrate of Arabia, a tax-gatherer, a nickname applied to Pompey, who largely increased the revenue by his Eastern conquests*, Cic

ălăbaster -stri, m., and **ălăbastrum** -i, n. (ἀλάβαστρος and -ον), 1, *a pear-shaped perfume casket*, Cic.; 2, *a rose-bud*, Plin

ălăcer -cris -cre and (rarely) **ălăcris** -e, adj. with compar I. Gen., *excited*, multos alacres exspectare quid statuetur, Cic II. *quick, cheerful, lively*, a, of men, Catilina alacer atque laetus, Cic., with ad and the gerund, ad bella suscipienda Gallorum alacer et promptus est animus, Caes; voluptas, Verg; b, of animals, equus, Cic

ălăcrĭtas -ātis, f (alacer), *quickness, briskness, eagerness, alacrity*, 1, of men, quae alacritas civitatis fuit? Cic; with genit., reipublicae defendendae, Cic., ad and gerund, mira alacritate ad litigandum, Cic., 2, of animals, canum tanta alacritas in venando, Cic.

Ălămanni (Ălămāni, Alĕmanni) -ōrum, m *name of a German confederacy between the Danube and the Rhine*

Ălāni -ōrum, m *a Scythian race*, originally from the Caucasus

ălăpa ae, f *a box on the ear*, Juv., given by a master to his slave on the manumission of the slave, hence, multo majoris alapae mecum veneunt, *I sell freedom at a much higher price*, Phaedr

ālārĭus -a -um, and **ālāris** -e (ala), *belonging to the wings of an army*, equites, Liv; cohortes, Cic; hence **ālārĭi**, *allied troops*, Caes. See ala II B

ālātus -a -um (ala), *winged*, Verg

ălauda ae, f (a Keltic word), *a lark* I. Lit., Plin II. Transf., *the name of a legion formed by Caesar in Gaul*, Suet; hence, *the soldiers of the legion*, Alaudae, Cic.

ălāzōn -ŏnis, m (ἀλαζών), *a braggart, boaster*, Plaut

Alba -ae, f (connected with albus, ἀλφός, alp, *a high mountain*) A. *Alba Longa*, the oldest Latin town, according to the legend built by Ascanius on a ridge of the Mons Albanus, the mother city of Rome, said to have been destroyed by Tullus Hostilius, hence, a, **Albānus** a -um, *Alban*, mons, *a holy mountain of the Latins* (now *Monte Cavo*), lacus, *the lake at the foot of mons Albanus* (now *Lago di Albano*), municipium, *a later town, not far from the site of Alba Longa*, **Albanum** -i, n (sc praedium), *name of the villa of Pompeius*, and afterwards of Nero and Domitian; b, **Albenses** populi, *the people of Latium*, who kept the feriae Latinae B. *Alba Fucentis* or *Albensium Alba, a town of the Marsi*, afterwards a Roman colony, in Samnium; hence **Albensis** -e, *belonging to Alba F.*

1 **Albāni**, sc Alba.

2 **Albāni** -ōrum, m *the Albanians*, inhabitants of Albania, hence, a, **Albānĭa** -ae, f *a country on the west of the Caspian sea* (*now Daghestan*), b, **Albānus** -a -um, *Albanian.*

albātus -a -um (albus), *clothed in white*, Cic

albĕo, 2 (albus), *to be white*; membra in eum pallorem albentia ut, etc., Tac., albente coelo, *at daybreak*, Caes

albesco, 3 (albeo), *to become white*, albescens capillus, Hor., lux albescit, *day dawns*, Verg

albĭcĕrātus -a -um, or **albĭcēris** -e, or **albĭcērus** -a um, *whitish yellow*, Plin.

albĭco, 1 (albus), 1, *to make white*, Varr; 2, *to be white*, prata canis albicant pruinis, Hor.

albĭdus -a um (albus), *whitish*, Ov

Albĭnŏvānus -i, m. I. C Pedo Albinovanus, *an epic poet, contemporary and friend of Ovid* II. Celsus Albinovanus, *a secretary in the retinue of Tiberius, to whom Horace addressed one of his Epistles*

Albīnus i, m *the name of a family of the Gens Postumia.* Aulus Postumius Albinus, consul 151 B.C., *writer of a Roman history in Greek*

Albĭon -ŏnis, f (from alb, i.e. *high*), *the "high" country, old name of Britain, from its cliffs*, Plin

Albis -is, m *the Elbe*, Tac

albĭtūdo -inis, f. (albus), *whiteness*, Plaut

Albĭus -ii, m *name of a Roman gens*; 1, Albius Tibullus, *the celebrated Roman elegiac poet*; 2, Statius Albius Oppianicus, *of Laterium, whom Cluentius was accused of murdering*; hence adj., **Albĭānus** -a -um, *relating to Albius.*

albŏr ŏris, m (albus), *the white of an egg*, Plin

albŭlus -a -um (dim of albus), *whitish*, columbus, Cat freta, *foaming*, Mart., hence as proper name, **I. Albŭla** -ae, f (sc aqua), *old name of the Tiber*, fluvius Albula quem nunc Tiberim vocant, Liv. **II. Albŭla** ae, m and f or **Albŭlae** aquae, or **Albŭlae** -arum, f *medicinal springs near Tiber* (Tivoli), now *Solfatara di Tivoli*, or *Acqua Zolfa*

album -i, n, v. albus

Albūnĕa -ae, f *a prophetic nymph to whom was dedicated a fountain and grotto at Tibur.*

Alburnus i, m *a high mountain of Lucania, near Paestum* (now *Monte di Postiglione*)

albus -a -um (root ALB, connected with ἀλφός), *white, dead white* (opp candidus = *glittering white*) I Adj, **A.** Lit, 1, *white*, equi, Liv, nuper in hanc urbem pedibus qui venerant albis, *slaves who came to Rome with feet chalked* to show they were for sale, Juv, prov, alba avis, *a white bird, a rarity*, Cic, albis dentibus deridere, *to laugh so as to show the teeth, i e heartily*, Plaut, filius albae gallinae, *a lucky fellow*, Juv, albis equis praecurrere, *to surpass greatly* (referring to the triumphing general whose car was driven by a white horse), Hor, 2, *grey*, barba, Plaut **B.** Esp, 1, *pale*, albus ora pallor inficit, Hor., 2, *bright*, admisso Lucifer albus equo, Ov., so *making bright*, notus, Hor, and fig, *fortunate*, stella, Hor **II.** Subst, **album** -i, n **A.** *white colour*, alba discernere et atra non posse, Cic, esp, 1, *white paint or cement*, columnas albo polire, Liv, 2, *a white spot in the eye*, Col, 3, album oculi, *the white of the eye*, Cels, 4, album ovi, *the white of an egg*, Cels **B.** *a white tablet*, esp, 1, *the tablet on which the pontifex maximus at Rome published the events of the year*, Cic, 2, album (praetoris), *the tablet on which the praetor published his edict*, 3, album senatorium, *the list of senators*, Tac, album judicum, *the jury-list*, Suet

Alcaeus i, m (Ἀλκαῖος), *a Greek lyric poet of Mytilene, flourishing about* 610-602 B C, hence **Alcăĭcus** a -um, metrum, *a metre named after him*

Alcăměnēs is, m (Ἀλκαμένης), *a sculptor scholar of Phidias*

Alcăthŏē -ēs, f (Ἀλκαθόη), *a mountain in Megara named after Alcathous*, poet for the whole district of Megaris, Ov

Alcăthŏus -i, m (Ἀλκάθοος), *son of Pelops rebuilder of Megara after it had been destroyed by the Cretans*, hence urbs Alcathoi, *Megara*, Ov

Alcē ēs, f (Ἄλκη), *town of the Carpetani in Hispania Tarraconensis.*

alcēdo inis, f (= alcyon, ἀλκυών), *the kingfisher*, Plaut, hence **alcēdōnia** ōrum, n (sc tempora) **I.** *the fourteen days of winter, during which the kingfisher is hatching its eggs, and the sea was believed to be calm* **II.** Transf, *quietness, calm*, Plaut

alces -is, f *the elk*, Caes

Alcestis idis, f and **Alcestē** -ēs f (Ἄλκηστις or Ἀλκήστη), *wife of Admetus, king of Pherae*, whose life she was said to have saved by dying for him, sent back to life by Proserpina, or, as in another legend, rescued from Hades by Hercules

Alcēus ĕi and -ĕos, m (Ἀλκεύς), *son of Perseus, father of Amphitryon, grandfather of Hercules*, hence **Alcīdēs** ae, m *a descendant of Alceus, Hercules*, Verg

Alcĭbĭădēs -is, m (Ἀλκιβιάδης) **I** *an Athenian, son of Clenias, cousin of Pericles, pupil of Socrates* **II.** *a Lacedaemonian living at the time of the war of the Romans with the Achaeans.*

Alcĭdămas -antis, m (Ἀλκιδάμας), *a Greek rhetorician of Elaea in Aeolis, pupil of Gorgias*

Alcĭmĕdē -ēs, f (Ἀλκιμέδη), *daughter of Autolycus, wife of Aeson, mother of Jason.*

Alcĭnŏus -i, m (Ἀλκίνοος), *king of the Phaeacians, the host of Odysseus*, noted for his gardens and orchards, hence poma dare Alcinoo, *to carry coals to Newcastle*, Ov; Alcinoi silvae, *orchards*, Verg., juventus, *luxurious young men*, Hor

Alcmaeo and **Alcmaeōn**, lengthened to **Alcŭmaeo** (Alcŭmĕo, Alcumĕo) -ŏnis, m, and **Alcŭmĕus** -i, m (Ἀλκμαίων) **I.** *son of Amphiaraus and Eriphyle*, who murdered his mother at the wish of his father and with the approval of the oracle, and was afterwards driven mad, hence adj, **Alcmaeŏnĭus** -a -um **II.** *a Greek philosopher and physician of Crotona, pupil of Pythagoras*

Alcmān ānis, m (Ἀλκμάν), *an old Greek poet of Sardis, in Lydia* (circ 670-640 B C)

Alcmēna -ae, f, and **Alcmēnē** -ēs, f, lengthened to **Alcŭmēna** ae, f (Ἀλκμήνη), *wife of the Theban Amphitryon and mother of Hercules by Jupiter.*

Alco and **Alcōn** -ōnis, m (Ἄλκων) **I.** *a son of Atreus*, Cic **II.** *a sculptor of Sicily*, Ov **III.** *a shepherd*, Verg **IV.** *a slave's name*, Hor **V.** *a Saguntine*, Liv

alcyŏn, alcyŏnĭa = alcedo, alcedonia (q v)

Alcyŏnē -ēs, f (Ἀλκυόνη), *daughter of Aeolus, who jumped into the sea on seeing her husband, Ceyx, drowned, and was changed with her husband into a kingfisher*

ālĕa -ae, f **1,** *a game with dice, hazard*; ludere alea, Cic, aleam exercere, Tac, de alea condemnatus (dice-playing being forbidden at Rome by the Lex Titia et Publicia et Cornelia, except during the Saturnalia), Cic, **2,** Transf, *chance, risk, uncertainty*, rem in aleam dare, *to risk*, Liv, subire, Cic, in dubiam imperii servitiique aleam ire, Liv

ālĕātor ōris, m (alea), *a dicer, hazard-player*, Cic

ālĕātōrĭus -a -um (aleator), *relating to a dicer*, damna, *losses at play*, Cic

ālec (allec) -ēcis, n *a sauce prepared from fish*, Hor, Plin.

Ălectō (Allecto), acc ō, f (Ἀληκτώ, or Ἀλληκτώ), *one of the three furies* (Only found in nom and acc)

āles, ālĭtis (gen pl alituum, Verg) (ala) **I.** Adj, *winged* **A.** Lit, *winged*, Pegasus, Ov.; deus, *Mercury*, Ov, puer, *Cupid*, Hor **B.** Transf, *swift, quick*, auster, Verg, passu alite, Ov **II** Subst, f *bird* (in only in poetry) mostly of large birds, regia, *the eagle*, Ov, Phoebeius, *the raven*, Ov, Daulias, *the nightingale*, Ov, Junonia, *the peacock*, Ov, imitatrix, rara, *the parrot*, Ov, sacer, *the hawk*, Verg, cristatus, *the cock*, Ov, Palladis, *the owl*, Ov, Caystrius, *the swan*, Ov, ales Maeonii carminis, *a poet of Homeric strain*, Hor In augury, *birds whose flight was examined* (while oscines = birds whose note was observed), Cic, hence, poet, *a sign, an omen*, so bona or secunda alite, *with favourable omen*, Hor

ălesco, 3 (alo), *to grow up*, Lucr

Ălĕsĭa -ae, f *town of the Mandubii in Gallia Lugdunensis*, now *St Reine d'Alise*

Ălēsus, v. Halesus

Aletrium (Alatrium) -ii, n *an old town of the Hernici in Latium*, afterwards a Roman colony and municipium, now *Alatri*, hence **Alētrīnās** -ātis, *relating to Aletrium*

Ălēvās -ae, m. (Ἀλεύας), *a descendant of Hercules who ruled in Larissa.*

Alexander -dri, m. (Ἀλέξανδρος). **I.** Mythol., *Paris, son of Priam, king of Troy.* **II.** Hist., **1,** *Alexander of Pherae, tyrant in Thessaly from* 370–357 B.C.; **2,** *Alexander, son of Neoptolemus, prince of the Molossi, uncle of Alexander the Great;* **3,** *Alexander the Great* (b. 356, d. 323 B.C.), *king of Macedonia, who conquered the Persians and extended the Macedonian empire to the Indus;* hence **A. Alexandrīa** or **-ēa** -ae, f. (Ἀλεξάνδρεια), *name of several cities founded by Alexander, the most famous of which was the Egyptian city, at the Canopic mouth of the Nile, capital of the kingdom of the Ptolemies.* **B. Alexandrēus** -a -um. **C. Alexandrīnus** -a -um, *belonging to Alexandria.*

alga -ae, f. **1,** *sea-weed,* Hor.; used for *a thing of little worth;* vilior algâ, Hor.; **2,** *the sea-coast,* Juv.

algens -tis (partic. of algeo), *cold, cool,* Plin.

algĕo, alsi, 2. *to be cold,* Juv.; transf., probitas laudatur et alget, i.e. *is neglected.*

algesco, alsi, 3. (inch. of algeo), *to become cold,* Ter.

1. **algĭdus** -a -um (algeo), *cold,* Cat.

2. **Algĭdus** -i, m. (sc. mons), *a range of mountains in Latium, from Tusculum to Praeneste* (now *Monte Compatri*); hence, **a, Algĭdum** -i, n. *a town of the Aequi on one of the mountains in this range;* **b, Algĭdus** -a -um, *belonging to Algidus.*

algor -ōris, m. (algeo). **I.** *the sensation of cold,* Sall. **II.** *that which causes cold, frost,* Lucr.

algōsus -a -um (alga), *abounding in sea-weed,* Plin.

algus -ūs, m. = algor (q.v.).

ălĭā, adv. (alius), sc. via, *by another way,* Liv.

ălĭās (sc. vices), adv. **I.** *at another time,* Cic.; alias . . . alias, *at one time . . . at another time,* Cic.; alius alias, *one person at one time, another at another,* Cic. **II.** Transf., **1,** *elsewhere,* Cic.; **2,** non alias quam, *on no other condition than,* Tac.; non alias nisi, *not otherwise than, as if,* Tac.

ălĭbī, adv. (alius), **1,** *elsewhere, at another place,* Cic.; alibi . . . alibi, *here . . . there,* Liv.; alibi alius, *one here, the other there,* Liv.; alibi atque alibi, *now here, now there,* Plin.; **2,** *in other respects,* Liv.

ălĭca (hălĭca) -ae f. **1,** *spelt, a kind of grain,* Plin.; **2,** *a drink prepared from spelt,* Mart.

ălĭcārĭus (hălĭcārĭus) -a -um, *belonging to spelt.* Subst., **a, ălĭcārĭus** -ĭi, m. *one who grinds spelt;* **b, ălĭcārĭa** -ae, f. *a prostitute; one who sat before the spelt-mills,* Plaut.

ălĭcŭbī, adv. (aliquis and ubi), *anywhere, somewhere,* Cic.

ālĭcŭla -ae, f. (ἄλλιξ), *a light upper garment,* Mart.

ălĭcundĕ, adv. (aliquis and unde), *from anywhere, from somewhere,* Cic.

ălĭēnātĭo -ōnis, f. (alieno). **I.** Active, *a transference* or *alienation of property;* sacrorum, *transfer of the sacra gentilicia from one gens to another,* Cic. **II.** Middle, **1,** mentis, *mental alienation, loss of reason,* Plin.; **2,** *a separation between persons, a desertion, enmity, alienation of feeling;* tua a me alienatio, Cic.

ălĭēnĭgĕna -ae, m. (alienus and gigno), *strange, foreign;* hostis, Cic. Subst., *a foreigner;* quid alienigenae de vobis loqui soleant, Cic.

ălĭēnĭgĕnus -a -um (alienus and geno = gigno), *of different elements, heterogeneous,* Lucr.

ălĭēno, 1. (alienus), *to make something another's.* **I.** Lit., **A.** *to take away;* usus fructus jam mihi harum aedium alienatus est, Plaut. **B. 1,** legal term, *to transfer property;* vectigalia, Cic.; **2,** *to sell* a child or slave to a new family, Liv.; **3,** alicuius mentem, *to cause a person to lose his reason;* Junonis iram ob spoliatum templum alienasse mentem ferebant, Liv.; oftener in pass., alienari, *to go out of one's mind;* mente alienata, Caes.; velut alienatis sensibus, Plin. **II.** Transf., **A.** *to remove from the mind, to banish;* alienatis a memoria periculi animis, *having forgotten danger,* Liv. **B.** *to estrange, put at variance;* omnes a se bonos, Cic.; with dat., alienati Romanis, Liv.; alienari ab interitu, *to have a repugnance to, to shun,* Cic.

ălĭēnus -a -um, adj. with compar. and superl. (alius), *that which belongs* or *relates to another* (opp. meus, tuus, suus, proprius). **I.** Lit., **A.** Gen., domus, Cic.; aes, *debt,* Cic.; nomina, *debts contracted in the names of others,* Sall.; alienis mensibus aestas, *the winter months,* Verg.; alieno vulnere, *a wound meant for another,* Verg. Subst., **ălĭēnum** -i, n. *another man's property,* Cic. **B. 1,** *not related* (opp. propinquus); with dat., non alienus sanguine regibus, Liv.; with a and the abl., alienissimus a Clodio, Cic.; **2,** *foreign;* domi atque in patria mallem, quam in externis atque alienis locis, Cic. Subst., **ălĭēnus** -i, m. **a,** *a stranger,* cives potiores quam peregrini, propinqui quam alieni; **b,** *a foreigner,* Plin. **II.** Transf., **A.** Of persons, **1,** *not at home in, not acquainted with, strange to;* in physicis totus alienus est, Cic.; **2,** *estranged, unfriendly;* with ab and the abl., ab aliquo or ab aliqua re, Cic.; with dat., homo mihi alienissimus, Cic. **B.** Of things, *unfavourable;* alieno loco proelium committere, *in a disadvantageous place,* Caes.; aliena verba, *unsuitable,* Cic.; non alienum est, followed by the infin., *it is not out of place to,* etc., Cic.; aliena loqui, *to talk nonsense,* Ov.; with ab and the abl., labor alienus non ab aetate solum nostra, verum etiam a dignitate, Cic.; with simple abl., dignitate imperii, Cic.; with dat., quod maxime huic causae est alienum, Cic.; with genit., aliena firmae et constantis assensionis, Cic.; with ad and the acc., ad committendum proelium tempus alienum, Cic.

ālĭgĕr -gĕra -gĕrum (ala and gero), *winged;* amor, Verg.

ălĭmentārĭus -a -um, *relating to food;* lex, *with regard to a distribution of bread among the poor,* ap. Cic.

ălĭmentum -i, n. (alo), **1,** *food* (gen. used in the plural); alimenta corporis, Cic. alimenta arcu expedire, *to get food by the bow,* Tac.; used of fire, ignis, Liv.; transf., seditionis, Tac.; **2,** *maintenance,* hence (like Gr. τροφεῖα), *the return due by children to their parents for their bringing up,* Cic.

ălĭmōnĭum -ĭi, n. (alo), *nourishment,* Tac.

ălĭō, adv. (alius), *to another place.* **I.** Lit., si offendet me loci celebritas, alio me conferam, Cic.; alius alio, *one in this direction, the other in that,* Cic. **II.** Transf., **1,** *to another person;* quo alio nisi ad nos socios confugerent, Liv.; **2,** *for another end;* nusquam alio natus quam ad serviendum, *born only for slavery,* Liv.; **3,** *to another object;* si placet sermonem alio transferemus, *to another topic,* Cic.

ălĭōquī (ălĭōquin), adv. (alius and quoi or qui, alius and quoine or quine). **I. 1,** *otherwise, in other respects,* introducing an exception; nunc pudore a fuga contineri, alioquin pro victis haberi, Liv.; **2,** concessive, triumphatum de Tiburtibus, alioquin mitis victoria fuit, Liv. **II.**

yet, besides, moreover, else, in general; Caesar Vanidus alioquin spernendis honoribus, Tac

ălĭorsum and **ălĭorsus,** adv (contr from aliovorsum (alioversum) and aliovorsus (aliover-sus)), 1, *in another direction, elsewhere,* mater ancillas jubet aliam aliorsum ire, *in different directions,* Plaut., 2, *in another manner,* Ter

ālĭpēs -pĕdis (ala and pes), 1, *having wings on the feet,* deus, or absol, *Mercury,* Ov; 2, *swift of foot* equi, Verg Subst, **ālĭpĕdes,** *horses,* Verg.

Aliphēra -ae, f (Ἀλίφηρα or Ἀλίφειρα), *a town of Arcadia not far from the border of Elis*

ălipta -ae, m, and **ăliptēs** -ae, m (ἀλείπτης), *the anointer in the wrestling-school or the baths,* hence *the master of the wrestling school,* Cic

ălĭquā (aliquis), adv I. *by some road,* evolare, Cic II. *in some way,* nocere, Verg

ălĭquamdĭū, adv (aliqui and diu), *for a moderately long time,* Cic

ălĭquammultus or **aliquam** (sc partem) **multus** -a -um (aliqui and multus), *considerable in number or quantity a pretty good many,* vestrum aliquam multi, Cic.

ălĭquandŏ, adv (aliquis) I. 1, *at any time, at some time, once,* scio, verum aliquando tamen, Cic, si forte aliquando, *if by chance ever,* Cic, 2, *once,* dicendum aliquando est, Cic, 3, *sometimes, occasionally,* scribe aliquando ad nos quid agas, Cic II. *at times, on some occasion.* aliquando ... aliquando, *at times ... at times,* Cic

ălĭquantillus -a -um (dim of aliquantus), *a very little,* Plaut

ălĭquantispĕr, adv. (aliquantus and per), *a moderately long time,* Plaut

ălĭquanto, ălĭquantum, v aliquantus

ălĭquantŭlus -a -um (dim of aliquantus), *little, small* Adv, **ălĭquantŭlum,** *a little,* Cic.

ălĭquantus -a -um (alius and quantus), *moderate, not small,* timor aliquantus spes amplior, Sall Subst, **ălĭquantum** -i, n *a good deal,* nummorum, Cic, temporis, Liv, acc aliquantum and abl aliquanto, *considerably, somewhat,* qui processit aliquantum ad virtutis aditum, *had made considerable progress towards,* Cic, epulamur intra legem et quidem aliquando, *not sparingly,* Cic, esp with comparative, aliquanto majorem locum occuparis, Cic, aliquanto post or ante, *some time after or before,* Cic

ălĭquātĕnus, adv (sc parte, from aliquis and tenus), *to a certain degree, in some measure,* Sen

ălĭqui, aliquae, aliquod (alius and qui), *some, any,* 1, masc, dolor aliqui, Cic, aliqui ex nostris, Caes, 2, fem, aliquae res, Lucr, 3, neut, simulacrum aliquod, Cic (For other cases see aliquis)

ălĭquis, aliqua, aliquid, pron indef (alius-quis), *some one, something, any one, anything* I. Gen, 1, used by itself, a, subst, quisquis est ille, si modo aliquis, *if he be any one at all,* Cic, b, adj, aliquis deus, Cic, aliquā republicā, *if only the state is in existence at all,* Cic, 2, strengthened by alius, aliquid aliud videbimus, Cic, 3, by unus, aliquis unus pluresve divitiores, Cic, 4, partitive with ex, aliquis ex vobis, Cic; 5, like the Gr τις (Engl *some*), to express an unascertained number, tres aliqui aut quattuor, Cic, 6, aliquid with genit of a subst. or adj, aliquid virium, Cic, falsi aliquid, Cic, 7, with adj, aliquid divinum, Cic 8, with si or nisi, acc aliquid, *in any respect* si in me aliquid offendistis, Cic II. Esp, 1, *some person or other,* dixerit hic aliquis, Cic, 2, *somebody or something great or significant;* si nunc aliquid assequi se putant, Cic, hence, a, esse aliquem or aliquid, *to be somebody, to be something,* Cic, est aliquid nupsisse Jovi, Ov, b, dicere aliquid, *to say something weighty,* Cic; Vestorio aliquid significes, *say something agreeable,* Cic

ălĭquō, adv (aliquis), *some or any whither;* aliquem secum rus aliquo educere, *in some direction or other,* Cic, aliquo concedere ab eorum oculis, Cic

ălĭquŏt, numer indef indecl, *some, several;* aliquot epistolae, Cic, aliquot diebus ante, Cic

ălĭquŏtĭēs, adv (aliquot), *several times,* aliquoties ex aliquo audisse, Cic

ălis, alid, old form of alius, aliud

ălĭtĕr, adv (from alis = alius), 1, *otherwise, in another way,* non fuit faciendum aliter, Cic, alius aliter, *in different ways,* Cic, in comparisons, aliter ... atque, aliter rem cecidisse atque opinatus sis, *in a different way from what you expected,* Cic, so aliter ... quam, Cic, aliter ... atque ut, Cic, non (or haud) aliter ... quam si, quam quum, ac si, *just as,* Ov, non aliter ... nisi, Cic, quod certe scio longe aliter esse, *is far from being the case,* Cic, aliter evenire, *to happen differently,* Sall, 2, *otherwise, else;* jus semper est quaesitum aequabile neque enim aliter jus esset, Cic

ălĭŭbī, adv (alius and ubi), *elsewhere,* Plin

ălĭundĕ, adv (alius and unde), *from some other direction,* alii aliunde coibant, *from different directions,* Liv, aliunde quam, *from a different direction from,* Cic, aliunde ... aliunde, Liv

ălĭus -a -ud (genit alius) *another, other* I. Lit, A. Gen, 1, distributively, *one, another,* aliud est maledicere, aliud accusare, Cic, alii ... alii, *some ... others* Cic, also, alii ... reliqui, Cic, alii ... quidam, Liv, alii ... pars, Sall, alii ... alii quidam, Cic, aliud alio melius, *one is better than the other,* Cic, alius alia via, *the one in this way, the other in that,* Liv, alius ex alio, Cic, super alium, Liv; post alium, *one after another,* Sall, alius atque alius, *now this, now that,* Cic, 2, followed by ac, atque, et, after a negative by nisi, quam, praeter, or the abl, lux longe alia est solis et lychnorum, *there is a great difference between the light of the sun and of lamps,* Cic, alius essem atque nunc sum, Cic; nec quidquam aliud philosophia est praeter studium sapientiae, Cic, nec quidquam aliud libertate quaesisse, *anything else but liberty,* Cic, tribunatus Sestii nihil aliud nisi meum nomen causamque sustinuit, Cic; 3, plur, alia, subst, si alia desint, Liv, acc plur, alia, *in other respects,* alia clarus, Tac; 4, aliud, subst with genit, aliud commodi, Cic B. Esp, 1, of auguries, alio die, si unus augur alio die dixerit, *if an augur pronounces the word "on another day,"* i e *postpones the comitia on the ground of unfavourable omens,* Cic, 2, *of another nature, different,* alium facere, *to change, transform,* Plaut, alium fieri, *to be transformed,* Cic, in alia omnia ire, discedere, transire, *to dissent from a proposition, be of a contrary opinion* (in the Roman senate), Cic II. Transf, 1, *the rest,* Divitiaco ex aliis (Gallis) maximam fidem habebat, Caes, 2, = alter, *one of two,* alius Augustus, *a second Augustus,* Tac, duo Romani super alium alius corruerunt, Liv

ălĭusmŏdi (alius and modus), *of another kind,* Cic.

allābor -lapsus, 3 *to glide to come to flow to,* angues duo ex occulto allapsi, Liv, with dat. and acc., antiquis allabimur oris, *we land on*, Verg.; fama allabitur aures, Verg.

allăbōro (ad-lăbōro), 1. *to labour at*, Hor.

allăcrĭmo (ad-lăcrimo), 1. *to weep at*, Verg.

allapsus -ūs, m. (allabor), *a gliding approach*, Hor.

allātro (ad-lātro), 1. *to bark at; fig., to rail at;* magnitudinem Africani, Liv.

allaudābĭlis (ad-laudābĭlis) -e, *praiseworthy*, Lucr.

allaudo, 1. *to praise*, Plaut.

allec, v. alec.

allecto (allicio), 1. *to entice*, Cic.

allectus -a -um (partic. of 2. allego), plur., *members elected into any collegium*, Varr.; under the empire, *persons raised by the emperor to a higher rank*, Plin.

allēgātĭo -ōnis, f. (1. allego), *a sending of a person on a mission;* quum sibi omnes ad istum allegationes difficiles viderent, Cic.

allēgātus, abl. -ū, m. (1. allego), *instigation*, Plaut.

1. **allēgo** (ad-lēgo), 1. **I. A.** *to send on private business, to commission* (lego of state business); aliquem ad aliquem or alicui, Cic.; patrem allegando fatigare, *by sending messages*, Cic.; allegati, *deputies*, Cic. **B.** *to instigate, to suborn*, Ter. **II.** Transf., *to adduce or allege in excuse;* munera, preces, mandata regis sui Scyrothemidi allegant, Tac.

2. **allĕgo** (ad-lĕgo) -lēgi -lectum, 3. *to choose, to elect;* de plebe omnes, Liv.; with in and the acc., aliquem in senatum, Suet.

allĕvāmentum -i, n. (allevo), *a means of alleviation*, Cic.

allĕvātĭo -ōnis, f. **A.** Lit., *a lifting up*, Quint. **B.** Transf., *alleviation;* doloris, Cic.

allĕvo (ad-lĕvo), 1. **A.** Lit., *to lift up, to erect;* circumstantium humeris, Tac. **B.** Transf., *to lighten, to alleviate;* sollicitudines, Cic.; pass., allevari, *to be cheered;* allevor, quum loquor tecum absens, Cic.

Allĭa (Alia) -ae, f. *river in Latium, flowing into the Tiber*, near which the Romans were defeated by the Gauls, B.C. 389; infaustum Alliae nomen, Verg. Adj., **Allĭensis** -e.

allĭcĕfăcĭo, 3. *to entice*, Sen.

allĭcĭo -lexi -lectum, 3 (ad and * lacio), *to allure, entice, draw to oneself;* ad se allicere et attrahere ferrum (of the magnet), Cic.; fig., oratione benigna multitudinis animos ad benevolentiam, Cic.

allīdo -līsi -līsum, 3. (ad and laedo). **A.** Lit., *to strike against, dash against;* allidi ad scopulos, Caes. **B.** Transf., allidi, *to suffer damage;* in quibus (damnationibus) Servius allisus est, Cic.

Allīfae -ārum, f. *a town of the Samnites on the left bank of the Vulturnus*, now *Alife* in the *Terra di Lavoro;* hence **Allīfānus** -a -um, *relating to Allifae.* Subst., **Allīfāna** -ōrum, n. (sc. pocula), *earthenware drinking-vessels of some size*, Hor.

allĭgo (ad-ligo), 1. *to tie to, bind to.* **I.** Lit., **A.** Gen., aliquem ad palum, *bind a criminal to the stake for punishment*, Cic. **B.** Esp., **1**, *to make fast;* unco dente velut manu ferrea injecta alligavit alterius proram, Liv.; unco non alligat (naves) ancora morsu, Verg.; **2**, *to bind by a fastening*, **a**, of a wound, vulnus, Cic.; **b**, of fetters, Tac. **II.** Transf., **A.** Gen., *to fetter, bind;* videas civitatis voluntatem solutam, virtutem alligatam, Cic.; tristi palus inamabilis unda alligat, *confines, imprisons*, Verg. **B.** Esp., **1**, *to bind by friendship or obligations;* non modo beneficio sed etiam benevolentia alligari, Cic.; **2**, in rhet., of the constraints of metre, ut verba neque alligata sint quasi certa lege versus, Cic.; **3**, *to bind by promise, oath*, etc.; lex omnes mortales alligat, Cic.; sacris alligari, *to pledge oneself to perform* the sacra gentilicia, Cic.; alligare se scelere, *to become an accomplice in a crime*, Cic.; alligatus, *implicated* or *involved* in a crime, Cic.

allĭno (ad-lĭno) -lēvi -lĭtum, 3. *to smear on*, or *over, to bedaub*, Cic.

allĭum -i, n. *garlic*, Plin.

Allŏbrŏges -um, m. *the Allobroges, a Gallic people between the Rhone and the Isère*; nom. sing., **Allŏbrox**, Hor.; Ciceronem Allobroga (i.e. *speaking bad Latin*) dixit, Juv. Adj., **Allŏbrŏgĭcus** -a -um, as *a surname of Q. Fabius Maximus*, conqueror of the Allobroges.

allŏcūtĭo -ōnis, f. (alloquor), *an address, a speaking to*, Plin.

allŏquĭum -i, n. (alloquor), *exhortation, encouragement, consolation;* benigni voltus et alloquia, Liv.; alloquio firmare militem, Tac.

allŏquor -lŏcūtus sum, 3. *to address, exhort, encourage*, Cic.; aliquem benigne, leniter, Liv.; patriam maesta voce ita miseriter, Cat.

allŭbesco, 3. inch. (ad and lubet), *to begin to please*, Plaut.

allūcĕo -luxi, 2. *to shine at, or upon;* Fortuna facu̇lam tibi allucet, *offers thee a favourable opportunity*, Plaut.

alludo (ad-lūdo) -lūsi -lūsum, 3. **1**, *to jest at, to sport with*; Galba alludens varie et copiose, Cic.; **2**, of waves, *to play* or *dash upon;* alludentibus undis, Ov.; quae fluctus salis alludebant, Cat.

allŭo (ad-lŭo) -ŭi, 3. *to wash;* used of the sea, alluuntur a mari moenia, Cic.; fig., Massilia quum barbariae fluctibus alluatur, *exposed to barbarians*, Cic.

allŭvĭēs -ēi, f. (alluo), *a pool caused by the overflow of a river*, Liv.

allŭvĭo -ōnis, f. (alluo), *alluvial land, earth deposited by water*, Cic.

Almo -ōnis, m. *a small brook on the south side of Rome*, now *Aquataccio.*

almus -a -um (alo), *nourishing;* ager, Verg.; *fair, gracious, propitious, kind;* Venus, Hor.

alnus -i, f. *the alder.* **I.** Lit., Plin. **II.** Meton., *a ship of alderwood*, Verg.

ălo, ălŭi, altum and ălĭtum, 3. *to nourish, support.* **I.** Lit., **A.** Of living things, **1**, *to rear;* altus educatusque inter arma, Liv.; **2**, *to keep;* anseres in Capitolio, Cic.; magnum numerum equitatus suo sumptu, Caes.; se alere or ali, with abl., or ex and the abl., *to support oneself;* se suosque latrociniis, *to live by brigandage*, Caes. **B.** Of things, **1**, of land, etc., *to provide means of existence;* cum agellus eum non satis aleret, Cic.; venatus viros pariter ac feminas alit, Tac.; **2**, of the earth, *to nourish;* tellus humida majores herbas alit, Verg.; **3**, *to support;* **a**, plants, gramen erat circa quod proximus humor alebat, Ov.; **b**, of rivers, amnis imbres quem super notas aluere ripas, *have swollen*, Hor.; idem (Libanus mons) amnem Jordanem alit funditque, Tac.; **c**, of fire, flammas, Ov.; **4**, of the means that support the body, *to give strength to;* otia corpus alunt, Ov. **II.** Transf., *to increase, promote, advance;* honos alit artes, Cic.; hos successus alit, *encourages*, Verg.; civitatem, *promote the good of the state*, Caes.; alere spem mollibus sententiis, Cic.

ălŏē -ēs, f. (ἀλόη), *the aloe;* transf., *bitterness;* plus aloes quam mellis habet, Juv.

Ălōĕūs -ĕi, m (Ἀλωεύς), *a giant, son of Neptune* **Alōīdae** -arum, m *sons of Aloeus (Otus and Ephialtes), giants who tried to storm heaven*

Alōīdae -ārum, m. (Ἀλωεῖδαι), v Aloeus

Ălŏpē -ēs, f (Ἀλόπη), *a town in Opuntian Locris*

Alpēs -ium, f (Keltic alb, alp = *height, high mountain*), *the Alps*, hence **A. Alpīnus** -a -um **B. Alpĭcus** -a -um, *Alpine*

alpha, indecl n (ἄλφα), *the name of the first letter in the Greek alphabet*, Juv , prov , *the first*, Mart

Alphēus -i, m (Ἀλφειός), *the principal river of the Peloponnesus flowing through Elis to the sea*, the river god Alpheus was said to have dived under the sea in pursuit of the nymph Arethusa, and to have come up in Sicily, hence **Alphēias** -ădis, f *surname of the nymph Arethusa* Adj , **Alphēus** -a -um, *belonging to the river Alpheus*, Verg

Alsĭum -ii, n *one of the oldest towns in Etruria* (now the village *Palo*), near which Pompeius had an estate, hence adj , **Alsĭensis** e, *belonging to Alsium*, villa (*of Pompeius*), Cic Subst., **Alsiense** -is, n (sc praedium), *the estate of Pompeius*, Cic

alsĭus (alsus) a -um, *frosty, cold*, Lucr , Cic

altānus -i, m *a S W wind*, Suet

altārĭa -ium, n (altus) **I.** *the slab upon the altar (ara), on which the fire is lighted*, Quint. **II.** *a high altar*, ecce duas tibi, Daphni, duas altaria Phoebo, Verg , *an altar*, Cic

altē, adv (altus) **I.** *on high, highly* **A.** Lit , cadere, *from a height*, Cic **B.** Transf spectare, *to have high aims*, Cic **II.** *deeply* **A.** Lit , sulcus altius impressus, Cic **B.** Transf , quod verbum in Jugurthae pectus altius quam quisquam ratus erat descendit, Sall , petere, *to seek far and wide*, Cic , altius perspicere, *to see farther*, Cic

altĕr -tĕra -tĕrum (genit , altĕrīus, in poetry also altĕrĭus, dat , alteri), *one of two, the one, the other* **I.** Lit , **A.** Gen , consulum alter, Liv , alter . alter, *the one* . *the other*, so alter ille or hic or iste, or a subst , in plur , alteri dimicant, alteri victorem timent, Cic , with the second alter in a different case, alter alterius ova frangit, Cic **B.** Esp , **1,** alter ambove, S E V , a form in the senate, *one of the consuls, or both*, si eis videbitur, Cic . **2,** *the second*; fortunate puer, tu nunc eris alter ab illo, *you will be second to him*, Verg , unus et alter dies, *one or two*, Cic , **3,** used appellat , *another, a second*, me sicut alterum parentem diligit, *a second parent*, Cic , tanquam alter idem, *a second self*, Cic , **4,** *the other*, i e *the opposite*, ripa, Caes , pars, *the opposite faction*, Cic , quoties te speculo videris alterum, *changed*, Hor **II.** Transf , *another*, in the sense of your *neighbour, fellow creature*, qui nihil alterius causa facit, Cic

altercātĭo -ōnis, f (altercor), **1,** *a dispute, wrangling, debate*; magna non disceptatio modo, sed etiam altercatio, Liv , **2,** legal t. t , *cross-examination* in a court of justice, Cic

altercātor -ōris, m (altercor), *a disputant*, Quint

altercor, 1, dep (alter), *to dispute, contend in words, quarrel* **I.** Gen , **A** Lit , altercari cum aliquo, Caes **B** Transf , poet , altercante libidinibus pavore, *contending with*, Hor **II.** Legal t t *to cross examine, to cross-question*, in altercando invenit parem neminem, Cic

alterno, 1 (alternus) **A.** Trans., *to do first one thing, then another*, fidem, *make at one time credible, at another not*, Ov , vices, Ov **II.** Intrans , **A** Lit *to change*: illi alternantes magna vi proelia miscent *changing sides*, Verg **B.** Transf , *to hesitate*, haec alternanti potior sententia visa est, Verg

alternus -a um (alter) **I.** *one after the other, by turns, alternate, interchanging*, sermones, *dialogue*, Hor ; versibus, *in alternate song*, Verg ; alterni metus, *mutual fear*, Liv , alterno pede terram quatiunt, *first with one foot then with another*, Hor , alterna loqui cum aliquo, *to hold a conversation with*, Hor **II., A.** Of metre, *elegiac verse*, where hexameter and pentameter alternate , pedes alternos esse oportebit, Cic , canere alterno carmine, Ov **B** Legal t t , rejicere alterna consilia or alternos judices (of plaintiff and defendant), *to challenge a number of jurors*, Cic

altĕrūtĕr, altĕrutra (altera utra), alterutrum (alterum utrum), genit , altĕrutrius, *one of two*, Cic

Althaea -ae, f (Ἀλθαία), *wife of Oeneus, king of Calydon, mother of Meleager*

altĭcinctus -a -um (altus and cingo), *high girt*, hence *busy*, Phaedr

altĭlis -e (alo) **A.** Of domestic animals, *fattened, fed up*, hence subst , **altĭlis**, f (sc avis), *a fowl*, Hor **B.** Transf , *rich*, Plaut

altĭsŏnus a -um (alte and sono) **I.** *sounding from on high*, Juppiter, Cic **II.** Transf , *high-sounding, sublime*, Maronis altisoni carmina, Juv

altĭtŏnans -tis, *thundering from on high*, Lucr

altĭtūdo -inis, f (altus). **I.** *height* **A.** Lit , montium, Cic **B.** Transf , *sublimity*, orationis, Cic **II.** *depth* **A.** Lit., fluminis, Caes **B.** Transf , altitudo animi, *secrecy, reserve*, Cic

altĭuscŭlus -a um (dim of altius), *a little too high*, Suet

altĭvŏlans -antis (altus and volo), *flying high*, Lucr

altor ōris, m. (alo), *a nourisher, a foster-father*, omnium rerum seminator et sator et parens, ut ita dicam, atque educator et altor est mundus, Cic

altrinsĕcŭs, adv (alter and secus), *on the other side*, Plaut

altrix -icis, f (altor), *a nurse, foster mother* ; terra altrix nostra, Cic

altrōvorsum, adv (alter and versus), *on the other side*, Plaut

altus a -um (alo), **I.** *high* **A** Lit Cic , Caes , with acc of measure, signum septem pedes altum, Liv Subst , **altum** -i, n *height*, **a,** aedificia in altum edita, Tac , **b,** esp , *the height of the heavens*, ab alto, Verg **B.** Transf , **1,** of position, altior dignitatis gradus Cic **2,** of the voice, *shrill*, altiore voce, Quint , **3,** of gods and exalted persons, Apollo, Verg , Caesar, Hor , Aeneas, *high-born*, Verg , **4,** of speech, *elevated*, nimis altam et exaggeratam (orationem), Cic , **5,** of character or intellect, *lofty*, te natura excelsum quendam et altum genuit, Cic , vultus, *a lofty mien*, Hor ; **6,** *ancient*, altior memoria, Cic ; aliquid ex alto petere, Verg **II.** *deep* **A.** Lit., flumen, Caes , with acc of measure, quinquaginta cubita altum mare, Plin Subst , **altum** -i, n *depth*, esp *the deep sea*, in portum ex alto provehi, Cic **B.** Transf , **1,** of quiet, etc , *deep*, somnus altus, Liv , **2,** *deep-seated*, pavor, Tac ; **3,** *secret*, si altior istis sub precibus venia ulla latet, Verg , **4,** *depth* (of mind), ex alto dissimulare, *to dissimulate profoundly*, Ov

ālūcĭnātĭo -ōnis, f (alucinor), *hallucination, delusion*, Sen

ălūcĭnor, 1. dep. (connected with ἀλύω), *to wander in mind, dream, to talk idly;* ego tamen suspicor, hunc, ut solet, alucinari, Cic.

ălumna -ae, f., v. alumnus.

ălumnus -a -um (alo), *a nursling, a foster-son.* **I.** Masc., **A.** Lit., *child of a country, inhabitant,* Verg.; Italia alumnum suum videret, Cic.; sutrinae tabernae, *a cobbler,* Tac.; legionum, *brought up in the camp,* Tac.; of animals, parvi alumni, *the young of the flock,* Hor. **B.** Transf., *pupil, disciple;* Platonis, Cic.; fig., ego, ut ita dicam, pacis alumnus, Cic. **II. A.** Fem., *foster-child;* nostra haec alumna et tua profecto filia, Plaut.; aquae dulcis alumnae, *frogs,* Cic. poet. **B.** Transf., bene constitutae civitatis quasi alumna quaedam eloquentia, Cic. **III.** Neut., numen alumnum, Ov.

Ăluntĭum (Haluntium) -ii, n. (Ἀλούντιον), *a town on the north coast of Sicily,* now *Caronia.* Adj., **Aluntīnus** -a -um.

ălūta, -ae, f. *a kind of soft leather,* Caes.; hence, meton., **1,** *a shoe,* Ov.; **2,** *a purse,* Juv.; **3,** *an ornamental patch,* Ov.

alvĕārĭum -ii, n. *a beehive,* Verg.

alvĕātus -a -um (alveus), *hollowed like a trough,* Cato.

alvĕŏlus -i, m. (dim. of alveus), **1,** *a little hollow, a tray, trough, bucket,* Juv., Liv.; **2,** *a gaming board,* Cic.

alvĕus -i, m. (connected with alo), *a hollow, an excavation;* **1,** *a trough,* Liv.; **2,** *a boat,* Verg.; *the hold of a ship,* Sall.; **3,** *a bathing-tub,* Ov.; **4,** *the bed of a stream;* quia sicco alveo transiri poterat, Liv.; **5,** *a beehive,* Tib.; vitiosae ilicis alveo, *the hollow of a tree in which bees settled,* Verg.; **6,** *a gaming-table,* Plin.

alvus -i, f. (alo). **I.** *the belly.* **A.** Lit., purgatio alvi, Cic. **B.** Transf., **1,** *the womb,* Cic.; **2,** *the stomach,* Cic. **II.** *the hold of a ship,* Tac. **III.** *a bee-hive,* Plin.

Ălyattēs -is or -ĕi, m. (Ἀλυάττης), *king of Lydia, father of Croesus.*

Alyzĭa -ae, f. (Ἀλυζία), *a small town of Acarnania,* with a temple of Hercules, now *Porto Candello.*

ămābĭlis -e (amo), *amiable, lovable;* amabilior mihi Velia fuit, quod te ab ea amari sensi, Cic.; amabile carmen, *lovely,* Hor.

ămābĭlĭtas -ātis (amabilis), *amiableness,* Plaut.

ămābĭlĭtĕr, adv. (amabilis), **1,** *amiably,* Hor.; **2,** *lovingly,* Cic.

Ămalthēa -ae, f. (Ἀμάλθεια), *a nymph, the nurse of Jupiter in Crete,* according to others, the goat on the milk of which Jupiter was reared; the cornu Amaltheae or Copiae was placed among the stars; hence **Amalthēa** -ae, f., and **Amalthēum** or **Amalthīum** -i, n. *a sanctuary of Amalthea, in Epirus,* near to the estate of Atticus.

āmandātĭo -ōnis, f. (amando), *a sending away,* Cic.

āmando, 1. *to send away, to send to a distance;* aliquem Lilybaeum, Cic.; transf., natura res similes procul amandavit a sensibus, Cic.

ămans -antis, p. adj. (amo), **1,** *loving, fond, affectionate.* **I.** Adj., **A.** Lit., pater amantissimus, Cic.; with gen., amantissimus reipublicae, Cic. **B.** Transf., of things, mea fidelissima atque amantissima consilia, Cic. **II.** Subst., c. *a lover,* Cic.

ămantĕr, adv. (amans), *lovingly,* Cic.

Amantĭa -ae, f. (Ἀμαντία), *a town in Illyria,* now *Nivitza;* hence **Amantĭāni** -ōrum *the inhabitants of Amantia.*

āmănŭensis -is, m. = a manu servus, *a secretary, clerk,* Suet.

Ămānus -i, m. (Ἄμανος), *a range of mountains in Asia Minor, dividing Cilicia from Syria* (now *Alma Dagh*); hence **Amānienses** -ium, m. *the mountaineers of Mount Amanus.*

ămārăcĭnus -a -um, *made of marjoram.* Subst., **ămārăcĭnum** -i, n. (sc. unguentum), *marjoram ointment,* Lucr.

ămārăcus -i, c., and **ămārăcum** -i, n. (ἀμάρακος), *marjoram,* Verg.

ămărantus -i, m. (ἀμάραντος, *unfading*), *the amaranth,* Ov.

ămārē, adv. (amarus), *bitterly,* Sen.

ămārĭtūdo -ĭnis, f. (amarus). **I.** Lit., *bitterness of taste,* Varr. **II.** Transf., **a,** *that which is bitter, unpleasant,* Plin.; **b,** in rhet., vocis, *an excessive vehemence, harshness of voice,* Quint.

ămāror -ōris, m. (amarus), *bitterness,* Lucr., Verg.

ămārus -a -um, *bitter.* **A.** Lit., **1,** of taste, Cic.; **2,** of smell, *pungent;* fumus, Verg.; **B.** Transf., **1,** *disagreeable, unpleasant;* historiae, *tedious,* Hor.; curae, Ov. Neut. plur., **ămāra** -ōrum, *what is unpleasant,* Hor.; **2,** *irritable, susceptible;* amariorem me senectus facit, Verg.; **3,** of speech, *biting, acrimonious;* lingua, Ov.

Ămăryllis -ĭdis, acc. -ĭda, f. (Ἀμαρυλλίς), *name of a shepherdess.*

Ămărynthĭs -ĭdis, f. *surname of Diana,* from Amarynthos, a place in Euboea where Diana was worshipped.

Ămăsēnus -i, m. *a river in Latium,* now *Amaseno.*

Ămāsis, acc. -im, abl. -i, -e, or -ĭdĕ, m. (Ἄμασις), *one of the Egyptian Pharaohs.*

ămāsius -ii, m. (amo), *a lover,* Plaut.

Ămastris -ĭdis, f. (Ἄμαστρις), *a town in Paphlagonia,* now *Amasserah;* hence **Amastrĭăcus** -a -um, *belonging to Amastris;* orae, *coasts of Pontus,* Ov.

Ămāta -ae, f. myth., *wife of king Latinus, mother of Lavinia.*

Ămăthūs -untis, f. (Ἀμαθοῦς), *a city of Cyprus,* famous for the worship of Venus; hence **Ămăthūsĭa,** *Venus;* **Ămăthūsĭăcus** -a -um, *Amathusian.*

ămātĭo -ōnis, f. (amo), *love-making, intrigue,* Plaut.

ămātor -ōris, m. (amo), **1,** *one who loves, a friend;* vir bonus amatorque noster, Cic.; amatores huic (Catoni) desunt, *admirers, readers of his works,* Cic.; so of a thing, puri sermonis, Caes.; sapientiae, pacis, Cic.; **2,** *lover of a woman, paramour;* virginem ab amatorum impetu prohibere, Cic.

ămātorcŭlus -i, m. (dim. of amator), *a little lover,* Plaut.

ămātōrĭē, adv. (amatorius), *amorously,* Cic.

ămātōrĭus -a -um (amator), *loving, amorous;* sermo, Cic.; poesis (Anacreontis), Cic.; frui voluptate amatoria, Cic.

ămātrix -īcis, f. (amator), *a mistress, sweetheart,* Plaut.

Ămāzon -ŏnis, f., gen. in plur., **Amāzŏnes** -um (Ἀμαζόνες), myth. *nation of female warriors;* hence, **1, Amāzŏnis** -ĭdis, f. = Amazon, Verg.; **2, Amāzŏnĭcus** -a -um, *Amazonian;* **3, Amāzŏnĭus** -a -um, *Amazonian;* vir, *Hippolytus,* son of an Amazon by Theseus, Ov.

amb, ambi, and **ambe,** an inseparable [illegible] sition, entering into the composition of [illegible] *about* (as in ambedo, etc.).

ambactus -i, m *a vassal*, Caes

ambădĕdo, 3 *to eat round, consume utterly*, Plaut.

ambāges, abl -e, f (of sing. only abl. found, complete in the plur), *going round, roundabout way, winding* I. Lit, variarum ambage viarum, *of a labyrinth*, Ov II. Transf, A. *circumlocution*, missis ambagibus, *without circumlocution*, Hor. B. *obscurity, ambiguity*, ambages canere, *of the Sibyl*, Verg, immemor ambagum, *of the Sphinx*, Ov, C. *shifts, prevarication*, falsi positis ambagibus oris, Ov

Ambarri -ōrum, m *a Gallic people east of the Aedui, with whom they were related*

ambĕdo ēdi ēsum, 3 *to eat round, consume*, Verg

Ambĭāni -ōrum, m *people in North Gaul, on the Somme*

Ambibarii -ōrum, m *Gallic people in Normandy* (whence the modern *Ambieres*)

ambĭgo, 3 (amb and ago) I. Lit, *to go about or round* II. Transf, A. *to doubt, hesitate, be uncertain*; jus quod ambigitur, Cic, ambigitur, impers, followed by de and the abl, or with relative or infinitive clause, or with negative followed by quin and the subj, quum de vero ambigetur, Cic B. *to dispute, contend*, at law or otherwise, cum eo qui heres est, Cic, de hereditate, Cic

ambĭgŭē, adv (ambiguus), 1, *ambiguously*, scribere, Cic, 2, *indecisively*, equites ambigue certavere, Tac.

ambĭgŭĭtas -ātis, f (ambiguus), *ambiguity*, verborum, Cic

ambĭgŭus -a -um (ambigo) I. *moving from side to side, of doubtful nature*, Proteus, Ov, virgo, *Siren* or *Sphinx*, Ov.; viri, *Centaurs*, Ov, ambiguam promisit Salamina, *a second Salamis*, Hor II. Transf, A. *uncertain, doubtful*, ambiguus tanti certaminis heres, Ov, imperandi, *not resolved on*, Tac Subst., **ambĭgŭum** -i, n *uncertainty*, non habui ambiguum *I had no doubt*, Cic, relinquere in ambiguo, Lucr B. Of speech, *ambiguous, obscure*, oracula, Cic Subst, **ambĭgŭum** -i, n *ambiguity*, ex ambiguo dicta, Cic C. *uncertain, untrustworthy*, fides, Liv, tribuni, Tac, res possessionis haud ambiguae, *with a clear title*, Liv, res, *insecure*, Tac, aquae, *changing*, Ov

Ambiliati ōrum, m *a Gallic people on the Somme*

ambĭo -īvi and ĭi -ītum, 4 (amb and eo, but conjugated regularly acc to the 4th conjug except imperf ambibat, Liv) I. *to go round* A. Lit, ut terram lunae cursus proxime ambiret, Cic B. Transf, *to surround*, silvas profunda palus ambibat, Tac, vallum armis, Tac II. A. *to go round canvassing for votes, or help*, ad id quod agi videbatur ambientes, Liv, pass, populus facit eos a quibus est maxime ambitus, Cic, B. *to address individuals*, reginam affatu, Verg, te pauper ambit sollicita prece ruris colonus, *approaches with prayer*, Hor

Ambĭŏrix -rīgis, m *prince of the Eburones in Gallia Belgica*

ambĭtĭo -ōnis, f (ambio) A. *a canvassing for office in a lawful manner*, opp ambitus (q v), me ambitio et forensis labor ab omni illa cogitatione abstrahebat, Cic B. Transf, *striving after honours*, 1, after public office *desire for office*, me ambitio quaedam ad honorum studium duxit, Cic 2, *desire for fame, display, pomp*; funerum nulla ambitio, *no empty pomp*, Tac, 3, *factiousness*, non puto existimare te ambitione me labi, Cic, 4, *striving after something*, conciliandae provinciae ad novas spes, Tac

ambĭtĭōsē, adv (ambitiosus), 1, *aspiringly*; petere regnum, Liv, 2, *with a view to one's interest, selfishly*, non vulgariter nec ambitiose scribere, Cic

ambĭtĭōsus -a -um (ambitio) 1, *twining around*, lascivis hederis ambitiosior, Hor, ambitiosa ornamenta, *excessive*, Hor, 2, a, *eager for public office, ambitious*; patres mollem consulem et ambitiosum rati, Liv, b, *vain, ostentatious, pretentious*, amicitiae, *interested*, Cic, mors, *ostentatious, studied*, Tac, c, *eager to win favour*, seeking *after popularity*, dux indulgens ambitiosusque, Liv, rogationes, *meant to win popularity*, Cic, d, *striving after anything*; Musa nec in plausus ambitiosa mea est, Ov, amor, Ov

ambĭtus ūs, m (ambio), *a going round* I. Gen, A. Abstr, *circuit, revolution*, siderum, Cic B. Concr, 1, *course, orbit*, stellarum rotundi ambitus, Cic, transf, *circumlocution*, multos circa unam rem ambitus facere, Liv, 2, *circle, edge*, extremus ambitus campi, Tac, esp, *the space left round a house*, Cic, 3, *extent*, castra lato ambitu, Tac II. *going round to entreat* A. Lit, *illegal canvassing for office, bribery*, lex de ambitu, Cic, ambitus aliquem accusare, damnare, Cic B. Transf, *striving after honours*, Plin, *popularity hunting*, Tac C. *striving for*, with genit, ambitu remanendi aut eundi, Tac

Ambivareti ōrum, m *a Gallic people, allies of the Aedui*

Ambivariti -ōrum, m *a Gallic people on the Maas*, near modern Breda

Ambĭvĭus, L Ambivius Turpio, *a celebrated actor in Rome*, contemporary of Terence

ambō -ae ō (ἄμφω), *both, two together* (uterque, *two considered separately*) hic qui utrumque probat, ambobus debuit uti, Cic

Ambrăcĭa -ae f (Ἀμβρακία), *town on the south border of Epirus, near the sea*, now *Arta*, hence, 1, adj, **Ambrăcĭensis** e, *Ambracian*, 2, **Ambrăcĭus** a um, *Ambracian*, 3, subst, **Ambrăcĭōtēs** -ae, m *inhabitant of Ambracia*

Ambrōnes um, m *a Keltic people defeated by Marius in the war with the Cimbri*

ambrŏsĭa -ae, f (ἀμβροσία), 1, *ambrosia, the food of the gods*, Cic, orator ambrosia alendus, *of a distinguished orator*, Cic, 2, *a miraculous unguent, giving divine beauty and making immortal*, Verg

ambrŏsĭus -a -um (ἀμβρόσιος), *divine, immortal, ambrosial*, dapes, Mart, comae, *anointed with ambrosia*, Verg

Ambrȳsus -i, f *a town in Phocis*, now *Dystomo*

ambūbājae ārum, f (Syrian abub, anbub, the flute), *Syrian music women and prostitutes in Rome*, Hor

ambŭlācrum -i, n *a walk shaded with trees*, Plaut

ambŭlātĭo ōnis, f (ambulo), 1, *a walk*, Cic, 2, *a place for walking, a promenade*, Cic

ambŭlātĭuncŭla -ae, f 1, *a little walk*, Cic, 2, *a little promenade*, Cic

ambŭlātor ōris, m (ambulo), *one who walks about, a lounger*, Cato, *pedlar*, Mart

ambŭlātōrĭus a -um (ambulo), *movable*, Plin

ambŭlātrix -īcis, f *a gadding woman*, Cato.

ambŭlo, 1 (dim of ambio) I. *to go backwards and forwards, to walk*, Cic, defessus sum ambulando, Ter, bene ambula, *bon voyage*, Plaut, ergo ambula, *be off with you*, Plaut, ambulare in jus, *to go to law*, Plaut, of soldiers, *to march*, eodem modo ambulat

Caesar ut, etc., Cic.; *to travel over, to traverse;* with acc., quum (Xerxes) maria ambulavisset, Cic. **II.** Transf., **A.** Of things, Nilus immenso longitudinis spatio ambulans, Plin. **B.** *to go for a walk,* in hortis cum Galba, Cic.

ambūro -ussi -ustum, 3. **I. A.** *to burn round, to scorch, to burn up;* ille domi suae vivus exustus est; hic sociorum *ambustus* incendio tamen ex illa flamma periculoque evasit, Cic.; ambusta tigna, Liv.; of lightning, *to scorch;* ambustus Phaethon, Hor. Subst., **ambustum** -i, n. *a burn,* Plin. **B.** Of cold, *to nip, numb;* ambusti multorum artus vi frigoris, Tac. **II.** Transf., *to injure;* ambustas fortunarum mearum reliquias, Cic.; damnatione collegae et sua prope ambustus evaserat, Liv.

ambustus -a -um, partic. of amburo.

ămellus -i, m. *the purple Italian starwort,* Verg.

Ămĕnānus -i, m. (Ἀμένανος), *a river of Sicily,* now *Indicello;* also used as an adject., Amenana flumina, Ov.

āmens -entis, *mad, insane, senseless;* metu, Liv.; animi, *in mind,* Verg.; homo audacissimus atque amentissimus, Cic.; consilium amentissimum, Cic.

āmentĭa -ae, f. (amens), *insanity, madness, folly;* in istam amentiam incidere, Cic.

āmento, 1. (amentum), *to furnish with a strap;* hastae, Cic.; and (in a figure) hastae amentatae, *ready-made arguments,* Cic.

āmentum -i, n. (for agimentum). **I.** *a strap, thong,* Caes. **II.** *a shoe-tie,* Plin.

Ămĕrĭa -ae, f. *a town in Umbria,* now *Amelia;* hence adj., **Ămĕrīnus** -a -um, *belonging to Ameria.*

Ămĕrĭola -ae, f. *a town in the Sabine country.*

āmĕs -itis, m. *a forked pole,* for suspending fowlers' nets, Hor.

Ămestrătus -i, f. (Ἀμήστρατος), *a town on the north coast of Sicily, on the Halaesus,* now *Mestretta;* hence **Ămestrătīnus** -a -um, *belonging to Amestratus.*

ămĕthystĭnus -a -um, **1,** *amethyst-coloured;* vestes, Mart. Subst., **ămĕthystĭna** -ōrum, n. (sc. vestimenta), *dresses of that colour,* Juv.; **2,** *set with amethysts,* Mart.

ămĕthystus -i, f. (ἀμέθυστος), *an amethyst,* Plin.

amfractus = anfractus (q.v.).

ămīca -ae, f. (v. amicus).

ămīcē, adv. (amicus), *in a friendly manner;* amice facis, Cic.; amice pauperiem pati, *willingly,* Hor.; with dat., vivere vitae hominum amice, *as the friend of man,* Cic.

ămĭcĭo -icui and -ixi -ictum, 4. **1,** *to clothe, wrap round;* amictus toga, laena, pallio, Cic.; **2,** Transf., *to cover, conceal;* nube cava amictus, Verg.; piper et quidquid chartis amicitur ineptis, *wrapped up in,* Hor.

ămīcĭtĕr = amice (q.v.).

ămīcĭtĭa -ae, f. (amicus), *friendship.* **I.** Lit., **A.** *friendship* between persons; est mihi amicitia cum aliquo, Cic.; amicitiam facere, jungere, gerere, dimittere, dissociare, dissolvere, Cic. **B.** In politics, *friendship* between states; omni tempore in fide atque amicitia civitatis Aeduae fuisse, Caes.; in amicitiam populi Romani venire, Liv.; **C.** Of inanimate things, *sympathy,* Plin. **II.** Meton., *friends;* parcet amicitiis et dignitatibus, Cic.

ămīcĭtĭes -ēi, f. = amicitia (q.v.).

ămictus -ūs, m. (amicio). **A.** *putting on of a garment,* Cic.; esp., *the manner of wearing the toga;* nihil est facilius quam amictum imitari alicuius aut statum aut motum, Cic. **B.** Meton., **1,** *a garment,* Verg.; **2,** *covering;* nebulae amictus, Verg.

ămĭcŭla -ae, f. v. amiculus.

ămĭcŭlum -i, n. (amicio), *a mantle, cloak,* Cic.

ămīcŭlus -i, m.; and **ămīcŭla** -ae, f. (dim. of amicus), *a little friend,* Cic.

ămīcus -a -um (amo). **I.** *friendly, well-wishing, inclined, favourable to.* **A.** Absol., amicus amicissimus animus, Cic.; homines sibi conciliare amiciores, Cic. **B.** With inter se, or erga aliquem, or dat., velim ut tibi amicus sit, Cic.; amica luto sus, Hor.; of things, silentia lunae, Verg.; amicum est mihi, *it pleases me;* secundum te nihil est mihi amicius solitudine, Cic. **II.** Subst.; **A. ămīcus** -i, m., **a,** *a friend;* intimus, Cic.; veritatis, Cic.; of states, socius atque amicus, Cic.; **b,** in plur., *the retinue of a Roman governor,* Suet.; *the courtiers of the emperor,* Suet. **B. ămīca** -ae, f. *a friend* or *a mistress,* Cic.

Ămīnaeus -a -um, *belonging to Aminaea, a district of Picenum, famous for its wine,* Verg.

Amīsĭa -ae. **I.** m. (ὁ Ἀμισίας), *a river in North Germany,* now the *Ems.* **II.** f. *a place at the mouth of the Ems.*

āmissĭo -ōnis, f. (amitto), *a loss;* oppidorum, Cic.; esp. *of a loss through death;* liberorum, Cic.

āmissus -ūs, m. = amissio (q.v.).

Ămīsus (Amisos) -i, f. (Ἀμισός), and **Ămīsum** -i, n. *a town in Pontus,* now *Samsun.*

ămĭta -ae, f. *a father's sister* (opp. matertera, q.v.), *an aunt,* Cic.

Ămĭternum -i, n. *a town in the Sabine country,* birthplace of the historian Sallust; hence adj., **Ămĭternīnus** -a -um, and **Ămĭternus** -a -um, *Amiternian.*

āmitto -mīsi -missum, 3. *to send away, to let go.* **I. A.** Lit., Plaut. **B.** Transf., *to give up;* omnes has provincias, Cic. **II.** *to let go, to let slip.* **A.** Lit., praedam de manibus, Cic.; occasionem, Cic.; tempus, Cic. **B.** *to lose;* vitam, Cic.; litem, Cic.; mentem, Cic.; fidem, *credit,* Phaedr.; esp. *to lose by death;* filium consularem, Cic.

Ammĭānus Marcellīnus -i, m. *historian of the fourth century* A.D., who wrote a history of Rome from Nerva to Valens (91–378 A.D.), the first books of which are lost.

Ammōn (Hammon) -ōnis, m. (Ἄμμων), *a Libyan deity,* with a temple in the Oasis of Siwah, worshipped in Rome under the name of Jupiter Ammon, Cic. Adj., **Ammōnĭăcus** -a -um.

amnĭcŏla -ae, c. (amnis and colo), *dwelling by the river-side;* salix, Ov.

amnĭcŭlus -i, m. (dim. of amnis), *a little river,* Liv.

amnis -is, m. (orig. apnis, from same root as Lat. aqua, Skr. ap.). **A.** *a stream of water, a river;* non tenuis rivulus sed abundantissimus amnis, Cic. **B.** Poet., *the stream;* secundo amni, *down stream,* Verg.; *the ocean,* Verg.; *a torrent;* ruunt de montibus amnes, Verg.; *water,* Verg.

ămo, 1. *to love from inclination* or *passion* (diligere, *to love from esteem*); me non diligi solum, verum etiam amari, Cic.; **1, a,** aliquem mirifice, Cic.; **b,** amare se, *to love oneself selfishly,* Cic.; **c,** aliquem de, or in aliqua re or quod, *to feel obliged* or *bound to a person;* te multum amamus, quod ea abs te diligenter parvoque curata sunt, Cic.; amabo te, or amabo, *please, be so good*, amabo te, advola, Cic, **d**, *to love something*; amas I amorem tuum prout ipse amabat litteris, Cic, amat janua limen, *clings to*, Hor, with infin, hic ames dici pater atque princeps, Hor; **e**, *to be wont, accustomed*, quae ira fieri amat, Sall, **2**, *to love passionately, sensually*, ibi primum insuevit exercitus populi Romani amare, *to lust*, Sall

ămoenē, adv (amoenus), *pleasantly*, Plaut

ămoenĭtas ātis, f (amoenus) **I.** Gen, *pleasantness* **II.** Esp, **a**, of situation, hortorum, Cic urbium, Liv, plur, amoenitates orarum ac litorum, Cic, absol, *pleasant situation*, Cic, **b**, of other things, vitae, Tac, as a term of endearment, mea amoenitas, Plaut

ămoenus a -um **I.** Gen, *pleasant, delightful* **II.** Esp, **a**, of place, locus, Cic Subst, **ămoena** -orum, n *pleasant places*, Tac, **b**, of other things, vita, Tac, cultus, *luxurious, splendid*, Liv, **c**, of persons, Venus, Plaut

āmōlĭor, 4 dep *to remove* **I.** Lit, objecta onera, Liv, se, *to take oneself off*, Plaut **II.** *to get rid of* **A.** Of persons, Octaviam uxorem, Tac. **B.** Of something unpleasant, *to remove*, dedecus, Tac. **C.** In speech, *to pass over*, amolior et amoveo nomen meum, Liv

ămōmum i, n (ἄμωμον), *a shrub, from which a costly balsam was prepared*, Verg

ămŏr (amos) -ōris, m (amo), *love from inclination* (caritas, *love from esteem*) **I. A.** Lit, noster in te amor, Cic, amplecti or prosequi aliquem amore, Cic, habere aliquem in amore, Cic, habere amorem erga aliquem, Cic, in amore esse alicui, *to be loved by some one*, Cic, in a bad sense, *passion*; amore perdita est, Plaut, plur, amores hominum in te, Cic, mihi est in amoribus, *he is loved by me*, Cic; in a bad sense, amores et hae deliciae quae vocantur, Cic, personif, *the god Cupid*, Verg **B.** Meton, *the object of love, darling*, amor et deliciae generis humani (Titus), Suet, esp in plur, amores et deliciae tuae, Cic. **II.** *love for something desire*, consulatus, Cic, cognitionis, Cic, scribendi, Hor

āmōtĭo -ōnis, f (amoveo), *a removing*, doloris, Cic

āmŏvĕo -mōvi -mōtum, 2 *to move away, remove* **I.** Lit, **A.** Gen, **1**, of things, neque in amovendo neque in exportando frumento, Cic, **2**, of persons, aliquem ex istis locis, Cic, aliquem ab altaribus, Liv, amoto patre, *in the absence of the father*, Tac, se amovere, *to depart*, Ter **B.** Esp, **1**, euphem, *to steal*, boves per dolum amotas, Hor, **2**, *to banish*, in insulam, Tac **II** Transf, **A.** Gen, *to remove something unpleasant*, ab se culpam Liv **B.** Partic, **1**, of things, sensum doloris mei a sententia dicenda amovebo, Cic, **2**, of persons, *to remove from a post*, Saturninum quaestorem a sua frumentaria procuratione, Cic.

Amphĭărāus -i, m (Ἀμφιάραος), *a celebrated Argive soothsayer, son of Oicles* (or Apollo) *and Hypermnestra, husband of Eriphyle, father of Alcmaeon and Amphilochus*, participator against his will in the expedition of the Seven against Thebes, when flying from Polyclymenus he was, by the order of Zeus, taken up from the earth and made immortal, hence, **a**, **Amphĭărāēus** a -um, *belonging to Amphiaraus*, **b**, **Amphĭărēĭădēs** ae, m *son of Amphiaraus* = Alcmaeon, Ov.

amphĭbŏlĭa -ae, f (ἀμφιβολία), *ambiguity, double meaning*, Cic

Amphictyŏnes um, m (Ἀμφικτύονες), *the Amphictyons, a religious assembly of representatives of the Greek states*, held first at Thermopylae and afterwards at Delphi.

Amphĭlŏchi ōrum, m *a people in Acarnania*, hence **Amphĭlŏchĭa** -ae, f *their country*, and **Argos Amphĭlŏchĭum**, or **Amphĭlŏchĭcum** -i, n *its chief town*, now *Philoḱia*

Amphīon -ŏnis, m (Ἀμφίων), *king of Thebes, and husband of Niobe*, said to have raised the walls of Thebes by the magical power of his lyre, hence arces Amphionis, i e *Thebes*, Ov Adj, **Amphīŏnĭus** a -um, *belonging to Amphion*

Amphĭpŏlis, acc -im, f (Ἀμφίπολις), *Athenian colony in Macedonia, on the Strymon*

amphisbaena -ae, f (ἀμφίσβαινα), *a kind of African snake*, Plin

Amphissa -ae, f (Ἄμφισσα), *a town of the Ozolian Locrians*, near modern Salona, hence **Amphissĭus** a -um

amphĭthĕātrālis e (amphitheatrum), *belonging to the amphitheatre*, spectaculum, Plin

amphĭthĕātrĭcus a -um = amphitheatralis (q v)

amphĭthĕātrum -i, n (ἀμφιθέατρον), *an amphitheatre, an oval building for gladiatorial shows and public spectacles*, Tac

Amphĭtrītē ēs, f (Ἀμφιτρίτη) *the wife of Neptune, goddess of the sea*, hence, *the sea*, Ov

Amphĭtryŏn and **Amphĭtrŭo** -ōnis, m. (Ἀμφιτρύων), *king of Thebes, and husband of Alcmena, the mother of Hercules by Jupiter*, hence **Amphĭtryŏnĭădēs** -ae, m *the son of Amphitryon*, i e *Hercules*, Verg

amphŏra -ae, f (ἀμφορεύς) **A.** *a two-handled vase, pitcher, or jug*, generally made of clay or glass, chiefly used for wine, Hor, hence, meton, *wine*, Hor, used also for honey, Cic, oil, Cato **B. 1**, *a measure for liquids*, 2 urnae or 8 congii or 48 sextarii, about 5¾ gallons, **2**, *measure of the tonnage of a ship*, as we use ton, about 80 Roman pounds, naves onerariae quarum minor nulla erat duum millium amphorum, Cic

amphŏrālis e (amphora), *containing an amphora*, Plin

Amphrȳsŏs -i, m (Ἄμφρυσος), *a stream in Phthiotis*, near which Apollo kept the flocks of Admetus, pastor ab Amphryso, *Apollo*, Verg Adj, **Amphrȳsĭus** -a -um, Amphrysia vates, *the Sibyl* (beloved by Apollo), Verg

amplē, adv (amplus) **I.** *richly, amply*, amplissime dare agrum, *most liberally*, Cic **II.** *magnificently, splendidly*, exornare triclinium, Cic, of oratory elate et ample loqui, *with dignity and weight*, Cic Esp in compar, **amplius**, **I.** *more*, amplius aequo lamentari, Lucr **II. A.** Of space or time, *more, further*, non luctabor tecum amplius, Cic, **a**, amplius pronuntiare, a judicial formula, *to adjourn the hearing of a case*, quum consules re audita amplius de consilii sententia pronuntiavissent, Cic, **b**, a formula in contracts, sales, etc, amplius non peti, *that no further claim is made*, Cic, **c**, esp of definite measures of time, with nom, acc, abl, genit, generally without quam, amplius centum cives Romani, Cic, non amplius pedum DC, Caes, triennio amplius, Cic, absol, xii non amplius legiones, 12 *legions and no more*, Liv **B.** *further, more, in addition*, quid est quod jam amplius exspectes, Cic, hence the formulae, **a**, non dico amplius, *I say nothing further*, Cic, **b**, hoc or eo amplius, *besides, moreover*, esp t t in the senate, Servilio assentior et hoc amplius censeo, *I give my adhesion to Servilius' proposal but make an addition to it*, Cic

amplector -plexus sum -plecti, 3 dep (amb and plecto) **I.** Lit *to surround, encircle* **A.** with the arms or hands, *to embrace*, **1**, aram,

Tac. ; dextram, Verg. ; **2,** *to embrace lovingly*, Ov. **B.** *to surround*; tellurem alis (of night), *to cover*, Verg. ; hostium aciem, Liv. ; of fire, ignis proxima quaeque et deinceps continua amplexus, Liv. **II.** Transf., **A.** *to welcome, receive*; libenter talem amicum, Cic. **B. 1,** *to love, esteem*; aliquem amore, Cic. ; **2,** *to prize*; tanto amore suas possessiones, Cic. ; **3,** *to embrace in thought, to consider*; si judex non omnia amplectetur consilio, Cic. ; **4,** *to embrace*, in the sense of *to include* or *comprise*; quod idem interdum virtutis nomine amplectimur, Cic. ; **5,** *to embrace* or *touch on* in discourse; argumentum pluribus verbis, Cic. ; omnia communiter, Liv.

amplexor, 1. dep. (intens. of amplector); **1,** *to surround, encircle, embrace*, Cic. ; transf., Appius totum me amplexatur, Cic. ; **2,** *to honour, esteem*; aequabilitatem juris, Cic.

amplexus -ūs, m. (amplector). **A.** *a surrounding, encircling, embrace*; draconis or serpentis, Cic. ; aliquem amplexibus necare (of a snake), Ov. **B.** Transf., terrarum amplexu, *the circuit of the earth*, Liv.

amplĭātĭo -ōnis, f. (amplio), *the adjournment of a suit*, Sen.

amplĭfĭcātĭo -ōnis, f. (amplifico), *an enlarging, increasing*. **I.** Lit., rei familiaris, Cic. **II.** Transf., **a,** *an enlarging, heightening*; honoris et gloriae, Cic. ; **b,** in rhetoric, *enlargement, amplification*, Cic.

amplĭfĭcātor -ōris, m. (amplifico), *one who enlarges*; dignitatis, Cic.

amplĭfĭco 1. (amplus and facio), *to enlarge*. **A.** Lit., civitatem, Cic. ; divitias, Cic. **B.** Transf., **1,** *to increase*; voluptatem, Cic. ; **2,** in rhetoric, *to dilate upon, magnify*; aliquid dicendo amplificare atque ornare, Cic.

amplĭo, 1. (amplus), *to make wide, enlarge, increase*. **I.** Lit., civitatem, Plin. ; equitum centurias, Liv. **II.** Transf., **a,** *to glorify*; nomen, Mart. ; **b,** legal t.t., *to adjourn the hearing of a case* (see under ample II. A.a); causam, Cic.

amplĭtĕr, adv. = ample (q.v.).

amplĭtūdo -ĭnis, f. (amplus), *breadth, size*. **A.** Lit., simulacrum modica amplitudine, Cic. **B.** Transf., **1,** amplitudines quaedam bonorum, *increase of property*, Cic. ; **2,** *greatness*; nominis, Cic. ; **3,** *dignity, grandeur*; maxima cum gloria ad summam amplitudinem pervenire, Cic. ; **4,** *dignity of expression*; Platonis, Cic.

amplus -a -um, adj. with compar. and superl., *large, spacious, ample*. **A.** Lit., **1,** of space, size, etc. ; domus, Cic. ; **2,** of number, height, quantity, etc. ; pecunia amplissima, Cic. ; ampliores copiae, Caes. Neut. subst., **amplius,** imponebat amplius quam ferre possent, Cic. ; with genit., si amplius obsidum dare velit, Caes. **B.** Transf., **1,** *great, important*; occasio, Cic. ; ampla spes, Sall. ; **2,** *honourable*; praemia, Cic. ; amplum Tuscis ratus, *thinking it an honour for the Etruscans*, Liv. ; **3,** *excellent, highly esteemed*; amplae et honestae familiae, Cic. ; amplissimi viri, *men of the highest position*, Cic. ; especially of public offices, amplissimus honor, *the consulship*, Cic.

Ampsancti (sc. lacus), or **Ampsanctus** -i, m. *a lake in the country of the Hirpini*, said to be one of the entrances to the lower world.

ampulla -ae, f. (dim. of amphora; amp(h)orula, amporla, ampurla, ampulla). **A.** *a flask, bottle*, Cic. **B.** Transf., *bombast*; projicit ampullas, Hor.

ampullācĕus -a -um (ampulla), *bottle-shaped*, Plin.

ampullārĭus -i, m. (ampulla), *a bottle-maker*, Plaut.

ampullor, 1. dep. (ampulla, B.), *to speak bombastically*, Hor.

ampŭtātĭo -ōnis, f. (amputo), *a cutting off, pruning*, Cic.

ampŭto, 1. *to cut off*. **A.** Lit., **1,** of plants or trees, *to lop or prune*; ramos inutiles, Hor. ; fig., non solum ramos amputare miseriarum, Cic. ; **2,** *to cut off a part of the body*; caput, Tac. ; as medical t. t., *to amputate*; in corpore quidquid est pestiferum, Cic. **B. 1,** *to shorten, diminish*; multitudinem sententiarum, Cic. ; **2,** amputata loqui, *to speak disconnectedly*, Cic.

Ampȳcus -i, m. (Ἄμπυκος). **I.** *son of Iapetus, a singer and priest of Ceres*, killed at the wedding of Perseus by Pettalus. **II.** *one of the Lapithae, father of Mopsus*; hence, **Ampȳcĭdēs** -ae, m. *a descendant of Ampycus*, i.e. *Mopsus*.

Ampyx -pȳcis, m. (Ἄμπυξ). **I.** *a comrade of Phineus, turned into stone by the Medusa's head at the wedding of Perseus.* **II.** *one of the Lapithae, killed by the centaur Oiclus at the wedding of Pirithous.*

ămŭlētum -i, n. (Arab. hamalet = *a pendant*), *a charm, amulet*, Plin.

Ămūlĭus -ii, m. *king of Alba Longa*, who drove his elder brother, Numitor, from the throne, and exposed in the Tiber Numitor's grandsons, Romulus and Remus.

ămurca -ae, f. (ἀμόργη), *the oil-lees*, Plin.

ămussis (acc. -im), f. *a carpenter's rule*; ad amussim, *exactly*, Varr.

Amȳclae -ārum, f. (Ἀμύκλαι). **I.** *a town in Laconia, south-east of Sparta*: myth., *home of the Dioscuri and of Helena.* **II.** *an old town in Latium* (said to have been founded from Amyclae I.). Adj. **Amȳclaeus** -a -um, *belonging to Amyclae, Amyclaean*; pluma, *of the swan*, in allusion to the story of Juppiter and Leda, Mart. ; fratres, *the Dioscuri*, Verg. ; hence poet. *Laconian*; canis, Verg.

ămygdălum -i. n. (ἀμύγδαλον), *an almond*, Ov.

Ămȳmōnē -ēs, f. (Ἀμυμώνη), *daughter of Danaus, beloved by Neptune*, who in her honour caused a fountain to spring out of the rock near Argos.

Amyntas -ae, m. (Ἀμύντας), *name of several Macedonian kings*, the most famous of whom was Amyntas II., *father of Philip of Macedon, and grandfather of Alexander the Great*; hence **Amyntĭădēs** -ae, m. *Philip.*

Ămyntōr -ōris, m. (Ἀμύντωρ), *king of the Dolopes, father of Phoenix*; hence **Ămyntŏrĭdēs** -ae, m. *a son of Amyntor = Phoenix*, Ov.

ămystis -idis, f. (ἄμυστις), *the emptying of a goblet at a draught*, Hor.

Ămȳthāōn -ŏnis, m. (Ἀμυθάων) *father of Melampus, Bias, and Aeolia*; hence, **Amȳthāŏnĭus** -a -um, *son of Amythaon*.

ăn, conj. *or, whether*, introduces the second clause of a direct or indirect double question, or of a sentence implying doubt. **I. A.** Of sentences implying doubt; **1,** after utrum, utrumne and ne, honestumne factu sit an turpe, dubitant, Cic. ; **2,** without a verb of doubt, *or rather*; non plus duobus an tribus mensibus, Cic. **B.** Elliptically, where the first clause is to be understood, dubito an, haud scio an, or nescio an, *I don't know whether it is not, perhaps, possibly*; haud scio an satis sit, eum qui lacesserit, injuriae suae poenitere, Cic. ; with a negative, *I don't know whether it is*; dubitet an turpe non sit, *whether it is base*, Cic. **C.** Like num, *whether* (poet or in post-Augustan prose), quis scit an adjiciant hodiernae crastina summae tempora di superi, Hor **II.** In direct or indirect questions **A.** Where both sentences are expressed; **1,** in direct questions, utrum ea vestra an nostra culpa est, Cic; **2,** in indirect questions, id utrum Romano more locutus sit an quo modo Stoici dicunt, postea videro, Cic **B.** Elliptically, where the first part of the question is suppressed, often to express irony or astonishment, *or then?*, an etiam id dubium est? Cic, an censes nihil inter nos convenire? Cic

ănăbathrum -i, n (ἀναβαθροι), *a raised seat*, Juv

Ănăcharsis -idis, m (Ἀνάχαρσις), *a Scythian who, it was said, visited Athens in the time of Solon*

Ănacrĕōn -ontis, m (Ἀνακρεων), *a lyric poet of Teos in Ionia* (559—478 B.C.) Adj, **Anacrĕontius** -a -um, *Anacreontic*

ănădēma ătis, n (ανάδημα), *an ornament or fillet for the head*, Lucr

Ănagnĭa -ae, f (Αναγνια), *a town in Latium, capital of the Hernici, now Anagni* Adj, **Anagnīnus** -a -um, *belonging to Anagnia.*

ănagnostēs -ae, m (ἀναγνωστης), *a reader*, Cic.

ănălecta -ae, m (ἀναλεγω), *a slave whose duty it was to collect and remove crumbs after a meal*, Mart.

ănălŏgĭa -ae, f (ἀναλογία), *proportion, comparison, analogy*, Varr, Quint

ănancaeum i, n (ἀναγκαῖον, *unavoidable*), *a large drinking cup, bumper*, Plaut

ănăpaestus -a -um (ανάπαιστος), pes, or simply anapaestus, *a metrical foot, an anapaest* (◡◡–), Cic. Subst, **a, anapaestus** -i, m *a verse composed of anapaests*, Cic, **b, anapaestum** -i, n., *a poem in anapaestic verse*, Cic

ănăphŏră -ae f (ἀναφορα), **1,** *the rising of the heavenly bodies*, Plin, **2,** in rhetoric, *the repetition of a word at the beginning of several sentences* (as in Cic Verr ii 26)

Ănăphē -ēs, f (Ἀναφη), *an island east of Thera, one of the Sporades, now Namfi, or Anafi*

Ănāpus, i, m (Ἄναπος), *a river in Sicily, near Syracuse, now Anapo*

Anartes -ium, m (Ἀναρτοι), *a people in Dacia*

1 **Ănās** -ae, m (Ἀνας), *a river in Spain, now Wadi ana or Guadiana.*

2 **ănas,** ănătis, f *a duck*, Cic.

ănătĭcŭla -ae, f. (dim. of anas), *a little duck*, Cic.

ănătŏcismus -i, m (ἀνατοκισμός), *compound interest*, Cic

Ănaxăgŏras -ae, m (Ἀναξαγόρας), *a philosopher of the old Ionian school, friend and teacher of Pericles and Euripides*

Ănaxarchus -i, m (Ἀνάξαρχος), *a philosopher of Abdera*

Ănaxĭmander dri, m. (Ἀναξιμανδρος), *a philosopher of Miletus, pupil of Thales*

Ănaxĭmĕnes -is, m (Ἀναξιμενης), *a philosopher of Miletus, pupil of Anaximander*

anceps cĭpĭtis, abl sing -cipiti (am and caput). **I.** Lit., *two headed*, Janus, Ov, acumen montis, *two peaked*, Ov. **II.** Transf *with two sides* **A.** *two edged*, securis, Ov **B. 1,** *coming on both sides, behind and before*, quum anceps hostis et a fronte et a tergo urgeret, Liv, anceps proelium, *a battle when the enemy attack on both sides*, Caes; anceps metus et ab cive et ab hoste, Liv; **2,** *of two natures*, bestiae quasi ancipites, *amphibious*, Cic, anceps faciendi dicendique sapientia, Cic **C. 1,** *ambiguous*, oraculum, Liv., **2,** *uncertain, undecided*, belli fortuna, Cic; proelium, Liv; **3,** *unsettled*, Lucanus an Apulus anceps, *uncertain whether a Lucanian or an Apulian*, Hor, **4,** *dangerous*, hic locus tam anceps, Cic.

Anchĭălos (ūs) i, f (Ἀγχίαλος), *a small town of Thrace on the Pontus Euxinus, now Akiali.*

Anchīsēs -ae, m (Ἀγχίσης), *son of Capys and father of Aeneas*; hence **1,** adj, **Anchīsēus** -a -um, *belonging to Anchises*, **2, Anchīsĭădēs** -ae, m *a descendant of Anchises*, i e *Aeneas*, Verg

ancīle -is, n (connected with *ancus, curved), **1,** *a shield which fell from heaven in the time of Numa, on the preservation of which the safety of the Roman empire was supposed to depend*, Liv, **2,** *any oval shield*, Verg (heterocl. genit plur anciliorum, Hor)

ancilla -ae, f. *a maid-servant, female slave*, Cic, used as an attrib, mulier ancilla, Sall

ancillārĭŏlus -i, m (ancilla), *a lover of maid-servants*, Mart.

ancillāris e (ancilla), *relating to a maid-servant*, artificium, Cic

ancillor, 1, dep (ancilla), *to serve as a maid-servant*, hence, *to serve slavishly*, Plin

ancillŭla -ae, f. (dim of ancilla), *a little maid-servant*, Liv, fig, idcirco istam juris scientiam tamquam ancillulam pedisequamque adjunxisti, Cic

ancīsus a -um (amb and caedo), *cut round*, Lucr.

Ancōn -ōnis, f (Ἀγκών, *elbow*), and **Ancōna** -ae, f *a town in Picenum, on the Adriatic Sea*, hence **Ancōnĭtānus** -i, m *an inhabitant of Ancona*

ancŏra -ae, f (ἄγκυρα), *an anchor*, ancoram jacere, Caes, figere, pangere, *to cast anchor*, Ov, tollere, *to weigh anchor*, Caes., consistere ad ancoram, in ancoris, *to lie at anchor*, Caes

ancŏrāle -is, n (ancora), *a cable*, Liv

ancŏrārĭus a -um (ancora), *belonging to an anchor*, funis, Caes

Ancus (see Marcius)

Ancȳra -ae, f (Ἄγκυρα) **I.** *the chief town of the Tectosages, capital of Galatia, now Angora*, hence, **Ancȳrānus** -a -um, *belonging to Ancyra*, Ancyranum monumentum, *an inscription put up by Augustus at the entrance to his temple at Ancyra, relating the chief events of his life* **II.** *a town in Phrygia, on the borders of Mysia and Lydia.*

andăbătă -ae, m *a kind of gladiator who fought with a helmet that had no openings for the eyes*, Cic

Andanĭa -ae, f (Ἀνδανια), *an old town in Messenia, between Megalopolis and Messene, now Andorossa*

Andecavi ōrum, m and **Andes** -ium, m *a Gallic people on the Loire with a town of the same name, now Angers*

1 **Andes,** v Andecavi

2 **Andēs** -ium, f *town in the Mantuan country, birthplace of Virgil, now Pietola*

Andraemōn ŏnis, m (Ἀνδραίμων) **I.** *father of Amphissus, husband of Dryope* **II.** (also Andremon) *king of Calydon, father of Thoas*

Andriscus -i, m (Ἄνδρισκος), *a slave who gave himself out to be the son of the Macedonian king Perseus, and caused the third Macedonian War, which ended with the reduction of Macedonia into a Roman province by Metellus,*

Andrŏgĕōs, or **-gĕus** -i, m (Ἀνδρογεως), *son of Minos and Pasiphae, killed by the Athenians, who were consequently attacked and subdued by Minos, and forced to pay a tribute of youths and maidens to the Minotaur*

andrŏgy̆nus -i, m (ἀνδρόγυνος), *a hermaphrodite*, Liv, Cic

Andrŏmăchē -ēs and **-cha** -ae, f. (Ἀνδρομαχη), *wife of Hector, and, after the capture of Troy, the captive of Pyrrhus and subsequently wife of Helenus*, appell, *a young and beautiful wife*, Mart

Andrŏmĕdē -ēs, f, and **-da** -ae, f (Ἀνδρομεδη), *daughter of the Aethiopian king Cepheus and of Cassiopeia, exposed to a sea-monster, but rescued by Perseus* (acc -an, Ov., Met iv 671, and Ars Am i 53)

Andrŏnīcus -i, m (Ἀνδρονίκος), L or T, Livius, *the earliest of the Roman tragic poets, a native of Magna Graecia, the slave of M Livius Salinator* (about 240 B C)

Andrŏs and **Andrus** -i, f (Ἄνδρος), *the most northerly of the Cyclades, now Andro*, hence adj, **Andrĭus** -a -um, *Andrian*, subst, **Andria** -ae, f *the Woman of Andros, name of one of Terence's comedies*

ănellus i, m (dim of anulus), *a little ring* Hor

ănēthum i, n. (ἄνηθον), *dill, anise*, Verg.

anfractus -ūs, m (an and frango) **A.** *a turning, bending*, solis, *revolution*, Cic, anfractus curvus vallis, *winding*, Verg, recta regione, si nullus anfractus intercederet, *no tortuous windings*, Caes **B.** Transf, **a,** *legal intricacies*, judiciorum, Cic, **b,** *prolixity*, Cic

angellus i, m (dim of angulus) *a little corner*, Lucr

angīna -ae, f (ἀγχόνη), *the quinsy*, Plaut.

angĭportum -i, n and (rarely) **angĭportus** -ūs, m (ango and portus), *a narrow street*, Cic

Angĭtĭa (Ancĭtĭa, Anguĭtĭa) -ae, f *a goddess of the dwellers round the lake Fucinus* (now *Lago di Celano*), *of the Marsi and Marrubii*, nemus Angitiae, *a grove on the west bank of lake Fucinus* (now *Selva d'Albi*)

Anglĭi -ōrum, m *a branch of the Suevi, living in modern Altmark*

ango, 3 (root ANG, Gr ΑΓΧ, whence angulus, angustus, ἄγχω) **I.** *to press together, to throttle*, **a,** guttur, Verg; **b,** *to distress*, ea collisio mistorum omnis generis animantium odore insolito urbanos et agrestem confertum in arta tecta aestu ac vigiliis angebat, Liv **II.** *to torment, make anxious*, alicuius animum and aliquem, Cic, angebant ingentis spiritus virum Sicilia Sardiniaque amissae, Liv, pass, angi animi or animo or simply angi, *to be grieved* or *troubled*, alicuius decessu, Cic, de Statio manumisso et nonnullis aliis rebus, Cic, me angit or angor, followed by quod, or the acc and the infin, Cic.

angor -ōris, m. (ango) **I. 1,** *a pressing together of the gullet, throttling*, Plin; **2,** *physical distress*, aestu et angore vexata, Liv. **II.** *mental distress, anguish, trouble*, confici angoribus, Cic

Angrivarĭi -ōrum, m *a German tribe on the Weser*

anguĭcŏmus -a -um (anguis and coma), *having snaky hair*, Ov

anguĭcŭlus i, m (dim of anguis), *a little snake*, Ov

anguĭfer -fĕra fĕrum (anguis and fero), *snake-bearing*; Gorgo, Prop.

anguĭgĕna -ae, c (anguis and geno = gigno), *snake born*, Ov

anguilla -ae, f *an eel*, Plaut

anguĭmănus -ūs, m *snake-handed*, elephantus (so called from the snake-like movements of its trunk), Lucr

anguĭnĕus -a -um (anguis), *pertaining to a snake, snaky*, Ov

anguīnus -a -um = anguineus (q v)

anguĭpes -pĕdis (anguis and pes), *snake-footed*, Ov

anguis -is, c (ango) **I.** *a snake*, Cic., prov, frigidus latet anguis in herba, *there is danger*, Verg **II. 1,** *the constellation Draco*, Verg; **2,** *the constellation Ophiuchus*, Ov (abl. angue, rarely—but sometimes in Cicero—angui)

Anguĭtĕnens -entis, m (anguis and teneo, translation of Gr Ὀφιοῦχος) *the Snake-holder*, *the constellation Ophiuchus*, Cic

Anguĭtĭa, v Angitia

angŭlātus -a -um (angulus), *angular, cornered*, Cic

angŭlōsus -a -um (angulus), *full of corners*, Plin

angŭlus -i m (root ANG, Gr ΑΓΧ, whence ango, angustus, ἄγχω) **A.** *a corner, angle*, Caes. **B. 1,** *an angle in mathematics*, Cic, **2,** *the extremity or corner of a country*, extremus angulus agri Bruttii, Liv; **3,** *a bastion*, Liv, **4,** *a retired spot*, in ullo angulo Italiae, Cic, fig, ad istas verborum angustias et ad omnes litterarum angulos, Cic

angustē, adv with compar. and superl. (angustus), *narrowly, in a confined manner* **I.** Lit, **A.** of space, sedere, Cic **B.** Of number or quantity, *sparingly*, uti re frumentaria, Caes. **II. A.** *in a narrow, circumscribed manner*; angustius apud Graecos valere, Cic. **B.** *briefly*, dicere, Cic

angustĭa -ae, f, gen pl **angŭstĭae** -ārum, f (angustus), *narrowness* **A.** Lit., fretorum, Cic, spiritus, *shortness of breath*, Cic.; absol, *defiles, narrow passes*, Caes **B.** Transf, **1,** *obscure or narrow reasoning*, tantas in angustias et stoicorum dumeta (orationem) compellimus, Cic, **2,** of time, *shortness*, angustiae temporis, Cic; **3,** of circumstances, *straitened condition, poverty*, pecuniae, aerarii, rei familiaris, Cic, absol, *poverty*, ap Cic, **4,** *difficulty, distress*, in angustias adduci, Cic; **5,** of disposition, *narrow-mindedness*, Cic

angustĭclāvĭus ii, m. (angustus and clavus), *wearing a narrow stripe of purple on his tunic;* epithet of a plebeian military tribune, Suet

angustus -a -um (root ANG, Gr. ΑΓΧ, whence ango, ἄγχω, angulus), *narrow* **A.** Lit, **1,** of space, *narrow, strait* (opp latus); pons, Cic., **2,** of other things, habenae, *tightly drawn*, Tib, spiritus angustior, *short breath*, Cic Subst, **angustum** -i, n *a narrow space*, in angusto tendere, *to encamp in a narrow space*, Liv, angusta viarum, Verg **B.** Transf, **1,** in angustum deducere perturbationes, *to bridle*, Cic; in angustum concludere, *to confine, limit*, Cic., **2,** of time, *short*, nox, Ov, **3,** of circumstances, *straitened, poor, scarce*, res frumentaria, Caes; angustas civium domos, Tac., liberalitas angustior, Cic., **4,** of other things, *precarious, critical, uncertain*, res angustae, Cic, fides angustior, Caes.; **5,** of character, *narrow-minded;* alii minuti et angusti, Cic, of perception, sensus, Cic, **6,** of speech, **a,** *concise*, disputationes, Cic; **b,** *petty, narrow, subtle*, concertationes, Cic Subst, **angustum** -i, n. *difficulty*, res est in angusto, Caes.

ănhēlātĭo -ōnis = anhelitus (q v).

ănhēlātor -ōris, m (anhelo), *one who breathes with difficulty*, Plin.

ănhēlītus ūs, m (anhelo) **A.** *short, quick breathing, puffing, panting*, anhelitum ducere, Plaut , anhelitus moventur, Cic , *asthma*, Plin **B.** Transf , **1,** *breath*, Ov , **2,** *exhalation, vapour*, terrae Cic

ănhēlo, 1 (am and helo) **I** Intransit , *to draw a heavy breath, puff, pant* **A.** Lit , Verg. **B.** Of lifeless objects, *to roar*, fornacibus ignis anhelat, Verg **II.** Transit , **A.** *to produce with panting*, verba inflata et quasi anhelata gravius, Cic **B.** *to pant for, desire eagerly*, scelus, Cic

ănhēlus -a -um (anhelo) = anhelans **I.** *puffing, panting*, equi, Verg **II** Meton , *causing to pant*, febris, Ov

ănĭcŭla ae, f (dim of anus), *a little old woman*, Cic

Ănĭēn -ēnis, v Anio

Ănĭensis, Ănĭēnus, v Anio

Ănĭgrŏs -i, m. (Ἄνιγρος), *a river in Triphylia (Elis)*

ănīlis -e (anus), *belonging to or like an old woman*, vultus, Verg , rugae, Ov , esp. with the notion of superstition or folly, superstitio, Cic. , fabellae, *old wives' tales*, Cic

ănīlĭtas ātis, f (anilis), *old age* (of women), Cat

ănīlĭtĕr, adv (anilis), *like an old woman*, id dicitis superstitiose atque aniliter, Cic

ănĭma -ae, f (connected with ἄω, ἄημι) **I.** Lit **A.** *wind*, impellunt animae lintea Thraciae, *the north winds*, Hor , quantum ignes animaeque valent, of Vulcan's bellows, Verg **B.** **1,** *the air as an element*, Cic , **2,** *the breath*, animam ducere, Cic , continere, Cic **II.** Transf , **A.** *the vital principle, the soul* (anima, *physical*, animus, *spiritual*), **1,** Lit , **a,** neque in homine inesse animum vel animam nec in bestia, Cic , *the spirits of the dead*, Suet , *the vital principle in plants*, Plin , **b,** *life*, animam edere, *to give up the ghost*, Cic , animam agere, *to be in the agonies of death*, Cic , trahere, *to drag on existence*, Liv , dum anima est, *as long as he is alive*, Cic , of the blood as the source of life, purpuream vomit animam, *life-blood*, Verg , **2,** Meton , *a living being*, ova parire, non animam, Enn , used as a term of endearment, *soul*, vos meae carissimae animae, Cic , egregiae animae, Verg **B.** (Like animus), *the rational soul*, anima rationis consilique particeps, Cic

ănĭmābĭlis, -e (animo), *animating, giving life*, natura, Cic

ănĭmadversĭo -ōnis, f (animadverto) **I.** *perception, observation*, excitare animadversionem et diligentiam ut ne, &c , Cic **II.** Transf **A** *punishment*; censoria, Cic , Dolabellae in audaces sceleratos, Cic , vitiorum, Cic , used euphem for *capital punishment*, Cic **B.** *censure, blame*, Cic.

ănĭmadversor ōris, m. (animadverto), *an observer*, Cic

ănĭmadverto (ănĭmadvorto), verti (vorti), -versum (-vorsum), 3 (for animum adverto) **I.** *to take notice of, attend to*, non animadverti in pace, Cic , followed by relat sent , ut animadvertam quae fiant, Cic , by ut or ne and the subj , animadvertant ne callida assentatione capiantur, Cic , t t , of the lictor, *to clear the road for the consul*, consul animadvertere proximum lictorem jussit, Liv **II.** Transf **A** *to perceive* eequid animadvertis horum silentium, Cic , with acc. and infin , animadvertit Caesar unos Sequanos nihil earum rerum facere, Caes , with rel sent , animadvertant quid de religione existimandum sit, Cic , with quum and the subj , animadversum saepe est, quum cor animantis alicujus evulsum palpitaret, Cic **B.** **1,** *to take notice of*, i e *to take measures against, to punish*, generally followed by in , in judices quosdam, Cic , res animadvertenda, Cic , euphem *to punish with death*, Tac , **2,** *to blame*, ea sunt animadvertenda peccata maxime, Cic

ănĭmal -ālis, n (for animale, from anima), **1,** *a living being, animal*, quum inter inanimum atque animal hoc maximum intersit, quod animal agit aliquid, Cic , **2,** *an animal*, as opposed to a man, Cic , so contemptuously of an animal ((like English *brute, beast*), funestum illud animal, Cic

ănĭmālis e (anima), **1,** *consisting of air, airy* natura, Cic , **2,** belonging to life, *living*, intelligentia Cic , exemplum, Cic.

ănĭmans -antis (p adj from animo), *living* **I.** Adj , mundus, Cic **II** Subst , masc , fem , and neut , *a living being, animal*. masc , alius animans, Cic , fem , ceterae animantes, Cic , neut , animantia omnia, Cic

ănĭmātĭo -ōnis, f (animo) **I.** Lit , *an animating* **II.** Meton (= animal), *a living being*, divinae animationis species, Cic

1 **ănĭmātus** -a -um (p adj from animo), **1,** *alive, animated*, anteponantur animata inanimis, Cic. , **2,** *disposed in mind, inclined*, **a,** morally or politically, Pompeius animatus melius quam paratus, Cic , with erga and acc , Cic , with in and acc , Cic , **b,** *courageously inclined, courageous*, Cic

2 **ănĭmātus** -ūs, m (animo), *life, animation*, Plin

ănĭmo, 1 (anima and animus), **1,** *to animate, give life to*, omnia animat, format, alit, Cic , animare in, with acc , *to change a lifeless into a living thing*, guttas animant in angues, Ov , **2,** *to endow with a particular disposition*, pueros orientes animari atque formari, Cic

ănĭmōsē, adv (animosus), *courageously*; animose et fortiter facere aliquid, Cic

ănĭmōsus -a um (animus), *courageous, high-spirited, ardent, passionate, furious* **I.** Gen , **A.** Lit., fortis et animosus vir, Cic , equus, Ov. **B.** Transf , of winds, poet , ventus, Ov , Euri, Verg , with abl , *proud of*, animosus spoliis, Ov **II.** Esp , *intent on*, corruptor, *a briber who spares no expense*, Tac

ănĭmŭla ae, f (dim of anima) **I.** *a little soul*, ap Cic **II.** *a little life*, tuae litterae quae mihi quidquam quasi animulae instillarunt, *have refreshed me a little*, Cic

ănĭmŭlus -i, m (dim of animus), *a term of endearment*, mi animule, *my life*, Plaut

ănĭmus -i, m (root AN, connected with anima and ἄνεμος) **I** *the spiritual principle of life in man*, opposed to corpus, *the body*, and to anima, *the principle of physical life*, credo deos immortales sparsisse animos in corpora humana, Cic , rarely of animals, bestiae quarum animi sunt rationis expertes, Cic **II** **A.** *the soul as the seat of feeling*, **1,** animus alius ad alia vitia propensior, Cic , genit animi (almost pleonastic) with adj. or subst , aeger animi, Liv , dubius animi, Verg , animi motus, Cic , with animo or animi and a verb, animo tremere, Cic , animi or animis pendere, *to be anxious*, Cic , **2,** *character, disposition*, apertus et simplex, Cic ;—esse angusti animi atque demissi, Cic , poet , transf , *nature*, exuerint silvestrem animum, Verg , **3,** *inclination towards some* *one;* bono (or alieno) animo esse in aliquem, Caes.; mi anime, "*my dear,*" Plaut.; **4,** *courage, confidence, spirit;* fac animo magno fortique sis, Cic.; neutris animus est ad pugnandum, Liv.; so in plur., animi cadunt, *courage sinks,* Cic.; transf., *fire* or *vivacity* in a speech, quae vis, qui animus, quae dignitas illi oratori defuit, Cic.; poet., of a top, dant animos plagae, Verg.; so (esp. in plural) *pride, arrogance,* uxor, inflata adhuc regiis animis et muliebri spiritu, Liv.; jam insolentiam noratis hominis, noratis animos ejus et spiritus tribunicios, Cic.; pone animos, Verg.; **5,** *wish, desire;* militum animis expletis, Liv.; animi voluptatisque causa, Caes. **B.** *the soul as the seat of the will;* ad omnia et animo et consilio paratus, Cic.; eo ad te animo venimus ut, &c., *with the resolve to,* &c., Cic.; habeo in animo, with infin., *I am resolved,* Cic.; so in animum habeo, Liv.; est mihi in animo, Cic.; avet animus, with infin., Cic.; inclinat animus, with ut and the subj., Liv.; ex animo, *willingly,* Cic. **C.** *the soul as the seat of the thoughts;* **1,** omnium mentes animosque perturbare, Caes.; **2,** *consciousness;* deficientibus animis, Liv.; *thought,* memor in bene meritos animus, Cic.

Anio -ōnis (or -ēnis from original Sabine form **Aniēn**), m., poet., **Aniēnus** -i, m. *the Anio, a river, tributary to the Tiber.* Adj., **1, Aniensis** -e, **2, Aniēnus** -a -um, *belonging to the Anio.*

Ănius -ii, m. *priest of Apollo, and king of the island of Delos, friend of Anchises and Aeneas.*

Anna -ae, f., **a,** *sister of Dido;* **b,** Anna Perenna, *a Roman goddess.*

annālis -e (annus). **I.** Adj., **A.** *lasting a year,* Varr. **B.** *relating to a year;* lex, *the law which determined the minimum age for the great offices of state,* Cic. **II.** Subst., **annālis** -is, m. (sc. liber) and plur. **annāles** -ium, m. (libri) *yearly records, annals,* in early times kept by the Pontifices (hence annales pontificum or annales maximi), in later times composed by the so-called annalists (as Q. Fabius Pictor), Cic.

annăto, 1. (ad-nato), **1,** *to swim to,* Plin.; **2,** *to swim by the side of,* Sen.

annāvĭgo, 1. (ad-navigo), *to voyage to,* Plin.

annecto (ad-necto) -nexŭi -nexum, 3. *to bind to, connect with.* **I.** Lit., stomachus ad linguam annectitur, Cic. **II.** Transf., **1,** physically, animos corporibus, Lucr.; **2,** *to connect,* in a speech, rebus praesentibus futuras adjungere atque annectere, Cic.

annexus -ūs, m. (annecto), *a binding to, a connection,* Tac.

Annĭbal, v. Hannibal.

Annĭcĕrii -ōrum, m. (Ἀννικέρειοι), *a sect of Cyrenaic philosophers.*

annĭcŭlus -a -um (annus), *one year old;* neptis, Nep.

annītor (ad-nitor) -nisus or -nixus, 3, dep. **I.** Lit., *to lean upon;* ad aliquod tamquam adminiculum, Cic. **II.** Transf., *to strive after;* de triumpho, Cic.; with ad and the acc. of the gerund, ad obtinendum hesternum decus, Liv.; foll. by ut or ne, with the subj., Liv.; also by the infin., Liv.

Annĭus -a -um, gens, *an old plebeian family at Rome,* of which T. Annius Milo was a member, v. Milo. Adj. **Anniānus** -a -um, *belonging to an Annius or Annia.*

annĭversārĭus -a -um (annus and verto), *recurring every year;* sacra, Cic.; arma, Liv.

1. **anno** (ad-no), 1. **I.** *to swim to,* or *near;* with acc., naves, Caes.; with dat., vestris oris, Verg.; navibus, Liv.; generally with ad and the acc., ad eam urbem, Cic. **II.** *to swim with,* or *alongside of;* peditos annantes equis, Tac.

2. **Anno,** v. Hanno.

annōna -ae, f. (annus). **I.** *yearly produce, crop;* **1,** Gen., Col.; **2,** *means of subsistence,* esp. *grain;* annonae caritas, *dearness,* Cic.: vilitas, *cheapness,* Cic. **II.** Meton., *price of provisions;* annona salaria, *price of salt,* Liv.; esp. of corn; annonae varietas, *fluctuation in the price of corn,* Cic.; esp. *high price of corn;* solatium annonae, Cic.; annonam queri, *to complain of the high price of corn,* Liv.; fig., vilis amicorum annona, *friends are to be had cheap,* Hor.

annōsus -a -um (annus), *full of years, long-lived;* cornix, Hor.

annŏtātĭo (ad-notatio) -ōnis, f. (annoto), *remark, annotation,* Plin.

annŏtātor -ōris, m. (annoto), *one who remarks, an observer,* Plin.

annŏtĭnus -a -um (annus), *a year old, belonging to last year;* naves, Caes.

annŏto (ad-noto), 1. *to note down.* **I.** Lit., annotatum est, with acc. and infin., Tac.; librum, *to make remarks on a book,*. Plin. **II.** Transf. *to remark, take notice of,* Plin.

annŭmĕro (ad-numero), 1. **I.** *to count out, pay;* tibi denarios, Cic. **II.** *to reckon with;* with dat., aliquem his duobus, Cic.; with in and the abl., aliquem patronorum in grege, Cic.

annuntio (ad-nuntio), 1. *to announce, tell, relate,* Plin.

annŭo (ad-nuo) -ŭi, 3. **I.** *to nod to;* simul atque sibi annuisset, Cic. **II. A.** *to assent by a nod or sign;* id toto capite, Cic.; with dat., of person, petenti, Verg.; of the thing, quibus (praemiis) etiam rex ipse annuerat, Liv.; annue coeptis, *be favourable to our undertaking,* Verg.; with fut. infin., quum annuisset se venturum, Liv. **B.** alicui aliquid, *to promise;* caeli arcem, Verg. **C.** *to point out by a sign;* quos iste annuerat, Cic.

annus -i, m. (root AN connected with anulus); *revolution of time,* hence *year.* **I.** Lit., exeunte anno, Cic.; anno superiore, Cic.; omnibus annis, *annually,* Caes.; tempus anni, *time of the year, season,* Cic.; adv. phrases, **1,** anno, *a whole year,* Liv.; *in each year, yearly,* Liv.; so, in anno, *in each year,* Cic.; annum, *a full year,* Cic.; in annum, *for a year,* Liv.; ad annum, *next year,* Cic.; intra annum, *within the space of a year,* Liv.; **2,** of the years of a person's life; annos LXX natus, *seventy years old;* Cic.; Hannibal annorum ferme novem, *when nine years old,* Caes.; habere annos viginti, Cic.; annum agere quartum et octogesimum, Cic.; hence, like aetas, *old age,* confectus annis, Sall.; **3,** *the year of a person's life at which he could stand for a magistracy;* is enim erat annus quo per leges ei consulem fieri liceret, Caes.; annus meus, tuus, suus, Cic.; so, *the year of office;* prorogare annum, Cic.; **4,** *a year with relation to the weather, healthiness,* &c.; locuples frugibus, Hor.; gravissimus et pestilentissimus, Cic.; **5,** annus magnus, *a cycle of years,* Cic. **II.** Transf. (poet.), **1,** *time of year;* pomifer, *autumn;* hibernus, *winter,* Hor.; **2,** *the growth of a year,* Cic.

annŭto (ad-nuto), 1. (intens. of annuo), *to nod to, make a sign to,* Plaut.

annŭtrio (ad-nutrio), 4. *to nourish at* or *near to,* Plin.

annŭus -a -um (annus). **I.** *lasting for a year;* magistratus, Caes. **II.** *returning every year, annual;* labor agricolarum, Cic.; hence, subst., **annŭum** -i, n. or **annŭa** -ōrum, n. *a yearly salary, pension, annuity,* Plin.

anquīro -quīsīvi -quīsītum (an and quaero), 3 *to search carefully, to inquire after* I. Lit., omnia quae sunt ad vivendum necessaria anquirere et parare, Cic II. Transf , A. Transit , *to investigate*, mens semper aliquid anquirit aut agit, Cic B. Intransit , legal t. t *to set an inquiry on foot*, de perduellione, Liv , capite or capitis, *on a charge involving capital punishment*, Liv.

ansa -ae, f *a handle, haft* I Lit , ansa poculi, canthari, Verg. , crepidae, *the eye through which a shoe-tie is passed*, Tib II. Transf , *occasion, opportunity*, habere reprehensionis ansam aliquam, Cic

Ansancti, v Ampsancti

ansātus -a -um (ansa), *provided with a handle*, homo, *a man with handles*, i e , *with arms akimbo*, Plaut

1 **anser**,-ĕris, m *a goose*, Cic.

2 **Anser** -ĕris, m *a wanton poet, friend of the triumvir Antonius*

ansĕrīnus -a -um (anser), *relating or belonging to a goose*, Plin

Antaeus -i, m (Ἀνταῖος), *a powerful giant, ruler of Libya, who compelled all strangers coming to his country to wrestle with him, at last slain by Hercules, who, observing that each time Antaeus fell on the earth he gained new force, held him aloft in the air and so killed him*

Antandros (us) -i, f (Ἄντανδρος), *a town of Mysia, now Antandro*, hence adj , **Antandrius** -a -um, *of Antandros*

antĕ (old form, anti, whence antidea, antideo, connected with ἄντα, ἀντί, ἄντην), prep & adv *before* I. Adv , A Of place, ante aut post pugnare, Liv B. Of time, a, *before*; multis ante saeculis, Cic , ante quam, *before that*, ut te ante videret quam a vita discederet, Cic , anno ante quam mortuus est, Cic , b, very rarely used as adj , neque ignari sumus ante malorum (= τῶν πρὶν κακῶν), *of former sufferings*, Verg II. Prep , *before* A. Of place, 1, Lit , ante pedes, Cic , causam ante aliquem dicere, *before a judge*, Cic , 2, Transf , of preference, quem ante me diligo, *whom I love more than myself*, Cic , so ante alios, Liv , ante omnes, Tac B. of time, ante lucem, Cic , ante me, *before my time*, Cic ; often with a partic , ante urbem conditam, *before the founding of the city*, Cic , esp a, ante annum *a year ago*, Plin , b, ante rem, *before the fight*, Liv ; ante tempus, *before the right time*, Liv , c, ante diem, (α) *before the day*, Ov , (β) *before the day fixed by fate*, Ov , d, ante id tempus, *up to the present time*, Caes , e, ante certam diem, *within a fixed time*, equites ante certam diem decederent, Cic , f, so to mark the date, ante diem quartum Idus Martias (a d IV Id Mart), *the fourth day before the Ides of March*, i e *the twelfth of March*, Cic

antĕā (ante and abl eā), adv , *before, formerly*, Cic , followed by quam, Cic

antĕambŭlo ōnis, m (ante and ambulare), *a running footman to clear the way*, Mart

antĕcănem (translation of προκύων), *a star, the little dog*, Cic

antĕcăpio -cēpi -ceptum, 3 I. Lit , *to seize beforehand*, pontem Mosae fluminis, Tac , locum castris, Sall II Transf , a, *to anticipate, to prepare beforehand*, quae bello usui forent, Sall , *to excite*, or *provoke beforehand*, ea omnia (famem aut sitim, etc.) luxu, Sall , *to use beforehand*, noctem, *not to wait for*, Sall , b, philosoph t t., anteceptam animo rei quandam informationem, *preconceived idea*, Cic

antĕcēdens entis, p adj (from antecedo), *preceding* I. Plin II. Esp , philosoph t. t , causa, *the antecedent cause* Subst , **antĕcēdens**, *the antecedent cause*; oftener in plur. antecedentia, Cic

antĕcēdo cessi -cessum, 3 *to go before, precede* I Gen , A. Lit , in space, agmen, Caes , absol , stellae tum antecedunt, tum subsequuntur, Cic B. Transf , in time (with dat and acc), alicui aetate paulum, Cic II. Esp *to hasten before, to o*[illegible] A. Lit , nuntios oppugnati oppidi fam[illegible] , Caes B. Transf , *to excel*, with dat , quantum natura hominis pecudibus reliquisque bestiis antecedat, Cic ; with acc , aliquem scientia atque usu nauticarum rerum, Caes , absol , et auctoritate et aetate et usu rerum, Cic

antĕcello -ĕre, no perf or sup , *to distinguish oneself, excel*, 1 of persons, with dat of person and abl of thing, omnibus ingenii gloria, Cic , with acc of the person and abl of the thing, omnes fortuna, Tac , with abl of thing alone, militari laude, Cic , 2, of things, duae aedes sacrae quae longe ceteris antecellant, Cic

antĕcessio ōnis, f (antecedo), 1, *a preceding* or *going before*, quae in orbibus conversiones antecessionesque eveniunt, Cic 2, *the antecedent cause*, homo causas rerum videt earumque praegressus et quasi antecessiones non ignorat, Cic

antĕcessus ūs, m (antecedo), *a going before*, in antecessum, *in advance*, Sen

antĕcursor -ōris, m (antecurro), *one who runs before*, plur *pioneers, advance guard of an army*, Caes

antĕĕo -ivi (and gen) ii, -īre (old form, antideo), *to go before* I Lit , alicui, Cic , aliquem, Hor II. Transf , A. *to go before* in time , alicui aetate, Cic , aliquem aetate, Cic , si anteissent delicta, *had happened before*, Tac B. 1, *to excel*, alicui sapientia, Cic , omnes intelligentia, Cic , absol , *to distinguish oneself*, operibus, *by actions*, Cic , 2, *to anticipate*, damnationem veneno Tac (in poets and post Augustan prose, the syllable after ante disappears, antīat, Ov ; antibo, Tac)

antĕfĕro -tŭli -lātum, -ferre I *to carry before*, viginti clarissimarum familiarum imagines, Tac II. Transf , A. *to prefer* , longe omnibus unum Demosthenem, Cic , iniquissimam pacem justissimo bello, Cic B. *to anticipate, consider beforehand*, quod est dies allatura, id consilio anteferre debemus, Cic

antĕfixus -a um, *fastened in front*, truncis arborum antefixa ora, Tac Subst , **antĕfixa** -ōrum, n *ornaments fixed on the roofs and gutters of houses*, antefixa fictilia deorum Romanorum, Liv

antĕgrĕdior -gressus gredi, dep (ante and gradior), *to go before* I. Lit , stella Veneris antegreditur solem, Cic. II. Transf , causae antegressae, *antecedent causes*, Cic

antĕhăbĕo, 2 *to prefer*, Tac

antĕhāc (old form, antidhac), adv (ante and abl hāc), *before this time, formerly*, Cic.

antĕlātus -a -um, v antefero

antĕlūcānus -a -um (ante and lux), *happening before daybreak*, tempus, Cic , cena, Cic

antĕmĕrīdiānus -a -um, *before noon*, Cic

antĕmitto, more properly separated, ante and mitto q v

Antemnae -ārum, f *Sabine town at the junction of the Anio with the Tiber*, hence, **Antemnātes** -ium, m *the inhabitants of Antemnae*

antenna (antemna) ae, f. (an = ἀνά and tendere), *a sail-yard*, antennas ad malos destinare, Caes

Antēnor -ŏris, m. (Ἀντήνωρ) *a Trojan, the legendary founder of Patavium* (Padua); hence, 1, **Antēnŏrĕus** -a -um, *belonging to Antenor, Patavian;* 2, **Antēnŏrĭdes** -ae, m. (Ἀντηνορίδης), *a descendant of Antenor.*

antĕpagmentum -i, n. *the lining of a door or post, a jamb,* Cato.

antĕpēs -pĕdis, m. *the forefoot,* Cic.

antĕpīlāni -ōrum, m. *the soldiers who fought in front of the pilani* or *triarii,* i.e. *the hastati and principes,* Liv.

antĕpōno -pŏsŭi -pŏsĭtum, 3. I. *to place before;* alicui prandium, Plaut. II. *to place in front.* A. Lit., equitum locos sedilibus plebis, Tac. B. Transf., *to prefer;* se alicui, Cic.; amicitiam omnibus rebus humanis, Cic.

antĕpŏtens -entis, *very powerful, very fortunate,* Plaut.

Antĕrōs -ōtis, m. (Ἀντέρως), 1, *the genius or avenger of slighted love,* Cic.; 2, *a kind of amethyst,* Plin.

antes -ium, m. *rows or ranks,* e.g. of vines, Verg.

antĕsignānus -i, m. (ante and signum), plur. antesignani, *chosen soldiers who fought in front of the line* to support the cavalry, *skirmishers,* Caes.; hence, sing., *a leader,* Cic.

antĕsto (antisto) -stĭti, 1. *to stand before;* transf., *to surpass;* with dat. of person and abl. of thing, multum omnibus (dat.) corporum viribus (abl.), Cic.; absol., *to be prominent,* Cic.

antestor, 1. dep. (contr. from antetestor), legal t. t., *to call to witness,* Hor. The formula was "licet antestari?" used by the demandant, and the person whose witness was required held up the lap of his ear to express his consent: used once by Cicero without reference to judicial proceedings.

antĕvĕnĭo -vēni -ventum, 4. I. Lit., A. *to come before, to get the start of;* per tramites occultos exercitum Metelli, Sall. II. Transf., A. *to anticipate, prevent;* consilia et insidias hostium, Sall. B. *to excel;* per virtutem nobilitatem, Sall.

antĕverto, antĕvorto -verti (-vorti) -versum (-vorsum), 3. and dep. **antĕvortor** -vorti. I. Lit., *to come or go before, to precede;* stella tum antevertens tum subsequens, Cic. II. Transf., A. *to anticipate, hinder by anticipating;* atque id ipsum quum tecum agere conarer, Fannius antevertit, Cic. B. *to prefer;* Caesar omnibus consiliis antevertendum existimavit ut Narbonem proficisceretur, Caes.

Anthēdōn -ŏnis, f. (Ἀνθηδών), *town and state of the Boeotian league on the river Messapius,* now *Lukisi.*

Anthĕmūsĭa -ae, f. and **Anthĕmūsĭas** -ădis, f. *a town in Mesopotamia.*

anthĭās -ae, m. (ἀνθίας), *a sea-fish,* Ov.

anthŏlŏgĭca, genit. -ōn, n. (ἀνθολογικά), *anthology, a collection of extracts and small poems,* Plin.

Antĭānus, Antĭas, v. Antium.

Antĭcăto -ōnis, m. *the Anticato, a work of C. Jul. Caesar in two books,* in answer to Cicero's Cato, Juv.

antĭcĭpātĭo -ōnis, f. (anticipo), *a preconception, innate idea,* Cic.

antĭcĭpo, 1. (ante and capio), 1, *to take or receive before, anticipate;* quod ita sit informatum anticipatumque mentibus nostris, Cic.; viam, *to travel over before,* Ov.; ludos, *to celebrate before their time,* Suet.; 2, *to come before,* Lucr.

Antĭclēa and **-clīa** -ae, f. (Ἀντίκλεια), *daughter of Autolycus, wife of Laertes, mother of Ulysses.*

antīcus -a -um (ante), *forward, in front* (opp. posticus), pars, Cic.

Antĭcȳra -ae, f. (Ἀντίκυρα), *a town in Phocis, famous for its hellebore,* now *Aspro Spiti,* Hor.

antidea, antideo, antidhac, v. antea, anteeo, antehac.

antĭdŏtum -i, n. (ἀντίδοτον), *an antidote,* Suet.

Antĭgĕnēs -is, m. (Ἀντιγένης). I. *a general of Alexander the Great,* Nep. II. *a shepherd,* Verg.

Antĭgĕnĭdas -ae, m. and **-ĭdēs** -ae, m. (Ἀντιγενίδης), *name of two celebrated flute-players, one of whom, a Theban, flourished about 440* B.C., *the other, a son of Dionysius, about 338* B.C.

Antĭgŏnē -ēs, f. and **Antĭgŏna** -ae, f. (Ἀντιγόνη). I. *daughter of Oedipus, sister of Polynices and Eteocles, put to death for burying her brother against the command of the king of Thebes.* II. *daughter of Laomedon, king of Troy, changed into a stork by Hera.*

Antĭgŏnēa -ae, f. (Ἀντιγόνεια or Ἀντιγονία) *name of several towns, the most important of which were*—a, *a town on the Celydnus, in Epirus;* hence, **Antĭgŏnensis** -e, *belonging to Antigonia;* b, *a town in Macedonia.*

Antĭgŏnus -i, m. (Ἀντίγονος), *name of several of the successors of Alexander the Great, the most celebrated of whom was* Antigonus I., *born* 385 B.C., *father of Demetrius Poliorcetes, ruler of Phrygia, and, after Alexander's death, of Pamphylia and Lycia, killed at Ipsus* 301 B.C.

Antĭlĭbănus -i, m. (Ἀντιλίβανος) *a mountain range in Phoenicia, running parallel to Mount Libanus,* now *Dschebel Escharki.*

Antĭlŏchus -i, m. (Ἀντίλοχος), *son of Nestor, friend of Achilles.*

Antĭmăchus -i, m. (Ἀντίμαχος), *a Greek poet, contemporary with Plato.*

Antĭnŏus -i, m. (Ἀντινόος), *a beautiful youth, beloved by the emperor Hadrian, who gave him divine honours on his early death.*

Antĭŏchīa -ae, f. (Ἀντιόχεια), *name of several towns.* I. *Antiochia Epidaphnes* (ἡ ἐπὶ Δάφνης, Plin.), *capital of Syria, on the river Orontes,* now *Antakia.* II. *town of Caria, on the Maeander;* hence, adj., **Antĭŏchensis** -e and **Antĭŏchīnus** -a -um, *belonging to Antioch.*

Antĭŏchus -i, m. (Ἀντίοχος). I. *name of thirteen Syrian kings, the most important of whom were*—a, Antiochus III., *Magnus, protector of Hannibal in his exile, conquered by L. Corn. Scipio;* b, Antiochus IV., *Epiphanes, who was deterred by the Roman envoy, L. Popilius, from seizing Egypt;* c, Antiochus X., *whose son,* Antiochus XIII., *came to Rome with his brother to uphold their claims on Egypt.* II. *name of several kings of Commagene.* III. Antiochus of Ascalon, *the last philosopher of the Academic school of philosophers, teacher of Varro and Cicero;* hence 1, **Antĭŏchīus** -a -um, *belonging to the philosopher Antiochus.* Subst., a, **Antĭŏchii** -orum, m. *the disciples of Antiochus;* b, ista Antiochia, *the dogmas of Antiochus;* 2, **Antĭŏchīnus** -a -um, a, *belonging to Antiochus III.;* b, *belonging to the philosopher Antiochus.*

Antĭŏpa -ae, f. and **Antĭŏpē** -ēs, f. (Ἀντιόπη), 1, *daughter of Nycteus, mother of Amphion and Zethus;* 2, *mother of the Pierides.*

Antĭpătĕr -tri, m. (Ἀντίπατρος). I. *name of several kings of Macedonia, the most important of whom was the confidant of Philip and Alexander the Great, king of Macedonia after Alexan-*

der's death **II.** *name of several Greek philosophers,* **a,** Antipater Cyrenaicus, *a disciple of the elder Aristippus,* **b,** Antipater of Tarsus, *a Stoic, teacher of Panaetius* **III.** L Caelius Antipater, v Caelius

Antipătrĭa -ae, f (Ἀντιπατρία), *a town in Macedonia, on the border of Illyria*

Antiphătēs -ae, m (Ἀντιφάτης) **I.** *ruler of the cannibal Laestrygones* **II** *a son of Sarpedon, killed by Turnus*

Antĭphōn -ontis (Ἀντιφῶν) **1,** *a celebrated Athenian orator,* 479–411 B.C , **2,** *a sophist, contemporary and adversary of Socrates,* **3,** *a freedman and actor*

Antĭpŏlis -is, f (Ἀντίπολις), *town of the Massilians in Gallia Narbonensis,* now *Antibes*

antīquārĭus -a -um (antiquus), *belonging to antiquity* Subst , **antīquārĭus** -ii, m and **antīquārĭa** -ae, f , *an antiquary,* Juv , Suet

antīquē, adv (antiquus), *in an ancient manner,* Hor

antīquĭtas -ātis, f (antiquus) **I.** *antiquity, ancient times,* Cic **II.** Meton , **1,** *the history of ancient times,* Cic , hence plur *the ancients,* Cic. , **2,** *the good old times, primitive virtue, integrity,* Cic , **3,** *great age,* generis, Cic

antīquĭtŭs, adv (antiquus), **1,** *formerly, in ancient times,* Caes ; **2,** *from antiquity,* Liv

antīquo, 1 (antiquus), *to leave in its former state,* hence, *to reject a bill,* legem, rogationem, Cic

antīquus -a -um (for anticus, from ante) **I.** *that which excels all other things in worth,* in compar and superl , *more* or *most weighty, important, preferable,* id antiquius consuli fuit, *the consul preferred that,* Liv , ne quid vita existimem antiquius, *more important,* Cic , nihil ei fuisset antiquius quam (followed by the infin), Cic , navalis apparatus ei semper antiquissima cura fuit, Cic **II.** *that which is before in point of time* **A.** Relative, *old, ancient previous, once existing,* **a,** antiquae munitiones, Caes , causa antiquior memoria tua, Cic , subst , nam illa nimis antiqua praetereo, Cic , **b,** (with the notion of what is *simple, pure, innocent,* antiqui homines, Cic **B.** Absol , *having existed for a long time, old, ancient, venerable;* tuus antiquissimus amicus, Cic , esp. of towns, urbs, Verg Subst , **antīqui** -orum m *the people of old time, ancient authors, old statesmen, men of old,* Cic

Antissa -ae, f (Ἄντισσα), *a town on a small island near Lesbos,* hence, **Antissaei** -orum m *the Antissaeans*

antistĕs -stitis, c (antisto) **I.** *a presiding priest* or *priestess,* sacrorum, Cic **II.** Transf , *master in any art,* artis dicendi, Cic

Antisthĕnēs -is and -ae, m (Ἀντισθένης), *a Greek philosopher, founder of the Cynic school*

antistĭta -ae, f (antistes), *a presiding priestess,* Cic , Ov

antisto, v antesto

antithĕton -i, n (ἀντίθετον), *a figure of rhetoric, antithesis, opposition,* Cic

Antĭum -ii, n (Ἄντιον), *an old town of Latium on the sea coast,* now *Torre* or *Porto d'Anzio,* hence, **1, Antĭānus** -a -um , **2, Antĭās** -ātis, *belonging to Antium*

antlĭa -ae, f (ἀντλίον) *a pump,* Mart

Antōnĭaster -tri, m *an imitator of the oratory of Antonius,* Cic

Antōnīnus -i, m *a name of several Roman emperors, the most notable of whom are,* **1,** Antoninus Pius, *ruled from* 138–161 A.D , **2,** M Aurelius Antoninus Philosophus, *son-in-law and adopted son of the former, ruled from* 161–180 A D , **3,** M Aurelius Antoninus, v Heliogabalus

Antōnĭus -a -um, gens, *the name of a Roman family, the most distinguished members of which were* (1) M Antonius, *surnamed Orator, born* B C 144, *put to death by Marius and Cinna* 88 , *introduced by Cicero as a speaker in the dialogue* De Oratore (2) M Antonius Creticus, *son of* (1) *despatched against the pirates of the eastern Mediterranean in* 74 B C (3) C Antonius, *second son of the preceding, the accomplice of Catiline, colleague with Cicero in the consulship,* B C 63 (4) M Antonius Triumvir, *son of* (2), *born* B C 83, *the bitter enemy of Cicero, after Caesar's death triumvir with Octavianus and Lepidus, defeated by Octavianus at the battle of Actium* (B C 31), *killed himself shortly after* (5) Iulus Antonius, *son of* (4), *by Fulvia, brought up by the elder Octavia,* hence, adj , **Antōnĭānus** -a -um, *of* or *relating to Antonius*

antrum -i, n (ἄντρον), *a cave,* Ov , Verg , transf , *the hollow of a tree,* exesae arboris antro, Verg , of a litter vehi clauso antro, Juv

Anūbis -bidis, m (Ἄνουβις, Egyptian Anup, or Anpu), *an Egyptian god, represented with a dog's head,* latrator A , Verg

ānŭlārĭus -a -um (anulus), *belonging to a seal ring,* scalae, *a place in Rome,* Suet Subst , **anularius** -i, m *a ring maker,* Cic

ānŭlātus -a -um (anulus), *beringed, ornamented with rings,* aures, Plaut

ānŭlus, annŭlus -i, m (1 anus), *a ring,* Esp **I** *a finger* or *signet ring,* in ejusmodi cera centum sigilla imprimere hoc anulo, Cic , vilissimi utensilium anulo clausa, *sealed up,* Tac , anulus equestris *the gold ring which was the sign of a knight in Rome,* Hor , anulum invenire, *to be raised to the rank of a knight,* Cic **II.** Of objects similar in form, **1,** *a curtain ring,* Plin , **2,** *the link of a fetter,* Plin , **3,** *a ringlet of hair,* Mart

1 **ānus** -i, m *the fundament,* Cic

2 **ănus** -ūs, f *an old woman,* Cic , anus Cumaea, *the Sibyl,* Ov , in apposition, *old,* sacerdos, Verg , of animals and things, cerva, Ov , amphora, Mart ; Appia via, Prop

anxĭē, adv (anxius), *anxiously,* Sall

anxĭĕtas -ātis, f (anxius) **I.** *anxiety, anxiousness,* as a trait in a person's character, while angor is the transitory feeling of anxiety, Cic ; also = angor, *grief, anguish,* Ov **II.** Transf *painful accuracy,* Quint

anxĭfer -fĕra -fĕrum (anxius and fero), *causing anxiety,* Cic

anxĭtūdo -inis, f (anxius), *anxiousness,* Cic

anxĭus -a -um (ango) **I.** *anxious, uneasy,* anxii senes, Cic , anxium habere aliquem, *to make anxious,* Tac , anxius animo, Sall , with abl of cause, ira et metu, Sall , with genit , furti, Ov , with de and the abl , de successore, Suet , with pro, pro mundi regno, Ov , followed by ne, Sall , an . . . an, Tac , -ne (enclitic) . . . an, Sall , quonam modo, Tac , unde, Hor **II** Transf , *causing anxiety* or *anguish,* aegritudines, Cic

Anxŭr -ŭris, m and n **I.** m Anxur (Axur), and Anxurus, *a deity of the Volscians, identified with the Etruscan Vejovis,* Anxurus Juppiter, Verg **II.** n *an old town of the Volsci, on the sea-coast, afterwards called Terracina* Adj , **Anxurnās** -ātis, *belonging to Anxur*

Āŏn -ŏnis, m (Ἄων), *son of Poseidon, an old Boeotian hero,* hence **1, Āŏnes** -um, acc -as, m (Ἄονες), *Boeotians,* **2, Āŏnĭa** -ae, f (Ἀονία), *mythic name of Boeotia, in which were*

the mountain Helicon and the spring Aganippe, the resort of the Muses; 3, **Aŏnĭdĕs** -um, f. *the Muses;* 4, **Aŏnĭus** -a -um (Ἀόνιος) *belonging to Aonia;* vertex, *Helicon,* Verg.; vir, *Hercules, born at Thebes,* Ov.; juvenis, *Hippomenes,* Ov.; deus, *Bacchus,* Ov.; fons and aquae, *Aganippe,* Ov.; sorores, *the Muses,* Ov.; vates, *a poet,* Ov.

Ăornos -i, m. and f. (ἄορνος, *without birds*), *the lake of Avernus,* Verg.

Ăōus -i, m. (Ἀῷος), *a river in Illyria, now Viosa* or *Vovussa.*

ăpăgĕ, interj., *away with thee! be off!* Ter., Plaut.

Ăpămēa and **-īa** -ae, f. (Ἀπάμεια), **1,** *a town of Syria on the Orontes,* now *Afamiah* or *Famit;* **2,** *a town of Phrygia on the Maeander;* **3,** *a town of Bithynia.* Adj., **Ăpămensis** -e and **Ăpămēnus** -a -um, *belonging to Apamea.*

Ăpellēs -is, m. (Ἀπελλῆς), *one of the greatest Greek painters, friend of Alexander the Great.* Adj., **Ăpellēus** -a -um.

Āpennīnĭcŏla -ae, c. (Apenninus and colo), *an inhabitant of the Apennines,* Verg.

Āpennīnĭgĕna -ae, c. (Apenninus and gigno), *one born upon the Apennines,* Ov.

Āpennīnus -i, m. (connected with Keltic Pen, a mountain-top), *the chain of the Apennines,* a mountain range running down through the centre of Italy.

ăper, apri, m. *a wild boar,* Cic.; prov., uno in saltu duos apros capere, *to kill two birds with one stone,* Plaut.; apros immittere liquidis fontibus, *to do something absurd and perverse,* Verg.

Ăperantĭi -ōrum, m. (Ἀπεραντοί), *a people in northern Aetolia;* hence **Ăperantĭa** -ae, f. *their country.*

ăpĕrio -pĕrŭi -pertum, 4. (ad-pario, from root PAR, whence pario). **I.** *to uncover, to lay bare, to expose to view.* **A.** Lit., caput, *to uncover,* Cic. **B.** Transf., occulta, *to make known,* Cic.; sententiam suam, *to pronounce,* Cic.; casus futuros, *to predict,* Ov.; refl., se aperire and middle aperiri, *to reveal one's true character;* studioque aperimur in ipso, Ov.; memet ipse aperio quis sim, Liv. **II.** *to open what was shut, to unclose.* **A.** Lit., fores, Cic.; epistolam, Cic.; fundamenta templi, *to excavate,* Liv.; fig., fontes eloquentiae, Cic. **B.** Transf., *to open up a country, render it accessible;* Pontum, Cic.; Syriam, Tac.; locum asylum, *to throw open as an asylum,* Liv; ludum, *to open a school,* Cic.; annum, *to begin the year* (poet., of the constellation Aries, because, on the entry of the sun into it the new year began for the farmer), Verg.

ăpertē, adv., with compar. and superl. (apertus), **a,** *openly;* mentiri, Cic.; **b,** *without concealment, straightforwardly;* scribere, Cic.; dicere, Cic.

ăperto, 1. (intens. of aperio), *to lay bare,* Plaut.

ăpertus -a -um, p. adj., with compar. and superl. (from aperio), *open, uncovered.* **I. A.** Lit., aether, caelum, *clear,* Verg.; naut. t.t., naves, *undecked,* Cic.; milit. t.t., *undefended;* latus, humerus, *unshielded, exposed,* Caes. **B.** Transf. *clear, unconcealed, manifest;* **a,** actio, Cic.; apertum latrocinium, Cic.; apertum est, *it is clear,* followed by acc. and infin., esse aliquod numen praestantissimae mentis, Cic.; in aperto esse, (α), *to be evident;* quo ad cognoscendum omnia illustria magis magisque in aperto sint, Sall.; (β), *to be practicable;* fessos hiemo hostes aggredi, Tac.; **b,** of speech, *clear, intelligible, unconcealed;* narratio aperta, Cic.; apertis or apertissimis verbis, Cic.; **c,** of character, *frank, straightforward, open;* animus, Cic.; homo, Cic. **II.** *unclosed, open, free, unhindered, accessible.* **A.** Lit., **a,** vastum atque apertum mare, Caes.; campi ad dimicandum aperti, Liv. Subst., **ăpertum** -i, n. *an open space;* in aperto castra locare, Liv.; **b,** milit. t.t., *open;* proelium, Liv. **B.** Transf. *open, accessible;* beate vivendi via, Cic.

ăpex -icis, m. *the top* or *summit.* **I.** Gen., montis, Ov.; flammae, Ov. **II.** Esp., **A.** *the top of the conical cap of the Roman flamines,* hence *the cap itself;* lanigeri apices, Verg.; apicem Dialem alicui imponere, *to make a person flamen of Jove,* Liv.; also *the tiara of eastern kings and satraps,* regum apices, Hor.; so fig., *crown;* apex senectutis est auctoritas, Cic. **B.** *a helmet,* Verg. **C.** Gramm., *the long mark over a vowel,* Quint.

ăphaerēma -ătis, n. (ἀφαίρεμα), *a coarse kind of grits,* Plin.

Ăphărcus, -ĕi, m. (Ἀφαρεύς). **I.** *a king of the Messenians, father of Lynceus and Idas;* hence **Aphareīus** -a -um, *belonging to Aphareus.* **II.** *a Centaur, whose arm was broken by Theseus at the wedding of Pirithous.*

aphractus -i, f. (ἄφρακτος), *a long undecked boat,* Cic.

Ăphrŏdīsĭa -ōrum, n. (Ἀφροδίσια), *the festival of Aphrodite,* Plaut.

Ăphrŏdīsĭas -ădis, f. (Ἀφροδισιάς), *name of several towns;* **1,** *a town on the borders of Phrygia and Caria,* now *Gheira;* hence **Ăphrŏdīsĭenses** -ium, m. *the people of Aphrodisias;* **2,** *a harbour in Cilicia, near Porto Cavaliere.*

ăpĭăcus -a -um (apium), *like parsley,* Cato.

ăpĭānus -a -um (apis), *relating* or *belonging to bees,* Plin.

ăpĭārĭus -ii, m. (apis), *a bee-keeper,* Plin.

ăpĭcātus -a -um (apex), *adorned with the priest's cap,* Ov.

Ăpīcĭus -ii, m. *a Roman name;* M. Gabius Apicius, *a celebrated epicure in the time of Tiberius.*

Ăpĭdănus -i, m. (Ἀπιδανός), *a river in Thessaly, tributary of the Peneus.*

ăpĭnae -ārum, f. *trifles,* Mart.

Apĭŏlae -ārum, f. *a town in Latium.*

Āpĭōn -ōnis, m. *surname of Ptolemaeus, king of Cyrene.*

1. **ăpis** -is, f. (ἐμπίς), *a bee,* Cic., Verg.

2. **Āpis** -is, acc. -im, m. (Ἆπις), *a sacred bull of the Egyptians at Memphis.*

ăpiscor, aptus, 3. dep. **I.** *to attain to, come up to, reach;* mare, Cic. **II.** Transf., **1,** *to lay hold of, grasp,* Lucr.; **2,** *to attain to* (the object of one's desire), cujus (finis bonorum) apiscendi causa, Cic.; summum honorem, Liv.; once in Tac., with genit., dominationis.

ăpĭum -ii, n. *parsley,* Hor.

ăplustrĕ -is, n. (ἄφλαστον), generally plur. aplustria -ium, n. and aplustra -ōrum, n. *the carved stern of a ship, with its ornaments,* Lucr.

ăpŏclēti -ōrum, m. (ἀπόκλητοι), *the supreme council of the Aetolian League,* Liv.

ăpŏdȳtērium -i, n. (ἀποδυτήριον), *the dressing-room in a bath,* Cic.

Ăpollo -inis (-ōnis), m. (Ἀπόλλων), *Apollo, son of Jupiter and Latona, brother of Diana, god of archery, music, poetry, prophesying, and the sun, born at Delos;* hence, Delius vates, Verg.; and simply Delius, Cic.; ad Apollinis (sc. aedem) *to the temple of Apollo,* Liv.; aperitur Apollo, *the temple of Apollo becomes visible,* Verg.; promontorium Apollinis, *a promontory north of Utica, over against Sardinia,* now *Cape Zibib,* Liv.; hence, **A.** Adj., **Ăpollĭnāris** -e, *sacred* *to Apollo*, ludi, *games held in honour of Apollo on the 5th of July*, Cic Subst., **Ăpollĭnāre** is, n *a place sacred to Apollo*, Liv, **B. Ăpollĭnĕus** -a -um, *pertaining to Apollo*, urbs, *Delos*, Ov; proles, *Aesculapius*, Ov; vates, *Orpheus*, Ov.; ars, *prophecy* or *medicine*, Ov

Ăpollŏdōrus -i, m (Ἀπολλόδωρος). 1, *a rhetorician of Pergamum, teacher of Augustus*, 2, *grammarian and mythological writer of Athens, about* 140 B C

Ăpollōnia ae, f (Ἀπολλωνία), 1, *citadel near Naupactus*, Liv, 2, *town in Illyria*, now *Polonia* or *Polina*, Cic, 3, *town in Macedonia*, now *Polina*, Liv; hence, a, **Ăpollōnĭātes** -ae, m *an inhabitant of Apollonia*, b, **Ăpollōniensis** -e, *belonging to Apollonia*.

Ăpollōnis -idis, f (Ἀπολλωνίς), *a town in Lydia*, hence **Ăpollōnĭdensis** -e, *belonging to Apollonis*

Ăpollōnĭus -ii, m (Ἀπολλώνιος), 1, Apollonius Alabandensis, *Greek rhetorician, living about* 120 B C; 2, Apollonius Molo, *a Greek rhetorician, living about* 110 B.C, 3, Apollonius Rhodius, *author of the Argonautica*, 4, Apollonius Tyaneus, *philosopher and magician in 1st cent* A D

ăpŏlŏgus i, m (ἀπόλογος), *a narrative, a fable, in the manner of Aesop*, Cic

ăpŏphŏrēta ōrum, n (ἀποφόρητα), *presents given to guests, especially at the time of the Saturnalia*, Suet

ăpŏprŏēgmĕna -ōrum, n plur (ἀποπροηγμένα), in the philosophy of the Stoics, *that which is to be rejected* (opp to proegmena), Cic.

ăpŏthēca -ae, f (ἀποθήκη), *a store-room, magazine*, especially for wine, Cic

appărātē, adv with compar (apparatus), *with much preparation, splendidly*, opipare et apparate edere et bibere, Cic

appărātĭo -ōnis, f (apparo), *preparation*, popularium munerum, Cic.

1. **appărātus** -ūs, m (apparo) I Abstr. *a preparation, preparing*, operis, Cic, belli, Liv, II. Concr, *preparation, provision, equipment* A. Gen tenuiculus, Cic, omnis apparatus oppugnandarum urbium, Liv, plur. apparatus regii, Cic. B Esp *brilliant preparations, splendour, magnificence, pomp*, 1, Lit *pomp*, regius, Cic 2, Transf, of a speech, *display, parade*, dixit causam illam nullo apparatu pure et dilucide, Cic

2 **appărātus** -a -um, p adj with compar and superl (from apparo), *prepared, ready*, of things, *well supplied, sumptuous, splendid*, domus apparatior, Cic

appārĕo (ad-pārĕo) -ŭi -itum, 2 *to become visible, to appear* I. Gen A. Lit equus mecum demersus rursum apparuit, Cic, with dat of person, anguis ille, qui Sullae apparuit immolanti, Cic, so of appearance before a court of justice, in his subselliis me apparere nollem, Cic, of daylight, stars, &c., Tib B. Transf, 1, *to be visible, to show itself, be manifest*, non apparere labores nostros, Hor, 2, res apparet and apparet, with acc and infin or relat sentence, *it is clear, plain, manifest*, Cic II. Esp *to appear as a servant* to some person in authority, or deity, *to serve*, a, saevi in limine regis apparent, Cic, b, *to serve* a magistrate, as lictor, clerk, &c., with dat of person, consulibus, Liv, with dat. of thing, quaestioni, Cic.

appărĭo, 3 *to get, obtain*, Lucr

appārĭtĭo -ōnis, f (appareo, No II) A. *A waiting upon, serving*, Cic B. Meton plur = apparitores, *servants*, Cic.

appārĭtor ōris, m (appareo, No II), *a servant*, esp *a public servant*, e g, *a lictor*, etc, Cic.

appăro (ad-păro), 1 *to prepare for, get ready for, provide*, convivium, Cic, bellum, iter, ludos, Cic., crimina in aliquem, *get up charges*, Cic; foll by infin, Caes

appellātĭo -ōnis, f (1 appello), *an addressing* I. with words, *speaking to* A. Gen hanc nactus appellationis causam, Caes B. Legal t t, *appeal*, tribunorum, *to the tribunes*, Cic, II. Of sounds A *Pronunciation* litterarum, Cic B. *Naming*, hence, meton = nomen, *name, title*, inanis, Cic, plur, regum appellationes, Cic

appellātor -ōris, m (1 appello), *an appellant*, Cic

appellĭto 1 (freq of 1 appello), *to be accustomed to name*, Tac

1 **appello** 1 (intens of 2 appello). I. *to address, accost*, with words A. Gen 1, singulos appellare, Cic, nominatim, Caes, 2, *to ask a person to do something, to make a proposal to a person*, a, aliquem, Cic, aliquem de proditione, Liv, b, legal t t, *to appeal to*, praetorem, Cic, tribunos, Liv, a praetore tribunos, Cic, de aestimatione et solutionibus, Caes, c, *to apply to for payment*, aliquem de pecunia, Cic, d, *to sue*, cavendum est ne isdem de causis alii plectantur, alii ne appellentur quidem, Cic, II. Of sounds, 1, *to pronounce*, litteras, Cic, 2, *to name, entitle*, aliquem sapientem, Cic, appellata est ex viro virtus, Cic, (Scipio) Africanus ob egregiam victoriam de Hannibale Poenisque appellatus, Liv, hence, *to mention by name*, quos idcirco non appello hoc loco, Cic, aliquem nutu significationeque, *to make known*, Cic

2 **appello** (ad-pello), pŭli -pulsum, 3 *to drive to, bring to* I. Gen A. Lit. turres ad opera Caesaris, Caes B. Transf, animum or mentem ad aliquid, *to direct the mind to something*, mentem ad philosophiam, Cic II. Esp, Nautical t t, *to bring to land*, navem ad ripam, Cic, classem in insulam, Liv, poet, aliquem, with dat, hinc me digressum vestris Deus appulit oris, Verg, pass, appelli, of the ship, navis appellitur ad villam, Cic, of the persons in the ship, alios ad Siciliam appulsos esse, Cic, refl, se appellere, in portum classe, Liv, absol, huc appelle, *put in here*, Hor

appendĭcŭla -ae, f, (dim of appendix), *a little addition*, Cic.

appendix -īcis, f (appendo), *an appendage, addition, an appendix to anything*, vidit enim appendicem animi esse corpus, Cic, appendices Olcadum, *smaller contingents*, Liv

appendo (ad pendo), -pendi -pensum, 3 *to weigh to*, aurum alicui, Cic, transf, non enim ea verba me annumerare, *pay out*, like small coin, lectori putavi oportere, sed tamquam appendere, *weigh out*, like whole bars, Cic

appĕtens -entis, p adj with compar and superl (from appeto), 1, *desirous of*, gloriae, Cic, 2, *desirous of gold, avaricious*, homo non cupidus neque appetens, Cic

appĕtenter, adv (appetens), *greedily*, Cic

appĕtentĭa -ae, f (appetens), *desire, longing*, laudis, Cic

appĕtītĭo -ōnis, f (appeto), 1, *grasping at*, Cic, 2 *longing for, desire*, with genit principatus, Cic

appĕtītus ūs, m (appeto), *a passionate longing, passion, appetite*, voluptatis, Cic

appĕto (ad peto), -īvi and -ĭi, ītum, 3 *to reach to* I. Gen *to grasp at seize on*, A Lit, solem manibus, Cic, haec enim ipsa sunt honorabilia, salutari, appeti, *to have their hands* *kissed*, Cic **B** Transf, *to desire, seek;* regnum, Cic, with infin, ut appetat animus aliquid agere semper, Cic **II.** Esp **A** *to make for* or *go to a place, to go to, arrive at*, Europam, Cic, mare terram appetens, *pressing on the land*, Cic **B.** *to attack*, aliquem lapidibus, Cic, transf, ignominiis omnibus appetitus, Cic. **C.** *to draw near*, of time, dies appetebat septimus, quem constituerat, Cic.

1. **Appĭa (Apĭa)** -ae, f. *a town in Phrygia*, hence **Appĭānus** -a -um, *of Appia, Appian*

2 **Appĭa,** fem of Appius.

appingo (ad-pingo) -pinxi -pictum, 3 *to paint to*, or *upon* **I.** Lit. delphinum silvis, Hor **II.** Transf, *to write in addition*, aliquid novi, Cic

Appĭus -ii, m, **Appĭa** -ae, f *a Roman praenomen, common in the gens Claudia*, v Claudius, hence, **1, Appĭus** a -um, *Appian*, via, *the celebrated road from Rome to Capua afterwards extended to Brundisium, constructed* A U C. 442 *by the Censor, App Claudius Caecus*, aqua, *a conduit constructed by the same*, Liv, Appii Forum, v forum; **2, Appĭas** -ădis, f a, *the statue of a nymph which stood at the commencement of the above-mentioned aqueduct*, Ov, **b,** Appiades deae, *statues in the temple of Venus, which stood near this aqueduct*, Ov **3, Appĭānus** -a -um, *belonging to an Appius, Appian*, libido (of the Decemvir App Claudius), Liv

Appĭĕtas ātis, f *the antiquity of the Appian family, a word invented by Cicero to flatter Appius*

applaudo (ad plaudo) -plausi -plausum, 3 **I** Trans, *to strike upon to clap*, cavis applauso corpore palmis, Ov **II.** Intrans *to applaud*, Plaut

applĭcātĭo -ōnis, f (applico) **I.** *inclination;* animi, Cic **II.** jus applicationis, *the rights springing from the relation of patron and client*, Cic

applĭcātus a um, p adj (from applico), *applied to, lying near*, Varr

applĭco (ad-plico), -āvi -ātum and -ŭi ĭtum, 1 **I.** *to add to, apply to, place to* or *near, join to, put to* **A.** Lit, **a,** se ad flammam, Cic, oscula feretro, *to kiss*, Ov; ensem capulo tenus, *to drive in*, Verg, milit t t, corpora corporibus, *to close up the ranks* Liv, **b,** in passive, esp. in partic perf, *lying near, situated near, built near*, Leucas colli applicata, Liv **B.** Transf, **1,** *to connect*, voluptatem ad honestatem, Cic, **2,** se ad and se alicui, *to attach oneself to*, se ad aliquem quasi patronum, Cic, se ad alicujus familiaritatem, or amicitiam, or societatem, Cic **II.** *to turn* or *direct towards.* **A.** Lit nautical t t, *to steer a ship towards, to bring to land*, naves ad terram, Caes, navem ad aliquem, Cic, absol, *to land*, quocumque litore applicuisse naves hostium audissent, Liv **B.** Transf, *to devote oneself to*, se ad eloquentiam, Cic, (perf applicui, only once in Cic, sup applicitum and partic applicitus not used by Cic).

applōro, 1 *to lament, deplore*, Hor

appōno (ad-pono) -pŏsŭi -pŏsĭtum, 3 **I** *to place near, to put to* **A.** Gen gladium, Cic **B.** Esp, **a,** *to serve, put on the table*, patellam, Cic, apposita secunda mensa, Cic., **b,** in writing, *to place near*, notam ad versum, or epistolis, Cic **II.** Transf **A.** a, *to appoint*, custodem me Tullio, Cic, **b,** *to procure, suborn*, calumniatores, Cic **B.** *to put to, add to*, **1,** Gen, annos alicui, Hor, vitiis modum, Cic, lucro, *reckon as a gain*, Hor, **2,** *to add*, by way of command, aqua et igni interdictum reo appositumque, ut teneretur insula, Tac

apporrectus -a -um (ad and porrigo), *extended near*, Ov.

apporto (ad-porto), 1. *to carry, bring to;* lapidem, signa, Cic

apposco (ad posco), 3 *to ask in addition*, Hor

appŏsĭtē, adv (appositus), *appropriately, appositely*, dicere apposite ad persuasionem, Cic

appŏsĭtus -a -um, p adj with compar and superl (from appono), *placed near.* **I.** Lit., *situated*, or *lying near*, castellum flumini app, Tac **II.** Transf, **A.** Gen, audacia fidentiae non contrarium sed appositum et propinquum, Cic, **B.** Esp, *fit, appropriate, apposite*, menses appositi ad agendum, Cic, homo bene appositus ad istius audaciam, Cic

appōtus (ad-pōtus) -a um, *very drunk*, Plaut.

apprĕcor (ad-prĕcor), 1, dep *to worship, pray to*, rite deos, Hor.

apprĕhendo (ad-prĕhendo) -prĕhendi -prĕhensum, 3 and poet **apprendo** (ad-prendo) prendi -prensum, 3 *to seize, lay hold of* **I.** Lit, **A.** Gen, claviculis adminicula tamquam manibus, Cic **B.** Esp, *to take possession of*, Hispanias, Cic **II.** Transf, of discourse, *to bring forward, allege*, ut quidquid ego apprehenderam, statim accusator extorquebat, Cic

apprīmē (apprimus), adv, *by far, above all, exceedingly*, Plaut, Nep

apprĭmo -pressi, -pressum, 3 (ad and premo), *to press to*, dextram alicujus, Tac

apprŏbātĭo ōnis, f (approbo) **I.** *approbation, approval, assent*, Cic **II.** Esp, philosoph t t, *proof*, quae (propositio) non indiget approbatione, Cic

apprŏbātor -ōris, m (approbo), *one who approves or assents*, profectionis meae, Cic

apprŏbē, adv. (ad and probus), *very well*, illum novisse, Plaut

apprŏbo (ad-prŏbo) 1 **1,** *to approve of, assent to*, consilium alicujus, Cic, esp of a deity, *to bless, approve of*, quod actum est dii approbent, Cic, **2,** *to prove, to establish*, propositionem app et firmare, Cic

apprōmitto (ad promitto) -misi -missum, 3 *to promise in addition*, i e *to promise also in one's own name*, Cic

apprŏpĕro (ad propĕro) -āvi, ātūm, -āre. **I.** Trans, *to hasten*, coeptum opus, Liv; **II.** Intrans, *to hasten*, approperate, Cic, appr ad cogitatum facinus, Cic

apprŏpinquātĭo -ōnis, f (appropinquo), *approach*, mortis, Cic

apprŏpĭnquo (ad-prŏpinquo), 1 *to approach, draw near.* **I.** Of place, ad summam aquam, Cic, with dat. januae, Liv; Oceano, Caes **II.** Transf, **a,** of time, hiems appropinquat, Caes, illi poena, nobis libertas appropinquat, Cic, **b,** of persons, qui jam appropinquat ut videat, *is near to seeing*, Cic

appugno (ad pugno), 1 *to storm, assault*, castra, Tac

Appŭlējus, or **Āpŭlējus** -i, m *a Roman name*, **1,** L Appulejus Saturninus, *tribune of the people*, 100 B.C, **2,** *a Roman writer, born about* 130 A D, *at Madaura, in Africa* Adj, **1, Appŭlējus** a -um, *of or belonging to Appulejus*, lex (de majestate) introduced by the tribune Appulejus, **2, Appŭlējānus** -a -um, *of or belonging to Appulejus*

Appŭlĭa, Āpŭlĭa ae, f *a country in the south of Italy* Adj, **a, Appŭlĭcus** -a -um, mare, *the Adriatic Sea*, Hor, **b, Appŭlus** -a -um, *Apulian*

appulsus -ūs, m (2 appello) **I.** *a driving towards.* **A.** *an approach*, quod pars earum (regionum) appulsu solis exarserit, Cic. **B,** *in-*

fluence produced by approach, caloris, Cic **II.** *landing on, landing*, litorum, Liv

ăprīcātĭo -ōnis, f. (apricor), *a basking in the sun*, Cic

ăprīcĭtas -atis, f (apricus), *sunniness, sunshine, warmth*, Plin

ăprīcor, 1, dep (apricus), *to sun oneself*, Cic

ăprīcus -a um, adj with compar and superl. (for apericus, from aperio) **I.** Lit., Of places, *open to the sun, sunny*, locus, Cic, in apricum proferre, *to bring to light*, Hor **II.** Transf, *loving the sun*, flores, Hor, mergi, Verg, senes, Pers

Aprīlis -e (aperio), Aprilis mensis or subst, *the month of April*, Cic

ăprīnus -a um (aper), *relating* or *belonging to a wild boar*, Plin

ăprūgnus -a -um (aper), *belonging to a wild boar*, Plaut

Apsus -i, m (Ἄψος), *a river of Illyria*, now *Berzatino*

aptatus -a -um (partic of apto), *fitted, appropriate*, Cic

aptē, adv, with compar and superl (aptus), *fitly, appropriately*, tacere, dicere, Cic

apto, 1 (intens of *apo), *to fit to, adapt to, adjust* **I.** Gen, corpori arma, Liv, enses dexteris, Hor **II.** *to prepare, get ready* **A.** Lit, arma, Liv, classem velis, Verg, se armis, Liv **B.** Transf, *to make fit or appropriate*, hoc verbum est ad id aptatum quod, etc, Cic

aptus -a -um, 1 (partic of obsolete verb, *apo) **I.** Partic, **1,** Lit, *fastened to*, gladius e lacunari seta equina aptus, Cic, **2,** Transf, *depending upon*, honestum ex quo aptum est officium, Cic, with abl alone, rudentibus apta fortuna, Cic **B.** *connected, joined, allied*, **1,** Lit, **a,** omnia inter se connexa et apta, Cic, **b,** *prepared, equipped, fitted out*, omnia sibi esse ad bellum apta et parata, Cic, caelum stellis fulgentibus aptum, *adorned with*, Verg, **2,** Transf, Thucydides verbis aptus et pressus, Cic **II.** Adj, with compar and superl, *suitable, appropriate, fitting*, with ad and the acc, milites minus apti ad hujus generis hostem, Cic, id pallium esse aptum ad omne anni tempus, Cic, with in and the acc, in quod (genus) minus apti sunt, Liv, with dat, haec genera dicendi aptiora sunt adolescentibus, Cic, absol, verbis quam maxime aptis, Cic

ăpŭd (aput), prep, with acc (root AP, whence apo, aptus, apud thus meaning *being fastened to, near to*), *at, near, by, with*, chiefly used of persons **I.** Of nearness to persons, **1,** apud aliquem sedere, *near*, Cic, plus apud me antiquorum auctoritas valet, Cic, hence **a,** apud me, *at my house* Cic, apud se esse (fig), *to be in possession of one's faculties*, Plaut, **b,** apud exercitum esse, *to be serving as a soldier*, Cic; **2,** *before, in the presence of*, apud judices, Cic., **3,** *with*, consequi gratiam apud bonos viros, Cic, hence, *with = in the time of*, apud patres nostros, Cic, **4,** of an author, *in the works of*, apud Xenophontem, Cic **5,** *to*, apud aliquem queri, Cic **II.** Of places, **1,** *in the neighbourhood of*, apud Alyziam, Cic, **2,** *at, in*, apud villam, Cic.

Ăpŭlējus, v Appulejus

Ăpŭlia, v Appulia

ăqua -ae, f (akin to Keltic ach and Sanscrit apa = *water*), *water* **I** Lit, **A** *water* in the broadest meaning of the word, pluvia, Cic, marina, Cic, plur, aquae dulces, Cic, special phrases, **a,** aspergere alicui aquam, *to re-animate*, Plaut, **b,** aquam praebere, *to entertain*, Hor, **c,** aqua et ignis, *the necessaries of life*, non aqua, non igni, ut aiunt, locis pluribus utimur quam amicitia, Cic, hence, (α) aqua et igni interdicere alicui, Cic, or aqua et igni aliquem arcere, Tac, *to banish*, (β) aquam terramque petere or poscere ab aliquo, *to demand submission from the enemy*, a Persian custom, Liv, **d,** aqua haeret, *there is a difficulty or a hitch*, Cic; **e,** in aqua scribere, *to write in water*, Cat **B.** *water* in a narrower sense, **1, a,** *the sea*, ad aquam, *on the sea-coast* Cic, **b,** *a lake*, Albanae aquae deductio, Cic **c,** *a river*, secunda aqua, *down stream*, Liv, **2,** *rain*, Hor, **3,** plur, aquae, **a,** *springs*, Verg, **b,** *hot medicinal springs*, ad aquas venire, Cic, hence as a proper name, Aquae Sextiae, &c, **4,** of an aqueduct, aquam ducere non longe a villa, Cic, **5,** *water in the water-clock*, hence, aquam dare, *to give time*, Plin, aquam perdere *to lose time*, Quint, **6,** *tears*, Prop **II.** Transf, Aqua, *a constellation*, Cic poet

ăquaeductus -ūs, m, **1,** *an aqueduct*, Cic, **2,** *the right of conveying water to a place*, Cic

ăquālĭcŭlus -i, m (dim of aqualis), *a small water-vessel*, hence, *the belly*, Pers

ăquālis -e (aqua), *watery* Subst, **ăquālis** is, c *a wash-bowl*, Plaut

ăquārĭus a -um (aqua), *belonging to water* **I.** Adj, provincia, *superintendence of the supply of water*, Cic **II.** Subst, **ăquārĭus** -ii, m **1,** *a water-carrier*, Juv, **2,** *an inspector of conduits*, ap Cic, **3,** *the constellation so called*, Hor

ăquātĭcus -a -um (aqua) **I.** *living in water, aquatic*, lotos, Ov **II.** *full of water, watery*, auster, *bringing rain*, Ov

ăquātĭlis -e (aqua), *living* or *growing in the water*, Cic

ăquātĭo -ōnis f (aquor) **A.** *A fetching of water*, Caes **B.** Meton, *a place whence water may be fetched, a watering place*, Plin

ăquātŏr -ōris, m (aquor), *a person that fetches water*, Caes

ăquĭla -ae, f (perhaps fem of aquilus), *an eagle* **I.** Lit., in mythology, the bearer of the lightning of Jove, Cic **II.** Transf, **1,** *an eagle as the standard of each Roman legion*, Cic, Meton, **a,** *a legion*, Plin, **b,** *the post of standard bearer*, Juv, **2,** *the Eagle, a constellation*, Cic **3,** plur aquilae *the eagle on the front and rear of the temple of Jupiter Capitolinus, which seemed to support the gable*, Tac

Ăquĭlēja -ae, f *a town in the north of Italy*, now *Aquileja* or *Aglar*, hence adj, **Ăquĭlējensis** -e, *of or belonging to Aquileja*

ăquĭlĭfer fĕri (aquila and fero), m *an eagle* or *standard bearer*, Cic

ăquĭlīnus -a -um (aquila), *relating to an eagle*, Plaut

Ăquīlĭus a -um, *name of a Roman gens, the most celebrated members of which were*—**1,** C Aquilius Gallus, *friend of and colleague with Cicero in the praetorship* (66 B C), *a famous orator and jurist*, **2,** Aquilius Regulus, *an informer under the empire*, hence, **Ăquīlĭānus** -a -um, *belonging to Aquilius*

ăquĭlo ōnis m (connected with aquilus, *the black stormy one*); **1,** *the north wind*, Cic; meton, *the north*, Cic, **2,** *Aquilo, as a myth person, husband of Orithyia, father of Calais and Zetes*

ăquĭlōnālis, e (aquilo), *northern*, Cic

Ăquĭlōnia ae, f *a town in the country of the Hirpini*, now *Carbonara*

ăquĭlōnĭus -a -um, **1,** *northern*, Cic, **2,** *belonging to Aquilo* (2), proles, *Calais and Zetes*, Prop

ăquĭlus -a -um, *dark-coloured, blackish*, Plaut.

Aquīnum -i, n. *town in Latium*, now *Aquino*. Adj., **Aquīnās** -ātis, *belonging to Aquinum.*

Ăquītāni -ōrum, m. *inhabitants of Aquitania;* hence **Ăquītānĭa** -ae, f. *Aquitania, the south-west part of Gaul, between the Garonne and the Pyrenees.*

ăquor, 1. dep. (aqua), *to fetch water*, Caes.

ăquōsus -a -um, adj. with compar. and superl. (aqua), *full of water, watery;* Orion, Verg.; Eurus, *rain-bringing*, Hor.; mater, *Thetis*, Ov.

ăquŭla -ae, f. (dim. of aqua), *a little water, a small stream*, Cic.

āra -ae, f. (connected with αἴρω, *I raise*); **1**, *an elevation of earth, stone*, &c.; **a**, ara sepulcri, *a funeral pyre*, Verg.; **2**, plur., arae, *rocks*, Verg.; **3**, *a monument of stone;* virtutis, Cic.; **4**, *an altar;* **a**, aram consecrare deo, Cic.; pro aris et focis, *for hearths and homes*, Cic.; fig., *a refuge, protection;* legum, Cic.; **b**, transf. *a constellation*, Cic. poet.

Ărăbarchēs -ae, m. (Ἀραβάρχης), *an Egyptian magistrate, a superior tax-collector*, Juv.; used sarcastically of Pompey (who by his conquests increased the tribute paid to Rome), Cic.

Ărăbes -um, m. (Ἄραβες), *the inhabitants of Arabia, the Arabs;* hence, **1**, **Ărabs** -ăbis, *Arabian;* **2**, **Ărăbĭa** -ae, f. (Ἀραβία), *the country of Arabia, in the south-west of Asia*, used loosely for any country inhabited by nomadic tribes akin to the Arabs; **3**, **Ărăbĭcus** -a -um, *Arabian;* **4**, **Ărăbĭus** -a -um, *Arabian;* **5**, **Ărăbus** -a -um, *Arabian.*

ărābĭlis -e (aro), *that can be ploughed, arable.* Plin.

Ărachnē, -ēs, f. (Ἀράχνη), *a Lydian maiden who entered into a contest in spinning with Minerva and was turned into a spider.*

Ărădus -i, f. (Ἄραδος), *a Phoenician town*, now *Ruad.* Adj., **Ărădĭus** -a -um.

ărānĕa -ae f. (ἀράχνη), **1**, *a spider;* **2**, *the spider's web*, Plaut.

ărānĕŏla -ae, f. (dim. of aranea), *a little spider*, Cic.

ărānĕŏlus -i, m. (dim. of aranea), *a little spider*, Verg.

ărānĕōsus -a -um (aranea), **1**, *full of cobwebs*, Cat.; **2**, *like a cobweb*, Plin.

1. **ărānĕus** -i, m. *a spider*, Lucr.

2. **ărānĕus** -a -um, *relating to a spider*, Plin. Subst., **ărānĕum** -i, n. *a cobweb*, Phaedr.

Ărăr and **Ărăris**, -is, m. *a river in Gaul, the Saone.*

ărātĭo -ōnis, f. (aro). **I.** *ploughing, agriculture*, Cic. **II.** Meton., *a ploughed field*, Plaut.; esp., arationes = *the public domains let at a rent of one-tenth of their produce*, Cic.

ărātor -ōris, m. **1**, *a ploughman, a husbandman*, Cic.; appel. taurus, Ov.; **2**, aratores, *tenants of the arationes*, q.v., Cic.

ărātrum -i, n. *the plough;* aratrum circumducere, Cic.; aliquem ab aratro arcessere, Cic.

Ăratthus -i, m. (Ἄρατθος), *a river in Epirus*, now *Arta.*

Ărātus -i, m. (Ἄρατος). **I.** *a Greek poet, born in Cilicia, whose astronomical poem Φαινόμενα was translated by Cicero.* Adj., **Ărātēus** and **Ărātĭus** -a -um, *belonging to Aratus;* carmina, Cic.; and absol., nostra quaedam Aratea, Cicero's translation of the poem, Cic. **II.** *a celebrated Greek general, founder of the Achaean League.*

Ăraxēs -is, m. (Ἀράξης), *a river in Armenia.*

arbĭtĕr -tri, m. (from ar = ad, and bitere, *to go*). **I.** *a witness, spectator, hearer;* locus ab arbitris remotus, Cic.; remotis arbitris, Cic. **II.** **A.** Legal t. t., *an umpire, arbitrator;* arbiter litis, Cic.; aliquem arbitrum adigere, Cic.; arbitrum dare, Cic.; sumere, Cic.; esse in aliquam rem arbitrum, Cic.; ad arbitrum confugere, Cic.; uti aliquo arbitro, Cic. **B.** Transf., **1**, *a judge of any matter;* formae (of Paris), Ov.; armorum, Ov.; **2**, *ruler, lord, master;* bibendi, Hor.; Adriae, *the south wind*, Hor.; elegantiae, Tac.

arbĭtra -ae, f. (arbiter) *a female witness*, Hor.

arbĭtrārĭus -a -um, *depending on the will, arbitrary, uncertain*, Plaut.

arbĭtrātus -ūs, m. *approval, will, choice, wish;* tuo arbitratu, Cic.; cujus arbitratu sit educatus, Cic.

arbĭtrĭum -i, n. **A.** *The umpire's decision;* aliud est judicium, aliud arbitrium; judicium est pecuniae certae, arbitrium incertae, Cic. **B.** Transf., **1**, *any decision, judgment, free choice;* arbitrium eligendi, Tac.; libera arbitria de aliquo agere, Liv.; res ab opinionis arbitrio sejunctae, Cic.; arbitria funeris, *the expenses of a funeral*, Cic.; **2**, *might, mastery, authority;* arbitrio suo, Cic.

arbĭtror, 1. dep. (pass. Plaut., Cic., arbitro, Plaut.). **I.** *to hear, perceive*, Plaut. **II.** Transf., *to express an opinion as witness*, Cic.; hence, *to think, be of opinion;* qui se natos ad homines juvandos arbitrantur, Cic.; with acc. and infin., ut quisque minimum in se esse arbitraretur, Cic.

arbŏr (arbos) -ŏris, f. *a tree.* **A.** Lit., fici, *a fig tree*, Cic.; Jovis, *the oak*, Ov.; Phoebi, *the laurel*, Ov.; Palladis, *the olive*, Ov. **B.** Meton., infelix, *the gallows*, Cic.; mali, *a mast*, Verg.; arbor, *an oar*, Verg.; *a ship*, Pelias, *the Argo*, Ov.

arbŏrĕus -a -um, *relating to trees*, Verg.; cornua, *branching*, Verg.

arbustum -i, n. (arbor), *a plantation, a vineyard planted with trees*, Cic.

arbustus -a -um, *full of trees;* ager, Cic.

arbŭtĕus -a -um, *relating to the arbutus*, Ov., Verg.

arbŭtum -i, n., **1**, *the fruit of the wild strawberry or arbutus tree*, Verg.; **2**, *the wild strawberry tree* or *arbutus*, Verg.

arbŭtus -i, f. *the wild strawberry* or *arbutus tree*, Verg.

arca -ae, f. (root ARC, whence also arceo). **I.** *a chest, box.* **A.** Gen., Cic. **B.** Esp., **a**, *a coffin*, Liv.; **b**, *money coffer*, Cic.; meton. = *the money in the coffer;* arcae nostrae confidito, Cic. **II.** *a cell for close imprisonment*, Cic.

Arcădĭa -ae, f. (Ἀρκαδία), *a country of the Peloponnesus.* Adj., **1**, **Arcădĭus** -a -um; **2**, **Arcădĭcus** -a -um; deus, *Pan*, Prop.; juvenis, *a simpleton*, Juv.; virgo, *Arethusa*, Ov.; **3**, **Arcăs** -ădis, tyrannus, *Lycaon*, Ov. Subst., **Arcăs** -ădis, *Mercury*, Mart.; **Arcădes** -um, m. *the Arcadians*, Cic.

arcānō, adv., *secretly*, Cic.

arcānus -a -um (arca, arceo), **1**, *silent;* homo, Plaut.; nox, Ov.; **2**, *secret*, Cic.; arcana consilia, Liv.; sacra, Ov. Subst., **arcānum** -i, n. *a secret*, Liv., Juv.

Arcăs -ădis, m. (Ἀρκάς), *son of Jupiter and Callisto, placed in the heavens as the star Arctophylax.*

arcĕo -cŭi, 2. (root ARC, whence arca). **I.** *to shut in, shut up;* alvus arcet et continet quod recipit, Cic. **II.** **A.** *to prohibit access to, to keep at a distance, to hinder, prevent;* copias hostium, Cic.; followed by ne with subj., Liv.; with the acc and ab with the abl, aliquem ab urbe, Cic, with the acc and abl alone, hostem Gallia, Cic, with dat, Verg **B.** *to protect from*, aliquem periclis, Verg

Arcĕsĭlās -ae, m (Ἀρκεσίλας) and **Arcĕsĭlāus** -i, m (Ἀρκεσίλαος), *a Greek philosopher of Pitane in Aeolia* (316-241 B C), *founder of the Middle Academy*

Arcĕsĭus -ii, m (Ἀρκείσιος), *father of Laertes, and grandfather of Ulysses*

arcessītor -ōris, m *one who calls or fetches*, Plin

arcessītus, abl -ū, m *calling for, summons*, ipsius rogatu arcessituque, Cic.

arcesso (accerso) -īvi -ītum, 3 (accedo), *to fetch* or *call to a place, to summon*, **I** Gen **A.** Lit., aliquem litteris Capua, Cic, aliquem in senatum, Cic, sacra ab exteris nationibus asciscere et arcessere, Cic **B.** Transf, of a thought, *to bring, derive*, argumentum usque a capite, Cic, hence arcessitus, *strained, far-fetched;* dictum, Cic **II.** Esp **1,** *to bring the dead from the lower world*, Verg, **2,** *to bring the bride to the bridegroom s house*, Ter, **3,** legal t t, *to summon bring before a court of justice*, aliquem judicio capitis, Cic, aliquem capitis, Cic

Archĕlāus -i, m (Ἀρχέλαος) **I.** *a Greek philosopher of Miletus* **II.** *King of Macedonia from* 413 B C, *friend of Euripides* **III.** *General of Mithridates* **IV.** *Son of* **III.**, *husband of Berenice.* **V.** *the grandson of* **IV.**, *the last king of Cappadocia*

archĕtȳpus -a -um (ἀρχέτυπος), *original*, Juv

Archĭās -ae, m (Ἀρχίας) **I.** Aulus Licinius, *a Greek poet of Antioch, defended by Cicero* **II.** *a celebrated cabinet-maker*, hence **Archĭăcus** -a -um, *of or belonging to Archias*

archĭgallus -i, m *a high priest of Cybele*, Plin

Archĭlŏchus -i, m (Ἀρχίλοχος), *a Greek satiric poet, inventor of iambic verse* Adj, **Archĭlŏchĭus** -a -um, *Archilochian*, appel, *sharp, biting*, Cic

archĭmăgīrus -i, m (ἀρχιμάγειρος), *head cook*, Ov

Archĭmēdes -is, m (Ἀρχιμήδης), *celebrated mathematical and mechanical philosopher, killed on the capture of Syracuse by Marcellus* (212 B C)

archĭmīmus -i, m (ἀρχίμιμος), *chief mime or buffoon*, Suet

archĭpīrāta -ae, m (ἀρχιπειρατής), *chief pirate*, Cic

archĭtectōn -ŏnis, m (ἀρχιτέκτων), **1,** *master builder*, Plaut, **2,** *a master in cunning*, Plaut

archĭtector, 1 dep **A.** *to build* **B.** Transf, *to devise, to prepare, provide*, voluptates, Cic

architectūra -ae, f *architecture*, Cic

archĭtectus -i, m (ἀρχιτέκτων), **1,** *an architect, master-builder*, architecti operum, Cic, **2,** Transf, *an inventor, author, maker*, hujus legis, Cic, quasi arch beatae vitae, Cic

archōn -ontis, m (ἄρχων), *an archon, one of the chief magistrates of Athens*, Cic

Archȳtās -ae, m (Ἀρχύτας), *a philosopher of Tarentum* (about 400-365 B C)

arcĭtĕnens -entis (arcus and teneo), *holding the bow, epithet of Apollo and Diana*, Verg, Ov

arct = art . . . q v

Arctŏs -i, f (ἄρκτος), **1,** *the great and little bear*, Verg, Ov, juncta Aquilonibus Arctos, *the North Pole*, Ov, opacam excipere Arcton, *to be towards the North*, Hor, **2,** *the night*, Prop

Arctōus -a -um (ἀρκτῷος) *belonging to the north pole, northern*, Mart.

Arctūrus -i, m (ἀρκτοῦρος), **1,** *the brightest star of the constellation Bootes*, Cic, **2,** *Bootes*, Verg

arcŭātus -a -um (partic of arcuo), *bent like a bow, curved*, currus, Liv

arcŭla -ae, f (dim of arca), **1,** *a casket for money, jewels, or perfume*, arculae muliebres, Cic, **2,** Transf, *rhetorical ornament*, omnes (Isocrati) discipulorum arculae, Cic

arcŭlārĭus -i, m *a casket maker*, Plaut

arcŭo, 1 *to bend or shape like a bow*, Plin

arcŭs -ūs m **I** *a bow*, **a,** arcum intendere, Cic, adducere, Verg, arcus Haemonii, *the constellation Sagittarius*, Ov, **b,** *the rainbow*, Cic, **c,** *an arch, vault, triumphal arch*, Suet **II.** Transf, **1,** *anything arched or curved*, Verg, Ov, **2,** *a mathematical arc*, Sen, *the parallel circles which bound the zones of the earth*, Ov

1 **ardĕa** -ae, f *a heron*, Verg

2 **Ardĕa** -ae, f (Ἀρδέα), *town of the Rutuli in Latium* Adj, **a,** **Ardĕās** -ātis, **b,** **Ardĕātīnus** -a -um *of or belonging to Ardea*

ardĕlio -ōnis, m *a busybody*, Mart

ardens -entis, p adj with compar and superl (ardeo), *hot, glowing* **A.** Lit., lapides, Liv **B.** Transf, **a,** of the eyes, *glowing*, oculi, Verg, **b,** of colour, *glittering*, apes ardentes auro, Verg, **c,** of wine, *strong, fiery*, Falernum, Hor, **d,** of passions, &c, *burning, eager, hot*, odium, Liv, avaritia, Cic, ardentes in aliquem litterae, Cic., ardentes equi, *spirited*, Verg, **e,** of oratory, *fiery*, orator, Cic; oratio, actio, Cic

ardentĕr, adv, with compar and superl (ardens), *hotly, violently*, cupere, Cic.

ardĕo, arsi, arsum, 2 *to burn, glow, be on fire* **I.** Lit, faces, Cic, domus, Cic, mare arsit eo anno, Liv, jam proximus ardet Ucalegon, *the house of U*, Verg, ardent altaria Verg **II.** Transf, **1,** of the eyes, *to glow*, Cic, **2,** of colours, *to flash, sparkle, glow*, ardebat murice laena, Verg, **3,** of feelings **a,** of the body, quum omnes artus ardere viderentur, *be in pain*, Cic, **b,** of the mind amore, dolore, furore, Cic, ardere in proelia, *eagerly to desire fight*, Verg, esp in poets *to burn with love*, ardere aliqua or in aliqua or aliquam, Hor, Verg, Ov, ardere invidia, *to be heated*, Cic, **c,** of conspiracies, wars, &c, *to burst out*, quum arderet conjuratio, Cic, quum arderet Syria bello, *be in a state of excitement* Cic

ardĕŏla -ae, f (dim of ardea), *a heron*, Plin

ardesco, arsi, 3 (inch of ardeo), *to take fire, kindle* **I.** Lit, arsit arundo, Verg **II.** Transf, **1,** *to glitter*, fulmineis ignibus ardescunt undae, Ov, **2,** of the passions, *to become inflamed*, tuendo, Verg, libidinibus, Tac

ardor -ōris, m *flame, burning heat* **I.** Lit, solis, Cic **II.** Transf, **1,** the glow of the eyes, oculorum, Cic, **2,** *gleam, glimmer*, stellarum Cic, **3,** of the feelings or passions, *ardour, fierceness* cupiditatum, Cic, animorum et armorum, Cic pugnandi, *for fighting* Liv, with ad and the acc, mentis ad gloriam, Cic, ad bellum armaque, Liv; esp *the passion of love*, Ov, virginis, *for a maiden*, Ov

Ardŭenna -ae, f *a forest in Gallia Belgica*, now *the forest of Ardennes*

ardŭus -a -um, adj with compar and superl (root AR Gr AP whence arca ἄρδαι), *steep* **I.** Lit, **A.** collis, Liv, ascensus difficilis atque arduus, Cic Subst, **ardŭum** -i, n *a steep place*, per arduum ducuntur, Liv **B.** Poet, *lofty*, aether, Ov, nubes, Hor, sese arduus infert (Turnus), *with proud mien*, Verg **II.** Transf, *difficult to undertake or reach*, res arduae ac difficiles, Cic.; arduum videtur, *or* est followed by infin., Sall., Liv. Subst., **arduum** -i, n. *what is difficult to accomplish*, Hor., Ov.

ārĕa -ae, f. (Root AR, Gr. AP, whence arduus and ἄραι), *a high-lying open space, surface.* **I.** Gen. collemque super planissima campi area, Ov. **II.** Esp., **1,** *an open space in a town*, Liv.; **2,** *a site for a house*, Cic.; **3,** *the court-yard*, Liv.; **4,** *threshing-floor*, Cic.; **5,** *the part of the circus where the games were held*; fig., *sphere, scope*, Ov.

ārĕfăcĭo -fēci -factum, 3. *to make dry*, Lucr.

Ărĕlātĕ, n. and **Ărĕlās** -ātis, f. *town in Gallia Narbonensis, now Arles.* Adj., **Ărĕlātensis** -e.

Ărēmŏrĭcus -a -um (from Keltic are = *on*, and mor = *sea*), *lying on the sea*; civitates, *Gallic states on the coast of the English Channel.*

ărēna -ae, f. *sand.* **I.** Lit., saxa globosa arenae immixta, Liv.; arenae carae, *the sands of Pactolus*, Ov.; prov., arenae mandare semina, *to sow the sand*, of a fruitless work, Ov. **II.** Meton., **1,** *a sandy place*; arenam aliquam aut paludes emere, Cic.; **2,** *the sea-shore*; optata potiri arena, Verg.; **3,** *the arena in the amphitheatre* (covered with sand); promittere operas arenae, Tac. **III.** Transf., *the scene of any contention* or *struggle*, Plin.

ărēnārĭus -a -um, *relating to sand, sandy.* Subst., **ărēnārĭa** -ae, f. (sc. fodina), *a sand pit*, Cic.

ărēnōsus -a -um, *sandy*, Verg.

ārens -entis, p. adj. (areo), *dry.* **I.** Gen. rivus, Verg. **II.** *dry with thirst*; ora, Ov.; poet. sitis, Ov.

ārĕo, 2. **A.** *to be dry*; aret ager, Verg. **B.** Esp., *to be dry with thirst*, Liv.

ārĕŏla -ae, f. (dim. of area), *a little open space*, Plin.

Ărēŏpăgus -i, m. (Ἄρειος πάγος), *Mars' hill at Athens, upon which the court called Areopagus held its sittings*, Cic.; hence, **Ărēŏpăgītēs** -ae, m. *a member of the court*, Cic.

Ăres -is, m. (Ἄρης), *the Greek god of war*, appell., *a warrior*, Plaut.

āresco, 3. (inch. of areo), *to become dry*; cito arescit lacrima, Cic.

Ărestŏrĭdēs -ae, m. (Ἀρεστορίδης), *a descendant of Arestor, i.e., Argus, his son.*

ărĕtālŏgus -i, m. (ἀρεταλόγος), *a babbler about virtue, a kind of philosophical buffoon*, Juv.

Ărĕthūsa -ae, f. (Ἀρέθουσα), *a fountain in the island of Ortygia at Syracuse*; myth. *a Nereid beloved by the river Alpheus, who dived under the sea in pursuit of her.* Adj., **1, Ărĕthūsis** -idis; **2, Ărĕthūsĭus** -a -um, *of* or *belonging to Arethusa.*

Ărēus -a -um, *relating to Mars*; judicium, *the Areopagus*, Tac.

Arganthōnĭus -ii, m. (Ἀργανθώνιος), *a king of Tartessus, who lived to a great age.*

Argēi -ōrum, m. 1, *chapels of local deities in Rome*; **2,** *figures of men, thrown into the Tiber every year on the Ides of May.*

Argentānum -i, n. *a town in Bruttium, now Argentino.*

argentārĭus -a -um, 1, *relating to silver*; metalla, *silver mines*, Plin.; **2,** *relating to money*; inopia, Plaut.; taberna, *a banker's stall*, Liv. Subst., **A. argentārĭus** -ii, m. *a money-changer, banker*, Cic. **B. argentārĭa** -ae, f. **1,** (sc. taberna), *a banker's office*, Liv.; **2,** (sc. ars), *a banker's trade*, Cic.; **3,** (sc. fodina), *a silver mine*, Liv.

argentātus -a -um, **1,** *ornamented with silver*; milites, *with silvered shields*, Liv.; **2,** *provided with money*, Plaut.

argentĕus -a -um, **I. 1,** *made of silver*; aquila, Cic.; nummus, Varr.; denarius, Plin.; or simply argenteus, Tac.; **2,** *ornamented* or *covered with silver*; scena, Cic.; **3,** *of the colour of silver*; anser, Verg. **II.** Transf., *belonging to the Silver Age*; proles, Ov.

argentĭfŏdīna -ae, f. *a silver mine*, Varr., Plin.

argentōsus -a -um, *full of silver, rich in silver*, Plin.

argentum -i, n. (ἀργής), *silver*; **I.** signatum, *stamped with a pattern*, Cic.; **II.** Esp., **1,** *silver plate*, Cic.; **2,** *silver coin*, and generally *money*, Cic., Liv.

Argīlētum -i, n. *a part of Rome where were many booksellers' shops.* Adj., **Argīlētānus** -a -um, *of* or *belonging to Argiletum.*

argilla, -ae, f. (ἄργιλλος), *white clay, potter's clay*, Cic.

argillācĕus -a -um, *clayey, of clay*, Plin.

Argĭnussae (Argĭnūsae) -ārum, f. (Ἀργινοῦσσαι), *islands on the coast of Aeolis, scene of a naval victory of the Athenians over the Spartans.*

Argō -ūs, f. (Ἀργώ), *the ship Argo, in which many Greek heroes sailed to Colchis, under Jason, to fetch the Golden Fleece.* Adj., **Argōus** -a -um.

Argŏnautae -ārum, m. (Ἀργοναῦται), *the Argonauts, the heroes who sailed in the Argo.*

Argŏs, n. and **Argi** -ōrum, m. **I.** *the capital of Argolis, a country of the Peloponnese.* Adj., **A. Argēus** -a -um. **B. Argīvus** -a -um, *Argive*; augur, *Amphiaraus*, Hor.; plur. subst., Argivi -orum, and poet. -um, m. *the Argives.* **C. Argŏlis** -idis, f. 1, Adj., *Argolic*; **2,** Subst., *the district Argolis*; hence adj., **Argŏlĭcus** -a -um, *Argolic.* **II.** Argos Amphilochium, *a town in Epirus.*

argūmentātĭo -ōnis, f. *the bringing forward of a proof*; argumentatio est explicatio argumenti, Cic.

argūmentor, 1, dep. **I.** Intransit. *to bring forward a proof*; quid porro argumenter, qua de re dubitare nemo possit, Cic. **II.** Transit. *to allege as a proof*, Liv.

argūmentum -i, n. (arguo), **1,** *an argument, proof*, Cic.; afferre argumenta, Cic.; multis argumentis deos esse docere, Cic.; argumenta atque indicia sceleris, Cic.; **2,** *subject, contents, matter*; **a,** epistolae, Cic.; **b,** *subject of a drama*; fabulae, Ter.; **c,** *a drama itself*; explicare argumenti exitum, Cic.; **d,** *subject of a work of art*, ex ebore diligentissime perfecta argumenta erant in valvis (*bas-reliefs*), Cic.

argŭo -ŭi -ūtum, 3. (connected with ἀργός), *to put in clear light.* **I.** Gen. **A.** Lit. *to maintain, prove*; speculatores non legatos venisse, Liv. **B.** Transf., *to betray, prove*; degeneres animos timor arguit, Verg.; laudibus arguitur vini vinosus Homerus, Hor. **II.** Esp. **A.** *to charge, accuse, expose, convict*; with gen., summi sceleris, Cic.; with abl., hoc crimine te non arguo, Cic.; with double acc., id quod me arguis, Cic.; with infin., Roscius arguitur occidisse patrem, Cic. **B.** *to censure, complain of*; culpa, quam arguo, Liv.

Argus -i, m. (Ἄργος), *the hundred-eyed guardian of Io, slain by Mercury.*

argūtātĭo -ōnis, f. *a rustling*, Cat.

argūtē, adv., with compar. and superl. (argutus), *sagaciously, acutely*; callide arguteque dicere, Cic.

argūtĭae -ārum, f. **1,** *liveliness, animation*; digitorum, *quick movement of the fingers*, Cic.;

2, a, *cleverness, subtlety, sagacity*, hujus orationes tantum argutiarum, tantum urbanitatis habent, Cic, b, in a bad sense, *cunning, quibbling*, Cic

argūtor, 1 dep *to chatter*, Plaut

argūtŭlus -a -um, *somewhat acute*, libri, Cic

argūtus a -um, p adj with compar and superl (arguo), 1, in relation to the senses a, to the eye, *expressive, lively*, manus, oculi, Cic, b, to the ear, *piercing, penetrating, shrill*, hirundo, Verg, forum, *noisy*, Ov, poeta, *melodious*, Hor, 2, relating to the mind, a, *significant, clear*, of omens, argutissima exta, Cic; b, of the understanding, α, in a good sense, *sagacious, acute*, argutus orator, Cic, β, in a bad sense, *sly, cunning*, meretrix, Hor

argyraspĭdes -pidum, m (αργυρασπιδες), *name of a picked corps in the Macedonian army, the wearers of the silver shield*, Liv

Ărĭadna ae, & **Ărĭadnē** ēs, f (Ἀριάδνη), *daughter of Minos and Pasiphae, who helped Theseus to slay the Minotaur, but was deserted by him and then beloved by Bacchus*

Ărĭărăthēs -is, m (Ἀριαράθης), *name of several kings of Cappadocia*

Ărīcĭa -ae, f *town in Latium at the foot of the Alban Mount* Adj **Ărīcīnus** a -um, *belonging to Aricia*

ārĭdŭlus -a um (dim of aridus), *somewhat dry*, Cat

ārĭdus a -um, adj with compar and superl (areo), *dry, arid* I. Lit, 1, folia, Cic, poet sonus, *a dry, crackling sound*, Verg, 2, *dry with thirst*, viator, Verg, 3, *shrivelled, fleshless*, crura, Ov, absol, exsiccati atque aridi, Cic Subst, **aridum** i, n *dry ground*, naves in aridum subducere, Caes II. Transf, 1, of manner of living, *poor, meagre*, vita, Cic, 2, *intellectually dry, jejune*; genus orationis, Cic, 3, *avaricious*, Ter

ărĭēs ĕtis, m (ἄρην, ἄρρην) I. Lit *a ram*, Cic II. Transf A. *a battering ram*, Caes B. *a prop, beam*, Caes C. *one of the signs of the zodiac*, Cic

ărĭĕtātĭo -ōnis, f *a butting like a ram*, Sen

ărĭĕto, 1 *to butt like a ram*, Verg

Ărīmĭnum -i, n *town and river in Umbria* Adj, **Ărīmĭnensis** e, *belonging to Ariminum*

Ărĭŏbarzānēs -is, m (Ἀριοβαρζάνης), *name of several kings of Cappadocia, and of one of Armenia*

Ărīōn or **Ărīo** ŏnis, m. (Ἀριων) I. Myth *a harp-player, saved from drowning by a dolphin.* Adj, **Ărīŏnĭus** a, -um, *belonging to Arion* II. *a Pythagorean philosopher, contemporary of Plato*

Ariovistus -i, m *a German prince, conquered by Caesar*

Ărisba -ae, and **Ărisbē** -ēs, f (Ἀρισβη), *town in the Troad*

ărista -ae, f I. A. *the point of an ear of corn*, Cic B. Meton, *the ear itself*, Verg II. Transf, *bristly hair*, Pers

Ăristaeus -i, m (Ἀρισταῖος), *son of Apollo and Cyrene, legendary introducer of bee-keeping*

Ăristarchus i, m (Ἀρισταρχος), *a celebrated grammarian and critic of Alexandria*, appell *a severe critic*, Cic

Ăristīdēs -is, m (Ἀριστειδης), I. *a celebrated Athenian statesman and general, rival of Themistocles* II. *a poet of Miletus*

Ăristippus -i, m (Ἀριστιππος), *a philosopher of Cyrene (about 380 B C) founder of the Cyrenaic school* Adj, **Aristippēus** a -um, *of or belonging to Aristippus.*

Ăristo and **Ăristōn** ōnis, m (Ἀριστων), *a philosopher of Chios, pupil of Zeno, contemporary with Caesar*, hence adj, **Aristōnēus** a -um, *of or belonging to Aristo*

Ăristŏdēmus i, m (Ἀριστόδημος) I. *a tragic actor at Athens* II. *a tyrant of Cumae in Campania, about 502 B C*

aristŏlŏchĭa ae, f (ἀριστολοχια), *a plant useful in childbirth*, Cic

Ăristŏphănēs -is, m (Ἀριστοφάνης) I. *the great Athenian comic dramatist* Adj, **Ăristŏphănēus** -a um, *of or relating to Aristophanes* II. *a celebrated grammarian, pupil of Eratosthenes*

Ăristŏtĕlēs is and -i, m (Ἀριστοτελης), *the celebrated Greek philosopher, founder of the Peripatetic school* Adj, **Ăristŏtĕlēus** a -um, *of or relating to Aristotle*

ărithmētĭca ae and **-ē** ēs, f (αριθμητική, sc τεχνη), *arithmetic*, Sen

ărithmētĭca ōrum, n *arithmetic*, Cic

ārĭtūdo inis, f *dryness*, Plaut

arma -ōrum, n (Root AR, Greek AP, cf τα ἄρμενα), *tools, implements* I. Gen, arma equestria, *the fittings of a horse*, Liv, cerealia, *implements for grinding and baking corn*, Verg, *building tools*, Cic II. *implements of war* A. In the broadest sense, Liv B. In a narrower meaning, *defensive armour* (tela, *offensive weapons*), 1, Lit arma his imperata, galea, clypeum, ocreae, lorica, omnia ex aere, Liv, arma capere, sumere, Cic, ad arma ire, Cic, armis decertare or decernere, Cic, in armis esse or stare, *to be under arms*, Liv, CL milia habere in armis, Liv, arma deponere, Liv, tradere, Liv, ad arma "*to arms*," Caes, 2, Meton, *war*, arma civilia, Cic, 3, *military power*, Romana arma ingruere, Liv, 4, *soldiers*, levia, *light armed troops*, Liv, 5, Fig *defence*, arma prudentiae, Cic

armāmenta -ōrum, n *implements, tackle*, esp of a ship, vela armamentaque, Caes

armāmentārĭum -i, n *an armoury*, Cic

armārĭŏlum -i, n (dim of armarium), *a little cupboard*, Plaut

armārĭum -i, n *a cupboard, chest*, Cic

armātūra -ae, f. A. *equipment, armour*, Numidae levis armaturae, *light armed*, Caes B. Meton, *armed soldiers*, armatura levis, *light-armed troops*, Cic

1 **armātus**, abl -ū, m. *armour* A. Lit, haud dispari armatu, Liv B. Meton, *armed troops*, gravis, *heavy armed troops*, Liv

2 **armātus** -a um, p adj with superl (armo), *armed, equipped* A. Lit, armatus togatusque, *both in war and in peace*, Liv, armatae classes, Verg B. Transf, erat incredibili armatus audacia, Cic

Armĕnĭa -ae, f (Ἀρμενία), *a country in Asia*, hence, **Armĕnĭus** a um A. Adj, *Armenian* B. Subst, *an Armenian*

armentālis -e, *belonging to a herd*, equae, Verg

armentum -i, n *cattle living in herds*, Esp *oxen and horses*, 1, sing collective, *a herd*, Pan erat armenti custos, Ov, 2, plur, *oxen*, greges armentorum reliquique pecoris, Cic

armĭfĕr fĕra -fĕrum (arma and fero), *bearing arms, warlike*, Ov

armĭgĕr -gĕra gerum (arma and gero), *bearing arms*, Subst, a, armiger -geri, m *an armour-bearer*, Cic, Jovis, *the eagle*, Verg, Catilinae, *adherent*, Cic, b, armigera -ae, f *a female armour-bearer*, Ov

armilla -ae, f *a bracelet*, worn by both men and women, Cic., Liv

armillātus -a -um, *adorned with a bracelet*, Suet. ; canes, *wearing a collar*, Prop.

armĭlustrĭum -ii, n. (arma and lustro), *a festival at which arms were consecrated*, celebrated at a spot in Rome called Armilustrum.

armĭpŏtens -entis, *mighty in arms, warlike;* Mars, Verg. ; diva, *Minerva*, Verg.

armĭsŏnus -a -um, *resounding with arms*, Verg.

armo, 1., **1**, *to provide with implements, to equip;* naves, Caes. ; **2**, *to arm, prepare for battle;* **a**, aliquem in rempublicam, Cic. ; milites, Caes. ; servum in or contra dominum, Cic. ; equum bello, *for battle*, Verg. : gladiis dextras, Liv. ; **b**, transf. *to supply, arm;* multitudinem auctoritate publica, Cic. ; se eloquentia, Cic.

armŏrăcĭa -ae, f. (-cium -ii, n.), *horse-radish* (cochlearia armoracia, Linn.), Plin.

armus -i, m. (ἁρμός), **1**, *the shoulder-blade;* latos huic hasta per armos tremit, Verg. ; in animals, *the shoulder;* ex humeris armi fiunt, Ov. ; **2**, *the side of an animal*, Verg.

Arnus -i, m. (Ἄρνος), *the chief river of Etruria*, now the *Arno*. Adj., **Arnĭensis**, -e.

ăro, 1. (ἀρόω), *to plough.* **A.** Lit., **1**, arare terram et sulcum altius imprimere, Cic. ; prov., non profecturis litora bubus aras, *to labour uselessly*, Ov. ; **2**, *to farm, cultivate;* Falerni mille fundi jugera, Hor. ; absol., cives Romani qui arant in Sicilia, *tenants of the domain-lands*, (cf. aratio), Cic. **B.** Transf., **1**, *to furrow, wrinkle;* rugae quae tibi corpus arent, Ov. ; **2**, of ships, *to plough the sea;* vastum maris aequor, Verg.

Arpi -ōrum, m. *a town in Apulia.* Adj., **Arpīnus** -a -um, *of* or *belonging to Arpi.*

Arpīnum -i, n. *a town in Latium, birthplace of Cicero and Marius.* Adj., **Arpīnās** -ātis, **Arpīnus** -a -um, *of* or *belonging to Arpinum.*

arquātus, v. arcuatus.

arra, v. arrha.

arrectus -a -um, p. adj. with compar. (from arrigo), *steep*, Liv.

arrēpo (ad-repo), -repsi, -reptum, 3. *to creep to, to glide gently to;* quibus rebus non sensim atque moderate ad amicitiam adrepserat, Cic.

Arrētĭum -ii, n. *a town in Etruria, birthplace of Maecenas.*

arrha -ae, f., and **arrhăbo** -ōnis, m. *earnest money*, Plaut., Ter.

arrīdĕo (ad-rīdĕo), -rīsi -rīsum, 2. *to laugh to;* **I.** *to laugh with;* ridentibus arrident, Hor. **II.** *to laugh at*, either in approval or ridicule. **A.** Lit., with dat. of pers., vix notis familiariter arridere, Liv. ; with acc. of the thing, video quid arriseris, Cic. **B.** Transf., **a**, *to be favourable;* quum tempestas arridet, Lucr. ; **b**, *to please;* "inhibere" illud tuum quod mihi valde arriserat, Cic.

arrĭgo -rexi -rectum, 3. (ad and rego). **A.** *to erect, lift up;* aures, comas, Verg. **B.** Transf., **a**, *to excite;* arrexere animos Itali, Verg. ; **b**, *to encourage, animate;* aliquem oratione, Sall.

arrĭpio -rĭpŭi -reptum, 3. (ad and rapio). **I.** *to seize on, lay hold of, snatch.* **A.** Gen. arma, Liv. ; cibum unguium tenacitate, Cic. ; aliquem manu, Liv. ; tabulam de naufragio, Cic. ; cohortes arreptas in urbem inducere, Liv. ; terram velis, *to sail quickly to*, Verg. **B.** Transf., **a**, *to seize upon, appropriate, take;* facultatem laedendi, quaecumque detur, Cic. ; maledicta ex trivio, Cic. ; **b**, *to comprehend quickly;* celeriter res innumerabiles, Cic. ; litteras Graecas, *take to with zeal*, Cic. ; **II.** *to seize with violence;* **a**, of diseases, &c., dolor, qui simul arripuit interficit, Cic. ; **b**, legal t.t. *to drag before a tribunal, accuse*, Cic. ; **c**, transf., *to satirize;* primores populi populumque, Hor.

arrīsor -ōris, m. *one who smiles approvingly, a flatterer*, Sen.

arrōdo (ad-rōdo) -rōsi -rōsum, 3. *to gnaw at;* mures Antii coronam auream arrosere, Liv. ; fig., ut illa ex vepreculis extracta nitedula rempublicam conaretur arrodere, Cic.

arrŏgans -antis, p. adj. with compar. and superl. (from arrogo), *assuming, arrogant, haughty;* Indutiomarus iste minax atque arrogans, Cic.

arrŏgantĕr, adv. *arrogantly, haughtily;* dicere aliquid, Cic. ; scribere ad aliquem, Cic. ; facere, Caes.

arrŏgantia -ae, f. *arrogance, assumption pride, haughtiness;* ex arrogantia odium, ex insolentia arrogantia oritur, Cic.

arrŏgo (ad-rŏgo), 1. **I. 1**, sibi aliquid, *to appropriate to oneself something to which one has no claim;* sibi sapientiam, Cic. ; **2**, alicui aliquid, *to claim, confer upon;* decus imperiis, Hor. **II. 1**, *to ask*, Plaut. ; **2**, *to associate one public officer with another;* cui unico consuli dictatorem arrogari haud satis decorum visum est patribus, Liv.

arrōsor -ōris, m. *one who gnaws at*, Sen.

Arrūns (Āruns) -ūntis, m, *name of a younger son of Tarquinius Superbus.*

ars -tis, f. (stem AR, whence ar- -mus, ar- -tus; Gr. ΑΡΩ, ἀρτύω, ἀρετή). **I. A.** *a trade, profession, art;* disserendi, *dialectics*, Cic ; artes sordidae, *mean occupations*, those of slaves, Cic. ; ingenuae, liberales, *honourable occupations*, Cic. ; urbanae, *jurisprudence and rhetoric*, Liv. ; artem aliquam factitare, Cic. ; exercere, *to practise, pursue*, Hor. **B.** Meton., **1**, *art, knowledge, theory* (opp. *practice*); res mihi videtur esse facultate (*in practice*) praeclara, arte (*in theory*) mediocris, Cic. ; ex arte (dicere, scribere, &c.), *according to the rules of art*, Cic. ; hence as title of treatises on a subject, artes oratoriae, Cic. ; **2**, *skill, cleverness;* opus est vel arte vel diligentia, Cic. ; arte laboratae vestes, Verg. ; arte canere, Ov. ; **3**, plur., artes, *works of art*, Cic. ; **4**, Artes, *the Muses*, Phaed. **II.** Transf., **1**, *conduct, character, method of acting*, good or bad ; bonae artes, *good qualities*, Sall. ; hac arte Pollux attigit arces igneas, Hor. ; **2**, absol., *cunning, deceit*, Verg.

Arsăcēs -is, m. (Ἀρσάκης), *the first king of the Parthians;* hence, **1**, **Arsăcĭdes** -ae, m. *a descendant of Arsaces;* **2**, **Arsăcĭus** -a -um, *Parthian.*

Artaxăta -ōrum, n. (-a -ae, f., Tac.), *capital of Armenia on the Araxes.*

Artaxerxēs -is,{m. (Ἀρταξέρξης), *name of three Persian kings.*

artē (arctē), adv. with compar. and superl. (artus), *narrowly, tightly, closely.* **I.** Lit. artius complecti aliquem, Cic. ; signa artius collocare, Sall. ; fig., artius astringere rationem, Cic. **II.** Transf., **a**, *fast, soundly;* dormire, Cic. ; **b**, *shortly;* artius appellare aliquem, *to cut a name short*, Ov. ; aliquem arte colere, *stingily*, Sall.

artērĭa -ae, f. (ἀρτηρία), **1**, *the wind-pipe*, Cic. ; neut. plur., heterocl. arteria, Lucr. ; **2**, *an artery*, Cic.

arthrītĭcus -a -um (ἀρθριτικός), *gouty*, Cic.

artĭcŭlāris -e, *relating to the joints;* morbus, *gout*, Suet.

artĭcŭlātim, adv. **A.** *limb by limb, piecemeal*, Plaut. **B.** Transf., *in a manner properly divided, distinctly;* articulatim distincteque dici, Cic.

artĭcŭlo, 1. *to articulate, speak distinctly*, Lucr.

artĭcŭlus -i, m. (dim. of artus). **I.** Lit. **1**, *a joint;* articulorum dolores, *gouty* or *rheumatic* *pains*, Cic ; plur meton , *the limbs*, esp , *the fingers*, Lucr , Ov ; 2, of plants, *a knob, knot*, Cic II. Transf , 1, *a division of a discourse*, articuli membraque, Cic , 2, of time, *a moment, crisis*, in ipso articulo temporis, Cic , 3, of other abstractions, *part, division, point*, per eosdem articulos et gradus, Suet.

artifex -ficis (ars and facio) I. 1, *an artist, artificer, painter, sculptor*, artifices scenici, *actors*, Cic , artifex equus, *a trained horse*, Ov , with genit of gerund ; Graeci dicendi artifices et doctores, Cic , 2, *the maker, author, contriver*, probus ejus (mundi) artifex, Cic , 3, *a master of any art*, tractandi animos artifices, Liv , artifex conquirendae et comparandae voluptatis, Cic , artifices ad corrumpendum judicium, Cic II. Of inanimate objects, 1, active, *clever, skilled*, artifex stilus, Cic , 2, passive, *skilfully wrought or made*, artifices boves, Prop

artĭfĭcĭōsē, adv *skilfully*, id multo artificiosius efficere, Cic

artĭfĭcĭōsus -a -um A. *skilful, accomplished*, rhetores artificiosissimi, Cic , opus, Cic B. Transf., *artificial* (opp to natural), ea genera divinandi non naturalia, sed artificiosa dicuntur, Cic

artĭfĭcĭum -i, n I. *an occupation, handicraft*, ancillare, Cic II. Esp , A. *theory, system*, componere artificium de jure civili, Cic B. a, *cleverness, skill, art*, simulacrum Dianae singulari opere artificioque perfectum, Cic , b, *dexterity*, and, in a bad sense, *cunning, craft*, artificio simulationis, Cic , c, *work of art*, haec opera atque artificia, Cic

arto (arcto), 1 (artus), 1, *to press together, reduce to small compass*, Lucr , 2, *to abridge, curtail*, in praemiis, in honoribus omnia artata, Liv

artŏlăgănus i, m (ἀρτολάγανος), *a cake made of meal, wine, milk, oil, lard, and pepper*, Cic

artopta -ae, m (ἀρτόπτης), 1, *a baker*, Juv , 2, *a baker's vessel*, Plin

1 **artus** (arctus), -a -um, adj , with compar and superl (root AR, Gr AP, whence 2 artus, arma, &c), *narrow, tight, close* I. Lit , catena, Ov , vinculum ad astringendam fidem artius, Cic , vallis, Liv Subst , **artum** i, n , *narrow space*, pugna in arto, Tac II. Transf , a, *fast, sound* somnus, Cic , b, *oppressed by care*, animus, Hor , c, *small, meagre*, numerus, Tac ; commeatus, Liv , d, *difficult, distressing*, res, Ov Subst., quum in arto res esset, Liv

2 **artus** -ūs, m (root AR, Gr ἄρθρον) usually plur , artūs -ŭum, *the joints*, dolor artuum, *gout*, Cic , omnibus artubus contremisco, *I tremble in all my limbs*, Cic , fig , nervi atque artus sapientiae, Cic , poet , *limbs*, salsus per artus sudor iit, Verg

ārŭla -ae, f , (dim of ara), *a little altar*, Cic

ărundĭfer -fĕra -fĕrum (arundo and fero), *reed-bearing*, caput, Ov

ărundĭnĕus -a -um, *reedy*, canales, Verg , carmen, *a shepherd's song*, Ov

ărundĭnōsus -a -um, *full of reeds*, Cat

ărundo inis, f *a reed* A Lit , crines umbrosa tegebat arundo, Verg , casae ex arundine textae, Liv B Meton , for an object made of reeds ; 1, *a fishing rod*, moderator arundinis, *a fisherman*, Ov , 2, *limed twigs for catching birds*, Plaut , 3, *a pen*, tristis, *a severe style*, Mart , 4, *the shaft of an arrow*, Ov , poet , *the arrow itself*, Verg ; 5, *a shepherd's pipe*, Verg., 6, *a flute*, Ov , 7, *a weaver's comb*, Ov , 8, *a scare crow*, Hor , 9, *a plaything for children, a hobby horse*, Hor

arvĕho = adveho

Arverni ōrum, m *a Gallic people in Aquitaine, in what is now Auvergne* Adj , **Arvernus** -a -um, *Arvernian*

arvīna -ae, f *fat, lard*, Verg

arvum -i, n (aro), 1, *a ploughed or sown field*, Verg 2, *a country, region*, arva laeta, Verg , arva Neptunia, *the sea*, Verg

arvus -a -um, *ploughed*, Cic

arx -cis, f (from ARC, root of arceo), *a fortress, citadel, stronghold* I. Lit , A. In the narrow sense, ne quando arx hostium esset, Liv ; at Rome the arx was *the S. W. height of the Capitol*, ne quis patricius in arce aut in Capitolio habitaret, Liv , used also of the whole hill , Capitolina, Liv , *the stronghold or chief place of a town*, amisso oppido fugerat in arcem, Cic , *the stronghold of a kingdom*, ad caput arcemque regni Pergamum, Liv , prov , arcem facere e cloaca, *to make a mountain of a mole hill*, Cic , B. In wider sense, *the height of heaven*, siderea arx, Ov ; *temples of the gods*, Hor , (of towers), beatae arces, Corinth, Hor , *the height of a mountain*, Parnassi arx, Ov II. Transf A. *refuge, bulwark, protection*, haec urbs arx omnium gentium, Cic B. *head quarters, chief place*, ubi Hannibal sit, ibi caput atque arcem totius belli esse, Liv.

as, assis, m (εἷς), *the whole as unity*, divided into twelve unciae, called uncia $\frac{1}{12}$, sextans $\frac{1}{6}$, quadrans $\frac{1}{4}$, triens $\frac{1}{3}$, quincunx $\frac{5}{12}$, semis $\frac{1}{2}$, septunx $\frac{7}{12}$, bes $\frac{2}{3}$, dodrans $\frac{3}{4}$, dextans $\frac{5}{6}$, deunx $\frac{11}{12}$ A. Gen , esp in terms relating to inheritance, haeres ex asse, *sole heir*, Plin B. Esp , 1, as a coin, *the as*, which originally consisted of a pound of copper, but was ultimately reduced to $\frac{1}{24}$ lb , and from the time of the second Punic war was worth a little over a farthing , hence prov , omnia ad assem perdere, *to the last farthing*, Hor , non assis facere, *not to estimate at a farthing*, Cat , 2, as a weight, *a pound*, Ov , 3, *an acre*, Plin

asbestĭnum -i, n sc linum (ἀσβέστινον), *incombustible cloth*, Plin

1 **Ascănĭus** -ii, m *son of Aeneas and Creusa*, Verg , or of Lavinia, Liv

2 **Ascănĭus**, ii, m *a river in Bithynia, now Ishakbgha Su*

ascaules is, m (ἀσκαύλης), *a bag piper*, Mart

ascendo -scendi -scensum, 3. (ad and scando), *to mount, ascend, go up* I. Lit with in and the acc , in murum, Cic , in equum, Cic , in concionem, *to go up to speak to the people*, Cic , with ad, ad Gitanas, Liv , with acc alone, murum, Caes , ripam equo, Cic II. Transf , *to rise*, in tantum honorem, Cic , altiorem gradum, Cic , gradatim ascendere vocem utile et suave est, *the voice rising higher and higher*, Cic

ascensĭo ōnis, f *an ascent*, Plaut , transf , oratorum, *lofty flight*, Cic

ascensus -ūs, m *a going up, climbing up, ascent* I. A. Lit , in Capitolium, Cic B Transf , primus ad honoris gradum, Cic II. Meton , *the place for ascending*, difficilis atque arduus, Cic

ascĭa -ae, f *a carpenter's axe or adze*, ap Cic

ascīo, (ad-scio), 4 *to take to oneself, adopt as one's own*, socios, Verg , asciri per adoptionem, Tac

ascisco (adscisco), ascīvi, ascītum, 3 (ascio) *to receive, admit* I. Lit , with ad and the acc , ad hoc sceleris foedus, Cic , with in, aliquem in numerum civium, Cic , with inter, inter patricios, Tac.; with dat., superis ascitus, Caesar, Ov.; with double acc., aliquem patronum, Cic. **II.** Transf. **A.** *to adopt*, hanc consuetudinem, Cic. **B.** *to approve of*; quas (leges) Latini voluerunt, asciverunt, Cic.; **2,** *to claim for oneself*, sibi sapientiam, Cic.

1. **ascītus** -a -um (partic. of ascisco), *foreign, derived from without* (opp. nativus), Nep.

2. **ascītus** -us, m. *an acceptance, reception*, Cic.

ascŏpēra -ae, f. (ἀσκοπήρα), *a leather knapsack*, Suet.

Ascra -ae, f. (Ἄσκρα), *a small town in Boeotia, near Mount Helicon, the home of Hesiod.* Adj., **Ascraeus** -a -um; **a,** *Ascraean, of Ascra*; poeta, Prop.; senex, Verg.; simply Ascraeus = *Hesiod*, Ov.; **b,** carmen, *Hesiodic*, or *rural*, Verg.; **c,** fontes, *Heliconian*, Prop.

ascrībo (ad-scribo) -scripsi -scriptum, 3. (ad and scribo), *to write to*, or *in addition.* **A.** Lit. **1,** with dat., poenam foederibus, Cic.; with in and the acc., aliquid in eandem legem, Cic.; **2,** *to fix, appoint*; aliquem tutorem liberis, Cic.; **3,** *to enrol*; aliquem in civitatem, Cic.; esp., *a*, *as a colonist*, colonos, Liv.; with acc., of the colony, colonos Venusiam, Liv.; *β*, *to enrol as a soldier*; urbanae militiae ascribi, Tac. **B.** Transf. **1,** *to reckon under a class, include*; with ad or in and the acc., or with the dat., tu vero me ascribe in talem numerum, Cic.; aliquem ordinibus deorum, Hor.; with two acc., opinio socium me ascribit tuis laudibus, Cic.; **2,** *to attribute, impute*, alicui incommodum, Cic.

ascriptīcĭus -a -um, *one who is enrolled as a member of a community*, Cic.

ascriptĭo -ōnis, f. *an addition in writing*, Cic.

ascriptīvus -a -um, *enrolled as a supernumerary*, Plaut.

ascriptor -ōris, m. *one who willingly adds his name, one who approves of*; legis agrariae, Cic.

Ascŭlum -i, n. *town of the Picentines.* Adj., **Ascŭlānus** -a -um, *of* or *belonging to Asculum.*

ăsella -ae, f. (dim. of asina), *a little she-ass*, Ov.

ăsellus -i, m. (dim. of asinus), *a little ass*, Cic.

Āsĭa -ae, f. (Ἀσία). **I.** *the district in Lydia near the river Cayster.* **II.** *The continent of Asia.* **III.** *The peninsula of Asia Minor*; sometimes used specially for the kingdom of Pergamus (Liv.), or of the Troad (Ov.). **IV.** In the narrowest sense (the ordinary meaning of the word), *the Roman province of Asia, formed out of the kingdom of Pergamus*; hence, **1, Āsĭăgĕnes** -is, m. *surname of L. Corn. Scipio*; **2, Āsĭānus** -a -um, *belonging to the province of Asia.* Plur. subst., **Āsĭani** -orum, m. *the farmers of the taxes of the province of Asia*, Cic.; **3, Āsĭātĭcus** -a -um, *Asiatic, surname of L. Corn. Scipio*; Asiatici oratores, *bombastic, ornate*, Cic.; **4, Āsĭs** -ĭdis, f. *Asiatic*; **5, Āsĭus** -a -um, palus, *the marsh round Ephesus*, Verg.

ăsīlus -i, m. *the gad-fly*, Verg.

ăsĭna -ae, f. *a she ass*, Varr.

ăsĭnīnus -a -um, *belonging to an ass*, Plin.

Āsĭnĭus -a -um, *name of a Roman gens, of which the most celebrated was* C. Asinius Pollio, *friend of J. Caesar and Augustus, statesman, orator, poet, historian.*

ăsĭnus -i, m. **A.** *an ass*, Cic. **B.** Transf., *a dolt, blockhead*; quid nunc te, asine, litteras doceam, Cic.

Āsōpus -i, m. (Ἀσωπός). **I. a,** *a river in Boeotia*; **b,** *the river-god Asopus*; hence, **A. Āsōpĭădēs** -ae, m. *a descendant of Asopus* (Aeacus), Ov. **B. Āsōpis** -ĭdis, f. **1,** *Aegina, daughter of Asopus, mother of Aeacus by Jupiter*, Ov.; **2,** *Evadne, daughter of Aegina*, Ov. **II.** *a river in Phthiotis.*

ăsōtus -i, m. (ἄσωτος), *a sensualist, libertine*, Cic.

aspărăgus -i, m. (ἀσπάραγος), *asparagus*, Suet.

aspargo, v. aspergo.

Aspāsĭa -ae, f. (Ἀσπασία), *the most celebrated of the Greek hetaerae, mistress of Pericles.*

aspectābĭlis -e, *visible*, Cic.

aspecto, 1. **I.** *to look at earnestly*, or *with respect*; **a,** quid me aspectas, Cic.; **b,** of place, *to lie towards, to face*; mare quod Hiberniam insulam aspectat, Tac. **II.** *to observe, attend to*; jussa principis, Tac.

aspectus -us, m. **A.** Act. **1,** *a seeing, looking, sight*; uno aspectu, Cic.; oculi mobiles ut aspectum quo vellent facile converterent, Cic.; **2,** *view, limit of vision*; orbes qui aspectum nostrum definiunt, Cic.; **3,** *power of vision*; omnia quae sub aspectum cadunt, Cic. **B.** Pass. **1,** *sight, power of being seen*; patriam privare aspectu tuo, Cic.; situs Syracusarum laetus ad aspectum, Cic.; **2,** *look, aspect, appearance*; pomorum jucundus aspectus, Cic.

aspello -pŭli -pulsum (abs and pello), 3. *to drive away*, Plaut.

Aspendus -i, f. (Ἄσπενδος), *a town in Pamphylia.* Adj., **Aspendĭus** -a -um, *of* or *belonging to Aspendus.*

asper -ĕra -ĕrum (-pra -prum, Verg.), *rough*; **1,** physically, **a,** to the sense of touch; loca, *uneven*, Caes.; mare, *stormy*, Liv.; aspera caelo, *inclement in climate*, Liv. Subst., **aspĕrum** -i, n. *roughness, a rough place*, Tac.; **b,** to the senses of taste and smell, *pungent, sour*; vinum, Ter.; **c,** to the sense of hearing, *harsh, grating*, Cic.; litera aspera, *the letter R*, Ov.; **2,** morally, *rough, wild, harsh*; homo asper et durus, Cic.; of animals, *fierce*, anguis asper siti, Verg.; of events, *adverse, troublous, dangerous*; res, tempora, Cic.; sententia, *severe*, Liv.; of speech, *harsh, bitter*; facetiae, Cic.

aspĕrē, adv. (asper), *roughly*; loqui, Cic.; scribere, Cic.

1. **aspergo** (aspargo) -spersi -spersum, 3. (ad and spargo). **I.** *to sprinkle*; **a,** guttam bulbo, Cic.; virus pecori, Verg.; **b,** *to cast upon, mingle with, add*; sapores huc, Verg.; transf., alicui molestiam, Cic. **II.** *to bespatter*; **a,** aram sanguine, Cic.; transf., *to sully, stain, asperse*; splendorem vitae maculis, Cic.; **b,** *to strew over*; olivam sale, Plin.; transf., aliquid mendaciunculis, Cic.

2. **aspergo** (aspargo) -ĭnis, f. *a sprinkling, besprinkling, spray*; aquarum, Ov.; salsa adspargo, Verg.

aspĕrĭtas -ātis, f. *roughness.* **I.** Lit. **1,** to the touch, *unevenness*; saxorum, Cic.; **2,** to the taste, *sourness*; vini, Plin.; **3,** to the ear, *harshness*; soni, Tac. **II.** Transf., **1,** of character, *harshness, fierceness, severity, austerity*; Stoicorum, Cic.; **2,** of inanimate things, *severity*; frigorum, *severe cold*, Sall.; of circumstances, *calamity, difficulty*; rerum, Cic.; of speech, *harshness*; judicialis verborum, Cic.

aspernātĭo -ōnis, f. *contempt*, Cic.

aspernor, 1. dep. *to despise, contemn, reject, spurn*; aspernatur dolorem ut malum, Cic.; amicitiam alicujus, Cic.; with a and the abl., proscriptionem nisi hoc judicio a vobis rejicitis atque aspernamini, Cic.

aspĕro, 1. *to make rough.* **I.** Lit., **a,** glacialis hiems aquilonibus asperat undas, *make stormy*, Verg.; **b,** *to sharpen, whet*; sagittas ossibus, Tac II. Transf., *to excite, arouse*, aliquem in saevitiam, Tac

aspersio -ōnis, f *a sprinkling*, aquae, Cic

aspersus ūs, m *a sprinkling*, Plin

aspicio -spexi -spectum, 3 (ad and specio) I. *to look at, behold, see* A. Lit, 1, a, of persons, lucem aspicere vix possum, *endure the light of day, live*, Cic, b, of places, *to look towards, to face*, ea pars Britanniae quae Hiberniam aspicit, Tac, 2, a, *to survey, inspect*; tabulas, Cic, b, *to look straight in the face, to withstand, confront*, aliquem in acie, Nep, hostem aspicere non possunt, Cic B. Transf, 1, *to weigh, consider*, neque tanta est in rebus obscuritas, ut eas non penitus vir ingenio cernat, si modo aspexerit, Cic, 2, *to investigate*, res sociorum, Liv II. Inchoative, *to perceive*, simulac Lentulum aspexit, Cic

aspiratio ōnis, f 1, *a breathing*, aëris, Cic, 2, *exhalation*, terrarum, Cic, 3, *the pronunciation of the letter H, aspiration*, Cic

aspiro, 1 *to breathe, blow upon* I. Intransit, *to breathe or blow upon* A. Lit, pulmones se contrahunt aspirantes, *exhaling*, Cic, aspirant aurae in noctem, *towards evening*, Verg B. Transf, 1, *to be favourable to, assist*, aspiravit nemo eorum, Cic, with dat, vos, Calliope, aspirate canenti, Verg, 2, *to approach*, Februario mense aspiravit in Curiam, Cic, 3, *to climb up to, to endeavour to obtain, to reach to* (in Cic only with negatives), ex bellica laude ad Africanum aspirare nemo potest, Cic II. Transit, *to breathe upon, blow on* A. Lit, Juno ventos aspirat eunti, *gives them a favourable wind*, Verg B. Transf, *to infuse*, divinum amorem dictis, Verg

aspis -idis f (ἀσπίς), *an adder, asp*, Cic

asportatio ōnis, f *a taking away, carrying off*, signorum Cic

asporto, 1 (abs and porto), *to carry off, take away*, multa de suis rebus secum, Cic, abreptam ex eo loco virginem secum, Cic

asprētum -i, n (asper), *a rough, uneven spot*, Liv

Assăracus -i, m (Ἀσσάρακος), *a mythical king of Phrygia, son of Tros, brother of Ganymede, grandfather of Anchises*, Assaraci nurus, *Venus*, Ov, domus Assaraci, *the Romans*, Verg, Assaraci tellus, *Troy*, Hor

assĕcla (assĕcŭla) ae, m (assequor), *a follower, servant, sycophant*, assentatores eorum atque asseculae, Cic

assectātio ōnis, f *respectful attendance*, e g, of a client on a patron, Cic

assectātor -ōris, m, 1, *a companion, follower*, cum ducibus ipsis, non cum comitatu assectatoribusque confligant, Cic, 2, *a disciple*, philosophiae, Plin

assector, 1, dep, *to follow, attend assiduously* (esp of friends of candidates), quum aedilitatem P Crassus peteret eumque Ser Galba assectaretur, Cic

assensio -ōnis, 1, *assent, agreement, applause*, popularis, Cic, rem assensione comprobare, Cic, plur, crebrae assensiones, Cic; 2, as philosoph t t, *belief in the reality of sensible appearances* (Gr συγκατάθεσις), Cic

assensor ōris, m *one who assents or agrees*, quotidie commemorabam te unum in tanto exercitu mihi fuisse assensorem, Cic

assensus -ūs, m I. *assent, agreement*, assensu omnium dicere, Cic II. Esp A. Philosoph t t *belief in the reality of sensible appearances*, assensum retinere, Cic B. Poet, *echo*, nemorum, Verg

assentātio -ōnis, f. *a flattering assent or applause, flattery*, faceta parasitorum, Cic; nullam in amicitiis pestem esse majorem quam adulationem, blanditiam, assentationem, Cic, plur, blanditiae et assentationes, Cic

assentātiuncŭla -ae, f (dim of assentatio), *trivial flattery*, Cic

assentātor ōris, m (assentor), *a flatterer*, cavendum est ne assentatoribus patefaciamus aures, Cic

assentātōrĭē, adv (assentator), *flatteringly* Cic

assentātrix -tricis, f (assentator), *a female flatterer*, Plaut

assentio -sensi sensum, 4 and (gen in classical authors) **assentior** -sensus sum, sentiri (ad and sentio), *to assent to, agree with*, a, deponent form, gov dat of pers, de Vennonianis rebus tibi assentior, Cic, with dat of the thing, ut ego assentior orationi, Cic, with acc of obj, ego illud assentior Theophrasto, Cic, b, active form, cavendum est ne his rebus temere assentiamus, Cic, c, pass, neque percepta neque assensa, Cic, assentiendum temporibus, *we must accommodate ourselves to the times*, Cic

assentor, 1 dep (intens of assentior), *to assent constantly, to flatter*, benevolentiam civium blanditiis et assentando colligere, Cic, with obj in acc, ut nihil nobis assentati esse videamur, Cic, Baiae tibi assentantur, *wooes thee*, Cic

assĕquor cūtus sum, 3 dep, *to follow* I. Lit, Porcius deinde assecutus cum levi armatura, Liv II. Transf, *to reach by following, come up to, attain*, a, aliquem, Cic, merita alicujus non assequi, Cic, b, esp, *to gain or attain to something for which one strives*, eosdem honorum gradus, Cic, immortalitatem, Cic, foll by ut or ne with the subj, Cic, or by the infin, Cic, c, of the mind, *to grasp, comprehend*, aliquid cogitatione, Cic

asser -ĕris, m (root ASS, whence also assis or axis) *a stake, a pole* A. Gen, Caes B Esp, *a pole for carrying a litter*, Suet

assercŭlum -i, n, or us -i, m, *a small stake or pole*, Cato

1. **assĕro** sēvi -situm 3 (ad and sero), *to plant at or near*, populus assita limitibus, Hor

2 **assĕro** -sĕrui -sertum, 3 (ad and sero), *to join to* I. Legal t t, A *to lay hold of a slave, and thereby declare him free*, in libertatem, Liv, aliquem manu liberali causa, Plaut, aliquem in liberali causa, Cic, assero jam me, *I have freed myself*, Ov B. *to claim as a slave*, aliquem in servitutem, Liv II. Transf, A. *to set free from, protect*, se a mortalitate, Plin B. *to claim*, alicui regnum, Liv, aliquem caelo, *declare the celestial origin of a person*, Ov

assertio ōnis, f *a formal declaration as to freedom*, Suet

assertor ōris, m (2 assero), *one who asserts that another person is free or a slave* I. Lit, A. *one who defends the liberty of another*, assertor libertatis, Plin B. *one who asserts that another is a slave*, assertor puellae, Liv II. Transf, *a liberator, saviour*, Ov

asservio, 4 *to assist, help*, toto corpore contentioni vocis, Cic

asservo, 1, a, *to preserve*, tabulas negligentius, Cic, aliquem domi suae, Cic, b, *to watch, observe*, oram, Caes, fig, *to attend to*, jus negligentius, Cic

assessio -ōnis, f (assideo), *a sitting by the side of one* (to console), quae tua fuerit assessio, oratio, confirmatio animi mei fracti, Cic

assessor -ōris, m (assideo), *one who sits by the side to assist*, Lacedaemonii regibus suis augurem assessorem dederunt, esp, *an assistant, a judicial assessor*, Suet

assessus, abl ū, m (assideo), *a sitting by the side of*, Prop

assĕvĕrantĕr, adv, with compar (asseverans), *earnestly, emphatically*, loqui, Cic

assĕvērātĭo -ōnis, f (assevero), 1, *earnestness in action*, multa asseveratione coguntur patres, Tac, 2, *vehement assertion, asseveration*, omni asseveratione tibi affirmo (foll by acc. with infin), Cic

assĕvēro, 1 (ad and severus), 1, *to act with earnestness*, bella ironia, si jocaremur, sin asseveramus, vide ne, &c, Cic, 2, *to assert confidently, strongly*, with acc and infin, idque se facturum asseveravit, Cic., with de and the abl, nemo de ulla re potest contendere neque asseverare, Cic

assĭdeo sēdi, -sessum, 2 (ad and sedeo), *to sit near*, or *by the side of* **I.** Gen, **A.** Lit, Sthenius est, is qui nobis assidet, Cic **B.** Transf, *to be next door to*, parcus assidet insano, Hor **II.** Esp, **A.** *to sit at a person's side, to give comfort, advice, protection*, &c, in carcere mater noctes diesque assidebat, Cic, assidere aegro collegae, *to sit at the bedside of*, Liv, quum, Cn Pompeius Lentulo frequens assideret, Cic, judiciis assidebat, *frequented*, Tac, tota vita litteris, *to devote oneself to*, Plin **B.** Milit t t *to besiege, blockade*, with dat, intactis muris, Liv, assidens Casilino, Liv

assīdo (ad-sīdo) -sēdi -sessum, 3 *to sit down*, in bibliotheca, Cic, super aspidem, Cic, propter Tuberonem, Cic, of an orator, *to break down in a speech*, subito assedit, Cic

assĭdŭē, adv (assiduus), *continuously, without remission*, voces quas audio assidue, Cic, quibus (litteris) assidue utor, Cic

assĭdŭĭtas -ātis, f (assiduus) **I.** *continual presence, attention of friends, clients, candidates*, quotidiana amicorum assiduitas et frequentia, Cic, medici, Cic **II.** Transf, **A.** *constancy*, id assiduitate et virtute consequere, Cic **B.** *constant repetition*, epistolarum, *unintermittent correspondence*, Cic, molestiarum, Cic, bellorum, Cic

assiduo = assidue, q v.

assĭdŭus -a, um (assideo) **I.** *sitting in a place constantly, established* Political t t, **assiduus** i, m *a settled* and hence *a well-to-do, taxpaying citizen*, gen in plur assidui, *the citizens of the upper classes*, opp to proletarii (who paid no taxes), Cic **II.** *continuously in one place*, or *engaged in one occupation*, a, ruri assiduum semper vivere, Cic, audivi Romae esse hominem et fuisse assiduum, Cic, esp of the friends who attended candidates and magistrates, mecum fuit assiduus praetore me, Cic; b, *constant, steady*, qui filios suos agricolas assiduos esse cupiunt, Cic, c, of things, *constant, unceasing*, imbres, Cic., homines labore assiduo et quotidiano assueti, Cic

assignātĭo -ōnis, f *assignment, allotment*, agrorum, Cic

assigno, 1 *to assign to any one, allot* **I.** **A.** Lit., inferiorem aedium partem alicui, Cic, esp, of allotting lands to colonists, loca, Cic, agros colonis, Cic, agrum militibus, Cic **B.** Transf, munus humanum a deo assignatum, Cic **C.** *to ascribe*, hoc preceptum deo, Cic, aliquid homini, non tempori, Cic **II.** *to seal*, Pers

assĭlĭo -silŭi, 4 (ad and salio), *to leap to*, or *on* **I.** Gen., a, of persons moenibus, Ov, b, of water, *to dash up*, assiliens aqua, Ov **II.** Transf, *to jump to*, neque assiliendum statim est ad genus illud orationis, Cic

assĭmĭlis -e, *like, similar*, with dat, assimilis spongiis mollitudo, Cic, with gen, Ov

assĭmĭlĭtĕr, adv (assimilis), *in like manner*, Plaut

assĭmŭlātus -a -um (partic of assimulo), 1, *similar*, Lucr, 2, *feigned, pretended, simulated*, virtus, Cic

assĭmŭlo, 1 *to make like* **I.** **A.** deos in humani oris speciem, Tac litterae lituraeque omnes assimulatae, Cic **B.** *to compare*, Cic, formam totius Britanniae auctores oblongae scutulae vel bipenni assimulavere, Tac **II.** *to imitate, counterfeit, pretend*, anum, Ov; with acc and infin, Plaut., with quasi and the subj, Plaut

assisto, astĭti, no sup, 3 *to place oneself, take up a position* **I.** Lit, a, ad fores, Cic; b, *to stand by*, foribus principum, Cic, ad epulas regis, Cic **II.** Transf *to help*, Tac

assŏlĕo, 2 *to be accustomed*; used only in the third person sing and plur, deinde quae assolent (scribi), Cic, ut assolet, *as is usual*, Cic

assŏno, 1 *to answer with a sound*, plangentibus assonat echo, Ov

assuēfăcĭo -fēci -factum, 3 (*assueo and facio), *to accustom to*, ad supplicia patrum plebem, Liv, with abl, quorum sermone qui assuefacti erant, Cic, with dat, pedites operi aliisque justis militaribus, Liv., with infin., equos eodem remanere vestigio, Caes

assuesco suēvi suetum, 3 (*assueo). **I.** Transit, *to accustom*, qui pluribus assuerit mentem, Hor **II.** Intransit, *to accustom oneself*, assuevi, *I am wont*, Cic, assuetus, *accustomed*, with in and the acc, in omnia familiaria jura assuetus, Liv, with abl, homines labore assiduo et quotidiano assueti, Cic, with dat, quaestui Liv, with acc., ne tanta animis assuescite bella, Verg, with infin, assueti vinci, Liv (syncop perf forms assuesti, assuerim, assueram, assuesse).

assuētūdo -inis, f 1, *custom, use*, Liv, 2, *carnal intercourse*, Tac

assuētus -a -um, adj (from assuesco), 1, *used to, accustomed to*, assueta oculis regio, Liv, 2, *usual*, assueti collis cultores, Liv

assūgo -suctum, 3 *to suck*, Lucr

assŭla ae, f *a shaving, chip*, Plaut

assŭlātim, adv (assula), *in shivers* or *splinters*, Plaut

assŭlōsē, adv. (assula), *splinter-wise*, Plin

assulto, 1 (Intens of assilio), *to leap violently upon* **I.** Gen, feminae assultabant ut sacrificantes aut insanientes Bacchae, Tac. **II.** Esp, *to attack, assault*, tergis pugnantium, Tac; latera et frontem (agminis), Tac

assultus -ū, m. (assilio), *a leaping upon, assault*, Verg

assum (adsum), affŭi (ad fŭi), adesse, *to be present, to be at.* **I.** Gen, **A.** Of persons, 1, of bodily presence, heri quum non adessetis, Cic, omnes qui aderant, Caes, mane ad portam adesse, Cic, in foro, Liv, ante oculos, Verg; portis (dat), Verg, huc ades, *come here*, Verg, 2, of the mind, in the phrase adesse animo *or* animis, *to attend*, adestote omnes animis, Cic, also, *to be of good courage*, ades animo et omitte timorem, Cic **B.** Of things, *to be near, at hand*, frumentum conferri, comportari, adesse, Caes; tanti aderant morbi, Cic, adesse Romanis ultimum diem, Liv. **II.** *to be present with a fixed object, to be in one's place* **A.** 1, of men, primum me ipsum vigilare, adesse, Cic, adversus hostes, Sall, jam omnes feroces aderant, Sall.; num ades ad parendum vel ad imperandum potius, Cic; 2, of deities, adsis placidusque juves, Verg.;

rebus Romanis, *to be favourable to*, Liv., si fortuna coeptis affuerit, Tac **B** Esp, **1**, *to be present to witness*, or *to share in*, ad sultingam, Cic, with dat, comitiis, Cic, pugnae, Liv, adesse scribendo senatus consulto or decreto, *to witness*, Cic, **2**, *to be present to help* or *defend*, semper absenti Deiotaro, Cic, alicujus rebus, Cic, alicui adesse in consilio, *to be an assessor to*, Cic, *to support* or *defend in the law courts*, adesse Quinctio, Cic; contra Satrium, Cic, **3**, *to be present in a court of justice*, **a**, *as the accused*, adesse juberi, Cic, or **b**, *as the accuser*, adesse in judicio, Cic

assūmo -sumpsi -sumptum, 3 *to take to oneself* **A.** Lit novas humeris alas, Ov, pluma sibi assumunt quam de se corpora mittunt, Lucr **B** Transf, **1**, *to take for one's assistance*, **a**, of persons, legiones in Italia, Cic, aliquem in nomen societatem armorum, Liv, aliquem in nomen familiamque, Tac, **b**, of things, aliquantum noctis, Cic, assumpta verba, *words borrowed from another source*, Cic; auxilia extrinsecus, Cic, **2**, *to appropriate to oneself, to take*, **a**, regni insignia, Tac, Cereris sacra de Graecia, Cic, **b**, *to claim*, in eo sibi praecipuam laudem assumere, Liv, **3**, *to take in addition to*, **a**, si quis in aliqua arte excellens aliam quoque artem sibi assumpserit, Cic, **b**, logical t t *to state the minor premises of a syllogism*, Cic

assumptĭo -ōnis, f (assumo), **1**, *choice, adoption*, Cic, **2**, *the minor premises of a syllogism*, Cic

assumptīvus a um (assumo), *which derives a defence from an extraneous cause*, causa, Cic

assŭo, 3 *to sew on*, unus et alter assuitur pannus, Hor

assurgo -surrexi surrectum, 3 *to rise up, stand up* **I** Of persons, **A.** Gen, assurgentem regem umbone resupinat, Liv, quae dum recitatur, vos quaeso, qui eam detulistis, assurgite, Cic, assurgere alicui, *to rise up in the presence of*, as a sign of respect, Cic, pass, haec ipsa sunt honorabilia, salutari, appeti, decedi, assurgi, Cic, (himissima vina, Tmolius assurgit quibus et rex ipse Phanaeus, *yields the preference*, Verg **B** Esp, **a**, *to rise from a sick bed*, ne assurrexisse quidem ex morbo, Liv, **b**, *to rise to give more force to a blow*, quantus in clipeum assurgat, Verg, **c**, *to rise into the air*, assurgere in auras, Verg, **d**, querelis haud justis assurgis, *break out into*, Verg **II.** Of things, *to rise* **A.** colles assurgunt, Liv **B** *to appear, show itself*, non coeptae assurgent turres, Verg

assus a um (from areo, as cassus from careo), *dried* **I** Lit, **a**, *roasted*, Plaut, assum vitulinum, *roast veal*, Cic, **b**, of bathing, sol, *basking in the sun* without being anointed, Cic, balnearia assa, *a sweating bath*, Cic. **II.** Transf, nutrix, *a dry-nurse*, Juv

Assȳrĭa -ae, f (Ἀσσυρία), *a country in Asia between Media, Mesopotamia, and Babylon* Adj, **Assȳrĭus** -a -um, *Assyrian*, poet, for *Median, Phrygian, Phoenician, Indian*, &c, **Assȳrĭi** -orum, m *the Assyrians*

ast = at, q v

Asta -ae, f (Ἄστα), *a town in Hispania Baetica*, now *Mesa de Asta*, hence adj, **Astensis** -e, *of or belonging to Asta*.

Astăcus -i, m *father of Melanippus*, hence, **Astăcĭdēs** -ae, m *the son of Astacus*

Astăpa -ae, f *town in Hispania Baetica*, now *Estepa*.

Astĕrĭa -ae, f, and -ĭē ēs, f (Ἀστερίη) **I.** *daughter of Coeus and Phoebe, changed into an island, first called Asteria, afterwards Ortygia, and later still Delos.* **II.** (Asterie), *a woman's name*, Hor

asterno, 3 *to scatter upon*, pass *to be stretched out*, asternuntur sepulchro, Ov

astĭpŭlātĭo -ōnis, f, **1**, *the assenting to, confirmation of*, Plin

astĭpŭlātor -ōris m **A.** Legal t t, at Rome, *one who joined another* (the stipulator) *in the Roman contract called* stipulatio **B.** Transf, *a supporter*, Stoici et eorum astipulator Antiochus, Cic

astĭpŭlor, 1, dep *to assent to*, Liv

astĭtŭo -ŭi ŭtum, m (ad and statuo), 3 *to put*, or *place somewhere*, Plaut

asto stiti, no sup, 1 **I.** *to stand by* **A** Gen alicui, Plaut, astante et inspectante ipso, Caes, astat in conspectu meo, Cic **B.** *to stand by the side to help, to assist*, Plaut **II.** *to stand upright*, Verg

Astraea ae f (Ἀστραία), *Astraea, goddess of justice who left the earth in the iron age, and was placed among the stars under the name Virgo*

astrĕpo (ad-strepo), -strĕpŭi -strĕpĭtum, 3, **1**, *to make a noise at*, astrepebat vulgus, Tac, **2**, *to applaud*, haec dicenti, Tac

astrictē, adv (astrictus), of discourse, *concisely, briefly*, Cic

astrictus -a -um, p adj with compar (from astringo), *tight, compressed, drawn together* **A** Lit, limen, *shut*, Ov, non astrictus soccus, *negligent, slatternly writing*, Hor, frons, *wrinkled*, Mart, aquae, *frozen*, Ov **B** Transf, **1**, *close-fisted, avaricious*, pater, Prop, mos, Tac, **2**, of oratory, **a**, *bound by the limits of rhythm*, numero et astricto et soluto, Cic, **b**, *concise*; contracta et astricta eloquentia, Cic

astrĭfer -fĕra -fĕrum (astrum and fero), *starry, placed among the stars*, Mart

astringo -strinxi -strictum, 3 **I** Lit *to tighten, draw together, compress, contract, bind together*, **a**, quae (vinculum) astringit Cic, aliquem ad statuam, Cic, **b**, of cold, *to contract*, Ov **II.** Transf, **a**, *to draw tight*, pater nimis indulgens quidquid ego astrinxi relaxat, Cic, **b**, of writing or speech, *to compress*, breviter argumenta Cic, **c**, *to bind, fetter, oblige*, vel armis vel legibus totum Galliam sempiternis vinculis, Cic, se videre astringere or astringi, *to commit oneself to, become guilty of*, Cic

astrŏlŏgĭa ae, f (ἀστρολογία), *astronomy*, Cic

astrŏlŏgus i, m (ἀστρολόγος), **1**, *an astronomer*, Cic, **2**, *an astrologer*, Cic

astrum -i, n (ἄστρον), *a star, a constellation* **A.** Lit, cognitio astrorum, Cic, astrum natale, Hor, poet, of a great height, turris educta ad astra, Verg **B.** Transf, tollere in astra, *to exalt sky high*, Cic, ex astris decidere, *from the highest glory*, Cic, sic itur ad astra, *thus is immortality gained*, Verg

astrŭo (ad and struo), -struxi -structum, 3. **I** Gen *to build to* or *near, to build in addition*, gradus, Liv **II** Transf, *to add to*, formae animum, Ov

astu (asty), only acc and abl astū, n (ἄστυ), *the city* (only used of Athens), Cic

astŭpĕo, 2 *to be astonished at*, Ov

Astŭra -ae, f (Ἄστυρα), *a river in Latium*, still called *Astura*

asturco -ōnis, m *an Asturian horse*, Plin

Astŭres um, m (Ἄστυρες), *the Asturians, a people in Spain*, sing **Astŭr** -ŭris, m, hence, **a**, **Astŭrĭa** -ae, f *the country of the Astures*, **b**, **Astŭrĭcus** -a -um, *Asturian*

astus ūs, m *cleverness, adroitness, cunning*, Verg, Liv

astūtē, adv, with compar and superl (astutus), *cunningly, astutely*, Cic

astūtĭa -ae, f. *adroitness, astuteness, craft*, Cic.

astūtus -a -um (astus), *adroit, clever, astute, cunning, crafty*, Cic.

Astȳăges -is, m. (Ἀστυάγης). **I.** *King of Media, grandfather of the elder Cyrus.* **II.** *a companion of Phineus.*

Astȳănax -actis, m. (Ἀστυάναξ). **I.** *son of Hector and Andromache.* **II.** *a tragic actor of Cicero's time.*

Astȳpălaea -ae, f. (Ἀστυπάλαια), *island near Crete.* Adj., 1, **Astȳpălaeensis** -e; 2, **Astȳpălēĭus** -a -um, *belonging to Astypalaea.*

ăsȳlum -i, n. (ἄσυλον), *a sanctuary, place of refuge, asylum*, Cic.; templa quae asyla Graeci appellant, Liv.

ăsymbŏlus -a -um (ἀσύμβολος), *one who contributes nothing to the cost of an entertainment*, Ter.

at (ast), conj., *but, moreover.* **I.** To introduce an idea different from, but not entirely opposed to, one that has gone before. **A.** una (navis) cum Nasidianis profugit, at ex reliquis una praemissa Massiliam, Cic. **B.** 1, in prayers, exhortations, etc., at videte hominis intolerabilem audaciam, Cic.; 2, in expressions of astonishment or impatience, at per deos immortales quid est quod dici possit, Cic. **II.** To express an idea entirely opposed to the preceding one. **A.** non cognoscebantur foris, at domi, Cic.; strengthened, at contra, Cic.; at etiam, Cic.; at vero, Cic. **B.** 1, to introduce an imaginary objection in an argument, factumne sit? at constat, Cic.; 2, *but at least, yet at least*; non est, inquit, in parietibus respublica, at in aris et focis, Cic.

ătābŭlus -i, m. *a hot wind in Apulia, the sirocco*, Hor.

Ătălanta -ae and -ē -ēs, f. (Ἀταλάντη), *a maiden of Boeotia* or *Arcadia, famous for her speed in running; she refused to marry any one except the person who could beat her in a race; finally conquered by Milanion by the aid of Aphrodite.* Adj., **Ătălantaeus** -a, m. *of or belonging to Atalanta.*

ătăt, attat, attatae, attattatae, etc. (ἀτταταί), an interjection expressive of pain, astonishment, fear, warning, etc., *oh! ah! alas!* Plaut., Ter.

ătăvus -i, m. **I.** *the father of the abavus or great-great-grandfather*, Cic. **II.** atavi, plur. = *ancestors*, Maecenas atavis edite regibus, Hor.

Ātella -ae, f. *a very ancient city of Campania.* Adj., a, **Ātellānus** -a, -um; fabella, or gen. simply **Ātellāna** -ae, f. *a species of popular farce, long popular in Rome*, Liv., Juv.; hence, a, **Ātellānus** -i, m. *a player in these dramas*; b, **Ātellānius** -a -um; **Ātellānĭcus** -a -um.

āter, atra, atrum, *black, dark* (*dead black*, while *niger* is *shining black*). **I.** Lit., nemus, Verg.; mare, *stormy*, Hor.; alba discernere et atra non posse, Cic.; poet. = atratus, *clothed in black*; lictores, Hor. **II.** Transf. **A.** *black*, as a sign of mourning, calamity, etc.; *dark, gloomy, sad, unfortunate*, mors, cura, Hor.; atri dies, *in the Roman calendar, those on which the republic had suffered a great misfortune*, Liv. **B.** *malicious, poisonous*; atro dente petere aliquem, Hor.

Ăthămānes -um, m. (Ἀθαμᾶνες), *the Athamanes, inhabitants of Athamania*; hence **Ăthămānĭa** -ae, f. *a country in the south of Epirus.*

Ăthămas -antis, m. (Ἀθάμας), *son of Aeolus and king of Thessaly, father of Phrixus and Helle, Melicerta and Learchus*; hence, a, **Ăthămantēus** -a -um, aurum, *the golden fleece*, Mart.; b, **Ăthămantĭădes** -ae, m. Palaemon, Ov.; c, **Ăthămantis** -idis, f. *Helle*, Ov.

Ăthēnae -ārum, f. (Ἀθῆναι), *Athens*; meton., *learning*, Juv.; hence, a, **Ăthēnaeus** -a -um; b, **Ăthēnĭensis** -e, *Athenian.* Subst., **Ăthēnĭenses** -ium, m. *the Athenians.*

Ăthēnĭo -ōnis, m. *a Sicilian shepherd, leader of the slaves in the 2nd Slave War* (102 B.C.).

ăthĕos and **ăthĕus** -i, m. (ἄθεος), *an atheist*, Cic.

Athĕsis, acc. -sim, abl. -si, m. (Ἄθεσις), *a river in Rhaetia*, now *Adige, Etsch.*

athlēta -ae, m. (ἀθλητής), *one who contends in the public games, wrestler, athlete*, Cic.

athlētĭcus -a -um (ἀθλητικός), *relating to an athlete.*

Ăthōs, dat. -o, acc. -o, and -on, abl. -o (Ἄθως), and **Ătho** or **Ăthōn** -ōnis, m. *a rocky mountain at the end of the peninsula of Chalcidice.*

Ătīlĭus -a -um, *name of a Roman gens*; 1, M. Atilius Regulus (see Regulus): 2, M. Atilius, *an early Roman poet.* Adj., **Ătīlĭānus** -a -um.

Ātīna -ae, f. *a town in Latium*, still called *Atina*; hence **Ātīnas** -ātis, *belonging to Atina.*

Atlās -antis, m. (Ἄτλας), 1, *a high mountain in Africa, on which the sky was supposed to rest*; 2, *a mythical king and giant, son of Iapetus and Clymene, king of Mauretania, changed into a mountain by Perseus*; hence, a, **Atlantis** -idis, f. *a female descendant of Atlas, Electra*, Ov.; *Calypso*, Tib.; plur., Atlantides, *the Pleiades and Hyades*; b, **Atlantĭcus** -a -um, mare, *the Atlantic ocean*; c, **Atlantēus** -a -um, finis, *Libyan*, Hor.; d, **Atlantĭădes** -ae, m. *a descendant of Atlas, Mercury* (*son of Maia, daughter of Atlas*); or *Hermaphroditus* (*son of Mercury and great-grandson of Atlas*).

ătŏmus -i, f. (ἄτομος), *that which is incapable of division, an atom*, Cic.

atque, or **ac** (ac only before consonants), *and, and also.* **A.** Joining single words; 1, Gen., spargere ac disseminare, Cic.; a, *and also*; nobiles atque ignobiles, Sall.; b, *and moreover, and even*; alii intra moenia atque in sinu urbis sunt hostes, Sall.; with the pron., hic, is, idem, etc., negotium magnum est navigare atque id mense Quintili, *and especially*, Cic.; so atque etiam, Cic.; 2, with comparisons; a, with words expressing comparison, as aeque, aequus, idem, item, juxta, par, proxime, similis, similiter, talis, totidem; or expressing dissimilarity, as aliter, aliorsum, alius, contra, contrarius, dissimilis, secus; b, with comparatives, for quam, artius atque hedera procera astringitur ilex, Hor.; c, simul atque, *as soon as*, Cic.; 3, with negatives, *and not rather* (also with potius); si hoc dissuadere est, ac non disturbare atque pervertere, Cic. **B.** Joining sentences, *and so*; 1, atque illi omnes sine dubitatione condemnant, Cic.; 2, to join a more important thought, *and especially*; id estne numerandum in bonis? Ac maximis quidem, Cic.; 3, to introduce an adversative clause, ac tamen, Cic.; 4, to introduce an objection raised by the speaker or writer himself, ac ne sine causa videretur edixisse, Cic.; 5, in narration, *and so*; atque iis, quos nominavi, Cic.; 6, at the end of a speech or treatise, ac de primo quidem officii fonte diximus, Cic. **C.** Particular connections and phrases; 1, alius atque alius, *now this, now that*, Liv.; 2, atque utinam, to express a wish, Cic.; 3, to make an assertion general, atque omnia, or omnes, atque haec omnia verbo continentur, Cic.; 4, with other conjunctions, after et, non minis et vi ac metu, Cic.; after que (Gr. τε . . . καί), submoverique atque in castra redigi, Liv.; with nec, Mart.; repeated in poetry, atque deos atque astra, Verg.

atqui, conj (at and qui = quoi = quo), *nevertheless, notwithstanding* **I.** Gen, atqui non ego te frangere persequor, Hor, *indeed, certainly*, Cic **II.** Esp in logical conclusions, to introduce the minor premise, *but now, now*, Cic

ātrāmentum -i, n (ater), **1**, *any black fluid*, sepiae, Cic, **2**, *ink*, Cic, **3**, *blue vitriol, shoemaker's black*, sutorium atramentum, Cic

ātrātus -a um (ater), *clothed in black, in mourning*, Cic

Atrax -ăcis (Ἄτραξ), **1**, *a river in Aetolia*, **2**, *a city in Thessaly*, hence, a, **Atrăcĭdes** -ae, m *the Thessalian Caeneus*, Ov, **Atrăcis** idis, f *Hippodamia*, Ov

Atrĕbătes -um, m. *a people in Gallia Belgica*, sing, **Atrĕbas** -bătis, m, Caes

Atreus -ĕi, m (Ἀτρεύς), *son of Pelops, king of Argos and Mycenae, father of Agamemnon and Menelaus*, hence, **Atrīdes** -ae, m *Agamemnon* or *Menelaus*, plur, Atridae, *Agamemnon and Menelaus*

ātrĭensis -is, m (atrium), *a head slave, steward*, Cic

ātrĭŏlum -i, n (dim of atrium), *a little atrium*, or *fore court*, Cic

ātrĭtas -ātis, f (ater), *blackness*, Plaut

ātrĭum -ii, n (ater), *the room blackened by smoke, the open court in a Roman house, into which opened the janua*, or *gate*, plur, atria -orum, n = atrium, Verg, meton, *a house*, Ov, *the halls of the gods*, Ov, *the hall of a temple or public building*, atrium Libertatis, Cic, auctionarium, *an auctioneer's sale room*, Cic

ătrōcĭtas -ātis, f (atrox) **A.** *fierceness, harshness, cruelty*, ipsius facti atrocitas aut indignitas, Cic, habet atrocitatis aliquid legatio, *has a threatening aspect*, Cic **B.** Transf *severity, barbarity*, invidiosa atrocitas verborum, Cic, atrocitas ista quo modo in veterem Academiam irruperit, Cic

ătrōcĭtĕr, adv, with compar and superl (atrox), *severely, harshly, cruelly*, Verri nimis atrociter minitans, Cic

Atrŏpŏs i, f (ἄ-τροπος, *not to be averted*), *one of the three Parcae*

ătrox -ōcis (from ater, as ferox from ferus). **I.** Lit, *terrible, fearful, cruel, horrible*; res scelesta, atrox, nefaria, Cic, of war, proelium, Liv, of the seasons, hora flagrantis Caniculae, Hor, of commands, *threatening*, imperium, Liv, atrocissimae litterae, Cic, of speeches, *violent*, vehemens atque atrox orationis genus, Cic **II.** Transf, of persons and character, *gloomy, morose, severe*, Agrippina semper atrox, Tac, animus Catonis, *unbending* Hor

Atta -ae, m *a Roman surname*, C Quintius Atta, *a comic poet* (d 102 B C)

attactus -ūs, m (attingo), *a touching, touch, contact*, Verg

attăgēn ēnis, m (ἀτταγήν), *a woodcock*, Hor

Attălus i, m (Ἄτταλος), *the name of several kings of Pergamos, the last of whom*, Attalus III, *left his territory to the Romans* hence, a, **Attălĭcus** a -um, *belonging to Pergamos*, agri, Cic hence *rich, splendid*, conditiones, Hor, peripetasmata, *woven with threads of gold*, Cic, b, **Attălis** idis, f (Ἀτταλίς), *name of a guild at Athens*

attămĕn, conj *but yet*, Cic

attat = **atat.**

attĕgia -ae, f *a hut*, Juv

attempĕrātē, adv (attemperatus), *in a fit or appropriate manner*, Ter

attempĕro (ad and tempero), 1. *to fit to, adjust to*, Sen.

attendo (ad and tendo) tendi -tentum, 3 *to stretch to*, animum, or absol, attendere, *to direct the attention towards, attend to*, with ad and the acc, attendite animos ad ea quae consequuntur, Cic, with acc, primum versum legis, Cic, with acc and infin, non attendere superius illud ea re a se esse concessum Cic, with rel sent, si paulo diligentius, quid de his rebus dicat attenderis, Cic, with de and the abl, animus tamen erit sollicitus, ut nihil possit de oneris legationis attendere, Cic

attentē, adv, with compar and superl (attentus), *attentively, carefully*, audire, Cic, cogitare, Cic

attentĭo -ōnis, f (attendo), *attentiveness, attention*, animi, Cic

attento (ad tento), or **attempto** (ad-tempto), 1 *to strive after, to attempt*, **1**, ut praeterire omnino fuerit satius quam attentatum deseri, Cic, **2**, *to tamper with, try to corrupt*, classem, Cic, **3**, *to attack*, aliquid lingua, Cic, aliquem vi, Tac

attentus (ad tentus) -a um **I.** Partic of attendo and attineo **II.** Adj with compar and superl (attendo), **1**, *attentive*, animus, Cic, cogitatio Cic, auditor, Cic, judex, Cic, **2**, *careful after one's property*, attentus quaesitis, Hor, paterfamilias, Hor, attenta vita et rusticana, Cic

attĕnŭātē, adv (attenuatus), *simply, without ornament*, dicere, Cic

attĕnŭātus -a -um, p adj with superl (from attenuo), *made weak*, of discourse, *abbreviated*, ipsa illa pro Roscio juvenilis abundantia multa habet attenuata, Cic, *over-refined*, ejus oratio nimia religione attenuata, Cic

attĕnŭo (ad-tĕnŭo), 1 *to make thin* **A.** Lit, **1**, corpus, Ov, **2**, of number, *to lessen*, legio proeliis attenuata, Caes, **3**, of strength, *to weaken*, vires diutino morbo attenuatae, Liv; **4**, of the voice, *to make shrill*, Cic **B** Transf, curas, Ov, insignem, *degrade*, Hor

attĕro (ad and tĕro) trivi (tĕrŭi) -tritum, 3. **A.** Lit, **1**, *to rub against*, leniter caudam, Hor **2**, *to rub* or *wear away*, attrita ansa, Verg **B.** Transf, *to weaken, ruin*, opes, Sall, aliquem, Sall

attestor (ad and testor), 1 dep *to attest, bear witness to*, Phaedr

attexo (ad and texo) -texŭi -textum, 3 *to weave or plait on or to* **A.** Lit, loricas ex cratibus, Caes **B.** Transf, *to add*, vos ad id, quod erit immortale, partem attexitote mortalem, Cic

Atthis -ĭdis, f (Ἀτθίς), *Attic, Athenian*, Mart Subst, f **1**, *Attica*, Lucr, **2**, *nightingale* or *swallow*, Mart, **3**, *name of a friend of Sappho*, Ov

Attĭca -ae, f (Ἀττική), *Attica, the most celebrated country of Greece, with Athens for its capital*

Attĭcē, adv (Atticus), *in the Attic or Athenian manner*, dicere, Cic

atticisso, 1 (ἀττικίζω), *to imitate the Athenian mode of speaking*, Plaut.

Attĭcus -a -um (Ἀττικός), **1**, *belonging to Attica or Athens, Attic, Athenian*, virgo, i e, *Canephoros*, Hor, pelex, *Philomela*, Mart Plur **Attĭci** -orum, m *the Athenians*, Cic, **2**, *Attic, Athenian*, with reference to style, art etc, stilus, *simple*, Cic, aures, *delicate*, Cic, hence Attici = *the Athenian orators*, Cic

Attĭcus, T Pomponius, *the intimate friend of Cicero*, who received his surname of Atticus from his long residence in Athens

attĭnĕo -tĭnŭi -tentum, 2 (ad and teneo), **I.** Transit, *to hold near, keep* **A.** Lit, aliquem castris, carcere, publica custodia, Tac. **B.**

Transf, simul Romanum et Numidam spe pacis, *to amuse*, Sall **II.** Intransit, *to pertain to, or concern*, only in 3rd person, cetera quae ad colendam vitem attinebunt, Cic, esp in the expression, quod attinet ad aliquem or aliquid, *in respect to*, qui omnes, quod ad me attinet, vellem viverent, *as far as I am concerned*, Cic, nihil attinet me plura scribere, *it is of no use*, Cic

attingo -tigi -tactum, 3 (ad and tango), *to touch* **A.** Lit, **1,** digito se caelum attigisse putare, Cic, **2,** *to arrive at a place*, Italiam, Cic, arces igneas, Hor, **3,** of places, *to touch upon, border upon*, Cappadociae regio ea quae Ciliciam attingit, Cic, **4,** *to attack*, Sulla quem primum hostes attigerant, Sall, **5,** *to touch*, i e, *to appropriate to oneself*, de praeda mea nec teruncium attigit, Cic, **6,** *to strike*, si digito quem attigisset, poenas dedisset, Cic, **7,** *to embrace*, Ov **B.** Transf, **1,** *to touch*, of sensations, voluptas aut dolor aliquem attingit, Cic, **2,** *to have to do with, to touch, to reach to*, corporis similitudo attingit naturam animi, Cic, attingere aliquem necessitudine, *to be closely connected with*, Cic, **3, a,** *to handle, manage, devote oneself to*, rempublicam, Cic, Graecas literas, Cic, rem militarem, Caes, **b,** *to glance at cursorily*, librum strictim, Cic, **4,** in writing or speech, *to mention;* illam injuriam non attingere, Cic

Attis (Atthis and **Atys)** -idis, m *a Phrygian shepherd, beloved by Cybele*

Attĭus -a -um, *name of a Roman gens, the most famous member of which was P Attius Varus, a praetor in Africa at the time of the war between Caesar and Pompeius, a supporter of the latter*, hence adj, **Attiānus** -a -um, *Attian*

attollo, no perf or sup, 3 *to raise up, lift up* **I.** Lit **A.** vix prae lacrimis oculos, Liv, minas, iras (of a snake raising its head in anger), Verg, se attollere, or middle, attolli, *to raise oneself*, Verg **B.** *to erect, raise*, molem, Verg, terra se attollere tandem visa, *to rise, appear*, Verg **II.** Transf, *to raise, elevate*, **a,** vocem, Quint., **b,** *to elevate, excite, distinguish*, animos ad spem consulatus, Liv, rempublicam bello armisque, Tac

attondĕo -tondi -tonsum, 2 **I.** Lit *to shear, shave, cut*, vitem, Verg **II.** Transf, *to make less, diminish*, Cic, poet

attŏnĭtus -a -um, p adj (from attono), *struck by thunder*, hence, **1,** *stunned, terrified, senseless*, magna pars integris corporibus attoniti concidunt, Liv., **2,** *inspired*, vates, Hor, attonitae Baccho matres, Verg

attŏno -tŏnŭi -tŏnĭtum, 1 *to strike with thunder, stun, make senseless*, Ov

attorquĕo, 2 *to whirl, swing upward*, Verg

attrăctĭo -ōnis, f (attraho), *a drawing to oneself*, hence, litterarum, *assimilation*, Varr

attrăho -traxi -tractum, 3 *to draw to, attract* **I.** Lit **A.** Of things, magnes lapis, qui ferrum ad se alliciat et attrahat, Cic **B.** Of persons, *to drag*, tribunos attrahi ad se jussit, Liv **II.** Transf, **1,** *to attract*, nihil esse quod ad se rem ullam tam alliciat et tam attrahat quam ad amicitiam similitudo, Cic, **2,** *to take with one*, aliquem Romam, Cic

attrectātus -ū, m (attrecto), *a handling, touching*, ap. Cic

attrecto, 1 (ad and tracto), *to touch, handle* **I.** Gen, blanditia popularis aspicitur, non attrectatur, Cic **II. A.** *to touch unlawfully, in an improper manner*, libros (Sibyllinos) contaminatis manibus attrectare, Cic **B.** *to lay hands on, to appropriate*, gazas, Liv.

attrĕpĭdo, 1 *to stumble along*, Plaut

attrĭbŭo -ŭi -ūtum, 3 *to allot to, assign to.* **A.** Lit **1,** servos, pastores armat atque iis equos attribuit, Caes, **2,** of money, *to assign, lend;* si modo attribuetur, quantum debetur, Cic, so of money paid from the public treasury, pecunia attributa, numerata est, Cic, **3,** *to assign* (to some one to keep or do something), attribuit nos trucidandos Cethego, Cic, esp of a military command, oppidum civibus Romanis, Caes, **4,** of a country, *to annex, subject*, insulae, quae erant a Sulla Rhodiis attributae, Cic **B.** Transf, **1,** *to add, give, cause*, summus timor quem mihi natura pudorque meus attribuit, Cic, **2,** gramm t t *to add as an attribute*, Cic, **3,** *to ascribe, impute*, bonos exitus diis immortalibus, Cic

attrĭbūtĭo -ōnis, f (attribuo), **1,** *the assignment of a debt*, Cic, **2,** rhet t t, *an accessory or attribute*, Cic

attrĭbūtum, -i, n (attribuo), *the predicate*, Cic

attrītus -a -um, p adj, with compar (from attero) **A.** *rubbed away, worn out*, Cic **B.** Transf, frons, *shameless*, Juv.

Attus Navĭus, *a celebrated augur of the time of Tarquinius Priscus*

Ătys (Attys) -yos, abl -ye, m (Ἄτυς, Ἄττυς) **I.** *a son of Hercules and Omphale, father of Tyrrhenus and Lydus, myth ancestor of the Lydian kings* **II.** *the founder of the gens Atia*

au, interj, *oh! ha!* Plaut

auceps -cŭpis, m (for aviceps, from avis and capio) **I.** Lit, *a fowler, bird-catcher*, Plaut., Hor **II.** Transf, peritissimum voluptatum aucupem sapientem esse, Cic; syllabarum, *a quibbling critic, caviller*, Cic

auctārĭum -i, n (augeo), *an increase* Plaut

auctĭo -ōnis, f (augeo), **1,** *an auction;* auctionem facere, constituere, *to appoint an auction*, Cic; praedicare, proscribere, Cic., proponere, *to announce publicly*, Quint, proferre, *to put off*, Cic, **2,** *that which is sold by auction*, auctionem vendere, Cic

auctĭōnārĭus -a um (auctio), *relating to an auction*, atrium, *auction-room*, Cic

auctĭōnor, 1 (auctio) *to hold an auction*, Cic

auctĭto, 1 (freq of augeo), *to increase very much*, Tac

aucto, 1 = auctito, Plaut, Lucr

auctŏr -ōris, m (augeo) **A.** *originator, causer, doer*, incendii, Cic; vulneris, Verg, esp, **1,** *the producer of a work of art, artist*, templi, *architect*, Liv, **2,** *the founder of a family, ancestor*, praeclarus auctor nobilitatis tuae, Cic, **3,** *writer, author*, carminis, Hor **B.** *the originator of a proposal or undertaking, leader, beginner*, nec auctor quamvis audaci facinori deerat, Liv, me auctore, *at my request*, Cic, auctor interficiendi alicuius, Cic with dat, ille legibus Caecilii Metelli contra auspicia ferendis auctor, Cic, with ad and the acc, ad instituendam (rem), Cic, with in and the abl, in restituendo auctorem fuisse, Cic, alicui auctorem esse *to advise, recommend*, semper senatui auctor pacis fui, Cic, foll by ut or ne with the subj, Cic **C.** *the author of a piece of information, warrant for its truth*, **a,** certis auctoribus comperisse, Cic., **b,** *an authority*, malus auctor Latinitatis, Cic, Cratippo auctore, *on the authority of Cratippus*, Cic; non sordidus auctor naturae verique, *investigator*, Hor, **c,** *an author of note*, Homerus optimus auctor, Cic, auctor rerum Romanarum, *historian*, Cic, hence, auctorem esse, *to answer for, state positively*, nec pauci sunt auctores Cn Flavium scribam libros protulisse, Cic. **D.** Esp, **1,** auctor legis or senatus consulti, *proposer*, Liv ; 2, *supporter of a law*, multarum legum aut auctor aut dissuasor, Cic , 3, auctores fiunt patres, *the senators sanction a law*, Cic 4, *defender, protector*, praeclarus iste auctor suae civitatis, Cic., 5, *the guarantee of a right to an estate*, a malo auctore emere, Cic , 6, of a guardian, etc , *approver, sanctioner*, quod mulier sine tutore auctore promiserit, *without the approval of her guardian*, Cic

auctōrāmentum -i, n (auctoro), *the pay or hire for the performance of any duty*, Cic

auctōrĭtas -ātis, f (auctor) *continuance, a causing to continue* **I. A.** *validity*, 1, in the case of property, usus et auctoritas, or simply auctoritas, *valid right to property arising from prescription*, usus et auctoritas fundi, Cic , 2, in case of an assertion, *attestation, security, authority*, publicarum tabularum, Cic , 3, *example*, majorum, Cic , alicuius auctoritatem sequi, Cic **B.** *the origination of a proposal or proceeding, support, aid*, cuius auctoritas multum apud me valet, Cic. **C.** *the expression of approval or assent, resolve*, 1, hominum consilia et auctoritates, Cic , 2, of the will of the people, populi Romani, Cic , 3, of public bodies or magistrates, collegii, Liv , 4, of the senate, a, *a measure to which the senate has assented, the approval of the senate*, auctoritatem senatus, jussa populi Romani vendere, Cic , b, *a resolution of the senate*, prevented from being made a decree by the veto of the tribunes, si quis huic senatus consulto intercessisset, auctoritas perscriberetur, Cic **D** *authorisation, full power*, legatos cum auctoritate mittere, Cic , hence, *power, might, command*, manere in alicuius auctoritate, Liv **II.** *influence, authority*, 1, of a person, a, lit , auctoritatem habere apud aliquem, Cic , auctoritatem restituere, levare, amittere, Cic , b, meton , *a person in authority, an influential person*, Cic , 2, of things, legum, Cic , orationis, Cic

auctōro, 1 (auctor) **I.** *to hire for money*, refl auctorare se, or pass *to hire, engage oneself*, Hor **II** Transf *to bind oneself*, eo pignore velut auctoratum sibi proditorem ratus est, Liv.

auctumnālis -e (auctumnus), *autumnal*, Liv

1 **auctumnus** -i m (augeo), *autumn*, Cic ; meton , septem auctumni = *seven years*, Ov

2 **auctumnus** -a um (1 auctumnus), *autumnal*, frigus, Ov

1 **auctus** -a -um, p adj (from augeo), only used in compar , *increased, enlarged, enriched*, majestas auctior, Liv , socii honore auctiores, Caes

2 **auctus** -ūs, m (augeo), *an increase, enlargement, growth*, corporis, Lucr , fluminum, Tac , imperii, Tac , maximis auctibus crescere, Liv

aucŭpātĭo -ōnis, f (aucupor), *fowling, bird-catching*, Quint

aucŭpātōrĭus -a -um (aucupor), *relating to fowling*, Plin.

aucŭpĭum -i, n (auceps), *bird-catching, fowling* **I. A.** Lit , vitam propagare aucupio, Cic **B.** Meton , *the birds caught*, Cat **II** Transf *hunting after anything*, delectationis, *after pleasure*, Cic ; aucupia verborum, *cavilling, quibbling*, Cic.

aucŭpor, 1 dep (auceps) **I.** Lit *to catch birds*, Varr **II.** Transf *to chase, strive for, lie in wait for*, verba, Cic , errores hominum, Cic., inanem rumorem, Cic , tempestates, *to wait for finer weather*, Cic

audācĭa -ae, f (audax), 1, *courage, boldness, daring*, audacia in bello, Sall , 2, *audacity, impudence, temerity*, audacia et impudentia fretus, Cic , alicuius audaciam debilitare, Cic ; frangere, Liv , contundere et frangere, Cic , plur audaciae, *audacious deeds*, Cic

audācĭtĕr, and **audactĕr**, adv , with compar and superl (audax), *boldly* (in a good or bad sense), *audaciously, rashly, impudently*, Cic

audax -ācis, adj , with compar and superl (audeo), *daring* (in a good or bad sense), *bold, courageous, audacious, rash, foolhardy*, a, of persons, Verres homo audacissimus atque amentissimus, Cic , paulo ad facinus audacior, Cic , audax in convocandis hominibus et armandis, Cic , b, of things, consilium prima specie temerarium magis quam audax, Liv

audens -entis, p adj , with compar and superl (from audeo), *daring, bold*, Verg

audentĕr, adv (audens), *boldly*, Tac

audentĭa -ae, f (audens), *boldness, courage*, Cic

audĕo, ausus sum, 2 (connected with avidus), *to dare, venture*, audeo dicere, *I venture to assert*, Cic , with acc , tantum facinus, Liv , proelium, aciem, Tac , with in and the abl , ausurum se in tribunis, quod princeps familiae suae ausus in regibus esset, Liv , with pro and the abl , pro vita majora audere probavi, Verg , absol , quod sperant, quod audent, omne Caesari acceptum referre possunt, Cic , adversus Neronem ausus, Tac , audere in proelia, Verg

audĭens -entis **I.** Partic of audio (q v) **II.** Subst *a hearer*, Cic.

audĭentĭa -ae, f (audio), *hearing, listening, attention*, alicui audientiam facere, *to get a hearing for any one by commanding silence*, Cic , Liv

audĭo, 4 (connected with auris), *to hear* **I.** *to have the power of hearing*, audiendi sensu carere, Cic **II.** *to hear something* **A.** clamorem, Caes , galli cantum, Cic , with double acc , te, ut spero, propediem censorem audiemus, Cic , with acc and infin , saepe hoc majores natu dicere audivi, Cic , with acc and partic , idque Socratem audio dicentem, Cic , with relative clause, audire cupio quid non probes, Cic , with de and the abl , multa falsa de me audierunt, Cic , the person from whom a thing is heard is put in the abl with ab or de, Cic Perf partic , as subst , **audītum** -i, n *hearsay*, nihil habeo praeter auditum, Cic. **B** *to listen to*, a, aliquem libenter studioseque, Cic , of judges, *to hear a case*, audire de ambitu, Cic , of pupils, *to listen to a master, to attend the classes or lectures of a professor*, annum jam audire Cratippum, Cic , b, *to listen to requests*, preces, Cic , c, of stories or persons, *to listen to*, i e , *to give credence to*, si fabulas audire volumus, Cic , audio, *I believe it*, Cic , d, *to obey, to follow*, aliquem amicissime monentem, Cic , dicto audientem esse, with dat , *to obey*, non fore dicto audientes milites, Caes **C.** *to be called* (like Gr ἀκουω), Matutine pater, seu Jane libentius audis, Hor , bene audire, *to be well spoken of*, a propinquis, Cic

audītĭo -ōnis, f 1, (audio), *hearing, listening*, aliquid multa lectione atque auditione assequi, Cic , 2, *hearsay report*, levem auditionem habere pro re comperta, Cic , plur., fictae auditiones, Cic

audītŏr -ōris, m (audio), *a hearer, auditor, scholar*, alicui auditorem venire, Cic

audītōrĭum -i, n (audio) *a place of audience, lecture room, court of justice, etc* , Tac , *a school*, Quint , *circle of listeners*, Plin

audītus -ūs, m (audio) **I.** Gen , *hearing, the sense of hearing*, Cic **II.** Esp , *listening*, Tac

aufero, auferre, abstŭli, ablātum, 3 (ab and fero) **I.** *to carry away, carry off remove* **A.**

Lit., inter manus e convicio tamquam e proelio auferri, Cic.; se e conspectu alicuius, Cic.; auferor in scopulos, Ov. **B.** Transf., *to draw away from one's aim, seduce;* ne te auferant aliorum consilia, Cic. **II.** *to take away with, bear off;* sometimes in good, but oftener in bad sense, *to rob, steal.* **A.** Lit., **a,** of persons; multa palam domum, Cic.; auriculam mordicus, *to bite off,* Cic.; **b,** of things; hi ludi XV. dies auferent, Cic.; mors Achillem abstulit, Hor. **B.** Transf., **1,** illa autem, quae contrariis commotionibus auferenda sunt, Cic.; **2,** *to carry off,* i.e. *to gain, obtain;* tantum abstulit quantum petiit, Cic.; responsum ab aliquo, Cic.; **3,** *to lay aside, cease from;* aufer abhinc lacrimas, Lucr.

Aufidēna -ae, f. *a town in Samnium,* now *Alfidena.*

Aufĭdĭus -a -um, *name of a Roman gens.*

Aufĭdus -i, m. *a river in Apulia,* now *Ofanto.*

aufŭgĭo -fūgi, 3. (ab and fugio), *to flee away,* Cic.

Augē -ēs, f. (Αὔγη), *daughter of Aleus and Neaera, mother of Telephus by Hercules.*

Augēas and **Augīas** -ae, m. (Αὐγείας), *king of the Epeans in Elis,* the cleansing of whose stable, which had not been cleansed for thirty years, was one of the labours of Hercules.

augĕo, auxi, auctum, 2. (connected with αὐξάνω), *to make to increase.* **I.** *to cause to grow, to fertilise;* aer humorem colligens terram auget imbribus, *makes fertile,* Cic. **II.** In a wide sense, *to make larger;* **a,** *to strengthen,* has munitiones, Caes.; **b,** of rivers, *to cause to rise,* gen. in pass., augeri = *to be swollen;* amnis nimbis hiemalibus auctus, Ov.; **c,** of number or quantity, *to increase;* numerum legatorum, Cic.; **d,** of degree, vitium ventris et gutturis, Cic.; populi Romani imperium, Cic.; **e,** of moral or intellectual qualities or feelings, benevolentiam, Cic.; luctum, Cic.; **f,** in speech, *to extol, set forth;* hostium vim et copias et felicitatem, Cic.; **g,** *to enrich, to honour;* cives suos copia rerum, Cic.; augeri cognomento Augustae, Tac.

augesco, auxi, 3. (inch. of augeo), *to begin to grow, to increase;* **a,** quae (uva) et suco terrae et calore solis augescens primo est peracerba gustu, Cic.; **b,** politically, *to increase in strength;* quum hostium res tantis augescere rebus cerneret, Liv.

augmĕn -ĭnis, n. (augeo), *an increase, growth,* Lucr.

augur -ŭris, c. *an augur, soothsayer, seer,* Cic.; aquae augur annosa cornix, *prophetess of rain,* Hor.

augŭrālis -e (augur), *relating to an augur or augury;* coena, Cic. Subst., **augŭrāle** -is, n. *the part of the Roman camp where the auguries were taken,* Tac.

augŭrātĭo -ōnis, f. (auguro), *divining, soothsaying,* Cic.

augŭrātus -ūs, m. (auguro), *the office of an augur,* Cic.

augŭrĭum -i, n. (augur), *the observation and interpretation of omens, augury.* **I. A.** Lit., augurium capere, Liv.; salutis, *an augury in time of peace* (to inquire if it were permitted to pray to the gods de salute reipublicae), Cic. **B.** Transf., **a,** *any kind of prophecy;* o mea frustra semper verissima auguria rerum futurarum, Cic.; **b,** *presentiment;* inhaeret in mentibus quasi saeculorum quoddam augurium futurorum, Cic. **II.** Meton., **A.** Subject., *the science of augury;* Apollo augurium citharamque dabat, Verg. **B.** Object., **1,** *an omen;* augurium accipere, Liv.; **2,** *a sign, token,* Ov.

augŭrĭus -a -um (augur), *relating to an augur,* jus, Cic.

augŭro, 1. (augur). **I.** *to act as an augur;* sacerdotes salutem populi auguranto, *take the auguries for,* etc., Cic.; pass., locus auguratur, *the place is consecrated by auguries,* Cic.; augurato (abl. absol.), *after taking the auguries,* Liv. **II.** Transf. **A.** *to prophesy,* Cic. **B.** *to have a foreboding or presentiment;* praesentit animus et augurat quodammodo, quae futura sit suavitas Cic.

augŭror, 1. dep. (augur). **I.** *to perform the functions of an augur, to foretell by auguries;* ex passerum numero belli Trojani annos, Cic. **II.** Transf., **1,** *to foretell;* alicui mortem, Cic.; **2,** *to guess;* quantum auguror conjectura aut opinione, Cic.; quum ex nomine istius, quid in provincia facturus esset, perridicule homines augurarentur, Cic.

Augusta -ae, f. **I.** *name of the wife, daughter, mother, or sister of the Roman Emperor.* **II.** *name of several towns named after the emperor,* Augusta Taurinorum (*Turin*), Augusta Praetoria (*Aosta*), Augusta Treverorum (*Treves*), Augusta Emerita (*Merida*), Augusta Vindelicum (*Augsburg*).

Augustālis -e (Augustus), *belonging to or in honour of the Emperor Augustus.*

augustē, adv. with compar. (augustus), *reverentially;* auguste et sancte venerari deos, Cic.

Augustŏdūnum -i, *town of the Aedui in Gaul,* now *Autun.*

1. **augustus** -a -um, adj. with compar. and superl. (augeo), **1,** *consecrated, holy;* Eleusis sancta illa et augusta, Cic.; **2,** *majestic, dignified;* vestis augustissima, Liv.

2. **Augustus** -i, m. *surname of Octavianus after his elevation to the imperial power, and of all subsequent Roman emperors.*

3. **Augustus** -a -um, *relating to Augustus;* pax, Ov.; mensis, *August,* formerly called Sextilis, changed to Augustus in honour of the emperor.

aula -ae, f. (αὐλή). **I.** *the fore-court in a building,* Hor.; *yard for cattle,* Prop. **II.** = atrium, *an inner court,* Verg. **III.** *a palace.* **A.** Lit., aula Priami, Hor.; so of the dwellings of the gods, illa se jactet in aula Aeolus, Verg.; of the lower world, immanis janitor aulae (of Cerberus), Verg.; of a bee-hive, Verg. **B.** Meton., **a,** *the court, courtiers;* puer ex aula, Hor.; divisa et discors aula erat, Tac.; **b,** *princely power;* auctoritate aulae constitutā, Cic.

aulaeum -i, n. (αὐλαία), usually plur., **1,** *curtain, tapestry;* aulaea superba, Verg.; **2,** *a canopy,* Hor.; **3,** *curtain of a theatre,* fastened below and let down at the beginning of a piece, and drawn up at the end; aulaeum tollitur, Cic.; **4,** *an embroidered upper garment,* Juv.

Aulerci -orum, m. *a people of Gallia Celtica,* divided into four branches; **a,** Aulerci Eburovīces, in modern Normandy; **b,** Aulerci Cenomani, in modern Dép. de la Sarthe; **c,** Aulerci Brannovices, on the Loire; **d,** Aulerci Diablintes or Diablinti, in Modern Dép. de la Maine.

aulĭcus -a -um, (αὐλή), *belonging to the court, princely,* Suet. Subst., **aulici** -orum, m. *courtiers,* Nep.

Aulis -ĭdis, f. (Αὐλίς), *a port in Boeotia,* where the Greek fleet collected before sailing to Troy.

auloedus -i, m. (αὐλῳδός), *one who sings to the flute,* Cic.

Aulōn -ōnis, m. *a celebrated wine-district near Tarentum.*

Aulŭlarĭa -ae, f. *the title of a comedy of Plautus.*

aura -ae, old genit. auraï (αὔρα), *air*. **A. 1,** *the motion of the air, wind*; nocturna aura uti (of ships), Caes.; venti et aurae cient mare, Liv.; **2,** meton., plur. aurae, **a,** *the heavens*; cursum per auras dirigere, Verg.; stat ferrea turris ad auras, Verg.; **b,** *the world above*; venire superas ad auras, *the light of day*, Verg.; ferre sub auras, *to make known*, Verg.; **3,** transf., *breath, sign*; rumoris, Cic.; aura popularis, *the breath of popular favour*, Cic.; **4,** *the air that we breathe*; auris vitalibus vesci, Verg. **B. 1,** *smell*, Verg.; **2,** *glitter*; auri, Verg.; **3,** *echo*, Prop.

aurārĭus -a -um (aurum), *golden, relating to gold*, Plin. Subst., **auraria** -ae, f. (sc. fodina), *a gold mine*, Tac.

aurātus -a -um (aurum), *golden, gilt*; tecta, Cic.; vestis, Ov.

Aurēlĭus -a -um, *name of a Roman plebeian gens* (with the surnames Cotta, Orestes, Scaurus).

Aurēlius, M., v. Antoninus.

aurĕŏlus -a -um (dim. of aureus). **A.** Lit., *golden*, Plaut. **B.** Transf., *glittering, splendid, beautiful*; libellus, Cic.

aurĕus -a -um (aurum), *golden*. **I. 1,** *made of gold*; **a,** lit., anulus, Cic.; nummus, and absol., *a golden coin*, Cic.; **b,** transf., *excellent, beautiful*; Venus, Verg.; mores, Hor.; **2,** *gilt, ornamented with gold*; amiculum, Cic.; sella, Cic.; currus, *the triumphal car*, Cic.; Pactolus, *with golden sands*, Ov. **II.** *of the colour of gold*; color, Ov.; caesaries, Verg.

aurichalchum = orichalchum (q.v.).

aurĭcŏmus -a -um (aurum and coma). **I.** *golden-haired*, P. Aug. **II.** Transf., *golden-leaved*; fetus arboris, Verg.

aurĭcŭla -ae, f. (dim. of auris), *the lobe of the ear, the ear*. **I.** Lit., auricula infima, Cic.; auriculam mordicus auferre, Cic.; praeceptum auriculis instillare, Hor. **II.** Meton., plur. = *favourable hearing*, Pers.

aurĭfer -fĕra -fĕrum (aurum and fero). **I.** *gold-bearing, gold-producing*, arbor (of a tree in the garden of the Hesperides), Cic. poet. **II.** *bringing gold*; Tagus, Ov.; amnis, Cat.

aurĭfex -ficis, m. (aurum and facio), *a goldsmith*, Cic.

aurĭfŏdīna -ae, f. *a gold mine*, Plin.

aurīga -ae, c. (from old aurea = *reins* and ago), *charioteer, driver*. **I.** Lit., Verg., Caes.; esp. *one who contends in the chariot race in the circus*, Cic. **II.** Transf., poet., *a helmsman*, Ov.

Aurĭgĕna -ae, c. (aurum and gigno), *begotten of gold*; epithet of Perseus, son of Danaë, Ov.

aurĭger -gĕra -gĕrum (aurum and gero), *gold-bearing*; taurus, *with gilt horns*, Cic. poet.

aurīgo, 1. (auriga), *to be a charioteer, contend in the chariot race*, Suet.

aurĭpigmentum -i, n. *orpiment*, Plin.

auris -is, f. (connected with audio), *the ear*. **I. A.** Lit., aures; erigere, Cic., arrigere, Ter., *to prick up the ears*; adhibere, admovere, Cic., applicare, Hor., *to listen*; praebere aures conviciis adolescentium, Liv.; dare, Cic., *to give a hearing to*; accipere auribus, Cic.; aliquem admonere ad aurem, *to whisper advice in the ear*, Cic.; claudere aures alicui, Cic.; demittere aures (as a sign of submission), Hor.; dicere in aurem alicui aliquid, Cic.; insusurrare ad aurem or in aures, Cic.; offendere aures, Cic.; aures refercire aliqua re, Cic.; aures respuunt aliquid, Cic.; servire alicuius auribus, *to speak according to the wish of*, Caes.; dormire in utramvis aurem, *to sleep soundly, be without anxiety*, Ter. **B.** Meton., **a,** *the hearing*, as judging of the merits of a [illegible], Atticorum aures teretes et religiosae, Cic. **II.** Transf., aures; *the earth or mould-boards of a plough*, Verg.

auriscalpĭum -i, n. *an ear-pick*, Mart.

aurītŭlus -i, m. (dim. of auritus), *the long-eared one*, i.e., *the ass*, Phaedr.

aurītus -a -um (auris). **A.** Lit., *long-eared*; lepus, Verg. **B.** Transf., *attentive*, Hor.; testis auritus, *a hearsay witness*, Plaut.

aurōra -ae, f. (αὔως, ἀώς, ἠώς), *the break of day, redness of morning*. **I.** Lit., **A.** Gen., Verg., Liv. **B.** Personified, *Aurora, goddess of morning*, Ov. **II.** Meton., *the east*, Ov.

aurum -i, n. *gold*. **I. A.** Lit., Cic. **B.** Meton., *something made of gold, gold plate*, Lucr.; *a golden goblet*, Verg.; *chain, necklace*, Verg.; *ring*, Juv.; *bit*, Verg.; *the golden fleece*, Ov.; *gold coin, money*, Cic. **II.** Transf., **A.** *the colour or glittering of gold*, Ov. **B.** *the golden age*, Hor.

Aurunci -orum, m. *the people of Aurunca*; **Aurunca** -ae, f. *a town in Campania*. Adj., **Auruncus** -a -um, *Auruncian*.

Ausci -ōrum, m. *a people in Aquitania*.

auscultātĭo -ōnis, f. (ausculto); **1,** *a listening*, Sen.; **2,** *obedience*, Plaut.

auscultātor -ōris, m. (ausculto), *a listener*, Cic.

ausculto, 1. (for ausiculito, from ausicula = auricula). **I.** *to hear attentively*; populum, Cat. **II.** Esp., **A.** *to listen in secret, to overhear*, Plaut.; in a good sense, *to attend, wait at the door*, Hor. **B.** *to obey*; mihi ausculta; vide ne tibi desis, Cic.

Ausētāni -ōrum, m. *a Spanish people in modern Catalonia*; hence adj., **Ausētānus** -a -um, *Ausetanian*.

Ausŏnes -um, m. (Αὔσονες), *aborigines of Central and Southern Italy*; hence, **A. Ausŏnĭa** -ae, f. *Ausonia, Lower Italy*, Ov.; *Italy*, Verg. **B.** Adj., **Ausŏnĭus** -a -um; poet., *Italian*, Verg. Subst., **Ausŏnĭi** = Ausones, Verg. **C. Ausŏnĭdae** -ārum, m. *the inhabitants of Ausonia*, or generally *of Italy*, Verg. **D. Ausŏnis** -ĭdis, *Ausonian, Italian*, Verg.

auspex -ĭcis, c. (for avispex, from avis and specio). **I.** *one who observes the habits of birds for purposes of divination*; latores et auspices legis curiatae (Caesar and Pompeius), Cic. **II.** Transf., **A.** *favourer, protector, leader*; Teucro duce et auspice Teucro, Hor. **B.** *a person who witnessed the marriage contract, best man, bridegroom's friend*, etc. (παράνυμφος), Cic.

auspĭcātō, adv. (lit. abl. absol. of auspico), *in a fortunate hour*; urbem condere, Cic.

auspĭcātus -a -um (auspico), **1,** *consecrated by auguries*, Cic.; **2,** *favourable, auspicious*; initium, Tac.

auspĭcĭum -ii, n. (for avispicium), *divination by means of birds*. **I. A.** Lit., in auspicio esse, *to act as augur*, Cic.; praeesse auspiciis, Cic.; adhibere aliquem in auspicium, Cic.; auspicio uti, Cic.; auspicia dissolvere, Cic.; esp., *the right to take auspices*, propraetores auspicia non habent, Cic.; auspicia ponere, *to lay down a magistracy*, Cic.; imperio atque auspicio alicuius, *under the command of* (in war the commander-in-chief alone had the right of taking the auspices), Liv. **B.** Transf., *control, protection, guidance*; suis auspiciis ducere vitam, Verg. **II.** Meton., *an omen, sign*; optimum, Cic.; aves auspicium ratum fecere, Cic.

auspĭco, 1. (auspex), *to take the auspices*; aliquid, *to accept as an omen*, Plaut.

auspĭcor, 1. dep. (auspex), **1,** *to take the auspices*; auspicari oblitus est, Cic.; **2,** *to begin under good auspices*, Tac.; *to begin*, Suet.

auster -stri, m. **I.** *the south wind*, Cic. **II.** Meton., *the south*, Verg.

austērē adv. (austerus), *severely, gravely, austerely*, Cic.

austērĭtas -ātis, f. (austerus). **I.** Lit., **a,** *harshness, sourness of taste*, Plin.; **b,** *darkness of colour*, Plin. **II.** Transf., *strictness, austerity*, Quint.

austērus -a -um (αὐστηρός). **I.** *sour, harsh in taste*, Plin. **II.** Transf., **1,** *strict, severe, austere*; illo austero more ac modo, Cic.; **2,** *sad, gloomy, melancholy, burdensome*; labor, Hor.

austrālis -e (auster), *southern*, Cic.

austrīnus -a -um (auster), *southern*, Verg.

ausum -i, n. (ausus, from audeo), *a daring deed, undertaking*, Verg.

aut, conj. disjunct., *or, or else, or rather*, Cic.; aut . . . aut, *either . . . or*, Cic.; neque . . . aut, = neque . . . neque, poet.; aut vero, *or indeed* (used ironically), Cic.; aut certe, *or at least*, Cic.; aut saltem, aut potius, aut etiam, Cic.

autem, conj. adversat. (αὖτε), *but, on the contrary, however, moreover*; never used at the beginning of a clause; joined with adeo, porro, tum, ast, even with sed; when used to correct a word before used = *did I say?* num quis testis Postumum appellavit? Testis autem? Num accusator? Cic.

authepsa -ae, f. (αὐτός and ἕψω), *a cooking-stove*, Cic.

autŏgrăphus -a -um (αὐτόγραφος), *written with one's own hand*, Suet.

Autŏlycus -i, m. (Αὐτόλυκος), *son of Mercury, famous for his thefts.*

autŏmătus (ŏs) -a -um (-ŏn), adj. (αὐτόματος), *self-acting*, Petr. Subst., **autŏmăton** -i, n. *an automaton*, Suet.

Autŏmĕdōn -ontis, m. (Αὐτομέδων), *the charioteer of Achilles*; appell., *a charioteer*, Cic.

Autŏnŏē -ēs, f. (Αὐτονόη), *mother of Actaeon.* Adj., **Autŏnēius** -a -um, heros, *Actaeon*, Ov.

autumnus, etc., v. auctumnus.

autŭmo, 1. (orig. aitumo, from aio), *to say, assert*, Plaut., Ter.

auxĭlĭāris -e (auxilium), *giving help, assisting, auxiliary.* **I.** Gen., Ov. **II.** Esp., auxiliares, (sc. milites, cohortes), *auxiliary or allied troops*, Caes., Tac.; hence, *belonging to the allied troops*; auxiliaria stipendia, Tac.

auxĭlĭārius -a -um (auxilium), **1,** *helping, auxiliary*, Plaut.; **2,** milit. t. t., milites, *auxiliary troops*, Cic.

auxĭlĭātor -ōris, m. (auxilior), *a helper, assister*, Tac.

auxĭlĭātus -ūs, m. (auxilior), *help, assistance*, Lucr.

auxĭlior, 1. dep. (auxilium), *to help, assist, support*; alicui, Cic.; especially used of medical aid, Ov.

auxĭlium -i, n. (augeo), *help, aid, assistance.* **I.** Gen., adjungere sibi auxilium, Cic.; arcessere aliquem auxilio, *to help*, Caes.; ad auxilium convenire, Caes.; dare adversus aliquem auxilium, Liv.; esse auxilio alicui, Caes.; consuli adversus intercessionem collegae auxilio esse, Liv.; alicui nemo auxilio est, quin, etc., Liv.; auxilio ei futurum ne causam dicat, Liv.; expetere auxilium ab aliquo, Cic.; exspectare vestrum auxilium, Cic.; alicui ferre auxilium, Cic.; ferre alicui auxilium contra tantam vim, Cic.; implorare auxilium alicuius, Cic.; aliquem auxilio mittere, Cic.; petere auxilium ab aliquo, Cic.; polliceri auxilium alicui rei, Cic.; venire auxilio alicui, Caes.; plur., illorum auxiliis uti, Cic. **II.** Esp., plur., **a,** *military power*; equitum peditumque, Caes.; **b,** auxilia, *auxiliary troops*, Cic., Caes.

ăvārē, adv. with compar. and superl. (avarus), *avariciously, covetously*, Cic.

Avăricum -i, n. *capital of the Bituriges Cubi in Aquitania*, now *Bourges.*

ăvārĭtĕr, adv. (avarus), *greedily*, Plaut.

ăvārĭtia -ae (**ăvārĭtiēs** -ei, Lucr.), f. *avarice, cupidity, covetousness*; ardere avaritia, Cic.; avaritia perire, Cic.; plur., omnes avaritiae, *all kinds of avarice*, Cic.

ăvārus -a -um (connected with aveo and avidus). **I.** Gen., *covetous, greedy*; mare, Hor.; with genit., publicae pecuniae avarus, Tac. **II.** Esp., *greedy after money, avaricious*; homo avarus et furax, Cic. Subst., **avarus** -i, m. *the avaricious man*, Hor.

āvĕho -vexi -vectum, 3. *to carry off, bear away*, Verg., Liv.; pass. *to ride off*, Liv.

āvello -velli and -vulsi (-volsi) -vulsum (-volsum), 3. *to tear away, pluck away.* **I.** Lit., poma ex arboribus, cruda si sint, vi avelluntur, Cic.; sive secetur aliquid sive avellatur a corpore, Cic. **II.** *to take away with violence, separate.* **A.** Lit., de matris complexu avellere atque abstrahere, Cic.; ex complexu avelli, Cic.; avulsus a meis, Cic. **B.** Transf., aliquem convicio ab errore, Cic.

ăvēna -ae, f. **I. a,** *oats*, Verg.; **b,** *wild oats*, Cic.; steriles, Verg. **II.** Transf., *the shepherd's pipe*, Ov.; plur., junctae avenae or structae avenae, *the Pan-pipes*, Ov.

ăvēnācĕus -a -um (avena), *oaten*; farina, Plin.

ăvēnārius -a -um, *relating* or *belonging to oats*, Plin.

Ăventīnum -i, n. and **Ăventīnus** -i, m. *the Aventine, one of the hills of Rome*, Cic. Adj., **Ăventīnus** -a -um, *of* or *belonging to the Aventine.*

1. **ăvĕo,** 2. (cf. Sanskr. av, *to wish*), lit., *to pant after*; hence, *to desire*; aveo genus legationis, Cic.; gen. with infin., valde aveo scire quid agas, Cic.

2. **ăvĕo (hăvĕo),** 2. *to be well*; found only in the imp. ave, aveto, avete, *hail! farewell!* a formula of greeting and farewell used by the Romans, Cic.

Ăvernus -a -um (ἄορνος), *without birds*; loca, *places where birds cannot live on account of the pestilential exhalations*, Lucr. Subst., **Ăvernus** -i, *the lake Avernus*, near Cumae, said to be the entrance to the infernal regions; *the infernal regions themselves*, Ov.; hence, adj., **Ăvernus** -a -um, **Ăvernālis** -e, *relating to Avernus, or the lower world.*

āverrunco, 1. *to turn away, avert*; iram deorum, Liv.

āversābilis (aversor), *that from which one must turn away, horrible*, Lucr.

1. **āversor,** dep. (averto). **A.** *to turn away* (on account of shame, disgust, etc.); aversari advocati, vix etiam ferre posse, Cic.; with acc., filium, Liv. **B.** Transf., *to repel, turn away, avoid, shun*; principes Syracusanorum, Liv.; preces, Liv.; aliquem ut parricidam liberum, Liv.

2. **āversor** -ōris, m. (averto), *an embezzler*; pecuniae publicae, Cic.

āversus -a -um, p. adj. (from averto). **A.** *turned away, backward, behind* (opp. adversus); adversus et aversus impudicus es, *before and behind*, Cic.; quendam actorem aversum (*turning his back on the people*) solitum esse dicere,

Cic, aversos boves in speluncam traxit, Liv Plur subst., **āversa** -orum, n *the back parts*, urbis, Liv **B.** *disinclined, unfavourable to, averse from*, aversus a vero, Cic, with dat, aversus mercaturis, Hor.

āverto (āvorto) -verti (-vorti) versum (-vorsum), 3 *to turn away, turn off, remove* **I.** Lit, **A.** Gen Lepidus se avertit, Cic; aliquid ab oculis, Cic, flumina, *divert*, Cic, iter, Caes, Liv, hence, **1,** pass, averti (as middle), aversus ab suo itinere, *turning away*, Liv, **2,** active, as reflexive, prora avertit, Verg **B.** Esp **1,** *to drive away by violence*, barbaros a portis castrorum, Caes, **2,** *to carry off, appropriate to oneself, embezzle*, pecuniam publicam, Cic, hereditatem, Cic; quatuor tauros a stabulis, Verg **II.** Transf, **A.** Gen, **1,** *to keep off something dangerous*, pestem ab Aegyptus, Cic, quod omen dii avertant, Cic, **2,** *to keep something dangerous* or *disgraceful off some one*, qui me a tanta infamia averterit, Cic **B.** Esp, **1,** *to turn away, divert* (thoughts or wishes, etc), Antonii furorem a pernicie reipublicae, Cic, cogitationem a miseriis, Cic; aliquem a consiliis pacis, **2,** *to estrange*, alicuius animum a se, Cic

ăvĭa -ae, f (avus), *a grandmother*, Cic

ăvĭārĭus -a -um (avis), *relating to birds*, rete, Varr Subst, **ăvĭārĭum** -ii, n, **a,** *a place where birds are kept, an aviary*, Cic, **b,** *the haunts of wild birds in the woods*, Verg

ăvĭdē, adv (avidus), *greedily*, exspectare, appetere, arripere, Cic

ăvĭdĭtas -ātis (avidus), f. **A.** Gen, *vehement desire, avidity*, cibi, pecuniae, *for food, money*, Cic; legendi, Cic. **B.** Esp, *desire of money, avarice*, Cic

ăvĭdus -a -um (1 aveo), *vehemently desiring, greedy* **I. a,** with genit, cibi, Ter, laudis, Cic., novarum rerum, Liv., belli gerendi, Sall., **b,** with infin, Verg, **c,** with in and the acc, Liv, **d,** with ad and the acc, Liv, **e,** with in and the abl, in pecuniis locupletium, Cic **II.** Absol. **A.** Lit, **a,** *covetous, greedy of money*, heres, Hor, subst, *a miser*, Cic, **b,** *greedy in respect of food, gluttonous*, conviva, Hor, leones, *bloodthirsty*, Ov, **c,** transf, aures avidae, *eager to hear*, Cic, libido, *insatiable*, Cic, mare, Hor, **d,** *hot, ardent, eager to fight*, legiones, Tac **B.** Fig, *wide, large, vast*, Lucr

ăvis -is, f (connected with ἄημι) **I.** Gen, *a bird*, and coll *the whole race of birds*, Cic **II** Esp, *omen*, as the chief method of divination among the Romans was by birds, avibus bonis Ov, secundis, Liv, *with good omens*, avi mala, Hor, sinistra, Plaut; adversa, *with bad omen* Cic

ăvītus -a -um (avus), *relating to a grandfather, ancestral*, bona paterna et avita, Cic, merum, *very old*, Ov

āvĭus -a -um (a and via) **I.** *out of the right way, untrodden*, avii saltus montesque, Liv Subst, **āvĭum** -ii, n *a by way, a solitary place*, avia dum sequor, Verg **II.** Poet, **A.** *out of the way, wandering, remote*, in montes se avius abdidit alios, Verg **B.** Transf, *straying, wandering*, a vera ratione, Lucr

āvŏcātĭo -ōnis, f (avoco), *a calling away from*, a cogitanda molestia, Cic

āvŏco, 1 *to call away, or off.* **A.** Lit, populum ab armis, Liv **B.** Transf, **1,** *to withdraw, remove, divert;* Socrates videtur primus a rebus occultis avocasse philosophiam, Cic, senectus avocat a rebus gerendis, Cic; **2,** *to relieve*, luctum lusibus, Sen

āvŏlo, 1 *to fly away* **A.** Lit, Cat **B.** Transf, *to hasten away*, experiar certe ut hinc avolem, so of the dying, hinc avolare, Cic

ăvuncŭlus -i, m (dim of avus), *a mother's brother, uncle* (patruus, *a father's brother*), magnus, *a grandmother's brother, a great-uncle*, Cic

ăvus -i, m *a grandfather*, Cic; generally *an ancestor*, Hor

Axĕnus (ἄξεινος, *inhospitable*), *earlier name of the Pontus Euxinus*, Ov

1 **axis** -is, m (root AC, AG, whence ago, Gr ἄξων), *an axle tree* **I. A.** Lit., Verg **B.** Meton, *a chariot, waggon*, Ov **II** Transf, **A** *the axis of the earth*, terra circum axem se convertit, Cic **B** Meton, **a,** *the north pole*, Verg, **b,** *the heavens*, sub axe, *in the open air*, Verg., **c,** *a part of the heavens*, boreus, *the north*, Ov

2 **axis** (assis) -is, m (root AC, whence ἄγνυμι, ἄγμα), *a board, plank*, Caes

Axŏna -ae, m. *a river in Gallia Belgica*, now *the Aisne*

B

B, b, the second letter of the Latin Alphabet, corresponding with the Greek beta (β)

băbae (βαβαί, or παπαί), an exclamation of astonishment or joy, *wonderful!* Plaut

Băbȳlo -ōnis, m *a Babylonian*, appell. = *a nabob*, Ter

Băbȳlōn -ōnis, f (Βαβυλών), *a city of Asia on the Euphrates* Hence, **A. Băbȳlōnĭa** -ae, f *a tract of country extending between the Euphrates and the Tigris*, of which the aforenamed city was the capital **B. Băbȳlōnĭcus** -a -um, *Babylonian*, Babylonica peristromata, *embroidered tapestry*, Plaut **C. Băbȳlōnĭus** -a -um, numeri, *astrological calculations, for which the Babylonians* (or more properly the Chaldeans) *were noted*, Hor, Babylonii, *inhabitants of Babylon* **D. Băbȳlōnĭensis** -e, *Babylonian*

bacca (bāca) -ae, f *a berry* **I.** Lit, **A.** Gen, lauri baccae, Verg **B.** Esp, *the fruit of the olive:* bicolor bacca Minervae, Ov **II.** Transf, **A.** *any fruit of a round shape*, arborum baccae, Cic **B.** *anything of the shape of a berry, a pearl*, Hor

baccar (bacchar) -ăris, n and **baccăris** -is, f (βάκκαρις), the Valeriana Celtica of Linnaeus, also called nardum rusticum, *a plant which yielded a kind of oil*, *Celtic Valerian*, Verg

baccātus -a -um, *set with pearls*, Verg

Baccha -ae, f *a Bacchante*, Ov, Bacchis aliquem initiare, *to initiate any one into the festival of Bacchus*, Liv

Bacchānal -is, n *the place where the festival of Bacchus was held*, Plaut, plur **Bacchānālĭa**, *the (Greek) festival of Bacchus* (not to be confounded with the Roman feast of Liber), celebrated at Rome every three years and suppressed by a decree of the senate, B C 186, Bacchanalia vivere, poet, *to live riotously or wantonly*, Juv

bacchātĭo -ōnis, f **1,** *the celebration of the Bacchanalia*, P Aug, **2,** *Bacchanalian revelling*, Cic

Bacchēĭus -a -um, *belonging to Bacchus*, dona, Verg

Bacchēus -a -um (Βακχεῖος), *belonging to Bacchus*, sacra, Ov, ululatus, *of the Bacchantes*, Ov

Bacchĭădae -ārum, m (Βακχιάδαι), *the Bacchiadae, an ancient noble family of Corinth*

Bacchis -idis, f. = Baccha.

Bacchĭus -a -um, *belonging to Bacchus*, sacra, Ov.

bacchor, 1. dep. (Bacchus). **I.** Intransit., **A. 1,** *to celebrate the festival of Bacchus*, Plaut.; partic. Bacchantes = Bacchae, Ov.; **2,** *to rage;* tum baccharis, tum furis, Cic.; quanta in voluptate bacchabere, Cic. **B.** *to run about in a furious manner, to rave;* totam per urbem, Verg.; of a fiery orator, eos furere et bacchari arbitraretur, Cic.; of prophetic inspiration, in antro, Verg.; of lifeless objects, the wind, Hor.; rumour, fama bacchatur per urbem, Verg. **II.** Transit., **A.** *to raise the Bacchic cry;* bacchari Evoë, Cat. **B.** Pass., of places, *to be made the scene of Bacchic revels;* bacchata jugis Naxos, Verg.; virginibus bacchata Lacaenis Taygeta, Verg.

Bacchus -i, m. (Βάκχος). **A.** *the god of wine, son of Jupiter and Semele.* **B.** Meton., **1,** *the vine*, Verg.; **2,** more frequently, *wine*, Verg.; **3,** *the Bacchic cry* (Io Bacche); Baccho audito, Verg.

baccĭfer -fĕra -fĕrum, **1,** *bearing berries*, Sen.; **2,** *bearing olive berries*, Pallas, Ov.

Băcēnis -is, f. *a forest in Germany*, probably the west part of the Thuringian Forest.

băcillum -i, n. (dim. of baculum), **1,** *a little staff*, Cic.: **2,** *the lictor's staff*, Cic.

Bactra -ōrum n. (Βάκτρα), *the chief city of Bactria, now Balk;* hence **Bactri** -ōrum, m. *inhabitants of Bactria;* **Bactria** -ae, f. *the country of the Bactri;* **Bactriānus** -a -um, **Bactrīnus** -a -um, *Bactrian*.

băcŭlum -i, n. and **băcŭlus** -i, m. (connected with βάκτρον, from βάω, βάζω, *to go*), *a stick, staff*, Liv.; *a shepherd's staff*, Ov.; *an augur's staff*, Liv.; *a walking-stick*, Liv.

bădisso, 1. (βαδίζω), *to walk, march*, Plaut.

Baebĭus -a -um, adj., *name of a plebeian Roman gens*, with the surnames Dives, Sulca, Tamphilus; hence, lex Baebia (de praetoribus creandis).

Baecŭla ae, f. *a town in Hispania Baetica.*

Baetis -is, m. *a river in Spain, the Guadalquivir;* hence, **Baetĭgĕna** -ae, *born on the Baetis;* **Baetĭcŏla** -ae, *living near the Baetis;* **Baetĭcus** -a -um, *relating to the Baetis;* Baetica provincia, now *Andalusia and a part of Granada;* **Baetĭci** -ōrum, m. *inhabitants of Baetica;* **Baetĭcātus** -a -um, *clothed in Baetican wool*, Mart.

Băgōus -i, m. and **Băgōas** -ae, m. (Βαγώας), *a eunuch at the Persian court;* hence *any person set to guard women*, Ov.

Băgrăda -ae, m. (Βαγράδας), *a river near Carthage.*

Bājae -ārum, f. **I.** *a town on the coast of Campania, a favourite resort of the Romans, celebrated for its baths.* **II.** Meton., *any watering place*, Cic. Adj., **Bājānus** -a -um, *belonging to Bajae.*

bājŭlo, 1. (bajulus), *to carry a burden*, Plaut.

bājŭlus -i, m. *a porter*, Plaut., Cic.

bālaena -ae, f. (φάλαινα), *a whale*, Ov.

bălănātus -a -um (balanus), *anointed with balsam, embalmed*, Pers.

bălănus -i, f. rarely m. (βάλανος), **1,** *an acorn*, Plin.; **2,** *any fruit of similar form*, e.g. *a kind of large chestnut*, Plin.; *a date*, Plin.; *a fruit, the Arabian behen-nut*, from which an ointment was extracted, Hor.; or *the tree which produces it*, usually called myrobalanus, Plin.

bălătro -ōnis, m. *a buffoon, jester*, Hor.

bālātus -ūs, m. (balo), *the bleating of sheep and goats*, Verg., Ov.

balbē, adv. (balbus), *in a stammering manner*, Lucr.

1. **balbus** -a -um (connected with balare), *stammering* (opp. planus); quum (Demosthenes) ita balbus esset ut, etc., Cic.; verba balba, Hor.

2. **Balbus** -i, m. *surname of the Attii, Cornelii*, etc.

balbūtĭo, 4. (balbus). **I.** Intransit., **A.** *to stammer, stutter*, Cels. **B.** Transf., *to speak obscurely;* desinant balbutire, aperteque et clara voce audeant dicere, Cic. **II.** Transit., *to stammer* or *stutter out;* illum balbutit Scaurum, Hor.

Bălĕāres -ium, f. (Βαλιαρεῖς), insulae, or absol., *the Balearic Islands, Majorca, Minorca;* hence, adj., **Bălĕāris** -e, **Bălĕārĭcus** -a -um.

bălĭnĕum or **balnĕum** -i, n., **bălĭnĕa** or **balnĕa** -ōrum, n.; heteroclite pl. **bălĭnĕae** or **balnĕae** -ārum (βαλανεῖον), *a bath, bathing place*, Cic.; a balineo or a balineis, *after bathing*, Plin.

Ballĭo -ōnis, m. *a worthless fellow*, from a character so named in the Pseudolus of Plautus, Cic.

ballista (bălista), -ae, f. (βάλλω). **A.** *a military engine for throwing large stones*, Cic., Caes. **B.** Transf., *the missiles thrown*, Plaut.

ballistārĭum -i, n. = ballista (q.v.).

balnĕae, v. balineum.

balnĕārĭus -a -um (balneum), *belonging to the bath;* fur, *lurking about baths*, Cat. Subst., **balnĕārĭa** -ōrum, n. *baths, bathing-rooms*, Cic.

balnĕātor -ōris, m. (balneum), *the keeper of a bath*, Cic.

balnĕŏlum -i, n. (dim. of balneum), *a little bath*, Cic.

balnĕum, v. balineum.

bālo, 1. *to bleat*, Plaut.; partic. balantes -ium and um, f. = oves, Verg.

balsămum -i n. (βάλσαμον), **1,** *the sweet-smelling gum of the balsam-tree*, Verg.; **2,** *the tree itself*, Tac.

balteus -i, m. (-um -i, n.), *the girdle;* **a,** esp., as serving to hold a weapon; sutilis, Verg.; **b,** *a woman's girdle*, Mart. (baltei dissyll., Verg. 10,496).

Bandŭsĭa -ae, f. *a fountain near Venusia, the birthplace of Horace.*

Bantĭa -ae, f. (Βαντία), *town of Apulia, near Venusia.* Adj., **Bantīnus** -a -um.

Baptae -ārum, m. (Βάπται = *baptists*, from the rite of initiation), *priests of the Thracian goddess Cotytto*, Juv.

baptistērĭum -i, n. (βαπτιστήριον), *a cold plunging bath*, Plin.

bărăthrum -i, n. (βάραθρον), **A.** *the abyss, the lower world*, Plaut.; barathro donare (*to squander*), Hor. **B.** Transf., barathrum macelli (of a greedy man), *the abyss of the market*, Hor.

bărăthrus -i, m. (βάραθρος), *worthless fellow*, Lucr.

barba -ae, f. *the beard.* **I.** Lit. **A.** of men, promittere barbam, *to let the beard grow*, Liv.; barbam tondere, Cic.; barbam ponere, Hor. **B.** of animals, lupi, Hor. **II.** Transf., of plants, nucum, Plin.

barbărē, adv. (barbarus), **1,** *like a foreigner;* loqui, Cic.; **2,** *cruelly, barbarously*, laedere oscula, Hor.

barbărĭa -ae, f. and **barbărĭēs**, acc. -em, abl. -e, f. (barbarus), **I.** *a foreign country*, as opposed to Greece and Rome; a quo non solum Graecia et Italia sed etiam omnis barbaries commota est, Cic.; *Persia*, Cic.; *Phrygia*, Hor.; *Gallia*, Cic.; *Scythia* and *Britannia*, Cic. **II.** Meton., **A.** *want of culture, rudeness, roughness;*

haec turba et barbaries forensis, Cic ; so of mistakes in speech, nec eos aliqua barbaries domestica infuscaverat, Cic **B.** *savageness*, inveteratam quandam barbariam ex Gaditanorum moribus disciplina delevit, Cic.

barbărĭcus, -a -um, *foreign*, i e, not Greek or Roman, supellex, Liv , esp , *eastern*, aurum, Verg , ope barbarica, Verg , manus (of the Phrygian Briseis), Ov

barbărus -a -um (βάρβαρος) **I.** *foreign*, as opposed to Greek, *Italian*, *Roman*, poeta (Naevius), Plaut ; used for *Phrygian*, carmen, Hor , for *Persian*, Nep Subst , *a foreigner*, one strange to Greek or Roman life, Cic **II.** Transf , **1**, *intellectually uncultivated*, *rough*, homines barbari atque imperiti, Caes , **2**, *morally rough*, *savage*, homines feri ac barbari, Caes

barbātŭlus a um (dim of barbatus), *with a slight beard*, juvenis, Cic

barbātus a -um (barba), *bearded* **I.** Of living beings **A.** Of men, **1**, quos aut imberbes aut bene barbatos videtis, Cic ; si quem delectet barbatum, *a man grown up*, Hor , **2**, esp , **a**, of men of the old Roman time, when the beard was worn, unus aliquis ex barbatis illis, Cic , **b**, barbatus magister, *a philosopher*, Pers **B.** Of animals, hircus, Cat. **II.** Transf , of plants, nux, Plin

barbĭgĕr -gĕra, -gĕrum (barba and gero), *wearing a beard*, Lucr

barbĭtŏs i, m and f (βάρβιτος). **A.** *the lyre*, Hor **B.** Meton , *the song sung to the lyre*, Ov

barbŭla -ae, f (dim of barba), *a little beard*, Cic.

Barcās -ae, m (Βάρκας, connected with Hebrew Barak, *lightning*), *the founder of the Barcine family of Carthage, to which belonged Hannibal and Hamilcar;* hence, adj , **Barcīnus** -a -um, *Barcine*

Barcē -ēs, f (Βάρκη), *town in Cyrenaica*, **Barcaei** -ōrum, m. *the inhabitants of Barce*

Bardaei -orum, m *a people of Illyria* Adj , **Bardaĭcus** -a -um, calceus, *a kind of soldier's boot*, in jest = *a centurion*, Juv

bardŏcŭcullus i, m *a Gallic overcoat with a hood made of wool*, Mart

1 **bardus** -a -um (βραδύς), *stupid*, *slow*, *dull*, Cic

2 **bardus** -i, m. *a bard*, *a poet among the Gauls*, Lucan

Bargȳlīae -ārum, f and **Bargȳlĭa** ōrum, n (Βαργυλία), *a town in Caria*. Hence, **a**, **Bargȳlētae** ārum, m *the inhabitants of Bargyliae*, **b**, **Bargȳlĭētĭcus** -a -um, *relating to Bargyliae*

bāris -ĭdos, f *a small Egyptian skiff*, Prop

barītus v barritus.

Bārĭum -ii, n (Βάριον), *a port in Apulia, on the Adriatic*

bāro -ōnis, m *a blockhead*, *simpleton*, Cic

barrĭo ire (barrus), *to roar* (of elephants), Suet

barrītus -ūs, m (barrio), **1**, *the roar of an elephant*, **2**, *the cry of the Germans*, Tac

barrus -i, m (an Indian word), *the elephant*, Hor

bascauda -ae, f. *a basket*, Mart , Juv.

bāsiātĭo -ōnis, f (basio), *kissing*, *a kiss*, Cat

bāsiātor -is, m. (basio), *a kisser*, Mart

băsĭlĭcē, adv (basilicus), *royally*, *splendidly*, Plaut.

băsĭlĭcus -a -um (βασιλικός) **I.** Adj *royal*, *kingly*, *princely*, Plaut. , vitis, *a kind of vine*, Plin **II.** Subst **A.** **băsĭlĭcus** -i, m (sc jactus), *the best cast of the dice*, Plaut **B.** **băsĭlĭca** -ae, f. (βασιλική sc οἰκία or στοά), *a basilica*, *the name of a building* (in Rome and other towns) *usually adorned with a double row of columns, and situated near the forum, used as a meeting-place of merchants and for the administration of justice*, qui forum et basilicas non spoliis provinciarum, sed ornamentis amicorum ornarent, Cic , basilicam habeo, non villam, frequentia Formianorum (of a much frequented place), Cic **C.** **băsĭlĭcum** i, n *a splendid dress*, Plaut

basiliscus -i, m (βασιλίσκος), *a kind of lizard*, *a basilisk*, Plin

bāsio, 1 *to kiss*, Cat., Mart

băsis -is and ĕos, f (βάσις), **1**, *a pedestal*, *base*, statuae, Cic. , **2**, *foundation*, *wall*, villae, Cic , **3**, mathemat t t , trianguli, *base*, Cic

bāsium ii, n *a kiss*, either of the hand or lip, Cat , basia jactare, *to throw kisses*, Juv

Bassăreus -ei, m (Βασσαρεύς, from βασσάρα, *a fox-skin*, as forming part of the clothing of the Bacchantes), *a name of Bacchus*, Hor , hence, **Bassărĭcus** -a -um, adj , Prop , **Bassăris** -idis, f *a Bacchante*, Pers

Bastarnae and **Basternae** -ārum, m *a German people near the mouth of the Danube*

Bătāvĭa -ae, f *the peninsula Batavia*, *Holland*, **Bătāvi** -orum, m *inhabitants of Batavia*, **Bătāvus** -a -um, *Batavian*, Batavorum insula = *Batavia*, Tac

bătillum (vatillum), -i, n *a chafing dish*, Hor

bătiŏla -ae, f *a small drinking-vessel*, Plin.

battŭo (**bātuo**), 3 *to beat*, *knock*, Plaut.

Battus -i m (Βάττος), *the founder of the African city Cyrene*, hence **Battĭădes** -ae, m *an inhabitant of Cyrene*, especially applied to the poet Callimachus, a native of Cyrene, Ov.

baubor, 1 dep., *to bark*, Lucr

bĕātē, adv (beatus), *happily*, bene et beate vivere, Cic

bĕātĭtas -ātis, f. (beatus), *happiness*, *blessedness*, Cic

bĕātĭtūdo -inis, f (beatus), *happiness*, *beatitude*, Cic

bĕātŭlus -a -um (dim of beatus), *somewhat happy*, Pers

bĕātus a um, p adj (from beo), *happy*, *blessed*. **I.** Gen **1**, of persons, qui beatus est, non intelligo quid requirat, ut sit beatior , si est enim quod desit, ne beatus quidem est, Cic , agricolae parvo beati, *happy on little means*, Hor , **2**, of events or circumstances, beata mors, Cic Neut subst , **bĕātum** i *happiness*, Cic **II.** Esp **A.** *wealthy*, *prosperous*, **1**, of persons, qui se locupletes, honoratos, beatos putant, Cic , **2**, of states, Dionysius tyrannus opulentissimae et beatissimae civitatis, Cic , **3**, of property, possessions, gazae beatae Arabum, Hor **B.** beatorum insulae, *the islands of the blest*, Cic.

Bebrȳces um, m (Βέβρυκες), *people in Bithynia* Adj , **Bebrȳcius** a -um, *Bebrycian*

Belgae -ārum, m *the Belgae*, *a warlike people of German and Celtic race, inhabiting the north of Gaul* Adj , **Belgicus** -a -um, *Belgic*, hence, Gallia Belgica, or simply Belgica, *the country between the Rhine, the Seine, the Marne, and the German Ocean*

bellārĭa -ōrum, n (bellus), *dessert*, *including fruit*, *nuts*, *confectionery*, *sweet wine*, Plaut

bellātor -ōris, m (bello), *a warrior*, Cic , used adj , *warlike*, *courageous*, deus, *Mars*, Verg , equus, Verg , also absol , *a war horse*, Juv

bellātōrius -a -um (bello), *skilled in carrying on war;* stilus, *a pugnacious, controversial style,* Plin.

bellātrix -īcis, f. (bellator), *a female warrior;* poet., adj., *warlike;* diva, *Pallas,* Ov.; Roma, Ov.; ira, Cic

bellātŭlus -a -um (dim., jocosely formed from bellus), *pretty,* Plaut.

bellē, adv. (bellus), *finely, prettily, elegantly, neatly.* **I.** Gen. scribere, Cic.; dicere, Cic.; negare, *politely,* Cic.; bellissime navigare, Cic.; praediola belle aedificata, Cic. **II.** belle se habere, or esse, *to be in good health,* Cic.

Bellĕrŏphōn -ontis, m. (Βελλεροφῶν), or **Bellĕrŏphontēs** -ae, m. (Βελλεροφόντης), *the slayer of the Chimaera.* Adj., **Bellĕrŏphontēus** -a -um, equus, *Pegasus,* Prop.

bellĭcōsus -a -um (bellicus), *warlike, bellicose.* **A.** gentes immanes et barbarae et bellicosae, Cic. **B.** Transf., differre sibi consulatum in bellicosiorem annum, *a more warlike year,* Liv.

bellĭcus -a -um (bellum), *relating to war.* **I.** disciplina, Cic.; virtus, Cic. Subst., **bellĭcum** -i, n. *the signal for the attack;* **a,** bellicum canere, Cic.; **b,** transf., *to excite,* Cic. **II.** Transf., **1,** *vigorous, fiery* (of style), alter (Thucydides) incitatior fertur et de bellicis rebus canit etiam quodammodo bellicum, Cic.; **2,** *warlike;* dea, *Pallas,* Ov.

bellĭger -gĕra -gĕrum (bellum and gero), *warlike, fond of war;* poet., gentes, Ov.; of inanimate things, hasta, Mart.; manus, Ov.

bellĭgĕro, 1. (bellum and gero), *to wage war;* qui isti par in belligerando esse possit, Cic.

bellĭpŏtens -entis (bellum and potens), *mighty in war.* Poet., subst. = *Mars,* Verg.

bello, 1. (**bellor,** dep., Verg.). **A.** *to wage war;* cum aliquo, Cic.; adversus aliquem, Nep.; bellare bellum, Liv. **B.** Transf., *to fight;* pictis armis, Verg.

Bellōna -ae f. (bellum), *the goddess of war,* Verg.

Bellŏvăci -ōrum, m. *a people in Gallia Belgica, near modern Beauvais.*

bellŭa, v. belua.

bellŭlus -a -um (dim. of bellus), *pretty, elegant, beautiful.*

bellum -i, n. (old form, **duellum,** *a contest between two*), *war.* **I.** Lit. domesticum, Cic.; sociale, Liv.; piraticum, Cic.; civile, Cic.; navale, Cic.; terrestre, Liv.; concitare, excitare, suscitare, Cic.; movere, commovere, conflare, Cic.; parare or comparare, Cic.; in bellum incumbere, Caes.; instruere, Cic.; nuntiare, denuntiare, indicere, *to declare war,* Cic.; suscipere, Cic.; indicare, Cic.; alicui inferre, Cic.: inferre contra patriam, Cic.; prorogare, Cic.; alere, Cic.; trahere, *to prolong,* Cic.; ducere, Caes.; deponere, Cic.; componere, Cic.; conficere, Cic.; exstinguere, restinguere, delere, Cic.; renovare, Cic.; impendet, Cic.; oritur, Cic.; renascitur, Cic.; in bello, *in time of war,* Cic.; locative, belli, *in time of war,* Cic.; vel domi vel belli, Cic. **II.** Transf., **a,** tribunicium, *contest,* Liv.; **b,** bellum indicere philosophis, Cic. **III.** Fig., *contention, fight,* Sall.

bellus -a -um (contr. from benulus, dim. of benus, i.e., bonus), *pretty, handsome, charming, neat, agreeable;* homo, Cic.; epistola, Cic.; locus, Cic.; vultu et fronte, *cheerful,* Cic.; *cheerful from good health;* fac bellus revertare, Cic.

bēlŭa -ae, f. (stem FE, whence fera and θήρ), **1,** *any very large animal,* e.g. *the elephant, lion, whale;* quantum natura hominis pecudibus reliquisque beluis antecedat, Cic.; belua fera et immanis, Cic.; esp. of the elephant, Ov.; **2,** as a term of reproach, *monster, brute, beast;* taetram et pestiferam beluam, Caes.

bēlŭātus -a -um (belua), *covered with figures of animals,* of tapestry, Plin.

bēlŭōsus -a -um (belua), *full of monsters;* Oceanus, Hor.

Bēlus -i, m., Myth. *an Asiatic king, founder of Babylon, father of Danaüs and Aegyptus;* hence, **A. Bēlis** -idis, f., gen. plur., **Bēlĭdes** -um, *the grand-daughters of Belus, the Danaides,* Ov. **B. Bēlīdēs** -ae, m. *Lynceus, son of Aegyptus,* Ov.

bĕnĕ, adv. (from benus for bonus), comp. melius, superl. optime. **I.** *well, rightly, honourably;* coenare, Hor.; habitare, Nep.; narrare, Cic.; promittere, Cic.; polliceri, Sall. **II.** Particular phrases. **A.** With verbs, **1,** bene agere, *to act fairly,* Cic.; **2,** bene audire, cf. audio; **3,** bene dicere; **a,** *to speak well;* bene dicere, id est, Attice dicere, Cic.; **b,** *to speak words of good omen* (εὐφημεῖν), Plaut.; **c,** *to speak well* of a person, *to commend,* Cic.; absol., Hor.; **4,** bene facere; **a,** *to do well,* Cic.; hence, bene facta, *famous deeds;* **b,** med., *to be of good effect,* Cato; **c,** bene facis, *excellent, I am much obliged,* Plaut.; **d,** *to do good to,* Cic., hence bene facta, *benefits,* Plaut.; **5,** bene est or bene habet; **a,** alicui, *it is well with,* Pompeio melius est factum, *Pompeius is better in health,* Cic.; **b,** *it is well, I am pleased,* Cic.; si bene habet, bene agitur, Cic.; **6,** bene vivere, *to live well,* i.e., **a,** *luxuriously,* Ter.; **b,** *happily,* Cic.; vivitur parvo bene, Hor.; **7,** bene vocas, *you are very kind* (polite refusal), Plaut.; **8,** bene vendere, *to sell dear,* Plaut.; emere, *to sell cheap,* Plaut. **B.** As an exclamation, *good, excellent,* Cic.; with acc. and dat., *good health to you,* Plaut. **III.** With adj. and adv., *well, thoroughly,* bene robustus, Cic.; bene penitus, Cic.; bene mane, Cic.

bĕnĕdictum -i, n. (benedico), *praise,* Plaut.

bĕnĕfăcio -fēci, -factum, 3. v. bene.

bĕnĕfactum -i, n. v. bene.

bĕnĕfĭcentĭa -ae, f. (beneficus), *kindness, liberality, beneficence,* Cic.

bĕnĕfĭcĭārĭus -a -um (beneficium), *relating to a favour,* Sen. Subst., **bĕnĕfĭcĭārĭi** -ōrum, m. *soldiers who by favour of their commanders were exempt from the severer military labours,* as throwing up intrenchments, fetching wood, water, etc.; *privileged soldiers,* Caes.

bĕnĕfĭcĭum -ii, n. (bene and facio), *a kindness, favour, benefit, service.* **I.** Gen. alicui beneficium dare, tribuere, Cic.; in aliquem conferre Cic.; apud aliquem collocare, Cic.; aliquem beneficio afficere, complecti, ornare, *to do any one a service,* Cic.; beneficium accipere, *to receive a kindness,* Cic.; beneficium tueri, *to be mindful of a service,* Cic.; in beneficio, Liv.; in beneficii loco, beneficii causa, per beneficium, *as a kindness, service,* Cic.; beneficio tuo, *by your kindness,* Cic.; deorum beneficio, sortium beneficio, Caes. **II.** In political life. **A.** *a favour, grant, distinction, promotion;* populi, *favour of the people,* Cic.; centuriones sui beneficii, *his creatures,* Suet.; quum suo magno beneficio esset, *since he owed much to his recommendation,* Cic.; used of military promotions, tribuni militum quae antea dictatorum fuerant beneficia, Liv.; in beneficiis delatus est, *among those recommended for promotion,* Cic. **B.** *privilege, exemption;* liberorum, *exemption from the judicial office in consequence of having a specified number of children,* Suet.

bĕnĕfĭcus -a -um, comp. -entior, superl. -entissimus (beneficissimus, Cat.), (bene and facio), *kind, generous, obliging,* Cic.

Bĕnĕventum -i, n. *a town of the Hirpini in*

Samnium, seat of a Roman colony (modern *Benevento*); hence, **Bĕnĕventānus** -a -um, *belonging to Beneventum*, in plur **Bĕnĕventāni** -orum, m *the people of Beneventum*

bĕnĕvŏlē, adv (benevolus), *benevolently, kindly*, Cic.

bĕnĕvŏlens -entis **A.** Adj *well-wishing, benevolent, obliging*, Plaut **B.** Subst, *friend, patron*, Plaut., Ter

bĕnĕvŏlentĭa -ae, f (benevolens), *good-will, friendly disposition, kindness, friendship, benevolence*, alicui praestare, conferre, Cic, colligere, Caes, erga aliquem habere, conferre, Cic

bĕnĕvŏlus -a -um (comp -entior, superl -entissimus), (bene and volo), *kind, obliging*, alicui, Cic, erga aliquem, Plaut, servus benevolus domino, *a faithful slave*, Cic

bĕnignē, adv (benignus), 1, *kindly, obligingly, willingly*, benigne respondere, Liv, benigne attenteque audire, Cic, arma capere, Liv, benigne dicis, or absol, benigne, *much obliged*, a phrase used either in accepting or refusing an offer, Cic, 2, *generously*, pecuniam praebere, Plaut, benigne facere alicui, *to confer benefits on a person*, Cic

bĕnignĭtas -ātis, f (benignus), 1, *kindness, mildness*, Cic, 2, *liberality, generosity*, Cic

bĕnignĭter = benigne, q v

bĕnignus -a um, adj with compar and superl, (contr from benigenus, from bonus and genus) **I.** *kindly, friendly, mild, pleasing* **A.** homines benefici et benigni, Cic, vultus benigni, Liv, dies, *fortunate*, Stat **II.** *liberal, generous*, **A.** erga aliquem, Plaut, alicui, Plaut, Hor, vini somnique benignus, *indulging in wine and sleep*, Hor, *prodigal*, Plaut; **B.** *rich, abundant*, ager, Ov, daps, Hor

bĕo, 1 (connected with benus, bonus), 1, *to bless, make happy*; beas or beasti, *that pleases me, I'm glad of it*, Ter, 2, *to make rich*, aliquem munere, Hor

Bĕrĕcyntus -i, m. *a mountain of Phrygia, sacred to Cybele*, hence adj, **Bĕrĕcyntĭus** -a um, mater, *Cybele*, Verg, heros, *Midas, son of Cybele*, Ov, tibia, *the flute used at the festivals of Cybele*, Hor.

Bĕrĕnīcē -ēs, f (Βερενίκη), 1, *queen of Ptolemy Euergetes, whose hair was placed among the stars as a constellation*, 2, *daughter of the Jewish king Agrippa I, mistress of Titus*

Bĕroea -ae, f (Βέροια) *a town in Macedonia* Hence, **Bĕroeaeus** -i, m, and **Bĕroeensis** -is, m *an inhabitant of Beroea*

bēryllus -i, c (βήρυλλος) **A.** *a beryl, a precious stone, of a sea-green colour, found in India*, Juv **B.** Meton, *a ring set with a beryl*, Prop

Bērȳtus -i, f (Βηρυτός), *an old Phoenician town, afterwards a Roman colony, and under the empire seat of a law school*, modern *Beyrout* Adj, **Bērȳtĭus** -a -um, and **Bērȳtensis** e

bēs, bessis, m (for be -is = binae partes assis), *two thirds* (= *eight* unciae) of any whole composed of twelve parts **A.** Lit., a, of a pound, *eight ounces*, Plin, b, of the as (as a coin), fenus ex triente Id Quint. factum erat bessibus, *the interest was raised from one-third per cent for the month to two thirds per cent*—i e, from 4 per cent for the year to 8 per cent., Cic **B.** Meton = *eight*, Mart

bessālis -e (bes), *containing the number 8*

Bessi -ōrum, m (Βέσσοι), *a people in Thrace* Adj, **Bessĭcus** -a um

Bessus -i, m *satrap of Bactria, who murdered Darius Codomannus*,

bestĭa ae, f (from stem FE, whence belua and fera), *an animal without reason* (opp homo), *beast* **A.** Gen, bestiae mutae, Cic, mala bestia, as a term of reproach, Plaut **B.** Particularly used of the animals exhibited in the amphitheatre, aliquem ad bestias mittere, *to condemn to be devoured by the beasts of the amphitheatre*, Cic

bestĭārĭus -a -um (bestia), *belonging to animals*, ludus, *a fight with wild beasts at a show*, Sen Subst., **bestĭārĭus** -ii, m *one who fought with wild beasts at the public shows*, Cic

bestĭŏla -ae, f (dim of bestia), *a small animal*, Cic

1 **bēta** -ae, f *a vegetable, beet*, Cic

2 **bēta**, indecl (βῆτα), *the beta, the second letter in the Greek alphabet*, sometimes used prov for *the second*, Mart

bēto (baeto, bito), 3 *to go*, Plaut

Bĭās -antis, m (Βίας), *a philosopher of Priene in Ionia, contemporary of Croesus of Lydia, one of the so-called seven wise men of Greece*

bĭblĭŏpōla ae, m (βιβλιοπώλης), *a bookseller*, Plin

bĭblĭŏthēca ae, f, and **bĭblĭŏthēcē** -ēs, f (βιβλιοθήκη), 1, *a collection of books, a library*, 2, *the place where books are kept*, Cic.

bĭbo, bibi, bibitum, 3 **I.** Lit, *to drink* (from natural desire), gemmā, *from a cup set with jewels*, Verg, sanguinem alicuius, Cic, dare bibere, *to give to drink*, Cic **II.** Particular phrases, a, aut bibat aut abeat (transl of Greek ἢ πῖθι ἢ ἄπιθι), Cic; b, Graeco more, *to drink to one*, Cic, c, ad numerum, *according to the number of years that a person wishes to live*, Ov, d, poet, bibere flumen, *to live on the banks of a river*, Verg, Danuvium, *to dwell on the banks of the Danube*, Hor **II. A.** Of things, *to drink in*, sat prata biberunt, Verg, hortus aquas bibit, Ov, arcus bibit, *the rainbow draws up water*, Verg **B.** Of persons, fig, amorem, Verg, aure (of attentive listeners), *to drink in*, Hor

Bĭbracte -is, n *a town in Gaul, capital of the Aedui on the modern Mount Beubray*

Bibrax actis, f *fortress of the Remi in Gaul*

bĭbŭlus -a -um (bibo), *fond of drinking* **I.** Act, *fond of drinking*, 1, with genit, Falerni, Hor, 2, of inanimate things, lapis, *sandstone*, Verg, lana, Ov, nubes, Ov, charta, *blotting paper*, Plin **II** Pass. *drinkable*, Falernum, Hor

bĭceps cipitis (bis and caput), *having two heads, two-headed* **A.** Lit, puer, Cic, Janus, Ov **B.** Poet, Parnassus, *double-peaked*, Ov

bĭclīnĭum -ii, n (bis and κλίνη), *a dining sofa for the use of two persons*, Plaut

bĭcŏlor -ōris (bis and color), *of two colours*, equus, Verg, myrtus, Ov

bĭcornĭger -gĕri, m (bis and corniger), *two horned*, an epithet of Bacchus, Ov.

bĭcornis -e (bis and cornu), *two horned*, Ov; poet, luna, *the new moon*, Hor, furcae bicornes, *two-pronged forks*, Verg, Rhenus, *with two mouths*, Verg

bĭcorpor -ŏris (bis and corpus), *having two bodies*, Cic poet

bĭdens entis (bis and dens), *having two teeth*, forfex, Verg, ancora, Plin Subst, a, m *a hoe with two crooked teeth for breaking clods*, Verg, b, f *an animal for sacrifice whose two rows of teeth were complete*, Verg, Ov; and esp, *a sheep*, Phaedr

bĭdental -ālis n (bidens), *a place struck with lightning, which was afterwards consecrated by the sacrifice of a sheep* (bidens), *and enclosed*, Hor,

Bidis -is, f. *a town in Sicily, north-west of Syracuse.* Hence, **Bidinus** -a -um, *belonging to Bidis.*

bīduum -i, n. (bis and dies), *the space of two days;* in iis operibus consiliisque biduum consumitur, Caes.; aliquem biduum cibo tectoque prohibere, Cic.; abl. biduo, *in the course of two days,* Cic.; eo biduo, *in the course of these two days,* Cic.; biduo aut summum triduo, *in two days or three at the most,* Cic.; biduo post, *two days afterwards,* Caes.; biduo quo haec gesta sunt, *two days after this was done,* Caes.; bidui iter abesse, *to be two days' march distant,* Caes.; so bidui by itself (iter understood), castra quae aberant bidui, Cic.

bĭennĭum -ii, n. (bis and annus), *a space of two years;* biennio jam confecto fere, Cic.; biennium jam factum est postquam abii domo, *it is now two years since I left home,* Plaut.; acc., biennium, *for the space of two years;* biennium provinciam obtinere, Cic.; abl., biennio, with compar., biennio major natu Domitius, *older by two years,* Tac.; biennio proximo, *in the course of two years,* Tac.; biennio ante, *two years before,* Cic.

bĭfārĭam, adv. (acc. of bifarius, *double*), *in two parts;* distribuere, Cic.; castra bifariam facta sunt, Liv.

bĭfer -fĕra -fĕrum (bis and fero), of a tree, *bearing fruit twice a year,* Verg.

bĭfĭdus -a -um (bis and findo), *split into two parts,* Ov.

bĭfŏris -e (bis and foris); **1,** *having two doors, valves,* or *openings;* valvae, Ov.; **2,** *with two openings;* ubi biforem dat tibia cantum, *the changing deep and high notes of the flute,* Verg.

bĭformātus -a -um, Cic. poet., v. biformis.

bĭformis -e (**bĭformātus** -a -um), *of double form;* Janus, Ov.; vates, *the poet turned into a swan,* Hor.

bĭfrons -frontis (bis and frons), *with double forehead* or *countenance,* epithet of Janus, Verg.

bĭfurcus -a -um (bis and furca), *having two prongs,* or *forks;* valli, Liv.; ramus, Ov.

bīgae -ārum, f. and P. Aug. **bīga** -ae, f. (contr. from bijugae or bijuga), *a pair of horses,* Liv., Verg.

bīgātus -a -um (bigae), *stamped with a pair of horses;* argentum, Liv. Subst., **bīgāti** -orum, m. sc. nummi, *silver denarii so marked.*

bĭjŭgis -e, v. bijugus.

bĭjŭgus a- -um (bis and jugum), *yoked two together;* certamen, *a race between two-horse chariots,* Verg. Subst., **bĭjŭgi** -ōrum, m. *a pair of horses,* Verg.

bĭlībra -ae, f. (bis and libra), *a mass of two pounds weight,* Liv.

bĭlībris -e (bis and libra), **1,** *weighing two pounds;* offae, Plin.; **2,** *containing two pounds;* cornu, Hor.

bĭlinguis -e (bis and lingua), *having two tongues;* **a,** *speaking two languages;* canusini more bilinguis, Hor.; **b,** *double-tongued, treacherous,* Verg.

bīlis -is, f. *gall, bile.* **I.** Lit., Cic.; suffusa, *jaundice,* Plin. **II.** Fig., **a,** *anger, displeasure;* commovere, Cic.; **b,** atra bilis (Gr. μελαγχολία), *black bile*—i.e., *melancholy,* Cic.; *madness,* Plaut.

bĭlix -icis (bis and licium), only acc. sing. bilicem found, *having a double thread,* Verg.

bĭlustris -e (bis and lustrum), *lasting ten years,* Ov.

bĭmăris -e (bis and mare), *lying on two seas;* Corinthus, Hor.; isthmus, Ov.

bĭmărītus, m. (bis and maritus), *the husband of two wives,* ap. Cic.

bĭmātĕr -tris, m. (bis and mater), *having two mothers;* epithet of Bacchus, Ov.

bīmātus -ūs, m. (bimus), *the age of two years* (of plants and animals), Plin.

bĭmembris -e (bis and membrum), *having double members, half man, half animal;* forma, used of the Centaurs, Ov.; bimembres, subst., *Centaurs,* Verg.

bĭmestris -e (bis and mensis), *lasting two months;* consulatus, ap. Cic.; porcus, *a pig two months old,* Hor.; stipendium, *pay for two months,* Liv.

bīmŭlus -a -um (dim. of bimus), *two years old,* Cat., Suet.

bīmus -a -um (bis and annus), *two years old;* equus, Plin.; vix bimum hunc Tiberium Caesarem, Vell.; legio, *a legion that had served for two years,* Cic.; merum, Hor.; nix, *snow lying for two years,* Ov.; honor, *office conferred for two years,* Ov.; sententia, *a vote of the senate prolonging a governor's time to two years,* ap. Cic.

bīni -ae -a (sing., binus -a -um, Lucr.), *two by two,* Lucr.; **1,** *two apiece,* sometimes simply *two;* unicuique binos pedes assignare, *two feet each,* Cic.; binos imperatores, *two consuls a year,* Sall.; with substt. that are used only in the plur., or that have a different meaning in the plur., *two;* bina castra, Cic.; binae litterae, Cic.; with other numerals, bina millia passuum, *two miles,* Quint.; **2,** of things that match, boves, *a yoke of oxen,* Plin.; scyphi, *a pair of goblets,* Cic.; neut. plur. subst., findi in bina, *to be cleft in twain,* Lucr.; si bis bina quot essent didicisset, *if he had learnt that twice two is four,* Cic.

bĭnoctĭum -ii, n. (bis and nox), *a space of two nights,* Tac.

bĭnōmĭnis -e (bis and nomen), *having two names;* Ascanius (because also called Iulus), Ov.; Ister (because also called Danuvius), Ov.

Bĭōn -ōnis, m. (Βίων), *a satirical philosopher, first of the Cyrenaic, then of the Stoic school;* hence **Bĭōnēus** -a -um, sermones, *witty, caustic,* Hor.

bĭŏs -ii, m. (βίος, *life,* cf. eau de vie), *a celebrated Greek wine,* Plin.

bĭpalmis -e (bis and palmus), *two palms or spans long* or *broad,* Liv.

bĭpartĭo, or **bĭpertĭo** (-ivi), -ītum, 4. (bis and partio), *to divide into two parts,* Cic.

bĭpartītō, adv., from partic. of bipartio, *in two parts, in two ways;* distribuere, Cic.; inferre signa, Caes.

bĭpătens -entis (bis and patens), *doubly open; open in two directions;* portis bipatentibus, Verg.

bĭpĕdālis -e (bis and pedalis), *two feet long, broad, thick,* or *high;* trabes, Caes.

bĭpennĭfer -fĕra -fĕrum, *armed with a two-edged axe* (bipennis), Ov.

bĭpennis -e (bis and penna), **1,** *having two wings,* Plin.; **2,** transf., *double-edged;* ferrum, Verg. Subst., **bĭpennis** -is, f. (sc. securis), *a double-edged axe,* Verg., Hor.

bĭpēs -ĕdis (bis and pes), *having two feet, biped,* Cic., Verg. Subst. plur., used contemptuously, *men;* omnium non bipedum solum, sed etiam quadrupedum impurissimus, Cic.

bĭrēmis -e (bis and remus). **I.** *two-oared,* Liv. Subst., **bĭrēmis** -is, f. *a skiff with two oars,* Lucan. **II.** *with two banks of oars;* used only as subst., *a ship with two banks of oars,* Cic.

bis, adv *twice, in two ways,* bis terque, Cic ; bis terve, Cic , *twice or thrice;* bis die, Cic ; bis consul, *a man who has been consul twice* (iterum consul, *a man who is consul for the second time*), Cic , bis tanto or tantum, *twice as great,* Plaut , with distributive numerals, bis bina, Cic , with cardinal numerals, only in poet , bis quinque viri (the decem viri), Hor , prov , bis ad eundem (sc lapidem offendere), *to make the same mistake twice,* Cic

Bistŏnes -um, m (Βίστονες), *the Bistones, a Thracian people settled not far from Abdera,* used poet for *Thracians,* hence adj , **Bistŏnius** -a -um, *Bistonian* or *Thracian,* tyrannus, *Diomedes,* Ov., chelys, *the lyre of Orpheus,* Claud , turbo, *violent north wind,* Lucan , Minerva, *goddess of the warlike Thracians,* Ov Subst., **Bistŏnia** -ae, f *Thrace,* **Bistŏnis** idis, f *a Thracian woman* = Bacchante, Hor , ales, *Procne, wife of the Thracian king Tereus,* Sen poet

bĭsulcis -e (bis and sulcus), *cloven* **A.** bisulci lingua (anguis), Pac **B.** Meton , *a double-tongued person, a hypocrite,* Plaut.

bĭsulcus a -um (bis and sulcus), *split into two parts,* lingua, *forked,* Ov , ungula, *cloven hoof,* Plin , pes, Lucr , Plin Subst , **bisulca** -ōrum, n *animals with cloven hoofs* (opp solipedes), Plin

Bĭthȳnia ae, f *a country of Asia Minor, between the sea of Marmora and the Black Sea,* hence adj , **Bĭthȳnicus** -a -um, *surname of Pompeius, conqueror of the Bithynians, and of his son,* Cic , **Bĭthȳnius** a -um , **Bĭthȳnus** -a um, *Bithynian,* **Bĭthȳnii** ōrum, m , Plin , **Bĭthȳni** -ōrum, m *the Bithynians,* Tac , **Bĭthȳnis** -idis, f *a Bithynian woman,* Ov

bĭtūmen -inis, n. *asphaltum, bitumen,* Verg , Ov

bĭtūmĭnĕus a -um (bitumen), *bituminous,* Ov

Bĭtūriges -um, m *a people of Aquitanian Gaul, near the modern town Bourges,* Caes

bĭvium ii, n *a place where two roads meet,* Verg , in bivio distineri, *to be distracted by a love for two persons,* Ov

bĭvius -a -um, *having two ways* or *passages,* Verg

blaesus -a -um (βλαισός), *lisping, indistinct,* lingua, sonus, Ov , used of the talk of a parrot, Ov Subst., madidi et blaesi, *drunken men,* Juv

blandē, adv (blandus), *caressingly, softly, tenderly, flatteringly,* rogare, Cic., blandissime appellare hominem, Cic

blandĭdĭcus -a -um (blande and dico), *flatteringly,* Plaut

blandĭlŏquentŭlus -a -um, *talking flatteringly,* Plaut

blandĭlŏquus -a um (blande and loquor), *flattering, fair-spoken,* Plaut

blandīmentum i, n (blandior) **I.** *flattery,* usually plur , blandimentis corrumpere, Cic , blandimenta muliebria, Tac **II. 1,** *whatever pleases the senses, an allurement,* sine blandimentis expellunt famem, *without sauces, delicacies,* Tac., **2,** *careful tending,* of a plant, Plin

blandĭor, 4 dep *to flatter, caress, coax* **A.** Lit , governing the dative, mihi et per se et per Pompeium blanditur Appius, Cic , Hannibalem pueriliter blandientem patri Hamilcari, ut duceretur in Hispaniam, Liv , auribus, *to tickle the ears,* Plin , sibi, *to deceive oneself,* Sen , votis meis, *to delude oneself into believing what one wishes,* Ov **B.** Transf , of things, blandiebatur coeptis fortuna, *fortune favoured his undertakings,* Tac , voluptas sensibus blanditur, Cic , blandiente inertia, *idleness pleasing him,* Tac Hence past partic , **blandītus** -a -um, *charming,* Prop

blandĭter = blande (q.v)

blandĭtĭa -ae, f (blandus), *a caress, flattery,* used in both a good and a bad and not always in an invidious sense, as assentatio, and adulatio **A.** Lit , popularis, Cic , plur benevolentiam civium blanditiis et assentando colligere, Cic , adhibere, Ov , muliebres, Liv **B.** *that which is alluring* or *attractive,* blanditiae praesentium voluptatum, Cic

blandĭtĭēs ei, f = blanditia (q v)

blandus a -um, *flattering, fondling, caressing,* **1,** blandum amicum a vero secernere, Cic , voluptates, blandissimae dominae, Cic , with dat , blandiores alienis quam vestris, Liv , **2,** of things, *enticing, alluring, tempting,* litterae, Cic ; somni, Ov , oculi, Plin , otium consuetudine in dies blandius, *ease becoming by habit every day more attractive,* Liv

blătĕro, 1 *to chatter, babble,* Hor

blătĭo, 4 *to talk idly, babble,* nugas, Plaut

blatta -ae f *a cockroach, chafer of uncertain species,* Verg , Hor

blennus i, m (βλεννός), *a stupid fellow,* Plaut

blĭtum -i, n (βλίτον), *a tasteless herb used in salad,* Plaut ; hence adj , **blĭtĕus** a- um, *insipid, silly,* Plaut

bŏārius, and **bŏvārius** a -um (bos), *relating to oxen,* forum, *the cattle market,* Liv

Boccar ăris m *a king of Mauritania at the time of the second Punic war ,* hence = *an African,* Juv

Bocchus -i, **1,** *king of Mauritania, the friend and afterwards the betrayer of Jugurtha,* **2,** *a plant named after him,* Verg

Boebe -ēs, f (Βοίβη), *a lake in Thessaly and also a place on its shores,* hence **Boebēis** idis and idos, f *the lake Boebe* Adj , **Boebēius** -a um

boeōtarchēs -ae, m (Βοιωτάρχης), *the highest magistrate of Boeotia,* Liv

Boeōti -ōrum, m (Βοιωτοί), and **Boeōtii** ōrum, m *the inhabitants of Boeotia, proverbial for their dulness,* hence **Boeōtia** -ae, f *a country in Greece, north west of Attica ,* **Bŏeōtĭcus** a -um, *Boeotian ,* **Boeōtis** idis, f *Boeotia ,* **Boeōtius** -a um, *Boeotian,* moenia, *Thebes,* Ov , **Boeōtus** a -um, *Boeotian*

Bŏēthĭus -ii, m (Anicius Manlius Torquatus Severus), *a distinguished Roman philosopher and theologian of the post-classical period,* beheaded in prison (where he wrote his most celebrated work, De Consolatione Philosophiae Libri v) 524 A D

Bŏgud -ŭdis, m. *son of Bocchus and king of Mauritania Tingitana,* ally of Caesar and afterwards of Antonius, taken prisoner by Agrippa and executed (B C. 31)

bŏjae -ārum, f , plur , *a species of collar,* of wood or iron, for slaves and criminals, Plaut

Bŏji (Bŏii), and **Bŏi** -ōrum, m *a Celtic people, settled partly in north Italy, partly in central Germany, partly in central Gaul* Sing , **Bŏius** -i, m *one of the Boii,* **Bŏia,** -ae, f *a woman of the Boii,* hence, **a, Bŏia** ae, f *the country of the Boii,* **b, Bŏiohaemum** -i, n (Germ Boienheim), *the land of the Boii* (hence modern Bohemia)

Bŏla -ae, f *a town of the Aequi in Latium,* now Lugnano Hence **Bŏlānus** a -um, *relating to Bola*

Bolbĭtīnē ēs, f. (Βολβιτίνη), *town in Upper*

Egypt, now *Rosetta;* hence **Bolbitīnus** a um, *of Bolbitine*, ostium, *the Rosetta mouth of the Nile*, Plin

bōlētus -i, m (βωλιτης), *the best kind of mushroom*, Plin

bŏlus -i, m (βολος), *a throw* (classical jactus), 1, of dice, Plaut, 2, of a fishing net, and hence a, *what is caught at one throw*, bolum emere, Suet; b, fig, *a good haul, gain*, is primus bolu 'st, Plaut, bolo tangere, or multare, or emungere aliquem, *to cheat a man of his game*, Plaut

bombax, interj (βόμβαξ), an exclamation of ironical astonishment; *is it possible?* Plaut

bombȳcīnus -a -um (bombyx), *silken*, Plin Plur subst., **bombȳcina** -ōrum, n *silken garments*, Mart

bombyx -ȳcis, m and f (βόμβυξ) I. *the silkworm*, Plin II. *silk, silk-stuff*, Prop

Bŏna Dĕa, *the good goddess*, the deity of fertility, worshipped by the Roman women

bŏnĭtas -ātis, f (bonus), *goodness, excellence*. I. Of material things, agrorum, praediorum, vocis, Cic II. A. Of abstract things, naturae bonitate, Cic; bonitas et aequitas causae, Cic, bonitas verborum, Cic B. Of character, *goodness, kindness, integrity*, bonitas et beneficentia, Cic, facit parentes bonitas (*parental love*), non necessitas, Phaedr, with in or erga followed by the acc, bonitas in suos, Cic, divina bonitate erga homines, Cic

Bŏnōnĭa -ae, f (Βονωνια), 1, *a town in Cisalpine Gaul* (now *Bologna*), hence adj **Bŏnōnĭensis** -e, 2, *a port in Gallia Belgica* (now *Boulogne*), 3, *a town on the Danube* (now *Banostor*)

bŏnum -i, n *good*, material or moral, 1, material, generally plural, **bŏna** -ōrum, *property*, bona fortunaeque, Cic, bonorum omnium heres, *sole heir*, Liv., esse in bonis, *to be in possession*, Cic; 2, moral, bonum mentis est virtus, Cic, summum bonum, *the supreme good* (in philosoph sense), Cic; bona pacis, *the blessings of peace*, Tac, bonum naturale, *inborn talent*, Cic, 3, *profit, advantage*, bonum publicum, *the common weal*, Liv; bono esse alicui, *to profit one*, Cic, cui bono fuisset, *for whose advantage*, Cic

bŏnus -a -um (old form, **duonus**), compar melior -ius, gen -ōris, superl optimus a -um (from opto), *good* I. Physically and mentally, 1, *good in itself*, nummi boni, *genuine coin*, Cic, bona voce, Plaut, dicta, *good things* = *jests*, Enn; bona indole, Cic, esp, a, *beautiful*, forma bona, Ter, cervix, Suet, b, *of good birth*, bono genere natus, Cic, c, *able, clever*, imperator, Cic; poeta, Cic; jaculo, *good at hurting the javelin*, Verg, hence, subst, **bŏni**, *able men*, Cic, d, in war, *brave*, vir pace belloque bonus, Liv, bonus militia, Sall., 2, *good* as regards the sensations, position, etc., a, physically, of health, valetudo bona, Cic, mens bona, Liv, bono animo, *of good courage*, Cic; b, of physical qualities, color, *good complexion*, Lucr, aetas bona, *youth*, Cic, of the weather, bona tempestas, Cic, c, *pleasant to the senses*, bonae res, *good things, delicacies*, Nep, d, of news, bona fama, *good news*, Cic, e, of human actions, etc, bonum exemplum, Tac, navigatio, *a good voyage*, Cic, mors, *a happy death*, Plin, bona gratia, *in all kindness*, Cic; bona venia, *with your permission*, Cic, bonae res, *good fortune*, Cic., in bonam partem accipere, *to take in good part*, Cic, f, of time, *lucky* (poet), dies, Verg, g, of good omen, auspicium, Cic, bona verba, *auspicious words*, Ov, quod bonum felix faustumque sit, Cic.; 3, *good*, with regard to some object; aetas tironum plerumque melior, Cic; with ad, ad proelium boni, Tac; with dat, civitatibus suis, Cic; optimum factu, Cic., 4, as regards number or quantity, bona pars hominum, Hor., bonam partem sermonis, Cic II. Morally, *honest, faithful* A. Gen, viri boni est misereri, Cic; often ironical, homines optimi, Cic, bona atque honesta amicitia, Cic, in vocative, as a familiar greeting, O bone! *my good fellow*, Hor B. Esp a, with regard to the state, *patriotic, loyal*, bonus et fortis civis, Cic, and often in Cic and Sall. boni = *conservatives, the supporters of the existing system*, b, *chaste*, femina, Cic; c, *kind*, bonus atque benignus, Hor; di boni, *gracious gods!* Cic, with dat, tuis, Verg, with in and the acc, in me, Cic., d, name of Juppiter, Optimus Maximus, Cic

bŏo, 1 (βοάω), *to shout, roar*, of places, *to echo*, redde meum! toto voce boante foro, Ov.

Bŏōtes -ae and -is, m (Βοώτης, *the ox-driver*), *a constellation in the northern hemisphere*, also called Arctophylax.

Bŏrĕās -ae, m (Βορεας) A. *the north wind*, Verg (Class Lat. aquilo) B. Meton, *the north*, Hor. B. Mythol, *the husband of Orithyia, and father of Calais and Zetes*, hence adj, **Bŏrĕus** -a -um, *northern*

bŏrĭa ae, f *a kind of jasper*, Plin

Bŏrysthĕnēs -is, m (Βορυσθενης), *a large river in Sarmatia* (now *the Dnieper*), hence **Bŏrysthĕnĭdae** or **-ītae** ārum, m *dwellers on the Borysthenes* **Bŏrysthĕnis** -idis, f *a Greek colony on the Borysthenes*, **Bŏrysthĕnĭus** -a -um, *belonging to the Borysthenes*

bōs, bŏvis, c. (βοῦς), 1, *ox, bullock, cow*, Cic; Liv., bos Luca *an elephant*, Lucr, prov, bovi clitellas imponere, *to saddle an ox*, i e *to impose on any one an office for which he is not fit*, ap Cic, 2, *a kind of flat fish*, Ov

Bospŏrus (Bosphorus), -i, m (Βοσπορος), 1, Bosporus Thracius, *the straits between Thrace and Asia Minor* (now *the Straits of Constantinople*), 2, Bosporus Cimmerius, *off the Crimea* (now *the Straits of Yenikale*), hence a, adj, **Bospŏrānus** -a um, *belonging to the Bosphorus*, subst *a dweller on the Bosphorus* b, **Bospŏrĭus** and **Bospŏrĕus** -a -um, *belonging to the Bosphorus*

Bostra -ae, f *capital of the Roman province of Arabia* (the Bozrah of the Bible), hence **Bostrēnus** -a -um, *of or belonging to Bostra*.

Bottĭaea -ae, f (Βοττιαία), *a district of Macedonia*, hence **Bottĭaei** ōrum, m *the inhabitants of the district*.

Bŏvĭānum -i, n (Βουιανον), *town in Samnium* (now *Bojano*), hence adj, **Bŏvĭānĭus** -a -um

bŏvīle = bubile (q v.)

Bŏvillae -ārum, f 1, *town in Latium, not far from Rome, near which Clodius was murdered by Milo*, hence adj, **Bŏvillānus** -a -um, pugna (with a play on the word bovillus), *the murder of Clodius*, Cic.; 2, *town in the district of Arpinum*

bŏvillus -a um (bos), an old form of bubulus, *relating to oxen*, grex, ap Liv

brăbeuta -ae, m (βραβευτης), *a judge, umpire in the public games*, Suet

brăcae (braccae) -ārum, f pl (sing once in Ov), *breeches, trousers, hose;* originally worn by Persians, Gauls, and Germans, Tac, Ov.

brăcātus (braccātus) -a -um (bracae) I. Lit, *wearing breeches* II. Transf, A. *foreign, barbarian, effeminate*, natio, Cic. B. As geograph.

name = transalpinus, Gallia bracata, *Gaul on the north side of the Alps, the old name of Gallia Narbonensis*, Plin, cognatio bracata, *kindred with people of Transalpine Gaul*, Cic

braces, acc -em, f *a kind of corn*, Plin

brăchĭālis e (brachium), *belonging to the arm*, Plaut.

brăchĭŏlum -i, n (dim of brachium), *a small delicate arm*, Cat.

brăchĭum li, n (βραχίων) **I.** *the arm from the elbow to the wrist* (lacertus = *the fore-arm*), brachia et lacerti, Ov **II.** Gen, *the whole arm* **A.** Lit, brachium frangere, Cic; diu jactato brachio scutum emittere, Caes; dare collo brachia, *to embrace*, Verg, as used in speaking, porrectio brachii, Cic; in dancing, brachia numeris movere, Ov, prov, esp, brachia sua praebere sceleri, *to assist in a crime*, Ov, levi brachio agere, *to act without energy*, Cic, molli brachio objurgare, *to upbraid lightly*, Cic, dirigere brachia contra torrentem, *to swim against the stream*, Juv **B.** Transf, **1,** *the limbs of animals, the claw of a crab*, Ov, *the thigh of an elephant*, Plin, *the leg of a lion*, Plin, *the claw of the nautilus*, Plin, used of the sign Cancer, Ov, and Scorpio, Verg, **2,** of things resembling the arm, *the branch of a tree*, Verg, *arm of the sea*, Ov, *the spur of a mountain chain*, Plin, *the yard of a sail* = antenna, Verg, *an outwork connecting two points of a fortification*, Liv, *the long walls connecting Athens with the Piraeus*, Liv

bractĕa (brattĕa) -ae, f *a thin plate of metal, gold leaf*, Luci, Verg, Ov

bractĕātus -a -um **A.** Lit *covered with gold leaf* **B.** Transf **1,** *gilt, glittering like gold, magnificent*, **2,** *glittering, unreal delusive*, felicitas, Sen

bractĕŏla -ae, f (dim of bractea), *a little leaf of gold* Juv

Branchus -i, m (Βράγχος), *a Greek to whom Apollo gave the gift of prophecy*, hence **Branchidae** -ārum, m (Βραγχίδαι), *descendants of Branchus, the hereditary caste of priests at the temple of Apollo at Didyma, near Miletus*

brassĭca -ae, f *cabbage*, Plaut

Bratuspantium -ii, n *town in Gallia Belgica*, now ruins of *Bratuspante, near Breteuil*

Brennus -i, m (Βρέννος), **1,** *leader of the Senonian Gauls who took and burned Rome*, B.C. 389, **2,** *leader of a Gallic horde who invaded Greece* Adj **Brennĭcus** -a -um

brĕvĭārĭus -a -um (brevis), *abridged* Subst, **brĕviārium** -i, n *short summary, report, epitome*, ...cem, *statistical report*, Suet.

brĕvĭcŭlus -a -um (dim of brevis), *somewhat short or little*, Plaut

brĕvĭlŏquens -entis (brevis and loquor), *brief in speech*, Cic

brĕvĭlŏquentĭa -ae, f (breviloquens), *brevity of speech*, Cic

brĕvis -e (βραχύς) **A.** In regard to space, **1,** as to length and breadth (opp to longus, latus), *short*, via, Verg, in breve cogere, *to contract into a small space*, Hor, **2,** as to height (opp to longus, altus, procerus), judex brevior quam testis, *of shorter stature*, Cic, **3,** as to depth (opp to profundus), *shallow*, brevia vada, Verg Subst, **brĕvĭa** -ium, n *shallows*, Verg, Tac, and sing, *a shoal*, Tac **B.** In regard to time (opp to longus), **1,** *short*, ad breve tempus, Cic, brevi post, *shortly afterwards*, Liv, brevi, *for a little time*, Ov, **2,** *of short duration*, vitae curriculum, Cic; rosa, flos, lilium, *blooming only for a short time*, Hor, breves populi Romani amores, *short lived*, Tac, **3,** of the quantity of syllables, *short*, syllaba, Cic, **4,** of discourse or writing, *short, concise*, breves litterae tuae, Cic, brevis narratio, Cic, brevi, *in a few words*, Cic, breve faciam, *I will make it short*, Cic, in breve cogere, *to shorten*, Cic; so meton. of persons, quum se breves putent esse, longissimi sint, Cic; brevis esse laboro, Hor

brĕvĭtas -ātis, f (brevis), *shortness* **I.** Of space, **1,** in regard to length or breadth, spatii, Caes, **2,** of height, brevitas nostra, *our short stature*, Caes **II.** Of time, **A.** Lit, temporis, diei, Cic **B.** Transf, **a,** of the quantity of syllables, syllabarum Cic, **b,** of speech and writing, *brevity, conciseness* litterarum Cic, orationis, Cic, brevitati servire, *to study brevity*, Cic.

brĕvĭtĕr, adv (brevis) *shortly* **I.** of space, Tib **II.** Transf, **a,** of the quantity of syllables, Cic, **b,** of conciseness in speaking or writing, *briefly* rem breviter narrare, Cic

Brĭărĕus -ĕi, m (Βριαρεύς) also called Aegaeon, *son of Uranus, a giant with a hundred arms and fifty heads*, centimgeminus, Verg Hence **Brĭărēĭus** -a -um

Brĭgantes -um, m *a tribe in the north of Britain, in Northumberland or Cumberland*, hence adj, **Brĭgantĭcus** -a -um, *surname of Julius, nephew of Civilis*

Brĭgantĭa -ae, f *town of the Vindelici on the lake of Constance (now Bregenz)*, hence adj, **Brĭgantīnus** -a -um, *Brigantine*

Brīmo -ūs, f (Βριμώ), *the terrible one*, epithet of Hecate, used of Proserpina, Prop

Brĭtannĭa -ae, f and plur **Brĭtannĭae** -arum, used both of *Great Britain* and *the British Isles*, hence adj, **1, Brĭtannĭcus** -a -um, herba, *the plant water-dock*, Plin, **2, Brĭtannus** -a -um, and subst, **Brĭtannus** -i, m *a Briton*, Hor, plur **Brĭtanni** -orum, m *the Britons*, Caes, **Brĭto** -onis, m *a Briton*, Juv, *a Breton*, poet for *a Gaul*, Mart

Brĭtannĭcus -i, m *the son of Claudius and Messalina, born A.D. 42*, so called from his father's pretended victories in Britain He was set aside from the succession in favour of Nero the son of his step-mother Agrippina, and murdered after Nero became Emperor

Brĭtŏmartis -is, f (Βριτόμαρτις), *a Cretan deity, afterwards identified with Diana*

Brixĭa -ae, f *town in Cisalpine Gaul (now Brescia) the mother city of Verona* Hence adj, **Brixĭānus** -a -um *of or relating to Brixia*

brocchĭtās -ātis, f *projection of the teeth in animals*, Plin

brocchus, (brochus, bronchus), *projecting* (of teeth), of men and animals, *having projecting teeth*, Plaut

Brŏmĭus -ii, m (Βρόμιος, *the noisy*), *a surname of Bacchus*, Plaut, Ov

Bructeri -ōrum, m *a people of North Germany*

brūma -ae, f (for brevima, contracted from brevissima, sc dies), *the time of the shortest day of the year the winter solstice* **I.** Lit, ante brumam, Cic, sub bruma, Caes **II.** Poet, *winter, wintry cold*, bruma recurrit iners, Hor, **III.** Meton, *the year*, Mart

brūmālis -e (bruma), **1,** *relating to the shortest day*, dies, Cic, signum, *Capricorn*, Cic, **2,** *wintry* horae, Ov, frigus, Verg

Brundĭsium -i, n *a town in Calabria*, with an excellent harbour, the port most used by the Romans for journeys to Greece and the East (now *Brindisi*), hence adj, **Brundĭsīnus** -a -um, *Brundisian*.

Bruttii (Brūtii, Brittii) -ōrum, m. *the Bruttii, the inhabitants of the southern extremity of Italy* (now *Calabria Ulteriore*); hence adj., **Bruttius** -a -um, *Bruttian.*

1. **brūtus** -a -um (connected with βαρύς and βριθύς), **1,** *heavy, immoveable;* pondus, Lucr.; **2,** *dull, insensible, without feeling or reason;* aliorum brutorum qui se cautos ac sapientes putant, Cic.

2. **Brūtus** -i, m. *a cognomen of the Roman Gens Junia.* **1,** L. Junius Brutus, *relative of Tarquinius Superbus, feigned idiocy, freed Rome from the kingly power,* B.C. 509. **2,** M. Junius Brutus, *nephew of Cato Uticensis, one of the murderers of Julius Caesar, intimate friend of Cicero, philosopher and orator.* **3,** D. Junius Brutus, *fellow conspirator with 2.* Adj., **Brūtīnus** -a -um, *belonging to* (M. Junius) *Brutus;* consilia Brutina, Cic.

Būbastis -is, f. (Βούβαστις), *an Egyptian goddess, represented with the head of a cat.*

būbīle -is, n. (bos), *an ox-stall,* Plaut.

būbo -ōnis, m. (βύας, βύζα), *the screech owl,* Verg.

bŭbulcĭtor, 1. dep., and **bŭbulcĭto,** 1. *to be a cow-herd,* Plaut.

bŭbulcus -i, m. (bos), *one who ploughs with oxen,* Cic.

būbŭlus -a -um (bos), *relating to cows or oxen;* caro, Plin. Subst., **būbŭla** -ae, f. (sc. caro), *beef,* Plaut.

būcaeda -ae, m. (bos and caedo), *one who has been beaten with thongs of ox hide,* Plaut.

bucca -ae, f. *the cheek;* esp. when puffed out. **I.** Lit., buccas inflare, *to swell with rage,* Hor.; prov., quod in buccam venerit, scribito, *whatever comes into your mouth,* Cic. **II.** Meton., **1,** *a declaimer, bawler,* Juv.; **2,** *one who fills his mouth very full, a parasite,* Petr.; **3,** *a mouthful,* Mart.; **4,** *a person with swollen cheeks* (of a trumpeter), Juv.

buccella -ae, f. (dim. of bucca), *a little mouthful,* Mart.

buccĭna, buccĭnator, etc., v. bucina, etc.

bucco -ōnis, m. (bucca), *a babbling foolish fellow,* Plaut.

buccŭla -ae, f. (dim. of bucca); **1,** *the cheek, jaw,* Plaut.; **2,** *the beaver, the visor, the part of a helmet which covers the cheeks,* Liv.

buccŭlentus -a -um (bucca), *puffy-cheeked,* Plaut.

Būcĕphălās -ae, acc. -an, and **-us** -i, m. (Macedonian Βουκεφάλας, Gr. Βουκέφαλος), *the horse of Alexander the Great.* **Būcĕphăla** -ae, f. and **Būcĕphălē** -ēs, f. (Βουκεφάλη), *a town founded in its honour on the Hydaspes.*

būcĕrōs -ōn, and **būcĕrĭus** -a -um, Lucr. (βούκερως), *having ox's horns,* Ov.

būcĭna -ae, f. (from the sound bu and cano, or contr. from bovicina, from bos and cano). **I.** *a crooked trumpet;* **a,** *the shepherd's horn,* Prop.; **b,** *a military trumpet,* Cic.; used as a signal for relieving guard, hence ad tertiam bucinam (= vigiliam), Liv.; **c,** *the trumpet used to summon the popular assemblies,* Prop. **II.** *Triton's horn,* Ov.

būcĭnātor -ōris, m. *a trumpeter,* Caes.

būcĭnum -i, n. **1,** *the sound of a trumpet,* Plin.; **2,** *a shell fish,* Plin.

būcŏlĭcus -a -um, and **-ŏs** -ŏ -ŏn (βουκολικός), *relating to shepherds, rural;* modi, Ov.

būcŭla -ae, f. (dim. of bos), *a heifer,* Verg., Cic.

būfo -ōnis, m. *a toad,* Verg.

bulbus -i, m. (βολβός), *an onion,* Ov.

būleutērĭon -ii, n. (βουλευτήριον), *the place of meeting of a Greek senate,* Cic.

bulla -ae, f. *a hollow swelling, a bladder, bubble.* **I.** Lit., *a water bubble;* ut pluvio per lucida caelo surgere bulla solet, Ov. **II.** Transf., **A.** *a boss, stud;* **1,** on girdles, aurea bullis cingula, Verg.; **2,** on doors, bullas aureas omnes ex his valvis non dubitavit auferre, Cic. **B.** bulla aurea, *a golden ornament, an amulet* (of Etruscan origin), worn by triumphing generals and by boys of good family, laid aside by the latter when the toga virilis was put on; hence dignus bulla = *childish,* Juv.

bullātus -a -um (bulla). **I.** *inflated, bombastic,* or *perishable, transitory,* Pers. **II.** Transf., **1,** *furnished with a* bulla, in the sense of *a boss, knob,* cingulum, Varr.; **2,** *wearing the bulla,* and consequently not yet arrived at years of discretion, heres, Juv.

bullĭo, 4. (bulla), *to well up, bubble up, boil up,* Pers.

Bullis (Byllis) -idis, f. *an Illyrian town and district between Dyrrhachium and Apollonia;* hence **Bullĭdenses** -ium, m. *inhabitants of Bullis;* also **Bulienses** -ium, m. and **Bullīni** -ōrum, m.

būmastus -i, f. *a kind of vine bearing very large grapes,* Verg.

Būra -ae, f. (Βοῦρα), and **Būris** -is, f. *a town in Achaia, forty stadia from the sea.*

Burdĭgăla -ae, f. *a town in Aquitania* (now *Bordeaux*).

būris -is, m. *the crooked hinder part of the plough,* Verg.

Būsīris -rīdis, m. (Βούσιρις), *an old king of Egypt who sacrificed all foreigners who came to his country.*

bustĭrăpus -i, m. (bustum and rapio), *a robber of tombs,* Plaut.

bustŭārĭus -a -um (bustum), *belonging to the place where corpses were burned;* gladiator, *one who fought at a funeral pile in honour of the dead,* Cic.

bustum -i, n. (from buro, old Lat. for uro). **I.** *the place where corpses where burned,* Lucr. **II.** *a grave, sepulchre.* **A.** Lit., Cic. **B.** Fig., tu bustum reipublicae, *the destroyer of the State,* Cic.; bustum miserabile nati, *Tereus who ate his own son,* Ov.

Buthrōtum -i, n. and **-tŏs** -i, f. (Βουθρωτόν and -τός), *a town on the coast of Epirus, opposite Corcyra,* now *Butrinto.*

būthȳsĭa -ae, f. (βουθυσία), *a sacrifice of oxen,* Suet.

Butrōtus -i, m. *a river in Bruttium,* now *Bruciano.*

Buxentum -i, n. *a town in Lucania,* now *Policastro.*

buxĭfĕr -a -um (buxus and fero), *producing the box-tree,* Cat.

buxus -i, f. and **buxum** i. n. (πύξος). **I. 1,** *the evergreen box-tree,* Ov.; **2,** *box-wood,* Verg. **II.** Meton., *articles made of box-wood—e.g., flute,* Verg.; *top,* Verg.; *comb,* Ov.; *writing-tablets,* Prop.

Byrsa -ae, f. (Βύρσα), *the citadel of Carthage.*

Byzantĭum -ii, n. (Βυζάντιον), *Byzantium, a city in Thrace on the Bosphorus, opposite the Asiatic Chalcedon* (now *Constantinople*). Adj., **Byzantīnus** -a -um, **Byzantĭus** -a -um *Byzantine.*

C

C c, the third letter of the Latin Alphabet, corresponding in place and originally in sound with the Greek Γ, γ At an early period it was substituted for K, which, except in a few instances, disappeared from the language

căballīnus a um, *belonging to a horse*, fons (in jest) = *Hippocrene*, Pers.

căballus -i, m. *a pack-horse, nag*, Hor , Juv

Cābillonum i, n. *a town of the Aedui in Gallia Lugdunensis*, now *Châlons sur-Saône*.

Căbīri ōrum, m (Κάβειροι), *gods honoured by secret rites in Lemnos and Samothrace*

căchinnātĭo ōnis, f. *a violent laughing, cachinnation*, Cic

1 **căchinno**, 1 (cachinnus), *to laugh aloud*, ridere convivae, cachinnare ipse Apronius, Cic

2 **căchinno** -ōnis, m (cachinnus), *one who laughs heartily, a jester*, Plaut. , *scoffer*, Pers

căchinnus -i m (καγχασμός), *loud laughter, jeering*, cachinnos irridentium commovere, Cic , poet transf , *the splashing of the sea*, Cat

căco, 1 (κακόω), 1, *to void the excrement*, Hor , 2, *to defile with excrement*, Cat

căcŏēthēs -is, n (κακοηθες), *an obstinate disease, an itch* or *incurable passion*, scribendi, *an incurable itch to write*, Juv

căcŭla ae, m *a soldier's* or *officer's servant*, Plaut

căcūmen -inis, n 1, *the extreme point, top, summit*, montis, Cat. , arboris, Verg. , ramorum, Caes , 2, *height, perfection*, alescendi, *the greatest growth*, Lucr

căcūmĭno, 1 (cacumen), *to point, make pointed*, Ov

Căcus -i, m (Κᾶκος), *son of Vulcan, an Italian cattle robber slain by Hercules*

cădāver ĕris (cado), n *a dead body, carcass*, of men or animals I. Lit , Cic , as a term of reproach, ab hoc ejecto cadavere quidquam mihi aut opis aut ornamenti expetebam, Cic II. Transf , of the ruins of towns, cadavera oppidūm, ap Cic

cădāvĕrōsus -a -um (cadaver), *like a corpse, cadaverous*, Ter

Cadmus -i, m. (Κάδμος), *the son of Agenor, king of Phoenicia and brother of Europa, father of Polydorus, Ino, Semele, Autonoe, and Agave, founder of Thebes in Boeotia* Adj , **Cadmēus** -a -um, Thebae, Prop ; hence subst , **Cadmēa** -ae, f *the citadel of Thebes*, Nep ; **Cadmēis** -idis, f arx, *Theban*, Ov , and subst , *a female descendant of Cadmus*, Ov

cădo, cĕcĭdi, cāsum, 3 *to fall* I. Gen , A. Lit , 1, of lifeless things, arma alicui cadunt de manibus, Cic , of weapons, levius, *with less violence*, Caes , of thunderbolts, caelo cadunt fulmina, Petr , of dice, ut (talus) cadat rectus, Cic ; of sails, vela cadunt, are *furled*, Verg , of rain, snow, tears, and other liquids, guttae cadentes, Cic ; of shadows, altis de montibus, Verg , of things which naturally fall—e g., fruit, leaves, &c , motis poma cadunt ramis, Ov , barba cadit, Verg ; of the sun, stars, the day, etc , *to set*, sol cadens, poet , *the west*, juxta solem cadentem, Verg , of winds, *to be lulled*, cadente jam euro, Liv , of words, *to fall from the mouth*, verba cadentia tollit, Hor ; grammat and rhet t t , *to come to an end*, verba melius in syllabas longiores cadunt, Cic 2, of living things, si prolapsus cecidisset, Liv , in terram, Cic , de equo, Cic B. Transf., 1, of payments, *to fall due*, in eam diem cadere nummos qui a Quinto debentur, Cic ; 2, of perception, *to fall to the notice of*, sub oculos, Cic , 3, *to fall under a certain class*; in idem genus orationis, Cic ; 4, *to fall under*, in unius potestatem, Cic , 5, *to agree with, be consistent with*, non cadit in hos mores, non in hunc hominem ista suspicio, Cic , 6, *to happen*; si quid adversi casurum foret, Liv , fortuito, Cic ; male, Caes , cadere ad or in irritum, *to become of no effect*, Liv , insperanti mihi cecidit ut, etc , Cic , 7, *to fall*, in power, honour, etc , tam graviter, Cic , *to lose* or *be cast in* a law-suit, in judicio, Cic , causa, Cic , *to lose courage*, non debemus ita cadere animis quasi, etc , Cic II. Esp , A. *to be destroyed*, non tota cadet Troja, Ov B. Of persons, *to be killed*, pauci de nostris cadunt, Caes ; in acie, Cic , sua manu, *to commit suicide*, Tac , of the victims of a sacrifice, ovis cadit deo, Ov

cādūcĕātor ōris, m (caduceus), *a herald*, Liv

cādūcĕus -i, m *a herald's staff*, Cic , *the wand* or *staff of Mercury*, Suet

cādūcĭfĕr fĕri (caduceus and fero), *he that bears the caduceus*, surname of Mercury, Ov , absol , Ov

cădūcus -a -um (cado), *that which has fallen or is falling* I. A. Lit , bello, *fallen in war*, Verg B. Transf , legal t t , bona, *a legacy rendered void by the death or legal incapacity of the legatee, which fell to other heirs or to the exchequer*, Cic , legatum omne capis necnon et dulce caducum, Juv II. A. Lit , *inclined or ready to fall*, 1, gen , vitis, Cic , flos, Ov , 2, esp , *destined to die, devoted to death*, juvenis Verg B. Transf , *frail, perishable, transitory*, res humanae fragiles caducaeque, Cic

Cădurci ōrum, m *a Gaulish people in Aquitania, famous for their linen manufactures*, hence a, adj , **Cădurcus** -a, -um , b, subst , **Cădurcum** -i, n (sc stragulum) A *a coverlet of Cadurcian linen* B. Meton., *the marriage-bed*, Juv

cădus -i, m (κάδος), *a wine jar* , capite sistere, *to overturn*, Plaut , meton , *wine*, Hor , also used for other purposes, for honey, Mart , = urna, *a funeral urn*, Verg

Cadūsii -ōrum, m (Καδούσιοι), *a warlike nation on the Caspian Sea*

caecias -ae, m (καικίας), *a north east wind*, Plin

caecĭgĕnus a -um (caecus and gigno), *born blind*, Lucr

Caecĭlius -a -um, *name of a celebrated plebeian gens*, the most important family of which was the Metelli , of these the most illustrious were 1, Qu Caec Metellus, *praetor* B C 148, *surnamed Macedonicus, for his conquests in Macedonia*, 2, his son, Qu Caec Metellus, *consul* B C 123, *surnamed Balearicus for his victories over the Baleares*; 3, Caecilia, *the daughter of Balearicus, the mother of the tribune Clodius*, 4, C Caecilius Statius, *Roman comic poet, contemporary of Ennius, died about* 168 B C Adj , **Caecĭlius** -a um, *Caecilian*, lex (de ambitu), Cic , **Caecĭliānus** -a -um, fabula, *of Caecilius Statius*, Cic , senex, *in a play of the same*, Cic

caecĭtas -ātis, f (caecus), *blindness*, Cic , fig , of the mind, an tibi luminis obesset caecitas plus quam libidinis ? Cic

caeco, 1 *to make blind*, Lucr , fig , largitione mentes imperitorum, Cic , celeritate caecata oratio, *made obscure*, Cic

Caecŭbum -i, n and **Caecŭbus ager**, *a district in Latium, famed for its wine*, hence adj , **Caecŭbus** -a um, *Caecuban*, vinum Caecubum and simply Caecubum *wine of Caecubum*, Hor

caecus -a -um, adj. with compar. **I.** Active. **A.** Lit., *blind, not seeing;* ille qui caecus factus est, Cic.; subst., apparet id etiam caeco, Liv. **B.** Transf., *intellectually* or *morally blind, blinded;* **1,** of persons, caecus animi, Cic.; **2,** of passions, timor, Cic. **II.** Passive. **A.** Lit., **1,** of places that have no light, *dark;* domus, Cic.; **2,** of objects, appearances, etc., *invisible, unseen;* fores, Verg.; pericula, Cic. **B.** Transf., **1,** *dark, unintelligible, unknown;* fata, Hor.; **2,** *blind, uncertain, objectless;* caeca expectatione, Cic.

caedes -is, f. (caedo). **A.** *a cutting off, a cutting down, killing, slaughter, carnage;* **a,** caedem facere, Cic.; plur. multae et atroces inter se caedes, Liv.; **b,** *killing of victims for sacrifice;* bidentium, Hor. **B.** Meton., **a,** *the persons slain;* caedis acervi, Verg.; **b,** *blood shed in slaughter,* (currus) respersus fraterna caede, Cat.

caedo, cĕcīdi, caesum, 3. *to hew, fell, cut down, hew in pieces, strike, beat.* **I. A.** januam saxis, Cic.; aliquem virgis, Cic.; silvam, Caes. **B.** Transf., testibus caedi, *to be hard pressed,* Cic. **II. A.** *to kill;* consulem exercitumque, Liv.; poet., caesi acervi, *heaps of the slain,* Cat.; caesus sanguis, *the blood of the slain,* Verg.; of sacrificial victims, hostias, Cic. **B.** *to cut out,* securibus humida vina (of wine when frozen), Verg.; latius (murus) quam caederetur ruebat, Liv.

caelāmĕn -inis (caelo), n. *a bas-relief,* Ov.

caelātor -ōris, m. (caelo), *a chaser, graver,* or *carver,* Cic.

caelātūra -ae, f. (caelo), *the art of engraving* or *chasing,* chiefly in metals or ivory, Quint.; meton., *an engraving,* Suet.

caelebs -libis, *unmarried, single* (of the man). **I. A.** Lit., se rectius viduam et illum caelibem esse futurum, Liv. **B.** Meton., vita (of an unmarried man), Hor. **II.** Transf., of trees, platanus, *to which no vine is trained,* Hor.

caelĕs -itis (caelum), *heavenly;* regna, Ov. Subst., *a god,* Ov.; oftener in plur., **caelites,** *the gods,* Cic.

caelestis -e (caelum), **a,** *belonging to heaven, heavenly;* corpora, Cic.; hence subst., **caelestia** -ium, n. *things in heaven, the heavenly bodies,* Cic; **b,** *coming from the heavens* or *seen in the heavens;* aqua, Hor.; spiritus, Cic.; **c,** *belonging to heaven as the seat of the gods, celestial, divine;* dii, Cic.; sapientia, Cic.; quem prope caelestem fecerint, *whom they almost deified,* Liv.; hence subst., **caelestis** -is, f. *a goddess,* Tib.; plur., m. and f. *the gods,* Cic.; transf. for what is excellent, *glorious, superhuman;* ingenium, Ov.

caelĭbātus -ūs, m. (caelebs), *celibacy,* Suet.

caelĭcŏla -ae, m. (caelum and colo), *a dweller in heaven;* poet., *a god,* Verg.

caelĭfĕr -fĕra -fĕrum, *bearing the heavens;* Atlas, Verg.

Caelius -a -um. **I.** *name of a Roman plebeian gens, the most celebrated members of which were:* **1,** C. Caelius Caldus, *Roman orator and lawyer;* **2,** L. Caelius Antipater, *annalist of the Second Punic War, contemporary of the Gracchi;* **3,** M. Caelius Rufus, *intimate friend and client of Cicero.* **II.** Caelius Mons, *a hill in Rome south of the Palatine and east of the Aventine* (now *the Lateran*). Adj., **Caeliānus** -a -um, *Caelian.*

caelo, 1. (1. caelum), **1,** *to engrave* or *chase metals* or *ivory, to carve in bas-relief;* speciem caelare argento, Cic.; vasa caelata, Cic.; **2,** of poetry, caelatum novem Musis opus, *adorned by,* Hor.

1. **caelum** -i, n. (caedo), *the burin* or *engraving-tool,* Mart.

2. **caelum** -i, n. (connected with Gr. κοῖλος, *hollow*), **1,** *the heavens;* caelum totum astris distinctum et ornatum, Cic.; non de caelo demissos, sed qui patrem ciere possent, Liv.; caelum ac terras miscere, Liv.; findere caelum aratro, *to do something impossible,* Ov.; hence, **a,** of a great height, it caelo clamor, Verg.; juncta caelo montium juga, Liv.; minari in caelum, Verg.: **b,** fig., as the height of joy, renown, etc., esse in caelo, Cic.; aliquem or aliquid ferre ad or in caelum, Cic.; **2,** *the heavens,* **a,** as the home of light, clouds, etc., caelum nocte atque nubibus obscuratum, Sall.; de caelo cadere (of meteors), Liv.; caelum discedit, *light,* Cic.; ictus e caelo, Cic.; **b,** *the air,* caelum liberum, Cic.; of climate, gravitas huius caeli, *unhealthiness,* Cic.; caelum crassum, Cic.; **3,** *heaven* as the home of the gods, de caelo delapsus, *a messenger of the gods,* Cic.; non ad mortem trudi, verum in caelum videri escendere, Cic.; quid me caelum sperare jubebas, *marriage with a god,* Verg.

Caelus -i, m. = Caelum *personified as a god, son of Aether and Dies.*

caementum -i, n. (caedo), *rough stone from the quarry,* Cic.

Caeneus -ĕi, m. (Καινεύς), *originally a maiden, daughter of Elatus, changed by Neptune into a boy and then into a bird.*

Caenīna -ae, f. (Καινίνη), *town in Latium;* hence adj., **Caenīnensis** -e and **Caenīnus** -a -um, *of or belonging to Caenina.*

caenōsus -a -um (caenum), *muddy,* Juv.

caenum -i, n. (connected with in-quino), *mud, dirt, filth;* male olere omne caenum, Cic.; as a term of reproach, labes illa atque caenum, Cic.

caepa (cēpa) -ae, f. and **caepe** (cēpe) -is, n. *an onion,* Hor.

Caepĭo -ōnis, m. *the cognomen of a patrician branch of the gens Servilia.*

Caerĕ, n. indecl., and **Caerēs** -ĭtis or -ētis, f. *a very old city of Etruria, whose inhabitants received the Roman citizenship, except the right of voting;* hence, **Caerēs** -ĭtis and -ētis, *belonging to Caere;* subst., **Caerĭtes** or **Caerētes** -um, m. *the inhabitants of Caere;* Caerite cera (i.e., tabula) digni = *deserving of civic degradation,* Hor.

caerĭmōnĭa -ae, f. **I.** *holiness, sacredness;* deorum, Cic.; legationis, Cic. **II. 1,** *holy awe, reverence;* summa religione caerimoniaque sacra conficere, Cic.; **2,** *religious usage, sacred ceremony* (gen. in plur.), Cic.

Caeroesi -ōrum, m. *a people in Gallia Belgica, near modern Luxemburg* or *Lüttich.*

caerŭlĕus (poet. **caerŭlus**) -a -um (connected with caesius). **I.** *dark-coloured, dark blue,* epithet of the sea and sky; **a,** of the sky, caerula caeli, or simply caerula, *the azure of the sky,* Lucr., Ov.; **b,** of the sea, aquae, Ov.; **caerŭla** -orum, n. *the sea,* Enn.; of sea-gods, deus, *Neptune,* Ov.; mater, *Thetis,* Ov.; equi, *of Triton,* Ov.; via, Ov.; puppis, Ov.; **c,** of rivers, Thybris, Verg.; **d,** of other things, angues, Verg.; Germanorum pubes, *blue-eyed,* Hor. Subst., **caerŭlĕum** -i, *a blue colour,* Plin. **II.** Poet., *dark green,* Ov.; *dark,* Verg.

Caesar -ăris, m. *a Roman family name of the gens Julia, the most famous of which were,* **1,** C. Julius Caesar, *who conquered Pompeius, overthrew the power of the senate, was made Dictator with supreme power, and was murdered by Brutus and Cassius,* 44 B.C.; **2,** *his nephew,* Octavius, *who took his name, with the addition of Octavianus, and established the empire.* After him all the emperors bore the name of Caesar with the title Augustus, till, under Hadrian, a distinction was made, and the reigning emperor was called Caesar Augustus, and the appointed heir Caesar Adj, **A. Caesărĕus** -a um, *belonging to Julius Caesar*, sanguis, Ov **B. Caesărĭānus** -a -um, *Caesarian*, subst Caesariani, *the partisans of Caesar.* **C. Caesăriensis** e, Mauritania, *the east part of Mauritania* **D. Caesărīnus** a -um, *of* (Julius) *Caesar*, celeritas, Cic

Caesarēa -ae, f (Καισάρεια), *name of several towns*, 1, *in Palestine*; 2, *in Mauritania Caesariensis*, 3, *in Cappadocia*, 4, *in Phoenicia*

caesărĭātus -a -um (caesaries), *long-haired*, Plaut

caesărĭēs -ēi, f *a bushy head of hair*, Verg, barbae, *the hair of the beard*, Ov

caesim, adv (caedo) **A.** *with cutting, with the edge of the sword* (opp to punctim, *with the point*), petere hostem, Liv **B.** Transf, of discourse, *in short sentences*; membratim adhuc, deinde caesim diximus, Cic.

caesĭus -a -um, *bluish grey*, used of the colour of the eyes, caesios oculos Minervae, caeruleos Neptuni, Cic, leo, *with grey eyes*, Cat

caespes (cespes) -itis (caedo), *grass that has been cut* **I. A.** Lit *turf*, used for altars, tombs, mounds, primum exstruendo tumulo caespitem Caesar posuit, Tac; plur, gladiis caespites circumcidere, Caes, non esse arma caespites neque glebas, Cic **B.** Meton, a, *a hut of turf*, Hor, b, *an altar of turf*, Hor, c, *a clump of plants*, Verg **II.** Transf. *grassy sward*, gramineus, Verg

1 **caestus** ūs, m (caedo), *gauntlet for boxers*, made of leathern thongs, Cic.

2 **caestus** -i, m, v cestus

caeterus, etc v. ceterus, etc

Caīcus -i, m (Κάικος), *a river in Mysia flowing into the Sinus Elaiticus*

Cājēta -ae (and ē -ēs), f **I.** *the nurse of Aeneas* **II.** *a town on the sea-coast, on the borders of Latium and Campania, now Gaeta*

Cājus (poet **Cāius**), -i, m, and **Cāja** ae, f, 1, *a common praenomen among the Romans* At a wedding, the bride and bridegroom were called by these names, and the bride said ubi tu Cajus, ego Caja, 2, *the name of a celebrated Roman jurist*, more frequently written Gaius, who flourished under the Antonines at the beginning of the second century.

Călabri -ōrum, m *inhabitants of Calabria*, hence, **Călăber** bra brum, *belonging to Calabria*, poet, Pierides, *the poems of Ennius*, Hor, **Călabrĭa** -ae, f *the peninsula at the south-east extremity of Italy*

Călactē -ēs, f (Καλὴ ἀκτή), *a town on the north coast of Sicily*, hence, **Călactīnus** -a um, *of or belonging to Calacte*

Călăgurris is, f *a town in Spain, now Loharre*; hence **Călăgurrĭtāni** -ōrum, m *the inhabitants of Calagurris*

Călăis, acc -in, abl -i, m (Κάλαϊς) *son of Boreas and Orithyia, brothers of Zetes, who accompanied the Argonauts and drove off the Harpies*

Călămis midis, m (Κάλαμις), *one of the greatest sculptors of the age of Phidias*

călămister tri, m and **călămistrum** -tri, n (calamus) **A.** *a curling iron for the hair*, frons calamistri notata vestigiis, Cic **B.** Transf *excessive ornament or flourish in discourse*, ineptis fortasse gratum fecit, qui volent illa calamistris inurere, Cic

călămistrātus -a -um *curled with the curling-iron*; coma, Cic., saltator, Cic

călămĭtas -ātis, f **A.** *damage, loss, failure*, especially in agriculture, Cic **B.** Transf *misfortune, damage, calamity, loss*, calamitatem tolerare, Cic, calamitate prohibere aliquem, Cic, plur, calamitates reipublicae, especially *misfortune, reverse in war*, Cannensis illa calamitas, Cic

călămĭtōsē, adv (calamitosus), *unfortunately*, vivere, Cic

călămĭtōsus a -um (calamitas), **1**, act, *causing loss, destructive*, tempestas, Cic, bellum, *calamitous*, Cic, **2**, pass, *suffering great loss, miserable*, agri vectigal, *oppressive*, Cic, homines miseri et fortuna magis quam culpa calamitosi, Cic

călămus -i, m, (κάλαμος), **I.** *a reed* **A.** Lit, Ov **B.** Meton, various articles made of reed, *a writing reed, pen*, Cic, *a reed-pipe, Pan-pipe*, Verg, *an arrow*, Hor, *a fishing rod*, Ov; *a limed twig for fowling*, Prop **II.** *any reed-shaped stalk*, Verg

călăthiscus -i, m (dim of calathus), *a small wicker basket*, Cat

călăthus -i, m (κάλαθος), **1**, *a wicker basket*, used for fruit or flowers, Verg, for spinning Ov, **2**, *a vessel of similar form* of metal or wood, *a cheese basket*, Verg, *a wine-bowl*, Verg

Călātĭa ae, and **Călātĭae** ārum, f *a town in Campania* Adj, **Călātīnus** a um, *Calatine*

călātor -ōris, m (1 calo), *a servant, attendant upon priests*, Suet

călautĭca -ae, f *a kind of female headdress with pendent lappets*, Cic

calcānĕum -i, n *the heel*, Verg (?)

calcar āris, n (calx), *a spur* **I.** Lit equo calcaria subdere, Liv, equum calcaribus concitare, Liv, prov, addere calcaria sponte currenti, *to spur the willing horse*, Plin **II.** Transf *stimulus, incitement*, admovere, Cic, gen. in plur, alter frenis eget, alter calcaribus, Cic, calcaria adhibere, Cic

calceāmentum -i, n (calceo), *a covering for the foot*, calceamentum solorum callum, Cic

calcĕārĭum i, n (calceus), *shoe money*, Suet

calceātus -ūs, m = calceamentum (q v)

calceo, 1 *to shoe, provide with shoes*, homines non satis commode calceati et vestiti, Cic

calceŏlārĭus -i, m (calceolus), *a shoemaker*, Plaut.

calceŏlus -i, m (dim. of calceus), *a half shoe*, Cic

calceus -i, m (calx, *the heel*), *a shoe*, distinguished from the sandal (solea) as covering the whole foot, Cic, calcei Sicyonii, *of Sicyonian leather*, Cic, (as the Romans took off their shoes when reclining at dinner), calceos poscere = *to rise from table*, Plin, calceos mutare, *to become a senator* (from a particular kind of shoe worn only by senators), Cic

Calchās (Calcās) antis, acc -antem and -anta, m. (Κάλχας), *son of Thestor, soothsayer to the Greeks before Troy*

Calchēdon -ŏnis and -ŏnos, acc -ŏnem and -ŏna, f (Χαλκηδών), *town in Bithynia on the Propontis, opposite Byzantium* Adj, **Calchēdŏnĭus** -a um, *Calchedonian*

calcio = calceo (q v)

calcĭtrātus ūs, m *a kicking*, Plin

1 **calcĭtro**, 1 (1 calx) **A.** Lit *to strike with the heel, kick*, Plin **B.** Transf *to oppose perversely and obstinately*, Cic

2 **calcĭtro** ōnis, m (1 calcitro), *a kicker*, Varr, of men, *a bully, blusterer*, Plin,

calco, 1. (1. calx), *to tread, to tread upon.* **I.** Gen. **A.** Lit. aliquem pede, Tac. **B.** Transf., **a,** *to trample under foot, conquer;* amorem, Ov.; **b,** *to mock, insult,* Prop. **II.** Esp. **A.** *to tread upon* (grapes) *in the wine-press;* uvas, Ov. **B.** *to stamp, compress,* Verg. **C.** *to visit* (a place); viam, Hor.

calcŭlātor -ōris, m. *a calculator, bookkeeper, accountant,* Mart.

calcŭlus -i, m. (dim. of 2. calx), *a little stone, pebble.* **I.** Gen., Cic.; collectively, *gravel,* Verg. **II.** Esp., **a,** *a piece used in the Roman game of* Latrunculi or Duodecim scripta; calculum reducere, *to retract a move,* Cic.; **b,** *a voting pebble,* a white one being thrown into the urn to acquit or to affirm, a black one to condemn or to negative; album calculum adjicere errori nostro, Plin.; **c,** *a counter for reckoning,* hence *a calculation;* ad calculos vocare aliquid, *to subject to a strict reckoning,* Cic.

caldus = calidus (q.v.).

Călēdŏnes -um, acc. -as, m. *the inhabitants of Caledonia.* Hence **A. Călēdŏnĭa** -ae, f. *the north-west of Scotland.* **B.** Adj., **Călēdŏnĭus** -a -um, *Caledonian.*

călĕfăcio (calfacio) -fēci -factum, 3., pass. **călĕfīo** (calfio) -factus sum -fieri. **A.** Lit., *to make warm, heat;* **1,** of things, balineum calfieri jubebo, Cic.; **2,** of animals, corpus, Cic. **B.** Transf., *to disturb, excite;* Gabinium ad populum luculente calefecerat Mummius, Cic.; calefacta corda tumultu, Verg.

călĕfacto, 1. (intens. of calefacio), *to make warm, heat,* Hor.

Călendae (Kălendae) -ārum, f. (from calare, *to call,* the calends being the day on which the times of the Nones and the festivals were proclaimed); **1,** *the first day of the month:* Cal. Februariae, *the first of February;* femineae Calendae, *the first of March, the day of the Matronalia, when Roman matrons sacrificed to Juno,* Juv.; on the calends, interest of money was paid; hence tristes Calendae — i.e., for debtors—Hor.; as there were no calends in the Greek year, ad Graecas Calendas solvere = *never to pay,* Suet.; **2;** *month,* Ov.

Călēnus, v. Cales.

călĕo -ui, 2. (connected with καίω), *to be warm, hot, to glow.* **I.** Lit., **A.** Of physical heat, ignis calet, Cic.; centum Sabaeo ture calent arae, Verg.; terrae alio sole calentes, Hor. **B.** Of animal heat, os calet tibi, Plaut. **II.** Transf., **A.** Of persons, *to be inflamed, aroused, excited;* calebat in agendo, *he was all fire in acting,* Cic.; Romani calentes adhuc ab recenti pugna, Liv.; cupidine laudis, Ov.; so of love, *to be in love with;* juvene, femina, Hor. **B.** Of things, **1,** *to be urged on zealously;* indicia calent, Cic.; res calet, *is ripe for execution,* Cic.; **2,** *to be yet warm, fresh of interest;* illud crimen de nummis caluit re recenti, Cic.

Călēs -ium, f. *town in Campania, famous for its wine, now Calvi.* Adj., **Călēnus** -a -um, *of* or *belonging to Cales.*

călesco, 3. (inch. of caleo), *to become warm, to grow hot;* calescere vel apricatione vel igni, Cic.; tunc primum radiis gelidi caluere triones, Ov.; fig., of love, quo propior nunc es, flamma propiore calesco, Ov.

Calēti -ōrum and **Calētes** -um, m. *a Gallic tribe in Normandy on the Seine.*

călĭandrum -i, n. v. caliendrum.

călĭdē, adv., with superl. (calidus), *warmly, speedily,* Plaut.

călĭdus (caldus) -a -um, *warm, hot.* **A,** Lit., dies, Cic. Subst., **a, călĭda** -ae, f. (sc. aqua), *warm water,* Plin.; **b, călĭdum** -i, n. *warm wine and water,* Plaut. **B. 1,** *hot, fiery, passionate, violent;* equus, Verg.; calidus juventa, Hor.; consilium calidum, Cic.; **2,** *quick, speedy,* Plaut.

călĭendrum -i, n. *a head-dress of Roman women,* Hor.

călĭga -ae, f. (connected with calceus and calx, *heel*), *a stout shoe, esp. soldier's shoe,* Cic.

călĭgātus -a -um, *wearing the caliga;* caligatum venire, *booted and spurred,* Juv. Subst. m., *a common soldier,* Suet.

cālīgĭnōsus -a -um (1. caligo). **I.** Lit., *foggy, misty;* caelum nebulosum et caliginosum, Cic. **II.** Transf., *dark;* nox, *the unknown future,* Hor.

1. **cālīgo** -ĭnis, f. **I.** *fog, mist, vapour;* fulvae nubis caligo crassa, Verg. **II.** Meton., *darkness.* **A.** Lit., **1,** gen., tetrae tenebrae et caligo, Cic.; **2,** esp., *mist before the eyes;* aliquid cernere quasi per caliginem, Cic. **B.** Transf., **1,** *mental darkness, dulness;* haec indoctorum animis offusa caligo, Cic.; **2,** *calamity;* superioris anni caligo et tenebrae, Cic.; **3,** *gloominess, sadness,* Cic.

2. **cālīgo,** 1. (1. caligo). **I.** *to spread a dark mist around,* Verg.; meton., caligantes fenestrae, *making dizzy,* Juv. **II.** *to be dark;* caligans lucus, Verg. **II.** Esp., of the eyes, *to be misty;* caligant oculi, Lucr.; transf., *to be in darkness,* Plin.; prov., caligare in sole, *to grope in daylight,* Quint.

Călĭgŭla -ae, m. (dim. of caliga, lit., *a little soldier's shoe*), *nickname of C. Caesar, the third Roman Emperor, so called because when a boy in the camp of his father Germanicus he was dressed as a common soldier.*

călix -ĭcis, m. (κύλιξ), **1,** *a goblet, drinking vessel;* calix mulsi, Cic.; **2,** *a cooking vessel,* Ov.

Callaeci (Gallaeci) -ōrum, m. *a people in the north-west of Spain.* Hence **Callaecĭa** (Gallaecĭa) -ae, f., *the country of the Callaeci;* adj., **Callaecus** -a -um and **Callăĭcus** -a -um.

callĕo, 2. (callum). **I.** *to be thick-skinned,* Plaut. **II.** Transf., **A.** Intransit., *to be clever, experienced,* ap. Cic.; usu alicuius rei, Liv. **B.** Transit., *to know by experience, understand;* Poenorum jura, Liv.

Callicrătĭdās -ae, m. (Καλλικρατίδας), *a Spartan commander, killed at the battle of Arginusae.*

Callicŭla -ae, f. *a small hill in Campania.*

callĭdē, adv. (callidus), in a good sense, *cleverly;* in a bad sense, *cunningly, slyly;* callide arguteque dicere, Cic.; omnia decreta eius peritissime et callidissime venditare, Cic.

callĭdĭtas -ātis, f. **I.** In a good sense, *expertness, cleverness;* vincere omnes calliditate et celeritate ingenii, Nep. **II.** More frequently in a bad sense, *cunning, craft, artifice;* scientia quae est remota ab justitia calliditas potius quam sapientia appellanda, Cic.; *stratagem in war,* Liv.; in oratory, *artifice;* genus eiusmodi calliditatis atque calumniae, Cic.

callĭdus -a -um (calleo), **1,** *clever by reason of experience, dexterous, skilful, sly, cunning;* **a,** absol., agitator (equi), Cic.; artifex, Cic.; legum scriptor peritus et callidus, Cic.; *a connoisseur in art,* Hor.; **b,** with ad and the acc., ad fraudem, Cic.; **c,** with in and the abl., in dicendo vehemens et callidus, Cic.; **d,** with the genit., rei militaris, Tac.; **e,** with the abl., homines callidi usu, Cic.; **2,** *of things, cunningly* or *slyly devised;* audacia, Cic.; nimis callida juris interpretatio, *too subtle,* Cic.

Callifae -ārum, f. *a town in Samnium.*

Callĭmăchus -i, m (Καλλίμαχος), *a celebrated Greek poet of Cyrene*

Callĭŏpē -ēs, f (Καλλιόπη, *the beautiful-voiced*), and **Callĭŏpēa** -ae, f **I.** *Calliope, the Muse of epic poetry,* or *of poetry in general*, Hor, Ov **II.** Meton, 1, vos, O Calliope, etc, *all the Muses collectively*, Verg, **2,** *poetry*, Ov.

Callĭpŏlis is, f (Καλλίπολις) **I.** *a town on the Thracian Chersonese, now Gallipoli.* **II.** *a town in the Tauric Chersonese*

Callirrhŏē -ēs, f (Καλλιρρόη), **1,** *daughter of the river Achelous, wife of Alcmaeon*, **2,** *a well at Athens, on the south side of the Acropolis*

callis is, m and (in prose, gen) f *a narrow track, footpath, cattle track;* Italiae calles et pastorum stabula, Cic

Callisthĕnēs is, m (Καλλισθένης), *a philosopher of Olynthus, who accompanied Alexander the Great into Asia, and died a violent death there*

Callistō -ūs, f (Καλλιστώ), *daughter of the Arcadian king Lycaon, mother of Arcas by Jupiter, changed by Juno into a bear, and placed by Jupiter among the stars as Ursa Major* or *Helice*

callōsus -a -um (callum), *having a hard skin, hard*, ova, Hor

callum -i, n and **callus** i, m **I.** *the hard skin of animals;* calceamentum callum soleorum, Cic **II.** Transf, *insensibility*, ipse labor quasi callum quoddam obducit dolori, Cic, quorum animis diuturna cogitatio callum vetustatis obduxerat, Cic

1 **călo,** 1 (καλῶ), *to call, summon*, t t of religious ceremonies, Quint, comitia calata, *an assembly of the curiae for merely formal business*, Cic

2 **cālo** -ōnis, m (perhaps contr for caballo, from caballus), *a horse-boy, groom, a litter-bearer*, Cic, *a soldier's slave, camp menial*, Caes

1 **călor** -ōris, m (caleo), *warmth, heat* **I.** Phys, **A.** Gen, vis frigoris et caloris, Cic **B.** Esp, *heat of the sun* or *day*, vitandi caloris causa Lanuvii tres horas acquieveram, Cic, calores maximi, Cic., mediis caloribus, *in full summer*, Liv **C.** *heat of a hot wind*, calores austrini, Verg **II.** *animal heat.* **A.** Lit, Tib **B.** Transf, *love*, Ov, Hor

2 **Călŏr** -ōris, m *a river in Samnium, now Calore*

Calpē -ēs, f (Κάλπη), *one of the pillars of Hercules, now Gibraltar*

Calpurnĭus -a um, *name of a Roman plebeian gens, the families of which bore the names of* Flaminia, Asprenas, Piso, Bestia, Bibulus *The most remarkable of this gens were* **1,** C Calp Piso, *praetor and propraetor in Spain*, 186 A C; **2,** L Calp Piso, *consul in* 112 A C, **3,** L. Calp Frugi, *tribune* 149 A C, *consul* 133 A C, **4,** L Calp Bestia, *tribune* 121, *consul* 111, *and general against Jugurtha*, **5,** L Calp Bibulus, *step-son of M. Brutus*, **6,** C Calp. Piso, *son-in-law of Cicero*, **7,** L Calp Piso Caesoninus, *father-in law of Caesar*, **8,** Calpurnia, *wife of Caesar*, **9,** T Calp Siculus, *Roman bucolic poet of third century* A C Adj, *Calpurnian*, Calpurnia lex, **a,** de repetundis of L Calp Piso Frugi, **b,** de ambitu of the consul C Calp Piso

caltha -ae, f *a plant*, prob *the common marigold*, Verg

calthŭla -ae, f (caltha), *a woman's robe of a yellow colour*, Plaut

călumnia -ae, f (Old Lat calvĕre, connected with carpere), *trick, artifice, chicane, craft*, **a,** Gen, inimicorum calumnia, Cic, religionis calumnia, *deceitful pretence*, Cic., calumniam adhibere, Cic; in hac calumnia timoris, *misgiving caused by ill grounded fear*, Cic, **b,** esp, *false accusation, malicious prosecution*, calumnia litium alienos fundos petere, Cic, calumniam jurare, *to swear that an accusation is not malicious*, Cic, meton, *action for false accusation*, calumniam privato judicio non effugere, Cic

călumnĭātor ōris, m (calumnior), *an intriguer, pettifogger*, scriptum sequi calumniatoris esse, boni judicis, voluntatem scriptoris auctoritatemque defendere, Cic

călumnĭor, 1 dep (calumnia), *to contrive tricks, to attack with artifices*, jacet res in controversiis isto calumniante biennium, Cic, calumniabar ipse, putabam, etc, *I made myself unnecessarily anxious*, Cic

calva -ae, f (calvus), *the bald scalp of the head*, Liv

calvĕo, 2 *to be bare of hair, bald*, Plin.

Calvĭsĭus -ii, m *Roman name*, **1,** C Calv Sabinus, *legate of Caesar*, **2,** Calvisius, *the accuser of Agrippina, the mother of Nero*

calvĭtĭēs -ei, f (calvus), *baldness*, Suet.

calvĭtĭum -ii, n (calvus), *baldness*, Cic

calvor, 3 dep *to form intrigues, deceive*, Plaut

calvus -a -um, *bald, without hair*, Plaut

Calvus, *the name of a family of the gens Licinia*, v Licinius

1 **calx** -cis, f *the heel;* certare pugnis, calcibus, Cic; calcem terere calce, *to tread close on the heels*, Verg, calces remittere, *to kick*, Nep, prov, adversus stimulum calces (sc jactare), *to kick against the pricks*, Ter.

2 **calx** -cis, f and (rarely) m (χάλιξ), *a stone* **I.** *a pebble used as a counter in various games*, Plaut **II.** *lime, chalk*, lintribus in eam insulam materiam, calcem, caementa convehere, Cic, as the goal in a racecourse was marked with chalk, meton = *a goal, end* (opp carceres, *the starting-point*), quibuscum tamquam e carceribus emissus sis, cum iisdem ad calcem, ut dicitur, pervenire, Cic; ad carceres a calce revocari, *to turn back from the end to the beginning*, Cic

Călўcadnus -i, m (Καλύκαδνος) **I.** *a river in Cilicia* **II.** *promontory in Cilicia at the mouth of the river of the same name*

Călўdon -ōnis, f (Καλυδών), *a very ancient city in Aetolia* Hence adj, **1, Călўdōnius** a -um, *Calydonian*, heros, *Meleager*, Ov, amnis, *the Achelous*, Ov, regna, *the kingdom of Diomedes in Lower Italy*, Ov, sus, aper, *the boar slain by Meleager*, Mart, **2, Călўdōnis** -idis, f *Calydonian;* subst = *Deianira*, Ov

Călypsō -ūs, acc o f (Καλυψώ), *a nymph, daughter of Atlas, who entertained Ulysses in the island of Ortygia, and kept him there seven years*

cămăra = camera (q v)

Cămărīna (Cămĕrīna) ae, f (Καμάρινα), *town in the south-west of Sicily, now Camerina* or *Camarana*

Cambūnii montes, m *mountains forming the boundary between Thessaly and Macedonia*

Cambȳsēs is, m (Καμβύσης), **1,** *husband of Mandane, father of Cyrus the Elder*, **2,** *son and successor of Cyrus the Elder*

camĕlla -ae, f (dim of camera), *a kind of goblet*, Ov

cămēlus -i, m and f (κάμηλος), *a camel*, Cic

Cămēna (Camoena), ae, f (from cano, orig casmena, then carmena), gen plur *the prophesying goddesses of springs*, in later times identified with the Greek Muses, meton, *poetry*, Hor

cămĕra (camara) -ae, f (καμάρα), **1,** *a vaulted*

chamber, vault, Cic, **2,** *a kind of flat covered boat*, Tac

Cămĕrĭa ae, f and **Cămĕrĭum** -ii, n *town in Latium* Adj., **Cămĕrīnus** a um, *of* or *belonging to Cameria*

Cămillus i, m *cognomen of several members of the gens* Furia, *the most famous of whom*, M Furius Camillus, *took Veii, and freed Rome from the Gauls* Appell, *a saviour of one's country*, novus Camillus, Liv

cămīnus -i, m (κάμινος), **1,** *a forge*, Ov, prov, semper ardente camino, *with ceaseless industry*, Juv, **2,** *a fire place*, Hor, meton, *fire*, luculentus, Cic, prov, oleum addere camino, *to aggravate an evil*, Hor

cammărus -i, m (κάμμαρος), *a crab lobster*, Juv.

Campānĭa ae, f (campus, cf Fr champagne, *the level country*), *a district of Central Italy, the capital of which was Capua*, now *Terra di Lavoro* Adj, **Campānus** -a um, *Campanian*, via, *a by road connected with the via Appia*, Suet, morbus, *a kind of wart on the face common in Campania*, Hor, pons, *the bridge over the Savo (Saona)*, Hor., colonia, *Capua*, Cic, arrogantia, Cic Subst, **Campāni** ōrum, m *the inhabitants of Campania*, Cic.

campester -tris -tre (campus), **1,** *relating to level country, flat*, loca campestria, Liv, iter, *march in a level country*, Caes, hence subst, **campestria** -ium, n *a plain*, Tac, **2, a,** *relating to the Campus Martius and its gymnastic exercises*, ludus, Cic, hence subst, **campestre** is, n (sc velamentum), *a covering worn by wrestlers round their loins*, Hor, **b,** *relating to the comitia*, certamen, Liv, quaestus, Cic

campus -i, m (connected with κῆπος), **1,** *a flat spot, a plain;* campos et montes peragrare, Cic, hence, *a meadow, field*, herbidus aquosusque, Liv, *field of battle*, Liv, poet, *a level surface of any kind, the sea*, Verg., so of the level surface of a rock, Verg, **2,** *the Campus, or Campus Martius at Rome, the place of meeting of the* comitia centuriata, hence meton, *the comitia*, fors domina campi, Cic; also used as a place of exercise, Cic, meton, *any free space, field*, or *theatre of action*, quum sit campus, in quo exsultare possit oratio, Cic

Camulŏdūnum -i, n *a town of the Trinobantes in Britain*, now *Colchester*

cămŭr -a -um (connected with κάμπτω), *hooked, curved*, Verg

Cănăcē -ēs, f (Κανάκη), *daughter of Aeolus*

Canae -ārum, f *a coast town in Aeolis*, now *Kanot Koei*.

cănālis -is, m (orig adj of canna, *in the shape of a reed*), *a waterpipe, channel, canal*, Verg, Caes.

cănārĭus a -um (canis), *relating to a dog, canine*, Plin Adj prop, **Cănārĭa** (insula), *one of the Happy Islands in the Atlantic*, plur **Canārĭae**, *the Canaries*

cancelli -ōrum, m (dim of cancer), *a lattice, grating*, or *trellis-work* **A.** Lit, fori, *the bar of a tribunal*, Cic **B.** Transf, *bounds, limits*, extra cancellos egredi, Cic

cancer -cri, m (connected with καρκίνος) **A.** *the crab, the sign of the zodiac in which the sun is at the summer solstice*, Ov **B.** Meton, **a,** *the south*, Ov, **b,** *summer heat*, Ov

Candāvĭa -ae, f (Κανδαουΐα), *a mountainous district of Illyria*

candĕfăcĭo -fēci factum (candeo and facio), *to make of a shining white*, Plaut

candēla ae, f (candeo), **1,** *a wax* or *tallow candle, taper*, candelam apponere valvis, *to set the house on fire*, Juv, **2,** *a rope coated with wax to preserve it from decay*, fasces involuti candelis, Liv

candēlābrum -i, n (candela), *a candlestick, candelabrum*, Cic

candĕo -ŭi, 2 (from caneo as ardeo from areo) **A.** *to be of a shining white, to shine, glitter*, candet ebur soliis, Cat **B.** Esp., *to glow with heat*, candente carbone, Cic

candesco, 3 (inch of candeo), **1,** *to begin to shine*, Ov, **2,** *to begin to glow with heat*, Lucr.

candĭdātōrĭus -a -um, *relating to a candidate*, munus, Cic

candĭdātus -a -um (candidus), *clothed in white*, Plaut Subst, **candĭdātus** -i, m *a candidate for office, who, among the Romans, was always clothed in white*, consularis, *for the consulship*, Cic

candĭdē, adv (candidus), **1,** *in white*, Plaut, **2,** *clearly, candidly*, ap Cic

candĭdŭlus -a -um, (dim. of candidus), *shining, dazzling*, dentes, Cic.

candĭdus a -um (candeo), *shining white, glittering white* (albus, *dead white*) **I.** Lit., **a,** lilia, Verg, tunicae linteae, Liv., tentoria, Ov, candidum altā nive Soracte, Hor, hence subst., **candĭdum** -i, n *white colour*, Ov, candidum ovi, *the white of the egg*, Plin, **b,** of the hair or beard, *silver white, silver grey*, barba, Verg, **c,** of the body, *snow-white*, corpora (Gallorum), Liv, brachia candidiora nive, Ov, *of dazzling beauty*, puer, Hor, of animals, avis, *the stork*, Verg, of deities, Bassareus, *of heavenly beauty*, Hor., **d,** of the stars or the day, *bright*, luna, Verg, dies, Ov, **e,** of the white toga of candidates, Cic, **f,** of a white stone, (α) candida sententia, *an acquittal*, Ov, (β) *a sign of a lucky day*, candidiore or candidissimo calculo notare diem, Cat **II.** Transf, **a,** of time, *happy*, hora, Ov; **b,** of writing, *clear, lucid*, genus dicendi, Cic, **c,** of character, *honest, straightforward*; pauperis ingenium, Hor

candor -ōris m. (candeo), *dazzling white colour* **I.** Of paint, fucati medicamenta candoris et ruboris, Cic **II.** As a quality, *whiteness, lustre* **A.** candor marmoreus, Lucr, **1,** of the body, candor huius et proceritas, Cic, **2,** of the sun or stars, solis, Cic; of the Milky Way, via candore notabilis ipso, Ov **B.** Transf, of character, *sincerity, candour*, animi, Ov

canens -entis, partic of caneo and cano.

cănĕo -ŭi, 2 (from canus, as albeo from albus), *to be white* or *hoary*, temporibus geminis canebat sparsa senectus, Verg, gramina canent, *of dew*, Verg, partic canens, *hoary*

cănēphŏros -i, f (κανηφόρος), *a basket-bearer*, and plur **cănēphŏroe** (κανηφόροι), *statues by Greek sculptors representing Athenian maidens bearing sacrificial baskets*

cānesco, 3 (inch of caneo), *to become white* or *hoary* **I.** canescunt aequora, Ov **II.** Transf, *to become old*, Ov, fig, quum oratio nostra jam canesceret, Cic

cănīcŭla -ae, f (dim of canis) **I. A.** *a little dog*, Plin **B.** Appell, *a violent woman*, Plaut **II. A.** *the dog-star, Sirius*, canicula exoritur, Cic, sitiens, Hor **B.** *the worst throw upon the dice, all aces*, Pers.

cănīnus -a -um (canis) **A.** *relating to a dog, canine;* lac, Ov **B.** Transf, **1,** littera, *the letter R*, Pers, **2,** of character, *snarling, spiteful*, latrare canina verba in foro, Ov

cănis -is, c *a dog* **I.** Lit, venaticus, Cic; alere canes in Capitolio, Cic., cave canem, beware *of the dog*, inscription on a house door, Varr, prov., cane pejus et angue vitare, Hor **II.** Transf, a, as a term of reproach, *a malicious, spiteful person*, of accusers, Cic, *a parasite, hanger on*, Clodianus canis, Cic, b, as a star, canis major, Verg, canis minor, Ov, c, *the sea dog*, Plin, canes, *the dogs of Scylla*, Verg, d, in dice, *the worst throw*, canes damnosi, Prop

cănistra ōrum, n (κανάστρα), *a bread, fruit, or flower basket*, Cic

cānitiēs, acc -em, abl -e, f (canus), **A.** *a whitish grey colour*, esp of the hair **B.** Meton, *grey hair*, Verg, *old age*, Hor

canna ae, f (κάννα) **A.** *a reed*, palustris, Ov **B.** Meton, *a reed-pipe*, Ov, *a small boat*, Juv

cannăbis is, acc im, abl i, f, (κάνναβις), **cannăbus** -i, m, **cannăbum** i, n *hemp*, Plin

Cannae ārum, f *a small town in Apulia, near the Aufidus, scene of a defeat of the Romans by Hannibal 216* A C Adj, **Cannensis** e *of or belonging to Cannae*, prov, pugna, *any disastrous slaughter* (e g, *the proscription of Sulla*), Cic

căno, cĕcĭni, cantum, 3 *to sing* **I.** Intransit **A.** 1, of men, voce, Cic, ad tibicinem, Cic, in oratory of a sing-song delivery, inclinata ululantique voce more Asiatico canere, Cic, 2, of animals, of the cock, *to crow*, Cic, of frogs, *to croak*, Plin **B.** *to play*, 1, of men, fidibus, Cic, canere receptui, *to sound the signal for retreat*, Liv, 2, of instruments, tubae cornuaque cecinerunt, Liv, classicum canit, Liv **II.** Transit., **A.** *to sing with the voice*, 1, carmen, Cic, 2, a, *to sing of, to celebrate in song*, ad tibiam clarorum virorum laudes atque virtutes, Cic, b, of animals, *to give warning by a cry*, anser Gallos adesse canebat **B.** *to play on a musical instrument*, signum canere, Liv, prov, hoc carmen hic tribunus plebis non vobis, sed sibi intus canit, *thinks only of his own advantage*, Cic **C.** Of gods, oracles, seers, *to prophesy*, ut haec quae fiunt canere di immortales viderentur, Cic, with acc and infin, te mihi mater, veridica interpres deum, aucturum caelestium numerum cecinit, Liv, of fame, *to announce*, ficta facta atque infecta canens, Verg

Cănōpus -i, m (Κάνωβος), *a city in Lower Egypt*, hence meton, *Lower Egypt*, Verg, and *Egypt* generally, Juv Adj, **Cănōpēus** -a um, *of or belonging to Canopus*, **Cănōpītae** -ārum, m *inhabitants of Canopus*, Cic

cănor ōris, m (cano), *melody, song, sound*, Martius aeris rauci, Verg

cănōrus -a -um (canor), *melodious, harmonious, sweet-sounding* **I.** Neut, profluens quiddam habuit Carbo et canorum, Cic, so of a fault in delivery, *of a sing song pronunciation*, vox nec languens nec canora, Cic Subst, **cănōrum** -i, n *harmonious sound*, Cic **II.** Act, of men, orator, Cic, of animals, ales, *the swan*, Hor, gallus, Cic, of instruments, aes, *the trumpet*, Verg

Cantăbri ōrum, m (Κάνταβροι), *a people in the north of Spain, not subdued till the reign of Augustus* Sing, **Cantăber** -bri, m *Cantabrian*; hence, **Cantăbrĭa** ae, f (Κανταβρία), *the country of the Cantabri*, adj, **Cantăbrĭcus** -a um, *Cantabrian*

cantāmen inis, n (canto), *incantation*, Prop

cantātor -ōris, m *a singer*, Mart

cantērīnus (canthērīnus) a um (canterius), *relating to a horse, equine*, Plaut

cantērius (canthērius) i, m (perhaps κανθήλιος), *a beast of burden, a gelding, nag*, Cic, canterius in fossa, *a person in a helpless condition*, Liv, meton, *an impotent person*, Plaut

canthăris -ĭdis, f (κανθαρίς), *a beetle, the Spanish fly*, Cic

canthărus -i, m (κάνθαρος), 1, *a large goblet with handles, a tankard*, Plaut, 2, *a kind of sea fish*, Ov

canthus -i, m (κανθός), *the tire of a wheel*, meton, *a wheel*, Pers

cantĭcum i, n (cano), 1, *a scene in the Roman comedy, enacted by one person and accompanied by music and dancing*, Cic, cantica agere, Liv, 2, *a song*, Mart, *a sing song delivery in an orator*, Cic

cantĭlēna -ae, f *an old song, twaddle, chatter*, ut crebro mihi insusurret cantilenam suam, Cic

cantĭo -ōnis, f (cano), 1, *a song*, Plaut, 2, *an incantation, enchantment*, veneficia et cantiones, Cic

cantĭto, 1 (freq of canto), *to sing repeatedly*, carmina in epulis, Cic

Cantĭum -ii, n (Κάντιον), *a district on the south east coast of Britain*, now *Kent*

cantĭuncŭla -ae, f (dim of cantio), *a flattering, enticing song*, si cantiunculis tantus vir irretitus teneretur, Cic

canto āvi ātum -are (intens of cano), *to sing or play* **I.** Intransit **A.** Of the voice, *to sing*, 1, of men, ad manum histrionum, *to sing and play to the dumb show of an actor*, Cic, 2, of birds, cantantes aves, Prop, of the cock, *to crow*, Cic **B.** *to play on an instrument*, avenis, Ov, of the instrument itself, bucina cantat, Ov **C.** *to sing an incantation*, Verg **II.** Transit, **A.** *to sing or play*, 1, with cognate object, carmina, Hor, doctum Catullum, *the songs of Catullus*, Hor, 2, *to celebrate in singing*, convivia, Hor, cantari dignus, *worthy to be celebrated in song*, Verg, so *to praise*, tam ut scis, jam pridem istum canto Caesarem, Cic, 3, *to recite*, elegos, Juv **B.** *to announce, tell*, vera cantas, Plaut **C.** *to sing an incantation*, carmen, Ov, hence, *to bewitch*, cantatae herbae, Ov

cantor ōris, m (cano), 1, *a singer, poet*; cantor Apollo, *player on the harp*, Hor, contemptuously, cantor formularum, Cic; cantores Euphorionis, *eulogists*, Cic, 2, *an actor*, esp *the actor who cried plaudite at the end of the piece*, Hor

cantrix -īcis, f (cantor), *a female singer*, Plaut

cantus ūs, m (cano) **I.** *song, melody, poetry*, Lucr **II.** Concrete, *a song, a melody* **A.** Gen, a, of persons, Sirenum, Cic, b, of animals, avium, Cic, c, of an instrument, *playing*, *music*, bucinarum, Cic **B.** Esp, a, *prophecy*, veridici cantus, Cat, b, *incantation*, Ov

Canulējus i, m *name of a Roman plebeian gens, to which belonged* C Canulejus, *tribune of the people* 445 B C, *author of the law permitting marriages between plebeians and patricians*

cānus a -um **I.** Lit, *whitish grey, grey*; fluctus, Lucr, lupus, Verg, esp of hair, capilli, Hor Subst, **cāni** ōrum (sc capilli), *grey hair*, Cic **II.** Meton, *old, aged*, senectus, Cat

Cănŭsium -ii, n *a town of Apulia* (now *Canosa*) Adj, **Cănŭsīnus** -a um, *Canusian*; lana, *Canusian wool*, which was very celebrated, Plin, hence, **Cănŭsīna** -ae, f (sc vestis), *a garment of Canusian wool*, Mart, **Cănŭsīnātus** -a um, *clothed in such a garment*, Suet

căpācĭtas -ātis, f (capax), *breadth, roominess*, Cic.

Căpăneus -ĕi, acc -ĕa, voc -eu, m (Καπανεύς), *one of the seven princes who besieged Thebes, killed by Jupiter with a thunderbolt*

căpax -ācis (capio), *able to hold* **I.** Lit, *able to hold much, broad, wide, roomy*, urbs, Ov, with genit, circus capax populi, Ov, cibi vinique capacissimus, Liv. **II.** Transf, *able to grasp, apt, capable, fit for*, aures avidae et capaces, Cic, with genit, capax imperii, Tac, with ad and the acc, animus ad praecepta capax, Ov.

căpēdo -inis, f (capis), *a bowl used in sacrifices*, Cic

căpēduncŭla -ae, f (dim of capedo), *a small bowl*, Cic

căpella -ae, f (dim of capra), **1,** *a she-goat*, Cic, **2,** *a constellation so called*, Ov

Căpēna -ae, f *a town in Etruria, at the foot of Mount Soracte* Adj, **Căpēnās** -ātis, **Căpēnus** -a -um, *of or belonging to Capena*, porta Capena, *a gate in Rome at the commencement of the via Appia.*

căper -ri, m **A.** Lit, *a he-goat*, Verg **B.** Meton., *the smell under the arm-pits*, Ov

căpĕro, 1. (caper), *to be wrinkled*, Plaut

căpesso -ivi and -ii -itum, 3 (desider of capio), *to seize, lay hold of eagerly* **I. A.** Lit, arma, Verg, cibum oris hiatu et dentibus (of animals), Cic. **B.** Transf, *to take to, to gain*, **a,** fugam, Liv, libertatem, Cic, **b,** *to take in hand, busy oneself with*, rempublicam, *to enter public life*, Cic, so magistratus, imperium, honores, provincias, Tac, bellum, Liv **II.** *to strive to reach, to hasten, to make for*, omnes mundi partes medium locum capessentes, Cic, animus superiora capessat necesse est, *aims after*, Cic, Melitam, Cic, Italiam, Verg, reflex, se in altum, Plaut (perf infin, capessisse, Liv).

Căphāreus and **Căphēreus,** or **Căpōreus** -ĕi and -éos, acc -ĕa, voc -eu, m (ὁ Καφηρεύς), *a dangerous promontory on the south coast of Euboea, where the Greek fleet on returning from Troy was shipwrecked* Adj, **Căphārēus** -a -um, *of or belonging to Caphareus.*

căpillātus -a -um (capillus), *hairy, having hair*, adolescens bene capillatus, Cic; vinum capillato diffusum consule, *made when long hair was worn* (i e, *very old*), Juv

căpillus -i, m. (dim form from root CAP, whence caput, and κεφαλή, prop adj sc crinis) **A.** *the hair of the head or of the beard* (crinis, *any hair*), compositus, Cic, plur, compti capilli, Cic **B.** Transf, *the hair of animals*, Cat

căpĭo, cēpi, captum, 3 (obs fut capso, Plaut), **I.** *to take, to seize* **A.** Lit, **a,** with the hand, arma, Cic; **b,** *to take possession of*, esp as milit t t, collem, Caes, *to arrive at*, esp. of ships, portum, Caes, *to select* a place, locum oculis, Verg, locum castris, Liv, so of auguries, templa ad inaugurandum, Liv **B.** Transf, **a,** of acts, *to take in hand, to begin*, fugam, Caes, consulatum, Cic, **b,** of an opportunity, satis scite et commode tempus ad aliquem adeundi, Cic, **c,** *to take* as an example or proof, documentum ex aliquo, Cic; **d,** of a quality, *to take, adopt*, avi prudentiam, Cic, **e,** *to take* as a companion, aliquem consilii socium, Verg; *to select* out of a number, in singulos annos sacerdotem Jovis sortito, Cic, aliquem flaminem, *as a flamen*, Liv **C** *to take possession of by force, in a hostile manner*, **1,** lit, **a,** lubido reipublicae capiundae, Sall, **b,** in war, (α) *to take booty*, etc, agros de hostibus, Cic; (β) *to take a town*, etc, urbem, castra hostium, Cic, (γ) *to take prisoner*, belli nefarios duces, Cic, partic as subst, **captus** -i, m (= captivus) *a captive*, Nep; **c,** *to take* animals, pisces, Cic; **2,** transf, **a,** *to seize, take possession of*; admiratio, metus capit aliquem, Liv., nos post reges exactos servitutis oblivio ceperat, Cic, **b,** esp, *to attack, to injure*, pass capi, *to be injured or diseased*, oculis et auribus captus, *blind and deaf*, Cic; captus mente, *distracted*, Cic, **c,** *to deceive*, adolescentium animos dolis, Sall, adversarium, Cic; capere aliquem sua humanitate, Nep **II.** *to take, receive* **A.** Lit., **a,** with the hand, per aliquem aut honores aut divitias, Cic., pecuniam, *to take money by force or bribery*, per vim atque injuriam, Cic, legal t t, *to take as heir*, ex hereditate nihil, Cic, of tribute, pay, etc, stipendium jure belli, Caes, **b,** *to receive into one's body*, cibum, Sall **B.** Transf., *to receive, suffer, undergo*, somnum capere non posse, Cic., aliquid detrimenti (esp in the formula, videant consules ne quid respublica detrimenti capiat), Cic, laetitiam, Cic **III.** *to contain* **A.** Lit, una domo capi non possunt, Cic **B.** Transf, *to allow of, to comprehend*, nullam esse gratiam tantam quam non capere animus meus posset, Cic

căpis -idis, f (capio), *a one-handled vessel*, used in sacrifices, Liv

căpistro, 1. (capistrum), *to fasten with a halter*, Cic

căpistrum -i, n *a halter*, Verg

căpĭtal -ālis, n (capitalis), sc facinus, *a capital crime*, Cic

căpĭtālis -e (caput), **1,** *relating to the head, relating to life, that which imperils a man's life*, or caput (i e, *social position* and *civil rights* in Rome), esp used of capital crimes, res, Cic, inimicus, *a deadly enemy*, Cic, odium, *mortal hatred*, Cic, oratio, *dangerous*, Cic, **2,** *first, chief, distinguished*, Siculus ille capitalis, creber, acutus, Cic., ingenium, Ov

căpĭto -ōnis, m (caput), *a man with a large head*, Cic

Căpĭtōlium -ii, n (caput), *the temple of Jupiter built upon the Tarpeian rock at Rome, the Capitol*, used often of the whole hill or mons Capitolinus Adj, **Căpĭtōlīnus** -a -um, *Capitoline*, ludi, *in honour of Jupiter Capitolinus*, Liv, hence subst, **Căpĭtōlīni** -ōrum, m *the superintendents of these games*, Cic

căpĭtŭlātim, adv (capitulum), *briefly, summarily*, Nep.

căpĭtŭlum -i, n (dim of caput), *a little head*, Plaut.

Cappădŏces -um, m (Καππαδόκες), *the inhabitants of Cappadocia*, sing, **Cappădox** -ŏcis, m *a Cappadocian*; **Cappădŏcia** -ae, f *a district of Asia Minor, the most eastern Asiatic province of the Romans.* Adj, **Cappădŏcius** and **Cappădŏcus** -a -um, *Cappadocian*

capra -ae, f (caper) **I.** *a she-goat* **A.** Lit, Cic, ferae, perhaps *chamois*, Verg **B.** Meton, *the odour under the armpits*, Hor **II.** Transf., **A.** *a constellation*, Cic. **B.** Caprae palus, *the place in Rome where Romulus disappeared*, Liv.

căprĕa -ae, f (capra), *a roe, roebuck*, Verg, prov, prius jungentur capreae lupis quam, etc. (of an impossibility), Hor

Caprĕae -ārum, f (Καπρέαι), *small island on the Campanian coast off Puteoli, to which Tiberius retired at the end of his life*, now *Capri*

caprĕŏlus -i, m (caper) **I.** *a roebuck*, Verg **II.** Meton, plur, *props, supports*, Caes

căprĭcornus -i, m *a sign of the Zodiac, Capricorn*, Hor

căprĭfīcus -i, m. *the wild fig tree, and its fruit*, Pers.

căprigĕnus -a -um (caper and gigno), *born of goats*, Verg

căprimulgus -i, m (capra and mulgeo), *a goat-milker*—i e , *a countryman*, Cat

căprīnus -a -um (caper), *relating to a goat*, pellis, Cic , prov , de lana caprina rixari, *to contend about trifles*, Hor

căprĭpes -pĕdis (caper and pes), *goat-footed*, satyri, Hor.

1 **capsa** -ae, f (capio), *a box or case for books*, Cic

2 **Capsa** -ae, f (Καψα), *a town in Byzacium, now Kafsa* (south of Tunis), hence, **Capsenses** -ium, m *the inhabitants of Capsa*

capsārius -i, m (capsa), *a slave who carried to school his young master's satchel*, Suet

capsŭla -ae, f (dim of capsa), *a little chest*, Cat

captātio -ōnis, f (capto), *an eager seizing, a catching*, verborum, *quibbling, logomachy*, Cic

captātor -ōris, m (capto), *one who eagerly seizes*, aurae popularis, *eager after favour of the people*, Liv , absol *a legacy-hunter*, Hor , Juv

captio -ōnis, f (capio), **a,** *a cheat, deception*, in parvula re captionis aliquid vereri, Cic ; meton , *harm, loss*, mea captio est, si, etc , Cic , **b,** *a fallacy, sophism*, quanta esset in verbis captio, si, etc , Cic , captiones discutere, explicare, repellere, Cic

captiōsē, adv (captiosus), *insidiously*, interrogare, Cic

captiōsus -a -um (captio), **1,** *deceitful*, societatem captiosam et indignam, Cic , **2,** *sophistical, captious, insidious*, captiosissimo genere interrogationis uti, Cic Subst , **captiōsa** -ōrum, n *sophistries*, Cic

captiuncŭla -ae, f (dim of captio), *fallacy, quibble*, omnes captiunculas pertimescere, Cic

captīvitas -ātis, f (captivus), *captivity*, Tac., urbium, *conquest*, Tac.

captīvus -a um (captus, capio), *taken, captured* **I.** *taken in war, captive*, **a,** of persons, cives Romani, Cic , gen subst , **captivus** -i, m , **captīva** -ae, f *a captive*, Cic , poet *relating to a prisoner*, sanguis, Verg , crines, Ov , **b,** used of inanimate things, *conquered, obtained as a prey*, naves, Caes , agri, Tac **II.** Gen , *captured, taken*, pisces, Ov

capto, 1 (intens of capio), *to seize, catch at, lay hold of, hunt* **I.** Lit , feras, Verg **II.** Transf **A.** Gen *to strive after, desire, seek*, sermonem alicuius, Plaut , plausus, risus, Cic **B.** Esp *to seek to win, entice, allure craftily*, insidiis hostem, Liv , testamenta, *to hunt for legacies*, Hor.

captus -ūs, m (capio) **1,** *a catching, taking*, meton , *that which is taken*, Plin , **2,** *power of comprehension, manner of comprehension, idea*, ut est captus hominum, Cic , Germanorum, Caes

Căpŭa -ae, f (Καπυη), *chief town of Campania* Adj , **Căpuānus** -a -um

căpŭlus -i, m (capio) **I.** *a coffin*, ire ad capulum, *to go to the grave*, Lucr **II.** *a handle* **A.** Gen , aratri, Ov. **B.** Esp *the hilt of a sword*, Cic

caput -itis, n (root CAP, connected with κεφαλη), *the head* **I.** Lit and Meton **A.** Of living things, **1,** of men, **a,** lit , *the head*, capite operto, obvoluto, involuto, Cic , caput alicui auferre, abscidere, praecidere, percutere, Liv , capita conferre, *to put their heads together* (of secret conversation), Liv , per caputque pedesque ire praecipitem in lutum, *to go over head and heels*, Cat ; nec caput nec pedes (habere), prov , of a business which one does not know how to begin with, Cic ; supra caput esse, of enemies, *to threaten*, Cic , caput extollere, *to raise one's head again*, Cic , **b,** meton , *a person*; caput liberum, Cic , carum caput, Verg and Hor , in counting numbers, capitum Helvetiorum milia cclxiii , Caes ; exactio capitum, *poll-tax*, Cic , of curses, quod illorum capiti sit, *may it fall on their heads*, ap Cic , **c,** *life, existence*, conjuratio in tyranni caput facta, Liv , esp in Rome, *a man's political and social rights*, judicium capitis, *a sentence involving loss of* caput—i e , *not necessarily of life, but of citizenship*, e g , *exile*, so capitis damnare, Cic , capite damnari, Cic , capitis minor, *a person who has suffered a loss of* caput, Hor , so capite deminui or minui, *to lose* caput, *to suffer a loss of status, to suffer a loss of political or social rights*, Cic , **2,** of animals, jumenti, Nep , belua multorum es capitum, Hor , meton , *a head of cattle* bina boum capita, Verg **B.** Of things without life, *the top, summit, outside*, papaveris, Liv , arcus capita, *the ends*, Verg , capita aspera montis, Verg , of rivers, *the source*, amnis, Verg , Rheni, Caes , fig , *the source*, quo invento ab eo quasi capite disputatio ducitur, Cic , in ea est fons miseriarum et caput, Cic **II.** Transf , **1,** of persons, *the head, chief*, omnium Graecorum concitandorum, Cic , **2, a,** of things without life, *the chief, principal*, cenae, *the main dish*, Cic ; civilis prudentiae, *leading principle*, Cic , **b,** in laws and writings, *the most important part*, legis, Cic , **c,** of money, *capital*, de capite ipso demere, Cic , **d,** of places, *the capital*, Roma caput orbis terrarum, Liv

Căpўs -yis, acc. yn, abl -ўe or -y, m (Καπυς), **1,** *son of Assaracus, father of Anchises*, **2,** *king of Alba*, **3,** *a companion of Aeneas*, **4,** *a king of Capua*

Cărălis -is, f (Κάραλις), and plur , **Cărăles** -ium, f *a town and promontory of the same name in Sardinia, now Cagliari*, hence **Cărălitānus** -a -um, *of or belonging to Caralis*

carbăsĕus -a -um (carbasus), *made of canvas*, vela, Cic

carbăsus -i, m (καρπασος), plur heterocl gen , **carbăsa** -ōrum, *fine Spanish flax*, gen meton , *articles produced from it, a linen garment, a sail*, Verg.

carbătĭnus (carpatinus), -a -um (καρβατινος), *of untanned leather*, crepidae, *rustic shoes*, Cat

carbo -ōnis, m **I.** *coal, charcoal*, candens, Cic , fig , carbone notare, *to mark with black*, i e , *think ill of any one*, Hor , prov carbonem pro thesauro invenire, *to find something of little value*, Phaedr **II.** *cognomen of the Papirii*

carbōnārius -ii, m (carbo), *a charcoal burner*, Plaut

carbuncŭlus -i, m (dim of carbo). **I.** Lit *a little coal*, Plaut **II.** Transf **A.** *a kind of stone*, Plin **B.** *a carbuncle*, Plin.

carcer -ĕris, m (connected with arceo and Gr ἕρκος), **1,** *a prison, jail, cell*, in carcerem ducere, condere, conjicere, contrudere, includere, Cic., emitti e carcere, Cic , fig , qui e corporum vinculis tamquam e carcere evolaverunt, Cic , meton , *the prisoners confined in a jail*, in me carcerem effudistis, *you have emptied the prison on me*, Cic , **2,** gen used in plur carceres, *the starting place of a racecourse* (opp meta, calx); e carceribus emitti cum aliquo, Cic ; ad carceres a calce revocari, *to begin life anew*, Cic

carcĕrārius -a -um (carcer), *belonging to a prison*, Plaut

Carchēdŏnius -a -um (Καρχηδονιος), *Carthaginian*, Plaut

carchēsium -ii, n. (καρχήσιον), *a goblet with handles, contracted in the middle*, Verg.

cardăces -um, m. (Persian carda, *brave, warlike*), *a Persian troop*, Nep.

cardĭăcus -a -um (καρδιακός), *pertaining to the stomach;* of persons, *suffering from a disease of the stomach;* amicus, Juv. Subst., **cardĭăcus** -i, m. *one who so suffers*, Cic.

cardo -ĭnis, m. (connected with Gr. κραδάω, κραδαίνω, *to swing*). **I.** Lit. **A.** *the hinge of a door;* cardinem versare, *to open a door*, Ov. **B.** *the point round which anything turns, a pole of the heavens;* cardo duplex, *the ends of the earth's axis*, Cic; poet., *a point through which a line is drawn from north to south*, Liv.; quatuor cardines mundi, *the four cardinal points*, Quint. **II.** Transf. *a chief circumstance*, or *consideration upon which many others depend;* haud tanto cessabit cardine rerum, Verg.

cardŭus -i, m. *a thistle*, Verg.

cārē, adv. (carus), *dearly, at a high price;* aestimare, ap. Cic.

cārectum -i, n. (for caricetum, from carex), *a sedgy spot*, Verg.

cărĕo -ŭi -ĭtūrus, 2. *to be without, destitute of, to want;* gov. the abl. **I.** Gen. **A.** of persons, dolore, febri, Cic. **B.** of things, lege carens civitas, *lawless*, Cic. **II.** Esp. **A.** *to make no use of:* temeto, Cic.; hence, of a place, *to absent oneself from;* foro, senatu, publico, Cic.; patria, *to leave Rome*, Tac. **B.** *to be deprived of, to miss;* consuetudine amicorum, Cic.; libertate, Hor.; absol., quamquam non caret is qui non desiderat, Cic.

Cāres -um, m. (Κᾶρες), *inhabitants of Caria;* sing., **Căr**, Cāris. Hence, **Cārĭa** -ae, f. (Καρία), *the most southerly district of Asia Minor.* **Cārĭcus** -a -um, *Carian.* Subst., **Cārĭca** -ae, f. (sc. ficus), *a kind of dried fig*, Cic.

cārex -ĭcis, f. *sedge*, Verg.

cărĭēs, acc. -em, abl. -e (other cases not found), f. *rottenness, decay*, Ov.

cărīna -ae, f. **I.** *the keel of a ship.* **A.** Lit., carinae aliquanto planiores quam nostrarum navium, Caes. **B.** Meton., *a ship, vessel*, Verg. **II.** Transf. plur., **Cărīnae** -ārum, f. *a spot in Rome on the Esquiline where Pompey's house stood.*

cărĭōsus -a -um (caries), *rotten, decayed, carious;* dentes, Plin.; transf., senectus, Ov.

cāris -ĭdis, f. (καρίς), *a kind of crab*, Ov.

cărĭstĭa = charistia (q.v.).

cārĭtas -ātis, f. (carus), *dearness, high price.* **I.** Lit., nummorum, *scarcity of money*, Cic.; absol. (sc. annonae), *high price of the necessaries of life;* annus in summa caritate est, *it is a very dear year*, Cic. **II.** Transf. *affection, love, esteem;* in caritate et honore esse, Liv.; complecti aliquem amicitia et caritate, Cic.; benevolentiā devincire homines et caritate, Cic.; civium, *esteem of the citizens*, Cic.; in pastores, Cic.; inter natos et parentes, Cic.; liberorum, *for one's children*, Cic.; in plur., omnes omnium caritates patria una complexa est, Cic.

carmen -ĭnis, n. (from cano and suffix -men, orig. canmen, then casmen, then carmen), *a song, tune*, either vocal or instrumental. **I.** Gen. carmina vocum, Ov.; *the song of the swan*, Ov.; *the screech of the owl*, Verg. **II.** Esp. **A.** *poetry, a poem of any kind;* **a,** fundere, condere, contexere, Cic.; componere, fingere, scribere, Hor.; facere, Verg.; **b,** *lyric poetry*, Hor.; amabile, *erotic poetry*, Hor.; **c,** *a part of a poem*, Lucr.; *a passage in a poem;* illud mollissimum carmen, Cic.; **d,** *a prediction, oracular declaration*, Liv. **B.** *incantation*, Verg. **C.** *a religious* or *legal formula*, in ancient times composed in verse; cruciatus, Cic.; lex horrendi carminis, Liv.

Carmentis -is, f., and **Carmenta** -ae, f. (carmen = *oracle*), *a prophetess, the mother of Evander, who came with him to Latium, prophesied on the Capitoline hill, and was afterwards reverenced as a deity.* Adj., **Carmentalis** -e, *of* or *belonging to Carmentis;* porta, *a gate of Rome near the temple of Carmentis, the right arch of which was called the* porta scelerata, *because the Fabii went through it on their journey to Cremera, where they were destroyed;* plur., **Carmentalia** -ium, n. *the festival of Carmentis.*

Carmo -ōnis, f. *town in Hispania Baetica*, now *Carmone, in Andalusia.*

Carna -ae, f. (caro), *the tutelary goddess of the nobler parts of the body, the heart*, etc., confused by Ovid with Cardea, *the goddess of hinges.*

carnarium -ii, n. (caro), *the larder, pantry*, Plaut.; *a frame provided with hooks to which provisions were hung*, Plaut.

Carnĕădēs -is, m. (Καρνεάδης), *philosopher of Cyrene, founder of the third Academic school, opponent of Zeno.*

carnĭfex -ficis, m. (2. caro and facio), *the public executioner, hangman*, Cic.; used also as a term of reproach, *tormentor*, carnifex civium sociorumque, Cic.

carnĭfĭcīna -ae, f. (carnifex), **1,** *the hangman's office*, Plaut.; **2,** *place of torture*, Liv.; transf., *torture*, Cic.

carnĭfĭco, 1. (carnifex), *to slay, behead*, Liv.

Carnūtes -um, m. *people in the middle of Gaul, whose chief town was Genabum*, the modern *Orleans*, Caes.

1\. **cāro,** 3. *to card wool*, Plaut.

2\. **căro,** carnis, f. *flesh.* **I.** Lit. **A.** lacte et carne vivere, Cic.; plur., carnes vipereae, Ov. **B.** Meton., used contemptuously of a man, ista pecus et caro putida, Cic. **II.** Transf. *the pulpy parts of fruit*, Plin. (old nom. carnis, Liv.).

Carpăthus (-ŏs) -i, f. (Κάρπαθος), *an island in the Aegaean sea*, now *Scarpanto.* Adj., **Carpăthĭus** -a -um; vates, senex, *Proteus*, Ov.

carpentum -i, n. **1,** *a two-wheeled carriage, a coach;* carpento in forum invehi, Liv.; **2,** *a baggage waggon;* carpenta Gallica multa praeda onerata, Liv.

Carpetāni -ōrum, m. *the Carpetani, a Spanish tribe in modern Castile and Estremadura, with chief town Toletum* (now *Toledo*).

carpo -psi -ptum, 3. (connected with κάρφω, ἁρπάζω), **I.** *to pluck, pluck off.* **A.** Lit. **1,** with the hand, flores ex arbore, Ov.; uvam de palmite, Verg.; pensum, *to spin*, Hor.; **2,** with the mouth, **a,** *to take something as food;* gramen, *to graze*, of a horse, Verg.; thyma, of bees, *to suck*, Hor.; **b,** *to tear, pull to pieces;* cibum, Ov. **B.** Transf., **1,** *to pluck off;* **a,** *to select, choose out;* flosculos, Cic.; paucos ad ignominiam, Cic.; **b,** poet., (α) *to enjoy;* diem, Hor.; auras vitales, Verg.; (β) of places, *to pass over, hasten over;* prata fuga, Verg.; mare, Ov.; **2, a,** *to carp at, slander, calumniate;* aliquem maledico dente, Cic.; **b,** milit. t.t., *to annoy, harass;* equitatu agmen adversariorum, Caes.; **c,** *to weaken;* vires paulatim, Verg. **II. A.** Lit. *to rend;* jecur, Ov. **B.** Transf. *to separate, divide;* in multas parvasque partes exercitum, Liv.

carptim, adv. (carptus, carpo), **1,** *in pieces, in single portions, in small parts*, Sall.; **2,** *in different places;* aggredi, Liv.; **3,** *at different times;* dimissi carptim et singuli, Tac.

carptor -ōris, m. (carpo), *one who carves food*, Juv.

carrūca -ae, f. *a kind of four-wheeled carriage*, Suet.

carrus -i, m (carrum -i, n), *a kind of four-wheeled baggage waggon*, Caes

Carsĕŏli (Carsioli) -ōrum, m (Καρσέολοι), *a town in Latium, now Arsoli*, hence, **Carsĕŏlānus** -a -um, *of or belonging to Carseoli*

Cartēja -ae, f, 1, *a town in Hispania Baetica*, hence, adj, **Cartējānus** -a -um, 2, *town of the Olcades in Hispania Tarraconensis*

Carthaea -ae, f (Καρθαία), *town on the south coast of the island Cea*; hence adj, **Carthaeus** -a -um, and **Carthēus** -a -um, *of or belonging to Carthaea*

Carthāgo -inis, f, 1, *the city of Carthage in N. Africa*, 2, Carthago (Nova), *colony of the Carthaginians in Hispania Tarraconensis, now Carthagena*. Adj, **Carthāginiensis** -e, *Carthaginian*

căruncŭla -ae, f (dim of caro), *a small piece of flesh*, Cic

cārus -a -um, 1, *high priced, dear*, annona carior, annona carissima, Cic, 2, *dear, beloved, esteemed*, patria, quae est mihi vita mea multo carior, Cic, carum habere, *to love, esteem*, Cic

Căryae -ārum, f (Καρύαι), *town in Laconia, with a temple to Artemis* (Diana), hence, **Căryātides**, acc -idas, f *the Laconian maidens who served in the temple of Artemis*, hence, in architecture, *the figures of women in the place of pillars*, Vitr

Cărystŏs -i, f (Κάρυστος), 1, *town on the south coast of Euboea, famous for its marble*, hence adj, **Cărystēus** -a -um, and **Cărystius** -a -um, *of or belonging to Carystos*, 2, *town of the Ligurians*

căsa -ae, f (root CAS, whence castrum), *a hut, cottage, cabin*, Cic, *barrack*, Caes

cāsĕŏlus -i, m (dim of caseus), *a little cheese*, Verg

cāsĕus -i, m (**cāsĕum** -i, n, Plaut), *a cheese*, caseum premere, *to make cheese*, Verg, collect, villa abundat caseo, Cic

căsĭa -ae, f (κασία), 1, *a tree with an aromatic bark, like cinnamon*, Verg, 2, *the sweet-smelling mezereon*, Verg.

Căsĭlīnum, -i, n *a town in Campania on the Volturnus*, hence, **Căsĭlīnātes** -um, and **Căsĭlīnenses** -ium, m *inhabitants of Casilinum*

Căsīnum -i, n *a town in Latium*. Adj, **Căsīnas** -ātis, *of or belonging to Casinum*

Caspĭum mărĕ or **pĕlăgus**, and **Caspĭus ōcĕănus** (τὸ Κάσπιον πέλαγος), *the Caspian Sea*. Adj, **Caspĭus** -a -um, *Caspian*

Cassandra -ae, f (Κασσάνδρα), *daughter of Priam, on whom the gift of prophecy was conferred by Apollo, with the reservation that no one should believe her*

Cassandrēa and **īa**, -ae, f (Κασσάνδρεια), *the town of Potidaea in Chalcidice, destroyed by Philip, re-built and re-named by Cassander*, hence, a, **Cassandrenses** -ium, m *the inhabitants of Cassandrea*, b, **Cassandreus** -ĕi, m (Κασσανδρεύς) = *Apollodorus, tyrant of Cassandrea*, Ov.

cassē, adv (cassus), *in vain, without result*, Liv

cassĭda -ae, f *a helmet*, Verg

1 **Cassĭŏpē** -ēs, f (Κασσιόπη), *wife of Cepheus, mother of Andromeda, changed into a star*

2 **Cassĭŏpē** -ēs, f (Κασσιόπη), *town in Corcyra*

1 **cassis** -idis, f A. *a metal helmet*, Caes B. Meton, *war*, Juv

2 **cassis** -is, gen plur **casses** -ium, m *a net* I. A. *a hunter's net*, casses ponere, Ov. B. Transf, *a trap, a snare*, Ov II. *a spider's web*, Verg

cassĭtĕrum -i, n. (κασσίτερος), *tin*, hence **Cassĭtĕrides** -um, f (Κασσιτερίδες), *the tin islands, the Scilly Isles*, Plin

Cassĭus -a -um, *name of a Roman gens, originally patrician, afterwards plebeian*. The most notable members were, 1, L Cassius Longinus Ravilla, *celebrated as an upright judge, author of the lex tabellaria Cassia, that jurymen should vote by ballot*, hence **Cassĭānus** -a -um *Cassian*, judex *an upright judge* Cic 2, *the consul L Cassius, conquered and killed by the Helvetii*, 107 A C, 3, C Cassius Longinus, *one of the murderers of Caesar*, 4, Cassius Parmensis, *a poet, another of Caesar's murderers*, 5, C Cassius Longinus, *a celebrated lawyer under Tiberius*

cassus -a -um (perhaps from careo) I. Lit, *empty, hollow*, nux, Plaut, poet, with abl or genit, *deprived of*, lumine cassus or aethere cassus, *dead*, Verg II. Transf *worthless, useless, vain*, cassum quiddam et inani vocis sono decoratum, Cic., in cassum, *in vain*, Liv

Castălĭa -ae, f (Κασταλία), *a spring on Mount Parnassus, sacred to Apollo and the Muses*. Adj, **Castălĭus** -a -um, and **Castălis** -idis, f *Castalian*, sorores, *the Muses*, Mart

castănĕa -ae, f, 1, *the chestnut-tree*, Col; 2, *the chestnut*, castaneae nuces, Verg

castē, adv (castus) I. *purely, spotlessly*; caste et integre vivere, Cic II. a, *innocently, chastely*, Cic, b, *piously, religiously*; caste ad deos adire, Cic

castellānus -a -um (castellum), *relating to a fortress*, triumphi, *on the capture of fortresses*, Cic Subst, **castellāni** -ōrum, m *the garrison of a fortress*, Sall

castellātim, adv (castellum), *in single fortresses*, dissipati, Liv

castellum -i, n (dim of castrum) I. A. *a castle, fortress, fort*, Cic B. Transf *protection, refuge*, omnium scelerum, Liv II. *a dwelling on a height*, Verg

castērĭa -ae, f *a portion of a ship, used as a resting-place for rowers*, Plaut

castīgābĭlis -e (castigo), *worthy of punishment*, Plaut

castīgātĭo -ōnis, f (castigo), *punishment, chastisement, reproof*, afficere aliquem castigationibus, Cic, verborum, Liv

castīgātor -ōris, m (castigo), *one who reproves or punishes*, Liv

castīgatōrĭus -a -um (castigo), *correcting*, Plin

castīgātus -a -um (partic of castigo), *checked, restrained*, hence *small, neat*, as a term of praise; pectus, Ov

castīgo (castum ago, as purgo = purum ago), 1 *to reprove, chasten, punish* I. Lit, pueros verbis, verberibus, Cic II. Transf, a, *to correct, amend*, carmen, Hor, b, *to check, restrain*, fig examen in trutina, *to amend one's opinion*, Pers

castĭmōnĭa -ae, f (castus), 1, *bodily purity*, Cic, 2, *moral purity*, Cic

castĭtas -ātis, f (castus), *abstinence from sensual pleasure, chastity*, Cic

1 **castor** -oris, m (κάστωρ), *the beaver*, Cic

2 **Castor** -ŏris, m (Κάστωρ), *the son of Tyndarus and Leda, twin-brother of Pollux and Helen*. Ecastor, mecastor, *By Castor!* a common form of oath in Rome

castŏrĕum, -i, n *an aromatic secretion obtained from the beaver*, Verg

castrensis -e (castra), *pertaining to a camp*, Cic

castro, 1, *to castrate*, Plaut

castrum -i, n (root CAS, whence casa) **I.** Sing, *a castle, fort, fortress*, Nep, oftener in sing as a proper name, e g, Castrum Inui in Latium **II.** Plur, **castra** -ōrum, n. **A.** Lit, **1,** *a camp fortified by a ditch* (fossa) *and a mound* (agger) *surmounted by palisades* (vallum), stativa, *permanent*, Cic; aestiva, *summer quarters*, Suet, hiberna, *winter quarters*, Liv, navalia, *a naval encampment*, when the ships were drawn up on the beach and protected by an entrenchment, Caes, ponere, Liv; locare, facere, *to encamp*, Cic, movere, *to break up the camp*, Caes; promovere, *to advance*, Caes, removere, or movere retro, *to retreat*, Liv, hostium castris exuere, *to take the enemy's camp*, Liv., fig, like the English *camp*, of a party, in Epicuri nos adversarii nostri castra conjecimus, Cic, **2,** esp, **a,** *the camp of the praetorian guard* at Rome, praetoriana, Suet; **b,** as a proper name, Castra Cornelia, *a height near Utica* **B.** Transf, of a bee-hive, cerea castra, Verg **C.** Meton, **1,** *a day's march*, tertiis castris pervenit, Liv, **2,** *martial service*, magnum in castris usum habere, Caes

castus -a -um (connected with Gr καθαρος) **I.** *pure, spotless, innocent*, homo castissimus, Cic **II.** Esp **A.** 1, *temperate, unselfish*, homo castus ac non cupidus, Cic, **2,** *chaste*, matronarum castissima, Cic **B.** Transf, of things, Cassii castissima domus, Cic **C.** of religion, *pious, religious, holy;* hac casti maneant in religione nepotes, Verg, castam contionem, sanctum campum defendo, Cic

căsŭla -ae, f (dim of casa), *a little hut, cottage*, Plin

cāsus -ūs, m (cado), *a falling, fall*, Liv **I.** Gen **A.** Lit, **a,** nivis, Liv, **b,** of a season, *end*, extremae sub casum hiemis, Verg, **c,** in grammar, *case*, casus rectus, *the nominative*, Cic **B.** Transf, **a,** *fall*, quum gravis casus in servitium ex regno foret, Sall; **b,** *occasion, opportunity*, aut vi aut dolis se casum victoriae inventurum, Sall, **c,** *accident, event, occurrence;* novi casus temporum, Cic, abl casu, *by chance*, evenire non temere nec casu, Cic., **d,** *disaster, mishap*, meus ille casus tam horribilis, tam gravis, etc, Cic, reipublicae, Sall **II.** *destruction, ruin*, **a,** of things, urbis Trojanae, Verg, **b,** of persons, *violent death*, Saturnini atque Gracchorum casus (plur), Caes

Cătăbathmŏs -i, m (Καταβαθμός), *a valley on the borders of Africa and Asia*, now *the valley of Akabah*

cătădrŏmus -i, m (κατάδρομος), *a rope for rope-dancing*, Suet

Cătădūpa -ōrum, n (Κατάδουπα) *the Nile cataracts on the Ethiopian frontier*, now *cataracts of Wady Halfa*

cătăgĕlăsĭmus a -um (καταγελάσιμος), *serving as a subject of jest*, Plaut

cătăgrăphus a -um (καταγραφος), *painted, parti coloured*, Cat

Cătămītus i, m *the Latin name for Ganymedes*

Cātăŏnĭa -ae, f *a district of the Roman province Cappadocia*

cătăphractes -ae, m (καταφρακτής), *a breast plate of iron scales*, Tac, hence, adj, **cătăphractus** -a um, *mail-clad*, Liv.

cătăplūs -i, m (καταπλους), *the arrival of a ship*, hence meton, *a ship that is arriving*, Cic

cătăpulta -ae, f. (καταπελτης), *an engine of war for throwing arrows, a catapult*, Liv

cătăpultārĭus -a -um (catapulta), *relating to a catapult*, Plaut.

cătăracta (catarr) -ae, f, and **cătăractes** -ae, m (καταῤῥακτης), **1,** *a waterfall*, esp *a cataract of the Nile*, Sen, **2,** *a sluice* or *floodgate*, Plin, **3,** *a portcullis*, Liv

cătasta -ae, f (καταστασις), *a stage upon which slaves were exposed in the market*, Pers.

cătē, adv (catus), *skilfully, cleverly*, Cic.

cătēja -ae, f *a kind of dart*, Verg

1 **catella** -ae, f (dim of catula), *a little bitch*, Juv

2 **cătella** -ae, f (dim of catena), *a little chain*, Liv

cătellus i, m (dim of catulus), *a little dog*, Cic.

cătēna -ae f (root CAT, CAS, whence cassis), **1,** *a chain, fetter*, aliquem catenis vincire, Liv., aliquem in catenas conjicere, Liv, alicui catenas injicere, Cic, in catenis tenere, Caes; fig, *restraint*, legum catenae, Cic, **2,** *a chain, series*, Lucr.

cătēnātus -a -um (catena), *chained, bound;* Britannus, Hor, labores, *unremitting*, Mart

căterva -ae, f. *crowd, troop* **I.** Of men, **A.** Gen, magna togatorum, Cic **B.** Esp, **1,** *a troop of soldiers*, esp of barbarian soldiers, of mercenaries as opp to Roman legionaries, Hor, Tac, **2,** *a company of actors*, Cic: **3,** *the chorus in the drama*, Cic. **II.** Of animals, Verg

cătervārĭus a -um (caterva), *belonging to a troop*, Suet

cătervātim, adv (caterva), *in troops, in masses*, Sall, Lucr

căthĕdra ae, f (καθεδρα) **I. A.** *a chair*, principally used by ladies, Hor, also, *a litter for women*, Juv **B.** Meton, cathedrae molles, *luxurious women*, Juv **II.** *a professor's chair*, Juv

Cătĭlīna -ae, m, L Sergius, *a Roman of noble birth, who headed a conspiracy against the state, and was killed in battle at Faesulae*, B C 62; hence adj, **Cătĭlīnārĭus** -a -um, *Catilinarian*

cătillo, 1 (catillus), *to lick plates*, Plaut

1 **cătillus** -i, m (dim of catinus), *a small dish or plate*, Hor

2 **Cātillus** -i, m *son of Amphiaraus, one of the legendary founders of Tibur.*

Cătĭna -ae, f (Κατάνη), and **Cătănē** -ēs, f *a town on the east coast of Sicily, at the foot of Mount Aetna*, now *Catania* Adj., **Cătĭnensis** -e, *of or belonging to Catina*

cătīnum -i, n and **cătīnus** i, m *a broad, flat dish*, Hor

Căto -ōnis, m **I.** *a cognomen belonging to the plebeian gens Porcia* **1,** M Porcius Cato Censorius (235–147 B C), *celebrated for his uprightness and strenuous support of the old Roman simplicity and discipline, author of several works, among which the most noted are the* Origines *and* de Re rustica; **2,** M Porcius Cato the younger, *leader of the senatorial party on the death of Pompeius, killed himself at Utica*, B C 46, *on the final ruin of his party* (hence called Uticensis) Adj, **Cătōnĭānus** -a -um, *Catonian* Subst, **Cătōnīni** orum, m *the party of the younger Cato* Plin, **Cătōnes,** *men of the old Roman type, like Cato*, Cic **II.** M Valerius Cato, *a freedman of Gaul, grammarian and poet in the time of Sulla*

cătōnĭum -i, n. (κάτω), *the lower world*, with

a play on the word Cato, vereor ne in catonium Catoninos, Cic

catta -ae, f *cat* or *weasel*, Mart.

cătŭla -ae, f *a little bitch*, Prop.

cătŭlīnus -a -um (catulus), *relating to a dog*, caro, Plaut, or subst, **cătŭlīna** -ae, f *dog's flesh*, Plin

Cătullus -i, m, Q Valerius Catullus, *a celebrated Roman elegiac and epigrammatic poet, born in or near Verona*, B.C. 87. Adj, **Cătulliānus** -a -um

1 **cătŭlus** -i, m (dim of catus), *a young animal*, esp of the dog or cat kind, **a**, suis, Plaut; leonis, Hor., lupi, Verg, ursae, Ov., **b**, esp *a young dog, whelp, puppy*, Cic

2 **Cătŭlus** -i, m, *the name of a branch of the plebeian gens Lutatia* **I.** C Lutatius Catulus, *consul* B C 242, *who brought the First Punic War to a close by the victory of Aegusa*, B C 241 **II.** Q Lutatius Catulus, *consul with Marius*, B C 102, *defeated the Cimbri at the battle of Vercellae, perished in the proscription of Sulla*, B C 87 **III.** Q Lutatius Catulus, *son of the preceding, an honest and popular aristocratic statesman, contemporary with Cicero, consul*, B C 78, *died* B C 60

cătus -a -um, **1**, *sagacious, acute, clever* (opp stultus), Cic, **2**, *cunning, sly*, in a bad sense, Hor

Caucăsus -i, m (Καύκασος), *mountains separating Asia from Europe* Adj, **Caucăsius** -a -um, *Caucasian*

cauda -ae, f *the tail of an animal*; **1**, leonis, Cic, caudam trahere, *to wear a tail, a fool's cap*, Hor, **2**, cauda Verrina, *the appendage to the name of Verres which was changed to Verrucius*, with a play on the word verres (*boar*)

caudĕus -a -um, *made of rushes*, Plaut

caudex (codex) -icis, m *the stem* or *trunk of a tree*, Verg

caudĭcālis -e (caudex), *relating to wood*, Plaut.

caudĭcārius, v codicarius

Caudĭum -ii, n *an old city in Samnium, near the pass of the Caudine Forks, in which the Roman army was enclosed by the Samnites*, B C 321 Adj, **Caudīnus** -a -um, *Caudine*, furculae, Liv, proelium, Cic

caulae -ārum, f (contr for cavillae, from cavus), **1**, *a hole, opening*, Lucr, **2**, *a sheep-fold*, Verg

caulis -is, m (connected with καυλός) **A.** *the stalk of a plant*, esp *the cabbage-plant*, Plin **B.** Transf, *anything of similar form*; pennae, *a quill*, Plin

Caulōn -ōnis, m and **Caulōnia** -ae, f (Καυλών), *Italian town in Bruttii*

Caunus (Caunŏs) -i, f (Καῦνος), *a town in Caria* Adj, **Caunĕus** or -**ius** -a -um

caupo -ōnis, m *a small shopkeeper*, or *innkeeper*, Cic

caupōna -ae, f (caupo), *a tavern, inn*, Cic, Hor.

caupōnius -a -um (caupo), *belonging to an innkeeper*, Plaut

caupōnor, 1. dep (caupo), *to trade in anything*, Enn

caupōnŭla -ae, f (dim of caupo), *a little inn*, Cic.

caurus (cōrus), -i, m *the north west wind*, Verg, Caes

causa (caussa) -ae, f (cado), *a cause, reason, motive, inducement* **A. 1**, magna, levis, justa, Cic, cum causa, *with good reason*, Cic, sine causa, *without reason*, Cic, with genit, causa belli, Cic; with infin (poet), quae causa fuit consurgere in arma, Verg, ob eam causam quia, etc, Cic, quidnam esse causae cur, etc, Cic, propter hanc causam quod, etc, Cic, ea est causa ut (with subj), Liv, quid est causae quin (with subj), Cic, eis causis quominus (with subj), Caes, in causa haec sunt, Cic, afferre causam, Cic, alicui inferre causam, Cic, alicui causam alicuius rei dare, Cic, causae esse, Caes, causam alicuius rei sustinere, *to bear the blame*, Cic, **2**, *excuse*, causam accipere, Cic, **3**, *pretext*, causas novarum postulationum quaerere, Cic, fingere causam, Cic, **4**, *cause of a disease*, Cic, **5**, abl, causa, *on account of*, joci causa, Cic, verbi causa, *for example*, Cic, mea causa, Cic, so tua, nostra, etc **B. 1**, *case*, armis inferiores, non causa fiunt, Cic, **2**, *situation condition*, erat in meliore causa, Cic, **3**, *side, party*, causa quam Pompeius susceperat, Cic, **4**, *point in an argument, subject*, causam disserendi, Cic, **5**, *lawsuit*, causa capitis, Cic, causae dictio, *pleading*, Cic, causam defendere, Cic, causam dicere, *to plead*, Cic, causam surripere, Cic, causam perdere or causa cadere, *to lose a suit*, Cic

causārius -a -um (causa A 4), *sickly, diseased*, Sen; hence subst, **causārii** -orum, m milit. t t, *invalided, discharged on account of illness*, Liv

causia -ae, f (καυσία), *a white broad brimmed Macedonian hat*, Plaut

causĭdĭcus -i, m (causa and dico), *an advocate, barrister*, used contemptuously to denote one who pleads for money and without skill, distinguished from orator, Cic

causĭfĭcor, 1 (causa and facio), *to bring forward as a reason or pretext*, Plaut

causor, 1 dep (causa), *to give as a reason, or pretext, to plead, pretend*, multa, Lucr, consensum patrum, Liv; valetudinem, Tac

caustĭcus -a -um (καυστικός), *burning, caustic* Subst, **caustĭcum** -i, n *caustic*, Plin

causŭla -ae, f (dim of causa), **1**, *a little lawsuit*, Cic., **2**, *a slight occasion*, Auct B Afr

cautē, adv (cautus), *cautiously, carefully*; caute pedetemptimque dicere, Cic

cautēs (cōtes) -is, f *a rough sharp rock*, Caes, Verg

cautim, adv (cautus), *cautiously, carefully*, Ter

cautĭo -ōnis, f (contr from cavitio, from caveo) **I.** *caution, care, foresight, precaution*; cautionem adhibere, Cic; hence, res cautionem habet, **a**, *the affair needs caution*, Cic, **b**, *allows of foresight*, Cic **II.** Legal t t, *security, bail, bond*, Cic., chirographi, *written*, Cic

cautor -ōris, m (caveo), **1**, *one who is on his guard*, Plaut, **2**, *one who gives bail for another*, Cic

cautus -a -um (caveo), **1**, **a**, *cautious, wary, careful, circumspect*, parum putantur cauti providique fuisse, Cic, in scribendo, Cic, consilia cautiora, Cic, **b**, *sly*, vulpes, Hor, **2**, of property, *made safe, secured*, quo mulieri esset res cautior, Cic

căvaedĭum -i, n = cavum aedium, *the open quadrangle formed by the inner walls of a house*, Plin

căvĕa -ae, f (cavus) **I.** *a hollow place, cavity*, Plin **II.** Esp **A.** *an inclosure, a den for wild animals*, Luc, esp **a**, *a birdcage*, Cic, **b**, *a beehive*, Verg **B a**, *the seats in a theatre or amphitheatre*, prima, *the first tier, the place of honour where the knights sat*, media, summa, *less distinguished seats*, Cic., **b**, *the whole theatre*, Cic

căvĕo, cāvi, cautum, 2. *to be on one's guard*, **I.** *to guard against, beware, avoid*; absol., nisi cavetis, Cic.; with ab, ab aliquo, Cic.; with acc., aliquem, *to be on one's guard against*, Cic.; pass., cavenda etiam gloriae cupiditas, *we must be on our guard against*, Cic.; with infin., in quibus cave vereri ne, etc., Cic.; with ne, ut ne, and the subj., quod ut ne accidat cavendum est, Cic.; with subj. alone, cave ignoscas, Cic.; with ut and the subj., Cic. **II.** *to take precautions*. **A.** With dat. of persons for whom, qui in Oratore tuo caves tibi per Brutum, Cic.; with ad, satis cautum tibi ad defensionem, Cic.; with ut and the subj., *to take care*, Cic. **B.** Esp., legal t.t., **1**, *to give security for*; praedibus et praediis populo, Cic.; **2**, *to get security*; ab sese caveat, Cic.; **3**, *to provide for in writing, to order*; **a**, by will, heredi velle cavere, Cic.; **b**, in a treaty, de quibus cautum sit foedere, Cic.; **c**, in a law, cautum est in legibus Scipionis ne, etc., Cic. (Imper. căvĕ sometimes in poet.)

căverna -ae, f. (cavus), *a hollow place, grotto, cavern*, Cic.; navis, *the hold*, Cic.; coeli, *the vault of heaven*, Lucr.

căvilla -ae, f. (dim. of cavus), *empty jesting, raillery, scoffing*, Plaut.

căvillātio -ōnis, f. (cavillor), *raillery, jesting, irony*, Cic.

căvillātor -ōris, m. (cavillor), *a jester, joker, humourist*, Cic.

căvillor, 1. dep. (cavilla), *to jest, joke, satirise, make game of*; **1**, cum aliquo, Cic.; in eo cavillatus est, Cic.; alicuius praetextam, Cic.; tribunos plebei cavillans, Liv.; **2**, *to make captious objections*; cavillari tribuni, Liv.

căvillŭla -ae, f. (dim. of cavilla), *a little jest*, Plaut.

căvo, 1. (cavus), *to hollow, make hollow, excavate*; naves ex arboribus, Liv.; oppida cuniculis, *to undermine*, Plin.; parmam gladio, *to pierce*, Verg.; luna cavans cornua, *waning*, Plin. Partic., **căvātus** -a -um, *hollowed out, hollow*; rupes, Verg.

căvum, -i, n. (cavus), *a hole, cavity, cave*, Liv.

căvus -a -um, *hollow, concave* (opp. plenus). **I.** Lit., vena, Cic.; vallis, Liv.; nubes, Verg.; flumina, *deep-channelled*, Verg.; luna, *waning*, Plin. **II.** Meton., *empty*; imago formae, Verg.

Căystrus -i, m. (Κάϋστρος), *a river in Lydia, famous for its swans*; hence adj., **Căystrius** -a -um, *Caystrian*; ales, *the swan*, Ov.

cĕ, an inseparable particle joined on to pronouns and adverbs—e.g., hisce, Cic.

Cĕa -ae, f. and **Cĕŏs**, acc. Ceo (Κέως), *one of the Cyclades Islands, birthplace of the poet Simonides*. Adj., **Cēus** -a -um, *Cean*, Camenae, *the poetry of Simonides*, Hor.

Cebenna (Gebenna) mons, m. *a mountain-chain in Gaul* (now *the Cevennes*).

Cĕbrēn -ēnis, m. (Κεβρήν), *a river-god in Troas, father of Oenone and Hesperie*. Hence, **Cĕbrēnis** -ĭdis, f. *the daughter of Cebren*, i.e., *Hesperie*, Ov.

Cĕcrops -ŏpis, m. (Κέκροψ), *the first king of Attica, mythical founder of Athens*; hence, **a**, **Cĕcrŏpĭdēs** -ae, m. *descendant of Cecrops*, e.g., *Theseus*, Ov.; plur. *the Athenians*, Verg.; **b**, **Cĕcrŏpis** -ĭdis, f. *a female descendant of Cecrops*, e.g., *Aglauros, daughter of Cecrops*, Ov.; *Procne and Philomela, daughters of Pandion*, Ov.; adj., terra, *Attica*, Ov.; ales, *Procne*, Ov.; **c**, **Cĕcrŏpĭus** -a -um, *Cecropian*, arx, Ov.; and subst., **Cĕcrŏpĭa** -ae, f. *the citadel of Athens*, Plin.; also, *relating to Attica and Athens*; *Athenian, Attic*.

1. **cēdo**, cessi, cessum, 3. **I.** Gen., *to go, proceed*. **A.** Lit., per ora, Hor. **B.** Transf., **1**, *to come to something, to turn out, to happen*; alicui male, Ov.; **2**, *to fall to the lot of*; ut etiam is quaestus huic cederet, Cic.; res omnis Albana in Romanum cedit imperium, Liv.; **3**, *to change to, to become*; huc omnis aratri cessit honos, Verg. **II.** Esp., **A.** Lit., *to give ground, retire*; cedam atque abibo, Cic.; horas cedunt et dies, Cic.; e patria, or (simply) patria, Cic.; ab or de oppido, Cic.; e vita or vita, Cic.; e memoria or memoria, Liv.; with dat. of the person before whom one retreats, infenso hosti, Liv. **B.** Transf., **1**, *to submit, yield*; minis alicuius, Cic.; tempori, Cic.; precibus alicuius, Cic.; **2**, *to be inferior to*; alicui virtute, Caes.; **3**, *to give up a right or some property*; with abl. and dat., alicui possessione bonorum, Cic.; with acc., multa multis de jure, Cic.; *permitto* aliquid iracundiae tuae, *do* adolescentiae, *cedo* amicitiae, *tribuo* parenti, Cic.

2. **cĕdŏ** and plur. **cettĕ** (contracted from cedito and cedite), **1**, *here with it! give here*; cedo aquam manibus, Plaut.; cedo ut bibam, Plaut.; **2**, *out with it! let us hear, tell us*; also, cedo dum, Plaut., Ter.; **3**, to call attention, *see here*; cedo mihi leges Atinias, Furias, Cic.

cĕdrus -i, f. (κέδρος). **I.** *the cedar*, or *juniper tree*, Plin. **II.** Meton., **A.** *cedar-wood*, Verg. **B.** *cedar oil*; carmina linenda cedro, *worthy of immortality* (as the cedar oil preserved from decay), Hor.

Cĕlaenae -ārum, f. (Κελαιναί), *a town in Phrygia, near the Maeander*, Liv. Adj., **Cĕlaenaeus** -a -um, *Celaenean*.

Cĕlaeno -ūs, f. (Κελαινώ). **I.** *daughter of Atlas, placed in the sky as one of the Pleiades*. **II.** *one of the Harpies*. Appell., *a covetous woman*, Juv.

cēlātor -ōris, m. (celo), *a concealer*, Lucr.

cĕlĕber -bris -bre and **cĕlĕbris** -e, *numerous*. **I.** Of places, meetings, etc., **A.** Lit., *much frequented*; portus, Cic. **B.** Transf., **1**, *honoured*; funus fit regium, magis amore civium et caritate quam cura suorum celebre, Liv.; **2**, *renowned, distinguished, well-known*; **a**, of things, res tota Sicilia celeberrima atque notissima, Cic.; **b**, of persons, *famous*; clarissimarum urbium excidio celeberrimi viri, Liv. **II.** *often repeated*; vox celeberrima, Ov.

cĕlĕbrātio -ōnis, f. (celebro), **1**, *a numerous assembly*; quae celebratio quotidiana, Cic.; **2**, *numerous attendance upon a festival, celebration*; ludorum, Cic.

cĕlĕbrātor -ōris, m. (celebro), *one who praises or extols*, Mart.

cĕlĕbrātus -a -um, p. adj. (from celebro), **1**, *numerously attended*; **a**, of places, *much frequented*; forum rerum venalium totius regni maxime celebratum, Sall.; **b**, of festivals, *kept solemn, festive*; dies festus celebratusque per omnem Africam, Liv.; **2**, *known*; **a**, res celebratissimae omnium sermone, Cic.; **b**, *praised, honoured*; eloquentia, Tac.

cĕlĕbrĭtas -ātis, f. (celeber), **1**, *a frequenting in large numbers, numerous attendance at*; loci, Cic.; of a festival, *celebration*; supremi diei, *at a funeral*, Cic.; **2**, *a multitude, concourse*; virorum ac mulierum, Cic.; **3**, *fame, renown*; celebritatem sermonis hominum consequi, Cic.

cĕlĕbro, 1. (celeber), **1** *to visit frequently, or in large numbers*; domum alicuius, Cic.; sepulcrum hominum conventu epulisque, Cic.; **2**, *to celebrate, solemnise*; festos dies ludorum, Cic.; celebratur omnium sermone laetitiaque convivium, Cic.; **3**, *to publish, make known*; factum esse consulem Murenam nuntii litteraeque celebrassent, Cic, 4, *to praise, honour*, egressum aliquius ornare atque celebrare, Cic, nomen alicuius scriptis, Cic, 5, *to practise often, exercise*, artes, Cic, nec unum genus est divinationis publice privatimque celebratum, Cic

Cĕlemna -ae, f *a town in Campania*, not far from Teanum

cĕler -ĕris, -ĕre (root CEL, connected with cello, celox, κελω, κελης), *swift, quick, rapid* I. Lit, navis, Ov II. Transf, A. 1, in a good sense, mens qua nihil est celerius, Cic, 2, in a bad sense, *hasty, rash, precipitate*, consilia celeriora, *over hasty plans*, Liv

cĕlĕrĕ, adv (celer), *quickly, swiftly*, Plaut

Cĕlĕres -um, m (connected with κέλης), *the name of the body-guard of the Roman kings*, Liv

cĕlĕrĭpes -pĕdis (celer and pes), *swift-footed*, Cic

cĕlĕrĭtas ātis, f (celer), *quickness, swiftness, celerity* I. Lit, equorum, Cic II. Transf, orationis, Cic, actionis, Cic, animorum, Cic

cĕlĕrĭtĕr, adv (celer), *quickly, swiftly*, Cic

cĕlĕro, 1 (celer) I. Transit, *to make quick, hasten, accelerate*, fugam, Verg II. Intransit, *to hasten*, Lucr, Cat

Cĕlĕus -i, m (Κελεος), *king in Eleusis, who hospitably entertained Ceres, and was taught by her agriculture and the mysteries of her worship*.

cella -ae, f *a room* I. In a Roman house A. Of a town house, 1, *a room for persons*, esp *the servants' rooms*, Cic, 2, *a storehouse*, with or without penaria, Cic, in cellam dare, imperare, emere, *to give out, order, buy things for the house*, Cic B. Of a country-house, 1, *storehouse*, penaria, *for corn*, olearia, *for oil*, vinaria, *for wine*, Cic, transf, Capua cella atque horreum Campani agri, Cic, 2, *place for keeping birds*, Col C. In a lodging-house, *a mean apartment*, Mart II. In a temple, *the shrine of the god's image*, Cic III. *the cell of a beehive*, Verg

cellārĭus a -um (cella), *relating to a store-room*, Plaut Subst, **cellārĭus** -i, m *a store-keeper, cellarer*, Plaut

cellŭla -ae, f (dim of cella), *a little chamber, or cell*, Ter.

cēlo, 1 *to hide conceal, keep secret*, sententiam suam, Cic, dolorem vultu tegere et taciturnitate celare, Cic, with acc of the thing concealed and acc of person from whom it is concealed, non te celavi sermonem T Ampii, Cic, with de and the abl of the person, de insidiis te celare noluit, Cic

cĕlox -ōcis, f (root CEL, v celer), *a swift vessel, or yacht*, Liv, publica, *packet boat*, Plaut

1. **celsus** -a um (from *cello, lit *driven up on high*), *high, upright* A. Lit., natura homines humo excitatos celsos et erectos constituit, Cic B. Transf, 1, of rank, *eminent*, celsissima sedes dignitatis et honoris, Cic, 2, morally, *lofty, elevated*, celsus et erectus, Cic, 3, in a bad sense, *proud, haughty*, Cic, celsi Ramnes, Hor.

2 **Celsus** i, m A Cornelius, *a Latin writer on medicine*

Celtae ārum, m *the Celts*. Adj, **Celtĭcus** a um, *Celtic*

Celtĭbēri -ōrum, m *the Celtiberians, a race in the middle of Spain of mixed Celtic and Iberian blood* Adj, **Celtĭbēr** -ēra -ērum and **Celtĭbērĭcus** -a -um, *Celtiberian* Subst, **Celtĭbērĭa** -ae, f *the land of the Celtiberi*

cēna -ae, f *the principal meal of the Romans, taken about three or four o'clock in the afternoon, dinner, supper*, I. Lit, cena recta, *a complete dinner of three courses*, Suet; caput cenae, *the chief dish*, Cic, inter cenam, *at dinner-time*, Cic, invitare ad cenam, *to ask to dinner*, Cic, obire cenas, itare ad cenas, Cic, cenam alicui dare, *to give any one a dinner*, Cic venire ad cenam, Cic, redire a cena, Cic II. Meton a, *the courses at a dinner*, prima, altera, tertia, Mart, b, *the company invited*, ingens cena sedet, Juv, c, *the place where the dinner is given*, Plin

cēnācŭlum i, n (ceno), *literally an eating-room*, Varr, and as these were often in the upper storey, *the upper storey of a house, the garret, attic*, Roma cenaculis sublata atque suspensa, Cic, mutat cenacula, Hor

Cēnaeum i, n (Κηναῖον ἄκρον), *the north-western promontory of Euboea, on which was a temple of Jupiter*, hence, adj, **Cēnaeus** -a -um, *of Cenaeum*, Juppiter, Ov

cēnātĭcus a -um (cena), *relating to dinner*; spes, Plaut

cēnātĭo -ōnis, f (cena), *an eating-room, dining hall*, Plin

cēnātōrĭus a -um (cena), *relating to dinner* Subst, **cēnātōrĭa** -ōrum n *clothes to dine in*, Petr

cēnātŭrĭo, 4 (ceno), *to wish to dine*, Mart

cēnātus -a -um, v ceno.

Cenchrĕae ārum, f (Κεγχρέαι), *port of the Corinthians on the Saronic gulf* Adj, **Cenchrēus** -a um, *Cenchrean*

cēnĭto, 1 (freq of ceno), *to dine often, be accustomed to dine*, apud aliquem, Cic

cēno, 1 (cena) I Intransit, *to take the cena, to dine, sup, eat*, cenare bene, Cic, cenare apud aliquem, Cic, impers, quum cenaretur apud Vitellios, Liv, partic perf, cenatus, with a middle meaning, *having dined, after dinner*, cenati discubuerunt ibidem, Cic II. Transit., *to dine on, to eat*, aprum, Hor

Cenomāni -ōrum, *a Celtic people in Gaul* Adj, **Cenomānus** -a -um, *Cenomanian*

censĕo sŭi -sum, 2 (root CENS, CONS, whence consulo), *to give an opinion* I. Gen, *to appraise, estimate* A. Lit, 1, si censenda nobis atque aestimanda res sit, Cic, 2, esp of the censor at Rome, a, *to take an account of the names and property of Roman citizens*, censores populi aevitates, suboles, familias pecuniasque censento, Cic, capite censi, *the lowest class of Roman citizens, whose persons only were counted*, Sall, sintne ista praedia censui censendo? *are those estates fit to be put on the censor's list?* (as the property of the possessors), Cic, b, *to make a return to the censor*, in qua tribu denique ista praedia censuisti, Cic B. Transf, censeri de aliquo, *to be regarded as belonging to a certain person*, Ov II. A. *to express an opinion, be of an opinion*, ita prorsus censeo, Cic, tibi igitur hoc censeo, Cic, with ut and the subj, Cic, with the subj alone, magno opere censeo desistas, Cic, with infin, delubra esse in urbibus censeo, Cic B. *to vote, recommend by vote or advice*, captivos reddendos in senatu non censuit, Cic, pars deditionem, pars eruptionem censebant, Caes C. Of the senate (as jubere for the populus), *to resolve, order*, senatus censuit uti, etc, Caes

censĭo -ōnis, f (censeo) A. *an assessment, estimate*, esp *the censor's estimate*, Plaut B. Transf, in jest, bubula, *a scourging*, Plaut

censor -ōris, m (censeo), *the censor* I. Lit, *a Roman magistrate, of whom two were elected, originally at intervals of five years, afterwards of one year and a half* Their business was a, to hold the census, b, to punish persons for offences against morals by degradation to a lower rank; c, to look after the roads and bridges, public buildings, and the revenues of the state. **II.** Transf., *a severe judge, a rigid moralist, a censurer*, Cic.; castigator censorque minorum, Hor.

censōrĭus -a -um. **A.** *relating to the censor*; homo, *one who has filled the office of censor*, Cic.; tabulae, *the censor's lists*, Cic.; lex, locatio, *a contract relating to building* or *to the public revenue*, Cic.; opus, *a fault which was punished by the censor*, Cic. **B.** Transf., *rigid, severe*, Quint.

censūra -ae, f. (censor), *the censor's dignity, the censorship*; censuram gerere, Cic.

census -ūs, m. (censeo). **A.** *the enrolment of the names and the assessment of the property of all Roman citizens, the census*; censum habere, Cic.; agere, *to take a census*, Liv.; censu prohibere, Cic.; censu excludere, *to refuse to enrol in the census*, Liv.; censum perficere, Liv.; censum accipere, Liv.; censum alicuius augere, extenuare, Cic. **B.** Meton., a, *the censor's list*, Cic.; b, *the amount of property necessary for enrolment in a certain rank*; senatorius = 800,000 *sesterces*, Suet.; equester = 400,000 *sesterces*, Suet.; homo sine censu, *a poor man*, Cic.; dat census honores, Ov.

centaurēum -ēi, n. and **centaurĭum** -ĭi, n. (κενταύρειον), *the plant centaury*, Verg.

Centaurus -i, m. (Κένταυρος). **I.** *a centaur, a monster, half man and half horse*, Verg.; nobilis, *Chiron*, Hor.; hence adj., **Centaurēus** -a -um. **II.** f. *the name of a ship*, Verg.

centēnārĭus -a -um (centenus), *containing a hundred, relating to a hundred*, Varr., Plin.

centēnus -a -um (centum). **I.** Sing., used collectively, *a hundred*; centena arbore, Verg. **II.** Plur., num. distrib., *a hundred each*, Cic.

centēsĭmus -a -um, num. ordin. (centum), *the hundredth*; lux ab interitu Clodii, Cic. Subst., **centēsĭma** -ae, f. (sc. pars), *the hundredth part*; a, *a tax of one per cent.*, Cic.; b, of interest of money, *one per cent.* (reckoned at Rome by the month, therefore = 12 *per cent. per annum*); binae centesimae = 24 *per cent.*; quaternae, Cic.; perpetuae, *compound interest*, Cic.

centĭceps -cĭpĭtis (centum and caput), *hundred-headed*; belua, *Cerberus*, Hor.

centĭens or **centĭēs**, adv. (centum), *a hundred times*; HS. centies (sc. centena milia), *ten million sesterces*, Cic.

centĭmănus -a -um (centum and manus), *hundred-handed*, Hor., Ov.

centĭplex, v. centuplex.

cento -ōnis, m. (κέντρων), *patchwork, a covering of rags*; in war, *coverings to ward off missiles* or *extinguish fires*, Caes.

centum, indecl. numer., 1, *a hundred*, Cic.; 2, hyperbol., *any indefinitely large number*; centum puer artium, Hor.

centumgĕmĭnus -a -um, *hundred-fold*; Briareus, *hundred-armed*, Verg.

centumpondĭum -ĭi, n. *a weight of a hundred pounds*, Plaut.

centumvir -i, m., plur. **centumvĭri** -ōrum, m. *a college of 105 magistrates* (increased under the emperors to 180), *yearly elected at Rome, having jurisdiction over cases relating to inheritance*, Cic.

centumvĭrālis -e, *relating to the centumviri*; causa, *heard before the centumviri*, Cic.

centuncŭlus -i, m. (dim. of cento), *a little patch*, or *patchwork*, Liv.

centŭplex -ĭcis, *a hundred-fold*, Plaut.

centŭrĭa -ae, f. (centum), *a division of 100*; 1, *a company of soldiers*, originally 100, afterwards 60, Liv.; 2, *a century, one of the 193 divisions into which Servius Tullius distributed the Roman people*; praerogativa, *the century which obtained by lot the privilege of first voting*, Cic.

centŭrĭātim, adv. (centuria), *by centuries* or *companies*, Caes., Cic.

1. **centŭrĭātus** -ūs, m. (1. centurio), *the division into companies* or *centuries*, Liv.

2. **centŭrĭātus** -ūs, m. (2. centurio), *the centurion's office*, Cic.

1. **centŭrĭo**, 1. (centuria), *to divide into centuries*; juventutem, Liv.; comitia centuriata, *the assembly in which the whole Roman people voted in their centuries* (e.g., at the election of a consul), Cic.; lex centuriata, *a law passed in such an assembly*, Cic.

2. **centŭrĭo** -ōnis, m. (centuria), *a commander of a century, a centurion*, Cic.

centŭrĭōnātus -ūs, m. (2. centurio), *the election of centurions*, Tac.

Centŭrĭpae -ārum, f. and **Centŭrĭpa** -ōrum, n. (τὰ Κεντόριπα), *a town in Sicily*, now *Centorbi*; hence, **Centŭrĭpīnus** -a -um, *of* or *belonging to Centuripa*.

centussis -is, m. (centum and as), *a hundred asses*, Pers.

cēnŭla -ae, f. (dim. of cena), *a little meal*, Cic.

cēnum, v. caenum.

Cĕōs, v. Cea.

cēpa, v. caepa.

Cĕphallēnĭa -ae, f. (Κεφαλληνία), *island in the Ionic Sea* (now *Cefalonia*); hence, **Cĕphallēnes** -um, m. *inhabitants of Cephallenia*.

Cĕphăloedis -ĭdis, f. (-ĭum -ĭi, n.), *town on the north coast of Sicily*. Adj., **Cĕphăloedĭtānus** -a -um, *of* or *belonging to Cephaloedis*.

Cēphēnes -um, m. (Κηφῆνες), *a people of Aethiopia*, hence adj., **Cēphēnus** -a -um, *Cephenian*.

Cēpheus -ĕi, m. (Κηφεύς), *a mythical king of Aethiopia, husband of Cassiope, father of Andromeda*. Adj., **Cēphēĭus** -a -um, *of* or *belonging to Cepheus*; virgo, *Andromeda*, Ov.; arva, *Aethiopia*, Ov.; **Cēphēus** -a -um, *Ethiopian*; also, **Cēphēis** -ĭdos, f. *Andromeda*, Ov.

Cēphīsus, or **Cēphissus** -i, m. (Κηφισός, Κηφισσός). **I.** *a river in Boeotia*, and, as a river-god, *the father of Narcissus*; hence, **Cēphīsĭus** -ĭi, m. = *Narcissus*, Ov. Adj., **Cēphīsis** -ĭdis, f. *of* or *belonging to Cephisus*; undae, Ov. **II.** *a river of Attica*, Ov. Adj., **Cēphīsĭas** -ădis, f. *of* or *belonging to the Cephisus*.

cēra -ae, f. (connected with κηρός), *wax*. **A.** Lit., mollissima, Cic.; ceras excudere (of bees making their hive), Verg. **B.** Meton., *articles made of wax*; a, *writing-tablets coated with wax*, Cic.; b, *a waxen seal*, Cic.; c, *a waxen image*, Sall.

Cĕrămīcus -i, m. (Κεραμεικός), lit., *the pottery market, the name of two places at Athens, one within, the other without the wall, in the latter of which statues were erected to the heroes who fell in war*.

cērārĭum -ĭ, n. (cera), *a fee for sealing a document*, Cic.

cĕrastēs -ae, m. (κεράστης), *the horned snake*, Plin.

1. **cĕrăsus** -i, f. (κέρασος), 1, *a cherry-tree*, Ov.; 2, *a cherry*, Prop.

2. **Cĕrăsus** -untis, f. (Κερασοῦς), *a town in Pontus, whence came the cherry*.

cĕraunĭus -a -um (κεραύνιος), ceraunia gemma, or subst , **cĕraunĭum** -i, n , *a kind of precious stone*, Plin

Cĕraunĭi montes, and alone **Cĕraunĭa** ōrum, n *mountains in Epirus.*

Cerbĕrŏs and **us** -i, m (Κέρβερος), *the three-headed dog at the gates of Tartarus* Adj , **Cerbĕrĕus** a -um, *of* or *belonging to Cerberus*

Cercīna -ae, f (Κερκίνα), *a large island off the African coast*, now *Kerkine* or *Cherkara* or *Zerbi*

cercŏpĭthēcŏs and **us** -i, m (κερκοπίθηκος), *a kind of long tailed ape*, Mart , Juv

cercūrus -i, m (κέρκουρος), **1**, *a light species of vessel peculiar to Cyprus*, Liv , **2**, *a kind of sea-fish*, Ov

Cercȳo ŏnis, m (Κερκύων), *a brigand in Attica, killed by Theseus* Adj , **Cercȳŏnēus** -a -um, *of* or *belonging to Cercyo.*

cerdo ōnis, m (κέρδος), *a handicraftsman, artisan*, Juv , sutor cerdo, *a cobbler*, Mart

cĕrĕbrōsus -a -um (cerebrum), *hot brained, hot-tempered*, Hor

cĕrĕbrum -i, n **A.** *the brain*, Cic **B.** Meton , **a**, *the understanding*, Hor , **b**, *anger*, Hor

Cĕrēs -ĕris (root CER, CRE, whence creo) **I.** *the Roman goddess of agriculture, the daughter of Saturn and Ops, sister of Jupiter and Pluto, and mother of Proserpine*, prov , Cerem has nuptias facere, i e , *without wine*, Plaut **II.** Meton , *grain, corn*, Verg , Hor , whence the proverb, sine Cerere et Libero friget Venus, Ter Adj , **Cĕrĕālis** -e, *relating to Ceres, relating to cultivation and agriculture*, Ov., papaver, *the emblem of Ceres*, Verg , cenae, *splendid, as at the festival of Ceres*, Plaut. ; aediles, *who superintended the supply of provisions*, hence subst , **Cĕrĕālĭa** -ium, n *the festival of Ceres*

cĕrĕus -a -um (cera) **I.** *waxen*, Cic ; castra, *the cells of a hive*, Verg Subst , **cĕrĕus** i, m *a wax taper*, Cic **II.** Meton , **1**, *wax-coloured*, pruna, Verg , brachia Telephi, *smooth as wax*, Hor , **2**, *flexible like wax*, cereus in vitium flecti, Hor

cĕrintha ae, f (κηρίνθη), *the wax flower, a plant of which bees are fond*, Verg

cērĭnus -a -um (κήρινος), *wax-coloured*, Plin

cerno, crēvi, crētum, 3 (Root CRE, CRI, Gr ΚΡΙ, whence κρίνω, cribrum) **I.** *to separate, sift*, aliquid in cribris, Ov **II.** Transf **A.** *to distinguish*, **1**, with the senses, **a**, ut non sensu, sed mente cernatur, Cic , **b**, esp of the eyes, acies ipsa, qua cernimus, quae pupula vocatur, Cic ; with acc , Pompeianum non cerno, Cic , with acc and infin , cernebatur novissimos illorum premi, Caes , **2**, with the mind, **a**, *to perceive*, animus plus cernit et longius, Cic , **b**, cerni in aliqua re, *to show oneself, to be shown*; fortis animus et magnus duobus rebus maxime cernitur, Cic **B.** *to decide*, **1**, in battle = *to contend*, magnis in rebus inter se, Lucr ; **2**, *to resolve, determine*, quodcumque senatus creverit, agunto, Cic , **3**, as legal t t , *to accept an inheritance*, hereditatem cernere, Cic , fig , hanc quasi falsam hereditatem alienae gloriae, Cic

cernŭus -a -um, *falling headlong, with the face towards the ground*, equus, Verg

cēro, 1 *to smear* or *cover with wax*, gen in perf partic pass , cerata tabella, Cic

cērōma -ătis, n (κήρωμα) **A.** *an ointment of oil and wax used by wrestlers*, Juv. **B.** Meton , **a**, *the arena for wrestling*, Plin ; **b**, *wrestling itself*, Mart

cērōmătĭcus -a um (κηρωματικός), *anointed with the ceroma*, Juv.

cerrītus -a -um (contracted from cerebritus, from cerebrum), *frantic, mad*, Plaut , Hor

cerrus -i, m *a kind of oak, the Turkey oak*, Plin

certāmen -ĭnis, n. (2 certo), *contest*, **a**, *in gymnastics*, gladiatorum vitae, Cic ; **b**, *any kind of rivalry*, honoris et gloriae, Cic , in certamen virtutis venire, Cic., **c**, *a fight*, proelii, Cic , vario certamine pugnatum est, Caes , **d**, *contention, rivalry*, est mihi tecum pro aris et focis certamen, Cic

certātim, adv (certatus, from 2 certo), *emulously, eagerly, as if striving for a prize*, Cic

certātio -ōnis, f (2 certo), *a contest*, **a**, in games, corporum, Cic , **b**, in words or actions, virtuti cum voluptate certatio, Cic , **c**, *a legal contest*, multae poenae, *as to the amount of a fine to be inflicted*, Cic , **d**, *emulation*, certatio honesta inter amicos, Cic

certē, adv (certus) **I. a**, *certainly, assuredly*, ea quae certe vera sunt, Cic , in answers, *without doubt*, Cic , **b**, certe scio, *certainly, I know it*, Cic **II.** *at least, at all events*, mihi certe, Cic , certe tamen, Cic

1 **certō**, adv (certus), *certainly, assuredly, undoubtedly*, nihil ita exspectare quasi certo futurum, Cic , esp in phrase, certo scio, *I am sure of it*, Cic

2 **certo**, 1 (Root CER, whence cerno and cretus), *to contend, struggle* (with the idea of rivalry) **A.** Lit , de imperio cum populo Romano, Cic **B.** Transf , **1**, in words, verbis, oratione, Liv , **2**, of law, *to dispute*, inter se, Cic ; **3**, *to vie with*, officiis inter se, Cic , foll. by infin , vincere, Verg

certus -a -um (cerno) **I.** Lit , *separated*, Cato **II.** Transf , **A.** *certain, definite, fixed, decided*, **1**, certum est mihi consilium, Plaut , certum est (mihi, etc), *I am resolved*, sibi certum esse a judiciis causisque discedere, Cic , **2**, of persons, certus mori, *determined to die*, Verg ; certus eundi, *determined to go*, Verg **B. 1**, *certain, fixed*, certus ac definitus locus, Cic , certi homines, *certain men*, Cic , **2**, *secure, to be depended on*, bona et certa tempestate, Cic , certissima populi Romani vectigalia, Cic , of persons, homo certissimus, *to be depended upon*, Cic , **3**, *true, undoubted, sure*, argumentum odii certius, Cic , certum est, *it is certain*, est certum quid respondeam, Cic , aliquid certi est, *something is certain*, si quicquam humanorum certi est, Liv , certum scio, *I know it for certain*; quamdiu affutura sunt, certum sciri nullo modo potest, Cic , certum habeo, *I have it for certain*, Cic , certum inveniri non potest (followed by ne (enclit) an), Caes , certum respondeo, Cic , pro certo scio, Liv , pro certo habeo, Cic., pro certo puto, ap Cic , pro certo nego, Cic , polliceor Cic ; dico, Cic , affirmo, Liv , pono, Liv , creditum, Sall , ad certum redigere, *to make it certain*, Liv , certum (as adv), nondum certum constituerat, Cic , of persons, certi patres, *undoubted*, Cic ; **4**, *certain of a thing*, certi sumus perisse omnia, Cic , certum facere aliquem, *to inform*, Verg , in prose, certiorem facere aliquem , with genit , sui consilii, Cic , with de, de Germanorum discessu, Caes , with acc and infin , P Africanum simulacrum Dianae majoribus suis restitutisse, Cic , with rel sent., quid egerim, Cic , with subj (without a particle), paulisper intermitterent proelium, *gives orders to*, etc , Cic

cērŭla ae, f (dim. of cera), *a little piece of wax*, miniata, *a kind of red pencil for marking errors in MSS* , Cic ; cerulas tuas miniatulas extimescebam, *criticisms*, Cic

cerva -ae, f (cervus), *a hind*, Liv , poet., *deer*, Verg.

cervārius -a -um (cervus), *relating to deer*, Plin.

cervīcal -ālis n. (cervix), *a cushion for the head, a pillow, bolster*, Plin.

cervīcŭla -ae, f. (dim. of cervix), *a little neck*, Cic.

cervīnus -a -um (cervus), *relating to a stag*; pellis, Hor.; senectus, *extreme old age*, because the stag was believed to be very long-lived, Juv.

cervix -icis, f. *the nape of the neck, the neck*. **I.** Of living beings, Cic.; alicui cervicem frangere, *to break the neck of any one*, Cic.; dare cervices alicui, *to submit to death*, Cic.; also, cervices securi subjicere, Cic.; fig., imponere in cervicibus alicuius sempiternum dominium, *to lay the yoke of mastery on*, Cic.; in cervicibus alicuius esse, *to be in burdensome and dangerous proximity*, Liv. **II.** Used of inanimate things, amphorae, Mart.; Peloponnesi, *the Isthmus of Corinth*, Plin.

cervus -i, m. (κεραός), *a stag*. **A.** Lit., Cic. **B.** Transf., cervi, military t.t., *branches of trees stuck in the ground as a palisade, to impede the advance of an enemy*, Caes.

cespes, v. caespes.

cessātio -ōnis, f. (cesso), 1, *a delaying*, Plaut.; 2, *inactivity, cessation, laziness, leaving off, idleness;* libera atque otiosa, Cic.

cessātor -ōris, m. (cesso), *one who loiters and lingers;* cessatorem esse solere, praesertim in litteris, Cic.

cessio -ōnis, f. (cedo), *a giving up, a cession;* legal t.t., in jure cessio, *a fictitious surrender*, Cic.

cesso, 1. (freq. of cedo). **I.** Lit., *to leave off, linger, delay, cease;* si tabellarii non cessarint, Cic. **II.** Transf., **1,** *to loiter, to be idle;* **a,** quid cessarent, Liv.; in suo studio atque opere, Cic.; **b,** *to be negligent in one's duty*, Hor.; **2, a,** *to rest, to take rest;* non nocte, non die unquam cessaverunt ab opere, Liv.; non cessare with infin., *not to cease;* ille in Achaia non cessat de nobis detrahere, Cic.; **b,** *to be idle, make holiday, do nothing;* cur tam multos deos nihil agere et cessare patitur, Cic.; cessasse Letoidos aras, *remained unvisited*, Ov.; of land, *to lie fallow;* alternis cessare novales, Verg.

cestrosphendŏnē -ēs, f. (κεστροσφενδόνη), *an engine for hurling stones*, Liv.

1. **cestus** -i, m. (κεστός), *a girdle*, esp. *the girdle of Venus*, Mart.

2. **cēstus** -ūs, m. v. caestus.

cētārius -a -um (cetus), *relating to sea-fish*, particularly *to the tunny-fish*. **I.** Adj., Tac. **II.** Subst. **A. cētārius** -ii, m. *a fishmonger, a dealer in sea-fish*, particularly *tunny-fish*, Ter. **B. cētāria** -ae, f. and **cētārium** -ii, n. (κητεία), *a bay in the sea where the tunny-fish collected and were caught*, Hor.

cēte, v. cetus.

cētĕroqui or **cētĕroquin**, adv. *otherwise, else*, Cic.

cētĕrus -a -um (= ἕτερος), *the other, the rest;* (sing. only used collectively, cetera classis, Liv.; nom. sing. masc. not found); usually found in the plur. **cētĕri** -ae -a; omnes ceterae res, Cic.; et cetera or simply cetera, *and so on*, Cic.; adv., ceterum, *for the rest, moreover*, Cic.; cetera, *besides*, Cic.; so, de cetero, Cic.; ad cetera, Liv.

Cĕthēgus -i, m. *the name of an old patrician family of the* gens Cornelia, *to which belonged* C. Cornelius Cethegus, *a conspirator with Catiline, put to death by Cicero.*

cētra -ae, f. *a small Spanish shield*, Verg., Liv.

cētrātus -a -um (cetra), *armed with the cetra*, Caes., Liv.

cette, v. cĕdo.

cētus (κῆτος), -i, m. and cētos, plur. cēte, n. (κήτεα, contr. κήτη), *any large sea-fish, the whale, dolphin;* used esp. of *the tunny-fish*, Verg.

ceu, adv. (contr. from ce-ve, as neu from neve), *as, like as;* ceu quum, *as when*, Verg.; ceu si, *as if*, Verg.; esp. in comparison, *as if;* per aperta volans, ceu liber habenis, aequora, Verg.

Ceutrōnes -um, acc. -as, m. **1,** *a people in Gallia provincia;* **2,** *a people in Gallia Belgica.*

Cēyx -ȳcis, m. (Κήϋξ). **I.** *king of Trachin, husband of Alcyone, changed with her into a kingfisher*, Ov. **II.** Plur., appel. **cēyces** -um, m., *the male kingfishers*, Plin.

Chaerōnēa -ae, f. (Χαιρώνεια), *a town in Boeotia, birth-place of Plutarch, scene of a victory of Philip of Macedon over the Athenians.*

Chalcĭoecŏs -i, f. (Χαλκίοικος, *with the brazen house*, name of the Greek Athena), *the temple of Minerva.*

Chalcĭŏpē -ēs, f. (Χαλκιόπη), *daughter of Aeetes, sister of Medea, wife of Phryxus.*

Chalcis -idis, f. (Χαλκίς), *the chief city of Euboea, on the banks of the Euripus;* hence adj., **Chalcĭdĭcus** -a -um, *Chalcidian;* versus, *poems of Euphorion, born at Chalcis*, Verg.; arx, *Cumae, said to have been a colony of Chalcis*, Verg.; **Chalcĭdensis** -e, *Chalcidian.*

chalcītis -idis, f. (χαλκῖτις), *copper ore*, Plin.

Chaldaea -ae, f. (Χαλδαία), *the south-west part of Babylonia from the Euphrates to the Arabian desert*, the inhabitants of which were famous for astrology and soothsaying; hence, **a, Chaldaeus** -a -um, *Chaldaean;* subst., **Chaldaei** -ōrum, m. (Χαλδαῖοι), *soothsayers*, Cic.; **b, Chaldaeĭcus** -a -um, *Chaldaic.*

chălȳbēĭus -a -um, *made of steel*, Ov.

Chălȳbes -um, m. (Χάλυβες), *a people in Pontus, famous for their steel.*

chălybs -ȳbis, m. (χάλυψ). **A.** *steel;* vulnificus, Verg. **B.** Meton., *articles made of steel; a sword*, Sen.; *a horse's bit*, Lucr.; *the tip of an arrow*, Lucr.

chamaelĕon -ōnis and -ontis m. (χαμαιλέων), *the chamaeleon*, Plin.

Chăŏnes -um, m. (Χάονες), *a people of north-western Epirus;* hence adj., **Chăŏnius** -a -um, *Epirote;* pater, *Jupiter, whose oracle was at Dodona*, Verg.; **Chăŏnis** -idis, f. *Chaonian;* ales, *the pigeon of Dodona*, Ov.; arbos, *the oak*, Ov. **Chăŏnia** -ae, f. *the district of Chaonia.*

chăos, acc. chaos, abl. chao (other cases not found), n. (χάος), **1,** *the lower world*, Ov.; personified, *the father of Night and Erebus*, Verg.; **2,** *the shapeless mass out of which the universe was made, chaos*, Ov.

chara -ae, f. *a root*, perhaps *wild cabbage*, Caes.

Chărīstĭa (cărīstia) -ōrum, n. (χαρίστια), *a festival celebrated among the Romans on the 22nd of February, the chief object of which was the reconcilement of family disagreements*, Ov.

Chărĭtes -um, f. (Χάριτες), *the Graces* (pure Lat. Gratiae), *Aglaia, Euphrosyne, and Thalia*, Ov.

Charmădās -ae, m. (Χαρμάδας), *a disciple of Carneades, belonging to the Academic school* (teaching at Athens, 109 B.C.).

Chărōn -ontis, m. (Χάρων), *Charon, the ferryman, who took the souls of the dead over the river Styx.*

Chărondās -ae, m. (Χαρώνδας), *a celebrated*

legislator of Catana, living about the middle of the seventh century B.C.

charta -ae, f. (χάρτης), *a leaf of the Egyptian papyrus, paper*. **I. A.** Lit., charta dentata, *smoothed*, Cic. **B.** Meton., **a**, *the papyrus plant*, Plin.; **b**, *that which is written upon it, a letter, poem, etc.*; ne charta nos prodat, Cic. **II.** Transf., *a thin leaf of any substance*, plumbea, Suet.

chartŭla -ae, f. (dim. of charta), *a little paper, a small writing*, Cic.

Chărybdis -is, f. (Χάρυβδις), *a dangerous whirlpool in the Sicilian straits, opposite the rock Scylla*, Cic.; fig., *anything voracious, greedy, or destructive*; Charybdim bonorum, voraginem potius dixerim, Cic.; quanta laborabas Charybdi, Hor.

Chatti (Catthi, Catti) -ōrum, m. (Χάττοι), *a German people* (in modern Hesse).

Chauci -ōrum, m. *a German people on the sea-coast*.

chēlē -ēs, f. (χηλή), plur. chēlae, *the arms of the Scorpion in the signs of the Zodiac*, and (since these reach into the constellation of Libra) *Libra*, Verg.

Chĕlīdŏnĭae insulae, *islands on the coast of Lycia* (lit. *swallow islands*), facing the Chelidonium or Chelidonium promontorium.

chĕlȳdrus -i, m. (χέλυδρος), *an amphibious snake*, Verg.

chĕlys, acc. -yn and -yn, voc. -y, f. (χέλυς), **1**, *the tortoise*, Petr.; and hence, **2**, *the lyre made of its shell* (pure Latin, testudo), Ov.

Cherrŏnēsus and **Chersŏnēsus** -i, f. (Χερρόνησος), **1**, *a peninsula*, Cic.; **2**, Thracia, *the Thracian peninsula on the Hellespont*, Cic.

Chĕrusci -ōrum, m. *a people in North Germany*.

chīlĭarchus -i, m. (χιλιάρχης), **1**, *a commander of 1,000 soldiers*, Tac.; **2**, among the Persians, *the chancellor, or prime minister*, Nep.

Chĭmaera -ae, f. (χίμαιρα, *a goat*), *a fire-breathing monster with the fore parts of a lion, the middle of a goat, and the hind parts of a dragon, killed by Bellerophon*. Adj., **Chĭmaerēus** -a -um.

chĭmaerĭfĕr -fĕra, -fĕrum (Chimaera and fero), *producing the Chimaera, an epithet of Lycia*.

Chĭŏnē -ēs, f. (Χιόνη), **1**, *mother of Eumolpus by Neptune*; whence **Chĭŏnĭdēs** -ae, m. = *Eumolpus*, Ov.; **2**, *mother of Autolycus by Mercury*.

Chĭos or **Chĭus** -i, f. (Χίος), *an island in the Aegean Sea (now Scio), famous for its wine*; hence adj., **Chĭus** -a -um, *Chian*, vinum, Plaut.; or subst., **Chĭum** -i, n. *Chian wine*, Hor.; **Chĭi** -ōrum, m. *the Chians*, Cic.

chīrāgra -ae, f. (χειράγρα), *the gout in the hands*, Hor., Mart.

chīrŏgrăphum -i, n. (χειρόγραφον), *an autograph, a person's own handwriting*; alicuius chirographum imitari, Cic.

Chīrōn, Chīro -ōnis, m. (Χείρων), *a centaur, son of Saturn and Phillyra, the preceptor of Aesculapius, Jason, and Achilles, killed by Hercules*.

chīrŏnŏmos -i, c., and **chīrŏnŏmōn** -ontis, m. (χειρονόμος, χειρονομῶν), *one who uses the hands skilfully, a mime*, Juv.

chīrurgĭa -ae, f. (χειρουργία), *surgery*; fig., sed ego diaeta curare incipio, chirurgiae taedet, *violent remedies*, Cic.

chlămȳdātus -a -um (chlamys), *clothed in the chlamys*, Cic.

chlămys -ȳdis, f., and **chlamȳda** -ae, f. (χλαμύς), *a large upper garment of wool*, often of purple and gold, worn in Greece, Cic., Verg.

Chlōris -idis, f. (Χλῶρις, *the green one*), **a**, = Lat. Flora, *the goddess of flowers*, Ov.; **b**, *a Greek female name*, Hor.

Choerĭlus -i, m. (Χοιρίλος), *a poet who accompanied Alexander the Great in his Persian expedition*.

chŏrāgĭum -ii, n. (χορήγιον), *the training of a chorus*, Plaut.

chŏrāgus -i, m. (χορηγός), *he who supplies the chorus and all appurtenances*, Plaut.

chŏraulēs -ae, m. (χοραύλης), *a flute-player*, Mart.

chorda -ae, f. (χορδή), *string, cat-gut* (of a musical instrument), Cic.

chŏrēa -ae, f. (χορεία), *a dance to the sound of the dancers' voices*, Verg.

chŏrēus -i, m., and **chŏrīus** -i, m. (χορεῖος), *the metrical foot* — ⏑, afterwards called a trochee, Cic.

chŏrŏcĭthărista -ae, m. (χοροκιθαριστής), *one who accompanies a chorus on the cithara*, Suet.

chŏrus -i, m. (χορός). **I.** *a dance in a circle, a choral dance*, agitare, exercere, Verg. **II.** Meton., *the persons singing and dancing, the chorus*, Cic. **A.** Lit., Dryadum, Verg.; Nereidum, Verg.; *the chorus of a tragedy*, Hor. **B.** Transf., *a crowd, troop of any kind*, Catilinam stipatum choro juventutis, Cic.

Chrĕmēs -mētis, m. *an old miser in several of the plays of Terence*.

Christĭānus -i, m. (Χριστιανός), *a Christian*, Tac.

Christus -i, m. (Χριστός), *Christ*, Tac., Plin.

chrŏmis -is, m. (χρόμις), *a sea fish*, Ov.

Chrȳsa -ae, f. and **Chrȳsē** -ēs, f. (Χρύση), *a town in Mysia, near which was a temple of Apollo Smintheus*.

Chrȳsās -ae, m. *a river in Sicily, now Dittaino*.

Chrȳsēs -ae, m. (Χρύσης), *the priest of Apollo at Chrysa, whose daughter was carried off by the Greeks*; hence, **Chrȳsēis** -idos, f. (Χρυσηΐς), *the daughter of Chryses = Astynome*.

Chrȳsippus -i, m. (Χρύσι-ππος), **1**, *Stoic philosopher of Soli in Cilicia*, b. 282, B.C.; **2**, *a freedman of Cicero's*. Adj., **Chrȳsippēus** -a -um, *of or belonging to Chrysippus*.

Chrȳsis -idis, f. (Χρυσίς), *name of one of the female characters in the Andria of Terence*.

chrȳsŏlīthus -i, m. and f. (χρυσόλιθος), *chrysolite, or topaz*, Plin.

chrȳsŏphrys, acc. -yn, f. (χρυσόφρυς), *a kind of sea fish with a golden spot over each eye*, Ov.

chrȳsos -i, m. (χρυσός), *gold*, Plaut.

chus, v. congius.

cĭbārĭus -a -um (cibus), *relating to food*. **A.** Lit., uva, *used for eating only*, not for wine, Plaut. Subst., **cĭbārĭa** -ōrum, n. *food, rations, fodder*, *corn allowed to provincial magistrates*, Cic.; *rations for soldiers*, Caes. **B.** Meton. (from the food usually given to servants), *ordinary, common*, panis, *black bread*, Cic.

cĭbātus -ūs, m. (cibo), *food, nourishment*, Plaut.

cĭbo, 1. (cibus), *to feed*, Suet.

cĭbōrĭum -ii, n. (κιβώριον), and **cĭbōrĭa** -ae, f. literally, *the seed pod of the Egyptian bean*, and hence, *a large drinking vessel of similar shape*, Hor.

cĭbus -i, m *food for man and beast, nourishment, fodder* **I.** Lit , **A.** Gen , cibum sumere, Nep , subducere, Cic **B.** Esp , **a,** animalis, *nourishment that the lungs draw from the air,* Cic , **b,** *bait,* fallax, Ov **II.** Transf , *sustenance,* quasi quidam humanitatis cibus, Cic

Cĭbyra -ae, f (Κίβυρα), *a town in Pisidia,* hence, **A. Cĭbyrātes** -ae, c *of Cibyra* **B. Cĭbyrātĭcus** -a -um, *of or belonging to Cibyra*

cīcāda -ae, f *a cicada, or tree cricket,* Verg , expectate cicadas, *summer,* Juv

cĭcātrīcōsus -a -um (cicatrix), *covered with scars,* Plaut

cĭcātrix -icis, f *a scar, cicatrice,* adversae or exceptae corpore adverso, *wounds received in front,* and therefore *honourable,* Cic , *the marks of incisions in plants,* Verg ; *the patch upon an old shoe,* Juv , fig , refricare obductam jam reipublicae cicatricem, Cic.

cicĭum -i, n (κίκκος), *the core of a pomegranate,* hence *something worthless,* ciccum non interduim, Plaut

cĭcer -ĕris, n *a chick-pea,* Hor

Cĭcĕro -ōnis, m *name of a family of the gens Tullia,* to which belonged, **1,** M Tullius Cicero, *the greatest Roman orator and writer,* born A C 106, *at Arpinum, murdered at the command of Antonius* A C 43, **2,** Qu Tullius Cicero, *brother of the above* Hence adj , **Cĭcĕrōnĭānus** -a -um, *Ciceronian*

Cĭcŏnes -um, m (Κίκονες), *a Thracian people*

cĭcōnĭa -ae, f **1,** *a stork,* Hor , Ov , **2,** *a gesture of ridicule, made by bending the fore-finger into the shape of a stork's neck,* Pers

cĭcur -ŭris, *tame;* bestia, Cic

cĭcūta -ae, f **A.** *hemlock,* Hor **B.** Meton , **1,** *poison extracted from the hemlock,* Hor , **2,** *a shepherd's pipe, made from the hemlock stalk,* Verg

cĭĕo, civi, citum, 2 (connected with κίω, κινέω), *to cause to move, to move, shake* **I. a,** natura omnia ciens et agitans motibus et mutationibus suis, Cic , **b,** legal t t , herctum ciere, *to divide the inheritance,* Cic , **c,** pugnam ciere, *to give new impulse to the battle,* Liv , **d,** *to disturb, agitate,* mare venti et aurae cient, Liv , **e,** *to summon to battle,* aliquem ad arma, Liv , **f,** *to summon to help* nocturnos manes carminibus, Verg **II. a,** *to excite, to arouse,* procellas proelia atque acies, Liv , seditiones, Liv , **b,** *to utter,* gemitus, Verg , **c,** *to call by name,* aliquem magna voce, Verg , patrem, *name one's father, i e , prove one's free birth,* Liv

Cĭlĭcĭa -ae, f (Κιλικία), *a country of Asia Minor,* hence adj , **1, Cĭlix** -icis, *Cilician,* pl **Cĭlĭces** -um, m *the Cilicians,* **Cĭlissa** -ae, f , *Cilician,* spica, *saffron,* Ov , **2, Cĭlĭcĭus** -a -um, *Cilician.* Subst , **Cĭlĭcĭum** -ii, n, *a coarse cloth, or covering made of Cilician goats' hair*

cĭlĭum -ii, n *the eye lid,* Plin.

Cilla -ae, acc -an, f (Κίλλα), *a town in Aeolis*

Cilnius -a -um, Cilnia gens, *a distinguished Etruscan family, from which Maecenas was descended*

Cimbri -ōrum, m (Κίμβροι), *the Cimbrians, a German tribe who invaded the Roman Empire and were defeated by Marius,* sing , **Cimber** -bri, m *a Cimbrian* Adj , **Cimbrĭcus** -a -um, *Cimbrian*

cīmex -icis, m *a bug,* Cat , as a term of reproach, Hor

Cĭmĭnus -i, m and **Cĭmĭnĭus** lacus, *a lake in Etruria near to a mountain of the same name.*

Cimmĕrĭi -ōrum, m (Κιμμέριοι) **I.** *a Thracian people, living on the Dnieper.* Adj , **Cimmĕrĭus** -a -um, *Cimmerian.* **II.** *a mythical people, living in the extreme west in darkness and mist* Adj , **Cimmĕrĭus** -a -um, *Cimmerian = dark,* lacus, *the lower world,* Tib

Cĭmōlus -i, f (Κίμωλος), *one of the Cyclades Islands*

Cĭmōn -ōnis, m (Κίμων), *an Athenian general*

cĭnaedĭcus -a -um (cinaedus), *unchaste,* Plaut

cĭnaedus -i, m (κίναιδος), *one who indulges in unnatural lust,* **a,** Plaut , Cat Adj , **cĭnaedus** -a -um = *bold, shameless,* homo cinaeda fronte, Mart , **b,** *a wanton dancer,* Plaut

Cĭnăra -ae, f (Κινάρα), **a,** *an island in the Aegaean Sea,* **b,** *a woman's name,* Hor

1 **cincinnātus** -a -um (cincinnus), *having curled hair,* Cic , of comets, stellae eas quas Graeci cometas, nostri cincinnatas vocant, Cic.

2 **Cincinnātus** -i, m *the name of a patrician family of the gens Quinctia,* to which belonged L Quinctius Cincinnatus, *a type of old Roman honesty and simplicity, consul* 460 B C , *in* 458 B C *called from the plough to be dictator.*

cincinnus -i, m, (κίκιννος) **A.** *curled hair, a lock of hair,* Cic **B.** Transf , *artificial rhetorical ornament,* Cic.

Cincĭus -a -um, *name of a Roman gens* **I.** L. Cincius Alimentus, *annalist at the time of the Second Punic War* **II.** M Cincius Alimentus, *tribune of the people,* 205 B C , *author of the lex Cincia forbidding advocates to receive pay*

cinctūra -ae, f (cingo), *a girdle,* Suet

cinctus -ūs, m (cingo), *a girding;* **1,** Gabinus, *a particular way of wearing the toga, at religious festivals, in which one end was thrown over the head, and the other passed round the waist, so as to look like a girdle,* Liv , **2,** *a girdle,* Suet

cinctūtus -a -um (cinctus), *girded,* Hor , Ov

cĭnĕfactus -a -um (cinis and facio), *changed into ashes,* Lucr

cĭnĕrārĭus -ii, m (cinis), *a slave who heated in hot ashes the irons for the hair dresser,* Cat.

Cinga -ae, m *a tributary of the Iberus in Hispania Tarraconensis,* now *Cinca*

Cingĕtŏrix -rīgis, m **I.** *a prince of the Treveri in Gaul* **II.** *a prince in Britain*

cingo, cinxi, cinctum, 3, *to surround* **I.** in a narrow sense, **1,** *to surround the body with a girdle, to gird,* pass cingi, as middle, *to gird oneself,* **a,** cincta conjux Dialis, Ov , **b,** *to gird oneself with a weapon;* ense, Ov , gladio, Liv , poet with acc , inutile ferrum cingitur, Verg , hence cingor, *to be prepared, ready,* Plaut ; **2,** *to surround the head with a chaplet, to crown,* cinge tempora lauro, Hor , anuli cingunt lacertos, Mart **II.** in a wider sense, *to surround, encircle,* **1,** of localities, *to surround, inclose;* tellus oras maris undique cingens, Lucr , colles cingunt oppidum, Caes ; milit t t , *to surround with hostile intent or for protection,* hiberna castra vallo, Caes., urbem obsidione, Verg ; transf , Sicilia multis undique cincta periculis, Cic , **2,** *to surround a person in society, accompany,* cingere alicui latus, Liv , **3,** *to circle, round a place,* polum coetu (of swans), Verg

cingŭla -ae, f (cingo), *a girdle,* Ov

1 **cingŭlum** -i, n (cingo), *a girdle, a sword-belt* (plur), Verg

2 **Cingŭlum** -i, n *a town in Picenum*

cingŭlus -i, m (cingo), *a girdle of the earth, a zone,* Cic.

cĭnĭflo -ōnis, m = cinerarius, Hor

cĭnis -ĕris, m, rarely f (connected with κόνις), *ashes* **I.** Lit, **A.** Gen, in cinerem dilabi, *to become ashes*, Hor, from the use of ashes for scouring came the prov hunus sermo cinerem haud quaeritat, Plaut. **B.** Esp, **1,** *the ashes of a corpse after being burned*, cinis atque ossa alicuius, Cic, **2,** *ruins of a city that has been burnt*, patriae cineres, Verg **II.** Transf, *as a symbol of destruction*, Troja virûm atque virtutum omnium acerba cinis, *the grave*, Cat

Cinna ae, m *the name of a family of the Cornelii and Helvii* **I.** L. Cornelius Cinna, *partisan of Marius in the civil war against Sulla, noted for his cruelty* Adj, **Cinnānus** a -um, *Cinnan* **II.** *son of I, one of Caesar's murderers* **III.** *son of II, twice pardoned by Augustus* **IV.** C Helvius Cinna, *a poet, the friend of Catullus.*

cinnămōmum or **cinnămum** -i, n (κιννάμωμον, κίνναμον), *cinnamon*, Ov; *as a term of endearment*, Plaut

Cīnyps -ȳphis, m (Κῖνυψ), *a river in Libya, between the two Syrtes*, hence adj, **Cīnȳphius** a -um, **1,** *relating* or *belonging to the Cinyps*, Verg, **2,** *African*, Ov

Cĭnȳras -ae, m (Κινύρας), *a mythical king of Assyria* or *Cyprus, father of Myrrha, and by her of Adonis* Adj, **Cĭnȳrēius** -a um, *Cinyrean*, virgo, *Myrrha*, Ov, juvenis, *Adonis*, Ov

Cĭos and **Cius** -ii, f (ἡ Κίος), *a town in Bithynia*, now *Ghio*, hence, **Cĭāni** -ōrum, m *the inhabitants of Cios.*

cippus -i, m **1,** *a tombstone* or *small tomb*, Hor, **2,** plur. milit t. t, *palisades*, Caes.

circā (contr for circum ea) **I.** Adv, *round about*; gramen erat circa, Ov, hence, circa esse, *to be round about, in the neighbourhood*, Liv, sometimes directly connected with the subst without esse, multarum circa civitatum, Liv, omnia circa or circa undique, *all things around*, Liv **II.** Prep with acc, **1,** of space, **a,** *around*, *at the side of*, ligna contulerunt circa casam, Nep, **b,** *round about to*, legatos circa vicinas gentes misit, Liv; **c,** *in the neighbourhood of, near to*, templa circa forum, Cic., **d,** *around* or *in company of a person*, trecentos juvenes circa se habebat, Liv, **2,** of time, *about*, circa eandem horam, Liv, lucem, Suet; Demetrium, *about the time of Demetrius*, Quint, **3,** of number = circiter, *about*, ea fuere oppida circa septuaginta, Liv, **4,** *about*, *in respect to*, circa bonas artes publica socordia, Tac.

circāmoerium -ii, n = pomoerium (q v), Liv

Circē -ēs and ae, acc -am, abl -a, f (Κίρκη), *an enchantress who lived in the neighbourhood of Circeji, where she turned her victims into swine, mother of Telegonus by Ulysses*, hence adj, **Circaeus** -a -um, *Circean*, poculum, *enchanted*, Cic, moenia, *Tusculum*, *said to have been built by Telegonus*, Hor, litus, *the promontory of Circeji*, Ov.

Circēji -ōrum, m *the town of Circeji on a promontory of the same name in Latium* Adj, **Circējensis** -e, *of* or *belonging to Circeji*

circensis -e (circus), *belonging to the circus*, ludi, *the games in the circus*, Cic. Subst, **circenses** -ium, m (sc ludi), *the circus games*, Sen

circĭno, 1 (circinus), *to make round, to form into a circle*, Plin; poet, easdem circinat auras, *flies through in a circle*, Ov

circĭnus i, m (κίρκινος), *a pair of compasses for describing a circle*, Caes

circĭtĕr, adv (circus) **I.** Of place, *about, near*, Plaut. **II.** Transf, **1,** of time, **a,** adv with abl, media circiter nocte, Caes, **b,** prep with acc, circiter Calendas, Cic, **2,** of number, *about*, circiter CCXX naves, Caes

circlus = circulus (q v)

circŭeo, v circumeo

circŭĭtĭo and **circŭmĭtĭo** -ōnis, f (circueo, circumeo), **1,** *a going round*, milit t t *patrol*, Liv, **2,** *a roundabout way of speaking* or *acting*, quid opus est circumitione et amfractu, Cic

circŭĭtus (circŭmĭtus), ūs, m (circueo = circumeo), *a going round in a circle*, *circuit*, *revolution* **I.** Abstract, **A.** Lit, circuitus orbis, Cic. **B.** Transf, mihi sunt orbes et quasi circuitus in rebus publicis commutationum et vicissitudinum, Cic. **II.** Concrete, **a,** *the path traversed in going round*, *a roundabout way*, *circuitous course*, longo circuitu petere aliquem locum, Caes, Liv, **b,** in rhetoric, *a period*, Cic, **c,** *compass, circumference, extent*; eius munitionis circuitus XI milia passuum tenebat, Caes

circŭlātim, adv (circulor), *circle-wise, in a circle*, Suet

circŭlor, 1 dep (circulus), **a,** *to gather in groups for conversation*, Caes, **b,** *to enter a group, to converse*, Cic

circŭlus (syncop circlus) i, m (dim of circus), *a circle, circular figure* **I.** circulus aut orbis, qui κύκλος Graece dicitur, Cic, priusquam hoc circulo excedas, Liv, hence, *the orbit of a planet*, stellae circulos suos orbesque conficiunt celeritate mirabili, Cic **II.** Esp, **a,** *any circular body*, flexilis obtorti circulus auri, poet = *a golden collar*, Verg, circulus muri exterior, Liv, **b,** *a circle* or *group for conversation*, circulos aliquos et sessiunculas consectari, Cic

circum (prop acc of circus = κίρκος, *in a circle*) **I.** Adv *round about, around*, quae circum essent, Caes, circum sub moenibus, Verg, circum undique, *round about, on all sides*, Verg **II.** Prep with acc **A.** *round about* terra circum axem se convertit, Cic **B.** *round about, near, in the vicinity of, around*, circum aliquem esse, *to be in any one's company*, Cic, habere aliquem circum se, Sall, circum haec loca commorabor, Cic, urbes quae circum Capuam sunt, Cic; circum pedes, *in attendance*, Cic; used with verbs of motion, circum villulas nostras errare, Cic, legatio circum insulas missa, Liv (circum sometimes after the subst which it governs, Cic, often in Verg)

circumactus a -um, partic of circumago

circŭmăgo -ēgi -actum, 3 **I. A.** *to drive* or *turn round, to drive in a circle*, hence a technical term for the manumission of a slave, because his master took him by the right hand, and turned him round, Sen **B.** Transf, of time, circumagi or circumagere se, *to pass away, to be spent*, annus se circumegit, Liv **II.** *to turn* or *twist round* **A.** Lit, equos frenis, Liv, circumagente se vento, Liv **B.** Transf, quo te circumagas? *how wilt thou evade the difficulty?* Juv **III.** *to lead* or *drive about from one place to another* **A.** Lit, huc illuc clamoribus hostium circumagi, Tac, nihil opus est te circumagi, *follow me about*, Hor **B.** Transf, *to drive about, distract, mislead*, rumoribus vulgi circumagi, Liv

circumăro, *to plough round*, Liv

circumcaesūra ae, f *the external outline of a body*, Lucr

circumcīdo -cīdi -cīsum, 3 (circum and caedo), *to cut round, to cut, trim* **A.** Lit, ars agricolarum quae circumcidat, Cic, caespitem gladiis, Caes **B.** Transf, *to make less, by cutting, diminish, cut off*, multitudinem, Cic; sumptus, Liv

circumcircā, adv., *all round about*, ap Cic., Plaut

circumcīsus -a -um, p adj (from circumcīdo), of localities, *abrupt, steep, inaccessible*, saxum, Cic, collis ex omni parte circumcisus, Caes

circumclūdo -clūsi -clūsum, 3 1, *to shut in, enclose on all sides, surround*, cornua argento, Caes, 2, *to surround* in a hostile manner, circumcludi duobus exercitibus, Caes, transf, Catilina meis praesidiis, meā diligentiā circumclusus, Cic

circumcŏlo, 3 *to dwell around, dwell near*, Liv

circumcurso, 1 (intens of circumcurro), *to run round*, Plaut, Lucr, Cat

circumdo -dĕdi -dătum, 1, *surround* **I. A.** *to put something round something else*, with acc, of the thing placed, and dat, of the thing round which it is placed, tectis ac moenibus subjicere ignes circumdareque, Cic, arma humeris, Verg, in tmesis, collo dare brachia circum, Verg **B.** Transf *to supply*, paci egregiam famam, Tac **C.** *to build or place round*, murum, Caes, equites cornibus, Liv **II.** *to surround something with something else*, with acc and abl **A.** Lit animum corpore, Liv, tempora vittis, Ov, regio insulis circumdata, Cic **B.** *to surround* in a hostile manner, omnem aciem suam redis et carris, Caes, oppidum coronā, Liv **C** Transf, exiguis quibusdam finibus totum oratoris munus, Cic

circumdūco -duxi -ductum, 3 **I.** *to lead round, move or drive round* **A.** exercitum, Plaut, aratrum (of the founding of a colony when a plough was driven around the site of the wall), Cic, flumen ut circino circumductum, Caes. **B.** *to lead round, to lead by a round-about course* 1, lit, cohortes quatuor longiore itinere, Caes, absol, praeter castra hostium circumducit, *he marches round*, Liv, 2, transf, a, *to lead astray, deceive*, Plaut, b, of discourse, *to extend, amplify*, Quint **II.** *to lead round about, to take round*, aliquem omnia sua praesidia circumducere, atque ostentare, Caes

circumductĭo -ōnis, f (circumduco), *cheating, deceiving*, Plaut

circumductus -a -um, partic of circumduco

circumĕo (circuĕo) -ivi or -ii -itum -ire, *to go, travel, or walk round* **I. A** Gen, 1, *in a circle*, flagrantes aras, Ov, hostium castra, Caes, 2, a, *to go round in a curve*, metam ferventi rota, Ov, b, transf, (α) *to cheat*, Ter, (β) *to express by circumlocution*, Vespasiani nomen suspensi et vitabundi circumibant, *avoided mentioning*, Tac **B.** *to enclose, surround*, aciem a latere aperto, Caes, fig, in pass, circumiri totius belli fluctibus, Cic **II.** *to go the round, go about* **A.** ipse equo circumiens unum quemque nominans appellat, Sall; urbem, Liv, plebem, Liv, praedia, *to visit*, Cic, oram maris, Cic, vigilias, Liv. **B.** Esp, *to go round to canvass or solicit*, senatum cum veste sordida, Liv, circumire ordines et hortari, Caes

circŭmĕquito, 1 *to ride round*; moenia, Liv

circŭmerro, 1 *to wander round*, Sen.

circumfĕro -tŭli -lātum -ferre, *to carry round, bring round*. **I.** 1, circumferuntur tabulae inspiciendi nominis causa, Cic, poculum circumfertur, Liv, 2, *to spread around*, circa ea omnia templa infestos ignes, Liv, incendia et caedes et terrorem, Tac, bellum, Liv, 3, *to move round, turn in all directions* (of a part of the body, esp. the eyes); oculos, Liv; 4, *to spread a report, disseminate news*; quae se circumferat esse Corinnam, Ov **II.** *to carry round in a circle*, 1, middle, sol ut circumferatur, *revolves*, Cic, 2, religious t t, *to lustrate, purify*, by carrying round consecrated objects; socios pura circumtulit unda, Verg

circumflecto -flexi -flexum, 3 *to bend round, to turn about*, longos cursus, Verg

circumflo, 1, *to blow round*, fig, ut ab omnibus ventis invidiae circumflari posse videatur, Cic

circumflŭo -fluxi -fluxum, 3 **I.** *to flow round*, Ov **II. A.** *to overflow*, fig, nec ea redundans tamen nec circumfluens oratio *diffuse*, Cic **B.** Transf *to abound in*, circumfluere omnibus copiis Cic, gloria, Cic

circumflŭus -a -um (circumfluo), 1, act, *flowing round, circumfluent*, humor, Ov; 2, pass, *flowed round, surrounded by water*, insula, Ov

circumfŏrānĕus -a -um (circum and forum), 1, *round the forum*, aes, *money borrowed from the bankers whose shops were round the forum = debt*, Cic, 2, *attending at markets*, pharmacopola, Cic

circumfundo -fūdi -fūsum, 3 *to pour around* **I. A.** Lit, gen in pass, circumfundi, or reflexive, se circumfundere, *to be poured round = to surround*, with dat, amnis circumfunditur parvae insulae, Liv **B.** Transf, of persons, refl, se circumfundere, or simply circumfundere, *to flock round*, with dat, equites Hannoni Afrisque se circumfudere, Liv., so pass., as middle, circumfunditur equitatus Caesaris, Caes; of things, undique circumfusis molestiis or voluptatibus, Cic **II.** *to encompass, surround* **A.** Lit, 1, act mortuum cera, Nep; 2, pass, *to be washed by*, parva quaedam insula est circumfusa illo mari quem oceanum appellatis, Cic **B.** Transf, *to surround, encircle, hem in*, praefectum castrorum et legionarios milites circumfundunt, Tac, gen in pass, multis circumfusus Stoicorum libris, Cic.

circumgĕmo, 3 *to growl round about*; ovile, Hor

circumgesto, 1. *to carry round*, epistolam, Cic

circumgrĕdĭor -gressus sum -grĕdi (circum and gradior), *to go round, travel round*, especially with hostile intent, exercitum, Sall; terga, Tac

circumĭcĭo = circumjicio (q v)

circuminjĭcĭo, 3 *to throw around*, vallum, Liv

circumjăcĕo, 2 *to lie round about, adjoin*; quaeque circumjacent Europae, Liv

circumjectus -ūs, m (circumjicio) **I.** *a surrounding, enclosing*, qui (aether) tenero terram circumjectu amplectitur, Cic **II.** Meton, ut ita munita arx circumjectu arduo niteretur, Cic

circumjĭcĭo -jēci -jectum, 3 (circum and jacio), 1, *to throw round, put round*, multitudinem hominum totis moenibus, Caes, hence of localities, **circumjectus** -a -um, *surrounding, adjacent*, nationes, Tac., aedificia circumjecta muris, Liv., 2, aliquid aliquā re, *to surround, enclose with anything*, Cic, circumjicere extremitatem coeli rotundo ambitu, Cic

circumlăvo -āre and -ĕre, *to wash round, to overflow round*, Sall

circumlĭgo, 1 1, *to bind round, bind to*; natum mediae hastae, Verg; 2, *to bind round with*, ferrum stuppa, Liv; circumligatum esse angui, Cic

circumlĭno, no perf -litum, 3. and also

circumlĭnĭo -lĭnĭ, 4 1, *to smear anything on anything*, sulfura taedis, Ov, 2, *to besmear with anything, to cover*, circumlitus auro, Ov.; circumlita saxa musco, Hor

circumlŭo, 3 *to wash round, flow round*, quo (mari) in paeninsulae modum pars major (arcis) circumluitur, Liv

circumlustrans -antis, *illuminating all round*, Lucr

circumlŭvĭo ōnis, f (circumluo), *the formation of an island by the encroachment of a river*, Cic

circummitto mīsī -missum, 3 **I.** *to send by a roundabout way, to send round*, tribuno cum duorum signorum militibus circummisso, Liv **II.** *to send round about, to send in all directions*, legationes, Caes

circummūnĭo (circummoenio, Plaut), 4 *to fortify round, to wall round, to shut in by lines of circumvallation*, Uticam vallo, Caes

circummūnītĭo -ōnis, f (circummunio), *the investing or circumvallation of a fortress*, Caes

circumpădānus -a -um, *round about the Po, near the river Po*, campi, Liv

circumplaudo, 3 *to clap or applaud on all sides*, aliquem, Ov

circumplector -plexus, 3 dep. *to embrace, enclose, surround*, domini patrimonium circumplexus quasi thesaurum draco, Cic, collem opere, Caes

circumplĭco, 1 *to fold round, wind round*, si anguem vectis circumplicavisset, Cic

circumpōno pŏsŭi -pŏsĭtum, 3 *to place or put round, encircle*, nemus stagno, Tac, piper catillis, Hor.

circumpōtātĭo ōnis, f (circum and poto), *drinking round in succession*, ap Cic.

circumrētĭo, 4 (circum and rete), *to enclose in a net, ensnare*, transf, aliquem, Lucr, te circumretitum frequentiā populi Romani video, Cic

circumrōdo -rōsi, 3 *to gnaw round* escam, Plin, transf, dudum enim circumrodo quod devorandum est, *I have long hesitated to speak out*, Cic, qui dente Theonino quum circumroditur, *slandered*, Hor

circumsaepĭo -saeptus, 4 *to hedge round, enclose*, corpus armatis, Liv.

circumscindo, 3 *to tear off, strip*, quo ferocius clamitabat, eo infestius circumscindere et spoliare lictor, Liv

circumscrībo scripsi -scriptum, 3 *to describe a circle round, to enclose in a circular line* **I.** Lit, orbem, Cic, stantem virgula, Cic **II.** Transf **A.** *to draw the outline of an object, to fix the boundaries of*, locum habitandi alicui, Cic **B.** *to draw together, confine, limit, circumscribe, hamper, restrain*, tribunum plebis, Cic **C. 1**, *to take in, deceive, circumvent, ensnare*, fallaciis et captiosis interrogationibus circumscripti, Cic, **2**, *to defraud*, adolescentulos, Cic, vectigalia, *to embezzle*, Quint. **3**, *to put aside as invalid, invalidate, annul*, sententias, Cic

circumscriptē, adv (circumscriptus), *in rhetorical periods*, circumscripte numeroseque dicere, Cic

circumscriptĭo -ōnis, f (circumscribo), *encircling* **I.** Lit, concrete, *circumference*, Cic **II.** Transf, **A.** *outline, boundary*, **1**, gen, terrae, Cic, temporis, *limit*, Cic, **2**, in rhetoric, *a period*, Cic **B.** *deceit, swindling, defrauding*, esp in pecuniary matters, adolescentium, Cic

circumscriptor -ōris, m (circumscribo), *a cheat swindler*, Cic.

circumscriptus -a -um p adj (from circumscribo), *concise*, brevis et circumscripta quaedam explicatio, Cic

circumsĕco -sectum, 1 *to cut round about*; aliquid serra, Cic

circumsĕdĕo -sēdi sessum, 2 **I.** Gen, *to sit round*, Sen **II.** Esp, *to surround with hostile intent, besiege, beleaguer*, aliquem vallo, Cic, transf, a lacrimis omnium circumsessus, *assailed*, Cic

circumsessĭo -ōnis, f (circumsedeo), *an encircling with hostile intent, a beleaguering*, Cic.

circumsīdo -sēdi, 3 *to sit down before a place, besiege*, oppidum, Sall

circumsĭlĭo, 4 (circum and salio), *to leap or jump round*, (passer) circumsiliens, Cat, transf, *to surround*, morborum omne genus, Juv

circumsisto stĕti, or (more rarely) -stĭti, 3 *to place oneself round, to surround* **A.** Gen, aliquem, Caes **B** Esp, *to surround hostilely, press round*, plures paucos circumsistebant, Caes, sex lictores circumsistunt, Cic

circumsŏno -sŏnŭi sŏnātum, **1, a**, *to sound around*, clamor hostes circumsonat, Liv, **b**, *to echo with*, locus qui circumsonat ululatibus, Liv, talibus aures tuas vocibus undique circumsonare, Cic

circumsŏnus -a -um (circumsono), *sounding around*, turba canum, Ov

circumspectātrix -īcis, f (circumspecto), *a female who looks round about*, Plaut

circumspectĭo -ōnis, f (circumspicio), *foresight, circumspection, caution*, circumspectio aliqua et accurata consideratio, Cic

circumspecto, 1 (freq of circumspicio), *to look around* **I.** Intransit, *to look round repeatedly*, circumspectant bestiae in pastu, Cic; fig, dubitans, circumspectans, haesitans, Cic **II.** Transit, **a**, *to look round at*, esp with anxiety or suspicion, omnia, Cic, patriciorum vultus, Liv, **b**, *to look round to seek for something or somebody*, circumspectare omnibus fori partibus senatorem raroque usquam noscitare, Liv; **c**, *to wait for, watch for*, defectionis tempus, Liv

1 **circumspectus** -a -um, p adj with compar and superl (from circumspicio), **1**, pass, of things, *deliberate, well considered*, verba circumspecta, Ov, **2**, active, of persons, *circumspect, cautious*, Sen

2 **circumspectus** -ūs, m (circumspicio), **1**, *looking round*, Plin, transf, *attention to*, detinere aliquem ab circumspectu rerum aliarum, Liv, **2**, *prospect, view on every side*, Cic

circumspĭcĭo -spexi -spectum, 3 *to look round* **I.** intransit **A** qui in auspicium adhibetur nec suspicit nec circumspicit, Cic, circumspicit (*looks round anxiously*), aestuat, Cic **B.** Transf, *to consider*, circumspicite celeriter animo qui sint rerum exitus consecuti, Cic **II.** Transit, *to look round at* **A. 1**, lit., urbis situm, Liv, **2**, transf, *to consider carefully*, omnia pericula, Cic **B.** *to look around for*, **1**, lit, Caes, saxum ingens, Verg, **2**, transf, *to look for, seek for*, externa auxilia, Tac

circumsto -stĕti, 1 **I.** *to stand round or in a circle, to surround, encircle*, sellam, Liv, hence partic subst, circumstantes, *the bystanders*, Liv **II.** *to surround with hostile intent, to beleaguer* **A.** Lit, circumstare tribunal praetoris urbani, obsidere cum gladiis curiam, Cic **B.** Transf quum tanti undique terrores circumstarent, Liv

circumstrĕpo -strĕpŭi -strĕpĭtum, 3 *to roar, make a noise round, shout clamorously around*, legatus clamore seditiosorum circum-strepitu, Tac., with acc, quidam atrociora circumstrepebant, Tac

circumstrŭo struxi -structum, 3 *to build round*, Suet.

circumsurgens -entis, *rising round*, Tac

circumtĕgo, 3 *to cover all round*, Lucr (?)

circumtĕro, 3 *to rub against on all sides, poet, to crowd round*, Tib

circumtextus -a -um, *woven all round*, circumtextum croceo velamen acantho, Verg

circumtŏno -tŏnŭi, 1 *to thunder round*, qua totum Nereus circumtonat orbem, Ov

circumtonsus -a -um, 1, *shaven or shorn all round*, Suet, 2, transf, of discourse, *artificial*, Sen

circumvado -vāsi, 3 *to attack from every side, to surround* I. Lit, immobiles naves circumvadunt, Liv II. Transf, cum terror circumvasisset aciem, Liv.

circumvăgus -a -um, *wandering round*, or *in a circle*, Oceanus, Hor

circumvallo, 1 *to surround with a wall*, or *fortification, to blockade, beleaguer*, oppidum, Caes, Pompeium, Cic, fig, tot res repente circumvallant, Ter.

circumvectio -ōnis, f (circumvehor), 1, *a carrying round of merchandise*, portorium circumvectionis, *transit dues*, Cic, 2, solis, *circuit, revolution*, Cic

circumvector, 1 dep (intens of circumvehor), 1, *to ride or sail round*, Ligurum oras, Liv, 2, poet, *to go through, describe*, singula dum circumvectamur, Verg

circumvĕhor -vectus, 3. dep, 1, *to ride or sail round*, jubet circumvectos (equites), ab tergo Gallicam invadere aciem, Liv, navibus circumvecti, Caes, with acc, cum classe Corsicae oram, Liv, transf, frustra circumvehor omnia verbis, *try to describe at once*, Verg, 2, *to ride or sail in every direction*, Liv

circumvēlo, 1 *to veil or conceal on all sides*, aurato circumvelatur amictu, Ov

circumvĕnio -vēni -ventum, 4. *to come round, surround, encircle*. I. Gen. A. Of persons, homines circumventi flamma, Caes B. Of places, Rhenus modicas insulas circumveniens, Tac II. *to surround with hostile intent*. A. Lit., 1, of persons, hostes a tergo, Caes; 2, of things, cuncta moenia exercitu, Sall B. Transf, 1, *to beset, oppress, assail*, aliquem judicio capitis, Cic, 2, *to cheat*, innocentem pecunia, Cic

circumversor, 1 dep, *to twist or turn round*, Lucr

circumverto (-vorto) -verti (-vorti) -versum (-vorsum), 3 A. *to turn, twist round*, rota perpetuum qua circumvertitur axem, Ov, mancipium, *to manumit*, Quint B. Transf, *to defraud*, qui me argento circumvortant, Plaut.

circumvestio, 4 *to clothe all round*, poet., ap Cic

circumvincio -vinctus, 4. *to bind all round*, Plaut

circumvīso, 3 *to look all round*, Plaut.

circumvŏlĭto, 1. 1, *to fly round*, lacus circumvolitavit hirundo, Verg, 2, transf, *to rove about, hover round*, circumvolitant equites, Lucr

circumvŏlo, 1. *to fly round*, aliquem atris alis (of death), Hor

circumvolvo -volvi -vŏlūtum, 3 *to roll round*, sol magnum circumvolvitur annum, *completes its annual course*, Verg

circus -i m (κίρκος) I. *a circular line*; candens, *the milky way*, Cic II. *a circus, hippodrome*. A. *in Rome*, 1, Circus Maximus, or Circus, *the great circus or racecourse in Rome, surrounded by galleries which accommodated 150,000 spectators*, Liv; 2, Circus Flaminius, outside the town, Cic B. *a circus in other places*, 1, Circus maritimus at Anagnia, Liv; 2, *any circus or place where games are held*, Verg

cīris -is, f (κεῖρις), *a bird, into which Scylla, daughter of Nisus, was transformed*, Ov

cirrātus -a -um (cirrus), *curled, crisped*, Mart

Cirrha -ae, f (Κίῤῥα), *a city of Phocis, the port of Delphi, sacred to Apollo*, hence, **Cirrhaeus** -a -um, *relating to Cirrha or Apollo*

cirrus -i, m, 1, *a lock, curl, or ringlet of hair*, Juv, 2, *the fringe of a garment*, Phaedr.

Cirta -ae, f (Κίρτα), *a town of Numidia*.

cis, prep, with acc (connected with is and hic, with demonstrative c prefixed), *on this side*; 1, of place, cis Taurum, Cic., 2, of time, cis dies paucos, *within a few days*, Sall.

cisalpīnus -a -um, *on this side (the Roman), i.e, the south side of the Alps*, Gallia, Caes

cĭsĭum -ii, n *a light two-wheeled gig*, Cic.

cisrhēnānus -a um, *on this side the Rhine*, Germani, Caes

Cisseus -ĕi, m (Κισσεύς), *king of Thrace, father of Hecuba*; hence **Cissēis** -idis, f (Κισσηΐς), *daughter of Cisseus, Hecuba*

cista -ae, f (κίστη), *a chest, casket* for keeping money, fruit, books, etc, Cic, for sacred utensils, Tib, *a ballot-box*, Plin.

cistella ae, f (dim of cista), *a little chest*, or *casket*, Plaut

cistellātrix -īcis, f (cistella), *the female slave whose business it was to keep the cash-box*, Plaut.

cistellŭla ae, f (dim of cistella), *a little casket*, Plaut.

cisterna -ae, f *a subterranean reservoir, a cistern*, piscinae cisternaeque servandis imbribus, Tac

cistĭfer fĕri, m (cista and fero), *one who carries a box or chest*, Mart.

cistŏphŏrus -i, m (κιστοφόρος), *an Asiatic coin worth about four drachmae, so called from the impression of a cista upon it*, in cistophoro in Asia habeo ad HS bis et vicies, *in Asiatic coinage*, Cic

cistŭla -ae, f (dim of cista), *a casket*, Plaut

cĭtātim, adv (citatus), *quickly, hastily*, Cic

cĭtātus a -um, p adj with compar and superl (from cito), *quick, rapid, speedy*; Rhenus per fines Trevirorum citatus fertur, Caes, citato equo or citatis equis, *at full gallop*, Liv.

cĭtĕr -tra -trum (cis), *on this side* I. Positive, Cato II. Compar., **cĭtĕrĭor** us, genit. -ōris, *on this side* A. Gallia, Cic B. Transf, 1, ad haec citeriora veniam et notiora nobis, *more closely concerning us*, Cic; 2, of time, *earlier*, citeriores nondum audiebamus, Cic. III. Superl, **cĭtĭmus** or **cĭtŭmus** -a -um, *very near, nearest*, stella ultima a caelo citima terris, Cic

Cĭthaerōn -ōnis, m. (Κιθαιρών), *a mountain in the south-west of Boeotia, scene of the Bacchic orgies*

cĭthăra -ae, f (κιθάρα) A. *a four-stringed instrument*, Hor B. Meton, 1, *the music of the cithara*, Hor; 2, *the art of playing the cithara*, Hor.

cĭthărista -ae, m (κιθαριστής), *a player on the cithara*, Ter.

cĭthăristria -ae, f (κιθαρίστρια), *a female player on the cithara*, Ter

cĭthărizo, 1. (κιθαρίζω), *to play the cithara*, Nep

cĭthăroedĭcus -a -um (κιθαρῳδικός), *relating to the citharoedus*, Suet.

cĭthăroedus -i, m. (κιθαρῳδός), *one who sings to the cithara*, Cic.

Cĭtĭum -ii, n (Κίτιον), *a maritime city of Cyprus, birthplace of the Stoic philosopher, Zeno*, hence, **A. Cĭtĭensis** -e, *belonging to Citium*. **B. Cĭtĭēus** -a -um, *belonging to Citium* **C. Cĭtĭĕus** -ĕi, m. *of Citium*, Zeno, Cic.

1 **cĭtŏ**, comp **cĭtius**, sup **cĭtissime**, adv (citus). **A.** *quickly, speedily*, Cic, cito discere aliquid, Cic **B.** Transf, **a**, non cito, *not easily*, Cic, **b**, compar, citius quam, *sooner than*, Cic

2 **cĭto**, 1 (freq of cio = cieo) **I.** *to put into violent motion*, hence *to cite, summon*, **a**, *the senate*, patres in curiam, Liv, **b**, *the people to vote;* in campo Martio centuriatim populum, Liv; **c**, *the knights*, "Cita," inquit Nero, "M Livium," Liv, **d**, *the citizens to take the oath of military allegiance*, citati milites nominatim apud tribunos militum in verba P Scipionis juraverunt, Liv; **e**, in a court of justice, (α) *the jury*, si Lysiades citatus judex non responderit, Cic, (β) *the prosecutor or defendant*, citat reum, non respondet, citat accusatorem, Cic, omnes ii ab te capitis C Rabirii nomine citantur, Cic; (γ) *a witness*, in hanc rem te, Naevi, testem citabo, Cic, transf, quamvis citetur Salamis clarissimae testis victoriae, Cic, (δ) *the condemned;* praeconis audita vox citantis nomina damnatorum, Liv., **f**, *to call upon a god for help*, aliquem falso, Ov **II. a**, *to shout out*, paeanem, Cic., **b**, *to call forth, to produce*, isque (animi) motus aut boni aut mali opinione citatur, Cic

cĭtrā, adv and prep with acc (from citer) **I.** *on this side*, citra Veliam, Cic., citra Rhenum, Caes **II.** Transf, **A.** *on this side of* (a certain boundary), *within, before*, **1**, of space, paucis citra milibus, Liv., citra tertiam syllabam, *before the third syllable*, Cic; **2**, of time, *within*, citra Trojana tempora, Ov **B.** = sine, praeter, *without, except*, citra vulnus, Plin

cĭtrĕus a -um (citrus), **1**, *belonging to the citrus tree*, mensa, *made of citrus wood*, Cic, **2**, *belonging to the citron tree*, citrea, *the citron tree*, Plin, citreum, *the citron*, Plin

cĭtrō, adv (citer), found only in combination with ultro, ultro et citro, ultro citroque, ultro citro, ultro ac citro, *up and down, hither and thither*, Cic

cĭtrum i, n *citrus wood*, Plin

cĭtrus -i, m. *the citrus, a kind of African cypress*, from the aromatic timber of which the Romans manufactured costly articles of furniture (perhaps Thuia orientalis, Linn), Plin

cĭtus -a -um, p adj (from cieo), *quick, speedy*, vox, Cic., incessus, Sall, pes, *the iambus*, Ov

cīvĭcus -a -um (civis), *relating to a citizen, civic;* bella, *civil war*, Ov, corona, and simply **cīvĭca** -ae, f *the civic crown, a chaplet of oak leaves presented to one who had saved the life of a Roman citizen in war, bearing the inscription*, ob civem servatum, Cic

cīvīlis e (civis) **I.** *relating to a citizen, civic, civil* **A.** Lit, conjuratio, Cic, discordia, Sall, quercus = corona civica (v civicus), Verg; jus, either *the civil law of the Romans* (opp jus naturale) or *the law of private rights* (opp jus publicum), Cic; dies, *from midnight to midnight*, as opp to the naturalis dies, *from sunrise to sunset*, Varr **B.** Transf, **a**, *becoming a citizen, befitting a citizen*, nulli civilis animus, Liv., **b**, *popular, affable, courteous*, quid civilius illo, Ov. **II.** *relating to public life or the state;* **a**, scientia, Cic.; civilium rerum peritus, Tac, **b**, *civil*, as opp to military, non militaria solum sed civilia quoque munera, Liv.

cīvīlĭtas -ātis, f (civilis), **1**, *the science of politics*, used by Quint. as a translation of ἡ πολιτική, **2**, *politeness, condescension, civility*, Suet.

cīvīlĭtĕr, adv (civilis), **1**, *like a citizen;* vivere, Cic.; **2**, *politely*, Ov

cīvis -is, c (from cio or cieo, *summoned*) **I.** *a citizen* (opp hostis or peregrinus), civis Romanus, Cic, aliquem civem asciscere, Cic.; fieri civem Romanum, Cic, fem, civis Attica, Ter **II. A.** *fellow citizen*, cives mei, Cic **B.** *subject*, imperare corpori ut rex civibus suis, Cic

cīvĭtas -ātis, f (civis) **I.** Abstr, *citizenship, the condition or rights of a citizen*, civitatem dare alicui, Cic, amittere, Cic, aliquem civitate donare, Cic, aliquem in civitatem asciscere, Cic, in populi Romani civitatem suscipi, Cic, civitatem consequi, adipisci, habere, impetrare, adimere, Cic, civitate mutari, Cic **II.** Concr **A.** *a union of citizens, a state, commonwealth*, civitates aut nationes, *civilised states* or *barbarous tribes*, Cic, civitatem instituere, administrare, Cic, civitates condere, Cic **B.** Meton, *a town, city*, Cic

clādēs -is, f (connected with gladius), *destruction* **I.** *destruction* of plants, etc, by hail or rain, *loss, damage*, Plaut, *loss of a limb*, dextrae manus, Liv **II. A.** *disaster, injury*, civitatis, Cic **B.** Meton, *persons who cause the disaster*, militum clades, Cic, geminos Scipiadas cladem Libyae, Verg **C.** Esp, *misfortune in war, defeat*, cladem inferre, Liv; facere, Sall., accipere, Liv., hosti inferre, Cic.

clam (old Lat călam or călim, from root CAL, CEL, whence cel -o) **I.** Adv, *secretly* (opp. palam), *in secret*, esse, *to remain incognito*, Liv; plura clam removere, Cic **II.** Prep **a**, with abl, clam vobis, Caes, clam istis, Cic, **b**, gen with acc, clam me est, *it is unknown to me*, Cic

clāmātor ōris, m (clamo), *a shouter, a bawler, noisy declaimer*, Cic

clāmĭto, 1 (intens of clamo), *to cry loudly, shout violently*, **1**, absol or with acc, Cauneas clamitabat, *cried figs of Caunus*, Cic, of things, nonne ipsum caput et supercilia illa penitus abrasa clamitare calliditatem videntur, Cic, **2**, followed by an exclamation in direct speech, ad arma! clamitans, Liv, **3**, foll by acc and infin in indirect speech, saepe clamitans liberum se liberaeque civitatis esse, Caes, **4**, with the acc, aliquem sycophantam, Ter

clāmo, 1 (connected with καλέω) **I.** Intransit, *to shout, cry aloud* **A.** Of men, loqui omnes et clamare coeperunt, Cic, de suo et uxoris interitu, Cic **B.** Of animals, anseres qui tantummodo clamant, nocere non possunt, Cic. **II.** Transit, **1**, *to call to* or *upon*, comites, Ov.; morientem nomine, Verg, with double acc, *to call aloud*, aliquem furem, Hor, **2**, *to proclaim aloud*, **a**, with acc, hoc de pecunia, Cic, **b**, in direct speech, infantem Io triumphe! clamasse, Liv, **c**, in indirect speech, clamare ille quum raperetur, nihil se miserum fecisse, Cic, **d**, with ut and the subj, clamare coeperunt, sibi ut haberet hereditatem, Cic.

clāmor -ōris, m *a loud shouting, cry* **A.** Of men, clamor populi infestus atque inimicus, Cic, clamorem edere, tollere, Cic excitare, Liv, clamor oritur, Sall, auditur, Caes, esp, **1**, *shout of applause*, haec sunt, quae clamores et admirationes in bonis oratoribus efficiunt, Cic, **2**, *wild cry*, aliquem clamoribus et con vicis et sibilis consectari, Cic. 3, *war-cry;* clamorem tollere, Caes.; **4,** *cry of sorrow;* lamentantium militum, Liv. **B.** Of animals, gruum, Lucr. **C.** *a sound* of lifeless things; montium, Hor.

clāmōsus -a -um (clamo), **1,** act., *noisy, clamorous,* Quint.; **2,** pass., *filled with noise;* circus, Mart.

clancŭlum, adv. (clam), *secretly, in secret,* Plaut., Ter.; prep. with acc., clanculum patres, Ter.

clandestīnus -a -um (clam), *secret, concealed, hidden, clandestine;* colloquia cum hostibus, Cic.

clangor -ōris, m. *a sound, clang, noise;* **1,** *the cry of birds,* Ov.; of the eagle, Cic. poet.; *the hissing of geese,* Liv.; **2,** *the sound of a trumpet,* Verg.

Clănis -is, m. *a river of Etruria.*

Clănĭus -ii, m. *a river of Campania.*

clārē, adv. (clarus). **I.** Lit. **A.** As regards sight, *clearly, brightly;* videre, Plaut.; fulgere, Cat. **B.** As regards hearing, *aloud;* plaudere, dicere, Plaut.; gemere, Cic. **II.** Transf. **A.** *clearly, distinctly;* apparere, ap. Cic.; ostendere, Quint. **B.** *illustriously;* explendescere, Nep.

clārĕo, 2. (clarus). **I.** *to be bright, to shine,* Cic. poet. **II.** Transf. **A.** *to be clear to the mind, be evident,* Lucr. **B.** *to be distinguished, illustrious,* Enn.

clāresco, clārŭi, 3. (inch. of clareo). **I. A.** *to become clear, bright,* Tac. **B.** *to sound* or *resound clearly;* clarescunt sonitus, Verg. **II.** Transf. **A.** *to become clear to the mind, become evident,* Lucr. **B.** *to become illustrious,* Tac.; ex gente Domitiā duae familiae claruerunt, Suet.

clārĭgātĭo -ōnis, f. (clarigo), **1,** *the demand of satisfaction and declaration of war by a Fetialis,* Plin.; **2,** *the fine imposed on a man caught beyond the limits within which he has been ordered to remain,* Liv.

clārĭgo (clare—i.e., clara voce—and ago), 1. *to declare war,* used of the Fetialis, Plin.

clārĭsŏnus -a -um (clarus and sono), *clearly sounding;* vox, Cat.

clārĭtas -ātis, f. (clarus). **I.** Lit. **A.** Of the sight, *clearness, brightness, brilliancy,* Plin. **B.** Of the voice, vocis, Cic. **II.** Transf. **A.** *clearness to the mind, plainness,* Quint. **B.** *fame, celebrity, renown;* hominis, Cic.

clārĭtūdo -inis, f. (clarus), *clearness, brilliancy.* **I.** Lit., of the sight, deae (i.e., lunae), Tac. **II.** Transf., *fame, renown, celebrity,* Sall.

clāro, 1. (clarus). **I.** *to make clear, make bright,* Cic. poet. **II.** Transf. **A.** *to make plain, evident;* animi naturam versibus, Lucr. **B.** *to make illustrious, renowned,* Hor.

clāror -ōris, m. (clarus), *brightness,* Plaut.

Clărŏs, i, f. (Κλάρος), *a small town in Ionia, on a promontory near Colophon, famous for a temple and oracle of Apollo;* hence **Clărĭus** -a -um (Κλάριος), *Clarian, surname of Apollo,* Ov.; poeta, *the poet Antimachus, born at Claros.*

clārus -a -um (connected with κλεεινός), *clear, bright* (opp. obscurus, caecus). **I.** Lit. **A.** In regard to objects of sight, *bright, shining, brilliant;* lumina mundi, Verg.; locus, Cic.; poet., of the wind, *making clear, bringing fair weather;* aquilo, Verg. **B.** In regard to objects of hearing, *clear, loud;* voce, Cic. **II.** Transf. **A.** *clear, evident, plain;* luce sunt clariora nobis tua consilia, Cic. **B. 1,** *illustrious, renowned, distinguished;* **a,** of persons, vir clarissimus, Cic.; clarus gloriā, Cic.; clarus in philosophia et nobilis, Cic.; ex doctrina nobilis et clarus, Cic.; **b,** of things oppidum Cic.; victoria clarissima, Cic.; **2,** in a bad sense, *notorious;* illa oppugnatio fani antiquissimi quam clara apud omnes, Cic.; populus luxuriā superbiāque clarus, Liv.

classĭārĭus -i, m. (classis), **1** (sc. miles), *a soldier on board ship, a marine,* Tac.; **2** (sc. nauta), *a rower,* or *sailor, on board a war galley,* Caes.

classĭcŭla -ae, f. (dim. of classis), *a little fleet, flotilla,* Cic.

classĭcus -a -um (classis). **I. A.** *relating to the classes into which the Roman citizens were distributed;* hence, **classĭcus** -i, m. *a citizen of the first* or *highest class.* **B.** Transf., classicus scriptor, *an author of the first rank,* Gell. **II.** *relating to the army* or *the fleet.* **A.** *relating to the army;* subst., **classĭcum** -i, n. *the signal of engagement given by a trumpet;* classicum canit, Liv.; or *the signal by which the classes were called to the comitia;* classico ad contionem convocat, Liv.; and meton., *the trumpet itself;* classicum inflare, Verg. **B.** *relating to the fleet;* milites, Liv.; bella, *naval war,* Prop.; and subst., **classĭci** -ōrum, m. *marines,* Tac.

classis -is, f. (connected with κλάσις, κλήσω, from κλέω, and calo, *to summon,* lit. *the multitude summoned*). **I.** *a class.* **A.** Lit., *one of the divisions into which Servius Tullius divided the whole Roman people;* hence fig., quintae classis, *of the lowest rank,* Cic. **B.** Transf., *any division;* servorum, Petr. **II.** In milit. lang., *the forces.* **A.** *a land army;* Hortinae classes, Verg. **B.** *the fleet;* classem facere, comparare, aedificare, *to build a fleet,* Cic.; instruere atque ornare, *to fit out a fleet,* Cic.; classem appellere ad Delum, *to land,* Cic.; poet., *a ship,* Hor., Verg.; hence, plur. classes = naves, Verg. Aen. ii. 30.

Clastĭdĭum -ii, n. *a town in Gallia Cispadana,* now *Casteggio* or *Chiateggio.*

Clăterna -ae, f., *stronghold in Cispadane Gaul* (now *Maggio*).

clātri -ōrum, m. and **clātra** -ōrum, n. (κλῇθρα), *a trellis* or *grating,* Hor.

clatro, 1. (clatri), *to provide* or *cover with a trellis* or *grating,* Plaut.

claudĕo -ēre, 2. and gen. **claudo,** clausurus, 3. (claudus), *to limp, halt, be lame;* gen. used fig., si (beata vita) una ex parte clauderet, Cic.; esp. of orators, in quacunque enim una (parte) plane clauderet, orator esse non posset, Cic.

Claudĭānus -i, m. (Claudius), *a Latin poet, who lived in the reigns of Theodosius the Great, and his sons Arcadius and Honorius.*

claudĭcātĭo -ōnis, f. (claudico), *a limping,* Cic.

claudĭco, 1. (claudus), *to limp, be lame;* graviter claudicare ex vulnere ob rempublicam accepto, Cic.; claudicat axis mundi, *inclines,* Lucr.; fig., *to halt, waver, be defective;* tota res vacillat et claudicat, Cic.; esp. of speech, nihil curtum, nihil claudicans, Cic.

Claudĭus (Clōdĭus) -a -um, *the name of a Roman family, both patrician and plebeian, of whom the most celebrated members were:*—**I.** Appius Claudius Sabinus Regillensis, *the founder of the family, a Sabine of Regillum, whose name was said to have been originally Attus Clausus.* **II.** Appius Claudius Crassus, *the most notorious of the decemvirs.* **III.** Appius Claudius Caecus, *censor* 312 B.C., *the builder of several great public works.* **IV.** Publius Clodius Pulcher, *tribune of the people, murdered by Milo,* B.C. 52. **V.** Tiberius Claudius Drusus Nero Germanicus, *the fourth Roman emperor.* Adj., **Claudĭānus** -a -um, **Claudĭālis** -e, **Clōdĭānus** -a -um, *Claudian.*

1 **claudo**, clausi, clausum, 3 and **clūdo**, clūsi, clusum, 3. (root CLA, whence clavis, Gr Dor κλαΐς = κλεΐς). **I.** Gen, *to shut close* (opp aperire). **A.** Lit, **1**, forem cubiculi, Cic; portas alicui, Caes, Janum, *to close the gates of the temple of Janus*, Liv, fig, claudere aures alicui rei, Cic., in ipsius consuetudinem, quam adhuc meus pudor mihi clausit, me insinuabo, Cic, **2**, *to close up a road or a country, to make inaccessible*, omnes aditus claudentur, Cic, quod clausae hieme Alpes essent, Liv, adhuc clausum fuisse mare scio, Cic, **3**, *to close up*, **a**, geograph t t, insula ea sinum ab alto claudit, **b**, milit. t t, agmen claudere, *to bring up the rear*, Caes Subst, **clausum** -i, n *a bolt* or *lock*; clausa effringere, Sall., **B.** Transf, **1**, *to bring to an end*, opus, Ov; octavum lustrum, Hor, **2**, of character, partic clausus, *secret, close*, Tiberius, Tac **II. A.** = intercludere, *to dam up, stop, intercept*, rivos, Verg, commeatus, Liv, horum ferocia vocem Evandri clausit, Liv **B.** = concludere, includere, **1**, lit, **a** *to shut up in*, aliquem in curiam or in curia, Liv, **b**, milit t t, *to invest*, oppidum undique, Sall, of hunting, nemorum saltus, Verg, **c**, *to encompass, surround*, urbs loci natura terra marique clauditur, Cic, **2**, transf, **a**, aliud clausum in pectore, aliud in lingua promptum habere, **b**, as rhet t t, sententias numeris, Cic

2. **claudo** = claudeo (q v.)

claudus (cludus) -a -um **I.** Lit, *limping, halting, lame*, claudus altero pede, *lame on one foot*, Nep, claudi ac debiles equi, Liv, prov, iste claudus pilam, *one who can make proper use of nothing*, Cic **II.** Transf **A.** *crippled, defective, wavering*, naves, Liv; poet., carmina alterno versu, *elegiac verse*, Ov **B** *wavering, insecure*, clauda nec officii pars erit ulla tui, Ov

claustrum -i, n (claudo), gen plur **I.** *a bolt, bar*, claustra revellere, Cic, laxare, Verg, relaxare, Ov, fig, portarum naturae effringere, *to lay bare the secrets of nature*, Lucr **II.** *a gate, inclosure, dam, limit, boundary*, **a**, venti circum claustra fremunt, Verg, **b**, *custody, confinement*, of animals, *a den, cage*, diu claustris retentae ferae, Liv, **c**, *a pass or narrow place*, claustra montium, Tac, milit t t, *the key or critical point of a position*, terra claustra locorum tenet; claustra Aegypti, Liv., fig, claustra ista (*barrier*) nobilitatis refregissem, Cic.

clausŭla -ae, f (claudo), *the end, conclusion* **A.** Gen, epistolae, Cic **B.** Esp. **1**, *the closing scene* or *closing word in a drama*, in quo (mimo) quum clausula non invenitur, Cic., **2**, in rhet., *the close of a period*, Cic

clāva -ae, f (clavus), *a knotty staff or cudgel*, Cic; also *the staff used in the drill of recruits or in exercises in the use of weapons*, Cic; *the club of Hercules*, Verg, Ov.

clāvārĭum -i, n (clavus), *a gift of money to Roman soldiers*, Tac.

clāvātor -ōris, m (clava), *one who carries the clava*, Plaut

clāvĭcŭla -ae, f (dim of clavis, *a little key*), hence, *the twig* or *tendril by which the vine clings to its prop*, Cic

1 **clāvĭger** -gĕri, m (clava and gero), *the club bearer*, epithet of Hercules, Ov.

2 **clāvĭger** -gĕri, m (clavis and gero), *the key-carrier*, epithet of Janus as god of doors, Ov

clāvis -is, f (κλαΐς, κλείς), **1**, *a key*, adulterina portarum, *a false* or *skeleton key*, Sall, claves adimere uxori, *to separate from one's wife*, Cic, **2**, *a lock*, alias claves omnibus portis imponere, Liv., **3**, clavis adunca trochi, *a stick for trundling a hoop*, Prop.

clāvus -i, m *a nail* **A.** Lit, clavis ferreis confixa transtra, Caes; clavus trabalis, *a spike*, as a sign of firmness, an attribute of Necessitas, Hor, hence, prov, trabali clavo figere, *to fix firmly*, Cic, annalis, *the nail which on the ides of September every year was driven into the wall of the temple of Jupiter Capitolinus at Rome*, hence fig, ex hoc die clavum anni movebis, *reckon the beginning of the year* Cic **B.** Transf, **1**, *a helm, rudder*, Verg, fig, clavum imperii tenere, Cic; **2**, *a stripe of purple on the tunic, worn broad by the senators* (latus), *narrow by the knights* (angustus), latum clavum a Caesare impetravi, *I have become a senator*, Plin, the latus clavus was also worn by the boys of noble families at Rome, Ov., meton, clavus = *the tunic with the broad* or *narrow stripe*, Hor

Clāzŏmĕnae -ārum, f (Κλαζομεναί), *one of the twelve Ionic towns in Asia Minor*

Clĕanthēs -is, m (Κλεάνθης), *a Stoic philosopher, pupil of Zeno*, hence adj, **Clĕanthēus** -a um, *Stoic*, Pers

clēmens -entis, adj with compar and superl., *mild, placid, kind, merciful* **I. a**, of persons, clementes judices et misericordes, Cic, ab innocentia clementissimus, Cic, **b**, of circumstances, events, etc, castigatio, Cic **II.** Transf, **a**, of the weather, *mild*, flamen, Cat, **b**, of water, *quiet, calm*, amnis clementissimus, *still*, Ov

clēmentĕr, adv with compar and superl (clemens), *mildly, gently, mercifully.* **I.** Lit, clementer facere or ferre aliquid, Cic, clementer et moderate jus dicere, Caes, clementer ductis militibus, *without plundering*, Liv **II.** Transf, of places, *gently rising*, clementer editum jugum, Tac

clēmentĭa -ae, f (clemens) **A.** *mildness, mercy, clemency*, clementia mansuetudoque, Cic, confugere in clementiam alicuius, Cic, clementia uti, Cic. **B.** Transf, *mildness of weather*, aestatis, Plin

Clĕombrŏtus -i, m (Κλεόμβροτος), **1**, *a general of the Lacedaemonians*, **2**, *a Greek philosopher of Ambracia*

Clĕōn -ōnis, m (Κλέων), *a celebrated Athenian demagogue*

Clĕōnae -ārum, f (Κλεωναί), *a city in Argolis, near Nemea*, hence adj **Clĕōnaeus** -a um, *Cleonean*

Clĕŏpātra -ae, f **I.** *the daughter of Philip of Macedon and of Olympias, wife of Alexander I of Epirus* **II.** *the daughter of Ptolemy Auletes, queen of Egypt, the mistress of Antonius, whose forces allied with hers were overthrown by Augustus at Actium*

clĕpo, clepsi, cleptum, 3 (κλέπτω), *to steal*, ap Cic, se, *to conceal oneself*, Sen.

clepsȳdra -ae, f (κλεψύδρα), *the water clock used to measure the time during which an orator spoke*, binas clepsydras petere, *to wish to speak for the length of two clepsydrae*, Plin, dare, *to give leave to speak*, Plin, cras ergo ad clepsydram, *rhetorical exercises*, Cic, so, aliquem ad clepsydram latrare docere, Cic

clepta -ae, m (κλέπτης), *a thief*, Plaut

clībănus -i, m (κλίβανος), *an earthen or iron vessel perforated with small holes used for baking bread*, Plin

clĭens -entis, m (archaic cluens, from cluo, κλύω, *to hear*, lit *a listener*) **I.** In Rome, *a client, dependent, one under the protection of a patronus* **II.** Transf, **1**, in Gaul and Germany, *a vassal*, used of entire nations, *allies*, Caes, **2**, *the worshipper of a god*; Bacchi, Hor

clienta -ae, f. (cliens), *a female client*, Hor,

clientēla -ae, f. (cliens). I. A. *clientship, the relation between the client and his patron;* esse in alicuius clientela, Cic.; in alicuius clientelam se conferre, Cic. B. Meton. (gen. in plur.), *clients,* Cic. II. *the relation of a weaker nation to a more powerful one, dependence;* magnae eorum erant clientelae, Caes.; dicare se alicui in clientelam, Caes.

clientŭlus -i, m. (dim. of cliens), *a little client,* Tac.

clīnāmen -ĭnis, n. (*clino), *the inclination of a thing,* Lucr.

clīnātus -a -um (partic. from obsolete verb clino = κλίνω), *inclined, bent, leaning,* Lucr., Cic. poet.

Clīnĭas -ae, m. (Κλεινίας), *the father of Alcibiades;* hence, **Clīnĭădes** -ae, m. *Alcibiades.*

Clīō -ūs, f. (Κλειώ), 1, *the Muse of history;* 2, *a daughter of Oceanus.*

clĭpĕo (clupeo), 1. *to provide with a shield;* clipeata agmina, Verg. Subst., **clĭpĕāti** -ōrum, m. *soldiers bearing shields,* Liv.

clĭpĕus (clŭpĕus) -i, m. and **clĭpĕum** (clŭpĕum) -i, n. *the round metal shield of the Roman soldiers.* I. Lit., Cic.; prov., clipeum post vulnera sumere, *to do anything too late,* Ov. II. Transf., of objects resembling a shield in shape, a, *the disk of the sun,* Ov.; b (gen. clipeum), *a medallion portrait of a god or distinguished man,* Liv., Tac.

Clisthĕnēs -is, m. (Κλεισθένης), *an Athenian statesman.*

Clītarchus -i, m. (Κλείταρχος), *a Greek historian who accompanied Alexander the Great on his expeditions.*

clītellae -ārum, f. (*clino), *a pack saddle, a pair of panniers,* Cic.

clītellārĭus -a -um (clitellae), *belonging or relating to a pack saddle,* Cic.

Clīternum -i, n. *a town of the Aequi.* Adj., **Clīternīnus** -a -um, *Cliternian.*

Clītŏmăchus -i, m. (Κλειτόμαχος), *an Academic philosopher, pupil of Carneades.*

Clītŏr -ŏris, m. (Κλείτωρ) and **Clītŏrĭum** -ii, n. *a town in Arcadia.* Adj., **Clītŏrĭus** -a -um, *Clitorian.*

Clītumnus -i, m. *a river in Umbria, now Clitunno.*

clīvōsus -a -um (clivus), *hilly, steep, precipitous,* rus, Verg.; Olympus, Ov.

clīvus -i, m. (from root CLI, whence acclivis and declivis, and clino in acclino, etc.), *a gentle ascent or elevation, a hill;* lenis ab tergo clivus erat, Liv.; clivum mollire, Caes.; clivus Capitolinus, *the ascent from the forum to the Capitoline hill, and the Capitoline hill itself,* Liv.; so clivus sacer, Hor.; prov. for *an obstacle which is to be surmounted;* clivo sudamus in imo, Ov.

clŏāca -ae, f. (from cluo = *I cleanse*), a, *a sewer or drain;* fossas cloacasque exhaurire, Liv.; b, cloaca maxima, *the sewer constructed by Tarquinius Priscus, through which the filth of Rome was discharged into the Tiber,* Liv.

Clŏăcīna -ae, f. (from cluo, *I cleanse*), *the cleanser, surname of Venus whose image stood at the place where the Romans and Sabines were reconciled after the rape of the Sabine women, and where they purified themselves with myrtle boughs.*

Clōdĭus = Claudius (q.v.).

Cloelĭus (Cluilĭus) -a -um, *name of an Alban and afterwards of a Roman gens, the most celebrated of the name being:* 1, Cluilius or Cloelius, *the last king of Alba, who invaded the Roman territory and made the Cluilia fossa or fossae Cloeliae,* Liv.; 2, **Cloelĭa** -ae, f. *a Roman maiden, hostage to Porsena, who swam back across the Tiber to Rome.*

Clōthō -ūs, f. (Κλωθώ), *the spinner, one of the Parcae.*

clŭĕo, 2. (κλύω), *I hear myself called, I am called, am named;* quaecunque cluent, *whatever has a name,* Lucr.

clūnis -is, m. and f. *the buttocks, hinder parts,* Hor., Liv.

Clŭpĕa (Clўpĕa) -ae, f. and plur. **Clŭpĕae** -ārum, f. (translation of Gr. Ἀσπίς), *a promontory and town in Byzacium in Africa.*

Clūsĭum -ii, n. *a town of Etruria.* Adj., **Clūsīnus** -a -um, *of Clusium.*

Clūsĭus -ii, m. (cludo), *the shutter,* epithet of Janus.

Clўmĕnē -ēs, f. (Κλυμένη), *the wife of the Aethiopian king Merops, and mother of Phaethon;* hence adj., **Clўmĕnēĭus** -a -um; proles, *Phaethon,* Ov.

clystēr -ēris, m. (κλυστήρ), 1, *a clyster,* Suet.; 2, *syringe,* Suet.

Clўtaemnestra -ae, f. (Κλυταιμνήστρα), *daughter of Leda, sister of Helen, Castor, and Pollux, wife of Agamemnon and mother of Orestes, Electra, and Iphigenia, slew her husband with the help of Aegisthus.*

Clўtĭē -ēs, f. (Κλυτίη), *daughter of Oceanus, beloved by Apollo, changed into the flower heliotropium.*

Cnĭdus (-ŏs), or **Gnĭdus** (-ŏs), -i, f. (Κνίδος), *a town in Caria, famed for the worship of Venus.* Adj., **Cnĭdĭus** -a -um, *Cnidian.*

cŏăcervātĭo -ōnis, f. (coacervo), *a heaping up* (of proofs), Cic.

cŏăcervo, 1. *to heap up, accumulate;* pecuniae coacervantur, Cic.; transf., argumenta, Cic.

cŏăcesco -ăcŭi, 3. *to become thoroughly sour;* ut enim non omne vinum, sic non omnis natura vetustate coacescit, Cic.; fig., quam valde eam (gentem Sardorum) putamus tot transfusionibus coacuisse, Cic.

cŏactĭo -ōnis, f. (cogo), *a collecting;* coactiones argentarias factitavit, Suet.

cŏacto, 1. (intens. of cogo), *to compel,* Lucr.

cŏactor -ōris, m. (cogo). I. Lit., a, *a collector of rents, money at auctions,* etc., Hor.; b, coactores agminis, *the rear-guard,* Tac. II. Transf., *one who compels,* Sen.

cŏactum -i, n. (cogo), *a coverlet of thick cloth,* Caes.

cŏactus -ūs, m. (cogo), *a compulsion, compelling;* coactu atque efflagitatu meo, Cic.

cŏaddo, 3. *to add in with,* Plaut.

cŏaedĭfĭco, 1. *to build on;* campum Martium, Cic.

cŏaequo, 1. *to level, make plain, even.* A. montes, Sall. B. Transf., omnia ad libidines suas, *placed on the same footing,* Cic.

cŏagmentātĭo -ōnis (coagmento), *a connection, binding together;* corporis, Cic.

cŏagmento, 1. (coagmentum), *to fix together, stick together, join together.* I. Lit., opus ipsa suum eadem, quae coagmentavit, natura dissolvit, Cic. II. Transf., verba compone et quasi coagmenta, Cic.; pacem, *to conclude,* Cic.

cŏagmentum -i, n. (cogo), *a joining together, a joint;* lapidum, Caes.

cŏāgŭlum -i, n. (cogo), 1, *that which causes to curdle, rennet,* Plin.; 2, meton., *curds,* Plin.

cŏălesco -ălŭi, -ălĭtum, 3. (com and alesco),

1, *to grow together, to become one in growth, to coalesce, unite*, saxa vides sola coalescere calce, Lucr, fig, sic brevi spatio novi veteresque (milites) coaluere, Sall, ut cum Patribus coalescant animi plebis, Liv; followed by in, in hunc consensum, Tac; 2, of plants, *to grow*, dum novus in viridi coalescit cortice ramus, Ov, *to take root*, grandis ilex coaluerat inter saxa, Sall, 3, of wounds, *to close, be healed, grow together*, fig, vixdum coalescens foventis regnum, Liv

cŏangusto, 1 *to narrow, limit, confine*, haec lex coangustari potest, Cic

coarcto, etc = coarto, etc. (q v)

cŏargŭo gŭi gūtum, but -gŭiturus, 3 (com and arguo), *to show in a clear light* **I.** Gen, *to demonstrate fully, to prove by evidence*; certum crimen multis suspicionibus, Cic, perfidiam alicuius, Cic, sin autem fuga laboris desidiam, repudiatio supplicum superbiam coarguit, Cic **II. A.** *to prove to be false*, 1, of things, id quidem coarguere nihil attinuere ratus, Liv, 2, *to prove a person to be wrong, to convict a person of an error, to confute*, quo (decreto) maxime et refelli et coargui potest, Cic **B.** *to prove a person to be guilty, to convict of a crime*, aliquem, Cic, with abl of means, criminibus coarguitur, Cic, with genit, of crime, aliquem avaritiae, Cic

cŏartātio -ōnis, f (coarto), *a drawing together, a confining* or *straightening in a small space*, Liv.

cŏarto, 1 *to confine, draw together* (opp laxare, dilatare) **A.** Lit, Thermopylarum saltum, ubi angustae fauces coartant iter, Liv **B.** Transf, 1, of discourse, *to compress, abbreviate*, ut quae coartavit, dilatet nobis, Cic, 2, of time, *to shorten*, consulatum aliorum, Tac

cŏaxo, 1 (onomatop), *to croak* (of a frog), Suet

coccĭnātus -a -um (coccinus), *clad in scarlet*, Suet.

coccĭnĕus a -um (coccum), *scarlet coloured*, Petr

coccĭnus -a -um (coccum), *scarlet coloured*, Juv Subst, **coccina** orum, n *scarlet clothes*, Mart

coccum -i, n (κοκκος) **A.** *the berry of the scarlet oak* (quercus coccifera, Linn) used as a scarlet dye by the ancients (the real source of the dye has since been discovered to be an insect), Plin. **B.** Meton, 1, *scarlet hue*, Hor, 2, *scarlet cloth* or *garments*, Suet.

cochlĕa -ae, f (κοχλιας) **A.** *a snail*, Cic **B.** Meton *the snail shell*, Mart

cochlĕar āris, n and **cochlĕārium** -ii, n Plin, and **cochlĕāre** -is, n Mart (cochlea), *a spoon*, Mart

Cocles -itis, m *the one-eyed man*, Plaut, esp Horatius Cocles, *the Roman who defended the bridge over the Tiber against the army of Porsena*

coctana = cottana (q v)

coctĭlis -e (coquo), *baked*, lateres, Varr, muri Babylonis, *made of burnt brick*, Ov

Cōcȳtŏs and ŭs, -i, m. (Κωκυτός, *the stream of wailing*), *a river of the Lower World* Adj, **Cōcȳtus** and **Cōcȳtius** -a -um, *Cocytian*, virgo, *Alecto*, Verg

cōda = cauda, (q v)

cōdex dicis m = caudex **I.** *the trunk of a tree*, Ov **II.** Meton, *a book, composed of wooden tablets, covered with wax* **A.** Gen, *a book, writing, document*, c falsus, Cic **B.** Esp, codex accepti et expensi, *an account book, a ledger* (adversaria, *a day-book*, the accounts from which were entered into the codex every month), in codicem referre, Cic

cōdĭcārius (caudĭcārius) -a -um (codex), *made of wooden blocks*, naves, Sall

cōdĭcilli ōrum, m (dim of codex), 1, *small tablets upon which to make memoranda*, in codicillis exarare, Cic, 2, *something written on tablets*, **a**, *a letter*, Cic, **b**, *a petition*, Tac, **c**, *a codicil*, Tac, **d**, *an imperial rescript or order*, Tac

Codrus -i, m (Κοδρος), *the last king of Athens, who was said to have voluntarily sought death in order to obtain victory for the Athenians over the Spartans*

Coelē Sўrĭa -ae, f (Κοιλη Συρια, *hollow Syria*), *the district between Libanus and Antilibanus*

coelebs = caelebs

coeles -itis, v caeles

coelestis e, v caelestis.

coelĭcŏla ae, v caelicola

coelifer, v caelifer

Coelius, v Caelius

coelo = caelo, q v.

coelum -i, v caelum

cŏĕmo ēmi emptum, 3 *to buy in large quantities, buy up*, te quae te delectarint coemisse, Cic

cŏemptio -ōnis, f (coemo), 1, *a form of marriage which consisted in a reciprocal sale of the parties to one another*, Cic, 2, *a fictitious marriage to enable a woman to acquire certain rights*, Cic

cŏemptiōnālis -e (coemptio), *relating to a coemptio*, senex, *an old man used for a fictitious marriage*, Cic

coena, &c, v cena

coenōsus a -um, v caenosus

coenŭla ae, f, v cenula

coenum, v caenum

cŏĕo -ii (rarely -ivi) -itum, 4 (com and eo), *to go together, come together, assemble* **I.** Gen, **A.** Of persons, 1, as friends, Capuae, Liv, 2, as enemies, *to engage* inter se coisse viros et cernere ferro, Verg **B.** Of things, vix memini nobis verba coisse decem, *that ten words have been exchanged between us*, Prop **II.** *to unite so as to form a whole, to combine* **A.** Of persons, 1, milit t t, coire inter se, Caes, in unum, Liv, in orbem, Liv, 2, *to unite in some relation*, **a**, politically, cum hoc tu coire ausus es, ut, etc, Cic, adversus rempublicam, Liv, with acc, societatem vel periculi vel laboris, Cic, in pass, societas coitur, Cic, **b**, *to unite in marriage*, hac gener atque socer coeant mercede suorum, Verg **B.** Of things, *to unite together*, 1, ut placidis coeant immitia, Hor, 2, of wounds, neve retractando nondum coeuntia rumpam vulnera, Ov, 3, *to curdle*, coit formidine sanguis, Verg 4, *to be frozen*, mentiar, an coeat duratus frigore pontus, Ov

coepĭo, coepi, coeptum, 3 (the present tenses very rare and only A Aug, the perfect tenses more commonly used), v transit and intransit (com and apio = apo) *to begin, commence* **I.** Transit, **A.** Act, coepit quum talia vates, Verg, dicere coepi, Cic, si quae rapinae fieri coeperunt, Cic, fut partic, coepturus, with acc, Romanos omnibus instructiores rebus coepturos bellum, Liv **B.** Pass, only in perf, lapides jaci coepti sunt, Caes, postquam armis disceptari coeptum sit, Cic, partic, coeptum bellum, Sall, nocte coepta, Tac **II.** Intransit, *to begin, arise*, quoniam coepit Graecorum mentio, Juv, ubi dies coepit, Sall.

coepto, 1. (intens. of coepi). **A.** Transit. *to begin* or *undertake eagerly;* with infin., coercere seditionem, Tac.; appetere ea, Cic. **B.** Intransit., coeptantem conjurationem disjecit, Tac.

coeptum -i, n. (coepi), *a beginning, undertaking,* Liv.

coeptus -ūs, m. (coepi), *a beginning, undertaking,* Cic.

coēpŭlōnus -i, m. *a fellow-reveller,* Plaut.

cŏercĕo -cŭi -citum, 2. (com and arceo). **I.** Gen., *to enclose on all sides and hold fast, to encompass, enclose;* mundus omnia complexu suo coercet et continet, Cic. **II.** Esp., **1,** *to confine, restrain;* (aqua) jubetur coerceri, Cic.; quibus (operibus) intra muros coercetur hostis, Liv.; **2,** *to keep in order;* virgā levem aureā turbam, Hor.; **3,** *to prune;* vitem ferro amputans coercet, Cic.; **4,** *to check, curb;* cupiditates, Cic.; seditionem, Liv.; **5,** *to punish;* magistratus noxium civem multā, vinculis verberibusque coerceto, Cic.

coërcĭtĭo -ōnis, f. (coerceo), **1,** *a confining, restraining;* profusarum cupiditatum, Tac.; **2,** *punishing;* magistratus, Liv.

coeruleus = caeruleus (q.v.).

coetus -ūs, m. (for coitus, from coeo). **I.** *a meeting together,* Lucr. **II.** *a meeting, assemblage;* in a bad sense, *a seditious meeting;* coetus nocturni, Liv.; coetum or coetus celebrare, *to assemble in large numbers,* Verg., Cic. poet.

Coeus -i, m. (Κοῖος), *a Titan, father of Latona.*

cōgĭtātē, adv. (cogitatus, from cogito), *carefully, thoughtfully, with consideration;* scribere, Cic.

cōgĭtātĭo -ōnis, f. (cogito), *thinking.* **I.** Gen., **A.** Act., **a,** *the act of thinking, conception;* dicebas, speciem dei percipi cogitatione, non sensu, Cic.; ea quae cogitatione depingimus, Cic.; **b,** *reflection, meditation, consideration, reasoning;* ad hanc causam non sine aliqua spe et cogitatione venerunt, Cic.; ad reliquam cogitationem belli se recepit, Caes. **B.** Pass., *a thought, idea;* num ullam cogitationem habuisse videantur ii, etc., Cic.; esp. in plur., mandare litteris cogitationes suas, Cic.; posteriores enim cogitationes sapientiores solent esse, Cic. **II.** Esp., **1,** *a thinking of, intention, design;* accusationis cogitatio, Cic.; **2,** pass., *a thought, plan, purpose;* minor cogitatio intervenit majori, Liv.; magnae cogitationis manifestis, Tac.; **3,** *the faculty of thought and reflection;* homo solus particeps rationis et cogitationis, Cic.

cōgĭtātus -a -um (partic. of cogito). Subst., **cōgĭtāta** -ōrum, n. *thoughts, reflections, ideas,* Cic.

cōgĭto, 1. (co-igito, for com and agito), *to put together in the mind, to think, reflect, consider.* **A.** Gen., cui vivere est cogitare, Cic.; with acc., beneficia alicuius, Cic.; Scipionem, Cic.; with acc. and infin., homines ea si bis accidere posse non cogitant, Cic.; with de and the abl., de deo, Cic.; with relative sentence, cogita qui sis, Cic.; with ad and the acc., ad haec igitur cogita, Cic.; with ut or ne and the subj., Caes. **B. a,** *to think of, intend, plan;* nihil cogitant nisi caedes, nisi incendia, Caes.; qui noceri alteri cogitat, Cic.; de parricidio, Cic.; ellipt. (in letters), inde ad Taurum cogitabam, *I intended to go,* Cic.; **b,** *to be disposed to;* si humaniter et sapienter et amabiliter in me cogitare vis, Cic.

cognātĭo -ōnis, f. (com and gnascor = nascor). **I.** Lit., *relationship, connexion by blood.* **A.** Lit., cognatio quae mihi tecum est, Cic.; cognatione cum aliquo conjunctum esse, Cic.; aliquem cognatione attingere, Cic. **B.** Meton., *persons related, kindred, family;* cognationis magnae homo, *with a large connexion,* Caes. **II.** Transf., *connexion, agreement, resemblance;* studiorum et artium, Cic.

cognātus -a -um (gnatus = natus, from nascor). **A.** *related, connected by blood,* Cic. Subst., **cognātus** -i, m., **cognāta** -ae, f. *a relation either on the father* or *mother's side,* Cic. **B.** Transf., *related, similar, cognate;* nihil est tam cognatum mentibus nostris quam numeri, Cic.

cognĭtĭo -ōnis, f. (cognosco). **I.** *knowledge,* **A.** *knowledge of* or *acquaintance with a thing* or *person;* aliquem cognitione atque hospitio dignum habere, Cic. **B.** *knowledge of, study of;* **1,** gen., cognitio contemplatioque naturae, Cic.; plur., meton., *an idea, a conception;* insitas deorum vel potius innatas cognitiones habemus, Cic.; **2,** legal t. t., *a legal investigation;* consulibus cognitionem dare, Cic.; cognitionem de existimatione alicuius constituere, Cic. **II.** = agnitio, *recognition,* Ter.

cognĭtor -ōris, m. (cognosco). **I.** Legal t. t., **1,** *a witness to the identity of a Roman citizen in a foreign country,* Cic. **II. 1,** *the procurator* or *attorney who took charge of an action at law,* Cic.; transf., huius sententiae, *voucher for,* Cic.; **2,** *a kind of public prosecutor in fiscal matters,* Ov.

cognĭtus -a -um, p. adj. with compar. and superl. (from cognosco), *known, tried, proved;* homo virtute cognitā, Cic.

cognōmĕn -inis, n. (com and gnomen = nomen). **A.** *a surname, family name, the name following the name of the* gens (e.g., Cicero); alicui cognomen Coriolano or Capitoni est, Cic., Liv.; cognomen habere sapientis, Cic.; cognomen sumere or trahere or sibi arripere ex aliqua re, Cic. **B.** *name of a place;* Hesperiam Graji cognomine dicunt, Verg.

cognōmentum -i, n. **1,** *a surname,* Plaut.; **2,** *a name,* Tac.

cognōmĭnātus -a -um (com and nominatus) = συνώνυμος, *of the same meaning;* verba, *synonyms.*

cognōmĭnis -e (cognomen), *having the same name;* gaudet cognomine terra, Verg.; with dat., cognomine Insubribus pago, Liv.

cognōmĭno, 1. (cognomen), *to give a surname to, call by a surname,* Varr.

cognosco -gnōvi -gnĭtum (com and gnosco = nosco), 3. *to become acquainted with, remark, notice, perceive, see;* and in the perf. tenses, *to know.* **I.** Gen., with acc., cognoscere naturam rerum, Cic.; aliquem bene cognovisse, Cic.; with abl. of means, aliquid experiendo magis quam discendo, Cic.; with per, homo per se cognitus, Cic.; with ab or ex, aliquem ex litteris alicuius, Cic.; with two accusatives, aliquem hominem pudentem et officiosum, Cic.; with acc. and infin., Attici nostri te valde studiosum esse cognovi, Cic.; abl. absol., cognito, *it being known,* cognito vivere Ptolemaeum, Liv.; with relative sentence, cognoscite nunc, quae potestas decemviris et quanta detur, Cic. **II. a,** *to recognise;* quum eum Syracusis amplius centum cives Romani cognoscerent, Cic.; **b,** *to study;* Demosthenem totum, Cic.; **c,** of judges, *to hear, decide;* causa cognita, Cic.; cognoscere de actis Caesaris, Cic.

cōgo, cŏēgi, cŏactum, 3. (coigo for com and ago). **I.** *to bring, drive,* or *draw to one point, to collect.* **A.** Lit., **a,** pecudes stabulis, Verg.; esp. as milit. t. t., exercitum magnasque copias, Caes.; **b,** political t. t., *to assemble a public body;* senatum, Cic.; judices, Cic.; comitium, Caes.; **c,** *to bring together* gifts or money; pecuniam ex decumis, Cic.; **d,** *to unite, gather together;* nubes imbres ventique coguntur, Cic.;

of liquids, or of a thin material, *to thicken;* ingoro mella cogit hiems, Verg, lac coactum, *curdled,* Ov., subst., **cŏacta** -ōrum, n *thick woven cloth, felt,* Caes; e, milit t t., agmen cogere, *to bring up the rear,* Caes, fig, *to be the last,* ut nec duces simus nec agmen cogamus, Cic **B.** Transf, a, *to unite, collect,* jus civile in certa genera, Cic; b, *to infer, conclude, prove;* hoc cogere volebat falsas litteras esse, Cic. **II.** *to drive, force into a narrow space* **A.** Lit., a, vi et necessario sumus in portum coacti, Cic; b, of liquids and places, *to confine,* in artissimas ripas Aous cogitur amnis, Liv **B.** Transf; a, *to force,* Boios in jus judiciumque populi Romani, Liv, b, *to compel to do something;* aliquem ad militiam, Sall.; with infin., te emere coegit, Cic; with ut and the subj, cogere incipit eos ut absentem Heraclium condemnarent, Cic., with acc of the thing one is compelled to do, cogere cives id omnes, Cic, partic, coactus, *constrained,* invitus et coactus, Cic.

cŏhaerentĭa -ae, f (cohaereo), *a coherence, connexion;* mundi, Cic.

cŏhaerĕo -haesi -haesum, 2 **I. A.** *to adhere to, hang together, be closely connected with,* cohaerens cum corpore membrum, Cic, nec equo mea membra cohaerent, Ov **B.** Transf, haec ratio pecuniarum implicita est cum illis pecuniis Asiaticis et cohaeret, Cic **II. A.** *to have coherence, subsist, hold together,* mundus ita apte cohaeret, ut dissolvi nullo modo queat, Cic **B** Transf, vix diserti adolescentis cohaerebat oratio, Cic.

cŏhaeresco -haesi, 3 (inchoat of cohaereo), *to hang together, mutually adhere,* atomi inter se cohaerentes, Cic

cŏhērēs ēdis, m *a coheir,* Cic

cŏhĭbĕo -ŭi -ĭtum, 2. (com and habeo) **I.** *to hold, contain, hold together,* brachium togā, Cic, omnes naturas ipsa (natura) cohibet et continet, Cic **II.** *to confine, restrain* **A.** Lit, ventos carcere, Ov, crinem nodo, *to tie,* Hor **B.** Transf, *to hinder, hold back, control, repress,* conatus alicuius, Cic; manum, oculos, animum ab auro gazaque regia, Cic; foll by quominus and the subj, Tac

cŏhŏnesto, 1 (com and honesto), *to honour* or *reverence,* statuas, Cic

cŏhorresco -horrŭi, 3 (com and horresco), *to shudder* or *shiver,* quo (sudore) quum cohorruisset, Cic, esp, *to shudder from fright, to be horrified at;* quem ut agnovi, equidem cohorrui, Cic.

cŏhors (cors, chors) -tis, f (connected with χόρτος) **I.** *an enclosure for cattle,* Ov **II.** Meton, **A.** *a troop, throng;* fratrum stipata, Verg; febrium, Hor **B.** Esp milit t t, 1, *a cohort, a division of the Roman army, being the tenth part of a legion,* Caes, often = *the auxiliary forces of the allies,* Sall, 2, praetoria cohors, a, *a body guard for the general,* Caes; b, *the retinue of the governor of a province,* Cic

cŏhortātĭo ōnis, f (cohortor), *an exhortation, encouragement,* cohortatio quaedam judicum ad honeste judicandum, Cic.

cŏhortĭcŭla -ae, f (dim of cohors), *a little cohort,* ap Cic

cŏhortor, 1 dep (com and hortor), *to encourage, incite, exhort;* used esp of the general's speech to his soldiers before a battle, aliquem ad virtutis studium, Cic, exercitum more militari ad pugnam, Caes; foll by ut or ne with the subj, or by the subj alone, Cic, Caes, with ad and the gerund, aliquem ad honorandum Serv Sulpicium, Cic

cŏinquino, 1 no perf, *to pollute, defile.* Col

cŏitĭo -ōnis, f (coeo), **1,** *a coming together, meeting,* Ter; **2,** *a faction, party, coalition, conspiracy,* suspicio coitionis, Cic, coitiones tribunorum adversus nobilium juventutem ortae, Liv.

cŏĭtus -ūs, m (coeo), *a coming together, union, connexion,* Ov

cŏlăphus -i, m (κόλαφος), *a box on the ear;* colapho icere, or ferire aliquem, Plaut, Nep

Colchis -ĭdis, f (Κολχίς), *Colchis, a country on the eastern shore of the Black Sea,* hence adj, **Colchis** -ĭdis, f *Colchian,* and used subst = *Medea,* Hor., **Colchus** -a -um, *Colchian,* venena (of Medea), Ov Subst, **Colchus** -i, m *a Colchian,* and appell = *a barbarian,* Hor

cŏlēns -entis, p adj (colo), *honouring, reverent,* qui sunt religionum colentes (cives), Cic

cōlĕus -i, m *a testicle,* Cic

cōlĭphia (colyphia) -ōrum, n *a kind of nourishing food used by wrestlers,* Juv.

cōlis = caulis (q v)

collăbasco, 3 (com and labasco), *to begin to fall, to totter,* Plaut

collăbĕfacto, 1 (com and labefacto), *to cause to totter,* Ov, used also of the liquefaction of hard bodies, Lucr.

collăbĕfīo -factus -fĭĕri (com and labefacio) **A.** Lit, *to be made to totter* or *fall,* altera (navis), praefracto rostro tota collabefieret, *was dashed to pieces,* igni collabefacta, *melted,* Lucr **B.** Transf, a Themistocle collabefactus, *overthrown,* Nep

collābor -lapsus sum, -lābi, dep. (com and labor), *to fall down, sink down, collapse,* a, of buildings, towns, etc, collapsa quaedam ruinis sunt, Liv, b, of persons, *to fall down in a swoon* or *death,* cecidit collapsus in artus, Verg.

collăcĕrātus -a -um (com and lacero), *very much lacerated* or *torn,* corpus, Tac.

collăcrĭmātĭo -ōnis, f (collacrimo), *a weeping,* Cic

collăcrĭmo, 1 (com and lacrimo), *to break out into tears,* Cic, with acc *to bemoan, weep for very much,* histrio casum meum totiens collacrimavit, Cic

collactĕus -i, m **-a** -ae, f *a foster-brother,* or *sister,* Juv

collāre -is, n (collum), *an iron collar* or *chain for the neck,* Plaut

Collātĭa -ae, f *town of the Sabines near Rome;* hence, **Collātīnus** -a -um, *belonging to Collatia, surname of L Tarquinius, the husband of Lucretia, native of Collatia*

collātĭo -ōnis, f (confero) **A.** Lit *a bringing together,* a, signorum, *a hostile collision in the field,* Cic, b, *a contribution, collection,* stipis aut decimae, Liv, *a present for the emperor,* Tac **B.** Transf *comparison, simile,* collatio est oratio rem cum re ex similitudine conferens, Cic

collātīvus a -um (collatus), *brought together, united,* venter, *swollen,* Plaut

collātor -ōris, m (confero), *a contributor,* Plaut

collātus -a um, partic of confero

collaudātĭo -ōnis, f (collaudo), *strong,* or *hearty praise,* Cic

collaudo, 1 (com and laudo), *to praise very much,* orationem satis multis verbis, Cic

collaxo, 1 (com and laxo), *to widen, extend,* Lucr

collecta -ae, f (collectus, from 1 colligo), *a contribution in money,* collectam a conviva exigere, Cic

collectīcĭus (collectitius) -a -um (1 colligo), *gathered together;* exercitus, *quickly levied*, Cic.

collectĭo -ōnis, f. (1. colligo). **I.** *a collecting, gathering together, collection;* membrorum, Cic. **II.** Transf., **1,** in rhetoric, *a brief recapitulation*, Cic.; **2,** in logic, *a conclusion, inference*, Sen.

collectus -a -um, p. adj. with compar. and superl. (1. colligo), *contracted, concise, concentrated;* dicendi genus, Tac.

collēga -ae, m. (com and lēgo), **1,** *one who is deputed with another, a colleague, partner in office;* alicuius collegam in questura fuisse, Cic.; **2,** *a comrade*, Juv.

collēgĭum -ii, n. (collega). **I.** Abstract, *colleagueship, the connexion between colleagues, between those who jointly fill the same office;* P. Decius per tot collegia expertus, Liv. **II.** Concrete, *persons united in colleagueship, a body, guild, corporation, college;* **a,** of magistrates, praetorum, tribunorum, Cic.; **b,** of priests, pontificum, augurum, Cic.; **c,** *a political club;* innumerabilia quaedam collegia ex omni faece urbis ac servitio constituta, Cic.; **d,** *a trade guild;* mercatorum, Liv.; **e,** *a band, body;* ambubajarum, Hor.

collībertus -i, m. (com and libertus), *a fellow freedman*, Cic.

collĭbet, or **collŭbet** -būit or -bĭtum est, 2. (com and lubet or libet), impers. *it pleases, is agreeable;* simul ac mihi collibitum sit de te cogitare, Cic.

collīdo -līsi -līsum (com and laedo), 3. *to strike together, dash together;* **1,** humor ita mollis est, ut facile comprimi collidique possit, Cic.; **2,** pass. *to come into hostile collision;* Graecia barbariae lento collisa duello, Hor.

collĭgātĭo -ōnis, f. (2. colligo), *a binding together, connexion;* causarum omnium, Cic.

1. **collĭgo** -lēgi -lectum, 3. (com and lĕgo), *to bring together, collect.* **I.** Lit., **a,** radices, Cic.; vasa, *to pack up*, Liv.; **b,** *to bring together, assemble;* ex agris ingentem numerum perditorum hominum, Cic.; milites, Cic.; **c,** *to gather into a smaller space, contract;* se colligere or colligi in arma, *to cover oneself with a shield*, Verg. **II.** Transf., **a,** *to gather together;* multa in conventu vitia in aliquem, Cic.; **b,** *to gain, acquire;* ex hoc labore magnam gratiam magnamque dignitatem, Cic.; **c,** colligere se, or animum, or mentem, *to compose oneself, gain courage;* se ex timore, Caes.; **d,** in speech, *to bring together, tell of;* omnia bella civilia, Cic.; **e,** *to think of;* quum maximarum civitatum veteres animo calamitates colligo, Cic.; **f,** of numbers, *to reckon;* centum et viginti anni ab interitu Ciceronis in hunc diem colliguntur, Tac.; **g,** *to infer, conclude;* bene etiam colligit haec pueris et mulierculis esse grata, Cic.

2. **collĭgo,** 1. (com and ligo), *to bind, tie, fasten together.* **I. A.** Lit., manus, Cic. **B.** Transf., **a,** *to connect;* (mens) homines antea dissociatos jucundissimo inter se sermonis vinculo colligavit, Cic.; gen. in pass., res omnes inter se aptae colligataeque, Cic.; **b,** *to join together in writing;* ut verbis colligentur sententiae, Cic.; **c,** *to join politically;* se cum multis, Cic.; **d,** *to detain;* aliquem in Graecia, Cic. **II.** *to bind together* the parts of a thing. **A.** Lit., omne colligatum solvi potest, Cic. **B.** Transf., **a,** *to join together* in narration; septingentorum annorum memoriam uno libro, Cic.; **b,** *to hinder, stop;* impetum furentis vitae suae periculo, Cic.

collīnĕo, 1. (com and lineo), *to direct in a straight line;* hastam aut sagittam, Cic.; absol., quis est enim qui totum diem jaculans non aliquando collineet, *hits the mark*, Cic.

collĭno -levi -litum, 3. (com and lino), *to besmear, daub;* aliquid aliqua re, Hor.

collīnus -a -um (collis). **I.** *hilly, relating to a hill, situate on a hill.* **II.** Esp. **Collīnus,** *of or on the Quirinal hill;* tribus, Cic.; esp., porta Collina, *a gate of Rome near the Quirinal Hill*, Liv.; herbae, *growing near the Porta Collina*, Prop.

collĭquĕfactus -a -um (com and liquefio), *liquefied, melted*, Cic.

collis -is, m. *a hill, high ground*, Cic.

collŏcātĭo -ōnis, f. (colloco). **I.** Act., *a placing*, esp. *a giving in marriage;* filiae, Cic. **II.** Pass., *a position;* **a,** siderum, Cic.; **b,** rhet. t. t., *position, arrangement, order;* verborum, Cic.; argumentorum, Cic.; bene structam collocationem dissolvere, Cic.

collŏco (con-loco), 1. *to place, lay, set.* **I.** Gen. **A.** Lit., **1,** tabulas bene pictas in bono lumine, Cic.; simulacrum Victoriae ante ipsam Minervam, Caes.; aliquem in curru, Cic.; **2,** milit. t.t., *to station;* duas legiones et omnia auxilia in summo jugo, Caes.; alicui insidias ante fundum suum, Cic. **B.** Transf., **1,** *to place, lay, put;* res eae, quae agentur aut dicentur, suo loco collocandae, Cic.; **2,** *to place, cause to rest;* in aliquo magnam spem dignitatis suae, *to build hopes on*, Cic.; **3,** of time, *to pass;* adolescentiam suam in amore atque voluptatibus, Cic. **II.** Esp. **A.** Lit., **1,** *to set up in a particular place, erect;* sedes ac domicilium, Cic.; **2,** chlamydem, ut pendeat apte, *to arrange*, Ov.; **3,** of persons, *to settle, station;* in eius tetrarchia unum ex Graecis comitibus suis, Cic.; colonias, Cic.; milit. t.t. *to billet, quarter;* exercitum in Aulercis Lexoviisque in hibernis, Caes.; **4,** *to settle in possession or property;* aliquem in patrimonio suo, Cic. **B.** Transf., **1,** *to place;* aliquem in amplissimo consilio et in altissimo gradu dignitatis, Cic.; **2,** of women, *to settle in marriage;* aliquam in matrimonium, Cic.; alicuius filio filiam suam, Cic.; **3,** of money, *to invest;* pecuniam in praediis collocare, Cic.; or *to employ, spend;* patrimonium in reipublicae salute, Cic.; **4,** *to arrange in proper order;* verba diligenter collocata, Cic.; **5,** *to direct, manage;* rem militarem, Cic.

collŏcŭplēto, 1. (com and locupleto), *to enrich exceedingly*, Ter.

collŏcūtĭo -ōnis, f. (colloquor), *conversation;* collocutiones familiarissimae cum aliquo, Cic.

collŏquĭum -ii, n. (colloquor), *talk, conversation, colloquy, conference;* colloquia secreta serere cum aliquo, Liv.; clandestina colloquia cum hostibus, Cic.; colloquium expetere, Caes.; dare, Liv.; crebra colloquia inter se habere, Caes.; per colloquia de pace agere, Caes.; aliquem ad colloquium evocare, Cic.; ad colloquium congredi, Liv.; dirimere, Caes.; interrumpere, Caes.; in alicuius congressum colloquiumque pervenire, Cic.

collŏquor -cūtus or -quūtus sum, -loqui (com and loquor), 3. dep. *to speak, talk, converse with any one, to treat* or *negotiate with;* cum aliquo, Cic.; inter se, Cic.; cum aliquo per litteras, Cic.

collūcĕo, 2. (com and luceo), *to shine on all sides, to be completely illuminated.* **I.** Lit., sol qui tam longe lateque colluceat, Cic.; collucent moenia flammis, Verg. **II.** Transf., vidi collucere omnia furtis tuis, Cic.

collūdo -lūsi -lūsum, 3. (com and ludo). **A.** Lit. *to play with;* paribus, Hor. **B.** Transf. *to have a secret understanding with another person, to act collusively*, Cic.

collum -i, n. (**collus** -i, m.), *the neck;* **1,** of men and animals, in collum invasit, *fell on his neck*, Cic , collum torquere, *to drag before a tribunal, or to prison*, Liv , posuit collum in pulvere, Hor , **2,** *the neck* of a bottle, Phaedr ; of a poppy, Verg

collŭo -lŭi -lūtum, 3 (com and luo), *to wash thoroughly, rinse*, os, Plin , ora, *to quench the thirst*, Ov

collus i, m = collum (q v)

collūsĭo -ōnis, f (colludo), *collusion, a secret understanding*, cum aliquo, Cic

collūsor ōris, m (colludo), **a,** *a play fellow*, Juv , **b,** *a fellow-gambler*, Cic

collustro, 1 (com and lustro) **A.** *to illuminate on all sides;* sol omnia clarissimā luce collustrans, Cic ; in picturis alios opaca, alios collustrata delectant, *brilliant colouring*, Cic **B.** Transf , *to survey, look at on all sides*, omnia oculis, Cic

collŭtŭlento, 1, *to dirty or defile all over*, Plaut

collŭvĭo ōnis, and **collŭvĭēs** -ēi, f (colluo) **A.** *a flowing together, or collection of impurities, filth*, Plin **B.** Transf , *rabble, medley, offscourings*, omnium scelerum, Cic , quum ex hac turba et colluvione discedam, Cic

collȳbus -i, m (κόλλυβος) **A.** *the agio or percentage charged in money changing*, Cic. **B.** Transf , *the money changer s occupation*, Cic

collȳra ae, f (κολλυρα), *a kind of cake or bun which was broken into broth*, Plaut

collȳrĭcus -a -um, jus *the broth with which the collyra was eaten*, Plaut

collȳrĭum ii, n (κολλυριον), *eye salve*, Hor

cŏlo, cŏlui, cultum, 3 **I. 1,** *to cultivate, till the ground, farm*, agrum, Cic , praedia studiose Cic , vitem, Cic , **2,** *to dwell in a place, inhabit*, urbem, Cic , insulas, Liv absol , circa utramque ripam Rhodani, Liv **II. 1,** *to take care of, attend to;* formam augere colendo, Ov , **2,** *to cultivate, practise, study*, studium philosophiae a prima adolescentia, Cic , fidem, virtutem, sapientiam, Cic ; **3,** *to pay respect to*, **a,** of deities, *to worship*, deos, Cic , Musarum delubra, Cic , templum miro honore, Verg ; **b,** of men, *to honour, reverence, court*, aliquem summā observantiā, Cic

cŏlŏcāsĭa ae, f and **cŏlŏcāsĭum** -ii, n (κολοκασια), *the Egyptian bean*, Verg

cŏlōna -ae, f (colonus), *a country woman*, Ov

Cŏlōnae ārum, f (Κολωναί), *a town in Troas*

Cŏlōnēus -a -um, *belonging to the Attic deme Colonos;* Oedipus Coloneus, *a tragedy of Sophocles*

cŏlōnĭa -ae, f (colonus) **I.** *a farm, estate*, Col **II.** *a colony* **A.** Lit , constituere coloniam, Cic , colonos deducere in colonias, Cic **B.** Meton , *the colonists*, deducere, Cic ; mittere in locum, Cic

cŏlōnĭcus a um (colonus), **1,** *relating or belonging to agriculture or a farm*, leges, Varr , **2,** *relating or belonging to a colony, colonial*, cohortes, *levied in Roman colonies*, Caes

cŏlōnus i, m (colo), **1,** *a farmer, agriculturist*, Cic , **2,** *a colonist, inhabitant of a colony*, Cic , poet. transf = *inhabitant*, Verg

Cŏlŏphōn -ōnis, f (Κολοφών), *one of the twelve Ionian towns on the coast of Lydia, famed for its cavalry* Adj , **Cŏlŏphōnĭăcus** -a -um, **Cŏlŏphōnĭus** a -um, *Colophonian*

cŏlor (colos) -ōris, m (colo) **I.** Lit , **A.** Gen *colour, tint, hue*, Cic , colorem ducere, of the grape, *to become coloured*, Verg **B.** Esp **1,** *complexion*, verus, *real*, Ter.; fucatus, *artificial*, Hor , mutare, *to change colour*, Hor , Ov.; **2,** *beautiful complexion, beauty;* nimium ne crede colori, Verg **II.** Transf , **1,** *outward show, external appearance*, civitatis, Cic , **2,** esp of oratory or speech, *cast, character, tone* color urbanitatis, Cic **3,** *ornament, embellishment* flos et color pigmentorum, Cic , **4,** *an artful excuse, or colouring of a questionable action*, Juv

cŏlōrātus -a um (partic of coloro), **1,** *coloured*, arcus, Cic , **2,** *red, embrowned*, Tac

cŏlōro, 1 (color) **A.** Lit , *to colour*, **a,** corpora, Cic , **b,** *to tan* (of the sun), quum in sole ambulem naturā fit ut colorer, Cic **B.** Transf , *to give tone or colour to style*, urbanitate quadam quasi colorata oratio, Cic

cŏlossēus -a -um (κολοσσαῖος) *colossal, gigantic*, Plin

cŏlossĭcus a um (κολοσσικος), *colossal, gigantic*, Plin

cŏlossus -i m (κολοσσος) *a colossus, a statue larger than life*, esp applied to the gigantic statue of Apollo at the entrance of the harbour of Rhodes, Plin

cŏlostra -ae, f (**cŏlostra** -ōrum, n), *the first milk after calving, biestings*, Mart , used as a term of endearment, Plaut

cŏlŭber bri, m *a serpent, snake*, Verg , Ov

cŏlŭbra -ae, f *a female serpent, a snake* Hor

cŏlŭbrĭfer fĕra fĕrum (coluber and fero), *snake bearing, snaky-haired*, epithet of Medusa, Ov

cŏlŭbrīnus a -um (coluber), *snake like; transf , cunning, wily*, Plaut

cōlum -i, n *a colander, sieve, strainer*, Verg

cŏlumba -ae, f (columbus), *a pigeon, dove*, Cic , Cythereiades (as sacred to Venus), Ov

cŏlumbar āris, n (columba), *a kind of collar for slaves like a pigeon hole*, Plaut

cŏlumbīnus a -um (columba), *relating or belonging to a pigeon*, pulli, Cic.

cŏlumbŭlus i, m (dim of columbus), *a little pigeon*, Plin

cŏlumbus i, m *a male dove or pigeon*, Hor

1 **cŏlŭmella** ae, f (dim of columna), *a little column*, Cic

2 **Cŏlŭmella** ae, m L Junius Moderatus, *a Roman writer upon agriculture, native of Cadiz, contemporary of Seneca and Celsus.*

cŏlŭmen inis, n (* cello, *that which is raised on high*) **I.** *a height* **A.** Lit , sub altis Phrygiae columinibus, *mountains*, Cat **B.** Transf , of persons, *the chief, most distinguished*, columen amicorum Antonii Cotyla Varius, Cic **II.** *a pillar* **A.** Lit , Cic poet **B.** Transf , columen reipublicae, *support*, Cic

cŏlumna ae, f (connected with columen), *a pillar, column* **A.** Lit , marmorea, Cic , prov , incurrere amentem in columnas, *to run one s head against a stone wall*, Cic , columna rostrata, *a column adorned with beaks of ships erected in honour of the victory of Duilius over the Carthaginians*, Quint , columna Maenia, *a pillar in the Roman forum to which thieves and slaves were tied to receive punishment*, Cic ; hence, adhaerescere ad columnam, Cic , ad columnam pervenire, Cic , columnae, *the pillars in Rome round which books were exposed for sale*, Hor , columnae Protei, *the boundaries of Egypt* (columns being used to mark boundaries), Verg , columnae Herculis, *the mountains of Calpe and Abyla at the straits of Gibraltar*, Plin. **B.** Transf , **a,** *a support, pillar of the state*, injurioso ne pede proruas stantem columnam, Hor ; **b,** *a water-spout*, Lucr

cŏlumnārĭus -a -um (columna), *belonging*

to a pillar. Subst., **1, cŏlumnārĭi** -ōrum, m. *those who have been punished at the* columna Maenia (v. columna), *rascals, thieves*, ap. Cic.; **2, cŏlumnārĭum** -ĭi, n. *a tax on pillars*, Cic.

cŏlumnātus -a -um (columna), *supported on columns*, Varr.; os, *resting on the hand*, Plaut.

cŏlurnus -a -um (for corulnus, from corulus), *made of hazel wood;* hastilia, Verg.

cŏlus -i and -ūs, abl. colo, f. (m. Cat., Ov.), *a distaff*, Cic.

com, old Latin = cum, in classical Latin; only found in composition.

cŏma -ae, f. (κόμη). **A.** Lit., *the hair of the head*, Cic. **B.** Transf., **1,** *the leaves of trees*, Hor.; **2,** *the wool of sheep*, ap. Cic.

cŏmans -antis (coma), *hairy;* colla equorum, Verg.; galea, *crested*, Verg.; stella, *a comet*, Ov.; narcissus sera comans, *covered with leaves*, Verg.

cōmarchus -i, m. (κώμαρχος), *the mayor or chief officer of a village*, Plaut.

cŏmātus -a -um (coma), **1,** *hairy*, Mart.; comata Gallia = *Transalpina*, Plin.; **2,** silva, *in full leaf*, Cat.

1. **combĭbo** -bĭbi, 3. *to drink in, suck up, imbibe.* **A.** Lit., venenum corpore, Hor. **B.** Fig., quas (artes) si dum est tener combiberit, Cic.

2. **combĭbo** -ōnis, m. *a boon companion, comrade in drinking*, Cic.

Combultĕrĭa -ae, f. *town of the Samnites on the south-west borders of Campania.*

combūro -bussi -bustum, 3. (com and uro). **A.** Lit., *to burn up, consume entirely;* libros, Caes.; aliquem vivum, Cic.; of the burning of the dead, aliquem in foro, Cic. **B.** Transf., aliquem judicio, *to ruin*, Cic.; diem, *to consume in revelling*, Plaut.

combustum -i, n. *a burn* or *scald*, Plin.

Cōmē -ēs, f. (κώμη, *village*). **I.** Hiera Come, *a place in Caria.* **II.** Xyline Come, *a place in Pisidia.* **III.** Antoridos Come, *a place in Phrygia.*

cŏmĕdo -ēdi -ēsum (-essum) or -estum, 3. *to eat up, consume entirely.* **A.** Lit., ex se natos (of Saturn), Cic. **B.** Transf., aliquem oculis, *to devour with one's eyes*, Mart.; se, *to consume oneself in grief*, Cic. **C.** *to consume, waste, squander;* patrimonium, Cic.

cŏmes -ĭtis, c. (com and eo or meo), **1,** *a companion, comrade, associate;* seditionum, Tac.; fugae, Cic.; victoriae, Caes.; esse comitem alicuius, Cic.; aliquem comitem habere, Cic.; non praebere se comitem illius furoris sed ducem, Cic.; used of things and abstractions, mortis comes gloria, Cic.; **2,** esp. *an attendant;* **a,** *the attendant* or *tutor of a boy*, Verg.; **b,** plur., comites, *the retinue which accompanied a Roman magistrate into his province*, and generally, *any body of attendants;* comites omnes magistratuum, Cic.; in later times, *the body of courtiers, the imperial court*, Suet.

cŏmētēs -ae, m. (κομήτης), *a comet*, Cic.

cōmĭcē, adv. (comicus), *in the manner of comedy;* comice res tragicas tractare, Cic.

cōmĭcus -a -um (κωμικός). **A.** Adj., **a,** *relating to comedy, comic;* poeta, Cic.; **b,** *represented in comedy;* senes, Cic.; adolescens, Cic. **B.** Subst., **a,** *an actor in comedy*, Plaut.; **b,** *a comic poet*, Cic.

cominus = comminus (q.v.).

cōmis -e (como), *courteous, kind, friendly, obliging, amiable;* **a,** of persons, dominus, Cic.; in amicis tuendis, Cic.; erga aliquem, Cic.; **b,** of things, comi hospitio accipi, Liv.; sermo, Tac.

cōmissābundus -a -um (comissor), *revelling, rioting;* temulento agmine per Indiam comissabundus incessit, Liv.

cōmmissātĭo -ōnis, f. (comissor), *a revel, riotous feasting*, Cic.

cōmissātor -ōris, m. (comissor), *a reveller, riotous feaster*, Cic.; transf., comissatores conjurationis, *accomplices*, Cic.

cōmissor (κωμάζω), 1, dep. *to make a joyful procession with music and dancing, to revel, feast riotously;* comissatum ire ad aliquem, Liv.; comissari in domum Pauli, Hor.

cōmĭtas -ātis, f. (comis), *courtesy, friendliness, obligingness, civility* (opp. gravitas, severitas); comitas affabilitasque sermonis, Cic.

cŏmĭtātus -ūs, m. (comitor), **1,** *attendance, companionship;* optimorum et clarissimorum civium, Cic.; transf., tanto virtutum comitatu (opus est), Cic.; **2,** *a train, retinue, following;* praedonis improbissimi societas atque comitatus, Cic.; esp. **a,** in imperial times, *the court, imperial suite*, Tac.; **b,** *a caravan, convoy;* magnus, Caes.

cōmĭtĕr, adv. (comis), *courteously, civilly, kindly, affably*, Cic.

cŏmĭtĭa, v. comitium.

cŏmĭtĭālis -e (comitia), *relating to the comitia;* dies, mensis, *when the comitia were held*, Cic.; homines, *men constantly in attendance on the comitia, and ready to sell their votes*, Plaut.; morbus, *epilepsy, so called because its occurrence put a stop to the* comitia, Cels.; hence subst., **cŏmĭtĭālis** -is, m. *one afflicted with epilepsy*, Plin.

cŏmĭtĭātus -ūs, m. (comitia), *the assembly of the people in the comitia*, Cic.

cŏmĭtĭum -ĭi, n. (comeo = coeo). **I.** Sing. *an enclosed place in or near the Roman forum, where the comitia were held.* **II.** Plur. **cŏmĭtĭa** -ōrum, n. *the assembly of the Roman people*, under three distinct forms; centuriata, *an assembly according to the centuries instituted by Servius Tullius;* curiata, *an assembly of the curies, in later times rarely held except formally;* tributa, *the assembly of the people in their tribes;* comitia habere, *to hold an assembly of the people*, Cic.; consularia, *assembly for the purpose of electing a consul*, Liv.; tribunicia quaestoria, Cic.; comitia instituere, obire, dimittere, Cic.

cŏmĭto, 1. = comitor, partic. comitatus, *accompanied;* with abl., alicuis viris, Cic.; dolore, Ov.; abs. bene comitare, Cic.

cŏmĭtor, 1. dep. (comes), **1,** *to join as a companion* or *follower, to accompany, to follow;* aliquem, Caes.; nautas fuga, Verg.; absol., magna comitante caterva, Verg.; with dat., tardis mentibus virtus non facile comitatur, Cic.; **2,** *to follow to the grave;* aliquem, Nep., Verg.

commăcŭlo, 1. *to spot all over, pollute* **I.** Lit., manus sanguine, Verg. **II.** Transf., se isto infinito ambitu, Cic.

Commăgēnē -ēs, f. (Κομμαγηνή), *a province of Syria* (capital Samosata), now *Camush.* Adj., **Commăgēnus** -a -um, *Commagenian.*

commănĭpŭlāris -is, m. *a soldier belonging to the same maniple* or *company, a comrade*, Tac.

commĕātus -ūs, m. (commeo). **I.** *free passage, going and coming*, Plaut. **II.** Meton., **1,** *liberty to go unhindered;* milit. t. t., *leave of absence, furlough;* sumere, dare, Liv.; in commeatu esse, *to be on furlough*, Liv.; cum commeatu Syracusis remanere, Cic; **2,** *that which is going or coming;* **a,** *a company of merchants, caravan;* Londinium copiā negotiatorum et commeatuum maxime celebre, Tac.; **b,** *supply of provisions, food, forage;* commeatum or commeatus parare, Liv., Sall , accipere, arcessere, convehere, advehere, portare, Liv ; petere, Caes , aliquem commeatu prohibere, Caes , aliquem commeatu et reliquis copiis intercludere, Cic.

comměditor, 1, dep *to remind, call to remembrance,* Lucr

comměmini -isse, *to remember fully,* utrum hoc tu parum commeministi, an ego non satis intellexi? Cic.

comměmŏrābilis e (commemoro), *worthy of remembrance, worthy of mention, memorable,* pietas, Cic

comměmŏrātio -ōnis, f (commemoro), *remembrance, mention, reminding,* officiorum, Cic

comměmŏro, 1 **I.** *to call to mind, recollect,* quid quoque die dixerim, audierim, egerim, commemoro vesperi, Cic **II. a,** *to remind another person of something, to bring to another person's remembrance,* gratiam, amicitiam cognationemque, Cic ; **b,** *to mention, relate, recount,* humanam societatem, Cic , Critolaus iste, quem cum Diogene venisse commemoras, Cic , de alicuius virtute, Cic

commendābilis -e (commendo), *commendable, praiseworthy,* nec illo commendabilis merito, Liv

commendātīcius a -um (commendatus), *relating to a recommendation,* literae, *a letter of introduction,* Cic

commendātio -ōnis, f (commendo), **1,** *recommendation, commendation,* commendatio nostra ceterorumque amicorum, Cic , **2,** *that which recommends, excellence,* ingenii, liberalitatis, Cic

commendātrix -īcis, f (commendo), *that which commends,* legem commendatricem virtutum, Cic

commendātus -a um, p adj (from commendo), **1,** *recommended, commended,* quae (res) commendatior erit memoriae hominum? Cic , **2,** *esteemed, prized, valued,* Plin

commendo, 1 (com and mando), *to commit to the care, keeping,* or *protection of any one* **I.** Lit , tibi eius omnia negotia, Cic **II.** Transf , **A.** Gen , nomen suum immortalitati, Cic , aliquid literis, *to commit to writing,* ap Cic. **B.** Esp **a,** *to recommend,* aliquem alicui diligenter, Cic , se Caesari, Caes , **b,** *to set off, grace, render agreeable,* nulla re una magis orationem commendari quam verborum splendore et copia, Cic

commensus, partic of commetior

commentārĭŏlum i, n (dim of commentarius), *a short treatise,* Cic

commentārĭus ii, m and **commentārĭum** ii, n (commentus, from comminiscor), **1,** *a memorandum,* or *note book, a diary,* in commentarium referre, Cic , commentarii belli Gallici, *the notes of Caesar on the Gallic war,* Cic , **2,** legal t. t , *a brief,* Cic

commentātio ōnis, f (commentor), **1,** *deep reflection, careful consideration, meditation,* tota philosophorum vita commentatio mortis est, Cic , **2,** *practice, study of an orator,* commentationes quotidianae, Cic , **3,** *a dissertation,* Plin

commentīcius -a um (commentus, from comminiscor), *invented, fictitious,* nominibus novis et commenticiis appellata, Cic , civitas Platonis, *ideal,* Cic , crimen, *false,* Cic

1 **commentor,** 1 dep (com and MEN, root of mens) **A** *to consider thoroughly, reflect upon deeply,* futuras secum miserias, Cic , de populi Romani libertate, Cic , with rel clause, ut ante commentemur inter nos qua ratione nobis traducendum sit hoc tempus, Cic **B.** Esp , *to study, practise, prepare for ;* commentabar declamitans saepe cum M Pisone et cum Q Pompeio quotidie, Cic., with acc , commentari orationem in Verrem, Cic , partic. perf passive, commentata oratio, Cic , neut plur subst , sua et commentata et scripta, Cic **C.** *to sketch, compose, write down,* mimos, Cic

2 **commentor** -ōris, m (comminiscor), *a discoverer, inventor,* uvae, *Bacchus,* Ov

commentum -i, n (commentus from comminiscor), **1,** *a fiction, an invention, contrivance,* opinionum commenta, *fancies,* Cic , miraculi, Liv , **2,** *a lie, falsehood,* mille rumorum commenta, Ov

commĕo, 1 *to go up and down, come and go, visit frequently,* vulgatum erat inter Veios Romamque nuncios commeare, Liv ; ut tuto ab repentino hostium incursu etiam singuli commeare possent, Caes , Delos quo omnes undique cum mercibus atque oneribus commeabant, Cic , of ships, navis, quae ad ea furta, quae reliquisses, commearet, Cic , of the heavenly bodies, sursum deorsum, ultro citro, Cic , of letters, crebro enim illius litterae ab aliis ad nos commeant, *find their way to us,* Cic

commercium ii, n (com and merx) **I. A.** *trade, commerce,* commercio prohibere aliquem, Sall **B.** Meton **a,** *the right of trade,* commercium in eo agro nemini est, Cic , salis commercium dedit, Liv , **b,** *an article of traffic,* Plin , **c,** *a place of trade, commercial depôt,* Plin **II.** *intercourse, communication, correspondence,* commercium sermonum facere, Liv , commercium belli, *negotiations as to ransom of prisoners, truces,* etc , Tac , habere commercium cum aliquo, Cic

commercor, 1 dep *to buy together, buy up,* arma, tela alia, Sall

commĕrĕo -ŭi itum, 2 (commereor, dep Plaut), **1,** *to deserve fully ;* aestimationem (poenae), Cic. , **2,** *to commit a fault,* culpam, Plaut

commētĭor mensus, 4 **1,** *to measure,* siderum ambitus, Cic ; **2,** *to measure with anything, compare,* negotium cum tempore, Cic

commēto, 1 (intens of commeo), *to go frequently,* Ter

commīgro, 1 *to remove in a body, to migrate;* in domum suam, Cic

commīlĭtium -ii, n (com and miles) **A.** *a companionship in war* or *military service,* Tac **B.** Transf , *companionship, fellowship,* Ov

commīlĭto -ōnis, m (com and milito), *a companion* or *comrade in war,* Cic

commĭnātio -ōnis, f (comminor), *a threatening, threat,* Cic

commingo minxi minctum or mictum, 3 *to make water on,* Hor , transf , *to defile,* Cat

commĭniscor mentus, 3 dep *to feign, invent,* monogrammos deos, Cic , mendacium, Plaut , perf partic pass , *feigned, invented,* commenta funera, Ov

commĭnor, 1 dep *to threaten,* comminati inter se, Liv , with acc , pugnam, obsidionem, oppugnationem, Liv

commĭnŭo ui -ūtum, 3 **A.** *to make small lessen, break into small pieces, crush to pieces,* statuam, anulum, Cic **B.** Transf , *to lessen, diminish, to weaken, deprive of strength,* opes civitatis, Cic , vires ingenii, Ov

commĭnus, adv (con and manus) **A** Lit , **a,** milit t t (opp eminus), *hand to hand, in close combat* nec eminus hastis aut comminus gladiis uteretur, Cic , comminus acriter instare, Sall , manum comminus conserere, Liv , of hunting, comminus ire in apros, Ov , **b.** gen., *close at hand*, comminus ad aliquem accedere, Cic B. Transf, *face to face*, comminus aspicere aliquem, Ov

commis, commi, cummis = gummi (q v)

commiscĕo -miscŭi mixtum, or mistum, 2 *to mix together, to mix up* **A.** Lit , ignem Vestae cum communi urbis incendio, Cic , commixta frusta mero cruento, Verg **B.** Transf , temeritatem cum sapientia, Cic

commĭsĕrātĭo -ōnis, f (commiseror), in rhetoric, *the part of an oration intended to excite pity*, Cic , absol , *an affecting tone* (of voice), Cic

commĭsĕresco, 3. *to pity*, Ter

commĭsĕror, 1 dep **1,** *to pity, commiserate, bewail*, fortunam, Nep . **2,** of a speaker, *to excite pity*, quum commiserari, conqueri coeperit, Cic

commissĭo ōnis, f (committo) **A.** *a contest or struggle for a prize*, Cic **B.** Meton , *a showy declamation*, Sen

commissum -i, n (committo) **I.** *something undertaken, an undertaking*, supererat nihil aliud in temere commisso quam, etc , Liv , esp , **a,** *a crime, fault, transgression*, factum aut commissum audacius, Cic , **b,** *confiscation*, Quint **II.** *a secret*, commissa enuntiare, Cic

commissūra -ae, f (committo) **A.** *a joining together, connection, joint, knot*, molles digitorum, Cic **B.** Transf , *connexion of a speech, the thread of a discourse*, Quint

committo -misi -missum, 3 *to unite, connect, combine* **I.** Lit , duas noctes, Ov., opera, Liv , nondum commissa inter se munimenta, Liv **II.** Transf , **1, a,** *to begin, set on foot*, pugnam or pugnam cum aliquo, Cic , proelium, Caes , bellum, Liv , ludos, Cic , **b,** *to commit a crime*, tantum facinus, Cic , multa et in deos et in homines impie, Cic., **c,** absol , *to commit a crime, to sin*, nemo enim committeret, Cic , contra legem, Cic , with ut and the subj , *to bring it about that*, non committam posthac ut me accusare de epistolarum negligentia possis, Cic , **d,** *to incur a punishment*, poenam, Cic., perf partic , *forfeited*, hereditas Veneri Erycinae commissa, Cic , **e,** *to entrust, commit to*, reflex , *to venture, risk oneself*, se in senatum, Cic. , se urbi, Cic , aliquem fidei potestatique eius, Cic , collum tonsori, Cic , alicui rempublicam, Liv , committere alicui, ut videat ne quid res publica detrimenti capiat, Cic.

commŏdē, adv (commodus), **a,** *rightly, properly, fitly, appropriately*, dicere, Cic , minus commode audire, *to have an indifferent reputation*, Cic , **b,** *agreeably, pleasantly*, feceris igitur commode mihique gratum si, etc , Cic , **c,** *satisfactorily*, navigare, Cic.

commŏdĭtas -ātis, f (commodus) **I. a,** *proportion, symmetry*, corporis, Cic ; vitae, Cic , **b,** *convenience*, ob commoditatem itineris, Liv , **c,** *fitness, a fit occasion*, commoditas ad faciendum idonea, Cic , **d,** *advantage*, qui ex bestiis fructus, quae commoditas percipi potest, Cic **II.** of persons, *complaisance, kindness*, Ov

commŏdo, 1 (commodus), **1,** *to make fit, adapt, accommodate*, Plin , **2, a,** *to adapt oneself to suit another person, to please, oblige, serve*, ut eo libentius iis commodes, Cic., **b,** with acc , *to furnish, lend, give*, nomen suum alicui, Cic , reipublicae tempus, Liv , alicui aurem, Ov , *to lend* for a time , alicui aurum, Cic

1 **commŏdum,** adv (commodus), **a,** *at the right time, opportunely*, commodum enim egeram diligentissime, Cic , **b,** with quum or postquam and the indic., *just*, commodum discesseras heri, quum Trebatius venit, Cic

2 **commŏdum** -i n. (commodus), **a,** *convenience*, nostro commodo, *at our convenience*, Cic , commodo tuo, Cic , per commodum, Liv , quod commodo valetudinis tuae fiat, Cic , commodo reipublicae facere aliquid, Cic , commodum alicuius exspectare, Cic. , **b,** *use, advantage, convenience*, pacis, Cic , sui commodi causa nocere alteri, Cic , servire or consulere alicuius commodis, Cic , plur , *favour, privileges, prerogatives*, tribunatus (militum) commoda, Cic , **c,** *loan*, qui forum et basilicas commodis hospitum, non furtis nocentium ornarent, Cic

1 **commŏdus** -a um (com and modus) **I. a,** *proper, fit, appropriate, convenient, satisfactory*; valetudine minus commoda uti, Caes ; litterae satis commodae de Britannicis rebus, Cic , with dat , nulla lex satis commoda omnibus est, Cic ; commodum est, *it pleases, is agreeable*, si tibi erit commodum, Cic ; with acc and infin , nihil duco esse commodius, quam de his rebus nihil jam amplius scribere, Cic ; **b,** *easy, convenient*, iter, Liv **II.** *friendly, obliging, pleasant*, mores commodi, Cic.

2 **Commŏdus** -i, in *Roman emperor from* 186–192 A D

commōlĭor, 4 dep *to set in motion*, fulmina, Lucr

commŏnĕfăcĭo -fēci -factum, 3 , pass **commŏnĕfīo** factus sum, -fieri (commoneo and facio), *to remind, warn*, aliquem etiam atque etiam, Cic , aliquem beneficii sui, Sall , with acc of thing, istius turpem calamitosamque praeturam, Cic

commŏnĕo -ŭi -ĭtum, 2 *to remind, warn, impress upon, bring to one's recollection*, quod vos lex commonuit, Cic , quum is unoquoque gradu de avaritia tua commoneretur, Cic , non exprobrandi causa, sed commonendi gratia, Cic ; animos de periculo, Cic ; quum quidam ex illis amicis commonerent oportere decerni, Cic

commonstro, 1 *to show fully and distinctly*, aurum alicui, Cic

commŏrātĭo -ōnis, f (commoror), *a delaying, loitering, lingering*, tabellariorum, Cic ; rhet t t , *the dwelling for some time on one point*, Cic

commŏrĭor -mortuus, 3 dep *to die together with*, with dat., hostibus, Sall

commŏror, 1. dep *to delay, linger, make a stay in any place, sojourn, tarry, remain*, **a,** Romae, Cic ; unam noctem ad Helorum, Cic ; apud aliquem, Cic , fig , consilium tuum diutius in armis civilibus commorandi, Cic. , **b,** rhet. t t. *to dwell on*, pluribus verbis in eo, Cic.

commōtĭo -ōnis, f (commoveo), *an emotion, excitement*, animi, Cic

commōtĭuncŭla ae, f (dim of commotio), *a slight indisposition*, Cic

commōtus a -um, p adj (from commoveo), **1,** *tottering, insecure, unsteady*, aes alienum, Tac , genus (dicendi) in agendo, Cic , **2,** *moved in mind, excited*, animus commotior, Cic

commŏvĕo -mōvi -mōtum, 3 **I.** Lit *to move entirely or violently, to shake, to move from a place*, **1,** se ex eo loco, Cic ; castra ex eo loco, *to cause the army to advance*, Cic , sacra, *to carry about* (at festivals, etc) *the statues of the gods and the sacred utensils*, Verg , nummum, *to employ in commerce*, Cic. ; columnas, *to carry off*, Cic ; **2, a,** *to hunt*, cervum, Verg , **b,** *to cause to yield or give way*, hostium aciem, Liv. **II.** Transf , **1,** of the mind or the passions, *to move, influence, disturb*, his omnes, in quibus est virtutis indoles, commoventur, Cic , aut libidine aliqua aut metu commotum esse, Cic ; nova atque inusitata specie commotus, Caes ; eiusdem miseriis ac periculis commovetur, Cic. ; quum esset ex aere alieno commota civitas, Cic,

2, *to call forth, produce, cause*; risum, Cic, magnum et acerbum dolorem, Cic., bellum aut tumultum, Cic; 3, *to treat of*, nova quaedam, Cic (contracted perf forms commossem, commosset, commosse, Cic)

commūnĭcātĭo -ōnis, f (communico), 1, *a communicating, imparting*, consilii, Cic, 2, *a rhetorical figure* = ἀνακοίνωσις, *in which the orator pretends to consult the audience*, Cic

commūnĭco, 1. (communis), *to share, divide with, communicate*, 1, judicia cum equestri ordine communicata erant, Cic, rem cum aliquo, Cic, 2, *to communicate, impart, inform*, by speaking or writing, consilia, Caes; de societate multa inter se, Cic, *to take counsel with, confer with*, cum aliquo de maximis rebus, Cic, 3, *to join, unite*, quantas pecunias ab uxoribus dotis nomine acceperunt, tantas ex suis bonis aestimatione factā cum dotibus communicant, Caes, 4, *to share something with one*, curam doloris sui cum aliquo, Cic

1 **commūnĭo** -īvi or -ĭi ītum, 4 *to fortify thoroughly on all sides*, castella, Caes, transf, *to fortify, strengthen*, causam testimoniis, Cic

2 **commūnĭo** -ōnis, f (communis), *communion, mutual participation*, inter quos est communio legis, inter eos communio juris est, Cic

commūnis -e (old form commoinis, from com and root MOIN, MUN, whence moenia, munus) **A.** *common, general, universal, ordinary, usual, public* (opp proprius = *individual, private*), loca, *public places*, Cic, loci, *philosophical* or *rhetorical commonplaces*, Cic, with genit, communis hominum infirmitas, Cic, with dat, mors omni aetati est communis, Cic, with cum and the abl, quocum fuit et domus et militia communis Cic, with inter se, multa sunt civibus inter se communia, Cic, subst, **commūne** -is, n, 1, *the common property of a corporation*, quod jus statues communi dividundo, Cic, 2, *state, commonwealth*, Siciliae, Cic, in commune, adv a, *for the public good, for common use*, in commune conferre, Cic, b, *in general*, Tac **B.** Transf, of persons, *affable, condescending*, Cyrum minorem communem erga Lysandrum atque humanum fuisse, Cic.

commūnĭtas -ātis, f (communis) **I.** *community, fellowship*, nulla cum deo homini communitas, Cic **II.** Transf, a, *the desire for human society*, Cic, b, *condescension, affability*, Nep

commūnĭtĕr, adv (communis), *in common with others, jointly, generally*, Cic

commurmŭror, 1, dep *to mutter, murmur*, ut scriba secum ipse commurmuratus sit, Cic

commūtābĭlis, e (commuto), *changeable*, a, vitae ratio, Cic; b, rhet t. t, exordium, *such as could be easily adapted to a speech on the other side of the question*, Cic

commūtātĭo -ōnis, f (commuto), *a change, alteration*, temporum, Cic, aestuum, Caes

commūtātus -ūs, m, *a change, alteration*, Lucr

commūto, 1 **A.** *to change, alter entirely*, cursum, Cic, iter, Caes, tempora in horas commutantur, Cic, reipublicae statum, Cic, consilium, Caes, sententiam, Cic, nihil commutari animo, Cic **B.** *to exchange, change something for something else*, gloriam constantiae cum caritate vitae, Cic, fidem suam et religionem pecunia, *to barter*, Cic

cōmo, compsi, comptum, 3 (contr from coemo), *to place together* **I.** Gen, Lucr **II.** *to place together in order, to arrange, adorn*, especially of the hair, *to comb, plait, adorn*, capillos, Cic, longas compta puella comas, Ov; placemeti recto pueri comptique, Hor

cōmoedĭa -ae, f (κωμῳδία), *a comedy*, Cic

cōmoedus -a -um (κωμῳδός), *relating to a comedy, comic*, natio, Juv Subst, **cōmoedus** -i, m *a comic actor*, Cic

cŏmōsus -a -um (coma), *hairy*, Phaedr

compăciscor (compĕciscor), -pactus, or pectus paciscī 3, dep *to conclude an agreement, make a compact with any one*, Plaut

compactĭo -ōnis, f (compingo), *a putting or joining together*, membrorum, Cic

compactum -i, n (compaciscor), *a compact, agreement*, compacto, Cic., de compacto, Plaut, ex compacto, Suet, *according to agreement*

compactus -a -um, p adj (from compingo), *thick-set, compressed, compact*, Plin

compāges -is, f (compingo) **I.** *a joining together, connexion*, lapidum, Ov, quae (navis) per se ipsa omnibus compagibus aquam acciperet, Liv **II.** Transf, dum sumus in his inclusi compagibus corporis, *bodily structure*, Cic

compāgo -ĭnis, f = compages (q v).

compar -păris, *like, similar*, postulatio Latinorum, Liv, with dat, milites militibus compares, Liv Subst, **compar** -păris, c *a companion, equal consort, spouse*, Hor

compărābĭlis -e (2 comparo), *capable of comparison, comparable*, comparabile est, quod in rebus diversis similem aliquam rationem continet, Cic

compărātē, adv (2 comparo), *in comparison, by comparison*, Cic

1 **compărātĭo** -ōnis, f (1 comparo), *a preparing, preparation*, novi belli, Cic, veneni, Liv, criminis, *evidence necessary for an accusation*, Cic

2 **compărātĭo** -ōnis, f (2 comparo) **A.** *a comparing, comparison*, orationis suae cum scriptis alienis, Cic, utilitatum, Cic, comparatio quibus plurimum sit tribuendum, Cic **B.** In rhet, comparatio criminis, *the set off of a good motive against a crime*, Cic.

compărātīvus a -um (2 comparo), *relating to comparison, containing a comparison, comparative*, judicatio, Cic

comparco (comperco) -parsi, -parsum, 3 *to scrape together, to save up*, Ter

compārĕo -pārŭi, 2, 1, *to appear, be visible*, cum subito sole obscurato non comparuisset (Romulus), Cic, 2, *to be present, be in existence*, signa et dona comparere omnia, Cic

1 **compăro**, 1 **A.** *to prepare, get ready, provide, furnish*, convivium magnifice et ornate, Cic, se, *to make oneself ready*, Cic, insidias alicui, Cic classem Cic exercitum, Cic, rem frumentariam, Caes, animum auditoris idonee ad reliquam dictionem, Cic, alicui a civitatibus laudationes per vim et metum, Cic, bellum adversus aliquem, Caes **B.** *to arrange, settle, dispose*, 1, of character, sic fuimus semper comparati ut, etc, Cic, 2, of institutions, jura praeclara atque divinitus a nostris majoribus comparata, Cic.

2 **compăro**, 1 (compar) **I.** Lit, a, *to form into pairs, to unite in pairs*, Cic, labella labellis, Plaut b, *to bring together for a contest, to match*, compararii cum Aeserninum Samnitem, cum patrono disertissimo, Cic **II.** Transf, a, *to compare*, et se mihi comparat Ajax? Ov, homo similitudines comparat, Cic, Attico Liviae Catonem nostrum, Cic, meme factum cum tuo comparo, Cic, b, comparare provincias inter se, or comparare provincias, or simply

comparare inter se (of magistrates), *to come to an agreement as to their several duties*, Liv.

compasco -pāvi -pastum, 3. *to feed or graze together*; si compascuus ager est, jus est compascere, Cic.

compascŭus -a -um, *relating to common pasturage*; ager, *pasturage held in common*, Cic.

compĕdĭo, 4. (compes), *to fetter*, Plaut.

compellātĭo -ōnis, f. (2. compello), *an accosting, rebuking, reprimanding*; crebrae vel potius quotidianae compellationes, Cic.

1. **compello** -pŭli -pulsum, 3. **I.** *to drive to one place, collect*; pecus totius provinciae, Cic. **II.** *to drive, force*. **A.** Lit., consules e foro in curiam, Liv.; naves in portum, Caes.; Romanos in castra, Liv.; omne Auruncum bellum Pometiam compulsum est, *confined to*, Liv. **B.** Transf., *to force* or *impel a person to an action, to compel*; aliquem ad bellum, Ov.; in eundem metum, Liv.; in hunc sensum et allici beneficiis hominum et compelli injuriis, Cic.

2. **compello**, 1. (intens. of 1. compello). **I.** Gen., *to address, accost, call by name*; aliquem voce, Verg. **II. A.** *to address with blame and reproach, chide, rebuke*; aliquem edicto, Cic. **B.** Legal t. t., *to accuse before a court of justice*; judicem, Cic.

compendĭārĭus -a -um (compendium), *short*; via, Cic.

compendĭum -ĭi, n. (com and pendo, *to weigh together*). **A.** *saving, parsimony*, and hence, *gain, profit, advantage* (opp. dispendium); privato compendio servire, Caes.; in re uberrima turpe compendium effugere, Cic. **B.** *a short way, a short cut*; per compendia maris assequi aliquem, Tac.

compensātĭo -ōnis, f. (compenso), *a balancing of an account, compensation*; incommoda commodorum compensatione leniant, Cic.

compenso, 1. *to weigh together, to reckon one thing against another, to balance*; laetitiam cum doloribus, Cic.; summi labores nostri magnā compensati gloriā, Cic.

compĕrendĭnātĭo -ōnis, f. (comperendino), *a putting off a trial to the third day*, Tac.

compĕrendĭnātus -ūs, m. = comperendinatio (q.v.).

compĕrendĭno, 1. (com and perendinus), *to remand to the third day*; reum, Cic.; absol., ut ante primos ludos comperendinem, Cic.

compĕrĭo -pĕri -pertum, 4. (com and root PER, whence peritus, periculum, and reperio, experior), *to find out, discover, gain certain information of*; haec certis nuntiis, certis auctoribus comperisse, Cic.; partic. perf., *certain, undoubted*; levem auditionem pro re comperta habere, *for a certainty*, Caes.; ea dicimus quae comperta habemus, quae vidimus, Cic.; compertum narrare, Sall.; with acc. and infin., posteaquam comperit eum posse vivere, Cic.; abl. absol., comperto, *it having been discovered for certain*; satis comperto Eordaeam petituros Romanos, Liv.; with de and the abl., nihil de hoc comperi, Cic.; partic. perf., compertus (of persons), *convicted*; probri, Liv.

compĕrĭor = comperio.

compēs -pĕdis, f. *a fetter or foot shackle*, gen. found in the plur, Plaut.; transf., qui in compedibus corporis semper fuerunt, Cic.; Telephum tenet puella grata compede vinctum, Hor.

compesco -pescŭi, 3. (connected with compes, compedio), *to hold in, restrain, check, curb*; equum angustis habenis, Tib.; seditionem exercitus verbo uno, Tac.; clamorem, Hor.; ramos, Verg.

compĕtītor -ōris, m. *a competitor*, Cic.

compĕtītrix -īcis, f. (competitor), *a female competitor*, Cic.

compĕto -pĕtīvi and -pĕtĭi -pĕtītum 3. *to come together, to meet*. **A.** Lit., Varr. **B.** Transf., **1,** *to agree, coincide in point of time*; tempora cum Othonis exitu competisse, Tac.; **2,** *to be equal to, capable of*; ut vix ad arma capienda aptandaque pugnae competeret animus, Liv.; neque oculis neque auribus satis competebant, Tac.

compīlātĭo -ōnis, f. (compilo), *a pillaging*, hence (contemptuously), *a compilation*; Chresti, Cic.

compīlo, 1.(com and pilo = ψιλόω), *to plunder, rob*; fana, Cic.; fig., ab ipsis capsis juris, consultorum sapientiam, Cic.

compingo -pēgi -pactum, 3. (com and pango). **A.** *to put together, construct*; part. perf., compactus, *constructed*, Cic., Verg. **B.** *to confine, hide, conceal*; se in Apuliam, Cic.; fig., in judicia et contiunculas tamquam in aliquod pistrinum detrudi et compingi, Cic.

compĭtālĭcĭus -a -um (compitalis), *relating to the Compitalia*; dies, Cic.; ludi, Cic.

compĭtālis -e (compitum), *relating* or *belonging to cross roads*; Lares, *the deities who presided over cross roads*, Suet. Subst., **Compĭtālĭa** -ium, n. *the festival in honour of these deities, celebrated on the cross roads on a day appointed by the praetor, shortly after the Saturnalia*, Cic.

compĭtum -i, n. (competo), *a place where two or more roads meet, a cross road*, Cic.

complăcĕo -cŭi or -cĭtus sum, 2. **1,** *to please several persons at once*, Ter.; **2,** *to please exceedingly*, Plaut.

complāno, 1. *to level*; domum, *to raze*, Cic.

complector -plexus -plecti, 3. dep. (com and plecto). **I.** Lit., **1,** *to embrace, encircle, surround, encompass*; aliquem medium, Liv.; aliquem artius, Cic.; me artior somnus complexus est, Cic.; **2,** *to enclose, surround*; collem opere, Caes.; animum mundi caelo, Cic. **II.** Transf., **1,** *to hold fast, master*; quam (facultatem) quoniam complexus es, tene, Cic.; **2,** *to attach oneself to, esteem*; quos fortuna complexa est, *the favourites of fortune*, Cic.; aliquem summa benevolentia, Cic.; **3,** of the mind, *to embrace, grasp, comprehend*; omnia una comprehensione, Cic.; **4,** *to unite in oneself* or *itself*; omnes omnium caritates patria una complexa est, Cic.

complēmentum -i, n. (compleo), *that which completes* or *fills up, a complement*; inania quaedam verba quasi complementa numerorum, Cic.

complĕo -plēvi -plētum, 2. *to fill up*. **I.** Lit., **1,** fossas sarmentis et virgultis, Caes.; paginam, Cic.; multo cibo et potione completi, Cic.; with genit., convivium vicinorum quotidie compleo, Cic.; **2,** milit. t. t., *to complete the number of an army, fleet*, etc.; classem Romanam sociis navalibus, Liv.; **3,** *to fill* a space with light, smell, shout, clamour, etc.; omnia clamoribus, Liv.; sol cuncta sua luce lustrat et complet, Cic. **II.** Transf., **1,** civitatem summa spe et voluntate, Caes.; **2,** *to fulfil*; fata sua, Ov.; centum et septem annos complesse, Cic.; **3,** of a sum, *to make up*; neque est adhuc ea summa (imperati sumptus) completa, Cic.; **4,** *to complete, finish*; his rebus completis, Caes.

complētus -a -um, p. adj. (from compleo), *perfect, complete*; completus et perfectus verborum ambitus, Cic.

complexĭo -ōnis, f. (complector), **1,** *connexion, combination*; complexiones atomorum inter se, Cic, 2, of discourse, **a,** brevis totius negotii, *a short summary of the whole matter*, Cic, **b,** verborum, or absol, *a period*, Cic, **c,** in logic, *the conclusion of a syllogism*, Cic, **d,** *a dilemma*, Cic

complexus -ūs, m (complector) **A. a,** *an embrace*, aliquem de complexu matris avellere, Cic, currere ad alicuius complexum, Cic., meton, *a loved object*, de complexu eius ac sinu, *from his favourites and bosom friends*, Cic, **b,** *combat*, complexum armorum vitare, Tac, **c,** *surrounding, encompassing*, qui (mundus) omnia complexu suo coercet et continet, Cic **B.** Transf, *love for*, complexus totius gentis humanae, Cic.

complĭco -āvi -ātum (-ŭi -ĭtum), 1 *to fold together, fold up* **I.** Lit, epistolam, Cic **II.** Transf, complicata notio, *confused, intricate*, Cic

complōrātĭo -ōnis, f (comploro), *a lamentation, a weeping and bewailing*, mulierum comploratio sui patriaeque, Liv

complōrātus -ūs, m = comploratio (q v)

complōro, 1 *to bewail* or *weep, to lament loudly and violently*, mortem, Cic, desperata comploratаque res est publica, Liv

complūres, neut **complūra,** and (rarely) **complūrĭa** -ium, n *very many*, Cic Subst, *several*, complures ex iis, Caes

complūrĭens (complūrĭēs), adv (complures), *many times, frequently*, Plaut

compluscŭli -ae, a (complures), *a good many*, Plaut

complŭvĭum -ii, n (compluo, *to flow together*), *the quadrangular roofless space in the centre of a Roman house, through which the water collected on the roofs found its way to the* impluvium *below*, Varr

compōno -pŏsŭi -pŏsĭtum, 3 *to put, place, lay, bring together* **I.** Gen., **1,** in quo (loco) erant ea composita, quibus rex te munerare constituerat, Cic; manibus manus atque oribus ora, Verg, **2, a,** *to place together as opponents*, Cic, pergis pugnantia secum pontibus adversis componere, Hor, **b,** *to compare*, dignitati alicuius suam, Cic **II** Esp. **A.** *to collect together a whole from several parts, compose*, exercitus eius compositus ex variis gentibus, Sall., venena, Ov, aggerem tumuli, Verg, of writers, *to compose*, volumen de tuenda sanitate, Cic, orationem ad conciliandos plebis animos composita, Liv **B.** **1,** *to compose, settle, arrange*, arma, Hor, opes, Verg, cinerem, *the ashes of the dead*, Ov, se thalamo, Verg, **2,** *to quiet, settle, reconcile*, controversias regum, Caes, Armeniam, Tac, amicos aversos, Hor **C.** *to place in a certain order, arrange*, **1,** sidera, Cic, classiarios in numeros legionis, Tac, **2,** rhet t t, *to arrange words in their order*, verba componere et quasi coagmentare, Cic **D.** **1,** *to arrange, smooth*; comas, Ov, composito et delibuto capillo, Cic, togam, Hor, vultum, Tac, **2, a,** *to dispose, settle in a particular way*, itinera sic ut, etc, Cic., auspicia ad utilitatem reipublicae composita, Cic, diem rei gerendae, Liv; ex composito, *as we agreed*, Liv, **b,** *to invent, feign*, crimen et dolum, Tac

comporto, 1 *to carry, bring together, collect*, frumentum ab Asia, Caes, arma in templum, Cic

compŏs -pŏtis (com and potis), *having the mastery or control of, possessed of, sharing in*, animi, Ter, mentis, *in full possession of mental faculties*, Cic, voti, *one whose wish is fulfilled*, Hor, Liv; scientiae compotem esse, *to be able to know something*, Cic; rationis et consilii compos, Cic, qui me huius urbis compotem fecerunt, *enabled me to be in this city*, Cic, tum patriae compotem me numquam siris esse, Liv

compŏsĭte, adv (compositus), **1,** *in an orderly manner, in good order*, composite et apte dicere, Cic, **2,** *quietly*, Tac

compŏsĭtĭo -ōnis, f (compono), *a putting together* **I.** Gen, *a matching*, gladiatorum compositiones, Cic **II.** Esp **1,** *a composing*, **a,** unguentorum, Cic, **b,** of a book, juris pontificalis, Cic, **2,** *a settlement of differences*, pacis, concordiae, compositionis auctor esse non destiti, Cic, **3,** *arrangement*, **a,** membrorum, Cic, **b,** anni *of the calendar*, Cic, **c,** rhet t t, *the proper arrangement of words*, compositio apta, Cic

compŏsĭtor -ōris, m (compono), *an arranger, adjuster*, Cic

compŏsĭtūra -ae, f (compono), *a connexion, joining, a joint*, Lucr

compŏsĭtus -a -um, p adj with compar and superl (compono), *placed together*, **1,** *composed, quieted*, composito vultu, Tac, **2,** *well arranged*, composito agmine legiones ducere, Tac, so of oratory, oratio, Cic, and of the orator himself, orator, Cic, **3,** *peacefully governed, settled*, respublica, Cic, hence subst, **compŏsĭta,** -orum, n *the orderly condition of a state*, Sall, **4, a,** *prepared*, ut nemo unquam compositior ad judicium venisse videatur, Cic, **b,** *feigned, pretended, studied*, indignatio, Tac

compōtātĭo -ōnis, f *a drinking party* (translation of συμποσιον), Cic

compŏtĭo, 4 (compos), *to make partaker of*, Plaut, passive, *to become partaker of*, Plaut

compōtor -ōris, m *a drinking companion*, Cic

compōtrix -īcis, f (compotor), *a female drinking companion*, Ter

compransor -ōris, m *a dinner companion, boon companion*, Cic

comprĕcātĭo -ōnis, f (comprecor), *supplication of a deity*, haec sollemnis deorum comprecatio, Liv

comprĕcor, 1, dep *to pray to, supplicate*, caelestûm fidem, Cat, Cytherea, comprecor, ausis assit, Ov

comprĕhendo (comprendo) -prĕhendi (-prendi) -prĕhensum (-prensum), 3 *to seize, lay hold of* **A.** Lit, **1,** quid opus est manibus si nihil comprehendendum est? Cic, ignem, *to catch fire*, Verg, ignis robora comprendit, *seizes on*, Verg, avidis comprenditur ignibus agger, Ov, without igne, comprehensa aedificia, Liv, **2,** as a suppliant, *to seize a person's hand*, comprehendunt utrumque et orant, Caes, **3,** *to attack, lay hold of in a hostile manner, seize, capture*, **a,** persons, tam capitalem hostem, Cic, aliquem vivum in fuga, Caes, aliquem in furto, Cic, **b,** animals, etc, *to seize, carry off*, redis equosque, Caes, **c,** *to seize a place*, aliis comprehensis collibus, Caes, **4,** *to discover or reveal a crime*, nefandum adulterium, Cic **B.** Transf, **1,** *to embrace*, multos amicitia, Cic, **2,** *to comprise, include*, quae omnia una cum deorum notione comprehendimus, Cic, **3,** *to relate, express, tell in words or writing*, breviter comprehensa sententia, Cic, ne plura consecter, comprehendam brevi, Cic, **4,** aliquid numero, *to count, express in numbers*, Verg, **5,** *to comprehend, perceive*, sensu or sensibus, Cic, animo intelligentiam alicuius rei, Cic, intelligere et cogitatione comprehendere qualis sit animus, Cic., esse aliquid, quod comprehendi et percipi posset, Cic

comprĕhensĭbĭlis -e (comprehendo), *that which can be comprehended, comprehensible*, natura non comprehensibilis, Cic

comprĕhensĭo -ōnis, f (comprehendo), *a seizing with the hands, laying hold of* **A.** Lit.

1, Cic.; 2, *a hostile seizing, apprehending;* sontium, Cic. **B.** Transf., **1,** *a perceiving, comprehending, comprehension;* complecti omnia una comprehensione, Cic.; **2,** *a period, sentence;* verba comprehensione devincire, Cic.

comprendo = comprehendo (q.v.).

compressē, adv. (compressus), *briefly, concisely, succinctly,* Cic.; compressius loqui, Cic.

compressĭo -ōnis, f. (comprimo), *compression of style, conciseness;* compressione rerum breves, Cic.

1. **compressus** -a -um, partic. of comprimo.

2. **compressus,** abl. -u, m. (comprimo), *a pressing together, pressure, embrace,* Cic.

comprĭmo -pressi -pressum. 3. (com and premo), *to press, squeeze together, compress.* **A.** Lit., **1,** quum digitos compresserat et pugnum fecerat, Cic.; prov., compressis manibus sedere, *to sit with folded hands, idle,* Liv.; **2,** *to press together, make closer* or *tighter;* ordines, *to close the ranks,* Liv. **B.** Transf., **1,** *to hold back;* **a,** frumentum, *to keep in the garner, not to sell,* Cic.; **b,** *to suppress;* delicta magna, Cic.; **2,** *to check;* plausus ipse admiratione compressus est, Cic.; gressum, Verg.; **3,** *to crush, subdue;* furentis hominis conatum atque audaciam, Cic.; seditionem, Liv.

comprŏbātĭo -ōnis, f. (comprobo), *approval,* Cic.

comprŏbātor -ōris, m. (comprobo), *one who approves,* Cic.

comprŏbo, 1., **1,** *to approve fully;* orationem omnium assensu, Liv.; istam tuam sententiam laudo vehementissimeque comprobo, Cic.; **2,** *to confirm, prove, establish;* patris dictum sapiens temeritas filii comprobavit, Cic.

comprōmissum -i, n. (compromitto), *a mutual agreement to abide by the decision of an arbitrator;* de hac pecunia compromissum facere, Cic.

comprōmitto -misi -missum, 3. *to agree to refer a cause to arbitration,* Cic.

Compsa -ae, f. *town of the Hirpini in Samnium* (now *Conza*); hence, **Compsānus** -a -um, *of* or *belonging to Compsa.*

1. **comptus** -a -um, p. adj. with compar. and superl. (from como), *ornamented, adorned;* oratio, Cic.

2. **comptus** -ūs, m. (como). **I.** *a head-dress,* Lucr. **II.** *a band, tie,* Lucr.

compungo -punxi -punctum, 3. *to prick, puncture on all sides.* **I.** Phaedr.; fig., ipsi se compungunt suis acuminibus, Cic. **II.** *to mark;* barbarus compunctus notis Threiciis, *tattooed,* Cic.

compŭto, 1. *to reckon together, calculate, compute:* rationem digitis, Plaut.; facies tua computat annos, *shows thy age,* Juv.; absol., computarat, pecuniam impetrarat, Cic.

compŭtresco -pūtrŭi, 3. *to putrefy,* Lucr.

Cōmum -i, n. (Κῶμον), *a town in Cisalpine Gaul,* now *Como.* Adj., **Cōmensis** -e, *of* or *belonging to Comum.*

con = com (q.v.).

cōnāmen -minis, n. (conor), *an effort, endeavour,* Lucr., Ov.

cōnātum -i, n. (conor), *an undertaking;* gen. in plur., conata efficere, Cic.

cōnātus -ūs, m. (conor), **a,** *an attempt, effort, undertaking;* hoc conatu desistere, Cic.; compressi tuos nefarios conatus, Cic.; **b,** *trouble, difficulty, effort;* tumultus Gallicus haud magno conatu brevi oppressus est, Liv.; **c,** *impulse, inclination;* ut (beluae) conatum haberent ad naturales pastus capessendos, Cic.

concăco, 1. *to defile all over,* Phaedr.

concaedēs -ium, f. *a barricade of trees,* Tac.

concălĕfăcĭo (concalfăcio) -fēci -factum, 3., and pass. **concălĕfīo** (concalfio), -factus sum, *to warm thoroughly;* brachium, Cic.

concălĕo, 2. *to be warm through and through,* Plaut.

concălesco -călŭi (inchoat. of concaleo), 3. **A.** Lit., *to become thoroughly warm;* corpora nostra ardore animi concalescunt, Cic. **B.** Transf., *to glow with love,* Ter.

concallesco -callŭi, 3. **a,** *to become practised;* tamquam manus opere, sic animus usu concalluit, Cic.; **b,** *to become callous* or *without feeling,* Cic.

Concăni -ōrum, m. (sing., **Concănus,** Hor.), *a savage tribe in Spain, who drank horses' blood.*

concastīgo, 1. *to punish, chastise severely,* Plaut.

concăvo, 1. (concavus), *to hollow out, make hollow* or *concave;* brachia geminos in artus, *curves, bends,* Ov.

concăvus -a -um, *hollow, vaulted, arched, concave;* cymbala, Lucr.; altitudines speluncarum, Cic.; aqua, *welling up,* Ov.

concēdo -cessi -cessum, 3. *to go away, depart, retire, withdraw.* **I.** Lit., superis ab oris, Verg.; ab alicuius oculis aliquo, Cic.; cum conjugibus ac liberis in arcem Capitoliumque, Liv.; docet unde fulmen venerit, quo concesserit, Cic.; concedere vita, *to die,* Tac.; so absol., quando concessero, Tac. **II.** Transf., **1,** *to cease;* tumor omnis et irae concessere deûm, Verg.; **2, a,** *to submit;* in alicuius ditionem, Liv.; **b,** *to pass over to some one's side* or *party* or *view;* in Attali sententiam, Liv.; **3,** *to yield;* **a,** intransit, (α) voluptas concedit dignitati, Cic.; concedere naturae, *to die a natural death,* Sall.; (β) *to give in to;* alicuius postulationi, Cic.; (γ) *to pardon;* alienis peccatis, Cic.; **b,** transit., (α) *to yield, give up;* alicui libertatem in aliqua re, Cic.; concedant, ut hi viri boni fuerint, *let them admit,* Cic.; alicui primas in dicendo partes, Cic.; (β) reipublicae dolorem atque amicitias suas, *sacrifice,* Cic.

concĕlĕbro, 1. **I.** Lit., *to visit a place often, or in large companies,* Lucr. **II.** Transf., **A.** Of any occupation, *to pursue eagerly, assiduously;* studia per otium, Cic. **B.** *to celebrate a festivity;* diem natalem, Plaut.; spectaculum, Liv. **C.** *to praise, extol;* fama et litteris eius diei victoriam, Cic.

concēnātĭo -ōnis, f. (coeno), *a supping together* (translation of Gr. σύνδειπνον), Cic.

concentĭo -ōnis, f. (concino), *a singing together, harmony,* Cic.

concentus -ūs, m. (concino). **A.** *a singing together, harmony;* avium, Cic.; tubarum ac cornuum, Liv. **B.** Transf., *agreement, harmony of opinion, unity, concord;* melior actionum quam sonorum concentus, Cic.

conceptĭo -ōnis, f. (concipio). **1, a,** *conception, a becoming pregnant,* Cic.; **2,** *the drawing up of legal formulae,* Cic.

conceptus -ūs, m. (concipio), *a conceiving, pregnancy,* Cic.

concerpo -cerpsi -cerptum, 3. (com and carpo), *to pull, pluck, tear in pieces.* **I.** Lit., epistolas, Cic. **II.** Transf., aliquem ferventissime, ap. Cic.

concertātĭo -ōnis, f. (concerto), *contest, strife;* **1,** magistratuum, Cic.; **2,** *contest in words, wrangling, dispute;* sine jejuna concertatione verborum, Cic.

concertātor -ōris, m (concerto), *a rival*, Tac.

concertātōrĭus -a -um (concerto), *relating to a contest in words*, genus dicendi, Cic

concerto, 1 *to strive eagerly*, **1,** proelio, Cic , **2,** esp of dispute in words, nunquam accidit ut cum eo verbo uno concertarem, Cic

concessĭo -ōnis, f (concedo), *a yielding, granting*, **1,** agrorum, Cic , **2,** rhet t t , *an admission of a fault*, Cic

concesso, 1 *to cease, leave off*, Plaut.

concessus -ūs, m (concedo), *permission, leave*, gen in abl , concessu omnium, Cic

concha -ae, f (κογχη) **I.** Lit , **1,** *a mussel*, Cic , **2,** *a mussel-shell*, Cic , poet , *pearl*, conchae teretesque lapilli, Ov , **3,** *the shell fish which yielded the purple dye*, Lucr , poet , *purple dye*, Ov **II.** Meton., *a vessel in the shape of a shell*, **1,** concha salis puri, *salt-cellar*, Hor , funde capacibus unguenta de conchis, Hor , **2,** *the horn of Triton*, Ov

conchĕus -a -um (concha), *relating to a mussel-shell*, bacca, *a pearl*, Verg

conchis -is, f (κόγχος), *a kind of bean boiled with its pod*, Juv

conchīta -ae, m (κογχιτης), *a mussel gatherer*, Plaut

conchȳlĭātus -a -um (conchylium), *purple*, peristromata, Cic

conchȳlĭum -ii, n (κογχυλιον), *a mussel*, or gen *shell fish* **I.** Gen , Cic **II.** Esp , **1,** *an oyster*, Cic , **2,** *the shell fish which yielded a purple dye*, Lucr , meton , **a,** *purple dye*, vestis conchylio tincta, Cic ; **b,** *a purple garment*, Juv

1 **concĭdo** -idi, 3 (com and cado), *to fall down, tumble to the ground, sink down* **A.** Lit , **1,** of things, concidat caelum omne necesse est, Cic , repentinā ruinā pars eius turris concidit, Caes , **2,** of the winds, *to drop*, concidunt venti fugiuntque naves, Hor , equus eius ante signum Jovis Statoris sine causā concidit, Cic , in battle, ita pugnans concidit, Caes **B.** Transf , **1,** *to sink, perish, waste away*, neque enim tam facile opes Carthaginis tantae concidissent, Cic , tum ferocia omnis concidit, Liv , **2,** of persons, **a,** *to be ruined, overthrown, to fail*, malas causas semper obtinuit, in optimā concidit, Cic , at law, *to lose*, judicum vocibus fractus reus et una patroni omnes conciderunt, Cic , **b,** ne unā plagā acceptā patres conscripti conciderent, *be disheartened*, Cic

2 **concīdo** -cidi -cīsum, 3 (com and caedo) **I.** *to cut up, cut in pieces, cut down, strike to the ground* **A.** Lit , concisos equites nostros a barbaris nuntiabant, Cic **B.** *to overthrow, annihilate*, Antonium decretis suis, Cic **II A.** *to beat severely, cudgel*, aliquem virgis, Cic **B. 1, a,** *to cut in pieces*, nervos, Cic , **b,** *to cut through*, magnos scrobibus montes, Verg , pedestria itinera concisa aestuariis, Cic , **2,** rhet t t , *to divide too minutely*, Cic , **3,** logic t t , *to analyse*, Cic

concĭĕo -civi -citum, 2 and (in prose gen) concio -ivi -itum, 4 *to stir up*, **1,** Gen , **a,** *to move violently*, concita navis, Ov , concita flumina, Ov , **b,** of men, *to summon, bring together*, totam urbem, Liv , exercitum ex tota insula, Liv , **2,** *to excite, disturb*, **a,** concita freta, Verg , **b,** of men, *to rouse, stir up*, plebem contionibus, Liv , immani concitus ira, Verg , **c,** *to produce, cause, promote*, bellum in his provinciis, Liv

concĭlĭābŭlum -i, n (concilio), *a place of assembly, market place*, nundinas et conciliabula obire, Liv

concĭlĭātĭo -ōnis, f (concilio) **I.** *a uniting, joining*, **1,** communem totius generis hominum conciliationem et consociationem colere, Cic , **2, a,** *a uniting in opinion, conciliating*, aut conciliationis causā leniter aut permotionis vehementer aguntur, Cic , rhet t t, *the gaining the favour of the audience*, Cic , **b,** *inclination*, prima est enim conciliatio hominis ad ea, quae sunt secundum naturam, Cic **II.** *a procuring, acquiring*, gratiae, Cic

concĭlĭātor -ōris, m (concilio), *one who prepares, procures*, nuptiarum, *a match-maker*, Nep , proditionis, Liv

concĭlĭātrīcŭla -ae, f (dim of conciliatrix), *that which conciliates*, Cic

concĭlĭātrix -icis, f (conciliator) **I.** *one who unites, a match maker*, Cic **II.** Transf , *that which causes, promotes, brings about*, vis orationis conciliatrix humanae societatis, Cic

1 **concĭlĭātus** -a -um, p adj with compar and superl (from concilio), **1,** *beloved by*, Hamilcari conciliatus, Liv , **2,** *inclined to*, ut judex ad rem accipiendam fiat conciliatior, Cic

2 **concĭlĭātus,** abl -u, m *the union, connexion of atoms*, Lucr

concĭlĭo, 1 (concilium), *to bring together* **I.** *to unite, connect* **A.** corpora, Lucr **B.** *to unite in sentiment, win over*, **1,** gen , legiones sibi pecunia, Cic., animos plebis, Liv , **2,** *to recommend, make acceptable*, dictis artes conciliare suas, Ov **II. A.** *to procure, prepare, provide, furnish*, **1,** gen , pecunias, Cic , **2,** *to bring together, unite*, conciliari viro, Cat **B.** *to bring about, cause, procure*, sibi amorem ab omnibus, Cic , nuptias, Nep

concĭlĭum -ii, n (com and cio = cieo) **I.** *a union, connexion*, rerum, Lucr **II. 1,** *a coming together, assembling*, Camenarum cum Egeria, Liv , **2,** *an assembly*, **a,** pastorum, Cic , deorum, Cic , **b,** *an assembly for deliberation, a council*, (α) outside Rome, Gallorum, Liv , concilium Achaicum, *the Achaean League*, Liv., constituere diem concilio, Caes , cogere or convocare concilium, Caes , aliquem adhibere ad concilium, Caes , (β) in Rome, concilium sanctum patrum, Hor , concilium plebis habere, *to hold a meeting of the comitia tributa*, Liv , populi, *of the comitia centuriata*, Liv

concinnē, adv with compar (concinnus), *elegantly, neatly, finely, tastefully*, rogare, Cic , distribuere, *to arrange a speech artistically*, Cic

concinnĭtas -ātis, f (concinnus), *elegance and harmony of style*, verborum or sententiarum, Cic

concinnĭtūdo -inis, f = concinnitas (q v)

concinno, 1 (concinnus) **I.** *to put or fit together carefully, to arrange*, munusculum alicui, ap Cic **II.** Transf , *to produce, cause*, amorem, Lucr

concinnus -a -um, *well put together* **I.** *pleasing, that which pleases on account of harmony and proportion, elegant, neat* **A.** Gen , sat edepol concinna est virgo facie, Plaut , tectorium, Cic , helluo *elegant*, Cic **B.** Esp of discourse, *tasteful, polished*, oratio, Cic , concinnus et elegans Aristo, Cic **II.** *suited, fit, appropriate, pleasing*, concinnus amicis, Hor

concĭno -cinui -centum, 3 (com and cano), **I.** Intransit **A.** Lit , *to sing in chorus, play instruments in concert*, concinunt tubae, Liv , sic ad vada Maeandri concinit albus olor, Ov. **B.** Transf , **a,** *to join together in an utterance, to agree in saying*, ne juvet vox ista VETO, qua concinentes collegas auditis, Liv , **b,** *to agree together, harmonise*, cum Peripateticis re concinere, verbis discrepare, Cic **II** Transit **A.**

Lit., haec quum concinuntur, Cic.; carmen ad clausas fores, Ov. **B.** Transf. *to celebrate;* laetos dies, Hor. **C.** *to prophesy;* tristia omina, Ov.

1. **concĭo** = concieo (q.v.).

2. **concĭo** -ōnis = contio (q.v.).

concĭōnabundus -a -um, v. contionabundus.

concĭōnālis -e, v. contionalis.

concĭōnārĭus -a -um, v. contionarius.

concĭōnātor, v. contionator.

concĭōnor, v. contionor.

concĭpĭo -cēpi -ceptum, 3. (com and capio), *to take together, hold together.* **I.** Gen. **A.** Lit. *to contain, hold;* multum ignem trullis ferreis, Liv. **B.** Transf., of words, *to express in a certain form;* verba, jusjurandum, Liv.; quod EX ANIMI SENTENTIA juraris, sicut concipitur more nostro, *according to our customary form,* Cic.; conceptis verbis jurare, Cic.; vadimonium, Cic.; so, **1,** *to repeat words after another person,* Qu. Marcio Philippo praeeunte in foro votum, Liv.; preces, Ov.; **2,** *to publish, conclude;* foedus, Verg.; **3,** concipere summas, *to give the totals,* Liv. **II.** Esp. **A.** Lit., **1,** of fluids, *to take in, draw in, suck;* concipit Iris aquas, Ov.; terra caducas concepit lacrimas, Ov.; **2,** of fire, *to catch fire;* materies, quae nisi admoto igni ignem concipere possit, Cic.; fig., of love, quem mens mea concipit ignem, Ov.; **3,** of air, *to draw in;* pars (animae) concipitur cordis parte quadam, quem ventriculum cordis appellant, Cic.; **4,** *to conceive;* quum concepit mula, Cic.; fig., hoc quod conceptum respublica periculum parturit, Cic.; **5,** of physical qualities, *to take, gain;* alias aliasque vires, Ov. **B.** Transf., **1,** *to receive, incur, commit;* dedecus, Cic.; scelus, *perpetrate,* Cic.; **2,** *to feel;* iram intimo animo et corde, Cic.; spem regni, Liv.; **3,** *to fancy, imagine;* quid mirum si in auspiciis imbecilli animi superstitiosa ista concipiant, Cic.; **4,** *to comprehend, grasp;* rerum omnium quasi adumbratas intelligentias animo ac mente c., Cic.

concīsē, adv. (concisus), *in detached or minute portions;* hence, *concisely,* Quint.

concīsĭo -ōnis, f. (2. concido), rhet. t. t., *the breaking up of a clause into divisions,* Cic.

concīsus -a -um, p. adj. (from 2. concido), *divided into short sentences, brief, concise;* sententiae, Cic.

concĭtātĭo -ōnis, f. (concito), **1,** *quick movement;* remorum, Liv.; **2,** *tumult, sedition;* plebi contra patres concitatio et seditio, Cic.; **3,** *disturbance of the mind, passion;* ab omni concitatione animi semper vacare, Cic.

concĭtātor -ōris, m. (concito), *one who excites, stirs up;* seditionis, Cic.

concĭtātus -a -um, p. adj. with compar. and superl. (from concito), **1,** *quick, rapid;* conversio caeli, Cic.; quam concitatissimos equos immittere, *spur the horses to a full gallop,* Liv.; concitatior clamor, *louder,* Liv.; **2,** *excited, violent, passionate,* contio, Cic.

concĭto, 1. (freq. of concieo). **I. 1,** *to move quickly, violently, stir up, excite;* equum calcaribus, *to spur to a gallop,* Liv.; navem remis, Liv.; Eurus concitat aquas, Ov.; esp. *to summon by the voice;* servos ex omnibus vicis, Cic.; concitare aciem, *to move forward the army,* Liv.; se concitare in hostem, *to rush against the enemy,* Liv.; **2,** *to stir up, incite, impel;* Etruriam omnem adversus Romanos, Liv.; omnem Galliam ad suum auxilium, Caes.; animi quodam impetu concitatus, Cic. **II.** *to cause, produce;* seditionem ac discordiam, Cic.; invidiam in aliquem, Cic.

concĭtor -ōris, m. (concieo), *one who excites, stirs up;* belli, vulgi, Liv.

concĭuncŭla -ae = contiuncula (q.v.).

conclāmātĭo -ōnis, f. (conclamo), *an exclamation, shouting together;* universi exercitus, Caes.

conclāmĭto, 1. (intens. of conclamo), *to shout loudly, cry violently,* Plaut.

conclāmo, 1. **1,** *to shout together, in company;* ad arma, *to call to arms,* Liv.; vasa, *to give the signal for packing up baggage before a march,* Caes.; with acc. and infin., vos universi unā mente atque voce iterum a me conservatam esse rempublicam conclamastis, Cic.; with ut and the subj. *to demand loudly;* conclamaverunt, uti aliqui ex nostris ad colloquium prodirent, Caes.; with indirect question, conclamavit, quid ad se venirent, Caes.; esp. **a,** of a shout of joy; ad quorum casum quum conclamasset gaudio Albanus exercitus, Liv.; with acc., conclamare victoriam, Caes.; **b,** of a cry of grief, aliquem conclamare, *to bewail the death of some one,* Verg.; **2,** *to call together;* conclamare socios, Ov.

conclāve -is, n. (com and clavis), *a room, chamber, a dining-room, a bedroom,* Cic.

conclūdo -clūsi -clūsum, 3. (com and cludo = claudo). **A.** Lit. *to shut up, inclose, confine;* bestias delectationis causā, Cic.; mare conclusum, *an inland sea,* Caes. **B.** Transf., **1,** *to include, compress, confine;* aliquem in angustissimam formulam sponsionis concludere, Cic.; quartus dies hoc libro concluditur, *is comprised,* Cic.; **2,** *to bring to an end;* epistolam, Cic.; perorationem inflammantem restinguentemve concludere, Cic.; **3,** rhet. *to close rhythmically, to round off in a period;* sententias, Cic.; **4,** philosoph. t. t. *to bring to a conclusion, to argue, infer;* deinde concludebas summum malum esse dolorem, Cic.; absol., argumenta ratione concludentia, *reasonable, logical proofs,* Cic.

conclūsē, adv. (conclusus, from concludo), *with well-turned periods;* concluse apteque dicere, Cic.

conclūsĭo -ōnis, f. (concludo). **A.** Lit. *a shutting, closing,* and in military language, *a blockade,* Caes. **B.** Transf. *a close, conclusion;* **a,** conclusio muneris ac negotii tui, Cic.; **b,** rhet. t. t., *conclusion of a speech, peroration;* conclusio est exitus et determinatio totius orationis, Cic.; **c,** *a period;* verborum quaedam ad numerum conclusio, Cic.; **d,** philosoph. t. t., *conclusion in a syllogism, consequence;* rationis, Cic.

conclūsĭuncŭla -ae, f. (dim. of conclusio), *a foolish inference, paltry conclusion;* contortulae quaedam et minutulae conclusiunculae, Cic.

concoenātĭo -ōnis, f., v. concenatio.

concŏlor -ōris, *similar in colour;* humerus, Ov.; with dat., concolor est illis, Ov.

concŏquo -coxi -coctum, 3. **I.** Lit. *to boil together,* Lucr. **II.** *to digest.* **A.** Lit., cibum, Cic. **B.** Transf., **a,** *to bear, endure, stomach;* ut eius ista odia non sorbeam solum sed etiam concoquam, Cic.; aliquem senatorem (*as senator*) non concoquere, Liv.; **b,** *to consider maturely, deliberate upon;* tibi diu concoquendum est utrum, etc., Cic.; clandestina concocta sunt consilia, *have been concocted,* Liv.

1. **concordĭa** -ae, f. (concors), *agreement, union, harmony, concord, friendship, sympathy.* **I.** Lit., concordiam reconciliare, Liv.; concordiam confirmare cum aliquo, Cic.; concordiam conglutinare, Cic.; concordiam constituere, Cic.; meton., et cum Pirithoo felix concordia Theseus, *one heart and mind,* Ov. **II.** Transf., *harmony, sympathy;* concordia discors, Ov.

2. **Concordĭa** -ae, f. *the goddess Concord,* to

whom several temples in Rome were dedicated, in one of which the senate frequently held its sittings, Cic.

concorditer, adv, with compar and superl (concors), *harmoniously, with concord, amicably*, concordissime vivere cum aliquo, Cic

concordo, 1 (concors), *to agree, be in union*, quum animi judicia opinionesque concordant, with dat, concordant carmina nervis, Ov.

concors -dis, adj with compar and superl (com and cor), *of one mind or opinion, concordant, agreeing, harmonious*, fratres concordissimi, Cic ; concordes animae, Verg ; of inanimate objects, moderatus et concors civitatis status, Cic

concrebresco -brui, 3 *to increase*, Verg.

concredo -didi -ditum, 3 *to intrust, commit to*, rem et famam suam commendare et concredere alicui, Cic

concremo, 1 *to burn up, burn entirely*, omnia tecta, Liv.

concrepo -ui, 1 **I.** Intransit. *to rattle, creak, clash, grate*, scabilla concrepant, Cic, concrepuere arma, Liv, armis concrepat multitudo, Caes ; exercitus gladiis ad scuta concrepuit, Liv, si digitis concrepuerit, *at the least sign*, Cic. **II.** Transit *to rattle, strike upon*, aera, Ov.

concresco -crevi -cretum **A.** Gen *to become stiff, to congeal, curdle, harden*, lac, Verg, aer, Cic, nive pruinaque concrescit aqua, Cic, frigore sanguis, Verg, quum claram speciem concreto lumine luna abdidit, *with darkened light*, Cic. **B.** *to grow, collect, increase, be formed*, aut simplex est natura animantis aut concreta est ex pluribus naturis, Cic, de terris terram concrescere parvis, Lucr (infin perf syncop concresse, Ov)

concretio -onis, f (concresco), **1,** *a growing together, congealing, condensing*; corporum, Cic, **2,** *materiality, matter*, mortalis, Cic

concretus -a -um p adj (from concresco), *thickened, congealed, condensed, stiffened*, glacies, Liv, lac, Verg ; dolor, *hard, tearless*, Ov

concrucio, 1 *to torture violently*, Lucr

concubina -ae, f (concubo), *a concubine*

concubinatus -us, m (concubinus), *concubinage*, Plaut

concubinus -i, m *a man living in a state of concubinage*, Tac

concubitus -us, m. (concubo), **1,** *lying together* (at table), Prop, **2,** *copulation*, Cic

concubium -ii, n (concubius), noctis, *the dead of night, the time at which men are in deep sleep*, Plaut

concubius -a -um (concumbo), *relating to sleep*, found only in the phrase concubia nocte, *at the time of men's first sleep, at dead of night*, Cic

concubo, 1 = concumbo (q v)

conculco, 1 (com and calco) **A.** *to tread, trample under foot*, Cato **B.** Transf, *to misuse, to despise*, miseram Italiam, Cic ; Macedonicam lauream, Cic.

concumbo -cubui -cubitum, 3 (com and cumbo), *to lie with, have intercourse with*, Ov

concupisco -pivi or -pii -pitum, 3 (com and cupio), *to desire eagerly, covet, to endeavour after, aim at*; eandem mortem gloriosam, Cic, signa, tabulas, supellectilem, vestem infinite, Cic, with infin., ducere aliquam in matrimonium, Cic

concurro -curri (rarely -cucurri) -cursum, 3. **I.** *to run together, come together, flock to one spot*, tota Italia concurret, Cic.; ad arma, Caes, ad curiam, Cic, ad me restituendum Romam, Cic **II. 1,** a, *to meet together*, ut neve aspere (verba) concurrerent neve vastius diducantur, Cic, concurrit dextera laeva, *of clapping the hands for applause*, Hor ; b, *to happen at the same time*, quae ut concurrant omnia, optabile est, Cic, **2,** a, *to run, dash, strike together*, ne prorae concurrerent, Liv, b, *to rush to conflict, attack, engage*, concurrunt equites inter se, Caes ; omnia ventorum concurrere proelia vidi, Verg, cum acie legionum recta fronte, Liv, with dat., concurrere equitibus, Liv, adversus aliquem, Liv, in aliquem, Sall, transf, concurrentis belli minae, *war on the point of breaking out*, Tac

concursatio -onis, f (concurso), *a running together, concourse*, **1,** of persons, a, puerorum, Cic, b, *going round*, concursatio regis a Demetriade nunc Lamiam in concilium Aetolorum nunc Chalcidem, Liv ; c, *skirmishing of light troops*, Liv, **2,** of things without life, somniorum, Cic

concursator -oris, m (concurso), *a skirmisher* (opp statarius), Liv

concursio -onis, f (concurro), **1,** *a running together, concourse*, atomorum, Cic, **2,** *a figure of speech, in which the same word is frequently repeated* (Gr συμπλοκή), Cic

concurso, 1 **I.** Intransit *to run about, rush hither and thither*, **1,** of persons, a, tum trepidare et concursare, Caes, dies noctesque, Cic, b, *to skirmish*, inter saxa rupesque, Liv, c, *to travel about* (esp of the magistrates of provinces), *to make official visits* Cic, **2,** of things, ignes concursant, Lucr **II.** Transit *to visit*, omnes fere domos omnium, Cic

concursus -us, m (concurro) **I.** *a running together, concourse*, **1,** concursus hominum in forum, Cic, facere, *to cause a tumult or concourse*, **2,** of abstractions, *union*, honestissimorum studiorum, *co-operation in*, Cic **II. A.** *a striking together, meeting*, corpusculorum, Cic, verborum, Cic **B.** *a dashing together*, **1,** navium, Caes, *a hostile encounter*, concursus utriusque exercitus, Caes, **2,** fig, non posse sustinere concursum omnium philosophorum, Cic, **3,** of disasters, concursus calamitatum, *attack*, Cic

concussus, abl -u, m (concutio), *a shaking, concussion*, Lucr

concutio -cussi -cussum, 3 **I.** *to shake violently, agitate* **A.** Gen., a, lit, caput, Ov, terra concussa motu est, Liv ; b, transf, te ipsum concute, *search, examine yourself*, Hor **B.** a, *to shatter, disturb, impair*, rempublicam, Cic, b, *to alarm, trouble*, terrorem metum concutientem definiunt, Cic, casu concussus acerbo, Verg, c, *to urge, excite*, pectus, Verg **C.** *to strike together*, frameas, Tac

condecet, 2, impers *it is proper, fit, decent*, capies quod te condecet, Plaut

condecoro, 1. *to adorn carefully*, ludos scenicos, Ter

condemnator -oris, m (condemno), *an accuser*, Tac

condemno, 1 (com and damno) **I.** Of a judge, *to condemn, sentence* **A.** Lit., Cic, with genit, of the crime, aliquem injuriarum, Cic, of the punishment, capitis, Cic, with de, aliquem de alea, Cic, with abl of the penalty, denis millibus aeris, Liv **B.** a, *to accuse*, aliquem impudentiae, Cic ; b, *to disapprove*; tuum factum non esse condemnatum judicio amicorum, Cic **II.** Of an accuser, *to urge or effect the condemnation of a person*, condemnare aliquem uno hoc crimine, Cic

condenseo = condenso (q.v.).

condenso, 1. *to make thick, press close together*, Varr.

condensus -a -um, *dense, thick;* puppes litore, Verg.; vallis arboribus condensa, Liv.

condīco -dixi -dictum, **1,** *to make arrangement with, agree to, fix, appoint, settle;* diem, Plaut.; **2,** condicere alicui, *to invite oneself as a guest*, Cic.

condignus -a -um, *quite worthy, very worthy;* donum, Plaut.

condīmentum -i, n. (condio), *spice, seasoning, sauce, condiment.* **A.** Lit. cibi condimentum est fames, potionis sitis, Cic. **B.** Transf., facetiae omnium sermonum condimenta, Cic.; severitas alicuius multis condimentis humanitatis mitigatur, Cic.

condĭo -ivi or -ii -itum, **4.** *to pickle, to preserve.* **A.** Lit. **a,** in wine or vinegar, oleas, Cato; **b,** in spice, *to make savoury;* herbas, Cic.; hence, **c,** unguenta, *to make fragrant*, Cic.; **c,** *to embalm;* mortuos, Cic. **B.** Transf. *to season, ornament, make pleasant;* orationem, Cic.; *to soften, temper;* tristitiam temporum, Cic.

condiscĭpŭla -ae, f. *a female schoolfellow*, Mart.

condiscĭpŭlus -i, m. *a schoolfellow*, Cic.

condisco -didici, 3. *to learn thoroughly;* modos, Hor.; with infin., mihi paulo diligentius supplicare, Cic.

1. **condĭtĭo** -ōnis (condio), **1,** *pickling* or *preserving of fruits*, Cic.; **2,** *a seasoning, making savoury;* ciborum, Ov.

2. **condĭtĭo** -ōnis, f. (condo), **1,** *state, condition, external position, place, circumstances;* infima servorum, Cic.; eā conditione nati sumus ut, etc., Cic.; conditio imperii, Cic.; parem cum ceteris fortunae conditionem subire, Cic.; **2,** *a condition, stipulation, provision, proviso;* non respuit conditionem, Caes.; conditionem aequissimam repudiare, Cic.; conditionem accipere, Cic.; hāc, eā, istā conditione, his conditionibus, *on these terms*, Cic.; armis conditione positis, *under conditions of peace*, Cic.; **3,** esp. *conditions of marriage, marriage contract, marriage;* and meton. *the person married;* aliam conditionem quaerere, Cic.; conditionem filiae quaerere, Liv.; nullius conditionis non habere potestatem, Nep.; in a bad sense, *a gallant, paramour*, Cic.

condĭtor -ōris, m. (condo), *a founder, maker, contriver, composer, author;* Romanae arcis, Verg.; Romanae libertatis, Liv.; conditor et instructor convivii, Cic.; conditor, Romani anni, *chronicler*, Ov.

condĭtōrium -ii, n. (condo), *the place in which a corpse or its ashes are preserved*, Suet.

1. **condĭtus** -a -um, partic. of condo.

2. **condĭtus** -a -um, p. adj., with compar. (from condio), *seasoned, savoury.* **I.** Lit. conditiora haec facit venatio, Cic. **II.** Transf. *seasoned, ornamented;* oratio lepore et festivitate conditior, Cic.

condo -didi -ditum, 3. **I. a,** *to put together, form, establish;* urbem Romam, Cic.; Romanam gentem, Verg.; collegium ad id novum, Liv.; **b,** *to compose, write;* carmen, Cic.; leges, Liv.; hence, *to celebrate in song;* tristia bella, Verg.; Caesaris acta, Ov. **II.** *to put in.* **A.** *to thrust, press in;* ensem in pectus, Ov. **B. 1,** *to preserve, collect;* pecuniam, Cic.; litteras publicas in sanctiore aerario conditas habere, Cic.; aliquid domi suae conditum jam putare, Cic.; so esp. **a,** of wine, fruits, etc. *to store up;* frumentum, Cic.; fig., bonum in visceribus medullisque, Cic.; of fruits, *to preserve, pickle;* corna condita in liquida faece, Ov.; **b,** of persons, *to hide;* se deserto in litore, Verg.; *to put, place;* aliquem in carcerem, Cic.; **c,** *to bury;* aliquem in sepulcro, Cic.; **2,** transf., in causis conditae (*hidden*); sunt res futurae, Cic.; **3, a,** *to withdraw from sight;* caput inter nubila, Verg.; of persons, condere diem, *to pass the day;* longos soles cantando, Verg.; **b,** *to conceal, to cover;* caelum umbra, Verg.; transf., iram, Tac.

condŏcĕfăcĭo -fēci -factum, 3 (condoceo and facio), *to train, instruct, teach;* beluas, Cic.; animum, Cic.

condŏlesco -dŏlŭi (com and doleo), 3. *to suffer severely, to feel pain, to pain;* si pes condoluit, si dens, Cic.; latus ei dicenti condoluisse, Cic.

condōnātĭo -ōnis, f. (condono), *a giving away;* bonorum possessionumque, Cic.

condōno, 1., **1,** a, *to give away, present;* agros suis latronibus, Cic.; consuli totam Achaiam, Cic.; of the praetor, alicui hereditatem, *to award the inheritance*, Cic.; **b,** *to give up to, sacrifice to;* se vitamque suam reipublicae, Sall.; condonari libidini muliebri, Cic.; **2, a,** *to forgive a debt;* pecunias creditas debitoribus, Cic.; **b,** hence, *to overlook, forgive a fault;* alicui crimen, Cic.; *to forgive an injury for the sake of a third party;* praeterita se Divitiaco fratri condonare dicit, Caes.

Condrūsi -ōrum, m. *a German people in Gallia Belgica.*

condūcĭbĭlis -e (conduco), *profitable, useful;* consilium ad eam rem, Plaut.

condūco -duxi -ductum, 3. **I.** Transit. **A.** *to bring* or *lead together, collect;* **a,** of persons, exercitum in unum locum, Caes.; virgines unum in locum, Cic.; **b,** of things, *to bring together, unite, connect;* partes in unum, Lucr.; vineas, Cic.; cortice ramos, Ov.; transf., propositionem et assumptionem in unum, Cic. **B.** *to hire*, **a,** of persons, aliquem mercede, Cic.; consulem ad caedem faciendam, Cic.; esp. milit. t. t. *to hire soldiers;* homines, Caes.; milites Gallos mercede, Liv.; **b,** of things, *to hire for use* (opp. locare), domum, hortum, Cic.; esp. *to farm the taxes;* portorium, Cic.; **c,** *to undertake, contract for;* columnam faciendam, Cic. **II.** Intransit. *to be of use, to profit, to serve*, Cic.; with dat., quae saluti tuae conducere arbitror, Cic.; with ad and the acc., ad vitae commoditatem, Cic.; with acc. and infin., hoc maxime reipublicae conducit Syriam Macedoniamque decerni, Cic.

conductīcĭus -a -um (conduco), *hired;* exercitus, *mercenary*, Nep.

conductĭo -ōnis, f. (conduco), **1,** *a bringing together, uniting, recapitulation*, Cic.; **2,** *hiring, farming;* fundi, Cic.

conductor -ōris, m. (conduco), **1,** *one who hires;* mercedes habitationum annuas conductoribus donare, Caes.; **2,** *a contractor;* operis, Cic.

conductus -a -um, partic. of conduco.

condŭplĭco, 1. *to double;* divitias, Lucr.

condūro, 1. *to harden, make quite hard;* ferrum, Lucr.

cōnecto, cōnexio, v. connecto, connexio.

cōnesto, v. cohonesto.

confābŭlor, 1., dep. *to talk, converse*, Plaut.

confarrĕātĭo -ōnis, f. (confarreo), *an ancient and solemn form of the marriage ceremony among the Romans, in which* panis farreus *was used*, Plin.

confarrĕo, 1. (com and far), *to marry by the ceremony of* confarreatio; patricios confarreatis parentibus genitus, Tac.

confātālis -e, *determined by fate*, Cic.

confectĭo -ōnis, f (conficio), 1, a, *a making ready, preparation, producing, composing, completing*, muneris libri, Cic.; belli, Cic.; b, *exaction*, tributi, Cic.; 2, *consumption*, escarum, Cic.; valetudinis, *weakening*, Cic.

confector -ōris, m (conficio), 1, *one who prepares, completes, finishes*, negotiorum, Cic.; 2, *a destroyer, consumer*, confector et consumptor omnium ignis, Cic.

confercĭo fersi -fertum, 4 (com and farcio), *to press close together, compress, cram together*; confertae naves, Liv.

confĕro, contŭli, collātum (conlātum), conferre. I. *to bring together, collect*, 1, a, lit., sarcinas in unum locum, Caes.; b, transf., conferamus igitur in pauca, Cic. 2, *to bring together money, contribute*, tributa quotannis ex censu, Cic.; quadragena talenta quotannis Delum, Nep.; 3, *to unite, to join, connect*, vires in unum, Liv.; 4, *to place together* or *near*, a, lit. (α) in a friendly manner, capita, Cic.; gradum, Verg.; (β) as milit. t. t., *to bring into hostile contact* or *collision*, Galli cum Fontejo ferrum ac manus contulerunt, Cic.; pedem cum pede, or conferre pedem, *to fight foot to foot*, Liv., Cic.; signa conferre, *to engage*, Cic.; se viro vir contulit, *man fought with man*, Verg.; absol., mecum confer, ait, *fight with me*, Ov.; conferre lites, *to contend*, Hor.; b, transf., of speech, *to interchange, exchange, discuss*, sermonem cum aliquo, Cic.; consilia, Liv.; tum si quid res feret, coram conferemus, Cic.; 5, *to compare*, Gallicum cum Germanorum agro, Caes.; cum illius vita P. Sullae vobis notissimam, Cic.; parva magnis, Cic. II. *to bring to a place*, 1, *to remove, transfer*, a, lit., suas rationes et copias in illam provinciam, Cic.; esp., se conferre, *to betake oneself, flee*, se in astu, Cic.; b, transf. (α) se conferre, *to devote oneself, join oneself to*, conferre se ad pontificem Scaevolam, Cic.; se ad studium scribendi, Cic.; (β) *to put off, postpone*, aliquid in longiorem diem, Caes.; 2, *to apply*, a, lit., pecuniam ad beneficentiam, Cic.; b, transf. (α) of thoughts, etc., *to direct, use*, curam ad philosophiam, Cic.; (β) *to hand over*; rem ad aliquem, Cic.; (γ) *to impute, attribute*, permulta in Plancium quae ab eo dicta non sunt, Cic.; culpam in aliquem, Cic.; (δ) confert, *it is profitable*, Quint.

confertim, adv. (confertus), *densely, thickly, compactly*, pugnare, Liv.

confertus a -um, p. adj. with compar. and superl. (confercio), 1, *closely compressed, dense* (opp. rarus), confertae naves, Liv.; confertissima turba, Liv.; conferti milites, *in close formation*, Caes.; 2, with abl., *full of*, ingenti turbā conferta templa, Liv.; transf., vita, plena et conferta voluptatibus, Cic.

confervĕfăcĭo, 3 *to make very hot, to melt*, Lucr.

confervesco ferbŭi, 3 *to begin to boil, begin to glow*, transf., mea quum conferbuit ira, Hor.

confessĭo -ōnis, f (confiteor), *a confession, acknowledgment*, errati sui, Cic.; captae pecuniae, Cic.; adducere aliquem ad ignorationis confessionem, Cic.; exprimere ab aliquo confessionem culpae, Liv.; ea erat confessio caput rerum Romam esse, Liv.

confessus -a um (partic. of confiteor, with pass. meaning), *undoubted, acknowledged, certain*; res manifesta, confessa, Cic.; hence, ex confesso, *confessedly*, Quint.; in confesso esse, Tac.; in confessum venire, *to be generally acknowledged, universally known*, Plin.

confestim, adv., *immediately, without delay*, confestim huc advolare, Cic.; confestim consequi, Cic.; patres consulere, Liv.

confĭcĭens entis, p. adj. (from conficio), *that which causes, effects, effecting, efficient*, causae, Cic.; with genit., cum civitate mihi res est acerrima et conficientissima litterarum, *that notes down everything carefully*, Cic.

confĭcĭo feci -fectum, 3 (com and facio), *to make together*, hence, I. *to finish, make ready, bring about, accomplish*, 1, a, soccos suā manu, Cic.; litteras, Cic.; sacra, Cic.; tantum facinus, Cic.; bellum, Cic.; his rebus confectis, Caes.; b, of business, *to conclude a bargain or transaction*; negotium ex sententia, Cic.; rem sine pugna et sine vulnere, Caes.; pactiones, Cic.; pretium, *settle the price*, Cic.; absol., confice cum Apella de columnis, *settle, arrange*, Cic.; c, of a journey, *to bring to an end*, cursum, Cic.; iter ex sententia, Cic.; incredibili celeritate magnum spatium paucis diebus, Cic.; d, of time, *to complete*, prope centum confecisse annos, Cic.; extremum vitae diem morte, Cic.; nondum hieme confecta, Caes.; 2, a, *to procure*, permagnam ex illa re pecuniam confici posse, Caes.; frumentum, Liv.; milit. t. t., *to get soldiers*, reliquas legiones, quas ex novo delectu confecerat, Cic.; exercitus maximos, Cic.; tribum suam necessariis, *to gain over*, Cic.; b, *to produce, cause*, (α) alicui reditum, procur., Cic.; motus animorum, Cic.; (β) philosoph. t. t., *to prove*, ex quo conficitur ut, etc., *it follows from this*, Cic. II. 1, *to consume*, a, of food, etc. (α) *to chew, eat*, escas, Cic.; plures jam pavones confeci, quam tu pullos columbinos, Cic.; (β) *to digest*, confectus et consumptus cibus, Cic.; b, *to waste, destroy*, patrimonium suum, Cic.; 2, *to destroy, kill*, haec sica nuper ad regiam me paene confecit, Cic.; 3, *to subdue*, Britanniam, Cic.; 4, *to weaken*, a, vitae cupiditas, quae me conficit angoribus, Cic.; often in pass., confici fame, frigore, lacrimis, curis, dolore, Cic.; confectus macie et squalore, Cic.; vulneribus, Caes.; b, of states, praevalentis populi vires se ipse conficiunt, Liv.

confictĭo ōnis, f (confingo), *a fabrication, invention*, criminis, Cic.

confīdens -entis, p. adj. with compar. and superl. (from confido), *confident, self-reliant*, gen. in a bad sense, *shameless, impudent*, Cic.

confīdentĕr, adv., with compar. and superl. (confidens), *boldly, confidently*, confidentius dicere, Cic.

confīdentĭa -ae, f (confidens), a, *confidence*, confidentiam afferre hominibus, ap. Cic.; b, more frequently, *impudence, boldness, shamelessness*, confidentia et temeritas tua, Cic.

confīdo -fisus sum (confidi (?), Liv.), 3 *to trust, be assured, confide*, a, absol., nimis confidere, Cic.; b, with dat., sibi, Cic.; c, with abl., militum virtute non satis, Cic.; d, with de, de salute urbis, Caes.; e, with acc. and infin., *to believe firmly*, id ita futurum esse confido, Cic.

confīgo -fixi -fixum, 3 1, *to fasten together, nail together*, transtra clavis ferreis, Caes.; 2, *to pierce through, transfix with a weapon*, a, lit., filios suos sagittis, Cic.; b, transf., ducentis confixus senatus consultis, Cic.

confindo, 3. *to cleave asunder*, Tib.

confingo -finxi fictum, 3 1, *to construct* nidos, Plin.; 2, *to fabricate, feign, invent*, crimen incredibile, Cic.; crimina in aliquem, Cic.

confīnis -e A. Lit., *having the same boundary, conterminous, adjacent, near*, confines erant hi Senonibus, Caes.; caput confinis collo, Ov. Subst., **confinis** is, m *a neighbour*, Mart. B. Transf., *nearly allied, similar*, studio confinia carmina vestro, Ov.

confīnĭum ii, n (confinis) A. Lit., a

confine, common boundary, limit, border (of countries or estates); Trevirorum, Caes.; convenict in omni re contrahenda vicinitatibus et confiniis aequum et facilem esse, Cic. **B.** Transf., *the bordering line, nearness, close connexion;* confinia noctis, *twilight,* Ov.; breve confinium artis et falsi, Tac.

confirmātĭo -ōnis, f. (confirmo), **a,** *an establishing, making firm;* confirmatio perpetuae libertatis, Cic.; **b,** esp., *consolation, encouragement, support;* neque enim confirmatione nostrā egebat virtus tua, Cic.; **c,** *confirming* or *verifying a fact;* perfugae, Caes.; **d,** rhet. t. t., *adducing of proofs,* Cic.

confirmātor -ōris, m. (confirmo), *one who confirms, establishes;* pecuniae, *a surety,* Cic.

confirmātus -a -um, p. adj. with compar. and superl. (from confirmo), **1,** *encouraged, emboldened;* satis certus et confirmatus animus, Cic.; **2,** *certain, credible;* in quibus (litteris) erat confirmatius idem illud, Cic.

confirmo, 1. **I.** Lit., *to establish, make firm, confirm, strengthen;* hoc nervos confirmari putant, Caes.; valetudinem, *to recover health,* Cic.; se confirmare, *to recover strength,* Cic. **II.** Transf., **A.** Gen., *to strengthen, make lasting;* pacem, Cic.; consilia, *to support,* Caes.; confirmatis rebus, *firmly established,* Caes.; se transmarinis auxiliis, Caes.; polit. t. t., *to ratify;* acta Caesaris, Cic. **B.** Esp. **a,** *to confirm persons in allegiance,* etc.; jure jurando inter se, Caes.; **b,** *to strengthen, encourage;* confirmare et excitare afflictos animos, Cic.; erige te et confirma, *take courage;* animos Gallorum verbis, Caes.; **c,** *to confirm* or *establish the truth of an assertion;* nostra argumentis ac rationibus, Cic.; **d,** *to affirm, assert positively;* id omne ego me rei publicae causā suscepisse confirmo, Cic.

confisco, 1. (com and fiscus), **1,** *to lay up, preserve in a chest,* Suet.; **2,** *to appropriate to the imperial treasury, to confiscate,* Suet.

confīsĭo -ōnis, f. (confido), *confidence, assurance;* fidentia, id est firma animi confisio, Cic.

confĭtĕor -fessus sum, 2. dep. (com and fateor). **I.** Lit., *to confess, allow, acknowledge;* with acc., hoc crimen, Cic.; with acc. and dat., amorem nutrici, Ov.; with double acc., se victos, Caes.; with acc. and infin., multa se ignorare, Cic.; with de, aliquid de veneno, Cic. Partic. perf., **confessus, a,** act., *having confessed;* quinque homines comprehensi atque confessi, Cic.; **b,** pass., *confessed, acknowledged;* quam improbam, quam manifestam, quam confessam rem pecunia redimere conetur, Cic. **II.** Transf., *to reveal, make known;* se, Ov.; deam, *as a goddess,* Verg.

conflăgro, 1. *to be destroyed by fire, to be burnt up.* **A.** Lit., classis praedonum incendio conflagrabat, Cic.; fig., amoris flammā, Cic.; incendio invidiae, Cic. **B.** Transf., conflagrare invidiā, *to fall a victim to hatred,* Cic.

conflictĭo -ōnis, f. (confligo), *a striking together, collision, a conflict, combat;* transf., causarum, Cic.

conflicto, 1. (intens. of confligo), *to strike together violently;* thus pass., **a,** *to combat with, contend with;* conflictari cum adversā fortunā, Nep.; conflictari cum aliquo, Cic.; **b,** conflictari aliquā re, *to be grievously troubled, to suffer severely, to be harassed, tormented;* iniquissimis verbis, Cic.; magnā inopiā necessariarum rerum, Caes.; duriore fortunā, Cic.

conflictus -ūs, m. (confligo), *a striking together;* lapidum, Cic.

confligo -flixi -flictum, 3. **I.** Transit., *to strike, bring, join together;* corpora, Lucr.; transf., *to bring together in order to compare;* factum adversarii cum scripto, Cic. **II.** Intransit., **a,** *to strike together;* illae (naves) graviter inter se incitatae conflixerunt, Caes.; **b,** *to struggle, fight, contend;* cum hoste, Cic.; contra or adversus aliquem, Nep.

conflo, 1. **I.** *to blow together, to blow up, to kindle.* **A.** Lit., quorum operā id conflatum incendium, Liv. **B.** Transf., *to excite;* seditionem, Cic. **II.** *to melt.* **A.** Lit., **a,** of metals, Plin.; falces in enses, *to forge,* Verg.; **b,** of money, *to coin;* aut flare aut conflare pecuniam, Cic. **B.** Transf., **a,** *to unite;* horum consensus conspirans et paene conflatus, Cic.; **b,** *to rivet together, forge, produce;* ut una ex duabus naturis conflata videatur, Cic.; **c,** *to get together;* exercitus perditorum civium clandestino scelere conflatus, Cic.; **d,** *to forge, invent;* crimen, Cic.; alicui periculum, Cic.; **e,** *to brood over, meditate;* judicia domi conflabant, pronuntiabant in foro, Liv.

conflŭens -entis or **conflŭentes** -ium, m. *the confluence* or *place of junction of two rivers;* Mosae et Rheni, Caes.

conflŭo -fluxi, 3. **A.** *to flow together;* in unum, Cic.; a confluente Rhodano castra movi, *from the confluence of the Rhone with the Arar,* ap. Cic. **B.** Transf., **a,** of a crowd, *to stream* or *flock together;* Athenas, Cic.; ad haec studia, Cic.; **b,** of abstractions, ad ipsos laus, honos, dignitas confluit, Cic.

confŏdĭo -fōdi -fossum, 3. **a,** *to dig thoroughly;* hortum, Plaut.; **b,** *to stab, pierce, wound;* jacentem, Liv.; (Ciceronem) de improviso domi suae, Sall.; fig., tot judiciis confossi praedamnatique, Liv.

conformātĭo -ōnis, f. (conformo). **A.** Lit., *a form, shape, forming, conformation;* lineamentorum, Cic. **B.** Transf., **1,** gen., vocis, *expression;* verborum, *arrangement,* Cic.; **2,** esp., **a,** philosoph. t. t., conformatio animi, or simply conformatio, *an idea,* Cic.; **b,** in rhet. t. t., *a figure of speech,* Cic.

conformo, 1. *to form symmetrically, form, arrange.* **A.** Lit., mundum a natura conformatum esse, Cic.; ad majora quaedam nos natura genuit et conformavit, Cic. **B.** Transf., *to arrange fittingly;* vocem secundum rationem rerum, Cic.; se ad voluntatem alicuius, Cic.

confossus -a -um, partic. of confodio.

confrăgōsus -a -um, *rugged, uneven;* loca, via, Liv.; neut. plur. as subst., *uneven places,* Liv.

confrĕmo -frĕmŭi, 3. *to murmur, roar, make a loud noise;* confremuere omnes, Ov.

confrĭco -fricŭi -fricātum, 1. *to rub;* caput atque os suum unguento, Cic.

confringo -frēgi -fractum, 3. (com and frango). **A.** Lit., *to break in two, break in pieces;* digitos, Cic. **B.** Transf., *to destroy, bring to naught;* consilia senatoria, Cic.

confŭgĭo -fūgi, 3. **A.** Lit., *to fly to, take refuge;* ad aliquem, ad or in aram, Cic.; in naves, Caes. **B.** Transf., **a,** ad alicuius misericordiam, Cic.; ad opem judicum, Cic.; **b,** *to have recourse to;* patrias ad artes, Ov.; confugit illuc ut neget, etc., Cic.

confŭgĭum -ĭi, n. (confugio), *a place of refuge,* Ov.

confŭlcĭo -fultus, 4. *to prop up,* Lucr.

confundo -fūdi -fūsum, 3. **I.** *to pour together, mingle, mix.* **A.** Lit., cum alicuius lacrimis lacrimas confundere nostras, Ov.; quum ignis oculorum cum eo igni qui est ob os offusus se confudit et contulit, Cic. **B.** Transf., **1,** *to join together;* tantā multitudine confusā, Caes. . . . populi confusi in unum, Liv.; ea philosophia quae confundit vera cum falsis, Cic , in hac confusā et universā defensione, *complicated*, Cic , **2,** **a,** *to confuse, throw into disorder*, signa et ordines peditum atque equitum, Liv , jura gentium, Liv , particulas minutas primum confusas, postea in ordinem adductas a mente divina, Cic , **b,** (α) *to obscure*, vultum Lunae, Ov , (β) *to confuse, trouble, disturb* confusa pudore, Ov , audientium animos, Liv , maerore recenti confusus, Liv **II.** *to pour into*, cruor confusus in fossam, Hor , per quas lapsus cibus in eam venam confunditur, Cic , transf , est hoc quidem in totam orationem confundendum, nec minime in extremam, Cic

confūsē, adv. with compar (confusus), *confusedly, in a disorderly manner*; loqui, Cic

confūsĭo -ōnis, f (confundo), **1,** *a mixture, union, connexion*, haec conjunctio confusioque virtutum, Cic , **2,** **a,** *confusion, disorder*, suffragiorum, *voting not in the centuries, but man by man*, Cic , religionum, Cic , **b,** oris, *blushing*, Tac

confūsus -a -um, p adj , with compar and superl (confundo), **a,** *disorderly, confused*, ita confusa est oratio, ita perturbata, nihil ut sit primum, nihil secundum, Cic., strages Verg , **b,** *confused in appearance*, vultus, Liv , confusus animo, Liv

confūto, 1 *to check the boiling of a liquid*, hence transf , **a,** *to check, repress*, maximis doloribus affectus eos ipsos inventorum suorum memoriā et recordatione confutat, Cic , **b,** esp by speech, *to put down, silence, overthrow*, audaciam alicuius, Cic , argumenta Stoicorum, Cic

congĕlo, 1 **I.** Transit , *to freeze thoroughly* **A.** Lit , Mart **B.** Transf , *to harden thicken*, rictus in lapidem, Ov. **II.** Intransit , *to freeze*, Ister congelat, Ov , fig , congelasse nostrum amicum laetabar otio, *had become inactive*, Cic

congĕmĭno, 1 *to double, redouble*, ictus crebros ensibus, Verg

congĕmo -gĕmŭi, 3 **I** Intransit , *to sigh or groan loudly*, congemuit senatus frequens, Cic **II.** Transit , *to bewail, lament*, mortem, Lucr

congĕr and **gongĕr** -gri, m (γόγγρος), *a sea or conger eel*, Ov

congĕrĭes -ēi, f (congero) **A.** Gen , *a heap, mass*, lapidum, Liv **B.** Esp , **1,** *a heap of wood, a wood pile*, Ov , **2,** *the mass of chaos*, Ov

congĕro -gessi -gestum, 3 **A.** Lit *to carry together, bring together, collect*; **1,** undique quod idoneum ad muniendum putarent, Nep , salis magnam vim ex proximis salinis, Caes ; maximam vim auri atque argenti in regnum suum, Cic., oscula, *to add one to another*, Ov , **2,** **a,** *to prepare*, alicui viaticum, Cic , **b,** *to heap together*, auri pondus, Ov , **c,** *to build*, aram sepulcri arboribus, so of birds, locus aerius quo congessere palumbes, *have built their nests*, Verg **B.** Transf , **a,** in discourse, *to bring together, comprise*; turbam patronorum in hunc sermonem, Cic , **b,** *to heap together*, ingentia beneficia in aliquem, Liv , omnia ornamenta ad aliquem, Cic , maledicta in aliquem, Cic , omnes vastati agri periculorumque imminentium causas in aliquem, *to ascribe, impute*, Cic

congestīcĭus -a -um (congero), *heaped up, artificially brought together*, agger, Caes

congestus -ūs, m (congero), *a collecting, heaping together* **I.** Lit , **a,** gen , municipia congestu copiarum vastabantur, Tac , **b,** esp of birds, *building nests*, herbam (exstitisse) avium congestu, Cic **II.** Meton , *that which is brought together, a heap, mass*, lapidum, Tac.

congĭārĭum ii, n (sc donum), *a donation distributed by the consuls and emperors among the people*, so called from the fact that it originally consisted of a congius of wine, oil, etc , Liv , *a donation in money to the soldiery*, Cic , or *to private friends*, Cic

congĭus ii, m *a Roman measure for liquids, containing six sextarii*, Liv

conglăcĭo, 1 **I.** Intransit , **A.** Lit , *to freeze*, frigoribus conglaciat aqua, Cic **B.** Transf , Curioni nostro tribunatus conglaciat, *passes inactively*, ap Cic **II.** Transit , *to turn to ice*, Plin

conglŏbātĭo -ōnis, f (conglobo), *a heaping, pressing, crowding together*, Tac

conglŏbo, 1 (com and globus), **1,** *to form into a ball or sphere*; mare conglobatum undique aequabiliter, Cic , figura conglobata, Cic , **2,** *to press together in a mass or crowd*, **a,** lit , catervatim uti quosque fors conglobaverat, Sall , conglobata in unum multitudo, Liv , **b,** transf , maxime definitiones valent conglobatae, *accumulated*, Cic

conglŏmĕro, 1 *to roll, twist, entangle together*, Lucr

conglūtĭnātĭo -ōnis, f (conglutino), **1,** *a sticking, cementing together*, Cic , **2,** *connexion, joining together*, verborum, Cic

conglūtĭno, 1 **A.** *to stick together, cement together*, Plin **B.** Transf , *to connect, bind closely*, amicitias, Cic , voluntates nostras consuetudine, Cic

congrātŭlor, 1 dep *to wish joy, congratulate*, congratulantur libertatem concordiamque civitati restitutam, Liv

congrĕdĭor -gressus, 3 dep (com and gradior), **1,** *to meet*, cum aliquo, Cic , inter se, Liv , **2,** *to meet hostilely, in combat*, **a,** *to engage, contend*, locus, ubi congressi sunt, Cic ; congredi sua sponte cum finitimis proelio, Cic , with dat , impar congressus Achilli, Verg , **b,** *to dispute in words, argue*, congredi cum Academico, Cic

congrĕgābĭlis -e (congrego), *sociable, inclined to collect*, examina apium, Cic

congrĕgātĭo -ōnis, f (congrego), *an assembling together, society, union*, nos ad congregationem hominum et ad societatem communitatemque generis humani esse natos, Cic

congrĕgo, 1. (com and grex) **I.** Lit , **A.** *to collect into a flock*, oves, Plin ; refl , se congregare, or pass , congregari, in a middle sense, *to form into flocks* apium examina congregantur, *form themselves into swarms*, Cic **B.** Of men, *to collect gather together*, dispersos homines in unum locum, Cic , refl , se congregare, and pass , congregari, in middle sense, *to assemble*, congregari in fano commentandi causa, Cic **II.** Transf , of things, *to unite*, signa in unum locum, Tac

congressĭo -ōnis f (congredior), **1,** *a meeting*, Cic , **2,** *intercourse, society*, aliquem ab alicuius non modo familiaritate, sed etiam congressione prohibere, Cic

congressus -ūs, m (congredior), *a meeting*, **1,** *a friendly meeting, social intercourse, conversation*, alicuius aditum congressum, sermonem fugere, Cic , often in plur , congressus hominum fugere atque odisse, Cic , **2,** *a hostile meeting, combat*, ante congressum, Cic primo congressu terga vertere nostros cogere, Caes

congrŭens entis, p adj (congruo), **1,** *agreeing, fit, appropriate, suitable*, vultus et gestus congruens et apta Cic , with cum and the abl , gestus cum sententiis congruens, Cic , with dat , actiones virtutibus congruentes, Cic,,

2, *harmonious, accordant;* is concentus ex dissimillimarum vocum moderatione concors tamen efficitur et congruens, Cic.; clamor congruens, *unanimous*, Liv.

congrŭentĕr, adv. (congruens), *aptly, agreeably, suitably;* congruenter naturae convenienterque vivere, Cic.

congrŭentĭa -ae, f. (congruo), *agreement, harmony, symmetry, proportion,* Suet.

congruo -ŭi, 3. (com and *gruo, connected with ruo). **A.** Lit., *to run together, come together, meet;* ut vicesimo anno ad metam eandem solis, unde orsi essent, dies congruerent, Liv. **B.** Transf., a, of time, *to coincide;* qui suos dies mensesque congruere volunt cum solis lunaeque ratione, Cic.; b, *to be suited, fitted to, correspond with, agree;* sensus nostri ut in pace semper, sic tum etiam in bello congruebant, Cic.; with cum and the abl., eius sermo cum tuis litteris valde congruit, Cic.; with dat., non omni causae nec auditori neque personae neque tempori congruere orationis unum genus, Cic.; with inter se, multae causae inter se congruere videntur, Cic.

congrŭus -a -um = congruens (q.v.).

conĭcio = conjicio (q.v.).

cōnĭfĕr -fĕra -fĕrum (conus and fero), *cone-bearing;* cyparissi, Verg.

cōnĭgĕr (conus and gero) = conifer (q.v.).

cōnītor = connitor (q.v.).

cōnīvĕo = conniveo (q.v.).

conjectĭo -ōnis, f. (conjicio). **A.** *a hurling, throwing;* telorum, Cic. **B.** Transf., *conjectural interpretation;* somniorum, Cic.

conjecto, 1. (freq. of conjicio), *to throw together;* transf., *to conclude, infer, conjecture, surmise, guess at;* conjectantes iter, Liv.; rem eventu, Liv.; Caesar conjectans eum Aegyptum iter habere, Caes.

conjector -ōris, m. (conjicio), *an interpreter of dreams;* Isiaci conjectores, *the priests of Isis,* Cic.

conjectrix -īcis, f. (conjector), *a female interpreter of dreams,* Plaut.

conjectūra -ae, f. (conjicio), *a guess, conjecture, inference.* **I.** Gen., conjecturam adhibere, Cic.; aberrare conjecturā, *to be mistaken in,* Cic.; conjecturam facere or capere ex or de aliqua re, Cic.; afferre conjecturam, Cic.; conjectura assequi or consequi (foll. by relative clause), Cic.; quantum conjecturā auguramur, Cic. **II.** Esp. 1, *interpretation of dreams and omens, divination, soothsaying;* facilis conjectura huius somnii, Cic.; 2, rhet. t. t., *a part of the proof, conjecture, inference,* Cic.

conjectūrālis -e (conjectura), *relating to conjecture, conjectural;* controversia, Cic.

conjectus -ūs, m. (conjicio), *a throwing together.* **I.** Lit., a, materiai, Lucr.; b, *a throwing, casting, hurling;* lapidum, Cic.; venire ad teli conjectum, *to come within shot,* Liv.; ne primum quidem conjectum telorum ferre, Liv. **II.** Transf. *casting* or *directing towards;* vester in me animorum oculorumque conjectus, Cic.

conjĭcĭo -jēci -jectum, 3. (com and jacio). **I. A.** Lit., 1, *to throw, bring together, collect;* sarcinas in medium, Liv.; sortes in hydriam, Cic.; sortem conjicere, *to cast lots,* Cic.; aggerem in munitionem, Caes.; 2, of missiles, *to throw, cast, hurl;* tela in nostros, Caes.; fig., petitiones ita ut vitari non possint, Cic. **B.** Transf., 1, Gen., *to cast, direct;* oculos in aliquem, Cic.; maledicta in alicuius vitam, Cic.; 2, a, *to conjecture, guess;* de matre suavianda ex oraculo acute argutеque, Cic.; partic. perf. subst., bene conjecta, *clever surmises,* Cic.; b, *to interpret conjecturally;* omen, Cic. **II.** *to throw, to hurl.* **A.** Lit. 1, quum haec navis invitis nautis vi tempestatis in portum conjecta sit, Cic.; aliquem in carcerem, Cic.; in vincula, Cic.; in lautumias, Cic.; se conjicere, *to betake oneself, flee;* se in portum, Cic.; se in fugam, Cic.; se in castra alicuius, Cic.; 2, *to insert,* libellum in epistolam, Cic.; 3, of a weapon, *to thrust;* gladium in adversum os, Caes. **B.** Transf., 1, naves conjectae in noctem, *benighted,* Caes.; se in noctem, *to hasten away under cover of night,* Cic.; forensem turbam in quatuor tribus, *to divide,* Liv.; aliquem ex occultis insidiis ad apertum latrocinium, *to force,* Cic.; 2, *to spend;* tantam pecuniam in propylaea, Cic.; 3, *to introduce;* haec verba in interdictum, Cic.

conjŭgālis -e (conjux), *relating to marriage, conjugal;* amor, Tac.

conjŭgātĭo -ōnis, f. (conjugo), *the etymological connection of words,* Cic.

conjŭgātor -ōris, m. *one who connects, unites;* boni amoris, Cat.

conjŭgĭālis -e (conjugium), *relating to marriage, conjugal;* festa, Ov.

conjŭgĭum -ĭi, n. (conjungo), 1, *a close connexion, union;* corporis atque animae, Lucr.; 2, a, *marriage, wedlock;* Tulliae meae, Cic.; tota domus conjugio et stirpe conjungitur, Cic.; poet., of animals, Ov.; b, meton., *husband,* Verg.; *wife,* Verg.

conjŭgo, 1. (com and jugum), *to yoke together, to bind together, connect;* a, est ea jucundissima amicitia, quam similitudo morum conjugavit, Cic.; b, conjugata verba, *words etymologically connected,* Cic.

conjunctē, adv., with compar. and superl. (conjunctus), 1, *conjointly, in connexion;* conjuncte cum reliquis rebus nostra contexere, Cic.; elatum aliquid, *hypothetically* (opp. simpliciter, *categorically*), Cic.; 2, *intimately, on terms of friendship;* cum aliquo vivere conjunctissime et amantissime, Cic.

conjunctim, adv. (conjunctus), *conjointly, in common;* huius omnis pecuniae conjunctim ratio habetur, Caes.

conjunctĭo -ōnis, f. (conjungo), *uniting, joining together;* 1, portuum, Cic.; 2, a, of things, conjunctio confusioque naturae, Cic.; rhet. and philosoph. t. t. *connexion of ideas,* Cic.; grammat. t. t. *a connecting particle, conjunction;* quum demptis conjunctionibus dissolute plura dicuntur, Cic.; b, of persons, *union, connexion;* (α) gen. societas conjunctioque humana, Cic.; citius cum eo veterem conjunctionem dirimere quam novam conciliare, Cic.; Pompeium a Caesaris conjunctione avocare, Cic.; summa nostra conjunctio et familiaritas, Cic.; (β) *relationship through marriage,* or *relationship;* conjunctio sanguinis, Cic.; conjunctio affinitatis, Cic.

conjunctus -a -um, p. adj., with compar. and superl. (conjungo), *connected, joined;* 1, sublicae cum omni opere conjunctae, Caes.; with dat. *bordering on, near;* theatrum conjunctum domui, Caes.; Paphlagonia conjuncta Cappadociae, Nep.; 2, *contemporary with;* conjunctus igitur Sulpicii aetati P. Antistius fuit, Cic.; 3, a, *connected with, agreeing with, proportioned to;* prudentia cum justitiā, Cic.; talis simulatio est vanitati conjunctior, *is more nearly allied,* Cic.; continuata conjunctaque verba, Cic.; subst., **conjunctum** -i, n. *connection,* Cic.; b, of persons, *connected, allied, friendly;* homines benevolentiā conjuncti, Cic.; homo mihi conjunctus fidissimā gratiā, Cic.; et cum iis et inter se conjunctissimos fuisse M'. Curium, Ti. Coruncanium, Cic.; tam conjuncta populo Romano civitas, Caes ; sanguine conjuncti, Nep , civium Romanorum omnium sanguis conjunctus existimandus est, Cic

conjungo -junxi -junctum, 3 *to join together* constr with dat., cum and abl , inter se, or the abl. alone **I.** Lit., navi onerariae alteram, Caes , calamos plures cerā, Verg. **II** Transf , *to unite*, **1,** of space, **a,** of things, dextram dextrae, Ov ; eam epistolam cum hac epistola, Cic , hunc montem murus circumdatus arcem efficit et cum oppido conjungit, Caes , **b,** of persons, ut paulatim sese legiones conjungerent, Caes , se Hannibali, Liv , **2,** of time, noctem diei, *to travel far into the night*, Caes , **3,** *to bring into connexion, unite, join*, **a,** causam alicuius cum communi salute, Cic , conjungere bellum, *to undertake in common*, Cic , **b,** *to unite in marriage, friendship, alliance*, etc , filias suas filiis alicuius matrimonio, Liv , me tibi studia communia conjungunt, Cic , conjungere amicitias, Cic

conjunx = conjux (q v).

conjūrātĭo -ōnis, f (conjuro) **A.** *union confirmed by an oath*, conjuratio Acarnanica, Liv , conjurationem nobilitatis facere, Caes **B.** *a conspiracy, plot*, conjuratio Catilinae, Sall , in ea conjuratione esse, *to be implicated in*, Sall , conjurationem facere contra rempublicam, Cic **C.** Meton *the conspirators*, voces conjurationis tuae, Cic

conjūrātus a um (conjuro), *united by oath, allied:* subst , **conjūrāti** -ōrum, m *conspirators*, Cic

conjūro, 1 *to swear together* **I.** *to take the military oath*, ut omnes Italiae juniores conjurarent, Caes. **II.** *to unite together by oath* **A.** Gen , barbari conjurare, obsides inter se dare coeperunt, Caes , with acc and infin ; per suos principes inter se conjurant nihil nisi communi consilio acturos, Caes **B.** Esp *to plot, conspire*, conjurasse supra septem millia virorum ac mulierum, Liv., with cum and the abl , or with inter se, ii, quibuscum conjurasti, Cic , principes inter se conjurant, Sall , with adversus or contra and the acc , contra rempublicam, Cic , adversus patriam, Liv , with de and the abl , de interficiendo Pompejo, Cic , with in and the acc , cum aliquo in omne flagitium et facinus, Liv , with infin , patriam incendere, Sall , with ut and subj , urbem ut incenderent, Liv

conjux (conjunx) -jŭgis, c (conjungo), **1,** *spouse, wife*, Cic , more rarely, *husband*, Cic , pl *a married pair*, Cat , **2,** poet *a betrothed virgin, bride*, Verg , *a concubine*, Prop

conl . . = coll . (q v).

conm = comm (q v)

connecto nexŭi nexum, 3 *to fasten, tie together, connect, unite.* **A.** Lit illae (apes) pedibus connexae ad limina pendent, Verg **B.** Transf , **1,** of space, Mosellam atque Ararim factā inter utrumque fossā, Tac , **2,** of time, persequere connexos his funeribus dies, *close-following*, Cic , **3,** *to unite*, amicitia cum voluptate connectitur, Cic , esp **a,** *to unite in discourse* facilius est enim apta dissolvere quam dissipata connectere, Cic , **b,** of logical connexion, omne quod ipsum ex se connexum sit verum esse, Cic , **c,** *of relationship*, alicui connexus per affinitatem, Tac , partic perf subst , **connexum** i, n *logical conclusion*

1 **connexus** -ūs, m (connecto), *connexion, union*, Cic

2 **connexus** -a -um, partic. of connecto

connītor nisus or nixus sum, 3 dep **A.** Lit , **1,** *to lean* or *push against with violence;* valido connixus corpore taurus, Cic. poet., **2,** *to climb up*, in summum jugum, Caes , **3,** *to bring forth*, gemellos, Verg **B.** Transf , *to strive with all one's might*, with abl , quantum animo conniti potes, Cic , with in and the acc , in unum locum connixi, Liv , with ad and the acc , ad convincendum eum, Tac , with infin , invadere hostem, Liv , with ut and the subj , infantes connitantur, sese ut erigant, Cic.

connīvĕo -nīvi or -nixi, 2 *to close the eyes, to wink, blink with the eyes* **A.** Lit , oculis somno conniventibus, Cic , altero oculo, Cic , poet., of the sun or moon, quasi connivent, Lucr **B.** Transf , *to wink at, let pass unnoticed* consulibus si non adjuvantibus, at conniventibus certe, Cic , with in and the abl , quibusdam etiam in rebus conniveo, Cic

connūbĭālis -e (connubium), *relating to marriage, connubial*, Ov

connūbĭum -ii, n (com and nubo), **1, a,** *a legal Roman marriage*, sequuntur connubia et affinitates, Cic , poet , *marriage* in general, Pyrrhi connubia servare, Verg , **b,** *intercourse*, Ov , **2,** *the right of intermarriage*, connubium finitimis negare, Liv (in poets often trisyll , connubjo, Verg , Aen i 73, vii 96)

Cŏnōn -ōnis, m (Κόνων), **1,** *an Athenian general*, **2,** *a mathematician and astronomer of Samos*

cōnōpēum -i, n (κωνωπεῖον) or **cōnōpĭum** ii, n *a net to keep off gnats or mosquitoes*, Hor

cōnor, 1 dep *to undertake, endeavour, attempt, exert oneself, strive*, with acc , opus magnum, Cic , with infin , facere id quod constituerant, Caes , ii qui haec delere conati sunt, Cic

conp . = comp (q v)

conquassātĭo -ōnis, f (conquasso), *a violent shaking, shattering*, totius valetudinis corporis, Cic

conquasso, 1. *to shake thoroughly, shatter;* quum Apulia maximis terrae motibus conquassata esset, Cic transf , conquassatas exteras nationes illius anni furore, Cic.

conquĕror -questus, 3 dep *to bewail* or *complain loudly*, fortunas suas, Plaut , bonorum direptiones, Cic , de istius improbitate, Cic

conquestĭo -ōnis, f (conqueror) *a loud complaint, bewailing*, ubi nullum auxilium est, nulla conquestio, Cic , in rhet., conquestio est oratio auditorum misericordiam captans, Cic

conquestus, abl ū, m (conqueror), *a loud complaint*, Liv

conquĭesco -quiēvi quiētum, 3 *to rest thoroughly, take rest, repose* **A.** *to rest bodily*, videmus ut conquiescere ne infantes quidem possint, Cic , haec (impedimenta) conquiescere vetuit, *to rest from a march*, Caes , conquiescere meridie, *to sleep*, Caes **B** *to be still, quiet, to take repose, stop*, **a,** imbre conquiescente, Liv , conquiescit mercatorum navigatio, *is stopped*, Cic , conquiescere a continuis bellis et victoriis, Cic , **b,** *to find rest or recreation in*, in nostris studiis libentissime conquiescimus, Cic

conquīro -quīsīvi quīsītum, 3 (com and quaero) *to seek for, to bring together, to collect, get together* **A.** Lit , sagittarios, Caes , colonos Cic , pecuniam, Cic , aliquem tota provinciā, Cic **B.** Transf , voluptatem conquirere et comparare, Cic , solebat mecum interdum eiusmodi aliquid conquirere, Cic (contr. fut perf form, conquisierit, Cic)

conquīsītĭo -ōnis, f (conquaero), **1,** *search, collection*, pecuniarum, Tac , talium librorum, Liv , **2,** *a pressing* or *forcible enlistment of soldiers, conscription*, exercitus durissimā conquisitione confectus, Cic

conquisitor -ōris, m. (conquiro), *a recruiting officer*, Cic.

conquisitus -a -um, p. adj. with superl. (conquiro), *sought after, selected, chosen, costly, precious;* mensas conquisitissimis epulis exstruere, Cic.

conr . . . = corr . . . (q.v.).

consaepio -saepsi, -saeptum, 4. *to fence round, to hedge in*, Suet.; gen., partic., **consaeptus** -a -um, *fenced round;* ager, Cic.; subst., **consaeptum** -i, n. *an inclosure*, Liv.

consălūtātio -ōnis, f. (consaluto), *a salutation of several persons;* forensis, Cic.

consălūto, 1. *to greet together, hail, salute;* inter se amicissime, Cic.; with double acc., aliquem dictatorem, Liv.; eam Volumniam, Cic.

consānesco -sānŭi, 3. *to become healthy, to get well;* illa quae consanuisse videbantur, Cic.

consanguĭnĕus -a -um, *related by blood, brotherly, sisterly;* umbrae, Ov. Subst., **consanguĭnĕus** -i, m. *brother*, Cic.; **consanguĭnĕa** -ae, f. *sister*, Cat.; plur., **consanguĭnĕi** -orum, m. *relations;* Aedui Ambarri necessarii et consanguinei Aeduorum, Caes.; transf., consanguineus Leti Sopor, Verg.

consanguĭnĭtas -ātis, f. (consanguineus), *relationship by blood, consanguinity*, Liv.

consaucio, 1. *to wound severely*, Suet.

conscĕlĕrātus -a -um, p. adj. with superl. (conscelero), *wicked, villainous, depraved;* consceleratissimi filii, Cic.; transf. of things, mens, Cic.

conscĕlĕro, 1. *to defile with crime;* miseram domum, Cat.; oculos videndo, Ov.; aures paternas, Liv.

conscendo -scendi -scensum, 3. (com and scando). **A.** *to ascend, mount, go up;* with acc., equum, *to mount on horseback*, Liv.; vallum, Caes.; aequor navibus, Verg.; with in and the acc., in equos, Ov. **B.** Naut. t. t., *to go on board ship, embark;* with in and the acc., in navem, Caes.; with acc., navem, Caes.; absol., *to embark;* conscendere a Brundisio, Cic.

conscensio -ōnis, f. (conscendo), *an embarking, embarkation;* in naves, Cic.

conscientia -ae, f. (conscio). **I. A.** *a joint knowledge with some other person, being privy to;* horum omnium, Cic.; conjurationis, Tac.; eiusmodi facinorum, Cic.; absol. conscientiae contagio, Cic.; aliquem in conscientiam assumere, Tac. **II.** *knowledge in oneself.* **A.** Gen., virium nostrarum ac suarum, Liv.; absol., nostra stabilis conscientia, Cic. **B.** *consciousness of right or wrong;* **a**, conscientia bene actae vitae, Cic.; scelerum et fraudum suarum, Cic.; ex nulla conscientia de culpa, Sall.; **b**, *conscience;* animi conscientiā excruciari, Cic.; praeclarā conscientiā, Cic.; absol., (α) *a good conscience;* mea mihi conscientia pluris est quam omnium sermo, Cic.; (β), *a bad conscience;* angor conscientiae, Cic.; conscientiā ictus, Liv.

conscindo -scidi -scissum, 3. *to tear* or *rend in pieces.* **I.** Lit., epistolam, Cic. **II.** Transf., conscissi sibilis, *hissed at*, Cic.

conscio, 4. *to be conscious of guilt;* nil conscire sibi, Hor.

conscisco -scīvi and -scii -scītum, 3. **1**, *to agree on, resolve publicly, decree*, Cic.; bellum, Liv.; **2**, *to bring* or *inflict upon oneself, inflict upon;* sibi mortem, or simply mortem, necem, *to kill oneself*, Cic.; sibi exsilium, Liv. (syncop. perfect forms conscisse, Liv.; conscisset, Cic.).

conscius -a -um (com and scio), **1**, *having joint* or *common knowledge with another, privy to, cognisant of;* with genit., homo meorum in te studiorum et officiorum maxime conscius, Cic.; conjurationis, *conspirator*, Sall.; poet., conscia fati sidera, Verg.; alicui conscium esse facinoris, Tac.; with dat., conscius facinori, Cic.; with in and the abl., conscius in privatis rebus, Cic.; with de and the abl., his de rebus conscium esse Pisonem, Cic.; absol., sine ullo conscio, Cic.; **2**, *conscious to oneself;* **a**, with genit., si alicuius injuriae sibi conscius fuisset, Cic.; with acc. and infin., etsi mihi sum conscius me nimis cupidum fuisse vitae, Cic.; absol., conscii sibi, Sall.; poet., virtus conscia, Verg.; **b**, esp., *conscious of guilt;* animus, Sall.

conscrībillo, 1. (dim. of conscribo), *to scribble* or *scrawl all over*, Varr.; transf., nates, *to mark with bloody weals*, Cat.

conscrībo -scripsi -scriptum, 3. *to write together.* **I. A. 1**, milit. t. t., *to enrol, levy;* exercitus, Cic.; legiones, Caes.; **2**, politic. t. t., **a**, *to enrol in a particular class;* centuriae tres equitum conscriptae sunt, Liv.; Collinam (tribum) novam delectu perditissimorum civium conscribebat, Cic.; **b**, *to enrol as a senator;* hence the phrase, patres conscripti (for patres et conscripti), *senators*, Cic.; sing., *a senator*, Hor.; **c**, *to enrol as colonists*, Liv. **B. 1**, *to put together in writing, write, compose;* librum de consulatu, Cic.; epistolam, legem, Cic.; absol., *to write a letter;* de Antonio quoque Balbus ad me cum Oppio conscripsit, Cic.; **2**, esp. of physicians, *to prescribe;* pro salutaribus mortifera, Cic. **II.** *to write all over;* mensam vino, Ov.

conscriptio -ōnis, f. (conscribo), *a writing, composition, written paper;* falsae conscriptiones quaestionum, *forged minutes*, Cic.

conscriptus -a -um, partic. of conscribo.

consĕco -sĕcŭi -sectum, 1. *to cut in small pieces, dismember;* membra fratris, Ov.

consĕcrātio -ōnis, f. (consecro), **1**, **a**, *a consecration;* aedium, Cic.; **b**, *a dedication to the infernal gods, execration, curse;* capitis, Cic.; **2**, *deification of the emperors, apotheosis*, Tac.

consĕcro, (con-sacro), 1. **I. A.** *to consecrate, to dedicate to the service of a god;* totam Siciliam Cereri, Cic.; diem adventus alicuius, *make a feast-day*, Liv. **B.** *to consecrate to the gods below, to curse;* quum caput eius, qui contra fecerit, consecratur, Cic. **II. A.** *to deify, elevate to divine honours;* Liber quem nostri majores consecraverunt, Cic.; of the emperors, consecrare Claudium, Suet. **B.** Transf., *to make holy;* vetera jam ista et religione omnium consecrata, Cic. **C.** *to make immortal;* amplissimis monumentis memoriam nominis sui, Cic.

consectārius -a -um (consector), *following logically, consequent*, Cic. Subst., **consectāria** -orum, n. *logical conclusions, inferences*, Cic.

consectātio -ōnis, f. (consector), *the eager pursuit of anything, desire, effort, striving after;* concinnitatis, Cic.

consectātrix -icis, f. (consectator), *an eager pursuer, devoted friend;* consectatrices voluptatis libidines, Cic.

consectio -ōnis, f. (conseco), *a cutting up, cleaving to pieces;* arborum, Cic.

consector, 1. dep. (freq. of consequor). **I. A.** Lit., *to follow, pursue eagerly*, Ter.; tardi ingenii est rivulos consectari, fontes rerum non videre, Cic. **B.** Transf., *to pursue zealously, strive after, try to imitate* or *gain;* opes aut potentiam, Cic.; ubertatem orationis, Cic.; vitium de industriā, Cic. **II.** *to follow hostilely, pursue;* redeuntes equites, Caes.; aliquem et conviciis et sibilis, Cic.

consĕcūtio -ōnis, f. (consequor), **1**, philosoph. t. t., *that which follows, an effect, conse-*

quence, causas rerum et consecutiones videre, Cic., 2, rhet. t. t., *order, connexion, arrangement*, verborum, Cic.

*consĕnesco -sĕnŭi, 3. I. *to become old, grow grey*, hac casā, Ov. II. In a bad sense, *to become old, to lose one's strength, to decay*. A. Lit., 1, of persons, insontem, indemnatum in exsilio consenescere, Liv.; consenescere in Siciliā sub armis, Liv.; 2, of bodily strength, *to decay*, consenescunt vires atque deficiunt, Cic. B. Transf., 1, invidia habet repentinos impetus, interposito spatio et cognitā causā consenescit, Cic.; 2, in politics, *to lose power*, omnes illius partis auctores ac socios nullo adversario consenescere, Cic.

consensĭo -ōnis, f. (consentio). A. Gen., *agreement, harmony, consent*; a, of persons, omnium gentium, Cic.; nulla de illis magistratuum consensio, Cic.; b, of things, *harmony*, naturae, Cic. B. In a bad sense, *a plot, conspiracy*, consensio scelerata, Cic.

consensus -ūs, m. (consentio). I. *agreement, unanimity, concord, agreement*; a, of persons, omnium, Cic.; optimus in rempublicam consensus, Cic.; abl., consensu, *unanimously, by general consent*, resistere, Liv.; b, of things, mirus quidam omnium quasi consensus doctrinarum concentusque, Cic. II. *a secret agreement, conspiracy*, consensus audacium, Cic.

consentānĕus -a -um (consentio), *agreeing to, agreeable with, consonant with, fit, suitable*, cum iis litteris, Cic.; gen. with dat., Stoicorum rationi, Cic.; impers., consentaneum est, with infin. or acc. and infin., *it agrees, is reasonable, suitable*, Cic.

Consentes Dii, *the advisers, the twelve superior deities of the Romans—viz., Jupiter, Juno, Vesta, Ceres, Diana, Minerva, Venus, Mars, Mercurius, Neptunus, Vulcanus, Apollo*, Varr.

Consentĭa -ae, f. *a town in Bruttii, now Consenza*. Adj., **Consentīnus** -a -um.

consentĭo -sensi -sensum, 4. *to agree*. I. Lit., of persons. A. Gen., *to agree, to assent, to resolve unanimously*; absol., animi consentientes, Cic.; with dat. or cum and the abl., consentire superioribus judiciis, Cic.; cum populi Romani voluntatibus consentiant, Cic.; with de or in and the abl., Cic.; ad with the acc., Cic.; adversus with the acc., Liv.; cum aliquo de aliquā re, Cic.; with acc., Cic.; bellum, *to resolve upon war*, Liv.; with acc. and infin. or infin. alone, Cic. B. *to plot, conspire, form an unlawful union*, ad prodendam Hannibali urbem, Liv.; belli faciendi causā, Cic. II. Transf., of inanimate objects, *to agree, harmonise*, ratio nostra consentit, Cic.; pres. partic., **consentiens** -entis, *harmonious*, consentiens populi Romani universi voluntas, Cic.

consēpĭo = consaepio (q.v.).

consĕquens -quentis, p. adj. (consequor), a, grammat. t. t., *appropriate, of the right construction*, in conjunctis (verbis) quod non est consequens vituperandum est, Cic.; b, philosoph. t. t., *following logically, consequent*, consequens est, *it follows as a logical consequence*, Cic. Subst., **consĕquens** -quentis, n. *a logical consequence*, Cic.

consĕquentĭa -ae, f. (consequor), *a consequence, succession*, eventorum, Cic.

consĕquĭa -ae, f. = consequentia (q.v.).

consĕquor -sĕquūtus (-sĕcūtus), 3. dep. *to follow, go after*. I. Gen., A. Lit., 1, aliquem vestigiis, *on foot*, Cic.; 2, *to pursue*, consequi statim Hasdrubalem, Liv. B. Transf., 1, *to follow in point of time*, mors, quae brevi consecuta est, Cic.; quia libertatem pax consequebatur, Cic.; 2, a, *to follow as an effect or consequence, result from*, quam eorum opinionem magni errores consecuti sunt, Cic.; b, *to follow as a logical consequence*, fit etiam quod consequitur necessarium, Cic.; 3, *to follow a particular object or example*, consequi suum quoddam institutum, Cic. II. *to come up to by following, attain to, reach, obtain*. A. Lit., 1, si statim navigas, nos Leucade consequere, Cic.; 2, *to come up with in pursuit, overtake*, reliquos omnes equitatu, Caes. B. Transf., 1, *to attain to, obtain, get*, cujus rei tantae tamque difficilis facultatem consecutum esse me non profiteor, secutum esse prae me fero, Cic.; opes quam maximas, Cic.; amplissimos honores, Cic.; fructum amplissimum ex reipublicae causa, Cic.; omnia per senatum, Cic.; fortitudinis gloriam insidiis et malitia, Cic.; foll. by ut or ne with the subj., Cic.; 2, of objects, events, *to befall, happen to*, tanta prosperitas Caesarem est consecuta, Cic.; 3, *to come up to in any respect, to equal*; a, verborum prope numerum sententiarum numero, Cic.; b, esp., *to express adequately in words*, alicujus laudes verbis, Cic.; 4, *to come up to in speech or thought, to understand, grasp*, similitudinem veri, Cic.

1. **consĕro** -sēvi -sĭtum, 3. 1, *to sow, plant*; a, lit., agros, Cic.; b, transf., lumine arva (of the sun), *to cover*, Lucr.; 2, *to plant, place in*, arborem, Liv.

2. **consĕro** -sĕrŭi -sertum, 3. I. Gen., *to connect, tie, join, twine together*, lorica conserta hamis, Verg.; exodia conserere fabellis potissimum Atellanis, Liv. II. *to join in a hostile manner*. A. Milit. t. t., manum or manus conserere, *to engage*, Cic.; cum aliquo, Cic.; inter se, Sall.; conserere pugnam, Liv.; proelium, Liv.; navis conseritur, *the ship is engaged*, Liv.; absol., conserere cum levi armatura, Liv. B. Legal t. t., aliquem ex jure manum consertum vocare, *to commence an action concerning property by laying hands on it*, ap. Cic.

consertē, adv. (consertus from 2. consero), *connectedly*, Cic.

conserva -ae, f. *a fellow servant*, Plaut.; transf., conservae fores, *in the same service*, Ov.

conservans -antis, p. adj. (conservo), *preserving*, with genit., ea quae conservantia sunt ejus status, Cic.

conservātĭo -ōnis, f. (conservo), *a preservation, keeping, laying up*; a, frugum, Cic.; b, *observing, observance*, aequabilitatis, Cic.

conservātor -ōris, m. (conservo), *a preserver*, inimicorum, Cic.; reipublicae, Cic.

conservātrix -icis, f. (conservo), *she who preserves*, natura, Cic. (?)

conservo, 1. *to keep, preserve, maintain*; a, of concrete objects, cives suos, Cic.; omnes salvos, Cic.; rempublicam, Cic.; rem familiarem, Cic.; b, of abstract objects, *to preserve, maintain, observe*, pristinum animum, Liv.; jusjurandum, *to keep*, Cic.

conservus -i, m. *a fellow slave, servant*, Cic.

consessor -ōris, m. (consido), *one who sits near or with*; in a court of justice, *an assessor*, Cic.; *a neighbour* at a feast or spectacle, Cic.

consessus -ūs, m. (consido), *an assembly* (of persons sitting together); in ludo talario, Cic.; praeconum, Cic.; ludorum gladiatorumque, Cic.; plur., consessus theatrales gladiatoriique, Cic.

consīdĕrātē, adv., with compar. and superl. (consideratus), *thoughtfully, carefully*, agere, Cic.

consīdĕrātĭo -ōnis, f. (considero), *consideration, contemplation, thought, reflection*, considerationem intendere in aliquid, Cic.

consīdĕrātus -a -um, p. adj. with compar.

and superl (considero), a, pass, *thoroughly considered, well weighed, deliberate*, verbum, Cic., considerata atque provisa via vivendi, Cic, b, act, of persons, *cautious, wary, circumspect*, homo, Cic

consīdĕro, 1 (com and root SID, connected with ΕΙΔΩ, ΙΔΩ, VID eo) **A.** Lit, *to look at, regard carefully, contemplate*; considerare opus pictoris, Cic. **B.** Transf, *to consider, weigh, reflect upon*, with secum, cum animo suo, secum in animo, considerare secum eos casus, in quibus, etc, Cic, with rel sent, consideres quid agas, Cic, with de and the abl, nunc de praemiis consideremus, Cic, absol, ille (ait) se considerare velle, Cic

consīdo -sēdi -sessum, 3, neut. **I.** Lit, *to sit down* **A.** Of persons, hic in umbrā, Cic, in molli herbā, Cic, esp, **1,** *to sit down in a public assembly* or *court of justice*; ut primum judices consederunt, Cic; ad jus dicendum, Liv, **2,** milit t t, **a,** *to take up one's position*, triarii sub vexillis considebant sinistro crure porrecto, Liv, in insidiis, Liv, **b,** more commonly, *to stop, encamp*, considere non longius mille passibus a nostris munitionibus, Caes, **3,** *to stay*, and of passengers on board ship, *to land*, hic an Antii, Cic., Tarquiniis, Liv **B.** Of things, *to fall to the ground, settle, sink, subside*; quae (Alpes) jam licet considant, Cic, Ilion ardebat neque adhuc consederat ignis, Ov **II.** Transf, **A.** Of persons, considere in otio, *to rest*, Cic, totam videmus consedisse urbem luctu, *sunk in grief*, Verg **B.** Of things, **1,** *to stop, cease*, ardor animi consedit, Cic, **2,** *to fall into neglect*, consedit utriusque nomen in quaestura, Cic.

consigno, 1 **1,** *to seal, to affix a seal as an authentication*; tabulas signis, Cic; **2,** *to vouch for, authenticate*, aliquid litteris, Cic, transf., antiquitas clarissimis monumentis testata consignataque, Cic

consĭlĭārĭus -a -um (consilium), *relating to counsel, deliberating*, senatus, Plaut. Subst, **consĭlĭārĭus** -ii, m *an adviser, an assessor, assistant judge*, consiliario et auctore Vestorio, Cic, dari alicui consiliarium atque administrum, Cic, consiliarii regis, Cic

consĭlĭātor -ōris, m (consilior), *counsellor, adviser*, Phaedr

consĭlĭor, 1 dep (consilium), *to hold a consultation, consult, take counsel*, difficilis ad consiliandum legatio, Cic

consĭlium -ii, n (connected with consulo) **I** Act, **A. 1,** lit, *a deliberation, consultation, taking counsel*, consilium principum habere, *to hold a consultation with the chiefs*, Liv, quasi consilii sit res, *as if the matter allowed of consideration*, Caes, consiliis interesse, Cic; esp *the deliberation of a public body*, consilii publici participem fieri, Cic; consilium habere, Cic, adesse alicui in consilio, Cic, **2,** meton., *the assembly of persons giving advice, council*, esp, **a,** *the senate*, senatus, id est, orbis terrae consilium, Cic, **b,** *the body of judges*, ex senatu in hoc consilium delecti estis, Cic, **c,** *a council of war*; consilium convocare, Caes; rem ad consilium deferre, Caes **B.** *understanding, foresight, prudence*, vir maximi consilii, Caes, mulier imbecilli consilii, Cic **II.** Pass, *the advice or counsel given, a resolution, plan, conclusion*, **1,** **a,** capere consilium, *to form a resolution*, Cic, belli renovandi, Caes, subito consilium cepi, ut antequam luceret exirem, Cic, consilium consistit, *holds good*, Cic, est consilium, foll by infin, Cic, quid sui consilii sit proponit *he explains what his plan is*, Caes, inire consilium senatus interficiendi, Cic, abl, consilio, *intentionally, designedly*, Cic, privato consilio, privatis consiliis (opp publico consilio, publicis consiliis), *in the interests of private persons*, Cic, **b,** milit t t, *stratagem, device*; consilium imperatorium, Cic, **2,** *advice, suggestion*, alicui consilium dare, Cic., egere consilii or consilio, Cic

consĭmĭlis -e, *like in all parts, exactly similar*, with genit, causa consimilis earum causarum quae, etc., Cic., with dat, consimilis fugae profectio, Caes, absol., laus, Cic.

consĭpĭo, 3 (com and sapio), *to be in one's senses, to have possession of one's faculties*, Liv

consisto -stiti, 3 *to put oneself in any place.* **I.** Gen, *to take one's stand, place oneself* **A.** Lit, **1,** of persons, consistere ad mensam, Cic, in proximo consistere, Liv, esp **a,** as a listener, tota in illa contione Italia constitit, Cic., **b,** milit t t, *to place oneself for battle, take one's place*, ne saucio quidem eius loci, ubi constiterat, relinquendi facultas dabatur, Cic, **2,** of dice, *to fall*, quadringentis talis centum Venerios non posse casu consistere, Cic. **B.** Transf., *to agree with*, videsne igitur Zenonem tuum cum Aristone verbis consistere, re dissidere, Cic. **II.** Esp. *to stand still* **A.** *to stop, halt*, **1,** lit, **a,** of persons, constitit! Ov, consistere et commorari cogit, Cic, esp, (α) *to stop for conversation*, viatores etiam invitos consistere cogunt, Caes, (β) *to stop in wonder, curiosity*, etc, bestiae saepe immanes cantu flectuntur et consistunt, Cic; (γ) milit t t, *to halt*, prope hostem, Caes, (δ) of travellers, fugitives, etc, *to halt, stop, stay*, consistere unum diem Veliae, Cic, **b,** of things, vel concidat omne caelum omnisque natura consistat necesse est, Cic, esp of water, *to stop still*, ter frigore constitit Ister, *froze*, Ov; **2,** transf, **a,** *to stop, dwell in speech*, in uno nomine, Cic, **b,** *to rest, cease*, quum ad Trebiam terrestre constitisset bellum, Liv; **c,** *to rest, fall upon*, in quo (viro) non modo culpa nulla, sed ne suspicio quidem potuit consistere, Cic, **d,** *to consist, to be formed of*, major pars victus eorum in lacte, caseo, carne consistit, Caes **B.** **1,** *to stand firmly, keep one's ground, footing*, in fluctibus, Caes; vertice celso aeriae quercus constiterunt, *were firmly rooted*, Verg, **2,** transf, **a,** *to keep one's ground, to hold one's own*, in forensibus causis praeclare, Cic; **b,** *to be firm*, neque mens, neque vox neque lingua consistit, Cic

consĭtĭo -ōnis, f (consero), *a sowing, planting*, plur, *different kinds of sowing or planting*, Cic.

consĭtor -ōris, m (consero), *a sower, planter*; uvae, *Bacchus*, Ov

consĭtūra -ae, f (consero), *a sowing, planting*, agri, Cic

consōbrīnus -i, m and **consōbrīna** -ae, f *cousin on the mother's side*, Cic, *cousin*, Cic, and in a more extended sense, *second, third cousin*, Suet

consŏcer -cĕri, m *a joint father-in-law*, Suet

consŏcĭātĭo -ōnis, f (consocio), *union, connexion, association*, hominum, Cic

consŏcĭātus -a -um, p adj (from consocio), *united, harmonious*, consociatissima voluntas, Cic

consŏcĭo, 1 *to unite, connect, share, associate, make common*, consilia cum aliquo, Cic; injuriam cum amicis, Cic., animos eorum, Liv; nunquam tam vehementer cum senatu consociati fuistis, Cic.

consōlābĭlis -e (consolor), *consolable*, dolor, Cic

consōlātĭo -ōnis, f (consolor), *consolation, encouragement, comfort, alleviation*, **1,** communium malorum, Cic, timoris, Cic., adhibere aliquam modicam consolationem, Cic.; adhibere alicui consolationem, Cic num me una consolatio sustentat quod, etc , Cic., uti hac consolatione alicuius (foll by acc and infin), Cic., 2, *a consolatory treatise* or *discourse*, Cic.

consōlātor -ōris, m. (consolor), *a consoler*, Cic

consōlātōrĭus -a -um (consolator), *relating to consolation, consolatory*, litterae, Cic

consōlor, 1 dep **1,** of persons, *to console, comfort, to encourage*, se illo solatio quod, etc , Cic , se his (foll by acc and infin), Cic , aliquem de communibus miseriis, Cic , spes sola homines in miseriis consolari solet, Cic , absol , consolando levare dolorem, Cic , Caesar consolatus rogat (eum) finem orandi faciat, Caes , **2,** of things, *to alleviate, lighten, solace*, dolorem, Cic

consŏno sŏnŭi, 1 **1,** *to sound together, sound loudly*, **a,** consonante clamore nominatim Quinctium orare ut, etc , Liv , **b,** *to echo*, plausu fremituque virum consonat omne nemus, Verg , **2,** transf , *to harmonise, agree, be consonant with*, Quint

consŏnus -a -um **A.** Lit , *sounding together, harmonious*, fila lyrae, Ov **B.** Transf , *accordant, fit, suitable*, credo Platonem vix putasse satis consonum fore ut, etc , Cic

consōpĭo, 4 *to lull to sleep, stupefy*, somno consopiri sempiterno, Cic ; Endymion a Luna consopitus, Cic

consors -sortis, **1,** *having an equal share with, sharing in, partaking of*, with genit , socius et consors gloriosi laboris, Cic , mecum temporum illorum, Cic , tribuniciae potestatis, Tac , applied to inanimate objects, *common*, tecta, Verg , **2,** *having an equal share in property*, tres fratres consortes, *tenants in common*, Cic., poet , *brother* or *sister*, consors magni Jovis, *Juno*, Ov , adj = *brotherly, sisterly*, sanguis, Ov

consortĭo ōnis, f (consors), *companionship, community, partnership*, humana, Cic

consortĭum -ii, n (consors), **1,** *community of goods*, Suet , **2,** *fellowship, participation in*, si in consortio, si in societate reipublicae esse licet Liv.

1 **conspectus** a -um, p adj (from conspicio) **A.** Gen , *visible*, tumulus hosti conspectus, Liv **B.** (with compar) *striking, remarkable, distinguished* conspectus elatusque supra modum hominis, Liv , conspecta mors eius fuit, quia publico funere est elatus, Liv , turba conspectior, Liv

2 **conspectus** ūs, m (conspicio), *look, sight, view* **I.** Act , **A.** Lit , dare se alicui in conspectum, *to allow oneself to be seen by*, Cic , in conspectu alicuius esse, *to be within sight of*, Cic , e conspectu abire, Caes , adimere conspectum oculorum, Liv , cadere in conspectum, Cic , conspectus est in Capitolium, *the view is towards the Capitol*, Liv , conspectum alicuius fugere, Caes , privare aliquem omnium suorum consuetudine conspectuque, Cic , of things, in conspectu alicuius loci, *in sight of*, Cic **B.** Transf , *mental view, survey*, in hoc conspectu et cognitione naturae, Cic **II** Pass , *appearance*, Liv **A.** Lit., conspectu suo proelium restituit, Liv **B.** Meton , tuus jucundissimus conspectus, Cic

conspergo (con spargo), -spersi -spersum, 3 *to sprinkle, moisten by sprinkling*, me lacrimis, Cic , transf , ut oratio conspersa sit quasi verborum sententiarumque floribus, *interspersed with*, Cic

conspĭcĭendus -a um p adj (from conspicio), *worthy of being seen, noteworthy*, opus, Liv , templum, Ov

conspĭcĭo -spexi spectum, 3 (con and specio), **1,** *to look at, view, behold, to descry, perceive*, conspicere nostros equites, Caes ; infestis oculis omnium conspici, Cic , milites in summo colle, Caes , procul Ambiorigem suos cohortantem, Caes , with acc and infin , calones qui nostros victores flumen transisse conspexerant, Caes , **2,** *to look at with attention*, Demetrium ut pacis auctorem cum ingenti favore conspiciebant, Liv , locum insidiis, *for an ambush*, Verg , in pass , conspici, *to attract notice, to be gazed at, to be distinguished*, velit per urbem, conspici velle, Cic

conspĭcor, 1 dep (conspicio), *to catch sight of, perceive*, agmen Aeduorum, Caes , ex oppido caedem et fugam suorum, Caes

conspĭcŭus -a um (conspicio), *visible* **A.** Gen , conspicuus polus, Ov **B.** *remarkable, striking, conspicuous*, conspicuus late vertex, Hor , Romanis conspicuum eum novitas divitiaeque faciebant, Liv.

conspīrātĭo -ōnis, f (conspiro), **1,** *unison, harmony, agreement, union*, omnium bonorum, Cic , magnā amoris conspiratione consentientes amicorum greges, Cic , **2,** in a bad sense, *conspiracy, plot*, conspiratio certorum hominum contra dignitatem tuam, Cic

conspīrātus -a -um (partic of conspiro), *sworn together, united by an oath*, Phaedr Subst , **conspīrāti** -orum, m *conspirators*, Suet

conspīro, 1 (com and spiro), *to breathe together* **I A** *to blow together, sound together*, aereaque assensu conspirant cornua rauco, Verg **B.** *to agree, harmonise in opinion and feeling*, *to unite*, conspirate nobiscum, consentite cum bonis, Cic , milites legionis nonae subito conspirati (*with one accord*) pila conjecerunt, Cic **II.** In a bad sense, *to conspire, to form a plot*, priusquam plures civitates conspirarent, Caes

consponsor -ōris, m *a joint surety*, Cic

conspŭo spŭi spūtum, 3 *to spit upon*, Plaut , Juv

conspurco, 1 *to cover with dirt, defile*, Lucr

conspūto, 1 (inchoat of conspuo), *to spit upon contemptuously*, nostros, Cic

constans -antis, p adj with compar and superl (consto), **a,** *steady, firm, unchanging, immovable, constant* quae cursus constantes habent, Cic , pax, Liv , fides, Hor , constans jam aetas, quae media dicitur, Cic , **b,** of character, *firm, resolute, unchanging, constant*, sunt igitur firmi et stabiles et constantes (amici) eligendi, Cic , **c,** *consistent, harmonious*, oratio, Cic , **d,** *uniform, unanimous*, constanti famā atque omnium sermone celebrari, Cic

constantĕr, adv with compar and superl (constans), **a,** *firmly, consistently, constantly*, constanter in suo manere statu, Cic , constanter et non trepide pugnare, Caes , constanter et sedate ferre dolorem, Cic , **b,** *uniformly, harmoniously*, constanter omnes nuntiaverunt manus cogi, Caes , constanter sibi dicere, Cic

constantĭa -ae, f (constans), **a,** *unchangeableness*, dictorum conventorumque constantia, Cic , **b,** *perseverance, firmness*, pertinacia aut constantia intercessoris, Cic , **c,** *agreement, harmony*, testimoniorum, Cic

consternātĭo ōnis, f (consterno), **1,** *fear, dismay, consternation, confusion*, pavor et consternatio quadrigarum, Liv , pavor et consternatio mentis, Tac , **2,** *a mutiny, tumult*, vulgi, Tac , muliebris consternatio, Liv

1 **consterno** strāvi -strātum, 3 **A.** *to strew, scatter, cover by strewing*, tabernacula caespitibus Caes , omnia cadaveribus, Sall , constrata navis, *a decked boat*, Caes , subst , **constrāta**

-ōrum, n., pontis, *the flooring* or *gangway over a bridge of boats*, Liv. **B.** *to throw down;* tempestas aliquot signa constravit, Liv.

2. **consterno,** 1. (intens. of 1. consterno), **1,** *to cause confusion, consternation, fear, to frighten;* procella ita consternavit equos, Liv.; esp. in pass., equi consternati, *startled*, Liv.; pavida et consternata multitudo, Liv.; also, *to drive to flight by fear;* in fugam consternari, Liv.; **2,** *to excite to sedition* or *revolt;* metu servitutis ad arma consternati, Liv.

constīpo, 1. *to press, crowd together;* tantum numerum hominum in agrum Campanum, Cic.

constĭtŭo -stĭtŭi -stĭtūtum, 3. (com and statuo). **I.** *to cause to stand, place, put;* hominem ante pedes Q. Manilii, Cic.; milit. t. t., **a,** *to draw up in line, place, station, arrange;* signa ante tribunal, *to set up the standards*, Liv.; legionem Caesar constituit, *drew up*, Caes.; naves in alto, Caes.; intra silvas aciem ordinesque, Caes.; **b,** *to halt;* signa haud procul porta, Liv.; agmen, Sall. **II.** *to put in a particular place;* **1,** *to station, post, settle;* **a,** praesidia in Tolosatibus circumque Narbonem, Caes.; plebem in agris publicis, Cic.; **b,** *to appoint to an office;* regem, Cic.; aliquem sibi quaestoris in loco, Cic.; with the acc., Commium regem ibi, Caes.; **2,** *to found, establish;* **a,** of buildings, towns, etc., turres, Caes.; oppidum, Caes.; nidos, Cic.; hiberna omnium legionum in Belgis, Caes.; **b,** of institutions, taxes, etc., vectigal, Cic.; of magistracies, quae (potestates, imperia, curationes) constituuntur ad populi fructum, Cic.; **c,** of an undertaking, auctionem, Cic.; actionem, *to begin an action*, Cic.; crimen in aliquo, Cic.; quaestionem, Cic.; **d,** of relations, *to establish;* concordiam, Cic.; exemplum justitiae in hostem, Cic.; **e,** of persons, tres legiones, *to form*, Caes.; **3,** *to arrange, appoint, dispose, establish firmly;* **a,** of the body, is cui corpus bene constitutum sit, Cic.; **b,** of the character, animus bene constitutus, Cic.; **c,** of condition, situations, etc., rem familiarem, Cic.; **d,** of the state, bene constituta civitas, Cic.; **4,** *to fix, settle upon;* **a,** (α) tempus, diem, Cic., Caes.; mercedem funeris, Cic.; pretium frumento, Cic.; diem cum aliquo, Caes.; with rel. sent., armorum quantum quaeque civitas quodque ante tempus efficiat constituit, Caes; with acc. and infin., me hodie venturum esse, Cic.; with ut and the subj., ut L. Bestia quereretur de actionibus Ciceronis, Cic.; absol., ut erat constitutum, Cic.; (β) of persons, *to appoint, agree upon;* accusatorem, Cic.; **b,** (α) *to settle, determine;* nondum satis constitui molestiaene an plus voluptatis attulerit Trebatius noster; (β) *to determine at law, settle, decide;* controversiam, Cic.; de perspicuo jure, Cic.; **c,** *to come to a determination, to resolve;* haec ex re et ex tempore constitues, Cic.; with infin., bellum cum Germanis gerere, Caes.; with ut and the subj., ut pridie Idus Aquini manerem, Cic.

constĭtūtĭo -ōnis, f. (constituo), **1,** *constitution, condition, disposition, nature;* firma constitutio corporis, Cic.; reipublicae, Cic.; illa praeclara constitutio Romuli, Cic.; **2,** *fixing, determining;* **a,** *the definition* or *settling of something;* ea constitutio summi boni quae est praeposita, Cic.; **b,** rhet. t. t., *the point in dispute*, Cic.; **c,** *a regulation, order, ordinance;* cogebatur alia aut ex decreto priorum legatorum aut ex novā constitutione senatus facere, Cic.

constĭtūtum -i, n. (constitutus, from constituo), **1,** *a fixed place* or *time of meeting, rendezvous;* V. Calend. igitur ad constitutum, Cic.; constitutum factum esse cum servis, ut venirent, Cic.; **2,** *an agreement, appointment, compact;* ad constitutum experiendi gratiā venire, Cic.

constĭtūtus -a -um, partic. of constituo.

consto -stiti -stātūrus, 1. *to stand still.* **I.** Lit., Plaut. **II.** Transf., **A.** Gen., **1, a,** *to exist;* unde omnis rerum nunc constet summa creata, Lucr.; **b,** *to consist;* ex animo constamus et corpore, Cic.; **c,** *to depend upon, rest upon;* monuit eius diei victoriam in earum cohortium virtute constare, Caes.; **2,** *to cost;* ambulatiuncula prope dimidio minoris constabit isto loco, Cic. **B. 1,** *to stand firm, remain;* **a,** milit. t. t. *to hold one's ground, stand firm;* postquam nullo loco constabat acies, Liv.; **b,** of looks, speech, etc. *to remain the same, to be unaltered;* adeo perturbavit ea vox regem, ut non color, non vultus ei constaret, Liv.; **2,** *to be in good order;* postquam cuncta videt caelo constare sereno, Verg.; esp., ratio constat, *the account is correct*, Cic.; **3,** *to remain in the same state, continue;* nullum est genus rerum, quod avulsum a ceteris per se ipsum constare possit, Cic.; uti numerus legionum constare videretur, Caes.; **4,** *to remain in the same thought* or *opinion;* **a,** *to remain constant;* nec animum eius satis constare visum, Liv.; constare sibi or alicui rei, *to be true to;* reliqui sibi constiterunt, Cic.; constat humanitati suae, Cic.; of resolves, *to be fixed, firm;* animo constat sententia, Verg.; alicui constat, *a person is resolved;* mihi quidem constat nec meam contumeliam nec meorum ferre, ap. Cic.; **b,** of evidence, facts, etc., *to be certain, sure, well-known;* eorum quae constant exempla ponemus, horum quae dubia sunt exempla afferemus, Cic.; quod omnibus constabat hiemari in Gallia oportere, Caes.; mihi plane non satis constit, utrum sit melius, Cic.; quum de Magio constet, Cic.

constrātum -i, n., v. 1. consterno.

constringo -strinxi -strictum, 3. **A.** Lit., **a,** *to draw, bind together;* sarcinam, Plaut.; **b,** *to confine, fetter;* corpora vinculis, Cic. **B.** Transf., **a,** *to strengthen, fortify;* constringere fidem religione potius quam veritate, Cic.; **b,** *to confine, limit, fetter, restrain;* orbem terrarum novis legibus, Cic.; **c,** of discourse, *to compress, abbreviate;* sententiam aptis verbis, Cic.

constructĭo -ōnis, f. (construo), **1,** *a putting together, building, construction, making;* hominis, Cic.; **2,** rhet. t. t. *the proper connexion of words;* verborum apta et quasi rotunda, Cic.

constrŭo -struxi -structum, 3., **1, a,** *to heap up together;* acervos nummorum, Cic.; divitias, Hor.; **b,** *to construct, build up;* mundum, navem, aedificium, Cic.; **2,** *to arrange;* dentes in ore constructi, Cic.

constŭprātor -ōris, m. *a ravisher, defiler*, Liv.

constŭpro, 1, *to ravish, violate;* matronas, Liv.; fig., emptum constupratumque judicium, *corrupt*, Cic.

consuādĕo -si -sum, 2. *to advise earnestly*, Plaut.

Consŭālĭa, v. Consus.

consuāsor -ōris, m. (consuadeo), *an adviser*, Cic.

consūdo, 1. *to sweat profusely*, Plaut.

consuēfăcĭo -fēci -factum, 3. (*consueo and facio), *to accustom, habituate*, (Gaetulorum) multitudinem ordines habere, Sall.

consuesco -suēvi -suētum, 3. **I.** Transit., *to accustom to;* brachia, Lucr. **II.** Intransit., **a,** *to accustom oneself*, and often in perf., consuevi, *I am accustomed;* with infin., qui mentiri solet, pejerare consuevit, Cic.; with inanimate things as subjects, naves quae praesidii causā Alexandriae esse consuerant, Caes.; ut consuesti, *as you are accustomed*, Cic.; **b,** *to be intimate with;* cum aliquo, cum aliquā, Cic. (perf. forms often contr consuesti, consuestis, consuemus, consuerunt, consueram, consuerim, consuesse)

consuētūdo -inis, f (consuesco) **I.** *custom, usage, habit*, 1, mos consuetudoque civilis, Cic , with genit of subst , or gerund, consuetudo populi Romani, Cic , consuetudo sermonis nostri, Cic , consuetudo peccandi, Cic , consuetudo bona, Cic , adducere aliquem or se in eam consuetudinem ut, etc , Caes ab omnium Siculorum consuetudine discedere, Cic , non est meae consuetudinis rationem reddere, Cic , ut est consuetudo, *as is the usual practice*, Cic mutare consuetudinem dicendi, Cic , obdurescere alicuius rei consuetudine, Cic , tenere consuetudinem suam, Cic , in consuetudinem venire, *to become customary* Cic , ex consuetudine Caes ; consuetudine, *according to custom*, Cic . **2**, **a**, *manner of living*, ad superiorem consuetudinem reverti, Cic , **b**, *manner of speaking*, consuetudo indocta, Cic **II.** *social intercourse intimacy*, insinuare in consuetudinem alicuius, Cic , esp of lovers, stupri vetus consuetudo, *an intrigue of long standing*, Sall

consuētus -a -um **I.** Partic of consuesco (q v). **II.** P adj , *accustomed, customary, usual*, lubido, Sall

consul -sŭlis, m (root CONS, or from con and the root of salio, which is seen in praesul and exsul), *a consul*, pl consules, *the consuls* **I.** *the two chief magistrates of the Roman state, chosen by the* comitia centuriata, *originally from patricians only, but after 365 B C , also from the plebeians*, consul ordinarius, *one elected at the usual time* (opp consul suffectus, *one chosen in the course of the year to supply the place of a consul deceased*), Liv , consul designatus, *consul elect*, so called between the election in July and entrance upon office on the 1st of January, Cic , consul major, *the consul who had precedence of his colleague*, consul Flaminius consul iterum, Cic ; aliquem dicere consulem, Liv , the year was generally called by the consuls' names, e g , L Pisone et A Gabinio coss (i e consulibus), i e , 696 A U C., Caes, , consule Tullo, Hor , the name of the consul stamped on the cork marked the age of wine , Bibuli consulis amphora, Hor , pro consule, *an officer in the place of the consul, a governor of a country, province, a proconsul*, proconsule in Ciliciam proficisci, *to go as proconsul to Cilicia*, Cic **II.** Transf , in the historians used instead of proconsul, Liv.

consŭlāris -e (consul), *relating to a consul, consular* **A.** Adj , aetas, *the age (namely forty-three), at which a man might lawfully be chosen consul*, Cic , fasces, Liv , lictor, auctoritas, Cic , candidatus, Cic , familia, Cic , imperium, Cic , locus, *place in the senate*, Cic , provincia, Caes **B.** Subst , **consularis** -is m *one who had been a consul, an ex consul*, Cic , in the imperial period, *a governor of consular rank*, Tac

consŭlārĭtĕr, adv (consularis), *in a manner worthy of a consul*, vita omnis consulariter acta, Liv

consŭlātus -ūs, m (consul), *the office of consul, the consulship*, abdicare se consulatu, Cic , abdicare consulatum, Liv ; abire consulatu, Liv , adipisci consulatum, Cic , afferre consulatum in eam familiam, Cic , petere consulatum, Cic , peracto consulatu, Caes

consŭlo -sŭlŭi -sultum, 3 (root CONS, CENS, or from con and the root of salio) **I. a**, *to reflect, weigh, deliberate, consider, consult*, in commune, *for the common good*, Liv , in longitudinem, *for the future*, Ter . facto non consulto in tali periculo opus esse, Sall , re consulta et explorata, Cic ; quid agant consulunt, Caes , **b**, *to come to a conclusion, to take measures*, libere consulere ad summam rem, Caes , quae reges atque populi male consuluerint, Sall , obsecro ne quid gravius de salute et incolumitate tua consulas, Caes , consulere in, *to take measures against*; nihil in quemquam superbe ac violenter, Liv , **c**, *to take counsel for some person or thing, to have regard for the interests of, look to*, with dat , partium consulere, partim negligere, Cic , sibi, Cic , dignitati alicuius, Cic , alicui optime, Cic , with ut, ne, or (with preced neg) quominus and the subj , Cic , **d**, aliquid boni consulere, *to take in good part*, haec missa, Ov **II.** *to ask the advice of, consult*, nec te id consulo, *consult about that*, Cic , quod me de Antonio consulis, Cic , quid mihi faciendum esse censeat, Cic , **a**, *to ask the opinion of the senate, to bring a matter before the senate*, senatus a Bestia consultus est, placeretne legatos Jugurthae recipi moenibus, Sall , **b**, *to lay a matter before the people*, seniores de tribus consulendum dixerunt esse, Liv , **c**, *to take legal advice*, qui de jure civili consuli solent, Cic , **d**, *to consult an oracle, or deity*, haruspicem, Cic , Phoebi oracula, Ov , exta, Verg , Apollinem Pythium quas potissimum regiones tenerent, Cic , id possetne fieri, consuluit, Cic

consultātĭo -ōnis, f (2 consulto), 1, *a full consideration, deliberation*, **a**, venit aliquid in consultationem, Cic , consultationem raptim transigere, Liv , **b**, *a case proposed for consideration*, Quint , **2**, *an asking for advice, inquiry*, consultationi alicuius respondere, Cic

consultē, adv , with compar and superl (consultus), *advisedly, after consideration*, caute ac consulte gerere aliquid, Liv

1 **consultō**, adv (abl of consultum), *deliberately designedly*, consulto fecisse aliquid, Cic , non consulto sed casu in eorum mentionem incidere, Cic

2 **consulto**, 1 (freq of consulo) **I.** *to consider maturely, weigh, ponder* **A.** Gen , de officio, Cic , triduum ad consultandum dare, Liv , in longius, *for the future*, Tac , in medium, *for the common good*, Sall ; consultabat, utrum Romam proficisceretur, an Capuam teneret, Cic **B.** alicui, *to consult for, provide for*, reipublicae, Sall **II.** *to consult, ask advice of*, aliquem, Tib , vates ad eam rem consultandam ex Etruria accire, Liv

consultor -ōris, m (consulo), 1, *an adviser*, egomet in agmine, in proelio consultor idem et socius periculi vobiscum adero, Sall , **2**, *one who asks advice, especially legal advice, a client*, consultoribus suis respondere, Cic

consultrix -īcis, f (consultor), *one who consults cares for, provides*, natura consultrix et provida utilitatum, Cic

consultum -i, n (consultus, from consulo) *resolution, plan, decision* . **a**, consulto collegae, virtute militum victoria parta est, Liv , facta et consulta fortium et sapientium, Cic , **b**, esp *a decree* of the senate at Rome, senatus consultum (shortened to S C), senatus consultum facere, Cic S C facere in aliquem, Liv , S C facere ut, etc , Cic , alicui senatus consulto scribendo adesse, Cic , consulta patrum, Hor , **c**, *the decree* of a Sicilian senate (βουλή), Cic , **d**, *the answer of an oracle*, dum consulta petis, Verg

1 **consultus** -a -um, p adj with compar and superl (consulo), **a**, *well considered, deliberated upon, well weighed* omnia consulta ad nos et exquisita deferunt, Cic , **b**, of persons, *experienced*, esp in law, with genit , juris consultus (adj or subst), *some one learned in the law*, Cic , consultissimus vir omnis divini et humani juris, Liv , consultus insanientis sapientiae, Hor , with abl , jure consultus, Cic. Subst , **consultus** -i, m *a lawyer* Hor

2. **consultus** -ūs, m. (consulo) = consultum (q.v.).

consum -fui -futurum -fore, *to be, to happen,* Plaut., Ter.

consummātĭo -ōnis, f. (consummo), **1,** *a summing up, adding up,* Plin.; **2,** *a finishing, completion, consummation;* maximarum rerum, Sen.

consummātus -a -um, p. adj. with superl. (consummo), *complete, perfect, consummate;* eloquentia, Quint.; orator, Quint.

consummo, 1. (com and summa), **1,** *to add together, sum up;* transf., *to form a whole, complete;* quae consummatur partibus, una dies (of an intercalary day), Ov.; in suum decus nomenque velut consummata eius belli gloria, Liv.; **2,** *to complete, finish;* eam rem, Liv.

consūmo -sumpsi -sumptum, 3. *to take altogether, consume.* **A.** In doing something, *to spend, employ;* pecuniam in agrorum coemptionibus, Cic.; omne tempus in litteris, Cic.; ingenium in musicis, Cic.; omnem laborem, operam, curam, studium in salute alicuius, Cic. **B.** *to destroy, waste, bring to an end;* **a,** omnia tela, *to shoot away,* Caes.; of provisions, omne frumentum, Caes.; of property, patrimonia, Cic.; omnes fortunas sociorum, Caes.; of time, *to spend, pass;* magna diei parte consumpta, Caes.; aestatem in Treviris, Caes.; consumendi otii causa, Cic.; horas multas saepe suavissimo sermone, Cic.; of resources or activity, *to waste, consume in vain;* multam operam frustra, Cic.; **b,** *to waste,* or *wear away, destroy;* quum eam (quercum) tempestas vetustasve consumpserit, Cic.; in pass., consumi incendio, or flamma, *to be destroyed by fire;* quae (aedes) priore anno incendio consumptae erant, Liv.; of life, *to destroy, kill;* si me vis aliqua morbi aut natura ipsa consumpsisset, Cic.; totidem plagis hostem, Hor.; garrulus hunc consumet, *will be the death of him,* Hor.; fame consumi, *to die of hunger,* Caes.

consumptĭo -ōnis, f. (consumo), *a consumption, consuming, destroying,* Cic.

consumptor -ōris, m. (consumo), *a consumer, destroyer;* confector et consumptor omnium, Cic.

consŭo -sŭi -sūtum, 3. *to sew together, stitch together,* Plaut.

consurgo -surrexi -surrectum, 3. *to rise up, stand up.* **I.** Lit., **1,** of persons, **a,** lying down; consolatus (ad terram projectos) consurgere jussit, Caes.; **b,** sitting; senatus cunctus consurgit, Cic.; esp. of an orator, *to rise up to speak;* consurgit P. Scaptius de plebe et inquit, Liv.; *to rise up in honour of some one;* consurrexisse omnes et senem sessum recepisse, Cic.; **c,** of persons kneeling, paulisper addubitavit an consurgendi jam triariis tempus esset, Liv.; **d,** of persons fighting, *to raise oneself to give more force to a blow;* ad iterandum ictum, Liv.; **2,** of things without life, consurgunt venti, Verg.; consurgunt geminae quercus, Verg. **II.** Transf., **1,** of persons, *to rise for any action, join in an insurrection;* magno tumultu ad bellum, Liv.; **2,** of things, *to break out;* novum bellum, Verg.

consurrectĭo -ōnis, f. (consurgo), *a rising up from a seat;* judicum, Cic.

Consus -i, m. *an ancient Roman deity,* whose worship was said to have been introduced by Romulus; hence, **Consŭālĭa** -ium, n. *games in honour of Consus,* on the 21st of August and 15th of December.

consŭsurro, 1. *to whisper together,* Ter.

contābĕfăcĭo, 3. *to consume, cause to waste away,* Plaut.

contābesco -tābŭi, 3. *to waste away, wear away gradually;* Artemisia luctu confecta contabuit, Cic.

contābŭlātĭo -ōnis, f. (contabulo), *a covering with boards, planking, floor,* Caes.

contābŭlo, 1. *to cover with boards, to plank;* turrem, Caes.

contābundus = cunctabundus (q.v.).

contactus -ūs, m. (contingo), **1,** *a contact, touching, touch;* sanguinis, Ov.; **2,** *a touching of something unclean, contagion;* contactus aegrorum vulgabat morbos, Liv.; transf., oculos a contactu dominationis inviolatos, Tac.

contāges -is, f. (contingo), *a touch, touching,* Lucr.

contāgĭo -ōnis, f. (contingo), *a touching, connexion;* **1,** gen., quum est somno sevocatus animus a societate et contagione corporis, Cic.; **2,** *a touching of something unclean, contagion, infection;* **a,** physical, contagio pestifera, Liv.; **b,** moral, *bad companionship, evil example;* turpitudinis, Cic.; furoris, Liv.

contāgĭum -ii, n. (contingo), **1,** *touch,* Lucr.; **2,** *infection, contagion;* **a,** physical, mala vicini pecoris contagia, Verg.; **b,** moral, contagia lucri, Hor.

contāmĭnātus -a -um, p. adj. with superl. (contamino), *unclean, contaminated,* Cic.

contāmĭno, 1. (com and TAG -o, tango), *to render unclean by contact or mixture, contaminate;* sanguinem, Liv.; se scelere, Cic.; veritatem aliquo mendacio, Cic.

contātĭo, contātus, etc. = cunctatio, cunctatus, etc. (q.v.).

contechnor, 1. dep. *to devise a trick,* Plaut.

contĕgo -texi -tectum, 3. *to cover.* **A.** Lit., **a,** locum linteis, Liv.; eos uno tumulo, *to bury,* Liv.; **b,** *to conceal;* corporis partes, quae aspectum sint deformem habiturae, contegere atque abdere, Cic. **B.** Transf., *to conceal;* libidines fronte et supercilio, non pudore et temperantiā, Cic.

contĕmĕro, 1. *to pollute, defile,* Ov.

contemno -tempsi -temptum, 3. *to think meanly of, despise, contemn.* **I.** Gen., casus humanos, Cic.; Romam prae sua Capua irridere atque contemnere, Cic.; with infin., contemnere coronari, Hor.; with acc. and infin., ut ipsum vinci contemnerent, Cic. **II.** Esp., *to ridicule, make little of;* Adherbalis dicta, Sall.; se non contemnere, *to have a high opinion of oneself,* Cic.

contemplātĭo -ōnis, f. (contemplor), *attentive or eager looking at, contemplation.* **A.** Lit., caeli, Cic. **B.** Transf., naturae, Cic.

contemplātor -ōris, m. (contemplor), *one who attentively looks at or contemplates;* caeli, Cic.

contemplātus, abl. -ū, m. (contemplor), *a looking at, contemplation,* Ov.

contemplor (contemplo), 1. dep. (com and templum), *to look at attentively or minutely, regard, contemplate.* **A.** Lit., coelum suspicere coelestiaque contemplari, Cic.; situm Carthaginis, Liv. **B.** Transf., *to consider carefully;* ut totam causam quam maxime intentis oculis, ut aiunt, acerrime contemplemini, Cic.

contemptim, adv. with compar. (contemptus), *contemptuously;* de Romanis loqui, Cic.

contemptĭo -ōnis, f. (contemno), *contempt, scorn, disdain;* pecuniae, Cic.

contemptor -ōris, m. (contemno), *one who contemns or despises;* divitiarum, Liv.; divum, Verg.; attrib., nemo tam contemptor famae est, Liv.; contemptor lucis animus, Verg.; contemptor animus, Sall.

1. **contemptus** -a um, p adj with compar and superl (contemno), *despised, despicable, contemptible;* **a,** of things, vita contempta ac sordida, Cic, **b,** of persons, homo contemptus et abjectus, Cic

2 **contemptus** -ūs, m (contemno), *a mean opinion, contempt, disdain,* **a,** pass, hominibus Gallis prae magnitudine corporum suorum brevitas nostra contemptui est, Caes, **b,** act, contemptus moriendi, Tac

contendo -tendi tentum, 3 **I.** Lit *to stretch forcibly,* arcum, Verg, ballistas lapidum et reliqua tormenta telorum contendere atque adducere, Cic; and hence of missiles, *to shoot, cast,* tela, Verg **II.** Transf, **A.** *to strive with all one's bodily or mental power, to strain, exert oneself,* **1** of the bodily powers, **a,** gen, (α) transit, summas vires, Lucr, (β) intransit, eniti et contendere debet ut vincat, Cic, fuga salutem petere contendunt, Caes, **b,** *to hasten on a journey, try to reach,* Bibracte ire contendit, Caes, fig, si potuissemus, quo contendimus pervenire, Cic, **2,** of the mental powers, **a,** *to exert oneself,* (α) transit, contendit omnes nervos Chrysippus ut, etc., Cic, (β) intransit, maximis laboribus et periculis ad summam laudem gloriamque, Cic, ob eam causam contendi, ut plura dicerem, Cic; **b,** *to strive to obtain something, strive for;* non erat causa, cur hoc tempore aliquid a te contenderem, Cic, ab aliquo valde de reditu in gratiam, Cic, vehementer contendere ab aliquo ut, etc, Cic, **c,** *to assert with confidence, maintain,* contendentes numquam eam urbem fuisse ex Triphylia, Liv **B.** *to strive with some one else,* **1, a,** cum victore, Caes; contra Paridem, Verg, pro vitulis contra leones, Cic, inter se de principatu, Caes, cum Libone de mittendis legatis, Caes, **b,** at an auction, *to bid against,* Cic, **2,** *to compare, contrast;* ipsas causas, quae inter se confligunt, Cic

1 **contentē,** adv, with compar and superl (1 contentus), *eagerly, earnestly;* contente pro se dicere, Cic.

2 **contentē,** adv. (2 contentus), *strictly, sparingly,* Plaut.

contentĭo -ōnis, f (contendo), *the full exercise of the powers, effort, striving* **I.** Gen, vocis, *the raising or straining of the voice,* Cic, animi, Cic **II.** **1,** *combat, contest, contention, strife,* magna contentio belli, Cic, adversus procuratores contentio dicendi, Cic, in contentionem honoris incidere, *rivalry in seeking a public office,* Cic., contentiones habere cum aliquo, Caes, **2, a,** *a contrast, comparison;* hominum ipsorum or fortunarum contentionem facere, Cic, **b,** rhet t t, *antithesis, juxtaposition of opposed ideas,* Quint

contentĭōsus a um (contentio), *pertaining to a contest, contentious, quarrelsome,* Plin

1 **contentus** a -um, p adj (contendo), *stretched, tense* **A.** Lit, funis, Hor **B.** Transf, **a,** onera contentis corporibus facilius feruntur, remissis opprimunt, Cic., **b,** *eager, zealous,* ad tribunatum contento studio cursuque veniamus, Cic

2 **contentus** a -um, p adj with compar (contineo), *contented, satisfied,* with abl, suis rebus, Cic, ea victoria, Cic., contentus quod, etc, Cic, with infin, Ov

contermĭnus -a -um, *having the same boundary, conterminous, near,* conterminа stabula ripae, Ov Subst., **contermĭnum** -i, n *an adjoining region, a confine,* Tac

contĕro -trivi -tritum, 3 **I.** In narrow sense, *to rub away, reduce to small portions by rubbing, to grind, pound,* cornua cervi, Ov. **II.** In wider sense, **1,** *to destroy, wear away,* eius omnes injurias voluntariā quādam oblivione, Cic; reliqua conterere et contemnere, *trample under foot,* Cic, ferrum, *to wear away by using,* Ov, se in musicis, geometriā, astris, Cic, **2,** of time, *to consume, spend,* omne otiosum tempus in studiis, Cic, bonum otium socordiā atque desidiā, Sall

conterrĕo -terrui -territum, 2 *to terrify, frighten exceedingly,* conterrere loquacitatem alicuius vultu ipso aspectuque, Cic, his nuntiis senatus conterritus, Liv

contestātĭo -ōnis, f (contestor), *an earnest supplication, eager request,* Cic

contestor, 1 dep **1,** *to call to witness,* deos hominesque, Cic, **2, a,** litem, *to set an action on foot, inaugurate an action by calling witnesses,* Cic, **b,** transf, virtus contestata, *approved,* Cic

contexo texui textum, 3. **I.** Lit, *to weave together, twine together, connect, unite,* lilia amaranthis, Tib, ovium villis contextis homines vestiuntur, Cic **II.** Transf, **1,** *to connect, unite,* extrema cum primis, Cic, **2,** *to continue,* carmen longius, Cic, **3,** *to build, construct, put together,* sic deinceps omne opus contexitur, Caes, equum trabibus acernis, Verg; **4,** *to devise, invent,* crimen, Cic

contextē, adv (contextus), *in close connexion,* Cic

1 **contextus** -a -um, p adj (from contexo), *interwoven, connected, united,* **a,** contexta condensaque corpora, Lucr, **b,** perpetuae et contextae voluptates, *an unbroken series of pleasures,* Cic, **c,** contexta historia eorum temporum, *continuous,* Nep

2 **contextus** -ūs, m (contexo), *uniting, connexion,* **a,** contextum corporum dissolvere, Lucr, **b,** of abstractions, mirabilis contextus rerum, Cic, **c,** of oratory, totius quasi contextus orationis, Cic

contĭcesco -ticui, 3 (inchoat of conticeo), *to become silent, to be dumb, silent* **I.** Lit, **a,** of persons, conscientiā convictus repente conticuit, Cic, **b,** of personifications, neque ulla aetas de tuis laudibus conticescet, Cic **II.** Transf, *to become still or quiet, to abate, cease,* illae scilicet litterae conticuerunt forenses et senatoriae, Cic

contignātĭo -ōnis, f (contigno), *woodwork, a flooring, joists, storey,* Caes

contigno, 1 (com and tignum), *to put planks together, to floor,* Cic.

contĭgŭus -a -um (contingo) **I** Act, *that which touches another, contiguous, near,* domus, Ov, pars circi quae Aventino contigua, Tac, Cappadoces, Tac **II.** Pass with dat, *within reach of,* contiguus missae hastae, Verg

contĭnens -entis, p adj with compar (contineo) **I. 1,** *lying near, adjacent, bordering upon,* praedia continentia huic fundo, Cic; continentibus diebus, *in the days immediately following,* Caes; **2, a,** *hanging together, unbroken,* agmen, Liv, terra continens, *the mainland,* Cic, subst, **contĭnens** -entis, f *a continent,* Caes; **b,** of time, *continuous, unbroken,* e continenti genere, *in unbroken genealogical succession,* Cic, totius diei continens labor, Caes, continenti cursu, Liv **II.** *temperate, continent,* puer, Cic, ne continentior in vita hominum, quam in pecuniā fuisse videatur, Caes **III.** Rhet t t, subst, **contĭnens** entis, f *the main point,* causae, Cic

contĭnentĕr, adv (continens) **1 a** of space, *in close succession,* sedetis, Cat, **b,** of time, *continuously, without cessation;* totā nocte ierunt, Caes, **2,** *continently, temperately,* vivere, Cic

contĭnentĭa ae, f (contineo), *continence, self restraint, moderation, temperance,* continentia in omni victu cultuque corporis, Cic.

contineo -tinui -tentum, 2. (com and teneo). **I.** *to keep together*; **1, a,** *to bind together, hold fast*; quum agger altiore aquā contineri non posset, Caes.; transf., nec enim ulla res vehementius rempublicam continet quam fides, Cic.; **b,** *to keep together, unseparated*; legiones uno in loco, Caes.; **c,** *to connect, join*; quod oppidum Genabum pons fluminis Ligeris continebat, Caes.; **2, a,** *to keep in, surround, contain, limit*; mundus qui omnia complexu suo coercet et continet, Cic.; *to confine*; beluas immanes saeptis, Cic.; milit. t. t., *to shut in*; Pompejum quam augustissime, Caes.; **b,** *to contain, comprehend, comprise*; tales res quales hic liber continet, Cic.; de summo bono quod continet philosophiam, *which is the main point in philosophy*, Cic.; status reipublicae maxime judicatis rebus continetur, *is involved in, depends upon*, Cic. **II.** *to keep, maintain*; **1, a,** *to keep firm*; naves minus commode copulis continebantur; **b,** *to keep what has been taken* or *received*; alvus arcet et continet quod recipit, Cic.; **2, a,** *to keep in a place* or *occupation*; milites sub pellibus, Caes.; se suo loco, Caes.; se in suis perennibus studiis, Cic.; Belgas in officio, *to maintain in allegiance*, Caes.; **b,** *to keep back, be silent about*; petimus ab Antonio, ut ea quae continet neque adhuc protulit explicet nobis, Cic.; **3,** *to restrain, confine, keep back*; **a,** lit., risum, Cic.; gradum, *to check*, Verg.; **b,** transf., *to keep some one from some thing*; suos a proelio, Caes.; contineo me ab exemplis, Cic.; *to keep obedient, hold in check*; et usus non tam armis, quam judiciorum terrore, Liv.; **c,** morally, *to restrain, curb, repress*; omnes cupiditates, Cic.; non posse milites contineri quin, etc., Caes.

1. **contingo** (contingue), 3. *to wet, moisten*, Lucr.

2. **contingo** -tigi -tactum, 3. (com and tango). **I.** Transit., *to touch*. **A.** Lit., **a,** terram osculo, Liv.; paene terram (of the moon), Cic.; **b,** *to grasp*; dextram, Liv.; **c,** poet., *to touch, taste*; cibos ore, Ov.; **d,** *to sprinkle*; ora nati sacro medicamine, Ov.; **e,** *to reach to, touch*; nullas profecto terras caelum contingere, Liv.; esp. geograph. t. t., *to border on, touch*; quorum agri non contingunt mare, Cic.; **f,** *to reach*; (α) an aim with a missile, ex tantā altitudine contingere hostem non posse, Liv.; (β) an object desired, optatam cursu metam, Hor.; Italiam, Verg.; (γ) of the voice, *to reach the ear of*; nec contigit ullum vox mea mortalem, Ov. **B.** Transf., **a,** *to be related to*; aliquem sanguine ac genere, Liv.; *to concern, affect*; Romanos nihil (consultatio) contingit, nisi quatenus, etc., Liv.; **b,** *to pollute, defile*; milites contacti sacrilegio, Liv. **II.** Intransit., *to happen, to befall*; with dat., mihi omnia, quae opto, contingant, Cic.; with infin., celeriter antecellere omnibus ingenii gloriā contigit, Cic.; with ut and the subj., quoniam autem, tecum ut essem, non contigit, Cic.

contĭnŭātio -ōnis, f. (continuo). **I.** Act., *an unbroken continuance, continuing*; tribunatus, Liv. **II.** Pass., **A.** *connexion, continuation, unbroken succession*; causarum, Cic.; rhet. t. t., *a period*; nimis longa continuatio verborum, Cic. **B.** *an unbroken succession, continuance in time*; imbrium, Caes.

contĭnŭĭtas -ātis, f. (continuus), *continuity, unbroken succession*, Varr.

1. **contĭnŭō,** adv. (continuus), **1,** *immediately, at once*, Cic.; **2,** in conjunction with a negative, *not immediately = not necessarily*; in a question = *perhaps then?* non continuo si me in gregem sicariorum contuli, sum sicarius, Cic.

2. **contĭnŭo,** 1. (continuus). **I.** Of space, *to bring into connexion, connect, unite*; aër mari continuatus est, Cic.; Suionibus Sitonum gentes continuantur, *are adjacent to*, Tac.; verba, *to form into a sentence*, Cic.; binas aut amplius domos, Sall.; aedificia moenibus, Liv.; agmen latissime, *to extend*, Cic. **II.** Of time, **a,** *to do in rapid succession, to keep on doing*; prope continuatis funeribus, *the funerals following close on one another*, Liv.; **b,** *to continue without interruption*; diem noctemque potando, *continue drinking day and night*, Tac.; iter die et nocte, Caes.; militiam, Liv.; magistratum, *to prolong*, Sall.; alicui consulatum, Liv.

contĭnŭus -a -um (contineo), *connected with, hanging together, continuous, unbroken, uninterrupted*. **I.** Of space, **a,** Leucada continuam veteres habuere coloni, *connected with the main land*, Ov.; transf. of persons, Nerva, continuus principi, *standing next to*, Tac.; **b,** *unseparated, undivided*; Rhenus uno alveo continuus, Tac.; translationes, Cic. **II.** Of time, *successive, following on, uninterrupted*; secutae sunt continuos complures dies tempestates, Caes.; superiora continuorum annorum decreta, Cic.; oppugnatio, Liv.

contĭo -ōnis, f. (contr. from conventio), **1,** *an assembly of the people* or *of the soldiers, a public meeting*; contionem advocare, Cic.; advocare contionem populi or militum, Caes.; vocare ad contionem, Liv.; habere, Cic.; dimittere, Liv.; dare alicui contionem (of a magistrate, who called the meeting), Cic.; prodire in contionem, Cic.; producere aliquem in contionem, Liv.; aliquid in contione dicere, Cic.; in contionem ascendere or escendere, *to go up to the platform to speak*, Liv.; **2,** meton., *the speech made in such an assembly*; contiones turbulentae Metelli, temerariae Appii, furiosissimae Publii, Cic.; habere contiones in Caesarem graves, Caes.; funebris, *a funeral oration*, Cic.

contĭōnābundus -a -um (contionor), *haranguing, speaking in public*, Liv.

contĭōnālis -e (contio), *relating to a public assembly*; contionalis prope clamor senatus, Cic.; illa contionalis hirudo aerarii, *that bloodsucker and demagogue*, Cic.

contĭōnārius -a -um (contio), *relating to a public assembly*; ille contionarius populus, Cic.

contĭōnātor -ōris, m. (contionor), *a popular orator, demagogue*, Cic.

contĭōnor, 1. dep. (contio), **a,** *to form, compose an assembly*; nunc illi vos singuli universos contionantes timent, Liv.; **b,** *to speak in public before an assembly*; apud milites, Caes.; superiore e loco, Cic.; also *to proclaim publicly, speak with a loud voice*; C. Cato contionatus est se comitia haberi non siturum, Cic.

contĭuncŭla -ae, f. (dim. of contio), **1,** *a small assembly*, Cic.; **2,** *a short harangue*, Cic.

contollo, 3. (obsol. for confero), gradum, *to betake oneself*, Plaut.

contŏnat, impers. *it thunders violently*, Plaut.

contor = cunctor (q.v.).

contorquĕo -torsi -tortum, 2. **I.** *to twist, whirl, turn violently, contort*; gubernaclum, Lucr.; membra quocunque vult, *to direct, turn*, Cic.; proram ad laevas undas, Verg. **II.** Esp. *to brandish, to hurl*, contorquere hastam in latus, Verg.; transf., verba, *to hurl forth*, Cic.

contortē, adv. with compar. (contortus), *in distorted order, in a constrained manner, ambiguously*; dicere, Cic.

contortĭo -ōnis, f. (contorqueo), *a swinging, twisting*; contortiones orationis, *distorted expressions*, Cic.

contortor -ōris, m. (contorqueo), *one who contorts or perverts*; legum, Ter.

contortŭlus -a -um (dim of contortus), *somewhat intricate, obscure*, Cic

contortus -a -um (p adj from contorqueo), 1, *intricate, confused, complicated*, contortae et difficiles res, Cic , 2, *powerful, vigorous*, oratio, Cic.

contrā (from com, as extra from ex). **I.** Adv , **A.** Of place, *opposite, over against, on the opposite side*, ulmus erat contra, Ov , omnia contra circaque plena hostium erant, Liv **B.** Of actions, **1,** which answer to one another, *in return*, quum hic nugatur, contra nugari lubet, Plaut ; **2,** which are opposed to one another, *on the other side, on the contrary*, alia aestimabilia, alia contra, Cic , foll by atque, or quam, simulacrum Jovis contra atque antea fuerat convertere, Cic , quum contra fecerint quam polliciti sunt, Cic , **3,** used of hostile opposition, *against*, pugnare, Lucr , consistere, Caes , dicere, Cic **II.** Prep with acc , **1,** *opposite to, over against*, insula quae contra Brundusinum portum est, Caes ; **2,** *against, in opposition to, contrary to*, vim atque impetum fluminis, Caes , opinionem, Cic. contra ea, *on the contrary, on the other hand*, Caes , **3,** *against*, in the sense of hostility; contra populum Romanum conjurasse, Caes , contra deos disputare, Cic (Contra occasionally is placed after its acc in the case of a noun, Verg , of a rel. pronoun, quos contra, Cic)

contractĭo -ōnis, f (contraho), *a drawing together, contraction*. **A.** Lit , contractio et porrectio digitorum, Cic , frontis, Cic **B.** Transf , **1,** *abbreviation, shortness*, orationis, Cic , syllabae, Cic , **2,** *anxiety, depression*, animi, Cic

contractiuncŭla -ae, f (dim of contractio), *dejection, sadness* , animi, Cic

contractus -a -um, p adj with compar (contraho), *drawn in, contracted, narrow*, **a,** of places, locus exiguus atque contractus, Verg , **b,** of time, *shorter*, his jam contractioribus noctibus, Cic , **c,** of the voice, contractum genus vocis, Cic , **d,** of orators, dialectica quasi contracta et astricta eloquentia putanda est, Cic ; **e,** of circumstances, *straitened;* paupertas, Hor , **f,** *retired, quiet;* contractus leget, Hor

contrādīco -dixi -dictum, 3 *to gainsay, speak against, contradict*, sententiis aliorum, Tac , nec contradici quin amicitia de integro reconcilietur, Liv

contradictĭo -ōnis, f (contradico), *a speaking against, contradiction*, Quint

contrăho traxi tractum, 3 **I.** *to draw together, collect, unite* (opp. dissipare) **A.** Lit , **a,** milit t t , cohortes ex finitimis regionibus, Caes , magnam classem, Nep , Luceriam omnes copias, Cic ; omnes or omnia ad unum, Cic , **b,** *to bring together for conversation*, etc , Scipionem et Hasdrubalem ad colloquium dirimendarum simultatum causa, Liv **B.** Transf , **a,** *to unite*, contrahit celeriter similitudo eos, Liv , contrahere amicitiam, *to form friendship*, Cic , **b,** *to complete a business arrangement*, rem, rationem, negotium, Cic , contrahere magnam rationem cum Mauritaniae rege, Cic ; **c,** *to cause, bring on, bring about*, aes alienum, *to contract debt*, Cic , bellum, Liv , lites, Cic , porca contracta, *due to expiate a crime*, Cic ; offensionem, Cic **II** *to draw together by way of shortening* **A.** Lit , **a,** frontem, Cic , collum, Cic , pulmones se contrahunt, Cic , contractum aliquo morbo bovis cor, Cic , vela, *to furl one's sails*, fig , *to be moderate*, Cic , **b,** of limbs, parts of the body, *to contract* (from cold, death, etc), contracto frigore pigrae, *numbing*, Verg **B** Transf , *to shorten, reduce, draw in, draw together* , **a,** castra, Caes ; of the moon, orbem, Ov , **b,** of speech, *to shorten*, orationem in verbum contrahere, Cic , **c,** of appetites *to repress*, appetitus omnes contrahere, Cic , **d,** of courage, etc , *to lower, lessen*, animum, Cic

contrārĭē, adv (contrarius), *in an opposite direction or manner*, sidera contrarie procedentia, Cic , verba relata contrarie, Cic

contrārĭus -a um (contra) **I.** Of place, *opposite, over against*, collis nascebatur adversus huic et contrarius, Caes , vulnera, *wounds in front*, Tac **II. A.** *coming from the opposite direction*, contrarius ictus, *a blow from an enemy*, Cic., in contrarias partes fluere, Cic , classi contraria flamina, *contrary winds*, Ov , in comparison, followed by atque, qui versantur contrario motu atque caelum, Cic **B.** 1 *opposed, contrary to*, contrariae epistolae, *contradictory*, Cic , in contrarias partes disputare or disserere de aliquā re, *to speak for and against*, Cic , with genit , hujus virtutis contraria est vitiositas, Cic , with dat , nihil malum esse, nisi quod virtuti contrarium esset, Cic , subst , **contrārĭum** -ii, n *the opposite*, in contrarium disputare, Tac , followed by atque or ac, contrarium decernebat ac paulo ante decreverat, Cic , adv , ex contrario, *against, on the other side*, ut ego hoc ex contrario contendo, Cic , plur , comparare contraria, Cic , **2,** esp **a,** *opposed to in a hostile manner*, arma, Ov , **b,** *injurious*, otium maxime contrarium esse, Caes

contrectābĭlĭtĕr, adv (contrectabilis), *with feeling*, Lucr

contrectātĭo -ōnis, f (contrecto), *a touching, handling*, Cic

contrecto, 1 (contracto), *to touch, feel, handle* **I. A.** Lit , vulnus, Ov **B.** Transf , totaque mente contrectare varias voluptates, *consider*, Cic **II.** *to dishonour*, Tac

contrĕmisco (contrĕmesco), -trĕmŭi, 3 **a,** *to tremble violently, to quake*, contremiscere tota mente atque artubus omnibus, Cic , **b,** *to tremble before, be afraid of*, periculum, Hor

contrĕmo, 3 *to tremble violently, quake*, Lucr

contrĭbŭo -tribŭi -tribūtum, 3 , **a,** *to contribute to in common with others* nec non Peneae nec Spercheides undae contribuere aliquid, Ov , **b,** *to annex, incorporate with, unite*, Calagurritani qui erant cum Oscensibus contributi, Caes , Ambracia quae tum contribuerat se Aetolis, Liv

contristo, 1 (com and tristo), *to make sad, make sorrowful, sadden*, **a,** pluvio frigore caelum, *make gloomy*, Verg , **b,** contristat haec sententia Balbum Cornelium, ap Cic

contrītus -a -um, p adj (from contero), *worn out, well used common, trite*, proverbium, Cic

contrōversĭa -ae, f (controversus), *debate, dispute, controversy*, hereditatis, *about an inheritance*, Cic , controversiam habere de re cum aliquo, Cic , controversia est inter aliquos de re, Cic , in controversiā versari, esse, Cic , rem adducere in controversiam, deducere in controversiam, vocare in controversiam, *to make matter of debate*, Cic , sine controversiā, *without dispute*, Cic , sine controversiā solvere, Cic , sine controversiā vicimus, *we have undoubtedly conquered*, Cic , controversia non erat quin, *there was no doubt that*, etc , Cic

contrōversĭōsus a um (controversia), *controverted, strongly disputed*, res, Liv

contrōversor, 1 dep (controversus), *to contend, dispute, debate*, inter se de hujuscemodi rebus controversari, Cic

contrōversus a -um (contro, like contra, from com = *with, against*), 1, pass , *that which is a subject of debate, controverted*, res, Cic , **2,** act *disputatious, fond of controversy;* gens, Cic

contrŭcīdo 1 *to cut in pieces, cut down*,

hew down, slay; debilitato corpore et contrucidato, Cic.; fig., rempublicam, Cic.

contrūdo -trūsi -trūsum, 3. **1,** *to thrust, push together*; nubes in unum, Lucr.; **2,** *to thrust, crowd into any place*; aliquos in balneas, Cic.

contrunco, 1. *to cut in pieces*; cibum, Plaut.

contŭbernālis -is, c. (com and taberna). **I.** **a,** *a messmate, comrade, one who shares the same tent*; domi una eruditi, militiae contubernales, Cic.; **b,** *a young man who accompanied a general to learn the art of war*; fuit in Cretā postea contubernalis Saturnini, Cic.; so in public affairs, *supporter*; alicui contubernalem in consulatu fuisse, Cic. **II.** **a,** *comrade, mate, constant companion*; habuisses non hospitem sed contubernalem, Cic.; **b,** *the husband* or *wife of a slave*, Plin.

contŭbernĭum -i, n. (com and taberna). **I.** Concr., **1,** *a hut*, or *tent in which ten men and an officer lodged*; deponere in contubernio arma, Caes.; **2,** *the common dwelling of a male and female slave*, Tac. **II.** Abstr., **1,** *a sharing in the same tent, comradeship*; militum, Tac.; **2,** *the attendance of a young man on a general to learn the art of war*; contubernii necessitudo, Cic.; **3,** *companionship, intimacy*, Suet.; **4,** esp. *the living together of slaves as man and wife*, Col.; and gen. *concubinage*, Cic.

contŭĕor -tŭĭtus sum, 2. *to regard on all sides, look at attentively*. **A.** Lit., aspicite ipsum, contuemini os, Cic. **B.** Transf. *to consider, reflect upon*; quum (revocatio illa) a contuendis nos malis avocat, Cic.

contŭĭtus, abl. -ū, m. (contueor), *a beholding, attentive looking at*, Plin.

contŭmācĭa -ae, f. (contumax), *stubbornness, obstinacy, insolence, haughtiness*; gen. in a bad sense, insolentia, superbia, contumacia, Cic.; in a good sense, *firmness*; libera contumacia (of Socrates), Cic.

contŭmācĭtĕr, adv. (contumax), *obstinately, stubbornly, insolently*; scribere, Cic.

contŭmax -ācis (com and TEM -o, temno), *haughty, insolent, stubborn, obstinate*; quis contumacior? quis inhumanior? quis superbior, Cic.; in a good sense, *firm, unyielding*; contumax etiam adversus tormenta servorum fides, Tac.

contŭmēlĭa -ae, f. (com and TEM -o, temno), *insult, affront, outrage, contumely*. **I.** Lit. **A.** contumeliam jacĕre in aliquem, Cic.; lacerare aliquem contumeliis, Cic.; onerare aliquem contumeliis, Cic.; vexare aliquem omnibus contumeliis, Cic.; contumeliae causa aliquem describere, Cic.; contumelia appellare aliquem perfugam, *insultingly*, Caes.; vertere aliquid in contumeliam suam, *to take as an insult*, Caes. **B.** *dishonour*, Cic. **II.** Transf. *damage, injury*; naves totae factae ex robore ad quamvis vim et contumeliam perferendam, Caes.

contŭmēlĭōsē, adv., with compar. and superl. (contumeliosus), *insolently, abusively*; contumeliose dicere, laedere, Cic.

contŭmēlĭōsus -a -um, adj., with compar. and superl. (contumelia), *insulting, abusive*; epistolae in aliquem contumeliosae, Cic.; id contumeliosum est plebi (followed by acc. and infin.), Liv.

contŭmŭlo, 1., **1,** *to heap up in a mound*, Plin.; **2,** *to bury, inter*, Ov.

contundo -tŭdi -tūsum, 3. **I.** *to bruise, crush, pound, break to pieces*; allia serpyllumque, Verg. **II.** *to crush, bruise, beat*. **A.** Lit., anum saxis, Hor.; pugiles caestibus contusi, Cic.; contusi ac debilitati inter saxa rupesque, Liv. **B.** **1,** *to destroy, subdue, crush, demolish*; ferocem Hannibalem, Liv.; animum, Cic.; audaciam alicuius contundere et frangere, Cic.; calumniam stultitiamque alicuius obterere ac contundere, Cic.

contŭo, contŭor, 3. = contueor (q.v.).

conturbātĭo -ōnis, f. (conturbo), *disorder, confusion, perturbation of mind*; mentis, Cic.

conturbo, 1., **1,** *to disturb, throw into disorder, confusion*; ordines Romanorum, Sall.; rempublicam, Sall.; **2,** *to disturb in mind, cause anxiety*; valetudo tua me valde conturbat, Cic.; rationes, or absol., conturbare, Cic., *to bring money matters into confusion, to ruin, make bankrupt*; conturbare putat sibi licere, Cic.

contus -i, m. (κοντός), **1,** *a pole used for pushing a boat along*, Verg.; **2,** *a long spear or pike*, Tac.

cōnus -i, m. (κῶνος). **1,** *a cone*, Cic.; **2,** *the apex of a helmet*, Verg.

convălesco -vălŭi, 3. *to become strong*. **I.** Gen. **A.** Lit., of things, postquam pestifer ignis convaluit, *blazed up*, Ov. **B.** Transf., **a,** *to gain strength*; quum mala per longas convaluere moras, *have become rooted*, Ov.; **b,** of persons or states, *to gain strength* or *power*; Milo in dies convalescebat, Cic.; his ille (Caesar) rebus ita convaluit ut, etc., Cic.; nimis vicinas prope se convalescere opes rati, Cic. **II.** Esp. **A.** *to recover from a disease, gain strength, get well*; non aegri omnes convalescunt, Cic.; ex morbo, Cic. **B.** Transf., ut tandem sensus convaluere mei, Ov.

convallis -is, f. *a valley shut in on all sides*, Cic.

convāso, 1. (com and vasa), *to pack up baggage*, Ter.

convecto, 1. (intens. of conveho), *to bring together, collect*; praedam, Verg.

convector -ōris, m. (conveho), *a fellow-voyager*, Cic.

convĕho -vexi -vectum, 3. *to bring together, carry into one place*; frumentum ex finitimis regionibus in urbem, Caes.; lintribus in eam insulam materiem, calcem, caementa, arma, Cic.

convello -velli, and (rarely) -vulsi (-volsi) -vulsum (-volsum), 3. *to tear, pluck, pull away, wrench off*. **I.** Lit., **1,** repagula, Cic.; gradus Castoris, Cic.; Herculem ex suis sedibus convellere atque auferre, Cic.; viridem ab humo silvam, Verg.; dapes avido dente, *devour*, Ov.; **2,** milit. t. t., convellere signa, *to pluck up the standards, to decamp*, Cic. **II.** Transf. *to weaken, overthrow, destroy*; cuncta auxilia reipublicae labefactari convellique, Cic.; si eam opinionem ratio convellet, Cic.; quo judicio convulsam penitus scimus esse rempublicam, Cic.

convĕna -ae, c. adj. (convenio), *coming together*, Plaut.; in plur. subst. *a concourse of strangers, assembled multitude*; pastores et convenas congregare, Cic.

convĕnĭens -entis, p. adj. (from convenio), **1,** *agreeing, unanimous, concordant*; bene convenientes propinqui, Cic.; **2,** *fit for, appropriate, suitable*; conveniens decretis eius, Cic.; oratio tempori conveniens, Liv.; nihil est enim tam naturae aptum, tam conveniens ad res vel secundas vel adversas, Cic.

convĕnĭentĕr, adv. (conveniens), *agreeably with, suitably to*; convenienter cum naturā vivere, Cic.; constanter convenienterque sibi dicere, Cic.

convĕnĭentĭa -ae, f. (conveniens), *agreement, harmony, conformity with*; quaedam convenientia et conjunctio naturae, Cic.

convĕnĭo -vēni -ventum, 4. **I.** Gen. **A.** Intransit., **1,** *to come together, collect*; ex pr-

viros, Caes., ad hoc judicium, Cic, celeriter ad clamorem hominum circiter millia sex convenerant, Caes., uno tempore undique comitiorum ludorum censendique causa, Cic, 2, civitates quae in id forum conveniunt, *who belong to that district*, Cic, 3, legal t t. convenire in manum (of the wife, *to come into the power of her husband by marriage*), Cic **B.** Transit, *to visit, meet, call upon*, quotidie plurimos, Cic, convento Cn Octavio Demetriade, Cic, tribunum plebis non desistebant clam inter se convenire, Cic **II.** *to fit* **A. 1,** Lit, si cothurni laus illa esset ad pedem apte convenire, Cic, **2,** Transf, *to agree with, be congenial to, harmonise, be fitting*, haec tua deliberatio non convenit cum oratione Largi, Cic, non in omnes omnia convenire, Cic, with infin or acc and infin, illicone ad praetorem ire convenit? Cic, impers, minime miror caelum et terram, si tibi ita conveniat, dimittere, Cic **B.** *to unite*, **1,** lit., Lucr, **2,** transf, **a,** res convenit, or impers, convenit, *a thing is agreed upon*, id signum quod convenerat, *which had been agreed upon*, Caes, pax convenit, Liv., convenit (*it is asserted*) jam inde per consules reliqua belli perfecta (esse), Liv, mihi cum Deiotaro convenit, ut ille in meis castris esset cum suis copiis, Cic, impers, quum de facto conveniret, Cic, **b,** bene (optime) convenit (alicui) cum aliquo, *to be on good terms with*, sorori vir, quicum optime convenisset, Cic

conventicium -ii, n (convenio), sc aes = το εκκλησιαστικον, *the money received by Greek citizens for attendance in the popular assembly*, Cic

conventiculum -i, n (dim of conventus), **a,** *a coming together, assembly, association*, conventicula hominum, quae postea civitates nominatae sunt, Cic, **b,** *a place of meeting*, Tac

conventio -ōnis, f (convenio), **1,** *an assembly*, Varr, **2,** *an agreement, compact*, Liv

conventum -i, n (convenio), *a covenant, agreement, compact*, pactum, conventum, stipulatio, Cic

conventus -ūs, m (convenio) **I.** Lit, **A.** *a coming together, an assembly*, **a,** virorum mulierumque celeberrimus, Cic, **b,** *an illegal assembly*, in nocturno conventu fuisse apud M Laecam, Cic, **c,** *a congress of states*, omnium sociorum civitatum, Liv, **d,** *the assembly of the inhabitants of a province held by the praetor* conventum agere, *to hold the assizes*, Cic, hence *the district of the province for which such an assembly was held*, homo omnium ex illo conventu quadruplatorum deterrimus, Cic, **e,** *the union of Roman citizens in a province forming a corporation*, conventus Syracusanus, Cic **B.** Of atoms, *union*, Lucr, **II.** Transf, *agreement*, Cic

converbero, 1 *to beat violently*, Plin

converro (-vorro) -verri (-vorri) -versum (-vorsum), 3 *to sweep together, brush out*, Plaut, transf, hereditates omnium, *scrape together*, Cic

conversatio -ōnis, f (conversor) **I.** *frequent use, a frequent sojourn in a place*, Plin **II.** *intercourse, conversation*, Tac

conversio -ōnis, f (converto) **A.** Lit, *a turning round*, coeli, Cic, mensium annorumque conversiones, *periodical return*, Cic **B.** in rhet, **1,** *the rounding off of a period*, ut (oratio) conversiones habeat absolutas, Cic, **2,** *the repetition of the same word at the end of a clause*, Cic, **3,** *change*, naturales esse quasdam conversiones rerum publicarum, Cic.

converso (intens of converto), 1 *to turn round frequently*, animus se ipse conversans, Cic

converto (-vorto) -verti (-vorti) -versum (-vorsum), 3 *to turn round, whirl round* **I.** Lit, **A.** *to turn round to the other side*, **1,** palma ad palmam, Cic, naves in eam partem, quo ventus fert, Caes, esp milit t t, signa convertere, *to wheel round*, Caes, terga or se convertere, *to flee*, Caes, **2, a,** in motion, *to turn round, change one's direction*; vox boum Herculem convertit, *makes Hercules turn round*, Liv, iter convertere, Caes, reflex, se ad montes, Caes, or without se, cum paucis ad equites, Sall, **b,** convertere pecuniam publicam domum suam, *to embezzle*, Cic, **3,** geograph t t *to face, be directed towards, lie towards*, spelunca conversa ad aquilonem, Cic **B.** *to turn round in a circle, to revolve*, quae (terra) circum axem se summa celeritate convertit et torquet, Cic, **II.** Transf, **1,** *to direct towards*, convertere in se unum omnium vires, Liv, in ceteros ordines easdem vitae conditiones, Cic, **2,** *to direct one's attention or looks towards*, video in me omnium vestrum ora atque oculos esse conversos, Cic, **3,** *to direct one's inclination, mind, etc, towards*, omne studium curamque ad hanc scribendi operam, Cic, reflex, se ad otium pacemque, Cic, se in or ad aliquem, *to attach oneself to*, Cic, **4,** *to devote to some object*, rationem in fraudem malitiamque, Cic, **5,** *to convert, pervert*, ad terum (auxilium) ad perniciem meam erat a vobis consulibus conversum, Cic, **6, a,** *to change, alter*, mirum in modum conversae sunt omnium mentes, Caes, cavendum ne in graves inimicitias convertant se amicitiae, Cic, Hecubam in canem esse conversam, Cic **b,** librum e Graeco in Latinum, *to translate*, Cic

convestio, 4 *to clothe* **A.** Lit, Enn **B.** Transf, *to cover, surround*, domus duobus lucis convestita, Cic

convexitas -ātis, f (convexus), *convexity*, mundi, Plin

convexus a -um (conveho), **1,** *vaulted, arched, convex*, orbis lunae, Cic Subst, **convexum** i, n, and commonly in plur, **convexa** -orum, n *an arch*, convexa coeli, Verg, **2,** *sloping, steep*, iter, Ov

conviciator -ōris, m (convicior), *a railer, slanderer, reviler*, Cic

convicior, 1 dep (convicium), *to rail at, revile, reproach*, Liv

convicium ii, n (= convocium, from com and vox), **1,** *a loud cry, shout, clamour*, mulierum, Cic, **2,** *violent reproach, reviling, insult*, clamore et conviciis et sibilis consectari, Cic, alicui convicium facere, Cic, non modo acclamatione sed convicio et maledictis impediri, Cic, verberavi te cogitationis tacito dumtaxat convicio, Cic; meton, nemorum convicia, picae, *mocking birds*, Ov

convictio ōnis, f (convivo), *social intercourse, familiarity*, Cic

convictor -ōris, m (convivo), *one who lives with another, constant associate*, ap Cic

convictus -ūs, m (convivo), **1,** *a living together, constant intercourse*, conventus hominum ac societas, Cic, **2,** *entertainment, feast*, Tac

convinco vici victum, 3 **1,** *to convict of a crime or mistake*, aliquem summae negligentiae, Cic, multis avaritiae criminibus, Cic, convictus in hoc scelere, Cic, with infin, or acc and infin, Liv, Sall, **2,** *to prove conclusively, demonstrate*, errores Epicuri, Cic, inauditum facinus ipsius qui commisit voce convinci, Cic with acc and infin, Stoicos nihil de diis explicare convincit, Cic

conviso, 3 *to behold attentively, examine*, omnia loca oculis, Lucr; poet (of the sun, etc), *to beam upon*, Lucr

convitiator, . conviciator,

convītĭor, v. convicior.

convītĭum, v. convicium.

convīva -ae, c. (com and vivo), *a guest*; hilarus et bene acceptus, Cic.

convīvālis -e (convivium), *relating to a feast or banquet*, Liv.

convīvātor -ōris, m. (convivor), *one who gives a feast, a host*, Hor., Liv.

convīvĭum -ii, n. (com and vivo). **A.** *a feast, entertainment, banquet*; accipere aliquem convivio, Cic.; adhibere aliquem convivio or in convivium, Cic.; convivium apparare opipare, Cic.; dimittere convivium, Liv.; discedere de convivio, Cic.; inire convivium publicum, Cic.; interesse in convivio, Cic.; producere convivium vario sermone ad multam noctem, Cic.; venire in convivium, Cic. **B.** Meton., *the company assembled, guests*; vinosa convivia, Ov.

convīvor, 1. dep. (conviva), *to eat and drink in company, feast, revel*; non solum in publico, sed etiam de publico, Cic.

convŏcātĭo -ōnis, f. (convoco), *a calling together*; populi Romani ad rempublicam defendendam, Cic.

convŏco, 1. *to call together, assemble, convoke*; dissipatos homines, Cic.; principes ad se, Caes.; ad concionem, Liv.

convolnĕro, v. convulnero.

convŏlo, 1. *to fly together, run together, come together hastily*; cuncta ex Italia ad aliquem revocandum, Cic.

convolsus, v. convulsus.

convolvo -volvi -vŏlutum, 3. **1,** *to roll round*; sol se convolvens, Cic.; in lucem lubrica terga, Verg.; **2,** *to cover*; testudo convoluta omnibus rebus, quibus ignis jactus et lapides defendi possent, Caes.

convŏmo, 1. *to vomit all over*, Cic.

convulnĕro, 1. *to wound severely*, Plin.

convulsus -a -um, partic. of convello.

cŏŏlesco = coalesco (q.v.).

cŏŏpĕrĭo -pĕrŭi -pertum, 4. (com and operio), *to cover entirely, envelop*; aliquem lapidibus, *to stone to death*, Cic.; Decii corpus coopertum telis, Liv.; transf., partic., coopertus, *overwhelmed*; flagitiis atque facinoribus, Sall.

cŏoptātĭo -ōnis, f. (coopto), *choice, election, co-optation*; collegiorum, Cic.; censoria, *filling up of the senate by the censors*, Cic.

cŏopto (com and opto), 1. *to choose, elect*, esp. to a public office or dignity, *to coopt*; senatores, Cic.; tres sibi collegas, Liv.; aliquem in paternum auguratus locum, Cic.; aliquem magistrum equitum, Liv.

cŏŏrĭor -ortus sum, 4. *to arise, come forth at once, appear.* **I. a,** of storms, etc., *to break out*; tum subito tempestates sunt coortae maximae, Lucr.; **b,** of fires, quod pluribus simul locis ignes coorti essent, Liv.; **c,** of disease, pestilentia coorta, minacior quam periculosior, Liv.; **d,** of political events, of war, sedition, etc., *to break out*; seditio tum inter Antiates Latinosque coorta, Liv.; **e,** of laughing or weeping, risus, Nep.; libero conquestu coortae voces sunt, Liv. **II.** *to rise for insurrection or fight*; sed adeo infensa erat coorta plebs ut, etc., Liv.; Volscos summa vi ad bellum coortos, Liv.

cŏortus -ūs, m. (coorior), *an arising, breaking forth*, Lucr.

Cŏos (Cŏus) -i, f., and **Cōs** -o, f. (Κόως and Κῶς), *a small island in the Aegean Sea, off the coast of Caria.* Adj., **Cōus** -a -um, *Coan*; poeta, *Philetas*, Ov.; artifex, *Apelles, whose picture of Venus Anadyomene was at Coos*, Ov.; Venus, *the Venus Anadyomene of Apelles*, Cic. Subst., **Cōum** -i, n. *Coan wine*; **Cōi** -orum, m. *the inhabitants of Coos*; **Cōa** -orum, n. *Coan garments.*

cōpa -ae, f. *the hostess of a wine-shop*, Verg.

Cōpāis -idis, f. (Κωπαΐς), palus, *a lake in Boeotia.*

cŏphĭnus -i, m. (κοφινος), *a large basket or hamper*, Juv.

cōpĭa -ae, f. (cŏŏpia, from com and ops), *plenty, abundance.* **I.** Lit., **1, a,** of things, agri, vectigalium, pecuniae, Cic.; frumenti, Caes.; copia cum egestate confligit, Cic.; in plur., omnium rerum affluentes copiae, Cic.; milit. t. t., *supplies, provisions*; copias Dyrrhachii comparare, Caes.; **b,** of persons, virorum fortium atque innocentium tanta copia, Cic.; esp. milit. t. t., *troops, forces*; (α) sing., omnis armatorum copia, Cic.; augebatur illis copia, Caes.; (β) plur., copiae peditum equitumque, Liv.; terrestres navalesque, Liv.; copias magnas cogere, Caes.; comparare, Cic.; contrahere, Cic.; dimittere, Caes.; educere castris, e castris, Caes.; **2,** of abstractions, copia dicendi or orationis, *fulness of expression*, Cic. **II.** Transf., *ability, power, opportunity*; est alicui copia somni, Liv.; dimicandi cum hoste, Liv.; ab hoste copia pugnandi fit, Sall.; facere alicui consilii sui copiam, *to be accessible to a person asking one's advice*, Cic.; habere copiam alicuius, *to have some one in one's power*, Sall.

cōpĭōsē, adv. (copiosus), **1,** *abundantly, plentifully*; large et copiose comparare pastum, Cic.; senatorum urna copiose absolvit, *with a large majority*, Cic.; **2,** of discourse, *copiously*; dicere, Cic.

cōpĭōsus -a -um (copia), **1,** *richly provided, wealthy*; urbs celebris et copiosa, Cic.; copiosus a frumento locus, *rich in*, Cic.; opulenti homines et copiosi, Cic.; **2,** *copious of speech, eloquent*; homo copiosus ad dicendum, Cic.; oratio multa et varia et copiosa, Cic.; lingua copiosa, Cic.

cōpis -e = copiosus (q.v.).

cōpo, cōpona = caupo, caupona (q.v.).

coprĕa (copria) -ae, m. (κοπρίας), *a low buffoon*, Suet.

copta -ae, f. (κόπτη), *a hard cake or biscuit*, Mart.

Coptos -i, f. (Κοπτός), *a town of Upper Egypt*, now *Coft* or *Keft.*

cōpŭla -ae, f. (com and * apio). **A.** *a rope, band, tie*; dura copula canem tenet, *a leash*, Ov.; plur., copulae, *fastenings, grapnels*, Caes. **B.** Transf., *a bond, connexion*; quos irrupta tenet copula, Hor.

cōpŭlātĭo -ōnis, f. (copula), *a union, connexion*; atomorum inter se, Cic.

cōpŭlātus -a -um, p. adj. (from copulo), *connected, united, coupled*; quaedam sunt in rebus simplicia, quaedam copulata, Cic.; transf., nihil est amabilius neque copulatius quam morum similitudo, *tending to unite*, Cic.

cōpŭlo, 1. (copula), *to join together, connect, unite.* **A.** Lit., altera ratis huic copulata est, Liv. **B.** Transf., copulati in jus pervenimus, Cic.; copulare honestatem cum voluptate, Cic.; an haec inter se jungi copularique possint, Cic.; equester ordo qui tum cum senatu copulatus fuit, *were in harmony with*, Cic.

cŏqua -ae, f. (coquus), *a female cook*, Plaut.

cŏquīno, 1. (coquo), *to cook*, Plaut.

cŏquo, coxi, coctum, 3. *to cook, prepare food.* **I.** Lit., **1,** is qui illa coxerat, Cic.; cibaria, Liv.; **2,** *to bake, burn*; coquit glebas aestas matutinis solibus, Verg.; **3,** *to ripen*; poma matura et cocta, Cic.; **4,** *to warm*; calore et spiritu omnia cocta et confecta, Cic. **II.** Transf., **1,** *to think* *of, meditate, contrive*: consilia secreto ab aliis, Liv.; **2,** *to disturb*; femineae ardentem curaeque iraeque coquebant, Verg.

cŏquus (cocus) -i, m. (coquo), *a cook*, Cic.

cŏr, cordis, n. (root CORD, Gr. καρδ-ία). **I. A.** Lit., *the heart*; cor palpitat, Cic.; fig., **a,** *the heart as the seat of the feelings, the soul, feeling*; exsultantia corda, Verg.; cordi est aliquis or aliquid, *is dear to*; quum audirem eam (sponsam) tibi cordi esse, Liv.; idque eo mihi magis est cordi quod, etc., Cic.; with acc. and infin., Liv.; **b,** *the heart as the seat of thought, the mind, judgment*; qui propter haesitantiam linguae stuporemque cordis cognomen ex contumelia traxerit, Cic. **B.** Meton., *a person*; lecti juvenes, fortissima corda, Verg. **II.** Transf., *the stomach*, Hor., Lucr.

Cŏra -ae, f. (Κόρα), *an old town in Latium, now Core or Cori.* Adj., **Cŏrānus** -a -um.

cŏrallium -ii, n. (κοράλλιον), *red coral*, Lucr.

cōram (com and os, oris). **I.** Adv., **1,** *in presence of, in face of, before*; commodius fecissent, si quae apud vos de me deferunt, ea coram potius me praesente dixissent, Cic.; **2,** *personally, in one's own person, oneself*; intueri aliquid, *to behold with one's own eyes*, Cic.; agere, *to transact personally, i.e., not by letters*, Cic.; quum coram sumus, *personally present*, Cic. **II.** Prep. with abl., *in presence of*; genero meo, Cic.; populo, Hor.

Corbĭo -ōnis, f. **1,** *a town of the Aequi*; **2,** *a town in Hispania Tarraconensis.*

corbis -is, m. and f. *a wicker basket*; messoria, Cic.

corbīta -ae, f. *a slow-sailing merchant vessel*, Cic.

corbŭla -ae, f. (dim. of corbis), *a little basket*, Plaut.

corcŭlum -i, n. (dim. of cor), *a little heart*, used as a term of endearment, Plaut.

Corcȳra -ae, f. (Κόρκυρα), *Corcyra, an island in the Ionian Sea,* identified with the Homeric Scheria, the home of Alcinous, now *Corfu*; hence adj., **Corcȳraeus** -a -um, *Corcyraean*; horti, *the gardens of Alcinous*, Mart.

cordātē, adv. (cordatus), *wisely, prudently*, Plaut.

cordātus -a -um (cor), *prudent, sagacious, wise*, Sen.

cordax -dăcis (κόρδαξ), *a licentious dance*, Petr.; transf. of the trochaic rhythm, Cic.

cordŏlium -ii, n. (cor and doleo), *heartache*, Plaut.

Cordŭba -ae, f. *a town in Hispania Boetica, now Cordova.* Adj., **Cordŭbensis** -e.

cordȳla -ae, f. (κορδύλη), *the fry of the tunny fish*, Mart.

Corfīnium -ii, n. *a town of the Peligni in Samnium.* Adj., **Corfīniensis** -e, *Corfinian.*

Cŏrinna -ae, f. (Κόριννα), **1,** *a Greek poetess of Tanagra, contemporary with Pindar*; **2,** *the feigned name of Ovid's mistress.*

Cŏrinthus -i, f. (Κόρινθος), *Corinth, a city of Greece on the Isthmus of Corinth.* Hence, **A.** Adj., **Cŏrinthĭus** -a -um, *Corinthian*; aes, *a mixed metal of gold, silver, and copper,* greatly prized by the ancients, Cic.; vasa, supellex, *made of Corinthian brass*, Cic.; and absol., **Cŏrinthia** -orum, n. (sc. vasa), Cic. **B. Cŏrinthĭārius** -ii, m. *an artificer in Corinthian brass, a nickname of Augustus*, Suet. **C. Cŏrinthĭăcus** -a -um, *Corinthian.* **D. Cŏrinthiensis** -e, *Corinthian.*

Cŏrĭŏli -ōrum, m. *a town of the Volsci in Latium.* Adj., **Cŏrĭŏlānus** -a -um, *belonging to Corioli*; Coriolanus, Cn. Marcius, *the capturer of Corioli*; **Cŏrĭŏlāni** -orum, m. *the inhabitants of Corioli.*

cŏrium (cŏrius) -ii, n. (χόριον), **1,** *hide, skin, leather*; animantium aliae coriis tectae sunt, Cic.; petere corium, *to thrash*, Cic.; prov., canis a corio nunquam absterrebitur uncto, *it is difficult to change a confirmed habit*, Hor.; **2,** *a leathern thong, strap, lash*, Plaut.

Cornēlius -a -um, *name of a Roman gens, the most famous members of which were,* **1,** P. Corn. Scipio Africanus major, the conqueror of Hannibal; **2,** P. Corn. Scipio Aemilianus Africanus minor, son of L. Aemilius Paulus, adopted by P. Corn. Scipio (son of Africanus major), the destroyer of Carthage; **3,** Cornelia, the youngest daughter of Africanus major, wife of Tib. Sempronius Gracchus, the mother of the Gracchi; **4,** Cornelia, the daughter of Qu. Metellus Scipio, wife first of P. Licin. Crassus, afterwards of Pompejus. Adj., **Cornēliānus** -a -um, *Cornelian.*

Cornēlius Nĕpos, v. Nepos.

cornĕŏlus -a -um (dim. of 1. corneus), *horny*, Cic.

1. **cornĕus** -a -um (cornu), **1,** *horny, made of horn*; rostrum, Cic.; **2, a,** *like horn, hard*; cornea fibra, Pers.; **b,** *horn-coloured*, Plin.

2. **cornĕus** -a -um (cornus), *relating or belonging to the cornel tree*; virgulta, Verg.

cornĭcĕn -cinis, m. (cornu and cano), *a horn-blower*, Cic.

cornīcor, 1. dep. (cornix), *to caw like a crow*, Pers.

cornīcŭla -ae, f. (dim. of cornix), *a little crow*, Hor.

cornĭcŭlārius -ii, m. (corniculum), *a soldier who has been presented with the* corniculum, *an adjutant*, Suet.

1. **cornĭcŭlum** -i, n. (dim. of cornu), **1,** *a little horn*, Plin.; **2,** *an ornament on the helmet given to deserving soldiers*, Liv.

2. **Cornĭcŭlum** -i, n. *a town in Latium.* Adj., **Cornĭcŭlānus** -a -um, *Corniculan.*

cornĭger -gĕra -gĕrum (cornu and gero), *horned*, Cic. Subst., **cornĭgera** -orum, n. *horned cattle*, Plin.

cornĭpēs -pĕdis (cornu and pes), *horn-footed, hoofed*; equi, Verg.

cornix -icis, f. (root COR, whence κορώνη, corvus, curvus, *crooked*), *the crow*; natura cervis et cornicibus vitam diuturnam dedit, Cic.; garrula, Ov.; annosa, Hor.; prov., cornicum oculos configere, and ellipt., qui cornici oculum, ut dicitur, *to deceive the sagacious*, Cic.

cornū -ūs and (rarely) -ū, n. (κέρας). **I.** Lit., **1,** *the horn of animals*, of the bull, ram, goat, stag, etc., Cic.; Cornu Copiae (Cornucopia), *the horn of the goat Amalthea, the sign of plenty*, Hor.; cornu, poet. for *strength, courage*; tollere cornua in aliquem, Hor.; cornua sumere, *gain courage*, Ov.; **2, a,** of things of similar material, *a hoof*, Verg.; *a beak of a bird*, Ov.; **b,** of things resembling a horn in shape, *the elephant's tusk*, Varr.; **c,** of things made of horn, *a bow*, Verg.; *a large curved trumpet, or horn*, Cic.; *a lantern*, Plaut.; *an oil cruet*, Hor.; *a funnel*, Verg. **II.** Transf., **A.** The horn as the point or end of anything, *the top of the helmet*, Verg.; *the ends of the sail-yards*, Verg.; *the ends of the staff round which parchments were rolled*, Ov.; *the horns of the moon*, Cic.; *the arm of a river*, Ov.; *the end of a promontory*, Liv.; *the corner or extremity of a country*, Liv.; *the wing of an army*, dextrum, sinistrum, Caes. **B.** *a growth like a horn, a large wart on the head*, Hor. (acc. cornum, Ov.).

Cornūcōpĭa -ae, v cornu

cornum -i, n (cornus), **1,** *the fruit of the cornel*, Verg , **2,** *the wood of the cornel tree*, meton *a spear made of cornel-wood*, Ov

cornus i, and ūs, f (cornu), lit *the horn-tree*, **1,** *the cornel tree* (cornus mascula, Linn), so called from the toughness of its wood, **2,** *the wood of the cornel-tree* and meton *a javelin made of cornel wood*, Ov

cornūtus -a -um (cornu), *horned*, aves, Ov

cŏrolla -ae, f (dim of corona), *a little crown*, Cat

Cŏroebus -i, m *a Phrygian, son of Mygdon.*

cŏrollārĭum -ĭi, n (corolla), originally, *a garland of flowers*, then, *a garland of gilt* or *silvered flowers given away to actors*, etc , Varr , hence, *a present, douceur, gratuity*, Cic

cŏrōna -ae, f. (κορώνη) **I.** Lit *a wreath, garland, chaplet, crown*, Cic , castrensis, triumphalis, navalis, civica, obsidionalis, muralis, navalis, Cic , sub corona vendere, *to sell into slavery prisoners of war* who wore chaplets, Cic , also, sub corona venire, Liv , regni corona, *a diadem*, Verg **II.** Transf , **1,** *a constellation, the northern crown*, Cic , **2,** *a circle, assembly of men*, Cic , milit t t *the besiegers of a city*, (urbem) coronā cingere, *to invest*, Caes , or, *the defenders of a city*, or *place*, coronā vallum defendere, Liv , **3,** *the halo round the sun*, Sen

cŏrōnārĭus a um (corona), *relating to a garland*, Plin , aurum, originally, *the golden crown sent by the provinces to a victorious general*, afterwards changed to *a sum of money*, Cic

Cŏrōnē -ēs, f (Κορώνη), *a town in Messenia* Adj , **Cŏrōnaeus** a -um, *Coronaean*

Cŏrōnēa -ae, f (Κορώνεια), *a town in Boeotia.* Adj , **Cŏrōnaeus** a -um, *Coronaean*

Cŏrōneus ĕi, m *king in Phocis, father of Corone*

Cŏrōnis -ĭdis, f (Κορωνίς), *daughter of Phlegyas, mother of Aesculapius*, hence **Cŏrōnīdes** -ae, m *Aesculapius*

cŏrōno, 1 (corona) **I.** Lit *to wreathe, crown with a garland*, aras, Prop , puppim, Ov , cratera, Verg , sequebantur epulae, quas inibant propinqui coronati, Cic , quis magna coronari contemnat Olympia, *to be crowned as conqueror at the Olympic games*, Hor **II.** Transf *to surround, enclose in the form of a circle*, coronant myrteta summum lacum, Ov , omnem abitum custode, Verg

corpŏrālis -e (corpus), *relating to the body, corporeal*, Sen

corpŏrĕus -a -um (corpus), **1,** *relating to the body, corporeal*, ille corporeus (ignis), Cic., **2,** *fleshy, consisting of flesh*, humerus, Ov

corpŏro, 1 (corpus), *to form into a body, provide with a body*, mundus corporatus, Cic

corpŭlentĭa -ae, f (corpulentus), *fatness, corpulence*, Plin

corpŭlentus -a -um, adj with compar (corpus), *fat, stout, corpulent*, Plaut

corpus pŏris, n (root COR, as in cortex). **I.** Lit **A.** Gen **1,** *a body, substance* (opp animus, anima), *the body of men and animals*, animi voluptates et dolores nasci e corporis voluptatibus et doloribus, Cic , hence, *a person*; delecta virum corpora, Verg , unum vile atque infame corpus, Liv , **2,** *a lifeless substance, mass*, individua corpora, *the atoms*, Cic **B.** Esp **1,** *flesh*, ossa subjecta corpori, Cic , corpus amittere, *to lose flesh*, Cic , abit corpusque colorque, Ov , **2,** *a corpse*, Caes , poet *of the souls of the dead*, Verg ; **3,** *the trunk*, Ov **II.** Transf *any whole like a body*, **1,** *the framework of a ship*, Caes., **2,** *the "body politic,"* totum corpus reipublicae, Cic , **3,** *any whole, collection, mass*, **a,** of military works, Caes , **b,** of the world, universitatis corpus, Cic , **c,** of a book, corpus omnis juris Romani, Liv ; **d,** *a collection of persons*, (α) of the state, ejusdem corporis, Liv , corpus nullum civitatis, Liv , (β) of a corporation, *a political union*, Liv

corpuscŭlum -i, n (dim of corpus), *a little body, corpuscle, atom*, Cic.

corrādo rāsi -rāsum, 3 (com and rado), *to scrape or rake together* **A** Lit , Lucr. **B.** Transf *to scrape together money*, Plaut.

correctĭo -ōnis, f (corrigo), **1,** *improvement, amendment*, correctio philosophiae veteris et emendatio, Cic , **2,** in rhet , *a figure of speech, in which an expression already used is replaced by a stronger one* (Gr ἐπανόρθωσις), Cic

corrector ōris, m (corrigo), *an improver, amender, corrector*, corrector atque emendator nostrae civitatis, Cic., emendator et corrector noster, Cic

corrēpo -repsi -reptum, 3 (com and repo), *to creep or crawl together, to slink in*, in onerariam (navem), Cic ; quoi non correpunt membra pavore, *whose limbs do not shrink with fear?* Lucr

correptē, adv with compar (correptus, from corripio), *shortly*, correptius exit syllaba, Ov

corrīdĕo, 2 (com and rideo), *to laugh together, laugh loudly*, Lucr.

corrigĭa -ae, f *a shoe-string, boot-lace*, Cic

corrigo rexi -rectum, 3 (com & rego), *to make straight, reduce to order, set right* **I.** Gen inde aegre cursum, Liv **II. a,** *to correct, improve, amend*, praeterita magis reprehendi possunt quam corrigi, Liv ; mores, Cic , alicuius sententiam, Cic , non modo superiores sed etiam se ipse correxerat, Cic , **b,** of writing, *to correct*, eas epistolas ego oportet perspiciam, corrigam, Cic , laudationem Porciae tibi correctam misi, Cic

corrĭpĭo -rĭpŭi -reptum, 3 (com and rapio). **I.** *to seize violently, lay hold of, take up.* **A.** Lit , hominem corripi jussit, Cic , arcumque manu celeresque sagittas, Verg.; se corripere, *to hasten away*, Verg , corpus corripere, *to start up*, Verg **B.** Transf , **a,** *to plunder, carry off*, pecuniam, Cic , **b,** *to accuse, bring to trial*, statim corripit reum, Tac., **c,** *to blame, rebuke*, consules, Liv ; voce magistri corripi, Hor , **d,** of disease, etc. *to attack*, nec singula morbi corpora corripiunt, Verg , **e,** of the passions, *to overcome*, visae correptus imagine formae, Ov **II** *to gather together*, **1,** of motion, *to hasten*, tarda necessitas leti corripuit gradum, Hor , viam, *to hasten over*, Verg , campum, Verg , **2,** of time, *to shorten*, numina corripiant moras, Ov

corrōbŏro, 1 (com and roboro) **A.** Lit *to strengthen, invigorate*, se corroborare, *to gain strength*, quum is se corroboravisset et vir inter viros esset, Cic **B.** Transf., conjurationem non credendo corroborare, Cic

corrōdo -rōsi -rōsum, 3 (com and rodo), *to gnaw away*, Platonis Politiam nuper apud me mures corroserunt, Cic

corrŏgo, 1. (com and rogo), *to bring together, collect by begging*, nummulos de nepotum donis, Cic , auxilia ab sociis, Liv

corrūgo, 1 (com and rugo) *to wrinkle up*; ne sordida mappa corruget nares, *make you turn up your nose in disgust*, Hor

corrumpo rūpi -ruptum, 3 **I.** *to destroy, annihilate*, sua frumenta corrumpere et aedificia incendere, Caes , vineas igni et lapidibus,

Sall ; res familiares, Sall , libertatem, Tac , multo dolore corrupta voluptas, Hor **II.** *to spoil, mar, make worse, deteriorate*, **a,** physically, conclusa aqua facile corrumpitur, Cic , Ceres corrupta undis, *corn spoiled by sea-water*, Verg ; of animals and men, *to weaken*, corrupti equi macie, Caes , **b,** of pronunciation, *to corrupt*, nomen eorum paulatim Libyes corrupere, barbarā linguā Mauros pro Medis appellantes, Sall , **c,** of writings, etc , *to falsify*, tabulas publicas municipii manu sua corrumpere, Cic , **d,** morally, *to corrupt*, mores civitatis, Cic , huius urbis jura et exempla corrumpere Cic , milites soluto imperio licentia atque lascivia corruperat, Sall ; corrumpere aliquem pecuniā, *to bribe*, Cic

corrŭo -rŭi, 3 (com and ruo) **I.** Intransit , *to fall to the ground, fall together, sink down* **A.** Lit , **a,** corruerunt aedes, Cic , conclave illud proxima nocte corruit, Cic ; **b,** of persons, paene ille timore, ego risu corrui, Cic , esp , *to fall in battle*, ubi vero corruit telis obrutus, Liv **B.** Transf , illa plaga pestifera qua Lacedaemoniorum opes corruerunt, Cic ; of persons, *to be ruined*, si uno meo fato et tu et omnes mei corruistis, Cic **II.** Transit , *to throw down, overthrow*, hanc rerum summam, Lucr

corruptē, adv with compar and superl (corruptus), *corruptly, incorrectly*, neque depravate judicare neque corrupte, Cic

corruptēla -ae, f (corruptus), *the means of corruption, corruption, bribery, seduction*, mores hac dulcedine corruptelaque depravati, Cic , pecuniosi rei corruptelam judicii molientes, Cic

corruptĭo -ōnis, f (corrumpo), *corruption, a corrupting*, corporis, Cic ; opinionum, Cic.

corruptor -ōris, m (corrumpo), *a corrupter, seducer, briber*, juventutis, Cic , tribus, *briber*, Cic , exercitus, Liv

corruptrix -icis, f (fem of corruptor), *one that corrupts* or *seduces*, attrib = *corrupting*, tam corruptrice provinciā, Cic

corruptus -a -um, p adj with compar and superl (corrumpo), *spoiled, damaged, corrupted, corrupt* **I.** Lit., physically, hordeum, Caes **II.** Transf , morally, civitas, Sall , judicia, Cic , adulescentulus, Cic

cors = cohors (q v)

Corsĭca -ae, f. *the island of Corsica in the Mediterranean Sea* Adj , **Corsus** a -um, and **Corsĭcus** -a -um, *Corsican*

cortex -ticis, m and f *bark, rind, shell*, **a,** *the bark of trees*, obducuntur libro aut cortice trunci (liber = *the inner bark*), Cic , **b,** esp , *the bark of the cork tree, cork*, Hor , prov , nare sine cortice, *to swim without corks*, i e , *to need no assistance*, Hor , levior cortice, Hor

cortīna -ae, f **1,** *a round kettle* or *caldron*, Plaut , esp *the caldron-shaped Delphic tripod*, cortina Phoebi, *the oracle of Apollo*, Verg , **2,** *anything in the shape of a caldron, a circle of hearers*, Tac.

Cortōna ae, f (Κόρτωνα), *Cortona, a town of Etruria* Adj , **Cortōnensis** e, *of* or *belonging to Cortona.*

cŏrŭlus = corylus (q v)

cōrus = caurus (q v).

cŏrusco, 1 (connected with κορύσσω). **I.** *to butt with the horns*, Cic **II. A.** Transit , *to move quickly, shake*, telum, Verg , of snakes, linguas, Ov. **B.** Intransit , **a,** coruscant (apes) pennis, *flutter*, Verg., coruscat abies, Juv , **b,** *to shine, flash, glitter*; apes fulgore coruscant, Verg.

cŏruscus -a -um (corusco), **1,** *shaking, trembling* silvae, Verg , **2,** *gleaming, flashing*, fulgura, Lucr , sol, Verg ; juvenes auro corusci, Verg

1 **corvus** i, m (κόραξ), *a raven*, Cic , prov , in cruce corvos pascere, *to be food for the crows, to be crucified*, Hor.

2 **Corvus** -i, m *a surname of a family of the gens Valeria*, Cic

Cŏrÿbās -bantis, m (Κορύβας), gen in plur , **Cŏrÿbantes** -ium, m *priests of Cybele* Adj , **Cŏrÿbantĭus** -a -um, *Corybantian*

Cōrÿcĭdes, nymphae, (Κωρυκίδες), *daughter of Plistus*

1 **Cōrÿcĭus** -a -um (Κωρύκιος) *belonging to the Corycian caves on Mount Parnassus*

2 **Cōrÿcĭus** -a -um, v Corycos, 1

1 **Cōrÿcos** or **-us** i, f (Κώρυκος), **1,** *a mountain and city of Cilicia, celebrated for a cave and the cultivation of saffron*, hence adj , **Cōrÿcĭus** -a -um, *Corycian*, crocum, Hor , senex, *Cilician*, Verg , **2,** *a promontory on the coast of Ionia*

2 **cōrÿcus** -i, m (κώρυκος), *a sand-bag in the palaestra, which the athletes struck to exercise their strength*, fig , corycus laterum et vocis meae, Bestia, Cic

cŏrÿlētum -i, n (corylus), *a hazel copse*, Ov

cŏrÿlus -i, f (* κόρυλος), *a hazel tree*, Verg , Ov

cŏrymbĭfĕr -fĕra -fĕrum (corymbus and fero), *carrying bunches of ivy berries*, epithet of Bacchus, Ov

cŏrymbus -i, m (κόρυμβος), *a bunch of flowers or fruit*, esp *a cluster of ivy berries*, Verg

cŏrÿphaeus i, m (κορυφαῖος), *the leader, chief, head*, Epicureorum Zeno, Cic

Cŏrÿthus -i (Κόρυθος), **1,** f *a town in Etruria*, afterwards *Cortona*, **2,** m *the legendary founder of Corythus.*

cōrÿtus -i, m (γωρυτός), *a quiver*, Verg

1 **cōs,** cōtis, f *any hard, flinty stone*, Cic , esp *a whetstone, grindstone*, Hor , Cic

2 **Cōs,** v Coos

Cŏsa (Cossa) -ae, f (Κόσσα) and **Cossae** -ārum, f (Κόσσαι), **1,** *a town in Etruria* Adj , **Cŏsānus** -a -um, *Cosan* , **2,** *a town in Lucania*

cosmētēs -ae, m (κοσμητής), *the slave who had charge of his mistress's wardrobe and toilet*, Juv

cosmĭcos -ŏn (κοσμικός), *belonging to the world* Subst , *a citizen of the world*, Mart

Cossÿra (Cŏsÿra) and **Cossūra (Cŏsūra)** -ae, f (Κόσσυρα), *a small island between Sicily and Africa*, now *Pantalaria*

costa -ae, f **1,** *a rib*, Verg , **2,** *a side*, aeni, Verg

costum -i, n (κόστος), *an eastern aromatic plant*, employed in the preparation of unguents, Hor

Cŏsūra and **Cŏsÿra** = Cossyra (q v.)

cŏthurnātus a -um (cothurnus), *provided with a buskin*, hence *sublime, tragic*, deae, Ov

cŏthurnus -i, m (κόθορνος) **I.** *a large hunting boot, reaching to the calf, and laced up the front*, Verg **II.** *the thick-soled boot worn by tragic actors* **A.** Lit , cothurnus tragicus, Hor , cothurnus major, minor, Cic **B.** Transf , **a,** *tragedy*, Hor , **b,** *a tragic, elevated style*, sola Sophocleo tua carmina digna cothurno, Verg

cotidianus, cotidie = quotidianus, etc (q v)

Cŏtōnĕus, v Cydonea.

Cotta - -- *a cognomen of a family of the* gens Aurelia.

cottăbus -i, m. (κότταβος), *a game played by throwing heeltaps of wine into a brazen basin;* hence, from the similarity of sound, *the crack of a whip,* Plaut.

cottăna (cotŏna, coctŏna, coctăna) -ōrum, n. (κόττανα), *a kind of small Syrian fig,* Juv.

Cottĭus -ii, m. *name of the kings of two Ligurian peoples in the Cottian Alps,* so called after them. Adj., **Cottĭānus** -a -um, *Cottian.*

cŏtŭla or **cŏtўla** -ae, f. (κοτύλη), *a measure of capacity, half a sextarius,* Mart.

cōturnix -īcis, f. *a quail,* Ov.

Cŏtўs -tўis, acc. -tyn, voc. -tў, abl. -tўe, m. (Κότυς), **1,** *name of several Thracian princes;* **2,** *brother of Mithridates, prince of the Bosporus.*

Cŏtyttō -ūs, f. (Κοτυττώ), *the goddess of unchastity, originally worshipped in Thrace, afterwards in Athens and Corinth also.* **Cŏtyttĭa** -ōrum, n. *the festival of Cotytto,* Hor.

cŏvĭnārĭus and **cŏvinnārĭus** -ii, m. *one who fights from a war chariot,* Tac.

cŏvĭnus (cŏvinnus), i., m. (a Celtic word), **1,** *the war-chariot of the ancient Britons and Belgians,* Luc.; **2,** *a travelling-chariot,* Mart.

cōxa -ae, f. *the hip-bone,* Plin.

coxendix -īcis, f. (coxa), *the hip, the hip-bone,* Plin.

Crabra or **Aqua Crabra,** *a small river near Tusculum.*

crabro -ōnis, m. *a hornet,* Verg.

Crăgus -i, m. (Κράγος), *a promontory of Lycia.*

crambē -ēs, f. (κράμβη), *cabbage,* Plin.; crambe repetita, *cold cabbage warmed up,* i.e. *stale repetitions,* Juv.

Crānōn (Crannōn) -ōnis, f. (Κρανών, or Κραννών), *a town in Thessaly.* Adj. **Crānōnĭus** (Κρανώνιος) -a -um, *Cranonian.*

Crantor -ŏris, m. **I.** Myth., *the armour-bearer of Peleus.* **II.** Hist., *a philosopher of the old Academy.*

Cranĭi -ōrum, m. *a town on the island of Cephallenia.*

crāpŭla -ae, f. (κραιπάλη), *intoxication, drunkenness, drunken revel;* crapulam edormire et exhalare, Cic.

cras, adv., **1,** *to-morrow;* scies igitur fortasse cras, Cic.; subst., cras istud, quando venit, Mart.; **2,** *in the future;* quod sit futurum cras, fuge quaerere, Hor.

crassē, adv., with compar. (crassus), *grossly, rudely, roughly;* crasse compositum poema, Hor.

crassĭtūdo -ĭnis, f. (crassus), *thickness;* parietum, Caes.; aëris, *density,* Cic.

1. **crassus** -a -um, *thick, dense, solid.* **A.** Lit., unguentum, Hor.; aër, *misty,* Cic.; filum, Cic.; toga, *course-grained,* Hor.; ager, *fruitful,* Cic. **B.** Transf., Ofellus rusticus crassā Minervā, *of sound common sense,* Hor.; turba, *rude, uncultivated,* Mart.

2. **Crassus** -i, m. *name of a family of the gens Licinia* (q.v.).

crastĭnus -a -um (cras), *relating to to-morrow;* dies crastinus, Cic.; die crastinā, *to-morrow,* Liv. Subst., **crastĭnum** -i, n. *the morrow;* in crastinum differre aliquid, Cic.

Crătaeis -ĭdis, f. (Κραταιΐς), *mother of Scylla, a nymph.*

crātēr -ēris, m. (κρατήρ) = cratera (q.v.).

crātēra -ae, f. **I.** Lit., *a large bowl in which wine was mixed with water,* Cic. **II.** Transf., **1,** *an oil-cruet,* Verg.; **2,** *the crater of a volcano,* Lucr., or *a volcanic fissure in the earth,* Ov.; **3,** *a constellation, the cup,* Ov.

Crătĕrus -i, m. (Κρατερός), **1,** *a general of Alexander the Great;* **2,** *a celebrated physician in the time of Cicero;* appellat. = *a skilled physician,* Hor.

Crăthis -thĭdis, m. (Κρᾶθις), *a river near Thurii, between Lucania and Bruttium,* now *Crati.*

Crătīnus -i, m. (Κρατῖνος), *an Athenian comic poet, contemporary of Aristophanes.*

Crătippus -i, m. (Κράτιππος), *a peripatetic philosopher of Athens, teacher of Cicero's son.*

crātis -is. **A.** Lit. *a frame or basket made of hurdles;* also, *a harrow,* Verg.; milit. t.t, *fascines,* Caes.; sub crate necari, *an old method of capital punishment, by which the accused was placed under a hurdle, and pressed to death with great stones,* Liv. **B.** Transf., favorum, *honeycomb,* Verg.; spinae, *the joints of the backbone,* Ov.

crĕātĭo -ōnis, f. (creo), *choice, election;* magistratuum, Cic.

crĕātor -ōris, m. (creo), *the creator, maker, founder;* huius urbis Romulus creator, Cic.; *father,* Ov.

crĕātrix -īcis, f. (creator), *she who brings forth or produces, a mother;* natura rerum, Lucr.; diva, Verg.

crēber -bra -brum, adj. with compar. and superl. (root CRE, whence creo, cresco). **I.** Of space, *thick, crowded together, close, pressed together;* **a,** creberrima aedificia, Caes.; creberrima grando, Liv.; crebri ignes, Sall.; **b,** *thick with, full of;* with abl., creber arundinibus lacus, Ov.; qui (Thucydides), ita creber est rerum frequentiā, Cic. **II.** Of time, *repeated, numerous, frequent;* **a,** crebra inter se colloquia habere, Caes.; crebri ictus, Verg.; creberrimus sermo, Cic.; **b,** creber pulsat, *he beats repeatedly,* Verg.; Africus creber procellis, *abounding in,* Verg.; in scribendo multo essem crebrior quam tu, Cic.

crēbresco (crēbesco), -brŭi (-bŭi), 3. (creber), *to become frequent, increase, gather strength, extend;* seditio crebrescens, Tac.; horror, Verg.; crebrescunt optatae aurae, Verg.; crebrescit vivere Agrippam, *the report is spread abroad that,* etc., Tac.

crēbrĭtas -ātis, f. (creber), *thickness, closeness, frequency;* sententiarum, Cic.; officiorum, Cic.

crēbro, adv., with compar. crebrius and superl. creberrime (creber), *repeatedly, frequently, very often;* ad aliquem crebrius litteras mittere, Cic.; crebro respicere Romam, Ov.

crēdĭbĭlis -e, adj. with compar. (credo), *credible, worthy of belief;* narrationes credibiles sint, Cic.; credibile est (fit, videtur), followed by acc. and infin., ita fit credibile deorum et hominum causā factum esse mundum, Cic.; vix credibile est, Hor.

crēdĭbĭlĭter, adv. with compar. (credibilis), *credibly,* Cic.

crēdĭtor -ōris, m. (credo), *a creditor;* tabulae creditoris, Cic.; fraudare creditores.

crēdĭtum -i, n. (credo), *a loan,* Sall.

crēdo -didi -ditum, 3. **I.** *to trust;* **1,** *to confide, trust in, rely upon, place confidence in;* with dat. of person, credere eorum nemini, Cic.; with dat. of thing, praesenti fortunae non credere, Liv.; **2,** *to believe, give credence to;* his auctoribus temere credens, Caes.; often parenthetic, mihi crede or crede mihi, *believe me, take my advice;* venies, mihi crede, exspectatus, Cic.; with dat. of thing, fabulis, Cic.; lacrimis, Ov.; somniis,

Cic, with de, non credis de numero militum, Cic II. *to trust*, in relation to something; 1, *to entrust, commit, trust something to some one*, a, arma militi, Liv, alicui res omnes, Cic, se perfidis hostibus, Ov, aciem campo, Verg, b, *to entrust to the secrecy of some one*, alicui arcanos sensus, Verg, c, *to lend*, alicui pecuniam, Cic, absol, *to lend*, credendi modum constituere, Cic, often in partic perf, pecunia credita or res creditae, *loans*, Cic, 2, *to believe something*, a, *to be convinced of as true*, fere libenter homines id quod volunt credunt, Caes, esp parenthetic, quod quidem magis credo, Cic, with acc and infin, Caes, Cic, or relative sentence, Hor, b, *to think, to be of the opinion* with acc and infin, credo ego vos, judices, mirari, Cic, moesti (crederes victos) redeunt in castra, *you would think*, Liv, in pass, with nom and infin, pro certo creditur necato filio vacuam domum scelestis nuptiis fecisse, Sall, with acc and infin, quorum neminem nisi juvante deo talem fuisse credendum est, Cic, parenthetic, credo, *I believe, I think*, male, credo, mererer de meis civibus, si, etc, Cic

crēdŭlĭtas -ātis, f (credulus), *credulity*, ap Cic

crēdŭlus a um (credo) A. Act *believing easily, credulous, confiding*, alicui, Verg, in aliquid, Ov; stultus et credulus auditor, Cic B Pass *easily believed*, fama, Tac

Crĕmĕra ae, m *a river in Etruria, near which 300 Fabii were killed* Adj, **Crĕmĕrensis** e

crĕmo, 1 *to burn, consume by fire*, a, libros in conspectu populi, Liv, regalia tecta, Ov, b, esp, of the burning of the bodies of the dead, Sulla primus e patriciis Corneliis igni voluit cremari, Cic, corpus alicuius, Cic, c, of sacrifices, crematos igni vitulos, Ov

Crĕmōna ae, f *Cremona, a town in N Italy*. Adj **Cremōnensis**, e, *of Cremona*

Crĕmōnis jugum, *a mountain range in the Pennine Alps*

crĕmor -ōris, m *the thick juice obtained from animal or vegetable substances, pulp, cream*, etc, Ov

1. **crĕo**, 1. (root CER, CRE, whence cresco), *to make, create, produce* I. Gen, a, omnes res quas et creat natura et tuetur, Cic, alicui periculum, Cic; b, *to beget a child*, Cic, pass partic, creatus with abl, of father or mother = *daughter* or *son*, Telamone creatus, Ov II. a, *to institute an office or magistracy*, tribuniciam potestatem, Liv, b, *to elect a magistrate* or *priest*, consules, Cic, with double acc, Ancum Marcium regem populus creavit, Liv

2 **Crĕo** ōnis, and **Crĕōn** -ontis, m *king of Corinth, whose daughter Creusa was betrothed to Jason*

crĕper -pĕra pĕrum (Sabine word connected with κνέφας), *dark, obscure, uncertain*, Luci

crĕpĭda -ae, f (κρηπίς), *a sandal*, Cic, prov ne sutor ultra crepidam, *shoemaker, stick to your last*, Plin

crĕpĭdātus -a -um (crepida), *wearing sandals*, Cic

crĕpīdo inis, f (κρηπίς), 1, *a base, foundation, pedestal*, Cic, 2, *a quay, pier*, Cic

crĕpĭtăcillum -i, n (dim of crepitaculum), *a little rattle*, Luci

crĕpĭtācŭlum -i, n (crepito), *a rattle*, Quint

crĕpĭto, 1 (freq of crepo), *to rattle, creak, crackle, rustle, clatter*; crepitantia arma, Ov, lenis crepitans auster, *rustling*, Verg, multā grandine nimbi culminibus crepitant, Verg

crĕpĭtus ūs, m (crepo), *a rattling, creaking, rustling, clattering*, digitorum, *snapping the fingers*, Mart, pedum, Cic, dentium, Cic, aeris, Liv, viridis materiae flagrantis, Liv, alarum, Liv

crĕpo -pŭi -pĭtum, 1 I. Intransit, *to creak, rattle, rustle, crackle*, digiti crepantis signa, *a snapping of the fingers to call a servant's attention*, Mart, acuto in murice remi obnixi crepuere, *crashed*, Verg, crepat in mediis laurus adusta focis, *crackle*, Ov. II Transit, a, *to cause to resound, rattle*, quum populus frequens laetum theatris ter crepuit sonum, Hor, *to talk much of, chatter about, prate about*, sulcos, Hor, b, immunda ignominiosaque verba, Hor, post vina gravem militiam aut pauperiem, Hor

crĕpundĭa -ōrum, n (crepo), *child's playthings, rattle*, nescio aliquo aut crepundiis aliquem cognoscere, Cic

crĕpuscŭlum -i, n (creper), *twilight* I. Gen, dubiae crepuscula lucis, Ov II. Esp, *evening twilight*, inducunt obscura crepuscula noctem, Ov

Crēs ētis, m, v 1 Creta

cresco, crēvi, crētum, 3 (inchoat from root CER, whence creo, creare) I. *to grow up, spring forth, arise*, quaecunque e terra corpora crescunt, Lucr, crescentes segetes, Ov, in past partic, cretus, *sprung from*, mortali semine, Ov, Trojano a sanguine, Verg II. *to grow, increase in size*, 1, a, fruges, arbusta, animantes Lucr; in longitudinem, Plin, ut cum luna pariter crescant pariterque decrescant, Cic, b, esp of boys, *to grow up*, toti salutifer orbi cresce, puer, Ov, 2, *to increase in height, number*, etc, Roma interim crescit Albae ruinis, Liv, quum Albanus lacus praeter modum crevisset, Cic, luna crescens, *waxing*, Cic, crescit in dies singulos hostium numerus, Cic; crescentes morbi, Cic, crescebat in eos odium, Cic, 3, *to grow great, increase in fame, power*, etc, patet per se crevisset, Caes

1 **Crēta** ae, f and **Crētē** ēs, f (Κρήτη), *the Mediterranean island of Crete*, now *Candia*, hence, 1, **Crēs** -ētis, m, *Cretan*, subst, *a Cretan*, plur, **Crētes** -um, m *the Cretans*, 2, **Cressa** -ae, f *Cretan*, Cressa nota, *of Cretan chalk*, Hor; bos, *Pasiphaë*, Prop, subst, *Ariadne, Aerope*, Ov, 3, **Crēsius** a -um, *Cretan*, 4, **Crētaeus** a -um *Cretan*, subst *Epimenides*, Prop, 5, **Crētānus** -i, m *a Cretan*, 6, **Crētensis** -is, *Cretan*, 7, **Crētĭcus** -a -um, *Cretan*, subst, *the surname of Q Metellus from his conquest of the island*, 8, **Crētis** -tĭdis, f *Cretan*

2 **crēta** ae, f (prop adj of 1 Creta), *Cretan earth, chalk*, or *a kind of fuller's earth*, used for cleansing garments, Plaut, used also for painting the face, Hor, for seals, Cic

crētātus -a -um (2 creta), *chalked*, fascia, Cic, transf, ambitio, *the canvassing of the white robed candidates*, Prop

crētĕus -a -um (2 creta), *made of chalk* or *Cretan earth*, Luci

crētĭo ōnis, f (cerno), *a declaration of an heir accepting an inheritance*.

crētŭla -ae, f (dim of creta), *white clay for sealing*, Cic

Crĕūsa -ae, f (Κρέουσα), 1, *daughter of Creon, king of Corinth, wife of Jason*, 2, *daughter of Priam, wife of Aeneas*, 3, *a port in Boeotia*

cribrum -i, n (from root CRE, CRI, whence also cerno), *a sieve*, Cic

crimen inis, n (from root CRE, CRI, Gr. ΚΡΙ, whence cerno, κρίνω) I A. Lit., *accusation, complaint, reproach, calumny*, esse in crimine, *to be accused*, Cic, dare alicui aliquid crimini,

Cic , propulsare, defendere, *to repel, confute*, Cic **B.** Meton , *an object of reproach*, perpetuae criminis posteritatis eris, Ov **II.** *the fault, guilt, crime, with which a person is charged* **A.** Lit , haec causa est omnium horum scelerum atque criminum, Cic **B.** Meton, **a,** *an object representing a crime*, pictas caelestia crimina vestes, Ov , **b,** *cause of crime*, se causam clamat crimenque caputque malorum, Verg

crīmĭnātĭo -ōnis, f (criminor), *an accusation, calumny, charge*, illa criminatio quā in me absentem usus est, Cic

crīmĭnātor -ōris, m (criminor), *an accuser, calumniator*, Tac

crīmĭnor, 1 dep (crimino, Plaut , criminor, pass , Cic ?), **1,** *to accuse, charge a person with a crime, to calumniate*, patres apud populum, Liv , nihil Sistium, Cic , Q Metellum apud populum Romanum criminatus est bellum ducere, Cic , **2,** *to charge with, to lay something to the blame of some one, to complain of;* non licet omnia criminari, Cic , contiones quibus quotidie meam potentiam invidiose criminabatur, Cic , with acc and infin , me esse gratum criminaris, Cic , absol , *to reproach*, argumentando criminari, Cic

crīmĭnōsē, adv , with compar and superl (criminosus), *by way of accusation, reproachfully*, qui suspiciosius aut criminosius diceret, Cic.

crīmĭnōsus -a -um (crimen), *reproachful, calumnious, slanderous*, ille acerbus criminosus popularis homo ac turbulentus, Cic ; criminosum nomen, Cic ; iambi, Hor , criminosum est or fit or habetur, *blameworthy*, Cic

Crīmissus (Crīmīsus) -i, m (Κριμισσος, Κριμισος), *a river in the south-west of Sicily*.

crīnālis -e, (crinis), *relating to the hair*, vitta, Ov Subst , **crīnāle** is, n *a hair-band*, curvum, *a diadem*, Ov.

crīnis -is, m (root CER, CRE, whence cerno, creo, cresco) **A.** *the hair*, esp of the head, Cic , crines sparsi, Liv , crinibus passis, Liv **B.** Transf , *the tail of a comet*, Verg

crīnītus -a -um (crinis), *provided with hair, hairy, with long hair* **A.** Lit., Apollo, Verg **B.** Transf , stella crinita, *a comet*, Cic

crispisulcans antis (crispus and sulco), *serpentine*, ap. Cic

crispo, 1 (crispus), **1,** *to curl, crisp;* capillum, Plin , **2,** *to move rapidly up and down, brandish*, hastilia manu, Verg

crispŭlus -a -um (dim of crispus), *curly-haired, curly*, Mart

crispus -a -um, **1,** *curly, curly-headed*, Plaut , Ter , **2,** *in trembling motion, trembling, quivering*, latus, Verg , pecten, Juv.

crista -ae, f (connected with cresco, crinis), **1,** *the crest of a bird, the comb of a cock*, Juv ; **2,** *the crest or plume of a helmet*, Verg , Liv

cristātus a -um, (crista), *crested*, **a,** draco, Ov , aves, cocks, Mart , **b,** *having a crest or plume;* galeae, Liv

Crithōtē -es, f (Κριθωτη), *a town on the east coast of the Thracian Chersonese*

Critĭas -ae, m (Κριτιας), *one of the Thirty Tyrants at Athens*

crĭtĭcus -i, m (κριτικός), *a critic*, Cic.

Crīto -ōnis, m (Κριτων), *a disciple and friend of Socrates*

Critŏbūlus -i, m (Κριτοβουλος), *a disciple of Socrates*

Critŏlāus -i, m. (Κριτολαος), **1,** *a peripatetic philosopher, ambassador from Athens to Rome, 155 B.C.;* **2,** *a general of the Achaean League*

crŏcĕus a -um (crocus), **1,** *belonging to saffron, saffron*, odores, Verg ; **2,** *saffron-coloured, golden, yellow*, flores, Verg

crŏcĭnus a -um (κροκινος), *belonging to saffron, saffron-coloured, yellow*, tunica, Cat. Subst , **crŏcĭnum** -i, n. (sc. oleum), *saffron-oil*, Prop

crōcio, 4. (κρωζω), *to caw like a crow*, Plaut

crŏcŏdīlus -i, m (κροκόδειλος), *a crocodile*, Cic

crŏcōta -ae, f (sc vestis, Gr ὁ κροκωτος, sc χιτών), *a saffron coloured robe worn by women*, Cic.

crŏcōtŭla -ae, f (dim. of crocota), *a little saffron coloured robe*, Plaut

crŏcus i, m , **crŏcum** -i, n (κροκος and κρόκον) **I.** *saffron*, used by the ancients not only as a spice and in medicine, but in the preparation of perfumes, Ov , personified, *Crocus, a young man changed into a saffron flower*, Ov **II.** Meton , *the colour of saffron, yellow*, Verg.

Croesus -i, m (Κροῖσος), *a king of Lydia famous for his wealth*, appell.=*a rich man*, Ov. Adj , **Croesĭus** -a -um, *of Croesus*.

Crŏmyŏn -ōnis, f (Κρομυων), *a village in Megaris*

crŏtălĭa -ōrum, n (κροταλια), *an earring consisting of several pendant pearls*, Pers

crŏtălistrĭa -ae, f *a female dancer and performer on the castanets*, Prop.

crŏtălum i, n (κρόταλον), *a castanet*, Verg

Crŏto (Crŏtōn) -ōnis, c. (Κροτων), *a town on the east coast of Bruttium*, now *Crotone* Hence **1, Crŏtōnĭātes** -ae, m (Κροτωνιάτης), *an inhabitant of Crotona*, **2,** adj , **Crŏtōnĭensis** -e, *of Crotona*.

Crŏtŏpĭădes -ae, m (Κροτωπιαδης), *the poet Linus, grandson, on the mother's side, of Crotopus, king of Argos*, Ov

crŭcĭāmentum -i, n. (crucio), *torture, torment*, Cic

crŭcĭātus -ūs, m. (crucio), *torture, torment, execution*, omnes animi cruciatus et corporis, Cic , per cruciatum interficere, Caes , quin tu abi in malam pestem malumque cruciatum, *go and be hanged*, Cic

crŭcĭo, 1 (crux), *to torture, torment*, quum vigiliis atque fame cruciaretur, Cic , aliquem, Cic

crūdēlis -e (crudus), *unfeeling, unmerciful, cruel, inhuman, hardhearted*, **a,** of persons, crudelissimus tyrannus, Cic , Lepidus crudelis in liberos, Cic ; in hominis consularis calamitate crudelis, Cic., **b,** of things, funus, Verg., bellum, Cic , consilia crudelissima, Cic

crūdēlĭtas -ātis, f (crudelis), *cruelty, inhumanity*, importuna in me crudelitas, Cic.

crūdēlĭtĕr, adv (crudelis), *cruelly, inhumanly*, imperare, Caes , aliquem crudelissime interficere, Cic.

crudesco -dŭi, 3 *to become hard, violent*, crudescit morbus, Verg ; seditio, Tac

crūdĭtas -ātis, f (crudus), *overloading of the stomach, indigestion*, Cic

crūdus -a um (contr. from cruidus, from root CRU, whence cruor), *raw* **I.** Lit , **1,** *not prepared by fire, uncooked, raw*, exta cruda victimae, Liv , **2,** *not ripened by the sun, unripe*, poma, Cic , **3, a,** *undigested*, pavo, Juv , **b,** *suffering from indigestion*, Roscius crudior fuit, Cic. , **4,** *raw, not healed*, vulnera, Ov , **5,** *unprepared, rough*, cortice crudo hasta, Verg **II.** Transf., **1,** *not ready, immature, fresh*, servitium, Tac.; **2,** *vigorous, fresh;* senectus cruda viridisque, Verg.; **3,** *rough, cruel;* Getae, Ov, ensis, Verg

crŭento, 1 (cruentus), *to make bloody, to stain with blood*, manus sanguine, Nep, gladium, Cic, fig, haec te lacerat, haec cruentat oratio, *wounds*, Cic

crŭentus -a -um (cruor), *bloody* I. Gen a, *mixed with blood*, guttae imbrium quasi cruentae, Cic, b, *blood-red*, myrta, Verg II. In a bad sense, *bloody through murder* A. Lit, *covered, stained, spotted with blood, bloody*, cruentus sanguine civium Romanorum, Cic, cadaver, Cic, gaudens Bellona cruentis, *in the shedding of blood*, Hor B. Transf, a, *wounding*, dens, Hor, b, *rejoicing in blood, bloodthirsty, cruel*, ira, Hor

crŭmēna -ae, f *a leathern pouch for money, carried by a strap round the neck* A. Lit, Plaut B. Transf *money*, non deficiente crumena, Hor

crŭor -ōris, m (root CRU, whence also crudus), *the blood which flows from a wound, gore*, cruor inimici recentissimus, Cic, fig, *murder, slaughter*, cruor Cinnanus, *the slaughter of Cinna*, Cic, castus a cruore civili, Cic, ad caedem et cruorem abstrahi, Cic

cruppellārii -ōrum, m *Gaulish gladiators, who fought in full armour*, Tac

crūs, crūris, n 1, *the shin, shin bone, leg*, frangere alicui crus or crura (of persons crucified), Cic, rigida crura, Cic, succidere crura equo, Liv, 2, plur, *the supports of a bridge*, Cat

crusta -ae, f 1, *the crust, rind, shell, bark of any substance*, concrescunt subitae currenti in flumine crustae, *coating of ice*, Verg, 2, *mosaic, inlaid work on walls, bas relief, or embossing on silver plate*, Cic

crustŭlum -i, n (dim of crustum), *a little cake*, Hor

crustum i, n. (crusta), *anything baked, bread, cake*, Verg

Crustŭmĕrĭa -ae, f (Κρουστομερία) (-mĕrĭum -ii, n, -mĕrĭi -ōrum, m -mĭum -ii, n), *a town of the Sabines, near the sources of the Allia* Hence adj, 1, **Crustŭmīnus** -a -um, 2, **Crustŭmĭus** -a -um, *of Crustumeria*

crux, crŭcis, f *a cross*, agere aliquem in crucem, Cic, affigere aliquem cruci, Liv, detrahere aliquem ex cruce, Cic, minari alicui crucem, Cic, rapere aliquem in crucem, Cic, abi in malam crucem, *go and be hanged!* Plaut

crypta -ae, f (κρύπτη), *a subterranean gallery, vault, crypt, grotto*, Juv

crystallĭnus -a -um (κρυστάλλινος), *crystalline, made of crystal*, Plin Subst, **crystallĭna** -ōrum, n. (sc vasa), *crystal vases*, Juv

crystallus -i, f and (rarely) m (κρύσταλλος) (heterocl plur, crystalla) A. Lit, *crystal* B. Meton, a, *a crystal drinking vessel*, Mart, b, *the glittering, precious stone in a ring*, Prop

Ctēsĭphōn -phontis, m (Κτησιφῶν), *an Athenian statesman, friend of Demosthenes, who defended him when accused by Aeschines*

cŭbĭcŭlāris -e (cubiculum), *relating to a sleeping-room*, lectus, Cic

cŭbĭcŭlārĭus -a -um (cubiculum), *belonging to a sleeping room* Subst, **cŭbĭcŭlārĭus** -ii, m *a chamber servant*, Cic

cŭbĭcŭlum -i, n (cubo), *a sleeping-room, bedroom*, Cic

cŭbīle (cubo), 1, *a bed*, esp *the marriage bed*, 2, *the resting place of animals, lair, den*, ferarum bestiarum, Liv, rimosa cubilia, of bees, *hives*, Verg, construere sibi cubilia nidos, Verg, fig, *the seat of an evil*, ut omnes mortales istius avaritiae non jam vestigia, sed ipsa cubilia videre

cŭbĭtal -tālis, n (cubitum), *an elbow cushion*, Hor

cŭbĭtālis -e (cubitum), *of the length of a cubit*, cubitalis fere cava, Liv

cŭbĭto, 1 (freq of cubo), *to lie down often, be accustomed to lie*, Cic

cŭbĭtum i, n and **cŭbĭtus** -i, m (cubo), 1, *the elbow*, cubito remanere presso, Hor; 2, *a cubit, an ell*, Cic

cŭbo ŭi -ĭtum, 1 1, a, *to lie down, recline*, in lectica, Cic, b, esp *to lie down to sleep*, cubitum ire, *to go to bed*, Cic, c, *to recline at table* quod meminisset quo eorum loco quisque cubuisset, Cic, d, *to lie down from illness, to lie in bed ill*, cubantem disputare de aliqua re, Cic, 2, applied to inanimate objects, partic cubans, *sloping*, Ustica, Hor

cŭcullus -i, m *a hood, cowl*, Juv

cŭcŭlus i, m (κόκκυξ), *the cuckoo*, Plaut; as a term of reproach, Plaut, Hor

cŭcŭmis -mĕris, m *a cucumber*, Verg

cŭcurbĭta ae, f 1, *a gourd*, Plin, 2, *a cupping-glass*, Juv

cūdo, 3 1, *to beat, pound*, fabas, *to thresh*, prov, istaec in me cudetur faba, *I shall suffer for that*, Ter, 2, of metals, *to stamp, beat out, coin*, plumbeos nummos, Plaut

cuicuimodi = cujus cujus-modi, *of what kind soever*, Cic

cūjās -ātis and **cūjātis** -is (cujus from qui), *of what country? whence?* Cic

cūjūs -a um, 1 (cujus from qui), 1, interrog pron *to whom belonging? whose?* cujum pecus? *whose flock?* Verg; 2, relat. pron. *whose*, is cuja res sit, Cic

cūjuscĕmŏdi (qui, ce, and modus), *of whatever kind*, Cic

cūjusdam-mŏdi, *of a certain kind*, Cic

cūjusmŏdi (quis and modus), *of what kind?* Cic

cūjusquĕmŏdi (quisque and modus), *of every kind*, Cic

culcĭta ae, f (calco), *a mattress, bolster, pillow*, plumea, Cic

cūlĕus (cullĕus) -i, m (root CU, whence cupa), *a large leathern sack*, Nep, aliquem insuere in culeum (the punishment of parricides), Cic

cŭlex ĭcis, m *a gnat, midge*, Hor

cŭlīna ae, f (contr from coquilina), a, *a kitchen*, tua (philosophia) in culina, mea in palaestra est, Cic, b, meton, *food, fare, victuals*, Murena praebente domum, Capitone culinam, Hor

cullĕus, v culeus

culmen -ĭnis, n (for columen from *cello), *the top, summit* I. A. Lit, 1, culmen Alpium, Caes, 2, *the ridge of a roof*, culmen tecti, Verg B. Transf, *summit*, summum culmen fortunae, Liv II. Poet. = culmus, *haulm*, Ov

culmus i, m (from *cello, like culmen), *a stalk, haulm*, esp of grain, Cic, *thatch*, Romuleo recens horrebat regia culmo, Verg

culpa -ae, f *fault, error* I. Lit, 1, culpa delicti, Cic, a, abl, culpā, *by one's own fault*, Cic, so mea culpa, tua culpa, etc, abesse a culpa or culpa, Cic, non abhorrere a tali culpa, Cic, uni culpam attribuere, Cic, committere culpam, Cic, dare alicui summam laudem vitio et culpae, Cic; est culpa mea, Cic, est culpa in aliquo or in aliqua re, Cic esse in culpa, Cic, extra culpam esse, Cic, liberare aliquem culpa, Cic, b, praestare culpam, *to make oneself responsible for* Cic; in se suscipere istius culpam, Cic, vacare culpa, Cic, 2, esp a, *the* *fault of negligence*, Hor. ; **b,** *unchastity*, Ov. **II.** Meton., *the cause of error* or *sin;* culpam ferro compesce, Verg.

culpātus -a -um, p. adj. (from culpo), *blameworthy;* Paris, Verg.

culpo, 1. (culpa), **1,** *to blame, find fault with, accuse, disapprove;* laudatur ab his, culpatur ab illis, Hor. ; **2,** *to lay blame on;* arbore nunc aquas culpante, Hor.

cultē, adv. with compar. (1. cultus), *elegantly;* loqui, Ov.

cultellus -i, m. (dim. of culter), *a little knife*, Hor.

culter -tri, m. (connected with Skr. kar, *to wound*, and Gr. κείρω), *a knife;* cultri tonsorii, *razors*, Cic. ; *a ploughshare, coulter*, Plin. ; prov., me sub cultro linquit, *leaves me under the knife*, i.e., *in the greatest peril*, Hor.

cultor -ōris, m. (colo), *a cultivator, planter, labourer.* **I.** Lit., **A.** Gen., terrae, Cic. ; agrorum, Liv. **B. 1,** absol., *husbandman*, Sall. ; **2,** with genit., *an inhabitant, occupier;* eius terrae, Sall. **II.** Transf., **1,** gen., *a friend, supporter;* bonorum (*of the optimates*), Liv. ; veritatis, Cic. ; **2,** esp., *a worshipper;* deorum, Hor. ; religionum, Liv.

cultrix -icis, f. (cultor), **1,** *she who tends* or *takes care of*, Cic. ; **2,** *inhabitant;* nemorum Latonia virgo, Verg.

cultūra -ae, f. (colo), *culture, cultivation.* **I.** Lit., **1,** gen., agri, Cic. ; vitis, Cic. ; **2,** *agriculture, husbandry*, Hor. **II. 1,** *mental culture, cultivation;* animi, Cic. ; **2,** *reverence, respect, courting;* potentis amici, Hor.

1. **cultus** -a -um, p. adj. with compar. and superl. (colo). **A.** *cultivated, tilled, planted;* loci culti, Cic. ; ager cultissimus, Cic. Subst., **culta** -orum. n. *cultivated land;* an culta ex silvestribus facere potui? Liv. **B. a,** *ornamented, adorned;* femina cultissima, Ov. ; **b,** *polished, elegant;* sonum linguae et corporum habitum et nitorem cultiora quam pastoralia esse, Liv. ; culta carmina, Ov.

2. **cultus** -ūs, m. (colo). **I.** *cultivation:* agrorum, Liv., Cic. **II. A.** *physical* or *mental cultivation;* **1, a,** *physical cultivation, care, tending;* corporis, Cic. ; **b,** *adornment, dress;* cultus Punicus, habitusque, Liv. ; **2,** *mental culture, training, education;* animi, ingenii, Cic. **B.** *reverence, respect, worship;* **a,** of the gods, cultus deorum, Cic. ; **b,** *respect paid to men;* benevolis officium et diligens tribuitur cultus, Cic.

cŭlullus -i, m. *a drinking-vessel*, Hor.

cūlus -i, m. *the fundament*, Cat.

1. **cum,** conj. = quum (q.v.).

2. **cum,** prep. with abl. *with.* **I.** In space, **1,** *together with;* esse, vivere, agitare, habitare, cessare, dormire, ire, abire, redire, mittere cum aliquo; cum impedimentis venire, Caes. ; esp. **a,** *in the company of a general;* cum Magone equites Hispanorum praemissos, Liv.; **b,** of some office held in common with some one else, unum imperium unumque magistratum habere cum ipsis, Liv. ; **c,** *in relation with, in company with;* cum aliquo se delectare, Cic. ; **2,** *adorned with, provided with;* cum pallio purpureo versabatur in conviviis, Cic. ; legatos cum auctoritate mittere, Cic. **II.** Of time, **1,** *at the same time with;* cum primā luce Pomponi domum venire, Cic. ; **2,** *together with;* aliquid magno cum gemitu civitatis sufferre, Cic. ; cum eo quod, ut, or ne, *on the condition that;* sit sane sed tamen cum eo, credo, quod sine peccato meo fiat, Cic. (Cum, when used with the personal pronoun, is always, and when used with relative pronouns generally, placed after its case. mecum, quocum, etc.)

Cūmae -ārum, f. (Κύμη), *an ancient city of Campania, famous as the residence of the Sibyl.* Adj. **Cūmānus** -a -um; **Cūmaeus** -a -um, *Cumaean;* virgo, *the Sibyl*, Ov.

cumba = cymba (q.v.).

cŭmĕra -ae, f. *a corn-chest*, Hor.

cŭmīnum -i, n. (κύμινον), *the herb cummin*, Hor.

cummi, v. gummi.

cumprīmis, v. primus.

cumque (cunque, quomque), an adverb usually found in composition, e.g., quicumque, ubicumque, etc., signifying *however, whatever, whenever;* sometimes standing by itself; quae demant quomque dolorem, *pain in general*, Lucr.; mihi cumque salve rite vocanti, *whenever I call*, Hor.

cŭmŭlāte, adv. with compar. and superl. (cumulatus), *abundantly, copiously;* gratias agere, Cic.

cŭmŭlātus -a -um, p. adj. with compar. and superl. (cumulo), **1,** *heaped up, increased, enlarged;* Hesiodus eādem mensurā reddere jubet, quā acceperis, aut etiam cumulatiore, si possis, Cic. ; **2,** *perfect;* hoc sentire et facere perfectae cumulataeque virtutis est, Cic.

cŭmŭlo, 1. (cumulus). **I. A.** Lit., *to heap up, pile up;* cetera omnis generis arma in acervum, Liv. **B.** Transf., quum aliae super alias clades cumularentur, Liv. ; omnes in aliquem honores, Tac. **II. a,** *to fill by heaping up, fill up, overload;* fossas corporibus, Tac. ; altaria donis, Verg. ; **b,** confiteor me cumulari maximo gaudio, Cic. ; cumulatus laude, *loaded with praise*, Cic. ; **c,** *to increase, heighten;* invidiam, Liv. ; cumulare eloquentiā bellicam gloriam, Cic.; **d,** *to bring to perfection;* cumulata erant officia vitae, *perfectly fulfilled*, Cic.

cŭmŭlus -i, m. (connected with culmen and culmus). **A.** Lit., *a heap, pile, mass;* hostium coacervatorum, Liv. ; aquarum, Ov. **B.** Transf., *addition, increase, surplus, summit;* commendationis tuae, Cic.; alicui afferre cumulum gaudii, Cic.

cūnābŭla -ōrum, n. (cunae). **A.** Lit., *a cradle;* **a,** esse in cunabulis, Cic. ; **b,** *the bed of the young of bees*, Verg. **B.** Meton., *the earliest abode;* gentis, Verg.

cūnae -ārum, f. (cubo, * cumbo), *a cradle;* **a,** in cunis dormire, Cic. ; primis cunis, *in earliest childhood*, Ov. ; **b,** *the nest of young birds*, Ov.

cunctābundus -a -um (cunctor), *loitering, delaying, dilatory*, Liv., Tac.

cunctans -antis, p. adj. with compar. (cunctor), *loitering, lingering, slow*, Plin.; ilex glebae, *tenacious*, Verg.

cunctantĕr, adv. with compar. (cunctans), *slowly, lingeringly*, Liv.

cunctātĭo -ōnis, f. (cunctor), *a delay, lingering, hesitation;* invadendi, Liv. ; sine cunctatione, Cic. ; abjecta omni cunctatione, Cic.

cunctātor -ōris, m. (cunctor), *one who delays, lingers, hesitates;* cunctatorem ex acerrimo bellatore factum, Liv.; *a surname of the dictator*, Q. Fabius Maximus.

cunctor, 1. dep. *to delay;* **1,** of motion, *to stay, tarry;* cunctari diutius in vita, Cic. ; tardum cunctatur olivum, *drops slowly*, Lucr. ; **2,** of action, *to hesitate, linger, be slow;* sedendo et cunctando bellum gerebat, Liv. ; with infin., non est cunctandum profiteri hunc mundum animal esse, Cic. ; non cunctor, foll. by quin and the subj. ; non cunctandum existimavit, quin pugnā decertaret, *there ought to be no delay in*, etc., Caes. ; impers. pass., nec cunctatum apud latera, Tac.

cunctus -a -um (contr. from

convinctus), *all, all collectively, the whole*, **a**, sing, senatus, Cic, orbis terrarum, Verg, **b**, plur, **cuncti** -ae -a, cives, Cic, in poet sometimes foll by genit., hominum, Ov

cŭnĕātim, adv (cuneo), *in shape of a wedge*, Caes

cŭnĕātus a -um, p adj with compar (cuneo), *pointed like a wedge*, jugum in angustum dorsum cuneatum, Liv

cŭnĕo, 1 (cuneus), *to drive in a wedge, to wedge in*, Plin

cŭnĕŏlus -i, m (dim of cuneus), *a little wedge*, Cic

cŭnĕus i, m *a wedge* **I.** Lit, **A.** cuneis scindere fissile lignum, Verg **B.** *a wedge as a triangular figure*, Britannia in cuneum tenuatur, *is narrowed in the shape of a wedge*, Tac **II.** Transf, **A.** *troops drawn up in form of a wedge, a wedge*, cuneum facere, Caes **B.** *the wedge-shaped compartments into which the seats of the amphitheatre were divided*, Verg, cuneis omnibus, *to all the spectators*, Phaed

cŭnīcŭlōsus a um (cuniculus), *full of holes and caverns*, Cat.

cŭnīcŭlus i, m **1,** *a rabbit, cony*, Cat., **2,** *an underground passage*, omne genus cuniculorum apud eos notum atque usitatum est, Caes, esp milit. t. t, *a mine*, agere cuniculum, Caes, aperire cuniculum, Caes

cunnus i, f =pudendum muliebre, meton, *a prostitute*, Hor

cūpa -ae, f (root CU, whence culeus), *a cask or butt*, Cic

cŭpēdĭa -ae, f *daintiness, fondness for dainties*, Cic

cŭpĭdē, adv with compar and superl (cupidus), *eagerly, passionately, hotly, vehemently, warmly*, cupide appetere aliquid, Cic, cupide proficisci, Cic., cupidius aliquid dicere, Cic, ego vero cupide et libenter mentiar tuā causā, Cic

cŭpĭdĭtas -ātis, f (cupidus), *eager desire*, and in a bad sense, *passionate longing, vehement desire* **I.** Gen, cupiditas inexplebilis, insana, nimia, Cic, with obj genit., pecuniae, Cic, dominandi, Cic, with ad, tanta cupiditas ad reditum, Cic, ardere cupiditate, Cic, coercere cupiditates, Cic, explere cupiditates, Cic, incitare aliquem cupiditate imitandi, Cic, servire cupiditatibus, Cic **II.** Esp, **a,** *ambition*, popularis (of a demagogue), Cic., **b,** *desire for money, avarice*, sine cupiditate vixisse, Cic.; **c,** *factiousness, party spirit*, cupiditatis atque inimicitiarum suspicio, Cic

cŭpīdo -inis, f (m only in poet) (cupio), *longing, desire* **I.** Gen, Sall, with genit, auri, Tac, pecuniae, honoris, Sall, flagrare cupidine regni, Liv, Hannibalem ingens cupido incesserat Tarenti potiendi, Liv **II.** Esp, **a,** *physical desire*, somni, Sall, **b,** *love*, cupido visae virginis, Ov; hence personified, **Cŭpīdo** -inis, m *Cupid, the god of love, son of Venus*, Cic, plur, **Cŭpīdines**, *Cupids* **c,** *avarice*, cupido sordidus, Hor., **d,** *ambition*, ita cupidine atque irā, pessimis consultoribus, grassari, Sall

cŭpĭdus -a -um, adj with compar and superl (cupio), *desirous, wishful, eager, fond* **I.** Gen, **a,** absol, consul non cupidus, Cic, **b,** with genit of object, pecuniae, Cic., novarum rerum, Cic, te audiendi, Cic., **c,** with in and the abl; in perspicienda cognoscendaque rerum natura, Cic **II.** Esp, **a,** *longing for, loving*, Ov; **b,** *avaricious*, homo non cupidus neque appetens, Cic, **c,** (α) in a good sense, *devoted to*, homo tui cupidus, Cic.; (β) in a bad sense, *factious, partial*, quaestores vehementer istius cupidi, Cic, absol, judex cupidus, Cic

cŭpĭens -entis, p adj with compar and superl (cupio), *desiring, longing, wishing, eager*, novarum rerum, Tac cupientissimā plebe, Sall

cŭpĭentĕr, adv (cupiens), *eagerly*, Plaut

cŭpĭo ivi or ii, itum, 3 *to desire, long for, wish for* **I.** Gen, **a,** with acc, is quem cupimus optamusque vestitus, Cic, pacem, Liv, partic perf, res cupita, Liv, **b,** with infin, cupiens ad suos redire, Cic, **c,** with acc and infin, equidem cupio Antonium haec quam primum audire, Cic **II.** Esp, alicui or alicuius causae, *to favour, support, wish well to*, quid? ego Fundanio non cupio? non amicus sum? Cic

cŭpītor ōris, m (cupio), *one who desires*; matrimonii, Tac

cuppēdĭa, v cupedia

cŭpressētum -i, n (cupressus), *a cypress wood*, Cic

cŭpressĕus -a -um (cupressus), *made of cypress wood*, signa Junonis, Liv

cŭpressĭfer fĕra -fĕrum (cupressus and fero), *cypress-bearing*, Ov

cŭpressus i, f -ūs, m (κυπάρισσος) **A.** *the cypress*, sacred to Pluto, used at funerals, Verg **B.** Meton, *a casket of cypress wood*, Hor

cŭprĕus a um, v cypreus

cūr (orig quoirei, cuirei, then cuire, cui, cur), adv *why? wherefore? for what reason?* **1,** rel, duae sunt causae, cur, etc, Cic, **2,** interrog, cur non assum? Cic

cūra -ae, f *care* **I. A.** Gen, *carefulness, solicitude, pains, trouble* (opp negligentia), *attention*, magna cum cura et diligentia scribere aliquid, Cic, with genit, rerum alienarum cura (difficilis) est, Cic, cura colendi, Verg, with de, studium tuum curaque de salute mea, Cic, verbal constructions, adhibere curam in capris et ovibus parandis, Cic, agere curam civium, Liv, conferre magnam curam in alicuius salutem, Cic, non dimittere istam curam, Cic, maxima erat cura duci ne, etc, Liv, salutem eius regis senatui populoque Romano magnae curae esse, Cic, imprimis tibi curae sit ne mihi tempus prorogetur, Cic, habere curam rerum divinarum, Liv, incumbe in eam curam, *devote yourself to*, Cic, ponere curam alicuius rei, *to lay aside*, Liv, ponere curam in aliqua re, *to devote one's attention to* Cic, suscipere curam, Cic, sustinere maximam curam belli, Cic **B.** *care for something, attending, caring, minding*, **1,** of husbandry, quae cura boum, Verg, **2,** *the adornment of the body*, cura cultusque feminarum, Liv, **3,** *healing, cure*, simplex illa jam cura doloris tui, Cic, **4,** *the worship of the gods*, deorum, Liv, **5,** *taking care of a person*, suum sororisque filios in eadem cura habere, Liv, meton, *the object of attention*, tua cura, palumbes, Verg, **6,** *care for, management, administration*, esp of public affairs, cura reipublicae, Liv, cura navium, *of the fleet*, Tac, meton, *business, administration*, quum sumus necessariis negotiis curisque vacui, Cic **II.** *care, anxiety, solicitude, disquiet*, **1,** sine cura, Cic, afferre alicui curam, Cic, afficere aliquem aliquā curā, Cic, confici curis, Cic, priusquam ea cura decederet patribus Romanis, Liv, liberare aliquem curā, Cic, et curā vacare et negotio, Cic; **2,** of the disquiet of love, juvenum curae Hor; meton, *the object of love*, tua cura, Lycoris Verg

cūrābĭlis e (cura), *exciting care or fear*; vindicta, Juv

cūrālium -ii = corallium (q v)

cūrātē, (curatus), adv *carefully*, compar, curatius legi, *between the lines*, Tac,

cūrātio -ōnis, f. (curo). **I.** Gen., *a taking care*, Plaut. **II.** Esp. *attention, management*; **1, a,** with genit., curatio corporis, Cic.; **b,** *medical attention, healing, cure*; curatio medici, Cic.; curatio valetudinis, Cic.; adhibere curationem, Cic.; praescribere curationem, Cic.; **2,** *management, administration*; esp. of a public office, curatio Nemeorum, *of the Nemean games*, Liv.; Asiatica curatio frumenti, *commission to buy corn*, Cic.; curatio agraria, *commission to divide land*, Cic.; curationem suscipere, Cic.; aedes Telluris est curationis meae, Cic.

cūrātor -ōris, m. (curo), *one who takes care*; **1,** *a guardian, overlooker, curator*; viae Flaminiae Cic.; muris reficiendis sunto aediles curatores urbis annonae ludorumque sollemnium, Cic.; legibus agrariis curatores constituere, Cic.; **2,** legal t. t., *guardian of a minor* or *idiot* or *prodigal*; alicui curatorem dare (of the praetor), Hor.

cūrātus -a -um, p. adj. (curo), *carefully prepared*; curatissimae preces, Tac.

curcŭlio -ōnis, m. *a weevil, corn-worm*, Verg.

Cŭrēs -ium, f. *an ancient town of the Sabines*; meton., *the inhabitants of Cures*, Ov. Hence **A.** Adj., **Cŭrensis** -e, *of Cures*. **B. Cŭres** -ētis, m. *an inhabitant of Cures*.

Cūrētes -um, m. (Κουρῆτες), *the ancient inhabitants of Crete, who celebrated a frantic worship of Jupiter, like that of Cybele by the Corybantes*. Adj., **Cūrētis** -idis, poet. = *Cretan*, Ov.

cūrĭa -ae, f. (connected with Quiris). **I.** *a curia, one of thirty divisions into which the Roman patricians were distributed by Romulus*, Liv. **II.** Meton., **A.** *the meeting-place of a curia*, Tac. **B. a,** *the building in which the senate met*, usually the Curia Hostilia, afterwards the Curia Pompeja or Curia Julia; **b,** Curia Saliorum, *the house of the Salii on the Palatine*, Cic.; **c,** *the senate*; aliquem in curiam introducere, Liv.; **d,** *the senate-house of non-Roman nations*—e.g., at Salamis, Cic.; Syracuse, Cic.; Troy, Ov.; Athens, *the Areopagus*, Juv.

cūrĭālis -e (curia), *belonging to the same curia*, Cic.

cūrĭātim, adv. (curia), *by curiae*; populum consuluit, Cic.

Cūrĭātii -ōrum, m. *name of an Alban gens, three of which fought with the Horatii*.

cūrĭātus -a -um (curia), *relating to the curiae*; comitia curiata, *the original assembly of the Roman people, in which they voted by curiae*, Cic.; lex, *a law passed in the comitia curiata*, Cic.

Cūricta -ae, f. *an island on the Illyrian coast, now Veglia*.

1. **cūrĭo** -ōnis, m. (curia), **1,** *the priest of a curia*, Varr.; maximus, *the head of the college formed by the thirty curiones*, Liv.; **2,** *a herald, crier*, Mart.

2. **Cūrĭo** -ōnis, m. *the name of a family of the gens Scribonia*.

cūrĭōsē, adv., with compar. and superl. (curiosus), **1,** *carefully*; conquirere ista curiosius, Cic.; **2,** *inquisitively*; curiosius id faciunt quam necesse est, Cic.

cūrĭōsitas -ātis, f. (curiosus), *inquisitiveness, curiosity*.

Curiosolītes -um, m. *a people in Brittany, near modern Corseult*.

cūrĭōsus -a -um, adj. with compar. and superl. (cura), *careful*; **1,** *attentive, diligent*; curiosis oculis perspici non posse, Cic.; permulta alia colligit Chrysippus, ut est in omni historia curiosus, Cic.; **2,** *inquisitive, curious*; isti curiosi, Cic.

cŭris -is, f. (a Sabine word) = hasta, *a lance, or javelin*, Ov.

Cŭrĭus -a -um, *name of a plebeian gens, of which the most illustrious member was* M'. Curius Dentatus, *the conqueror of the Sabines, Samnites, and of Pyrrhus, celebrated for his temperance*; hence appell. *a brave and temperate man*, Hor. Adj., **Cŭrĭānus** -a -um, *of* or *belonging to Curius*.

cūro, 1. (cura). **I.** Gen. *to care for, pay attention to, tend*; **a,** with acc., negotia aliena, Cic.; **b,** with acc. and gerundive, in Sicilia frumentum emendum et ad urbem mittendum curare, *to get bought and sent*, Cic.; **c,** with infin., qui res istas scire curavit, Cic.; non curare, *not to care, to decline, refuse*; in Siciliam ire non curat, Cic.; **d,** followed by ut, ne, ut ne and the subj., or the subj. alone, Cic.; so in letters, cura ut valeas, Cic.; **e,** with de, Quintus de emendo nihil curat hoc tempore, Cic. **II.** Esp., **1,** *to attend to, take care of*; se, Cic.; membra, Hor.; *to attend to, cure an invalid, or a disease*; curare corpora, Cic.; curari non posse, Caes.; **2,** *to attend to religious observances*; sacra, Cic.; **3,** *to provide* or *procure a sum of money*; jube sodes nummos curari, Cic.; **4,** *to administer, manage*; res Romae, Liv.; absol. *to command*; curare Romae, Tac. (Archaic forms, coiravi, coirandi, ap. Cic.)

curricŭlum -i, n. (curro). **I.** Act., **A,** Abstr., **1,** *running*, Plaut.; **2,** esp. **a,** *a contest in running, a race*, Cic.; **b,** *a course, orbit of heavenly bodies*; solis et lunae, Cic. **B.** Concr., *the chariot used in races*; in curriculum quadrigarum incurrere, Cic. **II.** Pass. *the raceground*; athletae se in curriculo exercentes, Cic.; often fig., exiguum vitae curriculum natura circumscripsit, immensum gloriae, Cic.

curro, cŭcurri, cursum, 3. *to run, hasten*; pass. impers., curritur, *one runs*, Cic.; curritur ad praetorium, Cic.; pro se quisque currere ad sua tutanda, Liv.; with cognate acc., eosdem cursus currere, Cic.; prov., currentem hortari, incitare or instigare, *to spur the willing horse*, Cic.; esp. **a,** *to run in a race*; currere bene, Ov.; with acc. of place, qui stadium currit, Cic.; **b,** of ships, *to sail*; per omne mare, Hor.; with acc., currere cavā trabe vastum aequor, Verg.; **c,** of a wheel, si mea sincero curreret axe rota, Ov.; **d,** of water, currentes aquae, Ov.; **e,** of the heavenly bodies, libera currebant et inobservata per annum sidera, Ov.; **f,** of the hem of a garment, quam plurima circum purpura Maeandro duplici Meliboea cucurrit, Verg.; **g,** of fright, cold, shame, etc., varius per ora cucurrit Ausonidum turbata fremor, Verg.; **h,** of time, *to pass*; currit ferox aetas, Hor.; **i,** fig., of discourse, *to march easily*; perfacile currens oratio, Cic.

currus -ūs, m. (curro). **I. A.** *a chariot, car*, esp. *a triumphal car*; escendere in currum, Cic.; flectere currum de foro in Capitolium, Cic.; invehi curru Capitolium, Cic. **B.** Meton., **a,** *the horses, the team*; neque audit currus habenas, Verg.; **b,** *triumph*; quem ego currum aut quam lauream cum tua laudatione conferrem? Cic. **II.** *a plough with wheels*, Verg. **III.** *a ship*, Cat. (syncop. genit. plur. currum, Verg., Aen. vi. 653).

cursim, adv. (curro), *hastily, quickly*; cursim agmen agere, Liv.; cursim dicere aliena, Cic.

cursĭto, 1. (intens. of curso), *to run up and down*; huc et illuc (of the atoms), Cic.

curso, 1. (freq. of curro), *to run hither and thither*; ultro et citro, Cic.

cursor -ōris, m. (curro). **I.** Lit. **A.** *a runner*, especially for a prize, Cic.; *one who contends in the chariot race*, Ov. **B.** [illegible] *postman*, Tac, 2, *a slave who ran before his master's carriage, a running footman*, Suet II. Transf. *surname of* L Papirius, *the conqueror of the Samnites*

cursus -ūs, m (curro), *a running, rapid motion on horseback, in a carriage, or ship*, milites cursu exanimatos, Caes, cursus equorum, Verg, longarum navium Caes, cursu tendere ad aliquem or ad locum, Liv, in cursu esse, *to travel in haste*, Cic; esp a, *chariot* or *horse race*, cursus certamen, Ov, fig *the race for office, honour*, etc, in eodem cursu fuisse a Sulla dictatore ad eosdem fere consules, Cic, b, *course, march, journey*; cursus maritimus, Cic, mihi cursus in Graeciam per tuam provinciam est, Cic, cursus dirigere, Liv; cursum secundum habere, Caes, cursum tenere Cic, fig, reliquus vitae cursus, Cic, c, *the course of water*, quosdam exaruisse amnes aut in alium cursum contortos et deflexos videmus, Cic, d, of heavenly bodies, annui cursus solis, Cic, e, of the voice, his per omnes sonos vocis cursus, Cic.

Curtĭus -a -um, *name of a Roman gens, the most noted members of which were*. a, M Curtius, *a Roman youth, said to have jumped into a chasm in the Roman forum, which then closed*, b, C Curtius Postumus, *an adherent of Caesar's*, Q Curtius Rufus, *the author of a Latin history of Alexander the Great, probably contemporary with Vespasian* Hence, Curtius lacus, *the chasm in the forum into which M Curtius was said to have jumped*.

curto, 1 (curtus), *to abridge, abbreviate, lessen*, Hor

curtus -a -um *shortened, mutilated, cut short*, res, Ov, mulus, Hor, transf, of discourse, *cut short*, curta sentiunt nec amant redundantia, Cic

cŭrūlis e (currus), *relating to a chariot*, equi, *the team of four horses provided out of the public purse for the Circensian games*, Liv, sella, *the curule chair adorned with ivory, the official seat of the* consuls, praetors, and curule aediles, Cic, curulis aedilis, *a curule aedile*, Liv

curvāmen -inis, n (curvo), *a curving, vaulting, arching*, Ov

curvātūra -ae, f (curvo), *a vault, arch*, Plin, rotae, *the rim*, Ov

curvo, 1 (curvus), *to bend, bow, curve*, curvare brachia longo circuitu, Ov, quum nux plurima curvabit ramos, *makes to bend*, Verg, tollimur in caelum curvato gurgite, Verg, curvare genua sua, Verg; Hadria curvans Calabros sinus, Hor, transf, *make to bend, move*, nec te vir Pieria pellice saucius curvat, Hor

curvus -a -um (κυρτος), *bent, bowed, arched, curved, crooked*, arbor, *bent with the weight of fruit*, Ov, aratrum, Verg, naves, Ov, litus, Hor, flumen, *winding*, Verg, curvus arator, *bowed down*, Verg, curva senecta, Ov, subst., **curvum** -i, n *what is crooked*, curvo dignoscere rectum, Hor

cuspis -ĭdis, f A. Lit *a point*, esp *the point or head of a spear*, asseres pedum XII cuspidibus praefixi, Caes, of the sting of a bee, Plin, of a scorpion, Ov B Meton a, *a lance, javelin*, infestis cuspidibus uti, Liv, b, *Neptune's trident*, cuspis triplex, Ov, c, *a spit*, Mart

custōdĭa -ae, f (custos) I. *a watching, guarding, custody, care* A. Lit, a, canum, Cic, aliquem diligenti custodiā asservare, Liv, b, milit t t *keeping guard, watching*, custodiae classium, Caes; committere custodiam corporis feris barbaris, Cic B. Meton, 1, *the watch, sentinels*, a, sing, in prose only collective, custodiam ex suis ac praesidium sex milia hominum ... Caes, b, plur., frequens custodiis locus, Liv, circumdare horribiles custodias, Cic, disponere custodias diligentius, Caes, 2, *the station of the guard, post*, haec mea sedes est, haec vigilia, haec custodia, Cic II. Esp *custody, safe-keeping*, custodia libera, *liberation on parole*, Liv, dare aliquem in custodiam, Cic, esse in custodia publica, Cic, necari in custodia, Caes

custōdĭo, 4 (custos). I Gen *to guard, watch, keep*, tuum corpus domumque, Cic, se diligentissime, Cic, custodire salutem alicuius, Cic, poma, of a dragon, Ov II. Esp a, *to keep in sight, observe, watch*, aliquem custodire ne quid auferat, Cic, A Terentius Varro ad custodiendum iter eorum missus, Liv, b, *to take care of*, liber tuus a me custoditur diligentissime, Cic, custodire aliquid litteris, Cic, c, *to keep in prison, hold captive*; ducem praedonum, Cic, obsides, Caes

custos -ōdis, c I. Gen *a guardian, watchman, keeper, preserver, attendant*, a, portae, Liv, custos defensorque provinciae, Cic, custos urbis, Cic, fortitudo custos dignitatis, Cic, b, *the guardian of a young man*, custos incorruptissimus, Hor, c, *the guardian of a woman*; nimium servat custos Junonius Io, Ov, d, *the officer in charge of the voting tablets*, custodes tabellarum, Cic, e, milit. t t, *a sentinel, guard*, custodes dare, Cic, disponere, Caes II. a, *an overseer, overlooker, spy*, custos ac vindex cupiditatum, Cic, b, *the gaoler, guard of a prisoner*, jugulari a custodibus, Nep.

cŭtĭcŭla ae, f (dim of cutis), *the skin, cuticle*, Juv

Cŭtilĭae -ārum, f *an old town in the country of the Sabines*

cŭtis -is, f (root CUT, Gr KYT, whence κύτος), *the skin*, Hor, *hide, leather*, Mart

Cўănē ēs, f (Κυάνη), *a nymph changed into a fountain for her grief at the loss of Proserpine*

Cўănēē -ēs, f (Κυανέη), *daughter of Maeander, mother of Caunus and Byblis*

cўăthus -i, m (κύαθος), 1, *a ladle for filling the goblets* (pocula) *with wine out of the crater*, Hor, 2, *a measure of capacity* = one-twelfth of a sextarius, Hor

cўbaeus -a -um, navis and absol, **cўbaea** -ae, f *a kind of transport or merchantman*, Cic

Cўbĕlē or **Cўbēbē** -ēs, f (Κυβέλη, Κυβήβη), 1, *a Phrygian goddess, afterwards worshipped at Rome under various names* (Rhea, Ops, Magna Mater, etc), *whose priests were called Galli*, adj, **Cўbĕlēĭus** a -um, *belonging to Cybele*, 2, *a mountain in Phrygia*

Cўbistra ōrum, n (τα Κύβιστρα), *a town in Cataonia, at the foot of Mount Taurus*

1 **cўclas** -ădis, f (κυκλάς), *a female robe of state, having a border of purple or gold embroidery*, Juv.

2 **Cўclas** ădis, f (sc insula), gen in plur **Cўclădes** -um, f (Κυκλαδες), *a group of islands in the Aegean Sea*

cўclĭcus a -um (κυκλικός), *cyclic*, scriptor, *an epic poet whose works formed a complete cycle of history*, Hor

Cўclops -clōpis, m (Κυκλωψ *round eyed*), *a Cyclops*, gen in plur, **Cўclōpes** clōpum, m. *the Cyclopes, a gigantic one eyed race, the workmen of Vulcan*, sing, *the Cyclops Polyphemus*, Hor Adj, **Cўclōpēus** -a -um, saxa, *Sicilian*, Verg

Cўcnēĭus -a -um, *belonging to the Boeotian Cycnus* Tempe, Ov

cўcnēus -a -um (κυκνειος), *belonging to the swan*, plumae, Ov, tamquam cycnea fuit divini hominis vox et oratio, *his swan's song*, Cic.

1. **cy̆cnus** -i, m (κύκνος), *the swan, famed in legend for its death-song, sacred to Apollo*, Cic, meton = *poet*, Dircaeus cycnus, *Pindar*, Hor

2 **Cy̆cnus** -i, m 1, *king of Liguria, son of Sthenelus, changed into a swan*. 2, *the son of Neptune by Calyce, changed into a swan*

Cy̆dōnēa -ae, f (Κυδώνεια), *an ancient city on the north coast of Crete*, hence, 1, **Cy̆dōn** -ōnis, m *a Cydonean*, 2, **Cy̆dōnĭātae** -ārum, m *inhabitants of Cydonea*, 3, **Cy̆dōnĭus** -a um, poet. for *Cretan*, Verg, 4, **Cy̆dōnēus** -a -um, poet for *Cretan*

cygn . . v cycn

cy̆lindrus -dri, m (κύλινδρος), 1, *a cylinder*, Cic, 2, *a roller for levelling the ground*, Verg

Cyllărŏs and **-ŭs** -i, m (Κύλλαρος), 1, *a Centaur*, 2, *the horse of Castor or Pollux*

Cyllēnē -ēs and -ae, f (Κυλλήνη) **I.** *a high mountain in north east Arcadia, where Mercury was born and reared* Hence, adj, 1, **Cyllēnĭus** -a -um, *Cyllenian* and *Mercurian*, proles, *Mercury*, Verg, also *Cephalus, son of Mercury*, Ov, ignis, *the planet Mercury*, Verg, subst., **Cyllēnius** -ii, m *Mercury*, Verg; 2, **Cyllēnēus** -a -um, *Cyllenian* or *Mercurian*, fides, *the lyre*, Hor, 3, **Cyllēnis** -idis, f *Cyllenian* or *Mercurian* **II.** *a town in the north of Elis*

cymba -ae, f (κύμβη), *a small boat, skiff*, Cic.; esp *the boat of Charon*, Verg

cymbălum -i, n (κύμβαλον), *a cymbal*, usually found in the plur, Cic

cymbĭum -ii, n (κυμβίον), *a small drinking-vessel*, Verg

Cy̆mē -ēs, f (Κύμη) **A.** *a town in Aeolis, mother-city of Cumae in Campania* Adj, **Cy̆maeus** -a -um, *Cymaean* **B.** = Cumae (q v).

Cy̆nāpēs, m *a river in Asia, falling into the Black Sea*

Cy̆nĭcus -i, m (Κυνικός), *a Cynic philosopher, a Cynic* Adj, **Cy̆nĭcus** -a -um, *Cynic*

cy̆nŏcĕphălus -i, m *an ape with a head like a dog's*, Cic

Cy̆nŏs and **-ŭs** -i, f (Κῦνος), *a town in Locris*

Cy̆nŏsargēs -is, n (Κυνόσαργες), *a gymnasium outside Athens, sacred to Hercules*

Cy̆noscĕphălae -ārum, f (Κυνὸς κεφαλαί, *dog's heads*), *two hills near Scotussa in Thessaly where the Romans defeated the Macedonians.*

Cy̆nŏsūra -ae, f (κυνόσουρα), *the constellation of the Little Bear, the pole star*, Cic Adj, **Cy̆nŏsūris** -idis, ursa, *the Little Bear*, Ov

Cy̆nŏsūrae -ārum, f (Κυνόσουρα), *a promontory in Attica*

Cynthus -i, m (Κύνθος), *a mountain in Delos, the birthplace of Apollo and Diana*, hence, **Cynthĭus** -ii, m *Apollo*, **Cynthĭa** -ae, f *Diana*

1 **Cy̆părissus** -i, m *a youth beloved by Apollo, changed into a cypress*

2 **cy̆părissus** = cupressus (q v)

Cyprus and **-os** -i f (Κύπρος), *the island of Cyprus*, hence adj, **Cy̆prius** -a -um, *Cyprian*, Cyprium aes, or subst, **Cy̆prium** -ii, n *copper*, Plin Subst, **Cy̆pria** -ae, f *Venus*, Tib, **Cy̆prii** -orum, m *the Cypriotes*

Cypsĕlus -i, m (Κύψελος), *a tyrant of Corinth*

Cy̆rēnē -ēs (**-ae** -ārum), f **I.** *a city of North Africa, birthplace of the poet Callimachus and of the philosopher Aristippus, founder of the Cyrenaic school.* Hence 1, adj, **Cy̆rēnaeus** a -um, *Cyrenaic*; **Cy̆rēnaei** -orum, m. *the Cyrenaic philosophers*, 2, **Cy̆rēnăĭcus** a -um, *Cyrenaic*, **Cy̆rēnăĭci** -orum, *the Cyrenaic philosophers*, 3, **Cy̆rēnensis** -e, *Cyrenaic* **II. Cy̆rēnē** -es, f *daughter of Hypseus, mother of Aristaeus by Apollo*

Cyrnŏs (Cyrnus) -i, f (Κύρνος), *the island of Corsica* Adj, **Cyrnaeus** -a -um, *Corsican*

Cyrtaei or **Cyrtii** -ōrum, m *a people in Persis and Media*

Cy̆rus -i, m (Κῦρος), 1, *the founder of the Persian Empire*, 2, Cyrus minor, *second son of Ochus, who fought with his brother, Artaxerxes Memnon, and was killed at Cunaxa*, 3, *an architect at Rome in the time of Cicero*, hence, **Cy̆rēa** -ōrum, n *the works of Cyrus*, Cic, 4, *a youth mentioned by Horace*

Cy̆tae -ārum, f. (Κύται), *a city in Colchis, birthplace of Medea* Adj, 1, **Cy̆taeus** -a -um, *Cytaean* = *Colchian*; 2, **Cy̆taeis** -idis, f *the Cytaean*, i e, *Medea*

Cy̆thēra -ōrum, n (Κύθηρα), *the island Cythera, sacred to Venus*, now *Cerigo*, hence, 1, **Cy̆thērēa** -ae, f *Venus*, 2, **Cy̆thĕrēĭus** -a -um, *Cytherean*, subst, **Cy̆thĕrēĭa** -ae, f, *Venus*, 3, **Cy̆thĕrēis** -idis, f *the Cytherean*, *Venus*; 4, **Cy̆thērĭăcus** -a -um, and 5, **Cy̆thĕrēĭăs** -ădis, f *sacred to Venus.*

Cythnŏs (Cythnus), -i, f (Κύθνος), *an island in the Aegean Sea*, now *Thermia.*

cy̆tĭsus -i, c and **cy̆tĭsum** -i, n (κύτισος), *a kind of clover or trefoil much valued by the ancients*, Verg

Cy̆tōrus -i, m (Κύτωρος), *a mountain and city in Paphlagonia, famous for box-trees* Adj, **Cy̆tōrĭăcus** a -um, *Cytorian*, pecten, *made of boxwood*, Ov.

Cyzĭcus (-os) -i, f (Κύζικος) and **Cyzĭcum** -i, n *a town on the Propontis* Adj, **Cyzĭcēnus** -a um, *Cyzicene*

D.

D d, the fourth letter of the Latin alphabet, corresponding in sound and alphabetical position with the Greek Δ, δ For its meaning as an abbreviation, see Table of Abbreviations

Dāci -ōrum, m *the Dacians, a warlike people on the Lower Danube*, hence, 1, **Dācĭa** -ae, f. *their country, Dacia*, 2, **Dācĭcus** -i, m (sc. nummus), *a gold coin of Domitian, the conqueror of the Dacians*

dactȳlĭcus -a um (δακτυλικός), *dactylic*; numerus, Cic

dactȳlĭŏthēca -ae, f (δακτυλιοθήκη), 1, *a casket for rings*, Mart, 2, *a collection of seal rings and gems*, Plin

dactȳlus (-os) -i, m (δάκτυλος) (lit *a finger*), *a metrical foot, consisting of one long, followed by two short syllables* (– ◡ ◡), *a dactyl*, Cic

Daedăla -ōrum, n *a stronghold in Caria*

1 **daedălus** -a -um (δαίδαλος), 1, act., *artful, full of art*, Circe, Verg, 2, pass, *artfully constructed*, tecta, Verg

2 **Daedălus** -i, m (Δαίδαλος), *a celebrated Athenian artificer, builder of the Cretan labyrinth*, hence adj, **Daedălēus** -a -um, *Daedalean*, iter, *the labyrinth*, Prop

Dăhae -ārum, m (Δάαι), *a Scythian tribe on the east side of the Caspian Sea.*

Dalmătae (Delmătae) -ārum, m. (Δαλμάται), *the Dalmatians, inhabitants of Dalmatia* Hence 1, **Dălmătia** ae, f *the country of Dalmatia on the east side of the Adriatic Sea*, 2, adj, **Dalmătĭcus** -a -um, *Dalmatian*, subst, **Dalmătĭcus** -i, m *surname of Metellus, conqueror of the Dalmatians*

dāma -ae, f (in Verg m), *a fallow deer*, Hor

Dămascus -i, f (Δαμασκός), *the Syrian city of Damascus* Adj, **Dămascēnus** a um, *Damascene*, pruna, *damsons*, Plin

Dămăsippus -i, m *cognomen in the gens Licinia.*

damma = dama (q v)

damnātĭo ōnis, f (damno), *condemnation*; ambitūs, *for bribery*, Cic., tantae pecuniae, *to pay*, etc, Cic.

damnātōrĭus -a -um (damno), *relating to condemnation, condemnatory*, Cic, judicium, Cic

damno, 1 (damnum) **I.** *to condemn declare guilty, sentence* **A.** Lit legal t t, aliquem ministros sociosque, Cic, with acc. of the cause, causa judicata atque damnata, Cic, with acc of person, aliquem inauditum, Tac., damnari inter sicarios, *to be condemned as an assassin*, Cic, damnari per arbitrum, Cic, damnari nullam aliam ob causam, Cic, with perf infin act, aut dabis aut contra edictum fecisse damnabere, Cic, with quod A Baebius unus est damnatus, quod milites Romanos praebuisset ad ministerium caedis, Liv, with abl of the motive, mutili pudore causam suam damnare, Liv, with abl of the accusation, damnari eo crimine, Cic., with abl of the law or formula, damnari suā lege, Cic, with abl of the court, damnari populi judicio, Cic, with abl of the punishment, damnare aliquem capite, *to loss of civil rights*, Cic, with genit of the crime, ambitus, Cic, with genit. of the punishment, damnari octupli, Cic, with de, damnari de vi, Cic, with ad, damnari ad mortem, Tac **B.** Transf, **a**, of deities, damnare aliquem voti or voto, *to grant a person's wish, and thereby compel him to keep his vow*, damnabis tu quoque votis, *you will grant prayer, and thereby bind the suppliant to keep his vow*, Verg, gen in pass, damnari voti or voto, *to attain one's wish*, bis ejusdem voti damnata respublica, Liv, **b**, of a testator, *to bind the heir*, Hor, **c**, *to sentence* to endure or suffer, damnare aeterna lumina nocte, Ov, **d**, *to condemn a person on account of, to inculpate*, aliquem summae stultitiae, Cic, **e**, *to blame, disapprove of*, nec mihi mens dubia est, quin te tua numina damnent, Ov, **f**, *to assign, devote to* (for destruction), Ilion, mihi castaeque damnatum Minervae, Hor **II.** *to procure the condemnation of a person*, hoc uno crimine illum, Cic

damnōsē, adv (damnosus), *ruinously*, bibere, *to the host's loss*, Hor

damnōsus -a -um, adj with compar and superl (damnum), *causing loss or damage, mischievous, ruinous, detrimental*, bellum sumptuosum et damnosum Romanis, Liv

damnum i, n (old form dampnum, from root DAP, connected with daps, Gr ΔΑΠ, whence δαπάνη, or else from dare — *the thing given as a punishment*), *loss, damage, injury* (opp lucrum) **I.** Gen contrahere, facere, *to suffer injury*, Cic, pati, Liv, damna caelestia lunae, *the waning of the moon*, Hor., maximis damnis affici, Cic, dare damnum, *to cause loss*, Cic, damnum naturae, *a natural defect*, Liv, stomachum suum damno Tulli (*to the injury of*) explere, Cic **II.** Esp, 1, *loss in war, defeat*, damna Romano accepta bello, Liv, 2, *a fine, pecuniary mulct*, Cic

Dămŏclēs -is, m (Δαμοκλῆς), *a friend of Dionysius, tyrant of Syracuse, who, on praising the tyrant's prosperity, was placed by Dionysius at a sumptuous feast, and a sword was let down so as to hang by a hair over his head*

Dāmōn ōnis m (Δάμων), 1, *a Pythagorean, famous for his friendship with Phintias*, 2, *a celebrated Athenian musician, teacher of Socrates*

Dănăē -ēs, f (Δανάη), *daughter of Acrisius, mother of Perseus by Zeus, who visited her in a shower of gold when shut up in a tower by her father*, hence, adj, **Dănăēĭus** -a -um, heros, *Perseus*, Ov

Dănăus -i, m (Δαναός), *son of Belus, brother of Aegyptus, and father of the fifty Danaides, the mythical founder of Argos*, hence, 1, adj, **Dănăus** -a -um, *Greek, Argive*, pl **Dănăi** ōrum, m *the Greeks*, 2, **Dănăĭdes** -um, f *the daughters of Danaus*

Dānūbĭus (Dānŭvĭus) -ii, m *the Danube* (in the upper part of its course, the lower part was called Ister)

dăno, v do

Daphnē -ēs f (Δάφνη), 1, *the daughter of the river-god Peneus, changed into a laurel tree*, 2, *a grove and temple to Apollo and Diana near Antiochia in Syria*

Daphnis -nĭdis, acc -nim and -nin (Δάφνις) *son of Mercury, a Sicilian shepherd, inventor of pastoral poetry, and the favourite of Pan*

daphnōn -ōnis, m (δαφνών), *a grove of laurels*, Mart

daps, dăpis, f (root DAP, Gr ΔΑΠ, whence δάπ-τω, δαπάνη), 1, *a sacrificial feast, religious banquet*, ergo obligatam redde Jovi dapem, Hor, 2, *a meal, feast, banquet*, amor dapis, Hor, humanā dape (*with human flesh*) pascere equos, Ov, plur, dapibus epulari opimis, Verg

dapsĭlis -e (δαψιλής), *sumptuous, plentiful, richly provided*, Plaut

Dardăni -ōrum, m (Δάρδανοι), *a people in Upper Moesia, the modern Servia*

Dardănus -i, m (Δάρδανος), *son of Jupiter and Electra of Arcadia, the mythical ancestor of the royal family of Troy*, hence 1, **Dardănus** a -um, *Trojan*, subst, **Dardăni** -ōrum, m *the Trojans*, 2, **Dardănĭus** -a -um, *Trojan*, subst, **Dardănia** ae, f *Troy*, 3, **Dardănides** ae, m. *a descendant of Dardanus, Aeneas*, Verg, *a Trojan*, Verg, 4, **Dardănis** -ĭdis, f *a Trojan woman*, Ov, *Creusa*, Verg

Dărēs -rētis, m (Δάρης), *a companion to Aeneas, a boxer*

Dārēus and **Dārīus** -i, m (Δαρεῖος), *name of several Persian kings*, 1, Darius Hystaspes, *died* 485 B C, 2, *son of Xerxes*, 3, Darius Ochus or Nothus, *died* 404 B C, 4, Darius Codomannus, *the last Persian king*

dătĭo -ōnis, f (do), 1, *a giving*, legum, Cic, 2, *the legal right of alienation*, Liv

Dātis -tĭdis, acc tim, m (Δᾶτις), *a Mede, general of Darius Hystaspis, defeated with Artaphernes at Marathon*

dător ōris, m (do), *a giver*, laetitiae, *Bacchus*, Verg

Daulis -ĭdis, f (Δαυλίς), *a city in Phocis*, adj, **Daulĭas** -ădis, f *Daulian* ales, *Procne*, Ov, Daulides puellae, *Procne and Philomela*, Verg

Daunus -i, m *a mythical king of Apulia, father (or ancestor) of Turnus, and father-in-law of Diomedes*, hence 1, **Daunĭus** -a -um *Daunian*;

heros, *Turnus*, Verg ; gens, *the Rutulians, of whom Turnus was king*, Verg , dea, *Juturna, sister of Turnus*, Verg ; Camena, *the Roman muse*, Hor , caedes, *Roman*, Hor., 2, **Daunias** -ădis, f *Apulia*, Hor

dē, prep , with abl , *from* **I.** In space, *from, away from, down from;* de altera parte agri Sequanos decedere juberet, Caes , de manibus effugere, Cic , de digito anulum detrahere, Cic. **II.** Transf , **A.** Of time, **1**, *in the course of, during*, de nocte venire, Cic , de die, *in the day time*, Hor , de mense Decembri navigare, Cic. , **2**, *from, immediately after* , statim de auctione venire, Cic , diem de die differre proferre, *to put off from day to day*, Liv **B. 1**, *from*, of the place from which a person comes , copo de via Latina, Cic , tabula de foro, Cic , Libyca de rupe Leones, *African lions*, Ov , **2**, to denote a body of persons *out of* which some one is taken , hominem certum misi de comitibus meis, Cic. , esp **a**, of the birth, origin, class to which a person belongs, homo de plebe, Cic , **b**, in the place of the partitive genit , de duobus honestis utrum honestius, Cic , **3**, *out of*, to express the material out of which a thing is made, de eodem oleo et opera exarare aliquid, Cic , esp **a**, of the change of one thing to another, de templo carcerem fieri, Cic , **b**, *from*, of the property which bears the cost of anything, de meo, de tuo, etc , *from my property*, de publico, *at the public expense*, Cic , **c**, of the part of the body which suffers punishment, de tergo satisfacere, Cic , **4**, of the ground, cause of a thing, *on account of*, gravi de causa, Cic , qua de causa, *on account of which*, Cic ; **5**, *in accordance with, in obedience to some form or example;* vix de mea sententia concessum est, Cic , **6**, *with relation to, concerning*, recte non credis de numero militum, Cic , **7**, with adj , to form an adverbial phrase, de improviso, *unexpectedly*, Cic , de integro, *anew*, Cic

dĕa -ae, f (dat and abl pl , dis, deis, deabus), *a goddess*, Cic , triplices, *the Parcae*, Ov , duae novem, *the Muses*, Ov

dĕalbo, 1 *to whitewash, plaster*, columnas, Cic

dĕambŭlo, 1 *to take a walk*, Suet

dĕarmo, 1. *to disarm*, quibus dearmatus exercitus hostium, Liv.

dēbacchor, 1 dep *to rave, rage furiously;* debacchantur ignes, Hor.

dēbellātor -ōris, m (debello), *a conqueror* , ferarum, Verg

dēbello, 1 **I.** Intransit. *to wage war to the end, finish a war*, neque priusquam debellavero absistam, Liv ; proelio uno debellatum est, Liv **II.** Transit., **a**, *to fight out*, rixa super mero debellata, Hor , **b**, *to conquer, overcome* , superbos, Verg

dēbĕo -ŭi -ĭtum, 2 (for dehibeo from de and habeo, *to have from a person*, i e. *to be bound to restore something)* **I.** Lit *to owe, be indebted*, alicui pecuniam, Cic ; talenta CC, Cic , illi quibus debeo, *my creditors*, Cic ; absol ii qui debent, *debtors*, Cic , subst, **dēbĭtum** -i, n *a debt;* debitum alicui solvere, Cic , debito fraudari, Cic. **II.** Transf , **A.** *to remain indebted*, quod praesenti tibi peste subnegaram, non tribueram certe, id absenti debere non potui, Cic **B.** *to owe, to be bound to repay*, **1**, morally, with acc , alicui gratiam, Cic ; with infin *to be bound, to be pledged* homines, qui te et maxime debuerunt et plurimum juvare potuerunt, Cic. , partic **dēbĭtus** -a -um, *bound, owed*, debitae poenae, Cic ; **2**, *to be bound* or *obliged by fate* or *circumstances*, tu, nisi ventis debes ludibrium, *if you are not bound to become*, Hor ; debitus destinatusque morti, Liv , vita quae fato debetur, Cic. , **3**, *to owe, to have to thank a person for, to be indebted to a person for*, alicui beneficium, Cic. , alicui vitam, Ov

dēbĭlis -e, adj with compar (orig dehibilis, from de and habilis), *feeble, weak* **A.** Lit , corpus, Cic , senex, Cic ; ferrum, Verg **B.** Transf., mancam ac debilem praeturam futuram suam, Cic

dēbĭlĭtas -ātis, f (debilis), *weakness, feebleness, debility* **A.** Lit , bonum integritas corporis, miserum debilitas, Cic. , linguae, Cic. **B.** Transf , animi, Cic

dēbĭlĭtātĭo -ōnis, f. (debilito), *a weakening, weakness* , animi, Cic

dēbĭlĭto, 1 (debilis), *to lame, weaken, cripple, disable* **A.** Lit , **a**, membra lapidibus, fustibus, Cic , gen in pass , esp in partic perf , debilitatum corpus et contrucidatum, Cic , **b**, of things, quae (hiems) nunc oppositis debilitat pumicibus mare Tyrrhenum, Hor. **B.** Transf *to enervate, break the force of, disable*, audaciam debilito, sceleri resisto, Cic , tribunicios furores, Cic. , debilitatum metu, Cic

dēbĭtĭo -ōnis, f (debeo), *an owing, debt* , pecuniae, Cic.

dēbĭtor -ōris, m (debeo), *one who owes, a debtor* **A.** Lit , addicere Futidium creditorem debitoribus suis, Cic **B.** Transf , mercede soluta non manet officio debitor ille tuo, Ov , vitae, *owing his life to*, Ov

dēbĭtum -i, n v debeo

dĕcanto, 1. **I.** Transit , **1**, *to sing, repeat in singing*, elegos, Hor ; **2**, *to repeat over and over again*, pervulgata praecepta, Cic **II.** Intransit , *to leave off singing*, sed jam decantaverant fortasse, Cic

dĕcēdo -cessi -cessum, 3 **I.** Lit , *to go forth, go away, depart* **A.** Gen , **a**, ex nostra provincia, Cic , decedere Italiā, Sall , of animals, decedere e pastu, Verg. , **b**, de via decedere, *to depart from one's course*, Cic ; naves imprudentiā aut tempestate paululum suo cursu decesserunt, Cic , fig , se nullā cupiditate inductum de via decessisse, Cic , alicui de via decedere, *to make way for*, as a sign of respect, Plaut. , salutari, appeti, decedi, *to have persons make way for you*, Cic , decedere canibus de via, *to get out of the way of*, Cic , *to yield to, get out of the way for, cease on account of*, serae decedere nocti, Verg , calori, Verg , **c**, milit t t , *to march away, to evacuate*, decedere atque exercitum deducere ex his regionibus, Caes ; pugnā, Liv , **d**, of the magistrate of a province, *to leave on the expiration of his term*, de or ex or (simply) provinciā, Cic , **e**, of actors, decedere de scena, Cic **B.** Esp , **a**, *to depart from life, to die*, decedere de vita, Cic ; or absol , decedere, Cic , pater nobis decessit a d III. Cal Dec , Cic , **b**, of things without life, (α) of water, *to retire*, quum decessisse inde aquam nuntiatum esset, Liv ; (β) of the sun and moon, *to set*, sol decedens, Verg ; (γ) of diseases, *to cease*, alteram quartanam mihi dixit decessisse, Cic **II.** Transf , **A.** Gen , **a**, *to abandon property;* de possessione, Cic , **b**, *to abandon a plan or opinion;* de sententia, Cic , **c**, *to swerve from duty*, de officio et dignitate, Cic , **d**, *to yield place to*, with dat , vivere si recte nescis, decede peritis, Hor **B.** **a**, *to decrease*, ut de causa periculi nihil decederet, Cic. , **b**, *to cease*, postquam invidia decesserat, Sall.

Dĕcĕlēa (-īa) ae, f (Δεκέλεια), *a town in Attica on the Boeotian border*

dĕcem (δέκα), *ten* **A.** Lit., Cic. **B.** Meton , *an indefinite number* , decem vitia, Hor

Dĕcember -bris -bre, abl -bri, (decem), **1**, mensis December, *the tenth month of the Roman year reckoned from March, December*, Cic , subst ,

Dĕcember -bris, m *December*, **2,** *belonging to the month December*, kalendae, Cic ; libertate Decembri utere, *the licence of December*, i e , *of the Saturnalia*, Hor

dĕcempĕda ae, f (decem and pes), *a measuring rod ten feet in length*, Cic

dĕcempĕdātor ōris, m (decempeda), *one who uses the decempeda, a land surveyor* aequissimus agri privati et publici decempedator, Cic

dĕcemplex -icis (decem and plex, from plico), *ten fold*, Nep

dĕcemprīmi -ōrum, m (often written in two words), *the ten chief men in the senate of a* municipium or colonia, Cic

dĕcemscalmus -a -um (decem and scalmus), *having ten thowls* or *rowlocks*, actuariolum, Cic

dĕcemvir -i, m , gen plur , **dĕcemvĭri** -ōrum or um, m *a college of ten magistrates at Rome*, **1,** decemviri legibus scribendis, *the magistrates who drew up the XII Tables*, **2,** decemviri sacrorum or sacris faciundis, *the guardians of the Sibylline Books* **3,** decemviri stlitibus (litibus) judicandis, *a judicial body who judged in cases affecting freedom and citizenship*, **4,** decemviri agris metiendis dividendisque, *commissioners for dividing public land*

dĕcemvĭrālis -e (decemvir), *relating to the decemvirs*, annus, Cic , potestas, Liv

dĕcemvĭrātus ūs, m (decemvir), *the office or dignity of a decemvir*, Cic

dĕcens entis, p adj with compar and superl (decet), **1,** *seemly, becoming, decent* amictus, Ov , quid verum atque decens curo atque rogo, Hor , **2,** *well-formed, handsome, comely*, facies, forma, Ov , malae, Hor , Venus, Hor

dĕcentia -ae, f (decet), *comeliness, decency*, figurarum venustas atque ordo, et ut ita dicam, decentia, Cic

dĕcerno crēvi crētum, 3 **I.** *to decide* **A.** *peacefully*, **1,** qui sine manibus et pedibus constare deum posse decreverunt, Cic , **2, a,** *to decide judicially*, quod iste aliter atque edixisset decrevisset, Cic , **b,** of the senate, etc , or of individual members of the senate, *to decree, propose*, si hic ordo (*the senate*) placere decreverat te ire in exsilium, obtemperaturum te esse dicis, Cic , pecunias ad templum monumentumque alicuius, Cic , D Junius Silanus primus sententiam rogatus supplicium sumendum decreverat, Sall , senatus decrevit, darent operam consules, ne quid respublica detrimenti caperet, Sall , alicui triumphum, Cic , **3,** *to decide in a hostile manner*, decernere pugnam, Liv , proelium, Cic , decernere armis, Cic , crastino die bene juvantibus diis acie decernamus, Liv **II.** *to resolve, form a resolution, settle*, gen. with infin , Caesar his de causis Rhenum transire decreverat, Caes , decreram cum eo familiariter vivere, Cic (syncop perf forms, decerno, decreram, decrero, decresset, decresse)

dĕcerpo -cerpsi -cerptum, 3 **A.** Lit , *to pluck off, pluck away*, arbore pomum, Ov **II.** **1,** transf , humanus animus decerptus ex mente divina, *a scion of*, Cic , **2,** *to take away*, ne quid jocus de gravitate decerperet, Cic

dĕcertātio ōnis, f (decerto), *a contest*, harum rerum omnium, Cic

dĕcerto, 1 *to contend, struggle vehemently, fight to a decision*, proeliis cum acerrimis nationibus, Cic , pugnā, Caes , armis, Caes , mecum contentione dicendi is locus, ubi Demosthenes et Aeschines inter se decertare soliti sunt, Cic , qua de re jure decertari oporteret, armis non contendere, Cic

dēcessio -ōnis, f (decedo), *a going away, departure* (opp accessio) **A.** Gen , tua decessio Cic **B.** Esp **1,** *the departure of a governor from his province* at the expiration of his year of office, Cic , **2,** *lessening, diminution* non enim tam cumulus bonorum jucundus esse potest quam molesta discessio, Cic.

dēcessor ōris, m (decedo), *one who retires from an office, a predecessor*, successori decessor invidit, Cic

dēcessus ūs, m (decedo), *a going away, departure* **I.** Gen , Dionysii, Nep **II.** Esp **A** *the retirement of a magistrate from office*, post M Bruti decessum, Cic **B.** **1,** *death*, amicorum, Cic , **2,** of water, *ebb*, aestus, Caes

dĕcet -cuit, 2 (root DEC or DIC, whence also dignus), *it becomes, it fits* **A.** Lit , quem decet muliebris ornatus, Cic , quem tenues decuere togae nitidique capilli Hor **B.** Transf , *it beseems, it is fitting it suits*, id enim maxime quemque decet, quod est cuiusque maxime suum, Cic , et quod decet honestum est et quod honestum est decet, Cic , oratorem irasci minime decet, Cic , with infin , exemplis grandioribus decuit uti, Cic ; absol , quo majorem spem habeo nihil fore aliter ac deceat, Cic

Decetia -ae, f *a town of the Aedui on the Liger, now Decize*

1 **dēcĭdo** -cidi, 3 (de and cado), *to fall down*, absol or with ex, ab, de, or abl alone **A.** Lit , **1,** of things, **a,** of water, si decidit imber, Hor , **b,** of things that fall naturally, poma, si matura et cocta, decidunt, Cic , fig , ficta omnia celeriter tamquam flosculi decidunt, Cic , **c,** of buildings, *to fall down*, celsae graviore casu decidunt turres, Hor , **2,** of persons, **a,** decidere equo, Caes , in praeceps, *headlong*, Ov , fig , ex astris decidere, *to fall from the height of happiness*, Cic , **b,** *to die* scriptor abhinc annos centum qui decidit, Hor **B.** Transf , *to sink, fall*, postquam a spe societatis Prusiae decidit, Liv , in hanc fraudem tuam tam scelestam ac tam nefariam decidisti, Cic

2 **dēcīdo** -cīdi -cīsum, 3 (de and caedo). **A.** Lit , *to hew off, cut off*, aures, Tac , pennas, Hor **B.** Transf , **a,** *to cut short*, post decisa negotia, Hor , **b,** *to decide* or *determine a dispute*, quibus omnibus rebus actis atque decisis, Cic , per te, C Aquili, decidit P Quinctius quid liberis eius dissolveret, Cic , sine me cum Flavio decidisti, Cic

dĕciēs (-iens), adv (decem), *ten times*, Cic

dĕcima (dĕcŭma) -ae, f (decimus), *a tenth part, tithe*, **a,** as an offering to the gods, Orestis nuper prandia in semitis decumae nomine magno honori fuerunt, Cic , **b,** *a tax paid by land owners in the provinces*, decuma hordei, Cic

dĕcĭmānus (dĕcŭmānus) a -um (decimus, decumus) **I.** **1,** *relating to the provincial tax of a tenth*, ager, *the land paying a tenth*, Cic , frumentum, *a tithe of corn*, Cic , subst , **dĕcĭmānus** -i, m *the farmer of such a tax*, Cic , mulier decumana or simply decumana -ae, f (sarcastically), *the wife of a farmer of the taxes*, Cic , **2,** milit t t , **a,** *belonging to the tenth legion*, Tac , **b,** *belonging to the tenth cohort*, porta, *the gate of a Roman camp farthest from the enemy*, so called because the tenth cohorts of the legions were there stationed **II.** Meton , *large, immense*, acipenser, ap Cic

dĕcĭmo (dĕcŭmo), 1 (decimus) *to select every tenth man for punishment, to decimate*, Suet

dĕcĭmus (dĕcŭmus) -a um **A.** Lit , *the tenth*, Cic , adv , decimum, *for the tenth time*, Liv **B.** Meton , *large, vast, great*, unda, Ov Subst , **dĕcĭmum** -i, n *tenfold*, ager efficit cum decimo, Cic

dēcĭpio cēpi -ceptum, 3 (de and capio) **I.**

to cheat, cozen, deceive; novem homines honestissimos, Cic.; exspectationes, Cic. **II.** Esp. of time, *to beguile*; sic tamen absumo decipioque diem, Ov.

dēcīsĭo -ōnis, f. (2. decido), *a decision*; decisionem facere, Cic.

Dĕcius -a -um, *name of a Roman gens, the most famous members of which, P. Decius Mus, father and son, devoted themselves to death in battle to save the state.*

dēclāmātĭo -ōnis, f. (declamo), **1,** *loud, violent speaking, declamation*; non placet mihi declamatio (candidati) potius quam persalutatio, Cic.; **2,** *practice in oratory*; quotidiana, Cic.

dēclāmātōrius -a -um (declamator), *relating to declamation, declamatory, rhetorical*, Cic.

dēclāmĭto, 1. (freq. of declamo), **a,** *to speak loudly, declaim*; Graece apud Cassium, Cic.; **b,** *to practise*; causas, *to plead for the sake of practice*, Cic.

dēclāmo, 1. **1,** *to speak loudly and violently*; contra me, *to declaim against*, Cic.; **2,** *to practise speaking in public*; **a,** intransit., ad fluctum aiunt declamare solitum Demosthenem, Cic.; **b,** transit., *to declaim*; quae mihi iste visus est ex alia oratione declamare, quam in alium reum commentaretur, Cic.

dēclārātĭo -ōnis, f. (declaro), *a declaration, revealing*; animi tui, Cic.

dēclāro, 1. *to make clear* or *distinct, reveal, declare.* **A.** Lit., **a,** praesentiam saepe divi suam declarant, Cic.; **b,** *to declare, pronounce, proclaim*; aliquem consulem, Cic.; Numa declaratus rex, Liv. **B.** transf., *to explain, make clear, declare*; **a,** volatibus avium res futuras declarari, Cic.; with infin., quod plurimis locis perorationes nostrae voluisse nos atque animo contendisse declarant, Cic.; with relat. sent., declaravit quanti me faceret, Cic.; absol., res declarat, Cic.; **b,** *to signify, mean*; verba idem declarantia, *synonyms*, Cic.

dēclīnātĭo -ōnis, f. (declino). **A.** Lit., *a bending away, a turning aside*; tuas petitiones parvā quādam declinatione effugi, Cic.; declinatio atomi, Cic. **B.** Transf., **a,** *an avoiding, declining, turning away from*; appetitio et declinatio naturalis, Cic.; **b,** rhet. t. t., *a digression*, declinatio brevis a proposito, Cic.

dēclīno, 1. *to bend aside, turn away.* **I.** Gen., **A.** Lit., **a,** transit., si quo ego inde agmen declinare voluissem, Liv.; **b,** intransit., Cumanae cohortes declinavere paululum, Liv.; declinare de via, Cic.; esp. of atoms, declinare dixit atomum perpaulum, Cic. **B.** Transf., **1,** transit., ut declinet a proposito deflectatque sententiam, Cic.; **2,** intransit., **a,** de statu suo, Cic.; a religione officii, Cic.; **b,** of orators, writers, *to digress*; aliquantum a proposito, Cic. **II.** *to avoid, shun*; **1,** lit., urbem unam mihi amoenissimam, Cic.; **2,** transf., vitia, Cic.

dēclīvis -e (de and clivus), *bent* or *inclined downwards, sloping*; collis aequaliter declivis ad flumen, Caes.; ripa, Ov. Subst., **dēclīve** -is, n. *a declivity*; per declive se recipere, Caes.

dēclīvĭtas -ātis, f. (declivis), *a declivity*, Caes.

dēcoctor -ōris, m. (decoquo), *a spendthrift, bankrupt*, Cic.

dēcollo, 1. (de and collum), *to behead*, Suet.

dēcŏlor -ōris, *discoloured.* **A.** Lit., decolor ipse suo sanguine Rhenus, Ov. **B.** Transf., *deteriorated*; deterior paulatim ac decolor aetas, Verg.

dēcŏlōrātĭo -ōnis, f. (decoloro), *a discolouring*, Cic.

dēcŏlōro, 1. (decolor), *to discolour*; quod mare Dauniae non decoloravere caedes, Hor.

dēcŏquo -coxi -coctum, 3. **I.** *to boil*; olus, Hor. **II. A.** Lit., of metals, *to melt away*; pars quarta argenti decocta erat, Liv.; fig., suavitas decocta, *insipid, washy*, Cic. **B.** Transf., absol., *to become bankrupt*; tenesne memoria praetextatum te decoxisse? Cic.

dĕcor -ōris, m. (decet), **1,** *grace, elegance*; mobilibus decor naturis dandus et annis, Hor.; **2,** *beauty*; te decor iste, quod optas, esse vetat, Ov.

dĕcōrē, adv. (decorus), **1,** *properly, fitly, becomingly*; ad rerum dignitatem apte et quasi decore loqui, Cic.; **2,** *beautifully*, Cic. poet.

dĕcŏro, 1. (decus). **A.** Lit., *to adorn, decorate*; oppidum monumentis, Cic.; templa novo saxo, Hor. **B.** Transf., *to honour*; quem populus Romanus singularibus honoribus decorasset, Cic.; haec omnia vitae decorabat dignitas et integritas, Cic.

dĕcōrus -a -um (decor). **A.** *fitting, seemly, becoming, decorous*; with infin., ut vix satis decorum videretur eum plures dies esse in Crassi Tusculano, Cic.; with dat., color albus praecipue decorus deo est, Cic.; with ad, ad ornatum decorus, Cic. Subst., **dĕcōrum** -i, n. *what is fitting, fitness, propriety*; πρέπον appellant hoc Graeci, nos dicamus sane decorum, Cic. **B.** *beautiful, graceful, handsome, adorned*; aedes, facies, Hor.; arma, Sall.

dĕcrĕpĭtus -a -um, *very old, infirm, decrepit*; aetas, Cic.

dēcresco -crēvi -crētum, 3. *to lessen, become gradually smaller, decrease*; ostreis et conchyliis omnibus contingere, ut cum luna pariter crescant pariterque decrescant, Cic.; decrescentia flumina, Hor.; cornua decrescunt, *become smaller and smaller, disappear*, Ov.; tantum animorum nobis in dies decrescit, Liv.

dēcrētum -i, n. (decerno), **1,** *a resolve, resolution, decree*; consulis, Liv.; senatus, Cic.; decreta facere, Cic.; **2,** philosoph. t. t. = δόγμα, *doctrine, principle*, Cic.

dĕcŭmānus, v. decimanus.

dĕcŭmātes -ium (decimus), *relating to tithes*; agri, *lands on which the tithe* or *land-tax was paid*, Tac.

dēcumbo -cŭbŭi, 3. (de and * cumbo), **1,** *to lie down*, either to sleep or at table, Cic.; **2,** *to fall, fall down*, used of a vanquished gladiator, Cic.

dĕcŭrĭa -ae, f. (decem), **1,** *a body of ten men*, Varr.; **2,** *a class, division*, esp. of jurors; judicum, Cic.; scribarum, Cic.

dĕcŭrĭātĭo -ōnis, f. (1. decurio), *a dividing into decuriae*, Cic.

dĕcŭrĭātus -ūs, m. (1. decurio), *a dividing into decuriae*, Liv.

1. **dĕcŭrĭo,** 1. (decuria), *to divide into bodies of ten*; equites decuriati, centuriati pedites conjurabant, Liv.; decuriare tribules, Cic.

2. **dĕcŭrĭo** -ōnis, m. (decuria), **1,** *the captain of a body of ten*; decurio equitum Gallorum, Caes.; **2,** *a senator of a municipium or colonia*, Cic.

dēcurro -curri (more rarely -cucurri) -cursum, 3. **I.** Lit., *to run down, hasten down*; summa decurrit ab arce, Verg.; ad naves, Caes.; decurro rus, Cic; esp., **1,** milit. t. t., *to make an evolution towards a lower place*; **a,** in practice or at a festival, *to manœuvre, charge*; pedites ordinatos instruendo et decurrendo signa sequi et servare ordines docuit, Liv.; mos erat lustrationis sacro peracto decurrere exercitum, Liv.; **b,** *to charge the enemy, to run down*; ex Capitolio in hostem, Liv.; ex omnibus partibus

Caes, 2, *to run in a race, run towards the goal*, nunc video calcem, ad quam quum sit decursum, nihil sit praeterea extimescendum, Cic., quasi decurso spatio, Cic, 3, of ships, *to sail*, ego puto te bellissime cum quaestore Mescinio decursurum, Cic., 4, of water, *to run down*, monte decurrens velut amnis, Hor. II. Transf, a, *to have recourse to, take refuge in*, decurrere ad istam cohortationem, Cic, ad miseras preces, Hor, b, *to finish*, prope acta jam aetate decursaque, Cic; inceptum unā decurre laborem, Verg, quae abs te breviter de me decursa sunt, *treated*, Cic

dēcursĭo -ōnis, f (decurro), *a military evolution or manœuvre, charge*, ap Cic

dēcursus -ūs, m. (decurro) I. Lit, *a running down*, in rus decurro atque in decursu, Cic; esp, 1, milit t t, a, *a manœuvre*, vilos decursu edere motus, Liv, b, *a charge, attack*, subitus ex collibus decursus, Liv, 2, of water, *running down*, aquarum, Ov II. Transf, *the completion of an office*, decursu honorum, *after filling every public office*, Cic

dēcurto, 1 *to cut off, abridge, curtail*, transf, of discourse, mutila sentit quaedam et quasi decurtata, Cic

dĕcus -ŏris, n (decet), *that which adorns* or *beautifies, an ornament, honour, glory, grace* I. Gen, A. Lit, a, of things, decora atque ornamenta fanorum, Cic, hominis decus ingenium, Cic; civitatis dignitatem et decus sustinere, Cic, b, of persons, *pride, glory*, imperii Romani decus ac lumen (of Pompey), Cic B. Meton, esp plur, decora, *exploits in war*, Liv, *renowned ancestors*, Tac II. Philosoph t. t., *moral dignity, virtue*, Cic

dĕcusso, 1 (decussis, *the intersection of two lines*), *to divide cross-wise in the shape of the letter* X, Cic

dēcŭtĭo -cussi -cussum, 3 (de and quatio) *to shake down, shake off, throw down, knock off* I. Lit., papaverum capita baculo, Liv, rorem, Verg, turres fulminibus, Liv, ariete decussi ruebant muri, Liv II. Transf, cetera aetate jam sunt decussa, *laid aside*, ap Cic

dēdĕcet -dĕcŭit, 2 *it is unbecoming, unsuitable to, unfitting*, gen with a negative A. Lit., neque te ministrum dedecet myrtus neque me, etc, Hor B. Transf, *it is unseemly, unfitting*, with infin, simulare non dedecet, Cic, falli, errare, labi, tam dedecet quam, etc, Cic, of persons, *to dishonour*, Pomponius Atticus Claudiorum imagines dedecere videbatur, Tac

dēdĕcor -ŏris, adj *unseemly, shameful, vile*, Sall

dēdĕcŏro, 1 (dedecus), *to dishonour, bring shame upon*, se flagitiis, Sall, et urbis auctoritatem et magistri, Cic

dēdĕcōrus -a -um, *shameful, dishonourable*, Tac

dēdĕcus -ŏris, n *shame, dishonour, disgrace* I. Gen, A. Lit, alicui dedecori esse or fieri, *to bring shame upon*, Cic, dedecus concipere, Cic B. Meton, *the crime, cause of disgrace*, nullo dedecore se abstinere, Cic.; dedecori militiae alicui objicere, *dishonourable conduct in the field*, Liv. II. Esp, philosoph t t, *evil, vice* (opp decus), Cic

dēdĭcātĭo -ōnis, f (dedico), *a consecration, dedication*, aedis, Liv

dēdĭco, 1 *to declare*, 1, naturam eius, Lucr., 2, *to make a return of property to the censor*, haec praedia in censu, Cic, 2, *to consecrate, dedicate a temple*, templum alicui, Cic, Junonem, *to dedicate the temple of Juno*, Cic

dēdignor, 1 dep *to disdain, scorn, reject as unworthy*, dedignari maritum, Ov, Nomades maritos, *as husbands*, Verg, with infin, sollicitare, Ov.

dēdisco -didici, 3 *to unlearn, forget*, nomen disciplinamque populi Romani, Caes, with infin, eloquentia loqui paene dedidicit, Cic

dēdītīcius -a -um (deditio), *relating to capitulation* or *surrender*, plur, deditici, *the subjects of Rome, those who had surrendered unconditionally* or *had no rights* (opp socii), Caes

dēdĭtĭo -ōnis (dedo), *surrender, capitulation*, aliquem in deditionem accipere, Caes, in deditionem venire, Liv, facere deditionem, Caes compellere in deditionem, Liv, deditionis conditio, Liv, agere de deditione, *to treat*, Caes, fit ad Poenos deditio, Liv

dēdĭtus -a -um (p adj with compar and superl), *given to, devoted to, zealous for, addicted to*, Coepio nimis equestri ordini deditus, Cic, adolescentulus mirifice studiis deditus, Cic, nimis voluptatibus esse deditum, Cic, ventri atque somno deditus, Sall

dēdo dĭdi -dĭtum, 3 I. Lit *to give up*, a, aliquem ad supplicium, Liv, aliquem telis militum, Cic., aliquem trucidandum populo Romano, Liv, b, of the conquered, *to give up, surrender*, esp, dedere se, or pass as middle, dedi, *to surrender*, dedere se populo Romano, Caes, se in arbitrium dicionemque populi Romani, Liv, se suaque omnia Caesari, Caes II. Transf *to give up to, dedicate, devote*, aures suas poetis, Cic, filium libidini Ap Claudii, Cic, se, *to devote oneself, give up oneself to*, se totum Catoni, Cic, se ei studio, Cic, deditā operā, *designedly, intentionally*, Cic

dēdŏcĕo, 2 *to cause to unlearn, to unteach*; aut docendus is est aut dedocendus, Cic; virtus populum falsis dedocet uti vocibus, *teaches them not to use*, Hor.

dēdŏlĕo -dolŭi, 2 *to make an end of grieving*, Ov

dēdūco -duxi ductum, 3 I. *to lead* or *bring down* A. Lit, 1, aliquem de rostris, Caes, ramos pondere suo, *to weigh down*, Ov, pectine crines, *to comb down*, Ov, 2, milit t t., *to lead down*, aciem in planum, Sall, 3, naut t t, a, *to spread sail*, tota carbasa malo, Ov, b, *to drag a ship down to the sea*, naves in aquam, Liv, 4, of enchantment, *to bring down*, Jovem caelo, Ov B. Transf, *to reduce*, universitatem generis humani ad singulos, Cic II. *to lead away* A. Lit, 1, aliquem ex ea via, Cic, aliquem in arcem, Liv, deducere atomos de via, Cic, 2, milit t t *to remove*, praesidia de its oppidis, Cic, legiones in hiberna Caes, 3, *to conduct, escort, accompany a person*, a, to an audience, transfuga deductus (sc) traditurum urbem promittit, Liv, b, *to accompany a person from the provinces to Rome*, aliquem secum Romam, Liv, aliquem deducere ex ultimis gentibus, Cic., c, *to take to a house as a guest*, aliquem ad Janitorem quendam hospitem, Cic, d, *to take under an escort* or *guard*, deducere Lentulum in carcerem, Sall, e, *to accompany* (as a sign of respect) *a statesman from his house to the forum* or *senate*, haec ipsa sunt honorabilia assurgi, deduci, reduci, Cic, magnam affert opinionem, magnam dignitatem quotidiana in deducendo frequentia, Cic, aliquem ad forum, Cic, f, *to accompany a bride to the house of a bridegroom*, virginem ad aliquem, Liv, 4, *to lead forth, conduct colonists, to found a colony*, coloniam, Cic, deducere colonos lege Julia Capuam, Caes, 5, *to bring before a court of law*, aliquem ad hoc judicium, Cic 6, of water, *to bring*, aquam Albanam id utilitatem agri suburbani, Cic, 7, *to dispossess*, ex ea possessione Antiochum, Liv, esp as legal t t, moribus deducere, *to make an entry on land for the sake of having the right* *possession tried*; aliquem de fundo (with or without moribus), Cic. **B.** Transf., **a,** *to lead away from, turn away from*; aliquem ab humanitate, Cic.; aliquem de sententia, Cic.; **b,** of things, *to bring to*; deducere rem ad arma, Caes.; **c,** *to derive one's origin*; nomen ab Anco, Ov. **C. a,** *to deduct, subtract*; centum nummos, Cic.; **b,** *to spin*; levi pollice filum, Ov.; transf., *to compose* (of writing), tenui deducta poemata filo, Hor.

dēductĭo -ōnis, f. (deduco), *a leading down.* **I.** Gen., **1,** *the quartering* or *billeting of soldiers*; in oppida militum crudelis et misera deductio, Cic.; **2,** *a conducting of colonists, a colonising*; quae erit in istos agros deductio, Cic.; **3,** *a fictitious ejectment from disputed property*, Cic.; **4,** *a bringing down of water*; rivorum a fonte, Cic. **II.** *a lessening, deduction*, Cic.

dēductor -ōris, m. (deduco), *a client or friend who accompanies a candidate*, ap. Cic.

dēductus -a -um, p. adj. with compar. (deduco), *thin, fine, slender*; carmen, *light, unambitious*, Verg.

dēerro, 1. *to wander from the right path, lose one's way.* **A.** Lit., in itinere, Cic.; in navigando a ceteris, Sall. **B.** Transf., magno opere a vero longe, Lucr.

dēfătīgātĭo -ōnis, f. (defatigo), *weariness, fatigue*; membrorum, Cic.; hostium, Caes.

dēfătīgo, 1. *to weary, fatigue, tire*; **a,** physically, exercitum quotidianis itineribus, Caes.; gen. in partic. pass., defatigatis in vicem integri succedunt, Caes.; **b,** mentally, te nec animi neque corporis laboribus defatigari, Cic.; non modo censores, sed etiam judices omnes potest defatigare, Cic.

dēfătiscor = defetiscor (q.v.).

dēfectĭo -ōnis, f. (deficio), **1,** *a desertion, defection, rebellion*; **a,** lit., defectio a populo Romano, Cic.; facere defectionem, Liv.; sollicitare aliquem ad defectionem, Liv.; sociorum, Cic.; **b,** transf., a tota ratione defectio, Cic.; **2,** *a ceasing, failure, vanishing, disappearing*; **a,** virium, Cic.; **b,** of light, defectiones solis et lunae, *eclipses*, Cic.; **c,** *weakness*; defectio manifesta, Tac.

dēfector -ōris, m. (deficio), *a rebel, deserter*, Tac.

1. **dēfectus** -a -um, partic. of deficio.

2. **dēfectus** -ūs, m. (deficio), *a failing, ceasing, disappearing*; **a,** aquarum, Liv.; **b,** *a failing of light, eclipse*; lunae, Cic.

dēfendo -fendi -fensum, 3. (de and * fendo). **I.** *to repel, repulse, ward off, drive away*; defendere ictus ac repellere, Caes.; nimios solis ardores (from the vines), Cic.; defendere civium pericula, Cic.; proximus a tectis ignis defenditur aegre, Ov. **II.** *to defend, protect, guard, watch over.* **A.** rempublicam, Cic.; se telo, Cic.; vitam ab inimicorum audaciā telisque, Cic.; castra, Caes.; senatum contra Antonium, Cic. **B.** In writing or speaking, *to defend*; **1, a,** acta illa Caesaris, Cic.; se adversus populum Romanum, Cic.; **b,** (α) *to defend before a court of law*, Sex. Roscium parricidii reum, Cic.; defendere crimen, *to defend a person on a charge of*, etc.; defendere crimen istius conjurationis, Cic.; aliquem de ambitu, *on a charge of*, Cic.; aliquem in capitis periculo, Cic.; (β) *to maintain* or *assert in defence*; id aliorum exempla se fecisse defendit, Cic.; **c,** *to maintain a proposition* or *statement*; defendere sententiam, Cic.; **2,** transf. *to sustain a part*; vicem rhetoris atque poetae, Hor.; defendere commune officium censurae, Cic.

dēfēnĕro, 1. *to plunge into debt*; dimissiones libertorum ad defenerandas diripiendasque provincias, Cic.

dēfensĭo -ōnis, f. (defendo), *a defence*; **a,** by arms, castrorum, Caes.; **b,** in speech or writing, defensio miserorum, Cic.; id ad suam defensionem offerre, Cic.; defensionem alicuius or alicuius rei suscipere, Cic.; **c,** *the speech* or *writing itself, defence*; defensionem causae suae scribere, Cic.

dēfensīto, 1. (freq. of defenso), *to be wont to defend, defend frequently*; causas, Cic.; haec non acrius accusavit in senectute quam antea defensitaverat, Cic.

dēfenso, 1. (intens. of defendo), *to protect, defend*; Italici, quorum virtute moenia defensabantur, Sall.

dēfensor -ōris, m. (defendo), **1,** *one who wards off* or *averts*; periculi, Cic.; **2,** *a defender*; **a,** in war, murus defensoribus nudatus, Caes.; **b,** *a defender, protector*; esp. in a court of law, adoptare sibi aliquem defensorem sui juris, Cic.; fieri defensorem alicuius, Cic.

dēfĕro -tŭli -lātum -ferre. **I.** *to bring, bear, carry down.* **A.** Gen. amoeno ex Helicone perenni [illegible]nde coronam, Lucr.; esp., **a,** of rivers, *to carry down with them*; excipere dolia quae amnis defert, Liv.; **b,** *to change, remove to a lower place*; aedes suas sub Veliam, Cic.; acies in campos delata est, Liv. **B.** Esp. *to carry down, bear down with violence*; ruinā tota prolapsa acies in praeceps deferri, Liv.; praeceps aerii speculā de montis in undas deferor, Verg. **II.** *to bear* or *bring from one place to another.* **A.** Lit., **1,** gen., **a,** ad causas judicia jam facta domo, Cic.; commeatum in viam, Liv.; alicui epistolam, Cic.; **b,** polit. t.t., deferre sitellam, de M. Octavio, *to bring the balloting-box for voting*, i.e. *to have the vote taken about*, etc., Cic.; deferre ex aerario or in aerarium, *to bring from* or *to the treasury* (where the standards, decrees of the senate, public accounts, etc., were kept), Liv.; deferre rationes, *to give in the accounts*, Cic.; deferre censum Romam, *to send the census-lists from the colonies to Rome*, Liv.; **2,** esp., **a,** *to take away violently from one place to another, to drive, carry*; hic rumor est Asinium delatum (esse) vivum in manus militum, Cic.; **b,** as naut. t.t. *to drive away, carry*, aliquem ex alto ignotas ad terras et in desertum litus, Cic. **B.** Transf., **1,** *to offer, hand over, refer*; si quid petet, ultro defer, Hor.; alicui praemium dignitatis, Cic.; totius belli summa ad hunc omnium voluntate defertur, Caes.; rem ad amicos, Cic.; rem ad senatum, Cic.; **2,** *to communicate, report, tell*; deferre falsum equitum numerum, Caes.; vehementer te esse sollicitum multi ad nos quotidie deferunt, Cic.; esp., **a,** as legal t.t., nomen alicuius, or alicuius rei, or nomen alicui, *to inform against, to set a prosecution on foot*; deferre nomen venefici cuiusdam, Cic.; deferre crimen, *to bring a charge*, Cic.; deferre aliquid, or de aliqua re, or de aliquo, *to inform*, Cic.; deferre aliquem, *to accuse*, Tac.; **b,** polit. t.t., ad aerarium deferre, *to register*; nomina judicum, Cic.; aliquem in beneficiis ad aerarium deferre, or simply deferre aliquem, *to recommend for reward*, Cic.

dēfervesco -fervi or -ferbŭi, 3. *to cease boiling*; of the heat of passion, *to cease to rage, diminish in violence*; quum adolescentiae cupiditatus defervissent, Cic.

dēfessus, v. defetiscor.

dēfĕtiscor (dēfătiscor) -fessus, 3. dep. *to become tired, grow weary*; gen. found in perf. partic., **dēfessus** -a -um, *weary, tired*; defessus cultu agrorum, Cic.

dēfĭcio -fēci -fectum 3. (de and facio). **I.** Intransit. or reflex., **1,** *to rebel, revolt*; **a,** lit., ab rege, Sall.; a republica, Cic.; ad Poenos, *to go over to the Carthaginians*, Liv.; **b,** transf., ab amicitia, Cic.; a virtute, Liv.; **2,** *to fail, cease, become less*; **a,** of the sun or moon, *to become eclipsed*; sol deficiens, Cic.; of fire, *to go out*; ubi ignem deficere extremum videbat, Verg ; of water, *to retire, fail*, utcumque exaestuat aut deficit mare, *flows or ebbs*, Liv ; deficiunt laesi carmine fontis aquae, Ov ; **b,** of number, quantity, etc *to become less, fail*, non materia, non frumentum deficere poterat, Caes ; nec vero levitatis Atheniensium exempla deficiunt, Cic ; **c,** of time, *to fail, to be too short for*, dies deficiat, si velim paupertatis causam defendere, Cic ; **d,** of strength, etc *to fail, become weak*, ne vox viresque deficerent, Cic ; nisi memoria defecerit, Cic., et simul lassitudine et procedente jam die fame etiam deficere, Liv ; animo deficere, *to lose heart*, Caes , Cic ; absol *to be disheartened*, ne unā plagā acceptā patres conscripti conciderent, ne deficerent, Cic **II.** Transit , **a,** act , *to abandon, leave, fail*, quoniam me Leontina civitas atque legatio propter eam quam dixi causam deficit, Cic., ipsos res frumentaria deficere coepit, Caes , dolor me non deficit, Cic ; **b,** pass defici *to be abandoned by, to be wanting in*, defici a viribus, Caes , mulier abundat audaciā, consilio et ratione deficitur, Cic., sanguine defecti artus, *bloodless*, Ov

dēfīgo -fixi -fixum, 3 *to fix* or *fasten into* **I.** Lit , sudes sub aqua, Caes , sicam in consulis corpore, Cic , tellure hastas, Verg **II.** Transf , **a,** *to fix the eyes* or *the mind on something*, omnes vigilias, curas, cogitationes in reipublicae salute defigere, Cic ; Libyae defixit lumina regnis, Verg , in cogitatione defixum esse, *to be deep in thought*, Cic., **b,** *to make fast*, virtus est una altissimis radicibus defixa, Cic ; **c,** *to fix in amazement, make motionless* with astonishment, etc ; defixerat pavor cum admiratione Gallos, Liv , partic , defixus, *motionless with astonishment, fear*, etc , quum silentio defixi stetissent, Liv ; **d,** *to imprint firmly ;* in oculis omnium sua furta atque flagitia defixurus sum, Cic ; **e,** religious t t *to declare, denounce*, quae augur injusta, nefasta, vitiosa, dira defixerit, Cic ; **f,** of enchantment, *to bind by a spell, to curse*, regis Iolciacis animum defigere votis, Verg

dēfingo -finxi -fictum, 3 *to form, mould, fashion*, Hor.

dēfīnĭo, 4 *to inclose within limits, to bound* **A.** Lit eius fundi extremam partem oleae directo ordine definiunt, Cic **B.** Transf , **1,** *to fix, define, determine*, ii qui mala dolore, bona voluptate definiunt, Cic , esp. **a,** logical t.t *to define, give a definition of*, rem definire verbis, Cic ; **b,** *to fix*, suum cuique locum, Caes ; **2,** *to confine within limits, restrain*, non vagabitur oratio mea longius atque eis fere ipsis definietur viris, etc , Cic

dēfīnītē, adv with superl. (definitus), *definitely, distinctly*, lex Gellia et Cornelia quae definite potestatem Pompejo civitatem donandi dederat, Cic

dēfīnītĭo -ōnis, f (definio), *a definition*, **a,** verborum omnium definitiones, Cic ; **b,** *a fixing*, judiciorum aequorum, Cic

dēfīnītīvus -a -um (definio), *relating to definition* or *explanation, explanatory*, constitutio, Cic

dēfīnītus -a -um, p adj (from definio), *definite, distinct*, constitutio, Cic , causa, Cic

dēfīo -fieri, pass. of deficio, *to fail*, numquamne causa defiet, cur victi pacto non stetis, Liv , lac mihi non aestate novum, non frigore defit, Verg

dēflăgrātĭo -ōnis, f (deflagro), *a burning, consuming by fire*, terrarum, Cic.

dēflăgro, 1 *to be burnt down, to be consumed by fire* **A.** Lit., quum curia Saliorum deflagrasset, Cic , Phaethon ictu fulminis deflagravit, Cic., part pass , deflagratus, *consumed*, Cic. **B.** Transf , *to cease burning, to abate cool*, interdum spes animum subibat deflagrare iras vestras, Liv ; deflagrante paulatim seditione, Tac

dēflecto -flexi -flexum, 3 **I.** Transit., **A.** Lit., **a,** *to bend down*, tenerum prono pondere corpus, Cat., **b,** *to turn aside*, amnes in alium cursum, Cic **B.** Transf , declinare a proposito et deflectere sententiam, Cic **II.** Intransit , *to turn aside, turn away*, **a,** de via, Cic , a veritate, Cic ; **b,** of speech, *to digress*, oratio redeat illuc unde deflexit, Cic

dēflĕo -flēvi -flētum, 2 **1,** *to bewail, weep for* impendentes casus inter se, Cic , alicuius mortem, Cic ; **2,** *to speak with tears*, haec ubi deflevit, Verg

dēflōresco -flōrui, 3 **A.** Lit , *to shed blossom, to fade*, idem (flos) quum tenui carptus defloruit ungui, Cat **B.** Transf , *to lose bloom, wither*, cum corporibus vigere et deflorescere animos, Liv , meton , amores mature et celeriter deflorescunt, Cic

dēflŭo -fluxi, 3 **I.** *to flow down* **A.** Lit , **a,** of water, etc , sudor a capite, Cic , humor saxis, Hor , Rhenus in plures defluit partes, Caes ; **b,** of things not liquid *to float ;* dolia medio amni defluxerunt, Liv , *to swim down*, secundo amni, Verg , *to sail down*, cum paucis navigiis secundo amni, Liv **B.** Transf , *to fall down, descend, glide down*, **1,** quum ipsae defluebant coronae, Cic , of dress, hair, etc , *to fall*, pedes vestis defluxit ad imos, Verg , rusticius tonso toga defluit, Hor , of horsemen, moribundus Romanus labentibus super corpus armis ad terram defluxit, Liv , **2,** abstr , **a,** *to be derived*, quodsi inest in hominum genere mens, fides, virtus, concordia, unde haec in terras nisi a superis defluere potuerunt, Cic , **b,** *to fall to the lot of*, multaque merces tibi defluat aequo ab Jove Neptunoque, Hor , **c,** *to change to*, a necessariis artificiis ad elegantiora defluximus, Cic **II.** *to flow away, disappear, be lost*, **a,** of hair, etc , extemplo tristi medicamine tactae defluxere comae, Ov , **b,** of persons, ex novem tribunis unus me absente defluxit, *has proved false to me*, Cic , **c,** of time, *to disappear, cease*, ubi salutatio defluxit ? Cic

dēfŏdĭo -fōdi -fossum, 3 **I.** **1,** *to dig in, to cover with earth*, signum septem pedes altum in terram defodi, Liv , **2,** *to conceal by digging, bury*, thesaurum sub lecto, Cic , aliquem humo, Ov , Menucia Vestalis viva defossa est scelerato campo, Liv **II** *to dig up*, terram, Hor

dēfōrmātĭo -ōnis, f (deformo), *a deforming, disfiguring* **I.** Lit., corporis et coloris, Cic **II.** Transf , tantae majestatis, *degradation*, Liv

dēformis -e, adj with compar and superl (de and forma), **I.** *deformed, misshapen, ugly* **A.** Lit , **a,** of persons or animals, *deformed in body*, deformem natum esse, Cic , jumenta parva atque deformia, Caes ; **b,** of things, *ugly, disgusting*, foeda omnia ac deformia visa, Liv , aspectus deformis atque turpis, Cic **B.** Transf , **a,** *disgraced, disgraceful*, patriae solum deformis belli malis, Liv , **b,** *hateful, foul, shameful*, ira, deforme malum, Ov , deforme est, foll by infin , Cic **II** *formless, shapeless*, deformes animae, Ov

dēformĭtas -ātis, f (deformis), *deformity, ugliness* **I** Lit , corporis, Cic , oris, Tac **II.** Transf , *disgrace, dishonour*, illius fugae negligentiaeque deformitas, Cic

1 **dēformo,** 1 *to form, fashion, delineate ;* transf , ille quem supra deformavi, *whom I have formerly described*, Cic

2 **dēformo,** 1 (de and forma) **A.** Lit , *to bring out of form and shape, disarrange*, **a,** of persons, deformatus corpore, *deformed in body*

Cic, **b,** of things, parietes nudos ac deformatos reliquit, Cic **B.** Transf, *to disgrace, dishonour*, victoriam clade, Liv, homo vitiis deformatus, Cic

dēfraudo, 1 *to deceive, defraud, cheat*, aures, Cic, aliquem, with abl of thing, aliquem ne andabatā quidem, Cic

dēfrēnātus -a -um (de and freno), *unbridled, unrestrained*, cursus, Ov

dēfrico -fricŭi -fricātum, and -frictum, 1 *to rub, rub hard* dentes, Ov, fig, urbem sale multo, *to satirise, lash*, Hor

dēfringo -frēgi -fractum, 3 (de and frango), *to break off*, ramum arboris, Cic, ferrum ab hasta, Verg

dēfrŭtum -i, n (for defervitum sc mustum), *must or new wine boiled down to a small portion of its original quantity*, Verg

dēfŭgio -fūgi, 3 **I.** Intransit, *to flee away*, armis abjectis totum sinistrum cornu defugit, Liv **II.** Transit., *to fly from, avoid, get out of the way of*, proelium, Caes, judicia, Cic, auctoritatem consulatus sui, Cic, eam disputationem, Cic

dēfundo -fūdi -fūsum, 3 *to pour down, pour out*, **a,** vinum, Hor, aurea fruges Italiae pleno defundit Copia cornu, Hor, **b,** *to pour a libation*, defunde merum pateris, Hor

dēfungor -functus sum, 3 dep *to finish, complete, discharge, perform, be relieved of an office or duty*, **a,** defunctus honoribus, *having filled all public offices*, Cic, periculis, Cic, proelio, bello, Liv, laboribus, Hor, defunctum bello barbiton, *discharged from the warfare of love*, Hor, **b,** vitā defungi, *to die*, Verg, absol, defuncta (est) virgo Vestalis Laelia, Tac

dēgĕnĕr -ĕris (de and genus) **A.** Lit, *unworthy of one's race, not genuine, degenerate;* Neoptolemus, *unworthy of his father*, Verg, hi jam degeneres sunt, mixti et Gallograeci vere, quod appellantur, Liv **B.** Transf, *morally degenerate, unworthy, ignoble*, patriae non degener artis, Ov, non degener ad pericula, Tac., ceterorum preces degeneres fuere ex metu, Tac

dēgĕnĕro, 1 (degener) **I.** Intransit, *to become unlike one's race or kind, to fall off, degenerate* **A.** Lit, Macedones in Syros Parthos Aegyptios degenerarunt, Liv, poma degenerant sucos oblita priores, Verg **B.** Transf, *to degenerate morally*, ab hac perenni contestataque virtute majorum, Cic., in Persarum mores, Liv. **II.** Transit, **a,** *to cause to degenerate*, ni degeneratum in aliis huic quoque decori offecisset, Liv, **b,** *to dishonour, stain by degeneracy;* propinquos, Prop

dēgo, dēgi, 3 (for deigo, from de and ago), *to pass time*, omne tempus aetatis sine molestia, Cic, vitam in egestate, Cic, in beatorum insulis immortale aevum, Cic, senectam turpem, Hor, absol, *to live*, ille potens sui laetusque deget, Hor.

dēgrandĭnat, impers *it ceases to hail*, Ov

dēgrăvo, 1 **A.** Lit, *to press down, oppress*, degravat Aetna caput, Ov, quae (duo millia) illatis ex transverso signis degravabant prope circumventum cornu, Liv **B.** Transf, *to weigh down, impede, distress*, quia vulnus degravabat, Liv

dēgrĕdior -gressus, 3 dep (de and gradior), *to step, march, walk down*, degressus ex arce, Liv, monte, colle, Sall, in aequum, Liv; in campum, Liv, ad pedes, *to dismount*, Liv

dēgusto, 1 **A.** Lit, *to taste*, **a,** of persons, inde, Sall, nec degustanti lotos amara fuit, Ov, **b,** of things, celeri flammā tigna trabesque (of fire), *to lick*, Lucr, of a weapon, *to graze;* summum vulnere corpus, Verg **B.** Transf, *to try, make a trial of*, genus hoc exercitationum, Cic, *to sound*, eorum, apud quos aliquid aget aut erit acturus, mentes sensusque degustet, Cic

dĕhinc, adv *from here, hence, henceforth* **I.** Of space **A.** Lit, Tac **B.** Transf, of the order of succession, *hereupon*, Hor **II.** Of time, **a,** *from this time, henceforth*, me L Tarquinium Superbum quacumque dehinc vi possum exsecuturum, Liv, **b,** *thereupon*, Eurum ad se Zephyrumque vocat, dehinc talia fatur, Verg; **c,** *then*, corresponding with primum, *in the second place*, Sall (dehinc sometimes one syllable, Verg Ov)

dĕhisco -hivi or hii, 3 *to gape, open, split*, terra dehiscat mihi, *may the earth swallow me up*, Verg, dehiscens intervallis hostium acies, Liv

dĕhŏnestāmentum -i, n (dehonesto), *a blemish, deformity, disgrace*, corporis, Sall, amicitiarum, Tac

dĕhŏnesto, 1 *to dishonour, disgrace*, famam, Tac, Liv

dĕhortor, 1 dep *to advise to the contrary, to dissuade*, aliquem, Cic, aliquem ab aliquo, Sall, with infin, plura scribere dehortatur me fortuna, Sall

Dēĭănīra -ae, f (Δηιάνειρα), *daughter of Oeneus, sister of Meleager, wife of Hercules, whose death she caused by sending him a garment poisoned with the blood of Nessus*

deicio, v dejicio

Dēĭdămīa -ae, f (Δηιδάμεια), *daughter of Lycomedes, king in Scyrus, mother of Pyrrhus by Achilles*

dĕin, v deinde

dĕinceps, adv (dein and capio), *one after another, successively* **a,** *in space*, tres deinceps turres cum ingenti fragore prociderunt, Liv, **b,** *in time*, quos (tres fratres) video deinceps tribunos plebis per triennium fore, Cic, **c,** *in order of succession*, P Sulpicius qui deinceps eum magistratum petiturus putabatur, Cic, corresponding to primus, primum est officium ut se conservet in naturae statu, deinceps ut, etc, Cic (deinceps, dissyll, Hor, Sat ii 8 80)

dĕindĕ and **dĕin** (for deim, from de and locat suff -im), adv **a,** of space, *thereupon, from that place*, via tantum interest perangusta, deinde paulo latior patescit campus, Liv, **b,** of time, *thereafter, thereupon, then, afterwards*, Cimbrum Gambrinium statim ad me vocavi, deinde item accessitur, etc, Cic, corresponding with primum, principio (initio), prius, inde, post, postremo, etc, Caesar primum suo, deinde omnium ex conspectu remotis equis, Caes, with other adverbs, tum deinde, Liv, deinde postea, Cic, etc, **c,** in narration or order of succession, *then, next;* ut a prima congressione maris ac feminae, deinde a progenie, etc., Cic., corresponding with primum, primum ... deinde, Cic (e. in classical poets, one syllable)

Dēĭŏnĭdes -ae, m (Δηϊονίδης), *son of Deione and Apollo, i e, Miletus*

Dēĭŏpēa -ae, f (Δηιόπεια), *one of the nymphs of Juno*

Dēĭphŏbē -ēs, f (Δηϊφόβη), *daughter of Glaucus*

Dēĭphŏbus -i, m (Δηΐφοβος), *son of Priam, husband of Helen after the death of Paris*

dējectio -ōnis, f (dejicio), *a throwing down*, legal t t *ejectment from property*, Cic

1 **dējectus** -a -um, p adj (from dejicio), **1,** *low lying*, equitatus noster dejectis locis constiterat, Caes; **2,** *dispirited, dejected*, Verg.

2 **dējectus** -ūs (dejicio), **1,** *a throwing down, hurling down*, arborum, Liv, **2,** *declivity, depression*, collis, Caes

dejĕro = dejuro (q v)

dējĭcĭo -jēci -jectum, 3 (de and jacio), *to throw, cast, hurl down* **I.** Lit **A.** Gen , aliquem de ponte in Tiberim, Cic , librum in mare, Cic **B.** Esp **1,** se dejicere, or pass dejici, *to rush down* venti ab utrimque terrae praealtis montibus subiti ac procellosi se dejiciunt, Liv , **2,** *to throw to the ground*, of trees, *to fell*, Liv , of statues, *to throw down*, Cic , of buildings, *to pull down*, turrim, Caes ; **3,** *to throw lots into an urn*, quum dejecta in id sors esset, Liv , **4,** milit t t. *to drive from a position*, nostros loco, Caes , **5,** pass , dejici, naut t t *to be driven away*, ad inferiorem partem insulae, Caes , **6,** of the head, eyes, &c *to let fall*, dejecto in pectora mento, Ov , vultum, Verg , **7,** legal t t *to eject, dispossess* aratores, Cic , aliquem de possessione fundi, Cic , **8,** *to kill*, paucis dejectis, Caes **II.** Transf , **1,** aliquem de sententia, *make a person change his opinion*, Cic , **2, a,** aliquem de honore, *to deprive*, Cic ; **b,** uxore dejectā, *carried off*, Tac

Dējŏtărus -i, m *one of the tetrarchs of Galatia, defended by Cicero on a charge of murder*

dējungo -junxi -junctum, 3 *to separate, sever*, Tac

dējūro, 1 *to swear solemnly, attest by an oath*, verbis conceptis dejurare ausim neminem inimicum tantum molestiae mihi tradidisse, Nep

dēlābor -lapsus sum, 3 dep **I.** *to glide down, fall down, sink*, **a,** signum de caelo delapsum, Cic , ex equo, Liv , **b,** *of a deity, to come down from heaven*, caelo, Verg , Liv ; aliquis de caelo delapsus, *a person who comes unexpectedly to one's assistance*, Cic , **c,** of liquids, *to flow down*, ex utraque parte tecti aqua delabitur, Cic **II.** *to glide away*, hence **1,** *to proceed from, be derived from*, illa sunt ab his delapsa plura genera (sc vocum), Cic , **2,** *to fall away* from the right path, *to fall away, to fall, to come to*, **a,** in eas difficultates, ut etc , Cic , in hoc vitium scurrile, Tac , **b,** *to digress*, nescio quo pacto ad praecipiendi rationem delapsa est oratio mea, Cic , a sapientum familiaritatibus ad vulgares amicitias oratio nostra delabitur, Cic , **3,** *to fall into unawares*, medios in hostes, Verg

dēlāmentor, 1 dep *to bewail, lament*, natam ademptam, Ov

dēlasso, 1 *to weary, tire out*, cetera de genere hoc loquacem delassare valent Fabium, Hor

dēlātĭo -ōnis, f (defero), *an information against any one, accusation, denunciation*, nominis, Cic , absol , dare alicui delationem, Cic

dēlātor -ōris, m (defero), *an accuser, informer, spy*, criminum auctores delatoresque, Liv , majestatis, *of high treason*, Tac

dēlēbĭlis -e (deleo), *that can be obliterated or destroyed*, liber, Mart.

dēlectābĭlis -e, adj with compar (delecto), *pleasant, delightful, agreeable*; cibus, Tac

dēlectāmentum -i, n (delecto), *delight, pleasure, amusement*, inania ista sunt delectamenta puerorum, Cic

dēlectātĭo -ōnis, f (delecto), *delight, pleasure*, mira quaedam in cognoscendo suavitas et delectatio, Cic ; magnam delectationem habere, Cic

dēlecto, 1 (intens of delicio), *to delight, cause pleasure or enjoyment*, **a,** act , ista me sapientiae fama delectat, Cic , with abl , of the cause, aut libris me delecto aut fluctus numero, Cic , with in and the abl , ille me delectat in omni genere, Cic , with infin , quum delectabat eum defectiones solis et lunae multo ante nobis praedicere, Cic , **b,** pass , *to take delight in*, with abl , jumentis, Caes , filiolā tuā te delectari laetor, Cic , criminibus inferendis, Cic , with in and the abl , in hac inani prudentiae laude delector, Cic , in hoc admodum delector, Cic ; in hoc admodum delector quod, etc , Cic , with infin., Hor

dēlectus -ūs, m (1 deligo) **I.** Gen *a choosing, choice, selection* verborum, *a choice of language*, Cic , sine ullo delectu, *without any choice*, Cic **II.** Milit t t , *a levy, recruiting of troops, conscription*, delectum habere, Cic , conficere Liv , delectus provincialis, *a levy in the provinces*, Cic

dēlēgātĭo -ōnis, f (2 deligo), *an assignment of a debt*, a mancipe annuā die, Cic

dēlēgo, 1, *to transfer, give in charge, to entrust, assign* **I.** Gen , ad senatum, Liv ; infantem nutricibus, Tac , hunc laborem alteri, ap Cic **II.** Esp **1,** mercantile t t *to assign a debt* or *to nominate some one else to pay a debt*, alicui, Cic , **2,** *to impute, attribute, ascribe a merit* or *a fault to any one*, crimen alicui, Cic , servati consulis decus ad servum, Liv

dēlēnīmentum -i, n (delenio), *anything that coaxes, soothes, caresses, a charm, blandishment*, delenimentum animis Volani agri divisionem obici, Liv

dēlēnĭo, 4 *to soothe, win, coax, caress, charm*, mulierem non nuptialibus donis, sed filiorum funeribus, Cic , aliquem blanditiis voluptatum, Cic , animos, Cic

dēlēnītor -ōris, m (delenio), *one who soothes, cajoles, wins over*, cujus (judicis) delenitor esse debet orator, Cic

dēlĕo -lēvi -lētum, 2 *to destroy, annihilate, abolish* **I.** Of things, **A.** Gen , urbes, Liv , Volsc um nomen, Liv , bella, *to bring to an end*, Cic , leges, Cic , improbitatem, Cic., ignominiam, Liv **B.** Esp *to efface or erase something engraved or written*, Cic , digito legata, Cic **II** Of persons, *to destroy, annihilate*, paene hostes, Caes , senatum, Cic , rarely of a single person, C Curionem delere voluisti, Cic , hostes, Caes

dēlētrix -trīcis (deleo), *that which destroys*, sica paena deletrix hujus imperii, Cic

Dēlĭa, v Delos

dēlīběrābundus a -um (delibero), *carefully considering, deliberating*, consules velut deliberabundi capita conferunt, Liv

dēlīběrātĭo -ōnis, f (delibero), *consideration, consultation, deliberation*, consilii capiendi, Cic , res habet deliberationem, *admits of*, cadit in deliberationem, Cic , habere deliberationes de aliqua re, Cic

dēlīběrātīvus -a -um (delibero), *relating to consideration or deliberation*, genus, Cic

dēlīběrātor ōris, m (delibero), *one who deliberates*, Cic

dēlīběrātus a -um, p adj (from delibero), *decided, resolved, certain*, Cic

dēlīběro, 1 (de and libra), *to weigh carefully, consider, consult about* **I.** Lit , maxima de re, Cic , deliberare de Corintho cum imperatore Romano, Liv , with rel clause, utri potissimum consulendum sit, deliberetur, Cic **II.** Transf **A.** *to ask advice*, esp of an oracle, Nep **B.** *to resolve, decide as a consequence of deliberation*, quod iste certe statuerat ac deliberaverat, non adesse, Cic

dēlībo, 1 *to take away a little, to taste* **I.** Lit , sol humoris parvam delibet partem, Lucr , oscula, Verg , fig , ut omnes undique flosculos carperem et delibem, Cic **II.** Transf **A** Gen , *to take from, to derive*, or *to enjoy*, ex universa mente divina delibatos animos habemus, Cic , novum honorem, Liv **B.** Esp , *to diminish, take away*, aliquid de gloria sua, Cic.

dēlibro 1 (de and liber), *to bark, peel the bark off*, Caes

dēlibŭo -ŭi ūtum, 3 (de and root LIB, Gr ΛΙΠ, whence λίπος, ἀλείφω) *to besmear, anoint*, multis medicamentis delibutus, Cic, delibutus capillus, Cic

dēlĭcātē, adv with compar (delicatus), *luxuriously*, delicate ac molliter vivere, Cic

dēlĭcātus -a um (adj with compar and superl (deliciae) **I.** *delightful, charming, alluring, luxurious*, comitatus, convivium, voluptas, Cic **II.** *soft, tender, delicate, voluptuous, luxurious* **A.** Lit., adolescens, Cic, capella, Cat; pueri, juventus, Cic **B.** Transf, *fastidious, dainty, nice*, est fastidii delicatissimi, Cic

dēlĭcĭae ārum, f (delicio, *to allure*), *pleasure, delight, charm, luxury* **A.** Lit, multarum deliciarum comes est extrema saltatio, Cic, ecce aliae deliciae (*pretensions*) equitum vix ferendae, Cic **B.** Transf. *the beloved object, darling, sweetheart*, amores ac deliciae tuae Roscius, Cic

dēlĭcĭŏlae -ārum, f (dim of deliciae), *a darling*, Tullia, deliciolae nostrae, Cic

dēlictum -i, n (delinquo), *a fault, crime, delinquency*, quo delictum majus est, eo poena est tardior, Cic

1 **dēlĭgo** -lēgi -lectum, 3. (de and lego), **1**, *to pick, pluck*, tenui primam ungue rosam, Ov; **2**, *to choose, select*, **a**, magistratus, consulem, Cic, aliquem potissimum generum, Cic, ad eas res conficiendas Orgetorix deligitur, Caes, optimum quemque, Cic, locum castris, Caes, **b**, *to pick out, send away*, longaevos senes ac fessas aequore matres, Verg

2 **dēlĭgo**, 1 *to bind, fasten, bind up*, naviculam ad ripam, Caes, aliquem ad palum, Cic

dēlĭno (-lēvi) -litum, 3 *to wipe off*, ex qua tantum tectorium vetus delitum sit, Cic

dēlinquo -liqui -lictum, 3 *to fail, be wanting*, esp *to fail in duty, commit a crime*, hac quoque in re eum deliquisse, Cic, ut nihil adhuc a me delictum putem, Cic, si quid deliquero, Cic, (miles) in bello propter hostium metum deliquerat, Cic

dēlĭquesco -licŭi, 3. *to melt, dissolve*; ubi delicuit nondum prior (nix) altera venit, Ov., transf, *to vanish, disappear*, nec alacritate futili gestiens deliquescat, Cic

dēlīrātĭo -ōnis, f (deliro), *folly, silliness, dotage*, ista senilis stultitia, quae deliratio appellari solet, Cic

dēlīro, 1 (de and lira, lit *to draw the furrow awry in ploughing*) *to be crazy, mad, insane, to rave*; delirare et mente captum esse, Cic, quidquid delirant reges plectuntur Achivi, *the people suffer for the mad acts of their kings*, Hor

dēlīrus a -um, adj with compar (deliro), *silly, crazy, doting*, senex, Cic

dēlĭtesco -tŭi, 3 (de and latesco), *to conceal oneself, lurk, lie hid* **A.** Lit, hostes noctu in silvis delituerant, Caes, in ulva, Verg, in cubilibus, Cic **B.** Transf, *to take refuge*, in alicuius auctoritate, Cic; in frigida calumnia, Cic, sub tribunicia umbra, Liv

dēlītĭgo, 1 *to scold furiously*, Hor

Dēlĭus, v. Delos

Dēlos -i, f (Δῆλος), *an island of the Aegean Sea, one of the Cyclades, and the birthplace of Apollo and Diana*, hence **1**, adj, **Dēlĭus** -a -um, *Delian*; folia, *the laurel*, Hor., tellus, *Delos*, Ov, subst, **Dēlĭus** -ii, m *Apollo*, Ov, **Dēlĭa** -ae, f *Diana*, Verg; **Dēlĭum** -ii, n *a place on the Boeotian coast where stood a temple of Apollo*; **2**, **Dēlĭăcus** -a -um, *Delian*, vasa, Cic, gallinarius Deliacus (the people of Delium being celebrated for their brazen vessels and for their poultry), Cic

Delphi ōrum, m (Δελφοί), *a town of Phocis, celebrated for its oracle of Apollo*, hence adj, **Delphĭcus** -a -um, *Delphian*, and subst, **Delphĭcus** i, m *Apollo*, Ov.

delphīnus i and **delphin** īnis, m (δελφίς), **1**, *a dolphin*, Cic, **2**, *a constellation so called*, Ov

Deltōton -i, n (Δελτωτόν), *the constellation called the Triangle*, Cic poet

dēlūbrum -i, n (de and luo), *a temple, shrine, as a place for expiation*, noctu ex delubro audita vox, Liv, gen in plur, *shrines, holy places*, deorum templa ac delubra, Cic

dēlūdo -lūsi -lūsum, 3 *to mock, cheat, delude, deceive*, corvum hiantem, Hor, et quae sopitos deludunt somnia sensus, Verg, absol, aliquanto lentius agere atque deludere, Cic

dēlumbis -e (de and lumbus), *nerveless, weak*, Pers

dēlumbo, 1 *to make weak and nerveless*, sententias, Cic

dēmădesco -mădŭi, 3 *to become wet*, Ov

dēmando, 1 *to entrust, give in charge*, pueros curae alicuius, Liv

Dēmărātus -i, m (Δημάρατος), *a Corinthian exile, father of Tarquinius Priscus*

dēmens -mentis, adj, with compar and superl, *out of one's mind, insane, foolish, senseless*, **a**, of persons, summos viros desipere, delirare, dementes esse dicebas, Cic., subst, in tranquillo tempestatem adversam optare dementis est, Cic, **b**, transf, of things, dementissimum consilium, Cic, minae, Hor

dēmentĕr, adv (demens), *foolishly, senselessly, madly*, Cic

dēmentĭa -ae, f (demens), *foolishness, madness, insanity*, Cic

dēmentĭo, 4 (demens), *to be mad, insane, to rave*, Lucr

dēmĕrĕo and dep **dēmĕrĕor**, 2 *to deserve well of, to oblige*; demerendi beneficio tam potentem populum occasio, Liv., servos, Ov

dēmergo -mersi -mersum, 3 **A.** Lit *to sink, to plunge into, dip under*, **1**, in water, **a**, C Marius in palude demersus, Cic, se demergere, Cic, **b**, of ships, *to sink*, tredecim capere naves, decem demergere, Liv, **2**, dapes avidam in alvum, *to swallow*, Ov; plebs in fossas cloacasque exhauriendas demersa, Liv **B.** Transf, est enim animus caelestis ex altissimo domicilio depressus et quasi demersus in terram, Cic, plebs aere alieno demersa, *over head and ears in debt*, Liv

dēmētĭor -mensus sum, 4 dep *to measure, measure out*, ut verba verbis quasi demensa et paria respondeant, Cic

dēmĕto -messŭi -messum, 3 *to mow, reap, cut down, or off*, fructus, Cic, frumentum, Liv, huic ense caput, Ov, agros, Cic.

dēmētor, dep. 1 *to measure off*, Cic

dēmīgrātĭo -ōnis, f (demigro), *emigration*, Nep

dēmīgro, 1 **1**, *to migrate, emigrate, remove or depart from a place*, ex his aedificiis, Caes, ex agris in urbem, Liv, in alia loca, Cic.; **2**, transf, hinc demigrare, *to die*, Cic, de meo statu demigro, Cic

dēmĭnŭo -minŭi -minūtum, 3 **A.** Lit, **1**, *to diminish, make less, lessen*, militum vires inopia frumenti deminuerat, Caes; aliquid de tempore, Cic, **2**, *to alienate*, praedia, Cic **B.** Transf, **a**, gen, aliquid de jure, de libertate,

Cic , **b,** esp legal t t , capite se deminuere or capite deminui, *to suffer a loss of civil rights*, Cic

dēminūtĭo -ōnis, f (deminuo), *a lessening, diminution* **A.** Lit , **1,** gen , accretio et deminutio luminis, Cic , deminutio vectigalium, Cic , **2,** legal t t , *right of alienation*, utique Fecenniae Hispalae datio deminutio esset, Liv **B.** Transf , **1,** gen., deminutio sui, *loss of honour, dignity*, etc , Tac , **2,** *loss of civil rights*, deminutio libertatis, Cic

dēmīror, 1 dep *to wonder at, to wonder*, quod demiror, Cic , with acc and infin , nihil te ad me postea scripsisse demiror, Cic

dēmissē, adv , with compar and superl (demissus) **A.** Lit , *low, near the ground*, volare, Ov **B.** Transf , *modestly, lowly, humbly, abjectly, meanly* suppliciter demisseque respondere, Cic , humiliter demisseque sentire, Cic

dēmissĭo -ōnis, f (demitto) **A.** Act., *a sinking, lowering*, storearum, Caes **B.** Pass *dejection*, animi, Cic

dēmissus -a -um, p. adj. (demitto) **I.** Lit , **a,** *hanging down*, aures, Verg , **b,** *sunken, low-lying*, loca demissa ac palustria, Caes **II.** Transf , **a,** *feeble, weak*, demissa voce loqui, Verg , **b,** *unassuming, modest*, sermo demissus atque humilis, Cic , **c,** *down-cast, dispirited*, animus, Cic , **d,** *poor, needy*, qui demissi in obscuro vitam habent, Sall

dēmītigo, 1 *to make mild, soften*, pass , *to become mild*, nosmetipsi quotidie demitigamur, Cic

dēmitto -misi -missum, 3. *to send down, to lower, let down, cast, thrust, throw, put down, cause to hang down* **I.** Lit , **A.** Gen , se manibus, *to let oneself down by the hands*, Liv , per manus, Caes , aliquem per tegulas, Cic , equum in flumen, Cic , imbrem caelo, Verg , caput ad fornicem, *to bend*, Cic , vultus, oculos, *to let fall, lower*, Ov , aures, Hor , fasces, *to lower*, Cic **B.** Esp , **1,** demittere agmen, exercitum, etc , *to lead an army to a lower position*, agmen in inferiorem campum, Liv , demittere se, *to march down*, Caes , **2,** naut t t., demittere antennas, *to lower sail*, Sall , **3,** navem demittere, *to sail down* (a river), Liv ; **4,** se demittere or demitti, *to flow down*, quo se demittere rivi assuerant pluvialis aquae, Ov , **5,** *to let the hair or beard grow long*, demissi capilli, Ov , **6,** of dress, *to let droop*, usque ad talos demissa purpura, Cic , tunica demissa, *hanging down, not girt up*, Hor , **7,** *to let fall to the ground*, sublicas in terram, Caes , **8,** *to plunge into* (of a weapon), ferrum in pectus, Tac , **9,** of places, *to let down, to cause to slope down*, molli jugum demittere clivo, Verg **II.** Transf , **a,** se animo, Caes., animum, Cic , mentem, Verg , *to lose heart, become discouraged*, aliquid in pectus, *to impress on one's mind*, Liv ; se in causam, *to engage in*, Cic , **b,** demitti ab aliquo, *to be descended from*, ab alto demissum genus Aeneae, Verg

dēmĭurgus -i, m (δημιουργός), *the highest magistrate in certain Greek states*, Liv

dēmo, dempsi, demptum, 3 (for deimo, from de and emo), *to take away* **A.** 1, lit , Publicola secures de fascibus demi jussit, Cic , barbam, Cic , 2. transf , sollicitudinem, Cic **B.** Esp , *to take away* from a whole, *to subtract, make less*, **1,** lit , partem solido de die, Hor , de capite medimna DC, Cic , **2,** transf , plus additum ad memoriam nominis nostri, quam demptum de fortuna

Dēmŏcrĭtus -i, m (Δημόκριτος), *a celebrated philosopher of Abdera, author of the Atomic theory*, hence adj , **Dēmŏcrĭtēus** (ius) -a -um, *Democritean* · subst , **a, Dēmŏcrĭtēa** -ōrum, n *the doctrines of Democritus*, Cic , **b, Dēmŏcrĭtii** -orum, m *the disciples of Democritus*, Cic.

dēmōlĭor, 4 dep **A.** Lit , *to throw down, to destroy utterly, demolish*, domum, parietem, statuas, Cic **B.** Transf , demolientes Bacchanalia, Liv.

dēmōlītĭo -ōnis, f (demolior), *a tearing down, demolition*, statuarum, Cic

dēmonstrātĭo -ōnis, f (demonstro) **I.** Lit , *a pointing out* (by the hand, by gestures, etc), Cic **II.** Transf **A.** Gen , *a representation, description*, Cic **B.** Esp rhet t t , *a laudatory style of oratory*, Cic

dēmonstrātīvus -a -um (demonstro) = ἐπιδεικτικός, *laudatory* or *declamatory*, genus orationis, Cic

dēmonstrātor -ōris, m (demonstro), *one who points out or indicates*, Simonides dicitur demonstrator uniuscujusque sepeliendi fuisse, Cic

dēmonstro, 1 *to show, indicate, point out* **I.** With the hand or by gesture, figuram digito, Cic , itinera, Cic **II.** *to point out by signs or words, indicate, describe, show* **A.** Gen , demonstrare rem, Cic , demonstravi haec Caecilio, Cic ; ad ea castra quae supra demonstravimus contendit, Caes , with acc and infin , mihi Fabius demonstravit te id cogitare facere, Cic , with rel sent , quanta praedae faciendae facultas daretur, demonstraverunt, Caes , esp in parenthetic sentences, ut supra or ante demonstravimus, ut demonstratum est, Caes **B.** Esp , **1,** legal t t., demonstrare fines, *to show a purchaser the extent of property and hand it over to him*, Cic , **2,** *to express, signify*, verba proprie demonstrantia ea quae significari ac declarari volemus, Cic

dēmŏrĭor mortuus, 3 dep *to die, die off* (used of one among a number), quum esset ex veterum numero quidam senator demortuus, Cic , in demortui locum censor sufficitur, Liv

dēmŏror, 1 dep **A.** Intransit , *to delay, loiter*, ille nihil demoratus (*without delay*) exsurgit, Tac **B.** Transit , *to stop, hinder, delay, retard*, aliquem diutius, Cic , iter, Caes , agmen novissimum, Caes , inutilis annos demoror, *drag on a useless existence*, Verg , Teucros quid demoror armis, *to restrain from battle*, Verg

Dēmosthĕnēs -is and -i, m (Δημοσθένης), *the celebrated Athenian orator*

dēmŏvĕo -movi -motum, 2 *to move away, remove* **I.** Gen , demoveri et depelli de loco, Cic , aliquem de sententia, *make a person change his opinion*, Cic **II.** Esp **A.** Milit t t or of gladiators, gradu aliquem *make a person give ground*, Liv , aliquem suo loco, Cic **B. a,** *to dispossess, remove from one's property*, populum Romanum de suis possessionibus, Cic , **b,** *to remove a person from an office*, aliquem praefecturā, Tac

dēmūgītus -a -um (de and mugio), *filled with the noise of lowing*, paludes, Ov

dēmulcĕo -mulsi -mulsum or -mulctum, 2 *to stroke down, caress by stroking*, dorsum (of horses), Liv

dēmum, adv (from de, connected with Gr δή) *at length, at last*, **1** with particles relating to time, nunc demum, *now at length*, Cic , jam demum, *now at last*, Ov , tum demum, *then indeed, then at length*, Caes , **2,** to express a climax or emphasis, esp with pron , ea demum firma amicitia est, *that and that alone*, Sall , hac demum terra, Verg

dēmurmŭro, 1 *to murmur* or *mutter over*, ter novies carmen magico ore, Ov

dēmūtātĭo -ōnis, f (demuto), *change, alteration*, morum, *deterioration*, Cic

dēmūto, 1 *to change*, animum, Plaut.

dēnārius a -um (deni), *containing the number ten*, nummus or subst, **denarius** -ii, m *a Roman silver coin, originally equivalent to ten, but afterwards to sixteen asses, worth about* 8½d *of English money*, alicui ad denarium solvere, *to pay in Roman currency*, Cic, ecquae spes sit denarii, *of being paid in denarii*, Cic

dēnarro, 1 *to narrate, tell, relate*, matri denarrat ut, etc Hor

dēnăto, 1 *to swim down*, Tusco alveo, Hor

dēnĕgo, 1 **1,** *to deny, say no*, Aquilium non arbitramur qui denegavit et juravit morbum, Cic, **2,** more frequently, *to deny, refuse, reject a request* operam reipublicae, Liv, id antea petenti denegavisse, Caes, potest enim mihi denegari occupatio tua, Cic

dēni -ae -a, num distrib (decem), **1,** *ten by ten, ten at a time, by tens*, uxores habent deni duodenique inter se communes, Caes, **2,** *ten*, bis deni, Verg

dēnĭcālis e (de and nex), *relating to death*, feriae, *a funeral feast or solemnity among the Romans* (at which the family of the person dead was purified), Cic

dēnĭque, adv **I. 1,** in the order of succession, *at last, at length*, Cic, **2,** to express a climax, qui non civium, non denique hominum numero essent, *even*, Liv, **3,** *in fine, in short*, omnia denique, Cic **II.** Like demum, nunc denique, *now indeed*, tum denique, *then indeed*, Cic

dēnōmĭno, 1 *to name*, hinc (ab Lamio) Lamias ferunt denominatos, Hor

dēnormo, 1 (de and norma), *to make irregular*, o si angulus ille proximus accedat, qui nunc denormat agellum, Hor

dēnŏto, 1 *to mark out, denote, designate precisely*, quum ei res similes occurrant, quas non habent denotatas, Cic, cives necandos denotavit, Cic

dens, dentis, m (connected with Gr ὀδούς) **A. 1,** *a tooth*, aprorum, Ov, dens eburneus, Liv, dentes genuini, *the grinders*, Cic, dentibus manditur atque extenuatur cibus, Cic, **2,** fig, **a,** *envy, ill-will, slander*, hoc maledico dente carpunt, Cic, dens invidus, *the tooth of envy*, Hor, atro dente aliquem petere, Hor, **b,** of time, vitiata dentibus aevi, Ov **B.** Transf, of things resembling a tooth, dens ancorae, Verg, dens vomeris, Verg, dens uncus, *mattock*, Verg, dens Saturni, *the sickle*, Verg

densē, adv, with compar and superl (densus), **1,** *densely*, Plin, **2,** of time, *frequently*, Cic

denseo = denso (q v)

Denselētae, v Dentheleti

denso, and **densĕo,** 2 (densus), *to make thick, to thicken, condense, press together* **I.** Gen, male densatus agger, Liv **II.** Esp, **a,** t t of weaving, *to make thick* with the reed, Ov, **b,** milit t t, *to press close together*, scuta super capita, Liv, ordines, Liv, catervas, Verg, **c,** mixta senum ac juvenum densentur funera, *are crowded together*, Hor

densus -a -um, adj, with compar and superl, *thick, close, dense* (opp rarus), **A.** Gen, silva, Cic, litus, Ov, imber densissimus, Verg, caput densum caesarie, Ov **B.** *crowded together, closely packed*, **1,** aristae, Verg, apes, Verg, frutices, Ov, **2,** of time, *following closely, uninterrupted, frequent*, ictus, Verg, amores, Verg, **3,** *vehement*, densa frigoris asperitas, Ov

dentālia -ium, n (dens), *ploughshare*, Verg

1 **dentātus** -a -um (dens) **I** *provided with teeth, toothed* **A.** Lit, si male dentata puella est, Ov. **B.** *toothed, spiked, pronged*, ex omni parte dentata et tortuosa serrula, Cic **II.** *smoothed with a tooth*, charta, Cic

2 **Dentatus,** v Curius

Denthēlēti -ōrum (Δανθηλῆται) and **Denselētae** -ārum, m *a Thracian people* living near the sources of Strymon

dentiscalpium ii, n (dens and scalpo), *a toothpick*, Mart

dēnūbo -nupsi -nuptum, 3 *to be married, to marry* (of the woman), nec Caenis in ullos denupsit thalamos, Ov, Julia, quondam Neronis uxor, denupsit in domum Rubellii Blandi, Tac

dēnūdo, 1 *to lay bare, uncover, denude*, **1,** ne Verres denudetur a pictore, Cic, transf, mihi suum consilium, Liv, **2,** *to rob, plunder*, cives Romanos, ap Cic, transf, suo eam (juris scientiam) concesso et tradito (ornatu) spoliare atque denudare, Cic

dēnuntiātio -ōnis, f (denuntio), *an announcement, intimation, declaration, threat* **I.** Gen, periculi, Cic **II.** Esp, **a,** polit t t, denuntiatio belli, *declaration of war*, Cic, **b,** legal t t, *summoning of a witness*, Cic, **c,** *warning*, quae est enim a dis profecta significatio et quasi denuntiatio calamitatum, Cic

dēnuntio, 1 **I.** Gen *to announce, intimate, declare, threaten, denounce*, proscriptionem, Cic; alicui mortem, Cic, illa arma, centuriones, cohortes non periculum nobis, sed praesidium denuntiant, Cic, with acc and infin., Gorgias se ad omnia esse paratum denuntiavit, Cic, with ut or ne with the subj, or subj. alone, Lupus mihi denuntiavit ut ad te scriberem, Cic.; with rel sent, ut denuntiet quid caveant, Cic **II.** Esp **a,** polit t. t, bellum denuntiare, *to declare war*, Cic, **b,** milit t t. *to give order*, denuntiare ut arma capiant, Liv, **c,** legal t t., of the prosecutor, (α) alicui testimonium denuntiare, *to summon a person as witness*, Cic; (β) denuntiare alicui, *to give notice of an action*, de isto fundo Caecinae, Cic, (γ) denuntiare in judicium, *to give notice to one's witnesses, friends, etc, to be present at the trial*, **d,** *to give warnings of, to forewarn*, qui (Hector) moriens propinquam Achilli mortem denuntiat, Cic., quibus portentis magna populo Romano bella perniciosaeque caedes denuntiabantur, Cic

dēnŭo, adv (for de novo), *anew, again*, **1,** = iterum, *again, a second time*; rebellare, Liv, **2,** = rursus, of that which is repeated any number of times, recita denuo, Cic.

Dēōis -idis, f (Δεωΐς), *daughter of Deo* (Δηώ, *Ceres*), i e, *Proserpina*, Ov

Dēōĭus -a -um, *sacred to Ceres*, quercus, Ov

dĕŏnĕro, 1 *to unload, disburden*, transf., ex illius invidia deonerare aliquid et in te trajecere coepit, Cic

dĕorsum, adv (for de-vorsum), *downwards* (opp sursum), indicating motion; sursum deorsum, *up and down, backwards and forwards*, naturis sursum deorsum, ultro citro commeantibus, Cic.

dēpăciscor (depĕciscor) pactus, 3 dep *to bargain for, make an agreement*, ipse tria praedia sibi depactus est, Cic, depaciscei cum aliquo ut, etc, Cic.

dēpango -pactum, 3 *to drive into the ground, to drive, fix in*, fig, vitae depactus terminus alte, Lucr

dēpasco -pāvi -pastum, 3, **1,** *to feed off, eat down*, saltus, Ov, luxuriem segetum, Verg, **2,** *to feed, graze, pasture* (found also in the dep form, **depascor** -pastus), agros, Cic, Hyblaeis apibus florem depasta salicti saepes, Verg, depasta altaria, poet = *food on the altars*, Verg;

transf, depascere luxuriem orationis stilo, *to prune down extravagance of language*, Cic, artus depascitur arida febris, Verg

dēpĕcīscor, v depaciscor.

dēpecto pexi -pexum, 3 *to comb, comb down*, crines buxo, Ov, vellera foliis tenuia, *to comb off*, Verg

dēpĕcūlātor -ōris, m (depeculor), *one who robs or embezzles*, aerarii, Cic

dēpĕcūlor, 1 dep (de and peculium), *to rob, plunder*, fana, Cic, aliquem omni argento spoliare atque depeculare, Cic, cui pro isto qui laudem honoremque familiae vestrae depeculatus est pugnas? Cic

dēpello -pŭli -pulsum, 3 **I.** *to drive away* (of shepherds), teneros fetus Mantuam, Verg **II.** *to drive down, cast down, expel, remove* **A.** Lit., **1**, gen., simulacra deorum depulsa, Cic, aliquem ex urbe, Cic, **2**, esp **a**, milit t t *to dislodge*, hostem loco, Caes, **b**, *to wean*, ab ubere matris, Verg; aliquem, Verg, **c**, naut t t, *to drive out of one's course*, aliquem obvii aquilones depellunt, Tac **B.** Transf *to drive away, keep off, turn away*, famem sitimque, Cic, suspicionem a se, Cic., aliquem de causa suscepta, Cic, de spe conatuque depulsus, Cic, aliquem tribunatu, Cic

dēpendĕo, 2 **A.** Lit *to hang down, hang from*, ex humeris dependet amictus, Verg, laqueo dependentem invenere, Liv **B.** Transf, *to depend upon*, **a**, fides dependet a die, Ov, **b**, *to be etymologically derived from*, huius et augurium dependet origine verbi, Ov

dēpendo -pendi -pensum, 3 *to weigh out* **A.** Lit *to pay*, dependendum tibi est quod mihi pro illo spopondisti, Cic **B.** Transf, poenas reipublicae, Cic

dēperdo perdĭdi perdĭtum, 3 **1**, *to spoil, ruin*, deperditus fletu, *exhausted*, Cat, deperditus in aliquā, *desperately in love with*, Cat, **2**, *to lose*, non solum bona sed etiam honestatem, Cic, paucos ex suis, Caes

dēpĕrĕo -pĕrĭi -pĕrĭtūrus, 4 *to perish or be ruined utterly*, tempestate deperierant naves, Caes, si servus deperisset, Cic, esp, deperire amore alicuius, *to be desperately in love with*, Liv, so aliquem (aliquam), Cat

dēpīlo, 1 *to deprive of hair, make bald*, Mart

dēpingo -pinxi pictum, 3 **A.** Lit *to paint, represent in painting, depict*, pugnam Marathoniam, Nep **B.** Transf, **1**, *to draw or depict in words*, vitam huius, Cic, nimium depicta, *too elaborately delineated*, Cic, **2**, *to picture to oneself in thought*, Cic

dēplango -planxi planctum, 3 *to bewail, lament*, Ov

dēplexus -a um, *clasping, embracing*, Lucr

dēplōro, 1 **I.** Intransit *to weep violently, to lament*, de suis incommodis, Cic **II.** Transit **A.** *to lament, bewail*, alicuius interitum, Cic **B.** Transf *to regard as lost, give up*, agros, Liv, spem Capuae retinendae deploratam apud Poenos esse, Liv

dēplŭo, 3 *to rain down*, Tib

dēpōno pŏsŭi pŏsĭtum, 3 *to put, place, lay down, put away, put aside* **I.** Gen **A** Lit, caput terrae, Ov, mentum in gremio, Cic, onus, Cic, arma, Caes, comas *to cut the hair*, Mart., plantas sulcis, Verg, aliquam, *to give birth to*, Cat, vitulam, *lay as a wager or as a prize*, Verg **B** Transf, **a**, *to renounce, lay aside, put an end to*, amicitias, simultates, Cic, adeundae Syriae consilium, Cic, memoriam alicuius rei, or aliquid ex memoria, *to forget*, Cic, **b**, *to lay down an office*, imperium, Cic, **c**, *to deprive of an honour or office*, triumphum, Liv **II.** Esp, *to deposit, lay up for preservation, commit to the charge of* **A.** Lit, pecuniam in delubro, Cic, obsides apud eos, Caes, pecuniam apud aliquem, Cic **B** Transf, jus populi Romani in vestra fide ac religione depono, Cic, hence **dēpŏsĭtus**, *laid out dead*, ut depositi proferret fata parentis, Verg, jam prope depositus, Ov

dēpŏpŭlātĭo -ōnis, f (depopulor), *a laying waste, plundering*, aedium sacrarum publicorumque operum, Cic

dēpŏpŭlātor -ōris, m (depopulor), *one who ravages or lays waste*, fori, Cic

dēpŏpŭlor, 1 dep *to lay waste, ravage*; Ambiorigis fines, Caes, agros, Cic (pass depopulatis agris, Caes, late depopulato agro, Liv)

dēporto, 1 *to bear, carry away, remove, convey away* **I** Gen, **a**, of persons and ships, frumentum in castra, Caes, Tertiam secum, Cic, Pleminium legatum vinctum Romam, Liv, **b**, of rivers, Nilus magnam vim seminum secum frumenti similium dicitur deportare, Cic **II.** Esp **a**, *to bring home from a province*, victorem exercitum, Cic, si nihil aliud de hac provincia nisi illius benevolentiam deportassem, Cic, **b**, *to banish for life* (with loss of civil rights and property), in insulam Amorgum deportari, Tac; Italia, Tac

dēposco -pŏposci, 3 *to ask, beg, beseech, demand earnestly* **I** Gen, certas sibi deposcit naves, Caes, unum ad id bellum imperatorem deposci atque expeti, Cic **II.** Esp **1**, *to ask an office or duty for oneself*, sibi id muneris, Caes, sibi partes istas, Cic, **2**, *to demand for punishment*, Hannibalem, Liv, aliquem ad mortem, Caes, aliquem morti, Tac, aliquem, Cic, **3**, *to challenge to combat*, aliquem sibi, Liv

dēprāvātē, adv (depravo), *unjustly, iniquitously*, judicare, Cic

dēprāvātĭo -ōnis, f (depravo), *a perverting, distorting* **A.** Lit, oris, Cic **B** Transf, animi, *depravity*, Cic

dēprāvo, 1 (de and pravus), *to pervert, distort, disfigure* **A.** Lit quaedam contra naturam depravata habere, Cic, depravata imitatio, *caricature*, Cic **B.** Transf *to spoil, corrupt, deprave*, pueri indulgentiā nostrā depravatus, Cic, mores dulcedine depravati, Cic, plebem consiliis, Liv

dēprĕcābundus a um (deprecor), *earnestly entreating* Tac

dēprĕcātĭo -ōnis, f (deprecor), **1**, *a warding off or averting by entreaty, deprecating*, periculi, Cic, in religious language, *an imprecation, curse*, deorum, *invoking the curse of the gods*, Cic, **2**, *an entreaty for forgiveness*, eius facti, Cic

dēprĕcātor -ōris, m (deprecor), *one who begs off, an intercessor*, huius periculi, Cic, eo deprecatore, *at his intercession*, Caes

dēprĕcor, 1 dep **I.** *to pray earnestly to some person or for something* **A.** Gen, **a**, aliquem, Cic, deprecari patres ne festinarent, Liv, non deprecor, foll by quominus, Liv; **b**, aliquid, *to beg for, entreat for*, pacem, Cic; with ne and the subj, unum petere ac deprecari ne, etc, Caes, primum deprecor ne putetis, etc, Cic, nihilum deprecans quin, etc, Liv; with infin = *to allege in excuse*, errasse regem, Sall, **c**, aliquid ab aliquo, *to beg for*, multorum vitam ab aliquo, Cic, civem a civibus, Cic, **d**, absol, *to intercede*, pro aliquo, Cic **B.** *to execrate, curse*, Cat **II.** *to avert by entreaty, beg off*, mortem, Caes, poenam, Liv

dēprĕhendo and **dēprendo** -prĕhendi (prendi) prĕhensum (prensum), 3 *to seize, lay* *hold of, catch* **I.** Lit, **A** Gen, tabellarios deprehendere litterasque intercipere, Caes, naves, Caes, of storms deprehensis nautis, *caught in a storm*, Verg **B.** Esp, *to surprise, catch, detect*, esp in a crime or fault, deprehendi in manifesto scelere, Cic, aliquem in adulterio, Cic **II.** Transf, **A.** *to perceive, observe, mark*, res magnas saepe in minimis rebus, Cic **B.** Pass, deprehendi, *to be surprised, embarrassed*, se deprehensum negare non potuisse, Cic

dēprĕhensĭo -ōnis, f (deprehendo), *detection*, veneni, Cic

dēpressus -a -um, p adj, with compar and superl. (deprimo), *low-lying, sunk down*, domus, Cic, convallis, Verg

dēprĭmo pressi pressum, 3 (de and premo), *to sink down, press down, depress* **I.** Lit, **A.** Gen, altero ad frontem sublato, altero ad mentum depresso supercilio, Cic, depresso aratro (sc in terram), Verg **B.** Esp **1,** *to plant or place deep in the ground, dig deep*, saxum in mirandum altitudinem depressus, Cic, **2,** of ships, *to sink*, naves, Caes, classem, Cic **II.** Transf, **A.** Gen, *to press down, depress, oppress*, fortunam meam, Cic, spes illius civitatis, Cic **B.** Esp *to put down by words*, multorum improbitate depressa veritas, Cic

dēproelĭor, 1 *to contend violently*, ventos aequore fervido deproeliantes, Hor

dēprōmo -prompsi -promptum, 3 *to bring forth, produce, fetch out*, pecuniam ex aerario, Cic, Caecubum cellis, Hor, transf, orationem ex jure civili, Cic, verba domo patroni, Cic.

dēprŏpĕro, *to hasten*, alicui coronas, *weave quickly*, Hor

dēpŭdet -puduit, 2 impers *to cease to be ashamed, to be shameless*, Ov

dēpūgis = depygis (q v)

dēpugno, 1 *to fight, struggle, contend violently*, ut acie instructā depugnarent, Caes; cum Hectore, Cic, transf, voluptas depugnat cum honestate, Cic

dēpulsĭo -ōnis, f (depello), **1,** *driving away, driving off*, luminum, Cic, doloris, Cic, **2,** in rhet, *defence*, Cic

dēpulsor -ōris, m (depello) *one who drives away, a destroyer*, dominatus, Cic.

dēpŭto, 1 *to prune, cut off*, umbras, *branches*, Ov

dēpȳgis is, *thin buttocked*, Hor.

deque, v susque deque

Dercĕtis is, f and **Dercĕtō** -ūs, f (Δερκετώ), *a Syrian goddess* (also called Atergatis), *identified with the Greek Aphrodite*

dērĕlictĭo -ōnis, f (derelinquo), *a deserting, forsaking*, communis utilitatis, Cic

dērĕlinquo -liqui -lictum, 3 *to forsake, desert entirely, abandon* **A.** Lit, totas arationes derelinquere, Cic, naves ab aestu derelictae, Caes **B.** Transf, derelictus ab amicis, Cic

dērĕpentĕ, adv, *suddenly*, ap Cic.

dērēpo -repsi, 3 *to creep, crawl down*, Phaedr

dērīdĕo -risi -risum, 2 *to laugh at, mock, deride, scoff at*, aliquem, Cic., absol, deridet, quum, etc, Cic

dērīdĭcŭlus -a -um (derideo), *very ridiculous, very laughable*, alterum deridiculum esse se reddere rationem, Liv, subst, **deridiculum** -i, n *ridicule, ridiculousness*, esse or haberi deridiculo, *to be an object of ridicule*, Tac

dērĭgesco (dirigesco) -rigui, 3 *to grow quite stiff, rigid*, derigescit cervix, Ov, deriguere oculi, Verg, Ov

dērĭpĭo -ripui -reptum, 3 (de and rapio), *to tear down, snatch away*, ensem vaginā, Verg; aliquid de manu, Cic, aliquem de provincia, Cic, (id) alteri, Cic, transf., quantum de mea auctoritate deripuisset, *curtailed*, Cic.

dērīsor -ōris, m (derideo), *one who mocks, derides, a mocker*, Hor.

dērīsus -ūs, m (derideo), *mockery, derision*, Phaedr, Tac

dērīvātĭo -ōnis, f (derivo), *a turning or drawing off of water*; aquae Albanae, Liv; derivationes fluminum, Cic

dērīvo, 1 **A.** *to turn, draw off water*; aquam ex flumine, Caes. **B.** Transf, *to turn off, divert*, crimen, Cic; responsionem alio, Cic; culpam in aliquem, Cic, partem curae in Asiam, Cic

dērŏgātĭo -ōnis f. (derogo), *the partial repeal of a law*, plur legum derogationes, Cic

dērŏgo, 1. **A.** Lit., *to repeal part of the provisions of a law, to restrict, modify a law*; huic legi nec obrogari fas est neque derogari ex hac aliquid licet neque tota abrogari potest, Cic **B.** Transf, *to diminish, take away, derogate from*, de honestate quiddam, Cic., fidem alicui or alicui rei, Cic

dērōsus -a -um (partic of an unused verb derodo), *gnawed away*, clipeos esse a muribus, Cic

dērŭo -rui -rutum, 3 *to cast down, overturn*, fig, cumulum de laudibus Dolabellae, Cic

dēruptus -a -um (*derumpo), *broken off*; hence, of places (conf abruptus), *precipitous, steep*, ripa, Liv., collis, Tac Subst., **derupta** -orum, n *precipices*, Liv

dēsaevĭo -ii -itum, 4 *to rage violently*; pelago desaevit hiems, Verg, toto Aeneas desaevit in aequore, Verg.

descendo -scendi -scensum, 3 (de and scando), *to step down, come down, descend* (opp ascendo) **I.** Of persons, **A.** Lit, **1,** gen, ex equo or equo, Sall; de rostris, Cic, monte, Verg, coelo ab alto, Verg., in ambulationem, Cic., ad naviculas, Cic., **2,** esp, **a,** descendere in or ad forum, or simply descendere, in Rome *to come down into the Forum*, in order to attend the Comitia, etc., hodie non descendit Antonius, Cic., **b,** of an army, *to descend from a height into the plain*, ex superioribus locis in planitiem, Caes, in aequum, Liv **B.** Transf, *to lower oneself, to have recourse to, to condescend to, agree to, give way to*, senes ad ludum adolescentium descendant, Cic, ad vim atque ad arma, Caes, in preces omnes, Verg. **II.** Of things, **A.** Lit, **a,** of weapons, *to pierce, to penetrate*; ferrum in corpus descendit, Liv, **b,** of mountains, *to slope down*, Caelius ex alto quā mons descendit in aequum, Ov, of the voice, *to sink*, Cic **B.** Transf, quod verbum in pectus Jugurthae altius quam quis ratus erat descendit, *sank deeper*, Sall

descensĭo -ōnis, f (descendo), *a going down, descending, descent*, Tiberina, *voyage down the Tiber*, Cic

descensus -ūs, m (descendo), *a descending, descent* **I.** Lit, descensus difficilis et artae viae, Liv, poet. with dat., facilis descensus Averni, Verg **II.** Meton, *a descending way*, descensus ripae utriusque in alveum trecentorum ferme passuum, Liv

descisco -scivi or -scii -scitum, 3 **A.** Lit, *to revolt from, desert to*, multae civitates ab Afranio desciscunt, Caes, desciscere a populo Romano, Liv, a senatu, Cic, ab Latinis ad Romanos, Liv **B.** *to withdraw, depart, diverge from, fall off from*, a pristina causa, Cic; a veritate, Cic, a se, *to be untrue to oneself*, Cic;

hence, *to fall into, degenerate to*, ad inclinatam fortunam, Cic.

descrībo -scripsi -scriptum, 3 **I.** *to transcribe, copy*, quintum "de Finibus" librum, Cic. **II.** *to describe, delineate*, or *represent in writing* or *by signs* **A.** Lit, geometricas formas in arena, Cic; carmina in foliis or in cortice, Verg **B.** Transf, **1,** *to represent in words, to describe*, **a,** of things, hominum sermones moresque, Cic, regionem aut pugnam, Cic, flumen Rhenum, Hor, **b,** of persons, *to portray*, conjugem sine contumelia, Cic, **2,** *to define, explain*, describere officia, Cic, **3,** *to mark out, arrange, classify*, rationem totius belli, Cic, jus civile generatim in ordines aetatesque, Cic, **4,** *to impose, appoint, fix, allot*; civitatibus pro numero militum pecuniarum summas, Cic, suum cuique munus, Cic, duodena in singulos homines jugera, Cic, **5,** *to divide, distribute*; populum censu, ordinibus, aetatibus, Cic

descriptē, adv (descriptus), *in order, systematically*, descripte et electe digerere, Cic

descriptĭo -ōnis, f (describo) **I.** *a copy*, descriptio imagoque tabularum, Cic **II.** *a representation by writing* or *signs* **A.** Lit, *a description, representation*, descriptio aedificandi, *plans*, Cic, numeri aut descriptiones, *geometric figures*, Cic **B.** Transf, **1,** *a representation in words, a description*, regionum, Cic, **2,** *a definition*, nominis brevis et aperta, Cic, **3,** *fixing, limiting*, expetendarum fugiendarumque rerum, Cic, **4,** *distribution*, possessionum, Cic, **5,** *arrangement, settling, division*, magistratuum, civitatis, Cic

descriptus a um, p adj with compar (from describo), *properly arranged*, ordo verborum, Cic

dēsĕco -sĕcŭi -sectum, 1 *to hew off, cut off*; partes ex toto, Cic., aures, Caes, segetem, Liv.

dēsĕnesco -sĕnŭi, 3 *to grow weaker by age*, ira belli, Sall

dēsĕro -sĕrŭi -sertum, 3 (de and sero, *to sever one's connexion with*), *to desert, forsake, abandon, leave* **I.** Gen, **1,** inamabile regnum desere, Ov, **2,** *to leave uninhabited*, agros latos ac fertiles deserere, Cic, insulas desertas, Cic **II.** *to abandon, be untrue to, desert* **A.** Lit, **1,** gen, cum amici partim deseruerint me, partim etiam prodiderint, Cic, pass, with abl alone, deseror conjuge, Ov, desertus suis, Tac, **2,** esp, milit t t, *to desert*, exercitum, Cic, exercitum ducesque, Caes, castra, Liv **B.** Transf, *to neglect, disregard*, **1,** gen, **a,** of persons, deserere officium, Cic, curam belli, Liv, nec fratris preces nec Sextii promissa nec spem mulieris, Cic, **b,** of things or abstractions, multo tardius fama deseret Curium Fabricium, Cic, a mente deseri, *to lose one's head*, Cic, **2,** esp., **a,** of religious rites, *to neglect*, publica sacra et Romanos deos in pace, Liv; **b,** legal t t, vadimonium, *to fail to appear*, Cic.

dēsertĭo -ōnis, f (desero), *neglect*, Liv (?)

dēsertor -ōris, m (desero), **1,** *one who forsakes, abandons, a deserter*, amicorum, Cic, desertor communis utilitatis, Cic, **2,** in milit t t, *a deserter*, Caes, poet, *a fugitive*, Ov, Verg

dēsertus -a um, p adj, with compar and superl (desero), *forsaken, abandoned, deserted*, locus, regio, Cic loca, Caes, deserta siti regio, Sall Subst, **dēserta** -ōrum, n *deserts, wildernesses*, Verg

dēservĭo, 4 *to serve zealously*; **a,** *to serve a person*, alicui, Cic., cunctis, Cic, **b,** *to be devoted to a thing*, divinis rebus, Cic, in a bad sense, *to be a slave to*, corpori Cic

dēsĕs -sĭdis, m (desideo), *idle, lazy, slothful, inactive*, sedemus desides domi, Liv, nec rem Romanam tam desidem umquam fuisse atque imbellem, Liv

dēsĭdĕo -sēdi -sessum, 2. *to sit idle, to be idle, slothful*, Ter

dēsīdĕrābĭlis -e, adj, with compar (desidero), *desirable*, nihil enim desiderabile concupiscunt, Cic.

dēsīdĕrātĭo -ōnis, f (desidero), *a desire, longing for anything*, Cic. (?)

dēsīdĕrĭum -ii, n (desidero) **I.** *desire* or *longing, yearning, grief for the absence* or *loss of a person* or *thing*, miserum me desiderium urbis tenet, Cic, esse in desiderio rerum sibi carissimarum Cic, me tanto desiderio afficis ut, etc, Cic, desiderio tabescere, Cic, desiderio alicuius mortuum esse, Cic, meton, *the object of desire*, desiderium meum, Cic **II.** Esp **A.** *natural desire*, cibi atque potionis, Liv **B.** *a wish, desire*, militum, Tac

dēsīdĕro, 1 (like considero, from root SID Gr ΙΔ, ΕΙΔ, *to look eagerly at*), *to long for some person* or *thing that is absent* or *lost, to wish for* **I.** Gen, **a,** of persons, aliquid, Cic, aliquid ab aliquo, Cic, aliquid in aliquo, Cic, with infin, haec scire desidero, Cic, **b,** of things, *to require, need*, res non modo tempus sed etiam animum vacuum desiderat, Cic **II.** Esp, **1,** with the notion of a fault, *to miss*, ex me audis quid in oratione tua desiderem, Cic, **2,** *to lose*, in eo proelio CC milites desideravit, Caes, quarta (legio) victrix desiderat neminem, Cic

dēsĭdĭa -ae, f (deses), *sloth, idleness, inactivity*, ne languori se desidiaeque dedat, Cic

dēsĭdĭōsē, adv (desidiosus) *slothfully, idly*, Lucr

dēsĭdĭōsus a um, adj with compar and superl (desidia), *slothful, idle, lazy*, **a,** of persons, qui nolet fieri desidiosus, amet, Ov, **b,** of things, *causing sloth*, illecebrae, Cic, delectatio, Cic, inertissimum et desidiosissimum otium, Cic

dēsīdo -sēdi and sīdi, 3 *to sink down, subside, settle*, terra, Cic, transf, *to diminish, deteriorate*, mores, Liv

dēsignātĭo -ōnis, f (designo) **I.** Lit, *a marking out, designing, describing*, personarum et temporum, Cic **II. 1,** *arrangement, order*, totius operis, Cic, **2,** *appointment to an office*, annua designatio, *nomination of consuls*, Tac

dēsignātor -ōris, m (designo), *one who arranges, an umpire at the public games*, Cic

dēsigno, 1 *to mark out, trace out* **I.** Lit, **a,** urbem aratro, Verg, fines templo Jovis, Liv, **b,** *to point out by signs*, aliquem digito, Ov, notare et designare aliquem oculis ad caedem, Cic; **c,** *to sketch, delineate*, Maeonis elusam imagine tauri Europam, Ov **II.** Transf, **A.** Gen, *to signify, allude to*, hac oratione Dumnorigem designari, Caes **B.** Esp, **1,** *to contrive, perpetrate*, quid non ebrietas designat? Hor, **2,** *to arrange, regulate*, constituere et designare, Cic, **3,** polit t t, *to nominate to an office, elect*, ut ii decemviratum habeant, quos plebs designaverit, Cic, esp, designatus, *elect*, consul designatus, *consul elect*, Cic, tribunus plebis, Cic, civis designatus (of a child not born), Cic.

dēsĭlĭo -sĭlŭi -sultum, 4 (de and salio), *to leap down*, de navibus, Caes, ex navi, Caes, ab equo, Verg, ad pedes, *dismount*, Caes, of things, ex alto desiliens aqua, Ov.

dēsĭno -sii -situm, 3 *to leave off, cease, give over, desist* (opp coepi) **I.** Transit artem, Cic, versus, Verg, poet (for desero) *to abandon*, dominam, Ov.; with infin. *to cease to;* desiit defendere, Cic.; illud timere desino, Cic.; with abl., desine quaeso communibus locis, Cic.; with genit., tandem mollium querelarum, Hor.; desinit in lacrimas, *ends by weeping,* Ov.; pass. impers., si esset factitatum, non esset desitum, Cic. **II.** Intransit. *to cease, stop, end;* in piscem, Ov.; rhet., of the close of a period, quae similiter desinunt aut quae cadunt similiter, Cic.

dēsĭpĭens -entis, p. adj. (desipio), *foolish,* Cic.

dēsĭpĭentĭa -ae, f. (desipiens), *foolishness, stupidity,* Lucr.

dēsĭpĭo -sĭpŭi, 3. (de and sapio), *to be foolish, silly, to act foolishly;* summos viros desipere, Cic.; dulce est desipere in loco, Hor.

dēsisto -stĭti -stĭtum, 3. *to desist, leave off, cease;* de illa mente, Cic.; a defensione, Caes.; conatu, Caes.; with infin. destiti stomachari, Cic.

dēsōlo, 1. *to leave solitary, to forsake;* ingentes agros, Verg.; frequently in perf. partic., **dēsōlātus** -a -um, *forsaken, desolate;* desolatae terrae, Ov.

despectĭo -ōnis, f. (despicio), *a looking down;* transf. *contempt;* humanarum opinionum, Cic.

despecto, 1. (intens of despicio), *to regard from above, look down upon.* **I.** Lit., **a,** of persons, terras, Verg.; **b,** of places, *to overlook;* quos despectant moenia Abellae, Verg. **II.** Transf., *to despise;* liberos ut multum infra, Tac.

1. **despectus** -a -um, p. adj., with compar. *despised, despicable,* Cic.

2. **despectus** -ūs, m. (despicio). **A.** *a looking down, downward view;* erat ex oppido Alesia despectus in campum, Caes. **B.** Transf., *contempt, despising;* alicui despectui esse, Tac.

despērantĕr, adv. (despero), *despairingly, hopelessly;* loqui, Cic.

despērātĭo -ōnis, f. (despero), *hopelessness, despair;* vitae, Cic.; recuperandi, Cic.

despērātus -a -um, p. adj. with compar. and superl. (despero), *desperate, hopeless;* aegrota ac paene desperata res publica, Cic.; morbi, Cic.; senes, Cic.; desperatissimo perfugio uti, Cic.

despēro, 1. *to be without hope, to despair, give up;* de republica, Cic.; honores, Cic.; sibi, Cic.; suis fortunis, Caes.; with acc. and infin., ista vera esse, Cic.; often in pass., desperatis nostris rebus, Caes.; desperatur turpiter quidquid fieri potest, Cic.

despĭcātĭo -ōnis, f. (despicor), *contempt;* in plur., odia, invidia, despicationes adversantur voluptatibus, Cic.

1. **despĭcātus** -a -um, p. adj. with superl. (despicor), *despised, despicable;* homo despicatissimus, Cic.

2. **despĭcātus** -ūs, m. (despicor), *contempt;* si quis despicatui ducitur, Cic.

despĭcĭentĭa -ae, f. (despicio), *contempt;* rerum humanarum, Cic.

despĭcĭo -spexi -spectum, 3. **I.** *to look down, regard from above.* **A.** Lit., **a,** intransit., de vertice montis in valles, Ov.; a summo caelo in aequora, Ov.; **b,** transit., Juppiter aethere summo despiciens mare, Verg.; varias gentes et urbes despicere et oculis collustrare, Cic. **B.** Transf., *to look down upon, despise;* despicere et contemnere aliquem, Cic.; partic. with gen., despiciens sui, Cic. **II.** Intransit., *to look away from,* Cic.

despŏlĭo, 1. *to plunder, despoil;* aliquem, Cic.; despoliandum templum Dianae, Cic.

despondĕo -spondi -sponsum, 2. **I.** *to promise.* **A.** Gen., Syriam homini, Cic. **B.** Esp., *to promise a maiden in marriage, betroth;* filiam alicui, Cic. **II.** Transf., **A.** Gen., *to promise, give up;* quaecumque (spes) est, ea despondetur anno consulatus tui, Cic. **B.** Esp., despondere animos, *to lose courage, despond,* Liv.

despūmo, 1. *to skim off;* foliis undam aheni, Verg.

despŭo -spŭi -spūtum, 3. **A.** Intransit., *to spit out* (a superstitious usage for averting evil); sacellum ubi despui religio est, Liv. **B.** Transit. fig., *to reject, abhor;* preces nostras, Cat.

desquāmo, 1. *to take off the scales, to scale,* Plaut.

desterto -tŭi, 3. *to finish snoring;* poet. *to finish dreaming,* Pers.

destillo, 1. *to drop down, distil;* lentum distillat ab inguine virus, Verg.

destĭnātĭo -ōnis, f. (destino), *a fixing, determination, resolution;* partium, quibus cessurus aut non cessurus esset, Liv.

destĭno, 1. (from root STAN, whence στανύω, ἱστάνω, lit. *to fix firm.*) **A.** *to make fast, bind, fasten;* antennas ad malos, Caes. **B.** Transf., **a,** *to fix, determine, settle;* tempus locumque ad certamen, Liv.; aliquem ad mortem, Liv.; debiti destinatique morti, Liv.; certae destinataeque sententiae, Cic.; with infin. *to resolve to do;* quae agere destinaverat, Caes.; quas urbes direpturos se destinaverant, Liv.; **b,** *to aim at with a missile;* locum oris, Liv.; **c,** *to fix upon, intend to buy,* Cic.; **d,** *to betroth, fix upon as a wife for some one;* Lepida destinata quondam uxor L. Caesari, Tac.; **e,** *to select, fix upon for an office;* destinare aliquem consulem, Liv.

destĭtŭo -stĭtŭi -stĭtūtum, 3. (de and statuo), *to set.* **I.** *to set down, to place.* **A.** aliquem ante tribunal regis, Liv. **B.** Transf., quum in hac miserrima fortuna destitutus sit, Cic. **II.** *to place on one side;* **1,** *to leave, abandon;* nudos in litore pisces, Verg.; aliquem in convivio, Cic.; **2,** *to leave in the lurch, forsake, desert;* aliquem in ipso discrimine periculi, Liv.; nudus paene est destitutus, Cic.; deos mercede pactā, *to cheat,* Hor.; spes destituit, Liv.; partic. perf. *abandoned;* ab omni spe destitutus, Liv.

destĭtūtus -a -um, partic. of destituo.

destĭtūtĭo -ōnis, f. (destituo), *a forsaking, abandoning,* Cic.

destrictus -a -um, p. adj. with compar. (destringo), *sharp, severe;* destrictior accusator, Tac.

destringo -strinxi -strictum. 3. **I.** *to strip off.* **A.** Gen., Quint. **B.** *to draw* or *bare the sword;* gladium, Cic. **II.** *to touch lightly, graze.* **A.** Lit., aequora alis, Ov.; pectora summa sagittā, Ov. **B.** Transf., *to satirise, censure;* aliquem mordaci carmine, Ov.

destrŭo -struxi -structum, 3. *to pull down.* **A.** Lit. *to destroy* (opp. construo); aedificium, Cic.; moenia, Verg. **B.** Transf. *to destroy, ruin;* jus destruere ac demoliri, Liv.; hostem, Tac.

dēsŭbĭto, adv. *suddenly,* Cic.

dēsūdo, 1. *to sweat violently;* transf. *to exert oneself, labour hard;* in aliqua re, Cic.

dēsuēfăcĭo -fēci -factum (* desueo and facio), *to disuse, make unaccustomed to;* multitudo desuefacta a contionibus, Cic.

dēsuesco -suēvi -suētum, 3. **A.** Transit. *to disuse, bring into disuse;* res desueta, Liv. **B.** Intransit. *to become unaccustomed to;* and in perf. *unused to;* desuetus triumphis, Verg.

dēsuētūdo -ĭnis, f. (desuesco), *disuse;* armorum, Liv.

dēsultor -ōris, m. (desilio), *a circus rider who leaped from one horse to another while both* *were at full speed*, Liv, transf *an inconstant person*, amoris, Ov.

dēsultōrius a -um (desultor), *relating to a desultor*, Cic

dēsum -fŭi -esse, *to be absent, away, wanting, to fail* **I.** Gen omnia deerant quae, etc, Caes, with dat, tibi nullum officium a me defuit, Cic, with in and the abl, desunt (verba) in C Laelii commendando, Cic, deesse, or non deesse, foll by quominus and the subj, duas sibi res, quominus in vulgus et in foro diceret defuisse, Cic, nihil deest, foll by quin, si tibi ipsi nihil deest, quod in forensibus civilibusque rebus versetur quin scias, Cic **II.** Esp **A.** *not to be present at*, convivio, Cic. **B.** *to fail, be wanting, not to keep, to leave in the lurch*, nullo loco deesse alicui, Cic, sibi, Cic; officio, Cic, non deesse, foll by quin, deesse mihi nolui, quin te admonerem, Cic, absol, nos consules desumus, *are wanting in our duty*, Cic

dēsūmo -sumpsi -sumptum, 3 *to choose, select*, sibi hostes, Liv

dēsŭpĕr, adv *from above, above*, Caes

dēsurgo surrexi -surrectum, 3 *to rise up, stand up*, coenā, Hor

dētĕgo -texi -tectum, 3, **1**, *to uncover, lay bare*, aedem, Liv, caput, Verg, quia possit fieri, ut (illa) patefacta et detecta mutentur, Cic, **2**, *to detect, disclose, betray*, insidias, consilium, Liv, culpam, Ov

dētendo (-tendi) -tensum, 3 *to unstretch*, tabernacula, *to strike the tents*, Caes

dētergĕo -tersi -tersum, 2 **I.** *to wipe off, wipe away*, lacrimas, Ov, primo anno LXXX detersimus, *got together*, Cic **II.** *to cleanse by wiping*, cloacas, Liv **III.** *to strip off, break off*, remos, Caes

dētĕrior -ĭus, genit -ōris, compar adj, with superl deterrimus (connected with detero), *worse, inferior, poorer*, vectigalia, Caes, aetas, Verg, peditatu, *weaker*, Nep, homo deterrimus, Cic, neut subst, in deterius, *for the worse*, in deterius mutare, Tac

dētĕrius, adv (deterior), *worse, in an inferior manner*, de male Graecis Latine scripta deterius, Cic

dētermĭnātio -ōnis, f (determino), *a boundary, end*, mundi, Cic, transf, orationis, Cic

dētermino, 1 *to bound, fix the limits of, determine* **I.** Lit, augur regiones ab oriente ad occasum determinavit, Liv **II.** Transf, id quod dicit spiritu non arte determinat, Cic

dētĕro -trivi -tritum, 3 **A.** Lit, *to rub off, rub away, wear out*, detrita tegmina, Tac **B** *to lessen in strength, to weaken*, laudes egregii Caesaris et tuas, Hor, si quid ardoris ac ferociae miles habuit, popinis et comissationibus et principis imitatione deteritur, Tac.

dēterrĕo -terrŭi -territum, 2 *to frighten from anything, deter by fear, discourage*, homines a scribendo, Cic, Stoicos de sententia, Cic, aliquem a dimicatione, Cic, aliquem multis verbis ne (with subj.), Caes, aliquem non deterrere quominus (with subj), Cic, nihil deterreri quominus, etc, Liv, aliquem non deterrere quin, etc, Caes; simply with acc, aliquem, Caes, with acc of thing, *to ward off*, vim a censoribus Liv

dētestābĭlis -e (detestor), adj, with compar (detestor), *abominable, detestable, horrible*, omen, Cic

dētestātio -ōnis, f (detestor), **1**, *cursing, execration, horror, detestation*, Liv, **2**, *a warding off, averting*, scelerum, Cic

dētestor, 1 dep **I. 1**, relig t t, *to invoke the curse of a god*, minas periculaque in alicuius caput, Liv, **2**, *to execrate, abominate, detest*, Ambiorigem, Caes, exitum belli civilis, Cic, partic perf (pass), bella matribus detestata, Hor **II.** Transf, *to avert, ward off*, o dii immortales, avertite et detestamini hoc omen, Cic

dētexo -texŭi -textum 3 **A.** *to plait, make by plaiting*, aliquid viminibus mollique junco, Verg **B.** Transf, *to finish* (of discourse), detexta prope retexere, Cic

dētĭnĕo -tĭnŭi -tentum, 2 (de and teneo), *to hold away, hold back, detain* **I.** Lit, novissimos proelio, Caes, Romano bello in Italia detineri, Liv, aliquem, Caes **II.** Transf, **1**, *to hold fast, fetter*, me grata detinuit compede Myrtale, Hor, **2**, *to occupy, engage*, in alienis negotiis detineri, Cic, aliquem de or ab aliqua re, *to detain from*, ab circumspectu aliarum rerum, Liv, **3**, detinere se, *to support existence*, se miserandis alimentis nonum ad diem, Tac **4**, *to detain possession of property*, pecuniam, Tac

dētondĕo tondi tonsum, 2 *to shear, clip* **A.** Lit, crines, Ov **B.** Transf, detonsae frigore frondes, *made leafless* Ov

dētŏno -tŏnŭi, 1 **I.** Lit, *to thunder, thunder down* hic (Juppiter) ubi detonuit, Ov **II.** *to cease to thunder*, transf = *cease to rage*, dum detonet omnis (nubes belli), Verg

dētorquĕo -torsi -tortum, 2 **I.** *to turn away, bend aside*, **a**, lit, ponticulum, Cic, habenas, Verg, in dextram partem, Cic, proram ad undas, Verg; **b**, transf, voluptates animos a virtute detorquent, Cic, **2**, *to twist anything out of its proper shape, distort*, corporis partes detortae, Cic, transf, calumniando omnia detorquendoque suspecta et invisa efficere, Liv.

dētractio -ōnis, f (detraho), *a drawing away, withdrawal, taking away* **I.** In a good sense, **A.** Lit, **1**, gen, doloris, Cic, **2**, esp medic t t, *a purging*, Cic **B.** Transf, *a taking away, withdrawal*, cuius loci detractionem fieri velit, Cic. **II** *taking away* (in a bad sense), detractio atque appetitio alieni, *of another person's property*, Cic.

dētracto = detrecto (q v)

dētractor -ōris, m (detraho), *one who makes less, a detractor*, sui, Tac

dētrăho -traxi tractum, 3 **I.** *to take down* **A.** Lit, aliquem de curru, Cic, aliquem equo, Liv, muros coronae, Tac **B.** Transf, *to lower, humiliate*, regum majestatem difficilius ad medium detrahi, etc, Liv. **II.** *to take away* **A.** **1**, lit, alicui de digito anulum, Cic, torquem hosti, Cic, vestem, Cic, pellem, Hor, **2**, transf, **a**, *to remove*, de homine sensus, Cic, **b**, milit t t, *to detach*, ex tertia acie singulas cohortes, Caes, **c**, numerically, *to subtract from a sum*, de tota summa binas quinquagesimas, Cic, **d**, *to take away some mental or moral evil or good*, alicui calamitatem, Cic., detracta opinione probitatis, Cic **B** *to take away, remove*, transl, **a**, inimicum ex Gallia, Cic, **b**, *to compel*, aliquem ad hanc accusationem, Cic **C.** *to drag away, take from*, **1**, lit, spolia hostium templis porticibusque, Liv, **2**, transf, **a**, alicui debitum honorem, Cic, multa de suis commodis, Cic, de honestate et de auctoritate alicuius, Cic, **b**, *to calumniate, slander*, de aliquo, Cic, absol, absentibus detrahendi causā maledice contumelioseque dicere, Cic

dētrectātio -ōnis, f (detrecto), *a refusal*, militiae, Liv

dētrectātor -ōris, m (detrecto), *a disparager, detractor*, laudum suarum, Liv

dētrecto, 1 (de-tracto), **1**, *to decline, refuse*, militiam, Caes, certamen, Liv, **2**, *to disparage, detract from, depreciate*, virtutes, Liv, bella facta Ov,

dētrīmentōsus -a -um (detrimentum), *detrimental, hurtful*, ab hoste discedere detrimentosum esse existimabat, Caes

dētrīmentum -i, n (detero), *damage, injury, detriment*, **a**, gen, detrimentum capere or accipere or facere, *to suffer*, Cic, alicui ornamento et praesidio non detrimento esse, Caes, **b**, polit t t, videant (provideant) consules or videat (consul) ne quid respublica detrimenti capiat or accipiat, Cic, **c**, milit t t., *loss, defeat*, magna detrimenta inferre, Caes, **d**, *loss of money, property*, etc, aestimando cuiusque detrimento quatuor progeneri Caesaris delecti, Tac

dētrītus -a -um, partic of detero

dētrūdo trūsi -trūsum, 3 **I.** Lit, **A.** Gen *to push away, push down, thrust down*, naves scopulo, Verg, scutis tegumenta, Caes **B.** Esp **1,** milit t t, *to dislodge an enemy from his position*, impetu conari detrudere virum, Liv., **2,** legal t t, *to dispossess, eject*, ex praedio vi, Cic **II.** Transf, **1,** *to force, compel*, aliquem de sua sententia, Cic., **2,** *to postpone*, comitia in mensem Martium, Cic

dētrunco, 1 **1,** *to lop or cut off*, arbores, Liv, **2,** *to mutilate, behead*, gladio detruncata corpora, Liv

dēturbo, 1 *to drive away with violence, cast down* **I.** Lit, **A.** Gen, aliquem de tribunali, Caes, aliquem tabula, Cic, alicuius statuam, Cic **B.** Esp, milit. t t, *to dislodge, drive off*, nostros de vallo lapidibus, Caes **II.** Transf, **A.** *to deprive*, aliquem de sanitate ac mente, Cic, deturbari ex magna spe, Cic **B.** Esp, legal t t, *to eject, dispossess*, aliquem possessione, Cic

Deucălĭōn -ōnis, m (Δευκαλίων), *son of Prometheus, king of Phthia in Thessaly, was saved alone with his wife Pyrrha from the deluge, re-peopled the world by throwing stones behind his back, which stones became men, while the stones that Pyrrha threw became women* Adj, **Deucălĭōnēus** -a -um, *Deucalionian*, undae, *the deluge*, Ov

dĕunx -uncis, m (de and uncia), *eleven-twelfths of unity*, heres ex deunce, Cic

dĕūro ussi -ustum, 3 **1,** *to burn down, burn utterly*, agros vicosque, Liv, **2,** of cold, *to destroy, nip*, hiems arbores deusserat, Liv

dĕus -i, m, nom plur dei, dii, and di, genit deorum or deum, dat deis, diis, and dis, voc sing deus (connected with Ζεύς), *a god, a deity* **A.** Lit, aliquem ut deum colere, Cic, dii hominesque, *the whole world*, Cic, of female deities, ducente deo, *Venus*, Verg; nec dextrae erranti deus afuit, *Allecto*, Ov, esp phrases, di or dii boni, Cic; (pro) dii immortales, Cic, pro deum atque hominum fidem, Cic, dii meliora (ferant), Cic, si dii volunt, Cic, si diis placet, Cic **B.** Transf, **a,** of distinguished persons, audiamus Platonem quasi quemdam deum philosophorum, Cic, **b,** of patrons, protectors, etc, P Lentulus cuius pater deus ac parens fortunae ac nominis mei, Cic

dĕūtor -ūti -ūsus, 3 dep *to misuse*, Nep

dēvasto, 1 *to lay waste, devastate*, agrum, fines, Liv

dēvĕho -vexi -vectum, 3 *to bear, carry away, convey away*, legionem equis, Caes, frumentum in Graeciam, Liv; pass., used as middle, develii (sc navi), *to sail*, Veliam devectus, Cic

dēvello -velli -vulsum, 3 *to pull, pluck, tear away*, ramum trunco, Ov.

dēvēlo, 1 *to unveil, uncover*, ora, Ov.

dēvĕnĕror, 1 dep *to venerate, worship*, deos cum prece, Ov.

dēvĕnĭo -vēni -ventum, 4 *to come to, arrive at, reach* **I.** Lit, ad senatum, Cic, poet with acc, speluncam, Verg **II.** Transf, in victoris manus, Cic, ad juris studium, Cic, in medium certamen, Cic.

1 **dēversor,** 1 dep *to lodge as a guest or stranger*, apud aliquem, Cic, in ea domo, Cic, absol, parum laute, Cic

2 **dēversor** -ōris, m (deverto), *a guest*, Cic

dēversōrĭŏlum -i, n (dim of deversorium), *a small lodging*, Cic

dēversōrĭus -a -um (deverto), *relating to the accommodation of strangers*, taberna, Plaut Subst, **dēversōrium** -ii, n *an inn, lodging*, peropportunum, Cic, emere deversorium Tarracinae, Cic, transf, *a place of resort, resting-place*, studiorum deversorium esse non libidinum, Cic

dēvertĭcŭlum (dēvortĭcŭlum) -i, n (deverto) **I. A.** Lit., *a by-way, by-path*, quae deverticula flexionesque quaesivisti, Cic **B.** Transf, *a digression*, Liv **II. a,** *an inn, lodging-place*, Liv; **b,** *a place of refuge, hiding-place*, Cic

dēverto (dēvorto) -verti (-vorti) -versum (-vorsum), 3 **I.** Transit, pass (in present tenses), devertor, with middle signification, *to turn aside from the way, betake oneself*, si qui Ebromago deverterentur, Cic, esp *to stay, lodge*, ut locum publice pararet, ubi deverteretur, Liv, fig, quid ad magicas deverteris artes, *have recourse to*, Ov **II.** Intransit., *to turn aside;* **a,** cum perpaucis via, Liv, transf, of discourse, *to digress*, redeamus ad illud unde devertimus, Cic, **b,** *to lodge, stay with, go to*, ad hospitem, Cic, ad villam alicuius, Cic.

devexus -a -um, adj with compar (de and veho), *going aside* **I.** Of motion, *moving away from, rolling from*, **a,** of space, amnis devexus ab Indis, Hor; Orion devexus, *sinking*, Hor; **b,** of time, aetas jam a diuturnis laboribus devexa ad otium, *inclining to*, Cic **II.** Of position, *sloping downwards, shelving, steep*, lucus devexus in novam viam, Cic.

dēvincĭo -vinxi -vinctum, 4 *to bind, tie fast.* **A.** Lit., aliquem fasciis, Cic **B.** Transf, *to bind, fasten, connect*, **a,** gen, illud vinculum quod primum homines inter se reipublicae societate devinxit, Cic, **b,** rhet t. t., *to connect*, verba comprehensione, Cic, **c,** *to fetter, bind* (by power eloquence, etc), urbem praesidiis, Cic, animos eorum, qui audiant, voluptate, Cic, **d,** morally, *to bind, pledge*, aliquem beneficio, Cic, se scelere, Cic

dēvinco -vici -victum, 3 **I.** *to conquer thoroughly, subjugate*, Galliam Germaniamque, Caes., Poenos classe, Cic **II.** Transf, Catonis sententia devicit, ut in decreto perscriberetur, Liv

dēvinctus -a -um, p. adj (from devincio), *bound to, devoted to*, iis studiis, Cic, devinctior alicui, Hor

dēvītātĭo -ōnis, f. (devito), *an avoiding*, legionum, Cic

dēvīto, 1 *to avoid;* procellam, Cic; dolorem, Cic

dēvĭus -a -um (de and via) **A.** Lit., **a,** *removed from the straight road, out of the way;* iter, Cic., oppidum, Cic, **b,** *living out of the way, retired, secluded;* devia et silvestris gens, Liv, esse devios, Cic, poet, *wandering*, mihi devio, Hor, uxores, *goats*, Hor **B.** Transf, *out of the way, erroneous, unreasonable*, homo in omnibus consiliis praeceps et devius, Cic.

dēvŏco, 1 **I.** *to call down;* suos ab tumulo, Liv, Jovem deosque ad auxilium, Liv, transf, philosophiam e caelo, Cic. **II.** *to call away call* *off, recall*, aliquem de provincia ad gloriam, Cic, transf, non avaritia ab instituto cursu ad praedam aliquam devocavit, Cic, sese suas exercitusque fortunas in dubium non devocaturum, Caes

dēvŏlo, 1 **I.** *to fly down* **A.** Lit., per caelum, (of Iris), Verg. **B.** Transf, *to hasten down*, alii praecipites in forum devolant, Liv **II.** *to fly away to* **A.** Lit., turdus devolat illuc, ubi, etc, Hor **B.** Transf, ad florentem (amicitiam), Cic

dēvolvo -volvi -vŏlūtum, 3 **A.** Lit **a,** *to roll down*, saxa musculum, Caes, corpora in humum, Ov, pass with middle signification, *to roll down, fall headlong*, veluti monte praecipiti devolutus torrens, Liv, **b,** *to roll off*, pensa fusis, *to spin off*, Verg **B** Transf, per audaces nova dithyrambos verba, Hor, pass, devolvi as middle, *to fall into*, ad spem estis inanem pacis devoluti, Cic

dēvŏro, 1 **I.** Lit, *to swallow, gulp down, devour*, id quod devoratum, Cic **II.** Transf, **A.** Of persons, **a,** of property, *to consume, waste*, pecuniam publicam, Cic, patrimonium, Cic, **b,** *to swallow, suppress*, lacrimas, Ov, **c,** *to devour, consume*, devorare spe et opinione praedam, Cic, **d,** *to devour eagerly* mentally, illos libros, Cic., **e,** *to swallow down, hear without understanding*, eius oratio a multitudine et a foro devorabatur, Cic., **f,** *to swallow anything unpleasant, to endure*, hominum ineptias ac stultitias, Cic **B.** Of things, me Zanclaea Charybdis devoret, Ov.

dēvortĭcŭlum, v deverticulum

dēvortĭum -ii, n (deverto), *a by-way, by-path*; itinerum, Tac

dēvōtĭo -ōnis, f (devoveo), **1,** *a consecrating, devoting* (esp to the infernal gods), vitae or capitis, Cic, P Decii consulis, Liv; plur Deciorum devotiones, Cic, **2,** *a curse*, Nep, esp *an enchantment, an incantation*, Tac, **3,** *a vow*, eius devotionis esse convictum, Cic

dēvōto, 1 (intens of devoveo), *to consecrate, devote to death*, quae vis patrem Decium, quae filium devotavit, Cic

dēvōtus a um, p adj with compar and superl (devoveo), *devoted*, **1,** to the infernal gods, *accursed*, arbor, sanguis, Hor, **2,** *devoted to any one, faithful, affectionate*, cliens, Juv; subst, **dēvōti** -ōrum, m *faithful followers* Caes

dēvŏvĕo -vōvi -vōtum, 2 *to consecrate, devote* **I.** Relig t t, *to devote to a deity* **A.** Gen, Dianae quod in suo regno pulcherrimum natum esset, Cic, Marti ea quae ceperunt, Caes **B.** Esp **1,** *to devote to the infernal gods, to devote to death*, se dis immortalibus pro republica, Cic., devota corpora (Deciorum), Liv, **2,** **a,** *to curse, execrate*, aliquem, Nep, **b,** *to bewitch, enchant*, Tib **II.** Transf, **1,** *to devote, give up*, devovere animam alicui, *for another*, Verg, **2,** se devovere alicui or alicui rei, *to devote, attach oneself*, se alicuius amicitiae, Caes

dextans -antis, m (de and sextans), *five-sixths*, Suet.

dextella -ae, f (dim of dextra), *a little right hand*; Quintus filius Antonii est dextella, Cic

dexter -tĕra tĕrum, or more freq -tra trum, comp **dextĕrior** -ius, superl. **dextĭmus** -a -um (δεξιτερός) **I.** Lit., **A.** Adj, *right, on the right hand, on the right side*, manus, Cic, latus, Hor; ab dextra parte, Caes, rota dexterior, Ov **B.** Subst, **1,** **dextera** or **dextra** -ae, f (sc. manus), *the right hand*, **a,** lit, ad dextram, *to the right*, Cic, a dextra, *on the right*, Caes, dexterā or dextrā, *on the right*, Caes, dextram dare, *to give the right hand* (as pledge of faith), Liv **b,** fig (α) *fidelity*, dominorum dextras fallere, *fidelity towards masters*, Verg (β) dextram alicui tendere or porrigere, *to help*, Cic, (γ) meā dextrā, *by my right hand, i e, power, bravery*, Ov, Hor, **2,** **dextera** or **dextra** orum, n *what is on the right, the right side*, Cic **II.** Transf, **a,** *propitious*, dexter adi, Verg, **b,** *skilful*, rem dexter egit, Liv

dextĕrē or **dextrē**, adv with compar (dexter), *dexterously, skilfully*, apud regem, liberaliter dextreque obire officia, Liv

dextĕrĭtas -ātis, f (dexter), *skilfulness, dexterity, readiness*, Liv

dextrorsum and **dextrorsus**, adv (from dextroversum), *on the right hand, towards the right*, Hor

Dīa -ae, f (Δῖα), *old name of the island of Naxos*

Diablintes -um and **Diablinti** -ōrum *m people in Gallia Lugdunensis, in what is now Dép de la Maine*

dĭădēma -ătis, n (διάδημα), *a royal head dress, diadem*, diadema alicui or capiti alicuius imponere, Cic, diadema ponere, Cic

dĭaeta -ae, f (δίαιτα), *a way of living prescribed by a physician, regimen, diet*, sed ego diaetā curare incipio, chirurgiae taedet, Cic

Dĭăgŏrās -ae, m (Διαγόρας), **1,** *a poet and philosopher of Melos, contemporary with Pindar and Simonides*, **2,** *an athlete of Rhodes, contemporary with Pindar*

1 **dĭălectĭcē**, adv. (dialecticus), *dialectically*, Cic

2 **dĭălectĭcē** -ēs, f. (διαλεκτική sc τέχνη), *the art of dialectic, logic*

dĭălectĭcus -a -um (διαλεκτικός) *relating to discussion, dialectical*, captiones, Cic; subst, **a,** **dĭălectĭca** -ae f (sc ars), *the art of dialectic*, Cic, **b,** **dĭălectĭca** ōrum, n *dialectical discussion*, Cic, **c,** **dĭălectĭcus** -i, m *a dialectician, logician*, Cic

Dĭālis -e (Διός = *Dis in Diespiter), *relating to Jupiter*, flamen, Liv, or simply Dialis, Tac, *the priest of Jupiter*, conjux sancta, *the wife of the priest of Jupiter*, Ov

dĭălŏgus i, m (διάλογος), *a philosophical dialogue or conversation*, Cic

Dīāna ae, f (old form for Jana, or Διώνη = *the daughter of Zeus*, orig Diviana = Diva Jana), *an Italian goddess, identified with the Greek Artemis, daughter of Jupiter and Latona, sister of Apollo, the virgin goddess of the moon and of hunting*, tria virginis ora Dianae, *the three forms of Diana, Luna in heaven, Diana on earth, Hecate in the lower world*, Verg, meton *the moon*, Ov, *the chase*, Mart Adj **Dīānĭus** a -um, *belonging to Diana*, Ov Subst, **Dīānĭum** -ii, n **a,** *a place dedicated to Diana*, **b,** *a promontory in Spain, now Denia*, Cic

dĭārĭum -ii, n (dies), *a day's allowance of provisions* for soldiers, Cic, slaves, Hor

dĭbăphus -um (later) a um (δίβαφος), *double dyed*, purpura, Plin Subst, **dĭbăphus** -i, f (sc. vestis), *the purple-striped robe of the higher magistrates at Rome*, Curtius dibaphum cogitat, *is longing for office*, Cic

dĭca -ae, f (δίκη), *a law-suit, action in a Greek court*, dicam scribere alicui, *to bring an action against*, Cic, dicam sortiri, *to select the jury by lot*, Cic.

dĭcācĭtas -ātis, f (dicax), *pungent wit, satire, raillery*, Cic

dĭcātĭo ōnis, f (1. dico), *settling as a citizen in another state*, Cic

dĭcax -ācis, adj with compar and superl.

(2. dico), *witty, satirical, ironical, sarcastic*; Demosthenes non tam dicax fuit quam facetus, Cic.

dĭchŏrēus -i, m. (διχορεῖος), *a double trochee*, Cic.

dĭcis, genit. (from unused nom. dix, from dico), found only in the phrases, dicis causā, dicis gratiā, *for form's sake, for appearance sake*, Cic.

1. **dĭco**, 1. (intens. of 2. dico). **A.** Lit., **a**, religious t. t., *to consecrate, dedicate, devote to the gods*; donum Jovi dicatum, Cic.; aram, Jovi, Liv.; templum, Ov.; **b**, *to deify, place among the gods*; inter numina dicatus Augustus, Tac. **B.** Transf., **a**, *to devote, give up to*; hunc totum diem tibi, Cic.; **b**, se alicui, *to devote oneself to*; se Crasso, Cic.; se alicui in clientelam, Caes.; se civitati or in civitatem, *to become a citizen of another state*, Cic.

2. **dīco**, dixi, dictum, 3. (root DIC or DEC, whence also dic-nus (dignus), dec-eo, δείκνυμι), *to say, relate, tell, mention*. **I.** Gen., ille, quem dixi, *he whom I have mentioned*, Cic.; illa quae dixi, Cic.; Hilarum dico, *I mean Hilarus*, Cic.; ne dicam, *not to say*; crudelem ne dicam sceleratum, Cic.; dicet aliquis, *one might say*, Cic.; nisi quid dicis, *if you have nothing to say against it*, Cic.; causam, *to plead a cause, answer an accusation*, Cic.; causas in foro, *to plead as an advocate*, Cic.; jus dicere, *to administer justice*, Cic.; sententiam (of a senator), *to vote*, Cic.; ut dixi, Cic.; ut dictum est, Caes.; foll. by ut or ne and the subj., *to command*, Cic.; pass., dicor, diceris, dicitur, etc., *it is said, the report is*; with nom. and infin., Aesculapius dicitur obligavisse, Cic.; dicto citius, *quicker than can be said, in a trice*, Verg. **II.** Esp. **a** (intransit.), *to speak, deliver an oration*; ars dicendi, *the art of eloquence*, Cic.; dicere pro reo, Cic.; contra aliquem pro aliquo apud centum viros, Cic.; **b**, *to name, call*; orbis qui κύκλος Graece dicitur, Cic.; with acc. of name, cui Ascanius parentes dixere nomen, Liv.; with double acc., quem dixere chaos, Ov.; **c**, *to sing, describe, celebrate in verse, compose*; versus, carmen, Verg., Hor.; carmina in imperatorem, Liv.; alicuius facta, Verg.; **d**, *to nominate, appoint*: dictatorem et magistrum equitum, Cic.; with double acc., aliquem dictatorem, Caes.; **e**, *to fix, appoint, settle*; diem operi, Cic.; **f**, *to say yes, affirm* (opp. nego); quem esse negas, eundem esse dico, Cic. (syncop. perf. dixti = dixisti, Cic., Ov.).

dicrŏtum -i, n. (δίκροτον), *a vessel having two banks of oars*, Cic.

dictamnum -i, n. and **dictamnus** -i, f. (δίκταμνον and -ος), *dittany, a plant found on Mount Dicte and Mount Ida* (Origanum dictamnum, Linn.), Cic.

dictāta -ōrum, n. (dicto), *that which is dictated by a teacher, precepts, rules*; iisdem de rebus semper quasi dictata decantare, Cic.

dictātor -ōris, m. (dicto). **I.** *a commander, dictator*; **a**, *the chief magistrate* in the Latin towns, Cic., Liv.; **b**, in Rome, *dictator, an extraordinary magistrate, elected in times of great emergency for six months, superseding all other magistrates, and armed with absolute power*. **II.** Transf., *the chief magistrate of Carthage, a suffete*, Liv.

dictātōrĭus -a -um (dictator), *relating or belonging to a dictator, dictatorial*; gladius, Cic.; invidia, *against the dictator*, Liv.; juvenis, *son of the dictator*, Liv.

dictātūra -ae, f. (dictator), *the office of dictator, dictatorship*; dictaturam gerere, Cic.; dictaturā se abdicare, Caes.; dictaturam abdicare, Liv.

Dictē -ēs, f. (Δίκτη), *a mountain in Crete on which Jupiter was reared*: adj., **Dictaeus** -a -um, arva, *Cretan*, Verg.; rex, *Jupiter*, Verg.; *Minos*, Ov.

dictĭo -ōnis, f. (2. dico). **I.** Gen., **A.** *a saying, speaking, uttering*; sententiae, Cic.; causae, *defence*, Cic.; multae, *fixing*, Cic. **B.** Meton., **a**, *the answer of an oracle*, Liv.; **b**, *conversation*, Tac. **II.** Esp. **A.** *declamation, elocution*; dictioni operam dare, Cic. **B.** Meton., **1**, *a speech*; dictiones subitae, *extemporised*, Cic.; **2**, *diction*; Attica, Cic.

dictĭto, 1. (freq. of 2. dico), **1**, *to say often*; *reiterate, assert repeatedly*; ut dictitabat, Caes.; quod levissimi ex Graecis dictitare solent, Liv.; with acc. and infin., Catilinam Massiliam ire, Cic.; with double acc., aliquem sanum recteque valentem, Hor.; **2**, esp. dictitare causas, *to plead causes frequently*, Cic.

dicto, 1. (intens. of 2. dico), *to reiterate, repeat, say often, to dictate to an amanuensis, pupil*, etc.; quod non modo tironi dictare, sed ne ipse quidem auderem scribere, Cic.; epistolam, Cic.; versus, Hor.; carmina Livii, Hor.

dictum -i, n. (2. dico), *a word, saying, speech*. **I.** Gen., nullum meum dictum, non modo factum, intercessit, quod, etc., Cic.; dicta tristia, *complaints, wailing*, Ov.; mutua dicta reddere, *to converse*, Liv. **II.** Esp., **1**, *a maxim, sentence, saying*; Catonis est dictum, *it is a maxim of Cato's*, Cic.; **2**, *a witty saying, a bon-mot*; dicta dicere in aliquem, Cic.; **3**, *a command, order*; dicto paruit consul, Liv.; **4**, *watch-word, password*, Nep.

Dictynna -ae, f. (Δίκτυννα), *surname of Artemis*. Hence, **Dictynnēum** -i, n. *temple of Artemis Dictynna, near Sparta.*

1. **Dīdō** -ūs or (gen.) -ōnis, f. (Διδώ), *the founder of Carthage, daughter of Belus, king of Tyre, sister of Pygmalion, wife of Sichaeus*; also called Elisa or Elissa.

2. **dīdo**, dīdĭdi, dīdĭtum, 3. (dis and do), **a**, *to divide, distribute*; dum munia didit, Hor.; **b**, *to spread, disseminate*; diditur hic subito Trojana per agmina rumor, Verg.

dīdūco -duxi -ductum, 3. (dis and duco). **I.** *to draw apart, stretch out, expand*; pugnum, Cic.; rictum, Hor.; fores, Tac. **II.** *to separate, divide*. **A.** Gen., **1**, **a**, assem in partes centum, Hor.; **b**, milit. t. t. (α) *to divide, distribute*; aciem in cornua, Liv.; (β) *to scatter the enemy, disperse*; adversariorum manus, Caes.; **2**, transf., oratio rivis diducta est, non fontibus, Cic.; vastius diducuntur verba, Cic. **B.** Esp., **1**, *to separate forcibly*; aliquem ab aliquo, Cic.; **2**, transf., animus varietate rerum diductus, *distracted*, Cic.

dīductĭo -ōnis, f. (diduco), *a separating*, Cic.

dĭēcŭla -ae, f. (dim. of dies), *a little day*; dieculam ducere, Cic.

dĭes -ēi, m. and f. in sing. (in Cic. fem. only when it applies to a fixed time or period of time or in the date of a letter), in plur. only masc. **I.** Gen., **A.** Lit., *a day*; hesterno, hodierno, crastino die, Cic.; postero die, Cic.; postera die, Sall.; diem de die, Liv., or diem ex die, Caes., *from day to day*; in dies, *daily*, Cic.; ad diem or ad certam diem, *for the appointed day*, Caes.; multo die, *late in the day*, Caes.; ad multum diem or ad multum diei, *till late in the day*, Liv.; bis in die, *twice a day*, Cic.; die et nocte, *a day and a night*, Cic.; noctes et dies, *night and day*, Cic.; so diem noctem, Cic. **B.** Meton., *the business* or *events of the day*; diei poenas dare, Cic.; exercere diem, *the day's work*, Verg.; *daylight*, Verg.; transf., videre diem, *to see the light of day*, Ov.; *a day's march*; dierum plus triginta in longitudinem patere, Liv. **II.** Esp., **A.** 1, gen., *a fixed day or time*; pecuniae, *pay-day*, Cic.; prodicere, *to put off a fixed day*, Liv.; diem ex die ducere, *to put off from one day to another*, Caes ; diem perexiguam postulavi, Cic., diem obire, *to wait for*, Cic., alios non solvere, aliorum diem nondum esse, *day for payment not arrived*, Cic , **2**, esp , *birthday*, dies meus, Cic , **3**, *the day of death*, obire diem supremum, Nep , **4**, *date of a letter*, in altera dies erat ascripta Nonarum Aprilium, etc , Cic **B.** *time*; quod est dies allatura, Cic

Diespiter tris, m (Umbrian = Δὶς πατήρ), *Jupiter*, Hor

diffāmo, 1. (dis and fama), *to spread abroad an evil report*, *to defame*, viros illustres procacibus scriptis, Tac

diffĕrens -entis, v differo

diffĕrentia -ae, f (differo), *difference*, *distinction*, honesti et decori, Cic

diffĕrĭtas -ātis, f. (differo), *difference*, Lucr

diffĕro, distŭli, dilātum, differre, 2 (dis and fero) **I.** Transit , **A.** *to carry in different directions, spread abroad, scatter*, **1**, lit , ulmos in versum, *to plant*, Verg , ignem, *to spread*, Caes , **2**, transf , a, (α) rumorem, *to spread*, Liv ; (β) aliquem variis rumoribus, *to malign*, Tac , b, of time, *to put off, delay, postpone*, tempus, Cic , bellum, Liv ; aliquem in tempus aliud, Cic , rem in aliud tempus, Caes , se differre, *to tarry*, Ov , with infin , nec differret obsides ab Arretinis accipere, Liv **B.** *to separate violently, disperse, scatter*, aquilo differt nubila, Verg , classem vis venti distulit, Hor **II.** Intransit (without perf or supine), *to differ*, *be different*, inter se, Cic , ab aliquo or ab aliqua re, Cic , cum aliqua re, Cic. ; nihil differt inter deum et deum, Cic

differtus a -um (dis and farcio), *stuffed full, crammed, full*, provincia differta praefectis atque exactoribus, Caes

diffĭcĭlis -e, adj with compar and superl (dis and facilis), *difficult*. **A.** Lit , res arduae ac difficiles, Cic ; of places, *difficult, dangerous*, iter, Sall , aditus, Caes , of time, *critical, dangerous*, tempus anni difficillimum, Cic ; est difficile with infin , est difficile confundere, Cic , with ad, difficilius ad eloquendum, Cic **B.** Transf., of character, *hard to please, surly, morose, captious, obstinate*, parens in liberos difficilis, Cic., difficilis alicui, Liv.

diffĭcĭlĭtĕr, adv with compar difficilius and superl difficillime (difficilis), *with difficulty*, Cic.

diffĭcultas -ātis, f (difficilis), *difficulty, need, peril, trouble, distress* **A.** Lit., dicendi, navigandi, Cic ; loci, Sall , magnam haec Caesari difficultatem ad consilium afferebat si, etc , Caes , nummaria, *pecuniary embarrassment*, Cic , domestica, *distressed circumstances*, Cic **B** Transf , *obstinacy, moroseness*, Cic.

diffĭcultĕr, adv. (difficilis), *with difficulty*, Caes

diffīdens, p adj (diffido) *distrustful, diffident*, Sall

diffīdentĕr, adv. (diffidens), *diffidently, without confidence*, altera timide et diffidenter attingere, Cic

diffīdentĭa -ae, f (diffidens), *want of confidence, diffidence, distrust, despair*, fidentiae contrarium est diffidentia, Cic , diffidentiam rei simulare, Sall

diffīdo -fīsus sum, 3 (dis and fido), *to have no confidence, mistrust, be hopeless, despair*, sibi, Cic ; suis rebus, Caes , virtuti militum, Sall ; with acc and infin , rem posse confici diffido, Cic , absol , jacet, diffidit, abjecit hastas, Cic

diffindo fĭdi -fissum, 3 (dis and findo), *to split, cleave* **A.** Lit , saxum, Cic , portas muneribus, *open*, Hor. **B** Transf , a, equidem nihil huic diffindere possum, *I have nothing to say against your opinion*, *I must agree to it*, Hor , **b**, legal t t , diem, *to postpone*, Liv.

diffingo -finxi fictum, 3 (dis and fingo), *to form again, forge anew*, ferrum incude, Hor , fig , *to change*, Hor

diffĭtĕor -ēri, 2 dep (dis and fateor), *to deny, disavow*, Ov

difflŭo -fluxi -fluxum, 3 (dis and fluo) **A** Lit , *to flow in different directions*, ut nos quasi extra ripas diffluentes coerceret, Cic **B.** a, juvenes sudore diffluentes, *dripping with sweat*, Phaedr , transf , otio, *to give oneself up to*, Cic , luxuria, Cic , b, *to dissolve, melt away*; diffluit acervus, Lucr , transf , uti per socordiam vires, tempus, ingenium diffluxere, Sall

diffŭgĭo -fūgi -fŭgitum, 3 (dis and fugio), *to fly apart, fly in different directions, to disperse*, metu perterriti repente diffugimus, Cic

diffŭgĭum -ii, n (diffugio), *a dispersion*, Tac

diffundo -fūdi -fūsum, 3 (dis and fundo) **I.** Lit , **A.** *to pour out on all sides, pour forth*, vina, Hor , sanguis per venas in omne corpus diffunditur, Cic **B.** *to spread, scatter, diffuse*, pass , diffundi, used as middle, lux diffusa toto caelo, Cic , diffusis capillis, Ov **II.** Transf , **A.** Gen , Claudia nunc a quo diffunditur et tribus et gens per Latium, *spread abroad*, Verg , error longe lateque diffusus, Cic. **B** Esp , *to brighten up, gladden*, diffundere animos munere Bacchi, Ov , ut bonis amici quasi diffundantur et incommodis contrahantur, Cic

diffūsē, adv (diffusus), *copiously, diffusely*; dicere aliquid, Cic

diffūsĭlis -e (diffundo), *easily extending itself, diffusive*, aether, Lucr

diffūsus -a -um, p adj. with compar (diffundo), *spread out, extensive, wide* **A.** Lit , platanus diffusa ramis, Cic **B.** Transf , jus civile quod nunc diffusum (*prolix*) et dissipatum est, in certa genera coacturum, Cic

dĭgamma, n indecl (δίγαμμα), or **dĭgamma** ae, f , or **dĭgammon** -i, n (δίγαμμον) or **dĭgammos** -i, f **I** *the Aeolic digamma* (Ϝ) **II.** (In jest) = *rental* or *investment book*, from F, the first letter of Fenus, tuum digamma videram, Cic

Dĭgentĭa ae, f *a brook flowing through Horace's estate into the Anio*, now *Licenza*

dīgĕro -gessi -gestum, 3 (dis and gero), *to carry apart in different directions, to separate, sunder, divide* **I.** Lit , **1**, *to plant out*, vacuos si sit digesta per agros (arbor), Verg , **2**, *to arrange, put in order*, capillos, Ov **II.** Transf , **1**, *to divide*, septem digestus in cornua Nilus, Ov , **2**, *to arrange*, jus civile in genera, Cic , rempublicam bene, Cic.; nomina in codicem accepti et expensi, Cic , **3**, *to count*, qui matris digerit annos, Ov

dīgestĭo -ōnis, f (digero), rhet fig = μερισμός, *distribution*, Cic

dīgestus -a um, v digero

dĭgĭtŭlus -i, m (dim of digitus), *a little finger*, Cic

dĭgĭtus -i, m (conn with δέχομαι) **I.** Lit **A.** *the finger*, pollex, *the thumb*, Caes ; index, Hor , digitos comprimere pugnumque facere, Cic , digitos extendere, Cic , concrepare digitis, Cic , digito se caelum attigisse putare, *to think himself almost in heaven* Cic , tuos digitos novi, *thy skill in counting*, Cic , liceri digito, Cic , tollere digitum, *to raise the finger as a sign of a bid at an auction*, Cic , ne digitum quidem alicuius rei causa porrigere, *not to move a finger*, Cic , digito aliquem attingere, *to touch gently*,

Cic , primoribus labris gustasse hoc genus vitae et extremis, ut dicitur, digitis attigisse, Cic **B.** *the toe*, insistere digitis, *to tread on the toes*, Ov , constitit in digitos arrectus, Verg **II.** Meton., as a measure, *a finger's breadth, an inch, the sixteenth part of a Roman foot*, quatuor patens digitos, Caes , prov , ab hac (regula) mihi non licet transversum, ut aiunt, digitum discedere, Cic

dīgladior, 1 dep (dis and gladius) **A.** Lit , *to fight for life and death, struggle fiercely*, inter se sicis, Cic **B.** Transf , *to dispute in words;* inter se de aliqua re, Cic , cum aliquo, Cic

dignātĭo -ōnis, f (dignor), *dignity, reputation, honour*, Liv

dignē, adv (dignus), *worthily*, quis de tali cive satis digne umquam loquetur? Cic

dignĭtas -ātis, f (dignus) **I.** *worth, worthiness, merit*, honos dignitate impetratus, Cic **II.** Meton **A.** *the consequence of worth*, **1,** *esteem, reputation, honour*, **a,** civitatis dignitatem et decus sustinere, Cic , **b,** *rank in the state, position*, altus dignitatis gradus, Cic , aliquem ad summam dignitatem perducere, Caes , **c,** *an office of honour* Cic , **d,** dignitates, *men of rank and position*, Cic , **2,** *honour, dignity*, agere cum dignitate, Cic **B.** Transf , of things that bring honour, **a,** of persons, *a dignified, seemly exterior*, in formis aliis dignitatem esse, aliis venustatem, Cic , **b,** of buildings, etc , *imposing appearance*, porticus, Cic , **c,** of expression, *dignity*, orationis, Tac

digno, 1 *to consider worthy*, quae consimili laude dignentur, Cic

dignor, 1 dep (dignus), **1,** *to consider worthy*, haud equidem tali me dignor honore, Verg , **2,** *to regard as worthy of oneself, to deign*, and with a neg , *to disdain*, Verg

dignosco -nōvi, 3 (dis and nosco), 3 *to recognise as different, to distinguish*, rectum curvo, Hor , non civem hoste, Hor ; geminos inter se similes vix dignoscere posse, Ov

dignus -a -um, adj with compar and superl (dic-nus, root DIC or DEK, whence deceo), *worthy, deserving* **I.** With abl laude, Cic , memoriā, Cic , with supine, dictu, Liv , followed by a relative qui aliquando imperet dignus, *worthy to command*, Cic ; with ut and the subj , quos ut socios haberes dignos duxisti, Liv , poet with infin , puer cantari dignus, Verg , with ad, amicus dignus huic ad imitandum, Cic , absol , diligere non dignos, Cic **II.** Transf , *worthy of a person or thing, becoming, suitable, fitting*, with abl., facere quid docto homine et amico dignum fuerit, Cic , with pro, quidnam pro offensione hominum dignum eloqui possim, Cic , absol , *fitting, suitable, sufficient*, qui maeror dignus in tanta calamitate inveniri potest, Cic , dignum est, foll by infin or acc. with infin , Cic

dīgrĕdĭor -gressus sum -grĕdi, (dis and gradior), 3 dep **A.** Lit , *to go apart, go asunder, separate, depart*, luna tum congrediens cum sole, tum digrediens, Cic ; ab aliquo, Cic , a Corcyra, Liv , ex loco, Caes , in urbem, Tac , viā, Liv , **B.** Transf , *to deviate*, **a,** de causa, Cic , a causa, Cic , **b,** of discourse, *to digress*, digredi ab eo quod proposueris, Cic

dīgressĭo -ōnis, f (digredior), **1,** *a separation, departure*, Cic , **2,** *a digression in discourse*, a proposita oratione, Cic

dīgressus -ūs, m (digredior), *a separation, departure*, digressus et discessus, Cic , digressus (lunae a sole), Cic

dījūdĭcātĭo -ōnis, f (dijudico), *an adjudication, decision*, Cic

dījūdĭco, 1 (dis and judico), **1,** *to decide, adjudicate, determine*, controversiam, Cic , litem, Hor , *to decide by arms*, dijudicatā belli fortunā, Caes ; **2,** *to distinguish, discern a difference*, vera et falsa, Cic , vera a falsis dijudicare et distinguere, Cic

dijun v disjun . .

dīlābor -lapsus sum, 3 dep (dis and labor) **I** *to glide apart* **A.** Lit , **a,** of houses, bodies, etc , *to fall to pieces, fall down*, aedis Jovi vetustate dilapsa, Liv , **b,** of fluids, *to melt, dissolve, disappear*, eadem (aqua conglaciata) admixto colore liquefacta et dilapsa, Cic . **B.** Transf , *to fall to decay, be ruined, disappear*, rem familiarem dilabi sinere, Cic , dilapsa esse robora corporum animorumque, Liv **II.** *to glide away from* **A.** Lit , *to slip away*, esp of soldiers, *to escape, disappear*, exercitus brevi dilabitur, Sall , nocte in sua tecta, Liv , of rivers, *to glide away*, Fibrenus rapide dilapsus, Cic **B.** Transf , *to vanish disappear;* **1,** sunt alii plures fortasse sed de mea memoria dilabuntur, Cic , **2,** esp of time, *to go by*, dilapso tempore, Sall

dīlăcĕro, 1 (dis and lacero), *to tear in pieces* **A.** Lit , aliquem, Ov **B.** Transf , rempublicam, Cic

dīlāmĭno, 1 (dis and lamina), *to split in two*, Ov

dīlănĭo, 1 (dis and lanio), *to tear in pieces*, cadaver, Cic

dīlargĭor, 4 dep. (dis and largior), *to lavish abroad, give liberally*, qui omnia quibus voluit dilargitus est, Cic

dīlātĭo -ōnis, f (differo), *a putting off, delaying, postponing*, temporis, Cic , belli, Liv ; sine dilatione Liv., res dilationem non recipit or non patitur, Liv

dīlāto (dis and latus), 1 *to spread out, extend* **I.** Lit , manum, Cic , aciem, Liv. **II.** Transf , **A.** Gen , nomen in continentibus terris, Cic , legem in ordinem cunctum, *to extend*, Cic **B.** Esp **1,** litteras, *to pronounce broadly*, Cic ; **2,** of speech, *to enlarge, amplify*, orationem, Cic

dīlātor -ōris, m. (differo), *a dilatory person, a loiterer*, Hor

dīlātus, v differo

dīlaudo, 1 (dis and laudo), *to praise highly;* libros, Cic

1 **dīlectus** -a -um, p adj with compar and superl (from diligo), *beloved, dear*, dilecti tibi poetae, Hor

2 **dīlectus** -ūs = delectus (q v)

dīlĭgens -entis, p adj with compar and superl (from diligo) **I.** Gen , *assiduous, accurate careful sedulous, diligent* (opp negligens), **a,** of persons, omnibus in rebus, Cic , with genit , diligentissimus omnis officii, Cic , with dat , Corinthios publicis equis assignandis fuisse diligentes, Cic , with ad and the gerund, ad custodiendum, Cic , **b,** of things which bear marks of attention, assidua ac diligens scriptura, Cic **II.** Esp. *careful in housekeeping, economical, saving*, homo frugi ac diligens, Cic , in re hereditaria, Cic.

dīlĭgentĕr, adv with compar and superl (diligens), *carefully, assiduously, accurately, diligently*, aliquem benigne et diligenter audire, Cic , iter caute diligenterque facere, Caes

dīlĭgentĭa -ae, f (diligo) **A.** Gen *carefulness, attentiveness, accuracy, diligence*, with obj genit , testamentorum, Cic ; with in and the abl , pro mea summa in republica diligentia, Cic ; non mediocrem adhibere diligentiam, Caes ; diligentiam adhibere ut or ne (with the subj), Cic , adhibere ad considerandas res et tempus et diligentiam, Cic ; omnia acerbissimā diligentiā perpendere, Cic **B.** Esp *care in management of a household, frugality*, res familiaris conservari (debet) diligentiā atque parsimoniā, Cic

dīlĭgo -lexi -lectum, 3 (dis and lego, *to choose*), *to prize, love, esteem highly*, aliquem, Cic , aliquem diligere et carum habere, aliquem colere atque diligere, Cic , se ipsum, Cic , inter se, Cic , of things, hunc locum, Cic , alicuius consilia, officia, *to be satisfied with*, Cic

dīlōrīco, 1 (dis and lorico), *to tear open*, tunicam, Cic

dīlūcĕo, 2 (dis and luceo) *to be clear, evident*, dilucere deinde fraus coepit, Liv

dīlūcesco luxi, 3 (inchoat of diluceo), *to grow light, become day*, **a**, pers , omnem crede diem tibi diluxisse supremum, Hor ; **b**, impers , quum jam dilucesceret, Cic.

dīlūcĭdē, adv with compar and superl (dilucidus), *clearly, plainly, lucidly*, plane et dilucide dicere, Cic

dīlūcĭdus a -um, *clear, lucid, plain*, oratio, Cic. , dilucidis verbis uti, Cic

dīlūcŭlum i, n (diluceo), *the break of day, dawn*, primo diluculo, Cic , diluculo, *at dawn*, Cic

dīlūdĭum ii, n (dis and ludus), *the period of rest for gladiators between the days of public exhibition*, transf , diludia posco, *breathing-time, rest*, Hor

dīlŭo -lŭi -lūtum, 3 (dis and luo), *to wash away, to dissolve* **A.** Lit , **a**, ne canalibus aqua immissa lateres diluere posset, Caes , unguenta lacrimis, Ov , **b**, *to dilute, temper*, vinum, Mart , venenum, Liv **B.** Transf , **a**, *to weaken the force of, lessen, impair*, molestias, Cic , curam multo mero, Ov , **b**, *to expose the falseness of a statement, refute*, crimen, Cic , diluere aliquid et falsum esse docere, Cic

dīlūtus -a um, v diluo

dīlŭvĭes -ēi, f (diluo), *a washing away, inundation*, Hor.

dīlŭvĭo, 1 (diluvium), *to overflow*, Lucr

dīlŭvĭum ii, n (diluo), *a flood, deluge, inundation*, Verg

dīmāno, 1 (dis and mano), *to flow in different directions, spread itself abroad*, fig meus hic forensis labor vitaeque ratio dimanavit ad existimationem hominum, Cic

dīmensĭo -ōnis, f (dimetior), *a measuring*, quadrati, Cic

dīmētĭor -mensus, 4 dep (dis and metior), *to measure out* **I.** Lit **A.** Gen , **a**, act , atque ego ista sum dimensus, Cic , **b**, pass , a quo essent illa dimensa atque descripta, Cic , tigna dimensa ad altitudinem fluminis, Caes **B.** Esp **a**, milit t t , *to measure out a place for a camp;* opere dimenso, Caes ; **b**, astronom t t , caelum atque terram, Cic , pass , certis dimensus partibus orbis, Verg , **c**, metric t t , syllabas, Cic , versum, Cic **II.** Transf , audiam civem digitis peccata dimetientem sua, Cic.

dīmēto, 1 (dis and meto), and dep **dīmētor**, 1 *to measure the boundaries of*, Cic , locum castris dimetari jussit, Liv , dep , eorum cursus (acc) dimetati, Cic

dīmĭcātĭo ōnis, f (dimico), **1**, *a fight, struggle, contest in arms*, proelii, Cic , **2**, *any contest or struggle*, vitae, *for life and death*, Cic , capitis, Cic

dīmĭco -āvi or ŭi, 1 (dis and mico) **A.** *to fight, contend, struggle in arms*, pro patria, Cic , proelio, Caes **B.** Transf , *to struggle, contend, strive*, omni ratione erit dimicandum ut, etc , Cic , de fama, de civitate, Cic

dīmĭdĭātus -a um (dimidium), *halved, divided, half*, mensis, Cic , partes versiculorum, Cic

dīmĭdĭus -a -um (dis and medius), *halved, divided in half*, gen with pars, dimidia pars, *the half*, Cic , terrae, Cic , of persons, frater meus dimidius major est quam totus, Cic Subst , **dīmĭdĭum** ii, n *the half*, pecuniae, Cic , dimidio with a compar , stultior, *by half*, Cic , prov , dimidium facti, qui coepit, habet, *well begun is half done*, Hor

dīmĭnūtĭo, v deminutio

dīmissĭo ōnis, f (dimitto), **1**, *a sending out*, libertorum ad provincias, Cic , **2**, *a dismissing, discharging*, remigum, Cic

dīmitto -mīsi -missum, 3 (dis and mitto) **I.** *to send forth, send in different directions*, pueros circum amicos, Cic , litteras per omnes provincias, Caes , nuntios in omnes partes, Caes , aciem (oculorum) in omnes partes, Ov **II.** *to send away from oneself, let go* **A.** Lit **1**, gen , **a**, legatos, Liv , tabellarium, Cic , hostem ex manibus, *let slip*, Caes , regem spoliatum, Cic , **b**, of things, *to let drop*, signa ex metu, Caes , librum e manibus, Cic , **2**, esp **a**, of persons (α) *to adjourn a meeting, dismiss*, senatum, Cic , (β) milit t t , *to discharge*, exercitum, Caes , **b**, of things, *to give up*, provinciam, Liv **B.** Transf , **1**, gen , quare istos sine ulla contumelia dimittamus, Cic , **2**, esp *to let drop, give up, renounce, abandon, leave*, oppugnationem, Caes , quaestionem, Cic ; injuriam ignominiamque nominis Romani multam impunitamque, Cic

dīmŏvĕo -mōvi mōtum, 2 (dis and moveo), *to move asunder, part, separate, divide* **A.** Lit , terram aratro, *to plough*, Verg , aquam corpore, Ov **B.** *to separate, remove, to take away*, **a**, spes societatis equites Romanos a plebe dimovet, Sall , **b**, statu sua sacra, Liv

Dīnarchus i, m (Δείναρχος), *an Athenian orator, contemporary with Demosthenes*

Dindȳmus i, m and **Dindȳma** ōrum, n (Δίνδυμος, Δίνδυμα τα), *a mountain in Mysia, sacred to Cybele*, hence **Dindȳmēnē** -ēs, f *Cybele*, Hor

dīnosco = dignosco (q v)

dīnŭmĕrātĭo -ōnis, f (dinumero), *an enumeration*, dierum ac noctium, Cic

dīnŭmĕro, 1 (dis and numero), *to count up, enumerate.* **A.** Gen , stellas, Cic , regis annos, Cic **B.** Esp *to count money, to pay*, centuriat Capuae, dinumerat, *counts out the gold*, Cic

Dĭŏdōrus -i, m (Διόδωρος) **I.** *a philosopher, contemporary of Ptolemaeus Soter* **II.** *a peripatetic philosopher, of Tyre, flourishing about* 109 B C **III.** (Siculus), *a Greek historian*

dĭoecēsis ĕos and is, f (διοίκησις), *the district of a magistrate*, Cic

dĭoecētes -ae, m (διοικητής), *a finance officer or treasurer*, Cic

Dĭŏgĕnēs -is, m (Διογένης), *the name of several Greek philosophers, the most notorious of whom was the Cynic philosopher of Sinope*

Dĭŏmēdēs is, m (Διομήδης), **1**, *a hero of the Trojan war, son of Tydeus, prince of Calydon, said to have subsequently settled in Apulia, and to have founded Arpi*, hence, adj , **Dĭŏmēdēus** -a um, *relating to Diomedes*, **2**, *king of the Bistones in Thrace, who gave his captives as food to his horses*

Dĭōn ōnis, m (Δίων), *brother-in-law of Dionysius I , tyrant of Syracuse, killed by a conspiracy*

Dĭōnē ēs, f and **Dĭōna** -ae, f (Διώνη), **1**, *the mother of Venus, daughter of Oceanus and Tethys or of Aether and Gaea*, **2**, *Venus* Adj ,

Dĭōnaeus -a -um, *relating to Dione*, or *Venus*, mater, i e *Venus*, Verg , Caesar (by the legend), *descendant of Aeneas, son of Venus*, Verg , antrum, *sacred to Venus*, Hor

Dĭŏnȳsius ii, m (Διονύσιος), 1, *the Elder, Tyrant of Syracuse* 406–367 B C , 2, *his son and successor, tyrant*, 367–356, B C

Dĭŏnȳsus -i, m (Διόνυσος), *the Greek name of Bacchus*, hence **Dĭŏnȳsia** -ōrum, n *the feast of Dionysus*

dĭōta -ae f (διώτη), *a two-handled wine-jar*, Hor

Dīphĭlus i, m (Δίφιλος), *a comic poet of Sinope, contemporary of Menander and Philemon, imitated by Plautus*

diplōma -ătis, n (δίπλωμα), literally, *a folded letter* ; 1, under the republic, *a circular letter of introduction given to travellers by the government, in order to facilitate their journey*, Cic , 2, under the empire, *a government document conferring privileges on the persons to whom it was addressed*, Tac.

Dīpȳlŏn, -i, n (Δίπυλον), *the double door, name of the Thriasian gate at Athens*

Dircē -ēs, f (Δίρκη). **I.** *the wife of Lycus king of Thebes, bound to a bull by Amphion and Zethus, and thrown* (or *changed*) *into the fountain named after her* **II.** *the fountain of Dirce, to the north-west of Thebes* Adj , **Dircaeus** a -um, *Dircean, Boeotian*, cygnus, *Pindar*, Hor

dīrectē, adv with compar (directus), *straightforward, in a straight line*, 1, horizontally, Cic ; transf , dicere, *directly*, Cic , 2, perpendicularly, directe ad perpendiculum, Caes.

dīrectō, adv (directus), *in a straightforward way, directly*, Cic.

dīrectus -a -um, p adj with compar (dirigo), 1, *straight, direct*, either in a horizontal or perpendicular direction , paries, Cic , iter, Cic , trabes, Caes , 2, *straightforward, plain, simple*, verba, Cic , homo, Cic

dīremptus -ūs, m (dirimo), *a separation*, Cic

dīreptĭo -ōnis, f (diripio), *a plundering, pillaging*, urbs relicta direptioni, Cic , bonorum direptio, Cic

dīreptor -ōris, m (diripio), *a plunderer, pillager*, Cic

dĭrĭbĕo -ŭi itum, 2 (for dis -hibeo, from habeo), *to sort the voting tickets which were cast into the balloting urn* , tabellas, Cic

dĭrĭbĭtĭo -ōnis, f (diribeo), *the sorting of the voting tickets*, Cic

dĭrĭbĭtor -ōris, m (diribeo), *the officer whose duty it was to sort the voting tickets*, Cic

dīrĭgo -rexi -rectum, 3 (dis and rego) **I.** *to set straight, arrange in a straight line*, pass dirigi, *to proceed in a straight line*, transf , dirigitur (argumentatio) quum proposuit aliquid quod probaret, Cic. **II.** *to arrange, direct* **A.** Lit , 1, as regards motion, **a**, of ships, carriages, journeys, etc , *to direct*, ad castra Corneliana vela, Caes , cursum eo (quo), Cic , iter ad Mutinam, Cic , **b**, of weapons, *to aim, direct*, hastam in aliquem, Ov ; **c**, of the sight, aciem ad aliquem, Cat , **2**, of position, **a**, *to arrange, order, dispose*, (α) in quincuncem ordines (arborum), Cic , (β) milit t t , *to draw up*, aciem, Caes , naves in pugnam, Liv , **b**, *to raise, erect*, opera, Caes **B.** Transf , **a**, *to direct, guide*, dirige vatis opus, Ov , intransit *to lead*, ad veritatem saepissime dirigit, Cic , **b**, *to direct the thoughts, attention*, etc , to something , suas cogitationes ad aliquid, Cic , **c**, *to direct a speech to, to address*, orationem ad aliquid, Cic , **d**, *to settle, arrange, fix, dispose* ; vitam ad certam rationis normam, Cic ; utilitate officium magis quam humanitate, Cic.

dĭrĭmo -ēmi -emptum, 3 (dis and emo) **I. 1**, *to part, separate, sunder, divide*, Sabinae mulieres ex transverso impetu facto dirimere infestas acies, dirimere iras, Liv ; **2**, *to interrupt, hinder, disturb, put off, break off*, **a**, an assembly or conversation, actum est de eo nihil ; nox diremit, Cic , ea res colloquium ut diremisset, Caes , esp of omens, *to interrupt* (as inauspicious), consilia, Liv , **b**, a fight, engagement, proelium, Liv , a war, contention, bellum inter Philippum atque Aetolos, Liv , **c**, an alliance, league, *to break up*, veterem conjunctionem civium, Cic **II.** *to divide*, quae urbs Volturno flumine dirempta Falernum a Campano agro dividit, Liv.

dīrĭpĭo -rĭpŭi -reptum, 3 (dis and rapio), **I** *to tear to pieces* **A.** Lit., Hippolytum, Ov. **B.** Transf *to plunder, pillage, destroy*, socios, Cic. **II.** *to tear away*, a pectore vestem, Ov , res pulcherrimas ex tota Asia, Cic

dīrĭtas -ātis, f (dirus), 1, *misfortune, disaster*, Cic poet , 2, *cruelty, fierceness*, quanta in altero diritas, in altero comitas, Cic.

dīrumpo rūpi ruptum, 3 *to break in pieces, shatter* **1.** Lit , tenuissimam quamque partem (nubis) dividere atque dirumpere, Tac. ; (homo) diruptus, *ruptured*, Cic **II.** Transf , **a**, dirupi me paene in judicio Galli Canini, *shouted myself hoarse in defending*, etc , Cic , middle, dirumpi, *to burst with envy, grief, anger*, etc , dirumpi plausu alicuius, *to burst with envy at the applause given to some one else*, Cic ; dolore, Cic ; **b**, *to sever, break up*; amicitiam, Cic., societatem, Cic

dīrŭo -ŭi ŭtum, 3 (dis and ruo), *to pull down, raze to the ground, destroy* **A.** Lit , urbem, Cic , agmina vasto impetu, *to scatter*, Hor **B.** Transf., aere dirui, *to be mulcted of one's pay*, Plin , in quibus (castris), quum frequens esset, tamen aere dirutus est, *ruined by gambling*, Cic , homo diruptus dirutusque, *bankrupt*, Cic

dīrus -a um (connected with δεινός), *fearful, horrible, dire* **A.** Of unfavourable omens, omen, Ov , subst , **dirae** -ārum, f *unlucky omens*, Cic , so **dira** ōrum, n , Cic **B.** Transf , *horrible, cruel, frightful*, **a**, of things, exsecratio, Verg , venena, Hor ; subst., **dirae** -ārum, f *curses*, diris agam vos, Hor., contingere funebribus diris signa tela arma hostium, Liv , **b**, of persons, *cruel, terrible*, dea, *Circe*, Ov ; Hannibal, Hor., subst , personif , **Dīra** -ae, f *a Fury*, Verg ; gen. plur often with ultrices, *Furies*, Verg

1 **dis**, inseparable particle, meaning *away from*, takes the form of dis-, di-, and dir-

2 **Dīs**, Ditis, m *a name of Pluto, god of the lower world*, Cic , domina Ditis, *Proserpina*, Verg.

3 **dīs**, ditis, adj with compar and superl , *rich.* **A.** Lit , dis hostis, Liv , apud Helvetios ditissimus fuit Orgetorix, Caes., with genit., ditissimus agri, Verg **B.** Transf *richly provided, making rich*, ditia stipendia, Liv

discēdo cessi -cessum, 3 **I.** *to go asunder, part, separate* ; in duas partes, Sall , caelum discedit, *the heavens open*, Cic ; transf , omnis Italia animis discedit, *is divided*, Sall **II. A.** Lit , 1, gen , *to depart, go away*, e Gallia, Cic., de foro, Cic. ; finibus Ausoniae, Ov. ; used impersonally, a contione disceditur, Caes , 2, esp **a**, milit t t (α) of troops, *to march away*, a Brundisio, Caes , ab signis, *to break the ranks, leave the line of battle*, Caes ; ab armis, *to lay down arms*, Caes , (β) *to come out of a contest, to come off*, victor, Caes ; victus, Sall , aequo Marte cum Volscis, *to have a drawn battle with*,

Liv , so *to come out of any contest* (e g in a court of law), superior discedit Cic , turpis sime, *to come off with disgrace*, Cic , b, *to abandon desert*, ab amicis, Cic , ab aliquo duce (of soldiers), Caes **B.** Transf , **1,** gen , ex vita tamquam ex hospitio, Cic , a vita, Caes , a re, *to digress* (of an orator), Cic , numquam ex animo meo discedit illius viri memoria, Cic , **2,** esp **a.** *to abandon a duty, deviate, swerve from principles*, etc ; ab officio, Cic , a consuetudine, Cic , **b,** polit t t of the senate, in aliquam sententiam discedere, *to support a resolution*, in alia omnia discedere, *to be quite of the contrary opinion*, Cic , **c,** discedere ab aliquo or ab aliqua re, *to except*, quum a vobis discessérim, *you excepted*, Cic

disceptātĭo -ōnis, f (discepto), **1,** *a debate, discussion, controversy*, cum quibus omnis fere nobis disceptatio contentioque est, Cic , with genit , disceptatio juris, Cic , **2,** *a judicial decision, award*, disceptationem ab rege ad Romanos revocabant, Liv

disceptātor -ōris, m (discepto), *an arbitrator, judge of a controversy*, domesticus, Cic , juris, Cic

disceptātrix trīcis, f (disceptator), *one who decides*, Cic

discepto. 1 (dis and capto), **1,** *to decide a suit or cause, adjudicate, determine*, controversias, Cic , inter populum et regem, Liv , **2,** *to dispute, debate, discuss*, verbis de jure, Liv , de controversiis apud se potius quam inter se armis, Caes , de jure publico armis, Cic , transf , in uno proelio omnis fortuna reipublicae disceptat, *depends upon*, Cic

discerno -crēvi crētum, 3 **A.** *to sever, separate*, mons qui fines eorum discerneret, Sall , duae urbes magno inter se maris terrarumque spatio discretae, Liv , discretae sedes piorum, *set apart*, Hor **B.** Transf , *to distinguish, discern*, alba et atra discernere non posse, Cic , with rel sent , animus discernit, quid sit ejusdem generis, quid alterius, Cic

discerpo cerpsi cerptum, 3 (dis and carpo) **A.** Lit *to pluck to pieces, tear in pieces, dismember*, membra gruis, Hor , animus nec dividi nec discerpi potest, Cic **B.** Transf , in a discourse, *to separate, divide*, qui quae complecti tota nequeunt, haec facilius divulsa et quasi discerpta contrectant, Cic

discessĭo -ōnis, f (discedo) **1,** *a going away, departure*, Tac , **2,** polit t t , *voting, division in the senate* (by going over to one side or the other), senatus consultum facere per discessionem, *without discussion*, Cic , discessionem facere, *to vote*, Cic , facta est discessio in sententiam alicuius, Cic

discessus ūs, m (discedo), **1,** *a parting, separation*, caeli, *lightning*, Cic , **2,** *a departure, going away*, ab urbe, Cic , e vita, Cic , esp , **a,** milit t t *marching off*, Caes ab Dyrrhachio discessus exercituum, Cic , **b,** euphem *banishment*, Cic

discĭdĭum -ii, n (discindo) **I.** *a tearing away, dividing*, nubis, Lucr **II.** *separation, division, parting* **A.** Lit conjugis miserae, *from a wife*, Cic , esp , of the parting of lovers or of divorce, Cic , divortia atque affinitatum discidia, Cic **B.** Transf *separation in feelings, dissension*, belli discidio, Cic , deorum odia, discidia, discordiae, Cic

discīdo, 3 (dis and caedo), *to cut in pieces, hew in pieces*, Lucr

discinctus -a um (p adj of discingo), *careless, reckless, dissolute, extravagant*, nepos, Hor , otia, Ov

discindo scidi -scissum, 3 (dis and scindo), **1,** *to cleave asunder, split*, cotem novaculā, Cic ; transf , amicitias, Cic , **2,** *to tear open*, tunicam, Cic

discingo cinxi -cinctum, 3 *to take off the girdle, ungird*, Afros, *to disarm*, Juv

discĭplīna ae, f (discipulus) **I** *instruction, teaching* **A.** Lit , litterae reliquaeque res quarum est disciplina, Cic , novum aliquem alumnum in disciplinam tradere Cic , ab aliquo disciplinam accipere, Cic , subj gen , disciplina majorum, Cic , obj gen , disciplina virtutis, Cic **B.** Meton , *that which is taught, learning, knowledge, science*, **a,** gen , bellica, *the art of war*, Cic , navalis, Cic , habere quasdam etiam domesticas disciplinas, Cic , juris civilis, Cic , **b,** *a philosophical school, a system*, philosophiae disciplina, Cic ; **c,** *a rhetorical school or system*, Hermagorae, Cic **II.** In a wider sense, *training, education*. **A.** Lit , **a,** gen , disciplina puerilis, *of boys*, Cic , disciplina familiae, *of slaves*, gravis et constans, Cic , **b,** esp *military training*, militaris Liv , militiae, Cic **B.** Meton , *the result of training, custom, habit, order*, **a,** gen , disciplinae sanctitas, Liv , certa vivendi disciplina, Cic , **b,** *the ordering of a state, constitution*, disciplina reipublicae, Cic , disciplinam dare, Cic , o morem praeclarum disciplinamque quam a majoribus accepimus, Cic

discĭpŭla -ae, f (discipulus), *a female scholar*, Hor

discĭpŭlus i, m (disco), *a scholar, pupil, disciple*, Cic

disclūdo -clūsi -clūsum, 3 (dis and claudo), *to shut up apart, to separate, divide* **I.** Nerea ponto, Verg , tigna, *keep at the proper distance*, Caes , mons qui Arvernos ab Helviis discludit, Caes **II.** Transf , morsus roboris, *to loosen*, Verg

disco, dĭdĭci, 3 **I.** *to learn* **A.** Gen , litteras Graecas, Cic , jus civile aut rem militarem, Cic , id quod ex pluribus testibus prioribus actionibus didicistis, Cic , ab eo Stoico dialecticam didicerat, Cic , apud aliquem litteras, Cic , in castris per laborem usum militiae, Sall , with infin , saltare, Cic , Latine loqui, Sall , quinqueremes gubernare didicisse, Cic , with rel clause, plures discent quem ad modum haec fiant quam quem ad modum his resistatur, Cic , ita didicisse a majoribus ut, etc , *to have so learnt to be accustomed to*, Caes , disco fidibus, *to learn to play on the lyre*, Cic , absol , valent pueri, studiose discunt, diligenter docentur, Cic , volunt is discendi, Cic **B** Esp , discere causam, legal t t , *to get up the facts of a case*, of an advocate, Cic **II.** *to become acquainted with* **1,** gen , me peritus discet Hiber Rhodanique potor, Hor , **2,** *to become acquainted with a fact, learn, find out*, didici ex tuis litteris te omnibus in rebus habuisse rationem, Cic

discŏlor ōris **A.** *of different colours*, signa, Cic , miles, *black and white* (of the men at draughts), Ov **B.** Transf , *different from, unlike to*, matrona meretrici dispar atque discolor, Hor

disconvĕnĭo, 4 *to disagree, not to harmonise*, vitae ordine toto, Hor , impers , eo disconvenit inter meque et te, Hor

discordĭa -ae, f (discors) **I. a,** *dissension, disagreement, discord*, haec discordia non rerum sed verborum, Cic , **b,** *dissension, sedition*, Tac **II.** Personif , Discordia, *the Goddess of Discord*, Verg

discordĭōsus a -um (discordia), *full of discord, mutinous*, vulgus seditiosum atque discordiosum fuit, Sall

discordo, 1 (discors), **1,** *to be at discord, to disagree*, cum Cheruscis, Tac , inter se dissidere atque discordare, Cic, animus a se dissidens secumque discordans, Cic, of soldiers, *to be mutinous*, Tac, 2, *to be unlike*, quantum discordet parum avaro, Hor

discors -cordis (dis and cor), 1 1, *disagreeing, inharmonious, discordant*, civitas secum ipsa discors, Liv, of inanimate objects, venti, Verg, bella, Ov, 2, *unlike, dissimilar, different*, tam discordia inter se responsa Liv

discrĕpantĭa ae, f (discrepo), *disagreement, difference*, scripti et voluntatis, Cic

discrĕpātĭo -ōnis, f (discrepo), *disagreement, disunion*, inter consules, Liv

discrĕpĭto, 1 (intens of discrepo), *to be entirely dissimilar, to be quite unlike*, Lucr

discrĕpo -pāvi, 1 *not to sound together* **A.** Lit, *to be out of time, to be discordant*, in fidibus aut in tibiis, Cic **B.** Transf, *to disagree, be different, be unlike*, cum aliquo or cum aliqua re, Cic, ab aliqua re, Cic, sibi, Cic; inter se, Cic, nunc in re, Cic, with dat, quantum simplex hilarisque nepoti discrepet, Hor, impers, discrepat, *there is a disagreement, people are not agreed*, discrepat inter scriptores, Liv, illud haudquaquam discrepat, Liv, with acc and infin, Liv, non or haud discrepat quin, etc, Liv

discrībo = describo (q v.)

discrīmen -inis, n (discerno), *that which divides* **I.** Lit, **A.** Concr, *the dividing line;* quum pertenui discrimine (duo maria) separarentur, Cic **B.** Abstr, **a,** *the space between*, spatium discrimina fallit, Ov; **b,** in music, *interval*, septem discrimina vocum (of the lyre with seven strings), Verg **II.** **a,** *separation, distinction, difference*, delectu omni et discrimine remoto, Cic, **b,** *turning-point, critical moment*, ea res nunc in discrimine versatur utrum possitne an, Cic, in discrimen adductum esse, Cic, **c,** *crisis, hazard, danger*, in tanto discrimine periculi, Liv, ad ipsum discrimen eius temporis, Cic, res esse in summo discrimine, Caes

discrīmĭno, 1 (discrimen), *to separate, sunder, divide*, Etruriam discriminat Cassia, Cic, vigiliarum somnique nec die nec nocte discriminata tempora, Liv

discriptĭo -ōnis, f (discribo), *a division*, Cic

discrŭcĭo, 1 *to torture vehemently, torment*, of bodily torture, discruciatos necare, Cic, of mental anguish, refl or pass, *to torment oneself, make oneself miserable*, Cic.

discumbo -cŭbŭi -cŭbĭtum, 3 *to lie down*, **a,** *to recline at table*, discubuimus omnes praeter illam, Cic, impers, discumbitur, *one goes to the table*, Cic, **b,** *to sleep, go to bed*, cenati discubuerunt ibidem, Cic

discŭpĭo -īvi -ītum, 3 *to desire vehemently*, Cat

discurro -cŭcurri and -curri -cursum, 3 *to run in different directions, run about, run to and fro*, in muris, Caes; circa deum delubra, Liv, ad arma, Liv, impers, totā discurritur urbe, Verg, of things, diversa ruens septem discurrit in ora, Verg, quum mens discurrit utroque, Ov

discursus -ūs, m (discurro), *a running up and down, a running about, running to and fro*, militum, Liv, lupi, Ov, of things, liber inter ordines discursus, of a ship, *unhindered motion*, Liv

discus -i, m (δίσκος), *a quoit*, discum audire quam philosophum malle, Cic.

discŭtĭo -cussi -cussum, 3 (dis and quatio), *to strike asunder* **I.** *to shatter, break down* tribus arietibus aliquantum muri, Liv. **II.** 1, *to disperse, scatter*, nubem, Ov, umbras, Verg, discussa est caligo, Cic, 2, *to frustrate, bring to nought, suppress*, eam rem, Liv, caedem, Cic; eorum captiones, Cic, eorum advocationem manibus, ferro, lapidibus, Cic

dĭsertē, adv with superl (disertus), *clearly, plainly, eloquently*, dicere, Cic

dĭsertus -a -um, p adj with compar and superl (dissero), *eloquent, well-expressed*, **a,** of the language, oratio Cic, historia, Cic, **b,** of the person speaking homo, Cic, disertissimus orator, Cic

disĭcĭo = disjicio (q v)

disjecto, 1 (intens of disjicio), *to cast about, scatter*, Lucr

1 **disjectus** -a -um, v disjicio

2 **disjectus** -ūs, m (disjicio), *a scattering, dispersing*, Lucr

disjĭcĭo -jēci -jectum, 3 (dis and jacio), *to cast asunder* **I.** Lit, **A.** Gen, of buildings, etc, *to throw down, destroy*, disjecta tempestate statua, Liv, disjecta aedificia, Caes **B.** *to scatter, disperse* naves or classem, Liv, disjecta comas, *with dishevelled hair*, Ov, disjecta membra poetae, Hor, disjecta manus, Cic, milit t t., *to scatter*, phalangem, Caes **II.** Transf, *to bring to naught, frustrate;* consilia ducis, Liv

disjunctĭo -ōnis, f (disjungo), *separation* **I.** Lit, meorum, Cic **II.** Transf, **1,** gen, *difference*, animorum, Cic, **2,** esp, **a,** in logic, *a disjunctive proposition*, Cic, **b,** in rhet *a series of sentences without connecting particles, asyndeton*, Cic

disjunctus -a -um, p adj with compar and superl (disjungo), *separated, sundered, distant* **I.** Lit., quae (Aetolia) procul barbaris disjuncta gentibus, Cic **II.** Transf, **A.** Gen, *remote from*, homines Graeci longe a nostrorum hominum gravitate disjuncti, Cic **B.** Esp, **1,** in logic, *disjunctive*, **2,** in rhet, *disconnected*, Cic.

disjungo -junxi -junctum, 3 *to unbind, loosen, separate* **I.** Lit, **a,** *to unyoke* or *unharness*, jumenta, Cic., **b,** *to separate, sunder, remove*, intervallo locorum et tempore disjuncti sumus, Cic; Italis disjungimur oris, Verg **II.** Transf., **A.** Gen, *to separate*, aliquem ab aliquo, Cic **B.** Esp, *to distinguish*, insaniam a furore, Cic.

dispālor, 1 dep *to wander about, to stray*, Nep

dispando -pandi -pansum, 3 *to expand, extend, stretch out*, Lucr

dispar -păris, *unlike, different, dissimilar, unequal*, fortuna, Cic, tempora, Cic, with dat, illa oratio huic dispar, Cic, with genit, quid quam dispar sui atque dissimile, Cic.

dispargo, v dispergo.

dispărīlis -e, *unlike, dissimilar, different, unequal*, disparilis exspiratio terrarum, Cic

dispăro, 1 *to separate, part, divide*, seniores a junioribus divisit eosque ita disparavit ut, etc, Cic, partic subst, **dispărātum** -i, n, rhet t t., *the contradictory proposition* (e g, sapere, non sapere), Cic

dispartĭo = dispertio (q v)

dispello -pŭli -pulsum, 3 **I.** *to drive in different directions*, pecudes, Cic. **II.** *to scatter, dispel*, umbras, Verg, transf, ab animo tamquam ab oculis caliginem, Cic

dispendĭum -ii, n (dispendo), *expenditure, expense, loss;* facere, *to suffer loss*, transf, dispendia morae, *loss of time*, Verg

1 **dispendo** = dispando (q v.)

2 **dispendo** -pensum, 3 *to weigh out*, Varr.

dispenno = dispando (q.v.)

dispensātĭo -ōnis, f (dispenso), 1, *management, economical administration*, aerarii, Cic, annonae, Liv, 2, *the office of a dispensator*, Cic, regia, *the office of treasurer to a king*, Cic

dispensātor ōris, m (dispenso), *a steward, bailiff, treasurer*, Cic

dispenso, 1 (intens of 2 dispendo) I. *to weigh out or pay away money*, Plaut, *to divide, distribute*, oscula per natos, Ov, laetitiam inter impotentes populi animos, Liv, in rhet., inventa non solum ordine, sed etiam momento quodam atque judicio, Cic II. a, gen, *to arrange*, annum intercalariis mensibus interponendis ita dispensavit ut, etc, Liv, b, esp, *to manage a household*, res domesticas, Cic

disperdĭtĭo ōnis, f (disperdo), *a total destruction, ruin*, Cic

disperdo dĭdi dĭtum, 3 *to destroy, ruin, annihilate*, possessiones, Cic

dispĕrĕo -ĭi, 4 *to perish utterly, be entirely ruined*, fundus disperit, Cic., dispeream, si, or nisi, *may I perish if* or *except*, Cat, Hor

dispergo -spersi -spersum, 3 (dis and spargo), *to scatter, spread abroad, disperse*, a, tam multa pestifera terrā marique, Cic., *to disperse an army*, Caes., b, rumores, *to spread abroad reports*, Tac

dispersē and **dispersim**, adv (dispersus), *in different places, dispersedly, here and there*, Cic

dispersĭo -ōnis, f (dispergo), *a scattering, destruction*, Cic

dispertĭo (dis-partio) -īvi and -ĭi -ītum, 4 *to separate, divide, distribute* A. Lit, pecuniam judicibus, Cic; exercitum per oppida, Liv B. Transf, tempora voluptatis laborisque, Cic, dep, **dispertĭor** -īri, aliquid in infinita, Cic, administrationem inter se, Liv

dispĭcĭo spexi -spectum, 3 (dis and specio) I. *to open the eyes and begin to see*, catuli qui jam dispecturi sint, Cic II. A. *to catch sight of, perceive*, 1, lit, Lucr; 2, transf, populus Romanus libertatem jam ex diutina servitute dispiciens, Cic B. 1, *to perceive mentally*, si dispicere quid coepero, Cic, with rel sent, sed ego quod sperem non dispicio, Cic, 2, *to reflect upon, consider*, res Romanas, Cic

displĭcĕo -plicŭi -plicitum, 2 (dis and placeo), *to displease* (opp placeo, complaceo), alicui, Cic, alicui de aliquo, Cic; mihi or alicui displicet, with infin, Cic, displicere sibi, *to be dissatisfied with oneself, to be melancholy, out of spirits*, Cic

displōdo -plōsi -plōsum, 3 *to spread out, dilate, burst*, Hor

dispōno -pŏsŭi pŏsĭtum, 3 (dis and pono), *to put in different places, to distribute*. I. Gen, A Lit, pocula Bacchi, Ov, signa ad omnes columnas, omnibus etiam intercolumniis, in silva denique disposita sub divo, Cic, milit. t t, portis stationes, Liv, praesidia ad ripas, Caes B. Transf, a, *to distribute on a definite plan*, imperii curas, Tac; b, rhet t t, verba ita, ut pictores varietatem colorum, Cic. II. *to arrange, dispose, set in order* A. Lit, Homeri libros antea confusos, Cic, bene dispositae comae, Ov B. Transf, disposita ad honorem studia, Cic

dispŏsĭtē, adv (dispositus), *in proper order, methodically*, accusare, Cic

dispŏsĭtĭo -ōnis, f (dispono), *a regular arrangement or order in a speech*, Cic

dispŏsĭtūra ae, f (dispono), *arrangement, order*, Lucr.

1 **dispŏsĭtus** -a um, p adj (dispono), *arranged*, Plin.

2 **dispŏsĭtus** -ūs, m (dispono), *arrangement*, Tac

dispŭtātĭo -ōnis, f (disputo), *an arguing, debating, argument, debate*, hāc in utramque partem disputatione habitā, Cic

dispŭtātor ōris, m (disputo), *a debater, disputant*, Cic

dispŭto, 1 *to discuss, weigh, debate, argue*, aliquid, Cic, de aliqua re, Cic, ad aliquam rem de aliqua re, Cic, pro omnibus et contra omnia, Cic, contra propositum, Cic, disputari in utramque partem, *for and against*, Cic, with rel sent, ego enim quid desiderem, non quid videam disputo, Cic

disquīro, 3 (dis and quaero), *to inquire into, investigate*, Hor

disquīsītĭo -ōnis, f (disquiro), *an inquiry, investigation*, Cic

dissaepĭo -saepsi -saeptum, 4 *to hedge off, separate, divide*, aliquid tenui muro, Cic

dissaeptĭo -ōnis, f (dissaepio), *a partition*, Liv (?)

dissaeptum -i, n (dissaepio), *a barrier, partition*, Lucr

dissēmĭno, 1 *to spread abroad, disseminate*, sermonem, Cic, malum, Cic

dissensĭo -ōnis, f (dissentio), *disagreement, variance* I. Of persons, a, in a friendly manner, inter homines de jure, Cic, est quaedam inter nos parva dissensio, Cic, b, in a hostile manner, *dissension, disunion*, dissensio ac discidium, Cic., dissensio civilis, Caes II. Of abstractions, *opposition* utilium cum honestis, Cic

dissensus ūs, m. (dissentio), *disunion, disagreement*, Verg

dissentānĕus -a -um (dissentio), *disagreeing, different* (opp consentaneus), alicui rei, Cic

dissentĭo -sensi -sensum, 4 *to be of a different opinion, not to agree* I. Lit, Of persons, a, in a friendly manner, ab aliquo, Cic, ab aliqua re, Cic, de aliqua re, Cic, cum aliquo, Cic, inter se, Cic, with dat, conditionibus foedis, Hor, b, in a hostile manner, *to be at variance*, acerrime dissentientes cives, Cic II. Transf, of things, *to be opposed, different*, a more, Cic, quid ipsum a se dissentiat, Cic

dissēp v dissaep.

dissĕrēnascit -āvit, impers (inchoat of disserenat, *it clears up* (of the weather), quum undique disserenavisset, Liv

dissĕrēnat, impers (dis and serenus), *it clears up*, Plin

1 **dissĕro** -sēvi sĭtum, 3, 1, *to scatter seed*, Plin, 2, *to plant at a distance in the ground*, taleas, Caes

2 **dissĕro** -sĕrŭi -sertum, 3 *to examine, treat of, discuss a subject*, with acc, ista, Cic, with acc and infin, Cic, with relative sentence (quomodo, qui, quid), Cic, with de, quae Socrates supremo vitae die de immortalitate animorum disseruisset, Cic

disserpo, 3 *to creep in different directions spread imperceptibly*, late disserpunt tremores, Lucr

dissertio, 1 (intens of 2 dissero), *to treat of discuss, argue*, aliquid, Tac

dissĭdĕo -sēdi -sessum, 2 (dis and sedeo), lit, *to sit apart* I. *to be drawn apart*, si toga dissidet impar, *sits unevenly*, Hor. II. *to be distant, to be separated* A. Lit, of places, quantum Hypanis Veneto dissidet Eridano, Prop B. Transf, *not to agree*, a, of persons, *to disagree, dissent, be of a different opinion*, inter se,

Cic.; ab aliquo, Cic.; cum aliquo, Cic.; de aliqua, Cic.; with dat., dissidens plebi virtus, Hor.; in a hostile sense, *to be at variance*, Cic.; b, of things, *to be opposed, contrary*; scriptum a sententia dissidet, Cic.; cupiditates inter se dissident et discordant, Cic.

dissĭdĭum -ĭi, n. (dissideo), *disagreement, disunion*, Cic.

dissĭlĭo -silŭi -sultum, 4. (dis and salio), *to leap apart, burst asunder*. **A.** Lit., haec loca dissiluisse feruut, Verg.; dissilit omne solum, Ov. **B.** Transf., gratia sic fratrum geminorum dissiluit, *was broken up*, Hor.

dissĭmĭlis -e, adj. with compar. and superl., *unlike, dissimilar*; with genit., verum tamen fuit tum sui dissimilis, Cic.; with dat., quies est tam dissimilis homini, qui non, etc., Cic.; with inter se, duo fuerunt per idem tempus dissimiles inter se, Cic.; with inter se and the genit., qui sunt et inter se dissimiles et aliorum, Cic.; with atque (ac) quam and et, dissimilis est militum causa et tua, Cic.; absol., naturae dissimiles, Cic.

dissĭmĭlĭtĕr, adv. (dissimilis), *differently, in a different manner*, Liv.

dissĭmĭlĭtūdo -ĭnis, f. (dissimilis), *unlikeness, difference*; locorum, Cic.; habet ab illis rebus dissimilitudinem, Cic.; dissimilitudinem non nullam habet cum illius administratione provinciae, Cic.; quum tanta sit inter oratores bonos dissimilitudo, Cic.

dissĭmŭlantĕr, adv. (dissimulo), *secretly, in a dissembling manner*; verba non aperte sed dissimulanter conclusa, Cic.; non or ne dissimulanter, *without dissembling*, Cic.

dissĭmŭlātĭo -ōnis, f. (dissimulo), *a concealing, dissembling, dissimulation*, Cic.; esp. *of irony* (in the Socratic sense), Cic.

dissĭmŭlātor -ōris, m. (dissimulo), *a dissembler, concealer*; opis propriae, Hor.

dissĭmŭlo, 1. *to make unlike*. **I.** *to conceal, to hide*; Achilles veste virum longā dissimulatus erat, *concealed his manhood beneath a woman's robe*, Ov. **II.** *to act or to speak as if a thing which is were not*. **A.** *to dissemble, disguise, keep secret*; aliquid silentio, Cic.; dissimulata deam, *concealing her divinity*, Ov.; with acc. and infin., Cic.; with ut and the subj., Cic.; non dissimulare, followed by quin, Cic.; dissimulare non sinit quin delector, Cic.; absol., *to dissemble*; non dissimulat, Cic. **B.** *to ignore, leave unnoticed*; dissimulare consulatum alicuius, Tac.

dissĭpābĭlis -e (dissipo), *that can be scattered*; ignis et aer, Cic.

dissĭpātĭo -ōnis, f. (dissipo). **I.** *scattering*; civium, Cic. **II. A.** *dispersion by sale*; praedae, Cic. **B.** Rhet. t. t., *the analysis of an idea*, Cic.

dissĭpātus -a -um, p. adj. (dissipo), *scattered, disconnected*; oratio, Cic.

dissĭpo, 1. (dis and * sipo). **I.** *to scatter, disperse, spread abroad*. **A.** Lit., membra fratris, Cic.; aliud alio, Cic. **B.** Transf., 1, ea contrahere amicitiam, dissipare discordiam, *put an end to*, Cic.: 2, famam, *spread abroad*, Cic. **II.** *to scatter by violence*; 1, lit., milit. t.t., *to rout, scatter*; hostes, Cic.; dissipata fuga, Liv.; 2, *to pull down, destroy*; statuam, Cic.; tecta, Liv.; 3, of property, *to squander, destroy*; patrimonium, Cic.; reliquias reipublicae, Cic.

dissĭtus, partic., v. 1. dissero.

dissŏcĭābĭlis -e (dissocio), 1, act. *that which separates*; oceanus, Hor.; 2, pass., *that which cannot be united*; res, Tac.

dissŏcĭātĭo -ōnis, f. (dissocio), *a separation, parting*; spiritus corporisque, Tac.

dissŏcĭo, 1. **I.** *to separate, sever, divide friendships, etc.*; morum dissimilitudo dissociat amicitias, Cic.; disertos a doctis, Cic. **II.** Of places, *to separate, divide*; ni (montes) dissocientur opacā valle, Hor.

dissŏlūbĭlis -e (dissolvo), *dissoluble, separable*; mortale omne animal et dissolubile et dividuum sit necesse est, Cic.

dissŏlūtē, adv. (dissolutus), 1, *disconnectedly, loosely*; dissolute dicere, *without connecting particles*, Cic.; 2, *carelessly, negligently, without energy*; minus severe quam decuit, non tamen omnino dissolute, Cic.

dissŏlūtĭo -ōnis, f. (dissolvo). **I.** Lit. *breaking up, dissolution, destruction, annihilation*; naturae, *death*, Cic.; navigii, *shipwreck*, Tac. **II.** Transf., 1, *destruction, abolition*; legum, judiciorum, Cic.; 2, *refutation* of a charge; criminum, Cic.; 3, *want of energy, weakness*; remissio animi ac dissolutio, Cic.; 4, in rhet., *want of connexion*, Cic.

dissŏlūtus -a -um, p. adj. with compar. and superl. (dissolvo). **I.** *not bound together, loosened*; navigium, *leaky*, Cic. **II.** Transf., 1, rhet. t. t., *disconnected, loose*, Cic.; 2, *wanting in energy, lax*; poterone esse in eum dissolutus qui, etc., Cic.; 3, *profligate, dissolute*; dissolutissimus hominum, Cic.

dissolvo -solvi -sŏlūtum, 3. **I.** *to loosen, unloose*. **A.** Lit., 1, gen., scopas, clipeum, Cic.; 2, esp. *to melt*; aes, Lucr. **B.** Transf., 1, gen., *to break up, destroy*; societatem, amicitiam, Cic.; leges, Cic.; 2, esp. a, rhet. t. t., *to divide*; orationem, Cic.; b, *to refute an assertion, charge*, etc.; criminationem, Cic. **II.** *to pay, discharge* a debt; aes alienum, Cic.; pecuniam publicam ulli civitati, Cic.

dissŏnus -a -um. **A.** *discordant, inharmonious, dissonant*; clamores, Liv. **B.** Transf., *different, disagreeing*; dissonae gentes sermone moribusque, Liv.

dissors -sortis, *having a different lot* or *fate*; ab omni milite dissors gloria, *not shared with*, Ov.

dissuādĕo -suāsi -suāsum, 2. *to advise against, oppose by argument*; legem agrariam, Cic.; de captivis, Cic.; with acc. and infin., Cic.; absol., dissuasimus nos, *I spoke against it*, Cic.

dissuāsĭo -ōnis, f. (dissuadeo), *advising to the contrary, speaking against*; rogationis eius, Cic.

dissuāsor -ōris, m. (dissuadeo), *one who advises to the contrary, one who speaks against*; rogationis, Cic.; legis agrariae, Liv.; transf., of things, Auster quasi dissuasor consilii mei, Cic.

dissuāvĭor, 1. dep. *to kiss eagerly*, ap. Cic.

dissulto, 1. (intens. of dissilio), *to leap apart, burst asunder*; nec fulmine tanti dissultant crepitus, Verg.; dissultant ripae, Verg.

dissŭo -sŭi -sūtum, 3. **A.** Lit., *to unstitch*. **B.** Transf., *to open wide*; sinum, Ov.; *to loosen gently* or *by degrees*; tales amicitiae dissuendae magis quam discindendae, Cic.

distantĭa -ae, f. (disto), *difference, diversity*; morum studiorumque, Cic.

distendo -tendi -tentum and -tensum, 3. *to stretch apart, expand, extend*. **I.** Gen., aciem, Caes.; brachia, Ov. **II.** 1, *to fill full, distend*; ubera cytiso, Verg.; horrea plena spicis, Tib.; 2, a, milit. t. t., *to divide, to distract the attention of the enemy by attacks in different places*; copias hostium, Liv.; b, *to distract, perplex*; distendit ea res animos Samnitium, Liv.

1. **distentus** -a -um, p. adj. (distendo) *distended, full*; ubera, Hor.

2 **distentus** a -um, p adj with superl (distineo), *busy, occupied*, tot tantisque negotiis, Cic

distermino, 1 *to separate by a boundary, divide*, Cic poet , quod (flumen) Dahas Ariosque disterminat, Tac

distichus a um (δίστιχος), *consisting of two rows*, subst **distichum** (-on) 1, n *a poem of two lines, a distich*, Mart.

distinctē, adv with compar. (distinctus), *clearly, definitely, distinctly*, dicere, Cic

distinctio -ōnis, f (distinguo), 1, *a separation in space*, solis lunae siderumque omnium, *different orbits*, Cic , 2, a, *distinguishing, discriminating*, facilis est distinctio ingenui et illiberalis joci, Cic , lex est justorum injustorumque distinctio, Cic , b, rhet t. t , *a distinguishing between the same word used in different ways*, or *between ideas nearly alike*, Cic . 3, a, *distinction, difference*, modo intelligatur, quae sit causarum distinctio et dissimilitudo, Cic , b, rhet t. t., *a pause, division*, Cic

1 **distinctus** a -um, p adj (distinguo), *separated, distinct*, urbs delubris distinctis spatiisque communibus, Cic

2. **distinctus,** abl -ū, m (distinguo), *difference, distinction*, Tac

distineo -tinui tentum, 2 (dis and teneo) I. A. Lit , *to hold asunder, keep apart, separate, divide*, tigna binis utrimque fibulis distinebantur, Caes B Transf , a, gen , duae senatum distinebant sententiae, Liv , b, esp , *to delay*, pacem, Cic II. *to prevent uniting together* A. Milit. t t , *to prevent the union of forces* , Caes . ans copias, Cic , Volscos, Liv B. *to prevent the concentration of one's thoughts, to distract*, maximis occupationibus distineri, Cic

distinguo stinxi stinctum, 3 (from dis and *stigo, stinguo, connected with στίζω) I. *to separate, divide* A. Lit ,onus numero distinxit eodem, Ov B. Transf , 1, *to separate, distinguish*, distinguere voces in partes, Cic , vera a falsis, Cic , impers , quid inter naturam et rationem intersit non distinguitur Cic , 2, grammat t t , *to punctuate*, Quint. II. Meton A. *to point out, mark out*, nigram medio frontem distinctus ab albo, Ov B. *to decorate, adorn*, pocula ex auro quae gemmis erant distincta clarissimis, Cic , of orator), oratio distinguitur atque illustratur aliquā re, Cic C. *to vary, change, give variety to*, historiam varietate locorum, Cic

disto, 1 (dis -sto). I. *to be apart, separate, distant*, 1, of space, quae turres pedes LXXX inter se distarent, Caes ; 2, of time quantum distet ab Inacho Codrus, Hor II. Transf , *to differ, be distinct*, inter se, Cic , ab aliquo, Cic , scurrae (dat), Hor , impers , distat, *there is a difference*, Cic

distorqueo -torsi -tortum, 2 *to twist apart, distort*, ora cachinno, Ov., oculos, Hor.

distortio -ōnis, f. (distorqueo), *distortion*, membrorum, Cic

distortus -a -um, p adj with compar and superl. (distorqueo), *distorted deformed* A. Lit , crura, Hor , of persons, distortus Gallus, Cic. B. Transf , of discourse, *perverse*, nullum (genus enuntiandi) distortius, Cic

distractio ōnis, f (distraho), 1, *a dividing, separating*, humanorum animorum, Cic , 2, *disunion, dissension*, nulla nobis societas cum tyrannis et potius summa distractio est, Cic

distrăho traxi -tractum, 3 I. *to pull apart, tear asunder, tear in pieces* A Lit , 1, gen , vallum, Liv , corpus, Cic ; equis distrahi, Verg , acies distrahitur, *is divided*, Caes , fuga distrahit aliquos, Cic , 2, esp , a, *to sell property by auction, to put up for sale*, agros, Tac , b, grammat t t , *to leave a hiatus in a verse*, voces, Cic B. Transf , 1, distrahi in contrarias partes (or sententias), Cic oratoris industriam in plura studia, *to distract*, Cic , 2, esp , a, *to dissolve a league or union*, omnem societatem civitatis, Cic , concilium Boeotorum, Liv , distrahi cum aliquo, *to fall out with some one*, Cic , b, *to bring to naught*, hanc rem, Caes , c *to settle a dispute*, controversias, Cic II. *to tear from something* A. Lit , aliquem a complexu suorum, Cic B. Transf , *to estrange*, aliquem ab aliquo, Cic

distrĭbŭo -ŭi -ūtum, 3 *to distribute, divide* I. Gen , populum in quinque classes, Cic , pecunias exercitui, Caes II. Esp , *to arrange or divide logically*, causam in crimen et in audaciam, Cic

distrĭbūtē, adv with compar (distributus), *methodically, with logical arrangement*, scribere, Cic

distrĭbūtio -ōnis, f (distribuo), a, *a division, distribution*, Cic , b, *logical arrangement of ideas*, Cic

distrĭbūtus -a -um, p adj (distribuo), *logically arranged*, expositio, Cic

districtus -a -um, p adj (from distringo), a, *busy, occupied, engaged*, contentione ancipiti, Cic , b, *severe*, Tac

distringo -strinxi -strictum, 3 A. Lit , *to draw apart, stretch out*, radiis rotarum districti pendent, Verg , fig , destrictus enim mihi videris esse, *to be on the rack*, Cic B. Transf , *to engage an enemy at different points, divert, occupy*, Hannibalem in Africam mittere ad distringendos Romanos, *to make a diversion*, Liv

disturbătio -ōnis, f (disturbo), *destruction*, Corinthi, Cic

disturbo, 1 *to drive apart, separate with violence, throw into confusion* I. Lit , A. Gen , contionem gladiis, Cic B. *to destroy, raze to the ground*, domum meam, Cic , aedes, Lucr. II. Transf , *to bring to naught, frustrate, ruin*, societatem, Cic , legem, Cic

dītesco, 3 (3 dis), *to become rich*, Hor

dīthy̆rambĭcus -a -um (διθυραμβικός), *dithyrambic*, poema, Cic

dīthy̆rambus -i, m (διθύραμβος), *a dithyrambic poem* (originally in honour of Bacchus), Cic

dĭtio (dĭcio) -ōnis, f *power, sovereignty, authority*, esse in ditione alicuius, *to be in the power of*, Cic , facere ditionis suae, Liv , redigere bellicosissimas gentes in ditionem huius imperii, Cic , urbes multas sub imperium populi Romani ditionemque subjungere, Cic , rem Nolanam in jus ditionemque dare Poeno, Liv

dītior, dītissĭmus, v 3 dis

1. **dītis,** v 3 dis

2 **Dītis,** v 2 dis

dīto, 1 (3 dis), *to enrich, make wealthy*, praemiis belli socios, Liv , militem ex hostibus, Liv , pass , ditari as middle, *to become rich*, Liv , transf , sermonem patrium, Hor

1 **dĭū,** adv. (old abl of dies) I. *by day*, diu noctuque, Tac. II. 1, *a long time, a long while, lasting for a long time*, tam diu, jam diu, Cic , diu multumque or multum diuque, Cic , 2, *a long time ago*, jam diu, Cic Compar , diutius; a, *longer*, Cic , b, *too long*, Cic , paulo diutius abesse, Liv Superl , diutissime, Cic , Caes

2 **dĭū,** v dius

diurnus -a -um (for diusnus, from dies) I. *lasting for a day*, opus, *a day's work*, Cic , cibus, *rations*, Liv Subst , a, **diurnum** -i, n *journal, account book of house expenditure kept or* *a slave*, Juv, b, **diurna** -orum, *v* acta **II.** *happening by day*, magna diurna nocturnaque itinera, Caes, metus diurni nocturnique, Cic

dius -a -um (archaic and poet form of divus), *god-like* **I.** Adj, **A.** Lit, dius Fidius, v Fidius **B.** Transf, 1, *noble*, dia Camilla, Verg, **2,** *beautiful, fine*, sententia dia Catonis, Hor **II.** Subst, **dium** -ii, n, sub dio, and (archaic) sub diu, *in the open air*, Lucr

diūtinus -a -um (diu), *lasting a long time, long*, servitus, Cic

diūtius, diūtissimē, v 1 diu

diūturnitas -ātis, f (diuturnus), *long duration*, temporis, Cic; belli, Caes

diūturnus -a -um (1 diu), *lasting a long time, of long duration;* gloria, bellum, Cic; of persons, quae nupsit, non diuturna fuit, *did not live long*, Ov, non potes esse diuturnus, *you cannot remain long in your position*, Cic

dīvārĭco, 1 *to stretch apart, spread out*, hominem, Cic

dīvello velli -vulsum (-volsum), 3 **I.** *to pluck apart, tear asunder, separate by force* **A.** Lit, suos artus lacero morsu, Ov **B.** Transf, 1, res a naturā copulatas, Cic, commoda civium, Cic, **2,** *to break up, destroy*, affinitatem, Cic, somnum, *interrupt*, Hor **II.** *to tear away, remove, separate* **A.** Lit, liberos a complexu parentum, Cic., se ab hoste, Liv. **B.** Transf, divelli, *to tear oneself away from*, ab otio, a voluptate, Cic

dīvendo (-vendĭdi) -vendĭtum, 3 *to sell in separate lots*, bona populi Romani, Cic

dīverbĕro, 1 *to strike apart, cleave, divide*, volucres auras sagittā, Verg

dīverbĭum -ii, n (dis and verbum), *a dialogue on the stage*, Liv

dīversē, adv with compar. and superl (diversus), *in different directions, differently, diversely*, inconstans est, quod ab eodem de eadem re diverse dicitur, Cic

dīversĭtas -ātis, f (diversus), **1,** *contrariety, disagreement*, inter exercitum imperatoremque, Tac., 2, *difference, diversity*, supplicii, Tac

dīversōrĭum, v deversorium

dīversus -a um, p adj with compar and superl (diverto), *turned in different directions* **I. A.** Lit, diversam aciem in duas partes constituere, Caes, diversi abeunt, *they go different ways*, Liv, ubi plures diversae semitae erant, *leading different ways*, Liv **B.** Transf, *inconstant, irresolute, wavering, undecisive*, metu ac libidine diversus agebatur, Sall, in diversum auctores trahunt utrum . . an, *are not agreed*, Liv **C.** *separate, isolated*, legatos alium ex alio diversos aggreditur, Sall, ex locis tam longinquis tamque diversis, Cic **II.** *turned away from, in a different direction* **A.** Lit., 1, quo diversus abis, Verg; diversis a flumine regionibus, Caes, **2,** *lying out of the way, remote*, de Achaiae urbibus regionis a se diversae, Liv.; arva colebat diversa Aetnae, Ov., **3,** *in an opposite direction*, equi in diversum iter concitati, Liv, anguli maxime inter se diversi, Cic **B.** *different, opposed*, **a,** *hostile*, acies, Tac, b, *different, opposed in character or nature*, with a or ab, haec videntur esse a proposita ratione diversa, Cic, with inter se, diversa inter se mala, luxuria atque avaritia, Sall; absol, varia et diversa studia et artes, Cic, of persons, *different in character*, ab aliquo, Cic

dīverto (dīvorto) -verti (-vorti), 3 *to turn away, to diverge from, differ*, Plaut.

dīves -vĭtis, compar **dīvĭtior** -ius, genit. -ōris, superl **dīvĭtissĭmus.** *rich, wealthy* **I.** Lit, **a,** of persons, ex pauperrimo dives factus est, Cic, with abl, agris, Hor; with genit, pecoris, Verg b, of things, terra dives amomo, Ov **II.** Transf, *rich*, **a,** epistola, *containing much*, Ov, lingua, *eloquent*, Hor, divitior fluxit dithyrambus, Cic, b, *precious, costly*, cultus, *rich dress*, Ov

dīvexo, 1 (dis and vexo), *to tear asunder, destroy, plunder*, agros civium optimorum, Cic

dīvĭdo -visi visum, 3 (from dis and root VID, whence viduus). **I.** *to separate, divide* **A.** Lit, **1,** gen, omne animal secari ac dividi potest, Cic, 2, *to destroy*, muros, Verg **B.** Transf, 1, **a,** *to divide into parts*, exercitum in duas partes, Caes, Gallia est omnis divisa in partes tres, Caes, populum in duas partes, Cic, b, of logical division, genus universum in species certas partiri et dividere, Cic, **c,** polit t t, sententiam, *to divide a resolution into parts so that each part can be voted on*, Cic, **2,** a, *to divide among persons, distribute, allot*, agrum, bona viritim, Cic., praedam per milites, Liv, b, *to separate a multitude into different places*, in hiberna exercitum Magnesiam et Tralles Ephesumque, Liv.; c, poet, imbelli citharā carmina, *to sing*, Hor **II.** *to separate two wholes from one another* **A.** Gen, **a,** lit, *to divide*, Gallos ab Aquitanis Garumna dividit, Caes, b, transf, *to distinguish*, legem bonam a mala, Cic **B.** *to adorn*, gemma fulvum quae dividit aurum, Verg

dīvĭdŭus -a um (divido), **1,** *divisible*, Cic; 2, *divided, parted*, aqua, Ov

dīvīnātĭo -ōnis, f (divino), **1,** *the gift of prophecy, divination*, Cic., 2, legal t. t, *the selection of a prosecutor out of several*, Cic

dīvīnē, adv (divinus), 1, *by divine inspiration, prophetically*, Cic.; 2, *divinely, admirably, excellently*, Cic.

dīvīnĭtas -ātis, f (divinus). **I.** *a divine nature, divinity*, Cic **II. A.** *the power of prophecy or divination*, Cic **B.** *excellence, surpassing merit* (of an orator), Cic

dīvīnĭtŭs, adv (divinus) **I.** Lit., *divinely, by divine influence*, Cic. **II.** Transf, **A.** *by inspiration, by means of divination*, Cic **B.** *admirably, nobly, divinely*, loqui, Cic.

dīvīno, 1. (divinus), *to foretell, prophesy, forebode, divine the future*, with acc., hoc, Cic, with rel sent, quid futurum sit latrocinio tribunorum non divino, Cic, absol., quiddam praesentiens atque divinans, Cic

dīvīnus a -um, adj with compar. and superl (divus) **I.** *belonging or relating to a deity, divine*, res divina, *the service of the gods*, Cic, so res divinae, but res divinae (also) = *natural objects* as opp to res humanae, and *natural law* as opp to res humanae, *positive law*, Cic Subst., **dīvīnum** -i, n *a sacrifice*, Liv, plur, divina, *divine things*, Liv, *the attributes of the gods*, Cic **II.** Transf, **A.** *divinely inspired, prophetic*, Cic vates, *a poet*, Hor., subst., **dīvīnus** -i, m *a seer*, Cic **B.** *divine, excellent, noble, admirable*, divinus ille vir, Cic.

dīvīsĭo -ōnis, f (divido), **1,** *division*, **a,** orbis terrae, Sall, b, rhet t t., *division of a subject*, Cic, **2,** *distribution*, agrorum, Tac

dīvīsor -ōris, m (divido), 1, *a divider, distributor*, esp. of lands in a colony, Cic, **2.** *a hired briber y agent*, Cic.

1 **dīvīsus** -a um, partic. of divido

2 **dīvīsus** -ūs, m (divido), *division*, Macedonia divisui facilis, Liv

dīvĭtĭae -ārum, f (dives), *riches, wealth*. **I.** Lit, superare Crassum divitiis, Cic, **II.** Transf., ingenii, Cic,

dīvortium -ii, n (diverto or divorto) **I.** Of things, **a,** of places, *the point where roads, etc. separate, cross roads,* divortia nota, Verg , **b,** *the boundary line between two continents* or *countries,* artissimum inter Europam Asiamque divortium, Tac **II.** Of persons, **a,** *a divorce,* divortium facere cum aliqua, Cic , **b,** *separation generally,* Cic.

divorto, v diverto

dīvulgātus -a -um, p adj (from divulgo), *spread abroad, made common* magistratus levissimus et divulgatissimus, Cic.

dīvulgo (divolgo), 1 (dis and vulgo or volgo), **1,** *to make public, publish, spread abroad,* librum, Cic , rem sermonibus, Cic , **2,** *to make common,* cuius primum tempus aetatis palam fuisset ad omnium libidines divulgatum, Cic

dīvus a -um (from deus) **I.** Adj , *belonging to the deity, divine,* diva parens, Verg **II.** Subst **A. dīvus** -i, m *a god,* Cic , **dīva** -ae, f *a goddess,* Liv ; in imperial times divus was the epithet of the deified emperors, divi genus, of Octavianus, Verg **B. dīvum** i, n *the sky,* only in the phrase, sub divo, *in the open air,* Cic

do, dĕdi, dătum, dăre, *to give, offer* **A.** aliquid , **1,** lit , dare donum, Cic , populo Romano arma, Cic , of letters, *send, despatch,* tres epistolae eodem abs te datae tempore, Cic , dare poenas, *to suffer punishment,* Cic , dare lora, *to let the reins loose,* Verg , vela dare ventis, *to sail,* Verg , dare alicui cervices, *to offer the neck for punishment,* Cic , **2,** transf , *to give, lend, bestow, offer* , alicui vitam, Cic , nomen alicui rei, Liv , dare alicui fasces, *consular power,* Cic , cum locum colloquio, *to fix,* Liv , accipio quod datur, *what is offered,* Cic , corpori omne tempus, Cic , id misericordiae, *to grant, give up,* Cic , dare alicui contionem, Cic , dare urbem excidio ac ruinis, Liv **B.** aliquem (also corpus, membra, animum), **1,** lit , dare arbitrum, Cic , natam genero, Verg., **2,** transf , aliquam in matrimonium, Caes , aliquem morti, Hor , **3,** dare se or pass. dari, *to give oneself up,* se dare alicui in conspectum, Cic , *to throw oneself,* se in viam, Cic , dare se (alicui) obvium, *to meet,* Liv , dare se somno, Cic , se labori et itineribus, Cic **C.** *to give something from oneself,* **1,** lit , clamorem, *to utter,* Verg , dare (alicui) responsum, Cic , dare litem secundum aliquem, *to decide in one's favour,* Cic , impetum in aliquem, Liv , **2,** transf , alicui dolorem, Cic , documenta dare, Cic

dŏcĕo, dŏcŭi, doctum, 2 (DOC -eo, causative of DIC-sco—i e , disco), *to teach, instruct* **I.** Gen , with acc , aliquem, Cic , aliquem equo armisque, Liv , aliquem fidibus, Cic , with ad, ad quam (legem) non docti, Cic , with adv , aliquem Latine, Cic , jus civile, Cic , with double acc , aliquem litteras, Cic ; de aliqua re, with infin , aliquem sapere, Cic , absol , quum doceo et explano, Cic **II.** Esp , **a,** theatr t t , docere fabulam, like διδάσκειν δρᾶμα (lit , *to teach a play to the actors*), *to bring out, exhibit,* Cic , **b,** *to bring a matter before a public body* or *patron,* judices de injuriis, Cic

dochmius -ii, m (δοχμιος, sc πους), *a species of foot in poetry, the dochmiac foot* (⏑ – – ⏑ –), Cic

dŏcĭlis -e, adj with compar (doceo), *teachable, docile, attentive,* attentus judex et docilis, Cic , docilis ad hanc disciplinam, Cic , with genit , modorum, Hor

dŏcĭlĭtas ātis, f (docilis), *teachableness, docility,* Cic

doctē, adv with compar and superl (doctus), *learnedly, skilfully,* luctari, Hor

doctor -ōris, m (doceo), *a teacher,* eiusdem sapientiae doctores, Cic

doctrīna ae, f (doceo), **1,** *teaching, instruction,* puerilis, Cic , honestarum rerum, Cic , **2,** *that which is imparted in teaching, knowledge, learning,* Piso Graecis doctrinis eruditus, Cic , animos nostros doctrinā excolere, Cic

doctus a um, p adj with compar and superl (from doceo), **1, a,** of persons, *learned, instructed, well-informed,* Graecis litteris et Latinis, Cic ex disciplina Stoicorum, Cic , subst , **docti** -orum, *learned men,* with genit , fandi, Verg , with acc , dulces modos, Hor , **b,** of things that show learning, ars, Ov , sermones, Cic , **2,** *experienced, clever, shrewd,* doctus usu, Caes ; actate et usu, Liv

dŏcŭmen inis, n = documentum (q v)

dŏcŭmentum -i, n (doceo), *example, pattern, warning, proof,* P Rutilius documentum fuit hominibus nostris virtutis, Cic ; alicui documento esse, Caes , documentum sui dare, Liv

Dōdōna -ae and -ē -ēs, f (Δωδώνη), *a city of Epirus, renowned for its oak groves and oracle,* hence adj , **1, Dōdōnaeus** -a um, *of Dodona,* **2, Dōdōnis** idis, f *of Dodona*

dōdrans antis, m (de and quadrans), *three-fourths;* **1,** gen , aedificii reliquum dodrantem emere, Cic., heres ex dodrante, *heir to three-fourths of the property,* Suet , **2,** esp , **a,** as a superficial measure = *three-fourths of an acre,* Liv ; **b,** as a measure of length, *nine inches, three-fourths of a foot,* Plin

dōdrantārĭus -a -um (dodrans), *belonging to three fourths,* tabulae, *the register of debts introduced by the* lex Valeria feneratoria, *whereby the debts were reduced to one fourth,* Cic

dogma ătis, n (δόγμα), *a philosophical doctrine, principle, dogma,* Cic

Dolabella ae, m *a Roman family name of the gens Cornelia, the best known member of which is* P Cornelius Dolabella, *the son in law of Cicero*

dŏlābra ae, f (1 dolo), *an axe, hatchet, a military implement,* Liv

dŏlentĕr, adv with compar (doleo), *painfully, sorrowfully,* hoc dicere, Cic

dŏlĕo -dŏlŭi, fut partic dŏlĭturus, 2 *to suffer pain* **I.** Of bodily pain, pes, caput dolet, Cic **II.** Mentally, **1,** of persons, *to suffer pain, to grieve, bewail,* de Hortensio, Cic , meum casum luctumque doluerunt, Cic , with acc and infin , se a suis superari, Cic , foll by quod, Caes , si, Hor , absol , aeque dolendo, Cic , **2,** of things, **a,** *to grieve,* injecta monstris terra dolet suis, Hor , **b,** *to cause pain;* nihil cuiquam doluit, Cic

dōlĭŏlum i, n (dim of dolium), *a little cask,* Liv

dōlĭum -ii, n *a large earthenware jar* or *wooden cask,* in which new wine was placed , de dolio haurire, *to drink new wine,* Cic

1 **dŏlo,** 1 **I.** *to hew with an axe,* robur, Cic , transf , alicuius caput lumbosque saligno fuste, *to cudgel,* Hor **II.** *to work with an axe,* non est (homo) e saxo sculptus aut e robore dolatus, Cic , transf , illud opus, *to work roughly,* Cic

2 **dŏlo** or **dŏlon** onis, m (δόλων), **1,** *a wooden staff with an iron point,* Verg , transf , *the sting of a fly,* Phaedr , **2,** *a small foresail,* Liv

Dŏlops -lŏpis and plur **Dŏlŏpes** um, acc -as, m (Δόλοπες), *the Dolopes, a people in Thessaly* Hence, **Dŏlŏpĭa** -ae, f (Δολοπία), *the country of the Dolopes*

dŏlor -ōris, m (doleo) **I.** *bodily pain,*

anguish; pedum, Cic.; laterum, Hor. **II.** *mental pain, grief, sorrow.* **A.** Lit., 1, gen., injuriae, Caes.; dolorem accipere aliquā re or ex aliqua re, Cic.; tanto dolore affici ut, etc., Cic.; dolorem alicui facere or efficere, or dare, or afferre, Cic.; hoc est mihi dolori, Cic.; **2,** *rancour, animosity,* Cic.; quo dolore exarsit, Caes. **B.** Meton., **a,** *the cause of sorrow,* Ov.; **b,** in rhet., *pathos,* Cic.

dŏlōsē, adv. (dolosus), *deceitfully, craftily;* agi dolose, Cic.

dŏlōsus -a -um (dolus), *crafty, deceitful, cunning;* consilia, Cic.

dŏlus -i, m. (δόλος). **I.** Legal t. t., dolus malus, *fraud;* quum ex eo quaereretur quid esset Dolus malus, respondebat quum esset aliud simulatum, aliud actum, Cic. **II. A.** *fraud, deceit, guile;* fraus ac dolus, Cic.; ut magis virtute quam dolo contenderent, Caes. **B.** Meton., *trick;* dolos (= retia) saltu deludit, Ov.

dŏmābĭlis -e (domo), *that can be tamed, tameable;* Cantaber, Hor.

dŏmestĭcus -a -um (domus). **I.** *belonging to the house* or *the family, domestic;* luctus, Cic.; difficultas, *poverty,* Cic.; tempus, *spent at home,* Cic.; domesticus homo, Cic., and subst. domesticus, Ov., *a friend of the house, member of a family;* plur., **dŏmestĭci** -ōrum, m. *the inmates of one's house, members of one's family,* Cic. **II.** Transf., *private, domestic, native* (opp. to *foreign* or *public*); crudelitas, *towards citizens,* Cic.; si superavissent vel domesticis opibus vel externis auxiliis, Caes.; bellum, *civil war,* Cic.

dŏmĭcĭlĭum -ii, n. (domus), *a place of residence, dwelling.* **A.** Lit., aliud domicilium, alias sedes parant, Caes.; domicilium collocare in aliquo loco, Cic. **B.** Transf., imperii, *Rome,* Cic.; superbiae, Cic.

dŏmĭna -ae, f. (dominus). **I.** *the mistress of a household, lady,* Verg. **II.** *mistress, queen, lady.* **A.** Lit., **a,** as a term of respect to goddesses, of Venus, Ov.; of Cybele, Verg.; **b,** like English mistress, *a sweetheart,* Tib. **B.** Transf., *ruler, controller;* justitia domina virtutum, Cic.; Fors domina campi, Cic.

dŏmĭnātĭo -ōnis, f. (domino), *irresponsible power, despotism, arbitrary government.* **I.** Lit., **A.** unius, Cic.; Cinnae, Cic. **B.** Meton. = dominantes, *absolute rulers,* Tac. **II.** Transf., *governing;* temperantia est rationis in libidinem firma et moderata dominatio, Cic.

dŏmĭnātor -ōris, m. (dominor), *ruler, governor;* rerum Deus, Cic.

dŏmĭnātrix -īcis, f. (fem. of dominator), *a despotic mistress;* transf., caeca ac temeraria animi cupiditas, Cic.

dŏmĭnātus -ūs, m. (dominor), **1,** *absolute power;* dominatus regius, Cic.; **2,** *rule;* dominatus cupiditatum, Cic.

dŏmĭnĭum -ii, n. (dominus), **1,** *rule, power,* Sen.; **2,** *a feast, banquet;* huius argento dominia vestra ornari, Cic.

dŏmĭnor, 1. dep. (dominus), *to rule, be lord or master, to domineer;* in adversarios, Liv.; summā arce, Verg.; dominari Alexandriae, Cic.; in suos, Cic.; in nobis, Cic.; in capite fortunisque hominum honestissimorum, Cic.; in judiciis, Cic.; transf., dominatur libido, Cic.; quod unum in oratore dominatur, *wherein the strength of the orator consists,* Cic.

dŏmĭnus -i, m. (domus). **I.** *the master of a house, the head of the household, lord, master;* plur., domini, *master and mistress,* Cic. **II.** **A.** Lit., **1,** *master, owner, possessor;* aedificii, navis, Cic.; **2,** *lord, ruler;* in aliquem, Cic.; gentium, Cic.; rei (of the judge), Cic.; esp., **a,** *a lover,* Ov.; **b,** attrib., *belonging to a master;* poet., manus dominae, Ov.; **3,** *the arranger, a person that orders something;* of gladiatorial games, Cic.; of an auction, Cic.; with or without convivii or epuli, *the person who arranges a feast, host,* Cic. **B.** Transf., *ruler;* vitae necisque, *over life and death,* Liv.; comitiorum dominum esse, Cic.

dŏmĭporta -ae, f. (domus and porto), *she who carries her house upon her back, the snail,* ap. Cic.

Dŏmĭtĭānus -i, m. *T. Flavius Domitianus Augustus, son of Vespasian, brother of Titus,* born 51 A.D., Emperor of Rome from 81 A.D. to 96 A.D.

Dŏmĭtĭus -a -um, *name of a plebeian gens at Rome, the most famous members of which were:—* Cn. Domitius Calvinus, *consul* 53 B.C.; Cn. Domitius Ahenobarbus, *consul* 122 B.C., *conqueror of the Allobroges;* Cn. Domitius Ahenobarbus, *tribune* 104 B.C., *proposer of the* lex Domitia de sacerdotiis (*by which the priesthoods were filled up by the votes of* 17 *tribes chosen by lot*); L. Domitius Ahenobarbus, *consul* 54 B.C., *general and adherent of Pompeius;* Cn. Domitius Ahenobarbus, *father of the Emperor Nero;* Cn. Domitius Corbulo, *successful general in Germany and Armenia under the Emperors Claudius and Nero.* Adj. = *Domitian;* via, *road in Gaul made by Domitius Ahenobarbus, the conqueror of the Allobroges,* Cic. Hence, **Dŏmĭtĭānus** -a -um, *of Domitius;* milites, *the soldiers of L. Domitius Ahenobarbus,* Caes.

dŏmĭto, 1. (intens. of domo), *to tame, subdue;* boves, Verg.

dŏmĭtor -ōris, m. (domo), *a tamer.* **I.** Lit., **a,** of animals, equorum, *a horse-breaker,* Cic.; **b,** of men, *conqueror, victor;* domitor Persarum, Cic. **II.** Transf., Saturnius domitor maris alti, Verg.

dŏmĭtrix -īcis, f. (fem. of domitor), *she who tames;* Epidaurus domitrix equorum, Verg.; clava domitrix ferarum, Ov.

dŏmĭtus, abl. -ū, m. (domo), *taming;* efficimus domitu nostro quadrupedum vectiones, Cic.

dŏmo, dŏmŭi, dŏmĭtum, 1. *to tame, break in.* **I.** Lit., **a,** animals, beluas, Cic.; equos stimulo et verbere, Ov.; **b,** men, peoples, countries, &c. *to conquer, subdue;* hasta pugnantem, Ov.; maximas nationes virtute, Cic. **II.** Transf., **a,** concrete objects, ipsius fluminis vim, Liv.; arbores multā mercede, Verg.; uvas prelo, *to press,* Hor.; **b,** abstract objects, domitas habere libidines, Cic.; invidiam, Hor.

dŏmus -ūs, f. (cf. Gk. root ΔΕΜ, δέμ-ω, whence δόμος). **I. A.** Lit., *a house* (as a dwelling-place, as a home, seat of family, etc., while aedes = house as a building), as opp. to insula (which was let out in flats or lodgings; domus = *a house with its outbuildings and garden;* domum aedificare, Cic.; aliquem tecto et domo invitare, Cic.; used adverbially, domi, *at home, in the house,* Cic.; meae domi (tuae, suae, nostrae, etc.), *at my house,* Cic.; alienae domi, *in the house of another,* Cic.; domi aliquid habere, *to have at home, to possess, be provided with,* Cic.; domum, *home, towards home, homeward,* Cic.; domo, *from home, out of the house,* Cic. **B.** Transf., poet. *a dwelling-place,* of birds, Verg.; of the gods, Verg.; of the spirits of the dead, Verg.; of the labyrinth, Verg. **II.** Meton., **A.** **1,** *inmates of a house, household,* Cic.; **2,** *a philosophical school or sect,* Cic.; Socratica domus, Hor. **B.** *a household, management of a house,* Cic. **C.** *home, native country;* domi, *at home, in one's own country,* Cic.; domi militiaeque, Cic., belli domique, Liv., *in peace and in war* (archaic genit. or locat.

domi in classical writers only = *at home*, dat domui, abl generally domo, also domu, plur nom domus, acc domus and domos, genit domuum and domorum, dat and abl. domibus)

dōnārium ii, n (donum), **1,** *temple, shrine, altar,* Verg, Ov., **2,** *a votive offering,* Liv.

dōnātĭo -ōnis, f (dono), *a giving, gift, present, donation,* Cic.

dōnātīvum -i, n (dono), *an imperial largess,* or *donative to the soldiery,* Tac

dōnĕc, conj (shortened from doneque, donique), **1,** *as long as, while,* Liv.; donec gratus eram tibi, Hor, **2,** *until,* Cic; with usque eo, Cic, or eo usque, Liv.

dōno, 1 (donum) **I.** (alicui aliquid), *to give as a present, to present* **A.** Gen, **1,** lit, non pauca suis adjutoribus, Cic., **2,** transf, **a,** *to grant, bestow,* alicui aeternam immortalitatem, Cic, poet., with infin, alicui divinare, Hor, **b,** *to sacrifice, give up to;* inimicitias reipublicae, Caes **B.** Esp, **1,** lit *to remit a debt* or *obligation,* alicui aes alienum, Cic, **2,** transf *to forgive, pardon* (for the sake of someone else), noxae damnatus donatur populo Romano, Liv **II.** (aliquem aliquā re), *to present a person with something,* cohortem militaribus donis, Caes

dōnum i n (dare), *a gift, present,* **1,** gen, dona nuptialia, Cic; dono dare, *to give as a present,* Ter, **2,** esp, *a gift to the gods, a votive offering,* Cic

Dŏnūsa -ae, f (Δονουσία), *an island in the Aegean Sea, east of Naxos*

dorcas -ădis, f (δορκάς), *a gazelle, antelope,* Mart.

Dōres -um, m. (Δωριεῖς), *the Dorians, one of the Hellenic races,* hence, **1,** adj, **Dōrĭcus** a -um, poet. = *Greek,* Verg; **2, Dōrĭus** a um, *Dorian,* **3, Dōris** -idis, f. *Dorian,* subst, **a,** *Doris, a country in the north of Greece,* **b,** *the wife of Nereus, and mother of the fifty Nereids,* meton *the sea,* Verg

1 **Dōris,** v Dores

2 **Dōris** -idis, f. (Δωρίς), *wife of Dionysius I. of Syracuse*

dormĭo -ivi or ii, itum, 4 **1,** *to sleep,* se dormitum conferre, Cic, ad dormiendum proficisci, Cic, dormientem excitare, Cic, innumerabilia saecula dormisse, Cic, **2,** *to rest, be inactive;* beneficia dormientibus deferuntur, Cic

dormīto, 1 (dormio), *to be sleepy, to begin to sleep* **A.** Lit, dormitanti mihi epistola illa reddita, Cic; jam dormitante lucernā, *just going out,* Ov **B.** *to dream, be lazy, inactive,* ista oscitans et dormitans sapientia Scaevolarum, Cic, quandoque bonus dormitat Homerus, *nods,* Hor

dormītor -ōris, m (dormio), *a sleeper,* Mart

dorsum -i, n (**dorsus** i, m) **A.** Lit, *the back,* either of men or animals, dorso onus subire, Hor, dorsum demulcere equis, Liv **B.** Transf *any elevation of similar form,* duplex (dentalium), *the projecting irons of a ploughshare,* Verg; immane dorsum, *a rock in the sea,* Verg, of mountains, *slope,* jugi, Caes.

Dŏrўlaeum -i, n (Δορύλαιον), *a town in Phrygia* Hence, **Dŏrўlenses** ium, m *the inhabitants of Dorylaeum*

dŏrўphŏrŏs i, m (δορυφόρος), *the lance-bearer,* the name of a celebrated statue by Polycletus, Cic

dōs, dōtis, f (δώς) **A.** Lit. *a dowry, portion;* accipere pecuniam ab uxore dotis nomine, Caes; filiae nubili dotem conficere non posse, Cic **B.** Transf, **a,** *a gift,* cuius artem quum indotatam esse et incomptam videres, verborum eam dote locupletasti et ornasti, Cic; **b,** *a quality, endowment,* dotes ingenii, Ov

dōtālis e (dos), *relating* or *belonging to a dowry,* praedium, Cic

dōtātus -a -um, p adj (from doto), *richly dowered* **A.** Lit, Aquilia, Cic **B.** Transf, *richly endowed,* Chione dotatissima forma, Ov

dōto, 1 (dos), *to provide with a dowry, endow,* sanguine Trojano et Rutulo dotabere, virgo, Verg

drachma -ae, f (δραχμή), **1,** *a small Greek coin, a drachm, about equal in value to a Roman denarius,* Cic, **2,** as a weight, ⅛ *of an uncia,* Plin

1 **drăco** -ōnis, m (δράκων), **A.** *a kind of snake, dragon,* Cic **B.** Meton, *a constellation so called,* Cic

2 **Drăco** -ōnis, m (Δράκων), *Draco, an Athenian legislator*

drăcōnĭgĕna -ae, c (draco and gigno) = δρακοντογενής, *dragon born, sprung from dragon-seed,* urbs, *Thebes,* Ov

Drĕpănum -i, n (Δρέπανον), and **Drĕpăna** -ōrum, n (Δρέπανα), *a town on the west coast of Sicily* (now *Trapani*) Adj **Drĕpănĭtānus** -a -um, *of* or *belonging to Drepanum*

drŏmas -ădis, m (δρομάς), *a dromedary,* Liv

drŏmos -i, m (δρόμος), *the race course of the Spartans,* Liv

Drŭentia -ae, f *a river in Gallia flowing into the Rhone,* now *the Durance*

Drŭĭdes -um, m, and **Drŭĭdae** -ārum, m (*derwydd* or *dryod,* old British = *wise man*), *the Druids, the priests of the Celtic nations,* Cic

Drūsus i, m. *a cognomen of the Gens Livia* and *Claudia* (1) M Livius Drusus, *murdered for attempting to revive some of the Gracchan laws,* (2) Nero, *son of the Empress Livia, by her first husband, Tiberius Claudius Nero* Hence **a,** adj, **Drūsiānus** a -um and **Drūsīnus** -a -um, *of* or *belonging to Drusus,* **b,** subst **Drūsilla** -ae, f *name of several females of the gens Livia*

1 **Drўăs** -ădis, f (Δρυάς), *a wood nymph, Dryad,* gen plur Dryades, Verg

2 **Drўās** antis, m (Δρύας), *father of Lycurgus, king of Thrace* Hence **Drўantīdes** -ae, m *the son of Dryas,* i e *Lycurgus,* Ov

Drўŏpes -um (Δρύοπες), *a Pelasgic people, who were driven southwards by the Dorians, and settled in Messenia*

dŭbĭē, adv (dubius), 1 **A.** *doubtfully, hesitatingly,* inter confessum dubie dubieque negantem, Ov **B** *doubtfully, uncertainly,* ut aliquod signum dubie datum pro certo sit acceptum, Cic, hence, haud dubie, nec dubie, non dubie, *certainly, without doubt,* Cic

Dūbis is, m *river in Gallia Belgica,* now *the Doubs*

dŭbĭtābĭlis e (dubito), *doubtful, uncertain,* Ov

dŭbĭtantĕr, adv (dubito), **1,** *doubtingly;* dubitanter unum quodque dicemus, Cic, **2,** *hesitatingly,* illud verecundi et dubitantes recepisse, Cic

dŭbĭtātĭo -ōnis, f (dubito) **I.** *doubt, uncertainty,* sine ulla dubitatione, *certainly,* Cic, res non habet dubitationem, *the matter admits of no doubt,* Cic, with obj genit, dubitatio adventus legionum, *doubt as to the coming,* Cic, with de, illa Socratica dubitatio de omnibus rebus, Cic, with rel sent, si quando dubitatio accidit, quale sit id, etc, Cic, followed by quin when a negative precedes, hic locus nihil habet dubitationis quin, etc *admits of no doubt that,* Cic, nulla dubitatio est quin, etc Cic nisi dubitationem affert quin, etc., Cic. **II.** *hesitation, wavering, irresolution;* dubitatio belli, *as to the conduct of the war*, Cic.; augunt me dubitationes tuae, Cic.

dŭbĭto, 1. (dubius). **I.** *to doubt, waver in opinion, be uncertain;* de hoc, Cic.; haec, Cic.; utrum sit utilius an, etc., Cic.; honestumne factu sit an turpe, Cic.; non dubito quid, etc.; non dubito quin, etc., *I have no doubt that*, Cic. **II.** *to waver in resolution, hesitate;* **a,** of persons, quid dubitas, Caes.; dubito, foll. by infin., Cic.; non dubito, foll. by infin., Cic.; non dubito, foll. by quin, Cic.; **b,** of things, dubitavit aciei pars, Sall.

dŭbĭus -a -um (duo). **I.** Subject., *doubting*. **A.** *wavering in opinion, doubting, doubtful, uncertain*, Cic.; with genit., sententiae, Liv.; haud dubius, foll. by acc. and infin., *confident that*, Liv. **B.** *wavering in resolve, hesitating, uncertain, irresolute;* dubius an transiret, Liv. **II.** Object., *doubted, doubtful*. **A.** *undecided, uncertain, doubtful;* genus causae, Cic.; victoria, Caes.; caelum, *cloudy*, Ov.; non est dubium quin, *there is no doubt that*, Cic.; dubiumne est or cui dubium est quin? Cic.; num or nemini dubium est, with acc. and infin., Cic.; neut. subst., generally with a prepos., in dubium vocare or revocare, *to make doubtful*, Cic.; sine dubio, Cic.; procul dubio, *without doubt*, Liv. **B.** Meton. *doubtful, dubious, dangerous, critical;* res dubia, Sall.; tempora, Hor.

dŭcēni -ae -a (distrib. of ducenti), *two hundred each*, Liv.

dŭcentēsĭma -ae, f. (fem. of ducentesimus, from ducenti, sc. pars), *the two hundredth part, as a tax, one-half per cent.*, Tac.

dŭcenti -ae -a (duo and centum), **1,** *two hundred*, Cic.; **2,** *generally any large number*, Hor.

dŭcentĭēs, adv. (ducenti), *two hundred times*, Cic.

dūco, duxi, ductum, 3. **I.** *to draw*. **A.** Gen., frena manu, Ov. **B.** Esp., **1,** *to drag behind;* sidera crinem ducunt, Verg.; **2,** *to draw towards oneself;* **a,** lit., ducere remos, *to row*, Ov.; colorem, *to get a darker colour*, Verg.; **b,** transf., (α) *to charm, attract;* fabellarum auditione ducuntur, Cic.; (β) *to draw away, mislead;* errore duci, Cic.; (γ) *to draw to, influence;* me ad credendum tua ducit oratio, Cic.; **3,** *to draw in;* aëra spiritu, Cic.; poet., somnos, *to sleep*, Verg.; *to quaff;* pocula Lesbii, Hor.; **4,** *to draw out;* ferrum vaginā, Ov.; sortes, Cic.; aliquid or aliquem sorte, Cic.; **5,** *to draw out, extend, make, build, fashion;* parietem, Cic.; murum, Liv.; vallum, Caes.; ocreas argento, Verg.; **6,** *to draw out a thread;* lanas, *to spin*, Ov.; transf., of a poet, carmina, *to make verses*, Hor.; **7,** *to prolong;* **a,** *to pass;* aetatem in litteris, Cic.; **b,** *to delay, protract;* bellum, Cic.; aliquem diem ex die, *to put off*, Caes.; **8,** *to distort;* os, Cic.; **9,** *to draw down;* transf., **a,** *to derive;* nomen ex aliqua re, Cic.; etymolog., ab eundo nomen (Jani) est ductum, Cic.; **b,** *to begin;* ab eodem verbo ducitur saepius oratio, Cic.; **10,** *to count, reckon;* fenus quaternis centesimis, Cic.; aliquem in hostium numero, Caes.; aliquid parvi, *to esteem little*, Cic.; pluris, Cic.; pro nihilo, Cic.; aliquem despicatui, *to despise*, Cic.; with accus. and infin., *to consider;* qui se regem esse ducebat, Cic. **II.** *to lead*. **A.** Gen., **1,** of persons, ducere equum, Liv.; **2,** of things, duxit via in leniter editum collem, Liv. **B.** Esp., **1,** polit. and legal t.t., *to lead before a court of justice*, or *to lead away for punishment;* aliquem in jus, Liv.; in carcerem, in vincula, Cic.; **2, a,** milit. t.t., *to march;* cohortes ad munitiones, Caes.; absol., ad hostem, Liv.; **b,** *to command;* exercitus, Caes.; transf., familiam, *to be the most celebrated of*, Cic.; **3,** uxorem ducere, *to marry;* ducere uxorem alicuius filiam, Cic.; absol., ducere ex plebe, *to marry from among the plebs*, Liv.; **4,** *to lead by the nose, cheat*, Ov.; **5,** of water, *to conduct;* aquam in urbem, Liv.; **6,** *to take with one;* suas mulierculas secum, Cic.; **7,** *to order, arrange;* alicui funus, Cic.

ducto, 1. (intens. of duco), *to lead;* exercitum, Sall.

ductor -ōris, m. (duco), *a leader, commander*, Cic.; ordinum ductor, *a centurion*, Liv.

ductus -ūs, m. (duco) **I.** *drawing;* **a,** oris, *the lineaments of the face*, Cic.; **b,** muri, *building*, Cic. **II.** *leading;* **1,** milit. t.t., *command, leadership;* alicuius ductu, Cic.; se ad ductum Pompeii applicare, Cic.; **2,** *conducting of water;* aquarum, Cic.

dūdum, adv. (from diu = die and dum), **1,** *a little while ago, not long since;* quod tibi dudum (*just now*) videbatur, Cic.; **2, a,** quam dudum, *as long as;* quam dudum nihil habeo quod ad te scribam, Cic.; **b,** jam dudum, *now for a long time;* quem jam dudum Cotta et Sulpicius expectat, Cic.

dŭellum, dŭellĭcus, dŭellātor = bellum, bellicus, bellator, q.v.

Dŭīlius -a -um, *name of a Roman gens, of which the most celebrated was* C. Duilius, *cons.* 261 B.C., *who gained a great naval victory over the Carthaginians, near the Liparean Islands*. The victory was commemorated by the erection in the forum of a column, adorned with the prows of ships (columna rostrata).

dulcĕ, adv. (dulcis), *sweetly;* canere, Hor.

dulcēdo -inis, f. (dulcis). **I.** Lit., *a sweet taste;* sanguinis, Ov. **II.** Transf., **a,** *sweetness, pleasantness, charm;* dulcedine quadam gloriae commoti, Cic.; dulcedine orationis, Cic.; **b,** *desire;* dulcedo invasit plebeios creandi, Liv.

dulcesco, 3. (dulcis), *to become sweet*, Cic.

dulcĭcŭlus -a -um (dim. of dulcis), *somewhat sweet;* potio, Cic.

dulcis -e, adj. with compar. and superl. (connected with γλυκύς). **I.** Lit. *sweet* (opp. amarus), vinum, Hor.; unda, *fresh water*, Ov. Subst., **dulcĕ** -is, n. *what is sweet*, Ov.; **dulcĭa** -ium, n. *sweet things*, Cic. **II.** Transf. **A.** *sweet, pleasant, delightful, agreeable;* nomen libertatis, Cic.; poemata, Hor.; orator, Cic. **B.** *friendly, dear, beloved;* amici, Cic.; used in addresses, dulcissime Attice, Cic.

dulcĭtĕr, adv. (dulcis), with compar. dulcius, superl. dulcissime, *sweetly*, Cic.

dulcĭtūdo -inis, f. (dulcis), *sweetness*, Cic.

Dūlĭchĭum -ii, n. (Δουλίχιον), *an island in the Ionian Sea, forming part of the kingdom of Ulysses*. Adj. **Dūlĭchĭus** -a -um, *Dulichian*, poet., *belonging to Ulysses;* rates, Verg.; dux, *Ulysses*, Ov.

dum (like quum and tum, the acc. of a pronoun). **I.** Adv., joined as an enclitic with other words, **a,** with non, nullus, haud, vix, nondum, *not yet*, Cic.; so necdum, neque dum, Cic.; nullusdum, *no one yet*, Liv.; vixdum, *scarcely yet*, Cic.; nihildum, *nothing yet*, Cic.; nedum (sc. dicam), *not to say*, Cic.; **b,** with imperat. *then;* age dum, Cic.; ite dum, **II.** Conj., **1,** *while;* generally with indic. **2,** *as long as;* with indicat., Cic. **3,** *until;* with subj., Cic.; **4,** *in so far as, provided that;* with the subj., Cic.; dum modo, dummodo, Cic.; dumne, *provided that not*, Cic.; dummodo ne, Cic.

dūmētum -i, n. (dumus), *a thicket*, Cic.; fig., cur eam tantas in spinas et Stoicorum dumeta compellimus,

dummŏdo, v dum.

Dumnŏrix -īgis, m *brother of the Aeduan Diviliacus*

dūmōsus a -um (dumus), *covered with thorn bushes, bushy*, Verg

dumtaxăt = duntaxat, q v

dūmus -i, m *a thorn bush, bramble*, Cic

duntaxăt (dumtaxat), adv (dum and taxo), *exactly, according to the right measure, not more and not less* **I.** nos animo duntaxat vigemus, *as far as the mind is concerned*, Cic **II. a,** *only, merely*, Cic , non duntaxat sed, *not only but*, Liv , **b,** *at least*, Cic **III.** *in so far*, exceptis duntaxat iis gentibus, quae regnantur, Tac.

dŭŏ -ae -ŏ (δυο), *two*, Cic

dŭŏ-dĕcĭēs, adv , *twelve times*, Cic

dŭŏ-dĕcim (duo and decem), *twelve*, tabulae, *the Twelve Tables*, Cic ; sometimes simply duodecim, *the Twelve*

dŭŏ-dĕcĭmus -a -um (duodecim), *the twelfth*, Caes

dŭŏ-dēni -ae -a, **1,** *twelve each*, Cic , **2,** *twelve*, Verg

dŭŏ-dē-quădrāgēsĭmus, *thirty-eighth*, Liv

dŭŏ-dē-quădrāginta, *thirty eight*, Cic

dŭŏ-dē-quinquāgēsĭmus -a -um, *the forty eighth*, Cic

dŭŏ-dē-trĭcĭens (tricies) adv , *twenty-eight times*, Cic

dŭŏ-dē-trĭginta, *twenty-eight*, Liv

dŭŏ-dē-vīcēni -ae -a, *eighteen each*, Liv

dŭŏ-dē-vīginti, *eighteen*, Cic

dŭŏ-et-vīcēsĭmāni ōrum, m *soldiers of the 22nd legion*, Tac

dŭŏ-et-vīcēsĭmus a -um, *the twenty-second* Tac

dŭplex -plĭcis (duo and plico), **1,** *double, two-fold*, amiculum, Nep, amictus, Verg, pannus, Hor., *a garment folded twice round the body*; palmae, *both hands*, Verg , **2, a,** *doubled, twice as much*, frumentum, stipendium, Caes , **b,** *double-faced, false, deceitful*, Hor

dŭplĭcārĭus -a -um (duplex), miles, *a soldier who gets double rations*, Liv

dŭplĭcĭtĕr, adv (duplex), *doubly*, Cic

dŭplĭco, 1 (duplex) **I.** Lit , *to fold in two, double up*, duplicatque virum (hasta), transfixa dolore, Verg **II.** Transf , **1, a,** *to double*, numerum dierum, Cic , **b,** duplicare verba, *to repeat*, Cic. , **2, a,** *to lengthen*, crescentes umbras (of the sun), Verg ; **b,** *to increase*, duplicari sollicitudines, Cic

dŭplus a -um (duo), *twice as much, double*, **1,** adj , pars, Cic. , pecunia, Liv , **2,** subst , **dŭplum** -i, n *the double*, esp *a double penalty*, in dupli subire or in duplum ire, Cic , [illegible]are in duplum, Cic

[illegible]ius -ii, m (= duo asses pondo), *a* [illegible]ses, Cic

[illegible] e (duro), *lasting, durable*, Ov

[illegible]lis, n (duro) *hardness*, aquarum,

[illegible]s -a -um (δουρατεος), *wooden*, applied [illegible] Trojan horse, Lucr.

[illegible]d **dūrĭtĕr**, adv with compar [illegible] dūrissĭmē (durus), *hardly* **I.** [illegible] respect to hearing, *unpleasantly*, dicere, Hor , **b,** of works of art, [illegible]y, quid sculptum infabre, quid [illegible] esset, Hor **II.** Transf , **a,** in [illegible] *awkwardly*, durius incedit, Ov , **b,** in conduct, *harshly, severely*, durius in deditos consulere, Liv , durius aliquid accipere, Cic

dūresco, dūrŭi, 3 (durus), *to grow hard*; frigoribus duresċit humor, *freezes*, Cic

dūrĭtas -ātis, f (durus), *harshness, unfriendliness*, Cic

dūrĭter = dure (q v)

dūrĭtĭa -ae, f and **dūrĭtĭēs** -ēi, f (durus), *hardness* **I.** Lit , of nature, atrae pellis, Ov **II.** Transf , **a,** *hardness, austerity*, duritia virilis, Cic , ab parvulis labori ac duritiae studere, Caes. , **b,** *harshness, severity*, animi, Cic , **c,** *severity, oppressiveness* operum, Tac , caeli militiaeque, Tac

dūro, 1 (durus) **I.** Transit **A.** Lit , *to make hard*, **1,** gen , caementa calce, Liv , enses in scopulos, Ov , **2,** esp , *to dry up, make dry*; terram (by heat), Verg , Albanam fumo uvam, Hor **B.** Transf , **1,** *to make hardy, inure*, se labore, Caes , in a bad sense, *to render callous*, ad omne facinus duratus, Tac , **2,** *to endure*, laborem, Verg , imperiosius aequor, Hor **II.** Intransit **A.** Lit , *to become hard or dry*, durare solum, Verg **B.** Transf , **1,** *to become hard or callous*, in nullius unquam suorum necem duravit, Tac , **2,** *to endure*, unam hiemem in castris, Liv , sub Jove, Ov , **3,** *to last, remain, continue*, durat simulacrum, Verg , totidem durare per annos, Verg

dūrus -a -um, adj with compar and superl , *hard*. **I.** Lit , **a,** *hard to the touch*, ferrum, Hor , **b,** *harsh to the taste*, sapor Bacchi, Verg , **c,** *harsh to the ear*, vocis genus, Cic , oratio, Cic , **d,** *rough to the eye, rude*, signa dura sed tamen molliora quam Canachi, Cic , **e,** of feeling, *hard, rough*, poeta durissimus, Cic **II.** Transf , **1,** *strong, enduring*, Scipiadae duri bello, Verg , **2,** in demeanour , **a,** *awkward, uncouth*, ut vitā sic oratione durus, incultus, horridus, Cic ; **b,** *shameless*, os, Ov , **3, a,** *hardy, austere*, homo durus ac priscus, Cic , **b,** *without taste for*, C Marius, qui durior ad haec studia videbatur, Cic , **4,** *feelingless, stern, severe*, Varius est habitus judex durior, Cic , **5, a,** of weather, *severe, tempestuous*, tempestates, Caes , **b,** of the soil, *hard, difficult to work*, glebae, Verg , **c,** of work, *hard, difficult*, subvectio, Caes , **d,** *hard, painful, unfavourable, adverse*, conditio durior, Verg , pauperies, Hor

dŭumvir and **dŭŏvir** -viri, m gen. plur , duumvirum or duovirum, *a pair of magistrates* **I.** In Rome **A.** duumviri perduellionis, *the magistrates who tried cases of* perduellio, Liv **B.** duumviri sacrorum or sacris faciundis, *keepers of the Sibylline books* (afterwards increased to [illegible], and then to fifteen), Liv **C.** duumviri aedi faciendae or locandae or dedicandae, *a commission for building or dedicating a temple*, Liv **D.** duumviri navales, *a commission for looking after the fleet*, Liv **II.** In the Roman municipia and coloniae, duumviri (juri dicundo), *the highest magistrates*, Cic.

dux, dŭcis, c **I.** *a leader, guide, conductor*, locorum, Liv , armenti, Ov , transf , impietatis, Cic , diis ducibus, *under the direction of the gods*, Cic **II.** *a ruler* **A.** Gen , superum, *Jupiter*, Verg **B.** Esp , **1,** *a military or naval commander*, dux praefectusque classis, Cic , **2,** *the emperor*, Ov

Dȳmās mantis, m (Δύμας), *father of Hecuba* Hence Dymantis proles, or subst **Dȳmantis** -tidis, f *Hecuba*, Ov

Dȳmē -ēs, f (Δύμη), and **Dȳmae** -ārum, f *a town in Achaia* Adj **Dȳmaeus** -a -um, *of or belonging to Dyme*

dȳnastes -is, m (δυναστης), *ruler, prince*, Cic

Dyrrăchium -ii, n. (Δυῤῥάχιον), *later name of Epidamnus, in Illyria, the port where ships landed coming from Brundisium to Greece,* now *Durazzo.* Hence **Dyrrăchini** (-ēni) -ōrum, m. *the people of Dyrrachium.*

E.

E e, the fifth letter of the Latin alphabet, corresponding in the Greek alphabet both to ε and η. For the meaning of E as an abbreviation, see Table of Abbreviations.

ē, prep. = ex (q.v.).

ĕā, adv. (abl of is, sc. parte), *there*, Liv.

ĕādem, adv. (abl. of idem, sc. viā), *by the same road*, Cic.

ĕā-propter = propterea.

ĕātĕnus = ea tenus (parte), adv., *so far*; foll. by qua, quoad, Cic.; by ut and the subj., Cic.

ĕbĕnus -i, m. (ἔβενος), *the ebony-tree, ebony*, Verg.

ēbĭbo -bibi -bĭtum, 3. **I.** Gen., *to drink up*; amnes (of the sea), Ov. **II. 1,** Nestoris annos, *to drink as many cups as the years of Nestor's age*, Ov.; **2,** *to squander*; ut haec ebibat, Hor.

ēblandĭor, 4., dep., *to obtain by flattery*; omnia, Liv.; enitere, elabora, vel potius eblandire, effice ut, etc., Cic.; partic. passive, eblandita illa non enucleata esse suffragia, Cic.

ēbrĭĕtas -ātis, f. (ebrius), *drunkenness, revelling*, Cic.

ēbrĭōsĭtas -ātis, f. (ebriosus), *the love of drink, habit of drunkenness*, Cic.

ēbrĭōsus -a -um (ebrius), *drink-loving*, Cic.

ēbrĭus -a -um, **1,** *drunk, intoxicated*, Cic.; **2,** transf., *intoxicated with, full of*; dulci fortunā, Hor.

ēbullĭo, 4. **I.** Intransit., *to boil up*, Sen. **II.** Transit., *to cause to boil up*; transf., *to boast of*; virtutes, Cic.

ēbŭlum -i, n. (-**us** -i, f.), *the dwarf elder-tree* (sambucus ebulus, Linn.), Verg.

ĕbur -ŏris, n. **A.** Lit., *ivory*; signum ex ebore, Cic. **B.** Meton., **a,** of things made of ivory, *a statue*, Verg.; *a flute*, Verg.; *the sheath of a sword*, Ov.; *the curule chair*, Hor.; **b,** *the elephant*, Juv.

ĕburnĕŏlus -a -um (dim. of eburneus), *made of ivory*; fistula, Cic.

ĕburnĕus (ĕburnus) -a -um (ebur). **A.** *made of ivory, ivory*; signum, Cic.; dens (of the elephant), Liv. **B.** Meton., *white as ivory*; brachia, cervix, Ov.

Ebūrōnes -um, m. *a German people in Gallia Belgica.*

Ebŭsus and **-ŏs** -i, f., *an island in the Mediterranean, off the Spanish coast,* now *Iviza* or *Yviça.*

ecastor, v. Castor.

eccĕ, adv. (for ence, from en and ce), *behold! lo! see!* ecce tuae litterae, Cic.; ecce tibi exortus est Isocrates, Cic.; ubi . . . ecce, Verg.; dum . . . ecce, Hor.; ecce autem, Cic.

ecdĭcus -i, m. (ἔκδικος), *among the Greeks, a public attorney or prosecutor*, Cic.

Ecĕtra -ae, f. *capital of the Volsci.* Hence **Ecĕtrānus** -i, m. *an inhabitant of Ecetra.*

ecf . . ., v. eff . . .

Echĕcrătēs -ae, m. (Ἐχεκράτης), *a Pythagorean philosopher, contemporary with Plato.*

ĕchĕnēis -idis, f. (ἐχενηΐς), *a sucking fish, remora* (echeneis remora, Linn.), Ov.

ĕchidna -ae, f. (ἔχιδνα). **I.** *the viper, adder, as an attribute of the Furies*, Ov. **II.** Proper noun, **A.** Echidna Lernaea, *the Lernaean hydra killed by Hercules*, Ov. **B.** *a monster of the lower world, mother of Cerberus and of the Lernaean hydra*, Ov. Adj. **Echidnēus** -a -um, canis echidneus, *Cerberus*, Ov.

Ĕchīnădes -um (Ἐχινάδες, Urchin Islands), *a group of five islands in the Ionian Sea at the mouth of the Achelous.*

ĕchīnus -i, m. (ἐχῖνος). **1,** *the edible sea-urchin* (echinus esculentus, Linn.), Hor.; **2,** *a brazen dish used for washing goblets*, Hor.

Ĕchīōn -ŏnis, m. (Ἐχίων). **I.** *one of the Theban heroes who sprang from the dragon's teeth sown by Cadmus, husband of Agave, father of Pentheus*; Echione natus, *Pentheus*, Ov. Hence, **1, Ĕchīŏnĭdēs** -ae, m. *a son of Echion—i.e., Pentheus*, Ov.; **2, Ĕchīŏnĭus** -a -um, *Echionian*, and poet. = *Cadmeian, Theban*, Verg. **II.** *son of Mercury, one of the Argonauts.* Hence adj., **Ĕchīŏnĭus** -a -um, *of or belonging to Echion.*

ēchō -ūs, f. (ἠχώ), **1,** *an echo*, Plin.; **2,** personif., *Echo, a wood-nymph*, Ov.

eclŏgārĭi -ōrum, m. = loci electi, *select passages or extracts*, Cic.

ec-quando, adv., **1,** *ever*, used in an impassioned interrogation, ecquando te rationem factorum tuorum redditurum putasti? Cic.; **2,** *ever*, indefinite, after nisi, Cic.

ec-qui, ecquae or ecqua, ecquod, pronoun interrog. adj. = numqui, *any*, used in an impassioned interrogation; ecqui pudor est? ecquae religio, Verres? Cic.; quaeris ecqua spes sit, Cic.

ec-quis, ec-quid, pron. interrog. subst. *whether any? any one? any thing?* in impassioned interrogation, ecquis retulit aliquid ad conjugem ac liberos, praeter odia? Liv.; with nam, ecquisnam tibi dixerit, Cic.; adj. = ecqui, ecquis Latini nominis populus defecerit ad nos? Liv.; used adverbially, **a,** ecquid, *whether*; fac sciam ecquid venturi sitis, Cic.; **b,** ecqui = num aliqui, Cat.; **c,** ecquo, *whither?* ecquo te tua virtus provexisset? Cic.

ĕcŭlĕus = equuleus (q.v.).

ĕdācĭtas -ātis, f. (edax), *greediness, gluttony*, Cic.

ĕdax -ācis, f. (1. edo), **1,** *greedy, gluttonous*; hospes, Cic.; **2,** transf., *destructive, consuming*; ignis, Verg.; curae edaces, "*eating cares*," Hor.; tempus edax rerum, Ov.

Ĕdessa -ae, f. (Ἔδεσσα), **1,** *town in Macedonia, residence of the old Macedonian kings.* Hence adj., **Ĕdessaeus** -a -um, *of or belonging to Edessa*; **2,** *capital of the province of Oshroene in Mesopotamia.*

ēdīco -dixi -dictum, 3. **1,** *to make known, publish, order, appoint*; hoc simul, Hor.; foll. by a rel. sent., Cic.; **2,** esp. *to publish openly* (by a herald or otherwise), *to decree, ordain by proclamation* (of magistrates); diem comitiis, Liv.; with acc. and infin., Cic.; with ut or ne and the subj., Cic.; with subj. alone, Cic.

ēdictum -i, n. (edico), *a decree, edict*; **a,** of a magistrate, general, king, etc., Archilochia in illum edicta Bibuli, Cic.; edictum constituere or proponere, Cic.; praemittere, Caes.; **b,** *the proclamation by a praetor on his entering office in which he published the principles that would govern his judicial decisions*, Cic.

ēdisco didici, 3 1, *to learn thoroughly, learn off by heart*, aliquid ad verbum, *word for word*, Cic , magnum numerum versuum, Caes , 2, *to learn, study*, istam artem, Cic

ēdissĕro -sĕrŭi sertum, 3 *to explain, set forth, relate fully*, res gestas, Liv , neque necesse est edisseri a nobis, quae finis funestae familiae fiat, Cic

ēdisserto, 1 (intens of edissero), *to set forth, explain, relate exactly*, neque aggrediar narrare quae edissertanda minora vero faciam, Liv

ēdĭtīcius -a -um (2 edo), *put forth, announced, proposed*, judices, *the panel of 125 judices (jury), of which the accused could reject 75*, Cic

ēdĭtĭo ōnis, f (2 edo), 1, *the publishing of a book*, maturare libri huius editionem, Tac , 2, *a statement;* in tam discrepante editione, Liv , 3, legal t t , editio tribuum, *the proposal of four tribes by the plaintiff or prosecutor, out of which the jury were to be chosen*

ēdĭtus -a -um, p adj with compar and superl. (2 edo), 1, *high, lofty*, collis, Caes , locus, Cic , subst , **ēdĭtum** -i, n *a lofty situation, height*, Tac , 2, transf , viribus editior, *mightier*, Hor

1 **ĕdo**, ēdi, ēsum, edere or esse (ἔδω), 1, *to eat*, nec esuriens Ptolemaeus ederat jucundius, Cic , multos modios salis simul edendos esse, ut amicitiae munus expletum sit, *many bushels of salt must be eaten together*, i e *the friendship must be of long standing*, Cic ; 2, of inanimate things, *to consume, eat away, corrode*, culmos edit or est robigo, Verg , si quid est animam, Hor (contracted forms, es, est, estis , subj essem, infin esse)

2 **ēdo** dĭdi -dĭtum, 3 *to give out* **I.** Gen , animam or extremum vitae spiritum, *to breathe one's last, to die*, Cic , of things, cuniculus armatos repente edidit, *brought to light*, Liv **II.** Esp , 1, *to bring into the world, to bring forth, give birth to ;* partum, Cic ; aliquem, Tac , edi in lucem, *to be brought into the world*, Cic , partic , Maecenas atavis edite regibus, *descended from*, Hor , of things, *to produce*, (terra) edit innumeras species, Ov ; 2, *to give forth from oneself, to utter*, clamorem majorem, Cic , 3, *to make known*, a, of writing, *to publish*, illos de republica libros, Cic ; b, *to spread a report*, quae opinio erat edita in vulgus, Cic , c, *to set forth, relate, tell, divulge*, ede illa quae coeperas, Cic , consilia hostium, Liv , esp (α) of the oracles, *to state, answer*, Apollo oraculum edidit Spartam periturам, Cic , (β) legal t t *to fix, determine*, judicium, Cic , tribus, *to nominate the tribes out of which the jury were to be chosen*, Cic , aliquem sibi socium in, etc , *to propose*, Cic , (γ) *to command*, ederet consul quid fieri vellet, Liv , partic subst , **ēdĭta** ōrum, n *commands*, Ov ; 4, *to bring about, cause, furnish*, a, ruinas, Cic , annuam operam, *to serve for a year*, Liv , magnam caedem, Liv ; b, of magistrates, *to provide games for the people*, ludos, spectaculum, Tac , 5, of time, *to close, bring to an end*, vitam, Cic

ēdŏcĕo -dŏcŭi -doctum, 2 *to teach, instruct thoroughly, to inform fully*, generally with double acc , juventutem multa facinora, Sall , with relat. sent , quos ille edocuerat quae fieri vellet, Caes , with infin , omnia venalia habere edocuit, Sall , with acc , of things, omnia ordine, Liv , freq in partic perf pass with acc , edoctus artes belli, Liv , of abstractions, with ut and the subj , edocuit ratio ut videremus, etc., Cic

ēdŏlo, 1 *to hew out with an axe, to bring into shape, complete*, quod jusseras edolavi, Cic

ēdŏmo -dŏmŭi -dŏmĭtum, 1. *to tame thoroughly, entirely subdue*, vitiosam naturam doctrinā, Cic , orbem (terrarum), Ov

Ēdōni -ōrum (Ἠδωνοί), *a Thracian people famed for the worship of Bacchus* Adj , 1, **Ēdōnus** a -um, poet , *Thracian*, Verg , 2, **Ēdōnis** nĭdis, f poet adj , *Thracian*, Ov , subst , *a Bacchanal*, Prop

ēdormĭo, 4 *to have one's sleep out* **I.** Intransit , *to sleep away, to sleep one's fill*, quum (vinolenti) edormiverunt, Cic **II.** Transit , a, *to sleep off*, crapulam, Cic , b, Fufius Ilionam edormit (of an actor), *sleeps through the part of Iliona*, Hor

ēdŭcātĭo -ōnis, f (educo), *bringing up, training, education*, of children, educatio liberorum, Cic , institutus liberaliter educatione doctrināque puerili, Cic

ēdŭcātor -ōris m (educo), *one who trains or brings up*, a, *a foster father*, Cic , b, *a tutor*, Tac

ēdŭcātrix īcis, f (educator), *a foster-mother, nurse*, transf , earum (rerum) parens est educatrixque sapientia, Cic

1 **ēdŭco**, 1 (intens of 2 educo), *to bring up, rear, educate*, a, of human beings, aliquem, Cic , caelum quo natus educatusque essem, Liv , homo ingenuus liberaliterque educatus, Cic , ad turpitudinem educatur, Cic , b, of animals, in educando perfacile apparet aliud quiddam iis (bestiis) propositum, Cic , c, of things, transf , educata huius nutrimentis eloquentia, Cic

2 **ēdūco** duxi -ductum, 3 **I.** *to draw out, lead out* **A.** *to draw out*, 1, gen , gladium e vagina, Cic , 2, esp , t t of drawing lots, sortem, Cic , aliquem ex urna, Cic **B.** *to lead out*, 1 gen , hominem de senatu, Cic , aliquem in provinciam, Cic , 2, esp , a, milit t t , *to march troops out*, cohortes ex urbe, Caes , exercitum in expeditionem, Cic , b, legal t t , *to lead before a court of law*, aliquem in jus, Cic , aliquem ad consules, Cic., or simply educere aliquem, Cic , c, naut t t , *to take a ship out of port*, naves ex portu, Caes , d, *to lead out of a country*, equos ex Italia, Liv , e, *to bring water (by aqueduct)*, lacum, Cic , f, *to build a wall on to a river*, moles quam eductam in Rhenum retulimus, Tac **II.** *to raise up* **A.** Lit , aliquem superas sub auras, Verg , fig , in astra, *to praise sky high*, Hor **B** Transf , a, turris summis sub astra educta tectis, Verg , b, *to bring up, rear a child*, aliquem, Cic **III** Of time, *to live, spend*, plures annos, Prop

ĕdūlis e (1 edo), *eatable*, Hor

ēdūro, 1 *to last, endure*, Tac

ēdūrus a um, *very hard*, pirus, Verg , transf , eduro ore negare, Ov

Ēĕtĭōn -ōnis, m (Ἠετίων), *father of Andromache, prince of Thebae in Cilicia* Hence adj , **Ēĕtĭōnēus** -a um, *of or belonging to Eetion*

effarcĭo fersi fertum, 4 (ex and farcio), *to stuff full*, intervalla grandibus saxis, Caes

effātum -i, n (n of partic of effor) 1, *an announcement, prediction*, fatidicorum et vatum, Cic , 2, *an axiom*, Cic

effectĭo ōnis, f (efficio), 1, *a doing, practising*, artis, Cic , 2, *an efficient cause*, Cic

effector -ōris, m (efficio), *one who produces, causes, originates*, effector mundi molitorque deus, Cic , of things, stilus optimus et praestantissimus dicendi effector ac magister, Cic

effectrix trīcis, f (effector), *she that causes or produces*, terra diei noctisque effectrix, Cic

1 **effectus** -a um, partic of efficio

2. **effectus** -ūs m. (efficio). **I.** Act , *doing,*

effecting, execution, performance; **1**, gen., conatus tam audax trajiciendarum Alpium et effectus, Liv.; in effectu esse, Cic.; postquam ad effectum operis ventum est, Liv.; **2**, esp., *the working*; quarum (herbarum) causam ignorare, vim et effectum videres, Cic. **II.** Pass., *effect, consequence*; effectus eloquentiae est audientium approbatio, Cic.; sine ullo effectu, Liv.

effēmĭnātē, adv. (effeminatus), *effeminately*, Cic.

effēmĭnātus -a -um, p. adj. with compar. and superl. (from effemino), *effeminate, womanish*; corpora, Liv.; opinio, Cic.; effeminatissimus languor, Cic.

effēmĭno, 1. (ex and femina), **1**, *to make into a woman*; effeminarunt eum (aërem) Junonique tribuerunt, Cic.; **2**, *to make effeminate, to enervate*; virum in dolore, Cic.; effeminari cogitationibus mollissimis.

effĕrātus -a -um, p. adj. with compar. and superl. (1. effero), *wild, savage*; mores ritusque, Liv.; gentes, Cic.

efferċio, v. effarcio.

effĕrĭtas -ātis, f. (efferus), *wildness, savageness*, Cic.

1. **effĕro**, 1. (efferus), *to make wild, make savage*. **A.** Lit., barba et capilli efferaverant speciem oris, Liv.; terram immanitate beluarum efferari, Cic. **B.** Transf., animos, Liv.; odio irāque efferati, Liv.

2. **effĕro** (ecfĕro), extŭli, ēlātum, efferre (ex and fero). **I.** *to bear, carry out, bring out*. **A.** Gen., **1**, lit., tela ex aedibus alicuius, Cic.; deam in terram, Liv.; esp., **a**, pedem or se efferre, *to betake oneself*; pedem portā non efferre, Cic.; **b**, milit. t.t., efferre signa (vexilla, arma), *to march out*; signa portis or extra urbem, Liv.; **c**, *to carry to the grave, bury*; aliquem, Cic.; pass., efferri, *to be borne out, burial*, Cic.; fig., ingens periculum manet ne libera respublica efferatur, Liv.; **d**, *to bring forth, bear*; uberiores fruges, Cic.; cum decimo, *tenfold*, Cic.; **2**, transf., *to utter*, **a**, *to express*; si graves sententiae inconditis verbis efferuntur, Cic.; **b**, *to publish, make known*; aliquid in vulgus, Cic.; ne has meas ineptias efferatis, Cic.; **c**, se, *to show itself*; volo enim se efferat in adolescente fecunditas, Cic. **B.** *to carry away*; **1**, lit., Messium impetus per hostes extulit ad castra, Liv.; **2**, transf., *to carry away, drive to*; si me efferet ad gloriam animi dolor, Cic.; se efferri aliquā re (laetitiā, dolore, studio, iracundiā), *to be carried away*, Cic. **II.** *to raise up, lift up*. **A.** Lit., **a**, scutum super caput, Liv.; **b**, *to make to appear*; lucem, Verg. **B.** Transf., **a**, *to raise*; aliquem ad summum imperium, Cic.; **b**, *to praise, extol*; aliquem or aliquid laudibus, Cic.; **c**, efferri or se efferre, *to pride oneself on, to be puffed up by*; efferre se insolenter, Cic.; partic., elatus, *puffed up*; recenti victoriā, Caes.

effertus -a -um, p. adj. (from effarcio), *stuffed full, full*; nimbus effertus tenebris, Lucr.

effĕrus -a -um (ex and ferus), *very wild, savage*; facta tyranni, Verg.

effervesco -ferbŭi and -fervi, 3. *to boil up, foam up, effervesce*. **A.** Lit., eae aquae, quae effervescunt subditis ignibus, Cic.; poet. of the stars, at the creation of the world, *to swarm forth, to break out into a glow*, Ov. **B.** Transf., **a**, Pontus armatus, effervescens in Asiam atque erumpens, *bursting forth*, Cic.; **b**, *to rage*, Cic.; esp. of an orator, *to be passionate*, Cic.

effervo, 3. (ex and fervo). **I.** *to boil up or over*; effervere in agros vidimus undantem Aetnam, Verg. **II.** *to swarm forth*, Verg.

effētus -a -um (ex and fetus, *having given birth to young*), *weakened, exhausted, effete*; corpus, Cic.; vires, Verg.; innumeris effetus laniger annis, Ov.; effeta veri senectus, *incapable of truth*, Verg.

effĭcācĭtas -ātis, f. (efficax), *efficacy, efficiency*, Cic.

effĭcācĭtĕr, adv. with compar. and superl. (efficax), *effectively, efficaciously*; id acturos efficacius rati, Liv.

effĭcax -ācis, adj. with compar. and superl. (efficio), *effective, efficient, efficacious*; **a**, of things, scientia, Hor.; with ad, quae maxime efficaces ad muliebre ingenium preces sunt, Liv.; with in and the abl., in quibus (rebus) peragendis continuatio ipsa efficacissima esset, Liv.; with infin., amara curarum eluere efficax, Hor.; **b**, of persons, Hercules, *active*, Hor.

effĭcĭens -entis, p. adj. (from efficio), *efficient, effective*; res, Cic.; causa, *efficient cause*, Cic.; with genit., efficiens voluptatis, *cause of*, Cic.

effĭcĭentĕr, adv. (efficiens), *efficiently, powerfully*, Cic.

effĭcĭentĭa -ae, f. (efficiens), *efficiency*, Cic.

effĭcĭo -fēci -fectum, 3. (ex and facio). **I.** *to produce, effect, make*. **A.** Gen., mundum, Cic.; magnas rerum commutationes, Caes. **B.** Esp., **a**, *to build, erect*; columnam, Cic.; **b**, of land, *to bear*; plurimum, Cic.; cum octavo, *eight-fold*, Cic.; **c**, of number, *to make up*; pass., effici, *come to*; ea tributa vix in fenus Pompeii quod satis est efficiunt, Cic.; **d**, *to bring together*; magnum cratium numerum, Caes.; duas legiones, Caes.; **e**, philosoph. t. t., *to prove, show*; minutis interrogationibus quod proposuit efficit, Cic.; ex quibus vult efficere, with acc. and infin., Cic.; ita efficitur ut, etc., Cic.; **f**, *to make*; Catilinam consulem, Cic.; hostes ad pugnam alacriores, Caes. **II.** *to bring to an end, accomplish, execute, complete*; **1**, omne opus, Caes.; sphaeram, Cic.; hoc, id, illud efficere ut, etc., Cic.; simply efficere ut, Cic.; non effici potest quin, etc., Cic.; **2**, *to accomplish* (of a march), quantumcumque itineris equitatu efficere potuerat, Caes.

effĭgĭēs -ēi, f. or **effĭgĭa** -ae, f. (effingo). **I.** Lit., **1**, *an image, likeness, effigy, portrait*; quaedam effigies spirantis mortui, Cic.; hanc pro Palladio effigiem statuere, Verg.; **2**, *form, shape*; **a**, simulacrum deae non effigie humana, Tac.; **b**, *a shade, ghost*; effigies, immo umbrae hominum, Liv. **II.** *abstract, copy, imitation, image*; et humanitatis et probitatis, Cic.; effigies justi imperii, *ideal*, Cic.

effingo -finxi -fictum, 3. (ex and fingo), **1**, *to wipe off, wipe out*; e foro sanguinem spongiis effingere, Cic.; **2**, **a**, *to form, fashion*; oris lineamenta, Cic.; **b**, *to represent*; (natura) speciem ita formavit oris ut in ea penitus reconditos mores effingeret, Cic.; so *to express in words*; alicuius mores, Cic.; **c**, *to imitate, strive to reach*; illum imitando, Cic.; *to conceive*; ea effingenda animo, Cic.

effīo -fĭĕri, pass. of efficio (q.v.).

efflāgĭtātĭo -ōnis, f. (efflagito), *an urgent demand*; efflagitatio ad coëundam societatem, Cic.

efflāgĭtātus -ūs, m. (efflagito), *an urgent request*; coactu atque efflagitatu meo, Cic.

efflāgĭto, 1. (ex and flagito), *to ask earnestly, demand, entreat*; nostram misericordiam, Cic.; ab ducibus signum pugnae, Liv.; epistolam, Cic.; ut se ad regem mitteret, Cic.

efflīgo -flixi -flictum, 3. (ex and fligo), *to kill, murder, slay*; Pompeium, Cic.

efflo, 1. (ex and flo), **1**, transit., *to blow out, breathe out*; ignes ore et naribus, Ov.; **2**, intransit, *to breathe forth*, Lucr, animam, Cic, extremum halitum, *to die*, Cic

efflōresco -flōrŭi, 3. (ex and floresco), *to blossom, break into bloom, flourish*, huic efflorescunt genera partesque virtutum, Cic si quidem efflorescit (illa aetas) ingenii laudibus, Cic

efflŭo (ecflŭo) -fluxi, 3 (ex and fluo), 3. *to flow out* **A.** una cum sanguine vita, Cic, aer effluens huc et illuc ventos efficit, Cic **B. 1,** *to vanish*, tanta est enim intimorum multitudo, ut ex his aliquis potius effluat quam novo sit aditus, Cic., **2, a,** *to vanish out of thought, to be forgotten*, effluere ex animo alicuius, Cic, absol, quod totum effluxerat, Cic, **b,** of thought, *to be lost, fail*, alicui ex tempore dicenti solet effluere mens, Cic, **c,** of time, *to disappear*; ne effluat aetas, Cic, **3,** *to come to light, become known*, effluunt multa ex vestra disciplina, quae etiam ad nostras aures saepe permanant, Cic

efflŭvium -ii, n (effluo), *flowing out, outlet*, convivium effluvio lacus appositum, Tac

effŏdio -fōdi -fossum, 3 (ex and fodio). **I.** *to dig out* **A.** Gen, ferrum e terra, Cic **B.** Esp, **1,** *to gouge out*, oculos, Cic, **2,** *to make by digging, to excavate*, portus Verg **II.** *to dig up* **A.** Gen, terram, Liv **B.** *to rummage*, domibus effossis, Caes

effor (ecfor), 1. dep. (ex and for) **I.** Gen, *to speak out, express, speak*, verbum, Cic, nefanda, Liv, tum ferunt ex oraclo ecfatam esse Pythiam, Cic. **II.** Esp, **A.** In logic, *to state a proposition*, Cic **B.** T t. of augury, *to fix or determine a place*, templum, Cic, partic, effatus (pass), *fixed, determined by the augurs*, Cic

effrēnātē, adv with compar (effrenatus), *unrestrainedly, violently*, Cic

effrēnātio ōnis, f *unbridled impetuosity*, animi impotentis, Cic

effrēnātus -a -um, p adj with compar and superl (from effreno, P Aug, *to let loose*), *unbridled*. **A.** Lit, equi, Liv **B.** Transf, *unrestrained, unchecked, violent*, furor, cupiditas, homo Cic, effrenatior vox, Cic; effrenata insolentiā multitudo, Cic

effrēnus -a um (ex and frenum), *unbridled*, **1,** lit, equus, Liv, **2,** transf, *unrestrained*, amor, Ov

effringo -frēgi -fractum (ex and frango), **1,** *to break open*, fores, Cic, januam, Cic, **2,** *to break off*, crus, Sall

effŭgio -fūgi fŭgitum, 3 (ex and fugio). **I.** Intransit, *to flee, fly away, escape, get off*, e proelio, Cic., a quibus (ludis) vix vivus effugit, Cic. **II.** Transit, *to escape from, avoid, flee from, shun*; equitatum Caesaris, Caes, alicuius impias manus, Cic, with ne and the subj, propinquae clade urbis ipsi, ne quid simile paterentur, effugerunt, Liv,, me effugit, *it escapes me, escapes my observation*, Cic

effŭgium -ii, n (effugio), *a flying away, flight* **I.** Lit, Lucr **II.** Meton, **A.** *an outlet for flight*, si effugium patuisset in publicum, Liv. **B.** *the means or opportunity of flight*, mortis, Cic, effugia pennarum habere, Cic

effulgĕo fulsi, 2 (ex and fulgeo), *to shine out, glitter* **A.** Lit, nova lux oculis effulsit, Verg, auro, *glitter with gold*, Verg **B** Transf, effulgebant Philippus ac magnus Alexander, Liv

effultus -a um (ex and fulcio), *resting upon, supported by*, velleribus, Verg

effundo -fūdi -fūsum, 3 (ex and fundo), *to pour out, pour forth, shed* **I. 1,** of liquids lacrimas, Cic, Tiberis effusus super ripas, Liv, imber effusus nubibus, Verg, **2,** of things not fluid, *to pour out, pour forth*, saccos nummorum, *to empty*, Hor **II. A 1,** *to throw down*, aliquem solo, Verg, esp of horses, *to throw their riders*, effundere consulem super caput, Liv, **2,** *to drive forth*, excutiat Teucros vallo atque effundat in aequum, Verg **B. 1,** *to loosen, let go*, iterum sinum, *unfold the toga*, Liv, navibus omnes habenas, Verg, **2,** *to pour, throw*, of weapons, telorum omnis generis vis ingens effusa est in eos, Liv, of other objects, primum impetum quem fervido ingenio et caecā irā effundunt, Liv, **3,** *to send forth* (a number of men), auxilium castris, Verg, reflex, se effundere, middle effundi, *to stream forth, pour forth*, cunctum senatum, totam Italiam esse effusam, Cic, Celtiberi omnes in fugam effunduntur, Liv, **4,** *to pour forth, give forth*, **a,** of sounds, tales voces, Verg, vox in coronam turbamque effunditur, Cic, **b,** of fruits, *to bring forth in abundance*, segetes effundunt fruges, Cic, **5,** of property, *to spend, squander*, patrimonia effundere largiendo, Cic **III.** Transf, **A.** *to pour out, tell, impart*, effudi vobis omnia quae sentiebam, Cic., in a bad sense, omnem suum vinolentum furorem in aliquem, *pour forth on*, Cic **B.** Esp. reflex and middle, *to give oneself up to indulge in*, effundere se in aliqua libidine, Cic, nimio successu in tantam licentiamque socordiamque effusus, Liv **C. 1,** *to use, expend, make full use of*; omnia reipublicae remedia, Cic, ibi omnis effusus labor, *wasted*, Verg, **2,** *to breathe forth*, spiritum extremum in victoria, *to die*, Cic

effūsē, adv with compar and superl (effusus) **I.** *far and wide*, ire, *in disorder*, Sall, vastare, Liv **II.** Transf, **1,** *profusely, lavishly*, donare, Cic, **2,** *unrestrainedly, immoderately*, exsultare, Cic

effūsio ōnis, f (effundo) **I.** Act **1,** *a pouring forth*, tutantur se atramenti effusione sepiae, Cic, **2,** *extravagance, prodigality*, hae pecuniarum effusiones, Cic, absol, liberalitatem effusio imitatur, Cic **II.** Middle, **1,** lit, **a,** aquae, Cic, **b,** *pouring out of people*, effusiones hominum ex oppidis, Cic, **2,** transf, *exuberance of spirits, excessive hilarity*, effusio animi in laetitia, Cic

effūsus -a -um, p adj with compar and superl (effundo), *poured forth* **I.** Lit, **1,** *let loose*, effusae comae, Ov, effuso cursu, *at full speed*, Liv, **2,** *wide spread*, mare late effusum, Hor, **3,** of soldiers, *disorderly* (in march), effuso agmine, Liv, fuga effusa, Liv **II.** Transf, **a,** *extravagant*, in largitione, Cic, **b,** *unrestrained, immoderate*, licentia, Liv

effūtio, 4 (ex and *futio, from root, FUD, FUT, whence fundo, futilis), *to blab out, chatter*, aliquid, Cic, de mundo, Cic, absol, ex tempore, Cic

effŭtŭo -ŭi, 3 *to squander in debauchery*, Cat

ĕgĕlĭdus -a -um, **1,** *with the chill off, lukewarm, tepid*, tepores, Cat, **2,** *cool, somewhat cold*, flumen, Verg

ĕgens -entis, p adj with compar and superl (egeo), *poor, needy, indigent* (opp locuples), egens quidam calumniator, Cic, with genit, verborum non egens, *not deficient in*, Cic

ĕgēnus -a -um (egeo), *needy, wanting, in need of* with genit, omnium egena corpora, Liv, of condition, *poor*, in rebus egenis, *poverty*, Verg

ĕgĕo -ŭi, 2 **I.** *to want, be in need, be destitute, be needy, poor*, **a,** absol, egebat? immo locuples erat, Cic, **b,** *to be in want of something*, with abl, medicinā, Cic; with genit, auxilii, Caes **II.** Transf, **1** (= careo), *to be without, not to have*, with abl, auctoritate, *to have no authority*, Cic; with genit, classis, Verg, **2,**

(= desiderio), *to desire, wish for, want;* with abl., pane, Hor.

Ēgĕria -ae, f. *an Italian nymph, the instructress of Numa Pompilius.*

ēgĕro -gessi -gestum, 3. *to carry, bear, bring, get out.* **A.** Lit., **1**, gen., tantum nivis, Liv.; **2**, esp., **a**, *to carry off,* as plunder, praedam ex hostium tectis, Liv.; **b**, dapes, *to vomit,* Ov. **B.** Transf., expletur lacrimis egeriturque dolor, *is expelled,* Ov.

ĕgestas -ātis, f. (for egentas from egeo). **I.** *extreme poverty, indigence, need.* **A.** Lit., ista paupertas vel potius egestas ac mendicitas, Cic. **B.** Transf., animi, Cic. **II.** *want of, deficiency in;* frumenti, Sall.

ēgigno, 3. *to produce out of,* Lucr.

Egnātia (Gnătia) -ae, f. *a town in Apulia Peucetia.*

ĕgŏ (ἐγώ), pron. pers. genit. mei, dat. mihi, acc. me, abl. me; plur. nom. nos, genit. nostrum and nostri, dat. nobis, acc. nos, abl. nobis, *I*, plur. *we.* **I.** Lit., **1**, gen., alter ego, *my second self,* Cic.; genit. nostrum partitive and possessive, nostri, objective, Cic.; **2**, esp., nos for ego, nobis consulibus, Cic. **II.** Meton., **A.** ad me, *to me, to my house,* Cic. **B.** a me, *from my property, at my expense;* se a me solvere, Cic. (ego, etc., strengthened by -met in all cases except genit. plur., egomet, etc.).

ēgrĕdĭor -gressus, 3. dep. (ex and gradior). **I.** Intransit., **A.** *to go out, pass out;* **1**, Lit., **a**, e cubiculo; **b**, milit. t.t., (α) *to leave the ranks;* egredi ordine, Sall.; (β) *to march out of camp;* e castris, Caes., or simply castris, Caes.; ad proelium, Caes.; **b**, naut. t.t. (α) egredi ex navi or simply navi, Cic., *to disembark;* so egredi in terram, Cic.; absol., Caes.; (β) egredi ex portu, *to sail away,* Cic.; **2**, in discourse, *to digress;* a proposito, Cic. **B.** *to go up, ascend;* ad summum montis, Sall. **II.** Transit., **A.** *to go out of;* urbem, Liv. **B.** Lit., **1**, *to pass beyond;* munitiones, Caes.; **2**, transf., *to overstep, pass;* medum, Tac.; *to go out of;* fines, Caes.

ēgrĕgĭē, adv. (egregius), *excellently, admirably, singularly;* with verbs, pingere, loqui, Cic.; with adjectives, egregie fortis imperator, Cic.; egregie subtilis scriptor et elegans, Cic.

ēgrĕgĭus -a -um, (ex and grex, lit., *not belonging to the common herd*), *admirable, excellent, extraordinary, distinguished;* civis, Cic.; with in and the abl., Laelius in bellica laude, Cic.; with ad, vir ad cetera egregius, Liv.; with abl., bello, Verg.; with genit., animi, Verg. Subst., **ēgrĕgĭa** -ōrum, n. *distinguished actions,* Sall.

ēgressus -ūs, m. (egredior). **I.** *a going out, departure;* vester, Cic.; ventos custodit et arcet Aeolus egressu, Ov. **II. A.** *a landing from a ship, disembarkation;* egressus optimus, Caes. **B.** *a passage out;* egressus obsidens, Tac.; poet., *the mouth of a river,* Ov.

ēheu, interj., expressing grief or pain, *alas! woe!* eheu me miserum; often followed by quam, Hor. (ēheu in epic and lyric poets).

ei (hei), interj., expressing pain, *ah! woe!* ei mihi conclamat, Ov.

eiă and **heiă** (εἶα), interj., exclamation of joy and surprise, *hallo! well then!* heia vero! Cic.; eia age, of exhortation, *quick! come then!* Verg.

ēĭcĭo = ejicio (q.v.).

ējăcŭlor, 1. dep., *to throw out, hurl out;* aquas, Ov.

ējectāmentum -i, n. (ejecto), *that which is thrown up;* maris, Tac.

ējectio -ōnis, f. (ejicio), *banishment, exile,* Cic.

ējecto, 1. (intens. of ejicio), *to throw, cast, hurl out, eject;* **1**, arenas, favillam, Ov.; **2**, *to vomit forth;* cruorem ore, Verg.

ējectus -ūs, m. (ejicio), *a casting out,* Lucr.

ējĭcĭo -jēci -jectum, 3. (ex and jacio), *to throw out, cast out, drive out, drive away, eject.* **I.** Gen., **A.** Lit., aliquem ex oppido, Caes.; multos sedibus ac fortunis, Cic.; se in terram e navi, Cic.; fig., si quidem hanc sentinam huius urbis ejecerit, Cic. **B.** Transf., amorem ex animo, Cic. **II.** Esp., **A.** *to cast forth, utter;* vocem, Cic. **B.** Milit. t.t., **a**, *to drive away;* cohortes, Caes.; **b**, se ejicere, *to rush forth;* se ex oppido, Caes. **C.** *to drive away;* **a**, from house or property, aliquem domo, Cic.; absol., damnato et ejecto, Cic.; of the wife (with or without domo), *to divorce,* Cic.; **b**, *to banish;* aliquem ex patria, Cic.; or simply ejicere aliquem, Cic.; **c**, *to remove from a magistracy, guild,* etc.; aliquem de collegio, Cic.; e senatu, Cic. **D.** Naut. t.t., **a**, *to bring to shore;* navem in terram, Caes.; **b**, in pass., *to be cast ashore, stranded;* classis ad Baleares ejicitur, Liv.; ejici in litore, Caes.; ejectus, *a shipwrecked person,* Cic. **E.** *to throw out a dead body, leave unburied;* ne corpus ejiciatur, Cic. **F.** **1**, *to stretch forth, thrust out;* linguam, Cic.; **2**, *to dislocate;* armum, Verg. **G.** *to hiss an actor off the stage,* Cic.; so transf., *to reject, disapprove of;* Cynicorum ratio tota est ejicienda, Cic.

ējŭlātĭo -ōnis, f. (ejulo), *wailing, a lamentation;* illa non virilis, Cic.

ējŭlātus -ūs, m. (ejulo), *a wailing, lamenting;* ejulatus ne mulieri quidem concessus est, Cic.

ējŭlo, 1. *to wail, lament;* magnitudine dolorum ejulans, Cic.

ējūro and **ējĕro**, 1. *to refuse or deny on oath.* **I.** Legal t. t., bonam copiam, *to swear that one is insolvent,* Cic.; forum sibi iniquum, provinciam sibi iniquam, aliquem (judicem) iniquum, *to declare by oath that a court or judge is partial, to challenge,* Cic.; magistratum, imperium, *to resign, abdicate, with an oath that the duties have been duly performed,* Tac. **II.** Transf., *to give up, abjure, abandon, disown;* patriam, Tac.

ējusdemmŏdi or **ējusdem mŏdi** (idem and modus), *in the same manner,* Cic.

ējusmŏdi or **ējus mŏdi** (is and modus). **I.** *of this kind, such;* genus belli est ejusmodi, Cic. **II.** = ita, *so,* quam viam tensarum atque pompae ejusmodi exegisti, ut, etc., Cic.

ēlābor -lapsus, 3. dep., *to glide out of, slide away from, escape, slip away.* **I.** Lit., **A.** Gen., anguis ex columna lignea elapsus, Liv.; quum se convolvens sol elaberetur et abiret, Cic. **B.** Esp., *to slip away, escape;* e manibus curantium, Liv.; animi corporibus elapsi, Cic.; with acc., custodias, Tac. **II.** Transf., **A.** Gen., disciplina elapsa est de manibus, Cic. **B.** Esp., *to be acquitted, escape from punishment, get off;* ex tot tantisque criminibus, Cic.

ēlăbŏro, 1. **I.** Intransit., *to labour hard, strive, take pains:* generally with in and the abl., in litteris, Cic.; with ut and the subj., in eo quoque elaborare ut, etc., Cic. **II.** Transit., *to labour on, work out, elaborate, produce;* causae diligenter elaboratae et tanquam elucubratae, Cic.; versus ornati elaboratique, *carefully worked out,* Cic.; as opp. to natural, *artificial;* elaborata concinnitas, Cic.

Ĕlaea -ae, f. (Ἐλαία), *a town in Aeolis.*

ēlāmentābilis -e, *very lamentable;* gemitus, Cic.

ēlanguesco -gŭi, 3. *to become weak, be relaxed, become languid;* alienā ignaviā, Liv.; differendo deinde elanguit res, Liv.

ēlargĭor, 4. *to lavish, give liberally* Pers.

ēlātē, adv (elatus), 1, *loftily*, loqui, Cic , 2, *arrogantly*, se gerere, Nep

Ĕlătēĭus -a um, *of or belonging to Elatus* Subst , *son of Elatus*, i e , *Caeneus*

ēlātĭo ōnis, f (effero), 1, *flight, soaring*, elatio et magnitudo animi, Cic ; elatio atque altitudo orationis suae, Cic ; 2, *elevation*, parium comparatio nec elationem habet nec summissionem, Cic

ēlātro, 1. *to bark out, cry out*, Hor

ēlātus -a -um (partic of 2 effero), *elevated, exalted*, of discourse, verba, Cic , of the mind, animus magnus elatusque, Cic

Ĕlăvĕr -ĕris, n *a tributary of the Liger*, now *the Allier*.

Ĕlĕa -ae, f (Ἐλέα), *town in Lower Italy* (Lat. *Velia*), *birthplace of Parmenides and Zeno, the founders of the Eleatic school of philosophy* Hence, **Ĕlĕātēs** -ae, m *Zeno*, Cic Adj , **Ĕlĕātĭcus** -a um, *Eleatic*, philosophi, Cic

ēlectē, adv with compar (electus) *choicely, selectly*, digerere, Cic

ēlectĭo -ōnis, f (eligo), *choice, selection*, a, of persons, senatus electionem (legatorum) Galbae permiserat, Tac , b, of things, judicium electioque verborum, Cic , iis trium conditionum electionem ferre, Liv

Ēlectra ae, f (Ἠλέκτρα), 1, *daughter of Atlas, one of the Pleiades, mother of Dardanus by Jupiter*, 2, *daughter of Agamemnon, wife of Pylades, sister of Orestes and Iphigenia*

ēlectrum -i, n (ἤλεκτρον), 1, *amber*, Verg , 2, *an alloy of gold and silver, resembling amber in colour*, Verg

1 **ēlectus** -a -um, p adj with compar and superl (eligo), *chosen, select*, a, of persons, manus, Tac , b, of things, verba electissima, *choice*, Cic

2 **ēlectus** -ūs, m (eligo), *choosing, choice*, necis, Ov

ēlĕgans -antis, adj with compar and superl (for eligens, from eligo), *choice, fine, neat, tasteful, elegant*, a, of persons, non parcus solum, sed etiam elegans, Cic , subst , elegantes, *fine folk*, Cic , b, of things, *tasteful*, artes, Cic , c, of oratory and diction, *fine, correct, elegant*, elegans in dicendo, Cic , subst , elegantes, *fine orators*, Cic , epistola elegantissima, Cic

ēlĕgantĕr, adv with compar and superl (elegans), *tastefully, choicely, neatly, elegantly*, scribere, Cic., scribere, psallere et saltare elegantius quam necesse est, Sall , Latine loqui elegantissime, Cic

ēlĕgantĭa -ae, f (elegans), a, *taste, refinement, grace, elegance*, integritas et elegantia alicuius, Cic , elegantia vitae, Cic , doctrinae, Cic., b, of oratory or diction, *grace, correctness, elegance, neatness*, elegantia loquendi, Cic , disserendi, Cic

ĕlŏgi -ōrum, m (ἔλεγοι), *elegiac verses*, Hor

ĕlĕgīa ae, f (ἐλεγεία), *a poem written in elegiac verse*, Ov

Ĕlĕlēŭs -ĕi, m (Ἐλελεύς, from ἐλελεῦ, the Bacchic cry), *a surname of Bacchus*, Ov., hence, **Ĕlĕlēĭdes** um, f *Bacchantes*, Ov

ĕlĕmentum i, n I. *an element first principle*, Plin , oftener in plur , Cic. II. Transf , plur elementa A. *the letters of the alphabet, and the alphabet itself*, Suet. B. *the rudiments or elements*, a, *in reading or writing*, pueros elementa docere, Hor , b, *the elements of any science or art*, loquendi, Cic., c, *the beginnings of other things*, prima Romae, Ov.

ĕlenchus -i, m (ἔλεγχος), *a pearl pendant worn as an earring*, Juv

Ĕlĕphantīnē -ēs, f (Ἐλεφαντίνη) and **Ĕlĕphantĭs** ĭdis (Ἐλεφαντίς), *an island in the Nile in Upper Egypt, opposite Syene*

ĕlĕphantus -i, c (in classical prose commoner than elephas in oblique cases), *an elephant*, elephanto beluarum nulla prudentior, Cic , meton , *ivory*, Verg

ĕlĕphās (-ans) -phantis, m (ἐλέφας) A. Lit , *the elephant*, Liv B. Meton , *the disease elephantiasis*, Lucr

Ēlēus -a -um, v Elis

Ĕleusin -īnis, f (Ἐλευσίν), *an ancient city in Attica, famous for the worship of Ceres and for the mysteries there celebrated* Adj , **Ĕleusīnus** -a -um, Eleusina mater, *Ceres*, Verg

Ēleuthĕrĭus -a um (Ἐλευθέριος), *making free* Subst I. m *the Liberator, a surname of Jupiter* II. **Ĕleuthĕrĭa** -ōrum, n (se sacra) *the festival of Jupiter Liberator*, Plaut

ēlĕvo, 1 (ex and levo) I. Lit , *to lift up, raise, elevate*, contabulationem, Caes II Transf , *to lessen*, a, in a bad sense, *to weaken, impair, disparage*, adversarium, Cic , res gestas, Liv ; b, in a good sense, *to alleviate, lighten*, suspiciones offensionesque, Cic

ēlĭcĭo -lĭcŭi -lĭcĭtum, 3 (ex and LAC -io), *to allure, entice out* I. Gen , A. Lit , 1, hostem ex paludibus silvisque, Caes ; 2, *to invoke the presence of a god or departed spirit*, inferorum animas, Cic B. *to invite, allure, induce* aliquem ad disputandum, Cic II. *to bring forth to the light of day* A. Lit , 1, gen , ferrum e terrae cavernis, Cic , 2, esp , *to produce, cause* lapidum ictu ignem, Cic B. Transf , 1, *to win from, gain*, alias litteras ab aliquo, Cic , 2, *to search out, find out*, causam alicuius rei, Cic sententiam meam, Cic , 3, *to awake*, misericordiam, Liv.

Ēlĭcĭus -ii, m (elicio) *a surname of Jupiter, he from whom a heavenly sign is called forth*, Liv

ēlīdo -līsi līsum, 3 (ex and laedo), *to strike, thrust, drive out* I. Lit , aurigam e curru, Cic , morbum, *to expel*, Hor II. *to dash to pieces, shatter*, naves, Caes , aliquem, Cic , caput pecudis saxo, Liv , fig nervos omnes virtutis, *to break*, Cic

ēlĭgo -lēgi -lectum, 3 (ex and lego) I. *to pick out, to choose, select*, amicos, Cic , ut de tribus Antoniis eligas quem velis, Cic , ex multis Isocratis libris triginta fortasse versus, Cic hunc urbi condendae locum, Liv II. *to root out*, fig , superstitionis stirpes omnes eligere, Cic

ēlīmĭno, 1 (ex and limen), *to carry over the threshold*, dicta foras, *to blab*, Hor

ēlīmo, 1 (ex and lima), *to file off, smoothe, polish* A. Lit , graciles ex aere catenas retiaque et laqueos, Ov B. Transf , *to polish, elaborate, perfect*, σχόλιον aliquod ad aliquem, Cic

ēlinguis -e (ex and lingua), 1, *speechless*, Cic , 2, *without eloquence*, Cic , mutus atque elinguis, Liv

Ēlĭs ĭdis, f (Ἦλις), *a territory of Western Peloponnesus, in which the Olympic games were solemnized*, hence adj , 1, **Ēlēus** -a um and **Ēlīus** a -um, *Elean, Olympic*, amnis, *the Alpheus*, Ov 2, **Ēlēis** -ĭdis, f *Elean* 3, **Ēlĭas** ădis, f *Elean, Olympic*, equa, *a horse running in the Olympic games*, Verg

Ēlissa (Ēlīsa) -ae, f (Ἔλισσα), *another name of Dido*.

ēlix -icis, m. (elicio), *a deep furrow, to withdraw moisture from the roots of plants*, Ov.

ēlixus -a -um (ex and lix), *boiled*, Hor.

ellĕbŏrus (hellĕbŏrus) -i, m. (ἐλλέβορος and ἑλλέβορος), and gen. **ellĕbŏrum (hellĕbŏrum)** -i, n. *hellebore*, a plant supposed to be a remedy for madness; expulit elleboro morbum bilemque meraco, Hor.

ēlŏco, 1. *to let, let on hire*; fundum, Cic.

ēlŏcūtĭo -ōnis, f. (eloquor), *oratorical delivery, elocution* (= φράσις), Cic.

ēlŏgĭum -ii, n. 1, *a short maxim, apophthegm*; Solonis, Cic.; 2, *an inscription on a gravestone, epitaph*, Cic.; 3, *a clause in a will, a codicil*, Cic.

ēlŏquens -entis, p. adj. with compar. and superl. (from eloquor), *eloquent*; omnium eloquentissimi Ti. et C. Sempronii, Cic.

ēlŏquentĭa -ae, f. (eloquens), *the art of speaking well, eloquence*, Cic.

ēlŏquĭum -ii, n. (eloquor), 1, *expression of thought, speech*; tulit eloquium insolitum facundia praeceps, Hor.; 2, *eloquence*; qui licet eloquio fidum quoque Nestora vincat, Ov.

ēlŏquor (ex-lŏquor), -lŏcūtus (-lŏquūtus) sum, 3. dep., *to speak out, say out, express*; id quod sentit, Cic.; cogitata praeclare, Cic.

Ĕlōrus (Hĕlōrus) -i, m. (Ἔλωρος) and **Ĕlōrum (Hĕlōrum)** -i, n. (Ἔλωρον), *river on the east coast of Sicily and a town of the same name*. Adj., 1, **Ĕlōrĭus (Hĕl-)** -a -um, *of or belonging to Elorus*; 2, **Ĕlōrīni** -ōrum, m. *inhabitants of the town*.

Elpēnor -ŏris, m. (Ἐλπήνωρ) *one of the companions of Ulysses, changed by Circe into a hog*.

ēlūcĕo -luxi, 2. (ex and luceo), *to beam forth, shine out, glitter*. **A.** Lit., splendidissimo candore inter flammas elucens circulus, Cic. **B.** Transf., quae (scintilla ingenii) jam tum elucebat in puero, Cic.

ēluctor, 1. dep. **I.** Intransit., *to struggle out, burst forth*. **A.** Lit., aqua eluctabitur omnis, Verg. **B.** Transf., velut eluctantia verba, Tac. **II.** Transit., *to struggle out of, surmount a difficulty*. **A.** Lit., quum tot ac tam validae manus eluctandae essent, Liv.; nives, Tac. **B.** Transf., locorum difficultates, Tac.

ēlūcŭbro, 1. *to compose by lamplight*; causae diligenter elaboratae et tanquam elucubratae, Cic. Dep. form, **ēlūcŭbror**, 1; epistolam, Cic.

ēlūdo -lūsi -lūsum, 3. (ex and ludo). **I.** Intransit., *to dash forth, play* (of the waves of the sea); ipsum autem mare sic terram appetens litoribus eludit, Cic.; litus qua fluctus eluderet, Cic. **II.** Transit., 1, *to parry a blow*; absol., quasi rudibus eius eludit oratio, Cic.; 2, *to evade, try to escape*; pugnam, Liv.; 3, *to mock, ridicule*, Cic.; aliquem omnibus contumeliis, Liv.

ēlūgĕo -luxi, 2. **I.** Intransit., *to mourn for any one during the prescribed period*, Liv. **II.** Transit., *to mourn for*; patriam, ap. Cic.

ēlumbis -e (ex and lumbus), *weak in the loins*; transf., of orators, *weak, feeble*, Tac.

ēlŭo -lŭi -lūtum, 3. *to wash out, wash clean, rinse, cleanse*. **A.** Lit., corpus, Ov.; sanguinem, Cic. **B.** Transf., *to wash away, efface, remove, get rid of*; maculas furtorum, Cic.; crimen, Ov.; amicitias remissione usus, *gradually loosen*, Cic.

ēlūtus -a -um, p. adj. with compar. (from eluo) *washed out, watery, insipid*; irriguo nihil est elutius horto, Hor.

ēlŭvĭes -ēi, f. (eluo). **I.** Middle, *a washing away, inundation, flood*; maris, Tac.; eluvie mons est deductus in aequor, Ov.; fig., illa labes atque eluvies civitatis, *impurity*, Cic. **II.** Pass., 1, *filth*; siccare eluviem, Juv.; 2, *a puddle, pond*; in proxima eluvie pueros exponunt, Liv.

ēlŭvĭo -ōnis, f. (eluo), *an inundation*, Cic.; plur. aquarum eluviones, Cic.; eluviones et exustiones terrarum, Cic.

Ĕlўmāïs -māïdis, f. (Ἐλυμαΐς), *a Persian district to the west of the present province of Iran*. Adj., **Ĕlўmaeus** -a -um, *Elymaean*.

Ēlўsĭum -ii, n. (Ἠλύσιον πεδίον), *Elysium, the abode of the blessed*; hence adj., **Ēlўsĭus** -a -um, *Elysian*, campi, Verg. Subst., **Ēlўsĭi**, m. *the Elysian fields*, Mart.

em, interj., *ha! indeed!* Cic.

ēmancĭpo (ēmancŭpo) 1. **I.** *to release or emancipate a son from the* patria potestas, Liv. **II. A.** *to transfer a son to the power of another*; filium alicui in adoptionem. **B.** Transf., *to make over, give up, transfer*; emancipatum esse alicui, Cic.

ēmāno (ex and mano). **A.** Lit., *to flow out*, Lucr. **B.** Transf., 1, *to arise, spring, emanate from*; alii quoque alio ex fonte praeceptores dicendi emanaverunt, Cic.; 2, *to spread abroad*; a, mala quae a Lacedaemoniis profecta emanarunt latius, Cic.; b, of speech, ne per nos his sermo tum emanet, Cic.; consilia tua emanare, Liv.; foll. by acc. and infin., Liv.

Ēmăthĭa -ae, f. (Ἠμαθία), *an old name for Macedonia*, Verg.; *a district of Macedonia*, Liv.; poet., *Thessaly*, Verg.; hence adj., 1, **Ēmăthĭus** -a -um, *Emathian, Macedonian*; dux, *Alexander*, Ov.; 2, **Ēmăthis** -idis, f. *Macedonian*; Emathides, *the Muses*, Ov.

ēmātūresco -tūrŭi, 3. **A.** Lit., *to become ripe*, Plin. **B.** Transf., *to become mild, be softened*; ira, Ov.

ĕmax -ācis (emo), *fond of buying*, Cic.

emblēma -ătis, n. (ἔμβλημα), 1, *inlaid or mosaic work*, ap. Cic.; 2, *raised or relief ornaments*, Cic.

embŏlĭum -ii, n. (ἐμβόλιον), *a dramatic interlude*, Cic.

ēmendābĭlis -e (emendo), *that may be amended*; error, Liv.

ēmendātē, adv. (emendatus), *correctly, faultlessly*; pure et emendate loqui, Cic.

ēmendātĭo -ōnis, f. (emendo), *improvement, emendation, amendment*; correctio philosophiae veteris et emendatio, Cic.

ēmendātor -ōris, m. (emendo), *an amender, corrector*; quasi emendator sermonis usitati, Cic.; emendator nostrae civitatis, Cic.

ēmendātrix -icis, f. (emendator), *she who corrects or amends*; vitiorum emendatricem legem esse oportet, Cic.; o praeclaram emendatricem vitae poeticam, Cic.

ēmendātus -a -um, p. adj. with compar. and superl. (from emendo), *free from mistakes, faultless, perfect*; a, intellectually, locutio, Cic.; carmina, Hor.; b, morally, mores, Cic.

ēmendo, 1. (ex and mendum), *to free from errors, emend, correct, improve*; a, intellectually, alicuius annales, Cic.; b, morally, civitatem, Cic.; conscius mihi sum corrigi me et emendari castigatione posse, Liv.; consuetudinem vitiosam, Cic.; res Italias legibus, Hor.

ēmentĭor -ītus, 4. dep., *to devise falsely, counterfeit, falsify, pretend*; auspicia, Cic.; falsa naufragia, Liv.; with acc. and infin., eo me beneficio obstrictum esse ementior, Cic.; absol., *to make false statements*; in aliquem, Cic.;

partic perf (pass), auspicia ementita, Cic, neut plur subst, ementita et falsa, Cic

ēmĕrĕo -ui -itum, 2 and **ēmĕrĕor** -itus, 2, dep **I. a,** *to deserve*, foll by infin, Ov; **b,** *to deserve well of a person*, aliquem, Ov **II** *to serve*, stipendia, Liv, partic, emeritus, *a soldier that has served his time, a veteran*, Suet, transf *old, disused* aratrum, Ov, pass, annuae operae emerentur, Cic, tempus emeritum, *ended*, Cic

ēmergo -mersi, -mersum (ex and mergo), 3 **I.** Transit, *to cause to rise up*, emergere se or emergi, *to rise up, emerge* **A.** Lit, serpens se emergit, Cic, emersus e flumine, Cic **B.** Transf, *to free oneself, to rise*, emergere se ex malis, Nep **II.** Intransit, *to come forth, come up, emerge* **A.** Lit, equus ex flumine emersit, Cic **B.** Lit, **1,** *to extricate oneself, get clear, emerge*, emergere ex judicio peculatus, Cic; ex paternis probris ac vitiis, Cic, **2,** *to come to light, appear*, emergit rursum dolor, Cic, ex quo magis emergit, quale sit decorum illud, Cic

ēmĕrĭtus -a -um (partic of emereo)

ĕmĕtĭca -ae, f (ἐμετική), *an emetic*, ap Cic

ēmētĭor mensus sum, 4 **I.** *to measure out* **A.** Lit, spatium oculis, Verg **B.** Transf, **a,** *to pass over, traverse*, una nocte aliquantum iter, Liv, partic perf pass, toto emenso spatio, Caes, **b,** *to pass through a space of time*, tres principes, *live through the reigns of*, Tac, partic perf pass, emensae in lucem noctes, Ov **II.** *to measure out, bestow*, ego autem voluntatem tibi profecto emetiar, Cic

ēmĕto (-messui) -messum, 3 *to reap, mow*, plus frumenti, Hor

ēmĭco -micui -micātum, 1 *to spring out, leap forth, appear quickly, dart forth* **I. A.** Lit, **1,** of lightning, flame, etc, flamma emicat ex oculis, Ov; **2,** of water, blood, etc, scaturigines tenues emicant, Liv **B.** Transf, **a,** *to break out*, alicui pavor emicat, Tac, **b,** *to shine forth, be distinguished*, inter quae verbum forte si emicuit decorum, Hor **II. 1,** of weapons, missiles, etc, *to whiz forth*, telum excussum velut glans emicabat, Liv, **2,** of persons, *to jump out*, in litus, Verg **III.** *to rush up*, **1,** of things, in superos ignes, Ov, **2,** of persons, *to jump up* solo, Verg

ēmĭgro, 1 *to remove from a place, wander forth, migrate, emigrate*, huc ex illa domo praetoria emigrabat, Cic, domo, Caes, transf, e vita, *to die*, Cic

ēmĭnens -entis, p adj (from emineo) **A.** Lit, *prominent, projecting, lofty*, promontoria, Caes; oculi, *standing out*, Cic; genae leniter eminentes, Cic **B.** Transf, *illustrious, distinguished, eminent*, oratores, Tac Subst, **ēmĭnentes** -ium, m *remarkable persons*, Tac

ēmĭnentĭa -ae, f (emineo), **a,** *protuberance, prominence*, nec habere ullam soliditatem nec eminentiam, Cic; **b,** in painting, *the lights of a picture*, Cic

ēmĭnĕo -minui, 2 (ex and mineo) **I.** Lit, **1,** *to project, stand out*, ex terra nihil eminet quod, etc, Cic, eminentibus oculis, *with projecting eyes*, Cic; jugum directum eminens in mare, Caes, **2,** of the lights of a picture, *to stand out*, magis id, quod erit illuminatum, exstare atque eminere videatur, Cic **II.** Transf, **1,** *to appear, become visible* toto ex ore crudelitas eminebat, Cic, eminente animo patrio inter publicae poenae ministerium, Liv, **2,** *to be conspicuous, remarkable, eminent*, Demosthenes unus eminet inter omnes in omni genere dicendi, Cic, tantum eminebat peregrina virtus, Liv

ēmĭnŭs, adv (e and manus, opp comminus), **1,** milit t t *at a distance, from a distance*, eminus hastis aut comminus gladiis uti, Cic; eminus pugnare, Caes, **2,** *at a distance, from afar*, Ov

ēmīror, 1 dep, *to wonder at exceedingly, be astonished at*, aequora, Hor

ēmissārĭum -ii, n (emitto), *an outlet for water*, Cic

ēmissārĭus -ii, m (emitto), *a person sent out to gain intelligence, an emissary, a spy*, Cic

ēmissĭo -ōnis, f (emitto), *a sending forth*, **1,** of missiles, balistae lapidum et reliqua tormenta eo graviores emissiones habent, quo sunt contenta atque adducta vehementius, **2,** *letting loose*, anguis, serpentis, Cic

ēmissus -ūs, m (emitto), *sending forth*, Lucr

ēmitto -misi -missum, 3 (ex and mitto) **I.** *to send forth, send out* **A.** Gen, equitatus pabulandi causā emissus, Caes **B.** Esp, **1,** milit t t, *to send out against an enemy*, cohortes ex statione et praesidio, Caes, equites in hostem, Liv, **2, a,** *to drive away*, aliquem ex domo, Cic, **b,** *to hurl forth*, hastam in fines eorum, Liv, **3,** *to send forth from oneself*, si nubium conflictu ardor expressus se emiserit, id esse fulmen, Cic, varios sonitus linguae, Lucr, **4,** of fluids, *to let forth*, aquam ex lacu Albano, Liv, lacum, *to draw off*, Cic, **5,** of a book, *to publish*, si quid dignum aliquid dignum nostro nomine emisimus, Cic **II.** *to let go, let loose* **A.** Gen, **1,** lit, aliquem noctu per vallum, Caes, manu arma, Caes, **2,** transf, aliquem de manibus, *to let slip*, Cic, emissa de manibus res est, Liv **B.** Esp, **1,** in the circus, *to start, send away*, quibuscum tanquam e carceribus emissus sis, Cic, **2, a,** *to let out of prison*, aliquem e or de carcere, Cic, **b,** *to let go*, aliquem, Cic, aliquem ex obsidione, Liv, aliquem sub jugum, *to send under the yoke*, Liv, legal t t, of slaves, aliquem manu, *to free*, Liv, of a debtor, libra et aere liberatum emittit, Liv

ĕmo, ēmi, emptum, 3 *to buy, purchase* **A.** Lit, domum de aliquo, Cic, aedes ab aliquo, Cic, with abl or genit (with adjectives and pronouns), of price, emere grandi pecuniā, Cic, magno, *dear*, Cic, parvo, *cheap*, Cic, emere domum prope dimidio carius quam aestimabatur, Cic, bene, *cheap*, Cic, male, *dear*, Cic, minoris, *cheaper*, Cic, pluris, *dearer*, Cic, bona de aliqua duobus millibus nummūm, Cic Subst, **emptum** -i, n *the contract of sale*, ex empto, Cic **B** Transf, *to bribe, buy*, judices, Cic, emptum judicium, Cic, empta dolore voluptas, Hor

ēmŏdĕror, 1 dep, *to moderate*; dolorem verbis, Ov

ēmŏdŭlor, 1 dep, *to sing, praise in verse*, Musam per undenos pedes, Ov

ēmōlīmentum = emolumentum (q v)

ēmollĭo -ivi -itum, 4 (ex and mollio), *to soften* **A.** Lit, fundas et amenta, Liv **B.** Transf, **a,** in a good sense, *to make mild, soften*, mores, Ov, **b,** in a bad sense, *to make effeminate*, exercitum, Liv

ēmŏlŭmentum -i, n (emolior, *to work out*), **1,** *effort, labour, exertion*, Caes, **2,** *the result of effort, gain, advantage*, emolumento esse, Cic, emolumenta rerum, Liv

ēmŏnĕo, 2 *to warn, admonish*, aliquem ut, etc, Cic

ēmŏrĭor mortuus sum mŏri, dep, *to die* **A.** Lit Of persons, pro aliquo Cic, non miserabiliter, Cic, per virtutem, *bravely*, Sall **B.** Transf, *to perish*, laus emori non potest, Cic

ēmŏvĕo -mōvi -mōtum, 2 **I.** *to move out*

move away, remove. **A.** Lit., multitudinem e foro, Liv.: aliquos senatu, Liv. **B.** Transf., curas dictis, Verg. **II.** *to shake, shatter;* muros fundamentaque, Verg.

Empĕdŏcles -is, m. (Ἐμπεδοκλῆς), *a poet and philosopher of Agrigentum;* hence adj., **Empĕdŏclēus** -a -um, *Empedoclean;* sanguis (acc. to the doctrines of Empedocles), *the soul,* Cic. Subst., **Empĕdŏclēa** -ōrum, n. *the doctrines of Empedocles,* Cic.

empīrĭcus -i, m. (ἐμπειρικός), *an unscientific physician, empiric,* Cic.

Empŏrĭae -ārum, f. (Ἐμπορίαι), *town in Hispania Tarraconensis, colony of the Phocaeans,* now *Ampurias.*

empŏrĭum -ĭi, n. (ἐμπόριον), *a place of trade, mart, emporium;* celebre et frequens emporium, Liv.

emptĭo -ōnis, f. (emo). **A.** *a buying, purchasing;* ista falsa et simulata emptio, Cic. **B.** Meton., *a purchase;* prorsus existis emptionibus nullam desidero, Cic.

emptĭto, 1. (freq. of emo), *to buy up, to buy,* ap. Tac.

emptor -ōris, m. (emo), *a buyer, purchaser;* emptor fundi, Cic.; emptores bonorum, Cic.; transf., dedecorum pretiosus emptor, Hor.

ēmulgĕo -mulsum, 2. *to milk out;* poet., transf., *to drain out, to exhaust;* paludem, Cat.

ēmungo -munxi -munctum, 3. (e and *mungo). **A.** Lit., *to blow the nose,* Juv. **B.** Transf., **a,** homo emunctae naris, *with a keen scent for other persons' faults,* Hor.; **b,** *to cheat, defraud, swindle;* aliquem, Hor.

ēmūnĭo -mūnīvi or -mūnĭi -mūnītum, 4. **1,** *to fortify, strengthen, make safe;* locum, murum, Liv.; **2,** *to make ready, prepare, make accessible;* silvas ac paludes, Tac.

ēn, interj., **1,** demonstr. with nom. or acc., *lo! behold! see!* en ego vester Ascanius, Verg.; en quatuor aras, Verg.; en causa, Cic.; absol., en, cui tu liberos committas, Cic.; with aspice, en aspice, Ov.; **2,** interrog., en, quid ago? Verg.; with unquam, en unquam futurum, etc., Liv.

ēnarrābĭlis -e (enarro), *that can be narrated or told,* Verg.

ēnarro, 1. *to tell, narrate;* enarrare alicui somnium, Cic.

ēnascor -nātus sum, 3. dep., *to grow out of, spring forth, arise from;* lauream in puppi navis longae enatam, Liv.

ēnăto, 1. *to swim from, escape by swimming.* **A.** Lit., si fractis enatat exspes navibus, Hor. **B.** Transf., *to extricate oneself from a difficulty;* reliqui habere se videntur angustius; enatant tamen, Cic.

ēnāvātus -a -um, *performed, finished,* Tac.

ēnāvĭgo, 1. **I.** Intransit., *to sail away;* fig., e quibus tanquam e scrupulosis cotibus enavigavit oratio, Cic. **II.** Transit., *to sail over, sail through;* undam, Hor.

Encĕlădus -i, m. (Ἐγκέλαδος), *one of the giants, slain by the lightning of Jupiter, and buried beneath Aetna.*

endo, archaic = in.

endrŏmis -ĭdis, f. (ἐνδρομίς), *a coarse woollen cloak worn after exercise in the palaestra,* Juv.

Endȳmĭōn -ōnis, m. (Ἐνδυμιών), *son of Aëthlius or of Zeus and Calyce, father of Aetolus, beloved by Selene and taken to Mount Latmos in Caria, and there lulled to perpetual sleep;* appell., *a beautiful youth,* Juv.

ēnĕco -nĕcŭi -nectum, 1. *to torment, torture;* siti enectus Tantalus, Cic.; fame, frigore, illuvie, squalore enecti, Liv.; provinciam enectam tradere, *exhausted,* Cic.

ēnervātus -a -um, p. adj. (enervo), *enervated, powerless, effeminate;* **a,** of persons, Cic.; **b,** of things, mollis et enervata oratio, Cic.; enervata muliebrisque sententia, Cic.

ēnervis -e (ex and nervus), *nerveless, powerless, weak;* orator, Tac.

ēnervo, 1. (enervis), *to render weak, powerless, effeminate, to enervate;* of age, aliquem, Cic.; of sleep, wine, etc., Liv.; bellum, Cic.; ut enervetur oratio compositione verborum, Cic.

Engyŏn -i, n. (Ἔγγυον), *a town in Sicily;* hence, **Engŭīnus** -a -um, *of or belonging to Engyon.*

ēnīco = eneco (q.v.).

ĕnim, conj. (from e and nam), *for;* **1,** to explain a previous statement or word, de corpusculorum (ita enim appellat atomos) concursione fortuita, Cic.; often where a sentence is to be understood, tum Socrates, non enim paruisti mihi revocanti, *that is not to be wondered at for,* etc., Cic.; **2,** to strengthen a previous statement, *truly, certainly;* in his est enim aliqua securitas, Cic.; with other conj., at enim, sed enim, *but then,* Cic. (enim generally the second or third word in its clause).

ĕnimvēro, 1, *to be sure, certainly,* Cic.; **2,** *but indeed;* stronger than at (to introduce an objection), Cic.

Enīpeus -pĕi and -pĕos, m. (Ἐνιπεύς), **1,** *a river in Thessaliotis, flowing into the Apidanus;* **2,** *a river in Pieria,* Liv.

ēnīsus, v. enixus and enitor.

ēnĭtĕo -ŭi, 2. *to shine out, shine forth, to glitter.* **A.** Lit., enitet campus, Verg. **B.** Transf., *to be conspicuous;* quo in bello virtus enituit egregia M. Catonis, Cic.

ēnĭtesco -tŭi, 3. (inchoat. of eniteo), *to gleam, shine forth.* **A.** Lit., enitescit pulchrior multo, Hor. **B.** Transf., bellum novum exoptabat, ubi virtus enitescere posset, Sall.

ēnītor -nīsus or -nixus, 3. dep. **I.** Intransit., **A.** *to work one's way up, to struggle up, ascend;* per adversos fluctus ingenti labore remigum, Liv.; in altiora, Tac. **B.** *to strive, struggle, make an effort;* with ut and the subj., Cic.; eniti et contendere, eniti et efficere ut, etc., Cic.; with ne and the subj., Sall.; pugnare et eniti ne, Cic.; with neut. acc., quod quidem certe enitar, Cic.; quid eniti et quid efficere possim, Cic.; with infin., Sall.; absol., in aliqua re, Cic.; ad dicendum, Cic. **II.** Transit., **1,** *to bring forth, bear;* partus plures, Liv.; **2,** *to climb;* aggerem, Tac.

ēnixē, adv. with compar. and superl. (enixus), *eagerly, strenuously, zealously;* enixe aliquem juvare, Caes.; enixe operam dare ut, etc., Liv. enixe obstare, Liv.

ēnixus (enīsus) -a -um, p. adj. (enitor), *strenuous, eager, zealous;* enixo studio, Liv.

Enna = Henna (q.v.).

Ennĭus -ĭi, m. *the most celebrated of the ante-Augustan poets, born at Rudiae in Calabria,* B.C. 239, *died* 169, *the creator of Roman epic poetry.*

Ennŏsĭgaeus -i, m. (Ἐννοσίγαιος), *the Earthshaker, surname of Neptune,* Juv.

ēno, 1. **A.** Lit., *to swim out;* **1,** e concha, Cic.; **2,** *to escape by swimming;* in terram, Liv. **B.** Transf., *to fly away;* insuetum per iter gelidas enavit ad Arctos, Verg.

ēnōdātē, adv. (enodatus), *clearly, plainly;* narrare, Cic.

ēnōdātĭo -ōnis, f. (enodo, *an untying*), *explanation, exposition;* cognitio enodationis indigens, Cic ; explicatio fabularum et enodatio nominum, Cic

ēnōdātus a -um, p. adj. (from enodo), *freed from knots, untied*, hence, *made clear, explained*, praecepta enodata diligenter, Cic

ēnōdis -e (ex and nodus), *without knots;* truncus, Verg ; abies, Ov

ēnōdo, 1 *to take out the knots;* transf , *to make clear, explain, expound ;* nomina, Cic.

ēnormis -e (ex and norma), **1,** *irregular, unusual;* vici, Tac.; **2,** *very large, immense, enormous*, hasta, gladius, Tac

ēnŏtesco -nŏtŭi, 3 *to become known, be made public*, quod ubi enotuit, Tac

ensĭfer -fĕra -fĕrum (ensis and fero), *sword bearing*, Orion, Ov

ensis -is, m *a sword*, Liv , Verg

Entella ae, f (Ἔντελλα), *a town in the interior of Sicily*, now *Entella* Adj., **Entellīnus** -a -um, *of or belonging to Entella.*

enthȳmēma -ătis, n (ἐνθύμημα), *a syllogism in which one of the three terms is unexpressed*, Cic

ēnūbo -nupsi -nuptum, 3 *to marry out of one's rank ;* e patribus, Liv., *from one town to another*, Liv

ēnŭclĕātē, adv (enucleatus), *clearly, plainly, concisely* (opp ornate), Cic.

ēnŭclĕātus -a -um, p adj (from enucleo), of discourse, *clear, plain, unadorned*, genus dicendi, Cic

ēnŭclĕo, 1 (ex and nucleus), *to take out the kernel*, transf , acu quaedam enucleata argumenta, Cic , eblandita illa, non enucleata esse suffragia, *given from conviction, free from corrupt motives*, Cic. ; haec nunc enucleare non ita necesse est, *explain in detail*, Cic

ēnŭmĕrātĭo ōnis, f (enumero), **1,** *a counting up, enumeration*, singulorum argumentorum, Cic , **2,** in rhetoric, *recapitulation*, Cic

ēnŭmĕro, 1 **1,** *to reckon, count up, enumerate*, pretium, *to compute, pay*, Cic , **2,** *to count up, enumerate in discourse, recapitulate*, multitudinem beneficiorum, Cic

ēnuntĭātĭo -ōnis, f (enuntio), *enunciation, proposition*, Cic

ēnuntĭātum i, n (enuntio), *a proposition*, Cic

ēnuntĭo, 1 **1,** *to tell, divulge, disclose ;* consilia adversariis, Cic ; enuntiare mysteria, Cic , silenda, Liv. , rem Helvetiis per indicium, Caes , dici rei sent , plane quid sentiam enuntiabo ad homines familiarissimos, Cic , **2,** *to de-, announce, express in words;* **a,** aliquid ..ris, Cic , **b,** logic t.t , *to state a proposition, predicate*, Cic

ēnuptĭo -ōnis, f (enubo), *marriage out of one's own condition*, gentis, *out of one's gens*, Liv

ēnūtrĭo -īvi -ītum, 4. *to nourish, rear, bring up*, puerum Ideis sub antris, Ov

1 **ĕo,** īvi and ii, itum, 4 (connected with Gr εἶμι) **I.** *to go* **A.** Of living beings, **1,** gen , domum, Plaut , ad forum, Plaut ; subsidio suis, Caes , novas vias, *to make a journey in unknown lands*, Prop , pedibus, *to go by land*, Liv. , maximis itineribus, *to make forced marches*, Liv ; cubitum, *to go to bed*, Cic , equis, *to ride*, Liv ; puppibus, *to make a voyage*, Ov , **2,** esp , **a,** ad arma, ap. Cic , and ad saga, Cic , *to fly to arms, prepare for war ;* **b,** in sententiam (with or without pedibus), *to support a motion in the senate*, Cic ; in alia omnia, *to oppose a motion, vote in the negative*, Cic , **c,** ire in aliquem, *to attack*, Liv., **d,** in poenas, *to punish*, Ov in scelus, *to commit a fault*, Ov , ire in duplum, *to give a double penalty*, Cic ; ierat in causam praeceps, Liv , **e,** ire per aliquid, *to go over*, ire per laudes tuorum, Ov **B.** of things, **a,** clamor it ad aethera, Verg , pugna it ad pedes, *they fight afoot*, Liv , **b,** *to move*, nec pes ire potest, Ov ; **c,** of missiles, *to go, pierce*, it hasta, Verg , **d,** of liquids, *to flow*, it naribus ater sanguis, Verg **II. 1,** *to pass away*, eunt anni, Ov , sic eat quaecumque Romana lugebit hostem, Liv , **2,** *to go, to happen*, incipit res melius ire, Cic , **3,** *to last*, si non tanta quies iret, Verg , **4,** ire in aliquid, *to be changed to* sanguis it in sucos, Ov (perf it, Verg *Aen* 9, 418, Ov *Met* 8, 349)

2 **ĕō,** adv **I.** Old dat of is, **a,** *thither, to that place;* pervenire, Cic , **b,** *so far, to such a pitch*, eo rem adducam ut, etc , Cic , with genit , eo consuetudinis adducta res est, Liv , eo usque, *to that point*, Cic **II.** Abl , **a,** *on that account*, eo quod, Cic , eo quia, Cic , eo ut, etc , Cic , non eo, dico, quo, Cic , **b,** with comparatives, eo magis, *the more*, Cic , **c,** *in that place*, eo loci, *at that very place*, Cic

ĕōdem, adv **I.** Old dat of idem, *to the same place, just so far*, eodem mittere, Caes , transf , eodem pertinere, Cic **II.** Abl , res est eodem loci ubi reliquisti, *in the same condition*, Cic

ĕopse = eo ipso

Ēōs (ἠώς) and **Ĕōs** (Ἕως) (occurs only in nom), f *the red of the morning, dawn*, hence adj , **Ēōus** and **Ĕōus** -a -um, *belonging to the morning* or *belonging to the East, eastern* Subst , **Ĕōus** -i, m **a,** *the morning star*, and meton , *the East or a dweller in the East*, Ov , **b,** *one of the horses of the sun*, Ov.

Ĕpămīnōndas -ae, m (Ἐπαμεινώνδας), *a celebrated general of the Thebans, killed in the hour of victory at Mantinea*

ēpastus a -um (pascor), *eaten up*, escae, Ov

Ĕpēŏs and -**ēus** (**Ĕpīus**) -i, m (Ἐπειός), *son of Panopeus, builder of the Trojan horse*

ĕphēbus -i, m (ἔφηβος), *a youth from his sixteenth to his twentieth year* (generally of Greeks), Cic

ĕphēmĕris -idis, f (ἐφημερίς), *a journal, diary*, Cic

Ĕphĕsus -i, m (Ἔφεσος), *one of the twelve Ionic towns in Asia Minor*, famous for its temple of Diana and school of rhetoric Hence, **Ĕphĕsius** -a um, *Ephesian*

Ĕphippĭātus -a -um (ephippium), *provided with an ephippium*

ĕphippĭum -i, n (ἐφίππιον), *a horse-cloth, housing, saddle*, Cic , prov , optat ephippia bos piger, optat arare caballus, *no one is content with his condition*, Hor.

1 **ĕphŏrus** -i, m (ἔφορος), *the ephor, a Spartan magistrate*, Cic

2 **Ĕphŏrus** -i, m (Ἔφορος), *a Greek historian of Cyme in Asia Minor, flourishing about 340 B C*

Ĕphȳra -ae, and **Ĕphȳrē** -ēs, (Ἐφύρα), f **I.** *a sea nymph*, Verg **II.** *the ancient name of Corinth*, hence, **Ĕphȳrēĭus** -a -um, *Corinthian*, Verg

Ĕpĭcharmus -i, m, (Ἐπίχαρμος), *a philosopher and poet of Cos, and afterwards of Syracuse, disciple of Pythagoras*

Ĕpĭclērŏs -i, f (Ἐπίκληρος), "*the Heiress,*" *name of a comedy of Menander*

ĕpĭcōpus -a -um (ἐπίκωπος), *provided with oars*, phaselus, Cic.

Ĕpĭcūrus -i, m (Ἐπίκουρος), *an Athenian philosopher, founder of the Epicurean school, which held that pleasure was the highest good* Hence adj, **Ĕpĭcūrēus** (-īus) -a -um, *Epicurean* Subst, **Ĕpĭcūrēi** -ōrum, m *the disciples of Epicurus*, Cic

ĕpĭcus -a -um (ἐπικός), *epic*, poeta, Cic, poema, Cic

Ĕpĭdaphna -ae, f, and **Ĕpĭdaphnēs**, *a place near Antioch in Syria*

Ĕpĭdauros -i, f (Ἐπίδαυρος), **1,** *a town in Dalmatia* **2,** *a town in Laconia*, **3,** *a town in Argolis, where Aesculapius was worshipped in the form of a serpent* Adj **Ĕpĭdaurĭus** -a -um, *Epidaurian* Subst, **Ĕpĭdaurĭus** -ii, m *Aesculapius*, Ov

Ĕpĭgŏni -ōrum, m (Ἐπίγονοι), *the after-born, sons of the Seven against Thebes, who renewed the war of their fathers*, *name of a tragedy of Aeschylus and of one of Accius*

ĕpĭgramma -ătis, n (ἐπίγραμμα), **1,** *an inscription on the base of a statue*, Cic, **2,** *an epigram*, Cic

ĕpĭlŏgus -i, m (ἐπίλογος), *a conclusion, peroration, epilogue*, Cic

Ĕpĭmĕnĭdes -is, m (Ἐπιμενίδης), *a Cretan, a poet contemporary with Solon*

Ĕpĭmētheus -ĕi and -ĕos, m (Ἐπιμηθεύς), *father of Pyrrha, son of Iapetus and brother of Prometheus* Hence **Ĕpĭmēthis** -thĭdis, f (Ἐπιμηθίς), *daughter of Epimetheus*—i e, *Pyrrha*, Ov

ĕpĭrēdĭum -ii, n (ἐπί and reda or raeda), *the strap by which a horse was fastened to a vehicle, trace*, Juv

Ēpīrus -i f (Ἤπειρος), *a country of Greece, between Macedonia, Thessaly and the Ionian Sea, part of the present Albania* Hence, **1, Ēpīrensis** -e, *of Epirus*, **2, Ēpīrōtes** -ae, m (Ἠπειρώτης), *an Epirote*, **3, Ēpīrōtĭcus** -a -um, *of Epirus*

ĕpistŏla -ae, f (ἐπιστολή), *a written communication, letter, epistle* epistola ab aliquo, Cic, ad aliquem, Cic, epistolam dare, *to send off or to deliver*, Cic, epistola Graecis litteris conscripta Caes, epistolam inscribere alicui, Cic

ĕpistŏlĭum -ii, n (ἐπιστόλιον), *a little letter, note*, Cat

ĕpĭtăphĭus -ii, m (ἐπιτάφιος), *a funeral oration*, Cic

ĕpĭtŏma -ae, and **ĕpĭtŏmē** -ēs, f (ἐπιτομή), *an abridgment, epitome*, Cic

ĕpŏdes -um, m *a kind of salt water fish*, Ov

Ĕpŏna -ae, f (epus = equus), *the protecting goddess of horses, asses, etc*, Juv

ĕpops -ŏpis, m (ἔποψ), *the hoopoe*, Verg

Ĕpŏrēdĭa -ae, f *a Roman colony in Gallia Transpadana, now Yvrea*

ĕpos, indecl n (ἔπος), *an epic poem, epos*, Hor

ēpōto -pōtāvi -pōtus and -pōtātūrus 1 (ex and poto), a *to drink up, drink out* (in class Lat only in partic perf), poculo epoto, Cic, epoto medicamento Liv, b, poet, *to suck up, swallow up*, terreno Lycus est epotus hiatu, Ov

ĕpŭlae -ārum, f *food, dishes* **I.** Gen, mensae conquisitissimis epulis exstruebantur, Cic **II.** Esp, *banquet, feast*, quotidianae epulae, Cic, funestas epulas fratri comparare, Cic, ad epulas regis assistere Cic, alicui epulas dare, Tac, fig (pass animi) satiata bonarum cogitationum epulis, Cic

ĕpŭlāris -e (epulae), *relating or belonging to a banquet*, accubitio amicorum, Cic, sacrificium, Cic

ĕpŭlātĭo -ōnis, f (epulor), *a feasting, revelling*, Cic

ĕpŭlo -ōnis, m (epulum), **1,** *a reveller, feaster*, Cic, **2,** Tresviri (and subsequently) Septemviri epulones, *a college of priests who had charge of the sacrificial feasts*, Cic, so simply epulones, Cic

ĕpŭlor, 1 dep (epulae), *to feast, eat.* **I** Intransit, unā, *together*, Cic, cum aliquo, Cic, modice, Cic, Saliarem in modum, *splendidly*, Cic, with abl, dapibus opimis, Verg **II.** Transit, aliquem epulandum ponere mensis, *to place on the table to be eaten*, Verg

ĕpŭlum -i, n *a solemn or public banquet, feast, entertainment*, epuli dominus, Cic, epulum populi Romani, Cic, alicui epulum dare nomine alicuius, Cic.

ĕqua -ae, f *a mare*, Cic (dat and abl plur generally equabus)

ĕques -itis, c (equus) **I.** Gen, *a horseman, rider*, illum equitem sex dierum spatio transcurrisse longitudinem Italiae, Liv **II.** Esp, **A.** *a horse-soldier*, Caes (opp pedes), and used collectively, *cavalry*, Liv **B.** equites, *the knights, a distinct order in the Roman commonwealth, between the senate and the plebs*, Cic

ĕquester -stris -stre (equus) **I. 1,** *relating to horsemen and horsemanship, equestrian*, statuae, Cic, **2,** *relating to horse soldiers and cavalry*, proelium, Caes, pugna, Cic **II.** *relating to the knights*, ordo, Cic, locus, Cic, census Cic Subst, **ĕquester** -stris, m *a knight*, Tac

ĕquĭdem (strengthened form of quidem by addition of demonstrative prefix e, cf enim and nam), a demonstrative particle, generally used with the first person, **1,** *indeed, truly*, nihil, inquit, equidem novi, Cic, equidem ego, Cic, certe equidem, Verg, **2,** in a concessive sense, *of course, certainly*, with sed, verum, sed tamen, Cic

ĕquīnus -a -um (equus), *relating to horses, equine*, seta, Cic, nervus, Verg

ĕquĭrĭa -um or -ōrum, n. (equus), *horse-races in honour of Mars, which took place at Rome, in the Campus Martius, every 27th of February and 14th of March*, Ov

ĕquĭtātus -ūs, m (equito), **1,** *cavalry* (opp peditatus), Cic, **2,** *the equestrian order*, Cic

ĕquĭto, 1 (eques). **A.** Lit, *to ride on horseback*, in equuleis, Cic **B.** Transf, of winds, *to rush*, Eurus per Siculas equitavit undas, Hor

ĕquŭlĕus -i, m (dim of equus) **A.** *a young horse, colt*, Cic **B.** *a wooden rack in the shape of a horse*, Cic

ĕquŭlus -i, m (dim of equus), *a colt*, Cic

ĕquus -i, m (ἵππος), *a horse* **I. A.** Lit, equorum domitores, Cic; equus bellator, *a war-horse*, Verg, equus publicus, *given by the state*, Liv, equum conscendere, Liv, in equum ascendere (opp ex equo descendere), Cic, in equum insilire, Liv sedere in equo, Cic; vehi in equo, Cic, equis insignibus et aurato curru reportari, *to ride in triumph*, Cic, merere equo, *to serve in the cavalry*, Caes, ad equum rescribere, *to make some one a knight*, Caes, equus Trojanus, *the Trojan horse*, Verg, fig, of a secret conspiracy, Cic **B.** Meton, plur, equi **1,** *a chariot*, Verg, **2,** *cavalry*, equi virique, Liv, so prov, equis viris or viris equisque, *with all one's might*, Cic **II.** Transf, of things like a horse **A.** equus bipes, *the sea horse*, Verg, **B.** *the constellation Pegasus* Cic poet. (genit plur, equum, Verg)

Equus Tūtĭcus -i, m *a small town in the country of the Hirpini in Lower Italy*

ērādo -rāsi -rāsum, 3, *to scratch out, to strike off.* **A.** Lit, aliquem albo senatorio, *from the senatorial list*, Tac **B.** Transf, *to destroy, eradicate*, elementa cupidinis pravi, Hor

Ĕrăna -ae, f (Ἔρανα), *capital of the Eleutherocilices on Mount Amanus*

Ĕrăsīnus -i, m (Ἐρασῖνος), *river in Argolis*, now *Kephalari*

Ĕrătō -ūs, f (Ἐρατώ), *the muse of amorous poetry*, Ov ; appell, *muse*, Verg

Ĕrătosthĕnēs -is, m (Ἐρατοσθένης), *a Greek philosopher and poet*

ercisco, erctum = hercisco, herctum (q v)

Ĕrĕbus -i, m (Ἔρεβος), **1,** *a god of the lower world, son of Chaos and brother of Nox*, Cic, **2,** *the lower world*, Verg Adj, **Ĕrĕbēus** -a -um, *belonging to the lower world*

Ĕrechthēūs -ĕi, m (Ἐρεχθεύς), *a mythical king of Athens, father of Orithyia and Procris*, hence, **1,** adj, **Ĕrechthēus** -a um, m *Athenian*, Ov, **2, Ĕrecthīdae** -arum, m *the Athenians*, Ov, **3, Ĕrechthis** idis, f *Orithyia*, Ov, *Procris*, Ov.

ērectus a -um, p adj with compar (from erigo), *set up* **I.** Lit, *upright, erect*, status, Cic **II.** Transf, **A.** Gen, *high, elevated*, **a,** in a good sense, celsus et erectus, Cic, **b,** in a bad sense, *proud*, erectus et celsus, Cic **B.** Esp **a,** *anxious, intent, with minds on the stretch*, judices, Cic, quum civitas in foro exspectatione erecta staret, *on the tiptoe of expectation*, Liv ; **b,** *resolute, lively, cheerful*, alacri animo et erecto, Cic

ērēpo -repsi -reptum, 1, *to creep through*, agrum, Juv ; **2,** *to climb*, montes quos nunquam erepsemus (= erepsissemus), Hor.

ēreptĭo -ōnis, f (eripio), *a taking by force, seizure*, Cic.

ēreptor -ōris, m (eripio), *one who takes away by force, a robber*, bonorum, Cic, libertatis, Cic

Ĕrĕtrĭa -ae, f (Ἐρέτρια) **I.** *a town near Pharsalus in Phthiotis* **II.** *a town in the island of Euboea, native town of the philosopher Menedemus, founder of the Eretrian school of philosophy* Adj, **a, Ĕrĕtrĭcus** a -um, subst, **Ĕrĕtrĭci** ōrum, m *the philosophers of the Eretrian school*, Cic, so **Ĕrĕtrĭăci** -ōrum, m Cic, **b, Ĕrĕtrĭensis** -e, *Eretrian*

Ērētum i, n (Ἤρητοι), *an old Sabine town on the Tiber*, now *Cretona* Adj, **Ērētīnus** -a -um, *Eretine*

ergā, prep with acc (root ERG, whence εἴργω), *towards*, **1,** *in relation to* ea prima Tiberio erga pecuniam alienam diligentia fuit, Tac, **2,** *in relation to, towards* (of one's feelings or attitude towards a person or thing), **a,** in a good sense, erga nos amice et benevole collegisti, Cic ; amor erga te suus, Cic, benevolentia erga aliquem, Cic., **b,** in a bad sense, odium erga aliquem, Nep ; invidia erga aliquem, Tac

ergastŭlum -i, n *a house of correction for slaves*, ille ex compedibus atque ergastulo, Cic, aliquem in ergastulum dare or ducere, Liv, apud aliquem in ergastulo esse, Cic, ergastula solvere, Caes

ergō, adv (ἔργῳ) **I.** With a genit preceding it, *on account of*, victoriae, non valetudinis ergo, Liv **II.** Absol, *consequently, therefore, accordingly, then* **A.** Gen, Cic, itaque ergo, Liv **B.** Esp, **a,** of logical consequences, *therefore*, ergo etiam, Cic, **b,** with questions, *then*, quid ergo? *why then?* Cic, **c,** with imperatives, *then, now*, Cic, **d,** to resume something that had been dropped, *well then, as I was saying*, Cic (sometimes ergŏ in meaning No II)

Ĕrichthō -ūs, f (Ἐριχθώ), *a Thessalian witch consulted by Pompey*, transf, *a witch*, Ov

Ĕrichthŏnĭus ii, m (Ἐριχθόνιος), **1,** *a mythical king of Athens, the first to yoke four horses in a chariot*, adj, **Erichthŏnĭus** -a -um, *Athenian*, **2,** *a mythical king of Troy, son of Dardanus, father of Tros*, hence, **Erichthŏnĭus** -a -um, *Trojan*

ērĭcĭus -ii, m (*a hedgehog*), milit t t., *a beam thickly studded with iron spikes, chevaux-de-frise*, Caes

Ērĭdănus -i, m (Ἠριδανός), **1,** *myth and poet name of the river Padus*, **2,** *a constellation*, Cic poet

ērĭgo -rexi -rectum, 3 (ex and rego), *to set up, place upright, lift up, erect* **I.** Lit, **A.** Gen, scalas ad moenia, Liv, malum, *a mast*, Cic, oculos, *to raise*, Cic, aures, *to prick up the ears*, Cic **B** Esp, **1,** *to raise in height*, **a,** of places, *to make higher*, donec erecta in arcem via est, Liv, so middle, *to rise*, insula Sicanium juxta latus erigitur, Verg ; **b,** *to raise, erect a building*, etc ; turrem, Caes, **2,** milit t t, *to march a body of soldiers up a height* agmen in adversum clivum, Liv, aciem in collem, Liv **II.** Transf, **A.** Gen, *to arouse, excite*, animum ad audiendum, Cic ; auditor erigatur, *be attentive*, Cic **B.** Esp, *to raise up, encourage cheer*, aliquem, Cic, aliquem ad spem belli, Tac, animum, Cic, se erigere, *to encourage oneself, be encouraged*, erigere se in spem legis, Liv, so pass, erigimur, Hor

Ērĭgŏnē ēs, f (Ἠριγόνη), *the daughter of Icarus, transformed into the constellation Virgo* hence adj, **Ērĭgŏnēĭus** -a -um, *belonging to Erigone*, canis, *the dog of Icarus, Maera, changed into the constellation Canicula*

Ĕrĭgōnus -i, m (Ἐρίγων), *a tributary of the Axius in Macedonia*, now *Tzerna*

Ērillus (Hērillus) -i, m (Ἤριλλος), *a Stoic philosopher of Carthage* **Ērillii** -ōrum, m *the disciples of Erillus*

Ĕrinnys (Erinys) -yos f (Ἐρινύς) **I.** *one of the Furies*, plur, Erinnyes, *the Furies* **II.** Transf, **A.** *scourge, curse*, patriae communis Erinys, Verg **B.** *fury, madness*, quo tristis Erinys, quo fremitus vocat, Verg

Ĕrĭphȳla ae, f and **Ĕrĭphȳlē** -ēs, f (Ἐριφύλη), *daughter of Talaus and Lysimache, wife of Amphiaraus, whom she betrayed to Polynices for a golden necklace, for which she was slain by her son Alcmaeon*

ērĭpĭo -ripŭi -reptum, 3 (ex and rapio), *to snatch away, tear out, pluck out take away*, constr with ex, ab, de with the abl or the abl alone, or with the dat (of the person) **I.** Gen, ensem vaginā, Verg, aliquem ex equo, Liv **II.** Esp, **A.** In a bad sense, *to tear away, snatch away by violence*, aliquem ex manibus populi Romani, Cic, hereditatem ab aliquo, Cic, aurum Gallis, Liv, Scipio quamquam est subito ereptus, *snatched away by death*, Cic, alicui vitam, Sall, omnem usum navium, Caes **B.** In a good sense, *to free, tear away*, aliquem e manibus hostium, *to rescue*, Caes, filium a morte, Cic, se ab illa miseria, Cic, aliquem ex servitute, Sall., alicui timorem, Cic ; eripe te morae, *away with delay*, Hor eripe fugam, *snatch the opportunity of flight*, Verg

ērōdo -rōsi rōsum, 3 (ex and rodo), *to gnaw away, gnaw into, eat into*, vites, Cic

ērŏgātio -ōnis, f. (erogo), *payment, expenditure*; pecuniae, Cic.

ērŏgo, 1. (ex and rogo), *to pay from the public treasury*; pecuniam ex aerario, Cic.; pecuniam in classem, Cic.

errābundus -a -um (1. erro), *wandering*; of persons, nunc errabundi domos suos pervagarentur, Liv.; of animals, etc., vestigia bovis, Verg.; odor, Lucr.

errātĭcus -a -um (1. erro), *wandering, erratic*; Delos, Ov.; vitis serpens multiplici lapsu et erratico, Cic.

errātio -ōnis, f. (1. erro), *a wandering, straying*; nulla in caelo erratio, Cic.; eum (caeli motum) ab omni erratione liberavit, Cic.

errātum -i, n. (1. erro), *a fault, error*; 1, technically, erratum fabrile, Cic.; erratum meum, tuum, etc., *mistake in reckoning*, Cic.; 2, morally, errata aetatis meae, *of my youth*, Cic.

errātus -ūs, m. (1. erro), *wandering about straying*; longis erratibus actus, Ov.

1. **erro**, 1. **I.** *to wander, stray, rove.* **A.** Lit., 1, intransit., quum vagus et exsul erraret, Cic.; of inanimate objects, stellae errantes, Cic.; 2, transit., terrae erratae, *wandered over*, Verg.; litora errata, Verg. **B.** Transf., ne vagari et errare cogatur oratio, Cic.; ne tuus erret honos, Ov.; sententia errans et vaga, *uncertain*, Cic. **II.** *to wander from the right path, lose one's way.* **A.** Lit., errare viā, Verg. **B.** Transf., *to err, be in error, be mistaken*; vehementer, valde, Cic.; si erratur in nomine, Cic.; cui, errato, nulla venia, *when a mistake is made*, Cic.

2. **erro** -ōnis, m. (1. erro), *a wanderer, rover, vagabond*; esp. of slaves, Hor.; of unfaithful lovers, Ov.

error -ōris, m. (1. erro), *a wandering about.* **I.** Gen., **A.** Lit., error ac dissipatio civium, Cic. **B.** Transf., *wavering, uncertainty*; qui tibi aestus, qui error, quae tenebrae erunt, Cic. **II.** Esp., *wandering from the right way.* **A.** Lit., errore viarum, Liv.; cursus errore facili, Cic. **B.** Transf., 1, *error, deception*; errore duci, Cic.; in errorem induci, rapi, Cic.; mentis, Cic.; 2, *mistake*; ferendus tibi in hoc meus error, Cic.

ērŭbesco -rŭbŭi, 3. *to grow red, blush*; **a**, erubuere genae, Ov.; **b**, *to grow red from shame, be ashamed*; ubi erubuit, Cic.; with in and the abl., Cic.; with abl., Liv.; with ut and the subj., Cic.; with infin., Liv.; **ērŭbescendus** -a -um, *of which one should be ashamed*; ignes, Hor.

ērūca -ae, f. *a kind of colewort*, Hor.

ēructo, 1. *to belch forth, throw up, vomit.* **A.** Lit., saniem, Verg.; fig., sermonibus suis caedem, *to talk of*, Cic. **B.** *to cast out, emit, eject*; arenam, Verg.

ērŭdio -īvi and -ĭi -ītum, 4. (ex and rudis), *to instruct, teach, educate*; aliquem, Cic.; with abl., aliquem artibus, Cic.; with in and the abl., aliquem in jure civili, Cic.; filios omnibus artibus ad Graecorum disciplinam, Cic.; with two acc., aliquem damnosas artes, Ov.; with infin., Ov.

ērŭdītē, adv., only used in compar. and superl. (eruditus), *learnedly*; eruditius disputare, Cic.

ērŭdītio -ōnis, f. (erudio), 1, *teaching, instruction*, Cic.; 2, *knowledge, learning, erudition*, eruditione atque doctrinā, Cic.

ērŭdītŭlus -i, m. (dim. of eruditus), *somewhat skilled*, Cat.

ērŭdītus -a -um, p. adj. with compar. and superl. (from erudio), *learned, instructed, polished, erudite*; homo, Cic.; eruditior litteris, Cic.; eruditissimus disciplinā juris, Cic. Subst.,

ērŭdīti -ōrum, m. *men of education*, Cic.; transf., of things, tempora, saecula, oratio, Cic.

ērumpo -rūpi -ruptum, 3. *to break out, break forth.* **I.** Transit., **A.** *to cause to burst forth*; 1, lit., gen. reflex., se erumpere, or pass., erumpi, *to burst forth*; portis se erumpere foras, Cic.; 2, transf., *to vent, discharge*; stomachum in aliquem, Cic. **B.** *to break through*; nubem, Verg. **II.** Intransit., *to burst forth, break out with violence.* **A.** Lit., ignes ex Aetnae vertice erumpunt, Cic.; milit. t. t., *to rush forth*; ex castris, Caes.; impers., duabus simul portis erumpitur, Liv. **B.** Transf., **a**, erumpat cum aliquando vera et me digna vox, Cic.; erupit deinde seditio, Liv.; **b**, *to break out into*; with in or ad and the acc., ad minas, Tac.; **c**, *to break out against*; sentire potuit sermones iniquorum in suum potissimum nomen erumpere, Cic.; **d**, *to come to light*; si illustrantur, si erumpunt omnia, Cic.; **e**, *to turn out, result*; haec quo sit eruptura timeo, Cic.; ad perniciem civitatis, Cic.

ērŭo -rŭi -rŭtum, 3. *to dig out.* **I.** Gen., **A.** Lit., 1, gen., mortuum, Cic.; aurum terrā, Ov.; 2, esp., **a**, *to dig up*; humum, Ov.; missā latus hastā, *to pierce*, Ov.; **b**, *to tear out, pluck away*; eruitur oculos, *his eyes are torn out*, Ov. **B.** Transf., **a**, memoriam alicuius ex annalium vetustate, *to bring forth*, Cic.; **b**, *to bring to the light of day, to search out, rummage out*; si quid indagaris, inveneris, ex tenebris erueris, Cic.; with rel. sent., mihi, sicunde potes, erues qui decem legati Mummio fuerint, Cic. **II.** *to destroy utterly, raze*; urbem, Verg.

ēruptio -ōnis, f. (erumpo), *a bursting or breaking forth.* **A.** Gen., eruptio Aetnaeorum ignium, Cic. **B.** Milit. t. t., *sally, attack*; eruptio ex oppido simul duabus portis, Liv.; eruptionem facere, Caes.

Ĕrȳcīna -ae, f. v. Eryx.

Ĕrȳmanthŏs -i, m. (Ἐρύμανθος). **I.** *a mountain in Arcadia, where Hercules slew the Erymanthian boar.* Hence, 1, **Ĕrȳmanthis** -ĭdis, f. (Ἐρυμανθίς), *Erymanthian*; custos ursae Erymanthidos (Callisto), i.e., *Bootes*, Ov.; 2, **Ĕrȳmanthĭus** -a -um (Ἐρυμάνθιος), *Erymanthian.* **II.** *a river on the borders of Elis, falling into the Alpheus.*

Ĕrȳsichthōn -thŏnis, m. (Ἐρυσίχθων), *the son of the Thessalian king Triopas, who was cursed by Ceres with a raging hunger for having cut down one of her groves, and who finally devoured his own flesh.*

Ĕrȳthēa (-īa) -ae, f. *a small island near Gades, where Hercules stole the oxen of Geryon.* Hence, **Ĕrȳthēis** -thēĭdis, f. *Erythean*; praeda, *the oxen of Geryon*, Ov.

ĕrȳthīnus -a -um (ἐρυθῖνος), *a kind of red barbel or mullet*, Ov.

Ĕrȳthrae -ārum, f. (Ἐρυθραί), 1, *a town in Boeotia*; 2, Erythrae Aetolorum, *a town in Aetolia*; 3, *one of the twelve Ionian towns in Asia Minor.* Hence adj., **Ĕrȳthraeus** -a -um, *Erythrean*; Erythraea terra, or simply **Ĕrȳthraea** -ae, f. *the district of Erythrae.*

ĕrȳthraeus -a -um (ἐρυθραῖος), *reddish*; mare Erythraeum, *the Indian Ocean*, Plin.

Ĕryx -rȳcis, m. (Ἔρυξ), *a mountain (also called Erycus mons), with a city of the same name on the north-west coast of Sicily, with a famous temple of Venus.* Adj., **Ĕrȳcīnus** -a -um, *of or belonging to Eryx*, Venus Erycina, Cic.; Erycina alone, *Venus*, Hor.

esca -ae, f. (1. edo), 1, *food, victuals, both of*

men and animals, Cic, **2**, *bait*, Ov., transf., voluptas esca malorum, Cic

escārĭus, -a -um, (esca), *relating or belonging to food*. Subst., **escārĭa** -ōrum, n. *eating utensils*, Juv.

escendo -scendi -scensum, 3 (ex and scando). **I.** Intransit., *to climb up, ascend*, **1**, in rotam, Cic., in rogum ardentem, Cic., in tribunal, Liv., in currum, Cic., **2**, *to go up from the sea-coast inland*, Ilium a mari, Liv. **II.** Transit., *to ascend*, Oetam, Liv., rostra, Tac.

escensĭo -ōnis, f. (escendo), *landing, disembarkation*, escensionem facere ab navibus in terram, Liv.

escensus, abl. -ū, m. (escendo), *climbing*, capta escensu munimenta, Tac.

escit, escunt = erit, erunt, v. sum

escul . . . v. aescul

escŭlentus -a -um (esca), *relating to eating, edible, esculent*, frusta, Cic.; subst., **escŭlenta** -orum, n. *eatables*, Cic.

Esquĭlĭae -ārum, f. (ex and colere, lit., *the outer town, the suburb*), *the most considerable of the hills on which Rome was built*, now *the height of S. Maria Maggiore*, hence, **1**, adj., **Esquĭlĭus** -a -um, **2**, **Esquĭlīnus** -a -um, *Esquiline*, subst., **Esquĭlīna** -ae, f. *the Esquiline gate*, Cic., **3**, **Esquĭlĭārĭus** -a -um, *Esquiline*

essĕda -ae, f. = essedum (q. v.)

essĕdārĭus -ii, m. (esseda), *a fighter in a British or Gallic war chariot*, Caes.

essĕdum -i, n. (a Celtic word), *a war chariot used among the Gauls and Britons, and afterwards adopted by the Romans in their public games*, Caes., *a travelling chariot*, Cic.

ēsŭrĭo, 4 (desider. of 1. edo). **A.** *to be hungry, desire food*, Cic. **B.** Transf., *to desire eagerly, long for*, nil ibi, quod nobis esuriatur, erit, Ov.

ēsŭrītĭo -ōnis, f. (esurio), *hunger*, Cat.

ēsus -a -um, partic. of 1. edo

ĕt, conj. (cf. Gr. ἔτι). **I.** *and* (joining single words and sentences), **1**, et . . . et, *both . . . and*, et in patre et in filios, Cic., so et . . . que, Cic., or que . . . et, Liv., **2**, nec (neque) . . . et, *not only not . . . but*, nec miror et gaudeo, Cic., et . . . nec (neque), *not only . . . but also not*, Cic., **3**, et quidem, *and indeed*, duo milia jugerum, et quidem immania, Cic., so et alone, *and indeed*, magna vis est conscientiae, et magna in utramque partem, Cic., **4**, et etiam, *and also*, auctoritate et consilio et etiam gratia, Cic., **5**, et vero, *and truly*, Cic., **6**, et non, *and not, and not rather*, dicam eos miseros, qui nati sunt, et non eos, qui mortui sunt, Cic., **7**, et deinde, *and then*, Liv. **II** *also*, addam et illud etiam, Cic. **III.** *but*, nullane habes vitia? imo alia, et fortasse minora, Hor.

ĕtĕnim, conj., **1** (explanatory), *namely*, Cic., **2** (strengthening a previous assertion), *truly and indeed*, Cic.

Ĕtĕŏclēs -is and -ĕos, m. (Ἐτεοκλῆς), myth., *son of Oedipus, brother of Polynices, killed in the siege of Thebes*

ĕtēsĭae -ārum, f. (ἐτησίαι, sc. ἄνεμοι), *winds which blow for forty days every year about the dog days, Etesian winds*, Cic.

ĕtēsĭus -a -um, *Etesian*, Lucr.

ēthŏlŏgus -i, m. (ἠθολόγος), *one who mimics in sport the peculiarities of others*, mimi ethologi, Cic.

ĕtĭam, conj. (= et jam), lit. *and already*. **I.** (to express duration of time), *as yet, still*, nondum etiam, vixdum etiam, *not yet, scarcely yet*, Cic., quum iste etiam cubaret, *when he was still*, &c., Cic. **II. 1**, in answer, *certainly, yes, indeed*, aut etiam aut non respondere, *to answer yes or no*, Cic., **2**, *certainly, by all means*, etiam inquit, beatam, sed non beatissimam, Cic., **3**, to express a climax, *even, nay even*, voce, motu, forma etiam magnifica, Cic., non solum . . . sed (or verum) etiam, *not only . . . but also*, Cic., tum (or quum) . . . tum etiam, *as well . . . as*, Cic., **4**, *even now*, tabulas nihil profuturas, etiam plus suspicionis futurum, Cic. **III.** *again*, dic etiam clarius, Cic., etiam atque etiam, *again and again*, rogare, considerare, Cic.

ĕtĭam-num and **ĕtĭam-nunc**, adv., *yet, still, till now*, de materia loqui orationis etiamnunc, non ipso de genere dicendi, Cic., nihil etiam nunc, *nothing further*, Cic.

ĕtĭam-si, conj., *even if, although*, Cic.

ĕtĭam-tum and **ĕtĭam tunc**, adv., *even then, till that time, till then*, Cic.

Etrūrĭa -ae, f. *a country in Central Italy, now Tuscany*. Adj., **Etruscus** -a -um, *Etruscan*

et-si, conj., **1**, *although, yet*, foll. by tamen, at, certe, etc., etsi non sapientissimi, at amicissimi hominis auctoritate, Cic., **2**, *and yet, notwithstanding*, do poenas temeritatis meae, etsi quae fuit ista temeritas, Cic.

ĕtymŏlŏgĭa -ae, f. (ἐτυμολογία), *etymology*, Cic.

eu (εὖ), interj., *good! well done!* an exclamation of joy and approval (sometimes ironical), Hor.

Euadnē -ēs, f. (Εὐάδνη), myth., *wife of Capaneus, one of the seven who fought against Thebes*

Euandĕr -dri, and **Euandrus** -i, m. (Εὔανδρος), myth., *son of Hermes and Carmentis, who led a colony from Pallantium in Arcadia, and built a town on the Palatine hill*. Adj., **Euandrĭus** -a -um, *Evandrian*, ensis, *of Pallas, son of Evander*

Euboea -ae, f. (Εὔβοια), *an island in the Aegean Sea*, hence adj., **Euboĭcus** -a -um, a, *Euboean*, cultor aquarum, *the sea-god Glaucus*, Verg., b, poet., *belonging to Cumae, a colony from Euboea*, urbs, *Cumae*, Ov.

Euclīdēs -is, m. (Εὐκλείδης), **1**, *a philosopher of Megara, founder of the Megarian school of philosophy*, **2**, *a mathematician of Alexandria*

Euēnus -i, m. (Εὔηνος), myth., *king of Aetolia, father of Marpessa, drowned in the river Lycormas, which received the name of Euenus*. Adj., **Euēnīnus** -a -um, *of or belonging to the (river) Euenus*

Eugănĕi -ōrum, m. *a people in Upper Italy, living near Patavium and Verona*. Adj., **Eugănĕus** -a -um, *Euganean*

ēugĕ, interj. (εὖγε), *well done!* (sometimes ironical), Pers.

euhan (euan), interj. (εὐὰν or εὐ ἄν), *shout of the Bacchanals*, euhan euhoe euhium, Enn.; personif., Iacchus et Euhan, Ov.

euhans (euans) -antis = εὐάζων, *shouting euhan*, of the Bacchanals, with acc., euhantes orgia, *celebrating the orgies of Bacchus*, Verg.

Euhēmĕrus -i, m. (Εὐήμερος), *Greek philosopher and historian of Agrigentum, flourishing about 315* B.C.

Euhĭas (Euĭas) -ădis, f. (εὔιος), *a Bacchante*.

Euhĭus (Euĭus) -ii, m. (Εὔιος), *surname of Bacchus*

euhoe, interj. (εὐοῖ), *shout of the Bacchantes*, euhoe Bacche, Verg.

Eumĕnēs -is, m. (Εὐμένης), *general of Alexander the Great, after his death governor of Cappadocia*

Euměnĭdes -um. f. (Εὐμενίδες), *Eumenides, the gracious ones,* euphem. name for the Furies.

Eumolpus -i, m. (Εὔμολπος), myth., *son of Poseidon and Chione, a Thracian priest of Demeter, founder of the Eleusinian mysteries.* Hence, **Eumolpĭdae** -ārum, m. (Εὐμολπίδαι), *a family in Athens from which the priests of Demeter were chosen.*

eunūchus -i, m. (εὐνοῦχος), *a eunuch,* Cic.

Euphorbus -i, m. (Εὔφορβος), *a Trojan, whose soul Pythagoras believed to have descended to himself.*

Euphŏrĭōn -ōnis, m. (Εὐφορίων), *a Greek poet of Chalcis in Euboea, flourishing about* 220 B.C.

Euphrātes -is (also -i and -ae), m. (Εὐφράτης), *the Euphrates, a river in Western Asia, rising in Armenia, joining the Tigris, and flowing into the Persian Gulf;* meton. *the dwellers on the Euphrates,* Verg.

Eupŏlis -pŏlĭdis, m. (Εὔπολις), *an Athenian comic poet, contemporary with Aristophanes.*

Eurīpĭdes -is and -i, m. (Εὐριπίδης), *the celebrated Athenian tragic poet.* Adj., **Eurīpĭdēus** -a -um, *of Euripides.*

Eurīpus -i, m. (Εὔριπος), **1,** *a channel, strait,* esp. *the strait between Euboea and the main land,* Cic.; **2,** *an artificial canal or water-course,* Cic.; *the ditch or moat constructed round the Circus Maximus,* Suet.

Eurōpa -ae, f., and **Eurōpē** -ēs, f. (Εὐρώπη). **I.** Myth., *daughter of Agenor, king of Phoenicia, mother of Sarpedon and Minos by Jupiter, who in the form of a bull carried her off to Crete.* **II.** Geogr., *the continent of Europe, said to have been named after Europa.* Adj., **Eurōpaeus** -a -um, *belonging to Europa;* dux, *Minos,* Ov.

Eurōtas -ae, m. (Εὐρώτας), *the chief river of Lacedaemonia,* now *Basilipotamo.*

eurōus -a -um (eurus), *eastern,* Verg.

eurus -i, m. (εὖρος), *a south-east wind,* Verg.; *an east wind.* Ov.; poet., *wind in general,* Verg.

Eurȳdĭcē -ēs, f. (Εὐρυδίκη), *wife of Orpheus, killed by a serpent's bite, recovered from Hades by Orpheus, but lost again by his looking back at her against his agreement with Pluto.*

Eurȳmĕdōn -ontis, m. (Εὐρυμέδων), *river in Pamphylia,* now *Kapri-Su.*

Eurȳmĭdes -ae, m. (Εὐρυμίδης), *son of Eurymus,* i.e., *Telephus.*

Eurȳnŏmē -ēs, f. (Εὐρυνόμη), *daughter of Oceanus and Tethys, mother of Leucothoë.*

Eurȳpȳlus -i, m. (Εὐρύπυλος), **1,** *a son of Hercules, and king of Cos;* **2,** *son of Euaemon, one of the Greek commanders before Troy.*

Eurystheus -ĕi, m. (Εὐρυσθεύς), myth., *son of Sthenelus, king in Mycenae, who imposed on Hercules his twelve labours.*

Eurȳtus -i, m. (Εὔρυτος), myth., *king in Oechalia, father of Iole and Dryope.* Hence, **Eurȳtis** -ĭdis, f. *daughter of Eurytus,* i.e., *Iole.*

Euterpē -ēs, f. (Εὐτέρπη), *the muse of harmony,* Hor.

Eutrŏpĭus -ĭi, m. *Flavius, a Roman historian of the fourth century* A.D.

Euxīnus -a -um (Εὔξεινος = *hospitable*), *an epithet of the Black Sea;* esp. in the phrase Pontus Euxinus; mare, aquae, Ov.

ēvādo -vāsi -vāsum, 3. *to go out, go forth.* **I.** Intransit., **A.** Lit., **1,** gen., ex balneis, Cic.; oppido, Sall.; per praeruptum saxum in Capitolium, Liv.; **2,** esp., *to escape, get off;* e manibus hostium, Liv.; e periculo, Cic. **B.** Transf., **a,** *to turn out, issue, become;* quos judicabat non posse oratores, evadere, Cic.; **b,** *to result, turn out;* quo evasura sint, Cic. **II.** Transit., **1,** *to climb, ascend;* gradus altos, Verg.; **2,** *to pass, travel over;* ripam, Verg.; evaserant media castra, Liv.; **3,** *to escape;* flammam, Verg. (syncop. perf., evasti, Hor.).

ēvăgor, 1. dep. **I.** Intransit., *to wander, stray away.* **A.** Lit., **a,** of plunderers, effuse, Liv.; **b,** milit. t. t., *to wheel to the right and left, manœuvre;* nullo ad evagandum relicto spatio, Liv. **B.** Transf., appetitus longius evagantur, Cic. **II.** Transit., *to overstep;* ordinem rectum, Hor.

ēvălesco -vălŭi, 3. *to grow strong;* **1,** in tumultum, *to grow into a tumult,* Tac.; **2,** *to prevail, come into vogue;* nationis nomen evaluisse paullatim, Tac.; **3,** *to have power, to be able;* with infin., sed non Dardanidae medicari cuspidis ictum evaluit, Verg.

ēvan, v. euhan.

Ēvander, v. Euander.

ēvānesco -vānŭi, 3. **A.** *to vanish, disappear, pass away;* evanescunt vinum et salsamentum vetustate, Cic. **B.** Transf., evanescit memoria alicuius, Cic.; spes, Cic.; rumor, Liv.

ēvānĭdus -a -um (evanesco), *vanishing, passing away;* pectora in tenues abeunt evanida rivos, Ov.

ēvans, v. euhans.

ēvasto, 1. *to devastate, lay waste utterly;* agrum, vallem, Liv.

ēvectus -a -um, partic. of eveho.

ēvĕho -vexi -vectum, 3. **I.** *to carry out, bear out.* **A.** Lit., aliquid plaustris ex fanis, Cic.; aquas ex planis locis, Liv.; pass., evehi (used as a middle); **1,** of ships, *to sail away;* in altum, Liv.; **2,** se evehere and evehi, *to ride away;* se incaute, Liv. **B.** Transf., middle evehi; **a,** e Piraeo eloquentia evecta est, Cic.; **b,** *to be carried away;* spe vanā, Liv.; **c,** fama eius evecta insulas, *spread abroad,* Tac. **II.** *to raise, lift up;* aliquem ad deos, *raises to the heaven,* Hor.; evehere aliquem ad consulatum, Tac.

ēvello -velli -vulsum, 3. **I.** *to tear out, pluck out.* **A.** Lit., alicui linguam, Cic.; arborem, Cic. **B.** Transf., *to tear out, erase, remove;* consules non modo e memoria sed etiam ex fastis evellendi, Cic.; alicui ex animo scrupulum, Cic. **II.** *to tear away;* emblema, Cic.

ēvĕnĭo -vēni -ventum, 4. *to come out, come forth.* **I.** Lit., merses profundo, pulchrior evenit, Hor. **II.** Transf., **1, a,** *to turn out, result;* bene, Cic.; alicui feliciter, Caes.; vides omnia fere contra ac dicta sint evenisse, Cic.; **b,** *to fall to the lot of;* provincia (sorte) evenit alicui, Liv.; **2,** *to happen, befall, occur;* pax evenit, Sall.; ut plerumque evenit, Cic.; forte evenit ut, etc., Cic.

ēventum -i, n. (evenio), **1,** *the issue, consequence of an action;* causarum cognitio cognitionem eventi facit, Cic.; **2,** *an event, occurrence;* causae eventorum magis me movent quam ipsa eventa, Cic.

ēventus -ūs, m. (evenio). **I.** *consequence, issue, result;* **1,** gen., eventus rei, Caes.; eventus rerum qui acciderunt, Cic.; eius diei, Caes.; belli eventus prosper, Liv.; **2,** esp., **a,** *issue, end, catastrophe;* (α) of a drama, semper ad eventum festinat, Hor.; (β) of persons, impiorum fratrum, Liv.; **b,** *favourable issue, success;* casus eventusque rerum, Tac.; nec eventus defuit, Tac. **II.** *an occurrence, event,* Cic.; *fate;* auditur Decii eventus, Liv.

ēverbĕro, 1. *to strike violently, flap;* clypeum alis, Verg.; cauda pendentem escam, Ov.

ēvergo, 3 *to send out, send forth*, nullos apertos rivos, Liv

ēverrĭcŭlum -i, n (everro), *a fishing-net, drag-net*, fig, quod umquam huiuscemodi everriculum ulla in provincia fuit (with a pun on the name of Verres), Cic, everriculum malitiarum omnium, judicium de dolo malo, Cic

ēverro -verri -versum, 3 (*to sweep out*), transf, *to plunder*, quod fanum non eversum atque extersum reliqueris (with a pun on the name of Verres), Cic.

ēversĭo -ōnis, f (everto), **1,** *an overturning*, columnae, Cic, **2,** transf, *a destruction, ruin*, vitae, Cic, patriae, rerum publicarum eversiones, Cic

ēversor -ōris, m (everto), *an overturner, destroyer*, civitatis, Cic

ēverto -verti -versum, 3 **I. A.** *to overturn, throw down*, **1,** lit, navem, Cic, arborem, Verg, hence, of a city, *to demolish, raze to the ground*, Carthaginem, Cic, **2,** transf, *to overthrow, destroy*, funditus civitates, Cic, constitutam philosophiam, Cic, aliquem, *to ruin politically*, Cic **B.** *to expel* or *eject from one's property*, aliquem bonis, Cic, perfidum fortunis patriis, Cic **II.** *to raise up*, aequora ventis, Verg

ēvestīgātus -a -um, *tracked out, discovered*, ingenuis evestigata priorum, Ov

Ēvĭas, v Euhias

ēvĭdens -entis, adj (ex and video), **1,** *visible*, mensura quaedam, Cic, **2,** transf, *clear, plain, evident*, res, Cic, evidentior causa victoriae, Liv, quid est evidentius? Cic

ēvĭdentĕr, adv (evidens), *visibly, manifestly*, evidenter praeniteré, Liv

ēvĭdentĭa -ae, f (evidens), *distinctness of language*, Cic

ēvĭgĭlo, 1 **I.** Intransit, *to watch, be vigilant*, in quo evigilaverunt curae et cogitationes meae? Cic **II.** Transit, **a,** *to watch through, pass in watching*, nox evigilanda, Tib, **b,** *to elaborate carefully*, libros, Ov, consilia evigilata cogitationibus, Cic

ēvīlesco -vilŭi, 3 *to become vile, worthless, contemptible*, Tac

ēvincĭo -vinxi -vinctum, 4 *to bind, bind round*, diademate caput Tiridatis evinxit, Tac; viridi evinctus oliva, Verg

ēvinco -vīci -victum, 3 *to conquer entirely, utterly subdue* **I.** Lit, imbelles Aeduos, Tac, evicit omnia assuetus praedae miles, Liv, platanus caelebs evincet ulmos, *will get the better of, drive away*, Hor, oppositas gurgite moles, *to get past* or *through*, Verg **II.** Transf, **A.** Gen, **a,** *to prevail upon a person*, lacrimis, dolore, precibus evinci, Verg, **b,** *to conquer a passion* or *feeling*, evicit miseratio justa sociorum superbiam ingenitam, Liv **B. a,** *to bring it about that*, with ut and the subj, summa ope evicerunt, ut M Furius Camillus crearetur, Liv, **b,** *to prove irresistibly*, si puerilius his ratio esse evincet amare, Hor

ēvīro, 1 (ex and vir), *to castrate*, Cat

ēviscĕro, 1 (ex and viscus), *to take out the bowels, eviscerate, tear in pieces*, (columbam) pedibus eviscerat uncis (of the hawk), Verg, evisceratum corpus patris, Cic

ēvītābĭlis -e (evito), *that can be avoided*, telum, Ov

ēvīto, 1 *to avoid, shun*, suspicionem, Cic

Ēvĭus, v Euhius

ēvŏcātor -ōris, m (evoco), *one who calls to arms*, servorum et civium perditorum, Cic

ēvŏcātus -a -um (partic of evoco), subst *a veteran who had served his time but was liable to be called upon in an emergency*, Caes

ēvŏco, 1 *to call out* **I.** Lit, **A.** Gen, aliquem e curia, Liv; mercatores undique ad se, Caes, aliquem litteris, Cic **B.** Esp, **1,** relig t t, **a,** *to summon the spirits of the dead*, aliquem ab inferis, Cic, **b,** *to call forth a deity from a besieged and hostile city by promising a temple at Rome* evocare deos, Liv, **2,** *to summon*, **a,** of magistrates, etc, aliquem ad se, Cic, aliquem ad colloquium, Liv, **b,** *to summon for military service*, legiones ex hibernis, Caes, **c,** *to summon to a place of honour*, aliquem ad eum honorem, Caes, **3,** *in a hostile manner, to call upon the enemy to come out to fight*, magna cum contumelia verborum nostros ad pugnam, Caes **II.** Transf, **a,** aliquam familiam abjectam et obscuram tenebris in lucem, Cic, **b,** *to call forth, produce*, misericordia tua nullius oratione evocata, Cic

ēvoe, v euhoe

ēvŏlo, 1 **I.** *to fly out, fly away* **A.** Lit, ex quercu, Cic **B.** Transf, *to come forth quickly, rush forth, hasten away*, ex corporum vinculis tanquam e carcere, Cic, e senatu, Cic, e conspectu, Cic fig, ex alicuius severitate, e poena, *to escape*, Cic. **II.** *to fly up*, concussisque levis pennis sic evolat ales, Ov

ēvŏlūtĭo -ōnis, f (evolvo), *the unrolling*, and hence, *reading of a book*, poetarum, Cic

ēvolvo -volvi -vŏlūtum, 3 **I. A.** Lit, *to roll out, roll forth*, **1,** per humum evolvi, Tac, **2,** of a river, se evolvere in mare, Verg, **3,** fig, evolutus illis integumentis dissimulationis, *unmasked*, Cic **B.** Transf, **1,** *to extricate*, se ex his turbis, Tac, **2,** *to deprive* illos ex praeda clandestina, *make to disgorge*, Liv, **3,** of news, evolvi, *to spread*, ad aures quoque militum dicta ferocia evolvebantur, Liv **II.** *to roll apart, open, unwind* **A.** Lit, **1,** gen, volumen epistolarum, Cic, **2, a,** of the fates, *to spin* fusos meos, Ov, **b,** *to read, study*, librum, Cic **B.** Transf, **1,** *to make clear, narrate*, aliquid accuratius in litteris, Cic, **2,** *to find out*, exitum criminis, Cic, **3,** *to think over, reflect upon*, haec sub antris, Verg

ēvŏmo -ŭi -itum, 3 *to vomit forth* **A.** Lit, conchas, Cic **B.** Transf, **a,** *to vomit forth, cast out*, quae (urbs) tantam pestem evomuit forasque projecit, Cic, in quo tu, acceptā et devoratā pecuniā, evomere non poteras, *disgorge*, Cic, **b,** of speech, in aliquem absentem orationem ex ore impurissimo, Cic

ēvulgo, 1 *to publish, make known*, jus civile, Liv, Octaviae injurias, Tac

ēvulsĭo -ōnis, f (evello), *a pulling out, plucking out*, dentis, Cic

ex, prep with abl (ἐξ, ἐκ), **e** before b, d, g, j, l, m, n, r, v, *from* or *out of* **I. 1,** In space, *out of, from*, exire ex urbe, e vita, Cic, milites ex eo loco deducere, Cic, delabi ex equo, Liv thus **a,** it follows verbs of taking, perceiving, questioning, and the like—e g, sumere, percipere, accipere, auferre, colligere, quaerere, percunctari, discere, intelligere, etc, **b,** so the phrase, ex persona alicuius, *under the mask*—i e, *in the character of any one*, ex sua persona, *in one's own name, for oneself*, Cic, **2,** to denote position, **a,** ex equo colloqui, Caes, qui nihil ex occulto agendum putant, Cic, **b,** laborare ex pedibus, *to suffer in the feet*, Cic **II.** Of time, **1,** *since*, ex eo tempore, Cic, esp, ex quo, *from which time, since* Liv, **2,** *on, at*, hunc judicem ex Kal Jan non habebimus, Cic, **3,** *after, immediately upon*, Cotta ex consulatu est profectus in Galliam, Cic, aliud ex alio, *one* *after another*, Cic.; diem ex die, *day after day*, Cic. **III.** To denote origin, *from, out of, of*; **1, a,** quidam ex Arcadia hospes, Nep.; virgines ex sacerdotio Vestae, *of the priesthood of Vesta*, Ter.; **b,** of etymological derivation, urbem quam e suo nomine Romam jussit nominari, Cic.; **2,** to denote the whole out of which any part is taken, unus ex meis intimis, Cic.; e numero, *of the number*, Cic.; hence, **a,** Q. Vettius Vettianus e Marsis, *a Marsian*, Cic.; **b,** in place of the genit., to denote that to which anything belongs, puppes e barbaris navibus, Caes.; **3,** to denote the material of which anything is made or compounded, pocula ex auro, Cic.; so of the source from which anything is paid or gained; largiri ex alieno, Liv.; vivere e rapto, Ov.; **4,** to denote the cause or occasion of anything, *from, on account of, by reason of*; ex eadem causa, Cic.; Demetrius e doctrina clarus, Cic.; esp. with conj. in the phrase, ex eo quod, ex eo quia, *on that account, because*, Cic.; ex eo factum est quod, *hence it came about that*, Cic.; ex quo, e quibus, *on account of which*, Cic.; e vulnere mori, Liv.; **5,** to denote a change from one condition or occupation to another, ex oratore arator factus, Cic.; **6,** *according to, in accordance with*; ex edicto, Cic.; ex decreto, Cic.; ex foedere, Liv.; ex re et ex tempore, *according to time and circumstance*, Cic.; esp. **a,** ex mea, tua re, *for my, thy advantage*, Cic.; e republica, *for the benefit of the republic*, Cic.; ex usu esse, *to be useful*, Cic.; **b,** ex animo, *heartily, earnestly*, Cic.; ex sententia, *satisfactorily*, Cic.; **7,** *in regard to, with respect to*; e ratione libertatis; e nostra dignitate, Cic. **IV.** Adv. phrases, ex industria, *designedly*, Cic.; e memoria, *from memory*, Cic.; ex parte, *in part*, Cic.; e vestigio, *forthwith*, Caes.; e regione, *opposite to*, Cic.; ex inopinato, *unexpectedly*, Cic.

exăcerbo, 1. *to irritate, provoke, exasperate, embitter*; contumeliis hostes, Liv.

exactio -ōnis, f. (exigo), **I.** *a driving out, expulsion*; regum, Cic. **II. 1,** *a demanding, exacting, collecting of debts, tribute*, etc.; **a,** act., nominum, Cic.; capitum, *poll-tax*, Cic.; **b,** pass., *that which is collected, income*; exactio prior, Cic.; **2,** *management, direction*; operum publicorum, Cic.

exactor -ōris, m. (exigo), **I.** *one who drives out, expels*; regum, Liv. **II. 1,** *one who demands or exacts, a collector of taxes*, Caes.; **2,** *an inspector, superintendent, overseer*; quum ipse imperator et exactor; circumiret, Liv.

exactus -a -um, p. adj. with compar. and superl. (from exigo), *accurate, precise, exact*; numerus, Liv.

exăcŭo -ŭi -ūtum, 3. *to sharpen to a point, make sharp*. **A.** Lit., furcas, Verg.; fig., mucronem aliquem tribunicium in nos, Cic. **B.** Transf., **a,** quum animus exacuerit illam, ut oculorum, sic ingenii aciem, Cic.; **b,** *to excite, stir up, inflame*; aliquem, Cic.; animos in bella, Hor.; irā exacui, Nep.

exadversum or **exadversŭs,** prep. with acc., *opposite*; exadversus eum locum, Cic.

exaedĭfĭcātio -ōnis, f. (exaedifico), *a building up*; fig., of an oration, ipsa autem exaedificatio posita est in rebus et verbis, Cic.

exaedĭfĭco, 1. *to build, build up, erect, finish building*; Capitolium, Cic.; domos et villas, Sall.; fig., *to finish*; exaedificare id opus quod instituisti, Cic.

exaequātio -ōnis, f. (exaequo), *a making equal, equality*, Liv.

exaequo, 1. **a,** *to place on a level, make equal*; jura, Cic.; facta dictis sunt exaequanda, *must be related in an adequate manner*, Sall.; **b,** *to compare*; se cum aliquo, Cic.; exaequari alicui, Cic.; **c,** *to equal*; aliquem, Ov.

exaestŭo, 1. **I.** Intransit., *to boil up, foam up*; mare, Liv.; unda ima verticibus, Verg.; transf., mens exaestuat irā, Verg. **II.** Transit., *to give forth*; hos igitur tellus omnes exaestuat aestus, Lucr.

exaggĕrātio -ōnis, f. (exaggero), *elevation, exaltation*; amplitudo et quasi quaedam exaggeratio quam altissima animi, Cic.

exaggĕro, 1. *to heap up*. **I.** Gen., **A.** Lit., Plin. **B.** Transf., *to raise, elevate*; animus virtutibus exaggeratus, Cic. **II.** *to heap up, increase*; **1,** gen., rem familiarem, Cic.; **2,** esp., by words, *to heighten, exalt, magnify*; beneficium verbis, Cic.; virtutem, Cic.

exăgitātor -ōris, m. (exagito), *one who blames, a censurer*; omnium rhetorum, Cic.

exăgĭto, 1. **I.** Lit., *to drive anything from its position*; **a,** of animals, *to hunt, chase*; et lepus hic aliis exagitatus erit, Ov.; **b,** of winds, *to raise*; quum vis (venti) exagitata foras erumpitur, Lucr. **II.** Transf., **1,** *to harass, disquiet, disturb, persecute*; exagitati istius injuriis, Cic.; ab Suebis complures annos exagitati bello premebantur, Caes.; quos illa quaestio exagitabat, Sall.; **2,** *to scold, blame, reproach, censure, criticise*; aliquem, Cic.; omnes eius fraudes, Cic.; *to disapprove of*; qui hanc dicendi exercitationem exagitarent atque contemnerent, Cic.; **3,** *to excite, irritate*; plebem, Sall.; maerorem, Cic.

exalbesco -bŭi, 3. *to grow white, turn pale with fright*, Cic.

exāmen -inis, n. (for exagimen, from ex and ago). **I.** *a swarm*. **A.** Lit., of bees, Cic.; of wasps, Liv. **B.** Transf., *a throng, crowd, shoal*; servorum, Cic. **II. A.** *the tongue of a balance*, Verg. **B.** Transf., *testing, consideration, investigation*; examina legum servare, *to apply*, Ov.

exāmino, 1. (examen), *to weigh*. **A.** Lit., ad certum pondus, Caes.; non aurificis staterā, sed quādam populari trutinā examinari, Cic. **B.** Transf., *to weigh, consider*; **a,** diligenter verborum omnium pondera, Cic.; with abl., haec meis ponderibus, Cic.; **b,** of judges, male verum examinat omnis corruptus judex, Hor.

ex-āmussim, *according to the square or rule, exactly, accurately*, Plaut.

exanclo, 1. *to exhaust, empty*. **A.** Lit., vinum poculo, Plaut. **B.** Transf., *to bear to the end, suffer, endure*; labores, Cic.

exănĭmātio -ōnis, f. (exanimo), *fright, terror*, Cic.

exănĭmis -e and gen. **exănĭmus** -a -um (ex and anima), **1,** *lifeless, dead*, Verg., Liv.; **2,** *lifeless, senseless with terror*, Verg.

exănĭmo, 1. (ex and anima or animus). **I.** *to deprive of breath*. **A. 1,** lit., duplici cursu exanimari, Caes.; milites cursu exanimati, *breathless*, Caes.; **2,** transf., *to make breathless with fear, to stun*; te metus exanimat, Cic. **B.** *to deprive of life, kill*; **1,** lit., aliquem, Cic.; **2,** transf., *to exhaust, weaken*; aliquem querelis, Hor. **II.** *to breathe out*; nolo verba exiliter exanimata exire, Cic.

exantlo = exanclo (q.v.).

exaptus -a -um, *fastened, attached*, Lucr.

exardesco -arsi -arsum, 3. **I.** Lit., **1,** *to take fire, kindle, burn up*; nulla materia tam facilis ad exardescendum est quae etc., Cic.; **2,** *to become hot, to glow*; aetherioque recens exarsit sidere limus, Ov. **II.** Transf., **1,** of persons, *to be violently excited, be inflamed*; iracundiā ac stomacho, Cic.; ad spem libertatis, Cic.; of love, *to burn*; imis tota exarsit medullis,

Cat., 2, of things, *to break out*, exarsit bellum, Cic

exāresco ārŭi, 3 *to dry, become quite dry.* **A.** Lit, exarescunt amnes, Cic, fontes, Caes, lacrimae, Cic **B.** Fig, *to dry up, become exhausted*, exaruit facultas orationis, Cic, vides enim exaruisse jam veterem urbanitatem, Cic

exarmo, 1. *to disarm, deprive of arms*, cohortes, Tac.

exăro, 1 **I.** *to plough up, dig up*, puerum, Cic **II.** *to gain by ploughing*, plus quam decem medimna ex agro, Cic **III.** *to plough*, **a,** lit, Varr; **b,** transf, frontem rugis, Hor; **c,** meton, *to write or note on waxen tablets*, exaravi ad te harum exemplum in codicillis, Cic

exaspĕro, 1 *to make rough* **A.** Lit, **a,** Plin; **b,** of the sea, *to make stormy;* exasperato fluctibus mari, Liv. **B.** Transf., **a,** *to make savage;* durati tot malis exasperatique, Liv, **b,** *to irritate, excite;* animos, Liv

exauctōro, 1 *to dismiss from military service, discharge*, aliquem, Liv, se exauctorare, *to leave the service*, Liv.

exaudĭo, 4 **I.** *to hear plainly*, maximā voce, ut omnes exaudire possint, dico, Cic, non exaudito tubae sono, Caes **II.** *to hear favourably, listen to*, **a,** aliquid, *to listen to prayers*, vota precesque, Verg, **b,** aliquem, *to obey*, monitor non exauditus, Hor

exaugĕo, 2 *to increase exceedingly*, radiorum ictum, Lucr

exaugŭrātĭo -ōnis, f (exauguro), *a profaning, desecrating*, sacellorum exaugurationes, Liv.

exaugŭro, 1 *to desecrate, profane*, fana, Liv

excaeco, 1 *to make blind.* **A.** Lit., aliquem, Cic **B.** Transf, *to stop a river or channel*, flumina, Ov.

excandescentĭa -ae, f (excandesco), *heat, irascibility*, Cic

excandesco -dŭi, 3 *to become hot with passion, to glow, burn*, absol, id postquam nescit, excanduit, ap. Cic, with abstractions, risi irā excanduerit fortitudo, Cic

excanto, 1 *to charm out, bring forth by incantations*, sidera excantata voce Thessalā, Hor

excarnĭfĭco, 1 *to tear to pieces*, aliquem, Cic

excăvo, 1 *to hollow out, excavate*, ex una gemma praegrandi trullā excavatā, Cic

excēdo -cessi -cessum, 3. **I.** Intransit, **A.** *to go out, go away, go from*, **1,** lit, viā, Liv, oppido, Caes, urbe, Cic; ex proelio, proelio, Caes; **2,** transf, **a,** ex ephebis, e pueris, *to pass out of the age of boyhood*, Cic, e memoria, *to pass out of memory*, Liv; e vita or simply vitā, *to die*, Cic, excedere palmā, *to resign the prize*, Verg, **b,** *to digress*, paullum ad enarrandum quam etc, Liv **B.** *to go beyond, exceed*, **1,** lit, ut nulla (pars) excederet ultra, Cic, **2,** transf, **a,** *to attain to*, eo laudis excedere quo, etc, Tac, **b,** *to result in, turn to;* ne in altercationem excederet res, Liv; **c,** *to pass beyond* quum libertas non ultra vocem excessisset, Liv, **d,** of events, *to happen*, insequentia excedunt in eum annum, etc, Liv **II.** Transit, **A.** Gen, *to leave*, curiam, urbem, Liv **B.** *to pass beyond*, modum, Liv, tempus finitum, Liv

excellens -entis, p adj with compar and superl (excello), *high, lofty, excellent, distinguished, remarkable*, Brutus excellens omni genere laudis, Cic., excellens pulchritudo muliebris formae, Cic.; una excellentissima virtus, justitia, Cic.

excellentĕr, adv (excellens), *excellently;* quae magno animo fortiter excellenterque gesta sunt, Cic

excellentĭa -ae, f (excellens), *excellence, distinguished merit;* animi excellentia magnitudoque, Cic; absol, propter excellentiam, *pre-eminently*, Cic.

excello (excellĕo), 3 *to excel, be distinguished, be eminent*, illud excellit regium nomen, Cic, with abl, animi magnitudine, Cic, with in and the abl, in qua parte excello ipse, Cic, with inter, inter quos posset excellere, Cic, with praeter, in eo genere praeter ceteros, Cic, with super, quia super ceteros excellat, Liv, with dat (of person excelled), ita figuratum esse corpus ut excellat ceteris, Cic, in quibus tu longe aliis excellis, Cic

excelsē, adv with compar and superl, (excelsus), *loftily*, dicere, *in a lofty style*, Cic

excelsĭtas -ātis, f (excelsus), *height*, transf, animi, *elevation*, Cic

excelsus -a -um, p adj with compar and superl (excello), *lofty, high, elevated* **A.** Lit, mons, Caes, locus, Cic Subst, **excelsum** -i, n *a lofty place* or *situation*, Cic **B.** Transf, *elevated above the common*, **1,** of position, *distinguished, eminent, illustrious*, in excelso et illustri loco sita laus tua, Cic, subst, **excelsum** -i, n *high dignity, lofty position*, **a,** sing, in excelso vitam agere, Sall, **b,** plur, excelsa et alta sperare, *high honours*, Liv., **2,** of the mind, *dignified, elevated*, magnus homo et excelsus, Cic, animus excelsus, Cic, **3,** of the style of a writer or speaker, *lofty, elevated*, orator grandior et quodammodo excelsior, Cic

exceptĭo -ōnis, f (excipio), **1,** *an exception, restriction, limitation*, cum exceptione, Cic, sine exceptione, Cic, quodsi exceptionem facit ne, etc, Cic, **2,** *an exception to the plaintiff's statement of a case tendered by the defendant* exceptionem alicui dare, Cic., exceptione excludi, Cic

excepto, 1 (intens of excipio), *to take out, catch up*, **1,** barbatulos mullos de piscina, Cic, singulos, Caes, **2,** auras, *to snuff up*, Verg

excerno -crēvi -crētum, 3 *to separate, sift, sort*, Saguntinos ex captorum numero, Liv, haedi excreti, *separated from their mothers*, Verg

excerpo -cerpsi -cerptum, 3 (ex and carpo), *to pick out* **I.** Lit, semina pomis, Hor, **II.** Transf, **A.** *to gather out, choose*, excerpere ex malis si quid inesset boni, Cic, excerpere nomina omnium ex juniorum tabulis, Liv **B.** *to put on one side, separate*, de numero, Cic, se numero illorum, Hor

excessus -ūs, m (excedo), *departure from life, death*, vitae, Cic, e vita, Cic, absol laeti excessu principes, Tac

excĕtra -ae, f *a snake*, Cic poet; transf, *a spiteful woman*, Liv

excĭdĭum -ii, n (excindo = exscindo), *destruction, annihilation*, **a,** of places, Libyae, Verg, excidia urbium relictarum, Liv, **b,** of persons, excidium meorum, Verg, legionum, Tac

1 **excĭdo** -cĭdi, 3 (ex and cado), *to fall out, fall down* **I.** Lit, **A.** Gen, sol excidisse mihi e mundo videtur, Cic, gladii de manibus exciderunt, poet, vinclis excides, *escape*, Verg **B.** Esp, **1,** of a lot, *to fall out* ut cuiusque sors exciderat, Liv.; **2,** *to fall out, be lost*, litteras excidisse in via, Cic. **II.** Transf, **A.** Gen, ut quodammodo victoria e manibus excideret, *slipped out*, Cic, in vitium libertas excidit, Hor **B.** Esp, **1,** *to slip out unawares, escape*, verbum ex ore alicuius or alicui, Cic, libellus me imprudente et invito excidit, Cic, **2,** *to vanish, disappear, pass away*, **a,** vultus, oratio, mens denique excidit, Cic; excidit illa metu, *lost consciousness*, Ov, **b,** esp, *to pass*

away from memory or *thought, be forgotten*; Carthaginem excidisse de memoria, Liv.; nomen tuum mihi excidit, Ov.; cogitatio mihi non excidit, Cic.; **3,** *to fail*; magnis excidit ausis, Ov.

2. **excīdo** -cīdi -cīsum, 3. (ex and caedo), *to cut out.* **I.** Lit., **A.** Gen., lapides e terra, Cic.; arbor excisa, non evulsa, Cic. **B.** Esp., **a,** *to hew out, excavate*; saxum, Cic.; **b,** *to destroy*; of places, portas, *force open*, Caes.; domos, Cic.; of persons, *to annihilate*; Sugambros, Tac. **II.** Transf., *to root out, banish*; illud tristissimum tempus ex anno, Cic.; causas bellorum, Tac.

excĭĕo -cīvi -cĭtum, 2. and (gen.) **excĭo** -cīvi and -cĭi -cĭtum, 4. *to call forth, summon out.* **I.** Of persons, **A.** Lit., **1,** gen., ea res ab stativis excivit Mettium, Liv.; artifices e Graecia, Liv.; animas imis sepulcris, Verg.; **2,** esp., *to summon to help*; Romanos ad auxilium urbis obsessae, Liv.; auxilia e Germania, Tac. **B.** Transf., **1,** *to provoke*; hostem ad dimicandum acie, Liv.; **2,** with or without somno or e somno, *to arouse, awake*, Liv., Sall.; **3,** *to frighten, alarm*; conscientia mentem excitam vastabat, Sall. **II.** Of things, **1,** *to call forth, excite, produce*; tumultum in portis, Liv.; timorem, Liv.; **2,** *to shake*; pulsuque pedum tremit excita tellus, Verg.

excĭpio -cēpi -ceptum, 3. (ex and capio). **I.** *to take out.* **A.** Lit., aliquem e mari, Cic. **B.** Transf., **a,** *to except*; hosce homines excipio et secerno, Cic.; excipere aliquem or excipi, foll. by ne, Cic.; non excipi quominus, Cic.; **b,** *to make a condition, state expressly*; lex exciperet ut, etc., Cic. **II.** *to take up, catch up.* **A.** Of things, **1,** sanguinem paterā, Cic.; **2,** *to catch up by listening, to listen, overhear*, Cic.; **3, a,** *to receive*; vulnera, Cic.; **b,** *to undertake*; labores magnos, Cic.; **c,** *to suffer, endure*; omnem diu collectam vim improborum, Cic. **B.** Of persons, **1,** *to catch*; moribundum, Liv.; se pedibus or in pedes, *to spring to the ground*, Liv.; **2,** *to catch* (in a hostile manner); **a,** lit., servos in pabulatione, Caes.; **b,** transf., *to snatch at*; voluntates hominum, Cic. **III.** *to receive.* **A.** Lit., **1,** excipi ab omnibus clamore, Cic.; **2,** *to entertain*; aliquem, Cic.; **3,** of places, illam (patriam) ubi excepti sumus, Cic.; **4,** *to attack*; **a,** Orestes excipit incautum, Verg.; **b,** *to wound*; aliquem in latus, Verg. **B.** Transf., **1,** *to hear, receive*; motus futuros, Verg.; assensu populi excepta vox, Liv.; **2,** *to await*; qui quosque eventus exciperent, Caes.; **3,** *to follow, succeed*; orationem Tullii exceperunt preces multitudinis, Liv.; Herculis vitam immortalitas excipit, Cic.; hunc excipit Labienus, *speaks next*, Caes.; **4,** *to continue, prolong*; memoriam viri, Cic.; **5,** poet., *to lie towards*; porticus excipit Arcton, Hor.

excīsĭo -ōnis (excīdo), *destruction*; tectorum, Cic.; urbium, Cic.

excĭtātus -a -um, p. adj. with compar. and superl. (from excĭto), *lively, animated, vigorous, loud*; sonus, Cic.; clamor, Liv.

excĭto, 1. **I.** *to rouse forth.* **A.** Of living creatures, **1,** feras, Cic.; **2,** *to call forth by shouting, to summon*; clamore excitatum praesidium Romanorum, Liv.; aliquem a mortuis or ab inferis, Cic. **B.** Transf., of things, alicui memoriam caram, *to renew*, Cic. **II.** *to rouse up.* **A.** of persons, **1, a,** lit., universi rursus prociderunt, tandem excitati curiā excesserunt, Liv.; **b,** transf., *to console, raise up*; animum amici jacentem, Cic.; afflictos, Cic.; **2,** *to summon*; triarios, Liv.; recitatores, lectores, Cic.; testes, Cic.; **3, a,** *to arouse from sleep*; aliquem e somno or somno, Cic.; **b,** *to arouse, animate*; trepido nuntio excitatus, Liv.; aliquem ad laborem et laudem, Cic. **B.** Of things, **1,** *to raise, erect*; turrem, Caes.; sepulcrum, Cic.; transf., excitata fortuna, *favourable*, Cic.; **2,** of a fire, *to kindle, inflame*; ignem, Caes.; incendium, Cic.; **3, a,** *to provoke, produce, call forth*; plausum, Cic.; fletum alicui, Cic.; **b,** *to provoke, cause*; amores, Cic.; indomitas iras, Verg.

exclāmātĭo -ōnis, f. (exclamo), in rhet., *an exclamation*, Cic.

exclāmo, 1. **I.** Intransit., *to shout, cry aloud*; in stadio cursores exclamant quam maxime possunt, Cic.; contiones saepe exclamare vidi, quum apte verba concidissent, Cic. **II.** Transit., **1,** *to shout out, call aloud by name*; Ciceronem, ap. Cic.; **2,** *to shout out*; mihi libet exclamare; pro Deum, etc., Cic.; with objective clause, quum magnā voce exclamasset ut, etc., Liv.

exclūdo -clūsi -clūsum, (ex and claudo), 3. **I.** *to shut out, exclude.* **A.** Lit., **a,** of persons, aliquem a domo sua, Cic.; aliquem moenibus, Cic.; ejicere nos magnum fuit, excludere facile, Cic.; **b,** of a place, *to cut off, separate*; locum, Liv. **B.** Transf., **a,** *to exclude*; ab hereditate paterna, Cic.; his praemiis et honoribus, Cic.; **b,** *to remove*; aliquem a republica, Cic.; **c,** *to prevent, hinder*; Romanos ab re frumentaria, *shut off*, Caes. **II.** of birds, *to hatch*; pullos suos in nido, Cic.

exclūsĭo -ōnis, f. (excludo), *a shutting out, exclusion*, Ter.

excōgĭtātĭo -ōnis, f. (excogito), *a contriving, devising*; illa vis quae tandem est, quae investigat occulta, quae inventio atque excogitatio dicitur, Cic.

excōgĭto, 1. *to scheme, devise, contrive, invent*; mira quaedam genera furandi, Cic.; with dat. of gerund, or ad with acc. (to express the object of the invention), alia tuendis urbibus excogitata, Cic.; excogitare multa ad avaritiam, Caes.; with relat. sentence, excogitat, sane acute quid decernat, Cic.; absol., ad haec igitur cogita, mi Attice, vel potius excogita, Cic.

excŏlo -cŏlŭi -cultum. 3. **A.** Lit., *to tend* or *cultivate carefully*; arva, Mart.; lanas rudes, *to spin*, Ov. **B.** Transf., **a,** *to adorn, polish, ennoble, refine*; Tuditanus omni vitā atque victu excultus, Cic.; animos doctrinā, Cic.; vitam per artes, Verg.; **b,** *to serve, honour*; quaeque tu, est pietas, ut te non excolat ipsum, Ov.

excŏquo -coxi -coctum, 3. *to boil down*; **1,** *to melt down, refine*; vitium metallis, Ov.; omne per ignes vitium, Verg.; **2,** *to bake, make hard*; terram sol excoquit, Lucr.

excors -cordis (ex and cor), *foolish, silly, without intelligence*; anus, Cic.; hoc qui non videt, excors est, Hor.

excrēmentum -i, n. (excerno), *excrement*; oris, *spittle*, Tac.; narium, Tac.

excresco -crēvi -crētum, 3. *to grow up, spring up*; in hos artus, in haec corpora, quae miramur, excrescunt, Tac.

excrētus -a -um, partic. of excerno or of excresco.

excrŭcĭābĭlis -e (excrucio), *deserving of torture*, Plaut.

excrŭcĭo, 1. *to torture, torment exceedingly.* **A.** Lit., servos fame vinculisque, Caes.; excruciare aliquem vinculis ac verberibus atque omni supplicio, Cic. **B.** Transf., **a,** of physical pain, fumo excruciatus, Cic.; **b,** of mental torture, meae me miseriae magis excruciant quam tuae, Cic.

excŭbĭae -ārum, f. (excubo). **A.** Lit., *a keeping watch, keeping guard*; o excubias tuas, o flebiles vigilias, Cic.; excubias agere alicui, *to keep watch over*, Tac.; of animals, excubiae vigilum canum, Hor.; poet., excubiae divûm aeterna, *the everlasting fire*, Verg **B.** Meton, *the persons who keep watch, watchmen, guard*, Cic

excŭbitor -ōris, m (excubo) *a sentinel, watchman, guard*, Caes, of birds, excubitor ales, *the cock*, Verg

excŭbo -bŭi -bĭtum, 1, *to lie*, or *sleep out of doors* **I.** Gen, in agris, Cic **II.** *to stand sentinel, keep watch*. **A.** Lit, in armis, Caes, pro castris, Caes, ad portum, Caes **B.** Transf, **a,** Cupido excubat in genis, Hor., **b,** *to be watchful, vigilant*, excubabo vigilaboque pro vobis, Cic

excūdo -cūdi -cūsum, 3 **I. A.** Lit, *to strike out*, scintillam silici, Verg **B.** Transf, *to hatch*, pullos ex ovis, Cic **II.** *to make ready by striking* **A.** *to hammer, forge*, spirantia mollius aera, Verg, of bees, *to mould*, recentes ceras, Verg **B.** Transf, *to compose* (of writing), aliquid, Cic.

exculco, 1 (ex and calco), *to trample firm, tread hard, stamp firm;* singuli ab infimo solo pedes terra exculcabantur, Cic

excurro -cŭcurri and -curri cursum, 3 **I.** *to run out, hasten forth* **A.** Gen, **1,** lit., excurrat aliquis (sc domo), Cic, **2,** transf, quorum animi spretis corporibus evolant atque excurrunt foras, Cic, campus in quo excurrere virtus possit, *show itself*, Cic **B** Esp **1,** milit t t, *to attack, make a sortie*, omnibus portis, Liv, ex Africa, Cic, **2,** transf, *to make a digression*, longius, Cic **II.** of places, *to run out, to project*, promontorium in altum excurrens, Liv; productiora alia et quasi immoderatius excurrentia, Cic

excursio -ōnis, f (excurro), **1,** *a stepping onward* (of an orator), excursio moderata eaque rara, Cic, **2,** *an attack, assault, sally*, excursionem facere ex oppido, Caes, excursiones et latrocinia hostium, Cic, fig, prima excursio orationis, Cic

excursor -ōris, m (excurro), *a scout, skirmisher*, Cic

excursus -ūs, m (excurro), **1,** *a running forth*, excursusque breves tentant (of bees), Verg.; **2,** milit. t t, *an attack, sally, assault*, excursus militum, Caes

excūsābilis -e (excuso), *excusable, deserving of excuse*, delicti pars, Ov.

excūsātio -ōnis (excuso) **I.** *an excuse* **1,** gen, with subject genit, Pompeii, Cic, with object genit, peccati, Cic, excusationem excipere, Cic, stultitia excusationem non habet, *finds no excuse*, Cic, excusationem probare, Cic, justā et idoneā uti excusatione intermissionis litterarum, Cic., plur, *grounds of excuse*, nullae istae excusationes sunt, Cic, **2,** esp, *refusal, declining*, excusatio Serv Sulpicii legationis, Cic **II.** *plea, defence*, excusationem oculorum accipere, Cic, excusatione uti temporis or valetudinis, *to allege in excuse*, Cic

excūso, 1 (ex and causa) **I.** *to excuse*, se apud aliquem or se alicui, Cic, se de aliqua re, Caes; tarditatem litterarum, Cic; excusare aliquem or se quod, etc, Cic, si Lysiades excusetur Areopagites esse, *is excused on the ground that he is* etc, Cic. **II.** *to allege in excuse, to plead*, **1,** morbum, Cic; valetudinem, aetatem, Liv, **2,** *to decline*, reflex, se excusare or pass, excusari with abl, *to be excused from, relieved from a duty*, etc, Tac

excussus a -um, partic of excutio

excŭtio -cussi -cussum, 3 (ex and quatio) **I.** *to shake out, strike out, throw out, drive out* **A.** Gen, **1,** lit, ancoram e nave, Liv, litteras in terram, Cic; **2,** transf, *to remove, drive away*, metum de corde, Ov., alicuius voces, *to pay no more heed to*, Verg **B.** Esp, **1,** *to tear away*, agnum ore lupi, Ov; transf, studia de manibus, Cic, **2, a,** of weapons, *to shoot*, glandem Liv, **b,** *to throw* (of a horse, etc), equus excussit equitem, Liv, **c,** *to drive away*, aliquem patriā, Verg, **3,** *to press out*, sudorem, Nep, transf, risum, *to force*, Hor, **4,** *to destroy, make void*, foedus, Verg, **5,** somno excuti, *to be disturbed from sleep*, Verg, **6,** *to spread out*, brachia, Ov **II.** *to shake violently* **A.** caesariem, Ov **B. 1,** *to search, examine* (by shaking a person's garments), non excutio te, si quid forte ferri habuisti, Cic, **2,** *to test, examine, weigh*, omnes eorum delicias, omnes ineptias, Cic

exec v exsec

exĕdo -ēdi -ēsum, 3 *to eat up, devour, consume* **I.** Lit, Plaut **II.** *to consume, destroy*, esp of the action of time, rust, etc; **a,** lit, exesis posterioribus partibus versiculorum, Cic, **b,** transf, of the mind, *to wear away, eat into, exhaust*, aegritudo exest animum, Cic

exĕdra ae, f (ἐξέδρα), *a room*, or *hall for conversation* or *debate*, Cic

exĕdrĭum -ii, n (ἐξέδριον), *a sitting-room*, Cic

exemplar -āris, n (**exemplāre** -is, n, Lucr) **I. A.** *a copy, transcript*, Cic **B.** *a pattern, model, exemplar, example*, Cic **II.** *an image, likeness*, Cic

exemplāris e (exemplum), *serving as a copy* Subst, **exemplāres**, *copies*, omnium litterarum, Tac

exemplum -i, n (for exempulum, from eximo, orig *something chosen from a number of the same kind*). **I.** *something similar*, **1,** *a copy, transcript*, Caesaris litterarum exemplum tibi misi, Cic, **2,** *manner, fashion*, quaestionem haberi eodem exemplo quo M Pomponius praetor habuisset, Liv **II.** *something to be imitated* **A.** Artistically, *an original, pattern*, in mutum simulacrum ab animali exemplo transfertur, Cic **B.** Morally, **1,** *a copy, model*, exemplum innocentiae, pudicitiae, Cic; exemplum capere or petere ab aliquo, Cic, **2,** *an example to be imitated* or *avoided*, aliquid aliorum exemplo institutoque facere, Cic, plus exemplo quam peccato nocent, Cic., **3,** *a warning and deterring example, exemplary punishment*, exemplum severitatis edere, Cic, exemplum statuere in aliquem or in aliquo, Cic **III.** *that which illustrates or explains, instance, example, proof*, magna exempla casuum humanorum, Liv, exempli causā, or gratiā, or in exemplum, *for example*, Cic

exemptus a -um, partic of eximo

exĕo -ii (-ivi) -itum, 4 **I.** Intransit., *to go out, go away, go forth* **A.** Lit, **1,** ex urbe Cic; ab urbe, Liv, de triclinio, Cic, domo, Cic, **2,** of things, **a,** of lots, cum de consularibus mea prima sors exisset, Cic, **b,** *to spring up, sprout forth* de stamine pampinus exit, Ov, **c,** *to rise in the air, ascend*, curribus auras in aetherias, Verg **B.** Transf, **1,** gen, de or e vita, *to die*, Cic, e patriciis, *to lose one's rank as a patrician*, Cic, exisse ex or de potestate (mentis), *to lose control over oneself*, Cic, **2,** esp, **a,** *to come out of*, aere alieno, Cic, **b,** *to become known*, exit oratio, Cic, **c,** of time, *to come to an end, pass away*, quinto anno exeunte, Cic **II.** Transit, **1,** *to pass over, beyond*, Avernas valles, Ov; transf, modum, Ov., **2,** *to ward off*, vim viribus, Verg

exeq v ex-seq

exercĕo -ui -itum, 2 (ex and ARC eo), *to work thoroughly, fatigue, weary* **I.** Lit, **a,** equos aequore campi, *to exercise*, Verg, indomitas qualis undas exercet Auster, Hor, **b,** *to occupy*, *employ the limbs in work;* assiduis brachia telis, Ov.; **c,** of slaves, animals, etc., *to employ in work;* famulas ad lumina longo penso, Verg.; **d,** *to work hard at;* solum presso sub vomere, *to cultivate diligently,* Verg. **II.** Transf., **A.** Gen., *to harass, trouble;* meos casus in quibus me fortuna vehementer exercuit, Cic.; exerceri poenis, Verg. **B.** *to occupy in some activity, to exercise, practise;* **a,** of the body, hoc vocem et vires suas, Cic.; milit. t. t., *to exercise in arms, drill;* copias, Caes.; reflex., se exercere and middle exerceri, *to practise, exercise;* of athletes, se in curriculo, Cic.; **b,** of the mind, memoriam, Cic.; adolescentes ad copiam rhetorum, Cic.; reflex., se exercere, or middle, exerceri, *to practise;* se quotidianis commentationibus acerrime, Cic. **C.** *to make use of* an instrument or weapon, *to employ, use;* **1,** gen., **a,** arma, Verg.; diem, *to do one's day's work,* Verg.; **b,** of politics, *to use, practise;* facilitatem et lenitudinem animi in aliquo, Cic.; graves inimicitias cum aliquo, Sall.; libidinem et avaritiam in socios, Liv.; **2,** esp., **a,** of land, *to cultivate;* praedia rustica, Liv.; of mines, *to work;* metalla auri atque argenti, Liv.; **b,** *to practise an art,* etc., medicinam, Cic.; **c,** legal t. t., (α) *to preside over, to conduct;* qui exercet judicium, Cic.; quaestionem inter sicarios, Cic.; (β) vectigalia, *to manage,* Cic.; (γ) *to bring a law into execution;* legem confestius exerceri, Liv.

exercĭtātĭo -ōnis, f. (exercito), *practise, exercise;* **a,** of the body, corpora nostra motu atque exercitatione recalescunt, Cic.; **b,** of the mind, with genit., dicendi, Cic.; juris civilis, Cic.; **c,** *practice;* virtutis, scelerum, Cic.

exercĭtātus -a -um, p. adj. with compar. and superl. (from exercito), **1,** *busied;* agris subigendis, Cic.; **2,** *practised, exercised;* **a,** of the body, homines in armis exercitati, Cic.; exercitatus in uxoribus necandis, Cic.; **b,** of the mind, in arithmeticis satis exercitatus, Cic. **II.** *troubled, harassed;* Syrtes exercitatae Noto, Hor.; curis agitatus et exercitatus animus, Cic.

exercĭtĭum -ĭi, n. (exerceo), *practice, exercise;* equitum, Tac.

exercĭto, 1. (intens. of exerceo), *to practise,* Varr.

1. **exercĭtus** -a -um, p. adj. (exerceo), **1,** *trained, schooled;* militiā, bello, Tac.; **2,** *severe, vexatious,* Tac.; **3,** *tried, harassed,* Cic.

2. **exercĭtus** -ūs, m. (exerceo), **a,** *a trained body of soldiers, army;* exercitus terrestris, navalis, Liv.; ducere exercitum, Cic.; conscribere, Cic.; parare or comparare, Cic.; conficere, Cic.; cogere, Caes.; repente conflare, Cic.; paucis diebus facere, Cic.; accipere, Cic.; exercitus alere, Cic.; exercitum ex castris educere, Caes.; exercitum exponere, *put on ship,* Caes.; esp., *the infantry;* exercitus equitatusque, Caes., Liv.; his omnibus diebus exercitum castris continuit, equestri proelio quotidie contendit, Caes.; **b,** poet., *crowd, swarm;* corvorum, Verg.

exēsor -ōris, m. (exedo), *one who gnaws or eats away,* Lucr.

exhālātĭo -ōnis, f. (exhalo), *an exhalation, vapour;* exhalationes terrae, Cic.

exhālo, 1. **I.** Transit., *to exhale, emit vapour,* **a,** of things, nebulam, Verg.; odores, Lucr.; **b,** of persons, vitam, Verg.; animam, Ov.; crapulam or vinum, Cic. **II.** Intransit., *to breathe forth,* Ov.

exhaurĭo -hausi -haustum, 4. **I.** *to draw out.* **A. 1,** of fluids, sentinam, Cic.; **2,** gen., *to take out;* terram manibus, Caes.; omnem pecuniam ex aerario, Cic. **B.** Transf., *to take away;* partem ex tuis laudibus, Cic. **II.** *to empty out.* **A.** Lit., fossas cloacasque, Liv.; puteos, poculum, vinum, *to empty by drinking,* Cic.; aerarium, Cic. **B.** Transf., **1,** *to exhaust, impoverish;* facultates patriae, Cic.; homines, Cic.; **2,** *to weaken, exhaust;* sermo hominum exhaustus est, Cic.; **3,** *to bring to an end, complete;* mandata, Cic.; **4,** *to endure, suffer;* labores, Liv.

exhērēdo, 1. (exheres), *to disinherit;* aliquem, Cic.

exhērēs -ēdis, *disinherited;* with genit., paternorum bonorum exheres, Cic.

exhĭbĕo -hibŭi -hibitum, 2. (ex and habeo). **I.** Gen., **a,** *to produce, bring forth;* esp., *to produce in a court of justice;* pupillum, fratres, Cic.; *to produce for proof,* etc., exhibe librarium illud legum vestrarum, Cic.; **b,** *to hand over, deliver;* omnia alicui integra, Cic. **II. 1,** *to show, display, exhibit;* **a,** dea formam removit anilem Palladaque exhibuit, Ov.; **b,** populo Romano philosophiam, *set forth, present,* Cic.; **2,** *to make, to cause;* alicui negotium, *to cause trouble,* Cic.; so alicui molestiam, Cic.; **3,** *to grant, allow;* toros, Ov.; exhibe liberam contionem vel Argis vel Lacedaemone, Liv.

exhĭlăro, 1. *to make cheerful;* miraris tam exhilaratam esse servitutem nostram, Cic.

exhorresco -horrŭi, 3. **I.** Intransit., *to shudder exceedingly, be terrified;* aequoris instar, Ov.; metu, Cic.; in aliquo, Cic. **II.** Transit., *to tremble at, to dread;* vultus, Verg.

exhortātĭo -ōnis, f. (exhortor), *exhortation, encouragement;* ducum, Tac.

exhortor, 1. dep., *to exhort, encourage;* natum, Verg.; foll. by ut and the subj., Tac.

exĭgo -ēgi -actum, 3. (ex and ago). **I.** *to drive out, drive away.* **A.** Lit., **1,** of living beings, reges ex civitate, Cic.; servam e montibus, Liv.; **2,** of things, **a,** sacer admissas exigit Hebrus aquas, *pours into the sea,* Ov.; **b,** agrorum fructus, *to sell,* Liv. **B.** Transf., otium, *to banish,* Hor. **II.** *to drive in, to thrust;* ensem per juvenem, Verg. **III.** *to complete, finish;* **a,** monumentum aere perennius, Hor.; opus, Ov.; **b,** of time, *to spend, pass;* exacto per scelera die, Tac.; *to complete, bring to an end;* exactis mensibus, Verg.; exactā aetate, *at the end of life,* Cic. **IV.** *to exact, demand.* **A.** Lit., **a,** of money, pecunias, Cic.; vectigalia, Cic.; **b,** of work, aedes privatas velut publicum opus, *superintend the execution of,* Liv.; esp., (α) *to require the building* or *making of something;* viam, Cic.; (β) *to make a requisition* or *demand for something;* equitum peditumque certum numerum a civitatibus, Caes. **B.** Transf., *to demand, require;* jusjurandum, Liv.; veritatem a teste, Cic.; promissum ab aliquo, Cic. **V.** *to measure, weigh, examine.* **A.** Lit., columnas ad perpendiculum, Cic. **B.** Transf., **1,** ad illam summam veritatem legitimum jus, Cic.; **2,** *to consider, reflect upon;* tempus secum ipsa opusque exigit, Verg.; non satis exactum quid agam, *not certain,* Cic.

exĭgŭē, adv. (exiguus), **1,** *sparingly, scantily, scarcely;* frumentum exigue dierum xxx habere, Caes.; nimis exigue et exiliter ad calculos revocare amicitiam, *too narrowly,* Cic.; **2,** *briefly;* exigue scripta est (epistola), Cic.

exĭgŭĭtas -ātis, f. (exiguus), **1,** of space, *smallness;* castrorum, Caes.; **2,** of number, *paucity;* copiarum, Cic.; **3,** of time, *shortness;* ut temporis exiguitas postulabat, Caes.

exĭgŭus -a -um (exigo), *small, little, scanty.* **I.** Of quantity, **A.** Of space, *small, little;* castra, Caes.; pars terrae, Cic.; neut. subst., **exĭgŭum** -i, n. *smallness;* spatii, Liv. **B.** Of number, *scanty, small;* numerus oratorum, Cic. **C.** Of time, *short, scanty;* vita, Cic. **II.** Of quality,

1, *thin, meagre*, corpus, Nep , 2, *sparing, scanty*, toga, Hor., laus, Cic , 3, of strength, *weak*, vires, Verg , vox, Ov

exīlis -e (for exiglis, from exigo), *little thin, slender, meagre, poor*, 1, of number, legiones, *weak, not of their proper number*, Cic , 2, of quality, a, *thin, slender, meagre*, cor, Cic , femur, Hor , b, of discourse, *meagre, dry*, genus sermonis, Cic ; c, *poor, insignificant, scanty*, solum, Cic , domus, Hor

exīlĭtas -ātis, f (exilis), *thinness, meagreness, weakness*, in dicendo, Cic

exīlĭtĕr, adv (exilis), *thinly, poorly, meagrely*; a, *sparingly, parsimoniously*, nimis exigue et exiliter ad calculos revocare amicitiam, Cic , b, *uninterestingly*, annales sine exiliter descripti, Cic , c, of strength, *weakly*, nolo verba exiliter exanimata exire, Cic

exĭmĭē, adv (eximius), *uncommonly, extraordinarily, extremely*, diligere, Cic , templum eximie ornatum, Liv

exĭmĭus -a -um (eximo) **I.** *excepted*, tu unus eximius eo, in quo hoc praecipuum ac singulare valeat, Liv , te illi unum eximium cui consuleret fuisse, Cic **II.** *exceptional, distinguished, extraordinary, uncommon*, facies, ingenium, spes, Cic , ironic , istae vestrae eximiae pulchraeque virtutes, Cic

exĭmo -ēmi -emptum, 3 (ex and emo), *to take out, take away* **I.** Lit , unam spinam de pluribus, Hor , aliquid tamquam e vinculis alicuius rei, Cic **II.** Transf , *to take away*, 1, a, aliquid ex rerum natura, Cic , unum diem ex mense, Cic , moram certaminis hosti, Liv , b, of time, *to delay, procrastinate, waste*, diem dicendo, Cic , c, of persons, aliquem ex or de reis, Cic , 2, *to take away from some evil*, a, aliquid de, *to free from*, agrum de vectigalibus, Cic ; b, aliquid alicui, *to take something away from*, alicui curas, Ov , c, of persons, aliquem ex with the abl , or with the abl alone, *to free from*, aliquem ex culpa, Cic , aliquem alicui rei, *to take away from*, aliquem vitae, Tac , Syracusas in libertatem, *to free*, Liv , d, *to except*, aliquem, Cic

exin = exinde (q v)

exĭnānĭo -ivi -itum, 4 *to empty*, navem, Cic , agros, gentes, *to plunder*, Cic

exindĕ (exin), adv **I.** Of place, *from there, thence, thereupon, next*, mari finitimus aer, Cic. **II.** Of time, 1, *thereupon, after that, then*, Cic , 2, in the enumeration of a series of facts, *then, next*, Verg , Liv

existĭmātĭo -ōnis, f (existimo) **I.** *the opinion that a man has of a thing* or *person, judgment*, non militis de imperatore existimationem esse, Liv. **II.** *the opinion that other persons have of a man*, esp morally, *reputation, good name, honour, character*; bona, integra, magna, Cic , alicuius existimationem offendere or oppugnare, Cic , venisse in eam existimationem, Cic

existĭmātor ōris, m (existimo), *one who forms or gives an opinion, a critic*, Cic

existĭmo (exaestumo, existumo), 1 *to judge a thing according to its value* **I** *to consider, hold, regard, esteem, deem*, with predic acc , existumare aliquem avarum, Cic , aliquem sapientem et appellare et existumare, Cic , in pass , homo, ut existimabatur, avarus et furax , with in and the abl , in hostium numero existimari, Cic **II.** Transf , **A.** *to think, be of opinion, hold*, with acc and infin , non possum existimare plus quemquam a se ipso quam me a te amari, Cic , Africano vim attulisse existimatus est, Cic , with pronoun acc quod ego nullo modo existimo , impers , ita intelligimus vulgo existimari, Cic **B.** *to judge, decide, pass judgment*, esp of critical judgment on literary works, with de and the abl , de scriptoribus, qui nondum ediderunt, existimare non possumus, Cic ; bene or male de aliquo, Cic , with rel sent , existimari non potest vix existimari potest utrum ... an, etc , Caes , Liv , absol partic subst , **existĭmantes** -ium, m *the critics*, Cic

exĭtĭābĭlis -e (exitium), *deadly, destructive*, bellum, Cic , tyrannus, Liv.

exĭtĭālis e (exitium), *destructive fatal, deadly*, exitus, Cic , donum Minervae, Verg

exĭtĭōsus a um, adj with compar and superl (exitium), *destructive, fatal, deadly*, conjuratio, Cic , exitiosum esse reipublicae, Cic

exĭtium ii, n (exeo, lit., *a going out* or *away*), *destruction, ruin*, 1, lit., huius urbis, Cic , exitio esse alicui, *to be fatal to*, Cic , omnia exitia publica, Cic , 2, meton , *the cause of destruction*, Hor

exĭtus -ūs, m (exeo), *a going out, a going forth* **I. A.** Lit , reditum mihi gloriosum injuria tua dedit, non exitum calamitosum, Cic , omni exitu et pabulatione interclusi, Caes , with ab, ne exitus inclusis ab urbe esset, Liv **B.** Meton , *a place of going out, exit*, quod (posticum) devium maxime atque occultissimi exitus erat, Liv **II.** Transf , **A.** Gen , quae plurimos exitus dant ad eiusmodi digressionem, *opportunities for digression*, Cic **B.** Esp , 1, *the end*, adducta ad exitum quaestio est, Cic , hic fuit exitus oppugnationis, Caes , tristes exitus habere, Cic , esp , a, of a tragedy, *the catastrophe*, ut tragici poetae, quum explicare argumenti exitum non potestis, Cic , b, *the end of life*, humanus, Cic , 2, *the result, consequence*, disceptatio sine exitu fuit, Liv , 3, *issue, result*, eventus atque exitus rerum, Cic , exitus futuri temporis, Hor

exlex -lēgis, *lawless, bound by no law*, exlegem esse Sullam, Cic

exmŏvĕo = emoveo (q v)

exŏdium ii, n (ἐξόδιον), *a comic afterpiece*, Liv , Juv

exŏlesco -lēvi lētum, 3 **I.** *to grow to full size*, only in perf partic , exoletus, Plaut **II.** *to pass away from use, be out of date, obsolete*, ne vetustissima Italiae disciplina per desidiam exolesceret, Tac , exoletum jam vetustate odium, Liv

exŏlētus a-um, partic of exolesco.

exŏnĕro, 1 **A.** Lit , *to unload, disburden*, a, Plaut , plenas colos, *to spin off*, Ov , b, *to remove, send away*, multitudinem in proximas terras, Tac **B** Transf , *to free, release, relieve*, civitatem metu, Liv , regnum praegravante multitudine, Liv

exoptātus -a um, p adj with compar and superl (exopto), *desired, wished for*, nuntius, Cic , nihil exoptatius adventu meo, Cic , exoptatissima gratulatio, Cic

exopto, 1 *to desire eagerly, earnestly wish for* exoptare ea maxime, Cic , Samnitium adventum, Liv , tibi pestem exoptant, *wish you*, Cic , with infin , Cic , with ut and the subj , Cic

exōrābĭlis -e, adj with compar (exoro), *easily entreated, placable*, Cic , Hor

exordĭor orsus sum, 4 dep , 1. *to lay a warp, begin to weave*, fig , pertexe quod exorsus es, Cic , 2, *to begin*, bellum ab causa tam nefanda, Liv , without acc , of orators, *to begin* ab ipsa re Cic , with infin , dicere, Cic Partic subst , **exorsa** ōrum, n *the beginning*, Cic

exordĭum -ii, n (exordior) 1, *the warp*

of a web, Quint.; **2, a,** *the beginning*; vitae, Cic.; plur., revocare exordia prima pugnae, Verg.; **b,** esp., *the beginning of a speech*; in dicendi exordio permoveri, Cic.; as a part of a speech, *the introduction*, Cic.

exŏrĭor -ortus sum -ŏrīri, dep. 3. and 4. **I.** *to rise, rise up.* **A.** Lit., omnes exorti, *sprang up*, Liv.; esp. of the sun, moon, and stars; post solstitium Canicula exoritur, Cic. **B.** Transf., **1,** *to appear, step forward, make one's appearance*; repentinus Sulla nobis exoritur, Cic.; exortus est servus, *as an accuser*, Cic.; of abstractions, exoritur Antipatri ratio ex altera parte, Cic.; **2,** *to rise up from a misfortune, breathe again*; ego nunc paulum exorior, Cic. **II.** *to arise, proceed, take rise.* **A.** exoritur ingens per litora flatus, Verg. **B.** Transf., **1,** exoritur fama alicuius rei or de aliqua re; with accus. and infin., Lucr.; **2,** *to proceed from*; honestum quod ex virtutibus exoritur, Cic.

exornātĭo -ōnis, f. (exorno), *adorning, ornament.* **A.** Lit., Cic. **B.** *embellishment of a speech*, Cic.

exornātor -ōris, m. (exorno), *one who adorns, an embellisher*; ceteri non exornatores rerum, sed tantummodo narratores fuerunt, Cic.

exorno, 1. *to furnish with, provide plentifully*; **1,** vicinitatem armis, Sall.; **2,** *to ornament, adorn*; **a,** lit., domum, Cic.; triclinium, Cic.; **b,** transf., Cic.; Graeciam praestantissimis artibus, Cic.; philosophiam falsā gloriā; of speech, orationem, Cic.

exōro, 1. **I.** *to entreat earnestly, obtain by entreaty, prevail upon*; exora supplice prece deos, Ov.; exorare pacem divûm, Verg.; with ut and the subj., denique exoravit tyrannum ut abire liceret, Cic. **II.** *to propitiate, move*; carmina exorant deos, Ov.; exorare aliquem or exorari foll. by ut or ne and the subj., Cic.; non exorari by quin, Cic.; absol., viri non esse neque exorari neque placari, Cic.

1\. **exorsus** -a -um, partic. of exordior.

2\. **exorsus** -ūs, m. (exordior), *a beginning*; orationis meae, Cic.

exos -ossis, *without bones*, Lucr.

exoscŭlor, 1., dep., *to kiss frequently*; alicuius manum, Tac.

exosso, 1. (exos), *to bone, take out the bones*, Ter.; exossatum pectus, *boneless, flexible*, Lucr.

exostra -ae, f. (ἐξώστρα), *a theatrical machine, by which the inside of a house was revealed to the spectators*, Cic.

exōsus -a -um (ex and odi), *hating exceedingly*; exosus Trojanos, Verg.; templa oculos exosa viriles, Ov.

exōtĭcus -a -um (ἐξωτικός), *foreign, outlandish, exotic*, Plaut.

expallesco -lŭi, 3. *to become very pale, to grow white*; toto ore, Ov.; poet., with acc., Pindarici fontis haustus, *to dread*, Hor.

expando -pansi -pansum and -passum, 3. *to stretch out, expand, spread out.* **A.** Lit., expassae delubri fores, *opened*, Tac. **B.** Transf., *to explain*; rerum naturam dictis, Lucr.

expătro, 1. *to squander*, Cat.

expăvesco -pāvi, 3. *to be exceedingly terrified*; ad id, Liv.; with acc., ensem, *to dread exceedingly*, Hor.

expĕdĭo -īvi and -ĭi -ītum, 4. (ex and pes). **I.** *to disengage, disentangle, set free.* **A.** Lit., se ex laqueo, Cic. **B.** Transf., *to free, help out, bring off*; se ab omni occupatione, Cic.; **a,** Claudias manus per acuta belli, *lead successfully*, Hor.; jaculum trans finem, *to throw*, Hor.; **b,** *to despatch, settle, execute*; negotia, Cic.; rem frumentariam, Caes.; **c,** *to explain, show*; omnem expediat morbi causam, Verg.; prinsquam huiusmodi rei initium expediam, Sall.; ea de re quam verissime expediam, Tac. **II. A.** *to bring forth, provide*; **1,** lit., virgas, Cic.; Cererem canistris, Verg.; **2,** transf., **a,** milit. t. t., *to make ready*; naves or classem, Caes.; se ad pugnam, Liv.; **b,** *to find out, discover*; alicui vicarium, Liv. **B.** res expedit, or impers. expedit, *it is expedient, useful, advantageous*; non quominus expediat quidquam Caesari ad diuturnitatem dominationis, Cic.; with acc. and infin. or the infin. simply, omnibus bonis expedit salvam esse rempublicam, Cic.; with ut and the subj., Tac.

expĕdītē, adv. with compar. and superl. (expeditus), **1,** *quickly*; expeditius navigare, Cic.; **2,** *without difficulty, easily*; explicare, Cic.

expĕdītĭo -ōnis, f. (expedio), *an undertaking against an enemy, expedition*; milites ex hibernis in expeditionem evocare, Sall.; milites equitesque in expeditionem mittere, Caes.; in expeditionem exercitum educere, Cic.

expĕdītus -a -um, p. adj. (from expedio). **I.** *unimpeded, unshackled*; **a,** *lightly clad*; Clodius, Cic.; jaculatores, Liv.; hence, subst., **expĕdītus** -i, m. *a light-armed foot-soldier*, Caes.; expediti, *not burdened with baggage*, Liv.; **b,** *without obstacles, easy*; via, Liv.; locus, Caes.; **c,** *not hindered by obstacles, easy, quick*; ad suos receptus, Caes.; expedita et facile currens oratio, Cic.; **d,** *not hindered by business, free*; ut expeditus in Galliam proficisci posset, Cic.; **e,** *ready, prepared*; expeditus homo et paratus, Cic.; ad dicendum, Cic.; of soldiers, *ready for fight*; copiae, Caes.; copias in expedito habere ad, etc., Liv. **II.** *disentangled*; **a,** *put in order, settled*; negotia, Cic.; **b,** *decisive*; victoria, Caes.

expello -pŭli -pulsum, 3. *to drive out, away.* **I.** Of animals, pecus portā Esquilinā, Liv. **II.** **1,** *to drive away, expel, throw away*; **a,** lit., genis oculos, *to tear*, Ov.; **b,** transf., naturam furcā, Hor.; **2,** *to drive forth, thrust forth*; **a,** lit., ab litore naves in altum, Liv.; sagittam arcu, Ov.; aliquem aethere toto, Ov.; (α) esp. milit. t.t., *to drive out*; aliquem ex oppido, Caes.; Romanos castris, Caes.; (β) *to drive out of a house or country, to banish*; aliquem domo suā, Cic.; patriā, Cic.; ex urbe, Cic.; aliquem bonis, *from one's property*, Cic.; *to drive out kings, tyrants, etc.*, aliquem regno, Cic.; (γ) esp., *to divorce*; filiam ex matrimonio, Cic.; **b,** transf., (α) aliquem vitā, *to bring about a person's death*, Cic.; (β) *to drive away, banish*; omnem dubitationem, Caes.; somnum or quietem, Verg.

expendo -pendi -pensum, 3. *to weigh.* **I. A.** Lit., ut jam expendantur non numerentur pecuniae, Cic. **B.** Transf., *to weigh, examine, test*; expendere atque aestimare voluptates, Cic.; testem, Cic. **II.** *to weigh out, pay out money, to pay.* **A.** Lit., auri pondo centum, Cic.; esp., ferre alicui expensum, *to put down in one's account book a payment to some one else*, Cic. **B.** Transf., *to pay*; poenas scelerum, Verg.

expergēfăcĭo -fēci -factum, 3. *to wake up.* **I.** Lit., Suet. **II.** Transf., *to rouse, excite*; se, Cic.

expergiscor -perrectus sum, 3. dep., *to awake, wake up, rise from sleep.* **A.** Lit., si dormis, expergiscere, Cic. **B.** Transf., *to awake, rouse oneself*; experrecta nobilitas, Cic.

expĕrĭens -entis, p. adj. with compar. and superl. (from experior), *active, industrious, enterprising, experienced in*; promptus homo et experiens, Cic.; with genit., experiens laborum, Ov.

expĕrĭentĭa -ae, f. (experior), **1,** *trial, ex-*

periment, with genit., patrimonii amplificandi, Cic., 2, *the knowledge gained by experiment, experience*, multarum rerum experientiā cognitus, Tac

expĕrīmentum -i, n (experior), *trial, experiment*, hoc maximum est experimentum, Cic ; Metello experimentis cognitum erat genus Numidarum perfidum esse, Sall

expĕrĭor -pertus sum, 4 dep (ex and root PER, whence com perio or perior, peritus, periculum) **I. A.** *to try, test, prove, put to the test*, 1, gen, alicuius amorem, Cic, vim veneni in servo, Cic, amicos, Cic, 2, esp, *to try in a hostile manner, to measure one's strength with another*, a, in battle, si iterum experiri velint, iterum paratum esse decertare, Caes, b, in a court of law, *to litigate*, cum aliquo, Cic **B.** *to try the success of something to risk, hazard, make a trial of*, 1, gen, experiri id nolent quod se assequi posse diffidant, Cic, rei eventum experiri, Caes, ultima audere atque experiri, Liv, with ut and the subj, experiar certe ut hinc avolem, Cic, 2, esp, experiri jus, *to go to law*, Cic, experiri judicium populi Romani, *to leave it to the decision of the Roman people*, Liv **II.** *to experience, find, or know by experience*, 1, omnia quae dico expertus in nobis, Cic, with predic acc, deos constantes inimicos, Ov, with acc and infin, jam antea expertus sum parum fidei miseris esse, Sall, equidem in me ipso saepissime experior, ut exalbescam in principio dicendi, Cic, with relat. sent, experiri libet quantum audeatis, Liv ; de me experior, *I experience it in myself*, Cic, 2, *to experience something unpleasant*, nondum alteram fortunam expertus Liv (pass, libertatis dulcedine nondum expertā, Liv.)

experrectus -a -um, partic of expergiscor

expers -pertis (ex and pars) **A.** *having no part in, not sharing in*, with genit, periculorum, publici consilii, Cic. **B.** Transf, *wanting in, destitute of*, with genit, omnis eruditionis, Cic ; viri, *without a husband*, Ov, with abl, famā atque fortunis, Sall

expertus a um, p adj with compar and superl (from experior), *that which has been often tested, tried, approved*, exercitus, Liv ; with genit, expertus belli, Verg, Tac, with abl, expertus tribuniciis certaminibus, Liv

expĕtendus -a -um, p adj (expeto), *to be desired, desirable*, gloriam expetendam putare, Cic

expĕtesso, 3 (expeto), *to desire, wish for*, Plaut.

expĕto -ivi -itum, 3 **I.** Transit, *to desire, wish, or long for*, vitam alicuius, Cic, auxilium ab aliquo, Cic., with infin, vincere illi expetunt, Cic, with acc and infin, nostram gloriam tuā virtute augeri expeto, Cic, with ut and the subj, Tac, of things, mare medium terrae locum expetens, *encroaching on*, Cic **II.** Intransit, *to fall upon, befall*; ut in eum omnes expetant huiusce clades belli, Liv

expĭātĭo -ōnis, f (expio), *atonement, expiation*, scelerum, Cic.

expīlātĭo -ōnis, f (expilo), *a plundering, robbing*, sociorum, Cic

expīlātor -ōris, m (expilo), *a plunderer, robber*, Cic

expīlo, 1 *to plunder, rob*, aerarium, Cic

expingo -pinxi -pictum, 3 *to paint, describe, depict in writing*, Cic

expĭo, 1 **I.** *to propitiate, appease* **A.** poenis manes mortuorum, Cic. **B.** *to avert an omen, or sign of the wrath of the gods*, prodigium, Liv **II. A.** *to purify*, forum a sceleris vestigiis, Cic, religionem aedium suarum, Cic **B.** *to atone for*, 1, lit, scelus supplicio, Cic, tua scelera di in nostros milites expiaverunt, *have avenged on our soldiers*, Cic, 2, transf, *to atone for, make amends for*, incommodum virtute, Caes

expiscor, 1, dep, *to fish out*, transf, *to search out, find out*, omnia ab aliquo, Cic

explānātē, adv with compar (explanatus), *clearly, plainly*, Cic

explānātĭo -ōnis, f (explano), 1, gen, *a making clear, explanation*, naturae, Cic, 2, esp, a, *interpretation*, portentorum, Cic, b, rhet t t., *illustration*, Cic

explānātor ōris, m (explano), *one who explains, an interpreter, expositor*, oraculorum et vaticinationum, Cic

explānātus -a -um, p adj (from explano), *clear, plain*, vocum impressio, Cic

explāno, 1 (ex and planus), *to explain, expound, make clear* 1, ille tibi omnia explanabit, Cic, 2, a, *to interpret*, carmen, Liv, b, *to set forth, state*, de cuius hominis moribus pauca prius explananda sunt, Sall

explaudo = explodo (q v)

explĕo -plēvi -plētum, 2 *to fill, fill up, complete by filling* **I.** Lit, paludem cratibus atque aggere, Caes, rimas, Cic **II.** Transf, 1, gen, sententias mollioribus numeris, Cic, 2, esp, a, *to amount to, make up*, aurum quod summam talenti Attici expleret, Liv ; milit t t, triam millium numerum, Liv b, *to fulfil, discharge*, munus, Cic, c, *to satisfy, quench, appease*, sitim, Cic, vereor ne non scribendo te expleam, Cic, with genit, animum ultionis flammae, Cic, d, *to make good*, ea damna, Liv, e, *to fill up, complete the number of*, centurias, tribus, Liv legiones, Caes, f, *to complete, perfect*, vitam beatam cumulate, Cic, g, of time, *to complete, finish*, expletum annum habeto Cic

explētĭo ōnis, f (expleo) *satisfying*, naturae, Cic

explētus a -um, p adj (from expleo), *perfect, complete* expletus omnibus suis partibus, Cic

explĭcātē, adv (explicatus), *plainly, clearly*, Cic

explĭcātĭo -ōnis, f (explico) **A** *an unfolding, uncoiling*, rudentis, Cic **B.** Transf, *explanation, exposition, interpretation*, in disserendo mira explicatio, Cic, explicatio fabularum, Cic

explĭcātor -ōris, m (explico), *an expounder, interpreter, explainer*, rerum explicator prudens, Cic.

1 **explĭcātus** a -um p adj with compar and superl (explico) **I.** *ordered, arranged*, provincia quam maxime apta explicataque, Cic **II.** *plain, clear*, litterae tuae, quibus nihil potest esse explicatius, Cic

2 **explĭcātus** ūs, m (explico), *explanation, exposition*, difficiles habere explicatus, Cic

explĭcĭtus a um, p adj (from explico), *straightforward, easy*, ex duobus consiliis propositis explicitius videbatur Ilerdam reverti, Caes

explĭco -ui -ātum, and (not in Cicero) -ui -itum, 1 *to unfold, unroll, disentangle* **I** Lit, **A.** volumen, Cic, suas pennas, Ov., frontem, *to unwrinkle*, Hor **B.** *to spread out, extend, expand*, forum laxare et usque ad atrium Libertatis explicare, Cic, Capua planissimo in loco explicata, Cic, esp as milit t t., *to extend the ranks, deploy*, agmen, aciem, ordines, Liv **II.** Transf, 1, explica atque excute intelligentiam tuam, Cic, 2, *to provide, arrange*; rem frumentariam, Caes, 3, *to set free*, numquam laborant, quem ad modum se probent, sed quem ad modum se explicent dicendo, Cic, 4, *to* *accomplish, execute, bring about;* rationes meas, *accounts,* Cic.; alicuius negotia, Cic.; mandata, Cic.; of a debt, *to pay off;* nomen, Cic.; 5, *to explain in discourse, expound, interpret;* causas rerum, Cic.; with relat. sent., explicare breviter quae mihi sit ratio et causa cum Caesare, Cic.; absol., explicare, de rerum natura, Cic.; 6, *to discover, find out;* ut explicarem quid optimum esset factu, Cic.

explōdo (explaudo) -plōsi -plōsum, 3. **I.** *to drive off with a noise,* Sen. **II.** *to hiss a player off the stage;* histrionem exsibilare et explodere, Cic.; transf., *to reject, disapprove;* sententiam, Cic.

explōrātē, adv. with compar. (exploratus), *certainly, surely, definitely;* ad te explorate scribo, Cic.

explōrātĭo -ōnis, f. (exploro), *an exploring, investigation;* occulta, Tac.

explōrātor -ōris, m. (exploro), *one who investigates, an explorer, scout, spy,* Caes.

explōrātus -a -um, p. adj. with compar. and superl. (exploro), *established, confirmed, certain, sure;* spes, Cic.; victoria, Caes.; de quo mihi exploratum est, *I am convinced, am sure,* foll. by acc. and infin., Cic.

explōro, 1. **I.** *to seek out, search out, investigate, explore.* **A.** Africam, Cic. **B.** Esp. **1,** milit. t. t., *to gain intelligence, spy out, reconnoitre;* hostium iter, Caes.; in abl. absol., explorato or explorato ante, *after intelligence had been gained,* Liv.; **2,** transf., **a,** *to search out, examine, investigate;* rem totam, Cic.; **b,** *to spy out for something;* fugam domini, Cic. **II.** *to test, try, put to proof;* explorat robora fumus, Verg.; epulas, cibos potusque, Tac.

explōsĭo -ōnis, f. (explodo), *a hissing off the stage,* ap. Cic.

expŏlĭo -ivi -itum, 4. *to smooth, polish, to polish, refine;* Dionem Plato doctrinis omnibus expolivit, Cic.; partes non eādem ratione, Cic.

expŏlītĭo -ōnis, f. (expolio), *a smoothing, polishing.* **A.** Lit., urbana, *of a town-house,* Cic. **B.** Transf., of discourse, *polishing, embellishing;* inventi artificiosa, Cic.

expŏlītus -a -um, p. adj. with compar. and superl. (expolio), **1,** *smooth, polished;* deus expolitior, Cat.; **2,** *polished, refined;* vir omni vitā excultus atque expolitus, Cic.

expōno -pŏsŭi -pŏsĭtum, 3. *to put out, place out, set out.* **I.** Lit., **A.** Gen., scalas, *put up,* Verg.; expositus, of places, *lying towards, placed near;* expositae prope in ipsis litoribus urbes, Liv.; super exposta (= exposita) ponto, Verg. **B.** Esp., **1,** *to put on land;* **a,** *to throw on the land;* os Orphei peregrinis arenis, Ov.; **b,** naut. t.t., *to land, disembark;* exponere frumentum, Cic.; esp. of troops, milites navibus, Caes.; **2,** *to expose openly;* aliquid venditioni, Tac.; esp. for show, vasa Samia, Cic.; aliquem populo videndum, Ov.; copias in omnibus collibus, *place openly,* Caes.; **3,** *to expose a child;* in proxima alluvie pueros, Liv. **II.** Transf., **1,** *to show, place before one;* praemia alicui, Cic.; per urbes benigne commeatus, Liv.; **2,** of discourse, *to set forth, exhibit, explain;* vitam alicuius totam, Cic.; with rel. sent. (with qui, quid, quemadmodum, etc.), Cic.; **3,** *to expose, leave unprotected;* mare nimiā propinquitate ad pericula classium externarum expositum, Liv.; libertas exposita ad injurias Masinissae, Liv. (syncop. perf. partic., expostus (for expositus), Verg.)

exporrĭgo -rexi -rectum, 3. *to stretch out, expand, extend,* Ter.

exportātĭo -ōnis, f. (exporto), *exportation;* earum rerum quibus abundaremus, Cic.

exporto, 1. *to carry out.* **I.** Gen., omnia signa ex fanis plaustris evecta exportataque, Cic. **II.** Esp., **a,** *to export;* aurum ex Italia quotannis Hierosolyma, Cic.; **b,** *to banish, drive away;* portentum in ultimas terras exportandum, Cic.

exposco -pŏposci, 3. **I.** *to demand vehemently, entreat earnestly.* **A.** Gen., signum proelii, Caes.; misericordiam, Cic.; with infin., Verg., Tac.; with acc. and infin., Verg.; with acc. of pers. and subj., precibus exposcere plebem, unum sibi civem donarent, Liv.; absol., exposcentibus militibus, Caes. **B.** Esp., **1,** *to ask of the gods, to pray for;* victoriam a diis, Caes.; **2,** *to demand the delivery of a person;* aliquem ad poenam, Tac. **II.** *to demand, require;* nec opes exposcere magnas, Ov.

expŏsĭtĭo -ōnis, f. (expono), of discourse, *a statement, setting forth, exposition, narration;* expositio sententiae suae, Cic.; plur., expositiones rerum, Cic.

expŏsĭtus -a -um, p. adj. (from expono), *exposed, open, accessible.* **A.** Lit., of places, mollibus expositum Zephyris Lilybaeon, Ov. **B.** Transf., *accessible;* domus patens atque adeo exposita cupiditati et voluptatibus, Cic. **C.** *vulgar,* Juv.

expostŭlātĭo -ōnis, f. (expostulo). **I.** *a demand;* bonorum, Cic. **II.** *complaint, expostulation;* expostulationem facere, Cic.; fuerunt nonnullae expostulationes cum absente Pompeio, Cic.

expostŭlo, 1. **I.** *to desire, demand earnestly.* **A.** Gen., aliquid ab aliquo, Cic.; foll. by ut or ne and the subj., Tac.; by acc. and infin., Tac. **B.** *to demand the delivery of a person;* aliquem ad supplicium, Tac. **II.** *to make a complaint, to expostulate;* cum aliquo de aliqua re, Cic.; cum aliquo aliquid or aliquem, *concerning a thing or person,* Cic.; expostulare et queri, foll. by acc. and infin., Cic.

expostus = expositus, v. expono.

expōtus = epotus (q.v.).

expressus -a -um, p. adj. with compar. (from exprimo). **I.** Of pronunciation, *clear, distinct,* Quint.; in a bad sense, *affected;* litterae neque expressae neque oppressae, Cic. **II.** *plain, evident, visible.* **A.** Lit., litterae lituraeque expressae, Cic. **B.** Transf., expressa sceleris vestigia, Cic.

exprĭmo -pressi -pressum, 3. (ex and premo), *to press out, force out.* **I. A.** Lit., **1,** sucina solis radiis expressa, Tac.; corporis pondere conisa tenuem jam spiritum expressit, Tac.; vestis exprimens singulos artus, *showing,* Tac.; **2,** of pronunciation, *to articulate distinctly;* exprimere litteras putidius, Cic. **B.** Transf., *to extort, wrest, squeeze out;* nummos ab aliquo blanditiis, Cic., expressi ut negaret, *made him deny,* Cic. **II.** *to express, model, portray, represent.* **A.** Lit., expressi vultus per ahenea signa, Hor. **B. 1,** *to express in words;* **a,** *describe;* mores alicuius oratione, Cic.; with rel. sent., qui crebro dicat diligenter oportere exprimi, quae vis subjecta sit vocibus, Cic.; **b,** *to translate;* aliquid Latine, Cic.; verbum e verbo, Cic.; ad verbum de Graecis, Cic., **2,** *to imitate, copy;* alicuius vitam et consuetudinem, Cic. **III.** *to raise up;* quantum bis quotidianus agger expresserat, Caes.

exprŏbrātĭo -ōnis, f. (exprobro), *reproach, upbraiding;* alicui veteris fortunae, Liv.

exprŏbro, 1. (ex and probrum), *to reproach, twit with, lay to the charge of;* with acc., officia, Cic.; ea (vitia) in adversariis, Cic.; with acc. and dat., haec hosti, Liv.; with dat. and de, with the abl., de uxore mihi exprobrare, Nep.;

with acc and infin, exprobrare nihilo plus sanitatis in curia quam in foro esse, Liv; with quod and the subj, quasi exprobrare quod in vita maneam, Cic; absol, circumstabant armati hostes exprobrantes eludentesque, Liv

exprōmo -prompsi promptum, 3 *to bring forth, produce* **I.** Lit, omnes apparatus supplicii, Liv **II.** Transf, **1,** *to fetch out, utter*, maestas voces, Verg; **2,** *to exhibit, display*, **a,** crudelitatem suam in aliquo, Cic; **b,** *to pronounce, set forth, state*, leges de religione, Cic; causas et ordinem belli, Liv; with rel sent, quanta vis sit (eius) eloquentiae expromere, Cic

expromptus -a um, partic of expromo

expugnābĭlis -e (expugno), *that may be besieged or captured*, urbs, Liv

expugnātĭo -ōnis, f (expugno), *the taking or capturing of any place by storm*, urbis, Caes; plur, expugnationes urbium, Cic

expugnātor -ōris, m (expugno), *a taker, capturer*, urbis, Cic; transf, pudicitiae, *violator*, Cic

expugno, 1 *to take, take by storm, capture, conquer, overcome* **A.** Lit, urbes, naves, Caes; urbem obsidione, Caes; tyrannos eius, non ipsam urbem, Liv; of things, fames obsessos expugnavit, *compelled to surrender*, Liv **B.** Transf, **a,** *to overcome, subdue*, animum, Cic; pertinaciam legatorum, Liv; **b,** *to destroy, violate*, quaestiones, *thwart*, Liv; pudicitiam, *violate*, Cic; **c,** *to force, compel*, legationem, Cic; with ut and the subj, *bring it about that*, etc, Cic; **d,** *to accomplish*, coepta, Ov

expulsĭo -ōnis, f (expello), *a driving out, expulsion*, Laenatis, Cic; plur, expulsiones vicinorum, Cic

expulso, 1 (intens of expello), *to drive out, drive back*, Mart

expulsor -ōris, m (expello), *one who drives out or expels*, iste homo acerrimus, bonorum possessor, expulsor, ereptor, Cic

expultrix -trīcis, f (expulsor), *one who expels*, philosophia expultrix vitiorum, Cic

expungo -punxi -punctum, 3 *to strike out, blot out, expunge*, Plaut.

expurgātĭo -ōnis, f (expurgo), *a vindication, justification*, Plaut.

expurgo, 1 *to cleanse, purify* **A.** Lit, quae poterunt umquam satis expurgare cicutae, Hor **B.** Transf, **a,** expurgandus est sermo, Cic; **b,** *to justify, defend*, dissimulandi causa aut sui expurgandi, Sall

expŭto, 1 *to comprehend*, ap Cic

exquaero = exquiro (q v)

Exquĭlĭae -ārum = Esquiliae (q v)

exquīro -quīsīvi -quīsītum, 3 (ex and quaero) **I.** *to seek out*, **1, a,** lit, antiquam matrem, Verg; iter per aliquem, Caes; **b,** transf, veritatem, verum, Cic; with rel sent, quid in omni genere vitae optimum et verissimum sit exquirere, Cic; **c,** *to ask, inquire*, exquirere palam pretia, Cic; a te nihil certi exquiro, Cic; ex aliquo causas alicuius rei, Cic; with rel sent, quid iis de quoque officii genere placeat exquirere, Cic; partic subst, **exquīsīta** -ōrum, n *inquiries*, Cic; **2,** *to choose, select*, verba ad (*according to*) sonum, Cic **II** *to search through* **A.** Lit, vescendi causā mari terraque omnia, Sall **B.** *to search, test*, facta alicuius ad antiquae religionis rationem, Cic **III.** *to ask for*, alicuius consilium, Cic

exquīsītē, adv with compar and superl (exquisitus), *accurately, carefully, admirably*, de eo crimine accurate et exquisite disputare, Cic

exquīsītus -a -um, p adj, with compar and superl (exquiro), **1,** *carefully sought, choice, exquisite, excellent, admirable*, sententiae, Cic; exquisitius dicendi genus, Cic; exquisitissimis verbis laudare, Cic; **2,** *artificial, far-fetched*, munditia exquisita nimis, Cic

exsăcrĭfĭco, 1 *to sacrifice*, ap Cic

exsaevĭo, 4 *to rage to an end, cease to rage*, dum reliquum tempestatis exsaeviret, Liv

exsanguis -e, *bloodless, without blood* **I.** Lit, umbrae, Verg **II.** Transf, **a,** *lifeless*, corpora mortuorum, Cic; **b,** *pale as a corpse, deathly pale*, Cic; color, Sall; **c,** *exhausted, weak*, Cic; of voice, speech, etc, Calvus exsanguis et aridus, Tac; **d,** act, *making pale*, cuminum, Hor

exsarcĭo (-sartūrus), 4 *to patch up, make good, repair*, Ter

exsătĭo, 1 *to satisfy thoroughly, satiate* **A.** Lit, vino ciboque, Liv **B.** Transf, morte alicuius exsatiari, Liv

exsătŭrābĭlis -e (exsaturo), *that can be satiated*, non exsaturabile pectus, Verg

exsătŭro, 1 *to satisfy, satiate* **A.** Lit, belua exsaturanda visceribus meis, Ov **B.** Transf, eius cruciatu atque supplicio pascere oculos animumque exsaturare, Cic

exscendo = escendo (q v)

exscensĭo = escensio (q v)

exscensus = escensus (q v)

exscindo -scidi -scissum, *to destroy utterly, raze to the ground*, Numantiam, Cic; of persons, *to destroy*, hostem, Tac

exscrĕo, 1 *to cough or hawk out*, totiens clausas ante fores, Ov

exscrībo -scripsi -scriptum, 3 **1,** *to copy*, litteras, Cic; **2,** *to note down, register*, ei sacra omnia exscripta exsignataque attribuit, Liv

exsculpo -sculpsi -sculptum, 3 **1,** *to scratch out, erase*, versus, Nep; **2,** *to cut out with a chisel, carve or scoop out*, aliquid e quercu, Cic

exsĕco -sĕcŭi -sectum, 1 *to cut out*, **1,** linguam, Cic; fig, vitiosas partes reipublicae, Cic; transf, quinas hic capiti mercedes exsecat, *deducts from the principal*, Hor; **2,** *to castrate*, Cic

exsĕcrābĭlis -e (exsecror), **1,** *deserving curses*, fortuna, Liv; **2,** *cursing, execrating*, carmen, Liv; hence, *deadly*, ira atque odium, Liv

exsĕcrātĭo -ōnis, f (exsecror), **1,** *a curse, execration*, Cic; **2,** *an oath containing an imprecation*, Cic

exsĕcrātus -a -um, p adj (from exsecror), *cursed, execrated*, exsecratus populo Romano, Cic

exsĕcror, 1 dep (ex and sacer) *to curse, execrate*, **1, a,** aliquem, Cic; consilia Catilinae, Sall; **b,** *to utter a curse*, in caput alicuius, Liv; exsecratur primum ut naufragio pereat, Cic; **2,** *to swear with an imprecation*, haec exsecrata civitas, Hor

exsectĭo -ōnis, f (exseco), *a cutting out*, linguae, Cic

exsĕcūtĭo -ōnis, f (exsequor), *performance, accomplishment*, negotii, Tac; exsecutio Syriae, *administration of*, Tac

exsĕquĭae -ārum, f (exsequor), *a funeral procession*, justa exsequiarum, *ceremonies of*, Cic; exsequias alicuius funeris prosequi, Cic; exsequias celebrare, Liv

exsĕquĭālis -e (exsequiae), *relating or belonging to a funeral procession*, carmina, Ov

exsĕquor -sĕcūtus sum, 3 dep **I.** *to follow a corpse to the grave*, Cic poet **II. A.** *to follow*, suam quisque spem sua consilia, communibus deploratis, exsequentes, Liv. **B. 1,** *to accomplish, execute;* **a,** mandata vestra, Cic.; officia, Cic.; **b,** *to assert, maintain;* jus suum armis, Caes.; **2,** *to follow revengefully, to avenge, punish;* jura violata, dolorem, Liv.; rem tam atrocem, Liv.; **3,** *to relate, describe, explain;* ea vix verbis exsequi posse, Cic.; viam consili, scelerati, Liv.; alicuius or alicuius rei laudes, *to spread abroad,* Liv.; with rel. sent., exsequebatur inde, quae sollemnis derivatio esset, Liv.; **4,** *to prosecute, carry out;* aliquid usque ad extremum, Cic.; **5,** *to ascertain, find out,* Liv.; **6,** *to suffer, endure;* cladem illam fugamque, Cic.

exsĕro -sĕrŭi -sertum, 3. **I.** Lit., **a,** *to stretch out, thrust out;* linguam, Liv.; caput ponto, Ov.; **b,** *to bare;* brachia, Ov.; Amazon unum exserta latus pugnae, Verg. **II.** Transf., *to free;* se aere alieno, Cic. (?)

exserto, 1. (intens. of exsero), *to stretch out;* ora, Verg.

exsertus -a -um, partic. of exsero.

exsībĭlo, 1. *to hiss an actor off the stage,* Cic.

exsiccātus -a -um, p. adj. (from exsicco), *dry, jejune;* genus orationis, Cic.

exsicco, 1. **1,** *to dry thoroughly;* arbores, Cic.; **2,** *to drain dry, to empty* by drinking; vina culullis, Hor.

exsigno, 1. *to put a mark upon, mark;* sacra omnia exscripta exsignataque, Liv.

exsĭlĭo -sĭlŭi -sultum, 4. (ex and salio), **1,** *to leap out, spring out;* in siccum (of a snake), Verg.; oculi exsiluere, Ov.; **2,** *to leap up, spring up;* de sella, Cic.; gaudio, *for joy,* Cic.; exsiluere loco silvae, Ov.

exsĭlĭum -ĭi, n. (exsul), **1,** lit., *banishment, exile;* exsilii poena, Cic.; aliquem exsilio afficere or multare, Cic.; in exsilium ire or pergere, Cic.; aliquem in exsilium mittere, Liv.; aliquem in exsilium ejicere or pellere, Cic., or agere, Liv.; aliquem reducere de exsilio, Cic.; **2,** meton., **a,** *the place of exile,* Cic.; **b,** exsilia = exules, plenum exsiliis mare, Tac.

exsisto (existo) -stĭti -stĭtum, 3. *to arise, come forth, appear.* **I.** ab ara, Cic.; of soldiers, *to start up;* e latebris, Liv.; of things, ab aede Junonis ex arce (of a voice), Cic. **II.** *to spring, arise, come into existence.* **A.** Lit., ex stirpe quadam, Cic.; in statuae capite, Cic. **B.** Transf., ut tyranni existerent, Cic.; exsistit motus, Caes.; ex luxuria existit avaritia, Cic.; with predic. nomin., ego huic causae patronus exstiti, Cic.; with ut and the subj. (of logical consequence), ex quo existet, ut de nihilo quippiam fiat, Cic.; with acc. and infin., exsistit illud, multa esse probabilia quae, etc., Cic.

exsolvo -solvi -sŏlūtum, 3. **I.** *to loosen, unloose, untie, unbind.* **A.** Lit., glaciem, *to dissolve,* Lucr.; fig., nodum huius erroris, Liv. **B.** Transf., exsoluti plerique legis nexus, Tac.; famem, *drive away,* Ov. **II.** *to set free, release.* **A.** Lit., se corpore, Verg. **B.** Transf., **1,** *to free;* plebem aere alieno, Liv.; se occupationibus, Cic.; **2,** **a,** *to pay;* nomina, Cic.; stipendium praeteritum cum fide, Tac.; **b,** *to discharge, to fulfil an engagement, perform a promise or something due;* quod promiserat, Cic.; jurandum, Liv.; poenas morte, Tac.

exsomnis -e (ex and somnus), *sleepless, wakeful,* Verg.

exsorbĕo -sorbŭi, 2. *to suck up, suck in.* **A.** Lit., sanguinem, Cic.; gustaras civilem sanguinem vel potius exsorbueras, Cic. **B.** Transf., **a,** *to endure;* multorum difficultatem, Cic.; **b,** *to swallow up, devour;* quantas iste Byzantiorum praedas exsorbuit, Cic.

exsors -sortis, *without lot;* **1,** *that for which no lot has been cast, specially chosen;* ducunt exsortem Aeneae (equum), Verg.; **2,** *having no share in, deprived of;* with genit., dulcis vitae, Verg.; amicitiae, Liv.

exspătĭor, 1. dep., *to digress from the path, deviate from the course;* exspatiantur equi, Ov.; of rivers, exspatiata ruunt per apertos flumina campos, Ov.

exspectābĭlis -e (exspecto), *that which is expected, probable,* Tac.

exspectātĭo -ōnis, f. (exspecto), *a waiting for, looking for, expectation;* with subj. genit., exspectatione hominum majore quam spe, Liv.; with obj. genit., exspectationem sui facere or concitare, Cic.; with de, quantum tu mihi moves exspectationem de sermone Bibuli, Cic.; with rel. sent., summa omnium exspectatio, quidnam sententiae ferrent judices, Cic.; absol., obscurā spe et caecā exspectatione pendere, Cic.

exspectātus -a -um, p. adj. with compar. and superl. (exspecto), *expected, wished for, welcome;* carus omnibus exspectatusque venies, Cic.; exspectati ad amplissimam dignitatem, *expected to arrive at the highest rank,* Cic.; litterae exspectatae, Cic.

exspecto, 1. *to wait for, look for, expect.* **I. 1,** gen., transitum tempestatis, Cic.; partic. perf. subst., ante exspectatum, *before it was expected,* Verg., Ov.; with rel. sent., exspecto quid tribunus plebis excogitet, Cic.; exspectare quam mox, etc., Cic.; with dum, exspectas fortasse dum dicat, Cic.; with quoad, Nep.; with si, Caes.; with ut and the subj., nisi forte exspectatis ut illa diluam, Cic.; non exspectare foll. by quin, Caes.; absol., *to wait, loiter;* ad portam, Cic.; **2,** esp., **a,** *to wait for a person or thing* (till it is ready or finished); oratores multas horas, Cic.; **b,** *to await;* me tranquilla senectus exspectat, Hor. **II.** *to wait with longing, fear, hope, desire,* etc., *to hope for, long, dread;* testamenta, Cic.; aliquid ab or ex with abl., a te hoc civitas vel potius omnes cives non exspectant solum sed etiam postulant, Cic.; with acc. and infin., quum exspectaret effusos omnibus portis Aetolos in fidem suam venturos (esse), Liv.

exspergo (ex-spargo), -spersum, 3. *to scatter,* Lucr.

exspes, adj. (only in nom. sing.), *without hope, hopeless;* errat inops, exspes, Ov.; with genit., exspes vitae, Tac.

exspīrātĭo -ōnis, f. (exspiro), *an exhalation;* terrae, Cic.

exspīro, 1. **I.** Transit., *to breathe out, exhale;* **a,** flammas pectore, Verg.; **b,** of the dying, animas, auras, Verg. **II.** Intransit., **1,** *to give up the ghost, to die;* in pugna et in acie, Liv.; fig., quid? si ego morerer, mecum exspiratura respublica erat, Liv.; **2,** *to blow forth, rush forth;* vis ventorum exspirare cupiens, Ov.

exspŏlĭo, 1. *to plunder, rob, despoil;* fana atque domos, Sall.; exercitu et provinciā Pompeium, Cic.

exspŭo -spŭi -spūtum, 3. *to spit out;* transf., *to get rid of, cast away;* hamum (of fishes), Ov.; rationem ex animo, Lucr.

exsterno, 1. *to frighten, terrify,* Ov., Cat.

exstillo, 1. *to drop moisture, drip, trickle,* Plaut., Ter.

exstĭmŭlātor -ōris, m. (exstimulo), *an inciter, instigator;* rebellionis, Tac.

exstĭmŭlo, 1. *to goad, to excite, instigate;* virum dictis, Ov.

extinctĭo -ōnis, f. (exstinguo), *annihilation, extinction,* Cic.

exstinctor -ōris, m. (exstinguo), **1,** *one who*

extinguishes, incendii, Cic, **2,** *one who destroys, annihilates*, patriae, Cic

exstinguo -stinxi -stinctum, 3 **I.** Lit, *to put out, extinguish*; incendium, Cic, middle, exstingui, *to go out*, consumptus ignis exstinguitur, Cic **II.** Transf, **1,** *to dry up*, aquam rivis, Liv **2,** *to quench*, sitim, Ov, **3,** *to kill*, invictum bello juvenem fortuna morbo exstinxit, Liv, middle, exstingui, *to die*, esp suddenly or prematurely, Cic, **4,** *to abolish, destroy, annihilate*, exstincto senatu, Cic, gratiam alicuius, Cic, esp, *to blot out the memory of something, to bring into oblivion*; memoriam publicam, crimina sua, Cic, middle, exstingui, *to be forgotten*, rumor exstinguitur, Cic (syncop pluperf, exstinxem, for exstinxissem, Verg)

exstirpo, 1 (ex and stirps) *to tear up by the root*, transf, *to root out, extirpate*, vitia, Cic, humanitatem ex animo, Cic

exsto (exto), 1 *to stand out, project* **I.** Lit, milites capite solo ex aqua exstant, Caes, quo altius ab aqua exstaret, Liv **II.** Transf, **A.** Gen, quo magis id quod erit illuminatum exstare atque eminere videatur, Cic **B. 1,** *to be visible, show itself, appear, exist*, exstant huius fortitudinis vestigia, Cic, exstat, impers with acc and infin, Cic, apparet atque exstat, utrum an, etc, Cic; **2,** *to be still in existence, to be extant*, exstant epistolae Philippi, Cic, non exstat alius, Liv.

exstructio -ōnis, f (exstruo), *a building up, erection*, ea exstructio quae, etc., Cic., plur, exstructiones tectorum, Cic

exstrŭo -struxi -structum, 3 *to heap up, pile up* **I.** Lit, rogum, Cic, magnum acervum librorum Dicaearchi sibi ante pedes, Cic, divitias in altum, Hor, focum lignis, Hor, mensae conquisitissimis epulis exstruebantur, Cic, mensae exstructae, *piled up with food*, Cic **II.** Transf, exstrue animo altitudinem excellentiamque virtutum, *build up*, Cic, accurate non modo fundata, verum etiam exstructa disciplina, Cic

exsuctus a -um, partic of exsugo

exsūdo, 1. **I.** Intransit, *to come out in sweat, exude*, inutilis humor, Verg **II.** Transit, *to sweat out* **A.** Lit, Plin **B.** Transf, *to sweat through, toil through, perform with great labour*, novum de integro laborem, Liv, certamen ingens, Liv

exsūgo -suxi -suctum, *to suck out, suck up*, ostrea vacuis exsucta medullis, Juv

exsul -sŭlis, c (from ex and the root of salio, cf con-sul, prae sul) **A.** *a banished or exiled person, an exile*, quum vagus et exsul erraret, Cic; exsules reducuntur, Cic, num qui exsules restituti, Cic.; with genit, patriae, Hor, with abl, exsul patriā, domo, Sall **B.** Transf, *deprived of*, with genit, exsul mentisque domusque, Ov.

exsŭlo (exŭlo), 1 (exsul), *to be banished, live in exile* **A.** Lit, Romae, *at Rome*, Cic, apud Prusiam, Cic, in Volscos exsulatum abire, Liv, aptis simus ad exsulandum locus, Cic **B.** Transf, meo discessu exsulasse rempublicam, Cic

exsultātio -ōnis, f (exsulto), *a leaping up* **I.** Lit, Plin **II.** Transf, *exultation, excessive rejoicing*, illa exsultatio Athamantis, Cic

exsultim, adv (exsilio) *friskingly*, Hor

exsulto (exulto), 1 (freq of exsilio), *to leap up frequently or violently* **I.** Lit., **a,** of living subjects, equi ferocitate exsultantes, Cic; in numerum, *to dance*, Lucr, medias inter caedes exsultat Amazon, Verg, **b,** of things, vada exsultant, *dash up*, Verg **II.** Transf, **A.** appetitus quasi exsultantes sive cupiendo sive fugiendo, Cic **B.** Esp **1,** *to rejoice exceedingly, triumph*, laetitiā or gaudio, Cic, in ruinis alterius, Cic, Graeci exsultant quod, etc, Cic, **2, a,** of orators and of discourse, *to run riot*, audacius, Cic, verborum audaciā exsultans, Cic, **b,** of discourse, *to move freely*, campus in quo exsultare possit oratio, Cic

exsŭpĕrābĭlis -e (exsupero), *that can be conquered or overcome*, non exsuperabile saxum (of Sisyphus), Verg

exsŭpĕrantĭa -ae, f (exsupero), *superiority, pre eminence*, virtutis, Cic

exsŭpĕro, 1 **I.** Intransit, **A.** Lit, *to mount up, appear above*, flammae, Verg **B.** Transf, **1,** *to be prominent, excel*, quantum feroci virtute exsuperas, Verg, **2,** in battle, *to get the upper hand, prevail*; si non poterunt exsuperare, cadant, Ov **II.** Transf, *to surmount something* **A.** Lit, **1,** *to surmount a height, to pass over or beyond*, jugum, Verg, an jam omnes angustiae exsuperatae, Liv, **2,** *to project above* angues exsuperant undas, Verg **B.** Transf, **1, a,** *to exceed*, magnitudo sceleris omnium ingenia exsuperat, *surpasses all thought*, Sall, **b,** *to surpass, go beyond*, omnes Tarquinios superbiā, Liv, **2,** *to overcome*, consilium caecum, Verg

exsurdo, 1 (ex and surdus), *to deafen* **I.** Lit, Plin **II.** Transf, of taste, *to make dull or blunt*, palatum, Hor

exsurgo -surrexi -surrectum, 3 *to rise up, lift oneself up, stand up* **I** Lit, **1,** of persons, quum exsurgeret, simul arridens, etc, Cic, exsurgit facem attollens, Verg; esp, *to raise oneself to one's full height to give force to a blow*, altior exsurgens, Verg, **2,** of things (Romam) tota simul exsurgere aedificiis, Liv **II.** Transf, **1,** *to rise up, to regain strength*, exsurgere atque erigere se, Cic, auctoritate vestrā respublica exsurget, Cic; **2,** of political risings, invidiā eorum exsurgere rursus plebem, Liv

exsuscĭto, 1. **I.** Lit, **a,** *to awaken from sleep*, te (juris consultum) gallorum, illum (imperatorem) bucinarum cantus exsuscitat, Cic; **b,** *to kindle fire*, flammam aurā, Ov **II.** Transf, *to excite, arouse*, quae cura etiam exsuscitat animos, Cic, se exsuscitare, *to arouse oneself, make an effort*, Cic

exta -ōrum, n *the entrails of animals*, esp, *the heart, lungs, liver*, etc, used by the Romans for divination, exta inspicere, Cic, si est in extis aliqua vis, quae declaret futura, Cic

extābesco -tābŭi, 3 *to waste away entirely* **A.** Lit, corpus macie extabuit, ap Cic **B.** Transf, *to vanish, disappear*, opiniones vetustate extabuisse, Cic

extemplo, adv (ex and templum), *immediately, directly, straightway*, Cic

extempŏrālis -e (ex and tempus), *extemporary, without preconsideration*, oratio, actio, Quint

extempŭlo = extemplo (q v)

extendo -tendi -tensum and -tentum, 3 *to stretch out, expand, extend* **I.** Lit **A. a,** brachium, Cic, extentum funem, *tight rope*, Hor, rigidā cervice et extento capite currere (of horses), Liv, milit t t, *to extend in order of battle*, aciem in radicibus montis, Liv, **b,** of time, *to extend, prolong*, ab hora tertia ad noctem pugnam, Liv, middle, *to last*, tamquam non longius, quam vitae humanae spatium est, cupiditas gloriae extenditur, Liv **B. 1,** *to stretch on the ground*, aliquem arenā, Verg, toto ingens extenditur (Cerberus) antro, *is stretched*, Verg, **2,** *to increase*, agros, Hor **II.** Transf, **1,** *to exert*, se supra vires, Liv, itinera, *to march at great speed*, Liv, avidos cursus, *to hasten eagerly*, Verg, **2,** *to extend*, nomen in ultimas oras,

Hor.; in Asiam quoque cognitionem, Liv.; famam factis, *to spread abroad*, Verg.

extento, 1. (intens. of extendo), *to stretch out, to extend*; nervos, Lucr.

extentus a -um, p. adj. with superl. (from extendo), *extended, wide*; stagna latius extenta Lucrino lacu, Hor.; castra quam extentissimā potest valle locat, Liv.

extěnŭātio -ōnis, f. (extenuo). **I.** *a making thin*, Plin. **II.** Rhet. t. t., a figure of speech, *a diminution, lessening* (Gr. μείωσις, opp. exaggeratio), Cic.

extěnŭātus -a -um, p. adj. (from extenuo), *weak, poor, slight*; vestigia, Cat.; copiolae extenuatissimae, ap. Cic.

extěnŭo, 1. *to make thin* or *small, to reduce, diminish*. **I.** Lit., **1,** aër extenuatus, *rarefied*, Cic.; dentibus extenuatur et molitur cibus, Cic.; extenuari in aquas, *dissolves into*, Ov.; **2,** milit. t. t., *to extend a line* or *column, make thin*; angustiae extenuabant agmen, Liv.; extenuatā suorum acie, Sall. **II.** Transf., **1,** *to lessen, weaken, diminish*; sumptus, Cic.; spem, crimen, Cic.; **2,** in speech, etc., *to disparage, depreciate*; suum munus, Cic.; famam belli, Liv.

exter and **extěrus** -a -um (from ex), *outward, foreign, strange*. **I.** Posit., jus nationum exterarum, Cic. **II.** Compar., **extěrĭor,** n. -ius, genit. -ōris; orbis, Cic.; hostis, Cic.; exteriorem ire alicui, *to go on the left side*, Hor. **III.** Superl. **A. extrēmus** -a -um, *the outermost*; **1,** lit., subst., **extrēmum** -i, n., **a,** *that which is outermost*; caelum quod extremum atque ultimum mundi est, Cic.; **b,** *the outermost, last*; pars, Cic.; vitae dies, Cic. Subst., **extrēmum** -i. n., *the end*; extremum habet, *has an end*, Cic.; aestatis, Sall.; *the end of life, death*, Verg.; ad extremum, adv., *to the end*; ad extremum reservatus, Cic.; *at the end*, Cic.; *entirely*; ad extremum perditus, Liv.; extremum, adv., *at the end*, Ov.; *for the last time*; extremum affari or alloqui aliquem, Verg.; extremo, *at the end*, Nep.; in extremo, *at the end of a letter*, Cic.; plur., **extrēma** -orum, n. *the end*; agri, Cic.; **2,** transf., **a,** *extreme*—i.e., only used in the greatest need; senatus consultum, Caes.; **b,** *extreme, greatest, most dangerous, most difficult*; tempora, *extreme need*, Cic.; extremum bonorum, malorum, *the highest good, evil*, Cic.; neut. subst., vitam ipsam in extremum adductam, Tac.; extrema pati, *the worst extremities*, Verg.; with genit., quotiens in extrema periculorum ventum, Liv.; **c,** *the lowest, worst*; haud Ligurum extremus, Verg.; extremi ingenii (*of the lowest understanding*) est qui, etc., Liv. **B. extīmus** -a -um, *the outermost*; orbis, Cic.

extěrěbro, 1. *to bore out, extract by boring*; ex eo auro, quod exterebratum esset, Cic.

extergěo -tersi -tersum, 2. *to wipe off, wipe dry*; transf., *to strip clean, plunder*; fanum quod non eversum atque extersum reliqueris, Cic.

extěrĭor, exterius, v. exter.

extermĭno, 1. (ex and terminus), *to drive beyond the boundaries*; hence, **1,** *to drive out, expel, banish*; aliquem ex urbe, Cic.; or urbe, Cic.; de civitate, Cic.; **2,** *to put aside, remove*; auctoritatem senatus e civitate, Cic.

externus -a -um (exter). **I.** *that which is outside, external*; tepor, Cic. Subst., **externa** -ōrum, n. *outward appearances*, Cic. **II.** *foreign, strange*; hostis, Cic.; amor (*of a foreigner*), Ov.; timor, terror (*of a foreign enemy*), Liv. Subst., **a, externus** -i, m. *a foreigner*, Liv.; *a stranger*; canum odium in externos, Cic.; **b, externa** -ōrum, n. *that which is foreign* or *strange*; externa (*foreign examples*) libentius in tali re quam domestica recordor. Cic.

extěro -trīvi -trītum, 3. *to rub out, rub off*, Lucr.

exterrěo -terrŭi -territum, 2. *to frighten suddenly, to terrify*; periculo suo aliquem, ut, etc., Liv.; in pass., praeter modum exterreri, Cic.; partic., exterritus aspectu, Cic.; of things, exterritus amnis, Verg.

extěrus, v. exter.

extĭmesco -timŭi, 3. **I.** Intransit., *to be greatly afraid, to be terrified*; de fortunis communibus extimescere, Cic.; foll. by ne and the subj., Cic. **II.** Transit., *to be greatly afraid of, to dread*; with acc. of the thing, adventum tuum, Cic.; with ne and the subj., unum illud extimescebam ne quid turpiter facerem, Cic.; with acc. of the person, victorem orbis terrarum, Cic.

extĭmus, v. exter.

extispex -spĭcis, m. (exta and *specio), *a soothsayer who predicts from the entrails of victims*, Cic.

extollo, extŭli, and rarely exsustŭli, 3. *to lift up, raise up*. **I.** Lit., cruentum pugionem, Cic. **II.** Transf., **1,** extollere animum or aliquem, *to raise, elevate, exalt*; extollere animos, *to become insolent*, Cic.; se extollere, Cic.; aliquem secundā oratione, Sall.; **2,** in words, *to raise*; aliquid verbis in majus, *to exaggerate*, Liv.; *to praise, celebrate, extol*; fortunam alicuius, Cic.; aliquem ad caelum, Cic.; **3,** *to adorn*; hortos a Lucullo coeptos insigni magnificentiā extollere, Tac.; **4,** *to raise to rank, power*, etc.; jacentem, Cic.

extorquěo -torsi -tortum, 2. *to twist out, wrest away, wrench out*. **I.** Gen., **A.** Lit., arma e manibus civium, Cic.; alicui sicam de manibus, Cic. **B.** Transf., *to obtain by force, extort*; a Caesare per Herodem talenta Attica L, Cic.; alicui veritatem, errorem, Cic.; ex animis cognitiones verborum, Cic.; with ut and the subj., extorsisti ut faterer, Cic. **II.** Esp., *to dislocate, put out of joint*; prava extortaque puella, *deformed*, Juv.; *to torture*, Liv.

extorris -e (ex and terra), *driven from the country, exiled, banished*; huic CXXXII patres familias extorres profugerunt, Cic.; with abl., agro Romano, Liv.; patriā, Sall.

extrā (= exterā sc. parte, from exter). **I.** Adv., **A.** Lit., *outside* (opp. intus); quae extra sunt, Cic.; quum extra et intus hostem haberent, Caes.; compar., exterius sitae (urbes), Ov. **B.** Transf., *except*; extra quam, extra quam si, *except, unless*, Cic. **II.** Prep. with acc., **A.** Lit., *beyond, outside of, without*; provinciam, Caes. **B. a,** *except, with the exception of*; extra ducem, Cic.; **b,** *beyond, outside*; extra modum, Cic.; extra ordinem, Cic.; **c,** *without*; extra jocum, *joking apart*, Cic.; esse extra culpam, Cic.

extrăho -traxi -tractum, 3. **I.** *to draw out, extract*. **A.** Lit., telum e corpore, Cic.; telum de vulnere, Ov.; vivum puerum alvo, Hor.; velut ab inferis extractus, Liv. **B.** Transf., **a,** *to extricate, free*; urbem ex periculis, Cic.; **b,** *to destroy, root out*; religionem ex animis, Cic. **II.** *to draw forth*; **1,** lit., aliquem turbā oppositis humeris, Hor.; aliquem vi in publicum, Liv.; aliquem domo, Cic.; milit. t. t., hostes invitos in aciem, Liv.; **2, a,** *to bring to light*; scelera in lucem, Liv.; **b,** *to bring out*; aliquem ad honorem, Liv. **III.** Of time, **1,** *to prolong, delay, protract*; res variis calumniis, Cic.; certamen usque ad noctem, Liv.; aliquem, *to put off*, Liv.; **2,** *to waste*; aestatem sine ullo effectu, Liv.

extrānĕus -a -um (extra), *that which is outside*. **I.** *not belonging to a thing* or *subject, extraneous*; res extraneae, Cic.; ornamenta, Cic. **II.** *not belonging to a house, family, or country*, *foreign, strange*, exercitatio forensis et extranea, Cic Subst, **extrānĕus** -i, m *a foreigner, stranger*, si extraneus deest, domi hostem quaerunt, Liv

extrā-ordĭnārĭus -a -um, *extraordinary, anomalous, irregular*, petitio consulatus, Cic, pecunia, *obtained by gift, legacy*, etc, Cic, cupiditates, *unnatural*, Cic, imperium, Cic, milit t t, equites, cohortes, or simply extra-ordinarii, *picked troops of the auxiliary forces*, Liv, porta, (= praetoria, near which the extra-ordinarii had their tents), Liv

extrārĭus -a -um (extra), 1, *outward, external, extrinsic*, utilitas aut in corpore posita est aut in extrariis rebus, Cic, 2, *strange, foreign* Subst, **extrārĭus** -i, m *a stranger*, Ter

extrēmĭtas -ātis, f (extremus), *the end, farthest portion, extremity*, mundi, Cic

extrēmus a -um v exter

extrīco, 1 (ex and tricor), *to disentangle, extricate* **A.** Lit, cervam plagis, Hor **B.** Transf, *to procure with difficulty*, nummos Hor

extrinsĕcŭs, adv. (extra and secus), **1**, *from without, from the outside*, Cic, **2**, *on the outside, outwardly*, columna extrinsecus inaurata, Cic

extrūdo -trūsi -trūsum, 3 *to push out, thrust out, extrude*, **a**, of persons, te in viam, Cic extrudi a senatu in Macedoniam, Cic, **b**, of things, mare aggere, *to dam out*, Caes

extundo -tŭdi, 3 **I.** *to beat out* **A.** Lit, *to form by beating with a hammer*, lapsa ancilia caelo extuderat, Verg **B.** *to invent, devise*, alicui artem, Verg **II.** *to beat out, force*, transf, *to drive away*, quum labor extuderit fastidia, Hor

exturbo, 1 *to drive away, thrust out* **A** Lit, homines e possessionibus, Cic, aliquem provinciā, Cic, aliquem e fortunis omnibus, Cic **B.** Transf, omnem spem pacis, Liv, mentem alicuius, *to put out of countenance*, Cic

exūbĕro, 1 **A.** Lit, of fluids, *to overflow*, alte spumis exuberat umbra, Verg **B.** Transf, *to abound*, si luxuriā foliorum exuberat amnis, Verg, pomis exuberat annus, Verg, tam lato te fenore exuberat, Tac

exul, v exsul

exulcĕro, 1 **I.** *to make sore* Plin **II.** Transf, **1**, *to make worse, aggravate*, ea quae sanare nequeunt, exulcerant, Cic, **2**, *to irritate, embitter*, ut in exulcerato animo facile fictum crimen insideret, Cic

exŭlŭlo, 1 *to howl out, howl loudly*, Ov, **exŭlŭlātus** -a -um, **a**, *having howled*, Ov **b**, *invoked with howlings*; mater Cybeleia, Ov.

exundo, 1 **1**, *to overflow, to flow out* or *over*, tura balsamaque vi tempestatum in adversa litora exundant, Tac, **2**, *to overflow, abound*, largus et exundans ingenii fons, Juv

exungo -unctus and **exungor** ungi, 3 *to anoint, besmear with unguents*, Plaut

exŭo -ŭi -ūtum, 3. (connected with ind—uo) **I.** *to draw out* or *off, to take out* **A.** se jugo, Liv; unum exuta pedem vinclis, Verg, se ex his laqueis, Cic **B.** Transf, **a**, hominem ex homine, *deprive of all human feeling*, Cic, mihi ex animo exui non potest esse deos, *I cannot but believe*, etc., Cic, **b**, *to deprive*; aliquem agro paterno, Liv.; milit. t t, *to strip an enemy of*, hostem impedimentis, castris, armis, praeda, Caes, Liv **II.** *to lay aside, put off, take off* **A.** Lit, ensem or pharetram, Verg, Ov **B.** Transf, **a**, *to lay aside*, torvam faciem, Verg, hominem, *human shape*, Ov, **b**, *to lay aside, remove, divest oneself of*, humanitatem omnem, Cic, servitutem muliebrem, Liv, magistros, *get rid of*, Tac

exūro -ussi -ustum 3 **I.** *to burn out*, aliis scelus exuritur igni, Verg **II.** *to burn up, consume entirely*, aliquem vivum, Cic, classem, Verg, exustus ager, *dried up*, Verg **III.** *to burn* **1**, sol graciles exurit artus, Tib, **2**, of thirst, *to burn*, sitis exurit miseros, Lucr, exustus flos siti veteris ubertatis exaruit Cic, **3**, *to heat*, **a**, antra positis exusta caminis, Ov, **b**, *to inflame with love*, Tib

exustĭo ōnis, f (exuro), *a burning up, conflagration*, terrarum, Cic

exŭvĭae -ārum, f (exuo), *that which is taken off from the body* **I.** Of men, **a**, *dress*, has enim exuvias mihi perfidus ille reliquit, Verg, **b**, *spoils taken from the enemy, arms*, etc, nauticae, Cic, tu ornatus exuviis huius, Cic **II.** Of animals, **a**, *the skin* or *slough which is laid aside* (naturally); exuvias ponere, Verg, **b**, *the skin captured and taken off, the hide*, leonis, Verg

F.

F, f, the sixth letter of the Latin Alphabet, corresponding in form with the Aeolic digamma (ϝ), though in sound most nearly represented by Φ, φ For the meaning of this letter when used as an abbreviation, see Table of Abbreviations

făba -ae, f. *a bean*, Cic; prov, isthaec in me cudetur faba, *I shall have to suffer for this*, Ter

făbālis -e (faba), *of* or *relating to beans*, stipulae, Ov

Făbăris -is, m, *a tributary of the Tiber in the Sabine country*, also called Farfarus, now *Farfa*

fābella -ae, f (dim of fabula) **I.** *a little story, little narrative*, fabellarum auditione duci, Cic **II.** Esp, **a**, *a fable*, Hor, **b**, *a little drama*, Cic

1 **făber** -bri, m (perhaps shortened for facier from facio), **1**, *a worker*, esp *in any hard material* tignarius, *a carpenter*, Cic, in the army, fabri, *the engineers*, Caes., praefectus fabrum, *commander of the engineers*, Caes, **2**, *a fish*, perhaps *the dory* Ov

2 **făber** -bra -brum, *ingenious, skilful*, ars, Ov

Făbĭus -a -um, *name of a Roman gens, of which the most famous were* **1**, Numerius Fabius Pictor, *Roman annalist at the beginning of the Second Punic war*, **2**, Qu Fabius Maximus Cunctator, *the opponent of Hannibal in the Second Punic war*, **3**, Qu Fabius Maximus Aemilianus, *son of L Aemilius Paullus, consul* 144 B C, **4**, Qu Fabius Maximus Allobrogicus, *son of the preceding, conqueror of the Allobroges, builder of a triumphal arch on the sacra via* (called fornix Fabii, fornix Fabius, fornix Fabianus, Cic), **5**, Servius Fabius Pictor, *celebrated lawyer, praetor* 145 B C Adj, **Fabius** a -um, *Fabian* Hence, **Făbĭānus** -a -um, *of* or *belonging to Fabius*

Fabrātĕrĭa ae, f *town of the Volsci on the river Trerus* Hence, **Fabrāternus** -a -um, *of* or *belonging to Fabrateria*

făbrē, adv (2 faber), *skilfully*, Plaut

făbrēfăcĭo -fēci -factum, 3 *to make* or *fashion skilfully*, ex aere multa fabrefacta, Liv.

făbrĭca ae, f (faber) **I.** (sc ars), *the art of a faber*, pictura et fabrica *architecture*, Cic **II.** *the work of a faber, working, making*, fabrica aeris et ferri, Cic. **III.** (sc. officina), *the workshop of a* faber, Cic.

făbrĭcātĭo -ōnis, f. (fabrico), **1,** *making, framing, construction;* hominis, Cic.; **2,** *artifice, device;* ne illa quidem traductio in verbo quandam fabricationem habet, Cic.

făbrĭcātor -ōris, m. (fabrico), *a maker, artificer, framer;* tanti operis, Cic.; ipse doli fabricator Epēos, Verg.

Făbrĭcĭus -a -um, *name of a Roman gens of which the most distinguished was* C. Fabricius, *consul 282 and 278 B.C., conqueror of Pyrrhus and the Samnites, famed for the simplicity of his life and the rigour of his censorship.* Adj., *Fabrician;* pons, *a bridge in Rome.* Hence, **Făbrĭcĭānus** -a -um, *of* or *belonging to Fabricius.*

făbrĭco, 1. (faber), *to form, make, forge out of hard materials;* arma, Hor.; pocula fago fabricata, Ov.

făbrĭcor, 1. dep. (faber), **1,** *to frame, make, forge out of a hard material;* gladium, fulmen, signa, Cic.; Capitolii fastigium, Cic.; **2,** *to fashion, form;* hominem, Cic.; verba, *invent new words,* Cic.

făbrīlis -e (faber), *relating or belonging to an artificer;* erratum, Cic.; scalprum, Liv.; [illegible], Verg.; neut. plur. subst., **făbrīlĭa** -ium, n., *tools,* Hor.

fābŭla -ae, f. (fari). **I,** *talk;* fabulam fieri or esse, *to be the common talk,* Cic.; *conversation;* fabulae conviviales, Tac. **II.** *a tale, narrative, story, fable.* **A.** Gen., 1, lit., fabula tantum sine auctore edita, Liv.; **2,** transf., fabulae manes, *the empty shades,* Hor. **B.** Esp., *the plot, story, of a drama,* Hor.; *a drama;* in iis quae ad scenam componuntur fabulis, Cic.

fābŭlor, 1. dep. (fabula), *to talk, converse, chatter;* quid Ser. Galba fabuletur, Liv.

fābŭlōsus -a -um (fabula), *renowned in story, fabled;* Hydaspes, Hor.; palumbes, Hor.

făcesso, făcessi, 3. (intens. of facio). **I.** Transit., *to do eagerly, perform, fulfil, accomplish;* jussa, Verg.; negotium, *to give trouble to,* Cic.; alieni periculum, Cic. **II.** Intransit., *to be off, go away, depart;* ab omni societate, reipublicae, Cic.; ex urbe, Liv.; urbe finibusque, Liv.

făcētē, adv. (facetus), *wittily, humorously;* si (contumelia) facetius jactatur, urbanitas dicitur, Cic.

făcētĭa -ae, f. (facetus). **I.** Sing., *wit,* Plaut. **II.** Plur., *wit, facetiousness, drollery, humour;* Scipio omnes sale facetiisque superabat, Cic.

făcētus -a -um (root FA, Skr. bha, Gk. φα, *shine,* whence also facies), **1,** *fine, elegant;* orator, Cic.; sermo, Cic.; **2,** *witty, facetious,* Cic.

făcĭes -ēi, f. (root FA). **I.** Abstr., **1,** *the external form* or *figure;* **a,** of persons, quem ne de facie quidem nosti, Cic.; **b,** of things, ceterum facies totius negotii varia, incerta, foeda atque miserabilis, Sall.; **2,** esp., **a,** *manner, kind;* in faciem hederae (*after the fashion of*), frondescere, Ov.; non una pugnae facies, Tac.; **b,** *beautiful exterior, beauty;* Tyndaridis, Verg. **II.** Concr., **1,** *figure, form;* Homeri, Cic.; se in omnes facies vertere, Verg.; **2,** *the face, countenance,* Cic.

făcĭlĕ, adv. (facilis). **I.** *easily, without difficulty;* **1,** gen., haec facile ediscere, Cic.; **2,** esp., *easily, indisputably, certainly;* facile primus, facile princeps, *indisputably first,* Cic.; facile doctissimus, Cic.; non facile or haud facile, *not easily, hardly,* Cic. **II.** *willingly;* pati, Cic.; facillime audiri, Cic.

făcĭlis -e (facio). **I.** Pass., **1,** *that which is easy to be done, easy;* ascensus, Caes.; aditus, Cic.; with ad and the acc., faciles ad receptum angustiae, Liv.; esp. with gerund, illud autem facile ad credendum est, Liv.; with in and the acc., altera crepido haud facilior in ascensum, Liv.; with the supine in u, or the abl., res cognitu facilis, Cic.; with infin., facile est perficere ut, etc., Cic.; with ut and the subj., quod ei fuit facillimum, ut in agrum Rutulorum procederet, Cic.; with dat., *suitable;* campus operi facilis, Liv.; neut. subst. with prep., in facili esse, *to be easy,* Liv.; e or ex facili, *easily,* Ov.; **2,** of circumstances, fortune, etc., *favourable;* quae (res et fortunae) quotidie faciliores mihi et meliores videntur, Cic. **II.** Act., **A. 1,** *that which does a thing easily, facile, skilful;* manu facili, Ov.; **2,** *dexterous, clever;* facilis et expeditus ad dicendum T. Junius, Cic. **B.** *ready, willing, inclined;* **1,** with dat., commercio facilis, Liv.; with ad, facili feminarum credulitate ad gaudia, Tac.; poet., with infin., Prop.; **2,** esp. of character, *courteous, accessible, affable, easy, good-natured;* facilis et liberalis pater, Cic.; mores facillimi, Cic.; with ad and the gerund, facilis ad concedendum, Cic.; with in and the abl., facilis in hominibus audiendis, Cic.; with in and the acc., si faciles habeas in tua vota deos, Ov.; with dat., si mihi di faciles et sunt in amore secundi, Ov.; with abl., facilis amicitiā, Sall.

făcĭlĭtas -ātis, f. (facilis). **I.** Pass., *easiness, ease;* facilitas camporum, *for marching,* Tac. **II.** Act., **1,** *readiness, disposition,* Cic.; **2,** *willingness, friendliness, affability, good-nature, courteousness;* facilitas in audiendo, Cic.

făcĭnŏrōsus -a -um (facinus), *full of shameful deeds, wicked, atrocious, nefarious;* vir, Cic.; vita, Cic.; plur. subst., facinorosi, *abandoned men,* Cic.

făcĭnus -ŏris, n. (facio), **1,** *a deed, action* (good or bad), pulcherrimum, Cic.; indignum, Cic.; **2,** *a bad deed, crime, villainy* (not so strong a word as scelus, which = *infamy*); facinus est vinciri civem Romanum, scelus verberari, Cic.; facinus facere, obire, committere, Cic.; in se admittere, Caes.; patrare, Sall.; meton., **a,** *the instrument of crime;* facinus excussit ab ore, *the poisoned cup,* Ov.; **b,** *a criminal;* omnium flagitiorum atque facinorum circum se stipatorum catervae, Cic.

făcĭo, fēci, factum, 3. **I.** Transit., **A. 1,** *to make, prepare, build;* alicui anulum, Cic.; castra, Caes.; hence, **a,** *to write down;* litteras ad aliquem, Cic.; **b,** *to perform some action of the body;* gradum, Cic.; impetum in hostes, *to attack,* Liv.; **2,** *to produce;* ignem ex lignis viridibus, Cic.; hence (of an orator, poet, etc.), *to compose;* orationem, versus, poema, Cic.; **3,** *to gain;* praedam, Caes.; lucrum, manubias sibi ex, etc., Cic.; stipendia, *to serve in war,* Sall.; **4,** *to raise, levy;* tributum, Cic.; auxilia mercede, Tac. **B. 1,** *to do, perform, accomplish, execute;* ego plus quam feci facere non possum, Cic.; caedem, furtum, fraudem, Cic.; alicui medicinam, *to cure,* Cic.; indutias, pacem, bellum, Cic.; fugam, *to take to flight,* or *to put to flight,* Sall., Liv.; facere de aliquo or de aliqua re, aliquo or aliquā re, alicui or alicui rei, cum aliqua re, *to do with,* or *do to;* quid hoc homine, or huic homini facias, Cic.; **2, a,** *to manage* or *hold a ceremony;* ludos, Cic.; sacra, or sacrificium, or res divinas, *to sacrifice,* Cic.; **b,** *to practise a profession;* praeconium, Cic.; **3,** *to procure;* orationi audientiam, Cic.; silentium, Liv.; **4,** *to grant;* potestatem, *permission,* Cic.; **5,** *to arouse* (some feeling, etc.); alicui dolorem, Cic.; spem, Cic.; **6,** *to cause, bring it about;* with ut and the subj., facis ut rursus plebes in Aventinum sevocanda esse videatur, Cic.; with subj. alone, di facerent, sine patre forem! Ov.; fac sciam, *let me know,* Cic.; facio, with ne or quo and the subj., non facere foll by quin or quominus and the subj , facere non possum quin quotidie ad te mittam (litteras), *I cannot but*, Cic , poet with acc and infin , illum forma timere facit, Ov , 7, *to make, represent*, with acc and infin (of artists and poets), quem tamen Homerus apud inferos conveniri facit ab Ulysse, Cic , 8, *to suppose, assume;* with acc and infin , esse deos faciamus Cic ; 9, with double acc , *to make*, aliquem consulem, Cic , me unum ex iis feci qui, etc , *made myself out to be, etc* , Cic , with adj , aliquem sanum, disertum, Cic , aliquem certiorem, v certus ; 10, *to make something the property of some one, to bring into the power of*, with genit , tota Asia populi Romani facta est, Cic , facere aliquid potestatis or ditionis suae, Cic , with pron possess , aliquam terram suam, *to subject*, Caes , 11, *to esteem, value*, with genit , parvi, minimi, pluris, maximi, nihili, Cic , aequi bonique facere aliquid, *to be content with*, Cic , 12, *to suffer*, naufragium facere, Cic ; damnum, detrimentum facere, *to suffer loss*, Cic , 13, *to do*, referring to another verb, me ut adhuc fecistis audiatis (where fecistis = audivistis), Cic **II.** Intransit , 1, *to act*, humaniter, bene, amice, Cic , 2, facere cum, or ab aliquo, *to act on the side of, support, be of the same party*, contra nos, *to be of the opposite party*, Cic , 3, *to sacrifice*, Junoni Sospitae, Cic ; 4, *to be suited for*, Medeae faciunt ad scelus omne manus, Ov , 5, *to be serviceable, advantageous to, to suit, to be of service*, nec caelum nec aquae faciunt nec terra nec aurae, Ov (archaic fut perf forms, faxo = fecero, Verg , Ov.; faxis, Hor , faxit, ap Liv , faxitis, ap Liv , faxint, Cic ; faxitur, ap. Liv The passive of facio is fio, q v).

făctĕŏn, a word formed from facio, in imitation of the Greek = faciendum, Cic

factĭo -ōnis, f (facio) **I.** *a making, doing*, 1, lit , Plaut , 2, transf , *the right of making or doing*, factionem testamenti non habere, *to be incapable of making a will*, Cic **II.** 1, *a political party, faction, side*, populus paucorum factione oppressus, Caes , feminta illorum consensus et factio, Cic , 2, a, *a faction or party in a theatre or circus*, Suet , b, *the parties into which the charioteers in the circus were divided*, Suet

factĭōsus -a -um (factio), *fond of power, factious*, adolescens nobilis, egens, factiosus, Sall , exsistunt in republica plerumque largiores et factiosi, Cic

factĭto, 1 (freq of facio) **I.** *to make, do frequently, be accustomed to make or do*, verba compone et quasi coagmenta, quod ne Graeci quidem veteres factitaverunt, Cic **II.** a, *to declare openly, to make or do*, quem palam heredem semper factitarat, Cic , b, *to follow a trade, practise a profession, make a trade of*, accusationem, Cic , delationem, Cic , c, *to celebrate usually*, sacrificia gentilicia illo ipso in sacello stato loco anniversaria, Cic

factum i, n (facio), *that which has been done, a deed, act, exploit;* bene facta, *good deeds*, Cic , recte facta, Liv , poet , facta boum, *the works of oxen—i e , a ploughed field*, Ov

factus -a -um, p adj (facio), 1, *wrought, worked*, argentum factum, *silver plate*, Cic , 2, *polished, refined* (of persons), qui illuc factus institutusque venisset, Cic , homo ad unguem factus, Hor

făcŭla ae, f (dim of fax), *a little torch*, Prop

făcultas -ātis, f (Old Lat facul = facile) **I. A.** *capacity, power, ability, capability*, facultas dicendi et copia, Cic , ingenii Cic **B.** Esp , *eloquence, oratorical power*, facultatis timor, Cic **II. A.** *possibility, opportunity, power, means*, Miloni manendi nulla facultas, Cic , dare alicui facultatem irridendi sui, Cic , habere efficiendi facultatem, Cic , res mihi videtur esse facultate (*in practice*) praeclara, arte (*in theory*) mediocris, Cic , alicui facultatem dare, offerre, concedere with ut and the subj , Cic **B** Transf , a, *abundance, great number*, omnium rerum in oppido summa facultas, Caes , b, *means, resources*, gen in plur , Cic

făcundē, adv with compar and superl (facundus), *eloquently, fluently*, alloqui hostem, Liv.

făcundĭa -ae, f (facundus), *eloquence, readiness of speech*, Romae Memmi facundia clara pollensque fuit, Sall

făcundus -a -um, adj with compar and superl (fari), *eloquent, fluent, ready of speech*, ingenia hominum sunt ad suam cuique levandam culpam nimio plus facunda, Liv , lingua, Hor , oratio, Sall

faecŭla -ae, f (dim of faex), *the tartar or crust of wine*, used either as a drug or condiment, Lucr , Hor

Faesŭlae -ārum, f *town in Etruria, at the foot of the Apennines*, now *Fiesole* Hence adj , **Faesulānus** a um, *of or belonging to Faesulae*

faex, faecis f **A.** *the dregs or refuse of any liquid*, Lucr Hor , *the tartar or crust of wine*, Hor , *the brine of pickles*, Ov **B.** Transf , *the dregs, the lower orders*, faex populi or plebis, Cic ; in Romuli faece, Cic

fāgĭnĕus -a -um (fagus), *beechen*, frons, Ov

fāgĭnus -a um (fagus), *beechen*, pocula, Verg

fāgus -i, f (φηγός), *the beech tree*, Caes ,Verg

făla ae, f 1, *a wooden tower from which missiles were thrown into a besieged city*, Plaut ; 2, *one of the seven wooden pillars on the spina or barrier of the circus*, Juv

fălārĭca (phălārĭca) -ae, f 1, *a huge spear hurled with the hand*, Verg , 2, *a missile covered with tow and pitch, hurled from the catapult, a brand*, Liv

falcārĭus -ii, m (falx), *a scythe or sickle-maker*, inter falcarios, *the street of the scythe-makers*, Cic

falcātus -a -um (falx), 1, *furnished with scythes*, currus, quadrigae, Liv , 2, *scythe-shaped*, ensis, Ov , sinus, *a bay*, Ov

falcĭfer fĕra fĕrum (falx and fero), *carrying a scythe or sickle*, senex, *Saturnus*, Ov

Fălĕrĭi -ōrum, m *the capital of the Falisci*.

Fălernus ager, *the Falernian country, at the foot of Mount Massicus, in Campania* Adj , **Fălernus** -a -um, *Falernian*, vites, uva, Hor Subst , **Fălernum** i, n *Falernian wine*, Hor.

Făliscī -ōrum, m *a people in Etruria* Adj , **Făliscus** -a -um, *Faliscan* Subst , **Făliscum** -i, n , *the territory of the Falisci*

fallācĭa -ae, f (fallax), *deceit, trick, fraud, artifice, craft*, sine fuco ac fallaciis, Cic

fallācĭlŏquus -a -um (fallax and loqui), *speaking falsely* or *deceitfully*, ap Cic

fallācĭtĕr, adv (fallax), *deceitfully, craftily, fallaciously*, Cic

fallax -ācis, adj (fallo), *deceitful, treacherous, false, fallacious*, homines, Cic., herbae non fallaces, *not disappointing the farmer*, Cic , spes, Cic , fallaces et captiosae interrogationes, Cic

fallo, fĕfelli, falsum, 3 (σφάλλω) **I.** *to make to slip*, glacies fallit pedes, Liv **II.** Transf , a, *to make invisible*, signa sequendi, Verg ; longe fallens sagitta, *coming unnoticed from afar*, Verg , aetas labitur occulte fallitque, *glides un-*

noticed, Ov.; **b,** *to make ineffective, to drive away, beguile;* infandum amorem, Verg.; curam vino et somno, Ov.; **c,** *to break* a promise, etc.; foedus ac fidem, Liv.; fidem hosti datam, Cic.; **d,** *to escape the notice of, be concealed from;* custodias, Liv.; non fefellere insidiae, Liv.; aliquem fallit or non fallit, with acc. and infin., Cic.; aliquem non fallit quin, Caes.; esp. (like Gr. λανθάνω) with a partic., hostis fallit incedens, *comes unnoticed*, Liv.; **e,** *to lead astray, to deceive;* pass., fallor as middle, *to make a mistake;* fallere alicuius spem or opinionem, Cic.; fallit me tempus, dies, *I am mistaken in*, Cic.; nisi me forte fallo, Cic.; non in sortitione fallere, Cic.; si fallo (in oaths), *if I do not keep my word*, Cic.; impers., me fallit, *I am mistaken, err;* quantum nos fefellerit, vides, Cic.; pass., potest fieri ut fallar, *I may be mistaken*, Cic.

falsō, adv. (falsus), *falsely*, Cic.

falsĭpărens -entis (falsus and parens), *having a putative father;* Amphitryoniades, *Hercules*, Cat.

falsō, adv. (falsus), *falsely, wrongly, erroneously, untruly*, Cic.

falsus -a -um, p. adj. (from fallo). **I.** *invented, feigned, false, untrue, spurious, made up;* gaudium, Cic.; Caesaris commentarii, Cic.; voculae, *falsetto*, Cic.; ora non falsa, *genuine*, Ov. Subst., **falsum** -i, n. *an untruth, something false, a lie;* ad te falsum scripseram, Cic.; falsum jurare, Cic.; falso, adv., *falsely*, Cic. **II.** *deceitful, false, hypocritical;* in amore, Tac.; lingua, Ov. Subst., **falsum** -i, n., **a,** *deceit, hypocrisy*, Tac.; **b,** tela in falsum jacere, *at random*, Tac.

falx, falcis, f. **1,** *a scythe, sickle, bill-hook, pruning-hook*, Cic.; **2,** *a sickle-shaped implement of war, used for tearing down stockades*, etc., Caes.

fāma -ae, f. (fari). **I.** *talk, tradition, a report, rumour, intelligence, unauthenticated news;* nulla adhuc fama venerat, Cic.; fama est, *there is a rumour*, Liv.; fama emergit, Cic.; fama nuntiabat, Cic.; fama manat, foll. by acc. and infin.; famā accipere, *to hear by rumour*, Caes.; personif., Fama, *a goddess, daughter of Terra*, Verg. **II.** *the opinion of the crowd, public opinion.* **A.** contra famam opinionemque omnium, Cic.; fama popularis, *popular favour*, Cic.; bona fama, *good opinion*, Cic.; mala fama, Sall.; fama sapientiae, Cic. **B.** *reputation;* **1,** *good name;* famae consulere, Cic.; famam sororis defendere, Cic.; **2,** *evil reputation;* moveri famā, Verg.

fāmātus -a -um (fama), *having an ill reputation*, Cic. (?).

fămēlĭcus -a -um (fames), *suffering hunger, hungry, famished;* armenta, Juv.

fămes -is, f. *hunger.* **I.** Gen., **A.** Lit., cibi condimentum esse famem, Cic.; aliquā re famem tolerare, Caes.; aliquā re famem depellere, *to satisfy*, Cic.; explere, Cic.; famem ab ore civium propulsare, Liv. **B.** Transf., **1,** *insatiable desire;* auri sacra fames, Verg.; **2,** *poverty of expression;* jejunitas et fames, Cic. **II.** *famine, time of famine;* in fame frumentum exportare, Cic.

fămĭlĭa -ae (-as after the words pater, mater, filius, filia), f. (from root FAM, whence famulus). **I.** *a household of slaves, household;* **a,** familiam intelligamus, quae constet ex servis pluribus, Cic.; emere eam familiam a Catone, Cic.; **b,** *a band of gladiators;* gladiatoria, Sall.; comparare familiam, Cic.; familiam ducere, *to be at the head, to take the first place*, Cic.; **c,** *the dependents, vassals of a noble*, Caes.; **d,** *the slaves of a temple.* **II.** Transf., **A.** *the entire household or family;* hence, paterfamilias, *the head of the household or family;* materfamilias, *a married woman who had passed in manum viri, or an unmarried woman whose father was dead*, Cic.; filiusfamilias, *the son still under his father's power*, Cic. **B.** *a family;* **1,** lit., **a,** in a wide sense, *race* (syn. with gens); familiam unam (sc. gentem Claudiam) subisse civitatis onus, Liv.; **b,** in a narrower sense, *a family*, as a subdivision of a gens; Laeliorum et Muciorum familiae, Cic.; **2,** transf., *sect;* tota Peripateticorum, Cic.

fămĭlĭāris -e (familia). **I.** *belonging to the slaves of a house*, Plaut. Subst., **fămĭlĭāris** -is, m., *a servant.*, plur., *the servants in a house*, Liv. **II.** *belonging or relating to a family or household.* **A.** Lit., **a,** *belonging to a household;* lares, Cic.; copiae, Liv.; res familiaris; (α) *the household*, Liv.; (β) *property*, Cic.; **b,** *belonging to a family;* funus, *a death in the family*, Cic. **B.** Transf., **a,** with compar. and superl., *known in the house or family, intimate, friendly;* biduo factus est mihi familiaris, Cic.; subst., **fămĭlĭāris** -is, m. *a friend;* so familiaris -is, f., *a female friend;* exclamat familiaris tua, Cic.; of things, *ordinary, familiar, confidential;* sermo, Cic.; aditus familiarior, Liv.; **b,** t. t. of augury, fissum familiare or pars familiaris, *the part of the entrails relating to the persons sacrificing*, Cic., Liv.

fămĭlĭārĭtas -ātis, f. (familiaris), **1,** *confidential friendship, intimacy, familiarity;* in alicuius familiaritatem venire or intrare, or se dare, Cic.; mihi cum aliquo familiaritas est or intercedit, Cic.; **2,** meton., *familiar friends;* e praecipua familiaritate Neronis, Tac.

fămĭlĭārĭtĕr, adv. with compar. and superl. (familiaris), *confidentially, familiarly, intimately;* familiariter cum aliquo vivere, Cic.

fāmōsus -a -um, adj. with compar. and superl. (fama). **I.** Pass., **a,** in a good sense, *much spoken of, renowned;* urbs (of Jerusalem), Tac.; mors, Hor.; **b,** in a bad sense, *infamous, notorious;* si qua erat famosa, Cic. **II.** Act., *libellous, defamatory;* versus, Hor.; libelli, Tac.

fămul, fămŭla, v. famulus.

fămŭlāris -e (famulus), *relating or belonging to servants or slaves;* vestis, Cic.; jura famularia dare, *to make slaves*, Ov.

fămŭlātus -ūs, m. (famulor), *service, servitude, slavery*, Cic.; transf., quam miser virtutis famulatus servientis voluptati, Cic.

fămŭlor, 1. dep. (famulus), *to be a servant, to serve any one*, Cic.; alicui, Cat.

fămŭlus -a -um (root FAM), *serving, servile;* vertex, Ov. Subst., **a,** **fămŭlus** -i, m. *a servant, slave;* of a man, Cic.; of a deity, Cic.; ante-class. form, **fămul**, Lucr.; **b,** **fămŭla** -ae, f. *a female slave, handmaid*, Verg., Ov.; transf., virtus famula fortunae est, Cic.

fānātĭcus a -um (fanum), *inspired by a deity, enthusiastic, raving.* **A.** Lit., of persons, Galli fanatici, Liv.; isti philosophi superstitiosi et paene fanatici, Cic. **B.** Transf. of things, vaticinantes carmine fanatico, Liv.; fanaticus error, Hor.

Fannĭus -a -um, *name of a Roman gens, of which the most famous were* C. Fannius, *an historian, and his uncle*, C. Fannius, *an orator, contemporaries of Scipio Aemilianus.* Hence adj., **Fannĭānus** -a -um, *of or relating to Fannius.*

fānum -i, n. (fari). **I.** **a,** *a place solemnly consecrated to a god*, Cic.; **b,** *a temple with the land round it, a holy place;* in sing. generally with the name of the deity, Apollinis, Cic.; fana spoliare, Cic. **II.** Proper name, **Fānum** -i, n. *town on the coast of Umbria*, now *Fano*.

făr, farris, n. **I.** Lit., *spelt* (triticum spelta, Linn.), farris seges, Liv.; farris acervus, Verg.

II. Transf, **a,** *meal,* percontor quanti olus et far, Hor, esp as used in sacrifices, far pium, Hor, **b,** *bread,* una farris libra, Hor

farcio, farsi, fartum, 4 (root FARC, Gr ΦΡΑΓ, φράγ-νυμι, φράσ-σω), *to fill full, stuff full,* pulvinus rosa fartus, Cic

Farfărus, v Fabaris

fărīna -ae, f (far), *meal, flour,* Plin, hence, *dust or powder of any kind,* Plin, fig, nostrae farinae, *of our kind or sort,* Pers

fărīnārĭus -a -um (farina), *relating to meal, made of meal,* Plin

farrācĕus (-ĭus) a -um (far), *of or belonging to spelt,* Plin.

farrāgo inis, f (far), **1,** *mixed fodder for cattle,* Verg, **2,** transf, *a medley, mixture,* nostri libelli, Juv

farrārĭus -a -um (far), *relating to spelt* or *to grain generally,* Cato

farrātus -a -um (far), **1,** *provided with grain,* Pers, **2,** *made of corn,* neut plur subst, farrata, *porridge,* Juv

farrĕus -a -um (far), *made of spelt or corn generally* Subst, **farrĕum** i, n *a spelt cake* Plin

fartor -ōris, m (farcio), *a fattener of fowls,* Hor

fartum -i, n and **fartus** -us, m (farcio), *the stuffing, the inside,* Plin

fās, n indecl (root FA, Gr ΦΑ-Ω, whence also fari, fatum), *something spoken* **I.** *divine law and right* (opp jus, *human law and right*), *divine command,* jus ac fas omne delere, Cic, contra jus fasque, Cic, personif, audi Juppiter, audite fines, audiat fas, Liv **II. A.** Gen, *that which is allowed, permitted, lawful, right* (opp nefas), per omne fas et nefas aliquem sequi Liv, fas est, *it is allowed, is lawful,* quod aut per naturam fas esset aut per leges liceret, Cic, si fas est, with infin, Cic, with supine, si hoc fas est dictu, Cic, fas est or non fas est, with infin, Cic, fas putare, with infin, Caes **B.** *fate, destiny,* fas obstat, Verg, fas est, with infin or acc and infin, si cadere fas est, *if I am destined to fall,* Ov

fascĭa -ae, f *a bandage, band* **I.** Lit, **1,** *a surgical bandage,* Cic, **2,** esp, **a,** *a woman's girdle,* Ov., **b,** *a bed-girth,* Cic **II.** Transf, *a streak of cloud in the sky,* Juv

fascĭcŭlus -i, m (dim of fascis), *a little bundle or packet,* epistolarum, Cic, librorum, Hor, florum, *a nosegay,* Cic

fascĭno, 1 (βασκαίνω), *to bewitch,* agnos, Verg

fascĭnum -i, n and **fascĭnus** -i, m (βάσκανον) **I.** *an enchanting, bewitching,* Plin **II.** = membrum virile, Hor

fascĭŏla -ae, f (dim of fascia), *a little bandage,* Hor., purpureae fasciolae, *bandages round the ankle worn by women,* Cic

fascis is, m *a bundle, packet* **I.** Gen, sarmentorum, Liv, ego hoc te fasce levabo, Verg **II.** Esp, plur **A.** Lit, fasces, *bundles of sticks with an axe projecting, carried by lictors before the chief Roman magistrates,* fasces praeferre, Liv, habere, Cic, dare alicui fasces, *the consulate,* Cic, summittere fasces, *to lower as a sign of respect,* Liv, fig, alicui, *to yield the preference to,* Cic, demissi populo fasces, *lowered before the people,* Cic **B.** Meton, *high office,* esp *the consulate,* Verg, Hor

făsēlus, făsēŏlus, etc = phaselus, etc (q v)

fasti ōrum, m, v fastus a -um

fastīdĭo -ivi -ītum 4 (fastidium), *to loathe, feel distaste or disgust* **I.** Lit, of physical loathing, olus, Hor, omnia praeter pavonem rhombumque, Hor **II.** Transf, *to be averse to, dislike, loathe,* etiam in recte factis saepe fastidiunt, Cic, preces alicuius, Liv, with infin, ne fastidieris nos in sacerdotum numerum accipere, Liv, with acc and infin, est aliquis, qui se inspici, aestimari fastidiat, Liv

fastīdĭōsē, adv with compar (fastidiosus), **1,** *with loathing, dislike,* huic ego jam stomachans fastidiose, immo ex Sicilia, inquam, Cic, **2, a,** *fastidiously, daintily,* quam diligenter et quam paene fastidiose judicamus, Cic, **b,** *disdainfully, contemptuously,* fastidiosius ad hoc genus sermonis accedere, Cic

fastīdĭōsus -a -um, adj with compar and superl (fastidium), *full of loathing* **I.** *feeling, loathing* **A.** Lit, *squeamish,* Varr **B.** Transf, **a,** *sick of, disgusted with, impatient of,* with genit, Latinarum (litterarum), Cic, terrae, Hor, **b,** esp, *nice, dainty, fastidious,* Antonius facilis in causis recipiendis erat, fastidiosior Crassus, sed tamen recipiebat, Cic, **c,** *contemptuous, disdainful,* Plin **II.** *causing loathing, disgusting, loathsome,* Hor

fastīdĭum ii, n (FAST-idium, of same root as 1 fastus), *loathing* **I.** Lit, *the loathing of food,* cibi satietas et fastidium, Cic **II.** Transf, **A.** *dislike, aversion, disgust,* domesticarum rerum, Cic **B. a,** *fastidiousness, hyper-criticism, fault-finding,* delicatissimum, Cic, audiendi, Cic, **b,** *scorn, haughtiness, pride,* fastidium et superbia, fastidium arrogantiaque, fastidium et contumacia, Cic, fastidium alicuius non posse ferre, Cic

fastīgātē, adv (fastigatus), *slantingly,* Caes

fastīgātus -a -um, partic of fastigo

fastīgĭum ii, n (FAST-igium, connected with ἄ-φλαστον) **I.** *a slope, declivity, descent,* ab oppido locus tenui fastigio vergebat, Caes **II.** *the extremity, either above or below* **A.** Lit, **1,** above, *height,* **a,** gen, *height, summit,* pari altitudinis fastigio, Caes, **b,** esp, *the summit of a roof,* both, (α) *the whole of the roof,* Cic, and (β) *the gable end, pediment,* fastigium Capitolii, Cic, operi inchoato, prope tamen absoluto, tamquam fastigium imponere, *put the last touch to,* Cic, **2,** below, *depth,* Caes **B.** Transf, **1,** *dignity, rank, position,* dictaturae altius fastigium, Liv, **2,** *principal point* (in writing), summa sequar fastigia rerum, Verg

fastīgo, 1 (fastigium), *to sharpen to a point,* **a,** upwards, collis est in modum metae in acutum cacumen a fundo satis lato fastigatus, Liv, **b,** *to slope down,* only in partic, fastigatus, collis leniter fastigatus, Caes

fastōsus -a -um (fastus), *proud, haughty,* Mart

1 **fastus** -ūs, m *pride, haughtiness, arrogance,* stirpis Achilleae fastus (plur), Verg, fastu erga patrias epulas, Tac

2 **fastus** a -um (root FA, Gr ΦΑ-ω, whence fatum, φάσκω, φημί), dies fastus, gen plur dies fasti, or simply fasti, *the days on which the praetor could administer justice* (opp nefasti) ille dies nefastus erit, per quem tria verba (do, dico, addico) silentur, fastus erit per quem lege licebit agi, Ov, *a list of these days, with the festivals, magistrates, chief events, etc, the Roman calendar,* fasti memores, Hor, *a poetical form of this calendar composed by Ovid,* fasti consulares or magistratuum, *a list of the highest magistrates at Rome from the earliest times,* Cic

fātālis -e (fatum), *relating to destiny or fate* **I. a,** *fated, destined by fate,* necessitas, Cic, annus ad interitum huius urbis fatalis, Cic, **b,** *fateful, connected with the fate of a person or thing,* pignora, *the Palladium,* Ov.; libri, *the*

Sibylline books, Liv ; bellum, Cic , deae, *the fates*, Ov **II.** In a bad sense, *deadly, fatal*, telum, Verg , jaculum, Ov

fātālĭtĕr, adv (fatalis), *according to fate or destiny*, definitum esse, Cic

fătĕor, fassus sum, 2 dep (root FA-, Gr ΦΑ-ω, whence also fari, φατίζω), 1, *to confess, admit, allow*, verum, Cic , de facto turpi , with acc and infin , si quis se amici causā fecisse fateatur, Cic , 2, *to discover, make known*, iram vultu Ov (pass , qui (ager) publicus esse fateatur, Cic)

fātĭcănus -a -um and **fātĭcĭnus** -a -um (fatum and cano), *prophetic*, Ov

fātĭdĭcus -a -um (fatum and dico), *announcing fate, prophesying, prophetic*, vates, Verg , anus, Cic , subst , *a soothsayer*, Cic

fātĭfĕr -fĕra -fĕrum (fatum and fero), *death-bringing, deadly, fatal*, arcus, Verg

fătīgātĭo -ōnis, f (fatigo), *weariness, fatigue;* cum fatigatione equorum atque hominum, Liv

fătīgo, 1 (perhaps connected with fatis, whence also affatim) **I.** *to weary, tire, fatigue*, cervos jaculo cursuque, Verg , se atroci pugnā, Liv , itinere, magno aestu fatigati, Caes **II.** Transf , *to vex, harass* **A.** Of the body, verberibus, tormentis, igni fatigati, Cic **B.** Of the mind, 1, animum, Sall , se, Sall ; qui punit aliquem aut verbis fatigat, Cic , 2, esp , *to tease, worry with entreaties*, etc , aliquem precibus, Liv , Vestam prece, Hor

fātĭlŏquus -a -um (fatum and loqui), *announcing fate, prophetic* Subst , *a prophet, prophetess*, Carmenta mater ... quam fatiloquam miratae hae gentes fuerant, Liv

fătis -is, f whence acc fatim, *sufficiently*, post-Aug

fătisco, 3 and **fătiscor**, 3 dep (χατέω, χατίσκω), 1, *to chink, gape, crack, open, part asunder*, naves rimis fatiscunt, Verg , 2, *to become weak, droop, decrease;* seditio fatiscit, Tac , dum copiā fatiscunt, Tac

fătŭĭtas -ātis, f (fatuus), *foolishness, simplicity*, Cic

fātum -i, n (for, fari), *an utterance* **I.** *the expressed will of a god, prophecy, prediction;* fata Sibyllina, Cic **II.** 1, *destiny, fate, the appointed order of the world, the fate, lot, or destiny of man*, omnia fato fieri, Cic , fato rerum prudentia major, Verg , alicui fatum est, with infin , Cic , alicuius or alicui fatum est, with acc and infin , Cic , fuit hoc sive meum sive rei publicae fatum ut, etc , Cic , *the will of a god*, sic fata Jovis poscunt, Verg , and personif , Fata, *the Parcae or Fates*, Prop , 2, a, *the natural term of life;* maturius exstingui quam fato suo, Cic , fato cedere, Liv , fato fungi, Ov , fato obire, *to die a natural death*, Tac , fata proferre, *to prolong life*, Verg., b, *misfortune, ruin, calamity*, impendet fatum aliquod, Cic , meton , *a cause of calamity or destruction*, duo illa reipublicae paene fata, Gabinius et Piso, Cic

fătŭus -a -um, *foolish, idiotic, fatuous*, a, of persons, puer, Cic , fatuus et amens es, Cic Subst, **fătŭus** -i, m *a fool, idiot*, Cat , b, of things, *foolish, insipid, perverse*, primas illas rabiosulas (litteras) sat fatuas dedisti, Cic

Faunus -i, m (root FAV-, faveo), *a mythic king of Latium, revered as a god of woods and fields*, subsequently identified with Pan , hence, **Fauni** = *forest gods*, Ov

faustē, adv (faustus), *happily, fortunately;* evenire, Cic

faustĭtas -ātis, f (faustus), *prosperity*, personif as a goddess of the fields, Hor

Faustŭlus -i, m. (root FAV-, whence faustus), myth , *the herdsman of the Alban Amulius, who saved and brought up Romulus and Remus*

faustus -a -um (root FAV-, faveo) **I.** *bringing luck or good fortune, fortunate, lucky, auspicious*, dies faustus alicui, Cic. **II.** As a proper name, Faustus, *a Roman surname* , L Corn Sulla Faustus, *son of the dictator Sulla* , Fausta, *daughter of the dictator Sulla, wife of Milo*

fautor -ōris, m (orig favitor, from faveo), *a favourer, protector, patron, promoter* , dignitatis, Cic , bonorum, Liv , absol , *an applauder*, Hor.

fautrix -trīcis, f (fautor), *a favourer, protector, promoter* , voluptatum, Cic , regio suorum fautrix, Cic

faux, faucis, f (usually plur. **fauces** -ium, f) **I.** Lit , *the jaws, gullet, throat*, arente fauce, Hor , sitis urit fauces, Hor , fig , quum inexplebiles populi fauces exaruerunt libertatis siti Cic ; Catilina cum exercitu faucibus urguet, *is at our throats*, Sall.; quum faucibus premeretur, *when the knife was at his throat*, Cic , premit fauces defensionis tuae, *strangles, makes impossible*, Cic.; urbem ex belli ore ac faucibus ereptam esse, Cic **II.** Transf , only in plur , **1,** *jaws, chasm*, patefactis terrae faucibus, Cic ; **2,** *entrance*, portus, Caes., macelli, Cic ; **3,** *a narrow pass, defile;* angustae, Liv , artae, Tac , Etruriae, Cic ; **4, a,** *isthmus, neck of land;* artae fauces (Isthmi), Liv , Graeciae, Cic., **b,** *straits*, Hellesponti, Liv

făvĕo, fāvi, fautum, 2 **I.** *to favour, be favourable or inclined to, help, protect*, with dat of person or party, faveas tu hosti, Cic , si tibi dei favent, Cat , favere suis, Cic , with dat of thing, favere enim pietati fideique deos, Liv ; favere et reipublicae et dignitati ac gloriae alicuius, Cic , isti sententiae, Cic , impers , non modo non invidetur illi aetati, verum etiam favetur, Cic , with pro and the abl , or contra and the acc , hac pro parte, Ov , qui Parthorum quoque contra Romanum nomen gloriae favent, Liv , with acc and infin , Ov , with neut acc (*as regards*), quod quidem ego favisse me tibi fateor, Cic , absol, dum favet nox et Venus, Hor , multitudo audiens favet, odit, Cic. **II.** Esp , *to favour* with the mouth, heart, etc , hence *to be silent*, favete linguis, Cic , ore favete, Verg , *be silent*, absol , celebrate faventes, Verg.

făvilla -ae, f. (faveo), *glowing ashes*, esp. *the still glowing ashes of the dead;* reliquias vino et bibulam lavēre favillam, Verg

făvĭtor -ōris, m = fautor (q v)

făvōnĭus -ii, m *the west wind or zephyr which blew at the beginning of spring*, Cic

făvor -ōris, m (faveo) **I.** *favour, goodwill, partiality, inclination*, with subject. genit , populi, Cic , with object genit., nominis, Liv ; with in and the acc , Liv., amplecti aliquem favore, Liv ; in favorem alicuius venire, Liv **II.** Esp , **a,** *attention at a religious ceremony;* pium praestate et mente et voce favorem, Ov ; **b,** *applause at the theatre, approbation, acclamation*, quod studium et quem favorem in scenam attulit Panurgus, Cic.

făvōrābĭlis -e, adj. with compar. (favor), *in favour, popular, beloved, pleasing*, oratio, Tac.

făvus -i, m *a honeycomb;* fingere favos, Cic ; poet , favos dilue Baccho, *honey*, Verg.

fax, făcis, f *a torch* **I. A.** Lit , faces incidere, Liv , faces nuptiales, Cic ; *a funeral torch*, Cic ; *a fire-brand;* faces incendere, Cic.; fig , eius omnium incendiorum fax, *Antonius*, Cic ; attribute of Cupid and the Furies, Ov , Verg. **B.** Fig , **1,** gen , faces dicendi, *fiery eloquence*, Cic ; alicui ad libidinem facem praeferre, *minister to*, Cic, facem bello praeferre, *to kindle the flame of war*, Tac; me torret face mutua Calais, *with the flame of love*, Hor, 2, esp, *that which provokes or causes, the author*, subjicere faces invidiae alicuius, Cic II. Transf, 1, *the light of the moon*, crescentem face Noctilucam, Hor, 2, *a fiery meteor, shooting star*, etc, faces caelestes or caeli, Cic

faxim, faxo = fecerim, fecero, v facio

fĕbrĭcŭla ae, f (dim of febris), *a slight fever, feverishness*, febricula incipit, Cic, febriculam habere, Cic

fĕbrĭcŭlōsus -a -um (febricula), *feverish*, Cat

fĕbris -is, f, acc -em or -im, abl -e or -i (for ferbis, from ferveo), *fever*, in febrim subito incidere, Cic, febrim habere, Cic, febri carere, Cic, Romam venisse cum febre, Cic, Febris personif as a goddess, with three temples in Rome

fĕbrŭārĭus -a -um (februus, februo, *to purify*), *relating to cleansing*, a, mensis Februarius or simply Februarius, *the cleansing month* (so called because of the purificatory sacrifices in its second half), up to 450 B C the last month of the year, in the time of Cicero the second, b, *belonging to the month February*, Kalendae Februariae, *the 1st of February*, Cic

fĕbrŭus -a -um, *purifying* (in the religious sense); subst **fĕbrŭum** -i, n *a means of religious purification*, hence, **Fĕbrŭa** -ōrum, n *the feast of purification held by the Romans at the end of February*

fētiālis = fetialis (q v).

fēcundĭtas -ātis, f (fecundus), *fruitfulness, fecundity* I. Lit, a, of persons, mulieris, Cic, b, of the earth, aquarum inundationibus terris fecunditatem damus, Cic, c, of the intellect, volo se efferat in adolescente fecunditas Cic II. Transf, *abundance*, Plin

fēcundo, 1 (fecundus), *to fructify, fertilise*, viridem Aegyptum nigrā arenā, Verg

fēcundus -a -um, p adj with compar and superl (FE o, whence fetus, femina, fenus) *fruitful, prolific* I. A. Lit, terra, Cic, conjux, Hor B. Fig, *rich, abounding in*, with genit, saecula fecunda culpae, Hor, with abl, gens inter accolas latrociniis fecunda, Tac II. Transf, 1, *abundant, full, plentiful*, quaestus, Cic; calices, Hor, with abl (specus) uberibus fecundus aquis, Ov, 2, *making fruitful*, fecundae verbera dextrae, Ov

fĕl, fellis, n *the gall, the gall bladder* A. Gen, 1, lit, fel gallinaceum, Cic, 2, fig, a, *bitterness*, Tib; b, *anger*, atrum fel, Verg B. Esp, *the venom of a serpent*, vipereo spicula felle linunt, Ov

fēles (faeles) -is, and **fēlis (faelis)** -is, f *a cat*, Cic

fēlīcitas -ātis, f (felix) I. *fertility*, Plin II. Transf, a, *happiness, felicity, good fortune, success*: perpetuā quādam felicitate usus ille excessit e vita, Cic; plur, incredibiles felicitates, Cic, personif, Felicitas, *Good Fortune as a goddess*, with a temple in Rome, b, *success*, esp in war, Helvetiorum, Caes

fēlīcĭtĕr, adv (felix), 1, *fruitfully*, illic veniunt felicius uvae, Verg, 2, *happily*, a, vivere, navigare, Cic, b, in a wish, *auspiciously, favourably*, precatus sum ut ea res mihi, populo plebique Romanae bene atque feliciter eveniret, Cic., c, *good luck!* feliciter velim, Cic.

fēlis = feles (q v)

fēlix -icis (root FE o, cf fecundus) I. *fruitful, fertile*, arbor, Liv, regio, Ov II. A. *fortunate, favourable, propitious, lucky*, 1, gen., Sulla felicissimus omnium, Cic; with genit, cerebri, Hor, with ad and the acc., ad casum fortunamque felix, Cic, with abl, morte felix, Verg, with abl gerund, tam felix vobis corrumpendis fuit, Liv, with in and the abl gerund, si minus felices in diligendo fuissemus, Cic, with ab and the abl, ille Graecus ab omni laude felicior, Cic, with infin, felicior ungere tela manu, Verg, Felix, *the Lucky One*, *surname of Sulla*, Liv, 2, esp, a, *rich*, tam felix esse, Ov, b, *successful*, seditio, Liv., arma, Verg B. Act, a, *bringing good luck*, omen, Ov, so the formula, quod bonum, faustum, felix fortunatumque sit, Cic, b, *blessed with healing power*, malum, Verg, c, *making joyful*, poma, Ov, d, *making fruitful*, limus, Verg

fēmella -ae, f (dim. of femina), *a young woman, a girl*, Cat

fĕmen = femur (q v)

fēmĭna -ae, f (root FE-o, cf fecundus), lit, *any female animal that bears young*, a, of human beings, *a woman*, Cic, b, of animals, *the female*, porcus femina, Cic

fēmĭnĕus -a -um (femina), 1, *relating to a woman, female, feminine*, calendae, *the 1st of March, when the Matronalia were celebrated*, Juv curae iraeque, Verg, 2, *womanish, effeminate*, amor, Verg, fuga, Ov

fĕmur -ŏris or (from femen) -inis, n (FE o, cf fecundus), *the upper part of the leg, the thigh*, Cic, femur utrumque, Caes

fēnĕbris -e (fenus), *relating to interest*, leges, Liv

fēnĕrātio -ōnis, f (fenero), *lending at interest, usury*, Cic

fēnĕrātor -ōris, m (fenero), *one who lends money at interest, money-lender, usurer*, fenerator acerbissimus, Cic

fēnĕro (faenĕro), 1 (fenus), *to lend money at interest*, ne fenerare liceret, Liv

fēnĕror (faenĕror), 1 dep (fenus), *to lend money at interest*, pecuniam binis centesimis, *at twenty-four per cent per annum*, Cic, provincias *to despoil by usury*, Cic, fig, beneficium, *to trade in*, Cic

fĕnestella -ae, f (dim of fenestra), *a little opening*, (porta) Fenestella, *a little gate in Rome*

fĕnestra -ae, f (connected with φαίνω) a, *a window*, Cic, b, *an opening*, lato dedit ore fenestram, Verg, esp, *a loophole for shooting*, fenestras ad tormenta mittenda in struendo reliquerunt, Caes

fēnĕus -a -um (fenum), *made of hay*, homines, *men of straw*, Cic.

fēnĭcŭlārĭus -a -um (feniculum), *belonging to fennel*, hence **Fēnĭcŭlārĭus** campus, *a district in Spain*, Cic

fēnĭcŭlum -i, n *fennel*, Plaut

fēnīlĭa -ium, n plur (fenum), *a hay-loft*, Verg

fēnĭsĕca -ae, m (fenum and seco), *a mower*, transf, *a countryman*, Pers

fēnum (faenum, foenum) -i, n (root FE o), *hay*, fenum alios esse oportere, *must eat hay*, i e, *be dolts*, Cic, prov, fenum habet in cornu, *he is dangerous* (the horns of vicious cattle were bound with hay), Hor

fēnus (faenus) -ŏris, n (root FE o), lit, *that which is produced* I. *interest of money*, pecuniam alicui dare fenore, *to lend at interest*, Cic, pecuniam accipere fenore, *to borrow*, Liv, pecuniam occupare grandi fenore, *to invest*, Cic II. Meton, 1, *debt, indebtedness*, fenore obrui, mersum esse, laborare, Liv, 2, *capital*, duas fenoris partes in agris collocare, Tac, 3, *usury*, fenore trucidare patrimonium or plebem, Cic,

fĕra -ae, f. v. ferus.

fĕrācĭtĕr, adv. with compar. (ferax), *fruitfully;* velut ab stirpibus laetius feraciusque renata urbs, Liv.

fērālis -e (root FER, whence also Feronia, in-fer-nus). **I.** *relating to the dead, funereal;* cupressus, Verg.; tempus or dies, = feralia, Ov. Subst., **fērālia** -ium, n., **a,** *the festival of the dead on the 10th of February,* Cic.; **b,** *things relating to the dead* or *to burial,* Tac. **II.** Transf., *death-bringing, deadly, fatal;* dona, Ov.; annus, Tac.

fĕrax -ācis (fero), *fruitful, fertile, prolific.* **A.** Lit., agri, Cic.; with genit., Iberia ferax venenorum, Hor.; with abl., feracior uvis, Ov.; **B.** Transf., nullus feracior in philosophia locus est quam de officiis, Cic.; with genit., illa aetate qua nulla virtutum feracior fuit, Liv.

ferbĕo = ferveo (q.v.).

ferculum and **fĕrĭcŭlum** -i, n. (fero), *a litter, bier, tray;* **a,** for carrying the spolia opima and the trophies at a triumph, Liv.; **b,** for carrying the images of the gods in processions, Cic.; **c,** for bringing in dishes; hence, meton., *a course,* Prop.

fĕrē, adv. (root FER-o), *almost, nearly.* **A.** Gen., totius fere Galliae legati, Caes.; omnes fere, Cic.; **a,** esp. with expression denoting time, quintā fere horā, Cic.; eādem fere horā quā veni, *about the same hour,* Cic.; **b,** with negatives, *scarcely, hardly;* aetates vestrae nihil aut non fere multum differunt, Cic. **B.** = semper fere, *nearly always, usually;* fit enim fere ut, etc., Cic.; with a negative, *seldom,* Cic.

fĕrentārĭus -ii, m. (fero), *a light-armed soldier who fought with missiles,* Sall.

Fĕrentīnum -i, n. **I.** *a town of the Hernici on the Via Latina,* now *Ferento;* adj., **a, Fĕrentīnus** -a -um, *Ferentine;* caput aquae Ferentinae, or simply caput Ferentinum, *the source of a stream running near Ferentinum,* Liv.; subst., **Fĕrentīna** -ae, f. *a goddess of Ferentinum;* **b, Fĕrentīnās** -ātis, *Ferentine.* **II.** *a town in Etruria,* now *Ferentino.*

Fĕrĕtrĭus -ii, m. (feretrum, fero), *a surname of Jupiter, to whom the* spolia opima *were dedicated,* Liv.

fĕrĕtrum -i, n. (fero), *a bier for carrying a corpse to the grave,* Ov., Verg.

fĕrĭae -ārum, f. for fesiae, same root as festus, *days of rest, holidays.* **I.** Lit., novendiales, Cic.; ferias agere, Liv. **II.** Transf., *rest,* Hor.

fĕrĭātus -a -um, p. adj. (from ferior), *keeping holiday, idle, unoccupied, disengaged, at leisure;* deus feriatus torpet, Cic.; with ab, feriatus a negotiis publicis, Cic.

fĕrĭcŭlum = ferculum (q.v.).

fĕrīnus -a -um (ferus), *relating to a wild beast, wild;* caro, Sall.; vellera, Ov. Subst., **fĕrīna** -ae, f. *flesh of wild animals, game,* Verg.

fĕrĭo, 4. *to strike, knock, beat, hit, smite.* **I. A.** Lit., murum arietibus, Sall.; frontem, Cic.; ferire mare, *to row,* Verg.; absol., contra ferire, Sall.; ferit sidera vertice, *reaches to the stars,* Hor. **B.** Transf., *to hit;* multa patent in eorum vita quae fortuna feriat, *influences,* Cic.; medium ferire, *to keep the middle of the road,* Cic. **II. 1,** *to strike dead, slay, kill;* hostem, Sall.; humilem agnam, Hor.; and hence, foedus, *to make a treaty* (because a sow was then slain), Cic.; **2,** *to cut in pieces;* stricto retinacula ferro, Verg.; **3,** *to bring out, utter;* verba palato, Hor. (syncop. imperf. feribant, Ov.).

fĕrĭor, 1. (feriae), *to keep holiday,* Varr.

fĕrĭtas -ātis, f. (ferus), *wildness, savageness;* hominis, Cic.; leonis, Ov.; loci, Ov.

fermē, adv. (superl. of fere = ferime), *almost, nearly, within a little.* **I.** haec ferme gesta, Liv.; **a,** of numbers, *about;* sex millia ferme passuum, Liv.; **b,** with negatives, *hardly, scarcely,* Cic. **II.** = semper ferme, *nearly always, usually;* ut ferme evenit, Cic.

fermento, 1. (fermentum), *to cause to ferment,* Plin.

fermentum -i, n. (for fervimentum, from ferveo), **1,** *that which causes fermentation, leaven, yeast,* Tac.; transf., *anger,* or *the cause of anger,* Plaut.; **2,** meton., *a kind of beer,* Verg.

fĕro, tŭli, lātum, ferre (root FER, Gr. ΦΕΡ, perf. tuli, from old form tulo, supine latum, orig. tlatum from old tlao, τλάω), *to bear, bring, carry.* **I.** Gen., **A.** Lit., **a,** *to bear;* faces in Capitolium, Cic.; (α) *to carry on one's person;* cervice jugum, Hor.; (β) ventrem, *to be pregnant,* Liv.; (γ) milit. t. t., arma contra aliquem, Cic.; signa in aliquem, *to attack,* Liv.; **b,** *to bring;* venenum, Liv.; alicui osculum, Ov.; alicui tributum, Liv.; *to offer* (to the gods); sacra divis, Verg. **B.** Transf., **a,** *to bear;* (α) nomen Aemilii Pauli, Liv.; aliquem in oculis or oculis, *to be very fond of,* Cic.; prae se ferre aliquid, *to display, make public,* Cic.; obscure ferre, *to conceal,* Cic.; (β) *to endure, submit to, bear;* contumaciam alicuius, Cic.; ea vina quae vetustatem ferunt, *which keep for a long time,* Cic.; with pers. obj., optimates quis ferat? Cic.; with acc. and infin., ferunt aures hominum illa laudari, Cic.; absol., non feram, non patiar, non sinam, Cic.; with adv., aliquid ferre aegre, moleste, graviter molesteque, *to take it ill, be vexed at,* Cic.; aequo or iniquo animo, Cic.; facile, clementer, fortiter ac sapienter, Cic.; with acc. and infin., si quis aegre ferat se pauperem esse, Cic.; partic., non ferendus, *intolerable;* facinus, Cic.; non ferendum, with acc. and infin., Cic.; **b,** *to bring;* (α) opem, auxilium, Cic.; alicui fraudem, Cic.; ferre responsa Turno, Verg.; conditionem ferre, *to propose terms,* Cic.; aliquam, *to propose some one as a wife,* Cic.; legal t. t., suffragium, *to vote,* Cic.; legem, *to propose a law,* Cic.; so ferre de aliqua re ut, etc., *to propose that,* Cic.; (alicui) judicem, of the prosecutor, *to propose a judge to the defendant,* Cic.; (β) of abstractions, *to demand, require, allow;* si ita res feret, Cic.; ut mea fert opinio, Cic. **II.** Esp., **A.** expensum ferre, *to set down in an account-book as paid,* Cic. **B.** *to spread abroad, report, speak of;* ferre haec omnibus sermonibus, Caes.; ferunt or pass. fertur, feruntur, *people say, it is reported,* with acc. and infin. or in pass. nom. and infin.; fama fert, *the story goes,* with acc., Liv.; ferre, with double acc., *to give a person out to be;* si te petitorem fero, Cic. **C,** *to think over, consider;* id consilio ante ferre debemus, Cic. **D.** *to carry off;* **1,** in a good sense, veniam peto feroque, Liv.; non tacitum feres, *I will not be silent about it,* Cic.; fructus ex republica, Cic.; gratiam (*thanks*) alicuius rei, Liv.; polit. t. t., repulsam (a populo), Cic.; centuriam, tribus, *to gain the votes of,* Cic.; **2,** in a bad sense, *to carry off violently;* te fata tulerunt, Verg.; ferre et agere, *to plunder,* Liv. **E.** *to bring forth;* terra fruges ferre potest, Cic. **F.** *to put in motion;* **1,** *to drive away, lead;* ferre se or middle ferri, *to hasten, rush,* and of things, *to flow, mount, sink;* **a,** lit., inde domum pedem, Verg.; milit. t. t., signa ferre, *to march away,* Liv.; se ferre alicui obviam, Cic.; se ferre aliquem, *to act as, to profess to be, to declare oneself to be;* libertum se populi Romani, Liv.; ad eum omni celeritate ferri, Caes.; Rhenus citatus fertur per, etc., *rushes quickly,* Caes.; **b,** transf., aliquem in or ad caelum laudibus, *to praise sky-high,* Cic.;

eloquentia quae cursu magno sonituque fertur, Cic, ferri aliqua re, *to be borne away by, to be possessed by*, crudelitate et scelere, Cic, 2, of a road, etc, *to lead to*, via fert Verruginem, Liv., transf, si qua ad verum via ferret inquirentem, Liv (archaic redupl perf tetulit, ap Cic)

fĕrōcia -ae, f (ferox), a, in a good sense, *high spirit, courage*, Cic, b, in a bad sense, *fierceness, ferocity*, Cic., transf, vini, *harshness, roughness*, Plaut

fĕrōcitas -ātis, f (ferox), a, *courage, untamed spirit*, Cic, b, in a bad sense, *fierceness, haughtiness*, Cic

fĕrōcitĕr, adv (ferox), a, in a good sense, *courageously, bravely*, Liv, b, in a bad sense, *rudely, roughly, fiercely*, Cic

Fērōnia -ae, f (root FER, cf feralis), *an old Italian goddess, patroness of freedmen.*

fĕrox ōcis (connected with ferus and Gr θηρ) **I.** In a good sense, *courageous, high-spirited, warlike, brave;* juvenis ferocissimus, Liv, feroces ad bellandum viri, Liv **II.** In a bad sense, *wild, unbridled, proud*, with abl, stolide ferox viribus suis, Liv, with genit, linguae, Tac, victoria eos ipsos ferociores impotentioresque reddit, Cic, of things, ferox aetas, Hor, oratio, Cic

ferrāmentum -i, n. (ferrum), *any instrument* or *tool*, esp in agriculture, *made of iron*, Cic

ferrāria -ae, f, v. ferrarius

ferrārius -a -um (ferrum), *relating* or *belonging to iron*, faber, *a blacksmith*, Plaut Subst, **ferrāria** -ae, f *iron mine*, Caes

ferrātus -a um (ferrum) **I.** *furnished* or *covered with iron*, Liv, hasta, Liv, agmina, *iron-clad*, Hor. **II.** *of iron, iron*, obices portarum, Tac

ferrĕus -a -um (ferrum), *iron* **A.** Lit, *made of iron*, clavi, Caes **B.** Meton, *like iron*, 1, *hard, stern, unfeeling, cruel*, Aristo Chius, praefractus, ferreus, Cic, os, Cic, 2, *lasting like iron, immovable, unyielding, firm*, corpus animusque Catonis, Liv, 3, *hard, oppressive*, sors vitae, Ov., somnus, *death*, Verg

ferrūginĕus -a um (ferrugo), *iron coloured, dusky*, hyacinthus, Verg, cymba, Verg

ferrūginus = ferrugineus (q v)

ferrūgo -inis, f (from ferrum, as aerugo from aes), 1, *iron rust*, Plin, 2, *the colour of iron rust, dusky (iron grey, dark blue, steel blue) colour*, viridis ferrugine barba, Ov

ferrum -i, n **I.** *iron in its rough state, ore* **A.** Lit, Cic **B.** Transf, *hard-heartedness, insensibility, cruelty*, in pectore ferrum gerit, Ov **II.** *iron worked up*, meton **A.** Gen, *any iron instrument, the plough*, Verg, *an axe*, Hor, *a stylus for writing*, Ov; *scissors for hair cutting*, Ov, *curling-irons*, Verg **B.** Esp, *a sword* ferrum stringere, Liv, aliquem cum ferro invadere, Cic, urbes ferro atque igni vastare, Liv, haec omnia flamma ac ferro delere, Cic

ferrūmen -inis, n, *cement*, Plin

ferrūmino, 1 (ferrumen), *to cement, bind together*, Plin

fertĭlis -e (fero), *fruitful, prolific, fertile*, 1, agri, Cic, with genit, multos fertiles agros alios aliorum fructuum, Cic, with abl, insula agro fertilis, Liv, transf, pectus, Ov 2, *fertilising, making fruitful*, dea, *Ceres*, Ov, Bacchus, Hor

fertĭlĭtas -ātis, f (fertilis), *fruitfulness, fertility;* with subject genit, agrorum, Cic, of persons, indoluit fertilitate sua, Ov

fertum (ferctum), -i, n, *a kind of sacrificial cake*, Pers.

fertus a-um (fero), *fruitful*, arva, ap Cic

fĕrŭla -ae, f (fero), 1, *the herb fennel*, 2, *a rod used to punish slight offences of slaves and children, a ferule*, Hor, used as a goad for cattle, Ov.

fĕrus -a um (root FER, connected with θήρ, Aeolic φήρ) **I** Lit., *wild, untamed, uncultivated;* bestiae, Cic, montes, Verg, silvae, Hor Subst., **a, fera** -ae, f (sc bestia), *a wild animal* (as opp to cicur, a domesticated animal), ferarum ritu, Liv, feras agitare, Cic; transf, of constellations, magna minorque ferae, *the Great and Little Bear*, Ov; **b, ferus** -i, m, *a wild beast, a wild boar*, Ov, *an ox*, Ov, *horse*, Verg, *stag*, Verg **II.** Transf, *wild, rough, savage, uncivilised, cruel*, gens, Cic, hostis, Cic, facinus, Liv

fervĕfăcio -fēci factum, 3 (ferveo and facio), *to make hot, heat, boil, melt*, pix fervefacta, Caes, jacula fervefacta, Caes

fervens -entis, abl -enti, p adj (from ferveo), *glowing, hot, heated* **I.** Lit, aqua, Cic, rota, Ov **II.** Transf, a, ira, Ov, b, of character, *impetuous, fiery*, fortis animus ferventior est, Cic, Cassi rapido ferventius amni ingenium, Hor

ferventĕr, adv (fervens), *hotly, warmly*, loqui, ap Cic

fervĕo, ferbŭi -ēre and (poet.) **fervo**, fervi -ĕre **I. A.** Lit, *to be boiling hot, to boil, seethe, glow*, Cic, validum posito medicamen aeno fervet, Ov **B.** Transf, a, *to glow with passion, etc, to be heated*, fervet avaritiā pectus, Hor qui usque fervet ferturque avaritiā ut etc Cic, b, *to be carried on briskly*, fervet opus, Verg, c, *to glitter*, jam fervĕre litora flammis, Verg **II.** 1, *to rage, foam, seethe, hiss*, a, lit, fervet fretis spirantibus aequor, Verg, b, transf, of a poet, monte decurrens velut amnis fervet (Pindarus), *rages*, Hor, 2, *to be in quick movement*, a, of a crowd, *to swarm forth*, fervĕre cum videas classem lateque vagari, Verg, b, of places, *to swarm with*, instructo Marte videres fervere Leucaten, Verg

fervesco, 3 (ferveo), *to become hot, begin to glow, begin to boil*, Lucr

fervĭdus a-um (ferveo) **I.** *boiling, seething* **A** 1, lit, humor, Ov, 2, transf, of orators, *passionate, excited*, paulo fervidior erat oratio, Cic **B.** *burning, glowing, hot*, 1, lit, pars mundi, Cic, vina, Hor, 2, transf, *fiery, hot*, fervidi animi vir, Liv, with abl, fervidus ira, Verg **II.** *raging, foaming*, vada, Verg

fervo = ferveo (q v)

fervor -ōris, m (ferveo) **I.** *boiling heat, raging heat* **A.** Lit, medius fervoribus, *in the heat of noon*, Verg, mundi, Cic **B.** Transf, *heat, ardour, passion*, mentis, animi, Cic **II** *raging, foaming*, Oceani, maris, Cic

Fescennia -ae, f, and **Fescennium** -ii, n, *a town in Etruria famous for the Fescennine verses* Adj, **Fescenninus** a um, *Fescennine*, Fescennini versus, *rude satirical verses*, hence licentia Fescennina, Hor

fessus a -um (fatiscor), *weary, tired, exhausted*, de via, Cic, militia, Hor, plorando, Cic, corpus fessum vulnere, Liv, in the genit, fessi rerum, Verg, fessa aetas, *old age*, Tac, res fessae, *distress*, Verg

festīnantĕr, adv (festino), *hastily, rapidly quickly*, nimium festinanter dictum, Cic

festīnātio -ōnis, f (festino), *haste, speed, hurry*, festinatio praepropera, Cic, with object genit, adipiscendi honoris, Cic, omni festinatione properare in patriam, Cic, plur, quid afferebat festinationum Cic

festīnāto, adv (festino), *hastily, rapidly*, Plin.

festīno, 1. (festinus). **I.** Intransit., *to be in rapid motion, to hasten, hurry;* plura scripsissem nisi tui festinarent, Cic.; with ad and the acc., ad effectum operis, Liv. **II.** Transit., *to hasten, accelerate;* profectionem, Sall.; fugam, Verg.; partic., festinatus, *hastened;* iter, Ov.: with infin., tanto opere migrare, Cic.

festīnus -a -um (fero), *hastening, hasty;* cursu festinus anhelo, Ov.

fēstīvē, adv. (festivus), *humorously, facetiously, wittily;* belle et festive, Cic.

festīvĭtas -ātis, f. (festivus). **I.** Object., **A.** *gaiety, pleasure*, Plaut. **B.** Esp., festivitates, *embellishments, ornaments* (of discourse), iis festivitatibus insolentius abutitur, Cic. **II.** Subject., *cheerfulness, humour, pleasantry;* lepos et festivitas, festivitas et facetiae, Cic.

festīvus -a -um (festus). **I.** Gen., **1,** *pleasant, agreeable, pretty;* poema, Cic.; copia librorum, Cic.; **2,** of places, *bright, pleasant*, Plaut. **II.** Esp., **1,** of character, *good-humoured, cheerful;* puer, Cic.; **2,** of discourse, or of speakers, *lively, bright, droll, amusing, humorous, witty;* oratio, Cic.; festivus homo, Cic.

festūca -ae, f. (fero). **A.** Lit., *a stalk, straw*, Plin. **B.** Transf., *the rod with which slaves were touched in the ceremony of manumission*, Plaut.

1. **festus** -a -um (root FE, whence also februus), *sacred, hallowed, devoted to festivals, festive;* dies, Cic.; chori, Ov.; lux (= dies), Ov.; tempus, Hor.; dies festos anniversarios agere, Cic. Subst., **festum** -i, n. *a feast*, Ov.

2. **Festus** -i, m. Sext. Pompeius, *a Latin grammarian, who lived probably at the end of the fourth century* A.D., *author of a work in twenty books*, "De Verborum Significatione."

fētĭālis -is, m. *a fetial*, plur. **fētĭāles,** *a college of heralds whose business it was to demand redress of grievances, declare war*, etc., Cic.; in sing., legatus fetialis, Liv. Adj., **fētĭālis** -e, *belonging to the fetiales;* jus fetiale, Cic.

fētūra -ae, f. (fetus). **A.** *the bearing or bringing forth of young, breeding*, Cic. **B.** Meton., *the young brood, offspring*, Ov., Verg.

1. **fētus** (foetus) -a -um (partic. of * feo). **I.** Pass., **A.** Lit., **1,** *pregnant;* pecus, Verg.; **2,** transf., **a,** *fruitful, fertile;* terra feta frugibus, Cic. **B.** Poet., *full of;* machina feta armis, Verg. **II.** Middle, *that has brought forth, newly delivered;* ursa, lupa, Ov.

2. **fētus** -ūs, m. (* feo, whence also fecundus), **I.** *the bearing, bringing forth, or hatching of young;* labor bestiarum in fetu, Cic.; of the soil, *bearing, producing;* quae frugibus atque baccis terrae fetu profunduntur, Cic.; fig., nec ullā aetate uberior oratorum fetus fuit, Cic. **II.** Meton., *that which is brought forth;* **a,** *offspring, brood;* Germania quos horrida parturit fetus, Hor.; fetus suis (*sucking-pig*), Verg.; **b,** of plants, *fruit, produce, shoot;* nucis, Verg.; meliores et grandiores fetus edere (of land), Cic.; fig., ex quo triplex ille animi fetus exsistet, Cic.

fĭber -bri, m., *a beaver*, Plin.

fībra -ae, f. (findo). **1,** *a fibre, filament*, in animals or plants; stirpium, radicum, Cic.; **2,** *the entrails of an animal;* bidentis, Ov.

Fĭbrēnus -i, m., *a river in Latium, near Arpinum, flowing into the Liris*, now *Fibreno.*

fĭbrīnus -a -um (fiber), *of or belonging to the beaver*, Plin.

fībŭla -ae, f. (contr. for figibula from figo), *a buckle, brooch, clasp*, Verg., Liv.; *an iron clamp fastening beams together*, Caes.

Fīcāna -ae, f., *a town in Latium on the road to Ostia.*

fīcēdŭla -ae, f. (ficus), *a small bird, the beccafico*, Plin.

fictē, adv. (fictus), *falsely, fictitiously;* ficte et fallaciter, Cic.

fictĭlis -e (fingo), *earthen, made of clay;* vasa, Cic.; figurae, Cic. Subst., **fictĭle** -is, n., usually plur., *earthenware, earthen vessels;* omnia (ponuntur) fictilibus, Ov.

fictor -ōris, m. (fingo), **1,** *an image-maker, a statuary;* pictores fictoresque, Cic.; **2,** *a feigner;* fandi fictor Ulysses, *master in deceit*, Verg.

fictrix -īcis, f. (fictor), *she that forms or fashions;* materiae fictrix et moderatrix divina est providentia, Cic.

fictūra -ae, f. (fingo), *a forming, fashioning*, Plaut.

fictus, partic. of fingo.

fīcŭla -ae, f. (dim. of ficus), *a little fig*, Plaut.

Fīcŭlĕa (Fīculnĕa) -ae, f. *town in the country of the Sabines on the* Via Nomentana. Adj., **Fīcŭlensis** -e, *Ficulean.*

fīculnus (fīculnĕus) -a -um (ficula), *of or relating to the fig-tree;* truncus, Hor.

fīcus -i and -ūs, f. (perhaps from fio, feo), **1,** *the fig-tree;* arbor fici, Cic.; **2,** *a fig*, Hor.

fīdē, adv. (fidus), *faithfully*, Cic.

fĭdĕīcommissum -i, n. (fides and committo), legal t. t., *a trust*, Quint.

fĭdēlĕ, adv. (fidelis), *faithfully*, Plaut.

fĭdēlĭa -ae, f. *an earthenware pot or vase*, Plaut.; *a pot for whitewash;* prov., duo parietes de eadem fidelia dealbare, *to kill two birds with one stone*, ap. Cic.

fĭdēlis -e (1. fides), *that can be trusted or relied upon, true, steadfast, faithful.* **A.** Of persons, socius, amicus, Cic.; alicui or in aliquem, Cic.; in amicitiis, Cic. Subst., **fĭdēles** -ium, m. *confidants, faithful friends*, Cic. **B.** Transf., of inanimate objects, consilium fidele, Cic.; lacrimae, *genuine*, Ov.; meton., *durable, lasting, strong;* lorica, Verg.

fĭdēlĭtas -ātis, f. (fidelis), *faithfulness, trustworthiness, fidelity*, Cic.; erga patriam, ap. Cic.

fĭdēlĭtĕr, adv. with compar. and superl. (fidelis). **1,** *faithfully, trustworthily, honestly, surely*, Cic.; per quorum loca fideliter (*free of danger*) mihi pateret iter, Cic.; **2,** meton., *properly, well;* ingenuas didicisse fideliter artes, Ov.

Fīdēnae -ārum, f. and **Fīdēna** -ae, f. *a town in Latium*, now *Castro Giubileo.* Adj., **Fīdēnas** -ātis, *of or belonging to Fidenae.*

fīdens -entis, abl. -enti, p. adj. (from fido), *without fear, confident, courageous;* homo, animus, Cic.; with genit., animi, Verg.; with abl., fidens et animo et viribus, Liv.

fīdentĕr, adv. with compar. (fidens), *confidently, courageously*, Cic.

1. **fīdentĭa** -ae, f. (fido), *confidence, courage, boldness*, Cic.

2. **Fīdentĭa** -ae, f. *town in Gallia Cispadana.*

1. **fīdes** -ĕi, f. (fido), *trust, confidence, reliance, credence, belief, faith.* **I.** Lit., **A.** Gen., fidem decipere, Liv., or fallere, Cic.; alicui or alicui rei fidem habere, *to place confidence in*, with acc. and infin., Cic.; alicui rei fidem tribuere, adjungere, Cic.; fidem facere, *to awake confidence*, Cic.; nuntiabantur haec eadem Curioni; sed aliquamdiu fides fieri non poterat, *no reliance was placed in the news*, Caes. **B.** Esp., mercantile t. t., *credit;* quum fides totā Italiā esset angustior, *impaired*, Caes.; fidem moliri, Liv.; fides concidit, *has fallen*, Cic.; fides de foro sublata est, Cic.; fidem renovare, Cic.; often with res, *property*, res et fides, Sall.

ubi res eos jam pridem, fides nuper deficere coepit, Cic ; homo sine re, sine fide, sine spe, Cic., transf, segetis certa fides meae, *produce, return*, Hor. **II.** Meton., **A.** *that which produces confidence, faithfulness, fidelity, conscientiousness, honesty, credibility, truthfulness;* **1,** gen, exemplum antiquae probitatis ac fidei, Cic., fidem praestare, *to be loyal*, Cic ; of faithfulness in treaties and political alliances pro vetere ac perpetua erga Romanum fide, Caes , **a,** in appeals and oaths, fidem vestram oro atque obsecro, judices, Cic.; pro deum atque hominum fidem, Cic , **b,** legal t t , ex bona fide or bonā fide, *in good faith, sincerely, honestly*, Cic , judicia de mala fide, *dishonesty*, Cic , Fides personif as a goddess, Cic ; **2,** esp , **a,** *a promise, assurance word of honour, engagement*, fidem fallere, frangere, violare, *to break a promise*, Cic , dare alicui, Cic , obligare, *to make an engagement*, Cic , liberare, servare, *to keep a promise*, Cic ; fidem prodere, Cic , fide meā, *on my word of honour*, Cic., **b,** fides publica or simply publica, *a promise of protection in the name of the state, a safe-conduct*, fidem publicam postulare, Cic , Lusitani contra interpositam fidem interfecti, Cic ; fide acceptā venerat in castra Romana, Liv , **c,** *faithful protection, constant help;* conferre se in alicuius fidem et clientelam, in alicuius amicitiam et fidem, Cic , se suaque omnia in fidem atque potestatem populi Romani permittere, Cic , venire in alicuius fidem, Liv , or in alicuius fidem ac potestatem, Caes , alicuius fidem sequi, Caes , aliquem in fidem recipere, Cic ; in alicuius fide et cl.c tela esse, Cic **B.** *credibility, trustworthiness*, .. reports, statements, etc ; **1,** fidem facit aliquid judicii mei, Cic.; tabularum, Cic , **2, a,** *proof*, manifesta fides publicā ope Volscos hostes adjutos, Liv , **b,** *certainty*, verba fides sequitur, Ov

2 **fides** -is, f, usually plur **fides** -ium (σφιδη, or perhaps from findo), lit. *a gut-string for a musical instrument;* hence, *a lyre, lute, harp*, discere, Cic., fidibus Latinis Thebanos aptare modos, Hor.; sing., fides Teia, Hor

fidicen -cinis, m (2 fides and cano), *a player on the harp, lyre, lute*, Cic , poet., *a lyric poet*, lyrae Romanae, Hor

fidicina -ae, f (fidicen), *a female player on the lute or harp*, Plaut.

fidicinus a -um (fidicen), *relating or belonging to harp playing*, Plaut.

fidicula -ae, f. and gen plur. **fidiculae** -ārum, f (dim of 2 fides), **1,** *a little lyre or lute*, Cic , **2,** *an instrument for torturing slaves*, Suet.

Fidius -ii, m (connected with fides, fido), in full Dius Fidius, *a Roman deity, personification of faith*, me Dius Fidius and medius fidius (ellipt = ita me Dius Fidius juvet), *So help me God!* Cic

fido, fisus sum, 3 (root FID, Gr ΠΙΘ, πείθ ω, πείθ-ομαι), *to trust, believe, confide in*, with dat. or abl., sibi, Cic ; nocti, Verg , prudentiā, Cic , with acc and infin , Liv

fiducia -ae, f (fido) **I.** Lit , **a,** *confidence, trust, reliance, assurance*, alicuius, *in some one*, Cic.; sui, *in oneself*, Liv , arcae nostrae, Cic , **b,** *self confidence, self reliance, courage, bravery*, Caes **II.** Legal t. t , *a contract by which a man temporarily transfers property to another, a pledging, pawning, mortgaging*, etc ; formula fiduciae, Cic , fiducia accepta, Cic

fiduciarius -a -um (fiducia), *entrusted, committed, given in trust*, urbs, Liv , opera, Caes

fidus -a -um (fido), *true, faithful, trusty, certain, sure*, **1,** of persons, amici fidi, Cic , with dat , Abe'nx fidus ante Poenis, Liv , with genit regina tui fidissima, Verg ; **2,** of inanimate objects, tam fida canum custodia, Cic , statio male fida carinis, *an insecure anchorage for ships*, Verg

figlinus (figulinus) -a -um (figulus), *of or belonging to a potter*, Plin Subst., **1, figlina** -ae, f **a,** *a potter's art or craft*, Plin ; **b,** *a potter's workshop, pottery*, Plin ; **2, figlinum** i, n. *earthenware*, Plin

figo, fixi, fixum, 3 **I.** *to fix, fasten, make fast, make firm, attach, affix* **A.** Lit , **a,** aliquem in cruce, Cic , caput legis in poste curiae, Cic ; arma ad postem, Cic , **b,** *to build*, moenia, Ov , **c,** oscula, *to imprint*, Verg **B.** Transf , **a,** nequitiae modum suae, *to set a limit*, Hor , **b,** vestigia, *to check one s steps*, Verg ; **c,** *to fix, make fast*, fixum et statutum est, Cic **II. A.** Lit , **a,** *to thrust in, drive in*, mucronem in hoste, Cic , **b,** *to transfix*, aliquem sagitti, Tac **B.** Transf , **a,** aliquem maledictis, *attack with reproaches*, Cic , **b,** *to fix*, oculos in terram, Liv , **c,** *to fix in one's attention*, illud fixum in animis vestris tenetote, Cic

figulāris -e (figulus), *relating or belonging to a potter*, Plaut

figulinus = figlinus (q v)

figulus -i, m (root FIG, whence fingo), *a worker in clay, a potter*, a figulis munitam urbem, *Babylon, made of brick*, Juv

figura -ae, f (fingo) **I.** *form, shape, figure*, **a,** hominis, Cic , **b,** *an atom*, Lucr , **c,** *shade of a dead person*, Verg **II. a,** *kind, nature, species, form*, negotii, Cic., **b,** in rhet , *a figure of speech*, Cic.

figurātus -a um, partic of figuro

figuro, 1 (figura), *to form, mould, shape;* **1,** ita figuratum corpus ut excellat aliis, Cic , **2,** transf , os tenerum pueri balbumque poeta figurat, Hor

filātim, adv (filum), *thread by thread*, Lucr

filia ae, f (filius), *a daughter*, Cic , virgo filia, Cic., poet transf , pinus silvae filia nobilis, Hor

filicātus -a um (filix), *adorned with ferns*, paterae, *embossed or chased with fern leaves*, Cic

filiola -ae, f (dim of filia), *a little daughter* Cic , sarcastically of an effeminate man, duce filiolā Curionis, Cic

filiolus -i, m. (dim of filius), *a little son*, Cic

filius -ii (voc sing fili), m (feo, whence fecundus, etc), *son*, Cic , terrae, *a man of mean origin, unknown person*, Cic , fortunae, *a child of fortune*, Hor

filix -ic s, f *fern*, Verg

filum -i, n (figo), *a thread* **I.** Lit , **a,** of wool, linen, etc , velamina filo pleno, Ov , prov , pendere filo (tenui), *to hang by a thread, be in great danger*, Ov , **b,** *a woollen fillet round the cap of the flamen*, capite velato filo, Liv , **c,** of other things, deducit aranea filum pede, Ov , **d,** *the thread of life* spun by the Parcae , sororum fila trium, Hor **II.** Transf , **a,** *the form, shape of anything*, Lucr , **b,** *the manner form, thread of discourse*, Cic

fimbriae -ārum, f plur , *fringe, border, edge*, madentes cincinnorum fimbriae, *extremities*, Cic

Fimbria -ae, m (G Flavius), *friend of Marius, general in the Mithridatic War.*

fimus -i, m. and **fimum** -i, n *dung, excrement, dirt*, Liv , Verg

findo, fidi, fissum, 3 *to split, cleave, separate, divide*, lignum, Verg , findere agros sarculo, Hor ; hāc insulā quasi rostro finditur Fibrenus Cic.

fingo, finxi, fictum, 3 (root FIG, whence figulus). **I.** *to stroke*, manus aegras manibus amici, Ov. **II. A.** *to fashion, form, mould;* **1,** lit., **a,** mollissimam ceram ad nostrum arbitrium formare et fingere, Cic.; **b,** imago ficta, *a statue,* Cic.; natura fingit hominem, Cic.; **2,** transf., **a,** *to imagine, conceive;* fingite igitur cogitatione imaginem huius conditionis meae, Cic.; with acc. and infin., finge aliquem fieri sapientem, Cic.; **b,** *to invent, fabricate, devise;* crimina, opprobria in aliquem, Cic.; partic., fictus, *invented, feigned;* ficta fabula, Cic.; hence subst., **fictum** -i, n. *something invented, a lie;* ficta loqui, Ov.; **c,** *to feign;* nihil fingam, nihil dissimulem, Cic. **B.** *to arrange, order;* **1,** lit., **a,** crinem fronde premit fingens, Verg.; **b,** fingere vultum, *to put on a friendly look,* Ov., or *to put on a brave look,* Caes.; ficto pectore fatus, Verg.; **2,** transf., *to form;* oratorem, Cic.; se totum ad arbitrium alicuius, Cic.

fīniens -entis (partic. of finio), sc. orbis or circulus, *the horizon,* Cic.

fīnio, 4. (finis). **I.** Transit., *to bound, limit, enclose within limits.* **A.** Lit., imperium populi Romani, Caes.; lingua finita dentibus, Cic. **B.** Transf., **1,** *to enclose within bounds, restrain;* an potest cupiditas finiri? Cic.; **2,** *to define, determine, prescribe, appoint;* sepulcris novis modum, Cic.; with ne and the subj., potuisse finire senatus consulto ne, etc., Liv.; **3, a,** gen., *to put an end to, conclude, end, finish;* bellum, Caes.; labores, Cic.; and pass., *to end, cease;* **b,** (α) finiri (middle), *to die,* Cic. poet.; finitā Claudiorum domo, *having become extinct,* Tac.; (β) *to finish speaking;* omnia finierat, Ov.; (γ) *to bring a period to a close;* ut sententiae verbis finiantur, Cic. **II.** Intransit., **a,** *to die;* sic Tiberius finivit, Tac.; **b,** *to finish speaking;* finierat Telamone satus, Ov.; *to bring a period to a close;* illi philosopho placet ordiri a superiore paeone, posteriore finire, Cic.

fīnis -is, m. and f. (findo). **I.** *the boundary, limit, border.* **A.** Lit., eius loci, Cic.; provinciae Galliae, Liv.; plur., *territory;* iter in Santonum fines facere, Caes. **B.** Transf., **a,** *boundary, limit;* mihi fines terminosque constituam, extra quos egredi non possum, Cic.; **b,** *term, limit;* ad eum finem, *so far,* Cic.; fine (fini), with genit., *as far as,* fine genus, Ov. **II.** *the end;* **a,** finis vitae, Cic.; ad finem venire, Liv.; finem facere, with genit. bellandi, Caes.; sollicitudinis, Cic.; finem facere, with dat. pretio, Cic.; finem capere, *come to an end,* Cic.; **b,** esp., (α) *death;* Neronis, Tac.; (β) *the highest, the extremity;* bonorum, malorum, *greatest good, greatest evil,* Cic.; **c,** *object, end, aim;* domus finis et usus, Cic. (abl. sing. fine and fini).

fīnītē, adv. (finitus, from finio), *moderately, within bounds,* Cic.

fīnĭtĭmus (fīnĭtŭmus) -a -um (finis), *neighbouring, adjacent.* **A.** Lit., Galli Belgis, Caes.; aër mari finitumus, Cic. Subst., **fīnĭtĭmi** -ōrum, m. *neighbours, neighbouring states,* Cic. **B.** Transf., *related to, resembling, similar;* vicina eius atque finitima dialecticorum scientia, Cic.; with dat., huic generi historia finitima est, Cic.

fīnītor -ōris, m. (finio), *one who determines boundaries, a land surveyor,* Cic.

fīnĭtŭmus = finitimus (q.v.).

fīnītus -a -um, partic. of finio.

fīo, factus sum, fieri (connected with φύω), pass. of facio. **I.** Lit., *to be made;* hic ubi fit doctā multa corona manu, Ov. **II.** Transf., **A.** Gen., **a,** *to be done, to arise;* fit clamor, Cic.; id ei loco nomen factum, Liv.; per aliquem fit quominus, etc., Cic.; **b,** *to happen;* (α) Pompeio melius est factum, Cic.; esp. with abl., quid illo fiet, *what will happen with him?* Cic.; with de, quid de Tulliola mea fiet? Cic.; ut fit, ut fieri solet, *as usual, as is often the case;* ut fit plerumque, Cic.; fit saepe ut non respondeant ad tempus, Cic.; potest fieri ut fallar, *I may be deceived,* Cic.; fieri non potest quin, etc., Cic.; ita fit ut, etc., Cic.; (β) *to follow;* ita fit ut sapientia sanitas sit animi, Cic.; (γ) *to be;* nec potest fieri me quidquam superbius, Cic. **B.** Esp., **a,** *to become something;* consules facti sunt, Cic.; **b,** *to be esteemed;* me a te plurimi fieri, Cic.; **c,** *to be sacrificed;* quum pro populo fieret, Cic.

firmāmen -inis, n. (firmo), *support, prop,* Ov.

firmāmentum -i, n. (firmo), *a means of support, a prop;* **1,** lit., transversaria tigna quae firmamento esse possint, Cic., Caes.; **2,** transf., **a,** reipublicae, Cic.; **b,** in rhet., *the main point of an argument,* Cic.

firmātor -ōris, m. (firmo), *one who makes firm or establishes,* Tac.

firmē, adv. (firmus), *firmly, steadfastly;* aliquid comprehendere, Cic.; firmissime asseverare, Cic.

firmĭtas -ātis, f. (firmus), *firmness, durability.* **A.** Lit., corporis, Cic. **B.** *firmness, strength of mind, constancy;* animi, Cic.

firmĭtĕr, adv. (firmus), *firmly, strongly;* firmiter insistere, Caes.; firmiter stabilire aliquem, Cic.

firmĭtūdo -dĭnis, f. (firmus), *firmness, strength.* **A.** Lit., operis, Caes. **B.** Transf., *strength, firmness, constancy;* animi, Cic.

firmo, 1. (firmus), *to make firm, strengthen.* **I.** Lit., urbem colonis, Cic.; castra munimentis, Liv. **II.** Transf., **a,** *to make durable, to make secure;* (α) vestigia pinu, *steady his steps by,* Verg.; (β) politically, rempublicam, Cic.; **b,** *to make strong, to strengthen;* (α) physically, vires, Verg.; vocem, Cic.; (β) morally, animum adolescentis nondum consilio et ratione firmatum, Cic.; (γ) *to encourage, cheer, animate;* nostros, Caes.; aliquem alloquio, Tac.; **c,** *to prove, establish;* aliquid rationibus or jurejurando, Cic.

Firmum -i, n. *a town in Picenum,* now *Fermo.* Adj., **Firmānus** -a -um, *of* or *belonging to Firmum.*

firmus -a -um, *firm, strong, stout.* **I.** Lit., ramus, Cic.; with dat., area firma templis ac porticibus sustinendis, Cic. **II.** Transf., **1,** *physically strong, powerful, healthy;* **a,** corpus, Cic.; **b,** milit., *strong;* equitatus et peditatus, Cic.; ad dimicandum, Caes.; **2,** of time, *durable, lasting;* firmissima vina, *which keep,* Verg.; transf., *lasting, valid;* acta Caesaris, Cic.; **3,** *morally and mentally strong;* **a,** *steadfast, firm, immovable;* animus, Cic.; accusator, Cic.; contra pericula, Sall.; firmior in sententia, Cic.; **b,** *sure, firm, to be relied upon;* litterae, Cic.; spes, Cic.; with abl., copiae et numero et genere et fidelitate firmissimae, Cic.; with ad and the acc., firmos (eos) milites ad tuendas nostras res efficere, Cic.

fiscella -ae, f. (dim. of fiscina), *a small rush* or *wicker basket,* Verg.

fiscĭna -ae, f. (fiscus), *a small basket of wicker-work,* Cic.

fiscus -i, m. *a wicker basket;* **1,** *a money-basket, money-bag, purse,* Cic.; meton. = *money,* Juv.; **2,** *the state treasury,* Cic.; **3,** under the empire, *the emperor's private purse* (opp. aerarium, *the state treasury*), Tac.

fissĭlis -e (findo), *that can be cloven* or *split;* lignum, Verg.

fissĭo -ōnis, f. (findo), *a splitting, cleaving, dividing;* glebarum, Cic.

fissum -i, n. (findo), *a split, cleft;* in augury, *a divided liver,* Cic.

fistūca or **festūca** -ae, f *a rammer, mallet*, Caes.

fistŭla -ae, f **I.** Lit, *a tube, pipe*, esp *a water pipe*, usually of lead; fistulas quibus aqua suppeditabatur Jovis templis, praecidere, Cic. **II.** Transf, **1,** *a reed-pipe, a shepherd's pipe, a reed*, eburneola, *a pitch pipe of ivory*, Cic.; **2,** *a kind of ulcer, fistula*, Nep

fistŭlātor -ōris, m (fistula), *one who plays upon the reed-pipe, one who gives a note with the pitch-pipe*, Cic

fixus -a -um, p adj. (from figo), *firm, fixed, immovable*, vestigia, Cic, fixum est, *it is fixed determined*, Cic, decretum, Cic

flābellum -i, n (dim of flabrum), *a small fan*, Prop, fig, cuius linguā quasi flabello seditionis illa tum est egentium contio ventilata, Cic

flābĭlis -e (flo), *airy*, Cic

flābrum -i, n (flo), gen in plur **flābra** -ōrum, *blasts of wind, breezes*, Verg

flaccĕo, 2 (flaccus), *to be faint weak, languid*, transf, *to fail* or *flag in an undertaking*, Messala flaccet, Cic

flaccesco, 3 (inch from flacceo), *to begin to fade, to become faint, weak, languid*, flaccescebat oratio, Cic

flaccĭdus a -um (flaccus), *withered, flabby, flaccid, weak, languid*, Lucr

1 **flaccus** -a -um, **1,** *flabby, flaccid*, Varr, **2,** of men, *flap-eared*, Cic

2. **Flaccus,** Q Horatius, v Horatius

3 **Flaccus,** C Valerius, v Valerius

flăgello, 1 (flagellum), *to whip, scourge, beat*, robora parte caudae, Ov.

flăgellum -i, n (dim of flagrum), *a whip, scourge* **I.** Lit, **a,** Cic, Hor, fig, *the scourge of conscience*, Juv, Lucr, **b,** *a riding-whip*, Verg **II.** Transf, **A.** *the thong of a javelin*, Verg **B.** *a young sprout, vine shoot*, Verg **C.** Plur, flagella, *the arms of a polypus*, Ov

flāgĭtātĭo -ōnis, f (flagito), *an earnest demand* or *entreaty*, Cic

flāgĭtātor -ōris, m (flagito), *one who earnestly demands* or *entreats*, Cic, with genit., pugnae, Liv

flāgĭtĭōsē, adv (flagitiosus), *shamefully, basely, disgracefully, infamously*; impure ac flagitiose vivere, Cic, sumus flagitiose imparati, Cic, alicuius amori flagitiosissime servire, Cic

flāgĭtĭōsus -a um (flagitium), *shameful, disgraceful, infamous*, flagitiosa atque vitiosa vita, Cic, flagitiosum est, with acc and infin, Sall; flagitiosum duco, with infin, Liv

flāgĭtĭum -ii, n. (root FLAG, whence flagito), **I.** *a disgraceful action, shameful crime, shame, disgrace, infamy*; factum flagitii plenum et dedecoris, Cic. ista flagitia Democriti, *shameful expressions*, Cic **II.** Meton, *scoundrel, rascal*, flagitia atque facinora, Cic

flāgĭto, 1 (root FLAG, whence also flagro) = flagranter posco, *to entreat, ask, demand earnestly* **I.** Gen, **a,** of persons, alicuius auxilium, Cic, mercedem gloriae ab aliquo Cic, with double acc, aliquem frumentum, Cic; with ut and the subj, semper flagitavi ut convocaremur, Cic, with infin, Hor, absol, flagitat tabellarius, Cic, **b,** of abstract subjects, quae tempus flagitat, Cic **II.** Esp, **a,** *to demand to know*, posco atque adeo flagito crimen, Cic; **b,** *to demand*, filium ab aliquo, Cic, **c,** *to summon before a court of justice*, aliquem peculatorem Tac

flagrans -antis, p adj (from flagro), *burning* **I.** Gen, **A.** Lit, telum, *lightning*, Verg, flagrantissimus aestus, Liv. **B.** Transf, *glowing with passion, eager, vehement, ardent*, cupiditate, Cic, multitudo, Cic **II.** Esp, **a,** of the eyes, *glowing*, oculi, Ov, **b,** of colour, *glittering*, flagrans sidereo clipeo, Verg

flăgrantĕr, adv (flagrans), *eagerly, ardently, vehemently*, cupere, Tac

flăgrantĭa -ae, f (flagro), *glowing*, oculorum, Cic

flăgro, 1 (root FLAG, Gk ΦΛΕΓ-ω, connected with FLA-re), *to blaze, burn, glow, flame* **I.** Lit., **1,** *to burn*, onerariae flagrantes, Cic, **2,** *to glow, glitter*, flagrant lumina nymphae, Ov **II.** Transf, **1,** of concrete subjects, esp of persons, **a,** Italia flagrans bello, Cic, invidiā propter interitum C Gracchi, Cic, **b,** *to glow or burn with passion, to be eager, vehement*, desiderio, amore, cupiditate, odio, studio dicendi, Cic, **2,** of abstract subj, flagrabant vitia libidinis apud illum, Cic

flăgrum -i, n (root FLAG, Gr ΠΛΗΓ or ΠΛΗΚ, πλησσω), *a scourge, whip*, used for punishing slaves, flagro caedi, Liv

1 **flāmen** -inis, m *the priest of some particular deity*, there were three flamines majores, Dialis *of Jupiter* (the highest in rank), Martialis, *of Mars*, and Quirinalis, *of Romulus*, and twelve flamines minores (Vulcani, Florae, etc), flaminem inaugurare, Liv.

2 **flāmen** -inis, n (flo) **I.** *a blowing, blast*, flamina venti, Lucr **II.** Meton, **A.** *the wind*; ferunt sua flamina classem, Verg **B.** (like πνευματα αὐλῶν) flamina tibiae, *the notes of a flute*, Hor

flāmĭnĭca -ae, f (sc uxor), *the wife of a flamen*, flaminica Dialis, Tac

Flāmĭnīnus, *a surname of the patrician Gens Quinctia*, v Quinctius

flāmĭnĭum -i, n (flamen, sc sacerdotium or munus), *the office or dignity of a flamen*, Cic

Flāmĭnĭus a -um, *name of a Roman gens, the most celebrated member of which was C Flaminius, who, when censor, built a circus and made one of the chief military roads in Italy, and who, when consul, was defeated by Hannibal at the battle of Lacus Trasimenus* Adj, *Flaminian* Hence, **Flāmĭnĭānus** a um, *of or belonging to Flaminius*

flamma -ae, f (for flag ma, from root FLAG, whence flagro), *a flame, blaze, blazing fire* **I.** Lit, **A.** Gen, effusa flamma pluribus locis reluxit, Liv; se flammā eripere, Cic, flammam concipere, *to catch fire*, Caes; prov, prius undis flamma (sc miscebitur), *sooner will fire mingle with water*, of something impossible, ap Cic **B.** Meton, **a,** *a flaming star, lightning*, Verg, **b,** *glitter*, galea flammas vomens, Verg **II.** Transf, **A.** Gen, belli, invidiae, Cic **B.** Esp, *the fire* or *glow of passion*, esp of love, amoris, Cic, gulae, *raging hunger*, Cic, ultrix flamma, *burning revenge*, Cic

flammĕŏlum -i, n (dim of flammeum), *a small bridal veil*, Juv

flammesco, 3 (flamma), *to become inflamed*, Lucr

flammĕus -a -um (flamma), *fiery flame like, flaming* **I** Adj, **A.** Lit, stella, Cic **B.** Transf, *flame-coloured, fiery red*, corpora, Lucr, vestigia, *in hot haste*, Cat **II.** Subst, **flammĕum** i, n *a flame coloured bridal veil*, flammeum capere, Cat

flammĭfer -fĕra fĕrum (flamma and fero), *flame-bearing, flaming, fiery*, Ov

flammo, 1 (flamma) **I.** Intransit, *to flame, blaze, burn*, flammantia lumina, *glittering*, Verg **II.** Transit, *to set on fire, inflame* **A.** Lit, ut interirent crucibus affixi aut flammandi,

Tac. **B.** Transf., flammato corde, *with angry passion*, Verg.

flammŭla -ae, f. (dim. of flamma), *a little flame*, Cic.

flātus -ūs, m. (flo), *a blowing, blast.* **I.** Gen., Alpini boreae, Verg.; fig., prospero flatu fortunae uti, Cic. **II.** *breathing.* **A.** Lit., **1,** flatus, *the breath*, Verg.; **2, a,** *snorting;* equorum, Verg.; **b,** *blowing on a flute*, Hor. **B.** Transf., *haughtiness, arrogance*, gen. in plur., Verg.

flāvĕo, 2. (flavus), *to be yellow* or *gold-coloured;* partic., flavens, *yellow, golden;* coma, Verg.; arena, Verg.

flāvesco, 3. (flaveo), *to become yellow* or *gold-coloured;* campus flavescet aristā, Verg.

Flāvīna -ae, f. *a town in Etruria.* Adj., **Flāvīnĭus** -a -um, *of* or *belonging to Flavina.*

Flāvĭus -a -um, *name of a Roman gens, to which the Emperors Vespasian, Titus, and Domitian belonged;* hence Flavius = *Domitian*, Juv.; Cn. Flavius, *a freedman of Appius Claudius Caecus, who first published the formulae used in law-suits.* Hence **1, Flāvĭālis** -is, m. (with or without flamen), *the flamen of the gens Flavia;* **2,** adj., **Flāvĭānus** -a -um, *Flavian.*

flāvus -a -um (root FLA, whence fla-gro), *golden-yellow, gold-coloured, yellow;* arva, Verg.; crines, Verg.; aurum, Verg.; decem flavi, *ten gold pieces*, Mart.

flēbĭlis -e (fleo) **I.** Pass., *lamentable, wretched, deserving tears;* illa species, Cic. **II.** Act., *causing lamentation* or *tears, tearful, doleful;* **a,** of things, gemitus, Cic.; **b,** of persons, *weeping;* Ino, Hor.

flēbĭlĭtĕr, adv. (flebilis), *tearfully, dolefully*, Cic.

flecto, flexi, flexum, 3. **I.** Transit., *to bend, bow, twist, curve.* **A. 1,** lit., membra, Cic.; iter suum or viam, *to diverge from one's march* or *journey*, Liv.; **2,** transf., **a,** *to modulate* (the voice), vocem, Cic.; flexus sonus, *a melancholy tone*, Cic.; **b,** *to change, alter;* vitam, Cic.; fata deum, Verg.; *to move, to make a person change his opinion;* animum or aliquem, Cic.; flecti misericordiā, Liv.; nihil flexerunt animos quin collem defenderent, Liv. **B.** *to bend, turn, direct;* **1,** lit., equos, Caes.; currum de foro in Capitolium, Cic.; acies (= oculos) huc, Verg.; middle, flecti in gyrum, *to turn round in a circle*, Ov.; transf., of places, flectere se or middle flecti, *to turn towards;* hinc (silva) se flectit sinistrorsus, Caes.; **2,** transf., *to turn from, dissuade from;* aliquem a proposito, Liv.; a studio ad imperium, Cic. **C.** *to double, sail round;* Leucatam, Cic. **II.** Intransit., **A.** *to turn, go;* ad Oceanum, Liv. **B.** Transf., ad sapientiam, Tac.

flĕo, flēvi, flētum, 2. **I.** Intransit., **a,** *to weep;* de filii morte, Cic.; lapides flere et lamentari cogere, Cic.; **b,** of fluids, *to trickle down*, Lucr. **II.** Transit., *to weep for, lament, bewail.* **A.** Lit., juvenem, Ov.; filii necem, Tac.; with acc. and infin., Verg.; flendus, *worthy of being lamented*, Ov.; fletus, *wept for, lamented*, Verg. **B.** Transf., cavā testudine amorem, *sing mournfully of*, Hor. (Syncop. perf. forms flesti, Ov.; flerunt, Verg.; flesse, Liv.).

1. **flētus** -a -um (partic. of fleo).

2. **flētus** -ūs, m. (fleo), *a weeping, bewailing;* prae fletu, Cic.; clamore et fletu omnia complere, Cic.; urbe totā fletus gemitusque fieret, Cic.

flexănĭmus -a -um (flecto and animus), **1,** *moving, affecting;* oratio, Cic.; **2,** *affected, touched, moved;* ap. Cic.

flexĭbĭlis -e (flecto), *that can be bent, flexible.* **A.** Lit., materia rerum, Cic. **B.** Transf., **a,** of the voice, vocis genus, Cic.; **b,** of speech, nihil est tam flexibile quam oratio, Cic.; **c,** of persons, *pliant, tractable*, or in a bad sense, *changeable;* aetas, Cic.; quid potest esse tam flexibile, Cic.

flexĭlis -e (flecto), *flexible, pliant, supple;* cornu, Ov.

flexĭlŏquus -a -um (flexus and loquor), *having two meanings, equivocal, ambiguous*, Cic.

flexĭo -ōnis, f. (flecto), *bending.* **I.** Gen., virili laterum flexione, Cic.; transf., vocis or modorum, *modulation of the voice*, Cic. **II.** Esp., *turning, winding;* deverticula flexionesque, Cic.

flexĭpes -pĕdis (flexus and pes), *crooked-footed;* hederae, *twining*, Ov.

flexŭōsus -a -um (flexus), *full of windings and turnings, crooked;* iter (of the ear), Cic.

flexūra -ae, f. (flecto), *a bending*, Lucr.

1. **flexus** -a -um, partic. of flecto.

2. **flexus** -ūs, m. (flecto), *a bending.* **I.** Middle, *bending oneself, turning, winding.* **A.** Gen., **1,** lit., **a,** cervicis, Ov.; **b,** *a turning of a road, by-path;* in quo flexus est ad iter Arpinas, Cic.; **2,** *variation, modification, change;* rerum publicarum, Cic. **B.** In the circus, *the turning round of the chariots towards the goal;* fig., in hoc flexu quasi aetatis, Cic. **II.** Pass., *being turned, turning, winding;* duros introitus habent (aures) multis cum flexibus, Cic.; flexus vallium, Liv.

flictus -ūs, m. (fligo), *a striking together, dashing against;* cavae dant sonitum flictu galeae, Verg.

fligo, 3. *to beat* or *dash down*, Lucr.

flo, flāvi, flātum, 1. **I.** Intransit., of winds, *to blow;* qui ventus in his locis flare consuevit, Cic.; ita belle nobis ab Epiro flavit Onchesmites, Cic.; of persons, scintillam levem flando accenderunt, Liv.; of the flute, protinus inflexo Berecyntia tibia cornu flabit, Ov. **II.** Transit., **A. a,** *to blow forth from the mouth;* flammam, Lucr.; **b,** *to blow an instrument;* furiosa tibia flatur, Ov. **B.** *to cast metals, to make into coin, to coin;* flare pecuniam, Cic.

floccus -i, m., *a lock of wool*, Varr.; non flocci facere, *to think nothing of*, Cic.

Flōra -ae, f. (flos), *the goddess of flowers.* Adj., **Flōrālis** -e, *belonging to Flora;* subst., **Flōrālĭa** -ium and -iōrum, n. *the festival of Flora on the 27th of April;* **Flōrālĭcĭus** -a -um, *relating to the festival of Flora.*

flōrens -entis, p. adj. (from floreo), *blooming;* **1,** *fresh, fine, vigorous;* **a,** of orators, etc., florens orationis genus, Cic.; **b,** of age, aetas, Cic.; **2,** *glittering, splendid, prosperous, flourishing;* (α) fortuna, Caes.; res publica florentissima, Cic.; (β) with abl., *distinguished for;* gratiā atque hospitiis florens hominum nobilissimorum, Cic.

Flōrentĭa -ae, f. *a town in Etruria, now Florence.* Adj., **Flōrentīnus** -a -um, *Florentine.*

flōrĕo -ŭi, 2. (flos). **I.** *to bloom, flower.* **A.** Lit., haec arbor ter floret, Cic. **B.** Fig., **a,** of things, verborum vetus interit aetas, et juvenum ritu florent modo nata virentque, Cic.; **b,** of persons, *to be in one's prime, to prosper, be flourishing, be in high repute;* floret Epicurus, Cic.; with abl., gratiā et auctoritate, Cic.; honoribus, Cic. **II.** Transf., **A.** Poet., *to be full of;* tibi pampineo gravidus auctumno floret ager, Verg. **B.** *to glitter;* florentes aere catervae, Verg. **C.** Of wine, *to froth*, Ov.

flōresco, 3. (inchoat. of floreo), *to begin to blossom, come into flower.* **A.** Lit., Cic. **B.** Transf., *to begin to flourish;* Sulpicius ad summam gloriam florescens, Cic.

flōrĕus -a -um (flos), 1, *made of flowers*, serta, Tib, 2, *rich in flowers, flowery;* rura, Verg.

flōrĭdŭlus -a -um (dim of floridus), *somewhat blooming*, Cat

flōrĭdus -a -um (flos), *flowery* **I.** Lit, **a**, *blossoming*, ramuli, Cat, **b**, *made of flowers*, serta, Ov, plur subst, florida et varia, Cic, **c**, *rich in flowers*, Hybla, Ov **II.** Transf, **a**, of age, *flourishing*, aetas, Cat, **b**, of expressions, *flowery, florid*, Demetrius est floridior, Cic

flōrĭfer -fĕra -fĕrum (flos and fero), *flower-bearing*, Lucr

flōrĭlĕgus -a -um (flos and lego), *culling flowers;* apes, Ov

Flōrus -i, m *a Roman historian of the time of Trajan and Hadrian, who composed an epitome of Roman history from the foundation of the city to the age of Augustus*

flōs, flōris (connected with φλόος), *a flower, blossom* **I. A.** Lit., florum omnium varietas, Cic **B.** Meton, flores, *the juice of flowers*, Verg **II.** Transf, **A.** *the prime, flower*, 1, gen, Graeciae, Cic, virium, Liv, 2, esp, flos aetatis, *the flower of youth*, Cic, so flos juventae, Liv **B.** *the flower = the best, the finest, the pride*, 1, gen, flos totius Italiae ac robur, Cic, florem et colorem defuisse, *grace of expression*, Cic, Bacchi, *strength*, Lucr, 2, esp, flos juvenilis, *the first beard, down*, so simply flos, Verg, flammae, *glitter*, Lucr

flōscŭlus -i, m (dim of flos), *a little flower* **I.** Lit, lecta omnia tamquam flosculi decerpunt, Cic, omni ex genere orationis flosculos carpam, Cic **II.** *pride*, o qui flosculus es Juventiorum, Cat

fluctĭfrăgus -a -um (fluctus and frango), *wave-breaking*, Lucr

fluctŭātĭo -ōnis, f (fluctuo), *a moving backwards and forwards, fluctuation* transf, *indecision*, animorum, Liv

fluctŭo, 1 (fluctus) **I.** *to be in wave-like motion, move up and down* **A.** Lit, mare, Plaut **B.** 1, *to heave, undulate*, fluctuat tellus aere renidenti, *shimmers*, Verg, 2, *to rage*, ira fluctuat, Verg **II.** *to move up and down in the sea, to be tossed about* **A.** Lit, of men and ships, Cic **B.** Transf, 1, *to waver*, acies fluctuans, Liv, of speech, oratio quasi fluctuans, Cic., 2, *to waver in resolve, to vacillate*, in suo decreto, Cic

fluctŭor -ātus sum, 1 dep, *to waver, vacillate*, fluctuatus animo est, utrum … an, Liv

fluctŭōsus -a -um (fluctus), *full of waves, stormy*, mare, Plant

fluctus -ūs, m (fluo) **I.** *a streaming, flowing*, Lucr **II.** *a wave, wave of the sea, billow*, **a**, sing, fluctu operiri, Cic, **b**, plur, fluctus sedare, Cic; prov, excitare fluctus in simpulo, *to make much ado about nothing*, Cic, fig, *commotion, disturbance*, fluctus contionum, Cic, irarum, Verg

flŭens entis, p adj (fluo) **I. A.** *flowing, easy, fluent*, tracta quaedam et fluens oratio, Cic **B.** *unrestrained, diffuse*, ut ne aut dissoluta aut fluens sit oratio, Cic **II.** *hanging down, flabby*, buccae fluentes, Cic

flŭentĕr, adv. (fluo), *in a flowing manner*, Lucr

flŭentĭsŏnus -a -um (fluentum and sono), *resounding with waves*, Cat

flŭentum -i, n (fluo) *running water, a stream*, rauca Cocyti, Verg

flŭĭdus -a -um (fluo), *flowing, fluid* **A.** Lit, cruor, Verg **B.** Transf, **a**, *lax, languid, flaccid*, frondes, Lucr, pendere lacertos, Ov, **b**, *dissolving*, calor, Ov.

flŭĭto, 1 (intens of fluo), *to flow hither and thither* **A.** Lit, **a**, of streams, waves, etc, fusile per rictus aurum fluitare videres, Ov, **b**, of ships, etc, *to float, move up and down, be tossed about on the water*, navem fluitantem in alto tempestatibus, Cic. **B.** Transf, **a**, *to waver*, fluitans testudo, Tac, **b**, *to flutter, flap about*, fluitantia vela, Ov, **c**, *to be uncertain, to vacillate, to be doubtful*, mobilia et caecā fluitantia sorte, Hor

flūmen inis, n (fluo), *flowing water, a stream* **I.** Lit, **A.** Gen, flumine vivo, *running water*, Verg; flumine secundo, *downstream*, Caes **B.** Esp, *a river, a stream*, Cic Garumna flumen, Caes **II.** Transf, 1, *a stream of anything*, of blood, Cic, of tears, Verg, 2, of the mind, **a**, *outpouring, flow*, nullius tantum flumen est ingenii, Cic, **b**, of oratory etc, *flood flow, stream*, flumen orationis aureum, Cic

Flūmentāna porta (flumen), *the river gate, a gate in Rome near the Campus Martius*

flūmĭnĕus -a -um (flumen), *of or relating to a river*, Ov

flŭo, fluxi, fluxum, 3 *to flow* **I.** Gen, **A.** Lit, of fluids and fluid bodies, 1, ut flumina in contrarias partes fluxerint, Cic, fluit de corpore sudor, Ov, 2, *to flow, drip with any liquid*, cruore, Ov, sudore, Ov **B.** Transf, 1, *to flow*, **a**, of air, wind, etc, venti fluunt, Lucr **b**, of clothes, *to flow down*, fluens vestis, Ov, **c**, of the neck, *to sink*, ad terram fluit cervix, Verg **d**, of branches, *to spread;* ramos compesce fluentes, Verg, 2, *to stream forth*, multa a luna manant et fluunt, Cic, of a crowd, turba fluit castris, Verg **C.** Fig, 1, *to be spread abroad*, Pythagorae doctrina quum longe lateque flueret, Cic; 2, *to be derived from*, haec omnia ex eodem fonte fluxerunt, Cic, 3, *to flow down*, **a**, *to proceed without interruption*, in rebus prosperis et ad voluntatem fluentibus, Cic, **b**, *to tend to*, res fluit ad interregnum, Cic, **c**, of oratory, *to be diffuse, lax*, Cic **II. A.** *to slacken, become weak*, mollitie or mollitiis, Cic, fluunt sudore et lassitudine membra, Liv **B.** 1, *to fall down*, fluent arma de manibus, Cic, 2, *to disappear, fall gradually*, **a**, lit, poma, Ov, **b**, fig, *to vanish*, fluit voluptas corporis, Cic

flūto, 1 (for fluito), *to flow, float, swim*, Lucr

flŭvĭālis -e (fluvius), *of or belonging to a river*, undae, Verg, anas, Ov

flŭvĭātĭlis -e (fluvius), *of or belonging to a river*, testudo, Cic

flŭvĭdus -a -um (fluo), *flowing, fluid*, Lucr

flŭvĭus -ii, m (fluo), 1, *flowing water*, Verg, 2, *stream, river*, fluvius Eurotas, Cic

fluxio -ōnis, f (fluo), *a flowing, flood*, Cic

1 **fluxus** -a -um p adj (fluo) *flowing* **A.** *waving, fluttering, loose*, crines, Tac, habena, Liv **B.** Transf, **a**, *uncertain, inconstant, changeable*, gloria, Sall, **b**, of character, *vacillating*, animus, Sall, **c**, *decaying, declining, tottering*, murorum aevo fluxa, Tac, res, Cic

2 **fluxus** -ūs, m (fluo), *a flowing*, Plin, transf, autumni, *the passing away of autumn*, Tac

fōcāle is, n (for faucale, from faux), *a wrapper for the neck*, Hor

fŏcŭlus -i, m (dim of focus), 1, *a small stove for cooking, brazier*, Juv, 2, *a small altar*, Cic

fŏcus -i, m (root FO, whence also foveo), *a fireplace* **A.** Gen, Ov **B.** Esp, 1, *the fireplace in a house, hearth*, **a**, lit, Cic, **b**, meton, *house, family, home*, domo et focis patriis aliquem ejicere, Cic, 2, *an altar*, Ov, 3, *the fire of a funeral pile* Verg

fŏdĭco, 1. (fodio), *to dig, pierce;* latus, *to dig in the ribs,* Hor.; transf., fodicantibus iis rebus quas malas esse opinemur, *troubling, vexing,* Cic.

fŏdĭo, fōdi, fossum, 3. (root FOD, Gr. ΒΟΘ, whence βόθρος), *to dig.* **I.** Intransit., fodit, invenit auri aliquantum, Cic. **II.** Transit., **A.** *to dig;* **1,** humum, Verg.; **2,** *to dig out;* argentum, Liv.; *to excavate;* puteum, Caes.; absol., fodientes, *miners,* Liv. **B.** *to pierce;* **1, a,** pectora telis, Ov.; aversos (elephantos) sub caudis, Liv.; **b,** *to gouge out;* lumina, Ov.: **2,** transf., of grief, pungit dolor . . . fodiat sane, Cic.

foecundus, foecundo = fecundus, fecundo (q.v.).

foedē, adv. (1. foedus), *foully, horribly, cruelly;* foede exercere victoriam, Liv.; foedius pulsi, Liv.; foedissime agere causam, Cic.

foedĕrātus -a -um (2. foedus), *confederate, allied;* civitates, Cic.

foedĭfrăgus -a -um (2. foedus and frango), *treaty-breaking;* Poeni, Cic.

foedĭtas -ātis, f. (1. foedus), *foulness, hideousness, filthiness;* **a,** physical, odoris intolerabilis foeditas, Cic.; vestitus, Cic.; **b,** moral, turpificati animi, Cic.; decreti, Liv.

foedo, 1. (1. foedus) *to make foul, make filthy, defile, pollute, deform, disfigure.* **A.** Lit., pectora pugnis, Verg.; canitiem pulvere, Ov.; aliquid sanguine, Ov.; serenos vultus, Verg.; agri foedati, *laid waste,* Liv. **B.** Transf., *to dishonour, disgrace;* aliquem nefario scelere, Cic.

1. **foedus** -a -um, *foul, filthy, horrible, abominable, detestable;* **a,** physically, monstrum foedissimum, Cic.; foedi oculi, *staring, bloodshot,* Sall.; with dat., pestilentia foeda homini, Liv.; with supine, rem non modo visu foedam sed etiam auditu, Cic.; **b,** morally, bellum foedissimum, Cic.; ludos vero non facere, quid foedius? Cic.; with supine, foedum inceptu, Liv.

2. **foedus** -ĕris, n. *a league.* **I.** Lit., **a,** between states, foedus facere cum aliquo, or icere, or ferire, Cic.; foedus frangere, rumpere, violare, Cic.; **b,** *a compact, covenant, agreement between individuals;* amorum, Cic.; scelerum, Cic. **II.** Poet., *a law,* Verg.

foem . . ., foen . . . v. fem . . ., fen . . .

foetĕo, 2. *to have a bad smell,* Plaut.

foetĭdus (faetĭdus, fētĭdus) -a -um, adj. with compar. (foeteo), *having a bad smell, stinking, fetid;* os, Cic.

foetor -ōris, m. (foeteo), *a bad smell, stink,* Cic.

foetus, v. fetus.

Fōlĭa -ae, f. *a witch of Ariminum.*

fŏlĭātum -i, n. (folium), *a salve* or *oil of spikenard leaves,* Juv.

fŏlĭum -ii, n. (connected with φύλλον, as alius with ἄλλος), *a leaf;* Sibyllae, *a prophecy, oracle written on leaves,* Juv.

follĭcŭlus -i, m. (dim. of follis), *a little sack* or *bag,* Cic.

follis -is, m. *a leather bag.* **I.** Gen., Plaut. **II.** Esp., **1,** *a pair of bellows,* Cic.; follis fabrilis, Liv.; transf., of the lungs, folles spirant mendacia, Juv.; **2,** *a leathern purse,* Juv.

fōmentum -i, n. (for fovimentum, from foveo); **1,** *a poultice, fomentation,* Hor.; **2,** transf., *alleviation;* summorum malorum, Cic.

fōmes -ĭtis, m. (foveo), *touchwood, tinder,* Verg.

1. **fons** -fontis, m. (orig. funs, from fundo), **1,** *a spring, well, fountain,* Cic.; meton. poet., *fresh* or *spring water,* Verg.; **2,** transf., *spring, origin, fountain, source;* philosophiae, Cic; juris, Liv.

2. **Fons,** Fontis, m., and **Fontus** -i, m. *the son of Janus, god of fountains.* Adj., **Fontĭnālis** -e, *belonging to Fons;* porta, *a gate in Rome on the Quirinal, near the Campus Martius,* Liv.

fontānus -a -um (fons), *belonging* or *relating to a spring* or *fountain;* unda, Ov.

Fontējus -a -um, *name of a Roman gens.*

fontĭcŭlus -i, m. (dim. of fons), *a little fountain* or *spring,* Hor.

Fontĭnālis, v. 2. Fons.

for, fātus, 1., dep. (φάω, φῶ), *to speak, say;* esp. of gods, oracles, seers, &c. **A.** Gen., *to speak, say;* ad aliquem, Cic.; aliquid, Verg.; fando audire, *hear by report,* Cic.; partic. **fandus** -a -um, *that which may be spoken,* hence, *right, lawful;* respersae fando nefandoque sanguine arae, Liv. **B.** Esp., **a,** of poets, *to sing of,* Prop.; **b,** *to prophesy,* Verg. (The forms which are found are fatur, fantur, fabor, fabitur, farer; partic. perf. fatus; perf. fatus sum and eram; imper. fare; infin. fari (farier, Verg.); gerund fandi, fando; supine fatu; partic. pres. fans).

fŏrābĭlis -e (foro), *that can be bored through, penetrable, vulnerable,* Ov.

fŏrāmen -ĭnis, n. (foro), *a hole, aperture, opening;* **a,** natural; foramina terrae, Lucr.; foramina illa quae patent ad animum a corpore, Cic.; **b,** artificial; convexa foramina retis, Ov.

fŏras, adv. (connected with foris), *out of doors, forth, out;* ire foras, Ov.; aliquem projicere foras, Cic.; portis se foras erumpere, Cic.; ea scripta foras dare, Cic.; quae (vestigia) ubi omnia foras versa vidit, Liv.

forceps -cĭpis, m. and f. *a pair of tongs, pincers,* Ov.

fordus -a -um (fero), *pregnant,* Ov. Subst. **forda** -ae, f. (sc. bos), *a cow in calf,* Ov.

fŏre, fŏrem, -es, etc. (for fuerem from old fuo, φύω, I am). **I.** forem, **1,** = essem, Sall.; **2,** = fuissem, Ov. **II.** Infin. fore, **1,** = futurum (-am, -os, etc.) esse, Cic.; **2,** = esse, Cic.

fŏrensis -e (forum), *relating to the market* or *forum.* **A.** Gen., **1,** *relating to the forum;* factio, turba, Liv.; vestitus, *dress worn out of doors, state dress,* Liv.; **2,** *relating to the forum as a place for administration of justice, legal;* causa, Cic.; Mars, *eloquence,* Ov.

Fŏrentum -i, n. *town in Apulia,* now *Forenzo,* Hor.

forfex -fĭcis, c. *a pair of shears* or *scissors,* Mart.

fŏrĭca -ae, f. = ἀφεδρών, Juv.

1. **fŏris** -is, f. (connected with 2. foris), **1,** *a door;* and plur., fores; *folding-doors;* claudere forem cubiculi, Cic.; fores aperire, Cic.; ad fores assistere, Cic.; **2,** *opening, entrance;* equi aenei, Cic.

2. **fŏris,** adv. (from obsolete nom. fora) **I.** *out of doors, outside, without.* **A.** Gen., aliquid quaere foris, Cic. **B.** Esp., **a,** *not at home;* foris cenare or cenitare, Cic.; foris valde plauditur, *among the people,* Cic.; foris esse Gabinium, *in debt,* Cic.; **b,** *outside the senate,* Cic.; **c,** *outside the state, outside Rome,* Cic. **II.** *from without, from abroad;* aliquid foris petere, Cic.

forma -ae, f. (fero), *form, figure, shape.* **I. A.** Lit., **1,** gen., corporis, Cic.; **2,** esp. **a,** *the face;* forma nostra reliquaque figura, Cic.; **b,** *beauty,* Cic. **B.** Transf., **1,** gen., *form = government, constitution;* forma rerum publicarum, Cic.; in formam provinciae redigere, Liv.; **2,** esp. *character, form, nature, kind, manner;* forma insolitae pugnae, Liv. **II.** *figure, image, likeness.* **A.** Lit., formae virorum, Cic.; formae quas in pulvere descripserat, Liv. **B.** Transf., **a,**

outline, sketch, totius negotii, Cic , b, in logic, *species* Cic **III.** *form as a model*, **a,** *a shoe-last*, Hor , **b,** *a mould, stamp for coining*, Ov

formāmentum -i, n (formo), *shape, form*, Lucr

formātūra ae, f (formo), *a form, forming, formation*, Lucr

Formiae ārum, f *town on the coast of Latium, famed for its wine*, now Mola di Gaeta Adj , **Formiānus** -a -um, *of or belonging to Formiae* Subst , **Formiānum** i, n (sc praedium), *an estate near Formiae*, Cic

formica ae, f (connected with μύρμηξ), *an ant*, Cic

formīdābilis -e (formido), *exciting terror, fearful, formidable*, lumen Ov

1. **formīdo**, 1. (perhaps connected with horreo), *to fear, be frightened, terrified, to dread*, omnia, Cic , with the infin , naribus uti, Hor , with ut and the subj , Tac

2 **formīdo** -inis, f (1 formido) **I.** Lit , **A.** *fear, dread terror*. Stoici definiunt formidinem metum permanentem, Cic , formidinem alicui injicere, Cic **B.** Esp , *religious awe*, existunt horribiles formidines, Cic **II.** Meton , *that which causes fear*, Cic , and esp *a scarecrow*, Hor

formīdŏlōsē, adv (formidolosus), *fearfully, terribly*, Cic

formīdŏlōsus -a -um (2 formido) **I.** Act , *exciting fear, terrible, fearful*, tempora, Cic ; bellum formidolosissimum, Cic **II** Neut , *fearful, timid*, with obj genit., formidolosior hostium, Tac

formo, 1 (forma) **I.** *to form, shape, fashion* **A.** Lit , materiam, Cic , orationem, Cic **B.** Transf , **1,** *to arrange, order, regulate*, formatis omnibus ad belli et pacis usus, Liv , **2,** *to fashion by education and habit, to accustom, shape;* novos collegas in suos mores, Liv , **3,** *to dispose, prepare*, animos, Cic **II.** *to fashion out of something* **A.** Lit , of sculptors, etc , signum in muliebrem figuram, Cic , classem, *to build*, Cic , personam novam, of actors, *to represent*, Hor **B** Transf , *to produce, form*, quattuor modis formatas in animis hominum deorum esse notiones, Cic

formons v formos .

formōsē, adv (formosus), *beautifully, gracefully*, Prop

formōsĭtas -ātis, f (formosus), *beauty*, Cic

formōsus a um (forma), *beautifully formed, beautiful;* virgines formosissimae, Cic , of abstractions, tempus, *spring*, Ov , virtute nihil est formosius, Cic

formŭla -ae, f (dim of forma), **1,** *a rule, pattern, scheme;* dicendi, Cic , ad formulam vivere, Cic , **2,** esp , **a,** *the form of an agreement between the Roman senate and its allies*, Lampsacenos in sociorum formulam referre, Liv , **b,** *the rating of the censor*, censum agere ex formula, Liv ; **c,** legal t t , *form of words, formula*, postulationum, testamentorum, Cic

fornācālis e (fornax), *relating to an oven*, dea, *the goddess of ovens* (Fornax) Ov Subst , **Fornācālia** -ium, n *the festival of the goddess Fornax, said to have been instituted by Numa*

fornācŭla -ae, f (dim of fornax), *a little oven*, Juv.

fornax -ācis, f (root FOR, connected with ferveo, θερ-μός), **1,** *an oven, furnace, kiln*, ardens, Cic , poet , Aetnae, *the crater*, Verg , **2,** personif , Fornax, *the goddess of ovens*, Ov

fornicātus -a -um (fornix), *arched, vaulted*, paries, Cic , via, Liv.

fornix icis, m *an arch, vault* **I.** Gen , parietis, Cic **II.** Esp , **A.** Fornix Fabii, *a triumphal arch erected by Q Fabius Maximus* **B.** Milit t t , **a,** *an arched sally port*, Liv , **b,** *a covered way* Liv **C.** *a brothel*, Hor

fornus = furnus (q v)

foro, 1 (cf Engl bore), *to pierce*, Plaut

fors, abl forte, f (fero), only in nom and abl sing , *chance, luck* **I. 1,** gen , sed haec ut fors tulerit, Cic **2,** esp , **a,** abl , forte, *by chance*, used with si, sin, ne, nisi, etc , Cic , **b,** adv fors = fortasse, *by chance*, Verg , **3,** fors fortuna, *good luck*, ensu aut forte fortuna, Cic **II.** Personif as a deity, dea Fors, Ov , esp , Fors Fortuna, Liv

forsăn, adv (= fors sit an), *perhaps*, Liv

forsit, adv (fors sit), *perhaps*, Hor

forsĭtăn, adv (fors sit an), *perhaps*, Cic

fortassĕ, adv (fors), *perhaps*, **a,** with verbs, dolent fortasse et anguntur, Cic , with subj , fortasse dixerit quispiam, Cic , **b,** with adj and adv , res fortasse verae, Cic ; incondite fortasse, Cic , **c,** with numbers, *about*, triginta fortasse versus, Cic

fortĕ, v fors

fortĭcŭlus a -um (dim of fortis), *tolerably strong, brave, courageous*, Cic

fortis -e (old form foretis = forectis, from fero, orig *one that can endure much*), *strong, powerful, durable* **I.** Lit , physically, *strong, durable, powerful, robust, stout*, ligna fortissima, Caes , coloni, Verg **II.** Transf , mentally, *brave, courageous, stout, steadfast*, **1,** of persons, horum omnium fortissimi sunt Belgae, Caes , fortior in dolore, Cic , vir fortissimus contra audaciam, Cic , fortis ad pericula, Cic , prov , fortes fortuna adjuvat, *fortune favours the brave*, Cic , so elliptically, fortes fortuna, Cic , **2,** of things, *courageous, energetic*, sententia, Cic , genus dicendi, Cic

fortĭtĕr, adv (fortis), **1,** *strongly, firmly*, fortius attrahere lora, Ov , **2,** *bravely, courageously, steadfastly*, ferre dolorem, Cic

fortĭtūdo inis, f (fortis), *bravery, courage, steadfastness, firmness, fortitude*, Cic , plur , fortitudines, *deeds of bravery*, Cic

fortŭĭto (fortŭĭtū), adv (fortuitus), *by chance, by accident, fortuitously*, Cic

fortŭĭtus a -um (fors), *accidental, casual, fortuitous*, concursus atomorum, Cic ; subita et fortuita oratio, *unpremeditated*, Cic Subst , **fortŭĭta** -ōrum n *chance occurrences*, Tac

fortūna -ae, f and plur **fortūnae** -ārum, f (fors), *chance, fate, lot, luck, fortune* **I.** Gen , **A.** **a,** sing , prospera, secunda, *good fortune*, Cic , adversa, *misfortune*, Cic , fortunae se or omnia committere, Cic , **b,** plur , fortunae secundae, Cic **B.** Personif , Fortuna, *the goddess of chance*, Cic , filius Fortunae, *a favourite of fortune*, Hor **II.** Esp , **A.** Without an epithet, **1,** = fortuna secunda, Cic , fortunam sibi ipsum facere, Liv , per fortunas ! *by thy good fortune ! for Heaven's sake !* Cic , **2,** = fortuna adversa, contra fortunam paratus armatusque, Cic **B. 1,** lit , **a,** *lot, condition, state, mode of life*, infima servorum, Cic magna, *a high position*, Liv , **b,** of things, bona belli, Cic , **2,** meton , **a,** *lot, share* cui cessit triplicis fortuna novissima regni, Ov **b,** *property, possessions*, gen plur , alicui bona fortunasque adimere, Cic

fortūnātē, adv (fortunatus), *happily, fortunately*, vivere, Cic

fortūnātus a -um, p adj (fortuno), *happy, lucky, fortunate*. **I.** Gen , homo, Cic , respub lica, Cic ; insulae, *the islands of the blest, Elysium*, Plin , so fortunata nemora, *Elysium*, Verg Subst , **fortūnātus** -i, m *a favourite of fortune*, Cic **II.** Esp , *well off, wealthy, rich*, Cic

fortūno, 1 (fortuna), *to make happy, bless, prosper* , tibi patrimonium dei fortunent, Cic

1 **fŏrŭli** -ōrum, m (dim of forus), *a bookcase*, Juv

2 **Fŏrŭli** -ōrum m *a place in the Sabine country*, now *Civita Tommasa*

fŏrum i, n (connected with foras and foris), *an open space.* **I.** *in front of a tomb*, ap Cic. **II. A.** *an open square, market-place*, Liv , esp at Rome, **1**, **a**, forum Romanum, or magnum, or vetus, or simply forum, *an open place at the foot of the Palatine and Capitoline hills, where legal, political, and commercial business was transacted*, Cic , **b**, forum Caesaris, *founded by J Caesar*, Suet , **c**, forum Augusti, *built by Augustus*, Ov , **d**, forum Trajani, *built by Trajan* , **2**, as mere market-places, **a**, forum boarium or boarium, *the cattle market*, Cic , **b**, forum olitorium, *vegetable market*, Liv , **c**, forum piscarium or piscatorium, *fish-market*, Liv , **3**, in reference to public business, law, and mercantile transactions, verba de foro arripere, *to use common and vulgar expressions*, Cic , annos jam triginta in foro versaris, *thou hast been in business thirty years already*, Cic , forum attingere, *to begin to apply oneself to public business*, esp legal, Cic **B.** Transf , **1**, *a place of trade*, Vacca, forum rerum venalium totius regni maxime celebratum, Sall , **2**, *the chief place or market-town of a district*, civitates quae in id forum conveniant, *which are in that district*, Cic , forum agere, *to hold an assize*, Cic Hence, the name of several towns, **a**, Forum Appii, *on the Via Appia in Latium*, **b**, Forum Aurelium, *in Etruria, on the Via Aurelia*, now *Monte Alto*, **c**, Forum Cornelii, *in Gallia Cispadana*, now *Imola*, **d**, Forum Julii or Julium *in Gallia Narbonensis*, now *Frejus* , **e**, Forum Voconii, *in Gallia Narbonensis*

fŏrus i, m **1**, *the gangway of a ship*, Cic ; **2**, plur , *a row of seats in the theatre*, Liv , **3**, plur , *the cells of bees*, Verg

Fosi -ōrum, m *a German people near the modern Hildesheim*, Tac

fossa -ae, f (fodio), *a ditch, trench* , **a**, fossam ducere, Caes , facere, fodere, Liv , obducere, praeducere, Cic , vallo et fossā cingere, Cic , fossas implere, Liv , **b**, *canal, bed of a river* , Rheni, Cic , fossae Cluiliae, Liv.

fossĭo -ōnis, f (fodio), *a digging, excavation*, Cic

fossor ōris, m (fodio), *a digger, delver*, Verg , poet , *a boor, clown*, Cat

fossūra -ae, f (fodio), *a digging*, Suet

fōtus, partic of foveo

fŏvĕa -ae, f *a pit as a trap for catching game, a pitfall*, in foveam incidere, Cic

fŏvĕo, fōvi, fōtum, 2 (root FO, whence fomes, fomentum), *to warm, keep warm.* **I. A.** Lit , **1**, esp of a bird keeping warm its eggs or young, pullos pennis, Cic ; **2**, *to bathe, foment a wound or part of the body*, vulnus lymphā, Verg , poet , **a**, *to heal*, ora, Verg , **b**, *to support*, colla, Verg **B.** Meton , **1**, *to stay constantly in a place*, castra, Verg , **2**, hiemem inter se luxu, *pass the winter*, Verg **II.** Transf , **1**, *to foster*, spem, Liv , **2**, *to cherish*, aliquem, Cic , **3**, *to support, favour* , voluntatem patrum, Liv

fractus a -um, p adj (frango), *weak, powerless*, animus, *broken down, spiritless*, Cic

fraeno, fraenum = freno, frenum (q v)

frāga -ōrum, n *strawberries*, Verg.

frăgĭlis e (frango) **I. A.** Lit , *easily broken, fragile*, rami, Verg **B.** Meton , *crackling*, laurus, Verg **II.** Transf , **a**, *frail, transitory*, corpus, Cic , res humanae, Cic ; **b**, *weak, nerveless*, anni, Ov ; Pediatia, Hor.

frăgĭlĭtas ātis, f (fragilis), *frailty, weakness*, humani generis, Cic.

fragmen -mĭnis, n (frango), *a piece broken off, fragment*, in plur , *ruins*, ingens montis, Verg , fragmina navigii, Ov.; *fragments, remains, ruins*, Verg , Ov

fragmentum i, n (frango), *a piece broken off, fragment*, plur , *ruins*, lapidis, Cic ; fragmenta saeptorum, Cic

frăgor -ōris, m. (frango), **1**, *breaking in pieces*, Lucr , **2**, *a loud noise, crash of falling houses*, Liv , *noise of the sea*, Verg , of thunder, Ov , fragorem dare, *to crash*, Ov

frăgōsus -a -um (fragor) **I.** *fragile*, **A.** Lit , Lucr **B.** Transf , *rough, uneven* silva, Ov **II.** *crashing, roaring* torrens, Verg

fragrans -antis, p. adj. (fragro), *sweet-scented*, mella, Verg

fragro, 1 *to smell sweet, be fragrant*, unguento, Sall

frāgum, v fraga

frango, frēgi, fractum, 3 (root FRAG, connected with ῥηγνυμι), *to break, break in pieces, shatter, dash to pieces* **I. A.** Lit , **1**, domum lapidum conjectu, Cic. , compluribus navibus fractis, *dashed to pieces*, Caes , gulam laqueo, *to strangle*, Sall ; glebas rastris, *to break small*, Verg , **2**, esp , **a**, *to grind*, fruges saxo, Verg , **b**, *to break* (a limb) , brachium, Cic **B.** Transf., **a**, reflex se frangere, *to break up* (of weather, cold, heat, etc), Cic , **b**, *to shorten time;* diem morantem mero, Hor **II.** Fig , **1**, *to weaken*, se laboribus, Cic. ; **2**, **a**, *to master, tame, subdue*, nationes, cupiditates, impetum, Cic ; **b**, *to discourage, dispirit, humble*, Clodium, Cic. , frangi animo or frangi, *to be discouraged*, Cic ; **3**, *to bend, touch, move*, te ut ulla res frangat, Cic , **4**, *to break, violate*, fidem, Cic.

frāter -tris, m , *a brother.* **I.** Lit , fratres gemini, *twin-brothers*, Cic , *Castor and Pollux*, Ov , fratres gemelli, Ov , germanus, *own brother*, Cic **II. A.** fratres (like ἀδελφοί), *brothers and sisters*, Tac **B.** **a**, frater patruelis, Cic , and simply frater, *cousin*, Cic , **b**, *brother-in-law*, Liv **C.** *brother* (as term of endearment), *friend*, Cic **D.** fratres, of things alike, positi ex ordine fratres (of writings), Ov

frātercŭlus -i, m (dim of frater), *a little brother* (as term of endearment) ; ap Cic.

frāternē, adv (fraternus), *in a brotherly manner, like a brother* **A.** Lit , facere, Cic **B.** Transf , *heartily*, ab aliquo amari, Cic

frāternĭtas -ātis, f (fraternus), *brotherhood, fraternity* Tac.

frāternus a -um (for fraterinus, from frater), *brotherly, fraternal* **I.** Lit., hereditas, *coming from a brother*, Cic , lyra, *received by Apollo from his brother Mercury*, Hor ; nex, *murder of a brother*, Hor **II.** Transf , **A.** *related*, sanguis, Verg , fraterna peto, *the arms of my cousin Achilles*, Ov **B.** *friendly* , amor in nos, Cic

frātrĭcīda -ae, m (from frater and caedo), *one who kills a brother, a fratricide*, Cic

fraudātĭo -ōnis, f (fraudo), *deceit, fraud*, Cic

fraudātor -ōris, m (fraudo), *a deceiver, defrauder* , creditorum, Cic

fraudo, 1 (fraus), *to cheat, defraud deceive.* **A.** Lit., with abl , Caecilium magnā pecuniā, Cic , milites praedā, Liv , creditores, Cic., aliquem in hereditaria societate, Cic, partic subst, **fraudāta** -ōrum, n *ill-gotten gains*, fraudata restituere, Caes, **B.** Transf, *to steal, embezzle*, stipendium equitum, Caes

fraudŭlentĭa ae, f (fraudulentus), *deceitfulness*, Plaut

fraudŭlentus a -um (fraus), *deceitful, fraudulent*, Carthaginienses, Cic, venditio, Cic

fraus, fraudis, f. *deceit, deception, fraud* I. **A.** Lit, **1**, fraus odio digni majore, Cic; sine fraude, *honourably*, Caes, fraudem facere legi, Liv, or contra legem, Liv, or senatus consulto, Cic, **2**, *self-deception, error*, in fraudem incidere, delabi, Cic **B.** Meton, *injury, damage, loss, caused by deception*, alicui fraudem ferre, or alicui fraudi esse, *to cause loss to*, Cic **II.** *a crime, offence*, fraudem suscipere, Cic, fraudem capitalem admittere or audere, Cic (genit plur fraudium and fraudum)

fraxĭnĕus -a -um (fraxinus), *of ash-wood, ashen*, trabes, Verg

1 **fraxĭnus** -a -um = fraxineus, Ov

2 **fraxĭnus** -i, f **1**, lit., *an ash tree*, Verg, **2**, meton, *a spear or javelin, the shaft of which was made of ash-wood*, Ov.

Frĕgellae -ārum, f, *town of the Volsci, in Latium, on the Liris, now Ceprano* Adj, **Frĕgellānus**, -a -um, *Fregellan*

Fregēnae -ārum, f *town of Etruria*

frĕmĕbundus -a -um (fremo), *growling, muttering, murmuring*, Ov

frĕmĭdus -a -um (fremo), *raging*, Ov

frĕmĭtus -ūs, m (fremo), *a low murmuring, muttering, growling noise, murmur, roar*, murmurantis maris, Cic, terrae, Cic, egentium, Cic, equorum, Liv, apum, Verg

frĕmo ŭi -ĭtum, 3 (βρέμω), *to roar, murmur, growl* **I** Intransit, **a**, of animals and things, leo, equus, Verg, fremunt ripae, *rustle*, Verg, **b**, of persons, laetitiā fremunt, Verg, adversus injuriam decreti fremere, Liv **II** Transit, **1** *to murmur out something, express in secret, grumble, complain*, uno omnes eadem ore fremebant, Verg, with acc and infin, falsas esse et a scriba vitiatas (litteras) fremebant, Liv, haec fremunt plebs, Liv, jam vero Arrius consulatum sibi ereptum fremit, Cic, **2**, *to demand, call for with tears or rage*, arma, Verg

frĕmor ōris, m (fremo), *murmuring*, varius, Verg

frendo, frēsum (fressum), ŏ, 3, intransit, with or without dentibus, *to gnash the teeth*, Cic.; **2**, transit, *to crush, bruise, grind*, fabam, Varr

frēni -ōrum, m v. frenum

frēno, 1 (frenum), *to bridle, curb*; **1**, lit, equos, Verg, **2**, transf, *to curb, restrain, check, hold in*, cursus aquarum, Verg, furores, Cic

Frentāni ōrum, m *a Samnite people on the east coast of Italy* Hence, adj, **Frentānus** -a, -um, *Frentanian*

frēnum -i, n, plur **frēna** ōrum, n, and **frēni** -ōrum, m (frendo), *bridle, reins, bit*, frena remittere, *to give the reins to*, Ov, so frena dare, Ov, frenos inhibere, *to draw in*, Liv, fig, frenos dare impotenti naturae, *to give full liberty to*, Liv, alicui frenos adhibere, *to bridle*, Cic, frenos recipere, *to submit to the rein*, Cic, frenum mordere, *to chafe against restraint*, Cic (in prose, nom pl, frena and acc plur frenos commoner than frena)

frĕquens entis **I** of space, **A.** Act, of a crowd, etc, *numerous, crowded*, legatio, Liv, senatus, Cic **B.** Pass, of places, *full, frequented, filled, populous*, theatrum, Cic, municipium, Cic, with abl, frequens custodiis locus, Liv **II.** of time, **A.** Act., *frequent, constant* Platonis auditor, Cic, cum aliquo frequentem esse, *to be often in a person's company*, Cic **B.** Pass, *frequently used, numerous*, pocula, Cic

frĕquentātĭo -ōnis, f (frequento), *frequency, frequent use*, argumentorum, Cic

frĕquentātus -a -um (partic of frequento), *full of, abounding in*, genus sententiis frequentatum, Cic

frĕquentĕr, adv (frequens), *frequently, numerously, in large numbers* **1**, quum ad eum frequenter per eos dies ventitaturos se esse dixissent, Cic; **2**, *frequently, often*, adhibendae frequentius etiam illa ornamenta rerum sunt, Cic

frĕquentĭa ae, f (frequens), **1**, *a large concourse, numerous assembly*, civium, Cic, frequentiā crescere, *to increase in population*, Liv, **2**, *a large number, abundance*, sepulcrorum, Cic

frĕquento, 1 (frequens) **I. A** a, of persons, *to collect in large numbers*, de domo scribas ad aerarium, Cic, **b**, transf, of things, multa acervatim, Cic **B.** *to visit in large numbers*, **a**, *to attend upon a person in large numbers*, Marium, Sall **b**, *to celebrate a festivity in large numbers*, ferias, Cic, **c**, *to make a place populous, to people*, urbes, Cic, solitudinem Italiae, Cic **II. A.** *to visit frequently, to frequent*, domum, Cic **B.** *to repeat constantly*; verba translationem, Cic

frēsus (fressus) -a -um, v frendo

frĕtum -i, n, and **frĕtus** ūs, m (connected with ῥέειν and ῥεῖθρον), **1**, **a**, lit, *the sea*, fretus Hadriae, Hor, **b**, *the spring* (as the time of transition from cold to heat), Lucr, **c**, *heat, violence, raging*, aetatis, Lucr **2**, *a strait sound, firth, channel*, gen, **a**, Siciliense, *the Straits of Messina*, Cic, nostri maris et oceani, *the Straits of Gibraltar*, Sall, **b**, esp, *the Straits of Messina*, Cic

1 **frētus** a um (from unused freo = *I strength-en*), *strengthened* hence *relying on, confiding in, trusting depending on* with the abl, vobis, Cic, intelligentiā vestrā, Cic, with dat, nulli rei, Liv, with acc and infin satis fretus esse etiamnunc tolerando certamini legatum, Liv

2 **frĕtus** -ūs, m = fretum (q v)

frĭco, fricŭi, frictum, and fricātum 1 *to rub, rub down*, (sus) fricat arbore costas, Verg

frīgĕo, 2 (ῥιγέω) **I.** *to be cold, be stiff with cold* (opp calere), corpus frigentis (of a dead person), Verg **II.** Transf, **A** *to be inactive, lifeless, languid, to flag*, quum omnia consilia frigerent, Cic **B.** *to be coldly received, fail of exciting approbation*, itaque (contio) frigebat, Cic

frīgĕro, 1 (frigus), *to cool, refresh*, Cat

frīgesco, frixi, 3 (frigeo) **I.** Lit *to become cold*; pedes manusque Tac **II.** Transf, *to become languid, inactive*, ap Cic

frīgĭdē, adv (frigidus), *coldly* hence transf, *languidly, feebly*, aliquid agere, ap Cic

frīgĭdŭlus a -um (dim of frigidus), **1**, *somewhat cold*, Verg, **2**, transf, *somewhat faint, languid*, Cat

frīgĭdus a um (frigeo), *cold, frigid, cool* **I. A.** Lit, flumen, Cic, rura, Verg, annus, *winter* Verg Subst plur, **frīgĭda** ōrum, n *cold*, Cic, of the chill of death or fright, Verg **B.** Transf, **1**, *cold, inactive, remiss, indolent*, accusator frigidissimus, Cic, litterae, Cic, **2**, of discourse, *frigid, dull*, calumnia, Cic **II.** Act, *causing cold*, sidera, Ov, mors, Verg, timor, *chilling, causing fright*, Hor

frīgo, frixi, frictum, 3 (φρύγω), *to roast, parch*, Hor

frīgus ŏris, n (ῥῖγος), *cold, coolness, coldness*,

I. Lit., **A.** *physical cold;* **1,** gen., vis frigoris et caloris, Cic.; **2,** esp., **a,** *the cold of winter;* propter frigora, Caes.; **b,** meton., (α) *winter,* Verg.; (β) *a cold place:* frigus non habitabile, Ov. **B.** *animal cold;* **a,** of death, Verg.; **b,** of fright, Verg. **II.** Transf., **a,** *coldness in action, indolence, remissness,* ap. Cic.; **b,** *coldness in behaviour, coolness, disfavour,* Hor.

frĭgūtĭo (frĭguttĭo), 4. **1,** *to twitter, chirp,* Suet.; **2,** *to stammer,* Plaut.

frĭo, 1. *to rub, crumble,* Lucr.

Frīsĭi -ōrum, m. *the Frisians.* Adj., **Frīsĭus** -a -um, *Frisian.*

frĭtillus -i, m. *a dice-box,* Juv.

frīvŏlus -a -um (frio), *silly, trifling, miserable, worthless,* Plin. Subst., **frīvŏla** -ōrum, n. *wretched furniture,* Juv.

frondātor -ōris, m. (1. frons), *one who cuts off leaves, a pruner of trees,* Verg.

frondĕo, 2. (1. frons), *to be in leaf, be leafy, green with leaves;* nunc frondent silvae, Verg.

frondesco, 3. (inchoat. of frondeo), *to come into leaf, put forth leaves,* Cic.

frondĕus -a -um (1. frons), *leafy, full of leaf, covered with leaves;* nemus, Verg.; tecta, *leafy coverts = trees in full leaf,* Verg.

frondĭfer -fĕra -fĕrum (1. frons and fero), *leaf-bearing, leafy,* Lucr.

frondōsus -a -um (1. frons), *full of leaves, leafy;* ramus, Verg.

1. **frons,** frondis, f. **A.** *a leaf, leafy twig or branch, foliage;* via interclusa frondibus et virgultis, Cic. **B.** Meton., *a chaplet* or *crown of leaves,* Hor.

2. **frons,** frontis, f. *the forehead, brow.* **I.** Lit., **a,** frontem contrahere, *to frown,* Cic.; explicare, *to unwrinkle the brow, become cheerful,* Hor.; frontem ferire or percutere, Cic.; **b,** *the forehead as a sign of the feelings;* laeta, Verg.; sollicita, proterva, Hor.; fronte occultare sententiam, Cic. **II.** Transf., **A.** *the outside;* **1,** gen., tabernae, Cat.; **2,** esp., *the edge of a roll* or *volume,* Ov. **B.** *the front, forepart;* **1,** gen., frons adversa (montis), Verg.; **2,** esp. milit. t. t., **a,** *the van;* et a fronte et a tergo circumire hostem, Caes.; a fronte instare, Liv.; **b,** *the front line in battle;* frontem aequare, Liv. **C.** *frontage* (in measuring land), Hor.

frontālĭa -ium, n. (2. frons), *the frontlet of a horse,* Liv.

fronto -ōnis, m. (2. frons). **I.** *a man with a broad forehead,* Cic. **II.** Fronto, a *Roman surname.*

fructŭārĭus -a -um (fructus), *fruit-bearing, fruitful;* agri quos fructuarios habent civitates, *for which a portion of the produce is paid,* ap. Cic.

fructŭōsus -a -um (fructus), *fruit-bearing, fruitful, fertile.* **A.** Lit., ager, Cic. **B.** Transf., tota philosophia frugifera et fructuosa, Cic.; fructuosum est, with infin., Cic.

fructus -ūs, m. (fruor). **I.** Abstr., *enjoyment, enjoying.* **A.** Lit., Plaut. **B.** Transf., ad animi mei fructum, *for my intellectual enjoyment,* Cic. **II.** Concr., *the proceeds, profit, produce, fruit, income.* **A.** Lit., praediorum, Cic.; fructus percipere, demetere, Cic.; fructui esse alicui, *to bring profit to,* Cic.; in fructu habere, *to consider profitable,* Cic. **B.** Transf., *advantage, gain, profit;* verae virtutis, Cic.; fructum ferre, or capere, or percipere ex aliqua re, Cic.

frugālis -e (frux), *frugal, sparing, economical, worthy, excellent;* colonus frugalissimus, Cic. (positive not used in class. Latin, frugi instead).

frūgālĭtas -ātis, f. (frugalis), *frugality, economy, worth, excellence,* Cic.; cognomen Frugalitatis, *the surname Frugi,* Cic.

frūgālĭtĕr, adv. (frugalis), *frugally, economically, worthily, honourably,* Cic.

frūgi, v. frux.

frūgĭfer -fĕra -fĕrum (frux and fero). **A.** Lit., *fruit-bearing, fruitful, fertile;* ager, Cic.; numen, *making fruitful,* Ov.; with abl., alimentis frugifera insula, Liv. **B.** Transf., *profitable, advantageous;* tota philosophia frugifera et fructuosa, Cic.

frūgĭfĕrens -entis (frux and fero), *fruitful, fertile,* Lucr.

frūgĭlĕgus -a -um (frux and lego), *collecting fruit;* formicae, Ov.

frūgĭpărus -a -um (frux and pario), *fruitful, prolific,* Lucr.

frŭĭtus, frŭĭtūrus, v. fruor.

frūmentārĭus -a -um (frumentum), *relating or belonging to grain* or *corn;* res, *the supply of corn,* Cic.; lex, *relating to the price of grain,* Cic. Subst., **frūmentārĭus** -ii, m. *a corn-merchant,* Cic.

frūmentātĭo -ōnis, f. (frumentor), *a foraging,* Caes.

frūmentātor -ōris, m. (frumentor), *a forager, provider of corn,* Liv.

frūmentor, 1. dep. (frumentum), *to forage, fetch corn;* frumentari in propinquo agro, Liv.

frūmentum -i, n. (fruor), *grain, corn,* Cic.

frŭor, fructus and frŭĭtus sum, 3. dep. **1,** *to enjoy, to delight in, to derive advantage from;* with abl., vitā, Cic.; voluptate, Cic.; votis, *to obtain one's wishes,* Ov.; amicitiae recordatione, *to take delight in,* Cic.; absol., jucundius est carere quam frui, Cic.; **2,** *to have the use and enjoyment of;* fundis certis, Cic.

Frŭsĭno -ōnis, m. *town of the Volsci in Latium,* now *Frosinone.* Hence, **Frŭsĭnās** -ātis, *of* or *belonging to Frusino.*

frustrā (for frustera, abl. of * frusterus, connected with fraudo), **1,** *in error;* frustra esse, *to be deceived, mistaken,* Sall.; **2,** *in vain, uselessly, without effect, unnecessarily,* Cic.; frustra esse (alicui), *to fail,* Sall.; frustra tempus contero, Cic.

frustrātĭo -ōnis, f. (frustro), *failure, disappointment;* tantae rei, Liv.

frustro, 1. and dep. **frustror,** 1. (frustra), *to cheat, deceive, trick;* nos falsā atque inani spe, Liv.; Coccejus vide ne frustretur, Cic.

frustum -i, n. (fruor), *a bit, piece, morsel of food;* frusta esculenta, Cic.; in frusta secare, Verg.

frŭtex -ĭcis, m. (perhaps connected with βρύω), **1,** *a shrub, bush,* Ov.; **2,** as a term of reproach, *blockhead,* Plaut.

frŭtĭcētum -i, n. (frutex), *a thicket,* Hor.

frŭtĭco and **frŭtĭcor,** 1. dep. (frutex), *to shoot out, become bushy;* quam fruticetur (arbor), vides, Cic.

frŭtĭcōsus -a -um, adj. with compar. and superl. (frutex), *bushy, thick with leaves, full of bushes,* Ov.

frux, frūgis (fruor). **A.** Lit., *fruit, produce;* non omnem frugem neque arborem in agro reperire, Cic.; plur., terrae fruges bacaeve arborum, Cic. **B.** Transf., **a,** *fruit;* fruges industriae, Cic.; bonam frugem libertatis ferre, Liv.; **b,** *moral excellence, virtue;* ad bonam frugem se recipere, *to improve oneself,* Cic.; **frūgi** used as an adj., *useful, worthy, honest, discreet, moderate, temperate;* homo, Cic.; permodestus et bonae frugi, Cic.

fūcātus a -um (p adj of fuco), *painted, counterfeited, simulated*, intor, Cic, omnia fucata et simulata a sinceris atque veris (secernere), Cic

Fūcīnus -i, m *a lake in Southern Italy, in the country of the Marsi, now Lago di Celano*

fūco, 1 (1 fucus), 1, *to colour, dye*, vellera hyali colore, Verg, 2, *to paint, rouge*, Ov, transf, iisdem ineptiis fucata sunt illa omnia, Cic

fūcōsus a -um (1 fucus), *painted, simulated, counterfeited*, merx, Cic, amicitia, Cic

1 **fūcus** i m (φῦκος), 1, *red or purple colour*, Hor, Ov, 2, = propolis, *the reddish substance with which bees stop up the entrance to their hives, bee-glue*, Verg, 3, *rouge*, 4, transf, *deceit, dissimulation, pretence*, sine fuco ac fallaciis, Cic

2 **fūcus** -i, m. *a drone bee*, Verg

Fūfius -a -um, *name of a Roman gens*

fŭga -ae, f (φυγή) I. A. Lit 1, gen, *flight, running away*, fuga ab urbe turpissima, Cic, ex fuga se recipere, Caes, esse in fuga, Cic.; hostes in fugam convertere, or dare, or conjicere, Caes, in fugam se dare, se conferre, se conjicere, Cic, fugae se mandare, Caes, or dare, Cic; fugam dare, *to flee*, Verg, or, *to let flee*, Verg, Hor, fugam facere, *to flee*, Sall, Liv.; or *to make to flee*, Cic, Liv, fugam sistere, *to stop*, Liv, plur, quintae in periculis fugae proximorum, Cic, 2, esp, *flight from one's country, exile, banishment*, fuga Metelli Cic, meton, *the place of exile*, Ov B. Transf, *disinclination to, avoidance of, aversion to* laboris, bellandi, Cic II. *flying, swift course*, Verg, of a ship, facilem fugam exspectare, Verg, transf, fuga temporum, *hastening*, Hor

fŭgācius, adv in compar (fugax), *in a manner more inclined to flight*, utrum a se audacius an fugacius ab hostibus geratur bellum, Liv

fŭgax -acis (fugio), 1, *ready to flee, flying, hastening*, Parthus, Ov, fugacissimus hostis, Liv, 2, transf, a, *fleeting, transitory*, anni Hor; haec omnia brevia, fugacia, caduca existima, Cic, b, with genit, *avoiding*, conditionis, Ov

fŭgiens entis, p adj (from fugio), *flying from, avoiding*, with genit, laboris, Caes

fŭgio, fūgi, fŭgitum 3 (φεύγω) I. Intransit A. *to flee, take to flight, run away*, 1, gen, a, lit, longe, Ov.; poet, of a bird, in auras, Verg, b, transf, omne animal appetit quaedam et fugit a quibusdam, Verg, 2, esp a, of soldiers, ex proelio, Cic, b, of fugitives, a Troja (of Aeneas), Cic, esp of exiles, a patria, Ov, c, of slaves, *to run away*, Hor. B. 1, *to hasten away, depart quickly*, fugientia flumina, Hor, Camilla super amnem fugit, Verg, 2, *to pass away, vanish, disappear*, fugiunt cum sanguine vires, Ov, vinum fugiens, *becoming flat*, Cic II. Transit, *to flee from* A. *to run away from*, cerva fugiens lupum, Liv, velut qui currebat fugiens hostem, Hor, patriam, Verg B. 1, *to avoid, shun*, a, lit, concilia conventusque hominum, Caes, b, transf, (α) ignominiam et dedecus, Cic; (β) *to decline, renounce, reject* aliquem judicem, Liv, neque illud fugerim dicere, Cic, fuge quaerere, *do not seek*, Hor, 2, *to escape from*, Acheronta, Hor.; scientiam alicuius, Cic, aliquid aliquem fugit, *escapes the notice of* Cic, with infin, de Dionysio fugit me ad te antea scribere, Cic

fŭgitans -antis, p adj (from fugito), *flying from, avoiding*, Ter

fŭgitīvus -a -um (fugio), 1, adj, *flying, fugitive*, a dominis, Cic, 2, subst, *a fugitive*, esp *a runaway slave*, Cic

fŭgito, 1 (intens. of fugio), *to fly from, avoid, shun*, quaestionem, Cic

fŭgo, 1 (fuga), 1, *to put to flight, chase away, drive away*, homines inermes, Cic, fundere atque fugare, Sall, 2, *to drive away*, a, aliquem, Cic; b, esp, *to drive into exile*, Ov

fulcīmen -inis, n. (fulcio), *a prop, support, pillar*, Ov

fulcio, fulsi, fultum, 4 I. *to prop up, support*, 1, lit, porticum, Cic., vitis fulta, Cic, 2, transf, *to support, stay, uphold* amicum Cic., labantem rempublicam, Cic, Thermum litteris, Cic II. *to strengthen, secure*, postes, Verg, januam sera, Ov

fulcrum i n (fulcio), 1, *a post or foot of a couch*, Verg, 2, meton, *a couch*, Juv.

Fulfŭlae -ārum, f *a town of the Samnites*

fulgĕo, fulsi, 2 (root FUL, whence also fulvus) I. *to lighten*, Jove, or caelo, fulgente, Cic II. Transf, A. Of Pericles, as a powerful orator, compared to Jupiter, fulgere, tonare, Cic B. 1, lit, *to shine, gleam, glitter*, auro, Cic, fulgebat luna, Hor, 2, transf, *to be distinguished, to shine*, virtus intaminatis fulget honoribus, Hor

fulgĭdus -a -um (fulgeo), *shining, gleaming, glittering*, Lucr

Fulgĭnia -ae, f *a town in Umbria, now Foligno* Adj, **Fulgĭniātis**, *of Fulginia*

fulgo, 3 = fulgeo (q v)

fulgor -ōris, m (fulgeo), 1, *lightning*, fulgores et tonitrua, Cic, 2, *glitter, brilliancy, brightness*, armorum, Hor, candelabri, Cic, 3, transf, *brightness, glory*, nominis, Ov, honoris, Tac

fulgŭr -ŭris, n (fulgeo) 1, *lightning*, Cic, 2, *a thunderbolt* Ov, condere fulgur, *to bury an object which has been struck by lightning*, Juv, 3, poet = fulgor, *brightness, brilliancy*, solis, Lucr, rapidum Aetnaeo fulgur ab igne jaci, Ov (plur fulgura, Cic)

fulgŭrālis -e (fulgur), *relating or belonging to lightning* libri, *treating of the* (religious) *significance of lightning*, Cic

fulgŭrātor -ōris, m (fulguro), *a haruspex who interpreted the omens from lightning*, Cic

fulgŭrītus a -um (fulgur), *struck by lightning*, Plaut

fulgŭro, 1 (fulgur), *to lighten*, Jove fulgurante, ap Cic

fŭlica -ae, f *a coot*, Verg

fūlīgo -inis, f (root FU, whence also fumus), 1, *soot*, Cic, 2, *a powder used for darkening the eyebrows*, Juv

fŭlix -icis, f = fulica (q v)

fullo -ōnis, m *a fuller, cloth fuller*, Plaut

fulmen -inis, n. (orig fulgmen, from fulgeo, and suffix men). I. *a flash of lightning which strikes something, a thunderbolt*, fulmine percussus, Cic, ictu fulminis deflagrare, Cic II. Transf, A. *a thunder-bolt, crushing calamity*, fortunae, Cic, duo fulmina domum perculerunt, Liv B. *mighty or irresistible power*, verborum, Cic, so of heroes, duo fulmina imperii nostri, *the two Scipios*, Cic

fulmĭnĕus -a -um (fulmen) A. Lit, *relating to lightning*, ignes, Ov, ictus Hor B. Transf, *slaying, murderous, destructive*, ensis, Verg, os apri, Ov

fulmĭno, 1 (fulmen), *to lighten, to thunder and lighten*, Juppiter fulminans, Hor; impers, boreae de parte trucis quum fulminat, Verg, transf, Caesar fulminat bello, Verg

fultūra -ae, f. (fulcio), *a support, prop stay* (of food), Hor

Fulviaster, v. Fulvius.

Fulvius -a -um, *name of a Roman gens of which the most celebrated members were* M. Fulvius Flaccus, *supporter of C. Gracchus*, and Fulvia, *wife of Clodius, and afterwards of Antonius.* **Fulviaster** -stri, m. *an imitator of* Fulvius (Postumius), Cic.

fulvus -a -um (root FUL, whence fulgeo), *dark* or *reddish yellow, tawny, yellowish brown* (of lions, wolves, sand, gold), Verg. ; caesaries, Verg. ; aquila or ales Jovis (because of its yellow eyes), Verg.

fūmĕus -a -um (fumus), *smoky, full of smoke*, Verg.

fūmĭdus -a -um (fumus), *smoky, full of smoke* ; taeda, Verg. ; altaria, Ov.

fūmĭfer -fĕra -fĕrum (fumus and fero), *smoke-bearing, smoky* ; ignes, nox, Verg.

fūmĭfĭcus -a -um (fumus and facio), *causing smoke*, Ov.

fūmo, 1. (fumus), *to smoke, steam* ; agger fumat, Caes. ; domus fumabat, *reeked with the odours of feasts*, Cic. ; equûm fumantia colla, Verg.

fūmōsus -a -um (fumus), *full of smoke, smoky, steaming, smoked* ; arae, Ov. ; imagines, *figures of ancestors*, Cic.

fūmus -i, m. (root FU, whence also fuligo), *smoke, steam, vapour* ; fumus ganearum, Cic. ; fumo excruciari, Cic. ; fumo dare signum, Liv. ; plur., fumi incendiorum procul videbantur, Caes. ; prov., vertere omne in fumum et cinerem, *to squander, consume*, Hor.

fūnālis -e (funis), *relating* or *belonging to a rope*. Subst., **fūnāle** -is, n., **1**, *the thong of a sling*, Liv. ; **2**, *a wax-torch*, Cic.

fūnambŭlus -i, m. (funis and ambulo), *a rope-dancer*, Ter.

functio -ōnis, f. (fungor), *a performance, performing, executing* ; muneris, Cic.

funda -ae, f. (2. fundo), **1**, *a sling*, Caes. ; fundā mittere glandes et lapides, Liv. ; **2**, *a casting-net*, Verg.

fundāmen -ĭnis, n. (1. fundo), *a foundation, base* ; ponere or jacere, Verg.

fundāmentum -i, n. (1. fundo), **1**, lit., *a foundation, base* ; fundamenta jacere, Cic. ; a fundamentis diruere Pteleum, Liv. ; **2**, transf., *foundation, basis* ; pietas fundamentum est omnium virtutum, Cic.

Fundānius -a -um, *name of a Roman gens.*

fundātor -ōris, m. (1. fundo), *a founder* ; urbis, Verg.

fundātus -a -um (p. adj. from 1. fundo), *firm, durable* ; fundatissima familia, Cic.

fundĭtor -ōris, m. (funda), *a light-armed soldier, furnished with a sling, a slinger*, gen. in plur., Caes. ; sing. collective, funditor Balearis, Liv.

fundĭtŭs, adv. (fundus). **I.** *from the ground*, **A.** Lit., monumenta delere, Cic. **B.** Transf., *completely, entirely* ; evertere amicitiam, Cic. **II.** *at the bottom, below*, Lucr.

1. **fundo**, 1. (fundus). **I.** *to lay the foundation of, to found* ; arces, Verg. ; urbem colonis, Verg. ; dente tenaci ancora fundabat naves, *fastened to the ground*, Verg. **II.** Transf., **A.** *to found* ; accurate non modo fundata verum etiam exstructa disciplina, Cic. **B.** *to make firm, to strengthen* ; urbem legibus, Verg. ; nostrum imperium, Cic.

2. **fundo**, fūdi, fūsum, 3. (root FUD, connected with χέω, χεύσω), *to pour, pour out.* **I.** Lit., **1**, of liquids, sanguinem e patera, Cic. ; liquorem de patera, Hor. ; lacrimas, Verg. ; middle, *to pour* ; ingentibus procellis fusus imber, Liv. ; **2**, of bodies not liquid, **a**, *to pour out* ; segetem in Tiberim, Liv. ; **b**, of metals, *to melt, cast* ; quid fusum durius, Hor. ; **c**, *to sprinkle* ; tempora multo mero, Tib. **II.** Transf., **A. 1**, *to throw to the ground*, often in partic., *thrown down, lying* ; fusi sub remis nautae, Verg. ; **2**, milit. t. t., *to rout, defeat, scatter, put to flight* ; hostes, Liv. ; middle, *to rush away* ; turpi fugā fundi, Liv. **B.** *to let loose* ; **1**, middle, fundi, *to spread* ; vitis funditur, Cic. ; **2**, **a**, *to discharge missiles* ; tela, Verg. ; **b**, luna per fenestram se fundebat, *streamed through*, Verg. ; **3**, of persons, reflex., *to rush out* ; plenis se portis, Verg. ; **4**, **a**, *to pour forth from the mouth, to utter* ; sonos inanes, Cic. ; esp. of poets, *to pour forth, compose* ; versus hexametros ex tempore, Cic. ; **b**, *to give forth, to produce* ; terra fundit fruges, Cic. ; quem Maia fudit, *gave birth to*, Verg. ; **c**, *to squander* ; opes, Hor. **III.** Fig., **a**, middle, fundi, *to spread* ; utrumque eorum fundi quodammodo et quasi dilatari, Cic. ; **b**, *to pour forth* ; multo vitam cum sanguine, Verg.

fundus -i, m. *the bottom* or *base of anything.* **I.** Gen., **1**, **a**, lit., armarii, Cic. ; aequora ciere fundo, *from the bottom*, Verg. ; **b**, transf., largitio non habet fundum, *knows no bounds*, Cic. ; fundum fieri legis, *to sanction, authorise*, Cic. **II.** Esp., *the soil, a farm, estate*, Cic.

fūnĕbris -e (funus), **1**, *relating* or *belonging to a funeral, funereal* ; epulum, contio, Cic. ; subst., **fūnĕbria** -ium, n. *funeral ceremonies*, Cic. ; **2**, *deadly, destructive, cruel, fatal* ; bellum, Hor. ; munera, Ov.

fūnĕrĕus -a -um (funus), **1**, *relating to a funeral, funereal* ; faces, Verg. ; **2**, *of that which causes* or *betokens death* ; dextra, Ov. ; bubo, *ill-omened*, Ov.

fūnĕro, 1. (funus), **1**, *to bury solemnly, inter with funeral rites*, Plin. ; **2**, *to kill*, Hor.

fūnesto, 1. (funestus), *to defile* or *pollute with murder* ; aras ac templa hostiis humanis, Cic.

fūnestus -a -um (funus). **I.** *filled with mourning, defiled by death* ; agros funestos reddere, *to pollute with blood*, Lucr. ; familia funesta, *in mourning*, Liv. **II.** *calamitous, mournful, disastrous, deadly* ; tribunatus, Cic. ; fax, Cic. ; with dat., funesta reipublicae pestis, Cic.

fungor, functus sum, 3. dep. *to be busy, occupy oneself, be engaged with anything, to perform, execute, accomplish.* **I.** Gen., **a**, with abl., muneribus corporis, Cic. ; virtute fungi, *to show bravery*, Hor. ; munere aedilicio, *discharge the office of aedile*, Cic. ; vice cotis, *to serve instead of*, Hor. ; dapibus, *to take food*, Ov. ; sepulcro, *to bury*, Ov. ; **b**, with acc., hominum officia, Tac. **II.** **a**, *to suffer* ; mala multa, Lucr. ; **b**, *to complete, finish* ; gen., functum esse morte, *to die*, Ov.

fungus -i, m. (σφόγγος, σπόγγος), **1**, *a mushroom, fungus*, Cic. ; as a term of reproach applied *to a dull, stupid fellow*, Plaut. ; **2**, *a thief in the wick of a candle, a candle-snuff*, Verg.

fūnĭcŭlus -i, m. (dim. of funis), *a thin rope, cord, string* ; funiculus a puppi religatus, Cic.

fūnis -is, m. (fem. Lucr. 2, 1154), *a rope, cord, line* ; per funem demitti, Verg. ; of ship's ropes, ancorarius funis, Caes. ; funes qui antemnas ad malos religabant, Caes. ; *the rope of a rope-dancer* ; per extentum funem ire, Hor. ; prov., ne currente retro funis eat rota, *that all your labour may not be wasted*, Hor. ; ducere, *to guide the rope*—i.e., *to command*, Hor. ; sequi, *to follow, obey*, Hor. ; reducere, *to change one's mind*, Pers.

fūnus -ĕris, n. *a funeral, obsequies, interment.* **I. A.** Lit., funus quo amici conveniunt ad exsequias cohonestandas, Cic. ; funus alicui facere,

Cic., ducere, Cic., in funus venire, Cic., funus celebrare, Liv. **B.** Meton., **1,** *the corpse*, lacerum, Verg.; **2,** *death*, crudeli funere exstinctus, Verg.; edere funera, *to kill*, Verg. **II.** Transf., *destruction*, *ruin*, reipublicae, Cic.; meton., *the persons who cause ruin*, paene funera reipublicae, *destroyers*, Cic.

fŭo, fŭi, fŭtūrus, etc., v. sum.

fūr, fūris, c. (φώρ), *a thief*, non fur, sed ereptor, Cic.; fur nocturnus, Cic.; as a term of reproach to slaves, Verg.

fūrācĭtĕr, adv. (furax), *thievishly*, domos furacissime scrutari, Cic.

fūrax -ācis (1. furor), *inclined to steal*, *thievish*, homo avarus et furax, Cic.

furca -ae, f. (fero). **I.** *a two-pronged fork*, *pitch-fork*, furcā detrudere aliquem, Liv.; prov., naturam expellas furcā, tamen usque recurret, Hor. **II.** Transf., **A.** *a fork-shaped prop* or *pole*, valli furcaeque bicornes, Verg.; furcas duodenos ab terra spectacula alta sustinentes pedes, Liv. **B.** *an instrument of punishment put over the neck, to the two prongs of which the arms were tied, used to punish slaves and parricides*, Liv.; fig., ire sub furcam, Hor. **C.** *a narrow pass*, Furcae Caudinae, v. Caudium.

furcĭfer -fĕra -fĕrum (furca and fero), *one who carries the furca as a punishment*, a term of reproach usually applied to slaves, *gallows-bird*, Cic.

furcilla -ae, f. (dim. of furca), *a little fork*, prov., furcillā extrudi, *to be expelled by force*, Cic.

furcŭla -ae, f. (dim. of furca), **1,** *a fork-shaped prop*, Liv.; **2,** *a narrow pass*, furculae Caudinae, Liv.

fŭrentĕr, adv. (furens), *furiously*, irasci, Cic.

furfur -ŭris, m. **1,** *bran*, Plaut.; **2,** *scales*, *scurf on the skin*, Plin.

fŭrĭa -ae, f., usually plur. (furo). **I.** *rage*, *madness*, *passion*, *fury*, muliebres furiae, Liv.; ventorum furiae, Verg. **II.** Personif., **Fŭrĭa** -ae, f. and gen. plur., **Fŭrĭae** -ārum, f. **A.** *the Furies* (Alecto, Megaera, Tisiphone), *the deities who avenged crimes and tormented criminals*, esp. *parricides*, eos (parricidas) agitent Furiae, Cic. **B.** Transf., of persons, **a,** illa Furia, *Clodius*, Cic.; **b,** *inciter to crime*, hunc juvenem tam quam furiam facemque huius belli, Liv.

fŭrĭālis -e (furia), **1,** *furious*, *raging*, *terrible*, vox, Cic.; incessus, Liv.; Erichtho, *inspired with Bacchic fury*, Ov.; **2,** *belonging to the Furies*, membra, Verg.

fŭrĭālĭtĕr, adv. (furialis), *furiously*, *madly*, Ov.

fŭrĭbundus -a -um (furo), **1,** *raging*, *furious*, furibundus homo ac perditus, Cic.; **2,** *inspired*, praedictio, Cic.

Fŭrīna -ae, f. *an ancient Roman goddess*, hence adj., **Fŭrīnālis** -e, *of* or *belonging to Furina*, subst., **Fŭrīnālĭa** -ium, n. *the festival of Furina*.

fŭrĭo, 1. (furia), *to make furious*, *cause to rage*, *infuriate*, matres equorum, Hor.; partic., furiatus, *raging*, mens, Verg.

fŭrĭōsē, adv. (furiosus), *furiously*, *madly*, aliquid furiose facere, Cic.

fŭrĭōsus -a -um, adj. with compar. and superl. (furia), *raging*, *raving*, *mad*, *furious*, mulier jam non morbo sed scelere furiosa, Cic.; transf., of things, cupiditas, Cic.; tibia, *inspiring*, Ov.

Fūrĭus -a -um, *name of a Roman gens, the most famous member of which was M. Furius Camillus, who freed Rome from the Gauls*. Adj., **Fūrĭānus** -a -um, *of* or *belonging to Furius*.

furnārĭa -ae, f. (furnus), *the trade of a baker*, Suet.

furnus -i, m. (root FOR, cf. fornus), *an oven*, *a bakehouse*, Ov., Hor.

fŭro, 3. (connected with θύω). **I.** *to rage*, *rave*, *be mad*, furere se simulavit, Cic. **II.** Transf., **A.** Of persons, **a,** *to rage*, *be furious*, Catilina furens audacia, Cic.; furens Neptunus, *the raging waves*, Hor.; with acc., furorem, Verg.; with acc. and infin., (Clodius) furebat a Racilio se contumaciter urbaneque vexatum, Cic.; **b,** *to give oneself up to any violent passion*, esp. *love*, libidinibus inflammatus et furens, Cic.; furere aliquā, *to be madly in love with*, Hor. **B.** Of inanimate objects, tempestas or ignis furit, Verg.

1. **fūror,** 1. dep. (fur), **1,** *to steal*, *pilfer*, haec quae rapuit et furatus est, Cic.; librum ab aliquo, (of plagiarists), Cic.; **2,** transf., **a,** *to obtain by stealth*, civitatem, Liv.; **b,** *to withdraw secretly*, oculos labori, Verg.; **c,** *to make secret attacks*, Tac.

2. **fŭror** -ōris, m. (furo). **I.** *madness*, *raving*, *insanity*, ira furor brevis est, Hor. **II.** Transf., **A.** Of persons, **1,** **a,** of the Bacchic fury, majorem orsa furorem, Verg.; fig., versatur mihi ante oculos aspectus Cethegi et furor in vestra caede bacchantis, Cic.; **b,** *inspiration*, *inspired rage*, negat sine furore Democritus poetam magnum esse posse, Cic.; **c,** of martial rage, sic animis juvenum furor additus, Verg.; personif., Furor, as an attendant of Mars, Verg.; **d,** *the rage of anger*, tum regia Juno acta furore gravi, Verg.; **e,** *passionate love*, intus erit furor igneus, Ov.; meton., *the object of passion*, sive mihi Phyllis, sive esset Amyntas, seu quicumque furor, Verg.; **2,** *delusion*, *frenzy*, *rage*, **a,** idem furor et Cretenses lacerabat, Liv.; **b,** *rage*, *tumult*, *sedition*, *revolt*, furor multitudinis, Cic.; alicuius furorem frangere, Cic. **B.** Of inanimate objects, furores et rabies tanta caeli marisque, Verg.

furtim, adv. (fur), *by stealth*, *stealthily*, *secretly* (opp. palam), Cic.

furtīvē, adv. (furtivus), *stealthily*, *secretly*, *furtively*, Ov.

furtīvus -a -um (furtum), **1,** *stolen*, strigilis, Hor.; **2,** *secret*, *concealed*, *furtive*, iter per Italiam, Cic.; amor, Verg.

furtum -i, n. (fur). **I. A.** Lit., *a theft*, furtum facere alicuius rei, Cic.; furti damnari, Cic. **B.** Meton., *the thing stolen*, furta reddere, Cic. **II.** Transf., **A.** *anything secret* or *concealed*, *hidden trick* or *deceit*, furto laetatus inani, Verg.; hence furto, adv. = furtim, *secretly*, Verg. **B. 1,** *secret* or *stolen love*, Verg.; **2,** in war, *a stratagem*, *secret attack*, parva furta per occasionem temptantes, Liv.

fūruncŭlus -i, m. (dim. of fur), *a little thief*, *a little rascal*, Cic.

furvus -a -um (from root FUR, whence also fuscus, connected with fumus, fuligo), *dark-coloured*, *dark*, *black*, **a,** gen., equus, Ov.; **b,** of the lower world and things relating to it, antrum, Ov.; Proserpina, Hor.

fuscĭna -ae, f. (connected with furca), *a three-pronged fork*, *trident*, Cic.

fusco, 1. act. (fuscus), *to make dark*, *darken*, *blacken*; dentes, Ov.

fuscus -a -um (orig. furscus from root FUR, whence furvus), **1,** *dark-coloured*, *dark*, *black*, cornix, Cic.; purpura paene fusca, Cic.; **2,** applied to the voice, *hoarse*, *rough*, genus vocis, Cic.

fūsē, adv. with compar. (fusus), *at length*, *copiously*, *diffusely*, dicere, Cic.

fūsĭlis -e (2. fundo), *melted*, *molten*, *liquid*, aurum, Ov.; ferventes fusili (*softened*), ex argilla glandes, Caes.

fūsĭo -ōnis, f (2 fundo), *a pouring-out, outpouring*, mundum esse eius (dei) animi fusionem universam, Cic

fustis -is, abl -i and -e, m *a stick, staff, cudgel, club*, Cic

fustŭārĭum -ii, n (sc supplicium, from fustis), *beating to death with sticks, the military punishment for desertion*, fustuarium merere or mereri, Cic

1 **fūsus** -a -um (p adj of 2 fundo), *spread out, extended*, **1, a,** of places, campi fusi in omnem partem, Verg , **b,** of bodies, sunt fusa et candida corpora, *fleshy*, Liv , **2,** *let loose;* **a,** *flowing free;* crines, Verg , **b,** of discourse, *diffuse*, genus sermonis, Cic

2 **fūsus** -i, m , *a spindle*, fusum versare, Ov , as an attribute of the Parcae, suis dixerunt, currite fusis, Verg

fūtĭlis -e (connected with 2 fundo), **1,** *that cannot hold* or *contain*, glacies, *brittle*, Verg , **2,** *vain, worthless, futile, good for nothing*, haruspices, Cic ; sententiae, Cic

fūtĭlĭtas -ātis, f (futilis), *worthlessness, folly, silliness*, Cic

fŭtūrus a -um (partic fut of fuo, used as the partic. of sum), *future, about to be*, res, Cic , tempus, Cic Subst , **fŭtūrum** i, n. *the future*, haud ignara futuri, Verg , videre in futurum, Liv ; plur , **fŭtūra** -ōrum, n *the future*, futura prospicere, Cic

G.

G, g, the seventh letter of the Latin alphabet, originally represented by C, introduced into the Latin alphabet about the time of the Second Punic War For the use of this letter in abbreviations, see Table of Abbreviations

Găbăli -ōrum, m and **Găbăles** -um, m *a people in the south-east of Gallia Aquitania*

Găbĭi -ōrum, m *a very ancient city of Latium, between Rome and Praeneste.* Adj , **Găbīnus** -a -um, *Gabinian*, via *from Gabii to Rome*, Liv ; Juno, *honoured in Gabii*, Verg , cinctus, *a particular mode of wearing the toga, in which one end was passed over the head, and the other round the waist*, Liv

Găbīnĭus -a -um, *name of a Roman gens, the most celebrated member of which was* A Gabinius, *who restored the Egyptian king Ptolemaeus Auletes to his kingdom*, hence adj , *Gabinian*, lex, *a law giving extraordinary military power to Pompeius* Adj , **Găbīnĭānus** a um, *of* or *belonging to Gabinius*

Gādēs and **Gādis** -ium, f *a town in the south west of Spain*, now *Cadiz* **Gādītānus** -a um, *of* or *belonging to Gades*

gaesum -i, n *a very strong and heavy javelin, originally a Gaulish weapon*, Caes

Gaetūli -ōrum, m *a people in north west Africa.* Adj , **Gaetūlus** -a -um, poet , *African, Libyan*

Gāius and **Gāia**, v. Caius

Gălaesus -i, m *a river in the south of Italy*, now *Galaso*

Gălătae ārum, m *a Celtic people settled in a part of Phrygia* Hence, **Gălātĭa** -ae, f *the country of the Galatae*

Galba -ae, m *a cognomen of the Sulpician gens.*

galbănĕus -a -um (galbanum), *of* or *relating to galbanum*, Verg.

galbănum -i, n (χαλβάνη), *the resinous sap of a Syrian plant* (bubon galbanum, Linn), Plin

galbănus -a -um, *greenish yellow, yellowish*, Juv

galbĕum -i, n *a kind of fillet* or *bandage for the arm*, Suet

galbĭnus a, -um, *greenish-yellow*, subst., **galbĭnum** -i, n *a greenish-yellow garment*, Juv

gălĕa -ae, f *a helmet* (orig of leather, opp cassis, of metal), Caes , Cic

gălĕo, 1 (galea), *to put on a helmet*, partic , galeatus, *armed with a helmet*, Minerva, Cic

Gălĕōtae -ārum, m (Γαλεῶται), *a body of Sicilian seers*, Cic

gălērĭcŭlum -i, n (dim of galerum), **1,** *a scull cap*, Mart , **2,** *a wig*, Suet

gălērītus -a -um (galerus), **1,** *wearing a skull cap of fur*, Prop ; **2,** transf , galerita avis, *the crested lark* (alauda cristata, Linn)

gălērum -i, n (**gălērus** -i, m.), **1,** *a cap of fur, skull cap*, Verg , **2,** *a wig*, Juv

Galesus = Galaesus (q.v.)

galla -ae, f *the gall-nut, oak-apple*, Verg

Galli -ōrum, m *the Gauls, a Celtic people, living to the west of the Rhine and in the north of Italy as well as in Phrygia ;* sing , **Gallus** -i, m *a Gaul*, and **Galla** -ae, f *a Gaulish woman* Hence, **A. Gallĭa** -ae, f *Gaul, the land of the Gauls*, cisalpina, or ulterior, *Lombardy*, transalpina, or ulterior, *Gaul north of the Alps*, Caes **B. Gallĭcānus** -a -um, *belonging to Gallia provincia, the south east part of Gaul.* **C. Gallĭcus** -a -um *Gaulish*

gallĭambus -i, m *a song of the priests of Cybele*, Mart

gallīna -ae, f (1 gallus), *a hen, fowl*, Cic

gallīnācĕus -a -um (gallina), *relating to poultry*, gallus, Cic , m *a cock.*

gallīnārĭus -a -um (gallina), *relating* or *belonging to poultry* Subst , **gallīnārĭus** -i, m *one who has the care of poultry*, Cic

Gallograecĭa -ae, f = Galatia (q v) Hence, **Gallograecus** a um, *Galatian*

1 **gallus** -i, m *a cock, dunghill cock*, gallorum cantus, *cock-crowing*, Cic

2 **Gallus**, *a Gaul*, v Galli

3 **Gallus** -i, m (Γάλλος), **1,** *a Phrygian river*, now *Kadshasu*. hence, adj , **Gallĭcus** -a -um, poet = *Phrygian, Trojan*, Prop ; **2** (hence), **Galli** ōrum, m *the priests of Cybele*, sing , **Gallus** -i, m and **Galla** -ae, f ; hence, adj , **Gallĭcus** -a -um, turba, *the priests of Isis*, whose worship resembled that of Cybele, Ov

4 **Gallus** -i, m Cornelius (69-26 B C), *a poet and orator, friend of Vergil*

Gămēlĭon -ōnis, m (Γαμηλιών), *the seventh month of the Attic year, corresponding to our January*, Cic

gānĕa -ae, f and **gānĕum** -i, n. (connected with γάνος, γάνυμαι), *a low eating house*, meton , *debauchery*, Cic

gānĕo -ōnis, m (ganea or ganeum), *a profligate person, debauchee, glutton*, Cic

Gangărĭdae and **Gangărĭdes** -um, m *a people in India, on the Ganges.*

Gangēs is, m (Γάγγης), *the river Ganges.* Adj , **Gangētĭcus** -a -um, and **Gangētis** -idis, f poet = *Indian*, Ov.

ganni 4 *to yelp, whine, to snarl, growl, grumble* Plaut , Ter.

gannītus -ūs, m (gannio), **1,** *a barking*.

yelping, snarling of dogs, Luc , 2, applied to men, Mart

Gănȳmēdēs is, m (Γανυμήδης), *son of the Trojan king Tros, carried off on account of his beauty to heaven by an eagle, and made the cup-bearer of Jove.*

Gărămantes -um, m (Γαραμαντες), *a people in the interior of Africa* Hence, **Gărămantis** idis, f = *African,* Verg

Gargānus -i, m *a mountain of Apulia,* now *Monte di S Angelo* Adj , **Gargānus** -a um, *of or belonging to Garganus*

Gargăphiē ēs, f (Γαργαφια), *a valley of Boeotia, sacred to Diana*

Gargăra -ōrum, n (Γάργαρα), *the highest peak of Mount Ida in Mysia, with a town of the same name*

Gargettus -i, m (Γαργηττός), *a deme in Attica, birthplace of Epicurus,* hence called Gargettius

Cargilius -ii, m *a Roman name*

găron = garum (q v)

garrio ivi and ii -itum, 4 (connected with γηρύω), *to chatter, prate, babble,* a, intransit , in iis philosophi garrire coeperunt, Cic , b, transit , quicquid in buccam (sc venerit), Cic

garrŭlitas -ātis, f (garrulus), *chattering,* of magpies, garrulitas rauca, Ov

garrŭlus a -um (garrio) I Lit , 1, of men, *talkative, garrulous, chattering, babbling,* garrula lingua, Ov , 2, applied to animals, cornix, Ov , hirundo, Verg II. Transf , *noisy, sounding,* rivus, Ov , lyra, Tib

Gărumna ae, f *a river in Gaul,* now *the Garonne* Hence, **Gărumni** -ōrum, m *the people living on the Garonne*

gărum (găron), -i, n *a costly fish sauce,* Ov

Gates -um, m *a people in Aquitania*

gaudĕo, gāvīsus sum, 2 (root GA, ΓΑ, whence γαιω, γαῦρος, γηθεω), *to rejoice, find pleasure* or *delight in anything, be glad, delight in* I. Lit , A. Gen , a, intransit , si est nunc ullus gaudendi locus, Cic ; poet with partic , gaudent scribentes, *write with pleasure,* Hor , mihi gaudeo *rejoice for my part,* Cic , gen with abl. of cause, correctione gaudere, Cic , b, transit , gen with acc and infin , quae perfecta esse gaudeo, Cic , poet with infin alone, laedere gaudes, Hor , with quod, sane gaudeo quod te interpellavi, Cic B. Esp , 1, in sinu gaudere, *to rejoice in secret,* Cic , 2, infin , gaudere as a salutation, Celso gaudere refer, *take my greeting to Celsus,* Hor II. Transf , of inanimate objects, *to delight in,* scena gaudens miraculis, Liv

gaudĭum -ii, n (gaudeo), *joy gladness, delight* (as an inward feeling, while laetitia denotes the external expression) I. Lit , gaudio, (*for joy*) lacrimare, triumphare, Cic , exsultare, Cic , aliquem gaudio afficere, Liv , gaudia corporis, Sall II Meton , *that which produces delight,* sua gaudia, Verg

Gaurus -i, m *a mountain in Campania,* now *Monte Gauro*

gausăpa -ae, f , and **gausăpĕ** -is, n , and **gausăpum** i, n , and **gausăpes** is, m (γαυσαπης) *a woollen cloth, with a long nap on one side, frieze,* Ov , Hor

gāza ae, f *the royal treasure of Persia treasure generally, riches, wealth,* regia, Cic

Gĕla ae f (Γελα), *town on the south coast of Sicily* Hence 1, adj , **Gĕlōus** -a um, *of or belonging to Gela,* 2, **Gĕlenses** -ium m *the inhabitants of Gela*

Gĕlās ae, voc Gela, m (Γελας), *a river on the south coast of Sicily*

gĕlăsīnus -i, m (γελασῖνος), *a dimple on the cheek,* Mart

gĕlĭdō, adv (gelidus), *coldly, languidly, feebly,* Hor

gĕlĭdus -a -um (gelu), *cold, icy-cold, frosty, icy* I. Lit , aqua, Cic , humor, *ice,* Verg Subst , **gĕlĭda** ae, f *ice cold water,* Hor II. Transf , applied to the chill of old age, fear, death, etc , sanguis, Verg , mors, Hor , metus, Ov

Gellius i um, *name of a Roman gens, the most famous member of which was A Gellius, a grammarian of the second century A D one of whose works,* Noctes Atticae, *is still extant*

gĕlo, 1 (gelu) I. Transit., *to cause to freeze, to freeze,* pavido gelantur pectore, Juv II. Intransit , *to freeze,* Plin

Gĕlōni -ōrum, m (Γελωνοί), *a Scythian or Sarmatian people on the Borysthenes, who tattooed themselves* Sing , **Gĕlōnus** -i, m , coll *the Geloni,* Verg

gĕlu, n , **gĕlus** -ūs, m , **gĕlum** -i n , 1, *frost, icy cold,* rura gelu claudit hiems, Verg , 2, *the chill of age, death, fear,* etc , Verg

gĕmĕbundus a -um (gemo), *groaning, sighing,* Ov

gĕmellĭpăra -ae, fem. adj (gemelli and pario), *twin bearing* , dea, or diva, Latona, Ov

gĕmellus a -um (dim of geminus), *twin, twin born* A. Lit , fratres, proles, Ov , hence subst , **gĕmellus** -i, m , *a twin,* Cat , plur , gemelli, *twins,* Ov B. Transf , a, *paired, double,* quam (legionem) factam ex duabus gemellam appellabat, Caes , b, *resembling each other like twins, similar* , par nobile fratrum nequitiā et nugis pravorum et amore gemellum, Hor

gĕmĭnātĭo ōnis, f (gemino), *a doubling;* verborum, Cic

gĕmĭno, 1 (geminus) I. Transit , 1, *to double,* victoriae laetitiam, Liv , aera, *to strike together,* Hor , partic **gĕmĭnātus** a -um, *doubled,* sol, Cic., 2, *to repeat, unite closely,* geminata ac duplicata ponantur, Cic , *to pair* , serpentes avibus, Hor II. Intransit , *to be double,* Lucr

gĕmĭnus -a um (perhaps from geno = gigno), *twin, twin-born* I Lit , fratres, Cic Subst , **gĕmĭni** -ōrum, m *twins, especially the twins Castor and Pollux* II Transf , A. a, *doubled, of double nature,* Chiron, *the Centaur, half man and half horse,* Ov ; Cecrops, *half Greek and half Egyptian,* Ov. , b, *doubled = two* , lumen, Cic , acies, Verg B. *similar, alike* , geminus et simillimus nequitiā, Cic

gĕmĭtus -ūs, m (gemo), *a sigh, groan* I. A. Lit , gemitus fit, Cic , gemitum or gemitus dare, Ov B. Meton., *pain,* Verg II. Transf , *a groaning, roaring* pelagi, Verg

gemma -ae, f, (probably connected with γεμω) I. *a bud or eye of a plant,* Cic II. *a jewel, gem, precious stone* A Lit , Cic B. Meton , 1, *a thing made of* or *adorned with jewels,* a, *a goblet,* bibere gemmā, Verg , b, *a seal ring, seal,* gemmā signari, Ov , 2, gemmae, *the eyes in a peacock's tail* Ov

gemmātus a -um (gemma), *set* or *adorned with jewels,* monilia, Ov

gemmĕus a um (gemma), *made or set with jewels, gemmed* , trulla, Cic

gemmĭfer -fĕra fĕrum (gemma and fero), *bearing or producing jewels* , mare, Prop

gemmo, 1 (gemma) I. *to bud* , vites, Cic,

II. A. *to be set with jewels*, sceptra gemmantia, Ov B. *to glitter like jewels*, herbae gemmantes rore recenti, Lucr

gĕmo ŭi -itum, 3. I. Intransit, A. Lit, *to sigh, groan*, desiderio alicuius, Cic B. poet, transf, a, of animals, of the lion, *to roar*, Lucr, of the turtle dove, *to coo*, Verg, b, of inanimate objects, *to groan, creak*, gementia litora Bospori, Hor, gemuit sub pondere cymba, Verg II. Transit, *to sigh or groan over, lament, bemoan*, aliquid, Cic., Ityn, Hor

Gĕmōniae -ārum, f (sc scalae), or more rarely Gemoniae scalae, *a flight of steps from the Aventine hill to the Tiber, down which the dead bodies of malefactors were thrown*

gĕna -ae, f usually plur (cf γένυς) I. *the cheek*, Cic II. Meton, a, *the eyelid*, Enn, b, *the eye-hole*, Ov, c, *the eyes*, et patiar fossis lumen abire genis, Ov

Gĕnăbum -i, n *a town in Gaul, the capital of the Carnutes*, now *Orleans*. Adj, **Gĕnăbensis** -e, *of or belonging to Genabum*.

Gĕnauni -ōrum, m (Γεναῦνοι), *a people in Vindelicia*

Genāva ae, f *a town of the Allobroges on the borders of the Helvetii*, now *Geneva*.

gĕnĕālŏgus -i, m (γενεαλόγος), *a genealogist*, Cic

gĕner -ĕri, m *a son in-law*, Cic, *granddaughter's husband*, Tac ; sometimes = *brother-in-law*, Nep

gĕnĕrālis -e (genus), 1, *relating* or *belonging to a kind or genus, generic*, constitutio, Cic, 2, *general*, quoddam decorum, Cic.

gĕnĕrālĭtĕr adv (generalis), *in general, generally*, Cic

gĕnĕrasco, 3. (genero), *to be generated, to be produced*, Lucr

gĕnĕrātim, adv (genus), 1, *according to kinds or classes*, copias generatim constituere, Caes, 2, *in general, generally*, loqui de aliqua re, Cic

gĕnĕrātor -ōris, m (genero), *a begetter, producer*, nosse generatores suos optime poterant, Cic

gĕnĕro, 1 (genus), *to beget, produce, create, cause to exist, bring to life, generate*, deus hominem generavit, Cic, Herculis stirpe generatus, Cic, quale portentum nec Jubae tellus generat, Hor

gĕnĕrōsē, adv. (generosus), *nobly*, perire, Hor

gĕnĕrōsus -a -um (genus) A. 1, *of noble birth, noble*, virgo, Cic, 2, applied to animals, plants, or inanimate objects, *excellent in kind, noble, of superior quality, well-bred*, pecus, Verg, vinum, Hor ; of abstractions, ortus amicitiae, Cic B. Transf, *noble, magnanimous*, virtus, Cic, mens, Ov

gĕnĕsis -is, f (γένεσις), *the constellation which presides over one's birth*, Juv

gĕnĕtīvus (gĕnĭtīvus) a -um (geno = gigno), 1, *inborn, innate*, imago, Ov, nomina, *family names*, Ov ; 2, casus, *the genitive case*

gĕnĕtrix tricis, f (genitor) A. *one who brings forth or bears, a mother*, magna deum genetrix, *Cybele*, Verg B. Transf, *she that produces*, frugum, *Ceres*, Ov

gĕnĭālis -e (genius), *of or belonging to the genius* I. *relating to the genius of marriage, nuptial*, lectus, *the marriage-bed*, Cic., and subst **gĕnĭālis** -is, m (sc torus), *the marriage-bed*, Liv II. *relating to the genius as partaking in enjoyment, pleasant, joyful, gay, delightful*; festum, Ov, hiems, Verg

gĕnĭālĭtĕr, adv (genialis), *joyfully, gaily*, Ov

gĕnĭcŭlātus -a um (geniculum), *knotty, full of knots*, culmus, Cic

gĕnĭcŭlum -i n (dim of genu), 1, *the knee*, Varr, 2, *a knot of a plant*, Plin

gĕnista (gĕnesta) -ae, f *the plant broom*, Verg

gĕnĭtābĭlis -e (geno = gigno), *relating to production or birth, fruitful, productive*, Lucr

gĕnĭtālis -e (geno = gigno), *belonging to birth, generation, generating, producing, fruitful*, 1, dies, *birthday*, Tac, 2, subst, **Gĕnĭtālis** -is, f *surname of Diana as presiding over births*, Hor

gĕnĭtālĭtĕr, adv (genitalis), *in a fruitful manner*, Lucr

gĕnĭtīvus, v gĕnĕtīvus

gĕnĭtor -ōris, m (geno = gigno), 1, *a begetter, father*, Cic, deum, *Jupiter*, Ov, urbis, *Romulus*, Ov, 2, *producer*, quae genitor produxerit usus, Hor

gĕnĭtūra -ae, f (geno = gigno), 1, *a begetting, engendering, bringing forth*, Plin ; 2, *the constellation which presides over a birth*, Suet.

gĕnĭus -ii, m (geno = gigno), 1, *the guardian spirit of a man or place, a genius*; genium piare or placare, Hor, genium curare vino, *to enjoy oneself with*, Hor, December geniis acceptus (because of rest from toil in the fields), Ov, 2, *talent, genius*, Juv

gĕno = gigno (q v).

gens, gentis, f (geno, old form of gigno) I. *a clan, a number of families connected together by a common descent and the use of the same gentile name* (orig only patrician, after the establishment of connubium between patricians and plebeians plebeian also). A. a, lit, vir patriciae gentis, Cic, gens Cornelia, Liv ; Peruvius, sine gente, *of low origin*, Hor ; patricii majorum (*senators appointed by Romulus*), et minorum (*appointed by Tarquin*), gentium, Cic, *a breed* or *species of animals*, Verg, b, transf, dii majorum gentium, *the supreme* or *superior gods*, Cic, dii minorum gentium, *the inferior*, Cic B. (Poet) Meton, *offspring, descendant*, vigilasne, deûm gens, Aenea? Verg II. *a people, tribe, nation* A. 1, lit, exterae nationes et gentes, Cic., Suevorum, Caes, 2, transf, a, *a district, canton*, ipsum in eam gentem iturum, Liv ; b, partitive genit ; ubinam gentium sumus? *where in the world are we?* Cic B. gentes, *foreigners*, Tac III. = genus, gens humana, *the human race*, Cic

genticus -a -um (gens), *belonging to a nation, national*, Tac

gentīlĭcius -a -um (gentilis), *belonging to a particular gens*, sacra, Liv., sacrificia, Cic

gentīlis e (gens) I. *belonging to a gens, gentile*, manus, *of the 300 Fabii*, Ov. Subst., **gentīlis** -is, m *a clansman, a person of the same gens*, Cic, plur, Cic II. *belonging to the same country, national*, religio, Tac

gentīlĭtas -ātis, f. (gentilis), *relationship between the members of a gens*, Cic

gĕnu -ūs, n (γόνυ), *the knee*, Cic, accidere genibus alicuius, Liv, attingere alicuius genu, Liv

Gĕnŭa ae, f *coast-town in Liguria*, now *Genoa*

gĕnŭāle is, n. (genu), *a knee-band, garter*, Ov

1 **gĕnŭīnus** -a -um (geno = gigno). *natural, innate*; genuinae domesticaeque virtutes, Cic

2 **gĕnŭīnus** -a -um (genae), *relating* or *belonging to the cheek* or *jaw*, dentes, *the back-teeth*, Cic Subst, **gĕnŭīnus** -i, m *a jaw tooth*, Juv

1 **gĕnus** -ĕris, n (root GEN, whence geno = gigno and γένος) **I.** *birth, descent, origin*, esp *of high birth*, generis auctor, *father*, Ov, genus patricium, Liv, plebeium, Liv, maternum, paternum, Cic, of animals, Ov **II.** *race* **A. 1,** *nation, stock*, Hispanum, Liv, **2,** **a,** *family, house*, genus Aemilium, Fabium, Liv, genere regio natum esse, Cic, **b,** *offspring, descendant*, and collectively, *descendants*, genus deorum (of Aeneas), Verg; **3,** *sex*, genus virile, muliebre, Cic **B. 1,** of living beings, **a,** *race, kind*, genus humanum, Cic, **b,** (α) of persons, *class, sort, kind*, omnis generis homines, Cic, (β) of animals, *species, class*, multa genera ferarum, Caes, **2,** of things, **a,** lit, *kind, variety, sort*, omne genus frugum, Liv, id genus imperii, Cic; philosoph t t, *genus* in logic, genus universum in species certas partiri, Cic, **b,** *fashion, manner, way*, tota domus in omni genere diligens, Cic

2 **gĕnus** -ūs = genu (q v)

Gĕnūsus -i, m *a river on the borders of Macedonia*, now *Iskumi*

gĕōgrăphĭa -ae, f (γεωγραφία), *geography*, Cic

gĕōmĕtres -ae, m (γεωμέτρης), *a geometer*, Cic

gĕōmĕtrĭa -ae, f (γεωμετρία), *geometry*, Cic

gĕōmĕtrĭcus -a -um (γεωμετρικός), *geometrical*, formae, *figures*, Cic Subst, **gĕōmĕtrĭca** -ōrum, n *geometry*, geometrica didicisse, Cic

gĕorgĭcus -a -um (γεωργικός), *agricultural* Subst, **Gĕorgĭca** -ōrum, n *the Georgics of Vergil*

Gĕraestĭcus portus, *a harbour near Teos, in Ionia*

Gĕraestŏs and **-ŭs** -i, f (Γεραιστός), *seaport town in Euboea*.

Gergŏvĭa -ae, f *town of the Arverni in Gallia Aquitania*

Germălus (**Cermălus**) -i, m *a part of the Palatine Hill at Rome*

germānē, adv (germanus), *faithfully, honestly*, rescribere, Cic

Germāni -ōrum, m *the Germans*, hence, 1 **Germānus** -a -um, *German*, 2 **Germānĭa** -ae, f *Germany*, superior, inferior, Tac, plur, Germaniae, Tac, 3 **Germānĭcus** -a -um, *German* Subst, **Germānĭcus** -i, m as a surname (on account of his victories over the Germans), Germanicus Caesar, *son of Drusus, and nephew of Tiberius*

germānĭtas -ātis (germanus), **1,** *the relationship between brothers and sisters, brotherhood, sisterhood*, Cic, **2,** *the connexion between cities which are colonies of the same mother-city*, Liv

1 **germānus** -a -um (like germen, from geno = gigno) **A.** *having the same parents* or *at least the same father*, frater, soror, Cic Subst, **a,** **germānus** -i, m *own brother*, **b,** **germāna** -ae, f *own sister*, Verg **B.** Transf, **a,** *brotherly, sisterly*, in germanum modum, Plaut, **b,** *genuine, real, true*, scio me asinum germanum fuisse, Cic, justitia, Cic

2 **Germānus** -a -um, v Germani

germen -ĭnis, n (perhaps from geno = gigno and suffix -men, orig genmen, then gesmen, germen, cf carmen), **1,** *a bud, sprout, twig*, Verg, **2,** *offspring*, Ov.

germĭno, 1 (germen) *to sprout forth*, Hor.

1 **gĕro**, gessi, gestum, 3 *to carry* **I** Gen, **A.** Lit, saxa in muros, Liv **B.** Transf, **1,** se gerere, *to behave oneself, to conduct oneself*, se honeste, Cic; with pro (= *as*) and the abl, ita se jam tum pro cive gessisse, Cic, **2,** *to conduct, manage*, quid negotii geritur, Cic, negotium, or rem, bene, or male gerere, Cic, rem or res gerere (of generals), *to hold the command*, Cnaeus terrā, Publius navibus rem gereret, Liv, also rem gerere, *to fight*, Liv, res gestae, *exploits*, esp, *warlike exploits*, Cic, negotii gerentes, *business people*, Cic, esp, **a,** *to hold some public office, to hold, to manage*, rempublicam gerere atque administrare, Cic, magistratum, Cic, **b,** bellum gerere, *to wage war*, cum aliquo, or adversus aliquem, or in aliquem, Cic, **3,** prae se gerere = prae se ferre, *to exhibit, manifest*, utilitatem, Cic **II.** Esp., *to carry on oneself, to have* **A.** Lit, **1,** gen, hastam, Verg, **2,** *to bear, produce*, platani malos gessere, Verg **B.** Transf, **1,** personam alicuius gerere *to act the part of*, Cic, **2,** amicitiam, *to entertain*, Cic

2 **gĕro** -ōnis, m (1 gero), *a carrier*, Plaut.

Gĕrōnĭum -ii, n *town in Apulia Daunia* or *Samnium*

gerrae -ārum, f (γέῤῥα), *wattled twigs*, Varr, transf, *trifles, nonsense*, Plaut

gerro -ōnis, m (gerrae), *a trifler, idler*, Ter

gĕrŭlus -i, m (1 gero), *a porter, carrier*, Hor

Gēryŏn (**Gēryo**) -ŏnis, m and **Gēryŏnēs** -ae, m (Γηρυών and Γηρυόνης), myth, *a king with three bodies, living in the island of Erythia, whose oxen were carried off by Hercules*

gestāmen -ĭnis, n (gesto), **1,** *that which is carried either as a burden or an ornament*, clipeus gestamen Abantis, Verg, **2,** *that in or on which anything is carried, a litter*, Tac

gestĭcŭlor, 1 dep (from gesticulus, dim of gestus), *to make pantomimic gestures, gesticulate, to represent or express by pantomime*, Suet

1 **gestĭo** -ōnis, f (1 gero), *management, performance*, negotii, Cic

2 **gestĭo** -īvi and -ii -ītum, 4 (gestus), **1,** *to exult, to be cheerful, lively, to be transported*, laetitiā, Cic, voluptate, Cic, animus gestiens rebus secundis, Liv, **2,** *to desire passionately, be eager*, with infin, scire omnia, Cic, absol, studio lavandi, Verg

gestĭto, 1 (freq of 1 gero), *to carry often, carry much, be accustomed to carry*, Plaut

gesto, 1 (intens of 1 gero), *to carry, bear, carry about one, wear*, clavos manu, Hor, caput in pilo, Cic

gestor -ōris, m (1 gero), *a tale-bearer, gossip*, Plaut

gestus -ūs, m (1 gero), **1,** *the carriage of the body*, corporis, Cic, **2,** esp, *the studied gestures of an actor or orator*, histrionum nonnulli gestus, Cic, in gestu peccare, Cic

Gĕtae -ārum, m (Γέται), *a people of Thrace living near the Danube* Sing, **Gĕta** -ae, m, and **Gĕtēs** -ae, m, gen collect, *the Getae*, hence, **a,** adj, **Gĕtes** -ae, m *Getic*; **b,** **Gĕtĭcus** -a -um, poet = *Thracian*, **c,** adv, **Gĕtĭcē**, *after the Getic fashion*, loqui, Ov

Gĕtūlus, etc = Gaetulus, etc (q v)

gibber -ĕra -ĕrum, *hump-backed*, Suet

gibbus -i, m (connected with κύπτω, κυφός), *a hump, hunch*, Juv

Gĭgas -gantis, m (Γίγας), *a giant*, gen plur, Gigantes, *sons of Terra, who stormed the heavens, but were killed by the lightning of Jupiter*,

Adj., **Gigantēus** -a -um, *relating to the giants, gigantic*, Verg.

gigno, gĕnŭi, gĕnĭtum, 3. (geno, connected with γίνομαι, γίγνομαι), *to beget, bear, bring forth*. **A.** Lit., Herculem Juppiter genuit, Cic.; Hecuba Alexandrum genuit, Cic. **B.** Transf., *to cause*; permotionem animorum, Cic.

gilvus -a -um, *pale yellow*, Verg.

gingīva -ae, f. *the gum*, Cat.

gĭnĭtrix = genetrix (q.v.).

glăber -bra -brum, *without hair, smooth-skinned*, Plaut.

glăciālis -e (glacies), *relating* or *pertaining to ice, icy*; hiems, Verg.; frigus, Ov.

glăcies -ēi, f. **1,** *ice*; dura et alte concreta glacies, Liv.; plur., glacies Hyperboreae, Verg.; **2,** *hardness*; aeris, Lucr.

glăcio, 1. (glacies), *to freeze*; nives, Hor.

glădiātor -ōris, m. (gladius), *one who was hired to fight at public shows, funerals*, etc., *a gladiator*. **A.** Lit., Cic.; as a term of reproach, *bandit, brigand*, Cic. **B.** Meton., gladiatores = *gladiatorial exhibition*; dare, Cic.; abl., gladiatoribus, *at the gladiatorial games*, Cic.

glădiātōrius -a -um (gladiator), **a,** *relating* or *pertaining to gladiators, gladiatorial*; ludus, Cic.; familia, *a troop* or *band of gladiators*, Cic.; locus, *the place of exhibition*, Cic.; consessus, *the assembled spectators*, Cic. munus, spectaculum, Cic.; **b,** transf., totius corporis firmitas, Cic. Subst., **glădiātōrium** -ii, n. *the pay of gladiators*, Liv.

glădiātūra -ae, f. (gladiator), *a combat of gladiators*, Tac.

glădius -ii, m. (root CLAD, whence also clades), *a sword, a short sword* (ensis, *a longer one*). **A.** Lit., gladius vaginā vacuus, *a naked sword*, Cic.; gladium stringere, Caes.; destringere, Cic.; educere, Caes.; nudare, *to draw the sword*, Ov.; aliquem gladio insequi, Cic.; alicui gladium intentare, Liv.; transfigere aliquem gladio per pectus, Liv.; prov., plumbeo gladio jugulari, *to be defeated with little trouble*, Cic. **B.** Meton., *that which is done by the sword*; tanta gladiorum impunitas, *of murder*, Cic.

glaeba = gleba (q.v.).

glaesum (glēsum) -i, n. *amber*, Tac.

glandĭfer -fĕra -fĕrum (glans and fero), *acorn-bearing*; quercus, Cic.

glans, glandis, f. (βάλανος), **1,** *an acorn*, and gen. *any fruit of similar shape*, Hor.; **2,** *a bullet discharged from a sling*; glandes fundis in casas jacĕre, Caes.

glārĕa -ae, f. *gravel*, Cic.

glārĕōsus -a -um (glarea), *gravelly, full of gravel*; saxa, Liv.

glaucōma -ătis, n. (γλαύκωμα), *a disease of the eye*, Plin.

1. **glaucus** -a -um (γλαυκός), *bluish-grey*; salix, Verg.; amictus Arethusae, Verg.

2. **Glaucus** -i, m. (Γλαυκός), **1,** *a fisherman of Anthedon, changed into a sea-god, the prophet of the Nereids*; **2,** *son of Sisyphus, torn to pieces by his own horses*.

glēba (glaeba) -ae, f. (connected with globus and glomus). **I.** *a lump* or *clod of earth*, Cic.; met., *land, soil*; terra potens ubere glebae, Verg. **II.** Transf., *a piece, lump of any substance*; picis, Caes.; turis, Lucr.

glēbŭla -ae, f. (dim. of gleba, *a little clod*), **1,** *a little farm* or *estate*, Juv.; **2,** *a small lump* or *bit of any substance*, Plin.

glēsum = glaesum (q.v.).

glis, gliris, m. *a dormouse*, Plin.

glisco, 3., **1,** *to grow up, swell up, blaze up*; ad juvenilem libidinem copia voluptatum gliscit illa, ut ignis oleo, Cic.; ignis sub pectore gliscens, Lucr.; **2,** *to increase, swell, spread*; ne glisceret negligendo bellum, Liv.; gliscente in dies seditione, Liv.; multitudo gliscit immensum, *increases very much*, Tac.

glŏbo, 1. (globus), **1,** *to form into a ball*, Plin.; **2,** *to form into a mass, to crowd together*, Plin.

glŏbōsus -a -um (globus), *spherical, globe-shaped*; terra, Cic.

glŏbŭlus -i, m. (dim. of globus), *a little round ball, globule*, Plin.

glŏbus -i, m. **1,** *a round ball, globe, sphere*; stellarum, Cic.; terrae, Cic.; **2, a,** *a round heap* or *mass*; flammarum, Verg.; **b,** *a troop, crowd, mass of people*; globus circumstans consulis corpus, Liv.

glŏmĕrāmen -inis, n. (glomero), *a round mass, globe*, Lucr.

glŏmĕro, 1. (glomus). **I.** Lit., **A.** *to wind round, make a ball, form into a sphere*; lanam in orbes, Ov. **B.** Of food, *to roll into a ball*; frusta mero glomerata, Ov. **II.** Transf., **A.** Of horsemen, superbos gressus, *to make a horse curvet* or *prance*, Verg. **B.** *to gather together, collect, form into a mass*; agmina, Verg.; glomerantur apes in orbem, Verg.

glŏmus -ĕris, n. (akin to globus), *clue, skein, ball of thread*; lanae, Hor.

glōria -ae, f. (root CLU, CLO; Gk. KΛΥ, KΛE, whence Latin laus, Gk. κλέος), *fame, renown, glory*. **I.** Lit., doctrinae et ingenii, Cic.; in summam gloriam venire, Cic.; gloriam habere, consequi, capere, acquirere, Cic.; gloriam sequi, Cic.; aliquem gloriā afficere, *to honour*, Cic.; plur., gloriae, *opportunities for fame*, Sall. **II.** Meton., **A. a,** *a glorious deed*, Tac.; **b,** *pride, glory*; taurus pecoris, or armenti, gloria, Ov. **B.** In a bad sense, *vain-glory, boasting, ambition, pride*, Cic.

glōrĭātĭo -ōnis, f. (glorior), *a glorying, boasting*, Cic.

glōrĭŏla -ae, f. (dim. of gloria), *a little glory*; hisce eum ornes gloriolae insignibus, Cic.

glōrĭor, 1. dep. (gloria), *to glory in, boast of, pride oneself on anything*; **1,** absol., hic tu me gloriari vetas, Cic.; with adverbs, nimis, Cic.; insolenter, Cic.; with adversus and the acc., ne adversus te quidem gloriabor, Liv.; with in and the abl., in victoria vel ignavis gloriari licet, Sall.; **2,** with abl., nominibus veterum, Cic.; suā victoriā tam insolenter, Caes.; **3,** with de and the abl., de tuis beneficiis intolerantissime gloriaris, Cic.; **4,** with acc. and infin., is mihi etiam gloriabitur se omnes magistratus sine repulsa assecutum, Cic.; **5,** with pronoun acc., vellem equidem idem posse gloriari quod Cyrus, Cic.; partic. fut. pass., gloriandus, *glorious, worthy to be boasted of*; beata vita glorianda et praedicanda est, Cic.

glōrĭōsē, adv. (gloriosus), **1,** *with glory, gloriously*; aliquid gloriosissime et magnificentissime conficere, Cic.; **2,** *vauntingly, boastingly*; mentiri, Cic.

glōrĭōsus -a -um (gloria). **I.** Object., *famous, glorious*; mors, Cic.; gloriosissimum factum, Cic. **II.** Subject., **a,** *ambitious*, Cic.; **b,** *pretentious, boastful*; miles, Cic.

glūbo, glupsi, gluptum, 3. **1,** *to peel, take off the rind* or *bark*, Varr.; **2,** transf., *to rob*; magnanimos Remi nepotes, Cat.

glūten -tinis, n. *glue*, Verg.

glūtĭnātor -ōris, m. (glutino), *one who glues together books, a bookbinder*, Cic.

glūtino, 1 (gluten), *to glue or paste together*, Plin

glūtio (gluttio) ivi or -ii itum, 4 *to swallow, gulp down*, epulas, Juv.

glūto (glutto) -ōnis, m (glutio), *a glutton*, Pers

Glycĕra -ae, f (Γλυκερα), *a woman's name*

Glyco and **Glycōn** -ōnis, m (Γλυκων), 1, *a celebrated athlete*, Hor , 2, *a physician*, Cic

Gnaeus -i, m *a Roman name*, shortened Cn

gnārĭtas -ātis, f (gnarus), *knowledge*, Sall

gnārus a -um (root GNA, whence also gnavus = navus), 1, *knowing, having knowledge of, acquainted with*, with genit., reipublicae, Cic ; Latinae linguae, Liv , with rel sent , eum gnarum fuisse, quibus orationis modis quaeque animorum partes pellerentur, Cic , with acc and infin , Hasdrubal satis gnarus Hannibalem transitus quosdam pretio mercatum (esse), Liv , 2, pass , *known*, gnarum id Caesari, Tac

Gnātho -ōnis, m *the name of a parasite in the Eunuchus of Terence*, hence = *parasite*, Cic , **Gnāthōnĭci** -ōrum, m *parasites like Gnatho*, Ter

Gnātĭa = Egnatia (q v)

gnātus, gnāvus = natus, navus (q v)

Gnĭdus = Cnidus (q v)

Gnōsus (Gnossus) i, f (Κνωσος, Κνωσσος), *an ancient city of Crete, the residence of Minos*, hence adj , 1, **Gnōsĭus** -a -um, *Gnosian, Cretan*, stella coronae, *crown of Ariadne*, Hor , subst , **Gnōsĭa** ae, f *Ariadne*, Prop , 2, **Gnōsĭăcus** -a -um, *Gnosian*, rex, *Minos*, Ov , c, **Gnōsĭas** -adis, f *Gnosian*, poet = *Cretan*, and subst. = *Ariadne*, d, **Gnōsis** -idis, f , corona, *the constellation of Ariadne's crown*, Ov , subst , *Ariadne*

gōbĭus (cōbĭus) -ii, m and **gōbĭo** -ōnis, m (κωβιός), *a gudgeon*, Ov

Gomphi -ōrum, m (Γόμφοι), *a town in Thessaly, on the Peneus* Hence **Gomphenses** -ium, m *the inhabitants of Gomphi*

gonger, v conger

Gordĭum -ii, n (Γόρδιον), *town in Phrygia*

Gordĭus -ii, m (Γορδιος), *a Phrygian king, famed for a knot on his chariot, the unfastener of which, according to a legend, would be the ruler of Asia. Alexander the Great cut the knot*

Gordĭutĭchos, n indecl (Γορδίου τεῖχος), *a place in Caria*

Gorgĭās -ae, m (Γοργιας), 1, *a Greek sophist of Leontini, contemporary of Socrates*, 2, *a rhetorician at Athens, contemporary of Cicero*

Gorgō -gŏnis, or -gūs, f (Γοργώ), plur , Gorgones, *the three daughters of Phorcus* (Stheno, Euryale, and Medusa), *monsters with snakes for hair, whose look turned persons to stone, the chief of whom, Medusa, was slain by Perseus, and her head set in Minerva's shield* Adj , **Gorgŏnĕus** a -um, *Gorgon* , equus, *the horse Pegasus*, Ov

Gorgobĭna ae, f *town of the Boii on the borders of Aquitania*

Gorgon, v Gorgo

Gortȳna -ae, f (Γορτυνα) *chief town of the island of Crete.* Adj , **Gortȳnĭus** -a -um, and **Gortȳnĭăcus** a -um, *Gortynian*

Gŏthini (Gŏtini) ōrum, m *a German people on the river March*

Gŏthōnes (Gŏtōnes) -um, m *a German people*

grăbātus -i m (κραββατος, a Macedonian word), *a low couch, a common, mean bedstead*, Cic

Gracchus i, m *the name of a family of the Gens Sempronia, the most famous members of which were Tib and C Sempronius Gracchus, sons of Tib Sempronius Gracchus and Cornelia, daughter of the elder Scipio Africanus* Adj , **Gracchānus** -a -um, *Gracchan*

grăcĭlis -e, *slender, thin, slim*, 1, lit , puer, Hor , capella, Ov , 2, transf , of discourse, *simple, without ornament* , materia, Ov

grăcĭlĭtas ātis, f (gracilis), *thinness, slimness, slenderness* , corporis, Cic

grăcŭlus -i, m *a jackdaw*, Phaedr

grădātim, adv (gradus), *step by step, by gradations, gradually, by degrees*, Cic

grădātĭo ōnis, f (gradus), in rhet , *climax*, Cic

grădĭor, gressus sum, grădi, dep , *to step, walk*, Cic

Grădīvus -i, m (gradior, *he that walks in battle*), *a surname of Mars*, Liv , Verg

grădus -ūs, m (gradior) **I.** *a step* **A.** Gen , **1**, lit , gradum facere, *to make a step*, Cic , celerare, Verg , corripere, Hor , addere, *to hasten*, Liv , gradu citato, pleno, *at quick march*, Liv , gradum referre, *to go back*, Liv , gradum inferre in hostes, *to advance against*, Liv , gradum conferre, *to come to close combat*, Liv , **2**, fig , **a**, *a step towards something*, primus gradus imperii factus est, Cic , gradum fecit ad censuram, Liv , **b**, *step, approach*, quem mortis timuit gradum, Hor **B.** *station, position, post* (of a combatant), aliquem gradu movere or demovere, *to drive from one's ground*, Liv , fig , aliquem de gradu dejicere or gradu depellere, Cic **II.** Meton , *step, stair, round of a ladder* **A.** Lit., **a**, gradus templorum, Cic , **b**, esp , gen in plur , *the rows of seats in a theatre*, etc , Tac , sing , at Novius collega gradu post me sedet uno, Hor **B.** Transf , **a**, music t t , *the gradations of sound*, sonorum gradus, Cic ; **b**, *degree, stage*, a virtute ad rationem video te venisse gradibus, *by stages*, Cic , omnes gradus aetatis, Cic , **c**, *degree of relationship*, necessitudinum gradus, Cic , **d**, *rank, position*, gradus senatorius, Cic , infimus fortunae gradus, Cic

Graeci -ōrum, m (Γραικοι), *the Greeks* sing , **Graecus** -i, m *a Greek*, Cic , and **Graeca** -ae, f *a Greek woman*, Liv Hence, **A. Graecus** a um, *Greek* , ad Graecas Calendas, v Calendae , subst , **Graecum** -i, *Greek language or literature*, adv **Graecē**, *in the Greek language* . **B. Graecĭa** -ae, f *Greece* (Ἑλλας), **1**, *Greece in the narrow sense*, **2**, Magna Graecia, *the Greek colonies in the south of Italy* **C. Graecŭlus** a -um, dim adj , *Greek* (gen used ironically) Subst , **Graecŭlus** i, m *a little Greek*, used contemptuously of the Greek philosophers and rhetoricians in the houses of the rich at Rome, Cic

graecor, 1 dep (Graecus), *to live in Greek fashion*, Hor

Graecostăsis is, f (Γραικοστασις), *a building in the Roman Forum, erected for the purpose of lodging Greek and other foreign ambassadors*, Cic

Grăii -ōrum (and poet -um), m = Graeci, *the Greeks*, Cic , sing , **Grăius** i, m *a Greek* Hence, **Grăius** a um, *Greek*

Grăiocĕli -ōrum, m *a Gallic people in the Graian Alps*

Grăiŭgĕna -ae, m (Graius and geno = gigno), *a Greek by birth, a Greek* , Verg

grāmen -ĭnis, n (root GER, CER, whence cresco), 1, *grass, turf*, Liv , Verg , 2, *plant, herb*, Verg

grāmĭnĕus -a -um (gramen). **I.** *made of grass.* **A.** Gen., corona obsidionalis, Liv. **B.** *made of cane* or *bamboo;* hasta, Cic. **II.** *grassy;* campus, Verg.

grammătĭca, v. grammaticus.

grammătĭcus -a -um (γραμματικός). **I.** Adj., *relating to grammar, grammatical;* tribus grammaticas adire, *the company of grammarians,* Hor. **II.** Subst., **a, grammătĭcus** -i, m. *a grammarian,* Cic.; **b, grammătĭca** -ae, f. and **grammătĭcē** -ēs, f. *grammar, philology,* Cic.; **c, grammătĭca** -ōrum, n. *grammar, philology,* Cic.

grammătista -ae, m. (γραμματιστής), *a teacher of grammar, teacher of languages,* Suet.

Grampĭus Mons, *a mountain in Scotland,* now *the Grampians.*

grānārĭum -ii, n. (granum), *a granary;* gen. in plur., Cic.

grandaevus -a -um (grandis and aevum), *very old;* Nereus, Verg.

grandĕsco, 3. (grandis), *to become great, increase in size,* Cic.

grandĭfer -fĕra -fĕrum (grandis and fero), *producing great profit* or *service,* Cic.

grandĭlŏquus -a -um (grandis and loquor), **1,** *speaking grandly,* Cic.; **2,** in a bad sense, *boastful, grandiloquent,* Cic.

grandĭnat, impers. *it hails,* Sen.

grandĭo, 4. (grandis). **I.** Transit., *to make great, increase,* Plaut. **II.** Intransit., *to become great,* Cato.

grandis -e. **I.** Lit., *great, large.* **A.** In extent, **1,** epistola, Cic.; **2,** in stature, *tall,* puer, Cic. **B.** Of weight, etc., *large;* pondus argenti, Cic. **C.** Of time, *old;* grandis natu, Cic. **II.** Transf., **A.** *great, important;* res grandiores, Cic. **B.** Esp., of style, *high, lofty, grand, elevated, sublime;* genus dicendi, Cic.; oratores grandes verbis, Cic.

grandĭtas -ātis, f. (grandis), of discourse, *loftiness, sublimity;* verborum, Cic.

grando -ĭnis, f. *hail, hail-storm,* Cic.

Grānĭcus -i, m. (Γρανικός), *river in Mysia, famous for one of Alexander's victories.*

grānĭfer -fĕra -fĕrum (granum and fero), *grain-carrying;* agmen, *ants,* Ov.

grānum -i, n. *a grain* or *seed;* uvae, Ov.; fici, Cic.

grăphĭārĭus -a -um (graphium), *relating to the graphium,* Suet.

grăphĭum -ii, n. (γραφίον), *a style* or *sharp-pointed instrument for writing on waxen tablets,* Ov.

grassātor -ōris, m. (grassor), **1,** *an idler,* Cato; **2,** *a nocturnal vagabond* or *rioter,* Cic.

grassor, 1. dep. (gradior). **I. 1,** *to advance, proceed;* ad gloriam virtutis viā, Sall.; in possessionem agri publici, Liv.; **2, a,** *to go to work, to proceed;* jure, non vi, Liv.; veneno, Tac.; **b,** esp., *to proceed violently, to rage;* ut paucorum potentia grassaretur, Tac. **II.** *to go about idly in the streets, to loiter, riot;* juventus grassans in Suburra, Liv.

grātē, adv. (gratus), **1,** *willingly, with pleasure,* Cic.; **2,** *thankfully;* et grate et pie facere, Cic.

grātes, acc. grates, abl. gratibus, f. (gratus), *thanks,* esp. to the gods; alicui grates agere, Cic.; laudes et grates alicui habere, Tac.

grātĭa -ae, f. (gratus), *agreeableness, pleasantness.* **I. A.** Lit., *that which is pleasing, charm;* gratia non deest verbis, Prop.; hence personif., Gratiae, *the Graces, daughters of Zeus and Eurynome* (Euphrosyne, Aglaia, and Thalia,) *the goddesses of grace, charm, agreeableness,* etc.). **B.** Transf., **1,** *favour, grace;* **a,** petivit in beneficii loco et gratiae, Cic.; gratiam dicendi facere, *to allow to speak,* Liv.; in gratiam alicuius, *to please someone,* Liv.; abl., gratiā, *on account of;* hominum gratiā, Cic.; exempli gratiā, *for example,* Cic.; **b,** *indulgence* (towards an offence); delicti gratiam facere, *to be indulgent to,* Sall.; **2,** *thankfulness, thanks;* gratiam ferre alicuius rei, Liv.; gratiam persolvere dils, Cic.; gratias agere, *to thank,* Cic.; alicui pro suo summo beneficio gratias agere, Cic.; gratiarum actio, *giving thanks,* Cic.; gratiam habere, *to be thankful,* Cic.; gratiam referre, *to make a return,* Cic.; gratiam reddere, Sall.; dis gratia or gratia dis, *thank God!* Ov.; abl. plur., gratiis or gratis, *without recompense, for nothing, gratis;* gratiis exaedificari atque effici navem, Cic. **II. A.** *favour with other persons, credit, influence;* gratiam alicuius sibi conciliare, Cic.; gratiam inire ab aliquo, Cic.; apud or ad aliquem, Liv.; in gratia esse, *to be beloved,* Cic. **B.** Transf., **1,** *friendship, regard;* in gratiam redire cum aliquo, Cic.; cum bona gratia aliquem demittere, Cic.; **2,** *power, dignity,* Cic.

grātĭfĭcātĭo -ōnis, f. (gratificor), *complaisance, obligingness, showing kindness;* Sullana, *of Sulla to his soldiers,* Cic.; impudens, Cic.; gratificatio et benevolentia, Cic.

grātĭfĭcor, 1. dep. (gratus and facio), **1,** *to act so as to please any one, to oblige, gratify, do a favour to;* alicui, Cic.; with de aliqua re, *to communicate;* qui de eo quod ipsis superat, aliis gratificari volunt, Cic.; **2,** with acc. of thing, *to give, present to;* populo aliena et sua, Cic.

grātĭis, v. gratia.

grātĭōsus -a -um (gratia), **1,** *enjoying favour, favoured, beloved;* apud omnes ordines, Cic.; in provincia, Cic.; **2,** *showing favour, complaisant;* gratiosi scribae sint in dando et cedendo loco, Cic.

grātis, v. gratia.

Grātĭus -ii, m. (Faliscus), *a Roman poet, contemporary of Ovid.*

grātor, 1. dep. (gratus), **1,** *to manifest joy, to congratulate any one;* alicui, Verg.; sibi, Ov.; gratatur reduces (sc. eos esse), Verg.; **2,** *to rejoice;* Jovis templum gratantes ovantesque adire, Liv.

grātŭīto, adv. (gratuitus), *without payment, gratuitously;* alicui gratuito civitatem impertire, Cic.

grātŭītus -a -um, *not paid for, gratuitous, free, spontaneous, voluntary;* suffragia, comitia, *unbribed,* Cic.; amicitia, Cic.; probitas, liberalitas, Cic.

grātŭlābundus -a -um (gratulor), *congratulating,* Liv.

grātŭlātĭo -ōnis, f. (gratulor), **1,** *a wishing joy, congratulation;* civium, Cic.; laudis nostrae, *because of,* Cic.; in sua gratulatione, *when he was being congratulated,* Cic.; **2,** *a thanksgiving festival;* reipublicae bene gestae, Cic.

grātŭlor, 1. dep. (gratus), **1,** *to manifest joy, to wish a person joy, congratulate;* alicui de reditu, Cic.; alicui in aliqua re, Cic.; with acc., alicui recuperatam libertatem, Cic.; with acc. of respect and infin., Cic.; alicui quod, etc., Cic.; with or without sibi, *to rejoice, wish oneself joy,* Cic.; **2,** *to give solemn thanks to a deity,* Ter.

grātus -a -um (root CRA, Gr. XAP, whence χαρτός, χάρις, χαίρω), *pleasing.* **I.** *charming, pleasant, agreeable;* Venus, Hor.; gratissima tellus, *Delos,* Verg. **II. 1, a,** *agreeable, welcome, beloved;* conviva, Hor.; gratissima victoria, Cic.;

b, *grateful, deserving thanks*, veritas etiamsi jucunda non est, mihi tamen grata est, Cic gratum est, with infin, Cic, 2, *grateful*, gratus in or erga aliquem, Cic Subst, **grātus** -i, m *grateful man*, Cic

grăvantĕr, adv (gravans, from gravor), *with difficulty*, reguli Gallorum haud gravanter ad Poenum venerunt, Liv

grăvātē, adv (gravor), *with difficulty, unwillingly*, gravate ille primo, Cic

grăvēdĭnōsus -a -um (gravedo), *subject to cold or catarrh*, Cic

grăvēdo -inis, f (gravis), *heaviness of the limbs and head, cold, catarrh*, Cic

grăvĕŏlens -lentis (grave and oleo), *strong smelling, rank*, Verg

grăvesco, 3 (gravis), 1, *to become grievous, grow worse*, aerumna, Lucr, 2, of animals, *to become pregnant*, Plin, transf, nemus fetu gravescit, *is laden with fruit*, Verg

grăvĭdĭtas -ātis, f (gravidus), *pregnancy*, Cic

grăvĭdo, 1 (gravidus), *to fructify*; terra gravidata seminibus, Cic

grăvĭdus -a -um (gravis), *pregnant* A. Lit, Cic B. *laden, filled, full*, with abl, pharetra sagittis, Hor, urbs bellis, Verg, tempestas fulminibus, Lucr

grăvis -e I. *heavy, weighty, burdensome* (opp levis) A. Lit, onus armorum, Caes, cibus, *heavy, hard to digest*, Cic, agmen, *heavy-armed*, Liv, aes grave, *heavy coin*, according to the old reckoning, in which an as weighed a pound, Liv B. Transf, a, of sound, *low, deep* (opp. acutus), vox, sonus, Cic; b, of persons or things relating to persons, *weighty, important*, testis, auctor, Cic, of style, *elevated, dignified*, genus epistolarum severum et grave, Cic, c, *grievous, painful, hard, harsh, severe, unpleasant*, tempestas, Cic, vulnus, Caes, ne quid gravius in fratrem statueret, *take harsh measures against*, Caes, d, (α) of smell, *strong, fetid*, odor caeni gravis, Verg, (β) *unwholesome, unhealthy*, anni tempus, Cic, (γ) *oppressive, troublesome, sad*, senectus, Cic, grave est, with infin, Cic II. *loaded with, laden with* A. Lit, agmen praedā grave, Liv B. Transf, a, *pregnant*, Verg, b, *heavy with sleep, food, wine*, etc, graves somno epulisque, Liv, c, *weak, ill*, morbo, Verg, d, *advanced in age*, gravis aetate, Liv

Grăviscae -ārum, f *a town in Etruria*

grăvĭtas -ātis, f (gravis) I. *weight* A. Lit, armorum, Caes B. Transf, a, *weight, consequence, importance*, sententiarum, Cic, b, *dignity, sublimity*, oris, Liv, esp of style, dicendi, Cic, c, *authority, seriousness, sternness, gravity*, cum gravitate et constantia vivere, Cic, d, (α) *high price*, annonae, Tac; (β) *unhealthiness*, caeli, Cic, (γ) *unpleasantness of smell*, odoris, Tac II. a, *pregnancy*, Ov, b, *dulness, heaviness, faintness*, corporis, Cic, linguae, Cic

grăvĭtĕr, adv (gravis), a, of sound, *deeply*, sonare, Cic, b, *impressively, with dignity*, orationem graviter habere et sententiis, Cic, c, *violently, vehemently*, graviter aegrotare, Cic, queri, conqueri, Cic, gravissime dolere, Caes, d, *in an unhealthy condition*, se non graviter habere, Cic, e, *irritably, hardly*, aliquid graviter accipere, ferre, *to be vexed with*, Cic.

grăvo, 1 (gravis) I. Act, *to load, burden* A. Lit, aliquem sarcinis, Tac B. Transf, a, *to heighten, exaggerate, increase*, invidiam matris, Tac, b, *to oppress, burden, trouble*, gravari injuriis militum, Liv. II. Pass gravor used as dep, *to bear or do unwillingly, to be troubled, annoyed, to refuse, decline*, with infin, rogo ut ne graveris exaedificare id opus quod instituisti, Cic,

grĕgālis -e (grex) I. *belonging to a herd*, Plin II. Transf, A. *belonging to the same company* as subst plur, **grĕgāles** -ium, m. *companions, associates, accomplices*, Catilinae, Cic B. *common, of a common kind*, amiculum, *of a private soldier*, Liv

grĕgārĭus -a um (grex), *belonging to the herd, common*, miles, *a private soldier*, Cic

grĕgātim, adv (grex) I. *in flocks or herds*, Plin II. Transf, *in troops or crowds*, videtis cives gregatim conjectos, Cic

grĕmium ii, n *the lap* A. Lit, in gremio matris sedere, Cic, fig, abstrahi e gremio patriae, Cic B. Transf, *centre, middle*, medio Graeciae gremio, Cic

gressus -ūs, m (gradior), *a step, course, way*, gressum tendere ad moenia, Verg, transf, of a ship, huc dirige gressum, Verg

grex, grĕgis, m I. *a herd, flock of any animals*, equarum, Cic, avium, Hor II. Transf, A. Of human beings, 1, gen, *troop, band, company*, sometimes contemptuously, *a herd*, amicorum, Cic, praedonum, Cic, 2, esp, a, *a philosophical sect*, philosophorum, Cic, b, of soldiers, *a troop*, often grege facto, *in close order*, Liv B. Of things without life, hyadum, Ov

grunnio (grundio) ivi or -ii -itum, 4 *to grunt like a pig*, Plin

grunnītus (grundītus) -ūs, m (grunnio), *the grunting of a pig*, Cic

grus, grŭis, m. and (gen) f *a crane*, Cic

gryllus -i, m (γρύλλος), *a cricket, grasshopper*, Plin

Grynēus -a um, v Grynia

Grynia -ae, f (Γρύνεια), and **Grynium** ii, n (Γρύνιον), *a town in Aeolis*, with a temple and oracle of Apollo Hence, **Grynēus** a -um, *Grynean*

gryps, grȳpis (gryphis), m (γρύψ), *a griffin*, Verg

gŭbernācŭlum (gŭbernāclum) i, n (guberno), *a rudder, helm*, 1, lit ad gubernaculum accedere, Cic, 2, transf, *direction, management, government*, esp of the state, accedere ad reipublicae gubernacula Cic, ad aliquem gubernacula reipublicae deferre, Cic, ad gubernacula reipublicae sedere, Cic, gubernacula reipublicae tractare, Cic, senatum a gubernaculis dejicere, Cic

gŭbernātio -ōnis, f (guberno), 1, lit, *steering, the art of steering*, Cic, 2, transf, *direction, government*, tantarum rerum, Cic

gŭbernātor -ōris, m (guberno), 1, *helmsman, steersman, pilot*, Cic, 2, transf, *leader, director, governor*, civitatis, Cic

gŭbernātrix -icis, f (gubernator), *she that leads, directs, governs*, ista praeclara gubernatrix civitatum, eloquentia, Cic

gŭberno, 1 (κυβερνάω) A. *to steer a ship*, Cic, prov, e terra, *from a place of safety to direct those who are in danger*, Liv B. Transf, a, intransit, *to sit at the helm, to steer*, jam pridem gubernare me taedebat, Cic, b, transit, *to guide, direct, govern*, rempublicam, Cic

gŭbernum i, n = gubernaculum (q v)

gŭla -ae, f 1, lit, *the gullet, throat*, obtorta gula, Cic, gulam laqueo frangere, *to strangle*, Sall, 2, meton, *greediness, gluttony*, Cic, irritamenta gulae, Sall, o gulam insulsam, Cic

gŭlōsus a um (gula), *gluttonous, greedy, dainty*, Mart

gŭmĭa ae, c *an epicure, gourmand*, ap Cic.

gummi, n indecl (κόμμι), *gum*, Plin

gurges -itis, m. (from root GAR, *to swallow*, whence also gula). **I.** *a whirlpool, eddy, abyss;* **a,** lit., Rheni, Cic.; **b,** fig., gurges libidinum, Cic.; gurges ac vorago patrimonii, *squanderer*, Cic.; tu gurges atque helluo, Cic. **II.** poet. transf., *any deep water, a stream, flood, sea;* Carpathius, Verg.

1. **gurgŭlĭo** -ōnis, f. (see gurges), *the windpipe*, Cic.

2. **gurgŭlĭo** -ōnis, m. v. curculio.

gurgustium -ii, n. *a hut, hovel*, Cic.

gustatus -ūs, m. (gusto), **1,** *taste, as one of the senses*, Cic.; fig., verae laudis gustatum non habere, *to have no taste for*, Cic.; **2,** *the taste, flavour of anything;* pomorum, Cic.

gusto, 1. *to taste, take a little of.* **A.** Lit., aquam, Cic.; gustare sanguinem alicuius, Cic.; absol., quorum nemo gustavit cubans, Cic. **B.** Transf., *to partake of, enjoy;* amorem vitae, Lucr.; lucellum, Hor.; Metrodorum, *listen to for a time*, Cic.

gustus -ūs, m. (root GU-o, ΓΥ-ω, whence also gusto, γεύω, γεύομαι, γεῦσις), **1,** *the tasting;* gustu explorare cibum, potum alicuius, Tac.; **2,** meton., **a,** *the whet* or *relish taken before a meal*, Mart.; **b,** *the taste* or *flavour of anything*, Plin.

gutta -ae, f. **A.** Lit., *a drop of any liquid;* guttae imbrium quasi cruentae, Cic. **B.** Transf., guttae, *spots* or *marks on animals, stones*, Verg., Ov.

guttur -ŭris, n. *the windpipe, throat;* **1,** lit., guttur alicui frangere, *to break a person's neck*, Hor.; **2,** meton., *gluttony*, Juv.

guttus -i, m. (gutta), *a narrow-necked jug*, Hor., Juv.

Gўăros -i, f. (Γύαρος), and **Gўăra** -ōrum, n. (Γύαρα), *an island in the Aegean Sea, one of the Cyclades*, now *Chiura*, or *Jura*.

Gўās -ae, acc. -an, and **Gўēs** -ae, acc. -en, m. (Γύης), **1,** *a giant with a hundred arms;* **2,** *a companion of Aeneas.*

Gўgēs -is and -ae, acc. -en, m. (Γύγης), **1,** *a favourite of Candaules, king of Lydia, whom he murdered and succeeded as king.* Adj., **Gўgaeus** -a -um, *of* or *belonging to Gyges.* **2,** *a youth mentioned by Horace.*

gymnăsĭarchus -i, m. (γυμνασίαρχος), *the master of a gymnasium*, Cic.

gymnăsĭum (gumnăsĭum) -ii, n. (γυμνάσιον), *a public school of gymnastics, gymnasium* (among the Greeks), Cic.; the gymnasia in Greece were frequented by philosophers and sophists, hence *a place for philosophical discussion*, Cic.

gymnastĭcus -a -um (γυμναστικός), *relating to gymnastic exercises*, Plaut.

gymnĭcus -a -um (γυμνικός), *gymnastic;* ludi, Cic.; certamen, Cic.

gўnaecēum -i, n., and **gўnaecīum** -i, n. (γυναικεῖον), *the women's apartments in a Greek house*, Cic.

gўnaecōnītis -idis, f. (γυναικωνῖτις) = gynaeceum (q.v.), Nep.

Gўndēs -is, m. (Γύνδης), *a river in Assyria*, now *Kerah*, or *Karah Su.*

gypso, 1. (gypsum), *to cover with gypsum;* partic. **gypsatus** -a -um, *covered with gypsum;* pes (the feet of slaves for sale being marked with gypsum), Ov.; gypsatissimis manibus, *with hands whitened with gypsum* (as of actors who played women's parts), Cic.

gypsum -i, n. (γύψος), **1,** *gypsum*, Plin.; **2,** meton., *a gypsum*, or *plaster figure*, Juv.

Gўrton -ōnis, f. (Γυρτών), and **Gyrtōnē** -ēs, f. (Γυρτώνη), *a town in Thessaly.*

gўrus -i, m. (γῦρος), *a circle, circular course;* **a,** gyrum trahere (of a snake), Verg.; gyros per aera ducere, *to wheel through the air* (of birds), Ov.; volat ingenti gyro (telum), Verg.; esp. of a horse, gyros dare, *to career, curvet*, Verg.; fig., in gyrum rationis et doctrinae duci, *to make a wide digression*, Cic.; ex ingenti quodam oratorem immensoque campo in exiguum gyrum compellere, Cic.; **b,** poet. (of time), *circuit;* bruma nivalem interiore diem gyro trahit, Hor.

Gythēum and **-īum** (Γύθειον), and **Gythĭum** -ii, n. (Γύθιον), *town in Laconia, the port of Sparta*, now *Paleopolis.*

H.

H, h, the eighth letter of the Latin Alphabet, corresponding to the Greek spiritus asper. Its position at the beginning of a word is often uncertain, as, for instance, we find aruspex for haruspex; and on the contrary, honus for onus, etc. In combination, h before t is sometimes changed into c, as traho, tractus, and with following s forms x, as traxi, vexi.

ha! an exclamation, *ha! hold! stop! ha! ha!* Plaut.

hăbēna -ae, f. (habeo), *that by which anything is held.* **I.** *a thong*, of a sling, Verg.; *a whip*, Hor. **II.** Esp., *the reins* (gen. in plur.). **A. 1,** lit., habenas fundere, dare, *to give the rein, to let loose the rein*, Verg.; habenas adducere, or premere, *to tighten*, Verg.; **2,** poet., transf., of sails, immittit habenas classi, *crowds on sail*, Verg. **B.** Fig., **1,** amicitiae habenas adducere, remittere, Cic.; **2,** *government, guidance;* rerum (of the state), Verg.

hăbĕo -ŭi -ĭtum, 2. (root HAB, connected with 'ΑΠ-ω, ἅπτω), *to have, hold.* **I.** Lit., **A. 1,** *to have*, in the hand or on the neck, etc.; *to carry, wear;* **a,** coronam in capite, Cic.; vestis bona quaerit haberi, *to be worn*, Ov.; of inanimate objects, altera vestes ripa meas habuit, *my clothes lay upon the other bank*, Ov.; **b,** *to have as part of oneself;* feminae duplices papillas habent, Cic.; **2,** of places, *to hold, have, contain, keep;* Tartara habent Panthoiden, Hor.; **3,** of the contents of a writing or book, nihil enim (epistola) habebat, quod, etc., Cic. **B.** In a wider sense, **1,** *to have possession of, have power over;* **a,** *to inhabit a place;* Capuam, *to inhabit*, Liv.; **b,** of an enemy, *to occupy;* hostis habet muros, *is in possession of*, Verg.; **c,** *to have as a ruler, to rule;* Romam a principio reges habuere, Tac.; animus habet cuncta neque ipse habetur, Sall.; **d,** *to have property in actual possession;* gemmas, argentum, Hor.; absol., *to possess property, to be wealthy;* habere in Bruttiis, Cic.; habet idem in nummis, habet in praediis urbanis, Cic.; habendi amor, Verg.; aliquid sibi, *to possess* or *keep for oneself;* sibi haberent honores, Cic.; hence the formula of divorce, res tuas tibi habeas (habe), Plaut.; istam suas res sibi habere jussit, *divorced*, Cic.; **e,** *to keep* cattle, animals; pecus, *to keep* or *possess a flock*, Verg.; so domi divisores, Cic.; **2,** *to keep constantly in some position, maintain;* **a,** around oneself, *to keep a person for a particular purpose;* aliquem secum, *to keep near oneself*, Nep.; catervas flagitiosorum circum se, Sall.; **b,** *to keep in some place;* milites in castris, *to keep the soldiers in camp*, Sall.; arma procul, *to keep arms at a distance*, i.e., *to avoid war*, Tac.; **c,** *to confine, to keep fast;* senatum in curia inclusum, Cic.; aliquem in vinculis, Sall.; in custodiam haberi, *to be placed in confinement*, Liv. **II.** Transf., **A.** In a narrower sense, **1**, generally, aliquid in manibus, *to have in hand*, Cic, aliquid in animo, *to have in the mind, intend*, with infin, Cic, aliquem in animo, *to have in one's thoughts*, Sall, **2**, of the condition of the mind or body, **a**, vulnus, *to be wounded*, Ov, febrem, Cic, animum fortem, Cic, bonum animum, *to be of good courage*, Sall, odium in aliquem, *to cherish hatred*, Cic, **b**, *to possess as a quality*; modestiam, Sall; Caesar hoc habebat, *had this custom*, Cic, **c**, *to draw after as a consequence, have as a result, to cause*, beneficium habet querelam, Cic, misericordiam, *to cause pity*, Cic **3**, **a**, *to bring into a certain condition*, mare infestum, *to make unsafe*, Cic, aliquem sollicitum, *to make anxious*, Cic; **b**, *to treat behave towards*, aliquem liberalissime, Cic, plebes servorum loco habetur, Cic, exercitum luxuriose, Sall, **c**, *to have or keep for some object*, aliquem ludibrio, *to make a mock of*, Cic, rempublicam quaestui, Cic, **4**, *to have, hold, consider, regard*, aliquem parentem, *in the light of a parent*, Cic, aliquem pro hoste, *as an enemy*, Liv, aliquid pro certo, Cic, (in) numero hostium, Cic, aliquid religioni, *to make a matter of conscience of*, Cic, paupertas probro haberi coepit, *to be considered a disgrace*, Sall, **5**, **a**, *to set about, order, hold, arrange*, concilium plebis, *to hold a council of the people*, Cic, iter Aegyptum, *to go to Egypt*, Cic; **b**, of speech, *to utter, deliver, propound*, orationem in senatu, *to deliver a speech*, Cic, sermonem cum aliquo, *to hold a conversation with*, Cic; habere verba, *to speak*, Cic, habere dialogum, *to compose*, Cic, **c**, of time, *to pass, spend*, aetatem, Sall, **6**, *to keep, observe*, ordines, Sall, **7**, alicui honorem, *to pay honour to*, Cic, **8**, reflex, se habere, or simply habere, *to fare, to be circumstanced, situated*, **a**, of persons, graviter se habere, *to be very ill*, Cic, singulos (saucios) ut se haberent rogitans, Liv, **b**, of things, res sic or ita se habet, or simply sic or ita se habet, Cic **B.** In a wider sense, **1**, gen, **a**, *to have, possess*, dimidium facti qui coepit habet, Hor, **b**, *to have, be informed of*, habes consilia nostra, Cic, **2**, *to have, experience*, nonnullam invidiam ex eo quod, etc, Cic, **3**, *to have in some relation or condition*, digni sumus quos habeas tui consilii participes, Cic, habeo aliquem acerbum, Cic, with pass partic, domitas habere libidines, Cic, **4**, **a**, nisi quid habes ad hanc, *have something to say*, Cic, **b**, *to be able, to be in a condition to*, habeo etiam dicere, Cic, nihil habeo quod incusem senectutem, Cic,

hăbĭlis -e (habeo) **I.** *easily managed, handy, supple*, arcus, Verg, currus, Ov **II.** Transf, *suitable, fit, convenient*, **a**, physically, vigor, Verg, with ad, calceus habilis et aptus ad pedem, Cic.; with dat, gens equis tantum habilis, Liv, **b**, mentally *skilful*, with dat of gerund, habilis capessendae reipublicae, Tac

hăbĭlĭtas -ātis, f (habilis), *aptitude, ability*, Cic

hăbĭtābĭlis e (habito), *habitable*, regio, Cic

hăbĭtātĭo -ōnis, f (habito), *dwelling, habitation*, sumptus habitationis, Cic

hăbĭtātor -ōris, m (habito), *one who dwells* or *inhabits*, **a**, of a house, habitatorem in hac caelesti ac divina domo, Cic, **b**, *dweller in a country*; sunt e terra homines non ut incolae et habitatores sed quasi, etc, Cic

hăbĭto, 1 (freq of habeo). **I.** Transit, *to inhabit*, urbes, Verg, in pass, *to be inhabited*, vix pars dimidia (urbis) habitabatur, Liv **II.** Intransit, **A.** *to dwell*, alibi, Liv., ad or apud aliquem, Cic, cum aliquo, Cic, in via, Cic, impers pass, habitari, ait Xenocrates, in luna, Cic., partic subst, habitantes, *the inhabitants*, Ov; fig, metus habitat in vita beata, Cic **B.** Transf, **a**, *to dwell, to be always in a place, to frequent*, in foro, Cic, quorum in vultu habitant oculi mei, Cic, **b**, *to dwell on a subject*, in eo genere rerum, Cic

hăbĭtūdo -inis f (habeo), *form, appearance*; corporis, Ter

1 **hăbĭtus** -a -um, p adj (from habeo), *formed, constituted*, Ter

2 **hăbĭtus** ūs, m (habeo) **I.** Lit, *the condition of the body, appearance* **A.** Gen, corporis, Cic, oris, Cic **B.** Esp, *the appearance of the dress of the body*, habitus atque vestitus, Cic, and meton, *dress itself*, Tac **II.** Transf., **A.** *the nature, condition*, pecuniarum, Cic, Italiae, Cic **B.** *disposition*, virtus est animi habitus naturae modo atque rationi consentaneus, Cic

hāc, adv (abl of hic, sc parte, or via), *here, this way, by this side*, Cic

hactĕnus, adv (lit, hāc parte tenus), *so far*. **I.** Lit, of place, *up to this point*, hactenus dominum est illa secuta suum, Ov **II.** Transf, **A.** In writing, discourse, etc, **1**, *up to this point*, hactenus mihi videor de amicitia quid sentirem potuisse dicere, Cic, often elliptically, to close a discussion, sed haec hactenus, Cic, or to pass on to something new, sed haec hactenus, nunc ad ostenta veniamus, Cic, **2**, *only so far, only this, only so much*, quare tibi hactenus mando, etc, Cic **3**, *in so far as*, with quoad, quod, etc, or with ut or ne, Cic **B.** Of time, *till now, hitherto*, Liv

Hadrĭa (Adrĭa) -ae, f, **1**, *a town in Picenum*, now *Atri*, **2**, *a town in the north of Italy between the Padus and the Athesis*, now *Adria*, **3**, generally masculine, *the Adriatic Sea* Hence, Adj **1**, **Hadrĭăcus (Adrĭăcus)**, a -um, *Hadriatic* **2**, **Hadrĭānus** -a -um, *belonging to Hadria* (No. 2), **3**, **Hadrĭātĭcus** -a -um, *Adriatic*

1 **Hadrĭānus** -a -um, v Hadria

2 **Hadrĭānus** -i, m, P Aelius Hadrianus, *Roman Emperor from* 117 *to* 138 A D

Hadrūmētum, v Adrumetum

haedīnus -a -um (haedus), *of or pertaining to a kid* pelliculae, Cic

haedŭlĕa -ae, f (dim of haedus), *a little kid*, Hor

haedŭlus -i, m (dim of haedus), *a little kid*, Juv

haedus i, m **1**, *a kid, young goat*, Cic, **2**, haedi, *the Kids, two stars of the constellation Auriga*, Cic

Haemŏnĭa -ae, f (Αἱμονία), Haemonia, *an old name of Thessaly* Adj **1**, **Haemŏnĭus** -a um, *Thessalian*, puppis, *the ship Argo*, Ov, juvenis, *Jason*, Ov, puer or heros, *Achilles*, Ov, meton, as Thessaly was notorious for witches, artes, *arts of enchantment*, Ov, **2**, **Haemŏnis** nidis, f *a Thessalian woman*, Ov

haerēdĭtas = hereditas (q v)

haerĕo, haesi, haesum, 2 *to hang to, stick to, cleave to, adhere* **I.** Gen, **A.** Lit, haerere in equo, Cic, or equo, Hor, terra radicibus suis haereat, Cic, fig, haerere visceribus civitatis, Liv **B.** Transf, **a**, *to remain in a place*, hic haereo, Cic, **b**, haerere alicui, *to keep close to a person, cleave to*, Verg in a hostile sense, haerere in tergo, or in tergis, or simply tergis hostium, *to hang upon the rear of an enemy*, Liv, **c**, *to remain fixed, to keep firm, not to leave*, haerere in jure ac praetorum tribunalibus, Cic, memoria rei in populo haerebit, Cic **II.** *to be rooted to a spot, to stand still* **A.** Lit, aspectu territus haesit continuitque gradum, Verg **B.** Transf,

a, *to be retarded, to cease;* Aeneae manu victoria haesit, Verg.; **b**, *to be in perplexity, to be embarrassed;* haerere homo, versari, rubere, Cic.

haeres = heres (q.v.).

haeresco, 3. (haereo), *to adhere, cleave, stick*, Lucr.

haerĕsis -ĕos, f. (αἵρεσις), *a philosophical sect*, Cic.

haesĭtantĭa -ae, f. (haesito), *a sticking fast;* linguae, *stammering*, Cic.

haesĭtātĭo -ōnis, f. (haesito), **1**, *a sticking fast, hesitation in speech, stammering;* quanta haesitatio tractusque verborum, Cic.; **2**, *perplexity, embarrassment, hesitation*, Cic.

haesĭto, 1. (intens. of haereo), *to stick fast, remain fast.* **I.** Lit., in vadis, Liv.; absol., Caes. **II.** Transf., *to stop.* **A.** Of the tongue, linguā, *to stammer*, Cic. **B.** *to be perplexed, embarrassed, to hesitate, be at a loss;* non haesitans respondebo, Cic.

Hălaesa, v. Halesa.

Hălaesus, v. Halesus.

halcēdo, v. alcedo.

halcўon, v. alcyon.

Halcўŏnē, v. Alcyone.

hālec, v. alec.

Hales -lētis, m. *river in Lucania*, now *Alento.*

Hălēsa (Hălaesa) -ae, f. (Ἅλαισα), *a town in Sicily.* Adj., **Hălēsīnus** -a -um, *of* or *belonging to Halesa.*

Hălēsus (Ălēsus) -i, m., *a descendant of Agamemnon.*

hālex, v. alec.

Hălĭacmōn (Ălĭacmōn) -mŏnis, m. *a river in Macedonia*, now *Vistriza.*

hălĭăĕtos and **hălĭaeĕtos** -i, m. (ἁλιαίετος), *the sea-eagle, osprey*, Ov.

Hălĭartus -i, f. (Ἁλίαρτος), *town in Boeotia on the lake Copais.* Hence, **Hălĭartĭi** -ōrum, m. *the inhabitants of Haliartus.*

Hălĭcarnassos -i, f. (Ἁλικαρνασσός), *town in Caria, birthplace of Herodotus, Hecataeus, and Callimachus.* Hence, **1**, **Hălĭcarnassenses** -ĭum, m. *the inhabitants of Halicarnassus;* **2**, **Hălĭcarnassĕus** -ĕi, m. (Ἁλικαρνασσεύς), *born in Halicarnassus;* **3**, **Hălĭcarnassĭi** -ōrum, m. *inhabitants of Halicarnassus.*

Hălĭcўae -ārum, f. (Ἁλικύαι), *town in Sicily, near Lilybaeum*, now *Salemi.* Hence adj., **Hălĭcўensis** -e, *of* or *belonging to Halicyae.*

hălĭeutĭca -ōn, n. (ἁλιευτικά), *the title of a poem of Ovid's on fishing.*

hālĭtus -ūs, m. (halo), *breath, exhalation*, Cic.

hallex, v. alec.

hālo, 1. **I.** Intransit., *to breathe, exhale, be fragrant;* arae sertis halant, Verg. **II.** Transit., *to breathe forth;* nectar, Lucr.

hālūc . . . v. aluc . . .

Hăluntĭum, v. Aluntium.

Hălus -i, f. *town in Assyria.*

Hălўattēs, v. Alyattes.

Hălўs -lўos, acc. -lyn, m. (Ἅλυς), *river in Asia Minor*, now *the Kisil-Irmak.*

hăma (ăma), -ae, f. (ἄμη), *a bucket*, esp. *a fireman's bucket*, Juv.

Hămādrўas (Ămādrўas) -ădis, f. (Ἁμαδρυάς), *a wood-nymph, hamadryad*, Verg.

hāmātus -a -um (hamus), **1**, *provided with hooks, hooked;* ungues, Ov.; **2**, *curved like a hook, hooked, crooked;* corpora, Cic.

Hămilcăr -căris, m. (Ἀμίλκας), *name of several Carthaginians*, (1) *the son of Gisgo, captured and killed by Agathocles;* (2) Hamilcar Barca, *Carthaginian general in the First Punic War, father of Hannibal.*

Hammon, v. Ammon.

hāmus -i, m. (perhaps from habeo, "*that which holds*"), *a hook.* **I.** Lit., **A.** Gen., hami ferrei, Caes.; hamis auroque trilix, *the links of a coat of mail*, Verg. **B.** Esp., *a fish-hook*, Cic. **II.** Transf., **a**, *the talons of a hawk*, Ov.; **b**, *a thorn*, Ov.

Hannĭbăl -bălis, m. (Ἀννίβας), *name of several Carthaginians, the most famous being* Hannibal, *son of Hamilcar Barca, general of the Carthaginians in the Second Punic War, defeated by Scipio at Zama.*

hăra -ae, f. *a pen or coop for domestic animals, a pig-sty*, Cic.

hărēna, v. arena.

hărĭŏlātĭo (ărĭŏlātĭo) -ōnis, f. *soothsaying*, ap. Cic.

hărĭŏlor (ărĭŏlor), 1. dep. (hariolus), **1**, *to utter prophecies, predict*, Cic.; **2**, *to talk nonsense, foolishness*, Plaut.

hărĭŏlus (ărĭŏlus) -i, m. (dim. of * harius, ἱερεύς), *a soothsayer, prophet*, Cic.

1. **harmŏnĭa** -ae, f. (ἁρμονία), **1**, *the agreement or skilful blending of sounds, harmony* (= concentus), Cic.; **2**, *concord, harmony*, Lucr.

2. **Harmŏnĭa** -ae, f. (Ἁρμονία), *daughter of Mars and Venus, wife of Cadmus, mother of Semele and Ino.*

harpăgo -ōnis, m. (ἁρπάγη), *a large hook, a drag, a grappling-iron*, Caes.; transf., *a rapacious person*, Plaut.

harpē -ēs, f. (ἅρπη), *a curved* or *sickle-shaped sword*, Ov.

Harpŏcrătes -is, m. (Ἁρποκράτης), *an Egyptian deity, the god of silence;* aliquem reddere Harpocratem, *to impose silence upon*, Cat.

Harpўiae (trisyll.) -ārum, f. (Ἅρπυιαι, *the snatchers*), *the Harpies, mythical monsters, half bird and half woman.*

Harūdes -um, m. *a German people between the Rhine, the Main, and the Danube.*

hărund . . . v. arund.

hăruspex (ăruspex) -spĭcis, m. (ἱερός, Boeotian ἱαρός, Etruscan harus and * specio), **1**, *a soothsayer, one who foretold the future from the inspection of entrails,* or *from the interpretation of natural phenomena, as thunder, lightning,* etc., Cic.; **2**, gen., *a seer, prophet*, Prop.

hăruspĭcīnus -a -um (haruspex), *relating to the inspection of entrails*, Cic. Subst., **hăruspĭcīna** -ae, f. (sc. ars), *the art of the haruspex, the art of inspecting entrails;* haruspicinam facere, *to practise the art of haruspex*, Cic.

hăruspĭcĭum -ĭi, n. (haruspex), *the inspection of entrails, divination*, Cat.

Hasdrŭbăl (Asdrŭbăl) -bălis, m. *name of several Carthaginians*, esp., **1**, *son of Mago, twelve times general, died* 480 A.C.; **2**, *son-in-law of Hamilcar Barca;* **3**, *son of Hamilcar Barca, brother of Hannibal, killed at the battle of the Metaurus;* **4**, *Carthaginian general in the Third Punic War.*

hasta -ae, f. **1**, *a spear, a pike, javelin;* amentata, *furnished with a thong to assist in throwing it*, Cic.; eminus hastis aut comminus gladio uti, Cic.; prov., hastas abjicere, *to lose* *courage*, Cic ; 2, a, a spear stuck in the ground was the token of a public auction, hence, sub hasta vendere, *to sell by auction*, Liv , emptio ab hasta, Cic , hasta venditionis, Cic , b, *a small spear, with which the bride's hair was parted on the wedding day*, Ov

hastātus a um (hasta) 1, *armed with a spear*, Tac , 2, subst , **hastāti** ōrum, m *the first line of the Roman army when drawn up in order of battle, the first rank, vanguard* hence, primus, secundus, etc , hastatus (sc ordo), *the first second, etc , of the companies into which the hastati were divided*, Liv.

hastīlĕ -is, n (hasta), 1, *the shaft of a spear*, Cic , 2, *the spear itself*, Verg , 3, *a piece of wood in the form of a shaft, a shoot, a prop for vines*, Verg

hau, interj *oh !* an exclamation of pain, Plaut

haud (haut), adv (an emphatic negative), *not, not at all, by no means*, 1, gen , a, with verbs, haud dubito, Cic , haud scio, Cic , haud scio an, etc , Cic , b, with adjectives, haud mediocris, Cic , c, with pronouns, haud alius, Liv , d, with subst , with or without a prep , haud injuriā, Liv , e, with adverbs, haud dubie, Sall , haud secus, Liv , haud longe, Caes , 2, in antitheses, hand .   sed, Cic , sed ut ita haud, Cic , 3, corresponding with other particles, hand   tam, Liv

hauddum (hautdum), adv *not at all as yet, not yet*, Liv

haudquāquam (hautquāquam), adv *by no means, not at all* Cic

haurĭo, hausi, haustum (fut partic hausurus, Verg), 4 (connected with ἀρύω and ἐπαυρέω), *to draw up, draw out* I. Gen , A. Of fluids, 1, lit , *to draw water*, aquam de puteo, Cic , 2, transf , a, *to draw or fetch a sigh*, suspiratus, Ov b, *to tear up* terram, Ov , c, *to shed blood*, sanguinem, Cic , d, *to collect together* pulvis haustus, Ov , 3, fig , a, hauris de faece, *you draw from the dregs, quote the worst orators*, Cic , b, *to take away*, sumptum ex aerario, Cic B Meton , *to drain dry, empty*, 1, lit , pocula ore, Ov , 2, transf , a, *to pierce*, latus gladio, Ov , b, *to squander*, sua, Tac , c, *to accomplish*, caelo medium sol igneus orbem hauserat, Verg , 3, fig , a, *to oppress ;* exsultantia haurit corda pavor pulsans, Verg , b, *to exhaust, weaken*, Italiam et provincias immenso fenore, Tac , c, *to suffer*, calamitates, Cic II. Esp , *to draw into oneself*, 1, lit , alveus haurit aquas, Ov , 2, transf , a, *to devour, consume*, multos hausit flamma, Liv , b, *to devour with the eyes or ears, to drink in*, vocem his auribus hausi, Verg , 3, fig , a, aliquid cogitatione, Cic , animo spem inanem, *drink in*, Verg , animo haurire, *to intend*, Tac , b, *to drink the cup of pleasure or pain*, voluptates, Cic , dolorem, Cic

haustrum i, n (haurio), *a machine for drawing water*, Lucr

haustus -ūs, m (haurio), *a drawing of water*, 1, legal t t , aquae, *the right of drawing water from a well*, Cic , 2, *drawing in*, a, of air, *inhaling*, apibus esse haustus aetherios, Verg , b, *drinking* and concrete, *a draught ;* aquae, Liv , fontis Pindarici, Hor , c, *a handful*, arenae, Ov

haut = haud (q v.)

hăvĕo, v aveo

hĕautontīmōrūmĕnos -i, m (ἑαυτὸν τιμωρούμενος), *the self tormentor, the title of one of Terence's comedies*

hebdŏmas -ădis, f (ἑβδομάς), *the seventh day of a disease* (supposed to be a critical period), Cic.

Hēbē -ēs, f (Ἥβη, *youth*), *the daughter of Jupiter, cup-bearer of the gods, wife of Hercules*

hĕbĕnus, v ebenus

hĕbĕo, 2 1, *to be blunt, dull*, ferrum, Liv , 2, transf , *to be dull heavy inactive*, sanguis hebet, Verg , sic mihi sensus hebet, Ov

hĕbĕs ĕtis, *blunt dull* I. Lit , a, Cic gladius, Ov , b, *blunted, stumpy*, lunae cornua, Cic , c, hebeti ictu, *a blow that bruises and does not pierce*, Ov II. Transf , a, of the senses, *dull*, aures, Cic , acies oculorum, Cic , b, of action, *sluggish, weak*, hebes ad sustinendum laborem miles, Sall , c, of colour, *dull*, color non hebes, Ov , d, *mentally dull, heavy, stupid ;* hebeti ingenio esse, Cic , homines hebetes, Cic

hĕbesco, 3 (inch from hebeo), *to become dull, blunt, dim*, mentis acies, Cic , auctoritatis acies, Cic

hĕbĕto, 1 (hebes), *to make dull, blunt* A. Lit , hastas, Liv B. Transf , *to make dull, blunt, to deaden, dim*, flammas, Ov , alicui visus, Verg

Hĕbraeus -a um, *Hebrew, Jewish*, Tac

Hebrus -i, m (Ἕβρος), *the chief river of Thrace, flowing into the Aegean Sea*

Hĕcăbē, v Hecuba

Hĕcălē ēs, f (Ἑκάλη), *a poor old woman who entertained Theseus*

Hĕcătē -ēs, f (Ἑκάτη) and **Hĕcăta** -ae, f *"she that works from afar," the goddess of magic and enchantment, often identified with Diana and Luna* Hence, adj , 1, **Hĕcătēĭus** -a um, and 2, **Hĕcătēis** -ĭdis, f *Hecatean*, hence = *magical*, Ov

hĕcătombē ēs, f (ἑκατόμβη), *a hecatomb, sacrifice of a hundred oxen*, Juv

Hector -ŏris, m (Ἕκτωρ), *son of Priam, husband of Andromache, the bravest of the Trojans, killed by Achilles* Adj , **Hectŏrĕus** a um (Ἑκτόρεος), *belonging to Hector*, poet = *Trojan*, Verg

Hĕcŭba ae, f and **Hĕcŭbē (Hĕcăbē)** -ēs, f (Ἑκάβη), *wife of Priam*

hĕdĕra -ae, f *ivy, a plant sacred to Bacchus*, Caes , Hor

hĕdĕrĭger gĕra -gĕrum (hedera and gero), *ivy-bearing, ivy crowned*, Cat

hĕdĕrōsus a -um (hedera), *ivied, full of ivy*, Prop

Hĕdessa, v Edessa

hēdȳchrum -i, n (ἡδύχρουν), *a fragrant salve*, Cic

hei, interj , *alas !* hei mihi, *woe is me*, Ov

Hĕlĕna ae, f and **Hĕlĕnē** -ēs, f (Ἑλένη), *daughter of Leda and Jupiter, sister of Castor, Pollux, and Clytemnestra, mother of Hermione, wife of Menelaus, carried off by Paris to Troy, and thus the cause of the Trojan war*

Hĕlĕnus i, m (Ἕλενος), *son of Priam, a soothsayer*

Hēlĭădes -um, f (Ἡλιάδες), *the daughters of the Sun, who, at the death of their brother Phaethon, were changed into poplars, and their tears into amber*, hence, nemus Heliadum, *a poplar grove*, Ov , Heliadum lacrimae, *amber*, Ov , geminae, *amber*, Mart.

hĕlĭca ae, f (ἑλίκη), *winding*, Cic

Hĕlĭcē -ēs, f (Ἑλίκη), 1, *a town in Achaia, destroyed by an earthquake*, 372 B C , 2, *a constellation, the Great Bear*, Cic

Hĕlĭcon -ōnis, m (Ἑλικών), *a hill of Boeotia, sacred to Apollo and the Muses*, Heliconis alumnae, *the Muses*, Ov Hence, 1, adj , **Hĕlĭcōnĭus** a -um, *Heliconian*, 2, **Hĕli-**

cōnĭădes -um, f and 3, **Hĕlĭcōnĭdes** -um, f *the Muses*

Hēlĭŏdōrus -i, m (Ἡλιόδωρος), *a celebrated rhetorician in the time of Horace*

Hēlĭŏpŏlis -ĕos, f (Ἡλιόπολις), 1, *a town in Coelesyria*, now *Baalbek*, 2, *a town in Lower Egypt*

Hellē -ēs, f (Ἕλλη), *daughter of Athamas and Nephele, who fled from her step mother Ino on a golden ram, and was drowned in the Hellespont, so named after her*

hĕlix ĭcis, f (ἕλιξ), *a kind of ivy*, Plin.

hellĕborus, v elleborus

Hellespontus -i, m (Ἑλλήσποντος), 1, *the Hellespont, Dardanelles*, 2, transf, *the coast on both sides of the Hellespont*, meton, *the inhabitants of this coast*, Nep Hence, adj, a, **Hellespontĭus** a -um, and b, **Hellespontĭăcus** -a um, *of or belonging to the Hellespont*

hĕlops (**ĕlops, ellops**), -ŏpis, m (ἔλλοψ), *a savoury fish*, perhaps *the sturgeon*, Ov

Hēlōtes, v Hilotae

hēlŭātĭo (**hēllŭātĭo**) ōnis, f (heluor), *gluttony*, Cic

hēlŭo (**hēllŭo**) -ōnis, m *a glutton, gormandiser*, Cic

hēlŭor (**hēllŭor**), 1 dep. (heluo), *to guzzle, gormandise*, Cic, transf, cum aliquo reipublicae sanguine, Cic

helvella -ae, f *a small pot-herb*, Cic.

Helvētĭi -ōrum m *the Helvetii, the inhabitants of the part of Gallia now called Switzerland* Hence, adj, **Helvētĭus** and **Helvētĭcus** -a um, *Helvetian*

Helvĭi (**Helvi**) -ōrum, m. *a people in Gallia Provincia*

hem, interj *ah! oh! well! only see! just look!* hem causam, Cic

hēmĕrŏdrŏmus -i, m. (ἡμεροδρόμος), *a special courier, express*, Liv.

hēmĭcillus -i, m (ἥμισυς and κίλλός), *half an ass*, a term of reproach Cic

hēmĭcyclĭum -ii, n (ἡμικύκλιον), *a semicircular settee for conversation*, Cic

hēmīna -ae, f (ἡμίνα), *a measure of capacity*, half a sextarius, nearly half a pint English, Plaut

hendĕcăsyllăbi -ōrum, m (ἑνδεκασύλλαβοι), *verses of eleven syllables*, Cat

Hĕnĕti -ōrum, m, v Veneti

Hēnĭŏchi -ōrum, m (Ἡνίοχοι), *a people of Asiatic Sarmatia* Hence adj, **Hēnĭŏchĭus** and **Hēnĭŏchus** a -um, *Heniochian*

Henna (**Enna**) -ae, f (Ἕννα), *an ancient city of Sicily, celebrated for a temple of Ceres* Hence adj, **Hennensis** -e, and **Hennaeus** -a um, *of or belonging to Henna.*

Hēphaestĭo ōnis, m (Ἡφαιστίων), *a general and friend of Alexander the Great*

heptēris -is, f (ἑπτήρης), *a galley with seven banks of oars*, Liv

1 **hĕra** (**ĕra**) ae, f (herus), 1, *the mistress of a house*, Plaut, Ter, 2, *mistress, queen, female ruler*, Cat, Ov.

2 **Hēra** -ae, f (Ἥρα), *the Greek goddess identified with the Roman Juno*, hence, **Hēraea** -ōrum, n (Ἡραῖα), *the festival of Hera*, Liv

Hērăclēa (-**īa**) -ae, f (Ἡράκλεια), *the city of Hercules* (Hercules), *name of several Greek towns*, 1, *a colony of the Tarentines in the south of Italy, on the river Siris*, 2, *a town in Phthiotis, near Thermopylae*, 3, *a town in Bithynia on the Black Sea*, now *Herakle* or *Erekli*, 4, *a town in Sicily on the Halycus, also called Minoa*, 5, Heraclea Sintica, *a town in Paeonia on the Strymon* Hence, a, **Hērăclĕenses** -ium, *the inhabitants of Heraclea*, b, **Hērăclĕōtes** ae, m *belonging to Heraclea*, plur, **Hērăclĕōtae** -ārum, m. *the inhabitants of Heraclea*

Hērăclēum i, n (Ἡράκλειον), *a town in Macedonia, on the borders of Thessaly*

Hērăclīa, v Heraclea

Hērăclīdēs -ae, m (Ἡρακλείδης), Ponticus, *a Greek philosopher*

Hērăclītus -i, m (Ἡράκλειτος), *a Greek philosopher of Ephesus*

1 **Hēraea** -ōrum, v Hera

2 **Hēraea** -ae, f (Ἡραία), *town in Arcadia on the Alpheus*

herba -ae, f (φερβ ω, φορβ-η, orig ferb-a, whence also febra, fibra), *a plant with stalks, grass, plant, herb* (sing often collective) I. Gen, stirpes et herbae, Cic, sing collective, in herba se abjicere, Cic II. Esp, a, *the stalk of wheat*, Cic, b, *tares*, officiant laetis ne frugibus herbae, Verg

herbĭdus -a -um (herba), *full of grass, grassy*, campus, Liv

herbĭfer -fĕra -fĕrum (herba and fero), *full of herbage, grassy*, colles, Ov

herbĭgrădus -a -um (herba and gradior), *going through the grass*, epithet of a snake, ap Cic

Herbīta -ae, f (Ἕρβιτα), *town in the interior of Sicily*, now *Nicosia.* Hence, adj, **Herbĭtensis** -e, *of or belonging to Herbita*

herbōsus -a -um (herba), *full of herbage, grassy*, campus, Hor

herbŭla -ae, f (dim of herba), *a little herb*, Cic

Hercēus -a -um (Ἑρκεῖος), *a surname of Jupiter as the protector of the house, courtyard*, etc

hercisco (**ercisco**), 3 (herctum), *to divide an inheritance*, Cic.

Hercle, v Hercules

herctum -i, n (probably connected with heres), *an inheritance* found only in the phrase herctum ciere, *to divide an inheritance*, Cic

Hercŭlānĕum -i, n I. *town in Campania, destroyed by an eruption of Vesuvius, under the emperor Titus* Hence, adj, 1, **Hercŭlānensis** -e, *of Herculaneum* Subst, in Herculanensi, *in the district of Herculaneum*, 2, **Hercŭlānĕus** and **Hercŭlānus** -a um, *of Herculaneum* II. *town in Samnium*

Hercŭles -is and i, m (Ἡρακλῆς), *the son of Jupiter and Alcmena, husband of Deianira and (after his deification) of Hebe, the national hero of the Boeotians, the performer of twelve labours imposed upon him by Eurystheus, regarded as the giver of riches and the guide of the Muses* Vocat. sing, Hercules or Hercule and Hercle (an oath of the Romans), *by Hercules*, Cic, also mehercules or mehercule, Cic, Hercle sane, Cic. Hence adj, **Hercŭlĕus** a -um, *Herculean*, arbor, *the poplar*, Verg

Hercȳnĭa silva -ae, f *the Hercynian forest, in Central Germany*, also, **Hercȳnĭa** -ae, f. *the Hercynian forest*, Tac

Herdŏnĭa -ae, f *town in Apulia, destroyed by Hannibal.*

hĕre = heri (q v.)

hērēdĭtārĭus -a -um (heres), 1, *relating to an inheritance*, auctio, Cic, 2, *inherited, hereditary*, cognomen, Cic., controversia, Cic,

hērēdĭtas -ātis, f (heres), *inheritance* **A.** Lit, hereditate possidere, Cic, hereditatem adire or cernere, Cic **B.** Transf, hereditas gloriae, Cic

Herennius a -um, *name of a Roman gens* Adj, **Herenniānus** a -um, *Herennian*

hērēdĭum -ii, n (heres), *a patrimony*, Nep

hēres (haeres) -ēdis, c (connected with hir, Greek χείρ), *an heir* **I.** Lit, heres esse alicui or alicuius, Cic, aliquem heredem scribere, facere, instituere, *to make a person one's heir*, Cic, secundus, *a person named to receive the inheritance if the original heir cannot inherit*, Cic **II.** Transf, *successor*, veteris Academiae, Cic

hĕri (hĕrĕ), adv (χθές, Lat. HES, whence first hesi, then heri), 1, *yesterday*, Cic, 2, *lately*, Cat

hĕrĭfŭga ae, m (herus and fugio), *a fugitive, runaway*, Cat

hĕrīlis -e (herus), *of or relating to the master or mistress of the house*, mensa, Verg

Hermaeum -i, n (Ἑρμαῖον), lit, *a temple of Hermes*, *a coast-town of Boeotia*

Hermăgŏrās -ae, m (Ἑρμαγόρας), *a Rhodian rhetorician of about the second half of the second century* A C

hermaphrŏdītus i, m (ἑρμαφρόδιτος), *an hermaphrodite*, Ov

Hermăthēna ae, f (Ἑρμαθήνη), *a double bust of Hermes and Athena, on the same pedestal*, Cic

Hermĕracles -is, m (Ἑρμηρακλῆς), *a double bust of Hermes and Hercules*, Cic

Hermes -ae, m (Ἑρμῆς, *the god Hermes, Mercury*), *a post, the top of which was carved into a head, placed in the streets, esp of Athens*

Hermĭŏnē ēs, f and **Hermĭŏna** -ae, f (Ἑρμιόνη), 1, *daughter of Menelaus and Helena, wife of Orestes*, 2, *town in Argolis, now Kastri* Hence, adj, **Hermĭŏnĭcus** -a um, *of or belonging to Hermione*

Hermĭŏnes -um, m *a people of Germany*

Hermundūri ōrum, m *a German tribe near the source of the Elbe*

Hermus -i, m (Ἕρμος), *a river in Lydia*

Hernĭci ōrum, m *a people in Latium* Adj, **Hernĭcus** -a -um, *Hernican*

Hērō -ūs, f (Ἡρώ), *a priestess of Aphrodite at Sestos, beloved by Leander*

Hērōdes -is m (Ἡρώδης), *Herod the Great, king of Judaea*

Hērŏdŏtus -i, m (Ἡρόδοτος), *the first great Greek historian, born* 484 A C

hērōĭcus -a um (ἡρωϊκός), *relating to the heroes, heroic*, tempora, Cic, personae, Cic

hērōīnē -ēs, f (ἡρωΐνη), *a demigoddess, heroine*, Prop

hērōis -idis, f (ἡρωΐς), *a demigoddess, heroine*, Ov (Gr dat plur, heroisin, Ov).

Hērŏphile -ēs, f (Ἡροφίλη), *a priestess of Apollo*

hērōs -ōis, m (ἥρως), 1, *a demigod, hero*, Cic, 2, *a distinguished man, hero*, noster Cato, Cic

hērōus -a -um (ἡρῷος), *relating to a hero, heroic*, pes, versus, *epic verse* (hexameter), Cic

Hersĭlĭa -ae, f *wife of Romulus*

hĕrus (ĕrus) i, m 1, *the master or head of a household*, Cic, 2, *master, owner, lord*, Hor

Hēsĭŏdus -i, m (Ἡσίοδος), *the oldest Greek poet after Homer* Adj, **Hēsĭŏdēus** -a -um, *Hesiodean*

Hēsĭŏna ae, f and **Hēsĭonē** ēs, f (Ἡσιόνη), *daughter of Laomedon, king of Troy, rescued by Hercules from a sea monster*

Hespĕris -idis, f (Ἑσπερίς), *western*, aquae, *Italian*, as Italy was to the west of Greece, Verg Subst, **Hespĕrĭdes** -um, f (αἱ Ἑσπερίδες Νύμφαι), *the Hesperides, daughters of the Evening, living in an island in the extreme west, in a garden with golden apples, guarded by a dragon*

Hespĕrĭus a -um (ἑσπέριος), *western*, terra, *Italy*, Verg Subst, **Hespĕrĭa** -ae, f *the western land, Italy*, Verg, *Spain*, Hor

Hespĕrus or **-os** i, m (Ἕσπερος), *the Evening Star*, Cic

hesternus -a -um (from root HES, whence heri), *of or relating to yesterday*, dies, Cic

hesterno, adv (hesternus), *yesterday*, Cic

hĕtaerĭcŏs -ē -ŏn (ἑταιρικός η ον), *relating to comradeship*, Nep

heu, interj *an exclamation of pain, oh! alas! woe!* heu! me miserum Cic

heus! interj *hallo! ho there! hark!* heus tu quid agis! Cic

hexămĕtĕr tra -trum (ἑξάμετρος), *with six feet* (of metre), hexameter versus, or versus hexameter, *a hexameter, a verse of six feet*, Cic

hexēris -is, f (ἑξήρης), *a galley with six banks of oars*, Liv

hĭātus ūs, m (hio) **A.** *a cleft, opening*, oris, Cic, terrae, Cic, absol, *the opening of the mouth, the open jaws*, Verg, quid dignum tanto feret hic promissor hiatu, *of such pompous language*, Hor **B.** Transf, **a**, *desire after*, praemiorum, Tac, **b**, in grammar, *a hiatus, the meeting of two vowels*, Cic

Hĭbēres um (Ἴβηρες), or generally **Hĭbēri** -ōrum, m *the Hiberians (Iberians)*, 1, *the inhabitants of Hiberia in Spain* sing, **Hĭber**, Hor, 2, *the inhabitants of Hiberia, in Asia* Hence, **A. Hĭbērĭa** -ae (Ἰβηρία), 1, *a part of Spain*, 2, *a district in Asia*, now *Georgia*, Hor **B.** Adj, 1, **Hĭbērĭcus** -a -um, and 2, **Hĭbērus** a -um, *Hiberian*, poet = *Spanish*, gurges (of the Western Ocean), Verg, pisces, *the scomber*, Hor, pastor triplex, *Geryon*, Ov, vaccae or boves, *belonging to Geryon*, Ov

hĭberna -ōrum, n, v hibernus

hĭbernācŭlum -i, n (hiberno), plur, hibernacula, *tents or huts for winter quarters*, Liv

Hĭbernĭa -ae, f *Ireland*

hĭberno, 1 (hibernus), *to winter, spend the winter*, 1, gen, in sicco (of ships), Liv, 2, esp as milit t t, *to keep in winter quarters*, Cic

hĭbernus -a-um (hiems) **I.** Lit, *wintry, winterly*, tempus, mensis, Cic, annus, *time of winter*, Hor, Alpes, *cold*, Hor, castra, *winter quarters*, Liv Subst, **hĭberna** -ōrum, n (sc castra), *winter quarters*, dies hibernorum, *time for going into winter quarters*, Caes, hiberna aedificare, Liv, cohortes in hiberna mittere, Cic, ibi hiberna habere, Liv, ex hibernis discedere, egredi, Cic **II.** Transf, *stormy*, mare, Hor, ventus, Verg

1 **Hĭbērus** -i, m (Ἴβηρ), *a river in Spain*, now *the Ebro*

2 **Hĭbērus**, v Hiberes

hĭbiscum -i, n (ἰβίσκος), *the marsh-mallow* Verg

hĭbrĭda (hȳbrĭda) -ae, c, 1, of animals, *a hybrid*, Plin, 2, of men, *the offspring of a Roman by a foreign woman*, or *of a freeman by a slave*, Hor

1. **hĭc,** haec, hōc, pron. demonstr. (from pro-

nominal stem I, whence also is, with demonstrative suffix ce), *this* **A.** Gen, hic avunculus, Cic, hic ipse, hic ille hic iste, hic talis, quidam hic, Cic., hic . ille, hic - iste, hic referring to the object which may be the remoter one in the sentence, but is the nearer in the speaker's thoughts, hoc, subst with genit, hoc commodi est, quod, etc, Cic, absol plur, haec, **a,** *this town, this state,* haec delere, haec vastare, Cic; **b,** *the whole visible world,* Cic **B.** Esp, **a,** hunc hominem = *me*, Hor, **b,** of time, *this, the present,* his temporibus, Cic, absol plur, haec, *the present state of affairs,* Cic

2 **hīc** and **heic,** adv *here* **I.** Lit., *in this place, in this spot,* Cic **II.** Transf, **A.** *herein, in this matter, on this occasion,* Cic **B.** Of time, *hereupon, here,* Cic

hīce, haece, hōce, pron demonstr (a more emphatic form of hic, haec, hoc), *this,* **a,** Cic, in questions with -ne, hicine, haecine, hocine, Cic, **b,** of time, *the present,* hunccine solem tam nigrum surrexe mihi, Hor

Hĭcĕtāon -ŏnis, m (Ἱκετάων), *son of Laomedon, king of Troy* Adj, **Hĭcĕtāŏnĭus** -a -um, Thymoetes, *son of Hicetaon,* Verg

Hĭcĕtas -ae, m (Ἱκέτας), *a Pythagorean of Syracuse*

hicine, v hice

hĭĕmālis -e (hiems), **1,** *wintry, winterly,* tempus, Cic, **2,** *stormy,* navigatio, Cic.

hĭĕmo, 1 (hiems) **A.** *to winter, spend the winter,* **a,** mediis in undis, Hor, **b,** esp of soldiers, *to keep in winter quarters;* hiemare in Gallia, Caes **B.** Transf, *to be stormy,* mare hiemat, Hor

hĭems (hĭemps) -ĕmis, f (χειμών) **I.** *rainy, stormy weather, storm,* hiemis magnitudo, Cic, dum pelago desaevit hiems, Verg **II. A.** *the rainy season, winter,* Arabes campos hieme et aestate peragrantes, Cic; personif, glacialis Hiems, Ov **B** Meton, **1,** *cold;* letalis hiems in pectora venit, Ov, **2,** *year,* post certas hiemes, Hor

Hĭĕro, and **Hĭĕrōn** -ōnis, m (Ἱέρων), **1,** Hiero I, *ruler of Syracuse* (477—467 B.C.); **2,** Hiero II, *ruler of Syracuse* (269—215 B.C.). Adj **Hĭĕrōnĭcus** -a -um, *of Hiero*

Hĭĕrŏcles -is, m (Ἱεροκλῆς), *a Greek rhetorician, contemporary of Cicero*

Hĭĕrōnȳmus -i, m (Ἱερώνυμος), **1,** *a ruler of Syracuse, successor of Hiero II,* **2,** *a Greek peripatetic philosopher*

Hĭĕrŏsŏlȳma -ōrum, n (Ἱεροσόλυμα), *the capital of Judaea* Hence, **Hĭĕrŏsŏlȳmārĭus,** *nickname of Pompey, "the hero of Jerusalem" (because of his priding himself on his oriental victories)*

hĭēto, 1 (intens. of hio for hiato), *to open the mouth, gape,* Plaut

hĭlărē, adv (hilarus), *cheerfully, merrily, blithely,* vivere, Cic, hilarius loqui, Cic

hĭlăris -e, and **hĭlărus** -a -um (ἱλαρός), *cheerful, merry, blithe, gay, jocund, jovial,* animus, vita, Cic, esse vultu hilari atque laeto, Cic., hilariores litterae, Cic

hĭlărĭtas -ātis, f (hilaris), *cheerfulness, mirth, gaiety, hilarity,* Cic

hĭlărĭtūdo -ĭnis, f = hilaritas (q v)

hĭlăro, 1 (hilarus), *to make joyful, cheerful, to cheer up, exhilarate,* huius suavitate maxime hilaratae Athenae sunt, Cic, multo convivia Baccho, Verg

hĭlărŭlus -a -um (dim of hilarus), *somewhat cheerful,* Cic.

hilla -ae, f (dim of hira), **1,** generally in plur, *the smaller intestines of all animals,* **2,** *a kind of sausage,* Hor

Hīlōtae, and **Īlōtae** -ārum, m (Εἱλῶται), *the Helots, slaves of the Spartans.*

hīlum -i, n (another form of filum), *a trifle;* neque (nec) hilum, *not a whit, not in the least,* Lucr

Hĭmella -ae, f *a stream in the Sabine country*

Hĭmĕra -ae, f (Ἱμέρα), **1,** *name of two rivers in Sicily;* **2,** *town on one of these rivers*

hinc, adv. *from here, hence* **I. A.** Lit, a nobis hinc profecti, Cic **B.** Transf., **1,** *from this cause,* Cic., hinc illae lacrimae, Ter, *from this matter,* hinc quantum cui videbitur decidere, Cic, **2,** of time, **a,** *henceforth,* quisquis es, amissos hinc jam obliviscere Graios, Verg; **b,** *thereupon,* hinc toto praeceps se corpore ad undas misit, Verg **II.** *on this side, in this direction,* hinc atque illinc, *on this side and on that,* Cic

hinnĭo, 4 *to neigh, whinny,* Lucr

hinnītus -ūs, m (hinnio), *a neighing,* Cic.

hinnŭlĕus (hinnŭlus), -i, m. (hinnus), *a young hind or fawn,* Hor

hinnus -i, m (ἴννος), *a mule, the offspring of a stallion and a she-ass* (mulus = *the offspring of a he-ass and a mare*), Varr.

hĭo, 1 (connected with χαίνω, χάσκω) **I.** Intransit, *to open, stand open, gape* **A.** Gen, **1,** lit, concha hians, Cic., **2,** transf, of discourse, *to be badly put together, hang together badly,* hiantia loqui, Cic **B.** Esp, *to open wide the mouth or jaws,* **1,** lit., Verg; **2,** transf, **a,** *to desire with open mouth, long for,* Verrem avaritiā hiante atque imminente fuisse, Cic, **b,** *to open the mouth in astonishment,* Verg **II.** Transit, *to pour forth;* carmen lyrā, Prop

hippăgōgoe -ōn, acc. -ūs, f (αἱ ἱππαγωγοί), *transports for cavalry,* Liv

Hippĭas -ae, m (Ἱππίας), **1,** *son of Pisistratus, tyrant of Athens;* **2,** *a sophist of Elis contemporary with Socrates*

Hippo -ōnis, m (Ἱππών), **1,** *Hippo regius town in Numidia,* now *Bona,* **2,** *town in Hispania Tarraconensis*

hippŏcentaurus -i, m (ἱπποκένταυρος), *a centaur,* Cic

Hippocrătēs -is, m (Ἱπποκράτης), *a physician of Cos* (flourishing about 436 B.C.)

Hippŏcrēnē -ēs, f (ἵππου κρήνη), *a fountain on Mount Helicon, produced by a blow from the hoof of Pegasus*

Hippŏdămē -ēs, f, and **Hippŏdămēa** or **-īa** -ae, f (Ἱπποδάμη, -δάμεια), **1,** *daughter of Oenomaus, king of Pisa in Elis;* **2,** *wife of Pirithous*

Hippŏdămus -i, m (Ἱππόδαμος), *the horse-tamer*—i.e., Castor; poet = *rider,* Mart.

hippŏdrŏmos -i, m (ἱππόδρομος), *a hippodrome, or racecourse for horses and chariots,* Plaut

Hippŏlȳtē -ēs, f, and **Hippŏlȳta** -ae, f. (Ἱππολύτη), **1,** *Queen of the Amazons, taken prisoner by Theseus,* **2,** *wife of Acastus, King of Magnesia*

Hippŏlȳtus -i, m (Ἱππόλυτος), *son of Theseus and Hippolyte,* or *Antiope*

hippŏmănes, n (ἱππομανές), **1,** *a slimy humour which flows from a mare when in heat,* Verg, **2,** *a membrane on the head of a new-born foal,* Plin, both 1 and 2 were used for love-potions, Juv.

Hippŏmĕnēs -ae, m (Ἱππομένης), 1, *the husband of Atalanta*, 2, *father of Limone*, whence **Hippŏmĕnēis** -nēidis, f = *Limone*

Hippōnax -nactis, m (Ἱππῶναξ), *a Greek satirical poet of the sixth century* B C Hence adj, **Hippōnactēus** -a um, *biting, satirical*, praeconium, Cic, Hipponacteos effugere vix posse, Cic

hippŏpŏtamus i, m (ἱπποπόταμος), *a river-horse, hippopotamus*, Plin

Hippŏtădes -ae, m (Ἱπποτάδης), *descendant of Hippotes, Aeolus* (*grandson of Hippotes*)

hippŏtoxŏta -ae, m (ἱπποτοξότης), *a mounted archer*, Caes

hippūrus, or -ŏs, i, m (ἵππουρος), *a fish, perhaps the gold fish*, Ov

hir and **ir**, indecl (connected with χείρ), *the hand*, ap Cic

hīra -ae, f *a gut, intestine*, Plaut.

hircīnus -a um (hircus), *of or relating to a he-goat*, folles, *made of goat skins*, Hor

hircōsus -a -um (hircus), *smelling like a goat, goatish*, Plaut

hircŭlus i, m (dim of hircus), *a little goat*, Cat

hircus i, m *a he-goat*, Verg, olere hircum, *to smell like a goat*, Hor; used as a term of reproach, *an old goat*, Cat

hirnĕa -ae, f *a can or jug*, Plaut

hirnŭla -ae, f (dim of hirnea), *a little can or jug*, Cic

Hirpīni -ōrum, m *a Samnite people of Lower Italy*, adj, **Hirpīnus** a -um, *Hirpine*

hirquus, hirquinus = hircus, hircinus (q v)

hirsūtus -a -um (conn with hirtus), 1, *covered with hair, hairy, hirsute, rough, shaggy, prickly*, supercilium, Verg, crines, Ov; aliae (annimantium) spinis hirsutae, Cic, 2, *rough, unadorned*, nihil est hirsutius illis (annalibus), Ov

Hirtĭus -a um, *name of a Roman gens, the most celebrated member of which was* A Hirtius, *the friend and follower of C Julius Caesar, slain at the battle of Modena, the author of the Eighth book of Caesar's* Bell Gall Hence, adj, **Hirtīnus** -a -um, *of or belonging to Hirtius*

hirtus a -um (root HIR), 1, *shaggy, rough, hairy prickly*, setae, Ov capellae, Ov, 2, transf, *rough, uncultivated*, ingenium, Hor

hīrūdo inis, f *a leech*, Plin, transf, aerarii, Cic

hirundĭnīnus -a -um (hirundo), *of or relating to swallows*, Plaut

hirundo -dinis, f (χελιδών), *a swallow*, Verg

hisco, 3 (contr for hiasco), 1, *to open, split open, gape*, Ov, 2, especially, *to open the mouth, to mutter*, respondebisne ad haec aut omnino hiscere audebis? Cic

Hispăl -pălis, n and (more commonly) **Hispălis** -is, f *town in Spain, now Seville* Hence, **Hispălienses** -ium, *the inhabitants of Hispalis*

Hispāni ōrum, m *the Spaniards*, hence **A. Hispānĭa** ae, f *the whole of the Spanish peninsula* (*including Portugal*) *divided into* citerior, *the eastern part* (later Hisp Tarraconensis), *and* ulterior, *the southern and western part* (later Lusitania and Baetica), hence plur Hispaniae **B. Hispāniensis** -e, and **C. Hispānus** -a um, *Spanish*

hispĭdus -a -um, *rough, shaggy, hairy, bristly*, facies, Hor, ager, *wild*, Hor

1 **hister** = histrio (q v.)

2 **Hister** -tri, m (Ἴστρος) *name of the lower part of the Danube*, binominis (as the upper part was called Danuvius), Ov

histŏrĭa -ae, f (ἱστορία), 1, *historical narrative, history* historia Graeca, *Roman history written in Greek*, Cic historia Italici belli et civilis, Cic, historiam scribere, Cic, 2, *narrative, narration*, historia dignum, *worthy of narration*, Cic

histŏrĭcus -a -um (ἱστορικός), *relating or belonging to history, historical* genus, Cic, subst, **histŏrĭcus** i, m *an historian*, Cic

Histri ōrum (Ἴστροι), *Istrians, inhabitants of Istria*, hence, **A. Histrĭa** ae, f (Ἰστρία), *Histria, a country near Illyria* **B. Histrĭcus** -a um, *Histrian*

histrĭcus -a um (hister), *of or relating to actors*, Plaut

histrĭo -ōnis, m *an actor*, Cic

histrĭōnālis -e (histrio), *of or relating to actors*, Tac

hĭulcē, adv (hiulcus), *in a disconnected manner*, loqui, Cic

hĭulco, 1 (hiulcus), *to cause to gape, to split*, Cat

hĭulcus -a -um (for hiulicus, from hio), *gaping, cleft, open* **I** Lit, hiulca siti arva, Verg **II.** Transf, a, of discourse, *ill put together, disconnected*, concursus verborum, Cic, b, *eager, longing*, Plaut

hŏdĭē, adv (hodie = hoc die), *to-day* (opp cras, heri) **I.** Lit, hodie sunt nonae Sextiles, Cic **II** Transf, a, *at the present time* Cic, b, *now, at present*, si hodie hanc gloriam atque hoc orbis terrae imperium teneremus, Cic, *up to to-day, up to the present time*, quem vivere hodie aiunt, Cic, c, = *at once, directly*, Cic

hŏdiernus a -um (hodie), *of or relating to to-day*, dies, Cic, edictum, Cic, ad hodiernum diem, *up to to-day* Cic

hoedus, hoedīnus, etc = haedus, haedinus, etc (q v)

Hŏmērus -i, m (Ὅμηρος), *the celebrated Greek epic poet*, hence, adj, **Hŏmērĭcus** -a um, *Homeric*

hŏmĭcīda -ae, c (homo and caedo) **I.** Lit, *a murderer, murderess, homicide*, Cic **II.** In a good sense (Gk ἀνδροφόνος), of Hector, *slayer of men*, Hor

hŏmĭcīdĭum ii, n (homicida) *murder, manslaughter, homicide*, Tac

hŏmo inis, m (old Latin hĕmo), *a human being, man* **I.** Gen, *man*, as opp to the beasts (vir, *man* as opp to woman); in plur, homines, *men in general, people* Cic, homo nemo, or nemo homo, *not a soul, no one*, Cic, odium hominis, *a hateful man*, Cic, inter homines esse, a, *to live*, Cic; b, *to mix in society, be in the world*, Cic **II.** Esp, **A.** a, *a man*, in the better sense of the word, nihil hominis esse, *to be without the better qualities of a man*, hominem ex homine tollere or exuere, *to take from a man that which constitutes a man*, Cic, si quidem homo esset *if he had the feelings of a man*, Cic, homines visi sumus, Cic, virum te putabo hominem non putabo, *I must praise your patience and not your taste*, Cic, b, *a man as liable to error, a mortal*, quia homo est, Cic **B.** Used in place of pronouns, valde hominem diligo, (where it stands for hunc, eum, or illum), Cic, hic homo = ego, Hor **C.** *a slave, servant*, Quintii, *Quintius's man*, Cic **D.** Plur, homines *infantry* (opp equites), Caes

hŏmoeŏmĕrīa -ae, f (ὁμοιομέρεια), *similarity of parts*, Lucr

Hŏmŏlē -ēs, f. (Ὁμόλη), *a mountain in Thessaly, where Pan was worshipped.*

hŏmullus -i, m. (dim. of homo), *a little man, manikin*, Cic.

hŏmuncĭo -ōnis, m. (dim. of homo), *a little man, manikin*, Cic.

homuncŭlus -i, m. (dim. of homo), *a little man, manikin*, Cic.

hŏnestas -ātis, f. (honestus). **I.** *honourable reputation, honour, respectability;* honestatem amittere, Cic.; appetens honestatis, Cic.; honestates civitatis, *notabilities*, Cic. **II.** *worth, virtue, honourable character, probity;* **1,** vitae, Cic.; hinc (pugnat) honestas, illinc turpitudo, Cic.; transf., of things, *beauty;* testudinis, Cic.; **2,** philosoph. t. t., *virtue*, Cic.

hŏnestē, adv. (honestus), **1,** *honourably, creditably, respectably;* cenare, Cic.; se gerere, Cic.; in pugna honeste cadere, Cic.; **2,** *honourably, nobly;* honeste geniti, *of noble birth*, Liv.

hŏnesto (honestus), *to honour, distinguish, adorn, dignify;* aliquem laude, honore, Cic.; domum, curiam, Cic.

hŏnestus -a -um (honor). **I.** *honourable; reputable, glorious;* **1,** gen., victoria, Liv.; dies honestissimus, Cic.; with sup., honestumne factu sit an turpe, Cic.; honestum est with acc. and infin., Cic.; subst., **hŏnestum** -i, n. *morality, virtue*, Cic.; **2,** esp., **a,** *fine, beautiful*, Ter.; subst., **hŏnestum** -i, n. *beauty*, Hor.; **b,** *specious, fine-sounding;* honestum et probabile nomen, Cic. **II.** *worthy of honour, distinguished;* familia, Cic.; honesto loco natus, Cic.; vir honestus or honestissimus (title of the knights), Cic.; subst., **hŏnesti** -ōrum, m. *people of distinction*, Hor.

hŏnor = honos (q.v.).

hŏnōrābĭlis -e (honor), *honourable;* haec ipsa sunt honorabilia, salutari, appeti, decedi, assurgi, etc., Cic.

hŏnōrārĭus -a -um (honor), *done or given in honour of, honorary;* vinum, frumentum, Cic.; opera, Cic.; delectare honorarium (est), *done out of respect for the audience*, Cic.

hŏnōrātē, adv. (honoratus), *with honour, honourably*, Tac.

hŏnōrātus -a -um, p. adj. with compar. and superl. (honoro), **1,** *honoured, distinguished, respected;* viri, Cic.; nusquam est senectus honoratior, Cic.; **2,** *honoured by a public office, placed in a high position, in office;* honorati quatuor filii, Cic.

hŏnōrĭfĭcē, adv., comp. honorificentius, superl. honorificentissime (honorificus), *with honour, in an honourable or respectful manner;* honorificentissime aliquem appellare, Caes.; aliquem honorificentissime tractare, Cic.

hŏnōrĭfĭcus -a -um, compar. honorificentior, superl. honorificentissimus (honor and facio), *causing honour, honourable, honouring;* senatus consultum, Cic.; senectus, Cic.

hŏnōro, 1. (honor), **1,** *to honour, show honour to;* aliquem, Cic.; **2,** *to adorn, dignify, honour with;* aliquem sellā curuli, Liv.

hŏnōrus -a -um (honor), *honourable*, Tac.

hŏnōs and **hŏnŏr** -ōris, m. **I.** *honour, honourable distinction.* **A.** Gen., honorem alicui habere, tribuere, Cic., praestare, Ov., honore aliquem afficere, *to show honour to*, Cic.; honore aliquem augere, Caes.; in honore habere, Cic.; esse, Cic.; esse alicui summo honori, *to prove honourable to*, Cic.; aliquid in honorem adducere, *to bring to honour*, Cic.; honori ducitur, *it is considered an honour*, Sall.; honorem praefari or dicere, *to say "by your leave,"* Cic.; honoris causā or gratiā, *out of respect;* quem honoris causā or gratiā nomino, Cic.; honoris Divitiaci et Aeduorum causā, Cic.; so, ad honorem alicuius, Cic.; ad honorem atque amplitudinem tuam, Cic.; supremus honos (*the last honour = burial*), Verg.; communi in morte honore carere, Cic.; mortis honore carere, Verg.; **B.** Esp., **a,** *an office of dignity, a public office;* ad honores ascendere, Cic.; honoribus amplissimis perfunctus, Cic.; **b,** *a title of honour;* honos militaris, Liv.; **c,** *a reward, fee;* honos medici, Cic.; **d,** *honour rendered to the gods, sacrifice*, Verg. **C.** Personif., Honor, *the god of honour.* **II.** Poet. transf., *beauty, grace, ornament;* honorum ruris, *crops*, Hor.; silvarum, *foliage*, Verg.

1. **hōra** -ae, f. (ὥρα). **I.** *time* in gen.; numquam te crastina fallet hora, Verg. **II.** *a definite space of time.* **A.** *a time of the year, season;* verni temporis hora, Hor. **B.** *a time of the day, hour;* **1,** lit., in horam vivere, *to live for the moment*, Cic.; horā amplius, *more than an hour*, Cic.; in hora, *in an hour*, Cic.; in horas, *hourly*, Cic.; hora quota est? *what's o'clock?* Hor.; horae legitimae, *hours fixed as limits to a speech*, Cic.; **2,** meton., **hōrae** -ārum, f. *a clock, dial*, mittere ad horas, Cic.

2. **Hŏra** -ae, f. *the name of Hersilia when deified, the celestial wife of Quirinus.*

Hōrae -ārum, f. (Ὧραι), *the Hours, goddesses who presided over the changes of the seasons, attendants on the sun-god.*

Hŏrātĭus -a -um, *name of a Roman gens to which belonged,* **1,** *the three* Horatii, *who fought against the three Alban Curiatii;* **2,** Horatius Cocles, *who defended the bridge over the Tiber against the army of Porsena;* **3,** Qu. Horatius Flaccus, *son of a freedman of the Horatian gens* (65-8 A.C.), *the celebrated Roman lyric poet.*

hordĕācĕus and **-cĭus** -a -um (hordeum), *of* or *relating to barley*, Plin.

hordĕārĭus -a -um (hordeum), *of* or *relating to barley*, Plin.

hordēĭus -a -um = hordeaceus (q.v.).

hordĕum (ordĕum) -i, n. *barley*, Liv., Caes.

hŏrĭa (ŏrĭa) -ae, f. *a small fishing-boat*, Plaut.

hŏrĭŏla (ŏrĭŏla) -ae, f. (dim. of oria), *a small fishing-boat*, Plaut.

hŏrĭor, 4. (connected with ὄρνυμι), *to urge, incite, encourage*, Enn.

hŏrīzon -ontis, m. (ὁρίζων), *the horizon*, Sen.

hornō, adv. (hornus), *this year*, Plaut.

hornōtĭnus -a -um (hornus), *of* or *relating to the present year;* frumentum, Cic.

hornus -a -um (for horinus, from hora), *of this year, this year's;* vina, Hor.

hōrŏlŏgĭum -ii, n. (ὡρολόγιον), *a clock, sundial,* or *water-clock*, Cic.

hōroscŏpŏs -ōn, m. (ὡροσκόπος), *a horoscope*, Pers.

horrendus -a -um (partic. of horreo), **1** *horrible, horrid, frightful, dreadful;* monstrum Verg.; Sibylla, Verg.; neut. as adv., horrendum stridens belua, Verg.; **2,** *worthy of reverence, venerable;* virgo, Verg.

horrĕo, 2. **I.** *to bristle.* **A.** Lit., **a,** horret seges aristis, Verg.; **b,** *to be hard and rough with frost;* terram uno tempore florere deinde vicissim horrere, Cic. **B.** Of hair, *to stand on end;* comae horrent, Ov.; partic., horrens, *prickly, rough;* rubi, Verg. **II.** Of persons, *to shiver or shudder with cold or fright.* **A.** Intransit., horreo animo, Cic. **B.** Transit., *to,* *shudder at*; crimen, Cic., with infin, non horreo in hunc locum progredi, Cic

horresco, horrŭi, 3. (horreo), 1, *to stand on end, bristle, be rough*; horruerunt que comae, Ov, mare coepit horrescere, *to be stormy*, Cic, 2, *to tremble, begin to shudder, begin to dread*, Cic; horresco referens, Verg; with acc, morsus futuros, Verg

horrĕum -i, n. *a barn, storehouse, magazine, granary*, Capua horreum Campani agri, Cic, poet., *a bee-hive*, Verg, *an ant-hill*, Ov.

horrĭbĭlis -e (horreo), 1, *horrible, frightful, dreadful, fearful*; pestis reipublicae, Cic, horribile est, with infin, Cic, 2, *astonishing, wonderful*, horribili vigilantiā, Cic

horrĭdē, adv (horridus), 1, *roughly, without embellishment*; dicere, Cic, horridius utetur ornamentis, Cic.; 2, *roughly, harshly*, alloqui, Tac

horrĭdŭlus -a -um (dim of horridus), 1, *somewhat rough, projecting*, Plaut, 2, transf, *somewhat rough, unadorned*, orationes, Cic

horrĭdus -a -um (horreo) **I.** *rough, shaggy, bristly* **A.** Lit, barba, Cic, sus, Verg **B.** Transf, a, *rough, wild, savage*, campus, Cic, b, *rough, without refinement, unpolished, uncouth*, Tubero vitā et oratione horridus, Cic. **II.** 1, *shuddering, trembling with cold*, si premerem ventosas horridus Alpes, Ov, 2, *dreadful, horrible*, procella, Verg

horrĭfer -fĕra -fĕrum (horror and fero), *causing dread, bringing fear, terrible*, boreas, Ov; Erinys, Ov.

horrĭfĭcē, adv (horrificus), *with dread*, Lucr.

horrĭfĭco, 1 (horrificus), 1, *to make rough*, Cat., 2, *to terrify*, Verg

horrĭfĭcus -a -um (horror and facio), *causing terror, horrible*, letum, Verg.

horrĭsŏnus -a -um (horreo and sono), *sounding horribly*, fremitus, Verg

horror -ōris, m (horreo), 1, *a shaking, shivering with cold, ague-fit*, quoniam jam sine horrore est, spero esse, ut volumus, Cic, 2, *trembling*, a, from dread, *terror, horror*, qui me horror perfudit, Cic, b, *religious dread, awe*, perfusus horrore venerabundusque, Liv.

horsum, adv (contr for hucvorsum), *in this direction, hitherward*, Plaut

Horta -ae, f *town in Etruria*, now *Orte* Adj, **Hortīnus** a -um, *of Horta*

hortāmen -ĭnis, n (hortor), *an encouragement, incitement, exhortation*, Liv.

hortāmentum -i, n (hortor), *encouragement, incitement*, Sall

hortātĭo -ōnis, f. (hortor), *exhortation, encouragement*, hortatione agere cum aliquo, Cic, plur, contiones hortationesque, Cic

hortātor -ōris, m (hortor), *an exhorter, encourager*; absol, isto hortatore, Cic, with genit, studii, *to study*, Cic; with ad and the acc gerund, auctores hortatoresque ad me restituendum, Cic, with ut and the subj, Cic, esp, as milit t t, *one who exhorts the soldiers*, Liv

hortātus -ūs, m (hortor), *incitement, exhortation*, id fecisse aliorum consilio, hortatu, Cic

Hortensĭus -a -um, *name of a Roman gens, the most famous member of which was* Qu Hortensius Hortalus, *an orator of the time of Cicero* Adj, **Hortensĭānus** -a um, *Hortensian*.

hortor, 1 dep (contr from horitor, intens of horior, *to encourage*, from the same root as ὄρνυμι), *to exhort, incite, encourage* **I.** Gen, a, of persons, aliquem, Cic, with ut and the subj, magno opere te hortor ut, etc Cic; with ne and the subj, hortatur eos ne animo deficiant, Caes, with subj alone, hortatur non solum ab eruptionibus caveant, etc, Caes, with infin, hortamur fari, Verg, with ad, populum ad vindicandum, Sall, with in and the acc, Gentium in amicitiam secum et cum Macedonibus jungendam, Liv, with de, de Aufidiano nomine nihil te hortor, Cic; with acc of thing, pacem, Cic, prov, hortari currentem, *to spur the willing horse*, Cic, b, of inanimate subjects, multae res ad hoc consilium Gallos hortabantur, Caes; with infin, reipublicae dignitas minora haec relinquere hortatur, Cic **II.** Esp, *to harangue soldiers before a battle*, suos, Caes

hortŭlus -i, m (dim of hortus), *a little garden*, Cat., gen plur, hortuli, *grounds, a small park*, Cic

hortus -i, m (χορτος), *garden*, Epicuri, (where Epicurus taught), Cic, meton, *garden produce*, Hor

hospes -pĭtis, c (akin to hostis), *a stranger, foreigner*, hence, *a guest, guest friend*, Cic, transf = *unknown, inexperienced in*, nec peregrinum atque hospitem in agendo esse debere, Cic

hospĭtālis e (hospes), 1, *relating to a guest or host*, cubiculum, *guest-chamber*, Liv, sedes, Cic, caedes, *murder of a guest*, Liv, Juppiter, *protector of guests*, Cic, 2, *friendly, hospitable*, domo hospitalissimus, Cic, with in and the acc, Cimonem in suos curiales Laciadas hospitalem Cic

hospĭtālĭtas -ātis, f (hospitalis), *hospitality*, Cic

hospĭtālĭtĕr, adv (hospitalis), *hospitably*, Liv

hospĭtĭum ii, n (hospes) **I.** *hospitality, the relation between host and guest*, mihi cum aliquo hospitium est, Cic, or intercedit, Caes, alicuius hospitio usus sum, Caes; hospitium cum aliquo facere, Cic, jungere, Liv **II.** *hospitality, friendliness, hospitable reception* **A.** aliquem hospitio magnificentissimo accipere, Cic, aliquem hospitio invitare, Cic **B.** Meton, *a guest-chamber, guest's lodging, inn*, hospitium parare, Cic, cohortes per hospitia dispersae, *billeted*, Tac, transf, *the resting-place of animals*, Verg

hospĭtus a um (hospes) **I.** *strange, foreign*, navis, Ov, aequora, Verg; conjunx hospita Teucris, Verg Subst, **hospĭta** -ae, f *a foreigner*, Cic **II.** *hospitable*, terra, Verg Subst, **hospĭta** ae, f *the hostess*, Cic

hostĭa -ae, f (from 2 hostio, lit, *the thing struck*), *an animal slain in sacrifice, a sin-offering*, humana, Cic; hostias immolare, Cic, or mactare, Verg

hostĭātus a -um (hostia), *provided with animals for sacrifice*, Plaut

hostĭcus -a -um (hostis), *relating or belonging to the enemy, hostile*, ager, Liv Subst, **hostĭcum** -i, n *the enemy's territory*, in hostico, Liv

hostĭfĭcus -a um (hostis and facio), *hostile*, Cic

hostīlis -e (hostis), 1, *of or relating to the enemy, hostile*, expugnatio, Cic, in augury, pars (opp familiaris), *the part of the entrails said to refer to the enemy*, Lucan, 2, *like an enemy, unfriendly, hostile*, hostili odio et crudelitate, Cic, multa hostiliter audere, Tac

hostīlĭtĕr, adv (hostilis), *hostilely, like an enemy*, quid ille fecit hostiliter, Cic

Hostīlĭus -ii, m Tullus, *third king of Rome* Adj, **Hostīlĭus** a -um, *Hostilian*, curia, *built by Tullus Hostilius*, Liv

hostimentum -i, n. (1. hostio), *compensation, requital*, Plaut.

1. **hostio,** 4. *to requite, recompense*, Plaut.

2. **hostio,** 4. *to strike*, Plaut.

hostis -is, c. originally *a stranger*, but afterwards *an enemy, a public foe* (opp. inimicus, *a private enemy*). **A.** Lit., cives hostesque, Liv.; omnes nos statuit ille non inimicos sed hostes, Cic.; populo Romano, adversus Romanos, Liv.; hostem aliquem judicare, *to denounce as an enemy to his country*, Cic.; sing. collect., capta hostis, *the female captives*, Liv. **B.** Transf., **1,** *a bitter foe in private life*; hostis omnium hominum, Cic.; **2,** *a rival in love*, Ov.

hūc, adv. (hic), *hither, to this place*, **1,** of space, huc ades, *come hither*, Verg.; tum huc tum illuc, Cic.; nunc huc nunc illuc, Verg.; huc et illuc, huc, illuc, Cic.; huc atque illuc, *hither and thither*, Cic.; **2,** not referring to place, *hither, thus far, to this point*; rem huc deduxi, Cic.; huc te pares, *for this object*, Cic.; accedat huc, Cic.

hūcine, adv. *so far? as far as this?* hucine tandem omnia reciderunt? Cic.

hŭi, interj., exclamation of astonishment, ridicule, etc., *eh! hullo!* hui, quam timeo quid existimes, Cic.

hūjusmŏdi or **hūjuscĕmŏdi,** *of this kind, of such a kind, such*; ex hujusmodi principio, Cic.

hūmānē, adv. (humanus), **1,** *humanly, like a human being*; morbos toleranter et humane ferre, Cic.; **2,** *humanely, kindly, courteously*; fecit humane, Cic.

hūmānĭtas -ātis, f. (humanus). **I.** *humanity, human nature, human feeling*; omnem humanitatem exuere, Cic.; fac, id quod est humanitatis tuae (*what you owe to yourself as a man*), ne quid aliud cures hoc tempore nisi ut quam commodissime convalescas, Cic. **II.** Esp., **A.** *humanity, human kindness, kindness, philanthropy, mildness*; edictorum, Cic. **B.** *refinement of education and taste, good breeding, mental cultivation, culture*; communium litterarum ac politioris humanitatis expers, Cic.

hūmānĭtĕr, adv. (humanus), **1,** *humanly, in a way becoming human nature*; vivere, Cic.; **2,** *politely, courteously, kindly*; litterae humaniter scriptae, Cic.

hūmānĭtŭs, adv. (humanus), *after the manner of men*; si quid mihi humanitus accidisset, i.e. *if I should die*, Cic.

hūmānus -a -um (homo), *human, of or relating to human beings*. **I.** Gen., genus, *the human race*, Cic.; facies, Cic.; res humanae, *human affairs*, Cic., or *things happening to man*, Cic.; hostia, *human sacrifice*, Cic.; scelus, *against men*, Liv.; humanum est, *it is human*, Cic.; subst., **a, humanus** -i, m. *one of the human race*, Ov.; **b, humana** -ōrum, n. *human affairs*; humana miscere divinis, Liv., or *things happening to man, the fate of man*; omnia humana tolerabilia ferre, Cic. **II.** Esp., **A.** *humane, kind, philanthropic*; erga aliquem, Cic. **B.** *civilised, refined*; gens humana atque docta, Cic.

hŭmātĭo -ōnis, f. (humo), *a burying, interment*, Cic.

hūmecto, 1. *to wet, moisten, water*; qua niger humectat flaventia culta Galesus, Verg.; vultum largo flumine, Verg.

hūmĕo, 2. *to be moist, wet*, Ov.; partic. pres., **hūmens** -entis, *moist, wet, dewy*; umbra, Verg.; oculi, Ov.

hŭmĕrus -i, m. *the shoulder*, **a,** of men, sagittae pendebant ab humero, Ov.; puerum in humeros suos efferre, Cic.; fig., comitia humeris suis sustinere, Cic.; **b,** of animals, *the shoulder, fore-quarter*, Cic.

hūmesco, 3. (humeo), *to become wet, grow moist*, Verg.

hūmĭdŭlus -a -um (dim. of humidus), *somewhat wet, moist*, Ov.

hūmĭdus -a -um (humeo), *wet, moist, humid*; ligna, Cic.; mella, *liquid*, Verg.; Ide, *rich in streams*, Ov. Subst., **hūmĭdum** -i, n. *a wet place*, Tac.; humida -ōrum, n. *wet parts*, Cic.

hūmĭfer -fĕra -fĕrum (humor and fero), *containing moisture, moist*, Cic. poet.

hŭmĭlis -e (humus), *low*. **I.** Lit., **a,** *low* (as opposed to high), arbores et vites et quae sunt humiliora, Cic.; staturā humili, Nep.; **b,** (as opposed to deep), *shallow*; fossa, Verg. **II.** Transf., **A.** Of position, rank, etc., *low, mean, humble, poor, insignificant*; humilibus parentibus natus, Cic.; humillimus de plebe, Liv.; subst., **humilis** -is, m. *a person of low rank*, Hor. **B.** Of character, **a,** *abject, base*; humili animo ferre, Cic.; **b,** *submissive, humble*; obsecratio humilis, Cic. **C.** Of expression, *mean, without elevation*; oratio humilis et abjecta, Cic.

hŭmĭlĭtas -ātis, f. (humilis). **I.** *smallness, lowness, nearness to the ground*; animalium, Cic. **II.** Transf., **A.** *lowness of birth or station, insignificance, obscurity*; alicuius humilitatem despicere, Cic. **B.** *humility of disposition, submissiveness, abjectness*; humilitas et obsecratio, Cic.

hŭmĭlĭtĕr, adv. with compar. and superl. (humilis), *humbly, meanly, abjectly*; sentire, Cic.; servire, Liv.

hŭmo, 1. (humus), **1,** *to cover with earth, bury*; aliquem, Cic.; **2,** transf., *to perform the funeral rites over a corpse (burn, etc.)*, Nep.

hūmor -ōris, m. (akin to χυμός, *a liquid*), *moisture, liquid, fluid*. **I.** Gen. Bacchi, *wine*, Verg.; lactens, *milk*, Ov.; circumfluus, *the sea*, Ov.; humor in genas labitur, *tears*, Hor.; plur., humores marini, Cic. **II.** Esp., *the sap of plants*, Verg.

hŭmus -i, f. (akin to χαμ-αί), *the ground, earth, soil*. **I.** Lit., humus injecta, Cic.; humi, *on the ground, on the floor*; jacere, Cic.; stratus humi, Cic.; humo, **a,** *from the ground*; surgere, Ov.; **b,** *on the ground*; sedere, Ov.; **c,** *out of the ground*; fundit humo facilem victum justissima tellus, Verg.; **d,** *in the ground*; figere plantas, Verg. **II.** Meton., *land, country*; Punica, Pontica, Ov.

hўăcinthĭnus -a -um (ὑακίνθινος), *hyacinthine, belonging to the hyacinth*; flos, Cat.

1. **Hўăcinthus (-ŏs)** -i, m. (Ὑάκινθος), *a beautiful Spartan youth, beloved of and accidentally killed by Apollo; from his blood sprang the flower called by his name*; hence, **Hўăcinthĭa** -ōrum, n. *a festival celebrated at Sparta*.

2. **hўăcinthus** -i, m. (ὑάκινθος), *a flower, the hyacinth* (not the flower so called by us), Verg.

Hўădes -um, f. (Ὑάδες), *the Hyades, a group of seven stars in the constellation Taurus*, Verg.

hўaena -ae, f. (ὕαινα), *the hyena*, Ov.

hўălus -i, m. (ὕαλος), *glass*; color hyali, *glass-green*, Verg.

Hўampŏlis -pŏlis, f. (Ὑάμπολις), *a city in the E. of Phocis*.

Hўantes -ium, m. (Ὕαντες), *an old name for the Boeotians*; adj., **a, Hўantēus** -a -um, *Boeotian*, Ov.; aqua, *Castalia*, Mart.; **b, Hўantĭus** -a -um, *Boeotian*; subst., **Hўantĭus** -ii, m. *Actaeon, grandson of Cadmus*, Ov.

Hyas antis, m (Ὑας), *son of Atlas, and brother (or father) of the Hyades*, sidus Hyantis, *the Hyades*, Ov (acc. sing, Hyan, Ov)

Hybla -ae, f and **Hyblē** ēs, f (Ὕβλα), 1, *a mountain of Sicily, famed for its bees*, adj, **Hyblaeus** -a -um, *Hyblaean*; 2, *name of three towns in Sicily* (parva, major, and minor), hence **Hyblenses** ium, m *the inhabitants of Hybla*

Hydaspēs pis, m (Ὑδάσπης), 1, *a river in India* now *Behut* or *Djelum* 2, *name of an Indian slave*

hydra -ae, f (ὕδρα), 1, *the many-headed water snake of the Lernaean Lake, slain by Hercules*, 2, *a constellation also called* Anguis, 3, *a monster of the lower world with fifty heads*

hydraulus i, m (ὕδραυλος), *a water organ*, Cic.

hydria -ae, f (ὑδρία), *an urn, water-jar*, Cic

hydrochous -i, m (ὑδροχόος), *the constellation Aquarius*, Cat

hydropicus -a -um (ὑδρωπικός), *dropsical*, Hor

hydrops ōpis, m (ὕδρωψ), *the dropsy*, Hor

1 **hydrus** -i m (ὕδρος), *a water-snake, hydra*, Verg, *applied to the hair of Medusa and the Furies*, Verg

2 **Hydrūs** druntis, f (Ὑδροῦς), and **Hydruntum** i, n *town on the E coast of Calabria*, now *Otranto*

hyems, hyĕmālis, etc = hiems, etc (q v)

Hylaeus i m (Ὑλαῖος), *a centaur slain by Atalanta*.

Hylās -ae, m (Ὕλας), *son of Thiodamas, a beautiful youth, the friend and companion of Hercules on the Argonautic expedition, carried off by the water-nymphs in Mysia*

Hyllus -i, m (Ὕλλος), *son of Hercules and Deianira*

Hymēn -ĕnis, m (Ὑμήν), 1, *the god of marriage*, Ov, 2, *the marriage song*, Ov.

hymĕnaeŏs or **-ŭs** -i, m (ὑμέναιος) **I** *the marriage song* **A.** Lit, hymenaeon canere Ov, canere hymenaeos, Verg **B.** (gen plur) meton, *the wedding*, Verg, transf, *the pairing of animals*, Verg **II** *Hymen, the god of marriage*, Ov

Hymettŏs and **Hymettus** -i, m (Ὑμηττός), *a mountain in Africa, famous for its bees and marble* Adj, **Hymettius** a -um, *Hymettian*

Hymnis -idis, f (Ὑμνίς), *name of a comedy of Caecilius Statius*

Hypaepa -ōrum, n (τὰ Ὕπαιπα), *a town in Lydia*, now *Birghe* or *Bereki*

Hypănis -is, m (Ὕπανις), *river in European Sarmatia*, now *the Bog*

Hypăta -ae, f (Ὕπατα), *town in Thessaly* Adj, 1, **Hypataeus** -a -um, 2, **Hypatensis** e, *of or belonging to Hypata*

Hypĕrbŏrĕi -ōrum, m (Ὑπερβόρεοι), *the Hyperboreans, a fabulous people dwelling at the extreme north* hence, adj, **Hypĕrbŏrĕus** a -um, *lying to the north, northern* Verg

Hypĕrides -ae, m (Ὑπερείδης), *an Athenian orator, contemporary with Demosthenes*

Hypĕrīon -ŏnis, m (Ὑπερίων), 1, *Hyperion, a Titan, father of the Sun* 2 *the Sun god himself*, hence, 1, **Hypĕrīŏnius** a -um, *of or belonging to Hyperion*. 2, **Hypĕrīŏnis** -idis, f *Aurora*, Ov

Hypermnestra -ae, and **-ē**, -ēs, f (Ὑπερμνήστρα), *the youngest of the Danaides, the only one who did not kill her husband (Lynceus)*

hypŏdĭdascălus i, m (ὑποδιδάσκαλος), *an under-teacher*, Cic

hypomnēma -mătis, n (ὑπόμνημα), *a memorandum, note*, ap Cic

hypŏthēca -ae, f (ὑποθήκη), *a pledge, security, mortgage*, Cic

Hypsĭpylē -ēs, f and **Hypsĭpyla** ae, f (Ὑψιπύλη), *queen of Lemnos, saved her father when the women of Lemnos killed all the men, received the Argonauts*

Hyrcāni -ōrum, m (Ὑρκανοί), *the inhabitants of Hyrcania* Hence 1, adj, **Hyrcānus** a um, *Hyrcanian*, 2, subst, **Hyrcānia** -ae, f *the land of the Hyrcani in Asia, between Media, Parthia, and the Caspian Sea*

Hyriē -ēs, f (Ὑρίη), *town and lake in Boeotia*

Hyrieus ĕi, m (Ὑριεύς), *father of Orion* Adj, **Hyrieus** -a -um, proles, *Orion*, Ov

Hyrtăcĭdēs -ae, m (Ὑρτακίδης), *the son of Hyrtacus, i e Nisus*

Hystaspēs -is, m (Ὑστάσπης), *father of the Persian king, Darius*

I.

I, i, *the ninth letter of the Latin alphabet* For meaning of I as an abbreviation, see Table of Abbreviations

Iacchus -i, m (Ἴακχος), 1, *a name of Bacchus*, 2, meton, *wine*, Verg

1 **Iālysus** i, m (Ἰάλυσος), *town in Rhodes*, now *Jaliso* Hence, **Iālysius** -a -um, poet = *Rhodian*, Ov

2 **Iālysus** -i m, *son of Sol*

iambēus a -um (ἰαμβεῖος), *iambic*, Hor

iambus i, m (ἴαμβος), 1, *an iambus, a metrical foot* (⏑ —), Hor, 2, *an iambic poem, iambic poetry*, Cic

ianthinus a -um (ἰάνθινος), *violet coloured*, Plin Subst, **ianthina** -ōrum, n *violet coloured clothes*, Mart

Iăpĕtus -i, m (Ἰαπετός), *a giant, father of Atlas, Epimetheus, and Prometheus*, genus Iapeti, *Prometheus*, Hor Hence, **Iăpĕtiŏnĭdēs** -ae, m *a son of Iapetus, i e Atlas*, Ov

Iăpydes -um, m (Ἰάπυδες), *a people in north-west Illyria* Hence, 1, **Iăpys** -pydis, *Iapydian*, 2, **Iapydia** ae, f *Iapydia*

Iăpyx -pўgis, m (Ἰάπυξ) **I.** *the son of Daedalus, who reigned in a part of Southern Italy, thence called Iapygia* **II. A.** *a west-north west wind, favourable for crossing from Brundusium to Greece* **B.** *a river in Apulia*, Iapygis arva, *Apulia*, Ov **C.** Adj, *Iapygian* Hence, **Iāpygia** -ae, f (Ἰαπυγία), *a district of Magna Graecia, part of Calabria*, now *Terra d'Otranto*

Iarba, and **Iarbas** -ae, m *an African king, rival of Aeneas* Hence, **Iarbita** -ae, m = *a Mauretanian*, Hor

Iardănis -idis, f *a daughter of Iardanus, i e, Omphale*, Ov

Iăsius -ii, m (Ἰάσιος), 1, *an Argive king, father of Atalanta*, 2, *a Cretan, beloved by Ceres* (also called Iăsĭōn) Hence, 1, **Iăsĭdes** -ae, m (Ἰασίδης), *a descendant of Iasius*, 2, **Iăsis** -idos, f *a daughter of Iasius, i e Atalanta*

Ĭāsōn -ŏnis, m. (Ἰάσων). **I.** *son of Aeson, king in Thessaly, leader of the expedition of the Argonauts to Colchis to fetch the golden fleece.* Adj., **Ĭāsŏnĭus** -a -um, *Jasonian;* carina, *the Argo,* Prop.; remex, *the Argonauts,* Ov. **II.** *a tyrant of Pherae, contemporary with Epaminondas.*

ĭaspis -ĭdis, f. (ἴασπις), *a jasper,* Verg.

Ĭassus (Ĭāsus) -i, f. (Ἴασσος), *a town in Caria;* hence, **Ĭassenses** -ium, m. *the inhabitants of Iassus.*

Ĭāzўges -um, m. (Ἰάζυγες), *a Sarmatian tribe on the Danube.* Sing., **Ĭāzyx** -zўgis, used as an adjective, *Iazygian.*

Ĭbēr . . . v. Hiber . . .

ĭbĭ, adv. (from pron. root I, whence is). **I.** *there, at that place,* Cic. **II.** Transf., **A.** Of time, *then, thereupon;* ibi infit, Liv. **B.** *in that thing, in that matter,* Cic.

ĭbīdem, adv. (ibi and demonstrat. suffix -dem, as in i-dem), **1,** *in the same place, in that very place;* hic ibidem, *on this very place,* Cic.; **2,** *moreover,* Cic. (ibīdem, Juv.).

ībis, genit. ibis and ibĭdis, f. (ἶβις), *the ibis, a sacred bird among the Egyptians,* Cic.

ĭbiscum, ibrĭda = hibiscum, hibrida (q.v.).

Ībўcus -i, m. (Ἴβυκος), *a Greek lyric poet, flourishing about* 540 A.C.

Ĭcădĭus -ĭi, m. (Ἰκάδιος), *a notorious pirate.*

Ĭcărĭus -ĭi, m. (Ἰκάριος), *the father of Penelope.* Hence, **Ĭcărĭōtis** -ĭdis, f., and **Ĭcăris** -ĭdis, f. *Penelope.*

Ĭcărus -i, m. (Ἴκαρος). **I.** *the son of Daedalus, drowned in the Aegean Sea, whilst flying from Crete with wings made by his father.* Hence adj., **Ĭcărĭus** -a -um, Icarium mare, or absol., **Ĭcărium** -ĭi, n. *the Icarian Sea, a part of the Aegean Sea.* **II.** *the father of Erigone, changed into the constellation Arcturus,* or *Bootes.* Adj., **Ĭcărĭus** -a -um, *Icarian;* canis, *the constellation Canis Major,* Ov.

iccirco = idcirco (q.v.).

Ĭcĕlos -i, m. (ἴκελος, *like*), *brother of Morpheus.*

Icēni -ōrum, m. *a people in Britain.*

ichneumon -ŏnis, m. (ἰχνεύμων), *the ichneumon,* Cic.

ĭcĭo, or **īco,** ici, ictum, 3. *to strike, hit, smite, stab.* **I. A.** Lit., lapide ictus, Caes.; e caelo ictus, *struck by lightning,* Cic. **B.** Meton., icere foedus, *to make a treaty,* Cic. **II.** Transf., partic., ictus, *affected, touched, moved, struck;* conscientiā ictus, Liv.; desideriis icta, Hor. (pres. also **īco,** Lucr.).

Ĭcŏnĭum -ĭi, n. (Ἰκόνιον), *town in Lycaonia.*

ictĕrĭcus -a -um (ἰκτερικός), *suffering from jaundice, jaundiced,* Juv.

ictus -ūs, m. (ico), *a blow, stroke, stab, hit, thrust.* **I.** Gen., **a,** lit., gladiatorius, Cic.; sagittarum ictus, Liv; lapidum, Caes.; apri, Ov.; pollicis, *the striking of the lyre,* Hor.; fulminis, *lightning-stroke,* Cic.; solis, *a sunbeam,* Hor.; **b,** transf., *blow;* novae calamitatis, Cic. **II.** Esp., **A.** *the charge* or *assault of an enemy;* sub ictum dari, *to be exposed to the attacks of the enemy,* Tac. **B.** In music, *beating time, beat,* Hor.

Īda -ae, f., and **Īdē** -ēs, f. (Ἴδα, Ἴδη). **I.** *a woman's name,* Verg. **II. A.** *a mountain near Troy.* **B.** *a mountain in Crete, where Jupiter was nursed.* Adj., **Īdaeus** -a -um, **a,** *relating to Mount Ida in Phrygia;* parens deum, Verg., or mater, Cic., *Cybele;* naves *Trojan,* Hor.; pastor, Cic., or judex, or hospes, Ov., *Paris;* **b,** *relating to Mount Ida in Crete.*

Īdălĭē -ēs, f. (Ἰδαλίη), *a surname of Venus, from Idalium.*

Īdălium -ĭi, n. (Ἰδάλιον), *promontory and town in Cyprus, with a temple of Venus.* Hence **1,** adj., **Īdălĭus** -a -um, poet., *belonging to Cyprus,* Venus, Verg.; **2,** subst., **Īdălĭa** -ae, f. (sc. terra), *the neighbourhood of Idalium.*

idcirco (iccirco), adj. (id and circa), *on that account, for that reason;* absol., Cic.; followed by quod or quia, Cic.; by si, Cic.; by ut or ne and the subj., Cic.; by qui and the subj., Cic.; by quo facilius and subj., Caes.

īdem, ĕădem, ĭdem (from is and suffix -dem), *the same;* idem velle atque idem nolle, *to have the same likes and dislikes,* Sall.; amicus est tamquam alter idem, *a second self,* Cic.; sometimes to be translated by *also;* suavissimus et idem facillimus, Cic.; followed by qui, atque (ac) et, ut, quam, quasi, cum, etc., eadem virtus, quae in proavo, Cic.; foll. by dat., idem facit occidenti, *he acted like,* etc., Hor.; neut. subst., idem juris, *the same right,* Cic.; eodem loci, *on the very spot,* Cic.; with et or que = *and indeed;* certissimi et iidem acerrimi, Cic. (abl. **ēōdemque, ēādemque,** trisyll., Verg.

ĭdentĭdem, adv. (idem -ti -dem), *repeatedly, again and again,* Cic.

ĭdĕō, adv. *on that account, therefore,* Cic.; followed by quod, quia, quoniam, by ut, or ne with the subj., Cic., or by quin with the subj., Liv.

ĭdĭōta (ĭdĭōtes) -ae, m. (ἰδιώτης), *an ignorant, uncultivated man,* Cic.

Idmōn -mŏnis, m. (Ἴδμων), *father of Arachne.* Adj., **Idmŏnĭus** -a -um, Arachne, *daughter of Idmon,* Ov.

Īdŏmĕneus -ei, m. (Ἰδομενεύς), *son of Deucalion, king of Crete.*

ĭdōnĕē, adv. (idoneus), *fitly, appropriately,* Cic.

ĭdōnĕus -a -um, *fit, appropriate.* **I.** Act., *fit to do something, capable, qualified, suitable;* constr., **a,** with dat., with ad or in and the acc., castris idoneum locum, Caes.; idonei ad hoc negotium, Cic.; idonei in eam rem, Liv.; **b,** with infin., fons rivo dare nomen idoneus, Hor.; **c,** absol., verba minus idonea, Cic.; of persons, *sufficient, satisfactory;* idonei auctores, Cic.; with infin., idoneum visum est dicere, Sall. **II.** Pass., *fit to suffer* or *receive something, worthy;* constr., **a,** gen., with qui and the subj. (like dignus), tibi fortasse nemo fuit quem imitere, Cic.; **b,** absol., minus idoneum praemio afficere, Cic.

Ĭdūmē -ēs, f. and **Ĭdūmaea** -ae, f. (Ἰδουμαία), *a district in Palestine, bordering on Judaea and Arabia Petraea.* Hence, **Ĭdūmaeus** -a -um, *Idumaean.*

īdus -ŭum, f. (root ID, VID, whence viduus and divido, *the dividing*), *the Ides, the middle of the Roman month, the fifteenth day in March, May, July, October; the thirteenth in the other months;* idus Martiae, *the 15th of March,* Cic.

Ĭdўĭa -ae, f. (Ἰδυῖα), *the mother of Medea.*

Igilium -ĭi, n. *a small island on the coast of Etruria,* now *Giglio.*

ĭgĭtur, adv. (from is and suffix -tur = -tus, as ita from i -s and suffix -ta), *then.* **A.** Of logical consequences, *so, therefore, then, accordingly;* si mentiris, mentiris. Mentiris autem; igitur mentiris, Cic. **B.** In asking questions, *then?* in quo igitur loco est? Cic.; ironically, haec igitur est tua disciplina? Cic. **C.** With imperatives, *then, so then;* fac igitur quod, etc., Cic.

D. After digressions, parentheses, etc to resume the argument, *so, as I was saying*, scripsi etiam (nam ab orationibus disjungo me fere), scripsi igitur, Cic **E.** In a climax, *then*, pro imperio, pro exercitu, pro provincia, etc, pro his igitur omnibus rebus, Cic. (Igitur stands most frequently second or third in its clause, but sometimes first, esp in Sallust)

ignārus -a -um (in and gnarus), **1,** *ignorant of, unacquainted with, inexperienced in,* with genit, faciendae orationis, Cic, mariti, *unmarried*, Hor, with acc and infin., non sumus ignari multos studiose contra esse dicturos, Cic, with rel sent., ignaro populo Romano quid ageretur, Cic, quid virtus valeret, Cic; multos esse dicturos, Cic; absol., Liv, **2,** pass, *unknown*, with dat., proles ignara parenti, Ov, regio hostibus ignara, Sall, absol, ignari montes, Verg

ignāvē and **ignāvĭtĕr,** adv (ignavus), *lazily, slothfully, without spirit*, dicere, Hor., facere, Cic

ignāvĭa -ae, f (ignavus), *idleness, laziness, listlessness, sloth, cowardice*, contraria fortitudini ignavia, Cic.

ignāvĭter = ignave (q v.)

ignāvus -a -um (in and gnavus) **I.** *idle, slothful, listless, inactive* (opp strenuus) **A.** Lit, **a,** homo, senectus, Cic., with genit, legiones operum et laboris ignavae, Tac; with ad and the acc, ignavissimus ad opera ac muniendum hostis, Liv, **b,** *cowardly*; miles, Cic, hostis, Liv., subst, **ignāvus** -i, m *a coward, poltroon*, Sall; plur, Cic **B.** Transf, of inanimate objects, *inert, sluggish*, nemus, *unfruitful*, Verg, lux, *a day in which one is lazy, an idle day*, Juv.; gravitas, *immovable*, Verg **II.** Act., *causing sloth and idleness*, frigus, Ov.; genus interrogationis, Cic

ignesco, 3 (ignis) **A.** *to kindle, catch fire*, Cic **B.** Transf, *to burn, glow with passion*, Rutulo ignescunt irae, Verg

ignĕus -a -um (ignis), *fiery, burning, glowing with heat* **I.** Lit., **a,** sidera, Cic, sol, Cic, **b,** *glowing like flame*, astra, Verg **II.** Transf, **A.** Of colours, *flaming, glowing*, Plin **B.** Fig, *glowing with passion, love, anger*, etc, furor, Ov; vigor, Verg, Tarchon, Verg

ignĭcŭlus -i, m (dim of ignis), *a little fire, little flame, spark*. **A.** Lit, Plin **B.** Transf, **a,** *ardour*, desiderii, Cic, **b,** *a spark, beginning*, virtutum, Cic, desiderii tui, *the ardour, glow*, Cic; ingenii, *sparks of talent*, Quint

ignĭfer -fĕra -fĕrum (ignis and fero), *fire bearing, fiery*, aether, Lucr, axis, Ov

ignĭgĕna -ae, m (ignis and geno = gigno), *born of fire*, epithet of Bacchus, Ov

ignĭpes -pĕdis (ignis and pes), *fiery footed*, equi, Ov

ignĭpŏtens -entis (ignis and potens), *mighty in fire, ruler of fire*, epithet of Vulcan, Verg

ignis -is, m *fire* **I.** Lit, **A. 1,** gen, ignem concipere, comprehendere, *to catch fire*, Cic, accendere, Verg, ignem ab igne capere, *to kindle*, Cic; operibus ignem inferre, Caes; aliquem igni cremare, necare, interficere, Caes. **2,** esp, **a,** *conflagration*, pluribus simul locis, et iis diversis, ignes coorti sunt, Liv., **b,** *a watch-fire*, ignibus exstinctis, Liv, **c,** *a fire-brand*, ignibus armata ingens multitudo, Liv, **d,** *the flames of the funeral pile*, ignes supremi, Ov, **e,** *lightning*, ignis coruscus, Hor, **f,** *light of the stars*, ignes curvati lunae, Hor **B. a,** *glow, heat*, solis, Ov, **b,** *glitter, fire*, of the eyes, Cic, **c,** *redness*, sacer ignis, *St Anthony's fire*, Verg **II.** Transf, **1,** hinc ordini novum ignem subjeci, *ground for hatred*, Cic, **2,** *glow of the passions of love or anger*, and meton, for the person beloved, meus ignis, Verg

ignōbĭlis -e (in and gnobilis = nobilis), **1,** *unknown, obscure, inglorious*, civitas, Caes, **2,** *of low birth, of mean extraction, ignoble*, familia, Cic, vulgus, Verg

ignōbĭlĭtas -ātis, f (ignobilis), **1,** *ingloriousness, obscurity*, Cic., **2,** *mean birth*, generis, Cic

ignōmĭnĭa -ae, f. (in and gnomen = nomen), *the deprivation of one's good name, disgrace, dishonour, ignominy*, ignominiam accipere, Cic, alicui injungere, inferre, Liv; inurere, Cic, ignominia aliquem afficere, Cic, ignominia notare, Cic, ignominiam habere, Cic, per ignominiam, Cic, with subj genit, senatus, *inflicted by the senate*, Cic

ignōmĭnĭōsus -a -um (ignominia), *full of disgrace, ignominious, disgraceful*, dominatio, Cic, fuga, Liv

ignōrābĭlis -e (ignoro), *unknown*, Cic

ignōrans -antis (partic of ignoro), *ignorant*, Caes

ignōrantĭa -ae, f (ignoro), *want of knowledge, ignorance*, loci, Caes, absol, Cic

ignōrātĭo -ōnis, f. (ignoro), *want of knowledge, ignorance*, locorum, Cic, sui, Cic, absol Cic

ignōrātus -a -um (partic of ignoro), *unknown*, ignoratum a Syracusanis sepulcrum, Cic,

ignōro, 1 (ignarus), *to be without knowledge, ignorant of, not to know*, **a,** with acc, causam, Cic, alicuius faciem, Sall, aliquem, Cic; **b,** with infin, Cic, **c,** with acc and infin, Cic, **d,** with rel sent, quum id quam vere sit ignores, Cic, **e,** with de and the abl, Cic, **f,** absol, Cic

ignoscens entis, (p adj of ignosco), *forgiving, placable*, Ter

ignosco -nōvi -nōtum, 3 (in and gnosco = nosco, *not to take notice of*), *to overlook, forgive, pardon*, with dat., haesitationi meae, Cic, orat ut sibi ignosceret, Caes; with neut acc, hoc, Cic, with si or quod, *that*, Cic

1 **ignōtus** -a -um, partic of ignosco

2 **ignōtus** -a -um (in and gnotus = notus) **I. 1,** *unknown*, with dat, plurimis ignotissimi gentibus, Cic, jus obscurum et ignotum, Cic, subst, **ignōtus** -i, m *an unknown person*, Cic, **2,** *ignoble, obscure* (opp generosus), mater, Hor, hic ignotissimus Phryx, Cic **II.** Act, *ignorant*, Cic

Ĭgŭvĭum -ii, n. *a town in Umbria*, now *Gubbio* or *Eugubio* Hence, **1, Ĭgŭvīni** -ōrum, m and **2, Ĭgŭvīnātes** -ium, m *the inhabitants of Iguvium*

Ĭlerda -ae, f *town in Hispania Tarraconensis*

Ilergăōnes -um, m and **Illurgavonenses** -ium, m *a people in the east of Hispania Tarraconensis*

Ilergētes -um, m *a people in Hispania Tarraconensis*

īlex ĭcis, f *the holm-oak*, Verg

1 **īlĭa** -ium, n **1,** *the part of the body between the ribs and thighs, the flank*, suffodere ilia equis, Liv, ima longo ilia singultu tendere, Verg, ducere, *to draw the flanks together, to become broken-winded*, Hor, rumpere, *to burst*, Verg, **2,** *the intestines of animals*, Hor

2 **Īlĭa** -ae, f v Ilion

Īlĭăcus, v Ilion

īlĭcet (= ire licet) **I. A.** Lit, *let us go, you may go*, a form of dismissal anciently used at the close of a meeting, Ter. **B.** Transf., *it is all over, all is lost,* Plaut., Ter. **II.** *immediately, forthwith, straightway,* Verg.

īlicētum -i, n. (ilex), *an ilex-grove,* Mart.

īlĭcō = illico.

Īliensis, v. Ilion.

īlignus -a -um (ilex), *belonging to the ilex;* glans, Hor.

Īlĭŏn or **Īlĭum** -ii, n. (Ἴλιον) and **Īlĭŏs** -ii, f. (Ἴλιος), *Troy;* hence, 1, adj., **Īlĭus** -a -um, *Trojan;* subst., a, **Īlĭi** -ōrum, m. *the Trojans;* b, **Īlĭa** -ae, f. *the Trojan woman = Rhea Sylvia, mother of Romulus and Remus,* Verg., and hence, **Īlĭădēs** -ae, m. *the descendant of Ilia = Romulus* or *Remus,* Ov.; 2, **Īlĭăcus** -a -um, *Trojan;* carmen, *on the Trojan war,* Hor.; 3, **Īlienses** -ium, m. *the inhabitants of Ilium;* 4, **Īlĭădēs** -ae, m. *Ganymede,* Ov.; 5, **Īlĭăs** -ădis, f. a, *a Trojan woman,* Verg.; b, *the Iliad of Homer,* Cic.

Īlĭŏna -ae, f. and **Īlĭŏnē** -ēs, f. 1, *the eldest daughter of king Priam, wife of Polymnestor, king in Thrace;* 2, = *Hecuba,* Cic.; Ilionam edormit, *the part of Hecuba,* Hor.

Īlīthȳia -ae, f. (Εἰλείθυια), *the goddess who aided women in child-birth.*

Iliturgi (Illiturgi) -ōrum, m. *a place in Hispania Baetica.* Hence, **Iliturgitāni** -ōrum, m. *the inhabitants of Iliturgi.*

illā (illic), adv. 1 (abl. of ille, sc. parte), *at that place,* Plaut., Tac.; 2 (dat. illai, sc. parti), *to that place,* Ov.

illăbĕfactus -a -um (in and labefacio), *unshaken, firm,* Ov.

illābor -lapsus, 3. dep. (in and labor), *to fall, glide, fall into, fall down;* 1, lit., si fractus illabatur orbis, Hor.; in stomacho illabuntur ea quae accepta sunt ore, Cic.; 2, transf., pernicies illapsa civium in animos, Cic.

illăbōro, 1. (in and laboro), *to work upon, labour at;* domibus, *in building houses,* Tac.

illāc, adv. (illic). **I.** (lit. abl.), *there, at this place;* hac atque illac, hac illac, Ter. **II.** (lit. dat.), *to that place;* transf., illac facere, *to stand on that side, belong to that party,* Cic.

illăcessītus -a -um (in and lacesso), *unattacked, unprovoked,* Tac.

illăcrĭmābilis -e (in and lacrimabilis), 1, *unwept;* omnes illacrimabiles urgentur, Hor.; 2, *not to be moved by tears, pitiless;* Pluto, Hor.

illăcrĭmo, 1. (in and lacrimo), *to weep, bewail;* with dat., errori, Liv.; absol., ebur maestum illacrimat templis, Verg.

illăcrĭmor, 1. dep. (in and lacrimor), *to weep over, bewail;* morti, Cic.

illaesus -a -um (in and laedo), *unhurt, uninjured,* Ov.

illaetābĭlis -e (in and laetabilis), *sorrowful, gloomy, cheerless;* ora, Verg.

illăquĕo (in and laqueo), *to entrap, ensnare, entangle;* fig., illaqueatus omnium legum periculis, Cic.

illaudātus -a -um (in and laudatus), *unpraised, obscure;* Busiris, Verg.

illautus = illotus (q.v.).

ille, illa, illud, genit. illīus, demonstr. pron. (perhaps for is-le, from is), *that;* a, ista beatitas cur aut in solem *illum* aut in *hunc* mundum cadere non potest, Cic.; of time, qui illorum temporum historiam reliquerunt, Cic.; b, *that glorious* or *notorious;* ille Epaminondas, Cic.; illa Medea, Cic.; hic ille, *this glorious,* etc.; hic nunc ille annus egregius, Cic.; c, ille quidem, *he indeed,* Cic.; non ille . . . sed hic, Cic.; d, referring to and preparing for what comes after, illud perlibenter audivi te esse, etc., Cic.; e, hic et (atque) ille, *the one and the other,* Hor.; ille aut (vel) ille, *this* or *that,* Cic.

illĕcĕbra -ae, f. (illicio), 1, *an allurement; enticement, attraction, charm;* voluptas est illecebra turpitudinis, Cic.; 2, meton., *an enticer, a decoy-bird,* Plaut.

1. **illectus** -a -um (in and lectus, from lego), *unread,* Ov.

2. **illectus** -ūs (illicio), m. *seduction, allurement,* Plaut.

3. **illectus** -a -um, partic. of illicio.

illĕpĭdē, adv. (illepidus), *ungracefully, inelegantly,* Plaut.

illĕpĭdus -a -um (in and lepidus), *ungraceful, inelegant, rude, unmannerly;* parens avarus, illepidus, in liberos difficilis, Cic.

1. **illex** -licis (illicio), *alluring;* subst., f. *a decoy-bird,* Plaut.

2. **illex** -lēgis (in and lex), *lawless,* Plaut.

illībātus -a -um (in and libo), *undiminished, uncurtailed, unimpaired;* divitiae, Cic.

illībĕrālis -e (in and liberalis), 1, *unworthy of a free man, ignoble;* te in me illiberalem putabit, Cic.; 2, transf., *low, mean;* quaestus, Cic.; genus jocandi, Cic.

illībĕrālĭtas -ātis, f. (illiberalis), *illiberality, stinginess, meanness;* illiberalitatis avaritiaeque suspicio, Cic.

illībĕrālĭtĕr (illiberalis), 1, *ignobly, meanly;* patris diligentiā non illiberaliter institutus, Cic.; 2, *in a sordid, niggardly manner;* facere, Cic.

1. **illic,** illaec, illŭc, pron. demonstr. (ille -ce), *that there;* in interrogative sentences, illiccine, Plaut.; illanccine, Ter.

2. **illīc,** adv. (1. illic), 1, *there, at that place,* Caes.; 2, transf., a, *on that side,* Tac.; b, *in that case,* Liv.

illĭcĭo -lexi -lectum, 3. (in and *lacio), *to entice, seduce, allure, decoy, inveigle;* conjugem in stuprum, Cic.; aliquem ad bellum, Sall.; with ut and the subj., Liv.

illĭcĭtātor -ōris, m. *a sham bidder at an auction, a puffer,* Cic.

illĭcĭtus -a -um (in and licitus), *not allowed, illicit, illegal;* exactiones, Tac.

illĭco (īlico), adv. (in loco), 1, *on the spot, in that very place,* Ter.; 2, transf., *on the spot, immediately,* Cic.

illīdo -lisi -lisum, 3. (in and laedo), 1, *to strike, knock, beat, dash against;* lateri algam, Verg.; saxeam pilam vadis, Verg.; illidere dentem, Hor.; 2, *to shatter, crush, dash to pieces;* serpens illisa morietur, Cic.

illĭgo, 1. (in and ligo), *to bind, tie, fasten.* **I. A.** aratra juvencis, Hor.; Mettium in currus, Liv. **B.** Transf., *to bind, to connect with oneself, bind to oneself;* aliquem pignoribus, Cic. **II. A.** *to fasten, attach;* a, lit., crustas in aureis poculis, Cic.; b, transf., sententiam verbis, Cic. **B.** *to entangle, impede;* a, lit., illigatur praedā, Tac.; b, transf., angustis et concisis disputationibus illigati, Cic.

illim, adv. = illinc, *from there, from that place,* Cic.

illīmis -e (in and limus), *free from mud, clear;* fons, Ov.

illinc, adv. (illim -ce). **I.** *from that place,* fugit illinc, Cic. **II.** Transf., *from that side, from that person, thence,* Cic.

illĭno lēvi -litum, 3 (in and lino), *to smear, daub, spread over*, 1, aurum vestibus illitum, Hor., quodcumque semel chartis illeverit, *has written, scribbled*, Hor., 2, *to cover with*, pocula ceris, Ov., fig., color venustatis non fuco illitus, Cic.

illĭquĕfactus -a -um (in and liquefacio), *molten, liquefied*, Cic.

illītĕrātus -a -um (in and literatus), *unlearned, ignorant, illiterate*, a, of persons, vir non illiteratus, Cic., b, of things, multa . . nec illiterata videantur, Cic.

illō, adv. (orig. illoi, dat. of ille), 1, *to that place, thither*, Cic., 2, transf., *to that matter or thing*, haec omnia eodem illo pertinere, Caes.

illōc, adv. (1. illic), *thither*, Ter.

illōtus (illautus, illūtus) -a -um (in and lotus, or lautus, from lavo), 1, *unwashed, unclean, impure*, Hor., 2, *not washed off*, sudor, Verg.

illūc, adv. (ille). **I.** Of space, *thither, to that place*. **A.** Lit., huc atque illuc, Cic. **B.** Transf., *to that matter*, or *person;* ut illuc revertar, Cic. **II.** Of time, *up to that time*, Tac.

illūcesco (illūcisco) -luxi, 3 (in and lucesco or lucisco). **I.** *to become light, begin to shine*. **A.** Lit., quum tertio die sol illuxisset, Cic., illucescet aliquando ille dies, Cic. **B.** Transf., *to show oneself, appear*, quum in tenebris vox consulis illuxerit, Cic. **II.** Impers., illucescit, *it grows light, is daylight*, ubi illuxit, Liv.

illūdo -lūsi -lūsum, 3 (in and ludo). **I.** *to play with, sport with;* chartis, *to play with paper*, i.e. *amuse oneself with writing*, Hor. **II.** In a bad sense, 1, *to mock at, laugh at, make a mock of;* a, with dat., capto, Verg., alicuius dignitati, Cic., rebus humanis, Hor., b, with the acc., miseros illudi nolunt, Cic.; eam artem, Cic., absol., illudens, *ironically, in ridicule*, Cic., 2, *to deceive*, Cretenses omnes, Nep., illusi pedes, *staggering*, Hor., 3, *to destroy, ruin, disgrace*, cui (frondi) silvestres uri illudunt, Verg.

illūmĭnātē, adv. (illumino), *luminously, clearly*, dicere, Cic.

illūmĭno, 1 (in and lumino). **A.** *to make light, enlighten, illuminate*, Cic., luna illuminata a sole, Cic. **B.** Of discourse, *to make clear, set off, adorn*, orationem sententiis, Cic.

illūsio -ōnis, f. (illudo), *irony*, as a rhetorical figure, Cic.

illustris -e (in and lustro), *light, full of light, bright, brilliant*. **A.** Lit., stella, lumen, locus, Cic. **B.** Transf., a, *clear, plain, evident*, oratio, res, Cic., b, *distinguished, celebrated, illustrious, famous, renowned*, illustriori loco natus, Caes., nomen illustrius, Cic., c, *remarkable*, res illustrior, Caes.

illustrĭus, adv. compar. and **illustrissĭmē**, adv. superl. (illustris), *more clearly, more distinctly*, dicere, Cic.

illustro, 1 (illustris), *to enlighten, make light*. **I.** Lit., sol cuncta suā luce illustrat, Cic. **II.** Transf., 1, *to bring to light, make known*, consilia, Cic., 2, *to explain, illustrate, elucidate*, jus obscurum, Cic., 3, *to adorn*, a, of speech, orationem sententiis, Cic., b, *to make illustrious, celebrate, do honour to;* aliquem laudibus, Cic.; aliquid Musā, Hor.

illŭvies -ēi, f. (illuo), a, *an inundation, flood*, Tac.; b, *dirt, mud;* morbo illuvieque peresus, Verg.

Illyrii -ōrum, m. *a people on the Adriatic Sea, in the modern Dalmatia and Albania*. Hence 1, adj., **Illȳrĭus** -a -um, *Illyrian;* 2, subst., **Illȳrĭa** -ae, f. *Illyria*, 3, **Illȳrĭcus** -a -um, *Illyrian*, subst., **Illȳrĭcum** -i, n. *Illyria*. 4, **Illȳris** -idis, f. *Illyrian*, subst., *Illyria*, Ov.

Ilōtae -ārum = Hilotae (q.v.).

Ĭlus -i, m. (Ἶλος), 1, *son of Tros, father of Laomedon, builder of Troy*, 2, = *Iulus*.

Ilva -ae, f. *an island to the west of Etruria*, now *Elba*.

Imăchăra -ae, f. *town on the east of Sicily*, now *Maccara*. Adj., **Imăchărensis** -e, *belonging to Imachara*.

im = **eum.**

ĭmāgĭnārĭus -a -um (imago), *imaginary*, fasces, Liv.

ĭmāgĭnātĭo -ōnis, f. (imaginor), *imagination, fancy*, provincias Orientis secretis imaginationibus agitare, Tac.

ĭmāgĭnor, 1. dep. (imago), *to imagine, conceive, picture to oneself*, pavorem, Tac.

ĭmāgo -inis, f. (root IM, whence also imitor and sim. ilis). **I.** Objective. **A.** Lit., 1, a, gen., *an image, representation, portrait, figure, bust, statue*, ficta, *a statue*, Cic., picta, *painted bust*, Cic.; *a portrait engraved on a seal-ring*, est signum notum, imago avi tui, Cic., b, esp., imagines (majorum), *waxen figures, portraits of ancestors* who had held curule offices, placed in the atria of Roman houses, and carried in funeral processions, Cic., 2, *a likeness, counterfeit:* imago animi et corporis tui, filius tuus, Cic., imago animi vultus est, Cic., 3, a, *the shade or ghost of a dead man*, imagines mortuorum, Cic., b, *a dream*, somni, noctis, *a dream*, Ov., c, in the Epicurean philosophy, *the mental idea* or *representation of a real object*, Cic., 4, *an echo*, laus bonorum virtuti resonat tamquam imago, Cic., 5, in discourse, *a metaphor, simile, image*, hac ego si compellor imagine, Hor. **B.** Transf., *the appearance, pretence*, pacis, Tac., decoris, Liv., imaginem reipublicae nullam reliquerunt, *they left no shadow or trace of the republic*, Cic. **II.** Subjective, 1, *the appearance*, imago venientis Turni, Verg., 2, *the image, idea, conception, mental representation of any object or event*, tantae caedis, Ov.; tantae pietatis, Verg.

imbēcillis, v. imbecillus.

imbēcillĭtas -ātis, f. (imbecillus), *weakness, imbecility, feebleness*. **A.** Lit., corporis, Cic. **B.** Transf., consilii, Cic., animi, Caes.

imbēcillĭus, adv. compar. (imbecillus), *somewhat weakly, feebly*, assentiri, Cic.

imbēcillus -a -um, *weak, feeble*. **A.** Lit., filius, Cic., imbecillior valetudine, Cic. **B.** Transf., a, regnum, Sall., b, of the mind, *weak, without energy*, animus, Cic., accusator, Cic.

imbellis -e (in and bellum). **I.** *unwarlike* 1, multitudo, Liv., telum, *feeble*, Verg., dii, *Venus and Cupid*, Ov., 2, *cowardly* res, *cowardly behaviour*, Cic. **II.** *without war, peaceful, quiet*, annus, Liv.

imber -bris, m. (ὄμβρος), *a shower or storm of rain, pelting rain* (pluvia, *gentle, fertilising rain*). **I.** Lit., magnus, maximus, Cic., so also lactis, sanguinis, lapidum, Cic. **II.** Transf., **A** *a storm, rain-cloud*, super caput astitit imber, Verg. **B.** *water or any fluid*, fluminis imber, Ov., tortus, *hail*, Verg. **C.** Of a shower of missiles, ferreus ingruit imber, Verg.

imberbis -e and **imberbus** -a -um (in and barba), *beardless*, Cic.

imbĭbo -bibi, 3. (in and bibo), 1, *to drink in, conceive*, de vobis malam opinionem animo, Cic., 2, *to resolve, to determine upon any thing;* memor eius quod initio consulatus imbiberat, Liv.

imbrex -ĭcis, c. (imber), *a hollow tile* (to keep the rain off), *used in roofing*, Verg.

imbrĭfer -fĕra -fĕrum (imber and fero), *rain-bringing;* ver, Verg.; auster, Ov.

Imbros and **Imbrus** -i, f. (Ἴμβρος), *an island in the Aegean Sea, near to Lemnos*, now *Embro.* Hence adj., **Imbrĭus** -a -um, *Imbrian.*

imbŭo -ŭi -ūtum, 3. (in and root BU, connected with BI in bibo), *to moisten, wet, steep, saturate.* **I.** Lit., vestem sanguine, Ov.; imbuti sanguine gladii, Cic. **II.** Transf., **A.** *to fill, stain, taint;* imbutus maculā sceleris, Cic.; imbutus superstitione, Cic. **B.** *to accustom, inure, initiate, instruct;* pectora religione, Cic.; imbutus cognitionibus verborum, Cic.; with ad and the acc., ad quam legem non instituti sed imbuti sumus, Cic. **C.** Poet., *to begin, make an essay of;* imbue opus tuum, Ov.

ĭmĭtābĭlis -e (imitor), *that can be imitated, imitable;* orationis subtilitas, Cic.

ĭmĭtāmen -ĭnis, n. (imitor), *an imitation, representation; image,* Ov.

ĭmĭtāmentum -i, n. (imitor), *an imitating, imitation;* lacrimae vel dolorum imitamenta, Tac.

ĭmĭtātĭo -ōnis, f. (imitor), *an imitation;* virtutis, Cic.

ĭmĭtātor -ōris, m. (imitor), *an imitator;* principum, Cic.

ĭmĭtātrix -īcis, f. (imitator), *she that imitates;* imitatrix boni, voluptas, Cic.

ĭmĭtor, 1. dep. (root IM, whence also imago). **I.** *to imitate, copy.* **A.** Lit., amictum alicuius aut statum aut motum, Cic.; praeclarum factum, Cic.; of things, *to be like, to resemble;* humor potest imitari sudorem, Cic. **B.** Transf., poet., *to replace,* or *supply by something similar;* pocula vitea acidis sorbis, Verg. **II.** *to represent, depict, express;* aliquid penicillo, Cic.; capillos aere, Hor.

immădesco -mădŭi, 3. (in and madesco), *to become moist* or *wet;* lacrimis immaduisse genas, Ov.

immānĕ, adv. (immanis), *frightfully, dreadfully, savagely;* leo immane hians, Verg.

immānis -e (in and root MA, whence also manus (= bonus), Manes, etc.). **I.** *enormous, vast, immense, monstrous;* corporum magnitudo, Caes.; ingens immanisque praeda, Cic.; antrum, Verg.; immane quantum discrepat, *differs to an enormous extent,* Hor. **II.** Transf., *frightful, savage, horrible, inhuman, fierce;* hostis gens, Cic.; belua, Cic.; flumen, Verg.

immānĭtas -ātis, f. (immanis), *savageness, fierceness, inhumanity, cruelty, barbarity, frightfulness;* vitiorum, facinoris, Cic.; meton., in hac tanta immanitate versari, *in the midst of these inhuman persons,* Cic.

immansuētus -a -um (in and mansuetus), *untamed, unrestrained, wild;* gens, Cic.

immātūrĭtas -ātis, f. (immaturus), *immaturity,* hence = *untimely haste,* Cic.

immātūrus -a -um (in -maturus), **1,** lit., *unripe, immature,* Plin.; **2,** transf., *untimely;* mors, Cic.; interitus C. Gracchi, Cic.; si filius immaturus obiisset, Hor.

immĕdĭcābĭlis -e (in and medicabilis), *that cannot be healed;* vulnus, Ov.; telum, *the wound from which cannot be healed,* Verg.

immĕmor -mŏris (in and memor), *unmindful, forgetful;* with genit., mandati, Cic.; nec Romanarum rerum immemor, *familiar with Roman history,* Cic.; libertatis, Liv.; poet., equus immemor herbae, *paying no heed to,* Verg.; absol., ingenium, Cic.

immĕmŏrābĭlis -e (in and memorabilis), **1,** *indescribable;* spatium, Lucr.; versus, *unworthy of representation,* Plaut.; **2,** *silent, uncommunicative,* Plaut.

immĕmŏrātus -a -um (in and memoro), *not mentioned, not narrated.* Plur. subst., **immĕmŏrāta** -ōrum, n. *new things, things not yet related,* Hor.

immensĭtas -ātis, f. (immensus), *immeasurableness, immensity;* latitudinum, altitudinum, Cic.

immensus -a -um (in and metior), *immeasurable, immense, vast, boundless;* magnitudo regionum, Cic.; mare, Cic. Subst., **immensum** -i, n. *immense size, immeasurable space, immensity;* altitudinis, *immeasurable depth,* Liv.; in immensum, *to an immense height,* Sall.; ad immensum, *to a vast extent;* augere, Liv.; immensum est dicere, *it is an endless task to tell,* Ov.; adv., immensum, *enormously;* crescere, Ov.

immĕrens -entis (in and mereo), *not deserving, innocent,* Ov.

immergo -mersi -mersum, 3. (in and mergo), **1,** lit., *to dip into, plunge into, immerse;* manus in aquam, Plin.; aliquem undā, Verg.; immersus in flumen, Cic.; **2,** transf., immergere se in consuetudinem alicuius, *to insinuate oneself into,* Cic.

immĕrĭto, v. immeritus.

immĕrĭtus -a -um (in and mereo), **1,** act., *not deserving* or *meriting, innocent;* gens, Verg.; mori, *that has not deserved to die,* Hor.; **2,** pass., *undeserved, unmerited;* laudes haud immeritae, Liv. **immĕrĭto,** adv. *undeservedly,* Cic.

immersābĭlis -e (in and merso), *that cannot be sunk;* adversis rerum immersabilis undis, *not to be overwhelmed by,* Hor.

immētātus -a -um (in and meto), *unmeasured;* jugera, Hor.

immĭgro, 1. (in and migro). **A.** Lit., *to remove into;* in domum et in paternos hortos, Cic. **B.** Transf., ut ea (translata) verba non irruisse in alienum locum, sed immigrasse in suum diceres, *to have fallen naturally into their place,* Cic.

immĭnĕo, 2. (in and mineo), *to hang, bend, incline over, project over, overhang.* **I.** Lit., quercus ingens arbor praetorio imminebat, Liv.; populus antro imminet, Verg.; collis urbi imminet, Verg.; carcer imminens foro, Liv.; lunā imminente, *by the light of the moon,* Hor. **II.** Transf., **A. a,** of evils, *to hang over threateningly, be imminent, threaten;* mors quae quotidie imminet, Cic.; imminentium nescius, *ignorant of the immediate future,* Tac.; **b,** *to be near with hostile intent, threaten;* castra Romana Carthaginis portis immineant, Liv.; videt hostes imminere, Caes.; gestus imminens, *threatening demeanour,* Cic. **B. a,** *to threaten, to be on the point of attacking;* imminent duo reges toti Asiae, Cic.; **b,** *to be on the watch for, to look out for;* in victoriam, Liv.; ad caedem, Cic.

immĭnŭo -ŭi -ūtum, 3. (in and minuo), *to lessen, diminish.* **I.** Gen., **A.** Lit., copias, Cic.; verbum imminutum, *abbreviated,* Cic. **B.** Transf., *to lessen, curtail;* imminuitur aliquid de voluptate, Cic. **II. A.** *to weaken;* corpus otio, animum libidinibus, Tac. **B.** Transf., *to weaken, destroy, injure;* majestatem, Liv.; auctoritatem, Cic.

immĭnūtĭo -ōnis, f. (imminuo), *a lessening, diminishing, weakening;* **1,** corporis, Cic.; **2,** transf., **a,** dignitatis, Cic.; **b,** a rhet. figure = λιτότης (e.g., non minime for maxime), Cic.

immiscĕo -miscŭi -mixtum or -mistum, 3. (in and misceo), *to mix in, mingle with, inter-*

mix I. Lit., a, of things, nives caelo prope immixtae, Liv, poet., immiscent manus manibus, *they fight hand to hand*, Verg, b, of persons, togati immisti turbae militum, Liv, se mediis armis, Verg II. Transf, *to join with, unite together*, a, of things, vota timori, Verg, sortem regni cum rebus Romanis, Liv; b, of persons, se colloquiis montanorum, Liv

immĭsĕrābĭlĭs e (in and miserabilis), *unlamented, unpitied*, Hor

immĭsĕrĭcors -cordis (in and misericors), *unmerciful*, Cic

immissĭo ōnis, f (immitto), *a letting grow*, sarmentorum, Cic

immītis -e (in and mitis), *sour, harsh* I. Lit, uva, Hor II. Transf, *rough, harsh, cruel, wild, pitiless, inexorable, stern*, tyrannus, Verg, immites oculi, Ov, lupus immitis, Ov, ara, *on which human sacrifices were offered*, Ov.

immitto -misi -missum, 3 (in and mitto) I. *to send in, cause* or *allow to go in* A. Lit, 1, servos ad spoliandum fanum, Cic, corpus in undam, Ov naves pice completas in classem Pompeianam, *let loose against*, Caes, 2, esp, a, milit t t, *to despatch, let go*, equitatum, Caes, se in hostes, *to attack*, Cic, b, *to discharge, shoot*, tela in aliquem, Caes, c, *to sink into, let into*, tigna machinationibus in flumen, Caes, d, *to conduct, convey*, aquam canalibus, Caes, e, *to engraft*, feraces plantas, Verg, f, *to work in*, lentum filis aurum, Ov, g, legal t t., *to put into possession of property*, tu praetor in mea bona quos voles immittes? Cic B. Transf, 1, hic corrector in eo ipso loco, quo reprehendit, immittit imprudens ipse senarium, *lets slip in*, Cic, 2, esp, a, *to send, incite*, immissus in rempublicam, Cic, b, *to cause*, Teucris fugam atrumque timorem, Verg II. A. *to let free*, juga, Verg; frena, Verg, habenas classi, *to crowd on sail*, Verg B. *to let grow*; palmes laxis immissus habenis, Verg, capilli, Ov

immissus a -um (immitto), *long, uncut*, barba, Verg

immixtus or **immistus**, v immisceo

immō (**īmō**), adv (for ipsimo), *yea, yes*, or *nay rather*, often with etiam, vero, enimvero, magis, potius, etc, vivit? immo in senatum venit, *nay more, he comes into the senate*, Cic, causa non bona est? immo optima, *yea, the very best*, Cic., familiarem? immo alienissimum, *nay, but rather*, Cic; non necesse esse? immo prorsus ita censeo, *nay, on the contrary*, Cic

immōbĭlĭs -e (in and mobilis), 1, *immovable*, terra, Cic; 2, transf, precibus, *inexorable*, Tac, Ausonia, *not agitated by war*, Verg

immŏdĕrātē, adv (immoderatus), 1, *without rule* or *measure*, moveri immoderate et fortuito, Cic; 2, *immoderately, intemperately*, vivere, Cic

immŏdĕrātĭo ōnis, f (immoderatus), *want of moderation, excess, intemperance*, efferri immoderatione verborum, Cic

immŏdĕrātus -a -um (in and moderatus), 1, *without measure, immeasurable, endless*, cursus, Cic, 2, transf, *immoderate, intemperate, unbridled, unrestrained*, libertas, Cic, oratio, Cic

immŏdestē, adv (immodestus), *immoderately, unbecomingly*, immodice immodesteque gloriari Hannibale victo a se, Liv

immŏdestĭa -ae, f (immodestus), 1, *intemperate conduct*, publicanorum, Tac, 2, *insubordination*, militum vestrorum, Nep

immŏdestus -a um (in and modestus), *intemperate, unbridled*, genus jocandi, Cic,

immŏdĭcē, adv (immodicus), *immoderately, intemperately*, hac potestate immodice ac superbe usum esse, Liv

immŏdĭcus a -um (in and modicus), *immoderate, excessive*, 1, lit, frigus, Ov, 2, transf, *unrestrained, unbridled*, a, of persons, with in and the abl in augendo numero, Liv, with abl, immodicus lingua, Liv, with genit, laetitiae, Tac, b, of things, imperia, Liv, cupido, Liv

immŏdŭlātus -a um (in and modulatus), *inharmonious*, Hor

immoenis, v immunis

immŏlātĭo -ōnis, f (immolo), *a sacrificing, immolation*, in ipso immolationis tempore, Cic

immŏlātor -ōris, m (immolo), *a sacrificer*, Cic

immōlĭtus -a -um (in and molior), *built up, erected*, quae in loca publica inaedificata immolitave privati habebant, Liv

immŏlo, 1 (in and molo), orig, *to sprinkle with sacred meal*, hence, *to sacrifice, immolate* A. Lit, bovem Dianae, vitulum Musis, Cic, with abl of the victim Jovi singulis bubus, Liv, absol in Capitolio, Liv B. Transf, *to devote to death, slay*, aliquem, Verg

immŏrior -mortŭus, 3 dep (in and morior), *to die in or upon*, sorori, *on his sister's body*, Ov, Euxinis aquis, Ov, transf, studiis, *to work oneself to death over*, Hor

immŏror, 1 (in and moror), *to stay, remain, linger in a place*, Plin

immorsus -a -um (in and mordeo) I. *bitten into, bitten*, immorso collo, Prop II. Transf, *macerated* (by sharp, biting food), stomachus, Hor

immortālis e (in and mortalis), *deathless, immortal* A. Lit., dii, Cic, subst, **immortālis** -is, m *an immortal*, Cic B. Transf, a, *everlasting, imperishable*, memoria et gloria, Cic, amicitiae immortales, inimicitiae mortales esse debent, Liv, b, *happy beyond measure, divinely blessed* Prop

immortālĭtas -ātis, f (immortalis), *immortality*, 1, lit, animorum, Cic; 2, transf, a, *everlasting renown, an immortality of fame*, gloriae, Cic, immortalitati commendare or tradere, *to make immortal*, Cic, b, *the highest happiness*, Ter

immortālĭtĕr, adv (immortalis), *infinitely*; gaudeo, Cic

immōtus a -um (in and motus), *unmoved, motionless* I. Lit, a, of things, arbores, *undisturbed*, Liv, dies, *calm, windless*, Tac with ab and the abl, portus ab accessu ventorum immotus, Verg, b, of persons, stat gravis Entellus nisuque immotus eodem, Verg, esp of soldiers in battle, adversus incitatas turmas stetit immota Samnitium acies, Liv II. Transf, a, *unchanged, unbroken*, pax, Tac; b, *fixed, firm, steadfast*, mens, fata, Verg

immūgĭo, 4 (in and mugio), *to bellow, roar, resound in*; immugiit Aetna cavernis, Verg

immulgĕo, 2 (in and mulgeo), *to milk into*, teneris immulgens ubera labris, Verg

immundĭtĭa -ae, f (immundus), *uncleanness, impurity*, Plaut

immundus a -um (in and 1 mundus) *unclean, impure, foul*, humus, Cic, canis, Hor, transf, dicta, Hor

immūnĭo, 4 (in and munio), *to fortify*, Tac

immūnis e (in and munis, from root MUN, whence also munus, munia), *free, exempt*, 1, with reference to the state, ager, *tax-free*, Cic, militia, *exempt from military service*, Liv, with genit., portoriorum, Liv.; immunes militarium operum, Liv.; **2,** gen., **a,** *free from work:* with genit., immunis operum, Ov.; **b,** *contributing nothing;* fucus, Verg.; non ego te meis immunem meditor tingere poculis, Hor.; quem scis immunem Cynarae placuisse rapaci, *without gifts,* Hor.; **c,** *inactive,* Cic.; **d,** *free from;* with genit., mali, Ov.; absol., manus, *stainless,* Hor.

immūnĭtas -ātis, f. (immunis), **1,** *exemption from public offices or burdens;* with genit., omnium rerum, Caes.; plur., immunitates dare, Cic.; **2,** *immunity, exemption;* magni muneris, Cic.

immūnītus -a -um (in and munitus), **1,** *unfortified;* oppida castellaque, Liv.; **2,** *unpaved;* via, Cic.

immurmŭro, 1. (in and murmuro), *to murmur in* or *at;* silvis immurmurat Auster, Verg.

immūtābĭlis -e (in and mutabilis), *immutable, unchangeable;* aeternitas, Cic.

immūtābĭlĭtas -ātis, f. (immutabilis), *immutability,* Cic.

immūtātĭo -ōnis, f. (immuto), **1,** *a change, alteration;* ordinis, Cic.; **2,** *metonymy,* Cic.

1. **immūtātus** -a -um (in and muto), *unchanged,* Cic.

2. **immūtātus** -a -um, partic. of immuto.

immūto, 1. (in and muto), **1,** *to change, alter;* ordinem verborum, Cic.; aliquid de institutis priorum, Cic.; of persons, prosperis rebus immutari, Cic.; **2, a,** in rhetoric, *to use by way of metonymy:* Ennius pro Afris immutat Africam, Cic.; **b,** *to use allegorically;* immutata oratio, *allegory,* Cic.

īmo = immo (q.v.).

impācātus -a -um (in and pacatus), *warlike, disinclined to peace, restless,* Verg.

impallesco, -pallŭi, 3. (in and pallesco), *to grow pale over;* nocturnis chartis, Pers.

impar -păris (in and par), **1, a,** *unequal, uneven;* par et impar ludere, *to play at odd and even,* Hor.; modi impares, *hexameter and pentameter,* Ov.; si toga dissidet impar, *sits awry,* Hor.; numeri impares an aequales, Cic.; **b,** transf., *different,* Cic.; **2, a,** *unequal in strength, not a match for;* impar congressus Achilli, Verg.; certamen, Ov.; **b,** *of unequal birth, of inferior birth;* maternum genus impar, Tac. (abl. sing. gen. impari, but impare, Verg. Ecl. 8. 75).

impărātus -a -um (in and paratus), *unprepared;* quum a militibus, tum a pecunia, *unprovided with,* Cic.; inermis atque imparatus, Caes.

impărĭtĕr, adv. (impar), *unevenly, unequally,* Hor.

impartĭo, impartĭor = impertio, impertior (q.v.).

impastus -a -um (in and pasco), *unfed, hungry;* leo, Verg.

impătĭbĭlis (impĕtĭbĭlis) -e (in and patibilis), *intolerable, insufferable;* dolor, Cic.

impătĭens -entis (in and patiens), *unable to bear* or *to endure, impatient;* **a,** of persons, laborum, Ov.; vulneris, Verg.; solis, Tac.; irae, *wrathful,* Tac.; **b,** applied to inanimate objects, cera impatiens caloris, Ov.; absol., impatiens animus, Ov.

impătĭentĕr adv. (impatiens), *impatiently, unwillingly,* Tac.

impătĭentĭa -ae f. (impatiens), *impatience, inability to endure;* silentii impatientiam, Tac.

impăvĭdē, adv. (impavidus), *fearlessly, undauntedly,* Liv.

impăvĭdus -a -um (in and pavidus), *fearless, courageous, undaunted;* vir, Hor.; pectora, Liv.

impĕdīmentum -i, n. (impedio). **I.** *a hindrance, impediment;* impedimentum alicui facere, inferre, Cic.; afferre, Tac.; esse impedimenti loco, or impedimento, Caes.; Gallis magno ad pugnam erat impedimento quod, etc., Caes. **II.** Esp., in plur., *the heavy baggage of an army* or *traveller, carried in waggons* or *on beasts of burden* (sarcina, *the soldier's knapsack*); impedimenta et sarcinas invadere, Liv.; impedimenta exspectanda sunt quae Anagniā veniunt, Cic.

impĕdĭo -īvi and -ĭi -ītum, 4. (in and PED, ΠΕΔ, whence also ped-s (pes), ποδ-ς (πούς), πεδ -άω). **I.** *to entangle, ensnare.* **A.** Lit. crura visceribus; esp., *to render a place impassable;* saltum munitionibus, Liv. **B.** Transf., **1,** *to embarrass, involve,* Tac.; mentem dolore, Cic.; **2,** *to hinder, impede, prevent, obstruct;* aliquem, Cic.; iter, Liv.; with ab and the abl., se a suo munere non impedit, Cic.; with abl., ne me dicendo impediat, Cic.; non or nihil impedire, foll. by quominus and the subj., Cic.; impedire, foll. by ne and the subj., Cic.; aliquid aliquem impedit, with infin., Cic.; with ad and the acc. gerund, Caes.; with in and the abl., Caes. **II.** *to surround, wrap round;* caput myrto, Hor.; equos frenis, *to bridle,* Ov.

impĕdītĭo -ōnis, f. (impedio), *a hindering, hindrance;* animus liber omni impeditione curarum, Cic.

impĕdītus -a -um (impedio), *hindered, impeded.* **I.** Lit., **a,** esp. as milit. t. t., *hindered by baggage, not ready for battle* (opp. expeditus); miles, Caes.; **b,** of places, *impassable, difficult of access;* silva, Caes. **II.** Transf., **a,** *hindered, encumbered;* solutio, Cic.; impeditis animis, *busy,* Caes.; **b,** *troublesome;* impeditus ancillarum puerorumque comitatus, Cic.; **c,** *embarrassed;* tempora reipublicae, Cic.

impello -pŭli -pulsum, 3. (in and pello). **I.** *to strike, strike upon;* chordas, Ov.; maternas impulit aures luctus Aristaei, Verg. **II.** *to push forward.* **A.** *to set in motion, drive on;* **1,** lit., navem remis, Verg.; aliquem in fugam, Cic.; **2,** transf., **a,** aliquem in hunc casum, Cic.; **b,** *to incite, urge on, impel;* aliquem ad scelus, Cic.; aliquem ut, etc., Cic.; aliquem with infin., Liv. **B.** *to throw to the ground;* **1,** esp. as milit. t. t., *to make to yield, to rout;* hostes, Liv.; **2,** transf., aliquem praecipitantem, *to give a push to some one falling, to complete a person's ruin,* Cic.

impendĕo, 2. (in and pendeo), *to hang over, overhang.* **A.** Lit., cervicibus, Cic.; saxum impendere Tantalo, Cic. **B.** Transf., *to impend* or *hang over menacingly, to threaten, be close at hand;* in me terrores impendent, Cic.; omnibus terror impendet, Cic.; magnum etiam bellum impendet a Parthis, Cic.

impendĭō, adv. (impendium), *much, very much;* with comparatives, magis, *far more,* Cic.

impendĭum -ii, n. (impendo), **1,** *expense, expenditure, outlay, cost;* impendio publico, *at the public expense,* Liv.; sine impendio, Cic.; **2,** *interest of money,* Cic.

impendo -pendi -pensum, 3. (in and pendo), *to expend, lay out;* **1,** lit., pecuniam in aliquam rem, Cic.; **2,** transf., ad incertum casum et eventum certus quotannis labor et certus sumptus impenditur, Cic.

impĕnĕtrābĭlis -e (in and penetrabilis), **1,** *impenetrable;* silex impenetrabilis ferro, Liv.; tegimen adversus ictus impenetrabile, Tac.; **2,** *unconquerable, invincible,* Tac.

impensa -ae, f. (impensus -a -um from

impendo), *expense, outlay, cost* 1, lit, impensam facere in aliquid, Cic, nullā impensā, Cic, 2, transf, applied to other than pecunia y outlay, cruoris, Ov; operum, Verg

impensē, adv (impensus) I. *at great cost,* Pers II. Transf, *urgently, eagerly, pressingly,* orare, Liv, nunc eo facio id impensius, Cic

impensus -a -um, p adj (from impendo), 1, lit, of price, *considerable, great*, impenso pretio, Cic, absol, impenso, *at a high price*, Hor, 2, transf, *strong, vehement*, voluntas erga aliquem, Liv, voluntas bonorum, Cic

impĕrātor ōris, m (impero), *a commander, leader* I Lit, A. Gen, populus est imperator omnium gentium, Cic, vitae, Sall B. *the commander-in-chief of an army,* Cic, hence, a title given to a general after a great success by the army and senate, Cic, added as a title to the name, e g Cn Pompeio Cn. F Magno imperatori, Cic II. Transf, A. name of Jupiter, Cic B. after Julius Caesar, a name of the Roman emperors, imperator Augustus, Suet, and absol, = *the Roman emperor,* Suet

impĕrātōrĭus -a -um (imperator) 1, *of or relating to a general*, nomen, Cic, jus, laus, labor, Cic, 2, *imperial*, uxor, Tac

impĕrātrix -icis f (imperator), *a female ruler* or *commander*, (sarcastically), *a general in petticoats,* Cic

imperceptus a -um (in and percipio), *unperceived, unknown*, fraus, Ov

impercussus -a -um (in and percutio), *not struck*, impercussos nocte movere pedes, *noiseless*, Ov.

imperdĭtus -a um (in and perdo), *not slain, undestroyed,* Verg

imperfectus -a -um (in and perficio) *incomplete, unfinished, imperfect*, verba, Ov, reliquum corpus imperfectum ac rude relinquere, Cic, neut. subst, imperfecto nec absoluto simile pulchrum esse nihil potest, Cic

imperfossus -a -um (in and perfodio), *unstabbed, unpierced*, ab omni ictu, Ov

impĕrĭōsus -a um (imperium), 1, *powerful, mighty, potent*, populus, Cic, virga, *the fasces,* Ov, sibi, *master of oneself*, Hor, 2, *masterful, imperious, tyrannical*, philosophus, Cic, cupiditas, Cic

impĕrītē, adv with compar and superl (imperitus), *unskilfully, ignorantly, clumsily*, imperite absurdeque fictum, Cic, quid potuit dici imperitius, Cic

impĕrītĭa -ae, f (imperitus), *want of skill and knowledge, inexperience, ignorance,* with subject genit, juvenum, Tac

impĕrĭto, 1 (intens of impero) I. Transit, *to command*, aequam rem imperito, Hor II. Intransit, *to have power over*; si Nero imperitaret, Tac, with dat., oppido, Liv

impĕrītus a -um (in and peritus), *unskilled, inexperienced, ignorant*, with genit, juris civilis non imperitus, Cic, absol, homines imperiti, Cic

impĕrĭum -ii, n (impero) I. *an order, command*, accipere, *to receive*, Liv, exsequi, *to execute*, Verg II. *the right* or *power of commanding, power, mastery, command* A. Gen, domesticum, Cic, animi imperio, corporis servitio magis utimur, *the mind as a master, the body as a slave*, Sall B Esp, 1, *the government* or *supreme authority in a state*, cadere sub P R imperium, Cic, sub P R imperium redigere, Cic, de imperio decertare, dimicare, Cic, of magistracies, in imperio esse, *to hold an office*, Cic., cum imperio esse, *to have unlimited power*, Cic., 2, *military power* or *command*, summum imperium, Cic, maritimum, *chief naval command*, Caes., imperia magistratusque, *civil and military honours*, Nep, alicui imperium prorogare, Cic C. Meton, 1, *the person or persons exercising authority*, erat plena lictorum et imperiorum provincia, Caes, imperia et potestates, *military and civil authorities*, Cic, 2, *the country governed, an empire*, finium imperii nostri propagatio, Cic

imperjūrātus -a -um (in and perjuro), *that by which no one has sworn or dares to swear falsely*, aquae, *the Styx*, Ov

impermissus a um (in and permitto), *forbidden* Hor

impĕro, 1 (in and paro), *to order, command* I. Gen, with acc, quae imperarentur facere dixerunt, Caes, partic subst, **impĕrātum** i, n *that which has been commanded*, imperatum, or imperata facere, Caes, with infin, flectere iter sociis, Verg pass infin, in easdem lautumias etiam ex ceteris oppidis deduci imperantur, Cic, with acc. and infin, esp with acc and pass infin, Cic, with ut and the subj, Cic, ne and the subj, Caes, with the subj alone, stringerent ferrum imperavit, Liv II. Esp, A. 1, *to rule over, govern, command*, Jugurtha omni Numidiae imperare parat, Sall, adesse ad imperandum, Cic, fig, sibi, Cic, cupiditatibus, Cic, 2, transf, of agriculture, *to work at* arvis, *compel to produce crops*, Verg B. *to order some action*, 1, of private life, cenam, Cic, 2, polit and milit t t, *to enjoin, prescribe, make a requisition for*, frumentum sibi in cellam, Cic, arma, Caes, (archaic form imperassit = imperaverit, Cic)

imperterrĭtus a -um (in and perterreo), *undaunted, fearless*, Verg

impertĭo (in-partio) -ivi and -ii itum (impertior, dep), 4 *to impart, communicate, share, bestow, give*, a, alicui de aliqua re or aliquid, indigentibus de re familiari, Cic, alicui civitatem, Cic, tempus cogitationi, Cic, b, aliquem aliquā re, Plaut, Ter, partic subst, **impertīta** -ōrum, n *favours, concessions*, Liv

imperturbātus a -um (in and perturbo), *undisturbed, calm*, os, Ov

impervĭus -a -um (in and pervius), *impassable, impervious*, iter, Tac, amnis, Ov

impes -pĕtis, m (in and peto) = impetus, *attack, onset, force*, impete vasto ferri, Ov

impĕtībĭlis -e = impatibilis (q v)

impĕtrābĭlis -e (impetro), 1, pass, *easy of attainment, attainable*, venia, Liv, pax, Liv, 2, act, *that obtains easily, successful*, orator, Plaut, transf, dies, *on which wishes have been fulfilled*, Plaut

impĕtrātĭo -ōnis, f (impetro), *an obtaining by asking*, Cic

impĕtrĭo, 4 (desider of impetro), *to seek to obtain a good omen, to obtain by favourable omens*, Cic

impĕtro, 1 (in and patro), *to get, obtain, accomplish, effect*, as a result of effort or entreaty, optatum, *to get one's wish*, Cic; alicui civitatem (*citizenship*) a Caesare, Cic, with ut and the subj, impetrabis a Caesare, ut tibi abesse liceat, Cic, absol, haec si tecum patria loquatur, nonne impetrare debeat? Cic

impĕtus -ūs, m (impes), *violent impulse, rapid motion, violence* I. quinqueremis praelata impetu, Liv II. *attack, assault, charge* A. Lit, 1, impetum facere in hostes, Caes, excipere, sustinere, ferre, *to receive an attack*, Caes, impetum dare, *to attack*, Liv, primo impetu pulsi, Caes, 2, of things, *force, vio-*

lence; in magno impetu maris atque aperto, Caes. **B.** Transf., **1**, of persons, **a**, *impulse, force;* impetus divinus, *inspiration*, Cic.; **b**, *inclination, violent desire;* imperii delendi, Cic.; **c**, *violence;* impetu magis quam consilio, Liv.; **2**, of things, tanti belli impetus, Cic.

impexus -a -um (in and pecto), **1**, *uncombed*, Verg.; **2**, transf., *rude, uncouth*, Tac.

impĭē, adv. (impius), *impiously, wickedly;* aliquid impie scelerateque committere, Cic.

impĭĕtas -ātis, f. (impius), *impiety, irreligion, ungodliness;* **a**, gen., Cic.; **b**, esp., *treason against the emperor*, Tac.

impĭger -gra -grum (in and piger), *unslothful, diligent, active;* in scribendo, Cic.; ad labores belli, Cic.; militiā, Liv.; with genit., militiae, Tac.; with infin., hostium vexare turmas, Hor.

impĭgrē, adv. (impiger), *actively, quickly;* impigre promittere auxilium, Liv.

impĭgrĭtas -ātis, f. (impiger), *activity, quickness*, Cic.

impingo -pēgi -pactum, 3. (in and pango), *to strike, beat, dash, drive, push against.* **I.** Lit., uncum alicui, Cic.; litoribus impactus, Tac. **II.** Transf., **A.** *to press upon one, to thrust into one's hand;* alicui calicem mulsi, Cic.; alicui epistolam, Cic. **B.** *to drive against;* agmina muris, Verg.; hostes in vallum, Tac.

impĭo, 1. (impius), *to render sinful, defile with sin;* se, *to sin*, Plaut.

impĭus -a -um (in and pius), *impious, godless, reprobate, undutiful, unpatriotic.* **I.** Lit., civis, Cic.; subst., nefarius impiusque, Cic. **II.** Transf., of things, bellum, Cic.; arma, Verg.

implăcābĭlis -e (in and placabilis), *implacable, irreconcileable;* alicui, Liv.; in aliquem, Cic.; of things, iracundiae, Cic.

implăcābĭlius, adv. in compar. (implacabilis), *more implacably;* implacabilius alicui irasci, Tac.

implăcātus -a -um (in and placo), *unappeased, unsatisfied;* Charybdis, Verg.

implăcĭdus -a -um (in and placidus), *rough, rude, harsh, savage, fierce;* genus, Hor.

implecto -plexi -plexum, 3. (in and plecto), *to interweave, weave*, or *twist with*, or *into;* **1**, lit., implexae crinibus angues Eumenides, *whose hair is interwoven with serpents*, Verg.; **2**, transf., vidua implexa luctu continuo, *plunged in*, Tac.

implĕo -plēvi -plētum, 2. (in and *pleo), *to fill, fill up, fill full.* **I. A.** Gen., **a**, lit., fossas, Liv.; with abl., gremium frustis, Cic.; mero pateram, Verg.; with genit., ollam denariorum, Cic.; with de, volumina de istis rebus, Cic.; **b**, transf., urbem lamentis, Liv.; implere aures alicuius Liv. **B.** Esp., **1**, *to fill with food, satiate;* implentur veteris Bacchi pinguisque ferinae, Verg.; **2**, *to make pregnant*, Ov.; **3**, *to fill a certain measure, to complete a number;* impleta ut essent sex milia armatorum, Liv.; of the moon, luna quater junctis implerat cornibus orbem, *had completed its circle*, Ov. **II.** Fig. **A.** omnia terrore, Liv. **B.** Esp., **1**, *to satisfy, content;* sese regum sanguine, Cic.; **2**, *to complete;* quater undenos decembres, *to have lived through*, Hor.; **3**, *to occupy a position;* locum principem, Tac.; **4**, *to fulfil, perform;* officium scribendi, Cic.; fata, Liv.

implexus -a um, partic. of implecto.

implĭcātĭo -ōnis, f. (implico), *an intertwining, interweaving;* **1**, lit., nervorum, Cic.; **2**, transf., **a**, *a weaving together;* locorum communium, Cic.; **b**, *embarrassment;* rei familiaris, Cic.

implĭcātus -a -um, p. adj. (from implico), *confused, entangled;* partes orationis, Cic.

implĭciscor, 3. dep. (implico), *to become confused, disordered*, Plaut.

implĭcitē, adv. (implicitus), *confusedly*, Cic.

implĭco -plĭcŭi -plĭcĭtum and -plĭcāvi -plĭcātum, 1. (in and plico). **I.** *to enfold, enwrap, entangle.* **A.** Gen., **1**, lit., se dextrae, *to cling to*, Verg.; implicari remis, Liv.; **2**, transf., implicari or implicare se aliquā re, *to be entangled in, engaged in;* implicari morbo or in morbum, *to be attacked by*, Caes.; negotiis, Cic.; se societate civium, Cic. **B.** *to confuse, perplex;* **a**, implicare ac perturbare aciem, Sall.; **b**, aliquem incertis responsis, Liv. **II. A.** *to twine around;* brachia collo, Verg. **B.** *to weave around, to surround;* tempora ramo, Verg.

implōrātĭo -ōnis, f. (imploro), *an imploring for help;* with subject. genit., illius, Cic.; with object. genit., deūm, Liv.

implōro, 1. (in and ploro). **I.** *to call upon with tears or entreaties.* **A.** Gen., nomen filii, Cic. **B.** Esp., *to beseech, implore;* deos, Cic.; alicuius auxilium, fidem, misericordiam, Cic. **II.** *to ask for;* auxilium ab aliquo, Cic., Caes.; with ne and the subj., Caes.

implūmis -e (in and pluma), *unfledged;* pulli, Hor.; fetus (avis), Verg.

implŭo -plŭi, 3. (in and pluo), *to rain upon;* with dat., Peneus summis aspergine silvis impluit, Ov.

implŭvĭum -ii, n. (impluo), *a square basin in the floor of the atrium of a Roman house, in which the rain-water, coming through the compluvium, was received*, Cic.

impŏlītē, adv. (impolitus), *plainly, without ornament;* dicere, Cic.

impŏlītus -a -um (in and polio), *rough, unpolished, unrefined, inelegant;* forma ingenii admodum impolita et plane rudis, Cic.; res, *unfinished*, Cic.

impollūtus -a -um (in and polluo), *unpolluted, undefiled*, Tac.

impōno -pŏsŭi -pŏsĭtum, 3. (in and pono). **I.** *to put, set, lay, place in;* aliquem sepulcro, *to bury*, Ov.; coloniam in agro Samnitium, Liv.; praesidium Abydi, *at Abydos*, Liv. **II.** *to put, lay, place upon.* **A.** Lit., **1**, gen., alicui coronam, Cic.; dextram in caput, Liv.; aliquem in rogum, Cic., rogo, Verg.; **2**, esp. as naut. t. t., imponere in naves or simply imponere, *to put on ship, to embark;* legiones equitesque in naves, Caes.; exercitum Brundisii, Cic. **B.** Transf., **1**, *to put over as master;* regem Macedoniae, consulem populo, Cic.; **2**, *to lay upon as a burden, impose;* frenos animo alicuius, Liv.; alicui onus, Cic.; invidiam belli consuli, Sall.; **3**, *to impose upon, cheat, deceive;* with dat., Catoni egregie, Cic. **III.** *to place on.* **A.** Lit., claves portis, Liv. **B.** Transf., **1**, manum extremam (summam, supremam) alicui rei, *to put the last touch to*, Verg.; finem imponere alicui rei, Liv.; modum alicui rei, *to put bounds to*, Liv.; **2**, *to add;* **a**, alicui nomen imponere (with genit. or acc. of the name); **b**, in a bad sense, *to cause;* alicui vulnus, Cic. (partic. perf. syncop. impostus, Verg.).

importo, 1. (in and porto), **1**, *to bring in, import;* vinum ad se importari omnino non sinunt, Caes.; **2**, transf., **a**, *to bring in, introduce;* importatis artibus, *foreign*, Cic.; **b**, *to bring upon, cause;* alicui detrimentum, Cic.

importūnē, adv. (importunus), *unseasonably, rudely, violently;* insistere, Cic.

importūnĭtas -ātis, f. (importunus), *rudeness, impoliteness, insolence, incivility;* animi, Cic.

importūnus -a -um (in and POR o, PORT o, whence portus, porta, etc), 1, lit., *unsuitable, ill-adapted*, loca machinationibus, Sall , 2. transf , a, of time, *unfavourable*, tempus, Cic , b, of circumstances, *troublesome, burdensome, oppressive*, pauperies, Hor , c, *rude, uncivil, unmannerly, churlish, savage*, mulier, hostis, libido, Cic

importŭōsus -a -um (in and portuosus), *without harbours*; mare, Sall ; litus, Liv

impos -pŏtis (in and POT, whence also potis), *having no power over*, animi, Plaut

impŏsitus -a -um, partic of impono

impŏtens -entis (in and potens) I. *weak, impotent, having no power*, homo, Cic , plur subst. **impŏtentes** -ium, *the weak*, Cic II. *having no power over, not master of* A. Gen with genit , equi regendi, Liv , irae, Liv B. *unable to command one's passions, violent, unrestrained, furious, outrageous*, a, lit , homo, Cic , animus, Cic ; b, transf , of the passions themselves, *unbridled*, injuria, Liv , laetitia, Cic

impŏtentĕr, adv. (impotens), 1, *weakly, powerlessly*, elephantos impotentius jam regi, Liv , 2, *intemperately, passionately*, Liv

impŏtentĭa -ae, f (impotens) I. *impotence*, Ter II. *passionateness, ungovernableness, intemperance, extravagant passion*, animi, Cic

impraesentĭārum (for in praesentiā rerum), *in present circumstances, for the present, at present*, Nep , Tac.

impransus -a -um (in and pransus), *that has not breakfasted, fasting*, Hor

imprĕcor, 1 dep (in and precor), *to wish any thing for any one, to call down upon, to imprecate*, litora litoribus contraria, Verg , alicui diras, Tac

impressĭo -ōnis, f (imprimo), 1, in rhetoric, a, *a distinct expression, emphasis, stress of voice*, explanata vocum impressio, Cic , b, impressiones, *raising and lowering of the voice*, Cic , 2, philosoph t t , *the impressions of outward things received through the senses*, Cic , 3, *a pressing-in-upon, an attack, assault*, non ferre impressionem Latinorum, Liv , of political contests, me vi et impressione evertere, Cic

imprīmis, adv (in and primus), *especially, first of all, principally*, Cic

imprĭmo -pressi -pressum, 3 (in and premo), *to press in or on* I. Gen , *to press upon, press into*, impresso genu, Verg II. a, *to press into, impress, drive in*, aratrum muris, Hor , sulcum altius, Cic , b, esp , *to stamp, make a mark*, sigillum in cera, Cic , c, transf , as philosoph. t t , of ideas, etc , *to impress on the mind*, quum visa in animis imprimantur, Cic , d, *to seal*, signo suo impressae tabellae, Liv , e, *to inlay, cover*; crater impressum signis, *chased, embossed*, Verg , f, fig , quae quum viderem tot vestigiis impressa, Cic.

imprŏbātĭo -ōnis, f (improbo), *disapprobation, blame*, improbatione hominis uti, Cic

imprŏbē, adv (improbus), 1, *wrongly, dishonestly, wickedly*, dicere, facere, Cic , 2, *wantonly, impudently*, improbissime respondere, Cic

imprŏbĭtas -ātis, f (improbus), *badness, wickedness, depravity*, alicuius, Cic , applied to animals, simiae (*roguery*), Cic

imprŏbo, 1 (in and probo), *to disapprove, blame, find fault with, reject*; multorum opera, Cic , with double acc , aliquem testem, Cic.

imprŏbŭlus -a -um (dim of improbus), *somewhat bad, wicked*, Juv

imprŏbus -a -um (in and probus) I. *bad, poor*, 1, lit , defensio, Cic , 2, transf , *morally bad, wicked, depraved, reprobate* homo, Cic , lex, Cic , subst., *a rogue*, Cic II. *beyond measure*; a, *beyond the usual size, enormous, immense*, labor, *never ending*, Verg , rabies ventris, *insatiable hunger*, Verg , anser, anguis, *voracious*, Verg , b, transf (α) *mischievous*, puer, Verg , (β) *bold*, Aeneas, Verg , *shameless, impudent*, siren, Hor , (γ) *lascivious, lewd*, carmina, Ov

imprōcērus -a -um (in and procerus), *small, low of stature*, pecora, Tac

impromptus -a -um (in and promptus), *not ready, not quick*, linguā, *slow of speech*, Liv

imprŏpĕrātus -a -um (in and propero), *not hasty, slow*, vestigia, Verg

improsper -ĕra -ĕrum (in and prosper), *unfortunate, unprosperous*, claritudo, Tac

improspĕrē, adv. (improsper), *unprosperously, unluckily*, Tac

imprōvĭdē, adv (improvidus), *without forethought, improvidently*, Liv

imprōvĭdus -a -um (in and providus). I. *not foreseeing*, improvidos incautosque hostes opprimere, Liv , with genit , improvidus futuri certaminis, Liv II *without forethought, incautious, heedless, improvident*, duces, Cic ; improvidi et creduli senes, Cic , with genit , improvidus futuri, Tac , transf , of things, improvida aetas (puerorum), Cic

imprōvīsō, adv (improvisus), *suddenly, unexpectedly*, Cic

imprōvīsus -a -um (in and provideo), *unforeseen, unanticipated, unexpected, sudden*, res, Cic , adventus, Cic , de or ex improviso, or improviso, *suddenly, unexpectedly*, Cic

imprūdens -entis (in and prudens) I. *not foreseeing, not expecting, not knowing*, aliquem imprudentem aggredi, *to attack unawares*, Caes , imprudente Sullā, *without the knowledge of Sulla* II. a, *ignorant of, not acquainted with*, legis, Cic , maris, Liv , b, *unwise, rash, imprudent*, Tac

imprūdentĕr, adv (imprudens) 1. *ignorantly, unwittingly, unawares, through ignorance*, Cic , 2, *imprudently, inconsiderately*, nihil imprudenter facere, ap Cic

imprūdentĭa -ae f (imprudens) I. *absence of design*, teli missi, Cic , quo ne imprudentiam quidem oculorum adjici fas fuit, *cast a look unawares*, Cic II. 1, *ignorance of*: eventus, Liv , 2, *want of foresight, imprudence, inadvertence*, per imprudentiam, *from imprudence*, Cic , propter imprudentiam labi, Caes

impūbes -bĕris and **impūbis** -e (in and pubes), *below the age of puberty, under age, youthful*, filius, Cic., anni, Ov , genae, *beardless*, Verg , qui diutissime impuberes permanserunt, *retained their chastity*, Caes plur , impuberes or impubes, *boys*, Liv , Caes

impŭdens -entis (in and pudens), *not ashamed, shameless, impudent*, tu es impudens! Cic , transf , mendacium, Cic , impudentissimae literae, Cic

impŭdentĕr, adv with compar and superl (impudens), *shamelessly, impudently*, mentiri, Cic

impŭdentĭa -ae, f (impudens), *shamelessness, impudence*, Cic

impŭdīcĭtĭa -ae, f (impudicus), *lewdness, incontinence, unchastity*, Tac

impŭdīcus -a -um (in and pudicus), *unchaste, lewd, incontinent*, homo, Cic , transf , P Clodii imperatoris impudentia, Cic

impugnātĭo -ōnis, f (impugno), *an assault, attack*, Cic

impugno, 1 (in and pugno), *to attack, as-*

sault, assail. **I.** Lit., as milit. t. t., terga hostium, Liv.; absol., Caes. **II.** Transf., **a,** *to contend, struggle against any one, attack, assail;* regem, Sall.; **b,** *to assail with words;* dignitatem alicuius, Cic.; sententiam, Tac.

impulsĭo -ōnis, f. (impello), **1,** *an external influence* or *force, an impression* or *impulse from without,* Cic.; **2,** *an instigation, incitement, impulse;* omnis ad omnem animi motum impulsio, Cic.

impulsor -ōris, m. (impello), *an instigator, inciter;* profectionis meae, Cic.; Caesare impulsore atque auctore, Cic.

impulsus -ūs, m. (impello). **I.** *an outward force, shock, pressure;* scutorum, Cic. **II. 1,** *an incitement, instigation;* impulsu meo, suo, vestro, Cic.; **2,** *an inward impulse, sudden passion,* Cic.

impūnĕ (impunis, from in and poena), adv. *with impunity, without punishment.* **A.** Lit., facere, Cic.; ferre, *to go unpunished,* Cic.; non impune abire, Caes. **B.** Transf., *without peril, safely;* in otio esse, Cic.; revisere aequor, Hor.

impūnĭtas -ātis, f. (impunis). **A.** Lit., *impunity, exemption from punishment;* peccandi, Cic.; alicui veniam et impunitatem dare, Cic.; impunitas non modo a judicio, sed etiam a sermone, Cic. **B.** Transf., *freedom, licence;* flagitiorum, Cic.; superfluens juvenili quādam impunitate et licentiā, Cic.

impūnītē, adv. (impunitus), *with impunity,* Cic.

impūnītus -a -um (in and punitus). **A.** *unpunished, exempt from punishment;* multorum impunita scelera ferre, Cic.; si istius haec injuria impunita discesserit, Cic.; aliquem impunitum dimittere, Sall. **B.** Transf., *unbridled, unrestrained;* mendacium, Cic.; omnium rerum libertas, Cic.

impūrātus -a -um (impuro), *vile, abandoned, infamous,* Plaut., Ter.

impūrē, adv. (impurus), *impurely, vilely, infamously, shamefully;* multa facere, Cic.; vivere, Cic.

impūrĭtas -ātis, f. (impurus), *moral impurity,* Cic.

impūrus -a -um (in and purus), **1,** lit., *unclean, stained, impure,* Ov.; **2,** usually in a moral sense, *impure, defiled, vile, shameful, infamous;* homo, Cic.; animus, Sall.; historia, Ov.

1. **impŭtātus** -a -um (in and puto), *unpruned, untrimmed;* vinea, Ov.

2. **impŭtātus** -a -um, partic. of imputo.

impŭto, 1. (in and puto), *to impute to, lay to the charge of any one, as a fault or merit, to account, reckon as a fault* or *merit;* **a,** as a merit, quis mihi plurimum imputet, Tac.; **b,** as a fault, alicui natum, Ov.

īmŭlus -a -um (dim. of imus), *lowest,* Cat.

īmus -a -um, superl. from inferus (q.v.).

1. **ĭn,** prep. with acc. = *into,* with abl. = *in.* **I.** With the acc. **A.** Of space, *into;* ad urbem vel potius in urbem exercitum adducere, Cic. **B.** Of time; **1,** *to;* dormire in lucem, Hor.; aliquid in omne tempus perdidisse, *for ever,* Cic.; **2,** *for, to;* magistratum creare in annum, Liv.; in multos annos praedicere, Cic.; in diem, **a,** *for a short time, for the day;* in diem vivere, *to live for the moment,* Cic.; **b,** *daily;* in diem rapto vivere, Liv.; **c,** *for the future;* in diem poenas praesentis fraudis dii reservant, Cic.; in dies or in singulos dies, (α) *from day to day,* Cic.; (β) *daily,* Cic.; in horas, *hourly,* Hor.; in singulos annos, *from year to year,* Liv. **C.** Of other relations; **1,** of dimension, *in;* murum in altitudinem pedum sedecim fossamque perducit, Caes.; **2,** of division, *into;* Gallia est omnis divisa in tres partes, Caes.; describere censores binos in singulas civitates, *two for each state,* Cic.; **3,** of object, *for;* nullam pecuniam Gabinio, nisi in rem militarem datam, Cic.; in hoc, *for this purpose,* Hor.; **4,** of manner, *according to;* tradere regnum in fidem alicuius, *on the word of,* Sall.; in eandem sententiam loqui, Cic.; jurare in verba alicuius, Hor.; in universum, *in general,* Liv.; in vicem, Cic., Caes., or in vices, Ov., *in turns;* **5,** of direction, **a,** *to, in the presence of, before;* de servis quaere in dominos, Cic.; **b,** *towards;* amor in patriam, Cic. **D.** Pregnant constr., aliquem in carcerem asservari jubere, *to be taken to prison and kept there,* Liv.; in Tusculanum futurum esse, *to wish to come to,* Cic. **II.** With abl., *in.* **A.** Of space; **1,** esse in Sicilia, Cic.; in oculis esse, *to be before one's eyes,* Cic.; **2,** esp. of dress, etc., esse in veste domestica, Ov.; excubare in armis, Caes. **B.** of time; **1,** *in the course of;* in sex mensibus, Cic.; in bello, Cic.; in deliberando, *during,* Cic.; **2,** *at;* in tali tempore, Liv.; in eo est nt, etc., *on the point of,* Liv.; in tempore, *at the right time,* Liv. **C.** Of other relations; **1,** of the condition in which one is, *in;* in hac solitudine, Cic.; with persons, *in the case of;* in hoc homine non accipio excusationem, Cic.; **2,** of action, etc., *in;* in motu esse, Cic.; **3,** of the subjects of education, *in;* erudire in jure civili, Cic.; **4,** *amongst the number of;* in quibus Catilina, Sall.

2. **in,** inseparable particle, with adjectives and participles, *without, not,* e.g., indoctus.

ĭnaccessus -a -um (in and accedo), *inaccessible;* lucus, Verg.

ĭnăcesco -ăcŭi, 3. *to become sour;* transf., haec tibi per totos inacescant omnia sensus, Ov.

Ĭnăchus (Ĭnăchos) -i, m. (Ἴναχος), *a mythical king of Argos, father of Io, after whom the river Inachus in Argolis was named;* hence **1,** adj., **Ĭnăchius** -a -um; **a,** *relating to Inachus;* juvenca, *Io,* Verg.; **b,** *Greek;* urbes, Verg.; **2,** **Ĭnăchĭdēs** -ae, m. *a descendant of Inachus, Perseus,* Ov.; *Epaphus,* Ov.; **3,** **Ĭnăchis** -ĭdis, f. *relating to Inachus;* ripa, *of the river Inachus,* Ov.; subst., *a daughter of Inachus, Io,* Prop.

ĭnădustus -a -um (in and aduro), *unburnt, unsinged,* Ov.

ĭnaedĭfĭco, 1. **1,** *to build in* or *upon;* sacellum in domo, Cic.; aliquid in locum, Liv.; **2,** *to build up, block up, barricade;* vicos plateasque, Caes.

ĭnaequābĭlis -e, **a,** *uneven;* solum, Liv.; **b,** *unequal, varying;* motus, Cic.

ĭnaequābĭlĭtĕr, adv. (inaequabilis), *unequally, variously,* Suet.

ĭnaequālis -e. **I.** *unequal, uneven, unlike, various;* **1,** lit., loca, Tac.; calices, *now full, now half full,* Hor.; **2,** transf., varietas, Cic. **II.** Act., *making unequal;* tonsor, Hor.; procellae, *disturbing the level of the sea,* Hor.

ĭnaequālĭtas -ātis, f. (inaequalis), *inequality, dissimilarity, irregularity,* Varr.

ĭnaequālĭtĕr, adv. (inaequalis), *unequally, unevenly;* inaequaliter eminentes rupes, Liv.

ĭnaequo, 1. *to make even* or *level;* haec levibus cratibus terrāque inaequat, Caes.

ĭnaestĭmābĭlis -e, **1, a,** *that cannot be estimated;* nihil tam incertum nec tam inaestimabile quam animi multitudinis, Liv.; **b,** *priceless, inestimable;* gaudium, Liv.; **2,** *having no (relative) value* (Gr. ἀπαξίαν ἔχων), Cic.; in a bad sense, *unworthy of being valued,* Cic.

ĭnaestŭo, 1. *to boil, rage in;* fig., si meis inaestuat praecordiis bilis, Hor.

Inaffectātus -a -um (in and affecto), *natural, unaffected*, Plin

Inalpīnus -a -um, *Alpine, dwelling in the Alps;* subst, **Inalpīni** -ōrum, *the dwellers in the Alps*, ap Cic

Inămābĭlis -e, *unpleasant, hateful, unlovely, odious*, palus (of the Styx), Verg.

Inămāresco, 3 *to become bitter*, Hor

Inambĭtĭōsus -a -um, *not ambitious, unpretentious*, Ov

Inambŭlātĭo -ōnis, f (inambulo), *a walking up and down*, Cic

Inambŭlo, 1 *to walk up and down* cum Cotta in porticu, Cic.

Inămoenus -a -um, *unpleasant, unlovely, dismal*, regna umbrarum, Ov.

Inānĭae -ārum, f (inanis), *emptiness*, Plaut

Inānĭlŏquus (inānĭlŏgus) -a -um (inanis and loquor), *speaking in vain or emptily*, Plaut

Inănĭmālis -e, *lifeless, inanimate*, animalia inanimaliaque omnia, Liv

Inănĭmātus -a -um, *lifeless, inanimate*, Cic (?)

Inānĭmentum -i, n (inanio), *emptiness*, Plaut

Inănĭmus -a -um (in and anima), *lifeless, inanimate*, neut subst., quum inter inanimum et animal hoc intersit, Cic.

Inānĭo -īvi -ītum, 4 (inanis), *to empty, make void*, Lucr

Inānis -e, *empty, void, vacant* (opp plenus, completus, confertus) **I.** Lit, **A.** Gen, vas, domus, Cic; equus, *without rider*, Cic, navis, *unloaded*, Caes, corpus, *soulless, dead*, Cic; lumina, *blind*, Ov., galea, *taken from the head*, Verg, with genit, Hor; with abl, epistola inanis aliquā re utili et suavi, Cic, subst, **Ināne** -is, n *space, empty space*, Cic **B.** 1, esp, *empty-handed:* a, redire, Cic; b, *poor, indigent;* civitas, Cic; **2,** *empty bellied, hungry*, Hor **II.** Transf, **1,** *empty, void of*, with genit, inanissima prudentiae, Cic, elocutio, Cic; subst, **Ināne** -is, n *vanity, emptiness*, Hor, **2,** *groundless, vain*, motus, Cic., **3,** *vain, useless;* contentiones, Cic, **4,** *vain, conceited*, animus, Cic

Inānĭtas -ātis, f (inanis), **1,** *emptiness, empty space*, Cic, **2,** transf, *worthlessness, inanity*, Cic

Inānĭtĕr, adv (inanis), *emptily, vainly, uselessly*, Cic

1 **Inărātus** -a -um (in and aro), *unploughed, fallow*, Verg

2. **Inărātus,** partic of inaro

Inardesco -arsi, 3 **I.** *to burn on*, humeris Herculis, Hor **II.** *to begin to glow, to kindle* **A.** Lit, nubes inardescit solis radiis, Verg **B.** Transf, of passions, *to glow, burn*, amor specie praesentis inarsit, Ov, specie juvenis, Ov

Inăresco ārŭi, 3 *to become dry*, vi solis, Tac.

Inargentātus -a -um, *silvered, plated with silver*, Plin

Inărĭmē -ēs, f = Aenaria

Inăro, 1 *to plough, to cultivate*, Plin

Inassuētus -a -um, *unaccustomed*, equus, Ov

Inattĕnŭātus (in and attenuo), *undiminished, unimpaired*, fames, *unappeased*, Ov

Inaudax -ācis, *timid, fearful*, Hor

Inaudĭo, 4. *to hear;* particularly, *to hear news, to hear a secret* aliquid de aliquo, Cic; de aliqua re ex aliquo, Cic

1 **Inaudītus** -a -um (in and audio), *unheard of*, **1,** a, inaudita criminatio, Cic, **b,** *unheard of, unusual*, agger inauditus, Caes, nomen est, non dico inusitatum, verum etiam inauditum, Cic, **2,** *unheard, without a hearing* (before a judge), aliquem inauditum et indefensum damnare, Tac

2 **Inaudītus** -a -um, partic of inaudio

Inaugŭrāto, adv (inauguro), *after having taken the auguries*, Liv

Inaugŭro, 1 **I.** Intransit, *to take the auguries, to divine*, Palatium Romulus, Remus Aventinum ad inaugurandum templa capiunt, Liv, with rel, sent, inaugura fierine possit, quod nunc ego mente concipio, Liv **II.** Transit, *to consecrate, instal, inaugurate*, templum, Cic, flaminem, Cic

Inaures -ium, f (in and aures), *earrings* Plaut

Inauro, 1 **I.** *to gild, cover with gold*, gen in partic, **inaurātus** a um, *gilt*, statua, Cic, vestis, *gold-worked*, Ov **II.** Transf (in jest), *to gild, enrich*, Cic.

Inauspĭcāto, adv (inauspicatus), *without consulting the auspices*, Cic

Inauspĭcātus a um **I** *without auspices* lex, *adopted without auspices*, Liv **II.** Transf, *unlucky, inauspicious*, Plin

Inausus -a -um (in and audeo), *not dared, not attempted*, ne quid inausum aut intractatum sceleris dolive fuisset, Verg

Incaedŭus -a um, *not cut down, unfelled*, lucus, Ov

Incălesco călŭi, 3 *to glow, become warm*, **a,** of things, incalescente sole, Liv, **b,** of persons, *to glow with wine or passion*, vino, Liv, esp of love, vidit et incaluit pelagi deus, Ov

Incalfăcĭo, 3 *to heat, warm, make hot*, Ov

Incallĭdē, adv (incallidus) *not cleverly, without ingenuity*, non incallide (= *skilfully*) tergiversari, Cic

Incallĭdus a -um, *not clever, without ingenuity*, servus non incallidus, Cic

Incandesco -candŭi, 3 *to begin to glow with heat, become very hot*, incandescit eundo (plumbum), Ov

Incānesco -cānŭi, 3, *to become white*, ornusque incanuit albo flore piri, Verg

Incantāmentum -i, n (incanto), *a charm, incantation*, Plin

Incanto, 1 *to consecrate with charms or spells*, vincula, Hor

Incānus -a -um, *quite grey*, menta, Verg

Incassum, adv (v. cassus), *in vain, vainly, uselessly*, Verg

Incastīgātus -a -um (in and castigo), *unchastised, uncorrected*, Hor

Incautē, adv (incautus), *incautiously, carelessly*, incaute et stulte, Cic, compar, incautius sequi, Caes

Incautus -a -um, **1,** *incautious, careless, heedless, unwary, inconsiderate*, homo incautus et rusticus, Cic, with ab and the abl, incautus a fraude, Liv, with genit, futuri, Hor; **2,** *not guarded against or that which cannot be guarded against, unforeseen, unexpected, uncertain, unprotected*, repente incautos agros invasit, Sall, iter hostibus incautum, Tac

Incēdo cessi cessum, 3 **I.** Intransit, *to walk, go, march, step in, enter* **A.** Lit, **a,** pedes, *on foot*, Liv, molliter, *with a light step*, Ov, quācumque incederet, Cic , b, as milit t. t , *to march, advance*, usque ad portas, Liv., in perculsos Romanos, *to come on*, Sall **B.** Transf, **a,** *to come on, break out*, postquam tenebrae incedebant, Liv , incessit in ea castra vis morbi, Liv , **b,** of news, reports, etc., occultus rumor incedebat (with acc and infin), Tac , **c,** of political events, *to take place, arise, spread abroad*, incessit timor Sabini belli, Liv , with dat. pers , *to seize on*, gravis cura patribus incessit, ut, etc , Liv **II.** Transit , **1,** *to walk on*, scenam, Tac , **2,** *to happen to, come to, befall*, aliquem valetudo adversa incessit, Tac

incĕlĕbrātus -a -um (in and celebro), *not made known, not spread abroad*, Tac

incendĭārĭus -a um (incendium), *relating to a conflagration, incendiary*, hence, subst , **incendĭārius** ii, m *an incendiary*, Tac

incendium -ii, n (incendo), *a conflagration, fire.* **I. 1,** lit , incendium facere, excitare, Cic , conflare, Liv , **2,** meton *fire-brand*, incendia poscit, Verg **II.** Transf , **1,** *fire, glow, heat* (of the passions); cupiditatum, Cic , **2,** *danger, destruction, ruin*, civitatis, Cic

incendo cendi -censum, 3 (in and *cando), *to kindle, set fire to, burn* **I. A.** Lit., **a,** tus et odores, Cic , **b,** *to set on fire*, urbem, Cic , **c,** medic t t , incensi aestus, *the burning heat of fever*, Verg **B.** Meton , **1,** *to kindle fire upon*, altaria, Verg , **2,** *to make bright, brilliant, to enlighten*, solis incensa radiis luna, Cic **II.** Transf , **1,** *to set on fire with passion, incite, excite, stir up, irritate, incense*, **a,** animos judicum in aliquem, Cic , desine me incendere querelis, Verg , esp , *to excite to love*, aliquem, Verg , incendi, *to burn, to glow, to be irritated, incensed*, amore, desiderio, Cic , incensus ira, Cic , **b,** of abstract objects, *to arouse*, cupiditatem, odia Cic , **2,** *to enhance, raise, increase*, luctum, Verg , **3,** *to fill* (as with fire), caelum clamore, Verg

incensĭo -ōnis, f (incendo), *a burning, conflagration*, Cic

1 **incensus** -a -um (in and censeo), *not enrolled by the censor, unassessed*, Cic

2 **incensus.** **I.** Partic of incendo **II.** P adj , fig , of orators, *fiery*, vehemens et incensus, Cic

inceptĭo ōnis, f (incipio), *a beginning, undertaking*; tam praeclari operis, Cic

incepto, 1 (intens of incipio), *to begin, undertake*, Plaut , Ter

inceptor -ōris m (incipio), *a beginner*, Ter

inceptum i, n (incipio), *an undertaking, beginning, enterprise*, inceptum non succedebat, Liv , incepta patrare, Sall , ab incepto desistere, Liv

inceptus -ūs, m = inceptum (q v)

incerno -crēvi -crētum, 3 *to sift upon, to bestrew by sifting*, piper album cum sale nigro incretum, Hor

incēro, 1 *to cover with wax*, in jest, genua deorum, *to cover with votive wax tablets*, i e , *to beseech, implore*, Juv

1 **incertō,** adv (incertus), *not certainly, doubtfully*, Plaut.

2 **incerto,** 1 (incertus), *to make uncertain or doubtful*, Plaut.

incertus a -um, *uncertain, doubtful, not sure* **I. A.** casus, Cic , responsum, Liv , rumores, Caes **B.** Esp , **a,** *not clearly visible, dim, dark*, luna, Verg , **b,** *not sure* (of a blow); securis, Verg , **c,** *disorderly*, crines, Ov., vultus, *disturbed*, Cic **II. A.** *undetermined*, os, *stammering*, Ov , with rel sent , incerti socii an hostes essent, Liv., subst., **incertum** -i, n *that which is uncertain, uncertainty*, ad or in incertum revocare, *to make uncertain*, Cic , plur , incerta belli, *the uncertainties of war*, Liv **B.** Transf , of persons, *uncertain, hesitating*, quum incertus essem ubi esses, Cic , with genit , rerum omnium, Liv

incesso cessi or -cessīvi, 3 (intens of incedo), *to attack, assail, fall upon* **A.** Lit , aliquem jaculis saxisque, Liv **B.** Transf , *to assail with reproaches*, reges dictis protervis, Ov , aliquem criminibus, Tac

incessus -ūs, m (incedo), *the gait, mode of walking* **I.** Lit , **A.** Gen., rarus incessus nec ita longus, Cic , incessus citus modo, modo tardus, Sall **B.** Esp , *a hostile attack, assault*; primo incessu solvit obsidium, Tac **II.** *entrance, approach*, alios incessus hostis claudere, Tac

incestē, adv (incestus), *impurely, sinfully*, Cic

incesto, 1 (incestus), **1,** *to defile, pollute*, classem funere, Verg , **2,** *to defile, dishonour*, Verg

incestum -i, n , v incestus

1 **incestus** a -um (in and castus), *impure, sinful, impious* **I.** Gen , os, Cic ; manus, Liv , subst , incestus, *a sinful person*, Hor **II.** Esp , *unchaste, lewd*, **a,** of persons, judex (of Paris), Hor , **b,** of things, flagitium, Cic , subst., **incestum** i, n *unchastity, lewdness, incest*; incestum facere, Cic.

2. **incestus** -ūs, m (1 incestus), *unchastity, incest*, Cic

inchŏo, 1 *to begin, commence* **A.** Gen , novum delubrum, Cic ; res quas (communis intelligentia) in animis nostris inchoavit, Cic. **B.** Esp , **1,** *to introduce, begin to treat of*; philosophiam multis locis, Cic ; **2,** *to bring a matter before the senate*, inchoante Caesare de, etc , Tac , **3,** partic perf , **inchŏātus** -a -um, *only begun, not finished, incomplete*, cognitio, officium, Cic

1 **incĭdo** -cĭdi, 3 (in and cado), *to fall in or on* **I.** Accidentally **A.** Lit , foveam, Cic., with dat , capitibus nostris, Liv **B.** Transf , **1,** *to fall into, to light upon*, in insidias, Cic., incidere alicui or in aliquem, *to meet unexpectedly*, Cic ; **2,** of time, *to fall upon, happen on*, in hunc diem incidunt mysteria, Cic., **3,** *to fall into a disease or some evil*; in morbum, Cic , in aes alienum, *to run into debt*, Cic., **4,** *to fall upon by chance*; **a,** of persons, casu in eorum mentionem, Cic ; in Diodorum, *to fall in with the opinion of*, Cic , **b,** of things, incidit mihi in mentem, *it comes into my mind*, Cic. ; **5,** *to happen, occur*; incidunt saepe tempora quum, etc , Cic., si qua clades incidisset, Liv , forte incidit ut with subj , Liv , with dat pers , *to happen to*, multis tales casus inciderunt, Cic **II.** Purposely **A.** Lit , into a place, *to burst into*, castris, Liv , in hostem, *to attack*, Liv. **B** Transf , *to fall upon, seize*, terror incidit exercitui, Caes.

2. **incīdo** -cīdi cīsum, 3 (in and caedo) **I.** *to cut into, make an incision, cut open*, **1,** gen , arbores, Caes ; pulmo incisus, Cic , **2,** esp , **a,** *to inscribe, engrave an inscription*, leges in aes, Cic , notum est carmen incisum in sepulcro, Cic , **b,** *to make by cutting*; faces, Verg , **c,** *to clip, prune, cut*; pinnas, Cic **II.** *to cut through* **A.** Lit , linum, Cic. **B.** Transf , **1,** *to cut short, bring to an end, break off*, poema quod institueram, Cic , sermonem, Liv ; genus vocis incidens, *broken off, interrupted*; **2,** *to take away*; spem omnem, Liv

inciens -entis (connected with ἐγκύμων, ἔγκυος), *pregnant, with young*, Plin.

incīlis -e (for incidilis from incīdo), *cut*, subst, **incīle** -is, n *a ditch or canal for carrying off water*; fig, tamquam in quodam incili jam omnia adhaeserunt, ap Cic

incīlo, 1. *to blame, scold, rebuke*, Lucr

incingo cinxi cinctum, 3 *to surround, engirdle*, incinctus cinctu Gabino, Liv, transf, urbes moenibus, Ov

incĭno, 3 (in and cano), *to sing*, Prop

incĭpĭo -cēpi -ceptum, 3. (in and capio), *to begin, commence* **I.** Transit., **A.** Gen with acc, pugnam, Liv, with infin., bella gerere, Cic, absol, ut incipiendi ratio fieret, Cic **B.** *to begin to speak*, sic statim rex incipit, Sall **II.** Intransit, *to commence*, tum incipere ver arbitrabatur, Cic

incĭpisso, 3. (incipio), *to begin, commence*, Plaut

incīsē and **incīsim**, adv (incido), *in short, disconnected sentences*, dicere, Cic

incīsĭo ōnis, f (incīdo), *a division or clause of a sentence*, Cic

incīsum -i, n. (incīdo), *a division of a sentence*, Cic

incīsūra ae, f (incīdo), *a cutting into, incision*, Plin

incĭtāmentum -i, n (incito), *an incitement, inducement, incentive*, incitamentum periculorum et laborum, Cic

incĭtātē, adv (incitatus), *hastily, violently*, incitatius ferri, fluere, of speech, Cic

incĭtātĭo -ōnis, f (incito), *an inciting, instigating, exciting* **I.** Act, languentis populi, Cic **II.** Pass **A.** *violent motion*, sol tantā incitatione fertur, Cic **B.** Transf, *excitement, ardour, energy, vehemence*, animi, Caes, mentis, Cic

incĭtātus a um, p adj (from incito) **A.** *rapid, vehement*, equo incitato, *at full gallop*, Cic **B.** Transf, cursus in oratione incitatior, Cic

incĭto, 1 *to put into rapid motion, urge on, to hasten* **I. A.** Lit, equos, Caes, prov, incitare currentem, *to spur the willing horse*, Cic, refl, se incitare, or middle incitari, *to quicken one's pace, to hasten*, alii ex castris se incitant, Caes **B.** Transf, *to incite, rouse, urge, spur on*, **1**, animos, ingenium, Cic, Caesarem ad id bellum, Caes, **2**, **a**, *to inspire*, terrae vis Pythiam incitabat, Cic, **b**, *to incite, make hostile, stir up*, aliquem in aliquem, Cic **II.** *to increase*, **1**, amnis incitatus pluviis, Liv, **2**, *to enhance*, eloquendi celeritatem, Cic.

1 **incĭtus** -a -um (in and cieo), *in rapid motion, rapid, swift*, Verg

2 **incĭtus** -a -um (in and cieo), *immovable*, esp used of a piece in the game of draughts, Plaut

incīvīlis -e, *unjust, tyrannical*, Eutr

inclāmĭto, 1 (intens of inclamo), *to call out against*, Plaut

inclāmo, 1 *to call upon loudly*, **1**, generally, aliquem nomine, Liv, comitem suum semel et saepius, Cic, with dat, Albanus exercitus inclamat Curiatiis, uti opem ferant fratri Liv, **2**, *to call upon for help*, nemo inclamavit patronum, Cic

inclāresco clārŭi, 3 *to become illustrious*, Tac

inclēmens entis, *unmerciful, not clement, harsh, rough*; dictator, Liv, inclementiori verbo appellare, Liv

inclēmentĕr, adv with compar (inclemens), *harshly, unmercifully, rigorously*, inclementius invehi in aliquem, Liv.

inclēmentĭa -ae, f (inclemens), *unmercifulness, rigour, harshness*, divum, Verg

inclīnātĭo -ōnis, f (inclino), *a leaning, bending, inclination* **I.** Lit, **A.** corporis, Cic **B.** *change of the voice*, Cic **II.** Transf, **1**, *a mental leaning, inclination*, ad meliorem spem, Cic, **2**, **a**, *inclination of will, good will, liking*, voluntatis, Cic, **b**, *change, alteration*, temporum, Cic

inclīnātus -a -um, p adj (from inclīno), *sunk* **I.** Lit, of the voice, *low, deep*, vox, Cic **II** Transf, **1**, *sunken, fallen*, fortuna, Cic, **2**, *inclined towards, favourable to*, ad pacem, Liv

inclīno, 1 (in and clino = κλίνω), *to bend bow, lean, incline.* **I.** Act., **A.** Lit, genua arenis, Ov, malos, *the masts* Liv **B** Transf **1**, *to incline turn away*; omnem culpam in aliquem, *to lay the blame on*, Cic, haec animum inclinant ut credam, *induce me to believe* Liv, **2**, **a**, *to cause to decline, change for the worse*, omnia simul inclinante fortunā, Liv, **b**, *to decide, give a decisive turn to*, fraus rem inclinavit, Liv **II.** Refl, se inclinare or simply inclinare, or middle inclinari, *to bend, incline* **A.** Lit, **1**, of an army, *to waver, yield*, acies inclinatur or inclinat, Liv, **2**, of the sun, or of time, inclinato in pomeridianum tempus die, *turning towards evening*, Cic **B.** Transf, **1**, paululum inclinari timore, *to waver*, Cic, **2**, **a**, *to incline in opinion* ad Stoicos, Cic, sententia senatus inclinat ad pacem, Cic, with ut and the subj, Liv, **b**, *to be favourable to*, pluribus hisce, Hor

inclūdo -clūsi -clūsum, 3 (in and cludo, claudo) **I.** *to shut up, shut in, enclose* **A.** Of personal objects, parietibus deos, Cic, aliquem in cella Concordiae, Cic **B.** Of inanimate objects, **1**, **a**, *to insert*, emblemata in scaphis aureis, Cic., verba versu, Cic, **b**, *to surround*, suras auro, Verg, *to insert as an episode*, aliquid orationi, Cic **II.** *to obstruct, hinder, stop*, vocem, Cic

inclūsĭo ōnis, f (includo), *a shutting up, confinement*, Cic

inclўtus (**inclŭtus**, **inclĭtus**) -a um (in and cluo) *celebrated, famous, renowned*, populi regesque, Liv, leges Solonis, Liv

1 **incoctus** -a -um (in and coquo), *uncooked, raw*, Plaut

2 **incoctus** -a -um, partic of incoquo

incōgĭtābĭlis -e, *thoughtless, inconsiderate*, Plaut

incōgĭtans -antis, *inconsiderate*, Ter

incōgĭtantĭa ae, f (incogitans), *thoughtlessness, heedlessness*, Plaut

incōgĭtātus -a -um, *inconsiderate*, Plaut

incōgĭto, 1 *to contrive, plan*, fraudem socio, Hor

incognĭtus a um **I.** *unknown* **A.** ne incognita pro cognitis habeamus, Cic **B.** Legal t t, *not examined*, incognitā re judicare, Cic **II.** *unclaimed*, Liv

incŏhĭbĕo, 2 *to hold together*, Lucr

incŏla -ae, c (incolo), *an inhabitant, dweller in any place* **I.** Gen **A** Of persons Pythagorei incolae paene nostri, *our fellow-countrymen*, Cic, with genit, mundi, Cic, poet, incolae turba, *natives*, Ov **B** Of animals, aquarum incolae Cic **C.** Of winds, *native*, aquilones, Hor **II.** Esp = μέτοικος, *a resident without full civic rights*, Cic

incŏlo -colŭi, -cultum, 3 **I.** Transit *to inhabit, dwell in*, eas urbes, Cic, partic subst, **incŏlentes** ium, m *the inhabitants*, Liv **II.** Intransit, *to dwell*, inter mare Alpesque, Liv

incŏlŭmis e (in and columis, from *cello),

uninjured, safe and sound, without damage, Cic.; naves, Caes.; with ab and the abl., incolumis a calamitate, Cic.

incŏlŭmĭtas -ātis, f. (incolumis), *safety, soundness, good condition, preservation;* mundi, Cic.; incolumitatem deditis polliceri, Caes.

incŏmĭtātus -a -um (in and comitor), *unaccompanied, without retinue, alone*, Verg.

incommendātus -a -um, *given up to, abandoned;* tellus incommendata ventis, Ov.

incommŏdē, adv. (incommodus), *inconveniently, unfitly, unsuitably, unseasonably;* venire, Cic.; incommodius mecum actum est, Cic.; incommodissime navigare, Cic.

incommŏdĭtas -ātis, f. (incommodus), *inconvenience, unsuitableness, disadvantage;* incommoditas alienati illius animi, Cic.; temporis, *unseasonableness*, Liv.

incommŏdo, 1. (incommodus), *to be unpleasant, burdensome, troublesome to any one, to incommode;* with dat., inimicis, Cic.; nihil alteri, Cic.

incommŏdum, v. incommodus.

incommŏdus -a -um, *inconvenient, unsuitable, unfit, troublesome, disagreeable*. **I.** Adj., a, of things, valetudo, *ill-health*, Cic.; compar., non incommodiore loco quam, etc., Cic.; superl., res eius incommodissimae, Cic.; **b**, of persons, *troublesome, annoying;* alicui incommodum esse, Cic. **II.** Subst., **incommŏdum** -i, n., a, *disadvantage;* incommodo tuo, Cic.; **b**, *injury, misfortune;* commoveri incommodo valetudinis tuae, Cic.; incommodo affici, Cic.; alicui incommodum ferre, Cic.; incommodum capere or accipere, Cic.

incommūtābĭlis -e, *unchangeable;* reipublicae status, Cic.

incompărābĭlis -e, *incomparable*, Plin.

incompertus -a -um (in and comperio), *unknown, not ascertained, uncertain;* inter cetera vetustate incomperta, Liv.

incompŏsĭtē, adv. (incompositus), *in a disorderly manner;* hostis negligenter et incomposite veniens, Liv.

incompŏsĭtus -a -um, *disordered, disorderly, irregular;* **1**, agmen, Liv.; hostes, Liv.; **2**, transf., of style, nempe incomposito pede currere versus Lucili, Hor.

incomprĕhensĭbĭlis -e, *that cannot be understood, incomprehensible*, Quint.

incomptus -a -um, **a**, *untended, untrimmed;* capilli, Hor.; **b**, *rude, artless*, Tac.; of style, *without ornament, rude, rough;* oratio, Cic.; versus, Verg.

inconcessus -a -um (in and concedo), *not allowed, forbidden;* hymenaei, Verg.

inconcĭlĭo, 1, *to win artfully to one's own side*, Plaut.

inconcinnus -a -um, *awkward, inelegant;* qui in aliquo genere inconcinnus et stultus est, Cic.

inconcussus -a -um, *unshaken, firm;* pax, Tac.

inconditē, adv. (inconditus), *confusedly;* versus Graecos dicere, Cic.

inconditus -a -um (in and condo), *disorderly, confused, irregular;* acies, Liv.; jus civile, *unarranged*, Cic.; genus dicendi, Cic.

incongrŭens -entis, *not agreeing, unsuitable*, Plin.

inconsīdĕrantĭa -ae, f. (in and considero), *thoughtlessness, inconsiderateness*, Cic.

inconsīdĕrātē, adv. (inconsideratus), *without consideration, rashly, inconsiderately;* agere, Cic.; dicere, Cic.

inconsīdĕrātus -a -um, **1**, *thoughtless, inconsiderate*, Cic.; **2**, *unadvised, unconsidered;* cupiditas, Cic.

inconsōlābĭlis -e, *inconsolable;* transf., vulnus, *incurable*, Ov.

inconstans -stantis, *changeable, unstable, inconstant;* mihi ridicule es visus esse inconstans, Cic.

inconstantĕr, adv. (inconstans), *inconstantly, inconsistently, capriciously;* loqui, Cic.; haec inconstantissime dicuntur, Cic.

inconstantĭa -ae, f. (inconstans), *changeableness, instability, inconstancy;* mentis, Cic.

inconsultē, adv. (inconsultus), *inconsiderately, unadvisedly;* inconsulte ac temere, Cic.

1. **inconsultus** -a -um (in and consulo), **1**, *not consulted;* inconsulto senatu, Liv.; **2**, *without advice, unadvised;* inconsulti adeunt, Verg.; **3**, *inconsiderate, imprudent, indiscreet;* homo inconsultus et temerarius, Cic.; ratio, Cic.

2. **inconsultus** -ūs, m. (in and consulo), *the not asking advice*, Plaut.

inconsumptus -a -um, *unconsumed, undiminished*, Ov.

incontāmĭnātus -a -um, (in and contamino), *unspotted, unpolluted, uncontaminated*, Liv.

incontentus -a -um (in and contendo), *not stretched;* fides, *out of tune*, Cic.

incontĭnens -entis, *incontinent, immoderate, intemperate;* Tityos, Hor.; manus, Hor.

incontĭnentĕr, adv. (incontinens), *immoderately, incontinently;* nihil incontinenter facere, Cic.

incontĭnentĭa -ae, f. (incontinens), *incontinence, intemperance*, Cic.

incontrōversus -a -um, *uncontroverted, undisputed*, Cic.

inconvĕnĭens -entis, *not agreeing with, dissimilar;* facta, ap. Cic.

incŏquo -coxi -coctum, 3. *to boil in* or *with*. **A.** radices Baccho, Verg. **B.** *to dye, colour;* vellera Tyrios incocta rubores, Verg.

incorrectus -a -um, *unamended, unimproved*, Ov.

incorruptē, adv. (incorruptus), *incorruptly, justly, impartially;* judicare, Cic.

incorruptus -a -um, *not corrupted*. **I.** Lit., sanguis, Cic.; templa, *not destroyed*, Liv.; incorruptā sanitate esse, Cic. **II.** Transf., *incorrupt, unbribed, genuine, uninjured, unimpaired;* testis, Cic.; virgo, *pure*, Cic.; judicium, *upright*, Liv.; integritas Latini sermonis, Cic.

increbresco -crēbrŭi, 3., and **incrēbesco** -crēbŭi, 3. *to become frequent, strong, prevalent; to increase, prevail;* ventus, Cic.; proverbio, *to become a proverb*, Liv.; quum hoc nescio quo modo increbruisset, with acc. and infin., Cic.

incrēdĭbĭlis -e, **1**, **a**, *incredible;* auditu, Cic.; dictu, Cic.; memoratu, Sall.; **b**, *extraordinary;* fides, Cic.; vis ingenii, Cic.; **2**, *not worthy of belief* (of persons), Plaut.

incrēdĭbĭlĭtĕr, adv. (incredibilis), *incredibly, extraordinarily;* delectari, Cic.; pertimescere, Cic.

incrēdŭlus -a -um, *incredulous*, Hor.

incrēmentum -i, n. (incresco), *the growth of plants* or *animals*. **I. A.** Lit., vitium, Cic. **B.** Transf., urbis, Liv. **II.** Meton., **1**, *that from* or *by which anything grows, increase;* incremento multitudinis, Liv.; dentes populi incrementa futuri, *the seed*, Ov, **2,** poet = *offspring;* Jovis, Verg

incrĕpĭto, 1 (intens of increpo) **I.** Intransit, *to call loudly to any one*, tum Bitiae dedit increpitans, Verg **II.** Transit, *to cry to, reproach, chide*, aliquem, Verg, increpitare vocibus quod, etc, Caes, increpitare Belgas qui (with subj), Caes, pertinaciam praetoris, Liv.

incrĕpo -ŭi (ăvi) -ĭtum (ātum), 1 **I.** Intransit **A.** *to rustle, rattle, whiz, rush, make a noise*, **1,** discus increpuit, Cic, **2,** *to be noised abroad, become known*, simulatque increpuit suspicio tumultūs, Cic, quicquid increpuerit, Catilinam timeri, Cic **B.** *to call upon*, increpat ultro, Verg **C.** With in and the acc, *to slander, revile*, in Fulvi similitudinem nominis, Liv **II** Transit, **A.** *to cause to sound, cause to be heard* lyram, Ov, tubā ingentem sonitum, Verg **B. a,** *to exclaim against, to blame, upbraid, chide, reproach, rebuke, reprove* Tullium nomine, Liv, aliquem graviter quod, etc, Liv, with acc and infin, *to shout out insultingly*, simul increpante qui vulneraverat habere quaestorem, Liv, with rel sent, quum undique duces, victisne cessuri essent, increparent, Liv, **b,** *to animate, excite*, morantes aeris rauci canor increpat, Verg, **c,** *to throw in one's teeth, to reproach a person with, to blame for*, perfidiam, Cic

incresco -crēvi, 3 **I.** *to grow in anything*, squamae cuti increscunt, Ov **II.** *to grow* **A.** (ferrea seges) jaculis increvit acutis, Verg **B.** Transf, increscit certamen, Liv

incrētus -a um, partic of incerno

incrŭentātus -a -um (in and cruento), *not bloody, not stained with blood*, Ov.

incrŭentus a -um, *bloodless*, proelium, victoria, Liv, exercitus, *that has lost no soldiers*, Sall

incrusto, 1 *to cover with a rind, encrust*, vas sincerum, *to bedaub*, Hor

incŭbātio -ōnis, f (incubo), *a sitting upon eggs, incubation*, Plin

incŭbo -āvi ātum and -ŭi ĭtum, 1 *to lie in or on* **I.** Gen, stramentis, Hor, cortici, Liv **II. A.** *to pass the night in a temple to receive a divine message or cure of a disease*, in Pasiphaae fano, Cic **B. 1,** lit, of birds, *to sit on or hatch eggs, to brood*, nidis, Ov, **2,** transf, *to brood over, earnestly watch over*, pecuniae, Cic, auro, divitiis, Verg **C** *to stay in a place*, Erymantho, Ov **D.** Transf, ponto nox incubat atra, *settles on*, Verg

incūdo -cūdi cūsum, 3 *to forge, fabricate*, lapis incusus, *a sharpened stone for a handmill*, Verg

inculco, 1 (in and calco), *to trample in* **A** *to foist in, mix in*, Graeca verba Cic **B.** Transf, **1,** *to impress upon, inculcate*, tradatur vel etiam inculcetur, Cic, with ut and the subj, Cic, **2,** *to force upon, obtrude upon*, se alicuius auribus, Cic

inculpātus -a um (in and culpo), *unblamed, blameless*, Ov

incultē, adv (1 incultus), **1,** *roughly, rudely*, vivere, Cic, incultius agere or agitare, Cic, **2,** of orators, *inelegantly, without refinement*, dicere, Cic

1 **incultus** a um, *uncultivated, untilled* **I.** Lit, **A.** ager, Cic Subst, **inculta** -ōrum, n *wastes, deserts*, Verg **B.** *unarranged, disordered, untidy*, comae, *uncombed*, Ov, homines intonsi et inculti, Liv **II.** Transf, *unpolished, unrefined, unadorned, rude*, homo, *without education*, Sall, inculta atque rusticana parsimonia, Hor, versus, *rough, unpolished*, Hor

2 **incultus** -ūs, m *neglect, want of cultivation*, suos honores desertos per incultum et negligentiam, Liv

incumbo -cŭbŭi cŭbĭtum, 3 *to lie upon, recline or lean upon, bend to* **I.** Lit **A.** remis, *to ply*, Verg, cumulatis in aqua sarcinis insuper, Liv, in gladium, Cic, ejecto (equiti) *to rush on*, Verg **B.** Esp, **1, a,** milit t t, *to throw oneself upon the enemy*, suo et armorum pondere in hostem, Liv, **b,** *to press hard on*, in aliquem, Cic, **2,** of things, **a,** *to overhang*, laurus incumbens arae, Verg **b,** *to burst upon, attack*, tempestas incubuit silvis, Verg **II.** Transf, **A.** *to apply oneself to anything, exert oneself, take pains with, lend one's mind to*, in bellum, Caes, in aliquod studium, Cic, ad laudem, Cic, novae cogitationi, Tac, with neut acc, haec incumbe, Cic, with infin, Verg, with subj, Liv **B.** *to press heavily upon*, ut jam inclinato (judici) reliqua incumbat oratio, Cic

incūnābŭla ōrum, n **I.** *swaddling-clothes*, Plaut **II.** Meton, **1,** *birthplace*, incunabula nostra, Cic, **2,** *origin, commencement, beginning*, incunabula nostrae veteris puerilisque doctrinae, Cic

incūrātus a -um, *uncared for, unhealed*, ulcera, Hor

incūria -ae, f (in and cura), *carelessness, neglect, negligence, indifference*, alicuius rei, Cic

incūrĭōsē, adv with compar (incuriosus), *negligently, carelessly*, agere, Liv

incūrĭōsus a -um **I.** Act, *careless, negligent*, serendis frugibus, Tac **II.** Pass, *neglected, careless*, finis, Tac

incurro curri (cŭcurri) -cursum, 3 **I** *to run purposely against something* **A.** Lit, **1,** incurrere in columnas, prov, *to run one's head against a stone wall*, Cic, **2,** as milit t t, **a,** *to assail, attack*, in Romanos, Liv, with dat, levi armaturae hostium, Liv, with simple acc, hostium latus, Liv, **b,** *to make an incursion into*, in Macedoniam, Liv **B.** Transf, *to attack, to inveigh against*, in tribunos militares, Liv **II.** *to run accidentally against* **A** lit, incurrere atque incidere in aliquem, Cic **B.** Transf, **1,** in oculos, *to meet the eye*, Cic **2,** of places, *to border on*, privati agri qui in publicum Cumanum incurrebant, Cic, **3,** of persons, **a,** *to stumble on something*, in aliquid, Cic, **b,** *to fall into any evil or misfortune*, in morbos, Cic, in odia hominum, *to incur the hatred of men*, Cic, **4,** of time, events, etc, **a,** *to happen*, occasiones incurrunt tempora, Cic, *to happen, happen to* casus qui in sapientem potest incidere, *may fall to the lot of the wise*, Cic, nec ulla est disputatio, in quam non aliquis locus incurrat, *does not occur*, Cic, **b,** *to fall on a certain time*, in aliquem diem, Cic

incursĭo -ōnis, f (incurro) **1,** *a running against, collision*, atomorum, Cic **2,** *a hostile attack*, incursio atque impetus armatorum, Cic, as milit t t, *an inroad, invasion*, incursionem facere in fines Romanos, Liv

incurso, 1 (intens of incurro) **I.** *to run against, strike against, attack* **A.** Lit, in agmen Romanum, Liv, agros Romanos, *to make an incursion into*, Liv **B.** Transf, incursabit in te dolor, Cic **II.** *to run against*, rupibus, Ov

incursus ūs, m (incurro), *an attack, assault, a pressing upon, incursion, influx* **I.** Lit, **a,** of things, aquarum, Ov, **b,** of persons and animals, *hostile attack*, luporum, Verg, esp as milit t t, aditus atque incursus ad defendendum, Caes **II.** Transf, incursus animus varios habet, *efforts, plans*, Ov

incurvo, 1 (incurvus), *to bend, curve, make*

crooked; bacillum, Cic.; arcum, Verg.; membra incurvata dolore, Ov.

incurvus -a -um, *bent, curved, crooked;* bacillum, Cic.

incus -cūdis, f. (incudo), *an anvil*, Cic.; prov., uno opere eandem incudem noctem diemque tundere, *to be always hammering at the same thing, to be always engaged in the same occupation*, Cic.

incūsātĭo -ōnis, f. (incuso), *blame, reproach, accusation*, Cic.

incūso, 1. (in and causa), *to accuse, blame, reproach, find fault with:* aliquem, Caes.; quietem Africani nostri somniantis, Cic.; with acc. and infin., Liv.; in pass., with nom. and infin., Tac.; with rel. sent., Verg.

incussus, only in abl. -ū, m. (incutio), *a beating* or *dashing against;* armorum, Tac.

incustōdītus -a -um (in and custodio). **I.** *unwatched, unguarded;* ovile, Ov.; urbs, Tac. **II.** Transf., **1**, *not observed, neglected;* observatio dierum, Tac.; **2**, *unconcealed;* amor, Tac.

incŭtĭo -cussi -cussum, 3. (in and quatio), *to strike, dash, beat against.* **I.** Lit., scipionem in caput alicuius, Liv. **II. A.** *to throw, hurl;* tela saxaque, Tac. **B.** *to strike into, inspire with, excite, produce;* terrorem alicui, Cic.; religionem animo, Liv.; desiderium urbis, Hor.

indāgātĭo -ōnis, f. (1. indago), *an inquiry, investigation;* veri, Cic.; initiorum, Cic.

indāgātor -ōris, m. (1. indago), *an investigator, explorer*, Plaut.

indāgātrix -trīcis, f. (indagator), *she who searches into* or *explores;* philosophia indagatrix virtutis, Cic.

1. **indāgo**, 1. **1**, *to follow a trail* or *scent, to track;* canis natus ad indagandum, Cic.; **2**, transf., *to search out, explore, investigate;* indicia, Cic.; with rel. sent., quid cuique esset necesse, Cic.

2. **indāgo** -inis, f. **1**, *a surrounding of any spot with nets* or *beaters so as to enclose the game;* saltus indagine cingere, Verg.; velut indagine dissipatos Samnites agere, Liv.; **2**, *investigation, research, inquiry*, Plin.

indĕ, adv. (from is, with adverbial ending), *thence, from there, from that place.* **I.** Of space, non exeo inde ante vesperum, Cic. **II.** Transf., **A. a**, *from thence, from that cause;* inde (i.e., ex audacia) omnia scelera gignuntur, Cic.; **b**, *from thence*, of persons, quod inde oriundus erat, Liv. **B.** Of time, **a**, *then, thereupon*, Caes.; **b**, *from that time forth*, Cic.; **c**, with ab and the abl., *from;* jam inde a principio, Liv.

indēbĭtus -a -um (in and debeo), *that which is not owed, not due;* non indebita posco, Verg.

indĕcens -centis, *unbecoming, unseemly, ugly, unsightly*, Mart.

indĕcentĕr, adv. (indecens), *unbecomingly, indecently*, Mart.

indēclīnātus -a -um (in and declino), *unchanged, firm;* amicitia, Ov.

indĕcōrē, adv. (indecorus), *unbecomingly, indecorously;* facere, Cic.

indĕcōris -e, *unbecoming, inglorious, shameful*, Verg.

indĕcŏro, 1. *to disgrace, dishonour*, Hor.

indĕcōrus -a -um, *unbecoming;* **a**, of outward appearance, *unseemly, unsightly;* motus, Liv.; **b**, morally, *indecorous, disgraceful;* si nihil malum, nisi quod turpe, inhonestum, indecorum, pravum, Cic.; indecorum est, with infin., Cic.

indēfensus -a -um (in and defendo), *undefended, unprotected;* Capua deserta indefensaque, Liv.

indēfessus -a -um, *unwearied, untired*, Verg.

indēflētus -a -um (in and defleo), *unwept*, Ov.

indējectus -a -um (in and dejicio), *not thrown down*, Ov.

indēlēbĭlis -e (in and deleo), *imperishable, indelible;* nomen, Ov.

indēlībātus -a -um (in and delibo), *untouched, uninjured, undiminished*, Ov.

indemnātus -a -um (in and damnatus, from damno), *uncondemned;* cives, Cic.

indēplōrātus -a -um (in and deploro), *unwept, unlamented*, Ov.

indēprĕhensus (indēprensus) -a -um (in and deprehendo or deprendo), *undiscovered, unobserved;* error, Verg.

indēsertus -a -um, *not forsaken*, Ov.

indestrictus -a -um (in and destringo), *untouched, unhurt*, Ov.

indētonsus -a -um (in and detondeo), *unshorn*, Ov.

indēvītātus -a -um (in and devito), *unavoided;* telum, Ov.

index -dĭcis, c. (indico). **I.** Lit., **A.** *one who informs* or *discloses*, Cic. **B.** In a bad sense, *an informer, traitor, spy*, Cic. **II.** Transf., **A.** Of things, *that which informs, a sign, token;* vox index stultitiae, Cic.; index digitus, Hor., or simply index, Cic., *the fore-finger.* **B. 1**, *the title* or *inscription on a book;* libri, Cic.; also on a statue, Liv.; **2**, *a touch-stone*, Ov.

Indi -ōrum, m. (Ἰνδοί), *the inhabitants of India, the Indians;* sing., **Indus** -i, m. *an Indian;* collective, Verg., Ov., and = *an elephant-driver, mahout*, Liv.; poet., **a**, = *Aethiopian*, Verg.; **b**, = *Arabian*, Ov. Hence, **A. India** -ae, f. (Ἰνδία), *India.* **B. Indĭcus** -a -um (Ἰνδικός), *Indian.* **C. Indus** -a -um (Ἰνδός), *Indian;* dens, *ivory*, Ov.; conchae, *pearls*, Prop.

indĭcātĭo -ōnis, f. (indico), *a setting a price upon anything, a valuing*, Plaut.

1. **indīcens** -entis (in and dico), *that does not say;* me indicente, *without my saying a word*, Liv.

2. **indīcens**, partic. of indico.

indĭcĭum -ĭi, n. (index). **I.** *a discovery, disclosure.* **A.** Lit., conjurationis, Cic.; indicia exponere et edere, Cic.; profiteri, *to make a confession before the judge*, Sall. **B.** Transf., **a**, *permission to confess;* indicium postulare, Cic.; **b**, *a reward for giving evidence;* partem indicii accipere, Cic. **II.** *a mark, sign, token, evidence;* sceleris, Cic.; indicio esse, *to be a sign of, serve to show*, Nep.

1. **indĭco**, 1. (intens. of 2. indico), *to disclose, declare, reveal, make known, betray, show, indicate.* **I.** Gen., rem dominae, Cic.; dolorem lacrimis, Cic.; vultus indicat mores, Cic.; se indicare, *to reveal one's own nature*, Cic.; in pass., with nom. and infin., Cic.; with rel. sent., Cic. **II. A.** *to inform against, give evidence about;* conscios, Cic. **B.** *to put a price on, value;* fundum alicui, Cic.

2. **indīco** -dixi -dictum, 3. *to make publicly known, announce, proclaim, fix, appoint.* **A.** Gen., alicui bellum, *to declare war*, Cic.; comitia, Liv.; diem comitiis, Liv.; exercitum Aquileiam, *order to*, Liv.; with ut and the subj., Liv. **B.** *to impose;* tributum, Liv.

1. **indictus** -a -um (in and dico), *not said, unsaid.* **A.** Lit., indictis carminibus nostris,

unsung, Verg B. Esp, *without a trial, without a hearing*, aliquem capitis condemnare, Cic

2 **indictus** a -um, partic of 2 indico

Indicus -a -um, v Indi

indidem, adv (inde and idem), 1, *from the same place, from that very place*, indidem Ameriā, Cic, 2, transf, *from the same matter*, Cic

indifferens entis (in and differo), *indifferent* (= ἀδιάφορον), *neither good nor bad*, Cic

indigena ae, c (indu and geno), *native, belonging to one's own country*, and subst. (opp advena), *a native*, ne majores quidem eorum *indigenas*, sed *advenas* Italiae cultores, Liv, of animals, bos, aper, Ov.

indigens, v indigeo

indigentia ae, f (indigeo), 1, *want, need*, Cic, 2, *insatiable desire*, Cic

indigeo -ŭi, 2. (indu = in and egeo) I. *to want, need, stand in need of, suffer want of*, with genit, Nep; with abl, iis rebus quae ad oppugnationem castrorum sunt usui, Caes Subst, **indigens** -entis, m *a needy person*, Cic II. *to need, require*, with genit, tui consilii, Cic; with abl, cohortatione non indigere, Cic

1 **Indiges** -gĕtis, m (indu = in and geno), *a native deity*, esp *Aeneas and the descendants of Aeneas, the fabled ancestors of the Romans* Sing, *Aeneas*, Verg, plur, *the descendants of Aeneas*, Liv, Verg.

2 **indiges** -is (indigeo), *needy*, ap Cic

indigestus -a -um (in and digero), *disordered, confused, unarranged*; chaos rudis indigestaque moles, Ov

Indigetes -um, m v Indiges

indignabundus a -um (indignor), *filled with indignation, greatly indignant*, Liv

indignandus a -um (partic of indignor), *deserving indignation, to be scorned*, Ov

indignans antis, p adj (from indignor), *impatient, indignant*, verba, Ov

indignatio -ōnis, f (indignor), 1, *indignation, disdain*, indignationem movere, Liv; 2, *the rhetorical exciting of indignation*, Cic

indigne, adv (indignus) I. *unworthily, disgracefully, dishonourably, undeservedly*, indignissime cervices frangere civium Romanorum, Cic II. *impatiently, unwillingly, indignantly*, indigne pati, with acc and infin, Cic, indigne ferre, with quod and the subj, Cic

indignitas -ātis, f (indignus), 1, *unworthiness, vileness*, hominis, accusatoris, Cic, 2, transf, a, *unworthy behaviour, meanness, indignity, baseness*, hominum insolentium, Cic, omnes indignitates perferre, Cic, b, meton, *indignation at unworthy treatment*, Cic

indignor, 1 dep (indignus), *to consider as unworthy or unbecoming, take as an indignity, be offended, indignant at*, aliquid, Cic, pro aliquo, Ov; foll by quod, Caes, by acc and infin, Caes, transf of things, pontem indignatus Araxes, Verg

indignus a -um I. *unworthy, not deserving*: a, with abl, omni honore indignissimus, Cic, b, with genit, magnorum avorum, Verg, c, with supine, id auditu dicere indignum esse, Liv, d, with rel sent, indigni erant qui impetrarent, *to obtain*, Cic, e, with ut and the subj, Liv, f, with infin, Ov, Hor, g, absol, divitias quivis, quamvis indignus, habere potest, Cic. II. Transf., *unworthy, unbecoming*, a, with abl indignum est sapientis gravitate et constantiā defendere, Cic, b, absol, *unworthy = disgraceful, shameful*; hoc uno sol non quidquam vidit indignius, Cic, indignum est, with infin or acc and infin, *it is unsuitable, inappropriate*, non indignum videtur memorare, Sall, *it is unworthy, disgraceful, shameful*, indignum est a pari vinci aut superiore, Cic facinus indignum or indignum facinus with infin or acc and infin as an exclamation, *it would be disgraceful*, facinus indignum! epistolam neminem reddidisse, Cic

indigus -a -um (indigeo), *needy, in want of*, with genit, nostrae opis, Verg, with abl, auxilio, Lucr

indiligens entis, *neglectful, negligent, heedless*, Caes

indiligenter, adv with compar (indiligens), *carelessly, heedlessly, negligently*, Cic

indiligentia -ae, f (indiligens), *carelessness, negligence*, Aeduorum, Caes, litterarum amissarum, Cic; veri, *in the investigation of truth*, Tac

indipiscor deptus sum, 3 dep (indu and apiscor), 1, *to reach, grasp, attain*, indeptum esse navem manu ferreā injectā, Liv; 2, *to obtain, attain, get*, Plaut

indireptus -a -um (in and diripio), *unpillaged*, Tac

indiscrēte, adv (indiscretus), *without difference or distinction* Plin

indiscrētus a um (in and discerno), 1, *unsevered, undivided*, Tac, 2, *undistinguished, indistinguishable, without difference*, proles indiscreta suis, Verg

indiserte, adv (indisertus), *ineloquently*, Cic

indisertus -a -um, *ineloquent*, homo, Cic

indispositus a -um, *disorderly, unarranged, confused*, Tac

indissolubilis -e, *indissoluble*, immortales et indissolubiles, Cic

indissolutus -a um (in and dissolvo), *undissolved*, Cic

indistinctus -a um, 1, *not separated, not arranged*, Cat, 2, transf, *unarranged, confused, indistinct, obscure*, Tac

individuus a um, 1, *indivisible* corpora, *atoms, monads of the Democritean system*, Cic, subst, **individuum** -i, n *an atom*, Cic; 2, *inseparable*, Tac

indivisus -a -um (in and divido), *undivided*, Plin

indo -didi -ditum, 3 I. *to put in or on, set or place in or on* A. Lit, aliquem lecticae, Tac B. Transf, 1, *to introduce*, novos ritus, Tac, 2, *to cause, occasion*, alicui pavorem, Tac II. *to place on something* A. Lit, castella rupibus, Tac B. *to give, impose a name*, with dat of the name, Superbo ei Romae inditum cognomen, Liv

indocilis -e I. A. *that cannot be taught, that learns with difficulty, unteachable, indocile*, 1, lit, homo, Cic, with infin, pauperiem pati, Hor, 2, *ignorant, inexperienced*, genus, Cic B. *that cannot be learned*, usus disciplina, Cic II. *untaught, unshown*, via, Prop, numerus, *artless*, Ov

indocte, adv (indoctus), *ignorantly, in an unlearned or inexperienced manner*, facere, Cic

indoctus -a -um, *untaught, unlearned, unskilled*, Cic, with genit, pilae discive, Hor, with infin, juga ferre nostra, Hor, canet indoctum, *without art*, Hor

indolentia -ae, f (in and doleo), *freedom from pain, absence of pain*, Cic

indoles -is, f (indu and alo), 1, *natural constitution or quality, nature*, servare indolem (of plants), Liv, 2, of men, *natural disposition,* *talents, inclination;* adolescentes bonā indole praediti, Cic.; indoles virtutis or ad virtutem, Cic.

indŏlesco -dŏlŭi, 3. (in and doleo), *to be pained, grieved at any thing,* Cic.; with acc. and infin., tam sero se cognoscere, Cic.; with abl., nostris malis, Ov.; with neut. acc., id ipsum indoluit Juno, Ov.; with quod or quia, Ov.

indŏmābĭlis -e, *that cannot be tamed, indomitable,* Plaut.

indŏmĭtus -a -um (in and domo), **1,** *untamed, unrestrained, wild;* **a,** of persons, pastores, Caes.; Mars, *furious fight,* Verg.; **b,** transf., of things, cupiditas, furor, libido, Cic.; **2,** *untameable, invincible;* mors, Hor.; Falernum, *indigestible,* Pers.; ira, Verg.

indormĭo -īvi -ītum, 4. *to sleep in* or *on anything;* with dat., congestis saccis, Hor.; fig. *to go to sleep over any occupation, be negligent in;* with dat. or in and the abl., tantae causae, Cic.; huic tempori, Cic.; in isto homine colendo tam indormivisse diu, Cic.

indōtātus -a -um, *without a dowry, portionless.* **I.** Lit., soror, Hor. **II.** Transf., corpora, *without funeral honours,* Ov.; ars, *unadorned, poor, without the gift of eloquence,* Cic.

indŭ, archaic form of in (q.v.).

indŭbĭtātē, adv. (indubitatus), *undoubtedly,* Liv.

indŭbĭtātus -a -um (in and dubito), *undoubted, not doubtful, certain,* Plin.

indŭbĭto, 1. *to doubt of;* with dat., suis viribus, Verg.

indŭbĭus -a -um, *not doubtful, certain,* Tac.

indūcĭae = indutiae (q.v.).

indūco -duxi -ductum, 3. **I.** *to draw over.* **A.** *to draw something over something else in order to cover it;* **1,** gen., tectorium, Cic.; varias plumas membris, Hor.; **2,** *to put on articles of clothing, arms,* etc.; manibus caestus, Verg.; poet. pass. with acc., toga inducitur artus, Verg. **B.** *to cover;* **1,** scuta pellibus, Caes.; **2,** *to erase writing on tablets, to draw a line through;* nomina, Cic.; *to revoke, make invalid;* senatus consultum, locationem, Cic. **C.** *to bring in, to reckon in one's account-book;* pecuniam in rationem, Cic. **II.** *to lead* or *bring in.* **A.** Lit., **1,** milites in pugnam, Liv.; **2,** esp. **a,** *to bring into a dwelling;* in regiam habitandi causā, Caes.; **b,** *to introduce* or *bring upon the stage* or *circus, produce on the stage;* gladiatores, Cic. **B.** Transf., **1,** gen., aliquem in errorem, Cic.; discordiam in civitatem, *to introduce,* Cic.; **2,** animum, or in animum; **a,** *to bring one's mind to, to resolve;* potuit inducere animum, ut patrem esse sese oblivisceretur, Cic.; **b,** *to direct one's attention to;* in spem cogitationemque meliorem, Cic.; **3,** *to induce, move, excite, persuade;* ad misericordiam, ad pigendum, Cic.; with ut and the subj., aliquem ut mentiatur, Cic.; with infin., Tac.; absol., inductus spe, cupiditate, *influenced by,* Cic.; **4,** *to bring in, introduce, represent in speaking* or *writing;* hinc ille Gyges inducitur a Platone, Cic.; **5,** *to bring in, introduce a custom;* morem novum judiciorum in rempublicam, Cic.

inductĭo -ōnis, f. (induco), *a leading* or *bringing to a place.* **A.** Lit., **1,** *into the arena;* juvenum armatorum, Liv.; **2,** of water, inductiones aquarum, Cic. **B.** Transf., **1,** animi, *resolve, determination, intention,* Cic.; **2,** erroris, *misleading,* Cic.; **3,** personarum ficta inductio, *feigned introduction of persons in a composition,* Cic.; **4,** *induction,* Cic.

inductor -ōris, m. (induco), *one who stirs up* or *rouses, a chastiser,* Plaut.

1. **inductus** -a -um (partic. of induco).

2. **inductus** -ūs, m. (induco), *inducement, instigation;* huius persuasu et inductu, Cic.

indŭgrĕdĭor = ingredior (q.v.).

indulgens -entis, p. adj. (from indulgeo), *kind, tender, indulgent;* peccatis, Cic.; in captivos, Liv.; irarum indulgentes ministri, Liv.

indulgentĕr, adv. (indulgens), *kindly, tenderly, obligingly, indulgently;* nimis indulgenter loqui, Cic.

indulgentĭa -ae, f. (indulgens), *kindness, tenderness, indulgence,* with obj. genit.; corporis, Cic.; with in and the acc., in captivos, Liv.

indulgĕo -dulsi -dultum, 2. (in and dulcis). **I.** Intransit., **A.** *to be complaisant, forbearing, indulgent, to indulge, gratify;* sibi, Cic.; sic sibi indulsit, *he allowed himself so many liberties,* Nep. **B.** Transf., **1,** *to give oneself up to, indulge in;* novis amicitiis, Cic.; vino, Verg.; ordinibus, *to enlarge,* Verg.; **2,** *to care for, attend to;* valetudini, Cic.; hospitio, Verg. **II.** Transit., *to give, to grant, allow, concede;* alicui sanguinem suum, Liv.; largitionem, Tac.

indŭo -dŭi -dūtum, 3. (= ἐνδύω), *to put on.* **I.** Lit., alicui tunicam, Cic.; pass. with abl., socci quibus indutus esset, Cic.; indutus duabus quasi personis, *with two masks,* i.e., *playing a double part,* Cic. **II.** Transf., **A. 1,** *to clothe, surround, cover;* dii induti specie humanā, *clothed in human form;* homines in vultus ferarum, *to change,* Verg.; arbor induit se in florem, Verg.; cratera coronā, *to crown with a garland,* Verg.; **2,** *to put on, assume;* personam judicis, Cic.; proditorem et hostem, *to play the part of,* Tac.; societatem, seditionem, *to engage in,* Tac.; sibi cognomen, Cic. **B. 1,** se in aliquid or alicui rei, *to fall into, fall on;* se hastis, Verg.; **2,** transf., *to entangle oneself in, become involved with;* se in captiones, Cic.; pass., indui confessione suā, *to be entangled in his own confession,* Cic.

indŭpĕdĭo, indŭpĕrātor = impedio, imperator (q.v.).

indūresco -dūrŭi, 3. *to become hard.* **I.** Lit., stiria induruit, Verg. **II.** Transf., miles induruerat pro Vitellio, *had become confirmed in attachment for Vitellius,* Tac.

indūro, 1. *to make hard, to harden.* **I.** Lit., nivem indurat Boreas, Ov. **II.** Transf., *to harden, to steel;* induratus resistendo hostium timor, Liv.

1. **Indus,** v. India.

2. **Indus** -i, m. (Ἰνδος), **1,** *a river of India,* now *Sind;* **2,** *a river of Phrygia and Caria.*

industrĭa -ae, f. (industrius), *industry, diligence;* in agendo, Cic.; industriam in aliqua re ponere, Cic.; de industria, Cic., ex industria, Liv., *on purpose, purposely, intentionally.*

industrĭē, adv. (industrius), *industriously, diligently, actively,* Caes.

industrĭus -a -um (for indu-starius, from industo = insto), *diligent, active, zealous, industrious, assiduous,* Cic.

indūtĭae -ārum, f. (from induo = tempus indutum, or insertum), *a truce, armistice, suspension of hostilities;* indutias facere, Cic.; dare, Liv.; violare, Caes.; rumpere, Liv.; postulare, Sall.; petere ab aliquo, Nep.; tollere, Liv.; per indutias, *during,* Sall.

Indutĭŏmărus -i, m. *prince of the Treveri.*

indūtus, only in dat. -ūi, abl. plur. -ĭbus, m. (induo), *a putting on a dress;* ea, quam indutui gerebat, vestis, Tac.

indŭvĭae -ārum, f. (induo), *clothes, clothing,* Plaut.

ĭnēbrĭo, 1., **1,** *to intoxicate, inebriate,* Plin.

2, *to saturate with*, aurem, *to fill full of idle talk*, Juv.

ĭnēdĭa -ae, f (in and edo), *fasting, abstinence from food*, vigiliis et inediā necatus, Cic , inediā consumi, Cic

ĭnēdĭtus a um (in and edo), *not published or made known*, juvenes, quorum inedita cura (*work*, i e *writings*), Ov

ĭneffābĭlis -e, *unutterable*, Plin

ĭnēlĕgans -antis, *inelegant, not choice, tasteless, not beautiful*, gen with negative, orationis copia, non inelegans, Cic

ĭnēlĕgantĕr, adv (inelegans), *inelegantly, tastelessly*, historia non ineleganter scripta, Cic , ineleganter dividere, *illogically*, Cic

ĭnēluctābĭlis -e, *that cannot be successfully struggled against, inevitable*, fatum, Verg

ĭnēmŏrĭor -ēmŏri, 3 dep , *to die in or at*, spectaculo, Hor

ĭnemptus (ĭnemtus) -a -um (in and emo), *unbought*, dapes, Verg

ĭnēnarrābĭlis -e, *indescribable, inexpressible*, labor, Liv

ĭnēnarrābĭlĭtĕr, adv (inenarrabilis), *indescribably*, Liv

ĭnēnōdābĭlis -e, (in and enodo), *inextricable*, res, *inexplicable*, Cic

ĭnĕo -ii (-ivi) -itum, 4 **I.** Intransit , *to go in, enter* **A.** Lit , in urbem, Liv **B.** Transf , of time, *to begin, commence*, iniens aetas, *youth*, Cic , ab ineunte aetate, *from youth*, Cic **II** Transit , *to go in, enter* **A.** Lit , domum, Cic , viam, *to enter upon, begin a journey*, Cic **B.** Transf , **1,** *to commence a period of time*, initā aestate, *at the beginning of*, Caes , **2,** of some kind of action, *to begin, to enter upon*, magistratum, Cic , proelium, Cic , **3,** *to undertake*, numerum, *to enumerate*, Liv , inire rationem, *to make an estimate*, Cic , and transf , *to consider*, Cic , societatem cum aliquo, *to enter into a league with*, Cic , consilium, *to form a plan*, Caes , gratiam ab aliquo, *to earn thanks from, conciliate the favour of*, Cic (pert init = iniit, Lucr 4,314)

ĭneptē, adv (ineptus), *unsuitably, inappropriately, absurdly, foolishly*, dicere, Cic.

ĭneptĭae -ārum, f (ineptus), *foolish behaviour, silliness, absurdity, foolery*, hominum ineptiae ac stultitiae, Cic , ut eos partim scelerum suorum, partim etiam ineptiarum poeniteat, Cic

ĭneptĭo, 4 (ineptus), *to talk foolishly, talk nonsense*, Cat

ĭneptus -a um (in and aptus), *unsuitable, inappropriate, tasteless, foolish, absurd, silly*, negotium, Cic , Graeculus, Cic , subst plur , **ĭnepti** -ōrum, *pedants*, Cic , compar , nam quid est ineptius quam, etc , Cic

ĭnermis -e, and **ĭnermus** -a -um (in and arma), *unarmed, weaponless* **I.** Lit , **a,** gen , Cic , gingiva, *toothless*, Juv , milites, Caes , **b,** of countries, *undefended by troops*, ager, Liv **II.** Transf , in philosophia, *not well versed in*, Cic , carmen, *inoffensive, offending no one*, Ov

1 **ĭnerrans** -antis (in and erro), *not wandering, fixed*, stellae inerrantes, Cic

2 **ĭnerrans** antis, partic of in erro

ĭnerro, 1 *to rove or wander about*, Plin

ĭners ertis (in and ars) **I.** *simple, unskilful*, poeta iners, Cic **II.** *inactive, lazy, idle, inert, sluggish, slothful* **A. a,** homo, senectus, Cic., **b,** transf of things and abstractions, (α) gen , otium, Cic , aqua, *stagnant*, Ov , aequora, *undisturbed by wind*, Lucr , stomachus, *not digesting*, Ov , terra, *immovable*, Hor , querelae, *useless*, Liv ; (β) of time during which nothing is done, *idle*, hora, Hor , tempus, Ov , (γ) of food, caro, *insipid*, Hor , (δ) act , *making idle or slothful*, frigus, Ov **B.** *cowardly*, Cic

ĭnertĭa -ae, f (iners), **1,** *unskilfulness, want of skill*, Cic **2,** *slothfulness, sluggishness*, laboris, *aversion to labour*, Cic

ĭnērŭdītus a -um, *unlearned, illiterate, ignorant*, Cic

ĭnesco, 1. *to allure with a bait*, transf *to entice, deceive*; nos caeci specie parvi beneficii inescamur, Liv

ĭnēvectus -a -um (in and eveho), *raised upon, borne upon*, Verg

ĭnēvītābĭlis e, *inevitable, unavoidable*, fulmen, Ov

ĭnexcītus -a -um (in and excieo), *unmoved, quiet*, Verg.

ĭnexcūsābĭlis -e, *without excuse, inexcusable*, Hor

ĭnexercĭtātus a um (in and exercito), *unexercised, unpractised*, miles, *undrilled*, Cic histrio, Cic , prompti et non inexercitati ad dicendum, Cic.

ĭnexhaustus -a um (in and exhaurio), *unexhausted, inexhaustible*, metalla, Verg , pubertas, *unenfeebled*, Tac

ĭnexōrābĭlis -e, *inexorable, not to be moved by entreaty*, **a,** of persons, in ceteros, Cic , adversus te, Liv , delictis, Tac , **b,** of things, disciplina, *severe*, Tac

ĭnexpĕdītus a um, *hampered*, pugna, Liv

ĭnexperrectus -a -um (in and expergiscor), *not awakened*, Ov

ĭnexpertus -a um **I.** Act , *inexperienced, unpractised, unacquainted with*, with genit , lascivia, Tac , with dat , bonis inexpertus atque insuetus, Liv , with ad and the acc , animus ad contumeliam inexpertus, Liv **II.** Pass , **1,** *untried, unattempted*, ne quid inexpertum relinquat, Verg , **2,** *untried, untested*, **a,** of persons, legiones bello civili inexpertae, Tac , **b,** of things, puppis, Ov , fides, Liv

ĭnexpĭābĭlis -e (in and expio), **1,** *inexpiable*; scelus, Cic , **2,** *implacable, irreconcilable*, homo, Cic , bellum, *obstinate*, Cic

ĭnexplēbĭlis -e (in and expleo), *insatiable, that cannot be satisfied*, **1,** lit , Sen , **2,** transf , **a,** of things, cupiditas, Cic , populi fauces, Cic , epularum foeda et inexplebilis libido, Tac , **b,** of persons, with genit , vir inexplebilis virtutis veraeque laudis, *with an insatiable desire for*, Liv

ĭnexplētus a um (in and expleo), *unfilled, insatiate, insatiable* inexpletus lacrimans, *that cannot be satisfied with weeping*, Verg

ĭnexplĭcābĭlis -e (*that cannot be untied*) transf , **1,** *intricate, impracticable, difficult*, inexplicabiles continuis imbribus viae, *impassable*, Liv ; legatio, *impracticable*, Cic ; res difficilis et inexplicabilis, Cic , facilitas, *leading to no result*, Liv , **2,** *inexplicable*, haec inexplicabilia esse dicitis, Cic

ĭnexplōrātō, adv (inexploratus), *without exploring, without reconnoitring*, proficisci, Liv

ĭnexplōrātus -a um (in and exploro), *unexplored, uninvestigated*, stagni vada, Liv

ĭnexpugnābĭlis e, *unconquerable, impregnable* **I.** Lit , **a,** arx, Liv , **b,** gramen, *that cannot be rooted out* Ov , via, *inaccessible*, Liv **II.** Transf , with dat , inexpugnabile amori pectus, Ov , of persons, volumus eum qui beatus sit tutum esse, inexpugnabilem, saeptum atque munitum, Cic

inexspectātus -a -um, *unlooked for, unexpected*, Cic.

inexstinctus -a -um (in and exstinguo), *unextinguished, inextinguishable*; **1**, lit., ignis, Ov.; **2**, transf., fames, libido, *insatiable*, Ov.; nomen, *immortal*, Ov.

inexsŭpĕrābĭlis -e, *that cannot be passed over or crossed, insurmountable*. **A.** Lit., Alpes, Liv.; paludes, Liv. **B.** Transf., **a**, *unsurpassable*, Liv.; **b**, *insuperable*; vis fati, Liv.

inextrīcābĭlis -e (in and extrico), *that cannot be disentangled, inextricable*; error, *mazes out of which it is impossible to find one's way*, Verg.

infăbrē, adv. *unskilfully, in an unworkmanlike manner*; vasa non infabre facta, Liv.

infăbrĭcātus -a -um (in and fabrico), *unwrought, unfashioned*; robora, Verg.

infăcētē (inficētē), adv. (infacetus), *tastelessly, coarsely, without humour*, Suet.

infăcētĭae (inficētĭae) -ārum, f. (infacetus), *coarse jests, poor wit*, Cat.

infăcētus and **inficētus** -a -um (in and facetus), *coarse, rude, unmannerly, unpolished, without humour or wit*; homo non infacetus, Cic.; transf., mendacium non infacetum, Cic.

infăcundus -a -um, *not eloquent*; vir acer nec infacundus, Liv.; compar., quia infacundior sit, Liv.

infāmĭa -ae, f. (infamis), *ill report, shame, dishonour, disgrace, ignominy, infamy*; **1**, lit., infamiam inferre, Cic.; movere, *to cause*, Liv.; infamiā aspergi, *to come into bad repute*, Nep.; infamiā flagrare, Caes.; infamiam habere, Caes.; subire infamiam sempiternam, Cic.; **2**, meton., *the cause of ill repute and infamy*; nostri saecli, *the disgrace of our age*, Ov.; infamia silvae (of Cacus), Ov.

infāmis -e (in and fama), **1**, *of ill repute, disreputable, infamous*; homines vitiis atque dedecore infames, Cic.; vita, Cic.; **2**, *bringing into ill repute, disgraceful*; nuptiae, Liv.

infāmo, 1. (infamis), **1**, *to bring into ill repute, make infamous, defame*; aliquem, Nep.; aliquid, Cic.; **2**, *to blame, accuse, find fault with*; rem, Liv.

infandus -a -um (in and fari), *unutterable, unspeakable, unheard of, unnatural, abominable*; corpus eius impurum et infandum, Cic.; caedes, Liv.; dolor, labores, dies, Verg. Subst., **infanda** -ōrum, n. *unheard-of enormities*, Liv.; infandum or infanda ! *abominable !* Verg.

infans -fantis (in and fari). **I. A.** *dumb, speechless*, Cic. **B.** Of children, *not able to speak*; adj. = *young*, subst. = *a little child*; **1**, **a**, lit., filius, Cic.; infantibus parcere, Caes.; **b**, meton., (α) poet., *belonging to a child*; pectora infantia, Ov.; (β) *childish, foolish*; omnia fuere infantia, Cic. **II.** *without the gift of speech, devoid of eloquence*; infantes et insipientes homines, Cic.; transf., pudor, *embarrassed*, Hor.; meton., historia, Cic.

infantĭa -ae, f. (infans). **I. A.** *inability to speak*; linguae, Lucr. **B.** *childhood* (up to the age of seven); prima ab infantia, Tac. **II.** Transf., *want of eloquence, slowness of speech*, Cic.

infarcĭo (infercĭo) -farsi (-fersi), -farsum (-fersum) and -fartum (-fertum), 4. (in and farcio), *to stuff in, cram in, stuff full of*; fig., neque inferciens verba quasi rimas expleat, Cic.

infătīgābĭlis -e, *that cannot be wearied, indefatigable*, Plin.

infătŭo, 1. (in and fatuus), *to make a fool of, infatuate*; aliquem mercede publicā, Cic.

infaustus -a -um, *unlucky, unfortunate*; auspicium, Verg.; dies, Tac.

infector -ōris, m. (inficio), *a dyer*, Cic.

1. **infectus** -a -um (in and facio). **I.** *unworked, unwrought*; argentum, Liv.; aurum, Verg. **II. A.** *undone, unfinished, incomplete*; pro infecto habere, *to consider as having never taken place*, Cic.; infectā re (*without having accomplished the business*) discedere, Caes., abducere exercitum, Liv.; infecto negotio, Sall.; infectā victoriā, Liv.; infectā pace, Liv.; infecto bello, Liv.; reddere infectum, *to make void*, Hor. **B.** Transf., *impracticable, impossible*; rex nihil infectum Metello credens, Sall.

2. **infectus**, partic. of inficio.

infēcundĭtas -ātis, f. (infecundus), *barrenness, sterility*; terrarum, Tac.

infēcundus -a -um, *unfruitful, barren, sterile*; ager, Sall.; fig., fons (ingenii), Ov.

infēlīcĭtas -ātis, f. (infelix), *ill-luck, unhappiness, misfortune*; haruspicum, Cic.; alicuius in liberis, Liv.

infēlīcĭtĕr, adv. (infelix), *unluckily, unfortunately*; totiens infeliciter temptata arma, Liv.

infēlīco, infēlīcito, 1. (infelix), *to make miserable*, Plaut.

infēlix -īcis. **I.** *unfruitful, barren*; tellus frugibus infelix, Verg. **II.** Transf., **A.** *unlucky, unhappy, miserable*; **a**, of persons, homo miserrimus atque infelicissimus, Cic.; infelicior domi quam militiae, Liv.; with genit., animi, *in mind*, Verg.; with abl., operis summā, Hor.; **b**, of things, patria, Verg. **B.** Act., *causing unhappiness, unfortunate, unlucky*; **1**, gen., **a**, of persons, qui reipublicae sit infelix, Cic.; **b**, of things, consilium, Liv.; **2**, esp., infelix arbor, *the gallows*, Cic.

infensē, adv. (infensus), *hostilely, acrimoniously*; infense invectus, Tac.; quis Isocrati est adversatus infensius, Cic.

infenso, 1. (infensus), *to treat in a hostile manner*; Armeniam bello, *to attack*, Tac.

infensus -a -um (in and *fendo), *hostile, full of hate and bitterness, enraged*; **a**, of persons, rex irā infensus, Liv.; with dat., infensus alicui, Verg.; with in and the acc., eo infensioribus in se quam in illum judicibus, Liv.; **b**, of things, animus, Cic.; opes principibus infensae, *dangerous*, Tac.

infer -a -um, **inferi** -ōrum, v. inferus.

infĕrĭae -ārum, f. (inferi), *sacrifices or offerings in honour of the dead*; alicui inferias afferre, Cic.

infercĭo, v. infarcio.

infĕrĭor, v. inferus.

infĕrĭus, **1**, adv., v. infra.; **2**, neut. adj., v. inferus.

infernē, adv. (infernus), *on the lower side, beneath, below*, Lucr.

infernus -a -um (infer), *that which is below, lower*. **I.** Gen., partes, Cic. **II.** Esp., **a**, *underground*; gurges, Ov.; **b**, *of or relating to the lower world, infernal*; rex, *Pluto*, Verg.; Juno, *Proserpine*, Verg.; palus, *the Styx*, Ov. Hence subst., **a**, **inferni** -ōrum, m. *the inhabitants of the lower world*, Prop.; **b**, **inferna** -ōrum, n. *the lower world, infernal regions*, Tac.

infĕro, intŭli, illātum, inferre, *to bring, bear, carry in, to put or place on*. **I.** Lit., **A.** Gen. templis ignes inferre, *to set fire to*, Cic.; aliquid in ignem, Caes.; in equum, *to put on horseback*, Caes. **B.** Esp., **a**, *to bury, inter*, Cic.; **b**, *to give in an account*; rationes, Cic.; sumptum civibus, *to charge, put to the account of*; **c**, *to sacrifice, pay*; honores Anchisae, Verg.; **d**, manus alicui or in aliquem, *to lay hands on*, Cic.; alicui vim, *to do violence to*, Cic.; **e**, signa in hostem, *to attack*, *charge*, Caes, f, bellum alicui, or contra aliquem, *to make war on, levy war against*, Cic, g, pedem, *to enter*, Cic, in a hostile meaning, *to attack*, alicui, Liv., so gradum, Liv, h, reflex and middle; (α) reflex, se inferre, *to betake oneself, to go*, lucus quo se persaepe inferebat, Liv, *to charge the enemy*, effusi se stantibus vobis intulerint, Liv, (β) middle, inferri in urbem, Liv **II.** Transf, **A.** se in periculum, *to fall into*, Cic **B.** a, *to produce, bring forward;* sermonem, *to speak*, Cic, mentionem, *to mention*, Liv; b, *to cause, occasion*, spem alicui, Caes; hostibus terrorem, Cic, periculum civibus, Cic; c, *to excite* or *seek to excite*, misericordiam, invidiam, Cic; d, *to infer, conclude*, Cic

infersus and **infertus**, v infarcio

infĕrus -a -um (connected with ἔνεροι), and **infĕr** -a -um, compar **infĕrior**, superl **infimus** and **imus** -a -um **I.** Positive, **infĕrus** -a -um, 1, *that which is below, lower* (opp superus); mare, *the Etruscan Sea* (opp mare Superum, *the Adriatic*), Cic, 2, *that which is in the lower world*, inferi dii, Cic Subst, **infĕri** ōrum and -ûm, m *the departed, the dead, the lower world*, ab inferis exsistere, *to rise from the dead*, Liv, apud inferos, *in the lower world*, Cic, elicere animas inferorum, Cic, ab inferis excitare or revocare, *to raise from the dead*, Cic **II.** Compar, **infĕrior**, neut **infĕrius**, genit -iōris, *the lower* (opp superior), 1, of position, labrum, *the under lip*, Caes, ex inferiori loco dicere, *to speak from the body of the court* (opp ex superiori loco, *from the tribunal*), Cic, 2, transf, a, of order, versus, *the pentameter*, Ov, b, of time, *later, younger*, aetate inferiores, Cic, c, of number, inferior numero navium, *weaker*, Caes, d, of rank, *lower, meaner, of less importance*, gradus, Cic, inferioris juris magistratus, Liv, e, of power, *weaker*, with abl, inferior animo, Caes; fortunā, *in fortune*, Cic., in jure civili, Cic **III.** Superl, **A. infĭmus (infŭmus)** a -um, *the lowest* (opp summus), 1, lit, a, solum, Caes, b, ad infimos montes, *at the bottom of the mountains*, Nep, ab infima ara, *from the bottom of the altar*, Cic, 2, transf, of position, *lowest, meanest*, infimo loco natus, Cic, faex populi, Cic, precibus infimis, *with abject prayers*, Liv **B. īmus** -a -um, *the lowest*, 1, lit, a, sedes ima, Cic, ab imo, *from the bottom*, Caes, ab imo suspirare, *to sigh deeply*, Ov, neut plur, **īma** ōrum, *the lower world*, Ov., b, ab imis unguibus ad verticem summum, Cic, gurges, *the bottom of*, Ov, 2, transf, a, of tone, *deepest, lowest*, vox ima, Hor, b, of position, superi imique deorum, Ov, c, *the last*, mensis, Ov, ad imum, *to the end*, Hor, and *at the end*, Hor

infervesco -ferbŭi, 3 *to begin to boil, grow hot, to be boiled down;* hoc ubi confusum sectis inferbuit herbis, Hor.

infestē, adv (infestus), *in a hostile manner*, Liv., compar, infestius atque inimicius, Liv, superl, inimicissime atque infestissime, Cic

infesto, 1 (infestus), *to attack, harass, disquiet*, latus dextrum, Ov

infestus -a -um (in and *fendo) **I.** Act, *hostile, inimical, dangerous, troublesome*, 1, of things, a, provincia Galliā, Cic with dat, alicui invisus infestusque, Cic, with in and the acc, infestus in suos, Cic, b, milit t t, *with hostile intent, in hostile array, prepared for battle;* ab Tibure infesto agmine profecti, Liv, 2, of things, infestis oculis conspici, Cic, infestis signis, *in hostile array*, Caes, hastā infestā, *with lance couched*, Liv, infestis pilis, *ready for the throw*, Caes. **II.** Pass, *made dangerous, unsafe, insecure, molested*, iter, Cic; mare infestum habere Cic, with abl, via illa incursionibus barbarorum infesta, Cic

inficētus, inficēte = infacetus, infacete (q v)

infĭcio -fēci fectum, 3 (in and facio) **I.** *to put or dip into anything*, hence, *to tinge, dye, stain, colour*, 1, lit, a, se vitro, Caes, rivos sanguine, Hor ora pallor albus inficit, *makes colourless*, Hor, b, *to mix with*, hoc (dictamno) fusum labris splendentibus amnem inficit, Verg 2, transf, *to imbue, instruct*, (puer) jam infici debet in artibus, etc, Cic **II.** 1, *to poison* Gorgoneis Alecto infecta venenis, Verg, 2, transf, *to taint, infect, corrupt*, ut cupiditatibus principum et vitiis infici solet tota civitas, Cic, poet, infectum scelus, *the crime with which they are stained*, Verg

infĭdēlis -e, *unfaithful, untrue, perfidious, faithless*, Cic, superl, infidelissimi socii, Cic

infĭdēlĭtas tātis, f (infidelis), *unfaithfulness, faithlessness*, amicitiarum, Cic.

infĭdēlĭtĕr, adv (infidelis), *unfaithfully, faithlessly*, Cic

infīdus -a -um, *unfaithful, faithless, untrue*, a, of persons, amici, Cic., b, of things, societas regni, Liv, nihil est enim stabile quod infidum est, Cic

infīgo -fixi -fixum, 3 *to fix, fasten to*, or *in, to thrust in* **I.** Lit, gladium hosti in pectus, Cic, hasta infigitur portae Verg **II.** Transf, *to imprint, impress, fix*, cura erit infixa animo, Cic, animus infixus est in patriae caritate, Cic, in hominum sensibus positum atque infixum est, Cic, infixum est, *it is fixed, finally resolved*, Tac

infĭmātis -is, m (infimus), *a person of the lowest condition*, Plaut

infĭmus a um, superl of inferus (q v)

infindo fĭdi -fissum, 3 *to cut in, cleave* sulcos telluri, Verg, poet, sulcos mari, *to sail through the sea*, Verg

infīnĭtas -tātis, f (in and finis), *infinity, endlessness* infinitas locorum, Cic, in infinitatem omnem peregrinari, Cic

infīnītē, adv (infinitus), *infinitely boundlessly, endlessly*, partes secare et dividere, Cic, concupiscere, Cic

infīnītĭo -ōnis, f (infinitus), *infinity*, Cic

infīnītus a -um (in and finio) **I.** 1, lit, of space, altitudo, Cic, 2, transf, a, of time, *endless, unceasing*, tempus, Cic, odium, Cic, b, of number, *countless*, infinita corporum varietas, Cic, c, of extent size, degree, *boundless, immense*, magnitudo, Caes, silva, Cic, infinitum est, with infin, Cic, subst, **infīnītum** -i, n *that which is boundless*, Cic **II.** *indefinite, general*, infinitior distributio, Cic

infirmātĭo -ōnis, f (infirmo), 1, *a refuting*, rationis, Cic, 2, *invalidating*, rerum judicatarum, Cic

infirmē, adv (infirmus), *weakly, faintly;* socii infirme animati, Cic

infirmĭtas -tātis, f (infirmus), *weakness, powerlessness, infirmity*, 1, corporis Cic, valetudinis, Cic, 2, transf, a, *mental weakness*, hominum, Cic, animi, *want of spirit, want of courage*, Cic, b, *instability, unsteadiness of character* Gallorum, Caes

infirmo, 1 (infirmus), *to weaken*, 1, lit, legiones, Tac 2, transf, a, *to shake*, fidem testis, Cic, b, *to refute*, res leves, Cic, c, *to annul*, acta illa atque omnes res superioris anni, Cic

infirmus a um, *weak, feeble, infirm* **I.**

Lit., physically, vires, Cic.; classis, Cic.; infirmi homines ad resistendum, Caes. **II.** Transf., **a,** *weak;* res infirma ad probandum, Cic.; **b,** mentally and morally, *weak, timorous;* animo infirmo esse, Cic.; *superstitious,* Hor.

infit, defective verb = incipit, **1,** *he or she begins;* with infin., Verg.; esp., **2,** *he or she begins to speak,* Verg.

infitiae, f. (in and fateor), *a denial;* found only in acc., infitias ire aliquid, *to deny anything,* Liv.; with acc. and infin., infitias eunt, *they deny,* mercedem se belli Romanis inferendi pactos (esse), Liv.

infitialis -e (infitiae), *negative, containing a denial;* quaestio, Cic.

infitiatio -ōnis, f. (infitior), *a denying;* negatio infitiatioque facti, Cic.

infitiator -ōris, m. (infitior), *one who denies or disavows a debt or deposit,* Cic.

infitior, 1. dep. (in and fateor), *to deny, disavow, not to confess;* **1,** with acc., verum, Cic.; with acc. and infin., neque ego in hoc me hominem esse infitiabor unquam, Cic.; **2,** *to deny a debt, refuse to restore a deposit;* quid si infitiatur? Cic.

inflammatio -ōnis, f. (inflammo), *a fire, conflagration;* inferre inflammationem tectis, Cic.; transf., animorum, *fire, inspiration,* Cic.

inflammo, 1. **A.** *to light up, kindle, set fire to;* taedas, Cic.; classem, Cic. **B.** Transf., *to inflame, excite, stir up, stimulate;* populum in improbos, Cic.; inflammari ad cupiditates, Cic.; inflammatus ipse (orator) et ardens, *fiery,* Cic.

inflatio -ōnis, f. (inflo), of the body, *a puffing up, blowing out, flatulence;* inflationem magnam habere, *to cause flatulence,* Cic.

inflatius, adv. in compar. (inflatus), *too pompously, proudly, haughtily;* haec ad eum latius atque inflatius perscribebat, Cic.

1. **inflatus** -a -um, p. adj. (from inflo). **A.** *swelling, swollen;* collum, Cic. **B.** Transf., **a,** *scornful;* animus, Cic.; **b,** *haughty, proud;* laetitiā, spe, Cic.

2. **inflatus** -ūs, m. (inflo), **1,** *a blowing into;* primo inflatu tibicinis, *at the first blast,* Cic.; **2,** *inspiration;* divinus, Cic.

inflecto -flexi -flexum, 3. *to bend, bow, curve.* **I.** Lit., bacillum, Cic.; quum ferrum se inflexisset, Caes.; inflectere nullum unquam vestigium sui cursus, Cic.; oculos, Cic.; middle, inflecti, *to curve;* sinus ab litore in urbem inflectitur, Cic. **II.** Transf., **a,** jus civile, *to warp,* Cic.; **b,** *to modulate the voice;* inflexā ad miserabilem sonum voce, Cic.; **c,** *to alter a name;* suum nomen ex Graeco, Cic.; **d,** of persons, *to change, move, affect;* aliquem leviter, Cic.; sensus animumque labantem, Cic.

infletus -a -um (in and fleo), *unwept, unlamented,* Verg.

inflexibilis -e, *that cannot be bent, inflexible,* Plin.

inflexio -ōnis, f. (inflecto), *a bending, swaying;* laterum inflexio fortis ac virilis, Cic.

inflexus -ūs, m. (inflecto), *a bending, curving,* Juv.

infligo -flixi -flictum, 3. **I.** *to strike, knock, dash against;* alicui securim, Cic.; puppis inflicta vadis, *dashed on,* Verg. **II.** *to inflict, cause hurt or damage;* mortiferam plagam, Cic.; alicui turpitudinem, Cic.

inflo, 1. **I.** *to blow on or in;* **a,** *to play on wind instruments;* calamos leves, Verg.; tibias, Cic.; and absol., *to give a blast;* simul inflavit tibicen, Cic.; **b,** *to produce by blowing;* sonum, Cic. **II.** *to blow out;* **1,** lit., **a,** *to puff out, to swell;* ambas buccas, Hor.; amnis inflatus (aquis), Liv.; **b,** *to blow out a sound fully;* aliquid extenuatur, inflatur, Cic.; **2,** transf., *to puff up, make proud or arrogant, elate;* animos falsā spe, Liv.; inflatus laetitiā, Cic.

influo -fluxi -fluxum, 3. *to flow in, stream in.* Caes. **A.** Lit., non longe a mari, quo Rhenus influit, Rhenus in Oceanum influit, Caes.; with simple acc., lacum, Caes. **B.** Transf., **1,** *to come in unawares, to steal in;* in aures, Cic.; in animos, Cic.; **2,** *to stream in, rush in, flow in;* in Italiam Gallorum copiae, Cic.

infodio -fōdi -fossum, 3. *to dig in, bury;* corpora terrae, Verg.; taleas in terram, Caes.

informatio -ōnis, f. (informo), *a conception, idea;* Dei, Cic.; antecepta animo rei, *an à priori idea,* Cic.

informis -e (in and forma), **1,** *formless, unformed;* alvei, Liv.; **2,** *unshapely, misformed, deformed, hideous;* cadaver, Verg.; hiems, Hor.

informo, 1. *to give form and shape to, to form, fashion.* **I.** Lit., clipeum, Verg. **II.** Transf., **a,** *to form;* animus a natura bene informatus, Cic.; **b,** *to form by instruction, instruct;* artes quibus aetas puerilis ad humanitatem informari solet, Cic.; **c,** *to sketch, represent, depict;* oratorem, Cic.; causam, Cic.; **d,** *to form an idea, conception, image of anything;* eos (deos) ne conjecturā quidem informare posse, *form a conjectural idea of,* Cic.

infortunatus -a -um, *unfortunate, unhappy, miserable;* nihil me infortunatius, Cic.

infortunium -ii, n. (in and fortuna), *misfortune, ill luck,* Hor., Liv.

infra (for inferā, sc. parte, from inferus). **I.** Adv., **1,** lit., **a,** gen. (α) posit. *on the under side, below, beneath;* innumeros supra infra, dextra sinistra deos esse, Cic.; *in writing,* earum (litterarum) exemplum infra scripsi or scriptum est, Cic.; (β) compar. inferius, *lower down;* inferius suis fraternos currere Luna admiratur equos, Ov.; **b,** *in the lower world,* Tib.; **2,** transf., *below* (in rank), nec fere unquam infra ita descenderent ut ad infimos pervenirent, Liv. **II.** Prepos. with acc.; **1,** lit., in space, *beneath, below;* mare infra oppidum, Cic.; infra eum locum ubi pons erat, Caes.; **2,** transf., **a,** of size, hi sunt magnitudine paulo infra (*less than*) elephantos, Caes.; **b,** of time, *later than;* Homerus non infra superiorem Lycurgum fuit, Cic.; **c,** *beneath, below,* in rank, estimation; res humanas infra se positas arbitrari, Cic.

infractio -ōnis, f. (infringo), *breaking;* transf., animi, *dejection,* Cic.

infractus -a -um (p. adj. from infringo), **1,** *broken,* Plin.; **2, a,** *broken, exhausted;* animos, *dejected,* Liv.; **b,** infracta loqui, *to speak disconnectedly,* Cic.

infragilis -e, **1,** *not fragile, that cannot be broken,* Plin.; **2,** *strong;* vox, Ov.

infremo -fremui, 3. *to roar, growl;* aper, Verg.

1. **infrenatus** -a -um (in and freno), *without bridle;* equites, *riding without a bridle,* Liv.

2. **infrenatus** -a -um, partic of infreno.

infrendeo, 2. *to gnash with the teeth;* dentibus, Verg.

infrenis -e and **infrenus** -a -um (in and frenum), *without bridle, unbridled;* equus, Verg.; Numidae, *riding without bridle,* Verg.

infreno, 1. **1,** lit., *to bridle;* equos, Liv.; currus, *to harness the horses to the chariot,* Verg.; **2,** transf., *to restrain, hold back, check;* horum alterum sic fuisse infrenatum conscientiā scelerum et fraudium suarum ut, etc., Cic.

infrĕquens -entis, *infrequent* **I.** Of space **A.** *not numerous, few in number*, hostes, Liv; copiae infrequentiores, Caes, senatus infrequens, Cic **B.** Of places, *not full, scantily populated*, pars urbis infrequens aedificiis erat, Liv, causa, *attended by few hearers*, Cic, subst, infrequentissima urbis, *the least populous parts of the city*, Liv **II.** Of time, of persons, *not doing a thing often, infrequent, occasional*, deorum cultor, Hor

infrĕquentĭa -ae, f (infrequens), **1,** *fewness, scantiness of number, thinness*, senatus, Cic, **2,** *solitude, loneliness*, locorum, Tac

infrĭco -fricŭi -frictum and -frĭcātum, 1 *to rub in or on*, Plin

infringo -frēgi -fractum, 3 (in and frango) **I.** *to break, break off, break in pieces* **A.** Lit, remum, Cic, hastam, Liv **B.** Transf, *to break, destroy, impair, check, enfeeble, cast down*; vim militum, Caes, spem, Cic, conatus adversariorum, Caes, animum, Liv; Samnitium vires, Liv **II** *to knock against*, liminibus lumbos, Hor

infrons -frondis, *leafless*, ager, *treeless*, Ov.

infructŭōsus -a -um, *unfruitful*, transf, *unproductive, fruitless, useless*, militia, Tac, laus, Tac

infūcātus -a um (in and fuco), *rouged, painted*, fig vitia, Cic

infŭla -ae, f *a band or fillet made of locks of wool, knotted at intervals, worn by priests and Vestal virgins, and used to decorate victims, altars, etc*, Cic, also worn by suppliants, Caes, hence, *something holy*, his insignibus atque infulis imperii Romani venditis, *the inalienable public land*, Cic

infŭlātus a um (infula), *adorned with or wearing the* infula, Suet

infulcĭo -fulsi -fultum, 4 *to stuff in, cram in*, Suet

infundo -fūdi -fūsum, 3 **I.** *to pour in or on* **A.** Lit, **1,** aliquid in vas, Cic, **2,** *to administer*, alicui venenum, Cic, alicui poculum, *to present*, Hor **B.** Transf **a,** of a crowd of people, gen reflex, se infundere or passive infundi as middle = *to pour in, stream in*, infusus populus, *collected in large numbers*, Verg, **b,** of wind, sound, etc, *to pour into, to allow to penetrate*, passive as middle = *to penetrate*, Cic, vitia in civitatem, Cic **II.** *to pour on or over* **A.** Lit, **a,** of liquids, largos humeris rores, Verg, **b,** of bodies not liquid, ignis infusus, Liv. **B.** Transf, infusus with dat, *spread, lying on*, gremio, Verg

infusco, 1. *to make dark or black, to obscure, blacken* **I.** Lit, vellera, arenam, Verg **II.** Transf, *to disfigure, corrupt, stain*, vicinitas non infuscata malevolentiā, Cic, eos barbaries infuscaverat, Cic

infūsĭo -ōnis, f (infundo), *a pouring in or on, infusion*, Plin.

Ingaevŏnes um, m *a German tribe on the shores of the North Sea*

Ingauni -ōrum, m *a Ligurian tribe*

ingĕmĭno, 1 **I.** Transit, *to double, redouble*, ictus, voces, Verg **II.** Intransit, *to become double, to increase*, imber, clamor, Verg

ingĕmisco (ingĕmosco) -gĕmŭi, 3 **I** Intransit, *to sigh or groan*, absol, nemo ingemuit, Cic, with in and the abl, in quo tu quoque ingemiscis, Cic, with dat, eius minis, Liv **II.** Transit, *to sigh or groan over*, with acc, quid ingemiscis hostem Dolabellam, Cic

ingĕmo, 3 *to sigh, groan over*, with dat, laboribus, Hor, aratro, Verg.

ingĕnĕro, 1 **I.** *to implant in, generate, produce* natura ingenerat amorem, Cic, partic, **ingĕnĕrātus** -a -um, *implanted by nature, innate, natural*, familiae frugalitas, Cic **II.** *to create*, animum esse ingeneratum a Deo, Cic

ingĕnĭātus a -um (ingenium), *endowed by nature*, Plaut

ingĕnĭōsē, adv (ingeniosus), *acutely, cleverly, ingeniously*, ista tractare, Cic

ingĕnĭōsus -a -um (ingenium), **1,** *naturally clever, talented, acute, able, ingenious*, quo quisque est sollertior et ingeniosior, Cic, **2,** of inanimate objects, *fit for, adapted to*, terra colenti, Ov, ad segetes ager, Ov

ingĕnĭtus -a um, partic of ingigno

ingĕnĭum -ii, n (in and geno = gigno), *nature, natural constitution* **I.** Of things, arvorum, Verg **II.** Of men **A.** *natural disposition, temperament, character*, ingenio suo vivere, *after one's own inclination*, Liv **B.** **a,** esp, *cleverness, talent, mental power, genius*, docilitas, memoria, quae fere appellantur uno ingenii nomine Cic, tardum, acerrimum acutum, magnum, Cic, ad fingendum, Cic, **b,** meton, *a man of genius, a genius*, Cic

ingens -entis (in and geno = gigno, lit, *grown to a great size*), *vast, immense, enormous* **I.** Lit, pecunia, campus, numerus, Cic **II.** Transf, exitus, Verg, bellum, Ov, with abl, ingens viribus, Liv, with genit, femina ingens animi, Tac

ingĕnŭē, adv (ingenuus), **1,** *nobly, liberally*, educatus, Cic, **2,** *freely, frankly*, confiteri, Cic

ingĕnŭĭtas -tātis, f (ingenuus), **1,** *the condition of a freeman, free birth*, Cic, ornamenta ingenuitatis, Cic, **2,** *noble-mindedness, uprightness, frankness*, Cic

ingĕnŭus -a -um (in and geno) **I.** *native, not foreign*, fons, Lucr **II.** *natural, innate*, color, Prop **III.** *free born, of free birth* **A.** Lit, Cic **B.** Transf, **a,** *that which becomes a free man, noble, honourable*, vita, artes, Cic, **b,** *frank, sincere*, homo, Cic, **c,** *weak, delicate*, Ov

ingĕro -gessi -gestum, 3 **I.** Lit, *to carry, throw, put, pour in or upon* ligna foco, Tib, hastas in tergum fugientibus, Verg, saxa in subeuntes, *to hurl at*, Liv **II.** Transf, **a,** *to heap on, to utter*, probra, Liv, convicia alicui, Hor., **b,** *to press upon, force upon*, alicui nomen, Tac, aliquem (*as judge*), Cic

ingestābĭlis -e, *unbearable, intolerable*, onus, Plin

ingigno -gĕnŭi -gĕnitum, 3 *to implant by birth or nature*, natura cupiditatem homini ingenuit veri videndi, Cic, partic, **ingĕnĭtus** -a um, *innate, inborn*, ut habeat quiddam ingenitum quasi civile atque populare, Cic

inglōrĭus a -um (in and gloria), *without fame or glory, inglorious*, vita, Cic, rex apum, *undistinguished*, Verg

inglŭvĭes -ēi, f (for ingulvies from in and gula), **1,** *the craw or crop of birds, the maw of animals*, Verg, **2,** meton, *gluttony*, Hor

ingrātē, adv (ingratus), **1,** *unpleasantly*, Ov, **2,** *ungratefully*, Cic

ingrātĭa ae, f (ingratus), *unthankfulness*, in class Lat only in abl, ingratiis (ingratis), *against the will of, unwillingly*, Cic

ingrātis, v ingratia

ingrātus a -um, **1,** *unpleasant, unpleasing* ne invisa diis immortalibus oratio nostra aut ingrata esse videatur, Cic, **2,** **a,** *unthankful, ungrateful*, homo, Cic, ingrati animi crimen horreo, Cic, with in and the acc, ingratus in Democritum, Cic, with genit, salutis, on *account of*, Verg.; with in and the abl., ingratus in referenda gratia, Caes.; of things, ingluvies, *insatiable*, Hor.; b, *unprofitable*, *thankless*; labor, Sall.; pericula, Verg.

ingrăvesco, 3. 1, lit., *to become heavy*, Plin.; 2, transf., a, in a good sense, hoc (philosophiae), studium cotidie ingravescit, *is followed more seriously*, Cic.; b, in a bad sense; (a) *to become annoying, troublesome*; annona ingravescit, *becomes dearer*, Cic.; ingravescit in dies malum intestinum, Cic.; (β) *to be oppressed, wearied*; corpora exercitationum defatigatione ingravescunt, Cic.

ingrăvo, 1. *to make heavy, to oppress, trouble, aggravate, render worse*; illa (conjugis imago) meos casus ingravat, Cic.; ingravat haec Drances, Verg.

ingrĕdĭor -gressus sum, 3. (in and gradior). I. Intransit., A. *to enter, go in*; a, lit., in navem, in templum, in fundum, Cic.; intra munitiones, Caes.; b, transf., *to enter on*; in bellum, Cic.; in eam orationem, Cic.; in spem libertatis, Cic. B. *to go forth, walk*; tardius, Cic.; per nudam infra glaciem, Liv. II. Transit., A. *to enter*; domum, Cic.; curiam, Liv. B. Of time, *to begin*; a, iter, Cic.: b, *to commence*; orationem, Cic.; with infin., dicere, Cic.

ingressĭo -ōnis, f. (ingredior), 1, *an entering, going in*; a, lit., fori, Cic.; b, transf., *a beginning*, Cic.; 2, *gait, pace*, Cic.

ingressus -ūs, m. (ingredior). I. *a going into, an entering*. A. Lit., *a hostile entrance, an inroad*; ingressus hostiles praesidiis intercipere, Tac. B. Transf., *a beginning*; ingressus capere, *to begin*, Verg. II. *walking, going, stepping*; ingressus, cursus, accubitio, inclinatio, sessio, Cic.; ingressu prohiberi, *not to be able to move*, Caes.

ingrŭo -ŭi, 3. (in and *gruo, connected with ruo), a, of persons, *to break in, fall upon violently*; ingruit Æneas Italis, Verg.; b, transf., of things, *to assault, attack*; periculum, bellum ingruit, Liv.; morbi ingruunt in remiges, Liv.; si nullus ingruat metus, Plin.

inguen -guĭnis, n. *the groin*, Verg.

ingurgĭto, 1. (in and gurges), 1, *to plunge*; se in tot flagitia, *to plunge into the whirlpool of vice*, Cic.; 2, esp. refl., se ingurgitare, *to glut* or *gorge oneself, to gormandise*, Cic.

ingustābĭlis -e (in and gusto), *that cannot be tasted*, Plin.

ingustātus -a -um (in and gusto), *untasted, not tasted before*; ilia rhombi, Hor.

ĭnhăbĭlis -e. I. *that cannot be handled* or *managed, unmanageable*; navis, Liv.; telum ad remittendum inhabile imperitis, Liv. II. *useless, unfit for, ill adapted to*; tegimen inhabile ad resurgendum, Tac.; multitudo inhabilis ad consensum, Liv.

ĭnhăbĭtābĭlis -e, *uninhabitable*; maximae regiones inhabitabiles, Cic.

ĭnhăbĭto, 1. *to inhabit*; eum secessum, Ov.

ĭnhaerĕo -haesi -haesum, 2. *to stick in, cleave to, remain fast to*; 1, lit., ad saxa, Cic.; visceribus, Cic.; sidera sedibus suis inhaerent, Cic.; 2, transf., inhaeret in mentibus quoddam augurium, Cic.; virtutes semper voluptatibus inhaerent, *are always connected with*, Cic.; semper alicui, *to be always in the company of*, Ov.

ĭnhaeresco -haesi -haesum, 3. (inchoat. of inhaereo), *to remain fast, to cleave to*; in mentibus, Cic.

ĭnhālo, 1. *to breathe upon*; quum isto ore foetido teterrimam nobis popinam inhalasses, Cic.

ĭnhĭbĕo -ŭi -ĭtum, 2. (in and habeo). I. *to hold in, hold back, check, restrain*; tela, Liv.; equos, Ov.; si te illius acerba imploratio et vox miserabilis non inhibebat, Cic.; as naut. t. t., inhibere remis, Cic., or navem retro inhibere, Liv., *to row a boat backwards, to row a boat stern first, to back water*. II. *to exercise, practise, use, employ*; supplicia nobis, Cic.; imperium in deditos, Liv.

ĭnhĭbĭtĭo -ōnis, f. (inhibeo), *a restraining*; remigum, *a rowing backwards*, Cic.

inhĭo, 1. I. *to gape, gape with wonder*; tenuit inhians tria Cerberus ora, Verg. II. *to gape for, open the mouth with desire*; Romulus lactens uberibus lupinis inhians, Cic.; fig. with dat., *to covet, desire, long for*; alicuius hortis, opibus, Tac.; varios pulchrā testudine postes, *look with desire upon*, Verg.

ĭnhŏnestē, adv. (inhonestus), *dishonourably, disgracefully*; aliquem accusare, Cic.

ĭnhŏnesto, 1. (inhonestus), *to disgrace, dishonour*; palmas, Ov.

ĭnhŏnestus -a -um, 1, *dishonourable, shameful, disgraceful*; homo, Cic.; vulnera, Ov.; inhonestissima cupiditas, Cic.; 2, *ugly, unsightly*; vulnus, Verg.

ĭnhŏnōrātus -a -um, 1, *not honoured, honoured by no public office, private, retired*; vita, Cic.; honoratus atque inhonoratus, Liv.; inhonoratior triumphus, Liv.; 2, *unrewarded, without gifts*; aliquem inhonoratum dimittere, Liv.

ĭnhŏnōrus -a -um, 1, *unhonoured, undistinguished*, Plin.; 2, *ugly, unsightly*, Tac.

ĭnhorrĕo -ŭi, 2. *to bristle with*; haud secus quam vallo saepta inhorreret acies, Liv.

ĭnhorresco -horrŭi, 3. I. *to begin to bristle, to bristle up*; a, aper inhorruit armos, Verg.; spicea jam campis messis inhorruit, Verg.; inhorruit unda tenebris, Verg.; b, *to be rough with frost*; quum tristis hiems aquilonis inhorruit alis, Ov. II. *to shudder, shiver, from cold, fever, fright*, etc.; 1, lit., dicitur inhorruisse civitas, Cic.; 2, transf., of things, *to shake, tremble*; aer, Ov.

ĭnhospĭtālis -e, *inhospitable*; Caucasus, Hor.

ĭnhospĭtālĭtas -tātis, f. (inhospitalis), *want of hospitality*, Cic.

ĭnhospĭtus -a -um, *inhospitable*; tecta, Ov.; Syrtis, Verg.

ĭnhūmānē, adv. (inhumanus), *inhumanly*; inhumanius dicere, Cic.

ĭnhūmānĭtas -tātis, f. (inhumanus), 1, *cruelty, inhumanity*, Cic.; 2, a, *incivility, discourtesy, disobligingness*, Cic.; b, *stinginess, niggardliness*, Cic.

ĭnhūmānĭtĕr, adv. (inhumanus), *uncivilly, rudely, discourteously*, Cic.

ĭnhūmānus -a -um, 1, *cruel, barbarous, inhuman*; homo, scelus, Cic.; quis inhumanior? Cic.; 2, a, *rude, uncourteous, uncivil, unmannerly*, Cic.; b, *uncultivated*; aures, Cic.

ĭnhŭmātus -a -um (in and humo), *unburied*, Cic.

ĭnhŭmo, 1. *to cover with earth*, Plin.

ĭnĭbī, adv. 1, of place, *therein, in that place, in that matter*, Cic.; 2, of time, *almost, nearly, on the point of*; inibi est, *it is on the point of taking place*; aut inibi esse aut jam esse confectum, Cic.

ĭnĭcĭo = injicio.

ĭnīmīcē, adv. (inimicus), *hostilely, in an unfriendly manner*; insectari aliquem, Cic.

inimicitia -ae, f. (inimicus), *enmity*, Cic., gen in plur, cum aliquo mihi inimicitiae sunt, or intercedunt, Cic., inimicitias gerere, Cic, exercere, Cic, suscipere, Cic

inimico, 1 (inimicus), *to make hostile, set at enmity*, ira miseras inimicat urbes, Hor.

inimicus -a -um (in and amicus) **I.** Act, *unfriendly, inimical, adverse* **A.** Lit., **a**, adj., inimicus alicui, Cic.; inimicus cenis sumptuosis, Cic, of inanimate objects, *hurtful, prejudicial;* odor nervis inimicus, Hor, **b**, subst, **inimicus** -i, m, *an enemy, foe*, Cic, **inimica** -ae, f. *a female foe*, Cic; inimicissimi Sthenii, *the bitterest foes of S*, Cic. **B.** Poet., transf. = hostilis, terra inimica, Verg **II.** Pass = *hated*, gener invisus inimici soceri, Tac.

inintelligens -entis, *unintelligent*, Cic

inique, adv (iniquus), **1**, *unequally;* iniquissime comparatum est, Cic., **2**, *unfairly, unjustly*, Cic

iniquitas -tātis, f (iniquus) **I.** *unevenness*, **a**, lit, loci, Caes; **b**, transf, *unfavourableness, difficulty, unpropitiousness*, temporis, Cic., rerum, Caes **II.** *unfairness, injustice, unreasonableness*, hominis, Cic, iniquitates maximae, Cic

iniquus a -um (in and aequus) **I.** *uneven*, **1**, lit, locus, Liv, **2**, transf, **a**, *unfavourable, disadvantageous;* locus, Caes, defensio angustior et iniquior, *on unfavourable ground*, Cic, **b**, of time, *unpropitious*, tempus, Liv., **c**, of character, *impatient, discontented*, animo iniquo ferre, with acc, *to be vexed at*, Cic, animo iniquissimo mori, *to die most reluctantly*, Cic **II.** *unequal*, **1**, lit., *too great*, pondus, Verg, sol, *too hot*, Verg, **2**, transf, **a**, *unjust, unfair*, pacem iniquā conditione retinere, Cic, **b**, *hostile, adverse*, animo iniquissimo infestissimoque aliquem intueri, Cic; subst., **iniqui** -ōrum, m *enemies*, Cic; aequi iniqui, or aequi iniquique, *friends and foes*, Liv.

initio, 1 (initium), *to initiate into a secret worship*, aliquem Cereri, Cic; aliquem Bacchis, *as one of the Bacchantes*, Liv

initium -ii, n (ineo), *a beginning, commencement* **I.** Gen., initium dicendi sumere Cic; initium caedis or confligendi facere, Cic, initium capere ab or ex, etc, Cic, ab initio, *from the beginning*, Cic, initio, *in the beginning, at the commencement*, Cic **II.** Esp, gen in plur **A.** *the elements* or *first principles of a science*, initia mathematicorum, Cic **B.** In natural philosophy, *elements*, Cic **C.** *the beginning of a reign*, initiis Tiberii auditis, Tac **D.** *a principle*, initium cognoscendi, Cic **E.** In plur, *a secret worship, hidden rites, mysteries*, Cic, and meton, *things used in such rites*, Cat.

initus -ūs, m (ineo), **1**, *an arrival, entrance*, Lucr; **2**, *a beginning*, Lucr, **3**, *copulation*, Ov

injectio -ōnis, f. (injicio), *a laying on*, manus, Quint

injectus -ūs, m (injicio), **1**, *a throwing on, throwing over*, injectu multae vestis, Tac, **2**, *a putting in, inserting*, Lucr

injicio -jēci -jectum, 3 (in and jacio) **I.** *to throw in* or *into, cast* or *put in* or *into*, **1**, lit, manum foculo, Liv., se in medios hostes, *to throw oneself into the midst of the enemy*, Cic, **2**, transf, **a**, *to cause, inspire, infuse, occasion*, alicui timorem, Cic; alicui mentem, ut audeat, etc., Cic; **b**, in conversation, *to mention, let drop, throw in*, alicui nomen cuiuspiam, Cic, quum mihi in sermone injecisset, with acc and infin, Cic **II.** *to throw* or *place on.* **A.** pontem flumini, Liv., brachia collo, *to embrace*, Cic, **B.** Esp, **1**, *to throw* or *cast on*, pallium alicui, Cic; sibi vestem, Ov, vincula animo, Cic, **2**, transf, injicere alicui manus, *to lay hands on*, fig, mihi veritas manum injecit, Cic, esp, *to lay hands on in order to appropriate what is one's own, to take possession of*, manum virgini venienti, Liv, fig, manum Parcae, Verg

injucunde, adv only in compar. (injucundus), *unpleasantly, in an unfriendly manner*, res injucundius actae Cic

injucunditas -tātis, f (injucundus), *unpleasantness*, ne quid habeat injucunditatis oratio, Cic

injucundus -a -um, *unpleasant, displeasing*, minime nobis injucundus labor, Cic., adversus malos injucundus, *unfriendly*, Cic

injudicatus -a -um (in and judico), *untried, uncondemned, undecided*, Quint

injungo -junxi -junctum, 3 **I.** *to join to, fasten to*, tignos in asseres, Liv **II. A.** Lit., *to join, unite, connect with*, vineas et aggerem muro, Liv **B.** Transf, **1**, *to cause*, alicui injuriam, Liv, **2**, *to inflict upon, occasion, bring upon, to lay* or *impose upon, charge, enjoin*, alicui munus, Liv, civitatibus servitutem, Caes, alicui laborem, onus, leges, Liv

injuratus -a -um, *unsworn, not having taken an oath*, Cic

injuria -ae, f (injurius), *an injury, injustice, wrong* **I.** Lit, **A.** injuriam alicui inferre, imponere, facere, Cic, in aliquem immittere, jacere, *to commit, inflict an injury on*, Cic; accipere, *to suffer wrong*, Cic, propulsare, Cic, defendere, Caes, *to repel*, etc, per injuriam, *wrongfully*, Cic, injuriā, Cic **B. 1**, *an insult*, spretae formae, Verg, **2**, legal t t, *damage, harm, injury, affront*, actio injuriarum, Cic **II** Meton, **1**, *a possession wrongfully obtained;* pertinaces ad obtinendam injuriam, Liv, **2**, *revenge for an affront*, consulis, Liv

injuriose, adv. (injuriosus), *illegally, wrongfully, injuriously*, in magistratus decernere, Cic, mercatores injuriosius tractare, Cic

injuriosus -a -um (injuria), *acting wrongfully, unjust, wrongful, unlawful*, vita, Cic, injuriosi in proximos, Cic

injurius -a -um (in and jus), *wrongful, unjust*, quia sit injurium, Cic

injurus a -um = injurius (q v)

1 **injussus** -a -um (in and jubeo), *uncommanded, unbidden, spontaneous*, gramina virescunt, *without cultivation*, Verg

2 **injussus**, m found only in abl injussu, *without orders*, injussu imperatoris, Cic, injussu suo, Cic, or simply injussu, e g, pugnare, Liv

injuste, adv (injustus), *unjustly, unfairly;* facere, Cic

injustitia -ae, f (injustus), *injustice, unjust proceeding*, totius injustitiae nulla est capitalior, Cic

injustus -a -um, **1**, *unfair, unjust*, homo, Cic, noverca, *harsh, severe*, Verg, regna, *unjustly acquired*, Ov, subst, **injustum** -i, n *injustice*, metu injusti, Hor, **2**, *heavy, burdensome, oppressive*, onus, Cic, fascis, Verg

inl v ill

inm v imm

innabilis e (in and no), *that cannot be swum in*, unda, Ov

innascor -nātus 3 dep **I.** *to be born, grow, arise in* or *upon*, neglectis filix innascitur agris, Hor salicta innata ripis, Liv **II** Transf, *to be produced, arise*, in hac elatione animi cupiditas innascitur, Cic., partic., in-

nātus -a -um, *innate, inborn*; insita quaedam vel potius innata cupiditas, Cic.

innăto, 1. **I.** *to swim into*; in concham hiantem, Cic. **II. A.** *to swim* or *float in* or *upon*; with dat., lactuca acri innatat stomacho, Hor.; with acc., undam innatat alnus, Verg. **B.** Transf., *to flow into* or *over*; innatat unda dulcis freto, Ov.

innātus, partic. of innascor.

innăvīgābĭlis -e, *not navigable*, Liv.

innecto -nexŭi -nexum, 3. *to tie, bind, fasten, weave together*. **I.** Lit., comas, Verg.; fauces laqueo, Ov.; palmas armis, Verg.; inter se innexi rami, Tac. **II.** Transf., **A.** causas morandi, *to bring forward one after the other*, Verg. **B.** Esp., **1,** *to entangle, implicate*; innexus conscientiae alicuius, Tac.; **2,** *to connect*; Hyrcanis per affinitatem innexus erat, Tac.

innītor -nixus sum, 3. dep. *to lean upon, rest upon, support oneself by*. **I.** Lit., scutis, Caes.; hastā, Liv.; alis, *to fly*, Ov. **II.** Transf., uni viro, Messio, fortuna hostium innititur, Liv.

inno, 1. *to swim in* or *on*. **I.** fluitantes et innantes beluae, Cic.; with dat., aquae, Liv.; with acc., fluvium, Verg. **II. a,** *to flow over*, Hor.; **b,** *to sail over, navigate*; Stygios lacus, Verg.

innŏcens -entis, *harmless, not hurtful*. **I.** Lit., innocentis pocula Lesbii, Hor. **II.** Transf., **A.** epistola, Cic. **B.** *innocent, harmless, inoffensive, blameless*; innocens is dicitur qui nihil nocet, Cic.; factorum, Tac.

innŏcentĕr, adv. (innocens), *innocently, blamelessly, inoffensively, irreproachably*; innocentius agere, Tac.

innŏcentĭa -ae, f. (innocens). **I.** *harmlessness*; ferorum animalium, Plin. **II.** *innocence, blamelessness, inoffensiveness, disinterestedness*, Cic.; meton., = *the innocent*; innocentiam judiciorum poenā liberare, Cic.

innŏcŭē, adv. (innocuus), *harmlessly, innocently*; vivere, Ov.

innŏcŭus -a -um. **I.** Act., *innocuous, harmless*. **A.** Lit., herba, Ov.; litus, *safe*, Verg. **B.** Transf., *innocent, harmless, blameless*; homo, Ov. **II.** Passive, *unhurt, unharmed*; carinae, Verg.

innōtesco -nōtŭi, 3. *to become known* or *noted*; nostris innotuit illa libellis, Ov.; quod ubi innotuit, Liv.

innŏvo, 1. *to renew*; se ad suam intemperantiam, *to return to*, Cic.

innoxĭus -a -um. **I.** Act. **A.** *innoxious, harmless*; anguis, Verg. **B.** Transf., *innocent*; criminis innoxia, Liv. **II.** Pass., **A.** *unhurt, unharmed*; ipsi innoxii, Sall. **B.** *undeserved*; paupertas, Tac.

innūbĭlus -a -um, *unclouded, clear*, Lucr.

innūbo -nupsi -nuptum, 3. *to marry into, connect oneself with by marriage*; quo innupsisset, Liv.

innŭbus -a -um (in and nubo), *unmarried, without a husband*; Sibylla, Ov.; laurus (because Daphne, while still a virgin, was changed into a laurel), Ov.

innŭmĕrābĭlis -e, *that cannot be counted, innumerable*; multitudo, Cic.

innŭmĕrābĭlĭtas -atis, f. (innumerabilis), *an infinite number, innumerableness*; mundorum, Cic.

innŭmĕrābĭlĭtĕr, adv. (innumerabilis), *innumerably*, Cic.

innŭmĕrālis -e, *countless, innumerable*, Lucr.

innŭmĕrus -a -um, *countless, innumerable*; gentes, Verg.

innŭo -ŭi, 3. *to give a nod to, make a sign or signal to*; alicui, Plaut., Ter.; ubi innuerint, Liv.

innuptus -a -um (in and nubo), **1,** *unmarried, having no husband*, Verg.; subst., **innupta** -ae, f. *a virgin, young damsel*, Verg.; **2,** meton., nuptiae innuptae (γάμος ἄγαμος), *a marriage that is no marriage, an unhappy marriage*; ap. Cic.

innūtrĭo, 4. *to bring up, educate with* or *among*; innutritus pessimis, Tac.

Īnō -ūs and -ōnis, f. (Ἰνώ), *daughter of Cadmus, wife of Athamas*; adj., **Īnōus** -a -um, *of* or *belonging to Ino*.

ĭnoblītus -a -um (in and obliviscor), *mindful, not forgetful*, Ov.

ĭnobrūtus -a -um (in and obruo), *not overwhelmed*, Ov.

ĭnobservābĭlis -e, *not to be observed, imperceptible*, Cat.

ĭnobservantĭa -ae, f. *negligence, carelessness, inattention*, Suet.

ĭnobservātus -a -um, *unobserved, unperceived*; sidera, Ov.

ĭnŏcŭlātĭo -ōnis, f. *an engrafting*, Plin.

ĭnŏdōror, 1. dep., *to trace out anything, to smell out*, Cic. (?).

ĭnŏdōrus -a -um, *without smell, inodorous*, Pers.

ĭnoffensus -a -um, *without stumbling, unrestrained, unhindered, unobstructed*; mare, Verg.; cursus honorum, *uninterrupted*, Tac.

ĭnoffĭcĭōsus -a -um, **1,** *contrary to* or *neglectful of duty*; testamentum, *in which the nearest relatives are passed over*, Cic.; **2,** *disobliging*; in aliquem, Cic.

ĭnŏlens -entis, *without smell, inodorous*, Lucr.

ĭnŏlesco -ŏlēvi -ŏlĭtum, 3. *to grow in* or *on*; **1,** lit., udo libro, Verg.; **2,** transf., penitusque necesse est multa (mala) diu concreta modis inolescere miris, Verg.

ĭnōmĭnātus -a -um (in and omen), *ill-omened, unlucky*, Hor.

ĭnŏpĭa -ae, f. (inops). **I.** *want, need*; in Rhodiorum inopia (*want of food*) et fame, Cic.; frumentaria, Caes.; with genit., frugum, Cic.; transf., consilii, Cic. **II.** *helplessness*, Cic.

ĭnŏpīnans -antis, *not expecting, unexpected, unawares*; aliquem inopinantem aggredi, Caes.

ĭnŏpīnantĕr (inopinans), *unexpectedly*, Suet.

ĭnŏpīnātō, adv. (inopinatus), *unexpectedly*, Liv.

ĭnŏpīnātus -a -um. **I.** Pass., *unexpected, unlooked for*; res, Cic.; malum, Caes.; subst., **ĭnŏpīnātum** -i, n. *an unexpected event*, Cic.; ex inopinato, Cic., inopinato, Liv., *unexpectedly*. **II.** Act., *not expecting*; inopinatos invadere, Liv.

ĭnŏpīnus -a -um (in and opinus, from opinor), *unexpected, unlooked for*; visus, Ov.; quies, Verg.

ĭnŏpĭōsus -a -um (inopia), *needy, in want of*; consilii, Plaut.

inopportūnus -a -um, *inopportune, unseasonable*, Cic.

ĭnops -ŏpis. **I.** *without means*. **A.** *poor*; **1, a,** lit., aerarium inops et exhaustum, Cic.; **b,** transf., *poor in words* or *thoughts*; lingua, oratio, Cic.; **2,** *poor in something, wanting in*; with genit. or abl., or ab and the abl., pecuniae, Liv.; verborum, verbis, Cic.; amicorum, ab amicis, Cic.; transf., humanitatis, Cic. **B.** *powerless, weak*, Liv. **II.** *helpless*; inopes relicti a duce, Cic.

inōrātus -a -um (in and oro), *not formally brought forward and heard*; re inorată, Cic

inordinātus -a um, *disorderly, in confusion*, dispersi, inordinati exibant, Liv, subst, **inordinātum** -i, n *disorder*, ex inordinato in ordinem adducere, Cic

inŏrior, 4 dep, *to arise, appear*, Tac (?)

inornātus a -um, *unadorned* **I.** Lit, mulieres, Cic. **II.** Transf, **A.** orator, Cic **B.** *unpraised, uncelebrated*, Hor.

inp = imp (q v)

inquam is -it, perf, inquii, v def (connected with ἐνέπω), *I say*, **a**, in quoting the words of a speaker, est vero, inquam signum, Cic, with dat, inquit mihi, Cic, **b**, in repetition, for the sake of emphasis, hunc unum diem, hunc unum, inquam, diem, Cic, **c**, in objections, non solemus, inquit, ostendere, Cic (The forms found are inquam, Cic, inquit, Cic, inquimus, Hor, inquiunt, Cic, inquiebat, Cic, inquii, Cat, inquisti, Cic, inquies, Cat, inquiet, Cic, inque, Plaut., inquito, Plaut)

1 **inquies** -ētis, f *disquiet, want of rest*, Plin

2 **inquies** ētis, *unquiet, restless*, homo, Sall, nox, dies, Tac

inquiēto, 1 (inquietus), *to disquiet, disturb*, victoriam, Tac

inquiētus -a -um, *unquiet, restless* **I.** Lit, Hadria, *stormy*, Hor, nox inquieta, Liv **II.** Transf, **a**, *restless in disposition*, inquietus animus, Liv, **b**, *politically restless*, Liv

inquilīnus -i, m *one who dwells in a place not his own, a tenant lodger*, transf, inquilinus civis Romae (said of Cicero, who was not born in Rome), Sall

inquĭnātē, adv (inquinatus), *filthily, impurely*, loqui, Cic

inquĭnātus -a -um, p adj (from inquino), *dirtied, befouled, defiled, polluted, contaminated, sordid, shameful*, homo vita omni inquinatus, Cic, sermo inquinatissimus, Cic

inquĭno, 1 (connected with coenum), *to befoul, pollute, defile, stain, contaminate*, **1**, lit, aqua turbida et cadaveribus inquinata, Cic, aquas venenis, Ov, **2**, transf, *to corrupt, defile*, omnem splendorem honestatis, Cic, se parricidio, Cic

inquīro -quisivi -quisitum, 3 (in and quaero) **I** *to seek for, search for*, corpus alicuius, Liv **II. A.** *to investigate, inquire into*, diligenter in ea, Cic, in eum quid agat, quem ad modum vivat, inquiritur, Cic, omnia ordine, Liv **B.** Legal t t, *to search for evidence against any one*, in competitores, Cic (pluperf subj, inquisissent, Liv, perf infin, inquisisse, Liv)

inquīsītio -ōnis, f (inquiro) **I.** *a searching after, looking for*, corporum, Plin **II. A.** *investigation, inquiry*, veri inquisitio atque investigatio, Cic **B.** Legal t t, *the search for evidence against any one*, candidati, *against a candidate*, Cic.

inquīsītor -ōris, m (inquiro), *an inquirer* **I.** *a spy*, Suet **II. A.** Philosoph t t, *an investigator*, rerum, Cic **B.** *one who searches for evidence to support an accusation*, Cic

inr v irr

insălūbris e, **1**, *unhealthy*, Plin, **2**, *unserviceable, unprofitable*, Plin

insălūtātus -a um, *ungreeted, of whom no farewell has been taken*, in the tmesis, inque salutatam linquo, Verg

insānābilis e, *incurable*, **1**, l t, morbus, Cic, **2**, transf, contumeliae, Cic.

insānē, adv (insanus), *madly, insanely*, in silvam ne ligna feras insanius, Hor

insānĭa ae, f (insanus), *madness, loss of reason, insanity*, **1**, **a**, lit, nomen insaniae significat mentis aegrotationem et morbum, Cic, concupiscere aliquid ad insaniam, *madly*, Cic, **b**, transf, *mad desire, mad, senseless excess, senseless extravagance*, libidinum, Cic, **2**, *poetical rapture or inspiration*, amabilis, Hor

insānĭo ivi and ii -itum, 4 (insanus), *to rage, be seized with madness or frenzy*; **a**, lit, ex injuria, Liv, nisi ego insanio, Cic, of things, insaniens Bosporus, *raging*, Hor, **b**, transf, *to act like a madman, to rave*, insanit statuas emendo, Hor, with acc, similem (errorem), Hor, sollemnia, *to be fashionably mad*, Hor

insānĭtas -ātis, f (insanus), *mental disease, insanity*, Cic

insānus -a -um **I.** *of unsound mind, mad, insane* **A.** Lit, Cic **B.** **1**, *acting like a madman, raging, senseless*, homo flagitiis insanus, Cic, contio, Cic, of things, **a**, *raging*, fluctus, Verg, **b**, *of great size or violence*, moles, Cic, cupiditas insanior, Cic, **2**, *inspired*, vates, Verg **II.** Act., *making mad*, aqua, Ov

insătĭābĭlis -e (in and satio) **I.** Pass, *that cannot be satisfied, insatiable*, cupiditas, Cic **II** Act, *that does not satiate, uncloying, unwearying*, pulchritudo, Cic, insatiabilior species, Cic

insătĭābĭlĭtĕr, adv (insatiabilis), *insatiably*, Lucr

insătĭĕtas -ātis, f *insatiableness*, Plaut

insătŭrābĭlis -e (in and saturo), *insatiable*, abdomen, Cic

insătŭrābĭlĭtĕr, adv (insaturabilis), *insatiably*, Cic

inscalpo, 1 *to engrave*, Plin

inscendo -scendi -scensum, 3 (in and scando), *to ascend, mount, go up*, in rogum ardentem, Cic, navem, Plaut

inscensĭo -ōnis, f (inscendo), *a going on board*, in navem, Plaut

insciens -entis, *ignorant, unaware*, me insciente factum, *done without my knowledge*, Cic

inscientĕr, adv. (insciens), *ignorantly, stupidly, foolishly*, facere, Cic

inscientĭa -ae, f (insciens), **1**, *ignorance, inexperience, want of acquaintance with*, inscientia mea, nostra, Cic, foll by genit. of the subject, vulgi, Caes, of the object, locorum, Caes, dicendi, Cic, **2**, philosoph t t, *want of certain knowledge* (opp scientia), Cic

inscītē, adv (inscitus), *clumsily, awkwardly, unskilfully*, inscite aliquid comparare cum aliqua re, Cic

inscītĭa ae, f (inscitus), **1**, *clumsiness, awkwardness, inexperience, ignorance*, with genit of subject, barbarorum, Cic, of object, negotii gerendi, Cic, disserendi, Cic, **2**, *ignorance, stupidity*, legionum, Tac, erga domum suam, Tac

inscītus -a -um, *ignorant, unskilful, absurd, silly*, quid autem est inscitius quam, etc, Cic

inscĭus a -um, *ignorant, not knowing*, medici inscii imperitique, Cic, followed by genit, omnium rerum, Cic, culpae, *free from*, Verg, equus inscius aevi, *not confident of its strength*, Verg; with rel sent, inscii quid in Aeduis gereretur, Caes

inscrībo -scripsi -scriptum, 3 **I.** *to write in or on, inscribe*, **1**, lit, aliquid in basi tropaeorum, Cic, nomen monumentis, Cic, librum, *to give a title to a book*, Cic, fig, *to impress*, orationem in animo, Cic, **2**, transf, **a**, *to assign*, sibi nomen philosophi, *to assume*, Cic.; **b,** *to ascribe;* deos sceleri, *to charge the gods with crime*, Ov. **II. A.** *to give an inscription or title to;* inscribo epistolam patri, *to address*, Cic.; liber qui Oeconomicus inscribitur, *is entitled*, Cic.; flores inscripti nomina regum, *marked with*, Verg.; versā pulvis inscribitur hastā, *is marked with*, Verg. **B.** *to brand*, Juv.

inscriptio -ōnis, f. (inscribo), *a writing in or upon;* **1,** nominis, Cic.; **2,** *the inscription on a statue, the title of a book*, Cic.

1. **inscriptus** -a -um (in and scribo), *unwritten*, Quint.

2. **inscriptus** -a -um, partic. of inscribo.

insculpo -sculpsi -sculptum, 3. *to cut or carve in, engrave;* **1,** lit., summam patrimonii saxo, Hor.; foedus columnā aeneā, Liv.; **2,** transf., *to impress;* natura insculpsit in mentibus, Cic.

insĕcābilis -e, *that cannot be cut, inseparable, indivisible*, Quint.

insĕco -sĕcŭi -sectum, 1. *to cut into, cut to pieces;* gurg[illegible]ones, Cic.; cutem, *to make an incision in*, Liv.

insectātio -ōnis, f. (insector), **1,** lit., *a following, pursuit*, Liv.; **2,** transf., *railing at, deriding, insulting;* alicuius, Liv.

insectātor -ōris, m. (insector), *a pursuer, persecutor;* plebis, Liv.

insector, 1. dep., *to follow, pursue;* **1,** lit., aquila insectans alias aves, Cic.; **2,** transf., *to pursue with harsh words, reproach, inveigh against, rail at;* aliquem maledictis, Cic.; audaciam improborum, Cic.

insēdābilitĕr, adv. (in and sedo), *inextinguishably, unquenchably*, Lucr.

insĕnesco -sĕnŭi, 3. *to grow old at or among;* libris et curis, Hor.

insensilis -e, *insensible, imperceptible*, Lucr.

1. **insĕpultus** -a -um (partic. of insepelio).

2. **insĕpultus** -a -um (in and sepelio), *unburied;* acervi civium, Cic.; aliquem insepultum projicere, Liv.; sepultura, *burial without the customary solemnities*, Cic.

insĕquor -sĕcūtus or -sĕquūtus sum, 3. *to follow after, follow on, succeed.* **I. A.** Lit., insequitur acies ornata armataque, Liv.; with acc., temere insecutae Orphea silvae, Hor. **B.** Transf., **a,** mors insecuta est Gracchum, *overtook*, Cic.; **b,** of time, *to follow;* hunc proximo saeculo Themistocles insecutus est, Cic.; annus insequens, Liv.; **c,** *to pursue a subject;* insequar longius, Cic. **II.** *to follow or pursue with hostile intent.* **A.** Lit., aliquem gladio stricto, Cic.; clamore et minis, Cic. **B.** Transf., **a,** *to press hard;* homines benevolos contumeliā, Cic.; **b,** *to censure, reproach, attack;* aliquem irridendo, Cic.; vitae eius turpitudinem, Cic.

1. **insĕro** -sēvi -sĭtum, 3. **1,** *to sow in, plant in*, Plin.; **2,** *to implant;* inserit novas opiniones, evellit insitas, Cic.; partic., **insitus** -a -um, *implanted, innate, inborn;* insitus menti cognitionis amor, Cic.; **3,** *to unite;* corpora animis, Cic.

2. **insĕro** -sĕrŭi -sertum, 3. *to put, place, set in, insert.* **I.** Lit., collum in laqueum, Cic.; oculos in alicuius pectora, *to fix the gaze upon*, Ov. **II.** Transf., **A.** Meton., *to introduce, insert into, intermingle with;* jocos historiae, Ov.; deos minimis rebus, Liv.; se alicui rei, *to meddle with*, Ov. **B.** *to incorporate with, place among;* aliquem vatibus, Hor.

insertim, adv. *by insertion*, Lucr.

inserto, 1. (intens. of 2. insero), *to insert, put into;* clypeo sinistram, Verg.

inservio, 4. *to serve.* **I.** Lit., as a vassal or subject, reges inservientes, Tac. **II.** Transf., *to serve.* **A.** *to be devoted to, to pay attention to:* alicui, Cic.; nihil est inservitum a me temporis causā, Cic. **B.** *to be devoted to a thing, to take care of;* inservi (valetudini), Cic.

insessus, partic. of insideo and insido.

insībilo, 1. *to hiss, pipe, whistle in*, Ov.

insĭdĕo -sēdi -sessum, 2. (in and sedeo). **I.** Intransit., *to sit upon.* **A.** Lit., **a,** with dat., or abl., immani et vastae beluae, Cic.; equo, Cic.; **b,** *to have one's seat or place* (of the Penates), Cic. **B.** Transf., **a,** insidens capulo manus, *resting upon*, Tac.; **b,** *to be settled, to dwell, remain;* insidet quaedam in optimo quoque virtus, Cic. **II.** Transit., **a,** *to take possession of, occupy;* locum, Liv.; **b,** *to inhabit;* ea loca, Tac.

insĭdiae -ārum, f. (insideo), *an ambush.* **I.** Lit., **a,** insidias locare, Liv.; collocare, Caes.: **b,** of the place of ambush, milites in insidiis collocare, Caes. **II.** Transf., **a,** *a snare, trap, treachery, deceit, plot;* insidias vitae ponere or facere, Cic.; insidias ponere contra aliquem, Cic.; insidias alicui parare, Cic.; insidias opponere, tendere, collocare, struere, adhibere, comparare, Cic.; insidias componere, Tac.; per insidias, ex insidiis, or insidiis, *treacherously*, Cic.; **b,** *illusion, deception;* noctis, Verg.

insĭdiātor -ōris, m. (insidior), *a spy, waylayer, lurker, traitor*, Cic.; viae, Cic.

insĭdĭor, 1. dep. (insidiae). **I.** *to lie in ambush against, lie in wait for*, Caes.; hostibus, Ov.; ovili, Verg. **II. a,** *to plot against the life of;* alicui, Cic.; **b,** *to watch for, wait for;* somno maritorum, Cic.; tempori, *to wait for the fitting opportunity*, Liv.

insĭdiōsē, adv. with superl. (insidiosus), *deceitfully, treacherously, insidiously*, Cic.

insĭdiōsus -a -um (insidiae), *deceitful, cunning, treacherous, full of snares;* **a,** of inanimate objects, insidiosus et plenus latronum locus, Cic.; clementia alicuius, Cic.; **b,** of persons, quis insidiosior? Cic.

insīdo -sēdi -sessum, 3. *to sit, settle, perch upon.* **I.** floribus (of bees), Verg.; digitos membris, *sink into*, Ov. **II. A.** *to settle, dwell;* jugis, Verg.; with acc., cineres patriae, Verg. **B. 1,** *to beset a place, take up one's post at;* with dat., silvestribus locis, Liv.; with acc., tumulos, Liv.; of things, semen in locis insedit, *takes root in*, Cic.; **2,** transf., *to sink deep;* in animo, Cic.

insignĕ -is, n. (insignis), *a signal, token.* **A.** Gen., Cic.; nocturnum, *a night-signal*, Liv. **B.** Esp., **1,** *the official badge of a magistracy;* insigne regium, Cic.; more commonly plur., insignia, *badges, insignia;* imperatoris, Caes.; sacerdotum, Liv.; regia, Cic.; transf., insignia virtutis, laudis, Cic.; **2,** orationis lumina et quoddammodo insignia, *beauties*, Liv.

insignio, 4. (insignis), **1,** *to put a mark, sign, or token upon, to impress;* in animis tamquam insignitae notae veritatis, Cic.; **2, a,** *to distinguish;* aliquem notā, Liv.; cum omnis annus funeribus et cladibus insigniretur, *was remarkable for*, Tac.; **b,** *to adorn;* agros tropaeis, Verg.; clipeum Io auro insignibat, Verg.

insignis -e (in and signum), *distinguished by a token, remarkable, noted, notable;* **1,** lit., bos maculis insignis, Verg.; uxores insignes auro et purpurā, Liv.; Phoebus insignis crinibus, Ov.; insignis ad deformitatem, *remarkably ugly*, Cic.; **2,** transf., *remarkable, eminent, distinguished, extraordinary;* improbitas, Cic.; virtus Scipionis, Cic.; insigne ad irridendum vitium, Cic.

insignītē, adv. with compar. (insignitus), *remarkably, extraordinarily*, Cic.

insignītĕr, adv with compar (insignis), *remarkably, extraordinarily*, Cic

insignītus a -um (p adj from insignio), 1, *marked so as to be known, noticeable, plain*, imago, Cic, notae veritatis, Cic, 2, *striking, remarkable, unexampled* imagines, Cic, insignitior contumelia, Liv

insīlĕ -is, n *the spool* or *bobbin* on which the yarn was twisted in weaving, Lucr

insĭlĭo -silŭi -sultum, 4 (in and salio), *to leap, spring, jump in* or *on*, in phalangas, Caes, in equum, Liv, tergo, Ov, with accus, Aetnam, Hor, undas, Ov (perf insilivit, Liv)

insĭmŭlātĭo -ōnis, f (insimulo), *an accusation, charge*, probrorum, Cic

insĭmŭlo, 1 *to charge, accuse, blame*, with acc of pers, aliquem falso, Cic with accus and infin, quod eos insimulemus omnia incerta dicere, Cic; with acc of pers and genit, se peccati quod, etc, Cic, with simple acc, quod ego insimulo, Cic

insincērus a um, *tainted, putrefying*, cruor, Verg

insĭnŭātĭo -ōnis, f (insinuo), rhet t t, *the gaining the favour of the audience*, Cic

insĭnŭo, 1 *to introduce by windings* or *turnings, to insinuate* **A.** Lit, Romani quacumque data intervalla essent, insinuabant ordines suos, *pushed forward their files into the gaps of the enemy*, Liv, refl, se insinuare, or simply insinuare, and middle insinuari, *to penetrate, work one's way in, to insinuate oneself*, insinuare in forum, Cic, se inter equitum turmas, Caes, qua se inter valles flumen insinuat, Liv **B.** Transf, se in familiaritatem alicuius, Cic, insinuare se in philosophiam, Cic, se insinuare, or insinuare alicui, *to gain the good will of*, Cic, penitus in causam, *to get to know thoroughly*, Cic

insĭpĭens -entis (in and sapiens), *foolish, stupid*, Cic

insĭpĭentĕr, adv (insipiens), *foolishly, stupidly*, Plaut

insĭpĭentĭa -ae, f (insipiens), *foolishness, stupidity*, Cic

insisto -stiti, 3 **I.** *to stand on, set foot on, tread on, place oneself on* **A.** Lit, 1, cingulus lunae in quo qui insistunt, etc, Cic, digitis, *to stand on the tip of one's toes*, Ov, limen, Verg, pedum primis vestigia plantis, Cic, insistere vestigiis alicuius, *to tread in the steps of* (fig), Cic, 2, esp, a, *to enter on a journey, pursue*; iter, Liv, b, *to follow hard on*, referentibus pedem, Liv **B.** Transf, 1, perge tenere istam viam quam institisti, Cic, 2, esp, *to follow any object* or *occupation eagerly, persist in*, totus et mente et animo in bellum insistit, Caes, with acc, rationem belli, *to follow out the plan of the war*, Caes, munus, Cic, with dat, ei rei, Liv **II.** *to remain still, stand still* **A.** Lit, stellae insistunt, Cic **B.** Transf, 1, a, *to stop, pause*, in speech, quae quum dixisset paulumque institisset, "Quid est," inquit, Cic b, *to pause over, dwell upon*, singulis peccatorum gradibus, Cic, 2, *to be fixed* or *obstinate in*, importune, Cic, crudelitati, Tac, with infin, sequi, Cic, 3, *to be at a stand = to doubt*, in reliquis rebus, Cic

insĭtīcĭus -a -um (1 insero), *engrafted, foreign*, Plin

insĭtĭo ōnis, f (1 insero), 1, *a grafting, budding*, plur, insitiones, *the kinds of grafting*, Cic, 2, meton, *the grafting season*, Ov

insĭtīvus a -um (1 insero), *grafted, engrafted* 1, lit, pira, Hor, 2, transf, a, *foreign*, quaedam disciplinae, Cic.; b, *supposititious, not genuine*, Phaedr

insĭtor ōris, m (1 insero), *a grafter*, Prop.

insĭtus -a -um, partic of 1 insero

insŏcĭābĭlis e, *that cannot be joined together, unsociable, unsocial*, gens, Liv., with dat, hominis generi humano insociabiles, Liv

insōlābĭlĭtĕr, adv. (in and solor), *inconsolably*, Hor

insŏlens entis (in and soleo) **I.** *unusual, contrary to custom*, quid tu Athenas insolens? Ter **II. A.** *unaccustomed to, unused to*, infamiae, Cic, in dicendo, Cic **B.** 1, *unusual, extravagant* verbum, Cic, 2, of behaviour, a, *prodigal*, non fuisse insolentem in pecunia, Cic, b, *proud, haughty, arrogant, insolent*, exercitus, *flushed with victory*, Hor, ostentatio, Cic

insŏlentĕr, adv (insolens), 1, *unusually, in a way contrary to custom*, evenire vulgo soleat, an insolenter et raro, Cic, 2, a, *immoderately, excessively*, his festivitatibus insolentius abuti, Cic, b, *haughtily, arrogantly, insolently*, se efferre, Cic

insŏlentĭa ae, f (insolens) **I.** *the not being accustomed to a thing, inexperience in, strangeness*, huius disputationis, Cic **II. A.** *strangeness, affectation, novelty of diction*, verborum, Cic **B.** *extravagance, profuseness*, Cic **C.** *pride, arrogance, insolence*, Cic

insŏlesco, 3 (in and soleo), a, *to behave extravagantly*, magis insolescente Plancina, Tac, b, *to become haughty* or *insolent, be elated*, per licentiam insolescere animum humanum, Sall

insŏlĭdus a -um, *weak, soft, tender*, herba, Ov

insŏlĭtus -a -um **I.** Act, *unaccustomed to*, ad laborem, Caes, with genit, rerum bellicarum, Sall **II.** Pass, a, *unusual, strange*, haec insolita mihi ex hoc loco ratio dicendi Cic, b, *uncommon, unusual*, insolita mihi loquacitas, Cic, verbum, Cic

insŏlūbĭlis -e, 1, *that cannot be paid*, Sen, 2, *incontrovertible, indubitable*, Quint

insomnĭa -ae, f (insomnis), *sleeplessness, loss of sleep*, gen in plur, insomniis carere, Cic

insomnis -e (in and somnus), *sleepless*, insomnes magis quam pervigiles, Tac, draco, Ov, of things, nox, Verg

1 **insomnĭum** -ĭi, n (in and somnus), *sleeplessness*, Plin

2 **insomnĭum** -ĭi, n (in and somnus), *a dream*, sing, Tac, plur, Verg

insŏno -sŏnŭi -sŏnitum, 1 **I.** Intransit, *to make a noise in, sound, resound*, insonuere cavernae, Verg, flagello, *to crack a whip*, Verg **II.** Transit, *to make to sound*, verbera, Verg

insons sontis, 1, *innocent, guiltless*, insontes sicut sontes circumvenire, Sall, 2, poet, transf, *harmless*, Cerberus, Hor

insōpītus -a -um (in and sopio), *not lulled to sleep, wakeful, watchful*, draco, Ov

inspargo = inspergo (q v)

inspecto, 1 (intens of inspicio), *to look at* or *in, observe, view*, inspectata spolia Samnitium, Liv, inspectante exercitu interfici, Cic

inspērans -antis (in and spero) *not hoping, not expecting*, insperanti mihi sed valde optanti cecidit ut, etc, Cic

inspērātō, adv (insperatus), *unexpectedly*, Plaut

inspērātus a -um (in and spero), *unhoped for, unexpected*, pecuniae, Cic, malum, Cic, ex insperato, *unexpectedly*, Liv.

inspergo and **inspargo,** -spersi (-sparsi), -spersum (-sparsum), 3. (in and spargo). **I.** *to strew, sprinkle in or on;* molam et vinum, Cic. **II.** *to besprinkle,* Plin.

inspĭcĭo -spexi -spectum, 3. (in and specio). **I.** *to look, see in or on.* **A.** Lit., **1,** faciem, Ov.; speculum, Phaedr.; **2,** *to look into, read;* leges, Cic.; verba, Ov. **B.** Transf., *to examine, look into, become acquainted with;* aliquem a puero, Cic. **II.** *to contemplate, view, observe;* **1,** gen., signum publicum, Cic.; **2,** esp., **a,** as buyer, *to inspect;* candelabrum, Cic.; **b,** as a messenger, *to investigate;* sociorum res, Liv.; **c,** as an inspector, milit. t. t., *to inspect;* arma militis, Cic.; viros, Liv.; **d,** as a sacrificer, fibras, Ov.; **e,** as a spy, domos, Verg.

inspīco, 1. *to sharpen a point,* Verg.

inspīro, 1. **1,** intransit., *to breathe upon, to blow upon;* conchae, Ov.; **2,** transit., **a,** lit., *to breathe, blow in or on;* venenum morsibus, Verg.; **b,** transf., *to breathe into, inspire, rouse, inflame;* alicui occultum ignem, Verg.

inspŏlĭātus -a -um (in and spolio), *not despoiled, not plundered;* arma, Verg.

inspŭo -spŭi -spŭtum, 3. *to spit in or upon,* Plin.

inspūto, 1. *to spit upon,* Plaut.

instăbĭlis -e. **I.** Act., **A.** *that does not stand firm, unstable, tottering;* pedes instabilis ac vix vado fidens, Liv. **B.** Transf., **a,** *unsteady, not keeping its ground;* hostis instabilis ad conferendas manus, Liv.; **b,** *unstable, inconstant, changeable;* motus, Caes.; animus, Verg. **II.** Pass., *on which it is impossible to stand, insecure;* tellus, Ov.

instăbĭlĭtas -ātis, f. (instabilis), *instability,* Plin.

instans -antis, p. adj. (from insto), **1,** *present;* subst., **instans** -antis, n. *the immediate present,* Cic.; **2,** *pressing, urgent;* instantior cura, Tac.

instantĕr, adv. (instans), *urgently, earnestly, vehemently;* instantius concurrere, Tac.

instantĭa -ae, f. (insto), *the present time,* Cic.

instar, n. indecl., *an image, likeness, picture, sketch;* **a,** quantum instar in ipso! *what an imposing presence,* Verg.; gen. with genit., *like to, as great as, after the fashion of;* navis cybaea maxima triremis instar, Cic.; instar montis equus, Verg.; instar alicuius or alicuius rei esse, instar habere, instar obtinere, *to be like, to be as good as, to be in the place of;* Erana quae fuit non vici instar sed urbis, Cic.; Plato mihi unus est instar omnium, Cic.; alicuius rei instar putare or reri, *to think a thing as good as, consider it equal to;* idque si accidat, mortis instar putemus, Cic.; **b,** of number, *as many as, as large as;* cohortes quaedam quod instar legionis videretur, Caes.

instaurātĭo -ōnis, f. (instauro), *repetition, renewal;* ludorum, Cic.

instaurātīvus -a -um (instauro), *renewed, repeated;* ludi, Cic.

instauro, 1. (in and * stauro from sto, stare). **I.** *to renew, repeat, begin anew;* **1, a,** of public solemnities and ceremonies, sacrificium, Cic.; **b,** of any kind of action, scelus, caedem, Cic.; novum de integro bellum, Liv.; **2, a,** *to reanimate, restore;* instaurati (sunt) animi, Verg.; **b,** *to repay, requite;* talia Graiis, Verg. **II.** *to set about, prepare;* choros, Verg.

instorno -strāvi -strātum, 3. **I.** *to strew over, cover over;* equum, *to saddle or cover with a saddle-cloth,* Liv. **II.** *to spread over;* modicis tignis, Hor.

instīgātor -ōris, m. (instigo), *an instigator, stimulator;* sibi quisque dux et instigator, Tac.

instīgātrix -tricis, f. (instigator), *she that instigates,* Tac.

instīgo, 1. (in and STIG-o = στίζω whence also instinguo), *to instigate, incite, stimulate;* aliquem in aliquem, Liv.; absol., instigante te, *at your instigation,* Cic.

instillātĭo -ōnis, f. (instillo), *a dropping into,* Plin.

instillo, 1. *to drop in, pour in by drops;* oleum lumini, Cic.; transf., *to instil;* praeceptum auriculis, Hor.

instĭmŭlātor -ōris, m. (instimulo), *an instigator;* seditionis, Cic.

instĭmŭlo, 1. *to stimulate, arouse, incite,* Ov.

instinctor -ōris, m. (instinguo), *an inciter, instigator;* sceleris, Tac.

instinctus -ūs, m. (instinguo), *instigation, incitement;* instinctu divino, Cic.

instinguo -stinxi -stinctum, 3. (in and STIG-o = στίζω, whence also instigo), *to instigate, incite;* gen. in partic., **instinctus** -a -um, *incited, impelled;* furore, Cic.

instĭpŭlor, 1. dep., *to stipulate or bargain for,* Plaut.

instĭta -ae, f. *a seam, border, or flounce on a lady's robe;* meton., *a lady;* nulla, Ov.

instĭtĭo -ōnis, f. (insisto), *a standing still;* stellarum, Cic.

instĭtor -ōris, m. (insto), *a broker, factor, huckster, pedlar;* mercis, Liv.

instĭtōrĭum -ĭi, n. (institor), *the business of a hawker,* Suet.

instĭtŭo -ŭi -ūtum, 3. (in and statuo). **I.** *to put or place into;* vestigia nuda sinistri pedis, Verg. **II.** *to arrange.* **A.** Lit., **1,** milit. t. t., *draw up in order;* aciem duplicem, Caes.; **2,** *to prepare, make ready, build, construct;* turrim, pontes, naves, Caes.; vineas, Cic.; dapes, Verg. **B.** Transf., **1,** *to make arrangements for, begin, undertake;* historiam, Cic.; iter, Cic.; with infin., *to resolve upon, determine;* oppidum oppugnare, Cic.; historias scribere, Nep.; **2, a,** *to appoint, ordain, establish, introduce, institute;* portorium, Cic.; dies festos, Liv.; ludos, Ov.; with ut and the subj., *to arrange that,* etc., Cic.; with infin., Caes.; **b,** *to settle, to administer;* civitates, Cic.; **c,** *to instruct, teach, educate for a particular purpose;* aliquem ad dicendum, Cic.

instĭtūtĭo -ōnis, f. (instituo), **1,** *arrangement;* rerum, Cic.; institutionem suam conservare, *method,* Cic.; **2,** *instruction;* doctoris, Cic.; Cynica, *the principles of the Cynic philosophy,* Tac.

instĭtūtum -i, n. (instituo), **1,** *an undertaking, purpose;* non ad nostrum institutum pertinet, Cic.; **2,** *an old-established custom, arrangement, institution;* majorum, Cic.; institutum vitae capere, *to adopt a rule of life,* Cic.; ex instituto, *according to custom, order,* Liv.; **3,** *instruction, precept;* philosophiae, Cic.

insto -stĭti -stātūrus, 1. **I.** *to stand in or on;* rectam instas viam, Plaut. **II. A.** *to be close to, follow closely;* **1,** lit., vestigiis, Liv.; **2,** transf., **a,** *to press upon, pursue eagerly, urge, harass;* absol., Cic.; with dat., adversario, Cic.; hosti, Liv.; **b,** currum, *to be zealous in building,* Verg.; *to pursue or devote oneself eagerly to anything;* operi, Verg.; with following infin., *to persist, not to cease, to persevere;* poscere recuperatores, Cic.; **c,** *to persist, insist, ask pressingly;* alicui instare ut, with subj., Cic.; **d,** of time, *to approach, draw nigh, threaten;* dies instat quo, etc., Cic. **B.** *to stand upon, be fixed;* jugis, Verg.

1 **instrātus** -a -um (in and sterno), *uncovered*, Verg

2 **instrātus**, partic of insterno

instrēnŭus -a -um, *inactive, lazy, idle*, Plaut

instrĕpo -ŭi -ĭtum, 3 *to make a noise, rattle, clatter, creak*, sub pondere axis instrepat, Verg

instringo -strinxi strictum, 3 *to bind*, instricta fides gemmis, Ov

instructē, adv with compar (instructius), *with great preparation*, ludos instructius fecit, Liv

instructio -ōnis, f (instruo), *a setting in array, drawing up in order*, militum, Cic

instructor -ōris, m (instruo), *a preparer*, convivii, Cic

1 **instructus** -a -um, p adj (from instruo), 1, *provided with, furnished*, Graecia instructa copiis, Cic, 2, *instructed, learned*, in jure civili, Cic, instructior a jure civili, Cic

2. **instructus** -ūs, m (instruo), *a preparation, provision*, fig = *matter* (in a speech), while ornatus = *rhetorical ornament*, quocumque (oratio) ingreditur, eodem est instructu ornatuque comitata Cic

instrūmentum -i, n (instruo) **I.** *a tool, implement, instrument*; **a**, sing, instrumentum villae, *implements of husbandry*, Cic, militare, Caes, belli, Cic, **b**, plur, instrumenta anilia, *dress*, Ov. **II.** Transf, 1, *store, stock*, oratoris, Cic, 2, *means to an end*, instrumenta ad obtinendam sapientiam, Cic

instrŭo struxi structum, 3 **I.** *to build in or into*, contabulationes in parietes, Caes **II.** **A.** *to set up, build*, muros, Nep **B.** *to arrange, prepare*, **a**, lit., apud aliquem epulas instruere, Liv; **b**, transf, instruere fraudem, Liv **C.** *to furnish, equip, provide*, 1, gen, **a**, lit, domum suam in provincia, Cic, domus instructa or aedes instructae, *a furnished house*, Cic, **b**, transf accusationem et petitionem adornare atque instruere, Cic, of persons, aliquem mandatis Liv, 2, esp, **a**, milit t t, (α) *to arm*, exercitum, Liv, (β) *to draw up in order of battle, to post*, exercitum, aciem, Cic, **b**, *to teach, instruct*, aliquem ad omne officii munus, Cic

insuāvis -e, *not sweet, unpleasant, disagreeable*, littera insuavissima, *ill-sounding*, Cic, homo, Hor, vita, Cic

Insŭbres -ium and -um, m *the Insubrians, a people in Cisalpine Gaul, whose capital was* Mediolanum (*Milan*), sing, **Insŭbĕr** -bris, m *an Insubrian* Adj, **Insŭbĕr** bris -bre, *Insubrian*

Insŭbĕr, v Insubres

insūdo, 1 *to sweat in or at*, libellis insudat manus, Hor

insuēfactus -a -um (in -sueo and facio), *accustomed to, inured to*, Caes

insuesco -suēvi -suētum, 3 **I.** Intransit, *to accustom oneself to, to become used to*, corpori, Tac, ad disciplinam, Liv, with infin, victoriā frui, Liv **II.** Transit, *to accustom, habituate any one to*, insuevit pater hoc me, Hor

1 **insuētus** -a -um (in and suesco), 1, *unaccustomed to, unused to*, with genit, laboris, Caes, with dat., moribus Romanis, Liv, with ad and the acc, ad stabilem pugnam, Liv, with infin, vera audire, Liv, 2, pass, *unusual, unwonted*, solitudo, Liv, poet, insueta (neut plur) as adv, *unusually*, rudere, Verg

2 **insuētus** -a -um, partic of insuesco

insŭla -ae, f 1, *an island*, Cic, 2, *a detached house or building, let out to several poor families*, Cic, *a hired lodging*, Tac, Suet

insŭlānus -i, m (insula), *an islander*, Cic

insulsē, adv (insulsus), *insipidly, tastelessly, sillily, absurdly*, loqui, Cic

insulsĭtas -ātis, f (insulsus), *insipidity, tastelessness, absurdity*, Graecorum, Cic

insulsus -a -um (in and salsus), 1, *unsalted, insipid*, O gulam insulsam, *pleased with tasteless food*, Cic, 2, *insipid, tasteless, absurd, foolish*, genus ridiculi, Cic, adolescens, Cic

insulto, 1 (intens of insilio), 1, *to leap at or on*, busta, Hor, nemora, *dance through*, Verg, 2, *to scoff at, revile, insult, deride*, alicui in calamitate, Cic, multos bonos, Sall in rempublicam, Cic

insultūra -ae, f (insilio), *a leaping at or on anything*, Plaut

insum -fŭi -esse, *to be in or on*, 1, lit, comae insunt capiti, Ov, ferrum quale hastis velitaribus inest, Liv., 2, transf, *to be in, to be contained in, to belong to*, with in and the abl, superstitio in qua inest inanis timor, Cic; vitium aliquod inesse in moribus, Cic, with dat, cui virile ingenium inest, Sall.

insūmo -sumpsi -sumptum, 3 *to take for anything, expend*, teruncium in aliquem, Cic, sumptum in rem, Cic, paucos dies reficiendae classi, Tac, operam libellis accusatorum, Tac

insŭo -sŭi -sūtum, 3 *to sew in, sew up, sew on*, aliquem in culeum, Cic, insutum vestibus aurum, *embroidered, sewn on*, Ov

insŭpĕr. **I.** Adv **A.** Lit, 1, *above, over, overhead*, insuper inicere centones, Caes, 2, *from above*, jugum insuper imminens, Liv **B.** Transf, *over and above, in addition, moreover, besides*, insuper etiam, Liv, insuper quam, Liv **II.** Prepos with acc, Cato

insŭpĕrābĭlis -e, 1, *insurmountable, impassable*, via, Liv, 2, transf, *unconquerable* genus insuperabile bello, Verg, fatum, *inevitable*, Ov

insurgo -surrexi -surrectum, 3 *to rise up, raise oneself up* **I.** Lit **A.** Of persons, *to rise to one's full height*, in order to give more force to some action of the body, arduus insurgens, Liv, of rowers, insurgite remis, *put all your strength into the stroke*, Verg **B.** Of things, inde colles insurgunt, Liv, of the wind, aquilo, Hor, of water, vastius insurgens decimae ruit impetus undae, Ov **II.** Transf, **a**, *to increase in power*, Caesar paulatim insurgere, Tac, **b**, *to rise up against* suis regnis, Ov

insŭsurro, 1 *to whisper, whisper in the ear*, **a**, intransit, alicui, Cic, in aurem alicuius, Cic; **b**, transit, alicui cantilenam, Cic

intābesco -tābŭi, 3 1, *to pine, waste, wither away gradually*, diuturno morbo, Cic, 2, *to become liquid, melt*, cera igni, Ov

intactĭlis -e, *that cannot be touched*, Lucr

1 **intactus** -a -um (in and tango), *untouched* **I.** Gen, nix, *virgin*, Liv, cervix juvencae, *untouched by the yoke*, Verg, Britannus, *unconquered*, Hor, intactum Graecis carmen, *not attempted by*, Hor **II.** Esp, **a**, *unhurt*, prope intacti evasere, Liv, **b**, *pure, chaste*, Pallas, Hor, **c**, intactus aliqua re or ab aliqua re, *free from*, infamiā, cupiditate, Liv

2 **intactus** ūs, m *intangibility*, Lucr

intāmĭnātus -a -um (in and *tamino, whence also contamino), *unstained, unspotted*, honores, Hor

1 **intectus** -a -um, 1, *uncovered, unclothed, unarmed*, pedes, Tac, dux, Tac, 2, *open, frank*, Tac

2 **intectus** -a -um, partic of intego.

intĕgellus -a -um (dim. of integer), *tolerably uninjured, pretty safe*, Cic.

intĕger -gra -grum (for intager, from in and TAG-o, tango), *whole, entire, undiminished*. **I.** Physically, **a,** *unharmed, unwounded*, Cic., integros pro sauciis arcessere, Sall.; **b,** of food, *fresh, untainted*, aper, Hor.; **c,** *unhurt, undiminished, whole*, sublicae quarum pars inferior integra remanebat, Caes.; opes integrae, Hor.; existimatio, Cic.; **d,** *unmixed, pure*, fontes, Hor.; **e,** of strength, *fresh, unweakened, unexhausted, vigorous*, integris viribus repugnare, Caes.; **f,** *chaste, pure*, virgo, Cat.; **g,** of health or age, *sound, blooming*, valetudo, Cic.; integer aevi, *in the prime of life*, Verg.; **h,** of time, *entire*, annus, Cic.; **i,** *undiminished, fresh*, integram famem ad ovum affero, Cic.; de integro, *anew*, Cic.; so ab integro, Cic.; as legal t. t., in integrum restituere, *to restore a thing to its former condition*, praedia, Cic. **II.** Morally and intellectually. **A.** Intellectually, **a,** *undecided, undetermined*, rem integram relinquere, Cic.; causam integram reservare alicui, Cic.; in integro mihi res est, or integrum est mihi, *I am fully at liberty*, Cic.; foll. by infin. or ut and the subj., Cic.; sibi integrum reservare de aliquo or de aliqua re, *to reserve one's freedom of action*, Cic.; dare, *to leave or grant full liberty*, Cic.; **b,** *unexperienced*, rudem me et integrum discipulum accipe, Cic.; **c,** *intellectually whole, unbiassed, impartial, free from prejudice*; integri testes, Cic.; integrum se servare, Cic. **B.** Morally, **a,** *uncorrupted*, se integros castosque conservare, Cic.; **b,** *blameless, innocent, pure*, nemo integrior, Cic.; integer vitae scelerisque purus, Hor.; **c,** *inviolate*; fides, Tac.; jus, Cic.

intĕgo -texi -tectum, 3. *to cover*, turres coriis, Caes.

intĕgrasco, 3. (integro), *to break out afresh*, Ter.

intĕgrātio -ōnis, f. (integro), *a renewing, renewal*, Ter.

intĕgrē, adv. (integer). **I.** *purely, correctly*, dicere, Cic. **II. a,** *honestly, uprightly, impartially*, judicare, Cic.; **b,** *disinterestedly*, in privatorum periculis caste integreque versari, Cic.

intĕgrĭtas -ātis, f. (integer). **I. a,** *unimpaired condition, soundness, health*, corporis, Cic.; valetudinis, Cic.; **b,** *purity, correctness*, incorrupta quaedam sermonis Latini integritas, Cic. **II.** *honesty, uprightness, integrity*; integritas vitae, Cic.

intĕgro, 1. (integer). **I. a,** *to renew, repeat, begin afresh*, pugnam, Liv.; lacrimas, Liv.; **b,** *to heal*, elapsos in pravum artus, Tac. **II.** *to refresh*, animus integratur, Cic.

intĕgŭmentum -i, n. (intego). **I.** *a covering*, lanx cum integumentis, Liv. **II.** Transf., *a cloak, disguise*, haec flagitiorum integumenta, Cic.; evolutum illis integumentis dissimulationis tuae, Cic.

intellectus -ūs, m. (intelligo). **I.** *a perceiving, perception, sensation*, Plin. **II.** *an understanding, comprehension*, boni, mali, Tac.; intellectum habere, *to be understood*, Tac.

intellĭgens -entis, p. adj. (from intelligo), **1,** *intelligent, understanding or well acquainted with anything*, **a,** of persons, vir, Cic.; cuiusvis generis eius intelligens, Cic.; **b,** of things, judicium, Cic.; **2,** *a connoisseur*; homo ingeniosus et intelligens (opp. idiota), Cic.; in hisce rebus intelligens esse, Cic.

intellĭgentĕr, adv. (intelligens), *intelligently, with understanding*; audiri, Cic.

intellĭgentĭa -ae, f. (intelligens). **I.** *a conception, idea*, Cic. **II.** *insight, intelligence, knowledge*. **A.** quia difficilis erat animi, quid aut qualis esset intelligentia, Cic.; intelligentiam juris habere, Cic. **B. a,** *the knowledge of a connoisseur in some art, taste*, Cic.; **b,** *understanding*, fretus intelligentiā vestrā, Cic.; quod in nostram intelligentiam cadit, Cic.; res sub intelligentiam cadentes, Cic.

intellĭgo (**intellĕgo**) -lexi -lectum, 3. (inter and lego), *to understand, comprehend*. **I.** By the senses or understanding, *to mark, perceive, observe, feel*; de gestu intelligo quid respondeas, Cic.; intellexi ex tuis litteris, te audisse, Cic.; ex quo intelligitur or intelligendum est, or intelligi potest, with acc. and infin. or rel. sent. (with quam, quantus, etc.), Cic. **II.** *to form an idea or conception, to think, to understand*. **A.** corpus quid sit intelligo, Cic.; with acc. and infin., *to be of the opinion, to think*, ipsi intelligamus naturā gigni sensum diligendi, Cic. **B.** Esp., **1,** *to be a connoisseur*; tamen non multum in istis rebus intelligo, Cic.; **2,** *to understand a person's character, judge, appreciate*, aliquis falsus intelligitur, Tac. (syncop. perf., intellexti, Cic.)

Intĕmĕlii (**Intĭmĕlii**) -ōrum, m. *a people on the east side of the Alps, a branch of the Ligurians*. Hence, **Intĕmĕlium** -ii, n. *the chief town of the Intemelii*.

intĕmĕrātus -a -um (in and temero), *unspotted, undefiled, inviolate*, fides, Verg.

intempĕrans -antis, **1,** *extravagant, immoderate, intemperate*; intemperantis est, with infin., Cic.; in augendo eo intemperantior, Liv.; of things, libertas, gloria, Cic.; **2,** esp., *incontinent*, in aliqua re, Cic.; of things, intemperantissimae perpotationes, Cic.

intempĕrantĕr, adv. (intemperans), *immoderately, extravagantly, intemperately*, intemperantius opibus suis uti, Cic.

intempĕrantĭa -ae, f. (intemperans), **a,** *want of moderation, immoderateness, excess, intemperance*, libidinum, Cic.; vini, *immoderate indulgence in*, Liv.; **b,** *insubordination, insolence, haughtiness, arrogance*, Cic.

intempĕrātē, adv. (intemperatus), *intemperately*; vivere, Cic.

intempĕrātus -a -um, *intemperate, immoderate*, intemperata quaedam benevolentia, Cic.; intemperatā nocte, *in the dead of night*, Ov.

intempĕrĭae -ārum, f. (intempero), *inclement, unfavourable weather*; transf., quae te intemperiae tenent? *are you crazy?* Plaut.

intempĕrĭes -ēi, f. **I.** *inclement, unseasonable weather*, caeli, Liv.; aquarum, *excessive fall of rain*, Liv. **II.** Transf., **A.** *intemperate behaviour, outrageous conduct, insubordination*, amici, Cic.; cohortium, Tac. **B.** *incontinence, intemperance*, unius ex illis viris, Cic.

intempestīvē, adv. (intempestivus), *unseasonably*, accedere, Cic.

intempestīvus -a -um, *unseasonable, untimely, inopportune*, epistola, Cic.

intempestus -a -um (in and tempus or tempestas), **1,** *unseasonable*, intempesta nox, *the dead of night*, Cic.; personified, Nox intempesta, *the mother of the Furies*, Verg.; **2,** *unwholesome, unhealthy*; Graviscae, Verg.

intendo -tendi -tentum, 3. **I.** *to stretch out, extend*. **A.** Lit., **1,** dextram ad statuam, Cic.; **2,** of weapons, *to aim, direct*; tela, Cic. **B.** Transf., **1,** transit., **a,** *to move in any direction, to direct towards*; iter in or ad locum, *to direct one's course towards*, Liv.; **b,** *to apply the mind, direct the thoughts to*, animum eo, Cic.; animum or mentem in aliquid, Cic, oculos mentesque ad pugnam, Caes; **c**, *to direct with hostile intention, to excite*, eo bellum, Liv, periculum alicui or in aliquem, Cic; alicui litem, Cic; **2**, intransit or reflex, **a**, *to direct one's course*, quo intenderat in Manliana castra pervenit, Cic; **b**, *to direct one's efforts*, quocumque intenderat, res adversae erant, Sall; **c**, *to devote oneself to*, ad publicas curas, Tac **II.** *to stretch* **A.** Lit, arcum, Cic; vincula stupea collo, *stretch round*, Verg, tabernacula carbaseis velis, *to pitch*, Cic **B.** Transf, **1**, *to exert*, se ad firmitatem, Cic; **2**, *to intend*, quod animo intenderat, Cic, **3**, *to raise*; vocem, Verg; **4**, *to maintain, try to prove*, id quod intenderat confirmare, Cic

1 **intentātus** a -um (in and tento), *untouched, untried*, nil intentatum nostri liquere poetae, *unattempted*, Hor

2 **intentātus** -a -um, partic. of intento

intentē, adv (intentus), *carefully, diligently, attentively, vigorously*, aliquem intentius admonere, Liv

intentĭo -ōnis, f (intendo) **I.** *a directing, attention*, absol, Cic, with subject genit, vultus, Tac., with object genit, lusus, Liv **II.** *stretching*, **a**, corporis, Cic, **b**, of the mind, *an effort, exertion*, animi cogitationum, Cic, **c**, *intention*, adversariorum, Cic

intento, 1 (intens of intendo), **1**, *to stretch towards or against, to stretch out threateningly*, manus in aliquem, Liv, sicam alicui, Cic, **2**, *to threaten with hostile purpose*, arma Latinis, *to threaten with war*, Cic

1 **intentus** -ūs, m (intendo), *a stretching out*, palmarum, Cic

2 **intentus** -a -um **I.** Partic of intendo **II.** P adj (from intendo), **a**, *anxious, intent, full of expectation*, omnes milites intenti pugnae proventum exspectabant, Caes; with ad or adversus aliquid, or with dat, *attentive to, waiting eagerly for*, in omnem occasionem, Liv, **b**, with dat., or ad, or in with the acc, *attentive to, intent upon, busied with, zealous in*, operi agresti, Liv; esp of soldiers, *ready for battle*, paratus et intentus, Liv, **c**, *active, unceasing, vigorous*, intentissima cura, Liv., **d**, *rigorous*, disciplina, Tac

intĕpĕo, 2 *to be lukewarm*, Prop

intĕpesco tĕpŭi, 3 (inchoat of intepeo), *to become lukewarm, grow gradually warm*, Ov

intĕr (in with adverbial ending ter), prep. with acc *between, among, amid* **A.** Of space, **1**, of rest, moror inter aras, templa, Cic, quum (Hercules) inter homines esset, *among the number of*, Cic., inter falcarios, *in the street of the sickle-makers*, Cic, **2**, of motion, inter stationes hostium emissi, Liv **B.** Transf, of time, **1**, *between*, inter horam tertiam et quartam, Liv, **2**, *during, in the course of*, inter decem annos, Cic, inter cenam, Cic, inter agendum, Verg **C. 1**, *among a class*, adolescens inter suos, Cic; **2**, *between* (parties, adversaries, etc), inter Marcellos et Claudios patricios judicare, Cic., **3**, of division, portion, inter se, *between one another*, Cic, **4**, *between* (of friendship, hostility, etc), amicitiam nisi inter bonos esse non posse, Cic **5**, with pronouns, inter se, inter nos, inter vos, inter ipsos, *between one another, mutually*, amare inter se, *to love one another*, Cic **D.** Particular phrases, **a**, inter sicarios accusare, *to accuse of murder*, Cic, **b**, inter pauca and inter paucos, *especially, particularly*, Liv, **c**, inter cuncta, *before all*, Hor; **d**, inter haec, *meanwhile*, Liv (inter sometimes put after its case, quos inter, Cic)

intĕrāmenta -ōrum, n (inter), *the woodwork of a ship*, Liv.

Intĕramna -ae, f, **1**, *a town in Umbria*, now *Terni*, **2**, *a town in Latium*, now *Teramo*, Hence, adj, **1**, **Intĕramnānus** -a -um; **2**, **Intĕramnās** -ātis, *belonging to Interamna* Subst, **Intĕramnātes** -ium, m *the people of Interamna*

intĕrāresco, 3. *to become dry, to dry up, decay*, transf, Cic

interbĭbo, 3 *to drink up*, Plaut

interbīto, 3 *to perish*, Plaut

intercălāris -e (intercalo), *intercalary*, calendae, *the first day of an intercalary month*, Cic

intercălārĭus -a -um (intercalo), *intercalary*, mensis, Cic

intercălo, 1 (lit, *to call out that something is inserted*), **1**, *to insert* or *intercalate a day or month in the calendar*, si scies Romae intercalatum sit necne, Cic, **2**, *to defer, put off*, poenam, Liv

intercăpēdo -inis, f (intercapio), *an interval, intermission, pause, respite*, molestiae, Cic

intercēdo cessi -cessum, 3 *to go between, come between* **I.** Lit, inter singulas legiones impedimentorum magnum numerum intercedere, Caes **II.** Transf, **A.** **a**, of places, *to stand or lie between*, palus quae perpetua intercedebat, Caes, **b**, hence of time, *to intervene*, nox nulla intercessit, Cic, **c**, of events, *to happen between*, saepe in bello parvis momentis magni casus intercedunt, Caes, **d**, of relations, *to be between* inter nos vetus usus intercedit, Cic **B.** Of persons, *to step between*, **a**, by way of hindrance, *to interpose, withstand, protest against* (of the tribunes when they exercised their veto), legi, Cic, alicui, Cic, **b**, as a mediator, *to interpose*, quum vestra auctoritas intercessisset ut, etc, Cic, in money transactions, *to stand surety*, pro aliquo, Cic., magnam pecuniam pro aliquo, *in a large sum for*, Cic

interceptĭo ōnis, f (intercipio), *a taking away*, poculi, Cic

interceptor -ōris, m (intercipio), *one who takes away, an embezzler*, praedae, Liv

intercessĭo ōnis, f (intercedo), **1**, *an intercession, interposition, suretyship for any one*, Cic, **2**, *a protest or exercise by the tribunes of their veto*, Cic

intercessor ōris, m (intercedo), **1**, *a surety, bail*, Cic; **2**, *one who protests against, opposes, withstands* (of a tribune in the exercise of his veto), legis, Cic

1 **intercīdo** cidi -cīsum, 3 (inter and caedo), *to cut off, cut asunder*, pontem, *to demolish, pull down*, Liv; montem, *to cut through*, Cic

2. **intercĭdo** cidi, 3 (inter and cado), **1**, *to fall between*, Liv, **2**, transf, **a**, *to happen, occur*, si quae interciderunt, Cic; **b**, *to become lost, decay, perish*, inimici, ap Cic, memoriā, *be forgotten*, Liv, intercidit mihi aliquid, *I have forgotten something*, Hor

intercĭno, 1 (inter and cano), *to sing between*, medios actus, Hor

intercĭpĭo -cēpi -ceptum, 3 (inter and capio), *to take by the way, intercept* **I.** Lit litteras, Cic, commeatus, Liv **II.** Transf, **1**, *to deprive of, rob, steal*, agrum ab aliquo, Liv, aliquem neci, Ov, **2**, *to snatch away, carry off prematurely*, aliquem veneno, Tac, **3**, *to cut off*, iter, Liv

intercīsē, adv (intercisus), *confusedly, interruptedly*, dicere, Cic

interclūdo -clūsi -clūsum, 3 (inter and cludo, claudo) **I.** *to block up, hinder*, alicui fugam, Cic, fig, omnes seditionum vias, Cic

II. A. *to cut off, separate from*; aliquem ab exercitu, Caes.; aliquem re frumentaria, Caes.; fig., intercludor dolore quominus, etc., *I am prevented by grief*, Cic. **B.** *to enclose, shut in*; aliquem in iis insidiis quas, etc., Cic; angustiis intercludi, Caes.

interclūsĭo -ōnis, f. (intercludo), *a stopping or blocking up*; animae, Cic.

intercŏlumnĭum -ii, n. (inter and columna), *the space between two columns*, Cic.

intercurro -cŭcurri and -curri -cursum, 3. **I. 1,** *to run between*, Lucr.; **2,** fig., **a,** *to step between, intercede*, Cic.; **b,** *to run along with, be among, mingle with*; his laboriosis exercitationibus et dolor intercurrit, Cic. **II.** *to run or hasten to in the meanwhile*; Veios ad confirmandos militum animos, Liv.

intercurso, 1. (intens. of intercurro), *to run between*, Liv.

intercursus -ūs, m. (intercurro), *a running between, interposition*; intercursu consulum, suorum, Liv.

intercus -cŭtis (inter and cutis), *under the skin*; aqua, *the dropsy*, Cic.

interdătus -a -um, partic. of interdo.

interdīco -dixi -dictum, 3. **I.** *to forbid, prohibit*. **A.** Gen., **a,** alicui aliquā re or aliquo; Romanis omni Galliā, Caes.; **b,** alicui aliquid; alicui orbem, Ov.; **c,** with or without dat. of person, foll. by ne or ut, etc., and the subj., interdicit atque imperat Cassivellauno ne Mandubracio noceat, Caes.; in pass., Pythagoreis interdictum ne fabā vescerentur, Cic. **B.** Esp., **1,** as legal t. t., interdicere alicui aquā et igni, *to banish*, Cic.; **2,** sacrificiis interdicere, Caes. **II.** *to order, command*; **1,** with ut and the subj., familiae valde interdicere ut uni dicto audiens sit, Cic.; **2,** of the praetor, *to make a provisional or interlocutory decree*; de vi, Cic.; praetor interdixit ut unde dejectus esset eo restitueretur, Cic.

interdictĭo -ōnis, f. (interdico), *a forbidding, prohibition*; aquae et ignis, *banishing*, Cic.

interdictum -i, n. (interdico), **1,** *a prohibition*; with subject. genit., Caesaris, Cic.; **2,** *a praetor's interdict or provisional order*, Cic.

interdĭu (interdĭus), adv. *in the daytime, by day*; nocte an interdiu, Liv.

interdo -didi -dătum, 1. *to give between, distribute*, Lucr.

interdŭātim = interdum (q.v.).

interductus -ūs, m. (*interduco), *interpunctuation*, Cic.

interdum, adv. **1,** *sometimes, occasionally, now and then*; interdum . . . interdum, Cic.; **2,** *meanwhile*, Tac.

interdŭo = interdo (q. v.).

intĕrĕā, adv. (inter and abl. eā), **1,** *in the meantime, meanwhile*, Cic.; interea quum, Cic.; **2,** *nevertheless, notwithstanding*, Cic.; quum interea, Cic.

intĕremptĭo -ōnis, f. (interimo), *slaughter, slaying*, Cic.

intĕrĕo -ii -ĭtum, 4. *to perish, to be lost among*. **I.** Lit., muriae stilla interit magnitudine maris, Cic. **II.** Transf., *to perish, be destroyed, be lost*; **a,** of things, intereunt sacra, Cic.; **b,** of men, *to die*; fame aut ferro, Caes. (syncop. perf. forms, interisse, interissent, Cic.).

intĕrĕquito, 1. *to ride between*; ordines, Liv.

interfātĭo -ōnis, f. (interfor), *a speaking between, interruption in discourse*, Cic.

interfectĭo -ōnis, f. (interficio), *a slaying*, ap. Cic.

interfector -ōris, m. (interficio), *a murderer, slayer*, Cic.

interfectrix -trīcis, f. (interfector), *a murderess*, Tac.

interfĭcĭo -fēci -fectum, 3. (inter and facio), *to destroy, put an end to, bring to naught*; **a,** of things, messes, Verg.; herbas, Cic.; **b,** of persons, *to murder, to slay, kill*; aliquem insidiis, Cic.; Crassum suāpte interfectum manu, Cic.

interfīo -fiĕri (pass. of interficio = interficior), *to perish*, Plaut.

interflŭo -fluxi -fluxum, 3. *to flow between*; Naupactum et Patras, Liv.

interflŭus -a -um (interfluo), *flowing between*, Plin.

interfŏdĭo -fōdi -fossum, 3. *to dig into, pierce*, Lucr.

interfor -fātus sum, 1. dep., *to speak between, interrupt in discourse*; aliquem, Liv.; or absol., Liv., Verg. (1st pers. pres. not found).

interfŭgĭo, 3. *to flee between*, Lucr.

interfulgens -entis, *shining or gleaming among or between*, Liv.

interfundo -fūdi -fūsum, 3. *to pour between*; middle, interfundi, *to flow between*; noviens Styx interfusa, Verg.; transf., maculis interfusa genas, *stained with*, Verg.

intĕrĭbi, adv., *meanwhile, in the meantime*, Plaut.

intĕrĭcĭo = interjicio (q.v.).

intĕrim, adv., **1,** *meanwhile, in the meantime*, Cic.; **2,** *however*, Cic.

intĕrĭmo -ēmi -emptum, 3. (inter and emo), *to take away out of the midst*; **1,** of things, *to destroy, annihilate, make an end of*; sacra, Cic.; **2,** of persons, *to put out of the way, to kill, slay, murder*; aliquem, Cic.; stirpem fratris virilem, Liv.; se, *to commit suicide*, Cic.; transf., me examinant et interimunt hae voces Milonis, Cic.

intĕrĭor, intĕrĭus -ōris, compar. adj., **intĭmus** -a -um, superl. (in-ter). **I.** Compar. interior. **A.** Lit., **1,** *inner, interior*; pars aedium, Cic.; interiore epistolā, *in the middle of the letter*, Cic.; Falernum interiore notā, *from the depth of the cellar*, Hor.; interior ictibus, *within shot*, Liv.; **2, a,** *remote from the sea, inland*; nationes, Cic.; interiora regni, *the interior of the kingdom*, Liv.; **b,** *nearer, shorter* (of the racecourse); gyrus, *on the inside of the course*, Hor.; cursus, *shorter*, Cic. **B.** Transf., **1,** interior periculo vulneris, *too near to be in danger of a wound*, Liv.; **2, a,** *more secret, more confidential*; amicitia, Cic.; **b,** *deeper*; (α) timor, Cic.; (β) *more erudite, profound*; interiores et reconditae litterae, Cic. **II.** Superl., intĭmus -a -um, *inmost*. **A.** Lit., intima Macedonia, *the very centre of Macedonia*, Cic. **B.** Transf., **1,** *deepest, most profound*; disputatio, philosophia, Cic.; **2,** *most secret, confidential, intimate*; amicus, Cic.; intimus alicui, Cic.; familiaritas, Nep. Subst., **intĭmus** -i, m. *an intimate friend*, Cic.

intĕrĭtĭo -ōnis, f. (intereo), *destruction, ruin*; aratorum, Cic.

intĕrĭtus -ūs, m. (intereo), *destruction, ruin, annihilation*; **a,** of things, legum, Cic.; **b,** of persons, consulum, Cic.; with abl., exercitus nostri interitus ferro, fame, frigore, Cic.

intĕrĭus, 1, compar. adj., v. interior; **2,** compar. of intra, v. intra.

interjăcĕo, 2. *to lie between or among*; absol., interjacebat campus, Liv.; with dat., campus interjacens Tiberi ac moenibus Romanis, Liv

interjectus -ūs, m (interjicio), *a putting between*, a, of place, interpositu interjectuque terrae, *between the sun and the moon*, Cic, b, of time, *an interval;* interjectu noctis, *after an interval of a night*, Tac

interjĭcĭo (interjăcĭo) -jēci jectum, 3 *to throw, cast, place, put among*, or *between* I. Lit, legionarias cohortes, Caes. Partic, **interjectus** a -um, *interposed, thrown between*, nasus, quasi murus oculis interjectus, Cic II. Transf, 1, idque interjecit inter individuum atque id, etc, Cic, interjectus inter philosophos et eos, *standing between*, Cic, 2, a, of time, *to put in between;* moram, Tac, anno interjecto, *after the interval of a year*, Cic, b, of words, *to intermingle*, pleraque Latino sermone, Cic

interjungo -junxi -junctum, 3 *to join together, unite, connect*, dextras, Liv.

interlābor -labi, 3 dep, *to glide, fall, flow between*, in tmesis, inter enim labentur aquae, Verg

interlĕgo, 3. *to pluck, gather here and there*, Verg

interlĭno -lēvi -lĭtum, 3 I. *to daub between*, caementa interlita luto, Liv II. *to erase, cancel, to falsify by erasure*, testamentum, Cic

interlŏquor -lŏcūtus (loquūtus) sum, 3 dep, *to interrupt a person speaking*, Ter

interlūcĕo luxi, 2 I. *to shine, gleam between*, terrena quaedam atque etiam volucria animalia plerumque interlucent (in amber), Tac, impers, noctu interluxisse, *there had been intervals of light*, Liv II. A. *to shine forth*, quibus inter gradus dignitatis et fortunae aliquid interlucet, Liv B. *to be transparent, capable of being seen through* (on account of small numbers), interlucet corona (militum), Verg

interlūnĭum -ii, n (inter and luna), *the change of the moon, time of new moon*, Hor

interlŭo -ŭi, 3 *to flow between, wash between*, fretum quod Capreas et Surrentum interluit, Tac

intermenstrŭus -a -um, *between two months*, intermenstruo tempore, *at the time of the change of the moon*, Cic, subst, **intermenstrŭum** -i, n (sc tempus), *the time of the new moon*, Cic

1 **intermĭnātus** -a -um (in and termino), *unbounded, boundless*, magnitudo regionum, Cic

2 **intermĭnātus** a -um, v interminor

intermĭnor, 1 dep, *to threaten, forbid with threats*, Plaut, partic perf pass, cibus interminatus, *forbidden with threats*, Hor

intermiscĕo -miscŭi mixtum, 2 *to mix with, intermix*, with dat., turbam indignorum intermiscere dignis, Liv, intermixti hostibus, Liv

intermissĭo -ōnis, f (intermitto) I. *leaving off*, epistolarum, Cic, officii, Cic II. *respite, interruption, interval*, verborum, Cic, sine ulla temporis intermissione, Cic

intermissus -a -um, partic of intermitto

intermitto -misi -missum, 3 I. Transit, A. *to place between*, trabes paribus intermissae spatiis, Caes B. *to leave a space between, leave free, unoccupied, unsurrounded*, 1, lit, pars oppidi a flumine intermissa, Caes, loca custodibus intermissa, Liv, 2, transf, a, *to leave off for a time, give over, break off, interrupt, neglect*, studia, Cic, proelium, Caes, with infin, alicui litteras mittere, Cic: vento intermisso, *the wind having dropped*, Caes, verba ab usu quotidiani sermonis intermissa, *obsolete*, Cic., b, of time, *to let pass;* ne quem diem intermitterem, Cic.; with ab and the abl, ut reliquum tempus ab labore intermitteretur, Caes, with ad and the acc, nulla pars nocturni temporis ad laborem intermittitur, Caes, with a negat foll by quin and the subj, neque ullum fere diem intermittebat quin perspiceret, *without examining*, Caes, c, *to discontinue, suspend an office* intermissis magistratibus, Cic II. Intransit, *to cease, leave off*, qua flumen intermittit, Caes

intermŏrĭor -mortŭus sum, 3 dep, *to die, perish, decay*, 1, lit., Suet 2, transf, a, intermoriuntur reliquiae conjurationis, Cic, civitas intermoritur, Liv, contiones intermortuae, *lifeless*, Cic, b, *to faint away*, Liv

intermundĭa -ōrum, n (inter and mundus), *spaces between the worlds* (according to Epicurus, *the abode of the gods*), Cic.

intermūrālis -e, *between walls*, amnis, Liv

internascor -nātus sum, 3 dep, *to grow between*, internata virgulta, Liv

internĕcīnus -a -um, v internecivus

internĕcĭo (internĭcĭo) -ōnis, f (interneco), *entire destruction, extermination, massacre, carnage*, civium, Cic; ad internecionem adducere gentem, *to annihilate*, Liv

internĕcīvus (internĕcīnus) -a -um (interneco), *murderous, mortal, deadly, internecine*, bellum, Cic

internĕco, 1 *to destroy utterly, exterminate*, hostes, Plaut

internecto, 3 *to bind together, to bind up;* ut fibula crinem auro internectat, Verg.

internĭcĭo = internecio (q v)

internĭtĕo -nitŭi, 2 *to shine among, gleam through*, Plin

internōdĭum -ii, n (inter and nodus), *the space between two knots or joints*, Ov

internosco -nōvi -nōtum, 3 *to distinguish between*, geminos, Cic, quae internosci a falsis non possunt, Cic

internuntĭa, v internuntius

internuntĭo, 1 *to send messengers between two parties*, Liv

internuntĭus -a -um, adj, used as subst, *a messenger, negotiator, go between*, a, masc, Jovis interpretes internuntiique (of the augurs), Cic, b, fem, aves internuntiae Jovis, Cic

internus -a -um, *inward, internal, civil*, discordiae, Tac.

intĕro -trīvi -trītum, 3 *to rub, crumble, pound in anything*, Plin

interpellātĭo -ōnis, f (interpello), *interruption, hindrance, disturbance*, especially in a speech, Cic

interpellātor -ōris, m. (interpello), *an interrupter, disturber*, Cic

interpello, 1 (inter and *pello are, intens of **pello** -ĕre), 1, *to interrupt a speaker*, crebro dicentem, Cic, 2, *to disturb hinder, impede*. a, of persons, aliquem in jure suo, Cic, aliquem ne etc, Liv; comitia, Liv; b, of things, haec tota res interpellata bello, Cic

interpŏlātĭo -ōnis, f (interpolo), *an alteration*, Plin

interpŏlis -e (inter and polio), *furbished, vamped up, repaired;* hence, *not genuine*, Plaut, Plin

interpŏlo, 1 (interpolis), 1, *to alter, furbish, repair, vamp up*, togam praetextam, *to re dye*, Cic, 2, *to spoil, corrupt, falsify*, semper aliquid demendo, mutando, interpolando, Cic

interpōno -pŏsŭi -pŏsĭtum, 3 *to put, place, lay between or among, interpose* **I.** Lit , **1,** elephantos, Liv , **2, a,** *to insert, intercalate*, menses intercalarios, Liv , **b,** *to insert in discourse*, ne inquinum saepius interponerétur, Cic. **II.** Transf , **A.** Of time, *to allow an interval to pass between*, spatium ad recreandos animos, Caes , spatio interposito, *after some time*, Cic , moram, Cic , cunctationem, Tac , *to interpose, delay* **B** *to cause to come between, to interpose*, operam, studium, laborem, *to use, apply*, Cic **C.** *to introduce, bring forward*, **a,** judicium, edictum, *to bring forward*, Cic , **b,** *to bring forward, allege as a reason or pretext*, gladiatores interpositi sunt, Cic ; **c,** *to pledge one's word*, in aliquid or in aliqua re fidem suam, Caes **D.** *to admit as a helper, participator, etc* , **1,** judices testes, Cic , **2,** se interponere in aliquid or alicui, *to engage in, have to do with, meddle*, se in pacificationem, Cic ; se audaciae alicuius, Cic **E.** *to falsify*, rationes populorum, Cic.

interpŏsĭtĭo -ōnis, f (interpono), **1,** *a bringing forward, introducing* (in a speech), multarum personarum, Cic ; **2,** *a putting in, insertion*, Cic

interpŏsĭtus, abl -ū, m (interpono), *a putting between, interposition*, luna interpositu terrae deficit, Cic

interpres -prĕtis, c (inter and PRET, ΦΡΑΔ, φραζω) **I.** *a negotiator, mediator, messenger*, judicii corrumpendi, Cic , divûm, *Mercury*, Verg **II. A.** *an expounder, explainer*; juris, Cic , poetarum, Cic , divûm, *prophet, prophetess*, Verg , Liv , interpretes comitiorum, *the haruspices, who declare whether the comitia have been rightly held*, Cic **B. a,** *an interpreter*, appellare or alloqui aliquem per interpretem, Cic , **b,** *a translator*, nec converti (orationes) ut interpres, sed ut orator, Cic

interprĕtātĭo -ōnis, f (interpretor) **I.** *explanation, exposition, interpretation* **A.** Gen , juris, Cic , verborum, Cic **B.** Esp , *translation*, Plin , concr = *that which is translated*, foederis, Cic **II.** *meaning, understanding*, nec interpretatio est facilis, Liv.

interprĕtor, 1 dep. (interpres), *to explain, expound, interpret, translate* **A.** Lit , **1,** jus alicui, Cic , fulgura, somnia, Cic , **2,** *to translate*, epistolam, scriptores, Cic. **B.** Transf , **1,** *to put an interpretation on, to understand in a certain manner*, male, Cic , aliquid mitiorem in partem, Cic , with acc and infin , reditum in castra liberatum se esse jurejurando interpretabatur, Cic , **2,** *to understand, grasp, comprehend*, recte alicuius sententiam, Cic , **3,** *to decide, determine*, neque, recte an perperam, interpretor, Cic (pass , Cic , esp in perf partic)

interpunctĭo -ōnis, f (interpungo), *punctuation*, verborum, Cic.

interpungo -punxi -punctum, 3 *to punctuate, point*, narratio interpuncta, *well-divided*, Cic , partic subst , clausulae atque interpuncta verborum, *divisions*, Cic

interquĕror -questus sum, 3 dep , *to interrupt with complaints*, Liv. (?)

interquĭesco -quiēvi -quiētum, 3 *to pause between, rest in the mean time*, quum haec dixissem et paulum interquievissem, Cic

interregnum -i, n *a period between two reigns, an interregnum* Cic ; under the republic at Rome, *the time during the absence of the consuls, or between the death or retirement of the consuls and the choice of successors*, Cic

interrex -regis, m *a regent, person temporarily invested with royal authority*, Cic , in later times *a person appointed in the absence of the consuls to hold the comitia for the election of their successors*, Cic.

interrĭtus -a -um (in and territo), *unterrified, undaunted*, Verg

interrŏgātĭo -ōnis f (interrogo), *a question, questioning, interrogation*, Cic , esp **a,** legal t t , *the examination of witnesses*, testium, Tac. ; absol , Cic , **b,** logic t t *an argument, syllogism*, apta interrogatione concludere, Cic

interrŏgātĭuncŭla -ae, f (dim of interrogatio), *a short syllogism or argument*, minutae interrogatiunculae, Cic

interrŏgo, 1 **I.** *to ask, question, interrogate* te eisdem de rebus, Cic , interrogabat suos quis esset, Cic , interrogans solerentne veterani milites fugere, Caes , with double acc , pusionem quendam interrogavit quaedam geometrica, Cic , interrogatus sententiam, *being asked his opinion*, Liv , partic subst , **interrŏgātum** -i, n *a question*, ad interrogata respondere, Cic **II.** Esp , **a,** *to interrogate judicially, to examine*, testem, Cic , **b,** *to accuse, bring an action against*, aliquem legibus ambitus, Sall.

interrumpo -rūpi -ruptum, 3 *to break down, break in the middle, break asunder* **I. A.** pontem, Caes , aciem hostium, Liv **B.** *to separate*, interrupti ignes, *isolated*, Verg , interruptae voces, *broken*, Cic **II.** Transf , *to interrupt, disturb*, **a,** gen , iter amoris et officii, Cic. , **b,** *to interrupt a speech*, orationem, Cic

interruptē, adv (interruptus from interrumpo), *interruptedly, disconnectedly*, non interrupte narrare, Cic

intersaepĭo -saepsi -saeptum, 4 *to hedge or fence in, inclose, hem in, block up.* **I.** Lit , foramina, Cic , quaedam operibus, Liv **II** Transf , *cut off, separate*, urbem vallo ab arce, Liv , iter, Cic

interscindo -scidi -scissum, 3 *to cut or hew asunder* **I.** Lit , pontem, Cic. , venas, *to open*, Tac **II.** Transf , *to cut off, separate*, Chalcis arcto interscinditur freto, Liv

intersēpĭo = intersaepio (q v)

1. **intersĕro** -sēvi -sĭtum, 3 *to sow or plant between*, Lucr

2. **intersĕro,** 3. *to put or place between*, oscula mediis verbis, Ov , transf , causam interserens, *alleging*, Nep

interspīrātĭo -ōnis, f *a breathing between, a taking breath*, Cic

1 **interstinguo** -stinctus, 3 *to cover with spots or speckles*, facies interstincta medicaminibus, Tac.

2 **interstinguo,** 3 *to extinguish*, ignem, Lucr

interstrĕpo, 3 *to roar, make a noise in the midst of*, Verg.

interstringo, 3 *to squeeze tight*, alicui gulam, *to throttle*, Plaut.

intersum -fŭi -esse. **I. A.** *to be between*, **a,** of space, ut Tiberis inter eos interesset, Cic ; **b,** of time, *to intervene*, inter primum et sextum consulatum XLVI anni interfuerunt, Cic **B.** *to be different, be distinguished from*, ut inter eos ne minimum quidem intersit, Cic., inter hominem et beluam hoc maxime interest Cic., quod ab eo nihil intersit, Cic **C.** *to be present, take part in*; with in and the abl , in convivio, Cic ; with dat , convivio, Cic **II.** Impers , interest, *it concerns, it imports, it is of importance*, constr. : (α) with genit of person or thing, or with the fem abl of the possess pron., meā, tuā, suā, nostrā, vestrā, cujā, nam eorum quoque vehementer interest, Cic , vestra hoc maxime interest, Cic , (β) with ad and the acc of the thing, ad nostram laudem non multum interesse, Cic ; (γ) with the neut , multum, quantum, tantum, plus, plurimum, or with adv., maxime, ve-

vehementer, magnopere, or with genit of value, magni, parvi, minoris, pluris, magni, Cic , (δ) with infin , or acc. and infin , or ut or ne, or with rel sent , magni interest meā unā nos esse, Cic , illud magni meā interest ut te videam, Cic , nunquam enim interest uter sit eorum in pede extremo, Cic

intertexo texŭi textum, 3 *to weave together, interweave* flores hederis intertexti, Ov , chlamys auro intertexta, Verg

intertrăho traxi, 3 *to take away*, Plaut

intertrīmentum -i, n (inter and tero) **I.** *loss by friction, loss in working gold and silver*, argenti, Liv. **II.** Transf , *loss, damage*, sine ullo intertrimento, Cic

interturbātĭo -ōnis, f *disturbance, disquiet*, Liv

intervallum i, n (inter and vallus), *a space between two palisades*, hence, **I. A.** *an intervening space, interval, distance*, pari intervallo, *at an equal distance*, Caes , locorum, Cic **B.** *an interval of time*, literarum, Cic , sine intervallo loquacitas, *without intermission*, Cic , longo intervallo, *after a long time*, Cic **II.** *difference, unlikeness*, Cic , as t t of music, intervalla = *distinctions between high and low notes*, Cic

intervello -vulsi -vulsum, 3 *to pull or pluck out here and there, to thin*, Plin

intervĕnĭo -vēni -ventum 4 *to come between, come up while anything is doing, to intervene* **I.** verens ne molesti vobis interveniremus, Cic , huic orationi, Liv **II.** Transf , a, of time, *to intervene, to interrupt*, with dat , nox intervenit proelio, Liv , b, of events, *to happen while something else is being done, and so to interrupt*, with dat , intervenit deinde his cogitationibus avitum malum, Liv , exigua fortuna intervenit sapienti, *opposes*, Cic

interventor -ōris, m (intervenio), *an interrupter, a visitor*, magis vacuo ab interventoribus die, Cic

interventus -ūs, m (intervenio), *intervention, interposition, interference*, hominis, Cic , noctis, Caes

interverto (-vorto) -verti (-vorti) -versum (-vorsum), 3 (*to turn aside*), *to embezzle, appropriate to one's own use, purloin* , **1,** regale donum, Cic , **2,** transf , *to take away, deprive of, defraud of*, promissum et receptum (consulatum) intervertere et ad se transferre, Cic , **3,** *to spend, lavish*, Tac

intervīso -visi visum, 3 **1,** *to look after, inspect secretly*, crebro interviso, Cic , **2,** *to visit from time to time*, aliquem, Cic

intervŏlĭto, 1 *to fly about among*, Liv

intervŏmo, 3 *to pour forth among*, Lucr

intestābĭlis -e, *disqualified from being a witness or from making a will*, hence *dishonourable, disgraceful, infamous, execrable*, Hor , Sall , perjurium, Liv

intestātus -a -um, **1,** *having made no will, intestate*, adv , intestato or ab intestato, *intestate*, mori, Cic., **2,** *not convicted by witnesses*, Plaut

intestīnum -i, v intestinus

intestīnus -a um (intus) **I.** *inward, internal* subst , **intestīnum** i, n *an intestine*, and plur , **intestīna** -orum, n *the intestines*, intestinum medium, Cic , ex intestinis laborare, *to have a pain in the bowels*, Cic **II.** a, *domestic, internal, civil*, intestinum ac domesticum malum, Cic ; bellum, Cic , b, *subjective* (opp oblatus, *objective*), Cic

intexo -texŭi -textum, 3 **I** *to weave in, plait in, interweave*, **1,** lit., purpureas notas filis, Ov., vimina, Caes , **2,** a, *to interlace;* venae toto corpore intextae, Cic , b, *to interweave in discourse*, parva magnis, Cic **II.** *to weave around, to wind around, to surround*, hastas foliis, Verg , hederae solent intexere truncos, Ov

intĭbum (intŭbum, intŭbum) -i, n and **intĭbus (intўbus, intŭbus)** -i, c *endive, succory*, Verg

intĭmē, adv (intimus), **1,** *confidentially, intimately*, Nep , **2,** *cordially, strongly*, commendari ab aliquo, Cic

intĭmus, superl from interior (q v)

intingo (intinguo) -tinxi -tinctum, 3 *to dip in*, faces sanguine, Ov

intŏlĕrābĭlis -e, *unbearable, intolerable;* frigus, dolor, Cic , saevitia, Liv

intŏlĕrandus a um, *unbearable, unendurable*, Cic

intŏlĕrans -antis **I.** Act , *impatient of, unable to bear*, with genit , corpora intolerantissima laboris, Liv **II.** Pass , *unbearable, intolerable*, subjectis intolerantior, Tac

intŏlĕrantĕr, adv (intolerans), *immoderately, excessively, impatiently*, dolere, Cic , intolerantius se jactare, Cic , intolerantissime gloriari, Cic

intŏlĕrantĭa -ae, f (intolerans), *intolerable, insufferable conduct, insolence*, regis, Cic , illa superbia atque intolerantia, Cic

intŏno -tŏnŭi tŏnātum, 1 **I.** Intransit , *to thunder* **A.** Lit , pater omnipotens ter caelo clarus ab alto intonuit, Verg **B.** Transf , a, *to thunder, make a thundering noise*, especially of a speaker , jam hesternā concione intonuit vox perniciosa tribuni, Cic , b, *to clash*, Aeneas horrendum intonat armis, Verg **II.** Transit , a, *to thunder forth*, quum haec intonuisset plenus irae, Liv , minas, Ov , b, *to make to roar upon*, Fors intonata fluctibus hiems, *raging on*, Hor (partic perf pass , intonatus, Hor)

intonsus a -um (in and tondeo), *unshorn* **I.** Lit , caput, Ov , of animals, intonsa bidens, Verg , of persons, *with long hair or beard*, deus, *Apollo*, Ov., of the old Romans, intonsi avi, Ov , Numa, Ov , Cato, Hor , of savage nations, homines intonsi et inculti, Liv , intonsi Getae, Ov **II.** *wooded, leafy, not cleared of trees*, montes, Verg

intorquĕo torsi -tortum, 2 **I.** *to twist or turn round* **A.** Gen **1,** paludamentum circum brachium, Liv , **2,** *to wind*, rudentes intorti, Ov **B.** *to hurl*, telum in hostem, Verg , transf , ardentes oculos, *to roll*, Verg , intorquentur inter fratres gravissimae contumeliae, Cic **II.** *to twist aside, turn, writhe* **A.** intorti capillis Eumenidum angues, Hor , navis vertice retro intorta, Liv **B.** *to distort, turn away*, mentum in dicendo, Cic

intortus a -um (partic of intorqueo).

intrā (for interā sc. parte, from *interus -a um) **I.** Adv (compar interius, superl intimē), *within*, compar , rapiat sitiens interiusque recondat, Verg **II.** Prepos with acc , *within* **A.** Lit , of space, **1,** intra parietes, Cic , **2,** *into*, ingredi intra finem loci, Cic. **B.** Transf , **1,** of time, *within, in the space of*, intra tot annos, Cic , intra annos XIV, Caes , foll by quam, intra decimum diem quam Pheras venerat, *in less than ten days after his arrival*, Liv , **2,** with numerals, intra centum, *less than a hundred*, Liv , **3,** of other words expressing boundary, etc , cedere intra finem juris, Liv , intra legem epulari, *within the bounds prescribed by law*, Cic.

intrābĭlis -e (intro), *that can be entered, accessible;* amnis os multis simul venientibus haud sane intrabile, Liv.

intractābĭlis -e, *unmanageable, intractable, ungovernable, rough:* genus intractabile bello, *unconquered,* Verg.; bruma, *rough,* Verg.

intractātus -a -um, *not handled.* **I.** Lit., equus intractatus et novus, Cic. **II.** Transf., *unattempted;* scelus, Verg.

intrĕmisco -trĕmŭi, 3. (inchoat. of intremo), *to begin to tremble;* genua timore intremuere, Cic.

intrĕmo, 3. *to tremble, quake,* Verg.

intrĕpĭdē, adv. (intrepidus), *without trembling, undauntedly, intrepidly,* Liv.

intrĕpĭdus -a -um. **I.** *not trembling, undaunted, intrepid;* dux, Ov.; with dat., intrepidus minantibus, Tac. **II.** *free from care or alarm;* hiems, *undisturbed by war,* Tac.

intrīco, 1. (in and tricae), *to confuse, entangle, bring into confusion;* Chrysippus intricatur, Cic.

intrinsĕcŭs, adv. (intra and secus), *inside, inwardly, internally,* Cato.

1. **intrītus** -a -um (in and tero), *not worn away;* transf., *unexhausted;* cohortes intritae ab labore, Caes.

2. **intrītus** -a -um, partic. of intero.

1. **intrō,** adv. (for intero sc. loco from *interus -a -um), *within;* intro ire, Caes.; filiam intro vocare, Cic.

2. **intro,** 1. (*interus), *to go into, enter.* **A.** Lit., regnum, pomoerium, Cic.; in hortos, Ov.; ad munimenta, Liv.; intra praesidia, Caes. **B.** Transf., **a,** *to enter, penetrate;* in rerum naturam, Cic.; in alicuius familiaritatem, Cic.; **b,** of things, quo non modo improbitas sed ne imprudentia quidem possit intrare, Cic.

intrōdūco -duxi -ductum, 3. *to lead or conduct into.* **I.** Lit., copias in fines Bellovacorum, Caes.; exercitum in Ligures, Liv. **II.** Transf., **A.** *to bring in, introduce;* philosophiam in domos, Cic.; consuetudinem, Cic. **B. 1,** *to introduce in speech;* introducta rei similitudo, Cic.; **2,** *to maintain;* with acc. and infin., Cic.

intrōductĭo -ōnis, f. (introduco), *bringing in, introduction;* adolescentulorum, Cic.

intrŏĕo -ivi and -ĭi -ĭtum, 4. *to go into, enter;* in urbem, Cic.; domum, Cic.; portā, *by the gate,* Cic.; transf., in vitam, Cic.

intrōfĕro -tŭli -ferre, *to bear, carry in;* liberis cibum, Cic.

intrōgrĕdĭor -gressus sum, 3. dep. (intro and gradior), *to enter,* Verg.

intrŏĭtus -ūs, m. (introeo), *an entrance.* **I. 1,** lit., Smyrnam, Cic.; in urbem, Cic.; **2,** transf., *beginning, introduction, preamble;* fabulae Clodianae, defensionis, Cic. **II.** Meton., *a place of entrance, passage,* Cic.

intrōmitto -misi -missum, 3. *to send in, cause to enter;* legiones, Caes.

introrsŭs (introrsum), adv. (for introversus), **1,** *towards the inside, inwards,* Caes.; **2,** *inwardly, internally,* Hor., Liv.

intrōrumpo -rūpi -ruptum, 3. *to break in, enter by force;* eā, Caes.

introspĭcĭo -spexi -spectum, 3. (intro and specio), *to look into, look within;* **1,** lit., domum tuam, Cic.; **2,** transf., *to look attentively, observe, examine;* in omnes reipublicae partes, Cic.; introspice in mentem tuam ipse, *cast a look within,* Cic.; aliorum felicitatem, Tac.

intrōversus = introrsus (q.v.).

intrŏvŏco, 1. *to call in, call within,* Cic.

intrūdo -trūsi -trūsum, 3. *to thrust in;* se, *to intrude,* Cic.

intŭbum -i, n., **intŭbus** -i, m., v. intibum.

intŭĕor -tŭitus sum, 2. dep. *to look at attentively, gaze at.* **I.** Lit., solem, Cic.; in aliquem contra, *right in the face,* Liv. **II. A.** *to consider, contemplate, pay attention to;* aliquid, Cic. **B.** *to look with astonishment or admiration at;* Pompeium, Cic.

intŭĭtus -a -um, partic. of intueor.

intŭmesco -tŭmŭi, 3. *to swell, swell up.* **I. A.** Lit., intumuit venter, Ov. **B.** Transf., vox, Tac.; intumescente motu, Tac. **II.** Fig., **a,** *to swell with pride;* superbiā, Tac.; **b,** *to swell with anger, be angry;* intumuit Juppiter, Ov.

intŭmŭlātus -a -um (in and tumulo), *unburied,* Ov.

intŭor, 3. dep. = intueor (q.v.).

inturbĭdus -a -um, **1,** pass., *undisturbed, quiet;* annus, Tac.; **2,** act., *not turbulent;* vir, Tac.

intŭs, adv. (in and -tus, cp. ἐντός), *within, inside.* **I. 1,** ea quae sunt intus in corpore, Cic.; poet., with abl., tali intus templo, Verg.; **2,** transf., *within the heart;* intus in animis inclusae (cupiditates), Cic. **II.** With verbs of motion, *into, to the inside;* duci intus, Ov.

intūtus -a -um, *unprotected, unsafe.* **I.** Pass., castra, Liv.; intuta moenium, *the unprotected parts of the walls,* Tac. **II.** Act., *unsafe, insecure;* latebrae, Tac.; amicitia, Tac.

ĭnŭla -ae, f. *the plant elecampane,* Hor.

ĭnultus -a -um (in and ulciscor). **I.** *unavenged;* injuriae, Cic.; ne inultus esset, Cic. **II.** *unpunished;* aliquem inultum sinere, or inultum esse pati, Cic.

ĭnumbro, 1. *to shade, overshadow, cover with shade;* vestibulum, Verg.; inumbrante vesperā, *as the shades of evening were coming on,* Tac.; ora coronis, Lucr.

ĭnunctĭo -ōnis, f. (inungo), *an anointing with salve or ointment,* Plin.

ĭnundātĭo -ōnis, f. (inundo), *an inundation, flood;* inundatio ex lacu Albano, Liv.

ĭnundo, 1. **I.** Transit., *to overflow, inundate.* **A.** Lit., hanc (terram) inundat aqua, Cic.; vestro sanguine Enna inundabitur, Liv. **B.** Transf., *to stream over like a torrent;* hinc densi cursus inundant Troes, Verg. **II.** Intransit., *to overflow with;* inundant sanguine fossae, Verg.

ĭnungo -unxi -unctum, 3. *to anoint, smear with ointment;* oculos, Hor.

ĭnurbānē, adv. (inurbanus), *unpolitely, inelegantly, without wit or humour,* Cic.

ĭnurbānus -a -um, *rude, unpolished, rough, clownish, boorish;* **1,** in demeanour, Cic.; **2,** in speech, *unrefined,* Cic.

ĭnurgĕo -ursi, 2. *to push, thrust against,* Lucr.

ĭnūro -ussi -ustum, 3. **I.** *to burn in.* **A.** Lit., notam, Verg. **B.** Transf., *to imprint indelibly, brand;* notam turpitudinis vitae alicuius, Cic.; alicui dolorem, Cic.; inuri notā censoriae severitatis, Cic. **II. a,** *to burn, burn up;* vulnere sanguis inustus, Ov.; **b,** *to burn or singe with the curling-irons, to curl;* fig., illa calamistris, *to adorn elaborately,* Cic.

ĭnūsĭtātē, adv. (inusitatus), *unusually, strangely;* inusitate loqui, Cic.; inusitatius contrahere, Cic.

ĭnūsĭtātus -a -um, *unusual, strange, uncommon;* res inusitata ac nova, Cic.; species navium inusitatior, Cic.; with dat., inusitatus nostris oratoribus lepos, Cic.; inusitatum est with infin., or with ut and the subj., Cic.

inustus -a -um, partic. of inuro

inūtilis -e **I.** *useless, unserviceable, unprofitable*, homo, Cic.; with dat., valetudine aut aetate inutiles bello, Caes.; with ad and the acc., ad usus civium non inutile, Cic.; inutile est with infin., Cic. **II.** *hurtful, injurious, harmful*, seditiosus et inutilis civis, Cic.; oratio inutilis sibi et civitati suae, Liv.

inūtilitas -ātis, f. (inutilis), *uselessness, unprofitableness*, Cic.

inūtilitĕr, adv. (inutilis), **1,** *uselessly, unprofitably*, Liv.; **2,** *hurtfully, injuriously*, Cic.

invādo -vāsi -vāsum, 3. **I.** *to go in, enter, come in*, **a,** in eas urbes, Cic.; with simple acc., portum, Verg.; tria milia stadiorum, *to advance*, Tac.; **b,** transf., *to undertake boldly*, aliquid magnum, Verg. **II. A.** *to attack, assault, fall upon, assail, invade*, **1,** lit., **a,** of persons, in hostem, Cic.; urbem, Verg.; **b,** of inanimate objects, *to penetrate, attack*, quocumque ignis invasit, Cic.; **2,** transf., **a,** with words, *to attack, assault*, aliquem minaciter, Tac.; **b,** of diseases, pestilentia populum invasit, Liv.; **c,** of passions and other evils, *to attack, befall*, pestis in vitam invasit, Cic.; furor invaserat improbis, Cic.; aliquem lubido invadit, Sall. **B.** *to fall upon in order to get possession of, usurp, seize*, in alicuius praedia, Cic.

invălesco -vălŭi, 3. (inchoat. of invaleo), *to gather strength, become strong*, tantum opibus invaluit, Cic.

invălētūdo -ĭnis, f. *indisposition*, Cic.

invălĭdus -a -um, **1,** *weak, powerless, feeble, impotent, indisposed, ill*, milites, Liv.; with ad and the acc., ad munera corporis senecta invalidus, Liv.; **2,** transf., *weak to resist*, exercitus, Liv.; moenia invalida adversus irrumpentes, Tac.

invectĭo -ōnis, f. (inveho), **1,** *importation*, Cic.; **2,** *an inveighing against, invective*, Cic.

invĕho -vexi -vectum, 3. **I.** Act., *to carry, bear, bring in*, **1,** lit., **a,** pecuniam in aerarium, Cic.; **b,** *to import*, vinum in Galliam, Liv.; **2,** transf., *to introduce, bring along with*, quae (mala) tibi casus invexerat, Liv.; divitiae avaritiam invexere, Liv. **II.** Middle, invehi, **A.** *to ride or travel on horseback, in a vehicle, in a ship*, curru in capitolium, Cic.; equo, Liv.; flumine, *to sail on*, Cic. **B.** Refl., se invehere and middle invehi, *to penetrate, burst into, attack*, **1,** lit., Romana se invexit acies, Liv.; quum utrinque invehi hostem nunciaretur, Liv.; **2,** transf., in aliquem or aliquid, *to attack with words, assail, inveigh against*, petulanter in aliquem, Cic.

invendĭbĭlis -e, *unsaleable*, Plaut.

invĕnĭo -vēni -ventum, 4. **I.** *to come or light upon, find, meet with*. **A.** Lit., **1,** aliquem, Cic.; naves, Caes.; **2,** *to find written, come upon in reading*, de aliqua re nulla littera in veteribus libris invenitur, Cic. **B.** Transf., **1,** *to find out*, ipsis durior inventus est, Caes.; **2,** *to procure, acquire, get, earn*, hoc cognomen, Cic.; gloriam ex culpa, Sall. **II.** *to find out, discover*. **A.** Lit., argenti venas, Cic. **B.** Transf., **1,** *to effect, bring about*, per me inventa salus, Cic.; **2,** *to find out from others, learn*, conjurationem, Cic.; inventum est with acc. and infin., Cic.; with rel. sent., non inveniebat quomodo, etc., Cic.; dolor se invenit, *shows itself*, Ov.

inventĭo -ōnis, f. (invenio), **1,** *invention*, Cic.; **2,** *the inventive faculty*, Cic.

inventor -ōris, m. (invenio), *an inventor, finder out*, novorum verborum, Cic.

inventrix -trīcis, f. (inventor), *she that finds out*, oleae Minerva inventrix, Verg.; illae omnium doctrinarum inventrices Athenae, Cic.

inventum -i, n. (invenio), *an invention, discovery*, Cic.

invĕnustē, adv. (invenustus), *ungracefully, inelegantly*, Plin.

invĕnustus -a -um, **1,** *inelegant, ungraceful*, Cic.; **2,** *unhappy in love*, Ter.

invĕrēcundus -a -um, *shameless, impudent*; deus, *Bacchus*, Hor.

invergo, 3. *to pour upon*, fronti vina, Verg.

inversĭo -ōnis, f. (inverto), *irony*, Cic.

inversus -a -um, partic. of inverto.

inverto -verti -versum, 3. *to turn over, turn about*. **I.** Lit., **A.** in locum anulum, Cic.; poet., inversum contristat Aquarius annum, *completed*, Cic. **B.** Esp., **1,** *to turn over*, **a,** of the plough, vomere terras graves, Verg.; **b,** of the winds, *to upturn*, Hor.; **2,** *to turn upside down, empty*, vinaria tota, Hor. **II.** Transf., **A.** *to invert, turn upside down, change, transpose, alter, pervert*, ordinem, Cic.; inversi mores, Hor. **B.** *to pervert, give a different meaning to*, verba, Cic.

invespĕrascit, 3. impers. *it grows dark, becomes twilight*, Liv.

investīgātĭo -ōnis, f. (investigo), *an inquiring into, investigation*, veri, Cic.

investīgātor -ōris, m. (investigo), *an inquirer, investigator*, antiquitatis, Cic.; conjurationis, Cic.

investīgo, 1. *to search out, track out*. **I.** Of dogs, canum tam incredibilis ad investigandum sagacitas narium, Cic. **II.** Of men, **a,** aliquem, Cic.; **b,** conjurationem, Cic.; verum, Cic.

invĕtĕrasco -āvi, 3. (invetero), *to become old, grow old*. **I. a,** *to grow old in*; inveteraverunt hi omnes compluribus Alexandriae bellis, Caes.; **b,** *to become obsolete*, si (res) inveteravit, actum est, Cic. **II.** *to become old, become established, become fixed, to be rooted*, inveteravit jam opinio, Cic.; with dat., quorum nomen et honos inveteravit et huic urbi et hominum famae et sermonibus, Cic.; of persons, *to be firmly established*, exercitum hiemare atque inveterascere in Gallia, Caes.

invĕtĕrātĭo -ōnis, f. (invetero), *a becoming old, an inveterate disease or mistake*, Cic.

invĕtĕro, 1. *to allow to become old*, and pass., **invĕtĕrāri**, *to grow old, become old*. **I.** conglutinatio inveterata, *of long standing*, Cic. **II.** Middle, inveterari, *to become established, firmly rooted*, opinio inveterari potuisset, Cic.; often in partic., **invĕtĕrātus**, *old, established*, amicitia, Cic.; ira, Cic.

invĭcem, adv. (in and vicis), *by turns, alternately*. **I.** hi rursus invicem anno post in armis sunt, illi domi remanent, Caes. **II.** Transf., **a,** *mutually, reciprocally*, invicem inter se gratantes, Liv.; **b,** *on both sides*, multae invicem clades, Tac.

invictus -a -um (in and vinco), *unconquered, unsubdued, unconquerable, invincible*, a labore, Cic.; ad laborem, Liv.; adversum aliquid, Tac.; Hannibal armis invictus, Liv.; absol., imperator, Cic.; defensio, *unanswerable*, Cic.

invĭdentĭa -ae, f. (invideo), *envying, envy*, Cic.

invĭdĕo -vīdi -vīsum, 2. **I.** *to look upon with the evil eye*, Cat. **II.** *to envy, grudge, be envious of*, **a,** with dat., paribus aut inferioribus, Cic.; honori, Cic.; in impers. pass., superioribus saepe invidetur, Cic.; **b,** alicui aliquid or simply aliquid, alicui honorem, Hor.; quoad id ipsi invidere dei, Liv.; **c,** alicui in aliqua re, in qua tibi invideo, Cic.; **d,** alicui aliqua re, non invideo laude sua mulieribus, Liv.; **e,** poet., alicui alicuius rei, illi ciceris, Hor.; **f,** with infin., or acc. and infin., Liburnis deduci triumpho, Hor.; **g,** with ut or ne and the subj., Verg.; **h,** absol., Cic.

invĭdĭa -ae, f. (invidus). **I.** *envy, grudging*, Nep. **II. 1, a,** *hatred, jealousy, ill-will, odium, unpopularity;* invidiam alicui facere, conflare, *to excite ill-will against*, Cic.; habere, *to be unpopular*, Cic.; in invidiam venire, Cic.; invidiam in aliquem commovere, concitare, excitare, Cic.; invidiam lenire, Cic.; absit invidia verbo, Liv.; **b,** meton. (α) *jealous* or *envious persons*, Verg.; (β) *something envied;* invidiae aut pestilentiae possessores, Cic.; **2,** *reproach;* invidiae erat amissum Cremerae praesidium, Liv.

invĭdĭōsē, adv. (invidiosus), *enviously, jealously, bitterly*, Cic.

invĭdĭōsus -a -um (invidia). **I.** *full of envy;* **1,** *envious;* omnes malevoli, iniqui, invidiosi, Cic.; **2,** *causing envy, envied;* invidiosae opes, Tac.; non invidiosa voluptas, Ov. **II.** *full of hate;* **1,** *feeling hate, hating*, Ov.; **2, a,** *causing hate, producing odium* or *ill-feeling;* crimen, Cic.; with in and the acc., ut invidiosum sit in eos, Cic.; with dat., hoc ipsis judicibus invidiosissimum futurum, Cic.; **b,** *hateful, detested;* senatus potentia, Cic.

invĭdus -a -um (invideo), *envious;* **I.** Lit., Cic.; subst., *an envier;* laudis, Cic.; obtrectatores et invidi Scipionis, Cic. **II.** Transf., of things, cura, aetas, Hor.; nox coeptis invida nostris, *unfavourable to*, Ov.

invĭgĭlo, 1. *to watch in* or *over, be watchful* or *wakeful over; give great attention and care to;* venatu, Verg.; reipublicae, Cic.

invĭŏlābĭlis -e, *inviolable, that cannot be injured;* pignus, Verg.

invĭŏlātē, adv. (inviolatus), *inviolately:* memoriam nostri pie inviolateque servabitis, Cic.

invĭŏlātus -a -um, **1,** *uninjured, unhurt;* invulnerati inviolatique vixerunt, Cic.; inviolatā vestrā amicitiā, Cic.; **2,** *inviolable;* tribunus plebis, Liv.

invīsĭtātus -a -um, *not seen;* hence, *unusual, strange;* magnitudo, Cic.; forma, Cic.; nova acies, Liv.

invīso, 1. **I.** *to go to see, to visit.* **A.** domum nostram quoad poteris invisas, Cic. **B.** *to visit a person* or *place;* aliquem, Cic.; suos, Liv.; Delum, Verg. **II.** *to perceive, get a sight of*, Cat.

1. **invīsus** -a -um (in and video), *unseen, secret:* sacra occulta et maribus non solum invisa sed etiam inaudita, Cic.

2. **invīsus** -a -um (invideo). **I.** Pass., *hated;* **a,** of persons, Cic.; with dat., invisus deo, Cic.; **b,** of things, cupressi, negotia, Hor.; judicium invisum etiam judicibus, Liv. **II.** Act., *hating, hostile;* invisum quem tu tibi fingis, Verg.

invītāmentum -i, n. (invito), *an invitation, attraction, allurement;* with subject. genit., naturae, Cic.; with object. genit., temeritatis invitamenta, Liv.; with ad and the acc., multa ad luxuriam invitamenta perniciosa, Cic.

invītātĭo -ōnis, f. (invito), *invitation;* with subject. genit., hospitum, Cic.; in Epirum, Cic.; ut biberetur, Cic.; ad dolendum, Cic.

invītātus -ū, m. (invito), *an invitation;* invitatu tuo, Cic.

invītē, adv. (invitus), *unwillingly, involuntarily, against one's will;* invite cepi Capuam, Cic.; vel pudentius vel invitius ad hoc genus sermonis accedere, Cic.

invīto, 1. *to invite, request civilly.* **I.** Lit., **A.** aliquem in legationem, *to invite one to undertake an embassy*, Cic. **B.** Esp., *to invite as a guest;* **a,** aliquem ad cenam, Cic.; aliquem domum suam, Cic.; aliquem tecto ac domo, Cic.; **b,** invitare se, *to take one's fill;* se cibo vinoque, Sall. **II.** *to invite, allure, entice;* aliquem praemiis ad rem, Cic.; somnos, *to invite, allure to sleep*, Hor.

invītus -a -um. **I.** *unwilling, against one's will;* invitus facio ut, etc., Cic.; eum invitissimum dimisi, Cic.; me, te, se invito, *against my, thy will*, etc.; invitissimis Stoicis, *spite of the opposition of the Stoics*, Cic.; of things, invitā lege agere, Cic. **II.** Poet., *given unwillingly;* invitā ope, Ov.

invĭus -a -um (in and via), *impassable;* saltus, Liv.; maria invia Teucris, Verg.; invia virtuti nulla est via, Ov. Subst., **invĭa** -ōrum, n., *impassable places*, Liv.; poet., lorica invia sagittis, *impenetrable*, Mart.

invŏcātĭo -ōnis, f. (invoco), *a calling upon, invocation;* deorum, Quint.

1. **invŏcātus** -a -um (in and voco), *uncalled*, Cic.

2. **invŏcātus** -a -um, partic. of invoco.

invŏco, 1. *to call in, call upon, call for help, invoke;* Junonem, Cic.; aliquem advocatum ad communem imperatorum fortunam defendendam, Cic.

invŏlātus -ūs, m. (involo), *a flying, flight*, Cic. (only found in abl. sing.).

invŏlĭto, 1. *to fly in;* transf., of the hair, *to float or wave over;* comae involitant humeris, Hor.

invŏlo, 1., **1,** *to fly at, attack furiously;* castra, Tac.; **2,** *to seize* or *pounce upon, take possession of;* in possessionem quasi caducam ac vacuam, Cic.; provinciam, Cic.

invŏlūcre -is, n. (involvo), *a napkin*, Plaut.

invŏlūcrum -i, n. (involvo), *a wrapper, cover, case;* **1,** lit., candelabri, Cic.; **2,** transf., involucris simulationum tegi, Cic.

invŏlūtus -a -um, p. adj. (from involvo), *obscure, confused, involved;* res involutas definiendo explicare, Cic.

involvo -volvi -vŏlūtum, 3. **I.** *to roll in;* igni suo involvunt, Tac. **II.** *to roll along;* silvas armenta virosque, Verg. **III.** *to roll over;* cupae involutae labuntur, Caes.; with dat., *to roll upon;* Olympum Ossae, Verg. **IV. a,** *to roll up, wrap up, cover;* sinistras sagis, Caes.; nox involvit umbrā diem, Verg.; **b,** transf., se litteris, *to bury oneself in, devote oneself to;* se suā virtute, Hor.; bellum pacis nomine involutum, *concealed under*, Cic.

involvŭlus -i, m. (involvo), *a caterpillar which wraps itself up in leaves* Plaut.

invulgo, 1. *to depose, give evidence*, Cic. (?)

invulnĕrātus -a -um (in and vulnero), *unwounded*, Cic.

1. **ĭō,** interj., an exclamation of joy and triumph, *hurrah!* Verg., Hor.; or of pain, *oh!* Ov.

2. **Īo (Ion)** -ūs and -ōnis, f. (Ἰώ), *daughter of the Argive king, Inachus, beloved by Jupiter, changed by Juno into a cow;* identified with the Egyptian goddess, Isis.

Ĭŏlāus -i, m. (Ἰόλαος), *son of Iphiclus, the constant companion of Hercules.*

Ĭolcus (-ŏs) -i, f. (Ἰωλκός), *town in Thessaly, the home of Jason.* Hence, adj., **Ĭolcĭăcus** -a -um, *of* or *belonging to Iolcus.*

Ĭŏlē -ēs, f. (Ἰόλη), *daughter of Eurytus, given by Hercules to his son Hyllus.*

1. **ĭon,** -ĭi, n. (ἴον), **1,** *the blue violet*, Plin.; **2,** *a precious stone of similar colour*, Plin.

2. **Īon** -ōnis, f., v. Io.

Īōnes -um, m. (Ἴωνες), *the Ionians, a people of Greece, one of the four Greek races;* hence, **1,**

adj , **Ĭōnĭăcus** -a -um, *Ionian* ; 2, **Ĭōnĭcus** -a -um, *Ionian*, 3, **Ĭōnĭus** -a -um, *Ionian*, *Ionic*; mare Ionium, *the sea between Italy and Greece*, Liv , so aequor Ionium, Ov , sinus Ionius, Hor , or simply Ionium -ii, n , Verg Subst , **Ĭōnĭa** ae, f *a district in Asia Minor between Caria and Aeolis*

Iōta n indecl (ἰῶτα), *the name of the Greek vowel*, I, ι, Cic.

Īphĭănassa ae, f = Iphigenia, Lucr

Īphĭās -ădis, f (Ἰφιάς), *daughter of Iphis*, i e , *Euadne*

Īphĭgĕnīa -ae, f (Ἰφιγένεια), *daughter of Agamemnon, sacrificed by her father to appease the wrath of Diana*, or, according to another legend, *saved by Diana, and carried away, and made her priestess in Tauris*

ipse a um, genit ipsius (poet , ipsĭus), dat. ipsi (is and -pse), *self* I. Gen , ille ipse, etc , Cic , ego ipse, *I myself*, Cic , ipse interviso, Cic , in me ipso probavi, *in myself*, Cic., et ipse, *also, too*, victor ex Aequis in Volscos transiit et ipsos bellum molientes, *who on their side were preparing war*, Liv II. Esp , A. *very, identical, exactly*, a, eaque ipsa causa belli fuit, *and that very thing was the cause of the war*, Liv , natali suo ipso die, *just on her birthday*, Cic , b, with numerals = *just, exactly*, ipso vicesimo anno, Cic , eā ipsā horā, Cic B. ipse, ipsa, used emphatically of a *master, mistress, teacher*, etc , ipse dixit, *the master* (i e *Pythagoras*) *has said it*, Cic C. = *spontaneously, of one's own accord*, valvae se ipsae aperuerunt, Cic. D. *alone, with oneself*, genitor secum ipse volutat, Verg , ipse per se, and simply ipse, *of himself, by himself, alone*, moventur ipsa per se, Cic. E. Used for the reflexive pronoun, quem si parum pudor ipsius defendebat, Cic , ipse with suffix met, ipsimet (nom plur), Cic (Superlative, ipsissimus, *one's very self*, Plaut).

īra -ae, f I. *wrath, anger, ire*, Cic , iram evomere in aliquem, Tac , irae indulgere, Liv , irae caelestes, *divine wrath*, Liv , with genit of the cause of anger, dictatoris creati, Liv , ira adversus Romanos, Liv veteres in populum Romanum irae, Liv , transf., of inanimate objects, *violence, rage*, belli, Sall. II. Meton , *the cause of anger*, Ov

īrācundē, adv with compar (iracundus), *wrathfully, angrily, passionately*, Cic

īrācundĭa -ae, f (iracundus) I. *an angry disposition, passionateness, irascibility*, Cic. II. *anger, fury, wrath*, iracundiam cohibere, Cic ; excitare, Cic , plur , iracundiae implacabiles, Cic

īrācundus -a um (irascor), *inclined to anger, irascible, passionate, angry, wrathful*, Cic , in aliquem, Cic

īrascor, 3 dep (ira), *to be angry, wrathful*, alicui, Cic , of a bull, in cornua, *to charge wrathfully with the horns*, Verg

īrātē, adv (iratus), *angrily*, Phaedr

īrātus -a um (irascor), *angry, full of wrath*, alicui, *with any one*, iratior, iratissimus alicui, Cic , quam iratus de judicio, Cic , of inanimate objects, *raging*, mare, venter, Hor.

Īris -ridis, f (Ἶρις), *the messenger of the gods, the goddess of the rainbow* (acc Irim, Verg , voc Iri, Verg , Ov)

irnĕa = hirnea (q v)

īrōnīa -ae, f (εἰρωνεία), *irony*, Cic

Irpini = Hirpini (q v).

irrāsus -a -um (in and rado), *unshaved*, Plaut.

irraucesco, or **irraucĭo** -rausi, 3 (in and raucus), *to become hoarse*, Cic.

irrĕlĭgātus -a -um (in and religo), *unbound*; croceas irreligata comas, Ov

irrĕlĭgĭōsē, adv with compar (irreligiosus), *irreligiously, impiously*, Tac

irrĕlĭgĭōsus -a um (in and religiosus), *irreligious, impious*, irreligiosum ratus, with infin , Liv

irrĕmĕābĭlis e (in and remeabilis), *from which there is no return*, unda, Verg

irrĕpărābĭlis e (in and reparabilis), *that cannot be restored, irreparable, irrecoverable*, tempus, Verg

irrĕpertus -a -um (in and reperio), *not discovered, not found out*, aurum, Hor

irrēpo -repsi -reptum, 3 *to creep, crawl in*; interim (Gabinius) ipso decimo die irrepsit, *came creeping in*, Cic , transf , *to creep in, insinuate oneself into*, in mentes hominum, Cic ; in testamenta locupletium, Cic

irrĕprĕhensus -a um (in and reprehendo), *unblamed, blameless*, Ov

irrĕquĭētus -a um (in and requietus), *restless, troubled*, Charybdis, Ov

irrĕsectus -a um (in and reseco), *uncut*; pollex, Hor

irrĕsŏlūtus -a -um (in and resolvo), *not loosed, not slackened*, vincula, Ov

irrētĭo, 4. (in and * retio, from rete), *to catch, entangle in a net*, a, lit , aliquem Cic , b, fig , aliquem corruptelarum illecebris, *to ensnare*, Cic

irrĕtortus -a -um (in and retorqueo), *not turned or twisted back*, oculo irretorto, Hor

irrĕvĕrentĭa -ae, f (irreverens from in and reverens), *want of respect, irreverence*, juventutis, Tac , adversus fas nefasque, Tac

irrĕvŏcābĭlis -e (in revocabilis), *that cannot be called back, irrevocable* I. Lit , aetas, Lucr , verbum, Hor II Transf , A. *unalterable*, casus, Liv B. *implacable*, Tac

irrĕvŏcātus -a um (in and revoco), 1, *not called back*, i e , *not asked to repeat anything*, Hor , 2, *not to be called or held back*, Ov. (?)

irrīdĕo -risi -risum, 2 (in and rideo) I. Intransit , *to laugh at, jeer at*, Cic II. Transit , *to mock, ridicule, deride*, deos, Cic

irrīdĭcŭlē, adv (in and ridicule), *without wit or humour*, non irridicule dixit, Caes

irrīdĭcŭlum -i, n (irrideo), *a laughing-stock*, irridiculo haberi (esse), *to be made game of*, Plaut

irrĭgātĭo -ōnis, f (irrigo) *a watering, irrigation*, agri, Cic

irrĭgo (in rigo), 1 I. *to conduct water or any other liquid to any place*, imbres, Verg , transf , *to diffuse*, per membra quietem, Verg II *to water, irrigate*, Aegyptum Nilus irrigat, Cic , hortulos fontibus, Cic , transf , fessos sopor irrigat artus, *overspreads, refreshes*, Verg

irrĭgŭus -a -um (irrigo) I. Act , *watering, irrigating*, fons, Verg , transf , somnus, *strengthening, refreshing*, Pers II Pass , *watered*, hortus, Hor , corpus irriguum mero, *soaked*, Hor

irrīsĭo -ōnis, f (irrideo), *a laughing at, mocking, derision*, with subject genit , omnium, Cic

irrīsor -ōris, m (irrideo), *a laugher, mocker, derider*, with object genit , hujus orationis, Cic

irrīsus -ūs, m (irrideo), *laughter, mockery, derision*, irrisui esse, *to be a laughing-stock*, Caes ; ab irrisu (*in derision*) linguam exserere, Liv

irrītābĭlis e (irrito), *irritable, easily roused*;

irritabiles sunt animi optimorum, Cic.; genus vatum, Hor.

irrītāmen -inis, n. (irrito), *an incitement, inducement;* amoris, Ov.

irrītāmentum -i, n. (irrito), *incitement, inducement, provocation, incentive;* with object. genit., certaminum, Liv.; libidinum, Tac.; with dat., luxui, Tac.

irrītātio -ōnis, f. (irrito), *a stirring up, provoking, irritating, irritation;* with subject. genit., nullis conviviorum irritationibus, Tac.; irritatio quidem animorum ea prima fuit, Liv.

irrītātus -a -um, partic. of irrito.

irrīto, 1. (in and *rito). **I.** *to stir up, stimulate, incite, excite;* aliquem ad certamen, Liv.; iram et odium, Liv. **II.** *to excite to anger, irritate;* aliquem, Cic.; animos barbarorum, Liv.

irrĭtus -a -um (in and ratus). **I.** *void, invalid;* testamentum facere irritum, Cic. **II.** *vain;* **a,** of things, *vain, ineffectual, without effect;* inceptum, Liv.; dona, tela, Verg.; remedium, Tac.; subst., **irritum** -i, n. *that which is vain;* spes ad irritum cadit, *is disappointed,* Liv.; **b,** transf., of persons, *without doing anything;* irriti legati remittuntur, Tac.; with genit. of the object., legationis, Tac.

irrŏgātio -ōnis, f. (irrogo), *the imposing of a fine or penalty;* multae, Tac.

irrŏgo (in-rŏgo), 1. **I.** *to propose to the people a measure against anyone;* alicui legem, privilegium, Cic.; alicui multam, poenam, Cic. **II.** *to inflict, impose;* poenas peccatis, Hor. (irrogassit = irrogaverit, Cic.).

irrōro (in-rōro), 1. *to moisten with dew.* **I.** *to wet, moisten;* crinem aquis, Ov.; lacrimae irrorant foliis, *trickle down upon,* Ov. **II.** *to sprinkle upon;* liquores vestibus et capiti, Ov.

irrumpo -rūpi -ruptum, 3. (in and rumpo), *to break in, burst into, rush in.* **I.** Lit., **1,** in castra, Cic.; with dat., thalamo, Verg.; with acc., portam, Sall.; **2,** *to rush into, seize upon;* in nostrum patrimonium, Cic. **II.** Transf., luxuries quam in domum irrupit, Cic.; imagines in animos per corpus irrumpunt, Cic.; *to break in upon, seek to prevent;* in nostrum fletum irrumpes, Cic. (?)

irrŭo (in-rŭo) -rŭi, 3. *to rush into, rush upon.* **A.** Lit., **1,** in aciem, Liv.; in aliquem, Cic.; **2,** *to rush and seize upon, take possession of;* in alienas possessiones, Cic. **B.** Transf., ne quo irruas, *make some blunder,* Cic.; in odium offensionemque populi Romani, *rush blindly into,* Cic.

irruptio -ōnis, f. (irrumpo), *a breaking, bursting into, irruption;* etiamsi irruptio nulla facta est, Cic.

irruptus -a -um (in and rumpo), *unbroken, unsevered;* copula, Hor.

Īrus -i, m. (Ἶρος), *the name of a beggar in Ithaca;* appell. = *a poor man* (opp. to Croesus), Ov.

ĭs, ĕa, ĭd. I. *he, she, it; this* or *that person* or *thing* (the demonstrative pronoun chiefly used to refer to something already mentioned). **A. a,** subst., mihi venit obviam puer tuus; is mihi literas reddidit, Cic.; **b,** adj., in eum locum, Caes.; ob eam causam, Nep. **B. a,** referring to a following subst., ea libera conjectura est, Liv.; **b,** used pleonastically for the sake of emphasis (α) with the relat., quod ne id facere posses, Cic.; esp. in apposition to a clause, si nos, id quod debet, nostra patria delectat, Cic.; (β) with a noun, urbem novam, conditam vi et armis, jure eam condere parat, Liv.; **c,** id subst.; id temporis, id aetatis, *at that age,* Cic.; id gaudeo, *I rejoice because of that,* Cic.; in eo est, or res in eo est, *it is on the point of,* etc., Liv.; **d,** id est, *that is,* in explanation, hodie, id est, Cal. Oct., Cic.; **e,** et is, isque, atque is, *and that too, and indeed;* Antonius cum una legione, eāque vacillante, *and that vacillating,* Cic. **II.** *that,* as the correlative of qui, quae, quod; is qui physicus appellatur, Cic. **III.** *such, of such a kind;* **a,** subst., neque is es, qui, quid sis, nescias, Cic.; **b,** cuius ea stultitia ut, etc., Cic.

Īsăra -ae, f. *a river in Gaul,* now *the Isère.*

Īsauri -ōrum, m. (Ἴσαυροι), *the Isaurians.* Hence, **A. Īsauria** -ae, f. (Ἰσαυρία), *a mountainous country of Asia Minor, north of Cilicia.* **B. Īsaurĭcus** -a -um, *surname of P. Servilius Vatia, the conqueror of the Isauri.* **C. Īsaurus** -a -um, *Isaurian.*

Īsis -idis, f. (Ἶσις), *the Egyptian goddess Isis.* Adj., **Īsĭăcus** -a -um, *of* or *belonging to Isis.*

Ismărus -i, m. (Ἴσμαρος), and **Ismăra** -ōrum, n. *a mountain in Thrace.* Adj., **Ismărius** -a -um, poet. = *Thracian;* tyrannus, *Tereus,* Ov.

Ismēnus (-ŏs) -i, m. (Ἰσμηνός), *a river in Boeotia.* Hence, **A. Ismēnis** -idis, f. poet. = *a Theban woman.* **B. Ismēnius** -a -um, poet. = *Theban.*

Īsŏcrătēs -is, m. (Ἰσοκράτης), *a celebrated Athenian orator.* Adj., **Īsŏcrătēus** and **Īsŏcrătīus** -a -um, *Isocratean.*

Issa -ae, f. (Ἴσσα), *an island in the Adriatic Sea, off the coast of Dalmatia,* now *Lissa.* Adj., **A. Issensis** -e. **B. Issaeus** -a -um. **C. Issăĭcus** -a -um, *of* or *belonging to Issa.*

istāc, adv. *by that way,* Ter.

istactĕnus, adv. *thus far,* Plaut.

istĕ, ista, istŭd, pron. demonstr. (is and -te), *this* or *that person* or *thing* (applies to the person spoken to). **I.** Gen., quid quod adventu tuo ista subsellia (*those seats where you sit*) vacuefacta sunt, Cic. **II. a,** in letters, relating to places or conditions in which the person addressed is, perfer istam militiam, *your military service,* Cic.; **b,** emphatic, referring to something said by the person addressed, Att. "Platonem videlicet dicis." M. "*istum* ipsum," Cic.; ista quae dicitis, Cic.; **c,** in speeches, referring to the accused, Cic.; **d,** ironical or contemptuous, ex quibus generibus hominum istae copiae comparentur, Cic.

Ister = Hister.

Isthmus -i, m. (ἰσθμός), *an isthmus;* **a,** *the isthmus on which Cyzicus was situated,* Prop.; **b,** especially *the Isthmus of Corinth,* Caes. Adj., **Isthmius** -a -um, *Isthmian;* labor, *in the Isthmian games,* Hor.; plur. subst., **Isthmia** -ōrum, n. *the Isthmian Games,* Liv.

istī, adv. (iste), *there,* Verg.

1. **istĭc (isthĭc),** istaec, istŏc or istŭc (isto and hic), *this same, this very person* or *thing;* istic labor, Plaut.; subst., istuc considerabo, Cic.; in interrogative sentences, istice, etc., Plaut.

2. **istīc (isthīc),** (iste and adv. hic), **1,** *there,* denotes the place of the person spoken to, *here, there;* quoniam istic sedes, Cic.; scribite quid istic (= *in Rome*) agatur, Cic.; **2,** *in this matter, in this affair,* Cic.; istic sum, *I am all ears,* Cic.

istim, adv. (iste), *from there,* Cic.

istinc (isthinc), adv. (iste and hinc), *thence, from thence.* **A.** Lit., alludes to the place where the person spoken to may be; qui istinc veniunt, Cic. **B.** Transf., of that thing, *thence,* Hor.

istiusmŏdi, *of that kind* or *sort, such;* ratio istiusmodi, Cic.

istō, adv (iste) **I.** *thither, to that place, to the place where you are;* venire, Cic **II.** Transf, *thereunto, into that thing,* admiscere aliquem, Cic.

istōc, adv (1 istic) **I.** *thither,* Plaut **II.** *from that place,* Ter

istorsum, adv (istoversum), *thitherwards, in that direction,* Ter

Istri, v Histri

1 **istūc,** n of 1. istic (q v)

2 **istūc (isthūc),** adv (iste and huc), *thither,* venire, Cic

ĭtă, adv (i-s and -ta), *so, thus, in such wise* **I.** Gen, **a,** te ita velle certe scio, Cic., **b,** intro ducing a following thought, with acc and infin, Cic, **c,** est ita or factum est ita, in answers, *so it is,* Cic, ita prorsus, ita plane, *certainly,* Cic, **d,** interrogative, itane? *really?* Cic; quid ita? *why so?* Cic. **II.** Esp, **A.** With comparisons, **a,** gen with ut, more rarely with quemadmodum, quomodo, quasi, etc *so . . as, in such a manner . as,* me consulem ita fecistis quo modo pauci facti sunt, Cic; **b,** in asseitions and adjurations, ita vivam ut maximos sumptus facio, Cic; saepe, ita me dii juvent, te desideravi, Cic **B** *of such a kind, such, in such a condition;* ita sunt res nostrae, Cic **C.** *and so, consequently, and then,* aliquot dies aegrotasse et ita esse mortuum, Cic. **D.** To express condition or limitation, ita . . ut, *to the extent that, only that,* ita tamen ut tibi nolim molestus esse, Cic **E.** *with the object that,* duobus consulibus ita missis, ut alter Mithridatem persequeretur, Cic **F.** To express degree, *so, to such an extent,* ita mendose scribuntur, Cic

Ĭtăli -ōrum and ûm, m. *the inhabitants of Italy, the Italians* Hence, **A. Ĭtălĭa** -ae, f. *Italy* **B. Ĭtălĭcus** -a -um, *Italian;* subst, **Ĭtălĭca** -ae, f *a town in Hispania Baetica* **C. Ĭtălus** -a -um, *Italian* **D. Ĭtălis** -ĭdis, f, *Italian* Plur, Italides = *Italian women,* Verg

ĭtăquĕ, adv., 1, *and thus, and so,* Cic, 2, *therefore, for that reason, on that account,* Cic., 3, after a digression, to resume the thread of discourse, *so,* Cic

ĭtem, adv. (i s and -tem) **I.** *also, likewise, in like manner,* Romulus augur cum fratre item augure, Cic. **II. A.** In comparisons, *in like manner, as,* fecisti item ut praedones, Cic **B.** et item, itemque, *and also and even,* solis defectiones itemque lunae, Cic

ĭtĕr, ĭtĭnĕris, n (connected with ire, itum). **I.** *a going, walk, way* **A. 1,** in diversum iter equi concitati, Liv, **2, a,** *a going, a journey, a march,* iter facere in Apuliam, Cic; iter ingredi, Cic, in itinere, *on the march,* Caes, **b,** *a march,* considered as a measure of distance, cum abessem ab Amano iter unius diei, *one day's journey,* Cic.; quam maximis itineribus potest, *with the longest possible stages,* Caes, **3, a,** *a legal right of way,* Cic., **b,** *permission to march,* negat se posse iter ulli per provinciam dare, Caes **B.** Fig, defessus labore atque itinere disputationis, Cic. **II.** Concrete. **A.** Lit, *a way, road;* iter angustum et difficile, Caes **B.** Fig, **1,** *way, course* iter amoris nostri et officii mei, Cic, **2,** *method,* naturam suo quodam itinere ad ultimum pervenire, Cic

ĭtĕrātĭo -ōnis, f (itero), *a repetition, iteration,* verborum, Cic.

ĭtĕro, 1 *to do a second time, repeat* **I.** pugnam, *to renew,* Liv; aequor, *to take ship again,* Hor. **II. A.** *to plough again,* agrum non semel arare sed iterare, Cic **B.** *to repeat* (words), verba, Cic

ĭtĕrum, adv **I. a,** *again, a second time;* C Flaminius consul iterum, Cic, **b,** of repeated actions, semel atque iterum, Cic, iterum atque iterum, *again and again,* Hor, **c,** in order of events, *secondly,* semel . . iterum, Cic **II.** *on the other hand,* pares iterum accusandi causas esse, Tac

Ĭthăca -ae, and **Ĭthăcē** -ēs, f (Ἰθάκη), *an island in the Ionian Sea, the home of Ulysses* Hence, adj, **A. Ĭthăcensis** -e, *Ithacan* **B. Ĭthăcus** -a -um, *Ithacan* Subst, **Ĭthăcus** -i, m *Ulysses,* Verg

ĭtĭdem, adv (item dem), *in like manner, likewise,* Cic

ĭtĭo -ōnis, f (eo), *a going, travelling,* domum itio, Cic

Ĭtĭus portus, *a port of the Morini from which Caesar crossed over to Britain, perhaps Wit Sand, Sandgatte, or Boulogne*

ĭto, 1 (intens of eo), *to go;* ad coenas, Cic

Ĭtōnē -ēs, f (Ἰτώνη) and **Ĭtōnus** -i, m (Ἴτωνος), *a town in Boeotia, with a temple of Athene* Hence, adj, **Ĭtōnĭus** -a -um, *Itonian*

Ĭtūraei -ōrum, m (Ἰτουραῖοι), *a people in the north-east of Palestine* Hence, adj, **Ĭtūraeus** -a -um *Ituraean*

ĭtus -ūs, m (eo), *a going, departure,* noster itus, reditus, Cic.

Ĭtўlus -i, m (Ἴτυλος), *son of the Theban king Zetheus and Aedon, killed by his own mother*

Ĭtўs -ўos, dat -ty, acc -tyn and -tym, abl -ty, m (Ἴτυς), *son of Tereus and Procne, killed by his mother and served up for food to his father.*

Ĭūlēus = Julius **I.** *named after Iulus, son of Aeneas,* avi, Ov **II.** *belonging to Julius Caesar,* Calendae, *1st of July,* Ov

Ĭūlus -i, m *son of Aeneas, also called Ascanius*

Ixīōn -ŏnis, m (Ἰξίων), *king of the Lapithae in Thessaly, father of Pirithous, for an insult to Juno he was hurled down to Tartarus, and bound to a perpetually revolving wheel* Hence, **A.** Adj, **Ixīŏnĭus** -a -um, *of Ixion* **B. Ixīŏnĭdēs** -ae, m (Ἰξιονίδης), *a son of Ixion, Pirithous,* Ov

J.

J, j, a consonant, originally written with the same sign as the vowel I, i, yet recognised by the ancients as a different letter.

jăcĕo -cŭi -citūrus, 2. (akin to jacio), *to lie* (opp stare, pendere) **I.** Lit, **A.** Gen, humi, Cic, in limine, Cic, lecto, Ov, super corpus alicuius, Ov, ad alicuius pedes, Cic. **B.** Esp, **1,** *to lie resting;* **a,** of persons, *to sleep,* in lecto, Cic, **b,** *to recline at table,* Ov, **c,** *to lie sick, be ill,* te jacente, *while you are ill in bed,* Cic, **2,** *to lie thrown to the ground,* **a,** Arge, jaces, Ov, **b,** *to lie dead, be slain,* pro patria, Ov; **3,** *to lie or remain for a long time,* Brundusii, Cic; **4, a,** *to lie geographically, be situate,* jacet inter eos campus, Liv, **b,** *to lie low, be flat,* domus depressa, caeca, jacens, Cic, **c,** *to lie in ruins,* jacet Ilion ingens, Ov, **d,** of clothes, *to hang loosely, be loose,* praeverrunt latas veste jacente vias, Ov, **e,** *to be cast down,* vultus attolle jacentes, Ov **II.** Fig, **A.** priora tempora in ruinis reipublicae nostrisque jacuerunt, *were united with,* Cic. **B. 1,** *to be sunk* *in*; in maerore, Cic.; **2, a,** *to be overcome, powerless*; (α) jacere Caesarem offensione populari, Cic.; (β) *to be hopeless, dispirited*: jacet, diffidit, abjecit hastas, Cic.; (γ) *to be neglected* or *despised*; philosophia jacuit usque ad hanc aetatem, Cic.; **b,** *to be overthrown, put out of court*; jacent hi suis testibus, Cic.; jacet igitur tota conclusio, Cic.; **c,** *to cease*: judicia jacebant, Cic.; **d,** *to be low in price*; jacent pretia praediorum, Cic.; **3,** of words, *to be in common use*; (verba) jacentia, Cic.

Jăcĕtāni -ōrum, m. *a people in the north of Hispania ulterior.*

jăcĭo, jēci, jactum, 3. *to throw, cast, hurl.* **I. A.** Lit., **1,** gen., in aliquem scyphum, Cic.; materiam de muro in aggerem, Caes.; se in profundum, Cic.; **2,** esp., **a,** *to throw dice*; talum, Cic.; **b,** *to throw out an anchor*; ancoram, Caes.; **c,** *to fling away*; vestem procul, Ov.; **d,** *to scatter, diffuse*: flores, Verg. **B.** Fig., **1,** *to throw, cast*; contumeliam in aliquem, Cic.; **2,** *to let fall in speaking, to utter*; assiduas ore querelas, Cic.; suspicionem, Cic.; de habitu cultuque et institutis eius, Tac. **II.** *to lay, build, erect*; aggerem, Caes.; fundamenta urbi, Liv.; fig., fundamenta pacis, Cic.

jactans -antis, p. adj. (from jacto), *boastful, vainglorious*, Cic.

jactantĕr, adv. with compar. (jactans), *boastfully, vaingloriously*, Tac.

jactantĭa -ae, f. (jacto), *boasting, bragging, vainglory*; sui, *about oneself*, Tac.

jactātĭo -ōnis, f. (jacto). **I.** Act., *a throwing, shaking, violently moving up and down*; **a,** corporis, Cic.; **b,** *extolling, belauding*; cultus, Tac. **II.** Pass., **1,** *being tossed about, tossing*; **a,** navis, Cic.; **b,** transf., *violent emotions*, Cic.; **2,** *applause*; jactationem habere in populo, Cic.; **3,** *vainglory*; alicuius, Cic.

jactātor -ōris, m. (jacto), *a boaster, ostentatious person*, Cic.

jactātus -ūs, m. (jacto), *a shaking, moving quickly up and down*; pennarum, Ov.

jactīto, 1. (intens. of jacto), *to produce in public, to utter*; ridicula, Liv.

jacto, 1. (intens. of jacio), *to throw, cast.* **I. A.** Lit., **1,** gen., faces in vicinorum tecta, Cic.; vestem de muro, Caes.; **2, a,** *to cast dice*; numeros eburnos, Ov.; **b,** *to throw away*; arma multa passim, Liv.; **c,** *to diffuse, spread, scatter*; odorem late, Verg. **B.** Transf., *to throw, utter, hurl*; minas, Cic.; jocosa dicta in adversarios, Liv. **II.** *to move up and down, throw about, drive about, toss.* **A.** Lit., **1,** brachia, Ov.; cerviculam, Cic.; cum adversā tempestate in alto jactarentur, Cic.; aestu febrique jactari, Cic.; **2,** esp., *to throw about, gesticulating*; se, Cic. **B.** Transf., **1,** gen., *to drive hither and thither*; curas pectore, Verg.; middle, jactabatur nummus, *fluctuated*, Cic.; refl., se jactare or middle jactari; se in causis centumviralibus, *to busy oneself with*, Cic.; **2,** esp., **a,** *to torment, disquiet*; jactatur domi suae, Cic.; **b,** *to talk about repeatedly, discuss, speak of*; rem in contione, Cic.; **c,** *to boast of, vaunt*; gratiam urbanam, Caes.; genus et nomen, Hor.; **d,** reflex., jactare se; (α) *to boast, brag*, Cic.; (β) *to behave oneself in a certain way*; se magnificentissime, Cic.

jactūra -ae, f. (jacio). **I.** *a throwing, throwing away*; in mari jacturam facere, *to throw overboard*, Cic. **II.** Transf., **A.** *loss, sacrifice*; jacturae rei familiaris erunt faciendae, Cic.; jacturam criminum facere, *to forego, pass over*, Cic. **B.** *cost, expense*, Cic.

jactus -ūs, m. (jacio), *a throwing, cast, throw.* **I.** fulminum, Cic.; intra teli jactum, *within shot*, Verg. **II.** *the throw of the dice*; tesserarum prosper jactus, Liv.

jăcŭlābĭlis -e (jaculor), *that can be thrown or cast*; telum, Ov.

jăcŭlātĭo -onis, f. (jaculor), *a throwing, hurling*, Plin.

jăcŭlātor -ōris, m. (jaculor), **1,** *a thrower, hurler*, Hor.; **2,** *a javelin-man, a light-armed soldier*, Liv.

jăcŭlātrix -icis, f. (jaculator), *she that hurls, the huntress (Diana)*, Ov.

jăcŭlor, 1. (jaculum). **I.** Intransit., **1,** lit., *to throw a javelin*; totum diem jaculari, Cic.; **2,** transf., *to make an attack with words*; probris procacibus in aliquem, Cic. **II.** Transit., **A.** *to cast, hurl*; **1,** lit., ignes, Verg.; silicem in hostes, Ov.; **2,** transf., verbum, Lucr. **B.** *to shoot at*; **1,** lit., cervos, Hor.; **2,** transf., *to aim at, strive after*; multa, Hor.

jăcŭlum -i, n. (jacio, *the thing thrown*), **1,** *a dart, javelin*; fervefacta jacula in castra jacĕre, Caes.; **2,** *a casting-net*, Ov.

jam, adv. (is), *now, already.* **I.** Temporal, **A. a,** of the immediate present, *just now*; non quia jam sint, sed quia saepe sint, Cic.; jam jamque, *directly*, Cic.; jam nunc, *just now*, Cic.; jam tum, *just then*, Cic.; **b,** of time just passed, *just lately*; illa his quae jam posui consequentia, Cic.; **c,** of future time, *immediately, directly, presently*: quam pulchra sint ipse jam dicet, Cic.; thus (α) *soon*; jam te premet nox, Hor.; (β) of commands, *now, at once*; sed jam age, carpe viam, Verg. **B. a,** *till now, up to the present time*; septingentos jam annos amplius unis moribus vivunt, Cic.; jam diu, jam dudum, jam pridem, *now for a long time*, Cic.; **b,** *from now*; jam concedo non esse miseros qui mortui sunt, Cic.; jam non, *not from this time*, Cic. **C.** To express something that happens unexpectedly early or late; **a,** *already*; omnes jam istius generis legationes erant constitutae, Cic.; **b,** *at last*; te aliquando jam rem transigere, Cic. **II.** Of other relations. **A.** *then certainly, now certainly*; da mihi hoc, jam tibi maximam partem defensionis praecideris, Cic.; thus used to express the consequence of something, *now indeed, so indeed*; id tu jam intelliges quum in Galliam veneris, Cic. **B.** To introduce something new, *further, moreover*; et aures . . . itemque nares . . . jam gustatus, Cic. **C.** To emphasise or limit statements, *just, indeed*; **a,** with pronoun, jam illud non sunt admonendi, Cic.; **b,** with adj., non scire quidem barbarum jam videtur, Cic.; **c,** of numerals, *just*; sunt duo menses jam, Cic.; **d,** with particles, non jam, *not indeed*, Cic.; nunc jam, *even now*, Cic.; tum jam, *just then*, Cic.

jamdūdum, jamprīdem, v. jam.

Jānālis, v. Janus.

Jānĭcŭlum -i, n. (Janus), *one of the hills of Rome, on the left side of the Tiber.*

Jānĭgĕna -ae, c. (Janus and gigno), *child of Janus*, Ov.

jānĭtor -ōris, m. (janua), *a door-keeper, porter.* **I.** Gen., janitor carceris, Cic. **II.** Esp., **A.** Of Janus, coelestis aulae, Ov. **B.** Of Cerberus, janitor immanis aulae, Hor.

jānĭtrix -īcis, f. (janitor), *a portress*, Plaut.

jānŭa -ae, f. (*see* Janus), **1,** *the outer door of a house*; januam claudere, Cic.; quaerere aliquem a janua, *to ask at the door for some one*, Cic.; **2,** transf., *entrance, passage*; Ditis, Verg.; maris gemini, *of the Bosphorus*, Ov.; eam urbem sibi Asiae januam fore, Cic.; fig., quā nolui januā sum ingressus in causam, Cic.

Jānŭārĭus -a -um (Janus), *belonging to*

Janus, Januarius mensis, *the month January*, Cic, or simply Januarius Caes, calendae Januariae, *the 1st of January*, Cic

Jānus -i, m (root i, *to go*, whence also janua). **I.** *an old Italian deity, the god of the year, represented with two faces looking in opposite directions* **II 1,** *a covered passage*, esp **a,** *one at the foot of the Argiletum, adorned with statues of Janus;* **b,** *one of the portals of the* porta Carmentalis, Liv, **c,** *one of the arcades in the forum at Rome*, of which there were three, Janus summus, imus, and medius, where the merchants, bankers, and booksellers had their shops, **2,** poet, *the month of January*, Ov. Hence, adj, **Jānālis** -e, *belonging to Janus*

jĕcur, genit jĕcŏris and jĕcĭnŏris, n, and **jŏcŭr,** genit jŏcĭnĕris, n, *the liver*, Cic, as *the seat of the passions* (according to the belief of the ancients), fervens difficili bile tumet jecur, Hor (Varro and Cic use the form jecoris, Livy jocineris)

jĕcuscŭlum (jŏcuscŭlum) -i, n (dim. of jecur), *a little liver*, Cic

jējūnē, adv (jejunus), of style, *dryly, meagrely, frigidly, without energy or taste*, de aliqua re jejune et exiliter disputare, Cic, haec dicuntur fortasse jejunius, Cic

jējūnĭōsus -a um (jejunium), *hungry, fasting*, Plaut

jējūnĭtas -ātis, f (jejunus) **I.** *hungriness, emptiness*, Plaut **II.** Transf, of discourse, *dryness, meagreness, frigidity, plainness*, inopia et jejunitas, Cic

jējūnĭum -ii, n. (jejunus) **I.** *a fast, abstinence from food*, **1,** lit. jejunium Cereri instituere, Liv, **2,** *hunger*, jejunia pascere, satiare, solvere, sedare placare, *to satisfy hunger*, Ov **II.** Transf, *leanness*, Verg

jējūnus a -um, *fasting* **I 1** lit., ita jejunus ut ne aquam quidem gustarim, Cic, **2,** meton, **a,** *hungry*, Cic, **b,** *thirsty*, Prop, **3, a,** *empty*, corpora suco jejuna, Lucr, **b,** *unfruitful*, ager, Cic, **c,** *scanty* sanies, Verg **II.** Fig, **A.** jejunae hujus orationis aures, *unacquainted with*, Cic. **B. a,** *poor, mean*, calumnia, Cic, **b** *dry, meagre, weak*, oratio Cic, **c,** *pitiful, insipid* illud vero pusilli animi et ipsa malevolentia jejuni et inanis, Cic

jentăcŭlum i, n (jento), *a breakfast*, Plaut

jento, 1 *to breakfast*, Suet

jŏcātĭo -ōnis, f (jocor), *a joke, jest*, Cic.

jŏcor, 1 dep (jocus) **I.** Intransit, *to joke, jest*, cum aliquo per litteras, Cic., me appellabat jocans, Cic **II.** Transit, *to say in jest*, haec jocatus sum, Cic

jŏcōsē, adv (jocosus), *in jest*, jocosius scribere, Cic

jŏcōsus -a um (jocus), *jocose, humorous, witty, sportive merry, facetious*, Maecenas, Hor, res, Cic; transf, imago (vocis), *the sportive echo*, Hor

jŏcŭlāris -e (joculus), *jocular, laughable, ludicrous*, licentia, Cic, subst, n pl, **jŏcŭlāria** -ium, n *jests*, Hor

jŏcŭlārĭter, adv (jocularis), *jocularly, jestingly*, Plin

jŏcŭlātor -ōris, m (joculor), *a joker, jocular person*, Cic

jŏcŭlor, 1 dep (joculus) *to joke, jest, speak jocosely*; quaedam militariter joculantes, *making rude soldier-jests*, Liv

jŏcŭlus -i, 1 (dim of jocus) *a little joke or jest*, Plaut

jŏcur, v jecur

jŏcus -i, m (plur joci and joca) **I.** *a joke jest* joci causa, *for the jest's sake*, Cic, per jocum, *in jest*, Cic, extra jocum, remoto joco, *joking apart* Cic **II.** Transf, **a,** *a game*, Ov, **b,** *toying*, Ov, **c,** *a subject for jesting*, Hor

1 **jŭba** ae, f, **1,** *the mane of any animal*, Cic, **2,** *the crest of a helmet*, Verg

2 **Jŭba** -ae, m, (Ἰόβας), *son of Hiempsal, king of Numidia, one of the supporters of Pompeius*

jŭbar -ăris, n (= jubare (sc lumen) from jubar), *a beaming light, radiance*, esp of the heavenly bodies, **a,** lit, *the light of the sun*, Ov, *of the moon*, Ov, *of fire*, Ov, **b,** meton, *a star*, esp, *the morning star*, Varr

jŭbātus -a -um (juba), *having a mane, crested*, anguis, Liv

jŭbĕo, jussi, jussum, 2 *to order, command* **I.** Gen constr, **a,** with accus and infin; Caesar te sine cura esse jussit, *told you not to be troubled*, Cic, Dionysium jube salvere, *greet*, Cic, pontem jubet rescindi, Caes, in pass with infin alone, consules jubentur scribere, Liv, **b,** with infin alone, receptui canere jubet, Caes, **c,** with ut and the subj, jubere ut haec quoque referret, Caes, **d,** with subj alone, Tac, **e,** with accus alone, fratris necem, Tac, **f,** absol, defessa jubendo est saeva Jovis conjux, Ov **II. A.** Of physicians, *to prescribe*, aegrotus qui jussus sit vinum sumere, Cic **B** As political t t, **a,** of the Roman senate and people, *to order*, senatus decrevit populusque jussit, Cic, senatus dictatorem dici jussit, Cic, legem, Cic, populus jussit de bello, Liv, **b,** transf, of a law, lex jubet aut vetat, Cic

jūcundē (jōcundē), adv. (jucundus), *pleasantly, agreeably, delightfully*, vivere, Cic, jucundius bibere, Cic

jūcundĭtas (jōcundĭtas) -ātis, f (jucundus), *pleasantness, agreeableness, delightfulness, pleasure*, vitae, Cic, dare se jucunditati, *to give oneself up to pleasure*, Cic

jūcundus (jocundus) a -um (for juvicundus, from juvo) *pleasant, agreeable, delightful, pleasing*, est mihi jucunda in malis vestra erga me voluntas, Cic, comes alicui jucundus, Cic, verba ad audiendum jucunda, Cic

Jūdaea ae, f (Ἰουδαία), *Judaea* or (sometimes) *Palestine*, hence, **1** adj, **Jūdaeus** -a -um, *Jewish*, and subst, **Jūdaei** ōrum, m *the Jews*, **2, Jūdāĭcus** a um, *Jewish*

jūdex -ĭcis, m (jus dicere = judicare), *a judge* **I.** selecti judices, *chosen by the praetor*, Cic, judex quaestionis, *a judge chosen to preside at a trial*, Cic, dare judicem, *to appoint a judge* (said of the praetor), Cic, judicem alicui ferre, of the plaintiff, *to propose a judge*, Cic judicem dicere, of the defendant, Liv, aliquem judicem sumere, or habere, Cic, judices rejicere, *to object to*, Cic, apud judicem causam agere, Cic, judicem esse de aliqua re, Cic, used with feminine nouns, dialectica veri et falsi quasi disceptatrix et judex, Cic; hac judice, Ov **II.** Transf, of a person who judges or decides on anything, aequissimus eorum studiorum aestimator et judex Cic

jūdĭcātĭo onis, f (judico), **1,** *a judicial investigation*, Cic, in a speech, *the examination of the defendant's plea*, Cic, **2,** *a judgment, opinion*, Cic

jūdĭcātum -i, n (judico), *a decided case, judgment, decision*, judicatum non facere, Cic, judicatum negare, Cic

jūdĭcātus -ūs, m. (judico), *the office or business of a judge*, Cic.

jūdĭcĭālis e (judicium), *relating to a court of justice, judicial*, causa, Cic.

jūdĭcĭārĭus -a -um (judicium), *relating to a court of justice;* quaestus, Cic.

jūdĭcĭum -ii, n. (judex). **I. 1,** *a trial, legal investigation;* judicium dare or reddere, Cic.; qui judicium exercet, i.e., *the praetor,* Cic.; **2,** meton., **a,** *a law-suit,* Cic.; **b,** *the judicial office,* Sall.; **c,** *the place of trial,* Nep.; **d,** *the judges;* judicium sortiri, Cic. **II.** *judgment, decision.* **A.** Lit., of an authority or superior, Cic.; senatus, Caes. **B.** Transf., **1,** *opinion, view;* judicium facere, *to decide,* Cic.; meo judicio, *in my opinion,* Cic.; **2, a,** *the judgment, power of judging, discernment, understanding;* intelligens, Cic.; subtile, Hor.; **b,** *reflection, consideration;* judicio aliquid facere, Cic.

jūdĭco, 1. (jus dico). **I.** *to investigate judicially, to be a judge,* Cic. **II.** *to judge, decide.* **A.** Lit., rem, Cic.; lites, Cic.; aliquid contra aliquem, Cic.; with acc. and infin., deberi dotem, Cic.; judicata res, *a decided case,* Cic. **B.** Transf., **1,** *to determine, decide;* judicatum est, Cic.; **2,** *to judge;* **a,** ii quos ego posse judicare arbitrarer, Cic.; **b,** *to esteem, value;* prudentem non ex ipsius habitu sed ex aliqua re externa, Cic.; **c,** *to be of an opinion;* quod ante judicaram, Cic.; with acc. and infin., judico neminem tanta habuisse ornamenta, Cic.; or in pass., with nom. and infin.; nos bene emisse judicati sumus, Cic.; **d,** *to declare openly;* Dolabellā hoste judicato, Cic.

jŭgālis -e (jugum), *yoked together;* **a,** subst., **jŭgāles** -ium, m. *a team or yoke,* Verg.; **b,** *matrimonial, nuptial;* vinculum, Verg.; dona, Ov.

Jŭgārĭus vicus, *a part of Rome, at the foot of the capitol, named after Juno Juga, who had an altar there.*

jŭgātĭo -ōnis, f. (jugo), *the training of vines on a trellis,* Cic.

jūgĕrum -i, n., plur. according to the 3rd declension (jugis), **1,** *a plot of land 240 feet long by 120 broad,* and containing therefore 28,800 square feet, Cic.; **2,** as a translation of the Greek πλέθρον, a measure of length, containing 100 Greek or 104 Roman feet, Plin.

jūgis -e (jungo), *joined together;* **a,** juge auspicium, *an auspice marred by the dunging of yoked oxen,* Cic.; **b,** *perpetual, continuous, neverfailing;* aqua, Cic.; puteus, Cic.

jūglans -glandis, f. (=Jovis glans), *a walnut,* Cic.

jŭgo, 1. (jugum), *to bind together, connect;* **a,** virtutes inter se jugatae sunt, Cic.; **b,** *to marry, give in marriage,* Verg.; aliquem or aliquam alicui, Verg.

jŭgōsus -a -um (jugum), *mountainous,* Ov.

jŭgŭlae -ārum, f. (jugulus = junctus), *the three stars which form the belt of the constellation Orion,* Plaut.

jŭgŭlo, 1. (jugulum), *to cut the throat, slay, kill.* **I.** Lit., suem, Cic.; cives optimos, Cic. **II.** *to ruin, destroy;* aliquem factis decretisque, Cic.; jugulari suā confessione, Cic.

jŭgŭlum -i, n. and **jŭgŭlus** -i, m. (jungo). **I.** *the collar-bone,* Plin. **II.** *the hollow above the collar-bone, the throat;* jugula concava, Cic.; jugulum dare (alicui), Cic., or porrigere, Hor.; of the defeated gladiator, *to present his throat to his adversary's stroke.*

jŭgum -i, n. (root JUG, whence also jungo; Gk. ΖΥΓ, whence ζυγόν, ζεύγνυμι). **I.** *a yoke passing over the necks of two oxen, a horse's collar.* **A. 1,** lit., juga imponere bestiis, Cic.; **2,** meton., **a,** *a team or yoke of oxen,* Cic.; **b,** *a team of horses,* Verg.; **c,** transf., *a pair, a couple;* impiorum (of Antonius and Dolabella), Cic. **B.** Fig., **1,** ferre jugum pariter, *to love in adversity as well as in prosperity,* Hor.; **2, a,** *the marriage-tie,* Ov.; **b,** *the yoke of slavery;* jugum accipere, Liv. **II. 1,** *the yoke under which the Romans compelled their vanquished enemies to pass in token of submission;* mittere sub jugum, Cic., Liv. **2, a,** *the constellation Libra,* Cic.; **b,** *the beam of a pair of scales,* Liv.; **3,** *the beam of a weaver's loom,* Ov.; **4,** juga, *the rowers' benches,* Verg.; **5,** *a ridge or summit of a mountain;* summum jugum montis, Caes.

Jŭgurtha -ae, m. *king of Numidia, who carried on a long war with the Romans, and was conquered by Marius.* Hence, adj., **Jŭgurthīnus** -a -um, *Jugurthine.*

Jūlĭus -a -um, *name of a Roman gens, the most celebrated members of which were* **a,** C. Julius Caesar; **b,** *his adopted son* Octavius; and **c,** Julia, *daughter of Augustus, wife of Marcellus, Agrippa, and Tiberius.* Adj., *Julian;* lex, *of Julius Caesar,* Cic.; mensis Julius or simply Julius, *the month of July,* so called in honour of Julius Caesar, formerly called Quinctilis.

jūmentum -i, n. (= jugmentum from jungo, as examen = exagmen), *an animal used for carrying or drawing, beast of burden,* Cic.

juncĕus -a -um (juncus), *of or relating to rushes, made of rushes;* vincula, Ov.

juncōsus -a -um (juncus), *full of rushes, rushy;* litora, Ov.

junctim, adv. (junctus), *successively, both together,* Suet.

junctĭo -ōnis, f. (jungo), *a joining, connexion;* eorum verborum, Cic.

junctūra -ae, f. (jungo), *a joining.* **A.** Lit., *a joint;* tignorum, Caes.; laterum, Verg. **B.** Transf., **1,** generis, *relationship,* Ov.; **2,** *rhetorical combination, putting together,* Hor.

junctus -a -um, p. adj. (from jungo), *joined together, yoked together, connected, united.* **I.** junctior cum exitu, Cic. **II. 1,** *joined by affection, relationship,* etc.; junctissimus, *most nearly connected, very intimate,* Ov.; **2,** rhet. t. t., *well put together;* oratio, Cic.

juncus -i, m. (σχοῖνος), *a rush, bulrush;* limosus, Verg.; junci palustres, Ov.

jungo, junxi, junctum, 3. (root JUG, Gk. ΖΥΓ, whence ζεύγνυμι, ζυγόν), *to join, unite, connect.* **I.** Lit., **A.** res inter se, Cic.; aliquid cum aliqua re, Cic.; oscula, *to kiss,* Ov.; fluvium ponte, Liv., pontem, Tac., *to throw a bridge over a river.* **B.** Esp., **1,** *to yoke;* equos curru (dat.), Verg.; **2,** of places, in passive, *to border on;* Juno loca juncta, Ov.; **3,** milit. t. t., *to unite troops;* socia arma Rutulis, Liv. **II.** Transf., **A.** cum hominibus consuetudines jungebat, Cic.; with abl., improbitas scelere juncta, Cic.; with dat., indignatio juncta conquestioni, Cic. **B.** Esp., **1,** *to unite in marriage;* aliquem secum matrimonio, Liv.; alicui, Ov.; se alicui, Ov.; **2,** *to connect by affection, relationship, friendship;* se ad aliquem, Cic.; amicitiam cum aliquo, *to form,* Cic.; **3,** *to unite politically;* foedere or societate alicui jungi, Liv.; **4,** *to connect grammatically;* juncta verba, Cic.

jūnĭor, v. juvenis.

jūnĭpĕrus -i, f. *the juniper-tree,* Verg.

Jūnĭus -a -um, *the name of a Roman gens, the most famous members of which were* L. Junius Brutus *and the two* Bruti, M. Jun. Brutus and D. Jun. Brutus, *the murderers of Caesar;* adj., *Junian;* mensis Junius or simply Junius, *the month of June.*

Jūno -ōnis, f. (= Jovino), *the goddess Juno, daughter of Saturn, sister and wife of Jupiter;* Juno inferna, *Proserpine,* Verg.; so Juno Averna,

Ov , inlis Junonis, *Argus*, Ov Hence, **A. Jūnōnālis** e, *relating or belonging to Juno*, tempus, *the month of June*, Ov **B. Jūnōnius** -a -um, *Junonian*, hospitia, *Carthage*, Verg , ales, *the peacock*, Ov , custos, *Argus*, Ov , mensis, *June*, Ov **C. Jūnōnĭcŏla** ae, c *a worshipper of Juno* **D. Jūnōnĭgĕna** ae, m *son of Juno, of Vulcan*, Ov

Juppĭter, Jŏvis, m (prop , Diuspater, Diespiter, Diespiter, *the father of the heavens*), *Jupiter*, 1, *the supreme god among the Romans, brother and husband of Juno, corresponding to the Ζεύς of the Greeks*, Jovis satelles, Cic , ales, *the eagle*, Ov , Juppiter Stygius, *Pluto*, Verg.; 2, transf., a, *the planet Jupiter*, Cic , b, *air, sky, heavens*, sub Jove, *in the open air*, Ov

Jūra ae, m *a mountain-chain extending northwards from the banks of the Rhone*

jūrandum -i, n (juro), *an oath*, Ter

jūrātor -ōris, m (juro), *a sworn assessor, assistant of the censor*, Liv

1 **jūrātus** a um, partic of juro

2 **jūrātus** -a -um (jus), *sworn, bound by an oath*, jurati judices, Cic

jūrĕconsultus = jurisconsultus (q v.)

jūrĕjūro, 1 (jus and juro), *to swear by an oath*, Liv.

jūrĕpĕrītus = jurisperitus (q v)

jurgium -ii, n (jurgo), *altercation, verbal contention, strife, quarrel, brawl*, jurgio saepe contendere cum aliquo, Cic

jurgo, 1 (= jure ago) **I.** Intransit , *to quarrel, contend in words, brawl*, Cic **II.** Transit., *to scold*, Hor.

jūrĭdĭcĭālis -e (juridicus), *relating to right or justice*, constitutio, Cic

jūrisconsultus i, m *one learned in the law, a lawyer*, Cic

jūrisdictĭo -ōnis, f **I.** *the administration of justice by the praetor, judicial authority*, Cic , jurisdictio urbana et peregrina (of the praetor urbanus and peregrinus), Liv , jurisdictio in libera civitate contra leges senatusque consulta. Cic **II.** Meton , *a place where justice is administered, an assize-town*, Tac

jūrispĕrītus -i, m *one skilled or experienced in the law*, Cic

jūro, 1 (2 jus) **I.** Intransit., *to swear, take an oath.* **A.** ex animi mei sententia, Cic , per deos, Sall , pro aliquo, *in the place of some one*, Liv **B.** in verba alicuius, *to swear after a certain formula*, Liv , in certa verba, Cic , in legem, *to swear to*, Cic , omnis exercitus in se quisque jurat, *each soldier took the oath separately*, Liv **II.** Transit , **A.** *to swear*, jurasi verissimum jusjurandum, Cic **B.** *to affirm on oath, to swear to*; morbum, *to the fact that one is ill*, Cic , falsum jurare, Cic , id in litem, *in support of a suit*, Cic , with acc and infin , Cic **C.** *to call the gods to witness*, deos, Ov. **D.** *to deny on oath*, calumniam in aliquem, Liv

jūror -ātus sum, dep 1 (= juro), *to swear*, quid juratus sit, Cic , partic. juratus, *sworn on oath*, si diceret juratus, Cic (only used in perf and partic perf)

1. **jūs,** jūris, n (connected with ζύος, from ζέω, ζύω), *broth, soup*, Cic

2. **jūs,** jūris, n (from the same root as jubeo, lit. = jussum), *right, law* **I. A.** As contained in statutes, etc , principia juris, Cic ; jus ac fas omne delere, Cic , jura dare, *to give laws*, Liv **B.** 1, *law*, as comprising rights , jus hominum, *natural law*, Cic , jus gentium, Cic , jus civile, *the common law* Cic , 2, a *law*, as opposed to equity , summum jus, summa injuria, Cic , jus dicere, *to declare the law to decide judicially* (said of the praetor), Cic , b, meton , *a court of justice*, in jus vocare, Cic , adire, Cic **II.** Transf , **A.** *right, law* as common to mankind ; divina ac humana jura, Cic , uxores eodem jure sunt quo viri, *have the same rights as*, Cic , jure optimo, *by the best of rights*, Cic ; jus est, with infin , *it is right*, Cic **B.** 1, *right, privilege*, jus civitatis Cic ; jus auxilii sui, Liv , 2, *legal right, authority*, jus agendi cum plebe, Cic ; sui juris esse, *to be independent*, Cic

jusjūrandum, jurisjurandi, n *an oath*, alicui jusjurandum dare, foll by acc and infin , *to promise on oath*, Cic , jusjurandum accipere, *to take an oath*, Caes , jusjurandum violare, Cic , conservare, Cic , fidem astringere jurejurando, Cic , aliquem jurejurando obstringere, with acc and infin , Caes (Sometimes separated, e g , jus igitur jurandum, Cic)

jussum -i, n (jubeo), gen in plur **I.** *a command, order*, Cic , jussa efficere, Sall **II. A.** *the prescription of a physician*, Ov **B** *the command of the Roman people*, perniciosa et injusta jussa, Cic

jussus -ū, m (jubeo), *a command, commanding*, vestro jussu, *by your order*, Cic

justē, adv (justus), *justly, rightly*, imperare, Cic , facilius fieri potuerit et justius, Cic , nimio justissime, Cic

justĭfĭcus -a um (justus and facio), *acting justly*, Cat

justĭtĭa -ae, f (justus), *justice, love of justice, equity*, justitiam colere, Cic , justitia erga deos, Cic , in hostem, Cic

justĭtĭum -ii, n (juris -stitium, from jus and sisto), *a suspension of business in the courts of law* **I.** a, justitium indicere, edicere, *to proclaim a suspension of legal business*; justitium remittere, *to close*, Liv , b, transf , *a pause, cessation, suspension*, omnium rerum, Liv **II.** *a public mourning*, Tac

justus -a -um (jus) **I.** Of persons, *just, upright, impartial*, judex, Cic **II.** Of objects, **A.** *just, equitable, fair*, supplicium,Cic , bellum Liv , hostis, *having the right on his side*, Cic , subst , justum colere, *to do what is right*, Cic **B.** Transf , 1, *well grounded, justifiable*, causa, Cic , ira, Ov , 2, *regular, proper, perfect, complete, suitable*, proelium, Liv , victoria, Cic , 3, *fitting, right, sufficient*, numerus, Liv , altitudo, Caes , neut subst , plus justo, *more than is right*, Hor. , so longior justo, Ov., plur , **justa** -orum, a, *what is fitting*, justa praebere servis, Cic , b, *due forms and observances*, esp *funeral rites*, justa facere alicui, Cic

Jūturna -ae, f (juvo), *the nymph of a spring in Latium, sister of Turnus, worshipped at Rome and sacrificed to in times of scarcity of water*. *a spring near the river Numicius, also worshipped*

1 **jŭvĕnālis** -e (juvenis), *youthful*, corpus, Verg ; ludus, Liv.

2 **Jŭvĕnālis** -is, m , D Junius, *a Roman writer of satires, contemporary of Domitian and Trajan*

jŭvĕnālĭtĕr, adv (1 juvenalis), *like a young man, with the strength of a young man*, Ov

jŭvencus -a -um (for juvenicus, from juvenis), *young* **I.** Adj , equus, Lucr **II.** Subst , **A. jŭvencus** -i, m , a, *a young man*, Hor ; b, *a young bullock or ox*, Verg **B. jŭvenca** ae, f , a, *a young woman, a maiden*, Hor , b, *a young cow, heifer*, Verg (genit plur , juvencūm, Verg)

jŭvenesco -vēnŭi, 3. (juvenis), 1, *to grow up to youth;* vitulus, Hor.; 2, *to become young again;* juvenescit homo, Ov.

jŭvĕnīlis -e (juvenis), *youthful, juvenile;* licentia, Cic.; redundantia, Cic.

jŭvĕnīlĭtĕr, adv. (juvenilis), *youthfully, like a youth;* Annibal juveniliter exsultans, Cic.

jŭvĕnis -is (juvo). **I.** Adj., *young, youthful;* anni, Ov.; compar., junior, Liv. **II.** Subst., **jŭvĕnis** -is, c., *a young man, young woman, one in the prime of life* (generally from the twentieth to the fortieth year), Cic.

jŭvĕnor, 1. dep. (juvenis), *to act like a youth, with youthful indiscretion and impetuosity,* Hor.

jŭventa -ae, f. (juvenis), *youth.* **I. 1,** lit., *the time of youth;* flos juventae, Liv.; **2,** meton., (α) *the youth = the young;* imbellis, docilis, Hor.; (β) prima juventa, *the down on a young man's cheeks,* Verg.; (γ) abstract, *the force of youth;* virtus et juventa, Liv. **II.** Personif., *the goddess of youth,* Ov.

jŭventas -ātis, f. (juvenis). **I.** *youth, the time of youth;* **1,** lit., Verg.; **2,** meton., a, prima juventas, *the down on a young man's cheeks,* Verg.; **b,** *the vigour of youth,* Hor. **II.** Person., *the goddess of youth, Hebe,* Cic.

jŭventus -ūtis, f. (juvenis), *youth, the period of life between the twentieth and the fortieth year.* **A.** Lit., ea quae juventute geruntur et viribus, Cic. **B.** Meton., *young men;* juventus Romana, Liv.; legendus est hic orator juventuti, Cic.; princeps juventutis, in republican times, *the first among the knights,* Cic.

jŭvo, jūvi, jūtum, fut. partic., jŭvātūrus, 1. **I.** *to help, assist, aid, be of service;* aliquem in aliqua re, Cic.; aliquem auxilio laboris, Cic.; hostes frumento, Caes.; juvante deo, diis juvantibus, *with God's help,* Cic. **II.** *to delight, please, gratify;* ut te juvit coena? Hor.; ita se dicent juvari, Cic.; often impers., juvat, with infin., *it delights, it pleases;* juvit me tibi tuas literas profuisse, Cic.; forsan et haec olim meminisse juvabit, Verg.

juxtā (connected with jungo). **I.** Adv., **A.** Of space, *close to, by the side of, near, hard by;* legio quae juxta constiterat, Caes.; sellam juxta ponere, Sall. **B.** Transf., *in like manner, equally;* vitam mortemque juxta aestimo, Sall.; aliaque castella juxta ignobilia, Liv.; juxta ac si hostes adessent, Liv.; juxta quam, Liv.; with dat., res parva ac juxta magnis difficilis, Liv.; with cum and the abl., juxta mecum omnes intelligitis, Sall. **II.** Prep. with acc. **A.** Of space, **1,** lit., *near to, hard by;* juxta murum castra posuit, Caes.; **2,** transf., *immediately after or upon, next to;* juxta deos in tuā manu positum est, Tac. **B.** Of time, *just before;* juxta finem vitae, Tac.

juxtim, adv. (connected with jungo), *near, close by,* Lucr.

K.

K, The letter K, k, was originally a part of the Latin Alphabet, but afterwards almost entirely disappeared from it, and was replaced by C. K was only used in abbreviations, as K. = Kaesar, Kal. = Kalendae.

Kălendae = Calendae (q.v.).

Karthāgo = Carthago (q.v.).

L.

L, l, corresponds to the Greek lambda (Λ, λ). For its use as an abbreviation, v. Table of Abbreviations.

lăbasco, 3. (labo), **1,** *to totter, threaten to fall,* Lucr.; **2,** *to give way,* Ter.

lăbea -ae, f., *the lip* = labia (q.v.).

lābēcŭla -ae, f. (dim. of labes), *a little spot or stain, a slight disgrace,* Cic.

lăbĕfăcio -fēci -factum, 3., pass., lăbĕfīo, -factus sum -fĭeri (labo and facio). **I.** *to make to totter, shake, loosen;* partem muri, Caes.; charta sit a vinclis non labefacta suis, *not opened,* Ov. **II.** Transf., **1, a,** *to weaken;* corpora aestus impatientia labefecit, Tac.; **b,** politically, *to shake, impair;* jura plebis, Liv.; **2,** *to cause to shake or waver;* quem nulla unquam vis, nullae minae, nulla invidia labefecit, Cic.

lăbĕfacto, 1. (intens. of labefacio), *to cause to totter, shake violently.* **I.** Lit., signum vectibus, Cic. **II.** Transf., **1, a,** animam sedibus intus, Lucr.; **b,** *to injure, weaken, destroy;* alicuius fidem pretio, *to corrupt,* Cic.; amicitiam aut justitiam, Cic.; vitas hominum, *to disturb, disquiet,* Cic.

1. **lăbellum** -i, n. (dim. of 1. labrum), *a little lip,* Cic.

2. **lābellum** -i, n. (dim. of 2. labrum), *a small bathing-vessel,* Cic.

Lăbĕrius -a -um, *name of a Roman gens, the most famous member of which was* D. Laberius, *a knight and writer of mimes, contemporary of Jul. Caesar.*

lābes -is, f. (1. labor), *a falling in, sinking in.* **I.** Lit., esp. of the earth, multis locis labes factae sint, Cic. **II.** Transf., **A.** prima labes mali, *the first mischance,* Verg. **B. 1,** *ruin, destruction;* innocentiae labes aut ruina, Cic.; applied to a person, labes atque pernicies provinciae Siciliae, Cic.; **2,** *a spot, stain, blemish;* **a,** physical, sine labe toga, Ov.; victima labe carens, Ov.; **b,** moral, *mark of disgrace, stain of infamy, disgrace, dishonour, ignominy;* illa labes atque ignominia reipublicae, Cic.; alicui labem inferre, Cic.

lăbĭa (lăbĕa) -ae, f. and **lăbĭum** -ii, n. (lambo), *a lip,* Plaut.

Lăbīci (Lăvīci) -ōrum, m. and **Lăbīcum** -i, n. *an old Latin town, fifteen miles south-east of Rome.* Hence, adj., **Lăbīcānus** -a -um, *of or belonging to Labicum;* subst., **a, Lăbīcānum** -i, n. *the territory of Labicum;* **b, Lăbīcāni** -orum, m. *the inhabitants of Labicum.*

Lăbĭēnus -i, m., T., *a legate of Julius Caesar, who deserted to Pompeius at the breaking out of the Civil War.*

lăbĭōsus -a -um (labium), *with large lips,* Lucr.

lăbĭum -ii, n. = labia (q.v.).

lăbo, 1. *to totter, waver, be about to fall, begin to sink.* **I.** Lit., signum labat, Cic.; labat ariete crebro janua, Verg.; labantem unā parte aciem, *wavering,* Liv. **II.** Transf., **1,** *to waver, totter;* omnes reipublicae partes aegras et labantes sanare et confirmare, Cic.; memoria labat, *is uncertain,* Liv.; **2,** *to waver in fidelity or opinion;* scito labare meum consilium, Cic.; fides sociorum labare coepit, Liv.

1. **lābor,** lapsus sum, 3. dep. *to glide, slide, fall down, slip.* **I. 1,** lit., ex equo, Liv.; humor in genas furtim labitur, Hor.; stellas praecipites coelo labi, Verg.; lapsi de fontibus amnes, Ov.;

quia continenter laberentur et fluerent omnia, Cic, 2, transf, a, *to glide, to run, to flow*, sed labor longius, ad propositum revertar, *I wander from the point*, Cic, oratio sedate placideque labitur, *flows along*, Cic, of time, *to pass away*, labuntur tempora, Hor, b, *to incline to, fall into*, labor eo ut assentiar Epicuro, *I feel myself drawn into*, etc, Cic, civitatum mores lapsi ad mollitiem, Cic **II. A.** *to glide down, glide off, deviate from*, ne adjectae voces laberentur atque errarent, Cic., hac spe lapsus, *deceived*, Cic. **B.** *to slip, to stumble*, 1, lit., agaso pede lapsus, Hor; 2, transf, **a**, *to make a slip, to make a mistake*, erravit, lapsus est, non putavit, Cic, in aliqua re, Cic, per errorem, Cic, propter imprudentiam, Cic, in officio, Cic, **b**, *to be on the point of falling*; labentem et prope cadentem rempublicam, Cic. **C.** *to glide out, to fall out*, viscera lapsa, Ov; of persons, *to slip away*, custodiā, Tac **D.** *to fall to the ground*, calor ossa reliquit, labitur, Verg; labentes deorum aedes, Hor, transf, *to fall, be destroyed*, lapsum genus, Verg

2 **lăbor** -ōris, m *work, labour, toil, effort* **I.** Lit, **a**, gen, res est magni laboris, *is difficult*, Cic; capere tantum laborem, Cic, impenditur labor ad incertum casum, Cic, laborem hominum periculis sublevandis impertire, Cic; laborem interponere pro aliquo, Cic, labor est, with infin, *it is a work of difficulty*, Liv, **b**, *activity, industry, capacity for work*, homo magni laboris, Cic., **2**, meton, **a**, *work, result of labour*, multorum mensium labor interiit, Caes, **b**, *deed, undertaking*, belli, Verg. **II. a**, *hardship, fatigue, need, distress, difficulty*; cuius erga me benevolentiam vel in labore meo vel in honore perspexi, Cic; poet, labores solis, *eclipse of the sun*, Verg, Lucinae, *pains of labour*, Verg, **b**, *sickness*, Plaut.

lăbōrĭfer -fĕra -fĕrum (labor and fero), *bearing toil and hardship*, Hercules, Ov

lăbōrĭōsē, adv (laboriosus), *laboriously, with toil and fatigue*, quo quisque est ingeniosior, hoc docet iracundius et laboriosius, Cic, diligentissime laboriosissimeque accusare, Cic

lăbōrĭōsus -a -um (2. labor) **I.** *full of toil, hardship trouble, laborious* **a**, vitae genus laboriosum sequi, Cic, **b**, of persons, *industrious*, Cic **II.** *troubled, harassed, undergoing trouble and hardship*, laboriosa cohors Ulixei, Hor, quid nobis duobus laboriosius, Cic

lăbōro, 1 (2. labor) **I.** Intransit, **A. a**, *to work, toil, labour, strive*. sibi et populo Romano, non Verri laborare, Cic, in aliqua re, Cic.; de aliqua re, Cic., de aliquo, Cic, in aliquid, Liv.; with ut or ne and the subj, Cic, non laboro, with infin, Cic, **b**, *to be troubled about, to be distressed, to care*, quorsum recidat responsum tuum, non magno opere laboro, Cic **B.** *to suffer, labour under anything, be oppressed with, afflicted with*, morbo, *to be ill*, Cic, ex intestinis, pedibus, renibus, *to suffer pain in*, Cic, ex invidia, Cic; a re frumentaria, Caes, in re familiari, Cic, absol, *to be in danger*, illi laboranti subvenire, Caes, of things, quod vehementer eius artus laborarent, *as he suffered from gout*, Cic, digitorum contractio nullo in motu laborat, *finds no difficulty in*, Cic, quum luna laboret, *is eclipsed*, Cic **II.** Transit, *to work out, to elaborate, prepare, form*, arte laboratae vestes, Verg, dona laboratae Cereris, *corn made into bread*, Verg

lăbos -ōris, m = 2 labor (q v.)

Lăbrŏs i, m (λαβρος), *name of a dog*, Ov

1 **lăbrum** -i n (lambo) *a lip*, superius, *the upper lip*, Caes; prov, primis labris gustasse physiologiam, *to have only a superficial knowledge of*, Cic; meton, *the edge, rim, lip*, fossae, Caes

2 **lābrum** -i, n (lavo), **a**, *a basin, vessel, tub*, Verg, **b**, especially, *a bathing vessel*, Cic, meton poet, labra Dianae, *bath*, Ov

lābrusca -ae, f *the wild vine*, Verg

lābruscum -i, n *the fruit of the wild vine*, Verg

lăburnum -i, n *the laburnum tree* (Cytisus Laburnum, Linn), Plin

lăbyrinthēus a -um (labyrinthus), *labyrinthine*, Cat

lăbyrinthus -i, m (λαβυρινθος), *a labyrinth*, esp *the labyrinth in Crete constructed by Daedalus*, Verg

lac, lactis, n (akin to γάλα, γάλακτος) *milk* **I.** Lit, Cic **II.** Transf, *the milky sap of plants*, Ov

Lăcaena -ae, f (Λακαινα), *Spartan, Lacedaemonian*; virgo, Verg, subst, *a Spartan woman*, esp, *Helen*, Verg, *Leda*, Mart

Lăcĕdaemon -ŏnis, f (Λακεδαιμων), *the city Lacedaemon or Sparta*, hence, adj, **Lăcĕdaemŏnius** -a -um, *Lacedaemonian*, Tarentum, *built by a colony from Sparta*, Hor

lăcer -cĕra -cĕrum **I.** Pass, *torn maimed, dismembered, torn to pieces*, corpus, Sall vestis, Tac **II.** Act, *tearing to pieces*, morsus, Ov

lăcĕrātio ōnis, f (lacero), *a tearing to pieces, maiming, mangling, laceration*, corporis, Cic

lăcerna -ae, f *a mantle worn over the toga on a journey or in bad weather*, Cic

lăcernātus -a um (lacerna), *clad in the lacerna*, Juv

lăcĕro, 1 (lacer), *to tear to pieces, maim, mangle, lacerate* **I.** Lit, alicuius corpus lacerare atque vexare, Cic, lacerare aliquem omni cruciatu, Cic, pontes, *to destroy* Liv **II.** Transf, **1**, *to wound deeply, ruin, destroy*, lacerare rempublicam, Cic., patriam scelere, Cic, esp, **a**, *to squander*, pecuniam, Cic, **b**, *to distress, torture*, meus me moeror quotidianus lacerat, Cic., **2**, *to wound with words, rail at, asperse, attack, rend*, haec te lacerat, haec cruentat oratio, Cic, aliquem probris, Liv

lăcerta -ae, f **I.** *a lizard*, Hor **II.** *a sea-fish*, Cic

lăcertōsus -a -um (lacertus), *muscular, powerful*, centuriones Cic

1 **lăcertus** -i, m gen plur = *the muscles* **I.** Gen, **1**, lit, lacertos exercitatio expressit, Quint, **2**, fig, of oratorical vigour, in Lysia sunt lacerti, Cic **II. 1**, *the muscles of the upper part of the arm* (from the shoulder to the elbow), Milo Crotoniates nobilitatus ex lateribus et lacertis suis, Cic, **2**, fig, of oratorical vigour, a quo quum amentatas hastas acceperit, ipse eas oratoris lacertis viribusque torquebit, Cic

2 **lăcertus** -i, m = lacerta (q v)

lăcesso -īvi and -ii -ītum, 3 (intens of *lacio), *to provoke, stimulate, excite, exasperate, irritate*, **a**, virum ferro, Cic, aliquem proelio, bello, Caes, aliquem ad pugnam, Liv, me scripto, *provoke me to write again*, Cic, so ad scribendum, Cic, aliquem injuriā, Cic, deos precibus, Hor, pelagus carinā, *to sail over*, Hor, **b**, with acc of thing, *to begin, occasion*, pugnam, Liv, sermonem, Cic

Lăcĕtāni -ōrum, m (Λακετανοι), *a people in Hispania Tarraconensis* Hence, **Lăcĕtānia** ae, f *the country of the Lacetani*

Lăchēs ētis, m (Λαχης), *son of Melanopus, general of the Athenians*, [illegible] (418 B C)

Lăchĕsis -is, f. (Λάχεσις), *the one of the three Parcae that spun the thread of life.*

lăchrĭma (lăchrȳma), v. lacrima.

lăchrĭmo (lăchrȳmo) and **-or,** v. lacrimo.

Lăcĭădēs -ae, m. (Λακιάδης), *belonging to the Lacian deme (in Attica),* Cic.

lăcĭnĭa -ae, f. (λακίς), *a lappet* or *flap of a garment;* prov., aliquid obtinere lacinia, *to hold by the extreme end, to have but an insecure hold,* Cic.; in lacinia servare ex mensa secunda semina, ap. Cic.

Lăcīnĭum -ĭi, n. (Λακίνιον ἄκρον), *a promontory in Bruttium, near Crotona,* where Juno Lacinia had a famous temple. Hence, adj., **Lăcīnĭus** -a -um, *Lacinian;* diva Lacinia, *the Lacinian goddess (Juno);* meton. = *the temple of Juno Lacinia,* Verg.

Lăco (Lăcōn) -ōnis, m. (Λάκων), *a Spartan, Lacedaemonian;* fulvus Laco, *a Spartan hound,* Hor.; plur., **Lăcōnes** -um, m. *the Lacedaemonians.* Hence, **1,** adj., **Lăcōnĭcus** -a -um, *Laconian.* Subst., **a, Lăcōnĭca** -ae, f. or **Lăcōnĭcē** -es, f. (Λακωνική), *the country of Laconia,* Nep.; **b, Lăcōnĭcum** -i, n. (sc. balneum), *a sweating-room in a bath,* Cic.; **2, Lăcōnĭs** -ĭdis, f. *Spartan;* mater, Ov.

lăcrĭma (lăcrŭma, lăchrĭma, or **lăchrȳma)** -ae, f. (δάκρυ, δάκρυμα). **I.** *a tear;* multis cum lacrimis, *with a flood of tears,* Cic.; lacrimas profundere, *to shed tears,* Cic.; prae lacrimis (*for tears*) loqui non possum, Cic.; debilitor lacrimis, *unmanned by,* Cic.; lacrimis gaudio effusis, Liv. **II.** *the exudation from certain plants;* turis, Ov.; Heliadum, *amber,* Ov.

lăcrĭmābĭlis (lăcrŭmābĭlis) -e (lacrimo), *deplorable, lamentable, woeful;* tempus, Ov.; bellum, Verg.

lăcrĭmābundus -a -um (lacrimo), *breaking into tears, weeping,* Liv.

lăcrĭmo (lăchrȳmo, lăcrŭmo), 1. *to weep, shed tears.* **I.** Lit., ecquis fuit quin lacrimaret? Cic. **II.** Of plants, *to exude, to drip, drop down;* partic. pass., lacrimatae cortice myrrhae, *dripping from,* Ov.

lăcrĭmōsus (lăcrŭmōsus) -a -um (lacrima). **I.** *tearful, shedding tears;* lumina vino lacrimosa, Ov.; voces, Verg. **II. a,** *causing tears;* fumus, Hor.; **b,** *mournful, piteous;* bellum, Hor.

lăcrĭmŭla -ae, f. (dim. of lacrima), *a little tear,* Cic.

lăcrŭma, etc., v. lacrima, etc.

lactĕo, 2. (lac). **I.** *to suck;* lactens Romulus, Cic.; lactens hostia, Cic. Subst., **lactentes** -ĭum, f. (sc. hostiae), *unweaned animals,* as victims for a sacrifice; lactentibus rem divinam facere, Liv. **II.** *to be milky, juicy, contain milk, to be full of sap;* frumenta, Verg.

lactĕŏlus -a -um, adj. (dim. of lacteus), *milk-white,* Cat.

lactes -ĭum, f. (lac), *the small intestines, guts,* Plaut.

lactesco, 3. (lacteo), *to become milk, be changed into milk;* omnis fere cibus matrum lactescere incipit, Cic.

lactĕus -a -um (lac). **I.** Lit., **1,** *milky;* humor, Ov.; **2,** *full of milk;* ubera, Verg. **II.** Meton., *milk-white;* cervix, Verg.; via lactea, Ov., or orbis lacteus, Cic., *the Milky Way.*

1. **lacto,** 1. (lac), *to give milk, to be full of milk,* Ov.

2. **lacto,** 1. (intens. of *lacio, *to entice*), *to allure, wheedle, dupe, deceive, cajole,* Plaut.

lactūca -ae, f. (lac), *a lettuce,* Hor.

lăcūna -ae, f. (for lacuina, from lacus). **I.** *a cavity, hollow, cavern;* **1, a,** lacunae salsae, *the salt depths of the sea,* Lucr.; **b,** in the body of animals, sint modici victus parvaeque utrimque lacunae, *dimples,* Ov.; **2,** *a pool, pond, ditch;* vastae lacunae Orci, Lucr.; cavae lacunae, Verg. **II.** Transf., *a gap, defect, loss;* ut illam lacunam rei familiaris expleant, Cic.

lăcūnar -āris, n. (lacuna), *a panelled ceiling,* Cic.; prov., spectare lacunar, *to gaze at the ceiling,* i.e., *to pretend not to see what is going on,* Juv.

lăcūno, 1. (lacuna), *to work in panels, to panel,* Ov.

lăcūnōsus -a -um (lacuna), *full of hollows* or *gaps;* nihil lacunosum, *defective,* Cic.

lăcus -ūs, m. (root LAC, whence also λάκκος, lacuna). **I.** *a lake,* Cic.; used poet. for *any large body of water,* Verg., Ov. **II.** *a water-trough* or *basin,* Hor.; *a blacksmith's trough,* Verg. **III.** *any large tank, vat, tub,* especially that into which the wine flows when pressed from the grapes; transf., nova ista quasi de musto ac lacu fervida oratio, Cic.

Lăcȳdēs -is, m. (Λακύδης), *an academic philosopher, founder of the New Academy.*

Lādās -ae, m. (Λάδας), *a Laconian athlete, whose speed in running was proverbial in antiquity,* Juv.

Lādōn -ōnis, m. (Λάδων), *a river in Arcadia.*

laedo, laesi, laesum, 3. *to hurt, injure, damage.* **I.** Lit., cursu aristas, Verg.; frondes, Ov.; zonā laedere collum, *to strangle,* Hor. **II.** Transf., *to trouble, offend, annoy, vex, calumniate, attack;* aliquem perjurio suo, Cic.; famam alicuius gravi opprobrio, Cic.

Laelĭus -a -um, *name of a Roman gens, the most prominent members of which were:* C. Laelius, *the friend of Scipio, and* D. Laelius, *a supporter of Pompeius.* Hence, adj., **Laelĭānus** -a -um, *Laelian.*

laena -ae, f. (χλαῖνα), *an upper garment of thick cloth,* Cic.

Lāërtēs -ae, m. (Λαέρτης), *the father of Ulysses;* hence, **1,** adj., **Lāërtĭus** -a -um, *Laertian;* regna, *Ithaca,* Verg.; heros, *Ulysses,* Ov.; **2, Lāërtĭădes** -ae, m. *the son of Laertes,* i.e., *Ulysses,* Hor.

laesĭo -ōnis, f. (laedo), rhet. t.t., *an oratorical attack,* Cic.

Laestrȳgŏnes -um, m. (Λαιστρύγονες), myth., *a race of cannibals in Sicily;* sing., **Laestrȳgōn** -ŏnis, m. *a Laestrygonian;* urbs Lami Laestrygonis (i.e., *Formiae*), Ov. Hence, adj., **Laestrȳgŏnĭus** -a -um, *Laestrygonian;* domus, *Formiae,* Ov.

laetābĭlis -e (laetor), *joyful, gladsome, joyous,* Cic.

laetātĭo -ōnis, f. (laetor), *a rejoicing, joy,* Caes.

laetē, adv. (laetus), *joyfully, gladly;* aliquid laete atque insolenter ferre, Cic.

laetĭfĭco, 1. (laetificus). **I.** *to cheer, gladden, delight, make joyful;* sol terram laetificat, Cic. **II.** *to fertilise;* agros aquā, Cic.

laetĭfĭcus -a -um (laetus and facio), *causing joy, gladdening, cheering, joyous,* Lucr.

laetĭtĭa -ae, f. (laetus). **I.** *joy, expressed and unrestrained gladness, delight;* laetitiam capere, percipere ex aliqua re, Cic.; dare alicui laetitiam, Cic.; laetitiam alicui afferre, Cic.; laetitiā frui maximae praeclarissimaeque pugnae, Cic. **II.** *a pleasing appearance, beauty, grace;* orationis, Tac.

laetor, 1. dep. (laetus), *to rejoice, be joyful, take delight, be glad;* **a,** with abl.; bonis rebus

Cic , b, with in and the abl , in communi gemitu, Cic , c, with de and the abl , de communi salute, Cic , d, with ex and the abl , Sall , e, with acc of the neut pron , utrumque laetor, Cic f, with acc and infin , filiola tua te delectari laetor, Cic , g, with quod, se laetari, quod effugissem duas maximas vituperationes, Cic , absol , laetanti animo, Cic

Laetōrius a -um, *name of a Roman plebeian gens*

laetus a um, *joyful, glad* **I. a,** lit , of persons, hi vagantur laeti atque erecti passim toto foro, Cic ; with abl , minime laetus origine novae urbis, Liv , with genit , laetus laborum, Verg , **b,** transf , of things, oratio, Liv ; vultus, Cic **II. A.** *making joyful, pleasing agreeable*, omnia erant facta laetiora, Cic **B.** Transf , 1, *favouring, fortunate, propitious*, augurium, Tac , 2, **a,** *fruitful*, pascua, Liv , laetae segetes, *rich*, Cic ; **b,** of animals, *fat*, Verg **c,** of orators, *copious, fluent, delightful;* nitidum quoddam genus est verborum et laetum, Cic

laevē, adv (laevus), *on the left hand*, hence *awkwardly*, Hor

laevus -a -um (λαιος), *left* **I** Lit , a, adj , manus, Cic , amnis, *the left bank*, Tac , **b,** subst , (α) **laeva** ae, f. (sc manus) *the left hand, the left;* ad laevam, *to the left*, Cic , (β) **laevum** -i, n *the left side*, in laevum flectere cursus, Ov , plur **laeva** -ōrum, *places lying to the left*, Ov **II.** Transf , 1, *left-handed, foolish, silly*, mens, Verg , et ego laevus ! *what a fool I am* ! Hor , 2, *unsuitable*, tempus, Hor , 3, *unlucky, unpropitious*, picus, Hor., 4, in augury, *favourable*, as the Roman augurs, looking south, had the east or lucky side on their left hand; laevum intonuit, *on the left*, Verg

lăgănum -i, n (λάγανον), *a cake made of flour and oil*, Hor.

lăgēna = lagoena (q v)

lăgēos -ēi, f (λάγειος), *a Greek kind of vine*, Verg

lăgoena -ae, f (λάγηνος), *a large earthen jar or bottle with handles and a narrow neck*, Cic

lăgōis -ĭdis, f (λαγωΐς), *a bird*, perhaps *a heathcock* or *grouse*, Hor.

lăguncŭla -ae, f. (dim of lagoena), *a little bottle* or *flask*, Plin

Lāgus -i, m *the father of Ptolemy, king of Egypt* Hence, adj , **Lāgēus** -a -um, poet = *Egyptian*, Mart.

Lāïs -ĭdis and -ĭdos, f (Λαΐς), *a celebrated Corinthian beauty*

Lāïus, or **Lājus** -i, m (Λάϊος), *son of Labdacus, father of Oedipus* Hence, **Lāïădēs** -ae, m *son of Laius, i e Oedipus*, Ov

lāma ae, f (perhaps connected with lacuna, lacus), *a bog, slough, ditch*, Hor

lambo, lambi, lambĭtum, 3 *to lick* **a,** of animals, tribunal meum, Cic , **b,** poet , transf , of things, quae loca fabulosus lambit Hydaspes, *bathes, washes*, Hor ; of fire, flamma summum properabat lambere tectum, Hor.

lāmentābĭlis e (lamentor) **I.** *lamentable, deplorable*, regnum, Verg **II.** *doleful, mournful*, vox, Cic , mulierum comploratio, Liv

lāmentātĭo -ōnis, f (lamentor), *a lamenting, weeping, wailing, lamentation*, plangore et lamentatione complere forum, Cic

lāmentor, 1, dep **I.** Intransit , *to weep, wail, lament*, flebiliter in vulnere, Cic **II.** Transit , *to bewail, weep over, lament*, caecitatem, Cic , with acc and infin , Hor

lāmentum -i, n. *a wailing, weeping, lamentation*, gen in plur , se lamentis muliebriter lacrimisque dedere, Cic

1 **lămĭa** -ae, f (λαμια), gen plur , lamiae, *witches believed to suck children's blood, vampires*, Hor

2 **Lămĭa** -ae, m *a cognomen of the Aelian gens*

3 **Lămĭa** -ae, f (Λαμια), *a town in Thessaly* (now *Zeitun* or *Zeituni*)

lāmĭna and **lamna** -ae, f (perhaps connected with latus, *broad*), *a plate or thin piece of metal or marble, etc* **I.** Lit 1, aenea, Liv , 2, **a,** *uncoined gold and silver*, inimicus lamnae, Hor , **b,** *a plate of iron, heated and used for torture*, laminae ardentes, Cic , **c,** *the blade of a sword*, Ov , **d,** *the blade of a saw*, Verg **II.** *a nutshell*, Ov

lampas -pădis, acc -păda, acc plur -pădes and -pădas, f (λαμπας), *a torch* **I** Lit , Verg , *a wedding torch*, Ter , also used at the torch race when one runner delivered his torch to another, hence, quasi cursores vitae lampada tradunt, *end the course of their life*, Lucr **II.** Meton , *brightness, brilliance*, Phoebaea, *the light of the sun*, Verg

Lampsăcum -i, n and **Lampsăcus** (os) -i, f (Λάμψακος), *a town of Mysia on the north-east part of the Hellespont* Hence, adj , **Lampsăcēnus** -a -um, *of or belonging to Lampsacus.*

Lămus -i, m (Λάμος), *king of the Laestrygones, founder of the town Formiae;* urbs Lami *Formiae*, Ov

lămўrus -i, m (λαμυρος), *an unknown seafish*, Ov

lāna -ae, f (λῆνος, Doric λᾶνος), *wool* **I.** Of animals, 1, **a,** lit , lanam ducere, Ov , trahere, *to spin*, Juv , lanam sufficere medicamentis quibusdam, Cic , **b,** meton , *wool spinning*, lanae dedita, Liv ; 2, *woolly hair*, prov , rixari de lana caprina, *to quarrel about nothing*, Hor **II.** *the down on leaves, fruit*, etc , Verg

lānārĭus -a -um (lana), *of or relating to wool, woollen*, Plin

lānātus -a -um (lana), *wool bearing, woolly* 1, lit , capras lanatas quibusdam factas (esse), Liv , subst , **lānātae** -ārum, f *sheep*, Juv , 2, *downy, covered with down*, Plin

lancĕa ae, f *a light spear* or *lance, with a leathern thong attached to it*, Lucr

lancĭno, 1 *to tear to pieces, mangle, rend in pieces*, 1, lit , Plin , 2, transf , paterna bona, *to squander*, Cat

lānĕus -a -um (lana), *made of wool, woollen*, 1, lit , pallium, Cic , 2, *soft as wool*, Cat

Langŏbardi -ōrum, m *a people in north Germany, on the west side of the Elbe*

languĕfăcĭo, 3 (langueo and facio), *to make languid or faint*, Cic

languĕo gŭi, 2 *to be faint, weak, languid* **I.** Physically, quum de via languerem, *weary with the journey*, Cic , partic , languens, *weak, faint, languid*, vox, Cic **II.** Transf , *to be languid, inert, inactive*, otio, in otio, Cic , languent vires, Cic , partic , languens, *inactive, inert*, languens labensque populus, Cic

languesco, langŭi, 3 (langueo), *to become faint, weak, languid, to languish* **I.** Lit , 1, corpore, Cic , senectute, Cic , Bacchus languescit in amphora, *becomes milder*, Hor , 2, *to become weak through illness*, nec mea consueto languescent corpora lecto, Ov **II.** *to become languid, inactive, listless*, Cic

languĭdē, adv (languidus), *faintly, languidly, feebly*, negant ab ullo philosopho quid, quam dictum esse languidius, Cic

languidŭlus -a -um, (dim. of languidus), *somewhat faint, languid, limp*, Cic.

languĭdus -a -um (langueo), *faint, weak, languid, dull.* **I.** Physically, **1**, gen., **a**, of persons, vino vigiliisque languidus, Cic.; **b**, of things, ventus, *gentle*, Ov.; aqua, *with gentle current*, Liv.; **2**, esp., of wine stored up, *mild, mellow*, Hor. **II.** Of activity, *sluggish, inactive;* **a**, pass., senectus non modo languida et iners non est, Cic.; studium, Cic.; **b**, act., languidae voluptates, *enervating*, Cic.

languor -ōris, m. (langueo), *faintness, languor, weariness, feebleness.* **I.** Physical, **1**, corporis, Cic.; **2**, *languor, weakness arising from ill-health, ill-health*; aquosus, *dropsy*, Hor. **II.** *listlessness, inactivity, idleness, sluggishness;* se languori dedere, Cic.; languorem alicui afferre, Cic.

lănĭātus -ūs, m. (lanio), *a mangling, tearing in pieces;* with subj. genit., ferarum, Cic.; fig., si recludantur tyrannorum mentes posse aspici laniatus et ictus, Tac.

lānĭcĭum, v. lanitium.

lănĭēna -ae, f. (lanius), *a butcher's shop, shambles*, Liv.

lānĭfĭcus -a -um (lana and facio), *working in wool, spinning* or *weaving wool;* ars, Ov.; sorores, *the Parcae*, Mart.

lānĭger -gĕra -gĕrum (lana and gero), *wool-bearing.* **I.** Adj., bidens, Verg.; poet., apices, *woollen*, Verg. **II.** Subst., **lānĭger** -gĕri, m. *a ram*, Ov.

lănĭo, 1. *to tear* or *cut to pieces, mangle, lacerate;* hominem, Cic.; aliquem bestiis, Liv.; crinem manibus, Ov.; transf., et tua sacrilegae laniarunt carmina linguae, Ov.

lănista -ae, m., **1**, *a trainer of gladiators*, Cic.; **2**, *an instigator, inciter*, Cic., Liv.

lānĭtĭum -ii, n. (lana), *wool*, Verg.

lănĭus -ii, m. (lanio), *a butcher*, Liv.; transf., *a hangman, executioner*, Plaut.

lanterna (lāterna) -ae, f. (conn. with λάμπω, λαμπάς), *a lantern, lamp*, Cic.

lanternārĭus -ii, m. (lanterna), *a lantern-bearer;* Catilinae, Cic.

lānūgo -inis, f. (lana), *the down of plants*, Plin.; *the first soft down of the beard;* flaventem primā lanugine malas, Verg.

Lānŭvĭum -ii, n. *a town in Latium, forty-eight miles south-east of Rome.* Hence, adj., **Lānŭvīnus** -a -um, *belonging to Lanuvium;* subst., **Lānŭvīnum** -i, n. *an estate near Lanuvium*, Cic.

lanx, lancis, f., **1**, *a plate, platter, a large flat dish*, Cic.; **2**, *the scale of a balance*, Cic.

Lāŏcŏōn -ontis, m. (Λαοκόων), *a priest of Neptune in Troy, who with his two sons was devoured by serpents.*

Lāŏdămīa -ae, f. (Λαοδάμεια), *daughter of Acastus and wife of Protesilaus, on whose death she slew herself.*

Lāŏdĭcēa -ae, f. (Λαοδίκεια), *name of several towns:* **1**, *a town in Phrygia Major*, now *Eski-Hissar;* **2**, *a town in Seleucis in Syria*, now *Ladikiyeh.* Hence, adj., **Lāŏdĭcensis** -e, *Laodicean.*

Lāŏmĕdōn -ontis, m. (Λαομέδων), *a king of Troy, father of Priam;* hence, **1**, adj., **Lāŏmĕdontēus** -a -um, *Laomedontean*, poet. = *Trojan*, Verg.; **2**, **Lāŏmĕdontĭus** -a -um, *Laomedontian;* **3**, subst., **Lāŏmĕdontĭădēs** -ae, m. *a male descendant of Laomedon (Priam)*, Verg.; plur., Laomedontiadae, *the Trojans*, Verg.

lăpăthum -i, n. and **lăpăthus** -i, f. (λάπαθον), *sorrel*, Hor.

lăpĭcīdīnae -ārum, f. (lapis and caedo), *the stone quarries as a place of punishment*, Cic.

lăpĭdārĭus -a -um (lapis), *of* or *relating to stone*, Plaut.

lăpĭdātĭo -ōnis, f. (lapis), *a throwing of stones;* facta est lapidatio, Cic.

lăpĭdātor -ōris, m. (lapido), *a thrower of stones*, Cic.

lăpĭdĕus -a -um (lapis), *made of stone, stone;* murus, Liv.; imber, *a shower of stones*, Cic.

lăpĭdo, 1. (lapis), **1**, *to throw stones at*, Suet.; **2**, impers., lapidat, *it rains stones;* Veiis de caelo lapidaverat, Liv.

lăpĭdōsus -a -um (lapis), **1**, *full of stones, stony;* montes, Ov.; **2**, *as hard as stone;* panis, Hor.

lăpillus -i, m. (dim. of lapis), *a little stone, pebble.* **I.** lapilli crepitantes, Ov.; white stones were used to mark lucky, and black stones unlucky days, hence, dies signanda melioribus lapillis, Mart. **II. 1**, *a precious stone, gem;* nivei viridesque lapilli, *pearls and emeralds*, Hor.; **2**, *a pebble used at trials* (a white one for acquittal, a black one for condemnation); lapilli nivei atrique, Ov.

lăpis -idis, m. (λᾶας), *a stone.* **I.** Gen., often collective, bibulus, *pumice-stone*, Verg.; ardens, *a meteoric stone*, Liv.; aliquem lapidibus prosequi, Cic.; lapidibus aliquem cooperire, or obruere, Cic.; lapidibus pluit, *it rains stones from the sky*, Liv.; lapide candidiore diem notare, *to mark a day as lucky* (cf. lapillus I.), Cat. **II.** Esp. **1**, *a boundary-stone*, Liv.; **2**, *a grave-stone*, Prop.; **3**, *a precious stone, jewel*, esp., *a pearl*, Hor.; **4**, *marble;* Parius, Verg.; albus, *a table of white marble*, Hor.; **5**, *a piece of mosaic*, Hor.; **6**, *a mile-stone;* intra vicesimum lapidem, Liv.; **7**, *the stone*, or *platform of stone on which the praeco stood at the slave-auctions;* duos de lapide emptos tribunos, Cic.; **8**, Juppiter lapis, *a stone held in the hand as a symbol of Jupiter, and sworn by;* Jovem lapidem jurare, Cic.

Lăpĭthēs -ae, m., plur., Lapithae (Λαπίθαι), *the Lapithae*, myth., *a savage mountain race, living near Olympus and Pelion in Thessaly, famous for their fight with the Centaurs at the wedding of Pirithous.* Hence, adj., **1**, **Lăpĭthaeus** -a -um; **2**, **Lăpĭthēĭus** -a -um, *of* or *belonging to the Lapithae.*

lappa -ae, f. *a bur*, Verg.

lapsĭo -ōnis, f. (1. labor), *a gliding, an inclination, tendency towards*, Cic.

lapso, 1. (intens. of 1. labor), *to totter;* Priamus lapsans, Verg.

lapsus -ūs, m. (1. labor). **I.** *a gradual motion, gliding, sliding*, Verg.; *the flowing of water;* si lacus emissus lapsu et cursu suo in mare profluxisset, Cic.; *the flight of birds;* volucrum lapsus atque cantus, Cic.; *the gliding of a snake*, Verg. **II.** *a falling, fall;* **1**, lapsus terrae, Cic.; **2**, *a moral fall, fault, error;* quum sint populares multi variique lapsus, Cic.

lăquĕar -āris and **lăquĕāre** -is, n. (laqueus), n. *a panel in a ceiling, panelled ceiling;* gen. plur., laquearia tecti, Verg.

lăquĕo, 1. (laqueus), *to adorn with a panelled ceiling;* only in partic. perf., laqueatus, laqueata tecta, Cic.

lăquĕus -i, m. *a noose, snare, trap;* **1**, lit., collum inserere in laqueum, Cic.; laqueo gulam frangere, Sall., or premere, Hor.; **2**, transf., *a snare, noose;* alicui laqueos ponere, *to lay snares for*, Ov.; in laqueos cadere, Ov.; laquei legum, interrogationum, Cic.

1. **Lar** or **Lars**, Lartis, m. *an Etruscan title*

signifying lord, found as a praenomen, Lars Tolumnius, Cic., Lars Porsena, Liv.

2 **Lār,** Lăris, m., usually plur., **Lăres** -um and (more rarely) -ium, *tutelary deities among the Romans,* Lares praestites, Ov., Lares domestici, familiares, privati, patrii, *domestic deities, the gods of the hearth,* Ov., permarini, *deities of the sea,* Liv., rurales, agri custodes, *guardians of agriculture,* Cic.; meton., *hearth, dwelling, home,* ad larem suum reverti, *home,* Cic.

Lăra and **Lărunda** -ae, f. *a nymph whom Jupiter deprived of her tongue because of her loquacity.*

Larcius -a -um, *name of a celebrated Roman gens, the most celebrated member of which was the first dictator,* T. Larcius Flavus, Cic.

lardum (lārĭdum) -i, n. (connected with λαρινός), *the fat of bacon, lard,* Ov.

Lărentālĭa -ium, n. *a feast in honour of Acca Larentia.*

Lārentia, v. Acca.

1 **Lăres,** v. 2 Lar.

2 **Lăres,** acc. Lares, abl. Laribus, f. *a town in Numidia, now Larbuss or Lorbus.*

largē, adv. (largus), *largely, plentifully, abundantly,* dare, Cic., large atque honorifice aliquid promittere, Cic., senatus consultum large factum, *with sweeping provisions,* Tac.

largĭfĭcus -a -um (largus and facio), *bountiful, liberal,* Lucr.

largĭflŭus -a -um (large and fluo), *flowing with full stream,* Lucr.

largĭlŏquus -a -um (large and loquor), *talkative, loquacious,* Plaut.

largĭor, 4. dep. (largus). **I.** *to give abundantly, bestow liberally, impart,* qui eripiunt aliis quod aliis largiantur, Cic.; absol., *to give liberal presents,* esp. for the purpose of bribing, ex alieno largiendo aliquid parare, *by means of bribery,* Cic. **II.** Transf., *to give, bestow, grant;* populo libertatem, Cic.; alicui civitatem, Cic., patriae suum sanguinem, Cic.

largĭtas -ātis, f. (largus), *liberality, bountifulness,* terra cum maxima largitate fruges fundit, Cic.

largĭtĕr, adv. (largus), *abundantly, plentifully, largely;* posse, *to be powerful,* Caes., de judicio largiter esse remissum, Cic.

largītĭo -ōnis, f. (largior), *a giving freely, liberality, spending freely, lavishing,* **1,** lit., a, in cives, Cic.; largitione benevolentiam alicuius consectari, Cic., prov., largitio non habet fundum, *giving has no limits,* Cic., b, *giving or spending in order to gain the favour of others, bribery;* largitionis suspicionem recipere, Cic.; **2,** *granting, bestowing,* civitatis, Cic., aequitatis, Cic.

largītor -ōris, m. (largior), *a liberal giver, spender,* praedae erat largitor, Liv.; absol., as attrib. = *generous,* Liv.; in a bad sense, *a briber,* Cic.

largus -a -um. **I.** *abundant, plentiful, numerous, copious,* quum sol terras largā luce compleverit, Cic.; imbres, Verg.; with genit., *rich in, abounding in,* opum, Verg. **II.** *liberal in giving and spending, bountiful, profuse,* qui si largissimus esse vellet, Cic., plur. subst., largi, *generous persons,* Cic., with abl., largus animo, *of a generous disposition,* Tac., promissis, *liberal in promises,* Tac.; with infin., spes donare novas, Hor.

lārĭdum -i, n. = lardum (q. v.)

Lārīnum -i, n. *town in Lower Italy, now Larino.* Hence, adj., **Lārīnās** -ātis, *of or belonging to Larinum.*

Lārīsa (Lārissa) -ae, f. (Λαρισα, Λάρισσα). **I.** *town in Pelasgiotis, in Thessaly, now Larisse.* Hence, a, **Lārīsaeus (Lārīssaeus)** -a -um, *Larissean = Thessalian,* Cic., Verg., b, **Lārīsenses** -ium, m. *the inhabitants of Larisa.* **II.** Larisa Cremaste, *town in Phthiotis, in Thessaly.* **III.** *a fortress of Argos.*

Lārĭus -ii, m. *name of a lake in north Italy, now Lago di Como.* Hence, adj., **Lārĭus** -a -um, *of or belonging to Larius.*

lărix -icis, f. (λάριξ), *the larch,* Plin.

Lars, v. 1 Lar.

Lărunda, v. Lara.

larva -ae, f. (2. Lar), 1, *a ghost, spectre,* Plaut.; 2, *a mask,* Hor.

Lās, acc. Lăn, f. (Λᾶς), *a town in Laconia, south-west of Gytheum.*

lăsănum -i, n. (λάσανον), *a cooking utensil,* Hor.

lascīvē, adv. (lascivus), *lasciviously, wantonly,* Mart.

lascīvia -ae, f. (lascivus), **1,** in a good sense, *playfulness, sportiveness, frolicsomeness,* hilaritas et lascivia, Cic., **2,** in a bad sense, *wantonness, licentiousness, lasciviousness, insolence,* quos soluto imperio licentia atque lascivia corruperat, Sall., lasciviam a vobis prohibetote, Liv.

lascīvĭbundus -a -um (lascivio), *wanton, sportive,* Plaut.

lascīvĭo -ii -ītum, 4 (lascivus), *to sport, play, be sportive, wanton, to be insolent,* agnus lascivit fugā, Ov., plebs lascivit, Liv.

lascīvus -a -um, **1,** in a good sense, *playful, sportive, frolicsome,* puella, Verg., aetas, Hor., **2,** in a bad sense, *wanton, licentious, lascivious, insolent, overbearing,* Epicrates, Cic., puella, Ov.

lăserpīcĭfer -fĕra -fĕrum, *producing the plant laserpitium,* Cat.

lăserpīcĭum (lăserpītĭum) -ii, n. *a plant called silphium,* used in medicine and in cooking, Plin.

lassĭtūdo -inis, f. (lassus), *weariness, lassitude,* Cic., lassitudine exanimari, confici, Caes.

lasso, 1. (lassus), *to make weary, tire, exhaust,* corpus, Ov.

lassŭlus -a -um (dim. of lassus), *somewhat weary, rather tired,* Cat.

lassus -a -um, *weary, tired, exhausted, faint, languid,* a, of persons, itinere atque opere castrorum et proelio fessi lassique erant, Sall.; ab equo domito, Hor., with genit., maris et viarum, Hor., b, applied to inanimate things, fructibus assiduis lassa humus, Ov., lasso papavera collo, *drooping,* Verg.

lātē, adv. (latus). **I.** *broadly, widely,* longe lateque, *far and wide,* Cic., vagari, *to wander far and wide,* Caes., populus late rex, Verg. **II.** Transf., 1, ars late patet, Cic., fidei bonum nomen latissime manat, Cic., **2,** *at length, amply, copiously,* fuse lateque dicere de aliqua re, Cic.

lătebra -ae, f. (lateo). **I.** *a concealment, hiding,* in quibus non invenio quae latebra togatis hominibus esse possit, Cic., lunae, *an eclipse of the moon,* Lucr. **II.** Concr. **A.** Lit., *hiding-place, lurking-place, covert,* latebrae ferarum, Cic., latebra teli, *the place where the arrow is embedded in the body,* Verg. **B.** Transf., **1,** *hidden place, secret retreat,* quum in animis hominum tantae latebrae sint, Cic., **2,** *a subterfuge, pretence, shift,* latebra mendacii, Cic.

lătebrĭcŏla -ae, c. (latebra and colo), *one who dwells in concealment,* Plaut.

lătĕbrōsē, adv. (latebrosus), *secretly, in a corner*, Plaut.

lătĕbrōsus -a -um (latebra), *full of hiding places, secret, retired*; via, Cic.; pumex, *porous*, Verg.

lătens -entis, p. adj. (from lateo), *concealed, hidden*; res, Cic.; causa, Verg.

lătentĕr, adv. (lateo), *secretly*, Cic.

lătĕo -tŭi, 2. (connected with λανθάνω). **I.** *to be hid, be concealed*; **1,** gen., in occulto, Cic.; abdite, Cic.; latet anguis in herba, Verg.; navis latet portu, Hor.; latet sub classibus aequor, *is concealed, covered*, Verg.; portus latet, *is screened from the winds*, Cic.; **2,** esp., **a,** *to keep out of sight*, in order not to appear in a court of justice, Cic.; **b,** *to live in obscurity*; bene qui latuit, bene vixit, Ov. **II.** Transf., **1,** *to be concealed*; scelus latere inter tot flagitia, Cic.; **2,** *to be concealed* or *safe from misfortune*; sub umbra amicitiae Romanae, Liv.; in tutela ac praesidio bellicae virtutis, Cic.; **3,** *to be unknown*; **a,** aliae (causae) sunt perspicuae, aliae latent, Cic.; **b,** res latet aliquem, *it is concealed from, unknown to, a secret to*, Verg.; so res latet alicui, Cic.

lăter -tĕris, m. *a brick, tile*, Cic., Caes.

lătĕrāmen -ĭnis, n. (later), *an earthen vessel*, Lucr.

Lătĕrānus -a -um, *family name in the gentes Claudia, Sextia, and Plautia.*

lătercŭlus -i, m. (dim. of later), *a brick, tile*, Caes.

lătĕrĭcius -a -um (later), *brick, built of brick*; turris, Caes.

Lătĕrium -ii, n. *an estate of Qu. Cicero at Arpinum*, Cic.

lāterna, v. lanterna.

lāternārius, v. lanternarius.

lătesco, 3. (lateo), *to hide oneself, be concealed*, Cic.

lătex -ticis, m. *a fluid, liquid*; used of water, occulti latices, Liv.; securi latices, Verg.; frugum laticumque cupido, *hunger and thirst*, Lucr.; also of wine, meri, Ov.; Lyaeus or Lenaeus, or simply latex, Verg.; latex absinthii, *wormwood juice*, Lucr.

Lătĭālis -e, v. Latium.

Lătĭāris -e, v. Latium.

lătĭbŭlum -i, n. (lateo), *a hiding-place, a lurking-place*. **I.** Lit., **a,** of animals, quum etiam ferae latibulis se tegant, Cic.; **b,** of men, latibula locorum occultorum, Cic. **II.** Transf., latibulum aut perfugium doloris mei, Cic.

lātĭclāvius -a -um, *having a broad purple stripe* (the distinguishing peculiarity of senators, equestrian military tribunes, and sons of noble families); tribunus, Suet.

lātĭfundium -ii, n. (latus and fundus), *a large landed estate*, Plin.

Lătīnē, v. Latium.

Lătīniensis, v. Latium.

Lătīnĭtas -ātis, f. (Latinus), **1,** *a pure Latin style, Latinity*, Cic.; **2,** = jus Latii, *Latin right, a condition intermediate between Roman citizenship and the condition of aliens*, Cic.

1. **Lătīnus** -a -um, v. Latium.

2. **Lătīnus** -i, m., *a king of the Laurentians, who received Aeneas hospitably, and gave him his daughter in marriage.*

lātĭo -ōnis, f. (fero), *a bringing*. **I.** auxilii, *rendering assistance*, Liv. **II. a,** legis, *a proposing, bringing forward*, Cic.; **b,** suffragii, *voting*, Liv.

lătĭto, 1. (intens. of lateo), *to lie hid, be concealed*; **a,** extrahitur domo latitans Oppianicus a Manlio, Cic.; invisae atque latitantes res, Caes.; **b,** esp., *to conceal oneself*, so as not to appear in court, Cic.

lātĭtūdo -ĭnis, f. (latus). **I.** *breadth*; **a,** fossae, Caes.; **b,** *extent, great size*; possessionum, Cic. **II.** *a broad pronunciation*; verborum, Cic.

Lătĭum -ii, n. **I.** *a district of Italy, in which Rome was situated*. **II.** Meton., **1,** *the Latins*; jus Latii (v. Latinitas), Tac.; **2,** = jus Latii or Latinitas, Tac. Hence, **a,** **Lătĭus** -a -um, *belonging to Latium, Latin*, poet. = *Roman*; forum, Ov.; **b,** **Lătīnus** -a -um, *Latin*; convertere in Latinum, *to translate into Latin*, Cic.; feriae Latinae, or simply Latinae, *the Latin games*, Liv.; **c,** adv., **Lătīnē**, *in Latin*; Latine loqui, Cic.; **d,** **Lătīniensis** -e, *Latin*; **e,** **Lătĭālis** -e, *Latin*; **f,** **Lătĭāris** -e, *Latin*; Juppiter, *as patron of the Latin league*. Hence, **Lătĭar** -āris, n. *a feast of Jupiter Latiaris.*

Latmus -i, m. (Λάτμος), *a mountain in Caria, where Selene laid Endymion to sleep.* Hence, adj., **Latmĭus** -a -um, *Latmian.*

Lātō -ūs, f. and **Lātōna** -ae, f. (Λητώ), *the mother of Apollo and Diana, whom she bore to Jupiter in the Island of Delos*; hence, **a,** **Lātōnĭus** -a -um, *Latonian*, Latonia virgo or simply Latonia, *Diana*, Verg.; **b,** **Lātōnĭgĕna** -ae, c. (Latona and gigno), *offspring of Latona*, Ov.; **c,** **Lātōĭus** and **Lētōĭus** -a -um, *Latonian*; proles, *Apollo and Diana*, Ov. Subst., **Lātōĭus** -ii, m. *Apollo*, and **Lātōĭa** -ae, f. *Diana*, Ov.; **d,** **Lātōis** or **Lētōis** -ĭdis, f., *Latonian*, Calaurea, *sacred to Latona*, Ov.; subst., *Diana*, Ov.; **e,** **Lātōus** -a -um, *Latonian.*

Latobrigi -ōrum, m. *a Gallic people, neighbours of the Helvetii.*

Lātōna, etc., v. Lato.

lātor -ōris, m. (fero), *the proposer of a law*; legis Semproniae, Cic.

Lātōus, v. Lato.

lātrātor -ōris, m. (1. latro), *a barker*; poet. = *dog*, Verg.

lātrātus -ūs, m. (1. latro), *a barking*, Verg.

1. **lātro**, 1. *to bark, bay*. **I.** Intransit., **1,** lit., quod si luce quoque canes latrent, Cic.; partic. subst., latrans, *a barker*, i.e., *a dog*, Ov.; **2,** transf., **a,** of men, *to bark, brawl, rant*; latrare ad clepsydram, Cic.; **b,** of inanimate objects, *to roar*; undae latrantes, Verg.; stomachus, *rumbling*, Hor. **II.** Transit., **1,** *to bark at*; senem, Hor.; **2,** transf., of men, *to shout out*; canina verba in foro, Ov.

2. **lātro** -ōnis, m. (λάτρις). **I.** *a hired servant, a mercenary soldier*, Plaut. **II.** Transf., **a,** *a robber, freebooter, bandit, brigand*; insidiosus et plenus latronum locus, Cic.; **b,** *a hunter*, Verg.; **c,** *a piece on a draught-board*, Ov.

lātrōcĭnium -ii, n. (latrocinor). **I.** *military service*, Plaut. **II.** **1,** *robbery, highway robbery, piracy*; **a,** lit., incursiones hostium et latrocinia, Cic.; transf., *villany, roguery*; quid futurum sit latrocinio tribunorum, Cic.; **b,** meton., *a band of robbers*; unus ex tanto latrocinio, Cic.; **2,** *a game of draughts*, Ov.

lātrōcĭnor, 1. dep. (2. latro). **I.** *to serve as a mercenary soldier*, Plaut. **II.** *to practise robbery, piracy, brigandage*, Cic.

lātruncŭlus -i, m. (dim. of 2. latro), *a highwayman, freebooter, bandit*, Cic.

1. **lātus** -a -um, partic. of fero.

2. **lātus** -a -um (orig. stlatus = *broadened out, extended*), *broad, wide* (opp. angustus). **I.** Lit.,

a, fossa XV pedes lata, Caes , via, Cic ; in latum crescere, *to grow broad*, Ov , **b,** *extensive, wide, large* , locus, Cic , latissimae solitudines, Caes , **c,** of persons, *proud, haughty*, latus ut in circo spatiere, Hor **II.** Transf , **a,** of pronunciation, *broad* , cuius tu illa lata non nunquam imitaris, Cic , **b,** *diffuse, copious, full, rich* , oratio, disputatio, Cic

3 **lătus** ĕris, n. *the side, flank* **I.** Of a body , **1, a,** of men, lateris dolor, Cic , in the action of an orator, virili laterum inflexione, Cic , latus dare, *to expose the side to* (*in boxing*), Tib , malo latus obdere apertum, Hor ab alicuius latere nunquam discedere, Cic., artifices lateris, *dancers who make pantomimic gestures*, Ov , **b,** of animals, cuius (equi aenei) in lateribus fores essent, Cic , **2,** esp , **a,** *the side*, as the seat of the bodily strength, neque enim ex te nobilitatus es sed ex lateribus et lacertis tuis, Cic , **b,** meton = *the body* , latus fessum longā militiā, Hor **II.** Of an object, *side, flank* (opp frons, tergum), **1,** latus castrorum, Caes , insula, cuius unum latus est contra Galliam, Caes , prora avertit et undis dat latus, Verg , **2,** milit t t , *the flank of an army* , nostros latere aperto aggressi, Caes , a latere, a lateribus, *on the flank* , Caes

lătuscŭlum -i, n (dim of 2 latus), *a little side*, Cat

laudābĭlis -e (laudo), **1,** *praiseworthy, laudable* vita, Cic , orator, Cic , **2,** *good in its kind, excellent* , vinum, Plin

laudābĭlĭter, adv (laudabilis), *laudably, in a praiseworthy manner* , vivere, Cic

laudandus -a -um, p adj (from laudo), *deserving praise, laudable*, Ov

laudātĭo -ōnis, f (laudo), *praise* **I.** *commendation* , laudatio tua, Cic **II. 1,** in a court of justice, *a testimony to character* , gravissima atque ornatissima, Cic , **2,** *a funeral oration or panegyric* , nonnullae mortuorum laudationes, Cic , **3,** *a vote of thanks to a provincial governor sent to the Roman senate*, Cic

laudātīvus -a -um (laudo), *laudatory*, Quint

laudātor -ōris, m (laudo) **I.** *a praiser* , temporis acti, Hor , pacis semper laudator, Cic **II. 1,** *a witness who bears favourable testimony to character*, Cic , **2,** *one who delivers a funeral panegyric*, Liv

laudātrix -icis, f (laudator), *a praiser* , vitiorum laudatrix fama popularis, Cic

laudātus a -um, p adj (from laudo), *praiseworthy, esteemed, excellent* , vir, Cic , vultus, Ov

laudo, 1 (laus) *to praise, laud, extol, commend* **I.** Lit., **A.** aliquem, Cic , laudare laudibus, Cic , foll by infin , extinxisse nefas laudabor, Verg **B.** Esp , **a,** *to bear favourable testimony to any one's character*, Cic , **b,** *to deliver a funeral panegyric over some one;* aliquem, Cic., **c,** *to call happy, consider fortunate* , agricolam laudat juris peritus, Hor **II.** Transf , *to name, mention, cite, quote* , aliquem auctorem, Cic

laurĕa -ae, f , v laureus

laurĕātus -a -um (laurea), *crowned with laurel, laurelled* (esp as a sign of victory), imago, Cic , fasces, lictores, Cic , literae, *bringing tidings of victory*, Liv

Laurentum -i, n *town in Latium, between Ostia and Lavinium* Hence, adj , **a, Laurens** -entis, *Laurentine* , **b, Laurentĭus** -a -um, *Laurentine*

laurĕŏla -ae, f (dim of laurea), *a laurel branch, laurel crown*, and meton , *triumph*, Cic , prov , laureolam in mustaceo quaerere, *to seek fame in trifles*, Cic.

Laurētum -i, n (laurus), *a grove of laurels, the name of a spot on the Aventine Hill*, Suet

laurĕus -a -um (laurus), *of or relating to the laurel* **I.** Adj , corona, Cic. **II.** Subst , **laurea** -ae, f **1,** *the laurel tree*, Liv , **2, a,** *the laurel crown or laurel branch, as a sign of victory;* decemviri laurea coronati, Liv , **b,** meton , *triumph, victory*, quam lauream cum tua laudatione conferrem, Cic

laurĭcŏmus -a -um (laurus and coma), *covered with laurel trees*, Lucr

laurĭger -gĕra -gĕrum (laurus and gero), *crowned with laurels, wearing laurels*, Ov.

laurus -i, f *the laurel or bay tree, sacred to Apollo, with which poets, triumphant generals, and, on certain occasions, flamens and ancestral busts were crowned*, Cic , hence, meton , *triumph, victory*, Cic (abl , lauru, Hor , nom and acc plur , laurus, Verg)

laus, laudis, f *praise, fame, glory, commendation* **A.** Lit , ad laudem, Cic ; canere ad tibiam clarorum virorum laudes, Cic capere (*to earn*) ex hac una re maximam laudem, Cic , celebrare alicuius laudes, Cic , cumulare aliquem omni laude, Cic , efferre aliquem laudibus ad caelum, Cic , in laude vivere, Cic alicuius laudes dicere, Verg , hoc in tua laude pono, *I consider this praiseworthy in thee*, Cic , non laudem habet de me, *he has nothing to boast of as far as I am concerned*, Ov **B** Meton **a,** *a praiseworthy action* , hae tantae summis in rebus laudes, Cic , **b,** plur , laudes = *praiseworthy qualities*, quarum laudum gloriam adamaris, Cic

lautē, adv. (lautus), **1,** *splendidly, brilliantly magnificently* , lautius res domesticas tueri, Cic **2,** *admirably, excellently, thoroughly* , hodie me emunxeris lautissime, ap Cic

lautĭa -ōrum, n (connected with lavo), *the entertainment given to foreign ambassadors at Rome*, Liv

lautĭtĭa -ae, f (lautus), *splendour, elegance, magnificence in one's manner of living* , mea nova lautitia, Cic

Lautŭlae (Lautŏlae) -ārum, f *a place of the Volscians between Anxur and Fundi*

lautŭmĭae (lātŏmĭae) -ārum, f (λατομίαι), *a stone quarry*, Plaut , *a prison or dungeon cut out of rock at Syracuse and Rome*, Cic , Liv

lautus -a -um, p adj (from lavo), lit , *washed, bathed* , and hence, **1,** *splendid, brilliant, elegant, sumptuous* , supellex, Cic , **2,** *illustrious, distinguished, grand* , homines lauti et urbani, Cic , lauta liberalitas, Cic

lăvābrum -i, n (lavo), *a bath*, Lucr

lăvātĭo -ōnis, f (lavo) **I.** *a washing, bathing*, Cic **II.** Meton , **1,** *bathing apparatus*, Phaedr , **2,** *water for bathing*, Cic

Lăverna -ae, f *the goddess of gain (just or unjust)*, hence, *protectress of thieves and cheats* , hence, adj , **Lăvernālis** -e, *belonging to Laverna*

Lavernĭum -ii, n *a place in Latium, near Formiae*

Lăvīci, etc , v Labici

Lāvīnĭa -ae, f *daughter of Latinus, wife of Aeneas*

Lāvīnĭum -ii, n *a town in Latium, built by Aeneas, and named after his wife Lavinia* (now Pratica) Hence, adj , **Lāvīnĭus** -a -um, and **Lāvīnus** -a -um, *Lavinian*

lăvo, lāvi, lautum, partic lautus and lōtus, lavĕre, and lăvātum and lăvāturus, lăvāre (λούω), *to wash, bathe* **I.** Gen , **1, a,** transit , manus, Cic , **b,** intransit lavare and pass lavari, *to wash oneself, bathe*, cum te lautum voluit, cenatum noluit occidere, Cic.; **2,** *to moisten, wet, bathe;* vultum lacrimis, Ov. **II.** *to wash away;* mala vino, *to drive away,* Hor.

laxāmentum -i, n. (laxo), *a widening, extending;* **1,** lit., gen.; **2,** transf., *a relaxing, mitigation, alleviation, respite;* si quid laxamenti a bello Samnitium esset, Liv.; laxamentum dare legi, *to release,* Cic.

laxē, adv. (laxus). **I.** *widely, spaciously, at wide intervals;* **1,** lit., habitare, Cic.; **2,** transf., of time, laxius proferre diem, *to put farther off,* Cic. **II.** *loosely;* **1,** lit., aliquem vincire, Liv.; **2,** transf., *loosely, without restraint;* vivere, Liv.

laxĭtas -ātis, f. (laxus), *wideness, roominess;* in domo clari hominis adhibenda cura est laxitatis, Cic.

laxo, 1. (laxus). **I.** *to widen, extend, enlarge;* forum, Cic.; manipulos, *to extend, leave a space between,* Caes. **II.** *to unloose, unfasten, slacken, relax;* **1,** vincula epistolae, Nep.; claustra, Verg.; **2,** *to set free from;* elatum pedem ab stricto nodo, Liv.; **3, a,** *to unbend, relax, refresh, amuse;* animos curamque, Cic.; quum laxati curis sumus, *free from,* Cic.; **b,** *to mitigate, relax, remit;* aliquid laboris, Liv.; annonam, *to lower the price of,* Liv.; intransit., annona haud multum laxaverat, *fallen in price,* Liv.; ubi laxatam pugnam vidit, Liv.

laxus -a -um. **I.** *wide, spacious;* **1,** lit., annulus, Ov.; spatium, Liv.; **2,** transf., of time, diem statuo satis laxum, *sufficiently distant,* Cic. **II.** *loose, lax, relaxed;* **1,** lit., arcus, Verg.; habenae, Verg.; funis, Hor.; male laxus in pede calceus haeret, Hor.; janua, *open,* Ov.; fig., laxissimas habenas habere amicitiae, Cic.; **2,** transf., annona laxior, *a lower price of provisions,* Liv.; milites laxiore imperio habere, Sall.

lĕa -ae, f. (leo), *a lioness,* Ov.

lĕaena -ae, f. (λέαινα), *a lioness,* Cic.

Lēander and **Lēandrus** -i, m. (Λείανδρος), *a youth of Abydos who swam nightly across the Hellespont to visit Hero at Sestos, till he was drowned in a storm.*

Lĕarchus -i, m. (Λέαρχος), *the son of Athamas and Ino, killed by his father in a fit of madness.* Hence, **Lĕarchēus** -a -um, *of* or *belonging to Learchus.*

Lĕbădīa -ae, f. (Λεβάδεια), *a town in Boeotia, famous for the Oracle and Grotto of Trophonius* (now *Livadia*), Cic.

Lĕbĕdŏs (-us) -i, f. (Λέβεδος), *a town in Ionia.*

lĕbēs -ētis, m. (λέβης), **1,** *a bronze kettle or cauldron,* often given as a prize in games, Verg.; **2,** *a metal vessel used for washing the hands,* Ov.

Lĕchaeum -i, n. (Λέχαιον), *the port of Corinth on the Corinthian Gulf.*

lectīca -ae, f. (lectus), *a palanquin or litter;* lecticā octophoro ferri, *a litter borne by eight slaves,* Cic.; cubare in lectica, Cic.

lectīcārĭus -ii, m. (lectica), *a litter-bearer, porter, chairman,* Cic.

lectīcŭla -ae, f. (dim. of lectica), *a small litter;* **1,** gen., lecticulā in curiam deferri, Cic.; **2,** *a bier,* Nep.

lectĭo -ōnis, f. (2. lego). **I.** *a picking out, selecting;* judicum, Cic. **II. A.** *a reading, perusal;* librorum, Cic.; lectio sine ulla delectatione, Cic. **B.** lectio senatus, *a reading out or calling over of the names of the senators* (by the censor, who at the same time struck from the list the names of those he considered unworthy), Liv.

lectisternĭum -ii, n. (lectus and sterno), *a feast offered to the gods, in which their images were placed on couches in the streets, and food put before them,* Liv.

lectĭto, 1. (intens. of 2. lego), *to read often, to read with eagerness and attention;* Platonem studiose, Cic.

lectĭuncŭla -ae, f. (dim. of lectio), *a short reading,* Cic.

Lecton and **Lectum** -i, n. (Λεκτόν), *a promontory in Mysia.*

lector -ōris, m. (2. lego), **1,** *a reader* of a book; aptus ad delectationem lectoris, Cic.; **2,** *a person who reads aloud,* Cic.

lectŭlus -i, m. (dim. of lectus), *a small bed, a bed, couch.* **I.** For sleeping, in lectulis suis mori, Cic. **II.** *a couch* for resting on; **a,** for reading, Cic.; **b,** for dining, stravit pelliculis haedinis lectulos Punicanos, Cic.; **c,** *a funeral bed, bed of state,* Tac.

1. **lectus** -a -um, p. adj. (from 2. lego), **1,** *chosen, selected;* verba, Cic.; **2,** transf., *choice, excellent;* adulescens, Cic.; femina lectior, Cic.; femina lectissima, Cic.

2. **lectus** -i, m. (2. lego), *a bed, couch.* **I.** For sleeping, *a bed;* **1,** gen., cubicularis, Cic.; lecto teneri, *to keep one's bed,* Cic.; **2,** *the marriage-bed;* genialis, Cic. **II.** *a couch* for resting on; **1,** *a dining-couch,* Cic.; **2,** *a funeral couch,* Tib.

Lēda -ae, f. and **Lēdē** -ēs, f. (Λήδη), *the wife of Tyndarus, who bore to Zeus Pollux and Helena, Castor and Clytemnestra.* Hence, adj., **Lēdaeus** -a -um, *of* or *belonging to Leda;* dei, *Castor and Pollux,* Ov.; poet. = *Spartan;* Helena, Verg.

lēgātārius -ii, m. (legatum), *a legatee,* Suet.

lēgātĭo -ōnis, f. (1. lego). **I.** *the sending of an embassy;* **1,** *the office of an ambassador, embassy, legation;* legationem suscipere, *to undertake,* Caes.; obire, Cic.; libera legatio, *permission given to a senator to travel with the privileges, yet without the duties, of an ambassador,* Cic.; votiva, *a* libera legatio, *which had for its object the fulfilment of a vow,* Cic.; **2,** meton., **a,** *the message or answer of an ambassador;* legationem renuntiare, Cic.; or referre, Liv.; **b,** *the persons attached to an embassy;* legatio Romam venit, Cic. **II.** *the office of legatus* (with a general or provincial governor); legationem obire, Cic.

lēgātor -ōris, m. (1. lego), *a testator, one who leaves something by will,* Suet.

lēgātōrĭus -a -um (legatus), *relating to an ambassador* or *legatus;* provincia, Cic.

lēgātum -i, n. (1. lego), *a legacy, bequest;* solutio legati, Cic.

lēgātus -i, m. (1. lego). **I.** *an ambassador;* legatos mittere, Cic. **II.** *a legate;* **a,** *a lieutenant, adjutant, second in command to a general,* Caes.; **b,** *the chief officer of the governor of a province;* legatum sibi legare, Cic.; **c,** in imperial times, *the general* or *governor sent by the emperor to take command of a province,* Tac.

lēgĭfer -fĕra -fĕrum (lex and fero), *law-giving;* Minos, Ov.

lĕgĭo -ōnis, f. (2. lego), *a legion, a division of the Roman army, consisting of ten cohorts of infantry, with an auxiliary force of 300 cavalry, altogether between 4,200 and 6,000 men,* Cic.; duas legiones ibi conscribere, Caes.; transf., **a,** of the troops of other nations, Liv.; **b,** *an army,* Verg.

lĕgĭōnārĭus -a -um (legio), *belonging or relating to a legion;* milites, Caes.; plur. subst., **lĕgĭōnārĭi** -ōrum, m. *legionary troops,* Liv.

lēgĭtĭmē, adv. (legitimus), **1,** *lawfully, legally,* Cic.; **2,** *rightly, properly,* Tac.

lēgĭtĭmus -a -um (lex) **I.** *lawful, legal, legitimate*, dies comitiis habendis, Cic.; controversiae, *legal, decided by law*, Cic. Subst., **lēgĭtĭma** -ōrum, n. *legal usages*, Nep. **II.** Transf., *right, fit, proper, just, appropriate*, numerus, Cic.; poema, Hor.

lĕgĭuncŭla -ae, f. (dim. of legio), *a small legion*, Liv.

1. **lēgo**, 1 (lex) **I. A.** *to send an ambassador*, aliquem, Cic. **B.** *to appoint as legate or second in command*, aliquem Caesari, Cic.; aliquem sibi, Cic. **II.** *to bequeath, leave as a legacy*, aliquid alicui ab aliquo, *to leave a legacy to be paid to the legatee by the heir*, Cic.; alicui pecuniam, Cic.

2. **lĕgo**, lēgi, lectum, 3 (λέγω), *to collect, gather together, to pick*. **I.** Lit., **1**, nuces, Cic.; spolia caesorum, Liv.; mala ex arbore, Verg.; legere ossa, *to collect the bones after a body has been burned*, Cic.; **2**, **a**, fila, of the Parcae, *to wind up, spin*, Verg.; vela, *to furl the sails*, Verg.; **b**, *to steal*, sacra divum, Hor.; **3**, **a**, *to pass or wander through a place*, saltus legit, Ov.; vestigia alicuius, *to follow or trace the footsteps of any one*, Verg.; tortos orbes, *to wander through*, Verg.; of ships, *to coast along*, oram Italiae, Liv.; **b**, *to choose, select, pick out*, judices, Cic.; viros ad bella, Ov.; aliquem in senatum, Cic. **II.** Transf., **1**, *to catch sight of, look at, regard*, omnes adversos, Verg.; **2**, **a**, *to read, peruse*, eos libros, Cic.; apud Clitomachum, *in the works of Clitomachus*, Cic.; partic. subst., **lĕgens** -entis, m. *a reader*, Ov.; **b**, *to read aloud, recite*, volumen suum, Cic.; hence, senatum legere, *to call over the senate, to go over the list of senators* with a view to erase the names of the unworthy, Liv.

lēgŭlējus -i, m. (lex), *a pettifogging lawyer*, Cic.

lĕgūmen -ĭnis, n. (lego), *pulse, or any leguminous plant*, Cic.; esp., *the bean*, Verg.

Lĕlĕges -um, m. (Λέλεγες), *a people, scattered in different places over Greece and Asia Minor*. Hence, **a**, **Lĕlĕgēis** -ĭdis, f. *Lelegean*; **b**, **Lĕlĕgēius** -a -um, *Lelegean*; litora, *coasts of Megara*, Ov.; moenia, *Megara*, Ov.

Lĕmannus (Lĕmānus) -i, m. (with or without lacus), *a lake in the country of the Helvetii, now the Lake of Geneva*.

lembus -i, m. (λέμβος), *a small, swift vessel, cutter, felucca*, Liv.

Lemnĭcŏla -ae, c. (Lemnus and colo), *an inhabitant of Lemnos* (of Vulcan), Lemnicolae stirps, i.e., *Erichthonius*, Ov.

lemniscātus -a -um (lemniscus), *adorned with ribbons*, palma, *a palm-branch ornamented with ribbons, the reward of a victor*, Cic.

lemniscus -i, m. (λημνίσκος), *a fillet, or ribbon given in token of honour*, usually affixed to a crown, palm-branch, etc., Liv.

Lemnŏs (-us) -i, f. (Λῆμνος), *the island of Lemnos in the Aegean Sea, the abode of Vulcan*. Hence, **a**, adj., **Lemnĭus** -a -um, *Lemnian*, Lemnius pater, Verg.; and subst., Lemnius, *Vulcan*, Ov.; furtum, *that of Prometheus, who stole fire from Vulcan at Lemnos*, Cic.; **b**, **Lemnĭās** -ădis, f. *a Lemnian woman*, Ov.; Greek dat. plur., Lemniasi, Ov.

Lemonĭa tribus, *a Roman country tribe on the via Latina*.

Lĕmŏvīces -um, m. *a Celtic people in the modern Limousin*.

lĕmūres -um, m. *the shades or spirits of the dead, ghosts, spectres*, Hor. Hence, **Lĕmūrĭa** -ōrum, n. *a festival held, to appease departed spirits, on the ninth of May*, Ov.

lēna -ae, f. (leno), **1**, *a procuress, bawd*, Ov.; **2**, *she that entices*, natura quasi sui lena, *enticing persons to her*, Cic.

Lēnaeus -a -um (Ληναῖος), *Bacchic*; latices, *wine*, Verg.; Lenaeus pater, or simply Lenaeus, *Bacchus*, Verg.

lēnĕ, adv. (lenis) = leniter, *gently, softly*, lene sonantis aquae, Ov.

lēnīmen -ĭnis, n. (lenio), *a means of alleviation, mitigation, assuaging*, testudo laborum dulce lenimen, Hor.

lēnīmentum -i, n. (lenio), *a mitigation, alleviation*, Tac.

lēnĭo -īvi and -ĭi, ītum, 4 (lenis), *to make mild, alleviate, mitigate, assuage, soothe, relieve*. **I.** Lit., stomachum latrantem, Hor.; vulnera, Prop. **II.** Transf., se consolatione, Cic.; aliquem iratum, Cic.; desiderium crebris epistolis, Cic. (imperf., lenibat, lenibant, Verg.)

lēnis -e, *smooth, soft, mild, gentle*. **I.** Lit., sensus judicat lene asperum, Cic.; venenum, *slight*, Cic.; vinum, *mellow*, Hor.; ventus lenissimus, Cic.; clivus, *rising gradually*, Liv.; stagnum, *flowing gently*, Liv. **II.** Transf., **A.** Populus Romanus in hostes lenissimus, Cic.; leniorem sententiam dicere, Caes. **B.** Of discourse, *mild, calm*, oratio placida, submissa, lenis, Cic.

lēnĭtas -ātis, f. (lenis), *gentleness, softness, mildness*. **I.** Lit., vocis, Cic.; Arar in Rhodanum influit incredibili lenitate, *slowness, gentleness*, Caes. **II.** Transf., **A.** *gentleness, lenity*, animi, Cic.; legum, Cic. **B.** Of discourse, *mildness, calmness*, verborum, Cic.

lēnĭtĕr, adv. (lenis), *softly, gently, gradually, mildly, quietly*. **I.** Lit., arridere, Cic.; iter facere, *slowly*, Caes.; collis leniter editus, or acclivis, *rising gradually*, Caes. **II.** Transf., **A.** *gently, mildly*, alloqui, *in a friendly manner*, Liv. **B.** Of discourse, dicere, Cic.

lēnĭtūdo -ĭnis, f. (lenis), *gentleness, mildness*, in aliquem, Cic.

lēno -ōnis, m. (lenio), *a procurer, pander, allurer, seducer*, Cic.

lēnōcĭnĭum -ii, n. (leno). **I.** *the trade of a procurer or bawd*, Cic. **II.** Transf., **1**, *an enticement, allurement*, Cic.; **2**, *finery in dress*, Cic.; **3**, of discourse, *meretricious ornament*, Tac.

lēnōcĭnor, 1 dep. (leno), *to pursue the trade of a procurer*; hence, transf., **1**, *to flatter basely, be meanly subservient to*, alicui, Cic.; **2**, *to advance, promote, increase*, feritati arte, Tac.

lēnōnĭus -a -um (leno), *relating or belonging to a procurer*, Plaut.

lens, lentis, f. *a lentil*, Verg.

lentē, adv. (lentus), **1**, *slowly*, procedunt, Caes.; currunt, Ov.; **2**, transf., **a**, *without animation, calmly, coolly, patiently*, aliquid ferre, Cic.; respondere, *quietly, phlegmatically*, Cic.; **b**, *deliberately*, lente ac fastidiose probare, Cic.

lentesco, 3 (lenteo) **1**, *to become pliant, soft, sticky*, tellus picis in morem ad digitos lentescit habendo, Verg.; **2**, *to slacken, relax, flag*, lentescunt tempore curae, Ov.

lentiscĭfer -fĕra -fĕrum (lentiscus and fero), *producing the mastich tree*, Ov.

lentiscus -i, f., and **lentiscum** -i, n. *the mastich-tree* (Pistacia lentiscus, Linn.), Cic.

lentĭtūdo -ĭnis, f. (lentus), **1**, *slowness, sluggishness*, Tac.; **2**, *insensibility, apathy*, Cic.

lento, 1 (lentus), *to make flexible, to bend*, lentandus remus in unda, *must be plied*, Verg.

Lentŭlĭtas -ātis, f., v. Lentulus.

1. **lentŭlus** -a -um (dim. of lentus), *somewhat slow (in paying)*, Cic.

2. **Lentŭlus** -i, m. *the name of one of the families of the patrician gens* Cornelia, *the most famous of the members of which were:* **1,** P. Cornelius Lentulus Sura, *a fellow-conspirator with Catiline;* **2,** P. Cornelius Lentulus Spinther, *who proposed the recall of Cicero from exile.* Hence, **Lentŭlitas** -ātis, f. *the family pride of the Lentuli* (a word coined in jest by Cic.).

lentus -a -um, *tough.* **I. 1,** gen., radix, Verg.; **2, a,** *pliant, flexible;* brachia, Hor.; lentior salicis ramis, Ov.; **b,** *sticky, clammy, tenacious;* gluten pice lentius, Cic.; **3,** fig., lentus abesto, *remain long away*, Ov. **II.** Transf., **1,** *slow, motionless, inactive;* marmor (of the sea), *unruffled*, Verg.; lento igne, Ov.; pugna lenta, Liv.; lentiorem facere spem, Ov.; **2, a,** *drawling;* in dicendo, Cic.; **b,** *lingering;* infitiator, *a bad payer*, Cic.; **c,** of character, *sluggish, apathetic, phlegmatic, insensible;* judex, Cic.; nihil illo lentius, Cic.; lentissima pectora, Ov.

lēnuncŭlus -i, m. (for lembunculus, dim. of lembus), *a small boat*, or *skiff*, Caes.

1. **lĕo** -ōnis, m. (λέων), *a lion;* **1,** lit., vis leonis, Cic.; **2,** transf., *the constellation Leo*, Hor.

2. ***leo** -ēre, *to blot out;* the root of deleo, letum, etc.

Lĕōcŏrĭon -ii, n. (Λεωκόριον), *temple at Athens to the three daughters of Leos, who sacrificed their lives for their country.*

Lĕōn -ontis, m. (Λέων), *a place in Sicily not far from Syracuse.*

Lĕōnĭdās -ae, m. (Λεωνίδας), *king of Sparta, killed at the defence of the pass of Thermopylae.*

lĕōnīnus -a -um (leo), *of* or *relating to a lion, leonine*, Plaut.

Lĕonnātus -i, m. (Λεοννάτος), *a general of Alexander the Great.*

Lĕontīni -ōrum, m. (Λεοντῖνοι), *a town on the east coast of Sicily.* Hence, adj., **Lĕontīnus** -a -um, *Leontine.*

Lĕontĭum -ii, f. (Λεόντιον), *an Athenian hetaira*, friend of Epicurus.

lĕpĭdē, adv. (lepidus). **I.** *pleasantly, agreeably, charmingly, capitally, prettily;* lepidissime, *excellently*, Plaut. **II.** Of style, *smartly, wittily*, Cic.

1. **lĕpĭdus** -a -um, **1,** *pleasant, charming, agreeable, elegant, neat, pretty*, Ter., Plaut.; in a bad sense, *nice, effeminate;* hi pueri tam lepidi ac delicati, Cic.; **2,** esp. of discourse, *witty, humorous;* dictum, Hor.

2. **Lĕpĭdus** -i, m. *the name of a family of the patrician gens Aemilia, the most famous members of which were:* **1,** M. Aemilius Lepidus, *praetor in Sicily, consul* B.C. 79, *the bitter enemy of Sulla, whose measures he proposed to annul, and thereby brought about a civil war;* **2,** M. Aemilius Lepidus, *Triumvir with Antonius and Octavianus*, B.C. 43.

Lĕpontĭi -ōrum, m. *an Alpine people in Cisalpine Gaul* (in modern *Val Leventina*).

lĕpor and **lĕpos** -ōris, m. **1,** *pleasantness, agreeableness, charm*, Cic.; **2,** of discourse, *pleasantry, wit, humour;* scurrilis, Cic.

lĕpos -ōris = lepor (q.v.).

Leptis -ptis, f. (Λέπτις), *Leptis, the name of two cities on the coast of Africa:* **1,** Magna, now *Lebida;* **2,** Minor, between Hadrumetum and Thapsus. Hence, **Leptĭtāni** -ōrum, m. *the inhabitants of Leptis.*

lĕpus -ŏris, m. and c. (akin to λαγώς), **1,** *a hare*, Verg.; prov., aliis leporem agitare, *to labour for another's advantage*, Ov.; **2,** *the constellation Lepus*, Cic.

lĕpuscŭlus -i, m. (dim. of lepus), *a little hare*, Cic.

Lerna -ae, f. and **Lernē** -ēs, f. (Λέρνη), *a marsh in Argolis, inhabited by the Lernaean Hydra slain by Hercules;* belua Lernae, Verg.; hence, adj., **Lernaeus** -a -um, *Lernaean.*

Lesbos -i, f. (Λέσβος), *an island in the Aegean Sea, birthplace of Pittacus, Alcaeus, Theophrastus, Arion, and Sappho, famous for its wine.* Hence, adj., **a, Lesbĭăcus** -a -um, *Lesbian;* libri (*dialogues of Dicaearchus*), Cic.; **b, Lesbĭas** -ădis, f. *Lesbian;* subst., *a Lesbian woman*, Ov.; **c, Lesbĭs** -ĭdis, f. *Lesbian;* lyra, *of Arion*, Ov.; Lesbis puella, or simply Lesbis, *Sappho*, Ov.; **d, Lesbĭus** -a -um, *Lesbian;* civis, *Alcaeus*, Hor.; plectrum, *lyric*, Hor.; pes, *lyric poetry*, Hor.; vates, *Sappho*, Ov.; subst., **Lesbĭum** -ii, n. *Lesbian wine*, Hor.; **e, Lesbōus** -a -um, *Lesbian.*

lessus, acc. -um (found only in acc. sing), m. *a mournful cry, lamentation for the dead*, ap. Cic.

lētālis -e (letum), *deadly, mortal, fatal;* arundo, Verg.

lēthargĭcus -a -um (ληθαργικός), *drowsy, lethargic.* Subst., **lēthargĭcus** -i, m. *a drowsy, lethargic person*, Hor.

lēthargus -i, m. (λήθαργος), *drowsiness, lethargy*, Hor.

Lēthē -ēs, f. (Λήθη), *a river in the infernal regions, the drinking of the waters of which produced complete forgetfulness of the past.* Hence, adj., **Lēthaeus** -a -um, **1,** *relating to Lethe* or *the infernal regions generally;* Lethaea vincula abrumpere alicui, *to restore to life*, Hor.; **2,** *causing forgetfulness;* somnus, Verg.; sucus, Ov.

lethum, v. letum.

lētĭfĕr -fĕra -fĕrum (letum and fero), *death-bringing, deadly, fatal, mortal;* arcus, Verg.; locus, *a place on the body where a wound is fatal*, Ov.

lēto, 1. (letum), *to kill, slay*, Ov.

Lētōis, Lētōĭus = Latois, Latoius (v. under Lato).

lētum -i, n. (*leo, whence deleo), **1,** *death;* turpi leto perire, Cic.; letum sibi parĕre manu, *to commit suicide*, Verg.; leto adimere aliquem, *to save from death*, Hor.; **2,** transf., of things, poet., *ruin, annihilation;* Teucrûm res eripe leto, Verg.

Leucădĭa -ae, f. (Λευκαδία), and **Leucăs** -ădis, f. (Λευκάς), *an island of the Ionian Sea, with a temple to Apollo* (now *S. Maura*). Hence, adj., **Leucădĭus** -a -um, *Leucadian;* deus, *Apollo*, Ov.; more Leucadio (in allusion to the Leucadian custom of throwing a man every year from a rock into the sea), Ov.; subst., **Leucădĭa** -ae, f. *name of a play of Turpilius*, Cic.; **Leucădĭi** -ōrum, m. *the Leucadians*, Liv.

Leucăs -ădis, f. (Λευκάς), **1,** *the island of Leucadia or its capital;* **2,** = *Leucatas.*

leucaspĭs -idis, f. (λεύκασπις), *having white shields;* phalanx, Liv.

Leucātās -ae, m. and **Leucātēs** -ae, m. (Λευκάτας), and **Leucăs** -cădis, f. *a promontory of the island Leucadia*, now *Capo Ducato.*

Leucē -ēs, f. (Λευκή), *a town in Laconia.*

Leuci -ōrum, m. *a people in Gallia Belgica.*

Leucippus -i, m. (Λεύκιππος). **I.** Myth., *father of Phoebe and Hilaira, who were carried off by Castor and Pollux.* Hence, **Leucippĭs**

-idis, f *a daughter of Leucippus* **II.** Hist, *a Greek philosopher, disciple of Zeno the Eleatic*

Leucŏpĕtra ae, f *a promontory in Bruttium*, now *Cap dell Armi*

Leucŏphrȳna -ae, f (λευκοφρύνη, i e *with white eyebrows*), *a surname of Diana among the Magnesians*

Leucōsĭa -ae, f (Λευκωσία), *an island near Paestum*, now *Licosia*

Leucŏthĕa ae, f and **Leucŏthĕē** -ēs, f (Λευκοθέα, i e *the white goddess*), *name of Ino, daughter of Cadmus, after she had been turned into a sea-deity, afterwards identified with the old Italian goddess, Matuta*

Leucŏthŏē -ēs, f *daughter of the eastern king Orchamus and Eurynome, beloved by Apollo*

Leuctra -ōrum, n (Λεῦκτρα), *a small town in Boeotia, where Epaminondas defeated the Spartans* Hence, **Leuctrĭcus** -a um, *Leuctrian*

lĕvāmen -ĭnis, n (1 levo), *a mitigation, alleviation, consolation, solace*, quod si esset aliquod levamen, id esset in te uno, Cic

lĕvāmentum -i, n (1 levo), *alleviation, mitigation, solace*, miseriarum, Cic

lĕvātĭo -ōnis, f (1 levo), **1,** *an alleviation, mitigation*, invenire levationem molestiis, Cic, **2,** *a diminution*, vitiorum, Cic

1 **lĕvātus** a -um, v 1 levo

2 **lēvātus (laevatus)** a um, v 2 levo

lĕvĭcŭlus a um (dim of 1. levis), *somewhat vain, light minded*, leviculus noster Demosthenes, Cic

lĕvĭdensis -e (1. levis), *lightly made, of thin texture*, transf, *slight, poor*, munusculum, Cic

lĕvĭpes -pĕdis (1 levis and pes), *light footed*, lepus, Cic

1 **lĕvis** e, *light, not heavy* (opp gravis) **I.** Lit, **1,** as regards weight, pondus, Ov, levis armatura, *light armour*, Caes, and concr = *light-armed soldiery*, Cic, **2,** *light or quick in movement, rapid, swift*, cervus, Verg, hora, *transitory*, Ov, **3,** *gentle, soft, mild*, somnus, Hor **II.** Transf, **1,** *light, trifling, unimportant, insignificant, of small value*, **a,** dolor, Cic, periculum levius, Caes, auditio, *a trifling, unfounded report*, Caes, subst., in levi habere, *to regard as a trifle*, Tac, **b,** of poetry, *light, unambitious* (of love songs, etc), Musa, Ov, **c,** *trivial, slight, insufficient*, levis causa belli, Liv, pecunia levissima, Cic, of persons, levis pauper, *whose credit is gone*, Hor, **2,** *light, mild, gentle*, reprehensio levior, Cic, **3,** *light, fickle, light-minded, unstable, unsteady*, homo, Cic, amicitia, Cic

2 **lēvis** (laevis) e (λεῖος), *smooth* (opp asper) **I.** Lit, **1,** corpuscula, Cic; **2,** **a,** *polished*, pocula, Verg, **b,** poet, *smooth, beardless* juventas, Hor, senex, *bald*, Ov, hence = *youthful*, pectus, Verg, vir, *decked out, spruce*, Ov, **c,** *slippery*, sanguis, Verg **II.** Of style, *flowing, smooth, polished*, oratio, Cic

lĕvĭsomnus a -um (1 levis and somnus), *lightly sleeping*, Lucr

1 **lĕvĭtas** -ātis, f (1. levis), *lightness* **I.** Lit, **1,** *lightness of weight*, armorum, Caes, **2,** *lightness in movement*, Lucr **II.** Transf, **1,** *lightness, levity, fickleness, changeableness, inconstancy*, levitatem alicuius experiri, Cic, levitatem insectari, Cic, **2,** *groundlessness*, opinionis, Cic

2 **lēvĭtas** -ātis, f (2 levis), **1,** *smoothness*, speculorum, Cic, **2,** *smoothness, polish (of style)*, Aeschini, Cic

lĕvĭtĕr, adv. (1 levis), **I.** *lightly, not heavily, softly*, levius casura pila sperabat, Caes **II.** Transf, **1,** *slightly, not much, somewhat* saucius, Cic, aegrotare, Cic, ut levissime dicam, *to speak in the mildest way*, Cic, **2,** *lightly, with equanimity*, ferre, Cic

1 **lĕvo,** 1 (1 levis) *to raise, lift up, elevate* **I.** Lit., se attollere ac levare, Liv, de caespite virgo se levat, Ov **II.** Transf, **1,** *to lighten make light, relieve from a weight*, ego te fasce levabo, Verg, aliquem metu, Cic, se aere alieno, *to free*, Cic, **2,** *to relieve, support, console, alleviate, mitigate*, curam et angorem animi mei, Cic, **3,** *to refresh, strengthen*, fessos corporis artus, Hor, **4,** *to diminish, weaken, impair*, fidem, Hor, auctoritatem, Cic

2 **lēvo,** 1 (2 levis), *to make smooth, polish* corpus, Cic, transf, of discourse, aspera, Hor

lēvor -ōris, m (2 levis), *smoothness*, Lucr

lex, lēgis, f (2 lego), *a set form of words* **I.** *a proposition made by a magistrate to the people, bill* **A.** Lit, legem ferre, rogare, *to propose a bill to the people*, Cic, sciscere, jubere (of the people), *to accept* or *pass a bill*, Cic, repudiare, antiquare, *to reject, throw out a bill*, Cic, promulgare, *to publish*, Cic **B.** *a law, legal enactment*, **1,** **a,** legem ferre, *to pass a law, enact*, Liv, abrogare, *to repeal*, Cic, leges duodecim tabularum, *the laws of the Twelve Tables, drawn up by the Decemvirs*, Cic, lege, legibus, used adv = *legally, according to law*, Nep, lege agere, (α) of the lictor, *to execute a sentence*, Liv, (β) *to bring an action*, Cic, lex est Lacedaemoniis or apud Rhodios (foll by ut and the subj), Cic, **b,** meton, (α) *law as written* (opp mores, consuetudo), Cic (β) *law generally*, including positive and natural law, Cic, **2,** *a law set by a man to himself*, legem sibi statuere, Cic, **3,** **a,** *a rule, principle, precept*, leges philosophiae, historiae, Cic, versibus est certa lex, Cic, **b,** *manner, way, nature, kind* ex lege loci, Ov, **c,** *order*, sine lege, *without order, irregularly* equi sine lege ruunt, Ov **II.** **A.** *a formula*, Manilianas venalium vendendorum leges ediscere, Cic **B** *a contract, covenant, agreement*, lex operi faciundo, *a building contract*, Cic, legem alicui scribere, Cic, leges pacis, *conditions of peace* Liv, hominis ea lege natos, *on these terms, on this condition*, Cic

Lexovii ōrum, m *a people of Gallia Lugdunensis on the Sequana* (Seine), whence the modern *Lisieux*

lībāmen -ĭnis, n (libo), **1,** *a libation, offering of wine made to the gods at a sacrifice*, Verg **2,** transf, *what is first taken, a sample, specimen*, in nova servatae carpes libamina famae, Ov

lībāmentum i, n (libo), *a libation*, Cic

lībātĭo ōnis, f (libo) *a libation*, Cic

lībella ae, f (dim of libra) **I.** **1,** *a small coin, 1-10th of a denarius, equal in value to the* as, prov, *a very small sum of money, a farthing, a mite*, hence, ad libellam, *exactly*, Cic, **2,** transf, heres ex libella, *heir to the whole property* (cp ex asse), Cic **II.** *a carpenter's level*, Plin

lĭbellus i, m (dim of liber), *a little book* **I.** scripsi etiam illud quodam in libello, Cic, pl meton, = *a bookseller's shop*, Cat **II.** Esp, **a,** *a note-book, memorandum book, diary*, retulit in libellum, Cic, **b,** *a memorial, a petition*, libellum composuit, Cic, **c,** *a note of invitation, programme*, gladiatorum libelli, Cic, **d,** *a placard, hand bill*, e g, announcing the sale of goods, dejicere libellos, *to put off the sale*, Cic, **e,** *a letter*, Cic, **f,** *a satire, a libel*, Suet

lĭbens and **lŭbens** -entis, p adj (libet), **1,** *willing, with good will, with pleasure*, libenti animo, *willingly*, Cic.; me libente, *with my goodwill*, Cic.; **2,** *joyful, pleased, glad*, Plaut., Ter.

lĭbentĕr (lŭbentĕr), adv. (libens, lubens), *willingly, with pleasure*; libenter uti verbo Catonis, Cic.; nusquam libentius cenare, *with better appetite*, Cic.; libentissime dare, Cic.

lĭbentĭa (lŭbentĭa) -ae, f. (libens, lubens), *cheerfulness, gladness*, Plaut.; personif., **Libentĭa** -ae, f. *the goddess of mirth*, Plaut.

Lĭbentīna (Lŭbentīna) -ae, f. (libens, lubens), *a name of Venus, as the goddess of sensual pleasure.*

1. **līber** -ĕra -ĕrum, *free.* **I. A.** *of free birth* (opp. servus), aliquem non liberum putare, Cic.; of states, *free, independent*; civitas, Caes.; subst., **līber** -eri, m. *a freedman*, Cic. **B.** Transf., **1,** *free from tax or tribute*; agri, Cic.; **2,** of houses and places, *free from inhabitants*; aedes, *uninhabited*, Liv.; **3,** *unencumbered with debt*; ut rei familiaris liberum quidquam sit, Cic. **II.** *free from fetters.* **A.** Lit., Plaut. **B.** Transf., **1,** *free from anything, without*; a delictis, Cic.; curā, Cic.; **2,** *free from restraint, unbridled*; **a,** adolescentia, Cic.; toga, vestis, *the toga virilis*, Ov.; custodia, *surveillance, confinement to a single house or town*, Cic.; fenus, *unlimited by law*, Liv.; liberum habere aliquid, *to have in complete possession*, Liv.; liberum est mihi, foll. by infin., *I am free to do*, Cic.; **b,** *free in thought* or *expression*; animus, Cic.; liberiores litterae, Cic.; **3,** *morally free*; **a,** *in the philosophical sense*, Cic.: **b,** in a bad sense, = *profligate, unbridled, unrestrained*; turba temulentorum, Cic.

2. **līber** -bri, m. **I.** *the inner bark of a tree*, Verg. **II.** And, as this was used by the ancients as a material upon which to write, *a book, writing, treatise*; **a,** librum inchoare, conficere, Cic.; libri Sibyllini, Cic.; nos autem in libris (*account books*) habemus, Cic.; **b,** *a book, a division into which a work is divided*; tres libri de Natura Deorum, Cic.; **c,** *a register, catalogue*, Cic.; **d,** *a letter*, Nep.

3. **Līber** -ĕri, m. **1,** *an old Italian deity, presiding over agriculture, and in later times identified with the Greek Bacchus*; **2,** meton., *wine*, Hor.

4. **līber** -ĕri, v. liberi -ōrum.

Lībĕra -ae, f. (3. Liber), **1,** *Proserpina, daughter of Ceres, sister of Liber*; **2,** *Ariadne, wife of Bacchus.*

Lībĕrālĭa -ium, n. (3. Liber), *the festival of Liber on the 17th of March, at which youths received the toga virilis*, Cic.

līběrālis -e (1. liber). **I.** *relating to freedom*; causa, *a lawsuit in which the freedom of some person is the matter in dispute*, Cic. **II.** *becoming or suitable to a freedman, noble*; **1,** mens, Cic.; artes liberales, *liberal arts, such as a freedman ought to be versed in*, Cic.; sumptus, *expenses to keep up station and appearances* (opp. necessarii), Cic.; **2, a,** *kind*; responsum, Cic.; **b,** *liberal, generous, giving freely*, Cic.; laudis avidi, pecuniae liberales erant, Sall.

līběrālitas -ātis, f. (liberalis), **1,** *a noble disposition or character, kind, friendly disposition*, Cic.; **2,** *liberality, generosity*, Cic.

līběrālitěr, adv. (liberalis), *in a manner becoming a freedman.* **I.** *nobly, becomingly*; vivere, Cic. **II.** Esp., **a,** *in a friendly manner, kindly, liberally*; liberalissime erat pollicitus omnibus, Cic.; **b,** *richly, bountifully*, Cic.

līběrātio -ōnis, f. (libero), **1,** *a setting free, releasing from*; culpae, Cic.; **2,** *a legal acquittal*, Cic.

līběrātor -ōris, m. (libero), *one who sets free, a liberator*; patriae, Cic.; attrib., liberator populus, Liv.

līběrē, adv. (1. liber). **I.** *like a freeman, liberally*, Ter. **II. 1,** *freely, without restraint, without hindrance*; vivere, Cic.; respirare, Cic.; **2, a,** *spontaneously*; tellus omnia liberius ferebat, Verg.; **b,** *frankly, openly, boldly*; loqui, Cic.

līběri -ĕrōrum and -ĕrum, m. (1. liber), **1,** *children*; liberos procreare, liberis operam dare, *to beget children*, Cic.; **2,** *the young of animals*, Plaut.

līběro, 1. (1. liber), *to set free, liberate.* **I.** From slavery, *to manumit*; aliquem, Cic. **II.** *to set free* from something that fetters. **A.** *to set free, liberate, deliver, release*; te ab eo vindico ac libero, Cic.; divinus animus liberatus a corpore, Cic.; aliquem culpā, Cic.; aliquem periculo, Caes.; obsidionem urbis, *to raise*, Liv. **B. 1,** *to set free from a debt* or *engagement*; aliquem, Cic.; aliquem eodem illo crimine, Cic.; with genit. of the debt or fault, aliquem culpae, Liv.; **2,** templa liberata, *having a free prospect, free from buildings which obstruct the view*, Cic.

līberta -ae, f., v. libertus.

lībertas -ātis, f. (1. liber). **I.** *freedom, liberty* (opp. slavery). **A.** Lit., **1,** se in libertatem vindicare, Cic.; **2, a,** *civil liberty*, as containing certain rights; ad usurpandam libertatem vocare, *to summon to the voting*, Cic.; libertatem eripere, *to take away political privileges*, Liv.; **b,** *national freedom, independence*; libertatem capessere, Cic.; perdere, Cic.; recipere, Cic. **B.** Transf., **1,** *freedom, liberty of action, freedom from restraint*; **a,** vivendi, loquendi, Cic.; dat populo libertatem ut quod velint faciant, Cic.; **b,** *licence*, Cic.; **2,** *freedom of speech, frankness, candour*; multa cum libertate dicere, Cic. **II.** Libertas, *personified as the goddess of Freedom, having a temple on the Aventine Hill*, Cic.

lībertīnus -a -um (libertus), *of or relating to the class of freedmen*, Cic.; hence, subst., **lībertīnus** -i, m. *a freedman*, Cic.; **lībertīna** -ae, f. *a freedwoman*, Hor.

lībertus -a -um (for liberatus), *placed in freedom*; subst., **a, lībertus** -i, m. *a freedman*, Cic.; **b, līberta** -ae, f. *a freedwoman*, Cic.

lĭbet (lŭbet) -būit or -bĭtum est, 2. impers., *it pleases, is agreeable*; mihi, tibi, etc., or absol., facite quod libet, Cic.; non libet plura scribere, Cic.

Lībēthra (Λειβῆθρα) -ōrum, n. and **Lībēthrus** -i, m. (Λειβηθρός), *a Thessalian spring, sacred to the Muses*; hence, adj., **Lībēthris** -ĭdis, f. nymphae Libethrides, *the Muses*, Verg.

lĭbīdĭnōsē, adv. (libidinosus), *lustfully, wilfully, wantonly*, Cic.

lĭbīdĭnōsus -a -um (libido), *full of desire, wilful, wanton, lustful*; homo, Cic.; caper, Hor.; applied to abstract things, libidinosissimas liberationes, Cic.; sententia, Cic.

lĭbīdo (lŭbīdo) -ĭnis, f. (libet), *violent desire, appetite, longing.* **I.** ad libidinem, *according to inclination*, Cic.; ex libidine, Sall.; libidine, *wantonly, out of mere caprice*, Cic.; libidinem habere in armis, *to take pleasure in*, Sall. **II. 1,** *immoderate or unrestrained desire, self-will, wilfulness, wantonness*; alicuius libidini adversari, obsistere, Cic.; libidines refrenare, Cic.; **2,** *sensual desire, lust, lewdness*; meton., libidines, *obscenities in painting and sculpture*, Cic.

Lĭbĭtīna -ae, f. **I.** *the goddess of corpses, in whose temple the requisites for a funeral were kept for hire, and the register of deaths was preserved.* **II.** Meton., **1,** *the requisites for a funeral*; pestilentia tanta erat, ut Libitina vix sufficeret, Liv 2, *death*, multaque pars mei vitabit Libitinam, Hor

lībo, 1 (λείβω) **I.** *to take away from* **A.** a natura deorum libatos animos habemus, Cic **B. 1,** *to taste* poem, Liv, hence **a,** *to touch*, cibos digitis, Ov, **b,** oscula natae, *to kiss*, Verg, **2,** *to pour a libation in honour of a god*, in mensam, Verg, **3,** *to sacrifice, offer, consecrate* diis dapes, Liv, frugem Cereri, Ov. **II.** *to diminish or injure by taking away*, vires, Liv

lībra -ae, f (λιτρα) **I.** *a balance, pair of scales*, **1, a,** lit, librae lanx, Cic, per aes et libram, aere et libra, *a fictitious form of sale used in making wills, adopting sons*, etc mercari aliquid aere et libra, *in due form*, Hor, **b,** meton, *the Roman pound of 12oz*, **2,** *the constellation called the Balance*, Verg **II.** *a level, a plummet level*, ad libram fecisse turres, Caes

lībrāmen inis, n (libro), *balance, poise*, Liv

lībrāmentum i, n (libro) **I.** *that which gives a thing a downward motion*, **a,** *weight*, Liv, **b,** *that which gives a missile its impetus*, tormentorum, *the thong*, Tac. **II.** Transf, *a horizontal plane, flat superficies*, Cic

lībrārĭa -ae, f (libra), *a female who weighed out the wool to the slaves*, Juv

lībrārĭŏlus -i, m (dim of librarius), **1,** *a transcriber, copyist, secretary*, Cic, **2,** *a bookseller*, Cic

lībrārĭum -ii, n, v librarius

lībrārĭus a -um (2 liber), *of or relating to books* **I.** Adj, taberna, *a bookshop*, Cic **II.** Subst, **1, lībrārĭus** -ii, m *a transcriber of books, a copyist*, Cic, **2, lībrārium** -ii, n *a place to keep books in, a bookcase*, Cic

lībrātor -ōris, m (libro) **1,** *a leveller or surveyor*, Plin, **2,** *one who hurls missiles by means of a machine*, Tac

lībrātus -a -um, p adj (from libro), *well-poised, swung, hurled with force*, glans, Liv, ictus, Liv

lībrīlis -e (libra), *of a pound weight*, fundae libriles, *slings, the stones of which weighed a pound*, Caes

lībro, 1 (libra), **a,** *to poise, keep in equilibrium*, terra librata ponderibus, Cic, **b,** *to swing, hurl, launch, brandish*, glandem, Liv, se, *to poise oneself in the air* (of bees), Verg, poet, corpus in herba, *to stretch out*, Ov, **c,** *to keep suspended, keep in its place*, vela librantur ab aura, Ov

lībs, libis, m (λίψ), *a west-south-west wind*, Plin

lībum -i, n *a cake offered to the gods, especially on a birthday*, Ov, Verg

Lĭburni ōrum, m *the Liburnians, a people inhabiting the modern Croatia*, sing, Liburnus, *a Liburnian slave*, Juv Hence, adj, **a, Lĭburnus** a -um, *Liburnian*, subst, **Liburna** ae, f *a light vessel of war, schooner, brigantine*, Caes, **b, Lĭburnĭcus** -a um, *Liburnian*

Lĭbўa -ae, f and **Lĭbўē** -ēs, f (Λιβύη), *Libya, the Northern part of Africa* Hence, **1, Lĭbўcus** -a -um, *Libyan*, fera, *lioness*, Ov, **2, Lĭbys** yos, *Libyan*, subst, Libys, *a Libyan*, Ov, **3, Lĭbyssa** -ae, f *Libyan*, arenae, Cat, **4, Lĭbystis** -idis, f *Libyan* ursa, Verg, **5, Lĭbўus** a -um, *Libyan*, **6, Lĭbystīnus** a um, *Libyan*.

Lĭbўphoenīces -um, m (Λιβυφοίνικες), *a Libyan people, descended from the Phoenicians, in Byzacium*.

lĭcens -entis **I.** Partic of liceor (q v). **II.** P adj (licet), *free, unrestrained, unbridled* Lupercus, Prop, of things, licentior dithyrambus, Cic

lĭcentĕr, adv (licens), *freely, according to one's own pleasure*, and in a bad sense, *boldly, impudently, unrestrainedly*, Cic, et dissoluta se, currere, *to wander on without rule or order*, Cic

lĭcentĭa -ae, f (licet), *freedom or permission to do what one pleases, leave, licence, liberty* **I.** pueris non omnem ludendi damus licentiam, Cic, tantum licentiae dabat gloria, Cic **II.** Esp, **a,** *freedom from restraint, licence* poetarum, Cic, verborum, Ov, **b,** *dissoluteness, licentiousness* comprimere hominum licentiam, Cic, personif, Licentia, as a goddess, *Licence*, Cic

lĭcĕo -ŭi -ĭtum, 2 *to be on sale, to be valued at, to be estimated at a price*, quanti licuisse tu scribis hortos *at what sum they were valued*, Cic

lĭcĕor citus sum 2 (liceo) *to bid for, offer a price for*, liciti sunt usque eo, Cic, followed by acc, hortos, Cic

lĭcet cŭit or citum est, 2, impers and intransit **I** *it is allowed, allowable, one can or may, one is at liberty*, with dat of pers or absol, **a,** with infin, as subject, licet rogare? *may I ask?* Cic, licet intelligi, *one can understand*, Cic, with acc and infin, nos frui liceret, Cic, with dat of predicate, Themistocli licet esse otioso, Cic, with acc of predicate, civi Romano licet esse Gaditanum, Cic, **b,** with a neuter pronoun or adj as subject, quid deceat vos, non quantum liceat vobis, spectare debetis, Cic, **c,** with subj, fremant omnes licet Cic, sequatur licebit, *he may follow*, Cic, with per and the acc, per me licet, *as far as I am concerned*, Cic **II.** Transf, *granted that, allowed that*, foll by the subj, omnia licet concurrant, Cic

Lĭchās -ae, m (Λίχας), *a servant of Hercules*

lĭchēn -ēnis, m (λειχήν), *moss or lichen*, Plin

Lĭcĭnĭus a -um, *name of a Roman gens, the most celebrated members of which were* **1,** C Licinius Crassus, *tribune of the people*, **2,** L Licinius Crassus *a celebrated orator*, **3,** M Licinius Crassus, *the triumvir*.

lĭcĭtātĭo ōnis, f (licitor), *a bidding, bid, at a sale or auction*, Cic

lĭcĭtor, 1 dep (intens of liceor), *to bid for*, Plaut

lĭcĭtus -a um (licet), *allowed, permitted*, sermo, Verg, neut. plur subst, *things permitted*, Tac

lĭcĭum ii, n *the thrum, or remnant of old web to which the weaver attaches the new fabric*, telae licia addere, Verg, in general, *a thread*, Ov

lictor ōris, m *a lictor*, plur lictores, *the lictors, the public attendants of the principal Roman magistrates, who bore before them the fasces as emblem of their criminal jurisdiction, and executed the sentences which they pronounced* Of these lictors, the dictator was attended by twenty-four, a consul by twelve, and a praetor by six lictor proximus, *the one nearest to the consul*, Cic

lĭen -ēnis, m or **lĭēnis** -is, m *the milt, or spleen*, Plaut

lĭēnōsus -a -um (lien), *splenetic*, Plaut

lĭgāmen inis, n (1 ligo), *a string, tie, bandage*, Ov

lĭgāmentum i, n (1 ligo), *a bandage*, Tac

Lĭgārĭus a -um, *the name of a Roman gens, the most famous member of which was* Q Ligarius, *a member of the Pompeian party, taken prisoner after the battle of Thapsus, and banished by Caesar*, *afterwards pardoned, defended by Cicero.* Hence, adj., **Lĭgārĭānus** -a -um, *relating to Ligarius;* oratio, Cic.; and subst., **Lĭgārĭāna** -ae, f. *Cicero's speech on behalf of Ligarius,* Cic.

Lĭgēa -ae, f. (Λίγεια, *the clear-voiced*), *name of a wood-nymph.*

Lĭgŏr -gĕris, m. *a river on the borders of Aquitania and Gallia Lugdunensis,* now the *Loire* (acc. Ligerem and Ligerim; abl. Ligere and Ligeri, Caes).

lignārĭus -ĭi, m. (lignum), *a carpenter;* inter lignarios, *in the wood-market,* Liv.

lignātĭo -ōnis, f. (lignor), *a felling of timber, wood-cutting,* Caes.

lignātor -ōris, m. (lignor), *a wood-cutter,* Caes.

lignĕŏlus -a -um (dim. of ligneus), *wooden,* Cic.

lignĕus -a -um (lignum), **1,** *made of wood, wooden;* ponticulus, Cic.; **2,** transf., *like wood, dry;* conjux, Cat.

lignor, 1. dep. (lignum), *to fetch wood;* lignari pabularique, Caes.

lignum -i, n. **I.** *wood,* esp., *firewood* (opp. materia, *wood used for building*); ignem ex lignis viridibus in loco angusto fieri jubere, Cic; prov., in silvam ligna ferre, *to carry coals to Newcastle,* Hor. **II.** Meton., **1,** *a writing-table of wood,* Juv.; **2,** = *a tree,* Verg.

1. **lĭgo,** 1. **I.** *to bind, tie;* aliquem vinculo, Tac.; manus post terga, Ov.; pisces in glacie ligati, *frozen fast,* Ov.; *to bind up, bandage;* vulnera veste, Ov. **II. 1, a,** *to harness;* mulam, Hor.; **b,** laqueo guttura, *to tie up, to bind around,* Ov.; **2,** transf., *to bind together, connect, unite;* dissociata locis concordi pace ligavit, Ov.

2. **lĭgo** -ōnis, m. **1,** *a hoe,* Hor.; **2,** meton., *tillage,* Juv.

lĭgŭla (lingŭla) -ae, f. (dim. of lingua). **I.** *a little tongue,* and hence, *a tongue of land, promontory,* Caes. **II.** *a shoe-strap,* Juv.

Lĭgŭres -um, m. *the Ligurians, a people in modern Piedmont;* sing., **Lĭgŭs (Lĭgŭr)** -gŭris, c. *a Ligurian;* adj. = *Ligurian.* Hence, **1, Lĭgŭrĭa** -ae, f. *the country of the Ligures;* **2, Lĭgustĭcus** -a -um, *Ligurian;* **3, Ligustinus** -a -um, *Ligurian.*

lĭgūrĭo (ligurrĭo), 4. (lingo), **1,** *to lick, lick up;* jus, Hor.; furta, *to feed upon, gloat over stealthily,* Hor.; **2,** *to lust after, long for;* lucra, Cic.

lĭgurrītĭo -ōnis, f. (ligurrio), *daintiness,* Cic.

Lĭgus -gŭris, m., v. Ligures.

Lĭgustĭcus -stinus, v. Ligures.

lĭgustrum -i, n. *privet,* Verg.

līlĭum -ĭi, n. (λείριον), *a lily;* **1,** lit., Verg.; **2,** transf., milit. t. t., *a kind of fortification consisting of low palisades,* Caes.

Lĭlўbaeŏn (-baeum) -i, n. (Λιλύβαιον), *a promontory in the west of Sicily,* now *Capo di Boco,* with a town of the same name. Adj., **a, Lĭlўbaeus** -a -um, **b, Lĭlўbēĭus** -a -um, and **c, Lĭlўbaetānus** -a -um, *Lilybaean.*

līma -ae, f. (limo), *a file,* Plaut.; fig., of style, *polishing, revision, correction;* defuit et scriptis ultima lima meis, Ov.

līmātē, adv. (limatus), *elaborately, elegantly,* Cic.

līmātŭlus -a -um (dim. of limatus), *polished, refined;* opus est huc limatulo et polito tuo judicio, Cic.

līmātus -a -um, p. adj. (limo), *polished, refined, elegant;* genus librorum limatius, Cic.

limbus -i, m. *a border, hem, selvage, fringe round the edge of a robe,* Verg.

līmen -inis, n. (connected with 1. limus and obliquus), *the threshold.* **I. A.** Lit., intrare limen, Cic. **B.** Meton., **1** = *house, dwelling;* limine contineri, Liv.; limine pelli, Verg.; **2,** *entrance;* in limine portus, Verg.; **3, a,** *the starting-point of a chariot-race in the circus;* limen relinquunt, Verg.; **b,** *border, boundary;* extra limen Apuliae, Hor. **II.** Fig., *a beginning;* belli, Tac.

līmes -ĭtis, m. (1. limus), *a cross path or by-way.* **I. A.** Lit., *the boundary between two fields indicated by a path or stone,* Verg. **B.** Meton., **1,** *a boundary-line;* partiri limite campum, Verg.; fig., *a distinction, difference;* judicium brevi limite falle tuum, Ov.; **2,** *a fortified boundary-line,* Tac. **II.** *a pathway, road;* Appiae, Liv.; acclivis, Ov.; transversus, Liv.; solitus limes fluminis, *river-bed,* Ov.; sectus, *the zodiac,* Ov.; quasi limes ad caeli aditum patet, Ov.

Limnaeum -i, n. (Λιμναία), *a town in Acarnania.*

Limnātĭs -tĭdis, f. (Λιμνᾶτις), *a surname of Diana, as the patroness of fishermen.*

līmo, 1. (lima), **I.** *to file;* **1,** lit., gemmas, Plin.; **2,** *to whet, sharpen,* Plaut.; **3,** fig., **a,** *to polish, finish;* quaedam institui, quae limantur a me politius, Cic.; **b,** *to investigate accurately;* veritatem, Cic. **II.** *to file off;* fig., *to take away from, to diminish;* alteri affinxit, de altero limavit, Cic.

līmōsus -a -um (2. limus), *slimy, miry, muddy;* lacus, Verg.; planities, Sall.

limpĭdus -a -um (connected with liquidus), *clear, limpid, pellucid;* lacus, Cat.

1. **līmus** -a -um (connected with limen and obliquus), of the eyes, *sidelong, looking sideways;* ocelli, Ov.

2. **līmus** -i, m. (lino), **1,** *slime, mud, mire,* Cic.; fig., malorum, Ov.; **2,** *dirt, filth,* Hor.

3. **līmus** -i, m. (1. ligo), *an apron trimmed with purple, worn by a priest when offering sacrifice,* Verg.

Lĭmўra -ōrum, n. (Λίμυρα, τά), and **Lĭmўra** -ae, f. or **Lĭmўrē** -ēs, f. (Λιμύρα, ἡ), *a town in the south of Lycia on the river Limyrus* or *Limyra.*

1. **linctus,** partic. of lingo.

2. **linctus** -ūs, m. (lingo), *a licking, taste,* Lucr.

Lindŏs and **-dus** -i, f. (Λίνδος), *a town in Rhodes.*

līnĕa -ae, f. (linum), *a linen thread.* **I.** Lit., **A.** Plin.; linea dives, *a string of pearls,* Mart. **B.** *a carpenter's plumb-line,* Cic.; lineā discere uti, Cic.; ad lineam, *exactly straight or perpendicular,* Cic. **II.** Transf., *a line made with a pen or pencil, geometrical line.* **A.** Gen., lineam scribere, Cic. **B. 1,** *a boundary-line in the circus, a starting-point or goal;* fig., si quidem est peccare tanquam transilire lineas, Cic.; mors ultima linea rerum est, *the final goal,* Hor.; **2,** *the line in the theatre by which the seats were separated;* cogit nos linea jungi, Ov.

līnĕāmentum -i, n. (linea), *a line drawn with pen or pencil, a geometrical line.* **I.** Lit., in geometria lineamenta, Cic. **II.** Transf., **1,** pl., *a drawing, delineation, sketch, outline;* tu operum lineamenta sollertissime perspicis, Cic.; **2,** *a feature, lineament;* corporis, Cic.

līnĕus -a -um (linum), *made of linen, linen;* vincula, Verg.; lanterna, Cic.

lingo, linxi, linctum, 3. (λείχω), *to lick,* Cat.

Lingŏnes -um, m. *a people in Gaul,* whence the modern *Langres.*

lingua ae, f *a tongue* **I. A.** Lit, linguam ab irrisu exserere, Liv, linguam ejicere, Cic **B.** Meton, **1,** *speech, language*, linguam diligentissime continere, *to restrain*, Cic, Aetolorum linguas retundere, *to silence*, Liv, transf, of the sounds of animals, linguae volucrum, Verg, **2, a,** *a language, tongue*, Latina, Cic, Gallica, Caes, utraque lingua, *Greek and Latin*, **b,** *a dialect*, disciplinis linguique divisa, Cic, **3,** *readiness of speech, eloquence*, est animus tibi, sunt mores et lingua fidesque, Hor, in a bad sense, *loquacity;* poenam linguae commeruisse, Ov, or *boasting*, Ov, or *bold talk*, Ov **II.** Transf, of tongue shaped objects, *a tongue of land, promontory*, Liv, tribus haec (Sicilia) excurrit in aequora linguis, Ov

linia, v linea

liniamentum, v lineamentum

liniger gera gerum (linum and gero), *clothed in linen*, applied to Isis and her priests, Ov

lino, livi and levi, litum, 3 **I.** *to smear upon, spread over*, medicamenta per corpora, Ov **II.** *to besmear, anoint*, **1,** spiramenta cerā, Verg, **2, a,** *to cover*, labra alicui, *to cheat, cozen*, Mart, tecta auro, Ov, **b,** *to rub over with the blunt end of the stylus what has been written on waxen tablets*, digna lini, *worthy of being erased*, Ov; **c,** *to besmear, dirty* ora luto, Ov, fig, splendida facta carmine foedo, Hor

linquo, liqui, 3 (λείπω), *to leave* **I.** Gen, **A.** Lit, socios ignotae terrae, Verg **B.** Transf, **1,** *to leave, give up, abandon*, haec, Cic, severa, Hor, **2,** with double acc, nil intentatum, Hor **II.** *to leave, depart from*, urbem, Cic, linqui, *to faint*, Ov, linquere dulces animas, *to die*, Verg

lintĕātus -a -um (linteum), *clothed in linen*, legio, *a Samnite legion, so called from the canvas covering of the place where they took the military oath*, Liv

lintĕŏlum -i, n (dim of linteum), *a small linen cloth*, Plaut.

linter tris, f **I.** *a boat, skiff, wherry*, prov, loqui e lintre (of an orator who sways his body up and down in speaking), ap Cic **II.** Transf, *a trough, tray, tub, vat*, used in the vintage, Verg

lintĕus a um (linum), *linen, made of linen*, vestis, Cic, libri, *written on linen*, Liv Subst, **lintĕum** i, n *linen cloth, linen*, merces linteis delatae, Cic, esp, *a sail*, dare lintea ventis, Ov

lintrĭcŭlus -i, m (dim of linter), *a small boat*, Cic

līnum -i, n (λίνον), *flax, linen* **I.** Lit, linum tenuissimum, Cic **II.** Meton, **1,** *a thread, line*, **a,** *the thread with which letters were tied up*, nos linum incidimus, legimus, Cic, **b,** *a fishing-line*, Ov, **2,** *a linen-cloth or garment*, Hor, **3,** *a rope, cable*, Ov, **4,** *a net for hunting or fishing*, Ov, Verg

Līnus (-ŏs) i, m (Λίνος), *Linus*. **I.** *son of Apollo and Psamathe, daughter of the Argive king, Crotopus, torn in pieces by dogs* **II.** *son of Apollo and the Muse Terpsichore, celebrated singer and poet, the teacher of Orpheus and Hercules, the latter of whom killed him with a blow of the lyre*

Lĭpăra ae, f and **Lĭpărē** ēs, f (Λιπάρα), *the largest of the Aeolian islands, north of Sicily*, now *Lipari*, plur, Liparae, *the Aeolian islands* Adj, **a, Lĭpăraeus** a um, **b, Lĭpărensis** -e, *Liparean*

lippio, 4 *to have sore eyes, be blear-eyed*, quum leviter lippirem, Cic

lippĭtūdo inis, f (lippus), *inflammation in the eyes*, Cic

lippus -a um, *having inflamed or watery eyes, blear eyed*, Hor, *sand-blind, half blind*, Juv

lĭquĕfăcĭo -fēci -factum, 3, pass, liquĕfīo factus sum fĭeri (liqueo and facio), *to melt, dissolve, make liquid* **I.** Lit, **1,** glacies liquefacta, Cic, **2,** *to putrefy*, viscera liquefacta, Verg **II.** Transf, *to make weak, enervate*, aliquem languidis voluptatibus, Cic

lĭquĕo, liqui or licŭi 2 (λείβω) **I.** *to be fluid, liquid*, concrescendi, liquendi, Cic, hence partic, liquens, *fluid, liquid*, vina, Verg, campi *the sea*, Verg **II** Transf, *to be clear, to be evident, apparent*, **a,** dixit sibi liquere, Cic, with accus and infin, cui neutrum licuerit nec esse deos nec non esse, Cic, **b,** legal t t, non liquet, *a phrase used by the jury when they declined to pronounce the accused person either innocent or guilty*, Cic

lĭquesco, licŭi, 3 (inchoat of liqueo), *to become fluid, to melt* **I.** Lit, **1,** cera liquescit, Verg **2,** *to putrefy*, liquescunt corpora, Ov **II** Transf, **1,** *to become effeminate* voluptate, Cic, **2,** *to melt or waste away* liquescit fortuna, Ov

lĭquĭdē, adv, with compar and superl (liquidus), *clearly, plainly, positively*, liquidius negare, Cic

lĭquĭdo, v liquidus

lĭquĭdus -a -um (liqueo), *fluid, flowing, liquid* **I. A.** Lit, odores, Hor, Nymphae, *nymphs of springs*, Ov **B.** Transf, genus sermonis, Cic **II.** *clear, bright*, **A.** Lit, fontes, Verg, aer, Verg, vox, Verg **B.** Transf **1,** *pure, clear*, liquida voluptas et libera, Cic, **2,** *calm*, mens, Cat, **3,** *clear, certain*, Plaut Subst, **lĭquĭdum** -i, n *certainty*, Liv, adv, liquido, *clearly, plainly*, dicere, Cic

lĭquo, 1 *to make liquid melt, liquefy* **I.** Lit, Cic poet **II.** *to strain, percolate, clarify*, vinum, Hor

1 **lĭquor,** 3 dep *to be fluid be liquid, flow, melt*, toto corpore sudor liquitur, Verg, transf, *to melt away, pass away;* in partem pejorem liquitur aetas, Lucr

2 **lĭquor** -ōris, m (liqueo), *liquidity, fluidity* **I.** Lit, Cic **II** Meton, *a liquid, fluid, liquor*, perlucidi amnium liquores, Cic, absol, *the sea*, Hor

Līrĭŏpē -ēs, f (Λειριόπη), *a sea-nymph, mother of Narcissus*

Līris is, acc -em and im, abl -i, m (Λεῖρις), *a river of Latium, flowing into the Sinus Cajetanus*, now the *Garigliano*

līs (old form, stlis), litis, f *a contention, strife, controversy, quarrel* **I.** Gen, aetatem in litibus conterere, Cic, lites eorum sedare, Cic, componere, *to settle*, Verg, discernere, *to decide*, Verg **II.** *a legal contention or controversy, an action, suit*, **1,** lit, litem alicui intendere, in aliquem inferre, *to bring an action against*, Cic, litem habere cum aliquo, Cic, litem suam facere, said of an advocate who neglects his client's business to defend himself, Cic, **2,** meton, *the subject or cause of a suit*, litem in rem suam vertere Liv litem lite resolvere, *to illustrate one obscure point by another*, Hor

Lissus -i, f *town in the south of Dalmatia*, now *Alessio*, or *Lesh*

Lĭtăna silva -ae f *a forest in Cisalpine Gaul where the Romans were defeated by the Gauls*, 216 A C

lĭtātĭo ōnis, f (lito), *an auspicious offering, successful sacrifice*, hostiae majores sine litatione caesae, Liv

lĭtĕra (littĕra) -ae, f. (1. lino), *a letter of the alphabet.* **I.** Lit., literarum notae, Cic.; homo trium literarum = fur, *a thief,* Plaut.; literae grandes, *uncial characters,* Cic.; tristis (C), which stood upon the balloting tickets for Condemno, salutaris (A), for Absolvo, Cic.; literas discere, *to learn to read,* Cic.; ad me literam nunquam misit, *not a line,* Cic.; literis parcere, *to be sparing with paper,* Cic. **II.** Meton., **A.** Sing., litera; **1,** *handwriting;* ad similitudinem literae tuae, Cic.; **2,** poet. for plur. literae, **a,** *a letter,* Ov.; **b,** *an epitaph,* Ov.; **c,** *a bond,* Ov. **B.** Plur. literae, *that which is written;* **1,** *written records;* quod parvae et rarae per eadem tempora literae fuere, Liv.; **2, a,** *writing, document, deed, contract;* litteras conquirere, Cic.; **b,** *a letter, private* or *official despatch, edict, decree, epistle;* dare alicui literas ad aliquem, *to give to a messenger a letter for a third person,* Cic.; liber literarum missarum et allatarum, *a book of letters despatched and received,* Cic.; **c,** *literature, letters, science, culture;* literis omnibus a pueritia deditus, Cic.; literis tinctus, Cic.

lĭtĕrārĭus -a -um (litera), *relating to reading and writing;* ludus, *an elementary school,* Tac.

lĭtĕrātē, adv. (literatus). **I.** *distinctly, clearly, legibly;* literate et scite perscriptae rationes, Cic. **II. 1,** *literally, word for word;* respondere, Cic.; **2,** *learnedly, scientifically;* dicta, Cic.

lĭtĕrātor -ōris, m. (litera), *a philologist, grammarian, critic.*

lĭtĕrātūra -ae, f. (literae). **I.** *a writing composed of letters:* **a,** *that which is written,* Cic.; **b,** *the alphabet,* Tac. **II.** *culture, learning, scholarship,* Sen.

lĭtĕrātus -a -um (literae). **I.** *lettered, inscribed with letters;* servus, *branded,* Plaut. **II.** *learned, liberally educated;* Canius nec infacetus et satis literatus, Cic.; transf., otium, *learned leisure,* Cic.

Līternum -i, n. *a town in Campania, north of the mouth of the river Liternus,* now *Patria.* Adj., **a, Līternus** -a -um; **b, Līternīnus** -a -um, *Liternian.* Subst., **Līternīnum** -i, n. *an estate near Liternum.*

lĭtĕrŭla -ae, f. (dim. of litera). **I.** *a little letter* (of the alphabet), literulae minutae, Cic. **II.** Plur., literulae, **1,** *a little letter, note,* Cic.; **2,** *letters, literature, literary and scientific culture,* Cic.

lĭtĭcen -cĭnis, m. (lituus and cano), *a trumpeter, clarion-blower,* Cic.

lĭtĭgātor -ōris, m. (litigo), *a party in a lawsuit, litigant,* Cic.

lĭtĭgĭōsus -a -um (litigium), *full of strife, contentious.* **I.** With comp. and superl., *fond of dispute, litigious;* homo minime litigiosus, Cic. **II.** Of things, **a,** *full of dispute, quarrelsome;* disputatio, Cic.; **b,** *contested at law;* praediolum, Cic.

lĭtĭgĭum -ii, n. (litigo), *a quarrel, contention,* Plaut.

lĭtĭgo, 1. (for litem ago), *to quarrel, dispute, brawl.* **I.** Gen., acerrime cum aliquo pro aliquo, Cic. **II.** Esp., *to go to law;* noli pati fratres litigare, Cic.

lĭto, 1. **I.** Intransit., **A.** *to bring an acceptable offering, to make an auspicious* or *accepted sacrifice, to obtain favourable omens;* alicui deo, Cic.; litemus Lentulo, *to appease, make an atonement to,* Cic.; with abl. of the sacrifice, proximā hostiā litatur saepe pulcherrime, Cic.; litato (abl. absol.), non auspicato nec litato aciem instruunt, *without having offered an auspicious sacrifice,* Liv. **B.** Of the victim, *to give a favourable omen, promise success;* victima nulla litat, Ov. **II.** Transit., *to sacrifice successfully;* sacris litatis, Verg.

lĭtŏrālis -e (litus), *of* or *relating to the shore;* dii, *gods of the shore,* Cat.

lĭtŏrĕus -a -um (litus), *of* or *belonging to the shore;* arena, Ov.; aves, Verg.

littĕra, etc., v. litera, etc.

lĭtūra -ae, f. (lino). **1,** *the drawing of the blunt end of the stylus over the waxen tablet to erase what has been written, an erasure, correction;* flagitiosa litura tabularum, Cic.; **2,** meton., *the passage erased;* nomen esse in litura, Cic.; poet. transf., *a blot,* Ov.

littus, etc., v. litus, etc.

lītus (littus) -tŏris, n. (lino). **I. 1,** *the seashore, beach, strand, coast;* litus insulae, Cic.; naves agere in litus, Liv.; prov., litus arare, *to plough the shore, to labour in vain,* Ov.; in litus arenas fundere, *to carry coals to Newcastle,* Ov.; **2,** *the sea-coast, territory near the coast;* cui litus arandum dedimus, Verg. **II.** Transf., *the shore of a lake,* Ov.; *of a river,* Cic.

lĭtŭus -i, m. (lito). **I.** *the curved staff* or *wand of an augur,* Cic. **II.** Transf., *a curved trumpet, clarion,* Cic.

līvens -entis, p. adj. (from liveo), **1,** *lead-coloured, bluish-grey;* plumbum, Verg.; crura compedibus, *livid, black and blue,* Ov.; **2,** *envious,* Mart.

līvĕo, 2. **1,** *to be of a bluish colour,* Ov.; **2,** transf., *to be envious, to envy;* alicui, Tac.

līvesco, 3. (liveo), *to become bluish, grow livid,* Lucr.

līvĭdŭlus -a -um (dim. of lividus) *somewhat envious,* Juv.

līvĭdus -a -um (liveo), *bluish, blue.* **I.** Lit., racemi, Hor.; vada (of the Styx), Verg.; esp. from blows, *livid, black and blue;* brachia, Hor. **II.** Transf., *envious, malicious, spiteful;* differ opus, livida lingua, tuum, Ov.; oblivio, Hor.

Līvĭus -a -um, *name of a Roman gens, the most celebrated members of which were:* **1,** C. or M. Livius, *surnamed Salinator, because of the salt-tax which he introduced when censor;* **2,** Livius Andronicus, of Tarentum, *slave of Livius Salinator, Roman tragic and comic poet;* **3,** T. Livius Patavinus, of Padua, *the great Roman historian, born 59* A.C., *died 16* A.D.; **4,** Livia Drusilla, *the second wife of the Emperor Augustus;* **5,** Livia Orestilla, *wife of the Emperor Caligula.* Adj., *Livian;* lex, Cic.; hence, **Līvĭānus** -a -um, *Livian;* fabulae, *of Livius Andronicus,* Cic.; exercitus, *of the consul M. Livius,* Liv.

līvor -ōris, m. (liveo), **1,** *a bluish colour, livid spot on the body;* niger livor in pectore, Ov.; **2,** *envy, spite, malice;* ap. Cic.

lixa -ae, m. *a sutler,* Liv.; plur., **lixae** -ārum, m. *camp-followers of every kind,* Sall.

lŏcātĭo -ōnis, f. (loco), *a letting out to hire, leasing;* **a,** lit., Cic.; **b,** meton., *a contract of letting and hiring, a lease,* Cic.

lŏcellus -i, m. (dim. of loculus), *a compartment in a chest,* Caes.

lŏcĭto, 1. (intens. of loco), *to let out to hire,* Ter.

lŏco, 1. (locus), *to place, lay, put, set.* **I.** Gen., **1,** lit., castra, Cic.; milites super vallum, Sall.; fundamenta urbis, Verg.; **2,** transf., *to place;* homines in amplissimo gradu dignitatis, Cic. **II.** Esp., **A.** *to give in marriage, bestow in marriage;* virginem in matrimonium, Plaut. **B. a,** *to let out to hire, to farm out taxes;* vectigalia, portorium, fundum, Cic.; agrum campanum fruendum, Liv.; with abl. of the price, agrum frumento, *for a tenth part of the produce,* Liv.; subst.,

lŏcātum -i, n *that which is let out to hire*, Cic, b, hence, *to give out on contract*, statuam faciendam, Cic.; c, *to hire out, let one's services on hire*, se, Plaut. C. *to lend money at interest*, Plaut., sc locare, *to yield an interest, profit*, disciplina quae erat ab hoc tradita locabat se non minus, etc, *produced no less than*, etc, Cic, fig, beneficia apud gratos, Liv (locassint for locaverint, Cic)

Lŏcri -ōrum, m (Λοκροί), 1, *the inhabitants of Locris, in Greece* Hence, a, **Lŏcrenses** -ium, m *the Locrians*, b, **Lŏcris** -idis and -idos, f *a Locrian woman*, Cat., *the country Locris*, Liv; 2, *the name of a town in Lower Italy, in Bruttium, with the name Epizephyrii, and also of its inhabitants, the Locrians*

lŏcŭlus -i, m (dim of locus), *a little place* Esp, 1, *a coffin*, Plin; 2, plur, loculi, *a box or chest containing many divisions, a coffer, casket*, nummum in loculos demittere, Hor

lŏcŭples -plētis (locus and * pleo) I. *possessing large landed property*, Cic II. *rich, wealthy, opulent*; 1, lit, a, of persons, mulier copiosa plane et locuples, Cic, with abl, copiis rei familiaris locupletes et pecuniosi, Cic, b, of things, villa tota locuples est, Cic, annus locuples frugibus, Hor. aquila, *the lucrative post of centurion*, Juv, 2, transf, a, *rich, abounding in*, Lysias oratione locuples, *of copious eloquence*, Cic, b, *credible, trusty, sufficient, satisfactory*, auctor, Cic, testis, Cic, tabellarius, Cic. (abl sing locuplete and gen (in Cic always) locupleti, genit plur locupletium, Cic, locupletum, Caes.).

lŏcŭplēto, 1 (locuples), *to enrich*, homines fortunis, Cic, templum picturis, Cic, transf, sapientem locupletat ipsa natura, Cic

lŏcus -i, m (plur loci, *single places*, loca, *places connected with one another, neighbourhood, region*) I. *a place* A. Gen., 1, lit, omnes copias in unum locum convenire, Cic, ex loco superiore agere, of a speaker from the rostra or of a judge who gives judgment from the bench; ex aequo loco, of a speaker in the senate, Cic; ex inferiore loco, of a pleader in a court of justice, Cic, 2, fig, locum dare, *to give occasion*, consilio, suspicioni, Cic, often with partic genit, quo loci, Cic, eo loci, Cic, so, a, *the right or proper place or occasion*, nec vero hic locus est, ut multa dicantur, Cic; dulce est desipere in loco, *in the right place*, Hor, b, *place in the order of succession*, secundo loco, *secondly*, Cic; loco dicere, *in his turn*, Cic, c, *position, degree, rank*, esse ex equestri loco, Cic, infimo loco natus, Cic; loco, with the genit, *in the place of*, alicui parentis loco esse, Cic B. Esp, 1, t t, of military or pugilistic language, *place, ground, post*, locum tenere, relinquere, Cic, fig, loco movere, *drive from one's position*, Cic., 2, *place, part of a book*, aliquot locis significavit, Cic., 3, loci, *means of proof*, locos nosse, Cic 4, *a piece of ground, an estate*, Cic; 5, a, *a dwelling, house*, loca et lautia, Liv, b, *place = town*; opportunitas loci, Cic, c, *neighbourhood*, ea loca incolere, Caes II. Transf, 1, *time*, a, ad id locorum, *up to that time*, Sall, b, *opportunity, occasion*, si est ullus gaudendi locus, Cic, 2, *condition, situation*, meliore loco erant res nostrae, Cic.

1. **lōcusta (lūcusta)** -ae, f 1, *a locust*, locustarum examina, Liv; 2, *a kind of lobster or crab*, Plin.

2. **Lōcusta** -ae, f *a woman in Rome, notorious for her skill in poisoning the contemporary and accomplice of Nero*

lŏcūtĭo (lŏquūtĭo) -ōnis, f (loquor), 1, *a speaking, speech*, Cic, 2, *pronunciation*, Cic

lōdix -dīcis, f *a rough blanket, rug, counterpane*, Juv

lŏgēum -ēi, n. and **lŏgĭum** -ii, n (λογεῖον and λόγιον), *archives*, Cic

lŏgĭca -ae, f and **lŏgĭcē** -ēs, f (λογική, sc τέχνη), *logic*, Cic

lŏgĭcus -a -um (λογικός), *logical*, subst, **lŏgĭca** -ōrum, n *logic*, Cic

lŏgos (-us) -i, m (λόγος), 1, *a word*, Plaut, 2, *a joke, jest, bon mot*, Cic

lōlīgo, v. lolligo

lŏlium -ii, n *darnel, cockle, tares*, Verg

lollīgo -ginis, f. *a cuttle fish*, Cic

Lollius a -um, *name of a Roman gens*, hence, **Lolliānus** -a -um, *Lollian*

lōmentum -i, n (lavo), *an unguent for the purpose of smoothing the skin, made of bean-meal and rice*, Mart, *a means of cleansing*, ap Cic

Londinium (Lundinium) -ii, n *London*

longaevus -a -um (longus and aevum), *aged, old*, parens, Verg, manus, Ov

longē, adv (longus), *long* I. In space A. *a long way off, far off, at a distance*, 1, lit, longe absum, Cic, longe videre, Cic, discedere, Cic; longe lateque, *far and wide*, Cic, 2, fig, a, *far off* longissime abesse a vero, Cic, ab aliquo longe abesse, *not to help*, Caes, b, *far*, longe dissimilis contentio, Cic; longe dissentire, with compar and superl, *by far* longe melior, Verg, longe maximus, Cic B. *from afar*, agnoscere regem, Verg, fig, tam longe repetita principia, *far-fetched*, Cic II. Transf, of time, *long, for a long time, far*, aetate longius provectus, Cic

longinquĭtas -ātis, f (longinquus) I. Lit, *length*, 1, itineris, Tac; 2, *distance, remoteness*, Cic II. Transf, of time, *length, duration*, temporum, Cic, morbi, Cic, bellorum, Liv

longinquus -a -um (longus), *long* I. Lit, 1, amnes, Tac, 2, a, *distant, far, remote*, hostis, Cic; Lacedaemon, Cic; e (ex) longinquo, *from a distance*, Tac., b, *living at a distance, foreign*, homo alienigena et longinquus, Cic, c, *standing at a distance*, Cic II. Transf, of time, 1, *long in duration, long*, observatio, Cic, morbus, Cic, 2, *distant*, in longinquum tempus aliquid differre, Cic

Longīnus -i, m *the name of a family of the gens* Cassia, v Cassius

longĭtĕr, adv (longus), *far*, ab leto errare, Lucr

longĭtūdo -inis, f (longus), *length* I. Lit, itineris, Cic II. Transf, *length of time*, noctis, Cic, orationis, Cic

longĭuscŭlus -a -um (dim of compar. longior), *somewhat long*, versus, Cic.

Longŭla -ae, f *a Volscian town not far from Corioli*

longŭlē, adv. (longulus), *somewhat far off, at a little distance*, ex hoc loco, Plaut

longŭlus -a -um (dim of longus), *somewhat long*, iter, Cic

longŭrius -ii, m (longus), *a long pole, rod, rail*, Caes

longus -a -um, *long* I. Lit, 1, gen, a, of things, epistola, Cic, spatium, Caes, navis *a man-of-war*, Liv, versus, *the hexameter*, ap Cic; with acc of length, ratis longa pedes centum, Liv, b, of persons, Cic, longus homo est, Cat, 2, esp poet., *vast, spacious*, freta, Ov, pontus, Hor II. Transf, of time, 1, gen, *long, of long duration, tedious*, horae quibus expectabam longae videbantur, Cic, longa mora, Cic, with acc., mensis XLV dies longus, Cic.; longum est dicere, *it is tedious to relate*, Cic.; ne longum sit, ne longum faciam, *to make a long story short, in brief*, Cic.; nihil est mihi longius, *I can hardly wait*, Cic.; in longum, *for a long time*, Verg.; ex longo, *for a long time back*, Verg.; as applied to persons, *prolix, tedious*; nolo esse longus, Cic.; **2**, esp., **a**, of syllables, *long*; syllaba, Cic.; **b**, *far-seeing, looking far into the future*; spes, Hor.; poet. transf., of persons, longus spe, *hoping to live long*, Hor.

lŏquācĭtas -ātis, f. (loquax), *talkativeness, loquacity*; mea, Cic.

lŏquācĭtĕr, adv. (loquax), *loquaciously, talkatively*; respondere, Cic.

lŏquācŭlus -a -um (dim. of loquax), *somewhat talkative*, Lucr.

lŏquax -quācis (loquor), *talkative, garrulous, loquacious*; **1**, of persons, homo omnium loquacissimus, Cic.; **2**, of animals, ranae, *croaking*, Verg.; **3**, transf., of things, nidus, *full of nestlings*, Verg.; stagna, *full of frogs*, Verg.; lymphae, *babbling*, Hor.; epistola, *gossiping*, Cic.; vultus, *expressive*, Ov.

lŏquēla (lŏquella) -ae, f. (loquor). **I.** *a speaking, speech, discourse*, Plaut. **II.** Transf., **1**, *a word*; fundit has ore loquelas, Verg.; **2**, *a speech, language*; Graja, Ov.

lŏquĭtor, 1. dep. (intens. of loquor), *to speak*, Plaut.

lŏquor, lŏcūtus (lŏquūtus) sum, 3. dep. (connected with λέγω), *to speak*. **I.** Intransit., *to speak* (of conversation; dicere, of an orator); **1**, lit., bene loqui de aliqua re, de aliquo, Cic.; cum aliquo, Cic.; pro aliquo (either = *in defence of* or *in the name of some one*), Cic.; apud (*before*) aliquem, Cic.; **2**, transf., ut consuetudo loquitur, Cic. **II.** Transit., **1**, *to say*; quid loquar de militari ratione, Cic.; loquuntur, *they say*, with acc. and infin., Cic.; **2**, *to talk of, speak of constantly*; classes, Cic.; proelia, Hor.; **3**, *to tell, mention*; pugnantia, Cic. (archaic locuntur = loquuntur, Cic.).

lōrātus -a -um (lorum), *bound with thongs*, Verg.

lōrĕus -a -um (lorum), *made of thongs*, Plaut.

lōrīca -ae, f. (lorum). **I.** *a leather cuirass, corselet*, Cic.; transf., libros mutare loricis, *to exchange study for war*, Hor. **II.** Milit. t.t., *a breastwork, parapet*, Caes.

lōrīco, 1. (lorica), *to arm with a corselet or cuirass*; gen. partic., **lōrīcātus** -a -um, *armed with a cuirass*, Liv.

lōrum -i, n. *a strap or thong of leather*. **I.** Lit., esp. for binding, quum apparitor Postumium laxe vinciret, 'Quin tu,' inquit, 'adducis lorum,' Liv. **II.** Meton., **1**, *the girdle of Venus*, Mart.; **2**, *a rein*; loris ducere equos, Liv.; lora dare, *to relax the reins*, Verg.; **3**, *a scourge, whip*; loris uri, Hor.; loris caedere aliquem, Cic.; **4**, *a leathern bulla* (v. bulla), Juv.

Lōtŏphăgi, genit. -phăgōn, m. (Λωτοφάγοι), myth., *the Lotus-eaters, a people in Africa*.

lōtŏs (-us) -i, f. (λωτός). **I.** *the Egyptian lotus*, Plin. **II.** *a tree growing in North Africa, said to have been the food of the Lotus-eaters*; transf., *the fruit of the lotus*, Ov.; meton., *a flute made of the lotus-tree wood*, Ov. **III.** m. and f. *an Italian plant* (Diospyros Lotos, Linn.), Cic. **IV.** *a plant used for fodder*, Verg.

1. **lōtus** -a -um, v. lavo.

2. **lōtus** -i, f., v. lotos.

Lŭa -ae, f. *a goddess to whom arms captured in war were dedicated*.

lŭbet, lubido, etc. = libet, libido, etc. (q.v.).

lūbrĭco, 1. (lubricus), *to make smooth or slippery*, Juv.

lūbrĭcus -a -um, *slippery*. **I.** Gen., **A.** Lit., glacies, Liv.; neut. subst., **lūbrĭcum** -i, n. *a slippery place*, Tac. **B.** Transf., *slippery, uncertain, insecure, tottering, perilous*; aetas puerilis maxime lubrica atque incerta, Cic.; lubrica defensionis ratio, Cic.; poet. with infin., vultus nimium lubricus aspici, *dangerous to look upon*, Hor.; in lubrico versari, Cic. **II.** Transf., **A.** *smooth, slimy*; anguis, Verg. **B.** *quickly moving, fleeting*; **1**, lit., amnis, Hor.; **2**, transf., annus, *quickly passing*, Ov.

1. **Lūca** -ae, f. *town in Etruria* (now *Lucca*). Hence, adj., **Lūcensis** -e, *of Luca*.

2. **Lūca,** v. Lucani.

Lūcāni -ōrum, m. (Λευκανοί), *an Italian people in Lower Italy*, and meton. = *the country of the Lucani*, Caes.; sing., Lucanus, collective, Liv. Hence, **1**, adj., **Lūcānus** -a -um, *Lucanian*; **2**, **Lūcānĭa** -ae, f. *the country of the Lucani*; **3**, **Lūcānĭcus** -a -um, *Lucanian*; subst., **Lūcānĭca** -ae, f. *a kind of sausage*, Cic.; **4**, **Lūca** -ae, m. *Lucanian*; Luca bos, *a Lucanian ox*, i.e., *an elephant*, because the Romans first saw elephants in Lucania with the army of Pyrrhus.

1. **Lūcānus** -a -um, v. Lucani.

2. **Lūcānus** -i, m., M. Annaeus, *a poet, native of Corduba in Spain, contemporary of the Emperor Nero, author of the still extant* Pharsalia.

lūcar -āris, n. (lucus), *the money paid to actors from the treasury, stipend, salary*, Tac.

lūcellum -i, n. (dim. of lucrum), *a little profit, a small gain*; Apronio aliquid lucelli jussi sunt dare, Cic.

Lūcensis, v. Luca.

lūcĕo, luxi, 2. (lux), *to be bright, shine, glitter*. **I.** stella lucet, Cic.; lucent oculi, Ov.; impers., lucet, *it is light, it is daylight, it is day*; nondum lucebat, *it was not yet light*, Cic. **II.** *to shine forth, be plain, evident*; nunc imperii nostri splendor illis gentibus lucet, Cic.; quum res ipsa tot, tam claris argumentis luceat, Cic.

Lūcĕres -um, m. *one of the three tribes into which the Romans of the age of Romulus are said to have been divided*.

Lūcĕrĭa -ae, f. *a town in Apulia* (now *Lucera*). Hence, **Lūcĕrīnus** -a -um, *of Luceria*.

lŭcerna -ae, f. (luceo), *a lamp, oil-lamp*; lumen lucernae, Cic.

lūcesco (lūcisco), luxi, 3. (inchoat. of luceo), *to begin to shine*; **a**, pers., novus sol lucescit, Verg.; cras lucescere Nonas, *appear*, Ov.; **b**, impers., lucescit, *it grows light, day is breaking*, Cic.

lūci = luce, v. lux.

lūcĭdē, adv. (lucidus), *clearly, plainly, lucidly*; definire verbum, Cic.

lūcĭdus -a -um (lux), *full of light, clear, bright, lucid*. **I.** Lit., **1**, amnis, Ov.; sidera, Hor.; adv., lucidum fulgentes oculi, Hor.; **2**, *bright, shining white*; ovis, Tib. **II.** Transf., *clear, plain, lucid*; ordo, Hor.

lūcĭfĕr -fĕra -fĕrum (lux and fero), *light-bearing, light-bringing*. **I.** Adj., **1**, gen., equi, *the horses of the moon*, Ov.; **2**, *bringing to light*; manus (of Lucina), Ov. **II.** Subst., **Lūcĭfĕr** -fĕri, m. *Lucifer, the morning star, the planet Venus*, Cic.; myth., *the son of Aurora, and father of Ceyx*; hence, Lucifero genitus (= *Ceyx*), Ov.; meton., *the day*; tot Luciferi, Ov.

lūcĭfŭgus -a -um (lux and fugio), *shunning the light*; blatta, Verg.; transf., homines, Cic.

Lūcīlĭus -a -um, *name of a Roman gens, the most celebrated members of which were* 1, Qu Lucilius Balbus, *a Stoic philosopher* 2, C Lucilius, *born at Suessa Aurunca*, B C 148, *died* B C 103, *a Roman knight, founder of Roman satiric poetry*

Lūcīna -ae f (lux), *"she that brings to light," the goddess of births, a surname of Juno or of Diana*, meton, *a bearing of children, birth*, Lucinam pati (of the cow), *to calve*, Verg

lūcisco = lucesco (q v)

Lūcĭus -ĭi, m *a common Roman praenomen* (gen abbreviated to L)

lŭcrātīvus -a -um (lucror), *attended with gain, profitable*, sol, Cic

Lŭcrētĭlis -is, m *a mountain in the Sabine country, part of the modern Monte Gennaro*

Lŭcrētĭus -a -um, *name of a Roman gens, the most famous members of which were* 1, Sp Lucretius Tricipitinus, *successor of L Junius Brutus in the consulate*, 2, *his daughter* Lucretia, *who, being ravished by Sextus, the son of Tarquinius Superbus, stabbed herself, and thereby led to the expulsion of the kings from Rome*, 3, T Lucretius Carus, *a Roman poet, contemporary of Cicero, author of the still extant poem* De rerum natura

lŭcrĭfăcio -fēci -factum, 3 (sometimes written separately lucri facio), *to gain, receive as profit*, pecuniam, Cic , tritici modios centum, Cic

lŭcrĭfĭcābĭlis -e, *gainful, profitable, lucrative*, Plaut.

lŭcrĭfĭcus -a -um (lucrum and facio), *gainful, profitable*, Plaut

lŭcrĭfŭga -ae, c (lucrum and fugio), *one who shuns gain*, Plaut

Lŭcrīnus -i, m (with or without lacus), *a lake on the coast of Campania, near Baiae* Hence, adj , a, **Lŭcrīnus** a -um, *Lucrine*, conchylia, Hor , and subst , **Lŭcrīna** -ōrum, n Mart , *Lucrine oysters*, celebrated for their flavour, b, **Lŭcrīnensis** -e, *Lucrine*, res, *oysters*, Cic

lŭcror, 1 dep (lucrum), *to get gain, to gain, profit* (opp perdere) **I.** Lit., auri pondo decem, Cic , stipendium, Cic **II.** Transf , nomen ab Africa, *to win*, Hor ; lucretur indicia veteris infamiae, *I will make him a present of*, i e , *I will say nothing about*, Cic

lŭcrōsus -a -um (lucrum), *full of gain, profitable, lucrative*, Ov

lŭcrum -i, n (cf λαύω), *gain, profit, advantage* (opp damnum) **I.** Lit , lucri causā, Cic , ad praedam lucrumque revocare, *to turn to one's profit*, Cic , ponere in lucro or in lucris, *to reckon a gain*, Cic lucra facere ex vectigalibus, Cic , lucri with dare, facere, addere, conferre, numerare, auferre, *as gain*, Cic , de lucro vivere, *to have to thank some one else for being alive*, Cic **II.** Meton , 1, *the love of gain, avarice*, Hor , 2, *lucre, riches*, Ov

luctāmen -ĭnis, n (luctor), *effort, exertion, struggling, toil*, Verg

luctātĭo -ōnis, f (luctor) **I.** *a wrestling*, Cic **II.** Transf , **A.** *a struggle, contest*, Liv **B.** *a contention in words, dispute, contest*, magna cum aliquo, Cic

luctātor -ōris, m. (luctor), *a wrestler*, Ov

luctĭfĭcus -a -um (luctus and facio), *causing grief, mournful, baleful*, Alecto, Verg

luctĭsŏnus -a -um (luctus and sono), *sorrowfully sounding*, mugitus, Ov.

luctor, 1 dep *to wrestle* **I.** Lit , fulvā arenā, Verg , luctabitur Olympiis Milo, Cic **II. A.** Physically, *to struggle, strive, contend with*, in arido solo, Liv , in turba, Hor with abl , Africus luctatur fluctibus, Hor , foll by infin , telum eripere, Verg **B** Intellectually, *to strive, struggle*, cum aliquo, Cic

luctŭōsē, adv (luctuosus), *mournfully, sorrowfully*, Liv

luctŭōsus -a -um (luctus), *mournful, sorrowful, lamentable, doleful baleful*, o diem illum reipublicae luctuosum, Cic , luctuosissimum bellum, Cic , misera tempora et luctuosa, Cic

luctus -ūs, m (lugeo) **I.** *mourning lamentation, especially for a bereavement* 1, lit , a, luctus domesticus, Cic , luctus publicus privatus, Liv , luctum minuere or levare, Cic , luctum ex aliqua re percipere or haurire, Cic , plur , *expressions of sorrow*, in maximos luctus incidere, Cic , b, *mourning apparel, mourning*, erat in luctu senatus, Cic , 2, meton , *the cause of sorrow*, tu . . . luctus eris levior, Ov **II.** personif , Luctus, *the god of mourning*, Verg

lūcŭbrātĭo -ōnis, f (lucubro), 1, *working by night or lamp-light, nocturnal study*, vix digna lucubratione anicularum, *to be told by old wives while spinning at night*, Cic , plur , lucubrationes detraxi et meridiationes addidi, Cic , 2, meton , *that which is produced by lamp-light, a lucubration*, lucubrationem meam perire, Cic

lūcŭbro, 1 (lux) **I.** Intransit , *to work by night*, inter lucubrantes ancillas sedere, Liv **II.** Transit , *to produce by night, to compose at night*, parvum opusculum, Cic

lūcŭlentē, adv (luculentus), *excellently, admirably, splendidly*, a, opus texere, Cic , ironic , calefacere, Cic , b, of style, *excellently*, scribere, dicere, Cic

lūcŭlentĕr, adv. (luculentus), *excellently, well*, Graece luculenter scire, Cic

lūcŭlentus -a -um (lux) **I.** *full of light, bright*, caminus, Cic **II.** Transf , *distinguished, splendid, excellent*, a, of outward appearance, forma, Ter , b, of importance, extent, plaga, Cic , patrimonium, Cic , c, of reputation, auctor, Cic , d, of style, oratio, Sall , verbis luculentioribus, Cic

Lūcullus -i, m *the name of a family of the gens Licinia* *The most distinguished of the Luculli was* L Licinius Lucullus, *general against Mithridates, notorious for his riches and lavish expenditure* Adj , 1, **Lūcullānus** -a -um 2, **Lūcullēus** -a -um, 3, **Lūcullīānus** -a -um, *Lucullan*

lūcŭlus -i, m (dim of lucus) *a little grove*, Suet

Lŭcŭmo and syncop , **Lucmō** or **Lucmōn** -ōnis, m (Etruscan Lauchme), plur , **Lŭcŭmōnes**, *the magnates of Etruria, who were also priests, an Etrurian prince and priest*, galeritus Lucmon = *an Etrurian*, Prop

1 **lūcus** -i, m *a sacred grove, consecrated wood*, Cic , poet , *a wood*, Verg

2 **lūcus** -ū, m (= lux), *light*, Ter

lūdĭa -ae, f (ludius), 1, *an actress or female dancer*, Mart , 2, *a gladiator's wife*, Juv

lūdĭbrĭum -ii, n (ludo), *derision, mockery, sport, jest* **I.** Lit , alicui esse ludibrio, Cic per ludibrium auditi dimissique, *heard and dismissed with scorn*, Hor **II.** *a laughing-stock plaything*, is ludibrium verius quam comes, Liv , fortunae, Cic , ludibria ventis, Verg

lūdĭbundus -a -um (ludo), 1, *playful, sportive*, Liv 2, transf , *playing*, i e , *with ease, without difficulty or danger*, coelo sereno in Italiam ludibundi pervenimus, Cic

lūdĭcer and **lūdĭcrus** -cra -crum (ludus), *done for sport or recreation, serving as sport or* *recreation, playful, sportive.* **I.** Adj., 1, gen., sermo, Cic.; ars ludicra armorum, Cic.; **2,** esp., *relating to the stage*; ars, *acting*, Cic. **II.** Subst., **lūdĭcrum** -i, n. **1,** gen., *a plaything*, Cat.; **2,** esp., *a theatrical performance, public spectacle*, Liv.

lūdĭfĭcātĭo -ōnis, f. (ludifico), *a making game of, deriding, deceiving*; quum omni morā, ludificatione, calumniā, senatus auctoritas impediretur, Cic.

lūdĭfĭcātor -ōris, m. (ludifico), *one who makes game of another, a derider*, Plaut.

lūdĭfĭco, 1. (ludus and facio), *to make game of, make a mock of, deride, cheat, cozen*; aliquem, Sall.; absol., Cic.

lūdĭfĭcor, 1. dep. (ludus and facio). **I.** *to make game of, make a mock of, deride, delude, cheat*; aliquem, Liv.; absol., Cic. **II.** Transf., *to make vain, frustrate by cunning*; ea quae hostes agerent, Liv.

lūdĭmăgister -tri, m. *a schoolmaster*, Cic.

lūdĭo -ōnis, m. *a pantomimic actor*, Liv.

lūdĭus -ĭi, m. **1,** *a pantomimic actor or dancer*, Cic.; **2,** *a gladiator*, Juv.

lūdo, lūsi, lūsum, 3. *to play*. **I.** Intransit., **A.** Lit., aleā, Cic.; trocho, Hor. **B.** Transf., **1,** *to play, sport, toy*; exempla honesta ludendi, Cic.; in numerum, *to dance*, Verg.; **2,** *to sport, amuse oneself*; lusisti satis, Hor. **II.** Transit., *to play*. **A.** Gen., proelia latronum, *chess*, Ov.; ludum insolentem ludere, Hor. **B.** 1, *to do for amusement, amuse oneself with doing, to play with*; opus, Hor.; causam illam disputationemque, Cic.; **2,** a, *to rally, banter*; aliquem, Cic.; b, *to deceive, delude*, Cic.

lūdus -i, m. *a game, sport, pastime*. **I.** Lit., 1, ludus campestris, Cic.; novum sibi aliquem excogitant in otio ludum, Cic.; dare ludum alicui, Cic.; **2,** esp., **a,** ludi, *public games or spectacles celebrated in honour of the gods*; ludos facere, *to give, celebrate*, Cic.; ludis, *at the time of the games*, Cic.; ludos committere, *to begin the games*, Cic.; b, *a satire*; in Naevii ludo, Cic. **II.** Transf., **A.** *a game, a child's game, a trifle*; illa perdiscere ludus esset, Cic. **B.** *a sport, jest, joke*; per ludum et jocum, Cic. **C.** *a place where the body or mind is exercised, a school*; gladiatorius, *for training gladiators*; esp., *a school for learning the elements of knowledge*, Cic.; ludus literarum, Liv.; ludum habere, *to keep a school*, Cic. (archaic form loedus, Cic.).

lŭēla (lŭella) -ae, f. (luo), *punishment, expiation*, Lucr.

lŭēs -is, f. (luo), *a plague, pestilence, contagious disease*, Verg.; transf., a, a word of reproach for criminals, *pest, plague*, Cic.; b, *any wide-spreading* or *universal calamity, destruction, war*, Tac.; *earthquake, tempest*, Tac.

Lugdūnum -i, n. *town on the north border of* Gallia Narbonensis *and* Gallia Lugdunensis (now *Lyons*). Adj., **Lugdūnensis** -e.

lūgĕo, luxi, luctum, 2. **I.** Intransit., *to mourn, be in mourning* (as shown by cries and outward signs, while maereo = *to be dejected*); luget senatus, Cic.; lugere pro aliquo, Cic.; campi lugentes, *places of mourning* (of the lower world), Verg. **II.** Transit., *to bewail, lament, deplore, to wear mourning for*; matronae annum, ut parentem, eum luxerunt, Liv.; aliquem, Cic.; mortem alicuius, Cic.

lūgŭbrĕ, adv. (lugubris), *mournfully, plaintively*, Verg.

lūgŭbris -e (lugeo), *relating to mourning, mournful*. **I.** Lit., lamentatio, *for the dead*, Cic.; domus, *a house of mourning*, Liv. Subst., **lūgŭbrĭa** -ium, n. *mourning attire*, Ov. **II.** 1, *causing mourning*; bellum, Hor.; **2,** *doleful, plaintive*; verba, Ov.

lumbus -i, m. *the loin*, Cic.

lūmen -ĭnis, n. (for lucmen, from luceo), *light*. **I.** Lit., **A.** Gen., tabulas collocare in bono lumine, *in a good light*, Cic.; lumen solis, Cic.; **B.** Esp. **1,** *a light, lamp, taper*; lumini oleum instillare, Cic.; sub lumina prima, *at twilight*, Cic.; **2,** *the light of day, day*; lumine quarto, Verg.; **3,** *the light of life, life*; relinquere, Verg.; 4, *the light of the eye, the eye*; luminibus amissis, *being blind*, Cic.; caecitas luminis, Cic.; lumina defixa tenere in aliqua re, Ov.; **5,** *light in a house*; luminibus obstruere, *to block up light by building*, Cic. **C.** Meton., *an opening through which light can enter*; **1,** duo lumina ab animo ad oculos perforata nos habere, Cic.; **2,** *a window*, Cic. **II.** Fig., **1,** *light, clearness, insight*; ordo maxime est, qui memoriae lumen affert, Cic.; **2,** *a light, a remarkable excellence, glory, ornament*; Corinthus totius Graeciae lumen, Cic.; lumina civitatis, Cic.

lūmĭnāre -āris, n. (lumen), *a window-shutter, window*; plur. Cic.

lūmĭnōsus -a -um (lumen), *full of light*; of discourse, *bright, luminous*, Cic.

1. **lūna** -ae, f. (for lucna, from luceo). **I.** *the moon*. **A.** Lit., plena, *full moon*, Caes.; ortus aut obitus lunae, Cic.; lunae defectus, Cic.; laborans, *the moon in eclipse*, Juv.; quarta luna, *the fourth day after new moon*, Cic.; luna crescit, Cic. **B.** Meton., **1,** *the night*; roscida, Verg.; **2,** *a half-moon, an ivory ornament in the shape of a half-moon, worn by Roman senators on their shoes*, Juv. **II.** Personif., Luna, *the goddess of the Moon*, afterwards identified with Diana.

2. **Lūna** -ae, f. *town on the borders of Liguria and Etruria*. Hence, adj., **Lūnensis** -e, *of Luna*.

lūnaris -e (luna), **1,** *relating to the moon, lunar*; cursus, Cic.; **2,** *like the moon*; cornua, Ov.

lūno, 1. (luna), *to bend into a crescent* or *half-moon*; arcum, Ov. Partic., **lūnātus** -a -um, *bent into a crescent, half-moon* or *sickle-shaped*; peltae Amazonidum, Verg.

1. **lŭo,** lŭi, 3. (λούω), *to wash*.

2. **lŭo,** lŭi, lŭitūrus, 3. (λύω), *to loose*; transf., **1,** *to expiate, atone for*; stuprum voluntariā morte, Cic.; **2,** *to pay*; luere poenam or poenas, *to suffer punishment, pay a penalty for*; itaque mei peccati luo poenas, Cic.; poenam pro caede, Ov.

lŭpa -ae, f. (lupus), **1,** *a she-wolf*, Liv.; **2,** *a prostitute*, Cic.

lŭpānar -āris, n. (lupa), *a brothel*, Juv.

lŭpātus -a -um (lupa), *provided with wolf's teeth—i.e., iron spikes*; frena, Hor. Hence, **lŭpāti** -ōrum, m. and **lŭpāta** -ōrum, n. *a curb with jagged spikes*, Verg.

Lŭpercal -cālis, n. (Lupercus). **I.** *a grotto on the Palatine Hill, sacred to Pan* or *Lupercus*, Verg. **II.** Plur., **Lŭpercālĭa** -ium, *the festival of Pan* or *Lupercus, celebrated in February*.

Lŭpercus -i, m. (lupus and arceo), "*the keeper off of wolves*," **1,** *an old Italian deity, protector of flocks against wolves, sometimes identified with the Arcadian Pan*; **2,** *a priest of Lupercus*, Cic.

Lupĭa -ae, m. *a river in North-west Germany*, now *the Lippe*.

lŭpīnus -a -um (lupus), *of* or *relating to a wolf, wolfish*. **I.** Adj., ubera, Cic. **II.** Subst., **lŭpīnum** -i, n. and **lŭpīnus** -i, m. *the lupine* (Lupinus albus, Linn.), used on the stage instead of coin; nec tamen ignorat quid distent aera lupinis, Hor.

lŭpus -i, m (λύκος), *a wolf* I. Lit, genus acre luporum atque canum, Verg, prov, lupus in fabula, *talk of the devil, and he'll appear*, Cic, hac urget lupus, hac canis angit, *to be between two fires*, Hor II. Transf, 1, *a voracious fish, the pike*, Hor; 2, a, *a horse's bit with jagged points*, Ov, b, *a hook*, ferrei, Liv

lurco -ōnis, m *a glutton, gormandiser*, Plaut

lūrĭdus -a -um, *pale yellow, lurid, livid, ghastly, deadly pale* I. Lit, pallor, Ov, dentes, Hor, sulfur, Ov II. Transf, *producing paleness*, horror, Ov, aconita, Ov

lūror -ōris, m *ghastliness, deathly paleness*, Lucr

luscĭnĭa -ae, f *the nightingale*, Hor

luscĭnĭŏla -ae, f (dim of luscinia), *a little nightingale*, Plaut

1 **luscīnus** -a -um (luscus), *one eyed*, Plin

2 **Luscīnus**, C Fabricius, v. Fabricius.

luscĭōsus and **luscĭtĭōsus** -a -um (luscus), *purblind, dim sighted*, Plaut

luscus -a -um, 1, *hollow eyed, blind*, statua, Juv, 2, *one eyed*, Cic, dux, *Hannibal*, Juv

lūsĭo -ōnis, f (ludo), *a playing, sport*, lusio pilae, Cic

Lūsĭtānĭa -ae f *the country of the Lusitani, between the Durius and the Tagus, the modern Portugal, with a part of the modern Spain* Hence, adj, **Lūsĭtānus** -a um, *Lusitanian*

lūsĭto, 1. (intens of ludo), *to play, sport*, Plaut

Lūsĭus -ii, m *a river of Arcadia*

lūsor -ōris, m (ludo) I. *one that plays, a player*, Ov II. a, *a playful or wanton writer*, tenerorum lusor amorum, Ov, b, *a mocker*, Plaut

lūsōrĭus a -um (lusor), *relating to play*, Plin

lustrālis -e (2 lustrum) I. *relating to expiation or atonement, expiatory, atoning*, sacrificium, Liv, exta, Verg II. *relating to a period of five years* (because of the quinquennial expiatory sacrifice at Rome), Tac

lustrātĭo -ōnis, f (lustro), 1, *a purification by sacrifice, expiation*; lustration sacrificio peracto, Liv, 2, *a going round, going over, traversing, wandering*, municipiorum, Cic, solis, Cic

lustro, 1 (connected with luceo) I. *to make bright, illumine* A. sol cuncta sua luce lustrat et complet, Cic B 1, *to look at, regard, observe, examine* quae sit me circum copia, lustro, Verg; alicuius vestigia, Verg, 2, *to wander over, traverse, pass through*, Aegyptum, Cic, aequor navibus, Verg II. *to purify, cleanse by sacrifices* A. Lit, populum, exercitum, Cic B. Meton 1, *to review, muster an army* (when a sacrifice was offered), exercitum, Cic, 2, *to go round, dance round, encircle*, aliquem choreis, Verg

1. **lustrum** -i, n (luo or lavo) I. *a bog, morass*, Varr II. Transf, 1, *the den or lair of a wild beast*, ferarum, Verg, 2, *a wood, forest*, Verg, 3, *a brothel*, Cic

2 **lustrum** -i, n (connected with 2 luo) I. *an expiatory sacrifice, offered every five years by the censors at the close of the census on behalf of the Roman people, at which an ox, sheep, and sow were sacrificed*, lustrum condere, *to offer the expiatory sacrifice*, Cic, sub lustrum censeri, *to be enrolled near the end of the census*, Cic II. Meton, *a period of five years, a lustre*, octavum claudere lustrum, Hor.

lūsus -ūs, m (ludo) I. *a playing, game, sport*, trigon, Hor II. Transf, *sport, amusement, trifling*, 1, per lusum atque lasciviam, Liv, 2, *dalliance*, Ov

Lŭtātĭus a um, *name of a Roman gens*, v Catulus

lūtĕŏlus -a -um (dim of luteus), *yellowish*; caltha, Verg

Lūtētĭa (Pārĭsĭōrum) -ae, f *town in Gallia Lugdunensis* (now *Paris*)

1 **lūtĕus** -a um (lutum), a, *of the colour of the plant lutum, yellow, saffron-yellow*, Aurora, Verg, b, *rose coloured*, soccus, Cat

2 **lŭtĕus** -a -um (lŭtum), 1, *of mud or clay*, Ov, transf, *worthless*, negotium, *a trifle*, Cic, 2, *dirty, covered with dirt*, Vulcanus, Juv

lŭto, 1 (lŭtum), *to besmear with mud or dirt*, Mart

lŭtŭlentus -a -um (lŭtum) 1, *muddy, dirty*, sus, Hor, humus erit lutulenta vino Cic, amnis, Ov, 2, fig, *filthy, dirty*, homo, Cic, vitia, Cic, esp, of style, *turbid, impure*, Hor

1 **lūtum** -i, n I. *a plant used for dyeing yellow, dyer's weed, weld*, Verg II. Meton, *yellow colour*, Verg

2 **lŭtum** -i, n (λύω) I. *mud, mire, dirt*, volutari in luto, Cic, crates luto contegere, Caes, prov, in luto esse, haerere, *to stick in the mud, be in great perplexity*, Plaut, Ter, used as a term of reproach, *filthy fellow, scum of the earth*, Cic II. *loam, clay*, caementa interlita luto, Liv

lux, lūcis, f *light* (root LUC, Gk λύκ η) I. A Lit, 1, gen, solis, Cic, lunae, Verg, lychnorum, Cic, 2, esp, *daylight, day*, cum prima luce, primā luce, *as soon as it was day*, Cic, ante lucem, Cic, ad lucem *in the morning*, Cic, luce or luci, *by day, by daylight*, Cic, meton, *a day* centesima lux ab interitu P Clodii, Cic B. Transf, 1, *a heavenly body*, Cic, 2, *the light* (of life), a, in lucem edi, Cic, b, meton, *life*, corpora luce carentum, Verg, 3, *the eye, eye sight*, Ov II. Transf, *the light*, 1, *publicity, the public view, the sight of men*, res occultas in lucem proferre, Cic, Isocrates luce forensi caruit, Cic 2, *light, illustration, elucidation* historia testis temporum, lux veritatis, Cic, 3, *light, help, succour*, lucem afferre reipublicae, Cic, 4, *light, ornament*, haec urbs, lux orbis terrarum, Cic

luxor, 1 dep (luxus), *to riot, revel*, Plaut

luxŭrĭa ae f and **luxŭrĭēs** -ei, f (luxus) I. Lit, of plants, *rankness, exuberant or luxuriant growth*, segetum, Verg, fig, Cic II. Transf, *excess, prodigality, dissipation, riotous living, luxury*, a, odit populus Romanus privatam luxuriam, publicam magnificentiam diligit, Cic, b, *unbridled insolence*, Liv

luxŭrĭo, 1 and **luxŭrĭor**, 1 dep I. *to be luxuriant, rank, abundant in growth*, humus, seges, Ov, transf, a, of animals, *to be playful, sportive, wanton*, ludit et in pratis luxuriatque pecus, Ov, b, *to be exuberant, abound in*, faciem decet deliciis luxuriare novis, Ov, *to swell, increase*, membra, Ov II. Transf, *to be luxurious, run riot, be dissolute*, ne luxuriarent otio animi, Liv, Capua luxurians felicitate, Cic

luxŭrĭōsē, adv (luxuriosus), *luxuriously, voluptuously*, vivere, Cic

luxŭrĭōsus -a um (luxuria) I. *luxuriant in growth*, frumenta, Cic II Fig, a, *immoderate, excessive*, laetitia, Liv, amor, Ov, b, *luxurious, dissolute, prodigal*, nihil luxuriosius (homine illo), Cic

1 **luxus** -a -um (λοξός), *dislocated*, pes, Sall

2 **luxus** ūs, m 1, *luxury, debauchery, sensual excess, revelling*, Cic, 2, *splendour*, Verg

Lўaeus -i, m (Λυαῖος), *the releaser from care, surname of Bacchus*, pater Lyaeus, Verg meton *wine;* uda Lyaei tempora, Hor.; attrib., latex Lyaeus, Verg.

Lўcaeus -i, m. (Λύκαιον), *a mountain in Arcadia, sacred to Jupiter and Pan.* Adj., **Lўcaeus** -a -um, *Lycaean.*

Lўcambes -ae, m. (Λυκάμβης), *a Theban who, for refusing his daughter in marriage to Archilochus, was attacked by the poet in such sarcastic verses that he and his daughter hanged themselves.* Hence, adj., **Lўcambēus** -a -um, *Lycambean.*

Lўcāon -ŏnis, m. (Λυκάων), *king of Arcadia, transformed by Jupiter into a wolf, father of Callisto.* Hence, **a,** adj., **Lўcāŏnius** -a -um; Arctos, *Callisto, as a constellation,* Ov.; whence axis, *the northern sky,* Ov.; **b, Lўcāŏnis** -idis, f. *Callisto, daughter of Lycaon,* Ov.

Lўcāŏnes -um, m. (Λυκάονες), *the Lycaonians, a people in Asia Minor between Cappadocia, Cilicia, and Pisidia.* Hence, adj., **Lўcāŏnius** -a -um, *Lycaonian.* Subst., **Lўcāŏnĭa** -ae, f. *the country of the Lycaones.*

Lўcēum -i, n. and **Lўcīum** -ii, n. (Λύκειον), **1,** *a gymnasium at Athens, at which Aristotle taught;* **2,** *a gymnasium with a library in Cicero's Tusculan villa.*

lychnūcus -i, m. (λυχνοῦχος), *a lamp-stand, candelabrum,* Cic.

lychnus -i, m. (λύχνος), *a lamp,* Cic.

Lўcĭa -ae, f. (Λυκία), *a country of Asia Minor between Caria and Pamphylia;* hence, adj., **Lўcĭus** -a -um, *Lycian;* deus, *Apollo,* Prop.; sortes, *the oracle of Apollo at Patara,* Verg.; hasta, *of the Lycian king Sarpedon,* Ov.; subst., **Lўcĭi** -ōrum, m. *the Lycians.*

Lўcīum = Lyceum (q.v.).

Lўcŏmēdēs -is, m. (Λυκομήδης), *king of the island of Scyros, where Achilles hid himself in female attire.*

Lўcŏphrōn -phrŏnis, m. (Λυκόφρων), *a Greek tragic poet of Chalcis in Euboea.*

Lўcōrĭās -ădis, f. (Λυκωριάς), *daughter of Nereus and Doris, a sea-nymph.*

Lўcōrĭs -ĭdis, f. *a freedwoman of Volumnius Eutrapelus, the mistress of the triumvir Antonius and of the poet L. Cornelius Gallus.*

Lўcormās -ae, m. (Λυκόρμας), *a river in Aetolia.*

Lyctus (-ŏs) -i, f. (Λύκτος), *a town in Crete.* Adj., **Lyctĭus** -a -um = *Cretan,* Verg.

Lўcurgus -i, m. (Λυκοῦργος). **I.** Myth., *son of Dryas, king of the Edoni in Thrace, who prohibited the worship of Bacchus among his subjects.* **II.** Myth., *son of Aleus and Neaera, father of Ancaeus, king in Arcadia;* hence, **Lўcurgīdēs** -ae, m. = *Ancaeus,* Ov. **III.** Hist., *an Athenian orator, famed for his severity;* hence **Lўcurgēi** -ōrum, m. (Λυκούργειοι) = *strict, inflexible citizens.* **IV.** Hist., *the celebrated Spartan legislator.*

Lўcus (-ŏs) -i, m. (Λύκος), *name of several rivers;* **1,** *a river in Paphlagonia, flowing into the Pontus Euxinus, near Heraclea (now Tarak);* **2,** *a river in Phrygia, flowing into the Maeander.*

Lўdĭa -ae, f. (Λυδία), *a country of Asia Minor, from which according to the legend the Etruscans originally came;* hence, adj., **A. Lўdĭus** -a -um, **a,** *Lydian;* aurifer amnis, *Pactolus,* Tib.; **b,** *Etruscan;* fluvius, *the Tiber,* Verg. **B. Lўdus** -a -um; **a,** *Lydian;* puella, *Omphale,* Verg.; **b,** *Etruscan;* plur., Lydi, *the Etruscans,* Cic.

lympha (limpha) -ae, f. *clear spring or river water,* Verg.; personif., **Lymphae** = *Nymphs of the springs,* Hor.

lymphātĭcus -a -um (lympha), *raving, raging, insane, mad, frantic;* pavor, *a panic terror,* Liv.

lympho, 1. (lympha), *to make mad, strike with frenzy,* Plin.; partic., **lymphātus** -a -um, *mad, frantic, insane;* lymphata mens, Hor.; lymphati, *struck with panic,* Liv.

Lyncestae -ārum, m. (Λυγκεσταί), *a people in the south-west of Macedonia near whom was a fountain, the waters of which caused drunkenness.* Adj., **Lyncestĭus** -a -um, *Lyncestian.*

Lynceūs -ĕi, m. (Λυγκεύς). **I.** *a Messenian hero, one of the Argonauts, renowned for the sharpness of his sight;* hence, **1,** adj., **Lyncēus** -a -um, **a,** *belonging to Lynceus,* Ov.; **b,** *sharp-sighted,* Cic.; **2, Lyncīdēs** -ae, m. *a descendant of Lynceus.* **II.** *a companion of Aeneas.*

Lyncus -i (Λύγκος). **I.** m. *a king in Scythia, changed into a lynx.* **II.** f. *the capital of the Lyncestae.*

lynx -cis, c. (λύγξ), *a lynx,* Verg.

lўra -ae, f. (λύρα). **I.** *the lyre, a stringed instrument;* quum (Themistocles) in epulis recusaret lyram, Cic. **II.** Transf., **1,** *lyric poetry, song;* Aeoliae lyrae amica, Ov.; **2,** *the constellation Lyra,* Ov.

Lyrcēĭus (**Lyrcēus**) -a -um, *belonging to the mountain Lyrceum between Arcadia and Argolis.*

lўrĭcus -a -um (λυρικός), *of or relating to the lyre, lyric;* vates, *a lyric poet,* Hor.

Lyrnēsos -i, f. (Λυρνησός), *town in the Troad, birthplace of Briseis.* Hence, **1, Lyrnēsis** -idis, subst., f. *Briseis;* **2, Lyrnēsĭus** -a -um, *Lyrnesian.*

Lўsander -dri, m. (Λύσανδρος), **1,** *a celebrated Spartan general, conqueror of the Athenians;* **2,** *an ephor of Sparta, friend of the king Agis.*

Lўsĭas -ae, m. (Λυσίας), *a celebrated Athenian orator, contemporary with Socrates.*

Lўsĭmăchīa -ae, f. (Λυσιμάχεια), *a town in Thrace, founded by Lysimachus.* Hence, **Lўsĭmăchienses** -ium, m. *the inhabitants of Lysimachia.*

Lўsĭmăchus -i, m. (Λυσίμαχος), *one of the generals of Alexander the Great, ruling after A.'s death in Thrace and Pontus.*

Lўsippus -i, m. (Λύσιππος), *a celebrated worker in metal of Sicyon.*

Lўsĭs -idis, m. (Λῦσις), **1,** *a Pythagorean philosopher of Tarentum, teacher of Epaminondas;* **2,** *a river in Asia.*

Lўsĭthŏē -ēs, f. (Λυσιθόη), *daughter of Oceanus.*

M.

M, m, the twelfth letter of the Latin Alphabet, corresponding in form and sound with the Greek M, μ. For M. as an abbreviation, see Table of Abbreviations.

Măcărĕūs -ĕi and -ĕos, m. (Μακαρεύς), *son of Aeolus, brother of Canace.* Hence, **Măcărēis** -idis, f. (Μακαρηΐς), *the daughter of Macareus (Isse).*

Măcĕdō (-ŏn) -dŏnis, m. (Μακεδών), *a Macedonian;* plur., **Măcĕdŏnes** -um, m. *the Macedonians.* Hence, **1, Măcĕdŏnĭa** -ae, f. (Μακεδονία), *a country between Thessaly and Thrace;*

2, **Măcĕdŏnĭcus** -a -um, *Macedonian*, 3, **Măcĕdŏnĭus** -a -um, *Macedonian*

măcellārĭus -a -um (macellum), *of or relating to the provision market*. Subst., **măcellārĭus** -ii, m *a victualler, provision-dealer*, Suet

măcellum -i, n *a provision-market, meat-market*, annonam in macello cariorem fore, Cic

măcĕo, 2 *to be lean*, Plaut

1 **măcĕr** -cra -crum, *lean*; taurus, Verg; transf, of soil, *poor*, solum, Cic; fig, me macrum reducit, Hor

2 **Măcĕr** -cri, m *a Roman family name*, 1, C Licinius Macer, *a Roman historian*, 2, Aemilius Macer, *a poet, friend of Vergil and Ovid*

mācĕrĭa -ae, f (μάκελος, or μακελλον, *an enclosure*), *a wall enclosing a garden, vineyard, or park*, Cic

mācĕro, 1 I *to soak, steep in water*, Ter II. Transf, 1, *to make weak, bring down, reduce*, aliquem fame, Liv, 2, *to torment, tease, vex*, quae vos, quum reliqueritis, macerent desiderio, Liv

măcesco, 3 (maceo), *to grow thin, become lean*, Plaut

măchaera -ae, f (μαχαιρα), *a sword, knife*, Plaut

măchaerŏphŏrus -i, m (μαχαιροφόρος), *armed with a sabre or machaera*, Cic

Măchāōn -ŏnis, m (Μαχάων), myth, *son of Aesculapius, celebrated physician*. Hence, adj, **Măchāŏnĭus** -a -um, *of or belonging to Machaon*

māchĭna -ae, f (μηχανή), 1, *a machine, any artificial contrivance for performing work*, especially *a machine for moving heavy weights*, Cic, *pulling down columns*, Cic, *drawing ships down to the sea*, Hor; fig, ut omnes adhibeam machinas ad tenendum adulescentulum, Cic, 2, *a military engine, a catapult, balista*, etc, Sall, 3, *a platform on which slaves were exposed for sale*, Q Cic, 4, *a device, contrivance, trick, stratagem*, Cic

māchĭnāmentum -i, n (machinor), *a machine, instrument*, Liv

māchĭnātĭo -ōnis, f (machinor), 1, *contrivance, machinery, mechanism*, cum machinatione quadam moveri aliquid videmus, Cic; transf *a cunning device, machination*, Cic, 2, meton, *a mechanical contrivance, a machine*, navalis, Caes

māchĭnātor -ōris, m (machinor), 1, *a maker of machines, architect*, tormentorum, Liv, 2, transf, in a bad sense, *a deviser, contriver, originator*, horum omnium scelerum, Cic, huius belli, Liv

māchĭnor, 1. dep (machina) 1, *to contrive, invent, devise*, opera, Cic, versum, Cic, 2, *to plot some evil, contrive*, pestem in aliquem, Cic

măcĭes -ēi, f (maceo), 1, *leanness, thinness*, a, of men, corpus macie intabuit, Cic, b, of soil or crops, *poverty, barrenness*, Ov, 2, transf, *meagreness of expression*, Tac.

măcĭlentus -a -um (macies), *thin, lean*, Plaut

Măcra -ae, 1, *a river in Italy, between Liguria and Etruria*, now *Magra*, 2, Măcra cōmē (Μακρα κωμη), *a place in Locris on the borders of Thessaly*

măcresco, macrui, 3 (macer), *to grow lean, become thin*, Hor

Măcri Campi and **Campi Măcri** -ōrum, m *a valley in Gallia Cispadane*

Măcrŏbĭus -ii, m, Aurelius Ambrosius Theodosius, *a grammarian of the fifth century* A D

măcrŏcollum -i, n (μακρόκωλοι), *paper of the largest size, royal paper*, Cic

mactābĭlis -e (macto), *deadly*, Lucr

mactātus -ū, m (macto), *a slaying, killing*, Lucr

macte, macti, v mactus

macto, 1 (intens of *mago, akin to mactus), *to honour, glorify*. I. *to honour a god with a sacrifice*, puerorum extis deos manes, Cic; transf, a, *to reward, honour with anything*, aliquem honoribus, Cic, b, in a bad sense, *to afflict, punish with*, aliquem summo supplicio, Cic II. *to sacrifice, offer*, hostiam, Hor; transf, *to devote*, aliquem Orco, Liv

mactus -a -um (from *mago, maxi, mactum = augeo), 1, found only in the forms macte, macti, joined with an abl and generally with the imper of the verb esse, *well done! bravo! all hail! good luck attend thee!* macte virtute! Cic, macte esto virtute! Hor, macte virtute diligentiāque esto! Liv, macti virtute, milites Romani, este! Liv, with genit, macte animi, Mart, 2, = mactatus, *sacrificed*, Lucr

măcŭla -ae, f (connected with maceo, macies, macer), 1, *a spot, mark*, equus albis maculis, Verg, 2, *the mesh of a net*, Cic, 3, transf, *a blot, stain, blemish, fault*, hunc tu vitae splendorem maculis aspergis tuis? Cic, familiae, Cic

măcŭlo, 1 (macula), *to cover with spots, to make spotted, stain, pollute*, 1, lit, terram tabo maculant, Verg, candor corporum magis sanguine atro maculabatur, Liv, 2, transf, *to stain, defile, pollute*, rex ille optimi regis caede maculatus, Cic, partus suos parricidio, Liv

măcŭlōsus -a -um (macula) *full of spots, spotted, speckled*, 1, lynx, Verg, 2, *stained, polluted, defiled*, vestis Pompeii, Cic; fig, *defiled, polluted*, senatores Cic, nefas, Hor

mădĕfăcĭo -fēci factum, 3, pass **mădĕfīo** factus sum fieri (madeo and facio), *to make wet, moisten, soak*, gladii sanguine madefacti, Cic, sanguis madefecerat herbas, Verg

mădĕo -ŭi 2 (μαδαω), *to be wet, moist, to drip, flow*. I. Lit, A. Gen, natabant pavimenta vino, madebant parietes, Cic, sanguine terra madet, Verg, partic, madens, *moist*, Cic B. Esp, 1, *to melt* (of snow), nix sole madens, Ov, 2, *to be drunk*, Plaut., 3, *to be boiled, to be made soft by boiling*, Verg II. Transf, *to be full of, abound in, overflow with*, pocula madent Baccho, Tib, Socraticis madet sermonibus, *steeped in*, Hor

mădesco, madŭi, 3 (madeo), *to become moist or wet*, semiusta madescunt robora, Verg

mădĭdus -a -um (madeo), *moist, wet*. I. Gen, fasciculus epistolarum totus aquā madidus, Cic, genae, *wet with tears*, Ov, vestis cocco madida, *dyed with*, Mart II. Esp, *drunk*, Plaut

mădor -ōris, m (madeo), *moisture, wetness*, Sall

Maeandĕr -dri, m and **Maeandrŏs** (-us) -dri, m (Μαίανδρος) I. *a river of Asia Minor, proverbial for its winding course*, now *Meinder*; *in the legend, father of Cyane, the mother of Caunus and Byblis*. II. Appellat, *a winding, turning*, a, of a road, Cic, b, *a winding border of a dress*, Verg Hence, adj, **Maeandrĭus** -a -um, *of or belonging to Maeander*, juvenis, *Caunus*, Ov

Maecēnās -ātis, m, C Cilnius, *a Roman knight, the friend of Augustus, and the patron of Horace and Vergil*

Maecĭus -a -um, *Maecian*. I. *name of a place in Latium, not far from Lanuvium*. II. *name of a Roman gens, of which the most celebrated member was* Sp Maecius Tarpa, *a celebrated Roman critic*.

Maedi -ōrum, m. (Μαῖδοι), *a Thracian people.* Adj., **Maedĭcus** -a -um, *belonging to the Maedi;* subst., **Maedĭca** -ae, f. *the country of the Maedi.*

Maelĭus -a -um, *name of a Roman gens, of which the most celebrated member was* Sp. Maelius, *slain, on suspicion of aiming at kingly power, by C. Servilius Ahala, master of the horse to the dictator Cincinnatus.*

maena (mēna) -ae, f. (μαίνη), *a kind of small sea-fish,* often salted, Cic.

Maenălus (-ŏs) -i, m. and **Maenăla** -ōrum, n. (Μαίναλον), *a mountain in Arcadia, sacred to Pan.* Hence, 1, **Maenălĭus** -a -um, *Maenalian, Arcadian;* deus, *Pan,* Ov.; versus, *pastoral poetry,* Verg.; 2, **Maenălĭs** -idis, f. *belonging or relating to Maenalus;* ursa, *Callisto,* Ov.; ora, *Arcadia,* Ov.

Maenăs -ădis, f. (μαινάς), 1, *a bacchante,* Ov.; transf., a, *a priestess of Priapus,* Juv.; b, *a priestess of Cybele,* Cat.; 2, *a prophetess* (*Cassandra*), Prop.

Maenădes, v. Maenas.

Maenĭus -a -um, *name of a Roman gens;* columna Maenia, v. columna. Hence, **Maenĭānus** -a -um, *Maenian.* Subst., **Maenĭānum** -i, n. *a projecting balcony,* first introduced by C. Maenius, Cic.

Maeŏnes -um, m. (Μαίονες), *the inhabitants of Maeonia, the Maeonians;* hence, a, **Maeŏnĭa** -ae, f. (Μαιονία), *Maeonia, a part of Lydia,* and, as the Etruscans were said to derive their origin from Lydia = *Etruria,* Verg.; b, **Maeŏnĭdēs** -ae, m., (α) *Homer,* as a native, according to some, of Colophon or Smyrna, Ov.; (β) *an Etruscan,* Verg.; c, **Maeŏnĭs** -idis, f. *a Lydian woman, Arachne,* Ov.; *Omphale,* Ov.; d, **Maeŏnĭus** -a -um, (α) *Maeonian, Lydian;* ripa (of the river Pactolus), Ov.; esp., senex or vates, *Homer,* Ov.; so *Homeric* or *heroic;* carmen, pes, chartae, Ov.; (β) *Etruscan;* nautae, Ov.

Maeōtae -ārum, m. (Μαιῶται), *a Scythian people on Lake Maeotis.* Hence, a, **Maeōtĭcus** -a -um, *Maeotic;* palus, *the Lake Maeotis,* Plin.; b, **Maeōtĭdae** -ārum, m. *the persons living on Lake Maeotis;* c, **Maeōtĭs** -idis, f. *relating to the Maeotae* or *to Lake Maeotis;* esp., Maeotis palus or lacus, now *the Sea of Azov;* d, **Maeōtĭus** -a -um, *Maeotian.*

maerĕo, 2. **I.** Intransit., *to be sad, mournful, to grieve, mourn, lament;* maeret Menelaus, Cic.; with abl. of cause, suo incommodo, Cic.; with abl. of instr., sono tenui, *in a gentle tone,* Ov.; maeret, foll. by quod, *he is pained that,* etc., Ov.; partic., maerens, *mournful, sorrowful;* quis Sullam nisi maerentem vidit? Cic. **II.** Transit., *to lament, mourn over, bewail;* casum, Cic.; filii mortem graviter, Cic.; with acc. and infin., Cic.; talia maerens, *uttering lamentations,* Ov.

maeror -ōris, m. (maereo), *mourning, grief, sorrow, sadness;* in maerore jacere, Cic.; maerorem minuere, Cic.

maestĭtĭa -ae, f. (maestus). **I.** *sadness, sorrowfulness, dejection, grief;* esse in maestitia, Cic. **II.** Transf., *gloominess;* orationis quasi maestitiam sequi, Cic.

maestĭtūdo -inis, f. (maestus), *sadness,* Plant.

maestus -a -um (maereo), *sad, sorrowful, dejected, cast down, melancholy.* **I.** Ulixes, Cic.; senex, Cic.; manus, Ov. **II.** Transf., 1, *gloomy;* neci maestum dimittit, Verg.; 2, *causing* or *indicating sorrow;* vestes, Prop.; funera, Ov.

Maevĭus -ii, m. *a bad poet of the time of Vergil.*

măga -ae, f. (magus), *the enchantress,* Ov. (?)

māgālĭa -ium, n. (*a Punic word*), *huts, cottages, hovels,* Verg.

măgĕ = magis (q.v.).

măgĭcus -a -um (μαγικός), *relating to magic* or *enchantment, magical;* artes, Verg.; dii, *gods invoked in enchantments* (as *Pluto, Hecate, Proserpina*), Tib.

măgis, adv. with compar. (from root MAC, with adverbial ending -is), *more.* **I.** Of degree, *more = in a higher degree.* **A.** Gen., 1, with adj. and adv., to form the comp. of adj. and adv. not inflected in the comp., magis necessarius, Cic.; 2, with verbs; a, foll. by quam, *more, rather . . . than;* sed praeterita magis reprehendi possunt quam corrigi, Cic.; b, sometimes without comparison, magis aedilis esse non potuisset, Cic. **B.** Particular combinations, a, non (neque) magis . . . quam, *not more . . . than, just as much . . . as,* Cic.; b, quo magis . . . eo magis, *the more . . . the more,* Cic.; quo magis . . . eo minus, Cic.; c, eo magis, *so much the more, all the more,* Cic.; d, with abl., impendio magis, *considerably more,* Cic.; multo magis, *much more, more by far,* Cic.; nihilo magis, *just as little,* Cic.; solito magis, *more than usual,* Liv.; e, magis etiam, *even more,* Cic.; f, magis magisque, magis et magis, *more and more,* Cic. **II.** = potius, *rather, more willingly.* **A.** Gen., magis id diceres, si, etc., Cic. **B.** Particular phrases, magis malle = potius malle, Cic.; magis est quod . . . quam quod, or magis est ut . . . quam ut, *it is more the cause that . . . than,* etc., Cic. Superl., **maxĭmē (maxŭmē,** adv. (for magissime, from old magus = magnus), *in the highest degree, most of all, especially, exceedingly, very.* **I.** Of degree, **A.** Gen., 1, with adj., a, maxime fidus, Cic.; b, to form the Superl. of adjectives which are not inflected in the superl., maxime necessarius, Cic.; c, to add force to a superl., aberratio maxime liberalissima, Cic.; 2, with verbs, a, cupere, velle, Cic.; b, where the meaning must in part be supplied, alicui confidere maxime, *implicitly,* Caes. **B.** Particular combinations, a, with unus, omnium, multo, *most of all, far before all the rest;* unus omnium maxime, Nep.; multo maxime, Cic.; b, quam maxime, *as much as possible,* Cic.; ut quisque . . . ita maxime, *the more . . . the more,* Cic.; hoc maxime officii est, ut quisque maxime opis indigeat, ita ea potissimum opitulari, Cic.; quum maxime, *just, precisely,* Liv.; quum maxime, *just now,* Cic.; c, quam or ut qui maxime, *in the highest possible degree,* Cic.; d, non maxime, *not altogether;* ingenium non maxime defuit, Cic. **II.** = potissimum, *principally, particularly, especially;* 1, quae ratio poëtas, maximeque Homerum impulit, *and most of all Homer,* Cic.; quum . . . tunc maxime, *both . . . and especially,* Cic.; 2, *just, exactly;* nunc quum maxime, Cic.; 3, in colloquial language maxime is used to express emphatic assent, and with immo, emphatic dissent; vos non timetis eam? Immo vero maxume, Sall.

măgister -tri, m. (root MAC, whence magnus), *master, ruler, president, chief, head, director, leader, superintendent.* **I.** Lit., 1, populi, *dictator,* Cic.; equitum, *master of the horse, the dictator's lieutenant,* Liv.; morum, *the censor,* Cic.; societatis, *the director of a company formed for farming the revenue,* Cic.; scripturae or in scriptura and portus (of a company that farmed the rents, tolls, etc.), Cic.; P. Terentius operas in portu et scriptura Asiae pro magistro dedit, *exercised the functions of vice-director,* Cic.; elephanti, *driver,* Liv.; auctionis, *director* or *conductor of a sale by auction,* Cic.; cenandi, *the president of a feast;* navis, a, *master, captain,*

Liv.; b, *helmsman*, Verg, ludi, *schoolmaster*, Cic, 2, a, *the trustee of a bankrupt's estate*, Cic, b, *a teacher*, artium, religionis, virtutis, Cic, usus est magister optimus, Cic, gladiatorium *a fencing-master*, Cic. II. Transf, *an instigator, inciter*, magister ad despoliandum Dianae templum, Cic

măgistĕrium ii, n (magister), *the office or power of a master, president, chief, director*, morum, *the censorship*, Cic, sacerdotii, *priesthood*, Liv; me magisteria (conviviorum) delectant, Cic

măgistra -ae, f (magister), *a mistress, directress, leader*, transf, lex aeterna quae quasi dux et magistra studiorum, Cic, arte magistrā, *by the help of art*, Verg

măgistrātus -ūs, m (magister). I. *the office or dignity of a magister, a magistracy, official dignity, office*, magistratum gerere, Cic, inire, ingredi, Sall; deponere, Caes, magistratu abire, Cic II. Meton, *a magistrate, high official* Magistrates in Rome were either ordinarii—e g, the praetors, consuls, etc; or extraordinarii—e g, dictator, master of the horse; curules or non curules, according to the seat on which they sat, patricii or plebeii, according as they were taken from the patricians or plebeians, majores or minores, the elections to the former taking place in the comitia centuriata, to the latter in the comitia tributa; est proprium munus magistratus intelligere se gerere personam civitatis, Cic, creare magistratus, Liv.

magnănĭmĭtas -ātis, f (magnanimus), *greatness of soul, magnanimity*, Cic

magnănĭmus -a -um (magnus and animus), *high-minded, courageous, high-spirited, magnanimous*, Cic. (genit. plur, magnanimūm, Verg)

Magnēs -nētis, v Magnesia

Magnēsĭa -ae, f (Μαγνησία) I. *a district of Thessaly* II. *a town in Caria on the Maeander* (now *Inek-bazar*) III. *a town in Lydia on Mount Sipylus* (now *Manissa*) Hence, 1, **Magnēs** -nētis, m (Μάγνης), *Magnesian*, esp, lapis Magnes or simply Magnes, *a loadstone, magnet*, plur subst., **Magnetes** -um, m *the Magnesians*, 2, **Magnēsius** -a -um, *Magnesian*; saxum, *the magnet*, Lucr, 3, **Magnessa** -ae, f *a Magnesian woman*, Hor, 4, **Magnētarchēs** -ae, m *the chief magistrate of the Magnesians*, Liv; 5, **Magnētis** -idis, f *Magnesian*, Argo, *built at Pagasae in Magnesia*, Ov

Magni Campi -ōrum, m *a place in Africa not far from Utica*

magnĭdĭcus a -um (magnus and dico), *boastful*, Plaut.

magnĭfĭcē, compar, **magnĭfĭcentius**; superl, **magnĭfĭcentissĭmē**, adv. (magnificus), a, *splendidly, nobly, grandly, pompously, magnificently*, habitare, vivere, Cic, b, *gloriously*, vincere, Cic, c, *eloquently, in a lofty strain*, collaudare aliquem, Liv, in a bad sense, *haughtily, proudly*, loqui de bello, Sall

magnĭfĭcentĭa ae, f (magnificus). I. Of persons, 1, *loftiness of thought and action, high mindedness, magnanimity*, Cic, and in a bad sense, *boasting, pomposity of language*, Cic, 2, *magnificence, splendour*, odit populus Romanus privatam luxuriam, publicam magnificentiam diligit, Cic II. Transf., of inanimate objects, *splendour, grandeur, magnificence*; epularum, villarum, Cic

magnĭfĭco, 1 (magnificus), *to prize highly, esteem greatly*, Plaut

magnĭfĭcus -a -um, compar., **magnĭfĭcentior**; superl, **magnĭfĭcentissimus** (magnus and facio) I. Of persons, a, *magnificent, fond of display*, in suppliciis deorum magnifici, domi parci, Sall, b, *glorious, distinguished*, vir factis magnificus, Liv, c, *imposing, dignified*, adhortator, Liv, d, *high-souled, lofty*, animo excelso magnificoque, Cic II. Transf, of things, a, *splendid, magnificent*, villa, Cic, b, *glorious*, aedilitas, Cic; c, *dignified, lofty* (of language), dicendi genus, Cic, and in a bad sense, *boastful, pompous*, alia magnifica pro se et illis dolentia, Sall, d, *famous, eminent, distinguished*, magnificentissimum decretum, Cic

magnĭlŏquentĭa -ae, f (magniloquus), 1, *lofty or elevated language*, Homeri, Cic; 2, *pompous, boastful language, magniloquence*, alicuius, Liv.

magnĭlŏquus -a -um (magnus and loquor), *pompous or boastful in talk, magniloquent*; os, Ov.

magnĭtūdo -inis, f (magnus), *greatness, size, magnitude* I. Lit, A. 1, of space, mundi, Cic, fluminis, Caes, 2, of number, *great quantity*, fructuum, Cic, pecuniae, Cic. II. Transf, 1, *size, importance*, a, beneficii, Cic; b, *power*, reipublicae, Sall, 2, *greatness, high degree*, amoris, Cic, animi, *magnanimity*, Cic

magnŏpĕrē, and separately **magno ŏpĕrē**, adv (magnus and opus), *greatly, exceedingly, very much*, nihil mirari, Cic, magnopere delectare, Cic; non magno opere laboro quorsum, etc, Cic, in the superl, maximopere, Cic, maximo opere, *very greatly*, Cic

magnus -a -um, compar, **mājor** -us; superl, **maxĭmus (maxŭmus)** -a -um (from root MAC, whence magis, mactus, macto = μέγας), *great, large* I. Lit, 1, of size, *large, great, tall, long, broad*, domus, Cic, montes, Cat, litterae maximae, Cic; magnae aquae, *an inundation*, Liv, 2, a, applied to number, bulk, mass, maximum pondus auri, magnum numerum frumenti, vim mellis maximam exportasse, Cic, multitudo peditatūs, Caes, b, of value, *high, great, considerable*, ornatus muliebris pretii majoris, Cic; thus abl magno and genit magni, *at a high value, dear*, magni aestimare, *to esteem highly*, Cic, magni, maximi facere, Cic, magno emere, Cic, 3, of sound, *loud*, vox, Cic; exclamare majus, *in a louder tone* Cic II. A. Of time, 1, *long*, annus, Verg, 2, magno natu, *of great age*, Liv, and esp in compar and superl, with or without natu or annis, *older*, natu major frater, Cic; annos natus major quadraginta, Cic, Fabii Ambusti filiae duae nuptae, Ser Sulpicio major, minor Licinio Stoloni erat, *the elder to Sulpicius, the younger to Licinius*, Liv, majores natu, *the older people*, Cic, esp = *the senate*, Cic; majores, *ancestors, forefathers*, Cic, maxima virgo, *the oldest of the Vestals*, Ov B. Of importance, 1, *great, important, significant*, magna et ampla negotia Cic, reipublicae magnum aliquod tempus, Cic, 2, a, *great, powerful, mighty*, propter summam nobilitatem et singularem potentiam magnus erat, Cic., b, of talents, ability, *distinguished, eminent, able*, nemo vir magnus sine aliquo afflatu divino unquam fuit, Cic, 3, *serious, heavy, severe*, periculum, Caes, infamia, Cic, 4, a, *strong, high, noble*, magno animo, Cic; b, *proud*, magna verba, Verg

Māgo (-ōn) -ōnis, m *brother of Hannibal*

1 **măgus** i, m (μάγος), *a learned man or magician among the Persians*, Cic

2 **măgus** -a -um, *magical*, artes, Ov.

Māja -ae, f (Μαῖα), *the daughter of Atlas, who bore Mercury to Jupiter, one of the Pleiades*, Majā genitus, Verg, Majā natus, Hor, Majā creatus, Ov, *Mercury* (acc, Majan, Ov).

mâjālis -is, m. *a gelded boar*, Varr.; used as a term of reproach, Cic.

mājestas -ātis, f. (majus = magnus). **I.** *grandeur, dignity, majesty;* applied to the gods, to all persons in high office, and frequently to the Roman people, dii non censent esse suae majestatis, *to be consistent with their majesty*, Cic.; consulis, Cic.; patria, *the paternal authority*, Liv.; populi Romani, Cic.; majestatem minuere, *to offend against the sovereignty of the people*, Cic.; crimen majestatis, *treason*, Cic.; lex majestatis, Cic. **II.** *honour, excellence, splendour;* matronarum, Liv.

mājor, majores, v. magnus.

Mājus -i, m. mensis Majus or simply Majus, *the month of May*, Cic.; used adj., Calendae Majae, Cic.

mājuscŭlus -a -um (dim. of major), *somewhat larger, somewhat greater;* in aliqua majuscula cura, Cic.

māla -ae, f. (contracted for mandela from mando, as scala for scandela from scando), **1,** *the cheek-bone, jaw-bone*, both in men and animals, Verg.; **2,** *the cheek;* malae decentes, Hor.

mălăcĭa -ae, f. (μαλακία), *a calm at sea;* tanta subito malacia ac tranquillitas exstitit ut, etc., Caes.

mălăcisso, 1. (μαλακίζω), *to soften, render pliable*, Plaut.

mălăcus -a -um (μαλακός), *soft, pliable*, Plaut.; fig., *effeminate, delicate*, Plaut.

mălĕ, adv., compar., **pējus;** superl., **pessime** (malus), *badly, ill.* **I.** Lit., **1,** male olere, Cic.; male vestitus, Cic.; L. Antonio male sit, *evil be to L. Antonius*, Cic.; male audire, *to be ill spoken of*, Cic.; **2,** a, *wrongly, improperly, badly;* male agere, Cic.; alicui male facere, Cic.; **b,** *unsuccessfully, unfortunately;* suos labores et apparatus male cecidisse, Cic.; **c,** *inopportunely, in the wrong place;* male salsus, Hor.; **d,** *dishonestly, wickedly;* male-agere, Cic.; Carthago jam diu male cogitans, Cic. **II.** Transf., **1,** *bitterly;* male odisse, Caes.; **2, a,** *too much, excessively;* male superbus, Caes., **b,** with adj. and partic., to give a directly opposite meaning, male sanus, Cic.; male gratus, *unthankful*, Ov.

Mălĕa -ae, acc. -an, f. (Μαλέα, Μάλεια), *promontory in Laconia* (now *Malio di S. Angelo.*)

mălĕdīcē, adv. (maledicus), *calumniously, abusively, scurrilously;* dicere, Cic.

mălĕdīcens -entis, p. adj. (from maledico), *evil-speaking, abusive, scurrilous;* maledicentissima civitas, Cic.

mălĕdīco -dixi -dictum, 3. *to speak ill, slander, asperse, abuse, revile;* alicui, Cic.

mălĕdictĭo -ōnis, f. (maledico), *a reviling, abusing*, Cic.

mălĕdictum -i, n. (maledico), *a railing accusation, foul, abusive language;* maledicta in vitam alicuius conjicere, Cic.; maledicta in aliquem dicere or conferre or congerere, Cic.

mălĕdĭcus -a -um (maledico), *abusive, scurrilous;* conviciator, Cic.

mălĕfăcĭo -fēci -factum, 3. *to do an injury, to injure;* alicui, Plaut.

mălĕfactor -ōris, m. (malefacio), *an evildoer, malefactor*, Plaut.

mălĕfactum -i, n. (malefacio), *an ill deed, injury*, Cic.

mălĕfĭcē, adv. (maleficus), *maliciously, mischievously*, Plaut.

mălĕfĭcĭum -ii, n. (maleficus), **1,** *an evil deed, crime, mischief;* maleficium committere, admittere, Cic.; se non maleficii causā (*with hostile intent*) ex provincia egressum, Caes.; sine ullo maleficio, *without doing any harm*, Caes.; **2,** *sorcery*, Tac.

mălĕfĭcus -a -um (malefacio), *wicked, malicious, mischievous;* homo, Cic.

mălĕsuādus -a -um (male and suadeo), *ill-advising, seductive, persuading to evil*, Verg.

Mălĕventum -i, n. *an old town of the Hirpini in Samnium, the name of which the Romans changed to Beneventum.*

mălĕvŏlens -entis (male and volo), *envious, malevolent*, Plaut.; superl., malevolentissimae obtrectationes, Cic.

mălĕvŏlentĭa -ae, f. (malevolens), *ill-will, malice, hatred, malevolence;* malevolentia est voluptas ex malo alterius sine emolumento suo, Cic.

mălĕvŏlus -a -um (male and volo), *ill-disposed, wishing evil, malicious, envious, spiteful, malevolent;* alicui, Cic.; in aliquem, Cic.; malevoli de me sermones, Cic. Superl., v. malevolens. Subst., **mălĕvŏli** -ōrum, m. *envious, ill-disposed persons*, Cic.

Mālĭăcus sinus (κόλπος Μαλιακός), *a gulf in Thessaly, opposite Euboea.* Hence, **Māliensis** -e, *Malian.*

mālĭfĕr -fĕra -fĕrum (malum and fero), *apple-bearing*, Verg.

mălignē, adv. (malignus), **1,** *maliciously, malignantly, enviously;* loqui, Cic.; **2,** *stingily, sparingly;* dividere, Liv.; laudare, Hor.

mălignĭtas -ātis, f. (malignus), **1,** *maliciousness, ill-nature, malignity, spite*, Liv.; **2,** *stinginess, niggardliness;* malignitas praedae partitae, Liv.

mălignus -a -um (opp. benignus, malus and gigno). **I.** *of bad disposition, ill-disposed, malicious, malignant, wicked;* vulgus, Hor.; oculis malignis spectare, Verg.; leges, Ov. **II. A. 1,** *stingy, niggardly;* caupo, Hor.; **2,** transf., **a,** *barren, unfruitful;* collis, Verg.; **b,** *small, little, scanty;* lux, Verg.; aditus, Verg. **B.** *coy, shy*, Ov.

mălĭtĭa -ae, f. (malus), *badness of quality.* **I.** *wickedness, vice*, Sall. **II.** *craft, cunning, malice;* malitia est versuta et fallax nocendi ratio, Cic.; sometimes used in a playful sense like our "*roguery;*" tamen a malitia non discedis, Cic.

mălĭtĭōsē, adv. with compar. (malitiosus), *wickedly, knavishly, perfidiously;* facere aliquid, Cic.

mălĭtĭōsus -a -um (malitia), *crafty, roguish, knavish, wicked;* homo, Cic.; juris interpretatio, Cic.

mallĕŏlus -i, m. (dim. of malleus), *a little hammer;* **1,** *a hammer-shaped slip* (of a vine), *a mallet-shoot for planting*, Cic.; **2,** *a kind of fire-dart*, Cic.

mallĕus -i, m. *a hammer, mallet;* **a,** gen., Liv.; **b,** esp., *the axe used for slaying animals offered in sacrifice*, Ov.

Malloea -ae, f. *town in Thessaly* (near modern *Mologhusta*).

mālo, mālŭi, malle (for mavolo, from magis volo), *to choose rather, prefer.* **I.** Gen., **a,** with acc., hunc animum, Cic.; **b,** with infin., servire quam pugnare, Cic.; **c,** with acc. and infin., malo me vinci quam vincere, Cic.; with potius, Uticae potius quam Romae esse maluisset, Cic.; with magis, Liv.; **d,** with nom. and infin., esse quam videri bonus malebat, Sall.; **e,** with subj., mallem cognoscerem, Cic. **II.** Esp., *to be more favourable to;* in hac re malo universae Asiae et negotiatoribus, Cic.

mālŏbăthron (-um) -i, n. (μαλόβαθρον);

I, *an Indian or Syrian plant, from which a costly ointment was prepared*, Plin , 2, meton , *the oil of the plant*, Hor

1 **mălum** -i, n , v malus

2 **mālum** -i, n (μῆλον), *an apple*, and generally any similar fruit, as the *quince, peach, pomegranate*, etc , Verg , prov , ab ovo usque ad mala *from beginning to end* (as the Roman dinner began with eggs and ended with fruit), Hor

1 **mălus** a um, comp , **pējor** -us, superl , **pessĭmus** a -um, *bad* I Subjective, A. *bad, physically and intellectually*, 1, mali versus, Cic ; loquendi consuetudo, Cic , 2, a, *incapable*, poeta, Cic , b, *cowardly, weak* , juxta boni malique, strenui et imbelles multi obtruncari, Sall B. Morally *bad, wicked* , 1, mala consuetudo, Cic , subst , malus, *a villain*, Cic , 2, in politics, *evil disposed, disloyal, demagogic*; cives, Sall II. Objective, 1, adj , a, *bad*, as regards condition, position, etc , mala valetudo, *ill health*, Cic , mala copia (*excess*) stomachum sollicitat, Hor , carmen, *a libel*, Hor , malam opinionem habere de aliquo, Cic , fama, *ill repute*, Sall. ; b, *unfavourable, unsuccessful, disadvantageous* , pugna, Cic , in pejus ruere, *to become worse*, Verg , auspicium, *ill omened*, Cic , 2, subst , **mălum** -i, n *an evil* , a, bona aut mala, *good qualities or faults*, Sall , b, *harm, disaster, evil* , ne malum habeat, Cic , mala civilia, Cic , malo esse alicui, Cic , as an interjection to express aversion or dislike, quae, malum, est ista tanta audacia atque amentia, *what in the world*, Cic

2 **mālus** i, f (2. malum), *an apple-tree*, Verg

3 **mālus** i, m (prob from root MAC, whence magnus), 1, *the mast of a ship*, malum erigere, Cic , 2, in the circus, *the pole to which the awnings were fastened*, Liv

malva -ae, f (μαλαχη, from μαλακος), *the mallow*, Cic

Māmers -mertis, m *the Oscan and Sabine name of Mars*, hence **Māmertīni** -ōrum, m (*sons of Mars*), *the name assumed by certain mercenary troops who seized Messana* Adj , **Māmertīnus** a -um, *Mamertine*, civitas, Messana, Cic

Māmĭlius -a -um, *name of a Roman gens*

mămilla ae, f (dim of mamma), *a breast, teat, pap*, Juv , used as a term of endearment, Plaut.

mamma ae, f (μάμμα) I. *a breast, teat* , a, of men, mamma et barba, Cic , b, of women, mammam matris appetere, Cic , c, of the females of animals, suibus mammarum data est multitudo, Cic II. *mother, mamma*, Mart

mammōsus -a um (mamma), *full breasted, having large breasts*, Lucr

Māmurra -ae, m *a Roman knight of Formiae*, praefectus fabrum in Caesar's army in Gaul, where he amassed great wealth, urbs Mamurrarum, *Formiae*, Hor

mānābĭlis -e (mano), *flowing, penetrating*, frigus, Lucr

manceps -cĭpis, m (manus and capio) I. *a person who bought anything at a public legal auction*, and esp , *one who publicly contracted to farm state property* , *a purchaser, farmer, contractor* , praedae, Cic , manceps fit Chrysogonus, Cic II. Transf , 1, *a tenant, lessee*, Plin , 2, *a surety*, Plaut

Mancīnus -i, m , C. Hostilius, *consul at Rome, delivered up to the Numantines in consequence of a dishonourable peace made by him with them, which the senate refused to ratify*

mancĭpātĭo -ōnis, f (mancipo), *a formal transfer of property* , also *purchase*, Plin

mancĭpātus -ūs, m (mancipo), *a sale*, Plin

mancĭpium (mancŭpium) -ii (manus and capio), *a taking by the hand*, an old form of purchase in Rome in the presence of five witnesses Hence, I. Lit , in Roman law *a formal, legal purchase of anything* lex mancipii (mancipi), *the contract of sale*, Cic mancipio dare, *to sell formally*, Cic , mancipio accipere, *to buy*, Cic , res mancipi, *property which could be acquired by the ceremony of* mancipium, Cic II. Meton , *a slave acquired by the process of* mancipium, Cic

mancĭpo (mancŭpo), 1 (manus and capio), 1 *to transfer by* mancipium *or formal sale, to sell formally*, alienos, Plaut , quaedam mancipat usus *gives a title to*, Hor , transf , *to give up to* , saginae mancipatus, Tac

mancus -a um, 1, *maimed, crippled, lame* mancus et omnibus membris captus ac debilis, Cic , 2, transf , *imperfect, incomplete, defective* , virtus, Cic , praetura, Cic

mandātor ōris, m (mando), *one who suborns accusers or informers*, Suet

mandātum -i, n (mando), *a commission, charge, injunction, order* , and esp , *a verbal commission, message* , a, dare alicui mandata ut, etc , Cic mandata efficere, Cic , perficere, Liv , *to execute a commission* , negligere, fallere *fail to execute*, Ov , mandato meo, *by my command*, Cic , b, mandati judicium, *an action for the non-performance of a commission*, Cic

mandātus, abl -ū, m found only in abl sing (mando), *a commission, order, injunction* , mandatu meo, Cic

Mandēla ae, f *a town in the Sabine country*

1 **mando**, 1 (perhaps for manui or in manum do) I *to commit to the charge of, entrust, deliver* , alicui magistratum, Cic , aliquem aeternis tenebris, Cic , corpus humo, *to bury* Verg , se fugae, *to take to flight*, Caes , aliquid memoriae, *to commit to memory*, Cic , litteris, scriptis, *to commit to writing* II. *to enjoin, order, command, commission* , a, with acc , typos tibi mando (sc comparandos, emendos), Cic , Rhodiaca vasa mandavi, *ordered*, Cic , b, with ut or ne and the subj , or simply the subj , tibi mandavit ut, etc , Cic , Trebonio mandaverat ne, etc , Cic , huic mandat, Remos adeat, Cic

2 **mando**, mandi, mansum, 3 (μαω, μάσσω), *to chew, masticate* I. animalia alia sugunt, alia carpunt, alia vorant, alia mandunt, Cic , equi fulvum mandunt sub dentibus aurum, *champ the bit*, Verg , humum, *to bite the ground* (cf mordere humum), of those who fall in battle, Verg II. *to eat, devour, consume* , lora, Liv

mandra ae, f (μανδρα), 1, *a stall, cattle pen*, Mart , 2, *a herd of cattle*, Juv , 3, *a row of pawns*, on a draught-board, Mart

Mandūbĭi -ōrum, m *a people in Gallia Celtica, with a capital Alesia* (now *Alise*)

mandūcus i, m (2 mando), *a mask to represent a glutton*, Plaut

Mandurĭa -ae, f *a town in Lower Italy, between Aletium and Tarentum*

mānĕ, subst. indecl n *the early morning, dawn of morning* , ad ipsum mane, Hor multo mane, *very early in the morning*, Cic Adv , *in the morning, at early morning* , hodie mane, *early this morning*, Cic , bene mane, *very early in the morning*, Cic

mănĕo, mansi mansum, 2 (μενω) I. Intransit., *to remain, stay in any place* A.

seu maneant, seu proficiscantur, Caes.; in patria, Cic.; ad exercitum, Caes. **B.** 1, *to stay the night;* apud me, Cic.; sub Jove frigido, Hor.; 2, a, *to remain, endure, last;* nihil suo statu manet, Cic.; b, *to remain fast, continue steadfast in;* in amicitia, Cic.; in voluntate, Cic.; in condicione, *to abide by,* Cic.; 3, *to wait,* Plaut.; transf., *to wait for, await;* cuius fatum tibi manet, Cic. **II.** Transit., a, *to wait for;* hostium adventum, Liv.; b, *to await as fate or destiny;* quis me manet exitus? Ov.

mānes -ium, m. (lit. = boni, *the good*). **I.** *the shades of the departed, the spirits of the dead;* dii manes, Cic.; of the shade of a single person, patris Anchisae, Verg. **II.** Transf., 1, poet., *the lower world, infernal regions,* Verg.; 2, *the punishment of the lower world;* quisque suos patimur manes, Verg.; 3, *corpse, ashes, remains;* accipiet manes parvula testa meos, Prop.; omnium nudatos manes, Liv.

mango -ōnis, m. (μάγγανον), 1, *a dealer in articles, which he seeks to sell by rubbing up, furbishing,* etc.; *a roguish dealer,* Plin., Quint.; 2, esp., *a slave-dealer,* Suet.

mănĭca -ae, f. (manus). **I.** *the long sleeve of the tunic reaching to the hand, and serving as a glove,* Cic. **II.** Transf., *handcuff, manacle,* Hor., Verg.

mănĭcātus -a -um (manica), *having long sleeves;* tunicae, Cic.

mănĭcŭla -ae, f. (dim. of manus), *a little hand,* Plaut.

mănĭfestārĭus -a -um (manifestus) *plain, visible, evident, manifest,* Plaut.

mănĭfestē, adv. (manifestus), *plainly, visibly, evidently, manifestly,* Verg.

1\. **mănĭfestō,** adv., v. manifestus.

2\. **mănĭfesto,** 1. (manifestus), *to manifest, show clearly, reveal, discover;* aliquem, Ov.

mănĭfestus -a -um (manus and *feudo, lit. *struck with the hand), clear, visible, evident, manifest.* **I.** manifestae et apertae res, Cic.; manifestum atque deprehensum scelus, Cic.; adv., manifesto, *clearly, plainly;* manifesto deprehendere, comprehendere, comperisse, Cic. **II.** *caught in, manifestly betraying;* uti eos maxime manifestos habeant, *caught in the act,* Sall.; with genit. of crime, rerum capitalium, Sall.; vitae, *giving evident signs of life,* Tac.

Mānīlĭus -a -um, *name of a Roman gens.* C. Manilius, *tribune of the people,* B.C. 67, *the author of the Lex Manilia, which gave to Pompeius the sole command in the Mithridatic War.*

mănĭprĕtium = manupretium (q.v.).

mănĭpŭlāris (mănĭplāris) -e (manipulus), *belonging to a maniple;* judex, *chosen from a maniple* (from the common soldiers), Cic. Subst., **mănĭpŭlāris** -is, m. *a common soldier,* Cic.

mănĭpŭlārĭus -a -um (manipulus), *belonging or relating to a private soldier,* Suet.

mănĭpŭlātim, adv. (manipulus), 1, *in bundles or handfuls,* Plin.; 2, milit. t. t., *in maniples;* manipulatim structa acies, Liv.

mănĭpŭlus (poet. **mănĭplus**) -i, m. (manus and *pleo), *a handful.* **I.** Lit., *a small bundle or handful;* filicum manipli, Verg. **II.** Transf., *a company of foot soldiers, a division of the Roman army, three maniples forming a cohort* (so called because in early times the standard was a pole with a bundle of hay at the top), Caes.

Manlĭus -a -um, *name of a Roman gens.* **I.** M. Manlius Capitolinus, *who repulsed the attack of the Gauls upon the Capitol, afterwards thrown from the Tarpeian rock, on suspicion of aiming at kingly power.* **II.** L. Manlius and his son T. Manlius, *who received the surname of* Imperiosus *from their severity.* Hence, adj., **Manlĭānus** -a -um, *Manlian, relating to Manlius;* turba, seditio, Liv.; Manliana imperia, *severe commands,* Liv. Subst., **Manlĭānum** -i, n. *an estate of Cicero's.*

1\. **mannus** -i, m. (a Celtic word), *a small horse of Gaulish breed, highly prized by the Romans for its swiftness,* Liv.

2\. **Mannus** -i, m. *a god of the Germans, son of Tuisco,* Tac.

māno, 1. **I.** Intransit., *to flow, run.* **A.** Of fluids, fons nigra sub ilice manat, Ov.; aliquā re, *to flow, run, drip with anything,* Cic.; Herculis simulacrum multo sudore manavit, Cic. **B.** Of the air and other things, *to flow, spread;* 1, aër, qui per maria manat, *diffuses itself,* Cic.; 2, transf., *to proceed, come from;* peccata ex vitiis manant, Cic.; 3, *to spread abroad, spread, be diffused;* malum manavit per Italiam, Cic. **II.** Transit., *to exude, give out;* lacrimas (of a statue), Ov.; fig., mella poëtica, Hor.

mansĭo -ōnis, f. (maneo). **I.** *a remaining, stay, sojourn;* in vita, Cic. **II.** *a station, halting-place, night-quarters,* Plin.

mansĭto, 1. (intens. of maneo), *to abide, stay, sojourn, remain;* sub eodem tecto, Tac.

mansuēfăcĭo -fēci -factum, 3., pass. **mansuēfīo** -factus sum -fiĕri (mansues and facio). **I.** Lit., of animals, *to tame;* uri mansuefieri non possunt, Caes. **II.** Of men, a, *to soften, pacify;* plebem, Liv.; b, *to civilise;* a quibus mansuefacti et exculti, Cic.

mansuēs -is or -ētis (manus and sueo), *tame,* Plaut.

mansuesco -suēvi -suētum, 3. (manus and suesco). **I.** Transit., *to tame,* Verg. **II.** Intransit., *to become tame, grow tame, to become mild, softened;* nesciaque humanis precibus mansuescere corda, Verg.

mansuētē, adv. (mansuetus), *mildly, gently, quietly,* Cic.

mansuētūdo -ĭnis, f. (mansuetus). **I.** *tameness,* Plin. **II.** Transf., *mildness, clemency, gentleness;* imperii, Cic.; uti clementiā et mansuetudine in aliquem, Caes.

mansuētus -a -um, p. adj. (from mansuesco), *tame.* **I.** Lit., of animals, sus, Liv. **II.** Transf., *mild, soft, gentle, quiet;* mansuetus in senatu, Cic.: ut mansuetissimus viderer, Cic.; Musae mansuetiores (of philosophy, rhetoric, etc., as opposed to contentious and political eloquence), Cic.

mantēlĕ (mantīlĕ) -is, n. and **mantēlĭum** -ii, n. (manus), *a towel, napkin,* Verg.

mantēlĭum -ii, n. = mantele (q.v.).

mantēlum (mantellum) -i, n. *a covering, veil, concealment,* Plaut.

mantĭca -ae, f. *a wallet, knapsack, saddle-bag,* Hor.

Mantĭnēa -ae, f. (Μαντίνεια), *a town in Arcadia, scene of the victory and death of Epaminondas.*

1\. **manto,** 1. (freq. of maneo), *to remain, wait, wait for,* Plaut.

2\. **Mantō** -ūs, f. (Μαντώ). **I.** *daughter of the Theban seer Tiresias, mother of the seer Mopsus.* **II.** *an Italian prophetess, mother of Ocnus, the founder of Mantua.*

Mantŭa -ae, f. *a town in north Italy, on the river Mincius, near to the birthplace of Vergil.*

mănŭālis -e (manus), *adapted, fitted to the hand, fitting the hand, relating to the hand;* saxa, *thrown by hand,* Tac.

mănŭbiae -ārum, f (manus), 1, *the money obtained from the sale of booty, esp the general's share, who usually spent it in erecting some public building*, porticum de manubiis Cimbricis fecit, Cic., transf, *the profits of an office*, manubias alicui concedere Cic, *plunder, booty*, Suet, 2, in augury, *a flash of lightning*, Sen

mănŭbiālis -e (manubiae), *of or relating to booty*, Suet

mănŭbiārius a -um (manubiae), *of or relating to booty*, Plaut

mănŭbrium ii, n (manus), *a haft, handle*, aureum vasis, Cic

mănŭf . . manu . .

mănŭlĕus -i, m (manus), *the long sleeve of a tunic*, Plaut

mănūmissio -ōnis, f (manumitto), *the emancipation or manumission of a slave*, Cic

mănūmitto -misi -missum (manus and mitto), 3 *to manumit, emancipate a slave*, aliquem, Cic

mănŭprĕtium (mănĭprĕtium) -ii, n (often found in two words, manus pretium), *wages, hire, pay*, Cic, transf, *a reward*, perditae civitatis, Cic

mănus ūs, f (connected with μάω, *to touch*), *the hand* **I.** Lit. and fig **A.** Gen, manus dextera, laeva, Cic, accipere aliquid manibus, Cic; manus adhibere vectigalibus, *lay hands on, rob*, Cic, conferre ferrum et manus, Cic, manus dare, *to surrender*, Cic, deponere aliquid de manibus, Cic, elabi de manibus, Cic, esse in manibus, 1, *to be in our hands*, oratio est in manibus, *can be read, is well known*, Cic, 2, *to be in preparation*; liber mihi est in manibus, Cic, 3, *to be near, to be present*, Caes, sed ecce in manibus vir et praestantissimo ingenio, etc, Cic; fugere e manibus, Cic, lavare manus, Cic, prehendere alicuius manum, Cic, aliquem manu, Cic, ne manum quidem vertere alicuius rei causā, *not to move a finger, not to take any trouble*, Cic. Particular phrases victoriam in manibus videre, *at hand*, Cic; ad manum esse, *to be near at hand*, Liv, servum sibi habere ad manum, *as a private secretary* Cic, de manu, *with one's own hand*, facere, Cic, de manu in manum tradere, *to give from one's hand into the hand of another*, Cic, plenā manu, *liberally*, plenā manu alicuius laudes in astra tollere, Cic, per manus, *with the hands*, trahere, Caes, *from hand to hand*, traditae per manus religiones, Liv, manibus aequis (*with equal advantage, after a drawn battle*) dirimere pugnam, Liv **B.** Esp 1, *the fist*, used for courage, force, violence, manu capere urbes, Sall; 2, *hand to hand fight*, res venit ad manus atque ad pugnam, Cic, 3, abl manu, *by manual labour, by art, artificially*, manu sata, *sown by hand*, Caes; urbs manu munitissima, Cic, 4, *power, jurisdiction*, haec non sunt in manu nostra, Cic. **II.** Meton, 1, *the hand*, i e, *the work of the artist or craftsman*, extrema, *the finishing touch*, Cic, extrema manus non accessit eius operibus, Cic, 2, *handwriting*, redeo ad meam manum, *I have begun again to write with my own hand*, Cic **III.** Transf, 1, *the trunk of an elephant*, Cic, 2, manus ferrea, *a grappling-iron used in naval warfare*, Caes, 3, a, *a band* or *body of men*, conjuratorum, Cic, b, *an armed band*, manum facere, Cic, conducere, Caes, cogere, Caes

măpālia ium, n (a Punic word), *huts, hovels, the movable habitations of the African Nomads*, Sall

mappa ae, f 1, *a table-napkin*, Hor, 2, *a cloth or napkin thrown down in the circus as a signal for the races to begin*, Juv

Mărăthōn -ōnis, m and f (Μαραθών), *a plain in Attica, where the Persian army was defeated by the Athenians* Adj, **Marathōnius** a -um, *Marathonian*

Mărăthos i, f (Μάραθος), *a Phoenician town opposite to the island of Aradus* Adj, **Mărăthēnus** -a -um, *belonging to Marathos*

mărăthrum -i, n (μάραθρον), *fennel*, Ov

Marcellus -i, m *the cognomen of an illustrious family of the gens Claudia* **I.** M. Claudius Marcellus, *the conqueror of Syracuse, defeated Hannibal at Nola, slew with his own hand* (?) *king of the Insubres with his own hand* **II.** M Claudius Marcellus, *an enemy of Caesar, but afterwards pardoned by him* **III.** M Claudius Marcellus, *nephew, adopted son, and son in law of the Emperor Augustus* Hence, **Marcellīa** -ōrum, n *the festival of Marcellus, a festival of the family of Marcellus in Sicily*, Liv

marcĕo, 2 **I.** *to wither, to droop*, Mart **II.** Transf, *to be faint, languid, feeble, lazy*, either from old age or indulgence, marcent luxuriā, Liv

marcesco, 3 (marceo) **I.** *to begin to droop*, Plin **II.** Transf, *to languish, grow weak, feeble*, vino, Ov, desidiā, Liv

marcĭdus a -um (marceo), 1, *faded, withering, drooping*, lilia, Ov, 2, transf, *enfeebled, languid, heavy, besotted from immoderate indulgence in eating, drinking, or sleeping*, somno aut libidinosis vigiliis, Tac

Marcĭus a um, *name of a Roman gens, the most celebrated members of which were* 1, Ancus Marcius, *fourth king of Rome*, 2, L Marcius, *a Roman knight, who commanded in Spain on the death of Scipio* Adj, *Marcium* aqua, *an aqueduct commenced by Ancus Marcius, restored by Q Marcius Rex*, saltus (in Liguria, so called from the defeat of Q Marcius, 188 B C), Liv Hence, **Marciānus** a -um, *Marcian*, foedus, *made by L Marcius with the inhabitants of Cadiz*

Marcŏmāni and **Marcŏmanni** -ōrum, m *a powerful German tribe*

marcor -ōris, m (marceo), *rottenness, decay, putrefaction*, Plin

Marcus i, m *a common Roman praenomen, gen abbreviated M*

măre is, n *the sea* **I.** Lit, mare Aegaeum, Cic., mare oceanus, Caes, nostrum mare, *the Mediterranean Sea*, Caes, superum, *the Adriatic*, Cic, inferum, *the Tuscan Sea*, Cic, conclusum, *inland sea*, Caes, clausum, *not navigable*, Cic, mare ingredi, *to go to sea*, Cic, mare infestum habere, *to infest the sea* (of pirates), Cic, terrā marique, *by sea and land*, Cic, polliceri maria et montes, *to make boundless promises*, Sall **II.** Meton, *sea water*, Chium maris expers, *unmixed with sea water*, Hor

Mărĕa ae, f or **Mărĕōta** -ae, f (Μάρεια), *a lake and city of Lower Egypt, famous for its wine*, hence, adj, 1, **Mărĕōtĭcus** -a -um, *Mareotic, Egyptian*, subst, **Mărĕōtĭcum** -i n *Mareotic wine*, 2, **Mărĕōtis** -idis, f poet = *Egyptian*, vites, Verg

margărīta -ae, f (μαργαρίτης) and **margărītum** i, n *a pearl*, Cic.

margĭno, 1 (margo), *to make a border to, to border*, Liv

margo -ĭnis, m and f **I.** *a border, edge*, scuti, Liv, fontis, Ov **II.** Transf, *boundary*, imperii, Ov

Mărīca ae, f *a nymph to whom a grove near Minturnae was sacred*, poet, *a lake near Minturnae named after her*, Hor.

mărīnus -a -um (mare), *of or relating to the sea, marine;* marini terrenique humores, Cic.; ros, *rosemary*, Hor.

mărisca -ae, f. **1,** *a large fig*, Mart.; **2,** *the piles*, Juv.

mărīta, v. maritus.

mărītālis -e (maritus), *relating to marriage or a married pair, conjugal, matrimonial, marital;* vestis, Ov.

mărĭtĭmus (mărĭtŭmus) -a -um (mare), **1,** *of* or *relating to the sea, marine, maritime;* praedo, *a pirate*, Cic.; imperium, *a naval command*, Cic.; **2,** *on the sea* or *on the sea-coast;* civitas, Caes.; silva, Cic. Subst., **mărĭtĭma** -ōrum, n. *maritime regions, places on the sea-coast*, Cic.

mărīto, 1. (maritus). **I.** *to wed, marry, give in marriage;* principem, Tac. **II.** Transf., of plants, *to bind one to another, to train one on another*, Hor.

mărītus -a -um (mas). **I.** Adj., **1,** lit., *of* or *relating to marriage, matrimonial, nuptial;* foedus, Ov.; Venus, *conjugal love*, Ov.; domus, *houses of married people*, Liv.; **2,** transf., of plants, *tied or trained together;* ulmus, Cat. **II.** Subst., **1, mărītus** -i, m. **a,** *a husband*, Cic.; **b,** *a lover, suitor*, Prop.; **c,** transf., of animals, maritus olens, *the he-goat*, Hor.; **2, mărīta** -ae, f. *a wife*, Hor.

Mărĭus -a -um, *the name of a Roman gens, the most distinguished member of which was* C. Marius, *seven times consul, conqueror of Jugurtha and the Cimbri, rival of Sulla, leader of the popular party at Rome.* Adj., *Marian.* Hence, **Mărĭānus** -a -um, *Marian.*

Marmărĭca -ae, f. *a district in Africa between Egypt and the Syrtes*, now *Barka.* Hence, **Marmărĭdēs** -ae, m. *a man of Marmarica.*

marmor -ŏris, n. (μάρμαρος). **I.** *marble.* **A.** Lit., Cic. **B.** Meton., **1,** *a marble statue*, Ov.; duo marmora, Ov.; in plur., *public monuments*, Hor.; **2,** *the white foamy surface of the sea;* marmor infidum, Verg. **II.** Transf., *stone generally*, Ov.

marmŏrĕus -a -um (marmor). **I.** *marble, made of marble;* signum, Cic.; aliquem marmoreum facere or ponere, *to make a marble statue of*, Verg. **II.** Transf., *like marble in smoothness* or *colour;* cervix, Verg.; gelu, Ov.; aequor, Verg.

Măro -ōnis, m. *the cognomen of the poet P. Vergilius*, v. Vergilius.

Marobodŭus -i, m. *king of the Suevi, who was defeated by Arminius, fled to Italy, and was kindly received by the Romans.*

Mărōnēa (-īa) -ae, f. (Μαρώνεια). **I.** *a town of Italy in the Samnite country*, now *Marano.* **II.** *a town in Thrace*, now *Marogna.* Hence, **Mărōnītēs** -ae, m. *a Maronite.*

Marpessus (Marpēsus) -i, m. *a mountain in the Island of Paros.* Adj., **Marpessĭus (Marpēsĭus)** -a -um, *Marpessian.*

marra -ae, f. *a hoe for rooting up weeds*, Juv.

Marrŭbĭum -ĭi, n., v. Marruvium.

Marrūcīni -ōrum, m. *a people on the coast of Latium, between the Frentani and the river Aternus.* Hence, adj., **Marrūcīnus** -a -um, *of or belonging to the Marrucini.*

Marrŭvĭum (Marrŭbĭum) -ĭi, n. *capital of the Marsi, on the banks of the Lacus Fucinus*, now *S. Benedetto.* Adj., **Marrŭvĭus** -a -um, *of or belonging to Marruvium.*

Mars, Martis, m. (poet. form. Māvors). **I.** *Mars, the god of war.* **A.** Lit., Mars Gradivus, Liv. **B.** Meton., **1,** *war, battle, fight;* **a,** lit., Hectoreus, *with Hector*, Ov.; invadunt martem, *begin the fray*, Verg.; suo marte cadunt, *in fight with one another*, Ov.; femineo marte cadere, *in fight with a woman*, Ov.; prov., suo marte, *by one's own resources*, rex suo marte res suas recuperavit, Cic.; esp., *manner of fighting;* equitem suo alienoque marte pugnare—i.e., *both on horse and on foot*, Liv.; **b,** transf., of legal disputes, forensis, Ov.; **2,** *the fortune* or *issue of war;* aequo marte, Liv.; mars belli communis, Cic.; **3,** *bravery, warlike spirit;* si patrii quid martis habes, Verg. **II.** Transf., *the planet Mars*, Cic. Adj., **Martĭus, Martĭālis** (q.v.).

Marsi -ōrum, m. **I.** *the Marsians, a people of Latium, notorious as sorcerers and snake-charmers.* Adj., **a, Marsĭcus** -a -um, *Marsic;* bellum, *the Social War*, Cic.; **b, Marsus** -a -um, *Marsian;* nenia, *enchantments*, Hor. **II.** *a people in Germany, between the Rhine, the Lippe, and the Ems.*

marsūpĭum -ĭi, n. (μαρσύπιον), *a money-bag, purse, pouch*, Plaut.

Marsўās -ae, m. and **Marsўa** -ae, m. (Μαρσύας). **I.** *a satyr, beaten in a musical contest with Apollo, who flayed him alive. A statue of Marsyas stood in the Roman forum, at the spot where lawyers transacted their business.* **II.** *a river in Phrygia Major, flowing into the Maeander.*

1. **Martĭālis** -e (Mars), **1,** *of* or *relating to Mars, consecrated to Mars;* flamen, Cic.; lupi, *sacred to Mars*, Hor.; plur. subst., **Martĭāles,** m. *the priests of Mars*, Cic.; **2,** *relating to the Legio Martia;* milites, Cic.

2. **Martĭālis** -is, m. M. Valerius, *the celebrated Roman epigrammatist of Bilbilis in Spain, who flourished under the emperors Domitian, Nerva, and Trajan.*

Martĭcŏla -ae, c. (Mars and colo), *a worshipper of Mars*, Ov.

Martĭgĕna -ae, c. (Mars and geno = gigno), *begotten of Mars, offspring of Mars*, Ov.

Martĭus -a -um (Mars). **I.** *of* or *relating to the god Mars, sacred to Mars;* **a,** lit., mensis, *the month of March*, Plin.; Calendae Martiae, *the 1st of March*, Cic.; proles, *Romulus and Remus*, Ov.; miles, *Roman* (as Mars was considered to be the ancestor of the Roman people), Ov.; Campus Martius, *the plain of Mars at Rome*, Cic.; gramine Martio, *on the Campus Martius*, Hor.; Martia legio, *name of a Roman legion*, Cic.; **b,** meton., *warlike;* Penthesilea, Verg.; Thebe, *scene of many wars*, Ov. **II.** Transf., *belonging to the planet Mars;* fulgor rutilus horribilisque terris quem Martium dicitis, Cic.

Marus -i, m. *a river in Dacia*, now *the Marosch.*

mas, măris, m. *the male* (opp. femina), applied to men, animals, and plants. **I.** Lit., a prima congressione maris et feminae, Cic.; mas vitellus, *a male yolk*, i.e., *that would produce a male chick*, Hor.; applied to plants, ure mares oleas, Ov. **II.** *manly, vigorous;* animi mares, Hor.; male mas, *unmanly, effeminate*, Cat.

Masaesўli and **Masaesўli** -ōrum and -ûm, m. *a people in Numidia.*

mascŭlīnus -a -um (masculus), *of the male sex, masculine*, Phaedr.

mascŭlus -a -um (dim. of mas), *of the male sex, male.* **I.** Lit., tura, Verg.; libido, Hor. Subst., **mascŭlus** -i, m. *a male*, Liv. **II.** Transf., *masculine, manly, bold, courageous;* proles, Hor.

Măsĭnissa -ae, m. *king of Numidia, father of Micipsa, grandfather of Jugurtha, ally of the Romans.*

massa -ae, f (μᾶζα), *a lump, mass*, picis, Verg, esp, **a,** lactis coacti, *of cheese*, Ov, **b,** of metals, Plin, absol, *a mass of gold*, Ov, *copper*, Verg, **c,** *chaos*, Ov

Massăgĕtes -ae, m (Μασσαγέτης), plur, Massagetae, *a Scythian people on the east coast of the Caspian Sea*

Massĭcus -i, m *a mountain in Campania, famous for its wine*, now *Monte Masso* or *Massico*, hence, Massicum vinum, or subst, **Massĭcum** -i, n *Massic wine*, Hor, so, humor Massicus, Verg

Massĭlĭa -ae, f *a celebrated town in Gallia Narbonensis, colonised from Phocaea in Asia Minor*, now *Marseilles* Adj, **Massĭlĭensis** -e, *of or belonging to Massilia*

Massȳli -ōrum, m and (poet) -um, *a people in Numidia* Adj, **Massȳlus** -a -um, poet = *African*, equites, Verg

mastīgĭa -ae, m (μαστιγίας), *a worthless fellow, scoundrel*, lit, *one who deserves a whipping*, Plaut

mastrūca (mastrūga) -ae, f. (a Sardinian word), *a rough garment of sheep-skin*, used as a term of reproach, Plaut

mastrūcātus -a -um (mastruca), *clothed in the mastruca*, Cic.

matăra -ae, f and **matăris (matĕris)** -is, f (a Celtic word), *a Gallic pike*, Caes

mătellĭo -ōnis, m. (dim of matula), *a small pot, vessel*, Cic

māter, mātris, f (μήτηρ), *a mother* **I** Lit, **1,** of men, **a,** de pietate in matrem, Cic, matrem fieri de Jove, *to become pregnant by*, Ov, **b,** esp, (α) = *woman, wife*, Liv, (β) applied to a nurse, Verg, (γ) to goddesses, Mater Terra, Liv, magna mater, Cic, or simply, mater (sc deorum), *Cybele*, Verg, Amorum, *Venus*, Ov, **2,** of animals, *dam, parent*, Verg, **3, a,** of plants, *the parent stem*, Verg, **b,** of towns, *mother city;* Populonia mater, Verg, **c,** of countries, haec terra quam matrem appellamus, Liv **II.** Meton, *motherly love*, simul matrem labare sensit, Ov. **III.** Fig, *source, origin*, mater omnium bonarum artium est sapientia, Cic, utilitas justi prope mater et aequi, Hc.

mātercŭla -ae, f (dim of mater), *a little mother*, Cic

mātĕrĭa -ae, f and **mātĕrĭes** -ēi, f (mater), *matter, material, stuff of which anything is composed* **I.** Lit, **A.** Gen, materia rerum, Cic, materiam praebet seges arida, *fuel*, Ov, materiam superabat opus, Ov, esp, *building materials*, delata materia omnis infra Veliam, Liv **B.** Esp **1,** *wood*, **a,** *green wood*, materies vitis, *the stem*, Cic, **b,** *wood for building, timber*, Cic, materiam caedere, Liv, **2,** *provisions*, Ov **II.** Transf, **1,** *matter, stuff, materials*, ad jocandum, Cic, artis, Cic, **2,** *incitement, occasion, cause*, seditionis, Cic, ... unum summi materies mali, Hor, materiam dare invidiae, Cic, **3,** *natural disposition, abilities*, Catonis, Cic

mātĕrĭārĭus -a -um (materia), *of or relating to timber*, Plin Subst, **mātĕrĭārĭus** -ii, m *a timber merchant*, Plaut

mātĕrĭes -ēi, f = materia (q v)

mātĕrĭo, 1 (materies), *to build, construct of wood*, aedes male materiatae, *of bad wood work*, Cic

mātĕrĭor, 1, dep (materia), *to fell wood, procure wood*, Caes

matĕris = matara (q v).

māternus -a um (mater), *of or relating to a mother, maternal;* sanguis, Cic; tempora, *period of pregnancy*, Ov, nobilitas, *on the mother's side*, Verg, Caesar cingens materna tempora myrto (i e, of Venus, mother of Aeneas and mythical ancestress of the Julian gens), Verg

mātertĕra -ae, f (mater), *a mother's sister, maternal aunt*, Cic

măthēmătĭcus -a -um (μαθηματικός) **I.** Adj, *mathematical*, Plin **II.** 1, subst, **măthēmătĭcus** -i, m, **a,** *a mathematician*, Cic, **b,** *an astrologer*, Tac, **2, măthēmătĭca** -ae, f, **a,** *mathematics*, Sen, **b,** *astrology*, Suet.

Mātīnus -i, m *a mountain in Apulia, famous for its honey* Hence, adj, **Mātīnus** -a -um, *Matine*

Matiscō -ōnis, f *town of the Aedui in Gaul*, now *Mâcon*

Mātĭus -a -um, *name of a Roman gens*

Mātrālĭa -ium, n (mater), *the annual festival of the Mater Matuta, celebrated on the 11th of June*, Ov

mātrĭcīda -ae, c (mater and caedo), *a person who murders his mother, a matricide*, Cic

mātrĭcīdĭum -ii, n (matricida), *the slaying of a mother by her son, matricide*, Cic

mātrĭmōnĭum -ii, n (mater) **I.** *marriage, matrimony*, aliquam in matrimonium ducere, *to marry*, Cic, dare alicui filiam in matrimonium, Cic, habere aliquam in matrimonio, Cic, aliquam ex matrimonio expellere, Cic **II.** Meton, matrimonia, *married women*, Tac

mātrīmus -a -um (mater), *having a mother still living*, Cic

1 **mātrōna** -ae, f (mater), *a married woman, matron*, esp, *an honourable, noble, respectable lady*, Cic, *an epithet of Juno*, Hor, more rarely = *wife*, Cic

2 **Mātrŏna** -ae, m *a river in Gallia Lugdunensis*, now the *Marne*

mātrōnālis -e (matrona), *of or relating to a married woman, fit for a matron, matronly*, decus, Liv, feriae Matronales, *a festival of the Roman matrons held in honour of* Juno Lucina *on the 1st of March* (hence called femineae calendae), Juv

matta -ae, f *a mat of rushes*, Ov

mattĕa -ae, f (ματτύα), *a dainty dish, a dainty*, Mart

Mattĭăcum -i, n *a town near the modern Wiesbaden*, hence, **Mattĭăcus** -a -um, *relating to Mattiacum*

mătŭla -ae, f *a vessel, pot*, as a term of reproach, *simpleton!* Plaut

mātūrātē, adv (maturatus from maturo), *quickly* Plaut

mātūrē, adv (maturus) **I** *at the right time, seasonably, opportunely* senatus, Cic, satis mature occurrere, Caes **II** 1, *in good time, betimes, soon, early*, senem fieri, Cic, maturius proficisci, Caes, maturissime rem vindicare, Cic, **2,** *too soon, prematurely*, mature decessit, Nep

mātūresco, mātūrŭi, 3 (maturus) **I.** *to ripen, become ripe*, quum maturescere frumenta inciperent, Caes **II** *to come to maturity*, partus maturescunt, Ov, nubilibus maturuit annis, Ov

mātūrĭtas -ātis f (maturus), *ripeness* **I.** Lit, of fruits, frugum, Cic **II.** Transf **a** *full development, ripeness, maturity* scelerum maturitas in nostri consulatūs tempus erupit, Cic *of the development of the mind*, aetatis ad prudentiam, Cic, **b,** *the right moment of time, fulness of time*, eius rei maturitas nequedum venit, Cic

mātūro, 1 (maturus) **I.** Transit, **A.** Lit. *to make fruits ripe, to ripen*, uvas, Tib, maturata uva, *ripe*, Cic. **B.** Transf., **1,** *to do early, betimes;* multa . . . quae maturare datur, Verg.; **2,** *to quicken, hasten, accelerate;* huic mortem, Cic.; insidias consuli, Sall.; iter, Caes.; fugam, Verg.; with infin., *to hasten, make haste to do anything;* flumen exercitum transducere maturavit, Caes.; oro ut matures venire, Cic.; ni Catilina maturasset signum dare, *had been too hasty in giving the signal*, Sall. **II.** Intransit., *to hasten, make haste;* successor tuus non potest ita maturare, Cic.

mātūrus -a -um. **I.** *ripe*, **A.** Of fruits, poma, Cic.; uva, Verg. **B.** *ripe, mature, perfect, seasonable;* **1,** lit., physically, **a,** maturi soles, *powerful*, Verg.; **b,** *ripe in point of age, grown up, marriageable;* virgo, Hor.; with dat., virgo matura viro, Verg.; progenies matura militiae, *ripe for*, Liv.; also *aged, of ripe years;* senex, Hor.; maturus aevi, Verg.; aetas, Hor.; **2,** transf., **a,** intellectually and morally, *ripe in understanding and character;* annis gravis atque animi maturus Aletes, Verg.; **b,** *ripe, developed, mature, timely;* gloria, Liv.; maturum videbatur (*it seemed the proper time*) repeti patriam, Liv. **II. 1,** *early;* hiems, Caes.; decessio, Cic.; **2,** transf., *quick, speedy;* judicium, Cic.

Mātūta -ae, f. *the goddess of the early morn;* gen., Matuta Mater, *an ancient Italian goddess, identified with Ino* or *Leucothea.*

mātūtīnus -a -um, *early in the morning, pertaining to the morning;* tempora, Cic.; equi, *horses of Aurora*, Ov.; pater, *Janus invoked in the morning*, Hor.

Mauri -ōrum, m. (Μαῦροι), *the Moors, inhabitants of Mauritania;* hence, **1, Maurus** -a -um, *Moorish;* poet., *African, Carthaginian;* **2, Mauritānĭa** -ae, f. *Mauritania, a district in Africa, between Numidia and the Atlantic Ocean.*

Maurūsĭa -ae, f. (Μαυρουσία), *Mauritania.* Adj., **Maurūsĭus** -a -um, *Mauritanian*, also poet. for *African.*

Mausōlus -i, m. (Μαύσωλος), *king of Caria, husband of Artemisia, who erected a splendid monument to his memory.* Adj., **Mausōlēus** -a -um, *belonging to Mausolus;* sepulchrum, or gen. subst., **Mausōlēum** -i, n. *the tomb of Mausolus;* or, in general, *any splendid sepulchre*, Suet.

māvŏlo = malo (q.v.).

Māvors -vortis, m., archaic and poet. for Mars. Adj., **Māvortĭus** -a -um, *belonging to Mars, Martial;* moenia, *Rome*, Ov.; tellus, *Thrace*, Verg.; proles, *the Thebans*, Ov.; subst., Mavortius, *Meleager, the son of Mars*, Ov.

maxilla -ae, f. (dim. of mala), *the jaw-bone, jaw*, Cic.

maxĭmē, superl. of magis (q.v.).

maxĭmĭtas -ātis, f. (maximus), *greatness, size*, Lucr.

maxĭmŏpĕrĕ, v. magnopere.

1. **maxĭmus,** superl. of magnus (q.v.).

2. **Maxĭmus,** v. Fabius.

māzŏnŏmus -i, m. (μαζονόμος), *a charger, large dish*, Hor.

mĕāmet, meapte, v. meus.

mĕātus -ūs, m. (meo), **1,** *a going, passing motion;* aquilae, *flight*, Tac.; **2,** *a way, path, passage;* Danubius in Ponticum mare sex meatibus (*mouths*) erumpit, Tac.

Mēcastor, v. Castor.

meddix -ĭcis, m. (Oscan metideicos, *giver of counsel*), *the name of a magistrate among the Oscans;* with the addition, tuticus, meddix tuticus, *chief magistrate*, Liv.

Mēdēa -ae, f. (Μήδεια), *an enchantress, daughter of king Aeetes in Colchis; helped Jason, the Argonaut, to obtain the golden fleece, fled away with him, afterwards deserted by him.*

Mēdēis -ĭdis, f. (Medea), *magical*, Ov.

mĕdens -entis, m. (partic. of medeor), subst., *a physician*, Ov.

mĕdĕor, 2. dep. *to heal, to cure;* **1,** lit., **a,** of persons, with dat., morbo, Cic.; **b,** prov., quum capiti mederi debeam, reduviam curo, *to neglect a great evil while taking care of a small one*, Cic.; of things, *to do good to, be good for*, Liv.; **2,** transf., *to heal, assist, alleviate;* incommodis omnium, Cic.; afflictae et perditae reipublicae, Cic.

Mēdi -ōrum, m. (Μῆδοι), *the Medes;* poet. = the *Persians, Assyrians, Parthians;* sing., Medus, *the Mede*, poet. = *Persian.* Hence, **a, Mēdĭa** -ae, f. (Μηδία), *Media*, a district of Asia; flumen, *Euphrates*, Hor.; **b, Mēdĭcus** -a -um, *Median;* transf., *Assyrian, Persian;* **c, Mēdus** -a -um, *Median*, poet. = *Persian, Assyrian.*

mĕdĭastīnus -i, m. (medius), *a slave who performed menial offices, a drudge*, Cic.

mēdĭca -ae, f. (Μηδική), *lucerne, clover*, Verg.

mĕdĭcābĭlis -e (medicor), *curable;* nullis amor est medicabilis herbis, Ov.

mĕdĭcāmen -ĭnis, n. (medicor), *a drug, medicine, medical substance.* **I.** Lit., **A.** In a good sense, Cic.; fig., iratae medicamina fortia praebe, Ov. **B.** In a bad sense, *poison, poisonous draught*, Tac. **II.** Transf., **1,** *colouring matter, dye*, and esp., *rouge, paint*, Cic.; **2,** *an artificial means of improving a natural product*, Plin.

mĕdĭcāmentum -i, n. (medicor), *a drug, medicine, remedy.* **I.** Lit., **A.** salutare, Cic.; fig., *remedy, cure;* doloris, Cic. **B.** *a poisonous drug, poison*, Cic.; coquere medicamenta, Liv. **II.** Transf., *a colouring substance, dye*, Cic.; fig., fucati medicamenta ruboris et candoris, Cic.

1. **mĕdĭcātus** -a -um, p. adj. (from medico), *healing, medicinal*, Plin.

2. **mĕdĭcātus** -ūs, m. (medicor), *a means of enchantment, charm*, Ov.

mĕdĭcīna -ae, f., v. medicinus.

mĕdĭcīnus -a -um (medicus), *relating* or *belonging to the art of healing.* **I.** Adj., Varr. **II.** Subst. **mĕdĭcīna** -ae, f. **A.** (sc. ars), *the art of healing;* medicinam exercere, *to practise medicine*, Cic.; medicinam facere alicui, *to heal*, Cic. **B.** (sc. res), *means of healing, medicine;* medicinam adhibere, Cic.; fig., *cure;* laboris, Cic.

mĕdĭco, 1. (medicus), *to heal, cure;* **1,** *to sprinkle with medicinal juices, to medicate, drug;* semina, Verg.; partic., medicatus, e.g., medicatae sedes, *medicated, sprinkled with a preparation*, Verg.; somnus, *procured by drugs* or *magic*, Ov.; **2,** *to dye;* capillos, Ov.

mĕdĭcor, 1. dep. (medicus), *to heal, cure;* alicui, Verg.; aliquid, Verg.

1. **mĕdĭcus** -a -um (medeor), *healing, wholesome, medicinal.* **I.** Adj., ars, Ov. **II.** Subst., **mĕdĭcus** -i, m. *a doctor, physician;* medicum ad aegrum adducere, Cic.

2. **Mēdĭcus,** v. Medi.

mĕdĭē, adv. (medius), *moderately*, Tac.

mĕdĭĕtas -ātis, f. (medius), *the middle, midst, that which is in the middle*, translation of the Greek μεσότης, Cic.

mĕdimnum -i, n. and **mĕdimnus** -i, m. (μέδιμνος), *a Greek measure of capacity, containing six Roman modii*, Cic. (genit. plur., gen. medimnûm).

mĕdĭŏcris -e (medius), *moderate, middling.*

I. Lit, spatium, Caes II. Transf 1, *middling, mediocre, tolerable, indifferent*, orator, vir, Cic, eloquentia, Cic, 2, *moderate, calm*, animus, Caes

mĕdĭŏcrĭtas -ātis, f (mediocris), 1, *moderation, medium, the mean between excess and defect*, mediocritatem illam tenere quae est inter nimium et parum, Cic, auream mediocritatem diligere, *the golden mean* Hor, plur, mediocritates probabant, *moderation in passion*, Cic, 2, *mediocrity, inferiority, insignificance*, ingenii, Cic

mĕdĭŏcrĭtĕr, adv (mediocris), 1, *moderately, tolerably, not extraordinarily*, nemo mediocriter doctus, Cic, in aliqua re mediocriter versatum esse Cic, 2, *with moderation*, aliquid non mediocriter ferre, Cic.

Mĕdĭŏlānum -i, n and **-lānium** -ii, n *town in Cisalpine Gaul* (now *Milan*) Hence, adj, **Mĕdĭŏlānensis** -e, *belonging to Mediolanum*

Mĕdĭŏmatrĭci -ōrum, m *a people in Gaul, on the Moselle*

Mĕdĭōn -ōnis, m (Μεδίων or Μεδέων), *town in Acarnania* Hence **Mĕdĭōnii** -ōrum, m *the inhabitants of Medion*

mĕdĭoxĭmus (mĕdĭoxŭmus) -a -um (medius), *that which is in the middle, the midmost*, dii superi atque inferi et medioxumi, *between the celestial and infernal deities*, Plaut

mĕdĭtāmentum -i, n (meditor), *a thinking upon anything, preparation*, in plur, belli meditamenta, Tac

mĕdĭtātē, adv (meditatus, from meditor), *with meditation, designedly, thoroughly*, Plaut.

mĕdĭtātĭo -ōnis, f (meditor) I *a thinking over anything, contemplation, meditation*, 1, gen, futuri mali, Cic, 2, esp, *a preparation for anything*, obeundi muneris, Cic II. *practice, exercise*, locos multā commentatione atque meditatione paratos atque expeditos habere, Cic

mĕdĭtātus a um, partic of meditor

mĕdĭterrānĕus -a -um (medius and terra), *inland, far from the sea* (opp maritimus), regiones, Caes, urbs, Cic, iter, Liv Subst, **mĕdĭterrānĕum** -i, n, gen plur, mediterranea, *inland country*, mediterranea Galliae petit, Liv

mĕdĭtor, 1 dep (connected with μελετάω, as lacrima with δάκρυον) I. *to think over, consider, meditate*, 1, gen, a, with acc, haec multa, Cic, b, with de and the abl, de sua ratione, Cic, c, with rel sent, mecum, quid dicerem, Cic., 2, esp, *to think upon anything in preparation, study, prepare oneself for, meditate, intend*, a, with acc, alicui pestem, Cic, accusationem, Cic, b, with ad and the acc, ad praedam, Cic, c, with in and the acc, in proelia, Verg, d, with infin, multos annos regnare, Cic II. Transf, *to practise, exercise oneself*, Demosthenes perfecit meditando, ut, etc, Cic, partic, **mĕdĭtātus** -a um, pass, *meditated, considered, reflected, prepared, devised*, meditatum et cogitatum scelus, Cic

mĕdĭum -ii, n *the middle*, v medius

mĕdĭus a um (connected with μέσος η -ον) *the middle, midmost, midst* I. Lit, 1, of space, a, gen, medius mundi locus, Cic, b, partitive, = *the middle of*, in foro medio, *the midst of the forum*, Cic, c, subst, **mĕdĭum** -ii, n *the midst, the middle point*, medium ferire, Cic, aliquem in medium accipere, *into their midst*, Liv, ob oculos voluptates faciles, communes, in medio sitas, *available to all*, Cic, tabulae sunt in medio, *in every one's view*, Cic, rem in medium vocare, *to bring before a court of law*, Cic, aliquem tollere de medio *to remove out of the way, to murder*, Cic 2, of time, a, gen, ultimum proximum, medium tempus, Cic, medius diebus, *in the intervening days*, Liv, of age, media aetas, *middle age*, Cic, b, partitive = *the middle of* medius dies, *the middle of the day*, Ov, c, subst, **mĕdĭum** -ii, n *the middle*, jam diei medium erat, Liv II. Fig, 1, *that which stands between two extremities*, a, gen, quum inter bellum et pacem medium nihil sit, *no middle thing no mean*, Cic, b, *standing between two views or parties, neutral, intermediate*, medium quendam cursum tenebant, Cic, medium se gerere, *to keep oneself neutral*, Cic, medios esse jam non licebit, Cic, c, *ordinary, common, usual, middling*, gratia non media, Liv, 2, a, *containing a mixture of two opposites*, medium erat in Anco ingenium, et Numae et Romuli memor, Liv, b, *acting as mediator*, medium se offert, Verg; medius fidus, Ov, 3, *coming between two persons to disturb or separate*, quos inter medius venit furor, Verg

mĕdĭus fĭdĭus, v fidius

medix, meddixtuticus, v meddix

mĕdulla ae, f (medius), *marrow of bones*, 1, lit, cum albis ossa medullis, Ov, 2, transf, *the inmost part*; mihi haeres in medullis, *I love you from the bottom of my heart*, Cic

Mĕdullĭa -ae, f *a town in Latium, colony of Alba* (now *St Angelo*) Hence, adj, **Mĕdullīnus** -a -um, *of or belonging to Medullia*

mĕdullĭtŭs, adv (medulla), *in the very marrow, fig, inwardly, cordially*, Plaut

mĕdullŭla -ae, f (dim of medulla), *marrow*, Cat

1 **Mēdus** -i, m, v Medi

2 **Mēdus** -i, m (Μῆδος) I. *a river in Persia*, now *Polvar* poet adj, Medum flumen, Hor II. *son of Medea, title of a tragedy by Pacuvius*

Mĕdūsa ae, f (Μέδουσα), *the daughter of Phorcus, mother of the horse Pegasus by Neptune, one of the Gorgons, slain by Perseus* Hence, adj, **Mĕdūsaeus** a um, *Medusean*, equus, *Pegasus*, Ov, fons, *Hippocrene*, Ov

Mĕgăbocchus (Mĕgăboccus) -i, m *Caius, fellow conspirator with Catiline*

Mĕgaera ae, f (Μέγαιρα), *one of the Furies*

Mĕgălē -ēs, f (Μεγάλη), *the Great One*, name of Cybele Hence, a, **Mĕgălensis** e, *belonging to the Magna Mater* (Cybele), gen subst, **Mĕgălensĭa** -ium, n and **Mĕgălēsĭa** -ium, n *the festival annually celebrated on the 4th of April, in honour of Cybele, the Magna Mater*; b, **Mĕgălēsĭăcus** -a -um, *relating to this festival*

Mĕgălŏpŏlis, acc -im, f and **Mĕgălē pŏlis**, acc -in, f (Μεγαλόπολις and Μεγάλη πόλις), *a town in Arcadia, birthplace of Polybius* Hence a, **Mĕgălŏpŏlitae** -ārum, m *the inhabitants of Megalopolis*, b, adj, **Mĕgălŏpŏlītānus** a -um, *of or belonging to Megalopolis*

Mĕgăra ae, f and **Mĕgăra** -ōrum, n (Μέγαρα, τά) I. *a town in Megaris* (now *Megara*) II. *a town in Sicily* (now *Cattaro*) Hence, a, adj **Mĕgărensis** -e, *Megarian*, b, **Mĕgărĕus** a um, *Megarian*, c, **Mĕgărĕus** -ĕi and ĕos, m *of Megara*; d, **Mĕgărĭcus** -a -um, *Megarian* Subst., **Mĕgărĭci** -ōrum, *philosophers of the Megaric school, disciples of Euclides*, c, **Mĕgărus** -a -um, *Megarian*

1 **Mĕgărĕus** v Megara

2 **Mĕgărĕus** -ĕos, m (Μεγαρεύς), *son of Neptune, father of Hippomenes* Hence, **Mĕgărēĭus** -a um *relating to Megareus*, heros *Hippomenes* Ov

Mĕgăris -idis, f. (Μεγαρίς). **I.** *a district in Greece.* **II.** *a town in Sicily,* also called *Megara.*

mĕgistānes -um, m. (μεγιστᾶνες), *grandees, magnates, nobles,* Tac.

mēhercle, mehercule, mehercules, v. Hercules.

mejo, 3. *to make water,* Hor.

mĕl, mellis, n. (μέλι), *honey.* **I.** Lit., stilla mellis, Cic.; plur., roscida mella, Verg.; prov., of a vain attempt, mella petere in medio flumine, Ov. **II.** Transf., *sweetness, pleasantness;* poetica mella, Hor.; hoc juvat et melli est, *is pleasant,* Hor.; as a term of endearment, Sempronius, mel ac deliciae tuae, ap. Cic.

Mĕla -ae, m., Pomponius, *a Roman writer on geography under the Emperor Claudius.*

Mĕlampūs -pŏdis, m. (Μελάμπους), *a celebrated physician and soothsayer, son of Amythaon.*

mĕlanchŏlĭcus -a -um (μελαγχολικός), *having black bile, melancholy,* Cic.

Mĕlanthĭus -ii, m. (Μελάνθιος), *the goatherd of Ulysses.*

Mĕlanthō -ūs, f. (Μελανθώ), *a sea-nymph, daughter of Deucalion.*

Mĕlanthus -i, m. (Μέλανθος). **I.** *a river of Sarmatia.* **II.** *king in Athens, father of Codrus.* Hence, adj., **Mĕlanthēus** -a -um, *of or relating to Melanthus.*

mĕlănūrus -i, m. (μελάνουρος), *a kind of sea-fish,* Ov.

Mĕlas, acc. -ăna and -an, m. (Μέλας). **I.** *a river of Sicily,* now *Mela.* **II.** *a river of Thessaly.* now *Mavra-neria.* **III.** *a river in Thrace,* now *Kavatch.*

melcŭlum -i, n. and **melcŭlus** -i, m. (mel), *little honey* (a term of endearment), Plaut.

Meldi -ōrum, m. *a people in Gallia Celtica.*

Mĕlĕăgĕr and **Mĕlĕăgrus (-ŏs)** -i, m. (Μελέαγρος), *son of Oeneus, king in Calydon, and of Althaea; his life depended on the preservation of an extinguished fire-brand, which was burnt by his mother in anger at the death of her brother by the hand of Meleager.* Hence, **Mĕlĕăgrĭs** -ĭdis, f., plur., **Mĕlĕăgrĭdes,** a, sc. aves or gallinae, *guinea-fowls,* Plin.; **b,** *the sisters of Meleager, who, according to the legend, were changed to guinea-fowls on his death.*

1. **Mĕlēs** -ētis, m. (Μέλης), *a river near Smyrna, where Homer is said to have been born.* Hence, adj., **a, Mĕlētēus** -a -um, *belonging to Meles,* poet., *Homeric;* **b, Mĕlētīnus** -a -um, *belonging to Meles.*

2. **Meles** -ium, f. *a place in Samnium.*

Mĕlĭboea -ae, f. (Μελίβοια), *a town in Thessaly on Mount Ossa, birthplace of Philoctetes.* Hence, adj., **Mĕlĭboeus** -a -um, *Meliboean;* dux, *Philoctetes,* Verg.

Mĕlĭcerta (-ēs) -ae, m. (Μελικέρτης), *son of Athamas and Ino; Ino plunged with him into the sea to escape the fury of her husband, and thereupon Melicerta was changed into a sea-god, called Palaemon by the Greeks and Portumnus by the Romans.*

mĕlĭcus -a -um (μελικός), *musical,* Lucr.; esp., *lyrical, lyric;* poema, Cic.

Mĕlĭē -ēs, f. (Μελία), *a nymph beloved by the river-god Inachus.*

mĕlĭlōtos -i, f. (μελίλωτος), *a species of clover,* Ov.

mĕlĭmēlum -i, n. (μελίμηλον), *a honey-apple, a kind of sweet apple,* Hor.

mĕlĭor -us, comp. of bonus (q.v.).

mĕlisphyllum and **mĕlissŏphyllŏn** -i, n. (μελισσόφυλλον), *balm, a plant of which bees are very fond,* Verg.

Mĕlissus -i, m. (Μέλισσος). **I.** *a Greek philosopher of Samos.* **II.** C. Maecenas Melissus, *the freedman of Maecenas, and librarian to Augustus.*

Mĕlĭta -ae, f. and **Mĕlĭtē** -ēs, f. (Μελίτη). **I.** *the island of Malta.* **II.** *an island near Dalmatia,* now *Meleda.* **III.** (form -ē) *a sea-nymph.* Adj., **Mĕlĭtensis** -e, *of or belonging to the island of Malta;* vestis, Cic.; and subst., **Mĕlĭtensĭa** -ium, n. *Maltese garments,* Cic.

mĕlĭuscŭlē, adv. (meliusculus), *somewhat better, pretty well* (in health); alicui est, Cic.

mĕlĭuscŭlus -a -um (dim. of compar. melior), *somewhat better in health,* Plaut.

Mella -ae, m. *a river in Upper Italy,* now *Mela.*

mellĭcŭlum -i, n. = melculum (q.v.).

mellĭfĕr -fĕra -fĕrum (mel and fero), *producing honey;* apes, Ov.

mellītus -a -um (mel), *sweetened with honey;* placenta, Hor.; transf., *as sweet as honey, pleasant, agreeable, delightful,* Cat.

1. **mĕlos,** n. (μέλος), *a tune, song, melody,* Hor.

2. **Mēlos** -i, f. (Μῆλος), *an island of the Aegaean Sea.* Hence, adj., **Mēlĭus** -a -um, *Melian.*

Melpŏmĕnē -ēs, f. (Μελπομένη), *the muse of tragic and lyric poetry.*

membrāna -ae, f. (membrum). **I.** *a skin, membrane, in the human* or *any animal body;* natura oculos membranis tenuissimis vestivit, Cic. **II.** Transf., **1,** *the skin* or *slough of a snake,* Ov.; **2,** esp., *skin prepared to write on, parchment,* Hor.; **3,** *surface of anything,* Lucr.

membrānŭla -ae, f. (dim. of membrana), *a little membrane;* transf., *parchment,* Cic.

membrātim, adv. (membrum), **1,** *limb by limb;* deperdere sensum, Lucr.; **2,** transf., *piecemeal, singly;* quasi membratim gestum negotium, Cic.; of discourse, *in short, detached sentences;* dicere, Cic.

membrum -i, n. **I.** *a limb* or *member of the body,* Cic.; captus (*crippled*) omnibus membris, Liv. **II.** Transf., **a,** *a limb, member, part, portion of anything;* omnes eius (philosophiae) partes atque omnia membra, Cic.; **b,** *an apartment of a house;* cubicula et eiusmodi membra, Cic.; **c,** *a clause in a sentence,* Cic.

mĕmĭni -isse (connected with moneo, mens, Gr. μέμνω, μνάω). **I.** *to remember, recollect, be mindful, bear in mind;* (α) with genit., vivorum memini, Cic.; (β) with acc., dicta, Cic.; (γ) with de, de Herode et Mettio meminero, Cic.; (δ) with rel. sent., meministi quanta esset, etc., Cic.; (ε) with acc. and infin., memini te narrare, Cic.; (ζ) with infin., Hor.; (η) absol., ut ego meminisse videor, Cic. **II.** Transf., *to make mention of, to mention;* de exsulibus, Cic.

Memmĭus -a -um, *name of a Roman gens, to which belonged* C. Memmius, *the friend of Cicero and Lucretius, who was condemned for bribery and went into exile at Athens.* Hence, **a, Memmĭădēs** -ae, m. *one of the Memmian gens, a Memmius;* **b, Memmĭānus** -a -um, *belonging to Memmius.*

Memnŏn -ŏnis, m. (Μέμνων), *king in Aethiopia, son of Tithonus and Aurora, killed before Troy by Achilles;* mater lutea Memnonis, *Aurora,* Ov.; Memnonis saxa effigies, *a statue of Memnon near Thebes, which gave forth a note on being struck by the first rays of the sun,* Tac. Hence, a, adj, **Memnŏnis** -ĭdis, f *of or relating to Memnon*, subst., **Memnŏnĭdes** -um, f *the birds of Memnon birds which arose from his ashes*, b, **Memnŏnius** -a -um, *Memnonian*, transf, *eastern, Moorish, black*

mĕmor -ŏris (memini) **I.** *mindful, not forgetful* **A.** Gen, **1,** of persons, (α) with genit, beneficii, Cic, (β) with rel sent, memor quae essent dicta, Cic, (γ) absol, memori animo notavi, Ov, **2,** transf, of things, memoris libertatis vox, Liv **B.** Esp, **1,** a, *remembering, thankful, grateful*, nimium memor nimiumque gratus, Cic, **b,** *unappeasable relentless*, memorem Junonis ob iram, Verg, **2,** *thoughtful*, Verg, **3,** *with a good memory, retentive*, memor an obliviosus sit, Cic **II.** Act., *reminding of, calling to mind*, indicii memor poema, Ov (abl sing, memori always)

mĕmŏrābĭlis -e, adj with compar (memoro), *remarkable, worthy of mention, memorable*, vir, Liv, virtus, Cic

mĕmŏrandus -a -um (memoro), *worthy of being remembered, memorable*, of persons, juvenis memorande, Verg, of things, proelium, Liv

mĕmŏrātor -ōris, m (memoro), *a narrator, relater*, Prop

1 **mĕmŏrātus** -a -um, p adj (from memoro), *celebrated, well known*, inter paucas memorata populi Romani clades, Liv

2 **mĕmŏrātus** -ūs, m (memoro), *a mention, mentioning*, Plaut

mĕmŏrĭa -ae, f (memor) **I.** Gen **A.** Lit, **1,** of the past, *remembrance, memory*, primam sacramenti memoriam, Caes; Pompeii memoriam amisisse, Cic, deponere, *to forget*, Caes memoria alicuius (rei) excidit, or abiit, or abolevit, *it has fallen into oblivion, it has been forgotten*, Liv, memoriae prodere, Cic and Nep, or tradere, Liv, *to commit to writing, to hand on record* (of historians), viri digni memoriā, *worthy of remembrance*, Cic, **2,** of the future, *thinking, thought*, periculi, Liv, **3,** meton, *recollection*, nostrā memoriā, *in our recollection*, Cic **B.** Transf, *handing down by word of mouth or by writing, tradition, history, information*, de hominum memoria (*oral evidence*) tacere, litterarum memoriam (*written evidence*) flagitare, Cic; aliquid prodere memoriā, *by word of mouth*, Caes, memoriā ac litteris, *by word of mouth and by writing*, Cic **II.** *capacity for remembering, memory*, memoria bona melior, Cic, aliquid memoriae mandare, Cic, memoriā comprehendere or complecti aliquid, *to remember*, Cic

mĕmŏrĭālis -e (memoria), *of or relating to memory or remembrance*, Suet

mĕmŏrĭŏla -ae, f (dim of memoria), *memory*, Cic

mĕmŏrĭtĕr, adv (memor), *by heart, from memory*, orationem memoriter habere, Cic

mĕmŏro, 1 (memor), *to mention, call to mind, recount, relate* (α) with acc, artibus quas supra memoravi Sall, (β) with de and the abl, de magna virtute, Sall; (γ) with acc and infin id factum per ambitionem consulis memorabant, Sall, in pass with nom and infin, ubi ea gesta esse memorantur, Cic

Memphis -idis, f (Μέμφις), *a celebrated city of Egypt* Hence, a, **Memphītes** -ae, m *belonging to Memphis*, bos, *Apis*, Tib **b, Memphĭtĭcus** -a -um, *belonging to Memphis*, c, **Memphītis** -idis, f *belonging to Memphis*, and poet = *Egyptian*, vacca (of Io), Ov

Mĕnae -ārum, f (Μέναι), *town in Sicily*, now *Meneo* Adj, **Mĕnaenus** -a -um, *of Menae*

Mĕnander -dri, m. (Μένανδρος), *a famous Greek comic poet, imitated by Terence* Adj, **Mĕnandrēus** -a -um, *Menandrian*

Mĕnăpĭi -ōrum, m *a people in Gallia Celtica, between the Meuse and the Scheldt*

menda -ae, f, v mendum

mendācĭum -ii, n (mendax) **I** *a lie, falsehood, untruth*, impudens, Cic, mendacium alicuius refellere et redarguere, Cic **II.** *deceit, deception*, oculorum reliquorumque sensuum mendacia, Cic

mendācĭuncŭlum -i, n (dim of mendacium), *a little lie*, Cic

mendax -ācis (mentior) **I.** *lying, mendacious*, homo, Cic subst, **mendax** -ācis, m. *a liar*, Cic **II.** Of inanimate objects, *deceitful, counterfeit, false, untrue*, visa, Cic, speculum, Ov, fundus, *bearing less than the expected crop*, Hor

Mendēs -ētis, f (Μένδης), *a town in Egypt on the Nile* Hence, adj, **Mendēsĭus** -a -um, *Mendesian*

mendīcābŭlum -i, n (mendico), *a beggar*, Plaut

mendīcĭtas -ātis, f (mendicus), *the condition of a beggar, indigence, poverty*, Cic

mendīco, 1 and **mendīcor**, 1 dep (mendicus) **I.** Intransit, *to beg, go begging*, Plaut **II.** Transit, *to beg for*, mendicatus cibus, Ov

mendīcŭlus -a -um (dim of mendicus), *belonging to a beggar*, Plaut

mendīcus -a -um, *poor as a beggar, beggarly, indigent* **I.** Lit, of persons, solos sapientes esse, si mendicissimi (sint), divites, Cic. Subst, **mendīcus** -i, m *a beggar*, Cic, plur, mendici, *the begging priests of Cybele*, Hor **II.** Transf, of things, *paltry, pitiful, beggarly*, instrumentum, Cic

mendōsē, adv (mendosus), *faultily, erroneously, incorrectly*, scribere, Cic, mendosissime scriptum esse, Cic

mendōsus -a -um (mendum) **I.** Pass, *full of faults*, a, *full of physical blemishes*, nec equi mendosa sub illo deteriorque viro facies, Ov, **b,** *full of inaccuracies* historia rerum nostrarum est facta mendosior, Cic, **c,** poet, *full of moral blemishes*, mendosi mores, Ov **II.** Act, *making a mistake*, cui servus semper in Verruca nomine mendosus esset, Cic

mendum -i, n and **menda** -ae, f **I** *a bodily defect, blemish*, Ov **II. a,** *an error, mistake in writing*, quod mendum ista litura correxit? Cic, **b,** *a mistake in reasoning or calculation*, Cic

Mĕnĕclēs -is, m (Μενεκλῆς), *an Asiatic rhetorician of Alabanda* Hence, adj, **Mĕnĕclīus** -a -um, *of or relating to Menecles*

Mĕnĕlāus (-ŏs) -i, m (Μενέλαος) *son of Atreus, brother of Agamemnon, husband of Helen* Hence, adj, **Mĕnĕlāēus** -a -um, *of or relating to Menelaus*

Mĕnēnĭus -a -um, *name of a Roman gens, to which belonged Menenius Agrippa, consul, said to have composed the differences between the patricians and the plebeians on the secession of the latter*

Mēninx (Mēnix) -ingis, f (Μῆνιγξ), *an island near Africa*, now *Jerbi*

Mĕnippus -i, m (Μένιππος) **I.** *a Cynic philosopher* **II.** *the greatest of the Asiatic orators of the time of Cicero*

Mĕnoecēus -ĕi and -ĕos m (Μενοικεύς), *son of the Theban king Creon, who sacrificed his life for his country in obedience to an oracle*

Mĕnoetĭădēs -ae, m. (Μενοιτιάδης), *the son of Menoetius, i.e., Patroclus*, Ov.

mens, mentis, f. (root MEN, whence memini), *the mind.* **I. A.** *the mind, opinion, way of thinking, character;* vestrae mentes atque sententiae, Cic. **B.** *the mind as the seat of feeling;* **1,** gen., mens mollis ad perferendas calamitates, Cic.; **2,** esp., *the conscience*, Cic. **II.** *the mind, understanding, reason, intellect, judgment.* **A.** Gen., mens cui regnum totius animi a natura tributum est, Cic.; mente complecti aliquid, *to comprehend*, Cic.; mentis suae esse, mentis compotem esse, *to be in possession of one's faculties*, Cic.; captus mente, *insane*, Cic. **B.** Esp., **1,** *reflection, insight;* sine ulla mente, Cic.; **2,** *courage;* addere mentem, *to inspire courage*, Hor.; demittere mentem, *to lose courage*, Verg.; **3,** *passion*, Hor.; **4,** *the thoughts;* **a,** venit (mihi) in mentem, *it occurs to me, I remember*, Cic.; temporis, Cic.; non venit in mentem pugna? Liv.; classem ea mente comparavit, ut, *with that intention*, Cic.; **b,** esp., *opinion, plan, resolve;* muta jam istam mentem, Cic. **C.** Person., Mens, *as goddess of understanding*, Cic.

mensa -ae f. (perhaps from root MEN, whence eminere, *anything raised up*), *a table*, **1,** esp., *a table for eating upon;* **a,** lit., mensas cibis exstruere, Cic.; mensam ponere, *to bring in dinner*, Ov.; tollere, Cic., removere, Verg., *to take dinner away;* **b,** meton., *a course;* mensa secunda, *dessert*, Cic.; **2, a,** *the table* or *counter of a money-changer, banker;* publica, *a public bank*, Cic.; **b,** *a sacrificial table, altar*, Verg.

mensārĭus -ii, m. (mensa), *a money-changer, banker*, esp., *a public banker who regulated the payments out of the treasury*, Cic.; mensarii tresviri, quinqueviri, Liv.

mensĭo -ōnis, f. (metior), *a measuring;* vocum, Cic.

mensis -is, m. (root MEN, whence μήν, μήνη, English *month*), *a month;* intercalarius, Cic.

mensor -ōris, m. (metior). **I.** *a measurer;* maris et terrae, Hor. **II.** *a measurer of land*, Ov.

menstrŭālis -e (menstruus), *monthly*, Plaut.

menstrŭus -a -um (mensis). **I.** *monthly;* usura, Cic. **II.** *lasting for a month;* spatium, Cic.; subst., **menstrŭum** -i, n. (sc. frumentum), *victuals, rations for a month*, Liv.

mensŭla -ae, f. (dim. of mensa), *a little table*, Plaut.

mensūra -ae, f. (metior), *a measuring.* **I.** Lit., mensuram alicuius rei facere, *to measure*, Ov. **II.** Meton., *a measure;* **1,** *length, thickness, size, circumference*, etc.; **a,** of space, nosse mensuras itinerum, Caes.; **b,** of time, alicui mensuram bibendi dare, Ov.; **2,** *a measure, that by which anything is measured;* majore mensurā reddere, Cic.; qui modus mensurae medimnus appellatur, *which species of measure*, Nep.; **3,** *measure = size, nature, character;* mensuram nominis implere, *to be worthy of one's name, character, capacity*, Ov.; legati, Tac.

menta (mentha) -ae, f. (μίνθη), *the herb mint*, Ov.

mentĭens -entis, m., partic. of mentior, as subst., *a fallacy, sophism*, Cic.

mentĭo -ōnis, f. (memini), *a speaking of, mention;* mentionem facere alicuius rei, or de aliqua re, or de aliquo, *to make mention of, to mention;* esp., *to bring before the senate*, Cic.; casu in eorum mentionem incidi, *I mentioned them accidentally*, Cic.; alicuius rei mentionem movere, *to mention*, Liv.

mentĭor, 4. dep. (mens), *to lie, utter that which is not true, whether intentionally or not.* **I.** Intransit., **A.** Gen., **1,** of persons, si te mentiri dicis, verumque dicis, mentiris, Cic.; aperte, Cic.; in aliqua re, de aliqua re, Cic.; **2,** transf., of inanimate objects, *to deceive, mislead;* frons, oculi, vultus persaepe mentiuntur, Cic. **B. 1,** of poets, *to feign, invent;* ita mentitur (Homerus), Hor.; **2,** *to fail in a promise, break one's word;* quod promisisti mihi, quod mentita, inimica es, Cat.; mentiri honestius, Cic. **II.** Transit., **A.** *to say something falsely, to invent;* **1,** gen., **a,** lit., Cic.; tantam rem, Sall.; res quas mentiris, Ov.; **b,** transf., of things, in quibus nihil umquam immensa et infinita vetustas mentita sit, Cic.; **2,** *to deceive, disappoint;* seges mentita spem, Hor. **B. 1,** *to allege falsely, speak falsely about;* auspicium, Liv.; **2,** *to counterfeit, put on, assume;* centum figuras, Ov.; partic., **mentītus** -a -um, as pass., *invented, feigned*, Verg.

Mentōr -ŏris, m. (Μέντωρ), *a celebrated artist in metal work.* Hence, adj., **Mentŏrĕus** -a -um, *of* or *relating to Mentor.*

mentum -i, n. *the chin*, Cic.

mĕo, 1. (connected with eo), *to go, pass;* **1,** of persons, domus Plutonia, quo simul mearis, Hor.; **2,** of inanimate objects, quum triremes huc illuc mearent, Tac.; meantia sidera, Ov.

mĕopte, v. meus.

mĕphītis -is, f. **1,** *a noxious exhalation from the earth, malaria*, Verg.; **2,** personif., Mephitis, *the goddess who protects against malaria*, Tac.

mĕrācŭlus -a -um (dim. of meracus), *tolerably pure, unmixed*, Plaut.

mĕrācus -a -um (merus), *pure, unmixed.* **I.** Lit., vinum meracius, Cic.; helleborum, Hor. **II.** Transf., *undiminished;* libertas, Cic.

mercābĭlis -e (mercor), *that can be bought*, Ov.

mercātor -ōris, m. (mercor). **I.** *a merchant, wholesale trader* (opp. caupo, *a shopkeeper, retailer*), Cic. **II.** Transf., *a buyer;* signorum, Cic.; transf., provinciarum, Cic.

mercātōrĭus -a -um (mercator), *relating to a trader;* navis, *a merchant-ship*, Plaut.

mercātūra -ae, f. (mercor), *trade, traffic;* mercaturas facere, *to carry on trade*, Cic.; transf., non erit ista amicitia, sed mercatura quaedam utilitatum suarum, Cic.

mercātus -ūs, m. (mercor). **I.** *trade, traffic, business*, Cic. **II.** *a market, fair, public place of business;* mercatum indicere, habere, Cic.; ad mercatum proficisci, Cic.; frequens, *a full market*, Liv.

mercēdŭla -ae, f. (dim. of merces), **1,** *a small reward, low wages;* mercedulā adducti, Cic.; **2,** *low rent;* praediorum, Cic.

mercennārĭus (mercēnārĭus) -a -um (orig. mercedinarius, then mercednarius, then assimilated mercennarius, from merces), *hired, paid, mercenary;* miles, Liv.; testes, *suborned*, Cic.; of things, arma, Liv.; liberalitas, Cic. Subst., **mercennārĭus** -ii, m. *a hired servant, hireling*, Cic.

mercēs -ēdis, f. (merco). **I.** *hire, pay, wages, reward, fee, salary;* **1,** gen., **a,** in a good sense, operae, Cic.; conducere aliquem mercede, Cic.; **b,** in a bad sense, *hire, bribe;* lingua astricta mercede, Cic.; **2,** esp., **a,** *the fee of a teacher;* mercede docere, Cic.; **b,** *the pay of soldiers;* mercede milites conducere, Liv.; **3,** transf., euphem., **a,** *pay = punishment;* temeritatis, Cic.; **b,** = *harm, loss;* istuc nihil dolere non sine magna mercede contingit, Cic. **II.** *Interest, rent, income;* praediorum, Cic.; insuarum, *rent*, Cic, quinas hic capiti mercedes exsecat, *5 per cent*, Hor

mercīmōnium -ii, n (merx), *goods, merchandise*, Plaut.

mercor, 1 dep (merx) **I.** Intransit, *to carry on trade, to traffic*, Plaut. **II.** Transit, *to buy*, **a**, lit, fundum de pupillo, Cic, aliquid ab aliquo, Cic, aliquid tanto pretio, Cic, **b**, transf, officia vitā, *with life*, Cic, hoc magno mercentur Atridae, *would give a high price for*, Verg

Mercŭrĭus -ii, m. **1**, Mercury, *identified with the Greek Hermes, son of Jupiter and Maia, the messenger of the gods, inventor of the lyre, god of oratory, conductor of the souls of the dead to the lower world, patron of merchants and thieves*, **2**, *the planet Mercury* Hence, adj, **Mercŭrĭālis** -e, *of* or *relating to Mercury; viri, lyric poets*, Hor. Subst, **Mercŭrĭāles** -ium, m *a corporation of traders at Rome*, Cic

merda -ae, f *excrement*, Hor.

mĕrē, adv (merus), *purely, without mixture*, Plaut.

mĕrenda -ae, f *an afternoon meal, taken between 4 and 5* P M

mĕrens -entis, partic of mereo

mĕrĕo -ŭi -ĭtum, 2 and **mĕrĕor** -ĭtus sum, 2 dep **I. A.** *to earn, obtain*, **1**, lit, mereri non amplius duodecim aeris, Cic, nardo vina, *to exchange*, Hor, **2**, transf, *to earn, win*, nullam gratiam hoc bello, Liv **B.** *to earn pay as a soldier = to serve as a soldier*, gen, merere or mereri stipendia, Cic; sub aliquo imperatore, Liv, equo, equis, *in the cavalry*, Cic, pedibus, *in the infantry*, Liv **II. A.** *to deserve, merit, be worthy of*, **1**, in a good sense, praemia, laudem, Caes, ut honoribus decoraretur, Cic, **2**, in a bad sense, *to merit* (punishment, etc), odium, Caes, poenam, Ov, fustuarium, Liv, meruisse mori, Ov, partic, **a**, merens, *deserving*, in a good sense *worthy*, in a bad sense *guilty*, Sall, **b**, meritus, (α) act, *deserving*, meriti juvenci, Verg, (β) pass, *deserved, merited*, dona, Liv, iracundia, Cic **B.** mereri de, *to deserve of*, in a good and bad sense, bene, optime de republica, Cic; male de civibus suis, Cic, ita se de populo Romano meritos esse ut, etc, Caes

mĕrĕtrīcĭē, adv (meretricius), *after the manner of a harlot*, Plaut.

mĕrĕtrīcĭus -a -um (meretrix), *of* or *relating to a harlot* or *prostitute*, amores, Cic

mĕrĕtrīcŭla -ae, f (dim of meretrix), *a public prostitute*, Cic

mĕrĕtrix -icis, f (mereo), *a public prostitute, harlot*, Cic

mergae -ārum, f. (mergo), *a two pronged fork*, Plaut

mergĕs -gitis, f *a sheaf of corn*, Verg

mergo, mersi, mersum, 3. **I.** *to dip, plunge into water, immerse* **A.** aves quae se in mari mergunt, Cic, nec me deus aequore mersit, Verg **B.** *to sink*, naves in alto, Liv **II.** Transf, **A. 1**, *to sink down, plunge in, fix in*, canes mersis in corpora rostris dilacerant dominum, Ov; caput in terram, Liv, middle, mergi, of stars, *to sink*, Ov, **2**, transf, *to sink, overwhelm, immerse*, me his malis, Verg, funere acerbo, *to destroy by a bitter death*, Verg.; se in voluptates, Liv, vino somnoque mersi jacent, *sunk in wine and sleep*, Liv **B** *to hide, conceal*, suos in cortice vultus, Ov

mergus -i, m (mergo), *a diver, gull*, Verg

mĕrīdĭānus -a -um (meridies) **I.** *of* or *relating to midday, meridian*, tempus, Cic, sol, Liv **II.** *southern*, regio, Liv, vallis, Liv

mĕrīdĭātĭo -ōnis, f (meridio), *a noontide repose, midday sleep, siesta* Cic

mĕrīdĭēs -ēi, m (for medidies, from medius and dies), **1**, *midday, noon*, Cic, **2**, *the south*; inflectens sol cursum tum ad septentriones, tum ad meridiem, Cic

mĕrīdĭo, 1 and **mĕrīdĭor**, 1, dep (meridies) *to take a siesta* or *midday sleep*, Cat

Mērĭŏnēs -ae, m (Μηριόνης), *a Cretan, friend and charioteer of Idomeneus.*

1 **mĕrĭto**, 1 (intens of mereo), *to earn*; fundus qui sestertia dena meritasset, *brought in*, Cic

2 **mĕrĭtō**, adv (meritus), *deservedly, with reason, rightly*, merito sum iratus Metello, Cic; merito ac jure laudari, Cic Superl, meritissimo, Cic.

mĕrĭtōrĭus -a -um (mereo) **I.** *that for which hire is paid or by which money is made*, rheda, *a hackney coach*, Suet Subst, **mĕrĭtōrĭa** -ōrum, n *lodgings*, Juv **II.** *gaining money by prostitution*, Cic

mĕrĭtum -i, n (mereo) **I.** *desert*, and hence, *reward, punishment*, merita invenire, Sall **II.** *desert, merit, any action which deserves thanks* or *reward* **A.** magnitudo tuorum in me meritorum, Cic **B 1**, *a good action, benefit*; dare et recipere merita, Cic, **2**, *demerit, blame, fault*, non meo merito, Cic, nullo meo in se merito, *though I am guilty of no offence against him*, Liv, **3**, *worth, value, importance of a thing*, quo sit merito quaeque notata dies, Ov

mĕrĭtus -a -um, partic of mereo (q v)

mĕrŏbĭbus -a -um (merum and bibo), *drinking wine unmixed*, Plaut

Mĕrŏē -ēs, f (Μερόη), *a large island in the Nile*

Mĕrŏpē -ēs, f (Μερόπη), *daughter of Atlas, wife of Sisyphus, one of the Pleiades, whose star is dimmer than the others because she married a mortal*

1 **Mĕrops** -ŏpis, m (Μέροψ), *king of Aethiopia, husband of Clymene, who bore Phaethon to Apollo*

2 **mĕrops** -ŏpis, f (μέροψ), *a bird, the bee-eater*, Verg

merso, 1 (intens of mergo), *to dip in, immerse*, gregem fluvio, Verg, transf, mersari civilibus undis, Hor

mĕrŭla -ae, f **1**, *a blackbird*, Cic, **2**, *a fish, the sea carp*, Ov

mĕrum -i, n, v merus

mĕrus -a -um **I.** *pure, unmixed*, esp applied to wine; vinum Ov, and subst, **mĕrum** -i, n *wine unmixed with water* (only drunk by the intemperate), Hor, undae, *water not mixed with wine*, Ov, fig, meram hauriens libertatem, *unrestrained*, Liv **II. A.** *naked, uncovered*, pes, Juv **B. 1**, *mere, only, nothing but*, Cic, merum bellum loqui, *to talk of nothing but war*, Cic; **2**, *real, genuine*; meri principes, Cic, libertas, Hor

merx, mercis, f *merchandise, goods, wares*, fallaces et fucosae, Cic, femineae, *for women*, Ov

Mĕsembrĭa -ae, f (Μεσημβρία), *a town in Thrace at the foot of Mount Haemus* Hence, adj, **Mĕsembrĭăcus** -a -um, *of* or *relating to Mesembria*

Mĕsŏpŏtămĭa -ae, f (Μεσοποταμία), *a country of Asia between the Euphrates and the Tigris*

Messalla (Messāla) -ae, m *a cognomen of the gens Valeria, the most celebrated members of which were* **1**, M Valerius Messalla Corvinus, *the patron of Tibullus, a skilled orator;* and **2,** Messalina, *the wife of the Emperor Claudius.*

Messāna -ae, f. *a town in Sicily, on the straits between Italy and Sicily,* now *Messina.* Hence, **Messēnius** -a -um, *Messenian.*

Messāpĭa -ae, f. *old name of a part of Lower Italy, Calabria.* Hence, **Messāpĭus** -a -um, *Messapian.*

Messēnē -ēs, f. (Μεσσήνη), *the chief town in the district of Messenia in the Peloponnese.* Hence, **Messēnĭus** -a -um, *Messenian.*

messis -is, f. (meto -ĕre), *harvest.* **I. A.** Lit., messem amittere, Cic.; *the gathering of honey,* Verg. **B.** Meton., **1, a,** *the grain gathered in, harvest;* illius immensae ruperunt horrea messes, Verg.; **b,** *the crop, standing crop,* Ov.; **2,** *the time of harvest, harvest-tide,* Verg; and poet., *the year;* sexagesima messis, Mart. **II.** Fig., illa Sullani temporis messis, Cic.

messor -ōris, m. (meto -ĕre), *a reaper, mower,* Cic.

messōrĭus -a -um (messor), *of* or *relating to a reaper;* corbis, Cic.

mēta -ae, f. *a conical* or *pyramid-shaped figure.* **I.** Gen., collis in modum metae in acutum cacumen fastigatus, Liv. **II.** Esp., **1,** *the pyramidal columns at the extremities of the Roman circus* (the race consisted in making the circuit seven times); metaque fervidis evitata rotis, Hor.; fig., in flexu aetatis haesit ad metas, *he was unfortunate,* Cic.; hence, **2, a,** *a place round which one has to go;* metas lustrare Pachyni, Verg.; **b,** *the goal, end, term, boundary;* mortis, aevi, Verg.; vitae metam tangere, Ov.

mĕtallum -i, n. (μέταλλον). **I.** *a metal, gold, silver, iron,* etc.; potior metallis libertas, *gold and silver,* Hor. **II.** Meton., *a mine, quarry;* reditus metallorum, *income,* Liv.; metalla instituit, Liv.

mĕtămorphōsis -is, f. (μεταμόρφωσις), *a transformation, metamorphosis;* plur., **Mĕtămorphōses** -ĕōn, *the title of a poem by Ovid.*

Mĕtăpontum -i, n. (Μεταπόντιον), *a Greek colony in Lucania.* Hence, adj. **Mĕtăpontīnus** -a -um, *Metapontine.*

mētātor -ōris, m. (metor), *a measurer, one who marks;* castrorum, Cic.; urbis, Cic.

Mĕtaurus -i, m. (Μέταυρος), *a river in Umbria, where Hasdrubal was defeated and slain* 207 A.C. Adj., poet., Metaurum flumen, Hor.

Mĕtellus -i, m. *a cognomen in the Caecilian gens, the most remarkable members of which were:* **1,** Qu. Metellus Macedonicus, *who made Macedonia a Roman province, proverbial for the success of his private and public life;* **2,** Qu. Caecilius Metellus Numidicus, *general in the war against Jugurtha;* **3,** C. Caecilius Metellus Celer, *a contemporary of Cicero, husband of Clodia;* **4,** Qu. Caecilius Metellus Pius (Scipio), *son of Scipio Nasica, adoptive son of Qu. Metellus Pius, father-in-law of Pompeius.* Hence, adj., **Mĕtellīnus** -a -um, *relating to Metellus;* oratio, *against Metellus Nepos, brother of Celer,* Cic.

Mĕtĕrēus -a -um, *Meterean;* turba, *a people near the Danube on the Black Sea,* Ov.

Mēthymna -ae, f. (Μήθυμνα), *a town in Lesbos.* Hence, adj., **a, Mēthymnaeus** -a -um; **b, Mēthymnĭăs** -ădis, f. *of* or *relating to Methymna.*

mĕtĭcŭlōsus -a -um (metus), **1,** *full of fear fearful,* Plaut.; **2,** *exciting fear, fearful,* Plaut.

mētĭor, mensus sum, 4. dep. *to measure.* **I.** Lit., **A.** agrum, Cic.; pedes syllabis, Cic. **B. 1,** *to measure out, distribute;* frumentorum exercitus, Cic.; **2,** *to measure, traverse, pass over;* aequor curru, Verg.; iter annium, Cat. **II.** Transf., *to measure according to a certain standard, to measure, estimate, judge of;* sonantia auribus, Cic.; oculo latus alicuius, Hor.; omnia quaestu, *estimate everything with reference to gain,* Cic.; odium aliorum suo odio, Liv.; fidelitatem ex mea conscientia, Cic.

Mĕtĭōsēdum -i, n. *town in Gallia Lugdunensis, in the country of the Senones.*

1. **mĕto,** messŭi, messum, 3. **I.** Intransit., *to reap, mow, gather harvest;* in metendo occupati, Caes.; applied to the vintage, Verg.; prov., ut sementem feceris, ita et metes, *as a man sows, so shall he reap,* Cic. **II.** Transit., **A.** *to mow, reap;* arva, Prop.; farra, Ov.; transf., of bees, apes metunt flores, Verg. **B. 1,** *to crop off, pluck off, cut off;* virgā lilia summa metit, Ov.; barbam forfice, Mart.; **2,** in battle, *to hew down, mow down;* proxima quaeque metit gladio, Verg.

2. **Mĕto (-ōn)** -ōnis, m. (Μέτων), *a celebrated Athenian astronomer.*

3. **mēto** -āre = metor.

mētor, 1. dep. (meta). **I.** *to measure;* caelum, Ov. **II.** *to measure off, lay out, define the boundaries of any spot;* regiones, Liv.; castra, Sall.; frontem castrorum, Liv.

mĕtrēta -ae, f. (μετρητής), **1,** *a Greek liquid measure, containing about nine English gallons;* **2,** *a large tub, cask,* Juv.

Mētrŏdōrus -i, m. (Μητρόδωρος). **I.** *a disciple of Epicurus.* **II.** *a rhetorician and philosopher of Skepsis in Mysia, disciple of Carneades.*

Mētrŏpŏlis, acc. -im, f. (Μητρόπολις), *town in Thessaly, between Pharsalus and Gomphi.* Hence, **a, Mētrŏpŏlītae** -ārum, m. (Μητροπολῖται), *inhabitants of Metropolis;* **b, Mētrŏpŏlītānus** -a -um, *belonging to Metropolis.*

mĕtrum -i, n. (μέτρον), *a measure;* and esp., *the measure of verses, metre,* Mart.

Mettĭus (Mētĭus) -ĭi, m. *a magistrate of the Albani.*

mĕtŭendus -a -um, p. adj. (from metuo), *fearful;* multae metuendaeque res, Cic.

mĕtŭens -entis, p. adj. (from metuo), *fearing, standing in awe of;* legum, Cic.

mĕtŭo -ŭi -ūtum, 3. (metus). **I.** Intransit., *to fear, be afraid* (esp. of some threatening evil, while timere is rather of fear of an object actually present); de sua vita, *for his life,* Cic.; ab Hannibale, Liv.; senectae, Verg. **II.** Transit., *to fear.* **A.** aliquem, Cic.; insidias ab aliquo, Cic.; metuit tangi, *he is afraid of being touched,* Hor.; metuo ne . . . *I fear that something will happen;* metuo ut . . . *I fear that something will not happen,* Cic. **B.** *to shun, seek to avoid;* nocentem corporibus Austrum, Hor.

mĕtus -ūs, m. *fear, apprehension, dread.* **I.** Lit., **1,** in metu esse, Cic.; adducere aliquem in eum metum ut, etc., Cic.; metum facere, *to cause fear,* Ov.; deponere metum, Cic.; with genit., existimationis, Cic.; with ab or ex, a Romanis, Liv.; with ne and the subj., Cic.; metus hostilis, *fear of an enemy,* Sall.; propter te, Cic.; de me, Cic.; **2,** *reverence, awe;* laurus multos metu servata per annos, Verg. **II.** Meton., **1,** *the object of fear,* Tac.; **2,** *danger, crisis;* metus maximi belli, Cic. (dat., metu, Verg., Tac.).

mĕus -a -um (root ME, MI), poss. pron. *my, mine, my own.* **I.** Adj., **1,** meum dictum consulis, Liv.; meum est with infin., *it is my duty, falls to my lot,* Cic.; meus hic est, *he is in my power,* Plaut.; nisi plane esse vellem meus, *except I wished to be quite original,* Cic.; Nero meus, *my friend Nero,* Cic.; **2,** *against me;* crimina mea, *charges against me*, Liv II. Subst, 1, **mĕa** -ae, f *my love*, Ov, 2, **mĕum** -i, n *mine own*, plur, **mĕa** -ōrum, n *my possessions*, Cic, 3, **mĕi** -ōrum, m *my attendants, slaves, my people*, Cic (voc, sing masc, mi, but also poet, meus, Verg, genit plur, meûm, Plaut The cases of meus are frequently strengthened by the enclitic additions, met, pte, meopte, meâpte, meāmet, Plaut)

Mēvānia ae, f *a town in Umbria, now Bevagna*

Mezentius -ii, m (lit, *a prince, ruler*), *name of a tyrant of Caere* or *Agylla*

mica -ae, f *a crumb, morsel, grain*, mica saliens (sc salis), Hor

Micipsa -ae, m *son of Masinissa, king of Numidia*.

micans -antis (partic of mico), *shining, glittering, sparkling*, Ov

mico -ŭi, 1 *to move rapidly up and down, tremble, beat like the pulse* I. 1, venae et arteriae micare non desinunt, Cic, micat (equus) auribus, Verg, corda timore micant, Ov, auribus, Verg. 2, micare digitis, *to play at a game which consisted in holding out the fingers suddenly that another might guess their number* (the Italian game of *alla mora*), quid enim sors est? Idem propemodum quod micare, Cic, prov, of a thoroughly honourable man, dignus quicum in tenebris mices, Cic II. *to shine, glitter, sparkle*, ignibus aether, Verg, micant gladii, Liv

Mīdās (Mīda) -ae, m. (Μίδας), *a king of Phrygia, who received from Bacchus the gift of turning to gold everything that he touched, as judge in a musical contest between Apollo and Pan he decided in favour of Pan, and Apollo punished him by changing his ears into those of an ass*

Migdilybs -lўbis, m (μίγδα and λίψ), *one of mixed African and Tyrian race, as the Carthaginians*, Plaut.

mĭgrātĭo -ōnis, f (migro), *a removal from one place of abode to another, migration*, Cic, transf, verbi migrationes (sunt) in alienum multae, *metaphorical uses*, Cic

mĭgro, 1 I. Intransit, *to remove from one place to another, quit a place, depart* A. Lit, etiam mures migrarunt, Cic, ab Tarquiniis, Liv B. Transf, 1, gen, de vita, ex vita, *to die*, Cic, 2, esp, *to change*, omnia migrant, *all things change*, Lucr, in colorem marmoreum, *to be changed into*, Lucr II. Transit, 1, *to remove from one place to another, transport*, migratu difficilia, *difficult of transportation*, Liv, 2, *to transgress*, jus civile, Cic (archaist, migrassit = migraverit, Cic)

mil v mill

Mīlănĭōn -ōnis, m (Μειλανίων), *husband of Atalanta*.

mīles -ĭtis, c (mille), *a soldier* I. Gen, a, lit., *a soldier*; scribere milites, *to enrol*, Liv; ordinare, *to draw up in order*, Liv, mercede conducere, *to take into pay*, Liv, dimittere milites, Cic; *a common soldier*, Liv, b, poet transf, (a) of persons, nova miles eram, Ov, (β) *a piece on a draught-board*, Ov II. milites = *infantry*, as opposed to cavalry, Caes, miles, used collectively, Liv.

Mīlētus i (Μίλητος) I. m, myth, *father of Caunus and Byblis, mythical founder of Miletus* II f *a town in Caria* Hence, adj, 1, **Mīlēsius** -a um, *Milesian*, 2, **Mīlētis** -idis f, a, *daughter of Miletus = Byblis*, Ov, b, *belonging to the town Miletus*, urbs, *Tomi, a colony of the Milesians*, Ov

mīlĭtāris e (miles), *of or relating to a soldier or to war, military*, tribuni, Cic; signa, Cic; aetas, *the legal period of military service, from the seventeenth*, namely, *to the forty-sixth year*, Tac Subst, **mīlĭtāris** -is, m. *a soldier, warrior*, Tac

mīlĭtārĭtĕr, adv. (militaris), *in a military or warlike manner*, tecta sibi militariter aedificare, Liv

mīlĭtĭa -ae, f (miles), *military service, warfare* I. Lit, munus militiae sustinere, Caes; discere, Sall, militiae vacatio, *exemption from military service*, Caes, domi militiaeque, domi et militiae, *at home and abroad, at peace and in war*, Cic II. Meton, *the military, soldiery*; cogere militiam, Liv

mīlĭto, 1 (miles), *to serve as a soldier, be a soldier*, in exercitu alicuius, Cic, sub signis alicuius, *under any one's command*, Liv; transf, *to serve under the banners of love*, militavi non sine gloria, Hor

mĭlĭum -ii, n (μελίνη), *millet*, Verg

millĕ, numeral, *a thousand* I. Adj, mille passibus, Caes II. Subst, *a thousand* A. Lit, sing, mille with genit, mille hominum versabatur, plur, millia or milia, viginti millibus peditum, quatuor equitum, Liv, esp, mille passuum, *a thousand paces, a mile* (among the Romans, less by 142 yards than the English mile), Cic B. Transf, *innumerable, countless*, mille pro uno Caesones exstitisse, Liv, temptat mille modis, Hor

millēsĭmus -a -um (mille), *the thousandth*, pars, Cic, adv, millesimum, *for the thousandth time*, Cic

millĭārĭus (mīlĭārĭus) -a -um (mille), *containing a thousand* I Gen, Plin II. Esp, *containing a thousand paces* Subst, **milliārium** -ii, n *a mile-stone*, Cic, aureum, *the central stone erected by Augustus in the forum, from which the miles were measured*, Tac

milliēs (mīlĭēs, miliens), adv (mille), 1, *a thousand times*, plus millies audivi, Ter; 2, *innumerable times, countless times*, millies melius, *a thousand times better*, Cic

1 **Mĭlo (-ōn)** ōnis, m (Μίλων), *of Crotona, a celebrated athlete*

2 **Mĭlo** -ōnis, m, T Annius Milo Papianus, *tribune of the people with Clodius* (57 B C), *whose adversary he was, and whom he slew in a street brawl on the Appian Way, on his trial for the murder he was defended by Cicero* Hence, **Mĭlōnĭānus** -a um, *relating to Milo*, subst, **Mĭlōnĭāna** ae, f, (sc oratio), *the speech of Cicero in defence of Milo*

Miltĭădēs -is and i, m (Μιλτιάδης), *a celebrated Athenian general who conquered the Persians at Marathon*

mĭlŭīnus (milvīnus) -a um (milvus), *of or relating to a kite*, pullus, *a young kite* (fig of the son of an avaricious man), Cic

mĭlŭus (milvus) i, m I. *a kite, hawk*, Cic II. Transf, 1, *a fish, the gurnard*, Ov., 2, *a star*, Ov

Mĭlyăs ădis, f. (Μιλυάς), *a district of Phrygia Major*

mīma -ae, f (mimus), *a female mime*, Cic

Mĭmallŏnis -idis, f *a Bacchante* Adj, **Mimallŏnĕus** a um, *Bacchanalian*

Mĭmās -antis, m (Μίμας) I. *a mountain in Ionia, opposite Chios* II. *a giant*.

mīmĭcē, adv (mimicus), *like a mime or buffoon*, Cat.

mīmĭcus a -um (μιμικός), 1, *mimic, farcical*, jocus, Cic, 2, *counterfeit, unreal* Plin

Mimnermus -i, m. (Μίμνερμος), *a Greek elegiac poet of Colophon.*

mīmŭla -ae, f. (dim. of mima), *a female mime*, Cic.

mīmus -i, m. (μῖμος). **I.** *a mime, mimic actor, pantomimist*, Cic. **II.** *a dramatic piece so called, broad farce;* persona de mimo, Cic.; fig., *a farce;* famam mimum facere, Cic.

min' = mihine, Pers.

mĭna -ae, f. (μνᾶ), **1,** *a Greek weight* = 100 *drachmae*, Plin.; **2,** *a Greek silver coin* = 100 *drachmae* or *Roman denarii*, Cic.

mĭnācĭae -ārum, f. (minax), *threats, menaces*, Plaut.

mĭnācĭtĕr, adv. (minax), *threateningly*, Cic.

mĭnae -ārum, f. (connected with mineo). **I.** *the battlements, parapets of a wall;* murorum, Verg. **II.** Transf., *threats, menaces;* minas iactare, *to threaten*, Cic.; of animals, Ov., Verg.; or of the wind, etc., Ov.

mĭnantĕr, adv. (1. minor), *threateningly*, Ov.

mĭnātĭo -ōnis, f. (1. minor), *a threatening, threat, menace* (plur)., Cic.

mĭnax -ācis, f. (1. minor). **I.** *overhanging;* scopulus, Verg. **II.** *threatening, full of threats;* homo, Cic.; vituli, Ov.; litterae, Cic.; fluvius, Verg.

Mincĭus -ii, m. *a river near Mantua*, now *Mincio.*

mĭnĕo, 2. *to project, overhang*, Lucr. (?)

Mĭnerva -ae, f. (Etruscan Menerfa or Meurfa), *the goddess Minerva, daughter of Jupiter, goddess of wisdom, and patroness of all the arts and sciences, identified with the Greek Athene;* prov., crassā (pingui) Minervā, *with homely mother-wit*, Cic.; sus Minervam (sc. docet), *when a foolish person begins to teach a wise one*, Cic.; invitā Minervā, *without ability*, Cic.; meton. = *working in wool*, Verg.

Mĭnervĭum -ii, n. (arx Minervae, Verg.), *a castle and temple to Minerva in Calabria.*

Mĭnervae prōmontōrium, *a promontory in Campania, south-east of Surrentum, the seat of the Sirens.*

mingo, minxi, minctum and mictum, 3. *to make water*, Hor.

mĭnĭātŭlus -a -um (dim. of miniatus), *somewhat coloured* or *tinged with cinnabar*, Cic.

mĭnĭātus -a -um, v. minio.

mĭnĭmē, v. parum.

mĭnĭmus, v. parvus.

1. **mĭnĭo**, 1. (minium), *to colour with cinnabar* or *red-lead*, Plin. Partic., **mĭnĭātus** -a -um, *coloured with cinnabar* or *red-lead, painted red*, Cic.

2. **Mĭnĭo (Mŭnĭo)** -ōnis, m. *a river in Etruria*, now *Mignone.*

mĭnister -tri, m. and **mĭnistra** -ae, f. (root MIN, whence also minus), *a servant, attendant, assistant;* **a,** in a house, minister cubiculi, Liv.; transf., virtutes voluptatum ministrae, Cic.; **b,** *a servant in a temple, the servant of a god;* Martis, Cic.; **c,** in a public office, ministri imperii tui, Cic.; **d,** *an assistant, supporter, aider, helper;* libidinis, Cic.; ministros se praebent in judiciis oratoribus, Cic.; ales minister fulminis, *Jupiter's eagle*, Hor.

mĭnistĕrĭum -ii, n. (minister). **I.** *service, assistance, attendance, office, employment, occupation*, Liv.; ministerio fungi, Liv. **II.** Meton., **a,** *servants*, Tac.; **b,** *retinue, personnel;* scribarum, Liv.

mĭnistra -ae, f., v. minister.

mĭnistrātor -ōris, m. (ministro), **1,** *a servant, attendant, assistant*, Suet.; **2,** esp., *one who supplied an advocate with the facts needed in his oration*, Cic.

mĭnistro, 1. (minister). **I.** *to serve, wait upon;* **1,** alicui, Cic.; **2,** esp., *to wait at table, to hand:* servi ministrant, Cic.; cibos, Tac.; pocula, Cic.; coenam, Hor. **II.** Transf., **1,** *to attend to, take care of, govern, direct:* velis, *to attend to the sails*, Verg.; jussa medicorum, Ov.; **2,** *to afford, procure, provide;* faces furiis Clodianis, Cic.; prolem, Tib.; furor arma ministrat, Verg.; vinum quod verba ministrat, Hor.

mĭnĭtābundus -a -um (minitor), *threatening, menacing*, Liv.

mĭnĭtor, 1. dep. (1. minor), *to threaten;* alicui mortem, Cic.; huic orbi ferro ignique, Cic.; minitans per litteras se omnia quae conarentur prohibiturum, Cic.

mĭnĭum -ii, n. (a Spanish word), *native cinnabar, red-lead, vermilion*, Verg.

1. **mĭnor**, 1. dep. (connected with minae and mineo). **I.** *to jut out, project, hang over;* gemini minantur in caelum scopuli, Verg. **II.** **1,** *to threaten, menace;* alicui, Cic.; alicui crucem, Cic.; **2,** *to promise boastfully;* multa, Hor.

2. **mĭnor** -ōris, compar., parvus (q.v.).

Mīnōs -ōis, acc. -ōem and -ōa, m. (Μίνως). **I.** *a mythical king and lawgiver in Crete, son of Zeus, and, after death, judge in Tartarus.* **II.** *Minos II., king of Crete, grandson of the preceding, husband of Pasiphaë, father of Ariadne, Phaedra, and Deucalion.* Hence, **a, Mīnōis** -idis, f. *a daughter of Minos, Ariadne*, Ov.; **b,** adj., **Mīnōĭus** -a -um, *relating to Minos, Cretan;* virgo, *Ariadne*, Ov.; **c, Mīnōus** -a -um, *relating to Minos;* poet. = *Cretan;* Thoas, *son of Ariadne*, Ov.; arenae, *shore of Crete*, Ov.

Mīnōtaurus -i, m. (Μινώταυρος), *a monster, half-bull, half-man, the offspring of Pasiphaë and a bull, slain by Theseus.*

mintha -ae, f. (μίνθα), *mint*, Plin.

Minturnae -ārum, f. *town in Latium, on the borders of Campania.* Hence, adj., **Minturnensis** -e, *relating to Minturnae.*

Mĭnŭcĭus -a -um, *name of a Roman gens, the most noted member of which was* M. Minucius Rufus, *magister equitum to the dictator Fabius Maximus Cunctator.*

mĭnŭme = minime (q.v.).

mĭnŭmus = minimus (q.v.).

mĭnŭo -ŭi -ūtum, 3. (root MIN, whence 2. minor, μινύω, μινύθω), *to make smaller.* **I.** *to cut up into small pieces, to chop up;* ligna, Ov. **II.** *to lessen, diminish;* **1,** lit., sumptus civitatum, Cic.; minuente aestu, *at the ebbing of the tide*, Caes.; **2,** transf., *to lessen, diminish, lower, reduce, limit;* gloriam alicuius, Cic.; molestias vitae, Cic.; ut controversiam minuam, *limit, confine to the point*, Cic.; majestatem P. R. per vim, *to offend against*, Cic.

mĭnus, compar. **I.** Adj., v. parvus. **II.** Adv., v. parum.

mĭnuscŭlus -a -um (dim. of compar. minor), *somewhat less, somewhat small*, Cic.

mĭnūtal -ālis, n. (minutus), *a dish of mincemeat*, Juv.

mĭnūtātim, adv. (minutus), *in small pieces, bit by bit, piecemeal, gradually;* aliquid addere, Cic.; interrogare, Cic.

mĭnūtē, adv. (minutus), *in small portions, meanly, pettily, paltrily;* res minutius tractare, Cic.

mĭnūtĭa -ae, f. (minutus), *smallness, littleness, minuteness*, Sen.

mĭnūtus -a -um, p. adj. (from minuo), *small, little, minute, unimportant, trifling*, res minutae, *trifles*, Cic.; philosophi, *petty, insignificant*, Cic.

Mĭnyās -ae, m. (Μινύας), *a rich king of Orchomenus, the fabulous ancestor of the Minyae* Hence, a, **Mĭnyae** -ārum, m. (Μινύαι), *the Argonauts, companions of Jason*; b, **Mĭnyēĭăs** -ădis, f. *daughter of Minyas*; c, **Mĭnyēĭus** -a -um, *belonging to Minyas*.

mīrābĭlis -e (miror). I. *wonderful, astonishing*, mirabile est, followed by quam and the subj., Cic.; by quomodo, Cic.; with 2. supine, auditu, Cic.; dictu, Cic. II. *extraordinary, unusual*, mirabilem in modum, Cic.

mīrābĭlĭtĕr, adv. (mirabilis), *wonderfully, marvellously, singularly, extraordinarily*, cupere, laetari, Cic.; mirabiliter moratus est, *is of an extraordinary disposition*, Cic.

mīrābundus -a -um (miror), *full of wonder, wondering*; mirabundi quidnam esset, Liv.

mīrācŭlum -i, n. (miror), *a wonderful thing, wonder, prodigy, miracle, marvellousness*, miracula philosophorum somniantium, *the wonderful opinions*, Cic.; adjiciunt miracula huic pugnae, *wonders*, Liv.; magnitudinis, *a wonder for size*, Liv.

mīrandus -a -um, p. adj. (from miror), *wonderful, singular*, mirandum in modum, Cic.

mīrātĭo -ōnis, f. (miror), *a wondering, wonder, astonishment*, Cic.

mīrātor -ōris, m. (miror), *an admirer*, Ov.

mīrē, adv. (mirus), *wonderfully, extraordinarily, astonishingly*, favere, Cic.; mire quam, *in a wonderful manner*, Cic.

mīrĭfĭcē, adv. (mirificus), *wonderfully, extraordinarily*, dolere, Cic.

mīrĭfĭcus -a -um (mirus and facio), *causing wonder, wonderful, astonishing*, homo, Cic.; turris mirificis operibus exstructa, Caes.; convicium, voluptas, Cic.

mirmillo (**murmillo**) -ōnis, m. *a kind of gladiator, generally matched with the Thraces or retiarii*, Cic.

mīror, 1. dep. I. *to wonder, be astonished at*, negligentiam hominis, Cic.; foll. by acc. and infin., me ad accusandum descendere, Cic.; foll. by quod, mirari quod non rideret haruspex, Cic.; with rel. sent., eius rei quae causa esset miratus, Caes.; foll. by si, miror illā superbiā si quemquam amicum habere potuit, Cic.; miror, *I wonder, I cannot understand, I am curious to know*, mirantes quid rei esset, Liv. II. *to admire, look on with admiration*, puerorum formas et corpora magno opere, Cic.; with genit. of cause, Verg.

mīrus -a -um, *wonderful, astonishing, extraordinary, very great*; desiderium urbis, Cic.; mirum quam inimicus erat, *it is wonderful how hostile, i.e., exceedingly hostile*, Cic.; se mirum quantum profuit, Liv.; mirum est ut, with subj., Cic.; quid mirum? *what wonder?* Ov.

Mīsargyrĭdēs -ae, m. (μισαργυρία, *hatred of money*), *a hater of money* (a name invented by Plautus and applied to a usurer), Plaut.

miscellānĕa -ōrum, n. (misceo), *a hash of different meats, hotchpotch, the food of gladiators*, Juv.

miscĕo, miscŭi, mixtum, and (later) mistum, 2. (μίσγω = μίγνυμι). I. Gen., *to mix, mingle*, 1, lit., mella Falerno, Hor.; 2, transf., a, *to blend, mingle*, gravitatem modestiae, Cic.; mixta metu spes, Liv.; b, *to unite*, sanguinem et genus cum aliquo, *to marry*, Liv.; se miscere viris, Verg.; corpus cum aliqua, Cic.; of battle, miscere certamina, Liv. II. 1, *to mix a beverage, prepare by mixing*, a, lit., mulsum, Cic.; pocula alicui, Ov.; b, *to stir up, excite*, incendia, Verg.; motus animorum, Cic.; 2, *to confuse, confound*, a, caelum terramque, *to raise a storm*, Verg.; b, of moral and political events, malis contionibus rempublicam, *to disturb*, Cic.; 3, *to fill*, domum gemitu, Verg.

mĭsellus -a -um (dim. of miser), *miserable, wretched, unhappy*, homo, Cic.; spes, Lucr.

Mīsēnus -i, m. *the trumpeter of Aeneas* Hence, **Mīsēnum** -i, n. *a promontory and town in Campania, now Capo di Miseno*, mons Misenus, Verg. Adj., **Mīsēnensis** -e, *relating to Misenum*.

mĭser -ĕra -ĕrum. I. *miserable, wretched, unhappy, pitiable, unfortunate, deplorable*, 1, of persons, hic miser atque infelix, Cic.; miserrimum habere aliquem, *to torment greatly*, Cic.; O me miserum! Cic.; 2, transf., of things, misera fortuna, Cic.; as parenthetical exclamation, miserum! *how wretched!* Verg. II. *suffering, ill*, miserum latus caputve, Hor.

mĭsĕrābĭlis -e, (miseror). I. *miserable, wretched, lamentable, deplorable*, aspectus, Cic.; squalor, Cic. II. *mournful, sad, plaintive*, vox, Cic.; elegi, Hor.

mĭsĕrābĭlĭtĕr, adv. (miserabilis). I. *miserably, lamentably, pitiably*, mori, Cic. II. *in a mournful or plaintive manner*, epistola miserabiliter scripta, Cic.

mĭsĕrandus -a -um (miseror), *pitiable, deplorable*; miserandum in modum, Cic.

mĭsĕrātĭo -ōnis, f. (miseror). I. *pity, compassion*; cum quadam miseratione, Cic. II. *pathetic or moving speech or tone*, uti miserationibus, Cic.

mĭsĕrē, adv. (miser). I. *wretchedly, pitiably, miserably*, vivere, Cic. II. *violently, exceedingly*, amare, Ter.; deperire amore, Plaut.

mĭsĕrĕo -sĕrŭi -sĕrĭtum and -sertum, 2. and **mĭsĕrĕor** -sĕrĭtus and -sertus sum, 2. dep. (miser). I. *to pity, have compassion on, commiserate*, sociorum, Cic.; laborum tantorum, Verg. II. Impers., miseret or miseretur me, *I pity, I am sorry for, I have compassion on*, me miseret tui, Cic.; cave, te fratrum pro fratris salute obsecrantium misereatur, Cic.

mĭsĕresco, 3. (misereo), 1, *to pity, have compassion on, commiserate*, regis, Verg.; 2, impers., me miserescit alicuius, *I am sorry for, have compassion on*, Plaut.

mĭsĕrĭa -ae, f. (miser). I. *wretchedness, unhappiness, misery, sorrow, grief, affliction, distress*, ubi virtus est, ibi esse miseria non potest, Cic.; in miseriis versari, Cic. II. Personif., Miseria, *the daughter of Erebus and Nox*.

mĭsĕrĭcordĭa -ae, f. (misericors), *pity, compassion, tenderness of heart, mercy*, populi, *on the part of the people*, Cic.; puerorum, *for boys*, Cic.; adhibere misericordiam, *to show*, Cic.; ad misericordiam inducere, Cic.; alicui suam misericordiam tribuere, Cic.

mĭsĕrĭcors -cordis (misereo and cor), *pitiful, compassionate, tender-hearted*, in aliquem, Cic.; quis misericordior inventus est? Cic.

mĭsĕrĭtus, v. misereor.

mĭsĕrĭtĕr, adv. (miser), *wretchedly, lamentably*, Cat.

mĭsĕror, 1. dep. (miser), *to pity, have compassion on, bewail, lament, deplore*, fortunam, Cic.; casum, Sall.

mĭsertus, v. misereor.

missīcĭus (**-tĭus**) -a -um (mitto), *discharged from military service*, Suet.

missile -is, v. missilis.

missilis -e (mitto), *that can be thrown, missile;* lapides, Liv.; ferrum, *a javelin,* Verg. Subst., gen. plur., **missilia** -ōrum, n. *missiles,* Liv.; res missiles, or subst., missilia, *gifts thrown among the people, donatives,* Suet.

missĭo -ōnis, f. (mitto). **I.** *a sending off, sending away;* legatorum, litterarum, Cic. **II.** *a letting go, releasing;* **1, a,** of a prisoner, Cic.; **b,** *a discharge* or *dismission from military service;* nondum justa, injusta, Liv.; honesta, *honourable discharge,* gratiosa, *out of favour,* Liv.; **c,** *a permission given to gladiators to cease fighting;* sine missione munus gladiatorium dare, *to exhibit gladiators who fought till death,* Liv.; **2,** *cessation, termination;* ludorum, Cic.

missĭto, 1. (freq. of mitto), *to send repeatedly;* auxilia, Liv.

missor -ōris, m. (mitto), *one who shoots, an archer,* Cic.

1. **missus** -ūs, m. (mitto). **I.** *a sending;* **1,** missu Caesaris ventitare, *having been sent by Caesar,* Caes.; **2,** *a throwing, shooting;* pili, Liv. **II. 1,** *a shot, the distance shot;* missus bis mille sagittae, Lucr.; **2,** in the public races, *a course, heat,* Suet.

2. **missus** -a -um, v. mitto.

mistim (mixtim), adv. (mistus or mixtus), *confusedly,* Lucr.

mistūra (mixtūra) -ae, f. (misceo), *a mixing, mixture;* rerum, Lucr.

mītĕ, adv. (mitis), *mildly, softly, gently;* mitius ferre, perire, Ov.

mĭtella -ae, f. (dim. of mitra), *a bandage for the head, head-dress, turban,* Cic.

mītesco, 3. (mitis), *to become mild.* **I.** Of fruits, *to ripen, become ripe,* Plin. **II. 1,** of the weather, *to become mild;* hiems, Liv.; frigora, Hor.; of abstract things, *to be allayed, to subside;* seditio, Tac.; discordiae, Liv.; ira, Ov.; **2,** *to become tame;* ferae quaedam nunquam mitescunt, Liv.

Mĭthrĭdātēs -is, m. (Μιθριδάτης), *king in Pontus (135–63* B.C.*), who waged a long war with the Romans, and was conquered by Pompeius.* Adj., **Mĭthrĭdātĭcus** -a -um, *Mithridatic.*

mītĭfĭco, 1. (mitificus), *to make mild, soft;* cibus mitificatus, *well digested,* Cic.

mītĭgātĭo -ōnis, f. (mitigo), *an assuaging, alleviating, appeasing,* Cic.

mītĭgo, 1. (= mitem ago), *to make mild, soft.* **I.** Lit., fruges, *to make ripe,* Cic.; cibum, *to make soft by cooking,* Cic.; agros, *to break up, loosen, till,* Cic. **II. a,** of character, *to soothe, make gentle, pacify;* animum alicuius, *to soothe,* Cic.; Lampsacenos in istum, Cic.; **b,** of things, *to soothe, assuage, alleviate, charm, enchant;* tristitiam et severitatem, Cic.; dolorem, Cic.

mītis -e, *mild, gentle, ripe.* **I.** Of fruits, poma, uva, Verg.; fig., of style, Thucydides fuisset maturior et mitior, Cic.; of climate, caelo mitissimo, Liv.; of water, wind, etc., fluvius, Verg. **II.** Transf., of character; **a,** of persons, *mild, gentle, free from harshness;* homo mitissimus atque lenissimus, Cic.; of animals, taurus, Ov.; **b,** of things, *mild, gentle;* dolor, Cic.; aliquid mitiorem in partem interpretari, *put a lenient interpretation upon,* Cic.; **c,** of speech, *mild;* mitis et compta oratio, Cic.

mĭtra -ae, f. (μίτρα), *a head-dress, in general use among Asiatic nations, but in Greece and Rome worn only by women and effeminate men,* Cic.

mĭtrātus -a -um (mitra), *wearing the mitra,* Prop.

mitto, misi, missum, 3. *to send, let go.* **I.** *to send, despatch.* **A.** Gen., **1,** lit., *to send away;* filium ad propinquum suum, Cic.; legatos de deditione ad eum, Caes.; misi, qui hoc diceret, Cic.; Deiotarus legatos ad me misit, se esse venturum, *with the intelligence that he was about to come,* Cic.; Curio misi, ut medico honos haberetur, *I sent word to Curius,* etc., Cic.; ad mortem, *to put to death,* Cic.; litteras ad aliquem or alicui, Cic.; **2,** transf., aliquem in possessionem, *to put in possession,* Cic.; funera Teucris, *to prepare,* Verg. **B. 1,** *to dedicate a book to a person;* librum ad aliquem, Cic.; **2,** *to conduct;* alias (animas) sub Tartara mittit (of Mercury), Verg.; **3,** *to send forth from oneself, give forth;* luna mittit lucem in terras, Cic.; vocem pro aliquo, *to speak for,* Cic.; **4,** *to push, throw;* pueros in profluentem aquam, Liv.; telum ex aliquo loco, Caes.; **5,** medic. t. t., *to let blood,* Sen.; fig., missus est sanguis invidiae sine dolore, Cic. **II. A.** *to let go, release, give up;* **1,** lit., Cat.; **2,** transf., mittere ac finire odium, Liv.; maestum timorem, Verg.; of orators, *to cease speaking, not to speak, to avoid, pass over;* mitto illud dicere, *I pass over that,* Cic.; mitto de amissa parte exercitūs, Cic. **B. 1,** in the race-course, *to start the competitors;* quadrigas, Liv.; **2,** *to dismiss an assembly;* senatum, Caes.; **3, a,** *to dismiss, discharge, send away;* esp. of soldiers, legiones missas fieri jubere, Cic.; **b,** *to release from imprisonment;* mitti eum jubere, Liv.

mītŭlus (mūtŭlus) -i, m. (μιτύλος), *a species of edible mussel,* Hor.

mixtūra, etc. = mistura (q.v.).

mna = mina (q.v.).

Mnēmŏnĭdes -um, f. *the Muses, daughters of Mnemosyne,* Ov.

Mnēmŏsȳnē -ēs, f. (Μνημοσύνη), *Mnemosyne, mother of the Muses.*

mnēmŏsȳnum -i, n. (μνημόσυνον), *a memorial,* Cat.

mōbĭlis -e (for movibilis, from moveo). **I.** *moveable, easy to be moved; not firm, not fixed;* **1,** lit., oculi, Cic.; **2,** transf., **a,** *excitable, pliable, flexible;* mobilis aetas, Verg.; gens ad omnem auram spei mobilis, Liv.; **b,** *changeable, inconstant;* animus, Cic.; Galli sunt in capiendis consiliis mobiles, Caes. **II.** *rapid;* rivi, Hor.

mōbĭlĭtas -ātis, f. (mobilis). **I.** *moveableness, mobility;* animal mobilitate celerrimā, Cic.; linguae, Cic.; transf., *inconstancy, changeableness;* alicuius, Cic. **II.** *rapidity;* equitum, Caes.

mōbĭlĭtĕr, adv. (mobilis), *rapidly, with quick motion;* palpitare, Cic.; ad bellum mobiliter excitari, *easily, quickly,* Caes.

mōbĭlĭto, 1. (mobilis), *to make moveable, put into motion,* Lucr.

mŏdĕrābĭlis -e (moderor), *moderate;* nihil moderabile suadere, Ov.

mŏdĕrāmen -ĭnis, n. (moderor), *a means of governing* or *guiding* (e.g., *a helm, rudder*); navis, Ov.; transf., rerum, *the management, government of the State,* Ov.

mŏdĕrantĕr, adv. (moderans from moderor), *moderately, with moderation,* Lucr.

mŏdĕrātē, adv. (moderatus), *moderately, with moderation;* moderatius id volunt fieri, Cic.

mŏdĕrātim, adv. (moderatus), *moderately, gradually,* Lucr.

mŏdĕrātĭo -ōnis, f. (moderor), *moderating.* **I. A.** *moderating, restraining;* effrenati populi, Cic. **B.** *government;* mundi, Cic. **II.** *moderation, temperance;* temperantia et moderatio naturae tuae, Cic.; vocis, *articulation,* Cic.

mŏdĕrātor -ōris, m (moderor), *a governor, guide, manager, ruler*, equorum, *a driver*, Ov , arundinis, *a fisher*, Ov , reipublicae, Cic

mŏdĕrātrix -icis, f (moderator), *she that rules or governs*, respublica moderatrix omnium factorum, Cic

mŏdĕrātus -a -um (moderor), *moderate, temperate, keeping within due measure*, of persons, frugi homo et in omnibus vitae partibus moderatus ac temperans, Cic , of things, convivium Cic , ventus, Ov , otium, Cic , oratio, Cic

mŏdĕro, 1 *to moderate, keep within bounds*, voci meae, Plaut.

mŏdĕror, 1 dep (modus) **I.** *to set bounds to, keep within bounds*, *to regulate, moderate, restrain*, (α) with dat , alicui, Cic , animo et orationi, Cic , irae, odio, Liv , (β) with acc , animos, Cic **II.** *to direct, guide* **A.** Lit , (α) with dat , navi funiculo, Cic , (β) with acc , habenas, Ov **B.** Transf , *to govern, rule, regulate*, (α) with dat , quibus totis moderatur oratio, Cic , (β) with acc , Deus qui regit et moderatur et movet id corpus, Cic cantus numerosque, Cic

mŏdestē, adv (modestus), *moderately, temperately, discreetly modestly*, Romam venire, Cic

mŏdestĭa -ae, f (modestus) **I. A** *moderation, temperance*, neque modum neque modestiam victores habere, Sall **B. 1**, applied to behaviour, *modesty, unassuming conduct*, in dicendo, Cic , **2**, *respect, obedience to authority*, in milite modestiam et continentiam desiderare, Caes , **3**, as translation of the Stoic phrase εὐταξία, *good, practical judgment*, Cic **II.** *mildness*, hiemis, Tac.

mŏdestus -a um (modus), *moderate, keeping within bounds, moderate in desires or passions, temperate* **A.** modestum ordinem, Cic **B. 1**, *modest, unassuming, unpretending*, adolescentuli modestissimi pudor, Cic , **2**, *modest chaste, virtuous*, videas dolere flagitiosis modestos, Cic

mŏdĭālis -e (modius), *containing a modius*, Plaut

mŏdĭcē, adv (modicus), *moderately*, **1**, *tolerably*, modice locuples *tolerably well off*, Liv , modice vinosus, *no great wine bibber*, Liv , **2**, *moderately, with moderation, temperately*, facere, agere, Cic

mŏdĭcus -a -um (modus) **I.** *moderate, not very large, middling, ordinary*, convivia, potiones, *not excessive*, Cic , fossa, *not very deep*, Liv , acervus, Hor , laus, Tac , equites, senatores *possessing moderate wealth*, Tac **II.** *moderate, keeping within bounds, temperate, modest, unpretending*, severitas, Cic , modicus voluptatum, *temperate in enjoyment*, Tac , animus belli ingens, domi modicus Sall

mŏdĭfĭco, 1 (modus and facio), *to measure off, measure, moderate*, verba ab oratore modificata, Cic

mŏdĭus -ii, m (modus), *a dry measure among the Romans* = 16 *sextarii, and containing somewhat less than two imperial gallons, a peck*, Cic , pleno modio *in full measure, abundantly*, Cic (genit plur , modium, Cic)

mŏdŏ, adv (modus), *only, alone, but* **I. A.** Gen , quod dixerit *solere* modo, non etiam *potuere*, Cic , nemo eorum progredi modo extra agmen audeat, *only to go, so much as to go*, Caes , ut ea modo exercitui satis superque foret, *that it alone was more than enough for the army*, Sall **B.** Esp , **1**, with wishes, commands, etc , *only, just* veniat modo, Cic vide modo, *only see*, Cic , **2**, **a**, in conditional sentences, modo ut, or modo alone with subj , *provided that, if only*, quos, valetudo modo bona sit, tenuitas ipsa delectat, *if the health be only good*, Cic , modo ne, *if only not, provided that not*, tertia aderit, modo ne Publius rogatus sit, Cic **b**, with relatives, servus nemo, qui modo tolerabili conditione sit servitutis, *if he only be, provided only that he is*, Cic , **c**, si modo *if only*, tu scis, si modo meministi, me tibi dixisse, Cic , **3**, in negative sentences, **a**, non modo . sed (verum), *not only but*, non modo sed (verum) etiam, *not only but also*, non modo sed (verum) ne quidem, *not only but not even*, Cic , **b**, non modo non sed, sed potius, sed etiam, *not only not but rather*, non modo non sed ne quidem, *not only not but not even*, Cic **II.** Transf , of time, **A. a**, *now, but now, just now, just*, advenis modo? *are you just come?* Ter , **b**, used also of a remoter past, *lately, some time ago*, modo hoc malum in rempublicam invasit (i e , *seventy years previously*), Cic **B.** modo modo, *sometimes sometimes, now now, at one time at another*, modo ait, modo negat, Cic , in place of the second modo is found nunc, Liv , interdum, Sall , aliquando, Tac , saepe, Sall , modo tum (deinde, paullo post, postremum, vicissim), *now then, in the first place in the second place, just afterwards*, Cic

mŏdŭlātē, adv with compar (modulatus), *in good time, in time* (of music), modulate canentes tibiae, Cic

mŏdŭlātor -ōris, m (modulor), *one who observes a regular rhythm, a musician*, Hor

mŏdŭlātus a -um, p adj (from modulor), *properly measured or modulated, in good time, rhythmical, melodious*, verba, Ov

mŏdŭlor, 1 dep (modus) **I.** *to measure, measure off, measure regularly*, Plin **II. 1**, t t of music, *to measure rhythmically, to modulate, to mark time*, vocem, Cic virgines sonum vocis pulsu pedum modulantes, Liv ; **2**, **a**, *to sing*, carmina, Verg , **b**, *to play*, lyram, Tib

mŏdŭlus -i, m (dim of modus) **I.** *a measure, standard of measurement*, metiri quendam suo modulo, Hor **II.** *rhythm, musical time, measure, melody*, Plin

mŏdus i, m *a measure, standard of measurement* **I.** Lit , Varr **II.** Transf **A.** *size, quantity, length*, etc , **1**, gen , agri certus modus, Caes , **2**, esp as musical t t , *rhythm, melody, time*, vertere modum, Hor , esp in plur , flebilibus modis concinere, Cic **B.** *a measure, bound, limit, boundary*, **1**, gen , modum imponere magistratui, Liv , modum lugendi aliquando facere, *to make an end of bewailing*, Cic , **2**, esp in action, *moderation, control*, imitari caelestium ordinem vitae modo et constantia, Cic , sine modo ac modestia, Sall **C.** *order, rule* alius modum pacis ac belli facere, Liv **D.** *manner, mode, fashion, way, method*, concludendi, Cic , servorum modo, *after the manner of slaves*, Liv , hostilem in modum, *in a hostile manner*, Cic , mirum in modum, Caes , quonam modo? Cic , eius modi, *in that manner, of that kind*, Cic , huius modi, Cic

moecha ae, f (moechus), *an adulteress*, Hor.

moechor, 1 dep (moechus), *to commit adultery*, Cat

moechus i, m (μοιχός), *a fornicator, adulterer*, Plaut , Ter.

moenĕra = munera (q v)

1 **moenĭa** -ium, n (connected with munio) **I.** *the walls or fortifications of a city*, sub ipsis Numantiae moenibus, Cic , transf , **a**, poet , *the walls, external compass, enclosure*, navis, Ov theatri, Lucr , caeli, Ov ; **b**, *defence, protection, bulwarks*, alpes moenia Italiae, Ov **II.** Meton , **1**, *the city enclosed within the walls*, Syracus-

arum moenia ac portus, Cic.; moenia triplici circumdata muro, Verg.; **2,** *mansion, dwelling;* Ditis, Verg.

2. **moenĭa** -ium, n. = munia (q.v.).

moenio = munio (q.v.).

1. **Moenus** -i, m. *the river Main.*

2. **moenus** = munus (q.v.).

moerus = murus (q.v.).

Moesi -ōrum, m. *a people in the modern Servia and Bulgaria;* hence **a, Moesĭa (Maesĭa)** -ae, f. *the country of the Moesi;* **b, Moesĭăcus** -a -um, *belonging to the Moesi.*

moerĕo, moeror, moestus = maereo, maeror, maestus (q.v.).

mŏla -ae, f. (molo), lit., *a mill-stone.* **A.** Hence, sing. and gen. plur., *the mill-stone = the mill* for grinding corn, olives, etc.; molis operam dare, Cic. **B.** Meton., *grits, coarse meal,* or *flour,* usually of spelt, which, mixed with salt, was sprinkled on victims before sacrifice; mola et vinum, Cic.

mŏlāris -e (mola). **I.** *of* or *relating to a mill;* **1,** lit., subst., **mŏlāris** -is m. *a mill-stone,* Verg.; **2,** transf., *as big as a mill-stone;* saxa, Sen.; subst., **mŏlāris** -is, m. *a huge block of stone,* Verg. **II.** *belonging to grinding;* subst., **mŏlāris** -is, m. *a molar tooth, grinder,* Juv.

mōles -is, f. *a mass, a heap.* **I.** Abstr. = *something heavy, weighty.* **A.** Lit., opposui molem clipei, *weighty shield,* Ov.; ingenti mole Latinus, Verg. **B.** Transf., **1,** *mass, heap = greatness, might, power;* tanti imperii, Liv.; pugnae, Liv.; **2,** *trouble, difficulty;* majore mole pugnare, Liv. **II.** Concr., **A.** *a heavy, shapeless mass;* chaos, rudis indigestaque moles, Ov. **B.** Esp., **1,** *a massive construction;* **a,** *a dam, mole;* oppositae fluctibus, Cic.; **b,** *a large building;* insanae substructionum moles, Cic.; **c,** moles belli, *large military machines, preparations for war, military works;* refectis vineis aliāque mole belli, Liv.; **2, a,** *a mass of men, large number;* hostes majorem molem haud facile sustinentes, Liv.; **b,** *a mass of clouds, storm,* Verg.

mŏlestē, adv. (molestus), **1,** *unwillingly, with vexation, with annoyance;* moleste fero, *I take it ill, I am annoyed, I am sorry;* with acc. and infin., te de praedio aviae exerceri moleste fero, Cic.; foll. by si, Cic.; by quod, Cic.; by acc., Cic.; **2,** *in a troublesome* or *disagreeable manner;* of discourse, gait, etc., *affectedly,* Cat.

mŏlestĭa -ae, f. (molestus), *annoyance, dissatisfaction, chagrin, disgust, dislike;* **1,** gen., fasces habent molestiam, *are attended with annoyance,* Cic.; sine molestia tua, *without trouble to yourself,* Cic.; ex pernicie reipublicae molestiam trahere, *to be chagrined at,* Cic.; molestiam alicui aspergere, *to cause annoyance to,* Cic.; **2,** *affectation, stiffness* (of style); Latine loquendi accurata et sine molestia diligens elegantia, Cic.

mŏlestus -a -um (moles), *burdensome, troublesome, annoying, irksome;* **1,** gen., labor, Cic.; nisi molestum est, exsurge, *if it be not inconvenient,* Cic.; tunica, *a dress of inflammable materials put on condemned criminals and set alight,* Juv.; **2,** of discourse, *affected, laboured;* veritas, Cic.

mōlīmen -ĭnis, n. (molior), *a great effort, exertion, undertaking;* res suo ipsa molimine gravis, Liv.; meton., *building;* molimine vasto, Ov.

mōlīmentum -i, n. (molior), *a great effort, exertion, endeavour;* sine magno commeatu atque molimento, Caes.; motam sede suā parvi molimenti adminiculis, *by machines of small power,* Liv.

mōlĭor, 4. dep. (moles). **I.** Transit., **A.** Gen., *to set in motion, remove, displace;* ancoras, *to weigh anchor,* Liv.; naves ab terra, *to unmoor,* Liv.; montes sede suā, Liv.; fulmina dextrā, *to hurl,* Verg.; habenas, *to guide, direct,* Verg. **B. 1,** *to cause to totter, undermine;* portam, Liv.; transf., fidem, *to undermine credit,* Liv.; **2,** *to work, cultivate the earth;* terram, Liv.; arva ferro, Lucr.; **3, a,** *to build, erect, rear, raise;* muros, arcem, Verg.; classem, Verg.; **b,** of abstract objects, *to undertake;* nulla opera, Cic.; **4,** *to cause, produce;* morbos, Verg.; sibi opem, Verg.; struere et moliri alicui aliquid calamitatis, *to plot, devise,* Cic.; alicui insidias, *to lay snares,* Cic.; peregrinum regnum, *to strive after, endeavour to obtain,* Liv. **II.** Reflex., *to toil, struggle, exert oneself.* **A.** Lit., in demoliendo signo permulti homines moliebantur, Cic. **B.** Transf., agam per me ipse et moliar, Cic.

mōlītĭo -ōnis, f. (molior), **1,** *a demolition, demolishing;* valli, Liv.; **2,** *an effort, laborious undertaking, preparation;* rerum, Cic.

mōlītor -ōris, m. (molior), *a builder, erector, producer, contriver, author;* mundi, Cic.

mollesco, 3. (mollio), **1,** *to become soft,* Ov.; **2,** transf., *to become soft, effeminate;* tum genus humanum primum mollescere coepit, Lucr.

mollĭcellus -a -um (dim. of mollis), *somewhat soft, somewhat tender,* Cat.

mollĭcŭlus -a -um (dim. of mollis), **1,** *somewhat soft* or *tender,* Plaut.; **2,** transf., *somewhat effeminate,* Cat.

mollĭo, 4. (mollis), *to make pliable, flexible, soft, supple.* **I. A.** Lit., lanam trahendo, *to spin,* Ov.; artus oleo, Liv.; ceram pollice, Ov.; cibum vapore, Lucr.; frigoribus durescit humor, et idem mollitur tepefactus, Cic.; glebas, *to loosen, soften,* Ov. **B.** Transf., **1,** clivum anfractibus modicis, *to diminish the steepness of the ascent,* Caes.; **2,** fructus feros colendo, *to render less harsh,* Verg. **II.** Fig., **A.** lacrimae meorum me interdum molliunt, Cic. **B. 1,** *to soften, to make milder, make gentle;* poetae molliunt animos nostros, Cic.; feroces militum animos, Sall.; vocem, *make womanish,* Cic.; ferro mollita juventus, *emasculated, castrated,* Lucr.; **2, a,** *to make milder, less disagreeable, render bearable;* verba usu, Cic.; poenam, Ov.; **b,** *to tame, restrain, keep within bounds;* Hannibalem exsultantem patientiā suā molliebat, Cic.; sedare motus et animos eorum mollire, Cic. (syncop. imperf., mollibat, Ov.).

*mollĭpes -pĕdis (mollis and pes), *soft-footed, i.e., having a trailing walk* (Gr. εἰλίπους), Cic.

mollis -e (= movilis, from moveo), *soft, tender, pliant, supple, flexible yielding.* **I. A. 1,** lit., juncus, acanthus, Verg.; crura, colla, Verg.; brachia, Ov.; arcus, *unstrung,* Ov.; zephyri, *gentle,* Ov.; **2,** transf., **a,** of works of art, *soft, not stiff, graceful;* signa, Cic.; of orators and poetry, oratio mollis et tenera, Cic.; **b,** of places, *with a gentle ascent;* fastigium, Caes. **B.** *soft to the touch;* **1,** lit., cervix, manus, Ov.; of the ground, mollis humus, Ov.; **2,** transf., *mild;* aestas, Verg.; vina, Verg. **II.** Fig. **A.** *gentle, sensitive, tender;* **1,** mollis animus ad accipiendam et ad deponendam offensionem, Cic.; homo mollissimo animo, Cic.; **2,** *effeminate, unmanly, weak;* philosophus, Cic.; disciplina, Cic.; vita, Ov. **B.** *gentle, mild, pleasant;* **1,** mollem ac jucundam efficere senectutem, Cic.; **2, a,** *compassionate, gentle, mild, complaisant, easy;* oratio, Cic.; jussa, Verg.; **b,** *tender, moving;* verbis mollibus lenire aliquem, Hor.; illud mollissimum carmen, Cic.

mollitĕr, adv. (mollis), **1,** *softly, easily, gently;* quis membra movere mollius possit, flor.; excellent spirantia mollius aera, *with more grace or skill*, Verg, 2, fig, a, *gently, easily*, quod ferendum est molliter sapienti, Cic, in a bad sense, *weakly, without energy*, nimis molliter aegritudinem pati, Sall, b, *effeminately*, delicate et molliter vivere, Cic, c, *mildly, compassionately*, feci parce et molliter, Cic.

mollĭtĭa -ae, f and **mollĭtĭes** -ēi, f (mollis) I. Lit, *softness, tenderness, flexibility, pliancy*, cervicum, Cic II. Fig, A. Gen, *tenderness, gentleness, mildness, sensibility*, animi, Cic, naturae, Cic B. Esp, *effeminacy, weakness*, civitatum mores lapsi ad mollitiam, Cic

mollĭtūdo -inis, f. (mollis) I. *softness, pliability, flexibility*, assimilis spongiis mollitudo, Cic II. Fig, *tenderness, softness, sensitiveness*, humanitatis, Cic

mŏlo -ŭi -ĭtum, 3 (mola), *to grind in a mill* Partic, **mŏlĭtus** -a -um, *ground*, cibaria molita, *meal*, Caes

Mŏlorchus -i, m (Μόλορχος), *a poor vine-dresser near Nemea, who hospitably received Hercules when about to slay the Nemean lion*, Molorchi luci, poet = *the Nemean woods*, Verg

Mŏlossi ōrum, m (Μολοσσοί), *the inhabitants of Molossia, a district of Eastern Epirus* Hence, adj, a, **Mŏlossus** -a -um, *Molossian*, canis, Hor, subst, **Mŏlossus** -i, m *a Molossian hound, in great request as a sporting dog*, Hor, b, **Mŏlossĭcus** -a -um, *Molossian*.

mōly -yos, n (μῶλυ), *the herb moly, given by Mercury to Ulysses as a counter charm against the enchantments of Circe*, Ov

mōmen inis, n (= movimen, from moveo), 1, *movement, motion*, e salso consurgere momine ponti, Lucr, 2, *momentum, impulse*, Lucr

mōmentum -i, n (= movimentum, from moveo) I. *movement, motion* A. 1, lit, astra forma ipsā figurāque suā momenta sustentant, Cic, 2, of time, *a small portion of time, minute, moment*, parvo momento, Caes, momento temporis, Liv, momento horae, *in the short space of an hour*, Liv, or simply momento, Liv. B. Fig, 1, *oscillation*, sine momento rerum, Lucr, 2, *change, alteration*, momentum facere annonae, Liv II. *that which puts in motion, impulse* A. Lit, ut (arbores) levi momento impulsae occiderent, Liv B. Fig, 1, *influence, cause*, parva momenta in spem metumque animum impellere, Liv, 2, *turning point, influencing cause*, a, parvo momento si adjuvissent, *with slight help*, Liv, b, *weight, importance, influence* si quid habeat momenti commendatio mea, Cic, esse maximi momenti et ponderis, Cic, argumentorum momenta, *decisive proofs*, Cic, juvenis egregius maximum momentum rerum eius civitatis, *a man of commanding influence*, Liv

Mŏna ae, f *an island off the coast of Britain* (*Anglesea* or *the Isle of Man*)

Mŏnaesēs is, m (Μοναίσης), *a general of the Parthians, who defeated the Romans*

mŏnēdŭla ae, f *a daw, jackdaw*, Cic

mŏnĕo -ŭi -ĭtum, 2 (from root MEN, whence mens), *to remind, admonish* I. Terentiam de testamento, Cic II. A. Lit, 1, a, *to warn, teach, admonish*, with de and the abl, aliquem de retinenda Sestii gratia, Cic, with acc of person and neut acc, id ipsum quod me mones, Cic, with acc and infin, magis idoneum tempus te esse ullum umquam reperturum, Cic, with rel sent, moneat quo statu sit res, Liv, b, *to advise, recommend*, with ut and the subj, ut magnam infamiam fugiat, Cic, with subj alone, eos hoc moneo desinant furere, Cic, with ne and the subj, ne id faceret, Cic, with infin, officium conservare, Cic, 2, *to instruct, prompt, suggest*; tu vatem, tu, diva, mone, Verg, de aliquare, Cic B. 1, *to admonish by punishment*, Tac, 2, *to urge on*, canes, Prop.

mŏnēris -is, f (μονήρης), *a vessel having only one bank of oars*, Liv.

Mŏnēta -ae, f (moneo) I. A. *the mother of the Muses* (= Μνημοσύνη) B *a surname of Juno*, and, as the Roman money was coined in the temple of Juno Moneta, hence, II. A. *the mint, the place where money was coined*, Cic B. Meton, 1, *coined metal, money*, Ov, 2, *the die or stamp with which money was coined*, Mart, transf, communi feriat carmen triviale moneta, Juv

mŏnētālis is, m (moneta), *relating to the mint*, in jest, *one who asks for money*, Cic

mŏnīle is, n *a necklace, a collar*, Cic

mŏnĭmentum = monumentum (q v)

mŏnĭta -ōrum, n (moneo), 1, *warning*, Cic, 2, *prophecies*, deorum, Cic

mŏnĭtĭo -ōnis, f (moneo), *a reminding, warning, admonishing, admonition*, Cic

mŏnĭtor -ōris, m (moneo) I *one who reminds* A. officii, Sall B. a, *one who supplies an orator with facts, an assistant, prompter*, Cic, b, *a nomenclator, who reminds one of persons' names*, Cic II. *an adviser, instructor*, fatuus, Cic

mŏnĭtus -ūs, m (moneo), 1, *a reminding, warning, admonition*, Ov, 2, *an intimation of the will of the gods by oracles, augury, portents, omens*, etc, monitus Fortunae, Cic

Mŏnoecus -i, m (Μόνοικος *he that dwells alone*), *surname of Hercules*; Monoeci Arx et Portus, *promontory and harbour on the coast of Liguria*, now *Monaco*

mŏnogrammos -on (μονόγραμμος), of pictures, *consisting only of outlines, sketched*. Epicurus monogrammos deos et nihil agentes commentus est, *incorporeal, shadowy*, Cic

mŏnŏpŏdĭum ii, n (μονοπόδιον), *a table with one foot* Liv

mŏnŏpōlĭum ii, n (μονοπώλιον), *a monopoly, sole right of sale*, Suet

mons, montis, m *a mountain* I. A Lit, mons impendens, Cic, prov of large promises followed by small performance, parturiunt montes, nascetur ridiculus mus, Hor B. Meton, *a rock*, improbus, Verg II Transf, *a large mass, great quantity*, mons aquarum Verg, maria montesque polliceri, *to make large promises*, Sall

monstrātor ōris, m (monstro), *a discoverer, teacher*, aratri, *Triptolemus*, Verg

monstrĭfĕr fĕra fĕrum (monstrum and fero), *producing monsters, horrible, monstrous*, Plin

monstro, 1 (= monestro, from moneo), *to show, point out* I. By signs or gestures, digito indice ad hoc, Hor, proceram palmam Deli monstrant, Cic II. By words, A. *to show, point out, teach, inform*, tu istic si quid librarii mea manu non intelligent monstrabis Cic B. 1, *to ordain, institute, appoint*, piacula, Verg, 2, *to inform against, denounce*, alii ab amicis monstrabantur, Tac, 3, *to advise, urge*, conferre manum pudor iraque monstrat, Verg

monstrum -i, n (= monestrum, from moneo) I. *a supernatural event, a prodigy, portent*, Cic II *a monster, monstrosity*, a, of persons, monstrum horrendum, *Polyphemus*, Verg, immanissimum ac foedissimum monstrum, *Clodius*, Cic, b, of things non mihi jam furtum, sed monstrum ac prodigium videbatur

batur, Cic.; esp., *wonders* or *marvels*; monstra nuntiare, Cic.

monstrŭōsē, adv. (monstruosus), *strangely, wonderfully, monstrously*, Cic.

monstrŭōsus -a -um (monstrum), *strange, singular, wonderful, monstrous*; monstruosissima bestia, Cic.

montānus -a -um (mons). **I.** *of* or *relating to a mountain, dwelling on mountains, found on mountains*; loca montana et aspera, Liv.; Ligures, Liv.; subst., **a, montānus** -i, m. *a mountaineer*, Caes.; **b, montāna** -ōrum, n. *mountainous districts*, Liv. **II.** *rich in mountains, mountainous*; Dalmatia, Ov.

montĭcŏla -ae, c. (mons and colo), *a dweller among the mountains, mountaineer*, Ov.

montĭvăgus -a -um (mons and vagus), *wandering over the mountains*; cursus, Cic.

montŭōsus -a -um (mons), *mountainous, full of mountains*; regio aspera et montuosa, Cic.; subst., **montŭōsa** -ōrum, n. *mountainous districts*, Plin.

mŏnŭmentum (mŏnĭmentum) -i, n. (moneo), *that which is intended to preserve the recollection of anything; a memorial, monument.* **I.** Lit., monumenti causā, Cic.; esp., **a,** *a building, statue, temple, gallery*, etc.; monumenta Africani, *statues*, Cic.; **b,** *a sepulchre*, Cic.; **c,** *written memorials, annals, memoirs*; monumenta rerum gestarum, Cic.; commendare aliquid monumentis, Cic. **II.** Transf., laudis, clementiae, furtorum, Cic.

Mopsĭi -ōrum, m. *a noble family in Compsa.* Hence, **Mopsĭāni** -ōrum, m. *the dependants of the Mopsii.*

Mopsŏpĭus -a -um (from Μοψοπία, *an ancient name of Attica*), *Attic, Athenian*; juvenis, *Triptolemus*, Ov.; muri, urbs, *Athens*, Ov.

Mopsuhestĭa (Mobsuëstĭa) -ae, f. *a town in Cilicia.*

Mopsus -i, m. (Μόψος). **I.** *the seer of the Argonauts.* **II.** *son of Apollo and Manto.* **III.** *name of a shepherd in Vergil.*

1. **mŏra** -ae, f. **I.** *delay.* **A.** Gen., moram alicui rei inferre, afferre, Cic.; creditoribus facere, *to put off the day of payment*, Cic.; trahere, Verg.; res habet (*suffers*) moram, Cic.; non (or nulla) mora est with quin or quominus and the subj., Cic.; sine mora, *without delay*, Cic. **B. 1,** *pause on a march*, Liv.; **2,** *a pause in discourse*, Cic. **II.** Transf., **1,** *space of time*, Ov.; **2,** *a hindrance*, Liv.

2. **mŏra** -ae, f. (μόρα), *a division of the Spartan army, of* 400, 500, 700, or 900 *men*, Nep.

mōrālis -e (mores), *moral, ethical*; philosophiae pars, Cic.

mŏrātor -ōris, m. (moror). **I.** *a loiterer* or *lagger behind*, Liv. **II.** *a delayer, retarder.* **A.** Gen., publici commodi, Liv. **B.** *an advocate who talked against time*, Cic.

1. **mŏrātus**, partic. of moror.

2. **mōrātus** -a -um (mores). **I.** *having certain manners* or *morals*; bene, melius, optime moratus, Cic. **II.** *adapted to manners* or *character, characteristic*; poema, Cic.; recte morata fabula, *in which the characters are correctly drawn*, Hor.

morbĭdus -a -um (morbus), **1,** *sickly, diseased, morbid*, Plin.; **2,** *unwholesome, causing disease*, Lucr.

morbōsus -a -um (morbus), *sickly, diseased, worn out*, Cat.

morbus -i, m. *disease, sickness.* **I.** Physical; **a,** mortifer, Cic.; in morbo esse, *to be sick*, Cic.; morbo laborare, opprimi, Cic.; conflictari, Nep.; morbus ingravescit, *grows worse, increases in violence*, Cic.; ex morbo convalescere, *to get well*, Cic.; morbum simulare, Cic.; **b,** personif., as a goddess, Verg. **II.** Of mental diseases, animi morbi sunt cupiditates immensae et inanes divitiarum gloriae, Cic.

mordācĭtĕr, adv. (mordax), *bitingly, sharply*; limā mordacius uti, Ov.

mordax -ācis (mordeo), *biting, given to biting, snappish.* **I. A.** Lit., canis, Plaut. **B.** Fig., **a,** *biting, satirical*; Cynicus, Hor.; carmen, Ov.; **b,** *wearing, corroding*; sollicitudines, "*eating cares*," Hor. **II. a,** *stinging*; urtica, Ov.; **b,** *sharp*; ferrum, Hor.; **c,** *pungent, biting in taste*; fel, Ov.

mordĕo, mŏmordi, morsum, 2. *to bite.* **I. A.** Lit., **1,** canes mordent, Cic.; **2,** *to bite, eat*; pabula dente, Ov. **B.** Transf., *to bite, sting, hurt, pain*; aliquem dictis, Ov.; conscientiā mordeor, Cic.; valde me momorderunt epistolae tuae, Cic. **II.** *to bite into, cut into, take fast hold of*; **a,** fibula mordet vestem, Ov.; **b,** of rivers, *to indent, wear away*; rura quae Liris quietā mordet aquā, Hor.; **c,** *to nip, bite, sting*; matutina parum cautos jam frigora mordent, Hor.

mordĭcĭtus = mordicus (q.v.).

mordĭcus, adv. (mordeo). **I.** Lit., *with the teeth, by biting*; auferre mordicus auriculam, Cic. **II.** Transf., tenere aliquid mordicus, *to keep fast hold of*; perspicuitatem, Cic.

mŏrētum -i, n. *a rustic salad made of garlic, parsley, vinegar, oil*, etc., Ov.

mŏrĭbundus -a -um (morior). **I.** Middle, **1,** *dying, expiring*; jacentem moribundumque vidisti, Cic.; **2,** *subject to death, mortal*; membra, Verg. **II.** Act., *causing death, deadly*, Cat.

mōrĭgĕror, 1. dep. (mos and gero), *to accommodate oneself to, comply with, gratify, subserve*; voluptati aurium morigerari debet oratio, Cic.

mōrĭgĕrus -a -um (mos and gero), *compliant, obedient, accommodating, obsequious*, Lucr.

Mŏrĭni -ōrum, m. *a people in Gallia Belgica.*

mŏrĭor, mortŭus sum, mŏrĭtūrus, 3. dep. *to die.* **I.** Lit., ex vulnere, Liv.; ferro, Liv.; hoc morbo, Cic.; fame, Cic.; frigore, Hor.; in suo lectulo, Cic.; voces morientes, *of a dying man*, Cic.; moriar si, *may I die if*, Cic. **II.** Transf., **A.** *to perish with love*, Ov. **B.** Of things and abstr. subjects, *to die away, wither away, decay*; **a,** segetes moriuntur in herbis, Ov.; **b,** of fire, *to be extinguished*; flammas et vidi nullo concutiente mori, Ov.; of parts of the body, *to lose strength*; at hi (lacerti) mortui jam sunt, Cic.; **c,** of abstractions, *to come to an end, perish*; suavissimi hominis memoria moritur, Cic.; p. adj., **mortŭus** -a -um, *dead*; subst., **mortŭus** -i, m. *a dead man*, Cic.

mormyr -ȳris, f. (μορμύρος), *a sea-fish*, Ov.

mōrŏlŏgus -a -um (μωρολόγος), *talking like a fool, foolish*; subst., *a fool*, Plaut.

1. **mŏror**, 1. dep. (mora), *to linger, loiter, tarry, delay.* **I. A.** Lucceius narravit Brutum valde morari, Cic.; with infin., alicui bellum inferre, Cic.; nihil moror, foll. by quominus and subj., Liv. **B.** *to stay, tarry in a place*; Brundisii, Cic.; in provincia, Cic. **II. 1,** *to cause delay to another, to delay, retard, keep back, detain, hinder*; impetum sustinere atque morari, Caes.; aliquem ab itinere, Liv.; **2, a,** esp. of the judge in acquitting and dismissing a person, C. Sempronium nihil moror, Liv.; **b,** as a formula, in breaking off a discourse; ne te morer, Hor.; **c,** nihil morari, (α) *to care nothing for*; nec

dona moror Verg, (β) *to have nothing to say against*, nihil moror, eos salvos esse, ap. Cic, 3, *to detain the attention of, fetter*, novitate morandus spectator, Hor

2 **mōror**, 1. dep (μωρος), *to be foolish, to be a fool*, Suet

mōrōsē, adv (morosus), *peevishly, captiously*, Cic

mōrōsĭtas -ātis, f (morosus), *peevishness, fretfulness, moroseness*, Cic, *pedantry, excessive fastidiousness in style*, Suet

mōrōsus -a -um (mos), *peevish, morose, capricious, captious, fretful*, senes, Cic, canities, Hor, morbus, *obstinate*, Ov

Morpheus ĕos, m (Μορφεύς), *god of dreams*

mors, mortis, f (root MOR, whence morior, connected with βροτος, μαραινω), *death* **I. A.** Lit, omnium rerum mors est extremum, Cic, mortem sibi consciscere, *to commit suicide*, Cic, mortem alicui inferre, *to slay, kill*, Cic; alicui morti esse, *cause a person's death*, Cic, aliquem ex media morte eripere, Cic, plur., mortes, *kinds of death*, clarae mortes pro patria oppetitae, Cic **B.** Personified as a goddess, *daughter of Erebus and Nox* **II.** Meton, 1, *a corpse*, Plin, 2, *life-blood*, ensem multā morte recepit, Verg, 3, *one who brings death* or *destruction*, mors terrorque sociorum lictor Sextius, Cic

morsus -ūs, m (mordeo), *a bite, biting* **I. A.** Lit, 1, serpentis, Cic, morsu dividere escas, Cic, 2, *eating*, mensarum, Verg **B.** Transf, 1, *a seizing, laying hold of*, like the bite of an anchor, Verg, and meton, *that which seizes*, morsus uncus, *the fluke of an anchor*, Verg, roboris, *the cleft of a tree holding fast a javelin*, Verg, 2, *a biting taste, pungency*, Mart **II.** Fig, 1, *a carping or malicious attack with words*, Hor; 2, *mental pain, vexation*, curarum, Ov, doloris, Cic

mortālis -e (mors), *subject to death, mortal* **I.** Lit, 1, omne animal esse mortale, Cic Subst., **a, mortālis** is, m, *a mortal man, a man*, and esp, plur, *mortals, men*, Cic, **b, mortāle** -is, n *that which is mortal* or *perishable*, Cic, 2, transf, *transitory, temporary, passing away*, leges, inimicitiae, Cic **II.** Transf, *relating or belonging to mortal men, mortal, human, earthly*; conditio vitae, Cic Subst, **mortālia** ium, n. *mortal things, mortal affairs*, and esp, *human sufferings*, et mentem mortalia tangunt. Verg

mortālĭtas ātis, f (mortalis) **I.** *the being subject to death*, Cic **II.** *human nature, the nature of man regarded as mortal*, mortalitatem explere, *to die*, Tac

mortārĭum -ii, n *a mortar*, Plin

mortĭcīnus a -um (mors), *dead*, Plin

mortĭfer -fĕra -fĕrum (mors and fero), *causing death, fatal, deadly, mortal*, vulnus, morbus, Cic

mortŭālĭa -ium, n (mortuus), *funeral songs, dirges*, Plaut

mortŭus -a -um, partic of morior (q v)

mōrum -i, n (μῶρον, μόρον), 1, *a mulberry*, Verg, 2, *a blackberry*, Ov

1 **mōrus** -i, f *a mulberry tree*, Ov

2 **mōrus** -a -um (μωρός), *silly, foolish*, Plaut

mos, mōris, m *the will of a person* **I.** *self-will, caprice* morem alicui gerere, *to comply with a person's wishes*, Cic **II. A.** Lit., *custom, usage, wont*, de more suo decedere, Cic, esse in more majorum, *traditional line of conduct*, Cic., mos est with genit gerund, mos est ita rogandi, Cic, with infin, magorum mos est non humare corpora, Cic, with acc and infin, mos est Athenis laudari in contione eos, etc, Cic, mos est or moris est with ut and the subj, mos est hominum ut nolint eundem pluribus rebus excellere, Cic, eum morem tenere, *to observe*, Cic, abl as adv, more majorum, *after the way of the ancestors*, Cic, meo, tuo, suo more, Cic, **b,** *fashion, mode*, quoniam ita se mores habent, Sall, 2, gen plur, *manners, character, disposition, morals*, suavissimi, justi, feri, Cic, totam vitam, naturam, moresque alicuius cognoscere, Cic, describere hominum sermones moresque, Cic **B.** Transf, 1, *quality nature, manner, use and wont*, siderum, Verg, more, ad morem or in morem, *after the fashion of*, foll by genit, Cic, 2, *rule, law*, mores viris ponere, Verg, sine more, *without rule or control*, Verg, quid ferri duritiā pugnacius? sed cedit et patitur mores, Plin

Mŏsa -ae, f *a river in Gallia Belgica*, now *the Meuse*

Moschus -i, m (Μοσχος), *a rhetorician of Pergamus, accused of poisoning*

Mŏsella -ae, f *a river in Gallia Belgica*, now *the Moselle*

Mostēni -ōrum, m *the inhabitants of the Lydian town Mostena* or *-en*

mōtĭo -ōnis, f (moveo) **I.** *movement, motion*, corporum, Cic **II.** Transf, *emotion, feeling*, motiones animi, Cic

mōto, 1 (intens of moveo), *to move up and down, move frequently*, lacertos, Ov, zephyris motantibus, Verg

1 **mōtus** -a -um, partic of moveo

2 **mōtus** -ūs, m (moveo) **I.** *a motion, movement* **A.** Lit., **a,** naturā omnia ciens motibus suis, Cic, **b,** terrae, *an earthquake*, Cic **c,** *motion of the body, movement, gesture*, esp of an orator, manuum motus teneant illud decorum, Cic, ex motus mei mediocritate, Cic, *the gestures of actors* or *pantomimic dancers*, haud indecoros motus more Tusco dare, Liv, dare motus Cereri, *to lead dances*, Verg **B.** Transf, **I,** *motion of the mind*, **a,** of the senses, dulcem motum afferent, Cic; **b,** of the mind, *activity* motus animorum duplices sunt, alteri cogitationis, alteri appetitūs, Cic, esp, (α) *movement of the passions* motus animi nimii, Cic (β) *motion of the will, impulse*, sine motu animi et cogitatione, Cic, 2, *political movement, insurrection, riot, commotion*, omnes Catilinae motus prohibere, Cic, motum afferre reipublicae, Cic **II.** *revolution in a state*, Cic

mŏvĕo, mōvi, mōtum, 2 (connected with mutare, ἀμείβειν, etc) **I.** *to move, set in motion, stir* **A.** Lit, **a,** caelum, Cic, reflex, terra movet, Liv, **b,** *to move the body*, se movere and moveri, *to dance*, Cic, **c,** milit t. t, movere arma, *to take up arms*, adversus aliquem, Liv **B.** Transf, **1,** *to produce a bad effect on the body, to attack, affect*, intoleranda vis aestus corpora movit, Liv., **2,** *to move mentally*, **a,** se ad motum fortunae, Caes, **b,** (α) *to influence, work upon, affect*, pulchritudo corporis movet oculos, Cic, moveri aliquā re, *to be disturbed, made anxious by*, Verg, (β) *to move compassion, move, affect*, Roscii morte moveri, Cic, (γ) *to work upon, induce*, with ut and the subj, Cic, **3,** politically, *to cause a commotion, arouse, excite*, omnia, Sall, **4,** *to change, shake, shatter*, alicuius sententiam, Cic, fidem, Ov **II.** *to move from a place* **A. a,** humum e gurgite, Ov, **b,** *to cause, produce, excite*, risum, Cic, misericordiam, Cic, **c,** *to bring to notice, bring before*, historias, Hor, **d,** *to begin* bellum, Cic **B.** *to remove, put out of its place* **a,** fundamenta loco, Cic, sede Commius, Cic, **b,** milit t t, movere signa, castra, or simply movere or moveri, *to march away, move from a place*, castra ex eo loco,

Caes ; **c,** *to dispossess*, aliquem ex agris, Cic , **d,** *to cause to move from one's position, dislodge*, hostem statu, Liv., **e,** *to expel*, aliquem de senatu, Cic , **f,** *to make a person change his opinion*, aliquem de sententia, Liv

mox, adv (moveo) **I.** Of future time, *soon, presently*, jussit mihi nunciari mox se venturum, Cic **II.** *then, thereupon*, mox rediit Cremonam reliquus populus, Tac , mox postremo, Liv

Mōysēs -is or i, m *Moses*

mūcĭdus a -um (mucus), *mouldy, musty*, Juv

Mūcĭus -a -um, *name of a Roman gens, the most celebrated members of which were* **1,** C Mucius Cordus (Scaevola), *a Roman who came to Porsena's camp to kill him, and being detected, thrust his right hand into the fire, and received the name of Scaevola (left-handed)*. **2,** P Mucius Scaevola, *friend of the Gracchi, enemy of the younger Scipio Africanus*, **3,** Qu Mucius Scaevola, *augur, husband of Laelia*, **4,** Qu Mucius Scaevola, *jurist and statesman, Pontifex Maximus, whose administration of the province of Asia was so upright that the Asiatics celebrated a festival in honour of him, called Mucia*, **5,** Mucia, *the wife of Cn Pompeius* Adj , *Mucian* subst., **Mūcĭa** ōrum, n *the festival instituted in honour of Mucius Scaevola (IV)* Hence, adj , **Mūcĭānus** -a -um, *relating to Mucius*, exitus, *death of Qu Mucius Scaevola (IV)*, murdered by Damasippus in the temple of Vesta

mūcro ōnis, m *a sharp point or edge* **A.** Lit , **a,** cultri, Juv , **b,** esp , *a sword's point or edge*, transf , *the sword*, mucrones militum tremere, Cic **B.** Transf , *sharpness, point*, tribunicius, Cic , defensionis tuae, Cic

mūcus i, m (mungo), *the mucous matter of the nose*, Cat

mūgil (mūgĭlis) is, m (μύξος), *a fish, perhaps the mullet*, Plin

mūgĭnor, 1 dep (mugio), *to loiter, trifle away time, dally*, dum tu muginaris, Cic

mūgĭo ivi and -ii -ītum, 4 (from sound mu, whence μυκάω), *to bellow as an ox, low* **I.** Lit., of cattle, Liv , subst , mugientes = *oxen*, Hor **II.** Transf , *to roar, bray, rumble, groan*, mugit tubae clangor, Verg , sub pedibus mugire solum, Verg , si mugiat Africis malus procellis, Hor

mūgītus -ūs, m (mugio) **I.** *the lowing, bellowing of cattle*, boum, Verg **II.** Transf , *a rumbling, groaning, creaking*, terrae, Cic.

mūla -ae, f (mulus), *a female mule*, Cic

mulcĕo, mulsi, mulsum, 2 *to stroke* **I. A.** Lit , manu mulcens barbam, Ov **B.** Transf , *to touch lightly*, virgā capillos, Ov **II.** Fig , **1,** *to charm, delight, enchant*, aliquem fistulā, Hor , **2,** *to soothe, appease*, tigres, Verg , et ipso mulcente et increpante Marcio, Liv , aliquem dictis, Ov , fluctus, iras, Verg , vulnera, *to allay pain*, Ov

Mulcĭbĕr ĕris and ĕri, m (mulceo, lit , *the melter*), **1,** *a surname of Vulcan*, Cic , Ov , **2,** meton , *fire*, Ov (genit. syncop , Mulcibri)

mulco, 1 (MULC, whence also mulc-eo, mulg-eo), *to thrash maltreat, cudgel, handle roughly*, male mulcati clavis ac fustibus repelluntur, Cic.

mulcta, mulcto, = multa, multo (q v)

mulctra ae, f. (mulgeo), *a milk-pail*, Verg

mulctrārĭum ii, n (mulgeo), *a milk pail*, Hor

mulctrum -i, n (mulgeo), *a milk-pail*, Hor

mulgĕo, mulsi, mulctum, 2 (root MULC, whence also mulceo), *to milk*, Verg , prov., mulgere hircos, of an impossible undertaking, Verg

mŭlĭebris -e (mulier). **I.** *of or relating to a woman, womanly, feminine*, vox, Cic , vestis, Nep , bellum, Cic., certamen, *on account of a woman*, Liv , Fortuna Muliebris, *revered in memory of the women who had appeased the anger of Coriolanus*, Liv **II.** Transf , *womanish, effeminate, unmanly*, sententia, Cic

mŭlĭebrĭtĕr, adv (muliebris), *after the manner of a woman, effeminately, womanishly* se lamentis muliebriter lacrimisque dedere, Cic

mŭlĭer -ĕris, f **I.** *a woman*, Cic **II.** *a wife, matron* virgo aut mulier, Cic , cras mulier erit, Cic

mŭlĭĕrārĭus -a -um (mulier), *womanish*, manus, *a troop of soldiers sent by a woman*, Cic

mŭlĭercŭla ae, f (dim of mulier), *a little woman*, used contemptuously, suas secum mulierculas in castra ducere, Cic

mŭlĭĕrōsĭtas -ātis, f (mulierosus), *excessive love of women*, Cic

mŭlĭĕrōsus a -um (mulier), *fond of women*, Cic

mūlīnus -a -um (mulus), *of or relating to a mule*, Juv

mūlĭo -ōnis, m (mulus), *a mule-keeper, mule driver, muleteer, one who lets mules to hire*, Cic

mūlĭōnĭus and (later) **mūlĭōnĭcus** a um (mulio), *of or relating to a muleteer*, Cic

mullus -i, m *the red mullet*, Cic

mulsus -a -um (mel), **1,** *mixed with honey sweetened with honey*, Plin , subst , **mulsum** -i, n *wine sweetened with honey*, calix mulsi, Cic , **2,** transf , *as sweet as honey*, dicta mulsa, *sweet words*, Plaut

multa (mulcta) -ae, f *a punishment consisting in loss of property* (originally a fine in cattle), usually *a money-fine, fine, mulct*, multam dicere, *to fix a fine*, Cic , multam petere, irrogare, *to propose that an accused person should be fined to a certain amount*, Cic , multam certare, *to discuss on both sides the amount of a fine*, Cic , aliquem multā multare, *to punish by a fine*, Cic , multam committere, *to incur a fine*, Cic

multangŭlus -a -um (multus and angulus), *many cornered, multangular*, Lucr

multātīcĭus -a um (multa), *belonging or relating to a fine*, pecunia, Liv

multātĭo -ōnis, f (1 multo), *a penalty, fine, mulct*, bonorum, Cic.

multēsĭmus -a -um (multus), *very small*; pars, Lucr

multĭcăvus -a -um (multus and cavus), *having many holes, porous*, pumex, Ov

multīcĭa -ōrum, n (multus and ico), *soft, finely woven garments*, Juv

multĭfārĭam, adv (multifarius from multus), *on many sides, in many places*, Cic

multĭfĭdus -a -um (multus and findo), *cloven into many parts*, faces, Ov , transf , Ister, *having many branches*, Mart.

multĭformis -e (multus and forma), *having many shapes, multiform, manifold, of many kinds*, qualitates, Cic

multĭfŏrus a -um (multus and foris), *having many openings, pierced with many holes*, multifori tibia buxi, Ov

multĭgĕnĕris -e (multus and genus), *of many kinds, of many sorts*, Plaut

multĭgĕnus a um = multigeneris (q v)

multĭjŭgus -a -um and **multĭjŭgis** -e (multus and jugum), *many-yoked, yoked many* *together* **I.** Lit, equi, Liv **II.** Transf, *manifold, of many sorts*, literae, Cic

multĭmŏdis, adv (for multis modis), *in many ways, variously*, Lucr

multĭmŏdus -a -um (multus and modus), *various, manifold*, Liv (?)

multĭplex -plĭcis (multus and plex, from plico), *having many folds* **I.** Lit, a, alvus est multiplex et tortuosa, Cic, **b**, *with many windings and turnings*, vitis serpens multiplici lapsu, Cic, **c**, *with many layers*, lorica, Verg, **d**, *having many parts*, corona, Cic, **e**, *manifold, many, numerous*, multiplices fetus, *numerous offspring*, Cic, **f**, *many times as large*, multiplex quam pro numero damnum est, Liv **II.** Transf, **A.** Of things, *of many different kinds, many-sided, manifold*, multiplex ratio disputandi, Cic **B.** Of persons, *many-sided*; varius et multiplex et copiosus, Cic, multiplices naturae, Cic, ingenium, *versatile, changeable*, Cic

multĭplĭcābĭlis -e (multiplico), *having many folds*, Cic

multĭplĭco, 1 (multiplex), *to increase many times, multiply*, aes alienum, Caes, flumina collectis multiplicantur aquis, Ov, domus multiplicata, *enlarged*, Cic

multĭtūdo -ĭnis, f (multus), *a large number, multitude* **I.** Gen, litterarum, Cic **II.** Esp, of men, **1**, *a large number of men, crowd, multitude*, tanta multitudo lapides ac tela jaciebat, Caes, **2**, in a contemptuous sense, *the common people, mob, multitude*, fama et multitudinis judicio moveri, Cic

multĭvŏlus -a -um (multus and volo), *having many wishes or desires*, Cat

1 **multo (mulcto)**, 1 (multa), *to punish*, aliquem morte, Cic, exsilio, Liv, vitia hominum damnis, ignominiis, vinculis, Cic, aliquem pecuniā, *to punish with a fine*, Nep, Veneri esse multatum, *punished with a fine paid to Venus*, Cic

2 **multo**, multum, used adv, v multus

multus -a -um, comp, **plūs**, plūris, superl, **plūrĭmus** -a -um, *much* **I.** Lit, **A.** Of number, *many, numerous*, multis verbis, Cic, viri, Cic, multi, *many persons*, Cic, minime multi, *exceedingly few*, Cic, quam minime multa vestigia, *as few as possible*, Nep, multis verbis, *diffusely, copiously*, Cic, elliptically, ne multa, ne multis, *briefly, in brief*, Cic, multi (= οἱ πολλοί), *the many, the multitude, the common herd*, unus de multis, Cic, orator e multis, Cic, compar, plures, genit plurium, *several, more than one*, Cic, quid plura? *in short*, Cic, pluribus verbis rogare, Cic, superl, plurimi, *very many, the most*, plurimis verbis, Cic, mons, *very large*, Verg, Aetna, *the greatest part of*, Ov **B.** Of strength or fulness, *much, great, strong, considerable*, **1**, multo labore, Cic, superl, plurimus sol, *very hot*, Ov, **2**, of time, ad multum diem, *till late in the day*, Cic, multā nocte, *late at night*, Cic, multo mane, *very early*, Cic **C.** Of space, *great*, multa pars Europae, Liv **II.** Transf, **A.** Of discourse, *copious, diffuse, prolix*, ne in re nota multus et insolens sim, Cic **B** Of an action, *busy, vigorous, zealous*, in eodem genere causarum multus erat T Juventius, Cic **C.** *obtrusive, troublesome*, qui in aliquo genere aut inconcinnus aut multus est Cic Hence, **multum**, compar, **plūs**, superl, **plūrĭmum**, *much, a great part* **I.** Subst, **A.** In nom or acc, with genit, ad multum diei, *till far in the day*, Liv, multum diei *a large part of the day*, Sall, compar, plus posse, plus facere, Cic, plus pecuniae, Cic, plurimum posse, Cic, plurimum gravitatis, Cic **B.** In genit, of price or value, pluris emere, vendere, *dearer, at a higher price*, Cic, mea mihi conscientia pluris est quam omnium sermo, *is of more value to me*, Cic, aliquem pluris aestimare, *to think more highly of*, Cic, superl, plurimi, *very dear*, esse, Cic **II.** Adv, **A. multo**, *by far*, with comparatives or words of similar force, multo pauciores, Cic, multo anteponere, Cic, non multo post, *not long after*, Cic **B. multum**; **1**, of degree, *much, very*, longe multumque superare, Cic, vir multum bonus, Cic, non multum est majus, Cic, **2**, of time, *often*, multum mecum loquuntur, Cic **C.** plus, **1**, of number, *more*, non plus quam semel, Cic, without quam, plus mille capti, Liv, with abl, nec esse plus uno, Cic, **2**, of degree, *more*, quem plus plusque in dies diligo, *more and more*, Cic **D.** plurimum, *most*, ut te plurimum diligam, Cic

Mulucha (Mulucha) -ae, m *a river in Mauritania*, now *Maluia* or *Molucha*

mūlus -i, m *a mule*, Cic

Mulvius -a -um, *Mulvian*, pons, *a bridge above Rome on the via Flaminia*, now *Ponte Molle*

Mummius -a -um, *name of a Roman gens, the most famous member of which was* L Mummius Achaicus, *the destroyer of Corinth*

Mūnātius -a -um, *name of a Roman gens, the most famous member of which was* L Munatius Plancus, *one of the legates of Caesar*

Munda -ae, f *town in Hispania Baetica, scene of a victory of Julius Caesar over the sons of Pompeius*, 45 B C

mundānus -a -um (mundus), *of or relating to the world, mundane* Subst, **mundānus** -i, m *a citizen of the world*, Cic

mundĭtĭa -ae, f and (not in Cic) **mundĭtĭes** -ēi, f (mundus), *cleanness* **I.** Lit, Plaut **II.** *neatness, spruceness, elegance*, **1**, non odiosa neque exquisita nimis, Cic munditiis capimur, Ov, simplex munditiis, Hor, **2**, *neatness, elegance of style*, quā munditiā, homines quā elegantiā, Cic

mundo, 1 (mundus), *to cleanse, purify*, Verg

1 **mundus** -a -um, *clean, neat, elegant* **I.** supellex, coena, Hor **II. 1**, of manner of life, *elegant, refined*, homo, Cic, cultus justo mundior, *too elegant apparel*, Liv, **2**, of discourse, *neat, elegant*, verba, Ov

2 **mundus** -i, m (1 mundus, like Gr κόσμος) **I.** *ornament*, muliebris, Liv **II.** *the universe, the world, and the heavenly bodies* **A.** hic ornatus mundi, *harmony of the universe*, Cic, mundi innumerabiles, Cic **B. 1**, *the heavens*, lucens, Cic, **2**, *the world, the earth*, **a**, lit, quicumque mundo terminus obstitit, Hor, **b**, meton, *the inhabitants of the world, mankind*, fastos evolvere mundi, Hor

mūnĕro, 1. (munus), *to give, present*, aliquem aliquā re, Cic

mūnĕror, 1 dep *to present*, natura aliud alii muneratur, Cic

mūnĭa -ium, n *duties, functions, official duties, official business*, candidatorum, Cic

mūnĭceps -cĭpis, c (munia and capio) **I.** *the citizen of a municipium*, municeps Cosanus, *of Cosa*, Cic **II.** *a fellow-citizen, countryman, fellow-countryman*, meus Cic, municipes Jovis advexisse lagoenas, *countrymen of Jupiter*, i e, *Cretan*, Juv

mūnĭcĭpālis -e (municipium), *relating or belonging to a municipium, municipal*, homines, Cic sometimes in a contemptuous sense, *provincial*, equites, Juv

mūnĭcĭpĭum -ii, n (municeps), *a town, usually in Italy, the inhabitants of which had the Roman citizenship, but were governed by their* *own magistrates and laws; a free town, municipal town*, Cic.

mūnĭfĭcē, adv. (munificus), *munificently, bountifully*, Cic.

mūnĭfĭcentĭa -ae, f. (munificus), *munificence, bountifulness*, Sall.

mūnĭfĭco, 1. (munificus), *to present, to give*, Lucr.

mūnĭfĭcus -a -um (munus and facio), *munificent, liberal*; in dando, Cic. (compar., munificentior, superl., munificentissimus).

mūnīmen -ĭnis, n. (munio), *a protection, defence, fortification*; munimine cingere fossas, Ov.; ad imbres, *against the rains*, Verg.

mūnīmentum -i, n. (munio). **I.** *a fortification, bulwark, defence, protection*; ut instar muri hae sepes munimenta praeberent, Caes.; tenere se munimentis, *entrenchments*, Tac. **II.** Fig., *protection*; rati noctem sibi munimento fore, Sall.

mūnĭo (moenĭo) -īvi and -ĭi -ītum, 4. (moenia). **I.** *to build, build with walls*; oppidum, Hor.; absol., *to build a wall*, Nep. **II. A.** *to surround with a wall, fortify*; **1, a,** lit., palatium, Nep.; montem, Caes.; castra vallo fossāque, Caes.; **b,** transf., *to protect, defend*; Alpibus Italiam munierat natura, Cic.; domum praesidiis, Cic.; quae (herbescens viriditas) contra avium morsus munitur vallo aristarum, Cic.; **2,** fig., *to secure, make sure*; munio me ad haec tempora, Cic. **B.** *to make* or *build a road, to pave a road*; viam, Cic.; itinera, Nep.; fig., munire alicui viam accusandi, *to prepare a way for*, Cic.

mūnītĭo -ōnis, f. (munio). **I.** *fortifying, entrenching*; **1,** lit., milites munitione prohibere, Caes.; **2,** meton., *a fortification, entrenchment*; urbem operibus munitionibusque saepire, Cic. **II.** *a making passable, paving of roads*; ex viarum munitione quaestum facere, Cic.; munitio fluminum, *bridging over*, Tac.

mūnīto, 1. (intens. of munio), *to pave, make passable*; viam, Cic.

mūnītor -ōris, m. (munio), *a builder of fortifications, a sapper and miner, military engineer*, Liv.

mūnītus -a -um, p. adj. (from munio), *fortified, made safe, secured*; oppidum munitissimum, Cic.

mūnus -ĕris, n. (moenus). **I.** *an office, function, employment, duty*; reipublicae, *a public office*, Cic.; officii, *the performance of a duty*, Cic.; tuum est hoc munus, Cic.; consulare munus sustinere, Cic.; belli munera inter se partiri, Liv. **II. A.** *an affectionate service, favour*; neque vero verbis auget suum munus, Cic.; munere alicuius rei (poet.), *by the help of*, Verg.; esp., *the last services to the dead, funeral honours, interment*; munere inani fungi, Verg. **B.** *a gift, present*; **1,** alicui munus mittere, Cic.; mittere alicui aliquid muneri, *to send or give as a present*, Caes.; munera Liberi, *wine*, Hor.; Cereris, *bread*, Ov.; transf., opusculum majorum vigiliarum munus, *the fruit of*, Cic.; **2, a,** *a sacrifice*; munera ferre templis, Verg.; **b,** *a public show, especially of gladiators, generally given by the aediles to the people*; munus magnificum dare, praebere, Cic.; munus gladiatorium, Cic.; hence, *a building* or *theatre erected for the people*, Ov.

mūnuscŭlum -i, n. (dim. of munus), *a small gift, little present*; alicui mittere munusculum levidense crasso filo, Cic.

Mūnȳchĭa -ae, f. (Μουνυχία), *one of the ports of Athens*. Adj., **Mūnȳchĭus** -a -um = *Athenian*, Ov.

1. **mūraena** = murena (q.v.).

2. **Mūraena** = Murena (q.v.).

mūrālis -e (murus), *of or relating to a wall, mural*; pila muralia, *used by those who defend a wall*, Caes.; falces, *hooks* or *grappling-irons for pulling down walls*, Caes.; corona, *the crown given to the one who first ascended the wall of a besieged city*, Liv.; also corona, *the diadem of Cybele, adorned with walls and towers*, Lucr.

Murcĭa (Murtĭa, Myrtĕa) -ae, f. *a surname of Venus*; ad Murciae (sc. aedem), or ad Murciam, *a valley separating the Palatine from the Aventine at Rome*, Liv.

1. **mūrēna (mūraena)** -ae, f. (μύραινα), *a sea-fish highly prized by the Romans*.

2. **Mūrēna** -ae, m. (1. murena), *a cognomen belonging to the gens Licinia, the most celebrated members of which were*: **1,** L. Licinius Murena, *defended by Cicero, in the extant oration* "Pro Murena," *on a charge of bribery*; **2,** L. Licinius Varro Murena, *friend of Cicero, executed for suspected complicity in a plot against Augustus*.

mūrex -ĭcis, m. **I.** *the purple-fish, a shell-fish from which the Tyrian dye was obtained*; the shell in poets is represented as the trumpet of Triton, Ov.; it was also used to adorn grottos, Ov.; meton., **1,** *the purple dye itself*, Tyrioque ardebat murice laena, Verg.; **2,** *a sharp stone, projecting rock*, resembling the murex in shape; acutus, Verg. **II.** *an edible shell-fish*; Baianus, Hor.

Murgantĭa -ae, f. **I.** *a town in Samnium, now Croce di Morcone*. **II.** *town in Sicily, now Mandri Bianchi*. Adj., **Murgantīnus** -a -um, *relating to Murgantia*.

murmillo = mirmillo (q.v.).

mŭrĭa -ae, f. (ἁλμυρίς), *brine, pickle*, Hor.

murmur -ŭris, n. (onomatop.), *a murmur, a humming, buzzing, roaring, growling noise*. **I.** of men and animals, populi, Liv.; of indistinct supplication, placare deos precibus et murmure longo, Ov.; *the humming of bees*, Verg.; *the roar of a lion*, Mart. **II.** Of things, of the sea, Cic.; of the wind, Verg.; of the sound of wind-instruments, cornuum, Hor.; inflati buxi, Ov.

murmŭro, 1. (murmur). **I.** *to murmur, make a humming, growling noise*; with acc., flebile lingua murmurat exanimis, Ov. **II.** Of things, *to roar*; mare murmurans, Cic.

1. **murrha (murra)** = 1. myrrha (q.v.).

2. **murrha (murra, myrrha)** -ae, f. *a mineral, perhaps fluor spar, out of which costly vases and goblets were made*; hence, poet., *the goblets themselves*, Mart.

1. **murrhĕus (murrĕus)** = 1. myrrheus (q.v.).

2. **murrhĕus (murrĕus, myrrhĕus)** -a -um (2. murrha), *made of fluor spar*, pocula, Prop.

1. **murrhĭnus (murrĭnus)** = 1. myrrhinus (q.v.).

2. **murrhĭnus (murrĭnus, myrrhĭnus)** -a -um (murrha), *made of* or *relating to the mineral called myrrha*, Plaut.

murt . . . v. myrt . . .

Murtĭa = Murcia (q.v.).

mūrus -i, m. *a wall*. **I. A.** Lit. **a,** *a wall round a city*; urbis, Cic.; muro lapideo urbem cingere, Cic.; **b,** *the wall of a private building*, Cic. **B.** Transf., **1,** *the wall of a building*, Cic.; **2,** *a bank or dyke of earth*, Varr.; **3,** *the rim or edge of a vessel*, Juv. **II.** *protection, defence*; lex Aelia et Fufia propugnacula murique tranquillitatis, Cic.; Graium murus Achilles, Ov.

1. **mūs**, mūris, c. (μῦς), *a mouse*; rusticus or agrestis, *field-mouse*, Hor.; non solum inquilini sed etiam mures migrarunt, Cic.; under

the word mus the Romans comprehended *the cat, marten, sable, ermine*, etc.

2 **Mūs,** Mūris, m *the name of a family of the gens Decia, two members of which, P. Decius Mus and his son of the same name, devoted themselves to death to gain victory for their country*

Mūsa -ae, f (Μοῦσα) **I.** *a muse, goddess of music, poetry, and generally of the fine arts* The Muses, usually said to be the daughters of Zeus and Mnemosyne, were nine in number, namely, Clio, Melpomene, Thalia, Euterpe, Terpsichore, Calliope, Erato, Urania, Polyhymnia **II.** Meton, **1,** *song, poetry*, pedestris, *poetry bordering on prose*, Hor, **2,** musae, *learning, studies*, agrestiores, Cic

1 **Mūsaeus** -i, m (Μουσαῖος), *a fabulous Greek poet*

2 **mūsaeus** -a -um (Musa), *poetical, musical*, Lucr

musca -ae, f. (μυῖσκα, dim of μυῖα), *a fly*, Cic; transf, *a troublesome, inquisitive person*, Plaut

muscārius a -um (musca), **1,** *of or relating to flies*, Plin, **2,** subst, **muscārium** -ii, n *a fly-flap, made of peacocks' feathers or an ox's or horse's tail*, Mart.

muscĭpŭla -ae, f and **muscĭpŭlum** -i, n. (mus and capio), *a mouse-trap*, Phaedr

muscōsus -a -um (muscus), *covered with moss, full of moss, mossy*, fontes, Verg, nihil muscosius, Cic

muscŭlus -i, m (dim of mus) **I.** *a little mouse*, Cic **II.** Transf, **1,** milit t t, *a shed, mantelet*, Caes, **2,** *a species of whale*, Plin

muscus -i, m *moss*, Hor

mūsēus a um = 2 musaeus (q v)

mūsica -ae, f and **mūsĭcē** -ēs, f (μουσική), *music*, musicam tractare, Cic

1 **mūsĭcē** -ēs, f = musica (q v)

2 **mūsĭcē**, adv (μουσικῶς), *splendidly, pleasantly, finely*, musice hercle aetatem agitis, Plaut

mūsĭcus a -um (μουσικός) **I.** *belonging or relating to music, musical*, leges, *rules of music*, Cic. Subst, **a,** **mūsĭcus** -i, m *a musician*, Cic, **b,** **mūsica** -ōrum, n *music*, Cic **II.** Esp, *relating to poetry, poetical*, Ter

mussĭto, 1 (intens of musso), *to murmur to oneself, to mutter to oneself*, Liv, clam mussito, Liv

musso, 1 (like mutio, from sound mu) **I.** **a,** *to murmur, mutter, whisper to oneself*, mussantes inter se rogitabant, Liv, **b,** *to hum, buzz*, of bees, mussant oras et limina circum, Verg **II.** *to be in fear and uncertainty*, mussat rex ipse Latinus, quos generos vocet, Verg

mustācĕum (mustācium) -i, n and **mustācĕus (mustācius)** -i, m (mustum) *a must-cake, a laurel-cake, a sort of wedding cake, mixed with must and baked on bay-leaves*, prov, laureolam in mustaceo quaerere, *to look for fame in trifles*, Cic

mustēla (mustella) -ae, f (dim of mus), *a weasel*, Cic

mustēlīnus (mustellīnus) -a um (mustela), *of or relating to a weasel*, Ter

mustum -i, n, v mustus

mustus a -um, *young, new, fresh* **I.** Adj, agna, Cato, vinum, *must*, Cato **II.** Subst, **mustum** -i, n *new wine, must*, Verg, fig, nova ista quasi de musto ac lacu fervida oratio, Cic, meton, ter centum musta videre, *vintages*, Ov

Musulāmi (Musulāmii) -ōrum, m *a warlike people of Numidia*

Mūta -ae, f (mutus), *a nymph, whom Jupiter made dumb because of her loquacity*

mūtābĭlis -e (muto), *changeable, variable, inconstant*, ea forma reipublicae mutabilis est, Cic

mūtābĭlĭtas -ātis, f (mutabilis), *changeableness, mutability*, mentis, Cic

mūtātĭo -ōnis (muto) **I.** *a changing, change, mutation*, facere mutationem alicuius rei, Cic **II.** *a mutual change, exchange*, officiorum, Cic

mŭtĭlo, 1 (mutilus) **I.** *to maim, mutilate, cut off*, nasoauribusque mutilatis, Liv, caudam colubrae, Ov **II.** Transf, *to curtail, diminish*, exercitum, Cic

mŭtĭlus a -um (μιτυλος, μυτιλος) **I.** *maimed, mutilated*, esp of animals which have lost one or both horns, alces mutilae sunt cornibus, Caes, so transf in jest, sic mutilus militabis, Hor **II.** Fig, of speech, mutila loqui, *briefly*, Cic

Mŭtĭna -ae, f *town in Cispadane Gaul*, now *Modena* Hence, adj, **Mŭtĭnensis** -e, *relating to Mutina*

mūtĭo (muttĭo), 4 (from sound mu), *to mutter, mumble, murmur*, Plaut, Ter

mūtĭtĭo (muttĭtĭo) -ōnis, f *a muttering, mumbling*, Plaut

mūto, 1 (for movito), *to move* **I.** *to move away, remove*, ne quis invitus civitate mutetur, *should be removed from the state*, Cic **II.** Transf, **A.** *to change, alter*, **1,** **a,** transit, sententiam, consilium, voluntatem, Cic, mutari alite, *to be changed into a bird*, Ov, **b,** reflex mutare, and pass mutari, *to be changed*, annona nihil mutavit, Liv, **2,** **a,** *to dye*, vellera luto, Verg, **b,** vinum mutatum, *spoiled, soured*, Hor **B.** *to change, exchange* **1,** jumenta, *to change horses*, Caes, but, mutare calceos et vestimenta, *to undress*, Cic, esp, mutare vestem, *to put on mourning*, Cic, mutare terram, *to go into another country*, Liv, mutata verba, *used metaphorically*, Cic, **2,** *to exchange, barter*, merces, Verg, res inter se, Sall

mūtŭātĭo -ōnis, f (mutuor), *a borrowing*, Cic

mūtŭē, adv (mutuus), *mutually, reciprocally, in return*, respondere, Cic

mūtŭō, adv (mutuus), *mutually, reciprocally*, aestus maritimi mutuo accedentes et recedentes, Cic

mūtŭor, 1 dep (mutuum), *to borrow* **I.** Lit, **a,** money, etc, pecunias, Caes, without acc ab aliquo, Cic, **b,** other things, auxilia ad bellum, Auct bell Gall **II.** Transf, orator subtilitatem ab Academicis mutuatur, Cic, verbum a simili, *to speak metaphorically*, Cic

mūtus a -um **I.** *unable to speak, not possessing the power of articulate speech, dumb*, bestia, Cic **II.** Transf, **A.** muta dolore lyra est, Ov **B.** *uttering no sound, mute, silent*, imago, Cic, artes quasi mutae, *the fine arts as opposed to rhetoric*, Cic **C.** **a,** of places whence no sound is heard, *still, quiet*, forum, Cic, **b,** of time, tempus mutum litteris, *when nothing is written*, Cic

mūtŭus -a -um (muto), lit, *given in exchange* **I.** *borrowed, lent*, pecuniam dare mutuam, *to lend*, Cic, sumere ab aliquo pecunias mutuas, *to borrow*, Cic Subst, **mūtŭum** -i, n *a loan*, Cic **II.** *mutual, reciprocal*, nox omnia erroris mutui implevit, *on both sides*, Liv, benevolentia, Cic Subst, **mūtŭum** -i, n *reciprocity*, mutuum in amicitia, Cic, pedibus per mutua nexis, *fastened on each other*, Verg

Mŭtyce -ēs, f *town in Sicily*, now *Modica* Hence, adj, **Mŭtycensis** -e, *relating to Mutyce*

Mўcălē -ēs, f. (Μυκάλη), *a promontory of Ionia, opposite the island of Samos.*

Mўcēnae -ārum, f., and **Mўcēna** -ae, f., and **Mўcēnē** -ēs, f. (Μυκῆναι, Μυκήνη), *a city in Argolis of which Agamemnon was king;* hence, 1, adj., **Mўcēnaeus** -a -um, *relating to Mycene or to Agamemnon;* 2, **Mўcēnenses** -ĭum, m. *inhabitants of Mycenae;* 3, **Mўcēnis** -ĭdis, f. *a Mycenian woman,* e.g., *Iphigeneia,* Ov.

Mўcŏnus (-ŏs) -i, f. (Μύκονος), *one of the Cyclades Islands in the Aegean Sea.*

Mygdŏnĕs -um, m. (Μυγδόνες), *a Thracian people who settled in Phrygia, Bithynia, and Mesopotamia.* Hence, 1, **Mygdŏnis** -ĭdis, f. = *Lydian,* Ov.; 2, **Mygdŏnĭus** -a -um = *Phrygian,* Hor.

Mygdŏnĭdēs -ae, m. *son of Mygdon, king of Phrygia.*

Mўlăsa -ōrum, n. (Μύλασα), *a town in Caria.* Hence, **A. Mўlăsēni** -ōrum, m. and **B. Mўlăsenses** -ĭum, m. *the inhabitants of Mylasa.* **C. Mўlăsēus** -ĕi, m. *an inhabitant of Mylasa.* **D. Mўlăsĭus** -a -um, *Mylasian.*

Myndus (-ŏs) -i, f. (Μύνδος), *sea-town in Caria.* Hence, **Myndĭi** -ōrum, m. *the inhabitants of Myndus.*

mўŏpăro -ōnis, m. (μυοπάρων), *a small piratical skiff,* Cic.

mўrīcē -ēs, f., and **mўrīca** -ae, f. (μυρίκη), *the tamarisk,* Verg.

Myrīna -ae, f. (Μυρίνα), *fortified sea-port of the Aeolians in Mysia.*

Myrmēcĭdēs -ae, m. (Μυρμηκίδης), *a celebrated sculptor.*

Myrmĭdŏnes -um, m. (Μυρμιδόνες), *the Myrmidons, a people in Thessalia Phthiotis under the rule of Achilles.*

myrmillo = mirmillo (q.v.).

Mўrō -ōnis, m. (Μύρων), *a celebrated Greek sculptor.*

mўrŏpōla -ae, m. (μυροπώλης), *a seller of unguents,* Plaut.

mўrŏpōlĭum -ĭi, n. (μυροπώλιον), *a shop where unguents are sold,* Plaut.

1. **myrrha (murrha, murra)** -ae, f. (μύῤῥα), 1, *the myrrh-tree,* Plin.; 2, *myrrh, a gum obtained from the myrrh-tree.*

2. **myrrha** = 2. murrha (q.v.).

3. **Myrrha** -ae, f. (Μύῤῥα), *the daughter of Cinyras, changed into a myrrh-tree.*

1. **myrrhĕus (murrhĕus, murrĕus)** -a -um (myrrha), 1, *perfumed or anointed with myrrh,* Hor.; 2, *myrrh-coloured, yellow,* Prop.

2. **myrrhĕus** = 2. murrheus (q.v.).

1. **myrrhĭnus (murrhĭnus, murrĭnus)** -a -um (1. myrrha), *of myrrh,* Plaut.

2. **myrrhĭnus** = 2. murrhinus (q.v.).

myrtētum (murtētum) -i, n. (myrtus), *a grove or thicket of myrtle-trees,* Sall.

myrtĕus (murtĕus) -a -um, 1, *of or relating to the myrtle,* Verg.; 2, *myrtle-coloured,* Tib.

myrtum -i, n. (μύρτον), *the myrtle-berry,* Verg.

myrtus -i and -us, f. (μύρτος), *the myrtle, myrtle-tree,* Verg.

Myrtĭlus -i, m. (Μυρτίλος), *the son of Mercury, who threw himself into the sea, hence according to some called* mare Myrtoum (but see under Myrtos).

Myrtos -i, f. (Μύρτος), *a small island near Euboea;* hence, adj., **Myrtōus** -a -um, mare Myrtoum, *a part of the Aegean sea between Crete, the Peloponnese, and Euboea.*

Myscĕlus -i, m. (Μύσκελος), *an Achaean, founder of Crotona.*

Mўsi -ōrum, m. (Μυσοί), *the people of Mysia in Asia Minor;* hence, 1, **Mўsĭa** -ae, f. *their country;* 2, **Mўsus** -a -um, *Mysian.*

mystăgōgus -i, m. (μυσταγωγός), *a priest or attendant who showed the temple to strangers; a cicerone,* Cic.

mystērĭum -ĭi, n. (μυστήριον). **I.** Sing., *a secret, secret science;* aliquid tacitum tamquam mysterium tenere, Cic. **II.** Plur., **mystērĭa** -ōrum, n. (μυστήρια). **A.** *mysteries or secret rites with which some gods of antiquity were worshipped;* especially *the Eleusinian worship of Ceres,* Cic. **B.** *secrets, mysteries* (of an art); mysteria rhetorum aperire, Cic.

mystēs -ae, m. (μύστης), *a priest at the mysteries,* Ov.

mystĭcus -a -um (μυστικός), *relating to the mysteries, secret, mystic,* Verg.

Mўtĭlēnae -ārum, f. and **Mўtĭlēnē** -ēs, f. (Μυτιλήνη), *capital of the island of Lesbos.* Hence, adj., **Mўtĭlēnaeus** -a -um, *Mytilenean.*

Myūs -untis, f. (Μυοῦς), *a town in Caria.*

mўtĭlus = mitulus (q.v.).

N.

N, n, the thirteenth letter of the Latin alphabet, corresponds in sound to the Greek nu (N, ν). For the uses of N. as an abbreviation, see Table of Abbreviations.

Năbătaei (Năbăthaei) -ōrum, m. (Ναβαταῖοι, Ναβαθαῖοι), *the Nabataeans in Arabia Petraea.* Hence, **Năbătaeus** -a -um, *Nabataean,* poet. = *Arabian, Eastern;* subst., **Năbătaea** -ae, f. (Ναβαταία), *a country of Arabia Petraea.*

Nābĭs -bĭdis, m. (Νάβις), *king of Sparta about 200* A.C.

nablĭum (naulĭum) -ĭi and **nablum** -i, n. *a stringed instrument of uncertain form; a kind of harp or lyre,* Ov.

nae = 1. ne (q.v.).

naenĭa = nenia (q.v.).

Naevĭus -a -um, *name of a Roman gens, of which the most notable member was* Cn. Naevius, *Roman dramatic and epic poet,* born about 274 A.C. Hence, **Naevĭānus** -a -um, *Naevian.*

naevus -i, m. *a mole on the body,* Cic.

Nahanarvali -ōrum, m. *a German tribe.*

Nāĭăs -ădis and **Nāĭs** -ĭdis (-ĭdos), acc. plur. -ĭdas, f. (Ναϊάς, Ναΐς, *a swimmer*), 1, *a water-nymph, Naiad;* used attrib., puellae Naiades, Verg.; 2, *a nymph, hamadryad, Nereid,* Ov. Hence, **Nāĭcus** -a -um, *belonging to the Naiads.*

nam, conj. *for* (differs from enim in standing at the beginning of a clause or proposition). **I.** Introducing an explanation, is pagus appellabatur Tigurinus; nam omnis civitas Helvetia in quatuor pagos divisa est, Caes.; hence, esp., **a,** sometimes introducing a parenthesis, in insula quae est in Tiberino (nam opinor illud alteri flumini nomen esse) sermoni demus operam, Cic.; **b,** or taking up the thought interrupted by a parenthesis, duplex inde Hannibali gaudium fuit (neque enim quidquam eorum, quae apud hostes agerentur, eum fallebat); nam et liberam Minucii temeritatem, etc., Liv.; also **c,**

introducing examples in illustration of a previous general assertion, vivo Catone minores natu multi uno tempore oratores floruerunt, nam et A Albinus et literatus et disertus fuit, Cic. **II.** Introducing a reason, argument, fact, a justification of a preceding statement, celebratote illos dies cum conjugibus ac liberis vestris, nam multi saepe honores dis immortalibus justi habiti sunt, sed profecto justiores numquam, Cic, also used in rhetorical questions to express a climax, numquam illum ne minimā quidem re offendi . una domus erat, idem victus isque communis, nam quid ego de studiis dicam? Cic, often found in connexion with hercle, mehercle, edepol, Cic **III.** Used to add emphasis to an interrogation, and in this application often enclitic, quis est nam ludus ii undis ! Verg

Namnētes -um, m *a people in Gallia Celtica near the modern Nantes.*

namquĕ, conj, a more emphatic form of nam (q v), standing like it at the beginning of a sentence or clause, though sometimes after the first or second word prodigium extemplo dedicationem secutum, namque lapidibus pluit, Liv, Alcibiades ad omnes res aptus consiliique plenus, namque imperator fuit summus mari et terrā Nep

nanciscor, nactus and nanctus sum, 3 dep. *to get, obtain, meet* **I.** Lit., *to find, fall on,* anulum, Ter, morbum, Nep, spem, Cic, fidem, Ov **II.** Transf, **A.** = *to reach,* vitis claviculis suis, quicquid est nacta, complectitur, Cic **B.** *to find, meet with,* aliquem, Cic, turbidam tempestatem, Caes

Nantŭātes -ium, m *a Celtic Alpine people*

nānus -i, m (νάννος, νᾶνος), *a dwarf,* Juv

năpaeus -a -um (να-αῖος), *of* or *relating to the forest;* subst, **năpaeae** ārum, f. *wood nymphs,* Verg

Nār, Nāris, m *a river of Italy, that flows into the Tiber,* now *Nera*

Narbo -ōnis, m *town in Gallia Narbonensis,* now *Narbonne* Hence, adj, **Narbōnensis** -e, *of* or *belonging to Narbo*

narcissus i, m (νάρκισσος) **I.** *the narcissus, daffodil,* Verg **II.** Proper name, *Narcissus, son of Cephisus and Liriope, a youth of remarkable beauty, who fell in love with his own reflection in a fountain, and wasted away till he was changed into the flower of the same name*

nardus i, f and **nardum** i, n (νάρδος), **1,** *nard, a name given by the ancients to various aromatic plants,* Plin, **2,** *the unguent* or *balsam of nard,* Hor

nāris -is, f *the nostril,* usually plur., **nāres**Ium, f *the nostrils* **A.** Gen, fasciculum ad nares commovere, Cic **B.** Esp, *the nose,* as expressive of sagacity or of scorn or anger, homo naris obesae, *a person of dull perception,* Hor, homo emunctae naris, *a man of keen perception,* Hor, naribus uti, *to laugh at, mock at,* Hor ne mappa nares corruget, *cause the guest to turn up his nose,* Hor

Narnĭa -ae, f. *a town in Umbria on the Nar,* now *Narni* Hence, adj, **Narniensis** -e, *relating to Narnia.*

narrābĭlis -e (narro), *that can be told* or *narrated,* Ov

narrātĭo ōnis, f. (narro), *a telling, narrating, relating, narration,* rem narrare ita ut verisimilis narratio sit, Cic

narrātor -ōris, m. (narro), *a relater, narrator,* Cic

narrātus -ūs, m (narro), *a narration, narrative,* Ov.

narro, 1 (for gnaro = gnarum facio), *to make known* **I.** *to relate, tell, narrate;* ego tibi ea narro, quae tu melius scis quam ipse qui narro, Cic; de mea sollicitudine, Cic, male bene, narrare, *to bring good* or *bad tidings,* Cic; with acc and infin, Cic, with rel sent, Cic, pass, narratur, with nom and infin, *it is narrated, it is told,* Liv **II** *to say, speak, tell,* narro tibi (a form of asseveration), *I assure you,* Cic

narthēcĭum -ii, n (ναρθήκιον), *a case for keeping perfumes and medicines,* Cic

narus = gnarus (q v)

Nārўcum -i, n and **Nāryx** -ўcis, f (Νάρυξ), *a town of the Ozolian Locrians, whence the town of Locri in Bruttium was founded* Adj, **Nārўcĭus** -a -um, *Narycian,* urbs, *Locri in Italy,* Ov

Năsămōnes -um, *a people in the south-west of Cyrenaica* Hence, adj, **Năsămōnĭăcus** a -um, *Nasamonian*

nascor (gnascor), nātus sum, 3 dep **I.** Lit, **A.** *to be born,* nasci patre certo, Cic, non nobis solum nati sumus, Cic; post hominum genus natum, *since the beginning of the world,* Cic **B.** *to descend from, spring from,* natus summo loco, *of a good family,* Cic **II.** Transf, *to arise, be produced, spring forth,* nascitur ibi plumbum, Caes, ab eo flumine collis nascebatur, *began to rise,* Cic, nulla tam detestabilis pestis est, quae non homini ab homine nascatur, Cic

Nāsīca -ae, m *name of a family of the Scipios, the most famous member of which, was* P. Cornel Scipio Nasica, *famous for his integrity*

Nāso -ōnis, m *the cognomen of the poet* P Ovidius, v. Ovidius

Nāsos -i f (νᾶσος = νῆσος, *island*), *a part of the city of Syracuse*

nassa (naxa) -ae, f *a narrow-necked basket for catching fish,* Plaut, fig, *a trap, net, snare,* ex hac naxa exire constitui, Cic

nasturcium (nasturtium) Ii, n *a kind of cress,* Cic

nāsus -i, m *the nose* **I.** Lit, **A** nasus ita locatus est, ut quasi murus oculis interjectus esse videatur, Cic **B.** *the nose,* a, as the seat of smell, nasus illis nullus erat, Hor, b, as expressing anger, scorn, etc, aliquem or aliquid naso suspendere adunco, *to turn up the nose at, ridicule, mock,* Hor **II.** Transf, *the nose, nozzle, spout of a vessel,* Juv

nāsūtus -a -um (nasus) **1,** *having a large nose,* Hor, **2,** *acute, sagacious, satirical,* Mart.

nāta -ae, f (nascor), *a daughter,* Verg

nātālĭcĭus -a -um (natalis), *of* or *relating to birth,* and esp *to the time of birth,* praedicta, *a horoscope,* Cic Subst, **nātālĭcĭa** -ōrum, n *a birthday festival,* Cic

nātālis -e (2 natus), *of* or *relating to birth, natal.* **I.** Adj, dies, Cic, lux, Ov, hora, Hor, diem natalem suum agere, *celebrate,* Cic, **II.** Subst, **nātālis** -is, m, a, *a birth place,* Delos natalis Apollinis, Hor.; b, *a birth-day,* Cic, natalis Romae, *festival of Palilia in honour of the founding of Rome,* Ov, plur **nātāles** -ium, m *birth, origin, condition,* Cornelius Fuscus, claris natalibus, *of illustrious origin,* Tac

nătans antis (partic of nato), *swimming,* poet subst f, natantes, *fishes,* Verg

nătātĭo -ōnis, f (nato), *swimming,* ap Cic

nătātor -ōris, m (nato), *a swimmer,* Ov

nătes, v. natis

nātĭo -ōnis, f (nascor) **I.** Abstr, *a being born, birth,* natione Numidā, Tac; hence, personif, Natio, *the goddess of birth,* Cic. **II.**

Conor., **A.** Lit., *a nation, people;* externae nationes et gentes, Cic. **B.** Transf., *a breed, race, species, stock, class;* candidatorum, Cic.; Epicureorum, Cic.; vestra natio (of the Stoics), Cic.

nătis -is, f., usually plur., **nătes** -ium, f. *the rump, buttocks,* Hor.

nātīvus -a -um (2. natus). **I.** *born, that which has come into existence by birth;* Anaximandri opinio est, nativos esse deos, Cic. **II.** *inborn, innate, native, natural, not artificial;* beluae nativis testis inhaerentes, Cic.

năto, 1. (from no, nare), *to swim.* **I.** Lit., studiosissimus homo natandi, Cic.; in oceano, Cic.; natant aequore pisces, Ov.; natat uncta carina, *floats,* Verg.; poet., followed by **acc.**, caeca freta, Verg. **II.** Transf., **A.** *to stream, spread abroad;* qua se Tiberinus in altum dividit et campo liberiore natat, Ov.; fig., *to totter = to be insecure:* tu mihi natare visus es, Cic. **B.** 1, *to swim with anything, be full of, overflow;* natabant pavimenta vino, Cic.; omnia plenis rura natant fossis, Verg.; **2,** of the eyes, *to swim, to be glassy;* vinis oculique animique natabant, Ov.

nătrix -icis, f. *a water-snake,* Cic.

nātūra -ae, f. (nascor). **I.** *birth,* Cic.; naturā frater, adoptione filius, Cic. **II.** *nature.* **A.** 1, *natural qualities of anything;* **a,** of things, haec est natura propria animae et vis, Cic.; montis, Caes.; loci, Caes.; **b,** of men, *nature, natural disposition, character;* quae tua natura est, Cic.; versare suam naturam, Cic.; naturam expellas furcā, tamen usque recurret, Hor.; **2,** *nature,* **a,** *the laws of nature, the order and constitution of the world;* quod rerum natura non patitur, Cic.; naturae satisfacere, *to pay the debt of nature, to die,* Cic.; naturae concedere, Sall.; **b,** *nature, possibility;* in rerum natura fuisse, *to be possible,* Cic. **B.** 1, **a,** *the world, creation;* in full, rerum natura, Cic.; **b,** *nature as the soul of the universe,* Cic.; **2,** *an element, substance, essence;* ex duabus naturis conflata, Cic.

nātūrālis -e (natura). **I.** *that which has arisen or been produced by birth, natural;* pater, *own father* (opp. *adoptive father*), Cic. **II.** 1, *natural;* societas, lex, Cic.; neut. plur. subst., naturalia anteponantur non naturalibus, *that which is natural to that which is not natural,* Cic.; **2,** *relating to nature;* quaestiones, Cic.

nātūrālĭtĕr, adv. (naturalis), *naturally, by nature, according to nature;* divinare, Cic.

1. **nātus** -a -um, p. adj. (from nascor). **I.** Adj., *born;* **1,** *born for, fitted by nature for:* with ad or in and the acc., or with dat., Judaei et Syrae nationes natae servituti, Cic.; poet. with inf., animal natum tolerare labores, Ov.; **2,** *naturally constituted;* ita natus locus est, Liv.; pro re nata, *under present circumstances, as things are now,* Cic.; **3,** with a date, expresses age, eques Romanus annos prope XC natus, *almost ninety years old,* Cic. **II.** Subst., **1, nātus** -i, m. *a son,* Cic.; **2, nāta** -ae, f. *a daughter,* Verg.

2. **nātus** -ū, m. (found only in the abl. sing.), (nascor), *birth* (particularly applied to denote age); magnus natu, grandis natu, *of considerable age,* Cic.; qui fuit major natu quam Plautus et Naevius, *older,* Cic.; ex his omnibus natu minimus, *the youngest,* Cic.

nauarchus -i, m. (ναύαρχος), *a captain of a ship,* Cic.

nauci, v. naucum.

Naucrătes, acc. -em, m. (Ναυκράτης), *a Greek orator, pupil of Isocrates.*

naucum -i, n., lit., *a nut-shell,* fig., *a trifle, something very small;* only used in such expressions as non nauci habere, *to esteem lightly,* Cic.

naufrăgium -ii, n. (for navifragium, from navis and frango), *a shipwreck.* **I.** Lit., naufragium (naufragia) facere, *to suffer shipwreck,* Cic.; naufragio interire, Caes.; perire, Cic.; prov., naufragia alicuius ex terra intueri, *to behold danger from a place of safety,* Cic.; fig., *misfortune, ruin, loss;* fortunarum, Cic.; patrimonii, Cic.; tabula ex naufragio, literally, *a plank from a shipwreck, a means of safety, way of deliverance,* Cic. **II.** Meton., *the remains of a shipwreck, wreckage;* fig., colligere naufragium reipublicae, Cic.

naufrăgus -a -um (for navifragus, from navis and frango). **I.** Pass., *that suffers or has suffered shipwreck;* Marium Africā devictā expulsum et naufragum vidit, Cic.; corpora, Verg.; puppis, Ov.; fig., patrimonio naufragus, Cic. **II.** Act., poet., *causing shipwreck;* mare, Hor.; unda, Tib.

naulĭum = nablium (q.v.).

naulum -i, n. (ναῦλον), *fare, passage-money,* Juv.

naumăchĭa -ae, f. (ναυμαχία), **1,** *a naval battle exhibited as a spectacle,* Suet.; **2,** *the place in which the spectacle was exhibited,* Suet.

naumăchĭārĭus -a -um (naumachia), *of or relating to a mock sea-fight,* Plin.; subst., **naumăchĭārĭus** -i, m. *one who fought in a mock sea-fight,* Suet.

Naupactus (-ŏs) -i, f. (Ναύπακτος), *a seaport on the Gulf of Corinth in Locri Ozolae, now Nepactos or Lepanto.* Hence, adj., **Naupactĭus** -a -um, *of or relating to Naupactus.*

Nauportus -i, f. *a town in Pannonia, now Ober-Laibach.*

nausĕa (nausĭa) -ae, f. (ναυσία), *sea-sickness;* navigamus sine timore et nausea, Cic.; transf., *sickness, nausea,* Hor.

nausĕo (nausĭo), 1. (nausea). **I.** *to be sea-sick;* epistola quam dedisti nauseans Buthroto, Cic.; transf., *to vomit, be sick;* quidlibet, modo ne nauseet, faciat, Cic. **II.** Transf., ista effutientem nauseare, *to belch out nonsense,* Cic.

nausĕŏla (nausĭŏla) -ae, f. (dim. of nausea), *a slight squeamishness,* Cic.

nauta -ae, m. (for navita, from navis), *a sailor, seaman, mariner,* Cic.

nautĭcus -a -um (ναυτικός), *of or relating to a sailor, nautical, naval;* verbum, Cic.; scientia atque usus nauticarum rerum, Caes.; subst., **nautĭci** -ōrum, m. *sailors,* Liv.

nāvālis -e (navis), **1,** adj., *of or relating to ships, naval, nautical;* bellum, pugna, Cic.; castra, *for the protection of ships when drawn upon shore,* Caes.; socii navales, *sailors* (chosen from the freedmen of the colonists and allies), Liv.; pedes navales, *galley-slaves,* Plaut.; **2,** subst., **a, nāvāle** -is, n. *a station for ships,* Ov.; **b, nāvālĭa** -ium, n., (α) *a dockyard,* and esp. *a place in Rome so called,* Liv.; (β) *materials for ship-building,* Liv.

nāvarchus = nauarchus (q.v.).

nāvē = naviter (q.v.).

nāvĭcŭla -ae, f. (dim. of navis), *a little ship, skiff, boat,* Cic.

nāvĭcŭlārĭus -a -um (navicula), *relating to small ships, boats.* **A. nāvĭcŭlārĭa** -ae, f. (sc. res), *the business of one who lets out ships for transport, the business of a ship-owner;* navicularium facere, Cic. **B. nāvĭcŭlārĭus** -ii, m. *one who lets out ships for transport, a ship-owner,* Cic.

nāvĭfrăgus -a -um (navis and frango), *causing shipwreck, ship-destroying*, Verg

nāvĭgābĭlis -e (navigo), *navigable*, mare, Liv.

nāvĭgātĭo -ōnis, f (navigo), *a sailing, voyage, navigation*, bona, Cic ; primam navigationem (*chance of sailing*) ne omiseris, Cic

nāvĭger -gĕra -gĕrum (navis and gero), *ship-bearing, navigable*, mare, Lucr

nāvĭgĭŏlum -i, n (dim of navigium), *a little ship, a bark*, ap Cic

nāvĭgĭum -ii, n (navigo), **1,** *a sailing, navigating*, Lucr , **2,** *a vessel, ship*, navigium facere, Cic.

nāvĭgo, 1 (navis) **I.** Intransit , *to sail, voyage.* **A.** ex Asia in Macedoniam, Cic , of ships, decrevimus, ut classis in Italiam navigaret, Cic **B.** Transf , of a naval war *to proceed, go*, quam celeriter, Cn Pompeio duce, belli impetus navigavit, Cic **II.** Transit , **1,** *to sail over, sail through, navigate*; terram, Cic., aequor, Verg , **2,** *to get* or *earn by navigation*, quae homines arant, navigant, aedificant, Sall

nāvis -is, f (ναῦς), *a ship, vessel* **I.** Lit , navis longa, *a man-of-war*, Liv , oneraria, *a ship of burden, transport ship*, Liv , praetoria, *admiral's ship, flag ship*, Liv , tecta, Liv , constrata, *decked*, Cic , aperta, *undecked*, Cic , navis auri, *laden with gold*, Cic ; navem deducere in aquam, *to launch*, Liv., subducere, *to drag on shore*, Caes , conscendere in navem, *to embark*, Cic ; prov , navibus et quadrigis, *with all one's might*, Hor **II.** Fig , of the state, una navis bonorum omnium, Cic , esse in eadem navi, *to be in the same boat with any one, to share a common lot*, Cic.

nāvĭta = nauta (q v)

nāvĭtas (gnāvĭtas) -ātis, f. (navus), *assiduity, zeal*, Cic

nāvĭtĕr, adv (navus), **1,** *assiduously, zealously, actively*, Liv , **2,** *entirely, quite*, impudens, Cic.

nāvo, 1. (navus), *to do anything zealously, actively, assiduously, diligently*, navare operam alicui, *to come to help, render assistance*, Cic , fortiter in acie navare operam, Liv , quam vellem Bruto studium tuum navare potuisses, Cic , bellum, *to carry on war with energy*, Tac , rempublicam, *to serve the state*, Cic

nāvus (gnāvus) -a -um, *active, diligent, energetic, assiduous*, homo navus et industrius, Cic

naxa -ae, f = nassa (q v)

Naxus (-ŏs) -i, f (Νάξος) *an island of the Aegean Sea, the largest of the Cyclades, now Naxia* or *Axia* Hence, **Naxius** -a -um, *Naxian.*

1 **nē (nae)**, adv. (νή), *yes, verily, truly*, ne illi multa saecula exspectanda fuerunt, Cic

2 **nē**, the original Latin particle of negation **I.** Adv , **A.** *not*, obsolete and rare in this sense, which however appears in compounds such as nemo (= ne hemo), ne-scio, etc , and in such phrases as **B. 1,** ne . . . quidem, *not even*, ne in oppidis quidem, Cic , **2,** ne . . . quoque = ne . . . quidem, ne quis, etc **C. a,** with the imper to express a prohibition, ne timete, Liv., **b,** with the subj , to express a prohibition, nobis nostras ne ademeris, Cic ; **c,** with subj , si certum est facere, facias, verum ne post conferas culpam in me, Tac , with a negative wish, ne id Juppiter Opt Max sinat, Liv ; illud utinam ne vere scriberem, Cic , ne vivam, si scio, *may I die if I know*, Cic **D. 1,** with compar , *not*, ut hoc desiderium ne plus sit annuum, Cic , **2,** in concessive and restrictive clauses, sint sane liberales ex sociorum fortunis, sint misericordes in furibus aerarii, ne illis sanguinem nostrum largiantur, *only let them not lavish our blood*, Sall **II.** Conj = *that not* **A.** to express purpose ; gallinae pennis fovent pullos, ne frigore laedantur, Cic , ne multa dicam, *in short*, Cic **B.** to express consequence , hoc te rogo ne demittas animum, Cic **C. 1,** ut ne, *that not*, quam plurimis de rebus ad me velim scribas, ut prorsus ne quid ignorem, Cic , **2,** ne non, *that not*, timeo ne non impetrem, Cic

3 **nĕ**, interrog and enclitic particle **I.** In simple questions , **1,** in direct questions, mittone alios, etiamne nobis expedit? Cic , **2,** in indirect questions, ut videamus, satisne ista sit defectio, Cic **II.** In compound questions ; **1,** in direct questions, satisne ergo pudori consulat, si quis sine teste libidini pareat, an est aliquid per se ipsum flagitiosum? Cic , **2,** in indirect questions, nescio gratulerne tibi an timeam, Cic

Nĕāpŏlis -pŏlis, acc -pŏlim, f (Νεάπολις) **I.** *a part of Syracuse* **II.** *a sea-port in Campania, now Naples.* Adj , **Nĕāpŏlītānus** -a -um, *Neapolitan*

nĕbŭla -ae, f (νεφέλη) **I.** Lit , **1,** *exhalation, fog, mist*, matutina, Liv , **2,** poet , *cloud*, Hor , pulveris, *a cloud of dust*, Lucr , **3,** *smoke*, Ov **II.** Transf , *anything soft and transparent*, vellera nebulas aequantia tactu, Ov.

nĕbŭlo -ōnis, m (nebula), *a good-for-nothing fellow, idle rascal, worthless wretch*, Cic

nĕbŭlōsus -a -um (nebula), *misty, foggy, cloudy, dark*, nebulosum et caliginosum caelum, Cic

nĕc and **nĕquĕ**, negative particles **I. A.** *and not*, quia non viderunt nec sciunt, Cic , neque vero, *and indeed not*, Cic , nec tamen, *and yet not*, Cic , neque etiam, *and indeed not*, Cic , nec enim, neque enim, *for not*, Cic , neque non, *and*, necnon, *and also, and indeed*, Cic **B. 1,** *and also not*, Stoicum est nec admodum credibile, Cic , **2,** *and indeed not*, nuntii nobis tristes nec varii venerunt, Cic , **3,** *and yet not*, conscripsi epistolam noctu, nec ille ad me rediit, Cic **II.** Joined with other particles ; **1,** nec . . . nec, or neque . . . neque, *neither . . . nor*, **2,** neque . . . et, *not only not . . . but also*, nec miror et gaudeo, Cic

necdum, adv *and not yet*, Cic

nĕcessārĭē, adv (necessarius), *necessarily, unavoidably*, Cic

nĕcessārĭō, adv. (necessarius), *necessarily, unavoidably*, Cic.

nĕcessārĭus -a -um (necesse), *necessary, unavoidable, inevitable* **I.** Adj , lex, Cic , mors, Cic , res, *necessity*, Caes., omnia quae sint ad vivendum necessaria Cic , quod mihi maxime necessarium, Cic , necessarium est, with infin , senatori necessarium est, nosse rempublicam, *it is necessary, indispensable*, Cic **II.** Transf *closely connected* or *related*, esp , subst , **nĕcessārĭus** -ii, m , **-a** -ae, f , *an intimate friend, connexion, near relation*, meus familiaris ac necessarius, Cic

nĕcessĕ, adj n (ne and cedo), found only in connexion with esse and habere, *necessary, fated, unavoidable, inevitable, indispensable*, nihil fit, quod necesse non fuerit, Cic , homini necesse est mori, Cic , necesse habere, *to consider necessary, be obliged*, eo minus habeo necesse scribere, Cic

nĕcessĭtas -ātis, f (necesse) **I.** Lit , **A** necessitati parere, Cic , necessitatem alicui imponere alicuius rei or aliquid faciendi, Cic **B. 1, a,** *that which is inevitable, fate*, mors est necessitas naturae, Cic , **b,** *want, need, poverty*,

Tac.; 2, plur., necessitates, *necessaries, accessary expenses*, Caes. **II.** Transf., *intimate connexion, friendship, relationship*; si nostram necessitatem familiaritatemque violasset, Cic.

nĕcessĭtūdo -inis, f. (necesse), *necessity, inevitableness*. **I.** Lit., puto hanc esse necessitudinem, cui nullā vi resisti potest, Cic. **II.** Transf., 1, of things, *close connexion*; rerum, Cic.; 2, *close connexion* or *relationship, intimate friendship*; liberorum necessitudo, Cic.; sunt mihi cum illo omnes amicitiae necessitudines, Cic.; familiaritatis et necessitudinis oblitus, Cic.; 3, plur., *intimate friends, near relations*, Suet.

nĕcessum and **nĕcessus** est = necesse est, *it is necessary*; with infin., Liv.; or acc. and infin., Liv.

necnĕ, *or not*. **I.** Generally in the second half of indirect questions, sintne dii necne, Cic. **II.** More rarely in direct questions, sunt haec tua verba necne? Cic.

necnon (neque non), v. nec.

nĕco, 1. (nex), *to kill, slay* (usually by hunger, poison, etc., rather than by a weapon); plebem fame, Cic.; aliquem igni, Caes.; aliquem verberibus, Cic.

nĕcŏpīnans -antis, *not expecting, unaware*; aliquem necopinantem liberare, Cic.

nĕcŏpīnāto, adv. (necopinatus), *unexpectedly*; si necopinato quid evenerit, Cic.

nĕcŏpīnātus -a -um, *unexpected*; bona, Cic.; ex necopinato, *unexpectedly*, Liv.

nĕcŏpīnus -a -um, 1, pass., *unexpected*; mors, Ov.; 2, act., *not expecting, careless*, Phaedr.

nectar -ăris, n. (νέκταρ). **I.** *nectar, the drink of the gods*, Cic. **II.** Applied to anything very sweet or pleasant; *honey*, Verg.; *milk*, Ov.

nectārĕus -a -um (νεκτάρεος), *sweet as nectar*; aqua, Ov.

necto, nexŭi and nexi, nexum, 3. **I.** Lit., **A.** *to tie, bind, fasten, connect, weave* or *fasten together*; catenas, coronam, Hor.; comam myrto, Ov. **B.** *to bind, fetter, enslave*, especially for debt; nexus, *a person enslaved in consequence of debt*, Liv.; eo anno plebi Romanae velut aliud initium libertatis factum est, quod necti desierunt, Liv. **II.** Transf., **A.** *to affix, attach*; ex hoc genere causarum ex aeternitate pendentium fatum a Stoicis nectitur, Cic. **B.** *to connect*; omnes virtutes inter se nexae et jugatae sunt, Cic.; dolum, *to plot*, Liv.; causas inanes, *bring forward*, Verg.; numeris verba, Ov.

nēcŭbi, adv. *lest anywhere, that nowhere*, Caes.

nēcundĕ, adv. *lest from any quarter, that from no direction*, Liv.

nēdum, adv. (lit. *while not*), 1, *much less, still less, to say nothing of*; foll. by subj., optimis temporibus nec P. Popilius nec Q. Metellus vim tribuniciam sustinere potuerunt, nedum his temporibus sine vestra sapientia salvi esse possimus, *much less at present*, Cic.; with ut and the subj., ne voce quidem incommodi, nedum ut ulla vis fieret, Liv.; 2, *much more*; consules bellicosi qui vel in pace tranquilla bellum excitare possent, nedum in bello respirare civitatem forent passuri, Liv.

nĕfandus -a -um (ne and fari), *not to be spoken of, impious, execrable, abominable*; scelus, Cic.; neut. subst., dii memores fandi atque nefandi, *of right and wrong*, Verg.

nĕfārĭē, adv. (nefarius), *impiously, abominably, execrably*; aliquid nefarie facere or committere, Cic.

nĕfārĭus -a -um (nefas), *impious, abominable, execrable, nefarious*; homo, Cic.; bellum, Cic.; subst., a, **nĕfārĭus** -ii, m. *a wicked person*, Cic.; b, **nĕfārĭum** -ii, n. *an abominable, execrable action*, Liv.

nĕfas, n. indecl., *that which is sinful, contrary to divine command, unlawful, wrong, an impious deed, a sin, crime*; 1, quicquid non licet, nefas putare debemus, Cic.; Mercurius, quem Aegyptii nefas habent nominare, Cic.; per fas et nefas, *by fair means or foul*, Liv.; in omne nefas se parare, Ov.; nefas est, *it is a sin*; with infin., indicare in vulgus nefas (est), Cic.; sometimes used as an interjection, *shocking, dreadful!* heu nefas! Hor.; 2, *a horrible thing*; exstinxisse nefas laudabor (Helen as the cause of the ruin of Troy), Verg.

nĕfastus -a -um, *forbidden, unholy*. **I.** Of time, a, religious t. t., dies nefasti, *on which no legal or public business could be transacted*, Liv.; b, *unlucky, inauspicious*; ille et nefasto te posuit die, Hor.; ne qua terra sit nefasta victoriae suae, Liv. **II.** Of action, *forbidden, sinful*; a, as religious t. t., quae augur injusta, nefasta dixerit, Cic.; b, transf., quid intactum nefasti liquimus? Hor.

nĕgantĭa -ae, f. (nego), *a denying*, Cic.

nĕgātĭo -ōnis, f. (nego), *a denying*; negatio infitiatioque facti, Cic.

nĕgito, 1. (intens. of nego), *to deny frequently, persist in denying*; quam multos annos esse negitavisset, Cic.

neglectĭo -ōnis, f. (negligo), *neglect*; amicorum, Cic.

1. **neglectus** -a -um, p. adj. (from negligo), *neglected, disregarded*; quum inter nos abjecti neglectique simus, Cic.

2. **neglectus** -ūs, m. (negligo), *a neglecting, neglect, disregard*, Ter.

neglĕg . . . v. neglig . . .

neglĭgens -entis, p. adj. (from negligo), 1, *negligent, careless, indifferent, unconcerned*; in amicis eligendis, Cic.; with genit., amicorum, Cic.; 2, esp. in regard to property, *careless, prodigal, extravagant*; adolescentia negligens luxuriosaque, Liv.

neglĭgentĕr, adv. (negligens), *carelessly, unconcernedly, negligently*; scribere, Cic.

neglĭgentĭa -ae, f. (negligens). **I.** *carelessness, negligence*; in accusando, Cic.; accusare aliquem de literarum negligentia, *of omitting to write a letter*, Cic. **II.** *neglect shown towards persons*; deûm, Liv.

neglĭgo (neglĕgo, neclĕgo) -lexi -lectum, 3. (nec and lego), *to neglect, disregard*. **I.** Unintentionally; mandatum, Cic.; with de and the abl., de Theopompo, summo homine, neglexĭmus, Cic.; with infin., obire diem edicti, Cic. **II.** Intentionally, 1, *to make light of, despise, pay no heed to*; periculum fortunarum et capitis sui, Cic.; 2, *to overlook, pass over*; injurias Aeduorum, Caes.

nĕgo, 1. (perhaps from ne and aio). **I.** Intransit., *to say no* (opp. aio, *to say yes*); Diogenes ait, Antipater negat, Cic.; with dat., saepius idem roganti, Cic. **II.** Transf., **A.** *to deny, to maintain* or *assert that a thing is not*; crimen, Cic.; with acc. and infin., Stoici negant, quicquam esse bonum nisi quod honestum sit, Cic.; pass., with nom. and infin., ibi vis facta (esse) negabitur, Cic.; non negare (foll. by quin and the subj.), negare non posse quin rectius sit exercitum mitti, Liv. **B.** *to deny a request, to refuse*; nunquam reo cuiquam tam praecise negavi, quam hic mihi, Cic.; of inanimate objects, poma negat regio, *refuses to produce apples*, Ov.

nĕgōtĭālis -e (negotium), *of or relating to business*, Cic

nĕgōtĭans -antis, m (partic of negotior as subst), *a wholesale dealer, merchant, banker*, Cic

nĕgōtĭātĭo -ōnis, f (negotior), *wholesale business, extensive trade, banker's business*, reliquiae negotiationis vestigia, Cic

nĕgōtĭātor -ōris, m (negotior), *a large wholesale dealer, extensive merchant, banker*, Cic.

nĕgōtĭŏlum -i, n (dim of negotium), *a small transaction, little business*, tua negotiola Ephesi curae mihi fuerunt, Cic

nĕgōtĭor, 1 dep (negotium) **I.** *to carry on business*, especially on a large scale, as e g , *a banker*, Patris, *at Patrae*, Cic **II.** *to trade*, Liv

nĕgōtĭōsus -a -um (negotium), *full of business, busy*, provincia, Cic , homo, Sall , dies, *working days*, Tac

nĕgōtĭum -ii, n (nec and otium), *absence of leisure, business, occupation, employment* **I.** satis negotii habui in sanandis vulneribus, Cic , neque esse quidquam negotii (*any difficulty*) hanc sub sarcinis adoriri, Caes , negotium alicui exhibere or facere, *to cause trouble to a person*, Cic **II.** Transf , **A.** *some single employment or occupation*, **1,** negotii privata, domestica, Cic , negotium suscipere, Cic , conficere, Caes , **2, a,** *public business*, negotia forensia, Cic , **b,** of a battle, *affair*, facies negotii, Sall , **c,** *money transactions*, habere negotii vetera in Sicilia, Cic , **d,** *management of a household*, negotium male gerere, Cic **B.** Meton , of men, Callisthenis quidem vulgare et notum negotium, Cic

Nēleus -ĕi, m (Νηλεύς), *a mythical king of Pylos, father of Nestor*. hence, **1,** adj , **Nēlēĭus** -a -um, and **2, Nēlēus** -a -um, *of or relating to Neleus or Nestor*, **3,** subst , **Nēlīdēs** -ae, m *a male descendant of Neleus, Nestor*, Ov

Nĕmĕa -ae, f (Νεμέα), and **Nĕmĕē** -ēs, f (Νεμέη), *a city of Argolis, near which Hercules killed the Nemean lion, and founded the Nemean games* Hence, **1,** adj , **Nĕmĕaeus** -a -um, *Nemean*, leo, Ov., **2,** subst , **Nĕmĕa** -ōrum, n *the Nemean games*, Liv

Nĕmĕsis -sĕos, f (Νέμεσις), *the goddess of justice and equity who punished pride and arrogance*, also called *Adrastea* and *Rhamnusia*

Nĕmĕtes -um, *a people in Gallia Belgica*

nēmo -ĭnis c (for nehemo, from ne and hemo = homo), *no man, no one, nobody* **I.** Subst , nemo omnium mortalium, Cic , nemo unus, Cic , nemo alius, *no one else*, Cic , nemo nec deus nec homo, *no god or mortal*, Cic , nemo est quin (with subj), *there is no one who does not*, etc , Cic , nemo non, *every one*, Cic , non nemo, *many a one*, Cic **II.** Adj = no, homo, Cic , civis Cic , Romanus, Liv (of the oblique cases only nemini and neminem are usually found)

nĕmŏrālis -e (nemus), *of or relating to woods or groves, sylvan*, umbrae, antrum, Ov

nĕmŏrensis -e (nemus), *belonging to a grove or wood*, esp , *of or relating to the grove of Diana at Aricia*, Suet

nĕmŏrĭcultrix -īcis, f (nemus and cultrix), *an inhabitant of the woods*, Phaedr

nĕmŏrĭvăgus -a -um (nemus and vagus), *wandering in the woods*, Cat

nĕmŏrōsus -a -um (nemus), **1,** *woody, full of groves*, Zacynthos, Verg , **2,** *thickly leaved, full of foliage*, silvae, Ov

nempĕ, conj (from nam and demonstrative suff -pe), *forsooth, truly, certainly, to be sure, namely*, nempe incomposito dixi pede currere versus Lucili, Hor , si dat tantam pecuniam Flacco, nempe idcirco dat, ut rata sit emptio, *of course*, Cic , nempe negas? Cic

nĕmus -ŏris, n (νέμος), *a wood with glades and pasture land for cattle, grove, forest*, **1,** agri et nemora, Cic , **2,** esp , *the grove at Aricia sacred to Diana*, Cic

nēnĭa (**naenĭa**) -ae, f *a funeral song, dirge* **1,** lit , Cic **2,** *any mournful song*, Hor , **3,** *a song of incantation, an incantation*, Hor , **4,** *a popular song, nursery song, lullaby*, Hor (nēnĭā (abl), dissyll , Ov Fast 6 142)

nĕo, nēvi, nētum, 2 (νέω) **I.** *to spin*, stamina, fila, esp of the Parcae, Ov **II.** *to weave interweave*, tunicam quam molli neverat auro Verg (syncop perf , nerunt, Ov)

Nĕŏcles -is and -i, m (Νεοκλῆς), *father of Themistocles* Hence, **Nĕŏclīdēs** -ae, m *son of Neocles, i e , Themistocles*

nĕpa -ae, f **1,** *a scorpion*, Cic , *the constellation so called*, Cic poet , **2,** *the crab*, Plaut , *the constellation so called*, Cic poet

Nĕpĕtĕ -is, n *a town of Etruria, now Nepi* Hence, adj **Nĕpĕtīnus** -a -um, *of or relating to Nepete*

Nĕphĕlē -ēs, f (Νεφέλη), *wife of Athamas, mother of Phrixus and Helle* Hence, **Nĕphĕlēis** -ēĭdos, f *a daughter of Nephele, Helle* Ov

1 **nĕpos** -ōtis, m and f *a grandchild* **I. A.** Lit , Q Pompeii ex filia nepos, Cic **B.** Transf , **1,** *a brother's or sister's child, nephew*, Suet , **2,** *a descendant*, Verg , Hor **II.** Meton , *a spendthrift, prodigal* (opp patruus), Cic

2 **Nĕpos** -pōtis, m , C Cornelius, *a Roman historian, friend of Atticus, Cicero, and Catullus, living probably between 94 and 24 B C , of whose works a part of the book* De Viris Illustribus *is extant*

nĕpōtŭlus -i, m (dim of nepos), *a little grandson*, Plaut

neptis -is, f (nepos), *a grand-daughter*, Cic , neptis Veneris, *Ino*, Ov , doctae neptes, *the Muses*, Ov

Neptūnīnē -ēs, f *a daughter or grand-daughter of Neptune*, Cat

Neptūnus -i, m *Neptune, god of the sea, brother of Jupiter, husband of Amphitrite, identified with the Greek Poseidon*, meton , *the sea*, Verg , hence, adj , **Neptūnĭus** -a -um, *Neptunian*, Troja, *built by Neptune*, Verg , heros, *Theseus*, Ov , dux, *Sext Pompeius*, Hor , aquae, *a well at Terracina*, Liv

nēquam, adj indecl , compar **nēquĭor**, superl **nēquissĭmus** (for ne aequum, from aequus), *worthless, good for nothing, useless, bad, wicked* quid est nequius effeminato viro? Cic , liberti nequam et improbi, Cic

nēquāquam, adv *by no means, in no wise*, Cic

nĕquĕ = nec (q v)

nĕquĕdum (**necdum**), adv *and not yet*, Cic

nĕquĕo -ivi and -ii -itum, 4 *to be unable*, actam aetatem meminisse nequimus, Lucr , cum Demosthenes rho dicere nequiret, Cic , pass , quicquid sine sanguine civium ulcisci nequitur, jure factum sit, Sall (imperf , nequibat, Sall , partic , nequiens, Sall)

nēquīquam (**nēquicquam, nēquidquam**), adv (ne and abl quiquam), *in vain, fruitlessly, to no purpose*, et sero et nequidquam pudet, Cic , alicuius auxilium implorare, Caes

nēquĭtĕr, adv (nequam), *worthlessly, wretchedly, badly, miserably*, ille porro male, prave nequiter, turpiter cenabat, Cic

nĕquĭtia -ae, f. and **nĕquĭtĭes** -ēi, f. (nequam), **1**, *worthlessness, laziness, idleness, inactivity;* inertissimi homines nescio qua singulari nequitiā praediti, Cic.; **2**, *extravagance, prodigality*, Cic.; **3**, *wantonness, profligacy;* uxor pauperis Ibyci, tandem nequitiae pone modum tuae, Hor.; **4**, *wickedness, villainy*, Cic.

Nĕrētum -i, n. *a town in Calabria*, now *Nardo*.

Nēreūs -ĕos and -ĕi, m. (Νηρεύς), *a sea-god, son of Oceanus and Tethys, father, by Doris, of the Nereids;* meton., *the sea*, Tib.; hence, **1**, **Nērēĭs** -ĭdis, f. *a daughter of Nereus, a Nereid*, Ov.; **2**, **Nērīnē** -ēs, f. *a Nereid*, Verg.; **3**, adj., **Nērēĭus** -a -um, *of* or *belonging to Nereus;* genitrix, *Thetis, mother of Achilles*, Ov.; nepos, *Achilles*, Ov.

Nērĭtus (-ŏs) -i, m. (Νήριτος), *a mountain of Ithaca*, also *the name of a small island near Ithaca;* hence, **Nērĭtĭus** -a -um, *Neritian;* ratis, *the ship of Ulysses*, Ov.; dux, *Ulysses*, Ov.

Nĕro -ōnis, m. *a family name of the gens Claudia, the most celebrated of which were:* **1**, C. Claudius Nero, *consul* 207 B.C., *who defeated Hasdrubal at the battle of the Metaurus:* **2**, C. Claudius Nero, *the fifth Roman emperor* (54–68 A.D.). Hence, adj., **1**, **Nĕrōnēus** -a -um, and **2**, **Nĕrōnĭānus** -a -um, *Neronian*.

Nersae -ārum, f. *a town in Italy, probably in Latium*.

Nĕrŭlum -i, n. *a fortified place in Lucania*.

Nervĭi -ōrum, m. *a warlike people in the north of Gallia Belgica*. Hence, adj., **Nervĭcus** -a -um, *Nervian*.

nervōsē, adv. (nervosus), *strongly, vigorously, energetically;* nervosius dicere, Cic.

nervōsus -a -um (nervus), *sinewy, nervous*. **I.** Lit., poples, Ov. **II.** Fig., of discourse, *vigorous, nervous in style;* quis Aristotele nervosior? Cic.

nervŭlus -i, m. (dim. of nervus), *nerve, strength;* in plur., nervulos adhibere, Cic.

nervus -i, m. (νεῦρον), *a sinew, tendon, nerve;* gen. plur., nervi, *the sinews, nerves*. **I. A.** Lit., nervi a quibus artus continentur, Cic. **B.** Transf., **1**, *the string of a musical instrument;* quotidiano cantu vocum et nervorum et tibiarum tota vicinitas personat, Cic.; **2**, *a bowstring;* nervo aptare sagittas, Verg.; **3**, *the leather with which shields are covered*, Tac.; **4**, *a strap or thong with which the limbs are bound, bonds, fetters*, and hence, *prison, imprisonment;* in nervis teneri, Liv. **II.** Fig., **A. 1**, *nerve, strength, vigour, effort;* in quo omnes nervos aetatis industriaeque meae contenderem, Cic.; **2**, esp., of discourse, *rigour, energy;* nervi oratorii, Cic. **B.** *the chief strength;* nervi belli pecunia, *money the sinews of war*, Cic.; nervi conjurationis, Liv.

nescĭo -īvi and -ĭi -ītum, 4. *not to know, to be ignorant of*. **I.** Gen., de Oropo opinor, sed certum nescio, *I do not certainly know*, Cic.; with rel. sent., nescis quanta cum exspectatione sim te auditurus, Cic.; quid nobis agendum sit, nescio, Cic.; nescio qui, quae, quod (interrog.), nescio quis, quid, *I know not who* or *what, somebody* or *something;* casu nescio quod, Cic.; in oppidum, nescio quod, Cic.; nescio quid exsculpserunt, Cic.; nescio quomodo, *I know not how, somehow or other*, Cic. **II.** Esp., **A.** *not to know* or *recognise a person* or *thing;* non nescire hiemem, Verg. **B.** *not to understand anything, to be unable to do anything, not to have learnt;* non tam praeclarum est scire Latine quam turpe nescire, Cic.; Stoici omnino irasci nesciunt, Cic.

nescĭus -a -um (ne and scio). **I.** Act., **A.** *not knowing, ignorant, unaware, unconscious;* nescia mens hominum fati sortisque futurae, Verg.; non sum nescius, ista inter Graecos dici, Cic. **B.** *not knowing how to do anything, unable to do anything;* pueri fari nescii, Hor.; cedere nescius, Hor. **II.** Pass., *unknown;* nescia tributa, Tac.; causa, Ov.

Nēsĭs -ĭdis, f. *an island in the Gulf of Puteoli*, now *Nisita*.

Nessus -i, m. (Νέσσος). **I.** *a river in Thrace*. **II.** *a Centaur killed by Hercules with a poisoned arrow*.

Nestŏr -ŏris, m. (Νέστωρ), *son of Neleus, king of Pylus, the oldest and most experienced of the Greek heroes before Troy*.

Nētum -i, n. *a town of Sicily, south-west of Syracuse*.

neu = neve (q.v.).

neuter -tra -trum (ne and uter), *neither of two*. **I.** Lit., quid bonum sit, quid malum, quid neutrum, Cic.; neutram in partem moveri, Cic.; neuter consulum, Liv. **II.** In grammar, nomina neutra, or simply neutra, *neuter nouns*, Cic.

neutĭquam, adv. *by no means, not at all;* monebas de Q. Cicerone ut eum quidem neutiquam relinquerem, Cic.

neutrō, adv. (neuter), *in neither direction, towards neither side;* neutro inclinata res, spes, Liv.

neutrŭbī, adv. (neuter and ubi), *in neither place*, Plaut.

nēvĕ or **neu**, adv. *and not, or not, nor* (follows ut or ne); rogo te, ne contrahas, neve sinas, Cic.; cohortatus est, uti suae pristinae virtutis memoriam retinerent, neu perturbarentur animo, Caes.; sometimes follows the subj. only, hic ames dici pater atque princeps, neu sinas Medos equitare inultos, Hor.; sometimes repeated, *neither . . . nor;* ut id neve in hoc, neve in alio requiras, Cic.

nēvis, nevult = nonvis, nonvult, v. nolo

nex, nĕcis, f. (cf. Gr. νέκυς). **I.** *violent death, murder;* necem sibi consciscere, *to commit suicide*, Cic.; vitae necisque potestatem habere in aliquem, Caes.; alicui necem inferre or offerre, Cic. **II.** Meton., *blood of the person slain;* manus nece Phrygiā imbutae, Ov.

nexĭlis -e (necto), *tied together, bound together;* sinus, Ov.

nexo, 1. (intens. of necto), *to tie together, bind together*, Lucr.

nexum -i, n. (necto), *a formal transaction between debtor and creditor, by which the debtor pledged his liberty as security for his debt*, Liv.; meton., *the obligation created by* nexum, Cic.; quum sunt propter unius libidinem, omnia nexa civium liberata nectierque postea desitum, Cic.

nexus -ūs, m. (necto). **I.** *a binding, tying together, entwining, connecting;* atomorum, Cic.; serpens, baculum qui nexibus ambit, Ov. **II.** Fig., **A.** legis nexus, Tac. **B.** *the relation* or *obligation arising from* nexum; nexu vincti, Liv.; se nexu obligare, Cic.

nī, adv. and conj. **I.** = ne in sentences with the subj., ni teneant cursus, Verg.; hence, quid ni? *why not?* Cic. **II.** = si non, *if not, except, unless;* moriar, ni puto, *I wish I may die if I don't think*, Cic.; plures cecidissent, ni nox praelio intervenisset, Liv.; excidium minitans, ni causam suam dissociarent, Tac.

Nīcaea -ae, f. (Νίκαια). **I.** *a town in Bithynia*, now *Isnik*. **II.** *a town in Locris, not far from Thermopylae*.

nīcaeus -a -um (νικαῖος, *victorious*), *epithet of Jupiter*

Nīcander -dri, m (Νίκανδρος), *poet, grammarian, and physician of Colophon*

nīcātor -ōris, acc. plur -oras, m (νικάτωρ), *the conqueror*, *soldier of a body-guard of Perseus, king of Macedonia*

Nīcēphŏrium (-ŏn) -ii, n (Νικηφόριον), **1,** *a grove near Pergamum*, **2,** *a town in Mesopotamia*

Nīcēphŏrius -ii, m *a river in Armenia*

nīcētērium -ii, n (νικητήριον), *the reward of victory, prize*, Juv

Nīcŏmēdēs -is, m (Νικομήδης), *name of several kings of Bithynia*

Nīcŏpŏlis, acc -im, f (Νικόπολις), *a town in Acarnania, founded by Augustus to commemorate his victory at Actium*

nicto, 1 and **nictor**, 1 dep (* nico, *to beckon*), **1,** *to move the eyelid up and down, to wink*, Plin **2,** *to wink with the eye, as a signal*, alicui, Plaut

nictus -ūs, m (* nico), *a winking with the eye*, Ov (?)

nīdāmentum -i, n (nidus), *the materials of a nest*, Plaut

nīdĭfĭco, 1 (nidus and facio), *to build a nest*, Plin.

nīdor -ōris, m (connected with κνίσσα), *a vapour, odour, steam arising from anything which is cooked*, ganearum, Cic

nīdŭlus i, m (dim of nidus), *a little nest*, Ithaca illa in asperrimis saxulis tamquam nidulus affixa, Cic

nīdus -i m *a nest* **I. 1,** lit, effingere et constituere nidos, Cic , nidum tignis suspendit hirundo, Verg , fig , me majores pennas nido extendisse, *to raise oneself above the condition in which one is born*, Hor , **2,** meton , *the young birds in the nest, nestlings*, nidi loquaces, Verg **II.** Transf , *a dwelling on a height*, celsae Acherontiae, Hor

nĭger -gra grum, *black, dark coloured* **I. A.** Lit , hederae, Verg , silvae, Hor , coelum pice nigrius, Ov , subst , **nĭgrum** -i, n *a black spot*, Ov **B.** Meton , *making black, blackening* Auster, Verg. **II.** Transf , **1,** *of or relating to death*, ignes, *the funeral pile*, Hor , dies, *the day of death*, Prop , **2, a,** *unlucky, unpropitious*, **b,** of character, *black = wicked*, Cic

nĭgrans -antis, p adj (from nigro), *black, dark-coloured*, Verg

nĭgresco -grŭi, 3 (* nigreo), *to become black, grow dark in colour, grow dark*, tenebris nigrescunt omnia circum, Verg

nĭgro, 1 (niger), *to be black*, Lucr

nĭgror -ōris, m (niger), *blackness*, mortis, Lucr

nĭhil and contr **nīl**, n indecl *nothing* **I.** Subst , **A.** *nothing*, nihil agere, Cic , with genit of subst or neut adj , nihil rerum humanarum, Cic , nihil mali, Cic , nihil est cur, quamobrem, quod, *there is no reason why*, nihil est cur gestias, Cic , nihil ad rem, *it has nothing to do with the business*, Cic , nihil non, *everything*, nihil mali non inest Cic , non nihil, *something*, Cic , nihil nisi, *nothing but*, Cic , nihil aliud nisi, *nothing else but*, Cic , nihil quin, e g , nihil agis quin ego audiam, *you do nothing that I do not hear of*, Cic **B.** *a nothing*, nihil esse, *to be good for nothing*, Cic , aliquem nihil putare, *to think nothing of*, Cic **II.** Adj in the phrases, nihil quidquam, nihil unum, Cic **III.** Adv , *not at all, in nothing*, de fratre nihil ego te accusavi, Cic , Thebani nihil moti sunt, Liv

nĭhildum, conj *nothing as yet*, Cic

nĭhĭlōmĭnus, v nihilum

nĭhĭlum -i, n (nihil) *nothing* **I.** Subst ex nihilo oriatur, Cic , ad nihilum venire or recidere, Cic , pro nihilo est, *it is as good as nothing*, Cic , nihili, the genit of price , facere, aestimare, *to think nothing of*, Cic ; de nihilo, *without ground or reason*, Liv , abl , nihilo, with compar , *by nothing, no*, nihilo benevolentior Cic , nihilo magis, Cic , nihilominus = *no less, nevertheless, notwithstanding*, nihilominus eloquentiae studendum est etsi ea quidam perverse abutuntur, Cic **II.** Adv , *in no way*, Hor , Liv

nīl = nihil (q v)

nīlum = nihilum (q v)

Nīlus -i, m (Νεῖλος), *the river Nile*, hence, **1,** adj , **Nīlĭăcus** -a -um, *belonging to the Nile*, fera, *a crocodile*, Mart , modi, *Egyptian*, Ov , **2, Nīlĭgĕna** -ae, m (Nilus and gigno), *one born on the Nile, an Egyptian*, **3,** transf = *a canal, aqueduct*, Cic

nimbātus -a -um (nimbus), *shrouded in cloud or mist*, Plaut

nimbĭfĕr -fĕra -fĕrum (nimbus and fero), *storm-bringing, stormy*, Ov

nimbōsus -a -um (nimbus), *rainy, stormy*, ventus, Ov

nimbus -i, m (connected with nubo) **I.** *a storm of rain, violent shower of rain*, **1,** lit , nimbus effusus, Liv , **2,** transf , ferreus, *shower of missiles*, Verg **II.** *a storm*, **1,** lit., **a,** Cic , **b,** *a storm wind* toto sonuerunt aethere nimbi, Verg **2,** fig , hunc quidem nimbum cito transisse laetor, Cic **III.** *a cloud*, **1,** *a black rain-cloud*, involvere diem nimbi, Verg , **2,** *a cloud, mist*, Liv , Verg , **3,** transf , **a,** fulvae nimbus arenae, Verg , **b,** of a large number of persons or things, *a cloud*, peditum, Verg

nĭmĭo, v nimius

nīmīrum, adv (ni = ne and mirum) *undoubtedly, doubtless, truly, certainly*, nimirum Themistocles est auctor adhibendus, Cic , often ironically, *doubtless, forsooth*, uni nimirum tibi recte semper erunt res, Hor

nĭmis, adv *too much, overmuch, excessively* valde, saepe, Cic , foll by genit , insidiarum, Cic , non nimis, *not particularly, not very much* praesidium non nimis firmum, Cic

nĭmĭum, v nimius

nĭmĭus -a -um (nimis), *too great*, *too much, excessive* **I.** Adj , **A.** Lit , **1,** gen , **a,** of things, celeritas, Cic , **b,** of persons, *intemperate, immoderate*, nimius in honoribus decernendis, Cic , with genit , imperii, Liv ; **2,** *too powerful, too great*, (legio) consularibus nimia, Tac **B.** Transf , *very large, excessively large*, nimium quantum, *to an extraordinary degree*, sales in dicendo nimium quantum valent, Cic **II** Subst , *excess, too much* nimium dixisse, Cic , nimium hostium, Liv **III.** Adv , **A.** nimio, *by far, very much, exceedingly* esp with compar , Albi, ne doleas plus nimio, Hor **B.** nimium, *too, too much*, nimium diu, *too long*, Cic , non nimium, *not particularly*, Cic

ningo (ningŭo), ninxi, 3 (nix), *to snow* **1,** usually impers , ningit, *it snows*, Verg , **2,** transf , ningunt floribus rosarum, Lucr

ninguis -is, f *snow*, Lucr

Nĭnus -i, (Νίνος) **I** m *king of Assyria, husband of Semiramis* **II.** f *Nineveh, the capital of Assyria*

Nĭŏbē -ēs, f and **Nĭŏba** -ae, f (Νιόβη), *daughter of Tantalus, wife of Amphion* Hence, adj , **Nĭŏbēus** -a -um, *of Niobe.*

Niphātes -ae, m. (Νιφάτης, *the snow-mountain*), *a mountain of the Taurus range in Armenia.*

Nīrĕus, acc. Nirĕa, m. (Νιρεύς), *son of Charopus, next to Achilles the most beautiful of all the Greek heroes at the siege of Troy.*

Nīsaeus, Niseis, Niseius, v. 1. Nisus.

nĭsi, conj. (for nī-si). **I.** *if not;* quod nisi esset, certe postea non discessisset, Cic. **II. A.** After negatives and questions, *except, unless;* hoc sentio, nisi in bonis, amicitiam non posse, Cic.; Labienus juravit se, nisi victorem, in castra non reversurum, Cic.; after nihil aliud, quid aliud, etc., nisi = *than, but;* erat historia nihil aliud nisi annalium confectio, Cic. **B.** nisi si, *except if, except in case that;* nisi si qui ad me plura scripsit, Cic.; nisi quod, *except that;* praedia me valde delectant, nisi quod illum aere alieno obruerunt, Cic.

Nĭsĭbis, acc. -in, f. (Νίσιβις), *capital of the province of Mygdonia in Mesopotamia.*

1. **Nīsus** -i, m. **I.** *king in Megara, father of Scylla, changed into a sparrow-hawk.* Hence, adj., **A. Nīsaeus** -a -um, *of Nisus;* canes (of Scylla, the daughter of Phorcus, confused with Scylla, daughter of Nisus), Ov. **B. Nīsĭăs** -ădis, f. = *Megarian,* Ov. **C. Nīsēĭs** -idis, f. *Scylla, daughter of Nisus.* **D. Nīsēĭus** -a -um, *of or relating to Nisus;* virgo, *Scylla,* Ov. **II.** *the friend of Euryalus* (*in Vergil's Aeneid*).

2. **nīsus (nixus)** -ūs, m. (1. nitor). **I.** *a step, tread;* stat gravis Entellus nisuque immotus eodem, *in the same posture,* Verg. **II. 1,** *an ascent;* nisus per saxa, Sall.; **2,** *flight,* Verg.; **3,** *the course of the stars,* Cic.; **4,** *the pains of labour, a giving birth,* Cic.

3. **nīsus** -a -um, v. 1. nitor.

nītēdŭla -ae, f. *a field-mouse, shrew-mouse,* Cic.

nītella = nitedula (q.v.).

1. **nĭtens** -entis, p. adj. (from niteo). **I. 1,** *shining, bright, glittering;* lacrimis oculos suffusa nitentes, Verg.; **2,** of animals, taurus, *sleek,* Verg.; **3,** of men, *bright, beautiful,* Cat.; **4,** of plants, *blooming;* nitentia culta, Verg. **II.** Fig., *brilliant;* oratio, Cic.

2. **nĭtens** -entis, partic. of nitor.

nĭtĕo -ŭi, 2. (nix), *to shine, glitter, be bright.* **I. A.** Lit., luna nitet, Lucr.; qui nitent unguentis, fulgent purpurā, Cic. **B.** Fig., *to be brilliant;* illorum vides quam niteat oratio, Cic. **II.** Transf., **1,** of men and animals, *to be sleek, appear in good condition, look bright or beautiful,* Hor.; **2,** of things, *to abound, to flourish;* vectigal in pace niteat, Cic.

nĭtesco, 3. (niteo), *to begin to shine, to be bright.* **I.** juventus nudatos humeros oleo perfusa nitescit, Verg. **II.** Of animals, *to be sleek, in good condition,* Plin.

nĭtĭdē, adv. (nitidus), *brilliantly, splendidly;* cenare, Plaut.

nĭtĭdĭuscŭlē, adv. (nitidiusculus), *somewhat splendidly, with moderate brilliance,* Plaut.

nĭtĭdĭuscŭlus -a -um (dim. of compar. nitidior), *somewhat splendid, somewhat brilliant,* Plaut.

nĭtĭdus -a -um (niteo), *bright, brilliant, shining, glittering.* **I. A.** Lit., ebur, Ov. **B.** Transf., **a,** of animals, *sleek, fat, in good condition;* vacca, Ov.; **b,** of men, (α) *sleek, healthy-looking;* me pinguem et nitidum bene curatā cute vises, Hor.; robur, Liv.; (β) *handsome, spruce, trim, elegant;* quos pexo capillo nitidos videtis, Cic.; ex nitido fit rusticus, Hor.; **c,** of fields and plants, *flourishing, blooming, luxuriant;* campi, Cic. **II.** Fig., *elegant, refined, polished, cultivated;* nitidum quoddam genus verborum et laetum, Cic.

Nitiobrīges -um, m. *a Celtic people in Aquitania.*

1. **nītor,** nisus or nixus sum, 3. dep. *to rest, lean, support oneself upon anything.* **I.** Gen., **A.** Lit., stirpibus suis, Cic.; hastili, Cic.; baculo, Ov.; in hastam, Verg. **B.** Transf., **1,** *to rest upon, depend upon;* in te nititur civitatis salus, Cic.; **2,** *to confide in, put one's trust in, lean upon;* consilio alicuius, Cic. **II. A.** Lit., **1,** *to tread, move;* simul ac primum niti possunt, Cic.; **2,** *to give birth to, bring forth,* Ov.; **3,** *to make an effort,* Caes.; **4,** of birds or winged creatures, *to fly,* Verg.; **5,** *to climb, ascend, push up towards a height;* gradibus, Verg. **B.** Transf., *to strain, strive, exert oneself, endeavour;* tantum, quantum potest, quisque nitatur, Cic.; pro libertate, Sall.; ad immortalitatem gloriae, Cic.; with acc. and infin., nitamur igitur nihil posse percipi, Cic.; with ut or ne and the subj., Nep., Sall.

2. **nĭtor** -ōris, m. (niteo), *brilliance, brightness, splendour.* **I.** Lit., diurnus, *daylight,* Ov.; argenti et auri, Ov.; *elegance, charm, beauty,* Cic.; urit me Glycerae nitor, Hor. **II.** Fig., *splendour, elegance of style;* orationis, Cic.; nitor et cultus descriptionum, Tac.

nĭtrum -i, n. (νίτρον), *natron, natural soda,* used for washing, ap. Cic.

nĭvālis -e (nix), *of or relating to snow, snowy.* **I. A.** Lit., dies, Liv. **B.** Meton., *snow-white;* equi candore nivali, Verg. **II.** *covered with snow;* Othrys, Verg.

nĭvātus -a -um (nix), *cooled with snow, iced,* Suet.

1. **nĭvĕ** = ni (q.v.).

2. **nĭvĕ** = neve (q.v.).

nĭvĕus -a -um (nix), *of or relating to snow, snowy.* **I.** Lit., agger, Verg.; mons, *covered with snow,* Cat. **II.** Meton., *white as snow, snowy;* lacerti, Verg.; lac, Verg.

nĭvōsus -a -um (nix), *abounding in snow, snowy;* grando, Liv.; hiems, Liv.

nix, nivis, f. (* νίψ, acc. νίφα). **I.** Lit., *snow,* Cic. **II.** = *grey hair;* nives capitis, Hor.

Nixi dii, *three images of gods in a kneeling position in the Capitol at Rome, invoked as the deities of child-birth.*

nixor, 1. dep. (intens. of nitor), *to lean upon, rest upon, to strive, strain,* Lucr., Verg.

1. **nixus** = 2. nisus (q.v.).

2. **nixus,** v. 1. nitor.

no, nāvi, nāre (νέω), *to swim.* **I.** Lit., bestiae nantes, Cic.; prov., nare sine cortice, *to be able to do without a guardian,* Hor. **II.** Transf., *to sail, float, flow, fly,* Verg., Cat.

nōbĭlis -e (nosco), *noticeable, well-known.* **I.** Gen., inimicitiae nobiles inter eos erant, Liv. **II. A.** *celebrated, renowned, well-known;* ex doctrina, Cic.; ut arcendis sceleribus exemplum nobile esset, Liv.; in a bad sense, *infamous, notorious;* nobilis clade Romanā Caudina pax, Liv. **B.** *of noble birth, noble, belonging to a family some members of which had held curule magistracies* (opp. novus or ignobilis), Cic.; nobili genere nati, Cic.; homo, Cic. **C.** *excellent, noble;* tres nobilissimi fundi, Cic.

nōbĭlĭtas -ātis, f. (nobilis). **I.** *fame, celebrity,* Cic. **II.** *noble birth, nobility;* genere et nobilitate sui municipii facile primus, Cic.; meton., *the aristocrats, the nobility;* omnis nostra nobilitas interiit, Caes. **III.** *excellence, worth, superiority;* signa summā nobilitate, Cic.

nōbĭlĭtĕr, adv (nobilis), *excellently, admirably, nobly*, Plin

nōbĭlĭto, 1 (nobilis), *to make known*. **I.** Gen, rem, Liv. **II.** *to make famous, renowned*, **a**, in a good sense, poetae post mortem nobilitari volunt, Cic, **b**, in a bad sense, *to make infamous, notorious;* Phalaris, cuius est praeter ceteros nobilitata crudelitas, Cic

nŏcens -entis, p adj (from noceo) **I.** Gen., *hurtful, injurious, noxious*, caules, Cic **II.** Esp, *culpable, criminal, guilty, wicked*, homo, Cic, subst. nocens, *a guilty person*, Cic.

nŏcĕo -ŭi -ĭtum, 2 *to hurt, injure, harm*, with dat, alteri, Cic; with dat and neut. acc, nihil iis, Caes., with acc. and infin, nocet esse deum, Ov., pass impers., ne quid eis noceatur, Cic

nŏcīvus -a -um (noceo), *hurtful, injurious*, Phaedr.

noctĭfĕr -fĕri, m (nox and fero), *the night bringer*, i e, *the Evening Star*, Cat

noctĭlūca -ae, f (nox and luceo, *something that shines by night*), *the moon*, Hor.

noctĭvăgus -a -um (nox and vagus), *wandering by night*, currus (of the moon), Verg.

noctū (another form of nocte), **a**, abl, hac noctu, Plaut., **b**, adv *by night, in the night* (opp interdiu, *by day*), Cic.

noctŭa -ae, f (*noctuus from nox), *the owl*, Verg

noctŭābundus -a -um (*noctuor from nox), *travelling by night*, tabellarius, Cic

noctŭīnus -a -um (noctua), *of* or *relating to the owl*, Plaut

nocturnus -a -um (noctu), *by night, nightly, nocturnal*, labores diurnos nocturnosque suscipere, Cic, fur, Cic, lupus, *preying by night*, Verg; Bacchus, *worshipped at night*, Verg, subst, **Nocturnus** -i, m *the god of night*, Plaut.

nŏcŭus -a -um (noceo), *hurtful, injurious*, Ov

nōdo, 1 (nodus), *to knot, tie in a knot* **I.** Lit, crines in aurum, Verg. **II.** Transf, *to fetter*, collum laqueo nodatus amator, Ov

nōdōsus a um (nodus), *full of knots, knotty* **I.** Lit, lina, *nets*, Ov **II.** Fig, *knotty, full of difficulties*, Sen, transf, Cicuta, *a usurer, cunning in ensnaring debtors*, Hor

nōdus -i, m *a knot* **I. A.** Lit, Cic **B.** Meton, **a**, *a girdle* Verg, anni, *the equator*, Lucr, **b**, *the knot into which the hair was sometimes collected*, Ov **C.** Fig, **1**, *a tie, bond, connexion*, amicitiae, Cic, **2**, **a**, *a bond, obligation, fetter*, exsolvere animos nodis religionum, Lucr, **b**, *a difficulty, entanglement, perplexity*, dum hic nodus expediatur, Cic **II.** Transf, **1**, *a knot or knob on the joint of an animal*, crura sine nodis articulisque habere, Caes, **2**, *a knot in the wood of plants*, Verg, Liv, **3**, *a star in the constellation Pisces*, Cic poet

Nōla -ae, f *a town in Campania*, now *Nola* Hence, adj, **Nōlānus** a -um, *belonging to Nola*, subst, **Nōlāni** ōrum, m *the inhabitants of Nola*, subst, in Nolano, *in the territory of Nola*, Cic

nōlo, nōlŭi, nolle (ne and volo). **I** *to be unwilling, not to wish*, with acc, quae etiamsi nolunt, Cic, with acc and infin, nolo enim, eundem populum imperatorem esse et portitorem terrarum, Cic, pluribus praesentibus eas res jactari nolebat, Caes, with infin, alienare nolui, Cic, with subj, nolo accusator in judicium potentiam afferat, Cic, the imper, noli, nolite, nolito, is frequently used with the infin. of another verb to form a periphrastic imper, noli putare, *don't imagine*, Cic; velle, Liv.; nollem, *I could wish not*, Carthaginem et Numantiam funditus sustulerunt, nollem Corinthum, Cic **II.** *to wish evil, to be unfavourable to;* alicui, Cic

Nŏmăs -ădis, c (νομάς), *pasturing*, hence, **1**, plur, Nomades, *nomads, nations who lead a migratory, pastoral life*, Plin, **2**, *the Numidians*, Verg

nōmen -ĭnis, n (from root GNO, whence nosco), *a name* **I. A.** Lit, gen, **1**, nomen est quod unicuique personae datur, quo suo quaeque proprio et certo vocabulo appellatur, Cic, imponere nova rebus nomina, Cic, appellare aliquem nomine, Cic, cantus cui nomen neniae, Cic.; nomen dare, Cic, edere, profiteri, Liv, *to give in one's name as a soldier, enlist*, Liv, **2**, esp, *the gentile name of a Roman*, as e g, Cornelius in P Cornelius Scipio, though sometimes used for the praenomen (Publius) or the cognomen (Scipio), Cic, **3**, meton, **a**, nomina tanta (like our *great names = great men*), Ov; **b**, nomen Romanum, *the Roman power* **B.** Fig, **1**, *name, fame, glory*, nomen habere, Cic, **2**, **a**, *name, cause*, nomine meo, tuo, *in my name, on my behalf*, Cic, nomine lucri, *for the sake of*, Cic, uno nomine, *at once*, accusati sunt uno nomine consulares, Cic, **b**, *ground, pretext;* nomen inductum fictae religionis, Cic, **3**, *the name* (as opposed to the thing), legionum, *the mere name*, Cic **II.** Transf, polit t t, **1**, nomen alicuius deferre, *to give information against, accuse judicially*, Cic., nomen recipere, *to receive an information*, Cic; **2**, *a security for a debt*, certis nominibus, *on good security*, Cic, nomina solvere, exsolvere, expedire, *to pay a debt*, Cic, nomina sua exigere, *to collect one's debts*, Cic, nomen facere, *to set down a debt in the account-book, to lend money*, Cic, meton, *a debtor*, bonum nomen, *a good payer*, Cic.

nōmenclātĭo -ōnis, f (*nomenclo, from nomen and calo = voco), *a calling by name, naming*, Qu Cic

nōmenclātor -ōris, m (*nomenclo), *a slave who told his master the names of his clients at his reception, or of the persons whom he met in the streets*, Cic

Nōmentum -i, n *a town fourteen miles north east of Rome* Hence, adj, **Nōmentānus** -a -um, *of* or *belonging to Nomentum*

nōmĭnātim, adv (nomino) *by name, expressly, particularly*, centuriones nominatim appellare, Caes, de aliquo nominatim decernere ut, etc., Cic

nōmĭnātĭo -ōnis, f (nomino), *a naming, nomination to a priesthood or other public office*, Cic

nōmĭnātus a -um, p adj (from nomino), *well known, noted, celebrated*, Cic

nōmĭnĭto, 1 (intens of nomino), *to name, call by name*, Lucr

nōmĭno, 1 (nomen) **I.** *to name, give a name to*, amore quo amicitia est nominata, Cic **II.** *to mention, speak about*, ad flumen Sabim quod supra nominavimus, Cic, Sulla quem honoris causā nomino, *whom I mention to do him honour*, Cic **III. A.** *to make famous, make renowned*, praedicari de se et nominari volunt omnes, Cic **B.** Polit t t, **a**, *to name, appoint, nominate to a priesthood or other office*, me augurem nominaverunt, Cic, **b**, *to accuse judicially, give information against*, aliquem apud dictatorem, Liv

Nŏmĭus (-ŏs) -ĭi, m (Νόμιος), *the pasturer, a name of Apollo (from his having fed the flocks of Admetus)*

nŏmisma (nūmisma) -mătis, n (νόμισμα), *a coin, a piece of money*, Hor

nōn, adv. (from old Latin noenum = ne unum). **I.** *not.* **A.** non est ita, judices, non est profecto, Cic.; before negatives, non forms a weak affirmative, e.g., non nihil, non nemo, non nullus, Cic.; after negatives the affirmative thus formed is emphatic, nihil non ad rationem dirigebat, Cic.; with affirmative adjectives the negative formed by non is emphatic, *by no means;* Cethegus homo non probatissimus, Cic.; homo non aptissimus ad jocandum, Cic.; non quod, non quo, *not that, not as if;* non quod sola ornent, sed quod excellant, Cic.; non nisi, *only;* non modum (solum), *not only,* Cic.; non ita, non tam, *not very, not particularly;* simulacra perampla, sed non ita antiqua, Cic. **B. 1,** non in questions = nonne? non idem fecit? Cic.; **2,** poet. = ne, non petito, Ov. **II.** Used in answers, *no;* aut etiam aut non respondere, Cic.

Nōnācris -is, f. (Νώνακρις), *a mountain in Arcadia.* Hence, adj., **1, Nōnācrīnus** -a -um, *Arcadian;* virgo, *Callisto,* Ov.; **2, Nōnācrĭus** -a -um, *Arcadian;* heros, *Evander,* Ov.; subst., **Nōnācrĭa** -ae, f. = *Atalanta,* Ov.

nōnae -ārum, f. (nonus), *the nones, the fifth day in all the months* (except March, May, and July, when it was the seventh), *so called from being the ninth day before the Ides.*

nōnāgēnārĭus -a -um (nonageni), *containing ninety,* Plin.

nōnāgēni -ae -a (nonaginta), *ninety each,* Plin.

nōnāgēsĭmus -a -um (nonaginta), *the ninetieth;* Cic.

nōnāgĭēs, adv. (nonaginta), *ninety times,* Cic.

nōnāginta, numer. *ninety,* Cic.

nōnānus -a -um (nona, sc. legio), *belonging to the ninth legion;* miles, Tac.; or subst., **nōnānus** -i, m. *a soldier of the ninth legion,* Tac.

nondum, adv. *not yet,* Cic.

nongenti -ae -a, *nine hundred,* Cic.

nonnĕ, interrog. adv., asks a question to which an affirmative answer is expected: **1,** in direct questions, nonne animadvertis? *do you not perceive?* Cic.; **2,** in indirect questions, quaero nonne id effecerit, Cic.

nonnēmo, nonnĭhil, v. nemo, nihil.

nonnullus (non nullus) -a -um, *some, several;* nonnulla in re, *in some respects,* Cic.; nonnulla pars militum, Caes.; non nullae cohortes, Caes.; subst., **nonnulli**, *some,* Cic.

nonnumquam (non numquam), adv. *sometimes,* Cic.

nonnusquam, adv. *in some places, in several places,* Plin.

nōnus -a -um (= novenus, from novem), *the ninth,* Cic.; subst., **nōna** -ae, f. *the ninth hour* (about three o'clock p.m.), when the chief meal (cena) was taken at Rome, Hor.

nōnusdĕcĭmus, nonadecima, nonumdecimum, *the nineteenth,* Tac.

Nōra -ōrum, n. **I.** *a town in Sardinia;* hence, **Nōrenses** -ium, *the inhabitants of Nora.* **II.** *a fort in Cappadocia.*

Norba -ae, f. *a town in Latium,* now *Alcantara.* Hence, adj., **Norbānus** -a -um, *of or belonging to Norba.*

Nōrēja -ae, f. *a town in Noricum,* now *Neumarkt.*

Nōrĭcum -i, n. *Noricum, a country south of the Danube.* Hence, adj., **Nōrĭcus** -a -um, *Noric.*

norma -ae, f. (nosco), **1,** *a carpenter's square for measuring right angles,* Plin.; **2,** *a rule, precept, model, pattern;* dirigere vitam ad certam rationis normam, Cic.

nōs, plur. of ego (q.v.).

Nortĭa -ae, f. (for Nevortia, from ne and vorto, Gk. Ἄτροπος, *the Unchangeable*), *an Etruscan goddess of fate, worshipped at Volsinii.*

noscĭto, 1. (intens. of nosco), *to get to know.* **I.** Lit., **A.** Gen., *to observe, perceive,* Liv. **B.** Esp., *to investigate, explore;* aedes, vestigia, Plaut. **II.** Transf., *to recognise again;* aliquem facie, Liv.

nosco, nōvi, nōtum, 3. (root NO, archaic GNO, whence gnosco; Gr. ΓΝΟ -Ω, whence γιγνώσκω). **I.** Lit., *to become acquainted with, get knowledge of;* and hence, in the perfect tenses, *to be acquainted with, to know;* (α) present tenses, studeo cursos istos mutationum noscere, Cic.; (β) perfect tenses, quam (virtutem) tu ne de facie quidem nosti, Cic.; si Caesarem bene novi, Cic. **II. A.** *to recognise;* ad res suas noscendas recipiendasque, Liv. **B.** Of a judge, *to investigate a case;* quae olim a praetoribus noscebantur, Tac. **C.** *to allow, admit, acknowledge a reason or excuse;* illam partem excusationis nec nosco, nec probo, Cic. (contracted perfect tenses, nosti, nostis, noram, noras, nosse).

noster -tra -trum (nos), *our, ours.* **I.** Gen., **a,** subject., provincia nostra, Caes.; **b,** object. (= *towards us*) amor noster, Cic. **II.** Esp., **A.** *our, our adherent or friend, on our side, one of us;* **a,** Furnius noster, *our friend Furnius,* Cic.; nostri, *our people,* Cic.; **b,** noster in jest = ego, Plaut. **B.** *favourable to us;* nostra loca, Liv.; noster Mars, Verg.

nostras -ātis (noster), *of our country, native;* mirifice capior facetiis, maxime nostratibus, Cic.; philosophi, Cic.

nŏta -ae, f. (nosco), *a mark, token, note, sign.* **I.** Gen., **1,** lit., signa et notae locorum, Cic.; **2,** fig., *distinguishing mark, sign;* notae argumentorum, Cic. **II. A.** *marks in writing;* **1,** *letters of the alphabet, numbers;* notae litterarum, Cic.; poet., meton., notae, *a writing, letter,* Hor., Ov.; **2,** notae librariorum, *marks of punctuation,* Cic. **B.** *marks on an object;* **1,** *marks on the body,* Hor.; **2,** *a branded mark, brand;* barbarus compunctus notis Thraeciis, *tattooed,* Cic.; fig., *disgrace, shame, ignominy;* quae nota domesticae turpitudinis non inusta vitae tuae est? Cic.; **3,** *a mark on a cask of wine or honey* (to mark the quality); **a,** interior nota Falerni, *a better kind,* Hor.; **b,** transf., *sort, quality;* aliquem de meliore nota commendare, Cic.; **4,** *a mark in a book* (to express approval or disapproval), Cic.; **5,** *the official censure of the senate;* motis senatu notas ascribere, Liv.; **6,** *a distinguishing name, mark of honour;* ille Numantina traxit ab urbe notam, Ov.

nŏtābĭlis -e (noto), *notable, remarkable, striking noteworthy;* exitus, Cic.

nŏtābĭlĭtĕr, adv. (notabilis), *notably, remarkably, extraordinarily,* Tac.

nŏtārĭus -ii, m. (nota), *a rapid writer, shorthand writer,* Quint.

nŏtātĭo -ōnis, f. (noto), *a marking.* **I.** Lit., tabellarum, *a marking of the voting-tickets with different coloured wax,* Cic. **II. 1,** *the stigma of the censor;* censoria, Cic.; **2,** *a choice;* judicum, Cic.; **3,** *the etymology of a word;* Cic.; **4,** *observing, noting, taking notice of;* naturae, Cic.

nŏtātus -a -um, p. adj. (from noto), *known, marked;* homo omnium scelerum libidinumque notis notatissimus, Cic.

nōtesco, nōtui, 3. (1. notus), *to become known,* Cat.

nŏthus -a -um (νόθος). **I.** Lit., **1,** of men, *illegitimate, bastard,* Verg.; **2,** of animals, *of mixed breed, hybrid, mongrel,* Verg. **II.** Transf., *not genuine, spurious,* Lucr., Cat.

nōtio -ōnis, f (nosco), *a making oneself acquainted with anything.* **I. 1**, lit, Plaut, **2**, transf, *an idea, notion of anything, image, mental conception*, deorum, Cic, rerum, Cic **II. A.** *an investigation*, pontificum, Cic **B.** *the investigation of the censor*, **1**, judicium et notio censoria, Cic; **2**, *the blame, animadversion of the censor*, notiones animadversionesque censorum, Cic

nōtitia -ae, f (1 notus), *a being known* **I.** Pass, **1**, hi propter notitiam sunt intromissi, Nep, **2**, *fame, celebrity*, Tac **II.** Act, **1**, *knowing, becoming acquainted with*, notitia nova mulieris, Cic.; **2**, **a**, *knowledge*, corporis sui, Cic, **b**, *an idea, notion, conception*, dei, Cic

nōtities -ēi, f. = notitia (q v)

nŏto, 1 (nota) **I.** *to mark* **A.** Lit, **1**, tabellam cerā, Cic, **2**, **a**, *to mark out*, notat et designat oculis ad caedem unumquemque nostrum, Cic, **b**, polit t. t, of the censor, *to place a mark against a Roman citizen's name in the burgess-list, to censure publicly, blame, reprimand*, quos censores furti et captarum pecuniarum nomine notaverunt, Cic **B.** Transf, **1**, *to mark, denote*, res nominibus, Cic, aliquid verbis Latinis, *to express*, Cic, **2**, *to mark out, make noticeable*, aliquem decore, Cic, **3**, *to blame, censure*, verbis aliquem, Cic **II.** *to express by signs.* **A. 1**, lit, *to unite*, litteram, Ov; **2**, **a**, *to point out shortly*, caput, Cic.; **b**, *to observe*, cantus avium, Cic. **B.** Fig, *to impress*, dicta memori pectore, Ov

nŏtŏs = 2 notus (q v)

1 **nōtus** -a -um, p adj (from nosco), *known* **I. 1**, lit, res nota, Cic, noti atque insignes latrones, Cic., aliquid notum habere, *to know*, Cic, subst., noti, *friends, acquaintances*, **2**, transf, **a**, = *friendly*; notis compellat vocibus, Verg., **b**, *customary*; ulmus nota quae sedes fuerat columbis, Hor **II. 1**, *distinguished, celebrated*; scriptor, Hor, **2**, *notorious*, mulier, Cic.

2 **nŏtus** (**ŏs**) -i, m (νότος), *the south wind*, **1**, lit, Verg, **2**, transf, *the wind*, Verg

nŏvācŭla -ae, f (novo), *a sharp knife* or *razor*, cotem novaculā praecidere, Cic

nŏvālis -is, f and **nŏvāle** is, n **1**, *fallow land*, Verg, **2**, *a cultivated field*; novalia culta, Verg

nŏvātrix icis, f (novator), *she that renews*, rerum, Ov

nŏvē, adv (novus) **I.** *newly, in a new and unusual manner*, Plaut. **II.** novissime: **a**, *lately, recently*, Sall, **b**, *lastly, in the last place*, Sall, Liv

nŏvellus -a -um (dim of novus), **a**, *new, young*, arbor, Cic., **b**, oppida, *lately conquered*, Liv

nŏvem, numer *nine*, Cic; decem novem, *nineteen*, Caes

Nŏvember -bris, m (novem and suffix -ber), *relating to the number nine*, **a**, mensis November, *the ninth month of the Roman year, November*, Cic., **b**, *belonging to the month of November*, kalendae Novembres, Cic

nŏvemdĕcim, numer (novem and decem) *nineteen*, Liv

nŏvendĭālis e (novem and dies), **1**, *that which happens on the ninth day*, coena, *a funeral banquet held on the ninth day after death*, Tac., pulveres = *new, fresh*, Hor, **2**, *that which lasts nine days*, feriae, *a nine days' festival celebrated on the occasion of any portent* (such as a shower of stones), Cic

Nŏvensĭles dii (novus and suffix -ensilis), *gods whose worship had been introduced from foreign countries* (opp indigetes, *native divinities*), Liv

nŏvēnus -a -um (novem), *nine each, nine*, Liv

nŏverca ae, f *a step-mother*, Cic, saeva, Verg; prov, apud novercam queri, i e, *in vain*, Plaut

nŏvercālis -e (noverca), *of* or *relating to a step-mother*, Juv, Tac

Nŏvesium -ii, n *fort of the Ubii on the Rhine*, now *Neuss*

nŏvĭcius -a -um (novus), *new, fresh*, Plaut, esp of *persons who have not long been enslaved*, subst, novicii, Syrum nescio quem de grege noviciorum factum esse consulem, Cic

nŏviēs, adv numer (novem), *nine times*, Verg

Nŏvĭŏdūnum -i, n, **1**, *a town of the Suessiones*, now *Soissons*, **2**, *a town of the Bituriges Cubi*, now *Nouan*

nŏvĭtas -ātis, f (novus), *newness* **I.** Lit **A.** anni, *the spring*, Ov, plur, novitates = *new acquaintances*, Cic **B.** *the condition of a* homo novus (v novus), *newness of nobility*, Cic **II.** *novelty, unusualness, strangeness*, terror quem tibi rei novitas attulerit, Cic.

nŏvo, 1 (novus) **I.** *to make new, renew* **A.** transtra, Verg., membra, *to revive*, Ov, ager novatus, *a field reploughed*, Cic **B.** Transf, **a**, *to revive, refresh*, (animus) risu novatur, Cic, **b**, *to change, alter*, aliquid in legibus Cic; novare res, *to alter the constitution of a state, make a revolution*, Liv **II.** *to invent something new*, verba, *invent new words*, Cic

nŏvus -a -um (νέος), superl, novissimus, *new, fresh, young* (opp vetus) **I** Lit, **A.** Gen miles, *a recruit*, Liv.; novae res, *novelties*, Cic, and esp, *political changes, revolutions*; rebus novis studere, Cic, lac, *new milk*, Verg, Subst, **nŏvum** -i, n *a new thing, novelty*, num quidnam novi? Cic **B.** Esp, **a**, novus homo or homo novus, *the first of a family who held a curule office in Rome*, e g, M T. Cicero, Cic, **b**, novae tabulae, *new account-books* (that is, *a total extinction of debts*), Cic, **c**, novae tabernae, or novae, *certain money-changers' shops in the forum which had been burnt down* A U C. 543, *and rebuilt*, sub Novis, Cic, **d**, Nova via, *a road in Rome leading down to the forum*, Liv **II.** Transf, **1**, *fresh, inexperienced*, equus, Cic, novus delictis, *inexperienced in crime*, Tac **2**, *new, novel, unusual, extraordinary*, genus dicendi, Cic, **3**, = alter, *a second*, Camillus, *a second Camillus*, Liv, novus Hannibal, Cic, **4**, of succession, the superl, **nŏvissimus** a um = (α) *the latest, last*, agmen, *the rear*, Caes, (β) *the extremest, severest*, exempla, Tac

nox, noctis, f (νύξ), *night* **I. A.** Lit, **1**, gen, nocte, or de nocte, *by night*, Cic, multā nocte, de multa nocte, *deep in the night, late at night* Cic, nocte mediā, de nocte media, *at midnight* Cic, noctes et dies urgeri, *night and day*, Cic., se conjicere in noctem, *to hasten away under shelter of night*, Cic, eam noctem pervigilare, Cic, **2**, personif, Nox, *the goddess Night, sister of Erebus*, Verg **B** Transf, **1**, meton, *sleep*, Verg, **2**, **a**, *the darkness of a storm*, Verg, **b**, *the lower world*, Verg; **c**, *death*, Verg, **d**, *blindness*, Ov **II.** Fig, **1**, *obscurity*, mei versus aliquantum noctis habebunt, Ov, **2**, *confusion, darkness, peril*, haec reipublicae nox, Cic

noxa ae, f, (noceo) **I.** *harm, injury, damage*; sine ullius urbis noxa, Liv **II.** Meton, **1**, *a crime, fault, offence*, in noxa esse, Liv., **2**, *punishment*, noxā liberari, Liv

noxia -ae, f. (sc causa, from noxius), *a fault, offence, crime*, alicui noxiae esse, *to be accounted a fault* Liv

noxĭus -a -um (noxa). **I.** *noxious, hurtful, injurious;* tela, Ov. **II.** *criminal, culpable, guilty;* aliquem noxium judicare, Liv.

nūbēcŭla -ae, f. (dim. of nubes). **I.** *a little cloud,* Plin. **II.** Fig., *a troubled, dark expression;* frontis, Cic.

nūbes -is, f. (cf. nubo), *a cloud.* **I. A.** Lit., aer concretus in nubes cogitur, Cic. **B.** Transf., 1, *a cloud,* e.g., of dust, pulveris, Liv.; **2,** *a great number, dense mass of any objects;* locustarum, Liv.; volucrum, Verg. **II.** Fig., 1, *a cloud,* or *dark expression on the countenance;* deme supercilio nubem, Hor.; **2,** *veil, concealment;* fraudibus objice nubem, Hor.; **3,** *a cloud,* i.e., *threatening* or *impending misfortune;* belli, Verg.; **4,** *a sad, miserable condition;* reipublicae, Cic.; **5,** *a cloud* (as emblem of something unsubstantial), *a phantom;* nubes et inania captare, Hor.

nūbĭfĕr -fĕra -fĕrum (nubes and fero), *cloud-bearing, cloud-bringing,* Ov.

nūbĭgĕna -ae, c. (nubes and gigno), *born of a cloud, produced from a cloud;* esp., of the Centaurs, *offspring of Ixion and a cloud;* Nubigenae alone = *Centaurs,* Verg.

nūbĭlis -e (nubo), *marriageable;* filia, Cic.

nūbĭlus -a -um (nubes), *covered with clouds, cloudy, overcast.* **I. A.** Lit., plur. subst., **nūbĭla** -ōrum, n. *clouds,* Hor. **B.** Transf., 1, act., *cloud-bringing;* Auster, Ov.; **2,** *dark;* via nubila taxo, Ov. **II.** Fig., **1,** of expression, *dark, gloomy;* toto nubila vultu, Ov.; **2,** *unfavourable;* nubila nascenti non mihi Parca fuit, Ov.; **3,** *dark, unhappy;* tempora, Ov.

nūbo, nupsi, nuptum, 3. (stem NUB, whence nubes), *to cover, veil;* and especially, of a bride, *to be married to, to marry any one;* virgo nupsit ei, cui Caecilia nupta fuerat, Cic.; nuptam esse cum aliquo, Cic.; nubere in familiam, *to marry into a family,* Cic.; aliquam nuptum collocare, *to give in marriage,* Caes.; partic., **nuptus** -a -um, *married;* filia, Cic.; subst., **nupta** -ae, f. *a wife,* Liv.

Nūcĕrĭa -ae, f. *a town in Campania,* now *Nocera.* Hence, adj., **Nūcĕrīnus** -a -um, *relating to Nuceria.*

nŭcĭfrangĭbŭlum -i, n. (nux and frango), *a nut-cracker* (in jest = *a tooth*), Plaut.

nŭclĕus -i, m. (nux). **I.** Lit., 1, *the kernel of a nut,* or *any nut-like fruit,* Plin.; **2,** *the stone* or *uneatable kernel of fruits,* Plin. **II.** Transf., *the kernel* or *inside of anything;* conchae, Plin.

nūdĭus = nunc dius (= dies), *it is now the . . . day since;* always with the ordinal numerals; nudius tertius, *the day before yesterday,* Cic.; nudius tertius decimus, *thirteen days ago,* Cic.

nūdo, 1. (nudus), *to make naked, to make bare, strip.* **I. A.** Lit., **1,** aliquem, Cic.; **2, a,** *to lay bare, uncover;* gladium, *to draw,* Liv.; murus nudatus defensoribus, Caes.; **b,** milit. t. t., *to lay bare, leave undefended;* castra nudentur, Caes. **B.** Transf., **1,** *to strip, make bare by robbery, to spoil, plunder;* spoliavit nudavitque omnia, Cic.; quem praeceps alea nudat, Hor.; **2,** *to deprive;* aliquem praesidio, Cic. **II.** Fig., **1,** *to strip, lay bare, expose;* nudata omnibus rebus tribunicia potestas, Caes.; vis ingenii scientiā juris nudata, Cic.; **2,** *to uncover, expose, make visible, reveal;* animos, Liv.

nūdus -a -um, *naked, unclothed, nude, bare.* **I. A.** Lit., **1,** Cic.; nudo capite, *bare-headed,* Sall.; **2,** *uncovered;* vertex, Verg.; subsellia, *vacant,* Cic.; terga, Liv. **B.** Transf., **1,** *deprived of;* with abl., praesidio, Cic.; with genit., loca nuda gignentium, Sall.; **2,** *without;* respublica nuda a magistratibus, Cic. **II.** Fig., **1,** *simple, unadorned, plain;* commentarii Caesaris, Cic.; **2,** *bare, mere, alone, only;* nuda ista, si ponas, Cic.; hoc nudum relinquitur, Cic.

nūgae -ārum, f. (naucum), *trifles, nonsense, stuff, trumpery.* **I.** Lit., huncecine hominem tantis delectatum esse nugis? Cic.; applied also to verses, nescio quid meditans nugarum, Hor. **II.** Transf., of persons, *a foolish, trifling fellow;* amicos habet meras nugas, Cic.

nūgātor -ōris, m. (nugor), *a trifler, foolish fellow, a jester,* Cic.

nūgātōrĭus -a -um (nugator), *trifling, good for nothing, frivolous, futile, nugatory;* mala nugatoriaque accusatio, Cic.

nūgax -ācis (nugor), *trifling, frivolous,* ap. Cic.

nūgor, 1. dep. (nugae), **1,** *to trifle, be frivolous, talk nonsense;* non inscite, Cic.; cum aliquo, Hor.; **2,** *to trick, cajole, make game of,* Plaut.

nullus -a -um (ne and ullus), *no, none, nobody, no one.* **I. A.** Lit., 1, adj., nullā unā re, Cic.; nullo modo, nullo pacto, *by no means,* Cic.; nullo certo ordine neque imperio, Caes.; **2,** subst., **a, nullus** = *nobody, no one,* Cic.; **b, nullum** -i, n. = *nothing,* Hor. **II.** Fig., **1,** nullus sum; **a,** *I am ruined, it is all over with me;* nullus repente fui, Liv.; **b,** of persons and things, *I am no longer in existence;* de mortuis loquor, qui nulli sunt, Cic.; nullus = mortuus, Ov.; vellera nulla, Ov.; **2,** *insignificant, of no importance, trifling, poor;* nullos judices habemus, Cic.; nullum argumentum est, Cic.

num, interrog. particle, asking a question to which a negative answer is expected. **A.** In direct questions, num censes etiam eosdem fuisse? Cic.; compounded with ne, deum ipsum numne vidisti? Cic.; num quid vis? *is there anything else which you want?* (a common form in leave-taking), Hor. **B.** In indirect questions, *whether;* quaero, num aliter ac nunc eveniunt evenirent? Cic.

Nŭma -ae, m., Pompilius, *the second king of Rome.*

Nŭmantĭa -ae, f. a *town in Hispania Tarraconensis, taken and destroyed by Scipio Africanus the younger.* Hence, adj., **Nŭmantīnus** -a -um, *Numantine.*

nŭmārĭus = nummarius (q.v.).

nŭmātus = nummatus (q.v.).

nūmen -ĭnis, n. (= nuimen, from nuo), *a nodding, beckoning with the head; a nod,* as sign of a command, *a command.* **I.** Gen., numen vestrum, Cic.; magnum numen senatūs, Cic. **II.** Esp., of a deity, **a,** *the divine will, divine command;* numen interdictumque deorum immortalium, Cic.; mundum censent regi numine deorum, Cic.; Jovis numina, Phoebi numina, Verg.; **b,** (α) *the might of a deity, majesty, divinity;* qui nullam vim esse dicit numenve divinum, Cic.; of deities themselves, conversa numina, pia numina, Verg.; (β) of the Roman emperors, violatum numen Augusti, Tac.

nŭmĕrābĭlis -e (numero), *that can be counted, enumerated,* Ov.

nŭmĕrātus -a -um, p. adj. (from numero), *counted, in hard cash, in ready money;* dos, pecunia, Cic.; subst., **nŭmĕrātum** -i, n. *hard cash, money down;* numerato solvere, Cic.

1. **nŭmĕro,** 1. (numerus), *to count.* **I.** Lit., **A.** aliquem a se primum, Cic.; aliquid per digitos, *on the fingers,* Ov.; consule et numera (senatum), *count the house* (with a view to determine whether a sufficient number to transact business were present), Cic. **B.** *to count,* i.e.,

to pay money, militibus stipendium, Cic. II. Transf, 1, to count up, reckon, enumerate, dies deficiat, si velim numerare, quibus bonis male evenerit, Cic, 2, to reckon under, class under; inter suos, Cic, inter honestos homines, Cic., mortem in beneficii loco, Cic., 3, with double acc, in pass with double nom, to count, esteem, hold, consider, Sulpicium accusatorem suum numerabat, non competitorem, Cic, sapientes cives, qualem me et esse, et numerari volo, Cic

2 **nŭmĕrō**, adv (lit, abl of numerus), 1, just, exactly, at the right time, Plaut; 2, quickly, soon, too quickly, too soon, Plaut

nŭmĕrōsē, adv (numerosus), 1, numerously, Plin, 2, rhythmically, harmoniously; circumscripte numeroseque dicere, Cic

nŭmĕrōsus -a -um (numerus) I. numerous, in great number, numerosissima civitas, populous, Tac II. rhythmical, harmonious, oratio, Cic.

nŭmĕrus -i, m. (connected with nummus), a number I. A. Lit, 1, numerum inire, to count, Caes; 2, a, a certain number, a number of persons or things, considered as a whole, ad pristinum numerum duo augures addidit, Cic, haec enim sunt tria numero, are three in number, Cic, numero quadraginta, forty in number, Sall, referre in deorum numero, to count as a god, Cic, b, an uncertain number, a heap, mass, hominum, Cic, innumerabilis frumenti numerus, an enormous quantity, Cic, c, a division of the army, company; sparsi per provinciam numeri, Tac, d, a cipher, i e, of no consequence, nos numerus sumus, Hor B. Meton, plur, numeri = 1, dice (as being marked with numbers), numerosque manu jactabit eburnos, Ov., 2, mathematics, Cic. II. Transf, 1, the part of a whole, elegans omni numero poema, in every respect, Cic; 2, a, melody, music, Verg, Ov, b, dance, Cic, c, a metrical foot, number, numeri ac modi Cic, poet, numeri graves, heroic verse, Ov, d, in oratory, harmony, oratorius, Cic, 3, rank, place, position, obtinere aliquem numerum, Cic., numero or in numero, in the post of, as, parentis numero esse, Cic, 4, order, rule, in numerum or numero, according to rule, Verg

Nŭmīcus (Nŭmīcĭus) -i, m a small river in Latium, flowing into the Tyrrhene sea near Ardea, now Numico

Nŭmĭda -ae, m. (nomas, νομάς), a Numidian, plur, **Nŭmĭdae** -ārum, the Numidians, attrib = Numidian Numidae jaculatores, Liv Hence, 1, **Nŭmĭdĭa** -ae, f a country in North Africa 2, **Nŭmĭdĭcus** a -um, Numidian

nŭmisma = nomisma (q v)

Nŭmistro -ōnis, f town in Lucania, on the borders of Apulia

Nŭmĭtor -ōris, m king of Alba, father of Ilia, grandfather of Romulus and Remus

nummārĭus -a -um (nummus). I. belonging to money, theca, Cic, difficultas nummaria or rei nummariae, scarcity of money, Cic II. bribed with money, venal, judex, Cic

nummātus -a -um (nummus), provided with money, rich, adolescens non minus bene nummatus quam capillatus, Cic

nummŭlus -i, m (dim of nummus), a little money, some money; nummulis acceptis jus ac fas omne delere, for a paltry sum, Cic.

nummus (nūmus) -i, m (νοῦμμος, Tarentine and Sicilian = νόμος, the regular silver currency) I. money, coin; adulterini nummi, bad money, Cic., habere in nummis, to have in cash, Cic II. Esp, the sesterce, a Roman coin worth about 2½d.; quinque milia nummum. Cic., transf., like the English penny, farthing (to express a very small sum), ad nummum convenit, it comes right to a farthing, Cic. (genit plur, gen nummum).

numquam, adv (ne and unquam), never, Cic, numquam adhuc, numquam ante, numquam alias, Cic, numquam non, always, Cic, non numquam, sometimes, Cic

nūmus = nummus (q v).

nunc, adv (νῦν) I. now, at present, at this moment, ut nunc est, as things are now, Cic, nunc ipsum, at this very moment, Cic, qui nunc sunt, the present generation, Cic, nunc . . . nunc, now now, at one time . at another, Liv II. but now, now however, Cic.

nunccĭne = nuncne?

nuncĭa = nuntia, v. nuntius.

nuncĭātĭo = nuntiatio (q v)

nuncĭo = nuntio.

nuncĭus = nuntius (q v)

nuncŭpātĭo -ōnis, f (nuncupo), a naming, the public offering or pronouncing of a vow, sollemnis nuncupatio votorum, Liv

nuncŭpo, 1 (nomine capio), to name, call by name I. aliquid nomine dei, Cic II. A. to pronounce solemnly and openly, a, vows, vota pro republica, Cic, b, an adoption, Tac B. to nominate as heir, heredem, Tac

nundĭnae, v nundinus

nundĭnātĭo -ōnis, f (nundinor), the holding of a market, trafficking, trade, business, fuit nundinatio aliqua, Cic

nundĭnor, 1 dep (nundinae) I. to transact business, trade, traffic A. Intransit, sedere nundinantem, Liv B. Transit., to buy, jus ab aliquo, Cic, totum imperium P. R, Cic II. Transf, to be present in great numbers (as at a market), ubi ad focum angues nundinari solent, Cic

nundĭnus a -um (lit., novendinus = novendinus, from novem and dies), belonging to the ninth day Subst, I. **nundĭnae** -ārum, f the market-day, held every ninth day, Cic; transf, a, the market place, illi Capuam nundinas rusticorum, horreum Campani agri esse voluerunt, Cic, b, traffic, trade, business, vectigalium flagitiosissimae nundinae, Cic II. **nundĭnum** -i n (sc tempus), the market time, trinum nundinum, the interval between one market-day and the next but one after (17-24 days), se praesentem trinum nundinum (on the three market days), petiturum, Cic, comitia in trinum nundinum indicere, Liv

nuntĭātĭo -ōnis, f (nuntio), religious t t, a declaration, announcement made by the augur of his observations, Cic

nuntĭo, 1 (nuntius), to announce, vera, Cic; qui nuntiarent prope omnes naves afflictas esse, Caes, oppugnata domus C Caesaris per multas noctis horas nuntiabatur, Cic with ut and the subj, paulo post ferunt nuntiatum Simonidi ut prodiret, Cic, absol, nuntiato, this being announced, Liv

nuntĭus -a -um (contr from noventius), announcing, bringing news I. Adj, rumor, Cic II. Subst, A. **nuntĭus** -ii, m. 1, messenger, announcer, facere aliquem certiorem per nuntium, Cic; 2, a, message, news, nuntium afferre, Cic, b, nuntium alicui remittere, to send one's wife a letter of divorce Cic transf, nuntium remittere virtuti, to renounce, Cic B. **nuntĭa** ae, f she that announces, historia nuntia veritatis, Cic C. **nuntĭum** -ii, n. message, news, Cat

nūpĕr, superl, **nūperrĭmē**, adv. (for

novper, from novus, *lately, not long ago;* qui nuper Romae fuit, Cic.; sometimes employed to denote a more distant period, nuper, id est, paucis ante seculis, Cic.

nupta -ae, f. (nubo), *a wife, spouse, bride*, Ov.

nuptĭae -ārum, f. (nubo), *marriage, nuptials;* Cornificia multarum nuptiarum, *often married*, Cic.; celebrare nuptias, Liv.; cenare apud aliquem in eius nuptiis, Cic.

nuptĭālis -e (nuptiae), *of* or *relating to a marriage;* cena, Liv.; donum, Cic.

nuptus -a -um (partic. of nubo), *married;* filia, mulier, Cic.

Nursĭa -ae, f. *a town in the west of the Sabine country*, now *Norcia*. Hence, adj., **Nursīnus** -a -um, *belonging to Nursia.*

nŭrus -ūs, f. (νυός), **1,** *a daughter-in-law, son's wife*, Cic.; **2,** poet., *a young matron, young married woman*, Ov.

nusquam, adv. (ne and usquam), *nowhere.* **I.** Lit., nusquam alibi, Cic. **II.** Transf., **1,** *in nothing, on no occasion;* praestabo sumptum nusquam melius poni posse, Cic.; **2,** *to nothing;* ut ad id omnia referri oporteat, ipsum autem nusquam, Cic.

nūto, 1. (*nuo). **I.** Gen., **1,** *to move up and down, totter, waver, nod;* ornus nutat, Verg.; nutant galeae, Liv.; **2,** transf., **a,** *to waver;* nutans acies, Tac.; **b,** *to waver, be uncertain in opinion;* etiam Democritus nutare videtur in natura deorum, Cic.; **c,** *to waver in fidelity;* Galliae nutantes, Tac. **II.** *to move the head up and down, to nod*, Plaut.; of persons, *sleeping*, Hor.

nūtrīcĭus -ii, m. (nutrix), *a foster-father, guardian*, Caes.

nūtrīco, 1. and **nūtrīcor,** 1. dep. (nutrix), *to suckle, nourish;* transf., *to support, sustain;* mundus omnia, sicut membra et partes suas, nutricatur, Cic.

nūtrīcŭla -ae, f. (dim. of nutrix), *nurse*, Hor.; transf., Gallia nutricula seditiosorum, Cic.

nūtrīmen -ĭnis, n. (nutrio), *nourishment*, Ov.

nūtrīmentum -i, n. (nutrio), *nourishment, nutriment;* transf., **a,** of fuel, arida nutrimenta, Verg.; **b,** *support, training;* educata huius nutrimentis eloquentia, Cic.

nūtrĭo -ivi and -ii -ītum, 4. (**nūtrĭor,** 4. dep., Verg.), *to give suck, suckle, nourish.* **I.** Lit., **A. a,** of animals, nutritus lacte ferino, Ov.; **b,** of plants, terra herbas nutrit, Ov.; **c,** of fire, ignes foliis, Ov. **B.** *to tend, wait upon;* corpora, Liv.; damnum naturae, *remove*, Liv. **II.** Transf., *to nourish, support, sustain;* amorem, Ov.; mens rite nutrita, *educated*, Hor.

nūtrix -īcis, f. (nutrio), *a nurse, foster-mother.* **I.** Lit., ut paene cum lacte nutricis errorem suxisse videamur, Cic.; meton., nutrices, *the breasts*, Cat. **II.** Transf., oratoris, Cic.; curarum maxima nutrix nox, Ov.

nūtus -ūs, m. (*nuo). **I.** *inclination, downward tendency, gravity*, Cic. **II.** *a nod, a signal, or beckoning of the head.* **A.** Lit., Liv. **B.** Transf., **1,** *command, will;* deorum nutu, Cic.; auctoritate nutuque deorum, Cic.; **2,** *assent;* annuite nutum numenque vestrum invictum Campanis, Liv.

nux, nŭcis, f. **I.** *a nut.* **A.** Lit., Liv.; prov., nux cassa, *something entirely worthless*, Hor. **B.** Transf., of similar fruit, castaneae nuces, *chestnuts*, Verg. **II. 1,** *the nut-tree*, Verg.; **2,** *an almond-tree*, Verg.

Nyctĕlĭus -i, m. (Νυκτέλιος), *nightly, a surname of Bacchus* (so called because his mysteries were celebrated by night), Ov.

nympha -ae, f. and **nymphē** -ēs, f. (νύμφη). **I.** *a bride, woman lately married*, Ov. **II.** Nymphae, *the Nymphs, beings of half-divine nature, believed to inhabit the seas, streams, woods*, etc., Verg.

Nymphaeum -i, n. (Νυμφαῖον), *a promontory and sea-port in Illyria.*

Nȳsa (Nyssa) -ae, f. (Νῦσα). **I.** *a town in Caria.* **II.** *a town in Palestine.* **III.** *a city in India, where Bacchus was said to have been brought up.* Hence, adj., **A. Nȳsaeus** -a -um, *Nysean.* **B. Nȳsēis** -ĭdis, f. *Nysean.* **C. Nȳsĭăs** -ădis, f. *of* or *relating to Bacchus.* **D. Nȳsĭgĕna** -ae, m. *born in Nysa.* **E. Nȳseus** -ĕi, *a surname of Bacchus.*

O.

1\. **O,** o, the fourteenth letter of the Latin alphabet, corresponding to the two Greek letters Omicron and Omega (Ο, ο, Ω, ω). For the use of O. in abbreviations, see Table of Abbreviations.

2\. **ō!** and **ōh!** interj. *an exclamation of joy, astonishment, derision, sorrow, pain*, etc., generally followed by voc. or acc.; o paterni generis oblite! Cic.; o me miserum! Cic.; sometimes with nom, o fortunata mors! Cic.; in wishes, o si, *if only!* Verg.; poet., put the second word of the clause, spes o fidissima Teucrum! Ov.

Ŏărīōn -ōnis, m. (Ὠαρίων) = Orion (q.v.).

Ŏaxes -is, m. (Ὄαξις), *a river in Crete.*

ob, prep. with acc. **I.** Of space, **a,** with verbs of motion, *towards, to;* ignis qui est ob os effusus, Cic.; **b,** with verbs not denoting motion, *at, before;* ob oculis versari, Cic. **II. 1,** *on account of;* ob rem judicandam pecuniam accipere, Cic.; unius ob iram prodimur, Verg.; ob eam rem, *on that account*, Cic.; quam ob rem, *on which account*, Caes.; ob id, ob id ipsum, ob hoc, ob haec, *on this account, therefore*, Liv.; ob metum, *out of fear*, Tac.; **2,** *in consideration of, for, as recompense for;* ager oppositus est pignori ob decem minas, Ter.; **3,** ob rem, *to the purpose, with advantage;* verum id frustra an ob rem faciam, in vestra manu situm est, Sall.

ŏbaerātus -a -um, adj. with compar. (ob and aes), *in debt*, Liv.; plur. subst., **ŏbaerāti** -ōrum, m. *debtors*, Cic.

ŏbambŭlo, 1. *to walk up and down, backwards and forwards;* with dat., muris, Liv.; with acc., Aetnam, Ov.; with prep., ante vallum, Liv.; in herbis, Ov.

ŏbarmo, 1. *to arm;* dextras securi, Hor.

ŏbăro, 1. *to plough up*, Liv.

1\. **obba** -ae, f. *a species of drinking-cup*, Pers.

2\. **Obba** -ae, f. *a town in Africa, near Carthage.*

obbrūtesco -tui, 3. *to become brutish, stupid*, Lucr.

obc . . . v. occ . . .

obdo -didi -ditum, 3. *to set, put, place before, put against;* pessulum ostio, *to bolt the door*, Ter.; fores, *to shut the door*, Ov.; nullique malo latus obdit apertum, *offers an unprotected side to no evil*, Hor.

obdormĭo -ivi and -ii -itum, 4. *to go to sleep*, Cic.

obdormisco, 3 (obdormio), *to go to sleep*, Cic

obdūco -duxi -ductum, 3 **I. A.** *to draw over, draw in front*, **1,** fossam, Caes , fig , callum dolori, Cic , **2,** *to cover*, trunci obducuntur libro aut cortice, Cic , transf , obducta cicatrix reipublicae, *closed wound*, Cic **B. 1,** *to drink*, venenum, Cic , **2,** *to wrinkle*, frontem, Hor **II** *to lead against*, Curium, *to bring forward, produce*, Cic , transf , *to pass, spend*, diem posterum, Cic

obductio -ōnis, f (obduco), *a covering*, capitis, Cic

obdūresco dūrŭi, 3 *to become hard, grow hard* **I.** Lit , Plaut **II.** Fig , *to become hard-hearted, to lose one's natural feeling, become obdurate*, ipse obdurui, Cic , ad dolorem novum, Cic

obdūro, 1 *to be hard*, fig , *to stand out, hold out, persist*, perfer et obdura, Ov , impers , obduretur hoc triduum, Cic

ŏbēdĭens (ŏboedĭens) -entis, p adj (from obedio), *obedient, compliant*, with dat nulli est naturae obediens aut subjectus deus, Cic , with ad and the acc , ad nova consilia, Liv Subst , **ŏbēdĭens,** *one who obeys, a dependant*, Cic

ŏbēdĭentĕr (ŏboedĭentĕr), adv (obediens), *obediently*, obedienter imperata facere, Liv

ŏbēdĭentĭa (ŏboedĭentĭa) -ae, f (obediens), *obedience, compliance*, Cic

ŏbēdĭo (ŏboedĭo) -ivi -itum, 4 (ob and audio) **I.** *to give ear to, listen to, follow a person's advice*, alicui, Nep **II.** *to obey*, praecepto, Cic , magistratibus, Cic., alicui ad verba, Cic

ŏbĕlīscus -i, m (ὀβελίσκος), *a pointed column, obelisk*, Plin

ŏbĕo -ivi and ii -itum, 4 **I.** Intransit , **A.** *to go to, come to, go to meet, go against*, ad omnes hostium conatus, *to oppose*, Liv., in infera loca, Cic **B. a,** of the heavenly bodies, *to set*, in reliquis orientis aut obeuntis solis partibus, Cic , **b,** *to die*, tecum vivere amem, tecum obeam libens, Hor **II.** Transit , **A. a,** *to go to, reach*, quantum flamma obire non potuisset, Cic. , **b,** *to go to, engage in, apply oneself to any business, to perform, execute, accomplish an object*, negotium, Cic , hereditatem, *to take possession of*, Cic , vadimonium, *to discharge one's bail, to appear at the fixed time*, Cic , diem supremum, *to die*, Nep , so obire mortem, Cic **B. 1,** *to visit, travel through*, provinciam, Cic , **2,** *to take part in*, comitia, Cic , **3,** *to surround*, clipeum obit pellis circumdata, Verg

ŏbĕquĭto, 1 *to ride up to*, castris Liv.

ŏberro, 1 *to wander about*, tentoriis, Tac , transf , chordā eādem, *to blunder*, Hor

ŏbēsĭtas -ātis, f (obesus), *fatness, corpulence, obesity*, Suet

ŏbēsus -a -um (ob and edo), **1,** *fat, plump*, turdus, Hor transf, *swollen*, fauces, Verg , **2,** *coarse, not delicate, unrefined, rude*, juvenis naris obesae, Hor

ōbex -icis, and objicis, m and f (objicio), **1,** *the fastening of a door, bolt, bar, barrier, barricade*, fultosque emunit objice postes, Verg , **2,** *an obstacle, hindrance*, Plin

obf . v off

obg . v. ogg . . .

ŏbhaerĕo, 2 *to stick to, cleave to*, Suet

ŏbhaeresco -haesi haesum, 3 *to stick fast, adhere to*, Lucr

ōbĭcio = objicio (q v).

ŏbīrascor -irātus sum, 3 dep *to be angry*, fortunae, *with fortune*, Liv.

ŏbīrātĭo -ōnis, f (obirascor), *a being angry, anger*, Cic

ŏbīrātus a -um, p adj (from obirascor), *angry, wrathful*, with dat , fortunae, Liv

ŏbĭtĕr, adv (ob), **1,** *on the way, in passing, on the journey*, Juv , **2,** *by the way, incidentally*, Juv

ŏbĭtus -ūs, m (obeo), **1,** *an approaching, going to*, Ter ; **2,** *a going down* (esp of the heavenly bodies), *setting*, siderum, Cic , **3,** *a downfall, ruin, destruction, death*, post obitum vel potius excessum Romuli, Cic

objăcĕo -jăcŭi, 2 *to lie at, against, in the way*, saxa objacentia pedibus, Liv.

objectātĭo -ōnis, f (objecto), *a reproach*, Caes

objecto, 1 (intens of objicio) **I.** *to put in the way, set against* **A.** Lit (of birds), caput fretis, *to dip, dive into*, Verg **B.** Transf , *to expose*, aliquem periculis, Sall , se hostium telis, Liv , moras, *to cause, interpose delay*, Ov **II.** Transf, *to reproach with anything, object anything to a person, throw in a person's teeth*, alicui probrum, Cic , with acc and infin , nobilitas objectare Fabio fugisse eum Ap Claudium collegam, Liv

1 **objectus** -a um, p adj (from objicio), **1,** *lying at, near, opposite to*, insula objecta Alexandriae, Caes , **2,** *exposed to*, fortunae, Cic , ad omnes casus, Cic

2 **objectus** ūs, m (objicio), *a placing at, before, opposite, a lying against, lying opposite*, insula portum efficit objectu laterum, Verg

objex = obex (q v)

objĭcĭo -jēci jectum, 3 (ob and jacio) **I.** *to throw in the way of* **A.** Lit , se telis hostium, Cic **B.** Transf , **1,** *to oppose*, Cic , **2,** *to expose*, consulem morti, Cic , se in dimicationes, Cic , **3,** *to cause, produce*, alicui errorem, Cic ; metum et dolorem, Cic , objicitur animo metus, *the heart is seized with fear*, Cic , hic aliud majus miseris objicitur, *presents itself*, Verg **II.** *to place before, throw before* **A.** Lit **1,** corpus feris, Cic , **2,** *to put before, hold before as a defence, protection*, Alpium vallum contra transgressionem Gallorum, *to oppose*, Cic., carros pro vallo, Caes **B. 1,** *to offer*, delenimentum animis, Liv , **2,** *to hold out as an example*, unum ex judicibus selectis, Hor , **3,** *to object to, reproach with, charge with*, alicui furta, Cic , with acc and infin , objicit mihi, me ad Baias fuisse, Cic with quod, non tibi objicio quod spoliasti, Cic

objurgātĭo -ōnis, f (objurgo), *a blaming, chiding, reproving*, Cic

objurgātor -ōris, m (objurgo), *a scolder, chider, reprover, blamer*, Cic

objurgātōrĭus -a um (objurgator), *scolding, chiding*, epistola, Cic

objurgo, 1 and **objurgor,** 1 dep *to scold, chide, reprove, reprimand, blame*, aliquem molli brachio de Pompeii familiaritate, Cic , verecundiam alicuius, Cic , quum objurgarer me, quod nimiā laetitiā paene desiperem, Cic

oblanguesco gŭi, 3 *to become languid*, Cic

oblātro, 1 *to bark at or against, to rail at, scold*, Suet

oblectāmen -inis, n (oblecto), *a delight, pleasure*, Ov

oblectāmentum -i, n (oblecto), *a delight, amusement, solace*, meae senectutis requies oblectamentumque, Cic

oblectātĭo -ōnis, f. (oblecto), *a delighting; pleasing*, animi, vitae Cic

oblecto, 1 (ob and lacto) **I.** *to delight, please, amuse*, quum eorum inventis scriptisque se oblectent, Cic.; senectutem, Cic.; legentium animos fictis, Tac.; me cum aliqua re, Cic.; se cum aliquo, Cic. **II.** *to pass time pleasantly, while away time*; lacrimabile tempus studio, Ov.

oblīcus, v. obliquus.

oblīdo -līsi -līsum, 3. (ob and laedo), *to squeeze together*; collum digitulis duobus, *to throttle*, Cic.; oblisis faucibus, *strangled*, Tac.

oblĭgātĭo -ōnis, f. (obligo), *a being bound, a legal obligation*; obligatio pecuniae, Cic.

oblĭgātus -a -um, p. adj. (from obligo), *bound, under an obligation to any one*; obligatus ei nihil eram, Cic.

oblĭgo, 1. *to bind, fasten to.* **I. A.** Lit., *to tie, bind up, bandage a wound*; vulnus, Cic.; medicum requirens a quo obligetur, Cic.; venas, Tac. **B.** Transf., *to bind, fetter by an oath, law, benefit, to bind, fetter, oblige, lay under an obligation, make liable*; **a,** se nexu, Cic.; aliquem sibi liberalitate, Cic.; poet., obligatam redde Jovi dapem, *that is due*, Hor.; **b,** *to pledge*; praedia obligata, *mortgaged*, Cic. **II.** *to make liable to punishment, make guilty*; aliquem scelere, Cic.; pass., obligari, *to commit an offence, be guilty*; obligari fraude impiā, Cic.

oblīmo, 1. (ob and limus). **I.** *to cover with slime or mud*; agros, Cic. **II.** *to lavish, squander*, Hor.

oblĭno -lēvi -litum, 3. **I.** *to smear, daub, besmear.* **A.** Lit., obliti unguentis, Cic.; oblitus faciem suo cruore, Cic. **B.** Transf., *to cover, load*; actor oblitus divitiis, Hor.; facetiae oblitae Latio, Cic. **II.** *to stain, pollute, defile*; oblitus parricidio, Cic.; sunt omnia summo dedecore oblita, Cic.; aliquem versibus atris, *to satirise, lampoon*, Hor.

oblīquē, adv. (obliquus), **1,** *sideways, athwart, aslant, obliquely*; ferri, Cic.; **2,** *indirectly, covertly, by implication*, Tac.

oblīquo, 1. (obliquus), *to make oblique, turn sideways, turn aside, slant, crook*; oculos, Ov.; ensem in latus, Ov.

oblīquus (oblīcus) -a -um (ob and liquis), *slanting, oblique, sideways, aslant, on one side.* **I.** Lit., hos partim obliquos, partim aversos, partim etiam adversos stare vobis, Cic.; amnis cursibus obliquis fluens, Ov.; ab obliquo, Ov., per obliquum, Hor., *sideways, obliquely.* **II.** Transf., **a,** of discourse, *indirect, covert*; insectatio, Tac.; **b,** *looking askance, envious*; invidia, Verg.

oblītĕrātĭo -ōnis, f. (oblitero), *a blotting out, obliteration*; and esp., *a blotting out from memory, total forgetfulness*, Plin.

oblītĕro, 1. (oblino), *to blot out, obliterate, to blot out of memory, bring to forgetfulness*; famam rei, Liv.; publici mei beneficii memoriā privatam offensionem obliterarunt, Cic.

oblītesco -tŭi, 3. (ob and latesco), *to hide, conceal oneself*; a nostro aspectu, Cic.

oblīvĭo -ōnis, f. (obliviscor), *forgetfulness, oblivion*; laudem alicuius ab oblivione atque a silentio vindicare, Cic.; dare aliquid oblivioni, *to bury in oblivion*, Liv.; in oblivionem negotii venire, *to forget*, Cic.

oblīvĭōsus -a -um (oblivio), **1,** *oblivious, forgetful*, Cic.; **2,** *causing forgetfulness*; Massicum, Hor.

oblīviscor, oblitus sum, 3. dep. (perhaps from oblino), *to forget.* **I.** Lit., with genit., temporum suorum, Cic.; with acc. of thing, injurias, Cic.; with infin., ne obliviscar vigilare, Cic.; with acc. and infin., obliviscor Roscium et Cluvium viros esse primarios, Cic. **II.** Transf., *to forget, lose sight of*; consuetudinis suae, Cic.; oblivisci sui, *to forget oneself*, Cic.

oblīvĭum -ii, n. (obliviscor), usually plur., *forgetfulness*; agere oblivia laudis, *to forget*, Ov.

oblongus -a -um, *rather long, oblong*, Liv.

oblŏquor -quūtus (-cūtus) sum, 3. dep. **I.** *to speak against, gainsay, contradict, interrupt*; **1,** gen., alicui, Cic.; **2,** esp., **a,** *to blame*, Tac.; **b,** *to chide*, Cat. **II.** *to join in singing, to accompany*; non avis obloquitur, Ov.

obluctor, 1. dep. *to struggle against, strive against*; genibus adversae arenae, Verg.

obmōlĭor, 4. dep. **I.** *to build or pile against* (as a defence); nec in promptu erat quod obmolirentur, Liv. **II.** *to obstruct, block up*, Liv.

obmurmŭro, 1. *to murmur against or at*; precibus, Ov.

obmūtesco -mūtŭi, 3. **I.** Lit., **A.** *to become dumb, become speechless* with astonishment, etc.; vocem mittenti non et linguam obmutuisse et manum obtorpuisse, Cic. **B.** = *to be silent*; ego neque Antonium verbum facere patiar et ipse obmutescam, Cic. **II.** Transf., *to cease*; dolor animi obmutuit, Cic.

obnātus -a -um (*obnascor), *growing on*; obnata ripis salicta, *growing on the bank*, Liv.

obnītor -nixus (-nisus) sum, 3. dep. *to push against, press against.* **I.** Lit., taurus arboris obnixus trunco, Verg.; scutis corporibusque ipsis obnixi, Liv. **II.** Transf., *to strive against, oppose*; consilio or manu hostibus, Tac.

obnixē, adv. (obnixus, from obnitor), *with all one's might, with all one's strength*, Ter.

obnixus -a -um, p. adj. (from obnitor), *steadfast, firm, unyielding*, Liv.

obnoxiē (obnoxius). **I.** *culpably*, Plaut. **II.** *slavishly, servilely, submissively*; sententias dicere, Liv.

obnoxiōsus -a -um (obnoxius), *submissive, compliant*, Plaut.

obnoxius -a -um (ob and noxa). **I.** *liable to punishment*; hence, *guilty of any crime, vice, etc.*; animus neque delicto neque lubidini obnoxius, Sall.; pecuniae debitae, *indebted*, Liv. **II. A.** *subject, obedient, compliant*; **1,** lit., subjecti atque obnoxii vobis, Liv.; **2, a,** *dependent upon*; luna radiis fratris obnoxia, Verg.; **b,** *slavish, servile, submissive*; pax obnoxia, Liv. **B.** *subject to, exposed to, obnoxious to*; arbores quae frigoribus obnoxiae sunt, Liv.; obnoxium est, *it is dangerous*, Tac.

obnūbo -nupsi -nuptum, 3. *to cover*; comas amictu, Verg.; caput, ap. Cic.

obnuntĭātĭo -ōnis, f. (obnuntio), in the language of augurs, *the announcement of an evil omen*, Cic.

obnuntĭo, 1. in the language of augurs, *to announce, report an unfavourable omen*; consuli, Cic.

obœd . . . v. oboed . . .

ŏbŏlĕo -ŭi, 2. *to smell of anything, emit an odour*, Plaut.

ŏbŏlus -i, m. (ὀβολός), *a Greek coin, in value one-sixth of a drachma*, rather more than 1½d. English, Ter.

ŏbŏrĭor -ortus sum -ōrīri, *to arise, appear*; bellum, Liv.; vide quanta lux liberalitatis et sapientiae tuae mihi apud te dicenti oboriatur, Cic.

obp . . . v. opp . . .

obrēpo -repsi -reptum, 3. *to creep, to crawl to.* **I.** Lit., ap. Cic. **II.** Transf., *to come up silently and unexpectedly, steal on imperceptibly, come on by surprise*; senectus adolescentiae obrepit, Cic.; ad honores, Cic.; imagines obrepunt in animos dormientium, Cic.

obreptus (partic of obrepo), *surreptitious*

obrētio, 4 (ob and rete), *to catch in a net*, Lucr.

obrĭgesco -rigŭi, 3 *to become stiff or frozen, to freeze*, nive pruināque, Cic

Obrĭmas -ae, m *a river in Phrygia*.

obrŏgo, 1 *to amend or repeal a law by another*, obrogare legibus Caesaris, Cic

obrŭo -rŭi -rŭtum, fut partic -rŭĭtūrus, 3 *to cover over, cover with earth, clothes, etc, to bury* I. Lit, A. se arenā, Cic, thesaurum, Cic, obruere aliquem vivum, Sall B. *to overload*, se vino, Cic II. Transf, A. testem omnium risus obruit, *overwhelmed*, Cic, obrui aere alieno, *plunged in debt*, Cic, obrutus criminibus, Cic B. 1, *to overwhelm, bury, ruin, consign to oblivion*, ut adversa quasi perpetuā oblivione obruamus, Cic; Marius talis viri interitu sex suos obruit consulatus, *obscured the fame of his six consulships*, Cic, 2, *to surpass, eclipse*, famam alicuius, Tac

obrussa -ae, f (ὄβρυζον), *the assaying of gold by fire*, Suet, fig, adhibenda tamquam obrussa ratio, *as a test*, Cic

obsaepĭo -saepsi -saeptum, 4 *to fence round, inclose, to block up, render access impossible* I. Lit, hostium agmina obsaepiunt iter, Liv II Fig, plebi iter ad curules magistratus, Liv

obsătŭro, 1 *to satisfy*, Ter

obscoenē (obscēnē), adv (obscoenus), *impurely, lewdly, immodestly, obscenely*, Cic

obscoenĭtas (obscēnĭtas) -ātis, f (obscoenus), *impurity, foulness, lewdness, obscenity*, verborum, Cic

obscoenus (obscēnus) -a -um (ob and coenum) I. *repulsive, filthy, disgusting, offensive*, volucres, *the Harpies*, Verg, risus, Ov II. Transf, A *morally disgusting, impure, lewd, foul, obscene*, voluptates, Cic, adulterium, Ov, jocandi genus, Cic B. *ill omened, unpropitious*, volucres, *owls*, Verg

obscūrātĭo -ōnis, f (obscuro), *an obscuring, darkening*, solis, Cic, fig, Cic

obscūrē, adv (obscurus) I. *darkly* Cic II. a, of discourse, *obscurely, unintelligibly*, disserere, Cic, b, *covertly, secretly, unobservedly*, aliquid non obscure ferre, Cic

obscūrĭtas -ātis, f (obscurus). I. *darkness, obscurity*: latebrarum, Tac, lucis, Liv II. Fig, a, of discourse, *obscurity, unintelligibleness, want of perspicuity*, oratio quae lumen adhibere rebus debet, ea obscuritatem affert, Cic, verborum, Cic, in ea obscuritate et dubitatione omnium, Cic b, of condition, *obscurity, low birth and station*, Cic

obscūro, 1 (obscurus) I. *to make dark, darken, obscure* A Lit, obscuratur luce solis lumen lucernae, Cic, caelum nocte atque nubibus obscuratum, Sall B a, of discourse, *to make dark, indistinct, unintelligible*, aliquid dicendo, *to pronounce indistinctly*, Cic, b, *to make obscure, keep in obscurity, cause to be forgotten*, fortuna res celebrat obscuratque, Sall, eorum memoria obscurata est, Cic II. Transf, *to conceal, hide*, magnitudinem periculi, Cic

obscūrus -a -um (perhaps for obscurus connected with occultus) I. *dark, obscure*, 1, lit, lucus, Verg, nox, Verg, subst, **obscūrum** -i, n *darkness*, sub obscurum noctis, Verg, applied to persons, ibant obscuri, *in the dark*, Verg, 2, fig, a, of discourse or a writer, *obscure, unintelligible, indistinct*, Heraclitus obscurus, Cic, brevis esse laboro, obscurus fio, Hor, b, *unknown, obscure, not celebrated*, Pompeius humili atque obscuro loco natus, *of humble origin*, Cic II. Transf, A. *dark, insecure* obscurā spe et caecā exspectatione, Cic B. *concealed, hidden*, 1, lit, locus, Liv, 2, fig, of character, *secret, reserved, close*, homo, Cic, odium, Cic

obsĕcrātĭo -ōnis, f (obsecro) I *an earnest entreaty, supplication, adjuration*, obsecratione humili ac supplici uti, Cic II. *a public prayer or supplication*, obsecratio a populo duumviris praeeuntibus facta, Liv

obsĕcro, 1 (ob and sacro), *to beseech earnestly, implore, adjure, entreat*, aliquem multis lacrimis, Cic, obsecro te, ut id facias, Cic, te hoc ut, etc, Cic, esp, as a polite phrase, *pray*, Attica, obsecro te, quid agit, Cic

obsĕcundo, 1 *to be subservient to, compliant with, fall in with*, voluntatibus alicuius, Cic

obsēpĭo = obsaepio (q v)

obsĕquēla -ae, f (obsequor), *compliance, yielding*, Plaut

obsĕquens -entis, p adj (from obsequor), 1, *compliant, yielding, obedient*, patri, Ter, 2, esp, an epithet applied to the gods, *favourable, gracious*, Plaut

obsĕquentĕr, adv (obsequens), *compliantly, obediently*, haec facere, Liv

obsĕquentĭa -ae, f (obsequens) *yielding, compliance, complaisance*, Caes

obsĕquĭōsus -a -um (obsequium), *compliant, yielding, obsequious*, Plaut

obsĕquĭum -ii n (obsequor), *compliance complaisance, deference to others, submission, obsequiousness* I. Gen, Cic, ventris, *gluttony*, Hor, transf, of inanimate objects, flectitur obsequio curvatus ab arbore ramus, Ov II. *obedience*, obsequium erga aliquem exuere, Tac

obsĕquor -cūtus (-quūtus) sum, 3 dep I. *to comply with, humour, gratify, obey* tibi roganti, Cic, neque, ubi de M Pomponio referrent, senatui obsequebantur, Liv II. Transf, *to give oneself up to anything*, tempestati, Cic; alicuius voluntati, Cic

1 **obsĕro**, 1 *to bolt, bar, fasten*, plebis aedificiis obseratis, Liv, transf, aures, Hor

2 **obsĕro** -sēvi -situm, 3 *to sow, plant*, terram frugibus, Cic Partic, **obsĭtus** -a -um, *sown with*, i e, *full of, covered with*, obsita pomis rura, Ov, vestis obsita squalore, Liv, legati obsiti squalore et sordibus, Liv

observans -antis, p adj, with compar and superl (observo), *attentive, respectful*, observantissimus mei, Cic

observantĭa -ae, f (observans), *respect, esteem, attention* observantia est, per quam aetate, aut sapientiā, aut honore, aut aliquā dignitate antecedentes veremur et colimus, Cic, in regem, Liv

observātĭo -ōnis, f (observo), 1, *an observing, observation*, siderum, Cic, 2, *care, accuracy, exactness, circumspection*, summa erat observatio in bello movendo, Cic

observātor -ōris, m (observo), *an observer, watcher*, Plin

observĭto, 1 (intens of observo), *to watch, observe diligently*, motus stellarum Cic

observo, 1 *to watch, observe, regard, attend to* I occupationem alicuius, Cic, tempus epistolae alicui reddendae, *to watch for*, Cic II. A. *to watch, guard, keep*, greges, Ov B. *to keep, obey, regard, observe a law, rule, precept*, leges, Cic, praeceptum, Caes, observare ne, with the subj, quod ne accidat observare nec potest nec necesse est, Cic C. *to respect, esteem, prize, honour*, me ut alterum patrem, Cic

obsĕs -sĭdis, c. (ob and sedeo). **I.** *a hostage;* obsides accipere, dare, Caes. **II.** *a surety, security, pledge;* seque eius rei obsidem fore, pollicitus est, *that he would be surety for that thing,* Nep.; obsides dare, *to give security,* with acc. and infin., Cic.

obsessĭo -ōnis, f. (obsideo), *a blockade, siege, encompassing;* viae, Cic.

obsessor -ōris, m. (obsideo), *one who sits or remains a long time in a place;* **1,** gen., vivarum obsessor aquarum (of the water-snake), Ov.; **2,** esp., *one who besieges* or *blockades;* curiae, Cic.; Luceriae, Liv.

obsĭdĕo -sēdi -sessum, 2. (ob and sedeo). **I.** Intransit., *to sit down, remain anywhere,* Ter. **II.** Transit., **A.** *to sit, remain in* or *on, haunt, frequent a place,* Plin. **B. 1,** lit., *to blockade, besiege, beset;* omnes aditus, Cic.; totam Italiam, Cic.; **2,** transf., **a,** *to occupy, fill;* corporibus omnis obsidetur locus, *every place is filled,* Cic.; **b,** *to be on the look-out for, watch for an opportunity;* jacere humi ad obsidendum stuprum, Cic.

obsĭdĭo -ōnis, f. (obsideo), *a blockade, siege.* **A.** Lit., obsidione urbes capere, Cic.; obsidione solvere or eximere, *to raise the siege of a place,* Liv. **B.** Transf., *pressing danger;* rempublicam liberare obsidione, Cic.

obsĭdĭōnālis -e (1. obsidium), *of or relating to a blockade, siege;* corona, *the honorary crown of grass given to the commander who had raised a siege,* Liv.

1. **obsĭdĭum** -ĭi, n. (obsideo), *a blockade, siege, besetting.* **I.** Lit., occupare obsidio Lacedaemonis exercitum, Liv. **II.** Fig., *danger,* Plaut.

2. **obsĭdĭum** -ĭi, n. (obses), *the condition of a hostage,* Tac.

obsīdo -sēdi -sessum, 3. *to blockade, besiege, invest, environ;* pontem, Sall.; milite campos, Verg.

obsignātor -ōris, m. (obsigno), *one who seals, a sealer;* literarum, Cic.; esp., *a witness who puts his seal to a will;* testamenti, Cic.

obsigno, 1. **I.** *to seal.* **A.** Gen., epistolam, Cic. **B.** Esp., **1,** of a witness, *to sign and seal a document;* prov., agere cum aliquo tabellis obsignatis, *to deal with any one in strict form of law,* Cic.; **2,** *to seal an accusation against any one;* contra Scaurum patrem suum, Cic. **II.** *to stamp, impress;* formam verbis, Lucr.

obsisto -stĭti, 3. **1,** *to stand, place oneself before* or *in the way of;* alicui abeunti, Liv.; **2,** *to oppose, withstand, resist;* omnibus eius consiliis, Cic.; alicui obsistere, foll. by quominus and the subj., Cic. Partic., **obstitus** -a -um (in the language of the augurs) = *struck with lightning,* Cic.

obsītus -a -um, partic. of 2. obsero (q.v.).

obsŏlĕfăcĭo -fēci -factum, 3. (obsoleo and facio), *to wear out, degrade, corrupt, make common;* obsolefiebant dignitatis insignia, Cic.

obsŏlesco -lēvi -lētum, 3. (obs and oleo), *to pass away by degrees, decay, wear out, fall into disuse, lose value;* oratio, Cic.; vectigal, Cic.

obsŏlētē, adv. (obsoletus), *poorly, meanly;* obsoletius vestitus, *shabbily dressed,* Cic.

obsŏlētus -a -um (partic. of obsolesco), *worn out, decayed;* **1,** lit., vestitu obsoletiore, Cic.; obsoletus Thessalonicam venisti, *dressed in old clothes,* Cic.; verba, *obsolete,* Cic.; **2,** *common, everyday;* crimina, Cic.; oratio, *ordinary,* Cic.

obsōnĭum -ĭi, n. (ὀψώνιον), *that which is eaten with bread,* e.g., *vegetables, fruit,* and esp. *fish,* Hor.

1. **obsōno** and **obsōnor,** 1. dep. (ὀψωνέω), *to buy for the kitchen, purvey;* **1,** lit., Plaut.; fig., ambulando famem, *to buy the sauce of hunger,* Cic.; **2,** *to give a feast,* Ter.

2. **obsŏno,** 1. *to interrupt a person speaking,* Plaut.

obsorbĕo -bŭi, 2. *to swallow, gulp down,* Plaut.

obstĕtrix -īcis, f. (obsto), *a midwife,* Hor.

obstĭnātē, adv. with compar. and superl. (obstinatus), *resolutely, persistently, obstinately;* negare, Caes.; credere, Liv.

obstĭnātĭo -ōnis, f. (obstino), *resolution, persistence, firmness, obstinacy;* sententiae, Cic.

obstĭnātus -a -um, p. adj. (from obstino), *firmly resolved, persistent, firm, obstinate;* obstinatior voluntas, Cic.; adversus obstinatior lacrimas muliebres, Liv.; ad decertandum obstinati mori, Liv.

obstĭno, 1. (ob and sto), *to persist in, be resolved on anything;* with infin., obstinaverant animis aut vincere aut mori, Liv.

obstĭpesco = obstupesco (q.v.).

obstĭpus -a -um, *leaning to either side* (opp. rectus); caput, Cic.; cervix, *thrown back* (said of a haughty person), Suet.; caput, *bent* or *bowed down,* Hor.

obsto -stĭti -stātūrus, 1. **I.** *to stand at, before, against,* Plaut. **II.** *to stand in opposition to, to oppose, resist, hinder, obstruct;* with dat., alicui, Cic.; vita cetera eorum huic sceleri obstat, *stands in opposition to, is inconsistent with,* Sall.; with quin, quominus, ne and the subj., quid obstat, quominus sit beatus? Cic.; ea ne impedirent tribuni, dictatoris obstitit metus, Liv. Partic. subst., **obstantĭa,** neut. plur., *hindrances, obstacles, impediments,* Tac.

obstrĕpo -strĕpŭi -strĕpĭtum, 3. **I.** *to make a noise, clamour at* or *against;* nihil sensere Poeni obstrepente pluviā, Liv.; with dat., fontesque lymphis obstrepunt manantibus, Hor.; obstrepunt portis, Liv. **II. 1,** *to disturb, interrupt a speaker by clamour;* alicui, Cic.; impers., decemviro obstrepitur, Liv.; **2,** *to disturb, molest;* tibi literis, Cic.

obstringo -strinxi -strictum, 3. *to bind to, fasten to, tie to, bind up, tie fast, keep bound.* **A.** ventos, Hor. **B.** Fig., **1,** *to bind, fetter, entangle, put under an obligation;* jurejurando, *to bind by an oath,* Caes.; aliquem legibus, Cic.; beneficio obstrictus, Cic.; **2,** *to entangle, involve;* aliquem aere alieno, *to entangle in debt,* Cic.; se parricidio, se scelere, *to be guilty of,* Cic.

obstructĭo -ōnis, f. (obstruo), *a hindrance, obstruction,* Cic.

obstrūdo = obtrudo (q.v.).

obstrŭo -struxi -structum, 3. **I.** *to build against, build before;* pro diruto novum murum, Liv.; luminibus alicuius, *to block up the light, build before the windows,* Cic. **II.** *to build up, block up, close;* **a,** portas, Caes.; aditus, Cic.; iter Poenis (*to the Carthaginians*) vel corporibus suis, Cic.; **b,** fig., obstruere perfugia improborum, Cic.

obstŭpĕfăcĭo -fēci -factum, *to bewilder, astound, stupefy, to render senseless, benumb;* pass., **obstŭpĕfīo** -factus sum -fiĕri, *to be bewildered, amazed;* ipso miraculo audaciae obstupefecit hostes, Liv.; obstupefactis hominibus ipsā admiratione, Cic.

obstŭpesco -stŭpŭi (-stĭpŭi), 3. *to become senseless, be stupefied, to be astounded, amazed;* quum eorum aspectu obstipuisset bubulcus, Cic.

obsum, obfŭi (offŭi) -esse, *to be in the way, hinder, impede, injure, be prejudicial to;* with dat., obsunt auctoribus artes, Ov., obest Clodii mors Miloni, Cic, non or nihil obest with infin, nihil obest dicere, Cic

obsŭo -sŭi -sūtum, 3. 1, *to sew on*, caput, Ov, 2, *to close up, stop up*, spiritus oris obsuitur, Verg

obsurdesco -dŭi, 3 *to become deaf, to be deaf*, 1, lit, hoc sonitu oppletae aures hominum obsurduerunt, Cic, 2, *to be deaf to warnings, etc, not to give ear to*, Cic

obtĕgo -texi tectum, 3 1, *to cover, protect*, se servorum et libertorum corporibus, Cic, eam partem castrorum vineis, Caes; 2, *to cover, conceal, hide, keep secret*, vitia multis virtutibus obtecta, Cic

obtempĕrātĭo -ōnis, f (obtempero), *compliance, obedience*, legibus, Cic

obtempĕro, 1 *to obey, comply with, conform to, submit to*: alicui, Cic, imperio populi Romani, Caes, ut ad verba nobis obediant, ad id, quod ex verbis intelligi possit, obtemperent, Cic

obtendo -tendi -tentum, 3 **I.** *to stretch before, spread before*, 1, pro viro nebulam, Verg, poet, obtentā nocte, *under the shelter of night*, Verg, obtendi = *to lie before, be over against*, Britannia Germaniae obtenditur, Tac, 2, *to put forward as an excuse, plead, allege*, matris preces, Tac, valetudinem corporis, Tac **II.** *to cover, conceal, hide*, diem nube atrā, Tac, fig., quasi velis quibusdam obtenditur unius cuiusque natura, Cic

1 **obtentus** -ūs, m (obtendo), 1, lit, *a stretching or spreading before*, frondis, Verg, 2, fig, *a pretext, pretence, excuse*, tempora reipublicae obtentui sumpta, *taken as an excuse*, Tac, sub eius obtentu cognominis, Liv

2 **obtentus** -a -um, 1, partic of obtineo, 2, partic of obtendo

obtĕro -trivi tritum, 3 *to trample, crush*, 1, lit, Cic, obtriti sunt plures quam ferro necati, Liv, 2, transf, *to crush, annihilate, destroy*: calumniam, Cic, jura populi, *trample under foot*, Liv (syncop pluperf, obtrisset, Liv)

obtestātĭo ōnis, f (obtestor), 1, *a solemn calling of God to witness, an adjuring in the name of the gods*, obtestatio et consecratio legis, Cic, tua obtestatio tibicinis, Cic, 2, *an earnest supplication, vehement entreaty*, Liv.

obtestor, 1 dep **I.** *to call to witness, protest before some person or thing*, deum hominumque fidem, Liv. **II.** 1, *to adjure, implore, entreat, supplicate in the name of the gods*, per omnes deos te obtestor ut, etc, Cic, quā re oro obtestorque vos, judices, ne, etc, Cic, 2, *to assert solemnly*, summam rempublicam agi obtestans, Tac

obtexo -texŭi -textum, 3 1, *to weave on, weave over*, Plin, 2, *to cover*, coelumque obtexitur umbrā, Verg

obtĭcĕo, 2 (ob and taceo), *to be silent*, Ter

obticesco -cŭi, 3 (obticeo), *to become quiet, grow silent*, Hor.

obtĭgo = obtego (q v)

obtĭneo -tinŭi -tentum, 2 (ob and teneo) **I.** *to hold with the hands*, obtine aures, Plaut **II.** *to hold, possess, keep possession of, occupy* **A.** suam domum, Cic, vada custodiis, Cic, citeriorem ripam armis, Liv. **B.** Transf, *to hold, occupy*, principem locum, *to hold the chief place*, Caes., secundum dignitatis locum, Caes, numerum deorum, *to be among the number of the gods*, Cic **III. A.** *to maintain, hold firmly*, pontem, Liv, hereditatem, Cic. **B.** Transf, **a,** jus suum contra aliquem, Cic, causam, *to carry one's point*, Cic; absol, obtinuit, with ut and the subj, *he carried his point that*, etc, Liv, **b,** *to maintain an assertion*, duas contrarias sententias, Cic **IV. a,** *to keep, observe*; silentium, Cic, vitam, Cic; lex quae in conviviis Graecorum obtinebatur, Cic, **b,** reflex, *to obtain, be held*, pro vero, Sall

obtingo -tigi, 3 (ob and tango), *to fall to the lot of any one, to happen, befall*, **a,** quod cuique obtigit, is quisque teneat, Cic, si quid mihi obtigerit, *if anything should happen to me, if I should die* Cic, **b,** esp as polit t t, of the casting of lots for public offices, alicui sorte obtingit provincia aquaria, Cic

obtorpesco -torpŭi, 3 *to become stiff, numb, torpid, insensible*, et linguam obmutuisse et manum obtorpuisse, Cic, manus prae metu, Liv, obtorpuerunt animi, Liv

obtorquĕo torsi -tortum, 2 *to turn or twist towards, to turn round, wrench, twist round* (usually found in partic perf), obtortā gulā in vincula abripi jussit, Cic

obtrectātĭo ōnis, f (obtrecto), *envious disparagement, detraction* obtrectatio est aegritudo ex eo, quod alter quoque potiatur eo, quod ipse concupiverit, Cic, laudis, Caes

obtrectātor ōris, m (obtrecto), *an envious detractor, disparager*, obtrectatores et invidi Scipionis, Cic

obtrecto, 1 (ob and tracto), *to disparage, detract from, enviously decry, to oppose, thwart, injure any one*, with dat, alicui, Cic, gloriae alicuius, Liv, inter se, Nep, legi alicuius, Cic, with acc, eius laudes, Liv

obtrūdo (obstrūdo) trūsi -trūsum, 1, *to gulp down, swallow down*, Plaut, 2, **a,** *to thrust, force, obtrude anything upon one*, virginem alicui, Ter, **b,** *to cover*, obstrusa carbasa pullo, *edged with*, Ov

obtrunco, 1 *to cut down, cut in pieces, slay*, regem, Liv

obtŭĕor 2 dep *to look at, gaze at, see, behold*, Plaut

obtundo -tŭdi tūsum, 3 **I.** *to beat upon, thump*; os mihi, Plaut **II.** *to make dull by striking* **A.** Lit, telum, Lucr **B.** Transf, 1, *to make blunt, dull, render obtuse, weaken*, obtundere aures, *to din into a person's ears*, obtuderunt eius aures te socium praetoris fuisse, Cic, obtundere vocem, of orators, *to speak hoarsely*, Cic, ingenia, *to make dull*, Cic, 2, *to weary*, aliquem longis epistolis, Cic

obturbo, 1 **I. A.** *to disturb, make turbid*, aquam, Plin **B.** *to disturb, put into confusion, perturb*, hostes, Tac **II.** Transf, **A.** *to deafen, stun*, **a,** with shouts, obturbabatur militum vocibus, Tac, **b,** mentally, me scriptio et literae non leniunt sed obturbant, *distract*, Cic **B.** *to disturb, break in upon*, solitudinem, Cic

obturgesco -tursi, 3 *to swell up*, Lucr

obtūro, 1 *to stop up* **I.** Lit, eas partes (corporis) obstructas et obturatas esse dicebat, Cic **II.** Transf, alicui aures, *to refuse to listen*, Hor

obtūsus -a -um, p adj (from obtundo), *blunt* **I.** Lit, pugio, Tac **II.** Transf, **a,** *darkened, dulled*, neque tum stellis acies obtusa videtur, Verg; **b,** of the intellect, *dulled, blunted*, cuius animis obtusior sit acies, Cic, **c,** of feeling, *insensible*, pectora Verg, **d,** *weak, powerless*, Verg

obtūtus -ūs, m (obtueor), *a looking at, beholding, look, gaze*, oculorum, Cic., dum stupet obtutuque haeret defixus in uno, Verg

ŏbumbro, 1 *to overshadow* **I.** Lit, humum, *to darken*, aethera telis, Verg **II.** Fig, 1, *to obscure, overcloud*, numquam obscura nomina, etsi aliquando obumbrentur, Tac.; **2,** *to conceal, protect, cover;* erroris sub imagine crimen, Ov.

ŏbuncus -a -um, *bent inwards, hooked inwards;* rostrum, Verg.

ŏbustus -a -um (ob and uro), *burnt, hardened in the fire;* sudes, Verg.; transf., gleba obusta (*pinched*) gelu, Ov.

obvallo, 1. *to surround with a wall, wall round;* fig., locus omni ratione obvallatus, Cic.

obvĕnĭo -vēni -ventum, 4. **I.** *to come in the way of, to meet;* se in tempore pugnae obventurum, Liv. **II.** Transf., **a,** *to fall in the way of, occur to, happen;* vitium obvenit consuli, Liv.; id obvenit vitium quod, etc., Liv.; **b,** *to fall to, fall to the lot of;* ei sorte provincia obvenit, Cic.

obversor, 1. dep. *to move up and down before; appear before, be before, go about, show oneself.* **A.** Lit., castris, Liv.; Appio in somnis eadem obversata species, *appeared,* Liv. **B.** Transf., sed mihi ante oculos obversatur reipublicae dignitas, *hovers before my eyes,* Cic.

obversus -a -um (partic. of obverto), *turned towards;* in agmen utrumque, Ov.

obverto (-vorto) -verti (-vorti) -versum (-vorsum), 3. *to turn towards, twist towards, direct towards.* **I.** Act., arcus in aliquem, Ov.; proras pelago, Verg. **II.** Middle, obverti, *to turn towards.* **A.** Lit., **a,** gen., in hostem, Liv.; **b,** esp., *to oppose;* profligatis obversis, *the opponents being scattered,* Tac. **B.** Transf., milite ad sanguinem et caedes obverso, Tac.

obvĭam, adv. *in the way, on the way;* hence, *towards, against, to meet* in a friendly or hostile manner; obviam alicui ire or prodire or procedere, Cic.; obviam alicui fieri, Cic.; obviam venire, *to come to meet,* Cic.; obviam ire alicui rei, *to oppose,* Cic.; cupiditati hominum, Cic.

obvĭus -a -um (ob and via), *in the way, meeting.* **I.** Lit., obvius esse alicui, Cic.; dare se obvium alicui, *to meet,* Liv.; obvias mihi literas mittas, Cic.; subst., obviis percunctari, Cic. **II.** Transf., **1,** *exposed to;* furiis ventorum, Verg.; **2,** *ready at hand;* testes, Tac.; **3,** *affable, courteous, easy of access;* comitas, Tac.

obvolvo -volvi -vŏlūtum, 3. *to roll up, wrap up, cover all round;* capite obvoluto, *with head muffled up,* Cic.; transf., verbisque decoris obvolvas vitium, Hor.

occaeco, 1. (ob and caeco). **I.** Lit., *to make blind, to blind;* **a,** lit., occaecatus pulvere effuso hostis, Liv.; **b,** transf., occaecati cupiditate, Cic. **II.** *to darken, overcloud;* **a,** lit., densa caligo occaecaverat diem, *to hide from sight;* **b,** transf., *to make obscure, unintelligible;* obscura narratio totam occaecat orationem, Cic. **III.** *to conceal, make invisible;* semen, Cic.

occallesco -callŭi, 3. (ob and calleo), *to become thick-skinned;* **1,** lit., Ov.; **2,** transf., *to become insensible, unfeeling,* Cic.

occăno -cănŭi, 3. (ob and cano), *to blow, sound;* cornua tubasque, Tac.

occāsĭo -ōnis, f. (from occasum, supine of occido), *a favourable moment, opportunity, occasion.* **I.** Gen., occasionem nancisci, Cic.; arripere, Liv.; amittere, Cic.; dimittere, Caes.; occasione datā, *when an opportunity is offered,* Cic.; ut primum occasio data est, *as soon as an opportunity offered,* Cic.; per occasionem, *on a favourable opportunity,* Liv.; quaerere criminandorum patrum occasiones, Liv. **II.** *an opportunity to make a coup-de-main;* occasionis esse rem, non proelii, Caes.

1. **occāsus** -a -um, partic. of occido.

2. **occāsus** -ūs, m. (occido), *the setting of the heavenly bodies.* **A.** Lit., **1,** solis, Caes.; **2,** *the west;* ab occasu, Verg. **B.** Transf., *fall, destruction, end, death;* occasus interitusque reipublicae, Cic.; occasus noster, *exile,* Cic.

occātĭo -ōnis, f. (occo), *a harrowing,* Cic.

occēdo -cessi -cessum, 3. (ob and cedo), *to go to, go towards, meet;* in conspectum alicuius, Plaut.

occento, 1. (ob and canto), **1,** *to sing to, sing a serenade to,* Plaut.; **2,** *to sing a lampoon* or *pasquinade against any one,* Cic.

occĭdens -entis, m. (lit., partic. of occīdo, sc. sol), *the evening, the west,* Cic.

occīdĭo -ōnis, f. (occīdo), *complete slaughter, extermination, utter destruction;* occidione occidere, *to destroy utterly, slay to the last man,* Cic.; occidione occumbere, *to be slain to the last man,* Tac.

1. **occīdo** -cīdi -cīsum, 3. (ob and caedo). **I.** *to knock down, beat to the ground;* Ctesipho me pugnis occidit, Ter. **II.** *to kill, slay.* **A.** Lit., L. Virginius filiam suā manu occidit, Cic.; ipse fortissime pugnans occiditur, Caes. **B.** *to plague to death, to torture, annoy, torment;* rogando, legendo, Hor.

2. **occĭdo** -cĭdi -cāsum, 3. (ob and cado). **I.** *to fall, fall down;* alia signa de coelo ad terram occidunt, Plaut. **II. A.** Of the heavenly bodies, *to set;* sol occidit, Liv.; ab orto usque ad occidentem solem, *from the east to the west,* Liv. **B.** *to die, perish;* **1,** lit., in bello, Cic.; suā dextrā, *to die by one's own hand,* Verg.; **2,** transf., *to perish, be ruined;* sin plane occidimus, Cic.; ornatus mundi occidat, Cic.; spes occidit, Hor.

occĭdŭus -a -um (occido). **I.** *setting;* **a,** lit., sol, Ov.; **b,** meton., *western, westerly,* Ov. **II.** Transf., *approaching death, near to dissolution,* Ov.

occĭno -cĕcĭni and -cĭnŭi, 3. (ob and cano), *to sing or chirp inauspiciously, to croak;* si occinuerit avis, Liv.

occĭpĭo -cēpi -ceptum, 3. (ob and capio). **I.** Intransit., *to begin;* a meridie nebula occepit, Liv. **II.** Transit., **A.** *to begin, commence;* quaestum, Ter.; with infin., regnare occepit, Liv. **B.** *to enter on;* magistratum, Liv.

occĭpĭtĭum -ĭi, n. (occiput), *the back of the head, occiput,* Plaut.

occĭput -ĭtis, n. (ob and caput), *the back of the head,* Pers.

occīsĭo -ōnis, f. (occīdo), *a slaying, killing, murdering, slaughter;* parentis, Cic.

occīsor -ōris, m. (occīdo), *a slayer, murderer,* Plaut.

occīsus -a -um, p. adj. (from occīdo), *ruined, unfortunate;* occisissimus sum omnium qui vivunt, Plaut

occlūdo -clūsi -clūsum, 3. (ob and claudo). **I.** *to shut up, close up;* tabernas, Cic. **II.** *to restrain, keep in;* furax servus, cui nihil sit obsignatum nec occlusum, Cic.

occlūsus -a -um, partic. of occludo.

occo, 1. *to harrow;* poet., segetem, *to till,* Hor.

occoepi -isse = occipio (q.v.).

occŭbo, 1. (ob and cubo), *to lie down,* esp., *to rest in the grave;* ad tumulum, quo maximus occubat Hector, Verg.

occulco, 1. (ob and calco), *to trample, tread in, trample down;* occulcare signa ordinesque (of elephants), Liv.

occŭlo -cŭlŭi -cultum, 3. (ob and root CUL, whence also cucullus), *to cover* (esp. for the purpose of hiding), *to hide, conceal;* aliquem,

Liv ; vulnera, Cic., transf, puncta argumentorum, Cic.

occultātĭo -ōnis, f (occulto), *a hiding, concealing, concealment*, occultatione se tutari, Cic

occultātor -ōris, m. (occulto), *a hider, concealer*, latronum, Cic

occultē, adv (occultus), *secretly, in secret, privately*, latēre, Cic, dicere, *obscurely*, Cic

occulto, 1 (intens of occulo), *to hide, conceal*, se latebris, Cic, transf., flagitia, Cic

occultus -a -um, p. adj (from occulo), *secret, hidden, concealed, private* **I.** Adj, **A.** Lit, occultissimus exitus, Liv **B.** Transf, occultior cupiditas, Cic., of persons, *secret, close, reserved*, si me astutum et occultum lubet fingere, Cic **II.** Subst, **a**, **occulta** -ōrum, *secret things, secrets*, Cic.; **b**, in adv. expressions, in occulto, Cic, per occultum, Tac, ex occulto, *secretly*, Cic

occumbo -cŭbŭi -cŭbĭtum, 3 (ob and cumbo), *to fall down, sink down*, usually, *to fall down in death, to die*, mortem, *to die*, Cic, poet., morti, Verg., or simply occumbere, aut occubuissem honeste, aut victores hodie viveremus, Cic

occŭpātĭo -ōnis, f (occupo) **I.** *a seizing, taking possession of, occupation*, fori, Cic **II.** *a business, employment, occupation*, occupationes reipublicae, Caes, maximis occupationibus impediri, distineri, Cic

occŭpātus -a -um, p. adj (from occupo), *busy, engaged, occupied*, in apparando bello, Cic.

occŭpo, 1 (ob and capio), *to take possession of, occupy, lay hold of, seize* **I.** Lit, **1**, totam Italiam suis praesidiis, Cic., tyrannidem, Cic, poet, aliquem amplexu, *to embrace*, Ov, **2**, *to fill, occupy with anything*, Tyrrhenum mare caementis, Hor; aream fundamentis, Liv. **II.** Transf, **1**, *to fall upon, attack*, aliquem gladio, Verg; **2**, *to anticipate, to do anything first*, with infin, occupant bellum facere, *first begin the war*, Liv, **3**, *to occupy, master*, pavor occupat animos, Liv, mentes Siculorum occupat superstitio, Cic, **4**, *to make busy, engage, occupy*, Liv, **5**, *to employ, occupy, to put out, invest money*, pecuniam grandi fenore, Cic

occurro -curri -cursum, 3 (ob and curro) **I.** *to run to meet, hasten to meet* **A.** 1, lit, **a**, gen, Caesari venienti, Caes, **b**, esp, *to fall upon, attack*; duabus legionibus, Caes, **2**, transf, of things, *to come in the way of*, in asperis locis silex saepe impenetrabilis ferro occurrebat, Liv **B.** Fig, **a**, *to work against, oppose, counteract*, omnibus eius consiliis, Cic, **b**, *to come to the help of, assist*, vestrae sapientiae, Cic **II. A.** *to be present at, engage in*, neutri proelio, Liv, negotiis, Cic **B** Fig, *to meet the eye, to come into the thoughts, to occur to any one to present itself, occur, happen*, animo, cogitationi, Cic, in mentem, Cic

occursātĭo -ōnis, f (occurso), *a going to meet a person, attention, officiousness*, facilis est illa occursatio et blanditia popularis, Cic

occurso, 1 (intens of occurro) **I.** *to go to meet, to meet* **A.** Lit, fugientibus, Tac **B.** *to oppose*, invidi, occursantes, factiosi, Sall **II.** *to rush upon, fall upon, attack*, occursat ocius gladio, Caes

occursus -ūs, m (occurro), *a meeting, a falling in with*; vacuae occursus hominum viae, Liv, alicuius occursum vitare, *to avoid meeting with any one*, Tac

Ōcĕănus -i, m (Ὠκεανός), **1**, *the ocean, the sea which encompasses the earth*, mare Oceanus, Caes, **2**, personified as a god, *the husband of Tethys and father of the Nymphs*, hence **Ōcĕănītis** -ĭdis, f. *a daughter of Oceanus*, Verg

ŏcellus -i, m. (dim of oculus), *a little eye*, Ov, fig, of something excellent, ocelli Italiae villulae nostrae, Cic

ōcĭor, ōcius, adj compar (ὠκίων), superl **ōcissĭmus** (ὤκιστος), *swifter, quicker, more rapid*, ocior cervis, Hor, ocior Euro, Hor

ōcĭus, adv. (= ὠκέως), superl. **ōcissĭmē**, *more quickly, swiftly, rapidly*, facere, Cic, recreari, Cic., serius, ocius, sors exitura, *sooner or later*, Hor

Ocnus -i, m ("Οκνος), *the founder of Mantua*

ŏcrĕa -ae, f *a metal greave*, Verg

ŏcrĕātus -a -um (ocrea), *wearing the ocrea*, Hor

Ocrĕsĭa -ae, f *mother of Servius Tullius*

Ocrĭcŭlum -i, n *a town in Umbria, on the Tiber, now Otricoli* Hence, adj, **Ocrĭcŭlānus** -a -um, *of or belonging to Ocriculum*

octăphŏros = octophoros (q v)

Octāvĭus -a -um, *name of a Roman gens* Hence, adj, **Octāvĭānus** -a -um, Octavianum, bellum, *of Cn Octavius with Cinna*, Cic, subst, **Octāvĭānus** -i, m *name of the Emperor Augustus after his adoption into the gens Julia*

octāvus -a -um (octo), *the eighth*, ager efficit cum octavo, *bears eight fold*, Cic, adv, octavum, *for the eighth time*, Liv, subst, **octāva** -ae, f (sc hora), *the eighth hour*, Juv

octāvusdĕcĭmus -a -um, *the eighteenth*, Tac

octĭes, adv (octo), *eight times*, Cic

octingĕnārĭus -a -um (octingeni), *consisting of eight hundred*, Varr

octingentēsĭmus -a -um (octingenti), *the eight hundredth*, Cic

octingenti -ae -a (octo and centum), *eight hundred*, Cic

octĭpes -pĕdis (octo and pes), *having eight feet*, Ov

octō (ὀκτώ), *eight*, Cic

Octōber -bris -bre, m (octo and suff -ber), *belonging to the number eight*, **a**, mensis October, *the eighth month of the Roman year*, reckoning from March, October, **b**, *belonging to the month of October*, Idus, Calendae, Cic

octōdĕcim, numer (octo and decem), *eighteen*, Liv

octōgēnārĭus -a -um (octogeni), *containing eighty, consisting of eighty*, Plin

octōgēni -ae -a, *eighty each*, Liv

octōgēsĭmus -a -um (octoginta), *the eightieth*, Cic

octōgĭes, adv *eighty times*, Cic

octōginta, numer *eighty* Cic

octōjŭgis -e (octo and jugum), *yoked eight together*, transf, octojuges ad imperia obtinenda ire, *eight together*, Liv

octōnārĭus -a -um (octoni), *consisting of eight, containing eight*, Plin

octōni -ae -a (octo), *eight each*, Caes

octōphŏros -on (* ὀκτώφορος), *borne by four*; lectica octophoro ferri, Cic Subst, **octōphŏrŏn** -i, n (ὀκτώφορον), *a litter carried by eight bearers*, Cic

octŭāgies, octuaginta = octogies, octoginta (q v)

octŭplĭcātus -a -um (octuplus), *increased eight fold*, Liv.

octŭplus -a -um (ὀκταπλοῦς), *eight-fold*, pars, Cic Subst, **octŭplum** -i, n *an eight-fold penalty*, damnari octupli, Cic.

octussis -is, m (octo and as), *eight asses*, Hor

ŏcŭlātus a um (oculus), *having eyes*, hence, 1, testis, *an eye witness*, Plaut , 2, *catching the eye, visible*, Cic (?)

ŏcŭlĕus -a -um (oculus), *having many eyes, sharp sighted*, Argus, Plaut

ŏcŭlus -i, m (dim of OC us, connected with ὄσσομαι, ὄσσε), *the eye* I. Lit , oculos amittere, *to lose one's sight*, Caes , cadere sub oculis, Cic , esse in oculis, *to be visible*, Cic , ante oculos ponere, proponere oculis, *to set before one's eyes*, Cic , res posita in oculis, *visible*, Cic , in oculis, *before one's eyes, in one's presence*, Cic , in oculis esse alicuius (alicui), *to be loved by*, Cic , so also aliquem in oculis ferre, *to esteem highly*, Cic , esse ante oculos, *to be visible*, Cic II. Transf , a, of something highly prized or excellent, illos oculos orae maritimae (Corinth and Carthage) effodere, Cic , b, *the spot upon a panther's skin or a peacock's tail*, Plin , c, *a bud or eye of a plant*, Verg

ōdi, ōdisse, partic. fut , ōsūrus. I. *to hate, detest*, aliquem acerbe, Cic II. *to dislike, be displeased with*, Persicos apparatus, Hor (perf , odivi, ap Cic)

ŏdĭōsē, adv (odiosus), *hatefully, odiously*, Cic

ŏdĭōsus a -um (odium), *hateful, odious, troublesome, irksome, vexatious, burdensome*, orator, *tedious*, Cic , verbum, Cic , cupidis rerum talium odiosum et molestum est carere, *it is annoying, unpleasant*, Cic

ŏdĭum -ii, n (odi), *hatred* I. Subject , a, odium in omnes, Cic odium mulierum, *towards women*, Cic , vestrum, *towards you*, Liv , in odium alicuius irruere, *to become hated by any one*, Cic , odium est mihi cum aliquo, *I am at enmity with*, Cic , esse odio alicui, *to be hated by*, Cic , in odio esse alicui or apud aliquem, *to be hated by*, Cic , odium saturare, *to satisfy one's hatred*, Cic , b, meton , *the object of hatred*, Antonius insigne odium omnium hominum, Cic II. Object , *offensive conduct, expression of hatred*, odio et strepitu senatus coactus est perorare, Cic

ŏdor and **ŏdōs** ōris m (ὄζω, ὀδμή), *a smell, odour* I. 1, lit , Cic , esp , a, *an unpleasant smell, stench, stink*, camera incultu, tenebris, odore foeda, Sall b, *a sweet smell*, Verg , c, *steam, vapour* insolitus, Liv , 2, transf , *a scent, suspicion, inkling, presentiment* , dictaturae, Cic , urbanitatis, Cic , suspicionis, Cic II. Meton , *perfume, incense*, and in plur , *perfumery, unguents, spices*, incendere odores, Cic

ŏdōrātĭo -ōnis, f (odoror), *a smelling, smell*, Cic

1 **ŏdōrātus** -ūs, m (odor), 1, *a smell, smelling*, Cic , 2, transf , a, *the sense of smell*, Cic , b, *an odour*, Plin

2 **ŏdōrātus** a -um (odor), *odorous, sweet smelling*, cedrus, Verg , capilli, Hor

3 **ŏdōrātus** a um, partic of odoror

ŏdōrĭfĕr fĕra -fĕrum (odor and fero), 1, *odoriferous, having a pleasant smell*, panacea, Verg , 2, *producing perfumes*; gens, Ov

ŏdōro, 1 (odor), *to make odorous*, odorant aera fumis, Ov

ŏdōror, 1 dep (odor) I. *to smell*; a, *to examine by smell*, aliquid, Plant ; b, *to scent, smell*, cibum, Hor II. Transf , a, *to sniff at, nose (as a dog), to aim at, aspire to*, quos odorari hunc decemviratum suspicamini, Cic , b, *to search into, track out, investigate*, quid sentiant, Cic , c, *only to smell of, to have the slightest smattering of*, philosophiam, Tac

ŏdōrus a um (odor), 1, *having a pleasant smell, sweet-smelling, odorous*, flos, Ov , 2, *keen-scented, tracking by smell*, odora canum vis, Verg

ŏdōs = odor (q v)

Ŏdrўsae -ārum, m (Ὀδρύσαι), *a people of Thrace*, hence, adj , **Ŏdrўsĭus** -a -um, poet = *Thracian*

Ŏdyssēa ae, f (Ὀδύσσεια), 1, *the Odyssey, a poem by Homer*, 2, Odysseae portus, *a promontory in the south of Sicily*

Oea -ae, f *a town in Africa*, now *Tripoli* Hence, adj , **Oeensis** -e, *of* or *belonging to Oea*

Oeăgrus -i, m (Οἴαγρος), *a mythical king of Thrace, father of Orpheus*, hence, adj , **Oeăgrĭus** a um, poet = *Thracian*

Oebălus i, m (Οἴβαλος), *a king of Sparta, father of Tyndarus, grandfather of Helen*. Hence, A. **Oebălĭdēs** ae, m *a descendant of Oebalus* = *a Spartan*, puer, *Hyacinthus*, Ov. ; plur , Oebalidae, *Castor and Pollux*, Ov B. **Oebălĭs** -idis, f *relating to Oebalus*, nympha, *Helen*, Ov , matres, *Sabine*, as the Sabines were supposed to be descended from the Spartans, Ov C. **Oebălĭus** -a -um, *relating to Oebalus*, vulnus, *of Hyacinthus*, Ov , **Oebălĭa** -ae, f *Tarentum* (colonised from Sparta), Verg.

Oechălĭa -ae, f (Οἰχαλία), *town in Euboea, residence of Eurytus, father of Iole* Hence, **Oechălĭs** -idis, f *Oechalian*

Oeclĕus -ĕi, m (Οἰκλεύς), *father of Amphiaraus* Hence, **Oeclīdēs** -ae, m. *son of Oecleus* = *Amphiaraus*.

oecŏnŏmĭcus -a -um (οἰκονομικός), *relating to domestic economy* Subst , **Oecŏnŏmĭcus** i, m *title of a book by Xenophon*, Cic.

Oedĭpūs -pŏdis, m (Οἰδίπους), *king of Thebes, son of Laius and Jocasta, fated to kill his father and to espouse his mother , known as having solved the riddle of the Theban Sphynx* · prov , Davus sum, non Oedipus, *I am no Oedipus to unriddle riddles*, Ter Hence, **Oedĭpŏdĭōnĭus** -a -um, *Oedipodean*, Ov

Oenĕus -ĕi or -ĕos m (Οἰνεύς), *king of Aetolia or Calydon, father of Meleager, Tydeus and Deianira* , hence, A. **Oenēĭus** -a -um and **Oenēus** a -um, *relating to Oeneus*, agri, *Aetolia*, Ov B. **Oenīdēs** ae, m *son of Oeneus, Meleager* , also *Diomedes, son of Tydeus, grandson of Oeneus*, Ov

Oenŏmăus -i, m (Οἰνόμαος), *king in Elis, father of Hippodamia, grandfather of Atreus and Thyestes*

Oenōnē -ēs, f (Οἰνώνη), *a Phrygian nymph, daughter of the river-god Cebrenus, beloved and afterwards deserted by Paris*

oenŏphŏrum -i, n (οἰνοφόρον), *a basket or hamper for wine*, Hor

Oenŏpĭa -ae, f (Οἰνοπία), *the island afterwards called Aegina* Hence, adj , **Oenŏpĭus** a um, *relating to Oenopia*

Oenŏpĭōn -ōnis, m. (Οἰνοπίων), *king in Chios, father of Merope*

oenŏpōlĭum -ii, n. (οἰνοπωλεῖον), *a wine-shop, tavern*, Plaut

Oenōtrĭa ae, f (Οἰνωτρία), *old name of the south east part of Italy*; hence, adj , **Oenōtrĭus** -a um and **Oenōtrus** -a um, *Oenotrian*; meton , *Italian, Roman*

1 **oenus** = unus (q v)

2 **Oenūs**, acc -unta, m. *a river in Laconia, falling into the Eurotas*.

oestrus -i, m (οἶστρος), *the gadfly, horsefly, breeze*, Verg

oesus = usus (q v)

oesypum -i, n (οἴσυπος), *the fat and dirt of unwashed wool*, Plin ; hence, *a cosmetic, used by Roman ladies, prepared from it*, Ov

Oeta -ae, f and **Oete** -ēs, f (Οἴτη), *the mountain chain between Thessaly and Macedonia, where Hercules burnt himself*; hence, adj , **Oetaeus** -a -um, *Oetean*, deus, Prop , and simply, Oetaeus, *Hercules*, Ov

ŏfella -ae, f (dim of offa as mamilla of mamma), *a bit, morsel*, Juv

offa -ae, f **I.** *a bit, morsel*, esp , *a ball or pellet of flour*, pultis, Cic **II.** Transf , **a,** *a piece, lump*, gummi in offas convolutum, Plin ; hence, *a swelling*, Juv , **b,** *an untimely birth, abortion*, Juv

offendo -fendi -fensum, 3 (ob and *fendo) **I.** Intransit , *to strike, knock, dash against* **A.** Lit , **1,** qui in tantis tenebris nihil offendat, Cic , **2,** *to suffer damage*, naves in redeundo offenderunt Caes **B.** Transf , **a,** *to make a mistake*, si quid offenderit, Cic , **b,** *to offend against a person*, si in me aliquid offendistis, Cic , **c,** *to come into danger, suffer reverse*, apud judices, *to be condemned*, Cic **II.** Transit , *to strike, knock against something* **A.** Lit , **1,** caput, Liv , **2, a,** *to hit upon a person, fall in with, come upon*, aliquem imparatum, *to come upon unawares, surprise*, Cic , **b,** *to injure*, latus vehementer, Cic. **B.** Transf , *to offend, displease*, aliquem or alicuius animum, Cic , animum in aliquo, *to feel hurt by some one*, Cic , eos splendor offendit, Cic , partic , **offensus** -a -um, **a,** *injured, hurt*, offensus animus, Cic , **b,** *repulsive*, civibus, Cic , subst , **offensum** -i, n *something causing offence*, Cic

offensa -ae, f (offendo) **I.** Lit *a striking against, knocking against*, Plin **II.** *dislike, hatred, enmity, affront, injury*, magna in offensa sum apud Pompeium, Cic , offensas vindicet ense suas, Ov

offensio -ōnis, f (offendo), *a striking against, hitting against* **I. a,** lit , pedis, *a stumbling*, Cic , **b,** meton , *that against which one stumbles, a stumbling block*, Cic **II. 1,** *indisposition, complaint*, corporum, Cic , **2, a,** *hatred, enmity, disfavour, aversion*, in alicuius offensionem cadere, Cic , effugere alicuius offensionem, Cic , **b,** *defeat, loss, misfortune*, offensionem timere, Cic

offensiuncŭla -ae, f (dim of offensio), **1,** *a slight offence, displeasure*, Cic , **2,** *a slight failure*, Cic

offenso, 1 (intens of offendo), *to strike, dash against*, capita, Liv

1 **offensus** -a -um, partic of offendo

2 **offensus** -ūs, m (offendo), **1,** *a dashing against, a shock*, Lucr , **2,** *offence, dislike*, Lucr

offĕro, obtŭli, oblātum, offerre (ob and fero), *to carry or bring to, place before, present, produce, offer* **I.** Lit , aciem strictam venientibus, Verg , os suum non modo ostendere, sed etiam offerre, Cic , reflex , **se** offerre, *to present oneself, appear*, pass , offerri, *to present oneself, offer oneself, appear*, multis in difficillimis rebus praesens auxilium eius numinis oblatum est, Cic **II.** Transf , **a,** *to offer, expose*, nos periculis sine causa, Cic , se morti, Caes , se ad mortem pro patria, Cic , vitam in discrimen, Cic , **b,** *to adduce, bring forward*, crimina, Cic , **c,** *to offer, proffer*, alicui operam suam, Liv , **d,** *to cause, occasion*, alicui beneficium, Cic , stuprum alicui, Cic , mortem alicui, Cic

offĭcīna -ae, f (= opificina, from opifex), *a workshop, manufactory, in which any handicraft is carried on*, armorum, *a manufactory of arms*, Caes , fig , *a workshop, laboratory*, falsorum commentariorum et chirographorum officina, Cic , discendi, Cic , nequitiae, sapientiae, Cic

offĭcio -fēci -fectum, 3 (ob and facio), *to be in the way of, impede, hinder* **A.** Lit , with dat , alicui apricanti, *to stand between any one and the sun*, Cic , ipsa umbra terrae soli officiens, *coming before the sun*, Cic **B** Transf , *to hinder, obstruct, be in the way of, to injure*, meis commodis, Cic , consiliis alicuius, Sall , officiunt laetis frugibus herbae, Verg

offĭcĭōsē, adv (officiosus), *obligingly, courteously*, hoc facere, Cic , sed illa officiosius, Cic

offĭcĭōsus -a -um (officium), *obliging, courteous attentive, kind, respectful* (especially used of the behaviour of inferiors to superiors), **1,** homo Cic in aliquem, Cic , **2,** *dutiful, conformable to duty*, dolor, Cic , labores, Cic

offĭcĭum -ii, n (perhaps for opificium) **I.** *duty, obligation, service, part* **A.** esse in officio, Cic , officio fungi, *to do one's duty*, Cic , officium praestare, Caes , officio suo deesse, *to fail in one's duty*, Cic **B.** *subjection allegiance*, in officio continere, Cic **II.** *dutiful action* **A.** meorum officiorum conscientia, Cic **B. 1,** *respect, courtesy, deference*, homo summo officio praeditus, Cic , **2,** *attention, complaisance, friendly service*, **a,** illius in ullum ordinem officia, Cic , **b,** *ceremony, attendance on some solemn occasion, service of honour*, urbana officia alicui praestare, ap Cic , officio togae virilis interfui, *I was present at the ceremony of taking the toga virilis*, Plin , suprema in aliquem officia, *the last offices, the ceremony of interment*, Tac , so officium triste, Ov , **3,** *service, business, official employment*, toti officio maritimo M Bibulus praepositus, *over the whole naval service*, Cic , confecto legationis officio, Cic

offīgo -fixi -fixum, 3 (ob and figo), *to fix in, fasten*, ita densos offigunt implicantque ramos, Liv

offirmātē, adv (offirmatus), *firmly, obstinately*, Suet

offirmātus -a -um (offirmo), *firm, steadfast, obstinate*, Cic

offirmo, 1 (ob and firmo), *to make firm, to fasten*, transf , *to make resolute, steadfast*, ne tam offirma te, *don't be so obstinate*, Ter

offūcia -ae, f (ob and fucus), **1,** *paint, rouge*, Plaut , **2,** transf , *deceit, deception*, Plaut

offulgĕo -fulsi, 2 (ob and fulgeo), *to shine upon, appear*, nova lux oculis offulsit, Verg

offundo -fūdi -fūsum, 3 (ob and fundo) **I.** *to pour before, pour around, pour out* **A.** Lit , Plaut **B.** Transf , pass , offundi, *to be poured out, to be poured round, to be spread around*, nobis aer crassus offunditur, *surrounds us*, Cic , fig , si quid tenebrarum offudit exsilium Cic , ne nimium terroris offundam, Liv , omnium rerum terrorem oculis auribusque est offusus, Liv **II.** *to spread over, to cover, conceal*, obscuratur et offunditur luce solis lumen lucernae, Cic ; fig offusus pavore, Tac

oggannio -ivi and -ii -itum, 4 (ob and gannio), *to yelp, growl at*, Plaut

Ōgȳgēs -is, m (Ὠγύγης), *a mythical king of Thebes* Hence, **Ōgȳgius** -a -um, *Theban*, deus, *Bacchus*, Ov

oh, interj *oh! ah!* Plaut

ŏhē, interj *ho! holloa!* Plaut

ŏho, interj *oho! aha!* Plaut

oi, interj *oh!* an exclamation of pain, Ter.

Oïlĕūs -ĕi and -ĕos, m. (Ὀϊλεύς), *king of Locris, father of Ajax* (who was also called *Ajax Oileus*).

Olbĭa -ae, f. (Ὀλβία), *a town on the east coast of Sardinia.* Hence, adj., **Olbĭensis** -e, *Olbian.*

ŏlĕa -ae, f. (ἐλαία), **1,** *the olive, the fruit of the olive-tree,* Varr.; **2,** *the olive-tree,* Cic.

ŏlĕāgĭnĕus (ŏlĕāgĭnus) -a -um (olea), *of or relating to the olive-tree,* Nep.

ŏlĕārĭus -a -um (oleum), *of or belonging to oil;* cella, Cic.

Ŏlĕărus (-ŏs) and **Ŏlĭăros** -i, f. (Ὠλέαρος), *one of the islands of the Sporades, now Antiparos.*

ŏlĕaster -tri, m. (olea), *the wild olive-tree,* Verg.

ŏlens -entis, p. adj. (from oleo), *smelling;* hence, **a,** *fragrant, sweet-smelling,* Ov.; **b,** *bad-smelling, stinking, fetid,* Verg.

Ōlĕnus (-ŏs) -i, f. (Ὤλενος). **I.** *a town in Achaia.* **II.** *a town in Aetolia.* Hence, **Ōlĕnĭus** -a -um = *Achaian;* capella or pecus, *the goat of Amalthea,* Ov.

ŏlĕo, ŏlŭi, 2. (cf. ὄζω, odor). **I.** *to emit an odour, smell.* **A.** bene, Cic.; with abl., sulfure, Ov.; with acc., crocum, *to smell of,* Cic.; nihil, Cic. **B.** Fig., *to smell of, to savour of, to smack of;* nihil ex Academia, Cic.; malitiam, Cic. **II.** *to be revealed* or *be betrayed by smell;* quid, illud non olet, unde sit, quod dicitur "cum illis?" Cic.

ŏlĕum -i, n. (ἔλαιον) *olive-oil, oil;* instillare oleum lumini, Cic.; prov., oleum et operam perdere, *to lose time and trouble,* Cic.; nitidum quoddam genus est verborum et laetum sed palaestrae magis et olei, etc., *shows signs of too much effort* (from the oil used in the palaestra by wrestlers), Cic.

olfăcĭo -fēci -factum, 3. (oleo and facio), *to smell.* **A.** Lit., ea quae gustamus, Cic. **B.** Fig., *to scent out, trace by smell, detect;* nummum, Cic.

olfacto, 1. (intens. of olfacio), *to smell at, smell,* Plaut.

ŏlĭdus -a -um (oleo), *smelling, emitting an odour;* capra, *stinking, fetid,* Hor.

ōlim, adv. (from ollus, old Lat. for ille). **I. A.** Of the past, *formerly, once upon a time, in times past;* qui mihi dixit olim, Cic. **B.** Of the future, *hereafter, at a future time:* non, si male nunc, et olim sic erit, Hor.; utinam coram tecum olim potius quam per epistolas, Cic. **II.** *at times, often;* ut pueris olim dant crustula blandi doctores, Hor.

ŏlĭtor -ōris, m. (olus), *cultivator of pot-herbs, kitchen-gardener,* Cic.

ŏlĭtōrĭus -a -um (olitor), *of or relating to culinary herbs;* forum, *vegetable market,* Liv.

ŏlīva -ae, f. **I.** *the olive,* Hor. **II.** *the olive-tree.* **A.** Lit., Cic. **B.** Meton., **1,** *an olive-branch,* Hor.; **2,** *a staff of olive-tree wood,* Ov.

ŏlīvētum -i, n. (oliva), *a place planted with olives, olive-garden,* Cic.

ŏlīvĭfĕr -fĕra -fĕrum (oliva and fero), *olive-bearing,* Verg., Ov.

ŏlīvum -i, n. (oliva), **1,** *olive-oil, oil,* Verg.; **2,** *oil for anointing, unguent,* Cat.

olla -ae, f. (orig. ola = aula), *an earthenware jar or pot,* Cic.

ollus, olle, obsolete form of ille -a -ud (q.v.).

ŏlo, 3. = oleo (q.v.).

ŏlor -ōris, m. *a swan,* Hor.

ŏlōrīnus -a -um (olor), *of or relating to a swan,* Verg.

ŏlus (hŏlus) -ĕris, n. *any kind of culinary vegetable, pot-herb,* Hor.

ŏluscŭlum -i, n. (dim. of olus), *a herb, vegetable,* Cic.

Olympĭa -ae, f. (Ὀλυμπία), *a holy city and territory in Elis, where stood the temple of Jupiter Olympius, and where the Olympic games were celebrated.* Hence, adj., **A. Ŏlympĭăcus** -a -um, *Olympian.* **B. Ŏlympĭcus** -a -um, *Olympian.* **C. Ŏlympĭus** -a -um, *Olympian.* Subst., **Ŏlympĭum** -ii, n. *the temple of Jupiter Olympius,* Liv.; **Ŏlympĭa** -ōrum, n. *the Olympic games,* Cic. **D. Ŏlympĭăs** -ădis, f. *an Olympiad or period of four years, elapsing between each celebration of the Olympic games,* Cic. **E. Ŏlympĭŏnīces** -ae, m. (Ὀλυμπιονίκης), *a victor at Olympia,* Cic.

1. **Ŏlympĭăs,** v. Olympia.

2. **Ŏlympĭăs** -ădis, f. (Ὀλυμπιάς), *daughter of Neoptolemus, king in Epirus, mother of Alexander the Great.*

Ŏlympus (-ŏs) -i, m. (Ὄλυμπος). **I.** m. **A.** *a mountain on the borders of Macedonia and Thessaly, supposed to be the habitation of the gods;* poet. = *heaven,* Verg. **B.** *a celebrated flute-player, the pupil of Marsyas.* **II.** f. *a town of Lycia on the Mount Olympus there.* Hence, **Ŏlympēni** -ōrum, m. *the inhabitants of Olympus.*

Ŏlynthus (-ŏs) -i, f. (Ὄλυνθος), *town in Chalcidice, on the borders of Macedonia.* Hence, adj., **Ŏlynthĭus** -a -um, *Olynthian.*

ŏmāsum -i, n. *bullocks' tripe;* transf., pingui tentus omaso, *with fat paunch,* Hor.

ōmĕn -inis, n. *an omen, sign, augury, prognostication.* **I.** Lit., **A.** hisce ominibus proficiscere, Cic.; ire secundo omine, *in God's name,* Hor.; omen avertere, *to avert an omen,* Cic.; accipere, *to accept,* Cic. **B.** *a wish,* as a good omen; optima omina, Cic. **II.** Meton., *that which is accompanied by auspices;* **1,** prima omina = nuptiae, Verg.; **2,** *a solemn usage,* Verg.

ōmentum -i, n. (= ob-mentum, connected with opimus), *the entrails, bowels,* Juv.

ōmĭnor, 1. dep. (omen). **I.** *to augur, presage, prophesy, predict;* malo alienae quam nostrae reipublicae ominari, Cic. **II.** *to speak words of* (good or bad) *omen;* ominari horreo, Liv.

ōmĭnōsus -a -um (omen), *foreboding, ominous,* Plin.

ŏmissus -a -um, p. adj. (from omitto), *neglectful, remiss,* Ter.

ŏmitto -mīsi -missum, 3. (= ommitto, from ob and mitto), *to let go, let alone, let fall.* **I.** Lit., arma, Liv.; habenas, Tac. **II.** Transf., **A.** *to give up, lay aside, leave off;* pietatem et humanitatem, *to put on one side,* Cic.; timorem Cic.; with infin., *to cease;* omittat urgere, Cic. **B.** Of discourse, *to leave unmentioned, to omit;* ut haec omittam, Cic.; de reditu, Cic.

omnĭfĕr -fĕra -fĕrum (omnis and fero), *bearing everything, all-bearing,* Ov.

omnĭgĕna -ae, genit. plur., -ûm, c. (omnis and genus), *of all sorts;* omnigenûm deum monstra, Verg.

omnĭgĕnus -a -um (= omne genus), *of all kinds,* Lucr.

omnĭmŏdis, adv. (omnis and modus), *in every way, wholly, entirely,* Lucr.

omnīnō, adv. (omnis), *altogether, entirely, wholly, totally.* **I.** quum senatoriis muneribus aut omnino aut magna ex parte essem liberatus, Cic ; esp , **a**, *in general, especially*, de hominum genere aut omnino de animalibus loquor, Cic , **b**, *in all, in the total*, quinque omnino fuerunt, Cic **II.** *utterly, entirely, at all*, fieri omnino neges, Cic , esp , **a**, with superl , miserrima est omnino ambitio, Cic , **b**, with negatives, is omnino servus in familia erat, Cic **III.** In concessive clauses foll by sed = *certainly but*, pugnas omnino sed cum adversario facili, Cic

omnĭpărens -entis (omnis and parens), *all producing, all-bearing*, terra, Verg

omnĭpŏtens -entis (omnis and potens), *almighty, all-powerful, omnipotent*, Verg

omnis -e, *all* **I.** Of number, **A.** omnis fortuna, Cic , leges aliae omnes, Cic , subst , omnes, *all men*, Cic , omnia, *everything*, Cic , so omnia, Cic , omnia facere *to do whatever is possible*, Cic , omnia mihi sunt cum aliquo, *I am quite in agreement with*, Cic , sic in eo sunt omnia, *everything depends upon that*, Cic , per omnia, *in every respect*, Liv , ante omnia, *especially*, Liv. **B. a**, *each, every, all*, omnis amans, *every lover*, Ov , omnibus mensibus, Cic . **b**, *of all kinds*, olus omne, Hor , omnibus precibus petere, Cic **II.** *the whole*, Gallia omnis, Caes , non omnis moriar, *not entirely*, Hor , sanguinem suum omnem effundere, Cic

omnĭtŭens -entis (omnis and tueor), *all-seeing, all beholding*, Lucr

omnĭvăgus a -um (omnis and vagus), *wandering everywhere*, Cic.

omnĭvŏlus -a -um (omnis and volo), *all willing, all-wishing*, Cat.

Omphălē ēs, f (Ὀμφάλη), *a queen of Lydia, whom Hercules served in woman's dress.*

ŏnăger and **ŏnāgrus** i, m *the wild ass*, Verg

ŏnĕrārĭus -a um (onus), *of or relating to freight, burden, etc.*, jumenta, *beasts of burden*, Liv Subst , **ŏnĕrārĭa**, ae, f *a merchant or transport ship*, Cic

ŏnĕro, 1 (onus) **I.** *to load, pack, freight, burden with anything* **A** Lit , **1**, naves, Caes , **2**, **a**, *to burden, trouble, tire, oppress, weigh down*, aures lapillis, Ov , hostes (saxis), Liv ; **b**, *to cover*, ossa aggere terrae, Verg , **c**, *to load, fill*, mensas dapibus, *to load the tables with victuals*, Verg , manus jaculis, Verg **B.** Fig , **1**, *to load, burden, oppress, overwhelm*, aliquem mendaciis, Cic , judicem argumentis, Cic , **2**, **a**, *to weary, tire*, aethera votis, Verg , **b**, *to overwhelm*, aliquem contumeliis, Cic , in a good sense, aliquem laudibus, Liv , **c**, *to make more burdensome, to aggravate*, curas, Tac , inopiam alicujus, Liv **II.** *to put into a cask, vessel*, etc , vina cadis, Verg

ŏnĕrōsus -a um (onus) **I.** *heavy, burdensome*, praeda, Verg **II.** Fig , *troublesome*, onerosior altera sors est, Ov

ŏnus -eris, n *a load, burden, freight* **I. A.** Lit , merces atque onera, Cic **B.** Transf , *any kind of burden, weight*; tanti oneris turrim in muros collocare, Caes **II.** Fig , **A.** *weight, burden, trouble, charge*, oneri esse, *to be burdensome*, Sall , Liv , plus oneris sustuli quam ferre me posse intelligo, Cic **B.** Esp , *a public burden, tax, charge*, his temporibus hoc munícipium maximis oneribus pressum, Cic , haec omnia in dites a pauperibus inclinata onera, Liv

ŏnustus a-um (onus), *laden, loaded, freighted* **I.** Lit., asellus onustus auro, Cic., naves onustae frumento, Cic. **II.** *full, filled*; onusti cibo et vino, Cic , pharetra onusta telis, Tac

ŏnyx -ychis (ὄνυξ) **I.** m **A.** *a kind of yellowish marble, onyx*, from which many articles of luxury were made, Plin **B.** Meton , *a box or casket of onyx*, Hor **II.** f *a precious stone of a yellowish colour, onyx*, Plin **III.** *a shell-fish*, Plin

ŏpācĭtas ātis, f (opacus), *a shade, shadiness* arborum, Tac.

ŏpāco, 1. (opacus), *to shade, overshadow* locum, Cic

ŏpācus a um **I.** Pass , *shaded, shady* **A.** Lit , ripa, Cic , neut subst , per opaca locorum, *shady places*, Verg **B.** Transf , *dark, shadowy, obscure* nox, Verg , mater, *the earth*, Verg **II.** Act , *casting a shade, shading, shady*, arbor, Verg

ŏpălus -i, m *a precious stone, the opal*, Plin

ŏpella ae, f (dim of opera), *a little work, little labour, trouble, service*, Lucr , Hor

ŏpĕra ae, f (1 opus), *trouble, pains, effort, exertion* **I.** Lit , **A.** Gen , laborem et operam in aliqua re consumere, Cic , operam tribuere reipublicae, *devote oneself to*, Cic , operam dare alicui rei *to work hard at*, Cic , operam dare, with ut or ne and the subj , *to do one's best to*, etc , Cic , non operae est, with infin , *it is not worth the while*, Liv **B.** Esp , *a service, doing service*, Cn Pompeius, qui est in operis eius societatis, *who is in the service of that company*, Cic , Musis operas reddere, *to serve the Muses*, Cic **II. 1**, *time for work*, deest mihi opera, Cic , **2**, *a day labourer, workman*, gen in plur , operae fabrorum, Cic , sometimes in a contemptuous sense, *mercenaries, hired assistants*, Cic , operae theatrales, *the claqueurs*, Tac

ŏpĕrārĭus a -um (opera), *of or relating to work*, homo, *a day labourer*, Cic Subst , **ŏpĕrārĭus** ii, m *a day-labourer, workman*, transf , quidam operarii linguā celeri et exercitatā (of bad orators), Cic

ŏpercŭlum -i, n (operio), *a lid, cover*, Cic , operculum dolii ferreum, Liv

ŏpĕrīmentum -i, n (operio), *a cover, covering*, Cic

ŏpĕrĭo pĕrŭi pertum, 4 (ob and pario) **I.** *to cover* **A. 1**, gen , amphoras auro, Nep , **2**, esp , **a**, *to cover with a garment*, esp with a toga, capite operto esse, Cic , **b**, *to cover with earth, to bury*, reliquias malae pugnae, Tac **B.** Fig , **1**, *to cover, load*, judicia operta dedecore, Cic , **2**, *to cover, conceal*, res opertae Cic **II.** *to close, shut up*, opertā lecticā latus est, Cic

ŏpĕror, 1 dep (opus), *to work, labour, be busied, occupied with*, followed by dat of the occupation, **1**, connubiis arvisque novis, Verg , materiis caedendis, Tac., **2**, esp *to be engaged in worship*, sacris, Liv ; with dat of deity, *to worship*, sacrifice, deo, Tib , absol , *to worship, sacrifice*, laetis operatus in arvis, Verg

ŏpĕrōsē, adv (operosus), *laboriously, carefully*, Cic

ŏpĕrōsus -a um (opera), *laborious, painstaking, industrious* **I.** Lit , **a**, senectus, Cic , colonus, Ov , **b**, of medicines, *active, powerful* herba, Ov **II.** *that which causes much labour or trouble, laborious, toilsome, difficult*, artes, Cic , moles mundi, Ov , carmina, Hor

ŏpertum i, n (operio), *a secret place* **I.** Bonae Deae, Cic **II.** *a secret*, operta Apollinis, *the mysterious oracles of Apollo*, Cic

ŏpes v ops

Ŏphīōn -ŏnis, m (Ὀφίων), *father of Amycus*, hence, **Ŏphīŏnĭdēs** ae, m *son of Ophion = Amycus*

Ŏphĭūchus -i, m (Ὀφιοῦχος), *the snake-holder, a constellation*, Cic.

Ophĭūsa -ae, f. (Ὀφίουσα), *old name of the island of Cyprus.* Hence, **Ŏphĭūsĭus** -a -um, *Ophiusian = Cypriote.*

Ŏpĭcus -a -um, *Oscan*; transf., *stupid, foolish, silly, clownish*, Juv.

ŏpĭfĕr -fĕra -fĕrum (ops and fero), *helpful, rendering help*; deus (of Aesculapius), Ov.

ŏpĭfex -fĭcis, c. (opus and facio), 1, *a worker, framer, fabricator*; mundi, Cic.; verborum, Cic.; 2, *a workman, artificer, artizan*, Cic.; opifices atque servitia, Sall.

ŏpĭfĭcīna = officina (q.v.).

ōpĭlĭo and **ūpĭlĭo** -ōnis, m. (for ovilio, from ovis), *a shepherd*, Verg.

ŏpīmē, adv. (opimus), *richly, splendidly*, Plaut.

ŏpīmĭtas -ātis, f. (opimus), *sumptuousness, splendour*, Plaut.

ŏpīmus -a -um (ops). **I.** Act., *fruitful, fertile*; ager, regio, Cic. **II.** Pass., *well-fed, fat.* **A. a,** lit., bos, Cic.; habitus corporis, Cic.; **b,** fig., of speech, *overloaded*; genus dictionis, Cic. **B.** Transf., **a,** *enriched, wealthy*; **b,** *splendid, sumptuous, abundant, rich, copious*, Verg.; praeda, Cic.; dapes, Verg.; esp., spolia opima, *the spoils taken from the enemy's general when slain by the commander of the army himself*, Liv.

ŏpīnābĭlis -e (opinor), *founded upon conjecture, conjectural*, Cic.

ŏpīnātĭo -ōnis, f. (opinor), *a supposing, supposition, conjecture*, Cic.

ŏpīnātor -ōris, m. (opinor), *one who supposes or conjectures*, Cic.

1. **ŏpīnātus** -a -um, p. adj. (from opinor), *conjectured, supposed, fancied*; bonum, Cic.

2. **ŏpīnātus** -ūs, m. (opinor), *a conjecture, supposition*, Lucr.

ŏpīnĭo -ōnis, f. (opinor), *an opinion, conjecture, supposition, belief, imagination.* **I.** Gen., with subj. genit., opinione vulgi, Cic.; with obj. genit., opinio eius diei, Cic.; with de, opinio de dis immortalibus, Cic.; adducere aliquem in opinionem ut putet, etc., Cic.; magna nobis pueris opinio fuit, with acc. and infin., Cic.; ut opinio nostra est (fert), *in my opinion*, Cic.; praeter opinionem, *contrary to expectation*, Cic.; celerius opinione, *quicker than was expected*, Cic. **II. A. 1,** *good opinion, favourable judgment*; opinione nonnullā, quam de meis moribus habebat, Cic.; **2, a,** *a good name, reputation*; propter eximiam opinionem virtutis, Caes.; **b,** *a bad name, notoriety*, Liv. **B.** *fame, report*; quae opinio erat edita in vulgus, Liv.

ŏpīnĭōsus -a -um (opinio), *full of conjectures or suppositions*, Cic.

ŏpīnor, 1. dep. (from opinus in nec-opinus, from root OP, connected with ὀφθῆναι, ὄπωπα), *to be of opinion, opine, believe, think, suppose*; me in provinciam exiturum, Cic.; de vobis non secus ac de teterrimis hostibus opinatur, Cic.; ut opinor (in a parenthesis), *as I hold*, Cic.

ŏpĭpărē, adv. (opiparus), *splendidly, sumptuously*; opipare apparatum convivium, Cic.

ŏpĭpărus -a -um (opes and paro), *splendid, sumptuous*, Plaut.

1. **Ōpis** -is, acc. -im, f. (Ὦπις), *a nymph in the train of Diana.*

2. **Ŏpis**, v. 1. Ops.

ŏpĭtŭlor, 1. dep. (ops and tulo = fero), *to help, aid, assist*; sontibus, Cic.

ŏpĭum -ĭi, n. (ὄπιον), *opium*, Plin.

ŏportet -tŭit, 2. impers. *it behoves, is needful, proper, it must be, ought to be*; foll. by the subj. alone, by the acc. and infin., by the infin., hoc fieri et oportet et opus est, Cic.; exstent oportet vestigia, Cic.; absol., quidquid veto non licet, certe non oportet, Cic.

oppēdo, 3. (op and pedo), *to mock, insult*; Judaeis, Hor.

oppĕrĭor -pertus and (more rarely) -pĕrītŭs sum, 4. (root PER, whence experior), *to wait.* **I.** Intransit., *to wait*; ibidem, Cic. **II.** Transit., *to expect*; agmen peditum, Liv.; abi intro, ibi me opperire, Ter.

oppĕto -īvi and -ĭi -ītum, 3. (ob and peto), *to go to meet, encounter* (especially an evil); pestem, Plaut.; mortem, *to die*, Cic.; or simply oppetere, Verg.

oppĭdānus -a -um (oppidum), *of or belonging to a town* (except Rome, of which urbanus was used), *belonging to a small town*; in a contemptuous sense, *provincial*; senex, Cic.; genus dicendi, Cic.; subst., **oppĭdāni** -ōrum, m. *the inhabitants of a town*, Caes.

oppĭdātim, adv. (oppidum), *in the towns, in all the towns*, Suet.

oppĭdo, adv. *very, very much, exceedingly*; ridiculus, Cic.; pauci, Cic.; in answers, *certainly*, Plaut.

oppĭdŭlum -i, n. (dim. of oppidum), *a little town*, Cic.

oppĭdum -i, n. (perhaps from ob and PED, whence Gr. πέδον, im-ped-ire, etc.), *a town* (urbs generally used for Rome); **a,** oppidum pervetus in Sicilia, Cic.; sanguine per triduum in oppido (*in town = in Rome*), pluisse, Liv.; with genit. of the name of the town, in oppido Antiochiae, Cic.; **b,** *a fortified wood in Britain*, Caes.

oppignĕro, 1. (ob and pignero), *to pledge, pawn, give in pledge*; libellos pro vino, Cic.

oppīlo, 1. (ob and pilo), *to stop up, close up, block up*; scalas tabernae librariae, Cic.

opplĕo -plēvi -plētum, 2. (ob and pleo), *to fill, fill up.* **I.** Lit., nives omnia oppleverant, Liv. **II.** Transf., nam vetus haec opinio Graeciam opplevit, Cic.

oppōno -pŏsŭi -pŏsĭtum (-postum, Lucr.), 3. (ob and pono), *to put or place opposite, before.* **I.** Lit., **A.** oculis manus, Ov.; luna subjecta atque opposita soli, Cic. **B.** *to place against or in the way of for protection*; **a,** omnes corpora nostra opponimus, Cic.; **b,** moles oppositae fluctibus, Cic.; se alicui, Caes. **II.** Transf., **1,** *to pledge against, mortgage for*; ager oppositus est pignori ob decem minas, Ter.; **2,** *to expose*; se periculis, Cic.; **3,** *to allege as an objection, to oppose, oppose in argument*; **a,** alicui nomen, valetudinem alicuius, Cic.; **b,** *to place one thing against another in the way of comparison, to contrast*; nunc omni virtuti vitium contrario nomine opponitur, Cic.

opportūnē, adv. (opportunus), *opportunely, seasonably, fitly, conveniently*; opportune adesse, Cic.

opportūnĭtas -ātis, f. (opportunus), *convenience, fitness, appropriateness, suitableness.* **I.** loci, Caes. **II. a,** *a fit time, right season, opportunity*; divina, Cic.; opportunitates ad cultum hominum, Cic.; **b,** *a fit state of the body or mind*; corporis, Cic.; **c,** *an advantage*, Cic.; opportunitate aliquā datā, Caes.

opportūnus -a -um (ob and POR-o, PORT-o, whence also portus, porta), *opportune, fit, suitable, appropriate, favourable.* **I. A.** Lit., loca, Sall. **B.** Transf., **a,** of time, *suitable, favourable*; tempus, Cic.; **b,** of nature, *serviceable, useful*; (a) of things, with dat. of object, ceterae res opportunae sunt singulae rebus fere singulis

Cic , (β) of persons, *suitable*, homines, Sall. **II.** *exposed to, liable to;* huic eruptioni, Liv., injuriae, Sall

oppŏsĭtĭo -ōnis, f (oppono), *opposing, opposition*, Cic

1 **oppŏsĭtus** -a -um, p adj (from oppono), *opposed, opposite, standing against*, Buthrotum oppositum Corcyrae, Caes

2 **oppŏsĭtus** -ūs, m (oppono), *a placing, setting against* or *opposite, interposition*, Cic

oppressĭo -ōnis, f (opprimo) **I.** *a pressing down, oppression;* legum et libertatis, Cic **II.** *a forcible taking possession of*, curiae, Cic

oppressor -ōris, m (opprimo), *a suppresser, crusher*, dominationis, ap Cic

1 **oppressus** -ūs, m. (opprimo), *a pressing down, pressure*, Lucr.

2 **oppressus** -a um, partic of opprimo

opprĭmo -pressi -pressum, 3 (ob and premo) **I. A.** Lit , **1,** *to press down, press together*, ora loquentis, Ov , **2, a,** *to crush*, opprimi ruinā conclavis, *to be crushed*, Cic , senem injectu multae vestis, *to stifle, smother*, Tac , **b,** of a flame, *to extinguish*, cum aquae multitudine vis flammae opprimitur, Cic , **c,** of a letter, *to slur over in pronunciation*, litterae neque expressae neque oppressae, Cic **B.** Transf , **1,** *to suppress*, **a,** dolorem, Cic , **b,** *to conceal*, insigne veri, Cic , **2,** *to crush, bear hard upon, weigh down*, opprimi aere alieno, Cic , **3,** *to crush an evil, suppress, stamp out*, perniciosam potentiam, Cic **4,** *to crush, subdue an adversary* **a,** in war, nationem Allobrogum, Cic , **b,** in politics, aliquem, Cic , **5,** *to hold firm, not to let go* , institit, oppressit non remisit, Cic. **II.** *to seize upon, fall upon, surprise* **A** Antonium mors oppressit, Cic , improvidos incautosque hostes, Liv **B.** Transf , numquam ille me opprimet consilio, Cic

opprŏbrāmentum i, n (opprobro), *a reproach, disgrace*, Plaut

opprŏbrĭum ii, n (ob and probrum), *a reproach, scandal, disgrace, opprobrium*, **1,** majoris fugiens opprobria culpae, Hor , **2,** meton , **a,** *a verbal reproach, taunt*, mordere opprobriis falsis, Hor , **b,** of persons, *shame, disgrace*, majorum, Tac

opprŏbro, 1 (ob and probrum), *to taunt, upbraid, reproach*, Plaut

oppugnātĭo ōnis, f (oppugno), *a storming, taking by storm;* oppidorum, Caes , oppugnationem sustinere, Caes , relinquere, Tac , judicium sine oppugnatione, *without opposition*, Cic

oppugnātor -ōris, m (oppugno), *one who storms, attacks, assaults*, fig , hostis et oppugnator patriae Antonius, Cic

1 **oppugno,** 1 (ob and pugno), *to attack, assault, storm, besiege* **I.** Lit , oppidum, Cic ; castra, Caes **II.** Transf , *to attack, lay siege to* , fig , aliquem clandestinis consiliis, Cic

2 **oppugno,** 1, (ob and pugnus), *to buffet with the fists*, Plaut

1 **Ops,** Opis, f = *the Earth, the goddess of abundance, wife of Saturn*, and *protectress of agriculture*

2 **ops,** ŏpis, f plur , **ŏpes** -um (sing only in genit , acc , and abl) **I.** *might, power* **a,** *resources*, opibus, armis, potentiā valere, Cic , **b,** *forces, troops*, tantas opes prostravit, Cic , **c,** *political power, influence*, alicuius opes evertere, Cic **II.** *physical power, might, strength* omni ope atque operā enitar, Cic , grates persolvere dignas non opis est nostrae, *is not in our power*, Verg **III.** *help, assistance, support*, opem petere ab aliquo, Cic , opem afferre, *to help*, Ov

ops . v. obs .

optābĭlis e (opto), *desirable, to be wished for* , mihi pax in primis fuit optabilis, Cic

optandus -a um, p adj (from opto), *to be wished for, desirable*, maxime fuit optandum Caecinae ut, etc , Cic

optātĭo ōnis, f (opto), *a wish* alicui tres optationes dare, Cic

optātō, adv. (optatus), *according to one's wish*, Cic

optātus a -um, p adj (from opto), *wished for, desired, pleasant, dear* , rumores, Cic frater, Cic Subst , **optātum** i, n *a wish* optatum impetrare, Cic

optĭmās ātis (optimus), *one of the best, aristocratic*, genus, Cic Subst , **optĭmās** ātis, m *an aristocrat*, ap Cic , gen plur , **optĭmātes** ium and um, m *the aristocratic party, the aristocrats*, Cic

optĭmē, superl of bene (q v)

optĭmus (optŭmus) -a -um, superl of bonus (q v)

1 **optĭo** -ōnis, f (* opo), *choice, free choice, option* , utro frui malis optio sit tua, Cic , si mihi optio daretur, utrum malim defendere, an, etc , Cic

2. **optĭo** ōnis, m in military language, *an adjutant*, Tac

optīvus a -um (opto), *chosen*, cognomen, Hor

opto, 1 (stem OP, Gr ΟΠΤ, whence ΟΠΤΩ, ὀψομαι) **I.** *to choose, elect, select*, ut in vis, opta, dum licet, Plaut , locum tecto, Verg , ut optet utrum malit an, etc , Cic **II.** *to wish for, desire* illam fortunam, Cic , with infin , tnem accusandi facere, Cic , with acc and infin , redire in me, Cic , with ut and the subj , optavit, ut in currum tolleretur, Cic , with subj alone, crescat tui civibus opto urbs, Ov , with acc and dat , alicui furorem et insaniam, Cic

ŏpŭlens -entis (opes), 1, *rich*, Nep , 2, *powerful*, civitas, Sall

ŏpŭlentē and **ŏpŭlentĕr**, adv (opulentus and opulens), *richly, splendidly, sumptuously*, ludos opulentius facere, Liv

ŏpŭlentĭa -ae, f (opulens), 1, *wealth, riches, opulence*, Sall , 2, *the power, greatness of a state*, Sall

ŏpŭlentĭtas -ātis, f (opulens), *riches, opulence*, Plaut

ŏpŭlento, 1. (opulens), *to make opulent, enrich*, Hor.

ŏpŭlentus -a -um (ops) **I.** *rich, wealthy, opulent* **A** civitas, Cic , oppidum, Caes ; Numidia agro virisque opulentior, Sall **B.** *rich splendid, sumptuous*, res haud opulenta, Liv **II.** *powerful, mighty*, reges, Sall , factio, Liv

Opuntiŭs, v 3 Opus

1 **ŏpus** -ĕris, n *a work, labour* **I. A.** Lit , **1,** opera nostrarum artium Cic., opus quaerere, *to seek for work*, Cic , **2, a,** *work in the fields*, facere patrio rure opus, Ov , **b,** *building*, lex operi faciundo, *building-contract*, Cic , **c,** milit. t t , *a military work, fortification, entrenchment*, operibus oppugnare urbem, Liv , Mutinam operibus munitionibusque sepsit, Cic , **d,** *work as opposed to nature, art*, nihil est opere aut manu factum, quod non aliquando consumat vetustas, Cic , **e,** *the work of an artist*, hydria Boethi manu facta praeclaro opere, *of admirable workmanship*, Cic **B.** Meton , **1, a,** *finished work* , opera magnifica atque praeclara, Cic , **b,** *a work of art*, Silanionis opus (of a statue), Cic , **c,** *a literary work* , opus habeo in manibus, Cic **II. a,** *action, work, business*, censorium,

Cic.; certatim ad hoc opus enitetur, Cic.; **b,** *an undertaking,* Liv.; **c,** *trouble;* magno opere, Cic.; nimio opere, Cic.

2. **ŏpus,** n. indecl., found in the phrases opus est, *there is need, it is needful, it is necessary;* with nom., dux nobis, et auctor opus est, Cic.; with abl. of the thing needed, opus est auctoritate tuā, Cic.; maturato opus est, *there is need of haste,* Liv.; with genit., quanti argenti opus fuit, Liv.; with acc., Plaut.; with infin., quid opus est affirmare, Cic.; with 2. supine, quod scitu opus est, Cic.

3. **Ŏpūs** -puntis, f. (Ὀποῦς), *town in Locris,* now *Talanta.* Adj., **Ŏpuntĭŭs** -a -um, *Opuntian.*

ŏpuscŭlum -i, n. (dim. of 1. opus), *a little work,* Cic.

1. **ōra** -ae, f. (1. os), *the edge, border, rim, boundary.* **I.** poculi, Lucr.; regionum, Cic.; clipei, Verg. **II. A.** *the coast, sea-coast;* Italiae, Cic. **B.** *a region, clime, country;* quăcumque in ora ac parte terrarum, Cic.; Acheruntis orae, *the lower world,* Lucr.; luminis orae, *the upper world,* Verg. **C.** *a zone, belt of the earth,* Cic.

2. **ōra** -ae, f. *a cable or hawser by which a ship was made fast to the shore,* Liv.

ōrācŭlum (ōrāclum) -i, n. (oro). **I.** *a place where an oracle is given, an oracle;* illud oraculum Delphis, Cic.; transf., domus jureconsulti oraculum civitatis, Cic. **II.** *an oracle, divine response;* **1,** oraculum edere, Cic.; petere a D lona, Cic.; **2, a,** *a prophecy;* oracula fundere, Cic.; **b,** *a wise speech, oracular declaration;* physicorum, Cic.

ōrātĭo -ōnis, f. (oro). **I.** *speaking, speech, language.* **A.** Gen., quae (ferae) sunt rationis et orationis expertes. **B.** *eloquence;* satis in eo fuit orationis, Cic. **II.** Meton., **A.** *speech, utterance;* orationem bonorum imitavi, Cic. **B. a,** *a set speech;* comparare ad id longam orationem, Cic.; habere orationem in senatu, Cic.; in extrema oratione nostra, *at the end of our speech,* Cic.; **b,** *prose* (as opp. to poetry); saepissime et in poematis et in oratione peccatur, Cic.

ōrātĭuncŭla -ae, f. (dim. of oratio), *a little speech, short oration,* Cic.

ōrātor -ōris, m. (oro), *speaker.* **I.** *the spokesman of an embassy,* Cic. **II.** *an orator,* Cic.

ōrātōrĭē, adv. (oratorius), *oratorically, like an orator,* Cic.

ōrātōrĭus -a -um (orator), *relating to an orator, oratorical;* ingenium, Cic.; ornamenta, Cic.

ōrātrix -icis, f. (orator), *a female suppliant;* virgines oratrices pacis, Cic.

ōrātus -ūs, m. (oro), *a request, entreaty;* oratu tuo, Cic.

orbātor -ōris, m. (orbo), *one who deprives another of children or parents,* Ov.

orbĭcŭlātus -a -um (orbiculus), *circular, round;* ap. Cic.

orbĭcŭlus -i, m. (dim. of orbis), *a little circle or disk,* Plin.

orbis -is, m. *a circle, ring, anything round.* **I. A.** Gen., torquere in orbem, Cic. **B.** Esp., **1,** milit. t. t., *a circle of soldiers;* in orbem consistere, Caes.; **2,** of the heavens, orbis signifer, *the zodiac,* Cic.; lacteus, *the Milky Way,* Cic.; **3,** *a circular motion, serpentine fold, winding;* immensis orbibus angues incumbunt pelago, Verg.; of the rounding off or period of a speech, orationis or verborum, Cic.; orbis terrarum, *the circle of the world, the world,* Cic. **II.** *a disk.* **A.** Gen., orbis mensae, *a round table,* Ov. **B.** Esp., **1, a,** *the disk of the sun* or *moon,* Liv.; **b,** *the heavens;* **c,** orbis terrae, *the earth,* (α) Cic.; (β) poet. = *land;* Eous, *the East,* Ov.; (γ) meton., *mankind;* orbis terrae judicio ac testimonio comprobari, Cic.; **2, a,** *a shield,* Verg.; **b,** *a wheel,* Verg.; *the wheel of fortune,* Ov.; **c,** *the hollow of the eye,* Ov. (locat., orbi terrarum, Cic.).

orbĭta -ae, f. (orbis), *a wheel-rut, mark of a wheel,* Cic.; fig., orbita veteris culpae, *bad example,* Juv.

orbĭtas -ātis, f. (orbus), *a bereaving, bereavement, loss of children or parents;* orbitates liberûm, Cic.; fig., orbitas reipublicae virorum talium, Cic.

orbo, 1. (orbus), *to bereave.* **I.** Gen., Italiam juventute, Cic. **II.** *to deprive of parents or children;* filio orbatus, Cic.

Orbōna -ae, f. (orbus), *the goddess invoked by bereaved parents,* Cic.

orbus -a -um (root ORB, Gk. ὈΡΦ-ανός), *deprived of.* **I.** Gen., *bereft, destitute;* with abl., rebus omnibus, Cic.; with genit., luminis, Ov. **II.** Esp., *deprived of parents* or *children, bereft, without parents* or *children;* orbus senex, Cic.; with abl., liberis, Liv.; with genit., Memnonis orba mei venio, Ov.; subst., **orbus** -i, m. and **orba** -ae, f. *an orphan,* Liv.; fig., respublica, Cic.; Sulpicius legationem orbam reliquit, Cic.

orca -ae, f. **1,** *a kind of whale,* Plin.; **2,** *an earthenware pot* or *jar with a large belly,* Hor.

Orcădes -um, f. *islands near Scotland,* now *the Orkneys.*

orchăs -ădis, f. (ὀρχάς), *a species of olive,* Verg.

orchestra -ae, f. (ὀρχήστρα), *the part of a Roman theatre reserved for the senators;* meton., *the senate,* Juv.

Orchŏmĕnus (-ŏs) -i, m. and **Orchŏmĕnum** -i, n. (Ὀρχομενός). **I.** *town in Boeotia.* **II.** *town in Arcadia.*

orcīnus -a -um (Orcus), *of or relating to Orcus or the dead;* senatores, *those who became senators by the will of Caesar,* Suet.

Orcus -i, m. (connected with ἕρκος and urgeo). **I.** *Orcus, the infernal regions.* **II. A.** *the god of the lower world, Pluto,* Cic. **B.** *death,* Hor.

orděum = hordeum (q.v.).

ordĭa prīma = primordia (q.v.).

ordĭnārĭus -a -um (ordo), *according to order, regular, ordinary;* consules, *elected in the regular manner* (opp. to suffecti), Liv.; ordinarii reipublicae usus, Liv.

ordĭnātim, adv. (ordinatus), **1,** *in order, in good order,* Caes.; **2,** *regularly, properly,* Caes.

ordĭnātĭo -ōnis, f. (ordino), *a setting in order, arrangement,* Plin.

ordĭnātus -a -um, p. adj. (from ordino), *set in order, arranged, orderly,* Cic.

ordĭno, 1. (ordo), *to set in order.* **I. a,** *to plant in rows;* latius arbusta sulcis, Hor.; **b,** *to arrange in rank* (of soldiers); agmina, Hor. **II.** Transf., **1,** *to settle;* aliter apud alios ordinatis magistratibus, Liv.; **2,** *to arrange, appoint, settle, dispose, classify;* partes orationis, Cic.; res publicas, *to narrate the history of the state,* Hor.

ordĭor, orsus sum, 4. dep. (connected with ordo), *to begin, commence.* **A.** Gen., alterius vitae quoddam initium, Cic. **B.** Esp., in speaking, *to begin;* with acc., sermonem, Cic.; with infin., de aliqua re disputare, Cic.; absol., de aliquo paulo altius, Cic.; sic orsus Apollo, *began to speak,* Verg.

ordo -ĭnis, m. (orior). **I.** *series, line, row, order.* **A.** Lit., olivarum, Cic.; ordine, (α) *in* *detail*, Cic ; (β) *in due order*, Cic ; ex ordine, *in succession*, Cic ; in ordinem, *in order*, Cic , nullo ordine, *without order, in a disorderly manner*, Caes ; extra ordinem, (α) *in an unusual, irregular manner* ; alicui provinciam decernere, Cic , (β) *extraordinarily, very greatly* Cic **B.** Meton., **1,** *a row of seats in a theatre*, Cic , *a row or bank of oars in a vessel*, Verg , **2,** milit t t , *rank, file*, ordines explicare, Liv ; ordine egredi, Sall , *a company*, ordinem ducere, *to be a centurion*, Caes , ordines primi, *commanders*, Caes ; **3, a,** politically, *an order, rank, class*, senatorius or amplissimus, *the senatorial body*, Cic ; equester, *the body of knights*, Cic., **b,** *a class, body of men*, publicanorum, Cic **II.** *order, arrangement*, nomina in ordinem referre, Cic., res in ordinem adducere, *to put into order*, Cic

Ordovīces -um, m *a people in Britain, opposite to the island of Mona*, now *Anglesea*

Ŏrēăs -ădis, f (Ὀρειάς), *a mountain nymph, Oread*, Verg

Ŏrestēs -ae and -is, m (Ὀρέστης), *son of Agamemnon and Clytaemnestra, brother of Iphigenia and Electra, who killed his mother, the murderess of his father, and with his friend Pylades and his sister Iphigenia (priestess of Diana in the Tauric Chersonese), carried away the image of Diana to Italy, near Aricia* Hence, adj , **Ŏrestēus** -a -um, *Orestean*

ŏrexis -is, f (ὄρεξις), *desire, appetite*, Juv

orgănĭcus a -um (ὀργανικός), *musical, relating to musical instruments*, Lucr ; subst , **orgănĭcus** -i, m *a musician*, Lucr

orgănum -i, n (ὄργανον), *any implement or instrument*, Plin , *a musical instrument, a water-organ*, Suet

Orgĕtŏrix -īgis, m *a celebrated Helvetian*

orgĭa ōrum, n (ὄργια), *nocturnal festivals in honour of Bacchus*, Verg , and hence, *any secret festival, orgies*, Juv

ŏrĭchalcum -i, n. (ὀρείχαλκος), *yellow copper ore* ; hence, *brass made from it*, Cic.

ōrĭcilla -ae, f (= auricilla), *an ear lap*, Cat.

Ōrĭcŏs i, f and **Ōrĭcum** -i, n *a town in Epirus*, now *Erico* Hence, **1,** adj , **Ōrĭcĭus** -a -um, *Orician*, and **2, Ōrĭcīni** -ōrum, m *the inhabitants of Oricum*.

ōrĭcŭla = auricula (q v)

ŏrĭens -entis, m (lit., partic of orior, sc sol) **I.** *the rising sun*, personif , *the sun god, day god*, Verg , Ov **II.** Meton , **1,** *the east*, as a part of the sky, Cic , **2,** *the east*, as a part of the world, Cic

ŏrīgo -ĭnis, f (orior) **I.** *origin, source*, principii nulla est origo, Cic **II.** *birth, descent* **A.** Lit , Ov **B.** Transf , **a,** *race*, Verg , **b,** *ancestor, founder of a race*, pater Aeneas Romanae stirpis origo, Verg

Ōrīōn -ōnis, m. (Ὠρίων), *the constellation Orion*

ŏrĭor, ortus sum, ŏrĭtūrus, ŏrīri, 4 dep (root OR, Gk ΟΡ, whence ὄρνυμι), *to rise* **I.** Of persons, quum consul oriens de nocte silentio diceret dictatorem, Liv **II.** Transf , *to arise = to become visible* **A.** Of the heavenly bodies, ortā luce, *in the morning*, Caes , oriens sol, *the East*, Cic **B.** *to arise, spring from, proceed from come forth*, Rhenus oritur ex Lepontiis, *takes its rise*, Caes , clamor, Caes , hence, **a,** *to be born*, equestri loco ortus, Cic , **b,** *to grow*, uva oriens, Cic , **c,** *to begin*, ab his sermo oritur, Cic (indic pres acc to 3rd conjug , orior, orĕris, oritur, orimur, orimini, so imperf subj., orĕretur)

Ōrīthȳia -ae, f (Ὠρείθυια), *daughter of Erechtheus, king of Athens, mother of Zethes and Calais by Boreas*

1 **ŏrĭundus** -a -um (orior), *arising from, springing from, born of*, ab ingenuis, Cic , ex Etruscis, Liv

2. **Ŏrĭundus** -i, m *a river in Illyria*

Ormĕnis -ĭdis, voc -i, f (Ὀρμενίς), *the Ormenid* (granddaughter of Ormenus) = *Astydamia*

ornāmentum -i, n (orno) **I.** *equipment, accoutrement, trappings, furniture* , certas copias et ornamenta vestra, Cic **II. A.** *ornament, decoration, embellishment* , omnia ornamenta ex fano Herculis in oppidum contulit, Caes ; fig , senectutis, Cic , esp , *rhetorical ornament*, oratoria ornamenta dicendi Cic **B.** *honour, ornament, distinction* , omnia ornamenta congerere ad aliquem, Cic

ornātē, adv with compar and superl (ornatus), *ornately, splendidly elegantly*, comparare convivium, Cic , loqui, Cic

ornātrix -īcis, f (ornator), *a female adorner, a tire woman*, Ov.

1 **ornātus** -ūs, m (orno) **I.** *dress, attire, equipment*, militaris, Cic , regalis, Cic **II.** *embellishment, decoration*, **1,** lit , urbis, Cic , **2,** fig , verborum, Cic , meton , of discourse, *embellishment, ornament*, ornatum afferre orationi, Cic ; **3,** as a translation of the Greek κόσμος, *the world*, Cic

2 **ornātus** -a um, p adj (from orno) **I.** *furnished, equipped, accoutred, provided*, scutis telisque parati ornatique sunt, Cic **II. a,** *adorned, decorated, embellished, beautiful*, oratio, Cic , so of persons, *adorned with all noble qualities, admirable, illustrious*, adolescens, Cic , **b,** *honoured*, honoribus, Cic.

orno, 1 **I.** *to equip, accoutre, provide with necessaries, fit out* ; aliquem armis, Verg , decemviros apparitoribus, Cic , classem, consules, Cic , provinciam, *to provide troops, money*, etc , *for the government of a province*, Cic **II.** *to adorn, decorate, embellish* **A.** Lit , **1,** domum suam, Cic , cornua sertis, Verg , **2,** *to praise, honour, show honour to*, fuit ornandus in Manilia lege Pompeius, Cic **B.** Transf , *to adorn, decorate honour, distinguish* ; civitatem omnibus rebus, Caes , aliquem laudibus, Cic

ornus i, f *the mountain-ash*, Verg

ōro, 1 (1 os) **I.** *to speak* , **a,** talibus orabat Juno, Verg , **b,** *to speak as an orator* , vestra in nos promerita complecti orando, Cic , ipse pro se oravit, *defended himself*, Liv , **c,** *to treat or handle in speech, to argue, plead*, capitis causam, Cic , litem, Cic **II.** *to beg, pray, entreat, beseech*, with acc. of the person entreated, principem, Tac , oro te (parenthetic), *I pray*, Cic , with acc of the thing, auxilium ad bellum, Liv , with acc of pers and acc of thing, auxilia regem, Liv , with ut or ne and the subj , or subj alone, oro ut homines conserves, Cic , with infin., Verg.

Ŏrōdēs -is and -i, m *king of the Parthians, who took Crassus prisoner*

Ŏrontēs -is, m (Ὀρόντης), *the chief river of Syria* Hence, adj , **Ŏrontēus** -a -um, poet. = *Syrian*

Orpheus ĕi and ĕos, acc ĕum and -ĕa, abl eo, m (Ὀρφεύς), *a celebrated mythical minstrel of Thrace, husband of Eurydice* Hence, adj , **1, Orphēus** a -um , and **2, Orphĭcus** a -um, *Orphic, of or relating to Orpheus.*

orphus -i, m (ὀρφός), *a sea fish*, Ov

orsa -ōrum, n (ordior), **1,** *a beginning, com*

mencement, undertaking, Liv.; **2,** poet., *speech, words*, Verg.

1. **orsus** -ūs, m. (ordior), *a beginning, undertaking*, Cic.

2. **orsus** -a -um, partic. of ordior.

orthŏgrăphĭa -ae, f. (ὀρθογραφία), *orthography*, Suet.

Ortōna -ae, f. *town of the Frentani in Latium*, now *Ortona*.

1. **ortus** -ūs, m. (orior). **I.** *a rising of the heavenly bodies*; **1,** lit., solis et lunae reliquorumque siderum ortus, Cic.; **2,** meton., solis, *the east*, Cic. **II. a,** *birth*; primo ortu, *immediately after birth*, Cic.; ortu Tusculanus, Cic.; ortum ducere ab Elide, Cic.; **b,** *origin, source*; tribuniciae potestatis, Cic.

2. **ortus** -a -um, partic. of orior.

Ortȳgĭa -ae, f. and **Ortȳgĭē** -ēs, f. (Ὀρτυγία). **I.** *an island forming part of Syracuse*. **II.** *the old name of the island of Delos*. Hence, adj., **Ortȳgĭus** -a -um, *Ortygian*.

ŏryx -ȳgis, m. (ὄρυξ), *a species of wild goat or gazelle*, Juv.

ŏrȳza -ae, f. (ὄρυζα), *rice*, Hor.

1. **ōs,** ōris, n. **I.** *the mouth*; **1,** lit., cadit frustum ex ore pulli, Cic.; aliquem semper in ore habere, *to be always talking about*, Cic.; in ore vulgi esse, Cic.; alicui esse ante os, *before one's eyes*, Cic.; uno ore, *unanimously*, Cic.; in ora vulgi (hominum) abire (pervenire), Cat.; **2,** transf., *mouth, opening*; portus, Cic.; dolii, Liv.; *source*, ora novem Timavi, Verg. **II.** *the face, countenance*. **A. 1,** lit., in ore hominum, *in the presence of men*, Cic.; **2,** meton., used for *impudence, shamelessness*; nostis os hominis, nostis audaciam, Cic. **B.** *a mask*; Gorgonis, Cic.

2. **ŏs,** ossis, n. *a bone*; dolorem cineri eius atque ossibus inussisti, Cic.; ossa legere, *to gather up the ashes of the bones after the burning of a corpse*, Cic.; tum vero exarsit juveni dolor ossibus ingens, *in his heart*, Verg.; fig., of orators, imitari non ossa solum sed etiam sanguinem, Cic.; of a meagre style, ossa nudare, Cic.

Osca -ae, f. *town in Hispania Tarraconensis*, now *Huesca*. Hence, adj., **Oscensis** -e, *belonging to Osca*.

oscen -inis, m. (= obscen from obs and cano), t. t. of augural language, *a bird from whose note auguries were taken* (e.g., the raven, owl, crow), Hor.

Osci -ōrum, *an ancient people of Italy*; hence, adj., **Oscus** -a -um, *Oscan*.

oscillum -i, n. (dim. of 1. os), *a little mask*, Verg.

oscĭtantĕr, adv. (oscito), *yawningly, carelessly, negligently*, Cic.

oscĭtātĭo -ōnis, f. (oscito), *the opening of the mouth, a gaping*, Plin.

oscĭto, 1. (perhaps from os and cieo = moveo), *to open the mouth, gape, yawn*, Cic.; fig., *to be lazy, idle, inactive*; oscitat Epicurus, Cic.

oscŭlābundus -a -um (osculor), *kissing*, Suet.

oscŭlātĭo -ōnis, f. (osculor), *a kissing*, Cic.

oscŭlor, 1. dep. (osculum), *to kiss*; consulem filium, Cic.; fig., *to caress, make much of, make a pet of*; scientiam juris tamquam filiolam osculari suam, Cic.

oscŭlum -i, n. (dim. of 1. os). **I.** *a little mouth*; oscula summa delibare, Verg. **II.** Meton., *a kiss*; oscula ferre, Cic.

Osīrĭs -ris, -rĭdis and -rĭdos, m. (Ὄσιρις), *husband of Isis, god of Egypt, the genius of the Nile*.

Ossa -ae, m. (Ὄσσα), *a high mountain in Thessaly*, now *Kissavo*. Adj., **Ossaeus** -a -um, *belonging to Ossa*.

ossĕus -a -um (2. os), *made of bone, like bone, bony*, Juv.

ossĭfrăgus -i, m. and **ossĭfrăga** -ae, f. (2. os and frango), *the sea-eagle, osprey*, Lucr.

ostendo -tendi -tentum and (later) -tensum, 3. (obs and tendo), *to show, display, exhibit, expose to view*. **I.** Lit., **a,** os suum populo Romano, Cic.; equites sese ostendunt, *come in sight*, Caes.; **b,** *to expose, lay open*; supinatas Aquiloni glebas, Verg. **II.** Fig., **1,** *to show, display*; spem, metum, Cic.; **2,** esp. of discourse, *to show, make plain, declare*; nihil sibi gratius ostendit futurum esse, Cic.; quid sui consilii sit ostendit, Caes.

ostentātĭo -ōnis, f. (ostento). **I.** *a showing, displaying, revealing*; ostentationis causâ latius vagari, Caes. **II.** Transf., **a,** *a boasting, display, ostentation*; ingenii, Cic.; **b,** *false, deceitful show, pretence*; consul veritate, non ostentatione popularis, Cic.

ostentātor -ōris, m. (ostento) *one who shows boastingly, a boaster, vaunter, parader*; factorum, Liv.

ostento, 1. (intens. of ostendo), *to hold out, offer*. **I.** Lit., **A.** alicui jugula sua pro capite alicuius, Cic. **B. a,** *to show publicly, display, exhibit*; passum capillum, Caes.; **b,** *to show boastingly*; equum armaque capta, Liv. **II.** Fig., **A.** *to hold before a person's eyes, to show boastingly, to proffer, promise*; agrum, Cic. **B. 1,** *to show off, display*; prudentiam, Cic.; **2,** *to hold out with a menace, threaten*; caedem, Cic.; **3,** *to show, reveal*; **a,** se in aliis rebus, Cic.; **b,** of discourse, *to show, declare, make known*; et simul ostentavi tibi me istis esse familiarem, Cic.

ostentum (ostendo) -i, n. *a prodigy, portent*; magnorum periculorum metus ex ostentis portenditur, Cic.

ostentus, dat. -ui, abl. -ū, m. (ostendo). **I.** *a showing, displaying*; corpora abjecta ostentui, *for a show*, Tac. **II. 1,** *outward show, parade*; illa deditionis signa ostentui esse, Tac.; **2,** *a sign, indication, proof*; ut Jugurthae scelerum ostentui essem, Sall.

Ostĭa -ae, f. and **Ostĭa** -ōrum, n. (ostium), *the harbour and port of Rome, situate at the mouth of the Tiber*. Hence, adj., **Ostĭensis** -e, *relating to Ostia*; incommodum, *the destruction of the Roman fleet by the pirates*, Cic.; provincia, *the office of the quaestor, who superintended the aqueducts and the supply of corn to the city*, Cic.

ostĭārĭus -a -um (ostium), *belonging to a door*; subst., **1, ostĭārĭus** -ii, m. *a doorkeeper, porter*, Varr.; **2, ostĭārĭum** -ii, n. (sc. tributum), *a tax upon doors, a door-tax*, Caes.

ostĭātim, adv. (ostium), *from door to door, from house to house*; compilare totum oppidum, Cic.

ostĭum -ii, n. (1. os), *the entrance*. **I.** portus, Cic.; fluminis Cydni, *mouth*, Cic.; Oceani, *Straits of Gibraltar*, Cic. **II.** *the door of a house*; exactio ostiorum, *the door-tax*, Cic.; aperto ostio dormire, Cic.

ostrĕa -ae, f. and **ostrĕum** -i, n. (ὄστρεον), *an oyster*, Hor.

ostrĕātus -a -um (ostrea), *rough like an oyster-shell*, Plaut.

ostrĕōsus -a -um (ostrea), *abounding in oysters*, Cat.

ostrĭfĕr -fĕra fĕrum (ostreum and fero), *producing oysters*, Verg

ostrīnus -a um (ostrum), *purple*, colores, Prop

ostrum -i, n (ὄστρεον), **1,** *the purple dye prepared from a shell-fish*, vestes ostro perfusae, Verg , **2,** *stuff dyed with purple, a purple dress*, Verg

ōsus -a um, partic of ōdi (q v)

Ŏtho -ōnis, m *a Roman name*, **1,** L Roscius Otho, *author of a law giving special seats in the theatre to the knights*. **2,** M Salvius Otho, *a Roman emperor who succeeded Galba* Hence,

Ŏthōniānus -a -um, *relating to Otho*

Othryădēs -ae, m (Ὀθρυάδης) **I.** *son of Othrys = Panthus* **II.** *a Spartan general, the sole survivor in a battle with the Argives*

Othrys̆ -yos, m (Ὄθρυς), *a high mountain in Thessaly*

ōtĭŏlum -i, n (dim of otium), *a little leisure*, ap Cic

ōtĭor, 1 dep (otium), *to be idle, to be at leisure*, quum se Syracusis otiandi non negotiandi causā contulisset, Cic

ōtĭōsē, adv (otiosus) **I.** *idly, without occupation*, Cic **II.** *leisurely, lazily, gently, quietly*, Cic

ōtĭōsus -a um (otium), *idle, at leisure without occupation* **I.** Lit , **a,** homo, Cic , tempus, Cic , **b,** *free from public duties, occupied in literary work only*, numquam se minus otiosum esse quam quum otiosus, Cic , **c,** *politically indifferent, neutral, quiet*, istos otiosos reddam, Cic **II.** Transf , *quiet, calm, undisturbed*, Cic

ōtĭum -ii, n (opp negotium), *idleness, leisure, ease*, **a,** otium inertissimum et desidiosissimum, Cic , hebescere et languescere in otio, Cic , **b,** *leisure, time for anything*, otium suum consumere in historia scribenda, Cic , otium litteratum, Cic , si modo tibi est otium, *if only thou hast time*, Cic , **c,** *peace, repose, quietness*, multitudo insolens belli diuturnitate otii, Caes , otium domesticum, Cic , valde me ad otium pacemque converto, Cic , ab hoste otium fuit, Liv

ŏvātĭo -ōnis, f (ovo), *an ovation, a kind of lesser triumph in which the victorious general proceeded to the Capitol on horseback or on foot*, Plin

Ŏvĭdĭus -ii, m , P Ovidius Naso, *the celebrated Roman poet, born at Sulmo*, B C 43, *died* A D 17

ŏvīle -is, n (ovis), **1,** *a sheepfold*, Verg , **2,** *an enclosed place in the Campus Martius, where votes were given at the Comitia*, Liv

ŏvillus -a um (ovis), *of or relating to sheep*, ap Liv

ŏvis -is f (ὄϊς), *a sheep* **I. a,** lit , pascere oves, Verg , **b,** transf , as a term of reproach, *simple foolish fellow*, Plaut **II** Meton , poet = *wool*, Tib

ŏvo, 1 (euoe, like Gr εὐάζω) **I.** *to rejoice, exult*, ovans victoriā, Liv **II.** *to celebrate an ovation*, ovantem in Capitolium ascendisse, Cic.

ōvum -i, n (ᾠόν), **1,** *an egg*, ovum gignere, or parere, *to lay an egg*, Cic., prov., integram famem ad ovum afferre, *to the beginning of the meal* (as Roman dinners often began with eggs), Cic , ab ovo usque ad mala, *from beginning to end*, Hor , **2,** transf , *one of the seven egg-shaped balls by which the heats in the circus were counted*, ova curriculis numerandis, Liv.

P.

P, p, the fifteenth letter of the Latin alphabet, corresponds with the Greek pi (Π, π) For the use of P in abbreviations, see Table of Abbreviations

pābŭlātĭo -ōnis, f (pabulor), *procuring of fodder, foraging*, pabulatione intercludi, Caes

pābŭlātor -ōris, m (pabulor) *a forager*, Caes

pābŭlor, 1 dep (pabulum), *to forage, seek fodder*, Caes

pābŭlum -i, n (pasco) **I.** Lit , **1,** *food, nutriment*; pabula caelestia, *ambrosia*, Ov , **2,** *the food of animals fodder*, pabulum secare, convehere, Caes **II.** Transf , *food, nourishment*, studii atque doctrinae, Cic

pācālis -e (pax), *belonging or relating to peace, peaceful*, laurus, Ov

pācātus -a -um, p adj (from paco), *pacified, made peaceful*, and hence, *peaceful, quiet*, **a,** lit , pacatae tranquillaeque civitates, Cic , mare, Hor , subst , **pācātum** -i, n *a peaceful, friendly country*, ex pacatis praedas agere, Sall , **b,** transf , illorum oratio pacatior, Cic

Păchy̆num -i, n and **Păchy̆nus** (-ŏs) -i, f (Πάχυνος), *the south-east promontory of Sicily*, now *Capo di Passaro*

pācĭfĕr -fĕra fĕrum (pax and fero), *peace bringing, establishing or announcing peace*, oliva, Verg , frequently used as an epithet of the gods, e g , of Mercury, Ov

pācĭfĭcātĭo -ōnis (pacifico) f *an establishing of peace, pacification*, Cic

pācĭfĭcātor -ōris (pacifico), m *one who establishes peace, a pacificator*, Cic

pācĭfĭcātōrĭus -a um (pacifico), *establishing peace, pacificatory*, legatio, Cic

pācĭfĭco, 1 (pax and facio), *to reconcile, appease, pacify*, caelestes heros, Cat

pācĭfĭcor, 1 dep (pax and facio), *to make peace*, pacificatum legati veniunt, Liv

pācĭfĭcus -a um (pax and facio), *peace-making, pacific*, persona, Cic

păciscor, pactus sum, 3 dep (root PAC, whence pac-s, * pago, pango), *to make a bargain, contract, agreement with any one, to agree stipulate about anything*, **a,** intransit , cum illo, Plaut , paciscitur magnā mercede cum Celtiberorum principibus, ut copias inde abducant, Liv paciscī cum decumano, Cic , **b,** transit provinciam, Cic , pretium, Cic , ex qua domo pactus esset (feminam), *betrothed himself*, Liv , with infin , *to bind oneself*, stipendium populo Romano dare, Liv Partic , **pactus** -a um, pass = *agreed upon, promised, appointed, settled*, pactam esse diem, Cic

pāco, 1 (pax), *to reduce to peace, pacify, make peaceful*, Cic , **a,** Amanum, Cic , omnem Galliam, Caes , **b,** poet , *to make fruitful*, incultae pacantur vomere silvae, Hor

Păcŏrus -i, m (Πάκορος), *son of Orodes king of Parthia, enemy of the Romans, born about* 68 B C

pacta -ae, f (paciscor), *a betrothed spouse*, Verg

pactĭo -ōnis, f (paciscor), *a bargain contract, covenant, agreement, treaty* **I.** Gen , facere pactionem de aliqua re, Cic. arma per pactionem dare, *to capitulate*, Liv **II. A.** *a contract between the farmers of the taxes of a province and its inhabitants*, pactiones conficere

Cic. **B.** *a fraudulent* or *collusive agreement*; pactionis suspicio, Cic.

Pactōlus -i, m. (Πακτωλός), *a river in Lydia, said to bring down golden sands, now Sarabat.* Adj., **Pactōlis** -idis, f. *of Pactolus*; Nymphae, Ov.

pactor -ōris, m. (paciscor), *one who makes a contract* or *treaty, negotiator*; societatis, Cic.

pactum -i, n. (paciscor), *a bargain, contract, agreement, covenant, treaty, pact*; manere in pacto, Cic.; transf., nullo pacto, *by no means*, Cic.; alio pacto, *in another way*, Cic.; isto pacto, *in that way*, Cic.

pactus -a -um, partic. of paciscor.

Pācŭvĭus -ii, m., M. Pacuvius, *a Roman tragic poet of Brundisium, nephew of Ennius, flourishing about the time of the Second Punic War; died at Tarentum, about* 132 B.C.

Pădus -i, m. *the largest river in Italy*, now *the Po.*

Pădūsa -ae, f. *a canal running from the Po to Ravenna*, now *Canali di S. Alberti.*

Paean -ānis, m. (Παιάν). **I.** Lit., *the Healer, a surname of Apollo*, Cic. **II.** Meton., *a hymn, paean, originally addressed to Apollo only, but afterwards to other deities*; conclamant socii laetum paeana secuti, Verg.

paedăgōgus -i, m. (παιδαγωγός), *a slave who accompanied children to and from school and had charge of them at home*, Cic.

paedor -ōris, m. *dirt, filth*, Cic.

paelex = pelex (q.v.)

Paeligni -ōrum, m. *an Italian tribe in Samnium*, in modern *Abruzzo Citeriore.* Hence, **Paelignus** -a -um, *Pelignian*; anus, *a witch*, Hor.

paene, adv. *nearly, almost*; paene amicus, Cic.

paeninsŭla -ae, f. (paene and insula), *a peninsula*, Liv.

paenŭla -ae, f. (φαινόλης), *a species of overcoat, without sleeves, and close to the body, worn on a journey*, or *in wet, cold weather*, Cic.; prov., paenulam alicui scindere, *to beg a guest very earnestly to remain*, Cic.

paenŭlātus -a -um (paenula), *clothed in the paenula*, Cic.

paeōn -ōnis, m. (παιών), *a metrical foot, consisting of three short syllables and one long*, Cic.

Paeŏnes -um, m. (Παίονες), *the Paeonians, the people of Paeonia*; sing., **Paeon** -ŏnis, m. Hence, **A. Paeŏnia** -ae, f. (Παιονία), *Paeonia, a district of Macedonia*, afterwards *Emathia.* **B. Paeŏnis**, f. *a Paeonian woman.*

Paeōnĭus -a -um (Παιώνιος), *relating to the god of healing, Apollo, medicinal*; herbae, Verg.

Paestum -i, n. *a town in Lucania, famous for its roses*, now *Pesto.* Hence, **Paestānus** -a -um, *of Paestum.*

paetŭlus -a -um (dim. of paetus), *having a slight cast in the eye*, Cic.

paetus -a -um, *having a cast in the eyes, blink-eyed*; and, as an epithet of Venus, *having an engaging leer, leering prettily*, Hor.

pāgānus -a -um (pagus), *belonging* or *relating to a village, rural*; focus, Ov.; and hence, **pāgānus** -i, m., subst., **1,** *a villager, countryman*, Cic.; **2,** *a person in civil life, a civilian*, (opp. miles), Tac.

Păgăsa -ae, f. and **Păgăsē** -ēs, f. and **Păgăsae** -ārum, f. (Παγασαί), *a seaport of Thessaly, where the ship Argo was built*; hence, adj., **Păgăsaeus** -a -um, *Pagasean*; puppis, carina, *the Argo*, Ov.; conjux, *Alcestis, daughter of the Thessalian king Pelias*, Ov.; Pagasaeus, *Jason, leader of the Argonauts*, Ov.

pāgātim, adv. (pagus), *in villages, by villages*, Liv.

pāgella -ae, f. (dim. of pagina), *a little page*, Cic.

pāgĭna -ae, f. (✓ pag-, pango). **I.** *a page* or *leaf of paper*, or *of a book*; complere paginam, Cic. **II.** Transf., *a leaf, slab, tablet*; pagina honorum, *a list of titles and honours on a statue*, Juv.

pāgĭnŭla -ae, f. (dim. of pagina), *a little page*, Cic.

păgur -i, m. *a fish of unknown species*, Ov.

pāgus -i, m. (pango). **I.** *a village*; **a,** as a place, Liv.; **b,** collectively, *the inhabitants of a village*; pagus agat festum, Ov. **II.** *a district, canton, province* (esp. of the Germans and Gauls); omnis civitas Helvetia in quatuor pagos divisa, Caes.

pāla -ae, f. (for pagela from pango). **I.** *a spade*, Liv. **II.** *the socket of a ring in which the jewel is set, the bezel of a ring*, Cic.

Pălaemōn -mŏnis, m. (Παλαίμων). **I.** *a sea-god, formerly called Melicerta.* **II.** *a shepherd*, Verg.

Pălaepharsālus -i, f. *Old Pharsalus, a town in Thessaly, near Pharsalus*, now *Farsa.*

Pălaeŏpŏlis, acc. -pŏlim, f. (Παλαιόπολις), *the older part of the town of Neapolis in Campania.* Hence, **Pălaeopŏlītāni** -ōrum, m. *the inhabitants of Palaeopolis.*

Pălaestē -ēs, f. (Παλαιστή), *a town of the province Chaonia in Epirus*, now *Palasa.* Hence, adj., **Pălaestīnus** -a -um, *relating to Palaeste.*

Pălaestīna -ae, f. and **Pălaestīnē** -ēs, f. (Παλαιστίνη), *Palestine*; hence, adj., **Pălaestīnus** -a -um, *relating to Palestine*; aqua, *the Euphrates*, Ov.; subst., **Pălaestīni** -ōrum, m. = *the Syrians*, Ov.

pălaestra -ae, f. (παλαίστρα). **I.** *a gymnasium* or *wrestling school*; **a,** lit., Cic.; **b,** transf., *a school of rhetoric*, Cic. **II.** Meton., **a,** *wrestling*; discere palaestram, Cic.; **b,** *exercise in the schools of rhetoric, rhetorical exercises, rhetorical practice*; quasi quandam palaestram et extrema lineamenta orationi attulit, Cic.; **c,** *art*; utemur eā palaestrā, Cic.

pălaestrĭcē, adv. (palaestricus), *after the manner of the palaestra*; spatiari in xysto, Cic.

pălaestrĭcus -a -um (παλαιστρικός), *of* or *relating to the palaestra*; motus, Cic.

pălaestrīta -ae, m. (παλαιστρίτης), *the superintendent of a palaestra*, Cic.

pălam (from same root as planus, πλατύς, pellis, etc.). **I.** Adv., *openly, publicly.* **A.** Lit., rem gerit, Cic. **B. 1,** *openly, without concealment*; palam agere et aperte dicere, Cic.; **2,** *openly, apparently, evidently*; palam proferre, Cic.; **3,** palam factum est (with acc. and infin.), *it is well known*, Cic. **II.** Prep. (= coram), with abl., *in the presence of*; populo, Liv.; me, Ov.

Pălămēdēs -is, m. (Παλαμήδης), *son of the Euboean king Nauplius, the mythical inventor of the balance, of dice, and of some of the Greek letters, one of the Greek heroes in the Trojan war, put to death through a false accusation by Ulysses.*

Pălātĭum -ii, n. **I.** *the Palatine Hill in Rome, on which Augustus had his house.* Hence, **II.** *a palace*; Palatia fulgent, Ov. Hence, adj., **Pălātīnus** -a -um, *Palatine*; **a,** *of or relating to the Palatine Hill*; Apollo, *whose temple was on the Palatine*, Hor.; Palatina tribus or subst., **Pălātīna** -ae, f. *the Palatine tribe*, Cic.; **b,** *relating to the imperial palace, imperial*, Ov.

pălātum -i, n and **pălātus** -i, m **I.** *the palate as the organ of taste*, quae voluptas palato percipiatur, Cic, fig, *taste, critical judgment, the palate as the organ of taste and judgment*, Epicurus dum palato quid sit optimum judicat, Cic, *the palate as the organ of speech*; ferire balba verba palato, Hor **II.** Transf, palatum caeli, *the vault of the heavens*, ap Cic

pălĕa -ae, f *chaff*, Cic.

pălĕar -āris, n *the dewlap of an ox*, gen plur, Verg

Păles -is, f (PA, ΠΑ-ω, pasco), *the tutelary goddess of herds and shepherds* Hence, adj, **Pălīlis** -e, *belonging to Pales*, flamma, *a fire of straw, part of the ceremonies at the feast of Pales*, subst, **Pălīlia** -ium, n *the feast of Pales on the 21st of April*.

Pălīci -ōrum, m (sing, Palicus, Verg, Ov), *twin sons of Jupiter by the nymph Aetna, worshipped as heroes in Sicily*

Pălīlis -e, v Pales

pălimpsestos -i, m (παλιμψηστος), *parchment, from which old writing has been erased for the purpose of using the parchment again, a palimpsest*, Cic

Pălinūrus -i, m (Παλινοῦρος) **I.** *the pilot of Aeneas who fell into the sea off the coast of Lucania* **II.** *a promontory on the west coast of Lucania*, now *Cap Palinuro*.

păliūrus -i, m (παλίουρος), *a plant, Christ's thorn* (Rhamnus Paliurus, Linn), Verg

palla -ae, f *a long and wide outer garment worn by Roman women, also by tragic actors*, Hor

pallăca -ae, f (παλλακη), *a concubine*, Suet

Pallacinē -ēs, f *a place in Rome*. Hence, **Pallacīnus** -a -um, *relating to Pallacine*

1 **Pallăs** -ădis and -ădos, f (Παλλας), *the Greek name of Minerva, goddess of wisdom, and discoverer of the olive*, Palladis ales, *the owl*, Ov; arbor, *the olive-tree*, Ov, meton, a, *the olive-tree*, Ov; b, *olive oil*, Ov., c, *the image of Pallas, the Palladium*, Ov, hence, adj, **Pallădĭus** -a -um, *of or relating to Pallas*, rami, *olive branches*, Verg, latices, *oil*, Ov, ratis, *the ship Argo*, Ov, arces, *Athens*, Ov, subst, **Pallădĭum** -ii, n *the image of Pallas in Troy, which fell from heaven*

2 **Pallas** -antis, m (Πάλλας) **I.** *son of Pandion, father (according to one legend) of Minerva* **II.** *grandfather or great-grandfather of Evander* **III.** *son of Evander* **IV.** *one of the giants* Hence, **A. Pallantēus** -a -um, *belonging to Pallas*, subst, **Pallantēum** -i (sc oppidum), a, *a town in Arcadia*, b, *a town in Italy on the site of Rome* **B. Pallantiăs** -ădis, f *Aurora, a descendant of Pallas* (IV.) **C. Pallantĭs** -ĭdos = Pallantias **D. Pallantĭus** -a -um, *relating to Pallas* (II or III), heros, *Evander*, Ov

pallens -entis, p adj (from palleo) **I. A.** *pale, wan*, umbrae Erebi, Verg **B** *pale or wan in colour, pale-yellow, pale green*, violae, Verg; hedera, Verg **II.** *making pale, causing paleness*, morbi, Verg

pallĕo -ŭi, 2 *to be pale* **I.** Gen, **A.** 1, lit, sudat pallet, Cic, 2, meton, a, *to be pale or sick with desire, to long for*, argenti pallet amore, Hor b, *to be pale with fear or anxiety*, ad omnia fulgura, Juv, pontum, *to pale at the sight of*, Hor **B.** Transf, *to lose one's natural colour*, Ov **II.** *to be yellow*, Ov

pallesco, pallŭi, 3 *to grow pale, turn pale, lose colour* **I.** Lit, nullā culpā, Hor **II.** Transf., *to grow yellow*, pallescunt frondes, Ov.

palliātus -a -um (pallium), *clad in a pallium, i e, as a Greek* (opp togatus, *clad as a Roman*), Graeculus, Cic

pallĭdŭlus -a -um (dim of pallidus), *somewhat pale*, Cat

pallĭdus -a -um (palleo), *pale, wan, pallid* **I.** Gen **1**, lit, pallida sedit, *pale with fright*, Ov, **2**, meton, pass, *causing paleness*, mors, Hor **II** *yellow olive green*, Cat

palliŏlātus -a -um (palliolum), *wearing a cloak, cape, or hood*, Suet

palliŏlum -i, n (dim of pallium), **1**, *a little Greek cloak or mantle*, Plaut, **2**, *a hood*, Ov

pallium -i, n **I.** *a coverlet*, Ov **II.** *a long Greek mantle*, Cic

pallor -ōris, m (palleo), *paleness, pallor*, **1**, lit, terrorem pallor consequitur, Cic, amantium, Hor, **2**, meton, *anxiety, fright*, personif as a goddess, Liv., **3**, *unsightliness, unpleasant colour*, Ov

palma -ae, f (παλάμη) **I.** *the palm of the hand*, **1**, lit, Cic, **2**, meton, **a**, *the whole hand, the hand*, Cic, **b**, *the blade of an oar*, Cat **II.** *the palm-tree*, **1**, lit, Plin, **2**, meton, **a**, *the fruit of the palm, a date*, Ov, **b**, *a palm branch, a besom or broom made of palm-branches*, Hor, *the palm branch* as a token of victory, Liv, hence, (α) *the reward of victory*, palmam dare, accipere, Cic, fig, palmam ferre, Cic, *fame*, Liv, (β) *victory*, alicui hanc palmam reservare, Cic **III.** *a shoot, twig*, palma stipitis, Liv

palmāris -e (palma), *deserving the palm or prize, excellent, admirable*, statua, Cic, sententia, Cic

palmārium -ii, n (palma), *a masterpiece*, Ter

palmātus -a -um (palma), *worked or embroidered with palm branches*, tunica (worn by triumphing generals), Liv

palmes -ĭtis, m (palma), *a young branch or shoot of a vine, a vine-sprout*, Verg

palmētum -i, n (palma), *a palm-grove*, Hor

palmĭfĕr -fĕra -fĕrum (palma and fero), *producing palm-trees, abounding in palm trees*, Ov

palmōsus -a -um (palma), *full of palms*, Verg

palmŭla -ae, f (dim of palma), *the blade of an oar, an oar*, Verg

palmus -i, m (palma), *the palm of the hand*, Plin, as a measure, *a span* (¼ of a Roman foot), Plin

pālor, 1 dep *to wander about, stray about*, agmen palatur per agros, Liv, palantia sidera, Lucr

palpĕbra -ae, f (palpo), *the eyelid*, gen. plur, palpebrae, *the eyelids*, Cic

palpĭto, 1 *to move quickly, tremble, palpitate, throb*, cor palpitat, Cic, esp of persons in death agony, Ov

1 **palpo**, 1 and **palpor**, 1 dep **I.** *to stroke or touch gently*, Ov **II.** Fig, *to coax, wheedle, caress*, with dat, scribenti palparer, ap Cic, with acc., quem munere palpat, Juv

2 **palpo** -ōnis, m. (1 palpo), *a coaxer, wheedler, flatterer*, Pers

pălūdāmentum -i, n *the military cloak, a soldier's cloak*, esp, *a general's cloak*, Liv

pălūdātus -a -um, *clad in the military cloak, dressed in a general's cloak*, Pansa noster paludatus profectus est, Cic

pălūdōsus -a -um (2. palus), *marshy, boggy*, Ov

pălumbes (pălumbis) -is, m. and f. *a wood-pigeon, ring-dove*, Verg.

1. **pālus** -i, m. (for paglus, from *pago, pango), *a pale or stake.* **I.** Gen., aliquem ad palum alligare or deligare, Cic. **II.** Milit. t. t., *a stake on which Roman recruits exercised their weapons;* aut quis non vidit vulnera pali? Juv.

2. **pălus** -ūdis, f. *stagnant water, a swamp, marsh, morass, bog, fen*, Cic.; tarda palus, *the Styx*, Verg.

păluster -tris -tre (2. palus). **I.** *marshy, boggy, fenny;* limus paluster, Liv.; plur., **pălustrĭa** -ĭum, n. *marshy places*, Plin. **II.** *found or living in marshes;* ranae, Hor.

Pamphȳlĭa -ae, f. (Παμφυλία), *a district in Asia Minor, between Cilicia and Lycia.* Adj., **Pamphȳlĭus** -a -um, *Pamphylian.*

pampĭnĕus -a -um (pampinus), *pertaining to or consisting of vine-tendrils or leaves;* hastae, *garlanded with vine-leaves*, Verg.; corona, *of vine-leaves*, Tac.

pampĭnus -i, m. and f. *a vine-tendril, vine-leaf;* uva vestita pampinis, Cic.

Pān, Pānis and Pānos, m. (Πάν), *the god of woods and shepherds;* plur., **Pānes,** *rural deities resembling Pan.*

pănăcēa -ae, f. and **pănăcēs** -is, n. and **pānax** -ăcis, m. (πανάκεια, πανάκες, πάναξ, lit., *all-healing*), *a fabulous plant, to which was attributed the power of healing all diseases, panacea, heal-all*, Verg.

Pănaetĭus -ii, m. (Παναίτιος), *a Stoic philosopher of Rhodes, teacher and friend of the younger Scipio Africanus*, 185–112 B.C.

Pănaetōlĭcus -a -um (Παναιτωλικός), *relating to the whole of Aetolia;* consilium, Liv.

Pănaetōlĭus -a -um (Παναιτώλιος), *relating to the whole of Aetolia;* consilium, Liv.

pānārĭum -ii, n. (panis), *a bread-basket*, Plin.

Pănăthēnāĭcus -a -um (Παναθηναϊκός), *of or relating to the Athenian festival of the Panathenaea;* hence, subst., **Pănăthēnāĭcus** -i, m. *an oration of Isocrates delivered at the Panathenaea*, Cic.

pănax = panacea (q.v.).

Panchāĭa -ae, f. (Παγχαΐα), *a fabulous island in the Indian Ocean, near Arabia, famous for its incense;* hence, adj., **Panchāĭus** and **Panchaeus** -a -um, *Panchean.*

panchrestus -a -um (πάγχρηστος), *good or useful for everything;* medicamentum, *sovereign remedy*, i.e., *gold*, Cic.

pancrătĭum (-ŏn) -ii, n. (παγκράτιον), *a gymnastic contest, including both boxing and wrestling*, Prop.

Pandātăria (Pandātĕrĭa) -ae, f. (Πανδαταρία), *an island in the bay of Naples, a place of exile under the Emperors*, now *Vandotina.*

Pandīōn -ŏnis, m. (Πανδίων), *a king of Athens, father of Progne and Philomela;* Pandionis populus, *the Athenians*, Lucr.; Pandione nata, *Progne* or *Philomela*, Ov.; hence, adj., **Pandīŏnĭus** -a -um, poet. = *Athenian.*

1. **pando**, 1. (pandus), *to bend, bow, curve*, Plin.

2. **pando**, pandi, pansum and passum, 3. **I.** *to stretch out, extend, expand;* **a,** lit., vela, Cic.; pennas ad solem, Verg.; crines passi, capillus passus, *dishevelled hair*, Caes.; passis manibus or palmis, *with outstretched hands*, Caes.; **b,** fig., alia divina bona longe lateque se pandunt, Cic. **II.** Transf., **A.** *to throw open;* and in pass., *to open itself, open;* **a,** lit., januam, Plaut.; moenia urbis, Verg.; panduntur inter ordines viae, Liv.; **b,** fig., (α) *to open, throw open;* viam alicui ad dominationem, Liv.; (β) *to lay open in speech, tell, announce, explain;* nomen, Ov.; res, Verg. **B.** *to spread out to dry in the sun;* racemi passi, Verg.; lac passum, *curdled*, Ov.

Pandrŏsos -i, f. (Πάνδροσος), *daughter of Cecrops.*

pandus -a -um, *bent, curved, bowed, crooked*, Verg.

pănēgȳrĭcus -i, m. (πανηγυρικός), *an oration of Isocrates, celebrating the glories of Athens*, Cic.

Pangaeus mons, m. and poet., **Pangaea** -ōrum, n. (τὸ Πάγγαιον), *a mountain of Macedonia on the Thracian borders.*

pango, panxi, panctum, and pēgi and pĕpigi, pactum, 3. (stem PAG, whence pac-s, paciscor, Gr. ΠΑΓ, whence πήγνυμι), *to fasten, fix, drive in.* **I.** Lit., clavum, Liv. **II.** Transf., **A. 1,** *to make, undertake;* neque prima per artem temptamenta tui pepigi, Verg.; **2,** *to compose, write;* versus de rerum natura, Lucr.; poëmata, Hor.; aliquid Sophocleum, Cic. **B.** *to fix;* **1,** terminos, fines, Cic.; **2,** *to agree upon, stipulate, contract;* **a,** pacem, Liv.; with genit. or abl. of price, tanti pepigerat, Liv.; pretium quo pepigerant, Liv.; with ut and the subj., ut vobis mitterem ad bellum auxilia pepigistis, Liv.; with infin., obsides dare pepigerant, Liv.; **b,** esp., used frequently of a contract of marriage, haec mihi se pepigit, pater hanc tibi, *has betrothed*, Ov.

pānĭcum -i, n. *the Italian panic grass, or wild millet* (panicum Italicum, Linn.), Caes.

pānis -is, m. (root PA, Gr. ΠΑ, whence pa-sco, πά-ομαι), *bread;* panis cibarius, *common bread*, Cic.; secundus, *black bread*, Hor.; plur., ex hoc (genere radicis) effecti panes, Caes.

Pānĭscus -i, m. (Πανίσκος), *a sylvan deity, a little Pan*, Cic.

pannĭcŭlus -i, m. (dim. of pannus), *a little rag;* bombycinus, *a thin and scanty garment*, Juv.

Pannŏnĭi -ōrum, m. *the Pannonians, inhabitants of Pannonia.* Hence, **Pannŏnĭa** -ae, f. *Pannonia, a district between Dacia, Noricum, and Illyria, part of modern Hungary, Slavonia and Bosnia.*

pannōsus -a -um (pannus), *ragged, tattered*, Cic.

pannūcĕus (-ĭus) -a -um (pannus), *wrinkled, shrivelled*, Pers.

pannus -i, m. (πῆνος). **I.** *a piece of cloth, garment;* assuitur pannus, Hor.; *a bandage for the head*, Ov.; in sing. or plur., used contemptuously, *shabby clothes, rags*, Hor. **II.** *a rag, shred*, Hor.

Pănomphaeus -i, m. (Πανομφαῖος), *the founder of oracles, surname of Jupiter.*

1. **Pănŏpē** -ēs, f. (Πανόπη), *an old town in Phocis, on the Cephisus.*

2. **Pănŏpē** -ēs, f. and **Pănŏpēa** -ae, f. *a sea-nymph.*

Pănormus -i, f. and **Pănormum** -i, n. *a town on the north coast of Sicily, colony of the Phoenicians, near modern Palermo.* Hence, adj., **Pănormĭtānus** -a -um, *belonging to Panormus.*

pansa -ae (pando), *splay-footed, having broad feet*, Plaut.

pansus -a -um, partic. of pando.

Pantăgĭēs (-ās) -ae, m. (Παντανγίης), *a small river on the east coast of Sicily.*

panthēra ae, f (πάνθηρα), *a panther*, Cic

Panthēum -i, n (Πάνθειον), *a temple of Jupiter at Rome, built by Agrippa*

Panthŏus (-ŏŏs) (Πάνθοος), and **Panthus** -i, m (Πανθους) *son of Othrys, father of Euphorbus* Hence, **Panthŏidēs** -ae, m *a descendant of Panthus*, a, *Euphorbus*, Ov, b, *Pythagoras* (who pretended that the soul of Euphorbus had passed into his), Hor

pantŏlăbus -i, m (παντολάβος, *taking everything*), *name of a parasite*

pantŏmīmus -i, m (παντόμιμος), 1, *a male dancer, mime*, Suet ; 2, *a ballet, pantomime*, Plin

păpae (παπαί), interj *wonderful ! indeed !* Ter

păpāver ĕris, n *the poppy*, Verg

păpāvĕrĕus -a um (papaver), *of* or *relating to the poppy*, comae, *the stamens of a poppy*, Ov.

Paphlăgō -ŏnis, m (Παφλαγών), *a Paphlagonian.* Hence, **Paphlăgŏnĭa** -ae, f (Παφλαγονία), *a district in Asia Minor, between Pontus and Bithynia*

Păphus (-ŏs) -i (Πάφος) I. m *son of Pygmalion, founder of the town of the same name* II. f *a town of Cyprus, sacred to Venus*; hence, adj, **Păphĭus** a -um, *Paphian*, heros, *Pygmalion, father of Paphos*, myrtus, *sacred to Venus*, Ov

pāpĭlio -ōnis, m *a butterfly* Ov.

păpilla -ae, f *a nipple, teat*, used of both human beings and animals, Plin ; meton = *the breast*, Verg

Păpīrĭus -a -um, *name of a Roman gens*, hence, **Păpīrĭānus** -a -um, *Papirian*

Papĭus -a -um, *name of a Roman gens*

păpŭla ae, f *a pimple, pustule*, Verg

păpyrĭfĕr fĕra -fĕrum (papyrus and fero), *producing the papyrus*, Nilus, Ov

păpȳrus -i, f and **păpȳrum** -i, n (πάπυρος) I. *the plant papyrus*, Sen II. Meton, A. *a garment made of the bark*, Juv B. *paper made of the papyrus bark*, Juv

pār, păris, *equal, like* I. *like* or *equal to another thing* or *person*. A. Gen, 1, adj, pari intervallo, Caes, est finitimus oratori poeta ac paene par, Cic, with in and the abl, ut sint pares in amore, Cic, with abl, libertate esse parem ceteris, Cic, with genit, cuius paucos pares tulit, *like to him*, Cic, with dat, hominem cuivis parem, Cic, with cum, quaedam ex eis paria cum Crasso, Cic with inter se, inter se aequales et pares, Cic, followed by conj, par atque, Cic., et, Cic.; quam, Liv., 2, subst, a, c, *a mate*, Ov, b, neut, (α), *the like*, par pari respondere, Cic, par impar ludere, *to play at odd and even*, Hor, (β) *a pair*, tria aut quatuor paria amicorum, Cic B. Esp, 1, *equally strong as*, c, adj, alicui, Caes ; b, subst, *an adversary*, Liv, 2, fig., *suitable, appropriate*, par est, with acc and infin, Cic II. *like to oneself, equal to oneself*, ut par sis in utriusque orationis facultate, Cic

părābĭlis -e (paro), *that can be easily procured, procurable*, divitiae, Cic

Păraetăcēnē -ēs, f (Παραιτακηνή), *a district on the borders of Media and Persia*; hence, **Păraetăcae** -ārum, m *the inhabitants of Paraetacene*

Păraetŏnĭum ii, n (Παραιτόνιον), *a frontier town of Egypt, on the sea*

părăsīta ae, f (parasitus), *a toady, parasite*, Hor

părăsītaster tri, m (parasitus) *a poor, contemptible parasite*, Ter.

părăsītĭcus -a um (παρασιτικός), *like a parasite, parasitic*, Plaut

părăsītor, 1 dep (parasitus), *to play the parasite*, Plaut

părăsītus -i, m (παράσιτος, *eating with another*), *a toady, parasite*, Cic

părātē, adv (paratus), *with preparation, readily*, ad dicendum venire magis audacter quam parate, Cic

părātĭo ōnis, f (paro), *a preparation, preparing for*, paratio regni, *a striving after sovereignty*, Sall

1 **părātus** -a -um, p adj (from 1 paro) I. *prepared, ready*, 1, victoria, *easily won*, Liv ; parata in agendo et in respondendo celeritas, Cic, 2, *ready for something*, a, of things, omnia sibi esse ad bellum apta ac parata, Caes ; b, of persons, *ready for, inclined to*, animo paratus, Caes ; ad omnia mulieris negotia paratus, Cic, acies parata neci, Verg, with infin, id quod parati sunt facere, Cic II. a, *well prepared* or *provided with anything, equipped*, adolescens et equitatu et peditatu et pecunia paratus, Cic, b, *instructed, prepared*, ad permovendos animos instructi et parati, Cic

2 **părātus** -ūs, m (1 paro), *preparation, fitting out, provision, equipment*, necessarius vitae cultus aut paratus, Cic

Parca -ae, f (connected with plec-to, amplec-tor, Gr πλεκ-ω, etc), *the goddess that allots the fate to each, the goddess of fate*, Hor. Plur, Parcae, *the three Fates*, Clotho, Lachesis, and Atropos, Cic

parcē, adv (parcus) I. *sparingly, frugally, economically*, frumentum parce metiri, Caes II. 1, *sparingly, moderately*, parcius dicere de laude alicuius, Cic, 2, *rarely, seldom*, parcius quatiunt fenestras, Hor

parco, pĕperci and parsi, parsum, 3 (parcus) I. *to spare, to be sparing, moderate, frugal with anything*, with dat., impensae, Liv sumptu, Cic, with acc, talenta gnatis parce tuis, Verg. II. Transf, A. *to spare, refrain from injuring*; aedificiis, Cic, sibi, Caes B. a, *to leave off, desist from, cease*, labori, Cic, with infin, parce fidem ac jura societatis jactare, Liv, b, *to refrain from, keep oneself from*, with dat, auxilio, *to make no use of proffered aid*, Cic, metu, Verg ; with ab and the abl, ab incendiis, Liv

parcus -a -um (connected with parum and παυρος) I. *sparing* (esp in expenditure), *frugal, thrifty, economical*, a, colonus, Cic ; with genit, donandi, Hor, b, *moderate, sparing*; in largienda civitate, Cic II. *scanty, small, little, slight*, parco sale contingere, Verg ; lucerna, Prop

pardus -i, m (πάρδος), *a panther, pard*, Juv

1 **pārens** -entis, p adj (from pareo), *obedient*, parentiores exercitus, Cic, subst, **pārentes** ium, m *subjects*, Sall

2 **părens** -entis, c (pario) I. *a parent, father, mother*, a, lit, Cic, usually plur, *the parents*, quae caritas est inter natos et parentes, Cic, alma parens Idaea deum, Hor, b, transf, (a) *author, cause, origin*, operum, Cic, parens lyrae, *Mercury*, Hor, (β) *a mother city*, Liv II. *a grandfather*, Ov, plur, *ancestors*, Verg

părentālis -e (2 parens) I *parental, of* or *relating to parents*, umbra, Ov II. *of* or *relating to the funeral of parents* or *other relations*, a, adj, dies, Ov, b, subst, **părentālĭa** -ium, n *a festival in honour of deceased parents* or *other relations*, Cic

părento, 1 (2 parens) I. *to celebrate the parentalia in honour of the dead*, Februario mense mortuis parentari voluerunt, Cic. **II.** Transf., *to bring an offering to the dead = to avenge the death of a person by that of another;* Cethego, Cic.

pārĕo -ŭi -Itum, 2. (akin to pario). **I.** *to appear, become visible.* **A.** Lit., Mart. **B.** Transf., *to be clear, evident;* impers. paret, a legal formula, *it is proved*, Cic. **II. 1,** *to obey, be obedient to;* **a,** voluntati, legibus, Cic.; ducibus, Liv.; **b,** *to be compliant, yield, give way to;* necessitati, Cic.; promissis, *to perform one's promises*, Ov.; **2,** *to be subject to, to serve;* neque uni neque paucis, Cic.

păries -ĕtis, m. *the wall of a house* (opp. murus, *the wall of a city*); nullo modo posse iisdem parietibus tuto esse tecum, *within the same house*, Cic.; prov., duo parietes de eadem fidelia dealbare, *to kill two birds with one stone*, ap. Cic.

părĭĕtĭnae -ārum, f. (paries), *old walls, ruined walls, ruins*, Cic.

Părīlĭa = Palilia (v. under Pales).

părīlis -e (par), *similar, like, equal;* aetas, Ov.; vox, Ov.

părĭo, pĕpĕri, partum, fut. partic., părĭtūrus, 3. (root PAR, whence 1. paro), *to bring forth.* **I.** Lit., quintum, *for the fifth time*, Cic.; of birds, ova, *to lay eggs*, Cic. **II.** Transf., **A.** *to bring forth, produce;* fruges et reliqua quae terra pariat, Cic. **B.** *to invent, compose;* verba, Cic. **C.** *to produce, occasion, bring forth, invent, devise, obtain;* **a,** in a good sense, sibi laudem, Cic.; consulatum, Cic.; parta bona, *acquired*, Cic.; plur. subst., **parta** -ōrum, n. *property that has been acquired;* **b,** in a bad sense, *to occasion, procure, cause;* suspicionem, Cic.

Părĭs -ĭdis, m. (Πάρις), *son of the Trojan king, Priam, the judge in the contest of beauty for the golden apple between Juno, Minerva, and Venus; carried away Helen from her husband Menelaus to Troy, and thus caused the Trojan war.*

Părīsĭi -ōrum, m. *a people in Gallia Celtica, whose capital was Lutetia (Parisiorum),* now *Paris.*

părĭtĕr, adv. (par). **I.** *in like manner, alike;* caritate non pariter omnes egemus, Cic.; followed by ut, atque, ac, et, Cic.; qualis, Sall.; by dat., Liv. **II.** Transf., **A.** *together with, at the same time as;* pariter cum luna crescere, Cic. **B.** *likewise, also*, Ov.

părĭto, 1. (intens. of 1. paro), *to prepare, to get ready to do anything*, Plaut.

1. **parma** -ae, f. (πάρμη), *the small round shield* or *buckler worn by light-armed troops and cavalry*, Liv.; poet., *any kind of shield*, Verg.

2. **Parma** -ae, f. *town in Gallia Cispadana, colony of the Etruscans,* now *Parma.* Hence, adj., **Parmensis** -e, *of* or *belonging to Parma.*

Parmĕnĭdēs -is, m. (Παρμενίδης), *a famous Greek philosopher of the Eleatic School.*

parmātus -a -um (parma), *armed with the parma*, Liv.

parmŭla -ae, f. (dim. of parma), *a small round shield, buckler*, Hor.

Parnāsus (**ŏs**) and **Parnassus** (**ŏs**) -i, m. (Παρνασός), *a mountain in Phocis, sacred to Apollo and the Muses;* hence, adj., **Parnāsĭus** (**Parnassĭus**) -a -um, *Parnassian, Delphian, relating to Apollo;* laurus, Verg.

1. **păro**, 1. (root PAR, whence pario). **I.** *to prepare, make ready, provide, furnish, equip;* convivium, Cic.; bellum, Caes.; alicui necem, Liv.; with infin., *to prepare to do something;* publicas litteras Romam mittere parabam, Cic.; foll. by ut with the subj., si ita naturā paratum esset, ut ea dormientes agerent, Cic. **II.** Transf., *to procure, get, obtain.* **A.** exercitum, copias, Sall.; non modo pacem sed etiam societatem, Liv.; praesidium senectuti, Cic. **B.** Esp., *to procure with money, buy;* hortos, Cic.

2. **păro**, 1. (par), **1,** *to prize* or *esteem equally;* eodem vos pono et paro, Plaut.; **2,** *to agree, arrange with;* se paraturum cum collega, Cic.

3. **păro** -ōnis, m. (παρών), *a small, light vessel, skiff*, Cic.

părŏchus -i, m. (πάροχος), **1,** *an officer in Italy or in the provinces who provided with necessaries ambassadors and magistrates when on a journey*, Cic.; **2,** transf., *one who gives an entertainment, a host*, Hor.

păropsis -ĭdis, f. (παροψίς), *a small dish, dessert-dish*, Juv.

Părus (**-ŏs**) -i, f. (Πάρος), *an island in the Aegean Sea, famous for its white marble.* Hence, **Părĭus** -a -um (Πάριος), *Parian;* lapis, *Parian marble*, Verg.; iambi, *of Archilochus, who was born at Paros*, Verg.

parra -ae, f. *a bird of ill omen*, according to some, *the owl*, to others, *the woodpecker*, Hor.

Parrhăsĭa -ae, f. (Παῤῥασία), *a district and city in Arcadia;* hence, adj., **1, Parrhăsis** -ĭdis, f. *Arcadian;* Arctos or ursa = *ursa major* or *Callisto;* subst., Parrhasis = *Callisto*, Ov.; **2, Parrhăsĭus** -a -um; **a,** *Arcadian;* virgo, *Callisto*, Ov.; dea, *Carmenta*, Ov.; **b,** *relating to the Palatine Hill, imperial* (because the Arcadian Evander was said to have settled upon the Palatine), Mart.

1. **Parrhăsĭus**, v. Parrhasia.

2. **Parrhăsĭus** -ii, m. (Παῤῥάσιος), *a celebrated Greek painter of Ephesus, rival of Zeuxis, flourishing about* 400 B.C.

parrĭcīda -ae, c. (perhaps from pater and caedo), *a parricide;* **a,** *one who murders his father* or *parents*, Cic.; **b,** *one who slays near relations;* parricida liberûm, *Virginius*, Liv.; **c,** *murderer of a free citizen;* parricida civium, Cic.; **d,** *murderer of the head of the state*, Cic.; **e,** *a traitor, betrayer of one's country, rebel;* parricidae reipublicae, Cic.

parrĭcīdĭum -ii, n. (parricida), **1,** *the murder of a father or parents, parricide; the murder of any near relation;* fratris, Liv.; patris et patrui, Cic.; **2,** *the murder of a free citizen*, Cic.; **3,** *high treason, the betraying of one's country;* parricidium patriae, Cic.

pars, partis, acc. partim and partem, f. *a part, portion, piece.* **I.** Gen., urbis, Cic.; partes facere, *to divide*, Cic.; partem habere in aliqua re, *to have a share in*, Cic. Especial phrases, **a,** pars . . . pars, *some . . . others*, Liv.; **b,** parte . . . parte, *partly . . . partly*, Ov.; pro parte or pro sua, mea, etc., parte, *for his part*, Cic.; **c,** ex aliqua parte, *in some degree*, Cic.; magna ex parte, *to a great extent*, Cic.; omni ex parte, *altogether*, Cic.; **d,** magnam partem, *to a great extent*, Cic.; **e,** acc. partim, *in part*, Cic.; **f,** multis partibus = *many times, much;* plures, Cic.; **g,** in eam partem, *in such a manner*, Cic., or *with a view to*, Cic.; in utramque partem (*on both sides*, pro and contra) disputare, Cic., or *in both cases*, Cic.; **h,** in omnes partes, *altogether, completely*, Cic.; **i,** in partem venire alicuius rei, *to take a share in*, Cic.; **j,** in parte, *in part*, Liv.; **k,** pro parte, *to the best of his ability*, Liv. **II. A.** *species*, Cic. **B.** *a party, faction;* nullius partis esse, *neutral*, Cic. **C.** *the part* or *rôle of an actor;* **a,** lit., primas partes agere, *the leading part*, Cic.; **b,** transf., *a part, office, function, duty;* tuum est hoc munus, tuae partes, Cic. **D.** *a part, portion, district of the earth;* partes orientis, Cic.

parsĭmōnĭa ae, f (parco), *thriftiness, parsimony*, Cic

Parthāōn -ŏnis, m (Παρθάων), *son of Agenor, king in Calydon, father of Oeneus*, Parthaone natus, *Oeneus*, Ov Adj, **Parthāŏnĭus** -a -um, *of Parthaon*, domus, *of Oeneus*, Ov

Parthēni (Parthīni) -ōrum, m *an Illyrian people near Dyrrhachium*

parthĕnīcē -ēs, f (παρθενική), *the plant parthenium*, Cat.

Parthĕnĭus -ii, m *a mountain on the borders of Argolis and Arcadia.*

Parthĕnŏpaeus -i, m (Παρθενοπαῖος), *one of the seven princes who fought against Thebes.*

Parthĕnŏpē -ēs, f (Παρθενόπη), *old name of the town of Neapolis, so called from the Siren Parthenope, who was said to have been buried there.* Adj, **Parthĕnŏpēius** -a -um, *Parthenopean*, poet = *Neapolitan*

Parthi -ōrum, m (Πάρθοι), *a Scythian nomadic people, famous for their archery, savage enemies of the Romans* Hence, **Parthĭcus** and **Parthus** -a -um, *Parthian*

partĭceps -cĭpis (pars and capio), *sharing, participating in*, animus rationis compos et particeps, Cic, praedae ac praemiorum, Caes, with dat., alicui ad omne secretum, Tac Subst, *a sharer, partaker, comrade*, huius belli ego particeps et socius et adjutor esse cogor, Cic

partĭcĭpo, 1 (particeps), *to cause to share, share with any one*, laudes cum aliquo, Liv, ad participandum alium alio communicandumque inter omnes jus, Cic

partĭcŭla -ae, f (dim of pars), *a small part, portion, particle*; caeli, Cic

partim, adv (acc of pars), *partly, in part*, Cic

partĭo, 4 and **partĭor**, 4 dep (pars), *to divide, subdivide*. **I.** genus universum in species certas partietur ac dividet, Cic **II.** *to divide, distribute, share*; consules designati provincias inter se partiverant, Sall, nonne aerarium cum eo partitus es? Cic.

partītē, adv. (partitus, from partior), *with proper divisions*; dicere, Cic.

partītĭo -ōnis, f. (partio) **I.** *a division*, 1, Graecos partitionem quandam artium fecisse video, Cic., 2, esp., *a logical or rhetorical division of a subject*, Cic **II.** *a division, distribution, partition*, aequabilis praedae partitio, Cic

partītus -a -um, partic of partior

partŭrĭo, 4 (desider of pario) **I.** *to desire to bring forth, have the pains of labour*, 1, lit, prov, parturiunt montes, nascetur ridiculus mus, Hor., 2, fig., a, *to be pregnant with any thing, to meditate, intend*, ut aliquando dolor P. R. pariat, quod jamdiu parturit! Cic., b, *to be anxious, troubled*, si tamquam parturiat unus pro pluribus, Cic. **II.** *to bear, bring forth, produce*; nunc omnis parturit arbos, Verg

partus -ūs, m. (pario) **I.** *a bearing, bringing forth young, a birth*, quum jam appropinquare partus putaretur, Cic; fig, Graeciae oratorum partus atque fontes, *beginnings*, Cic. **II.** Meton, **A.** *the time of bearing*, Cic **B.** *that which is brought forth, the fruit of the womb*; partum edere, *to give birth to*, Cic., partus terrae, *the giants*, Hor

părum, adv. (from same root as parvus and παῦρος), compar, **mĭnŭs**, superl, **mĭnĭmē**; *too little, not enough* (opp satis, nimium). **I.** Posit., parum id facio, *I make little account of that*, Sall.; parum est, foll. by quod, *it is not enough that*, etc, Cic, parum habere, *to think too little, be dissatisfied with*, foll by infin, Liv, parum diu, *too short*, Cic non parum saepe, *often enough*, Cic. **II.** Compar, minus **A.** *less*, minus ac minus, Plin minus minusque, *less and less*, Liv, nihil minus, *nothing less, not at all, by no means*, Cic, foll by quam, ac, atque Liv, with quam omitted, haud minus duo millia, *not less than two thousand*, Liv, foll by abl, minus triginta diebus, *in less than thirty days*, Cic, uno minus teste haberet, *one witness the less*, Cic, multo minus, *much less*, Cic; bis sex ceciderunt, me minus uno, *except me alone*, Ov. **B.** *not particularly*, minus multi, Cic **C.** *not*, **a**, after quo, *that*, prohibuisse, quo minus, etc, Cic; **b**, in the formulae, si minus, *if not*, sin minus, *but if not*, Cic. **D.** = parum, *too little*, dicere, Cic **III.** Superl., minime, *in the least degree, very little, least of all*; quod minime apparet et valet plurimum, Cic, with adjectives = *not at all, by no means*, homo minime ambitiosus, Cic, in answers, *by no means, not at all*, Cic, minime vero, Cic.

părumpĕr, adv (παῦρόν περ), *for a little while, a little space*, abduco parumper animum a molestiis, Cic

păruncŭlus -i, m (dim of 3 paro), *a little ship or vessel*, Cic.

Părus = Paros (q v)

parvĭtas -ātis, f (parvus), *littleness, smallness*, Cic.

parvŭlus -a -um (dim of parvus). **I.** *very small, very little, minute*; res, pecunia, Cic. **II.** Of age, *young, little*; filius, Cic, ab parvulis, *from childhood*, Caes

parvus -a -um (parvus, by change of consonants, from same root as παῦρος), compar, **minor**, superl, **minimus**; *little, small* **I.** Lit, **A.** Of size or extent, locus, Cic, navicula, Cic, minor capitis = capite deminutus (see deminuo), Hor. **B.** Of number or quantity, **a**, adj, minimus numerus, Liv, **b**, subst, **parvum** -i, n *a little*, contentus parvo, Cic; minus praedae, Liv., **c**, adv., **minimum**, *very little*, valere, Cic **II.** Transf, **A.** Of value, *slight, unimportant*, **a**, adj, parvo vendere pretio, Cic, **b**, subst, **parvum** -i, n *something little or slight*, parvi aestimo or duco, *I think little of*, Cic, minoris vendere, *cheaper*, Cic **B.** Of strength or degree, *slight, weak*; **a**, of the voice, etc, (α) *weak*, parvae murmura vocis, Ov, (β) *abject*, verbis minoribus uti, Ov, **b**, of the intellect, *poor, unproductive*, ingenium, Hor, **c**, of thought, will, etc, *little, abject, mean*; parvi animi, Cic, **d**, of circumstances, *trifling, unimportant, slight*, commodum, Cic, prov, minima de malis, *we must choose the least evil*, Cic, **e**, of persons, *poor in position, unimportant, low, insignificant*, domus, Ov Compar, minor, with abl, *inferior to, dependent on*, te minor, Hor **C.** Of time, 1, *short*, dies, Ov, 2, = *young*, minor natu, *younger*, Cic Subst, **parvus** -i, m *a little boy*, Cic, **parva** ae, f. *a little girl* Cic; a parvo, *from boyhood*, Cic, minores, *young people*, Hor, Ov

pasco, pāvi, pastum, 3 (root PA, whence panis, Gr ΠΑ, whence πάομαι) **I.** *to feed cattle, lead cattle to pasture* **A.** Lit., 1, sues, Cic; 2, hence, gen, *to feed, nourish, support*; of animals, ubi bestiae pastae sunt, Cic., of human beings, olusculis nos soles pascere, Cic, quot pascit servos, Juv. **B.** Transf, 1, *to feed, increase, enlarge, let grow*, barbam, Hor, crinem, Verg., 2, *to feed, feast, gratify*, oculos in aliqua re, Cic. **II.** = depascere. **A.** *to feed on*; asperrima (collium), Verg **B.** *to consume*, Ov. Hence, **pascor**, pastus sum, pasci, 3. dep **I.** 1, *to feed, eat, graze on*; boves pascuntur frondibus, Verg.; **2,** of the sacred chickens, *to eat;* quum pulli non pascerentur, *refused to eat,* Cic. **II.** With acc., *to feed on;* pascuntur silvas, Verg.

pascŭus -a -um (pasco), *fit for pasture* or *grazing;* ager, Cic.; hence, subst., **pascŭum** -i, n. *a pasture;* plur., **pascŭa** -ōrum, n. *pastures,* Cic.

Pāsĭphăē -ēs, f. and **Pāsĭphăa** -ae, f. (Πασιφάη), *daughter of Helios* (Sol), *sister of Circe, mother of the Minotaur, Androgeus, Phaedra, and Ariadne.* Adj., **Pāsĭphăēĭus** -a -um, *relating to Pasiphaë;* subst., **Pāsĭphăēĭa** -ae, f.= *Phaedra,* Ov.

Pāsĭthĕa -ae, f. and **Pāsĭthĕē** -ēs, f. (Πασιθέα, Πασιθέη), *one of the three Graces.*

passer -ĕris, m. (for panser, from pando), **1,** *a sparrow,* Cic., Cat.; **2,** *a sea-fish, a turbot* or *plaice,* Ov.

passercŭlus -i, m. (dim. of passer), *a little sparrow,* Cic.

passim, adv. (passus from pando). **I.** *here and there, up and down, far and wide, in a disorderly manner, confusedly;* Numidae nullis ordinibus passim consederant, Caes. **II.** *without distinction, indiscriminately, promiscuously;* scribimus indocti doctique poëmata passim, Hor.

passum -i, n. (pando, sc. vinum), *wine made of dried grapes, raisin-wine,* Verg.

1. **passus** -a -um, partic. of pando.

2. **passus** -a -um, partic. of patior.

3. **passus** -ūs, m. **I.** *a step, stride, pace.* **A.** **a,** lit., passus perpauculi, Cic.; **b,** fig., passibus ambiguis Fortuna errat, Ov. **B.** *a footstep, track;* passu stare tenaci, Ov. **II.** *the pace* (a Roman measure of length) = *five feet;* mille passus, *a mile,* Cic.

pastillus -i, m. (dim. of panis), *a lozenge used to give an agreeable smell to the breath,* Hor.

pastĭo -ōnis, f. (pasco), *a pasture,* Cic.

pastor -ōris, m. (pasco), *a herd;* esp., *a shepherd,* Cic.; pastorum domina, *Pales,* Ov.; pastorum dux geminus, *Romulus and Remus,* Cic.

pastōrālis -e (pastor), *of* or *relating to a shepherd, pastoral,* Cic.

pastōrĭcĭus -a -um (pastor), *relating to shepherds,* Cic.

pastōrĭus -a -um (pastor), *relating to shepherds,* Ov.

pastus -ūs, m. (pasco). **I.** *feeding.* **A.** Lit., ad pastum accedunt, Cic. **B.** Meton., *fodder, food;* pastum capessere et conficere, Cic. **II.** *pasture,* Verg.

Pătăra -ōrum, n. (Πάταρα), *a city in Lycia, with a celebrated oracle of Apollo;* hence, **1,** **Pătărĕus** -ĕi and -ĕos, m. *a surname of Apollo;* **2,** **Pătăraeus** -a -um, *Patarean;* **3,** **Pătărāni** -ōrum, m. *the inhabitants of Patara.*

Pătăvĭum -ii, n. *a town in Venetia, on the banks of the Medoacus, birth-place of the historian Livy,* now *Padua.* Adj., **Pătăvīnus** -a -um, *Patavinian.*

pătĕfăcĭo -fēci -factum, 3., pass., **pătĕfīo** -factus sum -fieri (pateo and facio), *to open, make open, lay open.* **I.** Lit., **A.** aures assentatoribus, Cic. **B.** **1.** *to make accessible, to open;* vias, iter, Caes.; *to open up a place,* patefactum nostris legionibus esse Pontum, Cic.; **2,** *to make visible,* Cic.; **3,** *to open* (by digging, etc.); presso sulcum aratro, Ov. **II.** Transf., *to bring to light, disclose, display, reveal;* odium suum in [illegible]ae, Cic.; comparationem, Cic.; rem, Cic.

pătĕfactĭo -ōnis, f. (patefacio), *a throwing open, disclosing;* rerum opertarum, Cic.

pătella -ae, f. (dim. of patera), **1,** *a dish, platter, plate* (used both in the cookery and serving up of food), Hor.; **2,** *a dish in which offerings were presented to the gods, a sacrificial dish,* Cic.

pătens -entis, p. adj. (from pateo). **I.** *open, unobstructed, accessible;* caelum, Cic.; loca, Caes. **II.** *open, exposed to;* domus patens cupiditati et voluptatibus, Cic.

pătentĕr, adv. (patens), *openly, evidently, clearly;* compar., patentius, Cic.

pătĕo -ŭi, 2. (perhaps connected with πετάννυμι), *to be open, stand open, lie open.* **I.** nares semper propter necessarias utilitates patent, Cic. **II.** **A.** *to be open, accessible;* **a,** lit., aditus patuit, Cic.; **b,** *to stand open, to be at the service of, to be in the power of;* honores patent alicui, Cic. **B.** *to lie open to, to be exposed to;* vulneri, Liv. **C.** *to lie open before the eyes, to be visible;* **a,** lit., nomen in adversariis patet, Cic.; **b,** transf., *to be revealed, disclosed, clear;* res patent, Cic. **D.** Geograph. t. t., **a,** lit., *to stretch out, extend;* Helvetiorum fines in longitudinem millia passuum CXL patebant, Cic.; **b,** transf., *to spread, extend itself;* in quo vitio latissime patet avaritia, Cic.

păter -tris, m. (πατήρ), *a father.* **I.** **A.** Lit., aliquem patris loco colere, Cic.; plur., patres, *parents,* Ov. **B.** Poet., meton., **1,** *fatherly love;* vex patrem vicit, Ov.; **2,** *the author or source of anything,* Verg. **II.** Transf., **A.** *father-in-law,* Tac. **B.** **a,** pater familias or familiae, *the head of a household,* Cic.; **b,** pater cenae, *the host,* Hor. **C.** patres, *fathers, ancestors;* aetas patrum nostrorum, Cic. **D.** Used as a title of honour; **a,** of the gods, Lemnius, *Vulcan,* Cic.; Lenaeus, *Bacchus,* Verg.; **b,** esp. the title by which the senators were addressed, patres conscripti, Cic.; **c,** pater patriae, *father of his country,* a name sometimes given to distinguished statesmen, Ov.; **d,** pater patratus, *the chief of the fetiales,* Cic.; **e,** used as a title of respect towards an old man, Verg.

pătĕră -ae, f. (pateo), *a shallow dish or saucer from which a libation was poured,* Cic.

Pătercŭlus -i, m. C. Velleius, *a Roman historian under Augustus and Tiberius.*

păternus -a -um (pater), **1,** *of or relating to a father, fatherly, paternal;* horti, Cic.; **2,** *of or relating to one's native country, native;* flumen, Hor.

pătesco, pătŭi, 3. (pateo), *to be opened, lie open.* **I.** Gen., **a,** lit., atria longa patescunt, Verg.; **b,** *to be revealed, disclosed;* Danaum patescunt invidiae, Verg. **II.** *to extend, stretch out;* deinde paulo latior patescit campus, Liv.

pătĭbĭlis -e (patior). **I.** Pass., *endurable, bearable;* dolores, Cic. **II.** Act., *sensitive;* natura, Cic.

pătĭbŭlum -i, n. *a fork-shaped yoke, an instrument of punishment fastened on the neck of slaves and criminals,* Cic.

pătĭens -entis, p. adj. (from patior). **I.** *bearing, enduring, capable of enduring.* **A.** Lit., with genit., patiens laborum, Sall.; amnis navium patiens, *navigable,* Liv.; animum patientem incommodorum, Cic. **B.** Poet., *firm, hard, unyielding;* aratrum, Ov. **II.** *enduring, patient;* ut ne offendam tuas patientissimas aures, Cic.

pătĭentĕr, adv. (patiens), *patiently;* ferre, Cic.

pătĭentĭa -ae, f. (patiens), *endurance.* **I.** famis, frigoris, Cic. **II.** **A.** *patience, long-suffer-*

ing; in cavendo, Cic. **B.** *indolence, faint-heartedness*, Tac. **C.** *subjection*, Tac.

pătina -ae, f. (πατάνη), *a dish*, Cic.

pătior, passus sum, 3. dep. (root PAT, connected with πάσχω, aor. ἔ-παθ-ον), *to suffer, bear, endure*. **I.** Lit., **A.** Gen., **a,** of persons, toleranter dolores, Cic.; gravissimum supplicium, Caes.; id damnum haud aegerrime pati, Liv.; **b,** of things, tunc patitur cultus ager, Ov. **B.** *to last, endure*; novem saecula (of the crow), Ov. **II.** Transf., **1,** *to suffer, experience*; multam repulsam, Ov.; **2,** *to suffer, permit, allow*; ista, Cic.; with acc. and infin., nullo se implicari negotio passus est, Cic.; with ut and the subj., quod si in turpi reo patiendum non esset ut arbitrarentur, Cic.; non patior, foll. by quin, nullam patiebatur esse diem quin in foro diceret, *he allowed no day to pass without speaking*, Cic.; with adv., facile, libenter, aequo animo, indigne pati, with acc. and infin., Cic.; with things as subjects, quantum patiebatur pudor, Cic.

Patrae -ārum, f. (Πάτραι), *a sea-port in Achaia*, now *Patras*. Adj., **Patrensis** -e, *relating to Patrae*.

pătrātor -ōris, m. (patro), *an accomplisher, achiever, effector*; necis, Tac.

pătria -ae, f. *father-land*, v. patrius.

pătrĭcĭātus -ūs, m. *the rank or condition of a patrician*, Suet.

pătrĭcīda (pater and caedo), *one who murders his father*, Cic.

pătrĭcĭus -a -um (patres, v. pater, II. D. b), *patrician, noble*; **1,** adj., familia, Cic.; **2,** subst., patricius, *a patrician*, and plur., patricii, *the Roman patricians or nobility*, Cic.; exire e patriciis, *to be adopted into a plebeian family*, Cic.

pătrĭmōnĭum -ii, n. (pater), *property inherited from a father, patrimony*; accipere duo lauta et copiosa patrimonia, Cic.; fig., filio meo satis amplum patrimonium relinquam, memoriam nominis mei, Cic.

pătrīmus -a -um (pater), *having a father still living*, Cic.

pătrītus -a -um (pater), *paternal*; patrita illa atque avita philosophia, Cic.

pătrĭus -a -um (pater), *of or relating to a father, fatherly, paternal*. **I.** Adj., animus, Cic.; amor, Ov.; res, *property inherited from one's father*, Cic.; mos, *ancestral, ancient*, Cic. **II.** Subst., **pătria** -ae, f. (sc. terra), *father-land, native land*; aliquem restituere in patriam, Cic.; hence, **pătrĭus** -a -um, *relating to one's native country*; ritus, Cic.

pătro, 1. *to accomplish, perform, execute, achieve*; promissa, Cic.; bellum, *to bring to an end*, Sall.; pacem, Liv.; jusjurandum, *to pronounce a solemn oath at the conclusion of a treaty*, Liv.

pătrōcĭnĭum -ii, n. (= patronocinium, from patronus). **I.** *protection, defence in a court of law*; controversiarum patrocinia suscipere, Cic.; meton., patrocinia = *clients*, ap. Cic. **II.** Transf., *defence, protection*; patrocinium voluptatis repudiare, Cic.

pătrōcĭnor, 1. dep. (patronus), *to protect, defend*; alicui, Ter.

Pătrŏclus -i, m. (Πάτροκλος), *son of Menoetius, friend and cousin of Achilles, slain by Hector before Troy*.

pătrōna -ae, f. (patronus), *a protectress, patroness*, Ter.; esp., *the mistress or protectress of a freedman*, Plin.; fig., *a protectress*; provocatio patrona illa civitatis et vindex libertatis, Cic.

pătrōnus -i, m. (pater). **I.** *the protector, defender, patron of a body of clients; the patron or powerful friend at Rome of a state or city*; *a defender, advocate before a court of justice*; patronus, defensor, custos coloniae, Cic.; huic causae patronum exsistere, Cic.; esp., *the protector of a freedman*, i.e., *his master before he was freed*, Cic. **II.** Transf., *a defender, protector*; plebis, Liv.; foederum, Cic.

pătrŭēlis -e (patruus). **I.** *descended from a father's brother*; frater patruelis, *cousin on the father's side*, Cic.; transf., *the son of a paternal aunt*, Cic. **II.** *of or relating to a cousin, cousinly*, Ov.

1. **pătrŭus** -i, m. (pater), *a father's brother, paternal uncle*; **a,** lit., Cic.; **b,** fig., *a severe reprover*, Cic.

2. **pătrŭus** -a -um (pater), *of or relating to an uncle*, Hor.

Pătulcius -ii, m. (pateo), *a surname of Janus, whose temple was always open in time of war*, Ov.

pătŭlus -a -um (pateo). **I.** *open, standing open*; pinna, Cic.; fenestrae, Ov. **II.** *wide-spreading, extended*; rami, Cic.; loca urbis, Tac.

paucitas -ātis, f. (paucus), *fewness, scarcity, paucity*; oratorum, Cic.; militum, Caes.

paucŭlus -a -um (dim. of paucus), *very small*; gen. in plur., *very few*; dies, Cic.

paucus -a -um, oftener plur., **pauci** -ae -a (connected with paulus and pauper, and Gr. παῦρος). **I.** *few, little*; pauco foramine (= paucis foraminibus), Hor.; paucis rebus, Cic.; pauciores viri, Cic. Plur. subst., **a, pauci** -ōrum, m. *a few*; esp., (α) (like οἱ ὀλίγοι), *the oligarchs*; (β) *the select few* (opp. populus), Cic.; **b, pauca** -ōrum, n. *a few words*; ut in pauca conferam, Cic. **II.** *a few*; paucis diebus, Cic.

paulātim (paullātim), adv. **I.** *gradually, little by little*; **a,** of place, paulatim ab imo acclivis, Caes.; **b,** of time, si paulatim haec consuetudo serpere ac prodire coeperit, Caes. **II.** *singly, one after another*; ex castris discedere coeperunt, Caes.

paulispĕr (paullispĕr), adv. *a little while, a short time*; partes alicuius suscipere, Cic.; foll. by dum, Cic.; donec, Liv.

paulo (paullo), v. paulus.

paulŭlo (paullŭlo), v. paululus.

paulŭlus (paullŭlus) -a -um (dim. of paulus), *very little, very small*; via, Liv.; neut., **paulŭlum** -i, n., **a,** subst., *a very little*; morae, Cic.; **b,** adv., *a little*; paululum respirare, Cic.; paululo with compar., paululo deterius, *a little worse*, ap. Cic.

1. **paulus (paullus)** -a -um (connected with paucus and pauper, and Gr. παῦρος), *little, small*; sumptus, Ter.; neut., paulum; **a,** subst., *a little*; paulum aliquid damni, Cic.; paulo, *by a little, a little*; with compar., paulo melior, Cic.; with adv., paulo secus, Cic.; **b,** adv., *a little*; paulum commorari, Cic.

2. **Paulus (Paullus)** -i, m. *the name of a family of the gens Aemilia, of which the most famous were*: **1,** L. Aemilius Paulus, *who commanded, with C. Terentius Varro, at Cannae, and was there slain*; **2,** L. Aemilius Paulus Macedonicus, *son of the preceding, the conqueror of Perseus, king of Macedonia*.

pauper -ĕris (contracted for pauci-per = πένης), *poor, not wealthy*; **a,** of persons, homo, Cic.; vir, Cic.; with genit., argenti, Hor.; subst., pauper, *a poor man*, Ov.; **b,** transf., of things, *poor, scanty, meagre*; domus, Verg.

paupercŭlus -a -um (dim. of pauper), *poor*, Hor.

pauperies -ēi, f. (pauper), *poverty, indigence,* Hor.

paupĕro, 1. (pauper). **I.** *to make poor,* Plaut. **II.** Transf., aliquem aliquā re, *to rob* or *deprive of anything,* Hor.

paupertas -ātis, f. (pauper), *poverty.* **A.** Lit., *humble circumstances* (opp. divitiae); paupertas vel potius egestas ac mendicitas, Cic. **B.** Transf. (= egestas, inopia), *need, want, indigence,* Cic.

pausa -ae, f. (παῦσις), *a pause, cessation, stoppage, end;* vitae, Lucr.

Pausănĭās -ae, m. (Παυσανίας), *son of Cleombrotus, commander of the Spartans at Plataea.*

pausĕa (pausia) and **pōsĕă** -ae, f. *a species of olive, which produced an excellent oil,* Verg.

Pausĭās -ae, acc. -an, m. (Παυσίας), *a Greek painter of Sicyon, contemporary with Apelles.* Adj., **Pausĭăcus** -a -um, *of* or *relating to Pausias;* tabella, Hor.

pausillŭlum = pauxillulum, v. under pauxillulus.

pauxillātim, adv. (pauxillus), *gradually, by degrees,* Plaut.

pauxillispĕr, adv. (pauxillus), *a little while,* Plaut.

pauxillŭlus -a -um (dim. of pauxillus), *very little, very small,* Plaut.; subst., **pauxillŭlum** -i, n. *a little,* Plaut.

pauxillus -a -um (dim. of paucus), *small, little,* Lucr.; subst., **pauxillum** -i, n. *a little,* Plaut.

păvĕfăcĭo, 3. (paveo and facio), *to frighten, terrify;* found only in partic., pavefactus, *terrified,* Ov.

păvĕo, pāvi, 2. *to fear, be afraid of, to quake with fear;* inde admiratione paventibus cunctis, Liv.; with acc., lupos, Hor.; varia miracula, Liv.; with ad and the acc., ad omnia, Liv.; with infin., Ov.

păvesco, 3. (paveo), *to fear, be afraid of, be terrified;* with abl. of cause, omni strepitu, Sall.; with acc., bellum, Tac.

păvĭdē, adv. (pavidus), *fearfully, in a state of terror;* fugere, Liv.

păvĭdus -a -um (paveo). **I.** *trembling, quaking, fearful, terrified;* castris se pavidus tenebat, Liv.; with ne and the subj., pavidi ne jam facta in urbem via esset, Liv.; with genit., offensionum, Tac. **II.** *causing terror, producing fear;* religiones, Lucr.; metus, Ov.

păvīmento, 1. (pavimentum), *to pave,* ap. Cic.

păvīmentum -i, n. (pavio), *a pavement of tiles, brick, stone, etc., laid in a bed of strong cement;* pavimentum facere, Cic.

păvĭo, 4. (παϝίω), *to beat;* terram, Cic.

păvĭto, 1. (intens. of paveo), **1,** *to tremble, quake with fear,* Verg.; **2,** *to quake, shiver with ague,* Ter.

pāvo -ōnis, m. (onomatop., root PA, cf. Gr. ταώς), *a peacock,* Cic.

păvor -ōris, m. (paveo). **I.** *a trembling* or *trepidation produced by fear, expectation, joy,* etc., Cic.; alicui pavorem injicere, incutere, *to cause fear,* Liv.; pavor est, pavor aliquem capit, foll. by ne and the subj., Liv. **II.** Personif., Pavor, *as a deity,* Liv.

pax, pācis, f. (root PAC, whence paciscor, pango, πήγνυμι), *peace.* **I.** Lit., pacem conciliare, conficere, facere cum aliquo, *to make peace,* Cic.; servare pacem cum aliquo, *to keep peace,* Cic.; uti pace, *to be at peace,* Cic.; turbare pacem, Liv. Plur., paces, *conditions* or *proposals of peace;* bella atque paces, Sall. Personif., Pax, *the goddess of Peace,* Ov. **II.** Transf., **1,** *peace, quiet;* **a,** of things, flumen cum pace delabens, *quietly,* Hor.; **b,** of looks or of feelings, semper in animo sapientis est placidissima pax, Cic.; pace tuā dixerim, *with your good leave,* Cic.; **2,** *favour* or *approval of the gods;* ab Jove ceterisque dis pacem ac veniam peto, Cic.

peccātum -i, n. (pecco), *a sin, crime, offence, fault;* peccatum suum confiteri, Cic.

peccātus -ū, m. (pecco), *a fault;* manifesto peccatu teneri, Cic.

pecco, 1. **I.** *to commit a fault* or *crime, to sin;* Empedocles multa alia peccat, Cic.; in se, Cic.; in servo necando, Cic. **II.** *to fail, to err, to go wrong;* in homine, Caes.; ne peccet equus, Hor.

pecten -inis, m. (pecto), *a comb.* **I.** Lit., *for combing the hair;* deducere pectine crines, Ov. **II.** Transf., **a,** *a weaver's comb,* Verg.; **b,** *a rake,* Ov.; **c,** *the clasping of the hands in trouble;* digiti inter se pectine juncti, Ov.; **d,** *an instrument with which the strings of the lyre were struck,* Verg.; meton., *song;* alterno pectine, *in elegiac verse* (first a hexameter, then a pentameter), Ov.; **e,** *a shell-fish, the scallop,* Hor.

pecto, pexi, pexum and pectitum, 3. (πεκτέω). **I.** *to comb;* comas, Ov. **II.** *to comb, card;* stuppam, Plin. Partic., **pexus** -a -um, *with the nap on, woolly;* tunica, *new,* Hor.

pectus -ŏris, n. *the breast in men and animals, the breast-bone.* **I.** Lit., Verg. **II.** Fig., **1,** *the breast as the seat of the affections, the heart, soul;* toto pectore amare, *to love with the whole heart,* Cic.; forti pectore, *courage,* Hor.; puro pectore, *with good conscience,* Hor.; **2,** *the breast, as the seat of reason, understanding;* toto pectore cogitare, Cic.; excidere pectore alicuius, *to be forgotten,* Ov.

pĕcu, dat. -ū, abl. -ū, nom. and acc. plur. pecua, n., genit. plur. pecuum (connected with pecus), *cattle,* Cic.

pĕcuārius -a -um (pecu), *of* or *relating to cattle.* **I.** Adj., res, *the breeding of cattle,* Cic. **II.** Subst., **A. pĕcuārius** -ii, m. *a breeder of cattle, grazier,* Cic. Plur., pecuarii, *the farmers of the public pastures* (in the provinces), Cic., Liv. **B. pĕcuāria** -ōrum, n. *herds of cattle,* Verg.

pĕcūlātor -ōris, m. (peculor), *one who embezzles the public money,* Cic.

pĕcūlātus -ūs, m. (peculor), *the embezzlement of the public money, peculation;* peculatum facere, Cic.

pĕcūlĭāris -e (peculium). **I.** *belonging to one's private property;* oves, Plaut. **II.** Transf., **a,** *proper, special, peculiar;* testis, Cic.; hoc mihi peculiare fuerit, Cic.; **b,** *peculiar, extraordinary, singular;* edictum, Cic.

pĕcūlĭo, 1. (peculium), *to provide with private property.* Partic., **pĕcūlĭātus** -a -um, *provided with property,* ap. Cic.

pĕcūlĭum -ii, n. (pecus), *property* (orig., *property in cattle*). **I.** Gen., cura peculi, Verg.; cupiditas peculii, Cic. **II.** Esp., *the private property possessed by a son or slave independent of the father* or *master;* peculium castrense, *earnings of the son on military service;* quasi castrense, *in other occupations;* profecticium, *property possessed by grant from the father;* adventicium, *by inheritance from the mother,* Cic., Liv.

pĕcūnia -ae, f. (pecus, orig. *property in cattle*). **I.** *property;* pecuniam facere, *to gain property,* Cic. **II.** Esp., *money, cash, sums of* *money*, accipere pecuniam, *to allow oneself to be bribed*, Cic ; coacervare pecuniam, *to heap money together*, Cic., flare et conflare pecuniam, *to make money, to become rich*, Cic , pecuniam mutuam sumere ab aliquo, *to borrow*, Cic.

pĕcūniārius -a -um (pecunia), *of or relating to money, pecuniary*, res pecuniaria, *a money-matter, business*, Cic , or simply = *money*, Cic.

pĕcūniōsus -a um (pecunia), *wealthy, rich*, homo pecuniosissimus, Cic

1. **pĕcus** -ŏris, n *cattle, a herd, flock* (collectively, while pecus ŭdis = *single head of cattle*). **I.** Lit., **A.** setigerum, *swine*, Ov ; lanigerum, *sheep*, Ov , applied also to *bees*, Verg , *fish*, Hor **B.** Esp , **1,** *a flock of sheep*, balatus pecorum, Ov , **2,** poet., pecus magnae parentis (of young lions), Ov **II.** Transf , applied contemptuously to human beings, imitatorum servum pecus, *a servile herd*, Hor

2. **pĕcus** -ŭdis, f (pecu, 1. pecus), *a single head of cattle, a beast, animal* **I.** Lit , **A.** quā pecude (sc. sue) nihil genuit natura fecundius, Cic.; solertia pecudum (of bees), Verg , pecudes et bestiae, *wild and domestic animals*, Cic **B.** Esp , **a,** *sheep*, pecus Helles, *the ram*, Ov., **b,** in plur , *land animals*, genus aequoreum, pecudes pictaeque volucres, Verg. **II.** Transf , contemptuously applied to a human being, stupor hominis, vel dicam pecudis? Cic.

pĕdālis -e (pes), *of the length of a foot*, Caes ; or *of the breadth* (in diameter) *of a foot*, Cic

pĕdārius -a um (pes), *relating to a foot*, senatores pedarii, *senators of inferior rank, who held no curule office*, Tac. Subst , **pĕdārii** -ōrum, m , Cic.

pĕdes -ĭtis, m (pes) **I.** *one who goes on foot*, quum pedes iret *on foot*, Verg , etiamsi pedes incedat, Liv **II.** Esp , *a foot soldier*, **a,** lit , Caes ; collect., *infantry*, Liv , **b,** transf , equites peditesque, *the whole people*, Cic

pĕdester -tris -tre (pes), *on foot, pedestrian* **I.** Lit , **A.** (opp equester), statua pedestris, Cic ; esp as milit t t , copiae, *infantry*, Caes , scutum, *infantry shield*, Liv **B.** *relating to land* (opp maritimus, navalis); iter, Caes , pugna, Cic **II.** Fig , **A.** Of style, *written in prose*; historiae, Hor **B.** *simple, ordinary, prosaic*, sermo, Hor , musa, Hor

pĕdĕtemptim, adv. (pes and tendo), *slowly, gradually, carefully, cautiously*, timide et pedetemptim, Cic

pĕdĭca -ae, f (pes), *a trap, snare, a fetter*, Liv.

pĕdĭsĕquus i, m. and **pĕdĭsĕqua** -ae, f (pes and sequor), *a servant whose business it was to attend upon the master* or *mistress*, *a lackey, footman*, and f *a waiting-woman*, Cic , fig , juris scientiam eloquentiae tamquam ancillulam pedisequamque adjunxisti, Cic ; transf., clamore pedisequorum nostrorum, *followers*, Cic

pĕdĭtātus -ūs, m (pedes), *infantry*, Caes

pēdo, pĕpēdi, pēditum, 3. *to break wind*, Hor

1 **pĕdum** -i, n. *a shepherd's crook*, Verg

2 **Pĕdum** -i, n *a town in Latium, ten miles south of Rome* Adj , **Pĕdānus** -a um, *of or relating to Pedum*, subst , **a,** **Pĕdānum** i, n *an estate near Pedum*; **b,** **Pĕdāni** -ōrum, m *the inhabitants of Pedum*.

1 **Pēgăsis,** v Pegasus

2 **Pēgăsis** -ĭdis, f. (πηγη), *a water nymph*

Pēgăsus (-ŏs) i, m. (Πηγασος), *the winged horse which sprang from the blood of Medusa, and produced the fountain Hippocrene by a blow from his hoof* Hence, adj , **A.** **Pēgăsēius** -a -um **B.** **Pēgăsēus** -a -um **C.** **Pēgăsis** -ĭdis, f *Pegasean*, undae, *fountains sacred to the Muses, Hippocrene, Aganippe* Plur , subst , Pegasides, *the Muses*, Ov

pegma ătis, n (πῆγμα), **1,** *a bookcase, shelf*, Cic ; **2,** *a theatrical machine*, Suet

pējĕro (perjĕro) and **perjūro, 1** *to commit perjury, forswear oneself*, verbis conceptis, Cic , jus perjeratum, *a false oath*, Hor., dii, *falsely sworn by*, Ov

pējor, comp of malus (q v)

pējūrus = perjurus (q v)

pĕlăgē, v pelagus.

pĕlăgĭus -a -um (πελάγιος) *of or relating to the sea, marine*, conchae, Plin , cursus, Phaedr

Pĕlăgŏnes -um, m (Πελαγονες), *the Pelagonians, a people in the north of Macedonia* Hence, **Pĕlăgŏnĭa** -ae, f , **a,** *the country of the Pelagones*, **b,** *a town in Pelagonia, now Bitoglia*

pĕlăgus -i, n (πέλαγος) **I.** *the sea, ocean*, Verg **II.** Poet , transf , *a mass of water like the sea, a flood*, pelago premit arva, *with its flood*, Verg (Greek plur , pelage, πελαγη, Lucr)

pēlămȳs ȳdis, f (πηλαμύς), *the young tunny-fish* (before it is a year old), Juv.

Pĕlasgi -ōrum and (poet) -ûm, m (Πελασγοί), *the oldest inhabitants of Greece*, and hence, poet., *the Greeks* Verg Hence, **A.** **Pĕlasgĭăs** ădis, f **B.** **Pĕlasgĭs** -ĭdis, f **C.** **Pĕlasgus** -a -um, *Pelasgian, Greek*.

Pĕlēthrŏnĭus -a -um, *of or belonging to the district of Thessaly, where the Lapithae lived, Pelethronian*.

Pēlĕus -ĕi and -ĕos, m (Πηλευς), *a mythical king of Thessaly husband of Thetis, father of Achilles*, hence, **Pēlīdēs** ae, m. *son of Peleus = Achilles*

pēlex (pellex) and **paelex** -lĭcis, f (πάλλαξ), *a mistress of a married man, a concubine*, Cic , Oebalia, *Helen*, Tyria, *Europa*, barbara, *Medea*, Ov

1 **Pēlĭăs,** v Pelion

2 **Pĕlĭās** ae, m (Πελίας), *king in Thessaly, half-brother of Aeson, whose son Jason he sent to fetch the golden fleece On Jason's return Pelias, at the instigation of Medea, was slain by his own daughters*.

pēlĭcātus (paelĭcātus) -us, m (pelex), *concubinage*, Cic.

Pēlīdēs, v Peleus.

Pēligni = Paeligni (q v)

Pēlĭon ii, n. (Πήλιον), and **Pēlĭus** ii, m. *a lofty mountain of Thessaly*. Hence, adj , **A.** **Pēlĭăcus** -a -um, *of or belonging to Pelion*; trabs, *the ship Argo* (the wood of which was cut from Mount Pelion), Prop , cuspis, *the shield of Achilles*, Ov. **B.** **Pēlĭăs** -ădis, *belonging to Pelion*.

Pella -ae, f and **Pellē** -ēs, f (Πελλα), *the chief city of Macedonia, birth-place of Alexander the Great*, hence, **Pellaeus** -a -um, *relating to Pella*, **a,** *Macedonian*, juvenis, *Alexander*, Juv , **b,** *relating to Alexandria in Egypt*, and hence, *Egyptian*, Verg

pellăcĭa -ae, f (pellax), *an enticing, alluring*, Lucr

pellax ācis (pellicio), *deceitful, seductive* Verg

pellectĭo (perlectĭo) -ōnis, f (pellego), *a reading through, perusing*, Cic.

pellĕgo = perlego (q v)

Pellēnē -ēs, f (Πελλήνη), *a town in Achaia*. Hence, adj , **Pellēnensis** -e, *Pellenian*

pellex = pelex (q.v.).

pellĭcātus = pelicatus (q.v.).

pellĭcĭo -lexi -lectum, 3. (per and lacio), *to entice, decoy, seduce.* **I.** Lit., mulierem ad se, Cic.; animum adolescentis, Cic.; populum in servitutem, Liv. **II.** Transf., multo majorem partem sententiarum suo lepore, *bring over to one's side*, Cic.

pellĭcŭla -ae, f. (dim. of pellis), *a little skin* or *hide;* haedina, Cic.; pelliculam curare, *to take care of one's skin*, Hor.

pellis -is, f. *a hide, skin.* **I.** Lit., caprina, Cic.; pelles pro velis tenuiter confectae, Caes.; fig., detrahere alicui pellem, *to disclose a person's faults*, Hor. **II.** Transf., **1,** *hide, leather;* **a,** as a covering for tents, sub pellibus, *in camp;* Caesar sub pellibus hiemare constituit, Caes.; **b,** as used for clothing, pellibus tecta tempora, *hood*, Ov.; **2,** meton., **a,** *a shoe-latchet*, Hor.; **b,** *a shoe*, Ov.

pellītus -a -um (pellis), *clothed in hides* or *skins;* Sardi, Liv.; testes, *from Sardinia*, Liv.; oves pellitae, *sheep with fine wool, covered with skins to protect the wool*, Hor.

pello, pĕpŭli, pulsum, 3. *to strike, knock, beat against.* **I. a,** lit., terram pede, Hor.; humum pedibus, Cat.; fores, *to knock at the door*, Cic.; puer pulsus, *beaten*, Cic.; **b,** transf., *to touch, move, make an impression upon;* quemadmodum visa non pellerent, Cic. **II.** Esp., **A.** *to put in motion by pushing* or *striking, to impel, propel, move;* sagittam, Verg.; nervos in fidibus, Cic. **B.** *to drive out, drive away, expel;* **1, a,** lit., quum viri boni lapidibus e foro pellerentur, Cic., uti omnes ex Galliae finibus pellerentur, Caes.; aliquem possessionibus, Cic.; aliquem civitate, Cic.; **b,** transf., maestitiam ex animis, *banish*, Cic.; curas vino, Hor.; **2,** transf., **a,** milit. t. t., *to repel, drive back an enemy;* hostes pelluntur, Caes.; **b,** legal t. t., *to banish, exile;* exsules pulsi, Liv.

pellūcĕo = perluceo (q.v.).

pellūcĭdŭlus = perlucidulus (q.v.).

pellūcĭdus = perlucidus (q.v.).

pellŭo = perluo (q.v.).

Pĕlŏponnēsus -i, f. (Πελοπόννησος), *the Peloponnesus*, now *the Morea;* hence, adj., **A. Pĕlŏponnēsĭus** -a -um. **B. Pĕlŏponnēsĭăcus** -a -um, *Peloponnesian.*

Pĕlops -ŏpis, m. (Πέλοψ), *a mythical king of Phrygia, son of Tantalus, father of Atreus and Thyestes, grandfather of Agamemnon and Menelaus; when a child he was killed by his father and served up as food to the gods; he was restored to life through the agency of Hermes (Mercury), and his shoulder, which had been eaten by Demeter (Ceres), was replaced by an ivory one.* Hence, **A. Pĕlŏpēĭăs** -ădis, f. *Pelopean, Peloponnesian;* Mycenae, Ov. **B. Pĕlŏpēĭus** -a -um, *relating to Pelops or his descendants;* virgo, *Iphigenia*, Ov.; arva, *Phrygia*, Ov. **C. Pĕlŏpēus** -a -um, *relating to Pelops;* moenia, *Argos*, Verg. **D.** subst., **Pĕlŏpĭdae** -ārum, m. *descendants of Pelops.*

pĕlōrĭs -ĭdis, f. (πελωρίς), *a large species of mussel*, Hor.

Pĕlōrus (-ŏs) -i, m. (Πέλωρος), and **Pĕlōrum** -i, n. *the north-east promontory of Sicily*, now *Capo di Faro* or *Faro di Messina.* Hence, adj., **1, Pĕlōrĭăs** -ădis, f.; and **2, Pĕlōrĭs** -ĭdis, f. *Pelorian.*

pelta -ae, f. (πέλτη), *a small, light, crescent-shaped shield*, Liv.

peltastae -ārum, m. (πελτασταί), *soldiers armed with the pelta*, Liv.

peltātus -a -um (pelta), *armed with the pelta*, Mart.

Pēlūsĭum -ii, n. (Πηλούσιον), *a town in Egypt on the Mediterranean Sea*, now *Castle of Tineh.* Hence, **Pēlūsĭăcus** -a -um, *Pelusian.*

pelvis -is, f. *a basin*, Plin.

pĕnārĭus (pĕnŭārĭus) -a -um (penus), *of* or *relating to provisions;* cella, *store-room*, Cic.

pĕnātes -ium, m., with or without dii (connected with pen-itus, pen-etro). **I.** *the household* or *family deities among the Romans;* publici or majores, *the guardian deities of the state*, Cic.; minores, familiares, privati, *of the family*, Cic. **II.** Meton., *the house, dwelling;* penates relinquere, Liv.; poet., *the cells of bees*, Verg.

pĕnātĭgĕr -gĕra -gĕrum (penates and gero), *carrying the Penates*, Ov.

pendĕo, pĕpendi, 2. (pendo), *to hang, hang down.* **I.** Lit., **A.** Gen., *ab* humero, Cic.; *ex* arbore, Cic.; *de* collo, Ov.; *in* arbore, Cic.; with abl. alone, tigno, Ov. **B.** Esp., **1,** *to be hung up;* pendebit fistula pinu, Verg.; **2,** of clothes, *to hang down, flow down;* ut pendeat apte (chlamys), Ov.; **3,** *to overhang;* **a,** *to hover;* dum nubila pendent, Verg.; **b,** *to hang in the air;* capellae pendent de rupe, Verg.; **c,** of birds, *to hover;* olor niveis pendebat in aere pennis, Ov.; **4,** transf., **a,** *to hang about a place, be continually there;* nostroque in limine pendes, Verg.; **b,** *to hang down* (from weakness); fluidos pendere lacertos, Ov. **II.** Fig., **A.** *to hang upon the lips of any one, listen* or *gaze attentively*, Verg.; narrantis conjux pendet ab ore viri, Ov. **B. 1,** *to be suspended, discontinued;* pendent opera interrupta, Verg.; **2,** *to be in suspense, be uncertain, undecided;* ne diutius pendeas, Cic.; frequently with animi, pendere animi exspectatione, Cic.; also with animo, Cic.; and animis, Cic.; **3,** *to depend upon;* **a,** spes pendet ex fortuna, Cic.; **b,** *to be a follower of a person, to imitate;* hinc omnis pendet Lucilius, Hor.

pendo, pĕpendi, pensum, 3. lit., *to cause to hang down;* hence, *to weigh.* **I.** Lit., **A. 1,** herbae pensae, Ov.; **2,** fig., **a,** *to weigh, consider, judge;* res, non verba, Cic.; **b,** *to value, esteem;* with genit., magni, *at a high price*, Hor. **B.** Esp., *to pay* (since money was originally paid by weight); **1,** lit., Achaei ingentem pecuniam pendunt L. Pisoni quotannis, Cic.; vectigal, Cic.; **2,** fig., poenas, supplicia, *to pay a penalty, suffer punishment*, Cic., Liv.; maximas poenas pendo temeritatis meae, Cic.; poenas capitis, Ov. **II.** Transf., intransit., *to weigh*, Liv.

pendŭlus -a -um (pendeo), **1,** *hanging, hanging down;* collum, Hor.; **2,** fig., *uncertain, undecided;* spe pendulus, Hor.

pēne = paene (q.v.).

Pēnēis, Peneius, v. Peneus.

Pēnĕlŏpa -ae, f. and **Pēnĕlŏpē** -ēs, f. (Πηνελόπεια, Πηνελόπη), *the wife of Ulysses, mother of Telemachus, famous for her chastity and constancy.* Hence, adj., **Pēnĕlŏpēus** -a -um, *of Penelope.*

pĕnĕs, prep. with acc. (from root PEN, whence penus, penates), *with, in possession of, in the power of;* **1,** penes quem est potestas, Cic.; penes se esse, *to be in one's senses*, Hor.; penes quos laus fuit, Cic.; **2,** *with;* penes Aetolos culpam belli esse, Liv.

Pĕnestae -ārum, m. (Πενέσται), *a people in Illyria.* Hence, **Pĕnestĭa** -ae, f. *the country of the Penestae.*

pĕnĕtrābĭlis -e (penetro). **I.** *that can be passed through, penetrable;* corpus nullo penetrabile telo, Ov II. Act, *easily penetrating, piercing*, frigus, Verg, fulmen, Ov

pĕnĕtrālis -e (penetro) I. *passing through, penetrating*, frigus, ignis, Lucr II. *inward, inside, internal, interior*, focus, Cic Subst,

pĕnĕtrāle and **pĕnĕtrăl** -ālis, n, gen plur,

pĕnĕtrālia -ium, n. 1, *the inner chambers, interior of a house or city*, penetrale urbis, Liv, penetralia regum, Verg; 2, esp, *the inmost part or shrine of a temple*, conditum in penetrali fatale pignus, Liv.

pĕnĕtro, 1 (penitus) I. Transit, *to set, place, put in* A. intra aedes penetravi pedem, Plaut B. *to pass through* or *into, to penetrate*, a, lit, Illyricos sinus, Verg, b, fig, id Tiberii animum altius penetravit, *sank deep into*, Tac II. Intransit, *to make one's way into, to enter, penetrate into*, sub terras, Cic., intra vallum, Liv; in urbem, Liv, transf, nulla res magis penetrat in animos, Cic

Pēnēus (-ēŏs) -i, m (Πηνειος), *the chief river of Thessaly, rising in Mount Pindus*, now *Salembria*, as a river-god, *father of Cyrene* Hence, adj, 1, **Pēnēis** -idis, f *of Peneus*, nympha, *Daphne*, Ov, 2, **Pēnēius** -a -um, *of* or *relating to Peneus*

pēnĭcillum -i, n and **pēnĭcillus** -i, m (dim. of peniculus), *a painter's brush* or *pencil*, Cic, meton, *painting*, Plin; and transf, *style of painting*, Cic.

pēnĭcŭlus -i, m (dim of penis), *a brush*, Plaut

pēnis -is, m. 1, *a tail*, Cic, 2, = membrum virile, Cic.

pĕnĭtē, adv. (penitus), *inwardly, internally*, Cat

1 **pĕnĭtus** a -um, *inward, interior, internal*, Plaut

2 **pĕnĭtŭs**, adv (root PEN), *internally* I. *in the inmost part, deep within*, 1, lit, periculum inclusum penitus in venis reipublicae, Cic, argentum penitus abditum, Cic, 2, transf, a, ea penitus animis vestris mandate, *impress deeply in your minds*, Cic, b, *accurately*, perspicere, Cic; nosse, Cic.; c, *through and through, thoroughly, entirely, wholly*, diffidere reipublicae, Cic, perdere se ipsos, Cic II. Transf, *far away, far removed*, penitus repostas gentes, Verg

Pĕnĭus ii, m (Πενιος), *a river in Colchis, flowing into the Black Sea*

penna -ae, f (old Lat pesna, root PET, whence peto, impetus, praepes), *a feather* I. Gen, 1, lit, Plin, 2, meton, a, *wing*, gen in plur, *wings* (of birds or insects), aves pullos pennis fovent, Cic, b, *a flying, flight*, Ov II. Poet, *the feathers on an arrow*, Ov, and hence, meton, *arrow*, Ov

pennātus -a -um (penna), *feathered, winged*, fama, Verg.

pennĭgĕr gĕra -gĕrum (penna and gero), *feathered, winged*, Cic.

pennĭpes -pĕdis (penna and pes), *wing footed*, Cat

pennĭpŏtens -entis (penna and potens), *able to fly, winged*, Lucr, subst, **pennĭpŏtentes** -ium, f = *birds*, Lucr

pennŭla -ae, f (dim of penna), *a little wing*, Cic

pensĭlis -e (pendeo), *hanging, hanging down, pendent*, Plaut; uva, *hung up to dry*, Hor

pensĭo -ōnis, f (pendo), *a paying, payment, day of payment*, 1, nihil debetur ei nisi ex tertia pensione, Cic.; 2, *rent*, Juv,

pensĭto, 1 (intens of penso), *to weigh* I. Transf, *to weigh, ponder, consider*, imperatoria consilia, Liv II. *to pay*, vectigalia, Cic, praedia quae pensitant, *are liable to taxes*, Cic

penso, 1 (intens of pendo) I *to weigh* A Lit, aurum, Liv, fig, Romanos scriptores eadem trutinā, Hor B. Transf, 1, *to weigh* = *to judge*, amicos ex factis, Liv, 2, a, *to ponder, consider, reflect upon*, consilium, Liv, b, *to weigh one thing against another, to compare*; adversa secundis, Liv II. *to counterbalance, repay, compensate, recompense, make good, requite*, a, lit, vulnus vulnere, Ov; transmarinae res quādam vice pensatae, Liv, b, transf, *to pay for, purchase with*, nece pudorem, Ov

pensum -i, n (pendo) I. *a portion of wool weighed out to a spinner as a day's work*, hence, *a day's work, task*, nocturna carpentes pensa puellae, Verg, mollia pensa, Verg II. Transf, *a task, a duty, engagement*, me ad meum munus pensumque revocabo, Cic

pensus -a -um, p adj (from pendo), *weighty, esteemed, valued, prized*, nihil pensi habere aliquid, *to put no value upon, be indifferent about*, Sall, alicui nec quicquam pensi est, Sall, illis nec quid dicerent nec quid facerent quicquam pensi fuisse, *they cared nothing what they did or said*, Liv

pentămĕter -tri, m (πεντάμετρος), *a pentameter verse*, Quint

Pentĕlĭcus mons (Πεντελικον ὄρος), *a mountain near Athens, celebrated for its marble quarries* Hence, **Pentĕlĭcus** -a -um, *belonging to Pentelicus*, Hermae Pentelici, *made of Pentelic marble*, Cic

Penthĕsĭlēa -ae, f (Πενθεσίλεια), *queen of the Amazons, ally of Priam against the Greeks in the Trojan War, slain by Achilles*

Penthēus -ĕi and ĕos, acc ĕum and ĕa (Πενθευς), *king of Thebes, grandson of Cadmus, who treated with contempt the worship of Bacchus, and was torn to pieces by his mother and her sisters in a Bacchic fury* Hence, A. **Penthēus** a -um, *of Pentheus* B. **Penthīdēs** -ae, m *a descendant of Pentheus* = *Lycurgus*, Ov.

Pentri ōrum, m *a people in Samnium, with a capital city Bovianum*

pēnūria -ae, f (πεῖνα), *want, need of any thing*, esp, *want of the necessaries of life, penury*, cibi, Lucr, victūs, Hor, sapientium civium bonorumque, Cic, liberorum, Sall

pĕnus -ūs and i, c, **pĕnum** -i, n, and **pĕnus** -ŏris, n (root PEN, whence penetro, penates, penitus, lit, *that which is kept within*), *provisions, store of food, victuals*, est enim omne, quo vescuntur homines, penus, Cic

Pĕpărēthus (-ŏs) -i, f (Πεπάρηθος), *an island of the Aegean Sea*, now *Scopelo*

peplum i, n and **peplus** -i, m (πεπλον, πεπλος), *the robe with which the statue of Athene at Athens was clad at the Panathenaea*, Cic

per, prep with acc I. Of space, *through*, a, *through* (of passage through), alterum iter per provinciam nostram multo facilius, Caes, b, *through, along, over*, coronam auream per forum ferre, Cic, per mare pauperiem fugiens, per saxa, per ignes, Hor c, *before, in the presence of*, incedunt per ora vestra magnifici, Sall, d, *over, about, all over*, equites per oram maritimam erant dispositi, Caes, qui per imperii tui provincias ei credidissent, Cic II. Transf, A. Of time, 1, *through, during*, ludi decem per dies facti sunt, Cic, 2, *in the course of*, per somnum, *in sleep*, Cic, 3, *during, under the influence of*, quod fecisset per iram, Cic. B. Of the means or instrument by which anything is done, *through by, by means of;* **1, a,** statuerunt istius injurias per vos ulcisci, Cic.; per se (te, etc.), *by oneself, alone, without help*, Cic.; per litteras, *by letter*, Cic.; **b,** *under pretence of, under shelter of;* fraudare aliquem per tutelam aut societatem, Cic.; **2,** *from motives of, on account of;* per avaritiam decipere, Cic.; per metum, *from fear*, Liv.; quum antea per aetatem nondum huius auctoritatem loci attingere auderem, *on account of age*, Cic.; **3,** *on account of, for the sake of, regarding;* per me vel stertas licet, *as far as I am concerned*, Cic.; cum per valetudinem posses, venire tamen noluisti, Cic.; hence, in entreaties, oaths, etc. = *by;* oro te per deos, Cic.; per tuam fidem perque huius solitudinem te obtestor; in this sense per is often separated from the noun which it governs, per ego te, fili, precor quaesoque, Liv.; per deos atque homines! *by gods and men!* Cic.

pēra -ae (πήρα), *a scrip* or *wallet*, Mart.

pĕrabsurdus -a -um, *excessively absurd*, Cic.

pĕraccommŏdātus -a -um, *very convenient;* (in tmesis) per fore accommodatum, Cic.

pĕrăcer -cris -cre, *very sharp;* judicium, Cic.

pĕrăcerbus -a -um, *very sour, harsh;* uva peracerba gustatu, Cic.

pĕrăcesco -ăcŭi, 3. *to become thoroughly sour;* transf., *to be exceedingly vexed*, Plaut.

pĕractio -ōnis, f. (perago), *a finishing, completion;* peractio fabulae, Cic.

pĕrăcūtē, adv. (peracutus), *very sharply, very acutely;* queri quod, etc., Cic.

pĕrăcūtus -a -um, *very sharp*. **I.** *very shrill, piercing;* vox, Cic. **II.** Transf., *sharp-witted, acute;* ad excogitandum, Cic.

pĕrădŏlescens -entis, *a very young man*, Cic.

pĕrădŏlescentŭlus -i, m. *a very young man*, Nep.

Pĕraea -ae, f. **I.** *a strip of land on the south coast of Caria, opposite Rhodes.* **II.** *a district in the south of Palestine.* **III.** *a town in Argolis.*

pĕraequē, adv. *quite alike, quite equally*, Cic.

pĕrăgĭto, 1. *to drive about violently, harass;* vehementius peragitati ab equitatu, Caes.

pĕrăgo -ēgi -actum, 3. **I.** *to pierce through, thrust through, transfix;* Theseus latus ense peregit, Ov. **II. A.** *to drive about, harass, disquiet;* **1,** agili freta remo, Ov.; agrum, *to till*, Ov.; **2,** fig., totum Sempronium usque eo perago ut, etc., ap. Cic. **B. 1,** *to bring to an end, complete, finish, accomplish;* navigationem, Cic.; inceptum, Liv.; concilium, Caes.; fabulam, *to play a drama through*, Cic.; transf., fabulam vitae, Cic.; as legal t. t., *to conduct a suit to the end;* causam rei, Hor.; reum, Liv.; **2,** *to go through, relate, go over, mention;* verbis auspicia, Liv.; postulata, Liv.; sententiam, Liv.

pĕrăgrātĭo -ōnis, f. (peragro), *a wandering through;* itinerum, Cic.

pĕrăgro, 1. (per and ager). **I.** *to wander through, pass through, travel through;* omnes provincias, Cic. **II.** Fig., *to search out, penetrate, examine;* omnes latebras suspicionum dicendo, Cic.

pĕrămans -antis, *very loving;* homo peramans semper nostri fuit, Cic.

pĕrămantĕr, adv. *very lovingly;* observare, Cic.

pĕrambŭlo, 1. *to walk through, pass through, travel through, perambulate;* rura, Hor.; transf., frigus perambulat artus, Ov.

pĕrămoenus -a -um, *very pleasant*, Tac.

pĕramplus -a -um, *very large*, Cic.

pĕrangustē, adv. *very narrowly*, Cic.

pĕrangustus -a -um, *very narrow, strait, confined;* fretum, Cic.; aditus, Caes.

pĕranno, 1. *to live through a year*, Suet.

pĕrantīquus -a -um, *very old;* sacrarium, Cic.

pĕrappŏsĭtus -a -um, *very fit, suitable;* alicui, Cic.

perardŭus -a -um, *very difficult;* mihi hoc perarduum est demonstrare, Cic.

pĕrargūtus -a -um, *very acute, clever, witty*, Cic.

pĕrăro, 1. *to plough through;* **1,** *to cover with wrinkles;* ora, Ov.; **2,** *to scratch letters with the stylus, to write on waxen tablets, to write;* litteram, Ov.

pĕrattentē, adv. *very attentively;* ab aliquo audiri, Cic.

pĕrattentus -a -um, *very attentive;* perattentos vestros animos habuimus, Cic.

perbacchor, 1. *to revel throughout* or *during;* multos dies, Cic.

perbĕātus -a -um, *very happy*, Cic.

perbellē, adv. *very prettily, very finely;* simulare, Cic.

pĕrbĕnĕ, adv. *very well;* loqui Latine, Cic.

perbĕnĕvŏlus -a -um, *very well wishing, very well disposed to;* alicui, Cic.

perbĕnignē, adv. *very kindly;* (in tmesis) per mihi benigne respondit, Cic.

perbĭbo -bibi, 3. *to drink in, drink up.* **I.** Lit., lacrimas, Ov. **II.** Fig., *to imbibe, take in mentally;* rabiem, Ov.

perblandus -a -um, *very charming, very engaging;* successor, Cic.

perbŏnus -a -um, *very good*, Cic.

perbrĕvis -e, *very short;* perbrevi tempore, or simply perbrevi, *in a very short time*, Cic.

perbrĕvĭtĕr, adv. *very shortly, very briefly*, Cic.

perca -ae, f. (πέρκη), *a fish, the perch*, Ov.

percălĕfăcĭo -fēci -factum, 3. *to make very warm;* pass., **percălĕfīo** -factus sum -fiĕri, *to become very warm, to be thoroughly heated*, Lucr.

percălesco -călŭi, 3. *to become very warm*, Ov.

percallesco -callŭi, 3. **I.** Intransit., *to lose all sensibility, become quite callous*, Cic. **II.** *to become experienced;* usu rerum, Cic.

percārus -a -um, **1,** *very dear, very costly*, Ter.; **2,** *very dear, much beloved*, Cic.

percautus -a -um, *very cautious*, Cic.

percĕlĕbro, 1. *to speak of very frequently, to talk of often;* in pass. = *to be in the mouths of people;* percelebrantur versus de, etc., Cic.

percĕlĕr -is -e, *very swift, very rapid;* alicuius interitus, Cic.

percĕlĕrĭtĕr, adv. (perceler), *very swiftly, very rapidly;* auferre diploma, Cic.

percello -cŭli -culsum, 3. (per and * cello). **I.** *to beat down, strike down, overturn, shatter.* **A. a,** lit., aliquem, Verg.; fig., quod duo fulmina domum meam per hos dies perculerint, Liv.; **b,** transf., eos vis Martis perculit, Cic. **B.** Fig., *to shatter;* **a,** *to ruin;* rempublicam, Tac.; **b,** *to cast down the courage of, dispirit, daunt;* aliquem, Liv.; timore perculsa civitas, Cic.; quos pavor perculerat in silvas, *driven to*, Liv. **II,** *to strike, push;* aliquem genu, Liv.

percensĕo -censŭi, 2 **I.** *to count through, count, reckon;* **a,** promerita, numerando, Cic, locos inveniendi, Cic, gentes, Liv, **b,** *to survey, review,* captivos, Liv.; fig, *to judge, criticise,* orationes, Liv. **II.** *to travel through,* Thessaliam, Liv.

perceptus a -um, partic. of percipio Subst, **percepta** -ōrum, n. *principles, rules,* artis, Cic.

perceptĭo ōnis, f (percipio) **I.** *a collecting, gathering together,* frugum fructuumque, Cic **II.** *perception, apprehension, comprehension,* perceptiones animi, Cic

percīdo cīdi -cisum, 3. (per and caedo), *to beat, cut to pieces,* Plaut

percĭo cīvi citum, 4 and **percĭēo** -cīēre, 2 **I.** *to stir up, set in motion;* se, Lucr., hence, **percĭtus** -a -um, **a,** *aroused, mad, excited,* Cic, **b,** *excitable, irritable,* ingenium, Liv **II.** *to call, name,* aliquem impudicum, Plaut

percĭpĭo cēpi -ceptum, 3 (per and capio) **I.** *to lay hold of, take possession of, seize,* percipit me voluptas atque horror, Lucr **II.** *to take to oneself* **A. 1,** sensus percipit rem in se, Lucr, **2,** *to get, receive, collect, gather,* fructus, Cic, praemia, Caes **B.** Transf, **1,** *to perceive, be sensible of, feel,* voluptatem, Cic., sonum, Cic, **2,** *to receive mentally,* **a,** *to learn,* and in perf tenses, *to know,* praecepta artis, Cic, omnia civium nomina perceperat, *he knew,* Cic, **b,** *to comprehend, understand,* aliquid animo, Cic.

percĭtus -a um, partic of percio

percīvīlis -e, *very condescending, very gracious, courteous,* Suet

1 **percōlo,** 1 **I.** *to strain through a sieve,* Cato **II.** *to allow to drain or pass through,* humor per terras percolatur, *percolates through,* Lucr

2 **percŏlo** cŏlŭi -cultum, 3 **I.** *to adorn, decorate,* quae priores nondum comperta eloquentiā percoluere, Tac **II.** *to honour, reverence exceedingly,* patrem, Plaut

percōmis -e, *very friendly, courteous,* Cic.

percommŏdē, adv *very conveniently, very appropriately,* percommode cadit, or accidit, or factum est quod, etc, Cic

percommŏdus a -um, *very convenient, fit, appropriate, opportune,* with dat, ipsis castris percommodum fuit, Liv.

percontātĭo (percunctātĭo) -ōnis, f. (percontor), *an inquiry, interrogation, question,* Cic, percontationem facere, Liv

percontātor (percunctātor) -ōris, m (percontor), *an inquirer, asker of questions,* Hor

percontor (percunctor), 1 dep (per and contus), *to ask, inquire, interrogate, question, investigate,* aliquem de aliqua re, Cic, aliquid ab or ex aliquo, Cic, aliquem aliquid, Liv, percontantes, quid praetor edixisset, ubi cenaret, quo denuntiasset, Cic

percontŭmax -ācis, *very obstinate,* Ter

percŏquo -coxi -coctum, 3 *to boil thoroughly* **I.** Lit, carnes Plin **II.** Transf, **A.** *to heat, make hot,* humorem, Lucr **B.** *to ripen, make ripe,* uvas, Ov, *to burn, blacken,* nigra virum percocto saecla colore, Lucr

percrēbresco brŭi, and **percrēbesco** bŭi, 3 *to become very frequent, be spread abroad, become prevalent, be well known;* res percrebuit, Cic, fama percrebruit, with acc and infin, Caes

percrĕpo -crĕpui -crĕpitum, 3 *to resound, ring with,* lucum illum percrepare mulierum vocibus, Cic

percunctor, percunctatio, etc = percontor, percontatio, etc (q v)

percŭpĭdus -a -um, *very fond of,* tui, Cic

percŭpĭo, 3 *to wish, desire exceedingly,* Plaut, Ter

percūrĭōsus a um, *very inquisitive,* Cic

percūro, 1 *to cure, heal thoroughly,* vixdum satis percurato vulnere Liv

percurro -cŭcurri or curri cursum, 3 **I.** Intransit, **A.** *to run along or over,* per temonem, Caes **B.** *to hasten to,* citato equo Cales, Liv **II.** Transit, *to run through, hasten through, travel through* **A.** Lit, omnem agrum Picenum, Caes **B.** Transf, **a,** of discourse, *to run through, discuss cursorily, mention in passing,* multas res oratione, Cic, **b,** *to run over in the mind or with the eye,* veloci percurrere oculo, Hor; multa animo et cogitatione, multa etiam legendo, Cic.

percursātĭo ōnis, f (percurso), *a running through, travelling through,* Italiae, Cic

percursĭo -ōnis, f (percurro) **I.** *a rapid consideration or reflection upon anything,* propter animi multarum rerum brevi tempore percursionem, Cic **II.** Rhet t t, *a rapid or hasty passing over a subject,* huic (commorationi) contraria saepe percursio est, Cic

percurso, 1 (percurro) **I.** Transit, *to ramble over or about,* ripas, Plin **II.** Intransit, *to rove about,* totis finibus nostris, Liv

percussĭo ōnis, f (percutio) **I.** *a striking, knocking against,* digitorum, *a snapping of the fingers,* Cic **II.** T t of music and rhet, *a beating time,* hence *time, rhythm,* numerorum percussiones, Cic

percussor -ōris, m (percutio), **1,** *a striker,* Plin, **2,** *a murderer, assassin,* Cic.

percussus -ūs, m (percutio), *a beating, knocking, striking,* percussu crebro, Ov

percŭtĭo -cussi -cussum, 3 (per and quatio). **I.** *to strike through, pierce, transfix;* rostro navem, Liv **II.** *to strike, beat, hit* **A.** Lit, **1,** aliquem lapide, Cic, forem virgā, Liv., turres de caelo percussae, *struck by lightning,* Cic; **2, a,** *to kill, slay,* aliquem securi, Cic, aliquem fulmine (of Jupiter), Cic, fulmine percussus, Cic, **b,** *to strike, play upon,* lyram, Ov; pennas, *to soar,* Ov **B.** Fig, **1,** non percussit locum, *he has missed the point,* Cic, **2, a,** *to affect, move, astound strike, shock,* percussus atrocissimis litteris, Cic, suspicione sum percussus, Cic., **b,** *to deceive,* aliquem strategemate, Cic, **c,** *to wound mentally, afflict,* percussus calamitate, Cic (syncop perf., percusti, Hor)

perdēlīrus -a um, *very silly, senseless,* Lucr

perdiffĭcĭlis -e, *very difficult,* navigatio, quaestio, Cic

perdiffĭcĭlĭtĕr, adv *with very great difficulty,* Cic

perdignus -a -um, *quite worthy of;* tua amicitiā, Cic

perdīlĭgens entis, *very careful, very diligent,* Cic

perdīlĭgentĕr, adv *very carefully, very diligently,* Cic

perdisco -didĭci, 3 *to learn thoroughly;* dictata, Cic, perf, perdidici, *to understand thoroughly,* with infin, hominis speciem pingere, Cic

perdisertē, adv *very eloquently,* Cic

perdĭtē, adv (perditus), **1,** *exceedingly, immoderately,* filiam amare, Ter, **2,** *in an abandoned manner, very badly,* se gerere, Cic.

perditor -ōris, m. (perdo), *a destroyer*; reipublicae, Cic.

perdĭtus -a -um, p. adj. (from perdo). **I.** *wretched, miserable, ruined*; valetudo, Cic.; res, Cic.; judicia, Cic. **II. A.** *immoderate*; amor, Cat.; perditus luctu, *sunk in grief*, Cic.; aere, Cic. **B.** *morally lost, abandoned, profligate*; adolescens perditus ac dissolutus, Cic.; homo perditissimus, Cic.

perdĭū, adv. *a very long time, for a very long time*, Cic.

perdĭŭturnus -a -um, *lasting a very long time, very tedious*, Cic.

perdīvĕs -vitis, *very rich*, Cic.

perdix -dīcis, c. (πέρδιξ), *a partridge*, Plin.

perdo -dĭdi -dĭtum, 3. (in pass., gen., pereo, perditus, perire). **I.** *to destroy, ruin.* **A.** funditus civitatem, Cic.; aliquem, Cic.; poet., perdere serpentem, *to kill*, Ov. **B.** *to waste, squander, spend uselessly*; operam, or oleum et operam, Cic.; tempus, Cic. **II.** Transf., **A.** *to lose*; liberos, Cic.; litem, *to lose a lawsuit*, Cic.; oculos, Cic.; vocem, Cic. **B.** *to lose money in gambling*; quod in alea perdiderat, Cic. (old subj. pres., perduim -is -it -int, esp. in the execration, di te perduint! Cic.).

perdŏcĕo -dŏcŭi -doctum, 2. *to teach, instruct thoroughly*; aliquem, Ov.; absol., res difficilis ad perdocendum, Cic.

perdocte, adv. *very learnedly, very skilfully*, Plaut.

perdoctus -a -um (perdoceo), *very learned, very skilful*, Cic.

perdŏlĕo -dŏlŭi -dŏlitum, 2. *to suffer great pain* or *grief*, Ter.

perdŏlesco -dŏlŭi, 3. *to suffer violent pain* or *grief*; suam virtutem irrisui fore perdoluerunt, Cic.

perdŏmo -dŏmŭi -dŏmitum, 1. *to tame thoroughly*; a, tauros feroces, Ov.; b, *to subdue thoroughly, to conquer*; Latium, Liv.

perdūco -duxi -ductum, 3. **I.** *to lead* or *bring to any place.* **A.** 1, aliquem Romam, Liv.; aliquem ad Caesarem, Caes.; bovem ad stabula, Verg.; 2, a, *to seduce a woman*, Cic.; b, *to carry or construct buildings, aqueducts*, etc., from one point to another; murum a lacu Lemano ad montem Juram, Caes.; viam a Bononia Arretium, Liv. **B.** Transf., *to bring to*; 1, ad dignitatem, Caes.; aliquem ad furorem, Cic.; ad exitum, Cic.; 2, a, *to bring over to one's opinion, induce to do anything*; aliquem ad suam sententiam, Cic.; aliquem ad ducenta (talenta), *to induce to pay*, Cic.; b, *to continue, prolong*; agri colendi studia ad centesimum annum, Cic. **II.** *to spread over, smear over*; totum nati corpus ambrosiae odore, Verg.

perductor -ōris, m. (perduco), *a pimp, pander*, Cic.

perdŭellĭo -ōnis, f. (perduellis), *a hostile attempt against the state, treason*, Cic.

perdŭellis -is, m. (per and duellum, archaic for bellum). **I.** *a public enemy, an enemy actually carrying on hostilities*, Cic. **II.** Transf., *a private* or *personal enemy*, Plaut.

perdŭim -is -it, etc., v. perdo.

perdulcis -e, *very sweet*, Lucr.

perdūro, 1. *to last a long time, endure*; probitas longum perdurat in aevum, Ov.

pĕrĕdo -ēdi -ēsum, 3. *to eat up, devour entirely*; a, cibum, Plaut.; b, of things, *to consume, destroy*; vellera morbo illuvieque peresa, Verg.; transf., quos durus amor crudeli tabe peredit, Verg.

pĕrĕgrē, adv. (per and ager), *in a foreign country, abroad*; a, habitare, Liv.; depugnare, Cic.; fig., animus est peregre, Hor.; b, *from abroad*; nuntiare, Liv.; c, *to a foreign country, abroad*; exire, Hor.

pĕrĕgrīnābundus -a -um (peregrinor), *travelling about*, Liv.

pĕrĕgrīnātĭo -ōnis, f. (peregrinor), *a travelling* or *sojourning in foreign countries*; omne tempus in peregrinatione consumere, Cic.

pĕrĕgrīnātor -ōris, m. (peregrinor), *one who travels about*, Cic.

pĕrĕgrīnĭtas -ātis, f. (peregrinus). **I.** *the condition of a foreigner* or *alien*, Suet. **II.** *foreign manners, customs*; quum in urbem nostram infusa est peregrinitas, Cic.

pĕrĕgrīnor, 1. dep. (peregrinus), *to sojourn* or *to travel in foreign countries.* **I.** Lit., totā Asiā, Cic.; in aliena civitate, Cic. **II.** Transf., **A.** a, of things, haec studia pernoctant nobiscum, peregrinantur, rusticantur, Cic.; b, of persons, *to stray, wander, ramble* (mentally); in infinitatem omnem, Cic. **B.** *to be strange, foreign*; philosophiam quae quidem peregrinari Romae videbatur, Cic.

pĕrĕgrīnus -a -um (peregre). **I.** *foreign, strange*; amores, *foreign sweethearts*, Ov.; terror, *caused by foreign enemies*, Liv.; subst., **pĕrĕgrīnus** -i, m. and **pĕrĕgrīna** -ae, f.; a, *a foreigner, stranger*, Cic.; b, esp., *a foreigner resident in Rome, an alien*; neque civis neque peregrinus, Cic. **II.** *strange to, inexperienced in*; in agendo, Cic.

pĕrēlĕgans -antis, *very pretty, neat, elegant*; oratio, Cic.

pĕrēlĕgantĕr, adv. *very prettily, elegantly*; dicere, Cic.

pĕrēlŏquens -entis, *very eloquent*, Cic.

pĕremnis -e (per and amnis), *relating to the crossing of a river*; auspicia, *the auspices taken on crossing a river or any running water*, Cic.

pĕremptus -a -um, partic. of perimo.

pĕrendĭē, adv. *the day after to-morrow*; scies igitur fortasse cras, summum perendie, Cic.

pĕrendĭnus -a -um (perendie), *relating to the day after to-morrow*; dies, *the day after to-morrow*, Cic.

pĕrennis -e (per and annus). **I.** *lasting* or *remaining throughout the year*; militia, Liv. **II.** *lasting, durable, perennial*; aquae, Cic.; cursus stellarum, Cic.; monumentum aere perennius, Hor.; virtus, Cic.; loquacitas, Cic.

pĕrennĭtas -ātis, f. (perennis), *duration, durableness, perpetuity*; fontium, Cic.

pĕrenno, 1. (perennis), *to last many years, be durable*; arte perennat amor, Ov.

pĕrĕo -ĭi and -īvi -ĭtum, 4. (*to go through*). **I.** *to pass away, vanish, disappear*; pereunt victae sole tepente nives, Ov.; dolium lymphae pereuntis, *passing through, moving away*, Hor. **II.** *to be lost, to perish.* **A.** Lit., a, of persons, *to perish, die*; foede, praeclare, Cic.; naufragio, Cic.; summo cruciatu supplicioque, Cic.; eodem leto, Cic.; b, of things, urbes pereunt funditus, Hor.; peritura regna, Verg. **B.** Transf., 1, *to pine away, waste away with love*; amore, Verg.; 2, *to be ruined politically*; meo vitio pereo, Cic.; perii! *I am undone!* Plaut., Ter.; peream si (nisi), etc., a common form of imprecation, *may I die if (if not)*, Ov.; 3, *to be lost*; a, *to be wasted, spent in vain*; ne oleum et opera philologiae nostrae perierit, Cic.; b, legal t. t., *to be extinguished, to be lost, to expire*; quia multis actiones et res peribant, Liv. (syncop. perf. infin., perisse, Ov., Liv.).

pĕrĕquito, 1 I. Intransit, *to ride through, ride round*, per omnes partes, Caes II. Transit., *to ride round*, aciem, Liv

pĕrerro, 1 *to wander, ramble, stray through*, totum Latium, Liv, forum, Hor, pass, pererrato ponto, Verg

pĕrērŭdītus -a -um, *very learned*, Cic

pĕrexĭguē, adv *very scantily, very sparingly*, Cic

pĕrexĭgŭus -a -um, *very small, very little, very scanty* I. Lit, 1, of space, loci spatium, Caes, 2, of number, quantity, etc, bona corporis, Cic II. Transf, of time, *very short*, dies, Cic

pĕrexpĕdītus -a um, *very easy*, Cic

perfăcētē, adv *very wittily*, perfacete dicta sunt, Cic

perfăcētus a -um, *very witty, facetious*, aliquid perfacetum dicere, Cic

perfăcĭlĕ, adv *very easily*, perfacile apparet, Cic

perfăcĭlis e I. *very easy*, erat perfacilis cognitu, Cic II. *very courteous*, in audiendo, Cic

perfămĭlĭāris e, *very intimate, familiar*, alicui, Cic, subst, m *a very intimate friend*, meus, Cic

perfectē, adv (perfectus), *perfectly, completely*, eruditus, Cic

perfectĭo -ōnis, f (perficio), *perfection, completeness, completion*, perfectio maximorum operum, Cic; hanc perfectionem absolutionemque in oratore desiderans, Cic

perfector -ōris, m (perficio), *a perfecter, completer, finisher*, dicendi, Cic

perfectus a um, p adj (from perficio), *perfect, complete, finished*, homo, orator, Cic, in dicendo, in arte, Cic, C Memmius perfectus litteris, Cic, eloquentia, Cic; valvas perfectiores nullas ullo unquam tempore fuisse, Cic, quod ego summum et perfectissimum judico, Cic

perfĕrens -entis, p adj (from perfero), *patient*, injuriarum, Cic

perfĕro tŭli -lātum -ferre, *to carry through, bear, bring to a certain place or end* I. Lit, A. nec pertulit ictum, *did not reach the mark*, Verg, alveus fluminis non pertulit gravissimas naves, *did not admit of*, Liv, reflex, se perferre hinc, *to betake oneself*, Verg B. a, *to carry, bring, bear, convey*, literas ad aliquem, Cic, alicui nuntium, Cic, pass, *to be brought, to reach*, quum ad eum fama perlata esset, Liv, b, esp, *to bring news* equites pertulere consulem obsideri, Liv II. Transf, A. *to maintain, preserve*, intrepidos ad fata novissima vultus, Ov B. 1, *to bring to an end, carry through, complete*, mandata, Liv, id quod suscepi, quoad potero, perferam, Cic, 2, *to carry through*, legem, rogationem, Cic, 3, *to bear, suffer, endure*, perfero et perpetior omnia, Cic, omnes indignitates contumeliasque, Caes

perfĭca ae, f (perficio), *she that accomplishes*, natura, Lucr

perfĭcĭo -fēci -fectum, 3 (per and facio) I. *to bring to an end, complete, finish*, 1, *to make ready, finish;* pontem, Caes, candelabrum, Cic, 2, *to accomplish a period of time, to live through*, centum qui perficit annos, Hor II. 1, a, *to accomplish, achieve*, cogitata, Cic, conata, Caes, scelus, Cic, b, *to bring to an end, to conduct to a close*, comitia, Liv, bellum, Liv, c, *to bring about, accomplish, effect;* perficiam ut, etc., Cic, omnia perfecit ne, etc, Cic, non perficio, foll by quominus, Cic, 2, *to make perfect*, Achillem cithara, Ov

perfĭdēlis e, *very faithful*, Cic

perfĭdĭa ae, f (perfidus), *faithlessness, perfidy, treachery, falsehood*, fraude et perfidia aliquem fallere, Cic

perfĭdĭōsē, adv (perfidiosus), *perfidiously, faithlessly, treacherously*, multa perfidiose facta, Cic

perfĭdĭōsus -a -um (perfidia), *perfidious, faithless, treacherous*, Cic

perfĭdus -a -um (per and fides), *perfidious, faithless, treacherous, false*, a, of persons, amicus, Cic, b, of inanimate objects, arma, verba, Ov, sacramentum, Hor

perfixus -a -um, *pierced through, transfixed*, Lucr

perflābĭlis -e (perflo), *that can be blown through*, dii, Cic

perflăgĭtĭōsus -a -um, *very shameful, very flagitious*, Cic

perflo, 1 *to blow through, blow over*, venti terras turbine perflant, Verg

perfluctŭo, 1 *to swarm all over*, Lucr

perflŭo fluxi -fluxum, 3 *to flow, stream through*, Lucr

perfŏdĭo -fōdi -fossum, 3 *to dig through, pierce through*, a, parietes, Cic, b, *to pierce through with the sword*, thoraca, Verg

perfŏro, 1. I. *to pierce through, perforate*, a, navem, Cic, operculum ferreum, Liv, b, *to pierce (with the sword)*, latus ense, Ov II. *to form by boring*, duo lumina ab animo ad oculos perforata, Cic

perfortĭtĕr, adv *very bravely*, Ter

perfrĕquens -entis, *much visited, much frequented*, emporium, Liv

perfrĭco -fricŭi fricātum and frictum, 1 I. *to rub over, to scratch*, caput sinistrā manu, Cic II. *to rub the face to hide the sign of blushing*, os, Cic, hence, *to lay aside shame* or *modesty*, Cic

perfrīgĭdus -a um, *very cold*, tempestas perfrigida, Cic

perfringo frēgi -fractum, 3 (per and frango) I. *to break through, break in pieces, shatter* A. Lit, saxum, Cic, naves perfregerant proras, Liv B. Fig, *to break through, set at nought, disregard, violate*, decreta senatus, Cic, leges, Cic II. *to break through, bear down* A. Lit, phalangem hostium, Caes B. Fig, omnes altitudines, Cic, animos, *to overpower*, Cic

perfrŭor -fructus sum, 3 dep I. *to enjoy thoroughly*, laetitiā, Cic, regali otio, Cic II. *to execute completely*, mandatis patris, Ov

perfŭga -ae, m (perfugio), *a deserter*, Cic

perfŭgĭo -fūgi -fŭgitum 3. *to flee away*, a, *to fly to any place, take refuge in any place*, ad aliquem, Liv, transf, ad otium, Cic, b, *to desert to the enemy*, quum paene quotidie a Pompeio ad Caesarem perfugerent, Caes

perfŭgĭum -ii, n (perfugio), *a place of refuge, refuge, asylum*, perfugium et praesidium salutis, Cic, plur, intercludere perfugia fortunae, Cic

perfunctĭo -ōnis, f (perfungor), *a performing, discharging*, honorum, Cic

perfundo fūdi -fūsum, 3 *to pour over* I. Lit, 1, *to moisten, wet*, a, aliquem sanguine, *besprinkle*, Tac, perfundi, *to be moistened with*, and in middle, *to bathe in, swim in*, aquā ferventi a Rubrio, Cic, vivo flumine, Liv, perfusus fletu, Liv, b, *to dye, stain*, ostro perfusae vestes, Verg, 2, *to sprinkle, bestrew;* Lethaeo perfusa papavera somno, Verg II. Fig, *to imbue or fill with anything*, qui me horror perfudit! Cic, sensus jucunditate quādam perfunditur, Cic.; timore, Liv.

perfungor functus sum, 3. dep., **a,** *to accomplish, perform, execute, discharge;* reipublicae muneribus, Cic.; rebus amplissimis, Cic.; **b,** *to go through, endure;* molestiā, Cic.; bello, Cic.; partic. pass., memoria perfuncti periculi, Cic.; absol., perfunctus sum, *I have endured,* Cic.; **c,** *to enjoy;* epulis, Ov.

perfŭro, 3. *to rage furiously,* Verg.

Pergămum -i, n. and **Pergămus (-ŏs)** -i, f. (Πέργαμος -ον). **I.** *The citadel of Troy:* gen. plur., **Pergăma** -ōrum, n. **II.** *a town in Mysia, on the river Caicus, capital of the kingdom of Pergamus, residence of the Attalian kings,* now *Bergamo.* Hence, **A. Pergămēnus** -a -um, *relating to Pergamum* (in Mysia). **B. Pergămĕus** -a -um, *relating to the citadel of Troy,* and hence, *Trojan.*

pergaudĕo, 2. *to rejoice exceedingly,* Cic.

pergo, perrexi, perrectum, 3. (per and rego). **I.** Lit., *to continue, proceed with, prosecute anything;* with acc., iter, Sall., Liv.; with infin., ad eum ire, Cic.; absol., perge porro, Cic.; in Macedoniam, Cic. **II.** Transf., **A.** Of abstract subjects, ut ad eas (virtutes) cursim perrectura beata vita videatur, Cic. **B.** Of persons, *to continue;* id agere perrexi, Cic.; perge quatuor mihi istas partes explicare, Cic.; absol., perge ut coeperas, Cic.

pergrandis -e, *very large, very great;* **a,** of size, gemma, Cic.; **b,** of value, pecuniae summa, Cic.; **c,** of time, pergrandis natu, *very old,* Liv.

pergrātus -a -um, *very pleasant, very delightful;* pergratum mihi feceris si, etc., *you would give me great pleasure if,* etc., Cic.

pergrăvis -e, *very weighty, very important;* oratio, Cic.

pergrăvitĕr, adv. *very seriously;* aliquem reprehendere, Cic.

pergŭla -ae, f. (pergo), **a,** *a shed or outhouse used for various purposes, a shop, workshop,* Plin.; **b,** *a school,* Juv.

pĕrhĭbĕo -ŭi -ĭtum, 2. (per and habeo). **I.** *to bring forward, propose;* quem Caecilius suo nomine perhiberet, Cic. **II. a,** *to speak, say;* ut Graii perhibent, *as the Greeks say,* Verg.; in pass., with nom. and infin., nuntii fuisse perhibentur; **b,** *to call, consider;* vatem hunc perhibebo optimum, Cic.

pĕrhīlum, *very little,* Lucr.

pĕrhŏnōrĭfĭcē, adv. *very respectfully,* Cic.

pĕrhŏnōrĭfĭcus -a -um, **1,** *very honourable;* discessus, Cic.; **2,** *very respectful;* collega in me perhonorificus, Cic.

pĕrhorrĕo, 2. *to shudder at, to dread,* Ov.

pĕrhorresco -horrŭi, 3. *to become rough.* **I.** Of water, *to be agitated;* aequor perhorruit, Ov. **II.** *to be filled with dread, to shudder.* **A.** Lit., **a,** intransit., recordatione consulatus vestri perhorrescere, Cic.; **b,** transit., *to shudder at;* tantam religionem, fugam virginum, Cic. **B.** Transf., *to tremble, quake;* clamore perhorruit Aetne, Ov.

pĕrhorrĭdus -a -um, *very dreadful;* silvae, Liv.

pĕrhūmānĭtĕr, adv. *very civilly, very kindly,* Cic.

pĕrhūmānus -a -um, *very friendly, kind, civil;* epistola, Cic.

Pĕrĭclēs -is, m. (Περικλῆς), *a celebrated Athenian statesman* (d. 429 B.C.).

pĕrīclĭtātĭo -ōnis, f. (periclitor), *a trial, experiment,* Cic.

pĕrīclĭtor, 1. dep. (periculum). **I.** Intransit., **A.** *to try, make a trial;* periclitemur in exemplis, Cic. **B.** *to be in danger, to be imperilled:* ut potius Gallorum vita quam legionariorum periclitaretur, Caes.; with abl., rebus suis, Liv. **II.** Transf., **A.** *to try, test, prove, put to the proof;* fortunam, Cic.; vires ingenii, Cic. **B.** *to risk;* non est salus periclitanda reipublicae, Cic.

Pĕrĭclȳmĕnus -i, m. (Περικλύμενος), *son of Neleus, an Argonaut.*

pĕrīcŭlōsē, adv. (periculosus), *dangerously;* aegrotare, Cic.

pĕrīcŭlōsus -a -um (periculum), *full of danger, threatening danger, dangerous, perilous;* vulnus, Cic.; with dat., periculosae libertati opes, Liv.

pĕrīcŭlum (contr. **pĕrīclum**) -i, n. (root PER, whence experior), *a trial, proof, test.* **I.** Gen., **1,** periculum facere, *to make a trial,* Caes.; with genit., fidei, Cic.; **2,** *an attempt in authorship* Cic. **II.** *danger, peril.* **A.** Gen., periculum facere alicuius rei, *to risk,* Liv.; salutem sociorum summum in periculum ac discrimen vocare, Cic.; capitis periculum adire, *danger of life,* Cic.; periculum subire pro amico, Cic.; periculum alicui creare, or conflare, or inferre, or injicere, or facessere, Cic.; periculum est, with ne and the subj., *there is danger that,* etc., Cic. **B.** Esp., *a trial, action, suit;* **a,** lit., Cic.; **b,** *a legal record or register;* pericula magistratuum, Cic.

pĕrĭdōnĕus -a -um, *very fit, suitable, appropriate;* locus peridoneus castris, Caes.

Pĕrillus -i, m. (Πέριλλος), *an artist in metal at Athens, who made for Phalaris of Agrigentum a brazen bull, in which criminals were to be shut up and roasted, and who was the first to suffer death by it.*

pĕrillustris -e, **1,** *very plain, very evident,* Nep.; **2,** *very distinguished,* Cic.

pĕrimbēcillus -a -um, *very weak,* Cic.

pĕrĭmo -ēmi -emptum, 3. (per and emo), *to destroy, ruin, annihilate.* **I.** Lit., **A.** sensu perempto, Cic.; Troja perempta, Verg.; corpus pallore et macie peremptum, Liv. **B.** Esp., *to kill a person;* aliquem, Ov.; partic. perf. = *slain,* Verg., Liv. **II.** Fig., *to hinder, thwart, frustrate;* reditum, consilium, Cic.; causam publicam, Cic.

pĕrincertus -a -um, *very uncertain,* Sall.

pĕrincommŏdē, adv. *very inconveniently, very inopportunely;* accidit incommode, Cic.

pĕrincommŏdus -a -um, *very inconvenient, very troublesome,* Liv.

pĕrindĕ, adv. *as, like as, just as, in a like manner;* foll. by ac si, Cic.; atque, Cic.; quasi, Cic.; tamquam, Cic.; ut, Cic.; perinde ut . . . ita, Liv.; perinde utcumque . . . ita, Cic.

pĕrindignē, adv. *very indignantly,* Suet.

pĕrindulgens -entis, *very indulgent, very tender,* Cic.

pĕrinfāmis -e, *very infamous,* Suet.

pĕrinfirmus -a -um, *very weak,* Cic.

pĕringĕnĭōsus -a -um, *very clever,* Cic.

pĕrīnīquus -a -um, **1,** *very unfair,* Cic.; **2,** *very discontented, very unwilling;* periniquo animo patior, with acc. and infin., Cic.

pĕrinsignis -e, *very conspicuous, very remarkable,* Cic.

Pĕrinthus (-ŏs) -i, f. (Πέρινθος), *a city in Thrace, afterwards called Heraclea,* now *Erekli.*

pĕrinvīsus -a -um, *much hated;* homo, Cic.

pĕrinvītus -a -um, *very unwilling,* Cic.

pĕrĭor, pĕritus sum, 4. *to experience, make a trial of,* Plaut.

Pĕrĭpătētĭcus -a -um (Περιπατητικός), *Peripatetic, belonging to the Peripatetic or Aristotelian* *school of philosophy*; subst, **Pĕrĭpătētĭci** ōrum, m *Peripatetic philosophers*

pĕrĭpĕtasma ătis, n (περιπέτασμα), *a curtain, hanging, covering*, Cic

pĕrīrātus a -um, *very angry*, Cic

pĕriscĕlĭs -ĭdis, f. (περισκελίς), *a garter or an anklet*, Hor.

pĕristrōma ătis, n (περίστρωμα), *a curtain, carpet, hanging*, Cic (abl. plur heterocl, peristromatis)

pĕristȳlum -i, n (περίστυλον), *a peristyle or court surrounded by a colonnade*, Cic.

pĕrītē, adv. (peritus), *skilfully, cleverly*, perite dicere, Cic; nihil (peritius) de foederibus, Cic.; peritissime venditare, Cic

pĕrītĭa -ae, f (peritus), *knowledge derived from experience, skill*, locorum ac militiae, Sall

pĕrīto, 1 *to perish utterly*, Lucr

pĕrītus -a -um (perior), *experienced, skilful, practised, expert*, absol, peritissimi duces, Caes, with genit., rerum, Cic, with abl, quis jure peritior? Cic., with ad and the acc, ad usum et disciplinam, Cic; with infin, cantare, Verg

perjĕro = pejero (q v)

perjūcundē, adv. *very pleasantly, very delightfully*, in aliqua re versari, Cic

perjūcundus -a -um, *very pleasant, very delightful*, litterae, disputatio, Cic

perjūrĭōsus -a -um (perjurium), *full of perjury, perjured*, Plaut

perjūrĭum -ii, n (perjurus), *false swearing, perjury*, Cic

perjūro = pejero (q v)

perjūrus (pējūrus) -a -um (per and jus), *perjured*, perjurus et mendax, Cic, leno perjurissimus, Cic., subst., *a perjured person*, Cic.

perlābor lapsus sum, 3 *to glide through, penetrate*, rotis summas levibus perlabitur undas, *glides along*, Verg, with ad and the acc, *to reach to*; inde perlapsus ad nos et usque ad Oceanum Hercules, Cic

perlaetus -a -um, *very joyful*, Liv

perlātē, adv *very widely, very extensively*, Cic

perlĕcĕbra (pellĕcĕbra) -ae, f (pellicio), *an enticing, alluring*, Plaut

perlectĭo = pellectio (q v)

perlĕgo (pellĕgo) -lēgi -lectum, 3 **I.** *to survey thoroughly, scan, examine accurately*, omnia oculis, Verg **II. A.** *to read through*, librum, Cic. **B.** *to read through, call over*, senatum, *to call over the roll of senators*, Liv

perlĕvis -e, *very light, very slight*, perlevi momento, Cic

perlĕvĭtĕr, adv *very slightly*, pungit animi dolor, Cic

perlĭbens (perlŭbens) -entis, *very willing*, Cic

perlĭbentĕr, adv *very willingly*, Cic

perlībĕrālis -e, *well brought up, well-bred*, Ter

perlībĕrālĭtĕr, adv *very liberally, very bountifully*, Cic

perlĭbet (perlŭbet) -buit, 3 *it is pleasing, very pleasant*, Plaut.

perlĭcĭo = pellicio (q v.)

perlĭto, 1 *to offer an auspicious sacrifice, to sacrifice with favourable omens*; primis hostiis, Liv.

perlongē, adv *very far*, Ter

perlongus a -um, **1,** *very long*; via, Cic, **2,** *lasting a long time, tedious*, Plaut

perlŭbet, etc = perlibet, etc (q v)

perlūcĕo (pellūcĕo) -luxi, 2 **I.** *to shine through, gleam through*, **1,** lit, lux perlucens, Liv, **2,** fig, *to shine through, be visible*; perlucet ex eis virtutibus, Cic **II.** *to be transparent*, pellucens, *transparent*, aether, Cic, fig, oratio, Cic.

perlūcĭdŭlus (pellūcĭdŭlus) -a -um (dim of perlucidus), *somewhat transparent*, lapis, *pearl*, Cat.

perlūcĭdus (pellūcĭdus) -a -um, *transparent*, membranae, Cic, transf, illustris et perlucida stella, *bright*, Cic

perluctŭōsus -a -um, *very mournful*, Cic

perlŭo -lŭi -lūtum, 3 *to wash, bathe*, manus unda, Ov, pass, perlui, as middle, *to bathe*, in fluminibus perluuntur, Caes; unda, Hor

perlustro, 1 **I.** *to pass, wander, range through*, agros, Liv **II.** *to regard, consider, examine*, omnia oculis, Liv, aliquid animo, Cic

permagnus -a -um, *very great, very large*, hereditas, Cic, permagnum est, with infin, Cic, subst, **permagnum** -i, n *a very great thing*, quod permagni interest, Cic

permălĕ, adv *very badly or unsuccessfully*; pugnare, Cic

permānantĕr, adv (permano), *by flowing through*, Lucr

permănĕo mansi mansum, 2 *to remain, stay, abide* **I.** Lit, Seleucus in maritima ora permanens, Liv **II. 1,** *to last, continue*, ut quam maxime permaneant diuturna corpora, Cic, **2,** *to abide, remain*, in mea pristina sententia, Cic

permāno, 1 **I.** *to flow through* **A.** Lit, in saxis ac speluncis permanat aquarum liquidus humor, Lucr **B** Transf, *to penetrate*, permanat frigus ad ossa, Lucr **II.** *to flow to* **A,** Lit, succus permanat ad jecur, Cic **B.** Transf, *to reach, penetrate, extend*, doctrina in civitatem, Cic, ad aures alicuius, Cic, conclusiunculae ad sensum non permanantes, Cic

permansĭo -ōnis, f (permaneo) **I.** *a remaining, abiding in a place*, quodvis enim supplicium levius est hac permansione, Cic **II.** *abiding in an opinion*, in una sententia, Cic.

permărīnus -a -um, *relating to the sea*; Lares, *guardian deities of those who travel by sea*, Liv

permātūresco -mātūrŭi, 3 *to become thoroughly ripe*, Ov

permĕdĭōcris -e, *very moderate*, Cic

permĕo, 1 **I.** *to go through, pass through, traverse*, maria ac terras, Ov **II.** *to penetrate or reach*, **1,** longius in hostes, Tac, **2,** *to pervade*, Cic

Permessus -i, m (Περμησσός), *a river in Boeotia, rising in the spring on Helicon, sacred to the Muses, and flowing into the Copaic lake*

permētĭor -mensus sum, 4 dep **I.** *to measure through, measure out*; solis magnitudinem, Cic **II.** *to traverse*, aequor, Verg

permĕtŭens -entis, *greatly fearing*, Verg.

permingo -minxi, 3 *to defile*, Hor

permĭnūtus -a -um, *very small, very trifling*, Cic

permīrus -a -um, *very wonderful*; illud mihi permirum accidit, with acc and infin, Cic

permiscĕo -miscŭi -mixtum or mistum, 2 *to mix, mingle thoroughly* **I.** Lit, naturam cum materia, Cic, permixti cum suis fugientibus, Caes **II.** Fig, **A.** fructus acerbitate permixti, Cic **B.** *to confound, confuse, bring into disorder*, omnia jura divina et humana, Caes; Graeciam, Cic.

permissio -ōnis, f. (permitto). **I.** *yielding, surrender*, Liv. **II.** *permission, leave;* mea permissio mansionis tuae, Cic.

permissus -ū, m. (permitto), *leave, permission;* only in abl., permissu legis, Cic.

permitto -mīsi -missum, 3. *to let go, let loose.* **A.** Lit., **1,** equos permittunt in hostem, Liv.; **2,** *to throw, hurl at a mark;* saxum in hostem, Ov. **B.** Fig., **1,** permittere tribunatum, *to make use of,* Liv.; **2, a,** *to give up, yield, cede, surrender;* alicui potestatem, Cic.; consulibus rempublicam, Cic.; se in fidem ac potestatem populi, Caes.; **b,** *to give up, sacrifice;* inimicitias patribus conscriptis, Cic.; permitto aliquid iracundiae tuae, *make some allowances for,* Cic.; **c,** *to allow, permit;* with infin., Liv.; with ut and the subj., Cic.; partic. subst., **permissum** -i, n. *permission,* Hor.

permixtē, adv. (permixtus, from permisceo), *in a mixed manner, confusedly,* Cic.

permixtio -ōnis, f. (permisceo), *a mixing, mixture,* Cic.

permŏdestus -a -um, *very modest, very moderate,* Cic.

permŏdĭcus -a -um, *very moderate, very small, very slight,* Suet.

permŏlestē, adv. (permolestus), *very hardly, with much difficulty;* permoleste tuli, *I was much vexed,* Cic.; with acc. and infin., Cic.

permŏlestus -a -um, *very troublesome, very burdensome,* Cic.

permōtĭo -ōnis, f. (permoveo). **I.** *a movement, motion, agitation;* animi, Cic. **II.** *an emotion,* Cic.

permŏvĕo -mōvi -mōtum, 2. *to move or stir up thoroughly.* **I.** Lit., mare permotum, *agitated,* Lucr. **II.** Transf., **A.** *to move, excite, agitate mentally;* **a,** *to persuade, induce, influence;* aliquem pollicitationibus, Caes.; nihil te curulis aedilitas permovit quominus ludos flagitio pollueres, Cic.; permotus auctoritate, injuriis, Cic.; **b,** *to move, affect;* mentem judicum, Cic.; permotus metu, dolore, iracundiā, odio, Cic. **B.** *to excite any particular passion or emotion;* invidiam, misericordiam, metum et iras, Tac.

permulcĕo -mulsi -mulsum and (rarely) -mulctum, 2. *to stroke.* **I. A.** Lit., aliquem manu, Ov.; barbam alicuius, Liv. **B.** Fig., **a,** *to charm, delight;* sensum voluptate, Cic.; **b,** *to soothe, tranquillise, soften;* senectutem, Cic.; iram alicuius, Cic. **II.** Transf., *to touch gently;* lumina virgā, Ov.

permultus -a -um, *very much, very many;* **a,** adj., viri, Cic.; **b,** subst., **permultum** -i, n. *much,* Cic.; hence, permulto, *by far, by much;* with compar., permulto clariora, Cic.; **c,** adv., permultum, *very much;* permultum ante, *long before,* Cic.

permūnĭo -ivi -ītum, 4. *to fortify completely, to finish fortifying;* quae munimenta inchoaverat, permunit, Liv.

permūtātĭo -ōnis, f. (permuto). **I.** *change, alteration;* coloris, Cic.; magna permutatio rerum, Cic. **II.** *an exchange, barter;* **1,** permutatio mercium, Tac.; plur., partim emptiones, partim permutationes, Cic.; **2,** *exchange of money;* publica, Cic.

permūto, 1. **I.** *to change completely;* sententiam, Cic.; dominos, Hor. **II.** *to exchange, barter;* **1,** nomina inter se, Plaut.; **2, a,** *to exchange money;* ut cum quaestu populi pecunia permutaretur, Cic.; **b,** *to exchange prisoners;* captivos, Liv.

perna -ae, f. (πέρνα), *a leg of pork, a ham,* or *gammon,* Hor.

pernĕcessārĭus -a -um. **I.** *very necessary;* tempus, Cic. **II.** *very intimate;* homo intimus ac mihi pernecessarius, Cic.

pernĕcessē, adv. *very necessary;* esse, Cic.

pernĕgo, 1. **I.** *to deny obstinately, persist in denying;* with acc. and infin., Cic. **II.** *to persist in refusing,* Plaut.

pernĭcĭābĭlis -e (pernicies), *deadly, destructive, fatal;* morbi, Liv.; id perniciabile reo, Tac.

pernĭcĭālis -e (pernicies), *deadly, fatal,* Lucr.

pernĭcĭes -ēi, f. (per and nex). **I.** *destruction, disaster, calamity, ruin;* perniciem afferre vitae alicuius, Cic.; incumbere ad alicuius perniciem, Cic.; moliri alicuius perniciem, Cic. **II.** Meton., *a dangerous person or thing;* pernicies provinciae Siciliae, Cic. (old genit., pernicii and dat., pernicie).

pernĭcĭōsē, adv. (perniciosus), *destructively, ruinously, calamitously, perniciously;* multa perniciose sciscuntur in populis, Cic.; quo perniciosius de republica merentur vitiosi homines, Cic.

pernĭcĭōsus -a -um (pernicies), *calamitous, pernicious, dangerous;* esp., *dangerous to the state;* exemplum, Cic.; lex, Cic.; morbi, Cic.

pernīcĭtas -ātis, f. (pernix), *swiftness, fleetness, agility,* Cic.

pernīcĭtĕr, adv. (pernix), *swiftly, actively, nimbly;* equo desilire, Liv.

pernĭmĭum, adv. *far too much,* Ter.

pernix -nīcis (* pernitor), *swift, nimble, agile, active;* corpus, Liv.

pernōbĭlis -e, *very celebrated;* epigramma Graecum, Cic.

pernocto, 1. (pernox), *to pass the night, spend the night;* ad ostium carceris, Cic.; in nive, Cic.; extra moenia, Liv.; fig., haec studia pernoctant nobiscum, Cic.

pernosco -nōvi -nōtum, 3. *to investigate thoroughly, to become thoroughly acquainted with;* hominum mores ex oculis, vultu, etc., Cic.

pernōtesco -nōtŭi, 3. *to become generally well known,* Tac.

pernox -nocte (only in nom. and abl.), *lasting all night;* luna pernox erat, Liv.

pernŭmĕro, 1. *to count out, reckon completely;* imperatam pecuniam, Liv.

1. **pēro** -ōnis, m. *a boot of rough leather or untanned hide,* Verg.

2. **Pērō** -ūs, f. (Πηρώ), *daughter of Neleus, sister of Nestor.*

pĕrobscūrus -a -um, *very obscure;* quaestio, Cic.

pĕrōdi -ōsus sum -ōdisse, *to hate exceedingly;* only in partic. perf., **pĕrōsus** -a -um, *hating, detesting;* decem virorum scelera, Liv.; lucem, *shunning the light,* Ov.; perosum esse, *to hate, detest;* plebs consulum nomen perosa erat, Liv.

pĕrōdĭōsus -a -um, *much hated, very troublesome,* Cic.

pĕroffĭcĭōsē, adv. *very obligingly, very attentively;* qui me perofficiose observant, Cic.

Pĕrŏlĕo, 2. *to emit a bad smell,* Lucr.

Pērōnātus -a -um (1. pero), *wearing boots of untanned leather,* Pers.

pĕropportūnē, adv. *very opportunely, very seasonably;* venire, Cic.

pĕropportūnus -a -um, *very opportune, very seasonable, very convenient;* deversorium, Cic.

pĕroptātō, adv. *according to one's desire,* Cic.

pĕrŏpŭs, adv. *very necessary,* Ter.

pĕrōrātĭo -ōnis, f (peroro), **a,** *the conclusion of a speech, peroration,* Cic ; **b,** *the closing speech,* Cic

perornātus a -um, *very ornate* (of an orator), Cic.

perorno, 1 *to adorn greatly,* senatum, Tac

pĕrōro, 1. **I.** *to speak from beginning to end, to plead a cause throughout, explain* or *state thoroughly* totam causam, Cic **II.** *to end, close* **a,** with accus , totum hoc crimen decumanum perorabo, Cic , res illis die non perorata, Cic , **b,** absol , *to conclude a speech, to wind up,* quoniam satis multa dixi est mihi perorandum, Cic , also *to close a case* (of the last speaker at a trial), Cic

pĕrōsus a -um, v perodi

perpāco, 1. *to pacify thoroughly, tranquillize* necdum omnia in Graecia perpacata erant, Liv

perparcē, adv *very sparingly, very frugally,* Ter

perparvŭlus -a -um, *very little,* sigilla, Cic

perparvus -a -um, *very little, very small,* perparva et tenuis civitas, Cic

perpastus a um (per and pasco), *well fed, fat,* canis, Phaedr

perpaucŭlus a um, *very few, very little,* passus, Cic

perpaucus a um *very few, very little,* **a,** adj , advocati, Cic , **b,** plur subst , (α) m , perpauci, *very few,* Cic , (β) n , perpauca dicere, Cic

perpaulŭlum (perpaullŭlum) i, n dim *a very, very little,* Cic

perpaulum (perpaullum), adv *a very little,* Cic

perpauper -ĕris, *very poor,* Cic

perpauxillum -i, n *a very little,* Plaut

perpăvĕfăcio, 3 *to terrify exceedingly,* Plaut

perpello -pŭli pulsum 3 **1,** *to drive, to urge, compel, prevail upon, constrain* urbem eo metu ad deditionem, Liv , gen with ut or ne and the subj , Sall , Liv , **2,** *to make a deep impression on,* candor huius te et proceritas, vultus oculique perpulerunt, Cic

perpendĭcŭlum -i, n (perpendo), *a plumb-line, plummet* ad perpendiculum columnas exigere, Cic , ad perpendiculum, *in a straight line,* Cic , Caes

perpendo -pendi -pensum, 3 *to weigh carefully, to consider, examine, investigate,* transf , aliquid ad disciplinae praecepta, Cic., perpenditur amicitia veritate, Cic.

perpĕram, adv *wrongly, falsely, untruly,* judicare, Cic , facere, Cic

perpĕs pĕtis (= perpetuus), *continuous, unbroken, perpetual,* noctem perpetem, *throughout the night,* Plaut

perpessĭo ōnis, f. (perpetior), *suffering, endurance,* laborum, Cic , dolorum, Cic

perpĕtĭor -pessus, 3 dep (per and patior), *to bear, endure, suffer steadfastly,* dolorem, Cic , with acc and infin , Verg

perpĕtro, 1 (per and patro), *to complete, accomplish, perform, commit, effect, bring about, finish,* caedem, sacrificium, Liv.

perpĕtŭĭtas ātis, f (perpetuus), *uninterrupted continuance, perpetuity, continuity,* vitae, Cic , orationis, Cic , ad perpetuitatem, *for ever,* Cic

1 **perpĕtŭō,** adv (perpetuus), *perpetually, for ever, uninterruptedly,* Cic

2 **perpĕtŭo,** 1. (perpetuus), *to make continual* or *perpetual continue, perpetuate,* verba, *to pronounce in unbroken succession,* Cic ; jus potestatem judicum, *to maintain unbroken,* Cic

perpĕtŭus -a um (peto), *continuous, uninterrupted, continual* **I. a,** of space, munitiones, Caes , oratio, Cic ; carmen, Hor , **b,** of time, *unbroken, continuing, lasting, perpetual,* ignis Vestae perpetuus ac sempiternus, Cic , quaestiones, *composed of a standing body of judges,* Cic , in perpetuum, *for ever,* Cic **II.** *universal, general,* jus, Cic

perplăcĕo, 2 *to please exceedingly,* ea (lex) mihi perplacet, Cic

perplexē, adv (perplexus), *confusedly, obscurely,* indicare, Liv

perplexus a um (partic of *perplecto), *confused, intricate, entangled* **I.** Lit , iter, Verg **II.** Transf , *confused, intricate, obscure, perplexed, dark, ambiguous* sermones, Liv , perplexum Punico astu responsum, Liv

perplĭcātus a um (per and plico), *entangled, involved,* Lucr

perplŭo, 3 *to let the rain through,* perpluunt tigna, Plaut , hence, *to rain into,* amor in pectus perpluit meum, Plaut

perpŏlĭo, 4 **I.** *to smooth, polish thoroughly,* Plin **II.** *to polish, perfect, complete* illam superiorem partem perpolire atque conficere, Cic

perpŏlītus -a um, p adj (from perpolio), *polished, accomplished, refined,* perfecti in dicendo et perpoliti homines, Cic , vita perpolita humanitate, Cic.

perpŏpŭlor, 1 dep *to lay waste, devastate completely,* Italiam, Liv

perporto, 1 *to carry, transport to any place,* Liv

perpōtātĭo ōnis, f (perpoto), *a continued drinking, drunken debauch,* plur , intemperantissimae perpotationes, Cic

perpōto, 1 **I.** *to continue drinking, to keep up a drunken debauch,* totos dies, Cic , perpotant ad vesperum Cic **II.** *to drink up* Lucr

perprĕmo — perprimo (q v)

perprĭmo pressi -pressum, 3 (per and premo), *to press hard,* cubilia, *to lie upon,* Hor

perprŏpinquus a um, *very nearly related ;* M Illius Auriu perpropinquus, Cic

perprosper -era erum, *very prosperous,* valetudo, *very good,* Suet.

perprūrisco, 3 *to itch all over,* Plaut

perpugnax ācis, *very pugnacious,* in disputando, Cic

perpulcher -chra chrum, *very beautiful,* Ter

perpurgo, 1 **I.** *to make thoroughly clean,* se quādam herbulā, Cic **II.** Fig , **1,** *to explain thoroughly, to clear up,* locum orationis, Cic , **2,** *to confute, refute,* crimina, Cic

perpŭsillus -a -um, *very small, very little,* in double sense, perpusillus testis processit non accusabis, perpusillum rogabo, i e , *I will ask a little question, I will question the little man,* Cic

perquam, adv (per and quam), *very much, extremely,* perquam grave est dictu, Cic , perquam breviter, Cic

perquīro sīvi -sītum, 3 (per and quaero), *to inquire earnestly, make accurate inquiries, search for eagerly,* vias, Caes , vasa, Cic , illa ab accusatore, Cic

perquīsītē, adv. (perquisitus, from perquiro), *accurately* in compar , perquisitius et diligentius conscribere, Cic

perrāro, adv. (perrarus), *very rarely, very seldom*, Cic.

perrārus -a -um, *very uncommon, very rare*, Liv.

perrĕcondĭtus -a -um, *very abstruse, very recondite*, Cic.

perrēpo -repsi -reptum, 3. *to crawl through, creep over*, Tib.

perrepto, 1. (intens. of perrepo), *to crawl about, to crawl through*, Plaut.

Perrhaebia -ae, f. (Περραιβία), *a district in Thessaly*. Adj., **Perrhaebus** -a -um, *Perrhaebian*, poet. = *Thessalian*.

perrīdĭcŭlē, adv. (perridiculus), *very laughably*, Cic.

perrīdĭcŭlus -a -um, *very laughable, very ridiculous*, Cic.

perrŏgo, 1. *to ask a number of persons in succession, to ask one after another*; sententiam, sententias, Liv.

perrumpo -rūpi -ruptum, 3. **I.** Intransit., *to break through, burst a way through*; per medios hostes, Caes.; per aciem, Liv. **II.** Transit., *to break through, burst through*. **A.** Lit., **1**, rates, Caes.; **2**, *to make a way through*; paludem, Caes.; cuneos hostium, Liv. **B.** Fig., *to break through, subdue, overpower, annihilate*; periculum, Cic.; quaestiones, Cic.

1\. **Persa** -ae, f. (Πέρση). **I.** *a nymph, mother of Aeetes, Circe, and Hecate by Sol.* Hence, adj., **Persēïs** -ĭdis, f. (Περσηΐς), = *magical*; herbae, Ov.; sc. Musa, *a poem*, Ov. **II.** *name of a little dog*, Cic.

2\. **Persa**, v. Persae.

Persae -ārum, m. (Πέρσαι), *the Persians*; sing., **Persa** -ae, m. and **Persēs** -ae, m.; hence, **A. Persĭa** -ae, f. *Persia*. **B. Persĭs** -ĭdis, f. **1**, adj., *Persian*, Ov.; **2**, subst., *Persia in a narrower sense, Persis, the district between Carmania, Media, and Susiana, now Fars or Farsistan*. **C.** Adj., **Persĭcus** -a -um, *Persian*; arbor, or simply **Persĭcus** -i, f. *the peach-tree*; **Persĭca** -ōrum, n. *Persian history*.

persaepĕ, adv. *very often*, Cic.

persalsē, adv. (persalsus), *very wittily*; persalse et humaniter gratias mihi agit, Cic.

persalsus -a -um, *very witty*, Cic.

persălūtātĭo -ōnis, f. (persaluto), *a greeting, salutation*, Cic.

persălūto, 1. *to greet a number in succession, greet all round*; omnes, Cic.

persanctē, adv. *very sacredly*, Ter.

persăpĭens -entis, *very wise*; homo, Cic.

persăpĭentĕr, adv. (persapiens), *very wisely*, Cic.

perscĭentĕr, adv. (per and scio), *very knowingly, very discreetly*, Cic.

perscindo -scĭdi -scissum, 3. *to tear to pieces*; omnia perscindente vento, Liv.

perscītus -a -um, *very fine, very clever, very pretty*; (in tmesis) per mihi scitum videtur, Cic.

perscrībo -scripsi -scriptum, 3. *to write down accurately, explicitly*. **A.** Gen., rationes sunt perscriptae scite et litterate, Cic. **B.** Esp., **1**, officially, *to note down, enter in a memorandum-book* or *register*; **a**, omnia judicum dicta, interrogata, responsa, Cic.; **b**, *to enter in an account-book*; falsum nomen, Cic.; **2**, *to notify, announce, relate in writing*; alicui mitissimam alicuius orationem, Cic.; de suis rebus ad Lollium, Cic.; **3**, *to make over* or *assign to in writing*; illam pecuniam in aedem sacram reficiendam perscribere, Cic.

perscriptĭo -ōnis, f. (perscribo). **I. a**, *an entering in a register*, Cic.; **b**, *an entering in an account-book*, Cic. **II.** *a making over or assigning by a written document*, Cic.

perscriptor -ōris, m. (perscribo), *one who writes down or makes an entry*, Cic.

perscrūtor, 1. dep. **I.** *to search through, look through, seek through*; arculas muliebres, Cic. **II.** Transf., *to examine into, to investigate*; naturam rationemque criminum, Cic.

persĕco -sĕcŭi -sectum, 1. *to cut off entirely, cut through, cut out*; **1**, id ne serperet iterum latius, Liv.; **2**, *to dissect, lay bare*; rerum naturas, Cic.

persector, 1. dep. **I.** *to follow, pursue eagerly*; accipitres persectantes, Lucr. **II.** Transf., *to investigate*; primordia, Lucr.

persĕcūtĭo -ōnis, f. (persequor), *a prosecution*, Cic.

persĕdĕo -sēdi -sessum, 2. *to remain sitting*; in equo dies noctesque persedendo, Liv.

persegnis -e, *very sluggish, very languid*; proelium, Liv.

persĕnex -is, *very old*, Suet.

persentĭo -sensi -sensum, 4. **1**, *to perceive distinctly*; eam tali peste teneri, Verg.; **2**, *to feel deeply*; magno pectore curas, Verg.

persentisco, 3. **1**, *to perceive distinctly*, Ter.; **2**, *to feel deeply*, Lucr.

Persĕphŏnē -ēs, f. (Περσεφόνη), *the Greek name of Proserpina* (q.v.); meton. = *death*, Ov.

persĕquor -sĕcūtus and -sĕquūtus sum, -sĕqui, 3. dep. **I.** *to follow constantly, pursue earnestly*. **A.** Lit., **1**, gen., vestigia alicuius, Cic.; **2**, esp., **a**, *to follow with hostile intent, pursue*; fugientes usque ad flumen, Caes.; **b**, *to search through a place*; omnes solitudines, Cic. **B.** Transf., **1**, omnes vias, *to use every method*, Cic.; **2**, **a**, *to strive after, seek to attain*; voluptates, Cic.; **b**, *to follow after, busy oneself with*; artes, Cic.; **c**, *to imitate*; ironiam, Cic.; aliquem, Cic.; **d**, *to belong to a sect, to be a follower of*; sectam et instituta alicuius, Cic.; Academiam veterem, Cic.; **e**, *to pursue hostilely, avenge, punish*; civitatem bello, Caes.; injurias, Cic.; mortem alicuius, *to avenge*, Cic.; **f**, *to prosecute judicially*; (α) a person, aliquem judicio, Cic.; (β) *to strive to obtain*; jus suum, Cic.; bona sua lite atque judicio, Cic.; **g**, *to follow up an act, bring about, accomplish, perform, execute*; mea mandata, Cic.; incepta, Liv.; **h**, *to treat of verbally* or *in writing*; *set forth, expound, describe*; quae versibus persecutus est Ennius, Cic.; Brutus philosophiam Latinis literis persequitur, Cic. **II.** *to reach to, attain to*. **A.** Lit., aliquem ne persequi quidem posse triginta diebus, Cic. **B.** Transf., **1**, *to collect, call in*; hereditates aut syngraphas, Cic.; **2**, *to write down, register*; quae dicuntur, Cic.

1\. **Persēs** -ae and **Persĕus** -ĕi, m. (Πέρσης), *the last king of Macedonia, defeated by the Roman general Aemilius Paulus* (168 B.C.). Hence, **1**, **Persĭcus** -a -um, *relating to Perseus*; **2**, **Persēïs**, acc. -ĭda, f. *a town in Macedonia*.

2\. **Persēs** -ae, m. *a Persian*, v. Persae.

Persĕus -ĕi and -ĕos, m. (Περσεύς), *son of Jupiter and Danaë, slayer of the Medusa and the monster to whom Andromeda was exposed*; hence, adj., **1**, **Persēus** -a -um; **2**, **Persēïus** -a -um, *relating to Perseus*.

persĕvērans -antis, p. adj. (from persevero), *holding out, enduring, persevering*, Liv.

persĕvērantĕr, adv. (perseverans), *perseveringly, persistently*; bene coeptam rem tueri, Liv.

persĕvērantĭa -ae, f. (persevero), *perseverance, endurance, persistence*, Cic.

persĕvēro, 1. (perseverus) **I.** Intransit, *to persist, remain constant, persevere in anything*, **a**, in sua sententia, Cic; pass used also impers, non est ab isto perseveratum, Cic, **b**, *to continue* or *finish a voyage* or *journey*, una navis perseveravit, Caes. **II.** Transit, *to proceed with, persist in*, id, Cic, with infin, injuriam facere fortissime, Cic, with acc and infin, *to maintain that*, perseverabat se esse Orestem, Cic.

persĕvērus a -um, *very strict*, imperium, Tac.

Persĭa, v Persae

Persĭcus, v Persae and Perses.

persĭdĕo -sēdi -sessum, 2 = persedeo (q v)

persīdo -sēdi sessum, 3. *to settle down*, Verg.

persigno, 1 *to note down, record*, dona, Liv

persĭmĭlis -e, *very like, very similar*, statua istius persimilis, Cic

persimplex -icis, *very simple*, Tac.

persisto, 3 *to remain constant, persist in anything*, in eadem impudentia, Liv. (for perfect form v persto)

Persĭus -ii, m **I.** *an orator, contemporary with Lucilius* **II.** *a celebrated Roman satirist in the reign of Nero*

persolla ae, f. (dim of persona), *a little mask*, hence, as a term of reproach, *a little fright*, Plaut

persolvo -solvi -sŏlūtum 3 **I** *to unloose*, fig, = *to explain, expound*, Cic. **II.** *to pay, pay off*; **a**, lit., stipendium militibus, Cic, aes alienum alienis nominibus suis copiis, *to pay the debts of others with one's own money*, Sall; **b**, transf, *to pay, give, render to any one his due, discharge an obligation*, grates, Verg, meritam diis immortalibus gratiam, Cic; poenas, *to suffer punishment*, Cic; epistolae, *to answer a letter*, Cic

persōna -ae, f. *the mask worn by the actors in the Greek and Roman drama* **I.** Lit, ut ex persona mihi ardere oculi hominis histrionis viderentur, Cic **II.** Meton, **1**, *the part, character, person represented by the actor*; persona de mimo, Cic; **2**, transf, **a**, *the part which any one plays, the character which he sustains in the world*, accusatoris, Cic, petitoris personam capere, Cic., personam in republica tueri principis, *to be a leading man in the state*, Cic, **b**, *a person in the abstract = a personality, individuality, character*, huius Staleni persona, Cic.

persōnātus -a -um (persona), **1**, *clad in a mask, masked*, Roscius, Cic, **2**, *fictitious, not genuine, counterfeited*, quid est, cur ego personatus ambulem, Cic

persŏno -sŏnui -sŏnitum, 1 **I.** Intransit, **A.** *to sound through, resound thoroughly*; domus cantu personabat, Cic, aures personant huiusmodi vocibus, Cic; id totis personabat castris, Liv.; of persons, *to shout*, Tac **B.** *to perform upon a musical instrument*; citharā Iopas personat, Verg **II.** Transit, **A.** *to fill with sound, cause to resound*; aequora conchā, Verg **B. a**, *to cry loudly*, with acc and infin, Cic, **b**, *to proclaim loudly*; quas (res) isti in angulis personant, Cic.

perspecto, 1. (intens of perspicio), **1**, *to look at to the end*, Suet, **2**, *to look all about*, Plaut

perspectus -a -um, p adj (from perspicio), *well known, fully known*, virtus, Cic, (superl), benevolentia perspectissima, Cic.

perspĕcŭlor, 1 dep *to investigate, explore thoroughly*, Suet.

perspergo, 3 (per and spargo), *to sprinkle, moisten* fig, quo tamquam sale perspergatur omnis oratio, Cic

perspĭcācĭtas -ātis, f (perspicax), *sharpsightedness*, Cic. (?)

perspĭcax -ācis (perspicio), *sharp-sighted, acute*, id quod acutum ac perspicax naturā est, Cic

perspĭcĭentĭa -ae, f (perspicio), *a perfect acquaintance with or knowledge of*, veri, Cic

perspĭcio -spexi -spectum, 3 (per and specio). **I.** Intransit, *to look into, to penetrate by the look*, quo non modo non intrari, sed ne perspici quidem posset, Cic **II.** Transit, **A.** *to see through, look through, behold*, ut prae densitate arborum perspici caelum vix posset, Liv **B. a**, *to look at attentively, survey, examine*, domum tuam, Cic, **b**, *to read through something written*, eas (epistolas) ego oportet perspiciam, Cic, **c**, *to regard mentally, note, observe, investigate, ascertain*, alicuius fidem, Cic, animos regum, Cic, with acc and infin, Cic, or pass, with nom and infin, Cic, with rel sent, ista veritas quae sit, non satis perspicio, Cic.

perspĭcŭē, adv (perspicuus), *clearly, plainly, evidently*, plane et perspicue expedire aliquid, Cic

perspĭcŭĭtas -ātis, f (perspicuus), **1**, *clearness, brightness, transparency*, Plin, **2**, transf, *clearness, perspicuity*, Cic

perspĭcŭus -a -um (perspicio) **I.** *transparent, bright, clear*, aquae, Ov **II.** Transf, *clear, evident, perspicuous*, utilitatis ratio aut perspicua nobis aut obscura, Cic

persterno -strāvi strātum, 3 *to make quite level, pave thoroughly*, viam silice, Liv.

pĕrstĭmŭlo, 1 *to goad on violently*, Tac

persto -stiti -stātūrus, 1 *to stand firm, remain standing* **I.** Lit armati omnes diem totum perstant, Liv **II.** Transf, **A.** *to remain unchanged, to last, endure*; nihil est quod toto perstet in orbe, Ov **B.** *to stand firm, persist, persevere*, in incepto, Liv, in sententia, Cic., with infin, si perstiteris corpus ad ea quae dixi referre, Cic.

perstrĕpo -ŭi, 3 *to make a great noise*, Ter.

perstringo strinxi strictum, 3 *to graze, graze against* **I.** Lit, **a**, portam aratro, Cic, solum aratro, *to plough*, Cic, **b**, esp, *to wound slightly*, femur, Cic **II.** Transf, **a**, *to touch, seize, lay hold of*, horror ingens spectantes perstringit, Liv, consulatus meus eum perstrinxerat, *had moved*, Cic, **b**, *to scold, blame, reproach*; voluntate [illegible] ctus, Cic, aliquem suspicione, Cic, **c**, [illegible] *upon in discourse, relate briefly*, tantummodo perstringere unamquamque rem, Cic

perstŭdĭōsē, adv (perstudiosus), *very eagerly, very willingly*, Cic

perstŭdĭōsus -a -um, *very eager, very desirous, very fond*, litterarum, Cic.

persuādĕo -suāsi suāsum, 2 **I.** *to convince*, with or without dat of pers, with accus and infin, or rel sent, or with de and the abl, velim tibi ita persuadeas me tuis consiliis nullo loco defuturum, Cic, imprimis hoc volunt persuadere, non interire animas, Caes; pass impers, hoc ipsis Siculis ita persuasum est, Cic **II.** *to persuade, prevail upon a person to adopt any course of action*, with or without dat of pers and with ut and the subj, or the subj alone, or with rel sent, or with the infin, huic persuadet uti ad hostes transeat, Caes, with accus of thing, quorum si utrumvis (Pompeio) persuasissem, Cic, pass impers, quibus persuasum est hostem persequi, Cic

persuāsĭo -ōnis, f. (persuadeo), **1**, *a con*

vincing, persuasion, Cic. ; **2**, *a conviction, belief, opinion ;* superstitionum persuasione, Tac.

persuāsus -ū, m. (persuadeo), *persuasion ;* huius persuasu, Cic.

persubtīlis -e, **1**, *very fine, very subtle*, Lucr. ; **2**, *very subtle, very refined ;* oratio, Cic.

persulto, 1. (salto). **I.** Intransit., *to leap, skip about a place ;* in agro, Liv. **II.** Transit., *to range through ;* captam Italiam, Tac.

pertaedet -taesum est, 2. impers. *to be weary of, disgusted with anything ;* pertaesum est levitatis, Cic. ; vos injuriae pertaesum est, Sall.

pertendo -tendi -tensum and -tentum, 3. **I.** *to continue, carry through ;* aliquid, Ter. **II.** *to direct one's steps anywhere, to go ;* pars maxima Romam pertenderunt, Liv.

pertento, 1. **I.** *to prove, test, try.* **A.** Lit., pugionem utrumque, Tac. **B.** Transf., **a**, *to put to the test ;* adolescentium animos, Liv. ; **b**, *to consider, to examine ;* perspice rem et pertenta, Cic. **II.** *to seize, lay hold of, affect ;* tremor pertentat corpora, Verg.

pertĕnŭis -e, **1**, *very fine, very small*, Plin. ; **2**, *very small, very slight ;* spes salutis, Cic. ; suspicio, Cic.

pertĕrĕbro, 1. *to bore through ;* columnam, Cic.

pertergĕo -tersi -tersum, 2. *to wipe off, wipe up.* **I.** Lit., gausape mensam, Hor. **II.** Transf., *to touch gently*, Lucr.

perterrĕfăcĭo (-fēci) -factum, 3. (perterreo and facio), *to frighten, terrify exceedingly*, Ter.

perterrĕo -terrŭi -territum, 2. *to frighten, terrify exceedingly ;* maleficii conscientiā perterritus, Cic.

perterrĭcrĕpus -a -um, *sounding, rattling terribly*, Lucr.

pertexo -texŭi -textum, 3. *to weave entirely ;* transf., *to complete, accomplish ;* pertexe modo quod exorsus es, Cic.

pertĭca -ae, f. *a long pole* or *rod*, Ov.

pertĭmĕfactus -a -um (pertimeo and facio), *frightened exceedingly*, ap. Cic.

pertĭmesco -timŭi, 3. (pertimeo), *to fear exceedingly, be very much afraid of ;* nullius potentiam, Cic. ; de suis periculis, Cic.

pertĭnācĭa -ae, f. (pertinax), *firmness, obstinacy, pertinacity ;* hominum nimia pertinacia et arrogantia, Caes. ; in pertinacia perstare, Liv. ; frangere pertinaciam, Liv.

pertĭnācĭtĕr, adv. (pertinax), *firmly, obstinately, pertinaciously ;* fusos insequi, Liv.

pertĭnax -ācis (per and tenax). **I.** *having a firm hold, tenacious ;* digito male pertinaci, Hor. **II.** *firm, persistent, persevering, pertinacious, obstinate ;* virtus, Liv. ; concertatio, Cic. ; pertinax ad obtinendam injuriam, Liv.

pertĭnĕo -tinŭi, 2. (per and teneo), *to reach to, extend to.* **I.** Lit., venae in omnes partes corporis pertinentes, Cic. ; Belgae pertinent ad inferiorem partem fluminis Rheni, Caes. **II.** Transf., **1**, *to reach, extend, spread ;* eadem bonitas ad multitudinem pertinet, Cic. ; **2**, *to tend towards, to have as an object* or *result ;* ea quae ad effeminandos animos pertinent, Caes. ; quorsum pertinet? *of what service is it? of what good is it?* Hor. ; **3**, *to relate, pertain, belong to ;* **a**, illa res ad officium meum pertinet, Cic. ; interpretando, quorsum quidque pertineat, Cic. ; **b**, *to attach to, to fall upon ;* ad quem suspicio malefici pertineat, Cic. ; **4**, *to have an influence upon, affect ;* si quid hoc ad rem pertinet, Cic. ; **5**, *to relate to ;* quod or quantum pertinet ad, with acc., *in relation to ;* quod ad populum pertinet, Cic.

pertingo, 3. (per and tango), *to stretch out, extend to ;* collis in immensum pertingens, Sall.

pertŏlĕro, 1. *to endure to the end, bear completely*, Lucr.

pertorquĕo, 2. *to twist, distort*, Lucr.

pertractātĭo -ōnis, f. (pertracto), *an occupying or busying oneself with, application to anything ;* rerum publicarum, Cic.

pertracto (pertrecto), 1. **I.** *to touch with the hands, lay hold of, handle, feel ;* barbatulos mullos exceptare de piscina et pertractare, Cic. **II.** Transf., **a**, *to busy oneself with, treat, study ;* philosophiam, Cic. ; **b**, *to influence, work upon ;* sensus mentesque hominum, Cic.

pertrăho -traxi -tractum, 3. *to drag to a place ;* **a**, *to forcibly conduct ;* aliquem in castra, Liv. ; **b**, *to entice* or *allure to a place ;* hostem ad insidiarum locum, Liv.

pertrecto = pertracto (q.v.).

pertristis -e, **1**, *very sorrowful*, ap. Cic. ; **2**, *very austere ;* quidam patruus, Cic.

pertŭmultŭōsē, adv. *in an agitated or tumultuous manner ;* nuntiare, Cic.

pertundo -tŭdi -tūsum (-tussum) and -tunsum, 3. *to bore through, thrust through, push through*, Cat.

perturbātē, adv. (perturbatus), *confusedly, in a disorderly manner ;* dicere, Cic.

perturbātĭo -ōnis, f. (perturbo), *confusion, disorder, disquiet.* **I.** Lit., caeli, *stormy weather*, Cic. **II.** Transf., **A.** *confusion, disorder ;* rationis atque ordinis, Cic. ; animorum, Cic. ; vitae, Cic. **B. 1**, *political disorder, disquiet, disturbance ;* magnā rerum perturbatione impendente, Cic. ; **2**, *passion, emotion ;* perturbationes sunt genere quatuor, aegritudo, formido, libido, laetitia, Cic.

perturbātrix -īcis, f. (perturbo), *she that disturbs*, Cic.

perturbātus -a -um, p. adj. (from perturbo), *confused, disquieted, disturbed ;* numquam vidi hominem perturbatiorem metu, Cic.

perturbo, 1. *to disturb greatly, bring into complete confusion.* **I.** Lit., aciem, Sall. ; ordines, Caes. **II.** Transf., **A.** *to disturb, confuse ;* conditiones factionesque bellicas perjurio, *to break*, Cic. **B. 1**, *to disturb politically ;* provinciam, Cic. ; **2**, *to disturb the feelings, to disquiet, alarm ;* de reipublicae salute perturbari, Cic. ; perturbari animo, Caes.

perturpis -e, *very base, very disgraceful*, Cic.

pertūsus -a -um, p. adj. (from pertundo), *bored through, perforated ;* dolium a fundo pertusum, Liv.

pĕrungo -unxi -unctum, 3. *to anoint thoroughly, besmear ;* corpora oleo, Cic.

pĕrurbānus -a -um, **1**, *very polite, refined, witty*, Cic. ; **2**, in a bad sense, *over-polite*, Cic.

pĕrurgĕo -ursi, 2. *to urge greatly, earnestly press upon*, Suet.

pĕrūro -ussi -ustum, 3. **I.** *to burn thoroughly, to burn up ;* agrum, Liv. **II. A.** *to inflame* (with love, etc.) ; perurimur aestu, Ov. ; perustus inani gloriā, Cic. **B. 1**, *to gall, chafe, inflame ;* subducant oneri colla perusta boves, Ov. ; **2**, *to pinch, nip with cold ;* terra perusta gelu, Ov.

Pĕrŭsĭa -ae, f. *one of the twelve allied Etruscan towns*, now *Perugia.* Hence, **Pĕrŭsīnus** -a -um, *belonging to Perusia.*

pĕrūtĭlis -e, *very useful*, Cic.

pervādo -vāsi -vāsum, 3. **I.** *to go through, come through, pass through.* **A.** Lit., incendium per agros pervasit, Cic , per aequa et iniqua loca, Liv **B.** Transf , *pervade*, opinio quae per animos gentium barbararum pervaserat, Cic **II.** *to attain, to reach to, to arrive at* **A.** Lit., in Italiam, Cic , ad castra, Liv **B.** Transf , *to reach to*, locus nullus est quo non hominum libido pervaserit, Cic

pervăgātus -a -um, p. adj (from pervagor) **I** *spread abroad, well known*, sermo, Cic , pervagatissimus versus, Cic , neut plur subst , ista communia et pervagata, *those well-known rules*, Cic **II.** *common, general*, pars est pervagatior, Cic

pervăger -ātus sum, 1 **I.** Intransit., *to wander, to rove about* **A.** Lit , omnibus in locis, Caes **B.** Transf , *to be widely spread*, **a,** = *to become known everywhere*, quod in exteris nationibus usque ad ultimas terras pervagatum est, Cic , **b,** *to become common*, ne is honos nimium pervagetur, Cic **II.** Transit , *to wander through* **A.** Lit , bello prope orbem terrarum, Liv. **B.** Transf , cupiditates, timores omnium mentes pervagantur, Cic

pervăgus -a -um, *wandering everywhere*, puer, Ov

pervălĕo ŭi, 2 *to be very strong*, Lucr

pervărĭē, adv *very variously*, Cic

pervasto, 1 *to devastate, lay waste completely*, omnia ferro flammāque, Liv

pervĕho -vexi vectum, 3 **I.** *to carry through, conduct through*, commeatus, Liv., pass , pervehi, as middle, *to travel, sail, pass through*, Tac **II.** *to carry, lead conduct, bring to a place*, virgines Caere, Liv , pass , pervehi, as middle = *to travel to*, Chalcidem, Liv , in portum (fig), Cic.

pervello -velli, 3 *to pluck, pull, twitch violently* **I.** Lit , aurem, Phaedr , stomachum, *to excite*, Hor **II.** Fig , *to pinch, hurt, pain*, si te forte dolor aliquis pervellerit, Cic , hence, *to disparage, revile*, jus civile, Cic

pervĕnĭo -vēni ventum, 4 *to arrive at, come to, reach*. **I.** Lit , Germani in fines Eburonum pervenerunt, Caes , ad portam, Cic **II.** Transf , **a,** of persons, *to attain to, to arrive at, reach*, in maximam invidiam, Cic , in senatum, *to become a senator*, Cic , in scripta alicuius, *to be mentioned by an author*, Cic , ad suum, *to obtain one's own*, Cic , ad primos comoedos, *to attain to the rank of*, Cic , **b,** of things, *to come to*, pecunia ad Verrem pervenit, Cic

perversē, adv (perversus), *wrongly, perversely*, interpretari, Cic , uti deorum beneficio, Cic

perversĭtas -ātis, f (perversus), *perversity*, hominum, Cic , opinionum, Cic

perversus a -um, p adj (from perverto), *crooked, awry, askew* **I.** Lit , perversissimi oculi, *squinting dreadfully*, Cic **II** *perverse, froward, wrong*, sapientia Tuberonis, Cic

perverto (pervorto) -verti (-vorti) versum (-vorsum), 3 *to turn upside down, overturn, overthrow* **I.** Lit , tecta, Cic **II.** Transf , **A.** *to invert, pervert*, perverso more, *against tradition, custom, etc* , Cic , perverso numine, *against the will of the gods*, Verg **B.** Meton , *to overthrow, destroy, pervert*, amicitiam aut justitiam, Cic , omnia jura divina atque humana, Cic **C.** *to trip up, put down* numquam (ille me) ullo artificio pervertet, Cic.

pervespĕri, adv *very late in the evening*, Cic

pervestīgātĭo -ōnis, f (pervestigo), *a tracking out, investigation*, Cic

pervestīgo, 1 *to track out* **I.** Lit., of hunting dogs, Cic **II.** Fig , *to investigate, search into*, pervestigare et cognoscere, Cic.

pervĕtus -ĕris, *very old*, rex, Cic , amicitia, Cic

pervĕtustus -a -um, *very old*, verba, Cic

pervĭcācĭa -ae, f (pervicax), *persistency*, usually in a bad sense, *obstinacy, stubbornness*, mulierositas, pervicacia, ligurritio Cic , pervicacia tua et superbia, Liv , pervicacia in hostem, *firmness*, Tac

pervĭcācĭtĕr, adv (pervicax), *firmly, obstinately, stubbornly*, compar , pervicacius, Liv

pervĭcax -ācis (*pervico for pervinco), *firm, unyielding*, in a bad sense, *stubborn, obstinate*, virtus, Liv , with genit , pervicax irae, Tac ; with adversus, adversus peritos pervicax, Tac

pervĭdĕo -vīdi -vīsum, 2 **I** *to overlook, look at, regard, behold*, **1,** lit , sol qui pervidet omnia, Ov , **2,** transf , **a,** cunctaque mens oculis pervidet usa suis, Ov , **b,** *to look over = to review*, quum tua pervideas oculis mala lippus inunctis, Hor **II** *to look through and through*, **1,** lit , *to distinguish*, ut neque quae cuiusque stipitis palma sit pervideri possit, Liv , **2,** transf , **a,** *to examine*, quid ea postulet pervidendum, Cic , **b,** *to look at, perceive, discern*, animi mei firmitatem, Cic , meton , *to consider, examine*, videbo te et pervidebo, Cic

pervĭgĕo -gŭi 2 *to flourish, bloom continually*, opibus atque honoribus perviguere, *remained long in possession of*, Tac

pervĭgil -ĭlis, *very watchful, always watching*, Ov

pervĭgĭlātĭo -ōnis, f (pervigilo), *a vigil, a religious watching*, Cic

pervĭgĭlĭum -ĭi, n **1,** *a watching throughout the night*, Plin , **2,** *a religious watching, vigil*, castra pervigilio neglecta, Liv , pervigilium celebrare, Tac

pervĭgĭlo, 1 *to watch, remain awake throughout the night*, noctem, Cic

pervīlis -e, *very cheap*, annona, Liv

pervinco -vīci victum, 3 **I.** Intransit , *to gain a complete victory* **A.** Lit , pervicit Vardanes, Tac **B.** Transf , *to carry one's point*, pervicit Cato, Cic **II.** Transit , *to conquer completely, subdue utterly* **A.** Lit , Plaut **B.** Transf , **1,** *to surpass, outdo*, voces pervincunt sonum, Hor , **2,** *to induce, prevail upon, succeed in prevailing*, with ut and the subj , multis rationibus pervicerat Rhodios ut Romanam societatem retinerent Liv , *to bring about with difficulty*, pervicerunt remis ut tenerent terram, Liv , **3,** *to prove, demonstrate*, aliquid dictis, Lucr

pervĭus -a -um (per and via), *passable, accessible, having a road through* **I.** Lit , loca equo pervia, Ov , transitiones, Cic Subst , **pervium** -ĭi, n *a passage*, Tac **II.** Fig , *accessible*, nihil ambitioni pervium, Tac

pervolgo = pervulgo (q v)

pervŏlĭto, 1 (intens of 1 pervolo), *to fly through or round, to flit about*, omnia late loca, Verg

1 **pervŏlo**, 1 **I.** *to fly through, fly round*; **1,** lit , aedes, Verg , iter aerium, Ov , **2,** transf , of any rapid motion, sex millia passuum cisiis, Cic **II.** *to fly to a place*, in hanc sedem, Cic

2 **pervŏlo** -vŏlŭi -velle, *to wish greatly, to be very desirous*, pervelim scire, Cic

pervŏlūto, 1 (intens of pervolvo), *to roll round*, esp , *to unroll, read a book*, libros, Cic.

pervŏlvo -volvi -vŏlūtum, 3 *to roll about*, **I.** Gen , **1,** lit , aliquem in luto, Ter , **2,** fig , ut in iis locis pervolvatur animus, *may be en-*

gaged in, Cic. **II.** *to turn over a book, to read*, Cat.

pervorsē, pervorsio, perverto, etc. = perverse, perversio, perverto, etc. (q.v.).

pervulgātus -a -um, p. adj. (from pervulgo), **1,** *very usual, very common;* consolatio, Cic.; **2,** *well known;* ista maledicta pervulgata in omnes, Cic.

pervulgo (pervolgo), 1. **I.** *to publish, make publicly known:* **1,** res in vulgus pervulgata, Cic.; illas tabulas pervulgari atque edi P. R. imperavi, Cic.; **2,** of a woman, se, *to prostitute herself*, Cic. **II.** *to visit* or *sojourn often in a place*, Lucr.

pēs, pĕdis, m. (πούς), *the foot* (used both of men and animals). **I.** Lit., **1,** calcei apti ad pedem, Cic.; pedem ferre, *to go*, Verg.; pedem portā non efferre, Cic.; pedem referre, Cic., revocare, *to go back, return*, Verg.; pedibus, *on foot*, also *by land*, Cic.; servus a pedibus, *an attendant, lackey*, Cic.; accidere ad pedes alicuius, Cic.; prohibiti estis in provincia vestra pedem ponere, Cic.; pede pulsare terram, *to dance*, Hor.; **2,** esp., **a,** milit. t. t., pedibus merere, *to serve in the infantry*, Liv.; descendere ad pedes (of cavalry), *to dismount*, Liv.; pedem conferre, *to fight hand to hand*, Liv.; **b,** as polit. t. t. (of senators), pedibus ire in sententiam alicuius, *to agree with, support some one's proposal*, Liv.; ne (quis) pedibus iret, *should vote*, Cic.; **3,** fig., sub pedibus, *under the power of*, Liv.; sub pedibus esse or jacere, *to be thought little of*, Ov.; so sub pede ponere, Hor.; pedem opponere, *to withstand*, Ov.; pedem trahere, *to limp* (of iambic verse), Ov.; per me ista trahantur pedibus, *may as far as I am concerned be turned topsy-turvy, may go to the dogs*, Cic.; ante pedes positum esse, *to be before one's feet* or *eyes*, Cic.; circum pedes = circum se, Cic.; ante pedes Manilii, *before Manilius*, Cic.; pes secundus, felix, dexter, *happy* or *fortunate arrival*, Verg., Ov. **II. A.** Transf., **1,** poet., of water, crepante lympha desilit pede, Hor.; of time, tacito pede lapsa vetustas, Ov.; **2, a,** *the foot of a chair, table,* or *other article of furniture*, Tac.; **b,** pes veli, *the rope* or *sheet attached to the lower edge of a sail, by which it was tightened* or *relaxed;* hence, pede aequo, *with fair wind*, Ov.; facere pedem, *to veer out the sheet to catch a side wind*, Verg.; **c,** *the pole on which a litter is carried*, Cat. **B.** Meton., **1,** pedibus vincere, *in a foot-race*, Ov.; **2,** esp., **a,** t. t. of poetry, *a metrical foot*, Cic.; **b,** *a metre, species of verse;* Lesbius, Hor.; **c,** *a foot*, as a measure of length; pedem non egressi sumus, Cic.

pessimus, pessime, v. malus.

Pessinūs (Pĕsinūs) -untis, f. (Πεσσινοῦς, Πεσινοῦς -οῦντος), *one of the most celebrated towns of Galatia, near Mount Dindymus, chief seat of the worship of Cybele,* now *Balahazar* or *Balahissar.* Adj., **Pessinuntius** -a -um, *relating to Pessinus.*

pessŭlus -i, m. (πάσσαλος), *a bolt;* pessulum ostio obdere, Ter.

pessum, adv. (for pedis versum), *to the ground, to the bottom, downwards;* pessum ire, *to sink to the ground*, Cic.; *to be ruined, to perish*, Tac. Esp., **pessum do** (or pessumdo, or pessundo) dĕdi, dătum, dăre, *to let fall to the ground, to destroy, ruin, put an end to*, Sall.; ad inertiam pessum datus est, *sunk into*, Sall.

pestifĕr -fĕra -fĕrum and **pestifĕrus** -a -um (pestis and fero), **1,** *pestiferous, pestilential;* odor corporum, Liv.; **2,** transf., *deadly, fatal, destructive, injurious;* vipera, Cic.; civis, Cic.

pestifĕrē, adv. (pestifer), *balefully, injuriously*, Cic.

pestilens -entis (pestis). **I.** *pestilential, unhealthy;* aedes, Cic.; annus pestilentissimus, Cic. **II.** Transf., *deadly, fatal, noxious;* homo pestilentior, Cic.

pestilentĭa -ae, f. (pestilens), *pestilence, plague, infectious disease.* **I.** Lit., and meton., **1,** lit., causa pestilentiae, Cic.; pestilentiā laborare, Liv.; **2,** meton., *unhealthy air, weather, place;* pestilentiae possessores (of unhealthy places), Cic.; autumni, Caes. **II.** Transf. (moral), *plague, pest*, Cat.

pestĭlitas -ātis, f. = pestilentia (q.v.).

pestis -is, f. **I.** *a pest, pestilence, plague, infectious disease, malaria;* pestem ab Aegypto avertere, Cic. **II.** Transf., **A.** *destruction, ruin, death;* pestem in aliquem machinari, Cic.; illam a republica pestem depellere, Cic. **B.** Meton., *an injurious thing* or *person, a pest, curse, bane;* illae inclusae in republica pestes, Cic.

pĕtăsātus -a -um (petasus), *wearing the petasus* (q.v.) = *equipped for a journey*, Cic.

pĕtăsĭo (pĕtăso) -ōnis, m. (πετασών), *a fore-quarter of pork*, Varr.

pĕtăsuncŭlus -i, m. (dim. of petaso), *a little fore-quarter of pork*, Juv.

pĕtăsus -i, m. (πέτασος), *a broad-brimmed felt hat, used by travellers*, Plaut.

pĕtaurum -i, n. (πέταυρον), *a spring-board used by tumblers and rope-dancers*, Juv.

Pĕtēlĭa (Pĕtīlia) -ae, f. *a town in the Bruttian territory colonised by the Lucanians,* now *Strongoli.* Hence, adj., **Pĕtēlīnus** -a -um, *Petelian.*

pĕtesso (pĕtisso), 3. (peto), *to desire, long for, strive after eagerly;* aliquid, Cic.

pĕtītĭo -ōnis, f. (peto). **I.** *an attack, thrust, blow;* tuas petitiones effugi, Cic.; *an attack in words;* novi omnes hominis petitiones rationesque dicendi, Cic. **II.** Transf., **1,** *a requesting;* **a,** petitio indutiarum, Liv.; **b,** *an application for office, candidature;* consulatūs, Caes.; dare se petitioni, Cic.; **2, a,** *a suit, legal claim*, Cic.; **b,** *a right of claim, a right to bring an action;* cuius sit petitio, Cic.

pĕtītor -ōris, m. (peto), *one who strives after anything.* **I.** *a candidate*, Hor. **II.** *the plaintiff in a civil* or *private suit*, Cic.

pĕtītūrĭo, 4. (desider. of peto), *to desire to become a candidate;* video hominem valde petiturire, Cic.

pĕtītus -ūs, m. (peto), *an inclining towards*, Lucr.

pĕto -īvi and -ĭi -ītum, 3. (root PET, whence impet-o, impes, impetus, Gk. ΠΕΤ, whence πέτο-μαι, πίπτω), *to reach towards.* **I.** Gen., **A.** Lit., **a,** with the hand, *to grasp;* Ilionea petit dextrā, Verg.; **b,** with a weapon, *to fall upon, attack, assail, aim at, thrust at;* caput et collum, Cic.; aliquem telis, Liv.; **c,** with the feet or with other kinds of motion, (α) *to make for, go to, hasten to;* Dyrrhachium, Cic.; loca calidiora, Cic.; caelum pennis, *to fly to*, Ov.; transf.; of inanimate objects, mons petit astra, *rears its head towards*, Ov.; (β) *to go to a person, to approach;* ut te supplex peterem, Verg.; (γ) *to take a certain direction, to take a road;* alium cursum petere, Cic. **B.** Transf., **1,** *to attack, assail:* qui me epistolā petivit, Cic.; aliquem fraude, Liv.; **2,** *to ask, require, claim, beg, beseech, request, entreat;* **a,** alicuius vitam, Cic.; pacem a Romanis, Caes.; with ut and the subj., peto a te ut, etc., Cic.; with subj. alone, abs te peto, efficias ut, etc., Cic.; with ne and the subj., peto a te ne me putes, etc., Cic.; transf., of inanimate objects, quantum res petit, *needs* or *demands*, Cic.; **b,** *to make a claim at* *law, to bring an action, to sue for*: hereditatis possessionem, Cic.; **c**, *to sue for, to solicit*, (α) *to become a candidate for public office*; consulatum, Cic.; (β) *to woo a maiden*, virginem petiere juvenes, Liv.; **3**, *to seek for*, **a**, sedes apibus statioque petenda, Verg.; **b**, *to seek, strive after, endeavour to obtain*: praedam pedibus, Ov.; sapientiam, Cic.; mortem, Cic.; with infin., Verg. **II.** *to fetch, derive*, **1**, lit., **a**, *to fetch*, cibum e flamma, Ter.; **b**, *to fetch, to bring forth*, gemitus alte de corde, Ov.; **2**, transf., a litteris oblivionem, Cic. (petit = petiit, Verg.)

pĕtorrītum (pĕtōrītum) -i, n. *an open, four wheeled Gallic carriage.*

1. **pĕtra** -ae, f. (πετρα), *a stone, rock*, Plin.

2. **Pĕtra** -ae, f. (Πετρα) **I.** *a town in Arabia Petraea, now ruins of Wady Musa.* **II.** *a town in Sicily.* Hence, **Pĕtrīni** -ōrum, m. *the inhabitants of Petra.*

Pĕtrējus -ii, m., M., *a Roman general, legate of Pompey in the Civil War.*

Pĕtrīnum -i, n. *an estate near Sinuessa in Campania.*

Pĕtrŏcŏrii -ōrum, m. *a Gallic tribe in Aquitania, in modern Perigord.*

Pĕtrōnius -ii, m., T. (or C.) Arbiter, *a Roman satirist under Nero.*

pĕtŭlans -antis (*petulo, from peto), *freakish, capricious, pert, wanton, froward, petulant*, and esp., *wanton, lustful*, homo, Cic.; genus dicendi, Cic.

pĕtŭlantĕr, adv. (petulans), *freakishly, capriciously, petulantly, frowardly, wantonly*, petulanter vivere, Cic.; petulantius jactari, Cic.; petulantissime fieri, Cic.

pĕtŭlantĭa -ae, f. (petulans), *capriciousness, freakishness, wantonness, petulance* (opp. pudor, modestia), Cic.

pĕtulcus -a -um (peto), *butting with the head*, agni, Lucr.; haedi, Verg.

Peucĕtĭa -ae, f. *a district of Apulia.* Adj., **Peucĕtĭus** -a -um, *Peucetian.*

pexus -a -um (partic. of pecto), *hairy, woolly, having a nap*; and hence (of a garment), *new*, Hor.

Phacus -i, m. (Φάκος), *stronghold of the Macedonian kings, near Pella.*

Phaeāces -ācum, m. (Φαίακες), *the Phaeacians, mythical inhabitants of the island of Scheria* (identified with *Corcyra*), *famed for their prosperity.* Sing., **Phaeax** -ācis, m. *a Phaeacian*, pinguis Phaeaxque, *a comfortable, luxurious person*, Hor. Hence, **A. Phaeācĭus** -a -um, *Phaeacian.* **B. Phaeācis** -ĭdis, f. *a poem on the stay of Ulysses among the Phaeacians.*

Phaedōn -ōnis, m. (Φαίδων), *disciple of Socrates and friend of Plato, who gave his name to a dialogue on the immortality of the soul.*

Phaedra -ae, f. (Φαίδρα), *daughter of Minos, sister of Ariadne and wife of Theseus; she fell in love with, and was* (by a false accusation) *the cause of the death of, her step-son Hippolytus.*

Phaedrus -i, m. (Φαῖδρος) **I.** *an Epicurean philosopher at Athens, teacher of Cicero.* **II.** *a disciple of Socrates.* **III.** *a freedman of Augustus, Thracian by birth, author of Latin fables.*

Phaestum -i, n. (Φαιστος) **I.** *a town on the south coast of Crete.* Hence, **Phaestĭăs** -ădis, f. *a dweller in Phaestum.* **II.** *a town in Thessaly.*

Phăĕthon -ontis, m. (Φαεθων), *the shining one.* **I.** Epithet of Helios, *the sun.* **II.** *the son of Helios and Clymene, who, attempting to drive the chariot of his father, set the world on fire, and was killed by a thunderbolt of Jupiter.* Hence, **A.** Adj., **Phăĕthontēus** -a -um, *relating to Phaethon.* **B.** Subst., **Phăĕthontĭăs** -ădis, f.; plur., **Phăĕthontĭădes** -um, f. *the sisters of Phaethon, who were turned into poplars.*

Phăĕthūsa -ae, f. (Φαέθουσα), *a sister of Phaethon.*

phăgĕr -gri, m. (φαγρος), *a fish*, Ov.

Phălaecus -i, m. (Φάλαικος), *a tyrant of the Phocaeans.* Hence, adj., **Phălaecēus** -a -um, *of Phalaecus.*

phălangae (pălangae) -ārum, f. (φάλαγγες), *rollers on which heavy bodies were moved*, Caes.

phălangītae -ārum, m. (φαλαγγῖται), *soldiers belonging to a phalanx*, Liv.

Phălantus -i, m. (Φάλαντος), *a Spartan who emigrated to Italy and founded Tarentum*, regnata Laconi rura Phalanto, *the Tarentine territory*, Hor.

phălanx -angis, f. (φάλαγξ) **I.** Gen., *a closely serried array of soldiers*, Verg. **II.** Esp., **a**, *a division of the Athenian and Spartan army drawn up in battle array, a phalanx*, Nep.; **b**, *the Macedonian phalanx, a body of men* (from eight to sixteen thousand strong) *drawn up in a close parallelogram, fifty men abreast and sixteen deep*; **c**, transf., *the order of battle array among the Gauls and Germans drawn up in a parallelogram*, phalange factā, *in close formation*, Cic.

Phălăra -ōrum, n. (Φάλαρα), *a port in Thessaly on the Sinus Maliacus, now Stylidha.*

Phălăris -ĭdis, m. (Φαλαρίς), *a tyrant of Agrigentum, notorious for his cruelty* (v. Perillus).

Phălăsarna -ae, f. (Φαλάσαρνα), *a town in Crete.* Adj., **Phălăsarnēus** -a -um, *of Phalasarna.*

phălĕrae (fălĕrae) -ārum, f. (φάλαρα) **I.** *a metal ornament worn on the breast as a military decoration*, Cic. **II.** *a trapping on a horse's head and breast*, Liv., Verg.

phălĕrātus -a -um (phalerae), *adorned with the phalerae*, equi, Liv.

Phălērum -i, n. (Φαληρον), *the oldest port of Athens, connected with the city by a long wall.* Hence, **A. Phălēreus** -ĕi and -ĕos, m. *belonging to Phalerum*, Demetrius Phalereus, or simply Phalereus, *regent of Athens* (about 300 B.C.). **B. Phălērĭcus** -a -um, *belonging to Phalerum*; subst., **Phălērĭcus** -i, m. (sc. portus), *the harbour of Phalerum.*

Phănae -ārum, f. (Φαναί), *harbour and promontory in the south of Chios, now Cap Mastico, the country near which was famous for its wine*; adj., **Phănaeus** -a -um, *Phanaean*, rex Phanaeus, poet. for *Phanaean wine* (as the king among wines), Verg.

Phantăsos -i, m. (Φαντασος), *a son of Somnus.*

Phăōn -ōnis, m. (Φάων), *a youth of Lesbos, beloved by Sappho.*

phărĕtra -ae, f. (φαρετρα), *a quiver*, Verg.

phărĕtrātus -a -um (pharetra), *furnished with a quiver, wearing a quiver*, virgo, *Diana*, Ov.; puer, *Cupid*, Ov.

pharmăceutrĭa -ae, f. (φαρμακεύτρια), *the sorceress* (title of Vergil's Eighth Eclogue).

phărmăcŏpōla (-ēs) -ae, m. (φαρμακοπώλης), *a seller of drugs, a quack*, Cic.

Pharnăcēs -is, m. (Φαρνάκης), *king in Pontus, son of Mithridates, conquered by Caesar.*

Pharsālus (-ŏs) -i, f. (Φάρσαλος), *a town in Thessaly, near which Pompeius was defeated by Caesar*, 48 B.C., now *Pharsa*. Hence, adj., **Pharsālĭcus** -a -um and **Pharsālĭus** -a -um, *Pharsalian*.

Phărus (-ŏs) -i, f. (Φάρος), *an island off Alexandria, where Ptolemy Philadelphus built a light-house*; adj., **Phărĭus** -a -um, a, *relating to Pharus*; b, *Egyptian*; juvenca, *Io*, Ov.; turba, *the priests of Isis*, Tib.; conjux, *Cleopatra*, Mart.

Phăsēlis -ĭdis, f. (Φασηλίς), *a town in Lycia, on the border of Pamphylia*. Hence, **Phăsēlitae** -ārum, m. *the inhabitants of Phaselis*.

phăsēlus (-ŏs) -i, m. and f. (φάσηλος), **1**, *an edible bean, the kidney-bean*, Verg.; **2**, *a kind of light skiff formed of osiers or papyrus, or burnt and painted clay*, Cic.

Phāsĭs -ĭdis and -ĭdos, m. (Φᾶσις), *a river in Colchis, falling into the Black Sea*, now *Rion* or *Rioni*. Hence, **A. Phāsĭs** -ĭdis, f. adj. *Phasian*, poet. = *Colchian*; volucres, *pheasants*, Mart.; subst., Phasis (sc. femina), *the Colchian woman = Medea*, Ov. **B. Phāsĭăcus** -a -um (Φασιακός), *Phasian*, poet. = *Colchian*. **C. Phāsĭānus (Fāsĭānus)** -a -um, avis, and simply Phasiana, Plin., or Phasianus, Suet., *a pheasant*. **D. Phāsĭăs** -ădis, f. (Φασιάς), *Phasian*, poet. = *Colchian*; puella, and simply Phasias, = *Medea*, Ov.

phasma -ătis, n. (φάσμα), *a ghost, spectre* (title of a comedy of Meander, and of a poem by Catullus), Ter., Juv.

phatnē -ēs, f. (φάτναι), *the Crib, a space between two stars of the constellation Cancer*, Cic.

Phēgeus -ĕi and -ĕos, m. (Φηγεύς), *king of Psophis*. Hence, **A.** Adj., **Phēgēĭus** -a -um, *belonging to Phegeus*. **B.** Subst., **Phēgĭs** -ĭdis, f. *the daughter of Phegeus*.

Phēmĭus -ĭi, m. (Φήμιος), *a celebrated harp-player in Ithaca*; hence, appell., *a good harp-player*, Ov.

Phĕnĕus (-ŏs) -i, f. (Φένεος), *a town in Arcadia*. Hence, **Phĕnĕātae** -ārum, m. *the inhabitants of Pheneos*.

phengītēs -ae, m. (φεγγίτης), *selenite or crystallised gypsum* (used for window panes), Suet.

Phĕrae -ārum, f. (Φέραι). **I.** *a town in Messenia*, near modern *Kalamata*. **II.** *a city in Thessaly, the residence of Admetus and of the tyrant Alexander*, now *Valestino*; hence, adj., **Phĕraeus** -a -um, *Pherean, or Thessalian*; vaccae, *of Admetus*, Ov.; gens, *a cruel race, like that of the tyrant Alexander of Pherae*, Ov.

Phĕrĕclus -i, m. (Φέρεκλος), *a ship-builder who built the ship in which Paris carried off Helen*. Hence, adj., **Phĕrĕclēus** -a -um, *of Phereclus*.

Phĕrĕcȳdēs -is, m. (Φερεκύδης). **I.** *a philosopher of Scyros, teacher of Pythagoras*. Hence, adj., **Phĕrĕcȳdēus** -a -um, *of Pherecydes*. **II.** *an Athenian chronicler*, flor. 480 B.C.

Phĕrēs -ētis, m. (Φέρης), *prince in Thessaly, father of Admetus*. Hence, **Phĕrētĭădēs** -ae, m. *son of Pheres = Admetus*.

phĭăla -ae, f. (φιάλη), *a drinking-vessel*, broad at the bottom, *bowl, saucer*, Juv.

Phīdĭās -ae, m. (Φειδίας), *a celebrated sculptor of Athens, contemporary of Pericles*. Hence, **Phīdĭăcus** -a -um, *of Phidias*.

Phĭlădelphēni (Phĭlădelphīni) -ōrum, m. *the inhabitants of Philadelphia in Asia Minor*.

Philaeni -ōrum, and Gr. -ōn, m. (Φίλαινοι), *two Carthaginian brothers who submitted to be buried alive for the sake of their country*; arae Philaenorum and Philaenon, *a port on the borders of Cyrene*.

Phĭlammōn -ōnis, m. (Φιλάμμων), *son of Apollo and Chione, a celebrated singer*.

Phĭlippi -ōrum, m. (Φίλιπποι), *a city in Macedonia, where Octavianus and Antony defeated Brutus and Cassius*, now *Filibah* or *Filibejik*; hence, adj., **A. Phĭlippensis** -e. **B. Phĭlippĭcus** -a -um, *relating to Philippi*.

Phĭlippŏpŏlis -ĕos, f. (Φιλιππόπολις), *a town in Thrace on the right bank of the Hebrus*, now *Philippopoli*.

Phĭlippus -i, m. (Φίλιππος). **I.** *the names of several kings of Macedon, the most celebrated of whom was the father of Alexander the Great*; meton., *a gold coin coined by Philip*, Hor.; hence, adj., **A. Phĭlippēus** -a -um, *belonging to Philip*; nummus, *a gold coin of King Philip, worth twenty drachmae*. **B. Phĭlippĭcus** -a -um, *relating to Philip*; orationes, *the speeches of Demosthenes against Philip*; subst., **Phĭlippĭcae** -ārum, f. *the speeches of Demosthenes against Philip, and of Cicero against Antonius*. **II.** *a Roman name, cognomen of the gens Marcia*.

Phĭlistus -i, m. (Φίλιστος), *a Greek historian of Syracuse, imitator of Thucydides*.

phĭlītĭa -ōrum, n. (φιλίτια), *the public meals of the Lacedaemonians*, Cic.

Phĭlo -ōnis, m. (Φίλων). **I.** *an academic philosopher*, flourishing at Athens, 91 B.C. **II.** *a celebrated Athenian architect*.

Phĭloctēta (-ēs) -ae, m. (Φιλοκτήτης), *son of Poeas, the companion of Hercules, whose bow and poisoned arrows he received after Hercules' death; joined in the expedition against Troy, but was left behind in the island of Lemnos wounded by a snake; brought to Troy in the tenth year of the war* (as Troy could not be taken without his arrows); *healed by Machaon; slew Paris*. Adj., **Phĭloctētaeus** -a -um, *belonging to Philoctetes*.

phĭlŏlŏgĭa -ae, f. (φιλολογία), *love of learning, study of letters*, Cic.

phĭlŏlŏgus -i, m. (φιλόλογος), *a learned man, a student of literature, a scholar*, Cic.

Phĭlŏmēla -ae, f. (Φιλομήλα). **I.** *the daughter of Pandion, king of Athens, turned into a nightingale*. **II.** Meton., *a nightingale*, Verg.

Phĭlŏmēlĭum -ĭi, n. (Φιλομήλιον), *a small town in the south-east of Phrygia, not far from the borders of Lycaonia*, now *Ak-cher*. Hence, **Phĭlŏmēlĭenses** -ium, m. *the inhabitants of Philomelium*.

Phĭlŏpoemēn -ĕnis, m. (Φιλοποίμην), *general of the Achaean League* (born 253 B.C.).

phĭlŏsŏphĭa -ae, f. (φιλοσοφία). **I.** *philosophy*, Cic. **II.** Meton., **A.** *a philosophical subject*, Nep. **B.** Plur., philosophiae, *philosophical sects or systems*, Cic.

phĭlŏsŏphor, 1. dep. *to philosophise, to apply oneself to philosophy*, Cic.

phĭlŏsŏphus -a -um (φιλόσοφος), *philosophic*. **I.** Adj., Cic. **II.** Subst., **A. phĭlŏsŏphus** -i, m. *a philosopher*, Cic. **B. phĭlŏsŏpha** -ae, f. *a female philosopher*, Cic.

philtrum -i, n. (φίλτρον), *a love-potion, philtre*, Ov.

1. **phĭlȳra** -ae, f. (φιλύρα), *the inner bark of the linden-tree, of which bands for chaplets were made*, Hor.

2 **Philyra** -ae, f (Φιλύρα), *a nymph, daughter of Oceanus, and mother of Chiron, changed into a linden tree* Hence, **A. Philyrēius** -a -um, *relating to Philyra*, heros, *Chiron*, Ov , tecta, *of Chiron*, Ov **B. Philyrides** -ae, m *son of Philyra = Chiron*, Ov

phīmus -i, m (φιμός), *a dice box*, Hor.

Phīnēus -ĕi and -ĕos, m (Φινεύς) **I.** *a king of Salmydessus in Thrace, who was deprived of sight and tormented by the Harpies for having put his sons to death on a false accusation.* Hence, **A. Phīnēius** and **Phīnēus** -a -um, *of or relating to Phineus* **B. Phīnīdēs** -ae m *a male descendant of Phineus* **II.** *brother of Cepheus, fought with Perseus about Andromeda*

Phintĭa -ae, f *a town in Sicily*

Phintĭās -ae, m (Φιντίας), *a Pythagorean, famous for his friendship with Damon*

Phlĕgĕthōn -ontis, m (Φλεγέθων, *burning*), *a river in the infernal regions, in which fire flowed instead of water* adj , **Phlĕgĕthontis** -idis, f *of Phlegethon*, lympha, Ov

Phlĕgra -ae, f (Φλέγρα = φλεγυρά *burning*), *a district in Macedonia, afterwards called Pallene, where the gods were said to have killed the giants with lightning* Hence, adj , **Phlĕgraeus** -a -um, *relating to Phlegra*, campi, Ov , transf , campus, *the field of Pharsalia* (because of the fierce battle fought there), Prop

Phlĕgȳās -ae, m (Φλεγύας) **I.** *king of the Lapithae, father of Ixion and Coronis* **II.** Plur , **Phlĕgȳae** ārum, m *a robber tribe in Thessaly*

Phlīūs -untis, f (Φλιοῦς), *a city in the Peloponnese between Sicyon and Argos* Hence, adj , **Phlīāsius** -a -um, *of Phlius*

Phŏbētŏr ŏris, m (Φοβήτωρ), *a son of Morpheus*

phōca -ae, f and **phōcē** -ēs, f (φώκη), *a seal, sea-dog, sea-calf*, Verg

Phōcaea ae, f (Φώκαια), *a sea-port in Ionia, mother city of Massilia, now Fouges* Hence, **A. Phōcaeensis** -e, *Phocaean* **B. Phōcaei** -ōrum, m *the Phocaeans* **C. Phōcāicus** a -um, *Phocaean*

Phōcis -idis and idos, f (Φωκίς), *Phocis, a district in the north of Greece, between Boeotia and Aetolia* Hence, **1, Phōcăicus** -a um, *Phocian*, **2, Phōcenses** ium m *the inhabitants of Phocis*, **3, Phōcēus** a -um, *Phocian*, juvenis Phoceus, or simply Phoceus, *the Phocian = Pylades, son of Strophius, king of Phocis*, Ov , **4, Phōcii** -ōrum, m *the Phocians*

Phōcus -i, m (Φῶκος), *son of Aeacus, brother of Peleus and Telamon*

Phoebē -ēs, f (Φοίβη) **I. a,** *the sister of Phoebus, the Moon-goddess, Diana*, **b,** meton , *Night*, Ov **II.** *daughter of Leucippus* **III.** *daughter of Leda and sister of Helena*

Phoebĭgĕna ae, m. (Phoebus and geno = gigno), *the son of Phoebus, Aesculapius*, Verg

Phoebus -i, m (Φοῖβος), *Apollo, the Sun-god*, poet = *sun*, fugat astra Phoebus, Hor , and = *quarter of the heavens*, sub utroque Phoebo, *in the east and west*, Ov Hence, **A. Phoebăs** ădis, f (Φοιβάς), *priestess of Phoebus, a prophetess* **B. Phoebēius** a -um and **Phoebēus** -a -um (Φοιβήιος, Φοιβεῖος), *of Phoebus*, juvenis, *Aesculapius*, Ov , ales, *the raven*, Ov., virgo, *Daphne*, and poet = *laurel crown*, Ov

Phoenīcē, v Phoenice.

Phoenīces um, m (Φοίνικες), *the Phoenicians, inhabitants of the district of Phoenicia, famous for their skill in navigation and commerce, founders of several colonies*, Carthage, Hippo, etc. Hence, **A. Phoenīcē** -ēs, f and **Phoenīca** ae, f (Φοινίκη), *Phoenicia, a small strip of the coast of Syria, with the chief towns Tyre and Sidon* **B. Phoenissa** -ae, f (Φοίνισσα), *Phoenician*, exsul, *Anna, sister of Dido*, Ov

phoenīcoptĕros -i, m (φοινικόπτερος), *the flamingo*, Juv

Phoenix -īcis, m (Φοῖνιξ) **I.** *son of Amyntor, companion of Achilles at the Trojan War* **II.** *a fabulous bird of Arabia, said to live 500 years, and then to be burnt to death, from the ashes of the dying bird a new phoenix was said to spring*

Phŏlŏē ēs, f (Φολόη), *a woody mountain in Arcadia, on the border of Elis, now Olona*

Phŏlus i, m (Φόλος), *a centaur*

° **Phorcus** -i, m (Φόρκος), **Phorcȳs** -cȳis m (Φόρκυς), and **Phorcyn** cȳnis, m (Φόρκυν) *a sea god, son of Neptune, father of Medusa and her sisters* Hence, **A. Phorcis** -idos, f *daughter of Phorcys* sorores Phorcides = *Graeae*, Ov **B. Phorcȳnis** idis, f *the daughter of Phorcus, Medusa*

Phŏrōnēus -ĕi and -ĕos, m (Φορωνεύς), *king of Argos, son of Inachus, brother of Io* Hence, **Phŏrōnis** idis, f = *Io*, Ov

Phrăātēs (Phrăhātēs) is, m *name of several Parthian kings*

phrĕnētĭcus -a -um (φρενητικός) and **phrĕnitĭcus** a -um (φρενιτικός), *mad, frantic*, Cic

Phrixus -i, m (Φρίξος), *son of Athamas and Nephele, brother of Helle, with whom he fled to Colchis on a ram with a golden fleece* Hence, adj , **Phrixēus** -a -um, *belonging to Phrixus*, stagna sororis Phrixeae, *the Hellespont*, Ov

Phrȳges -um, m (Φρύγες), *the Phrygians, the inhabitants of Phrygia, famous for their embroidery, but despised for their sloth and stupidity* Sing , **Phryx** -ȳgis, adj = *Phrygian*, subst , *a Phrygian*, esp , **a,** = *Aeneas*, Ov , **b,** = *a priest of Cybele*, Prop Hence, **A. Phrȳgĭa** -ae, f *the country of Phrygia, in Asia Minor* **B. Phrȳgĭus** -a -um (Φρύγιος), *Phrygian*, and poet = *Trojan*, maritus, *Aeneas*, Ov , *Pelops*, Prop , pastor, *Paris*, Verg , tyrannus, *Aeneas*, Verg Ov , *Laomedon*, Ov , mater *Cybele*, Verg , vestes, *embroidered*, Verg , buxum, *the Phrygian flute*, Ov , lapis, *Phrygian marble*, Ov.

1 **Phryx** -ȳgis m (Φρύξ), *a river in Lydia, now Ouletshuk-Su*

2 **Phryx,** v Phryges

Phryxēus, v Phrixus

Phthīa -ae, f (Φθία) *a town in Thessaly, birth place of Achilles* Hence, **A. Phthĭās** ădis f (Φθιάς), *a woman of Phthia* **B. Phthĭōtēs** -ae, m (Φθιώτης), *an inhabitant of Phthia* **C. Phthĭōtis** -idis, f (Φθιῶτις), *Phthiotis, the district of Thessaly in which Phthia is* **D. Phthĭōtĭcus** -a -um (Φθιωτικός), meton = *Thessalian* **E. Phthīus** -a, m (Φθῖος), *belonging to Phthia*, rex, *Peleus*, Ov , meton = *Thessalian*, Liv

Phȳlăcē -ēs, f (Φυλάκη) **I.** *a city in Thessaly, where Protesilaus reigned* Hence, **A. Phȳlăcēis** -idis, f *belonging to Phylace*, matres, *Thessalian*, Ov. **B. Phȳlăcēius** a -um, conjux, *Laodamia*, Ov. **II.** *a town in Molossis in Epirus*

Phȳlăcus i, m (Φύλακος) **I.** *founder of Phylace* **II.** *grandfather of Protesilaus* Hence,

Phy̆lăcĭdēs -ae, m. (φυλακίδης), *a descendant of Phylacus = Protesilaus*, Ov.

phy̆larchus -i, m. (φύλαρχος), *the head of a tribe, an emir*; Arabum, Cic.

Phyllŏs -i, f. (Φύλλος), *town in Thessaliotis*. Hence, **Phyllēĭus** -a -um (Φυλλήιος), poet. = *Thessalian*; juvenis, *Caeneus*, Ov.

phy̆sĭca -ae, f. and **phy̆sĭcē** -ēs, f. (φυσική), *physics, natural science*, Cic.

phy̆sĭcē, adv. *in the manner of the natural philosophers*; dicere, Cic.

phy̆sĭcus -a -um, *relating to physics or natural philosophy, physical*. **A.** Adj., ratio, Cic. **B.** Subst., **1**, **phy̆sĭcus** -i, m. *a natural philosopher*, Cic.; **2**, **phy̆sĭca** -ōrum, n. *natural philosophy, physics*, Cic.

physĭognōmōn -ŏnis, m. (φυσιογνώμων), *a physiognomist, one who judges men's characters by their features*, Cic.

phy̆sĭŏlŏgĭa -ae, f. (φυσιολογία), *natural philosophy*, Cic.

pĭābĭlis -e (pio), *expiable, that can be atoned for*; fulmen, Ov.

pĭācŭlāris -e (piaculum), *atoning, expiating*; sacrificia, and subst., **pĭācŭlārĭa** -ium, n. *expiatory sacrifices*, Liv.

pĭācŭlum -i, n. (pio). **I.** *any means of expiating sin or appeasing a deity*. **A.** *an expiatory sacrifice, a sin-offering*, Cic.; porco feminā piaculum pati, Cic.; transf., ut luendis periculis publicis piacula simus, Liv.; hence, *any means of healing, remedy*, Hor. **B.** *punishment*; gravia piacula exigere, Liv. **II.** *that which renders an offering necessary, a sin, crime, evil deed*; piaculum committere, Liv.

pĭāmen -inis, n. (pio), *a means of atonement or expiation*, Ov.

pīca -ae, f. *a pie, magpie*, Ov.

pĭcārĭa -ae, f. (pix), *a place where pitch is made, a pitch-hut*, Cic.

pĭcĕa -ae, f. (pix), *the pitch-pine* (pinus silvestris, Linn.), Verg.

Pīcēnum -i, n. *a district in the east of Italy on the Adriatic, famed for its oil*. Hence, **A.** **Pīcens** -entis, *belonging to Picenum*; **Pīcentes** -ium, m. *the people of Picenum*. **B.** **Pīcēnus** -a -um, *belonging to Picenum*.

pĭcĕus -a -um (pix), *pitchy, pitch-black*; caligo, Verg.

pĭco, 1. (pix), *to pitch, smear, cover with pitch*; cadus picatus, Verg.

Pictŏnes -um, m. *a people in Gallia Aquitania*, whence *Poitou*.

1. **pictor** -ōris, m. (pingo), *a painter*, Cic.

2. **Pictor** -ōris, m. *a surname in the gens Fabia*, v. Fabius.

pictūra -ae, f. (pingo). **I.** **A.** Lit., *painting, the art of painting*; ars ratioque picturae, Cic. **B.** Meton., *a painting, picture*; pictura textilis, *embroidery*, Cic. **II.** Fig., *a painting in words, picture, description*, Cic.

pictūrātus -a -um (pictura), *painted*; vestes, *embroidered*, Verg.

pictus -a -um, p. adj. (from pingo). **I.** Of style, *ornamental, ornate, artistic*; genus orationis, Cic. **II.** *unreal, vain*; metus, Prop.

1. **pīcus** -i, m. *a woodpecker*, Ov.

2. **Pīcus** -i, m. (Πῖκος), *an Italian deity, husband of Canens, father of Faunus; according to a later legend, changed by Circe into a woodpecker*.

pĭē, adv. (pius), *piously, dutifully* (opp. scelerate), Cic.

Pĭĕrĭa -ae, f. (Πιερία), *a district of Macedonia on the coast*.

Pĭĕrus (-ŏs) -i, m. (Πίερος). **I.** *king of Emathia, who gave his nine daughters the name of the nine Muses*. **II.** *a Macedonian, father of the nine Muses*. Hence, **A.** **Pĭĕrĭs** -ĭdis, f. (Πιερίς), *a Muse*. Plur., Pierides, *the Muses*. **B.** **Pĭĕrĭus** -a -um, *Pierian*; subst., Pieriae, *the Muses*, Cic.; hence, poet., via, *the study of poetry*, Ov.; modi, *poems*, Hor.

pĭĕtas -ātis, f. (pius), *dutifulness*. **I.** Lit., **a**, *towards the gods, piety*; est pietas justitia adversus deos, Cic.; **b**, *dutifulness towards parents, native country, benefactors; filial piety, gratitude, patriotism*; quid est pietas nisi voluntas grata in parentes? Cic.; in patrem patriamque, Liv.; **c**, *justice, equity*, Verg.; **d**, *kindness, compassion*, Verg. **II.** Pietas, personif. as *a goddess with two temples in Rome*.

pĭger -gra -grum (root PIG, whence piget), *disinclined, unwilling, lazy, slothful*. **I.** Lit., serpens frigore pigra, Ov.; with in and the abl., in labore militari, Cic.; with ad and the acc., gens pigerrima ad militaria opera, Liv.; with genit., militiae, Hor.; with infin., ferre laborem scribendi. **II.** Transf., **A.** *inactive, slow*; bellum, tedious, Ov.; campus, *unfruitful*, Hor.; pectora, *insensible*, Ov. **B.** Of waters, *flowing slowly, sluggish, stagnant*; palus, Ov.

pĭget -gŭit -gĭtum est, 2. impers. **I.** Lit., *it causes annoyance, it disgusts*; with acc. of pers. and genit. of thing, me pigeat stultitiae meae, Cic.; with infin., referre piget, Liv.; absol., oratione multitudo inducitur ad pigendum, Cic. **II.** Transf., **1**, *it repents*; illa me composuisse piget, *I repent that I*, etc., Ov.; **2**, *it causes shame*; with infin., fateri pigebat, Liv.

pigmentārĭus -ii, m. (pigmentum), *a seller of paints and unguents*, Cic.

pigmentum -i, n. (pingo), *a paint, colour, pigment*. **I.** Lit., aspersa temere pigmenta in tabula, Cic. **II.** Transf., of discourse, *ornament, decoration*; pigmenta Aristotelia, Cic.

pignĕro, 1. (pignus), *to give as a pledge, put in pledge, mortgage*; bona, Liv.; transf., quum velut obsidibus datis pigneratos haberent animos, Liv.

pignĕror, 1. dep. (pignus). **I.** *to take in pledge, appropriate as one's own*; Mars fortissimum quemque pignerari solet, Cic. **II.** *to accept as a pledge of certainty*; quod das mihi pigneror omen, *I take as a pledge of the fulfilment of my prayer*, Ov.

pignus -nŏris and -nĕris, n. (root PAG, pango, perf. pe-pig-i), *a pledge, pawn, security*. **I.** Lit., **A.** Gen., se pignori opponere, Plaut.; rem alicuius pignori accipere, Tac.; esp., *a security to enforce attendance of senators in the senate*; senatores pignoribus cogere, Cic. **B.** Esp., **1**, *a wager, bet, stake*; pignore certare cum aliquo, Verg.; **2**, *a pledge of love*, used of children and parents; pignora conjugum ac liberorum, Liv. **II.** Fig., *a pledge, token, assurance, proof*; voluntatis, injuriae, Cic.

pĭgrĭtĭa -ae, f. and **pĭgrĭtĭes** -ēi, f. (piger), *sluggishness, sloth, indolence*, Cic.; militandi, Liv.; ad sequendum, Liv.

pĭgro, 1. (piger), *to be sluggish, slothful, lazy*, Lucr.

pĭgror, 1. dep. (piger), *to be slow, sluggish*; with infin., scribere ne pigrere, Cic.

1. **pīla** -ae, f. (for pisula, from piso), *a mortar*, Ov.

2. **pīla** -ae, f. (for pigula, from pango), *a pillar*; nulla meos habeat pila libellos = *a bookstall*, books being sold in Rome round pillars of

buildings, Hor ; collect , saxea pila, *a pier or mole in the sea*, Verg

3 **pila** -ae, f *a ball* **I.** Lit , *a ball to play with*, pilā ludere, Cic , prov , claudus pilam, *one who cannot make a right use of a thing* Cic , meton , *a game at ball*, quantum alii tribuunt alveolo, quantum pilae, Cic **II.** Transf , *any ball or sphere-shaped substance, a balloting ball*, Prop

pilānus -i, m (pilum) = triarius (q v)

pilātus a -um (pilum), *armed with the pilum or javelin*, Verg

pilěātus -a -um (pileus), *wearing the pileus or felt cap*, fratres, *Castor and Pollux*, Cat , pileati epulati sunt, Liv , used of freedmen (slaves at their emancipation receiving the pileus), coloni, Liv , rex, Liv

pilentum -i, n *a carriage, coach*, esp used by Roman ladies, Liv

pilěŏlus -i, m and **pilěŏlum** i, n (dim of pileus), *a little cap, skull cap*, Hor

pilěus -i, m and **pilěum** -i, n (πῖλος), *a felt cap, fitting close to the head, worn at feasts, especially the Saturnalia, and by slaves in token of manumission*, Liv , servos ad pileos vocare, *to summon the slaves to freedom*, Liv

pilo, 1. (1 pilus), *to deprive of hair, make bald*, Mart

pilōsus -a -um (1 pilus), *covered with hair, hairy*, genae, Cic

pilum -i, n (piso, pinso), **1,** *a pestle*, Plin , **2,** *the short pike or javelin of the Roman infantry, used as a missile*, Cic , Liv , pila Horatia, *a place in Rome on the forum*, Liv

Pīlumnus -i, m *husband of Danae, father of Daunus, ancestor of Turnus*

1 **pīlus** -i, m *a single hair*, munitae sunt palpebrae vallo pilorum, Cic , fig , *a trifle* (usually with a negative), ego ne pilo quidem minus me amabo, *not a hair less*, Cic , non facit pili cohortem, Cat

2 **pīlus** -i, m (pilum) **I.** *a maniple of the triarii in the Roman army* primi pili centurio, Caes , aliquem ad primum pilum transducere, *to promote to be chief centurion*, Caes , primum pilum ducere, *to be the centurion of the first maniple of the triarii*, Caes **II.** Meton = *the centurion of the triarii*, primus pilus, *the centurion of the first maniple of the triarii* (the first of the sixty centurions of the legion), Liv

Pimpla -ae, f (Πίμπλα), *a place in Pieria, with a mountain and spring, sacred to the Muses* Hence, **A. Pimplēïs (Piplēïs)** -idis, f *a Muse*, Hor **B. Pimplēus** -a -um *sacred to the Muses*, mons, Cat. Subst , **Pimplēa** ae, f *a Muse*, Hor

pīnă = 2 pinna (q v)

Pīnārĭus a um, *name of a Roman gens The Pinarii and Potitii were the priests of Hercules at Rome*

Pindărus i, m (Πίνδαρος), *a celebrated lyric poet of Thebes in Boeotia, contemporary with Aeschylus* Adj , **Pindărĭcus** a -um, *of Pindar, Pindaric*

Pindĕnissus -i, f (Πινδένισσος), *a town in Sicily*, hence, **Pindĕnissītae** ārum, m *the inhabitants of Pindenissus*

Pindus -i, m (Πίνδος), *a mountain in Thessaly*, now *Mezzara*

pīnētum -i, n (pinus), *a pine wood*, Ov

pīnĕus a -um (pinus), *made of pine wood or deal*, claustra, *the wooden horse of Troy*, Verg ; plaga, *places where pines grow*, Verg , pineus ardor, *a fire of pine wood*, Verg

pingo, pinxi, pictum, 3 *to paint* **I.** Lit , **A. 1,** *to paint* hominis speciem, Cic **2,** esp , *to embroider*, with or without acu, Cic , toga picta, *the embroidered robe of the triumphing general*, Liv , picti reges, *clad in embroidered garments*, Mart **B** Transf , **1,** *to stain, dye, colour* , frontem moris, Verg , **2,** *to decorate, adorn* , bibliothecam, Cic **II.** Fig of speech, *to embellish, depict eloquently* , Britanniam pingam coloribus tuis penicillo meo, Cic

pinguesco, 3 (pinguis), *to become fat, grow fertile*, sanguine pinguescere campos, Verg

pinguis e (πίων), *fat* **I.** Lit , **a,** of animals, Thebani, Cic , pinguior agnus, Plaut Subst , **pingue** -is, n *fatness, fat*, Verg , **b,** of things, merum or vinum, *oily*, Hor , ara, *covered with fat of victims*, Verg , of soil, *rich*, pinguior campus, Hor **II.** Transf , **1,** *besmeared*, crura luto Juv , **2,** *thick, gross*, caelum, *air*, Cic , **3,** *without understanding heavy, stupid*, ingenium, Ov , **4,** of speech, *bombastic*, poetae pingue quiddam ... tes, Cic , **5,** *quiet, undisturbed*, somnus, Ov , amor, Ov

pīnĭfĕr -fĕra -fĕrum (pinus and fero), *producing pines*, Verg

pīnĭgĕr -gĕra -gĕrum (pinus and gero), *producing pines*, Ov

1 **pinna** ae, f (another form of penna), *a feather* **I. A.** Lit , *a feather*, and plur , *feathers*, esp , *the feathers in the wings and tail*, Tac **B.** Meton , **1,** = *the wing* praepetibus pennis, Cic , prov , alicui incidere pinnas, Cic **2,** poet = *flight*, Ov , **3,** *an arrow*, Ov **II.** Transf , **1,** *the fin of a fish*, Ov , **2,** *the battlement along the top of a wall*, Caes

2 **pinna (pīna)** -ae, f (πίννα), *a species of mussel*, Cic

pinnātus a -um (pinna), *feathered, winged*, Cic

pinnĭgĕr gĕra -gĕrum (pinna and gero), *having feathers, feathered, winged*, Lucr , transf , piscis, *having fins*, Ov

pinnĭrăpus -i, m (pinna and rapio), *a gladiator who fought against a Samnite having a peak to his helmet*, Juv

pinnŭla ae, f (dim of pinna) lit , *a small feather* , plur , meton , *small wings*, Cic

pīnŏtērēs (pīnŏthērās) -ae, m (πιννοτήρης), *the pinna-guard, a small crab found in the shell of the pinna*

pinso, pinsi and pinsŭi, pinsum, pinsĭtum, pistum and pisum 3 (root PIS, whence piso, Gk πίσσω, πτίσσω), *to stamp, pound, crush*, Plaut

pīnus -i and ūs, f (for pic-nus from pix, picis), *the pine, fir* (pinus silvestris, Linn) **A.** Lit , Verg **B** Meton = *something made of pine wood* , **a,** *a ship*, Verg , **b,** *a torch*, Verg , **c,** *a garland of pine-leaves*, Ov

pio, 1 (pius) **I.** *to seek to appease by an offering, to appease, propitiate* , Silvanum lacte, Hor **II.** Transf **A.** *to pay religious honours to, venerate*, Prop **B.** *to cleanse, purify*, Cic **C.** *to make good, atone for* , damna, Ov , fulmen, *to avert the misfortune portended by lightning*, Ov , nefas triste, Verg , culpam morte, Verg

pĭper, pĭpĕris, n (πέπερι), *pepper*, Hor

pīpĭlo, 1 *to twitter, chirp*, Cat

pīpŭlus i, m and **pīpŭlum** -i, n *a chirping*, hence, *an outcry, upbraiding*, Plaut

Pīraeēus -ĕi, m (Πειραιεύς), and **Pīraeus** i, m *the Piraeus, a port of Athens, connected with the city by long walls*, poet form in neut plur , Piraea tuta, Ov Adj , **Pīraeus** -a um, *belonging to the Piraeus*

pīrāta -ae, m. (πειρατής), *a pirate, corsair*, Cic.

pīrātĭcus -a -um (πειρατικός), *piratical*; myoparo, Cic.; subst., **pīrātĭca** -ae, f. *piracy*; piraticam facere, Cic.

Pīrēnē -ēs, f. (Πειρήνη), *a spring in Corinth, sacred to the Muses*. Hence, **Pīrēnĭs** -ĭdis, f. (Πειρηνίς), *Pirenian*; Pirenis Ephyre, *Corinth*, Ov.

Pīrĭthŏus -i, m. (Πειρίθοος), *son of Ixion, king of the Lapithae, husband of Hippodamia, friend of Theseus, with whom he went down to the lower world to carry off Proserpina*.

pĭrum -i, n. *a pear*, Verg.

pĭrus -i, f. *a pear-tree*, Verg.

Pīrustae -ārum, m. (Πιροῦσθαι), *an Illyrian robber-tribe*.

Pīsa -ae, f. (Πίσα), and **Pīsae** -ārum, f. **I.** *a town in Elis on the river Alpheus, where the Olympian games were held*. Hence, **Pīsaeus** -a -um, *Pisaean*; Arethusa, *because she came originally from Elis*, Ov.; hasta, *of Oenomaus*, Ov.; subst., **Pīsaea** -ae, f. = *Hippodamia*, Ov. **II. Pīsae** -ārum, f. *a town in Etruria, famous for its baths (now Pisa), said to be a colony of Pisa in Elis*. Hence, **Pīsānus** -a -um, *Pisan*.

Pīsandrus (-ŏs) -i, m. (Πείσανδρος), *son of Polyctor, one of the suitors of Penelope*.

Pĭsaurum -i, n. *a town in Umbria*, now *Pesaro*. Hence, adj., **Pĭsaurensis** -e, *Pisaurian*.

Pĭsaurus -i, m. *a river in Umbria, near Pisaurum*, now *Foglia*.

piscārĭus -a -um (piscis), *of or belonging to fish*; forum, *the fish-market*, Plaut.

piscātor -ōris, m. (piscor), *a fisherman, angler*, Cic.

piscātōrĭus -a -um (piscator), *of or relating to fishermen and fishing*; navis, *a fishing-smack*, Caes.; forum, *fish-market*, Liv.

piscātus -ūs, m. (piscor). **I.** *a fishing, catching of fish*, Cic. **II.** Meton., *fish*, Plaut.

piscĭcŭlus -i, m. (dim. of piscis), *a little fish*, Cic.

piscīna -ae, f. (piscis). **I.** *a tank for keeping fish, fish-pond*; mullos exceptare de piscina, Cic. **II.** Transf., **1**, *a tank for bathing, swimming-bath*, Plin.; **2**, *a reservoir*, Plin.

piscīnārĭus -ii, m. (piscina), *one fond of fish-ponds*, Cic.

piscis -is, m. *a fish*. **I.** Lit., pisces capere, Cic.; sing., used collectively, Ov. **II.** Transf., Pisces, *the sign of the zodiac so called*, Ov.; pisces gemini or gemelli, Ov.; piscis aquosus, Verg.

piscor, 1. dep. (piscis), *to fish*; ante hortulos alicuius, Cic.

piscōsus -a -um (piscis), *abounding in fish*; amnis, Ov.

piscŭlentus = piscosus (q.v.).

Pīsĭda -ae, m. (Πισίδης), *a Pisidian*; plur., Pisidae, *the Pisidians, inhabitants of Pisidia*. Hence, **Pīsĭdĭa** -ae, f. (Πισιδία), *a district in Asia Minor bordering on the east on Cilicia, on the north and west on Phrygia, Caria, and Lycia, on the south on Pamphylia*.

Pīsistrătus -i, m. (Πεισίστρατος), *tyrant at Athens, contemporary of Servius Tullius*. Hence, **Pīsistrătĭdae** -ārum, m. (Πεισιστρατίδαι), *the sons of Pisistratus*.

1. **pīso**, v. pinso.

2. **Pīso** -ōnis, m. *a surname in the gens Calpurnia*, v. *Calpurnius*.

pistillum -i, n. or **pistillus** -i, m. (pinso), *a pestle*, Plaut.

pistor -ōris, m. (pinso). **I.** *a grinder, miller*, Plaut. **II.** *a baker*, Cic.; Pistor, *surname of Jupiter*.

Pistōrĭum -ii, n. *a town in Etruria*, now *Pistoja*. Hence, **Pistōrĭensis** -e, *relating to Pistorium*.

pistrilla -ae, f. (dim. of pistrina), *a small mortar or mill*, Ter.

pistrīna -ae, f. (pinso), *a bakehouse*, Plin.

pistrīnum -i, n. (pinso), *a mill* (usually worked by horses and asses, though sometimes by slaves as a punishment); homo pistrino dignus, Ter.; transf., tibi mecum in eodem est pistrino vivendum, *in the same drudgery*, Cic.

pistris = pristis (q.v.).

pīsum -i, n. (πίσον), *the pea, pease*, Plin.

Pĭtănē -ēs, f. (Πιτάνη), *a town in Asia Minor*, now *Sandarlik*.

Pĭthēcūsa -ae, f. and **Pĭthēcūsae** -ārum, f. (Πιθηκοῦσα, Πιθηκοῦσαι), *an island in the Tyrrhene Sea, near Cumae*, now *Ischia*.

Pittăcus (-ŏs) -i, m. (Πίττακος), *a philosopher of Mitylene, one of the Seven Wise Men*.

Pittheūs -ĕi and -ĕos, m. (Πιτθεύς), *king in Troezen, father of Aethra, who was the wife of Aegeus and mother of Theseus*. Hence, **A. Pitthŏĭs** -ĭdos, f. (Πιτθηΐς), *a daughter of Pittheus = Aethra*, Ov. **B. Pitthēĭus** and **Pitthēus** -a -um, *belonging to Pittheus*.

pītŭīta -ae, f. *phlegm, rheum*; quum pituita redundat, Cic.

pītŭītōsus -a -um (pituita), *full of phlegm*; homo, Cic.

pitysma = pytisma (q.v.).

pĭus -a -um (superl. pissimus, condemned by Cicero). **I.** *acting dutifully, dutiful, pious*; **a**, *upright, God-fearing, virtuous*; homo, Cic.; pii, "*the blessed dead*," Cic.; transf., of things or actions, *upright*; pax, Cic.; subst., justum piumque, *justice and equity*, Ov.; pium est, with infin., Ov.; **b**, *affectionate towards one's parents, benefactors, relations, native country*, etc., *grateful, patriotic, obedient*; in parentes, Cic.; adversus sororem, Liv. **II.** Esp. (like φίλος), *kind, gentle*; pia testa (of wine), Hor.

pix, pĭcis, f. (πίσσα), *pitch*; aliquid pice linere, Liv.

plācābĭlis -e (placo), *easy to be appeased, easy of propitiation, placable*; homines, Cic.: with ad and the acc., placabile ad justas preces ingenium, Liv.; poet., transf., ara Dianae, Verg.

plācābĭlĭtas -ātis, f. (placabilis), *placability*, Cic.

plācāmen -ĭnis, n. (placo), *a means of appeasing, propitiating*; placamina irae, Liv.

plācāmentum -i, n. (placo), *a means of appeasing*, Tac.

plācātē, adv. (placatus), *calmly, composedly*; omnia humana placate et moderate ferre, Cic.

plācātĭo -ōnis, f. (placo), *a soothing, appeasing, propitiating*; deorum, Cic.

plācātus -a -um, p. adj. (from placo). **I.** *soothed, appeased, placable*; placatiore eo et suā et regis spe invento, Liv. **II.** *calm, gentle, quiet*; vita, Cic.; quies placatissima, Cic.; transf., mare, Verg.

plăcenta -ae, f. (πλακοῦς), *a cake*, Hor.

Plăcentĭa -ae, f. *a town in Gallia Cispadana*, now *Piacenza*. Hence, **Plăcentīnus** -a -um, *Placentine*.

plăcĕo -ŭi -ĭtum, 2 (root PLAC, cf. placo), *to please, be agreeable, acceptable to* **I.** Gen., **a**, of persons, velle placere alicui, Cic.; placere sibi, *to please, be satisfied with oneself*, Cic.; middle perf., placitus sum, *I am pleased*, Ov.; **b**, of things, placet hoc tibi? *does this please you?* Cic.; foll. by quod, sibi non placere quod tam cupide elaborasset, Nep. **II.** Esp., **A.** Of actors and artists, *to please, to win applause*, admodum placere in tragoediis, Cic. **B.** placet, with or without dat. of pers., *it pleases, it seems good, it is the opinion of, I hold*, **a**, ut doctissimis placuit, Cic.; with ut and the subj., his placuit ut tu in Cumanum venires, Cic.; with infin., nec mihi ipsi placebat diutius abesse, Cic.; with acc. and infin., placet Stoicis homines hominum causā esse generatos, Cic.; as a parenthesis, si placet, Cic.; si dis placet, Liv.; **b**, as legal t. t., *to seem good, resolve, order, command*, with ut and the subj., senatui placere ut, etc., Cic.; with acc. and infin., suggestum adornari placuit, Liv.

plăcĭdē, adv. (placidus), *quietly, gently, composedly, placidly*; ferre dolorem, Cic.

plăcĭdus -a -um (placeo), *quiet, still, placid, gentle*; reddere aliquem placidum, Cic.; senatus, Cic.; amnis, Ov.; placidior civitas, Liv.; placidissima pax, Cic.

plăcĭtum, v. placitus.

plăcĭtus -a -um, p. adj. (from placeo). **I.** Adj., *pleasing, pleasant, agreeable*; amor, Verg.; locus, Sall. **II.** Subst., **plăcĭtum** -i, n. **A.** *that which pleases one*; ultra placitum, *more than is agreeable*, Verg. **B.** *opinion, teaching*; placita maiorum, Tac.

plāco, 1 (causat. of placeo, as sedo of sedeo, connected with planus), *to soothe, appease, calm*. **I.** Lit., aequora tumida, Verg. **II.** Transf., *to assuage, reconcile, appease*; animum, animos, Cic.; aliquem, Cic.; aliquem alicui, Cic.; homo sibi ipse placatus, *of a quiet mind*, Cic.; transf., ventrem, Hor.

1. **plāga** -ae, f. (πληγή), *a blow, stroke*. **I.** Gen., Cic.; plagam ferre, Verg. **II.** Esp., *a stroke that wounds*, and meton. = *the wound itself*, plagam accipere, Cic.; infligere, imponere, Cic.; fig., oratio parem plagam facit, Cic.; levior est plaga ab amico, Cic.

2. **plăga** -ae, f. (root PLAC, whence placentum, Gr. ΠΛΑΚ, πλάξ), *a flat surface*. **I.** *a net for hunting boars and similar animals*, **1**, lit., plagas tendere, Cic.; in plagam cadere, Ov.; **2**, fig., *a net, snare, toil*; quas plagas ipsi contra se Stoici texuerunt, Cic.; Antonium conieci in Octaviani plagas, Cic. **II.** *a district, zone, tract, region*; caeli, Cic.; aetheria, *the air*, Verg.; quatuor plagae, *the four zones*, Verg.

plăgĭārĭus -ii, m. *a man stealer, kidnapper*, Cic.; hence, in jest, *a literary thief, plagiarist*, Mart.

plāgōsus -a -um (1. plaga), *fond of flogging*; Orbilius, Hor.

plăgŭla -ae, f. (dim. of 2. plaga), *a curtain, bed-curtain*, Liv.

Planasia -ae, f. (Πλανασία), *an island south of Elba in the Ligurian Sea, now Pianosa, place of banishment under the emperors*.

Plancius -a -um, *name of a Roman gens, the most celebrated member of which was Cn. Plancius, whom Cicero defended when tried for bribery*.

planctus -ūs, m. (plango), *a loud noise as of beating*, esp., *beating the breast, wailing, lamentation*; planctus et lamenta, Tac.

Plancus -i, m. (= πλατύπους, *broad footed*), *a family of the gens Munatia*.

plānē, adv. (planus). **I.** *plainly, simply, intelligibly*; loqui, Cic.; planius dicere, Cic.; planissime explicare, Cic. **II.** *wholly, entirely, quite, thoroughly*; plane eruditus, Cic.; si plane occidimus, Cic.; plane nihil sapit, Cic.

plango, planxi, planctum, 3 (root PLAC, Gk. ΠΛΑΓ, whence πλήσσω), *to beat, strike with a loud noise*. **I.** tympana palmis, Cat.; litora planguntur fluctu, Ov. **II.** Esp., *to strike the breast, head, etc., as a sign of grief*; pectora, Ov.; femur, Ov.; lacertos, Ov. **B.** Transf., as κόπτεσθαι, refl. plangere, middle plangi, *to bewail loudly*; planguntur matres, Ov.; agmina plangentia, Verg.

plangor -ōris, m. (plango), *a striking or beating accompanied by noise*. **I.** Gen., Ov. **II.** Esp., *the beating of the head and breast in token of grief, loud lamentation*; plangore et lamentatione implere, complere forum, Cic.; plangorem dare, Ov.

plangunculă -ae, f. (dim. of πλαγγών), *a wax doll*, Cic.

plānĭpes -pĕdis, m. (planus and pes), *a mime who played the part of slaves, etc., and wore no shoes*, Juv.

plānĭtas -ātis, f. (planus), *plainness, distinctness*, Tac.

plānĭtĭa -ae, f. and **plānĭtĭes** -ēi, f. (planus), *level surface, a plain*, Cic.

planta -ae, f. **I.** *a green twig, cutting, graft*, **a**, of the vine, Cic.; of trees, Verg.; **b**, *a slip for transplanting*, Ov. **II.** *the sole of the foot*, with or without pedis, Verg.

plantārĭa -ium, n. (planta), *young trees, slips*, Verg.

1. **plānus** -a -um (root PLA, whence placo), *level, flat*. **I.** Lit., locus, Cic.; filum, *thick*, Ov. Subst., **plānum** -i, n. *a plain, level ground*, Sall., Liv.; fig., via vitae plana et stabilis, Cic.; de plano, *easily, without trouble*, Lucr. **II.** Transf., *plain, clear, intelligible*; narratio, Cic.; planum facere, *to explain*, foll. by acc. and infin., Cic.

2. **plănus** -i, m. (πλάνος), *a vagrant, juggler, charlatan*, Cic.

Plătaeae -ārum, f. (Πλαταιαί), *a town in Boeotia, famed for a victory of the Greeks over the Persians (479 B.C.), now Palaeo-Castro*. Hence, **Plătaeenses** -ium, m. *the inhabitants of Plataea*.

plătălĕa -ae, f. *a water-bird, the spoonbill*, Cic.

plătănus -i, f. (πλάτανος), *the plane tree*, Cic.; caelebs, *not used to train the vine on* (like the elm), Hor.

plătēa -ae, f. (πλατεῖα), *a street*, Caes.

Plăto (-ōn) -ōnis, m. (Πλάτων). **I.** *a celebrated Greek philosopher, disciple of Socrates, founder of the Academic philosophy*. Hence, **Plătōnĭcus** -a -um, *Platonic*; homo, transf. = *a deep thinker*, Cic. Plur. subst., **Plătōnĭci** -ōrum, m. *the Platonists*, Cic. **II.** *an Epicurean of Sardis, living at Athens, in 59 B.C.*

plaudo (plōdo), plausi (plōsi), plausum (plōsum), 3. **I.** Intransit., *to clap, strike, beat*. **A.** Gen., alis, Verg.; pennis, Ov.; rostro, Ov. **B.** Esp., *to clap the hands in token of applause*, **a**, lit., manus in plaudendo consumere, Cic.; impers., huic ita plausum est ut, etc., Cic.; esp. in the theatre, plaudite (said at the end of a piece), Hor.; **b**, transf., *to give signs of approval, applaud, to approve*, ingeniis sepultis, Hor.; dis hominibusque plaudentibus, Cic.; hence plur., sibi, Hor. **II.** Transit., **A.** *to beat, clap*; pectora manu, Ov.; plausa colla equorum, Verg.; pedibus choreas, *to dance, stamping with* *the fist*, Verg B. *to strike together*, plausis alis, Ov

plausibilis e (plaudo), *worthy of applause*, Cic

plausor ōris, m (plaudo), *an applauder at the theatre*, Hor

plaustrum (plostrum) i, n I. *a wagon, cart*, omnia ex locis publicis plaustris coacta, Cic II. Transf, *Charles's Wain, the constellation of the Great Bear*, Ov

plausus ūs, m (plaudo), *the noise made by the striking together of two bodies* I. Gen, plausum dare pennis, Verg, ingenti sonuerunt omnia plausu, Verg II. Esp, *the clapping of the hands in sign of approval, applause*, accipere plausum, Cic, captare plausus, Cic, comprimitur plausus ipsā admiratione, Cic

Plautĭus (Plōtĭus) a um, *name of a Roman gens*, hence, adj, **Plautĭānus (Plōtĭānus)** a um, *Plautian*

Plautus i, m (lit *flat footed*), M Accius (or T Maccius), *a celebrated Roman comic poet, who died about eighty years before Cicero's birth*, hence, **Plautīnus** -a um, *relating to Plautus*, Plautinus pater, *in a comedy of Plautus*

plēbēcŭla ae, f (dim of plebs), *the common people, mob, rabble*, Cic

plēbēĭus -a -um (plebs) I. *relating or belonging to the plebs or people* (opp patricius), *plebeian*, familia, Cic, ludi, *games celebrated in honour of the driving out of the kings or of the return of the plebeians from their secession to the Aventine Hill*, Cic Subst, **plēbēĭus** -i, m *a plebeian*, and **plēbēĭa** ae, f *a plebeian woman*, Liv Plur, **plēbēĭi** or **plēbēi**, Cic II. *plebeian = common, vulgar, low, mean, inferior*, sermo, *of the lower classes*, Cic, purpura, Cic, philosophi, Cic

plēbes -ēi, f = plebs (q v)

plēbĭcŏla -ae, m (plebs and colo), *a friend of the common people*, Cic

plēbiscītum -i n (plebs and scisco), *a decree or ordinance of the people*, Cic

plebs, plēbis, f (root PLE, whence ple-o, ple nus, Gr ΠΛΕ, ΠΛΗ, whence πληθω, πλῆθος), *the multitude* Hence, I. As a political division, *the plebeians, the people* (opp patricii, patres, senatus, while populus includes both these and the plebeians), consulem de plebe non accipiebat, Cic II. Transf, *the common people, the multitude, mass of the people, the lower orders, rabble, mob*, plebs et infima multitudo, Cic, plebs eris, Hor, plebs deorum, *the lower order of deities*, Ov

1 **plecto**, plexi and plexŭi, plexum, 3 (root PLEC, Gr ΠΛΕΚ, πλεκω), *to plait, braid*, more frequently in partic, **plexus** a -um, *braided, plaited*, corollae, Lucr, flores, Cat

2 **plecto**, 3 (πλήττω), *to punish*, usually in pass, *to be punished with blows* A. Lit, tergo, Hor B. Transf, 1, *to be punished*, with abl of crime, negligentiā, Cic, 2, *to be blamed, censured*, Nep

plectrum -i, n (πλῆκτρον), *a short stick or quill with which the strings of a stringed instrument were struck* A. Lit, Cic B. Poet, meton, 1, *the lyre*, Hor, 2, *lyrical poetry*, Hor

Plēĭăs (Πληιας), **Plējăs**, and **Plīăs** (Πλειας) ădis, f *a Pleiad*, gen plur, **Plēĭădes (Plīădes)** and **Plējădes** -ădum, f *the Pleiads, the Seven Stars, according to the legend, the seven daughters of Atlas by Pleione* (Electra, Halcyone, Celaeno, Maia, Sterope, Taygete, Merope)

Plēĭŏnē ēs, f (Πληιονη), *the wife of Atlas, mother of the Pleiads*, Pleiones nepos, *Mercury, son of Maia*, Ov

Plēmȳrĭum (Plēmūrĭum) -ii, n (Πλημμυριον), *a promontory of Sicily, near Syracuse, now Punta di Gigante*

plēnē, adv (plenus), *fully*, fig, *fully, completely, wholly, abundantly*, plene perfectae munitiones, Caes, plene sapientes homines, Cic

plēnĭtūdo -inis, f (plenus), *fulness, completeness*, Plin

plēnus -a -um (root PLE, whence ple-o, Gr ΠΛΕ, πλεος), *full* I. Lit, A. Gen, a, lit, with genit, argenti, Cic, with abl, plena domus ornamentis, Cic, absol, plenissimis velis navigare, Cic, calcari ad plenum, *completely*, Verg, b, fig, plenus timoris, Caes, plenus expectatione, Cic, absol, plenā manu alicuius laudes in astra tollere, Cic B. Esp, 1, *plump, portly, stout*, homo, Cic, velamina filo pleno, *thick*, Ov, 2, *pregnant*, Cic, 3, *full, satiated*, plenus eras minimo, Ov, 4, *full of, richly provided with, rich in*, exercitus plenissimus praedā, Cic, fig, plenus inimicorum, Cic, negotiis, *occupied*, Cic, hence, absol = *well stocked, rich*, urbs, Cic, homo, Cic, epistola plenior, *full of matter*, Cic II. Transf, A. *full*, of quantity and number, 1, *numerous*, agmen, Ov, 2, = *complete, entire*, a, lit, annus, Cic, legio, Caes, b, fig, *complete, perfect*, gaudium, Cic, pleno gradu, *at quick step*, Liv B. Of strength, *strong, loud*, vox, Cic, pleniore voce, Cic

plērumquĕ, v plerusque

plērus = plerusque (q v)

plērusquĕ -răquĕ -rumquĕ, gen plur, **plērīquĕ** -raequĕ -răquĕ, *very many, a large part, the most, the greatest part, the majority* (opp unus, pauci) I. Plur, 1, absol, multi nihil prodesse philosophiam, plerique etiam obesse arbitrantur, Cic, plerique Belgae, Caes, in plerisque, *in the majority of cases*, Cic, 2, with genit, plerique Poenorum, Cic, 3, with the abl, plerique ex factione, Sall II. Sing, juventus, Sall, nobilitas, Sall, Africa, Sall. Neut, plerumque, a, subst, *the greater part*, noctis, Sall, per Europae plerumque, Liv, b, adv, *for the most part, mostly, generally, commonly*, Cic

Pleumoxĭi -ōrum, m *a people in Gallia Belgica*

Pleurōn ōnis, f (Πλευρων) *a town in Aetolia* Hence, adj, **Pleurōnĭus** -a -um, *Pleuronian*

plĭco -ŭi ātus, 1 (πλεκω) *to fold, double up, fold together*, se in sua membra, Verg

Plīnĭus a -um, *name of a Roman gens, the most famous members of which were* 1, C Plinius Secundus (Major, *the Elder*), *probably of Como, author of a Natural History in thirty seven books, killed 79* A D, *at the eruption of Mount Vesuvius*, 2, C Plinius Caecilius Secundus (Junior, *the Younger*), *governor under Trajan in Bithynia, author of letters and of a panegyric on Trajan*

Plisthĕnēs -is, m (Πλεισθενης) I. *son of Pelops, brother of Atreus and Thyestes, father of Agamemnon and Menelaus, who was brought up by his brother Atreus* Hence, **Plisthĕnĭcus** a -um, torus, *of Agamemnon*, Ov

plōdo = plaudo (q v)

plōrābĭlis -e (ploro), *deplorable, lamentable*, Pers

plōrātor ōris, m (ploro), *a wailer, howler, lamenter*, Mart

plōrātus -ūs, m (ploro), *a crying, weeping, lamenting*, gen in plur, audivi civitatum gemitus, ploratus, Cic

plōro, 1 I Intransit, *to lament, wail, cry aloud for grief*, plorando fessus sum, Cic, jubeo te plorare (= οἰμώζειν λέγω σοι, *bad luck to you!*), Hor II. Transit, *to weep over, to lament, deplore*, turpe commissum, Hor

plostellum -i, n (dim. of plostrum), *a little waggon*, Hor

plostrum = plaustrum (q v)

ploxĕmum (ploxĭmum, ploxĭnum) -i, n *a waggon box*, Cat

plŭit, v pluo

plūma -ae, f *the downy part of a feather, a small, soft feather*, plur = *down* I. Lit, plumae versicolores columbarum, Cic, in plumis delituisse Jovem, *to have been disguised in the form of a bird*, Ov, in plumam, *after the fashion of feathers*, Verg, used to stuff pillows, bolsters, etc, with, hence, meton = *bolster, feather-bed, pillow*, Juv, as an emblem of lightness fickleness, etc, plumā aut folio facilius moventur, Cic II. Transf, *the first down on the chin*, Hor

plūmātus -a -um (pluma), *covered with feathers*, Cic poet

plumbĕus -a -um (plumbum), *leaden, made of lead* I. Lit, glans, Lucr II. Transf, *leaden*, 1, = *blunt*, gladius, Cic, pugio, Cic, 2, = *bad*, vina, Mart, 3, *dull, stupid*, plumbeus in physicis, Cic, 4, *heavy, oppressive, burdensome*, auster, Hor

plumbum -i, n (akin to μόλιβδος), *lead* I. Lit, plumbum album, *tin*, Caes II. Meton, 1, *a bullet*, Verg, 2, *a leaden-pipe*, Hor

plūmĕus -a -um (pluma), *downy, consisting of, covered with fine feathers*, culcita, Cic, torus, Ov

plūmĭpes -pĕdis (pluma and pes), *feather footed*, Cat

plūmōsus -a -um (pluma), *feathered, covered with down, downy*, Prop

plŭo, plŭi, 3 (root PLU, connected with FLU-o, Gr ΠΛΥ, whence πλύνω), *to rain* I. Lit, impers, pluit, *it rains*, dum pluit, Verg, aqua, quae pluendo crevisset, Cic, with acc and abl of what falls, sanguine pluisse, Cic, lapides pluere, Liv II. Transf, *to fall down in a great mass or number*, tantum glandis pluit, Verg

plūrĭēs, adv (plus), *often, frequently*, Caes

plūrĭfārĭam (plus), *on many sides, in many places*, Suet

plūrĭmus, plurimum, v multus

plūs, pluris, v multus

plusculus -a -um (dim of plus), *somewhat more, rather many*, **plusculum** -i, n used subst, causae in quibus plusculum negotii est, Cic

plŭtĕus -i, m and **plŭtĕum** -i, n I. A. a, *a moveable penthouse, shed*, or *mantlet* (made of hurdles covered with hides to protect the besiegers of a town), Caes, b, *a breastwork, battlement on a tower*, Caes II. A. *the back board of a bed or sofa*, Mart B *the board on which a corpse is laid out*, Mart C. *a book-shelf, book case*, Juv

Plūto (-ōn) -ōnis, m (Πλούτων), *the king of the lower world, brother of Jupiter and Neptune husband of Proserpina* Hence, **Plūtōnĭus** -a -um, *belonging to Pluto* domus, *the grave*, Hor, plur subst, **Plūtōnĭa** -ōrum, n (sc loca), *a place in Asia Minor, perhaps in Lydia, where there was a temple to Pluto*

plŭvĭa -ae, f (pluvius), *rain*, pluvias metuo, Cic

plŭvĭālis -e (pluvia), *of or relating to rain rainy*, aquae Ov, fungi, *growing after rain*, Ov, auster, Verg

plŭvĭus -a um (pluo) *of or relating to rain, rainy, rain-bringing*, aquae, Cic Hyades, Verg, venti, Hor, arcus, *a rainbow*, Hor

pōcillum -i, n (dim of poculum), *a little drinking cup, goblet*, Jovi Victori pocillum mulsi facere, *to offer*, Liv

pōcŭlum -i, n (root PO, whence potus, poto), *a drinking cup, goblet* I. poculum impavide haurire, Liv, poculum mortis exhaurire, Cic, poscunt majoribus poculis (sc bibere), *to drink out of goblets*, Cic II. Meton, A. *a drink, draught*, ad pocula venire, Verg, amoris poculum, *a love-philtre*, Hor, in ipsis tuis immanibus poculis *in thy cups, in the midst of thy revels*, Cic B. Esp, *a poisonous draught*, Cic

pŏdăgra -ae, f (ποδάγρα), *the gout in the feet*, podagrae doloribus cruciari, Cic

Pŏdălīrĭus -ii, m (Ποδαλείριος) I *son of Aesculapius, a celebrated physician* II. *a Trojan*

pōdex -icis, m *the fundament*, Hor

pŏdĭum -ii, n (πόδιον), *a basement or balcony immediately above the arena in the amphitheatre, where the emperor and other distinguished persons sat*, Juv

Poeās (Paeās) -antis m (Ποίας) *the father of Philoctetes*, Poeante satus, *son of Poeas* = *Philoctetes*, Ov Hence, A adj, **Poeantĭus** -a um, proles or heros or simply Poeantius = *Philoctetes*, Ov B. **Poeantĭădēs** -ae, m *son of Poeas* = *Philoctetes*, Ov

pŏēma -ătis, n (ποίημα), *a poem*, poema facere, or componere, or condere, Cic, plur, poemata = *poetry* (opp oratio, *prose*), Cic

poena -ae, f (ποινή), *the fine paid for murder*, hence, *punishment, penalty, expiation, compensation* I. poena dupli, octupli, Cic, vitae, Cic, capitis, Caes, mortis, Cic, oculorum, *loss of eyesight*, Cic, votorum, *payment of one's vows*, Verg, poenas justas et debitas solvere, Cic, poenas expetere ab aliquo, Cic, poenas domestici sanguinis expetere, *to avenge the murder of a blood-relation*, Cic, poenas parentium a filiis expetere, *to visit the sins of the fathers on the children*, Cic, poenas capere pro aliquo, *to avenge some one*, Sall, poenam habere, *to be punished*, Liv, poenas habere ab aliquo, *to obtain vengeance from some one*, Liv; poenas dare, *to be punished*, Cic, poenā aliquem afficere or multare, Cic, poenam subire, ferre, perferre, luere, Cic, extra poenam esse, *to get off scot free*, Liv II. Personif, Poena, *the goddess of revenge or punishment*, Cic, plur, a liberum Poenis actum esse praecipitem, Cic

Poeni -ōrum, m *the Phoenicians* = *the Carthaginians* (colonists from Phoenicia), proverbial among the Romans for faithlessness and breach of treaties, Poeni foedifragi, Cic, sing, **Poenus** -i, m *a Phoenician, a Carthaginian*, used for *Hannibal*, Cic, collective, Poenus advena, Liv, Poenus uterque, *the Carthaginians in Africa and Spain*, Hor Hence, A **Poenus** -a -um, *Phoenician, Punic, Carthaginian*, navita, Hor, leones Verg B. **Pūnĭcus (Poenĭcus)** -a -um, *Phoenician, Punic, Carthaginian* a, lit, Punicum bellum, Cic, fides = *faithlessness*, Sall, so ars, Liv, b, poet, transf = *purple red*, sagum, Hor C. **Pūnĭcĕus (Poenĭcĕus)** and **Pūnĭcĭus (Poenĭcĭus)** -a um, a, *Punic, Carthaginian*, b, *purple red*

Poenīnus -a -um *Pennine*, Alpes or juga, *the Pennine Alps* Poeninus mons *the Great St Bernard*, or simply Poeninus, Liv

poenĭo, poenio = punio (q v).

poenitens -entis (partic. of poeniteo).

poenitentĭa (paenĭtentĭa) -ae, f. (poeniteo), *repentance, penitence*, Liv.

poenĭtĕo (paenĭtĕo) -ŭi, 2. (from poenire = punire; lit., *to punish*). **I.** *to displease*, Plaut. **II.** *to feel displeasure, to repent, to regret, to be sorry.* **A.** Pers., *to rue*; poenitens consilii, Sall.; si poenitere possint, Liv.; poenitens, Cic.; poeniturus, Sall.; poenitendo, *by repentance*, Cic. **B.** Impers., poenitet aliquem alicuius rei, etc., *it repents one, one is displeased, vexed*, etc.; (a) with acc. of pers. and genit. of thing, suae quemque fortunae poenitet, Cic.; me poenitet consilii, Cic.; without acc. of pers., tamquam poeniteat laboris, Liv.; (β) with acc. of pers. and nom. pron. neuter, nihil sane esset quod nos poeniteret, Cic.; with only nom. pron., nihil quod poenitere possit, *of which one could repent*, Cic.; (γ) with acc. of pers. and infin., non poenitet me vixisse, Cic.; or, (δ) simple infin., ut fortiter fecisse poeniteat, Cic.; or with acc. and infin., in posterum diem dilatum (esse) certamen, Liv.; (ε) with acc. of pers. and rel. sent., Quintum poenitet quod animum tuum offendit, Cic.; (ζ) or with rel. sent. alone, poenitet quod deduxisti, Liv.; (η) absol., poenitet et torqueor, Ov.

pŏēsis -is, acc. -in, f. (ποίησις), *poetry*, Cic.

pŏēta -ae, m. (ποιητής), *a poet*; poeta comicus, tragicus, Cic.

pŏētĭca -ae, f. and **pŏētĭcē** -ēs, f. (ποιητική, sc. τέχνη), *the art of poetry*, Cic.

pŏētĭcē, adv. (poeticus), *poetically, after the manner of a poet*; ut poetice loquar, Cic.

pŏētĭcus -a -um (ποιητικός), *poetical*; verbum, Cic.; facultas, Cic.

Poetovĭo -ōnis, f. *a town in Pannonia*, now *Pettau*.

pŏētrĭa -ae, f. (ποιήτρια), *a poetess*, Cic.

pol! interj. *by Pollux! truly! really!* Cic.

Pŏlĕmo (-ōn) -ōnis, m. (Πολέμων). **I.** *a Greek philosopher at Athens, pupil of Xenocrates, teacher of Zeno and Arcesilaus.* Hence, **Pŏlĕmōnēus** -a -um, *of Polemo*. **II.** *a king in Pontus*.

pŏlenta -ae, f. (root POL, POLL, whence pollen, Gr. ΠΑΛ, πάλη), *pearl-barley, barley-groats*, Ov.

pŏlĭo, 4. *to polish, file, make smooth.* **I. A. 1,** rogum asciā, Cic.; **2,** esp., *to cover with white mortar or gypsum, to whiten*; columnas albo, Liv. **II.** Fig., *to adorn, embellish, to polish, finish*; orationem, Cic.

pŏlītē, adv. (politus), *in a polished manner, elegantly*, Cic.; politius limare, Cic.

pŏlītīa -ae, acc. -an, f. (πολιτεία), **1,** *the state*; **2,** *the Republic* (title of a work by Plato), Cic.

pŏlītĭcus -a -um (πολιτικός), *of or relating to the state, political*; philosophi, Cic.

Pŏlītōrĭum -ii, n. *a town in Latium, south of the Tiber, according to the legend founded by the Trojan Polites, son of Priam.*

pŏlītus -a -um, p. adj. (from polio), *polished, refined, accomplished*; homo, Cic.; politior humanitas, Cic.; vir omni liberali doctrinā politissimus, Cic.

pollen -inis, n. and **pollis** -inis, c. (cf. polenta), *fine flour, meal*, Ter.

pollens -entis, p. adj. (from polleo), *strong, powerful, mighty*; matrona, Ov.; herbae, Ov.; with abl., viribus, Sall.

1. **pollentĭa** -ae, f. (polleo). **I.** *power, strength, might*, Plaut. **II.** Personif., *the goddess of might*, Pollentia, Liv.

2. **Pollentĭa** -ae, f. *a town in Liguria, famous for its wool*, now *Polenza*.

pollĕo, 2. (potis and valeo), *to be strong, mighty, powerful, able*; qui in republica plurimum pollebant, *had the most power*, Cic.; ubi plurimum pollet oratio, Cic.; with abl., scientia, Cic.

pollex -icis, m. (polleo), lit., *that which is strong.* **A.** *the thumb*; Aeginetis pollices praecidere, Cic.; as a measure, clavi ferrei digiti pollicis crassitudine, Caes. **B.** *the great toe*, Plin.

pollĭcĕor -citus sum, 2. dep. (pro and liceor), *to offer, promise, proffer.* **I.** Gen., **a,** with acc. of thing, pecuniam, Cic.; **b,** with acc. of thing and dat. of person, senatui frumentum, Cic.; maria montesque, *to make boundless promises*, Sall.; **c,** with double acc., sese itineris periculique ducem, Sall.; **d,** with de and the abl., with or without the acc., nihil ego tum de meis opibus pollicebar, Cic.; **e,** with infin., obsides dare, Caes.; **f,** with acc. and infin., gen. future, me tibi satisfacturum, Cic.; **g,** with rel. sent., quae meum tempus postularet, Cic.; **h,** with adv., ultro polliceri, Cic.; bene, Sall.; benigne, Liv.; liberaliter, Caes. **II.** Esp., of an orator at the beginning of his speech, *to promise, declare*; docui quod primum pollicitus sum, Cic. (partic. perf. pass., pollicita fides, Ov.).

pollĭcĭtātĭo -ōnis, f. (pollicitor), *an offer, proffer, promise*; magnis praemiis pollicitationibusque polliceri, Caes.

pollĭcĭtor, 1. dep. (intens. of polliceor), *to promise, proffer*, Sall.

pollĭcĭtum -i, n. (polliceor), *that which is promised, a promise*, Ov.

Pollĭo (Pōlĭo) -ōnis, m., C. Asinius, *the patron of Vergil.*

pollis = pollen -inis (q.v.).

pollūcĕo -luxi -luctum, 2. **I.** *to place something upon the altar as a sacrifice, to offer*; decumam partem Herculi, Plaut. **II.** *to put on the table as a dish*, Plaut.

pollŭo -ŭi -ūtum, 3. (pro and luo), *to befoul, defile, pollute.* **I.** Lit., ora cruore, Ov. **II.** Transf., *to defile morally, pollute, dishonour*; jura scelere, Cic.; caerimonias stupro, Cic.

pollūtus -a -um, p. adj. (from polluo), *morally defiled, polluted*; hence (of women), *unchaste*; femina, Liv.

Pollux -ūcis, m. (Πολυδεύκης), *the twin-brother of Castor, son of Tyndarus (or Jupiter) and Leda, renowned for his skill in boxing*, Cic.; Pollux uterque, *Castor and Pollux*, Hor.

pŏlus -i, m. (πόλος). **I.** *the pole of the earth*; polus gelidus, glacialis, and simply polus, *the north pole*, Ov.; polus australis, *the south pole*, Ov. **II.** Transf., *the sky, the heavens*, Verg., Hor.

Pŏlȳbĭus -ii, m. (Πολύβιος), *a Greek historian, contemporary and friend of Scipio Africanus Minor.*

Pŏlȳclītus (Pŏlȳclētus) -i, m. (Πολύκλειτος), *a celebrated Greek sculptor of Sicyon, contemporary of Pericles.*

Pŏlȳcrătes -is, m. (Πολυκράτης), *tyrant of Samos, famed for his prosperity, but crucified by the Persian satrap Orontes.*

Pŏlȳdămas -mantis, m. (Πολυδάμας), *a Trojan, friend of Hector.*

Pŏlȳdectēs -ae, m. (Πολυδέκτης), *king in Seriphos, who brought up Perseus.*

Pŏlȳdōrus -i, m. (Πολύδωρος), *son of Priam, entrusted to the care of Polymnestor, king in Thrace, but slain by him.*

Pŏlÿgnōtus -i, m (Πολύγνωτος), *a celebrated Greek painter of Thasos, contemporary with Socrates*

Pŏlÿhymnĭa -ae, f (Πολύμνια), *one of the Muses*

Pŏlÿmestōr (Pŏlymnestōr) ŏris, m (Πολυμήστωρ), *king in Thrace, husband of Ilione, daughter of Priam, the murderer of Polydorus.*

Pŏlÿphēmus (-ŏs) i, m (Πολύφημος), *the one eyed Cyclops in Sicily, son of Neptune, blinded by Ulysses*

pŏlÿpus i, m (πολύπους, Dor and Aeol, πωλύπος, hence with long ō in Horace) **I.** *the polypus, a marine animal*, Ov **II.** *a polypus in the nose*, Hor

Pŏlyxĕna ae, f (Πολυξένη), *daughter of Priam, sacrificed at the tomb of Achilles*

pōmārĭus a -um (pomum), *of or relating to fruit*, subst . **A. pōmārĭus** -ii, m *a fruiterer*, Hor **B. pomārĭum** -ii, n *a fruit garden, orchard*, Cic

pōmĕrīdĭānus = postmeridianus (q v)

pōmērĭum ii, n (orig pomoerium, post and moerus = murus), *a space left free from buildings for a certain breadth on each side the walls of a town, bounded by stones* (cippi or termini), pomerium intrare, transire, Cic

Pōmētĭa -ae, f and **Pōmētĭi** -ōrum, m *old town of the Volsci in Latium* Hence, **Pōmētīnus** -a -um, *Pometine*

pōmĭfĕr -fĕra -fĕrum (pomum and fero), *fruit bearing, fruit-bringing*, Hor

Pōmōna -ae, f (pomum), *the goddess of fruit and fruit trees*

pōmōsus a -um (pomum), *full of fruit, abounding in fruit*, Prop

pompa -ae, f (πομπή), *a solemn procession* **I. A.** Lit , **1,** gen , of funerals, Cic , pompam funeris ire, Ov , of a wedding, pompam ducit, Ov , of a triumph, Ov , pomparum ferculis similes esse, *to resemble in gait the bearers at a procession*, Cic , **2,** esp , *the procession at the Circensian games at which the images of the gods were carried* **B.** Transf , *a train, suite, retinue*, lictorum, Cic **II.** Fig , *display, parade, ostentation ;* genus (orationis) pompae quam pugnae aptius, Cic

Pompēji -ōrum, m *town in the south of Campania, destroyed by an eruption of Vesuvius*, 79 A D Hence, adj , **Pōmpējānus** -a -um, *belonging to Pompeji*, subst , a, **Pōmpējānum** -i, n (sc praedium), *an estate of Cicero, near Pompeji* , b, **Pōmpējāni** ōrum, m *the inhabitants of Pompeji*

Pompōjŏpŏlis -is, f (Πομπηιούπολις), *later name of the town Soli, destroyed by Tigranes, rebuilt by Pompejus*

Pompējus (Pompēĭus) -a um, *name of a Roman gens, the most famous members of which were* 1, Cn Pompejus, *triumvir with Caesar and Crassus, conqueror of Mithridates and the pirates, defeated by Caesar at Pharsalia and slain off Egypt* , 2, Pompeja, *wife of P Vatinius*, adj , *Pompeian*, domus, Cic , lex, *proposed by Cn Pompey* Hence, **Pompējānus** a um, *belonging to Pompey* , subst , **Pompējānus** -i, m *a member of the Pompeian party*

Pompĭlĭus -a um, *name of a Roman gens, to which belonged Numa Pompilius, second king of Rome, legendary founder of many religious rites at Rome* Adj , *Pompilian* , sanguis, *descendants of Numa Pompilius*, Hor

pompĭlus -i, m (πομπίλος), *the pilot-fish* , according to some, *the nautilus*, Ov

Pompōnĭus a -um, *the name of a Roman gens, the most famous member of which was* T. Pomponius Atticus, *friend of Cicero*

Pomptīnus (Pomtīnus) -a -um, *Pomptine or Pontine*, palus and paludes, *a marshy district, thirty miles long and twelve to thirteen miles wide, exposed to the inundation of the river Amaseaus and Ufens, on the Appian road* Subst , a, **Pomptīnum** -i, n *the neighbourhood of the Pontine marsh* , b, **Pomptīna** -ae, f *the upper end of the Pontine marsh*

pōmum i, n **I.** *any kind of fruit, a mulberry*, Ov , plur , poma, *fruit*, Verg , Hor **II.** Transf , *a fruit tree*, Verg

pondĕro, 1 (pondus) **I.** *to weigh*, Plaut **II.** Transf , *to weigh mentally, to consider, deliberate upon* , verborum delectum, Cic , causas, Cic

pondĕrōsus -a -um (pondus), *heavy, weighty, ponderous* **I.** Lit , Plin **II.** Transf , *weighty, significant* , epistola, Cic

pondo (abl of obsolete pondus -i), *in weight, heavy*, coronа libram pondo, *a pound in weight*, Liv , used as an indecl subst , *a pound, pounds* , argenti pondo viginti milia, Caes , auri quinque pondo, Cic

pondus -ĕris, n (pendo), *a weight* **I. A.** Lit , **1,** *a weight used in a pair of scales ;* pondera ab Gallis allata, Liv , **2,** *a pound weight, a pound*, Liv **B.** Transf , **1,** abstr , **a,** *the weight of any body* , moveri gravitate et pondere, Cic , **b,** *balance, equilibrium* , tertius motus oritur extra pondus et plagam, Cic , **2,** concr , **a,** *a heavy body, weight, load, burden* , in terram feruntur omnia pondera, Cic , **b,** *a mass = a quantity, sum* , auri pondus ingens, Liv **II.** Fig , **A.** In a good sense, **1,** *weight, gravity, authority, influence* , commendationem magnum apud te pondus habuisse, Cic , **2,** *weight* of words or thoughts , omnium verborum ponderibus est utendum, Cic **B.** In a bad sense, *an oppressive weight, burden* , pondera amara senectae Ov

pōnĕ (perhaps from posne, connected with ποτί, πρός) **I** Adv *behind, at the back* , moveri et ante et pone, Cic **II.** Prep with acc , *behind* , pone quos aut ante labantur, Cic

pōno, pŏsŭi (pŏsīvi), pŏsĭtum, 3 (for po-sino) *to lay down, put, place, lay* Constr with adv of place, with in and abl , with ad, ante, sub, super , poet with abl alone **I.** Gen , **A.** Lit , **1,** **a,** of things, vestigium, Cic , fig , pedem ubi ponat in suo (regno) non habet, Cic , ponere genu, *to kneel*, Ov ; ponere scalas, *to put up ladders*, Caes **b,** of persons, positi vernae circa Lares, Hor , **2,** of furniture or food, *to lay out, prepare*, mensam, Hor , casses, Ov , **3,** *to lay, stretch out*, artus in litore, Verg , somno positae, Verg , positae det oscula frater, *laid out, i e , dead*, Ov , **4,** *to erect a statue in honour of some one* , alicui statuam, Nep , esp , *to consecrate a gift to the gods* coronam auream in Capitolio, Liv , **5,** *to wager in play*, pocula fagina, Verg , **6,** t t of calculators, ponere calculum, *to calculate*, Juv , **7,** milit t t , *to station men, to place*, praesidium ibi, Caes , **8,** *to remove away to a distant place*, pone sub curru solis, Hor , **9,** *to publish* , edictum, Tac , **10,** *to put down in writing*, signa novis praeceptis, Hor , **11,** partic perf , **pŏsĭtus** -a -um, **a,** of snow, etc , *fallen* , posita nix, Hor , **b,** of places, *situated* , Roma in montibus posita Cic **B.** Transf , **1,** *to place, put, present* , aliquid sub uno aspectu, Cic , **2,** *to bring, put* , aliquem ponere in gratia apud aliquem, Cic , in laude positum esse, *to be famed* Cic , **3,** *to place, build, rest* , principi spem salutis in virtute, Cic , **4,** *to* *pass time in some occupation;* totum diem in consideranda causa, Cic.; **5,** *to reckon, count;* mortem in malis, Cic.; aliquid in beneficii loco, Cic.; haud in magno discrimine ponere, *to attach no great importance to,* Liv.; with double acc., *to hold, regard;* aliquem principem, Cic.; **6,** *to put down in writing, to remark, observe, mention;* cuius pauca exempla posui, Cic. **II. A.** *to lay, place by way of building, making,* etc.; **1,** lit. **a,** of building, *to erect;* urbem, Verg.; milit. t.t., castra in proximo colle, *to pitch one's camp,* Caes.; **b,** of an artist, *to represent, picture;* Orphea in medio silvasque sequentes, Verg.; ponere totum, *to present a whole,* Hor.; **2,** transf., **a,** *to found, place;* ponere initia male, Cic.; **b,** *to fix, settle;* leges in conviviis, Cic.; ponere praemium, *to promise a reward,* Cic.; **c,** *to maintain, lay down;* nosmet ipsos commendatos esse nobis, Cic.; **d,** *to put, ask;* quaestiunculam, Cic.; **e,** *to put a person in some position* or *office;* alicui custodem, Caes.; aliquem custodem in frumento publico, Cic. **B.** *to put food, dainties,* etc., *before one;* pavonem, merulas, Hor. **C.** *to plant;* piros, Verg. **D.** *to deposit;* tabulas testamenti in aerario, Caes. **E.** *to lay out money, to invest, lend;* pecuniam apud aliquem, Cic.; in praedio, Cic. **F.** *to arrange the hair;* comas, Ov. **G.** Of the winds, etc., *to lay, to soothe;* tollere seu ponere vult freta, Hor.; refl., ponere, of the winds, *to lull,* Verg. **H.** *to lay aside;* **1,** lit., librum de manibus, Cic.; arma, *to lay down,* Caes.; and hence, *to submit,* Caes.; **2,** transf., *to lay aside, remove, give up;* vitam, Cic.; vitia, Cic.; dolorem, Cic.; moras, Verg.; **3,** naut. t.t., *to throw out anchor;* ancoris positis, Liv. (syncop. perf. partic., postus, Lucr.).

1. **pons,** pontis, m. *a bridge,* Cic. **I.** facere pontem in flumine, *to bridge over a river,* Caes.; pontem facere in Tiberi, Liv.; pontem interscindere, *to cut down,* Cic. **II.** Esp., **A.** *a plank between a ship and the shore,* Verg. **B.** *a drawbridge,* Verg. **C.** *the bridge at the comitia over which the voters passed singly, to pass into the saepta,* Cic. **D. a,** *the deck of a ship,* Tac.; **b,** *the floor of a tower,* Verg.

2. **Pons,** Pontis, *as a geographical name.* **I.** Pons Argenteus, *a place and bridge over the river Argenteus in* Gallia Narbonensis. **II.** Pons Campanus, *a bridge on the* Via Appia.

Pontĭa -ae, f. *an Island off the coast of Latium,* now *Isola di Ponza.* Hence, **Pontĭāni** -ōrum, m. *the inhabitants of Pontia.*

pontĭcŭlus -i, m. (dim. of pons), *a little bridge,* Cic.

1. **Pontĭcus** -a -um, v. Pontus.

2. **Pontĭcus** -i, m. *a Roman poet, contemporary and friend of Propertius and Ovid.*

pontĭfex -ficis, m. (from pons and facio, or = pompifex, from pompa and facio), *a pontiff, a high priest, pontifex;* plur., pontifices, *a guild of priests at Rome, containing at first four, then eight, then fifteen members, the president of which was called* pontifex maximus; pontifices minores, *a lower class of pontiffs, assistants to the guild of* pontifices, Cic. Hence, **A. pontĭfĭcālis** -e, *pontifical;* auctoritas, Cic. **B. pontĭfĭcātus** -ūs, m. *the office of pontiff, the pontificate,* Cic. **C. pontĭfĭcĭus** -a -um, *relating to the pontificate;* libri, Cic; jus, Cic.

pontĭfĭcālis, v. pontifex.

pontĭfĭcātus, v. pontifex.

pontĭfĭcĭus, v. pontifex.

Pontĭus -a -um, *name of a gens, originally Samnite, afterwards Roman, the most famous members of which were:* **1,** C. Pontius, *commander of the Samnites at Caudium;* **2,** L. Pontius Aquila, *one of the murderers of Caesar;* **3,** Pontius Pilatus, *procurator of Judaea at the time of the crucifixion of Christ.*

ponto -ōnis, m. (pons), *a flat-bottomed boat, punt,* Caes.

1. **pontus** -i, m. (πόντος). **I.** *the deep, depth;* maris, Verg. **II.** Meton., **A.** *the deep sea,* Verg. **B.** *a wave of the sea,* Verg.

2. **Pontus** -i, m. (Πόντος). **I.** *the Black Sea.* **II.** Meton., **A.** *the country on the shores of the Black Sea.* **B.** Esp., *a district of Asia Minor between Bithynia and Armenia, the realm of Mithridates, later a Roman province, Pontus.* Hence, **Pontĭcus** -a -um (Ποντικός), *belonging to Pontus, Pontic;* mare, *the Black Sea,* Liv.; serpens, *the dragon that guarded the golden fleece at Colchis,* Juv.

pŏpa -ae, m. *the inferior priest* or *temple-servant who slew the victims,* Cic.

pŏpănum -i, n. (πόπανον), *a sacrificial cake,* Juv.

pŏpellus -i, m. (dim. of populus), *the common people, rabble,* Hor.

pŏpīna -ae, f. (πέπω, πέπτω, *to cook*). **I.** *a cook-shop, eating-house,* Cic. **II.** Meton., *the food sold at an eating-house,* Cic.

pŏpīno -ōnis, m. (popina), *the frequenter of eating-houses, glutton,* Hor.

poplĕs -ĭtis, m. **I.** *the ham, hough;* succidere poplitem, Verg.; femina poplitesque, Liv. **II.** Meton., *the knee;* duplicato poplite, *with bent knee,* Verg.; contento poplite, *with stiff knee,* Hor.

Poplĭcŏla = Publicola (q.v.).

poppysma -ătis, n. (πόππυσμα), and **poppysmus** -i, m. (ποππυσμός), *a clucking of the tongue as a sign of approbation,* Juv.

pŏpŭlābilis -e (populor), *that can be laid waste, devastated,* Ov.

pŏpŭlābundus -a -um (populor), *laying waste, devastating,* Liv.

pŏpŭlāris -e (1. populus), *belonging to the same people* or *country, native;* **1,** adj., flumina, Ov.; **2,** subst., **a,** lit. *a fellow-countryman;* Solon popularis tuus, Cic.; **b,** transf., *participator;* conjurationis, Sall. **II.** *belonging to the people, relating to the whole state, proceeding from the state;* **1,** gen., leges, Cic.; admiratio, Cic.; oratio, *to the people,* Cic.; **2,** esp., **a,** *popular, agreeable to the people, beloved by the people;* **b,** *of* or *relating to the people* (as opposed to the aristocracy), *popular, democratic;* popularis vir, *a friend of the people,* Liv.; homo, Cic. Subst., **pŏpŭlāres** -ium, m. *the popular party, the democracy,* Cic.

pŏpŭlārĭtas -ātis, f. (popularis), *desire to please the people, popular behaviour,* Tac.

pŏpŭlārĭtĕr, adv. (popularis). **I.** *after the manner of the people, commonly, vulgarly;* loqui, scribere, Cic. **II.** *after the fashion of a friend of the people, in a popular manner,* or, in a bad sense, *like a demagogue;* agere, Cic.

pŏpŭlātĭo -ōnis, f. (populor), *a laying waste, devastating, plundering;* populatio agrorum ceterorum, Liv.; ita libera populatio a tergo erat, Liv.; plur., Vejentes pleni jam populationum, *who had had their fill of plundering,* Liv.; hostem populationibus prohibere, Caes.

pŏpŭlātor -ōris, m. (populor), *a devastator, plunderer,* Liv.

pōpŭlĕus -a -um (2. populus), *of* or *relating to the poplar;* frondes, Verg.

pōpŭlĭfĕr -fĕra -fĕrum (2. populus and fero), *producing poplars,* Ov.

pŏpŭliscītum -i, n *a decree of the people,* Liv

Pŏpŭlōnĭa -ae, f, **Pŏpŭlōnĭum** -ii, n, and **Pŏpŭlōnii** -ōrum, m *a town in Etruria, now ruins of Poplonia*, hence, **Pŏpŭlōnĭenses** -ium, m *the inhabitants of Populonia*

pŏpŭlo, 1 and **pŏpŭlor**, 1 dep (1 populus), *to lay waste, devastate, plunder* I. Lit, agros, Caes, provinciae populatae Cic II. Poet transf, *to destroy, ruin, spoil, rob*, populat acervum curculio, Verg, populati s hamus, *robbed of the bait*, Ov

1 **pŏpŭlus** -i, m (connected with πλῆθος, plenus, etc, redupl populus, syncop poplus), *the people as forming a political community, a state.* I. Lit, 1, *the union of the inhabitants of a district, a state, a free state* populi liberi . . reges, Cic, reges et populi liberi, Sall, hence, meton, *a district, canton*, frequens cultoribus alius populus, Liv; 2, transf, *a crowd, host, multitude*, fratrum, Ov II In narrower sense, 1, *the sovereign body in a free state, the sovereign people*, a, civitas popularis in qua in populo sunt omnia, Cic, b, esp in Rome, originally *the patricians*, afterwards *the whole people*, as opp to the senate, often in the phrase, senatus populusque Romanus, Cic, et patres in populi potestate fore, Liv, as opp to the plebs, non populi sed plebis judicium esse, Liv, often, esp with historians, *the people as a party, the democratical party*, populum a senatu disjunctum, Cic, 2, *the people, multitude*, malus poeta de populo, Cic

2 **pōpŭlus** -i, f *the poplar tree*, Verg

porca -ae, f (porcus), *a sow*, sometimes poet, *a pig, hog*, Verg

porcīna -ae, f (sc caro), *pork*, Plaut

porcīnus a um, *of or relating to swine*, Plaut

Porcĭus a -um, *name of a Roman gens, the most famous members of which were* 1, M Porcius Cato Censorius or Major, *a severe Censor, after whom Cicero named his work on old age*, 2, M Porcius Cato, *the Younger, a contemporary of Cicero, called Uticensis, from his suicide at Utica*, 3, Porcia, *sister of the younger Cato, wife of Domitius Ahenobarbus* Adj, Porcian, lex, *forbidding corporal punishment of a Roman citizen*, Cic

porcŭlus -i, m (dim of porcus), *a young pig, porker*, Plaut

porcus -i, m *a pig, hog*, porcus femina, *a sow*, used as a term of reproach against a glutton, Epicuri de grege porcus, Hor

porgo = porrigo (q v)

Porphyrĭo (-ōn) -ōnis, m *one of the giants*

porrectĭo -ōnis, f (porrigo), *a stretching out, extension*

porrectus -a -um, p adj (from porrigo) I. *stretched out, extended, long*, porrectior acies, Tac II. Transf, poet of time, *long*, mora, Ov

porrĭcĭo -rēci and -rexi -rectum, 3 *to offer sacrifice to the gods*, prov, inter caesa et porrecta, *between the slaying and the offering of the victim*—i e, *at the eleventh hour*, Cic

1 **porrĭgo** -rexi -rectum, 3 (pro and rego), *to stretch out, reach out, extend* I. A. 1, lit, a, membra Cic, manum, Cic, medicum, porrigi, *to be stretched out, to lie stretched out* corpus porrigitur in novem jugera, Verg, b, milit t t, *to extend*, aciem, Sall, c, porrigere manum, *to hold up the hand in voting*, 2, transf, of position, scopulus frontem porrigit in aequor, Ov, porrecta in dorso urbs, Liv B. Fig, a, vectigalia, *to increase*, Hor, se porrigere, *to extend, reach*, quo se tua porrigat ira, Ov, b, syllabam, *to lengthen the quantity of a syllable*, Ov II. A. *to lay at full length, to lay low*, hostem, Liv, hence, partic, porrectus = *dead*, senex, Cat B. Meton, *to hold out to, reach to, offer to*, 1, lit, dextram regi Deiotaro, Cic, gladium nobis, Cic, 2, fig *to afford, supply* praesidium clientibus, Cic

2 **porrīgo** -ĭnis, f (= prurigo), *scurf, dandruff*, Hor

porro, adv (πόρρω), *forward, further* I. Of space, *at a distance, afar off*, a, with verbs of motion, ire, Liv, agere armentum, Liv, b, with verbs of rest, inscius Aeneas quae sint ea flumina porro, Verg II. Transf, A. Of time, *formerly* Cat B. To express advances from one thought to another, *then, next, further, again, in succession, in turn* saepe audivi a senioribus natu, qui se porro pueros a senibus audisse dicebant, Cic, sequitur porro, nihil deos ignorare, Cic

porrus -i, m and **porrum** -i, n (πράσον), *a leek*, Juv

Porsĕna (**Porsenna**) and **Porsīna** (**Porsinna**) ae, m (Πορσήνας, Πορσίνας), *king of Etruria, who attacked Rome in order to bring back Tarquinius Superbus* as a formula on the sale of booty, bona Porsinae regis veneunt, Liv

porta -ae, f (connected with περάω πορθμός, experior, etc), *a gate, city gate* I. A. Lit, with or without urbis, Cic, portas claudere, Caes, portā introire, Cic, pedem porta non extulisse, Cic B. Transf, *any place of ingress or egress, door, gate of a camp*, porta decumana, Caes, porta Taenaria (where Hercules entered the lower world), Ov, portae jecoris, Cic II. Fig, quibus e portis occurri cuique deceret, *in what ways or means*, Lucr

portātĭo -ōnis, f (porto), *a carrying, conveying*, armorum, Sall

portendo -tendi -tentum, 3 (pro-tendo), *to indicate, predict, presage, forbode, portend*, magnitudinem imperii portendens prodigium, Liv, dii periculum portendunt, Liv

portentĭfĭcus -fĕra -fĕrum (portentum and fero), *bringing prodigies*, Ov

portentĭfĭcus -a -um (portentum and facio), *extraordinary, supernatural, marvellous, miraculous*, venena, Ov

portentōsus -a -um (portentum), *extraordinary, prodigious, portentous, monstrous, unnatural*, nata, *abortions*, Cic

portentum -i, n (portendo) I. *a prodigy, portent*, Cic II. Transf A. *a wonderful story, extravagant tale*, poetarum et pictorum Cic B. *a monster, monstrosity*, hominum pecudumque portenta, Cic, so of "*a monster of depravity*," portentum reipublicae (of Piso), Cic

porthmĕus -ĕi and -ĕos, m (πορθμεύς), *a ferryman* (of Charon), Juv

portĭcŭla -ae, f (dim of porticus), *a little gallery or portico*, Cic

portĭcus -ūs, f (porta) *a portico, colonnade, arcade, gallery* I. 1, lit, a, quum paullulum inambulavisset in porticu, Cic b, *the hall of justice, tribunal of the praetor*, Cic, 2, meton, *the Stoic school* (so named from στοά, *a porch*), *the Stoics* clamat Zeno et tota illa porticus tumultuatur II. Transf, plur porticus, *galleries to protect the besiegers of a place* Caes

portĭo -ōnis, f (root POR, Gr ΠΟΡ ω) *a part, portion, section, division* I. Lit, Plin II. Transf, *proportion, ratio* pro portione, *in proportion, proportionally*, Cic

1. **portĭtor** -ōris, m. (portus), *a custom-house officer, collector of customs*, Cic.

2. **portĭtor** -ōris, m. (root POR-o, whence porto), *a carrier;* and usually, *a boatman, ferryman; Charon*, Verg.

porto, 1. (root POR-o, ΠΟΡ-ω, whence fero, portus), *to bear, carry, convey, bring.* **I.** Lit., concrete objects, **1,** gen., **a,** things, (*a*) onera, Caes.; omnia mecum porto mea, Cic.; with abl. or abl. and prep., in triumpho Massiliam, *a representation of Massilia*, Cic.; with adv., or prep., or acc., multa undique portari, Caes.; Romae domum ad Antonium frumentum, Cic.; viaticum ad hostem, Cic.; (β) of things as subjects, portans in corpore virus lolligo, Ov.; **b,** persons, lecticā portari, Cic. **II.** Transf., with abstract objects, sociis atque amicis auxilia portabant, Sall.; has spes cogitationesque secum portantes, Liv.

portōrĭum -ĭi, n. (POR-o, porto), *customs, tax on imported and exported goods;* portorium vini instituere, Cic.; exigere portorium, Cic.; portorium locare, *to let out the duties to farm*, Cic.

portŭla -ae, f. (dim. of porta), *a little gate, postern*, Liv.

Portūnus -i, m. (portus), *the god of harbours* (identified with the Greek Palaemon); hence, **Portūnālĭa** -ium, n. *the festival of Portunus, on the 17th of August.*

portŭōsus -a -um (portus), *having many harbours, abounding in ports;* superum mare, Cic.; navigatio minime portuosa, *without harbours*, Cic.

portus -ūs, m. (POR-o, whence porto), *a harbour, port, haven.* **I. 1,** lit., portus Caietae celeberrimus, Cic.; e portu solvere, Cic.; in portum pervehi, Cic.; as a place for levying duties, in portu operam dare, *to be a custom-house officer*, Cic.; prov., in portu esse, navigare, *to be out of danger*, Cic.; **2,** transf., *the estuary of a river*, Ov. **II.** Fig., *a place of refuge, harbour, haven;* nationum portus et refugium senatus, Cic.; se in philosophiae portum conferre, Cic.

poscaenĭum -ii, n. (post and scaena), *the theatre behind the scenes;* fig., poscaenia vitae, *the secret actions of men*, Lucr.

posco, pŏposci, 3. (pet-sco, from peto), *to ask earnestly, request strongly, demand.* **I.** Gen., **A.** Of persons, pugnam, Liv.; argentum, Cic.; with eth. dat., audaciae partes sibi, Cic.; with acc. and ab with abl., munus ab aliquo, Cic.; with double acc., magistratum Sicyonium nummos poposcit, Cic.; absol., poscimur, *we are asked for a song*, Hor.; with ut and the subj., Tac.; with acc. and infin., Ov. **B.** Transf., of things, *to demand, require;* quod res poscere videbatur, Caes. **II.** Esp., **A.** *to demand for judgment, require to be given up;* accusant ii, quos populus jussit, Cic. **B.** *to challenge to fight;* aliquem in proelia, Verg.; so absol., transf., poscunt majoribus poculis, *challenge one another*, Cic. **C.** *to inquire;* causas, Verg. **D.** *to call;* **1,** poscor Olympo, *heaven summons me to battle*, Verg.; **2,** *to call upon;* tua numina posco, Verg.

Pŏsīdōnĭus -ii, m. (Ποσειδώνιος), *a Stoic philosopher, pupil of Panaetius and teacher of Cicero.*

pŏsĭtĭo -ōnis, f. (pono), *a placing, putting;* caeli, *climate*, Tac.

pŏsĭtor -ōris, m. (pono), *a founder, builder*, Ov.

pŏsĭtūra -ae, f. (pono), *position, situation, place, posture*, Lucr.

posĭtus -ūs, m. (pono). **I.** *position, place;* urbis, Ov.; regionis, Tac. **II.** *arrangement of the hair*, Ov.

possessĭo -ōnis, f. (possideo). **I.** *possession;* **a,** lit., fundi, Cic.; possessionem hereditatis alicui dare, eripere, Cic.; aliquem movere, demovere de possessione, Cic.; **b,** fig., prudentiae doctrinaeque, Cic. **II.** Meton., *that which is possessed, a possession, property;* paternae atque avitae possessiones, Cic.

possessĭuncŭla -ae, f. (dim. of possessio), *a little possession, small property*, Cic.

possessor -ōris, m. (possideo), *a possessor.* **I.** Gen., locorum, Cic. **II.** Esp., *a possessor of land;* possessor agrorum, Liv.; absol., Cic.

possĭdĕo -sēdi -sessum, 2. (potis and sedeo), *to possess, have, hold.* **I. A.** Lit., ex edicto bona, Cic. **B.** Fig., ingenium, Cic. **II.** Transf., *to occupy a place by force, beset;* forum armatis catervis perditorum hominum, Cic.

possīdo -sēdi -sessum, 3. (potis and sido), *to take possession of, occupy.* **I.** Lit., bona sine testamento, Cic. **II.** Fig., totum hominem totamque eius praeturam, Cic.

possum, pŏtŭi, posse (potis and sum), *to be able, I (thou, he, etc.) can.* **I.** Gen., facere ut possem, Cic.; potest fieri ut fallar, *I may be mistaken*, Cic.; fieri non potest ut non or quin, *it cannot but be that*, Cic.; ut nihil ad te dem litterarum, facere non possum, *I cannot help writing to you*, Cic.; si potest, *if it is possible*, Cic.; qui potest? *how is it possible?* Cic.; with superl., Caesari commendavi ut gravissime potui, *as strongly as I could*, Cic. **II.** Esp., *to avail, be efficacious, have influence;* **a,** of persons, apud Sequanos plurimum, Caes.; quum omnia se posse censebat, *thought himself all-powerful*, Cic.; **b,** of things, plus potest apud te pecuniae cupiditas, Cic.

post (= ponst, from pone). **I.** Adv. *behind.* **A.** Of place, *behind, in the rear;* qui post erant, Cic. **B.** Transf., **1,** of time, *after, afterwards, subsequently;* multis post annis, *many years afterwards*, Cic.; aliquanto post, *shortly afterwards*, Cic.; multo post, *long after*, Cic.; **2,** of the order of succession, primo . . . post, Cic. **II.** Prep. with acc. **A.** Of place, *behind;* post nostra castra, Caes. **B.** Transf., **1,** of time, *after;* post Brutum consulem, Cic.; foll. by quam, post diem tertium . . . quam dixerat, Cic.; **2,** of order, *next to;* erat Lydia post Chloen, Hor.

postĕā, adv. (post and abl. eā), *after, after that, afterwards;* postea aliquanto, Cic.; quid postea? *what then? what next?* Cic.

postĕāquam, conj. *after that;* with indic.; (*a*) with perf., posteaquam victoria constituta est, Cic.; (β) with pluperf., posteaquam bis consul fuerat, Cic.; (γ) with imperf., posteaquam e scena explodebatur, Cic.; (δ) with pres., posteaquam in Formiano sum, Cic.

postĕri, v. posterus.

postĕrĭus, v. posterus.

postĕrĭtas -ātis, f. (posterus). **I.** *the future;* habere rationem posteritatis, Caes.; posteritatis otio consulere, Cic. **II.** *future generations, after-ages, posterity;* omnium seculorum, Cic.; posteritati servire, Cic.; invidia posteritatis, Cic.

postĕrus (poster) -a -um, compar., **postĕrĭor** -us; superl., **postrēmus** and **postŭmus** -a -um (post). **I.** Posit., *subsequent, ensuing, following, next, future;* lit., postero die, Cic.; in posterum, *for the next day*, and *for the future*, Cic.; subst., **postĕri** -ōrum, m. *posterity.* **II.** Compar., **postĕrĭor** -us, **1,** *following after,* *next in order, later, posterior;* posteriores cogitationes, *second thoughts,* Cic ; paulo aetate posterior, Cic , neut adv , posterius = *later,* Cic ; **2,** transf , *inferior, worse,* nihil posterius, Cic **III.** Superl **postrēmus** and **postŭmus** -a -um **A.** postremus, *the hindmost, last,* **1,** lit , pagina, Cic , acies, Sall , hoc non in postremis, Cic , abl , postremo *at last,* primum deinde postremo, Cic , postremum, *for the last time,* Cic , **2,** transf , of position and value, *the worst, most pitiable,* homines, Cic **B.** ad postremum *at last, lastly,* meton , *the last,* **postŭmus** -a -um, *the last, last born* (esp of children born after the father's will or death), *posthumous,* proles, Verg , subst , **postŭmus** -i, m , Cic

postfĕro -ferre, *to esteem less, consider of less account,* libertati plebis suas opes, Liv

postgĕnĭti -ōrum, m (post and gigno), *posterity, descendants,* Hor

posthăbĕo -ŭi -itum, 2 *to esteem less, make of less account,* omnibus rebus posthabitis, Cic

posthāc, adv *hereafter, after this, in future,* Cic

postĭcus -a -um (post), *hinder, back, behind* **I.** Adj , partes aedium, Liv **II.** Subst , posticum aedium, *a back door,* Liv

postĭlĭo -ōnis, f (postulo), *the demand of a deity for a sacrifice,* Cic

postillā, adv *after, afterwards,* Cat

postis -is, m *a post, door-post* **I.** Lit , postem tenere (of a person who consecrated a temple), Cic **II.** Plur , meton , poet , *a door, gate,* Verg

postlīmĭnĭum -ii, n (post and limen), *a return home, postliminy the resumption by a prisoner of war of his civil rights, which were in abeyance during his captivity,* ei esse postliminium, Cic , gen abl , postliminio, *by right of postliminy,* redire, Cic

postmĕrīdĭānus (pōmĕrīdĭānus) -a -um (post and meridianus), *belonging to the afternoon, afternoon,* tempus Cic

postmŏdŏ and **postmŏdum,** adv *after, afterwards,* Liv

postpōno -pŏsŭi -pŏsĭtum, 3 *to esteem less, consider of less account, put after,* omnia, Cic , aliquem alicui, Ov , omnibus rebus postpositis, Cic

postquam, conj *after, after that, as soon as;* **a,** with indic , (α) gen with perf , postquam Caesar pervenit, Caes , (β) with pluperf , undecimo die, postquam a te discesseram, Cic , (γ) with pres , Hostilia curia minor mihi esse videtur, postquam est major, Cic , (δ) with imperf , postquam amici non poterant vincere etc Cic , **b,** with historic infin , postquam exin aequalis, Tac

postrēmo, v posterus.

postrēmum, v posterus.

postrēmus -a um, superl of posterus (q v)

postrīdĭē, adv (for posteri diei), *the day after, the following day, on the next day,* prima luce postridie, Caes , foll by quam, postridie quam a vobis discessi, Cic , with acc , ludos, *the day after the games,* Cic , with genit , postridie ejus diei, Caes

postrīdŭo = postridie (q v)

postscrībo -scripsi -scriptum, 3 *to write after,* Tac

postŭlātĭo ōnis, f (postulo), *a request, entreaty, demand* **I.** Gen , ignoscendi, *for pardon,* Cic , concedere postulationi ejus, Cic **II.** Legal t t , *an application to the praetor to allow a complaint* or *charge to be brought,* Cic

postŭlātum -i, n (postulo), *a demand, request,* Cic

postŭlātus ūs, m (postulo) *a legal complaint, accusation,* Liv

postŭlĭo = postilio (q v)

postŭlo, 1 (= poscŭlo, from posco) *to demand, beg, entreat, ask, request* **I.** Gen , (α) with acc , auxilium, Cic , (β) with double acc , haec quum praetorem postulabas, Cic , (γ) with ut or ne or ut ne and the subj , postulat abs te ut Romam rem rejicias, Cic , with subj alone, qui postularent, eos sibi dederent, Caes , (δ) with infin , or acc and infin , dicendo vincere non postulo, Cic , hic postulat Romae se absolvi, Cic , with nom and infin pass , bona possideri postularentur, Cic , (ε) absol and transf , of things or subjects, quum tempus necessitasque postulat, Cic **II** Esp , legal t t , **a,** *to demand from the praetor against some one,* judicium, Cic , **b,** *to impeach, accuse* aliquem de ambitu, Cic , aliquem majestatis, Cic

Postŭmĭus -a -um, *name of a Roman gens, the most celebrated members of which were* **1,** *the consul* P Postumius Tubertus, *conqueror of the Sabines,* **2,** A Postumius Tubertus, *dictator, who ordered the execution of his own son for fighting against orders,* poet form, Postumus , adj , *Postumian,* and hence, **Pōstŭmĭānus** -a -um, *Postumian*

1 **postŭmus** -a um, superl of posterus (q v)

2 **Postŭmus,** v Postumius

Postverta (Postvorta) -ae, f (post and verto), *the goddess of childbirth, invoked in case of an irregular presentation,* Ov

pōtātĭo -ōnis, f (poto), *a drinking bout,* hesterna ex potatione oscitantes, Cic

pōtātor ōris, m (poto), *a drinker,* Plaut

pŏtĕ, v potis

pŏtens -entis, p adj (from possum) **I.** *powerful in, having power over* **A.** neque jubendi neque vetandi, Tac **B. 1,** *capable of,* armorum tenendorum, Liv , **2,** *mighty, influential* , civis, civitas, Cic , subst , *a powerful person,* Liv , plur., Cic , **3,** of things, *powerful, efficacious* , nihil est potentius auro, Ov ; **4,** *master of, lord of,* potentes rerum suarum et urbis, Liv , dum mei potens sum, *as long as I am my own master,* Liv , Diva potens Cypri, *ruling over Cyprus,* Hor , fig , potens sui, *having command over oneself, temperate,* Hor , potens irae, *able to control one's anger,* Liv **II.** *that which has obtained something,* voti, Ov , jussi, *having fulfilled the command,* Ov

pŏtentātus ūs, m (potens), *political power supremacy,* Cic

pŏtentĕr, adv (potens) **I.** *powerfully, strongly, efficaciously,* Hor **II.** *according to one's power,* Hor

1 **pŏtentĭa** -ae, f (potens), *power, might, ability* **I.** Physical, **1,** lit , solis, Verg , **2,** transf , *efficacy, potency,* herbarum, Ov **II** *political power* **a,** *influence, authority,* erant in magna potentia qui consulebantur, Cic , **b,** *supremacy, rule,* rerum, Cic

2 **Pŏtentĭa** -ae, f *a town in Picenum, on the river Flosis, now, perhaps, Monte Santo*

pŏtestas -ātis, f (possum), *power* **I.** Gen , *might, strength, efficacy,* herbarum, Verg **II.** *power to do something, power over something* **A. 1,** gen , habere potestatem vitae necisque in aliquem, Cic , esse in potestate senatūs, Cic , excedere ex or de potestate (sc. mentis), *to lose the control of one's reason*, Cic.; **2,** esp., **a,** *political power, supremacy, dominion*; esse in alicuius ditione ac potestate, Cic.; **b,** *the power, authority of a magistrate, official authority, office*; (α) lit., praetoria, Cic.; dare alicui potestatem legati, Cic.; (β) meton., *the magistracy itself*; imperia et potestates, *military and civil commands*, Cic. **B.** *might, power, ability, opportunity, possibility, occasion*; data est potestas augendae dignitatis, Cic.; facere potestatem alicui, (α) *to give an opportunity of fighting*, Caes.; (β) *to allow access to oneself, grant an interview*, Caes.; potestas est, *it is possible*, with infin., non fugis hinc praeceps dum praecipitare potestas, Verg.

1. **pōtĭo** -ōnis, f. (poto), *a drinking, draught, potion*. **I.** Gen., Cic. **II. a,** *a draught of poison*, Cic.; **b,** *a love-draught, philtre*, Hor.

2. **pŏtĭo,** 4. (potis), *to put any one in the power of*; aliquem servitutis, *to reduce to slavery*, Plaut.

1. **pŏtĭor,** 4. dep. (potis). **I.** *to get, get possession, become partaker of, obtain*; with abl., urbe, Cic.; victoriā, Caes.; with genit., illius regni, Cic.; with acc., urbem, Cic. **II.** *to possess, have, be master of*; with abl., mari, Liv.; with genit., rerum, Cic. (potior has some forms from the third conjug., potitur, Verg.; potĕremur, Ov.; potĕrentur, Liv.).

2. **pŏtĭor,** v. potis.

pŏtis, pŏtĕ (root POT, whence δεσ-πότης, compos, etc.). **I.** Adj., compar., **pŏtĭor** -us; superl., **pŏtissĭmus** -a -um. **A.** Posit., *able, capable*; usually in the phrase potis est, *he can, is able*; potis est vis ulla tenere, Verg.; nec potis est cerni, *nor is it possible to distinguish*, Lucr.; neut., pote est, Cat.; pote = pote esse, hoc quidquam pote impurius, Cic. **B.** Compar., **pŏtior** -us, *preferable, better*; cives potiores quam peregrini, Cic.; potior patre, Cic.; mors servitute potior, Cic. **C.** Superl., **pŏtissĭmus** -a -um, *best of all, chief, principal*; quid potissimum sit, Cic. **II.** Adv., only in compar., **pŏtĭus,** and superl., **pŏtissĭmum. A.** compar., potius, *rather, more, preferably*; magnus (homo) vel potius summus, Cic.; potius quam, foll. by ut and subj., or simply subj., Cic.; with verbs expressing a comparison, emori potius quam servire praestaret, Cic. **B.** Superl., **pŏtissĭmum (pŏtissĭme),** *chiefly, above all*, Cic.

pŏtissĭme, potissimum, v. potis.

pōtĭto, 1. (intens. of poto), *to drink frequently, drink hard*, Plaut.

pŏtĭus, v. potis.

Potnĭae -ārum, f. (Ποτνιαί), *a place in Boeotia on the river Asopus, the pastures of which were said to make animals that grazed them mad.* Hence, **Potnĭăs** -ădis, f. *belonging to Potniae*; equae, Ov., quadrigae, Verg., *the team of horses which threw out and killed their master Glaucus.*

pōto, pōtāvi, pōtātum and pōtum, 1. *to drink*. **I.** Lit., **1,** aquas, Ov.; absol., huc veniunt potum juvenci, Verg.; **2,** *to drink, revel*; totos dies potabatur, Cic. **II.** Transf., *to absorb, suck in*; potantia vellera fucum, Hor.; partic., **a, pōtus** -a -um, (α) pass., *drunk, drunk up, drained*; sanguine poto, Cic.; poti faece tenus cadi, Hor.; (β) act., *having drunk, drunken*; anus, Hor.; bene potus, Cic.; **b, pōtūrus** -a -um, Prop.

pōtor -ōris, m. (poto), *a drinker*. **I.** aquae, Hor.; Rhodani, *a dweller by the Rhone*, Hor. **II.** *a tippler, drunkard*, Hor.

pōtrix -īcis, f. (potor), *a female tippler*, Phaedr.

pōtŭlentus -a -um (poto), *drinkable, potable*; hence, subst., **pōtŭlenta** -ōrum, *things that can be drunk, drinkables*; esculenta et potulenta, Cic.

1. **pōtus,** v. poto.

2. **pōtus** -ūs, m. (poto). **I.** *a drinking*; immoderatus, Cic. **II.** Meton., *a draught, that which is drunk, drink*; cibi potusque, Ter.

prae, adv. and prep. (old dat. fem., like pro, dat. neut., from * prus -a -um, formed from per). **I.** Adv. *before, in front*; i prae, Plaut., Ter. **II.** Prep. with abl., **A.** *before*; prae se pugionem tulit, Cic.; prae se armentum agens, Liv.; fig., prae se ferre, *to show, exhibit, betray, discover, manifest*; scelus, Cic.; vocem, Cic. **B.** Transf., **1,** *in comparison with, compared with*; Atticos prae se agrestes putat, Cic.; prae nobis beatus, Cic.; **2,** *on account of, because of, in consequence of*; nec loqui prae maerore potuit, Cic.; prae metu, Cic.; prae ira, Liv.

praeăcŭo (-ŭi) -ūtum, 3. *to sharpen to a point*; gen. in partic., **praeăcūtus** -a -um, *sharpened to a point, pointed*; sudes, Sall.; stipites, Caes.

praealtus -a -um. **I.** *very high*; rupes, Liv. **II.** *very deep*; flumen, Liv.

praebĕo -bŭi -bĭtum (= praehibeo, from prae and habeo). **I.** *to offer, hold out*; crus alterum, Cic.; os ad contumeliam, Liv.; manum verberibus, Ov. **II.** Transf., **A.** *to expose*; se telis hostium, Liv. **B.** *to show, give*; operam alicui, *to serve*, Liv.; reflex., with or without se, *to show oneself, prove oneself*; with acc. of predicate, misericordem se praebuit, Cic.; se virum, Cic.; in eos se severum vehementemque, Cic.; utrisque se aequum, Cic. **C.** *to furnish, supply, afford*; alicui naves, Liv.; rebus adversis perfugium ac solatium, Cic.; hence, **a,** *to offer, present, cause, bring about*; speciem horribilem, Caes.; modum, *to make music*, Ov.; **b,** *to allow*; praebuit ipsa rapi, Ov.

praebĭbo -bĭbi, 3. *to drink before, to drink to*; ei cui venenum praebiberat, Cic.

praebĭtor -ōris, m. (praebeo) = πάροχος, *a furnisher, supplier, one who in the provinces furnished officials with necessaries*, Cic.

praecălĭdus -a -um, *very hot*, Tac.

praecānus -a -um, *prematurely grey*, Hor.

praecăvĕo -cāvi -cautum, 2. **I.** Intransit., *to take precaution beforehand, to be on one's guard, to be careful*; providens et praecavens, Cic.; ab insidiis, Liv.; with dat., *to take care for some person's safety*; decemviris ab ira et impetu multitudinis, Liv.; with ne and the subj., id ne accideret, sibi praecavendum existimabat, Caes. **II.** Transit., *to beware of, guard against beforehand, seek to avert*; quod a me ita praecautum est, Cic.; peccata, quae difficillime praecaventur, Cic.

praecēdo -cessi -cessum, 3. *to go before, precede*. **I.** Lit., **1,** intransit., praecedens consulis filius, Liv.; cum equite, Liv.; **2,** transit., agmen, Verg. **II.** Transf., **A.** Of time, *to go before, precede*; fama loquax praecessit ad aures tuas, Ov. **B.** Of rank, etc., *to surpass, be before*; reliquos Gallos virtute, Caes.; vestros honores rebus agendis, Liv.

praecellens -entis, p. adj. (from praecello), *excellent, admirable, distinguished, surpassing*; vir et animo et virtute praecellens, Cic.; vir omnibus rebus praecellentissimus, Cic.

praecello, 3. (prae and * cello), *to surpass, excel, exceed*; **a,** absol., gravitate morum, Tac.; **b,** with acc. or dat., aliquam fecunditate, Tac.; genti, *had the supremacy over*, Tac.

praecelsus -a -um, *very high, very lofty*, rupes, Verg

praecentĭo -ōnis, f (praecino), *a musical prelude, playing before a sacrifice*, Cic

praeceps -cĭpĭtis (prae and caput), *headlong, headforemost* **I.** Adj, **A.** Of motion, **1,** lit, **a,** of persons, (α) aliquem praecipitem dejicere, Cic, praeceps in terram datus, Liv, (β) *in haste, hasty, quick*, praecipites columbae, Verg, praecipites se fugae mandabant, Caes, praeceps fertur, Cic, **b,** transf, (α) of things, *hasty, precipitate*, profectio, Cic, celeritas dicendi, Cic, (β) of time, *declining*, praeceps dies, Liv, praeceps aetas, Sall, **2,** fig, **a,** of persons, *blind, rash, headlong*, agunt eum praecipitem poenae civium Romanorum Cic, homo in omnibus consiliis praeceps, Cic, praeceps in genio in iram, *inclined to*, Liv., **b,** of things, circumstances, etc, *dangerous*, libertas, Liv, lubricum genus orationis adulescenti non acriter intellegenti est saepe praeceps, Cic **B.** Of rest, **1,** adj, of places, *steep, precipitous*, locus, Caes, saxa, Liv, fig, iter ad finitimum malum praeceps ac lubricum, Cic, **2,** subst, **praeceps** -cĭpĭtis, n *a steep place, precipice*, in praeceps deferri, Liv, fig, *danger*, prope totam rempublicam in praeceps dederat, Liv **II.** Adv, vim mortalium praeceps trahit, *drags headlong*, Tac

praeceptĭo -ōnis, f (praecipio), **1,** *a preconception*, Cic, **2,** *a precept*, Stoicorum, Cic.

praeceptor -ōris, m (praecipio), *a teacher, instructor, preceptor*, vivendi atque dicendi, Cic

praeceptrix -trīcis, f (praeceptor), *she that teaches*, quā (sapientiā) praeceptrice, Cic

praeceptum -i, n (praecipio), *a precept, command, rule, ordinance, injunction*, medicorum, philosophorum, rhetorum, Cic, Latine loquendi, Cic, praecepta dare, Cic

praecerpo -cerpsi -cerptum, 3 (prae and carpo), *to pluck prematurely gather before the time* **I.** Lit, messes, Ov **II.** Fig, *to lessen or take away*, fructum officii tui, Cic

praecīdo -cīdi -cīsum, 3 (prae and caedo) **I.** *to cut off in front, cut off* **A.** Lit, alicui caput, Liv, fistulas (aquae), Cic, ancoras, *to cut the cables*, Cic **B.** Fig, **1,** *to cut short, to cut, abbreviate, abridge*, brevi praecidam, *I will express myself briefly*, Cic, praecide, *make it short*, Cic, **2,** *to take away, deprive of;* sibi reditum, Cic, **3,** *to refuse point blank*, plane sine exceptione, Cic **II.** *to cut in pieces* **A.** Lit, canem, Liv, cotem novaculā, Cic **B.** Fig, *to break off suddenly*, amicitias magis decere diluere quam repente praecidere, Cic.

praecinctus -a -um, partic of praecingo

praecingo -cinxi -cinctum, 3 *to gird, surround with a girdle*, middle, praecingi, *to gird oneself*, Cic Partic, recte praecincti pueri, Hor, altius ac nos praecincti, *girded higher up*, i e, *more rapid travellers*, Hor

praecĭno -cĕcĭni and -cĭnŭi -centum 3 (prae and cano) **I** Intransit, **A.** *to sing or play before*, **a,** of musical instruments (esp the flute), epulis magistratuum fides praecinunt, Cic, **b,** of flute-players, praecinere sacrificiis or sacris, Liv **B.** *to sing an incantation*, Tib **II** Transit, *to prophesy, predict*, magnum aliquid deos populo Romano praecinere, Cic

praecĭpes -is = praeceps (q v)

praecĭpĭo -cēpi -ceptum, 3 (prae and capio), *to take before, get before, receive in advance* **I.** Lit, pecuniam mutuam, Cic, iter, *to get the start*, Liv, si lac praeceperit aestus, *if the heat dries the milk beforehand*, Verg, praecipitur seges, *ripens too fast*, Ov **II.** Transit, **A.** *to take beforehand, anticipate*, praecipio gaudia suppliciorum vestrorum, *I enjoy in anticipation*, ap Cic, animo victoriam, Caes, consilia hostium, *know beforehand*, Cic **B.** Esp, *to tell beforehand, to write beforehand*, **a,** *to instruct, advise, warn, prescribe, admonish, charge, command*, hoc tibi praecipio, Cic, with ut or ne and the subj, illud potius praecipiendum fuit ut, etc, Cic, with subj alone Sall, with infin, temporibus parēre, Cic, absol, ut erat praeceptum, Caes, **b,** *to teach*, artem, Ov, alicui rationem tempestatum, Cic, praecipe cantus, Hor, absol, *to be a teacher, to give instruction*, de eloquentia, Cic

praecĭpĭtantĕr, adv (praecipito), *headlong, headforemost, precipitately*, Lucr

praecĭpĭto, 1 (praeceps) **I.** Transit, *to cast down headlong* **A.** **1,** lit, sese Leucade, Cic, sese in fossas, Caes, pass, praecipitari, in middle sense, *to cast oneself down*, Sall, poet, lux praecipitatur aquis, *sinks beneath the waves*, Ov, **2,** transf, partic praecipitatus, *drawing to a close* Ov, nox praecipitata, Ov **B.** Fig, **a,** *to cast down*, aliquem ex altissimo dignitatis gradu, Cic, *to cast to the ground, destroy, ruin* rempublicam, Liv, **b,** pass, praecipitari, as middle, *to rush into*, in insidias, Liv, hence, (α) *to hurry away*, furor iraque mentem praecipitant, Verg, (β) *to hasten* moras omnes, Verg, (γ) *to press on*, with infin, dare tempus sociis humandis, Verg **II.** Intransit, *to fall down, to sink violently* **A.** **1,** lit, Nilus praecipitat ex montibus, Cic, in fossam, Liv, **2,** transf, *to draw to a close, hasten to the end*, sol praecipitans, *declining*, Cic, hiems jam praecipitaverat, *was drawing to a close*, Caes **B.** Fig, **a,** praecipitantem impellere, *to give a push to a falling man, to knock a man when he is down*, Cic, praecipitare ad exitium, Cic, respublica praecipitans, *hastening to its fall*, Cic, **b,** *to fall into*, in amorem, *to fall in love*, Plaut

praecĭpŭē, adv (praecipuus), *especially, chiefly, particularly, principally*, Cic

praecĭpŭus -a -um (prae and capio) **I.** *peculiar, especial*, mihi consuli praecipuum fuit praeter alios, Cic, in communibus miseriis praecipuo quodam dolore angi, Cic Subst, **praecĭpŭum** -i, n *a special right, a prerogative*, Cic **II.** *excellent, distinguished, extraordinary, especial*, **a,** quos praecipuo semper honore Caesar habuit, Caes, natura ingenerat praecipuum quendam amorem, Cic, praecipuus toro (*distinguished by a seat of honour*) Aeneas, Verg Subst, **praecĭpŭum** -i, n *pre-eminence superiority*, homini praecipui a natura nihil datum esse, Cic, plur, **praecĭpŭa** -ōrum, n = προηγμενα, *things* (in the Stoic philosophy) *that come next to the greatest good*, **b,** *especially suited for*, praecipuus ad pericula, Tac

praecīsē, adv (praecisus) **I.** *briefly, in few words*, id praecise dicitur, Cic **II.** *absolutely, decidedly*, negare, Cic

praecīsus -a -um, p adj (from praecido) **I.** *steep, abrupt, precipitous*, saxa, Verg **II** Rhet t t, *short, brief, broken off*, Cic

praeclārē, adv (praeclarus) **I.** *very plainly, very clearly*, intellegere, Cic, explicare, Cic **II** *admirably, excellently*, gerere negotium, Cic meminisse, Cic, facere, *to do something remarkable*, Cic

praeclārus -a -um, *very bright, very brilliant* **I.** Lit, lux, Lucr **II.** Fig, **1,** *noble illustrious, remarkable, distinguished, excellent, admirable, famous*, gens bello praeclara, Verg, situs (urbis), Cic, indoles, Cic, praeclarissimi conatus, Cic, subst, **praeclāra** -ōrum, n *valuables*, Cic.; **2,** in a bad sense, *notorious*; sceleribus ferox atque praeclarus, Sall.

praeclūdo -clūsi -clūsum, 3. (prae and claudo). **I.** Lit., *to close in front, to shut up, to close*; praecludere portas consuli, Caes. **II.** Transf., *to close to any one, deprive of access to*; sibi curiam, Cic.; maritimos cursus, Cic.; vocem alicui, *to stop a person's mouth*, Liv.

praeco -ōnis, m. **I.** *a public crier, herald* (in a court of justice, at public assemblies, at auctions); per praeconem vendere aliquid, Cic.; fundum subjicere praeconi, *bring to the hammer*, Liv. **II.** Transf., *a publisher, herald, one who praises*; virtutis, Cic.

praecōgĭto, 1. *to think meditate, consider carefully beforehand*; multo ante facinus, Liv.

praecognosco (-cognōvi) -cognĭtum, 3. *to learn beforehand*; praecognito nostro adventu, ap. Cic.

praecŏlo -cŏlŭi -cultum, 3. *to cultivate before*, fig. **I.** animi praeculti rectis studiis et artibus, Cic. **II.** *to honour highly, to revere*; nova et ancipitia, Tac.

praecompŏsĭtus -a -um (prae and compono), *composed beforehand, studied*; os, *mien*, Ov.

praecōnĭus -a -um, *belonging to a praeco or crier*. **I.** Adj., quaestus, Cic. **II.** Subst., **praecōnĭum** -ĭi, n. **A.** *the office or business of a public crier*; praeconium facere, Cic. **B.** Transf., **1,** *a public crying, publishing, making known*; tibi praeconium deferam, Cic.; perago praeconia casus, Ov.; **2,** *a public laudation, commendation*; laborum suorum, Cic.

praeconsūmo -consumptus, 3. *to consume, exhaust beforehand*, Ov.

praecontrecto, 1. *to handle beforehand*, Ov.

praecŏquis -e and **praecŏquus** -a -um = praecox (q.v.).

praecordĭa -ōrum, n. (prae and cor). **I.** *the muscle separating the heart and lungs from the abdomen, the midriff, the diaphragm*, Cic. **II.** Transf., **A.** *the bowels, stomach*; anulus in praecordiis piscis inventus, Cic.; quid veneni saevit in praecordiis, Hor. **B.** *the breast, heart* (as the seat of feelings and passions); redit in praecordia virtus, Verg.; spiritus remanet in praecordiis, Liv.

praecorrumpo -rūpi -ruptum, 3. *to corrupt, bribe beforehand*; me donis, Ov.

praecox -cŏcis, **praecŏquis** -e, and **praecŏquus** -a -um (prae and coquo), *ripe before the time, premature*, Plin.

praecultus -a -um, partic. of praecolo.

praecurro -cŭcurri and -curri -cursum, 3. **I. A.** Lit., *to run before, hasten before*; praecurrit ante omnes, Caes.; ad aliquem, Caes.; aliquem equis albis, fig. = *to excel*, Hor. Partic. subst., **praecurrentĭa** -ium, n. *what goes before, antecedents*, Cic. **B.** Transf., **1,** *to go on before*; eo fama jam praecurrerat de praelio Dyrrhachino; **2,** of time, *to precede*; aliquem aetate, Cic.; with dat., ut certis rebus certa signa praecurrerent. **II.** Esp., *to surpass, exceed*; aliquem celeritate, Caes.

praecursĭo -ōnis f. (praecurro), *a going before*. **I.** Gen., sine praecursione visorum, Cic. **II.** In rhet., *the previous preparation of the hearer*, Cic.

praecursor -ōris, m. (praecurro), *a goer before, precursor*. **I.** Lit., **A.** Milit. t. t., praecursores, *the vanguard, advanced guard*, Liv. **II.** Transf., *a spy, scout*; in omni calumnia praecursorem habere, Cic.

praecŭtĭo -cussi -cussum, 3. (prae and quatio), *to shake before, brandish before*; taedas, Ov.

praeda -ae, f. (connected with prehendo), *spoils of war, plunder, booty*. **I.** Lit., praeda parta, Cic.; ingentes praedas facere, Liv. **II.** Transf., **A.** *the spoils of the chase, quarry, prey*; cervi luporum praeda rapacium, Hor. **B.** *plunder, gain*; maximos quaestus praedasque facere, Cic.

praedābundus -a -um (praedor), *plundering*, Sall.

praedamno, 1. **I.** *to condemn before*; aliquem. **II.** *to give up*; spem, Liv.

praedātĭo -ōnis, f. (praedor), *a plundering, pillaging*, Tac.

praedātor -ōris, m. (praedor). **I.** Lit., *a plunderer, pillager, robber*; vexatores ac praedatores, Cic. **II.** Transf., **A.** *a hunter*; caprorum, Ov. **B.** *a gain-loving, greedy person*, Tib.

praedātōrĭus -a -um (praedator), *plundering, pillaging, predatory*; classis, Liv.

praedēlasso, 1. *to weary, weaken beforehand*, Ov.

praedestĭno, 1. *to appoint, ordain beforehand*; sibi similes triumphos, Liv.

praedĭātor -ōris, m. (praedium), *a buyer of landed estates sold by auction, a dealer in estates*, Cic.

prediātōrĭus -a -um (praediator), *of or relating to the sale of land by auction*; jus, Cic.

praedĭcābĭlis -e (1. praedico), *praiseworthy*, Cic.

praedĭcātĭo -ōnis, f. (1. praedico). **I.** *a making publicly known, the public announcement of the praeco*, Cic. **II.** Transf., **1,** *a declaration, deposition*; nefariae societatis, *relating to*, Cic.; **2,** *a praising, commending, praise*, Cic.

praedĭcātor -ōris, m. (1. praedico), *a praiser, commender, public eulogist*, Cic.

1. **praedĭco,** 1. *to make publicly known, publish*. **I.** Lit., of the praeco, dimidias venire partes, Cic. **II.** Transf., **1,** *to declare, speak out, relate, proclaim, say, tell*; paucitatem nostrorum militum suis, Caes.; with acc. and infin., praedicantem contumeliam illam sibi a Cicerone impositam esse, Sall.; ea juventutis exercendae causā fieri praedicant, Caes.; praedicat se servo imperasse, Cic.; **2,** *to mention with praise, to commend, eulogise, boast*; virtutem, Cic.; falsa de se, Cic.; de suis laudibus, Cic.: with acc. and infin., Galli se omnes ab Dite patre prognatos praedicant, Caes.

2. **praedīco** -dixi -dictum, 3. **I.** *to say beforehand, speak before*; praedicta cornua quaerunt, Ov.; esp. of writers and orators, haec mihi praedicenda fuerunt, Cic. **II.** Esp., **A.** *to predict, foretell, prophesy*; defectiones solis, Cic.; futura, Cic.; with acc. and infin., nihil Antonium facturum (esse), Cic. **B. a,** *to fix, appoint beforehand*; diem (of the praetor), Tac.; **b,** *to warn, admonish, instruct, charge, command*; Pompeius suis praedixerat, ut Caesaris impetum exciperent, Caes.; Junonem praedicere, ne id faceret, Cic.

praedictĭo -ōnis, f. (2. praedico), *a prophesying, predicting*, Cic.

praedictum -i, n. (2. praedico), *a prophecy, prediction*, Cic. **II.** *an order, command*, Liv. **III.** *a concert, agreement*, Liv.

praedĭŏlum -i, n. (dim. of praedium), *a small landed estate, little farm*, Cic.

praedisco -didĭci, 3. *to learn before*; ea quae agenda sunt in foro, Cic.

praedispŏsĭtus -a -um, *arranged beforehand*; nuntii, Liv.

praedĭtus -a -um (prae and do), *endowed, furnished, provided with*, with abl , sensibus, Cic , virtute, Cic , amentiā, Cic , crudelitate, Cic

praedĭum -ii, n (praes), *a plot of land, landed estate*, rusticum, Cic , praedium vendere, Cic

praedīvĕs ītis, *very rich*, Liv

1 **praedo**, 1 = praedor (q v)

2 **praedo** ōnis, m (praeda), *a robber, pillager, plunderer*, urbis, Cic , maritimi, *pirates*, Nep , praedo maritus, *the husband that carried her off* (of Pluto), Ov

praedŏcĕo -doctus, 2 *to teach before, instruct before*, praedocti ab duce, Sall

praedŏmo -dŏmŭi, 1 *to tame before*, Sen

praedor, 1 dep (praeda) **I.** Intransit , **A.** Lit., praedatum exisse in agrum Latinum, Liv , milites praedantes, Caes **B.** Transf , *to rob, plunder, get gain*, in bonis alienis, Cic., de aratorum bonis, Cic , apud Mamertinos, Cic , ex alterius inscitia, Cic **II.** Transit , **A.** *to plunder, pillage, rob*, socios magis quam hostes, Tac **B.** 1, lit , *to carry off as prey*, ovem unam, Ov , **2,** transf , amores alicuius, *one's sweetheart*, Ov , singula de nobis anni praedantur, Hor

praedūco -duxi ductum, 3 *to lead forward, carry forward*, fossas viis, Caes , murum, Caes

praedulcis -e **I.** Lit , *very sweet*, Plin **II.** Transf , *very pleasant, very delightful*, decus Verg

praedūrus -a -um, *very hard, very strong*, homo praedurus viribus, Verg , corpora, Verg

praeēmĭnĕo (praemĭnĕo), 2 *to surpass, excel*, ceteros peritiā legum, Tac

praeĕo -īvi and -ii -itum, 4 *to go before, precede*. **I.** Lit , Laevinus Romam praeivit, Liv **II.** Fig , **A.** Gen , naturā praeeunte, Cic **B.** Esp , 1, *to say before, sing before, play before*, **a,** gen , ut vobis voce praeirent, quid judicaretis, Cic , **b,** religious and legal t t , *to dictate the words of an oath*, or *any solemn form of words*, verba praeire, Liv , carmen, Liv , praeire alicui, Cic , **2,** *to order, command*, omnia, ut decem viri praeierunt, facta, Liv

praefātĭo ōnis, f (praefor), *a religious or legal form of words, formula*, sacrorum, Liv., donationis, Cic.

praefectūra ae, f (praefectus), *the office of superintendent* or *overseer* **I.** Gen , annonae, Tac , vigilum, Tac **II.** Esp , 1, *the command of auxiliary troops*, esp of cavalry, Suet , **2,** *a subordinate provincial command*, praefecturam petere, Cic , **3,** meton , *an Italian town governed by a praefectus, a prefecture*, Cic

1 **praefectus** a -um, partic of praeficio

2 **praefectus** i, m (praeficio), *an overseer, superintendent* **I.** In private life, his utitur quasi praefectis libidinum suarum, Cic **II.** In political life, *a civil* or *military officer* or *superintendent* **A.** Gen , annonae, Liv , castrorum and castris, Tac , praefectus urbis, *governor of the city* (*Rome*), *and commander of the fire* cohortes urbanae, in the time of the republic only commanding in the place of the consul when absent, Liv

praefĕro -tŭli -lātum -ferre **I. A.** *to bear, carry before* or *in front*, ardentem facem, Cic , fasces praetoribus, Cic **B.** Fig , 1, gen , clarissimum lumen praetulistis menti meae, Cic , **2,** esp , **a,** *to bring to light, to show, manifest, display*, avaritiam, Cic , judicium, *express one's judgment*, Liv ; haec eius diei praefertur opinio, Caes , **b,** *to give the preference to, to prefer*, aliquem sibi, Cic , otium labori, Sall **II.** *to carry by*, middle, praeferri = *to hasten by, to ride by*, praeter castra praelati, Liv **III.** *to anticipate*, diem triumphi, Liv

praefĕrox -ōcis, *very bold, impetuous*, legati, Liv

praefervĭdus -a -um, *burning hot, very hot* **I.** Lit , balneum, Tac **II.** Fig , ira, Liv

praefestīno, 1 **I.** *to hasten exceedingly, hasten too much*, ne deficere praefestinarent, Liv. **II.** *to hasten by*, sinum, Tac

praefĭcĭo -fēci -fectum, 3 (prae and facio), *to set over, appoint as superintendent, overseer*, etc , aliquem pecori, Cic , bello gerendo or simply bello, Cic , legioni, Caes , praeficere aliquem in eo exercitu, Cic

praefīdens entis, *very confident, over confident*, Cic

praefīgo -fixi fixum, 3 *to fix in front, fasten before*, ripa sudibus praefixis munita, Caes , arma puppibus, Verg **II.** Transf , **A.** *to tip, point with*, jacula praefixa ferro, Liv **B.** *to pierce through, transfix*, Tib

praefīnĭo, 4 *to fix, prescribe, appoint beforehand*, diem, Cic , sumptum funerum, Cic , non praefinire, foll by quominus, Cic

praeflōro, 1 *to pluck the blossom prematurely*, fig , *to diminish, lessen*, gloriam eius victoriae praefloratam apud Thermopylas esse, Liv

praeflŭo, 3 *to flow past*, infimā valle, Liv , with acc of place, Tibur fertile, Hor , Noricam provinciam, Tac

praefōco, 1 (prae and faux), *to choke, suffocate*, viam animae, Ov

praefŏdĭo fōdi -fossum, 3 **I.** *to dig in front of*, portas, Verg **II.** *to bury previously*, aurum, Ov

praefor fātus sum fāri, *to speak before* **A. a,** *to utter beforehand*, majores nostri omnibus rebus agendis quod bonum, faustum, felix sit, praefabantur, Cic , carmen, Liv , so with acc of deity, divos, Verg , **b,** *to mention beforehand, to premise*, quae de deorum natura praefati sumus, Cic **B.** *to prophesy, foretell*, Liv

praefractē (praefractus), *sternly, resolutely*, nimis praefracte vectigalia defendere, Cic

praefractus -a -um, p adj with compar (from praefringo) **I.** Of written style, *abrupt, disconnected*, Thucydides praefractior, Cic **II.** Of character, *stern, severe, harsh*, Aristo Chius praefractus, ferreus, Cic

praefrīgĭdus -a -um, *very cold*, Ov

praefringo -frēgi -fractum, 3 (prae and frango), *to break off in front, break in pieces*, hastas Liv

praefulcĭo -fulsi -fultum, 4 *to support, prop up*, fig , illud praefulci atque praemuni ut, etc , Cic

praefulgĕo -fulsi, 2 *to gleam forth, shine forth* **I.** Lit , equus praefulgens dentibus aureis, Verg **II** Fig , triumphali decore praefulgens, *conspicuous, distinguished*, Tac

praegĕlĭdus -a -um, *very cold*, Alpes, Liv

praegestĭo, 4 *to desire exceedingly*, praegestit animus videre, Cic

praegnans (prae and root GNA, whence gnascor), *pregnant* **I.** Lit , Cic **II.** Fig , *full of*, fusus stamine, Juv.

praegrăcĭlis e, *very slim, slender, lank*, Tac

praegrăvis -e, *very heavy* **I.** Lit , **A.** Of weight, onus, Ov **B** Of movement, praegravis corpore, Liv **II.** Transf , of persons, *wearisome*, Tac.

praegrăvo, 1. *to press heavily upon, weigh upon, oppress, to weigh down.* **I.** Lit., praegravata inhaerentibus scuta, Liv. **II.** Fig., *to overwhelm, oppress, weigh down;* dantem et accipientem, Liv.; animum, Hor.

praegrĕdĭor -gressus sum, 3. dep. (prae and gradior). **I.** *to go before, precede;* praegredientes amici, Cic.; with acc., signa, agmen, Liv.; nuntios, famam, *outstrip*, Liv. **II.** *to pass by, march by;* ea (castra), Liv.

praegressĭo -ōnis, f. (praegredior), *a going before, precedence;* causae, Cic.

praegressus -ūs, m. (praegredior), *a going on before*, Cic.

praegustātor -ōris, m. (praegusto), *one who tastes before, a taster, foretaster.* **I.** Lit., Suet. **II.** Fig., libidinum tuarum, Cic.

praegusto, 1. *to taste before;* cibos, Ov.

praehĭbĕo -ŭi -ĭtum, 2. (prae and habeo), *to offer, hold out, afford, supply, furnish*, Plaut.

praejăcĕo, 2. *to lie before;* campus qui castra praejacet, Tac.

praejūdĭcātus -a -um, v. praejudico.

praejūdĭcĭum -ĭi, n. *a previous judgment, a preliminary decision* or *examination* (for the sake of investigating facts for subsequent proceedings). **I.** Lit., **a**, de quo non *praejudicium* sed plane *judicium* jam pactum putatur, Cic.; apud eosdem judices reus est factus, quum duobus jam praejudiciis damnatus esset, Cic.; **b**, transf., *a premature decision;* neminem praejudicium tantae rei afferre, Liv. **II.** Meton., *an example, precedent;* Pompeius vestri facti praejudicio demotus, *by your example*, Caes.

praejūdĭco, 1. *to decide beforehand, to give a preliminary judgment;* **a**, legal t. t., re semel atque iterum praejudicatā, Cic. Partic. perf. subst., **praejūdĭcātum** -i, n. = praejudicium, (I.); **b**, transf., in partic., **praejūdĭcātus** -a -um, *previously decided;* opinio praejudicata, Cic.

praejŭvo -jūvi, 1. *to assist before*, Tac.

praelābor -lapsus sum, 3. dep. *to glide before, flow, swim before* or *along;* insula in quam Germani nando praelabebantur, Tac.; with acc., praelabi flumina rotis, Verg.

praelambo -lambi, 3. *to lick before, taste before*, Hor.

praelargus -a -um, *very abundant*, Juv.

praelĕgo -lēgi -lectum, 3. *to sail past, coast along;* Campaniam, Tac.

praelĭgo, 1. **I.** *to bind in front;* sarmenta praeligantur cornibus boum, Liv. **II.** *to bind up;* os obvolutum est folliculo et praeligatum, Cic.

praelium, etc. = proelium, etc. (q.v.).

praelongus -a -um, *very long;* gladius, Liv.

praelūcĕo -luxi, 2. *to carry a light before;* lit., *to light before*. **I.** Lit., Suet. **II.** Fig., **1**, with acc. (amicitia) bonam spem praelucet in posterum, *sheds the kindly light of hope*, Cic.; **2**, *to outshine, surpass;* nullus sinus Baiis praelucet, Hor.

praelum = prelum (q.v.).

praelustris -e (prae and lustro), *very illustrious;* praelustri ab arce, Ov.

praemando, 1. *to order beforehand;* ut conquireretur, ap. Cic.; hence, **praemandāta** -ōrum, n. *a writ of arrest*, Cic.

praemātūrus -a -um, *too early, premature;* hiems, Tac.; canities, Tac.

praemĕdĭcātus -a -um, *protected by medicine* or *charms*, Ov.

praemĕdĭtātĭo -ōnis, f. (praemeditor), *considering beforehand;* futurorum malorum, Cic.

praemĕdĭtor, 1. dep. *to meditate upon, consider beforehand;* praemeditari quo animo accedam ad urbem, Cic.; with acc. and infin., id praemeditari ferundum modice esse, Cic.; partic. perf. pass., **praemĕdĭtātus** -a -um, *considered beforehand;* mala, Cic.

praemĕtŭens -entis, p. adj. (from praemetuo), *fearing beforehand*, Phaedr.

praemĕtŭentĕr, adv. (praemetuens), *apprehensively, anxiously*, Lucr.

praemĕtŭo, 3. *to fear beforehand, be apprehensive.* **I.** Intransit., alicui, Caes. **II.** Transit., *to fear beforehand;* deserti conjugis iras, Verg.

praemitto -mīsi -missum, 3. *to send before, send on, despatch before.* **I.** Lit., (α) of persons, aliquem, Cic.; legiones in Hispaniam, Caes.; without acc., *to send before;* ad eos equites, Caes.; (β) of things, alicui odiosas literas, Cic. **II.** Transf., *to send before;* haec favorabili oratione praemisit, Tac.

praemĭum -ĭi, n. (prae and emo), *that which is taken first.* **I.** Gen., *advantage, gain, profit;* omnia praemia donaque fortunae, Cic. **II.** Esp., **A.** *an honourable reward, recompense;* praemia bene de republica meritorum, Cic.; alicui praemium dare pro aliqua re, Cic.; praemium praeponere or exponere, *to promise*, Cic.; ironically = *punishment;* cape praemia facti, Ov. **B.** Esp., *booty;* in war, pugnae, Verg.; in the chase, leporem et gruem jucunda captat praemia, Hor.

praemŏlestĭa -ae, f. *trouble beforehand*, Cic.

praemōlĭor, 4. dep. *to prepare beforehand;* rem, Liv.

praemŏnĕo -ŭi -ĭtum, 2. *to warn, advise, admonish beforehand.* **I.** Gen., with acc., conatus hostis, *against hostile attempts*, Liv.; with ut and the subj., me, ut magnopere caverem, praemonebat, Cic. **II.** *to foretell, presage*, Ilion arsurum Ov.

praemŏnĭtus -ūs, m. (praemoneo), *a prediction, premonition*, Ov.

praemonstro, 1. **I.** *to show, point out before*, Lucr. **II.** *to prophesy, presage, predict;* magnum aliquid populo Romano, Cic.

praemordĕo -mordi -morsum, 2. *to bite off;* fig., *to pilfer;* aliquid ex aliquo, Juv.

praemŏrĭor -mortŭus sum -mŏri, 3. dep. *to die prematurely*, Ov.; transf., praemortui jam est pudoris, *his modesty is dead*, Liv.

praemūnĭo (praemoenio), 4. **I.** *to fortify in front;* aditus duos magnis operibus, Caes. **II.** Fig., *to fortify, secure, make safe;* genus dicendi praemunitum, Cic.; quae praemuniuntur sermoni, *premised to meet objections*, Cic.

praemūnītĭo -ōnis, f. (praemunio), *a fortifying beforehand;* rhet., fig., of an orator, *a preparation of the minds of his hearers*, Cic.

praenăto, 1. *to swim before, swim past, flow by*, Verg.

Praeneste -is, n. (f. in Verg.), *a town in Latium, famous for its roses, its nuts, and for the temple and oracle of Fortuna*, now *Palestrina.* Hence, **Praenestīnus** -a -um, *belonging to Praeneste;* sortes, *the utterances of the oracle there*, Cic.

praenĭtĕo -ŭi, 2. *to shine forth;* fig., cur tibi junior praeniteat, *outshines thee*, Hor.

praenōmen -ĭnis, n. *the name which stood before the gentile name, and distinguished the individual, the first name, the praenomen* (e.g., Caius, in C. J. Caesar; Marcus, in M. T. Cicero), Cic.

praenosco -nōvi -nōtum, 3. *to become acquainted with beforehand, foreknow*, futura, Cic

praenōtio -ōnis, f (praenosco), *preconception, innate idea* (translation of πρόληψις), Cic

praenūbĭlus a -um, *very cloudy, very dark*, Ov

praenuncĭa, etc = praenuntia, etc (q v)

praenuntĭa, v praenuntius

praenuntĭo, 1 *to announce, report, tell beforehand, foretell, predict*, futura, Cic

praenuntĭus -a -um, *foretelling*, subst (in f and n), *that which announces beforehand, a harbinger, sign, token, omen*, stellae calamitatum praenuntiae, Cic , ales praenuntius lucis, *the cock*, Ov

praeoccŭpātio ōnis, f (praeoccupo), *a taking possession of before*, locorum, Nep

praeoccŭpo, 1 **I.** *to take possession of before, seize before*, iter, Caes , loca, Liv **II.** Transf , **1,** *to take possession of beforehand, to preoccupy*, animos timor praeoccupaverat, Caes , **2,** *to anticipate, to surprise*, ne adventu Caesaris praeoccuparetur, Caes , with infin , legem ipsi praeoccupaverant ferre, Liv

praeopto, 1 **I.** *to prefer, wish rather, desire more*, nemo non illos sibi, quam vos, dominos praeoptet, Liv , with infin , nudo corpore pugnare, Caes **II.** aliquid alicui rei, *to prefer*, otium urbanum militiae laboribus, Liv.

praepando, 3 *to open wide in front, stretch open in front, extend before*, Cic

praepărātio ōnis, f (praeparo), *preparation*, ad minuendum dolorem, Cic

praepăro, 1 *to make ready, provide, prepare*, naves, Cic , res necessarias ad vitam degendam, Cic , animos ad sapientiam, Cic ; aures (auditorum) praeparatae, Liv

praepĕdĭo -ivi and -ii itum, 4 (prae and root PED) **I.** *to entangle by the feet, shackle, fetter*, praepeditis Numidarum equis, Tac **II.** Transf , *to hinder, impede, obstruct*, quum lassitudo ac vulnera fugam praepedissent, Liv , singultu medios praepediente sonos, Ov , praepediri valetudine, *to be hindered by ill health*, Tac

praependĕo -pendi, 2 intransit , *to hang before, hang in front*, Caes

praepĕs -pĕtis (prae and peto) **I.** Lit., t t of augury, of birds from whose flight favourable omens were gathered, *quick in flight, rapidly flying, swift*, praepes avis, and subst simply praepes, Cic , praepetibus pennis se credere caelo, Verg **II.** Transf , *quick in flight and motion*, **a,** adj , deus, *the winged god*—i e , *Cupid*, Ov , **b,** subst , *a bird*, Jovis, *the eagle*, Ov , Medusaeus (of Pegasus), Ov

praepīlātus -a um, *having a ball or button in front* (applied to foils or blunt weapons); missilia, Liv.

praepinguis e, *very fat, very rich*, solum, Verg

praepollĕo -pollui, 2 *to be very powerful, to excel* or *surpass in power*, vir virtute praepollens, Liv

praepondĕro, 1 *to outweigh*, fig , neque ea volunt praeponderari honestate, Cic

praepōno -pŏsui pŏsitum, 3 *to put before, place before* **I.** Lit , **A.** Gen , pauca (scribendo), Cic transf , praepositae causae, *antecedent*, Cic **B.** Esp , *to put over, set over as overseer, commander*, etc , aliquem bello, provinciae, navibus, Cic , militibus, Caes Partic subst , **praepŏsĭtus** -i, m *a commander*, Tac **II.** Fig , *to prefer*, salutem reipublicae vitae suae, Cic Partic. subst , **praepŏsĭtum** i, n (translation of προηγμένον), *something to be preferred, something advantageous, but not* (in the Stoic philosophy) *absolutely good*, e g , *riches*, etc , Cic.

praeporto, 1 *to carry before*, Lucr

praepŏsĭtio ōnis, f (praepono), *a placing before* **I.** 1, lit , negationis, Cic , **2,** meton , grammat t t , *a preposition*, Cic **II.** *a preferring, preference*, Cic

praepŏsĭtus, partic of praepono

praepossum pŏtui -posse, *to be very powerful, have the chief power*, Tac

praepostĕrē, adv (praeposterus), *in a reversed order, perversely, absurdly*, Cic

praepostĕrus a -um **I.** *having the last first, inverted, perverse, distorted, absurd*, gratulatio, Cic , consilia, Cic **II.** Transf , of persons, *perverse*, Cic

praepŏtens -entis, *very powerful, very mighty*, **a,** of persons, viri, Cic , Carthago praepotens terrā marique, Cic , with abl instr , praepotens armis Romanus, Liv , with genit , Juppiter omnium rerum praepotens, *ruling over*, Cic , **b,** transf , of things, philosophia, Cic

praeprŏpĕrantĕr, adv *very quickly, very hastily*, Lucr

praeprŏpĕrē, adv (praeproperus), *very hastily, too quickly*, festinare, Liv , agere, Liv

praeprŏpĕrus -a um, *exceedingly quick, too quick, overhasty, precipitate* **I.** Lit , festinatio, Cic , celeritas, Liv **II** Transf , ingenium, Liv

praepūtĭum -ii, n *the foreskin*, Juv

praequam, v prae.

praequĕror -questus sum queri, *to complain beforehand*, Ov

praerădĭo, 1 *to outshine*, Ov

praerăpĭdus -a -um, *very rapid*, gurges, Liv

praerĭgesco -rigui, 3 *to grow very stiff*, Tac

praerĭpĭo -ripui reptum, 3 (prae and rapio), *to snatch away, pluck from, tear away, carry off*. **I.** Gen , alicui arma, Ov , alicui laudem destinatam, Cic **II.** Esp , **a,** *to carry off before the time*, deorum beneficium festinatione, Cic , **b,** *to anticipate, forestall*, hostium consilia, Cic

praerōdo -rōdi rōsum, *to gnaw in front, to gnaw off, bite through*, Hor

praerŏgātīvus a -um (praerogo, *to ask beforehand*), *asked before others* (for vote, opinion, etc) **I.** Lit , polit t t , *voting first, voting before others*, centuria praerogativa, and gen subst , **praerŏgātīva** -ae, f *the century to which the lot fell of voting first in the comitia*, Cic , praerogativam referre, Cic , hence, omen praerogativae, *the omen given by the name of the prerogative century*, Cic **II** **praerŏgātīva** -ae, f **A.** *a previous choice*, Liv **B.** *a sure sign, indication, presage*, triumphi, Cic , voluntatis, Cic

praerumpo -rūpi -ruptum, 3 *to break off, tear off in front*, funes, Caes

praeruptus a um, p adj (from praerumpo), *broken off* **I.** Lit , of places, *steep, precipitous, overhanging*, saxa, Cic , mons, Verg Plur subst , **praerupta** -ōrum, n *precipices*, Liv **II.** Transf , juvenis animo praeruptus, *violent*, Tac , dominatio, *stern, severe*, Tac

praes, praedis, m (praevideo) **I.** *a surety, security*, praedem esse pro aliquo, Cic , praedes dare, Cic **II.** Metón , *the property of the security*, ne L Plancus praedes tuos venderet, Cic

praesaepes (**praesaepis**) -is, f , **praesaepe** is, n , and **praesaepium** -ii, n.

(praesaepio), *an inclosure.* **I.** *a crib, manger,* Ov., transf., certum praesaepe, contemptuously= *table,* Hor. **II.** *a stall,* Verg.; transf., praesaepibus arcent, *from the hives,* Verg.; in praesaepibus, *in low houses,* Cic.

praesaepio -saepsi -saeptum, 4. *to block up in front;* omnem aditum, Cic.

praesāgio, 4. **I.** *to presage, forebode, have a presentiment of;* praesagire, id est, futura ante sentire, Cic.; quasi praesagiret, Cic.; de fine belli, Liv. **II.** Transf., *to foreshow, predict,* Lucr.

praesāgitio -ōnis, f. (praesagio), *a premonition, foreboding, presentiment,* Cic.

praesāgium -ii, n. (praesagio). **I.** *a presage, presentiment, foreboding;* malorum, Tac. **II.** Transf., *a prediction, prophesying;* Tiberii de Servio Galba, Tac.

praesāgus -a -um. **I.** *presaging, foreboding;* pectora, Ov.; with genit., mens praesaga mali, Verg. **II.** Transf., *predicting;* fulmen, Verg.; verba, Ov.

praescisco -scivi, 3. *to learn, find out beforehand;* praesciscere quam quisque eorum provinciam, quem hostem haberet volebat, Liv.

praescius -a -um, *knowing beforehand, prescient;* corda, Verg.; with genit., periculorum, Tac.

praescrībo -scripsi -scriptum, 3. **I.** *to write before, set before in writing;* **1,** lit., sibi nomen, Verg.; auctoritates praescriptae, *the names of senators contained in a decree of the senate,* Cic.; **2,** transf., *to put forward* or *take as a pretext,* Tac. **II.** *to write down for imitation.* **A.** *to prescribe, ordain, define, direct beforehand;* jura civibus, Cic.; ne quid ageret, Cic. **B.** *to draw up an outline of,* Tac.

praescriptio -ōnis, f. (praescribo). **I.** Lit., *a writing before;* hence, meton., *a title, inscription, preamble, introduction;* legis, Cic. **II.** Transf., **1,** *a precept, rule, order;* rationis, Cic.; **2,** *limitation;* in hac praescriptione semihorae, Cic.; **3,** *a pretext;* honesta, Cic.; hence, legal t. t., *an objection, demurrer,* Cic.

praescriptum -i, n. (praescribo), *that which is written down.* **I.** Lit., **A.** *a prescribed limit;* intra praescriptum equitare, Hor. **II.** Fig., *an order, a precept, rule;* legum, Cic.

praesĕco -sĕcŭi -sĕcātum and -sectum, 1. *to cut in front;* crines, Caes.; fig., carmen praesectum, *pruned down,* Hor.

praesens -entis (praesum). **I.** Gen., *present, in person, at hand;* quo praesente, *in whose presence,* Cic.; praesens tecum egi, *in person,* Cic.; in praesenti (sc. tempore), *now,* Cic.; in praesens tempus, *for the present time,* Cic. Subst., **praesentĭa** -ium, n. *the present,* Ov. **II.** **1,** *on the spot, immediate, momentary, not delayed;* poena, *immediately following the offence,* Cic.; decretum, *passed instantly,* Liv.; **2,** *immediately efficacious, effective, powerful;* auxilium, Cic.; memoria praesentior, *more vivid,* Liv.; with infin., praesens imo tollere de gradu, *with power to,* Hor.; **3,** *open, visible;* ora, Verg.; transf., insidiae, *plain,* Cic.; **4,** *pressing, urgent;* jam praesentior res erat, Liv.; **5,** of character, *resolute, determined;* animus, Cic.; **6,** *present, aiding, propitious;* deus, Cic.

praesensio -ōnis, f. (praesentio), *a presentiment, foreboding, premonition;* rerum futurarum, Cic.

praesentĭa -ae, f. (praesens). **I.** *presence;* alicuius, Cic.; animi, *presence of mind, determination, courage,* Caes., Cic.; in praesentia, *for the present, now, at present,* Cic. **II.** *impression, effect;* veri, Ov.

praesentĭo -sensi -sensum, 4. *to feel or perceive beforehand, to have a presentiment* or *premonition;* animo providere et praesentire, Caes.; futura, Cic.

praesēpes, etc. = praesaepes, etc. (q.v.).

praesēpio = praesaepio (q.v.).

praesertim, adv. *especially, chiefly;* praesertim quum and quum praesertim, Cic.; praesertim si, Cic.; praesertim quod, Cic.

praesĕs -sidis, c. (praesideo), *sitting before* (i.e., *to protect, take care of*); hence, **I.** *protecting;* usually subst., *a protector, protectress;* reipublicae, Cic.; templorum, Cic. **II.** *a chief, ruler, president;* praeses belli, *goddess of war* (of Minerva), Verg.; praeside pendet ab uno, Ov.

praesĭdens -entis, m. (praesideo), *a president, ruler,* Tac.

praesĭdĕo -sēdi -sessum, 2. (prae and sedeo). **A.** *to sit before, protect, guard;* with dat., huic imperio, Cic.; urbi, Liv.; foribus caeli (of Janus), Ov.; with acc., Galliae litus, Tac. **B.** *to preside over, manage, direct, govern;* rebus urbanis, Caes.; orbi terrarum, Cic.; with acc., exercitum, Tac.

praesĭdĭārĭus -a -um (praesidium), *serving as a guard* or *protection;* milites, Liv.

praesĭdĭum -ii, n. (praeses), *a sitting before;* hence, **I.** Lit., *protection, defence;* **a,** alicui esse praesidio, Cic.; **b,** milit. t. t., *a guard, patrol, escort;* legiones quae praesidio impedimentis erant, Caes. **II.** Meton., **A.** *that which defends, protection, help;* **a,** classis praesidium provinciae, Cic.; **b,** milit. t. t., *the soldiers who form the guard;* praesidium agitare, *to set guards,* Liv.; praesidia in urbes inducere, Cic.; fig., in praesidio collocatus, Cic. **B.** *a place occupied by a garrison* or *guard, post, camp, fortification;* quum legio praesidium occupavisset, Caes.; in praesidiis esse, Cic.; praesidium communire, Liv.; fig., de praesidio et statione vitae decedere, Cic. **C.** *help, assistance, support;* magnum sibi praesidium ad beatam vitam comparare, Cic.

praesignĭfĭco, 1. *to signify, announce beforehand;* hominibus futura, Cic.

praesignis -e (signum), *distinguished, remarkable before others,* Ov.

praesŏno -sŏnŭi, 1. *to sound forth, resound,* Ov.

praespargo, 3. *to scatter, strew before,* Lucr.

praestābĭlis -e (praesto), *distinguished, preeminent, remarkable;* res magnitudine praestabiles, Cic.; melius fuisse et praestabilius me civem in hac civitate nasci, Cic.; nullam dignitatem praestabiliorem, Cic.

praestans -antis, p. adj. (from praesto), *excellent, distinguished, preeminent;* **a,** of persons, gen. with abl., or in with the abl., homo prudentiā praestans, Cic.; Aristoteles longe omnibus praestans et ingenio et diligentiā, Cic.; virginibus praestantior omnibus, Ov.; in illis artibus praestantissimus, Cic.; **b,** of things, praestanti et singulari fide, Cic.; praestanti corpore Nymphae, Verg.

praestantĭa -ae, f. (praestans), *superiority, excellence;* si quam praestantiam virtutis, ingenii, fortunae consecuti sunt, Cic.; mentis, Cic.

praesterno, 3. *to strew, spread before,* Plaut.

praestĕs -stitis, c. (2. praesto) = praeses, *a tutelary, protecting deity;* Lares, Ov.

praestīgĭa -ae, f., usually plur., **praestīgĭae** -ārum, f. (praestringo), *deception, illusion, juggling;* verborum, Cic.

praestĭtŭo -stitŭi -stitūtum, 3 (statuo), *to prescribe, appoint beforehand*, tempus alicui, Cic ; diem operi, Cic

1 **praestō**, adv (from praestus = praesitus, as repostus = repositus), *present, at hand, here, ready*, gen with esse, *to be at hand, to show oneself, to appear*, with the notion of, *to attend or to wait upon, to be at one's service*, alicui, *to appear to help one at a court of law*, Cic , quaestores consulibus ad ministeria belli praesto essent, Liv , praesto esse virtutes ut ancillulas, Cic , fig , praesto esse, *to serve*, alicui, Cic , saluti tuae, Cic

2 **praesto** stiti -stitum and stātum stātūrus, 1 **I.** Intransit , *to stand before, excel, be distinguished*, inter suos, Cic , aliquā re, Cic , with dat or acc of person, *to surpass, excel*, alicui, Cic , alicui aliquā re, Cic , aliquem aliquā re, Liv , praestat used impers , *it is better, it is preferable*, with infin , praestat in eandem recidere fortunam, Cic , with quam, mori millies praestitit, quam haec pati, Cic **II.** Transit , *to become surety or guarantee for answer for, be responsible for* **A.** Lit , Messallam Caesari, Cic , damnum emptori, Cic , a vi, *from violence*, Cic , de me, Cic , with acc and infin , nullos (praedones) fore quis praestare poterat, Cic **B.** Transf , **a,** *to perform, do, execute, fulfil*, suum munus, Cic , officium, Caes , **b,** *to keep, hold*, fidem, *to keep one's word*, Cic , **c,** *to preserve*, socios salvos, Cic , rem publicam, Cic , **d,** *to show, manifest, exhibit*, benevolentiam, Cic , se, with acc of predicate, *to show oneself, behave oneself as* se invictum, Ov , praesta te eum, Cic , **e,** *to give, evince*, honorem debitum patri, *to show proper respect*, Cic , sententiam, *to give one's opinion*, Cic

praestōlor, 1 dep (connected with 1 praesto), *to wait for, expect*, with dat , tibi ad forum Aurelium, Cic , with acc , huius adventum ad Clupeam, Cic

praestringo -strinxi -strictum, 3 **I.** *to bind up, tie up*, faucem laqueo, Ov , pollices nodo, Tac **II.** *to make blunt*, aciem oculorum, *to weaken, darken*, Liv , oculos, Cic ; fig , aciem animi or mentis, Cic

praestrŭo -struxi -structum, 3 **I.** *to build in front, construct before*, hence, *to block up, render impassable*, aditum montis, Ov **II.** *to prepare, make ready for anything*, fraus fidem sibi in parvis praestruit, *procures for itself credibility in little things* Liv.

praesŭl -sŭlis, c *one who jumps or dances before others, a dancer*, Cic

praesultātor -ōris, m (praesulto), *one who dances before others, a dancer*, Liv

praesulto, 1 (prae and salio), *to leap, spring before*, Liv.

praesum -fŭi -esse, *to be before* **I.** *to be over, be placed over, preside over*, **a,** sacris, Cic , navi faciendae, Cic , **b,** *to be placed over, to govern*; populo, Cic , magistratui, *to preside as a magistrate*, Cic , **c,** milit t t., *to command*, exercitui, Caes ; in Bruttiis, Liv **II.** Transf , *to be the chief person, to take the lead in*, temeritati T Gracchi, Cic , illi crudelitati, Cic

praesūmo -sumpsi -sumptum, 3 *to take beforehand* **I.** remedia, Tac , domi dapes, Ov **II.** Transf , **1,** *to enjoy beforehand, to anticipate*, fortunam principatūs, Tac , **2, a,** *to imagine, represent to oneself beforehand*, spe praesumite bellum, Verg , praesumptum habere, *to suppose, take for granted*, Tac , **b,** *to assume, presume, suppose, conjecture, believe*, Tac

praesumptus -a -um, p adj (from praesumo), *taken for granted, presumed*, suspicio, *a preconceived suspicion*, Tac

praesŭo -sūtus, 3 *to sew up, to cover, conceal*, praesuta foliis hasta, Ov

praetempto = praetento (q v)

praetendo -tendi -tentum, 3 **I.** *to stretch out before, extend backwards*, hastas dextris, Verg , ramum olivae manu, Verg , poet , nec conjugis umquam praetendi taedas, i e , *never laid claim to lawful wedlock*, Verg **II.** *to place before, hold, spread before* **A. 1,** lit , saepem segeti, Verg , **2,** transf , *to place before*, sermonem decreto, Liv , hence, praetendi, of places, *to lie before or in front*, praetentaque Syrtibus arva, Verg , absol , tenue praetentum litus esse, Liv **B.** Fig , *to hold before as a pretext, pretend*, hominis doctissimi nomen tuis immanibus et barbaris moribus, *allege in excuse for*, Cic , aliquid seditioni, Liv

praetento (praetempto), 1 *to feel, try, test beforehand* **A.** Lit , iter baculo, Ov **B.** Fig , vires, Ov

praetĕpesco -tĕpŭi, 3 *to glow beforehand*, fig , si praetepuisset amor, Ov

praeter (from prae and suffix -ter like inter propter) **I** Adv , **A.** With negatives, *more than, except, with exception of*, nil praeter canna fuit, Ov **B.** *more than*, foll by quam, praeter sapit quam, etc , Plaut **II.** Prep with acc , **A.** Of space, *past, by, beyond*, praeter castra Caesaris suas copias transduxit, Caes , praeter oculos Lollii haec omnia ferebant, *before the eyes of*, Cic **B.** Transf , **1,** *beyond, beside, contrary to*, praeter spem, Liv , praeter modum, *beyond measure*, Cic , praeter opinionem, Cic , praeter naturam, Cic , **2,** *beyond, more than*, praeter ceteros laborare, Cic , **3,** *except, with the exception of*, omnes praeter Hortensium, Cic , with preceding negatives, nihil praeter suum negotium agere, Cic , hence, sometimes = *besides, in addition to, with*; num quid aliud ferret praeter arcam? Cic , ut praeter se denos adduceret, Caes

praetĕrăgo, 3 *to drive past, drive by*, equum, Hor

praetĕrĕā (praeter and abl eā). **I.** *besides, beyond this, further*, Cic **II.** *henceforth, hereafter*, Verg

praetĕrĕo -ivi and oftener ii -itum -ire **I.** Intransit , *to go by, pass by*, unda praeterit, Ov , of time, *to pass, elapse*, hora, Ov **II.** Transit , *to go by, pass by* **A.** Gen , **1,** hortos, Cic ; of time, in pass partic., **praetĕrĭtus** -a um, *past*, Cic , **praetĕrĭta** -ōrum, n *the past*, Cic , **2,** fig , **a,** *to escape the notice of, be unknown to*, non me praeterit, *I am not unaware*, Cic , **b,** (*a*) *to pass, omit*, nullum genus crudelitatis praeterire, *leave unpractised*, Cic , ut nulla fere pars orationis silentio praeteriretur, *was unapplauded*, Cic , (*β*) *to omit, not to mention*, caedes praetereo, libidines praetereo, Cic , esp , of the Censor, *not to read the name of a senator at the census (to publish his expulsion from the senate)*, quatuor praeteriti sunt, Liv , (*γ*) *to forget to do* foll by quin and subj , praeterire non potui quin scriberem ad te, Cic , (*δ*) *to omit, leave out, take no notice of, pass over*, in presents, legacies, etc , Philippus et Marcellus praetereuntur, *are passed by, get nothing*, Caes , filium fratris (in a will), Cic **B.** Esp , **1,** *to pass in a race, outstrip*, jamque hos cursu, jam praeterit illos, Verg , **2,** fig , *to surpass*, virtus tua alios praeterit, Ov

praetĕrĕquĭto, 1 *to ride past, ride by*, Liv

praeterfĕro -tŭli -lātum -ferre, *to carry past*, pass , praeterferri, *to be carried past, to flow, drive, go past*, Liv

praeterflŭo, 3 *to flow past, flow by*, moenia,

Liv.; fig., nec praeteritam (voluptatem) praeterfluere sinere, *vanish from the recollection*, Cic.

praetergrĕdior -gressus sum, 3. dep. (praeter and gredior), *to pass by, go beyond*; castra, Cic.; primos suos, Sall.

praetĕrĭtus -a -um, partic. of praetereo.

praeterlābor -lapsus sum, 3. dep. **I.** *to glide by, flow by*; tumulum, Verg.; tellurem, *to sail by*, Lucr. **II.** Fig., *to slip away*; ante enim (definitio) praeterlabitur quam percepta est, Cic.

praetermĕo, 1. *to pass by, go by*, Lucr.

praetermissio -ōnis, f. (praetermitto). **I.** *a leaving out, omission*; sine ullius (formae) praetermissione, Cic. **II.** *a passing over, neglecting*; aedilitatis, Cic.

praetermitto -misi -missum, 3. *to let pass*. **A.** Lit., neminem, Cic. **B.** Transf., **1**, *to let pass time, opportunity*, etc.; diem, Cic.; occasiones, Caes.; **2**, *to neglect, omit*; gratulationem, Cic.; defensionem, Cic.; non or nihil praetermittere, foll. by quin, or nihil praetermittere, foll. by quominus, Cic.; **3**, in writing or speaking, *to pass over, omit*; quod dignum memoriā visum, praetermittendum non existimavimus, Caes.; verba, Cic.; tantam rem negligenter, Liv.; **4**, *to overlook, let pass unpunished*, Liv.

praeterquam, adv. *except*, Cic.; praeterquam quod, *except that*, Cic.; praeterquam . . . etiam, Liv.; nihil praeterquam, Liv.

praetervectio -ōnis, f. (praetervehor), *a passing by, travelling past*; in praetervectione omnium, Cic.

praetervĕhor -vectus sum, 3. dep. **I.** *to ride by, sail by, be carried past*, Cic.; naves Apolloniam praetervectae, Caes.; classis praetervehens, Liv.; praetervehens equo, Liv.; fig., locum cum silentio, *pass by in silence*, Cic.; oratio aures vestras praetervecta est, Cic. **II.** Of soldiers, *to march past*, Tac.

praetervŏlo, 1. *to fly past*. **I.** Lit., quem praetervolat ales, Cic. **II.** Fig., *to slip by, escape*; praetervolat numerus, Cic.; occasionis opportunitas praetervolat, Cic.

praetexo -texŭi -textum, 3. **I.** *to weave before, form an edge, border, fringe*; **1**, lit., purpura saepe tuos fulgens praetexit amictus, Ov.; toga or tunica purpurā praetexta, Liv.; or simply toga praetexta, Cic.; or subst., **praetexta** -ae, f. *an upper garment, bordered with purple*, worn by the magistrates at Rome and in the Italian municipia and coloniae, and by free-born children, till they assumed the toga virilis, Cic.; hence, meton., **praetexta** -ae, f. (sc. fabula), *a Roman national tragedy*, Hor.; **2**, transf., **a**, *to provide with a border, adorn*; *to provide, furnish with*; omnia lenioribus principiis natura praetexuit; **b**, *to fringe, cover*; puppes praetexunt litora, Verg.; fig., *to cover, conceal*; culpam nomine conjugii, Verg.; **c**, *to adorn*; Augusto praetextum nomine templum, Ov. **II.** *to put forward as a pretext*; cupiditatem triumphi, Cic.

praetexta, v. praetexo.

praetextātus -a -um (praetexta, from praetexo). **I.** *clad in the* praetexta, Cic. **II.** *licentious*; mores, Juv.

praetextum -i, n. (praetexo), *a pretence, pretext*, Tac.

praetextus -ū, m. (praetexo). **I.** *outward appearance, consideration, consequence*, Tac. **II.** *a pretext*; sub levi verborum praetextu, Liv.

praetingo -tinctus, 3. *to dip in or moisten beforehand*, Ov.

praetor -ōris, m. (for praeitor, from praeeo), lit., *one who goes before*; hence, *a leader, chief*. Hence, **I.** In civil business, *the praetor*; used of the chief magistrate at Capua, Cic.; of the Suffetes at Carthage, Nep.; of the consul at Rome (also called praetor maximus), Liv.; at Rome, esp., *one of the praetors*, the Roman magistrates who administered justice (orig. two, the praetor urbanus and the praetor peregrinus, of whom the former was judge in disputes between Roman citizens, the latter in disputes between foreigners and between Roman citizens and foreigners); praetor is also used for propraetor, a magistrate who, after he had been praetor, was sent as a governor to a province; praetor primus, *the praetor who headed the poll*, Cic. **II.** To translate Gr. στρατηγός, *a commander of the army of a non-Roman nation*, Cic.

praetōrĭānus -a -um (praetorium), *belonging to the imperial body-guard, praetorian*, Tac.; plur. subst., **praetōrĭāni** -ōrum, m. *the praetorian guard*, Tac.

praetōrĭum, v. praetorius.

praetōrĭus -a -um (praetor). **I.** Adj., **A.** *relating to the praetor, praetorian*; **a**, of the praetor at Rome, comitia, *election of the praetor*, Liv.; jus, *administered by the praetor*, Cic.; potestas, *office of praetor*, Cic.; **b**, *relating to a praetor or propraetor in the provinces*; domus, *dwelling of a propraetor*, Cic. **B.** *relating to a general or commander*, Cic.; navis, *the admiral's ship*, Liv.; imperium, *command of the fleet*, Cic.; porta, *the gate of the camp near the general's tent*, Caes.; cohors praetoria; (α) *the general's body-guard*, Caes.; ironically, scortatorum praetoria cohors, Cic.; (β) (in imperial Rome) *the emperor's body-guard, the praetorian guard*, Tac. **II.** Subst., **A.** **praetōrĭum** -ii, n. **1**, *the official residence of the praetor or propraetor in a province*, Cic.; hence, transf., *a palace*, Juv.; **2**, *the chief place in a Roman camp, where the general's tent was, and where the ara, the augurale, and the tribunal were, to which the soldiers were summoned to hear speeches from the general, the officers to hold a council of war*; fit celeriter concursus in praetorium, Caes.; praetorium mittere, dimittere, *to dismiss the council of war*, Liv.; poet., *the cell of the queen-bee*, Verg.; **3**, *the imperial body-guard*, Tac. **B.** **praetōrĭus** -ii, m. (sc. vir), *a past praetor*, Cic.

praetrĕpĭdo, 1. *to tremble exceedingly, to be hasty or impatient*; praetrepidans, *hasty*, Cat.

praetūra -ae, f. (praetor). **I.** *the office, dignity of a praetor at Rome*; praeturā se abdicare, Cic. **II.** = στρατηγία, *the dignity of a general in Greece*, Cic.

Praetūtĭi -ōrum, m. *a people in Italy, in Picenum*. Adj., **Praetūtĭānus** -a -um, *Praetutian*; ager, Liv.

praeumbro, 1. *to overshadow*; fig., *to obscure*, Tac.

praevălens -entis, partic. of praevaleo (q.v.).

praeuro -ussi -ustum, 3. *to burn at the end or tip*; hasta praeusta, Liv.; stipites ab summo praeacuti et praeusti, Caes.

praevălĕo -vălŭi, 2. **I.** *to be physically strong*; praevalens juvenis Romanus, Liv. **II.** Transf., *to be very strong or powerful, to have great influence, to be stronger, to have more influence than others, to prevail, to get the upper hand*; praevalens populus, Liv.; praevalet pugnā equestri, *to be stronger in*, Tac.

praevălĭdus -a -um. **I.** Lit., *very strong, very powerful*; juvenis, Liv. **II.** Fig., **a**, of persons, etc., Blaesus, Tac.; urbs, Liv.; **b**, of things, terra, *too fertile, too productive*, Verg.

praevārĭcātĭo -ōnis, f (praevaricor), *a violation of duty;* esp of an advocate who has an understanding with the opposite party, *collusion*, Cic

praevārĭcātor -ōris, m (praevaricor), *one who violates his duty,* esp of an advocate, accuser, etc, *one who has a secret understanding with the opposite party, a double dealer*, praevaricator significat eum qui in contrariis causis quasi varie esse positus videatur, Cic

praevārĭcor, 1 dep (varico) **I.** Lit *to go crooked, walk crookedly,* Plin **II.** Fig, *to play a false* or *double part*, esp of an advocate or accuser who has a secret understanding with the other side, *to be guilty of collusion*, Cic

praevārus -a -um, *very perverse*, Cic

praevĕhor vectus sum, 3 dep *to ride* or *be carried before, in front, past*, praevectus equo, *riding past*, Verg, Liv.

praevĕnĭo -vēni -ventum, 4 *to come before, anticipate, get the start of*, hostis breviore via praeventurus erat, Liv, with acc, hostem, Liv, morte praeventus, *overtaken by death*, Liv

praeverro, 3 *to sweep* or *brush before*, veste vias, Ov

praeverto (praevorto) verti (-vorti) versum (-vorsum), 3 and **praevertor** verti, 3 dep **I.** *to undertake before*, quod huic sermoni praevertendum, Cic **II.** *to go before, run before, outstrip* **A.** Lit, ventos, Verg **B.** Fig, **1,** *to anticipate*, with acc = *to hinder, make of no avail*, quorum usum opportunitas praevertit, Liv, **2,** *to lay hold of before, preoccupy*, praevertere animos amore, Verg, **3,** *to be of more importance, to surpass, to be weightier*, nec posse bello praevertisse quidquam, Liv, **4,** (dep praevertor only in present forms); **a,** *to turn to first, to take more notice of*, illuc praevertamur, Hor, **b,** *to go to, make a visit to*, in Thessaliam, Liv

praevĭdĕo -vidi -visum, 2 *to see before, foresee* **I.** Physically, ictum venientem, Verg **II.** Transf, respublica quam praevideo in summis periculis, Cic

praevĭtĭo, 1 *to corrupt* or *vitiate beforehand*, gurgitem, Ov

praevĭus -a -um (prae and via), *going before, preceding*, Ov

praevŏlo, 1. *to fly before*, praevolantes grues, Cic

pragmătĭcus a um (πραγματικος), *skilled in civil affairs, state business etc*, pragmatici homines, Cic, subst, **pragmătĭcus** -i, m *a person who supplied orators and advocates with materials for their speeches*, Cic

prandĕo, prandi, pransum, 2 (prandium), *to take breakfast, to breakfast*, Cic, with acc, *to breakfast on*, olus, luscinias, Hor

prandĭum -ii, n (conn with Dor πράν = πρωΐ), *a late breakfast* or *lunch, taken about noon, of bread, fish, cold meat, etc*, prandium (alicui) dare, Cic, aliquem ad prandium invitare, Cic

pransus -a -um (prandeo), *having lunched*, curatus et pransus (of soldiers), *ready for action, prepared for battle*, Liv, pransus, potus, *having eaten and drunk well*, Cic

prātensis e (pratum), *of* or *relating to a meadow, growing in a meadow*, fungus, Hor

prātŭlum -i, n (dim of pratum), *a little meadow*, Cic

prātum i, n **I.** *a meadow*, pratorum viriditas, Cic **II.** Meton, *meadow-grass*, Ov.

prāvē, adv (pravus), lit., *crookedly*, hence, *ill, wrongly*, Cic.

prāvĭtas ātis, f (pravus) **I.** *crookedness, irregularity, deformity*, membrorum, Cic, oris, *a distortion of the mouth in speaking*, Cic **II.** Transf, **A.** *irregularity, impropriety*, Cic **B.** *moral irregularity, wickedness, perversity, pravity*, mentis, Cic, consulum, Liv

prāvus -a -um, *crooked, irregular, misshapen deformed* **I.** Lit, membra, Cic **II.** Transf, *morally crooked, perverse, improper, wrong*, affectio, Cic, pravissima regula, Cic

Praxĭtĕlēs -is and i, m (Πραξιτελης), *a sculptor of Athens, especially famous for his statues of Aphrodite at Cnidus and of Eros at Thespiae* Hence, adj, **Praxĭtĕlīus** -a -um, *of Praxiteles*

prĕcārĭo, adv (precarius), *by entreaty*, rogare, Cic

prĕcārĭus a -um (precor), *begged for, asked for, obtained by entreaty* **I.** libertas, Liv, orare precariam opem, Liv **II.** Transf, *uncertain, insecure, precarious*, forma, Ov, imperium, Tac

prĕcātĭo ōnis, f (precor), *a begging, entreating, request, prayer*, illa sollemnis comitiorum precatio, Cic

preces, v prex

prĕcĭae (prĕtĭae) ārum, f *a kind of vine*, Verg

prĕcor (praecor), 1. dep (prex), *to beg, entreat, request, pray, invoke* **I.** Gen, (α) with acc of pers, deos, Cic (β) with acc of thing, opem, Liv, haec precatus sum Cic, (γ) with ut or ne, or ut ne or non precor, foll by quominus and subj, precor ab diis ut, etc, Cic, (δ) absol eum sororem dedisse Prusiae precanti atque oranti, Liv, used also of things, dextra precans, Verg **II.** *to wish good* or *evil*, bene precari, Liv, male precari, Cic; precari alicui, *to curse a person*, Cic (partic, precantia, three syllables, Verg)

prĕhendo, prĕhendi, prĕhensum, 3 and syncop, prendo, prendi, prensum (prae and HENDO, χανδανω), *to lay hold of, seize hold of, catch* **I.** aliquem manu, Cic, of the soil, tellus prehendit stirpes, Cic **II.** Esp, **A.** *to lay hold of, to catch, detain*, in order to speak to a person, aliquem, Cic **B.** *to catch, detect in any act*, in furto, Plaut. **C.** *to seize violently, to take hasty possession of*, Pharum, Caes **D.** Meton, *to reach*, oras Italiae, Verg, quum ipsum ea moderantem et regentem paene prendent, *observed* Cic

prĕhenso, and oftener **prenso** (intens of prehendo), 1 *to lay hold of, seize* **I.** manus, Liv **II.** Esp, **A.** *to lay hold of a person in order to speak to him, to make a request, etc*, genua, Tac, veteranos, Liv **B.** *to canvass for an office*, homines, Liv, patres, Liv, absol, prensat Galba, Cic

prēlum -i, n (premo), *a wine-press, olive-press*, Verg

prĕmo, pressi, pressum, 3 *to press* **I.** Gen, **1, a,** lit, ad pectora natos, Verg, vestigia alicuius, *to follow in any one's footsteps*, Tac, frena dente, *to champ*, Ov, **b,** fig, necessitas eum premebat, Cic, premi aere alieno, Cic, **2,** transf, **a,** *to touch*, litus, Hor, insulam premit amnis, *surrounds*, Ov, **b,** *to hold*, frena manu, Ov, **c,** locum, *to be often in a place, frequent*, forum, Cic, so *to press with the body, lie on* humum, Ov, ebur, poet = *the curule chair of ivory*, Ov, **d,** *to cover, conceal*, canitiem galea premimus, Verg, ossa, *to bury*, Ov, fig, (α) *to bury, wrap*, me pressit alta quies, Verg; (β) *to conceal, suppress*, curam sub corde, Verg; **e,** *to make something by pressing*, caseum, Verg, lac, *to make cheese*, Verg, **f,** *to press hard, to pursue closely, press upon*, hostes, Caes, oppidum obsidione, Caes.; cervum ad retia, *to drive into the nets*, Verg.; fig., *to pursue with words*; aliquem, Cic.; aliquem criminibus, Ov.; **g,** *to lade, to load*; carinae pressae, Verg. **II. A.** *to press in*; dentes in vite, Ov.; presso vestigio, Cic.; transf., *to mark*; rem notā, Ov. **B. a,** *to extinguish*; ignem, Verg.; **b,** *to press out*; oleum, Hor. **C.** *to press down*; **a,** lit., (α) currum, Ov.; aulaeum premitur, Hor.; (β) *to plant*; virgulta per agros, Verg.; (γ) *to strike to the ground*; tres famulos, Verg.; **b,** fig., (α) *to slander, depreciate*; aliquem, Liv.; humana omnia, *to despise*, Cic.; (β) *to surpass*; facta premant annos, Ov.; (γ) *to rule, keep within bounds*; populos ditione, Verg. **D.** *to press together*; **a,** alicui fauces, Ov.; collum laqueo, Hor.; **b,** *to draw in*; habenas, Verg.; equos currentes, *to check*, Verg.; **c,** *to pare down, prune*; umbram falce, Verg.; fig., *to shorten*; quae dilatantur a nobis, Zeno sic premebat, Cic. **E.** *to hold back*; cursum, *to check*, Cic.; vocem, *to be silent*, Verg.

prendo = prehendo (q.v.).

prensātĭo -ōnis, f. (prenso), *the canvassing for an office*, Cic.

prenso = prehenso (q.v.).

pressē, adv. (pressus), **a,** of pronunciation, *not broadly, neatly*; presse et aequabiliter et leniter, Cic.; **b,** of style, *briefly, concisely*; dicere, Cic.; **c,** *accurately, precisely*; pressius agere, Cic.

pressĭo -ōnis, f. (premo), in plur., *props, stays*, Caes.

presso, 1. (intens. of premo), *to press*; manu brachia, Hor.; ubera, *to milk*, Ov.

1. **pressus** -a -um, p. adj. (from premo). **I.** Lit., *slow, measured*; presso gradu, Liv. **II.** Transf., **1,** *measured*; of pronunciation, *slow, controlled, moderate*; soni, Cic.; **2,** *short, concise*; oratio, Cic.; orator, Cic.; **3,** *accurate, precise*; Thucydides verbis pressus, Cic.

2. **pressus** -ūs, m. (premo), *a pressing, pressure*; ponderum, Cic.

prestēr -ēris, m. (πρηστήρ), *a fiery whirlwind*, Lucr.

prĕtĭōsē, adv. (pretiosus), *in a costly manner, splendidly, magnificently*; vasa pretiose caelata, Cic.

prĕtĭōsus -a -um (pretium). **I.** *costly, precious, of great value*; equus, Cic.; fulvo pretiosior aere, Ov.; res pretiosissimae, Cic. **II.** Transf., **A.** *costly, high-priced, dear*, Prop. **B.** *extravagant, giving a high price for a thing*; emptor, Hor.

prĕtĭum -ĭi, n. (root PRET, ΦΡΑΔ, φράζω), *worth, value, price*. **I.** Lit. and fig., **1,** lit., pretium constituere, *to fix the price*, Cic.; pretium habere, *to be worth something*, Cic.; so esse in pretio, Liv.; parvi pretii esse, Cic.; **2,** fig., operae eorum pretium facere, *to prize*, Liv. **II.** Transf., **A.** *money*; pretio emere, *for money*, Cic.; esp., *ransom-money*; pactum pro capite pretium, Cic. **B.** *wages, pay*; **a,** manus, Cic.; fig., operae pretium est, or videtur, with infin., *it is worth the while*, Cic.; **b,** *prize, reward*; certaminis, Ov.; nullo satis digno morae pretio tempus terunt, Liv.; **c,** *pay = punishment*; et peccare nefas, aut pretium est mori, Hor.; **d,** *bribe*; adduci pretio ad hominem condemnandum, Cic.

prex, prĕcis, only in dat., acc., and abl., gen. plur., prĕces, prĕcum, f. *a request, entreaty*. **I.** Gen., preces adhibere, Cic.; prece humili, Cic.; omnibus precibus petere or orare ut, etc., Caes., Cic. **II.** Esp., **a,** *prayer*; eorum preces ac vota, Cic.; **b,** *a curse, execration*; omnibus precibus detestari aliquem, Caes.; **c,** *a wish*; damus alternas accipimusque preces, Ov.

Prĭămus -i, m. (Πρίαμος). **I.** *the last king of Troy, husband of Hecuba, father of Paris, Hector, Cassandra*, etc. Hence, **A. Prĭămēis** -ĭdis, f. *a daughter of Priam, Cassandra*, Ov. **B. Prĭămĭdēs** -ae, m. *a son of Priam*, Verg. **C.** Adj., **Prĭămēius** -a -um, *belonging to Priam*; hospes, *Paris*, Ov.; conjux, *Hecuba*, Ov. **II.** *grandson of foregoing, son of Polites.*

Prĭāpus (-ŏs) -i, m. (Πρίαπος), *the god of gardens and vineyards, the god of fertility*, orig. worshipped at Lampsacus.

prīdem, adv. (from old form pris, whence prior, pridie and -dem). **I.** *long ago, long since*; jam pridem, *long ago*, Cic.; non ita pridem, *not very long ago*, Cic. **II.** *formerly*, Cic.

prīdĭē, adv. (from old form pris, whence prior, pridem and dies), *on the day before yesterday*; with acc. or genit. of the day from which the reckoning is taken, or foll. by quam, pridie eum diem, Cic.; pridie eius diei, Cic.; pridie quam Athenas veni, Cic.

Prĭēnē -ēs, f. (Πριήνη), *a sea-port in Ionia, birthplace of Bias, now Samsun Kalesi.*

prīmaevus -a -um (primus and aevum), *young, youthful*; Helenor, Verg.

prīmānus -a -um (primus), *belonging to the first legion*. Subst., **prīmāni** -ōrum, m. *soldiers of the first legion*, Tac.

prīmārĭus -a -um (primus), *in the first rank, excellent, distinguished*; vir populi, Cic.

prīmĭgĕnĭus -a um (primus and geno = gigno), *original, primitive*, Varr. Subst., **Prīmĭgĕnĭa** -ae, f. *a surname of the goddess Fortune*, Cic.

prīmĭgĕnus -a -um (primus and geno = gigno), *original, primitive*, Lucr.

prīmĭpīlāris -is, m. (primipilus), *the centurion of the first maniple of the* triarii.

prīmĭpīlus, v. pilus.

prīmĭtĭae -ārum, f. (primus), *first-fruits*, Ov.; transf., metallorum, *the minerals first taken out of a mine*, Tac.; spolia et primitiae, *first-fruits of victory*, Verg.

prīmĭtŭs, adv. *first, for the first time*, Lucr.

prīmō, adv. (primus), *firstly, at first, in the beginning*; primo . . . dein or deinde, Cic.; primo . . . post, Liv.; quum primo, *as soon as*, Liv.

prīmor -ōris (primus), *the first*. **I.** *the foremost part, tip, end*; primori in acie versari, Tac.; sumere aliquid digitulis duobus primoribus, *with the tips of the fingers*, Plaut.; aliquid primoribus labris attingere, or gustare, *to touch with the lips, i.e., to treat superficially*, Cic. Subst., primores, *the foremost* (milit. t. t.); quum primores caderent, Liv. **II.** Transf., *the first in rank, most distinguished*; juventus, Liv. Subst., **prīmōres** -um, m. *the most illustrious*; civitatis, Liv.

prīmordĭum -ĭi, n. (primus and ordior), *the first beginning, commencement, origin*; urbis, Liv. Plur., primordia rerum, Cic.

prīmum, adv. (primus). **I.** *first, firstly, at first*; foll. by deinde, tum, etc., Cic. **II.** *for the first time*; quo die primum convocati sumus, Cic. **III.** With ut, ubi, quam, simulac, *as soon as*, Cic.; quam primum, *as soon as possible*, Cic.

prīmus, v. prior.

princeps -cĭpis, c. (primus and capio), adj. and subst. **I.** Lit., princeps est in agendo, Cic.; principes inveniendi, *first to discover*, Cic.; princeps senatūs, *the senator whose name stood first on the Censor's list*, Liv. **II.** *the chief, the most distinguished*. **A.** Gen., with genit., principes civitatis, Cic, principes conjurationis, *the heads*, Cic, rerum publicarum principes, Cic; esp, princeps juventutis, *one of the most distinguished of the patrician youth*, esp *among the patrician knights*, Cic, with in and the abl, in jure civili princeps, Cic, plur, principes, *distinguished men*, Cic **B.** Esp, **1,** *chief, leader, founder*, Zeno princeps Stoicorum, Cic, **2,** *a ruler, prince*, esp of the emperor at Rome, Ov, **3,** principes, orig *the first rank in a Roman army, afterwards the second line, between the* hastati and triarii, hence, princeps, **a,** *a maniple of the* principes, signum primi principis, Liv, **b,** *a centurion of the* principes, princeps prior, Caes

principālis e (princeps) **I.** *first, original*, causae, Cic **II.** Transf, *relating to the chief place in a Roman camp* (principia), via, porta, *the broad alley which passed through the centre of a Roman camp*, Liv, porta principalis, dextra, sinistra, *the gate on each side*, Liv

principātus -ūs, m (princeps), *the first place, preeminence* **I.** Gen, tenere principatum sententiae, *to have the right to vote first*, Cic **II.** Esp, **A.** *the first rank in the state* or *army*, and gen, *rule, dominion*, Cassio principatum dari, Cic, principatum in civitate obtinere, Cic **B.** In philosophy, *the governing principle of actions* (Gk τὸ ἡγεμονικόν), Cic **C.** *a beginning, origin*, Cic

principiālis -e (principium), *original*, Lucr

principium -ii, n (princeps), *a beginning, origin* **I.** Lit, principium dicendi, Cic, principio belli, Liv, ducere principium ab aliquo, *to make a beginning with*, Cic, (in) principio, *in the beginning, at first*, Cic, a principio, *from the beginning*, Cic **II.** Meton, **A.** *the groundwork, foundation*, id est principium urbis, Cic, plur, principia, *the elements, first principles*, juris, Cic **B. 1,** *the tribe* or *curia which voted first, the prerogative tribe*, etc, Faucia curia fuit principium, Liv, **2,** *the beginner, founder*, moris, Ov **C.** Milit t t, **principia** -ōrum, **1,** *the front ranks*, Sall, **2,** *the chief place, chief street in a camp, where stood the tents of the general, legates, and tribunes, and where speeches were delivered to the soldiers, the head-quarters*, in vestrorum castrorum principiis, Cic

prior -ius, genit -ōris, superl, **prīmus** -a -um (from old form pris, whence pridem, pridie, pristinus) **I** Compar, **A.** Lit, *the first, the first of two*, priores pedes, Nep **B.** Transf, **1,** *first in order of time, former, first of two*, comitia, Cic, consul anni prioris, Liv, priore aestate, *in the previous summer*, Cic, subst, **priōres** -um, m *ancestors*, Verg, **2,** *better, preferable, more excellent*, res nulla prior potiorque visa est, Liv, nihil prius nec potius est quam (foll by infin), Liv **II.** Superl, **primus** a um, *the first.* **A.** Of place, *the first, foremost*, **a,** adj, Eburonum fines, Caes; primis labris, *with the tips of the lips*, Cic, **b,** subst, primi, *the foremost*, Cic **B.** Transf, **1,** *first in order* or *in time*, **a,** adj, primae litterae, Cic, esp, (α) in poets, primus for primum, vix prima inceperat aestas, Verg, (β) partitive, primā nocte, *in the first part of the night*, Caes, **b,** subst, a primo, *from the beginning*, Cic, in primo, *at first*, Cic, plur, prima, *the beginning*, Liv, *the elements*, Lucr., in primis, *at the beginning*, Liv, **2,** of rank, station, etc., *first, most excellent, most distinguished*, homines primi, *the most illustrious*, Cic, comitia prima (i e., centuriata and tributa), Cic, primas tenere, *to hold the first place*, Verg, partes primae, or simply primae, *the leading part (on the stage)*, Cic; primas agere, Cic, primae, *the first prize*, primas ferre, deferre, Cic, in primis, *especially*, Cic

priscē, adv (priscus), *after the manner of the ancients, sternly, severely*, agere, Cic

priscus -a -um (from pris, cp Gk πρίν) **I.** *ancient, antique*, priscis viris, Cic, hence Tarquinius Priscus, *the first of his line*, Liv, esp with the notion of *ancient, venerable, belonging to the good old times*, priscam imitari severitatem, Cic **II.** Transf, **A.** *former, previous*, Venus, Hor **B.** *severe, stern*, Cat

pristīnus -a -um (from pris, cp Gk πρίν, as crastinus from cras), *former, previous, early, pristine* **I.** Gen, dignitas, Cic, suos, Cic, in pristinum statum redire, Caes **II.** *just past, of* or *relating to yesterday*, diei pristini, Caes

pristis -is, f and **pistrix** -tricis, f (πρίστις) **I.** *any sea monster, a whale, shark, saw-fish*, Verg **II.** Transf, **a,** *the constellation of the Whale*, Cic, **b,** *a small, swift-sailing ship of war*, Liv, *name of a ship*, Verg

priŭs, adv (prior) **I.** *before, previously*, Cic, foll by quam, *before that, before*, Cic. **II.** *formerly*, Cat

prīvātim, adv (privatus), *privately, as a private person, in private life* **I.** Lit, privatim aliquid gerere, Cic, si privatim mandasset, Cic **II.** Transf, *at home*, privatim se tenere, *to remain at home*, Liv

prīvātio -ōnis, f (privo), *a freeing from*, doloris, Cic

prīvātus -a -um (privo), *private, of* or *relating to a private individual* **I.** a, of things, privati et separati agri, Caes vita, Cic, neut subst, in privato, *at home*, Liv, privato consilio, *without the authority of the state, on one's own account*, Caes, in privatum vendere, *for private use*, Liv., tributum ex privato conferre, *from one's private property*, Liv, **b,** of persons, *as a private man*, Cic, vir privatus, Cic, and subst, privatus, *a private person*, Cic, reges, augures, privati, Cic **II.** Esp, in imperial times, *not belonging to the royal family*, Tac

Prīvernum -i, n *a town in Latium*, now *Piperno* Hence, **Prīvernās** -ātis, *relating to Privernum*, Cic, in Privernati, *in the county of Privernum*, Cic

prīvigna -ae, f (fem of privignus), *a step-daughter*, Cic

prīvignus -i, m (= privigenus, from privus and gigno, *one begotten separately*), *a step-son*, Cic

prīvilēgium -ii, n (privus and lex), *a law relating to one person only, a special law, private law*, privilegium ferre, irrogare, Cic

prīvo, 1 (privus) **I.** In a bad sense, *to deprive of*, aliquem vitā, Cic **II.** In a good sense, *to free from*, aliquem dolore, Cic

prīvus -a -um **I.** *single*, in dies privos, Lucr, homines, Cic **II.** Transf, **A.** *each, every*, Lucr, used distributively, *one each*, bubus privis binisque tunicis donati, Liv **B.** *particular, special, one's own*, priva triremis, Hor

1 **pro** (old abl neut of * prus -a -um, cp prae, connected with πρό), *before, for* **I.** Adv, only in phrases proquam, prout **II.** Prep with abl **A.** Lit., of space, **1,** *before, in front of*, **a,** in answer to the question, where? sedens pro aede, Cic, **b,** in answer to question, whither? Caesar pro castris suas copias produxit, **2,** *before, on, in*, pro tribunali, Cic **B.** Transf, **1,** *for, in behalf of, in favour of*, hoc non modo non pro me, sed contra me est, Cic, dimicare pro legibus, Cic, **2,** **a,** *in place of, for*, pro consule, Cic pro quaestore, Cic, **b,** *as, as good as*, pro damnato esse, *as good as condemned*, Cic, se pro cive gerere, *to behave as a citizen*, Cic, **3,** *for, as a reward*, or *as wages for*, (alicui) pro meritis gratiam referre, Cic, pro

vectura solvere, Cic.; aliquem pro scelere suo ulcisci, Caes.; **4,** *in proportion to, according to, conformably with, in consideration of;* pro multitudine hominum et pro gloria belli atque fortitudinis, Cic.; pro caritate reipublicae, Cic.; agere pro viribus, Cic.; pro virili parte, *to the best of one's abilities,* Cic.; pro tempore et re, *as the time and circumstances demanded,* Caes.; pro mea parte, *for my part,* Cic.; pro se quisque, *each one according to his strength,* Cic.; pro eo, *just as, according as;* foll. by ac and atque, or quam, quantum, etc., pro eo quanti te facio, *according to my estimation of you;* **5,** *through;* ut pro suffragio renuntiaretur, Cic.

2. **pro! (proh!),** interj. *oh! ah!* pro dii immortales, Cic.; pro deûm atque hominum fidem! Cic.; pro sancte Juppiter, Cic.

prŏāgŏrus -i, m. (προήγορος), *the chief magistrate in certain Sicilian cities,* Cic.

prŏăvītus -a -um (proavus), *of* or *relating to a great-grandfather, ancestral;* regna, Ov.

prŏăvus -i, m. **I.** *a great-grandfather,* Cic. **II.** Transf., *an ancestor, forefather,* Cic.

prŏbābĭlis -e (probo). **I.** *probable, credible, not impossible;* ratio, Cic. **II.** *pleasing, acceptable, worthy of approval, good;* probabilior populo orator, Cic.; vir ingenio sane probabili, Cic.

prŏbābĭlĭtas -ātis, f. (probabilis), *probability, credibility;* captiosa, Cic.

prŏbābĭlĭtĕr, adv. (probabilis), *probably, credibly;* dicere, Cic.; probabilius accusare, Cic.

prŏbātĭo -ōnis, f. (probo). **I.** *a proving, testing, test, trial, examination;* athletarum, Cic. **II.** *an approving, approval,* Cic.

prŏbātor -ōris, m. (probo), *one who approves, an approver;* facti, Cic.

prŏbātus -a -um, p. adj. (from probo). **A.** *approved, excellent;* ceterarum homines artium spectati et probati, Cic.; femina probatissima, Cic. **B.** *pleasant, agreeable;* ut nemo probatior primoribus patrum esset, Liv.; probatissimus alicui, Cic.

prŏbē, adv. (probus), *well, rightly, fitly, properly, excellently;* scire, nosse, meminisse, Cic.; de Servio probe dicis, Cic.; hoc probe stabilito et fixo, Cic.

prŏbĭtas -ātis, f. (probus), *honesty, uprightness, probity, worth, modesty,* Cic.

prŏbo, 1. (probus). **I. A.** *to try, test, prove, examine;* **a,** lit., munera, Tac.; opera quae locassent, Liv.; **b,** transf., amicitias utilitate, Ov. **B.** *to approve, be satisfied with, esteem good and serviceable;* (a) lit., domum tuam perspexi atque vehementer probavi, Cic.; (β) transf., *to approve of,* morally or intellectually; consilium, Cic.; causam et hominem, Caes.; aliquem judicem, Cic. **II.** *to recommend as good, represent as good, guarantee;* **a,** alicui libros oratorios, Cic.; obscurius vitium pro vero probatur, Cic.; se probare alicui, *to recommend oneself to some one, gain a person's approval;* se in legatione sociis, Cic.; in pass., probari alicui, *to appear worthy of approval,* Cic.; **b,** *to show, prove, demonstrate;* crimen, Cic.; causam, Cic.; with acc. and infin., probare judicibus Verrem pecunias cepisse, Cic.; absol., difficile est probatu, Cic.

prŏbrōsus -a -um (probrum), *shameful, disgraceful, infamous, ignominious;* crimen, Cic.; carmen, Tac.

prŏbrum -i, n. **I.** *a shameful, infamous deed;* **1,** gen., alicui probrum objectare, Cic.; emergere ex paternis probris ac vitiis, Cic.; **2,** esp., *unchastity;* probri insimulasti pudicissimam feminam, Cic. **II.** Transf., *shame, disgrace, infamy;* **1,** gen., probro esse, Cic.; probrum inferre alicui, Cic.; alicui ut probrum objicere quod, etc., Cic.; **2,** esp., *abuse, insult, libel;* epistolae plenae omnium in me probrorum, Cic.; multa objicere probra, Cic.

prŏbus -a -um, *good, excellent, fine;* **a,** physically or intellectually, res, Cic.; navigium, Cic.; ingenium, Cic.; **b,** morally, *good, upright, virtuous, honourable;* filius, Cic.; homo probior, Cic.

Prŏca (Prŏcās) -ae, m. *an old king of Alba.*

prŏcācĭtas -ātis, f. (procax), *shamelessness, impudence,* Cic.

prŏcācĭtĕr, adv. (procax), *shamelessly, impudently,* Liv.

prŏcax -cācis (proco), *shameless, bold, impudent, importunate, insolent;* **a,** of persons, in lacessendo, Cic.; procacius stipendium flagitare, Liv.; **b,** of things, sermo, Sall.; scripta, Tac.; auster, *blustering,* Verg.

prŏcēdo -cessi -cessum, 3. *to go forth, go before, proceed.* **I.** Lit. and transf., **A.** Gen., **1,** lit., **a,** e tabernaculo in solem, Cic.; alicui obviam procedere, *to go to meet,* Cic.; **b,** milit. t. t., *to advance;* lente atque paulatim, Caes.; ad dimicandum, Liv.; **c,** *to appear, show oneself, step forward;* procedere in medium, Cic.; esp., *to come forward to speak to an assembly;* procedere in contionem, Liv.; **2,** transf., *to advance;* **a,** of ships, quantum naves processissent, Caes.; **b,** of stars, *to appear;* processit Vesper, Verg. **B.** Transf., *to advance, progress,* of work, etc., magna pars operis Caesaris processerat, Caes. **II.** Fig., **A.** Gen., **a,** in dando et credendo longius procedere, *to go too far,* Cic.; eo processit vecordiae ut, etc., *he went to such a pitch of madness that,* etc., Sall.; esp., *to advance towards some good, go on, make progress;* in philosophia, Cic.; **b,** *to run on, continue, be counted up;* stipendia, aera alicui procedunt, Liv.; hence, transf., *to be of use to, do good to;* benefacta mea reipublicae procedunt, Sall.; **c,** of time, dies procedens, Cic.; si (puer) aetate processerit, Cic.; multum diei processerat, Sall. **B.** Of actions, etc., *to turn out in a certain way, to result;* si bene processit, Cic.; alicui bene, pulcherrime, Cic.; and absol., *to turn out well, to be prosperous;* si processit, Cic.

prŏcella -ae, f. (procello), *a storm, tempest, gale;* **1,** lit., nimbi, procellae, turbines, Cic.; **2,** transf., **a,** *a sudden charge of cavalry, onset, charge;* primam procellam eruptionis sustinere non posse, Liv.; **b,** procellae insidiarum, Cic.; procellam temporis devitare, Cic.

prŏcello, 3. (pro and cello), *to throw down, cast down,* Plaut.

prŏcellōsus -a -um (procella), *stormy, tempestuous,* Verg., Liv.

prŏcer -ĕris, m. *an illustrious person;* usually plur., **prŏcĕres** -um, m. *chiefs, nobles, princes;* audiebam enim nostros proceres clamitantes, Cic.

prōcērē, adv. (procerus), *far outstretched;* compar., brachium procerius projectum, Cic.

prōcērĭtas -ātis, f. (procerus), *height, slimness, slenderness.* **I.** Lit., cameli adjuvantur proceritate collorum, *by the length of their necks,* Cic.; arborum, Cic. **II.** Transf., *length* (of a syllable or foot in poetry); pedum, Cic.

prōcērus -a -um (pro and cerus, from root CER, CRE, whence cresco), *tall, slender, long.* **I.** Lit., of bodies, etc., collum, rostrum, Cic.; of trees, procerissima populus, Cic. **II.** Transf., in rhythm and pronunciation, *long;* procerior quidam numerus, Cic.

prōcessĭo -ōnis, f. (procedo), *a military advance,* Cic.

prōcessus -ūs, m (procedo), *a going forth, advance, course, progress*, gradus et quasi processus dicendi, Cic , tantos progressus efficiebat ut, etc , Cic

Prŏchўta -ae, f and **Prŏchўtē** -ēs, f (Προχύτη), *an island on the coast of Campania, now Procida*

prōcĭdo -cĭdi (pro and cado), 3 *to fall down forward, fall forward*, praeceps procidit ante proram, Liv

prōcinctus -ūs, m (procingo), *a being girded, hence, a being equipped for battle, readiness for battle*, in procinctu ac castris habiti, Tac , testamentum in procinctu facere, *on the battlefield*, Cic

proclāmātor -ōris, m (proclamo), *a bawler, vociferator* (of a bad advocate), Cic

proclāmo, 1 *to call out, cry out*, absol, Cic , with acc and infin , se filiam jure caesam judicare, Liv ; pro aliquo (contemptuously of an advocate), *to defend a person*, Liv

Prŏcles -is, m (Προκλῆς), *son of Aristodemus, brother of Eurysthenes king of Sparta, founder of the family of the Proclidae*

prōclīno, 1 act *to bend, incline forwards to bend*, mare in litora, Ov , transf , proclinatā jam re *approaching consummation*, Caes , adjuvare rem proclinatam, *tottering to its fall*, Caes

prōclīvĕ (prōclīvī), compar prōclīvius, adv (proclivis), *downwards*, proclivi currere, labi, Cic

prōclīvis -e and **prōclīvus** -a -um (pro and clivus), *inclined forwards, sloping downwards, steep* **I.** Lit , via proclivis Liv , subst per proclive, *downwards*, Liv **II.** Fig , 1, meton , *going downwards*, proclivi cursu et facili delabi, Cic , 2, *inclined to, ready for, prone to*, ad morbum Cic , ad comitatem, Cic , 3, *easy to do*, illa facilia, proclivia, jucunda, Cic alicui est proclive, with infin , Caes , dictu proclive est, *it is easy to say*, with acc and infin , Cic

prōclīvĭtas -ātis, f (proclivis), *a slope*, fig , *inclination, tendency, proneness*, ad morbos, Cic

prōclīvus = proclivis (q v)

Procnē (Prognē) -ēs, f (Πρόκνη) **I.** *daughter of Pandion, sister of Philomela and wife of Tereus, changed into a swallow* **II.** Meton , *a swallow*, Verg

prŏco, 1 and **prŏcor**, 1 dep *to ask, entreat*, Cic

prōconsul -sŭlis, m *a proconsul, one who after his consulship* (and sometimes without having been consul), *was governor of a province*, Cic

prōconsŭlāris -e (proconsul), *of or relating to a proconsul, proconsular*, Liv

prōconsŭlātus -ūs, m (proconsul), *the office or dignity of a proconsul*, Tac

prōcrastĭnātĭo -ōnis, f (procrastino), *a putting off from day to day, procrastination*, Cic

prōcrastĭno, 1 (pro and crastino), *to put off till to-morrow, procrastinate*, Cic

prōcrĕātĭo -ōnis, f (procreo), *begetting, procreation*, Cic

prōcrĕātor -ōris, m. (procreo), *a begetter*, mundi, *Creator*, Cic , procreatores = *parents*, Cic

prōcrĕātrix -īcis, f (procreator), *one that brings forth, mother*, transf , artium, Cic

prōcrĕo, 1 **I.** *to beget, procreate*, of animals, *to bring forth*, multiplices fetus, Cic **II.** Fig *to bring forth, produce, cause, make*, inter arma civium (tribunatum) procreatum, Cic.

prōcresco, 3 **I.** *to grow forth, arise*, Lucr. **II.** Fig , *to increase*, Lucr

Prŏcris -cris, f (Πρόκρις), *daughter of Erechtheus, wife of Cephalus, who killed her in a forest, mistaking her for an animal*

Prŏcrustēs -ae, m (Προκρούστης), *a robber in Attica, who tied his prisoners to a bed, stretching the limbs of those shorter than the bed, and cutting off the limbs of those who were taller, killed by Theseus*

prōcŭbo, 1 *to lie stretched out, to lie along*, ubi saxea procubet umbra, Verg

prōcūdo -cūsi -cūsum, 3 **I.** 1, *to thrust or drive forward*, Lucr , 2, *to forge*, enses, Hor **II.** Fig , linguam, *to form, train*, Cic

prŏcŭl, adv (from procello) **I.** *afar off, at a distance, far away*, non procul, sed hic, Cic , foll by a, ab, *far from*, procul a terra abripi, Cic , by abl alone, procul coetu hominum, Liv **II.** Transf , *far from, far away*, with abl , procul dubio, *without doubt*, Liv , haud procul est, with quin and subj , *it is not far from*, Liv , of time, haud procul occasu solis, *not long before*, Liv

prōculco, 1 (pro and calco) *to tread, trample upon*, 1 things, is (aper) modo crescentes segetes proculcat in herba, Ov , 2, persons, *to trample to the ground, to tread down*, aliquem, Tac

Prōcŭlēius -i, m *a Roman knight, friend of Augustus*

prōcumbo -cŭbŭi -cŭbĭtum, 3 *to lean or bend forward* **I.** Gen , **A.** 1, lit , of persons, olli certamine summo procumbunt (of rowers), Verg , 2, transf , of things, *to incline forward*, secundum naturam fluminis, Caes **II** *to fall down, sink down, to fall prostrate* **A.** 1, lit , of living beings, alces procumbunt, Caes , of persons in prayer, entreaty, etc , procumbere alicui ad pedes, Caes , ad genua alicuius, Liv , of persons wounded, vulneribus confectum procumbere, Caes , 2, transf , of things, frumenta imbribus procubuerant, *were laid low*, Caes **B.** Fig , *to sink, fall*, res procubuere meae, Ov

prōcūrātĭo -ōnis, f (procuro), *a taking care of, management, administration* **I.** Gen , reipublicae, Cic , mearum rerum, Cic , annonae, Cic **II.** Esp 1, under the empire, *the office of imperial procurator*, Tac , 2, *a religious act for the propitiation of an offended deity*, ut sue plena procuratio fieret, Cic

prōcūrātor -ōris, m (procuro), *a manager, administrator, agent, factor, deputy* **I.** Gen , regni, *a viceroy*, Caes , with genit of person, procurator P Quinctii, Cic **II.** Esp , 1, *a land steward, land agent*, Cic , 2, in imperial times, *a functionary who collected the imperial revenue both in Rome and in the provinces*, procurator Caesaris, Tac , procurator Judaeae, Tac

procūrātrix -trīcis f (procurator), *she that governs*, fig , sapientia totius hominis procuratrix, Cic

procūro, 1 *to take care of, look after, tend* **I.** Gen , corpus, Verg sacrificia, Caes **II.** Esp , 1, *to manage, administer any one's affairs*, alicuius negotia, Cic , hereditatem, Cic , 2, *to offer sacrifice in order to avert an evil omen*, monstra, Cic , prodigia, Cic

prōcurro -curri and -cŭcurri -cursum, 3 *to run forward, rush forward, charge* **I.** Lit , of persons, ex castris, Caes , in vias, Liv , ad repellendum hostem, Caes **II.** Transf , of places, *to project, jut out, run forward*, infelix saxis in procurrentibus haesit, Verg , terra procurrit in aequor, Ov.

prōcursātĭo -ōnis, f (procurso), *a running forward, charge*, velitum, Liv.

prōcursātor -ōris, m. (procurso), *one who runs forward;* milit. t. t., procursatores, *skirmishers*, Liv.

prōcurso, 1. (intens. of procurro), *to run forward, spring forward;* as milit. t. t., *to skirmish*, Liv.

prōcursus -ūs, m. (procurro), *a running forward;* and esp., in military language, *an advance, charge;* procursu militum, Liv.

prōcurvus -a -um, *bent forward, curved forward;* falx, Verg.; litora, *winding*, Verg.

prŏcus -i, m. (proco), *a wooer, suitor;* transf., impudentes proci, *candidates*, Cic.

Prŏcyŏn -ōnis, m. (Προκύων), *a constellation which rises before the Dog-star*, Cic.

prōd = pro (q.v.)

prōdĕo -ii -ĭtum, 4. *to go, come forth.* **I. A. 1**, lit., obviam mihi est proditum, Cic.; prodire ex portu, Caes.; in publicum, *to appear in public*, Cic.; in proelium, Caes.; **2**, esp., *to appear in some character, to come forth*, e.g., *as an actor;* in scenam, Cic. **B.** Fig., **a**, *to appear, show itself;* consuetudo prodire coepit, Cic.; **b**, *to go forth = to become;* prodis ex judice Dama turpis, Hor. **II.** *to advance, go forward.* **A. 1**, lit., longius, Caes.; **2**, transf., *to project;* rupes prodit in aequor, Verg. **B.** Fig., sumptu extra modum, *to exceed the mark*, Cic.

prōdīco -dixi -dictum, 3. **I.** *to say before*, Cic. (?) **II.** *to fix for a later time, put off;* diem in Quirinalia, Cic.

prōdictātor -ōris, m. *one who acts as dictator*, Liv. (?)

Prŏdĭcus -i, m. *a Greek sophist of Ceos, contemporary of Socrates.*

prōdĭgē, adv. (prodigus), *prodigally, extravagantly;* vivere, Cic.

prōdĭgentĭa -ae, f. (prodigo), *profusion, prodigality*, Tac.

prōdĭgĭālĭtĕr, adv. *strangely, wonderfully*, Hor.

prōdĭgĭōsus -a -um (prodigium), *unnatural, strange, wonderful, prodigious*, Ov.

prōdĭgĭum -ii, n. (prod and agere), *a prodigy, portent, omen, ominous sign.* **I.** Lit., multa prodigia eius vim declarant, Cic. **II.** Transf., **a**, *a monstrosity, something unnatural;* prodigium videbatur civitatum frumentum improbare, suum probare, Cic.; **b**, *a monster;* prodigium triplex, *Cerberus*, Ov.; fatali portentum prodigiumque reipublicae (of Clodius), Cic.

prōdĭgo -ēgi -actum, 3. (prod and ago), **I.** *to drive forth;* sues, Varr. **II.** Transf., *to spend, waste;* alienum, Sall.

prōdĭgus -a -um (prodigo), *prodigal, profuse, extravagant.* **I. a**, lit., Cic.; with genit., aeris, Hor.; **b**, fig., with genit., animae, *not sparing his own life*, Hor.; arcani, *revealing a secret*, Hor.; with in and the abl., in honoribus decernendis nimius et tamquam prodigus, Cic. **II.** Transf., *rich, abounding in;* locus prodigus herbae, Hor.

prōdĭtĭo -ōnis, f. (prodo), *a betraying, betrayal, treachery, treason;* amicitiarum proditiones et rerum publicarum, Cic.

prōdĭtor -ōris, m. (prodo), *a betrayer, traitor;* consulis, Cic.; transf., risus latentis puellae proditor, Hor.

prōdo -dĭdi -dĭtum, 3. **I.** *to put forth, bring forth.* **A.** Gen., *to bring forth;* fumoso condita vina cado, Ov.; suspiria pectore, Ov. **B.** Esp., **1**, **a**, *to give, show, publish;* decretum, Cic.; exemplum, Liv.; **b**, *to proclaim elected, to appoint;* flaminem, interregem, Cic.; **c**, *to relate;* quae scriptores prodiderunt, Cic.; **d**, *to reveal, betray something secret, to betray;* conscios, Cic.; crimen vultu, Ov.; **2**, *to give up, discover, betray treacherously;* classem praedonibus, Cic.; aliquem ad mortem, Verg.; utilitatem communem, Cic. **II. A.** *to hand over, deliver, transmit;* sacra suis posteris, Cic.; esp. in writing, memoriae prodere, *to commit to writing*, Cic.; memoriae prodiderunt, with acc. and infin., Cic. **B.** *to propagate;* genus, Verg.

prōdŏcĕo, 2. *to teach, inculcate*, Hor.

prŏdrŏmus -i, m. (πρόδρομος), *a messenger, forerunner.* **I.** Lit., Cic. **II.** Transf., *a north-north-east wind, said to blow for eight days before the rising of the Dog-star*, Cic.

prōdūco -duxi -ductum, 3. *to lead forth.* **I.** Gen., **A.** Lit., **1**, equos, jumenta, Caes.; **2**, milit. t. t., *to lead forth troops;* copias pro castris, Caes.; **3**, **a**, polit. t. t., *to bring before the public assembly or before a court of justice;* harum rerum omnium auctores testesque, Cic.; **b**, *to bring out of prison;* aliquem capite involuto ad necem, Cic.; **c**, *to bring forward on the stage, on the arena*, etc.; aliquem, Cic.; **3**, *to bring forth a corpse to the funeral pile;* aliquem funere, Verg.; **4**, *to entice forth;* aliquem dolo in proelium, Nep. **B.** Fig., *to bring before some one, reveal;* occulta ad patres crimina, Juv. **II. A.** Lit., **1**, *to advance;* unam navem longius, Caes.; *to draw out, stretch out, extend;* **a**, ferrum incude, Juv.; **b**, in pronunciation, *to lengthen out, make long;* litteram, Cic.; syllabam, Ov.; **2**, **a**, *to beget, produce;* fig., nova (vocabula) quae genitor produxerit usus, Hor.; **b**, *to rear, bring up;* subolem, Hor.; of plants, arborem, Hor. **B.** Fig., **1**, *to advance, promote;* aliquem ad dignitatem, Cic.; **2**, *to prolong* (in duration of time); **a**, *to continue, keep on;* sermonem longius in multam noctem, Cic.; **b**, *to put off, postpone;* rem in hiemem, Caes.; **c**, *to put off, delay;* conditionibus hunc, quoad potest, producit, Cic.

prōductē, adv. (productus), *in a lengthened manner, long* (of pronunciation); producte dici, Cic.

prōductĭo -ōnis, f. (produco), *an extending, lengthening;* **a**, of a word by the addition of a syllable, Cic.; **b**, of a syllable in pronunciation, Cic.; **c**, of time, *prolonging;* temporis, Cic.

prōductus -a -um, p. adj. (from produco). **I.** Adj., *extended, lengthened, prolonged;* productiore cornu sinistro, Tac.; quinto productior actu fabula, Hor.; of words, nomen, *lengthened by addition of a syllable*, Cic.; of syllables, *long* (in pronunciation); (syllaba) producta atque longa, Cic.; of time, *prolonged, drawn out;* dolores, Cic. **II.** Subst., **prōducta** -ōrum, n. (τὰ προηγμένα), *preferable things* (in the Stoic philosophy, things which, while not absolutely good, were to be preferred, e.g., beauty, health), Cic.

proelĭātor -ōris, m. (proelior), *a warrior, combatant*, Tac.

proelĭor, 1. dep. (proelium), *to give battle, fight;* ad Syracusas, Cic.; pedibus, Caes.; transf., vehementer proeliatus sum, *striven*, Cic.

proelĭum -ii, n. *a battle, fight.* **I. a**, lit., proelium facere, Cic.; redintegrare, Caes.; inire, Liv.; proelio abstinere, Caes.; **b**, transf., of a fight in words, proelia meā causā sustinere, Cic. **II.** Meton., proelia = *fighters, combatants*, Prop.

Proetus -i, m. (Προῖτος), *king in Tiryns, brother of Acrisius.* Hence, **Proetis** -ĭdis, f. *a daughter of Proetus;* plur., Proetides, *the daughters of Proetus, who were punished with madness, and imagined themselves to be cows.*

prŏfāno, 1 (profanus), *to profane, desecrate*, sacra, Liv, festum, Ov

prŏfānus -a -um (pro and fanum, lit, *lying before a temple*, i e, *outside it*), *not sacred, not consecrated* **I.** Gen, *common, profane*, **1**, lit, locus Cic, bubo, avis, *of evil omen*, Ov, subst, **prŏfānum** -i, n *that which is profane, unconsecrated*, Tac, **2**, transf, *profane, godless, impious*, verba, Ov **II.** Esp, **1**, *not initiated, uninitiated*, procul este profani, Verg, **2**, transf, *not initiated in the service of the Muses*, profanum vulgus, Hor

prŏfectio -ōnis, f (proficiscor), **1**, *a departure*, Cic, **2**, transf, *source, origin*, pecuniae, Cic

prŏfecto, adv (pro and factus) *truly, really, indeed*, Cic

prŏfĕro -tŭli -lātum -ferre **I.** *to carry forth, bring forth* (from a place), **1**, lit, **a**, nummos ex arca, Cic, pecuniam alicui, Cic, **b**, milit t t, *to deliver up, bring forth*, arma tormenta que ex oppido, Caes, **c**, *to raise a limb or part of the body*, caput, Ov, digitum, Cic **d**, *to bring forth, show*, proferre in conspectum liberos, Caes, of writings, *to publish, make known*, orationem, Cic, **2**, fig, **a**, *to bring to light, reveal*, (α) aliquid in medium, Cic, (β) as a discoverer, *to bring to light, produce*, aliquid proferre in aspectum lucemque, Cic proferre artem, Cic, **b**, *to bring forward, produce, cite, mention*, testes, Cic, nominatim multos, Cic, exempla omnium nota, Cic **II. 1**, *to advance, move forward*, **a**, milit t t, signa, *to march on*, Liv, inde castra, *to move from thence*, Liv, **b**, *to extend*, fines agri publici paulatim, Liv, fig, fines officiorum paulo longius, Cic, **2**, fig, **a**, of duration of time, *to extend, lengthen*, beatam vitam usque ad rogum, Cic, **b**, *to put off, postpone*, diem auctionis, Cic

prŏfessio -ōnis, f (profiteor), *acknowledgment, declaration, profession* **I.** Gen, bonae voluntatis, ap Cic. **II.** Esp, **A.** lit, *public declaration of one's name, property, occupation etc* haec pecunia ex eo genere est, ut professione non egeat Cic **B.** Meton, **1**, *the register of persons and their property*, Cic **2**, *an occupation, art, profession*, bene dicendi, Cic.

prŏfessōrius -a -um, *of or relating to a professor, professorial*, Tac

prŏfessus -a -um, partic of profiteor (q v)

prŏfestus -a -um, *not kept as a festival, common*, dies, *work-days, ordinary days*, Liv

prŏfĭcĭo -fēci -fectum, 3 (pro and facio) *to make progress, advance, gain ground, to get an advantage, to effect anything* **I.** Of persons, nihil in oppugnatione, Caes, aliquid in philosophia Cic **II.** Of things, **a**, *to be of use or advantage to, to assist, help*, nulla res tantum ad dicendum proficit, quantum scriptio, Cic, **b**, of medical remedies, herba proficiente nihil, Hor

prŏfĭciscor -fectus sum, ficisci, 3 dep (pro and facio, facesso, facisco), *to set out, depart go, travel, march, take a journey* **I.** Lit, ex portu, Caes, Aegyptum, Cic, ad or contra hostem, Caes, cum exercitus parte frumentatum, Liv **II.** Fig, **A.** *to go towards*, ad reliqua, Cic **B 1**, *to set out from, begin with*, a lege, Cic, ab hoc initio, Caes, **2**, meton, *to arise from, spring from, originate from* a natura, Cic, qui a Zenone profecti sunt, *Zeno's disciples*, Cic

prŏfĭtĕor -fessus sum, 2 dep (pro and fateor), *to acknowledge openly, confess, avow* **I.** Gen, fateor atque etiam profiteor, Cic; with acc and infin, profiteor me relaturum, Cic **II.** Esp, **A.** *to profess or declare oneself anything*; **a**, with double acc, of pers, se grammaticum, Cic, **b**, with acc and infin, me defensorem esse profiteor, Cic, **c**, with acc of thing, *to profess any science, art* etc, philosophiam, Cic, jus, Cic **B.** indicium, *to turn king's evidence*, Sall, Tac, *to offer, promise* operam, Cic, profitetur se venturum, Cic **C.** *to make a public statement of return of property*, etc, jugera, Cic, frumentum, Liv, nomen, Cic, and simply profiteri, *to announce oneself as a candidate*, Sall (Partic, **prŏfessus** -a um, pass, *known, acknowledged, avowed*, culpa, Ov)

prōflīgātor -ōris, m (profligo), *a spendthrift, prodigal*, Tac

prōflīgātus -a -um, p adj (from profligo), **1**, *cast down ruined, wretched*, Cic, **2**, *dissolute, profligate*, tu omnium mortalium profligatissime, Cic

prōflīgo, 1 (pro and fligere), *to strike to the ground* **I.** Lit, *to overthrow, overcome*, copias hostium, Cic, classem hostium, Caes **II.** Fig, **A. a**, politically, *to ruin*, rempublicam, Cic, **b**, *to lower, abase*, judicia senatoria, Cic, **c**, *to bring almost to an end, nearly finish*, profligatum bellum et paene sublatum, Cic, profligata jam haec, et paene ad exitum adducta quaestio est, Cic

prōflo, 1 *to blow forth, breathe forth*, flammas, Ov, fig, toto proflabat pectore somnum, Verg

prōflŭens -entis, p adj (from profluo), *flowing* **I.** Lit, aqua, Cic Subst, **prōflŭens** -entis, f *running water*, Cic **II.** Transf, of discourse, *flowing, fluent*, genus sermonis, Cic

prōflŭentĕr, adv (profluens), *flowingly, easily*, Cic

prōflŭo -fluxi -fluxum, 3 *to flow, flow forth* **I.** Lit, ex monte, Caes, in mare, Cic **II.** Fig, *to flow forth, proceed*, ab his fontibus profluxi ad hominum famam, Cic

prōflŭvium -ii, n (profluo), *a flowing forth*, sanguinis, Lucr

prōfor fātus sum, 1 dep **1**, *to say, speak*, Verg, **2**, *to foretell predict*, Lucr

prōfore, v prosum

prŏfŭgĭo -fūgi -fŭgitum, 3 **I.** Intransit, *to flee away, escape*, ex oppido, Caes, domo, Cic, absol, Catilina ipse pertimuit profugit, Cic **II.** *to flee away from*, agros, Hor

prŏfŭgus -a -um (profugio), *flying, fleeing, fugitive*, **a**, gen, (α) of persons, populus, Tac, poet, Scythae, *wandering, migratory, flying from one's native country, banished*, Hor, (β) of animals, taurus Tac, (γ) of things, currus, Ov, **b**, of soldiers, *flying from battle*, Sall, **c**, of exiles, with abl, patria profugus, Liv, ab Thebis, Liv, ex Peloponneso, Liv, subst, **prŏfŭgus** -i, m *a fugitive, exile*, Ov

prōfundo -fūdi -fūsum, 3 *to pour forth, shed abundantly, cause to flow* **I. A.** Lit, sanguinem suum omnem, Cic vim lacrimarum, Cic, reflex, se profundere, and middle, profundi, *to stream forth*, lacrimae se profuderunt, Cic **B** Transf, **1**, *to stretch at full length*, somnus membra profudit, Lucr, **2**, **a**, reflex, se profundere, or middle, profundi, *to pour out, rush forth*, omnis multitudo sagittariorum se profudit, Caes, of plants, quae (in vitibus) se nimium profuderunt, *have shot out*, Cic, **b**, *to utter*, clamorem, Cic, **c**, *to bring forth, produce*, ea quae frugibus atque bacis terrae fetu profunduntur, Cic, **3**, *to spend, sacrifice, give up*, pro patria vitam, Cic, in a bad sense, *to spend, lavish, squander*, pecuniam, Cic, patrimonia, Cic **II.** Fig, **a**, *to pour, vent, expend upon*, omne odium in me, Cic, **b**, reflex, se profundere, *to burst forth, to pour forth, rush forth*, voluptates subito se profuderunt, Cic

prŏfundus -a -um. **I.** *deep, profound*; **1,** lit., mare, Cic.; subst., **prŏfundum** -i, n. *the bottomless depth*; aquae, Cic.: absol., poet. = *the sea*, Verg.; **2,** fig., libidines, Cic.; avaritia, Sall. **II.** Transf., **A.** *high*; caelum, Verg. **B.** *deep, dense*; silvae, Lucr.

prŏfūsē, adv. (profusus). **I.** *in a disorderly manner*; profuse tendere in castra, Liv. **II.** Fig., *lavishly, extravagantly*; profusius sumptui deditus erat, Sall.

prŏfūsus -a -um, p. adj. (from profundo), *immoderate, extravagant*; **1,** gen., hilaritas, Cic.; **2,** esp., **a,** *immoderate in expenditure, extravagant*, Cic.; with genit., sui profusus, Sall.; **b,** transf., *costly*; epulae, Cic.

prōgĕner -i, *a grand-daughter's husband*, Tac.

prōgĕnĕro, 1. *to engender, produce*, Hor.

prōgĕnĭes -ēi, f. (progigno). **I.** *descent, race, lineage*, Cic. **II.** Meton., *progeny, offspring, descendants*; veteres, qui se deorum progeniem esse dicebant, Cic.

prōgĕnĭtor -ōris, m. (progigno), *the founder of a family, ancestor, progenitor*, Ov.

prōgigno -gĕnŭi -gĕnitum, 3. *to engender, bring forth, bear*, Cic.

prognātus -a -um (partic. of *prognoscor), *born, sprung from*; deo, Liv.; ex Cimbris, Caes.; ab Dite patre, Caes.

Prognē = Procne (q.v.).

prognostĭca -ōrum, n. (προγνωστικά), *signs of the weather*, a poem by Aratus, translated by Cicero, Cic.

prōgrĕdĭor -gressus sum -grĕdi, 3. dep. (pro and gradior). **I.** *to go forth, go out*; ex domo, Cic. **II.** *to go forwards, to advance*. **A.** Lit., of persons, regredi quam progredi mallent, Cic.; milit. t.t., *to advance*; longius a castris, Caes. **B.** Fig., *to proceed, advance*; **a,** quatenus amor in amicitia progredi debeat, Cic.; **b,** in a speech, etc., *to proceed to, go on*; ad reliqua, Cic.; **c,** of time, paulum aetate progressus, *advanced in years*, Cic.

prōgressĭo -ōnis, f. (progredior), *an advancing, progress, increase*; **a,** progressionem facere ad virtutem, Cic.; **b,** rhet. t. t., *a gradual strengthening of expression, climax*, Cic.

prōgressus -ūs, m. (progredior), *a going forwards, advance*. **I.** Lit., aliquem progressu arcere, Cic. **II.** Fig., **a,** *beginning of a speech*; primo progressu, Cic.; **b,** *progress, increase*; aetatis, Cic.; tantos progressus habebat in Stoicis, *progress in the Stoical philosophy*, Cic.; progressus facere in studiis, Cic.

proh! = pro! (q.v.).

prŏhĭbĕo -bŭi -bĭtum, 2. (pro and habeo). **I.** *to hold back, hold in, check, restrain, hinder*. **A.** Gen., praedones a Sicilia, Cic.; aliquem a familiaritate, Cic.; vim hostium ab oppidis, Caes.; se suosque ab injuria, Caes.; exercitum itinere, *to obstruct on the march*, Caes.; with infin., prohibeo aliquem exire domo, Cic.; with ne and the subj., potuisti prohibere ne fieret, Cic.; with quin and the subj., nec, quin erumperet, prohiberi poterat, Liv.; with quominus and the subj., prohibuisse, quominus de te certum haberemus, Cic.; with double acc., id eo ut prohiberet, Liv.; with simple acc., Caesarem, Caes.; conatus alicuius, Cic. **B.** *to hinder by words, forbid, prohibit*; lex recta imperans, prohibensque contraria, Cic. **II.** *to preserve, defend, protect*; a quo periculo prohibete rempublicam, Cic.

prŏhĭbĭtĭo -ōnis, f. (prohibeo), *a hindering, prohibition*; tollendi, Cic.

proĭcĭo = projicio (q.v.).

prŏin = proinde (q.v.).

prŏindĕ, adv. **I.** *just as, in the same manner, in like manner*; foll. by atque (ac), ut, quasi, quam, tamquam, Cic. **II.** *therefore, then, hence, accordingly*; esp. used in phrases of exhortation, encouragement, etc., Cic.

prōjectĭo -ōnis, f. (projicio), *a throwing forward, stretching out*; brachii, Cic.

1. **prōjectus** -ūs, m. (projicio), *a projecting, jutting out*, Lucr.

2. **prōjectus** -a -um, p. adj. (from projicio), *stretching out, jutting forward, projecting*; urbs, Cic.; saxa, Verg. **I.** Fig., **a,** *prominent*; audacia, Cic.; **b,** *addicted to*; homo ad audendum projectus, Cic. **II.** *stretched out, prostrate, lying*. **A.** Lit., ad terram, Caes.; in antro, Verg. **B.** Fig., **a,** *abject, base*; patientia, Tac.; **b,** *cast down*; vultus, Tac.

prōjĭcĭo -jēci -jectum, 3. (pro and jacio). **I.** *to throw, cast before, throw down*. **A.** Gen., cibum, Hor. **B.** Esp., **1,** *to stretch forth, throw out*; **a,** of limbs, brachium, Cic.; **b,** of buildings, pass., projici, *to project*; tectum projiceretur, Cic.; **c,** *to throw or place a weapon before one*; clipeum prae se, Liv.; **2,** *to push forth, drive forth*; **a,** aliquem foras, Cic.; aliquem ab urbe, Ov.; **b,** *to banish*; aliquem in insulam, Tac. **II.** *to throw out, throw in front*. **A.** Gen., crates, Caes.; se ad pedes alicuius, Cic.; projectā vilior algā, *cast upon the shore*, Verg. **B.** Esp. **1,** *to throw away*; arma, Caes.; fig., **a,** se projicere, *to lower oneself to, to stoop to*; in muliebres fletus, Liv.; **b,** *to reject, abandon*; libertatem, Cic.; **c,** *to expose, betray*; ab aliquo projici et prodi, Cic.; **2,** *to cast to the ground*; effigies, Tac.; **3,** *to put off*; aliquem ultra quinquennium, Tac.

prōlābor -lapsus sum -lābi, 3. **I.** *to glide forward, slide forward, slip along*. **A.** Lit. (elephanti) clunibus subsistentes prolabebantur, Liv. **B.** Fig., **1,** *to come to, fall into*; huc libido est prolapsa, Cic.; **2,** *to slip out, escape*; verbum a cupiditate prolapsum, Liv. **II.** *to fall down*. **A.** Lit., ex equo, Liv.; prolapsa Pergama, Verg. **B.** Fig., **1,** *to fail, to err*; cupiditate, timore, Cic.; **2,** *to fall, go to ruin, sink*; ita prolapsa est juventus ut, etc., Cic.

prōlapsĭo -ōnis, f. (prolabor), *a slipping, sliding*, Cic.

prōlātĭo -ōnis, f. (profero). **I.** *a bringing forward in discourse, mentioning*; exemplorum, Cic. **II.** **1,** *an extension*; finium, Liv.; **2,** *a putting off, deferring*; judicii, Cic.

prōlāto, 1. (intens. of profero). **I.** *to extend, enlarge, lengthen*; agros, Tac. **II.** Transf., **A.** *to put off, delay, defer*; comitia, Liv.; malum, Cic. **B.** *to prolong*; vitam, Tac.

prōlecto, 1. (intens. of prolicio), *to entice, allure*; egentes spe largitionis, Cic.

prōles -is, f. (pro and *aleo, alesco). **I.** *offspring, descendants, posterity*; **a,** of gods and men, illa futurorum hominum, *future generations*, Cic.; Apollinea, *Aesculapius*, Ov.; Latonia, *Apollo and Diana*, Ov.; **b,** of animals, Verg.; **c,** of plants, *fruit*, Verg. **II.** Transf., *youth, young men*; equitum peditumque, Cic.

prōlētārĭus -ii, m. (proles), *a citizen of the lowest class who served the state only by being the father of children*, Cic.

prōlĭcĭo, 3. (pro and lacio), *to lure forth, entice*, Ov.

prōlixē, adv. (prolixus). **I.** *abundantly, copiously*; id prolixe cumulateque fecit, Cic. **II.** *freely, willingly*; in delectu parum prolixe respondere, Cic.

prōlixus -a -um (pro and laxus), *widely extended, wide, broad, long*. **I.** Lit., Lucr. **II.**

Fig., 1, *willing, obliging*, tua prolixa beneficaque natura, Cic.; 2, *prosperous, fortunate*, cetera spero prolixa esse competitoribus, Cic.

prŏlŏgus -i, m. (πρόλογος), *a prologue*, Ter.

prōlŏquor -lŏcūtus (-lŏquūtus) sum -lŏqui, 3. dep. *to speak out, say out*. I. Gen., quod proloqui piget, Liv. II. Esp., *to prophesy, predict*, Prop.

prōlūdo -lūsi -lūsum, 3. *to play beforehand, to prelude, to practise beforehand*. I. Lit., ad pugnam, Ov. II. Fig., ut ipsis sententiis, quibus proluserint, vel pugnare possint, Cic.

prōlŭo -lŭi -lūtum, 3. I. *to wash forth* or *out*. A. *to cast up, to wash out*, genus omne natantum litore in extremo fluctus proluit, Verg. B. *to wash off*, tempestas ex omnibus montibus nives proluit, Caes. II. *to wash*, in vivo prolue rore manus, Ov.; leni praecordia mulso (of drinking), Hor.

prōlūsĭo -ōnis, f. (proludo), *a prelude, preliminary exercise, essay*, Cic.

prōlŭvĭes -ēi, f. (proluo). I. *an inundation*, Lucr. II. *excrement*, ventris, Verg.

prōmĕrĕo -ŭi -ĭtum, and **prōmĕrĕor** -ĭtus sum -ēri, 2. dep. *to deserve*. I. reus levius punitus quam sit ille promeritus, Cic.; suo beneficio promeruit, se ut ames, Cic.; partic. subst., **prōmĕrĭtum** -i, n. *deserts, merit*, vestra in nos universa promerita, Cic. II. (Gen. in form promereor), *to deserve (well) of*, promereri bene de multis, Cic.

Prŏmētheus -ĕi and -ĕos, m. (Προμηθεύς, *the Forethinker*), *son of Iapetus, brother of Epimetheus and father of Deucalion, the mythical hero, who made man of clay, and stole fire to animate his creation from heaven, for which he was bound to a rock in the Caucasus, where a vulture devoured his liver*. Hence, A. Adj., **Prŏmēthēus** -a -um, *Promethean*, juga, Prop.; rupes, *the Caucasus*, Mart. B. Subst., **Prŏmēthīădes** -ae, m. *son of Prometheus, Deucalion*.

prōmĭnens -entis (promineo), *jutting out, projecting*; subst., **prōmĭnens** -entis, n. *a projection*, in prominenti litoris, Tac.

prōmĭnĕo -minŭi, 2. *to stand out, jut out, project*. I. Lit., collis prominens, Liv.; prominet in altum, Liv.; pectore nudo prominentes, Caes. II. Fig. (justitia) foras tota promineat, *to step forth, be prominent*, Cic.; maxima pars (gloriae) in posteritatem prominet, *extends*, Liv.

prōmiscē, adv. (promiscus) = promiscue, Cic.

prōmiscŭē, adv. (promiscuus), *promiscuously, without distinction*, Caes.

prōmiscus = promiscuus (q.v.).

prōmiscŭus -a -um, *mixed, in common, indiscriminate, promiscuous*. I. Lit., comitia plebi et patribus promiscua, Liv.; connubia, *between patricians and plebeians*, Liv.; divina atque humana promiscua habere, *to make no distinction between*, Sall.; in promiscuo esse, *to be common*, Liv. II. Transf., *common, usual, general*, Tac.

prōmissĭo -ōnis, f. (promitto), *a promise*, auxilii, Cic.

prōmissor -ōris, m. (promitto), *a promiser*, esp. *one who promises boastingly, a boaster*, Hor.

prōmissum -i, n. (promitto), *a promise*, promissum facere, *to make a promise*, Hor.; promissa servare or promissis stare, *to keep promises*, Cic.; praemiorum promissa, Cic.

prōmissus -a -um, p. adj. (from promitto). I. *long, hanging down*, of hair, capillus, Caes.; caesaries, Liv.; barba, Liv. II. *producing much expectation*, carmen, Hor.

prōmitto -mīsi -missum, 3. *to let go forward, send forth*. I. *to grow*, capillum et barbam, *to let grow*, Liv. II. 1, *to promise, cause to expect, assure*, a, with acc. of thing and with or without acc. of person, si Neptunus quod Theseo promiserat, non fecisset, Cic.; with de and the abl., de horum erga me benevolentia promittebam, Cic.; with acc. and fut. infin., promitto tibi, si valebit, tegulam illum in Italia nullam relicturum, Cic.; b, *to vow, promise to a god*, donum Jovi dicatum et promissum, Cic.; c, promittere ad aliquem, ad cenam, *to accept an invitation to dine with*, ad fratrem promiserat, Cic.

prōmo, prompsi, promptum, 3. (for proimo, from pro and emo), *to bring forth, bring out, produce*. I. Lit., 1, gen., medicamenta de narthecio, Cic.; 2, esp., a, *to bring money out of a coffer, to produce*, aurum ex aerario, Cic.; esp. of the quaestor, alicui pecuniam ex aerario, Cic.; b, *to bring wine up out of the cellar*, vina, Hor.; c, *to bring weapons out*, tela e pharetra, Ov. II. Transf., 1, gen., *to bring forth, draw forth*, animus eruditus, qui semper ex se aliquid promat, quod delectet, Cic.; 2, *to bring forward, utter, express, mention*, plura adversus Cottam, Tac.

prōmŏnĕo, 2. *to warn*, t. t. of augury, de periculis promoneri, Cic.

prōmontōrĭum -ii, n. (promineo). I. *a mountain peak*, Liv. II. *a promontory*, Cic.

prōmōta -ōrum, n. (promoveo), (translation of the Greek προηγμένα), *preferable things, next in degree to the absolute good*, Cic.

prōmŏvĕo -mōvi -mōtum, 2. *to move forwards, push onwards*. I. Lit., A. Gen., a, of things, saxa vectibus, Caes.; castra ad Carthaginem, Liv.; b, of persons, promovere legiones, *cause to advance*, Caes. B. Esp., 1, *to advance a building in a certain direction, to push on*, aggerem in urbem, Liv.; assa in alterum angulum, *to remove*, Cic.; 2, *to extend*, imperium, Ov. II. Fig., A. Gen., promovere arcana loco, *to bring to light*, Hor. B. *to increase, improve*, doctrina vim promovet insitam, Hor.

promptē, adv. (promptus). I. *promptly, quickly, readily*, Tac. II. *easily*, Juv. III. *frankly, freely*, dicam paulo promptius, Cic.

1. **promptus** -a -um, p. adj. (from promo). I. *visible, apparent, manifest*, aliud clausum in pectore, aliud promptum in lingua habere, Sall.; prompta et aperta, Cic. II. Transf., *ready, at hand, prepared*. A. Of things, 1, gen., fidem suam populo Romano promptam, *at the disposition of*, Cic.; 2, esp., *easy*, defensio, Cic. B. Of persons, *ready, prepared, resolute, quick, disposed for*, promptissimus homo et expeditus, Cic.; with ad or in and the acc., ad vim promptus, Cic.; with abl., ingenio, linguā, Liv.; with genit. (of place), belli (*in war*) promptissimos, Sall.

2. **promptus** -ūs, m. (promo). I. *a being visible, visibility*, only in the phrases in promptu esse, *to be visible, manifest*, etc., Cic.; in promptu ponere, *to make manifest*, Cic.; in promptu habere, Sall. II. Transf., A. *readiness*, only in the phrases in promptu esse, *to be ready at hand*, Cic.; in promptu habere, *to have ready at hand*, Cic. B. *easiness*, only in phrases in promptu esse, *to be easy*, Sall.

prōmulgātĭo -ōnis, f. (promulgo), *a making publicly known, proclamation, promulgation* (of a proposed law), Cic.

prōmulgo, 1. (pro and mulco), *to publish, promulgate*. I. Lit., legal t. t., *to publish a proposed law* (on three market days), leges, Cic.; promulgare de aliquo, Cic. II. Transf., *to publish, make known*, proelia, Cic.

prōmulsĭs -ĭdis, f. (pro and mulsum), *a dish taken as a relish before a meal (eggs, salt-fish, radishes*, etc.), *a whet.*

prōmuntūrĭum = promontorium (q.v.).

prōmus -i, m. (promo), *the slave who had charge of the store-room and served out the daily supplies, steward, butler*, Hor.

prōmūtŭus -a -um, *advanced, paid beforehand*, Caes.

prōnē, adv. (pronus), *downwards, on an incline;* prone ac fastigate, Cic.

prŏnĕpos -pōtis, m. *a great-grandson*, Cic.

prŏneptis -is, f. *a great grand-daughter*, Pers.

prōnis = pronus, (q.v.).

prŏnoea -ae, f. (πρόνοια), *providence*, Cic.

prōnŭba -ae, f. (pro and nubo), *a matron who attended on a bride at a Roman wedding;* Juno Pronuba, *the goddess who presided over marriage;* transf., of Bellona, *as presiding over an unlucky marriage* (leading to war), Verg.; so of the Furies, Ov.

prōnuntĭātĭo -ōnis, f. (pronuntio). **I.** *making known publicly, publication*, Caes.; esp., *the decision of a judge, a judgment*, Cic. **II.** In logic, *a proposition*, Cic.

prōnuntĭātor -ōris, m. (pronuntio), *a relater;* rerum gestarum, Cic.

prōnuntĭātum -i, n. (pronuntio), in logic, *a proposition*, Cic.

prōnuntĭo, 1. *to make publicly known, publish.* **I.** Gen., *to proclaim, announce;* pronuntiare quae gesta sunt, Caes. **II. A.** Esp., polit. and milit. t. t., *to publish, proclaim, make known by proclamation;* **a,** in public gatherings, by the herald or crier at the command of the magistrate; te illo honore affici pronuntiavit, Cic.; pronuntiare aliquem praetorem, Liv.; so of a command given to the soldiers in a camp; pronuntiatur primā luce ituros, Caes.; so, *publicly to promise something to the people;* nummos in tribus, Cic.; **b,** in the senate, of the consul, *to announce a resolution and the name of its proposer;* Lentulus sententiam Calidii pronuntiaturum se negavit, Cic. **B.** Legal t. t., **a,** of judges, etc., (α) *to express;* graviorem sententiam, Caes.; (β) *to decide, pronounce a judgment;* de tribunali pronuntiavit sese recepturum, Cic.; **b,** in an agreement for a sale, *to make a statement as to the defects of the thing sold;* quum in vendendo rem eam scisset et non pronuntiasset, Cic. **C.** Rhet. t. t., *to declaim, recite, deliver;* summā voce versus multos uno spiritu, Cic.

prōnŭrus -ūs, f. *a grandson's wife*, Ov.

prōnus -a -um, *inclined forward, stooping forward, hanging down.* **I. A.** Adj., **a,** of persons, pronus pendens in verbera, *leaning forward to the blow*, Verg.; so of persons, *swiftly running*, Ov.; **b,** of the position of parts of the body, motu prono, Cic.; **c,** of things, amnis, *rushing down*, Verg.; **d,** transf., (α) of places, *sloping;* Anxur fuit urbs prona in paludes, Liv.; poet., *precipitous, steep;* via, Ov.; (β) of stars, *setting;* Orion, Hor.; (γ) of time, *hastening away;* menses, Hor. **B.** Subst., **prōnum** -i, n., nihil proni habere, Cic. **II.** Fig., **A.** *inclined towards;* **1,** to something good or bad; ad novas res, Tac.; in obsequium, Hor.; in hoc consilium, Liv.; **2,** *inclined, well-disposed, favourable;* in aliquem, Tac. **B.** Meton., *easy;* omnia virtuti prona, Sall.; id pronius ad fidem est, *is more creditable*, Liv.

prŏoemĭum -ĭi, n. (προοίμιον). **I.** *a preface, introduction, prelude*, Cic. **II.** *a beginning*, Juv.

prŏpăgātĭo -ōnis, f. (1. propago). **I.** *an extension, enlargement.* **A.** In space, imperii nostri, Cic. **B.** In time, *prolonging, extending;* temporis, Cic.; vitae, Cic. **II.** *planting, propagation*, Cic.; transf., of a race, Cic.; nominis, Cic.

prŏpāgātor -ōris, m. (1. propago), *an extender, enlarger;* provinciae, Cic.

1. **prŏpāgo,** 1. (pro and PAG-o, pango). **I.** Gen., **A.** *to extend, enlarge;* fines provinciae, Cic. **B.** *to extend in point of time, prolong;* bellum, Cic.; laudem alicuius ad sempiternam gloriam, Cic.; imperium consuli in annum, Liv.; multa saecula reipublicae, *to prolong the existence of the state by many centuries*, Cic. **II.** Esp., *to propagate, plant;* transf., of a race, stirpem, Cic.

2. **prōpāgo** -ĭnis, f. (1. propago). **I.** *a sucker, layer, shoot;* esp., of the vine, Cic. **II.** Transf., of men and animals, *offspring, progeny, race, posterity;* Romana, Verg.; catulorum, Lucr.; plur., clarorum virorum propagines, *genealogies*, Nep.

prōpălam, adv. *publicly, in public;* dicere, Liv.; collocare, Cic.

prōpătŭlus -a -um, *open, uncovered.* **I.** Adj., in aperto ac propatulo loco, Cic. **II.** Subst., **prōpătŭlum** -i, n. *an open place, unroofed space;* hence, in propatulo; **a,** *openly*, Cic.; transf., *visibly, publicly*, Sall.; **b,** esp., in propatulo aedium, *in the open fore-court of a house*, Liv.

prŏpĕ (from pro and pe, or else the neuter of an unused adj., propis). Compar., **prŏpĭus;** superl., **proxĭmē. I.** Adv., **A.** *near;* **1,** of space, *near;* volebam prope alicubi esse, Cic.; propius, *nearer;* accedere, Cic.; proxime, *next;* proxime trans Padum, Caes.; **2,** of time, *near;* hence, proxime, *a short time ago, just now;* quem proxime nominavi, Cic.; **3,** of other relations; **a,** of approximation to; (α) *nearly;* prope erat ut pelleretur, *he was near being*, etc., Liv.; propius nihil est factum quam ut occideretur, Cic.; (β) *nearly, almost;* annis prope quadraginta, Liv.; prope desperatis rebus, Cic.; prope adesse, *to be close at hand*, Cic.; (γ) *more closely, more accurately;* propius res aspice nostras, Verg.; (δ) of similarity, proxime atque (ac) ille, Cic.; **b,** of order, *near;* proxime a Lacyde, Cic. **B.** *near by, close to, hard by;* gen. with a and the abl., prope a Sicilia, Cic. **II.** Prep. with acc. (sometimes with dat.), **1,** of space, *near to;* prope me, Cic.; proxime hostem, *next the enemy*, Caes.; propius grammatico accessi, Cic.; **2,** of time, *near to, close on;* prope calendas Sext., Cic.; **3,** of approximation or similarity, *not far from, near to:* propius, *nearer to;* proxime, *nearest to, very like to;* prope secessionem plebis res venit, Liv.; propius fidem est, *it deserves more credit*, Liv.; proxime morem Romanum, Liv.

prŏpĕdĭem, adv. *at an early day, very soon*, Cic.

prōpello -pŭli -pulsum, 3. *to drive before one, drive forth, drive away.* **I.** Lit., **1,** of things, **a,** *to drive away, push away;* crates pro munitione objectas, Caes.; **b,** *to hurl down;* corpus alicuius e scopulo in profundum, Ov.; **c,** *to drive forward;* navem in altum, Ov.; **2, a,** of persons, *to drive away forcibly, repulse;* hostes, Caes.; **b,** of animals, *to drive away;* pecus extra portam, Liv. **II.** Fig., **a,** *to drive away;* vitae periculum ab aliquo, Liv.; **b,** *to drive forwards;* orationem dialecticorum remis, Cic.; **c,** *to drive, to compel;* aliquem ad voluntariam mortem, Tac.

prŏpĕmŏdŏ, adv. (prope and modus), *almost, nearly*, Liv.

prŏpŏmŏdum, adv. (prope and modus), *almost, nearly*, Cic.

prŏpendĕo pendi -pensum, 2 *to hang down* **I.** Lit, tantum propendere illam boni lancem ut, etc, Cic **II.** Fig, bona propendent, *to preponderate*, Cic, inclinatione voluntatis ad aliquem, *to be inclined to, favourable towards*, Cic

prōpensē, adv (propensus), *readily, willingly*, gen compar, propensius, Liv

prōpensio -ōnis, f (propendeo), *an inclination towards, propensity*, Cic

prōpensus a um, p adj (from propendeo), **1,** *inclined to, disposed to*, ad misericordiam, Cic, in alteram partem, Cic, **2,** *coming near to*, ad veritatis similitudinem, Cic

prŏpĕrantĕr, adv (propero), *hastily, quickly*, Tac, properantius, Sall, Ov

prŏpĕrantĭa ae, f (propero), *haste, rapidity*, Sall

prŏpĕrātĭo ōnis, f (propero) *haste*, Cic

prŏpĕrātō, adv (propero), *hastily, quickly*, Tac.

prŏpĕro, 1 (properus) **I.** Intransit, *to hasten* (from a particular point); **a,** of persons, Romam, Cic, with in and acc, in patriam, Caes, with ad and acc, ad aliquem, Caes, with adv, alio, Sall, with infin, redire, Cic, absol, properantes arma currunt, Sall, **b,** of things, properans aqua per agros, Hor **II.** Transit., *to haste something, to accelerate, complete quickly*, iter, Sall, mortem, Verg, opus, studium, Hor

Prŏpertĭus ii, m, Sex Aurelius, *a Roman elegiac poet, born in Umbria, educated in Rome* (about 49-15 B C)

prŏpĕrus a -um, *quick, rapid, hasty, bustling*, circumstant properi aurigae, Verg

prōpexus a -um (pro and pecto), *combed forwards, hanging down*, propexa in pectore barba, Verg., propexam ad pectora barbam, Ov

prŏpīnātĭo -ōnis, f (propino), *a drinking to one's health*, Sen

prŏpīno, 1 (προπίνω) **I.** *to drink to any one*, propino hoc pulchro Critiae, Cic **II.** Transf, *to give drink to any one*, Mart

prŏpinquē, adv (propinquus), *near, close by*, Plaut

prŏpinquĭtas ātis, f (propinquus) **I.** *nearness, proximity*, loci, Cic, hostium, Caes **II.** Transf, *relationship*, vinculis propinquitatis conjunctus, Cic

prŏpinquo, 1 (propinquus) **I.** Intransit *to come near, draw near, approach* **A.** Lit, **a,** of persons, with dat, scopulo, Verg, with acc, campos, Tac, **b,** of things, ignis domui alicuius propinquat, Tac **B** Transf, of time, *to draw near*, Parcarum dies et vis inimica propinquat, Verg **II.** Transit, *to bring near, hasten*, augurium, Verg

prŏpinquus a -um (prope), *near* **I.** Of space or position, *neighbouring, bordering*, provincia, Cic, with dat, propinquus cubiculo hortus, Liv, subst (in sing only with a prep), in propinquo esse, *to be near*, Liv, oppido propinqua, *the neighbourhood of the town*, Sall **II.** Transf, **A.** *near*, as regards time, reditus, Cic **B.** Of other relations, **a,** *similar*, quae propinqua videntur et finitima, Cic, **b,** *near in point of relationship, closely connected*, cognatio, Cic, with dat tibi genere propinqui, Sall, subst, *a kinsman*, Cic

prŏpior -us, genit -ōris, superl, **proxĭmus** a -um (prope) **I.** Compar, **prŏpior**, *nearer* **A.** Lit, of place, portus, Verg, pons, Caes, with dat, propior patriae, Ov, neut plur. subst, propiora, *the nearer regions*, Verg **B.** Transf, **1,** of time, *nearer, more recent*, epistola, Cic, with dat, propior leto, Ov, **2, a,** of relationship, *nearer, more closely connected*, societas, Cic, quibus propior P Quinctio nemo est, Cic, **b,** *nearer, more closely affecting*, sua sibi propiora esse pericula quam mea Cic, **c,** *nearer in point of likeness, more similar*, sceleri propiora, Cic, propius est vero, Ov, with acc and infin, Liv, **d,** *more suitable to*, portus propior huic aetati, Cic, **e,** *more inclined towards*, proprior Saturnia Turno, Ov **II.** Superl, **proximus** -a -um, *very near nearest* **A** Lit, of place, oppidum, Caes vicinus, Cic, with dat, huic proximus locus, Cic, with acc, proximus quisque hostem, Liv, with ab and the abl, dactylus proximus a postremo, Cic, subst, **a, proximi**, *those standing next*, Caes, or *those standing nearest*, Caes, **b, proximum** -i, n *the nearest, the neighbourhood*, e proximo, Nep, proxima Illyrici, Liv **B.** Transf, **1,** of time, **a,** of the future, *next, following*, nox, Caes, annus, Cic, **b,** of the past, *nearest, most recent*, quid proxima nocte egeris, Cic, proximis superioribus diebus, Caes, **2,** of succession, *next, following next* proximus post Lysandrum, Cic, proximum est, with infin, non nasci homini optimum est, proximum autem (*the next best thing*) quam primum mori, Cic, proximum est, with ut and the subj, *the next thing is to*, etc, proximum est ut doceam, Cic, **3,** *next in succession, in rank, in worth*, proximus est huic dignitati ordo equester, Cic, **4,** *nearest akin, most nearly related*, proximus cognatione, Cic, subst, **proximi** -ōrum, m *near relations*, Cic, **5,** *nearest in resemblance, most like*, deo proximum, Cic

prŏpĭtĭo, 1 (propitius), *to soothe, propitiate, appease*, Venerem, Plaut

prŏpĭtĭus -a -um (pro and peto, Gr προπετής) *favourably inclined, favourable, gracious, propitious*, dii, Cic, hunc propitium sperant, Cic

prŏpĭus, comp of prope (q v)

Prōpoetĭdes um, f *maidens of Cyprus who denied the divinity of Venus and were changed into stone*

prŏpōla -ae, m (προπώλης), *a forestaller, retailer, huckster*, Cic

prōpollŭo, 3 *to pollute greatly*, Tac

prōpōno pŏsŭi -pŏsitum, 3 **I.** *to put forth, place out, set in view, expose, display* **A.** Lit, vexillum, Caes, aliquid venale, *expose for sale*, Cic, oculis and ante oculos, *to place before the eyes*, Cic **B.** Fig, **1,** *to place before, set before*, aliquem sibi ad imitandum, Cic, **2,** *to bring forward*, proposita sententia, Cic, **3,** *to propose*, proponat quid dicturus sit, Cic, **4,** *to report, relate, tell*, rem gestam, Caes, **5,** *to make known*, epistolam in publico, Cic, hence, **a,** *to propose, promise, offer as a reward*, praemia alicui, Cic **b,** *to threaten, menace*, poenam improbis, Cic, **6,** *to propose a question for answer*, quaestionem, Nep, **7,** *to propose to oneself, purpose, intend*, consecutus id, quod animo proposuerat, Caes, with ut or ut ne and subj, quum mihi proposuissem ut commoverem, Cic, with infin, quibus propositum est contra omnes philosophos dicere, Cic **II.** *to state the premiss of a syllogism*, Cic

Prŏpontis idis and -idos, f (Προποντίς), *the Propontis, now the Sea of Marmora*, hence, **Prŏpontĭăcus** -a -um, *of or relating to the Propontis*

prŏporrō, adv *further, moreover*, Lucr

prŏportĭo -ōnis, f *proportion, relation, analogy, similarity*, Cic

prōpŏsĭtĭo -ōnis, f. (propono). **I.** *a setting before oneself;* **1,** *the representation which a man forms in his own mind of something;* animi, Cic.; vitae, Cic.; **2,** *the subject or theme of a discourse,* Cic. **II.** In logic, *the first proposition of a syllogism,* Cic.

prōpŏsĭtum -i, n, (propono). **I.** *that which is set before one:* **1,** *a design, plan, purpose, intention;* propositum assequi, *to accomplish a design,* Cic.; tenere, *to keep to a design,* Cic.; **2,** *the subject or theme of a discourse;* ad propositum redeamus, Cic. **II.** *the premiss of a syllogism,* Cic.

prōpraetor -ōris, m. and **pro praetōre,** *a propraetor, a Roman who, after having been praetor at Rome, was sent as governor to a province without a military command,* Cic.

prŏprĭē, adv. (proprius). **I.** Lit., *peculiarly, exclusively for oneself;* proprie parvā parte frui, Cic. **II.** Transf., **a,** *peculiarly, characteristically, personally;* quod tu ipse tum amandus es, id est proprie tuum, Cic.; **b,** *specially, expressly;* cuius causam neque senatus publice neque ullus ordo proprie susceperat, Cic.; **c,** *accurately, in a proper sense;* illud honestum quod proprie vereque dicitur, Cic.

prŏprĭĕtas -ātis, f. (proprius), *a property, peculiarity;* rerum, Cic.; plur., frugum proprietates, Liv.

prŏprĭtim (proprius), *properly, peculiarly,* Lucr.

prŏprĭus -a -um, *one's own, special, particular, peculiar.* **I.** Lit., **a,** opp. to communis; ista calamitas communis est utriusque nostrûm, sed culpa mea propria est, Cic; often with possess. pron., proprius et suus, suus proprius, noster proprius, Cic.; **b,** *one's own,* as opp. to alienus; assumpto aliunde uti bono, non proprio, non suo, Cic. **II.** Transf., **A.** *peculiar to a person* or *thing;* **a,** *characteristic of;* proprium est senectutis vitium, Cic.; proprium est alicuius, with acc. and infin., *it is the distinguishing mark of, it is peculiar to;* fuit hoc proprium populi Romani longe a domo bellare, Cic.; **b,** *special, exclusive;* nulla est in republica causa mea propria, Cic.; **c,** of words, *proper, peculiar;* discedebat a verbis propriis rerum ac suis, Cic. **B.** Esp., *lasting, permanent;* munera, Hor.; illud de duobus consulibus perenne ac proprium manere potuisset, Cic.

proptĕr (for propiter from prope), adv. **I.** *near, hard by;* quum duo reges cum maximis copiis prope assint, Cic. **II.** Prep. with acc. **A.** Lit., of a place, *near, hard by;* insulae propter Siciliam, Cic. **B.** Transf., *on account of, by reason of, because of, for, from;* metum, Cic.; frigora, Caes.; propter quos vivit, *by whose means he is alive, whom he has to thank for his life,* Cic. (propter sometimes put after its case, as quem propter, Cic.).

proptĕrĕā, adv. *on that account, therefore,* Cic.; foll. by quia, Cic.; quod, Cic.; ut or ne and the subj., Cic.

prōpŭdĭōsus -a -um (propudium), *covered with infamy, full of shame, infamous,* Plaut.

prōpŭdĭum -ii, n. (= quasi porro pudendum). **I.** *a shameful action,* Plaut. **II.** Meton., *a wretch, villain, rascal;* propudium illud et portentum L. Antonius, Cic.

prōpugnācŭlum -i, n. (propugno), *a fortification, rampart, fortress, defence.* **I.** Lit., moenium, Tac.; propugnaculum Siciliae, *of the fleet,* Cic.; propugnacula imperii, *fleets and armies,* Cic. **II.** Fig., **a,** lex Aelia et Fufia propugnacula tranquillitatis, Cic.; **b,** *grounds of defence;* firmissimo propugnaculo uti, Liv.

prōpugnātĭo -ōnis, f. (propugno), *defence, defending;* fig., nostra propugnatio et defensio dignitatis tuae, Cic.

prōpugnātor -ōris, m. (propugno), *a defender, combatant, soldier.* **I.** Lit., **a,** duplici propugnatorum ordine defendi, Caes.; **b,** *a marine;* dimissio propugnatorum, Cic. **II.** Fig., *a defender;* patrimonii sui, Cic.

prōpugno, 1. *to skirmish to the front.* **I.** Intransit., *to fight in defence, to defend oneself;* **a,** lit., uno tempore propugnare et munire, Caes.; e loco, Caes.; pro vallo, Liv.; pro suo partu (of animals), Cic.; partic. subst., propugnantes, *the defenders,* Caes.; **b,** transf., *to fight for something, to fight in defence;* pro fama alicuius, Cic. **II.** Transit., *to defend;* munimenta, Tac.

prōpulso, 1. (intens. of propello), *to drive back, repel, ward off.* **I.** Lit., hostem, Caes.; populum ab ingressione fori, Cic. **II.** Transf., frigus, famem, Cic.; suspicionem a se, Cic.

prŏpy̆laeon -i, n. (προπύλαιον), *a gateway, entrance;* plur., **Prŏpy̆laea** -ōrum, n. (τὰ προπύλαια), *the celebrated entrance to the Parthenon at Athens, built by Pericles.*

prō-quaestōre, *a proquaestor, a quaestor in a Roman province, who attended to the finances and pay of the army,* Cic.

prōquam, conj. *according as,* Lucr.

prōra -ae, f. (πρῴρα), *the prow, bow of a ship.* **I.** Lit., Caes.; prorae tutela = proreta, Ov. **II.** Meton. = *a ship,* Verg., Ov.

prōrēpo -repsi -reptum, 3. *to creep forward, crawl forth,* Hor.

prōrēta -ae, m. (πρωράτης), *the look-out man at the prow of a ship,* Plaut.

Prōreus -ĕi, m. (Πρωρεύς), *a Tyrrhene sailor,* Ov.

prōrĭpĭo -rĭpŭi -reptum (pro and rapio), 3. *to snatch, tear, drag forth;* hominem, Cic.; se proripere, *to rush forward, hurry;* se in publicum, Liv.; se ex curia, Cic.; se portā foras, Caes.; quo proripis (sc. te)? Verg.; fig., quae libido non se proripiet, Cic.

prōrŏgātĭo -ōnis, f. (prorogo), **1,** *a prolongation of a term of office,* Liv.; **2,** *a deferring of a fixed time, prorogation,* Cic.

prōrŏgo, 1. **1,** *to propose to the people an extension of something for some person, to prolong;* imperium alicui, Cic.; provinciam, Cic.; **2,** *to put off;* dies ad solvendum, Cic.

prorsum, adv. (pro and versum), *forwards.* **I.** Lit., **a,** Plaut.; **b,** *straightforwards, straight on,* Plaut. **II.** Transf., *at all,* Plaut., Ter.

prorsŭs, adv. (pro and versus), *turned forwards, forwards.* **I.** prorsus ibat res, Cic. **II.** Transf., **a,** *utterly, absolutely, wholly, entirely;* ita prorsus existimo, Cic.; prorsus assentior, Cic.; non prorsus, nullo modo prorsus, *not at all;* nullo modo prorsus assentior, Cic.; **b,** *in a word, to sum up,* Sall.

prōrumpo -rūpi -ruptum, 3. **I.** Transit., *to cause to break forth, thrust forth, send forth;* **1,** lit., nubem atram, Verg.; mare proruptum, *the sea breaking in front,* Verg.; transf., prorupta audacia, *unbridled,* Cic. **II.** Intransit., *to burst forth, break forth.* **A.** Lit., per medios, Cic. **B.** Transf., *to break out;* prorumpit pestis, Cic.; of persons, in scelera ac dedecora, Tac.

prōrŭo -rŭi -rŭtum, 3. **I.** Intransit., *to rush forth;* qua proruebat, Caes. **II.** Transit., *to overthrow, throw down, cast to the ground, destroy;* munitiones, Caes.; vallum, Liv.; Albam a fundamentis, Liv.; hostem profligare ac proruere, Tac.

prōsāpĭa -ae, f. *a family race, stock* (an archaic word), Sall., eorum, ut utamur veteri verbo, prosapiam, Cic.

proscaenium (proscēnium) -ĭi, n. (προσκήνιον), *the part of a theatre before the scenes, stage,* Liv.

proscindo -scĭdi -scissum, 3 *to tear off in front, to rend.* **I.** Lit., *to break up fallow land, plough up,* poet., *to plough,* terram, Verg.; meton., aequor, *to plough the waters,* Cat. **II.** Transf., *to censure, defame, satirise,* Ov.

proscrībo -scripsi -scriptum, 3. **I.** *to make publicly known, publish,* Cic., with acc. and infin., auctionem in Gallia Narbone se facturum esse, Cic. **II.** Esp., **A.** *to offer publicly for sale or hire, advertise,* insulam, bona, fundum, Cic. **B.** *to confiscate the property of any one,* possessiones, Cic.; Pompeium, *to confiscate the estates gained by Pompey,* Cic. **C.** *to proscribe, outlaw* (by publishing the person's name in a list), aliquem, Cic.; **proscripti** -ōrum, m. *the proscribed,* Sall.

proscriptĭo -ōnis, f. (proscribo), **1,** *an advertisement of sale,* bonorum, Cic.; **2,** *a proscription, outlawry,* Cic.

proscriptŭrĭo, 4 (desider. of prōscribo), *to desire to declare any one an outlaw,* Cic.

prōsĕco -sĕcŭi -sectum, 1. *to cut off in front, cut off,* esp., *to cut off the portions of a victim to be sacrificed,* exta, Liv.

prōsectum -i, n. (proseco), *the part of a victim cut off to be offered to a god, the entrails,* Ov.

prōsēmĭno, 1. *to sow.* **I.** Lit., vel in tegulis proseminare ostreas, Cic. **II.** Fig., *to disseminate, propagate,* Cic.

prōsĕquor -cūtus (-quūtus) sum -sĕqui, 3. dep. *to follow, accompany.* **I.** In a friendly sense, **A.** *to accompany, attend,* esp. of friends who "*see off*" a person going on a journey, aliquem usque ad agri fines, Cic.; prosequi exsequias, Cic.; transf., of things, ventus prosequitur euntes, Verg.; eos honos, memoria, desiderium prosequitur amicorum, Cic. **B.** Fig., **1,** *to accompany,* aliquem votis, ominibus, lacrimisque, Caes.; **2, a,** *to honour, adorn, or present with, treat with,* aliquem verbis honorificis, Cic.; aliquem beneficiis, Cic.; misericordiā, Cic.; **b,** of a discourse, *to go on with, continue,* quod non longius prosequar, Cic. **II.** In a hostile sense, *to attack, pursue,* hostem, Caes.; longius fugientes, Caes.

Prōserpĭna -ae, f. (Περσεφόνη), *the daughter of Ceres and Jupiter, carried off by Pluto to be queen of the lower world,* hence, meton., *the lower world,* Hor. (in Verg. and Ov. Prōserpĭna, in Hor. Prŏserpĭna).

prŏseucha -ae, f. (προσευχή), *a place of prayer for the Jews,* Juv.

prōsĭlĭo -ŭi (-īvi or -ĭi), 4. (pro and salio). **I.** *to spring, leap forth.* **A. 1,** lit., ex tabernaculo, Liv.; ab sede, Liv.; repente, Cic.; finibus suis, Verg.; **2,** of things, flumina prosiliunt, Ov. **B.** Fig., vaga prosiliet frenis natura remotis, Hor. **II.** *to spring forward to a place,* in contionem, Liv.

prōsŏcer -ĕri, m. *a wife's grandmother,* Ov.

prospecto, 1. (intens. of prospicio), *to look forward, look forth upon.* **I. A.** Lit., e puppi pontum, Ov.; euntem, Verg.; ex tectis fenestrisque, Liv. **B.** Transf., of places, *to look towards, be situate towards,* villa quae subjectos sinus prospectat, Tac. **II.** Fig., *to look for, hope, expect,* exsilium, Cic.; te quoque fata prospectant paria, *a like fate awaits,* Verg.

prospectus -ūs, m. (prospicio). **I.** *an outlook, view, prospect;* unde longe ac late prospectus erat, Liv.; prospectum impedire, Caes.; meton., *the sight;* aequora prospectu metior alta meo, Ov. **II.** Pass., *view, sight,* cum jam extremi essent in prospectu, *were within sight,* Caes.

prospĕcŭlor, 1. dep. **I.** Intransit., *to look out to a distance,* hence, *to explore, reconnoitre,* Liv. **II.** Transit., *to look for, wait for,* adventum imperatoris, Liv.

prosper (prospĕrus) -a -um (pro and spero) *according to one's hope,* hence, **I.** *fortunate, favourable, lucky, prosperous,* fortuna, Cic.; exitus, Cic.; subst., **prospĕra** -ōrum, n. *prosperity, good fortune,* Ov. **II.** Transit., *bringing good fortune, propitious,* Bellona, Ov.; with genit., prospera frugum, Hor.

prospĕrē, adv. (prosper), *prosperously, fortunately, favourably,* procedere prospere, Cic.

prospergo -spersi -sparsum, 3. (pro and spargo), *to sprinkle,* Tac.

prospĕrĭtas -ātis, f. (prosper), *prosperity, good fortune;* vitae, Cic.; plur., improborum prosperitates, Cic.

prospĕro, 1. (prosper), *to make fortunate or prosperous, to cause to succeed, to give a favourable issue to,* alicui victoriam, Liv.

prospĕrus = prosper (q.v.).

prospĭcĭentĭa -ae, f. (prospicio), *foresight, precaution,* Cic.

prospĭcĭo -spexi -spectum, 3. (pro and specio). **I.** Intransit., *to look forward, look into the distance.* **A.** Lit., **1,** ex castris in urbem, Caes.; multum, *to have a wide prospect,* Cic.; **2,** *to look out, be upon the watch,* Nep. **B.** Fig., *to exercise foresight, to take precaution,* with dat., consulite vobis, prospicite patriae, Cic.; with ut and the subj., Cic.; with ne and the subj., Caes. **II.** Transit., *to see, behold, gaze upon from afar.* **A.** Lit., **1,** Italiam ab unda, Verg.; **2,** transf., of places, *to look towards, be situate towards,* domus prospicit agros, Hor. **B.** Fig., **a,** *to foresee,* casus futuros, Cic.; **b,** *to look out for, provide, procure,* ferramenta, Cic.; commeatus, Liv.

prosterno -strāvi -strātum, 3. *to strew before, throw down in front, cast down.* **A.** Lit., **a,** circa viam corpora humi, Liv.; se ad pedes alicuius, Cic.; hence, **prostrātus** -a -um (sc. humi), *lying on the ground,* ad pedes, Cic.; **b,** *to throw down with violence,* hostem, Cic. **B.** Fig., **1,** se abjicere et prosternere, *to debase oneself,* Cic.; **2,** *to throw to the ground, overthrow, destroy, ruin,* omnia furore, Cic.; aliquem, Cic. (syncop. infin. perf., prostrasse = prostravisse, Ov.).

prostĭtŭo -stĭtŭi -stĭtūtum, 3. (pro and statuo), *to prostitute,* vocem ingrato foro, Ov.

prosto -stĭti, 1. *to stand before,* hence, **I.** *to stand forward, project,* Lucr. **II.** Of goods, *to be exposed for sale,* liber prostat, Hor.; vox prostitit, Cic.; *to sell one's person, prostitute oneself,* transf., illud amicitiae quondam venerabile nomen prostat, Hor.

prōsŭbĭgo, 3. *to dig up, throw up,* terram, Verg.

prōsum, prōfŭi, prōdesse, *to be useful, advantageous to,* illa quae prosunt aut quae nocent, Cic.; with dat., qui nec sibi nec alteri prosunt, dicere quod causae prosit, Cic.; with infin., multum prodest ea quae metuuntur ipsa contemnere, Cic.; quid mihi fingere prodest? Ov.

Prōtăgŏrās -ae, m. (Πρωταγόρας), *a Greek philosopher, of Abdera, contemporary with Socrates, banished from Attica on a charge of atheism.*

prŏtĕgo -texi -tectum, 3. **I.** *to cover in front.* **A.** Lit., tabernacula protecta hederā, Caes.; aliquem scuto, *protect,* Caes. **B.** Transf., *to cover, protect;* jacentem, Cic.; regem, Liv. **II.** *to furnish with a roof;* aedes, Cic.

prōtēlo, 1. (pro and telum), *to drive off, put to flight,* Ter.

prōtēlum -i, n. (protendo), *a yoke of oxen;* fig., *a series, succession,* Lucr.

prōtendo -tendi -tentum and -tensum, 3. *to stretch forward, stretch out;* brachia in mare, Ov.; cervicem, Tac.; temo protentus in octo pedes, *eight feet long,* Verg.

prōtĕnŭs (prōtĭnŭs), adv. *forward, further, further on.* **I.** Lit., protenus ago capellas, Verg.; quum ad alias angustias protenus pergerent, Liv. **II.** Transf., **A.** *without delay, straightway, on the spot;* Laodiceam protenus ire, Cic.; ut is ad te protenus mittat, Cic. **B.** *of unbroken extent, continuously;* quum protenus utraque tellus una foret, Verg. **C.** Of unbroken succession in time, **1,** *constantly, continuously;* quem (morem) protenus urbes Albanae coluere sacrum, Verg.; **2,** *immediately, at once;* **a,** protenus Carthaginem ituros, Liv.; protenus de via, Liv.; **b,** *immediately, at the beginning;* oratio protenus perficiens auditorem benevolum, Cic.

prōtĕro -trīvi -trītum, 3. **I.** *to trample under foot, tread down.* **A. a,** lit., equitatus aversos proterere incipit, Caes.; frumentum, Liv.; **b,** hence, *to overthrow in battle, rout, defeat;* Poenos, Hor. **B.** Fig., *to trample on, despise;* aliquem, Cic. **II.** *to drive away, push aside;* ver proterit aestas, Hor.

prōterrĕo -terrŭi -territum, 2. *to frighten away, scare away;* Themistoclem patriā pulsum atque proterritum, Cic.; aliquem verbis gravissimis, Cic.

prŏtervē, adv. (protervus), *boldly, impudently, shamelessly,* Ov.

prŏtervĭtas -ātis, f. (protervus), *boldness, impudence,* Cic.; and in a milder sense, *wantonness, pertness,* Hor.

prŏtervus -a -um (protero), *trampling upon everything;* hence, **I.** *violent, vehement;* venti, Hor.; stella canis, Ov. **II.** *bold, impudent, shameless,* and in a milder sense, *wanton, pert;* homo, Cic.; juvenes, Hor.

Prōtĕsĭlāus -i, m. (Πρωτεσίλαος), *the husband of Laodamia, the first Greek who landed before Troy in the Trojan war, and the first of the Greeks to be slain.* Adj., **Prōtĕsĭlāēus** -a -um, *belonging to Protesilaus.*

Prōtĕus -ĕi and -ĕos, m. (Πρωτεύς), *a god of the sea, the herdsman of Poseidon's sea-calves, a prophet who would not answer those who consulted him except when bound in chains, and who had the power of changing himself into different shapes;* Protei columnae, poet., *the borders of Egypt,* Verg.; appellat., *a changeable or a crafty man,* Hor.

prōtĭnam (prōtĕnam), adv. (protinus), *immediately, directly, at once,* Plaut.

prōtĭnus = protenus (q.v.).

Prōtŏgĕnēs -is, m. (Πρωτογένης), *a famous Greek painter of Caunos on the coast of Caria, flourishing about* 300 B.C.

prōtollo, 3. **I.** *to put forth, stretch forth,* Plaut. **II.** *to extend, lengthen, prolong,* Plaut.

prōtrăho -traxi -tractum, 3. *to draw, drag forth.* **I.** *to drag to a place.* **A.** Lit., aliquem hinc in convivium, Cic. **B.** Transf., **1,** *to draw forth;* **a,** aliquid in lucem, Lucr.; **b,** *to bring to light, to reveal, make known;* auctorem nefandi facinoris, Liv.; **2,** *to compel, force;* aliquem ad indicium, Liv. **II.** Transf., *to extend in point of time, protract, defer,* Suet.

prōtrūdo -trūsi -trūsum, 3. *to push forward, thrust forth.* **I.** Lit., cylindrum, Cic. **II.** Fig., *to put off, defer;* comitia in Januarium mensem, Cic.

prōturbo, 1. *to drive forward, drive away, repel;* **a,** of persons, equites, Caes.; hostes telis missilibusque saxis, Liv.; **b,** of things, pectore silvas, *to throw down,* Ov.

prŏŭt, conj. *according as;* prout res postulat, Cic.

prōvectus -a -um (p. adj. from proveho), *advanced in age;* longius aetate provectus, Cic.

prōvĕho -vexi -vectum, 3. *to carry forward, to lead forward.* **I.** Act., **A.** Lit., aër a tergo quasi provehit, Lucr. **B.** Fig., **1,** *to carry away, carry too far, lead on;* pass., provehi = *to be carried away, to allow oneself to be carried away;* vestra benignitas provexit orationem meam, Cic.; gaudio provehente (me), Liv.; studio rerum rusticarum provectus sum, Cic.; **2,** *to bring forwards, to advance, raise, promote;* aliquem ad summos honores, Liv. **II.** Pass., provehi, in a middle sense, *to go forward, ride forward, ride, drive, sail to a place.* **A.** Lit., of persons, esp. of persons in a ship or of the ship itself, Nasidius cum classe freto Siciliae provehitur, Caes. **B.** Fig., *to go too far;* sentio me esse longius provectum quam, etc., Cic.; longius in amicitia provehi, Cic.; quid ultra provehor? *why do I continue?* Verg.

prōvĕnio -vēni -ventum, 4. *to come forth.* **I.** Lit., in scenam, *to appear upon the stage,* Plaut. **II.** Transf., **A.** *to come up, shoot forth, grow;* frumentum propter siccitates angustius provenerat, Caes. **B.** Fig., *to result, turn out;* ut initia belli provenissent, Tac.; and esp., *to turn out well, succeed, prosper;* carmina proveniunt animo deducta sereno, Ov.

prōventus -ūs, m. (provenio). **I.** *a coming forth, growing.* **A.** Lit., Plin. **B.** Meton., *growth, product, crop;* proventu oneret sulcos, Verg. **II.** Fig., *the result, issue;* pugnae, Caes.; secundi rerum proventus, Caes.; esp., *fortunate result, success,* Liv.; temporis superioris, Caes.

prōverbĭum -ii, n. (pro and verbum), *a proverb;* in proverbii consuetudinem venit, *has become a proverb,* Cic.; vetere proverbio, *after the old proverb,* Cic.; ut est in proverbio, *as is said in the proverb,* Cic.; quod est Graecis hominibus in proverbio, *is a proverb among,* Cic.

prōvĭdens -entis, p. adj. (from provideo), *provident, prudent,* Cic.; quod est providentius, Cic.

prōvĭdentĕr, adv. (providens), *providently, with forethought,* Sall.; providentissime constituere aliquid, Cic.

prōvĭdentĭa -ae, f. (provideo). **I.** *foresight, foreknowledge;* providentia est, per quam futurum aliquid videtur ante quam factum sit, Cic. **II.** *forethought, providence;* deorum, Cic.

prōvĭdĕo -vīdi -vīsum, 2. *to look forward to, see at a distance.* **I.** Lit., aliquem non providisse, Hor.; quid petatur provideri, Liv. **II.** Transf., **1,** *to see beforehand, to foresee;* quod ego, priusquam loqui coepisti, sensi atque providi, Cic.; medicus morbum providet, Cic.; **2,** *to take precautions for or against something, to provide for, make preparation for, care for;* (α) with acc., rem frumentariam, Caes.; multa, Cic.; consilia in posterum, Cic.; (β) with de and the abl., de re frumentaria, Caes.; de Brundisio atque illa ora, Cic.; (γ) with dat., saluti hominum, Cic.; (δ) with ut or ne and the subj., ne quid ei desit, Cic.; ut res quam rectissime agantur, Cic.; (ε) absol., actum de te est, nisi provides, Cic.

1 **prōvĭdus** -a -um (provideo) **I.** *foreseeing*; rerum futurarum, Cic **II.** *caring beforehand*, 1, *providing for, taking measures for*, natura provida utilitatum, Cic, **2,** *cautious, provident, prudent*, orator, Cic

prōvincĭa -ae, f (perhaps pro and VIC, root of vices) **I.** *employment, charge, sphere of duty, office* illam officiosam provinciam ut me in lectulo trucidaret, Cic, quasi provincias atomis dare, Cic **II.** Polit t t, *the sphere of office assigned to a magistrate, a charge, office* **A. a,** of Roman magistrates, sortiri provincias (inter se), Liv, of the jurisdiction of the praetor urbanus and peregrinus, provincia urbana et peregrina, Liv, of a military command, Sicinio Volsci, Aquilio Hernici (nam hi quoque in armis erant) provincia evenit, Cic, of a command at sea, provincia classis, provincia maritima, Liv, **b,** of non-Roman magistrates, Hannonis cis Iberum provincia erat, *had the command*, Liv **B.** *the government of a province, a country outside the limits of Italy*, and meton, *the province itself*, primus annus provinciae erat, Cic, dare alicui provinciam, Cic, administrare provinciam, Cic, hence, provincia, *the province*, esp, either **a,** *the east part of Gallia Narbonensis*, Caes, or **b,** *the Roman province of Asia*, Caes

prōvinciālis -e, *of or relating to a province* **I.** Adj, scientia, *how to govern a province*, Cic, administratio, *government of a province*, Cic, abstinentia, *moderation in governing*, Cic **II.** Subst, **prōvinciāles** -ium, m *inhabitants of the provinces, provincials*, Cic

prōvīsĭo -ōnis, f (provideo), **1, a,** *a foreseeing, a foreknowledge*, animi, Cic, **b,** *foresight*, animi, Cic, **2,** *a providing, provision*, **a,** *for something*, temporis posteri, Cic, **b,** *against something*, vitiorum atque incommodorum, Cic

1 **prōvīso,** 3 *to look out for* go to see, Ter

2 **prōvīsō,** adv *with forethought, circumspectly*, Tac

prōvīsor -ōris, m (provideo), **1,** *one who foresees*, dominationum, Tac, **2,** *a provider*; utilium, Hor.

prōvīsus -ūs, m (provideo) **I.** *a looking before, a looking into the distance*, Tac **II.** Transf, **A.** *seeing beforehand, foreseeing*, periculi, Tac **B.** *a providing, provision*, provisus rei frumentariae, Tac

prōvīvo -vixisse, 3 *to live on, continue to live*, Tac

prōvŏcātĭo -ōnis, f (provoco), *a calling forth, an appeal to a higher court of law*, provocatio ad populum, Cic, magistratus sine provocatione, *from whose decision there is no appeal*, Liv, est provocatio, *an appeal is possible*, Liv

prōvŏcātor -ōris, m (provoco), *one who challenges or summons to fight*, esp, *a kind of gladiator*, Cic

prōvŏco, 1 *to call forth, call out* **I.** Gen, **a,** lit, herum, Plaut, **b,** transf, of things, *to cause to come forth*, roseo ore diem (of Aurora), Ov **II.** Esp, **A.** *to call forth, to excite, rouse*, and in a bad sense = *to provoke*, **1,** munificentiā nostrā provocemus plebem, Liv, beneficio provocati, Cic, **2,** *to challenge to a game, combat, drinking*, etc, ad pugnam, Cic, esp in pass, provocatus maledictis, injuriis, Cic **B.** Legal t. t., *to summon before a higher court, to appeal to a higher tribunal*, **a,** lit, ad populum, Cic, ab omni judicio poenāque provocari licere, Cic; **b,** transf, *to appeal to*, provocare ad Catonem, Cic

prōvŏlo, 1. *to fly forth*, transf., of men, *to rush forth, hasten forth*; subito, Caes; ad primores, Liv.

prōvolvo -volvi -vŏlūtum, 3. *to roll forward, roll along, roll over and over* **I.** Lit, **a,** gen, congestas lapidum moles, Tac, **b,** *to throw oneself down, fall down before*, se alicui ad pedes, Liv, provolvi ad genua alicuius, Liv **II** Fig **a,** multi fortunis provolvebantur, *were ruined*, Tac, **b,** middle = *to abase oneself*, Tac

prōvŏmo, 3 *to vomit forth*, Lucr

proxĭme, superl of prope (q v)

proxĭmĭtas -ātis, f (proximus) **I.** *nearness, vicinity, proximity*, Ov **II** Fig, **1,** *near relationship*, Ov, **2,** *similarity*, Ov

proxĭmo, adv (abl of proximus), *i.e.*, *lately*, Cic

proxĭmus -a -um, superl of propior (q v)

prūdens -entis (contr from providens), *foreseeing* **I** Partic = *knowing, with intention* quos prudens praetereo Hor, prudens et sciens sum profectus, Cic **II.** Adj, **A.** *versed, skilled, experienced, practised in anything*, rei militaris, Nep, locorum, Liv, with infin, prudens dissipare, Hor **B.** *prudent, discreet, wise, sagacious, judicious*, vir naturā peracutus et prudens, Cic, transf, of things, consilium, Cic, with genit., ceterarum rerum prudens, *in all other matters*, Cic, with de and the abl, in jure civili, Cic, in existimando admodum prudens, Cic

prūdentĕr, adv (prudens), *prudently, discreetly, sagaciously, wisely*, facere, Cic, intelligere, Cic

prūdentĭa -ae, f (prudens) **I.** *knowledge of any subject*, juris publici, Cic, physicorum, Cic **II.** *prudence, sagacity, practical wisdom, discretion*, prudentia est rerum expetendarum fugiendarumque scientia, Cic, prudentia cernitur in delectu bonorum et malorum, Cic

prŭīna -ae, f **I.** *hoar frost, rime*, Cic **II** Plur, pruinae, meton, **a,** = *winter*, Verg, **b,** = *snow*, Verg

prŭīnōsus -a -um (pruina), *full of hoar frost, covered with hoar-frost*, nox, Ov, axis (Aurorae) pruinosus = matutinus, Ov

prūna -ae, f *a live coal*, Hor

prūnĭcĕus -a um, *of plum-tree wood*, Ov

prūnum -i, n *a plum*, Hor

prūnus -i, f (προύνη), *a plum tree*, Plin

prūrīgo -ĭnis, f (prurio), *the itch*, Mart

prūrĭo, 4 *to itch*, Juv

Prūsĭās -ae, m *king in Bithynia, who received Hannibal, but afterwards betrayed him to the Romans*

prȳtănēum -i, n (πρυτανεῖον), *the town hall in certain Greek cities where the prytanes assembled and where persons who had done distinguished services to the state were entertained*, Cic

prȳtănis, acc -in, m (πρύτανις), *a chief magistrate in certain of the Greek states*, Liv

psallo, psalli, 3 (ψάλλω), *to play on, sing to a stringed instrument, especially the cithara*, psallere docta, *skilled in singing*, Hor

psaltērĭum -ii, n (ψαλτήριον), *a stringed instrument, the psaltery*, Cic

psaltrĭa -ae, f (ψάλτρια), *a female player on, or singer to the cithara*, Cic

Psămăthē -ēs, f **I** *daughter of the Argive king Crotopus*, Ov **II.** *a sea-nymph, mother of Phocus*, Ov.

1 **psĕcăs** -ădis, f (ψεκάς), *the female slave who anointed her mistress's hair*, Juv.

2 **Psĕcăs** -ădis, f *name of a nymph among the attendants of Diana.*

psēphisma ătis, n (ψήφισμα), *a decree of the people among the Greeks*, Cic

Pseudŏcăto -ōnis, m. *a sham Cato*, Cic.

Pseudŏdămăsippus -i, m. *a sham Damasippus*, Cic.

Pseudŏlus -i, m. *The Liar* (title of a comedy by Plautus), Cic.

pseudŏmĕnos -i, m. (ψευδόμενος), *a sophistical syllogism*, Cic.

Pseudŏphĭlippus -i, m. (Ψευδοφίλιππος), *a sham Philip*, i.e., Andriscus, *who gave himself out to be Philip, son of Perseus, king of Macedonia.*

pseudŏthўrum -i, n. (ψευδόθυρον), *a secret door;* fig., per pseudothyrum revertantur (nummi), *in a secret way*, Cic.

psĭthĭus (psўthĭus) -a -um, *psithian, name of a kind of Greek vine;* vitis, Verg.; subst., **psĭthĭa** -ae, f. (sc. vitis), Verg.

psittăcus -i, m. (ψίττακος), *a parrot;* loquax, Ov.

Psōphĭs -ĭdis, f. (Ψωφίς), *a town in Arcadia.*

psōra -ae, f. (ψῶρα), *the mange, itch*, Plin.

psўchŏmantīum -ii, n. (ψυχομαντεῖον), *the place where the souls of the dead were invoked, a place where necromancy is practised*, Cic.

psўthĭus = psithius (q.v.).

-**ptĕ**, enclit. particle appended to pers. and poss. pronouns in the abl., *self, our;* suopte pondere, Cic.; suāpte manu, Cic.

Ptĕlĕon (-um) -i, n. (Πτελεόν), *a town in Thessaly, over against Euboea*, now *Ftelia*, Liv.

ptĭsănārĭum -ii, n. *a decoction of crushed barley* or *rice*, Hor.

Ptŏlĕmaeus (Ptŏlŏmaeus) -i, m. (Πτολεμαῖος), *the first king of Egypt after Alexander's death with the surname* Lagi (sc. filius, i.e., *son of Lagus*); *after him each king of his line was called* Ptolemaeus. Hence, **1, Ptŏlĕmaeus** -a -um, *belonging to Ptolemy*, poet. = *Egyptian;* **2, Ptŏlĕmāis** -ĭdis, f. *name of several towns, one in Egypt, another in Phoenicia, another in Cyrene.*

pūbens -entis (* pubeo), *arrived at puberty;* transf., of plants, *in full growth, luxuriant*, Verg.

pūber -bĕris = 2. pubes (q.v.).

pūbertas -ātis, f. (puber), *puberty, the age of maturity.* **I.** Lit., nondum pubertatem ingressas, Tac. **II.** Meton., **A.** *the signs of puberty, the hair on the chin*, Cic. **B.** *virility*, Tac.

1. **pūbes** -is, f. **I.** *the signs of puberty, the hair on the chin*, Plin. **II.** Meton., **A.** *the pudenda*, Verg. **B. a,** *the youth, adult population;* omnis Italiae pubes, Verg.; **b,** transf., *people, folk;* agrestis, Verg.

2. **pūbes** -ĕris, *arrived at the age of puberty, adult.* **I.** Lit., prope puberem aetatem, Liv.; subst., **pūbĕres** -um, m. *the men, the adult population*, Caes. **II.** Transf., *downy, ripe;* folia, Verg.

pūbesco -bŭi, 3. (inchoat. of pubeo). **I.** *to become pubescent, arrive at the age of puberty.* **A.** Lit., Hercules, quum primum pubesceret, Cic. **B.** Transf., *to grow up, arrive at maturity;* quae terra gignit, maturata pubescunt, Cic. **II.** Esp., *to be covered with the signs of puberty;* transf., *to be covered or clothed with something;* prata pubescunt variorum flore colorum, Ov.

publĭcānus -a -um (publicum), *relating to the farming of the public taxes*, Cic.; gen. subst., **publĭcānus** -i, m. *a farmer of the Roman taxes* (generally of the equestrian order), Cic.

publĭcātĭo -ōnis, f. (publico), *a confiscation;* bonorum, Cic.

publĭcē, adv. (publicus). **I.** *publicly* (opp. privatim); **a,** *in the name or at the command of the state;* dicere, Cic.; venire, Cic.; **b,** *in the interest of the state, to the good of the state, for the state;* publice esse laudem, *it is an honour to the state*, Caes.; publice scribere or litteras mittere, Cic.; **c,** *at the cost of the state;* vesci, Liv. **II.** *generally, all together, without distinction;* publice ire exsulatum, Liv.

publĭcĭtŭs, adv. (publicus). **I.** *at the public expense, in the public service*, Plaut. **II.** Transf., *publicly, before all the world*, Plaut.

Publĭcĭus -a -um, *name of a Roman gens, the most famous members of which were the two brothers* L. and M. Publicii Malleoli, *both Aediles, who laid out and paved the Clivus Publicus, the chief entrance to the Aventine.* Hence, adj., **Publĭcĭānus** -a -um, *Publician.*

publĭco, 1. (publicus). **I.** *to appropriate to the public use, confiscate;* regnum, Caes.; privata, Cic. **II.** *to give over to the public use.* **A.** Gen., Aventinum, Liv. **B.** Esp., *to make public, publish*, Tac.

Publĭcŏla -ae, m. (also written Poplicola and Poplicula, from poplus (= populus) and colo), *the honourer of the people, the people's friend, a surname of* P. Valerius Publicola, *the first consul of the Roman republic.*

publĭcus -a -um (so poblicus and poplicus from poplus for populus), *belonging to the people, public.* **I.** *of* or *belonging to the commonwealth, in the name of* or *on account of the people, at the public expense.* **A.** Adj., loca, Cic.; sumptu publico, *at the cost of the state*, Cic.; bonum publicum, *the commonweal*, Liv. **B.** Subst., **publĭcum** -i, n., **a,** *the property of the state, public territory;* Campanum, Cic.; **b,** *the public revenue, the treasury;* convivari de publico, *at the cost of the state*, Cic.; in publicum emere, Liv.; dum in eo publico essent, *farming of the taxes*, Liv.; plur., societates publicorum, *companies of the farmers of the taxes*, Cic.; **c,** *the public stores;* in publicum conferre frumenti quod inventum est, Cic.; **d,** *publicity, an open place, the open street;* prodire in publicum, Cic.; blandiores in publico quam in privato, Liv.; publico carere, *to remain at home*, Cic.; legem proponere in publicum or in publico, *openly*, Liv., Cic. **II.** *universal, common, general, ordinary;* **a,** lit., verba, Cic.; lux publica mundi, *the sun*, Ov.; publica cura juvenum prodis, *general object of the care of*, etc., Hor.; **b,** poet., *common, bad, ordinary;* structura carminis, Ov.

Publĭlĭus -a -um, *name of a Roman gens, the most famous of which were:* Publilia, *the second wife of Cicero;* Publilius, *her father;* and Publius Publilius Lochius Syrus, *a celebrated mime and writer of mimes towards the end of the republic;* adj., *relating to the Publilian gens*, Liv.

Publĭus -ii, m. *a common Roman praenomen*, abbreviated P.

pŭdendus -a -um (partic. of pudeo), *of which one ought to be ashamed, shameful, disgraceful;* vita, Ov.; vulnera, Verg.

pŭdens -entis, p. adj. (from pudeo), *modest, shamefaced;* pudentes ac boni viri, Cic.; te videri pudentiorem fuisse, Cic.; femina pudentissima, Cic.

pŭdentĕr, adv. (pudens), *modestly, bashfully*, Cic.; pudentius ad hoc genus sermonis accedere, Cic.; pudentissime hoc Cicero petierat, Cic.

pŭdĕo -ŭi -ĭtum, 2. **I.** *to be ashamed;* induci ad pudendum, Cic.; partic. subst., pudentes, *modest persons*, Caes. **II.** *to cause shame, fill with shame.* **A.** Pers., me autem quid pudeat, qui, etc., Cic. **B.** Impers., *I (you, he, etc.) am ashamed*, with acc. of the pers.; ceteros pudeat, Cic ; and with genit. of the thing causing the shame, te huius templi pudet, Cic , with genit alone, pudet deorum hominumque, *it is a disgrace before God and men*, Liv , with infin , pudet dicere, Cic , dep , puditum est, nonne esset puditum si, etc ? *ought they not to be ashamed that*, etc ? Cic

pŭdĭbundus -a -um (pudeo), *shamefaced, modest, bashful*, matrona, Hor

pŭdīcē, adv. (pudicus), *modestly, virtuously, chastely*, Cat.

pŭdīcĭtĭa -ae, f (pudicus), *bashfulness, modesty, chastity, virtue*, Cic , Pudicitia, personif as a goddess (patrician and plebeian), Liv

pŭdīcus a -um (pudeo), *modest, bashful, chaste, virtuous*, **a,** of persons, Cic , **b,** transf , of things, mores, preces, Ov

pŭdor -ōris, m (pudeo), *the feeling of shame, shyness, bashfulness, modesty, decency* **I.** Lit , **a,** natura pudorque meus, *my natural modesty*, Cic , paupertatis, *on account of poverty*, Cic , famae, Cic , pudor est or pudori est with infin , *I am ashamed*, Ov , **b,** *chastity, purity*, pudorem projicere, Ov , Pudor, personif as a deity, Verg **II.** Meton , **A.** *that which causes shame, a disgrace*, pudori esse, Liv **B.** *the blush of shame*, famosus, Ov

pŭella -ae, f (puellus), *a girl, maiden* **I.** Lit , **A.** Gen , *a maiden*, Cic **B.** Esp , **1,** *a sweetheart*, Ov ; **2,** *a daughter*, Danai puellae, Hor. **II** Transf , *a young woman, a young wife*, used of Penelope, Ov , of Lucretia, Ov , puella Phasias, *Medea*, Ov , Lesbis, *Sappho*, Ov , Lydia, *Omphale*, Ov , Cressa, *Phaedra*, Ov

pŭellāris -e (puella), *of or belonging to a maiden or young woman, girlish, maidenly*, Ov.

pŭellŭla -ae, f (dim of puella), *a little girl*, Cat

pŭellus i, m (dim of puer, for puerulus), *a little boy*, Lucr

pŭer -i, m (root PU, whence Laconian πὸρ = παῖς) **I.** *a child*, plur , pueri = *children*, Cic **II.** Esp , *a male child, boy, lad* **A.** Lit , **a,** properly *a boy under seventeen*, Cic , but used also of Octavianus in his nineteenth year, Cic , and of Pallas, who commanded a company of soldiers, Verg ; puer sive jam adolescens, Cic , a puero, a pueris, *from boyhood*, Cic , ex pueris excedere, *to pass out of boyhood*, Cic., **b,** *boy = son*, Ascanius puer, Verg , Latonae, *Apollo*, Hor , Ledae pueri, *Castor and Pollux*, Hor. **B.** Transf , **1,** (like παῖς), *a waiter, serving-lad, a servant, slave*, tuus, Cic , pueri regii, *royal pages*, Liv , **2,** *an unmarried man, a bachelor*, Ov

pŭĕrīlis -e (puer), *youthful, boyish* **I.** Lit , aetas, Cic **II.** Transf , *puerile, childish, silly*, consilium, Cic si puerilius his ratio esse evincet amare, Hor

pŭĕrīlĭtĕr, adv (puerilis) **I.** *boyishly, like a boy*, blandiri, Liv. **II.** Transf , *childishly, foolishly*, facere, Cic

pŭĕrĭtĭa -ae, f (puer), *boyhood*, a pueritia, *from boyhood*, Cic

pŭerpĕrus -a um (puer and pario), *relating to child-birth*, verba, *words supposed to assist labour*, Ov

pŭerpĕrĭum -ii, n (puerperus), *a lying-in, labour, confinement*, Tac

pŭertĭa = pueritia (q v)

pŭĕrŭlus i, m (dim of puer), *a little boy, a young slave*, Cic

pūga (pȳga) ae, f (πυγή), *the rump, buttocks*, Hor

pŭgil ilis, m (connected with pugnus), *a boxer, fighter with the cestus pugilist* Cic

pŭgĭlātĭo ōnis, f (pugil), *a fight with the cestus*, Cic

pŭgĭlātus -ūs, m (pugil), *a fighting with the cestus*, Plaut

pŭgillāris e (pugillus), *that can be grasped with the fist*, Juv , subst , **pŭgillāres** ium, m (sc libelli or codicilli), *writing tablets, waxen tablets* Cat

pŭgillus -i, m (dim of pugnus), *a handful*, Plin

pŭgio ōnis, m (pungo), *a dagger, dirk, poniard* **I.** Lit , cruentum pugionem tenens, Cic **II.** Fig , plumbeus pugio, *a weak argument*, Cic

pŭgĭuncŭlus -i, m (dim of pugio), *a little dagger*, Cic

pugna -ae, f (connected with pugnus), *a fight, either of one man against another, or of several* (proelium, *a fight between armies*, cp diuturnitate pugnae defessi praelio excedebant, Caes) **I. A.** Lit , **a,** gen , equestris *cavalry engagement*, Cic , navalis, Cic , pugnam committere, Cic , cum aliquo, Cic , pugnā decertare, Caes , **b,** esp., *athletic games*, pugna quinquennis Graia Elide, Ov **B.** Meton , **a,** *the line or array of battle*, pugnam mediam tueri, Liv **II.** Transf , *contest, contention*, doctissimorum hominum, Cic

pugnācĭtas -ātis, f (pugnax), *desire of fighting, pugnacity*, Tac

pugnācĭtĕr (pugnax), *pugnaciously, obstinately*, certare cum aliquo, Cic , pugnacissime defendere sententiam, Cic

pugnātor -ōris, m (pugno), *a fighter, combatant, soldier*, Liv

pugnax ācis (pugno), *fond of fighting, combative, contentious, martial* **I.** Lit , pugnax Minerva, Ov , centurio, Cic **II.** Transf , **A.** *combative, contentious, polemical* exordium dicendi, Cic , oratio pugnacior, Cic **B.** Of discourse, *obstinate, refractory*, contra senatorem, Cic

pugno, 1 (pugna), *to fight, combat, give battle* **I.** Lit , both of single combatants and of whole armies, cum aliquo, Caes , ex equo, Cic , pro commodis patriae, Cic , pugna summā contentione pugnata, Cic , impers , pugnatur uno tempore omnibus locis, Caes , partic subst , pugnantes, *the combatants*, Caes **II.** Transf , **A.** *to struggle, to contend, fight*, pugnant Stoici cum Peripateticis, Cic sed ego tecum in eo non pugnabo, quominus utrum velis eligas, Cic , with acc and infin , *to maintain in dispute*, Cic , transf , of things, pugnat diu sententia secum, Ov **B.** Esp , **a,** *to contradict*, ut tota in oratione tua tecum ipse pugnares, Cic , **b,** *to strive, struggle, exert oneself*, followed by ut or ne or quominus with the subj , illud pugna et enitere ut, etc , Cic

pugnus -i, m (root PUG, Gr ΠΥΚ, whence πύξ), *the fist* pugnum facere, Cic , aliquem pugnis concidere, Cic

pulchellus -a -um (dim of pulcher), *very pretty*, Bacchae, Cic , used ironically of Clodius, with a pun on his surname Pulcher, Cic

1 **pulcher** -chra -chrum and **pulcer** cra crum (connected with polire, purus, etc), *beautiful, fair, lovely* **I.** Lit , puer, Cic , quid aspectu pulchrius ? Cic , urbs pulcherrima, Caes **II** Transf , **a,** *excellent, admirable, fine, glorious* exemplum, Caes , facinus, Sall , factum pulcherrimum, Sall , pulchrum est, *it is noble, glorious, fine*, with acc and infin , illis pulcherrimum fuit tantam vobis imperii gloriam tradere, Cic , **b,** *lucky, happy*, dies, Hor. ne pulchrum se ac beatum putaret Cic,

2. **Pulcher** -chri, m. **I.** *a Roman surname*, e.g., P. Claudius Pulcher. **II.** Pulchri Promontorium, *a promontory in Africa*, now *Cap Bono*.

pulchrē (pulcrē), adv. (pulcher), *beautifully, admirably, excellently, nobly;* dicere, Cic.; hostia litatur pulcherrime, *very favourably*, Cic.; pulchre est mihi, *all's well with me*, Cic.; used as an exclamation of approval, *bravo! well done!* Hor.

pulchrĭtūdo (pulcrĭtūdo) -inis, f. (pulcher), *beauty, excellence.* **I.** Lit., corporis. **II.** Fig., *excellence;* virtutis, Cic.; verborum, Cic.

pūlējum (pūlēgĭum) -ii, n. *fleabane, pennyroyal*, Cic.; fig., ad cuius rutam pulejo mihi tui sermonis utendum est, *sweetness*, Cic.

pūlex -icis, m. *a flea*, Plaut.

pullārĭus -ii, m. (pullus), *the feeder of the sacred chickens*, Cic.

pullātus -a -um (2. pullus), *clad in dirty* or *black garments* (of mourners); proceres, Juv.

pullŭlo, 1. *to shoot up, sprout out.* **A.** **a,** of plants, etc., Verg.; **b,** poet., transf., tot pullulat atra columbis, *burgeons with*, Verg. **B.** Fig., quae (luxuria) incipiebat pullulare, *luxuriate*, Nep.

1. **pullus** -i, m. (root PU, whence puer, Gr. πῶλος, etc.), *a young animal.* **I.** Lit., **a,** gen., columbinus, Cic.; pulli ex ovis orti, Cic.; **b,** esp., *a young cock* (whence Fr. poulet), Hor.; of the sacred chickens, Cic., Liv. **II.** Transf., of men; **a,** as a term of endearment, *chicken*, Hor.; **b,** pullus milvinus, *a young kite*, Cic.

2. **pullus** -a -um (connected with πελλός), *dark-coloured, blackish, greyish black;* capilli, Ov.; myrtus, *dark-green*, Hor.; esp., pulla vestis, *a garment of undyed wool, worn as mourning*, Cic.; poet., pulla stamina (of the threads of the Parcae), *sad, gloomy*, Ov.; subst., **pullum** -i, n. *a dark-coloured garment*, Ov.

pulmentārĭum -ii, n. (pulmentum), *a relish, anything eaten with bread;* pulmentaria quaere sudando, *get an appetite by hard work*, Hor.

pulmentum -i, n. (= pulpamentum, from pulpa), *a relish*, Hor.; in general, *food, victuals;* mullum in singula pulmenta minuere, *into small portions*, Hor.

pulmo -ōnis, m. (from πλεύμων = πνεύμων), *the lung;* usually pl., pulmones, *the lungs*, Cic.

pulmōnĕus -a -um, *of* or *relating to the lungs, pulmonary*, Plaut.

pulpa -ae, f. *flesh;* **a,** lit., Mart.; **b,** meton., pulpa scelerata, *the flesh as sign of sensuality*, Pers.

pulpāmentum -i, n. (pulpa). **I.** *flesh*, esp. of fish, Plin. **II.** *a relish;* mihi est pulpamentum fama, Cic.

pulpĭtum -i, n. *a platform, tribune for public readings, debates, etc.*, Hor.; for actors, "*the boards*" *of a theatre*, Ov.

puls, pultis, f. (πόλτος), *a porridge* or *pottage of flour, pulse, used as food for the sacred chickens*, Cic.

pulsātĭo -ōnis, f. (pulso), *a knocking, striking, beating*, Cic.; scutorum, Liv.

pulso, 1. (intens. of pello), *to strike, beat, knock.* **I.** Gen., **1,** lit., **a,** of stamping the ground, dancing, etc., pede libero tellurem, Hor.; of horses, pedibus spatium Olympi, poet. = *to hasten over*, Ov.; **b,** of knocking at the door, fores, Ov.; **c,** *to beat, ill-treat;* pulsare et verberare aliquem, Cic.; transf., of the wind, storms, etc., piniferum caput et vento pulsatur et imbri, Verg.; **d,** *to knock against, reach to;* ipse arduus alta pulsat sidera, Verg.; **e,** *to strike, touch*, of a musical instrument; septem discrimina vocum, Verg.; **2,** fig., **a,** *to move, affect;* dormientium animos externā et adventiciā visione pulsari, Cic.; **b,** *to alarm, agitate;* pavor pulsans, Verg. **II.** *to drive away;* sagittam, Verg.; divi pulsati, Verg.

pulsus -ūs, m. (pello), *a pushing, beating, striking, blow, push, stroke.* **I.** Gen., remorum, Cic.; pedum, *a footstep*, Verg.; lyrae, *a playing on the lyre*, Ov.; pulsum venarum attingere, *to feel the pulse*, Tac. **II.** *influence, impulse;* externus pulsus animos commovet, Cic.

pulto, 1. (= pulso), *to knock, beat, strike;* januam, Plaut.

pulvĕrĕus -a -um (pulvis). **I.** *full of dust, dusty;* nubes, *dust-clouds*, Verg.; solum, Ov. **II.** Act., *raising dust;* palla (Boreae), Ov.

pulvĕrŭlentus -a -um (pulvis), *full of dust, dusty.* **I.** Lit., via, Cic. **II.** Fig., *won by hard work;* praemia militiae, Ov.

pulvillus -i, m. (dim. of pulvinus), *a little pillow*, Hor.

pulvīnar -āris, n. (pulvinus). **I.** *a couch covered with cushions placed for the images of the gods at the Lectisternium* (q.v.), *a cushioned seat;* pulvinar suscipere, Liv.; dedicare, Cic.; meton., ad omnia pulvinaria supplicatio decreta est, *at all the temples*, Cic. **II.** Transf., *a state couch for any distinguished person*, Cic.

pulvīnārĭum -ii, n. (pulvinus), *a cushioned seat for the gods*, Liv.

pulvīnus -i, m. *a pillow, cushion*, Cic.

pulvis -ĕris, m. and rarely f. *dust.* **I.** Lit., **A.** multus erat in calceis pulvis, Cic.; pulvis eruditus, or simply pulvis, *the sand or dust in which the old mathematicians drew their diagrams*, Cic.; numquam eruditum illum pulverem attigistis, *you have never learnt mathematics*, Cic.; pulvis exiguus, *a handful of dust thrown on the dead*, Hor.; poet., pulvis hibernus, *dry winter*, Verg.; plur., novendiales pulveres, *dust nine days old* (= *fresh ashes of the dead*), Hor.; prov., sulcos in pulvere ducere, *to labour in vain*, Juv. **B.** Esp., *the dust of the circus* or *wrestling-place;* pulvis Olympicus, Hor.; hence, meton., *place of exercise, arena;* domitant in pulvere currus, Verg.; and fig., *scene of action;* doctrinam in solem atque pulverem produxit, *into public*, Cic.; sine pulvere palmae, *without effort*, Hor. **II.** Transf., *the earth*, Prop.

pūmex -icis, m. (f. Cat.), *pumice-stone.* **I.** Lit., esp. as used for polishing marble, books, etc., Cat., Ov. **II.** Transf., *any kind of soft, porous stone;* pumices cavi, Verg.

pūmicĕus -a -um (pumex), *made of pumice-stone*, Ov.

pūmico, 1. (pumex), *to polish with pumice-stone*, Cat.

pūmĭlio -ōnis, c. *a dwarf*, Lucr.

punctim, adv. (pungo), *by stabbing, by thrusting* (opp. caesim); petere hostem, Liv.

punctum -i, n. (pungo). **I.** *a little hole, small puncture*, Mart. **II.** **1,** lit., **a,** *a point*, and meton., *a division of a discourse, a short clause, section;* puncta argumentorum, Cic.; **b,** in the comitia, *the point made on a tablet as often as one of the candidates was voted for*, hence *a vote;* quot in ea tribu puncta tuleris, Cic.; hence, transf., *approval, applause;* discedo Alcaeus puncto illius, Hor.; omne tulit punctum qui miscuit utile dulci, Hor.; **2,** transf., *a mathematical point, the smallest quantity;* hence, **a,** *a very small space;* quasi punctum terrae, Cic.; **b,** *a small portion of time, a moment;* ad punctum temporis, *in a moment*, Cic.

pungo, pŭpŭgi, punctum, 3 *to prick, puncture, stab* **I.** **1,** lit, **a,** neminem, Cic, **b,** *to make by piercing*, vulnus quod acu punctum videretur, Cic, **2,** transf, **a,** *to penetrate, enter*, corpus, Lucr, **b,** *to touch, move*, sensum Lucr, **c,** *to point off*, hence, puncto tempore, *in a moment*, Lucr **II.** Fig, *to sting, vex, annoy, mortify*, epistola illa ita me pupugit, ut somnum mihi ademerit, Cic., si paupertas momordit, si ignominia pupugit, Cic

Pūnĭcĕus, v Poeni.

Pūnĭcus, Punice, v Poeni

pūnĭo (poenio) ivi and -ii itum -ire, and dep **pūnĭor (poenĭor)** -itus sum -iri (poena) **I.** *to punish*, sontes, Cic, maleficia, Cic, aliquem supplicio, Cic, dep, peccatum, Cic **II.** *to avenge*, dolorem, Cic, dep, necem, Cic

pūnītor -ōris, m (punio), *a punisher, avenger*, doloris, Cic

pūpa -ae, f (pupus) **I.** *a little girl*, Mart **II.** *a doll*, Pers

pūpilla -ae, f (dim of pupa) **I.** *an orphan girl, ward, minor*, Cic **II.** Transf (like Gr κόρη), *the pupil of the eye*, Cic

pūpillāris -e (pupillus), *of or relating to a ward*, pecuniae, Liv

pūpillus i, m (dim of pupulus), *an orphan, ward*, Cic

Pupinĭa ae, f. *the Pupinian country in Latium, a sterile tract of country*, hence, Pupiniensis ager, Liv

Pūpĭus a -um, *name of a Roman gens*, adj, lex Pupia *proposed by* Pupius, *a tribune, that the senate should not hold a meeting on the day of the Comitia*

puppis is, f *the poop or stern of a vessel* **I.** Lit, navem convertere ad puppim, Cic, ventus surgens a puppi, *from behind*, Verg, fig, sedebamus in puppi, *I sat at the helm of the state*, Cic **II.** Meton, *the whole ship*, Verg, *the constellation of the Ship*, Cic (abl sing, puppi, acc, puppim)

pūpŭla ae, f (dim of pupa), *the pupil of the eye*, Cic, meton, *the eye*, Hor

pūpŭlus -i, m (dim of pupus), *a little boy*, Cat

pūpus -i, m *a boy, child*, used as a term of endearment, Suet

pūrē and poet **pūrĭtĕr,** adv (purus) **I.** **A.** Lit, **a,** *purely, cleanly*, pure lauta corpora, Liv, **b,** *brightly*, splendens Pario marmore purius, Hor **B.** Transf, *clearly, naturally*, pure apparere, Hor **II.** Fig, **1,** gen, **a,** *uprightly, purely*, pure et eleganter acta vita, Cic, pure et caste deos venerari, Cic, **b,** of style, *purely, faultlessly*, pure et emendate loqui, Cic, **2,** esp, *finely, perfectly, entirely*, quid pure tranquillet, Hor

purgāmen -inis, n (purgo) **I.** *filth, dirt, sweepings*, Vestae, *that which was annually swept from the temple of Vesta*, Ov **II.** *a means of purgation or expiation*, mali, Ov, caedis, Ov

purgāmentum -i, n (purgo), *that which is cleaned out, swept away, sweepings, rubbish, filth*, urbis, Liv

purgātio ōnis, f (purgo), *a cleaning out, cleansing* **I.** **1,** lit, alvi, *purging*, Cic, **2,** meton, plur, purgationes, *purgatives*, Cic **II.** Transf, *excusing, justification*, Cic

purgo, 1 (purigo, from purus), *to clean, cleanse* **I.** Lit, **1,** locum, *to clean out, make ready for ploughing*, Cic, arva longis ligonibus, Ov, **2,** *to purge the body*, purgor bilem, *I free myself from gall*, Hor, purgatum te illius morbi, *healed*, Hor **II.** Transf, **1,** *to purge, cleanse, purify*, educ tecum omnes tuos, purga urbem, Cic, **2,** *to cleanse morally*, **a,** *to excuse, defend, justify*, aliquem de luxuria, Cic, civitatem facti dictique, Liv, crimen, *to confute*, Cic; with acc and infin, *to allege in defence*, Liv, **b,** *to purge, purify religiously*, populos, Ov, **c,** *to make good*, malum facinus forti facinore, Liv

pūrĭtĕr = pure (q v)

purpŭra -ae, f (πορφύρα) **I.** *the purple-fish*, Plin **II.** Meton, **A.** *the purple dye, purple*, Verg **B** *any stuff or texture dyed purple, purple cloth*, Cic.

purpŭrasco, 3 *to become purple or dark*, Cic

purpŭrātus a um (purpura), *clad in purple*. **I** Adj, mulier, Plant **II.** Subst., *a high dignitary among eastern princes (clad in purple)*, plur, *courtiers*, purpuratis tuis ista minitare, Cic

purpŭrĕus -a um (πορφύρεος) **I.** *purple*, and so of shades resembling purple, *blackish, dark red, dark-brown, dark-violet*, vestitus, Cic, rubor, *blush*, Ov, capillus, crinis, Verg, mare, Cic **II.** Meton, **A.** *clad in purple*, rex, Ov, tyrannus, Hor, transf, *adorned with purple*, torus, Ov, purpureis pennis, *with purple plumes*, Verg **B.** *bright, beautiful*, olores, Hor, ver, Verg

pūrus -a um, *clean, pure* **I.** **A.** Lit, **a,** unda, Verg, fons, Plaut, aere purior ignis, Ov, terra, *cleared of stones, stubble*, etc, Cic, **b,** of the air, sun, etc, *bright, clear* Cic, neut. subst, per purum, *the clear sky*, Verg **B.** Transf, *without addition, simple plain*, **a,** hasta, *without a head*, Verg, **b,** *unadorned, plain*, parma, Verg, argentum, *without reliefs*, Cic, of dress, *without ornament*, esp, among the Romans, *without a purple stripe*, vestis, Verg, toga, Phaedr, **c,** *clear, unmixed, unadulterated*, nardum, Tib, **d,** *clear (gain, profit)*, quid possit ad dominos puri ac reliqui pervenire, Cic **II.** Fig, **A.** Gen, **1,** *spotless*, **a,** *holy, upright*, purus et integer, Cic, **b,** *free from crime*, esp, *murder*, pura manus, Verg, with genit, sceleris, Hor, **c,** *free from sensuality, chaste, pure*, animam puram conservare, Cic; **d,** of discourse, *pure, faultless* pura et incorrupta consuetudo, Cic, **2,** **a,** religious t t, (α) *unconsecrated*, Cic (β) *untrodden, undefiled*, locus Liv, (γ) *free from mourning* (by completion of funeral rites), familia, Cic, (δ) act, *purifying*, arbor, Ov, **b,** rhet t t, *unadorned, natural, simple* purum genus dicendi, Cic, **c,** legal t t, *without conditions, absolute, unconditional*, judicium, Cic

pūs, pūris n *corrupt matter*, fig, *gall, venom*, Hor

pŭsillus -a -um, dim *very small, tiny, puny* **I.** Lit, testis, Cic, Roma, Cic, epistola, Cic Subst, **pŭsillum** -i, n *a trifle, a little*, ap. Cic **II.** Transf, **a,** of ability, *very insignificant*, ingenium, Mart, **b,** of courage, animus, *timid*, Hor, **c,** *petty, mean* animus, Cic; **d,** *little, insignificant*, causa, Ov

pūsio -ōnis, m *a little boy*, Cic

pŭtă (imper 2 puto), *for example, suppose, for instance*, Hor

pŭtāmen -inis, n (1 puto), *a cutting, paring, shred, shell*, Cic

pŭtĕal -ālis, n (puteus) **I.** *a stone curb round the mouth of a well* **II.** Transf, *a similar enclosure around a sacred place—e g*, the Puteal Libonis or Scribonianum at Rome, where the usurers carried on business in the Comitium, Cic,

pŭtĕālis -e (puteus), *of or relating to a well*, undae, Ov.; lymphae, Lucr.

pŭtĕārĭus -ii, m. (puteus), *a well-sinker*, Liv.

pūtĕo, 2 (root PUT, Gr. ΠΥΘ, whence πύθω, πύθομαι), *to stink*, Cic.

Pŭtĕŏli (**Pŏtĕŏli**) -ōrum, m. *a town in Campania on the coast, with many mineral springs, favourite resort of the Romans*, now *Pozzuolo*. Hence, **Pŭtĕŏlānus** a -um, *belonging to Puteoli*. Subst., a, **Pŭtĕŏlānum** -i, n. *an estate of Cicero, near Puteoli*; b, **Pŭtĕŏlāni** -ōrum, m. *the people of Puteoli*.

pŭter -tris -tre and **putris** -e. **I.** *rotten, putrid, stinking*; poma, Ov.; fervent examina putri de bove, Ov. **II.** Transf., *loose, flabby, crumbling, friable*; gleba, Verg.; campus, Verg.; mammae, Hor.; oculi, *languishing*, Hor.

pūtesco (**pūtisco**) -tŭi, 3 (puteo), *to decay, become rotten, grow putrid*, Cic.

pŭtĕus -i, m. (root PUT, connected with ΒΟΘ, whence βόθρος), *a pit*; a, in agriculture, *a pit, trench*, Verg.; b, *a well, spring*, Cic.

pūtĭdē, adv. (putidus), of discourse, *affectedly, disgustingly*; dicere, Cic.; putidius litteras exprimere, Cic.

pūtĭdĭuscŭlus -a -um (dim. of putidus), *somewhat affected, nauseous*, Cic.

pūtĭdus -a -um (puteo), *rotten, stinking, putrid*. **A.** Lit., caro, Cic. **B.** Transf., 1, cerebrum putidius, *addled*, Hor.; 2, *nauseous, troublesome, pedantic, affected*; haec satis spero vobis molesta et putida videri, Cic.; putidum est, with infin., *it is pedantic*, etc., Cic.; of orators, *affected, ornate*; Demosthenes, Cic.

1 **pŭto**, 1 (root PU, whence purus, putus), *to cleanse*; hence, *to lop, to prune trees*; vites, Verg.

2 **pŭto**, 1 (root PUT, Gr. ΠΥΘ, πυθέσθαι, aor. of πυνθάνομαι), *to reckon*. **I.** Gen., a, *to reckon, calculate, compute, to estimate, value at*, with genit. of value, magni putare honores, Cic.; with pro and the abl., aliquem pro nihilo, Cic.; with in and the abl., in hominum numero putabat, Cic.; with acc. of predicate, se solum beatum, Cic.; b, *to consider, hold, believe, suppose*; with acc., putare deos, *to believe in the gods*, Cic.; with acc. and infin., noli putare me maluisse, Cic.; absol., non putaram, Cic.; parenthet., puto or ut puto, *I suppose*, Cic. **II.** a, *to count over*; rationes cum publicanis, *settle accounts with*, Cic.; b, *to weigh, reflect*; debes putare comitiis studium esse populi, non judicium, Cic.

pūtor -ōris, m. (puteo), *bad smell, stink*, Lucr.

pŭtrĕfăcĭo -fēci -factum, 3, pass., **pŭtrĕfīo** -factus sum -fĭĕri (putreo and facio). **I.** *to make rotten*, and pass., *to become rotten, decay*; nudatum tectum patere imbribus putrefaciendum, Liv. **II.** *to make pliable, to soften*; ardentia saxa infuso aceto, Liv.

pŭtresco -trŭi, 3 (putreo), *to become rotten or decayed*, Hor.

pŭtrĭdus -a -um (putreo), 1, *rotten, decayed, putrid*; dentes, Cic.; 2, *loose, flabby*, Cat.

pŭtror -ōris, m. *rottenness, putridity*, Lucr.

pŭtus -a -um (root PU, whence puto, purus), *pure, unmixed, unadulterated*; usually found in connexion with purus, Plaut.; without purus, meae putissimae orationes, *brilliant*, Cic.

pycta (**-es**) -ae, m. (πύκτης), *a boxer, pugilist*, Phaedr.

Pydna -ae, f. (Πύδνα), *a town in Macedonia, where Aemilius Paulus defeated Perseus, king of Macedonia*, 168 B.C., perhaps modern *Ayan*. Hence, **Pydnaei** -ōrum, m. *the inhabitants of Pydna*.

pȳga = puga (q.v.).

pȳgargus -i, m. (πύγαργος), 1, *the fish eagle*, Plin.; 2, *a species of antelope*, Juv.

Pygmaei -ōrum, m. (Πυγμαῖοι), *the Pygmies, a race of dwarfs supposed to inhabit Africa, and to engage in war with cranes*. Hence, adj., **Pygmaeus** -a -um, *Pygmaean*; quae Pygmaeo sanguine gaudet avis, *the crane*, Ov.

Pygmălīōn -ōnis, m. (Πυγμαλίων). **I.** *grandson of Agenor, who fell in love with a beautiful statue which he had made, and which Venus at his prayer endowed with life*. **II.** *king in Tyre, brother of Dido, whose husband he slew*.

Pȳlădēs -ae and -is, m. (Πυλάδης), *son of Strophius, and the faithful friend of Orestes*; hence, prov. for *a faithful friend*, Ov. Hence, adj., **Pȳlădēus** -a -um, *Pyladean*; amicitia, i.e., *faithful, tender*, Cic.

pȳlae -ārum, f. (πύλαι, *gates*), *passes between mountains, defiles*. **I.** Gen., Tauri, *separating Cappadocia from Cilicia*, Cic. **II.** Esp., Pylae = *Thermopylae*, Liv. Hence, **Pȳlăĭcus** -a -um, *relating to Thermopylae*; concilium, conventio, *congress held at Thermopylae*, Liv.

Pȳlaemĕnēs -is, m. *an old king of the Heneti in Paphlagonia, killed before Troy*.

Pȳlĭus, Pylus.

Pȳlus (**-ŏs**) -i, f. (Πύλος), *name of two cities in the Peloponnesus, one in Messenia, the residence of Neleus*, now *Alt-Navarino*, *the other in Triphylia, the residence of Nestor, hence called* Nestorea, Ov.; hence, adj., **Pȳlĭus** -a -um, a, *relating to Pylus*; subst., **Pȳlĭus** -ii, m. *the Pylian*, i.e., *Nestor*; b, poet. = *of Nestor*; dies, Ov.

pȳra -ae, f. (πυρά). **I.** *a funeral pyre*, Verg. **II.** As a proper name, **Pyra** -ae, f. *a place on Mount Oeta, where Hercules burnt himself*.

Pȳracmōn -ŏnis, m. (Πυράκμων), *one of the Cyclopes of Vulcan*.

Pȳracmŏs -i, m. *one of the Centaurs at the wedding of Pirithous*.

pȳrămĭdātus -a -um, *pyramidal*, Cic.

pȳrămĭs -ĭdis, f. (πυραμίς), *a pyramid*, Cic.

1 **Pȳrămus** -i, m. (Πύραμος), *the lover of Thisbe, who stabbed herself in the belief that he was dead*.

2 **Pȳrămus** -i, m. (Πύραμος), *a river in Cilicia*, now *Geihun*.

Pȳrēne -ēs, f. (Πυρήνη), *daughter of Bebryx, beloved by Hercules, buried in the mountain called after her*; hence, **Pȳrēnaeus** -a -um, *belonging to Pyrene*; Pyrenaei Montes, *the Pyrenees, the mountains between Gaul and Spain*; so simply, **Pȳrēnaeus** -i, m., Liv. (Pȳrēnē, in Tib.)

pȳrĕthrum -i, n. (πύρεθρον), *a plant, pellitory*, Ov.

Pyrgi -ōrum, m. (Πύργοι = turres), *a town in Etruria*, now *the village of St. Severo*. Hence, **Pyrgensis** -e, *belonging to Pyrgi*.

Pyrgo -ūs, f. *the nurse of Priam's children*.

Pȳrĭphlĕgĕthōn -ontis, m. (Πυριφλεγέθων), *the fire-stream, a river in the lower world*, gen. simply *Phlegethon*.

Pȳrŏis (**-eis**) -entos, m. (πυρόεις), *fiery, one of the horses of the Sun*, Ov.

pȳrōpus -i, m. (πυρωπός), *a kind of mixed metal, bronze*, Ov.

Pyrrha ae, f (Πύῤῥα) **I.** *daughter of Prometheus, wife of Deucalion* **II.** *a town in Lesbos, now Caloni* Adj, **Pyrrhĭăs** ădis, f *relating to the town of Pyrrha*

Pyrrho (Pyrro) -ōnis, m (Πύῤῥων), *a Greek philosopher of Elis, founder of the so called Sceptical School, contemporary of Alexander the Great* Hence, **Pyrrhōnēi** ōrum, m *the followers of Pyrrho*

Pyrrhus i, m (Πύῤῥος) **I.** *son of Achilles and Deidamia of Scyrus* (also called Neoptolemos), *founder of a monarchy in Epirus, killed at Delphi by Orestes* **II.** *king in Epirus, enemy of the Romans* Hence, **Pyrrhēum** -i, n *the royal castle of Pyrrhus*

Pȳthăgŏrās ae, m (Πυθαγόρας), *Greek philosopher of Samos* (about 550 B C), *who afterwards settled in Lower Italy* (in Crotona and Metapontum), *and founded the school named after him* Hence, **Pȳthăgŏrēus** -a um, *Pythagorean*, and subst, *a Pythagorean*

Pȳtho -ūs, f (Πυθώ), *the old name of the part of Phocis at the foot of Parnassus where Delphi lay.* Hence, **A Pȳthĭcus** -a -um, *Pythian, Delphic, relating to Apollo* **B. Pȳthĭus** -a -um, *relating to Apollo, Delphic*, subst, **a, Pȳthĭa** ae, f *the priestess who delivered the oracles at Delphi*, **b, Pȳthĭa** -ōrum, n (τὰ Πύθια), *the Pythian games, celebrated every five years in the Cumaean plains near Delphi in honour of Apollo, who slew the Python*

Pȳthōn -ōnis, m (Πύθων), *a great snake killed by Apollo, near Delphi*

pȳtisma -ătis, n (πύτισμα), *the wine which is spit out or spurted through the lips* (in tasting), Juv

pȳtisso, 1 (πυτίζω), *to spit out wine* (in tasting), Ter

pyxis -ĭdis, f (πυξίς), *a little box, casket, used for drugs, etc*, venenı, Cic

Q.

Q, q, the sixteenth letter of the Roman alphabet, only used before u followed by a vowel It not unfrequently represents the Greek π, e g, quinque πέντε, equus ἵππος, sequor ἕπω For abbreviations in which Q is used, see Table of Abbreviations

quā, adv (from qui, quae, quod) **I** *on which side, where*; ad omnes introitus qua adiri poterat, Cic, corresp, ea ... qua, Caes **II.** Transf, **A.** partitive, qua ... qua, *partly ... partly, both ... as well as*, qua dominus qua advocatus Cic **B.** *in so far as, in as much as*, effuge qua potes, Ov, Cic **C.** *in what manner, how*, illuc qua veniam? Cic

quăcumque, adv (sc parte, from quicumque) **I.** *wherever, wheresoever*, quacumque iter fecit, Cic **II.** *by all means, in every manner*, Verg

quādamtĕnus, adv *to a certain point, so far*, found in the tmesis, est quadam prodire tenus, Hor

Quādi ōrum, m *a people in the south east of Germany in modern Moravia*

quădra, v quadrus

quădrāgēni -ae -a, num distrib (quadraginta), *forty each*, Cic

quădrāgēsĭmus -a -um (quadraginta), *the fortieth*, subst, **quădrāgēsĭma** ae, f *the fortieth part*, esp, *as a tax*, Tac

quădrāgĭes, adv *forty times*, Cic

quădrāginta, *forty*, Cic

quădrans -antis, m (quadro), *a fourth part, quarter*. **I.** heres ex quadrante, *to the fourth part of the property*, Suet **II.** As a coin, *the fourth part of an as, three unciae*, Liv, *the ordinary price of a bath* dum tu quadrante lavatum rex ibis, Hor.

quădrantal -ālis, n *a liquid measure containing 8 congii* Plaut

quădrantārĭus -a um (quadrans), *pertaining to a quarter* **I.** Gen, tabulae quadrantariae, *reduction of debts by a quarter in consequence of the lex Valeria feneratoria*, Cic **II.** Esp, *costing a quarter of an as*, Cic

quădrātus -a -um (quadro), *quadrangular, square* **A.** Adj, saxum, Liv, agmen, *a square of soldiers*, Cic **B.** Subst, **quădrātum** -i, n, **a**, *a square*, Cic, **b**, t t of astronomy *quadrature*, Cic

quădrīdŭum (quătrīdŭum, quattrīdŭum) -i, n (quattuor and dies), *a space of four days*, quadriduo quo haec gesta sunt, Cic

quădrĭennĭum ĭi, n (quattuor and annus), *a period of four years*, Cic

quădrĭfārĭam, adv (quattuor), *fourfold, in four parts*, Liv

quădrĭfĭdus a -um (quattuor and findo), *split into four portions*, Verg

quădrīgae -ārum, f (= quadriiugae, from quattuor and iugum), *a team of four horses abreast*, used of the animals alone, of the animals and the chariot, and of the chariot alone **I.** Lit, alborum equorum, Liv, esp, of racing chariots, curru quadrigarum vehi, Cic **II.** Fig, equis aut quadrigis poeticis, Cic

quădrīgārĭus -ĭi, m (quadriga), *the driver of four horses, a racing charioteer*, Cic

quădrīgātus -a -um (quadriga), *stamped with the figure of a quadriga*, nummi, *silver denarii*, Cic

quădrīgŭlae ārum, f (dim of quadriga), *a little team of four horses*, Cic

quădrĭjŭgis -e (quattuor and iugum), *yoked four together*, equi, Verg

quădrĭjŭgus ă -um (quattuor and iugum), *yoked four together*, equi, Ov, currus, Verg, subst, **quădrĭjŭgi** -ōrum, m *a team of four horses*, Ov

quădrīmus -a -um (quattuor), *four years old*, Cic

quădringēnārĭus a um (quadringeni), *of four hundred each*, Cic

quădringēni ae -a (quadringenti), num distrib, *four hundred each*, Liv

quădringentēni -ae -a, *four hundred each*, Liv

quădringentēsĭmus a -um (quadringenti), *the four hundredth*, Liv

quădringenti ae -a (quattuor and centum), *four hundred*, Cic

quădringentĭēs, *four hundred times*, Cic

quădrĭpartītō, *in four parts*, Co

quădrĭpartītus (quădrĭpertītus) -a um (quattuor and partior), *divided into four parts, fourfold*, distributio, Cic

quădrĭrēmis -e (quattuor and remus), *with four banks of oars*, quadriremis navis, and subst, **quădrĭrēmis** -is, f *a ship with four banks of oars*, Cic

quădrĭvĭum -ii, n (quatuor and via), *a place where four roads meet*, Cat

quădro, 1. (quadrus) **I.** Transit, *to make square, to square*, transf, *to join properly together, complete rhythmically*, quadrandae orationis industria, Cic. **II.** Intransit, *to be square*, **a**, *to fit exactly, to suit*, omnia in istam quadrant, *correspond with*, Cic, **b**, esp, of accounts, *to agree*, quo modo sexcenta eodem modo quadrarint, Cic

quădrum, v quadrus

quădrŭpĕdans -antis (quatuor and pes), *going on four feet, galloping;* **a**, adj, Echetlus, *a Centaur*, Ov, transf, sonitus (of a galloping horse), Verg, **b**, subst, *a horse*, Verg

quădrŭpes -pĕdis (quatuor and pes), *fourfooted*, usually subst, **quădrŭpes** -pĕdis, c *a fourfooted animal, quadruped*, (α) masc, saucius quadrupes, Verg, (β) fem, quadrupes nulla, Verg

quădrŭplātor -ōris, m (quadruplor), *an informer who received a fourth part of the penalty*, Cic

quădrŭplex -plicis (quatuor and plico), *fourfold, quadruple*, Liv

quădrŭplor, 1 dep *to be an informer*, Plaut (cf quadruplator)

quădrŭplus -a -um (quatuor and plus = πλοῦς = τετραπλοῦς), *fourfold* Subst, **quădrŭplum** -i, n *four times the amount, four times as much*, judicium dare in quadruplum, Cic

quădrus a -um (quatuor), *square* Subst, **A. quădra** -ae, f *a square*, **1**, *a square dining-table*, hence, *a piece of bread used as a plate*, Verg, alienā vivere quadrā, *to live at another person's table*, Juv, **2**, *a square piece* or *morsel*, Hor **B. quădrum** -i, n. *a square;* transf, redigere omnes in quadrum numerumque sententias, *proper order*, Cic

quaerito, 1 (intens of quaero) **I.** *to seek eagerly*, Plaut. **II.** *to inquire eagerly*, Plaut.

quaero, quaesīvi, quaesītum, 3 **I.** *to seek, search for*, **1**, lit, (α) of persons, suos, Caes, liberos ad necem, Cic portum, Caes, (β) of things, te decisa suum dextera quaerit, Verg, **2**, transf, (α) *to seek to obtain, strive to get*, alicui or sibi honores, Cic, gloriam bello, Cic, (β) *to prepare, make ready for*, fugam ex Italia, Cic, (γ) *to seek with longing, to miss, want*, Caesarem, Hor, eas balneas, Cic, with ut and the subj, quaeris ut suscipiam cogitationem, Cic, (δ) *to look round about for, think of*, omisso veteri consilio novum, Sall, (ε) with infin, *to seek to, wish to*, abrumpere lucem, Verg, **3**, *to investigate, make an examination of*, reliquorum sententiam, Cic, with de and the abl, de vita et de moribus, Cic, **4**, *to wish to know, to ask, to inquire*, aliquem a janua, *to ask after some one at the door of his house*, Cic, aliquid ex or de aliquo, gen with rel sent, de te quaero utrum an, Cic ; quaesivit si (*whether*) incolumis evasisset, Liv, partic subst, **quaesītum** -i, n *the question*, Ov, **5**, *to ask judicially, hold a judicial investigation, inquire into*, de morte alicuius, Cic ; de servo in dominum, *to interrogate the slave under torture about his master*, Cic. **II. a**, *to seek = to obtain* (by work, etc), *to win, gain;* nummos aratro et manu, Cic, jam diu nihil quaesivisse, Cic, partic subst, **quaesītum** -i, n and plur, **quaesīta** -ōrum, n *that which is gained, acquisition*, Ov, **b**, *to look round for in vain, to miss*, Siciliam in Sicilia, Cic, quaerit Boeotia Dircen, Ov ; **c**, *to demand, make necessary*, dictatoriam majestatem, Liv

quaesītĭo -ōnis, f (quaero), *an interrogation by torture*, Tac

quaesītor -ōris, m (quaero), *an investigator, inquirer*, esp, *a judicial investigator*, Cic ; criminum, Liv

quaesītum, v quaero

quaesītus -a -um, p adj (from quaero) **I.** *sought out, uncommon, select, extraordinary*, leges quaesitiores (opp. simplices), Tac **II.** *unnatural, affected;* comitas, Tac

quaeso -ivi, 3 (another form of quaero) **I.** *to seek for, strive to obtain*, Plaut **II.** *to beg, beseech, entreat*, with acc, ventorum paces, Lucr, with ut or ne and the subj., a vobis quaeso ut, etc, Cic ; absol, *I beg, I entreat;* tu, quaeso, scribe, Cic

quaestĭcŭlus -i, m (dim of quaestus), *a small gain, slight profit*, Cic

quaestĭo -ōnis, f (quaero), *a seeking, searching* **A.** *an asking, questioning*, captivorum, Caes **B. 1**, *an inquiring, investigating, inquiry*, tota fere quaestio tractata videtur, Cic, in quaestionem vocare, *to investigate*, Cic., **2**, meton, **a**, *the subject of inquiry*, de natura deorum, Cic, **b**, esp, rhet t. t, (α) *the subject of debate in a speech*, Cic., (β) *the main point, the issue*, Cic **C. 1**, *a public judicial inquiry, investigation*, often with torture, hae quaestiones in senatu habitae, Cic., quaestionem habere de viri morte, Cic, quaestionem habere de servis in filium, Liv, quaestionem inter sicarios exercere, *on an assassination*, Cic, quaestiones perpetuae, *standing courts of justice at Rome for the investigation of crime* (instituted 149 B.C.), **2**, meton, *record* (of such a court), fictam quaestionem conscribere, Cic

quaestĭuncŭla -ae, f. (dim. of quaestio), *a little question;* ponere alicui quaestiunculam, Cic.

quaestor ōris, m (for quaesitor, from quaero), *the quaestor*, in plur, *the quaestors, magistrates in Rome, originally two in number, who inquired into and punished capital crimes*, in full, quaestores parricidii; gen., simply quaestores, Cic, in later times there were other quaestors, quaestores aerarii and urbani, *the magistrates who took charge of the public treasury and expenditure*, other quaestors accompanied the consuls and praetors on military expeditions and to provincial commands, and acted as paymasters, the number of quaestors, originally two, was in the end raised to eighteen

quaestōrĭus -a -um (quaestor), *belonging or relating to a quaestor* **I.** Gen, **A.** Adj, comitia, *for choice of a quaestor*, Cic., officium, *duty of quaestor*, Cic ; scelus, *committed by a quaestor*, or *investigated by a quaestor*, Cic, porta, *gate in the camp near the quaestor's tent*, Liv. **B.** Subst, **quaestōrĭum** ii, n **1**, (sc. tentorium), *the quaestor's tent in camp*, Liv, **2**, (sc aedificium), *the quaestor's dwelling in a province*, Cic. **II.** Esp, *having the rank of a quaestor* **A.** Adj, legatus, Cic **B.** Subst, **quaestōrĭus** ii, m *one who had been quaestor*, Cic

quaestŭōsus -a -um (quaestus), *gainful, profitable* **I.** mercatura, Cic. **II.** Of persons, **1**, *fond of gain, eager after profit;* homo, Cic.; **2**, *having gained much, rich*, Tac.

quaestūra -ae f. (quaestor), *the office or dignity of the quaestor, quaestorship*, Cic

quaestus ūs, m. (quaero), *a gaining, getting, profit, gain, advantage*, quaestus ac lucrum unius agri et unius anni, Cic, quaestui deditum esse, *to be devoted to money getting*, Sall ; quaestui habere rempublicam, *to make the administra-*

tion of the state an occasion of profit, Cic , furtis quaestum facere, Cic , quaestu judiciario pasci, *to live on the pay of a judge*, Cic

quālĭbĕt (quālŭbĕt), adv (abl of quilibet) **I.** *wherever you like, everywhere*, Plaut **II.** *in any way you please*, Cat

quālis e (from quam, as talis from tam) = ποῖος, *of what sort, what kind of* **I.** Interrog , qualis est istorum oratio? Cic **II.** Rel , with corresponding talis, *as* , without talis, *of such a kind, such as*, qualem te praebuisti, talem te impertias, Cic , ut res non tales, quales ante habitae sint, habendae videantur, Cic , in hoc bello, quale bellum nulla barbaria gessit, *such a war as*, Caes , doce me quales sint, Cic **III.** Indef subst , quale, *having some quality or other* , illa quae appellant qualia, Cic

quālĭscumquĕ, quālĕcumquĕ **I.** Rel , *of whatever kind, of whatever sort*, homines qualescumque sunt, Cic **II.** Indef *any, without exception, any whatever*, sin qualemcumque locum sequimur, Cic

quālislĭbĕt, quālĕlĭbĕt, *of what sort you will*, formae litterarum vel aureae vel qualeslibet, Cic.

quālĭtas -ātis, f (qualis), *a quality, property*, Cic

quālĭtĕr, adv. (qualis), *as, just as*, Ov

quālus i, m and **quālum** i, n *a wicker-basket*, Verg

quam (acc of quae, analogous to tam), *how, in what way*, and emphatic, *how much* **I.** In correlation **A.** In comparison, **a**, with tam, v tam; with tam left out, homo non, quam isti sunt gloriosus, Liv , quam si = tamquam si, *as if*, Cic , often with superl quam maximā possum voce dico, *with as loud a voice as possible*, Cic , quam celerrime potuit, Caes , elliptically, without possum, *as much as possible, very* with adj and adv in posit. and superl , quam magnis itineribus, Caes , quam plurimo vendere, *as dear as possible*, Cic , quam saepissime, *as often as possible*, Cic , quam primum, *as soon as possible*, Cic , nocte quam longa est, *the whole long night through*, Verg , **b**, with tantus, v tantus , **c**, with sic, Verg , **d**, with comparatives or words implying comparison, *than, as*, nihil est magis timendum quam, etc , Cic , major sum quam cui possit, etc , *too great to be*, etc , Ov , with a second comparative following, longior quam latior, *more long than wide*, Cic , with a superl , to express an emphatic comparative, cum tyranno, quam qui umquam, saevissimo, Liv , with verbs implying a comparison, such as malle, potius malle, praestat, etc , Caes , and other words of similar meaning, as aeque, supra, ultra, secus, alius, aliter, alibi, dissimilis, diversus, etc , quam pro, foll by abl after a comparison , proelium atrocius quam pro numero pugnantium editur, *fiercer than you would expect from the number of the combatants*, Liv **B.** In phrases relating to time, *after that, that* , postero die or postridie quam, Cic **II.** To express degree, *how, how great, how little*, **a**, in indirect speech, (α) with adv and adj , memoriā teneatis quam valde admurmurarint, Cic , (β) with verbs, attende jam, quam ego defugiam auctoritatem consulatus mei, Cic , **b**, in direct speech, in questions and exclamations , (α) with adj and adv , quam multis, quam paucis, Cic , (β) with verbs, quam hoc non curo, Cic

quamdĭū, *so long as, as long as, until* , quamdiu potuit tacuit, Caes , disces quamdiu voles, Cic

quamlĭbĕt, adv **I.** *as you please, as you will*, Lucr **II.** *howsoever, ever so much*, manus quamlibet infirmae, Ov

quamobrem (quam ob rem), *on which account, for which reason, wherefore, why* **I.** Interrog , Cic **II.** Rel , si res reperietur quam ob rem videantur, Cic

quamprīmum, adv *as soon as possible, forthwith*, Cic

quamquam, conj *although, though*, and sometimes at the beginning of a sentence, *nevertheless, notwithstanding, and yet, yet* , gen with indic , only in classical prose with subj when the thought would require the subj even without quamquam , medici quamquam intelligunt saepe, tamen numquam aegris dicunt, Cic , at the beginning of a sentence, quamquam quis ignorat, Cic , with a partic , omnia illa quae sunt extra, quamquam expetenda, summo bono continerentur, Cic

quamvīs, **I.** Adv **A.** Gen , *as you will, as much as you please, ever so much* , quamvis multos nominatim proferre, Cic , et praeter eos quamvis enumeres multos licet, Cic **B.** *as much as possible, very much, exceedingly*, quamvis copiose, Cic **II.** Conj *however much, although, albeit*, gen with subj , quamvis prudens sis, tamen, etc , Cic , with an adj or partic without a verb, quamvis iniqua passi, Cic

quānam (abl of quinam), *where indeed, where*, Liv

quandŏ, adv and conj **I.** Adv , *when* **A.** *when = at what time*, **a**, interrog , quando enim me ista curasse arbitramini? Cic , **b**, rel , non intelligitur, quando obrepat senectus, Cic , **c**, indef , *at any time, ever*, quaestio num quando amici novi veteribus sint anteponendi, Cic. **B.** *when = in what circumstances*, Cic **II.** Conj , **a**, temporal = *when*, tum quando legatos Tyrum misimus, Cic , **b**, causal, *since, because*, quando ad majores quaedam nati sumus, Cic

quandŏcumquĕ, adv **I.** Rel , *whenever, as often as*, quandocumque trahunt invisa negotia Romam, Hor **II.** Indef , *at some time or other* , quandocumque mihi poenas dabis, Ov

quandōquĕ, adv **I.** Rel , *whenever as often as*, Cic **II.** Indef , *at some time or other*, Cic

quandŏquĭdem, conj *since, because*, Cic

quantillus -a -um (dim of quantulus), *how little! how small! how insignificant!* Plaut

quanto, v quantus

quantŏpĕrĕ (quanto ŏpĕrĕ), adv (quantus and opus), *with what great trouble* **I.** Lit , *with what care, how much* , quanto se opere custodiant bestiae, Cic **II.** Transf , *to what an extent, how much* , dici non potest, quanto opere gaudeant, Cic

quantŭlus -a -um (dim of quantus), *how little, how small, how unimportant* , quantulus sol nobis videtur! Cic , quantulum judicare possemus, Cic

quantŭluscumquĕ -ăcumquĕ -umcumquĕ, *how little soever, however small* , de hac mea, quantulacumque est, facultate, Cic , neut subst , *how little soever* , quantulumcumque dicebamus, Cic

quantum, v quantus

quantumvis. **I.** Adv *as much as you please, ever so much, very much*, Suet **II.** Conj *although* , ille catus quantumvis rusticus, Hor

quantus a um (from quam and adj ending tus), *of what size, how great* **I.** Rel = ὅσος **A** Gen of size, number, etc *how great* and (without corresponding tantus) *as great as*, of time, *how long, so long as* , of other relations *how important, as important as* , 1, adj , (α) with tantus or tam, v tantus, tam , (β) with correl left out, ut acciperent pecuniam quantam vellent, Cic.; nox acta, quanta fuit, *as long as it lasted, the whole long night*, Ov.; quantā maximā celeritate potui, *with the greatest possible speed*, Liv.; **2,** neut. subst., quantum; **a,** with genit. or absol., quantum est ex Sicilia frumenti, Cic.; quantum ego sentio, Cic.; quantum in me est, *as far as in me lies*, Cic.; in quantum, *in so far*, Ov.; **b,** genit. of price, *how dear, at what price;* quanti locaverint, tantam pecuniam solvendam, Cic.; quanti quanti, *at whatever price*, Cic.; **c,** abl., quanto in comparatives, *the more;* quanto longius discederent, eo, etc., Liv.; so, quanto ante, Cic.; **3,** neut., quantum, adv., **a,** *as far as;* nisi quantum usus necessario cogeret, Liv.; **b,** = quam, to strengthen a superl., quantum maxime accelerare poterat, Liv.; **c,** parenthet., ea, quantum potui, feci, *to the best of my power*, Cic. **II.** Interrog. = πόσος, *how great?* **A.** Gen., **1,** adj., (α) in direct questions, in exclamations, quanta notitia antiquitatis? Cic.; (β) in direct speech, quum ipsa pecunia numero et summa sua, quanta fuerit, ostendat, Cic.; **2,** neut. subst., genit. quanti, *at what a price? how dear?* in indirect questions, cum scias, quanti Tulliam faciam, *how highly I esteem*, Cic.; **3,** neut., quantum, adv., *how much;* quantum mutatus ab illo Hectore, Verg.; **B.** Emphatic, *how little!* **1,** adj., in indirect speech, me ipsum poenitet, quanta sint, Cic; **2,** subst., **a,** quantum, (α) in direct question, Ov.; (β) in indirect speech, quantum tu speres perspicio, Cic.; **b,** genit., quanti est ista hominum gloria quae, etc., Cic.

quantuscumquĕ -ăcumquĕ -umcumquĕ. **I.** *how great soever;* bona, quantacumque erant, Cic.; emphat., quantacumque victoria, Cic. **II.** *as much soever as;* quantumcumque possum, Cic.

quantuslĭbet -tălibet -tumlibet, *as great as you will, however great, however much;* ordo, Ov.; magnitudo hominis, Liv.

quantusvis -ăvis -umvis, *as great as you please, how great* or *how much soever;* quantasvis magnas copias sustineri posse, Caes.; portum satis amplum quantaevis classi, Liv.

quāpropter, *on which account, wherefore*, Cic.

quāquā (abl. of quisquis), *wherever, whithersoever*, Plaut.

quārē, adv. (qui and res). **I.** *by which means, whereby;* permulta sunt quae dici possunt, quare intelligatur, Cic. **II.** *wherefore, on which account.* **A.** Interrog., quare negasti, etc., Cic. **B.** Rel., utendum est excusatione, quare id necesse fuerit, Cic.

quartădĕcŭmāni -ōrum, m. (quartus decimus), *soldiers of the fourteenth legion*, Tac.

quartāna, v. quartanus.

quartānus -a -um (quartus), *relating to the fourth.* **I.** *relating to the fourth day;* febris quartana, Cic.; and subst. simply, **quartāna** -ae, f. *a quartan fever;* quartana ab aliquo discessit, Cic. **II.** *relating to the fourth legion;* **quartāni** -ōrum, m. *the soldiers of the fourth legion*, Tac.

quartārĭus -ii, m. (quartus), *the fourth part of a sextarius*, Liv.

quarto, v. quartus.

quartum, v. quartus.

quartus -a -um, *the fourth.* **I.** Adj., pars, Caes. **II.** Subst., **1,** **quartus** -i, m., (α) (sc. liber), *the fourth book;* in quarto accusationis, Cic.; (β) (sc. lapis), *the fourth milestone*, Tac.; **2,** **quarta** -ae, f. (sc. hora), *the fourth hour*, Hor. **III.** Adv., **1,** quartum, *for the fourth time*, Cic.; **2,** quarto, *for the fourth time*, Ov.

quartusdĕcĭmus -a -um, *the fourteenth*, Tac.

quăsi, adv. *as if.* **I.** Of the comparison of whole sentences; **1,** in hypothetical comparisons, *as if;* **a,** corresponding to ut, ita, tam, perinde, proinde, and idem, with subj., sensu amisso fit idem quasi natus non esset omnino, Cic.; with partic., quas ut avide arripui quasi sitim explere cupiens, Cic.; **b,** without any corresponding partic. in the subj., quid ego his testibus utor, quasi res dubia aut obscura sit, Cic.: often ironical, *as if, just as if;* medico tria millia jugerum (dedisti) quasi te sanasset, Cic.; with partic., hostes maximo clamore insecuti quasi partā jam atque exploratā victoriā, Cic.; **2,** in pure comparison, *as, like as;* with the indic., quasi poma ex arboribus, cruda si sunt, vix evelluntur ut, etc., Cic. **II.** To compare clauses or words; **1,** to soften an unusual expression, *as it were, a sort of;* philosophia procreatrix quaedam et quasi parens, Cic.; **2,** transf., *as it were, almost, all but;* quasi in extrema pagina, Cic.

quăsillus -i, m. and **quăsillum** -i, n. (dim. of qualus), *a little wicker-basket*, esp. for holding wool, Cic.

quassātio -ōnis, f. (quasso), *a shaking*, Liv.

quasso, 1. (intens. of quatio). **I.** Transf., *to shake violently.* **A.** Lit., **1,** gen., hastam, Verg.; **2,** esp., *to shatter, break in pieces, dash to pieces;* classis ventis quassata, Verg.; naves quassatae, Liv. **B.** Transf., *to shake, shatter;* rempublicam, Cic. **II.** Reflex., *to shake oneself, shake;* siliquā quassante, Verg.

quassus -a -um, partic. of quatio.

quătĕnŭs, adv. *how far.* **I.** Lit., quatenus progredi debeat, Cic.; ut nulla in re statuere possimus quatenus, Cic. **II.** Transf., **A.** Of time, *how long.* **B.** Of other relations, **1,** *in so far as*, Cic.; **2,** *since, seeing that*, Hor.

quătĕr, adv. numer. (quatuor), *four times*, Verg.; ter et quater, *again and again, often*, Hor., Verg.

quăterni -ae -a, num. distrib. (quatuor), *four each;* quaternae centesimae, *interest at four per cent. monthly*, Cic.

quătĭo, quassi, quassum, 3. *to shake.* **I.** Lit., **1,** gen., caput, Liv.; alas, Verg.; hastam, *to brandish*, Verg.; **2,** esp., **a,** *to convulse;* risu populum, *make their sides shake with laughing*, Hor.; **b,** *to strike, beat;* cymbala, Verg.; **c,** *to crash, shatter;* muros arietibus, Liv.; esp. partic., quassus; quassae naves, *leaky, shattered*, Liv. **II.** Transf., **a,** *to shake, agitate, trouble;* quod aegritudine quatiatur, Cic.; **b,** *to harass;* oppida bello, Verg.

quătrĭdŭum = quadriduum (q.v.).

quătŭor (quattŭor), adj. num. (τέσσαρες or τέτταρες), *four*, Cic.

quătŭordĕcim, adj. num. (quatuor and decem), *fourteen;* quatuordecim ordines, or simply quatuordecim, *the fourteen rows of seats reserved in the circus for the equites*, or *knights, at Rome;* in quatuordecim ordinibus sedere, *to be a knight*, Cic.

quătŭorvĭrātus -ūs, m. (quatuorviri), *the office of the* quatuorviri; ap. Cic.

quătŭorvĭri -ōrum, m. *a college of four magistrates;* e.g., in Rome, for the care of the streets; in municipia and coloniae, *the chief magistrates*, Cic.

-quĕ (Gr. τε) (an enclitic conj. always affixed to a word), *and;* teque hortor, Cic.; que . . . que, *both . . . and, and . . . and;* quique Romae quique in exercitu erant, Liv.; special uses of que, **a,** *and above all;* largitiones temeritatisque invitamenta, Liv , **b,** *and indeed,* Caes ; **c,** *and accordingly,* Cic , **d,** *and rather,* non nobis solum nati sumus ortusque nostri partem patria vindicat, Cic ; **e,** *also, moreover,* Trebatioque mandavi, Cic , **f,** *or,* uxores habent deni duodenique inter se communes, Caes

queis, quis = quibus, v qui

quĕmadmŏdum (quem ad mŏdum), *in what manner, how* **I.** Interrog , quemadmodum est asservatus? Cic **II.** Rel , **A.** Gen , semper vigilavi et providi, quemadmodum salvi esse possemus, Cic **B.** Esp , corresponding with sic, ita, item, etc , *as, just as,* quemadmodum socius in societate habet partem, sic heres in hereditate habet partem, Cic

quĕo, quivi and quii, quitum, quire, *to be able, I (thou, he, etc) can,* often with the negative non queo, esp. with Cicero, who never uses the 1st pers nequeo , non queo reliqua scribere, Cic

quercētum i, n (quercus), *an oak-wood,* Hor

quercĕus -a-um (quercus), *oaken* , coronae, *of oak-leaves,* Tac.

quercus ūs, f **I.** *the oak,* Cic **II.** Poet , meton , 1, *that which is made of oak* , quercus civilis, *a crown of oak-leaves for saving the life of a citizen in war,* Cic , 2, *an acorn,* Juv

quĕrēla (quĕrella) ae, f (queror), *a complaint* **I.** *as an expression of pain* , **a,** *wailing, cry* , maestis implere juga querelis, Ov , **b,** *a cry or plaintive sound of animals,* Verg ; **II.** *as an expression of sadness, complaint, complaining* , epistola plena querelarum, Cic vestrum beneficium nonnullam habet querelam, *gives some occasion of complaint,* Cic

quĕrĭbundus -a -um (queror), *complaining, plaintive* , vox, Cic

quĕrĭmōnĭa ae, f (queror), *a complaining, complaint* , de tuis injuriis, Cic

quĕrĭtor, 1 dep (intens of queror), *to complain excessively,* Tac

quernĕus -a um (for querceus from quercus), *of or relating to the oak, oaken* , frondes, Prop

quernus = querneus (q v)

quĕror, questus sum, 3 dep. *to complain, bewail* **I.** Gen , **a,** of birds, Hor , **b,** of musical instruments, flebile nescio quid queritur lyra, Ov **II.** *to lament or bewail something* , suum fatum, Caes , injurias Cic de Milone, Cic , cum patribus conscriptis, *to have a cause of complaint of, to complain of,* Liv , with acc and infin , se tum exstingui, Cic , with dat of pers and acc of thing, Oceano furta mariti, Ov

querquētŭlānus -a -um (querquetum), *of or belonging to an oak-wood* , Querquetulanus mons, *old name of the Caelius mons at Rome,* Tac

querquētum = quercetum (q v)

quĕrŭlus a -um (queror) **I.** *complaining, plaintive* , cicada, Verg , vox, Ov **II.** *complaining, querulous* , senex, Hor

questus -ūs, m (queror), *a complaining, complaint, lament* , **a,** of human beings, qui questus, qui maeror dignus inveniri in tanta calamitate potest, Cic , **b,** *of the nightingale's song,* Verg

1 **quī,** quae, quŏd **I.** Pron rel , *who, which, what, that* **A.** Agreement agrees in gender and number with its antecedent, but for case depends on its own verb, luna eam lucem, quam a sole accipit, mittit in terras, Cic Peculiarities **a,** qui sometimes has the same noun as the antecedent in its own clause, quas res violentissimas natura genuit, earum moderationem nos soli habemus, Cic , **b,** qui takes a subst as an attribute, ab Romanis cui uni fidebant auxilio, Liv , often used parenthetically with esse, spero, quae tua prudentia et temperantia est te valere, *such is your temperance,* Cic , **c,** with an adj as attribute, ad suas res revocet, quas aut tulerit acerbas aut timeat, Cic , **d,** qui often introduces a new sentence, *and this,* res loquitur ipsa, quae semper valet plurimum, Cic Irregularities **a,** qui in a different gender from its antecedent (*a*) with a verb of calling, when it agrees with an attrib subst in its own clause, agrum, quae postea sunt Mucia prata appellata, Liv , (*β*) quod with neut , referring to the whole previous sentence, Lacedaemonii regem, quod numquam antea apud eos acciderat, necaverunt, Cic , **b,** when qui is in a different number from its antecedent, (*a*) with a collective noun as antecedent, equitatum praemittit qui videant, Cic , (*β*) when the rel sent is more general than the antecedent clause, si tempus est ullum jure hominis necandi , quae multa sunt, Cic , **c,** qui is sometimes attracted into the case of its antecedent, illo augurio quo diximus Cic **B.** Mood 1, foll by the indic when a simple statement is made, mors quae naturā debita est, Cic , 2, by the subj, **a,** to express purpose, *that,* eripiunt aliis quod aliis largiantur, Cic , **b,** to express reason, *as,* recte Socrates exsecrari eum solebat, qui primus utilitatem a natura sejunxisset, Cic , **c,** with such words as is, talis, ejusmodi, tam and with adj , aptus, idoneus, dignus, ego is sum qui nihil fecerim, *the kind of man to,* etc , Cic , and with verbs such as habere, reperire, esse, and in the phrase, nemo est qui, nullus est qui, quotusquisque est qui, etc , quis est qui dicere audeat, Cic , also after a comparative, Liv **II.** Pron interrog , *who? which? what? what manner of? what kind of?* **A** In direct speech, **a,** adj , qui cantus dulcior inveniri potest? Cic , **b,** subst , qui primus Ameriam nuntiat, Cic **B.** In indirect speech, **a,** adj , scribis te velle scire, qui sit reipublicae status, Cic , **b,** subst , tu te collige, et qui sis considera, Cic **III.** Pron indef , qui, quae and qua, quod, **a,** adj , *any, some,* nisi qui deus subvenerit, Cic , **b,** subst , *any one,* si qui Romae esset demortuus, Cic (old form, abl qui with cum quicum = quocum, Cic , plur dat , queis, Verg , quis, Sall , Hor)

2 **quī** (old abl of qui) **I.** Rel , *wherewith, wherefrom,* in tanta paupertate decessit, ut qui efferretur vix reliquerit, Nep , habeo qui utar, Cic **II.** Interrog , **A.** In direct questions, *in what manner? how then?* deum nisi sempiternum intelligere qui possumus? Cic **B.** In indirect questions, Plaut

quĭă, conj (old neut plur of qui), *because* (used only of a reason that is certain), often with particles, ideo, idcirco, propterea, etc , quia mutari natura non potest, idcirco verae amicitiae sempiternae sunt, Cic , under the phrases, **a,** quiane, in questions, *is it because?* quiane juvat ante levatos, Verg , **b,** quianam = cur *why,* Verg

quīcumquĕ, quaecumquĕ, quodcumquĕ, *whoever, whichever, whatever* **I.** Gen , quicumque is est, ei, etc Cic , quācumque potui ratione, *in every possible way,* Cic , ut quodcumque vellet, liceret facere *everything that he chose,* Nep , neut , quodcumque, *however much,* hoc quodcumque est or vides, *the whole,* Verg **II.** = qualiscumque, *of whatever kind,* quaecumque mens illa fuit, Gabinii fuit, Cic , separated, qua re cumque possemus, Cic

quīdam, quaedam, quoddam, and subst , quiddam, *a certain person or thing* **I.** Lit , **a,** quaedam vox, Cic , quodam tempore, *at a certain* *time;* subst., quidam de collegis nostris, Cic.; neut., quiddam divinum, *something divine,* Cic.; with genit., quiddam mali, Cic.; **b,** quidam or quasi quidam, tamquam quidam, velut quidam, *a kind of, so to speak;* incredibilis quaedam magnitudo ingenii, Cic. **II.** Plur., quidam, quaedam, *some;* quidam dies, Cic.

quĭdem, conj. *indeed, even.* **I.** To strengthen an assertion, est illum quidem vel maximum animo ipso animum videre, Cic. **II.** Uniting an assertion, *at least, for certain;* non video causam, cur ita sit, hoc quidem tempore, Cic.; ne . . . quidem, *not even,* Caes. **III.** In explanation, *indeed, truly;* doleo ac mirifice quidem, Cic.

quidnī? *why not?* Cic.

quĭēs -ētis, f. *rest.* **I.** Gen., *repose, quiet;* **1,** lit., mors laborum ac miseriarum quies est, Cic.; quietem capere, *to enjoy,* Caes.; quies ab armis, Liv.; plur., somno et quietibus ceteris, *kinds of rest,* Cic.; **2,** meton., *a place of rest,* Lucr. **II.** Esp., **A.** *rest at night, sleep;* **1,** lit., **a,** gen., ire ad quietem, *to go to sleep,* Cic.; datur hora quieti, Verg.; **b,** *the sleep of death;* dura quies, Verg.; **2,** meton., **a,** *dream,* Tac.; **b,** *time of sleep, night,* Verg. **B.** *silence,* Tac. **C.** *keeping quiet;* **1,** lit., **a,** *peace,* Sall.; **b,** *neutrality,* Tac.; **c,** *quiet of the mind,* Ov.; **2,** transf., of things, *calm,* Verg.

quĭesco -ēvi -ētum, 3. (quies), *to rest, repose.* **I.** Gen., *to rest from work,* etc.; **a,** of living beings, ipse dux (gruum) revolat, ut ipse quoque quiescat, Cic.; **b,** transf., of things, prato gravia arma quiescunt, Verg. **II.** Esp., **A.** *to rest, to lie down,* Cic. **B.** *to rest = to sleep;* **a,** of the living, cenatus quiescebat, Cic.; **b,** of the dead, *to rest in the grave;* placidā compostus pace quiescit, Verg. **C.** *to keep quiet;* **1,** lit., **a,** *to be silent;* quiescebant voces hominum canumque, Ov.; **b,** *to remain quiet, to do nothing;* esp. in politics, (α) *to be inactive;* quiescere viginti dies, Cic.; (β) *to undertake no war,* etc., *to be at peace;* urbs illa non potest quiescere, Cic.; (γ) *not to mix in politics, to hold aloof, to be neutral;* quiescere in republica, Cic.; **2,** transf., of things; **a,** *to be still, calm;* alta quierunt aequora, Verg.; **b,** of the soil, *to remain fallow;* ager qui multos annos quiescit, Cic. **D.** *to remain free from trouble, to be peaceful, undisturbed;* numquamne quiescit civitas nostra a suppliciis? Liv. **E.** *to rest;* **a,** *to cease from some action, to leave off doing something,* Hor.; **b,** *to cease to be of any weight;* potentia quiescit, Cic. **F.** *to be quiet in mind,* Ter. (syncop. form, quierunt, quierim, quierint, quiessem, quiesse).

quĭētē, adv. (quietus), *quietly, peaceably;* vivere, Cic.; apte et quiete ferre aliquid, Cic.

quĭētus -a -um (quies), *quiet, peaceful.* **I.** Lit., *resting from activity.* **A.** Gen., aër, Verg. **B.** Esp., **1,** *resting, sleeping,* Tac.; **2,** *resting from tumult, uproar, combat,* etc.; **a,** *quiet, inactive;* (α) of persons, quieto sedente rege ad Enipeum, Liv.; (β) of places, *free from tumult, quiet, at peace;* quieta Gallia, Caes.; with ab and the abl., a seditione et a bello quietis rebus, Liv.; neut. plur. subst., quieta movere, Sall.; **b,** *neutral, quiet,* Liv.; **3,** *keeping aloof from politics, retired, living in peace;* (α) of persons, major cura efficiendi rempublicam gerentibus quam quietis, Cic.; (β) of situations, vita privata et quieta, Cic. **II.** Transf., of character, **1,** *quiet, peaceful, mild;* homo quietissimus, Cic.; animus quietus et solutus, Cic.; **2,** *deliberate, slow,* in a bad sense (opp. acer); quietus, imbellis, placido animo, Sall.

quĭlĭbet, quaelibet, quodlibet and subst., quidlibet, *any you will, any one, anything.* **I.** Gen., quaelibet minima res, *any the least thing,* Cic.; quibuslibet temporibus, *at all times,* Liv.; subst., quidlibet, *anything and everything,* Hor. **II.** Esp., with a contemptuous meaning, *the first that comes, any;* certo genere, non quolibet, Cic.

quīn (for quine, from qui and ne). **I.** In dependent sentence with a preceding negative. **A.** *that not, so that not, without;* numquam tam male est Siculis quin aliquid facete et commode dicant, Cic.; esp., with phrases nemo est, nihil est, quis est, quid est, nemo fuit quin illud viderit, Cic.; non quin ipse dissentiam, *not as if I did not disagree,* Cic. **B. a,** with verbs of hindering, neglecting, etc., to be translated into English by *without* and the present participle, nullum adhuc intermisi diem, quin aliquid ad te litterarum darem, Cic.; nihil abest quin sim miserrimus, Cic.; **b,** after verbs of doubting, ignorance, etc., *that, but that;* non dubitari debet quin fuerint ante Homerum poetae, Cic.; quis ignorat, quin tria Graecorum genera sint? *who does not know that?* Cic. **II.** In principal sentences. **A.** To express encouragement, exhortation, etc., *why not?* quin conscendimus equos, Liv. **B.** To add emphasis, *rather, yea rather;* quin contra si, etc., Liv.; quin etiam, quin immo, Cic.

quĭnam, quaenam, quodnam, pron. interrog., *who, which, what then?* **I.** In direct questions, sed quinam est ille epilogus, Cic. **II.** In indirect questions, quaesivit quasnam formosas virgines haberet, Cic.

Quinctĭus (Quintĭus) -a um, *name of a Roman gens, the most famous members of which were:* **1,** L. Quinctius Cincinnatus, *summoned from the plough to be dictator;* **2,** T. Quinctius Flamininus, *the conqueror of the Macedonian king Philip.* Adj. = *Quinctian;* gens, Liv. Hence, adj., **Quinctĭānus** -a -um, *Quinctian.*

quincunx -cuncis (quinque and uncia), *five-twelfths of a whole.* **I.** Lit., *five-twelfths of an as;* as a coin = *five unciae,* Hor. **II.** Transf., *the form of the five* ⁙ *spots on dice;* and hence applied to *a plantation in which rows of trees were so planted;* directi in quincuncem ordines, Cic.

quindĕcĭēs, adv. (quinque and decies), *fifteen times,* Cic.

quindĕcim, num. (quinque and decem), *fifteen,* Caes.

quindĕcimprīmi -ōrum, m. *the fifteen chief senators of a municipium,* Caes.

quindĕcimvir -i, m. and **quindĕcimvĭri** -ōrum and (gen.) -ûm, *a college of fifteen magistrates;* esp., quindecimviri sacris faciundis or quindecimviri sacrorum, or simply quindecimviri, *one of the three great priestly colleges, having the superintendence of the Sibylline books;* separated, quindecim Diana preces virorum curet, Hor.

quindĕcimvĭrālis -e, *of* or *relating to the quindecimviri,* Tac.

quingēni -ae -a, num. distrib. (quingenti), *five hundred each,* Cic.

quingentēsĭmus -a -um (quingenti), *the five hundredth,* Cic.

quingenti -ae -a, num. (quinque and centum), *five hundred,* Cic.

quingentĭēs, adv. (quingenti), *five hundred times,* Cic.

quini -ae -a, num. distrib. (quinque). **I.** *five each,* Cic. **II.** *five,* Liv.

quinidēni -ae -a, num. distrib. *fifteen each,* Liv.

quinivicēni -ae -a, num. distrib. *twenty-five each,* Liv.

quinquāgēni ae -a, num distrib. (quinquaginta), *fifty each*, Cic

quinquāgēsĭmus -a -um, num (quinquaginta), *the fiftieth*, Cic, subst, **quinquāgēsima** -ae, f (sc pars), *a fiftieth part*, as a tax, Cic

quinquāgies, adv *fifty times*, Plin

quinquāginta num (πεντήκοντα), *fifty*, Cic

quinquātrus -uum, f and **quinquātria** -ium, n *a festival of Minerva*, majores (celebrated from the 19th to the 23rd of March), minores, minusculae (on the 13th of July), Cic

quinquĕ, num (πέντε), *five*, Cic

Quinquĕgentiāni -ōrum, m *a people in Cyrenaica* (Pentapolitani)

quinquennālis -e (quinquennis) I. *happening every five years*, *quinquennial*, celebritas ludorum, Cic II. *lasting for five years*, censura, Liv.

quinquennis e (quinque and annus) I. *five years old*, vinum, Hor II. Transf, poet, *celebrated every five years*, Olympias, *the Olympic games*, Ov

quinquennium -ii, n (quinque and annus), *a period of five years*, quinquennii imperium, Cic, filius quinquennio major, *more than five years old*, Liv

quinquĕpertītus (**quinquĕpartītus**) -a -um, *divided into five portions*, *fivefold*, Cic

quinquĕprīmi -ōrum, m *the five chief senators in a municipium*, Cic

quinquĕrēmis e (quinque and remus) *having five banks of oars*, navis, Liv, oftener as subst, **quinquĕrēmis** is, f *a ship with five banks of oars*, *a quinquereme*, Cic

quinquĕvir -i, m, plur quinqueviri, *a commission or college of five persons*, e g, the agrarian commission for distributing the public land, Cic, for repairing fortifications, Liv, for helping the tresviri in the night police, Liv

quinquĕvĭrātus -ūs, m *the office or dignity of a quinquevir*, Cic

quinquies, adv *five times*, Cic

quinquiplico, 1 *to make fivefold*, Tac

quintădĕcimāni -ōrum, m *the soldiers of the fifteenth legion*, Tac

quintānus a -um (quintus), *of or relating to the fifth* I. Subst, **quintāna** ae, f *a road in a Roman camp which intersected the tents of the legionary soldiers, dividing the fifth maniple and the fifth turma from the sixth*, Liv II. *belonging to the fifth legion*, subst, **quintāni** -ōrum, m *soldiers of the fifth legion*, Tac

Quintĭliānus -i, m *a Roman name, the most celebrated bearer of which was* M Fabius Quintilianus, *the famous rhetorician, born at Calagurris in Spain, head of a school of rhetoric at Rome, teacher of Pliny the Younger and of Juvenal*

Quintīlis (**Quinctīlis**) -is, m (with or without mensis), *the fifth month* (reckoning from March as the first), *afterwards called Julius, in honour of Julius Caesar*, Cic

Quintīlius Vārus, *of Cremona, a friend of Horace and Vergil*

1. **quintus** a -um (quinque), adv. *the fifth*, Cic, quintum, quinto, *for the fifth time*, Liv

2 **Quintus**, fem **Quinta**, *a common Roman praenomen*, the masc usually abbreviated Q

quintusdĕcimus a -um, *the fifteenth*, Liv

quippĕ, conj (quia pe, as nempe from nam pe), *certainly, indeed, by all means, to be sure* I. Gen, a te quidem apte et rotunde (dicta sunt), quippe habes enim a rhetoribus, Cic, used with quod, Cic, quum, Cic, qui, quae, quod (and subj in Cic), quippe etiam, quippe et, Verg II. Esp, ironically, *forsooth*, quippe homini erudito, Cic

quippīni (**quippĕni**), adv *why not?* Plaut

Quĭrīnus -i, m (from Sabine curis, *a spear*, *the wielder of the spear, the warlike one*) I *the name of Romulus after his apotheosis*, populus Quirini, *the Romans*, Hor, gemini Quirini, *Romulus and Remus*, Juv II. *Janus*, Suet III. *Augustus*, Verg IV. *Antonius*, Prop; hence, A. **Quĭrīnus** a -um, *of or relating to Romulus*, collis, *the Quirinal*, Ov B. **Quĭrīnālis** e, *relating to Quirinus or Romulus*, trabea, Verg, collis, *the Quirinal Hill* (now *Monte Cavallo*), Cic, subst, **Quĭrīnālia** ium n *a festival in honour of Romulus, celebrated on the 17th of February*, Cic

1 **Quĭris**, v Quirites

2 **quĭris** -is, f (curis) (a Sabine word), *a spear*, Ov

quĭrītātio -ōnis, f (quirito), *a shriek, scream, cry of distress*, Liv

Quĭrītes -ium and um, m (Cures), *the inhabitants of the Sabine town Cures*, Verg, after the union of the Romans and Sabines the name Quirites was used of the citizens of Rome considered in their civic character, *Romani* of them in their political and military character found in the expressions, Populus Romanus Quiritium Populus Romanus Quiritesque, Quirites Romani, Liv, for a general to address his soldiers by the term Quirites was equivalent to a discharge, Tac, jus Quiritium, *full Roman citizenship*, sing, **Quĭris** itis, m *a Roman citizen*, Cic, plur, **Quĭrites**, poet, transf, of the bees in a hive, Verg

quĭrīto, 1 and **quĭrītor** -āri, 1 dep (Quirites), orig, *to call the Quirites to help*, hence, gen, *to utter a cry of distress, to shriek, scream, cry out*, vox quiritantium, Liv

1 **quis**, quid, pron interrog I. In direct questions, *who? what?* quis clarior Themistocle? Cic, quis tu? Cic, esp, quid, a, subst., *what?* quid tum? *what follows?* Cic, quid igitur est? *how stands it, then?* Cic, with genit = *how much? how many?* quid pictarum tabularum, Cic, b, adv, (α) to express surprise, quid! *what! how!* quid! eundem nonne destituisti? Cic, (β) *why? wherefore?* sed quid argumentor? Cic, quid ita? *why so? how so?* Cic, quidni? *why not?* Cic II. In indirect questions A. Subst, considera quis quem fraudasse dicatur, Cic B. Adj, rogitat, quis vir esset, Liv

2 **quis**, quid, pron indef, *any one, anybody, anything* potest quis errare aliquando, Cic

3 **quis** = quibus, v qui

quisnam, quidnam, pron interrog *who then? what then?* quisnam igitur tuebitur P Scipionis memoriam mortui? Cic, frequently joined with num, num quidnam novi (sc accidit)? Cic, sometimes separated with nam placed first or afterwards, quid se nam facturum arbitratus est? Cic, nam quis te nostras jussit adire domos? Verg

quispĭam, quaepiam quodpiam and subst, quidpiam or quippiam I. *any, any one, anything, some one, something*, quaepiam cohors, Caes, si cuipiam pecuniam ademit, Cic II. *many a one*; innocens est quispiam, Cic

quisquam, quaequam, quidquam (quicquam), *any person, anybody, any one, anything*, used chiefly in negative sentences, or in questions; esne quisquam qui, etc? Cic, nec quisquam, *and no one*, Cic, with genit, vestrum quisquam, Liv

quisquĕ, quaequĕ, quidquĕ and adj, quodque, *each, every, every one, everybody, everything*, often used with the plur of verbs, pro se quisque nostrum debemus, Cic, generally used with sui, sibi, se, suus, suo cuique judicio est utendum, *every one must use his own judgment*, Cic, suum quisque flagitium aliis objectantes, Tac, with comp, quo quisque est sollertior, hoc docet laboriosius, *the more the more*, Cic, with superl, doctissimus quisque, *all the most learned*, Cic, optimum quidque rarissimum est, Cic, so with numerals, quinto quoque anno, *every five years*, Cic, esp, primus quisque, (α), *the first possible, the very first*, primo quoque tempore, *on the very first occasion*, Cic, (β) *one after the other*, Cic

quisquiliae -ārum, f (perhaps from quisque, *any sort of thing*), *rubbish, sweepings, refuse, offscourings*, applied to persons, quisquiliae seditionis Clodianae, Cic

quisquis, quaequae, quidquid (quicquid), and adj quodquod **I.** *whoever, whichever, whatever*, quisquis ille est, *whoever he may be*, Cic, quoquo modo res se habeat, *however the affair may stand*, Cic, with genit, (α) masc, deorum quisquis amicior Attis, Hor, (β) neut, deorum quidquid regit terras, *all the gods who*, etc, Cic, acc, quidquid, adv, *how much soever*, quidquid progredior, Liv, abl, quoquo, adv, *whithersoever*, Cic **II.** *any one, anything, any*, quocumque in loco quisquis est, Cic

quīvis, quaevis, quidvis and adj, quodvis, *whoever, whatever you will, any one, anything whatever*, quivis ut perspicere possit, Cic, quodvis genus, Cic, quivis unus, *any one you please*, Cic, quidvis, *anything whatever, everything*, quidvis perpeti, *all possible evil*, Cic.

quīviscumquĕ, quaeviscumquĕ, quodviscumquĕ, *who or whatsoever you will*, Lucr

quō, adv (orig quoi, dat. and abl of neut of rel pron, qui) **I.** Indef, **A.** *any whither*, si quo erat prodeundum, Cic **B.** *anyhow*, Liv **II.** Rel, **A.** 1, lit., *whither*, ad partem provinciae venturum, quo te velle arbitrarer, Cic, eos quo se contulit (= ad quos), Cic, with genit, quo terrarum possent, Liv, 2, transf, a, *how far, to what extent*, scire quo amentiae progressi sitis, Liv, b, *to what end* quo tantam pecuniam, Cic **B.** Causal, 1, *because, as if*, non quo ipse audieris, Cic, 2, with compar, *to the end that, that the (more)*, Cic, 3, *wherefore, on which account*, in causa esse, quo serius, etc, Liv, quominus, *that not*, after verbs of hindering, such as impedire, deterrere, recusare, Liv, stetit per Trebonium quominus, etc, *it was owing to Trebonius that not*, Cic. **C.** *how*, Ov

quŏăd, adv **I.** Of space, *how far, as far as*, videte nunc quoad fecerit iter, Cic, quoad possem, Cic, quoad possunt ab homine cognosci, *as far as men can know them*, Cic, with genit of the object or limit, quoad eius facere possum, Cic **II.** Of time, **a,** *as long as*, quoad potui, Cic, b, *until, up to the time that*, (α) with indic, quoad senatus dimissus est, Cic, (β) with subj, quoad te videam, Cic (quoad one syllable, in Hor)

quŏcircā, conj *therefore, on that account* Cic, in tmesis, quo, bone, circa, Hor

quŏcumquĕ, adv *whithersoever*, Cic, in tmesis, num eam rationem, quo ea me cumque ducet, sequar? Cic

quod, orig neut of rel pron, qui **I.** Rel adv, **1,** *in which relation, wherein*; quod continens memoria sit, Liv; **2,** *why, on which account*, esp, est quod, *there is reason for*, etc, est magis quod gratuler, Cic, at the beginning of a new sentence, *therefore, thereby*, quod vobis venire in mentem necesse est, Cic, with other conjunctions, quod si, *but if*, Cic, quod utinam, *might it be so*, Cic, so also, quod ubi, Cic; quod quum, Caes **II.** Conj, **A.** 1, *because*, noctu ambulabat, quod somnum capere non posset, Cic, **2,** after verbs of rejoicing, praising, blaming, *that, because*, tibi agam gratias, quod me vivere coegisti, Cic **B.** 1, bene facis, quod me adjuvas, Cic, **2,** *as respects that, as to that*, quod scribis, Cic, **3,** *although*, Ov

quōdammŏdŏ, adv *in a certain way, in a certain measure*, Cic

quōlĭbĕt, adv (orig quoilibet, dat of quilibet), *whithersoever you please*, Ov

quōmĭnus, v quo

quōmŏdŏ, adv *in what manner, how* **I.** Interrog, a, in questions, quomodo? Cic, **b,** in exclamations, quomodo mortem filii tulit! Cic. **II.** Rel, haec negotia quomodo se habeant ne epistolā quidem narrare audeo, Cic, corresponding with sic or ita, Cic

quōmŏdŏcumquĕ, adv *in what way soever, howsoever*, Cic

quōmŏdŏnam, adv *how then?* Cic

quōnam, *whither then, whither pray*, Cic; quonam haec omnia nisi ad suam perniciem pertinere? *what end tend they to?* Caes

quondam, adv. (= quumdam) **I.** *at a certain time*, **a,** *once*, Cic; **b,** *at times*, Cic. **II.** Esp, **a,** of past time, *once*, Cic, **b,** of the future, *at some future time, sometime*, Verg

quŏnĭam, conj (quom = quum and jam), *since, seeing that, whereas, because*, Cic

quōquam, adv *to any place, any whither*, Lucr

1 **quŏquĕ**, adv (never at the beginning of a clause, but placed after the word to which it immediately refers), *also*, Cic, ne quoque = ne quidem, Liv

2 **quōquĕ**, **a,** from quisque (q v), **b,** = et quo, Liv

quōquō, v quisquis.

quōquōversŭs (quōquōvorsŭs) and **quōquōversum (quōquōvorsum)**, adv *in every direction*, Cic

quorsum (quorsŭs), adv (= quo versus), *whither, to what place?* transf, a, quorsum haec pertinent? Cic, b, *to what purpose? with what view? to what end?* quorsum igitur haec disputo, Cic

quŏt, adj plur indecl **I.** *how many*, **a,** interrog, *how many?* quot calamitates? Cic, **b,** rel, quot dies erimus in Tusculano, *as long as I shall be*, etc, Cic, in correlation with tot, *as many, so many*, quot homines, tot causae, Cic **II.** *all, every*, quot annis, *yearly*, Cic

quŏtannis, v quot

quotcumquĕ, *as many as, how many soever* Cic

quŏtēni -ae -a (quot), *how many each*, Cic

quŏtīdĭānus (cŏtīdĭānus, cottīdĭānus) -a um (quotidie) **I.** *every day, daily*, aspectus, Cic, exercitatio, Caes, vita, Cic, adv, quotidiano, *daily*, Cic **II.** Transf, *every day, common, ordinary*, verba, Cic, vis, Cic.

quŏtīdĭē (cŏtīdĭē, cottīdĭē), adv. *daily, every day*, Cic

quŏtĭēs (quŏtĭens), adv (quot) **I.** Interrog, *how often?* Cic **II.** Rel, in correlation, *as often . so often*, toties quoties, Cic.;

and with toties omitted, quoties mihi potestas erit, non praetermittam, Cic

quŏtiescumquĕ, adv *how often soever*, Cic

quotquŏt, num indecl *however many as many soever as*, Cic

quŏtus -a -um (quot), *what in number? of what number? how many?* quotus erit iste denarius qui non sit ferendus? Cic, hora quota est? *what o'clock is it?* Hor, tu, quotus esse velis, rescribe, *how many guests you would like to be invited with you*, Hor, quotusquisque, *how many*, ironically = *how few*, quotus enim quisque disertus, Cic

quŏtuscumquĕ -acumquĕ -umcumquĕ, *whatever in number, how great* or *how small soever*, Tib.

quŏtusquisque, v quotus

quŏusquĕ, adv *until when, how long, how far*, quo usque tandem abutere, Catilina, patientiā nostrā? Cic (separated, quo enim usque, Cic)

quum (cum), conj (an old acc neut from quus = qui). **I.** Of time, **A.** Gen, **1**, *when*, qui non defendit injuriam quum potest, injuste facit, Cic, esp. with tunc, tum, nunc, jam, quum primum, *as soon as*, Cic, with historic present or aorist perf or imperf, or with the historic infin, Liv, Cic; **2**, *as often as, whenever*, quum ad aliquod oppidum venerat, in cubiculum deferebatur, Cic, **3**, *since*, multi anni sunt, quum Fabius in aere meo est, Cic **B. 1**, used in a relative sense after a subst, *when, at which*, fuit quoddam tempus, quum homines vagabantur, Cic, with the subj, fuit quum arbitrarer, Cic, **2**, used in a causal sense, *when*, praeclare facis quum puerum diligis, Cic, quum ... tum, *when ... so also, both ... and, not only ... but also*, volvendi sunt libri, quum aliorum tum inprimis Catonis, Cic, quum maxime, *particularly, above all*, nunc quum maxime, Cic **II.** To express cause with subj, **A.** *as*, quum vita metus plena sit, Cic **B. 1**, with a mixture of connexion in time and in cause, esp in narrative, with imperf and pluperf, *as when*, Epaminondas quum vicisset Lacedaemonios, quaesivit, Cic, **2**, *although*, quum ipse litteram Socrates nullam reliquisset, Cic

R.

R, r, the seventeenth letter of the Latin alphabet, corresponds with the Greek rho (Ρ, ρ) On account of the aspirate which always accompanies the Greek letter, we find it represented by *rh* in some words derived from that language. The letters *r* and *s* seem to have been interchangeable to a great extent, as in arbor, arbos, honor, honos, quaeso for quaero, hesternus, from heri, etc, *r* is also assimilated with *l*, as in the diminutive libellus from liber, in intelligo from inter-lego, etc For abbreviations in which R is used, see Table of Abbreviations

răbĭdē, adv (rabidus), *madly, savagely, fiercely*, omnia appetere, Cic

răbĭdus -a -um (rabies), *raging, mad* **I.** In a narrow sense, Plin **II.** In a wider sense, *fierce, raving, savage* **A. 1**, lit, of animals, canes, Ov, leones, Hor, **2**, transf, of things, personal characteristics, *wild, savage*, mores, Ov., fames, Verg **B.** Of inspired madness, *raging*, os, ora, Verg

răbĭes ēi, f (rabio), *madness* **I.** In a narrow sense, as a disease, Ov, contacto eo scelere velut injectā rabie ad arma ituros, Liv **II.** In a wider sense. **A.** *raging, fierceness, fury, rage*, **a**, of persons, animi acerbitas quaedam et rabies, Cic, ira et rabies Latinorum, Liv, **b**, transf, of things, *fury, rage*, fatalis temporis, Liv, caeli marisque, Verg **B.** Esp, of the inspired madness of the Sibyl, Verg

răbĭo, 3 *to be mad*, Varr

răbĭōsē, adv (rabiosus), *madly, furiously*, Cic

răbĭōsŭlus -a -um (dim of rabiosus), *somewhat raging, furious*, Cic

răbĭōsus -a -um (rabies), *raging, mad* **I.** In a narrow sense, of madness as a disease, Plaut **II** In a wider sense, *furious, savage*, canis, Hor, transf, of things, vide ne fortitudo minime sit rabiosa, Cic

Răbīrĭus a -um, *name of a Roman gens, the most famous members of which were* **1**, C Rabirius Postumus, *accused of treason, and defended by Cicero*, **2**, Rabirius, *a poet, contemporary of Vergil* Adj **Răbīrĭānus** -a -um, *relating to Rabirius*

răbo = arrhabo (q v)

răbŭla -ae, m (rabio), *a bawling advocate, pettifogger*, Cic

răcēmĭfĕr -fĕra -fĕrum (racemus and fero). **1**, *bearing berries*, uva, Ov, **2**, *crowned with grapes*, capilli, Ov

răcēmus -i, m **I.** *the stalk of a cluster of grapes*, uva lentis racemis, Verg **II.** Meton, **A.** *a cluster of grapes*, Verg **B.** *the juice of the grape*, Ov

Răcĭlĭus a -um, *name of a Roman gens, the most famous member of which was* L Racilius, *a tribune of the people in the time of Cicero* **Răcĭlĭa** -ae, f *wife of the dictator* L Q Cincinnatus

rădĭātus (radius), *provided with rays, beaming*, sol, Cic; lumina, Ov

rādīcĭtŭs, adv (radix), *with the root* **I.** Lit, Plin **II.** Fig, *roots and all, utterly*, extrahere cupiditatem, Cic

rādīcŭla -ae, f (dim of radix), *a little root*, Cic

rădĭo, 1 and **rădĭor**, 1 dep (radius, *beam*), *to gleam, glitter, emit rays* or *beams, radiate*. argenti radiabant lumine valvae, Ov, partic, radians, *gleaming*, luna, Verg

rădĭus -ii, m *a staff, rod* **I.** Lit, **A.** Gen, acuti atque alius per alium immissi radii, Liv **B.** Esp, **1**, *the spoke of a wheel* Verg, **2**, mathem t t, *the staff that mathematicians used for drawing figures on the abacus*, **3**, t t of weaving, *a shuttle*, Verg, **4**, t t of zoology, **a**, *the sting of the fish* pastinaca, Plin, **b**, radii, *the spurs of birds*, Plin, **5**, t t of botany, *a kind of long olive*, Verg **II.** Transf, **1**, mathem t t, *the radius or semi diameter of a circle*, Cic, **2**, *a ray, beam of light*, radii solis, Cic

rādix -īcis, f (perh. connected with ῥίζα), *a root* **I.** Gen, **A. 1**, lit, *the root of a tree* or *plant*, cortices et radices, Cic, arbores ab radicibus subruere, Caes, **2**, transf, **a**, *the root* or *lowest part of anything* (of the tongue), Ov; of a feather, Ov, **b**, *the foot of a mountain*, in radicibus Caucasi natus, Cic **B.** Fig, **a**, *origin, source*, patientiae, Cic. ex iisdem, quibus nos, radicibus natum, *a native of the same place*, Cic **b**, *firm foundation*, Pompejus, eo robore vir iis radicibus, Cic **II.** Esp, **a**, *edible root*, a genus radicis quod appellatur chara, Caes, **b**, *a radish*, Hor

rādo, rāsi, rāsum, 3 *to scrape, scratch, shave* **I.** *to make smooth by scraping, shaving,* etc., lapides palmā, Hor **II.** *to graze, brush along, touch,* litora, Verg., terras, Hor **III.** *to scratch* or *scrape away erase,* **a,** nomen fastis, Tac., **b,** *to shave the hair with a razor* (tondere, *to cut it with scissors*), caput et supercilia, Cic., radere caput, as a sign of slavery, Liv., in pursuance of a vow, Juv

Raeti (Rhaeti) -ōrum, m *a people between the Danube, the Rhine, and the Lech, north of the Po* Hence, **A. Raetĭa** -ae, f *Raetia, their country* **B. Raetĭcus** -a -um, *Raetian* **C. Raetus** -a -um, *Raetian*

rāja -ae, f. *a fish, the ray,* Plin

rallum -i, n (rado), *a scraper for cleaning a ploughshare,* Plin

rallus -a -um (rad-lus, from rado), *thin, of fine texture,* Plaut.

rāmāle is, n (ramus), usually plur., *twigs, branches, brushwood,* Ov

rāmentum -i, n (for radmentum, from rado, as caementum from caedo) **I.** *a shaving, splinter, chip,* Lucr **II.** Transf., *a bit, morsel,* aurum cum ramento, *every halfpenny,* Plaut

rāmĕus -a -um (ramus), *of or relating to branches,* fragmenta, *brushwood,* Verg

rāmex -ĭcis, m **I.** *a rupture,* Plin **II.** ramices, *the blood-vessels of the lungs, the lungs,* Plaut

Ramnes ĭum, m (from ROM -us, Romulus), and **Ramnenses** ĭum, m **I.** *one of the three tribes into which the early Roman citizens were divided by Romulus according to their nationality* (Ramnes, the Latin stem, Titian, the Sabine, Luceres, the Etruscan), *and hence the name of one of the three centuries of cavalry instituted by Romulus* **II.** Poet., transf. = *nobles,* Hor

rāmōsus -a um (ramus), *full of boughs, branching, branchy.* **I.** Lit., arbor, Liv. **II.** Poet., transf., hydra ramosa natis e caede colubris, *the hydra, from whose trunk, as from a tree, grew young serpents,* Ov

rāmŭlus -i, m (dim of ramus), *a little branch, twig,* Cic

rāmus -i, m **I.** *a bough, branch, twig* **A.** Lit., in quibus non truncus, non rami, non folia, Cic **B.** Meton., **a,** *the fruit growing on a bough,* rami atque venatu alebat, Verg., **b,** *a branch of a stag's antlers,* Caes **II.** Transf., **1,** *branch of a mountain range,* Plin; **2,** rami, *the arms of the Greek letter Y, regarded by the Pythagoreans as symbolical of the two paths of life,* Samii rami, Pers

rāna ae, f *a frog* **I.** Lit., Verg., rana turpis, *a toad,* Hor **II.** Transf., rana marina, *a sea-fish* (Lophius piscatorius, Linn.), Cic

rancĕo, *to stink,* only in partic., **rancens** -entis, *stinking, putrid,* Lucr

rancĭdŭlus a -um (dim of rancidus) **I.** *somewhat stinking, putrid,* Juv **II.** Transf., *loathsome,* Pers

rancĭdus -a -um (ranceo), *stinking, rank* **I** Lit., aper, Hor **II.** Transf., *disgusting, offensive,* Juv

rānuncŭlus -i, m (dim of rana) **I.** *a little frog, a tadpole,* Cic., in jest, used of the inhabitants of Ulubrae which was near the Pomptine Marshes, Cic **II** *a plant,* perhaps *crowfoot,* Plin

rāpa ae, f = rapum (q v)

răpācĭda -ae, m (rapax), *a robber,* Plaut

răpācĭtas ātis, f (rapax), *greediness, rapacity,* quis in rapacitate avarior? Cic

răpax -ācis (rapio) **I.** *seizing to oneself, bearing or snatching away, furious, violent* **A.** Lit., ventus, Ov; fluvius, Lucr **B.** Transf., *grasping, prone to grasp,* nihil est appetentius, similius sui, nec rapacius quam natura, Cic **II.** *plundering, greedy of plunder* Subst., *a robber*: **a,** of persons, Cic., **b,** of animals, lupus, Hor; **c,** of abstr. personif., mors, Tib; Orcus, Hor

răphănīnus -a -um (ῥαφάνινος), *of radishes, made from radishes,* Plin

răphănītĭs -ĭdis, f (ῥαφανῖτις), *a sword-lily,* Plaut

răphănus -i, m and f (ῥάφανος), *a radish,* Cat

răpĭdē, adv (rapidus), *hurriedly, quickly, rapidly* **I.** Lit., rapide dilapsus fluvius, Cic **II.** Transf., quod quum rapide fertur, Cic

răpĭdĭtas ātis, f (rapidus), *rapid flow, rapidity,* fluminis, Caes

răpĭdus -a -um (rapio), *tearing, seizing* **I. a,** of living beings, *violent, savage,* ferae, Ov., **b,** of things, *consuming, devouring,* sol, Verg **II.** Of motion, *hurried, hasty, quick, rapid,* **1, a,** of living beings, Achates, Verg., equus, Ov., **b,** of things, amnis, Hor., torrens, Verg., **2,** transf., oratio, Cic

răpīna ae, f (rapio) **I.** Lit., *robbery, plundering, pillage,* gen in plur., Cic **II.** Meton., *booty, plunder,* Verg

răpĭo -răpŭi raptum, 3 (stem RAP, Gk APΠ in ἁρπάζω), *to snatch* **I.** Gen., **A.** Lit., **a,** *to snatch to oneself, seize hastily,* bipennem dextrā, Verg., **b,** *to drag away hastily,* corpus consulis, Liv., **c,** *to hurry away, lead away with haste, hurry off,* aliquem hinc, Liv., manipulos aliquot in primam aciem secum rapit, Verg., reflex., se rapere hinc ocius, *to hasten away,* Hor., inde se ad urbem, id est ad caedem optimi cujusque, Cic., **d,** (α) *to conquer hastily, overpower,* castra urbesque primo impetu, Liv., (β) *to hasten through,* densa ferarum tecta, Verg. **B.** Transf., **a,** *to snatch, to enjoy or use in haste,* occasionem de die, Hor., **b,** *to accomplish in haste, to hasten,* viam, Ov., nuptias, Liv **II.** *to take* or *snatch away by force* **A.** Lit., **a,** *to snatch away, carry off,* pilam, Cic., **b,** *to drag away by force, lead away,* in jus ad regem, Liv; e carcere ad palum et ad necem, Cic., **c,** *to carry off as plunder, to seize, rob,* quantum rapere potuisset, Cic., virgines, Cic. Subst., (α) **rapta** -ae, f *she that is carried off,* Ov., (β) **raptum** -i, n *that which is carried off, plunder, booty,* rapto gaudere, Liv., **d,** = diripere, *to plunder,* Armeniam, Tac., **e,** *to carry off prematurely,* of death or disease, improvisa leti vis rapuit gentes, Hor **B.** Transf., **a,** *to seize for oneself*; commoda ad se, Cic., **b,** *to carry off, take away,* almum quae rapit hora diem, Hor., **c,** *to carry away, lead astray,* ipsae res verba rapiunt, Cic., rapi in invidiam, Cic., **d,** *to transport, carry away*; in a bad sense, animus cupidine caecus ad inceptum scelus rapiebat, Sall., in a good sense, ad divinarum rerum cognitionem curā omni studioque rapi, Cic. (archaic fut perf., rapsit, ap Cic)

raptim, adv (raptus, from rapio), *violently, hastily, quickly, hurriedly,* haec scripsi raptim, Cic

raptĭo -ōnis f (rapio), *a carrying off, abduction,* Ter

rapto, 1 (intens of rapio) **I.** *to carry away in haste, hurry away,* huc illuc vexilla, Tac., transf., of things, me Parnasi deserta per ardua raptat amor, Verg **II.** *to carry off from, drag away violently* **A.** Lit., **a,** conjugem, Cic; Hectora circa muros, Verg., nubila caeli, Lucr; **b,** *to rob, plunder,* Tac. **B.** Fig., **a,** *to drag along*;

quid raptem in crimina divos, accuse, Prop , **b,** *to hurry along with passion*, Plaut

raptor -ōris, m (rapio). **A.** Lit., **a,** *a robber, plunderer*, Tac , attrib , lupi raptores, *ravenous*, Verg , **b,** *an abductor, ravisher*, Ov **B.** Transf , raptores alieni honoris, Ov

raptus -ūs, m (rapio) **I.** *a tearing off, rending away*, Ov **II. 1,** *a carrying off, abduction, rape*, Cic , **2,** *plundering*, Tac

rāpŭlum -i, n (dim of rapum), *a little turnip*, Hor

rāpum i, n (ῥάπυς), *a turnip*, Liv

rārō, adv. (rarus), *rarely, seldom*, Plaut

rārēfăcio -fēci -factum 3 (rarus and facio), *to make thin, rarefy* Lucr

rāresco, 3 (rarus) **I.** *to become thin to lose density*, humor aquai ab aestu, Lucr , ubi angusti rarescunt claustra Pelori, *open themselves, expand*, Verg **II.** Transf , *to become rarer, to diminish, to lessen*, paulatim rarescunt montes, Tac

rārĭtas ātis, f (rarus) **I** *want of density, thinness, looseness of texture, distance apart*, Cic **II.** Transf , *fewness, rarity*, dictorum, Cic

rārō, adv (rarus), *seldom, rarely*, ita raro, Cic , quod si rarius fiet, Cic

rārus a um, *loose in texture, loose, wide apart, thin* (opp densus) **I.** Lit , retia, Verg , cribrum, Ov **II.** Transf , **A. a,** *scattered, scanty, far apart*, vides habitari in terra raris et angustis in locis, Cic , **b,** milit t t , *scattered, wide apart, dispersed* (opp confertus), ipsi ex silvis rari propugnabant, Caes **B. 1,** gen , **a,** *few in number, rare*, raris ac prope nullis portibus, Caes , in omni arte optimum quidque rarissimum, Cic , Oceanus raris navibus aditur, Tac., neut plur subst , rara (anteponuntur) vulgaribus, Cic , **b,** of a man that does something rarely, nec Iliacos coetus nisi rarus adibat, *seldom*, Ov ; **2,** esp , *rare, extraordinary, distinguished in its kind*, rara quidem facie sed rarior arte canendi, Ov

rāsĭlis e (rado), *scraped, having a smooth surface, polished*, torno rasile buxum Verg

raster tri, m and **rastrum** -i n (rado), plur , gen **rastri** ōrum, m *an instrument for scraping, a toothed hoe, a rake, a mattock*, Verg

rătĭo -ōnis, f (reor), *a reckoning account, computation, calculation* **I A.** Lit , (α) sing , eius pecuniae, cuius ratio in aede Opis confecta est, Cic , auri ratio constat, *comes right, is correct*, Cic , rationem ducere, *to compute, calculate*, Cic , rationem referre, *give in an account*, Cic , (β) plur , rationes cum aliquo putare, Cic , rationes subducere, *to close*, Cic **B.** Transf , **1,** *a roll, register, a list, catalogue account*, rationem carceris, quae diligentissime conficitur, Cic , **2,** *a sum, number*, Plaut , **3,** *a business transaction, matter, affair*, de tota illa ratione atque re Gallicana, Cic , haec res non solum ex domestica est ratione, attingit etiam bellicam, Cic , fori iudiciique rationem Messala suscepit, *public and legal business*, Cic , meae (tuae, etc) rationes, *my (thy, etc) interest, advantage*, rationes meas vestrae saluti anteposuissem, Cic **II.** Fig , **A.** *an account, reckoning, calculation*, rationem habere, *to make a calculation*, Cic ; semper ita vivamus ut rationem reddendam nobis arbitremur, Cic **B.** Transf , **1, a,** *a relation with, reference to*, rationem habere, aliquid rationis habere cum aliquo, *to have relations with*, Cic , quae ratio tibi cum eo intercesserit? Cic , **b,** *respect, consideration, regard for anything*, vel dignitatis vel commodi rationem habere, Cic , suam rationem ducere, *to consider his own advantage* Cic , **c,** *plan, mode of procedure, method, manner, fashion, nature, kind, way*, ita fiet ut tua ista ratio existimetur astuta Cic , scribendi consilium ratioque, Cic , meae vitae rationes ab ineunte aetate susceptae, Cic , rationes belli gerendi, *principles*, Caes , **2,** esp , *the faculty of mind which calculates and plans, the reason*, homo rationis particeps, Cic , mens et ratio et consilium Cic , consilio et ratione, Cic ratio est, *it seems reasonable*, with infin , Cic , hence **a,** *reason, motive, ground*, (α) nostri confirmare argumentis ac rationibus, Cic , consilii causa ratioque, Cic , (β) rhet t t *ground or reason brought forward to support a proposition*, Cic , **b,** meton , *reasonableness, propriety, method, order, rule*, modo et ratione omnia facere, *moderately and reasonably*, Cic , **c,** *principle, view, tendency*, florens homo in populari ratione, *the most distinguished representative of the democratic view*, Cic , **d,** *theory, doctrine, system, knowledge*, Epicuri ratio, *philosophical system*, Cic , de ratione vivendi, *the art of living*, Cic , **e,** meton , *a view, opinion*, quam in eam rationem quisque loquatur, Cic , **f,** *an adducing of proof, reasoning*, concludatur igitur ratio, Cic

rătĭōcĭnātĭo ōnis, f (ratiocinor) **I.** *a careful and deliberate consideration and conclusion*, Cic **II** *a reasoning, ratiocination, argument, syllogism*, Cic

rătĭōcĭnātīvus -a -um (ratiocinor), *argumentative syllogistic*, Cic

rătĭōcĭnātor -ōris, m (ratiocinor), *a calculator, accountant*, Cic

rătĭōcĭnor, 1 dep (ratio), **1,** *to compute, calculate*, Cic , **2,** *to argue, infer, conclude*, inter se, with acc and infin , Cic

rătĭōnālis e (ratio), *reasonable, rational*, Quint

rătĭōnārĭum ii, n (ratio), *a statistical account*, imperii, Suet

rătis -is, f **I.** *a raft*, Cic , Caes , ratibus, quibus iunxerat flumen, resolutis, Liv , sing , collect = *a bridge of boats*, Liv **II.** Poet , transf , *a ship, boat, vessel*, Verg

rătĭuncŭla ae, f (dim of ratio) **I.** *a little reckoning, account*, Plaut **II.** Transf , **A.** *a poor, insufficient reason* huic incredibili sententiae ratiunculas suggerit, Cic **B.** *a petty syllogism*, concludunt ratiunculas Stoici, Cic

rătus a um, p adj (from reor) **I** *reckoned, calculated*, pro rata parte, or simply pro rata, *according to a fixed proportion, in proportion, proportionally*, Cic **II.** Transf , *determined, fixed, settled*, **a,** rati astrorum ordines, Cic , **b,** *valid, fixed, legal* id iussum ratum ac firmum futurum, Cic , ratum facere, *to ratify, confirm, make valid*, Cic , ratum habere ducere *to consider valid*, Cic , aliquid mihi ratum est, *I approve*, Cic

raucĭsŏnus a -um (raucus and sonus), *hoarse, hoarsely sounding*, Lucr

raucĭtas -ātis, f (raucus), *hoarseness*, Plin

raucus -a um (for ravicus, connected with ravis), *hoarse* **I.** Lit , **A.** *hoarse through illness*, fauces, Lucr **B** a, *hoarse through shouting*, nos raucos saepe attentissime audiri video, Cic , of birds, *screaming*, cornix, Lucr , palumbes, *cooing*, Verg , **b,** of sound, vox ranarum, Ov **II.** Poet , transf , *hoarse, hollow-sounding, deep or dull sounding*, cornu, Plaut , murmur undae, Verg

Raudĭus a -um, *Raudian*, Raudius Campus, and Raudii Campi, *a plain in Upper Italy, where Marius defeated the Cimbri*

raudus (rōdus, rūdus) ĕris, n *a rough*

mass or lump; esp., a piece of brass used as a coin, Liv.

raudusculum -i, n. (dim. of raudus), *a small sum of money;* transf., de raudusculo Numeriano, *the little debt of Numerius*, Cic.

Raurĭci -ōrum, m. *a Celtic people in Gaul, near modern Basle.*

Răvenna -ae, f. *a town in Gallia Cispadana, near the Adriatic, made a naval station by Augustus, now Ravenna.* Hence, **Răvennās** -ātis, m. *belonging to Ravenna.*

rāvĭo, 4. (ravis), *to talk oneself hoarse*, Plaut.

rāvis -is, f. (connected with raucus), *hoarseness*, Plaut.

rāvus -a -um, *grey, greyish*, Hor.

rĕ- prep. insepar., meaning sometimes *back*, as in recurro; sometimes *against*, as in reluctor; sometimes *again*, as restituo (orig. form red, which appears before vowels, e.g., redeo, sometimes lengthened, as redi-vivus).

1. **rĕa**, v. reus.

2. **Rēa** = Rhea (q.v.).

rēapsĕ, adv. (re and eapse, i.e., eā and suff. -pse), *indeed, in truth, really*, Cic.

Rĕātĕ, n. (defect., with same form for nom., acc., and abl.), *an old town in the Sabine country*, now *Rieti*. Adj., **Rĕātinus** -a -um, *Reatine;* subst., **Rĕātīni** -ōrum, m. *the people of Reate.*

rĕātus -ūs, m. (reus), *the state* or *condition of an accused person*, Mart.

rĕbellātĭo, = rebellio (q.v.).

rĕbellātrix -icis, f. (rebello), *renewing war, rising again;* Germania, Ov.

rĕbellĭo -ōnis, f. (rebellis), *a renewal of war by a conquered people;* rebellionem facere, Caes. Plur., Carthaginiensium rebelliones, Cic.

rĕbellis -e (re and bellum), *renewing a war, insurgent;* **1**, lit., colonia, Tac.; **2**, fig., amor, Ov.

rĕbellĭum = rebellio (q.v.).

rĕbello, 1. *to renew a war;* **a**, lit., septies rebellare, Liv.; **b**, poet., transf., *to renew the fight*, Ov.

rĕbīto, 3. *to go back, return*, Plaut.

rĕbŏo, 1. *to echo, resound*, Verg.

rĕcalcitro, 1. of a horse, *to kick backwards;* fig., *to deny access*, Hor.

rĕcălĕfăcĭo = recalfacio (q.v.).

rĕcălĕo, 2. *to be warm again;* recalent nostro Tiberina fluenta sanguine, Verg.

rĕcălesco -călŭi, 3. (recaleo), *to become warm again;* quum motu atque exercitatione recalescunt corpora, Cic.; fig., mens recalescit, Ov.

rĕcalfăcĭo (rĕcălĕfăcĭo) -fēci -factum, 3. *to make warm again*, Ov.

rĕcandesco -candŭi, 3. **I.** *to grow white;* recanduit unda, Ov. **II.** Transf., *to become hot, to begin to glow.* **A.** Lit., (tellus) recanduit aestu, Ov. **B.** Fig., recanduit ira, Ov.

rĕcanto, 1. **I.** Intransit., *to resound, echo*, Mart. **II.** Transit., **A.** *to recall, recant;* recantata opprobria, Hor. **B.** *to charm away;* curas, Ov.

rĕcēdo -cessi -cessum, 3. **I.** *to go back, draw back, recede, retreat, retire.* **A. 1**, lit., of persons, ex eo loco, Caes.; non modo e Gallia non discessisse, sed ne a Mutina quidem recessisse, Cic.; **2**, transf., of things, **a**, ut illae undae ad alios accedant, ab aliis autem recedant, Cic.; **b**, of places, *to retire, stand back;* Anchisae domus recessit, Verg.; **c**, *to recede in the distance, disappear from the view;* provehimur portu, terraeque urbesque recedunt, Verg. **B.** Fig., **1**, of persons, in otia tuta, Hor.; **2**, of things, anni recedentes, Hor. **II.** *to go away, depart, go to a distance.* **A. 1**, lit., of living beings, nec vero a stabulis recedunt longius (apes), Verg.; **2**, transf., of inanimate things, **a**, *to separate from;* recedit caput e cervice, Ov.; **b**, *to vanish, disappear;* in ventos vita or anima exhalata recessit, Verg., Ov. **B.** Fig., **1**, of persons, **a**, *to depart from, abandon;* ab officio, Cic.; **b**, *to depart from, give up, renounce;* ab armis, *to lay down arms*, Cic.; a vita, Cic.; **2**, transf., of things, **a**, *to depart from, lose;* res ab usitata consuetudine recessit, Cic.; **b**, *to vanish, disappear, cease;* et pariter Phoebes pariter maris ira recessit, Ov.; **c**, recedere ab aliquo, *to pass away from, be lost;* quum res (*property*) ab eo quicum contraxisset, recessisset et ad heredem pervenisset, Cic.

rĕcello, 3. *to spring back, fly back, bend back;* quum (ferrea) manus gravi libramento recelleret ad solum, Liv.

rĕcens -entis, *new, fresh, young, recent.* **I.** Adj., **A.** Lit., (α) absol., caespes, Caes.; his recentibus viris, *men of modern times*, Cic. Subst., recentiores, *later authors*, Cic.; recenti re, recenti negotio, *while the business is still fresh*, Cic.; injuriarum memoria, Caes.; (β) with ab and the abl., *fresh from, soon after, a little subsequent to;* Homerus, qui recens ab illorum aetate fuit, Cic.; (γ) with ex and the abl., quum e provincia recens esset, Cic.; (δ) with abl. alone, praeturā, Tac.; with abl. of name of town, Regini quidam eo venerunt, Romā sane recentes, *direct from Rome*, Cic. **B.** Transf., of strength, *fresh, vigorous;* of soldiers, integri et recentes, Caes.; of horses, Liv.; of things, animus (consulis), Liv. (abl. sing., gen. recenti, in poets sometimes recente; genit. plur., gen. recentium, in poets sometimes recentum). **II.** Adv., *lately, recently;* sole recens orto, Verg.; recens ad Regillum lacum accepta clades, Liv.

rĕcensĕo -censŭi -censītum and -censum, 2. *to review, muster, examine.* **I.** Lit., milit. t. t., exercitum, legiones, Liv.; polit. t. t., of the censor, equites, Liv. **II.** Transf., **A.** *to go through, pass through;* signa (of the sun), Ov. **B.** Esp., **1**, *to go over in thought, review;* fataque fortunasque virûm, Ov.; **2**, *to go over in words, recount;* fortia facta, Ov.

rĕcensĭo -ōnis, f. (recenseo), *a reviewing, mustering, enumeration by the censor*, Cic.

rĕcensus -ūs, m. (recenseo) = recensio, *a reviewing, mustering;* equitum recensum habere, *of the censor*, Liv.

rĕceptācŭlum -i, n. (recepto). **I.** *a magazine, reservoir, receptacle;* cibi et potionis (of the stomach), Cic.; cloaca maxima receptaculum omnium purgamentorum urbis, Liv. **II.** Esp., *a place of refuge, shelter, retreat:* militum Catilinae, Cic.; receptaculum esse classibus nostris, Cic.; fugientibus, Liv.

rĕceptĭo -ōnis, f. (recipio), *a receiving, reception*, Plaut.

rĕcepto, 1. (intens. of recipio). **I. A.** *to draw back;* **1**, transit., hastam, Verg.; **2**, reflex., se receptare, *to retire;* Saturni sese quo stella receptet, Verg. **B.** *to receive back*, Lucr. **II.** *to receive frequently;* mercatores, Liv.

rĕceptor -ōris, m. (recipio), *one who receives or harbours, a harbourer;* praedarum, Tac.; transf., ipse ille latronum occultator et receptor locus, Cic.

rĕceptrix -trīcis, f. (receptor), *a receiver* (of stolen goods); furtorum, Cic.

rĕceptus -ūs, m. (recipio). **I.** *a drawing back.* **A.** Lit., spiritus, Quint. **B.** Fig., *re-*

tractation, recantation, nimis pertinacis sententiae, Liv **II. A. a**, *a retreat*, non tutissimus a malis consiliis receptus, Liv, **b**, esp, *recourse to*, receptus ad Caesaris gratiam atque amicitiam, Caes **B.** Milit t t, *a retreat, falling back*, ut expeditum ad suos receptum habeant, Caes, Caesar receptui cani jussit, *ordered the signal of retreat*, Caes, fig, canere receptui a miseriis, Cic

rĕcessim, adv (recedo), *backwards*, Plaut

rĕcessus -ūs, m (recedo) **I.** *a going back, receding, retreating*, **1**, lit, lunae accessus et recessus, Cic, (aestuum maritimorum) accessus et recessus, *ebb and flow*, Cic, recessum primis ultimi non dabant, *chance of retreating*, Caes; **2**, fig., accessum ad res salutares, a pestiferis recessum *disinclination for*, Cic, ut metus recessum quendam animi et fugam efficiat, Cic. **II.** Meton, **1**, lit, **a**, *a hollow, recess*, Verg, **b**, *a place of retreat, quiet, retired place*, mihi solitudo et recessus provinciae est, Cic, **2**, fig, in animis hominum tanti sunt recessus, *corners, intricacies*, Cic

rĕcidīvus a -um (recido), *returning, repeated*, poet, Pergama, *rebuilt*, Verg

1 **rĕcĭdo** -cidi -cāsūrus, 3 (re and cado) **I.** *to fall back* **A.** Lit., recidunt omnia in terras, Cic **B.** Transf, **1, a**, *to relapse, sink*, in graviorem morbum, *to relapse*, Liv, in eandem fortunam, Cic, **b**, *to fall to*, cum ad eum potentatus omnis recidisset, Cic, **c**, *to fall upon, reach*, hunc casum ad ipsos recidere posse, Cic, esp, *to fall on the head of*, ut amentiae poena in ipsum eiusque familiam recidat, Cic, **2**, *to come to, fall to, sink to*, Cic, **3**, *to fall, happen, occur, light upon*, illa omnia ex laetitia ad lacrimas reciderunt, Cic; ad nihilum, *to come to naught*, Cic **II. 1**, *to fall into, to become*, quorsum recidat responsum tuum non magno opere laboro, Cic, **2**, *to fall within a certain time*, in nostrum annum, Cic

2 **rĕcīdo** -cīdi -cīsum, 3 (re and caedo). **I.** *to cut off, cut away*, **1**, caput, Ov, ceras inanes, Verg, **2**, transf, *to extirpate*, nationes, Cic **II.** *to cut away*, **1**, lit, barbam falce, Ov, **2**, transf, *to cut away, lop off, abbreviate, retrench*; ambitiosa ornamenta, Hor

rĕcingo -cinxi -cinctum, 3 *to ungird*, tunicas, Ov, pass as middle, recingor, *I ungird myself*, Ov

rĕcino, 3 (re and cano), *to resound, echo* **I.** Intransit., in vocibus nostrorum oratorum recinit quiddam et resonat urbanius, Cic, parra recinens, *shrieking*, Hor **II.** Transit, *to cause to resound*, **a**, of echo, cuius recinet jocosa nomen imago, *re echo*, Hor, **b**, of a poet, *to praise loudly on the lyre*, curva lyra Latonam, Hor

rĕcĭpĭo cēpi -ceptum, 3 (re and capio) **I.** *to take back* **A.** *to draw back, fetch back*, **1**, lit, **a**, of things, ensem, *to draw back, draw out*, Verg, **b**, of pers, aliquem medio ex hoste, Verg, esp as milit t t, *to draw back, cause to retreat*, milites defessos, Caes, reflex, se recipere, *to withdraw, retire, retreat, betake oneself to any place*, se ex hisce locis, Cic, se ad nos, Cic, esp as milit t t, se hinc, se inde, se ex aliquo loco, se ad or in aliquem locum, se aliquo ad aliquem, Caes, **2**, transf, **a**, vocem ab acutissimo sono usque ad gravissimum sonum, Cic, reflex, se recipere, *to turn to, to have recourse to*, se ad bonam frugem, Cic; se ad reliquam cogitationem belli, Caes, **b**, business t t, *to keep back, retain, reserve a portion*, ruta caesa, Cic, sibi aliquid, Cic, **c**, *to seize out of the hands of the enemy*, aliquem ex hostibus, Liv **B.** *to take back, receive again, receive*, **1**, lit, merita, Cic; arma, Liv, obsides, Caes, so *to reduce again by conquest, to recover*, Tarentum, Cic suas res amissas, Liv, **2**, transf, *to recover*, antiquam frequentiam, Liv, vitam herbis fortibus, Ov, animos ex pavore, *to regain courage*, Liv **II.** *to receive, accept, take to oneself*, **1**, lit, **a**, *to take in to oneself*, ferrum, gladium, *to receive the death-wound*, Cic, necesse erat ab latere aperto tela recipi, Caes, of animals, frenum, Hor, of rivers, Mosa parte quadam ex Rheno accepta quae, etc, Caes, **b**, *to receive into a place*, (α) with acc alone, of persons, Xerxen, Cic; aliquem libentissimo animo, Caes., of places, hos tutissimus portus recipiebat, Caes, (β) with ad and the acc, aliquem ad epulas, Cic, (γ) with in and the acc, Tarquinium in civitatem, Cic, (δ) with abl alone, exercitum tectis ac sedibus suis, Cic, (ε) with acc of place, aliquem domum suam, Cic, (ζ) with supine, senem sessum, Cic, (η) absol, qui receperant, Caes, **c**, *to take possession of, conquer*, oppidum, civitatem, Caes, **d**, *to receive money*, pecuniam ex novis vectigalibus, Cic, **2**, transf, **a**, *to receive into a certain rank or position*, aliquem in ordinem senatorium, Cic; aliquem in fidem, Cic, **b**, *to receive, accept, admit, allow*, fabulas, *to believe*, Cic, nec inconstantiam virtus recipit, *admits, allows of*, Cic, **c**, *to accept a task, undertake, take upon oneself*, causam Siculorum, Cic, officium, Cic, **d** hence, *to accept an obligation, guarantee, promise, be responsible for*, pro Cassio et te, si quid me velitis recipere, recipiam, Cic, ea quae tibi promitto ac recipio, Cic, partic subst, **rĕceptum** i, n *an engagement, guarantee*, **e**, legal t t, of the praetor, recipere nomen, *to entertain, receive an accusation against any one*, Cic

rĕcĭprŏcātĭo -ōnis, f (reciproco), *a returning by the same path*, Plin

rĕcĭprŏco, 1 (reciprocus) **I** Transit, *to move backwards, to move backwards and forwards*, animam, *to draw in and breathe out the air, to breathe*, Liv, quinqueremem in adversum aestum reciprocari non posse, *turned round and moved back*, Liv, esp of the ebb tide, in motu reciprocando, *of the ebb*, Cic, fig, si quidem ista reciprocantur, *if the proposition is converted or reversed*, Cic **II.** Intransit, *to move backwards and forwards*, fretum Euripi non septies die temporibus statis reciprocat, *ebbs and flows*, Liv

rĕcĭprŏcus -a -um, *returning, going back in the same path* **I.** Lit., mare, *ebbing*, Tac, vox, *echoing*, Plin **II.** Fig, ars, *alternating*, Plin

rĕcīsāmentum i, n (recido), *a chip, shaving*, Plin

rĕcīsĭo -ōnis, f (recido), *a cutting off*, Plin

rĕcīsus -a -um, partic of recido

rĕcĭtātĭo ōnis, f (recito), *a reading aloud*, **a**, of documents in legal proceedings, Cic, **b**, of literary works, Plin

rĕcĭtātor -ōris, m (recito), *a reader aloud*, **a**, of documents in legal proceedings Cic, **b**, of literary works, *a reciter*, Hor

rĕcĭto, 1 *to read, read aloud, read publicly*, **a**, legal t t, (α) *to read a document*, litteras in senatu, in contione, Cic, aliquid ex codice, Cic, (β) *to read out the name of a person*, testamento heredem aliquem, Cic, aliquem praeterire in recitando senatu, *in reading the list of senators*, Cic, (γ) *to read the words of an oath, to dictate*, Tac, **b**, *to read or recite one's literary works before friends*, Hor

rĕclāmātĭo ōnis, f (reclamo), *a crying out against, loud disapprobation*, Cic

rĕclāmĭto, 1 (intens of reclamo), *to cry out against loudly, violently contradict*, Cic

rĕclāmo, 1 *to cry out against, shout in disapprobation, contradict loudly* **I. A.** Lit, (a) absol., Cic.; (β) with dat. of pers., alicui, Cic.; of things, orationi, Cic.; alicuius promissis, Cic.; (γ) with ne and the subj., unā voce omnes judices, ne is juraret, reclamasse, Cic. **B.** Fig., quoniam ratio reclamat vera, Lucr. **II.** Poet., transf., *to reverberate, re-echo, resound;* with dat., scopulis reclamant aequora, Verg.

rĕclīnis -e (reclino), *leaning backwards, bent backwards, reclining,* Ov.

rĕclīno, 1. (re and * clino), *to bend back, cause to lean back.* **I.** Lit., se, Caes.; scuta, Verg.; **rĕclīnātus** -a -um, *bent back, reclined,* Caes. **II.** Transf., nullum ab labore me reclinat otium, *releases me from labour,* Hor.

rĕclūdo -clūsi -clūsum, 3. (re and claudo), *to unclose, to open.* **I. A.** Lit., portas hosti, Ov. **B.** Transf., **1,** *to bring to light, to disclose, reveal;* viam, Ov.; tellurem unco dente, *to turn over, cultivate,* Verg.; ensem, *to draw from the scabbard,* Verg.; **2,** *to open with a weapon = to pierce;* pectus mucrone, Verg. **II.** Fig., ebrietas operta recludit, *reveals,* Hor.; fata, *to relax,* Hor.

rĕcōgĭto, 1. *to think over again, consider, deliberate upon;* de re, Cic.

rĕcognĭtĭo -ōnis, f. (recognosco). **I.** *recollection;* scelerum suorum, Cic. **II.** *investigation, inspection, examining;* agri Campani, Liv.

rĕcognosco -nōvi -nĭtum, 3. **I. A.** *to recognise, to know again;* res, *as one's property,* Liv.; illa reminiscendo, Cic. **B.** *to recall, to go over again;* recognosce mecum noctem illam, Cic. **II. a,** *to inspect, examine, investigate;* agros, Liv.; **b,** *to examine critically, to revise, authenticate, certify;* decretum populi, Cic.; codicem, Cic.

rĕcollĭgo -lēgi -lectum, 3. *to collect again, gather together again;* fig., se, *to regain courage,* Ov.; primos annos, *to become young again,* Ov.; animum alicuius, *to reconcile,* Cic.

rĕcŏlo -cŏlŭi -cultum, 3. *to cultivate again.* **I.** Lit., desertam terram, Liv. **II.** Fig., **A.** Gen., **1,** *to practise again, resume;* artes, Cic.; studia, Cic.; **2,** *to set up again, renew, repair;* imagines subversas, Tac.; dignitatem, Cic.; **3,** *to honour again;* aliquem sacerdotiis, Tac. **B.** Esp., **1,** *to reflect upon again;* inclusas animas lustrabat studio recolens, Verg.; **2,** *to recollect, think over again;* quae si tecum ipse recolis, Cic.; **3,** *to call to mind, remember again,* Ov.

rĕcommĭniscor, 3. dep. *to recollect,* Plaut.

rĕcompōno (-pŏsŭi) -pŏsĭtum, 3. *to readjust, re-arrange;* comas, Ov.

rĕconcĭlĭātĭo -ōnis, f. (reconcilio). **I.** *a restoration, re-establishment;* concordiae, Cic. **II.** *reconciliation;* irridebatur haec illius reconciliatio, Cic.

rĕconcĭlĭātor -ōris, m. (reconcilio), *a restorer, re-establisher;* pacis, Liv.

rĕconcĭlĭo, 1. **I. A.** *to make good again, restore, repair;* diuturni laboris detrimentum sollertiā et virtute militum brevi reconciliatur, Caes. **B.** *to re-unite, bring together again;* **a,** inimicos in gratiam, Cic.; **b,** *to appease, to reconcile;* aliquem alicui, Cic. **II.** *to restore, re-establish;* existimationem judiciorum, Cic.

rĕconcinno, 1. *to restore, renovate, repair;* tribus locis aedifico, reliqua reconcinno, Cic.

rĕcondĭtus -a -um, p. adj. (from recondo), *far removed, secret, concealed.* **I.** Lit., locus, Cic.; neut. plur., occulta et recondita templi, *secret recesses,* Caes. **II.** Fig., **a,** *abstruse, profound;* reconditae abstrusaeque res, Cic.; **b,** of character, *reserved, mysterious;* naturā tristi ac reconditā fuit, Cic.

rĕcondo -dĭdi -dĭtum, 3. **I.** *to lay back, put back;* gladium in vaginam, Cic.; poet., oculos, *to close again,* Ov. **II.** *to lay aside.* **A.** Gen., **1,** lit., **a,** tamquam in vagina reconditum, Cic.; **b,** of provisions, treasure, etc., *to lay up in store, keep;* prome reconditum Caecubum, Hor.; recondita alia (medicamenta), Liv.; **2,** fig., mens alia recondit, e quibus memoria oritur, *lays up in store,* Cic. **B.** *to conceal, hide;* **1,** lit., **a,** quod celari opus erat habebant sepositum ac reconditum, Cic.; Ascanium curvā valle, Verg.; **b,** *to thrust,* etc.; ensem in pulmone, Verg.; **c,** *to devour;* volucres avidā alvo, Verg.; **2,** fig., *to conceal;* voluptates, Tac.

rĕcondūco -duxi -ductum, 3. *to bargain, contract for again,* Plin.

rĕconflo, 1. *to rekindle,* Lucr.

rĕcŏquo -coxi -coctum, 3. **I.** *to boil again;* Peliam (*in order to make young again*), Cic. **II.** *to melt, smelt, forge again.* **A.** Lit., enses, Verg. **B.** Fig., recoctus scriba ex quinqueviro, *new-moulded,* Hor.

rĕcordātĭo -ōnis, f. (recordor), *a recollection, remembrance;* ultimi temporis recordatio, Cic.; plur., recordationes fugio, Cic.

rĕcordor, 1. dep. (re and cor). **I.** *to remember, recollect;* (α) with genit., flagitiorum suorum, Cic.; (β) with acc., majorum diligentiam, Cic.; (γ) with acc. and infin., hoc genus poenae saepe in improbos cives esse usurpatum, Cic.; (δ) with rel. sent., non recordor, unde ceciderim, Cic.; (ε) with de and the abl., de ceteris, Cic.; (ζ) absol., si recordari volumus, Cic. **II.** *to think of something in the future, to ponder over;* quae sum passura recordor, Ov.

rĕcrastĭno, 1. (re and crastinus), *to put off from day to day,* Plin.

rĕcrĕātĭo -ōnis, f. (recreo), *a restoration, a recovery,* Plin.

rĕcrēmentum -i, n. (cerno), *dross, slag, refuse,* Plin.

rĕcrĕo, 1. **I.** *to create again,* Lucr. **II.** *to restore to a sound condition, to refresh, invigorate, revive;* reflex., se recreare and middle, recreari, *to revive, to recover, to be refreshed;* **a,** physically, voculae recreandae causā, Cic.; recreari ex vulnere, Cic.; ex vulneribus, Liv.; **b,** politically, provinciam afflictam et perditam erigere atque recreare, Cic.; middle, civitas recreatur, Cic.; **c,** mentally, afflictos animos, Cic.; recreare se ex magno timore, *to recover from,* Cic.

rĕcrĕpo, 1. *to echo, resound,* Cat.

rĕcresco -crēvi -crētum, 3. *to grow again,* Liv.

rĕcrūdesco -crūdŭi, 3. *to become raw again.* **I.** Of wounds, *to open afresh;* quae consanuisse videbantur, recrudescunt, Cic. **II.** Fig., *to break out again;* recrudescente Manlianā seditione, Liv.

rectā, adv. (sc. viā), *straightway, straightforward, right on, directly,* Cic.

rectē, adv. (rectus). **I.** *in a straight line,* in a straight (horizontal) direction; recte ferri, Cic. **II.** Fig., *rightly, properly, well, duly, suitably.* **A. a,** of conduct, behaviour, recte atque ordine facere, judicare, Cic.; recte et vere respondere, Cic.; **b,** of condition, *well;* apud matrem recte est, *it is all right with,* Cic.; **c,** of consequence, *well, favourably, safely;* se alicui recte committere, Caes.; quicum quidvis rectissime facere posset, Cic.; recte vendere, *at a high price,* Cic. **B.** Of degree, recte ambulare, Cic.

rectĭo -ōnis, f. (rego), *a ruling, governing;* rerum publicarum, Cic.

rector -ōris, m (rego), *a ruler, governor, director guide, leader* **I.** Lit, navis, *steersman*, Cic. **II.** Fig, rector et gubernator civitatis, Cic, of deities, *ruler*, Olympi, or superum, or deûm, *Jupiter*, Ov, maris, *Neptune*, Ov

rectrix -icis, f. (rector), *she that leads or guides*, Plin

rectus a -um, p adj (from rego), *straight* (whether horizontally or vertically), *upright* **I.** **1,** lit, **a,** *in a horizontal direction, straight*, recto itinere ad Iberum contendere, Caes, rectus cursus hinc ad Africam, Liv, recti oculi, *straight, steadfast look*, Cic; **b,** of vertical direction, *upright*, ita jacĕre talum, ut rectus assistat, Cic, **2,** transf, grammat t t, casus rectus, the nom (opp casus obliquus), Quint **II.** Fig, *right, correct, proper, suitable, due*, **a,** physically and intellectually, (a) rectum et justum proelium, Liv, (β) *simple, natural, plain, straightforward*, commentarii Caesaris, Cic, (γ) *right, free from mistakes*, quae sint in artibus ac rationibus recta ac prava, Cic, neut subst, recti ac pravi numque, Cic, **b,** morally, (a) *straightforward, honest, upright*, consilia recta, Liv, conscientia recta, Cic, praetor populi Romani rectissimus, Cic, (β) *right, virtuous dutiful*, in neut subst, *right, virtue, good*, neque quid quam nisi honestum et rectum alter ab altero postulabit, Cic, rectum est, *it is right*, with acc and infin, Cic

rĕcŭbĭtus -ūs, m (recumbo), *a falling down*, Plin

rĕcŭbo, 1 *to lie back, to lie on the back, recline*, in hortulis suis, Cic

rĕcumbo cŭbŭi, 3 *to lie backwards, recline* **I.** Of persons **A.** Gen, in cubiculo, Cic, in herba, Cic **B.** Esp, *to recline at table*, in triclinio, Cic **II.** Transf, of inanimate things, *to sink down fall down*, cervix in humeros, Verg

rĕcŭpĕrātĭo -ōnis f (recupero), *a recovery*, libertatis, Cic

rĕcŭpĕrātor ōris, m. (recupero) **I.** *a recoverer*, urbis, Tac **II.** Esp, recuperatores, *a college of three or five magistrates appointed by the praetor to decide causes which required speedy settlement*, Cic

rĕcŭpĕrātōrĭus a -um (recuperator), *of or relating to the* recuperatores, judicium, Cic

rĕcŭpĕro, 1 (recipio), *to get again, regain, recover* **I.** Lit, **a,** of things, villam suam ab aliquo, Cic, urbem, Liv, amissa, Caes, rempublicam, *supremacy in the state*, Cic, **b,** of persons, obsides, Caes, Cic, si vos et me ipsum recuperaro, Cic **II.** Transf, *to win again, recover again (a person's favour)*, voluntatem alicuius, Cic

rĕcūro, 1 *to restore, refresh*, Cat

rĕcurro -curri -cursum, 3 *to run back, hasten back* **I.** **a,** lit, of persons, ad aliquem, Cic, ad redam, Cic, in Tusculanum, Cic, rure, Hor, **b,** transf of things, luna tum crescendo tum defectionibus in initia recurrendo, Cic, bruma recurrit iners, Hor, esp, of the course of the sun and the year, *to roll round*, sol recurrens, Verg **II.** Fig, **A.** Gen, naturam expellas furcā, tamen usque recurret, Hor **B.** *to come back to, return to*, ad eisdem deditionis conditiones, Caes

rĕcurso, 1 (intens of recurro), *to run back, hasten back, return* **I.** Lit, Lucr **II.** Fig, cura recursat, Verg

rĕcursus ūs, m (recurro), *a return, coming back, retreat*, **a,** of persons, Liv, **b,** of water, etc, Ov

rĕcurvo, 1 (recurvus) *to bend or curve backwards*, colla equi, Ov, aquas in caput, *make to flow back*, Ov, undae recurvatae, *winding*, Ov.

rĕcurvus a -um, *bent or curved backwards*, cornu, Verg, tectum, *labyrinth*, Ov, aera, *hooks*, Ov, nexus hederae, *winding*, Ov

rĕcūsātĭo ōnis, f (recuso) **I.** *a refusal*, Cic, adimere alicui omnem recusationem, *possibility of refusing*, Cic **II.** Legal t t, *a protest*, Cic

rĕcūso, 1 (re and causa), *to refuse, decline, reject, be unwilling to do* **I.** Gen, (a) with acc, laborem, Caes, molestias non recuso, Cic, with double acc, populum Romanum disceptatorem, Cic, transf, of things, genu cursum recusant, Verg, (β) with infin, gen with preceding negative, non recuso mori, Caes, (γ) with ne and the subj, sententiam ne diceret recusavit, Cic, (δ) when a negative precedes, with quin or quominus and the subj, non possumus quin alii a nobis dissentiant recusare, Cic, non recusabo quominus omnes mea legant, Cic, (ε) with de and the abl, de judiciis transferendis, Cic, (ζ) absol, non recuso, non abnuo, Cic **II.** Esp, legal t t, *to object, take exception, plead in defence*, quoniam satis recusavi, Cic

rĕcussus -ūs, m (recutio), *a striking back, rebound, recoil*, Plin

rĕcŭtĭo -cussi -cussum, 3 (re and quatio) *to strike back, cause to rebound*, Verg

rĕcŭtītus a -um (re and cutis) **I.** *circumcised* Judaei, Mart **II.** *smooth shorn* Mart

rēda (rhēda) and **raeda** ae, f (a Gallic word), *a travelling carriage with four wheels*, vehi in reda, Cic

rĕdambŭlo, 1 *to walk back*, Plaut

rĕdămo, 1 *to love again, return love for love*, Cic

rĕdardesco, 3 *to break out again* (into flames), Ov

rĕdargŭo gŭi -gūtum, 3 *to confute, refute, disprove, contradict*, **a,** of persons, redargue me, si mentior, Cic, **b,** of things as objects, referre et redarguere mendacium alicuius, Cic, with things as subjects, improborum prosperitates redarguunt vires deorum, Cic

rēdārius ii, m (reda), *the driver of a reda, coachman*, Cic

rĕdauspĭco, 1 *to take fresh auspices*, jestingly = *to return*, Plaut

redditĭo -ōnis, f (reddo), *the consequent clause of a sentence, apodosis*, Quint

reddo didi -ditum, 3 **I.** *to give back, restore* **1,** *to restore* (the same object), (a) of concr obj, obsides, captivos, Caes, equos, Cic, alicui pecuniam, Cic, reflex, se reddere convivio, *to return to*, Liv, se terris, Verg, so pass, reddi, as middle, reddar tenebris, *I shall return to*, Verg, (β) of abstr obj, alicui patriam, Liv; **2,** *to give back something as an equivalent, to give back, requite, repay*, **a,** gen, (a) of concr obj, oscula, Ov, (β) of abstr obj, beneficium, Cic, pro vita hominis vitam, Caes, **b,** esp, (a) *to give back in another language = to translate, render, interpret*, quum ea quae legeram Graece, Latine redderem, Cic, (β) *to give back in utterances, to imitate*, verba bene (of a parrot), Ov, *to answer*, veras audire et reddere voces, Verg, **3,** *to represent, imitate, reflect, resemble*, qui te nomine reddet Silvius Aeneas, Verg, **4,** *to make, render cause to be*, with double acc aliquid or aliquem, foll by an adj, aliquem iratum, Cic, itinera infesta, Caes, with a subst, aliquem avem, Ov **II.** *to give forth from oneself, to give out*, **1,** *to give what is due or asked for or settled*, **a,** suum cuique, Cic, honorem, Cic, caute vota, *to fulfil*, Cic; rationem alicui, *to render an account*, Cic, so also (α) of the dying, eum spiritum, quem naturae debeo, patriae reddere, Cic, vitam naturae, Cic, (β) of persons sacrificing, *to offer*, liba deae, Ov, (γ) of persons writing or speaking, *to communicate*, sed perge, Pomponi, de Caesare et redde quae restant, Cic, **b**, (α) *to give, bestow, grant*, responsa, Verg, peccatis veniam, Hor, legal t t, reddere judicium, *to grant or appoint a judicial inquiry*, in aliquem, Caes, reddere jus, *to administer justice, pronounce sentence*, alicui petenti, Caes, (β) *to grant, allow, leave*, Thermitanis urbem, agros legesque suas, Cic, **2**, *to give forth from the body*, **a**, *to give out, give forth* (animam) a pulmonibus, Cic, sonum, *to sing or play*, Hor, **b**, *to repeat, recite, narrate*, ea sine scripto verbis iisdem, Cic, carmina, Hor

rĕdemptĭo -ōnis, f (redimo) **I.** *a buying up*, **a**, *bribing*, judicii, *a corrupting by bribery*, Cic, **b**, *a farming of taxes*, Cic **II.** *ransoming, redemption*, captivorum, Liv

rĕdempto, 1 (freq of redimo), *to ransom, redeem*, captivos, Tac

rĕdemptor ōris, m (redimo), *a buyer, contractor, farmer* (of taxes), Cic, frumenti, Liv

rĕdemptūra -ae, f (redimo), *a contracting, farming* (of taxes, etc), redempturis auxisse patrimonia, Liv

rĕdĕo -ii (-īvi) -ĭtum, 4 *to go back, come back, return* **I. A.** Lit, **a**, of persons, e provincia, Cic, a Caesare, Cic, Romam, Cic, domum, Caes, in proelium, Liv, ad suos, Caes, with predic nom, victor ex hac pugna redit, Liv, with 1 sup, spectatum e senatu, Cic, **b**, of things as subjects, redeunt humerique manusque, Ov, of water, flumen in eandem partem, ex qua venerat, redit, Caes, of the stars, day and night, etc, quum ad idem, unde profecta sunt, astra redierint, Cic, of places, collis paulatim ad planitiem redibat, *sloped down to*, Caes, poet, of plants, redeunt jam gramina campis, Hor of physical qualities, forma prior redit, Ov **B.** Transf, 1, gen, **a**, of persons, in pristinum statum, Caes, cum aliquo in gratiam, *to be reconciled with*, Cic, redire ad se, *to return to one's senses*, physically, Liv, and mentally, Cic, redire ad se atque ad mores suos, Cic, ad sanitatem, Cic, Caesar ad duas legiones redierat, *was reduced to*, Caes, **b**, of things, res redit, *the matter comes up again*, Cic, **2**, esp, of discourse, *to return to the previous subject*, sed de hoc alias, nunc redeo ad augurem, Cic. **II. A.** Of revenue, income, *to come in*, pecunia publica, quae ex metallis redibat, Nep **B.** *to come to be brought to, fall to*, **a**, pilis omissis, ad gladios redierunt, *they betook themselves to their swords*, Caes, **b**, of things, bona in tabulas publicas redierunt *have been registered in*, Cic, summa imperii, summa rerum redit ad aliquem, Caes, mortuo Tullo res (*government of the state*) ad patres redierat, Liv

rĕdhālo, 1 *to breathe out again*, Lucr

rĕdhĭbĕo -ui -ĭtum, 2 (re and habeo) **I.** *to give back, return*, Plaut. **II.** In business, *to give back, return a damaged article*, mancipium, Cic

rĕdĭgo -ēgi actum, 3 (re and ago) **I.** *to drive back, bring back, lead back* **A.** Lit, hostium equitatum in castra **B.** Fig, rem in pristinum belli rationem, Caes, in memoriam alicuius, *to a person's recollection* (foll by acc and infin), Cic. **II.** *to bring or carry to* **A.** Lit, *to draw in, call in, collect*, quantam (pecuniam) ex bonis patriis redegisset, Cic, omnem pecuniam Idibus, Hor, magnam pecuniam in aerarium, Liv, esp, aliquid in publicum redigere, *to deliver into the public treasury, to confiscate*, Liv, or simply redigere, Heracli bona verbo redigere, re dissipare, Cic **B.** Fig, **a**, *to bring or reduce to a state or condition to make, render such*, Aeduos in servitutem, Caes, civitatem in ditionem potestatemque populi Romani, Cic ad certum, *to make certain*, Liv, victoriam ad vanum et irritum, *make fruitless*, Liv, aliquem or aliquid eo ut, etc, *to bring to such a point that*, etc, Liv, with double acc, quae facilia ex difficillimis animi magnitudo redegerit, *had made difficulties easy*, Caes, in ordinem redigere, *reduce to order*, Liv, **b**, *to reduce in compass, number, value*, etc, *to lessen, bring down*, ex hominum millibus LX vix ad D, Caes, nobilissima familia jam ad paucos redacta, Cic, vilem ad assem redigi, Cic.

rĕdĭmīcŭlum -i, n (redimio), *a lappet or fillet, frontlet, necklace*, Cic

rĕdĭmĭo -ii -ītum, 4 *to bind round, tie round, wreathe round, crown*, sertis redimiri et rosā, Cic; tempora vittā, Verg, partic. perf, **rĕdĭmītus** -a um, silvis redimita loca, Cat (syncop imperf, redimibat, Verg)

rĕdĭmo ēmi -emptum (-emtum), 3 (re and emo) **I.** *to buy back*, domum, Cic, fundum, Cic **II.** *to buy*, **A.** Gen, 1, lit, necessaria ad cultum, Liv, vitam alicuius pretio, Cic, **2**, transf, *to buy*, i e, *to procure, obtain for a price*, pacem parte fructuum, Cic, pacem obsidibus, Caes **B.** Esp, polit and legal t t, **1**, *to farm, hire*, vectigalia, Caes, picarias, Cic, **2**, *to contract for*, opus, Cic **III.** *to ransom* **A.** *to set free by payment of money*, **1**, lit, captivos e servitute, Cic, **2**, transf, *to set free, deliver*, se pecuniā a judicibus, Cic, se a Gallis auro, Liv **B.** *to buy off, avert, remove*, acerbitatem a republica, Cic; litem, *to compromise*, Cic

rĕdintĕgro, 1 *to restore, renew, repair*, **a**, of persons, deminutas copias, Caes, proelium, Caes, memoriam auditoris, Cic, spem, Caes, pacem, Liv, **b**, of things as subjects, redintegravit luctum in castris consulum adventus, Liv

rĕdĭpiscor, 3 dep (re and apiscor), *to get, obtain again*, Plaut

rĕdĭtĭo -ōnis, f (redeo), *a going back, coming back, returning, return*, celeritas reditionis, Cic

rĕdĭtus -ūs, m (redeo) **I.** *a coming back, going back, return* **A.** Lit, **a**, of persons, domum, Cic, in urbem, Cic, ad aliquem, Cic, est hominibus reditus in curiam, *may return to*, Cic, intercludere alicuius reditum, Cic, plur, sanguine quaerendi reditus, Verg, **b**, transf, of the stars, Cic **B.** Fig, ad rem ad propositum, Cic, reditus in gratiam, *reconciliation*, Cic **II.** *returns, income, revenue*, sing, Nep; plur, reditus metallorum, Liv

rĕdĭvĭa = reduvia (q v)

rĕdĭvīvus -a -um (redi = re and vivus), *renewed, renovated*, applied to old building materials used a second time, lapis, Cic, subst., **rĕdĭvīvum** -i, n and **rĕdĭvīva** -ōrum, n *old building materials used again*, Cic

rĕdŏlĕo -ui, 2 *to emit an odour, diffuse an odour* **I.** Lit, redolent murrae, Ov; with abl, redolere thymo, *smell of thyme*, Verg with acc, vinum, *to smell of wine*, Cic **II.** Fig, ita domus ipsa fumabat, ut multa eius sermonis indicia redolerent, Cic, mihi quidem ex illius orationibus redolere ipsae Athenae videntur, Cic, with acc, doctrinam, Cic, antiquitatem, Cic

rĕdŏmĭtus -a -um, *tamed again, subdued again*, Cic

rĕdōno, 1 **I.** *to give back*, Hor **II.** *to pardon*, graves iras et invisum nepotem Marti redonabo, Hor.

rĕdordĭor, 4 dep *to unravel, unweave*, Plin

rĕdormĭo, 4 *to sleep again*, Plin

rĕdormītĭo -ōnis, f (redormio), *a going to sleep again*, Plin

rĕdūco -duxi ductum, 3 **I.** *to bring back, lead back* **A.** *to draw back, to draw backwards, draw towards oneself*, **1**, lit, **a**, gen, falces tormentis internis, Caes, remos ad pectora Ov, **b**, esp, (α) *to draw in*, auras naribus, Lucr, (β) *to extend a fortification*, reliquas omnes munitiones ab ea fossa pedes CCC reduxit, Caes, **2**, fig, **a**, *to rescue* socios a morte reduxi, Verg, **b**, *to keep back from*, meque ipse reduco a contemplatu dimoveoque mali, Ov **B.** *to lead back*, often with rursus or rursum, **1**, lit **a**, gen, (α) of persons as obj, aliquem domum, Cic, (β) of things, diem or lucem, Verg, **b**, esp, (α) *to accompany, to escort*, as a mark of respect, aliquem domum, Cic, (β) *to restore an exile*, aliquem de exsilio, Cic, regem, Cic, (γ) milit t t, *to draw back forces, withdraw, cause to retire, take back*, legiones ex Britannia, Caes, copias a munitionibus, Caes, victorem exercitum Romam, Liv, **2**, fig, **a**, aliquem in gratiam cum aliquo, Cic, aliquem ad officium sanitatemque, Cic, in memoriam, *to recall to recollection*, Cic, **b**, *to re-introduce*, legem majestatis, Tac. **II.** *to bring* or *reduce to a certain state or condition*, (carnem) lambendo mater in artus fingit et in formam reducit (of the she bear), Ov

rĕductĭo -ōnis, f (reduco), *a bringing back*, regis Alexandrini, *restoration*, Cic.

rĕductor -ōris (reduco), *one who brings back*; plebis Romanae in urbem, Liv

rĕductus -a -um, p adj (from reduco), *withdrawn, retired* **I.** Lit, of places, *retired, sequestered*, vallis, Verg **II.** Fig, virtus est medium vitiorum et utrimque reductum, *distant from both extremes*, Hor, applied to a painting, reductiora, *the background*, Quint, subst, **rĕducta** -ōrum, n (translation of ἀποπροηγμένα), in the language of the Stoics, *things which though not evils were to be regarded as inferior* (opp producta), Cic.

rĕduncus -a -um, *bent, bowed, curved*; rostrum (aquilae), Ov

rĕdundantĭa -ae, f (redundo), *an overflowing*, fig, of style, *redundancy*, Cic

rĕdundo, 1 (re and unda), *to overflow, stream over* **I. 1**, lit, of water, etc, lacus, Cic, pituita, Cic; partic perf, redundatus poet = redundans, *overflowing*, aquae, Ov, **2**, transf, *to overflow with*, foll by abl, Asia, quae eorum ipsorum sanguine redundat, Cic **II.** Fig, **1**, *to overflow, abound, flow forth freely*, **a**, nationes in provincias redundare poterant, Cic, infamia ad amicos redundat, Cic, **b**, of orators, Asiatici oratores nimis redundantes, *copious, diffuse*, Cic; **2**, *to be very abundant, abound*, ut neque in Antonio deesset hic ornatus orationis, neque in Crasso redundaret, Cic, with abl, *to abound in*; splendidissimorum hominum multitudine, Cic

rĕdŭvĭa (**rĕdĭvĭa**) -ae, f (from *reduo, as exuviae from exuo), *a hangnail, whitlow, a loosening of the skin round the nails*, prov, quum capiti mederi debeam, reduviam curem, *attend to a trifle*, Cic

rĕdux -dŭcis (reduco) **I.** Act, *bringing back, restoring*, epithet of Jupiter, Ov **II.** Pass, *brought back, returned*, reduces socii, Verg, me reducem esse voluistis, *returned from exile*, Cic (abl sing, reduci in poets, Ov)

rĕfectĭo -ōnis, f (reficio), *a repairing, restoration*, Suet.

rĕfector -ōris, m (reficio), *a repairer, restorer*, Suet

rĕfello -felli, 3 (re and fallo), *to refute, confute, disprove*, aliquem, Cic, refellere et redarguere mendacium alicuius, Cic, crimen commune ferro, Verg

rĕfercĭo -fersi -fertum, 4 (re and farcio), *to stuff quite full, fill full* **I.** Lit, cloacas corporibus civium, Cic **II.** Fig, **A.** Gen, complures aures istis sermonibus, Cic, libros puerilibus fabulis, Cic **B.** *to crowd together*, quae Crassus peranguste refersit in oratione sua, Cic.

rĕfĕrĭo, 4 **I.** *to strike back, strike again*, Plaut **II.** *to reflect*, speculi referitur imagine Phoebus, Ov

rĕfĕro tŭli -lātum -ferre **I.** *to carry back, bring back, bear back* **A. 1**, to a place, **a**, *to bring back, carry back*, candelabrum, Cic, pecunias in templum, Caes, esp, of the wounded, aliquem in castra, Liv, **b**, *to take back, restore what has been lent or stolen, give back* pateram, Cic, fig, ad equestrem ordinem judicia, Cic, **c**, *to give back from oneself*, (α) *to spit out*, cum sanguine mixta vina, Verg, (β) *to cause to sound back, to cause to echo*, in pass = *to echo, to resound*, theatri natura ita resonans, ut usque Romam significationes vocesque referantur, Cic, **d**, *to carry back = to make to return*, (α) of return, me referunt pedes in Tusculanum, Cic, esp, referre pedem, or referre se, or pass, referri, as middle, *to return, to turn back again, to return home*, se iterum Romam, Cic, classem relatam nuntio, Verg, esp, (αα) *to bring back time that is past*, o mihi praeteritos referat si Juppiter annos, Verg, (ββ) *to direct again one's look, energy*, etc, oculos animumque ad aliquem, Cic, animum ad studia, Cic, se ad philosophiam, Cic, (γγ) *to restore to a condition*, consilia in melius, Verg, (δδ) legal t t, *to bring again before a court of justice*, rem judicatam, Cic; (εε) *to refer to, to judge by, measure according to a certain standard*, omnia ad voluptatem, Cic., omnia consilia atque facta ad dignitatem et ad virtutem, Cic, (β) of retreat, *to move back*, castra, Liv, esp, referre pedem or vestigia, or gradum (gradus), or reflex, se referre and pass, referri, as middle, *to retreat, move back, yield*, esp as milit t t, paulatim cedere ac pedem referre, Caes, (γ) naut t t, *to drive back*, auster aliquem in Italiam refert, Cic, **2**, *to bring back from a place, as a trophy, present, discovery*, **a**, tabulas repertas ad Caesarem, Caes, pro re certa falsam spem domum, Cic, esp, milit t t, signa militaria sex, Caes, **b**, *to bring back a message, report*, etc, responsum, Cic, rumores, Cic, with acc. and infin, imminere Volscum bellum, Liv, **3**, *to bring back as equivalent, return, requite*, **a**, vicem, Ov, alicui plurimam salutem, Cic, **b**, gratiam, *to return thanks, to recompense*, Cic, **4**, *to turn back* (parts of the body), oculos ad terram identidem, Cic, os in se, Ov, **5**, *to repeat, renew, restore*; **a**, eandem totius caeli descriptionem, Cic, **b**, *to represent, be the image of, recall*, aliquem ore, Verg **II.** *to give away from oneself* **A.** *to give up, present, deliver*, frumentum omne ad se referri jubet, Caes, polit t t, hanc ex fenore pecuniam populo, *deliver into the public treasury*, Cic, rationes ad aerarium, Cic, esp, **a**, *to pay off*, octonis idibus aera, Hor; **b**, *to offer as a sacrifice*, sollemnia ludis, Verg, **c**, *to procure, confer upon*, consulatum ad patrem, Cic, **d**, *to report, relate by word of mouth or by writing*, certorum hominum sermones ad aliquem, Cic, haec mandata Caesari, Caes, aliquem in numero deorum, *to raise to*, Cic, with acc and infin, referunt Suebos ad extremos fines se recepisse, Caes, **e**, *to place before for advice, apply to, refer to*, de signo Concordiae dedicando ad pontificum collegium, Cic.; esp., **1**, referre ad senatum, *to bring a question before the senate;* ad senatum de legibus abrogandis, Cic.; **2**, *to register, record, enter;* judicium in tabulas publicas, Cic.; aliquid in commentarium, in libellum, Cic.; aliquem in proscriptos, *in the list of proscribed,* Cic.; esp., *to write in an account-book;* pecuniam operi publico, *under the head of a public work,* Cic.; aliquid in acceptum referre or acceptum referre, *to enter as paid,* Cic. (perf. and sup., rettuli and rellatum sometimes in poets to make the first syllable long).

rēfert, rētŭlit, rēferre, impers. (from re, for ex re and fert), *it matters, it concerns, is of use, is advantageous, is one's interest;* with meā, tuā, nostrā, vestrā, cujā; more rarely with ad and the acc., or only acc., or with genit.; **a**, with possess. pron., non ascripsi id, quod tuā nihil referebat, Cic.; non plus suā referre, quam si, etc., Cic.; **b**, without poss. pron., refert magno opere id ipsum; with infin. as subj., neque refert videre quid dicendum sit, Cic.; with depend. interrog. sent., quid refert, qua me ratione cogatis? Cic.; quid refert, utrum volueris fieri, an gaudeam factum? Cic.; **c**, with dat., quid referat intra naturae fines viventi, jugera centum an mille aret? Hor.; **d**, with genit., faciendum aliquid, quod illorum magis, quam suā retulisse videretur, Sall.; **e**, absol., tamquam referret, *as if it were of any consequence,* Tac.

rĕfertus -a -um, p. adj. (from refercio), *stuffed, crammed, filled, full;* (α) with abl., insula referta divitiis, Cic.; (β) with genit., mare refertum praedonum, Cic.; (γ) with de and the abl., cur de procemiis referti essent eorum libri, Cic.; (δ) absol., aerarium refertius, Cic.; theatrum refertissimum, Cic.

rĕfervĕo, 2. *to boil over;* fig., refervens falsum crimen, Cic.

rĕfervesco, 3. (referveo), *to boil up, bubble up;* sanguis refervescit, Cic.

rĕfĭcĭo -fēci -fectum, 3. (re and facio). **I.** *to make again.* **A.** *to make afresh, prepare again;* arma, Sall.; ea quae sunt omissa, Cic. **B.** *to choose again;* tribunos, Cic. **II.** *to re-establish, restore a thing to its previous condition;* salutem, Cic.; esp., **a**, *to build again;* pontem, Caes.; fana, Cic.; **b**, *to refit, repair;* naves, classem, Caes.; aedes, Cic.; **c**, *to light again, kindle again;* flammam, Ov.; **d**, *to restore in point of number, to fill up, complete;* exercitum, Liv.; copias, Caes.; **e**, *to restore health, heal, cure;* Tironis reficiendi spes, Cic.; **f**, *to restore (physically, politically, mentally), to refresh, revive;* reficere se et curare, Cic.; fessum viā ac vigiliis militem, Liv.; me recreat et reficit Pompeii consilium, *gives me strength,* Cic.; of things, herbas, Ov. **III.** *to get back again, receive, get;* plus mercedis ex fundo, Cic.

rĕfīgo -fixi -fixum, 3. *to tear, loose, pluck off, pluck apart, unfasten.* **I.** Lit., tabulas, Cic.; signa templis, Hor. **II.** Meton., **A.** *to take down the tables of the law,* i.e., *to repeal, abrogate;* leges, aera, Cic. **B.** *to pack up,* ap. Cic.

rĕfingo, 3. *to form anew;* cerea regna, Verg.

rĕflāgĭto, 1. *to ask back, demand again,* Cat.

rĕflātus -ū, m. (reflo). **I.** *a blowing against,* Plin. **II.** Meton., *a contrary wind;* naves delatas Uticam reflatu hoc, Cic.

rĕflecto -flexi -flexum, 3. *to turn back, bend back.* **I.** Lit., cervicem, Ov.; oculos, Ov.; pass., reflecti, as middle, tereti cervice reflexa, Verg.; longos reflectitur ungues, *bends his nails into long talons,* Ov. **II.** Fig., *to turn back, turn, divert;* animum, Cic.; mentes, Cic.; orsa in melius, Verg.

rĕflo, 1. **I.** Intransit., *to blow back, blow against, blow contrary;* etsi etesiae valde reflant, Cic. **II.** Transit., *to blow out, breathe out,* Lucr.

rĕflōresco -flōrŭi, 3. *to begin to bloom again,* Plin.

rĕflŭo -fluxi -fluxum, 3. *to flow back, to overflow;* Nilus refluit campis, Verg.

rĕflŭus -a -um (refluo), *flowing back;* mare, Ov.

rĕfŏdĭo -fōdi -fossum, 3. *to dig out, dig up,* Plin.

rĕformātor -ōris, m. (reformo), *one who forms again, a reviver, improver,* Plin.

rĕformīdātĭo -ōnis, f. (reformido), *excessive dread, fear, terror,* Cic.

rĕformīdo, 1. *to dread, fear, be afraid of, shun, avoid;* **a**, of persons, (α) with acc., aliquem, Cic.; bellum, Cic.; (β) with infin., refugit animus eaque dicere reformidat, Cic.; (γ) with rel. sent., nec, quid occurrat, reformidat, Cic.; (δ) absol., vide, quam non reformidem, Cic.; **b**, of things, ante (vites) reformidant ferrum, Verg.

rĕformo, 1. *to form again, mould anew, alter in form;* Iolcus reformatus in annos primos, Ov.

rĕfŏvĕo -fōvi -fōtum, 2. *to warm again, cherish again, revive, restore, refresh.* **I.** Lit., corpus, Ov.; vires, Tac.; ignes tepidos, Ov. **II.** Fig., provincias internis certaminibus fessas, Tac.

rĕfractārĭŏlus -a -um (dim. of refractarius), *somewhat contentious, stubborn;* hoc judiciale dicendi genus, Cic.

rĕfractārĭus -a -um (refragor), *stubborn refractory, contentious,* Sen.

rĕfrāgor, 1. dep. (opp. to suffragor), *to oppose, withstand, thwart;* petenti, Cic.; honori eius, Liv.; illa lex petitioni tuae refragata est, *is opposed to,* Cic.

rĕfrēno, 1. *to hold back, rein in;* transf., *to hold back, restrain, curb;* fluvios, Lucr.; aquas, Ov.; fig., animum, Cic.; juventutem, Cic.; adolescentes a gloria, Cic.

rĕfrĭco -fricŭi -fricātūrus, 1. *to rub again, scratch again, gall.* **I.** Lit., alicuius vulnera, *to tear open,* Cic.; cicatricem, Cic. **II.** Transf., *to excite again, renew;* pulcherrimi facti memoriam, Cic.; tuis sceleribus reipublicae praeterita fata refricabis, Cic.; dolorem, Cic.; crebro refricatur lippitudo, *breaks out afresh, appears again,* Cic.

rĕfrīgĕrātĭo -ōnis, f. (refrigero), *a cooling, coolness;* me delectant et refrigeratio et vicissim aut sol aut ignis hibernus, Cic.

rĕfrīgĕrātōrĭus -a -um (refrigero), *cooling,* Plin.

rĕfrīgĕrātrix -īcis, f. *cooling,* Plin.

rĕfrīgĕro, 1. *to make cool.* **I.** Lit., **a**, physically, stella Saturni refrigerat, Cic.; **b**, of animal heat, membra undā, Ov.; dei membra partim ardentia partim refrigerata dicenda sunt, Cic.; pass., refrigerari, as middle, *to cool oneself, grow cool;* umbris aquisve, Cic. **II.** Transf., *to cool, to deprive of warmth* or *zeal;* and hence, pass., *to be cold, exhausted, languid, to grow cool* or *languid;* refrigerata accusatio, Cic.; sermone refrigerato, Cic.

rĕfrīgesco -frixi, 3. *to grow cold, cool down, become cool.* **I.** Lit., cor corpore cum toto refrixit, Ov. **II.** Transf., *to lose warmth, vigour, zeal, grow cool, to flag, to fail, to abate, to grow stale;* illud crimen de nummis caluit re recenti, nunc in causa refrixit, Cic.; vereor ne hasta (*the public auction*) refrixerit, Cic.; of persons, Scaurus refrixerat, Cic.

rĕfringo -frēgi fractum, 3 (re and frango), *to break up, break open* **I.** Lit, claustra, Cic carcerem, Liv. **II.** Transf, *to break in pieces, to break, destroy*, vim fluminis, Caes, vim fortunae, Liv

rĕfŭgio fūgi fŭgitum, 3 **I.** Intransit, *to flee away, take to flight, escape* **A.** Lit, velocissime, Caes, ad suos, Caes, Syracusas, Cic, ex castris in montem, Caes **B.** Transf, **a,** *to turn away from, avoid*, vites a caulibus refugere dicuntur, Cic, **b,** of places, *to retire from, recede from*, refugit ab litore templum, Verg, **c,** *to take refuge with, have recourse to* ad legatos, Cic **II.** Transit, *to fly from, avoid, run away from* **A.** Lit, impetum, Cic **B.** Fig, *to avoid, shun*, judicem, Cic, ministeria, Verg

rĕfŭgium -ii, n (refugio), *a place of refuge, a refuge*, silvae dedere refugium, Liv, refugium populorum erat senatus, Cic

rĕfŭgus -a -um (refugio). **I.** *flying, fugitive, receding* quidam in castra refugi, Tac Subst, refugi, *fugitives*, Tac **II.** Poet, transf, *receding, recoiling*, unda, Ov

rĕfulgĕo fulsi, 2 *to gleam or glitter back, to shine brightly, to glitter.* **I.** Lit arma refulgentia, Liv, Jovis tutela refulgens (of Jupiter, as an auspicious birth-star), Hor **II.** Fig, splendidaque a docto fama refulget avo, Prop

rĕfundo -fūdi -fūsum, 3 **I.** *to pour back*, vapores eădem, Cic, aequor in aequor, Ov, refusus Oceanus, *ebbing and flowing*, Verg **II.** *to cause to flow forth*, pass, refundi, as middle, *to overflow*, stagna refusa vadis, Verg

rĕfūtātĭo -ōnis, f (refuto), *a refutation, confutation*, Cic

rĕfūtātus, abl -ū = refutatio (q v)

rĕfūto, 1 **I.** *to drive back, press back*, nationes bello, Cic **II.** Fig, *to resist, oppose, repel, repress* **A.** Gen, clamorem, Cic, cupiditatem, Cic, virtutem aspernari ac refutare, Cic **B.** Esp, *to confute, refute, disprove*, sceleratorum perjuria testimoniis, Cic, aliquos domesticis testibus, Cic, Fors dicta refutet! *may fate avert!* Verg

rēgālĭŏlus -i, m (dim of regalis) *a small bird, perhaps the wren*, Suet

rēgālis -e (rex), *royal, regal, kingly* **I.** Lit, genus civitatis, *monarchical*, Cic, nomen, Cic, carmen, *celebrating deeds of kings* Ov **II** Transf, *kingly, princely, worthy of a king*, ornatus, Cic, regalem animum in se esse, Liv

rēgālĭtĕr, adv (regalis) *royally, regally;* **a,** in good sense, centum hostias sacrificium regaliter Minervae conficere, Liv, **b,** in a bad sense, *despotically, tyrannically*, precibus minas regaliter addere, Ov

rĕgĕlo, 1 *to thaw, warm*, Mart

rĕgĕnĕro, 1 *to bring forth again to generate again, reproduce*, Plin

rĕgermĭnātĭo -ōnis, f (regermino) *a budding again, putting forth of buds again*, Plin

rĕgermĭno, 1 *to put forth buds again, germinate again*, Plin

rĕgĕro -gessi gestum, 3 *to carry back, bear back, bring back* **I.** Lit, quo regesta e fossa terra foret, Liv, tellurem, *to throw back again*, Ov **II.** Transf, *to throw back, return, retort*, convicia, Hor

rēgĭa, v regius

rēgĭē, adv (regius), *royally*, **a,** in a good sense, Plaut, **b,** in a bad sense, *arbitrarily, despotically, tyrannically*, crudeliter et regie fieri, Cic, ea quae regie seu potius tyrannice statuit in aratores, Cic.

rēgĭfĭcus -a -um (rex and facio), *royal, princely, splendid*, luxus, Verg

rĕgigno, 3 *to bring forth again, beget again*, Lucr

Rēgillus -i, m **I.** *a town in the country of the Sabines, from which Appius Claudius came to Rome* Hence, **Rēgillensis** e and **Rēgillānus** -a -um, *belonging to Regillus* **II.** *a small lake in Latium on the via Lavicana, scene of a victory of the Romans over the Latins, 496* B C Hence, **Rēgillensis** -e, *surname of the Postumii, as the Roman commander was the dictator Postumius.* **III.** *surname of the gens Aemilia*

rĕgĭmen -ĭnis, n (rego) **I.** *guiding, leading* **A.** Lit, equorum, Tac, navis, Tac, cohortium, Tac **B.** Fig, *guidance, rule, government, direction*, totius magistratus, Liv, absol, *the government of a state*, Tac **II.** *that which guides* **A.** Poet, *the rudder*, Ov **B.** Fig, *a ruler, governor*, rerum, *of a state*, Liv

rēgīna -ae, f (rex), *a queen* **I A** Lit, **1,** gen, Plaut, **2,** esp, of Cleopatra, Cic, of Dido, Verg **B.** Transf, **a,** of goddesses, regina Juno, Cic, **b,** *a king's daughter, a princess* (of Ariadne), Verg, of Medea, Ov **II.** Fig, *queen, mistress, sovereign*, haec una virtus (justitia) omnium est domina et regina virtutum, Cic, regina pecunia, Hor

Rēgīnus, v Regium

rĕgĭo -ōnis, f (rego) **I.** *a direction, line* **A.** Gen, si qui tantulum de recta regione deflexerit, Cic, haec eadem est nostra regio et via, Cic., oppidi murus rectā regione, si nullus anfractus intercederet, MCC passus aberat, Caes, rectā regione, *in a straight line*, Liv **B.** Esp e regione, adv, **a,** *in a straight line*, alterum e regione movetur, alterum declinat, Cic, **b,** *in the opposite direction, over, against*, (a) with genit, e regione solis, Cic, (β) with dat, esse e regione nobis e contraria parte terrae, Cic **II.** Transf, **A.** *a boundary line, boundary*, **1,** gen, **a,** lit., usually plur, res eas orbis terrae regionibus definiuntur, Cic, **b,** fig, sese regionibus officii continet, Cic, **2,** esp, **a,** t t of augurs' language, *the line of sight*, per lituum regionum facta descriptio, Cic, **b,** *a region of the heavens or earth*, regio aquilonia, australis Cic, **c,** *geographical position*, eam esse naturam et regionem provinciae tuae, Cic **B. 1,** *a region, country, territory, district*, **a,** lit, locus in regione pestilenti saluber, Cic **b,** fig, *sphere, department, territory*, bene dicere non habet definitam aliquam regionem, Cic, **2,** esp, **a,** *an administrative division, province, district*, principes regionum atque pagorum inter suos jus dicunt, Caes, **b,** *a division, quarter, ward, district of Rome*, Tac.

rĕgĭōnātim, adv (regio), *according to districts, provinces*, tribus describere, Liv

Rēgĭum -ii, n **I.** *a town of the Boii in Gallia Cispadana, now Reggio* Hence, **Rēgienses** -ium, m *the inhabitants of Regium* **II.** *a town of the Bruttii, at the south of Italy, near Sicily, now Reggio* Hence, **Rēgīnus** -a -um, *belonging to Regium*

rēgĭus a -um (rex), *royal, regal, kingly* **I.** Adj, **A.** Lit, anni, *the period of monarchy at Rome*, Cic, ales, *the eagle*, Cic, causa (of the installation of Ptolemaeus Auletes), Cic **B.** Transf, *royal, splendid, magnificent*, moles, Hor; morbus, *jaundice*, Hor **II** Subst, **A. rēgĭi** ōrum, m **1,** *the troops of the king*, Liv, **2,** *the satraps of the king*, Nep **B. rēgĭa** -ae, f **1,** *the royal dwelling, the palace*, **a,** gen, Cic, **b,** esp, a building in Rome on the Via Sacra, the palace of Numa, afterwards used by the priests,

Cic.; so atrium regium, Liv.; **c**, meton., *the court, the royal family*, Liv.; **2**, = basilica, *a public hall*, Suet.

rĕglūtĭno, 1. *to unglue, separate*, Cat.

regnātor -ōris, m. (regno), *a ruler, governor, king*; Olympi, *Jupiter*, Verg.; Asiae, Verg.

regnātrix -trīcis, f. (regnator), *ruling*; domus, Tac.

regno, 1. (regnum). **I.** Intransit., *to exercise royal authority, be a king, reign.* **A.** Lit., septem et triginta regnavisse annos, Cic.; impers., post Tatii mortem ab sua parte non erat regnatum, Liv. **B.** Transf., *to rule as a king*; **a**, of persons, *to be master, to have absolute sway, to play the lord*; partly in a good sense, Graeciā jam regnante, Cic.; partly in a bad sense, *to be a tyrant*; regnavit is quidem (Gracchus) paucos menses, Cic.; **b**, of things, *to rule, get the mastery*; ignis per alta cacumina regnat, Verg.; ardor edendi per viscera regnat, *rages*, Ov.; of abstractions, in quo uno regnat oratio, Cic. **II.** Transit., *to rule*; only in pass., regnandam accipere Albam, Verg.; with abl. of pers., terra regnata Lycurgo, Verg.; gentes quae regnantur, *which are ruled by kings*, Tac.

regnum -i, n. (rex), *royal power* or *authority, royalty, monarchy, the throne.* **I. A.** Lit., superbi regni initium, Cic.; regnum affectare, Liv. **B.** Transf., **1**, in a good sense, *authority, rule, unrestrained power*; alicui regnum deferre, Caes.; abuti ad omnia atomorum regno et licentiā, Cic.; **2**, in a bad sense, under the republic at Rome, *tyranny, despotism*; regnum appetere, Cic.; crimen regni, Ov.; regnum judiciorum, regnum forense, Cic. **II.** Meton., **A.** *a country ruled by a king, a kingdom*; fines regni, Caes. **B.** Transf., **1**, *the kingdom of the dead*, Verg.; **2**, *any possession, estate*; in tuo regno, Cic.; mea regna, Verg.

rĕgo, rexi, rectum, 3. *to guide, direct.* **I.** Lit., **A.** equum, Liv.; regit beluam quocumque vult, Cic. **B.** Legal t. t., regere fines, *to mark out boundaries*, Cic. **II.** Fig., **A.** *to guide, direct*; **a**, motum mundi, Cic.; juvenem, Cic.; **b**, esp., as a ruler, *to guide, direct, rule, govern, administer*; rempublicam, Cic.; Massilienses summā justitiā, Cic.; transf., of abstract objects, omnes animi partes, Cic.; suorum libidines, Cic. **B.** *to show the right way to, to set right*; errantem, Caes.; te regere possum, Cic.

rĕgrĕdĭor -gressus sum, 3. (re and gradior), *to go back, retreat, step back.* **I.** Lit., **a**, ut regredi quam progredi mallent, Cic.; **b**, as milit. t. t., *to retreat*, Caes. **II.** Fig., in illum annum, Cic.

rĕgressĭo -ōnis, f. (regredior), *a going back, repetition*, as a rhetorical figure, Quint.

rĕgressus -ūs, m. (regredior), *a going back, return.* **I.** Lit., **a**, Cic.; dare alicui regressum, Ov. Plur., conservare progressus et regressus, Cic.; **b**, milit. t. t., *a retreat*, Liv. **II.** Fig., **a**, *a return*; ab ira, Liv.; **b**, *refuge, recourse*; ad principem, Tac.

rēgŭla -ae, f. (rego), *a rule, a bar, staff, lath, stick.* **I.** Gen., Caes. **II.** Esp., **A.** Lit., *a rule*, Cic. **B.** Fig., *a rule, pattern, model*; juris, Cic.; regula ad quam omnia judicia rerum dirigentur, Cic.

1. **rēgŭlus** -i, m. (dim. of rex). **I.** *a petty king, prince*, Sall. **II.** *a king's son, prince*, Liv.

2. **Rēgŭlus**, *surname of the gens Atilia, the most famous member of which was the consul* M. Atilius Regulus, *famous for his devoted return into captivity in the First Punic War.*

rĕgusto, 1. *to taste again* or *repeatedly.* **I.** Lit., Pers. **II.** Fig., crebro litteras alicuius, *to take pleasure in reading over again*, Cic.; laudationem Lollii, Cic.

rĕĭcĭo = rejicio (q.v.).

rējectānĕus -a -um (rejicio), *to be rejected*: subst., **rējectānĕa** -ōrum, transl. of the Stoic ἀποπροηγμένα, *things which, though not evil, are to be rejected*, Cic.

rējectĭo -ōnis, f. (rejicio). **I.** Lit., *a throwing out, throwing back, throwing up*; sanguinis, *a spitting of blood*, Plin. **II.** Fig., **A.** *a casting out, rejection, despising*; **a**, huius civitatis, Cic.; **b**, esp., legal t. t., *the refusal to accept a particular judex, challenging a juryman*; judicum, Cic. **B.** In rhet., in alium, *a shifting off from oneself to another*, Cic.

rējecto, 1. (intens. of rejicio), *to cast back, throw back*, Lucr.

rējĭcĭo -jēci -jectum, 3. (re and jacio), *to throw back.* **I.** Gen., **A.** In a narrow sense, *to cast behind, throw behind*; **a**, scutum (to protect oneself), Cic.; esp., of a garment, *to throw behind*; togam ab humero, Liv.; paenulam, *to throw back on the shoulders* (to leave the hands free), Cic.; **b**, esp., (α) rejicere or pass., rejici, as middle, *to sink back*; se in alicuius gremium, Lucr.; (β) *to place behind*; accensos in postremam aciem, Liv.; rejecta mater, Cic. **B.** In a wider sense, *to cast back from oneself, throw away, repel, drive back*; **1**, lit., **a**, colubras ab ore, Ov.; oculos Rutulorum arvis, *turn from*, Verg.; esp., (α) *to throw away a garment*; vestem ex humeris, Ov.; sagulum, Cic.; (β) *to throw back, cause to echo*; gen., in pass., *to echo back*; imago rejecta, Lucr.; **b**, esp., (α) *to drive off* living beings; capellas a flumine, Verg.; esp., as milit. t. t., *to drive back*; equitatum, Caes.; hostes ab Antiochea, Cic.; fig., alicuius ferrum et audaciam in foro, Cic.; (β) as naut. t. t., of a storm, *to drive back, cast up*; naves tempestate rejectae, Caes.; rejici austro ad Leucopetram, Cic.; **2**, fig., **a**, *to drive off from oneself, remove, repulse*; hanc proscriptionem hoc judicio a se rejicere et aspernari, Cic.; **b**, esp., (α) *to reject with scorn, disdain, spurn*; bona diligere et rejicere contraria, Cic.; omnem istam disputationem, Cic.; as legal t. t., *to challenge* the judices or jury; judices, Cic.; recuperatores, Cic.; (β) *to refer to*; aliquem ad ipsam epistolam, Cic.; (γ) *to bring a matter before the senate*, or *a magistrate*; rem ad senatum, Liv.; (δ) *to put off*; totam rem in mensem Januarium, Cic. **II.** *to throw back at some one*; telum in hostem, Caes. (imper., reice, dissyll., Verg.).

rĕlābor -lapsus sum, 3. dep. *to slide, glide, flow, fall back.* **I.** Lit., prenso rudente relabi, Ov.; relabi montibus, Hor. **II.** Fig., tunc mens et sonus relapsus, Hor.; nunc in Aristippi furtim praecepta relabor, *come back to*, Hor.

rĕlanguesco -langui, 3. *to become faint, languid.* **I.** Physically, Ov. **II.** Morally or intellectually, **a**, *to be weakened, be made effeminate*; iis rebus relanguescere animos, Caes.; **b**, *to become relaxed, to abate*; taedio impetus relanguescit regis, Liv.; relanguisse se dicit, *his animosity had abated*, Liv.

rĕlātĭo -ōnis, f. (refero), *a carrying back, bringing back.* **I.** Lit., Quint. **II.** Fig., **A.** Legal t. t., criminis, *a retorting of the accusation upon the accuser*, Cic. **B.** **1**, polit. t. t., *a motion, proposal, proposition of a magistrate in the senate*, Cic.; **2**, grammat. t. t., *relation, reference, respect*, Cic.

rĕlātor -ōris, m. (refero), *a mover, proposer in the senate*, ap. Cic.

rĕlātus -ūs, m. (refero), *a bringing before.* **I.** *a narrative, recital*; quorum (carminum) relatus, Tac. **II.** *a proposal, report in the senate*, Tac.

rĕlaxātĭo -ōnis, f (relaxo), *a relaxation, easing*, animi, Cic

rĕlaxo, 1 **I.** *to loosen, widen enlarge, relax*, alvus tum astringitur, tum relaxatur, Cic, ora fontibus, Ov **II.** *to make slack, to ease, to open, unfasten* **A** Lit, claustra, Ov vias et caeca spiramenta, Verg **B.** Fig, *to ease, lighten, alleviate, assuage, relax*, a, gen, (a) transit, continuationem verborum modo relaxet, Cic, pater nimis indulgens quidquid astrinxi relaxat, *loosens the reins which I drew tight*, Cic, (risus) tristitiam ac severitatem mitigat et relaxat Cic, (β) reflex and middle, animi cum se plane corporis vinculis relaxaverint, *shall have freed themselves*, Cic, simply relaxare and middle, relaxari = *to slacken*, (dolor) levis dat intervalla et relaxat, Cic, insani quum relaxentur, *when they have a lucid interval*, Cic, **b**, esp, *to relax by way of recreation to lighten, enliven, cheer up*, (a) transit, animum, Cic, (β) reflex and middle, se istā occupatione, Cic, relaxari animo, Cic

rĕlēgātĭo -ōnis, f (1 relego), *a banishing, banishment, the mildest form of exile from Rome, by which the exile preserved his civil rights*, Cic

1 **rĕlēgo**, 1 *to send away* **I.** Lit, **1**, tauros procul atque in sola pascua, Verg, **2**, as a punishment, *to remove, banish*, filium ab hominibus, Cic, aliquem in exsilium, Liv, relegatus, non exsul dicor (the relegatio being the mildest form of banishment), O **II.** Transf, **a**, *to remove far away*, terris gens relegata ultimis, Cic, **b**, *to reject*, Samnitium dona, Cic

2 **rĕlĕgo** -lēgi -lectum, 3 **I.** *to gather up, collect again.* **A.** Lit, filo relecto, Ov **B.** Transf, *to travel, sail through, traverse again*, Hellespontiacas aquas, Ov **II.** *to go over again*, **a**, *to read over again*, Trojani belli scriptorem, Hor, scripta, Ov, **b**, *to talk over*, suos sermone labores, Ov

rĕlentesco, 3. *to become languid, feeble again*, amor, Ov

rĕlĕvo, 1 **I.** *to lift, raise up again*, e terra corpus, Ov **II** *to make light again, to lighten* **A.** Lit, epistolam graviorem pellectione, Cic, relevari longā catenā, *to be freed from*, Ov **B.** Fig, **1**, *to relieve, free from an evil, to lessen, diminish*, communem casum misericordiā hominum, Cic, morbum, Cic, **2**, *to lighten, alleviate, refresh*, pectora mero, Ov, potius relevare quam castigare, Cic, relevari, *to be relieved, refreshed*, relevata respublica, Cic

rĕlictĭo -ōnis, f (relinquo), *a leaving, deserting*, reipublicae, Cic

rĕlĭcŭus and **rĕlĭcus** = reliquus (q v)

rĕlĭgātĭo -ōnis, f. (religo), *a tying up, training*, vitium, Cic

rĕlĭgĭo (rellĭgĭo) -ōnis, f (perhaps from re ligo) **I.** Gen, *conscientiousness, scrupulousness, conscientious exactness*, hac ego religione non sum ab hoc conatu repulsus, Cic, nulla in judiciis severitas, nulla religio, Cic, with object genit, non nullius officii, privati officii, Cic, with subject genit, fides et religio judicis, Cic **II.** Esp, *respect for what is sacred* **A.** *conscientious scruples, respect for conscience* perturbari religione et metu, Cic, res in religionem alicui venit, *is a matter of conscience to*, Cic, religio alicui non est, quominus, etc, *a man is not prevented by conscience from*, etc, Cic, in plur, quas religiones, Cic **B.** *religious feeling, religious awe*, **1**, lit, **a**, in a good sense, inclita justitia religioque Numae Pompilii, Liv, in plur, hostis omnium religionum Cic, **b**, in a bad sense, *superstition*, animos multiplex religio et pleraque externa incessit, Liv, **2**, meton, *that which is holy or sacred*, **a**, gen (a) in a good sense, in sacerdotibus tanta offusa oculis animoque religio, Liv, (β) in a bad sense, *an insult to religion, sin, curse*, religio Clodiana, Cic, **b**, esp, (a) act, *religious obligation*, tantā religione obstricta tota provincia est, Cic, so of an oath, religio jurisjurandi, Cic, (β) *holiness, sanctity*, deorum, Cic, magistratus religione inviolati, Cic of a place, fani, sacrarii, Cic **C.** *religious worship, the worship of the gods, external religion* **1**, lit, religio, id est, cultus deorum, Cic, plur, religiones, *religious observances*, diligentissimus religionum cultor, Liv, **2**, meton, *an object of worship, holy thing*, religio domestica (of a statue), Cic, hence, *the sacred dwelling of a god*, a deorum religionibus demigrare, Cic (in poets the first syllable is long, hence written relligio)

rĕlĭgĭōsē (rellĭgĭōsē), adv (religiosus) **I.** *conscientiously scrupulously*, testimonium dicere, Cic **II.** *piously, religiously*, deos colere Liv, religiosissime templum colere, Cic

rĕlĭgĭōsus (rellĭgĭōsus) a um (religio) **I.** *conscientious, scrupulous*, testis, Cic **II. A.** *religiously scrupulous*, civitas, Liv, dies *a day of evil omen*, as the dies Alliensis, Cic **B.** a, in a good sense, *religious, god-fearing, pious*, (a) lit, qui omnia, quae ad cultum deorum pertinerent, diligenter retractarent et tamquam relegerent sunt dicti religiosi, Cic, (β) meton, *holy, sacred*, templum sanctum et religiosum, Cic, b, in a bad sense, *superstitious*, Ter

rĕlĭgo, 1 **I.** *to tie, fasten behind* **A.** Lit, **1**, virginem, Ov, rite equos, Verg, trabes axibus, Caes, aliquem ad currum, Cic, funera in stipite, Ov, funiculum a puppi, Cic, **2**, *to bind up the hair*, alicui, *for the sake of some one*, flavam comam, Hor, **3**, *to fasten a boat or ship to the bank, to moor*, naves ad terram, Caes, religata in litore pinus, Ov **B** Transf, quae (prudentia) si extrinsecus religata pendeat *connected with*, Cic **II.** *to unbind, unfasten*, Cat

rĕlĭno -lēvi litum, 3 *to unseal, open anything fastened by pitch*, etc, Verg, Ter

rĕlinquo -līqui lictum, 3 **I.** *to leave behind, leave* **A.** Gen, **1**, lit, aliquem in Gallia, Caes, **2**, fig, *to leave behind*, aculeos in animo alicuius, Cic **B** Esp, **1**, of a deceased person, *to leave, leave behind*, **a**, lit, heredem testamento reliquit hunc, Cic, so of posthumous work, scriptum in Originibus, Cic, **b**, fig, memoriam, Cic, nomen, Hor, **2**, *to leave over, leave to, to let remain* **a**, alicui ne paleas quidem ex omni fructu, Cic, equitatus partem alicui, Caes, relinquebatur una per Sequanos via, *there remained*, Caes, **b**, fig, populari reipublicae laudem, Cic, spes relinquitur, *remains*, Cic, Caes, urbem direptioni ac incendiis, Cic, relinquitur with ut and the subj, Cic, Caes, **3**, *to leave behind in a certain state, to let lie, leave* **a**, lit, aliquem insepultum, Cic, **b**, fig, rem integram, Cic, sine imperio tantas copias, Caes **II.** *to abandon, forsake, separate oneself from some one or something* **A.** Gen, **1**, lit, domum propinquosque, Caes, **2**, fig, **a** quartana aliquis relinquitur, Cic, vitam, Verg, relinquit aliquem animus, Caes, ab omni honestate relictus, Cic **B.** *to desert, abandon, leave in the lurch*, **1**, lit, equos Caes, signa, *desert*, Liv, **2**, fig, **a**, *to neglect, abandon, let go, take no thought for*, rem et causam et utilitatem communem, Cic, agrorum et armorum cultum, Cic, **b**, esp, (a) *to pass over, not to notice*, caedes relinquo, libidines praetereo, Cic, (β) *to leave unfinished*, artem inveniendi totam, Cic, (γ) *to leave unavenged, unpunished*, injurias suas, Cic

rĕlĭquĭae (rellĭquĭae) -ārum, f (reliquus), *remains, relics, remainder, remnant* **I.** Lit, **A.** Gen, conjurationis, Cic, Troas

Danaum reliquias, *remnant left by the Greeks*, Verg. **B.** Esp., **a,** *the fragments of food, remnants of a feast*, Plaut.; fig., vellem me ad cenam (*the murder of Caesar*) invitasses, reliquiarum nihil haberes (*had not left Antonius alive*), Cic.; **b,** *the remains of some one dead, carcass; humanorum corporum*, Tac.; **c,** *the remains, ashes of a corpse burnt on the funeral pyre*; Marii, Cic. **II.** Fig., pristinae fortunae reliquiae miserae, Cic. (in poets, to lengthen the first syllable, also written relliquiae).

rĕlĭquus (rĕlĭcus) -a -um (relinquo), *that which is left behind, remaining, left.* **I.** Lit., **A.** Gen., spes, Cic.; subst., (α) plur., **rĕlĭqui** -ōrum, m. *the rest*; with genit., reliqui peditum, Liv.; (β) **rĕlĭquum** -i, n. and **rĕlĭqua** -ōrum, n. *the rest, the remainder*; de reliquo, Cic.; reliqua belli perficere, Liv.; esp., reliquum est ut, foll. by subj. only, *it remains that*, Cic.; reliquum est with infin., Cic.; nihil est reliqui, *nothing remains*, Cic.; reliquum facere, *to leave remaining*; nullum munus cuique reliquum fecisti, *thou hast left no duty unperformed*, Cic.; nihil reliqui facere, *to leave nothing remaining*, Cic. **B.** Esp., **1,** t. t. of business language, *outstanding* (of a debt), *remaining*; pecuniam reliquam ad diem solvere, Cic.; subst., **rĕlĭquum** -i, n. and plur., **rĕlĭqua** -ōrum, n. *what is outstanding, remaining*; quum tanta reliqua sunt, Cic.; **2,** of time, *remaining, future*; gloria, Cic.; in reliquum tempus, Cic. **II.** Transf., *that which is left of a whole when the part is taken away, remaining*; reliqua pars exercitus, Caes.; reliqui omnes, *all the rest*, Cic.

rellĭgĭo, relligiosus, etc. = religio, etc. (q.v.).

rellĭquĭae = reliquiae (q.v.).

rĕlūcĕo -luxi, 2. *to gleam back, to glitter, shine*, Cic.

rĕlūcesco -luxi, 3. (inchoat. of reluceo), *to become bright again, begin to shine again*; imago solis reluxit, Ov.

rĕluctor, 1. dep. *to strive against, struggle against*; draco, Hor.

rĕmăcresco -crŭi, 3. *to grow thin again*, Suet.

rĕmălĕdīco, 3. *to revile again*, Suet.

rĕmando, 3. *to chew the cud, ruminate*, Plin.

rĕmănĕo -mansi -mansum, 2. *to remain behind, remain.* **I.** Gen., Romae, Cic.; in exercitu, Cic.; ad urbem, Caes.; domi, Cic.; apud aliquem, Caes. **II.** Esp., *to remain, abide, continue*; **1,** lit., animi remanent post mortem, Cic.; **2,** *to remain in a certain condition*; pars integra remanebat, Cic.

rĕmāno, 1. *to flow back*, Lucr.

rĕmansĭo -ōnis, f. (remaneo), *a remaining, continuing in one place*, Cic.

rĕmĕdĭum -ĭi, n. (re and medeor). **I.** *a means of healing, a cure, remedy, medicine*; remedium quoddam habere, Cic.; remedio quodam uti, Cic.; remedio esse, Cic. **II.** Transf., *a means of assistance* or *relief, a remedy*; injuriae tuae, Cic.; remedia incommodorum, Cic.; ad magnitudinem frigorum hoc sibi remedium comparare, Cic.

rĕmĕo, 1. *to go back, come back, return*; remeat victor, Verg.; aër, Cic.; with acc., urbes, Verg.; aevum peractum, *to live over again*, Hor.

rĕmētĭor -mensus sum, 4. *to measure over again, measure back.* **I.** Gen., astra rite, *to observe carefully*, Verg. **II.** *to go back*, Plin.; in pass. meaning, iter retro pari ratione remensum est, *has been traversed*, Lucr.

rēmex -igis, m. (remus and ago), *a rower*, Cic.; collectively = remiges, *the crew of rowers*, Verg.

Rēmi (Rhēmi) -ōrum, m. *a people of N. Gaul, between the Matrona* (Marne) *and the Axona* (Aisne), whence modern *Rheims*; sing., Iccius Remus, Caes.

rēmĭgātĭo -ōnis, f. (remigo), *a rowing*, Cic.

rēmĭgĭum -ĭi, n. (remex). **I.** *rowing.* **A.** Lit., Ov. **II.** Meton., **A.** *the oars*; **a,** lit., Verg.; **b,** transf., of the oar-like motion of wings, remigio alarum, Verg. **B.** *the crew of rowers, the oarsmen*, Liv.

rēmĭgo, 1. (remex), *to row*, Cic.

rĕmĭgro, 1. *to wander back, come back, return.* **I.** Lit., in domum suam, Cic.; Romam, Cic. **II.** Fig., ei ne integrum quidem erat, ut ad justitiam remigraret, Cic.

rĕmĭniscor, 3. dep. *to call to mind, recollect, remember*; absol., de quaestoribus reminiscentem recordari, Cic.; with genit., veteris incommodi populi Romani, Caes.; with acc., eas res, Cic.; with rel. sent., quae tradantur mysteriis, Cic.

rĕmiscĕo -miscŭi -mistum (-mixtum), 2. *to mix, mix up, mingle*; Lydis remixtum carmen tibiis, Hor.

rĕmissē, adv. (remissus). **I.** *loosely*; orationem non astricte, sed remissius numerosam esse oportere, Cic. **II.** *gently, mildly*; remissius disputare, Cic.

rĕmissĭo -ōnis, f. (remitto). **I.** *sending back*; obsidum captivorumque, Liv. **II.** *a letting down.* **A.** Lit., **1,** *a letting fall, lowering*; superciliorum, Cic.; **2,** *letting fall, lowering, sinking*; vocis contentiones et remissiones, Cic. **B.** Transf., **1,** *breaking off, interrupting, ceasing*; morbi, Cic.; usūs, Cic.; **2,** *a remitting*; tributi in triennium, Tac.; **3,** remissio animi; **a,** *relaxation, recreation*, Cic.; **b,** *quiet, tranquillity*; in acerbissima injuria remissio animi ac dissolutio, Cic.; **c,** *mildness*, Cic.

rĕmissus -a -um, p. adj. (from remitto), *relaxed, languid.* **I.** Lit., corpora, Cic. **II.** Fig.; **A.** In a bad sense, *negligent, remiss, inactive*; animus, Cic.; te remissiorem in petendo, Cic. **B.** In a good sense; **1,** *less severe*; ventus remissior, Caes.; frigora remissiora, Caes.; **2,** *mild, gentle*, Cic.; **3,** *cheerful, merry, lively*; homo, Cic.; jocus, Cic.

rĕmitto -misi -missum, 3. **I.** *to send back, send*; mulieres Romam, Cic.; obsides alicui, Caes.; nuntium, *to send a divorce to*, Cic.; so **1,** *to throw back*; pila, Caes.; **2,** *to give back, return*; alicui beneficium, Caes.; **3,** *to give back from oneself*; **a,** vocem nemora remittunt, *echo*, Verg.; **b,** *to cause, produce*; atramenta remittunt labem, Hor. **II.** *to let go back, relax*; habenas, Cic.; frena equo, Ov.; arcum, Hor.; so **1,** *to let sink down*; brachia, Verg.; tunica remissa, Ov.; **2,** *to loosen*; vincula, Ov.; esp., **a,** *to make liquid* (*again*); calor mella liquefacta remittit, Verg.; **b,** *to free*; vere remissus ager, *freed from ice and snow*, Ov.; **c,** *to cause to relax, to relieve, release, abate*; spes animos a certamine remisit, Liv.; se remittere, *to leave off work, refresh oneself*, Nep.; cantus remittunt animum, *relieve, enliven the mind*, Cic.; reflex., se remittere, or simply remittere, *to abate, become milder, cease*; quum remiserant dolores, Cic.; ventus remisit, Caes.; **3,** *to give free scope to*; animi appetitus, qui tum remitterentur, tum continerentur, Cic.; **4,** *to give up, to allow, forego, concede, grant*; **a,** omnia ista concedam et remittam, Cic.; provinciam remitto, exercitum depono, Cic.; **b,** *to renounce some work, punishment*, etc., *to remit, forego, give up*; navem in triennium, Cic.; Erycis tibi terga remitto, *make no use of*, Verg.;

inimicitias suas reipublicae, Liv ; **c**, *to abate, stop*, de celeritate, Cic , aliquantum, Cic , aliquid de severitate cogendi, Cic

rĕmōlior, 4 dep *to press back, push back, move back*, pondera terrae, Ov

rĕmollesco, 3 *to become soft again* **I.** Lit , cera remollescit sole, Ov **II.** Fig , **a**, *to be moved by*, precibus, Ov , **b**, *to become effeminate*, ea re ad laborem ferendum remollescere homines, Caes

rĕmollio, 4 *to make soft again*, fig , *to make effeminate, to weaken*, artus, Ov

rĕmŏra -ae, f *a delay, hindrance*, Plaut

rĕmŏrāmen -inis, n (remoror), *a delay*, Ov

rĕmordĕo -mordi -morsum, 2 *to bite again*, fig , *to annoy, disquiet, harass*, te cura remordet, Verg

rĕmŏror, 1 dep **I.** Intransit , *to remain behind, delay, dally, linger, loiter*, in Italia, Liv **II.** Transit , *to delay, obstruct, hinder*, aliquem, Cic , iter alicuius, Sall

rĕmōtē, adv (remotus), *afar off, at a distance*, aliae (stellae) propius a terris, aliae remotius eadem spatia conficiunt, Cic

rĕmōtĭo -ōnis, f (removeo), *a putting away, removing*, criminis, *repelling*, Cic

rĕmōtus a -um, p adj (from removeo) **I.** Lit , *distant, afar off, remote*, locus ab arbitris remotus, Cic , loci remoti a mari, Cic **II.** Fig , *removed from*, **a**, *free from*, ab suspicione remotissimus, Cic , a vulgari scientia remotiora, Cic , **b**, *disinclined to, averse from*, ab inani laude remotus, Cic , **c**, subst , **rĕmōta** ōrum, n = ἀποπροηγμένα, of the Stoics, *things to be rejected*, Cic

rĕmŏvĕo -mōvi mōtum, 2 *to move back, remove, take away, put away*, pecora, Caes , arbitros, Cic , aliquid ex oratione, Cic , aliquid de medio, Cic , aliquid ab oculis, Cic , equos ex conspectu, Caes , aliquem a republica, *to deprive of political rights*, Cic , aliquem senatu, Liv , removere se artibus, Cic

rĕmūgio, 4 **I.** *to bellow again, bellow back*, ad verba alicuius, Ov **II.** Transf , *to roar back, resound, echo*, vox assensu nemorum ingeminata remugit, Verg

rĕmulcĕo mulsi mulsum, 2 *to stroke back*, caudam, Verg

rĕmulcum -i, n (ῥυμουλκέω, for ῥυμὸν ἕλκω), *a tow-rope, towing cable*, navem remulco adducere, Caes

Rĕmŭlus -i, m **I.** *a king in Alba*, Ov **II.** *the name of a hero*, Verg

rĕmūnĕrātĭo -ōnis, f (remuneror), *a recompense, repaying, return*, benevolentiae, Cic , officiorum, Cic

rĕmūnĕror, 1 dep *to recompense, repay, reward*, (a) with acc. of pers , aliquem simillimo munere, Cic , aliquem magno praemio, Caes (β) with acc of thing, beneficia alicuius officiis, Cic , (γ) absol , in accipiendo remunerandoque, Cic

Rĕmūrĭa = Lemuria, v Lemures

rĕmurmŭro, 1 *to murmur against, murmur back*, nec fracta remurmurat unda, Verg

1 **rēmus** -i, m (ἐρετμός), *an oar* **I. A.** Lit , navigium remis incitare, Caes , prov , remis ventisque, or ventis remis, *by oars and sails, by all means in our power*, res velis, ut aiunt, remisque fugienda, Cic **B.** Fig , orationem dialecticorum remis propellere, Cic **II.** Transf , remi, *the hands and feet of a person swimming*, Ov , of the wings of a bird, alarum remis, Ov.

2 **Rĕmus** -i, m *the twin brother of Romulus, first king of Rome, who slew him in a dispute respecting the foundation of the city*

3 **Rēmus**, v Remi

rĕnarro, 1 *to relate again*, fata divum, Verg

rĕnascor -nātus sum, 3 dep *to be born again, arise, grow again* **I.** Lit , pinnae renascuntur, Cic **II.** Transf , **a**, of concr , ab secunda origine velut ab stirpibus laetius feraciusque renata urbs, Liv , **b**, of abstr , bellum istuc renatum, Cic

rĕnāvĭgo, 1 *to sail back*, in haec regna, Cic

rĕnĕo, 2 *to unspin, unravel that which has been spun*, dolent fila reneri, *that the destiny is reversed*, Ov

rēnes um and -ium, m *the kidneys*, Cic

rĕnīdĕo, 2 **I.** *to shine, gleam back, to glitter, be bright, to shimmer*, pura nocturno renidet luna mari, Hor , non ebur neque aureum mea renidet in domo lacunar, Hor **II** Meton , *to beam with joy, be joyful, cheerful, to laugh*, and in a bad sense *to laugh scornfully, to grin*, homo renidens, Liv ; adiecisse praedam torquibus exiguis renidet, Hor

rĕnīdesco, 3 (renideo), *to glitter*, Lucr

rĕnītor, 3 dep *to oppose, withstand, resist*, Liv

1 **rĕno**, 1 *to swim back*, Hor

2 **rēno (rhēno)** -ōnis, m *an animal of northern Europe*, perhaps *the reindeer*, Caes

rĕnōdo, 1 *to unbind, untie*, comam, Hor

rĕnŏvāmen -inis, n (renovo), *a renewal, new condition*, Ov

rĕnŏvātĭo -ōnis, f (renovo), *a renewing, renewal, renovation* **I.** Lit , mundi, Cic esp , renovatio singulorum annorum, *compound interest*, Cic **II.** Transf , renovatio timoris, Cic.

rĕnŏvo, 1 *to renew, renovate, restore* **I.** Lit , templum, Cic , agrum aratro, *to plough land that has been left fallow for some time*, Ov , esp , fenus in singulos annos, *to reckon compound interest*, Cic , centesimae quotannis renovatae Cic **II** Transf , a, *to renew*, scelus suum illud pristinum, Cic , bellum, Caes , ex morbo velut renovatus flos iuventae, Liv , animos ad odium renovare, *to inflame afresh to*, Cic , **b**, *to renew in thought or words, to repeat, recall*, renovabo illud quod initio dixi, Cic , **c**, *to refresh restore, renew in strength*, reficere et renovare rempublicam, Cic

rĕnŭmĕro, 1 *to count over, pay, pay back, repay*, Plaut.

rĕnuntĭātĭo -ōnis, f (renuntio), *a proclamation, declaration, public announcement*, with subject genit , eius, Cic , with object genit , suffragiorum, Cic

rĕnuntĭo (rĕnuncĭo), 1 **I.** *to bring back word, report, announce*, **a**, gen with acc , with de and the abl , with acc and infin , with dependent rel sent , assentior renuntioque vobis nihil esse quod, etc , Cic , renuntiatum est de obitu Tulliae filiae tuae, *I was informed*, ap Cic , **b**, *to make an official announcement or declaration, to report*, aliquid ad senatum, Cic ; **c**, *to make a thing publicly known, to announce*, e g , the election of a consul, etc , *to proclaim*, with double acc , L Murenam consulem, Cic , or in pass with double nom , sacerdos Climachias renuntiatus est, Cic **II.** *to disclaim, refuse, renounce*, amicitiam alicui, Liv , hospitium alicui, Cic ; decisionem tutoribus, Cic.

rĕnuntĭus ii, m *one who brings back word, a reporter*, Plaut

rĕnŭo -nŭi, 3. *to deny by a motion of the head, to refuse, deny, disapprove, reject;* renuit negitatque Sabellus, Hor.; with dat., huic decem millium crimini, *to deny,* Cic.; with acc., nullum convivium, *to decline,* Cic.

rĕnūto, 1. (intens. of renuo), *to refuse, deny, decline,* Lucr.

rĕnūtus, abl. -ū, m. (renuo), *a denial, refusal,* Plin.

rĕor, rătus sum, 2. dep. (root RE, Gr. ΡΕ-ω, *I say*), *to think, be of opinion, suppose, judge;* (α), with acc. and infin. or with infin. alone, rentur eos esse, quales se ipsi velint, Cic.; rebantur enim fore ut, etc., Cic.; (β) with double acc., alii rem incredibilem rati, Sall.; (γ) absol., reor in parenthesis, nam, reor, nullus posset esse jucundior, Cic.

rĕpāgŭla -ōrum, n. (repango). **I.** *the barrier in a circus or racecourse to keep in the horses,* Ov. **II.** *the bars or bolts fastening a door;* convulsis repagulis, Cic.; fig., omnia repagula pudoris officiique perfringere, *restraints, limits,* Cic.

rĕpandus -a -um, *bent backwards, turned up;* calceoli, Cic.

rĕpărābĭlis -e (reparo), *that can be repaired or restored;* damnum, Ov.

rĕparco (rĕperco), 3. *to spare, refrain from, abstain from;* id facere, Lucr.

rĕpăro, 1. **I.** *to prepare anew, repair, restore, renew.* **A.** Gen., perdere videbatur, quod reparare posset, Cic.; vires, Ov.; tribuniciam potestatem, Liv. **B.** Esp., *to fill up, complete;* exercitum, Liv.; damna caelestia lunae, Hor.; cornua (of the moon), Ov. **II.** *to barter for, purchase with;* vina Syrā reparata merce, Hor.

rĕpastĭnātĭo -ōnis, f. (repastino), *a digging up again,* Cic.

rĕpastĭno, 1. *to dig, trench, delve again,* Plin.

rĕpecto -pexus, 3. *to comb again;* coma repexa, Ov.

rĕpĕdo, 1. (pes), *to go back, retreat,* Lucr.

rĕpello, rĕpŭli (reppŭli) -pulsum, 3. **I.** *to drive back, drive away.* **A.** Lit., homines a templi aditu, Cic.; aliquem ex urbe, Cic.; hostes in silvas, Caes. **B.** Fig., *to drive away, banish, repel;* vim vi, Cic.; dolorem a se, Cic.; aliquem a spe, *deprive of hope,* Caes. **II.** *to push back, repulse.* **A.** Lit., repagula, Ov.; aliquem a genibus, Cic.; tellurem (sc. a mari), *to sail away from,* Ov.; amnes Oceani pede repellere, *to spurn* (of a star rising from the sea), Verg. **B.** Fig., **1,** criminationes, *to refute,* Cic.; **2,** *to spurn, scorn, repel;* connubia, Verg.; preces, Ov.; repulsi sunt ii, quos, etc., Cic.

rĕpendo -pendi -pensum, 3. **I.** *to weigh back again;* pensa, *to return an equal weight of,* Ov. **II.** *to weigh against.* **A.** Lit., **1,** aurum pro capite, Cic.; **2,** *to ransom;* miles auro repensus, Hor. **B.** Transf., *to repay, recompense, requite,;* gratiam, Ov.; si magna rependam, Verg.; pretium vitae, Prop.; damna formae ingenio, *make up for,* Ov.

rĕpens -entis (ῥέπω, i.e., vergo). **I.** *sudden, unexpected;* adventus, Cic.; adv., repens alia nuntiatur clades, Liv. **II.** (In Tacitus only), *new, fresh, recent;* perfidia, Tac.

rĕpenso, 1. (intens. of rependo), *to repay, requite, recompense, make up for,* Sen.

rĕpentĕ, adv. (repens), *suddenly, unexpectedly,* Cic.

rĕpentīnus -a -um (repens), *sudden, unlooked for, unexpected;* amor, Cic.; adventus, Caes.; venenum, *quick-working,* Tac.; ignoti homines et repentini, *upstarts,* Cic. Hence, adv., **rĕpentīno,** *suddenly, unexpectedly,* Cic.

rĕpercussio -ōnis, f. (repercutio), *a rebounding,* Sen.

rĕpercussus -ūs, m. (repercutio), *a rebounding, reverberation* (of sound, etc.), *echo, reflection;* quo plenior et gravior vox repercussu intumescat, Tac.

rĕpercŭtĭo -cussi -cussum, 3. *to strike back, drive back, cause to rebound* (of sound, etc.); discus repercussus in aëra, Ov.; esp., pass., repercuti, *to bound back,* and repercussus, *bounding back;* **a,** of sound, *to re-echo;* valles repercussae (clamoribus), Liv.; **b,** of light, *to be reflected;* lumen aquae sole repercussum, Verg.

rĕpĕrĭo, rĕpĕri (reppĕri) -pertum (re and PER-io, cf. comperio), 4. *to find, meet again.* **I.** Lit., mortui sunt reperti, Cic. **II.** Fig., **A. 1,** *to reveal, discover, ascertain, find out;* causas duas, Cic.; neque reperire poterat quanta esset, etc., Caes.; in pass. with double nom., *to be found out = to appear;* Stoici inopes reperiuntur, Cic.; improbus reperiebare, Cic.; with acc. and infin. = *to find out,* as stated in history; quem Tarentum venisse L. Camillo Appio Claudio consulibus reperio, Liv; in pass. with nom. and infin., in Italiae partes Pythagoras venisse reperitur, Cic.; **2,** *to find, acquire, gain;* sibi salutem, Caes.; nomen ex inventore, Cic. **B.** *to find out something new, discover, invent;* nihil novi, Cic.; viam quā, etc., Cic.

rĕpertor -ōris, m. (reperio), *a discoverer, inventor;* medicinae, Verg.; hominum rerumque, *Jupiter,* Verg.

rĕpertus -a -um, partic. of reperio.

rĕpĕtentĭa -ae, f. (repeto), *a recollection, remembrance,* Lucr. (?)

rĕpĕtītĭo -ōnis, f. (repeto), *repetition;* **a,** eiusdem verbi crebra repetitio, Cic.; **b,** as a figure of speech = ἀναφορά, *the repetition of the same word at the beginning of several sentences,* Cic.

rĕpĕtītor -ōris, m. (repeto), *one who reclaims or demands back again;* nuptae ademptae, Cic.

rĕpĕto -ivi and -ii -itum, 3. **I.** *to strive after again.* **A.** *to attack again, fall upon again;* regem repetitum saepius cuspide, Liv. **B.** *to go to again, turn to again, return to;* castra, Cic.; retro in Asiam, Liv. **II.** Transf., **A.** *to ask back or again;* **1,** *to ask again* or *anew, ask for;* Gallum ab eodem repetit, Caes.; **2,** *to ask back, demand back;* promissa, Cic.; Salaminii Homerum repetunt, *claim as their countryman,* Cic.; pecunias ereptas, Cic.; esp., **a,** res repetere, *to demand satisfaction of an enemy* (used of the Fetiales), Cic.; **b,** *to demand back again;* res, *to demand one's own property from a legal tribunal,* Cic.; pecuniae repetundae, or simply repetundae, *money extorted from the provinces by their governors;* meton., *extortion;* lex repetundarum pecuniarum, de pecuniis repetundis, *law against extortion,* Cic.; **3,** *to demand as one's right;* jus suum, Cic.; rationem ab aliquo, Cic. **B.** *to fetch back;* **1, a,** *to fetch afresh;* alii (elephanti) repetiti ac trajecti sunt, Liv.; **b,** *to renew, begin again;* pugnam, Liv.; studia, Caes.; partic., repetitus, poet., as an adv. = *anew, afresh;* repetita robora caedit, Ov.; **c,** *to think over again, recall, remember;* rei memoriam, Cic.; **2,** *to repeat by words or writing;* repete quae coepisti, Cic.; **3,** *to trace back from antiquity, deduce, fetch;* originem domūs, Verg.; aliquid alte, et a capite, Cic.; haec tam longe repetita principia, Cic.; **4,** *to regain, recover;* libertatem, Liv.; **5,** *to reckon again;* repetitis et enumeratis diebus, Caes.

rĕpĕtundae, v. repeto.

rĕplĕo -plēvi -plētum, 2 *to fill again, fill up* **I.** Lit., exhaustas domos, *complete, make good*, Cic., consumpta, Cic., exercitum, Liv. **II.** *to make full, fill, satisfy* **A.** corpora carne, Ov., exercitum frumento, *supply with*, Caes., fig., repleri scientiā juris, Cic., hence, **rĕplētus** -a -um, *filled, full*, lit. and fig., templa, Cic. **B.** *to infect*, ut curantes eādem vi morbi repletos secum traherent, Liv.

rĕplētus a -um, partic. of repleo (q. v.).

rĕplĭcātĭo -ōnis, f. (replico), *a rolling again, rolling round*, ut replicatione quādam mundi motum regat atque tueatur, Cic.

rĕplĭco, 1 *to fold back, unroll*, fig., *to unfold, unroll, turn over*, memoriam temporum, Cic., memoriam annalium, Cic., temporis primum quidque replicans, Cic.

rēpo, repsi, reptum, 3 (root REP, Gr. ΕΡΠ-ω), *to creep, crawl*, 1, lit., cochleae inter saxa repentes, Sall., 2, transf., of slow travellers, Hor., of clouds, Lucr., fire, Lucr., 3, fig., sermones repentes per humum, *a vulgar, prosaic style*, Hor.

rĕpōno pŏsŭi -pŏsĭtum (-postum), 3 **I.** *to place back, put behind*, 1, cervicem, *to bend back*, Lucr., 2, *to lay up in store, lay by, preserve*, pecuniam in thesauris, Liv., arma, Caes., fig., haec sensibus imis reponas, *impress deep in*, Verg., 3, *to lay aside, put on one side*, tela, Ov., faciemque deae vestemque, Verg., falcem arbusta reponunt, *make unnecessary*, Verg., transf., *to give up*, caestum artemque, Verg., 4, *to bury, lay in the earth*, tellure repostos, Verg. **II.** *to place a thing back in its former place, put back, restore*, 1, columnas, Cic., lapidem suo loco, Cic., se in cubitum *recline at table again, begin to eat*, Hor., 2, *to place on the table again*, plena pocula, Verg., 3, *to restore a thing to its former condition*, robora flammis ambesa, Verg., hence, *to restore a person*, aliquem in sceptra, Verg., 4, *to bring on the boards again, represent again*, Ialmlam, Hor. **III.** *to place one thing against another, in the place of another*, 1, *to put in the place of*, te meas epistolas delere, ut reponas tuas, Cic., 2, *to answer again*, ne tibi ego idem reponam, Cic., 3, *to requite, return* haec pro virginitate reponit, Verg. **IV.** *to place in or on*, 1, lit., quae sacra quaedam more Atheniensium virginum reposita in capitibus sustinebant, Cic., 2, transf., a, sidera in numero deorum, Cic., b, *to place, cause to rest*, spem in virtute, Caes., causam totam in judicum humanitate, Cic.

rĕporto, 1 *to bear back, bring back, carry back* **I.** Lit., **A.** exercitum Britanniā, Cic., milites navibus in Siciliam, Caes. **B.** *to bring back, to bring back home*, as victor, nihil ex praeda domum, Cic., victoriam, non pacem domum, Liv. **II.** Transf., 1, *to bring back, deliver*, adytis haec tristia dicta, Verg., 2, *to bring to a person*; alicui solatium aliquod, Cic.

rĕposco, 3 **I.** *to ask back again, demand back*, arma, Ov., alter a me Catilinam, alter Cethegum reposcebat, Cic., with double acc., *to ask back something from a person*, aliquem simulacrum, Cic., Parthos signa, Verg. **II.** *to demand as a right, claim* regem ad supplicium, Verg., ab aliquo rationem vitae, Cic., with double acc., quos illi poenas (*as a punishment*) reposcent, Verg.

rĕpŏsĭtōrĭum -ii, n. (repono), *a tray, waiter, stand*, Plin.

rĕpŏsĭtus (rĕpostus) -a -um **I.** Partic. of repono **II.** P. adj., *remote, distant*, terrae repostae, Verg.

rĕpostor -ōris, m. (repono) *a restorer*, templorum, Ov.

rĕpōtĭa -ōrum, n. (re and poto), *a drinking, revelling the day after an entertainment*, Hor.

rĕpraesentātĭo -ōnis, f. (repraesento) **I.** *a representation, a lively description*, Plin. **II.** *payment in cash*, Cic.

rĕpraesento, 1 **I.** *to represent, make present to the imagination, bring before the mind, show, make manifest*; a, quod ipsum templum repraesentabat memoriam consulatus mei, Cic., b, *to express, imitate*, virtutem moresque Catonis, Hor. **II.** *to perform immediately, hasten*, a, se repraesentaturum id, etc., Caes., medicinam, *use directly*, Cic., diem promissorum, Cic., si repraesentari morte mea libertas civitatis posset, *brought about at once*, Cic., b, esp. t. t. of commercial language, *to pay cash, pay ready money*, pecuniam, Cic.

rĕprĕhendo -prĕhendi -prĕhensum, 3 and **rĕprendo** prendi prensum, 3 *to catch, to hold back, to seize, hold fast, detain* **I.** Lit., quosdam manu, Liv., fig., revocat virtus vel potius reprehendit manu, Cic. **II.** Fig. **A.** Gen., genus pecuniae, Cic. **B.** Esp., 1, *to blame, censure, reprove, reprehend*; aliquem, Cic., aliquem in eo quod, etc., Cic.; id in me reprehendis, Cic., 2, rhet. t. t., *to refute*, Cic.

rĕprĕhensĭo -ōnis, f. (reprehendo). **I.** *a holding back*, fig., *a stopping or check in speaking*, sine reprehensione, Cic. **II.** Esp., 1, *blame, censure, reprehension*, culpae, vitae, Cic., plur., Cic., 2, rhet. t. t., *a refuting, refutation*, Cic.

rĕprĕhenso, 1 (freq. of reprehendo), *to hold back eagerly, to hold fast*, singulos, Liv.

rĕprĕhensor -ōris, m. (reprehendo) **I.** *a censurer, reprover*, Cic. **II.** *an improver, reformer*, comitiorum, Cic.

rĕpressor -ōris, m. (reprimo), *a represser, restrainer*, caedis quotidianae, Cic.

rĕprĭmo pressi -pressum, 3 (re and premo), *to hold back, restrain, hinder, repress* **I.** Lit., lacum Albanum, Cic., dextram, Verg., retro pedem, Verg., represso jam Lucterio ac remoto (in battle), Caes., (Mithridatem) repressum magna ex parte, non oppressum, Cic. **II.** Fig., *to keep under, check, curb, restrain, repress*, a, of things, furorem exsultantem, Cic., animi incitationem atque alacritatem, Caes., conatus alicuius, Cic., b, of persons as objects, se, *to restrain oneself*, Cic., concitatam multitudinem, Cic.

rĕprŏbo, 1 *to disapprove*, Cic. (?)

rĕprōmissĭo -ōnis, f. (repromitto), *a counter-promise*, Cic.

rĕprōmitto -misi -missum, 3 *to make a counter-promise, to promise in return*, Cic.

reptātĭo -ōnis, f. (repto), *a creeping, crawling*, Quint.

reptātus -ūs, m. (repto), *a creeping* (of plants), Plin.

repto, 1 (intens. of repo), *to creep, crawl*, applied to slow walkers or travellers, Hor.

rĕpŭdĭātĭo -ōnis, f. (repudio), *a refusal, rejecting, disdaining* supplicum, Cic.

rĕpŭdĭo, 1 (repudium) **I.** *to refuse, reject, disdain*, cuius vota et preces a vestris mentibus repudiare debetis, Cic., pacem, Cic., conditionem aequissimam, Cic. **II.** Esp. of married or betrothed persons, *to repudiate, divorce, separate oneself from*, uxorem, Suet.

rĕpŭdĭum -ii, n. (re and pes, as tripudium from terra and pes), *a separation between married or betrothed persons, repudiation, divorce*, alicui repudium renuntiare, or remittere, *to send a divorce to*, Plaut., repudium dicere, Tac.

rĕpŭĕrasco, 3. *to become a boy again, to sport, frolic like a child*, Cic.

rĕpugnans, p. adj. (from repugno), *contrary, opposed*; subst., **rĕpugnantĭa** -ium, n. *contradictory things*, Cic.

rĕpugnantĕr, adv. (repugnans), *unwillingly, with repugnance*, Cic.

rĕpugnantĭa -ae, f. (repugno). **I.** *resistance, means of resistance*; natura hanc dedit repugnantiam apibus, Plin. **II.** Fig., *a contrariety, discordance* (opp. concordia); rerum, Cic.

rĕpugno, 1. *to oppose, resist, withstand*. **I.** Lit., nostri primo fortiter repugnare, Caes. **II.** Transf., **A.** Gen., *to be opposed to, to oppose, resist*; contra veritatem, Caes.; quum huic (cupiditati) obsecutus sis, illi est repugnandum, Cic.; non repugno, foll. by quominus and subj., Cic. **B.** Esp., *to be naturally opposed or repugnant to, to be inconsistent with, incompatible with*; simulatio amicitiae repugnat maxime, Cic.; haec inter se quam repugnent, plerique non vident, Cic.

rĕpullŭlo, 1. *to sprout out again*, Plin.

rĕpulsa -ae, f. (repello). **I.** *a repulse in soliciting an office, a rejection*; repulsa consulatus, Cic.; aedilicia, Cic.; a populo repulsam ferre, or accipere, Cic. **II.** Transf., *a denial, refusal*; amor crescit dolore repulsae, Ov.

rĕpulso, 1. (intens. of repello), *to beat back*. **I.** colles verba repulsantes, *echoing*, Lucr. **II.** *to repel again and again*; vera repulsans pectus verba, Lucr.

1. **rĕpulsus** -a -um, p. adj. with compar. (repello), *removed*; quod procul a vera nimis est ratione repulsum, Lucr.

2. **rĕpulsus** -ūs, m. (repello), *a striking back*, hence, *the reflection of light, echoing of sound*; durioris materiae, *resistance*, Cic.

rĕpūmĭcātĭo -ōnis, f. (re and pumico), *a rubbing down again, repolishing*, Plin.

rĕpungo, 3. *to prick again, goad again*; fig., leviter illorum animos, Cic.

rĕpurgo, 1. *to cleanse again*. **I. A.** Lit., iter, Liv.; humum saxis, Ov. **B.** Transf., caelum, Ov. **II.** Meton., *to clear away, purge out*; quicquid in Aenea fuerat mortale repurgat, Ov.

rĕpŭtātĭo -ōnis, f. (reputo), *a consideration, reflecting upon, pondering*, Tac.

rĕpŭto, 1. **I.** *to reckon, count, compute*; ex hoc die superiores solis defectiones usque ad illam quae, etc., Cic. **II.** Transf., *to think over, consider, ponder*; horum nihil umquam, Cic.; with acc. and infin., cum tibi nihil merito accidisse reputabis, Cic.; with depend. interrog. sent., quid ille vellet, Cic.

rĕquĭes -ētis, f. *rest, repose*. **I.** Lit., non labor meus, non requies, Cic.; curarum, Cic.; animi et corporis, Cic. **II.** Meton., *a resting-place*, Hor. (dat. not used, acc., requietem and requiem, Cic.; abl., requiete, Cic. poet.; requie, Ov.).

rĕquĭesco -quiēvi -quiētum, 3. *to rest, repose*. **I.** Lit., **A.** Gen., **1,** of persons, in sella, Cic.; sub umbra, Verg.; a muneribus reipublicae, Cic.; **2,** of things, vixdum requiesse aures a strepitu et tumultu hostili, Liv.; requiescit vitis in ulmo, *rests upon, is supported by*, Cic. **B.** Esp., **1,** *to rest, to sleep*; lecto, Prop.; **2,** *to rest in the grave*; in sepulchro requiescere mortuum, Cic. **II.** Transf., *to repose, find rest*; animus ex multis miseriis atque periculis requievit, Sall.; in spe huius, Cic. (syncop. perf. form, requierunt, Verg.; requiesse, Cic.).

rĕquĭētus -a -um, p. adj. (from requiesco), *rested, refreshed*; miles, Liv.; ager, *fallow*, Ov.

rĕquīrĭto, 1. (intens. of requiro), *to inquire after*, Plaut.

rĕquīro -quīsīvi -quīsītum, 3. (re and quaero). **I.** *to seek, search for again*. **A.** Lit., libros, Cic. **B.** Transf., **1,** *to miss, need, feel the want of*; majorum prudentiam in aliqua re, Cic.; subsidia belli, Cic.; **2,** *to demand, to desire, consider necessary*; virtus nullam voluptatem requirit, Cic.; in hoc bello virtutes multae requiruntur, Cic. **II.** *to ask for, inquire after*. **A.** Gen., domum alicuius, Cic.; quae a me de Vatinio requiris, Cic.; quoniam nihil ex te hi majores natu requirunt, Cic.; with depend. interrog., illud quoque requirit, qua ratione fecerit, Cic. **B.** *to investigate*; rationes, Cic.

rĕquīsītum -i, n. (requiro), *need, necessity*, Sall.

rēs, rĕi, f. (connected with PE-ω, whence ῥῆμα), *a thing, object, matter, affair, circumstance*. **I.** Gen., divinae humanaeque res, natura rerum, *the world*, Cic.; genit., rerum, pleonastic, ficta rerum, Hor.; abdita rerum, Hor.; rerum, used to strengthen a superl., rerum pulcherrima, Roma, Verg.; si res postulabit, *if the position of affairs shall require*, Cic.; homines nullā re bonā digni, *good for nothing*, Cic.; re natā, Cic.; pro re, *according to circumstances*, Liv.; res populi Romani perscribere, *to narrate the affairs of the Roman people, write the history of Rome*, Liv. **II.** Esp., **A.** Emphatic, *the thing itself, the real thing, the reality*; rem opinor spectari oportere, non verba, Cic.; hos deos non re, sed opinione esse, Cic.; quantum distet argumentatio ab re ipsa atque a veritate, Cic.; et re vera, *and in truth*, Cic. **B.** *possessions, property, wealth*; rem facere, Hor.; augere, Cic.; plur., privatae res, Cic. **C.** *interest, advantage, benefit*; consulere suis rebus, Nep.; in rem suam convertere, Cic.; e or ex re publica (*to the advantage of the state*) fecisse, Cic.; ducere, Liv.; ex or e re publica est, with acc. and infin., *it is for the public benefit*, Cic.; ex re mea, *to my advantage*, Cic. **D.** *ground, reason*, only in the phrases, eā (hāc) re, ob eam (hanc) rem, *on this account, on that account*, Cic. **E.** *a matter of business, an affair*; rem cum aliquo transigere, Cic.; de tota illa ratione atque re Gallicana, Cic.; transf., res (alicui) est cum aliquo, *to have to do with*; tecum mihi res est, T. Rosci, quoniam, etc., Cic. **F.** *a lawsuit, cause, action*; utrum rem an litem dici oporteret, Cic. **G.** res publica, and (in histor.) simply res; **a,** res publica, *the republic, the state, commonwealth, government*; rem publicam sustinere, Cic.; **b,** simply res, res Romana, *the Roman state*, Liv.

rĕsăcro, 1. *to free from a curse*, Nep.

rĕsaevĭo, 4. *to rage again*, Ov.

rĕsălūtātĭo -ōnis, f. (resaluto), *a greeting in return*, Suet.

rĕsălūto, 1. *to salute again, return a greeting to*; aliquem, Cic.

rĕsānesco -sānŭi, 3. *to become sound again, to heal again*, Ov.

rĕsarcĭo -sarsi -sartum, 4. *to patch again, mend again, repair*. **I.** Lit., tecta, Liv. **II.** Fig., *to repair, restore*; detrimentum, Caes.

rescindo -scĭdi -scissum, 3. *to tear off again, tear away again, cut off, cut away*. **I. A.** Lit., vallum ac loricam falcibus, Caes.; pontem, *to break away*, Caes.; latebram teli, *to cut open*, Verg.; vulnus, *to open again*, Ov.; and fig., luctus obductos, *to renew*, Ov. **B.** Meton., hence, *to open*; locum firmatum, Cic. **II.** Transf., *to rescind, repeal, abrogate a law, decree*, etc.; acta M. Antonii, Cic.; totam triennii praeturam, Cic.

rescisco -scīvi and -scĭi -scītum, 3. *to find out, ascertain*; quum id rescierit, Cic.

rescrībo -scripsi -scriptum, 3 **I.** *to write again, to write anew*, ex eodem milite novas legiones *to enrol again*, Liv **II.** *to write back, answer in writing*, **1,** ad aliquem, Cic, alicui, Cic, **2,** litteris, ad litteras, or ad epistolam, Cic, of the emperor, *to answer a petition or inquiry in writing*, Suet., hence, **rescriptum** -i, n *an imperial rescript*, Tac. **III. a,** in book-keeping, *to enter to the credit of an account, to pay, repay*, reliqua rescribamus, Cic, quod tu numquam rescribero (*pay again*) possis, Hor; **b,** *to transfer from one class of soldiers to another*, ad equum, jestingly, with a double meaning, *to make cavalry* and *to place in the order of knights*, Caes

rĕsĕco -sĕcŭi -sectum, 1 *to cut off* **I.** Lit, linguam, Cic, partem de tergore, Ov **II.** Transf, *to cut off, put away, remove*, libidinem, Cic, spem longam, Hor.

rĕsĕcro, 1 (re and sacro), *to adjure repeatedly, implore again and again*, Plaut (another form resacro, q v)

rĕsēdo, 1 *to heal, assuage*, Plin

rĕsegmĭna -um, n (reseco), *cuttings, parings*, Plin

rĕsēmĭno, 1 *to beget, produce again*, Ov

rĕsĕquor -sĕcūtus (-sĕquūtus), 3 dep *to follow, pursue*, aliquem dictis, *to answer*, Ov

1 **rĕsĕro** -sēvi, 3 *to sow again, set again plant again*, Plin

2 **rĕsĕro,** 1. *to unclose, open* **I.** Lit, **A.** In a narrow sense, *to open a door*, fores, januam, Ov **B.** In a wider sense, *to open*, pectus, *to tear open*, Ov. **II.** Transf, **A.** *to open, make accessible*, Italiam exteris gentibus, Cic, aures, Liv **B.** *to reveal*, augustae oracula mentis, Ov **C.** *to open = to begin*, annum, Ov.

rĕservo, 1 **I.** *to lay up, keep back, reserve, keep*, hoc consilium ad extremum, Caes, in aliud tempus, Caes, cetera praesenti sermoni, Cic **II. a,** *to save*, omnes, Cic; **b,** *to retain, preserve*, nihil ad similitudinem hominis, *nothing human*, Cic

rĕses -sĭdis (resideo) **I.** *remaining, sitting, staying behind*, reses in urbe plebs, Liv **II.** *motionless, inactive, inert*, eum residem tempus terere, Liv, animus, Verg

rĕsĭdĕo -sēdi -sessum, 2 (re and sedeo), *to remain sitting, to abide, stay.* **I.** Lit., **a,** residamus, *let us sit down*, Cic, in equo, Ov, in republica, Cic, **b,** *to celebrate a festival or holiday*; denicales, quae a nece appellatae sunt, quia residentur mortuis, *kept in honour of the dead*, Cic **II.** Transf, in corpore nullum residere sensum, Cic, residet spes in tua virtute, *depends upon*, Cic, cuius culpa non magis in te resedit, Cic

rĕsīdo -sēdi -sessum, 3 **I.** *to sit down, place oneself*, **a,** *to sit down to rest*, Cic, mediis aedibus, Verg, **b,** *to settle*, Siculis arvis, Verg, **c,** *to stay in a place, remain*, in villa, Cic, in oppido aliquo, Cic **II.** Of inanimate things, *to sink down, settle* **A.** Gen, **1,** lit, si montes resedissent, Cic; **2,** fig, **a,** *to sink, to settle down, abate, grow quiet*, mens resedit, Caes, cum tumor animi resedisset, Cic, **b,** *to become tired, to be weary, exhausted*, longiore certamine sensim residere Samnitium animos, Liv **B.** *to sink down = to draw back, withdraw*, **a,** lit, maria in se ipsa residant, Verg, **b,** fig, sex mihi surgat opus numeris, in quinque residat, *interchange hexameter and pentameter*, Ov

rĕsĭdŭus a -um (resideo), *remaining, left behind, outstanding*, odium, Cic, simulatio, Liv, pecuniae, Cic; subst, **rĕsĭdŭum** -i, n *that which remains, the remainder, residue, rest*, Cic

rĕsigno, 1 **I.** *to unseal, open* **A.** Lit, litteras, Cic; testamenta, Hor **B.** Fig, **1,** *to open = to reveal*, venientia fata, Ov, **2,** *to cancel, annul, destroy*, omnem tabularum fidem, Cic, **3,** *to release, free*, lumina morte resignat (Mercurius), *releases from death*, Verg **II.** *to enter from one account-book into another, to give back, resign*, cuncta, Hor, quae dedit, Hor.

rĕsĭlĭo -sĭlŭi -sultum, 4 (re and salio), *to leap back, spring back*, in gelidos lacus, Ov, ad manipulos, Liv **I.** Of inanimate things, *to spring back, rebound*, resilit grando a culmine tecti, Ov, fig, ubi scopulum offendis eiusmodi, ut non modo ab hoc crimen resilire videas, verum etiam, etc, Cic **II.** Transf, *to contract, diminish*, in spatium breve, Ov

rĕsīmus -a -um, *bent backwards, turned up*, nares, Ov

rēsīna -ae, f (ῥητίνη), *resin*, Plin

rēsīnācĕus -a -um (resina), *resinous*, Plin

rēsīnātus a -um (resina) **I.** *flavoured with resin*, vinum, Mart. **II.** *smeared with resin*, juventus (to take hairs off the skin), Juv

rēsīnōsus a -um (resina), *full of resin, resinous*, Plin

rĕsĭpĭo, 3 (re and sapio), *to have a smack, taste, flavour of anything* **I.** Lit, Plin **II.** Fig, Epicurus minime resipiens patriam, *with no trace of the wit of his country*, i e, *Athens*, Cic

rĕsĭpisco -sīpŭi and -sīpii, also sipivi, 3 (resipio) **I.** *to recover one's senses, come to one self again* (from fainting, etc), Cic **II.** *to become rational again, come to one's right mind*, Cic (syncop perf, resipisset, Cic).

rĕsisto -stĭti, 3 **I.** *to remain standing* **A a,** in a position of rest, *to remain, continue*, ibi, Caes, Romae, Cic, **b,** after motion, *to stand still, halt*, Caes, virtus resistet extra fores carceris, Cic, negabat se umquam cum Curione restitisse, *had stopped to talk*, Cic **B.** Transf, **a,** of discourse, sed ego in hoc resisto, *stop here*, Cic, **b,** *to recover a footing, get to one's feet again*, ubi lapsi resistamus, Cic **II.** *to resist, oppose, withstand* **A.** Physically, **a,** of persons, hostibus, Caes, vi contra vim, Liv, **b,** of things, quae nunc immotae perstant ventisque resistunt, Ov, **c,** morally, dolori fortiter, Cic, lacrimis et precibus, Cic, resistere et pugnare contra veritatem, Cic, impers, omnibus his resistitur, Caes, foll by ne and the subj ne sibi statua poneretur, restitit, Nep, foll by quin and the subj, vix deorum opibus, quin obruatur Romana res, resisti potest, Liv; cui nullā vi resisti potest, foll by quo secius and subj, Cic, absol, restitit et pervicit Cato, Cic

rĕsŏlūtus -a -um, p. adj (from resolvo), *relaxed, effeminate*, Mart

rĕsolvo -solvi -sŏlūtum, 3 *to unbind, untie, loose, loosen, open* **I. A.** vestes, Ov, equos, *to unyoke*, Ov, puella resoluta capillos, *with dishevelled hair*, Ov **B.** Transf, **1,** gleba se resolvit, *becomes loose*, Verg, Cerberus immania terga resolvit fusus humi, *stretches out in sleep*, Verg, **2,** *to open*, litteras, Liv, fauces in verba, Ov, **3,** *to melt*, ignis aurum resolvit, Lucr, nivem, Ov, **4,** *to drive away, dissipate*, tenebras, Verg, nebulas, Ov **II.** Fig, **1,** *to end*, curas, Verg, litem lite, Hor, **2,** *to dissolve, to relax physically, weaken, make languid*, ut jacui totis resolutus medullis, Ov, **3,** *to abolish, destroy*, jura pudoris, Verg, **4,** *to free*, te piacula nulla resolvent, Hor, **5,** *to unravel, reveal*, dolos tecti (Labyrinthi) ambagesque, Verg, **6,** *to pay*, Plaut Cic

rĕsŏnābĭlis -e (resono), *resounding, echoing*, Ov.

rĕsŏno -sŏnŭi and -sŏnāvi, 1. **I.** Intransit., **A.** *to give back an echo, to resound, echo;* aedes plangoribus resonant, Verg.; resonans theatrum, Cic.; gloria virtuti resonat, *is an echo of,* Cic. **B.** *to sound again and again, to resound;* nervos resonare, Cic.; resonant avibus virgulta, Verg. **II.** Transf., **A.** *to re-echo, repeat;* doces silvas resonare Amaryllida, Verg.; umbrae resonarent triste et acutum, Hor.; in pass., in fidibus testudine resonatur (sonus), Cic. **B.** *to fill with sound;* lucos cantu, Verg.

rĕsŏnus -a -um (resono), *resounding, echoing;* voces, Ov.

rĕsorbĕo, 2. *to swallow, suck in, absorb again;* fluctus, Ov.

respecto, 1. (intens. of respicio). **I.** *to look eagerly back, look about for.* **A.** Lit., respectare ad tribunal, Liv.; with acc., arcem Romanam, Liv. **B.** Transf., verum haec ita praetereamus, ut tamen intuentes et respectantes relinquamus, Cic.; with acc., si qua pios respectant numina, *have regard for,* Cic. **II.** Meton., *to look for, expect;* par munus ab aliquo, Cic.

respectus -ūs, m. (respicio). **I.** *a looking back, looking around one.* **A.** Lit., sine respectu fugere, Liv.; incendiorum, *looking back upon,* Cic. **B.** Transf., *care, regard, respect, consideration towards;* Romanorum maxime respectus civitates movit, Liv.; sine respectu majestatis, Liv. **II.** Meton., *a place of refuge, a retreat;* quum respectum ad senatum non haberet, Cic.

respergo -spersi -spersum, 3. (re and spargo), *to besprinkle, sprinkle over;* manus sanguine, Cic.; aliquem cruore, Liv.; fig., servili probro respergi, Tac.

respersĭo -ōnis, f. (respergo), *a sprinkling over, besprinkling;* pigmentorum, Cic.; sumptuosa respersio, *sprinkling of the grave with incense and wine,* Cic.

respersus, abl. -ū, m. (respergo), *a sprinkling, besprinkling,* Plin.

respĭcĭo -spexi -spectum, 3. (re and specio), transit. and intransit., *to look behind, to look back.* **I.** Lit., Cic.; nusquam circumspiciens aut respiciens, Liv.; with acc., **a,** *to look back upon;* tribunal, Liv.; Eurydicen suam, Ov.; amicum, Verg.; **b,** *to see behind one, to observe;* quos ubi rex respexit, Liv.; angues a tergo, Verg.; with acc. and infin., respiciunt atram in nimbo volitare favillam, Verg. **II.** Transf., **a,** *to look back upon, reflect upon;* spatium praeteriti temporis, Cic.; **b,** *to have respect to;* (α) *to think upon, provide for;* ut respiciam generum meum, Caes.; (β) *to care for, consider;* rempublicam, Cic.; commoda populi, Cic.; **c,** *to belong to, fall to the care of;* ad hunc summa imperii respiciebat, Caes.; **d,** *to look towards with desire, to hope, expect;* spem ab Romanis, Liv.

respīrāmen -ĭnis, n. (respiro), *the windpipe,* Ov.

respīrātĭo -ōnis, f. (respiro). **I.** *a taking breath, respiration;* **1,** lit., Cic.; **2,** meton., *a pause in a speech where the speaker takes breath,* Cic. **II.** *an exhalation;* aquarum, Cic.

respīrātus -ū, m. (respiro), *a taking breath,* Cic.

respīro, 1. **I.** *to blow back, blow in a contrary direction;* of winds, Lucr. **II.** Esp., *to breathe back.* **A.** *to take breath, breathe, breathe out;* animam, Cic.; ex ea pars redditur respirando, Cic. **B.** *to take breath, recover oneself after any violent exertion;* **1,** lit., Cic.; **2,** fig., *to be relieved from fear, anxiety,* etc.; paulum a metu, Cic.; of abstractions, *to abate, decline;* cupiditas atque avaritia respiravit paulum, Cic.; oppugnatio respiravit, *took breath, declined in violence,* Cic.; pass. impers., ita respiratum est, Cic.

resplendĕo -ŭi, 2. *to glitter back, be bright, resplendent,* Verg.

respondĕo -spondi -sponsum, 2. **I.** *to promise in return,* Plaut. **II.** *to answer.* **A.** Lit., *to answer* (prop., *by word of mouth*); tibi non rescribam, sed respondeam, Sen.; *to answer by word of mouth* or *by writing;* epistolae, Cic.; ad haec, Cic.; alicui ad rogatum, Cic.; videat quid respondeat, Cic.; respondent "cui," Cic.; esp., **a,** of judges, *to give decisions;* de jure, Cic.; criminibus respondere, *to defend oneself against,* Cic.; of oracles and soothsayers, *to answer,* Cic.; transf., saxa respondent voci, *give an echo,* Cic.; **b,** *to answer to one's name,* hence, *to appear, be present;* quum ad nomen nemo responderet, Liv.; Verrem non responsurum, Cic.; so of soldiers, *to answer to one's name, take one's place;* ad nomina non respondere, Liv.; fig., pedes respondere non vocatos, *be in readiness,* Cic. **B.** Transf., **a,** *to correspond to, to answer to, to agree* or *accord with;* verba verbis respondeant, Cic.; tua virtus opinioni hominum respondet, Cic.; **b,** *to requite, return;* amori amore, Liv.; **c,** *to lie over against;* contra respondet tellus, Verg.; **d,** *to be punctual in paying;* ad tempus, Cic.; **e,** *to balance, correspond to in strength,* etc.; orationi illorum, Cic.

responsĭo -ōnis, f. (respondeo). **I.** *a reply, answer;* responsionem elicere, Cic. **II.** Rhet. t.t., sibi ipsi responsio, *a replying to one's own argument* (= ἀπόκρισις), Cic.

responsĭto, 1. (intens. of responso), *to give an answer, opinion* (of legal advisers), Cic.

responso, 1. (intens. of respondeo), *to answer, reply, respond.* **I. A.** Lit., Plaut. **B.** Transf., *to re-echo;* lucus ripaeque responsant circa, Verg. **II.** Fig., responsare cupidinibus, *to withstand,* Hor.; cenis, *to scorn,* Hor.; palato, *to defy,* Hor.

responsor -ōris, m. (respondeo), *one who answers,* Plaut.

responsum -i, n. (respondeo), *an answer.* **I.** Gen., responsum dare alicui, Cic.; reddere, Cic.; ferre, auferre, *obtain,* Cic. **II.** Esp., **a,** *the answer of an oracle or soothsayer;* haruspicum, Cic.; Sibyllae, Verg.; **b,** *the answer* or *opinion of a lawyer,* Cic.

respublĭca, v. res.

respŭo -ŭi, 3. **I.** Lit., *to spit back* or *out, to reject;* reliquiae cibi, quas natura respuit, Cic. **II.** Fig., *to reject, refuse, repel, disapprove of;* quum id dicat, quod omnium mentes aspernentur ac respuant, Cic.; defensionem, Cic.; poëtas, Hor.; conditionem, Caes.

restagnātĭo -ōnis, f. (restagno), *an overflowing;* Euphratis, Plin.

restagno, 1. *to overflow;* quas (paludes) restagnantes faciunt lacus, Liv.; restagnans mare, Ov.; transf., of places, *to be overflowed;* late is locus restagnat, Caes.

restauro, 1. (re and *stauro, from sto, whence instauro), *to restore, replace, repair, rebuild;* aedem, Tac.

restĭcŭla -ae, f. (dim. of restis), *a thin rope or cord,* Cic.

restillo, 1. *to drop back again;* fig., quae (litterae) mihi quiddam quasi animulae restillarunt, *have instilled,* Cic.

restinctĭo -ōnis, f. (restinguo), *a slaking, quenching;* sitis, Cic.

restinguo -stinxi -stinctum, 3. *to extinguish, quench.* **I.** Lit., ignem, Cic. **II.** Transf., **a,** *to quench, master, subdue, control;* sitim, Cic.; ardorem cupiditatum, Cic.; odium alicuius, Cic.;

b, *to extinguish, destroy, put an end to*, studia, Cic, animos hominum sensusque morte restingui, Cic

restĭo -ōnis, m (restis), *a rope-maker* Suet, in jest, *one who is scourged with ropes*, Plaut

restĭpŭlātĭo -ōnis, f (restipulor), *a counter engagement*, Cic

restĭpŭlor, 1 *to promise, engage in return*, Cic

restis -is, acc im and em, abl -e, f *a rope, cord*, per manus reste datā, *in a kind of dance where the rope ran through the hands of the dancers*, Liv

restĭto, 1 (freq of resto), *to remain behind, loiter, linger*, Liv

restĭtrix tricis, f (resisto or resto), *she that remains behind*, Plaut

restĭtŭo -ŭi -ūtum, 3 (re and statuo) **I.** *to put in its former place, replace, restore* **A.** Gen, statuam, Cic **B. a,** *to bring back again, restore*, causa restituendi mei, Cic, **b,** *to give back, give up again, restore*, agrum alicui, Liv, fig, se alicui, *to become friends again*, Cic **II.** *to restore, build again, bring a thing back to its previous condition*, oppida, Caes, provinciam in antiquum statum, Cic, aliquid in pristinam dignitatem, Cic, aliquem in amicitiam, Cic, aliquem, *to restore a person's property to him*, Cic, aliquem in integrum, *to place a man in his former condition*, Cic, rem, aciem, proelium, Liv, damna Romano bello accepta, *to repair*, Liv

restĭtūtĭo -ōnis, f (restituo) **I.** *a restoration*, Capitolii, Suet **II.** *a calling back again*, **a,** from banishment, *restoration of a person to his previous condition*, Cic, **b,** *a pardoning*, damnatorum, Cic

restĭtūtor -ōris, m (restituo), *a restorer*, templorum, Liv, salutis, Cic

resto -stiti, 1 **I.** *to remain behind, remain standing, stand still* **A.** Gen, Prop **B.** *to resist, oppose, withstand*, Liv, pass impers, quā minimā vi restatur, *where the least resistance is*, Liv **II.** *to remain, remain over* **A.** Gen, **1,** of things, hic restat actus, Cic, dona pelago et flammis restantia, *saved from*, Verg; restat ut, etc, *it remains that*, etc, Cic, non or nihil aliud restat nisi or quam, foll by infin, Liv, **2,** of persons, *to remain, be left*, (α) restabam solus de viginti, Ov, (β) *to remain alive*, qui pauci admodum restant, Cic **B.** With reference to the future, *to remain for, await*, placet (vobis) socios sic tractari, quod restat, ut per haec tempora tractatos videtis, *for the future*, Cic, hoc Latio restare canunt, with acc and infin, Verg

restrictē, adv (restrictus) **I.** *sparingly*, tam restricte facere id, Cic **II.** *accurately, strictly*, praecipere, Cic, observare, Cic

restrictus -a -um, p adj (from restringo) **I.** *close, tight*, toga, Suet **II.** Transf, **1,** *close, stingy*, homo, Cic, quum naturā semper ad largiendum ex alieno fuerim restrictior, Cic, **2,** *strict, severe*, imperium, Tac

restringo -strinxi strictum 3 **I.** *to bind back, bind fast, bind tight*, restrictis lacertis, Hor **II. 1,** *to draw back, confine, restrict, restrain*, Tac, **2,** *to draw back, to open*, dentes, Plaut

rĕsulto, 1 (intens of resilio), *to spring back, rebound* **I.** tela resultant galeā, Verg **II.** Of sound, *to echo, resound*, imago vocis resultat, Verg, transf, of places, *to resound*, pulsati colles clamore resultant, Verg

rĕsūmo sumpsi sumptum, 3 *to take again, take back* **I.** Lit tabellas, Ov **II.** Transf, **1,** *to renew, repeat*, pugnam, Tac, **2,** *to obtain again, to recover*, vires, Ov

rĕsŭpīno, 1 **I.** *to bend, turn backwards*; assurgentem umbone, *to strike back to the ground*, Liv, middle, resupinari, *to bend back*, resupinati Galli, *prostrate from intoxication*, Juv. **II.** Meton, *to break open*, valvas, Prop

rĕsŭpīnus -a -um, *bent backwards* **I A.** Gen, collum, Ov, resupinus haeret curru, Verg, resupinum aliquem fundere, *to lay low on the ground*, Ov **B.** Esp, *lying on one's back*, jacuit resupinus, Ov, resupini natant, *on their backs*, Ov **II.** Meton, *throwing back the head, with the nose high in the air* (of the proud), Ov

rĕsurgo -surrexi surrectum, 3 *to rise up again, appear again* **I. A.** Lit, herba resurgens, Ov, resurgam (from bed), Ov **B.** Fig, **1,** *to rise up again*, in ultionem, Tac, **2,** *to come up again, reappear*, amor, *re-awakens*, Verg, **3,** *to come forth again*, quum res Romana contra spem votaque eius velut resurgeret, Liv **II.** Meton, *to stand up again = to be built again*, resurgens urbs, Tac

rĕsuscĭto, 1 *to revive, resuscitate*, fig, veterem iram, Ov

rĕsūtus -a -um, *ripped open* Suet

rĕtardātĭo -ōnis, f (retardo), *a retarding, protracting, delay*, Cic

rĕtardo, 1 *to delay, protract, retard, impede, detain* **I.** Lit, aliquem in via, Cic, in middle signification, motus stellarum retardantur, *move slowly*, Cic **II.** Fig, *to hinder, prevent*, aliquem a scribendo, Cic

rĕtaxo, 1 *to censure in return*, Suet.

rētĕ is, n *a net* (both for fishes and for hunting animals with), retia ponere cervis, Verg, retia tendere, Ov, ex aranciolis aliae quasi rete texunt, Cic

rĕtĕgo -texi -tectum, 3 *to uncover, reveal, lay bare, to open* **I.** Lit, **A.** thecam nummariam, Cic, homo retectus, *not covered by a shield*, Verg **B.** Poet, *to make visible, to illuminate*, orbem radiis, Verg, jam rebus luce retectis, Verg **II.** Transf, *to reveal, discover*, arcanum consilium, Hor, scelus, Verg

rĕtendo -tendi -tensum and -tentum, 3 *to slacken, unbend*, arcum, Ov

rĕtentĭo -ōnis, f (retineo), *a keeping back, holding in* **I.** Lit, aurigae, Cic **II.** Transf, *a withholding*, assensionis, Cic

1 **rĕtento,** 1 (intens of retineo), *to hold firmly back, hold fast* **I.** Lit, Liv, caelum a terris, *to keep apart*, Lucr **II.** Transf, *to preserve, maintain*, sensus hominum vitasque, Cic poet

2 **rĕtento (rĕtempto),** 1 (re and tento), *to try, attempt again*, fila lyrae, Ov, foll by infin, Ov

rĕtentus -a -um **I.** Partic of retendo **II** Partic of retineo

rĕtexo texŭi textum, 3 **I.** *to unweave, unravel* **A.** Lit, quasi Penelope telam retexens, Cic **B.** Transf, **1,** gen, dum luna quater plenum tenuata retexuit orbem, *diminished again*, Ov **2,** esp, *to dissolve, cancel, annul, reverse*, praeturam, Cic, orationem, *retract*, Cic, scriptorum quaeque, *to revise, correct*, Hor **II.** *to weave again*, poet, transf, *to renew, repeat*, properata retexite fata, Ov

rētĭārĭus -ii, m (rete), *a fighter with a net, a gladiator furnished with a net with which he strove to entangle his adversary*, Suet

rĕtĭcentĭa ae, f (reticeo), *a keeping silent, silence* (opp locutio) **I** Gen, Cic, vestra virtus neque oblivione eorum qui nunc sunt, neque reticentiā posterorum sepulta esse poterit, Cic.; poena reticentiae, i.e., *for keeping silent about a defect in an object offered for sale*, Cic. **II.** As a figure of speech, *a sudden pause* (Gr. ἀποσιώπησις), Cic.

rĕtĭcĕo -cŭi, 2. (re and taceo). **I.** Intransit., *to be silent, keep silence;* (α) absol., quum Sulpicius reticuisset, Cic.; de injuriis, Cic.; (β) with dat., *to give no answer to*, Liv. **II.** Transit., *to keep secret, conceal;* cogitationes suas, Cic.; quod ii, qui ea patefacere possent, reticuissent, Cic.

rētĭcŭlātus -a -um (reticulum), *net-like, reticulated*, Plin.

rētĭcŭlus -i, m. and **rētĭcŭlum** -i, n. (dim. of rete), *a little net;* a, *for catching fish*, Plaut.; b, *a bag of net-work used for carrying certain articles;* reticulum plenum rosae, Cic.; reticulum panis, Hor.; **c,** *a net for the hair*, Juv.; **d,** *a racket for striking a ball*, Ov.

rĕtĭnācŭlum -i, n. (retineo), *a rope, a cable, cord*, Verg., Ov.

rĕtĭnens -entis, p. adj. (from retineo), *tenacious of anything;* sui juris dignitatisque, Cic.

rĕtĭnentĭa -ae, f. (retineo), *a retaining in the memory, recollection*, Lucr.

rĕtĭnĕo -tĭnŭi -tentum, 3. (re and teneo). **I.** *to hold back, hold fast, detain.* **A.** Lit., **1,** *to keep back;* **a,** of persons, concilium dimittit, Liscum retinet, Caes.; nisi jam profecti sunt, retinebis homines, Cic.; **b,** of things, lacrimas, Ov.; manus ab ore, Ov.; **2,** *to keep back, preserve, hold back;* armorum parte tertiā celatā atque in oppido retentā, Caes.; **3,** *to retain a conquest;* oppidum, Caes. **B.** Transf., **1,** *to keep within bounds, restrain;* moderari cursum atque in sua potestate retinere, Cic.; retinere in officio, Cic.; foll. by quin, aegre sunt retenti, quin oppidum irrumperent, Caes.; **2,** *to keep, preserve, hold fast;* ut amicos observantiā, rem parsimoniā retineret, Cic.; statum suum, Cic.; memoriam suae pristinae virtutis, Caes.; aliquid memoriā, Cic. **II.** *to hold fast.* **A.** Lit., arcum manu, Cic. **B.** Transf., ordo ipse annalium mediocriter nos retinet quasi enumeratione fastorum, Cic.

rĕtinnĭo, 4. *to resound, to ring again;* in vocibus nostrorum oratorum retinnit et resonat quiddam urbanius, Cic.

rētis -is, f. = rete (q.v.).

rĕtondĕo -tonsus, 2. *to reap, mow again*, Plin.

rĕtŏno, 1. *to thunder back, to resound*, Cat.

rĕtorquĕo -torsi -tortum, 2. *to twist back, bend back, turn back.* **I.** Lit., oculos saepe ad hanc urbem, Cic.; caput in sua terga, Ov.; brachia tergo, *to bind behind the back*, Hor. **II.** Transf., *to change;* mentem, Verg.

rĕtorrĭdus -a -um, *parched up, dried up*, Plin.

rĕtostus -a -um, *roasted*, Plin.

rĕtractātĭo -ōnis, f. (retracto), *refusal, denial;* sine ulla retractatione, Cic.

rĕtractātus -a -um, p. adj. (from retracto), *revised;* idem σύνταγμα misi ad te retractatius, Cic.

rĕtracto (rĕtrecto), 1. **I.** *to lay hold of, handle again, undertake anew.* **A.** Lit., ferrum, Verg.; arma, Liv.; cruda vulnera, *to open the old wounds*, Ov. **B.** Transf., **a,** *to take in hand again, retouch, use again;* verba desueta, Ov.; **b,** *to renew;* augere dolorem retractando, Cic.; **c,** *to think of again;* aliquid diligenter, Cic.; fata, Ov. **II.** *to draw back;* transf., **a,** *to recall, retract;* dicta, Verg.; **b,** *to refuse, be unwilling, be reluctant, decline*, Cic.; quid retractas, Verg.

rĕtractus -a -um, p. adj. (from retraho), *afar off, distant, remote;* retractior a mari murus, Liv.

rĕtrăho -traxi -tractum, 3. **I.** *to draw back.* **A.** *to draw backwards;* **1,** lit., **a,** manum, Cic.; Hannibalem in Africam, Cic.; se ab ictu, Ov.; **b,** *to fetch back a fugitive, bring back*, Cic.; aliquem ex fuga, Sall.; **2,** transf., **a,** *to keep back, prevent;* consules a foedere, Cic.; **b,** *to hold back, not to give out;* quos occulere aut retrahere aliquid suspicio fuit, Liv.; **c,** se, *to withdraw oneself;* quum se retraxit, ne pyxidem traderet, Cic. **B.** *to drag forth again, draw forth again;* Treveros in arma, Tac. **II.** *to draw towards;* fig., in odium judicis, Cic.

rĕtrĭbŭo -trĭbŭi -trĭbūtum, 3. **I.** *to give again.* **A.** *to give back, restore;* pro Siculo frumento acceptam pecuniam populo, Liv. **B.** *to give again, afresh*, Lucr. **II.** *to give back a man his due;* alicui fructum quem meruit, Cic.

rĕtrō (from re and pron. suff. ter, as citro, intro), adv. **I.** Lit., *backwards, back, behind;* redire, retro repetere, Liv.; retro respicere, Cic.; quod retro atque a tergo fieret, ne laboraret, Cic. **II.** Transf., **A.** Of time, *in times past, formerly, back;* et deinceps retro usque ad Romulum, Cic. **B.** Of other relations, **1,** *back, backwards;* retro ponere, *to postpone*, Cic.; **2,** *again, on the contrary, on the other hand*, Cic.

rĕtrŏăgo -ēgi -actum, 3. *to drive back, lead back, turn back*, Plin.

rĕtrŏĕo, 4. *to go back, return*, Plin.

rĕtrōgrădior -gressus sum, 3. dep. *to go backwards, move backwards*, Plin.

rĕtrōgrădus -a -um (retrogradior), *retrograde, going backwards*, Sen.

rĕtrorsum and **rĕtrorsŭs**, adv. (= retroversum [-vorsum] and retroversus [-vorsus]), *backwards, behind.* **I.** Lit., retrorsum vela dare, Hor. **II.** Transf., *in return, in reversed order;* deinde retrorsum vicissim, etc., Cic.

rĕtrorsus = retrorsum (q.v.).

rĕtrōversus -a -um (verto), *turned backwards, back*, Ov.

rĕtrūdo -trūsus, 3. *to push back, thrust back*, Plaut. Partic., **rĕtrūsus** -a -um, *remote, distant, sequestered, obscure;* simulacra deorum jacent in tenebris ab isto retrusa atque abdita, Cic.; voluntas abdita et retrusa, Cic.

rĕtundo, rĕtŭdi (rettŭdi) -tūsum (-tunsum), 3. *to beat back, to drive back.* **I. A.** Lit., Lucan. **B.** Transf., *to check, keep within bounds;* linguas Aetolorum, Liv. **II.** *to hammer back something sharp, to blunt, make dull.* **A.** Lit., tela, Ov.; fig., ferrum alicuius, *to frustrate a murderous attempt*, Cic. **B.** Transf., impetum, Liv.; mucronem stili, Cic.

rĕtūsus (rĕtunsus) -a -um, p. adj. (from retundo), *dull, blunt.* **I.** Lit., ferrum, Verg. **II.** Transf., *dull;* ingenium, Cic.

Reudigni -ōrum, m. *a people in the north of Germany.*

rĕus -i, m. and **rĕa** -ae, f. (res). **I.** *an accused person, prisoner, culprit, defendant;* gen. with acc. of the charge, more rarely with de and the abl., reum facere aliquem, *to accuse*, Cic.; reum fieri, *to be accused*, Cic.; referre in reos (of the praetor), *to enter a name on the list of accused persons*, Cic.; aliquem ex reis eximere, *to strike out the name of an accused person*, Cic.; Sextius qui est de vi reus, Cic.; used without reference to a court of justice, reus fortunae, *accused as responsible for ill fortune*, Liv.; reus sine te criminis huius agor, Ov.; plur., rei, *the parties to a suit, both plaintiff and defendant;*

reos appello quorum res est, Cic II. bound by, answerable for, voti, bound to fulfil my vow (i e, having obtained the object of my wishes), Verg, suae partis tutandae, answerable for, Liv

rĕvălesco -vălŭi, 3 to become well again, be restored to health I. Lit, ope qua revalescere possis, Ov II. Transf, to be restored, Laodicea revaluit propriis opibus, Tac

rĕvĕho -vexi -vectum, 3 to carry, bear, bring back I. Lit, a, act. and pass, tela ad Graios, Ov, praeda revecta, brought back, Liv, b, middle, reveh, to drive back, ride back, sail back, (with or without equo, curru, navi, etc) in castra, Liv, Ithacam, Hor II. Fig, ad superiorem aetatem revecti sumus (in discourse), have gone back, Cic

rĕvello -velli -vulsum, 3 I. to tear, pull, pluck away A Lit, tela de corpore, Cic, caput a cervice, Verg, saxum e monte, Ov, morte ab aliquo revelli, to be separated from, Ov B. Fig, to tear away, destroy, banish, consulatum ex omni memoria, Cic, omnes injurias, Cic II. to tear up, to open, humum dente curvo, to plough, Ov, cineres manesque, to disturb, violate a tomb, Verg

rĕvēlo, 1 to unveil, uncover, lay bare, frontem, Tac, os, Ov, sacra, Ov

rĕvĕnio -vēni -ventum, 4 to come back, return, domum, Cic, in urbem, Tac

rĕvērā, adv (re and vera), indeed, in truth, truly, Cic

rĕverbĕro, 1 to beat back, drive back, Sen

rĕvĕrendus -a -um, p adj (from revereor), inspiring awe, venerable, nox, Ov, facies, Juv

rĕvĕrens -entis, p adj (from revereor), respectful, reverent, erga patrem, Tac

rĕvĕrentĕr, adv (reverens), reverently, respectfully, Plin, reverentius, Tac, reverentis sime, Suet

rĕvĕrentĭa -ae, f (revereor), reverence, respect, fear, awe, adversus homines, Cic, legum, before the laws, Juv Personif, **Rĕvĕrentĭa** -ae, f a goddess, mother of Majestas by Honor

rĕvĕrĕor -vĕritus sum, 2 dep to feel awe or respect or shame before, to revere, reverence, respect, to fear, suspicionem, Cic, multa adversa, Cic, coetum virorum, Liv

rĕverro, 3 to sweep again, Plaut

rĕversĭo (rĕvorsĭo) -ōnis, f (revertor) I. a turning back on the way before a man has reached the end of his journey (while reditus = return after a man has reached his journey's end), Cic, reditu vel potius reversione, Cic, consilium profectionis et reversionis meae, Cic. II Transf, a return, recurrence, tertianae febris et quartanae reversio, Cic, plur, sol binas in singulis annis reversiones ab extremo contrarias facit, Cic

rĕverto (rĕvorto) verti (-vorti) versum (vorsum) -ĕre and **rĕvertor (rĕvortor)** versus (-vorsus) sum -verti (-vorti), dep. I. to turn back, return A. Lit., ex itinere, Cic, ad aliquem, Caes, Laodiceam, Cic, with double nom, quum victor a Mithridatico bello revertisset, Cic, poet, of things, Tiberim reverti, Hor B. Transf, to return, come back, ad sanitatem, to a better frame of mind, Cic, in gratiam cum aliquo, to be reconciled with, Liv, poena reversura est in caput tuum, doomed to fall, Ov esp, in discourse, to return, revert, rursus igitur eadem revertamur, Cic, ad propositum revertar, Cic, ad id, unde digressi sumus, revertamur, Cic II. reverti, to turn to, revertitur ad commodum, Cic (act not used in present tense in prose)

rĕvĭdĕo, 2 to see again, Plaut.

rĕvincio vinxi -vinctum, 4 I. to tie back, tie behind, juvenem manus post terga revinctum, Verg II. A. Lit, bind fast, bind round, trabes, Caes, zona de poste revincta, Ov B. Transf, mentem amore, Cat

rĕvinco -vīci -victum, 3 to reconquer, subdue again I. Lit catervae consiliis juvenis revictae, Hor II. Transf, A. Gen, revictam conjurationem, suppressed, Tac B. Esp, to confute, convict, aliquem, Cic

rĕvĭresco -virŭi, 3. (inchoat of revireo), to grow green again, to grow strong, flourish again, revive, senatum ad auctoritatis pristinae spem revirescere, Cic

rĕvīsĭto, 1 to visit repeatedly, Plin

rĕvīso visi -visum, 3 to look back at, come again to see, revisit I. Intransit., furor revisit, returns, Lucr II. Transit, revise nos aliquando, Cic, domos, Liv

rĕvīvisco -vixi, 3 to come to life again, revive I. Lit, Cic II. Transf, reviviscere memoriam ac desiderium mei, Cic

rĕvŏcābĭlis -e (revoco), that can be revoked or called back, Ov

rĕvŏcāmen inis, n (revoco), a calling back, recall, Ov

rĕvŏcātĭo ōnis, f (revoco) I a calling back A. Lit, a bello, Cic B. Fig, avocatio a cogitanda molestia et revocatio ad contemplandas voluptates, Cic II. In rhetoric, a withdrawal, withdrawing, revocation, verbi, Cic

rĕvŏco, 1. I. to call again A. 1, in suffragium, Liv, 2, legal t t, to summon again before a court of justice, to bring a fresh charge against, hominem revocat populus, Cic, 3, theatrical t t, to call again for a repetition of a speech, etc, to encore, quum saepius revocatus vocem obtudisset, Cic, with acc of thing to be repeated, to call for again, primos tres versus, Cic, impers, millies revocatum est, Cic, 4, milit t t., to summon again soldiers who had been discharged, milites, Cic B. 1, to call again, in turn, unde tu me vocasti, unde te ego revoco, Cic, 2, to invite back or again, qui non revocaturus esset, Cic II. to call back A. In a narrow sense, 1, lit, a, aliquem ex itinere, Cic, qui me revocastis, out of exile, Cic, with things as objects, oculos, Ov, pedem, Verg, gradum, Verg, to turn away, b, esp, milit t t, to recall soldiers from a march, expedition, etc, legiones ab opere, Caes, 2, transf a, to call back, bring back again, recover, renew, studia longo intervallo intermissa, to take up again, Cic, b, to call back, apply again, se ad industriam, Cic, se ad se revocare, or simply se revocare, to recover oneself, collect oneself, Cic hence, (α) to keep back, aliquem a tanto scelere, Cic, (β) to confine, comitia in unum domum, Cic, (γ) to recall, revoke, facta, Ov B. In a wider sense, to call to 1, lit, abi, quo blandae juvenum te revocant preces, Hor, 2, transf, a, to apply to, refer to, illam rem ad illam rationem conjecturamque revocabant, Cic; b, to bring to, in dubium, Cic, omnia ad suam potestatem Cic, c, to judge according to, omnia ad gloriam, Cic

rĕvŏlo, 1 to fly back I. Lit, dux gruum revolat, Cic II Transf, revolat telum, Ov

rĕvŏlūbĭlis e (revolvo), that can be rolled back, pondus, Ov

rĕvolvo -volvi -vŏlūtum, 3 to roll back, unroll I. A. Gen, 1, transit, Tac, poet, rursus iter omne, measure back again, traverse again, Verg, 2, reflex and middle, draco revolvens sese, Cic, revolutus equo, falling down from

Verg.; ter revoluta toro est, *sank back*, Verg.; revoluta dies, *returning*, Verg. **B.** Esp., *to unroll or open a book*; Origines (a work of Cato's), Liv. **II.** Fig., **A.** Gen., **1**, act. and pass., omnia ad communes rerum atque generum summas revolventur, *will be brought back to, reduced to*, Cic.; poet., iterum casus, *to undergo again*, Verg.; **2**, middle, revolvi, **a**, *to return to, in speaking or writing*; ut ad illa elementa revolvar, Cic.; **b**, *to come to (something bad)*; revolutus ad dispensationem inopiae, Liv. **B.** Esp., *to read again*; loca jam recitata, Hor.; *to think of again*; visa, Ov.; *to tell again*; haec, Verg.

rĕvŏmo -vŏmŭi, 3. *to vomit up, disgorge*; fluctus, Verg.

rĕvorsĭo = reversio (q.v.).

rĕvorsus, etc. = reversus, etc. (q.v.).

rĕvulsĭo -ōnis, f. (revello), *a tearing away*, Plin.

rex, rēgis, m. (rego), *ruler, prince.* **I.** Lit., rex Dejotarus, Cic.; rex regum (of Agamemnon), Liv.; simply rex, used of the Parthian king, Suet.; of the Persian king (like Gr. βασιλεύς), Nep.; regem deligere, creare, constituere, Cic.; poet. attrib., populus late rex, *ruling far*, Verg. **II.** Transf., **1**, of some of the gods, rex divum atque hominum, or deorum, *Jupiter*, Verg.; rex aquarum, *Neptune*, Ov.; rex Stygius, *Pluto*, Verg.; **2**, *the king and his consort*; reges excitos, Liv.; *the royal family*; direptis bonis regum, Liv.; **3**, during the republic at Rome, rex = *a despot, an absolute monarch, tyrant*; rex populi Romani, i.e., *Caesar*, Cic.; decem reges aerarii, Cic.; **4**, in the religious language, rex sacrorum, sacrificiorum, Cic., sacrificus, Liv., sacrificulus, Liv., *a priest who under the republic performed the sacrifices which formerly the kings performed*; **5**, gen. = *head, chief, leader*; **a**, of animals, rex apum, Verg.; **b**, of rivers, rex Eridanus (the chief stream in Italy), Verg.; **c**, of the patron of a parasite, Hor.; **d**, *the guide, tutor of a young man*; rex pueritiae, Hor.

rhăcŏma (rhēcŏma) -ae, f. *a root*, perhaps *rhubarb*, Plin.

Rhădămanthus (-ŏs) -i, m. (Ῥαδάμανθυς), *son of Jupiter, brother of Minos, judge in the lower world.*

Rhaeti = Raeti (q.v.).

rhăgădes -um, f. and **rhăgădĭa** -ōrum, n. (ῥαγάδες, ῥαγάδια) *a kind of sores or ulcers*, Plin.

rhăgĭon -ii, n. (ῥάγιον), *a kind of small spider*, Plin.

Rhamnes = Ramnes (q.v.).

rhamnos -i, f. (ῥάμνος), *buckthorn*, Plin.

Rhamnus -nuntis, f. (Ῥαμνοῦς), *a village of Attica, where the goddess Nemesis was worshipped*; hence, **A.** Adj., **Rhamnūsĭus** -a -um, virgo, Cat., or simply Rhamnusia, *Nemesis*, Ov. **B.** **Rhamnūsĭs** -ĭdis, f. *Nemesis*, Ov.

Rhamses -sesis, m. *an old king of Egypt.*

rhapsōdĭa -ae, f. (ῥαψῳδία), *a rhapsody*; secunda, *the second book of the Iliad*, Nep.

1. **Rhēa (Rēa)** -ae, f. Rhea Silvia, *daughter of King Numitor of Alba, mother of Romulus and Remus by Mars.*

2. **Rhĕa** -ae, f. (Ῥέα), *an old name of Cybele.*

rhēcŏma = rhacoma (q.v.).

rhēda = reda (q.v.).

rhēdārĭus = redarius (q.v.).

Rhēgĭum = Regium (q.v.).

Rhēmi = Remi (q.v.).

Rhēnus -i, m. *the Rhine*; poet. adj., flumen Rhenum, Hor.; in poets, meton. = *the people dwelling on the banks of the Rhine.* Adj., **Rhēnānus** -a -um, *belonging to the Rhine.*

Rhēsus -i, m. (Ῥῆσος), *king in Thrace, who came to the help of Troy; according to an oracle, the Greeks could not capture Troy if the horses of Rhesus tasted of Trojan pastures, so Diomedes and Ulysses stole the horses and killed Rhesus.*

rhētor -ŏris, m. (ῥήτωρ). **I.** *a teacher of rhetoric, a rhetorician*, Cic. **II.** *an orator*, Nep.

rhētŏrĭca v. rhetoricus.

1. **rhētŏrĭcē**, v. rhetoricus.

2. **rhētŏrĭcē**, adv. (rhetoricus), *rhetorically, oratorically*, Cic.

rhētŏrĭcus -a -um (ῥητορικός). **I.** *of or relating to a rhetorician, rhetorical*; mos, Cic.; ars, Cic.; whence subst., **rhētŏrĭca** -ae, f. and **rhētŏrĭcē** -ēs, f. (ῥητορική), Cic. **II.** *relating to rhetoric*; doctores, *teachers of rhetoric*, Cic.; libri rhetorici, *text-books of rhetoric*, Cic.; subst., **rhētŏrĭca** -ōrum, n. *rhetoric*, Cic.

rheumătismus -i, m. (ῥευματισμός), *rheum, catarrh*, Plin.

rhīna -ae, f. (ῥίνη), *a kind of shark*, Plin.

rhīnŏcĕrōs -ōtis, m. (ῥινόκερως). **I.** *a rhinoceros*, Plin.; prov., nasum rhinocerotis habere, *to turn up the nose, sneer at everything*, Mart. **II.** Meton., *a vessel made of the horn of the rhinoceros*, Juv.

Rhīnŏcŏlūra -ae, f. (Ῥινοκόλουρα), *a town on the coast of the Mediterranean between Egypt and Syria*, now *El-Arish (Arisch).*

Rhintōn -ōnis, m. (Ῥίνθων), *a tragic poet of Tarentum.*

Rhĭŏn (-um) -ii, n. (Ῥιόν), *a promontory in Achaia, opposite Antirrhium.*

Rhīphaeus = Riphaeus (q.v.).

Rhīzōn -ōnis, m. (Ῥίζων), *a town in Illyria*, now *Risano*; hence, **Rhīzōnītae** -ārum, m. *the inhabitants of Rhizon.*

rhō, n. indecl. (ῥῶ), *the Greek name of the letter R*, Cic.

Rhŏda -ae, f. *a town of the Indigetes in Hispania Tarraconensis*, now *Rosas.*

Rhŏdănus -i, m. (Ῥοδανός), *a river in Gaul*, now *the Rhone*; Rhodani potor, *a dweller on the banks of the Rhone*, Hor.

rhŏdĭnus -a -um (ῥόδινος), *made of roses*, Plin.

Rhŏdĭus, v. Rhodus.

rhŏdŏdaphnē -ēs, f. (ῥοδοδάφνη), *the oleander*, Plin.

rhŏdŏdendrŏs -i, f. and **rhŏdŏdendrŏn** -i, n. (ῥοδόδενδρον) = rhododaphne (q.v.).

Rhŏdŏpē -ēs, f. (Ῥοδόπη), *a mountain in Thrace*, now *Despoto* or *Despoti Dag*; meton. = *Thrace*, Verg.; hence, adj., **Rhŏdŏpēĭus** -a -um, *Thracian*; vates, heros, *Orpheus*, Ov.

Rhŏdus (-ŏs) -i, f. (Ῥόδος), *Rhodes, an island in the Carpathian Sea, off the coast of Asia Minor, famous for its trade, its school of rhetoric, and its colossus.* Hence, adj., **Rhŏdĭus** -a -um, *Rhodian*; plur. subst., **Rhŏdĭi** -ōrum, m. *the Rhodians*, Cic.

Rhoetēum (Ῥοίτειον), *a promontory in the Troad*; hence, **Rhoetēus** -a -um, *Rhoetean*, **a**, lit., profundum; and subst., **Rhoetēum** -i, n. *the sea near Rhoeteum*, Ov.; **b**, poet., transf. = *Trojan*; ductor, *Aeneas*, Verg.

Rhoetus (Rhoecus) -i, m. (Ῥοῖκος). **I.** *a giant*, Hor. **II.** *a centaur*, Verg.

rhombus (-ŏs) -i, m. (ῥόμβος). **I.** *a magician's circle*, Ov. **II.** *the turbot*, Hor.

rhomphaea -ae, f *a long missile weapon*

Rhōsus (-ŏs) -i, f (Ῥῶσος), *a sea port in Cilicia, famous for its pottery* Hence, **Rhōsĭăcus** -a um, *Rhosian*, vasa, Cic

Rhoxŏlāni (**Roxŏlāni**) -ōrum, m *a Scythian people in modern European Tartary*

rhythmĭcus -i, m (ῥυθμικός), *one who teaches the art of preserving rhythm in composition*, Cic

rhythmus -i, m (ῥυθμός), *rhythm, time* (either in music or discourse), Quint.

rhytium -ii, n (ῥύτιον), *a drinking-horn*, Mart.

rīca -ae, f. *a veil*, Plaut.

rīcinium -ii, n (rica), *a small veil worn especially as an article of mourning*, Cic

rictum = rictus (q v).

rictus -ūs, m and **rictum** -i, n (ringor), *the opening of the mouth, the open mouth*, **a**, of man, risu diducere rictum, Hor , **b**, of animals, *the expanded jaws*, rictus Cerberei, Ov.

rīdĕo, risi, risum, 2 **I.** Intransit , *to laugh* **A.** Gen , ridere convivae, *cachinnare* ipse Apronius, Cic , in stomacho ridere, *to laugh grimly*, Cic ; pass impers , ridetur, *there is laughter*, Hor **B.** Esp , **1,** *to laugh* or *smile in a friendly manner*, alicui or ad aliquem, *to smile upon*, cui non risere parentes, Verg , so transf , (*a*) *to laugh, to look cheerful, to look bright*, omnia nunc rident, Verg , domus ridet argento, Hor , (*β*) *to please*, ille terrarum mihi praeter omnes angulus ridet, Hor , **2,** *to laugh triumphantly, to triumph over*, muneribus aemuli, Hor **II.** Transit , *to laugh at* **A.** Gen , joca tua de haeresi Vestoriana risisse me, Cic , haec ego non rideo, *I do not jest*, Cic , pass , non sal sed natura ridetur, Cic **B.** Esp , *to ridicule* aliquem, Cic , pass , Pyrrhi ridetur largitas a consule, Cic

rīdĭbundus -a um (rideo), *laughing*, Plaut.

rīdĭcŭlārĭus -a um (ridiculus), *laughable, droll*, subst , **rīdĭcŭlārĭa** -ōrum, n *drolleries*, Plaut

rīdĭcŭlē, adv (ridiculus) **I.** In a good sense, *jokingly, humorously*, Cic **II.** In a bad sense, *ridiculously, absurdly*, homo ridicule insanus, Cic

rīdĭcŭlōsus -a um (ridiculus), *laughable, facetious*, Pers

rīdĭcŭlus (rideo), *exciting laughter* **I.** In a good sense, *droll, humorous, funny, facetious* **A.** Adj , cavillator facie magis quam facetiis ridiculus, Cic , poet with infin , (Porcius) ridiculus totas simul absorbere placentas, Hor **B** Subst , **a, rīdĭcŭlus** -i, m *a joker, jester*, Plaut , Ter , **b, rīdĭcŭlum** -i, n *a thing to laugh at, joke, jest*, per ridiculum dicere, Cic , plur , sententiose ridicula dicere, Cic **II.** In a bad sense, *laughable, absurd, ridiculous*, insania quae ridicula aliis, Cic , ridiculum poema, Hor , ridiculum est with infin , Cic

rĭgens -entis, p adj (from rigeo), *stiff, unbending*, aqua, *frozen*, Mart

rĭgĕo, 2 (root RIG, Gr. ΡΙΓ, connected with FRIG eo), *to be stiff, to stiffen* **I. A.** Lit , **1,** with cold, frost, etc , rigere frigore, Cic ; **2,** poet , *to be stiff, bend, unbending*; terga boum plumbo insuto ferroque rigebant, Verg ; **3,** poet., *to be stiffened*, auro or ex auro, Verg **B.** Transf , **1,** *to be stiff = to be immovable*, nervi rigent, Hor , **2,** *to stand stiff* or *upright*, cervix riget horrida, Ov , of hair, *to stand on end*, gelido comae terrore rigebant, Ov **II.** Fig , feritas immota riget, Mart

rĭgesco, rigŭi (inchoat of rigeo), 3 *to grow stiff, become stiff* **I.** Lit , with cold , vestes rigescunt, Verg **II.** Transf , of hair, *to stand on end* (from terror), metu capillos riguisse, Ov

rĭgĭdē, adv (rigidus), *stiffly*, fig , *rigorously, severely*, Ov

rĭgĭdus -a -um (rigeo), *stiff, unbending, rigid* **I. A.** Lit , from cold; tellurem Boreā rigidam movere, Verg , or by nature, *hard*, silex, Ov , ensis, Verg **B.** Transf , **1,** *stiff = standing upright*, columna, Ov ; capilli, Ov , **2,** *stiff stretched out*, crura, Cic ; cervix, Liv. **II.** Fig , **1,** *immovable, inflexible*, innocentia, Liv , vultus, Ov , **2,** *stiff, rough, unpolished;* mores, Ov., signa rigidiora, *not elaborated*, Cic., **3,** *stern, inflexible*, satelles, Hor , censor, Ov , **4,** *wild, savage*, ferae, Ov

rĭgo, 1 **I.** *to lead* or *conduct water to any place* **A.** Lit , aquam per agros, ap Liv **B.** Fig , hinc motus per membra rigantur, Lucr **II.** *to wet, moisten, bedew* **A. 1,** lit , lucum fons perenni rigabat aqua, Liv , **2,** poet , transf , *to bedew*, ora lacrimis, fletibus, Verg , Ov , **3,** fig , Prop.

Rigŏdūlum -i, n *a town in the country of the Treveri*, now *Ricol* or *Reol*.

rĭgor -ōris, m (rigeo), *stiffness, rigidity, hardness* **I.** Gen , **A.** Lit , of gold, Lucr of wood or iron, Verg **B.** Fig , **1,** *severity, harshness, sternness*, Tac , **2,** *roughness, rudeness, harshness of manner*, Ov **II.** Esp , *rigidity* or *numbness produced by cold*, torpentibus rigore membris, Liv

rĭgŭus -a -um (rigo) **I.** Act *watering, irrigating*, amnes, Verg **II.** Pass , *well-watered, irrigated*, hortus, Ov

rīma -ae, f *a crack, cleft, fissure*, rimas agere, Cic ; naves rimis dehiscunt, *spring a leak*, Verg , poet , ignea rima micans, *the lightning*, Verg

rīmor, 1 dep (rima), *to cleave* **I.** Gen *to turn up*, terram rastris, Verg **II.** Esp , *to grub up, burrow through, root up* **A.** Lit , of birds and other animals, Verg **B.** Transf , *to turn over, pry into, search, examine*, id quoque rimatur quantum potest, Cic , secreta, Tac

rīmōsus -a -um (rima), *full of cracks, chinks, fissures*, cymba, Verg , fig , quae rimosa bene deponuntur in aure, *that cannot keep a secret*, Hor

ringor, 3 dep *to show the teeth*, fig , *to snarl, growl, be angry at*, Hor

rīpa -ae, f *a bank* **I.** Lit , *the bank of a river* (litus, *the shore of the sea*, ora, *the sea-coast*), ripa magni fluminis, Cic , plur , ripae, of one of the banks of a river, Liv **II.** Poet and post classical, *the shore of the sea* Hor

Rīpaeus = Rhiphaeus (q v)

rīpārĭus -a um (ripa), *frequenting riverbanks*, hirundo, Plin

Rīphaeus (**Rhīphaeus**, **Rhīpaeus**, **Rīpaeus**) -a -um (Ῥιπαῖος), *name of a country in Sarmatia* or *Scythia*, arces, *the Riphaean mountains*, pruina, Verg

rīpŭla -ae, f (dim of ripa), *a little bank* (of a river), Cic

riscus -i, m (ῥίσκος), *a box, chest, trunk*, Ter

rīsĭo -ōnis, f (rideo), *laughing, laughter*, Plaut

rīsor -ōris, m (rideo), *a laugher, mocker*, Hor

rīsus -ūs, m (rideo), *laughing, laughter*, in a bad sense, *jeering, ridicule* **I.** Lit , hominum de te Cic , risus consecutus est, non in te, sed in errorem tuum, Cic , miros risus edere,

Cic ; risum movere, commovere, excitare, *to cause laughter*, Cic , risus captare, *to try to raise a laugh*, Cic , risum tenere, continere, *to check*, Cic **II.** Meton., *an object of laughter*, deus omnibus risus erat, Ov.

rītĕ, adv (root RI, Gr ΡΕ ω, whence ritus, prop abl , instead of ritu). **I.** *with suitable religious ceremonies*, deos colere, Cic **II.** Transf , **A.** *properly, duly, fitly, rightly*, deum rite beatum dicere, Cic., rebus rite paratis, Verg , poet , *fortunately, luckily*, propinqua augurium, Verg , **2,** *usually, in the ordinary manner*, quorum plaustra vagas rite trahunt domos, Hor

rĭtŭālis -e (ritus), *relating to religious usage*, libri, Cic.

rītus -ūs, m (root RI, Gr. ΡΕ-ω, lit., *course*) **I.** *religious custom, usage, ceremony, rite*, Cic **II.** Gen , *a custom, usage, observance*, ritus Cyclopum, Ov , esp abl , ritu, *after the manner of, as*, mulierum ritu, Liv , pecudum ritu, latronum ritu, Cic

rīvālis -e (rivus), *of* or *relating to a brook* or *canal* **I.** Adj , Col. **II.** Subst , **A.** Lit , *one who uses a brook* or *canal in common with another* **B.** Transf., *a rival in love, rival suitor*, Ov., prov , se amare sine rivali, *to have no rival to fear*, Cic

rīvālĭtas -ātis, f (rivalis), *rivalry* (in love), Cic

rīvŭlus i, m (dim of rivus), *a small brook, rivulet*, fig , Cic.

rīvus -i, m (root RI, Gr ΡΕ-ω, whence ῥεῦσαι), *a stream* **I. 1,** lit , **a,** *a brook* rivorum a fonte deductio, Cic ; **b,** *an artificial watercourse, channel, dyke*, rivos ducere, Ov , **2,** transf., *a stream*, of other fluids, such as blood, milk, etc , lacrimarum, Ov , rivis currentia vina, Verg **II.** Fig , *a stream, course*, fortunae, Hor

rixa ae, f (connected with ἔρις, ἐρίζω), *a quarrel, brawl, strife, dispute*, (α) between men , Academiae nostrae cum Zenone magna rixa est, Cic , (β) between animals, Ov

rixātor ōris, m (rixor), *a brawler*, Quint

rixor, 1 dep (rixa), *to quarrel, brawl*, cum aliquo de amicula, Cic.

rōbīgĭnōsus -a -um (robigo), *rusty*, Plaut , robiginosis dentibus cuncta rodit, *with envious teeth*, Mart.

1 **rōbīgo (rūbīgo)** -ĭnis, f (1 robus, ruber), *rust* **I.** Lit , scabra robigine pila, Verg , ferrum robigine roditur, Ov , poet , of the dark deposit on the teeth, Ov **II.** Fig , *the rust of inactivity* or *oblivion*, ingenium longā robigine laesum torpet, Ov

2 **Rōbīgo (Rūbīgo)** ĭnis, f and **Rōbīgus (Rūbīgus)** -i, m (1 robigo), *the deity invoked by the Romans to preserve their grain from mildew* Hence, **Rōbīgālĭa** -ium, n *the festival of the deity Robigo, celebrated annually on the 25th of April*

rōbŏr = robur (q v)

rōbŏrĕus -a um (robur), *oaken*, Ov

rōbŏro, 1 (robur), *to strengthen, make firm* **I.** Lit , artus, Lucr **II.** Fig., pectora, Hor , gravitatem (animi), Cic

rōbur (rōbus, archaic) -ŏris, n (root RO, Gr ῬΩ νυμι, ῬΩ μη), *strength* **I.** Lit., *hard wood*, esp , *oak, oak-wood*, **a,** gen , quercus antiquo robore, Verg , sapiens non est e saxo sculptus aut e robore dolatus, Cic , **b,** poet , of other hard wood, morsus roboris (of the oleaster), Verg **II.** Meton , **A.** Of things made of oak or other hard wood , **a,** in robore accumbunt, *on oaken benches*, Cic ; robur sacrum, *the Trojan horse*, Verg ; robur praefixum ferro, *a lance*, Verg , **b,** esp , *the underground cellar in the prison of Servius Tullius at Rome*, also called the Tullianum, Liv **B.** *hardness, strength, firmness ;* **1, a,** of physical strength, robur iuventae, Liv , **b,** of political power, neque his ipsis tantum umquam virium aut roboris fuit, Liv , **c,** of intellectual or moral strength, *firmness, constancy*, alter virtutis robore firmior quam aetatis, Cic , robur incredibile animi, Cic ; **2,** concr , *the strength, pith of anything*, **a,** versatus in optimorum civium vel flore vel robore, Cic ; **b,** of soldiers, *the flower of the army;* quod fuit roboris duobus proeliis interiit, Caes.

1 **rōbus** -a um, archaic = rufus, *red*, Juv.

2 **rōbus** -ŏris, n = robur (q v)

rōbustus -a -um (robur). **I.** *of hard wood, of oak, oaken*, stipites, Liv **II.** Transf , **1,** *strong, powerful, hard, firm, solid, robust ;* si esses usu atque aetate robustior, Cic , **2,** *intellectually strong, powerful*, animus, Cic , malum fit robustius, Cic

rōdo, rōsi, rōsum, 3 *to gnaw, nibble at* **I.** Lit , **1,** vivos ungues, Hor., **2,** fig , *to calumniate, disparage, backbite, slander*, absentem amicum, Hor , absol , in conviviis rodunt, Cic **II.** Transf , *to eat away, corrode, consume*, ferrum robigine roditur, Cic

1 **rōdus** = raudus (q v)

2 **rōdus** = rudus (q v)

rōduscŭlum = rauduseculum (q v)

rŏgālis -e (rogus), *of* or *relating to the funeral pile* Ov

rŏgātĭo -ōnis, f (rogo) **I.** *asking, question.* **A.** Act , *asking*, Cic **B.** Pass , *that which is asked, a question*, **a,** as a figure of speech, Cic , **b,** polit t t , *a proposal, proposition, project of law, bill laid before the people*, Caecilia, *proposed by Caecilius*, Cic , rogationem ad populum ferre, Caes , rogationem perferre, Cic **II.** *a request, entreaty*, Cic

rŏgātĭuncŭla -ae, f (dim of rogatio) **I.** *a little question*, Cic **II.** *an unimportant proposal* or *bill*, Cic

rŏgātor -ōris, m (rogo), *one who asks* **I.** *the proposer of a bill*, Cic. **II.** *an officer who took the votes in the comitia, a polling-clerk*, rogator primus, *the one who took the votes of the prerogative century*, Cic.

rŏgātus -ū, m (rogo), *a request, entreaty ;* rogatu tuo, Cic , eius rogatu, Cic

rŏgĭtātĭo -ōnis, f (rogito), *a proposition, project of law*, Plaut

rŏgĭto, 1. (freq of rogo), *to ask, inquire frequently* or *eagerly*, rogitantes alii alios, Liv ; quid rei sint, rogitant, Liv

rŏgo, 1 (root ROG, Gr ΟΡΓ, whence ὀρέγω, ὀρέγομαι), *to stretch after something, to fetch* **I.** Lit , Plaut **II.** Transf , **A.** *to ask, inquire, question*, **1,** gen , **a,** aliquem aliquid quid me istud rogas? Cic , **b,** with de and the abl , quae de te ipso rogaro, Cic , **c,** with dep interrog. sent , rogatus de cybaea, quid responderit, Cic , **2,** esp , **a,** polit t t , (α) aliquem sententiam or aliquem, *to ask a person his opinion*, quos priores sententiam rogabat, Cic , (β) rogare populum or legem or absol , lit , *to ask the people about a law*, hence, *to make a proposal, proposition, project of law*, etc , *to the people, to propose a bill*, rogare populum, Cic , rogare plebem, Cic., rogare legem, Cic ; (γ) rogare (populum) magistratum, *to propose a magistrate to the choice of the people, offer a person for election ;* ut consules roget praetor vel dictatorem dicat, Cic.; **b,** milit t t , rogare milites sacramento, *to administer an oath to the troops*, Caes **B.** *to ask* *entreat, beseech, request*, 1, gen, a, aliquem aliquid, Cic., b, aliquem, lautum de aqua per fundum eius ducenda, Cic ; c, with ut or ne and the subj, or the subj alone, id ut facias, te etiam atque etiam rogo, Cic ; Caesar consolatus rogat finem orandi faciat, Caes , d, absol, Cic , 2, esp , *to invite*, aliquem, Cic (archaic subj perf, rogassit, rogassint, Cic)

rŏgus i, m *a funeral pile*, rogum exstruere, Cic , aliquem in rogum imponere, Cic , poet , carmina diffugiunt rogos, *escape destruction*, Ov

Rōma -ae, f (Ῥώμη), *Rome, the chief city of Latium and the Roman empire, founded 753 or 754 B C , honoured as a goddess in a separate temple* Hence, **A. Rōmānus** -a um, **1**, *Roman* ludi *the oldest games at Rome* (also called ludi magni and maximi), Cic , Romano more, *straightforwardly, candidly*, Cic , Romanum est, *it is the Roman custom*, foll by acc. and infin , Liv , subst., a, **Rōmānus** -i, m , (a) sing collect = *the Romans*, Liv , (β) plur , Romani, *the Romans*, Cic , b, **Rōmāna** -ae, f *a Roman woman*, **2**, = *Latin*, lingua, Ov

Rōmŭlus -i, m *son of Ilia or Rhea Silvia and Mars, twin brother of Remus, the founder and first king of Rome, worshipped after his death under the name of Quirinus* Hence **A.** Adj , **Rōmŭlĕus** a -um, *of Romulus*, fera, *the she wolf which suckled Romulus*, Juv **B. Rōmŭlus** a -um, a, *belonging to Romulus*, ficus = Ruminalis, Ov , b, *Roman*, Verg. **C. Rōmŭlĭdēs** -ae, *a descendant of Romulus*, plur , **Rōmŭlĭdae** -ārum and -um, poet., *the Romans*, Verg

rōrārĭi -ōrum, m (sc milites), *a kind of light armed troops, skirmishers*, Liv

rōrĭdus -a -um (ros), *bedewed*, Prop

rōrĭfĕr -fĕra -fĕrum (ros and fero), *dew-bringing*, Lucr

rōro, 1 (ros) **I.** Intransit , *to cause dew, to drop or distil dew* **A.** Lit , quum rorare Tithonia conjux coeperit, Ov **B.** Transf , *to drip, drop, be moist*, rorant pennae, Ov ; capilli rorantes, Ov , rorabant sanguine vepres, Verg **II.** Transit , *to bedew, cover with dew* **A.** Lit , roratae rosae, Ov . **B.** Transf , 1, *to moisten, water*, ora lacrimis, Lucr ; 2, *to drip, let fall in drops*, roratae aquae, Ov , pocula rorantia, *which let fall the wine drop by drop*, Cic

rōrŭlentus a -um (ros), *bedewed, dewy*, Plin

rōs, rōris, m (connected with δρόσος), *dew* **I.** Lit , ros nocturnus, Caes **II.** Transf , **1**, poet , *any dripping moisture*, rores pluvii, *rain-clouds*, Hor , of tears, stillare ex oculis rorem, Hor , stillans, *blood*, Ov , of perfume, Arabus, Ov , **2**, ros marinus, or in one word rosmarinus, *rosemary*, Hor , poet , ros maris, Ov , or simply ros, Verg.

rŏsa -ae, f *a rose* **I. A.** As a flower, a, Cic , plena rosarum atria, Ov , b, collect = *roses, a garland of roses*. reticulum plenum rosae, Cic , in rosa, *crowned with roses*, Cic **B.** As a plant, flores rosae, Hor , Verg **II.** As term of endearment, mea rosa, *my rosebud*, Plaut

rŏsācĕus -a -um (rosa), *made of roses*, Plin , rosaceum oleum, or subst , **rŏsācĕum** -i, n *oil of roses*, Plin

rŏsārĭus -a -um (rosa), *made of roses*, Plin , subst , **rŏsārĭum** i, n *a rose garden, rosary*, Verg.

roscĭdus -a -um (ros), *bedewed, dewy* **I.** Lit , mala, Verg , mella, *dripping like dew*, Verg ; dea, *Aurora*, Ov **II.** Poet , transf , *moistened, watered*, Hernica saxa rivis, Verg

Roscĭus -a um, *name of a Roman gens, the most celebrated members of which were* **1**, Sex Roscius, *of Ameria, accused of the murder of his father, and defended by Cicero* ; **2**, Q Roscius, *of Lanuvium, a celebrated Roman actor, the contemporary and friend of Cicero*, appellat , *a Roscius = a master in his art*, hence, adj , **Roscĭānus** -a um, *Roscian*, imitatio, Cic , **3**, L Roscius Otho, *friend of Cicero, tribune of the people, proposer of the* lex Roscia , adj , **Roscĭus** -a um, *Roscian*, lex Roscia, *a law giving the equites special seats in the theatre*

Rōsĕa (Rōsĭa) ae, f *a district in the Sabine country, famous for the rearing of horses* Hence, adj , **Rōsĕus** -a -um, *Rosean*

rŏsētum -i, n (rosa), *a garden of roses*, Varr

1 **rŏsĕus** -a -um (rosa) **I.** *made of roses, full of roses*, strophium, Verg **II.** Meton , *rose coloured, rosy* ; rubor, Ov , poet , epithet of the deities of the morning and of light, dea, *Aurora*, Ov , Phoebus, Verg , so of anything young or fresh, *blooming*, esp , of parts of the body, cervix, os (of Venus), Verg

2 **Rōsĕus** -a um, v Rosea

rōsĭdus = roscidus (q v)

rōsĭo ōnis, f (rodo), *corrosion*, Plin

rosmărīnus, v ros

rostellum i, n (dim of rostrum), *a little beak or snout*, Plin

rostra ōrum, n , v. rostrum

rostrātus -a -um (rostrum), *having a beak or hook, beaked*, esp , of the beaked ornament of ships, *curved*, navis, Cic , corona, *a crown ornamented with small figures of the beaks of ships, given to the person who first boarded an enemy's ship*, Plin , hence, poet , transf , cui tempora navali fulgent rostrata corona, *with the crown of honour on his brow*, Verg , columna rostrata, *the pillar adorned with ships' prows, erected in the forum to commemorate the naval victory of Duilius*, Liv

rostrum -i, n (rodo), *that which gnaws* **I.** Lit , in birds, *the beak*, in other animals, *the snout*, Cic **II.** Transf , of things resembling a beak or snout , esp , **A.** *the curved end of a ship's prow, a ship's beak* (used for ramming other ships), Caes **B.** Meton , **1**, poet , *the prow of a ship*, Verg., **2**, **rostra** -ōrum, n *the speaker's platform or tribune in the forum* (so called because ornamented with the prows of the ships taken from the Antiates, 338 B C), escendere in rostra, Cic , descendere de rostris, Cic , in rostris, Hor

rŏta ae, f *a wheel* **I.** Lit , **A.** Gen , *the wheel of a carriage*, Lucr , *of a machine*, nec currente rotā funis eat retro, Hor **B.** Esp , **1**, *a wheel for torture* (Gr τροχός), in rotam ascendere, Cic , used often of the wheel of Ixion, rota orbis Ixionii, Verg , **2**, *a potter's wheel*, currente rotā cur urceus exit? Hor , **3**, *a wheel or roller for moving heavy weights*, Tac **II.** Transf , **1**, *the wheel of a chariot* meton , poet , *the chariot itself*, pedibusve rotāve, Ov ; plur , rotae, Verg , **2**, *the sun's disk*, Lucr , **3**, *the course in a circus*, Prop **III** Fig , **1**, fortunae rota, *the wheel, vicissitudes of fortune*, Cic , **2**, poet , imparibus vecta Thalia rotis, *in the unequal alternation of hexameter and pentameter, i e , in elegiac verse*, Ov

rŏto, 1 (rota) **I.** Transit , *to cause to turn round like a wheel, to whirl round, swing round* **A.** Lit , ensem fulmineum, *to brandish*, Verg , middle, rotari, *to revolve, to turn or roll round*, circum caput igne rotato, Ov **B.** Fig , Juv **II.** Intransit , *to turn or wheel round*, saxa rotantia, Verg

rŏtŭla ae, f (dim of rota), *a little wheel*, Plaut

rŏtundē, adv. (rotundus), *roundly; fig.*, of expression, *elegantly, smoothly*, Cic.

rŏtundĭtas -ātis, f. (rotundus), *roundness, rotundity*, Plin.

rŏtundo, 1. (rotundus), *to round, make round.* **I.** Lit., Cic. **II.** Transf., *to make up a round sum of money;* mille talenta rotundentur, Hor.

rŏtundus -a -um (rota), *round, circular, spherical.* **I.** Lit., caelum, Hor.; nihil rotundius, Cic.; prov., mutat quadrata rotundis, *turn everything upside down*, Hor. **II.** Transf., **1,** *round, perfect, complete, self-contained;* teres atque rotundus, Hor.; **2,** of style, *well-rounded, elegant, smooth, well-turned;* verborum apta et quasi rotunda constructio, Cic.

rŭbĕfăcĭo -fēci -factum, 3. (rubeo and facio), *to redden, make red*, Ov.

rŭbellus -a -um (dim. of ruber), *reddish, somewhat red*, Plin.

rŭbens -entis, p. adj. (from rubeo), *red, reddish;* **1,** gen., uva, Verg.; **2,** esp., *red with shame, blushing*, Tib.

rŭbĕo, 2. (v. ruber), **1,** *to be red;* sol rubere solitus, Liv.; **2,** *to be red with shame, blush*, Cic.

rŭber -bra -brum (root RU, whence rufus and rutilus), *red, ruddy.* **I.** Gen., flamma, Ov.; sanguis, Hor.; aequor rubrum oceani, *reddened by the setting sun*, Verg. **II.** Adj. proper, **A.** Rubrum Mare, *the Red Sea, the Arabian and Persian Gulfs*, Cic. **B.** Saxa Rubra, *a place in Etruria, not far from Cremera*, Cic.

rŭbesco -bŭi, 3. (rubeo), *to grow red, become red;* mare rubescebat radiis, Verg.

1. **rŭbēta** -ae, f. (rubus), *a species of toad found in bramble-bushes*, Juv.

2. **rŭbēta** -ōrum, n. (rubus), *bramble-bushes*, Ov.

1. **rŭbĕus (rŏbĕus)** -a -um (ruber), *red, reddish*, Varr.

2. **rŭbĕus** -a -um (rubus), *made of bramble, twigs;* virga, Verg.

Rŭbi -ōrum, m. *a town in Apulia*, now *Ruvo.*

rŭbĭa -ae, f. *madder*, Plin.

Rŭbĭco -ōnis, m. *a small river in Italy, south of Ravenna, which before the time of Augustus marked the boundary between Italia and Gallia Cisalpina, the crossing of which by Caesar was an act of war against the senate;* now *Pisatello*, also called *Rukon.*

rŭbĭcundŭlus -a -um (dim. of rubicundus), *somewhat red* (for shame), Juv.

rŭbĭcundus -a -um (rubeo), *red, reddish, ruddy, rubicund;* Priapus, *painted red*, Ov.; matrona, *browned by the sun*, Ov.; Ceres, *golden-red*, Verg.

rŭbĭdus -a -um (ruber), *red, reddish, ruddy*, Plaut.

Rŭbīgālĭa, v. 2. Robigo.

rŭbīgo = robigo (q.v.).

Rŭbīgus, v. 2. Robigo.

rŭbor -ōris, m. (rubeo), *redness.* **I. a,** *red paint, rouge;* fucati medicamenta candoris et ruboris, Cic.; **b,** *purple;* Tyrii rubores, Verg. **II.** As a quality, **1,** lasting, **a,** gen., Ov.; **b,** *the red tint of the skin, glow;* ille fusus et candore mixtus rubor, Cic.; **2,** momentary, **a,** *redness of the skin;* flammae latentis indicium rubor est, Ov.; **b,** *glow of the eyes in anger;* saepe suum fervens oculis dabat ira ruborem, Ov.; **c,** *reddening from shame, blush;* Masinissae rubor suffusus, Liv.; alicui non rubor est, with infin., *one need not blush that*, etc., Ov.; hence, meton., (α) *modesty*, Cic.; (β) *the cause of shame, disgrace*, Cic.

Rŭbra Saxa, v. ruber.

rŭbrīca -ae, f. **I.** *red earth*, and esp., *red ochre*, Hor. **II.** Meton., *the title of a law which was written in red, the rubric;* and hence, *the law itself*, Pers.

rŭbrīcōsus -a -um (rubrica), *full of red earth*, Plin.

rŭbus -i, m. (root RU, whence ruber), **1,** *a bramble-bush*, Caes.; **2,** *a blackberry*, Prop.

ructo, 1 and **ructor,** 1. dep. (root RUC, whence ructus, erugo, eructo), **1,** *to belch, eructate*, Cic.; **2,** *to belch out, vomit forth;* fig., versus, Hor.

ructor = ructo (q.v.).

ructus -ūs, m. (conn. with ructo), *belching, eructation*, Cic.

rŭdens -entis, m. (f. Plaut.), *a strong rope, cable;* rudentis explicatio, Cic.; stridor rudentum, Verg.

rŭdĕra -um, n., v. 1. rudus.

Rŭdĭae -ārum, f. *a town in Calabria, birthplace of Ennius*, now *Rotigliano* or *Ruge.* Hence, **Rŭdīnus** -a -um, *of Rudiae;* Rudinus homo, i.e., *Ennius*, Cic.

rŭdĭārĭus -ii, m. (2. rudis), *a gladiator who had been presented with a* rudis, i.e., *one who had served his time, a discharged gladiator*, Suet.

rŭdĭcŭla -ae, f. (dim. of 2. rudis), *a small wooden spoon, used in cooking*, Plin.

rŭdīmentum -i, n. (rudis), *the first trial* or *beginning in anything, an attempt, essay;* **a,** gen., primum regni puerilis, Liv.; **b,** in warfare, militare, Liv.; belli, Verg.; rudimentum adolescentiae ponere, Liv.

Rŭdīnus, v. Rudiae.

1. **rŭdis** -e, *rough, raw, rude, unwrought, uncultivated.* **I.** Lit., **a,** of things, rudis campus, Verg.; rudis indigestaque moles, *chaos*, Ov.; lana, *unspun*, Ov.; **b,** poet., of living creatures, *young, fresh*, Cat. **II.** Transf., *rude, uncultivated, unrefined, ignorant, unskilled, inexperienced;* (α) absol., forma quaedam ingenii admodum impolita et plane rudis, Cic.; rudis et integer discipulus, Cic.; (β) with in and the abl. or the abl. alone, in disserendo, Cic.; arte, Ov.; (γ) with ad and the acc., rudis ad pedestria bella gens, Ov.; (δ) with genit., Graecarum literarum, Cic.

2. **rŭdis** -is, f. *a small stick.* **I.** *a ladle, scoop*, used for stirring and mixing in cooking, Plin. **II.** *a staff used for soldiers and gladiators in fencing exercises, a foil*, Liv.; a staff of this kind was given to a gladiator on his discharge from service; tam bonus gladiator rudem tam cito accepisti? Cic.; hence, transf., rude donari, *to be discharged*, Ov.

rŭdo, rūdīvi, 3. *to bellow, roar.* **I.** Lit., of lions, Verg.; of asses, *to bray*, Ov. **II.** Transf., **a,** of men, Verg.; **b,** of things, prora rudens, *rattling*, Verg.

1. **rūdus (rōdus)** -ĕris, n. **1,** *broken fragments of stone used for making floors*, Plin.; **2,** *rubbish from ruined buildings*, Tac.

2. **rūdus** = raudus (q.v.).

rūduscŭlum = rauduscuIum (q.v.).

rūfesco, 3. (rufus), *to grow reddish*, Plin.

rūfo, 1. (rufus), *to make reddish*, Plin.

Rufrae -ārum, f. *a town in Campania, on the borders of Samnium.*

Rufrĭum -ii, n. *a town of the Hirpini*, now *Ruvo.*

rūfŭlus -a -um (dim. of rufus). **I.** *reddish, somewhat red*, Plaut. **II.** Rufuli, *those tribuni militum who were chosen by the army or general himself* (opp. comitiati), Liv.

rūfus -a -um (root RU, whence ruber and rutilus), *red, ruddy, reddish*, Plaut, Ter.

rūga -ae, f *a wrinkle in the face* **I.** Lit., Hor., sulcare rugis cutem, Ov, as a sign of age, non rugae auctoritatem arripere possunt, Cic, of sadness, nunc ruga tristis abit, Ov, of anger, *a frown*, rugas coegit, Ov., populum rugis supercilioque decepit, Cic. **II.** Transf, 1, nitidis rebus maculam ac rugam figere, *to disgrace, mar*, Juv, 2, *a crease, fold, plait of any kind*, Plin

Rŭgii -ōrum, m *a German people between the Elbe and the Weichsel, and on the island of Rugen*

rūgo, 1 (ruga) **I.** Transit, *to fold, wrinkle*, Plin **II.** Intransit, *to be wrinkled*, Plaut.

rūgōsus -a -um (ruga), *full of wrinkles, wrinkled*, genae, Ov., cortex, Ov, rugosus frigore pagus, *villagers*, Hor

rŭīna -ae, f (ruo), *a falling down, fall.* **I. A.** Lit, 1, jumentorum sarcinarumque, Liv, 2, esp., *the falling down of a building*, turris, Caes, eā ruinā oppressum interire, Cic, ruinam dare, *to fall down*, Verg **B.** Transf, *fall, ruin, disaster, calamity, catastrophe, destruction*, urbis, Liv, ruinae fortunarum tuarum, Cic, ille dies utramque ducet ruinam, *death*, Hor **II.** Meton, **A.** *that which falls down*, 1, caeli ruina, *a rain-storm*, Verg, 2, *the ruins of a building, rubbish*, gen in plur, ruinae templorum, Liv **B.** Of persons, *a destroyer, overthrower, bane*, reipublicae, Cic, ruinae publicanorum, *Piso and Gabinius*, Cic

rŭīnōsus -a -um (ruina), *going to ruin*, 1, *ruinous*, aedes, Cic, 2, *ruined, fallen*, domus, Ov

Rullus -i, m, *Servilius, tribune of the people, against whom Cicero delivered three speeches*

rūma = rumis (q v)

rūmen -inis, n *the gullet*

rūmex -icis, c *sorrel*, Plin

rūmĭfĭco, 1 (rumor and facio), *to report*, Plaut

Rūmīna -ae, f (ruma), *a Roman goddess, whose temple stood near the fig tree under which, according to the legend, the she-wolf had suckled Romulus and Remus* Hence, **Rūmīnālis** ficus, Liv, also called Rumina ficus, *the fig tree above-mentioned*, Ov

rūmĭnātĭo -ōnis, f (rumino), *a chewing the cud* **I. A.** Lit, Plin **B.** *a repetition, return*, Plin **II.** *turning over in the mind, ruminating upon*, Cic

rūmĭno, 1 and **rūmĭnor**, 1 dep (rumen), *to chew the cud, ruminate, chew over again*, pallentes herbas, Verg

rūmis -is, f and **rūma** -ae, f *the breast, teat*, Plin

rūmor -ōris, m *a dull noise* **I.** Gen, **a**, of things, *the noise of the oars*, Verg, **b**, *murmuring, murmur, confused cry*, rumore secundo = clamore secundo, *with favouring shout*, Hor **II. A.** *a report, rumour, common talk, hearsay*, rumores incerti, Caes, rumor multa fingit, Caes, rumor multa perfert, Cic, with genit of the cause, uno rumore periculi, Cic; with de and the abl, graves de te rumores, Cic, rumor est, with acc and infin, Cic, rumor vulgatur, Liv, crebri rumores afferebantur, Caes, increbrescit rumor, Liv **B.** *common or general opinion, popular judgment*, 1, gen, parva aura rumoris, Cic, 2, esp, *good opinion*, rumorem quendam et plausum popularem esse quaesitum, Cic

rumpo, rūpi, ruptum, 3 *to break, break in pieces, burst, rend, tear asunder.* **I.** Lit, **A.** Gen, 1, vincula, Cic., pontem, *to break down*, Liv, pass, rumpi = *to be burst*, inflatas rumpi vesiculas, Cic, 2, *to burst, split, injure, damage*, jecur, Juv, pass, rumpi, as middle = *to burst*, ut licentiā audaciaque, quā ante rumpebar (*burst with anger*), nunc ne movear quidem, Cic, 3, milit t t, *to break through*, ordines, mediam aciem, Liv, 4, poet, transf, unde tibi reditum certo subtemine Parcae rupere, *cut off*, Hor **B.** 1, *to break through, to force, make open*, ferro per hostes viam, Verg, eo cuneo viam, Liv, 2, *to cause to break forth*, a, fontem, Ov, often reflex, se rumpere, and middle, rumpi, *to break forth*, tantus se nubibus imber ruperat, Verg., b, *to cause a sound to burst forth, to utter*, questus, Verg **II.** Fig, *to break*, a, *to destroy, violate, annul, make void*, foedera, Cic, jus gentium, Liv, testamentum, Cic; **b**, *to break off, interrupt, disturb*, visum, Cic, somnum, Verg, silentia, Ov, rumpe moras, Verg

rūmuscŭlus -i, m (dim of rumor), *a trifling rumour, idle talk, gossip*, imperitorum hominum rumusculos aucupari, Cic

rūna -ae, f *a species of missile, a dart or javelin*, Cic (?)

runcĭno, 1 *to plane, plane off*, Plaut

runco, 1 *to weed, thin out*, Plin

rŭo, rŭi, rŭtum, but partic fut, rŭĭtūrus, 3 (connected with *ῥέω, to flow*), *to run, to rush, to hasten* **I.** Intransit, **A.** Gen, 1, lit, **a**, of persons, (Pompejum) ruere nuntiant et jam jamque adesse, Cic, in aquam caeci ruebant, Liv., **b**, of rivers, de montibus, Verg; **c**, of sounds, unde ruunt, *rush forth*, Verg, **d**, of night and day, ruit oceano nox, *hastens over*, Verg, (but) nox ruit, *hastens away*, Verg, 2, fig, **a**, in arma ac dimicationem, Liv, ad interitum, Cic, **b**, esp of over hasty actions, *to be hasty, precipitate*, ruere in agendo, in dicendo, Cic **B** *to fall down, sink, fall to the ground*, 1, lit, **a**, poet, of persons, ruebant victores victique, Verg, **b**, of things, ruere illa non possunt, ut haec non eodem labefacta motu non concidant, Cic, 2, transf, *to fall, be ruined*, ruere illam rempublicam, Cic **II.** Transf, **A. 1**, *to snatch up, pick up*, **a**, cinerem et confusa ossa focis, Verg, **b**, *to collect together, scrape together*, unde divitias aerisque ruam acervos, Hor, 2, *to cast up from below*, **a**, ruere spumas salis aere (of ships), Verg, **b**, legal t t, ruta et caesa, and by asyndeton, ruta caesa, *everything on an estate dug up* (ruta), *and fallen down* (caesa), *minerals and timber*, Cic **B.** *to cast down*, immanem molem volvuntque ruuntque, Verg

rūpes -is, f (rumpo), *a rock, cliff*, Caes, Liv

rūpĭcapra -ae, f (rupes and capra), *a chamois*, Plin

ruptor -ōris, m (rumpo), *a breaker, violator*, foederis, Liv

rūrĭcŏla -ae, c (rus and colo), *inhabiting, cultivating the country*, boves, Ov, deus, *Priapus*, Ov Subst, **rūrĭcŏla** -ae, m *a countryman, a tiller of the field*, poet, of an ox, Ov

rūrĭgĕna -ae, m (rus and gigno), *born in the country, rustic* Subst, **rūrĭgĕnae** -ārum, c, *the countryfolk*, Ov

rūro, 1 and **rūrŏr**, 1 dep (rus), *to live in the country*, Plaut

rursŭs and **rursum**, adv (contr for reversus, revorsum, i e, reversus, reversum) **I.** *backward, back*, rursum trahunt, Cic **II.** Transf, **A.** *on the other hand, on the contrary, in return*, rursus repudiaret, Cic **B.** To express repetition of a previous action, *again, once more, afresh*, rursus sevocanda videatur Cic, rursus resistens, Caes

rūs, rūris, n. *the country* (in opposition to the town), *lands, a country-seat, villa, farm.* **I.** Lit., habes rus amoenum, Cic.; acc., rus, *to the country*, Plaut.; plur., in sua rura venire, Cic.; abl., rure, and locat., ruri, *in the country;* ruri vivere, Cic. **II.** Meton., manent vestigia ruris, *traces of boorish nature*, Hor.

Ruscĭno -ōnis, f. *a town in Gallia Narbonensis, on a river of the same name*, now *Tour de Rousillon.*

ruscum -i, n. and **ruscus** -i, f. *butcher's broom*, Verg.

Rūsellae -ārum, f. *one of the twelve confederate towns of Etruria*, now ruins near *Roselle;* hence, adj., **Rūsellānus** -a -um, *belonging to Rusellae.*

russus -a -um, *red, russet*, Cat.

rustĭcānus -a -um (rusticus), *of or relating to the country, rustic;* vita rusticana, Cic.; homines rusticani, Cic.

rustĭcātĭo -ōnis, f. (rusticor). **I.** *a living in the country*, Cic. **II.** *agriculture*, Cic.

rustĭcē, adv. (rusticus). **I.** *like a rustic, in a countrified manner;* loqui, Cic. **II.** Meton., *clownishly, awkwardly;* facere, Cic.

rustĭcĭtas -ātis, f. (rusticus), **a**, *rustic manners, rusticity, awkwardness*, Ov.; **b**, *bashfulness, timidity*, Ov.

rustĭcor, 1. dep. (rusticus), *to live in the country, to rusticate;* absol., Cic.; cum aliquo, Cic.

rustĭcŭlus -a -um (dim. of rusticus), *somewhat rustic, boorish.* Subst., **rustĭcŭlus** -i, m. *a little countryman, a little rustic*, Cic.

rustĭcus -a -um (rus), *of or belonging to the country, rural, rustic.* **I.** Lit., **A.** Adj., praedium, Cic.; vita, Cic.; homo, *a countryman*, Cic. **B.** Subst., **rustĭcus** -i, m. *a countryman, a rustic*, Cic. **II.** Meton., *country-like.* **A.** In a good sense, *plain, simple, homely;* mores, Cic. **B.** In a bad sense, *clownish, countrified, awkward, boorish;* rustica vox et agrestis, Cic. Subst., **rustĭcus** -i, m. *a boor, clown;* **rustĭca** -ae, f. *a country-girl*, Ov.

1. **rūta** -ae, f. (ῥυτή), *the herb rue.* **I.** Lit., Cic.; plur., Ov. **II.** Fig., *bitterness, unpleasantness*, Cic.

2. **rūta** caesa, v. ruo.

rŭtābŭlum -i, n. (ruo), *a fire-shovel*, Suet.

rūtātus -a -um (1. ruta), *flavoured with rue*, Mart.

Rūtēni (**Rūthēni**) -ōrum, m. *a Celtic people in Gallia Aquitania*, in modern *Rovergue*, *with capital Segodunum*, now *Rhodez.*

rŭtĭlesco, 3. (rutilo), *to become reddish*, Plin.

Rŭtĭlĭus -a -um (orig. appellat. = *red*), *name of a Roman gens, the most celebrated member of which was* P. Rutilius Rufus, *an orator and historian, consul in the time of Marius.*

rŭtĭlo, 1. (rutilus). **I.** Intransit., *to shine with a reddish gleam, to glitter like gold;* arma rutilare vident, Verg. **II.** Transit., *to make reddish, to dye red;* comae rutilatae, Liv.

rŭtĭlus -a -um (root RU, whence ruber and rufus), *red, gold-red, golden, yellow, auburn;* capilli, Ov.; ignis, Verg.; cruor, Ov.; fulgor, Cic.

rūtrum -i, n. (ruo), *a spade, shovel*, Liv.

rŭtŭla -ae, f. (dim. of ruta), *a little bit of rue*, Cic.

Rŭtŭli -ōrum and (poet.) -ûm, m. *the Rutuli, an ancient people of Latium, whose capital was Ardea;* sing., **Rŭtŭlus** -i, m. *a Rutulian*, Verg.; Rutulus audax, *Turnus, king of the Rutuli*, Verg. Hence, adj., **Rŭtŭlus** -a -um, *Rutulian;* rex, *Turnus*, Verg.

Rŭtŭpĭae -ārum, f. *a town of the Caverni in Britain*, perhaps the modern *Richborough.* Hence, adj., **Rŭtŭpīnus** -a -um, *belonging to Rutupiae.*

S.

S, s, the eighteenth letter of the Latin alphabet, corresponding to the Greek sigma (Σ, σ, ς), sometimes representing the Greek aspirate, e.g., *sex* = ἕξ, *sal* = ἅλς, *serpo* = ἕρπω, ὑπέρ = *super.* It is occasionally interchanged with *t* (as mersare, pulsare, mertare, pultare), and *r* (as honor and honos). The poets of the older period often elided *s* before a consonant, e.g., vitā illā dignu' locoque; by assimilation, *s* before *f* becomes *f*, as difficilis; it often represents another consonant which has been assimilated to it, as jubeo, jussi (for jubsi), cedo, cessi (for cedsi), premo, pressi (for premsi), pando, passum (for pandsum). For abbreviations in which S. is used, v. Table of Abbreviations.

Săba -ae, f. (Σάβη), *a district in Arabia Felix, famous for its perfumes.* Hence, **Săbaeus** -a -um (Σαβαῖος), *Sabaean;* poet. = *Arabian.* Subst., **a**, **Săbaea** -ae, f. (sc. terra), *the country of Sabaea* (= *Arabia Felix*); **b**, **Săbaei** -ōrum, m. *the Sabaeans.*

Sābātē -ēs, f. *a town in Etruria, on a lake of the same name*, now *Lago di Bracciano.* Hence, adj., **Sābātīnus** -a -um, *of or relating to Sabate;* tribus, Liv.

Săbāzĭus (**Săbādĭus, Sŏbādĭus**) -ii, m. (Σαβάζιος), *a surname of Bacchus*, Cic. Hence, **Săbāzĭa** -ōrum, n. *a festival in honour of Bacchus.*

Sabbăta -ōrum, n. (Σάββατα), *the Sabbath, Jewish day of rest;* tricesima sabbata, either *the great Sabbath* (a Jewish festival in October), or else *the new moon*, Hor. Hence, **Sabbătārĭus** -a -um, *relating to the Sabbath.* Subst., **Sabbătārĭi** -ōrum, m. *the observers of the Sabbath, the Jews*, Mart.

Săbelli -ōrum, m. (dim. of Sabini), *a poetic name of the Sabines;* sing., Sabellus, *the Sabine* (i.e., Horace, as owner of an estate in the Sabine country), Hor. Hence, **A.** Adj., **Săbellus** -a -um, *Sabine.* **B.** **Săbellĭcus** -a -um, *Sabine.*

Săbīni -ōrum, m. *an ancient people of Italy, neighbours of the Latins;* meton. = *the country of the Sabines*, Liv.; sing., **Săbīnus** -i, m. *a Sabine*, Liv.; **Săbīna** -ae, f. *a Sabine woman*, Juv. Hence, adj., **Săbīnus** -a -um, *a Sabine.* Subst., **Săbīnum** -i. n. (sc. vinum), *Sabine wine*, Hor.

Sabis -is, acc. -im, m. *a river in Gallia Belgica*, now the *Sambre.*

săbŭlēta -ōrum, n. (sabulum), *sandy places*, Plin.

săbŭlo -ōnis, m. *gravel, sand*, Plin.

săbŭlōsus -a -um (sabulum), *abounding in sand, sandy, gravelly*, Plin.

săbŭlum -i, n. *gravel, sand*, Plin.

1. **săburra** -ae, f. *sand used as ballast*, Verg.

2. **Săburra** -ae, m. *a general of king Juba.*

· **săburro**, 1 (saburra) **I.** *to load with ballast*, Plin **II.** Transf, *to cram full* (with food), Plaut

sacal, indecl. (an Egyptian word), *Egyptian amber*, Plin

saccărius -a -um (saccus), *relating to sacks*, navis, *laden with sacks*, Quint

sacchăron -i, n (σάκχαρον), *a saccharine juice exuding from the joints of the bamboo*, Plin

saccipērium ii, n. (saccus and pera), *a pocket* or *fob for a purse*, Plaut

sacco, 1 (saccus), *to strain* or *filter through a bag*, Plin, transf, Lucr.

saccŭlus -i, m (dim of saccus), *a small bag*, Cic

saccus i, m (σάκκος), *a sack, bag*, Cic, esp, *a purse, money-bag*, Hor, also *a bag* (for straining wine through), Plin

săcellum -i, n (dim of sacrum), *a small shrine* or *chapel*, Cic

săcer -cra -crum (root SA, whence sancio, sanus, Gr σάος), *sacred, holy, consecrated* **I.** Adj, **A.** Gen, **a**, with dat. and genit, sacrum deae pecus, Liv, illa insula eorum deorum sacra putatur, Cic, **b**, absol, sacra aedes, Cic, vates, *sacred to Apollo*, Hor, poet, of deities themselves, Vesta, Prop, name of certain places, as sacer mons, *the holy hill, a hill in the Sabine country, three Roman miles from Rome, on the right bank of the Anio*, Liv, sacra via, *the holy street, a street in Rome beginning at the Sacellum Streniae and ending at the Capitol*, also sacer clivus, Hor **B** Esp, *consecrated to one of the infernal deities*, hence *accursed, devoted to destruction*, **a**, relig t t, eius caput Jovi (Stygio) sacrum esset, ap Liv, eum qui eorum cuiquam nocuerit sacrum sancire, Liv, **b**, transf, *detestable, accursed, horrible*, is intestabilis et sacer esto, Hor., auri sacra fames, Verg **II.** Subst., **săcrum** i, n, *that which is holy* **A.** *a holy thing*, **a**, lit, sacrum rapere, Cic, **b**, poet, transf, of poems, sacra caelestia, Ov **B.** *some holy observance, a festival, sacrifice*, **a**, lit., sacra Cereris, Cic, sacra facere Graeco Herculi, Liv, so of the private religious rites peculiar to each Roman gens, sacra gentilicia Liv, sacra interire majores noluerunt, Cic, eisdem uti sacris, Cic; **b**, transf, *a secret, mystery*, Ov

săcerdos -dōtis, c (sacer), *a priest, priestess*, sacerdotes populi Romani, Cic, in apposition, regina sacerdos, *Rhea, a vestal*, Verg

săcerdōtālis -e (sacerdos), *of* or *relating to a priest, priestly, sacerdotal*, Plin

săcerdōtium -ii, n (sacerdos), *the office* or *dignity of a priest, priesthood*, sacerdotium inire, Cic

săcōpēnium ii, n (σαγόπηνον), *the gum of an umbelliferous plant*, Plin

săcrāmentum -i, n (sacro), *that which binds* or *obliges a person* **I.** Legal t t, *the money deposited with the tresviri capitales by the parties in a suit, which the defeated party lost*, multae sacramenta, Cic, meton, *a kind of legal challenge* or *wager, a civil suit, process*, justo sacramento contendere cum aliquo, Cic **II.** Milit t t, *the engagement entered into by newly-enlisted soldiers, the military oath of allegiance*, **1**, **a**, lit, aliquem militiae sacramento obligare, Cic, milites sacramento rogare, Caes, Liv, or adigere, Liv, dicere sacramentum, Caes, or sacramento, Liv, alicui sacramento or sacramentum dicere, *to swear allegiance to*, Caes, **b**, meton, *military service*, Tac, **2**, transf, *an oath*, perfidum sacramentum dicere, Hor.

Săcrāni -ōrum, m *a people in Latium*; hence, **Săcrānus** -a -um, *of the Sacrani*, acies, Verg

săcrārium ii, n (sacrum) **I.** *a place where sacred things are kept, the sacristy of a temple*, Ov, Caere sacrarium populi Romani (as the Roman religious vessels, etc, were said to have once been taken to Caere), Liv **II.** *a place of worship, a chapel, temple*, Bonae Deae, Cic; *the chapel in a private house*, in tuo sacrario, Cic

săcrātus -a -um, p adj (from sacro), *sacred, holy, consecrated*, templum, Verg used esp of the Roman emperor, whose genius was worshipped, dux (i e, Augustus), Ov

săcricŏla ae c. (sacrum and colo), *a sacrificing priest* or *priestess*, Tac

săcrifĕr -fĕra -fĕrum (sacrum and fero), *carrying sacred things*, rates, Ov

săcrificālis (**săcrificiālis**) e (sacrificium), *of* or *relating to the sacrifices*, Tac

săcrificātio -ōnis, f (sacrifico), *a sacrificing*, Cic

săcrificium -ii, n (sacrifico), *a sacrifice*, facere sacrificium and sacrificia, Cic

săcrifico, 1 and **săcrificor**, 1 dep (sacrificus) **I.** Intransit, *to offer sacrifice, to sacrifice*, alicui majoribus hostiis, Liv, in sacrificando, Cic **II.** Transit, *to offer in sacrifice, to sacrifice*, suem, Ov, pecora, Liv

săcrificŭlus i, m (dim of sacrificus), *a sacrificing priest*, Liv, rex sacrificulus, *the priest in Rome under the Republic who offered the sacrifices previously offered by the kings*, Liv

săcrificus -a um (sacrum and facio) **I.** *sacrificing*, Ancus, Ov, rex (v sacrificulus), Liv **II.** *of* or *relating to a sacrifice*, ritus, Ov

săcrilĕgium -ii, n (sacrilegus) **I.** *robbery of a temple, stealing of sacred things, sacrilege*, sacrilegium prohibere, Liv **II.** *profanation of religious rites*, Nep.

săcrilĕgus -a -um (sacra and lego) **I.** *stealing sacred things, sacrilegious*, subst, *a temple-robber*, Cic **II.** *violating* or *profaning sacred things, irreligious, impious*, **a**, lit, used of Pentheus, who despised the worship of Bacchus, Ov, **b**, transf, *godless, impious, wicked*, linguae, manus, Ov

Săcriportus -ūs, m (sacer and portus) **I.** *a town not far from Rome in the Volscian country between Signia and Praeneste* **II.** *a town on the Tarentine Gulf*

săcrium -ii, n *Scythian amber*, Plin

săcro, 1 (sacer) **I.** *to dedicate to a god, consecrate* **A.** Lit, caput, Liv; aras, Verg **B.** Transf, **1**, *to devote, give, allot*, honorem alicui, Verg, **2**, meton, *to consecrate, make holy, make inviolable* foedus, Liv, lex sacrata, *a law the violation of which was punished by a curse*, Cic **II.** *to make imperishable, to immortalise*, aliquem Lesbio plectro, Hor, vivit eloquentia Catonis sacrata scriptis omnis generis, Liv

săcrōsanctus -a -um (sacer and sanctus), *consecrated with religious ceremonies*, hence, *holy, sacred, inviolable* (of the tribunes of the people), ut plebi sui magistratus essent sacrosancti, Liv, possessiones, Cic, potestas (of the tribune), Liv, alicuius memoria, Plin

săcrum, v sacer

Sădăla and **Sădălēs** -ae, m *a Thracian prince, son of Cotys III*

saeclum = saeculum (q v)

saecŭlāris (**sēcŭlāris**) e (saeculum), *relating to a saeculum* or *age*, ludi, *secular games* (celebrated at intervals of 110 years), Suet.; carmen, *a hymn sung at the secular games*, Suet.

saecŭlum (sēcŭlum, syncop. **saeclum, sēclum)** -i, n. (perhaps connected with 1. secus and with sexus). **I.** *race, sex, generation*; muliebre, Lucr. **II.** Transf., **A.** In a restricted sense, like γενεά, *the average duration of a man's life* (33⅓ years), *a generation, age*; **1,** lit., multa saecula hominum, Cic.; **2,** meton., **a,** *the human race living at any particular generation, the age, the times*; ipse fortasse in huius saeculi errore versor, Cic.; **b,** *the spirit of the age, the prevailing tone of manners*; mitescent saecula, Verg. **B.** In a wider sense, *the longest duration of a man's life, a hundred years, a century*; **1, a,** lit., duobus prope saecula ante, Cic.; **b,** transf., *an indefinitely long time, an age*; aliquot saeculis post, Cic.; saeclis effeta senectus, Verg.; **2,** meton., *the men living in a particular century, the century*; saeculorum reliquorum judicium, Cic.

saepĕ, adv., comp. saeplus, superl. saepissime, *often, oftentimes, frequently*, Cic.; bene saepe, Cic.; saepe et multum, Cic.; saepe multi, Cic.; saepenumero, *repeatedly, again and again*, Cic.

saepes (sēpes) -is, f. (σηκός), *a hedge, fence*.

saepĭa = sepia (q.v.).

saepĭcŭlē, adv. (dim. of saepe), *pretty often*, Plaut.

saepīmentum (sēpīmentum) -i, n. (saepio), *an inclosure*, Cic.

Saepīnum -i, n. *a small town in Samnium*, now *Sepino*.

saepĭo (sēpĭo), saepsi, saeptum, 4. (saepes), *to surround with a hedge, to hedge in, to inclose*. **I. a,** lit., vallum arboribus, Liv.; **b,** fig., locum cogitatione, Cic. **II.** Transf., **1,** *to shut in, to confine, to surround*; urbes moenibus, Cic.; se tectis, *to shut oneself up at home*, Verg.; **2, a,** *to beset, to occupy*; vias, Liv.; **b,** *to guard, to secure, protect*; natura oculos membranis vestivit et saepsit, Cic.

saepta -ōrum, n., v. saeptum.

saeptum (septum) -i, n. (saepio), *an inclosure, barrier*. **I.** Gen., quibus saeptis beluas continebimus, Cic. **II.** Esp., **saepta** -ōrum, n. *the inclosure where the Romans voted at the comitia, sometimes erected in the forum, sometimes in the Campus Martius*, Cic.

saet . . . v. set . . .

Saetăbis -bis. **I.** m. *a river in Spain*, now *Mijares* or *Myares*, or else *Cenia* or *Senia*. **II.** f. *a town in Hispania Tarraconensis, famous for its flax*. Adj., **Saetăbus** -a -um, *relating to Saetabis*.

saetĭger and **saetōsus** = setiger, setosus (q.v.).

saevē, adv. with compar. and superl. (saevus), *cruelly, barbarously, ferociously*, Hor.

saevĭdĭcus -a -um (saevus and dico), *angrily spoken*; dicta, Ter.

saevĭo -ii -itum, 4. (saevus), *to rage, be fierce, furious*. **I.** Lit., of animals, saevit lupus, Ov.; anguis, Verg.; saevire coepisse (of elephants), Liv.; in aliquem, Ov. **II.** Transf., a, of men, *to be furious, angry*; saevire in obsides, Liv.; impers., in ceteros saevitum esse, Liv.; **b,** of things and of abstractions, *to rage*; saevit pontus, Hor.; saevit venenum in praecordiis, Hor.; saevit amor ferri, Verg.

saevĭtĕr = saeve (q.v.).

saevĭtĭa -ae, f. (saevus), *ferocity*. **I.** Lit., of animals, canum, Plin. **II.** Transf., *fierceness, rage, cruelty, harshness, severity*; **a,** of men, judicis, Cic.; creditorum, Tac.; hostium, Sall.; **b,** of inanimate and abstract things; annonae, *high price of provisions*, Tac.

saevum = sebum (q.v.).

saevus -a -um, *raging, wild, violent, fierce*. **I.** Lit., of animals, leones, Lucr.; saevior leaena, Verg. **II.** Transf., *raging, fierce, cruel, savage, harsh*; **a,** of persons, Juno, Verg.; Aeneas saevus in armis, *terrible*, Verg.; poet. with the infin., quaelibet in quemvis opprobria fingere saevus, Hor.; **b,** of inanimate and abstract things, aequora, Verg.; ventus, Cic.; scopulus, Verg.; funera, Verg.

sāga -ae, f. (root SAC, whence sagio), *a female soothsayer, prophetess, fortune-teller*, Cic.

săgācĭtas -ātis, f. (sagax), **I.** *keenness, acuteness of the senses*; esp., *keenness of scent in dogs*; canum ad investigandum sagacitas narium, Cic. **II.** Transf., *mental acuteness, sagacity, shrewdness*; hominis, Cic.

săgācĭtĕr, adv. (sagax), *sharply, keenly*. **I.** Of the senses, *with keen scent*, Plin. **II.** Transf., of the mind, *acutely, sagaciously, shrewdly*; pervestigare, Cic.; tu sagacius odorabere, Cic.; ut odorer, quam sagacissime possim, quid sentiant, etc., Cic.

Săgăris, acc. -im, abl. -i, m. and **Sangărius** -ii, m. (Σαγγαριός), *a river in Phrygia and Bithynia, flowing into the Propontis*, now *Sakarja, Sakari*. Hence, **Săgărītis** -idis, f. *of or relating to Sagaris*; nympha, Ov.

săgātus -a -um (sagum), *clothed with a sagum*; esp., of a soldier in a military cloak, Cic.

săgax -ācis (sagio), *having keen senses*. **I.** *keen-scented*; canes, Cic.; *of quick hearing*; sagacior anser, Ov. **II.** Transf., of mental acuteness, *acute, clever*; mens, Cic.; sagacissimus ad suspicandum, Cic.; with infin., sagax quondam ventura videre, Ov.

săgīna -ae, f. (σάττω, *to fill*). **I.** *fattening, feeding, nourishing, stuffing, cramming*, Cic. **II.** Transf., *food, fodder, nourishment*, Tac.

săgīno, 1. (sagina), *to fatten, feed up, cram*. **I.** Lit., porcum, Prop.; quae copiā rerum omnium (illos Gallos) saginaret, Liv. **II.** Transf., sanguine reipublicae saginari, Cic.

săgĭo, 4. (root SAC, whence sagax, sagus), *to perceive quickly, feel keenly*; sagire sentire acute est, Cic.

săgitta -ae, f. *an arrow*. **I.** Lit., Cic. **II.** Transf., *the Arrow, a constellation*, Cic.

săgittārĭus -a -um (sagitta), *of or relating to arrows*; subst., **săgittārĭus** -ii, m. *an archer*; **a,** lit., Cic.; **b,** transf., *the constellation Sagittarius*, also called *Arcitenens*, Cic.

săgittĭfĕr -fĕra -fĕrum (sagitta and fero). **I.** *carrying arrows*; pharetra, Ov. **II.** *armed with arrows*; Geloni, Verg.

Săgittĭpŏtens -entis, m. (sagitta and potens), *the constellation Sagittarius*, Cic.

sagmen -ĭnis, n. (SAC, sacer, sancio), *a bunch of sacred herbs plucked in the citadel, by bearing which the persons of the Roman fetiales and ambassadors became inviolable*, Liv.

Sagra -ae, c. *a river in the country of the Bruttii, on the banks of which a battle was fought* 580 B.C., *between Croton and Locri*, now *Sacriano*.

săgŭlum -i, n. (dim. of sagum), *a small military cloak*, Cic.

săgum -i, n. (σάγος, a Celtic word), *a mantle made of coarse wool worn by slaves, also the plaid of the Celts*; esp., of soldiers, *a military cloak*, Caes.; hence, symbolical of war, as the toga of peace; hence, saga sumere, ad saga ire, *to take up arms, prepare for war*, Cic.; in sagis esse, *to* *be in arms*, Cic., saga ponere, *to lay down arms*, Liv

Saguntia, v Segontia

Săguntum -i, n and **Săguntus** (-ŏs) -i, f *a town in Spain, south of the Ebro, now Murviedro, the besieging of which by Hannibal led to the outbreak of the Second Punic War*. Hence, **A Săguntīnus** -a -um, *Saguntine* **B. Săguntii** -um, m *the people of Saguntum*

săgus a um (root SAG, whence sagio), *prophetical, soothsaying*, subst, **săga** ae, f *a fortune-teller*, Cic

Săis is, f (Σαϊς), *the old capital of Lower Egypt*, now ruins near *Sâ el Haggar* Hence, **Săitae** -ārum, m *the inhabitants of Sais*

săl, sălis, m and n, and plur, săles, m (root ΑΛ, ἅλς), *salt* **I. 1**, lit, multi modii salis, Cic, **2**, fig, *salt*, i e, *wit, facetiousness*, epistolae humanitatis sparsae sale, Cic, sale et facetiis Caesar vicit omnes, Cic **II.** Meton, **1**, *the salt sea*, campi salis, Verg, **2**, plur, sales, *salt taste*, Ov

Sălācia -ae, f (salum and cieo), *a sea-goddess, corresponding to the Greek Tethys, wife of Oceanus*

sălăco -ōnis, m (σαλάκων), *a swaggerer, boaster, braggart*, Cic

Sălămis -mīnis, acc -mīna, f (Σαλαμίς) **I.** *an island and town in the Saronic Gulf, over against Eleusis, scene of a naval victory of the Greeks over the Persians, now Koluri* **II.** *a town in Cyprus, built by Teucer* Hence, **Sălămīnius** a um, **a**, *relating to the island Salamis*, **Sălămīnii** -ōrum, m *the Salaminians, inhabitants of Salamis*, **b**, *relating to the town of Salamis in Cyprus*; subst, **Sălămīnii** ōrum, m *the inhabitants of Salamis in Cyprus*

Sălāpia -ae, f *a town in Apulia*, now *the village of Sapi* Hence, **Sălāpītāni** ōrum, m and **Sălāpīni (Salpīni)** ōrum, m *the inhabitants of Salapia*

sălăputtium (sălăpūtium) ii, n. *a little dwarf, manikin*, Cat

sălārius -a um (sal), *of or relating to salt* **I.** Adj, annona, *yearly revenue from salt*, Liv., adj prop, Salaria via, or simply Salaria, *a road beginning at the Porta Capena and leading into the Sabine country, the Salt Road*, so called because the Sabines used it for conveying their salt from the sea, Cic **II.** Subst, **sălārium** -ii, n *salt rations, money given to soldiers and officers for salt*, and hence, *allowance, pay, wages, salary*, Suet

Salassi -ōrum, m *the Salassi, an Alpine people in modern Savoy*

sălax -ācis (1 salio) **I** Of male animals, *lustful, lecherous*, aries, Ov **II.** Transf, *exciting lust*, eruca, Ov

sălebra -ae, f (1 salio), *a rough, uneven road*. **I.** Lit, Hor **II.** Fig, applied to discourse, *roughness, ruggedness*, oratio haeret in salebra, *sticks fast*, Cic

sălebrōsus a -um (salebra), *rugged, rough*, saxa, Ov

Sălentīni (Sallentīni) -ōrum, m *a people of Calabria on the coast* meton, *the country of the Salentini* Adj, **Sălentīnus** a um, *Salentinian*

Sălernum i, n *a town on the Adriatic Sea, in the Picentine country*, now *Salerno*

Săliāris, v Salii

Săliātus -ūs, m. (Salii), *the office* or *dignity of a priest of Mars*

sălicastrum i, n (salix), *a kind of vine growing wild among the willows*, Plin

sălictārius -a -um (salix), *of* or *relating to willows*, Plin

sălictum -i, n (syncop for salicetum, from salix), *a plantation of willows*, Cic

sălientes ium, m, v 2 salio

sălignus a -um (salix), *made of willow wood*, fustis, Hor

Sălii -ōrum, m (salio, i e, *the leapers* *jumpers*), *a college of priests of Mars, instituted by Numa, whose sacred processions, accompanied by singers and armed dancers, took place annually in the beginning of March* Hence, **Săliāris** e, **a**, lit, *relating to the Salii*, carmen Numae, Hor, **b**, transf, *splendid, magnificent* (from the sumptuous feasts that followed the procession of the Salii), epulari Saliarem in modum, Cic

sălillum -i, n (dim of salinum), *a little salt-cellar*, Cat

sălīnae ārum, f (sal), *salt-works, brine-pits* **I.** Gen, Cic, Caes, in jesting reference to sal (*wit*), possessio salinarum mearum, Cic **II.** Esp, **A.** *salt works on the banks of the Tiber*, in full, salinae Romanae, Liv **B** Salinae, *a place in Rome, near the Porta Trigemina*, Liv

sălīnum -i, n (sal), *a salt cellar*, Hor

1 **sălio (sallio)**, 4 (sal), *to salt, pickle*, Varr

2 **sălio**, sălŭi (sălii rare), saltum, 4 (root SAL, Gr 'ΑΛ, whence ἅλλομαι) **I** Intransit., *to spring, leap, jump, bound* **A.** Lit, of living beings, de muro, Liv, in aquas, Ov, super vallum, Liv, saliunt in gurgite ranae, Ov **B.** Transf, of things, **a**, salit grando Verg, sal or mica (salis) saliens, *sacrificial salt, which (as a good omen) leapt up when thrown into the fire*, farre pio et saliente mica, Hor, pectora trepido salientia motu, Ov, **b**, of water, *to spring, leap, flow*, dulcis aquae saliens rivus, Verg Partic. subst, **sălientes** -ium, m (sc fontes), *fountains*, Cic **II.** Transit, of animals, *to leap, to cover*, Ov

Sălisubsĭlus -i, m (= Salius subsiliens), *one of the Salii*, Cat

săliunca -ae, f *wild* or *Celtic nard*, Verg

săliva ae, f (connected with σίαλος), *spittle, saliva* **I. A.** Lit, Cat **B.** Meton, **1**, *appetite, desire*, Pers, **2**, *taste*, Prop **II.** Transf, *any similar moisture*, e g, *tears*, Plin, *honey*, Plin

sălīvārius -a -um (saliva), *slimy*, Plin

sălīvo, 1 (saliva), *to spit out*, Plin

sălīvōsus -a -um (saliva), *slimy*, Plin

sălix -icis, f *a willow*, Verg

Sallentīni = Salentini (q v)

sallio = 1 salio (q v).

Sallustius (Sālustius) -ii, m *a Roman name, the most celebrated bearers of which were* **1**, C Sallustius Crispus, of Amiternum, *the celebrated Latin historian, contemporary and opponent of Cicero*, **2**, Sallustius Crispus, *great nephew of the historian, friend of Augustus, famous for his great riches, the owner of splendid gardens at Rome* Hence, adj, **Sallustiānus (Sālustiānus)** -a -um, *Sallustian*

salmăcidus a -um, *salt* Plin

Salmăcis -idis, f (Σαλμακίς), *a fountain in Caria, fabled to make those who drank of it effeminate* Personif, *the nymph of this fountain*, Ov

salmo -ōnis, m *a salmon*, Plin

Salmōneus -ĕi and ĕos, m (Σαλμωνεύς), *son of Aeolus, brother of Sisyphus, king in Elis, founder of the town Salmone he imitated the thunder and lightning of Zeus, who on that account struck him with a thunderbolt, and hurled* *him down to Tartarus*. Hence, **Salmōnis** -ĭdis, f. (Σαλμωνίς), *the daughter of Salmoneus, i.e., Tyro, mother of Neleus and Pelias by Neptune, who took the form of the Enipeus.*

Sălōna -ae, f. and **Sălōnae** -ārum, f. *a seaport in Dalmatia.*

salpa -ae, f. *a kind of stock-fish*, Ov.

Salpĭa = Salapia (q.v.).

Salpīnātes -um, m. *a people of Etruria, near Volsinii.* Hence, adj., **Salpīnās** -ātis, *belonging to the Salpinates; ager*, Liv.

Salpīni = Salapini, v. Salapia.

salsāmentārĭus -a -um (salsamentum), *of or relating to salt-fish.* Subst., **salsāmentārĭus** -ii, m. *a dealer in salt-fish*, Suet.

salsāmentum -i, n. (* salso -āre), **1**, *fish-pickle, brine*, Cic.; **2**, *salted or pickled fish*, gen. in plur., Ter.

salsē, adv. with compar. and superl. (salsus), *wittily, humorously, facetiously; dicere*, Cic.

salsĭtūdo -ĭnis, f. (salsus), *saltness*, Plin.

salsūgo -ĭnis, f. (salsus), *saltness*, Plin.

salsūra -ae, f. (sal), *a salting, pickling*, Varr.; fig., meae animae salsura evenit, *I am in an ill-humour*, Plaut.

salsus -a -um, p. adj. (from sallo), *salted, salt.* **I. A.** Lit., fluctus salsi, *the sea*, Verg. **B.** Transf., *tasting like salt, sharp, biting;* lacrimae, Lucr.; robigo, *corrosive*, Verg. **II.** Fig., *witty, humorous, facetious, satirical;* inveni ridicula et salsa multa Graecorum, Cic.; male salsus, *with poor wit*, Hor.

saltātĭo -ōnis, f. (salto), *a dancing, pantomimic dance*, Cic.

saltātor -ōris, m. (salto), *a (pantomimic) dancer*, Cic.

saltātōrĭus -a -um (saltator), *of or relating to dancing; orbis*, Cic.

saltātrix -tricis, f. (saltator), *a female dancer, a dancing-girl*, Cic.

saltātus -ūs, m. (salto), *a dancing, dance*, Liv.

saltem, adv. (orig. salutim, from salus, as viritim, from vir), *at least, at all events.* **I.** Affirmative, **a**, with an antithetical sentence, eripe mihi hunc dolorem aut minue saltem, Cic.; **b**, without an antithetical sentence, nunc saltem ad illos calculos revertamur, Cic. **II.** With negatives, non, neque, *not even, nor even*, Liv.

salto, 1. (intens. of salio). **I.** Intransit., *to dance with pantomimic gestures.* **A.** Lit., ad tibicinis modos, Liv.; saltare in convivio, Cic.; discere saltare, *to learn to dance*, Cic. **B.** Transf., of orators, Hegesias saltat incidens particulas (of a jerking, hopping style), Cic. **II.** Transit., *to represent in pantomimic dancing;* Cyclopa, Hor.; carmina, poemata, *sing with gestures*, Ov.

saltŭōsus -a -um (saltus), *wooded, well wooded*, Sall.

1. **saltus** -ūs, m. (salio), *a spring, leap, bound*, Cic.; saltum and saltus dare, Ov.

2. **saltus** -ūs, m. (connected with ἄλσος, ἄλτις). **I.** *a pass through a mountain or forest, a dale, ravine, glade;* Thermopylarum, Liv.; saltus Pyrenaei, Caes. **II.** *a forest or mountain pasture, cattle-run;* saltibus in vacuis pascant, Verg.; sometimes, *an estate including a cattle-run;* de saltu agroque dejicitur, Cic.

sălūbris -e and **sălūber** -bris -bre (salus), *healthy.* **I.** *conducive to health, healthful, healthy, salubrious, wholesome.* **A.** Lit., natura loci, Cic.; annus salubris, Cic.; somnus, Verg. **B.** Transf., *sound, serviceable, useful;* consilia, Cic.; res salubrior, Liv; sententia reipublicae saluberrima, Cic. **II.** *healthy, strong, sound, vigorous.* **A.** Lit., corpora salubriora, Liv. **B.** Transf., *good, fit, suitable;* quidquid est salsum aut salubre in oratione, Cic.

sălūbrĭtas -ātis, f. (saluber). **I.** *wholesomeness, salubrity.* **A.** Lit., loci, Cic.; tum salubritatis tum pestilentiae signa, Cic. **B.** Fig., omnis illa salubritas Atticae dictionis et quasi sanitas, Cic. **II.** *soundness, healthiness, health;* corporum, Tac.

sălūbrĭtĕr, adv. (saluber). **I.** *healthfully, wholesomely;* salubrius refrigerari, Cic. **II.** *serviceably, advantageously;* bellum trahere, Liv.

sălum -i, n. (σάλος). **I.** **a**, *the open sea*, esp., *a place where ships lie anchored, a roadstead;* propter vim tempestatis stare ad ancoram in salo non posse, Liv.; **b**, poet., *the sea generally;* altum, Hor. **II.** *the rolling of a ship at sea, motion of a ship;* salo nauseāque confecti, Caes.

sălus -ūtis, f. (salvus), *health.* **I.** Gen., **1**, medicinā aliquem ad salutem reducere, Cic.; **2**, *welfare, well-being, weal, good fortune;* utilitati salutique servire, Cic.; spes salutis, Cic.; also *the civil well-being of a Roman citizen* (not in exile); restitutio salutis meae, *my recall from exile*, Cic.; hence, **a**, *a term of endearment*, Plaut.; **b**, personif., Salus, *the goddess of the public safety of Rome, whose temple was on the Quirinal*, Liv.; **c**, *deliverance from death, danger*, etc., ad salutem vocare, *to save*, Cic.; salutem afferre reipublicae, *to save*, Cic.; also *a means of deliverance;* nulla salus reipublicae reperiri potest, Cic.; una est salus, *there is one means of deliverance*, foll. by infin., Cic.; **d**, *security, safety;* fortunarum suarum salus in istius damnatione consistit, Cic. **II.** Esp., *a wish for a person's welfare* (spoken or written), *salutation, greeting;* salutem nuntiare, Cic.; ascribere, Cic.; alicui salutem dicere jubere, *to send a greeting to*, Plaut.; and ellipt., Anacharsis Hannoni salutem (sc. dicit), Cic.; fig., salutem dicere foro et curiae, *to bid farewell to, renounce*, Cic.

sălūtāris -e (salus), *healthful, beneficial, salutary, serviceable, wholesome, advantageous.* **I.** Gen., **a**, absol., (α) of things, ut quae mala perniciosaque sunt, habeantur pro bonis ac salutaribus, Cic.; herba salutaris, Ov.; salutares litterae, Cic. Subst., **sălūtārĭa** -ium, n. *remedies, medicines;* pro salutaribus mortifera conscribere, Cic.; (β) of persons, agri ipsi tam beneficum, tam salutarem, tam mansuetum civem desiderant, Cic.; **b**, with dat., and ad and acc., and contra and acc., consilium salutare utrique, Cic. **II.** Esp., **A.** Appell., salutaris littera—i.e., *the letter A*, abbreviation of absolvo (littera tristis, *C* = condemno, Cic). **B.** Adj. proper, **Sălūtāris**, as a surname of Jupiter (Gr. Σωτήρ, as a surname of Zeus).

sălūtārĭtĕr, adv. (salutaris), *beneficially, advantageously;* uti armis, Cic.; se recipere, Cic.

sălūtātĭo -ōnis, f. (saluto). **I.** *greeting, salutation*, Cic. **II.** Esp., *a greeting, salutation, a call, visit of ceremony, waiting upon a person;* dare se salutationi amicorum, Cic.; ubi salutatio defluxit, Cic.

sălūtātor -ōris, m. (saluto), *one who pays complimentary visits, a visitor, caller*, ap. Cic.

sălūtātōrĭus -a -um (salutator), *relating to greeting or visits;* cubicula, *hall of audience*, Plin.

sălūtātrix -trīcis, f. (salutator). **I.** *greeting, saluting*, Mart. **II.** Esp., *paying a visit, calling, waiting upon;* turba, Juv.

sălūtĭfĕr -fĕra -fĕrum (salus and fero), *health-bringing, salubrious;* puer, *Aesculapius*, Ov.; opem salutiferam dare, Ov.

sălūtĭgĕrŭlus -a -um (salus and gero), *carrying complimentary messages*, Plaut

sălūto, 1 (salveo), *to say* salve *to a person*, *to greet*, *salute* **I.** Gen, aliquem, Cic, sternutamentis, *to say "God bless you," when a person sneezes*, Plin; deos, *to pay respect to, to worship*, Cic, with double acc, *to greet as, to name*, aliquem imperatorem, Tac **II.** Esp, **1,** *to call upon, to pay court to, wait upon*, venit salutandi causā, Cic, **2,** *to greet a person*, **a,** *on his arrival*, Cic, **b,** *on his departure*, Plaut.

Sălŭvĭi (Sallŭvĭi) -ōrum and -ûm, m *a Ligurian people in modern Provence*

salvē, v salveo

salvĕo, 2 (salvus), *to be well in health*, found chiefly in the forms salve, salvete, salveto, salvebis, salvere (jubeo), used by the Romans as a greeting, *Good day! I hope you are well? How are you?* **a,** In welcoming a person, *Good day! good morning!* jubeo te salvere, *I greet you*, Cic., Dionysium velim salvere jubeas, *greet Dionysius for me*, Cic., salvebis a meo Cicerone, *my son Cicero sends you greeting*, Cic, so of greetings addressed to a distinguished person, or of respect paid to a deity, *hail!* salve vera Jovis proles, Verg, **b,** in taking farewell, *good-bye! God be with you!* vale, salve, Cic

salvĭa ae, f (salvus), *the herb sage*, Plin

salvus -a -um (root SAL, whence salus, connected with σαοω), *safe, unhurt, uninjured, well, sound* **I.** Gen, **a,** of persons, salvus atque incolumis, Caes, salvus revertor, Cic; se salvo, *while he is alive*, Cic, **b,** of things, clipeus, Cic, with abl absol, *saving, without infraction of*, Cic, salvo jure nostrae veteris amicitiae, Cic, salvo officio, Cic **II.** Esp formulae (of conversation), **a,** of persons, ne salvus sim, si, etc., *may I die if*, etc, Cic, salvus sis = salve! Plaut; **b,** of things, salva res est, *it is all right*, often in questions, satine or satin salvae? *Is all right (with you)?* Liv

Sămărĭa -ae, f (Σαμάρεια), *a district of Palestine* Hence, **Sămărītēs** -ae, m *a Samaritan*

Sămărŏbrīva -ae, f *a town in Gallia Belgica, chief town of the Ambiani*, now *Amiens*

sambūca -ae, f (σαμβυκη), *a species of harp*, Plaut

sambūcĕus -a -um (sambucus), *made of elder-wood*, Plin

sambūcĭna ae, f (sambuca and cano), *a female harp-player*, Plaut.

sambūcistrĭa -ae, f (σαμβυκίστρια), *a woman that plays on the* sambuca, Liv

sambūcus (săbūcus) -i, f *an elder-tree*, Plin

Sămē -ēs, f (Σάμη), *older name of the island Cephallenia*, now *Cefalonia* Another form, **Sămŏs** -i, f Hence, **Sămaei** -ōrum, m *the inhabitants of Same*

samĕra (samăra) -ae, f *the seed of the elm*, Plin

Sămĭŏlus, v Samos

Samnis, Samnites, v Samnium

Sămĭus, v Samos

Samnĭum -ii, n (syncop from Sabinium), *a mountainous region of central Italy between Campania and the Adriatic Sea* Hence, **A.** Adj, **Samnis** -itis, *Samnite*, subst, **a,** *a Samnite*, used collectively, *the Samnites*, Liv, **Samnītes** -ium, m *the Samnites*, **b,** *a gladiator armed with Samnite weapons*, Cic **B.** **Samnītĭcus** -a -um, *Samnite.*

1. **Sămŏs (-us)** -i, f (Σαμος), *an island in the Aegean Sea, off the coast of Asia Minor, opposite Ephesus, the birth place of Pythagoras, chief seat of the worship of Hera, famous for its clay and the vessels made from it*, now *Sussam* or *Sussam-Adassi*, Threicia Samus = *Samothrace*, Verg, Ov Hence, **A. Sămĭus** -a -um, *Samian*, vir, senex, *Pythagoras*, Ov, capedines, *made of Samian earthenware*, Cic, terra, *a part of the main-land of Asia Minor or belonging to Samos*, Liv, subst, **a,** **Sămĭus** -ii, m *the Samian* = *Pythagoras*, Ov, plur, **Sămĭi** -ōrum, m *the inhabitants of Samos, Samians*, Cic, **b,** **Sămĭa** -ōrum, n. (sc. vasa), *Samian ware* **B** **Sămĭŏlus** -a um, adj dim, *Samian*, Plaut.

2 **Sămŏs** = Same (q v)

Sămŏthrācē (Sămŏthrēcē) -ēs, f and **Sămŏthrāca** -ae, f (Σαμοθρακη), and **Sămŏthrācĭa** -ae, f *an island of the Aegean Sea on the coast of Thrace opposite the mouth of the Hebrus, famous for the mystic rites of the Cabiri*, now *Samothraki* Hence, **A. Sămŏthrāces** -um, m **a,** *the inhabitants of the island of Samothrace*, Ov, **b,** *the Cabiri*, Juv **B. Sămŏthrācĭus** -a -um, *Samothracian*

Sampsĭcĕrămus i, m *an Arab prince of Emesa in Libanus, whom Pompejus overcame*, hence, in jest, *a name for Pompejus himself*, Cic

sampsūchĭnus -a um (σαμψύχινος), *made of marjoram*, Plin

sampsūchum -i, n (σάμψυχον), *marjoram*, Plin

sānābĭlis -e (sano), *that can be healed, curable*, **a,** physically, vulnus, Ov., **b,** of the mind, iracundi sanabiles, Cic

sānātĭo -ōnis, f (sano), *a healing, curing*, corporum, Cic, fig, malorum, Cic

sancĭo, sanxi, sanctum, 4 (root SA, whence sacer, sanus, Gr σάος, σῶς, etc), *to make sacred or inviolable by a religious act* **I.** Lit, **a,** *to make irrevocable, to appoint, order* (of a law, league, etc), legem, Cic, foedus sanguine alicuius, Liv; Solon capite sanxit, si qui, etc, *Solon ordered, on pain of death*, Cic., **b,** *to sanction, render valid by law*, acta Caesaris, Cic **II.** Transf, *to forbid on pain of punishment, lay under a penalty*, incestum supplicio, Cic (partic sancitus, Lucr)

sanctē, adv (sanctus), *piously, conscientiously, scrupulously*, pie sancteque colere naturam, Cic, multa sunt severius scripta et sanctius, Cic; se sanctissime gerere, Cic, sanctissime observare promissa, *sacredly*, Cic

sanctĭmōnĭa ae, f (sanctus). **I.** *sanctity, sacredness*, ad deorum religionem et sanctimoniam demigrasse, Cic **II.** *purity, chastity, virtue*, domum habere clausam pudori et sanctimoniae, Cic

sanctĭo -ōnis, f (sancio) **I.** *the article or clause in a law which recites the penalty*, legum sanctionem poenamque recitare, Cic. **II.** In treaties, *a clause, proviso*, foederis, Cic

sanctĭtas -ātis, f (sanctus) **I.** *inviolability, sanctity*, tribunatus, Cic, templi insulaeque, *right of asylum*, Tac **II.** *piety, virtue, chastity*, **a,** matronarum, Cic, **b,** *piety towards the gods*, deos placatos pietas efficiet et sanctitas, Cic

sanctĭtūdo -inis, f = sanctitas (q v)

sanctor -ōris, m (sancio), *an ordainer*, legum, Tac

sanctŭārĭum ii, n (sanctus), *the private cabinet of a prince*, Plin

sanctus a -um, p adj (from sancio) **I.** *sacred, inviolable*, tribuni plebis, Cic, officium, Cic,

II. *venerable, holy, divine* **a**, of deities or distinguished men, stella Mercurii, Cic., sancte deorum, Verg, so, of the senate, sanctissimum orbis terrae consilium, Cic ; vates, *the Sibyl*, Verg, **b**, *pious, virtuous, holy, blameless*, nemo sanctior illo (viro), Cic ; homo sanctissimus, Cic, virgo, *a Vestal virgin*, Hor, conjux, *chaste*, Verg

Sancus -i and -ūs, m, also **Semo, Semo Sancus** or **Fidius Sancus**, *an Umbrian and Sabine deity*, probably=Ζεὺς Πίστιος, *afterwards identified with Hercules*

sandălĭārĭus -a -um (sandalium), *of or relating to sandals*, Apollo, *who had a statue in the Street of the Sandal-makers*, Suet

sandălĭgĕrŭlae -ārum, f (sandalium and gero), *female slaves who carried their mistresses' sandals*, Plaut

sandălis -idis, f *a kind of palm-tree*, Plin

sandălĭum -ii, n. (σανδάλιον), *a slipper, sandal*, Ter

sandăpĭla -ae, f *a kind of bier used by poor persons*, Juv

sandărăca ae, f (σανδαράκη), *sandarach, a kind of red dye*, Plin

sandărăcātus -a um (sandaraca), *mixed with sandarach*, Plin

sandarēsos -i, f *an oriental precious stone, perhaps a kind of cat's eye*, Plin

sandyx -dȳcis, c (σάνδυξ), *vermilion*, or *a similar colour*, Verg

sānē, adv (sanus) **I.** *soberly, rationally, sensibly* non ego sanius bacchabor Edonis, Hor **II.** Transf, **A.** *really, indeed* (used emphatically), sane vellem, *I would indeed wish*, Cic, hence, **a**, in answers, *surely, to be sure*, sane hercle or sane hercule, Cic, **b**, in concessions, *to be sure, certainly*, sint falsa sane, Cic, **c**, with imperatives, *then, if you will*, age sane, Cic **B.** *exceedingly*, bene sane or sane bene, Cic, sane quam, *exceedingly, extremely*, with verbs and adj, Cic.

Sangărĭus, v Sagaris

sanguĭnārĭus -a -um (sanguis), *of or relating to blood*, fig, *bloody, blood-thirsty, sanguinary*, juventus, Cic

sanguĭnĕus a -um (sanguis), *relating to blood* **I. A.** Lit, **1**, *of blood, bloody*, imber, Cic, guttae, Ov, **2**, *stained with blood*, caput, Ov, manus, Ov. **B.** Transf, **1**, *stained with blood shed, bloody*, rixa, Hor, **2**, *blood-red*, sagulum, Cic **II.** Fig, *bloody, blood-thirsty*, Mavors, Verg

sanguĭno, 1 (sanguis), *to be blood thirsty*, Tac

sanguĭnŏlentus (sanguĭnŭlentus) -a -um (sanguis), *bloody* **I.** *stained with blood, bloody*, 1, lit, conjugis imago, Ov., **2**, transf, *wounding, injuring*, nulla exstat littera Nasonis sanguinolenta legi, Ov **II.** *blood-red*, color, Ov.

sanguis (sanguen) -inis, m *blood, blood flowing in the veins of a living being*, while cruor = *blood of the dead* or *blood from wounds* **I. 1**, lit, tauri sanguis, Cic ; sanguinem mittere, *to let blood*, Cic, sanguinem effundere, *to shed one's blood*, Cic, **2**, fig, **a**, *vigour, strength, force* amisimus sucum et sanguinem, Cic, so of orators, verum sanguinem deperdebat, Cic, **b**, *property, money*, de sanguine aerarii detrahere, Cic **II.** Meton, **1**, *shedding of blood, murder*, odio civilis sanguinis, Cic, **2**, *blood relationship race, blood, family*, **a**, abstr, magnam possidet religionem paternus maternusque sanguis, Cic, **b**, concr, *a descendant, progeny*, regius sanguis, *Europa*, Hor, saevire in suum sanguinem, Liv

sānĭes -ēi, f (connected with sanguis) **I.** *diseased blood, bloody matter*, Verg **II.** Transf, *venom, poison, slaver*, perfusus sanie atroque veneno, Verg, sanies manat ore trilingui, Ov

sānĭtas -ātis, f (sanus), *health* **I.** Lit, *physical health*, Cic **II.** Transf, **1**, *a sound state of mind, reasonableness, good sense, sanity*, ad sanitatem se convertere or redire, Cic, **2**, of style, *soundness* or *correctness, purity*, orationis, Cic.

sanna ae, f (σάννας), *a mocking grimace*, Juv

sannĭo -ōnis, m (sanna), *one who makes grimaces, a buffoon*, Cic

sāno, 1 (sanus), *to heal, cure, restore to health* **I.** Lit, tumorem oculorum, Cic. **II.** Transf, physically and morally, *to heal, restore, repair, quiet*, partes aegras reipublicae, Cic, vulnera avaritiae, Liv, mentes eorum, *to change to right views*, Caes

Sanquālis (Sanguālis) -e (Sancus), *belonging to Sancus*, avis, *the bird sacred to Sancus, the osprey*

Santŏnes -um, m and **Santŏni** -ōrum, m *a people in Aquitanian Gaul*, whence *Saintonge* Hence, adj, **Santŏnĭcus** -a -um, *belonging to the Santones*

sānus -a -um, *sound, healthy*. **I.** Lit, pars corporis, Cic, aliquem sanum facere, Cic **II.** Transf, **a**, *sound, uninjured*, respublica, Cic, **b**, of sound mind, *rational, sane*, mens, homo, Cic, **c**, of discourse, *sound, sensible, natural*, genus dicendi, Cic

săpa -ae, f *must* or *new wine boiled to one-third of its bulk*, Ov.

Săpaei -ōrum, m *a Thracian people on the Propontis*, Ov

săperda -ae, m (σαπέρδης), *a small fish caught in the Palus Maeotis, a kind of herring*, Pers

săpĭens -entis, p adj (from sapio), *wise, sensible, prudent, judicious* **I.** Gen., rex aequus ac sapiens, Cic, quis sapientior ad conjecturam rerum futurarum, Cic, Cyrus ille Perses justissimus fuit sapientissimusque rex, Cic., of things, vera et sapiens animi magnitudo, Cic, subst, *a sensible, judicious person*, insani sapiens nomen ferat, Hor, used as a surname of the jurists, L Atilius, M Cato, etc, Cic **II.** Like the Greek σοφός, *wise*, subst, *a wise man, a practical philosopher, a sage*, septem sapientes, *The Seven Wise Men of Greece*, sometimes simply septem, Cic

săpĭenter, adv (sapiens), *wisely, discreetly, judiciously*, facere, Cic

săpĭentia -ae, f (sapiens) **I.** *good sense, discernment, prudence*; pro vestra sapientia, Cic **II.** (like σοφία,) *wisdom, esp, practical wisdom, knowledge of the world, knowledge of the art of government*, Cic, with genit, constituendae civitatis, Cic, plur, virtutes ebullire et sapientias, *rules of wisdom*, Cic

săpĭo -ii 3 **I.** *to taste, have a flavour* or *taste*, **a**, lit, Plin ; **b**, *to smell of something*, crocum, Cic **II.** *to taste, to have taste*; **a**, lit, ut, cui cor sapiat, ei non sapiat palatus, Cic, **b**, fig, *to discern, perceive, to be sensible, discreet, wise*, sapere eum plus quam ceteros, Cic, with acc, *to understand*, recta, Cic

sāpo -ōnis, m (a Celtic word), *soap used by the Gauls as a pomade for the hair*, Plin

săpor -ōris, m (sapio), *taste* **A.** *the taste of a thing*, **1**, **a**, lit, qui non sapore capiatur, Cic, **b**, fig, *elegance in discourse*, vernaculus, Cic, **2**, meton, *a delicacy, a titbit*, gallae admiscere saporem, Verg, **2**, transf, *scent*, Plin., meton., sapores, *pleasant odours*, Verg. **B.** *the taste which a person has*, 1, lit., Lucr.; 2, fig., *good taste in behaviour or discourse*, homo sine sapore, *without taste*, Cic.

Sapphĭcus a -um, v. Sappho.

sapphīrus (sappīrus) i, f. (σάπφειρος), *the sapphire*, Plin.

Sapphō ûs, f. (Σαπφώ), *a lyrical poetess of Mytilene in Lesbos, who threw herself into the sea on account of her unrequited love for Phaon*. Hence, adj., **Sapphĭcus** -a -um, *Sapphic*.

sappīrus = sapphirus (q. v.).

saprus -a -um (σαπρός), *putrid*, *rotten*, Plin.

sarcĭna -ae, f. (sarcio), *a bundle, pack, package, portable luggage of a person*. **I. A.** Lit., a, sing., Plaut.; b, plur., sarcinas conferre, Cic.; legionem sub sarcinis adoriri, Caes. **B.** Fig., *burden, load*, publica rerum, *burden of government*, Ov. **II.** Transf., *the fruit of the womb*, Ov.

sarcĭnārĭus a -um (sarcina), *pertaining to burdens or baggage*; jumenta, *pack-horses, beasts of burden*, Caes.

sarcĭnātor -ōris, m. (sarcio), *a patcher, mender, cobbler*, Plaut.

sarcĭnātus -a -um (sarcina), *loaded, burdened*, Plaut.

sarcĭnŭla -ae, f. (dim. of sarcina), *a little bundle or package*, gen. plur., Cat., Juv.

sarcĭo, sarsi, sartum, 4. *to mend, patch, repair*. **I.** Lit., tunicam, Juv. **II.** Fig., *to make good, repair*; damna, Cic.; detrimentum, Caes.; injuriam, Caes.; gratia male sarta, *not completely restored*, Hor. Partic., **sartus** a -um, with special phrase sartus et tectus or sartus tectus, *in good condition*; a, lit., of buildings, *in good repair, in good condition, well repaired or built*; aedem Castoris sartam tectam tradere, Cic.; omnia sarta tecta exigere, Cic.; b, fig., *in a good condition, well preserved, safe*; M. Curium sartum et tectum, ut aiunt, ab omni incommodo conserves, Cic.

sarcion ii, m. (σαρκίον), *a flaw in an emerald*, Plin.

sarcŏcolla -ae, f. (σαρκοκόλλα), *a kind of Persian gum*, Plin.

sarcŏphăgus -a -um (σαρκοφάγος), lit., *flesh-eating*; lapis, *a kind of stone used for coffins, which was believed to consume the body*; hence, subst., **sarcŏphăgus** -i, m. *a coffin, sarcophagus*, Juv.

sarcŭlātĭo -ōnis, f. (sarculum), *a hoeing*, Plin.

sarcŭlum -i, n. (sarrio), *a light hoe*, Hor.

sarda -ae, f. **I.** *a small fish which was pickled, perhaps a sardine*, Plin. **II.** *a precious stone, perhaps cornelian*, Plin.

Sardănăpālus (Sardănăpallus) -i, m. (Σαρδανάπαλος, Σαρδανάπαλλος), *the last king of the Assyrians, who, on a revolt against him, burnt himself with his seraglio and all his treasures*.

1. **Sardi**, v. Sardis.

2. **Sardi** -ōrum, m. (Σαρδώ = Sardinia), *the inhabitants of the island of Sardinia, the Sardinians, notorious for their perfidy*, Cic. Hence, **A. Sardus** a -um, *Sardinian*. **B. Sardŏnius** a -um, *Sardinian*; herba, v. Sardous. **C. Sardōus** (Σαρδῷος), *Sardinian*; herba, *a kind of poisonous crow's-foot*. **D. Sardĭnĭa** -ae, f. *the island of Sardinia*, Cic.; hence, **Sardiniensis** -e, *Sardinian*.

Sardīs ium, acc. is, f. (Σάρδεις), *Sardis, the old capital of Lydia on the Pactolus, residence of King Croesus, now Sart*. Hence, **A. Sardi** -ōrum, m. *the Sardians, Lydians*. **B. Sardiānus** a -um, *Sardian*; plur., **Sardiāni** -ōrum, m. *the Sardians*.

sardŏnyx -nўchis, (σαρδόνυξ), *a precious stone, the sardonyx*, Juv.

Sardōus, v. Sardi.

Sardus -a -um, v. 2. Sardi.

sargus i, m. *a salt-water fish much esteemed by the Romans*, Ov.

sărĭo = sarrio (q. v.).

sărīsa (sărissa) -ae, f. (σάρισσα), *the long Macedonian pike*, Liv.

sărīsŏphŏrus (sarissŏphŏrus) i, m. (σαρισσοφόρος), *a Macedonian pikeman*, Liv.

Sarmăta -ae, m. (Σαρμάτης), *a Sarmatian*; plur., Sarmatae, *the Sarmatians, a nation in modern Poland, Little Tartary and adjoining countries*. Hence, **A. Sarmătĭa** -ae, f. (Σαρματία), *Sarmatia, the country of the Sarmatae*. **B. Sarmătĭcus** a -um (Σαρματικός) *Sarmatic*; mare, *the Black Sea*, Ov.; adv., **Sarmătĭcē**, *after the Sarmatian manner*; loqui, Ov. **C. Sarmătĭs** -ĭdis, f. *Sarmatian*; tellus, Ov.

sarmen -ĭnis, n. = sarmentum (q. v.).

sarmentōsus -a -um (sarmentum), *full of twigs or small branches*, Plin.

sarmentum i, n. *twigs, loppings, small branches, brushwood*; a, green, of the vine, Cic.; b, dry = *brushwood, loppings, faggots*; fasces sarmentorum, *fascines*, Liv.; ligna et sarmenta circumdare, Cic.

Sarnus -i, m. *a river in Campania, on which was Pompeii, now Sarno*.

Sarpēdōn -ŏnis, m. (Σαρπηδών). **I.** *son of Jupiter, king in Lycia, who came to the help of the Trojans, and was slain by Patroclus*. **II.** *a promontory in Cilicia, now Lissan el Kahpe*.

Sarra -ae, f. *the Hebrew Zor, old name of the city of Tyre*; hence, adj., **Sarrānus** -a -um, *Tyrian, Phoenician*; ostrum, Verg.

sarrăcum -i, n. = serracum (q. v.).

Sarrānus a -um, v. Sarra.

Sarrastes -um, m. *a people in Campania, living on the Sarnus*.

sarrĭo (sărĭo) -ii and -ivi -itum, 4. *to hoe, and thence, to weed*, Plin.

sarrītor -ōris, m. (sarrio), *one who hoes up weeds, a hoer, weeder*, Varr.; syncop., sartor, fig., Plaut.

sartāgo ĭnis, f. *a frying pan*, Juv.; sartago loquendi, *medley, hotch potch*, Pers.

sartor = sarritor (q. v.).

sartus a -um, partic. of sarcio (q. v.).

săt = satis, *enough, sufficient*. **I.** Adj., *enough, sufficient*; tantum, quantum sat est, Cic.; foll. by genit., nec sat rationis in armis, Verg.; by infin., nonne id sat erat, accipere ab illo injuriam, Tac. **II.** Adv., a, with verbs, bibere, Verg.; b, with adj., bonus, Cic.; c, with another adv., sat diu, Cic.

sătăgĭto, 1. *to have enough to do, have one's hands full*, Plaut.

sătăgo, 3. **I.** *to satisfy or pay a creditor*, Plaut. **II.** *to be very busy, have enough to do, have one's hands full, be in trouble*, Petr.

sătellĕs ĭtis, c. **I.** *a guard, attendant*, and plur., *guards, escort, suite, train*, Cic. **II.** Transf., 1, *a companion, attendant*; Aurorae, *Lucifer*, Cic.; Orci *Charon*, Hor.; 2, esp., in a bad sense, *lackey, aider, accomplice, abettor*; audaciae, Cic.; scelerum, Cic.

sătĭas -ātis, f. (satis) = satietas. **I.** *a sufficiency, abundance*; cibi, Lucr. **II.** *satiety, satie-*

fied desire, loathing; quo de die epulatis jam vini satias esset, Liv.

Sătĭcŭla -ae, f. *a town of Samnium, near modern Caserta Vecchia.* Hence, **A. Sătĭcŭlānus** -a -um, *relating to Saticula.* **B. Sătĭcŭlus** -i, m. *an inhabitant of Saticula.*

sătĭĕtas -ātis, f. (satis). **I.** *a sufficiency, abundance,* Plaut. **II.** *satiety, loathing;* cibi, Cic.; fig., satietas provinciae, Cic.; studiorum omnium satietas vitae facit satietatem, Cic.

sătĭnĕ, *satin'* = satisne, v. satis.

1. **sătĭo,** 1. (satis), *to satisfy, satiate.* **I. 1,** lit., with food and drink, Ov.; **2,** transf., **a,** of natural desires, *to satisfy, appease;* desideria naturae, Cic.; sitim, Plaut.; **b,** of other things, ignes odoribus, Ov. **II.** Fig., **1,** *to satisfy, sate;* aviditatem legendi, Cic.; **2,** *to overfill, to cloy, to disgust, satiate;* numerus agnoscitur, deinde satiat, Cic.

2. **sătĭo** -ōnis, f. (sero). **I.** *a sowing;* plur., sationes, concr., *the sown fields,* Cic. **II.** *planting,* Verg., Liv.

sătĭra (sătŭra) -ae, f. (satur), *satirical poetry, satire,* Hor.

sătĭs, compar., **sătĭus,** *enough, sufficient.* **I.** In posit., **A.** Gen., **1,** adj., satis est alicui aliquid, Cic.; satis est foll. by si, Cic.; satis superque habere, *enough and more than enough,* Cic.; foll. by genit., ea amicitia non satis habet firmitatis, Cic.; ad dicendum temporis satis habere, Cic.; (non) satis est, foll. by infin., Cic.; satis habeo, with infin., Sall.; with quod, Liv.; **2,** adv. (often satine or satin'=satisne); **a,** with verbs, consequi, Cic.; satin' est id ad, etc., Cic.; **b,** with adj., satis multa restant, Cic.; **c,** with adv., honeste, Cic.; absol., de hoc satis, *enough of this,* Cic. **B.** Particular phrases; **a,** satis ago, *to have enough to do;* impers., agitur tamen satis, Cic. (cf. satagito and satago); **b,** legal t. t., satis accipere, *to take bail, security,* Cic. **II.** Compar., satius, *better, more advantageous;* satius est, or satius (esse) existimo, or satius puto; with infin., mori satius esse, Cic.

sătisdătĭo -ōnis, f. (satisdo), *a giving bail or security,* Cic.

sătisdo -dĕdi -dătum -dăre, 1. *to give bail or security;* with genit., damni infecti, Cic.; hence, satisdato, *by bail, by security;* debere, Cic.

sătisfăcĭo -fēci -factum, 3. *to satisfy, give satisfaction.* **I.** Gen., officio suo, Cic.; vitae satisfeci, *I have lived long enough,* Cic.; alicui aliquid petenti, Cic.; histriones satisfaciebant, Cic. **II.** Esp., **A.** *to satisfy, pay a creditor;* ipse Fufiis satisfacit, Cic. **B. a,** *to give satisfaction, make amends, make reparation;* alicui, Caes., Cic.; omnibus rationibus de injuriis, Caes.; **b,** *to prove sufficiently;* alicui with acc. and infin., Cic.

sătisfactĭo -ōnis, f. (satisfacio). **I.** *satisfaction, amends, reparation, excuse, apology;* satisfactionem alicuius accipere, Cic., Caes. **II.** *satisfaction by punishment,* Tac.; Caesar Ubiorum satisfactionem accepit, Cic.

sătĭus, comp. of satis (q.v.).

sătīvus -a -um (sero, sevi), *sown or planted,* Plin.

sător -ōris, m. (sero, sevi). **I.** *a sower, planter;* omnium rerum seminator et sator est mundus, Cic. **II.** Transf., *begetter, father, producer, causer;* sator hominum atque deorum, i.e., *Jupiter,* Verg.; so also litis, Liv.

sătrăpes -ae and -is, m., **sătrăpa** -ae, m., and **sătraps** -ăpis, m. (σατράπης, a Persian word), *the governor of a Persian province, satrap,* Nep.

sătrăpīa (sătrăpēa) -ae, f. (σατραπεία), *a province governed by a satrap, satrapy,* Plin.

Satrĭcum -i, n. *a Latin town on the Appian Road,* now *Casale di Conca.* Hence, **Satrĭcāni** -ōrum, m. *the inhabitants of Satricum.*

sătur -tŭra -tŭrum (satis), *full, sated, satiated.* **I. A.** Lit., pullus, Cic. **B.** Transf., **1,** *satisfied;* expleti atque saturi, Cic.; **2,** *rich, fertile;* Tarentum, Verg.; **3,** of colours, *deeply dyed, full, dark;* color, Verg. **II.** Fig., *rich, copious;* nec satura jejune (dicet), Cic.

sătŭra -ae, f. (sc. lanx), *a dish of various fruits annually offered to the gods;* hence, transf., *a mixture, medley;* per saturam, *indiscriminately, confusedly, pell-mell;* quasi per saturam sententias exquirere, Sall. Hence, satira (q.v.).

Sătŭrae palus, *a lake in Latium.*

sătŭrēja -ae, f. *the herb savory,* Plin.; heteroclite plur., **sătŭrēja** -ōrum, n. Ov.

Sătŭrējānus -a -um, *belonging to a district of Apulia,* hence, poet. = *Apulian,* Hor.

sătŭrĭtas -ātis, f. (satur). **I.** *satiety, repletion,* Plaut. **II.** Transf., *abundance;* saturitas copiaque rerum omnium, Cic.

Sāturnālĭa, etc., v. Saturnus.

Sāturnīnus -i, m., L. Apulejus, *tribune of the people, killed in a riot,* 100 B.C.

Sāturnus -i, m. (sero, sevi), *an old Latin god, honoured as the god of planting* (a satu or satione frugum); in later times identified with the Κρόνος of the Greeks; Saturni sacra dies, *Saturday,* Tib.; Saturni stella, Cic., or simply Saturnus, Hor., *the planet Saturn.* Hence, adj., **A. Sāturnĭus** -a -um, *Saturnian;* stella, *the planet Saturn,* Cic.; tellus, or arva, *Italy* (because Saturn was said to have reigned there), Verg.; gens, *the Italians,* Ov.; numerus, *the old Italian poetry,* Hor.; proles, *Picus, son of Saturn,* Ov.; domitor maris, *Neptune,* Verg.; virgo, *Vesta, daughter of Saturn,* Ov.; Saturnius pater, *Jupiter,* Verg.; and subst., **1, Sāturnĭus** -ii, m., (α) *Jupiter,* Ov.; (β) *Pluto;* **2, Sāturnĭa** -ae, f., (α) *Juno,* Verg.; (β), *an old mythical town on the Capitoline Hill,* Verg. **B. Sāturnālis** -e, *belonging to Saturn;* gen. subst. plur., **Sāturnālĭa** -ium, n. *the festival beginning with the 17th of December, at which there were public spectacles and banquets, presents were exchanged, slaves were waited upon by their masters:* the festival lasted several days, the first of which was called Saturnalia prima, the next Saturnalia secunda, and the third, Saturnalia tertia, Cic. Hence, adj., **Sāturnālĭcius** -a -um, *of or relating to the Saturnalia,* Mart.

sătŭro, 1. (satur), *to satisfy, satiate.* **I. A.** Lit., animalia ubertate mammarum, Cic. **B.** Transf., *to satisfy = to fill;* sola fimo, *to manure,* Verg. **II.** Fig., *to satiate, glut, appease, satisfy;* crudelitatem suam odiumque, Cic.; homines saturati honoribus, Cic.

1. **sătus** -a -um, partic. of 2. sero (q.v.).

2. **sătus** -ūs, m. (2. sero). **I.** *a sowing, setting, planting,* Cic.; fig., *seed;* haec preparat animos ad satus accipiendos, Cic. **II.** Transf., *begetting, origin, stock, race;* Hercules Jovis satu editus, Cic.; a primo satu, Cic.

Sătўrĭcus -a -um, v. Satyrus.

sătўrĭon -ii, n. (σατύριον), *the plant ragwort,* Plin.

Sătўriscus -i, m. (σατυρίσκος), *a little Satyr,* Cic.

Sătўrus -i, m. (Σάτυρος). **I.** *a Satyr, a companion of Bacchus, represented with long pointed ears, behind which were the stumps of horns, with the tail of a goat, bristly hair, and a* *flat nose*, in later times identified with the fauns of the Roman mythology, deities of the woods with horns and the feet of goats; Satyrus Phryx, *Marsyas*, Ov **II.** Transf, *Greek Satyric drama*, in which Satyrs formed the chorus; Satyrorum scriptor, Hor

sauciātio ōnis, f (saucio), *a wounding*, Cic

saucio 1 (saucius), *to wound, hurt* **I.** Lit, **a,** aliquem telis, Cic, **b,** *to let blood*, euphem, *to wound mortally*, Cic **II.** Transf, *to tear up the ground with the plough*, duram humum, Ov

saucius -a -um, *wounded, injured, hurt* **I.** Lit, graviter saucius, Cic, paucis saucius, Caes, plur subst, **saucii** -ōrum, m *the wounded*, Cic **II.** Transf, **a,** of inanimate objects, *injured*, malus saucius Africo, Hor., glacies saucia sole, Ov, **b,** *attacked by illness*, Prop, **c,** *drunken*, Mart, **d,** of accused persons, *half condemned*, de repetundis saucius, ap Cic, **e,** *wounded, injured in mind*, (α) *troubled, distressed*, animus eius Cic, (β) esp, *wounded by love*, regina saucia curā, Verg

saurion i, n (σαυριον), *mustard*, Plin

Sauroctŏnos -i, m (σαυροκτόνος), *the lizard-killer* (the name of a statue of Apollo by Praxiteles), Plin

Saurŏmătēs -ae, m (Σαυρομάτης), *a Sarmatian*, plur, **Saurŏmătae** ārum, *the Sarmatians*, Ov

sāvĭŏlum i, n (dim of savium), *a little kiss*, Cat

sāvĭor, 1 dep (savium), *to kiss*, aliquem, Cic

sāvĭum -ii, n **I.** *the mouth formed for kissing*, Plaut **II.** Meton, *a kiss*, Atticae meis verbis savium des volo, Cic

saxātĭlis e (saxum), *frequenting rocks, to be found among rocks*, Plin

saxētum -i, n (saxum) *a rocky place*, Cic

saxĕus a um (saxum), *made of rock or stone, rocky, stony*, scopulum, Ov, umbra, *cast by a rock*, Verg, Niobe saxea facta, *turned to stone*, Ov

saxĭfĭcus a -um (saxum and facio), *turning into stone, petrifying*, Medusa Ov

saxĭfrăgus -a -um (saxum and frango), *stone breaking, stone-crushing*, Plin

saxōsus -a -um (saxum) **I.** *full of rocks, rocky*, valles, Verg Subst, **saxōsa** -ōrum, n *rocky places*, Plin **II.** Transf *stony, flowing between rocks*, saxosus sonans Hypanis, Verg

saxŭlum i, n (dim of saxum), *a little rock*, Cic

saxum i, n *a rock or large stone, a detached fragment of rock* (rupes, *a cliff, precipitous rock*) **I.** Lit, **A** *a rock*, **1,** gen, saxo undique absciso rupes, Liv; saxa latentia, *reefs*, Verg, **2,** esp, **a,** Saxum sacrum, *the holy rock, the place on the Aventine where Remus took the auspices*, Cic, **b,** *the Tarpeian rock*, Cic, **c,** Saxa rubra, v ruber **B.** *a stone*, **a,** *a (large) stone*, saxa iacere, Cic, **b,** *a stone for building*, saxum quadratum, Liv, or for statues, non e saxo sculptus, Cic **II** Meton, **a,** *a stone wall*, saxo lucum circumdedit alto, Ov, **b,** *a stone building*, perrumpere amat saxa, Hor

scăbellum -i, n (dim of scamnum) **I** *a small stool, footstool*, Varr **II.** *a musical instrument played with the foot, used to accompany dancing*, Cic

scăber -bra brum (scabo), *rough, scurvy* **I.** Gen, unguis, Ov., robigo, Verg, of persons, *rough, untidy*, Hor. **II.** Esp, *scabby, mangy*; oves, Plaut.

scăbĭes ēi, f (scabo), *roughness* **I.** ferri Verg **II.** *the scab, mange, the itch* **A.** Lit Verg **B.** Fig, *an itch, itching desire for anything*, Cic, lucri, Hor

scăbĭōsus -a -um (scabies) **I.** *rough*, Plin **II.** *scabby, mangy*, Pers

scăbo, scābi, 3 (root SCAB, Gk ΣΚΑΠ-τω), *to scratch, rub*, caput, Hor

scăbrĭtĭa ae, f and **scăbrĭtĭes** -ēi, f (scaber), *roughness*, Plin

Scaea porta -ae, f and **Scaeae portae** (Σκαιαὶ πύλαι), *the west gate of Troy*

scaena (scēna) ae f (σκηνη), *the boards of the theatre, the stage, the scene, the theatre* **I.** **A.** Lit, de scaena decedere, *to go off the stage*, Cic, sphaeram in scenam afferre, Cic, Agamemnonius scaenis agitatus Orestes, *on the stage*, i e, *in the tragedies*, Verg **B.** Transf, of nature, *a background*, tum silvis scaena coruscis, Verg **II.** Fig, **A.** *the stage, the boards of any public action*, **a,** of the forum, etc, *publicity, the world* in scaena, id est, in contione, Cic., minus in scena esse, *to be less before the eyes of the world*, Cic, scaenae servire, Cic, **b,** of schools of rhetoric, Tac, **c,** gen, *scene, sphere*, scaena manet dotes grandis tuis, Ov **B.** *anything presented for outward display*, **a,** *parade, outward show*, (verba) ad scaenam pompamque sumuntur, Cic, **b,** *deception, fraud*, scena rei totius haec, ap Cic

scaenālis e (scena), *belonging to the theatre, theatrical*, Lucr (?)

scaenĭcus -a -um (σκηνικος), *belonging to the boards, scenic, theatrical* **A.** Adj, ludi, Liv, voluptas, Cic **B.** Subst, **scaenĭcus** -i, m *a stage-hero, an actor*, Cic

Scaevola ae, m (dim of scaevus, *the left-handed*), *a surname of the gens* Mucia, v Mucius

scaeva -ae, f (scaevus), *an omen, portent*, Plaut

scaevus a -um (σκαιός). **I.** *left, on the left hand*, Varr **II.** *awkward*, Sall

scālae -ārum, f (from scando, as ala from ago), *a flight of stairs, staircase, ladder*, se in scalas tabernae librariae conjicere, Cic, scalas admovere (muris or moenibus), *scaling ladders*, Caes, Liv, muros scalis aggredi, Sall

Scaldis -is, m *a river in Gallia Belgica, now the Scheldt*

scalmus -i, m (σκαλμος), *a thole or thole-pin, on which an oar works, a row lock*, navicula duorum scalmorum, *two oared*, Cic, scalmum nullum videt, *no trace of boats*, Cic

scalpellum -i, n (dim of scalprum), and **scalpellus** -i, m. *a small surgical knife, lancet, scalpel*, Cic

scalpo, scalpsi, scalptum, 3 (root SCALP, Gk ΓΛΑΦ-ω), *to scrape, scratch, tear* **I.** Gen, **a,** lit, terram unguibus, Hor, **b,** fig, *to tickle*, Pers **II.** Esp t t of art, *to scratch with a sharp tool, to engrave on wood, gems*, etc, apta manus est ad fingendum, ad scalpendum, Cic

scalprum i, n (scalpo), *a sharp, cutting instrument*, **a,** *a cobbler's awl*, Hor, **b,** *a chisel*, Liv, **c,** *a pen-knife*, Tac

scalptor ōris, m (scalpo), *a cutter, engraver*, Plin

scalptūra ae, f (scalpo) **I.** *a cutting, engraving*, gemmarum, Plin **II.** Meton, *a figure engraved, an engraving*, Suet

Scămander -dri, m (Σκαμανδρος), *a river in Troas, rising on Mount Ida and joining the Simois, called Xanthus, on account of its red colour*

scambus -a -um (σκαμβός), *crooked-legged*, Suet.

scammōnĭa (scămōnĭa) and **scammōnĕa** -ae, f. (σκαμμωνία, σκαμωνία), *scammony*, Cic.

scammōnītes -ae, m. *scammony-wine*, Plin.

scamnum -i, n. (root SCAP (cf. scabellum and scapus), Gr. ΣΚΗΠ, whence σκήπτω, σκῆπτρον, Doric, σκᾶπτρον), *a prop, bench, stool, step, footstool*; scamnum facere, Hor.; cava sub tenerum scamna dare pedem, Ov.; ante focos scamnis considere longis, Ov.

scandix -icis, f. (σκάνδιξ), *chervil*, Plin.

scando, scandi, scansum, 3. **I.** Intransit., *to climb*; **a**, lit., in aggerem, Liv.; in domos superas, Ov.; **b**, transf., *to raise oneself, to rise*; supra principem, Tac. **II.** Transit., *to ascend, to climb up*; malos, Cic.; muros, Liv.; Capitolium, Hor.; fig., scandit aeratas vitiosa naves cura, Hor.

scansĭlis -e (scando), *that can be climbed*; ficus, Plin.

scansĭo -ōnis, f. (scando), *a climbing up, ascending*, Varr.

Scantĭus -a -um, *name of a Roman gens*, Cic.; adj., Scantia silva, *a wood in Campania*, Cic.

scăpha -ae, f. (σκάφη), *a small boat, skiff*, Cic.

scăphĭum -ii, n. (σκαφίον), *a bowl in the shape of a boat*; esp., *a drinking-vessel*, Cic.

Scaptensŭla -ae, f. (Σκαπτὴ ὕλη), *a small town in Thrace near Abdera, famous for its gold and silver mines, and as the place of exile of Thucydides.*

Scaptĭa -ae, f. *a town in Latium*; hence, adj., **Scaptĭus** -a -um, *Scaptian*; tribus, Liv.

Scăpŭla -ae, m. *a surname of the Cornelian gens*; adj., **Scăpŭlānus** -a -um, *belonging to Scapula*; horti, Cic.

scăpŭlae -ārum, f. *the shoulder-blades, the shoulders, the back*, Plaut.

scāpus -i, m. (v. scamnum), *anything that supports*, e.g., **I.** *the stalk of plants*, Plin. **II.** *a weaver's beam*, Lucr. **III.** *the shaft* or *stem of a candelabrum*, Plin.

scărăbaeus -i, m. (*σκαράβαιος, from σκάραβος = κάραβος), *a beetle*, Plin.

scărīfātĭo (scărīfĭcātĭo) -ōnis, f. (scarifo), *a scratching up, scarifying*, Plin.

scărīfo (scărīfĭco), 1. (σκαριφάομαι), *to scratch up with any sharp-pointed instrument, scarify*, Plin.

scărus -i, m. (σκάρος), *a salt-water fish, much liked by the Romans, the parrot-fish*, Hor.

scătĕbra -ae, f. (scateo), *a spouting up, bubbling up of water*, Verg.

scătĕo, 2. and (archaic) **scăto**, 3. *to gush forth, spout out, bubble out.* **I.** Lit., Lucr. **II.** Meton., *to swarm, abound*; with abl., arx scatens fontibus, Liv.; with genit., terra ferarum scatet, Lucr.

scătūrīgo (scăturrīgo) -gĭnis, f. (scaturio), *a spring of bubbling water*; plur., scaturigines turbidae, Liv.

scătūrĭo (scăturrĭo), 4. (scateo), *to gush forth*; meton., Curio totus hoc scaturit, *is full of* (love for this party), ap. Cic.

scăturrex = scaturigo (q.v.).

scaurus -a -um (connected with σκάζειν). **I.** *having projecting* or *swollen ankles*, Hor. **II.** Scaurus, *a Roman surname of the gens Aemilia and Aurelia, the most famous bearer of the name being* M. Aemilius Scaurus, *whom Cicero defended.*

scazon -ontis, m. (σκάζων, *limping*), *an iambic trimeter with a spondee* or *trochee in the last foot*, Plin.

scĕlĕrātē, adv. (sceleratus), *impiously, wickedly*; facere, Cic.; dicere in aliquem, Cic.; domus sceleratius aedificata quam eversa, Cic.; sceleratissime machinari omnes insidias, Cic.

scĕlĕrātus -a -um, p. adj. (from scelero). **I.** *polluted, profaned by guilt*; terra, Verg.; limina Thracum, Ov.; esp., sceleratus vicus, *the accursed street, the highest point of the vicus Cyprius on the Esquiline, where Tullia, the daughter of Servius Tullius, drove over the corpse of her father*; sceleratus campus, *the accursed field, on the porta Collina, where unchaste Vestal virgins were buried alive*, Liv.; scelerata sedes, *the lower world*, Ov. **II.** Transf., **A.** *impious, wicked, profane, infamous, accursed*; hasta sceleratior, Cic.; homo sceleratissimus, Cic.; subst., **scĕlĕrāti** -ōrum, m. *villains, miscreants*, Cic.; poet., sceleratas sumere poenas, *for impiety, wickedness*, Verg. **B.** *wretched, unlucky, calamitous, noxious*; frigus, Verg.

scĕlĕro, 1. (scelus), *to pollute, profane with guilt*; manus, Verg.

scĕlĕrōsus -a -um (scelus), *full of guilt, wicked, impious, accursed*; facta, Lucr.

scĕlestē, adv. (scelestus), *wickedly, impiously*; facere, Liv.; suspicari, Cic.

scĕlestus -a -um (scelus). **I.** *wicked, accursed, infamous*; **a**, facinus, Cic.; sermo scelestior, Liv.; scelestissimum te arbitror, Plaut.; **b**, *knavish, roguish*, Plaut. **II.** Transf., *unlucky, wretched, pernicious*, Plaut.

scĕlus -ĕris, n. *wickedness*. **I.** Lit., subject., *impiety, wickedness*, Cic. **II.** Meton., object., **A.** *a crime, evil deed, impious action, heinous offence*; **1**, lit., scelus facere, admittere, committere, edere, concipere, in sese concipere or suscipere, Cic.; minister sceleris, Liv.; scelus est (civem Romanum) verberare, Cic.; **2**, transf., *misfortune, calamity*, Plaut. **B.** *a villain, scoundrel, rascal*; ne bestiis, quae tantum scelus attigissent, immanioribus uteremur, Cic.; scelus viri, *a rogue of a man*, Plaut.; so scelus artificis, Verg.

scēna = scaena (q.v.).

scēnālis = scaenalis (q.v.).

scēnĭcus = scaenicus (q.v.).

Scepsis -is, f. (Σκῆψις), *a town in Mysia*, now *Eskiupschi* or *Eski-Schupsche*. Hence, **Scepsĭus** -a -um, *of Scepsis*; Metrodorus, Cic.

sceptrĭfĕr -fĕra -fĕrum (sceptrum and fero), *sceptre-bearing*, Ov.

sceptrĭgĕr = sceptrifer (q.v.).

sceptrum -i, n. (σκῆπτρον), *a sceptre, royal wand* or *staff*. **I.** Lit., Cic.; so jestingly, paedagogorum, Mart. **II.** Transf., *dominion, kingdom, royal authority*; sceptra petit Evandri, Verg.

sceptūchus -i, m. (σκηπτοῦχος), *the wand-bearer, a high official in Eastern courts*, Tac.

schĕda (schĭda) and **scĭda** -ae, f. (σχίδη). **I.** *a strip of papyrus bark*, Plin. **II.** Transf., *a leaf of paper*; ut scida ne qua deperëat, Cic.

schēma -ae, f. and **schēma** -ătis, n. (σχῆμα), *shape, figure, form, fashion*, Quint.

schĭda = scheda (q.v.).

schistos -a -on (σχιστός), *cleft, cloven, split*, Plin.

Schoenēus -ĕi and -ĕos, m. (Σχοινεύς), *a king of Boeotia, father of Atalanta*; hence, **A.** Adj., **Schoenēĭus** -a -um, *belonging to Schoeneus*;

Schoeneia virgo or simply Schoeneis, *Atalanta*, Ov **B. Schoenēis** -ĭdis, f. *Atalanta*, Ov

schoenŏbătes ae, m (σχοινοβάτης), *a rope-walker, rope-dancer*, Juv

schoenus -i, m (σχοῖνος) **I.** *an aromatic reed used by the Romans to flavour wine, and as an ingredient in an unguent*, Cato **II.** Meton, **A.** *an ointment*, Plaut **B.** *a Persian measure of distance* (between 30 and 60 stadia), Plin

schŏla (scŏla) -ae, f (σχολή), *leisure, rest from work*, hence, **I.** *learned leisure, learned conversation, debate, dispute, lecture, dissertation*, certae scholae sunt de exsilio, de interitu patriae, etc, Cic, scholas Graecorum more habere, Cic, vertes te ad alteram scholam, *matter*, Cic **II.** Meton, **1,** **a,** *a place where learned disputations are carried on, a school*, Cic, **b,** transf, (α) *a gallery of works of art, used for such disputations and conferences*, Plin, (β) *a waiting room, room in a bath*, Vitr; **2,** *the disciples of a philosopher, a school, sect*, clamabant omnes philosophorum scholae, Cic

schŏlastĭcus a um (σχολαστικός), *of or relating to a school*, esp, *to a school of rhetoric or to rhetoric, rhetorical* **I.** Adj, controversia, Quint **II.** Subst, **A. schŏlastĭca** -ōrum, n *rhetorical exercises*, Quint **B. schŏlastĭcus** i, m **1,** *a student of rhetoric*, Quint., **2,** *a teacher of rhetoric, a professor*, Suet

scĭădeūs -ĕi, m and **sciaena** -ae, f (σκιαδεύς, σκίαινα), *the male and female of a salt-water fish*, perhaps Salmo Thymallus, Linn, Plin.

Scĭăthus (-ŏs) i, f (Σκίαθος), *an island in the Aegean Sea, north of Euboea*

scĭda = schida (q v)

scĭens -entis (scio) **I.** Partic, *knowing something*, Ter **II.** Adj, with compar and superl, **A.** = *purposely, knowingly*, ut offenderet sciens neminem, Cic **B.** *acquainted with a matter, knowing, understanding, versed in, acquainted with*, with genit, belli, Sall, citharae, Hor, scientissimus reipublicae gerendae, Cic, with infin, flectere equum sciens, Hor; absol, quis hoc homine scientior, Cic, scientissimus gubernator, Cic

scĭentĕr, adv (sciens), *skilfully, expertly*, dicere, Cic

scĭentĭa ae, f (sciens), *a knowing, knowledge of, acquaintance with* **I.** Gen, regionum, Cic, futurorum malorum Cic memoriā et scientiā comprehendisse, Cic **II** Esp, *theoretical, philosophical knowledge, theory science*, an, quum eā non utare, scientiā tamen ipsā teneri potest, Cic, scientia dialecticorum, juris, Cic, rei militaris, Cic, plur, tot artes, tantae scientiae, Cic

scĭlĭcĕt, adv (contr from scire licet) **I.** *actually, just think!* (to call attention to something strange), rogat et prece cogit, scilicet ut tibi se laudare et tradere cogar, etc, Hor, ter sunt conati Olympum scilicet atque Ossae frondosum involvere Olympum, Verg **II.** *of course, naturally, evidently* **A.** Gen, **a,** with acc and infin, Lucr, **b,** as a simple particle, cur igitur eos manumisit? metuebat scilicet, Cic **B.** Esp, **a,** *naturally, of course, undoubtedly*, with an adversative sent (gen with tamen, sed tamen, or sed), nihil scilicet novi, ea tamen, quae te ipsum probaturum confidam, Cic, **b,** ironically, *of course, to be sure, forsooth*, id populus curat scilicet, *much the people trouble themselves about that!* Ter, ego istius pecudis consilio scilicet aut praesidio uti volebam, Cic, **c,** *doubtless alas!* unda scilicet omnibus enaviganda, Hor, **III.** *to wit, namely*, Suet.

scilla (squilla) ae, f (σκίλλα), **1,** *a sea-leek, squill*, Plin, **2,** *a small sea crab*, Cic

scillīnus -a -um (scilla), *made of squills*, Plin

scillītes ae, m (σκιλλίτης), *flavoured with or made of squills*, Plin

scillītĭcus = scillinus (q v)

scin' = scisne (q v)

scincos i, m. (σκίγκος), *an Egyptian species of lizard* Plin

scindo, scĭdi, scissum, 3 (connected with σχίζω), *to tear, rend, tear asunder, break, split* **I** Lit, crines, Verg; mater scissa comam, *with torn hair*, Verg, epistolam, Cic vestem de corpore, Prop, lignum cuneis, *split, cleave*, Verg, prov, paenulam alicui, *to tear* (off a person's travelling cloak), i e, *to urge a person to stay*, Cic **II.** Transf, **1,** *to part, divide, separate*, genus amborum scindit se sanguine ab uno, Verg, pass, scindi, as middle, *to separate, part*, in contraria studia scinditur vulgus, Verg, **2,** esp, **a,** *to break off, interrupt*, verba fletu, Ov, **b,** *to destroy*, Plaut; **c,** (= rescindo) *to renew*, ne scindam ipse dolorem meum (from the metaphor of tearing open a wound), Cic

scintilla -ae, f *a spark* **I** Lit, Liv, silici scintillam excudere, Verg **II.** Fig, *a spark, glimmer, faint trace*, belli, Cic, ingenii, Cic

scintillātĭo ōnis, f (scintillo), *a sparkling*, Plin

scintillo, 1 (scintilla), *to sparkle, glitter*, scintillat oleum testā ardente, Verg

scintillŭla ae, f (dim of scintilla), *a little spark*, fig, virtutum quasi scintillulae, Cic

scĭo īvi and -ĭi -ītum, 4 *to know, to have knowledge of, to experience* **I** Gen (opp opinari, arbitrari), (α) with acc, istarum rerum nihil Cic, quod sciam, *as far as I know*, Cic, (β) with infin, scio tibi ita placere, Cic, scimus Atilium appellatum esse sapientem, Cic (γ) with dep rel or interrog sent, cum sciatis, quo quaeque res inclinet, Cic, (δ) absol, statim fac ut sciam, Cic, with de and the abl, cum is, qui de omnibus scierit, de Sulla se scire negavit, Cic **II.** Esp, **a,** *to know, have learned, be acquainted with*, (α) with acc, literas, Cic., (β) with infin, qui tractare et uti sciat, Cic, (γ) absol, scire Graece, Latine, *to understand Greek, Latin*, **b,** *to perceive, to mark*, Plaut (syncop perf, scisti, Ov; infin, scisse, Cic)

scĭŏthērĭcŏn i, n (σκιοθηρικόν), *a sun dial*, Plin

Scīpĭădas and **Scīpĭădes**, v 2 Scipio

1 **scīpĭo** ōnis, m (σκίπων, σκήπων), *a staff, wand*, Plaut, eburneus, carried by viri triumphales, Liv

2 **Scīpĭo** -ōnis, m (Σκιπίων, Σκηπίων), *a family name of the gens Cornelia*, v Cornelius Hence, **Scīpĭădas (-ēs)** ae, m (Σκιπιάδης), *one of the family of the Scipios, a Scipio*

Scīron -ōnis, m (Σκίρων, Σκείρων) **I.** *a noted robber on the coast between Megaris and Attica, killed by Theseus* **II.** (Sciron, Scyron, Siron, Syron), *an Epicurean philosopher, contemporary with Cicero and Vergil*

scirpĕus (sirpĕus) -a -um (scirpus), *made of rushes* **I.** Adj, imago or simulacrum (v Argei), Ov **II.** Subst, scirpea or sirpea (sirpia) -ae, f *basket work made of rushes* (to form the body of a waggon), Ov

scirpĭcŭlus (sirpĭcŭlus) -a um (scirpus), *made of rushes* Subst, **scirpĭcŭlus** -i, m *a rush-basket*, Prop

scirpus (sirpus) -i, m *a rush, bulrush*, Plin, prov, nodum in scirpo quaerere, *to find a difficulty where there is none*, Plin.

scirros -i, m. (σκιῤῥος), *a hard swelling*, Plin.

sciscitator -ōris, m. (sciscitor), *an inquirer, examiner*, Mart.

sciscĭtor, 1. dep. *to investigate, inquire into, examine into, ask, interrogate*; (α) with acc. of thing, consulis voluntatem, Liv.; (β) with acc. and ex and the abl., ex eo eius sententiam, Cic.; (γ) with de and the abl., sciscitari de victoria, Cic.; (δ) with acc. of person, *to consult*; deos, Liv.; (ε) with dep. interrog. sent., sciscitari, uter Porsena esset, Liv.; (ζ) absol., elicuit comiter sciscitando ut, etc., Liv.

scisco, scīvi, scītum, 3. (scio). **I.** *to seek to find out, investigate, inquire*, Plaut. **II.** Polit. t.t., *to approve of by voting, to vote, assent to*; **a,** of the people, *to ordain, resolve*; quae scisceret plebes, Cic.; with ut and the subj., Athenienses sciverunt ut, etc., Cic.; of an individual, *to vote for*; legem, Cic.

scissūra -ae, f. (scindo), *a splitting, cleaving, rending, separating, parting*, Plin.

scissus -a -um, p. adj. (from scindo), *torn, rent*; transf., genus vocum, *harsh, grating*, Cic.

scītāmenta -ōrum, n. (1. scitus), *dainties, titbits*, Plaut.

scītē, adv. (1. scitus), *cleverly, skilfully, tastefully, nicely, elegantly*; scite loqui, Liv.; capella scite facta, Cic.

scītor, 1. (scio), *to wish to know, inquire, ask*; aliquid, Verg.; aliquem de aliqua re, Ov.; oracula, *to consult*, Verg.; with dep. interrog., quid veniat, scitatur, Ov.

scītŭlus -a -um (dim. of scitus), *neat, pretty, elegant*; facies, Plaut.

scītum -i, n. (scisco). **I.** *a decree, statute, ordinance*; plebis scitum, populi scitum, Cic.; plebei and plebi scitum, Liv.; scita pontificis, Liv.; Ctesiphon scitum fecit ut, etc., Cic. **II.** *a philosophical tenet or maxim* (δόγμα), Sen.

1. **scītus** -a -um, p. adj. (from scisco). **I.** *clever, wise, shrewd, skilful, adroit*; sermo, Cic.; with genit., scitus vadorum, *acquainted with*, Ov.; lyrae, Ov.; hence, scitum est, *it is a clever saying*, Cic.; vetus illud Catonis admodum scitum est, Cic. **II.** Transf., *pretty, fine*, Plaut.

2. **scītus** -ū, m. (scisco), *a statute, decree*; plebi scitu, Cic.

sciūrus -i, m. (σκίουρος), *a squirrel*, Plin.

scĭus -a -um (scio), *knowing*, Petr.

scŏbīna -ae, f. (scobis), *a rasp, file*, Plin.

scŏbis -is, f. (scabo), *that which is scratched or scraped off, filings, cuttings, chips, shavings, sawdust*, Hor.

Scodra -ae, f. *a town in Macedonian Illyria, now Scodar or Scutari*. Hence, **Scodrenses** -ium, m. *the inhabitants of Scodra*.

Scodrus -i, m. mons, *the easterly continuation of the Dalmatian and Illyrian mountains, now Argentaro*.

scŏla, etc. = schola, etc. (q.v.).

scŏlŏpendra -ae, f. (σκολόπενδρα), *a kind of multipede, scolopendra*, Plin.

scŏlȳmus -i, m. (σκόλυμος), *a species of artichoke*, Plin.

scomber -bri, m. (σκόμβρος), *a sea-fish, a mackerel*, Plin.

scōpa -ae, f. **I.** *a thin twig, a sprig*, gen. in plur., Plin. **II.** Meton., plur., **scōpae** -ārum, f. *a besom or broom, made of a number of twigs or branches*; scopae viles, Hor.; hence, prov., scopas dissolvere, *to untie a broom*, i.e., *throw anything into confusion*, Cic.; scopae solutae = *a muddled, foolish man*, Cic.

Scŏpās -ae, m. (Σκόπας), *a famous sculptor of Paros*.

scōpes -um, f. (σκῶπες), *a kind of owl*, Plin.

scōpĭo -ōnis, f. *the stalk of a bunch of grapes*, Plin.

scŏpŭlōsus -a -um (scopulus), *rocky, full of cliffs, craggy*. **I.** Lit., mare, Cic. **II.** Fig., intelligo quam scopuloso difficilique in loco verser, Cic.

scŏpŭlus -i, m. (σκόπελος). **I.** *a rock, crag, cliff*; esp., *a rock in the sea*; ad scopulos allidi, Caes.; affligi, Cic.; poet., of a promontory, infames scopuli, Acroceraunia, Hor.; in comparisons, o scopulis undāque ferocior, Ov. **II.** Fig., **A.** Gen., ad scopulum ire, *to be ruined*, Lucr. **B.** Esp., *a rock, cliff* (as symbolical of danger, difficulty, peril); in hos scopulos incidere vitae, Cic.; of persons, vos geminae voragines scopulique reipublicae (of Piso and Gabinius), Cic.

scŏpus -i, m. (σκοπός), *a mark set up to shoot at*, Suet.

scordĭon -ii, n. (σκόρδιον), *a plant having an odour of garlic* (Teucrion scordium, Linn.), Plin.

Scordus -i, m. (τὸ Σκάρδον ὄρος), *a mountain in Illyria barbara or Romana, on the borders of Moesia and Macedonia*.

scōrĭa -ae, f. (σκωρία), *dross or slag* (of metals), Plin.

scorpaena -ae, f. (σκόρπαινα), *a sea-scorpion*, Plin.

scorpĭo -ōnis, m. and **scorpĭus** (-ŏs) -i, m. (σκορπίων). **I.** *a scorpion*, Ov. **II.** Transf., **a,** *the Scorpion, as one of the signs of the Zodiac*, **b,** *a military engine for throwing missiles*, Caes.; **c,** *a prickly salt-water fish* (Cottus scorpio, Linn.), Plaut.; **d,** *a prickly plant* (Spartium scorpius, Linn.), Plin.

scorpĭōnĭus -a -um (scorpio), *of or relating to a scorpion*, Plin.

scorpĭūron -i, n. (σκορπίουρον), *a plant, scorpion's tail, heliotrope*, Plin.

scortātor -ōris, m. (scortor), *a fornicator*, Hor.

scortĕus -a -um (scortum), *of or relating to hides, leathern, made of leather*, Mart.; subst., **scortĕa** -ae, f. *a leathern garment*, Mart.

scortillum -i, m. (dim. of scortum), *a little harlot*, Cat.

scortor, 1. dep. (scortum), *to whore*, Plaut.

scortum -i, n. **I.** *a skin, hide*, Varr. **II.** *a prostitute*, Cic.

scrĕātor -ōris, m. (screo), *one who hawks or hems*, Plaut.

scrĕātus -ūs, m. (screo), *a hawking, hemming*, Terr.

scrĕo, 1. *to hawk, hem*, Plaut.

scrība -ae, m. (scribo), *a clerk or secretary*; **a,** in a public capacity, *a clerk in the service of the senate or the higher magistrates*; scriba aedilicius, Cic.; **b,** of private persons, *private secretary*; scriba meus, Cic.

scriblīta -ae, f. *a kind of tart*, Plaut.

scrībo, scripsi, scriptum, 3. (root SCRIB, SCRIP, connected with ΓΡΑΦ-ω, as sculpo with γλύφω), *to engrave with a sharp-pointed pencil, draw lines*. **I. 1,** gen., lineam, Cic.; **2,** *to draw, sketch, make an outline of*; scribetur tibi forma et situs agri, Hor. **II.** *to write*. **A.** Gen., literam, Cic.; meā manu scriptae literae, Cic. **B.** Esp., **1,** *to write a letter to*; alicui, Cic.; ad aliquem, Cic.; ad aliquem de aliquo (*to recommend a person in writing to some one else*) accuratissime, Cic.; pass., with acc. and infin., scribitur nobis multitudinem convenisse, Cic, 2, *to beg, entreat, command by letter*, with ut or ne and the subj, velim domum ad te scribas ut mihi tui libri pateant, Cic, Scipioni scribendum, ne bellum remitteret, Liv, with subj alone, scribit Labieno, veniat, Caes, 3, *to write, put down in writing, compose, prepare*, libros, Cic, leges, Cic, senatus consultum, Cic., absol, (α) like the English, *to write*, i e, *to compose a literary work*, se ad scribendi studium contulit, Cic, (β) *to treat of in writing*, hac super re scribam ad te, Cic, (γ) *to compose a legal instrument, to draw up, write drafts*, haec urbana militia respondendi, scribendi, cavendi, Cic, 4, with double acc, *to appoint in writing*, aliquem heredem, Cic, 5, commercial t t, *to give an order for the payment of money*, scribe decem a Nerio, *let the debtor pay 10,000 sesterces through* (the money-changer) *Nerius*, Hor, 6, *to write about, describe, celebrate in writing*, Marium, Cic, scriberis Vario fortis, Hor, 7, polit t t, *to enrol soldiers, colonists, etc*, supplementum legionibus, Cic, quinque milia colonorum Capuam, Liv., transf, scribe tui gregis hunc, *enrol him as one of your friends*, Hor

scrīnium -ii, n *a cylindrical case, casket, or box for books, papers, unguents, etc*, Sall, Hor

Scrībōnius -a -um, *name of a Roman gens*

scriptio ōnis, f (scribo) **I.** *writing, the art of writing*, Cic **II.** Esp, *writing, written composition*, nulla res tantum ad dicendum proficit, quantum scriptio, Cic

scriptĭto, 1 (intens of scribo) **I.** *to write frequently*, et haec et si quid aliud ad me scribas velim vel potius scriptites, Cic **II** *to write, compose*, orationes multas, Cic

scriptor -ōris, m (scribo) **I.** *a writer, clerk, secretary*, Cic **II.** *a writer, author, composer, narrator*, 1, a, with genit, rerum suarum domestici scriptores et nuntii, Cic, scriptor rerum, *a historian*, Liv, b, absol, *an author, writer*, of orators, subtilis scriptor (Lysias), Cic, of historians, Sall, of poets, Hor, 2, polit t t, *a composer, one who draws up*, legis, Cic

scriptŭla -ōrum, n (dim of scriptum), *the lines on a draught-board*, Ov.

scriptum -i, n (scribo) **I.** *a line drawn on a draught board*, ludere duodecim scriptis, *to play at draughts*, Cic **II.** *anything written, a writing*, 1, gen, Latina scripta, Cic, mandare scriptis, Cic, 2, esp, a, *a written decree, a law*, Cic, b, *the text or letter of a work*, quum videtur scriptoris voluntas cum scripto ipso dissentire, Cic

scriptūra -ae, f (scribo), *a writing* **I.** Gen., Plin **II.** Esp., *a composing in writing, written composition* **A.** Lit, scriptura assidua ac diligens Cic, scriptura aliquid persequi, Cic **B.** Meton, 1, *the writing* or *work itself*, Tac, 2, *testamentary disposition*, deinde ex superiore et ex inferiore scriptura docendum id, quod quaeratur, Cic, 3, *a tax or rent paid for the public pastures*, vectigal ex scriptura, Cic, magistri scripturae, Cic

scrīpŭlum (scrūpŭlum) -i, n (another form of scrupulus), *a scruple, the smallest part of a weight* or *mass* **I.** Lit, $\frac{1}{24}$ *part of an uncia*, argenti scripulum, Cic **II.** Transf, *the smallest portion of a degree* (in astronomy), *a minute*, Plin

scrŏbĭcŭlus i, m (dim of scrobis), *a little ditch*, Plin

scrŏbis -is, c *a ditch*, Verg, *a grave*, Tac

scrōfa ae, f (γρομφάς), *a breeding sow*, Varr

scrōfĭpascus -i, m (scrofa and pasco), *a keeper of pigs*, Plaut

scrupĕda and **scrūpĭpĕda** ae, f *hobbling, limping*, Plaut

scrūpĕus a um (scrupus), *consisting of sharp stones, rugged, rough*, spelunca, Verg

scrūpōsus a -um (scrupus), *rough, rugged*, Lucr

scrūpŭlōsē, adv (scrupulosus), *accurately, exactly, scrupulously*, Quint

scrūpŭlōsus -a um (scrupulus) **I.** Lit, *full of sharp stones, rough, rugged*, cotes, Cic. **II.** Fig, *exact, accurate, scrupulous, precise*, Plin

scrūpŭlum = scripulum (q v)

scrūpŭlus -i, m (dim of scrupus), lit, *a small stone*, fig, *uneasiness, care, disquiet, anxiety, doubt, scruple*, scrupulum alicui injicere, Cic, scrupulus tenuissimus residet, Cic, scrupulum ex animo evellere, Cic

scrūpus i, m **I.** *a sharp stone*, Petr **II.** Fig, *anxiety, disquiet, care*, Cic

scrūta ōrum, n (γρυτη), *frippery, trash, trumpery*, Hor

scrūtātio -ōnis, m (scrutor), *a searching, investigating*, Quint

scrūtātor -ōris, m (scrutor), *one who searches, investigates, examines*, Suet

scrūtor, 1 dep (scruta) **I.** *to search into, search through, investigate accurately, examine, inspect* **A.** Lit, domos, naves, Cic, Alpes, Cic, abdita loca Sall **B** Fig, *to examine thoroughly, to seek for*, locos ex quibus argumenta eruamus, Cic **II.** *to search into, find out*, arcanum, Hor; mentes deûm, Ov

sculpo, sculpsi, sculptum, 3 (root SCULP, Gr ΓΛΥΦ, γλυφω), *to carve, hew, grave, cut, chisel*, ebur, *a statue of ivory*, Ov

sculpōnĕae ārum, f *wooden shoes*, Plaut

sculptĭlis e (sculpo), *carved, hewn, cut*, opus dentis Numidae, *work in ivory*, Ov

sculptūra ae, f (sculpo), *raised work in wood, ivory, marble, gems, sculpture*, Quint

scurra ae, m **I.** *a dandy, beau, man about town, a fine gentleman*, scurrae locupletes, Cic **II.** *a jester, buffoon, a parasite who earned his dinner at the tables of the great by witty conversation* Zeno Socratem scurram Atticum fuisse dicebat, Cic, scurra vagus, non qui certum praesepe teneret, Hor

scurrīlis -e (scurra), *like a buffoon, mocking, jeering*, jocus, Cic.; dicacitas, Cic

scurrīlĭtas -ātis, f (scurrilis), *buffoonery*, Tac.

scurrīlĭtĕr, adv. (scurrilis), *like a buffoon*, Plin

scurror, 1 dep (scurra), *to play the buffoon*; scurrantis speciem praebere, Hor

scūtāle -is, n (scutum), *the thong of a sling*, Liv

scūtārĭus -ii, m (scutum), *a shield-maker*, Plaut

scūtātus -a -um (scutum), *armed with a shield*, cohortes, Caes.

scŭtella -ae, f (dim of scutra), *a little flat dish or salver*, dulciculae potionis, Cic

scŭtĭca (scўtĭca) -ae, f (σκυτική, from σκῦτος, *leather*), *a whip, lash*, Hor

scūtĭgĕrŭlus -i, m (scutum and gero), *a shield bearer, armour-bearer*, Plaut

scŭtra -ae, f *a tray, dish, salver*, Plaut.

scŭtŭla -ae, f (σκυταλη) **I.** *a roller for moving heavy weights*, Caes **II.** *a small tray or dish*, Mart **III.** *a diamond or lozenge shaped figure*, Tac

scŭtŭlātus -a -um (scutula), *lozenge or diamond-shaped fabrics woven in checks*, Juv. Plur. subst., **scŭtŭlāta** -ōrum, n. (sc. vestimenta), *clothes made of such fabrics*, Juv.

scūtŭlum -i, n. (dim. of scutum), *a little shield*, Cic.

scūtum -i, n. (σκῦτος, *leather*), *a large quadrangular shield, made of wood covered with hides* (clipeus, *a smaller oval shield of metal*); pedestre (of a foot-soldier), Liv.; scutum abjicere, Cic.; scuto vobis magis quam gladio opus est, Liv.

Scȳlăcēum -i, n. *a town in Lower Italy*, now *Squillace*; navifragum, Verg.; hence, **Scȳlăcēus** -a -um, *relating to Scylaceum*; litora, Ov.

Scylla -ae, f. (Σκύλλα). **I.** *a lofty rock at the entrance to the straits between Sicily and Italy, opposite to the whirlpool Charybdis, dangerous for sailors*; personif., *daughter of Phorcus, changed by Circe into a monster, with dogs about the lower part of her body*. **II.** *daughter of Nisus, king in Megara, who cut off her father's hair, on which his happiness depended, and was turned into the bird Ciris*. Hence, **Scyllaeus** -a -um (Σκυλλαῖος), *belonging to Scylla* **I.** Subst., Scyllaeum = Scylla I., *a rock*; transf., Scyllaeum illud aeris alieni, Cic.

scymnus -i, m. (σκύμνος), *a young animal, whelp*; leonum, Lucr.

scȳphus -i, m. (σκύφος), *a drinking-cup, goblet*; inter scyphos, *over our wine, in our cups*, Cic.; vadit in eundem carcerem atque in eundem paucis post annis scyphum (*cup of poison*) Socrates, Cic.

Scȳrĭăs, v. Scyros.

Scȳrōn = II. Sciron (q.v.).

Scȳrus (-ŏs) -i, f. (Σκῦρος), *an island in the Aegean Sea, near Euboea*, now *Sciro*, *where Achilles concealed himself in woman's clothes, the residence of Lycomedes, whose daughter Deidamia was the mother of Pyrrhus by Achilles*. Hence, **A. Scȳrĭăs** -ădis, f. *of Scyrus*; puella, *Deidamia*, Ov. **B. Scȳrĭus** -a -um, *of Scyrus*; pubes, Verg.; membra (of Pyrrhus), Ov.

scȳtăla -ae, f. and **scȳtălē** -ēs, f. (σκυτάλη), *a roller*; hence, *the roller used by the Spartans*, around which they bound strips, and thus wrote their despatches, so that the despatches which were unwound could only be read by being rolled round a similar stick; hence, meton., *a secret despatch*, Nep.

Scȳthēs (Scȳtha) -ae, m. (Σκύθης), *a Scythian*. Plur., Scythae, *the Scythians, a name of various meaning, sometimes including all the nomadic tribes to the north of the Black and the Caspian Seas*. Hence, **A. Scȳthĭa** -ae, f. (Σκυθία), *Scythia*. **B. Scȳthĭcus** -a -um (Σκυθικός), *Scythian*; amnis, *the Tanais*, Hor. **C. Scȳthĭs** -ĭdis, f. *a Scythian woman*. **D. Scȳthissa** -ae, f. *a Scythian woman*.

1. **sē (sēd)**, prep. = *without*. **I.** With abl., se fraude esto, ap. Cic. **II.** Prep. insepar., **a**, = *without*, as securus (= sine cura); **b**, = *apart*, e.g., sepono.

2. **sē** = semi, *half*, as semodius.

3. **sē** = sex, *six*, as semestris.

4. **sē**, acc. and abl. of sui (q.v.).

Sēbēthos (Sēbētos) -i, m. *a river in Campania, near Neapolis*. Hence, **Sēbēthĭs (Sēbētis)** -ĭdis, f. *of Sebethos*; nympha, Verg.

sēbōsus -a -um (sebum), *full of tallow, tallowy*, Plin.

sēbum (sēvum) and **saevum** -i, n. *tallow, suet, fat, grease*, Caes.

sĕcāle -is, n. *a species of grain, perhaps rye*, Plin.

sĕcāmenta -ōrum, n. (seco), *carved work*, Plin.

sēcēdo -cessi -cessum, 3. *to go apart, go away, withdraw*. **I.** Gen., **a**, of persons, secedant improbi, Cic.; **b**, of things, *to be distant*; tantum secessit ab imis terra, Cic. **II.** Esp., **a**, *to withdraw, retire, go aside*; in abditam partem aedium, Sall.; ad deliberandum, Liv.; **b**, *to withdraw, secede*; plebs a patribus secessit, Sall.; in sacrum montem, Liv.

sēcerno -crēvi -crētum, 3. *to separate, sever, part, sunder, set apart*. **I.** Lit., nihil praedae in publicum, Liv.; with ab and the abl., se a bonis, Cic.; inermes ab armatis, Liv.; with ex and the abl., aliquem e grege imperatorem velut inaestimabilem, Liv. **II.** Fig., **A.** Gen., animum a corpore, Cic. **B.** Esp., **1**, *to distinguish*; blandum amicum a vero, Cic.; poet., with abl. alone, honestum turpi, Hor.; **2**, *to set aside, to reject*; frugalissimum quemque, Cic.; contraria non fugere, sed quasi secernere, Cic.

sĕcespĭta -ae, f. (seco), *a sacrificial knife*, Suet.

sēcessĭo -ōnis, f. (secedo). **I.** *a going on one side*; secessione factā, Liv.; esp. for a conference or parley, secessiones subscriptorum, Cic.; milites vesperi secessionem faciunt, *collect together*, Caes. **II.** *a political withdrawal, secession*; populi, Caes.; in Aventinum montem, Liv. Plur., secessiones plebei, Cic.

sēcessus -ūs, m. (secedo). **I.** *a going away*; avium, *migration*, Plin. **II.** *retirement, retreat*, Ov.; hence, meton., (α) *a place of retirement, a retreat*, esp., *a summer place of residence*, Verg.; (β) *a recess*; longus, *a bay running far into the land*, Verg.

sēclūdo -clūsi -clūsum, 3. (cludo, i.e., claudo), *to shut off*. **I.** *to shut away, shut up apart*; antro seclusa, Verg.; transf., inclusum supplicium atque a conspectu parentium ac liberûm seclusum, Cic. **II.** *to sever, separate, sunder*, Cic.; munitione flumen a monte, Caes.; transf., curas, *to banish*, Verg.

sēcius, v. secus.

sēclūsus -a -um, partic. of secludo.

sĕco, sĕcŭi, sectum, but sĕcātūrus, 1. (root SEC, connected with German sägen, English *to saw*), *to cut, cut off, cut in pieces*. **I.** Lit., **A.** Gen., pabula, Caes.; unguis sectus, Hor. **B.** Esp., **1**, medical t. t., *to cut off, amputate, to cut surgically*; varices Mario, Cic.; **2**, *to cut, geld, castrate*, Mart. **II.** Transf., **1**, *to tear, wound, scratch, injure, hurt*; secuerunt corpora vepres, Verg.; si quem podagra secat, *torments*, Cat.; **2**, *to cut through, run through, sail through, traverse*; avis secat aethera pennis, Verg.; aequor puppe, Ov. **III.** Fig., **1**, *to lash in words, satirise*; urbem, Pers.; **2**, *to divide*; causas in plura genera, Cic.; hence, **a**, *to settle, decide*; lites, Hor.; **b**, *to pursue, follow up*; spem secare, Verg.

sēcrētō, adv. (secretus), *separately*; consilia secreto ab aliis coquebant, Liv.; eadem secreto ab aliis quaerit, Caes.; secreto hoc audi, tecum habeto, Cic.

sēcrētus -a -um, p. adj. (from secerno), *separate, apart*. **I.** Adj., **A.** Lit., **1**, gen., arva, Verg.; imperium, Liv.; **2**, esp., *separate, solitary*; colles, Tac.; secreta petere loca, Hor. **B.** Fig., **a**, *deprived of*; with abl., secreta cibo natura, Lucr.; with genit., corpora secreta teporis, Lucr.; **b**, *secret*; artes, Ov.; nec quicquam secretum alter ab altero habent, Liv. **II.** Subst., **sēcrētum** -i, n. **1**, *retirement, solitude, a solitary place*; secreta Sibyllae, Verg.; abducere aliquem in secretum, Liv , in secreto, Liv , 2, *a secret, mystery*, omnium secreta rimari, Tac , in secretis eius, *in his private papers*, Suet

secta -ae, f (sequor), *a mode of life, procedure, conduct, plan* **I.** Gen , nos qui hanc sectam rationemque vitae secuti sumus, Cic **II.** Esp , 1, *political method, party*, sequi eius auctoritatem cuius sectam atque imperium secutus est, Cic ; 2, *a philosophical school, sect*, philosophorum sectam secutus es, Cic

sectārius a um (seco), *cut, gelded*, Plaut

sectātor -ōris, m (sector), *a follower, hanger on*, plur , *a suite of attendants, train, retinue* **A.** Gen., lex Fabia quae est de numero sectatorum, *dependents, clients*, Cic **B.** *a member of a sect or school*, Tac

sectīlis -e (seco). **I.** *cut, cloven* ebur, Ov , pavimenta, *made up of small pieces, mosaic*, Suet **II.** *that can be cut or cloven*, Mart

sectĭo -ōnis, f (seco) **I.** *a cutting, cutting up*, Plin **II.** *the buying up of confiscated property, both of the goods of proscribed persons and of booty taken in war, and of inheritances which lapsed to the state*, ad illud sectionis scelus accedere, Cic , exercendis apud aerarium sectionibus famosus, Cic , concr = *property of this kind put up to auction*, cuius praedae sectio non venierit, Cic , sectionem eius oppidi universam Caesar vendidit, Caes

sectīvus -a -um (seco), *that can be cut or chopped up*, Plin

1 **sector** -ōris, m (seco), 1, *a cutter*, collorum, *a cut throat*, Cic , 2, *a buyer of confiscated or other public property*, bonorum, Cic , Pompeji, *of the property of Pompey*, Cic

2 **sector**, 1 dep (intens of sequor), *to follow eagerly, continually* **I.** Lit , 1, in a friendly way, *to accompany constantly, run after*, **a**, aliquem totos dies, Cic , **b**, as a servant, *to be in the train of*, ii servi ubi sunt? Chrysogonum sectantur, Cic , 2, in a hostile manner, *to run after in order to ridicule, to harass*, **a**, ut pueri eum sectentur, Cic , **b**, *to follow animals in the chase, to hunt, pursue*, leporem, Hor , apros, Verg **II** Transf , 1, *to strive after, pursue eagerly*, praedam, Caes virtutes, Tac., 2, *to try to find out*, mitte sectari quo, etc , Hor

sectrix -trīcis, f (sector), *she that purchases the confiscated property of the proscribed*, Plin

sectūra -ae, f. (seco) **I.** *a cutting*, Plin **II.** Meton , *a place where something is cut or dug out* aerariae secturae, *copper-mines*, Caes

sĕcŭbĭtus -ūs, m (secumbo), *a sleeping alone*, Ov

sĕcŭbo -ŭi, 1 *to sleep alone, sleep by one's self* **I.** Lit., Ov , Liv **II.** *to live a solitary life*, Prop

sēcŭlāris = saecularis (q v)

sēcŭlum = saeculum (q v)

sēcum = cum se, v sui and cum

sĕcundāni -ōrum, m (secundus), *soldiers of the second legion*, Liv

sĕcundārius -a -um (secundus), *belonging to the second rank or class, of second-rate quality*, panis, Suet , of abstr , status de tribus secundarius, Cic , subst , **sĕcundārium** -ii, n *secondary matter of discussion*, Cic

1 **sĕcundō**, adv (secundus) **I** *in the second place*, Cic **II.** *for the second time*, Lucr

2 **sĕcundo**, 1 (secundus), *to make favourable, to favour, bless, assist, second*, di incepta secundent, Verg , secundante vento, Tac

sĕcundum, adv and prep (secundus) **I.** Adv , 1, *afterwards behind*, ite hac secundum, Plaut , 2, *secondly, in the next place*, Cic **II.** Prep with acc , *after* **A.** In space, 1, *close behind*, aram, Plaut , 2, *along, close along, by, near to*, secundum mare, Cic **B.** In time and order of events, 1, lit , a, of time, *after*, secundum comitia, Cic , secundum haec, *after this*, Liv , secundum quietem, *in a dream*, Cic ; b, of order, *after, next to*, secundum te, nihil mihi amicius est solitudine, Cic , heres secundum filiam, *next after the daughter*, Cic , 2, transf , a, *according to, in accordance with*, secundum naturam vivere, Cic , b, legal t t , *in favour of, to the advantage of*, decernere secundum aliquem, Cic.

sĕcundus -a -um (sequor), *following* **I.** Gen , 1, of time, lumine secundo, *on the following day*, Enn , mensa, *the dessert*, Cic , 2, *in succession, following the first, second*, **a**, lit , id secundum erat de tribus, Cic , heres, *a person to inherit in case the first heir dies*, Cic ; partes secundae, *the second rôle*, Cic , hence, subst , (α) **sĕcundae** -ārum, f *the second rôle*, agere, Sen , fuit M Crassi quasi secundarum, *was second fiddle to Crassus, followed after him*, Cic (β) **sĕcunda** -ae, f (sc hora), *the second hour* ad secundam, Hor , **b**, fig , (α) *second in rank, next, following*, secundus ad principatum, Cic , (β) *second in value, second rate, inferior*, panis, Hor , nulli Campanorum secundus, Liv **II.** Esp , *following easily or willingly* **A.** Lit , 1, of persons, dum ridetur fictus Balatrone secundo, Hor , 2, of wind or tide, *following* (i e , *favourable*), **a**, of water, secundo flumine, *with the stream*, Caes , **b**, of wind, navem secundis ventis cursum tenentem, Cic , vento secundissimo, Cic , **c**, of sails filled with a favourable wind, secunda vela dato, Ov ; 3, of things, currusque (dat) volans dat lora secundo, Verg **B** Fig , **a**, *favourable, favouring* voluntas contionis, Cic , secundo populo, *with the goodwill of the people*, Cic., secundo Marte, *with success in battle*, Verg ; leges secundissimae plebi, Liv , **b**, *fortunate, successful*, secundissimum proelium, Caes , res secundae, *prosperity*, Cic , subst , **sĕcundum** -i, n *prosperity*, Nep , plur , secunda, Hor.

sēcūrē, adv. (securus) **I.** *composedly, tranquilly, unconcernedly*, Suet **II.** *securely, safely*, Plin

sĕcūrĭcŭla -ae, f (dim of securis), *a little axe*, Plaut

sĕcūrĭfĕr -fĕra -fĕrum (securis and fero), *carrying an axe*, Ov

sĕcūrĭgĕr -gĕra gĕrum (securis and gero), *carrying an axe*, puellae, *the Amazons*, Ov

sĕcūris -is, acc -im, abl -i, f (seco), *an axe hatchet* **I. A** Lit , for felling trees, Verg , as a weapon of war, *a battle-axe*, Verg , for killing victims at a sacrifice, Verg , esp , for executing criminals, *the headsman's axe*, securi ferire, percutere, Cic , saevus securi Torquatus (who had his own son beheaded), Verg , prov , securi Tenediā (Τενεδία πελέκει) *with the extremest severity* (from king Tenes of Tenedos, who executed every person who accused an innocent man), Cic **B.** Fig , *wound, injury, disaster*, graviorem infligere securim reipublicae, Cic **II.** Meton , (as secures, fasces and virgae were carried by the lictors of the highest magistrates at Rome), *supreme power, Roman supremacy*, a, plur , Gallia securibus subjecta, *completely subdued*, Caes , **b**, sing , Germania colla Romanae praebens animosa securi, O

sĕcūrĭtas -ātis, f (securus) **I.** *freedom from care* **A.** In a good sense, *peace of mind, quiet*, Cic **B.** In a bad sense, *carelessness, indifference*, Tac **II.** Transf , *freedom from danger security*, Tac.

sēcūrus -a -um (1. se and cura), *free from care*. **I.** Lit., *unconcerned, fearless, tranquil*; **a**, of persons, animus securus de aliqua re, Cic.; securior ab aliquo, Liv.; with genit., amorum, Verg.; famae, Ov.; with dep. interrog. sent., quid Tiridaten terreat, unice securus, Hor.; non securus, followed by ne and the subj., ne quis etiam errore labatur vestrûm quoque non sum securus, Liv.; **b**, of inanimate things, (*a*) *untroubled, cheerful*; quies, Ov.; olus, *simple, plain meal*, Hor.; with genit., sint tua vota licet secura repulsae, *safe against*, Ov.; (*β*) in a bad sense, *negligent, careless*; castrensis jurisdictio, Tac. **II.** Transf., *safe, secure*; tempus, locus, Liv.

1. **sĕcus**, n. indecl. = sexus, *sex*; virile et muliebre secus, Liv.

2. **sĕcŭs**, adv. (root SEC, SEQ, whence sequor). **I.** Posit., **A.** Adv., **a**, *otherwise, not so*; secus est, non (haud) secus, *just as*, foll. by atque (ac) quam, etc.; longe secus, *far otherwise*, Cic.; **b**, *not right, not well, badly* (opposed to preceding recte, bene, beate, etc.); recte an secus, *rightly or wrongly*, Cic.; aut beate aut secus vivere, *happily or the reverse*, Cic.; secus existimare de aliquo, Cic.; **c**, *less*; neque multo secus in iis virium, Tac. **B.** Prep. with acc. = secundum, Cato. **II.** Compar., **sĕquius** (**sĕcius**) and **sectius** (**sētius**), **1**, *otherwise, not so*; non setius ut, *not otherwise than, just as*, Verg.; non setius uritur quam, Ov.; **2**, = minus, *less*; nilo and nihilo setius (sequius), *none the less*, Cic.; haud setius and non setius, Verg.; **3**, *less well, badly*; invitus quod sequius sit de meis civibus loquor, Liv.

sĕcūtor -ōris, m. (sequor), *a gladiator armed with a sword and shield who fought with a retiarius*, Juv.

1. **sĕd**, v. 1. se.

2. **sĕd** (old Latin sēt), conj. (connected with sĕd = se, *without*). **I.** *but, yet*; **1**, to limit or qualify a person's statement, Cic.; sed enim, Cic.; sed enimvero, Liv.; sed autem, Verg.; **2**, esp., **a**, to express an ascending climax, sed etiam, *but also, nay rather*; avarissimae sed etiam crudelissimae, Cic.; consilium defuit, sed etiam obfuit, Cic.; **b**, in transitions, *but, yet*; (*a*) in returning to a previous subject, sed redeamus ad Hortensium, Cic.; (*β*) in resuming a discourse after a parenthesis, ut peroravit (nam . . . peregerat), sed ut peroravit, etc., Cic.; **c**, in breaking off discourse, *but, yet*; sed haec hactenus, Cic. **II.** To limit or qualify a previous negative sent., *but*; esp., in the phrases non modo (non solum, non tantum), sed etiam (quoque), *not only . . . but also*; non modo (solum) . . . sed, *not only . . . but even*; negotiis non interfuit solum, sed praefuit, Cic.

sēdāmen -inis, n. (sedo), *a sedative*, Sen.

sēdātē, adv. (sedatus), *quietly, composedly, tranquilly*; placide atque sedate, constanter et sedate dolorem ferre, Cic.; of discourse, sedate placideque labi, Cic.

sēdātio -ōnis, f. (sedo), *an allaying, soothing, assuaging of violent emotion or passion*; animi, Cic.; maerendi, Cic.; plur., sedationes (animi), Cic.

sēdātus -a -um, p. adj. (from sedo), *quiet, composed, tranquil*; homo, Cic.; sedato gradu abire, Liv.; animus sedatior, Cic.

sēdĕcies, adv. (sedecim), *sixteen times*, Plin.

sēdĕcim and **sexdĕcim** (sex and decem), *sixteen*, Caes.

sēdĕcŭla -ae, f. (dim. of sedes), *a low seat or stool*, Cic.

sĕdentārius -a -um (sedens), *sitting, sedentary*; sutor, Plaut.

sĕdĕo, sēdi, 2. *to sit*. **I.** Gen., **A.** Lit., **1**, **a**, of persons, with in and the abl., in sella, in solio, in equo, Cic.; with abl. alone, carpento, sede regiā, Liv.; absol., quum tot summi oratores sederent, Cic.; **b**, of animals, *to settle*; cornix sedet in humo, Ov.; **2**, esp., of magistrates, *to sit in council, sit in judgment*; Scaevolā (tribuno) in rostris sedente, Cic.; pro tribunali, Cic.; in tribunali, Cic. **B.** Transf., of things, *to settle, sink down*; sedet nebula densior campo, Liv.; sedisse montes, Tac.; of food, *to settle, be digested*; esca quae tibi sederit, Hor. **II.** With a notion of endurance. **A.** Lit., **1**, *to remain in one place, settle, stay*; also with the notion of *to be inactive, idle*; in villa totos dies, Cic.; Corcyrae, Cic.; desidens domi, Liv.; sedit qui timuit, *remained at home*, Hor.; consulibus sedentibus, Cic.; prov., compressis manibus sedere, *to sit with folded hands*, Liv.; **2**, esp., **a**, *to sit as a suppliant at the altar of some god*; meliora deos sedet omnia poscens, Verg.; **b**, milit. t. t., *to remain encamped, to sit down before a place, to remain inactive*; Arretii ante moenia, Liv. **B.** Transf., **1**, lit., **a**, *to be firmly settled*; in liquido sederunt ossa cerebro, Ov.; **b**, of weapons, *to be fixed, be fastened, to stick*; clava sedet in ore viri, Ov.; **2**, fig., **a**, *to remain fast, unchanged*; pallor in ore sedet, Ov.; **b**, of resolves, *to be firmly determined, to remain fixed*; idque pio sedet Aeneae, Verg.

sēdes -is, f. (sedeo), *a seat*. **I.** Lit., *a stool, chair, throne*; sedes honoris, sella curulis, Cic.; sedes ponere, Liv.; priores sedes tenere, *the first rank*, Hor. **II.** Transf., **a**, *an abode, habitation, place of settlement, home*; sedes fundatur Veneri, *a temple*, Verg.; sceleratorum, *the infernal regions*, Cic.; eam sibi domum sedesque deligere, Cic.; plur., sedes sanctae penatium deorumque, Cic.; his sedibus sese continere, Cic.; esp., (*a*) *the grave*; sedibus hunc refer ante suis et conde sepulchro, Verg.; (*β*) *the dwelling-place of the soul, the body*; anima misera de sede volens exire, Ov.; **b**, of things, *place, seat, spot, base, foundation*; turrim convellimus altis sedibus, Verg.; suis sedibus convulsa Roma, Cic.; montes moliri sede suā, Liv.

sĕdīle -is, n. (sedeo), *a seat*; (*a*) sing., Verg.; (*β*) plur., sĕdilia, *a row of seats or benches in the theatre or elsewhere*, Hor.; *benches for rowers*, Verg.

sĕdīmentum -i, n. (sedeo), *a settling, sediment*, Plin.

sēditio -ōnis, f. (from sed = se, *apart*, and itio), *a dissension*. **I.** Between individuals, *dissension, quarrel*; domestica (of brothers), Liv.; crescit favore turbida seditio, Ov. **II.** Between members of a political union, esp., citizens and soldiers, *a civil or military revolt, insurrection, sedition, rising, mutiny*. **A. 1**, lit., militaris, Liv.; seditionem ac discordiam concitare, Cic.; seditionem concire, Liv.; conflare, Cic.; facere, Caes.; restinguere, Cic.; personif., *as an attendant of Fama*; Seditio repens, Ov.; **2**, meton., *the rebels*, Liv. **B.** Transf., *rising, tumult*; intestina corporis, Liv.; iracundia dissidens a ratione seditio quaedam, Cic.

sēditiōsē, adv. with compar. and superl. (seditiosus), *seditiously*, Cic.

sēditiōsus -a -um (seditio). **I.** *seditious, turbulent*; civis, Cic.; triumviri seditiosissimi Cic. **II.** *restless*; seditiosa ac tumultuosa vita, Cic.

sēdo, 1. (causat. of sedeo). **I.** Lit., *to cause to settle*; pulverem, Phaedr. **II.** *to settle, soothe, still, calm, allay, assuage, put an end to, extinguish*; bellum, pugnam, Cic.; incendia, Liv.; invidiam, Cic.; impetum populi, Cic.; iram, Plin.; seditionem, Cic.; lites eorum, Cic.

sēdūco duxi -ductum, 3 *to take or lead aside* I. Lit, a, in order to speak secretly to a person, aliquem, Cic, aliquem a debita peste, *to lead aside and so rescue from danger*, Cic, b, of things, vacuos ocellos, *to turn aside*, Prop, stipitem, *to push aside*, Ov, vini paulum seducta, *placed aside*, Ov II. Transf, a, poet, *to separate, sever*, seducit terras unda duas, Ov, seducunt castra, *divide into two*, Ov, b, *to exclude*, consilia seducta plurium conscientiā, Liv

sēductĭo -ōnis, f (seduco), *a leading or drawing aside*, testium, Cic

sēductus -a -um, p adj (from seduco), *remote, distant*, recessus gurgitis, Ov

sēdŭlē = sedulo (q v)

sēdŭlĭtas -ātis, f (sedulus), *assiduity, zeal, application*, Cic

sēdŭlō, adv (sedulus), a, *busily, zealously*, sedulo argumentaris, Cic, b, *purposely, designedly*, Liv

sēdŭlus -a um (from sedeo, as credulus from credo), *busy, diligent, assiduous, sedulous, earnest, zealous*, homo, Cic, apis, Cic, brachia, Ov

sĕdum i, n *the plant houseleek*, Plin

Sedūni -ōrum, m *a Helvetian people, near modern Sion*

sĕgĕs -ĕtis, f (perhaps from root SEC, Gr ΤΕΚ-ω, *that which is produced* I. *the seed in a field, from its being sown to the crop being reaped*, a, lit, laetae segetes, Cic, seges farris est matura messi, Liv, used of the vine, Verg, b, fig., *advantage*, quae inde seges, Juv, 2, transf, *a thickly packed mass or number*, seges clipeata virorum, Ov; telorum, Verg II Meton, *a sown field*, 1, a, lit, Cic, b, fig, *field, soil*, quid odisset Clodium Milo segetem ac materiem suae gloriae? Cic, 2, poet., transf, *fruitful plains, fields*, fert casiam non culta seges, Tib, ubi prima paretur arboribus seges, Cic

Sĕgesta -ae, f *Roman name of the old town Acesta* (Ἀκέστη), *on the north coast of Sicily, near Mount Eryx*, now *Castel a mare di Golfo* Hence, A. **Sĕgestāni** ōrum, m *the inhabitants of Segesta* B. **Sĕgestenses** -ium, m *the inhabitants of Segesta*

sĕgestre -is, n (στέγαστρον), *a covering, wrapper of straw matting or skins*, Plin

segmentātus -a -um (segmentum), *ornamented with a purple or gold border, bordered*, cunae, Juv

segmentum -i, n (root SEC, whence seco) I. *a piece cut off, cutting, shred*, 1, lit, Plin, 2, transf, *a zone or region of the earth*, Plin II. Plur, segmenta, *pieces of purple or cloth of gold sewn on the skirt of women's dresses, gold or purple border*, Ov.

segnĕ, adv, v segniter

segnĭpēs -pĕdis (segnis and pes), *slow-footed*, Juv.

segnis -e (root SEC, sequor), *slow, slothful, tardy, sluggish, dilatory*, a, absol., segniores castigat, Caes, bellum, *sluggishly prosecuted*, Liv, mors, *a lingering death by poison*, Liv, b, with ad and acc, segnior ad respondendum, Cic, nec ad citharam segnis nec ad arcum, Ov, c, with in and the acc, non in Venerem segnes, Verg, d, with genit, laborum, Tac, e, with infin, solvere nodum, Hor

segnĭtas -ātis, f (segnis), *sluggishness, tardiness, dilatoriness*, Cic

segnĭtĕr and **segnĕ** (segnis), *sluggishly, slothfully, slowly*, a, posit, Liv, b, compar, segnius, Liv, esp with preceding negative, nihilo segnius, Sall

segnĭtĭa -ae, f and **segnĭtĭēs** -ēi, f (segnis), *sluggishness, slothfulness, slowness, tardiness*, a, lit, Cic, b, transf, segnitia maris, *calmness*, Tac

Sĕgŏdūnum i, n *the chief town of the Ruteni, on the northern border of Gallia Narbonensis*, now *Rodez*, Cic

Segontĭa (Saguntĭa) and **Secontĭa** -ae, f *a town in Hispania Baetica, near modern Siguenza*

Segontĭăci -ōrum, m *a people in the south of Britain*

Segovax -actis, m *one of the British chiefs in Kent at the time of Caesar's invasion*

sēgrĕgo, 1 (grex) I. *to separate from the flock, segregate*; oves, Phaedr II. Transf, *to separate, sever, remove*, aliquem a numero civium, Cic, aliquem a se, Cic, virtutem a summo bono, Cic

Sĕgūsĭāvi (Sĕgūsĭāni) -ōrum, m *a people in Gallia Lugdunensis, in modern Feurs* (Dép de la Loire)

segutilum i, n. *the external indication of a gold-mine*, Plin

Sējānus, v Sējus

sējŭgātus -a um, *disjointed, separated*, animi partem ab actione corporis sejugatam, Cic.

sējŭges ium, m (sex and jugum), *a chariot drawn by six horses abreast*, Liv

sējunctim, adv (sejunctus), *separately*, Tib

sējunctĭo -ōnis, f (sejungo), *a separation, severance*, Cic

sējungo -junxi -junctum, 3 *to separate, sever, disjoin* I. Lit, Alpes Italiam a Gallia sejungunt, Nep, se ab aliquo, Cic II. Transf, 1, gen, se a libertate verborum, *to refrain from*, Cic, bonum quod non possit ab honestate sejungi, Cic, 2, esp, *to distinguish*, liberalitatem ac benignitatem ab ambitu atque largitione, Cic

Sējus i, m. *a Roman name, the most celebrated bearer of which was M Sejus, a friend of Atticus and Cicero* Hence, **Sējānus** -a -um, *relating to Sejus*, subst., as name, L Aelius Sejanus, *son of Sejus Strabo, the praefectus praetorii of Tiberius*

sĕlas, n (σέλας), *a species of fiery meteor*, Sen

sēlectĭo ōnis, f (seligo), *a choosing out, selection*, si selectio nulla sit ab iis rebus quae, etc, Cic

Sĕleucēa (Sĕleucīa) -ae, f (Σελεύκεια), *name of several towns* I. S Babylonia *a town near the Tigris, on the canal connecting it with the Euphrates built by Seleucus Nicator*, now *El-Madaien* II. S Pieria *a town in Syria, not far from the Orontes*, now ruins near *Kepse* III. S Trachēa *a town in Cilicia*, now *Selefkieh*

Sĕleucus -i, m (Σέλευκος), Nicator, *a famous general of Alexander the Great, king of Syria*

sēlībra -ae, f (for semilibra), *half a pound*, Liv

sēlĭgo -lēgi -lectum, 3 (se and lego), *to choose, choose out, select* I. Gen, exempla, Cic II. Esp, judices selecti, *the judges appointed by the praetor in a criminal case*, Cic

Sĕlīnūs nuntis, f (Σελινοῦς) I. *a sea port in Sicilia*, now *Selinonto* II *a town in Cilicia, afterwards called Trajanopolis*, now *Selenti*, Liv Hence, adj, **Sĕlīnūsĭus** -a -um, *belonging to Selinus*

sella -ae, f (for sedla, from sedeo), *a seat, stool, settle* I. Gen, in sella sedere, Cic II. Esp, 1. *a work-stool, a stool or bench on which handicraftsmen sit*, in foro sellam ponere, Cic.,

2, *the stool of a teacher*, Cic.; 3, *the curule stool*, in full, sella curulis, *on which the higher magistrates at Rome sat*, Cic.; 4, *a throne*, Nep.; 5, *a sedan-chair*; gestatoria, Suet.

sellārĭus -a -um (sella), *relating to a seat or stool*; subst., **sellārĭa** -ae, f. *a room furnished with seats, a sitting-room*, Plin.

sellisternĭum -ii, n. (sella and sterno), *a religious banquet in honour of goddesses, at which their images were placed on seats and food put before them*, Tac.

sellŭla -ae, f. (dim. of sella), *a little sedan-chair*, Tac.

sellŭlārĭus -a -um (sellula), *of or relating to a seat*; artifex, *a handicraftsman who sat at his work*; hence, subst., **sellŭlārĭus** -ii, m. *a handicraftsman*, Cic.

sĕmĕl, adv. numer. **I.** *once, a single time*; semel atque iterum, semel iterumque, *once and again, twice*, Cic.; semel atque iterum ac saepius, Cic.; plus quam semel, Cic.; non semel, Cic. **II.** Transf., **A.** *the first time, firstly*; foll. by iterum, deinde, item, etc., Cic. **B.** *once*; **a,** quoniam semel ita vobis placuit, Cic.; **b,** *once* (of things which cannot be altered); qui semel verecundiae fines transierit, eum bene et naviter oportet esse impudentem, Cic. **C.** *once, once for all*; **a,** semel exorari soles, Cic.; vitam semel finirent, Liv.; **b,** in discourse, *once for all, in a word, briefly*; ut fundus semel indicaretur, Cic.

Sĕmĕla -ae, f. and **Sĕmĕlē** -ēs, f. (Σεμέλη), *daughter of Cadmus, mother of Bacchus by Jupiter; she asked Jupiter to appear to her in his person as a god, and was consumed by the blaze of his majesty*; Semeles puer, *Bacchus*, Hor. Hence, **Sĕmĕlēĭus** and **Sĕmĕlēus** -a -um, *of Semele*; Semeleia proles, *Bacchus*, Hor.

sēmen -ĭnis, n. (root SE, whence se-ro, se-vi), *the seed*. **I. A.** Lit., **a,** of plants, semen manu spargere, Cic.; **b,** (α) of animals, creatae semine Saturni, Ov.; (β) of the elements of water, fire, stone, etc., Verg., Lucr. **B.** Meton., *the seed*; **1,** *the race*; Romanum, Cic.; regio semine orta, Liv.; **2,** *descendant, child, offspring*; caelestia semina, Ov.; semina Phoebi, *Aesculapius, son of Phoebus*, Ov. **II.** Fig., *seed = cause, origin, author, instigator*; stirps ac semen malorum omnium, Cic.

sēmentĭfĕr -fĕra -fĕrum (sementis and fero), *seed-bearing, fruitful*, Verg.

sēmentis -is, acc. -em and -im, f. (semen), *a sowing*. **I, a,** lit., sementes maximas facere, Cic.; prov., ut sementem feceris, ita metes, Cic.; **b,** fig., malorum sementim or proscriptionis sementem facere, Cic. **II.** Meton., sementes, *the young growing corn*, Ov.

sēmentīvus -a -um (sementis), *of or relating to seed or seed-time*; dies, Ov.

sēmento, 1. (sementis), *to bear seed*, Plin.

sēmestris (sēmenstris) -e (sex and mensis), *of six months, six-monthly*; **a,** = *six months old*; infans, Liv.; **b,** = *limited to six months*; regnum, Liv.; semestri vatum digitos circumligat auro, *the ring of the tribunes of the soldiers worn for six months*, Juv.

sēmēsus -a -um (semi and esus), *half-eaten, half-consumed*; praeda, ossa, Verg.

sēmĭădăpertus -a -um (semi and adaperio), *half-open*, Ov.

sēmĭambustus -a -um (semi and amburo), *half-burnt*, Suet.

sēmĭănĭmis -e and **sēmĭănĭmus** -a -um (semi and anima), *half-alive, half-dead*; corpora semianima, Liv.

sēmĭăpertus -a -um (semi and aperio), *half-open*; portarum fores, Liv.

sēmĭbarbărus -a -um, *semi-barbarous*, Suet.

sēmĭbos -bŏvis, m. *half-ox*; vir, *the Minotaur*, Ov.

sēmĭcăper -pri, m. *half-goat*, Ov.

sēmĭcinctĭum -ii, n. (semi and cinctus), *a narrow girdle or apron*, Mart.

sēmĭcircŭlus -i, m. *a semicircle*, Col.

sēmĭcoctus -a -um (semi and coquo), *half-cooked*, Plin.

sēmĭcrĕmātus -a -um (semi and cremo), *half-burnt*, Ov.

sēmĭcrĕmus (semi and cremo), *half-burnt*, Ov.

sēmĭcrūdus -a -um, *half-raw*, Suet.

sēmĭcŭbĭtālis -e, *half a cubit in length*, Liv.

sēmĭdĕus -a -um, *half-divine*; subst., *a demigod, demigoddess*; semideum genus, *the Nereids*, Ov.

sēmĭdoctus -a -um (semi and doceo), *half-taught, half-learned*; haec ut apud doctos et semidoctos ipse percurro, Cic.

sēmĭermis (sēmermis) -e and **sēmĭermus (sēmermus)** -a -um (semi and arma), *half-armed, half-equipped*, Liv.

sēmĭēsus = semesus (q.v.).

sēmĭfactus -a -um (semi and facio), *half-done, half-finished*, Tac.

sēmĭfĕr -fĕra -fĕrum (semi and ferus), *half-animal, half-bestial, half-man and half-animal*. **I.** Lit., pectus Tritonis, Verg.; subst., of the Centaurs, Ov. **II.** Transf., *half-wild, half-savage*. Subst., **sēmĭfĕr** -fĕri, m. *half a savage*, Verg.

sēmĭfultus -a -um (semi and fulcio), *half-propped*, Mart.

sēmĭgermānus -a -um, *half-German*, Liv.

sēmĭgraecus -a -um, *half-Greek*, Suet.

sēmĭgrăvis -e, *half-intoxicated*, Liv.

sēmĭgro, 1. *to go away, depart, remove from*; a patre, Cic.

sēmĭhĭans -antis (semi and hio), *half-open*; labellum, Cat.

sēmĭhŏmo -hŏmĭnis, m. *half a man*. **I.** *half a man and half an animal*; Centauri, Ov. **II.** Transf., *half-wild*; Cacus, Verg.

sēmĭhōra -ae, f. *half an hour*, Cic.

sēmĭlăcer -cĕra -cĕrum, *half-torn, half-mangled*, Cic.

sēmĭlautus -a -um, *half-washed*, Cat.

sēmĭlīber -bĕra -bĕrum, *half-free*, Cic.

sēmĭlixa -ae, m. *half a sutler*, used as a term of reproach, Liv.

sēmĭmărīnus -a -um, *half-marine, half in the sea*; corpora (Scyllarum), Lucr.

sēmĭmas -măris, m. **I.** *half-male, hermaphrodite*, Liv. **II.** *castrated*; oves, Ov.

sēmĭmortŭus -a -um, *half-dead*, Cat.

sēmĭnārĭus -a -um (semen), *of or relating to seed*; subst., **sēmĭnārĭum** -ii, n. *a plantation, nursery*; fig., equites seminarium senatus, Liv.; Catilinarum, Cic.; triumphorum, Cic.

sēmĭnātor -ōris, m. (semino), *a producer, begetter, author*; qui est verus omnium seminator malorum, Cic.

sēmĭnex -nĕcis, *half-dead*, Liv.

sēmĭnĭum -ii, n. (semen), *a race or breed of animals*, Lucr.

sēmĭno, 1. (semen) **I.** *to sow*, Col **II.** *to beget, produce*, Plaut, of plants, viscum, quod non sua seminat arbos, Verg

sēmĭnūdus -a -um, *half-naked*, Liv, pedes prope seminudus, *nearly defenceless, without arms*, Liv.

sēmĭpāgānus i, m *half a rustic*, Pers

sēmĭpĕdālis -e, *half a foot in dimension*, Plin

sēmĭpĕdānĕus = semipedalis (q v)

sēmĭperfectus -a um (semi and perficio), *half finished*, Suet

sēmĭpes -pĕdis, m *a half foot*, Plin

sēmĭplēnus -a um, *half-full*, naves, *half-manned*, Cic, stationes, Liv

sēmĭpŭtātus -a -um (semi and puto), *half pruned*, vitis, Verg

Sĕmīrămĭs (Sămīrămĭs, Sămērămĭs) -midis and -midos, f (Σεμιραμις), *wife and successor of Ninus, king of Assyria.*

sēmĭrāsus -a -um (semi and rado), *half-shaven, half shorn*, Cat

sēmĭrĕductus a um (semi and reduco), *half bent back*, Ov

sēmĭrĕfectus a -um (semi and reficio), *half-repaired*, Ov

sēmĭrŭtus -a -um (semi and ruo), *half ruined, half pulled down, half destroyed*, urbs, Liv, castella, Tac, plur subst, **sēmĭrŭta** ōrum, n *half-demolished places*, Liv

sēmis -issis, m and sometimes indecl (semis *half*, and as), *the half of anything*, esp, 1, *half an as*, Cic, 2, as a rate of interest, = 6 *per cent per annum*, semissibus magna copia, etc, *there is plenty of money to be had at 6 per cent*, Cic, 3, as a measure of land, *half a juger*, Liv

sēmĭsĕpultus a -um (semi and sepelio), *half buried*, Ov

sēmĭsomnus a -um, *half asleep, drowsy*, Cic

sēmĭsŭpīnus -a -um, *half-inclined backwards*, Ov.

sēmĭta -ae, f. *a narrow path, footpath, footway* **I.** Lit, angustissimae semitae, Cic, omnibus viis semitisque essedarios ex silvis emittebat, Cic **II.** Fig, Aesopi semitā feci viam, *I have amplified the materials in Aesop*, Phaedr, pecuniam, quae viā visa est exire ab isto, eandem semitā revertisse, Cic

sēmĭtactus a -um (semi and tango), *half-touched*, Mart

sēmĭtārĭus a um (semita), *frequenting lanes or by paths*, Cat

sēmĭtectus -a um (semi and tego), *half-covered*, Sen

sēmĭustŭlatus = semustulatus (q v)

sēmĭustus (sēmustus) a um (semi and uro), *half-burnt*, Enceladi semustum fulmine corpus, Verg, in fig, se populare incendium priore consulatu semiustum effugisse, Liv

sēmĭvir -viri, m *half-man* **I** Lit., 1, *half-man, half-animal*, Chiron, *the centaur*, Ov, bos, *the Minotaur*, Ov; 2, *a hermaphrodite*, Ov **II.** Transf, 1, *castrated, gelded*, Juv, 2, *effeminate, unmanly*, Verg

sēmĭvīvus a -um, *half-dead, almost dead* **I.** Lit, Cic **II.** Fig, voces, *faint*, Cic

sēmĭvōcālis -e, *half-sounding*, in grammar, subst, **sēmĭvōcāles** -ium, f (sc litterae), *semivowels*, Quint

Semnōnes -um, m *a German people between the Elbe and the Weichsel* Tac

sēmŏdĭus -ii, m (semi and modius), *a half-modius*, Mart

sēmōtus a -um, p adj (from semoveo), *remote, distant* **I.** Lit, locus a militibus semotus, Cic, neut plur subst, quae terris semota ridet, Hor **II.** Transf, a, *far from*, semotus a curis, Lucr, b, *distinct from, different from*, Lucr, c, *confidential*, arcana semotae dictionis, Tac

sēmŏvĕo -mōvi mōtum, 2 *to move away, set, separate* **I.** Lit qui voce praeconis a liberis semovebantur, Cic **II.** Transf, *to lay aside, exclude*, voluptatem, Cic, Strato ab ea disciplina omnino semovendus est *is not to be reckoned under that school*, Cic

sempĕr, adv (sem (= semel) and per, as nu (= nov) and per), *always, at all times* Cic, with subst, used almost as an adj, heri semper lenitas, *the constant mildness*, Ter, Hasdrubal pacis semper auctor, Liv

sempĭternus -a um (semper), *continual, perpetual, everlasting*, tempus, Cic, ignes Vestae, Cic, adv, **sempĭternum**, *for ever*, Plaut

Semprōnĭus a -um, *name of a gens at Rome, the most famous members of which were the brothers* Tib Sempronius Gracchus, and C Sempronius Gracchus, *tribunes of the people, who introduced agrarian laws and other reforms, but were both killed in riots provoked by the senatorial party* Adj, *Sempronian*, lex, Cic Hence, **Semprōnĭānus** -a um, *relating to Sempronius*, senatus consultum, *proposed by C Sempronius Rufus*, Cic, clades, *the defeat of the consul, C Sempronius Atratinus*

sēmuncĭa -ae, f (semi and uncia), *half an uncia*, $\frac{1}{24}$ *of an as*, 1, as a weight = $\frac{1}{24}$ *of a pound*, Cic, 2, to express the share of an inheritance, facit heredem ex deunce et semuncia Caecinam, Cic.

sēmuncĭārĭus -a um (semuncia), *relating to half an ounce*, fenus, $\frac{1}{24}$ *per cent monthly*, i e, *one-half per cent per annum*, Liv

sēmustŭlātus (sēmĭustŭlātus) and **sēmustilātus (sēmĭustilātus)** -a um (semi and ustulo, ustilo), *half-burnt*, Cic

Sēna -ae, f *a town in Umbria on the Adriatic Sea, where Livius Salinator defeated Hasdrubal, now Senigaglia* Hence, **Sēnensis** -e, *relating to Sena*, proelium, Cic

sĕnācŭlum i, n (senatus), *a senate-house, hall of council*, Liv

sēnārĭŏlus -i, m (dim of senarius), *a little trifling senarius*, Cic

sēnārĭus a um (seni), *composed of six*, senarius versus and subst **sēnārĭus** -ii, m *a verse of six feet* (generally iambic), Cic

sĕnātor ōris, m (senex), *a member of the Roman senate, senator*, Cic, transf, of the governing or deliberative bodies of other states of the Nervii, Caes, of the Rhodians, Cic, of the Macedonians, Liv

sĕnātōrĭus -a -um (senator), *of or relating to a senator, senatorial*, ordo, *the rank of senator*, Cic, consilium, *the panel of senators from which judges were chosen*, Cic

sĕnātus i and ūs, m **I.** *the Roman senate*, Cic, princeps senatus, *the senator whose name stood at the head of the censor's list*, Liv., in senatum venire, *to become a senator*, Cic, senatu movere, *to expel from the senate*, Cic, senatum legere, *to call over the senate*, Liv, so senatum recitare, Cic, senatum vocare, Liv, convocare, Cic, senatus (senati) consultum, *a formal resolution of the senate*, Cic used also of similar bodies in other nations, Carthaginiensis, Liv , Aeduos omnem senatum amisisse, Caes **II.** Meton , *a meeting, assembly of the senate*, senatum habere, dimittere Cic , frequens, *a full house*, Cic , datur alicui senatus, *obtains an audience of the senate*, Cic

sĕnātusconsultum, v senatus

Sĕnĕca ae, m *a family name of the Annaean gens, the most celebrated members of which were* 1, M Annaeus Seneca, *a rhetorician of Corduba in Spain*, 2, L Annaeus Seneca, *son of the foregoing, a celebrated philosopher, author of many works in prose and verse* (tragedies and epigrams), *the tutor of Nero, who compelled him to commit suicide*

sĕnecta, v 1 senectus

1 **sĕnectus** -a -um (senex), *old, aged* **I.** Adj , aetas, *old age*, Sall **II.** Subst , **sĕnecta** -ae, f *old age.* **A.** Lit , Liv , of animals, Verg , Ov **B.** *the slough of a serpent*, Plin

2 **sĕnectus** -ūtis, f (senex), *age, old age* **I. A.** Lit , vivere ad summam senectutem, Cic , of animals, Verg , in fig , of discourse, plena litteratae senectutis oratio, Cic **B.** Meton , 1, *gloom, moroseness*, Hor , 2, concr , a, *grey hair*, Verg , b, *old age = the old men* , senectus semper agens aliquid, Cic , c, *the slough of a serpent*, Plin **II.** Transf , of a thing, *old age, age*, vini, Juv , cariosa (tabellarum), Ov

sĕnĕo, 2 (senex), *to be old*, Cat

sĕnesco, sĕnŭi, 3 (seneo) **I** *to grow old in years, become old* , tacitis senescimus annis, Ov **II** *to grow old in strength* **A.** 1, of living beings, *to lose strength, become weak, waste away* , senescens equus, Hor , otio tam diutino, Liv , 2, of things, *to become old, to decay* , arbor hiemali tempore cum luna simul senescens, Cic **B.** Transf , a, *to wane, come to an end, flag, be relaxed* , luna senescens, Cic , hiems senescens, Cic , of abstractions, senescit laus, morbus, Cic , b, of polit power, *to wane, fade, lose power* , prope senescente Graeciā, Cic , senescit Hannibalis vis, Liv

sĕnex, sĕnis, compar , **sĕnĭor**, neut sĕnĭus, genit sĕniōris, *old, aged* **I.** Adj , a, of persons, miles, Ov , senem fieri, *to age*, Cic , of animals, cervus, Ov , of things, vis est senior quam, etc , Cic , b, fig , *ripe*, senior, ut ita dicam, quam illa aetas ferebat, oratio, Cic **II.** Subst , a, m *an old man, a man over sixty*, while senior = *a man between forty-five and sixty* (for which Hor and Liv sometimes use senex), Cic , b, f *an old woman*, Tib

sēni -ae -a (sex) **I.** *six each*, Cic **II.** *six*, Ov

sĕnīlis -e (senex), *of or relating to an old man, senile*, prudentia, Cic , stultitia, Cic ; statua incurva, Cic , animus, Liv , amor, Ov

sĕnīlĭtĕr, adv (senilis), *like an old man*, Quint

sĕnĭo ōnis, m (seni), *the number six upon dice*, Mart

sĕnĭor, compar of senex (q v)

sĕnium -ii, n (senex), *old age, the weakness, decay of old age* **I. A.** Lit , omni morbo senioque carere, Cic **B.** Transf , *decline, decay*, lentae velut tabis, Liv ; mundus se ipse consumptione et senio alebat sui, Cic **II.** Meton , **A.** Abstr , 1, *gloom, moroseness*, Hor , 2, *chagrin, vexation, sadness* , tota civitas confecta senio, Cic **B.** Concr , *an old man* , with in pron , illum senium, Ter

Sĕnŏnes -um, m **I.** *a people in Gallia Lugdunensis, with chief town Agendicum*, now *Sens* **II.** *a kindred people in northern Italy*

sensĭbĭlis e (sentio), *that can be perceived by the senses*, Suet.

sensĭcŭlus -i, m (dim of sensus), *a little sentence*, Quint

sensĭfĕr -fĕra -fĕrum (sensus and fero), *producing sensation*, Lucr

sensĭlis e (sentio), *endowed with sensation*, Lucr

sensim, adv (root SENS, whence sentio, sensi, sensus) *scarcely observably, gradually, by degrees, slowly* , sensim sine sensu, Cic , amicitias sensim dissuere, Cic

sensus -ūs, m (sentio). **I.** *perception, observation* , utere igitur argumento tute ipse sensus tui, Cic. **II.** *the power of perceiving* **A.** Physically, a, *feeling, consciousness* , sensus moriendi, Cic , voluptatis sensum capere, Cic , b, *a sense*; sensus videndi, audiendi, Cic , c, *feeling, consciousness*, in plur , *senses* , a mero redeunt in pectora sensus, Ov **B.** Morally, a, *emotion, sense, feeling* , amoris, amandi, diligendi, Cic ; b, *a manner of thinking, the sense, signification of a word, sentence, discourse, meaning* , verbi, Ov , testamenti, Hor

sententĭa -ae, f (sentio) **I.** *an opinion, thought, sentiment, meaning, purpose* (opp to expression) **A.** Gen , abundans sententiis, *rich in ideas*, Cic , sententiam fronte tegere, Cic , in sententia manere, Cic ; ex sententia, *to one's mind*, Cic , meā sententiā, *in my opinion*, Cic **B.** Esp , a, *an expressed opinion, vote of senators*; sententiam dicere, ferre, Cic , dare, Liv , in sententiam alicuius discedere, *to support a proposition*, Liv , so (pedibus) ire in sententiam, Liv , of judges, *decision, judgment* , sententiam dicere, Cic , sententiam ferre, Cic , b, as formula for an oath, ex animi mei sententia jurare, *to the best of my knowledge and belief*, Cic **II.** Transf , **A.** Abstr , a, *the meaning, signification of a word* or *sentence* , id habet hanc sententiam, Cic , b, *the purport of a speech* , contionis, Cic **B.** Concr , a, *a thought expressed in words, a sentence*, b, esp , *a maxim, aphorism* , acuta, Cic.

sententĭŏla -ae, f (dim of sententia), *a short sentence, maxim, aphorism*, Cic

sententĭōsē, adv (sententiosus), *sententiously*, dicere, Cic

sententĭōsus -a -um (sententia), *pithy, sententious* Cic

sentĭcētum -i, n (sentis), *a thorn-bush*, Plaut

sentīna ae, f *bilge water in the hold of a ship* **I.** Lit , sentinae vitiis conflictari, Caes **II.** Fig , 1, gen , sedebamus in puppi et clavum tenebamus, nunc autem vix est in sentina locus, *we can scarcely find room in the lowest part of the ship*, i e , *we are of next to no importance*, Cic , 2, esp , *the lowest of the people, rabble, dregs of the population* , reipublicae, Cic , urbis, Cic

Sentīnum -i, n *a town in Umbria.* Hence, adj , **Sentīnās** ātis, *belonging to Sentinum.*

sentĭo, sensi, sensum, 4 *to feel, perceive, have a sensation of* **I.** With the outward sense, **A.** Gen , suavitatem cibi, Cic , dolorem, Lucr , colorem, *to see*, Lucr , pass , posse prius ad angustias veniri quam sentirentur, Caes , with nom of partic , sensit medios delapsus in hostes, Verg **B.** *to feel, experience, learn* , (α) of persons. quod ipse sensisset ad Avaricum, Caes , (β) of things, ora senserat vastationem, Liv **II.** Mentally, *to feel* **A.** Lit , *to perceive, remark, observe, notice* , plus sentire, *have more insight*, Caes , quod quidem senserim, *as far as I have observed*, Cic , with acc and infin , sentit animus se moveri, Cic , with rel sent , quod sentio, quam sit exiguum, Cic , nec aliter sentire, foll. by quin and the subj , *to be convinced that*, Caes. , ex nocturno fremitu de profectione eorum senserunt, *observed their departure*, Caes , impers non ut dictum est in eo genere intelligitur, sed ut sensum est, Cic **B.** Transf , *to judge, think* , **a,** idem, Cic , recte, Cic , humiliter, Cic , cum aliquo, Cic , with double acc , *to consider* or *think a person something* , aliquem bonum civem, Cic , partic subst , **sensa** -ōrum, n *thoughts*, mentis, Cic , **b,** legal t t *to give one's opinion, to vote*, sentire lenissime, Cic

sentis -is, c *a thorn bush, briar*, usually plur , rubi sentesque, Caes

sentisco, 3 (inchoat of sentio), *to perceive, observe*, Lucr

sentus -a -um (sentis), *thorny, rough*, loca, Verg

sēnus -a -um, sing of seni (q v.).

sĕorsum (sĕorsŭs) and **sĕvorsŭs** (from se and vorto or verto), *especially, particularly*, omnibus gratiam habeo et seorsum tibi, Ter foll by ab, *apart from, separately from*, seorsum ab rege exercitum ductare, Sall , abs te seorsum sentio *I am of a different opinion*, Plaut , with abl alone, seorsus corpore, *without a body*, Lucr

sēpărātē, adv only in compar (separatus), *apart, particularly*, Cic

sēpărātim, adv (separatus), *apart, separately, distinctly differently*, separatim semel, iterum cum universis, Cic , nihil accidet ei separatim a reliquis civibus, Cic , castra separatim habebant, Liv , with ab and the abl , dii separatim ab universis singulos diligunt, Cic

sēpărātĭo -ōnis, f (separo) *separation, severance* **I.** Lit , distributio partium ac separatio, Cic **II.** Transf , sui facti ab illa definitione, Cic.

sēpărātus -a -um, p adj (from separo), *separated, severed, sundered, separate, apart, distinct*, volumen, Cic , exordium, Cic , separatis temporibus, *at different times*, Nep

sēpăro, 1 *to disjoin, sever, separate* **I** Lit (α) aliquem or aliquid ab, etc Cic , (β) aliquid aliquā re , Seston Abydenā separat urbe fretum, Ov , (γ) aliquid ex aliqua re or in aliquid, e potium magno numero ex omni populi summa separato, Cic , (δ) with acc alone, nec nos mare separat ingens, Ov **II.** Fig , *to separate, treat separately*, (α) with ab and the abl , a perpetuis suis historiis bella ea, Cic ; (β) with acc alone, utilitatem, Cic

sĕpĕlībĭlis -e (sepelio), *that can be buried*, fig , *that can be concealed*, Plaut

sĕpĕlĭo -pĕlīvi and -pĕlii -pultum, 4 (root SEP, connected with sop oi, sop io), *to lay to rest the remains of the dead, to bury* **I.** Lit , **a,** *to bury* ossa, Ov , **b,** *to burn*, Liv **II.** Fig , **1,** *to bury, put an end to, ruin, destroy*, patriam, Cic , dolorem, Cic , **2,** poet partic , sepultus, *buried, sunk, immersed in anything*, somno vinoque sepultus, Verg , inertia sepulta, Hor

sēpes = saepes (q v)

sēpĭa ae, f (σηπία), *the cuttle fish*, Cic

sēpīmentum = saepimentum (q v)

sēpĭo = saepio (q.v.)

sēpĭŏla -ae, f (dim. of sepia), *a small cuttle-fish*, Plaut.

Sēplăsĭa ae, f *a street in Capua, where unguents were sold*

sēpōno -pŏsŭi -pŏsĭtum, 3. *to put, lay on one side, place apart* **I.** Gen , **A.** Lit , aliquid ad fanum, Cic , captivam pecuniam in aedificationem templi, Liv. , primitias magno Jovi, Ov **B.** Transf , *to keep back, reserve* , ut alius aliam sibi partem, in qua elaboraret, seponeret, Cic **II.** Esp , **A.** *to separate*, **1,** lit , de mille sagittis unam, *to select*, Ov , **2,** transf , **a,** *to separate, divide*, a ceteris dictionibus eam partem dicendi, Cic , **b,** *to distinguish*, inurbanum lepido dicto, Hor **B** *to keep far off*, **1,** lit , **a,** interesse pugnae imperatorem an seponi melius foret dubitavere, Tac **b,** *to remove out of the way, banish* , aliquem in insulam, Tac , **2,** transf , graves curas, *to banish*, Ov

sēpŏsĭtus a um, p adj (from sepono) **I.** *distant, remote*, fons, Prop **II.** *choice, select*, vestis, Tib

1 **seps,** sēpis, c (σήψ) **I.** *a species of venomous lizard*, Plin **II.** *an insect, perhaps the woodlouse*, Plin

2 **seps** = saepes (q v)

sepsĕ = se ipse

septa, v saeptum

septem, numer (ἑπτά), *seven* **I.** Gen , Cic **II.** Esp **A.** septem (οἱ ἑπτά), *the Seven Wise Men of Greece*, Cic **B.** Septem Aquae, *the meeting of streams near Reate, now Lake Sta Susanna*

September -bris -bre, abl -bri (septem and suffix -ber), *belonging to September*, **a,** mensis September, *the seventh month of the Roman year* (reckoning from March), *September*, **b,** kalendae, nonae, idus (*the 1st, 5th 13th of September*), horae, *the unhealthy time of September*, Hor

septemdĕcim, numer *seventeen*, Cic

septemflŭus -a -um (fluo), *having a sevenfold flood, with seven mouths*, Nilus, Ov

septemgĕmĭnus a -um, *sevenfold, with seven mouths*, Nilus, Verg

septempĕdālis -e, *seven feet high*, Plaut

septemplex plicis (septem and plico), *sevenfold*, clipeus, *with seven layers of hides*, Verg , Nilus, *with seven mouths*, Verg , so Ister, Ov

septemtrĭo (septemptrĭo, septentrĭo) -ōnis, m , gen plur , septemtriones, *the seven plough-oxen* **I.** As a constellation *the Great Bear, the Wain* , septemtrio minor, *the Little Bear*, Cic **II** Meton , **a,** *the north* , (a) sing , septemtrio a Macedonia obicitur, Liv , in tmesis, septem subjecta trioni Verg , (β) plur , inflectens sol cursum tum ad meridiem, tum ad septemtriones, Cic , **b,** *the north wind*, Cic

septemtrĭōnālis -e (septemtrio), *northern*, subst , **septemtrĭōnālĭa** -ium, n *the northern regions*, Tac

septemvir -viri, m , plur , **septemvĭri** -ōrum and ûm, m *the seven men, a college or guild of seven persons* **I** Of the Epulones, v epulo **II.** *to divide public land among colonists*, Cic

septemvĭrālis -e, *of* or *relating to the septemviri*, auctoritas, Cic , subst , **septemvĭrāles** -ium, m = septemviri (q v)

septemvĭrātus -ūs, m *the office* or *dignity of a septemvir*, Cic

septēnārĭus -a um (septeni), *containing the number seven*, numerus, Plin , plur subst , **septēnārĭi,** m (sc versus), *verses containing seven feet*, Cic

septendĕcim = septemdecim (q v)

septēni ae a (septem) **I.** *seven each* duo fana septenos habere libros, Liv , genit plur septenûm, e g , pueri annorum senûm septenûmque denûm, Liv. **II.** *seven*, septena fila lyrae, Ov , sing , Lucr

septentrĭo = septemtrio (q v)

septentrĭōnālis = septemtrionalis (q v)

septĭcus -a -um (σηπτικός), *causing putrefaction*, Plin.

septĭēs (septĭens), adv. (septem), *seven times;* septiens milliens sestertium or simply septiens milliens, 700 *millions of sesterces,* Cic.

septĭmānus (septŭmānus) -a -um, *relating to the number seven.* **I.** Adj., nonae, *falling on the seventh day of the month,* Varr. **II.** Subst., **septĭmāni** -ōrum, m. *soldiers of the seventh legion,* Tac.

Septĭmontĭālis -e, *of* or *relating to the festival Septimontium,* Suet.

Septĭmontĭum -ĭi, n. (septem and mons). **I.** *the circuit of seven small hills round the Palatine, which became the germ of the city of Rome.* **II.** *a festival at Rome in December to celebrate the walling-in of these small hills and the formation of a city.*

septĭmus (septŭmus) -a -um (septem), *the seventh;* adv., **septĭmum,** *for the seventh time,* Cic.

septingēnārĭus -a -um (septingeni), *containing seven hundred,* Varr.

septingēni -ae -a (septingenti), *seven hundred each,* Plin.

septingentēsĭmus -a -um (septingenti), *the seven hundredth,* Liv.

septingenti -ae -a (septem and centum), *seven hundred,* Liv.

septingentĭēs, adv. (septingenti), *seven hundred times,* Plin.

Septizōnĭum -ĭi, n. (septem and zona), *a lofty building in Rome,* Suet.

septŭāgēni -ae -a (septuaginta), *seventy each,* Plin.

septŭāgēsĭmus -a -um (septuaginta), *the seventieth,* Cic.

septŭāgĭēs, adv. (septuaginta), *seventy times,* Col.

septŭāginta, numer. (ἑβδομήκοντα), *seventy,* Cic.

septŭennis -e (septem and annus), *of seven years, seven years old;* puer, Plaut.

septum = saeptum (q.v.)

septunx -uncis, m. (septem and uncia), *seven-twelfths of the as,* or *of any unity with twelve parts;* jugeri, Liv.; auri, *seven ounces,* Liv.

sepulch . . . v. sepulc . . .

sĕpulcrālis (sĕpulchrālis) -e (sepulcrum, sepulchrum), *of* or *belonging to a tomb, sepulchral;* arae, Ov.; fax, *funeral torch,* Ov.

sĕpulcrētum -i, n. *a burial-place, cemetery,* Cat.

sĕpulcrum (sĕpulchrum) -i, n. (from sĕpelio, as fulcrum from fulcio), *the resting-place.* **I. A.** Lit., *a place of burial;* **1, a,** *a grave, sepulchre;* monumenta sepulcrorum, Cic.; **b,** *the mound over a grave;* onerare membra sepulcro, Verg.; **2,** *the place where a corpse is burnt;* ara sepulcri, Verg. **B.** Transf., sepulcrum vetus, *of an old man,* Plaut. **II.** Meton. **A.** *the tomb,* including grave, monument, and inscription; sepulcrum facere, Cic.; legere sepulcra, *to read the epitaph on a grave-stone,* Cic. **B.** *the dead person;* placatis sepulcris, Ov.

sĕpultūra -ae, f. (sepelio), *the laying the body of a dead person to rest;* **a,** *a burying, burial, interment, sepulture;* sepulturā aliquem afficere, *to bury,* Cic.; **b,** *the burning of the body of the dead,* Tac.

Sēquăna -ae, m. *a river of Gaul, forming, with the Matrona, the boundary between the Celts and the Belgae,* now *the Seine.*

Sēquăni -ōrum, m. *a Gallic people in modern Burgundy and Franche-Comté.*

sĕquax -ācis (sequor). **I.** *following easily* or *quickly;* equus, Ov.; undae, *following each other rapidly,* Verg.; hederae, *quickly spreading itself,* Pers.; fumus, *penetrating,* Verg.; Latio (= Latinis) dant terga sequaci, *pursuing,* Verg. **II.** Transf., *easily worked, pliable, ductile;* materia sequacior, Plin.

sĕquester -tra -trum and **sĕquester** -tris -tre (from 2. secus, as magister from magis), *mediating.* **I.** Adj., pace sequestrā, *by the medium of peace,* Verg. **II.** Subst., **A. sĕquester** -tri or -tris, m. **a,** *a go-between* or *agent* (in cases of bribery); quo sequestre in illo judice corrumpendo dicebatur esse usus, Cic.; **b,** *a stakeholder, depositary, a person in whose hands the matter in dispute is deposited till the dispute is settled,* Plaut. **B. sĕquestrum** -i, n. and **sĕquestre** -is, n. *the deposit of the matter in dispute in the hands of a third person;* sequestro deponere, *by way of deposit,* Plaut.

sĕquĭus = secius, compar. of secus (q.v.).

sĕquor, sĕcūtus (sĕquūtus) sum, sĕqui, 3. dep. (root SEC, connected with ἝΠ-ομαι), *to follow, accompany.* **I. A.** Lit., **1,** gen., **a,** of persons, qui ex urbe amicitiae causā Caesarem secuti, Caes.; vestigia alicuius, Ov.; **b,** of things, zonā bene te secutā, Hor.; **2,** esp., **a,** *to follow with hostile intent, pursue;* hostes, Caes.; feras, Ov.; **b,** *to follow a person to a place;* Formias, Cic.; secutae sunt nares vicinitatem oris, *have sought for,* Cic. **B.** Transf., **a,** of time or order, *to follow, ensue;* sequitur hunc annum nobilis clade Caudinā pax, Liv.; sequenti anno, Liv.; sequenti die, Liv.; et quae sequentia, *and so on,* Cic.; **b,** *to fall to any one as an inheritance* or *possession, to fall to the share of;* urbes captae Aetolos sequerentur, Liv.; heredes monumentum ne sequeretur, Hor.; **c,** *to follow,* i.e., *to yield, to give way;* ipse (ramus) facilis sequetur, Verg. **II.** Fig., **A.** Gen., *to follow, follow after;* gloria virtutem tamquam umbra sequitur, Cic.; edictum, *the words of the edict,* Cic. **B.** Esp., **1,** *to follow a person's authority, example, opinion, to tread in the steps of, to agree to;* leges, Cic.; amicum, Cic.; liberi sequuntur patrem, *follow the rank of their father,* Liv.; **2,** *to strive after, aim at, seek to gain;* amicitiam fidemque populi Romani, Cic.; **3,** *to follow in discourse, ensue;* sequitur illa divisio, Cic.; sequitur ut doceam, Cic.; **4,** *to follow as a consequence, be the consequence of, be caused by;* moneo ne summa turpitudo sequatur, Cic.; poena quae illud scelus sequeretur, Cic.; esp., *to follow logically, be the logical consequence of,* gen. with ut and the subj.; si hoc enuntiatum verum non est, sequitur, ut falsum sit, Cic.; **5,** *to follow easily, come of itself;* non quaesitum esse numerum, sed secutum, Caes.

sĕra -ae, f. (root SER, whence 2. sero, series), *a moveable bar* or *bolt for fastening doors;* centum postibus addere seras, Ov.

Sĕrāpĭs (Sărāpĭs) -pis and -pĭdis, m. (Σεράπις, Σαράπις), *a deity of the Egyptians, in later times worshipped at Greece and at Rome.*

sĕrēnĭtas -ātis, f. (serenus), *clearness, serenity,* esp., *clear, bright, fair weather.* **I.** Lit., caeli, Cic. **II.** Fig., fortunae, Liv.

sĕrēno, 1. (serenus). **I.** *to make clear, serene, bright;* caelum, Verg. **II.** Fig., spem fronte, Verg.

sĕrēnus -a -um, *clear, bright, fair, serene.* **I. A.** Lit., caelum, Cic.; nox, Verg.; pelagus, Verg.; subst., **sĕrēnum** -i, n. *fair weather,* Plin.; aperta serena, Verg. **B.** Transf., **1,** *clear;* aqua, Mart.; vox, Pers.; **2,** act., *making bright, bringing fair weather;* Favonius, Plaut. **II.** Fig., *cheerful, tranquil, serene;* frons, Cic.

Sēres -um, m. (Σῆρες), *a people in eastern*

Asia, famous for their silken stuffs, the Chinese, hence, adj, **Sērĭcus** -a -um, *Chinese;* pulvillus, *silken*, Hor Subst, **Sērĭca** ōrum, n *silken garments*, Prop

1 **sĕresco**, 3 (serenus), *to become dry*, Lucr

2 **sēresco**, 3 (serum), *to turn to whey*, Plin

Sergĭus -a um, *name of a Roman gens, the most celebrated member of which was L Sergius Catilina, the head of a conspiracy suppressed in the consulship of Cicero*

1. **sērĭa** -ae, f *a large earthen jar for holding wine and oil*, Liv

2 **sērĭa**, v 1 serius

sērĭcātus -a -um (Seres), *clothed in silken garments*, Suet

Sērĭcus, v Seres

sĕrĭes, acc -em, abl e, genit and dat not found, f (root SER, whence 2 sero), *a row, succession, chain, series* **I.** Gen, **A.** Lit, juvenum, *dancing hand in hand*, Tib **B.** Fig, *a succession, series*, rerum, Cic, innumerabilis annorum, Hor **II.** Esp, *a line of descent, lineage*, digne vir hāc serie, Ov

sērĭo, v 1 **sērĭus.**

sērĭŏla -ae, f (dim of seria), *a small jar*, Pers

Sĕrīphus (-ŏs) -i, f (Σεριφος), *an island in the Aegean Sea, now Serfo or Serfanto* Adj, **Sĕrīphĭus** -a um, *Seriphian*, subst, **Sĕrīphĭus** ii, m *a Seriphian*

sĕris -idis, f (σερις), *a species of endive*, Plin

1 **sērĭus** -a um, *serious earnest* (used gen only of things, not of persons), res, Cic, with 2 supine, verba seria dictu, Hor Subst, **sērĭum** ii, n *earnestness, seriousness*, Plaut., hence, abl serio, *in earnest, earnestly, seriously*, serio audire, Liv, plur, seria, *serious things*, seria ac jocos celebrare, Liv, quam joca, seria, ut dicitur (sc agimus or aguntur), Cic

2 **sērĭŭs**, adv, v sero under serus

sermo ōnis, m (2 sero), *talk, conversation, discourse* **I.** Lit., **A.** Gen, 1, sermonem conferre cum aliquo, Cic, esse in sermone omnium, *the subject of every one's conversation*, Cic, jucundus mihi est sermo litterarum tuarum, Cic, 2, meton, *the subject of conversation*, Cataplus ille Puteolanus, sermo illius temporis, Cic **B.** Esp, 1, *learned conversation, discussion, dialogue*, sermonem cum aliquo habere de amicitia, Cic, 2, in writing or speaking, *a familiar, conversational style*, sermonis plenus orator, Cic, scribere sermoni propiora, Hor, hence, meton, a, in Horace, his *Letters* and *Satires* as opposed to his more ambitious poems, b, *spoken words, utterance*, multi et illustres et ex superiore et ex aequo loco sermones habiti, *utterances on the bench and in ordinary conversation*, Cic, 3, *the talk of the multitude about something, common talk, report, rumour*, vulgi, hominum, Cic **II.** Transf, 1, *manner of speaking, language, style, expression, diction*, sermo rusticus, urbanus, Liv; plebeius, Cic, sermonis error, Cic, 2, *language, dialect*, sermone debemus uti, qui natus est nobis, *our mother-tongue*, Cic, quae philosophi Graeco sermone tractavissent, *in the Greek language*, Cic

sermōcĭnātĭo ōnis, f (sermocinor), *a discussion, disputation, dialogue*, Quint

sermōcĭnātrix icis, f (sermocinor), *the art of conversation*, Quint

sermōcĭnor, 1 dep (sermo), *to converse, talk, discuss with any one* **I.** Gen, sermocinari cum isto diligenter, Cic **II.** Esp, *to hold a learned discourse or discussion*, Suet

sermuncŭlus i, m (dim of sermo), *a report, rumour, tittle tattle*, urbani malevolorum sermunculi, Cic

1 **sĕro**, sēvi, sătum, 3 (root SE-o, whence semen) **I.** *to sow, set, plant* **A.** 1, lit, oleam et vitem, Cic, frumenta, Caes, partic subst, **săta** ōrum, n *the sown fields, standing corn*, Verg, Liv, **2,** transf, *to beget, engender, bring forth*, genus humanum, Cic, partic, **sătus** a um, *sprung from, born of*, sato sanguine divum, Verg, matre satus terrā, Ov, Anchisā satus, *son of Anchises*, Verg, satus Nereide, *son of Thetis*, Ov, satae Peliā, *daughters of Pelias*, Ov **B.** Fig, *to plant, sow, spread abroad, disseminate, cause, occasion*, cum patribus certamina, Liv, discordias Liv, crimina, Liv, mentionem, *to make mention of*, Liv, mores, Cic, diuturnam rempublicam, Cic **II.** *to plant, sow, sow over*, agrum, Ov, jugera sunt sata, Cic

2 **sĕro** (sĕrŭi), sertum, 3 (root SER, Gr ΕΡ-ω, εἴρω), *to join together, weave together, entwine* **I.** Lit, only in the partic perf, **sertus** -a -um, loricae, *linked*, Nep **II.** Fig, *to join together, connect, combine*, ex aeternitate causa causam serens, Cic, fati lege immobilis rerum humanarum ordo seritur, Liv, fabulam argumento, Liv, colloquia cum hoste, Liv, multa inter sese vario sermone serebant, Verg

3 **sēro**, v serus

sērōtĭnus a um (3 sero), *late*, hiems, Plin

serpens -entis, c (serpo), *an animal that crawls* **I.** *a snake, serpent* **A.** Lit, Cic **B.** *a constellation in the northern hemisphere* (also called Draco and Anguis), Ov **II.** *a creeping insect on the human body, louse*, Plin

serpentĭgĕna ae, c (serpens and gigno), *offspring of a serpent*, Ov

serpentĭpes pedis (serpens and pes), *snake-footed*, Ov

serpĕrastra ōrum, n (sirpo *to bind*), *bandages or knee splints for straightening the crooked legs of children*, Varr, in jest, of officers who keep their soldiers in order, Cic

serpillum = serpyllum (q v)

serpo, serpsi, serptum 3 (ἕρπω), *to creep, crawl*. **I. A.** Lit, of animals, quaedam bestiae serpentes, quaedam gradientes, Cic, serpere per humum, Ov **B.** Transf, of any slow and imperceptible motion, vitis serpens multiplici lapsu et erratico, Cic, flamma per continua serpens, Liv, et (Ister) tectis in mare serpit aquis, Ov **II** Fig, **A** Gen of prosaic poetry, serpit humi tutus, Hor **B.** Esp, *to spread abroad, increase, extend imperceptibly*, serpit hoc malum longius quam putatis, Cic, si paullatim haec consuetudo serpere ac prodire coeperit, Cic, serpit hic rumor, foll by acc and infin, Cic

serpyllum (serpillum) and **serpullum** -i, n (ἕρπυλλον), *wild thyme* (Thymus serpyllum, Linn), Verg

serra -ae, f (sec ra, from seco = *that which cuts*), *a saw* **I.** Gen, Cic **II.** Transf, *a kind of saw fish*, Plin

serrăcum (sarrăcum) i, n **I.** *a kind of waggon used by the Roman peasants to carry their goods and families in*, Juv **II.** Transf, *a constellation, the Wain*, Juv

serrātŭla ae, f *betony*, Plin

serrātus a um (serra), *toothed like a saw, serrated*, dentes, Plin Subst, **serrāti** ōrum, m (sc nummi), *silver denarii notched on the edge*, Tac

serrŭla -ae, f (dim of serra) *a little saw*, Cic

serta, v sertum

Sertōrius -ii, m., Q., *a celebrated Roman general of the Marian faction, who, on Sulla gaining the upper hand in Rome, fled to Spain, and resisted there bravely and successfully till he was treacherously killed by Perperna.* Adj., **Sertōriānus** -a -um, *Sertorian.*

sertŭm -i, n., gen. plur., **serta** -ōrum, n., and **serta** -ae, f. (sero), *a garland of flowers;* sertis redimiri, Cic.; serta Campanica, and simply serta, *a plant* = melilotos, Cato.

1. **sĕrum** -i, n. **I.** *the watery part of curdled milk, whey,* Verg. **II.** *the watery part or serum of other things,* Plin.

2. **sērum,** v. serus.

sērus -a -um. **I.** *late.* **A.** Gen., gratulatio, Cic.; hora serior, Ov.; si hiems magis sera (= serior), Liv.; subst., **sērum** -i, n., rem in serum trahere, *to retard,* Liv.; serum diei, *late in the day, evening,* Liv.; abl., sero, adv. = *late,* Cic.; esp., *late = in the evening,* Cic.; compar., serius, *later;* biduo serius, Cic.; spe omnium serius (id bellum fuit), Liv.; serius ocius, *sooner or later,* Hor. **B.** Esp., **1,** *late in being fulfilled;* spes, Liv.; portenta, Cic.; **2,** *doing something late;* serus abi, *go late away,* Ov.; with genit., o seri studiorum! *late learned* (ὀψιμαθεῖς), Hor.; **3,** *aged, old;* platanus, Ov.; ulmus, Verg.; **4,** *lasting a long time;* bellum, Ov. **II.** *too late;* kalendae, Cic.; bellum, Sall.; sera assurgis, Verg.; abl., sero, adv. = *too late,* Cic.; prov., sero sapiunt (sc. Phryges, i.e., Trojani), Cic.; compar., serius, *somewhat too late;* venire, Cic.

serva, v. servus.

servābĭlis -e (servo), *that can be saved,* Ov.

servans -antis, p. adj. only in superl. (servo), *observing;* servantissimus aequi, Verg.

servātor -ōris, m. (servo), *a preserver, saviour;* reipublicae, Cic.; salutis, Ov.

servātrix -īcis, f. (servator), *she that preserves, a preserver, saviour,* Cic.

servīlis -e (servus), *of or relating to a slave, slavish, servile;* vestis, Cic.; tumultus, *a servile insurrection,* Cic.; terror, *dread of an insurrection of slaves,* Liv.

servīlĭtĕr, adv. (servilis), *slavishly, servilely;* ne quid serviliter muliebriterve faciamus, Cic.

Servīlĭus -a -um, *name of a Roman gens, the most celebrated members of which were:* **1,** C. Servilius Ahala, *who as magister equitum killed Maelius;* **2,** P. Servilius Rullus, *composer of the lex Servilia concerning the selling of the Italian public lands, against which Cicero delivered his agrarian speeches;* **3,** Servilia, *mother of Brutus, mistress of Caesar.* Adj., *Servilian;* lex, Cic.; lacus, *a piece of artificial water near the Capitol, where the heads of the proscribed were put up,* Cic.

servĭo -īvi and -ĭi -ītum, 4. (servus), *to serve, be a servant or slave.* **I. A.** Lit., alicui, Ter.; apud aliquem, Cic.; with cognate acc., servitutem, Cic. **B.** Transf., of things, **a,** of land, buildings, etc., *to be subject to certain rights of other persons than the owner, to be subject to an easement,* Caes.; (aedes) serviebant, Cic.; **b,** *to serve, be useful, serviceable for;* chartis serviunt calami, Plin. **II.** Fig., **1,** *to subserve, assist, comply with, accommodate, gratify;* alicui, Cic.; amori aliorum, Cic.; iracundiae, Cic.; **2, a,** *to care for, have regard to, devote one's attention to;* brevitati, Cic.; **b,** *to adapt oneself to, to allow oneself to be governed by;* incertis rumoribus, Caes.; tempori, Cic.

servĭtĭum -ii, n. (servus). **I.** *slavery, service, servitude, subjection;* ducere aliquem in servitium, Liv., civitatem a servitio abstrahere, Cic.; animi imperio, corporis servitio magis utimur, *the mind is the master, the body the slave,* Sall. **II.** Meton., *slaves, servants, a household of slaves;* used both sing. and plur., servitia sileant, Cic.; servitia concitare, Cic.; servitium in scaenam immissum, Cic.

servĭtrīcĭus -a -um (servus), *belonging to a slave,* Plaut.

servĭtūdo -inis, f. (servus), *slavery, servitude,* Liv.

servĭtus -ūtis, f. (servus), *the condition of a slave, slavery, servitude.* **I. A.** Lit., both of individuals and states, diutina, Cic.; perpetua, Caes.; aliquem in servitutem abducere, Cic.; addicere aliquem in servitutem, Cic., perpetuae servituti, Caes.; anteponere mortem servituti, Cic.; esse in servitute, *to be a slave,* Cic. **B.** Transf., **1,** *subjection, obedience;* of the wife towards the husband, muliebris, Liv.; officii, Cic.; **2,** of houses, lands, etc., *liability to certain burdens, easements,* e.g., a right of way, fundo servitutem imponere, Cic. **II.** Meton., *slaves;* servitus crescit nova (of the lovers of a maiden), Hor.

Servĭus -ii, n. (servus, *son of a slave*), *a Roman praenomen occurring in the name of the king Servius Tullius and in the Sulpician gens,* v. Sulpicius.

servo, 1. (root SERV, connected with 'ΕΡΥ-ω, ἐρύομαι). **I.** *to keep, preserve, save, rescue, deliver.* **A.** Gen., **1,** of concrete objects, populum, Cic.; aliquem ex judicio, Cic.; with double acc., se integros castosque, Cic.; **2,** of abstract objects, *to observe, pay heed to, keep;* ordinem, Liv.; ordines, Caes.; concentum, Cic.; amicitiam, Cic.; legem, Cic.; pacem cum aliquo, Cic.; fidem juris jurandi cum hoste, Cic.; foll. by ut or ne and the subj., quum ita priores decemviri servassent, ut unus fasces haberet, Liv. **B.** Esp., *to keep for the future, to lay up, keep, preserve, reserve;* Caecuba centum clavibus, Hor.; se ad tempora, Cic.; se ad majora, Liv.; eo me servavi, Cic.; with dat., res judicio voluntatique alicuius, Cic. **II.** Transf., **A.** *to give regard to, pay attention to, watch;* **1,** gen., me omnibus servat modis ne, etc., Plaut.; sidera, *to observe,* Verg.; ortum Caniculae, Cic.; servare de caelo, *to observe lightning* (the duty of the augurs), Cic.; *to keep watch;* cetera servabant atque in statione manebant, Ov.; **2,** esp., **a,** *to take care, take precautions;* servarent ne qui nocturni coetus fierent, Liv.; serva, *take care,* Hor.; **b,** *to watch, keep, detain, preserve;* (α) aliquem liberā custodiā, Cic.; limen, *stay at home,* Verg.; (β) *to dwell, remain in a place, inhabit;* silvas et flumina, Verg. **B.** *to keep, preserve;* quum populus suum servaret, Cic.

servŭlus (servŏlus) -i, m. (dim. of servus), *a young slave,* Cic.

servus -i, m. and **serva** -ae, f. *a slave, servant;* servi publici, *slaves of the state,* Cic.; Transf., servi cupiditatum, Cic.; legum, Cic. Hence, adj., **servus** -a -um, *servile, slavish;* **a,** gen., aqua, *drunk by slaves,* Cic.; civitas, Liv.; imitatorum servum pecus, Hor.; **b,** legal t. t., of lands or buildings, *subject to right of other persons than the owner, subject to a servitude or easement;* praedia serva, Cic.

sēsămĭnus -a -um (σησάμινος), *made of sesame,* Plin.

sēsămŏīdes -is, n. (σησαμοειδές), *a plant like sesame,* Plin.

sēsămum (-on) -i, n., **sīsămum** -i, n. and **sēsăma** -ae, f. (σήσαμον), *an oily plant, sesame,* Plaut.

sescennāris -e (sesqui and annus), *a year and a half old;* bos, Liv.

sescŭplus -a -um (sesqui), *one and a half times as much,* Quint.

sĕsĕlis -is, f. (σέσελις), *a plant, hartwort,* Cic.

Sĕsostrĭs -trĭdis and **Sĕsōsĭs** -sĭdis, m (Σεσωστρις), *a mythical king of Egypt.*

sesquĭ, adv. num (semis and qui), *one half more, half as much again*, sesqui major, Cic

sesquĭalter and syncop **sesqualter** -altera -alterum (Gr. ἐπιδευτερος), *one and a half*, Cic

sesquĭhōra -ae, f. *an hour and a half*, Plin

sesquĭjūgĕrum -i, n *an acre and a half*, Plin.

sesquĭlībra -ae, f *a pound and a half*, Cato

sesquĭmensis -is, m *a month and a half*, Varr

sesquĭmŏdĭus ii, m *a modius and a half*, Cic

sesquĭŏbŏlus i, m *an obolus and a half*, Plin

sesquĭoctāvus a -um, *containing* $\frac{9}{8}$ *of a thing*, Cic

sesquĭŏpus -ĕris, n *the work of a day and a half*, Plaut

sesquĭpĕdālis -e, *a foot and a half long*, tigna, Caes, hence, poet., *very long*, dentes, Cat., verba, Hor

sesquĭpĕdānĕus = sesquipedalis (q v)

sesquĭpēs -pĕdis, m *a foot and a half*, Plaut

sesquĭplāga ae, f *a blow and a half*, Tac.

sesquĭplex -plĭcis, *taken one and a half times*, Cic

sesquĭtertĭus a -um, *containing* $\frac{4}{3}$ *of any thing*, Cic

sessĭbŭlum -i, n (sedeo), *a seat, stool, chair* Plaut.

sessĭlis -e (sedeo), *fit for sitting upon* **I.** Pass, tergum (equi), Ov **II.** Act, of plants, *low, dwarf, spreading*, Plin

sessĭo ōnis, f (sedeo) **I. 1**, *sitting, the act of sitting;* status, incessio, sessio, Cic, sessiones quaedam (*postures in sitting*) contra naturam sunt, Cic, **2**, esp, **a**, *a sitting idle, loitering in a place*, Capitolina, Cic, **b**, *a sitting, session for discussion*, pomeridiana, Cic **II.** Meton, *a place for sitting, seat*, Cic

sessĭto, 1 (intens of sedeo) *to sit much, sit always*, quam deam (Suadam) in Periclı labris scripsit Eupolis sessitavisse, Cic

sessĭuncŭla -ae, f (dim of sessio), *a little company or assembly for conversation*, Cic

sessor ōris, m (sedeo) **I.** *one who sits, a sitter*, Hor **II.** *an inhabitant, dweller*, urbis, Nep

sestertĭus -a -um (semis tertius), *two and a half*, **sestertĭus** ii, m, and in full, sestertius nummus, genit plur sestertium nummûm, and simply sestertiûm and sestertiorum *a sesterce* **A.** *a silver coin*, in the time of the Republic = ¼ *denarius* = 2½ *asses* (= about 2½d), Cic, **1**, lit, sestertii duodeni, Cic; genit plur, sestertiûm (sc mille), treated as a neut noun, and so declined, = 1,000 *sesterces*, decies sestertiûm (sc. centena milia) = *a million sesterces*, centies sestertiûm = *ten million sesterces*, Cic, millies sestertiûm = 100 *millions*, Cic, **2**, transf, nummo sestertio or sestertio nummo, *for a mere trifle* nummo sestertio or sestertio nummo alicui addici, Cic **B.** In Imperial times, *a copper coin of the value of* 4 asses, Plin

Sestus (Sestŏs) -i, f (Σηστός), *a town in Thrace on the Hellespont, residence of Hero*, now, perhaps, *Jalova* Adj, **Sestus** -a um, *Sestian*, puella, *Hero*, Ov

set = sed (q v)

sēta (saeta) -ae, f **I.** *a bristle, stiff hair*, of pigs, Ov, seta equina, *horsehair*, Cic., of goats, cows, lions, Verg, of coarse, bristly, human hair Verg **II.** Meton, *part of an angler s line*, Ov

sētānĭa -ae, f and **sētānĭon** ii, n (σητανια) **I.** *a species of medlar*, Plin **II.** *a kind of onion*, Plin

sētĭgĕr (saetĭgĕr) -gĕra -gĕrum (seta and gero), *having bristles, bristly*, sus, Verg, subst., **sētĭgĕr** gĕri, m *a boar*, Ov

sētōsus (saetōsus) a -um (seta), *full of bristles, bristly*, aper, Verg

seu = sive (q v)

sĕvērē, adv with compar and superl (severus), *seriously, gravely, austerely, severely*, Cic

sĕvērĭtas -ātis, f (severus), *gravity, seriousness, severity austerity, sternness, strictness* censorum, censoria, Cic, severitatem in filio adhibere, Cic., severitatem adhibere reipublicae causā, Cic

sĕvērĭtūdo inis, f = severitas (q v)

1 **sĕvērus** a -um, *grave, serious, strict, rigid, stern, austere, severe* **I.** In a good sense **A.** Lit, **1**, of persons, Tubero vitā severus, Cic, familia quum ad ceteras res tum ad judicandum severissima, Cic, **2**, of things, frons, Ov, congressio, Cic, subst, **a**, **sĕvērus** i, m *a grave, serious man*, Hor, **b**, **sĕvēra** ōrum, n *serious things*, Hor **B.** Transf, Falernum (vinum), *harsh*, Hor, amnis Eumenidum or Cocyti, *awful*, Hor **II** In a bad sense, *hard, cruel*, **a**, lit, Neptunus saevus severusque, Plaut, turba Eumenidum, Prop, **b**, transf, uncus, Hor

2 **Sĕvērus** i, m *a Roman family name, the most celebrated persons bearing which were* **1**, Cornelius Severus, *epic poet in the time of Augustus, friend of Ovid*, **2**, L Septimius Severus, *emperor* 193 211 A D, **3**, Aurelius Alexander Severus, *emperor* 222 234 A D

3 **Sĕvērus** mons, *a mountain in the Sabine country, a branch of the Apennines*, now *Vissa*

sēvŏco, 1 *to call aside, call away* **I.** Lit, singulos, Caes, plebem in Aventinum, Cic **II.** Fig, *to call off, call away, separate*, animum a voluptate, Cic

sēvum, etc = sebum, etc. (q v).

sex, numer (ἕξ), *six*, Cic, sex septem, *six or seven*, Hor

sexāgēnārĭus -a -um (sexageni), *containing the number sixty*, and esp, *sixty years old*, Quint.

sexāgēni -ae a, genit -ēnûm (sexaginta), *sixty each*, Cic

sexāgēsĭmus -a -um (sexaginta), *the sixtieth*, Cic

sexāgĭēs (sexāgĭens), adv (sexaginta), *sixty times*, sestertium sexagies, *six millions of sesterces*, Cic, so simply sexagiens, Cic

sexāginta, num (ἑξήκοντα) **I.** *sixty*, Cic. **II.** = *very many*, Mart

sexangŭlus -a -um, *hexagonal*, Ov.

sexcēnārĭus a -um (sexceni), *consisting of six hundred*, cohortes, Caes

sexcēni (sescēni) ae a (sexcenti), *six hundred each*, Cic

sexcentēni = sexceni (q v)

sexcentēsĭmus a -um (sexcenti), *the six hundredth*, Cic

sexcenti -ae -a (sex and centum) **I.** *six hundred*, Cic **II.** To denote an indefinite round number = *countless*, epistolae, Cic

sexcentĭēs (sexcentĭens), adv (sexcenti), *six hundred times*, Cic.

sexcentŏplāgus -i, m. (sexcenti and plaga), *one who receives innumerable stripes*, Plaut.

sexdĕcim = sedecim (q.v.).

sexennis -e (sex and annis), *six years old*, Plaut.

sexennium -ii, n. (sexennis), *a period of six years*, Cic.

sexiēs (sexiens), adv. (sex), *six times*, Cic.

sexprīmi -ōrum, m. *the six highest magistrates in colonies and municipia*, Cic.

sextādĕcimāni -ōrum, m. (sextusdecimus), *soldiers of the 16th legion*, Tac.

sextans -antis, m. (sex), *the sixth part of an as*, Varr.; esp., **a**, as a coin, *two unciae*, Liv.; **b**, *the sixth part of an inheritance*; in sextante sunt ii, quorum pars, etc., Cic.; **c**, *the sixth part of a pound*, Ov., **d**, *of an acre*, Varr., **e**, *of a sextarius*, Mart.

sextantārius -a -um (sextans), *containing a sixth part*; asses sextantario pondere, *weighing only one-sixth of the former asses*, Plin.

sextāriŏlus -i, m. (dim. of sextarius), *a small liquid measure*, Suet.

sextārius -ii, m. (sextus), *the sixth part*. **I.** In liquid measure, *the sixth part of a congius* (about a pint), Cic. **II.** As a dry measure, *the sixteenth part of a modius*, Plin.

Sextīlis -is, m. (sextus), mensis, or simply Sextilis, *the sixth month of the Roman year* (reckoning from March), afterwards called *August*; kalendae Sextiles, *the 1st of August*, Cic.

Sextius (Sestius) -a -um, *name of a Roman gens, the most famous members of which were*: **1**, L. Sextius, *tribune of the people, the author of a law enacting that one of the consuls should always be a plebeian*; **2**, P. Sextius, *tribune of the people, who proposed the recall of Cicero from exile*. Adj., *Sextian*: lex, *the above-mentioned law of L. Sextius*; tabula, *of a banker named Sextius*, Cic.; esp., Aquae Sextiae, *Roman colony near Massilia, founded by C. Sextius Calvinus*, 123 B.C., now *Aix*. Hence, adj., **Sextiānus (Sestiānus)** -a -um, *Sextian*.

sextŭla -ae, f. (sc. pars, from sextulus, dim. of sextus), *the sixth part of an uncia, therefore* 1-72*nd of an as*, Varr.; 1-72*nd part of an inheritance*, Cic.

sextus -a -um (sex). **I.** *the sixth*, Cic.; adv., **sextum**, *for the sixth time*; sextum consul, Cic. **II.** Sextus, *a Roman name*.

sextusdĕcĭmus -a -um, *sixteenth*, Cic.

sexus -ūs, m. (another form of secus), *the male or female sex*; **a**, of men, hominum genus et in sexu consideratur, virile an muliebre sit, Cic.; **b**, of animals, Plin.; **c**, of plants, minerals, etc., Plin.

si, conj. (εἰ). **I.** A particle expressing condition, *if, in case that*; foll. by both indic. and subj. **A.** Gen., numquam labere, si te audies, Cic.; si minus, *if not*, Cic.; quod si, *and if, but if*, Cic. **B.** Esp., **a**, to confirm or explain or justify what has gone before, *if only, provided that*; delectus habetur, si hic delectus appellandus, Cic.; bellum vobis indictum est, magno eorum malo, qui indixere, si viri estis, Liv.; **b**, in wishes, *if only*; si nunc se ostendat, Verg.; **c**, in comparisons, *as if, just as if*; with subj., Cic., Liv.; **d**, to express a concession, *even if*; si omnes deos hominesque celare possumus, Cic. **II.** In indirect questions and dependent clauses, *whether, if*; conati, si possent, etc., Cic.; dicito, si etc., Cic.; castra movet, si . . . posset, *to try whether*, etc., Liv.

sībĭlo, 1. (sibilus). **I.** Intransit., *to hiss*; of snakes, Verg.; anguis sibilat, Ov.; transf., of red-hot iron plunged into water; in tepida submersum sibilat unda, Ov. **II.** Transf., *to hiss at, hiss down*; aliquem, Cic.

1. **sībĭlus** -i, m. (plur., sibili, and in poets, sibila), *a hissing, whistling, rustling*; austri, Verg.; of persons, *whistling*; sibilo signum dare, Liv.; esp., *a contemptuous hissing*; sibilum metuis? Cic.; sibilis conscindi, Cic.; sibilis aliquem explodere, Cic.

2. **sībĭlus** -a -um, *hissing*; colla (of a snake), Verg.; ora, Verg.

Sĭbylla -ae, f. (Σίβυλλα, from Σιὸς (= Διὸς) βουλή, *God's counsel*), *a prophetess and priestess of Apollo, a Sibyl*; *in the Roman mythol.*, esp., *the Sibyl of Cumae whom Aeneas consulted*; *another Sibyl of Cumae was said to have composed the Sibylline books, which were bought by Tarquin from an old woman, and kept in the Capitol, and consulted in time of danger*.

Sĭbyllīnus -a -um, *of or relating to the Sibyl, Sibylline*; libri, Cic.; vaticinatio, Cic.

sīc (from root i (whence is and ita), with the spirant prefixed and the demonstrative suffix -ce added, si-ce, which became sic), *so, thus, in this manner*. **I.** Gen., **a**, sive enim sic est, sive illo modo, Cic.; illa civitas popularis (sic enim appellant) in qua in populo sunt omnia, Cic.; **b**, to introduce something that follows, *thus, as follows*; ingressus est sic loqui Scipio, Cic.; esp., with acc. and infin., sic velim existimes, te nihil gratius facere posse, Cic.; **c**, in affirmative answers, sic est, etc.; sic plane judico, Cic. **II.** Esp., **A.** In comparisons, *so, as*; gen. corresponding to ut, more rarely to quemadmodum, tamquam, quasi, etc., Atticum sic amo, ut alterum fratrem, Cic.; quemadmodum . . . sic, Cic.; sic . . . tanquam, Cic.; sic . . . quasi, Cic.; in wishes, *so*; sic tua Cyrneas fugiant examina taxos, Verg. **B.** *of such a kind, of such a nature*; sic est vulgus; ex veritate pauca, ex opinione multa, existimant, Cic. **C. a**, *in such circumstances, in such a manner, so, and thus*; sic ad supplicium Numitori Remus deditur, Liv.; **b**, *consequently, in consequence*; quia non est obscura tua in me benevolentia, sic fit ut, etc., Cic. **D.** To express limitation or condition, *so* = *on condition that, in so far as*; gen. corresp. with ut, recordatione amicitiae sic fruor, ut beate vixisse videar, Cic.; sic . . . si, *then . . . if, only if*; decreverunt, id sic ratum esset, si patres auctores fierent, Liv. **E.** To express degree, *so much, to such a degree*; often foll. by ut, Caecinam a puero semper sic dilexi ut non ullo cum homine conjunctius viverem, Cic. **F.** To express carelessness, indifference, *thus, simply*; sic nudos (*naked as they are*) in flumen projicere, Cic.

sīca -ae, f. (seco). **I.** *a dagger, dirk, poniard*; maximus sicarum numerus et gladiorum, Cic. **II.** Meton., *assassination, murder*; hinc sicae, venena, falsa testamenta nascuntur, Cic.

Sĭcāni -ōrum, m. *a people of Celtic origin who originally inhabited the banks of the Tiber, and thence migrated to Sicily*. Hence, **A.** Adj., **Sĭcānus** -a -um, *Sicanian*, poet. = *Sicilian*. **B. Sĭcānius** -a -um, *Sicanian*, poet. = *Sicilian*. **C. Sĭcānis** -idis, f. adj., *Sicanian*, poet. = *Sicilian*. **D.** Subst., **Sĭcānia** -ae, f. *Sicania* = *Sicily*.

sīcārius -ii, m. (sica), *an assassin, murderer*; accusare aliquem inter sicarios, *of murder*, Cic.

Sicca -ae, f., Veneria, *an important town in Numidia, on the Bagradas, with a temple to Venus*, now *Keff*. Hence, **Siccenses** -ium, m. *the inhabitants of Sicca*.

siccānus -a -um (siccus), *dry*, Plin.

siccātĭo -ōnis, f (sicco), *a drying*, Plin

siccē, adv (siccus), *drily*, fig, of discourse, dicere *plainly, vigorously*, Cic

siccesco, 3 (siccus), *to become dry*, Plin

siccinĕ (sīcĭnĕ or **sīcin')**, adv (sic ce), interrog particle, *is it thus? thus? so?* Cat

siccĭtas -ātis, f (siccus) **I.** *dryness*, **a**, lit., paludum, Caes **b**, meton, *dryness of weather, drought*, Cic **II.** Transf, *freedom from humours, firm health*, **a**, lit, Cic, **b**, fig, of discourse, *plainness, simplicity, dryness* orationis, Cic

sicco, 1 (siccus), *to make dry, to dry* **I.** Transf, **A** Gen vellera, Verg, herbas, Ov, esp, *to dry up water or soil*, paludes, Cic **B.** **a**, *to drain dry, to drink up, empty*, calices, Hor, **b**, *to milk*, ovem, Ov, **c**, *to suck dry*, ubera, Verg **II.** Intransit and impers, siccat, *it dries up*, Cat

siccŏcŭlus -a -um (siccus and oculus), *having dry eyes*, Plaut

siccus -a um, *dry* **I. A.** Lit, **1**, gen, lignum, Verg, subst, **siccum** -i, n *the dry land*, in sicco hibernare, Liv, **2**, esp, **a**, *without tears, tearless*, oculi, Hor, **b**, *dry, thirsty*, siccus, inanis, Hor, poet, dies = *hot, thirsty*, Hor, meton, *temperate, abstinent*, Cic, **c**, *fasting, a poor starving wretch*, accedes siccus ad unctum, Hor, **d**, *bright, cloudless*, Prop **e**, *bright, rainless*, fervores, Ov **B** Fig, *dry, cold, impassive*, puella, Ov **II** Transf, **A** Of the body, *free from humours, in sound, vigorous health*, corpora, Plin **B.** Of discourse, *plain, simple*, oratio, Cic

sīcĕlĭcon -i, n (Σικελικόι), *the plant flea wort*, Plin

Sĭcĭlĭa ae, f (Σικελία), *the island of Sicily* Hence, **A. Sĭcĕlis** -idis, f *Sicilian* **B. Sĭcĭliensis** e, *Sicilian*

sĭcĭlĭcŭla -ae, f (dim of sicilis), *a small sickle*, Plaut

sīcĭlīcus -i, m (sicilis), **a**, *the 4th part of an uncia, and therefore 1 48th of an as*, **b**, *a quarter of an inch*, Plin, **c**, *1 48th of an hour*, Plin

sīcĭlĭo, 4 (sicilis), *to cut or mow with the sickle*, Plin

sīcĭlis is, f (seco), *a sickle*, Plin

Sĭcŏris is, m *a tributary of the Hiberus in Spain*, now *Segre*

sīcŭbī, adv (= si alicubi), *if anywhere*, Cic

Sĭcŭli -ōrum, m *a people of Celtic origin, akin to the Sicani, who settled on the coast of Italy, but were afterwards compelled to migrate to Sicily*, hence, transf, *the inhabitants of Sicily, the Sicilians*, Cic sing, **Sĭcŭlus** -i, m *a Sicilian*, Cic, hence, **Sĭcŭlus** a -um, *Sicilian*, tyrannus *Phalaris*, Ov

sīcundĕ, adv (= si alicunde), *if from anywhere*, Cic

sīcŭt and **sīcŭtī**, adv *as, just as* **I.** Gen, **a**, with a verb, sicut sapiens poeta dixit, Cic, foll by ita, itidem, sic, sicuti ita, Liv; sicuti sic, Caes, sicuti ita, Caes, **b**, without a verb, sicut apud nos, Cic, viri in uxores, sicut in liberos potestatem, Caes, foll by ita, sicuti in foro, item in theatro, Cic **II.** Esp, **1**, *inasmuch as*, sicuti cras aderit, hodie non venerit, Plaut, **2**, sicut est, sicut erat, *as the case really is, in fact*, quamvis felix sit, sicuti est, Cic, **3**, in a comparison, **a**, *as it were*, hic locus sicut aliquod fundamentum est huius constitutionis, Cic, **b**, *just as if*, sicuti foret lacessitus, Sall, **4**, to add an example, *as, as for example*, quibus in causis omnibus, sicuti in ipsa M Curii, Cic, **5**, to express a state or condition, *just as*, sicut eram, fugio, Ov

Sĭcyōn -ōnis, m and f (Σικυών), *a city of Peloponnesus*, hence, adj **Sĭcyōnĭus** -a -um, *Sicyonian*, calcei, Cic, and subst **Sĭcyōnĭa** ōrum, n *a kind of soft shoes from Sicyon*, Lucr

Sīda -ae, f (Σίδη), *a town in Pamphylia, west of the river Meles, now Eski-Adalia* Hence, **Sīdētae** -ārum, m *the inhabitants of Sida*

sīdĕrālis -e (sidus) *of or relating to the stars*, Plin

sīdĕrātĭo -ōnis, f (sideror), *a blast, blight upon plants, supposed to be produced by the influence of the stars*, Plin

sīdĕrĕus a um (sidus), *of or belonging to the stars, starry* **I.** Lit, **a**, caelum, *starry*, Ov, ignes, *the stars*, Ov, Canis, *the Dog star*, Ov, dea = Nox, Prop, conjux, *Ceyx* (as son of Lucifer), Ov **b**, esp, *of or relating to the sun, solar*, ignes, Ov, lux, Ov **II.** Transf, *gleaming, glittering*, clipeus, Verg

sīdērĭon ii, n (σιδήριον), *the plant vervain*, Plin

sīdērītes -ae, m (σιδηρίτης) = sideritis (q v)

sīdērītis is, f (σιδηρῖτις) **I.** *a stone*, **a**, *a magnet*, Plin, **b**, *a kind of diamond*, Plin **II.** *a plant, vervain*, Plin

sīdĕror, 1 (sidus) = sidere afflari, *to suffer from a sun-stroke, be planet-struck*, Plin

Sĭdĭcīni -ōrum, m *a people of Campania, whose chief town was Teanum* Hence, adj, **Sĭdĭcīnus** a um, *Sidicine*

sīdo, sidi and sēdi, sessum, 3 (ἵζω), *to sit down, settle, alight* **I** Lit, of living creatures, columbae super arbore sidunt, Verg, immo sessum? Cic **II** Transf, of inanimate things **A.** Gen, *to sink down, settle* orta ex lacu nebula campo quam montibus densior sederat, Liv **B.** Esp, **1**, *to remain lying or fixed, to settle*, **a**, quum sederit glans, Liv, **b**, naut t t, *to stick fast, to be stranded*, ubi cymbae siderent, Liv, **2**, *to sink = to vanish, disappear*, Prop, Tac

Sīdon -ŏnis, f (Σιδών), *a city of Phoenicia* Hence, adj, **A. Sīdŏnĭus** a um, *Phoenician, Sidonian*, amor, *of Jupiter for Europa*, Mart, esp, of purple, ostrum, Ov, subst, **Sīdŏnĭi** ōrum, m *the Sidonians or Tyrians* **B. Sīdŏnĭcus** -a um, *Sidonian* **C. Sīdŏnis** -idis, f *Sidonian, Tyrian*, concha, *Tyrian purple*, Ov, tellus, *Phoenicia*, Ov, subst = *the Sidonian woman* Europa, Ov, Dido, Ov, Anna, *sister of Dido*, Ov

sīdus -ĕris, n *a group of stars, constellation*, sometimes used of a single star **I. A.** Lit., **a**, (α) sing, sidus Vergiliarum, Liv, sidus aetherium, Ov, (β) plur, illi sempiterni ignes, quae sidera et stellas vocatis, Cic, **b**, poet, sidera solis (of the sun itself), Ov **B.** Meton, **1**, sing, **a**, *the time of year*, hiberno sidere, *in winter*, Verg, mutato sidere, *at another time of the year*, Verg **b**, *the day*, brumale, *the shortest day*, Ov, **c**, *climate, regions*, tot sidera emensae, Verg, **d**, *weather*, grave sidus et imber, Ov, Minervae, *storm raised by Minerva*, Verg, **e**, *a star, as bringing disaster* (cf sideratio), haud secus quam pestifero sidere icti, Liv, **2**, plur, *the heavens*, ad sidera missus, Juv, ad sidera ferre, *to praise to the skies*, Verg, poma ad sidera nituntur, *grow up*, Verg, sub sidera lapsae, Verg, vertice sidera tangere, Ov, or ferire, Hor, *to touch the stars, to be elevated in happiness or prosperity beyond measure*, sub pedibus videt nubes et sidera, *is raised to heaven*, Verg **II.** Transf, **1.** of beautiful eyes, geminum, sua lumina, sidus, Ov , **2,** *pride, glory*, O sidus Fabiae, Maxime, gentis, Ov

Sĭgambri = Sugambri (q v)

Sīgēum -i, n (Σίγειον), *a promontory and port in Troas, where was the grave of Achilles,* now *Jenischer* Hence, **A. Sīgēus** -a -um, *Sigean* **B. Sīgēĭus** -a -um, *Sigean*

sĭgilla -ōrum, n (dim of signum), *small figures, images*, patella in qua sigilla erant egregia, Cic ; *statuettes* Cic., *figures cut upon a signet-ring*, Cic , and hence, *a seal*, Hor

Sĭgillārĭa -ōrum, abl -iis and ibus, n (sigilla) **I.** *a festival in Rome, at which little figures were exchanged as presents*, Suet **II.** *the little images thus used*, Sen **III.** *a place in Rome where such images were sold*, Suet

sĭgillātus -a -um (sigilla), *ornamented with small figures*, scyphi, Cic

sĭgillum, v sigilla

sigma ătis, n (σίγμα), *the Greek letter sigma*, and hence, *a semicircular dining-couch in the original shape of a capital sigma* (C), Mart

signātor -ōris, m (signo), *one who seals a document as a witness*, **a,** *the witness to a will*, Suet signatores falsi, *forgers of wills*, Sall , **b,** *the witness to a marriage contract*, Juv.

Signĭa -ae, f *a city in Latium*, now *Segni*. Hence, adj , **Signīnus** -a -um, *of* or *belonging to Signia*, opus, or simply subst., **Signīnum** -i, n *a kind of plaster for walls and pavements*, plur subst , **Signīni** -ōrum, m *the inhabitants of Signia*

signĭfĕr -fĕra -fĕrum (signum and fero), *bearing figures, adorned with figures* **I.** Gen , puppis, Lucan **II.** Esp , **A.** *bearing stars, covered with constellations*, aether, Lucr , orbis, *the zodiac*, Cic **B.** Subst , **signĭfĕr** -fĕri, m , milit t t , *a standard bearer*, Caes , Cic , transf , *a leader, head*, calamitosorum, Cic., juventutis, Cic

signĭfĭcābĭlis -e (significo), *significant, conveying a meaning*, vox, Varr

signĭfĭcans -antis, p adj (from significo), *graphic, distinct, clear*, Quint

signĭfĭcantĕr, adv (significans), *plainly, distinctly, clearly*, acrius, apertius, significantius dignitatem alicuius defendere, Cic

signĭfĭcantĭa -ae, f (significo), *expressiveness, energy, distinctness*, Quint

signĭfĭcātĭo -ōnis, f (significo) **I.** *a showing, pointing out, indicating, sign, token, indication*, **a,** absol , declarare aliquid significatione, Cic , **b,** with subject genit , litterarum, Cic , **c,** with object genit , virtutis, Cic , **d,** with acc and infin significatio fit non adesse constantiam, Cic **II.** Esp , **1,** *a sign of assent, approbation, applause*, significatio omnium, Cic , significatione florere, Cic , **2,** *a sign, prognostic of a change of weather*, Plin , **3,** *emphasis*, Cic ; **4,** *the meaning, signification of a word*, scripti, Cic

signĭfĭcātus -ūs, m (significo), *a sign, prognostic of a change of weather*, Plin

signĭfĭco, 1 (signum and facio), *to give a sign, indication, to indicate, notify* **I.** Gen , **a,** with acc , hoc mihi significasse et annuisse visus est, Cic , **b,** with acc. and infin , omnes significabant ab eo se esse admodum delectatos, Cic , **c,** with ut and the subj , ut statim dimitterentur, Caes , **d,** with rel sent , litterae neque unde neque quo die datae essent significabant, Cic , **e,** with de and the abl , de fuga, Caes **II.** Esp , **A.** *to indicate that which is to come*, **a,** futura, Cic , **b,** *to give signs of, indicate a change of weather*, Plin **B.** Of words, *to mean, signify*; uno verbo significari res duas, Cic.

Signīnus, v Signia

signo, 1 (signum), *to put a mark upon, mark, designate* **I.** Lit , **A.** Gen , humum limite, Ov , caeli regionem in cortice signant, *cut in, inscribe*, Verg , sonos vocis, Cic , humum pede certo, *to tread on*, Hor **B.** Esp , **1,** *to mark with a seal, seal, seal up*, libellum, Cic , volumina, Hor , arcanas tabellas, Ov., **2,** *to coin, stamp money*, argentum signatum, Cic , **3,** *to adorn*, honore, Verg. **II.** Fig , **A.** Gen , signatum memori pectore nomen habe, Ov **B.** Esp , **1,** *to signify, express*, ossa nomen (Cajeta) signat, Verg , **2,** *to observe, notice*, ora sono discordia, Verg

signum -i, n (perhaps connected with εἰκών, εἰκος), *a sign, mark, token* **I.** Gen , signa et notae locorum, Cic , signum imprimere pecori, Verg., signa pedum sequi, *to follow the footsteps*, Ov , signa doloris ostendere, Cic. **II.** Esp , **A.** Milit t t , **1,** *a standard, flag, banner*, **a,** of large divisions of an army, *the legion*, etc , signa relinquere, *to desert*, Sall , signa ferre, *to march away*, Caes , signa convelli jubere, *to give the signal for marching away*, Liv , signa inferre, *to attack*, Caes , signa conferre, (α) *to bring the standards together*, Caes , (β) *to fight*, cum Alexandrinis, Cic , **b,** of small divisions, of cohorts and maniples, Cic , hence, transf = *a small division of the army, company*, signa et ordines, Liv , **2, a,** *the signal, order, command given by the general*, signum pugnae proponere, Liv , signum tubā dare, Caes , **b,** *a watchword, pass-word*, it bello tessera signum, Verg **B.** *the sign* or *signal in the circus given by the praetor* or *consul for the races to begin*, signum mittendis quadrigis dare, Liv **C.** *a sign, token, indication of the future*, signum se objicit, Cic , medici signa habent ex venis, Cic **D.** *a sign = a proof*, hoc signi est, id signi est, or signum est with acc and infin , Cic **E.** *a figure, image, statue*, signum aeneum, marmoreum, Cic ; hence, **a,** *a seal, signet*, Cic., **b,** *a group of stars, constellation*, Cic

sīl, silis, f *a kind of yellow earth, ochre*, Plin.

Sīla ae, f *a forest in Bruttii*

sīlācĕus -a -um (sil), *like ochre*, color, Plin

sīlānus -i, m (Σιληνος), *a fountain* (frequently made to issue from the head of Silenus), Lucr

Sĭlărus i, m *a river in Lucania*, now *Sele*

silaus -i, m *a species of parsley*, Plin

sĭlens, v. sileo

sĭlentĭum -ii, n (sileo), *silence, stillness, quietness* **I.** Lit , **A.** Gen , audire aliquid magno silentio, Cic , silentium fieri jubere, Cic , animadvertere cum silentio, *to notice in silence*, Ter ; silentio praeterire, Cic , silentium noctis, *the stillness of night*, Caes , ruris, Ov **B.** Esp., **a,** *freedom from disturbance*, and hence, *completeness, perfectness in taking the auspices*, id silentium dicimus in auspiciis, quod omni vitio caret, Cic , **b,** *obscurity, ingloriousness*, laudem eorum a silentio vindicare, Cic **II.** Transf , *quiet, repose, inactivity*, judiciorum ac fori, Cic ; vitam silentio transire, Sall

Sīlēnus i, m (Σειληνός), *the tutor and attendant of Bacchus, represented with a bald head, as always drunk, and riding on an ass*

sĭlĕo -ŭi, 2 *to be still, noiseless, silent* **I.** Lit , **1,** of persons, **a,** absol , or with de and the abl , optimum quemque silere, Liv ; ceteri de nobis silent, Cic., partic , silens, *silent*, umbrae silentes (of the dead), Verg , subst., **sĭlentes,** *the silent*, (α) = *the dead*, rex silentum (Pluto), Ov , (β) *the Pythagoreans*, coetus silentum, Ov , **b,** with acc , *to be silent about*, tu hoc silebis, Cic , neque te silebo, Hor , in pass , res siletur, Cic ; partic subst , **silenda** ōrum, n *things to be silent about, secrets, mysteries*, Liv , **2,** of things silet aer, Ov , aequor, Verg , nox, Verg , with foll rel sent , si chartae sileant quod bene feceris, Hor , partic , **silens,** *quiet, still*, nox, Verg , agmen, Liv **II.** Transf , *to rest, to be inactive*, **a,** of persons, silent diutius Musae quam solebant, Cic **b,** of things, si quando ambitus sileat, Cic (partic pres in abl , gen silente , syncop genit plur , silentum, Verg , Ov).

sĭler -ĕris, n *a species of willow, the brook willow*, Verg

sĭlesco, 3 (inchoat of sileo), *to become silent, grow still*, Verg

sĭlex Icis, m (rarely f), *any hard stone, flint, granite, basalt*, esp as material for pavement **I.** Lit , certo in loco silicem caedere, Cic , vias in urbe silice sternere, Liv , as fig of cruelty or hardheartedness, dicam silices pectus habere tuum, Ov **II** Poet , transf , = scopulus, *rock, cliff*; acuta silex praecisis undique saxis, Verg

Sĭlĭānus, v Silius

sĭlĭcernĭum ii, n *a funeral feast*, Varr ; hence, transf , as a term of abuse applied to an infirm old man, Ter

sĭlĭcĭa ae, f *the plant fenugreek*, Plin

sĭlĭcŭla -ae, f (dim of siliqua), *a little pod or husk*, Varr

sĭlīgĭnĕus -a -um (siligo), *made of wheat, wheaten*, Plin

sĭlīgo -inis, f. **1,** *a kind of very white wheat* (Triticum hibernum, Linn), Plin , **2,** meton , *wheaten flour*, Juv

sĭlĭqua -ae, f *a husk, pod, shell*, Verg , plur , **sĭlĭquae** ārum, *pulse*, Hor

sĭlĭquor, 1 dep (siliqua), *to put forth or get pods*, Plin

Sĭlĭus -a -um, *name of a Roman gens* **1,** A Silius, *a friend of Cicero*, **2,** P Silius Nerva, *propraetor in Bithynia and Pontus*, 51 B C , **3,** C Silius Italicus, *an epic poet of the first century A D , author of an epic poem on the Punic War in seventeen books* Hence, **Sĭlĭānus** a -um, *relating to Silius*

sillȳbus = sittybos (q v)

sĭlphĭum -ii, n (σίλφιον) = laserpitium (q v)

Sĭlūres -um, acc -as, *a people in Britain, to the west of the Severn and the Avon*

sĭlūrus i, m (σίλουρος), *a species of river-fish*, prob *the sheat fish*, Juv

sīlus -a -um (σιλλός and σιλός) = simus, *flat-nosed, snub-nosed, pug-nosed*, Cic

silva (sylva) -ae, f (connected with ὕλη) *a wood, forest* **I. 1,** lit , **a,** silva densa, Cic , silvarum dea, *Diana*, Ov , **b,** *a plantation, a grove, a park*, signa in silva disposita, Cic , **2,** meton , **a,** *a quantity of shrubs or plants, underwood*, Verg , **b,** poet , *a tree or trees*, Verg , Ov **II.** Transf , **1,** *a dense mass or quantity*, immanem aerato circumfert tegmine silvam, *a dense mass of spears*, Verg , **2,** *plentiful supply, abundance*, virtutum et vitiorum, Cic , esp , of materials for speaking and writing, silva rerum, Cic , omnis ubertas et quasi silva dicendi, Cic (silŭae, trisyll in Hor)

Silvānus -i, m (silva), *a Latin god of forests and the country*, plur , Silvani, *gods of the forests and the country*

silvātĭcus a um (silva), **1,** *of or relating to a forest or wood*, Varr ; **2,** of plants and animals, *wild*, Plin

silvesco, 3 (silva), of a vine, *to run wild, to run to wood*, Cic.

silvester -tris -tre and gen **silvestris** e (silva) **I.** *belonging to a wood or forest*, **a,** *covered with trees, wooded, woody*, collis, Caes , locus, Cic , subst , **silvestria** -ium, n *woody places*, **b,** *living or being in the woods*, belua, Cic , homines, Hor , cursus, Cic **II.** Transf , **A.** *growing wild, wild*, oliva, Ov **B** *rural, pastoral*, Musa, Verg

Silvia, v 1 Rhea

silvĭcŏla -ae, c (silva and colo), *an inhabitant of the woods*, Verg

silvĭcultrix tricis, f (silva and colo), *inhabiting the woods*, Cat

silvĭfrăgus a -um (silva and frango), *shattering the woods*, Lucr

silvĭgĕr gĕra -gĕrum (silva and gero), *wooded, covered with forests*, montes, Plin

silvōsus -a -um (silva), *well wooded, abounding in forests*, saltus, Liv

Simbrŭvium -ii, n *a district in the country of the Aequi* Hence, **Simbrŭīnus** -a um, *relating to Simbruvium*

sīmĭa ae, f and **sīmĭus** -i, m (simus) *an ape, monkey*, Cic , used as a term of abuse of men, simius iste, Hor

sĭmĭla -ae, f *the finest wheaten flour*, Mart

sĭmĭlāgo = simila (q v)

sĭmĭlis -e (connected with simul, simulare), *like, resembling, similar*, **a,** with genit (nearly always so in Cicero when used of persons) fratris, hominis, Cic , simile veri, Cic , non est veri simile ut occiderit, Cic , mihi minus simile veri visum est, with acc and infin , Liv , compar , veri similius, Liv , similiores Atticorum, Cic , superl , simillimum veri, Cic , **b,** with dat , si similes Icilio tribunos haberet, Liv , quid simile habet epistola aut judicio aut contioni, Cic , compar., similius id vero fecit, Liv , superl , simillimus deo, Cic , **c,** with dat. and genit together, similis illi similis deorum, Cic , **d,** with inter se, homines inter se quum formā tum moribus similes, Cic , **e,** foll by atque, ut si, tamquam si, Cic , **f,** absol , minus, Cic Subst , **sĭmĭle** -is, n *a resemblance*, Cic

sĭmĭlĭtĕr, adv (similis), *in like manner, similarly*, foll by atque, ut si, Cic

sĭmĭlĭtūdo inis f (similis), *likeness, similitude, resemblance* **I. 1,** gen , est inter ipsos similitudo, Cic , est homini cum deo similitudo, Cic , veri similitudo, *probability*, Cic , plur , similitudines, concr , *similar things*, Cic , **2,** esp , **a,** *likeness in a portrait*, Cic , **b,** *a metaphor, simile*, Cic **II.** Transf , **1,** *a comparison, similitude*, Cic , **2,** *uniformity*, Cic

sĭmĭlo = simulo (q v)

sīmĭŏlus -i, m (dim of simius), *a little ape* (of a man), Cic

sĭmĭtū, adv , old form of simul (q v)

Sĭmŏis -mŏentis, m (Σιμόεις), *a small stream in Troas, falling into the Scamander*

Sĭmōnĭdes -is, m (Σιμωνίδης), *a lyric poet of Cos* Adj , **Sĭmōnĭdēus** -a um, *Simonidean*

simplex -plĭcis (sim = *simple*, cf sincerus, and plex, from plico), *simple, uncompounded, unmixed* **I.** Lit., **a,** natura animantis, Cic , aqua, *pure*, Ov , jus, Hor , **b,** *single, one*, simplici ordine urbem intrare, Liv , plus vice simplici, *more than once*, Hor **II.** Transf , **A.** a, *plain, simple, not complicated*, causa, Cic , genus mortis, *without torture*, Liv.; necessitudo, *unconditional*, Cic.; **b**, *natural, simple;* ratio veritatis, Cic. **B.** Esp., *morally simple, straightforward, upright, guileless;* animus apertus ac simplex, Cic.

simplĭcĭtas -ātis, f. (simplex). **I.** *simplicity, simpleness*, Lucr. **II.** *moral simplicity, straightforwardness, guilelessness, honesty, candour;* puerilis, Liv.; sermo antiquae simplicitatis, Liv.

simplĭcĭtĕr, adv. (simplex). **I. a**, *plainly, straightforwardly, directly;* defendere, Cic.; sententiam referre, Cic.; **b**, *simply, without art, artlessly;* loqui, Cic. **II.** Esp., *frankly, candidly, honestly*, Tac.

simplus -a -um (ἁπλοῦς), *simple.* Subst., **simplum** -i, n. *that which is single* (opp. duplum), Cic.

simpŭlum -i, n. *a ladle;* prov., excitare fluctus in simpulo, *to make a storm in a tea-cup, to make much ado about nothing*, Cic.

simpŭvĭum -ii, n. *a sacrificial vessel*, Cic.

sĭmŭl (archaic **sĕmŭl**), adv. (connected with ἅμα), *at once, at the same time as.* **I.** Gen., **a**, absol., venire, Cic.; simul commonefacere, Caes.; **b**, with cum, testamentum simul obsignavi cum Clodio, Cic.; **c**, with et, que, atque, simul et ostendi, Cic.; simul inflatus exacerbatusque, Liv.; simul honoribus atque virtutibus, Liv.; **d**, with abl., simul septemviris, Tac.; simul his dictis, Verg. **II.** Special phrases. **A.** simul . . . simul, *not only . . . but at the same time, partly . . . partly* (ἅμα μὲν . . . ἅμα δὲ); increpando simul temeritatem, simul ignaviam, Liv.; foll. by ut or ne and subj., by quod and indic. or subj., simul sui purgandi causā, simul ut, etc., Caes. **B.** simulatque (simulac), *as soon as;* **a**, simulatque cognitum est, Cic.; **b**, with ut, simul ut experrecti sumus, Cic.; **c**, simul alone (as a conj.), simul inflavit tibicen, Cic. **C.** (Like Gr. ἅμα) with partic. pres., simul hoc dicens, *while saying this*, Verg.

sĭmŭlācrum -i, n. (from simulo, as lavacrum from lavo), *an image, likeness, portrait, effigy.* **I.** Lit., **1, a**, oppidorum, Cic.; Helenae, Cic.; **b**, *a doll;* simulacra cerea, Ov.; **2**, *a reflection in a mirror, a shadow, vision in a dream or seen in fancy;* **a**, *a reflection in a mirror or in water*, Lucr.; **b**, *a shade, ghost*, Ov.; **c**, *a vision in a dream;* vana (noctis), Ov.; **d**, t. t. of the Epicurean philosophy, *a conception of an object in the mind*, Lucr.; **e**, *the recollection of a thing*, Cic.; **3**, transf., in a discourse, *a character-picture*, Liv. **II.** Fig., as opposed to what is real, **1**, *a mere image, imitation;* simulacra virtutis, Cic.; **2**, esp., **a**, *a phantom, appearance;* religionis, Cic.; **b**, *a shade, ghost* (of something lost); auspiciorum, Cic.

sĭmŭlāmen -inis, n. (simulo), *an imitation*, Ov.

sĭmŭlans -antis, p. adj. (from simulo), only in compar., *imitating, imitative;* simulantior vocum ales, *the parrot*, Ov.

sĭmŭlātē, adv. (simulatus), *in appearance, feignedly*, Cic.

sĭmŭlātĭo -ōnis, f. (simulo), *the assumed appearance of anything, pretence, feint, simulation, false show;* imitatio simulatioque virtutis, Cic.; agere cum simulatione timoris, Cic.; absol., simulatio ficta, Cic.

sĭmŭlātor -ōris, m. (simulo). **I.** *an imitator;* figurae, Ov. **II.** Transf., *a hypocritical imitator, hypocrite, counterfeiter, feigner;* segnitiae, Tac.; cuius rei libet simulator ac dissimulator, Cic.; simulator in omni oratione, *a master in irony*, Cic.

sĭmŭlo, 1. (similis), *to make like.* **I.** Lit., **A.** Gen., Minerva simulata Mentori, Cic. **B.** Esp., **1**, *to present, represent;* cupressum, Hor.; **2**, *to imitate;* nimbos, Verg.; Catonem, Hor. **II.** Transf., *to put on the appearance of, simulate, feign, counterfeit;* simulare gaudia vultu, Ov.; lacrimas, Ov.; negotia, Sall.; aegrum, *to play the part of a sick man*, Liv.; aliud agentes, aliud simulantes, Cic.; with acc. and infin., se furere, Cic.; poet., with infin. alone, simulat Jove natus abire, Ov.; absol., non sui commodi causā simulare, Cic. Esp., partic., **sĭmŭlātus** -a -um, *feigned, counterfeit;* nec simulatum quidquam potest esse diurnum, *nothing counterfeit can be lasting*, Cic.

sĭmultas -ātis, f. (= similitas, as facultas = facilitas), *enmity towards some one who is like us, rivalry, jealousy, feud, animosity, dissension, hatred;* **a**, sing., simultatem deponere, Cic.; **b**, plur., simultates exercere cum aliquo, Cic.; simultates dirimere, Cic.

sīmŭlus -a -um (dim. of simus), *a little pugnosed, somewhat snub-nosed*, Lucr.

sīmus -a -um (σιμός), *flat-nosed, pug-nosed, snub-nosed*, Verg.

sīn, conj. *but if, if however.* **I.** With preceding particle, si, nisi, *if . . . but if*, Cic.; si . . . sin aliter, Cic.; si . . . sin autem, Cic.; sin minus, sin aliter, sin secus, ellipt., *but if not, if on the contrary*, Cic. **II.** Without preceding particle, Cic.; strengthened, sin autem, Cic.

sĭnāpi, indecl. n. and **sĭnāpis** -is, acc. -im, abl. -e and gen. -i, f. (σίναπι), *mustard*, Plin.

sincērē, adv. (sincerus), *honestly, frankly, sincerely;* loqui, Cic.; pronuntiare, Caes.

sincērĭtas -ātis, f. (sincerus). **I.** *purity, freedom from adulteration, clearness*, Plin. **II.** *uprightness, integrity*, Phaedr.

sincērus -a -um (from sin = *simple* and cerus, connected with cresco, cf. procerus = *simply grown*). **I.** *pure, unmixed, unadulterated, genuine;* **a**, lit., secernere fucata et simulata a sinceris atque veris, Cic.; genae, Ov.; **b**, transf., *upright, honourable, sincere;* nihil sinceri, Cic.: fides, Liv. **II.** *pure;* **1**, *sound, healthy;* **a**, lit., corpus, Ov.; sincerum integrumque conserva, Cic.; **b**, transf., *uninjured, undestroyed;* Minerva, Ov.; judicium, Cic.; **2**, *unmixed, pure, mere;* **a**, lit., proelium equestre, Liv.; **b**, fig., voluptas, Cic.; gaudium, Liv.

sincĭput -pĭtis, n. (for semi caput). **I.** *half a head;* esp., *the smoked chap of a pig*, Juv. **II.** Meton., *the brain*, Plaut.

sindon -ŏnis, f. (σινδών), *fine cotton cloth, muslin*, Mart.

sĭnĕ, prep. with abl., *without* (opp. cum), semper ille ante cum uxore, tum sine ea, Cic.; sine dubio, Cic.; sine ulla dubitatione, *without doubt*, Cic.; sometimes placed after its case, vitiis nemo sine nascitur, Hor.

singillārĭtĕr, adv. (singulus), *singly*, Lucr.

singillātim (singŭlātim), adv. (singulus), *singly, one by one*, Cic.

singŭlāris -e (singuli), *belonging to single persons or things.* **I.** Lit., **A.** gen., **a**, *single, individual;* ubi aliquos singulares ex nave egredi conspexerant, Caes.; non est singulare nec solivagum genus hoc, Cic.; **b**, *relating to an individual;* imperium, potentia, *absolute rule*, Cic. **B.** Esp., **1**, grammat. t. t., *singular, belonging to the singular number*, Quint.; **2**, subst., **singŭlāres** -ium, m. *a select body of life-guards in the imperial service*, Tac. **II.** Fig., *single in its kind, distinguished, eminent, singular, unique, extra-*

ordinary, **a,** in a good sense, ingenio atque animo singulares, Cic, Pompeii singularis eximiaque virtus, Cic, **b,** in a bad sense, *exceptional*, nequitia, Cic

singŭlārĭtĕr, adv (singularis) **I.** *singly*, **a,** Lucr, **b,** *in the singular number* Quint **II.** Transf, *particularly, singularly, extraordinarily*, aliquem diligere, Cic

singŭlārĭus -a -um (singularis), *single*, catenae, *once twisted* (or *one pound in weight*), Plaut.

singŭlātim = singillatim (q v)

singŭli, v singulus

singultim, adv (singultus), *in sobs*, transf = *stammeringly*, pauca loqui, Hor

singultĭo, 4 (singultus) **I.** *to hiccough*, Plin **II.** *to throb*, Pers

singulto, 1 (singultus) **I.** Intransit, *to hiccough, to sob*, Quint, of dying persons, *to rattle in the throat*, Verg **II.** Transit, *to sob out, gasp out*, animam, Ov

singultus -ūs m (singuli) **I.** *weeping, sobbing*, **a,** of persons, singultuque pias interrumpente querellas, Ov, multas lacrimas et fletum cum singultu videre potuisti, Cic, **b,** of persons dying, *rattling in the throat*, Verg **II.** Of similar sounds, *the croaking of a raven, the gurgling of water*, Plin

singŭlus -a um, more freq in plur, **singŭli** -ae -a (from sin = semel, *singly*, as simplex) **I.** *single, a single person* or *thing, one alone*, **a,** sing, singulum vestigium, Plaut, **b,** plur, frequentes an pauci an singuli, Cic **II.** Distributive, *one each* legiones singulas posuit Brundisii, Tarenti, etc, *one legion at Brundisium, one at Tarentum*, Cic, filiae singulos filios habentes, Liv

Sĭnis -is, m (Σίνις, i e., *he that injures*), *a robber on the isthmus of Corinth, killed by Theseus*

sĭnister tra trum, *left, on the left hand* **I** Lit, **A.** Adj, manus, Nep., ripa, Hor, compar, **sĭnistĕrĭor** us, rota, Ov **B.** Subst, **1,** **sĭnistra** -ae, f **a,** *the left hand*, Caes, used in stealing, natae ad furta sinistrae, Ov, **b** *the left side*, dextrā sinistrā, Cic, sub sinistra, Caes, **2,** **sĭnistri** -ōrum, m *the left wing of a line of battle*, Liv **II.** **1,** *awkward, wrong, perverse*, mores, Verg, **2,** *unfavourable, adverse*, signa, Ov, notus pecori sinister, Verg **3,** t t of augury, **a,** amongst the Romans, who, turning towards the south, had the east on the left *favourable*, tonitrus, Ov, **b,** among the Greeks, who, turning towards the north, had the east on the right, *unfavourable*, omen, Ov

sĭnistĕrĭtas -ātis, f (sinister), *left-handedness, awkwardness*, Plin

sĭnistrō, adv (sinister), *unfavourably, unpropitiously*, excipere, Hor, rescribere, Tac

sĭnistrorsus (sĭnistrorsum), adv. (for sinistroversus, sinistroversum), *on the left hand*, Caes, Hor

sĭno, sivi, sĭtum, 3 lit, *to place, put down, to set down*, only used in this sense in the partic situs, and in the compound pono (= posino). in the finite verb only transf, *to permit, allow, suffer* **I.** Gen, **a,** with acc and infin, vinum ad se importari omnino non sinunt, Caes, nos transalpinas gentes oleam et vitem serere non sinimus, Cic, in pass, with nom and infin, hic accusare eum moderate per senatus auctoritatem non est situs, Cic, **b,** with subj. alone, sine pascat aretque, Hor, **c,** with acc, sinite arma viris, Verg, **d,** absol, non feram, non patiar, non sinam Cic **II.** Esp, **A.** In conversation, sine, *let = may*, ferant sine litora fluctus, Verg, or simply sine, *good, be it so*, Plaut. **B.** ne di sinant (sirint), ne Juppiter sirit, *God forbid*, Liv (perf tenses syncop, sisti, sistis, siris, sirit, siritis, pluperf, sisset and sissent) Hence, **sĭtus** -a -um **I.** Partic, *placed, laid down*. **1,** gen, Plaut, **2,** esp **a,** *built*, Philippopolis a Philippo sita, Liv, **b,** *buried*, C Marii sitae reliquiae apud Anienem, Cic **II** P Adj = *lying, situate* **A.** Lit, **1,** gen, lingua in ore sita est, Cic, **2,** esp, of places, *situate*, locus situs in media insula, Cic **B.** Fig, **1,** gen, voluptates in medio sitas esse dicunt, Cic, **2,** esp situm esse in aliqua re or in aliquo, *to rest upon, depend upon*, assensio quae est in nostra potestate sita, Cic

Sĭnōpa -ae, f and **Sĭnōpē** -ēs, f (Σινώπη) **I.** *a town in Paphlagonia on the Black Sea, a colony from Miletus, birth place of the cynic Diogenes, now Sinap Sinoob, Sinub* Hence, **A.** **Sĭnōpensis** -e, *belonging to Sinope* **B** **Sĭnōpeus** -ĕi, m (Σινωπεύς), *the Sinopian*, Cynicus, *Diogenes*, Ov **C.** **Sĭnōpis** -idis, f *a kind of red ochre, found near Sinope* **II.** *a Greek town in Latium, afterwards called Sinuessa* (q v)

Sĭnŭessa -ae, f (Σινουεσσα or Σινύεσσα), *a town in Latium, formerly called Sinope, colonised by Romans, the neighbourhood of which was famous for its wine and warm baths* Adj, **Sĭnŭessānus** a -um, *of* or *belonging to Sinuessa*

sīnum, v 1 sinus

sĭnŭo, 1 (2 sinus), *to bend, curve*, terga, Verg, arcum, Ov, pass as middle, muri introrsus sinuati, *bent inwards*, Tac, serpens sinuatur in arcus, Ov

sĭnŭōsus a um (2 sinus) **I** *full of windings, bendings, curves, sinuous*, vestis, Ov, flexus (anguis), Verg **II.** Fig, of discourse, *diffuse, digressive*, Quint

1 **sīnus** -i, m and **sīnum** -i, n *a large bowl, a basin*, Verg

2 **sĭnus** -ūs, m *a bending, curve, fold* **I** Gen, of the windings of a snake, Cic, of the curls of hair, Ov, *the fold of a garment*, sinu ex toga facto, Liv, *the belly of a sail swollen by the wind*, sinus implere secundos, Verg pleno pandere vela sinu, Ov, cedendo sinum in medio dedit, *formed a curve*, Liv **II.** Esp, **A.** *the lap*, **1,** lit, **a,** sinum implere floribus, Ov, **b,** *the hanging fold of the toga, the bosom, lap*, litteras in sinu ponere, Liv, oblatum negotium sibi in sinum delatum esse dicebat, Cic, in sinu gaudere, *to rejoice in secret*, Cic, **2,** meton, *a garment*, indue regales sinus, Ov, **3,** **a,** *the bosom*, hence, *love, affection, affectionate protection*, in sinu est meo, *is my darling*, Cic, in sinu gestare, *to hold dear*, Cic, **b,** *the inmost part of anything, the heart*, in sinu urbis sunt hostes, Sall **B.** *a bay, gulf*, **a,** lit, maritimus, Cic, **b,** meton, *land on a bay or gulf*, Liv **C.** *a chasm in the earth*, Liv (dat and abl plur, always sinibus)

sīpărĭum -ii, n (dim of siparum = supparum) **I.** *a drop scene at a theatre*, **a,** lit, Cic, **b,** meton = *comedy*, Juv **II.** *a curtain to exclude the sun*, Quint

sīpho (sīpo) -ōnis, m (σίφων), *a siphon*, Juv

Sīpontum -i, n (Σιποῦς), *an important harbour in Apulia, now Maria de Siponto* Adj, **Sīpontīnus** a -um, *Sipontine*

siptachŏras ae, m *an Indian tree, supposed to yield amber*, Plin

Sĭpўlus i, m (Σίπυλος), *a mountain in Lydia, where, according to the legend, Niobe was turned into stone*

sīquandō, adv. *if ever*, Cic.

sīquĭdem, conj. **I.** *if indeed*, Cic. **II.** *since, because*, Cic.

sīraeum -i, n. (σίραιον) = sapa (q.v.).

sīremps and **sīrempse** (similis re ipsā), *the same;* sirempse legem, Plaut.

Sīrēn -ēnis, f., usually plur., **Sīrēnes** -um, f. (Σειρῆνες), *the Sirens, birds with the faces of women, on the coast of Southern Italy, who by their song lured mariners to destruction.* **Sīrēnum** scopuli, *three small rocky islands on the south-west coast of Campania, between Surrentum and Capreae;* transf., vitanda est improba Siren, desidia, Hor.

sīrĭăsis -is, f. (σειρίασις), *a disease in children, caused by excessive heat*, Plin.

sīrĭus -ii, m. (σείριος), *the dogstar*, Verg.; poet. attrib., sirius ardor, *of the dogstar*, Verg.

sirpĕa and **sirpĭa**, v. scirpeus.

sirpĭcŭlus = scirpiculus (q.v.).

sirpus = scirpus (q.v.).

sīrus -i, m. (σειρός), *a pit or cellar for keeping corn, a silo*, Plin.

sīs = si vis, v. 1. volo.

Sisapo -ōnis, f. *a town in Hispania Baetica, near which were gold-mines, now Guadalcanal.*

Sīsenna -ae, m. **I.** *L. Cornelius, a famous Roman orator and historian, contemporary of Cicero.* **II.** *a notorious slanderer in Rome in the time of Horace.*

sīser -ĕris, n. (σίσαρον), *a plant with an edible root* (Sium sisarum, Linn.), Plin.

sisto, stĭti and stĕti, stătum, 3. (reduplication of sto). **I.** Transit., **A.** *to cause to stand, put, place;* **1,** aciem in litore, Verg.; alicui jaculum in ore, *to hit on the mouth*, Verg.; **2,** esp., **a,** legal t. t., sistere se or aliquem, *to produce, cause to appear before a court of justice*, Cic.; vadimonium sistere, *to appear on the appointed day*, Cic.; **b,** *to erect;* effigiem, Tac. **B. 1,** *to stop, bring to a stand, check;* **a,** lit., legiones, Liv.; equos, Verg.; pedem or gradum, Verg.; **b,** fig., querelas, lacrimas, Ov.; fugam, Liv.; **2,** *to make firm, settle firmly, establish;* rem Romanam, Verg. **II.** Intransit., **A.** *to stand;* **1,** gen., Plaut.; **2,** esp., *to appear, present oneself in court*, Cic. **B.** *to stand still, to halt;* **1,** lit., ubi sistere detur, Verg.; **2,** *to stand firm;* rempublicam sistere negat posse, Cic.; impers., vix concordiā sisti posse, *one cannot hold out, one can stand it no longer*, Liv.; partic., **stătus** -a -um, *fixed, determined, recurring periodically;* dies, Liv.; sacrificium, Cic.

sistrātus -a -um (sistrum), *furnished with a sistrum*, Mart.

sistrum -i, n. (σεῖστρον), *a sort of rattle used in the worship of Isis*, Ov.

sĭsymbrĭum -ii, n. (σισύμβριον), *an aromatic herb sacred to Venus;* perhaps, *mint*, Ov.

Sīsўphus (-ŏs) -i, m. (Σίσυφος), *a son of Aeolus, brother of Salmoneus, a king of Corinth, a cunning robber, killed by Theseus, condemned in the lower world to roll up hill a great stone which constantly fell back.* Hence, **A.** Adj., **Sīsўphĭus** -a -um, **a,** *of or relating to Sisyphus*, Prop.; sanguine cretus Sisyphio, *Ulysses*, Ov.; **b,** *Corinthian*, Ov. **B.** Subst., **Sīsўphĭdēs** -ae, m. *Ulysses, said to be the son of Sisyphus.*

sītānĭus -a -um (σητάνιος), *of this year, this year's*, Plin.

sĭtella -ae, f. (dim. of situla), *an urn, used for drawing lots*, Liv., Cic.

Sīthōn -ŏnis, m. (Σίθων), *son of Neptune, king in the Thracian Chersonese.* Hence, **A.** **Sīthōn** -ŏnis, *Sithonian;* poet. = *Thracian.* **B.** **Sīthŏnis** -ĭdis, f., subst., *a Thracian woman*, Ov. **C.** **Sīthŏnĭus** -a -um, *Sithonian, Thracian;* subst., **Sīthŏnĭi** -ōrum, m. *the Thracians*, Hor.

sĭtīcŭlōsus -a -um (sitis), *very dry, parched*, Hor.

sĭtĭens, v. sitio.

sĭtĭentĕr, adv. (sitiens), *thirstily, greedily, eagerly;* expetere, Cic.

sĭtĭo -ivi and -ii -itum, 4. (sitis), *to thirst, be thirsty.* **I.** Intransit., **A. 1,** lit., Cic.; prov., sitire mediis in undis, *to starve in the midst of plenty*, Ov.; **2,** transf., **a,** of plants, the soil, etc., *to be dry, parched;* sitiunt agri, Cic.; tellus, Ov.; **b,** *to suffer from heat, to be situated in a hot climate;* Afri sitientes, Verg. **B.** Fig., *to be eager;* partic., **sĭtĭens,** *thirsting, eager;* eo gravius avidiusque sitiens, Cic.; fac venias ad sitientes aures, *languishing for news*, Cic. **II.** Transit., *to thirst for something.* **A.** Lit., Tagum, Mart.; pass., aquae sitiuntur, Ov. **B.** Fig., *to thirst after, eagerly desire;* sanguinem, Cic.; honores, Cic.; partic., sitiens, with genit., virtutis, Cic.

sĭtis -is, f. *thirst.* **I. 1,** lit., arentibus siti faucibus, Liv.; sitim colligere, *to feel thirst*, Ov., *to cause thirst*, Verg.; sitim explere, Cic., exstinguere, Ov., restinguere, Cic., depellere, Cic.; **2,** transf., of the earth or of plants, *dryness, drought;* deserta siti regio, Verg. **II.** Fig., *thirst, eager desire;* libertatis, Cic.; argenti, Hor.

sĭtītor -ōris, m. (sitio), *one who thirsts, a thirster*, Mart.

sittўbos (sittŭbos) -i, plur., **sittyboe,** m. (σίττυβος = σίττυβον), *a strip of parchment on which the title of a book was written*, Cic.

sĭtŭla -ae, f. and **sĭtŭlus** -i, m. **a,** *a small urn for drawing water*, Plaut.; **b,** *an urn used in drawing lots*, Plaut.

1. **sĭtus** -a -um, v. sino.

2. **sĭtus** -ūs, m. (sino). **I.** *the place, site, situation of anything;* **1,** lit., loci, urbis, Cic.; plur., situs oppidorum, castrorum, Caes.; terrarum, Cic.; **2,** meton., **a,** *situation = building;* monumentum regali situ pyramidum altius, Hor.; **b,** *a region of the earth, zone, quarter*, Plin. **II. A. 1,** lit., situ durescere campum, *rest*, Verg.; **2,** meton., **a,** *want of cultivation;* cessat terra situ, Ov.; **b,** *rust, mould, dirt caused by remaining in one place;* occupat arma situs, Tib.; canescunt tecta situ, Ov.; **c,** *filthiness of the body*, Ov. **B.** Fig., of the mind, *rusting, dulness, weakness;* marcescere otio situque civitatem, Liv.; senectus victa situ, Ov.

sīvĕ and **seu,** conj. **I.** *or if;* si omnes declinabunt, sive aliae declinabunt, Cic.; me, seu corpus spoliatum lumine mavis, redde meis, Verg. **II.** With a disjunctive sense; **a,** doubled, sive . . . sive, seu . . . seu, *whether . . . or, if . . . or if;* sive tu medicum adhibueris (fut. perf.) sive non adhibueris (fut. perf.), Cic.; sive fecisset sive voluisset, Cic.; sive deus sive natura ademerat, Cic.; sive casu, sive consilio deorum, Caes.; in the same sense, sive . . . seu, Verg., Liv.; seu . . . sive, Verg.; repeated several times, sive . . . sive . . . sive, Cic.; with other disjunct. particles, seu . . . aut, Verg.; with interrog. particles, -ne . . . seu, Verg.; sive . . . an, Tac.; **b,** *or;* regis Philippi sive Persae, Cic.

smărăgdus -i, m. and f. (σμάραγδος), *an emerald*, Lucr.

smectĭcus -a -um (σμηκτικός), *cleansing, cleaning;* vis, Plin.

smegma -ătis, n. (σμῆγμα), *a means of cleaning, detergent*, Plin

smīlax -ăcis, f (σμῖλαξ) **I.** *bindweed*, Plin **II.** Smilax, *a maiden changed into the plant of the same name*, Ov

Sminthĕus -ĕi, m (Σμινθεύς), *a surname of Apollo*, either from σμίνθος (in Cretan = *mouse*), *the mouse-killer*, or from Sminthia (Σμίνθη), a town in the Trojan country

1 **smyrna** -ae, f (σμυρνα), *myrrh*, Lucr

2 **Smyrna** -ae, f (Σμύρνα), *a famous trading town in Ionia, one of the places where Homer was said to have been born* Hence, **Smyrnaeus** -a -um, *of or belonging to Smyrna.*

smyrrhiza = myrrha, myrrhis (q v)

sŏbŏles, sobolesco = suboles, subolesco (q v)

sōbrĭē, adv (sobrius) **I.** *moderately, frugally, soberly*, vivere, Cic **II.** *prudently, carefully*, Plaut.

sōbrĭĕtas -ātis, f (sobrius), *moderation in drinking sobriety*, Sen

sōbrīna ae, f (sobrinus), *a cousin on the mother's side*, Tac

sōbrīnus -i, m (for sororinus, from soror), *a cousin on the mother's side*, Cic

sōbrĭus -a um (perhaps = se ebrius as socors = secors), *sober, not intoxicated* **I. a,** lit , of persons, Cic , **b,** meton , of inanimate things, lympha, Tib , nox, Prop **II. 1,** transf , *moderate, frugal, continent*, homines plane frugi ac sobrii, Cic , **2,** fig , *sober minded, prudent, reasonable, cautious*, orator, homo, Cic

soccātus -a -um (soccus), *wearing the soccus*, Sen

soccŭlus -i, m. (dim of soccus), *a little soccus*, Plin

soccus -i, m (συκχις, συγχις), *a light shoe or slipper in use among the Greeks*, Cic , esp , *the soccus* or *low shoe worn by comic actors* (as the cothurnus was worn by tragic actors), hence, meton , **a,** *comedy*, Hor , **b,** *comic style*, Hor

sŏcer -ĕri, m (ἑκυρος), *a father-in law*, Cic , plur , soceri, *the father- and mother in law*, Liv

sŏcĕra = socrus (q v)

sŏcĭa -ae, f , v socius

sŏcĭābĭlis -e (socio), *sociable, easily united or joined together*, consortio inter reges, Liv

sŏcĭālis e (socius) **I.** *social, sociable*, homo sociale animal, Sen **II.** Esp , **A.** *conjugal*, amor, Ov **B.** *of* or *relating to allies, allied*, exercitus, Liv., bellum, *the Social War*, Nep , lex, Cic

sŏcĭālĭtĕr, adv (socialis), *sociably*, Hor

sŏcĭennus -i, m (socius), *a companion, comrade*, Plaut

sŏcĭĕtas ātis, f (socius) **I.** *society, company, companionship, fellowship, association*, hominum inter ipsos, Cic , vitae, Cic , regni, Liv , sceleris, Cic , societatem coire, statuere, inire, conflare, Cic., venire in societatem laudum alicuius, Cic **II.** Esp , **1,** *commercial partnership*, **a,** societatem facere, Cic , gerere, Cic , judicium societatis, *relating to partnership*, Cic , **b,** *the partnership* or *company of the publicani to farm the taxes of the provinces*, Bithynica Cic , **2,** *a political alliance between states*, societatem belli facere, Cic

sŏcĭo, 1 (socius) **I.** *to unite, combine, associate, share*, vim rerum cum dicendi exercitatione, Cic , vitae suae periculum cum aliquo, *to risk one's life with any one*, Cic , sanguinem (of relationship), Liv , of things, omne genus hominum sociatum inter se esse, Cic ; nos urbe domo socias, *givest us a share in*, Verg **II.** Esp , *to accomplish in company with others*, sociati parte laboris fungi, Ov

sŏcĭŏfraudus -i, m (socius and fraudo), *one who cheats a comrade*, Plaut

sŏcĭus a um (from sequor, or else connected with sodalis) **I.** *taking part, sharing in*, subst = *a companion, comrade, associate, partner, sharer*, socii penates, Ov , socius regni, *fellow regent*, Cic , socius periculorum, Cic , belli, Cic , amentiae, Cic , nocte socia, *under the shelter of night*, Cic **II.** Esp , **1,** of relationship, socius sanguinis, *a brother*, Ov , **2,** of marriage, socius tori, *a husband*, Ov , socia tori, Ov and simply socia, Sall , *a wife*, **3,** *allied, confederate*, socii Carthaginiensium populi, Liv , classis socia, Ov , subst , **sŏcĭus** -ii, m *an ally*, huic populo socii fuerunt, Cic , Socii, *the Italian nations beyond the boundaries of Latium in alliance with the Romans, the allies*, Socii et Latini, Cic , Socii Latini nominis, *the Latin allies*, Liv , **4,** in relation to trade, **a,** *a partner*, judicium pro socio, *a judgment in a partnership suit*, Cic , pro socio damnari, *to be condemned for defrauding a partner*, Cic , **b,** socii = *the company of* publicani *for the purpose of farming the taxes*, Cic (genit plur , socium, Liv , Verg).

sōcordĭa ae, f (socors) **I.** *stupidity, folly, weakness of intellect*, Tac **II.** *carelessness, negligence, indolence, inactivity*, Liv

sōcordĭtĕr, adv only in compar (socors), *lazily, slothfully, carelessly*, ab Albanis socordius res acta, Liv

sōcors -cordis (se and cor) **I.** *weak minded, stupid, silly*, Cic **II.** *negligent, careless, slothful, inactive*, Sall

sŏcra = socrus (q v.)

Sōcrătēs -is, m (Σωκράτης), *the famous Athenian philosopher, contemporary of Xenophon and Alcibiades, put to death on a charge of impiety and of corrupting the youth by his teaching* Adj , **Sōcrătĭcus** -a -um, *Socratic*, chartae, *philosophy*, Hor Plur subst , **Sōcrătĭci** -ōrum, m *the pupils and followers of Socrates*

sŏcrus ūs, f (ἑκυρα), *a mother in-law*, Cic

sŏdālĭcĭus -a -um (sodalis), *of* or *relating to companionship* **I.** Adj , jure sodalicio, Ov **II.** Subst , **sŏdālĭcium** -ii, n **A.** *comradeship, intimacy*, Cat **B.** In a bad sense, *a secret society*, lex Licinia quae est de sodaliciis Cic

sŏdālis e, *relating to comradeship* **I.** Adj , turba, Ov **II.** Subst , **sŏdālis** is m **A** *a comrade, intimate associate, companion, mate, friend*, **1,** lit , Cic , **2,** transf , **a,** of things, *a companion, attendant on*, sodalis hiemis (of the Hebrus), Hor , **b,** *a sharer with* = *resembling*, sodalis istius erat in hoc morbo, Cic **B.** Esp , **1,** *a table companion, a boon companion*, Cic , **2,** *a member of a club, association, corporation*, **a,** in a good sense, of a college of priests, sibi in Lupercis sodalem esse, Cic , esp of the priests of the deified emperor, sodales Augustales, Tac , **b,** in a bad sense, *a member of a secret and illegal society*, Cic (abl , sodali, Cic)

sŏdālĭtas -ātis, f (sodalis) **I.** *companionship, intimate association*, officia sodalitatis familiaritatisque, Cic , homo summā sodalitate, Cic **II.** Esp , **1,** *a club for feasting*, Plin , Cic , **2,** *a club, association*, **a** in a good sense, *a religious brotherhood*, quaedam sodalitas Lupercorum, Cic , **b,** in a bad sense, *a secret, illegal society*, Cic

sōdēs (for si audes), *pray, if you please, with your leave, prithee*, jube sodes nummos curari, Cic , me, sodes (sc relinque), Hor

sōl, sōlis, m. *the sun.* **I. A.** Lit., **1**, sol praecipitans, *inclining towards evening*, Cic.; supremo sole, *at evening*, Hor.; sol mihi excidisse e mundo videtur, Cic.; prov., nondum omnium dierum sol occidit, *the sun has not yet set for ever*, Liv.; **2**, as a proper name, Sol, *the sun-god, the Phoebus of the Greeks, father of Phaethon, Pasiphae, Circe;* filia Solis, *Pasiphae*, Ov. **B.** Meton., **1**, *the light, warmth, heat of the sun;* plur., soles often = *sunny days;* sol nimius, Ov.; ambulare in sole, Cic.; hence, of work done in the sun (opp. to umbra), **a**, *military service;* cedat umbra (i.e., jurisprudentia) soli, Cic.; **b**, *appearance in public;* procedere in solem et publicum, Cic.; **2**, *the day;* tres soles erramus, Verg. **II.** Fig., *the sun*, of distinguished persons, P. Africanus sol alter, Cic.; solem Asiae Brutum appellat, Hor.

sōlācĭum = solatium (q.v.).

sōlāmen -ĭnis, n. (solor), *a means of consolation, comfort*, Verg.

sōlānum -i, n. *the plant nightshade*, Plin.

sōlāris -e (sol), *of* or *relating to the sun, solar;* lumen, Ov.

sōlārĭum -ĭi, n. (sol). **A.** *a sundial*, Plaut.; *a much frequented place in the forum, where a sundial stood;* non ad solarium versatus est, Cic. **B.** *a balcony, terrace exposed to the sun*, Plaut.

sōlātĭŏlum -i, n. (dim. of solatium), *a small consolation*, Cat.

sōlātĭum (sōlācĭum) -ĭi, n. (solor), *a consolation, comfort, solace, relief.* **I. 1**, lit., servitutis, Cic.; solatium afferre or praebere, Cic.; absenti magna solatia dedisse, Cic.; **2**, transf., **a**, *a means of help, refuge in need;* annonae, Cic.; **b**, *amends, compensation*, Tac. **II.** Meton., = *a consoler;* aves, solatia ruris, Ov.

sōlātor -ōris, m. (solor), *a consoler, comforter*, Tib.

sōlātus -a -um (sol), *sun-struck*, Plin.

soldurĭi -ōrum, m. (a Celtic word), *retainers, vassals*, Caes.

soldus = solidus (q.v.).

sŏlĕa -ae, f. (solum). **I.** *a leather sole strapped on the foot, a sandal;* soleas poscere (after dinner), Hor. **II.** Transf., **a**, *a species of clog* or *fetter*, Cic.; **b**, *a kind of shoe for animals, not nailed on, like our horse-shoes, but tied on*, Cat.; **c**, *a fish, the sole*, Ov.

sŏlĕārĭus -ĭi, m. (solea), *a sandal-maker*, Plaut.

sŏlĕātus -a -um (solea), *wearing sandals*, Cic.

sōlēn -ēnis, m. (σωλήν), *a species of mussel, the razor-fish*, Plin.

sōlennis, solennitas = sollemnis, etc. (q.v.).

sŏlĕo, sŏlĭtus sum, 2. *to be accustomed, be used, be wont;* with infin., mentiri, Cic.; ut soleo, ut solet (sc. facere), *as is my custom*, Cic.; ut solet (sc. fieri), *as is the custom*, Cic.

sōlers, solertia = sollers, sollertia (q.v.).

Sŏli (Sŏloe) -ōrum, m. (Σόλοι), *a town in Cilicia, a Greek colony, native place of the Stoic Chrysippus, of Menander, and of the astronomer Aratus.*

sŏlĭdē, adv. (solidus). **I.** *firmly, densely, solidly*, Col. **II.** *surely, certainly;* aliquid scire, Plaut.

sŏlĭdĭpes -pĕdis (solidus and pes), *not dividing the hoofs, having undivided hoofs*, Plin.

sŏlĭdĭtas -ātis, f. (solidus), *solidity;* nec dii habent ullam soliditatem nec eminentiam, Cic.

sŏlĭdo, 1. (solidus). **I. a**, *to make dense, solid;* aream cretā, Verg.; **b**, *to make firm;* muros, Tac. **II.** Transf., *to join together, to make whole*, Plin.

sŏlĭdus -a -um (Gr. ὅλος), *dense, firm, solid.* **I.** Lit., gen., **a**, paries, Cic.; subst., **sŏlĭdum** -i, n., (α) *firm ground*, Ov.; (β) *a thick body*, Verg.; **b**, of metals, *massive, solid;* crateres auro solidi, *of massive gold*, Verg.; **c**, *firm, hard;* ripa, Ov.; adamas, Verg.; subst., **sŏlĭdum** -i, n. *something firm*, Hor.; solido carere, Cic.; in solido, fig., *in safety;* aliquem in solido locare, Verg.; **d**, *thick, strong;* tori Herculis, Ov. **II.** Transf., **1**, *whole, complete, entire;* usura, Cic.; partem solido demere de die, Hor.; subst., **sŏlĭdum** -i, n. *the whole sum*, Cic.; **2**, *firm, enduring, real, substantial, solid;* laus, Cic.; utilitas, Cic.; subst., *that which is real* or *genuine*, Hor.; **3**, *firm, immovable;* mens, Hor.

sōlĭfĕr -fĕra -fĕrum (sol and fero), *sun-bringing*, Sen.

sōlĭfŭga -ae, f. (sol and fugio), *a kind of poisonous ant*, Plin.

sōlistĭmum (sollistŭmum) and **sollistŭmum tripudium**, *the good omen afforded when the sacred chickens ate so eagerly that the food fell out of their beaks*, Cic.

sōlĭtārĭus -a -um (solus), *standing alone;* **a**, *solitary, alone, lonely;* solitarius homo atque in agro vitam agens, Cic.; **b**, *single, alone, by itself;* quoniam solitaria non posset virtus ad ea pervenire, Cic.

sōlĭtūdo -ĭnis, f. (solus). **I.** *solitude, loneliness* (opp. frequentia, celebritas); loci, Cic.; in solitudine secum loqui, Cic.; plur., in animi doloribus solitudines captare, Cic. **II.** *a state of desertion, deprivation, want;* liberorum, Cic.

sŏlĭtus -a -um, p. adj. (from soleo), *usual, customary, wonted, habitual;* **a**, adj., locus, Ov.; solito matrum de more, Verg.; **b**, subst., **sŏlĭtum** -i, n. *that which is usual* or *customary, custom;* often with prep., praeter solitum, Hor.; in abl. with compar., major solito, Liv.; plus solito, Liv.

sŏlĭum -ĭi, n. **I.** *a chair of state, royal seat, throne;* **a**, for kings, regale, Liv.; meton. = *throne, regal power;* in paterno solio locare, Liv.; **b**, for the gods in the temples; deorum solio, Cic.; **c**, of jurists, *an arm-chair, seated in which they gave their opinion;* quo minus more patrio sedens in solio consulentibus responderem, Cic. **II.** *a bathing-tub of stone* or *wood*, Suet. **III.** *a stone coffin, sarcophagus*, Suet.

sōlĭvăgus -a -um (solus and vagus), *wandering alone.* **I.** Lit., bestiae, Cic. **II.** Fig., *solitary, lonely, single;* cognitio, Cic.

sollemnis (sōlemnis, sōlennis) -e (from sollus = totus and annus). **I.** *yearly, annual* (applied to annually recurring festivals); sacra, sacrificia, Cic. **II.** Transf., **A.** *solemn, festive, religious;* epulae, ludi, Cic.; subst., **sōlenne** -is, n. *a solemn feast, sacrifice, a religious rite;* sollemne clavi figendi, Liv.; esp., plur. = *the sacrificial victims;* extis sollemnibus vesci, Liv. **B.** *usual, customary, wonted, common;* lascivia militum, Liv.; officium, Cic.; subst., **sollemne** -is, n. *a custom;* nostrum illud solemne servemus, Cic.

sollemnĭtĕr (sōlemnĭtĕr, sōlennĭtĕr), adv. (sollemnis). **I.** *solemnly, religiously;* omnia peragere, Liv. **II.** *according to use, custom*, Plin.

sollers (sōlers) -ertis (sollus = totus and ars), lit., *possessed entirely of an art* (opp. iners), hence, *clever, skilful, adroit;* **a**, of persons, agricola, Cic.; Ulysses, Ov.; quo quisque est sollertior et ingeniosior, hoc, etc., Cic.; sollertissimus omnium, Sall , with infin , Hor , with genit , Musa lyrae sollers, Hor , b, of things, ingenious, intelligent, natura, Cic , descriptio, Cic (abl sing , gen sollertı , sollerte, Ov)

sollerter (sŏlertĕr), adv with compar. and superl , cleverly, skilfully, adroitly, Cic

sollertia (sŏlertia) ae, f (sollers), cleverness, skilfulness, inventiveness, adroitness, ingenuity, naturae, Cic , ingenii Sall , with object. genit , cogitandi, judicandi, Cic , in hac re tanta inest ratio atque sollertia ut, etc , Cic.

sollicitatio -ōnis, f (sollicito), an inciting, instigating, instigation, solicitation, Cic

sollicite, adv (sollicitus), anxiously, solicitously, carefully, Plin

sollicito, 1 (sollicitus), to move violently, shake, stir, agitate **I.** 1, lit, tellurem, to plough, Verg , freta remis, Verg , spicula, Verg , stamina docto pollice, to touch the strings, Ov , 2, transf , to weaken, disturb , mala copia aegrum stomachum, Hor **II.** Fig , 1, to disturb, trouble , pacem, Liv , 2, a, to agitate, vex, disquiet, annoy, haec cura me sollicitat, Cic , sollicitatus Juppiter, Liv , b, to stir up, incite, instigate to any action, solicit, tamper with, (α) in a bad sense, civitates, Caes , sollicitatus ab Arvernis pecuniā, Caes , poet , with a thing as object, sollicitare judicium donis, seek to obtain by bribery, Ov ; to express the object, with ad and the acc , causa and the genit , ut or ne and the subj , poet infin , servos ad hospitem necandum, Cic , dixit se sollicitatum esse, ut regnare vellet, Cic , (β) in a good sense, to persuade, solicit influence, Lucr

sollicitudo -inis, f (sollicitus) uneasiness, mental disturbance, anxiety, solicitude, care, trouble, a, sing , cura et sollicitudo, Cic , with object genit , provinciae, about the province, Cic , abstrahere se ab omni sollicitudine, Cic , demere sollicitudinem, Cic , sollicitudinis aliquid habere, Cic , b, plur , sollicitudines domesticae, Cic ; habere aliquem sollicitudinum socium, Cic

sollicitus -a -um (sollus = totus and cio), strongly moved, stirred up, agitated **I.** Lit , physically, mare, Verg **II.** Transf , **A.** politically disturbed, Sall **B.** mentally disturbed, anxious, uneasy, disturbed, solicitous, a, of the mind, anxius animus aut sollicitus, Cic , b, of living beings, (α) of persons, vehementer sollicitum esse, Cic , aliquem sollicitum habere, to trouble, Cic , with prep or with vicem, sollicitum esse de aliennis valetudine, Cic , pro Aetolis sollicitus, Liv , sollicitus propter difficultatem locorum, Liv , meam vicem sollicitus, Liv , with abl , sollicitus morte Tigelli, Hor , with ne and the subj , quae cruciatur et sollicita est, ne eundem paulo post spoliatum omni dignitate conspiciat, Cic , (β) of animals, canes, watchful, Ov ; c, of things, (α) pass , troubled, in vita omnia semper suspecta atque sollicita, Cic , (β) act , disquieting, causing trouble , amores, Verg

solliferreum (sŏliferreum) i, n (sollus = totus and ferrum), a javelin entirely of iron, Liv

sollistimus = solistimus (q v)

sollus a um (Oscan) = totus (q v)

1 **sōlo,** 1 (solus), to make solitary, make desert, Sen

2 **Sŏlo** = Solon (q v)

Sŏloe = Soli (q v)

sŏloecismus -i, m (σολοικισμός), a grammatical error, solecism, Quint

Sŏlon (Sŏlo) -ōnis, m (Σόλων), one of the Seven Wise Men of Greece, a famous Athenian legislator, living about 600 B C.

Solonius a um, name of a district in Latium

sōlor, 1 to comfort, console **I.** Lit , inopem, Hor **II.** Transf , a, to assuage, soothe, relieve, mitigate, famem, Verg , laborem cantu, Verg , aestum fluviis, Hor , b, to indemnify, to compensate, Tac

solstitialis e (solstitium) **I.** of or relating to the summer solstice, dies, the longest day, Cic , nox, the shortest night, Ov , orbis, the tropic of Cancer, Cic **II.** Meton , **A.** relating to summer or to the warmth of summer, solstitiali tempore, Liv **B.** of or relating to the sun, solar, orbis, Liv

solstitium -ii, n (sol and sisto) **I** a solstice, Plin **II.** Esp , the summer solstice, the longest day **A.** Lit , Cic **B.** Meton , summer, summer-heat, solstitium pecori defendite, Verg

1 **sŏlum** i, n the bottom or lowest part of anything **I.** Gen , a, lit, fossae, Caes , clivus ad solum exustus est, Liv , b, fig , ground, foundation, solum et quasi fundamentum oratoris, locutionem emendatam et Latinam, Cic **II.** Esp , 1, the floor of a room, Cic , 2, the sole of a foot, Cic , 3, of a shoe, Plin , 4, soil, ground, earth, land, a, macrum, Cic , prov , quodcunque in solum venit, whatever falls on the ground (i e , whatever comes into one's head), Cic , ellipt , ibi loquor, quod in solum, ut dicitur, Cic , b, soil, country, solum patriae, the soil of one's native country, Cic , solum vertere, mutare, to leave one's country, go into exile, Cic., 5, soil = that which is underneath, Cereale, a layer of biscuit underneath other food, Verg , substrahiturque solum (sc navi), sea, Verg , astra tenent caeleste solum, = heaven, Ov

2 **sōlum,** adv (solus), alone, only, a, una de re solum est dissensio, Cic , b in negat sent , non solum verum etiam, not only . but also, Cic , non solum sed etiam, Cic , non solum sed ne quidem, not only but not even, Cic , non solum sed vix, Cic

Sŏluntinus, v 2 Solus

1 **sōlus** -a -um genit. solius, dat soli (from so), alone, only, sole **I.** Gen , solum regnare, Cic , solos novem menses, only nine months, Cic **II.** Of places solitary, desert, uninhabited, quum in locis solis moestus errares, Cic

2 **Sŏlūs** untis, f (Σολοῦς), a town on the north coast of Sicily, east of Panormus, now Castello di Solanto Hence, **Sŏluntinus** -i, m an inhabitant of Solus

sŏlūtē, adv (solutus) **I.** a, without impediment, freely, moveri, Cic ; b, without difficulty, easily, Cic **II.** carelessly, negligently, Cic

sŏlūtilis e (solutus), easily coming to pieces, Suet

sŏlūtio ōnis, f (solvo) **I.** a loosening **A.** Lit , linguae, a loose, ready tongue, Cic **B.** Fig , 1, a paying, payment, legatorum, Cic ; 2, solutio rerum creditarum, Cic **II.** dissolution, a, totius hominis, Cic , b, explanation, Sen

sŏlūtus -a -um, p adj (from solvo), loosened **I.** loosened, unbound, free **A.** Lit , tunica, Quint **B.** Fig , unbound, free from fetters, free, independent, 1, in a good sense, a, solutus liberque animus, Cic , soluta optio eligendi, unhindered, Cic , with ab and the abl , soluti a cupiditatibus, Cic , with abl alone, ambitione, Hor , with genit , famuli operum soluti, Hor , b, free from debt or mortgage, unencumbered, praedia, Cic , c, of orators, fluent, ready, solutus atque expeditus ad dicendum, Cic , d, of discourse, unbound, (a) free from the fetters of metre, prose, soluta oratio (opp poemata), Cic ;

(β) *loose, flowing, not carefully constructed*, verba, Cic.; numeri, of Pindaric poetry, Hor.; 2, in a bad sense, **a,** *unrestrained, unbridled, unchecked, dissolute, licentious*, libido solutior, Liv.; praetura, Cic.; risus, Verg.; **b,** *lazy, sluggish;* Titius tam solutus et mollis in gestu, Cic.; **c,** *negligent*, Cic. **II.** Of soil, *loose, loosened*, terra, Plin.

solvo, solvi, sŏlūtum, 3 (1. se and luo), *to loosen.* **I.** *to loosen, untie, unbind.* **A.** 1, lit., funem a stipite, Ov.; corollas de nostra fronte, Prop.; crines, capillos, Hor.; nodum, Tib.; 2, transf., **a,** *to unbind, release, set free*, canem, Phaedr.; equum senescentem, *to unyoke*, Hor.; **b,** transf., *to untie, loosen, open*, epistolam, Cic.; ora, *open the mouth*, Ov.; **c,** naut. t. t., ancoram, navem, *to weigh anchor, set sail*, so solvere funem, Verg.; absol., naves a terra solverunt, Caes. **B.** Fig., **1,** commercial t. t., *to pay or discharge a debt*, **a,** lit. (a) aliquid, pecuniam debitam, Cic.; pro frumento nihil, Cic.; solvendo non erat, *he was insolvent*, Cic.; (β) aliquem, *to pay any one*, Plaut.; **b,** transf., *to perform a promise or duty, fulfil an engagement*, si solveris ea quae polliceris, Cic.; justa paterno funeri, Cic.; suprema alicui, Tac.; capite poenas, *to suffer capital punishment*, Sall.; **2,** *to set free, release*, aliquem curā et negotio, Cic.; civitatem, rempublicam religione, Cic.; per aes et libram heredes testamenti, Cic.; ut si solvas (*if you release from the fetter of verse, i.e., turn into prose*) "postquam Discordia," etc., Hor. **II.** *to break up, to loosen, break in pieces.* **A.** 1, lit., **a,** gen., *to break to pieces;* navem, *to dash to pieces*, Ov.; pontem, Tac.; **b,** *to melt, dissolve*, nivem, Ov.; solvuntur viscera, *putrefy*, Verg.; **2,** transf., **a,** *to part, separate*, agmina diductis choris, Verg.; **b,** *to weaken, relax*, homines solverat alta quies, Ov.; solvuntur frigore membra, Verg.; solvi morte, or solvi alone, *to die*, Ov. **B.** Fig., **1,** *to remove by breaking up*, **a,** *to bring to an end, terminate*, injuriam, Sall.; pass., hiems solvitur, *is broken up, disappears*, Hor.; **b,** *to break, to violate*, traditum a prioribus morem, Liv.; solventur risu tabulae (perhaps = *the laws will lose their force*, but see under tabulae, II. 1.), Hor.; **c,** *to banish, get rid of*, pudorem, Verg.; metum corde, Verg.; **2,** *to solve, explain*, juris nodos et legum aenigmata, Juv.; captiosa, Cic.

Sŏlymi -ōrum, m. (Σολυμοι), *the earliest inhabitants of Lycia, from whom, according to some, the Jews were descended, whence the name Hierosolyma, Jerusalem.* Hence, adj., **Sŏlymus** -a -um, *belonging to Jerusalem or the Jews.*

somnĭātor -ōris, m. (somnio), *a dreamer*, Sen.

somnĭcŭlōsē, adv. (somniculosus), *sleepily, lazily*, Plaut.

somnĭcŭlōsus -a -um (somnus), *sleepy, drowsy, sluggish*, senectus, Cic.

somnĭfer -fĕra -fĕrum (somnus and fero). **I.** *sleep-bringing, sleep-causing*, virga (Mercurii), Ov. **II.** *narcotic, deadly*, venenum, Ov.

somnĭfĭcus -a -um (somnus and facio), *bringing or causing sleep*, Plin.

somnĭo, 1. (somnium), *to dream.* **I.** Lit., totas noctes, Cic.; de aliquo, Cic.; with acc., *to dream of*, ovum, Cic.; with accus. and infin., ovum pendēre ex fascia lecti, Cic. **II.** Transf., *to dream, think, or imagine foolishly*, portenta non disserentium philosophorum, sed somniantium, Cic.; with acc. (= *of*, etc.), Trojanum, Cic.

somnĭum -ii, n. (somnus), *a dream*, **1,** lit., per somnia (*in a dream*) loqui, Cic.; **2,** transf., *vain imagination, foolishness, nonsense*, Ter.

somnus -i, m. (for sop-nus, root SOP, whence sopor and sopio), *sleep, slumber.* **I.** **A.** Lit., **1,** gen., Endymionis, *everlasting*, Cic.; somnum capere non posse, *not to be able to sleep*, Cic.; somnum tenere, *to keep oneself from sleeping*, Cic.; somnum alicui afferre, Cic.; somno consopiri sempiterno, Cic.; dare se somno, Cic.; aliquem ex somno excitare, Cic.; in somnis videre, Cic.; **2,** esp., *drowsiness, laziness, inactivity*, somno nati, Cic.; dediti somno, Sall. **B.** Transf., *the sleep of death*, longus, Hor. **II.** Meton., *night*, libra die (= diei) somnique pares ubi fecerit horas, Verg.

sŏnābĭlis -e (sono), *sounding, resounding*, sistrum, Ov.

sŏnans -antis, p. adj. (from sono) *sounding;* concha, Ov.; of words, ut sint alia (verba) sonantiora, *full sounding, sonorous*, Cic.

sŏnax -ācis (sono), *sounding, resounding*, Ov.

sonchos -i, m. (σογχος), *the plant sow-thistle*, Plin.

sŏnĭpēs -pĕdis (sonus and pes), *sounding with the feet*, usually subst., m. *the horse*, Verg.

sŏnĭtus -ūs, m. (sono), *a sound, noise;* Olympi, *thunder*, Verg.; sonitum reddere, Cic.

sŏnĭvĭus -a -um (sono), *sounding*, only used in augury in the phrase sonivium tripudium, *the noise of the food falling from the beaks of the sacred chickens*, Cic.

sŏno, sŏnŭi, sŏnĭtum, 1. (sonus). **I.** Intransit., **1,** *to sound, resound, make a noise*, **a,** sonuerunt tympana, Caes.; classica sonant, Verg.; sonare inani voce, *to produce an empty jingle of words*, Cic.; with acc. neut., amnis rauca sonans, *sounding harshly*, Verg.; **b,** esp., of discourse, *to sound*, bene, melius, optime sonare, Cic.; **2,** *to re-echo*, ripae sonant, Verg. **II.** Transit., *to sound*, **1, a,** *to produce a sound;* inconditis vocibus inchoatum quiddam atque peregrinum sonantes, Cic.; nec vox hominem sonat, *sounds human*, Verg.; **b,** *to betray by a sound*, furem sonuere juvenci, Prop.; **2,** *to mean*, quid sonet haec vox, Cic.; **3, a,** *to shout, cry, sing*, euhoe Bacche, Ov.; **b,** *to sing of;* bella, Ov.; **c,** *to celebrate*, atavos et atavorum antiqua nomina, Verg. (fut. partic., sonaturum, Hor.)

sŏnor -ōris, m. (sono), *sound, noise, din*, sonorem dant silvae, Verg.

sŏnōrus -a -um (sonor), *sounding, resonant, ringing, loud, sonorous*, cithara, Tib.; tempestas, Verg.

sons, sontis, *guilty, deserving of punishment;* anima, Verg.; sanguis, Ov.; subst., punire sontes, *the guilty*, Cic.

Sontĭātes -um, m. *a people in Gallia Aquitania, on the borders of Gallia Celtica.*

sontĭcus -a -um (sons), *dangerous*, morbus *dangerous* (such a disease as forms an excuse for not appearing in a court of law), hence, causa, *a weighty, serious, important excuse*, Tib.

sŏnus -i, m. *a noise, sound, din.* **I.** **1,** lit., **a,** dulcis, Cic.; ab acutissimo sono usque ad gravissimum sonum, *from the highest treble to the deepest bass*, Cic.; inanes sonos fundere, Cic.; **b,** esp., *a word*, ficti soni, Ov.; **2,** meton., *voice, speech*, tunc mens et sonus relapsus, Hor. **II.** Transf., *tone*, Cic.

sŏphĭa -ae, f. (σοφια), *wisdom*, Mart.

sŏphisma -ătis, n. (σοφισμα), *a sophism*, Sen.

sŏphista -ae, m. and **sŏphistes** -ae, m. (σοφιστής), *a sophist, a philosopher who taught for money eloquence, practical wisdom, the art of disputing, etc.*, hence often = *a quibbler, charlatan*, Cic.

Sŏphŏcles -is, m., voc. Sophocle (Σοφοκλῆς), *the famous Greek tragic poet.* Hence, adj.,

Sŏphŏclēus -a -um, *Sophoclean, relating to Sophocles*, Cic

Sŏphŏnība -ae, f (Σοφονίβα), *daughter of Hasdrubal, wife of the Numidian king, Syphax*

1 **sŏphus (-ŏs)** -i, m (σοφος), *wise*, Phaedr., subst, *a wise man*, Mart

2 **sŏphōs** (σοφῶς), adv *bravo, well done*, Mart

sōpĭo -ivi and -ii -ītum, 4. **I.** *to put to sleep, lull to sleep*, **1,** gen , **a,** of living beings, vino oneratos, Liv , pervigilem draconem herbis, Ov , partic , sopitus, *lulled to sleep*, vigiles, Liv , **b,** transf , of things, *to lull, quiet* , in pass , sopiri, sopitum esse = *to slumber, rest*, virtus sopita sit, Cic , ignis sopitus, *slumbering under the ashes*, Verg , 2, *to lull to an eternal sleep, kill*, quiete sopitus, Lucr **II.** Meton , *to stun, render senseless*, impactus ita est saxo, ut sopiretur, Liv

sŏpor ōris, m (root SOP, whence sopio and somnus), *deep sleep* **I.** Lit , **1,** gen , sopor aliquem opprimit, Liv , personif , Sopor, *the god of sleep*, Verg , **2,** *the sleep of death*, perpetuus sopor, Hor. **II.** Meton , 1, *sleepiness, laziness, inactivity*, Tac , **2,** *a sleeping draught*, patri soporem dare, Nep

sŏpōrātus -a -um, p adj (from soporo) **I.** *sleeping* hostes, Ov **II.** *provided with sleep giving power, stupefying*, ramus vi soporatus Stygiā, Verg

sŏpōrĭfĕr -fĕra -fĕrum (sopor and fero), *causing deep sleep, soporific*, Verg

sŏpōro, 1 (sopor), *to put to sleep, cast into a deep sleep*, Plin.

sŏpōrus -a -um (sopor), *sleep-bringing*, Nox, Verg

Sōra -ae, f *the most northerly town of the Volsci, in Latium, on the right bank of the Liris*, still called *Sora*. Hence, **Sōrānus** a -um, *belonging to Sora*

Sōractĕ (Sauractĕ) is, n *a mountain in Etruria, near Rome, on which stood a famous temple of Apollo*, now *Monte di S Silvestro*

Sōrānus -a um, v Sora

sōrăcum -i, n (σώρακος), *a pannier, hamper*, Plaut

sorbĕo, sorbŭi, 2 (root SORB, Gk POB, whence ροφεω), *to suck up, suck in, drink down, to swallow* **I** Lit , **a,** of persons, sanguinem, Plin , **b,** of things, Charybdis vastos sorbet in abruptum fluctus, Verg , sorbent avidae praecordia flammae, Ov **II.** Fig , odia, *to swallow, put up with*, Cic.

1 **sorbĭlo (sorbillo)**, 1 (dim of sorbeo), *to suck in, sip*, Ter

2 **sorbĭlo,** adv (sorbeo), *drop by drop*, Plaut

sorbĭtĭo -ōnis, f (sorbeo), *a draught, potion*, Pers

sorbum -i, n *the fruit of the* sorbus, *a service-berry*, Verg

sorbus i, f *the service-tree*, Plin

sordĕo, sordŭi, 2 (sordes) **I.** *to be dirty, filthy* cunctane prae campo sordent? Hor **II.** Fig , 1, *to be mean, sordid in appearance*, Plaut , **2,** *to be contemptible, be despised*, adeo se suis etiam sordere, Liv

sordes is, f and gen plur , **sordes** -ium, f *dirt, filth* **I. 1,** lit , **a,** sine sordibus ungues, Hor , in sordibus aurium inhaerescere, Cic , **b,** esp , *soiled or dirty garments, used by mourners and persons accused* , sordes lugubres, Cic , **2,** meton , of persons, O tenebrae, lutum, sordes, Cic , apud sordem urbis et faecem, *the dregs of the people*, Cic **II.** Transf , **1,** *meanness, baseness* , hominis, Cic ; fortunae et vitae, Cic ; **2,** *sordid frugality, stinginess, niggardliness* , **a,** rarely in sing , nulla in re familiari sordes, Cic , **b,** gen in plur , mens oppleta sordibus, Cic

sordesco, sordŭi, 3 (sordeo), *to become dirty*, Hor

sordĭdātus -a -um (sordidus), *wearing dirty clothes* , **a,** gen , Cic , **b,** (v sordes, 1 b), *clad in mourning*, Cic

sordĭdē, adv (sordidus). **I** *meanly, in a low station* , nasci, Tac **II.** Transf , **a,** *vulgarly, meanly* , dicere, Cic , **b,** *sordidly, stingily*, Cic

sordĭdŭlus -a -um (dim of sordidus), *somewhat dirty*, Juv

sordĭdus -a -um (sordeo), *dirty, filthy, unclean* **I.** Lit , **1,** gen , amictus, Verg , mappa, Hor , **2,** *in soiled or dirty clothes, as a sign of mourning* , squalore sordidus, Cic **II.** Transf , **1,** *poor, mean, base* (in rank or condition), *humble, small, paltry* , loco sordido ortus, Liv , reus, Cic , oratores sordidiores, artes sordidiores, Cic , ut quisque sordidissimus videbatur, Cic , **2,** *mean, base, vile, disgraceful* , iste omnium turpissimus et sordidissimus, Cic , esp , *stingy, sordid* , homo, Cic , cupido, Hor

sordĭtūdo -inis, f (sordes), *dirt, filth*, Plaut

sōrex icis, m (υραξ), *a shrew-mouse*, Plin

sōrĭcīnus -a -um (sorex), *of or relating to a shrew-mouse*, Plaut

sōrītes ae, m (σωρείτης), *a sorites, a sophism formed by accumulation of arguments*, Cic (dat , soriti, Cic , acc. sing , soritam, Cic)

sŏror (= sosor, connected with English *sister*, and German *schwester*), *a sister* **I.** Lit , **1,** gen , Cic , Phoebi, *Luna*, Ov ; magna soror matris Eumenidum, *the earth as sister of night*, Verg , plur , Sorores, *the Parcae*, Ov , so tres sorores, Hor *the Furies*, Ov , **2,** esp = soror patruelis, *aunt*, Cic , Ov **II.** Transf , **a,** as a term of endearment, *friend, playmate* , sorores meae, Verg , **b,** of things alike or connected, e g , the hair, Cat

sŏrōrĭcīda -ae, m (soror and caedo), *one who murders a sister*, Cic

sŏrōrĭo, 1 (soror), applied to the female breasts, *to grow up or swell together* , Plin

sŏrōrĭus -a um (soror), *of or relating to a sister, sisterly*, stupra, *incest*, Cic

sors, sortis, f (from 1 sero, as fors from fero), *a lot* **I. A.** Lit , **a,** conjicere sortes in hydriam, Cic , or simply, conjicere sortes, Cic , dejicere sortes, Cic , sors mea exit, *comes out*, Cic , ut sors excideret, Liv , **b,** esp , sortes, used as oracles, verses (from Vergil, etc), written on leaves and drawn by persons , sortes ducere, Juv **B.** Transf , res revocatur ad sortem, Cic , conjicere in sortem provincias, *to cast lots for*, Liv **II.** Meton , **1,** *an oracular response, prophecy* , sors oraculi, Liv , sors ad sortes referenda, Cic. , **2,** *official duty* , nunquam afuit nisi sorte, Cic , **3, a,** = *part* , in nullam sortem bonorum nato, Liv , Saturni sors prima, *first child*, Ov , **b,** *lot, fate, fortune, destiny* , nescia mens hominum fati sortisque futurae, Verg , illacrimare sorti humanae, Liv hence, esp , (α) *rank* or *station of a person* , prima, secunda, Liv , (β) *sex* , altera, *female*, Ov , (γ) *kind* , nova pugnae sors, Verg , **4,** *money, capital out at interest* , sorte caret, usurā nec eā solidā contentus est, Cic (archaic abl , sorti, Verg)

sortĭcŭla -ae, f (dim of sors), *a little lot or ticket*, Suet

sortĭlĕgus -a -um (sors and lego), *prophetic, oracular*, Hor Subst , **sortĭlĕgus** -i, m. *a soothsayer, fortune teller*, Cic

sortĭor, 4. dep. (sors). **I.** Intransit., *to cast lots*; inter se, Cic. **II.** Transit., **A.** *to decide by lot, cast lots for*; **1,** lit., provinciam, Cic.; consules sortiti, uter dedicaret, Liv.; quasi sortiri, quid loquare, Cic.; **2,** transf., **a,** *to choose, select*; subolem, Verg.; **b,** *to share, divide*; regnum in plebem, Liv. **B.** *to gain by lot*; **1,** lit., peregrinam (provinciam), Liv.; **2,** transf., *to gain by fate, to get, receive, obtain*; mediterranea Asiae, Liv.; amicum casu, Hor.; **sortītus** -a -um, pass., *gained by lot*, Cic.

sortītĭo -ōnis, f. (sortior), *a casting lots, deciding by casting lots*; judicium sortitio fit, Cic.

sortītō, adv. (abl. of sortitus, from sortior), *by lot*, Cic.

sortītor -ōris, m. (sortior), *one who draws lots*, Sen.

1. **sortītus** -ūs, m. (sortior), *a casting of lots, deciding by lot*, Cic., Verg.

2. **sortītus** -a -um, partic. of sortior.

sōry (sōri) -rĕōs, n. (σῶρυ), *inkstone, sory*, Plin.

sospĕs -ĭtis (root SOS, σῶς), *safe, unhurt, uninjured*. **I. a,** of persons, sospites brevi in patriam ad parentes restituunt, Liv.; **b,** of things, navis sospes ab ignibus, Hor. **II.** Transf. = *lucky, favourable*: cursus, Hor.

Sospĭta -ae, f. (sospes), *the Saviour*; Juno Sospita, *a goddess worshipped originally in Lanuvium, afterwards at Rome*; illa vestra Sospita, Cic.

sospĭtālis -e (sospes), *salutary*, Plaut.

sospĭto, 1. (sospes), *to keep safe, preserve*; suam progeniem, Liv.

sōtēr -tēris, acc. -tēra, m. (σωτήρ), *a saviour*, Cic.

sōtērĭa -ōrum, n. (σωτήρια), *presents given in celebration of a recovery from sickness*, Mart.

spādix -dīcis (σπάδιξ), *of the colour of a palm-branch with its fruit, chestnut-coloured*; equi, Verg.

spădo -ōnis, m. (σπάδων), *a eunuch*, Liv.

spădōnĭus -a -um (spado), *unfruitful, producing no seed*, Plin.

spargănĭon -ĭi, n. (σπαργάνιον), *the plant burweed*, Plin.

spargo, sparsi, sparsum, 3. (root SPAR, Gr. ΣΠΑΡ, whence σπείρω). **I.** *to scatter, strew, sprinkle*. **A.** Gen., nummos populo, Cic.; nuces, Verg. **B.** Esp., **1,** *to scatter seeds, to sow*; semina humo, Ov.; fig., animos in corpora, Cic.; **2,** *to throw, hurl, cast*; tela, Verg.; **3,** *to scatter, disperse, dissipate*; **a,** (α) of things, arma (*war*) per agros, Liv.; hence, *to scatter, spread abroad, circulate a report*; spargere voces in vulgum ambiguas, Verg.; Argolicas nomen per urbes Theseos, Ov.; (β) of things, *to divide, distribute*; per vias speculatores, Liv.; also, *to disperse, scatter in flight*; spargere se in fugam, Liv.; **b,** *to dissipate property*; spargas tua prodigus, Hor.; **c,** *to tear in pieces*; corpora, Ov. **II.** *to besprinkle, bestrew*; **1,** lit., humum foliis, Verg.; **2,** transf., **a,** *to besprinkle*; aurora spargebat lumine terras, Verg.; fig., litterae humanitatis sale sparsae, Cic.; **b,** *to bedew, moisten*; lacrimā favillam amici, Hor.; **c,** *to dash, speckle*; alas coloribus, Verg.

sparsĭo -ōnis, f. (spargo), *a sprinkling of perfumed waters in the theatre*, Sen.

sparsus -a -um, p. adj. (spargo). **I.** *spread out, scattered*; crines, *dishevelled*, Liv. **II.** *speckled, coloured, spotted*; anguis maculis sparsus, Liv.

Sparta -ae, f. and **Spartē** -ēs, f. (Σπάρτη), *Sparta, the capital of Laconia*, now *Misitra*. Hence, adj., **A. Spartānus** -a -um, *Spartan*; subst., **Spartānus** -i, m. *a Spartan*. **B. Spartĭcus** -a -um, *Spartan*. **C.** Subst., **Spartĭātes** -ae, m. *a Spartan*.

Spartăcus -i, m. *a gladiator, by birth a Thracian, head of the Gladiatorial War against the Romans*, 73–71 B.C., *defeated by Crassus*.

spartārĭus -a -um (spartum), *bearing esparto grass*, Plin.; plur. subst., **spartārĭa** -ōrum, n. (sc. loca), *places where esparto grass grows*, Plin.

spartum (-on) -i, n. (σπάρτον), **1,** *a kind of grass, esparto grass*, Liv., Plin.; **2,** *rope made of esparto grass*, Plin.

spărŭlus -i, m. (dim. of sparus), *a kind of fish, a bream*, Ov.

spărus -i, m. and **spărum** -i, n. *a small curved spear* or *javelin, a hunting-spear*, Verg., Sall.

spasmus -i, m. (σπασμός), and **spasma** -ătis, n. (σπάσμα), *a cramp, spasm*, Plin.

spastĭcus -a -um (σπαστικός), *seized with cramp* or *spasm*, Plin.

spătha -ae, f. (σπάθη). **I.** *a wooden instrument for stirring* or *mixing, a spatula*, Plin. **II.** *an instrument of like shape used by weavers*, Sen. **III.** *a broad two-edged sword without point*, Tac. **IV.** *the pedicle of the leaf* or *flower of a palm-tree*, Plin. **V.** *a kind of pine* or *fir*, also called elate, Plin.

spătĭor, 1. dep. (spatium), *to walk, walk about, to take a walk, to promenade*; in xysto, Cic.; in sicca arena, Verg.; transf., of things, *to spread out, expand*; alae spatiantes, Ov.

spătĭōsē, adv. (spatiosus). **I. a,** *widely, extensively*, Plin.; **b,** *greatly*; spatiosius increvit flumen, Ov. **II.** Fig., of time, *long*, Prop.

spătĭōsus -a -um (spatium). **I.** *occupying much space, wide, spacious, large*; taurus, Ov. **II.** Fig., of time, *long*; nox, Ov.

spătĭum -ĭi, n. (σπάδιον Dorian = στάδιον), *space, distance*, or *extension in length and breadth*. **I. A.** Gen., spatia locorum, Caes.; caeli spatium, Verg. **B.** Esp., *space* or *distance between two points*; **1, a,** *distance, interval*; paribus spatiis intermissae trabes, Caes.; **b,** *circumference, size, length*; oris et colli, Ov.; **2, a,** *tract, extent, course*; longum spatium itineris, Caes.; eadem spatia quinque stellae conficiunt, Cic.; **b,** *the course in a race*; spatia corripere, Verg.; fig., quasi decurso spatio, Cic.; **c,** *a walk*; (α) duobus spatiis tribusve factis, Cic.; (β) *a place for walking in, walk, promenade*; spatia silvestria, Cic. **II.** Transf., of time, **A.** Gen., **a,** *a division* or *space of time, time*; spatium preteriti temporis, Cic.; hoc interim spatio, Cic.; **b,** *duration of time, length of time*; spatio pugnae defatigati, Caes. **B.** Esp., **1,** *the time fixed for any action, time, leisure, opportunity*; nisi tempus et spatium datum sit, Cic.; irae spatium dare, *give the reins to*, Liv.; si mihi aliquid spatii ad scribendum dareut, Cic.; **2,** *metrical time, measure, quantity*, Cic.

spĕcĭālis -e (species), *individual, particular, special*, Quint.

spĕcĭes -ēi, f. (specio). **I.** Act., *a seeing, sight, view, look*; speciem aliquo vertere, Lucr. **II.** Pass. = **1,** *sight, look, appearance*, speciem boni viri prae se ferre, Cic.; speciem ridentis praebere, Liv.; **2,** *form, figure*, esp. of imposing appearance; humana, Cic.; divina, Liv.; **3,** *beautiful form, beauty*; vaccae, Ov.; esp. of outward ornament, *glitter, splendour*; triumpho maximam speciem captiva arma praebuere, Liv.; **4,** *that which a man sees mentally*; **a,** *model, ideal*; eloquentiae, Cic.; **b,** *idea, conception, notion*; boni viri, Cic.; **c,** *a vision seen in a dream, a dream, phantom*; consuli visa species uni, Liv ; d, *appearance, show*, speciem utilitatis habere, Cic , specie, *in appearance*, Cic , ad speciem, *for the sake of outward show* (to deceive), Cic , 5, *a statue, representation, image*, Cic , 6, *a kind, species, division of a genus*, Cic (genit and dat plur not used by classical authors)

spĕcillum -i, n (specio), *a surgeon's probe*, Cic

spĕcĭmen inis, n (specio), *that by which a thing is known, mark, token, sample specimen* I. Lit., ingenii, Cic , justitiae, Liv. II. Transf., *a pattern, example, ideal*, prudentiae, Cic , num dubitas quin specimen naturae capi debeat ex optima quaque natura, Cic (only used in the sing)

spĕcio (spĭcio), spexi, spectum (σκέπτω), *to look at, behold, see*, Plaut

spĕcĭōsē, adv (speciosus), *beautifully, splendidly, handsomely, showily*, speciosius instratus equus quam uxor vestita, Liv

spĕcĭōsus -a -um (species) I. *beautiful, splendid, handsome*, mulier, Ov , hence, a, *dazzling, well-sounding*, nomina, Tac , b, *imposing, distinguished*, opes, Tac , exemplum, Liv II. *plausible, specious*, vocabula, Hor , titulus, Liv., with 2 supine, si vera potius quam dictu speciosa dicenda sunt, Liv

spectābĭlis -e (specto), 1, *visible*, corpus, Cic , 2, *worth seeing, notable, remarkable*, heros, Ov

spectācŭlum -i, n (specto), *a sight, show, spectacle* I. Gen , luctuosum, Cic , rerum caelestium, Cic , alicui spectaculum praebere, Cic , spectaculo esse, Cic II. Esp , *a spectacle in the theatre or circus*, 1, lit , spectaculum apparatissimum, Cic., gladiatorium, Liv , 2, meton , *a place from which or where one can see a spectacle*, gen plur , spectacula, a, *the stage, the seats* spectacula sunt tributim data, Cic , b, *the theatre*, Suet

spectāmen -inis, n (specto), *a sign, token, proof*, Plaut

spectātē, adv , but only in superl (spectatus), *admirably, excellently*, Plin

spectātio -ōnis, f (specto), *a looking at, beholding, viewing* I. Gen , apparatus, Cic , animum spectatione levari, Cic II. *the inspection, testing of money*, Cic

spectātīvus -a um (specto), *contemplative* (opp. activus), *theoretical*, Quint

spectātor ōris, m (specto) I. *one who beholds, contemplates, a spectator, observer*, a, quasi spectatores superarum rerum atque caelestium, Cic , b, *a spectator at the theatre or public games*, Cic II. *an inspector, examiner*, formarum, *connoisseur*, Ter , acrior virtutis spectator ac judex, Liv

spectātrix -tricis, f (spectator), *a female spectator, beholder, observer*, Ov

spectātus a um, p adj (from specto) I. *proved, approved, tried*; homo, Cic , castitas, Liv II. Esp , *of tried abilities, excellent, respected, renowned*; vir spectatissimus, Cic

spectio -ōnis, f (specio), *the right of observing the auspices appertaining to certain of the higher magistrates*, nos (augures) nuntiationem solum habemus, consules et reliqui magistratus etiam spectionem, Cic

specto, 1 (intens of specio), *to look at carefully, contemplate, observe*. I. Lit., A. Gen , aliquid, Cic , tota domus quae spectat in nos solos, Cic , spectatumne huc venimus? Liv B. Esp , 1, *to be a spectator of a spectacle or play, to look at, look on at*, fabulam, ludos, Hor , Megalesia, Cic , 2, a, *to look at with wonder*, gaude quod spectent oculi te mille loquentem, Hor , b, *to look at for the purpose of examining or testing, to test, to examine*, spectatur in ignibus aurum, Ov , fig , hunc igni spectatum arbitrantur, *tried by fire*, Cic , 3, of places, *to look towards, lie towards, be situate towards*, collis ad orientem solem spectabat, Caes , spectare in Etruriam, Liv , spectare inter occasum solis et septentriones, Caes II. Fig , A. *to look at, contemplate, observe*, voluptatis procul specto, Cic. B. Esp , 1 *to look to as an aim or object, bear in mind, have a regard to strive after*, a, of persons, magna, Cic , ea quae sunt in usu vitaque communi, Cic fugam, Cic , with ut and the subj , spectavi semper ut possem, etc , Cic , with ad and the acc , ad imperatorias laudes, Cic , b, transf , *to tend to, incline to*, ad perniciem, Cic , ad bene beateque vivendum, Cic , quo igitur haec spectat oratio? *what is the aim (or tendency) of this speech?* Cic , 2, *to judge, test*, aliquem ex trunco corporis, Cic , non ex singulis vocibus philosophi spectanda sunt, Cic

spectrum -i, n (specio), *the appearance, image of anything, spectre, apparition*, Cic

1 **spĕcŭla** -ae, f (specio) I *a watch tower*, speculas per promuntoria omnia ponere, Liv , multo ante tamquam ex specula prospexi tempestatem futuram, Cic , fig , homines in speculis sunt, *on the watch*, Cic II. Transf , in speculis, *any lofty place*, Verg

2 **spēcŭla** -ae, f (dim of spes), *a little hope*, qui aliquid ex eius sermone speculae degustarat, Cic

spĕcŭlābundus -a um (speculor), *watching, on the watch*, Tac

spĕcŭlāris e (speculum), *of or relating to a mirror*, Sen , lapis, *a species of transparent stone, talc*, Plin Subst , **spĕcŭlāria** ium and ōrum, n *window-panes made of talc*, Plin

spĕcŭlātor -ōris, m (speculor) I. *a looker-out, scout, spy*, Caes , Cic II Transf , *an observer, investigator*, naturae, Cic

spĕcŭlātōrius -a -um (speculator), *of or relating to a looker out or scout*, navigia, Caes , naves, Liv , and subst , speculatoriae, *vessels on the look out, spy-boats*, Liv

spĕcŭlātrix icis, f (speculator), *she that observes, a looker out, observer, watcher*, Furiae sunt speculatrices et vindices facinorum et scelerum, Cic

spĕcŭlor, 1 dep (specio) I. Intransit , *to spy, to look about*, unde sedens partes speculatur in omnes, Ov II. Transit , *to look out, spy out, watch, observe, explore*, omnia, Cic , loca, Cic , alicuius consilia, Sall , with rel sent , quae fortuna esset, Liv

spĕcŭlum i, n (specio) *a mirror* (made of glittering plates of metal) I. Lit , speculorum levitas, Cic , speculo placere, *to be brilliantly adorned*, Ov , speculum suum consulere, Ov , se speculo videre alterum, Hor II. Fig = *an image, copy*, quae (parvos et bestias) putat esse specula naturae, Cic

spĕcus -ūs, m f and n (σπέος), *a cave* I. Lit , a, *a natural cave*, Hor , Liv , horrendum, Verg , b, *an artificial cave, excavation*, (α) in defossis specubus, Verg , (β) *a covered watercourse, culvert*, subterranei, Cic II. Transf , *a hole, hollow*, vulneris, Verg

spēlaeum -i, n (σπήλαιον), *a cave, grotto, hole, den*, ferarum, Verg

spēlunca -ae, f (σπῆλυγξ), *a cave, grotto*, Cic , Verg

spērābĭlis -e (spero), *that may be hoped for*, Plaut

Spercheos (-cheus) and **Sperchios** (-chius) -i, m. (Σπερχειός), *a river in Thessaly.* Hence, **A. Spercheïs** -ĭdis, f. *of Spercheus.* **B. Sperchīŏnīdes** -ae, m. *a person who lives near the Spercheus.* **C. Sperchiae** -ārum, f. *a town in the valley of the Spercheus.*

sperno, sprēvi, sprētum, 3. **I.** *to separate, remove,* Plaut. **II.** Transf., *to reject, to despise, contemn, scorn, spurn;* nos sprevit et pro nihilo putavit, Cic.; voluptatem, Hor.; poet. with infin., nec partem solido demere de die spernit, Hor.; partic., **sprētus** -a -um, *despised,* Cic., Liv.

spēro, 1. *to look for, to expect.* **I.** *to expect something favourable, to hope, hope for, promise oneself, flatter oneself;* bene or recte, *to have good hopes,* Cic.; ut spero (in a parenthesis), Cic.; de aliqua re, Cic.; pacem, Cic.; in pass., sperata gloria, Cic.; with acc. and fut. infin., sperant se maximum fructum esse capturos, Cic.; more rarely with pres. or perf. infin. (when there is no reference to the future), spero ex hoc ipso non esse obscurum, Cic.; de nostra Tullia spero cum Crassipede nos confecisse, Cic.; with ut and the subj., Liv.; partic. as subst., **spērāta** -ōrum, n. *one's hopes;* potiri speratis, *to realise one's hopes,* Liv. **II.** Like ἐλπίζω, *to expect something unfavourable, to forebode, fear;* id quod non spero, Cic.; with acc. and infin., haec spero vobis molesta videri, Cic.

spēs -ĕi, f. (root SPE, whence spero). **I.** *hope;* **1,** lit., **a,** spes est exspectatio boni, Cic.; spes emptionis, Cic.; summae spei adulescentes, *of great promise,* Caes.; spes est in vobis, *rests on you,* Cic.; omnem spem salutis in virtute ponere, Caes.; spem habere, in spem venire, ingredi, adduci, spes me tenet, *I hope,* foll. by acc. and infin., Cic.; si spem afferunt ut, etc., Cic.; spe duci, with acc. and infin., Cic.; spem alicui dare, *to infuse,* Cic.; pax fuit in spe, *was hoped for,* Cic.; spem abscidere, Liv., praecidere, Cic., fallere, Cic., eripere, Cic., adimere, Cic., perdere, Cic.; praeter spem, Cic.; contra spem, Liv.; plur., spes, Liv.; **b,** personif., Spes, *Hope as a goddess,* with several temples in Rome, and a festival on the 1st of August; **2,** meton., *that which is hoped for, hope;* spe potitur, *realises his hope,* Ov.; castra Achivom, vestras spes, uritis, Verg.; of living beings, spes gregis, Verg.; spes nostra reliqua, Cicero, Cic. **II.** *expectation of, fear of, foreboding;* mala res, spe multo asperior, Sall.

speustĭcus -a -um (σπευστικός), *made in haste,* Plin.

sphaera -ae, f. (σφαῖρα), *a globe, sphere.* **I.** Gen., Cic. **II.** **a,** *an astronomical globe or sphere,* Cic.; **b,** *the orbit of planets,* Cic.

sphaeristērĭum -ĭi, n. (σφαιριστήριον), *a place for playing ball,* Plin.

sphaerŏmăchĭa -ae, f. (σφαιρομαχία), *a kind of boxing in which the combatants had iron balls strapped to their hands,* Sen.

sphagnos -i, m. (σφάγνος), *a kind of aromatic moss,* Plin.

sphingĭon -ĭi, n. (σφίγγιον), *a species of ape,* Plin.

Sphinx, Sphingis, f. (Σφίγξ), *a female monster at Thebes, who proposed riddles to all the passers-by, and destroyed them if they could not answer the riddles;* represented among the Egyptians as a winged lion with a human head, among the Greeks and Romans as an unwinged lion with the head and breast of a maiden.

sphrāgis -ĭdis, f. (σφραγίς). **I.** *a species of stone used for seals,* Plin. **II.** *Lemnian earth, so called because sold with a seal on it,* Plin.

spīca -ae, f., **spīcus** -i, m., and **spīcum** -i, n. (from same root as spi-na); lit., *a spike;* hence, *an ear of corn.* **I.** Lit., ad spicam perducere fruges, Cic. **II.** Transf., **a,** *the brightest star in the constellation Virgo,* Cic.; **b,** *the tuft or head of other plants resembling the shape of an ear of corn,* Ov.

spīcĕus -a -um (spica), *consisting of ears of corn;* corona, Tib.; serta, Ov.

spīcĭfĕr -fĕra -fĕrum (spica and fero), *wearing or carrying ears of corn,* Mart.

spīcĭlĕgĭum -ĭi, n. (spica and lego), *a gleaning,* Varr.

spīco, 1. (spica), *to furnish with spikes or ears,* Plin.; partic., **spīcātus** -a -um, *having spikes or ears;* herbae spicatae, Plin.

spīcŭlo, 1. (spiculum), *to make pointed, sharpen to a point,* Plin.

spīcŭlum -i, n. (spicum), *a sharp point, sting;* **a,** lit., of bees, Verg.; of the scorpion, Ov.; *the point of a spear, arrow, javelin,* Cic., Liv., Hor.; **b,** poet., meton. = *a spear, javelin,* Verg., Ov.

spīcum, spicus = spica (q.v.).

spīna -ae, f. (from same root as spica). **I.** *a thorn.* **A.** Lit., Verg. **B.** Fig., **a,** spinae = *cares, anxieties;* spinas animo evellere, Hor.; **b,** *difficulties, subtleties, perplexities;* disserendi, Cic. **II.** Transf., **1,** *the prickle or spine of certain animals, the hedgehog, sea-urchin,* etc., Cic.; **2,** *the backbone,* Varr.; **3,** *a fish-bone,* Ov.

spīnĕa -ae, f. = spionia (q.v.).

spīnētum -i, n. (spina), *a thorn-hedge, thorn-bush* (only used in plur.), Verg.

spīnĕus -a -um (spina), *made of thorns, thorny,* Ov.

spīnĭgĕr -gĕra -gĕrum (spina and gero), *thorn-bearing,* Cic. poet.

spīnōsus -a -um (spina). **I.** *full of thorns, thorny, prickly,* Ov. **II.** Fig., **a,** of discourse, *thorny, crabbed, obscure;* disserendi genus, Cic.; **b,** *full of cares, anxiety,* Cat.

spinter -ēris, n. (σφιγκτήρ), *a bracelet, armlet,* Plaut.

spīnus -i, m. (spina), *the blackthorn,* Verg.

spionĭa -ae, f. *a kind of vine,* Plin.

spīra -ae, f. (σπεῖρα), *anything coiled, wreathed, twisted.* **I.** Gen., *the winding of a snake,* Verg. **II.** Esp., **1,** *the base of a column,* Plin.; **2,** *a string for fastening a hat or cap under the chin,* Juv.

spīrābĭlis -e (spiro). **I.** *that may be breathed;* **a,** natura, cui nomen est aër, Cic.; **b,** *sustaining life, vital;* lumen caeli, Verg. **II.** *fitted for breathing;* viscera, Plin.

spīrācŭlum -i, n. (spiro), *an air-hole, breathing-place,* Verg.

spīraea -ae, f. (σπειραία), *the plant meadow-sweet,* Plin.

spīrāmen -ĭnis, n. (spiro), *a breathing-hole, air-hole,* Lucan.

spīrāmentum -i, n. (spiro). **I.** *a breathing-hole, air-hole,* Verg. **II.** *breathing;* meton., *a breathing-time, short pause, interval;* temporum, Tac.

spīrĭtus -ūs, m. (spiro), *breathing.* **I.** **1,** *a gentle blowing, breath of air, air in gentle motion;* spiritus Boreae, Verg.; **2,** *the breathing in of the air, breath;* spiritum ducere, *to draw breath,* Cic.; **3,** *breath;* angustior, *short breath,* Cic.; esp., *the breath of life, life;* spiritum auferre, Cic.; extremum spiritum effundere in victoria, Cic.; hence, **a,** *a sigh,* Hor., Prop.; **b,** *the hissing of a snake,* Verg.; **c,** *the voice,* Quint.;

d, *breath*, Lucr **II.** *the spirit, soul* **A.** dum spiritus hos regit artus, Verg **B.** Fig, **1,** *a haughty spirit, pride, arrogance, high spirit, courage*, filia Hieronis, inflata muliebri spiritu, Liv, spiritus tribunicii, Cic, remittere spiritus, Cic, **2,** *opinion, feeling*, Liv, **3,** *irritation, animosity*, Tac, **4,** *divine or poetic inspiration*, divinus, Liv, carent libri spiritu illo, etc, Cic

spīro, 1. **I.** Intransit, **1,** *to blow gently, blow, breathe*, zephyri spirant, Verg, **2,** *to breathe*, poet = *to rush, to foam, ferment, roar*, freta spirantia, Verg, spirat e pectore flamina, Verg, with abl, spirare ignibus, *to breathe out flame*, Verg, **3,** *to breathe, to draw in breath*, dum spirare potero, Cic, hence transf, **a,** *to live, be alive*, ab eo spirante defendi, Cic, videtur Laelii mens spirare in scriptis, Cic, **b,** *to seem to live* of works of art, *to be depicted to the life, to breathe*, spirantia signa, Verg, **c,** *to have poetic inspiration, to be inspired*, quod spiro et placeo tuum est, Hor, **4,** *to breathe, to smell*, thymbra graviter spirans, Verg **II.** Transit, **1,** *to breathe, exhale*, Diomedis equi spirantes naribus ignem, Lucr, flammas spirantes, *breathing forth flames*, Liv; spirare ignem naribus, Verg, tunc immensa cavi spirant mendacia folles, Juv, transf, homo tribunatum etiamnunc spirans, *inspired with the spirit of a tribune*, Liv, tragicum satis, *to have tragic genius*, Hor, **2,** *to exhale, give forth*, divinum vertice odorem, Verg

spissāmentum -i, n. (spisso), *a stopper, plug*, Sen

spissē, adv (spissus) **I.** *densely, closely*, Plin **II** *slowly*, spisse atque vix ad aliquem pervenire, Cic

spissesco, 3 (spissus), *to become thick, thicken*, Lucr

spissĭgrădus a um (spisse and gradior), *walking slowly*, Plaut.

spissĭtas -ātis, f (spissus), *closeness, density*, Plin

spissĭtūdo -inis, f (spissus), *closeness, density*, Sen

spisso, 1 (spissus), *to make thick, thicken*, Ov

spissus a um, *close, dense, thick* **I.** Lit, nubes, Ov, theatrum, *full*, Hor, arena, Verg, with abl, corona spissa viris, Verg **II** Transf, *slow, tardy, difficult*, opus spissum et operosum, Cic, exitus spissi et producti, Cic

spĭthăma ae, f (σπιθαμή), *a span*, Plin

splēn, splēnis, m (σπλήν), *the spleen, milt*, Plin

splendĕo, 2 *to shine, glitter, be bright* **I** Lit, splendet tremulo sub lumine pontus, Verg **II.** Fig, *to be bright, illustrious*, virtus splendet per sese semper, Cic

splendesco dŭi, 3 (splendeo), *to become bright* **I.** Lit, Verg **II.** Fig, nihil est tam incultum, quod non splendescat oratione, Cic

splendĭdē, adv (splendidus). **I.** *splendidly, magnificently*, ornare convivium, Cic, acta aetas honeste ac splendide, Cic **II.** *clearly, plainly*, loqui, Cic

splendĭdus a -um (splendeo), *shining, bright, brilliant, splendid* **I. A.** Lit, fons splendidior vitro, Hor, brachia, Ov, splendidissimus candor, Cic **B.** Fig, **a,** *well-sounding*, nomen, Cic **b,** *brilliant, fine*, oratio, Cic, **c,** *illustrious, distinguished, renowned*, eques, Cic **II.** Transf, *clear*, vox, Cic

splendor -ōris, m (splendeo), *brilliance, brightness, lustre* **I. A.** Lit, flammae, Ov, argenti, Hor. **B.** Fig, **a,** *splendour, magnificence*, omnia ad gloriam splendoremque revocare, Cic, **b,** *splendour, lustre, honour, distinction*, animi et vitae, Cic, summorum hominum, Cic, eo negotio M Catonis splendorem maculare, Cic; **c,** *ornament, honour*, ordinis, Cic **II.** Transf, *clearness*, vocis, Cic.

splēnĭātus -a -um (splenium), *plastered*, Mart

splēnĭcus -a um (σπληνικός), *splenetic*, Plin

splēnium -ii, n (σπλήνιον) **I.** *spleenwort*, Plin **II.** *an adhesive plaster*, Mart

spŏdĭum -ii, n (σπόδιον) **I** *the dross of metals, slag*, Plin **II.** *ashes*, Plin

spŏdos i, f (σποδός), *the dross of metals, slag*, Plin

Spōlētium -ii, n *one of the most important towns of Umbria*, now *Spoleto* Hence, **Spōlētīnus** -a -um, *of or belonging to Spoletium, Spoletian*

spŏlĭārium -ii, n (spolium) **I.** *the place in the amphitheatre where the slain gladiators were stripped of their arms and clothing*, Sen **II.** Transf, *a den of robbers*, Sen

spŏlĭātĭo ōnis, f (spolio), *a plundering, spoliation*, omnium rerum, Cic, sacrorum, Cic, transf, *violent taking away*, consulatus, Cic, dignitatis, Cic

spŏlĭātor ōris, m (spolio), *a plunderer*, monumentorum, Cic, templorum, Liv

spŏlĭātrix trīcis, f (spoliator), *plundering, she that plunders*, Venus, Cic

spŏlĭātus -a -um, p adj with compar (from spolio), *plundered*, Cic

spŏlĭo, 1 (spolium). **I.** *to rob a man of his clothes, strip, despoil*; aliquem, Cic, corpus caesi hostis, Liv **II.** *to plunder, rob, despoil*, fana sociorum, Cic, hominem, Cic, with abl, aliquem argento, Cic, poet, with acc of respect, hiems spoliata suos capillos, Ov

spŏlĭum ii, n **I.** *the skin or hide stripped from an animal*, leonis, Ov **II.** Transf, gen plur, **1,** *arms taken from an enemy, booty* (opp praeda = *cattle*, etc.), spolia caesorum legere, Liv, spolia opima (v opimus), meton = *victory*, spolia ampla referre, Verg, **2,** transf, *booty*, **a,** *booty or plunder taken from an enemy, spoil*, spolia classium, Cic, **b,** *any kind of plunder or booty*, aliorum spoliis nostras facultates augeamus, Cic, sceleris, *the golden hair which Scylla robbed from her father*, Ov

sponda -ae, f **I.** *the frame of a bed or sofa, bedstead*, Ov. **II.** Meton, **a,** *a bed*, Hor, **b,** *a sofa*, Verg, **c,** *a bier*, Mart

spondālium (spondaulium) ii, n *a sacrificial hymn, accompanied on the flute*, Cic

spondĕo, spŏpondi, sponsum, 2 (root SPOND, Gr ΣΠΕΝΔ, σπένδω) *to pledge oneself, promise solemnly, engage*, **a,** political and legal t t of alliances, contracts, etc, quis spopondisse me dicit? Cic, with acc, quod spopondit, Cic, illis spondere pacem, Liv, with acc and infin, si spopondissemus urbem hanc relicturum populum Romanum, Liv, **b.** *to be a security or guarantee for any one*, se quisque paratum ad spondendum Icilio ostendere, Liv, hic sponsum (supine) vocat, Hor, with pro and the abl, pro multis, Cic, **c,** *to promise, betroth a daughter*, Ter, Plaut, partic subst, **sponsus** -i, m *a bridegroom*, and **sponsa** -ae, f *a bride*, Cic, **d,** *to promise, vow* (α) of persons, with acc his honores et praemia, Cic, with neut acc and de with the abl, quod de me tibi spondere possum, Cic, with acc and infin, promitto, recipio spondeo C Caesarem talem semper fore civem qualis, etc, Cic, (β), transf, of things, quod propediem futurum spondet et virtus et fortuna vestra, Liv

spondēus (spondīus) -i, m. (σπονδεῖος), *a spondee; a metrical foot consisting of two long syllables* (– –), Cic.

spondȳlē -ēs, f. (σφονδύλη), *an insect that lives upon roots*, Plin.

spondȳlium -ii, n. (σπονδύλιον), *bear's-foot*, Plin.

spondȳlus -i, m. (σπόνδυλος). **I.** *one of the upper vertebrae of the back*, Plin. **II.** *the fleshy part of the oyster* or *mussel*, Plin. **III.** *a kind of mussel*, Plin.

spongĭa (spongĕa) -ae, f. (σπογγιά), *a sponge*. **I.** Lit., raritas quaedam et assimilis spongiis mollitudo, Cic. **II.** Transf., **1,** *an open-worked cuirass*, Liv.; **2,** *the roots of the asparagus*, Plin.; **3,** spongiae, *pieces of iron melted together*, Plin.

spongĭŏla -ae, f. (spongia), *the gall-apple which grows upon rose-trees*, Plin.

spongĭōsus -a -um (spongia), *porous, spongy*, Plin.

spongītis -idis, f. (σπογγῖτις), *a kind of precious stone*, Plin.

spons, spontis, f. (from spondeo, as fors from fero), *free-will*; only found in genit. and abl. **I.** Abl., sponte alicuius, *with the free-will of some one*; sponte Antonii, Tac.; gen., sponte meā, tuā, suā, etc., or simply sponte; **a,** *of my, thy, his*, etc., *free-will, voluntarily, of one's own accord, willingly, freely*; meā sponte feceram, Cic.; **b,** *of oneself, of one's own knowledge*; neque id meā sponte (prospexi), Cic.; **c,** *of oneself alone, without assistance*; nec suā sponte sed eorum auxilio, Cic.; **d,** *of itself, merely, alone*; an est aliquid, quod te suā sponte delectet, Cic.; **e,** *first, without an example* or *precedent*; suā sponte instituisset, Cic. **II.** Genit., homo suae spontis, *one's own master*, Col.

sponsa, v. spondeo.

sponsālis -e (sponsa), *of* or *relating to a betrothal*. **I.** Adj., Varr. **II.** Subst., **sponsālĭa** -ium or -ōrum, n. *a betrothal*; sponsalia facere, Cic.; **b,** *a betrothal feast*, Cic.

sponsĭo -ōnis, f. (spondeo), *a solemn promise, engagement*. **I.** Of a vow, voti, Cic. **II.** *a solemn engagement between two parties*. **A.** In alliances, contracts, etc., *a solemn promise, pledge, surety, guarantee*; non foedere sed per sponsionem pax facta est, Liv. **B.** In civil process, *a solemn promise* or *engagement between the two parties that the loser shall forfeit a certain sum, a kind of legal wager*; quum sponsionem fecisset NI VIR BONUS ESSET, *he agreed to pay the stipulated sum if he was not*, etc., Cic.; vincere sponsionem or sponsione, Cic.

sponsor -ōris, m. (spondeo), *a surety, bail, guarantee*, Cic.

sponsum -i, n. (spondeo). **I.** *that which is promised* or *guaranteed, a covenant*; sponsum negare, Hor. **II.** = sponsio No. II., ex sponso agere, Cic.

1. **sponsus** -a -um, v. spondeo.

2. **sponsus** -ūs, m. (spondeo), *an engagement, suretyship*, Cic.

spontānĕus -a -um (spons), *voluntary, spontaneous*; Sen.

spontĕ, spontis, v. spons.

sporta -ae, f. (σπυρίς), *a basket, hamper*, Plin.

sportella -ae, f. (dim. of sporta), *a little basket, cake*, or *fruit-basket*, Cic.

sportŭla -ae, f. (dim. of sporta). **I.** *a little basket*, Plaut. **II.** *a provision-basket*. **A.** *the basket in which great men were accustomed to give to their clients and dependents provisions* or *an equivalent in money (gen. ten sesterces)*, Juv.; hence, *a gift, present*, Plin. **B.** = δεῖπνον ἀπὸ σπυρίδος, *a picnic*, Juv.

sprētĭo -ōnis, f. (sperno), *a despising, contemning*, Liv.

sprētor -ōris, m. (sperno), *a despiser*; deorum, Ov.

spūma -ae, f. (spuo), *foam, froth, scum*; cum spumas ageret in ore, Cic.; Venus spumā procreata, *from the foam of the sea*, Cic.; spuma argenti, *litharge of silver*, Verg.; spuma caustica, *a soap used by the Germans and Gauls for the purpose of giving a red tinge to the hair*, Mart.

spūmesco, 3. (spuma), *to begin to foam*, Ov.

spūmĕus -a -um (spuma), *foaming, frothy*, Verg.

spūmĭfĕr -fĕra -fĕrum (spuma and fero), *foam-bearing, foaming*; amnis, Ov.

spūmĭgĕr -gĕra -gĕrum (spuma and gero), *foaming*, Lucr.

spūmo, 1. (spuma). **I.** Intransit., *to foam, froth*; spumans aper, Verg. **II.** Transit., *to cover with foam*; partic., **spūmātus** -a -um, *covered with foam*; saxa, Cic. poet.

spūmōsus -a -um (spuma), *foaming, full of foam*, Ov.

spŭo, spŭi, spūtum, 3. (πτύω), *to spit out*; terram, Verg.

spurcē, adv. (spurcus), *filthily, dirtily*; fig., *basely, impurely*; quin in illam miseram tam spurce, tam impie dixeris, Cic.

spurcĭdĭcus -a -um (spurce and dico), *talking filthily, obscenely*, Plaut.

spurcĭfĭcus -a -um (spurce and facio), *making filthy, polluting*, Plaut.

spurcĭtĭa -ae, f. and **spurcĭtĭes** -ēi, f. (spurcus), *dirt, filth*, Lucr.

spurco, 1. (spurcus), *to defile, pollute*, Cat.; partic. adj. in superl., helluo spurcatissimus, Cic.

spurcus -a -um (perhaps connected with spargo), *swinish, dirty, filthy, unclean, impure*. **I.** Lit., Cat. **II.** Fig., of character or position, *mean, base, low, foul, impure*; homo spurcissimus, Cic.

spūtātĭlĭcĭus -a -um (sputo) = καταπτυστος, *abominable, detestable*, ap. Cic.

spūtātor -ōris, m. (sputo), *one who spits much, a spitter*, Cic.

spūto, 1. (intens. of spuo), *to spit, spit out*; cum atro mixtos sanguine dentes, Ov.

spūtum -i, n. (spuo), *spittle*. **I.** Lit., Lucr. **II.** Meton., *a very thin plate of metal*, Mart.

squālĕo, 2. *to be rough, stiff*. **I.** Gen., squalentes conchae, Verg.; with abl., *to be rough with, to be stiff with = to be thickly covered with*; tunica or lorica squalens auro, Verg. **II.** Esp., **1,** *to be rough from neglect, dirty, squalid, slovenly*; barba squalens, Verg.; coma squalens, Ov.; hence, meton., *to wear dirty apparel as a sign of mourning, to mourn*; squalent municipia, Cic.; **2,** of places, *to be uncultivated, untilled*; squalent abductis arva colonis, Verg.

squāles -is, f. (squaleo), *dirt, filth*, Varr.

squālĭdē, adv. (squalidus), *roughly, in a slovenly manner*; dicere, Cic.

squālĭdus -a -um (squaleo). **I.** *rough, stiff*; membra, Lucr.; fig., of discourse, *rough, unpolished*; quoniam suā sponte squalidiora sunt, Cic. **II.** Esp., *rough from want of attention, cultivation, squalid, dirty*; **1,** lit., corpora, Liv.; **2,** transf., **a,** *in mourning attire*; reus, Ov.; **b,** *waste, desert*; humus, Ov.

squālor -ōris, m. (squaleo). **I.** *roughness*, Lucr. **II.** *roughness arising from dirt and* *neglect, filthiness, squalor*, 1, lit., squaloris plenus ac pulveris, Cic, 2, transf, *dirty cloth ing worn as a sign of mourning*, squalor et maeror, Cic

squălus -i, m *a kind of salt water fish*, Ov

squāma -ae, f (squaleo), *a scale* I. Lit, of a fish, serpent, bee, etc, Cic II. Transf, a, of things like scales, e g, *scale armour*, Verg, b, meton, *a fish*, Juv

squāmātim, adv (squama), *like scales*, Plin

squāmĕus -a -um (squama), *scaly*, Verg

squāmĭfĕr -fĕra -fĕrum (squama and fero), *scale bearing, scaly*, Sen

squāmĭgĕr gĕra -gĕrum (squama and gero), *scale bearing, scaly*, Ov, subst, **squāmĭgĕri** -ōrum, m *fishes*, Lucr

squāmōsus -a -um (squama), *covered with scales, scaly*, Verg

squatina -ae, f *a salt-water fish, a species of shark*, Plin

st! interj *hush! hist!* Ter, Plaut

Stăbiae ārum, f *a town in Campania, between Pompeii and Surrentum, destroyed with Pompeii and Herculanum on the eruption of Mount Vesuvius* Hence, adj, **Stăbiānus** a -um, *belonging to Stabiae*, subst, **Stăbiānum** -i, n *an estate at Stabiae*

stăbĭlīmen -inis, n (stabilio), *a stay, support*, Cic

stăbĭlīmentum = stabilimen (q v)

stăbĭlio, 4 (stabilis), *to make firm* I. Lit stipites, Caes II. Fig, *to make stable, to establish*, leges, rempublicam, Cic

stăbĭlis e (sto), *firm, steadfast, stable* I. Lit, via, Cic, solum, Liv II. Fig, *firm, steadfast, stable, lasting, unwavering*, amici, Cic, matrimonium, Cic, oratio, Cic, with ad and the acc, nihil est tam ad diuturnitatem memoriae stabile, Cic; subst, **stăbĭlia** -ium, n *things that are stable*, Cic

stăbĭlĭtas -ātis, f (stabilis) *firmness, stability, steadfastness* I. Lit, peditum in proeliis, Caes, stirpes stabilitatem dant iis, quae sustinent Cic II. Fig, *durability, steadfastness*, amicitiae, Cic, fortunae, Cic

stăbĭlĭtĕr, adv (stabilis), *firmly, durably*, Suet.

stăbĭlītor ōris, m (stabilio), *one who makes firm, establishes*, Sen

stăbŭlārĭus ii, m (stabulum), *a low innkeeper*, Sen

stăbŭlo, 1 (stabulum), *to have a stall or abode, to stall*, in foribus (Orci), Verg

stăbŭlor, 1 dep (stabulum) of animals, *to stand, be stabled abide*, Ov

stăbŭlum -i, n (sto) I. *a place of abode, habitation*, Plaut II. *a place of abode for animals and men of the poorer class* A. Of animals, 1, of wild animals, *den, lair* ferarum stabula alta, Verg, 2, of tame animals *a stall, stable*, poet, of pasture, Verg, plur, stabula, *the stalls, cattle-yard*, as a place of abode for shepherds, pastorum stabula, Cic B Of men of the lower classes, *inn, tavern, pot house*, Cic

stăchys -yos, f (στάχυς), *horse mint*, Plin

stacta -ae, f and **stactē** -ēs, f (στακτή), *oil of myrrh*, Lucr

stădĭum ii, n (στάδιον) I *a Greek measure of length, being 625 feet = 606 English feet, and rather less than a furlong*, Cic II. Meton, *a race course* qui stadium currit, Cic, fig, *contest, emulation*, me adolescentem multos annos in stadio eiusdem laudis exercuit Cic,

Stăgīra ōrum, n (Στάγειρος), *a town in Macedonia birth place of Aristotle*, now *Libanora* Hence, **Stăgīrītēs** -ae, m (Σταγειρίτης), *the Stagirite, i e, Aristotle*

stagnātĭlis e (stagnum), *found in ponds or pools*, pisces, Plin

stagno, 1 (stagnum) I. Intransit, 1, of water, *to overflow*, stagnans flumine Nilus, Verg, 2, transf, of places, *to be overflowed, to stand under water*; orbis stagnat paludibus, Ov II. Transit, *to overflow, inundate*, Tiberis plana urbis stagnaverat, Tac

stagnum -i, n (root STAC, G. ΣΤΑΓ, whence στάζω, σταγών, σταγες), *water that overflows* I. Lit., *standing water, left by the overflow of the sea or of a river, a pool, pond, marsh, swamp*, fontes et stagna, Cic II. Transf, A. (poet), *a sluggish stream of water*, Phrixeae stagna sororis, *the Hellespont*, Ov B. *an artificial lake*, stagna et euripi, Ov

stăgŏnĭas ae, m (σταγονίας), *a species of frankincense*, Plin

stăgŏnītis -idis, f (σταγονῖτις), *the gum called galbanum*, Plin

stălagmĭas ae, m (σταλαγμίας), *natural vitriol*, Plin

stălagmĭum -ii, n (στάλαγμα), *an eardrop pendant*, Plin

stāmen -inis, n (from STA, root of sisto, as στήμων from ἵστημι) I. *the warp, which in the upright looms of the ancients was stretched in a vertical direction*, stamen secernit arundo, Ov II Transf, 1, *the thread*, a, *the thread on the spindle*, stamina ducere or torquere, *to spin*, Ov, *the thread spun by the Parcae*, Ov, hence, de nimio stamine queri, *of too long a life*, Juv, b, *a thread of another kind*, e g, *that by which Ariadne guided Theseus through the labyrinth*, Prop, of a spider, Ov, *the string of a lyre*, Ov, 2, meton, *cloth woven of thread*, hence, *the fillet worn by priests*, Prop

stāmĭnĕus -a -um (stamen), *full of threads*, Prop

stannĕus a um, *made of* stannum, Plin

stannum i, n *an alloy of silver and lead*, Plin

Stăta mater = Vesta, or simply Stata, Cic

stătārĭus -a -um (status), *standing firm, steady, stable, stationary*, miles, Liv, esp, statarii comoedia, *a quiet kind of comedy* (opp comoedia motoria), Ter, subst, **stătārii** -ōrum, m *the actors in the* comoedia stataria, Cic, transf, C Piso, statarius et sermonis plenus orator, *quiet composed*, Cic

Statellī and **Statiellī** -ōrum, m *a people in Liguria, whose chief town was* Aquae Statiell orum or Aquae Statiellae, now *Acqui*, hence, A. **Statellās** -ātis, *belonging to the Statelli* B. **Statiellenses** -ium, m *the inhabitants of* Aquae Statiellorum

stătēra -ae, f (στατήρ), *a steelyard, a balance*; aurificis, Cic

stătīcŭlum -i, n (statua), *a small statue*, Plin

stătīcŭlus i, m (dim of 2 status), *a kind of slow dance*, Plin

stătim, adv (sto) I. *without yielding, firmly, steadfastly*, rem gerere, Plaut II. Transf, *on the spot, immediately, at once*, ut statim alienatio disjunctioque facienda sit, Cic, foll by ac, atque, ut, quam, quum, simulac, *as soon as*, Cic

stătĭo -ōnis, f (sto) I. *a standing, standing still*, manere in statione, *to stand still*, Lucr II. Transf, *a place of abode or sojourn*, 1, gen, alternā fratrem statione redemit, Ov , **2,** esp , **a,** of soldiers, (α) *post, watch, picket, guard*, equites ex statione, Caes ; stationem portis disposuit, Liv , in statione and (of several cohorts) in stationibus esse, Caes , stationem relinquere, Verg , (β) *quarters*, fig , imperii, Ov , de praesidio et statione vitae decedere, Cic , **b,** *a place of abode, resting-place*, sedes apibus statioque petenda, Verg , in arce Athenis statio (*post*) mea nunc placet, Cic , **c,** *a roadstead, anchorage, bay*, Cic , fig , fluctibus ejectum tutā statione recepi, *haven*, Ov , **d,** *the proper place, order* (of things), comas ponere in statione, Ov

stătĭōnālis -e (statio), *standing still, stationary*, Plin

Stātĭus -ii, m **1,** Caecilius Statius, of Insubria, *a Roman comic poet, born* 168 B C , **2,** P Papinius Statius, *an Epic poet, under Domitian, composer of Silvae, a Thebais, and an unfinished Achilleis*

stătīvus -a -um (sto), *standing, standing still* **I.** Adj , praesidium, *picket*, Cic , castra, *fixed quarters*, Liv **II.** Subst , **stătīva** -ōrum, n (sc castra), *permanent camp*, Liv

1 **stător** ōris, m (sto), *a magistrate's servant or attendant*, Cic

2 **Stător** ōris, m (sisto), *the supporter, establisher, the stayer of flight, a surname of Jupiter*, Cic

stătŭa ae, f (statuo), *a statue, image* (of a man, while simulacrum = *statue of a god*), simulacra deorum, statuae veterum hominum, Cic , statuam alicui ponere or statuere, Cic

stătŭārĭus -a -um (statua), *of or relating to statues* **I.** Adj , Plin **II.** Subst , **1, stătŭārĭa** -ae, f (sc ars), *the art of casting statues*, Plin , **2, stătŭārĭus** -ii, m *a maker or caster of statues, a statuary*, Quint

stătūmen inis, n (statuo), *a stay, support, prop*, plur , *the ribs of a ship*, Caes

stătūmino, 1 (statumen), *to underprop*, Plin

stătŭo ŭi -ūtum, 3 (from statum, the supine of sisto), *to cause to stand, put, place, set, set up* **I.** Lit , **1,** gen , captivos in medio, Liv , crateras, Verg , **2,** esp , *to set up, erect, build*, statuam, Cic , tropaeum, Cic , tabernacula, *to pitch*, Caes , urbem, Verg , regnum, Cic **II.** Transf , 1, *to establish in one's mind, to consider, believe*, ut mihi statuo, Cic , laudem statuo esse maximam, Cic , **2,** *to resolve, determine, decide*, with de and the abl , de aliquo, Caes , de capite civis, Cic , with in and the acc , in aliquem aliquid gravius, Caes , with acc alone, stipendium alicui de publico, Liv , with rel sent , utrum diem tertium an perendinum dici oporteret, Cic , with infin , judices rejicere, Cic , with ut and the subj , ut naves conscenderent, Cic

stătūra -ae, f (sto), *stature, height, size of a man*, homines tantulae staturae, *of so small stature*, Caes , quā facie fuerit, quā staturā, Cic.

1 **stătus,** v sisto

2 **stătus** ūs, m (sto), *a standing, standing position* **I.** Lit , **1,** gen , status, incessus, sessio, Cic , erectus, Cic , **2,** esp , *posture, position*, minax, Hor , statu movere hostem, Liv **II.** Fig , **1,** gen , *position, condition, state*, adversarios de omni statu dejicere, Cic , restituere aliquem in pristinum statum, Cic , omnes vitae status, Cic , **2,** esp , **a,** *one's position in life as determined by birth*, agnationibus familiarum distinguuntur status, Cic , **b,** *a firm position, stability, prosperity*, civitatis, Cic , **c,** rhet. t. t , status causae, or simply status, *the state of the question, state of the case* = στάσις, Cic

stĕātōma -ătis, n (στεάτωμα), *a kind of fatty swelling*, Plin

stĕga -ae, f (στέγη), *a ship's deck*, Plaut

stegnus a -um (στεγνός), *causing costiveness*, Plin

stēla -ae, f (στήλη), *a pillar, column*, Plin

stēlis idis, f (στελίς), *mistletoe growing on firs and larches*, Plin

stella ae, f (= sterula, connected with ἀστήρ), *a star*. **I.** Lit , **1,** *a star, planet, comet*, stella Saturni, stella Jovis, *the planet Saturn, planet Jupiter*, Cic , stellae inerrantes, *fixed stars*, Cic , vagae, *planets*, Cic. ; stella comans, *a comet*, Ov , **2,** transf , **a,** *a figure in the form of a star*, Plin ; **b,** *a star-fish*, Plin **II.** In poets, **1,** = sidus, *constellation*, Verg , Ov , **2,** = *sun*, auget geminos stella serena polos, Ov.

stellans -antis (stella), **1,** *starry, set with stars*; caelum, Lucr , **2,** *bright, shining, glittering*, gemma, Ov

Stellātis campus or ager, *a very fruitful district in Campania* Hence, adj , **Stellātīnus** -a um, *Stellatian*

stellātus -a -um (stella), *set with stars, starry*, **a,** lit , Cepheus, Cic , **b,** transf , Argus, *having many eyes*, Ov , ensis, *bright, glittering*, Verg

stellĭfĕr fĕra -fĕrum (stella and fero), *star-bearing, starry*; stellifer cursus, Cic

stellĭgĕr -gĕra -gĕrum (stella and gero), *star-bearing, starry*, Varr

stellĭo (stēlĭo) ōnis, m *a lizard with spots on its back* (Lacerta gecko, Linn), Verg

stello, 1 (stella), *to set with stars*, Plin

stemma -ătis, n (στέμμα) **I.** *a crown, chaplet*, Sen **II.** Meton , *a genealogical tree*, Suet , transf , *nobility, high antiquity*, Mart

Stentor -ŏris, m (Στέντωρ), *one of the Greeks before Troy, famed for his loud voice and the strength of his lungs*

stĕphănēplŏcos -i, f (στεφανηπλόκος), *the weaver of chaplets, the name of a painting by Pausias*, Plin

stĕphănītis -ĭdis, f (στεφανῖτις), *a kind of vine*, Plin

stĕphănŏmĕlis -is, f *a plant which stops a bleeding at the nose*, Plin

stĕphănŏpōlis -is, f (στεφανόπωλις), *the seller of chaplets, the name of a picture by Pausias, also called* stephaneplocos, Plin

stĕphănos -i, m (στέφανος), lit , *a garland, chaplet, the name of several plants*, Plin

stercŏrārĭus -a -um (stercus), *of or relating to dung*, Varr

stercŏrātĭo -ōnis, f. (stercoro), *a manuring*, Varr.

stercŏrĕus -a -um (stercus), *filthy, stinking*; miles, Plaut

stercŏro, 1 (stercus), *to dung, manure*; agrum, Cic

stercus -ŏris, n *dung, muck, manure*, Cic ; as a term of reproach, stercus curiae, Cic

stergēthron -i, n (στέργηθρον), *a plant, great houseleek*, Plin

stĕrĭlesco, 3 (sterilis), *to become barren*, Plin

stĕrĭlis e (connected with Gr στερεός, στερρός) **I.** *barren, unfruitful, sterile* (applied to animals and plants). **A. a,** lit , ager, Verg ; vacca, Verg , **b,** transf. = *empty*, corpora sonitu sterila (= sterilia), Lucr. **B.** Fig., *unfruitful, empty, vain*; amor, *unrequited*, Ov **II** (Poet.) act *making unfruitful*, robigo, Hor.

stĕrĭlĭtas -ātis, f (sterilis), *unfruitfulness, sterility, barrenness*, agrorum, Cic , mulierum, Plin

stĕrĭlus = sterilis (q v)

sternax -ācis (sterno), *throwing to the ground*, equus, *throwing his rider*, Verg

sterno, strāvi, strātum, 3 (root STER, Gr ΣΤΟΡ, whence στορέννυμι) **I.** *to stretch out, spread out* **A.** Gen , vellus in duro solo, Ov , arenam, Ov , strata jacent passim sua quaque sub arbore poma, Verg **B.** Esp , **1, a,** *to stretch on the ground, lay down, throw down*, corpora passim, Liv , reflex , se sternere, *to lie down*, se somno in litore, Verg , so pass as middle, sterni passim ferarum ritu, Liv , partic , **strātus** -a um, *stretched out, prostrate*, humi, Cic , **b,** *to throw down violently, to strike to the ground, lay low*, (α) lit, caede viros, Verg , ingenti caede sterni, Liv , poet., ventos, *to calm*, Hor , (β) fig , *to overthrow, lay prostrate*, afflictos se et stratos esse, Cic , **2,** *to make smooth, level*, **a,** of the sea, (α) placidi straverunt aequora venti, Verg , (β) fig , *to calm, allay*, odia militum, Tac , **b,** *to make a rough road smooth, to level*, viam, Lucr esp , *to pave*, semitam saxo quadrato, Liv. **II.** Meton , *to cover, overlay with*, **a,** solum telis, Verg , **b,** esp , (α) *to cover with carpets*, etc , triclinium, Cic , (β) *to saddle a horse*, equum, Liv.

sternūmentum -i, n (sternuo), *a sneezing, sneeze*, Cic

sternŭo -ŭi, 3 (connected with πτάρνυμαι) **I.** Intransit , *to sneeze*, **a,** lit , Plin , **b,** transf , of a light, *to crackle, sputter*, Ov **II.** Transit , *to give by sneezing*, omen, Prop.

sternūtāmentum i, n (sternuo), *a sneezing, sneeze*, Sen

sterquĭlīnĭum -ĭi, n (stercus), *a dung pit*, Plaut

Stertĭnĭus ĭi, m *a Stoic philosopher* Hence, **Stertinius** a -um, *of Stertinius*

sterto, 3 (connected with δέρθω, δαρθάνω), *to snore*, Cic

Stēsĭchŏrus -i, m (Στησίχορος), *a Greek lyric poet of Himera* (632-553 B C), *contemporary of Sappho*

Sthĕnĕlus i, m (Σθένελος) **I.** *son of Capaneus and Euadne, one of the Epigoni, leader of the Argives against Troy under Diomedes* **II.** *king in Liguria, whose son Cycnus was changed into a swan* Hence, **A. Sthĕnĕlēĭus** a um, *Sthenelean*, hostis, *Eurystheus*, Ov , proles, *Cycnus*, Ov **B. Sthĕnĕlēis** -ĭdis, f *Sthenelean*, volucris, *the swan*, Ov

stĭbădĭum ĭi, n (στιβάδιον), *a semicircular sofa*, Plin

stĭbĭum ĭi, n (**stĭbi** and **stimmi** -is, n), *antimony*, used for dyeing the eyebrows black, and as an eye salve, Plin

stigma ătis, n (στίγμα) **I.** *a mark or brand put upon slaves*, **1,** lit , Sen , **2,** fig , *infamy, stigma*, Mart **II.** *a cut inflicted by an unskilful barber*, Mart

stigmătĭas -ae, m (στιγματίας), *a branded slave*, Cic

stilla -ae, f (dim of stiria), *a drop*, Cic

stillātĭcĭus -a -um (stillo), *dropping, dripping*, Plin

stillĭcĭdĭum -ĭi, n (stilla and cado) **I.** *a dripping or dropping moisture*, Lucr **II** Esp , *rain water falling from the eaves of houses*, Cic

stillo, 1 (stilla) **I** Intransit , *to drip drop*, de ilice stillabant mella, Ov , pugio stillans, *dripping with blood*, Cic **II.** Transit , *to drop, let drop*, **a,** lit , ex oculis rorem, Hor , **b,** fig , tuae litterae, quae mihi quiddam quasi animulae stillarunt, Cic

stĭlus (not **stȳlus**) -i, m (for stig lus , cf Gr στίζω, στίγ-μα) **I.** *a stake, pale*, Auct b Afr **II. 1,** *the pointed iron or bone instrument with which the Romans wrote on their waxen tablets*, Plin , as one end was flat, in order to erase the impression made by the other, vertere stilum = *to rub out, erase writing*, Hor , vertit stilum in tabulis suis, Cic , **2,** meton , *writing, composing, written composition*, and hence *mode of writing, speaking, style*, stilus exercitatus, *a practised pen*, Cic , unus sonus est totius orationis et idem stilus, Cic

stĭmŭlātĭo ōnis, f (stimulo), *a spurring on, stimulating*, Tac

stĭmŭlātrix īcis, f (stimulator), *she that goads on, stimulates*, Plaut

stĭmŭlĕus -a -um (stimulus), *relating to the goad*, supplicium, *punishment* (of slaves) *with the goad*, Plaut

stĭmŭlo, 1 (stimulus) **I.** *to goad, prick*, Lucan **II.** Fig , **1,** *to goad, disquiet, vex, annoy*, te conscientiae stimulant maleficiorum tuorum, Cic , **2,** *to goad, incite stir up, stimulate to any action*, (α) with acc , aliquem incitare et stimulare, Verg , (β) with ad and the acc ad huius salutem defendendam stimulari, Cic , (γ) with ut and the subj , ut caverem, Cic , (δ) poet , with infin , Verg

stĭmŭlus -i, m (root STIG, whence in stig o and 1 stinguo, Gr ΣΤΙΓ, whence στίζω, στιγμή) **I.** Milit t t , stimuli *pointed stakes to repel the advance of troops*, Caes **II.** *a goad used for driving cattle, slaves*, etc **A.** Lit , Plaut , used contemptuously, dum te stimulis fodiam, Cic **B.** Fig , **a,** *a sting, torment*, doloris, Cic , amoris, Liv , **b,** *a goad, spur, incentive, stimulus*, gloriae, Cic , alicui stimulos admovere, Cic

1 * **stinguo**, 3 *to goad*, a word only found in compounds, such as distinguo, instinguo, interstinguo (interstinctus)

2 **stinguo**, 3 *to extinguish, put out*, Lucr

stīpātĭo -ōnis, f (stipo), *a crowd of attendants round any one, numerous suite, retinue*, Cic

stīpātor -ōris, m (stipo), *an attendant, follower*, plur , *a suite, train, retinue*, Cic

stīpātus a um, p adj (from stipo)

stīpendĭārĭus -a um (stipendium) **I.** *liable to taxes or tribute, tributary*, Aeduos sibi stipendiarios factos, Cic , vectigal, *a yearly contribution*, Cic , subst , **stīpendĭārĭi** -ōrum, m *tributaries*, socii stipendiariique populi Romani, Cic **II.** Of soldiers, *serving for pay, mercenary*, Liv

stīpendĭor, 1 dep (stipendium), *to serve, serve for hire*, Plin

stīpendĭum -ĭi, n (= stipipendium, from stips and pendo) **I.** *a tax, tribute, contribution*, **a,** lit , stipendium imponere alicui, Caes , pacisci annuum stipendium, Liv , **b,** transf , *punishment*, quod me manet stipendium? Hor **II.** *pay of a soldier*, **a,** lit (in full, stipendium militare), stipendium alicui decernere Cic , persolvere, Cic , flagitare, Caes , stipendia merere and mereri, *to serve in the army*, Cic , **b,** meton , *military service*, finis stipendiorum, Cic ; esp , *a year's service, campaign*, septem et viginti enumerare stipendia, Liv , fig , tam quam emeritis stipendiis libidinis, ambitionis, etc , Cic

stīpes ĭtis, m (στύπος), *a log, stump, trunk of a tree*, **a,** in a rough state, Verg , poet , *a tree*, Ov , **b,** worked into something, *a stake, post*, Caes , poet , *a club*, Ov , as a term of reproach, *blockhead*, Ter

stīpo, 1. (connected with Gr. *στέφ-ω*, *στέφ-ανος*, etc.), *to press closely together, compress*. **I.** Gen., mella (of bees), Verg.; ita in arte stipatae erant naves ut, etc., Liv.; Graeci stipati, quini in lectulis, saepe plures, Cic. **II. A.** *to crowd a place;* curia quum patribus fuerit stipata, Ov. **B.** *to press round, accompany, surround, attend;* senatum armatis, Cic.; qui *stipatus* semper sicariis, *saeptus* armatis, *munitus* judicibus fuit, Cic.; senectus stipata studiis juventutis, Cic.

stips, stipis, f. *an offering, gift, donation in money, a religious offering, alms;* stipem conferre, Liv.; stipem cogere, Cic.; stipem aut stipes dare, Ov., Tac.; stipem tollere, *to put an end to begging*, Cic.

stĭpŭla -ae, f. *the stalk, haulm;* **a,** of corn; plur. = *straw*, Ov.; **b,** of a reed, contemptuously of a flute made of a reed, *a reed-pipe*, Verg.; **c,** of the bean, Ov.

stĭpŭlātĭo -ōnis, f. (stipulor), *a verbal agreement, covenant, stipulation*, Cic.

stĭpŭlātĭuncŭla -ae, f. (dim. of stipulatio), *an unimportant engagement* or *stipulation*, Cic.

stĭpŭlātor -ōris, m. (stipulor), *one who stipulates for* or *demands a formal agreement*, Suet.

stĭpŭlor, 1. dep. *to demand, stipulate for by a formal agreement*, Cic.

stīrĭa -ae, f. *an icicle*, Verg.

stirpesco, 3. (stirps), *to run to stalk*, Plin.

stirpĭtŭs, adv. (stirps), *root and branch, thoroughly, entirely*, Cic.

stirps (stirpes, stirpis), stirpis, f. **I.** *the stock or stem of a tree.* **A.** Lit., **a,** *the trunk with the root*, Cic.; **b,** *the trunk*, Verg.; **c,** *a branch, a young shoot* or *sprout*, Verg. **B.** Transf., **1,** of plants, **a,** *a plant, stalk, root;* stirpes et herbae, Cic.; **b,** *a twig*, Lucr.; **2,** of hair, *the root*, Prop.; **3,** of men, **a,** abstr., *the stem = the source, origin;* divina, Verg.; ne Italicae quidem stirpis, Liv.; a stirpe par, Verg.; **b,** concr., (α) *male offspring;* unum prope puberem aetate relictum stirpem genti Fabiae, Liv.; (β) *family, race;* Herculis, Cic.; (γ) *offspring;* stirpem ex se relinquere, Liv. **II.** Fig., *the root;* **1,** gen., ex hac nimia licentia ut ex stirpe quadam exsistere et quasi nasci tyrannum, Cic.; Carthago ab stirpe interiit, *root and branch*, Sall.; **2,** esp., **a,** *foundation, origin;* virtutis, Cic.; **b,** *original nature*, Cic. (stirps masc. once in Verg.).

stīva -ae, f. *a plough-handle*, Verg.

stlātārĭus -a -um (from stlata, *a kind of ship*), *brought by sea*, and therefore, *costly*, Juv.

stlīs, archaic = lis (q.v.).

stloppus -i, m. *the noise of a slap on the inflated cheeks*, Pers.

sto, stĕti, stātum, stātūrus, stāre (STA, root of ἵ-στη-μι), *to stand.* **I.** As opposed to sitting, *to remain standing.* **A.** Lit., **1,** gen., **a,** of persons, quum virgo staret, et Caecilia in sella sederet, Cic.; ad januam, Cic.; **b,** of things, quorum statuae steterunt in rostris, Cic.; **2,** esp., **a,** milit. t. t., *to stand, to be stationed;* pro porta, Liv.; **b,** of buildings, *to stand, to be built;* jam stabant Thebae, Ov.; **c,** of ships, *to be at anchor;* stant litore puppes, Verg.; stare ad ancoram in salo Romana classis non poterat, Liv.; **d,** *to stand upright, stand on end;* steteruntque comae, Verg.; **e,** with abl., *to stand stiff with, to be full of, loaded with;* stat nive candidum Soracte, Hor. **B.** Fig., **1,** gen., pericula stant circum aliquem, Verg.; **2,** *to stand at the side of, to support,* or *to stand opposite to as an enemy, to range oneself;* **a,** with ab and the abl., stare a se potius quam ab adversariis, Cic.; **b,** with cum and the abl., vobiscum me stetisse dicebat, Cic.; **c,** with pro and the abl., pro nobis, Ov.; **d,** with in or contra or adversus and acc., quum saepe a mendacio contra verum stare homines consuescerent, Cic.; **3,** *to rest upon;* omnis in Ascanio cari stat cura parentis, Verg.; **4,** = *to cost* (like English *stand*); centum talentis, Liv.; transf., multo sanguine ac vulneribus ea Poenis victoria stetit, Liv. **II. A.** Lit., **1,** as opposed to motion, *to stand still, not to move;* **a,** lit., (α) of animals, equus stare nescit, Ov.; (β) of things, e.g., of ships, videsne navem illam? *stare* nobis videtur, at iis qui in navi sunt *moveri* haec villa, Cic.; **b,** transf., of time, *to stop, stand still;* veluti stet volucris dies, Hor.; **2,** with the notion of steadfastness; **a,** milit. t. t., (α) *to stand, hold one's ground;* qui (miles) steterit, Cic.; stare in pugna, Liv.; (β) transf., of a battle, *to remain in a certain position, to waver, not to be decided;* diu pugna neutro inclinata stetit, Cic.; **b,** of buildings, rocks, etc., *to stand firm, last, endure, remain;* nec domus ulla nec urbs stare poterit, Cic.; **c,** of missiles, *to stick fast, remain;* hasta stetit medio tergo, Ov. **B.** Fig., **1,** gen., *to remain still, remain, continue;* utinam respublica stetisset quo coeperat statu, Cic.; **2,** stare per aliquem, *to happen through some one's fault*, Ter.; often stat or non (nihil) stat per aliquem, foll. by quominus and subj., *it is owing to some one that not*, etc., Cic., Liv.; stat per aliquem, foll. by quin or ne and subj., Liv.; **3,** with the notion of steadfastness or duration; **a,** *to remain steadfast, firm, immovable, to stand one's ground, hold out;* si stare non possunt, corruant, Cic.; stas animo, Hor.; stamus animis, Cic.; **b,** *to remain firm in something;* (α) *to remain in, continue in;* with in and the abl., in fide, Cic.; with abl. alone, suis stare judiciis, Cic.; (β) transf., *to be fixed* or *determined;* stat sua cuique dies, Verg.; tempus agendae rei nondum stare, Liv.; stat alicui sententia, with infin., *to be resolved* or *determined to*, Liv.; so stat alicui, or simply stat, Cic.; **c,** of a play or an actor, *to please, gain applause, keep the stage*, Hor. (perf., stĕtĕrunt, Verg., *Aen.* II. 774; III. 48).

Stōĭcē, adv. (Stoicus), *like a Stoic, stoically*, Cic.

Stōĭcĭda -ae, m. *a satirical name given to a voluptuary who pretended to be a Stoic*, Juv.

Stōĭcus -a -um (Στωϊκός), *of* or *relating to Stoic philosophy, Stoic;* schola, Cic. Subst., **a, Stōĭcus** -i, m. *a Stoic philosopher*, Cic.; **b, Stōĭca** -ōrum, n. *the Stoic philosophy*, Cic.

stŏla -ae, f. (στολή), *a long outer garment.* **I.** *the long outer garment worn by Roman ladies, robe*, Cic. **II.** Of men, *the robe of a flute-player at the festival of Minerva*, Ov.

stŏlātus -a -um (stola), *clad in a stola*, Suet.

stŏlĭdē, adv. (stolidus), *stupidly, foolishly, stolidly;* stolide laetus, Liv.; stolide ferox, Liv.

stŏlĭdus -a -um (connected with stultus). **I.** *stupid, foolish, dull, obtuse;* **a,** of persons, o vatum stolidissime, Ov.; **b,** of things, fiducia, superbia, Liv. **II.** *inactive, indolent*, Cic.

stŏlo -ōnis, m. *a useless sucker, superfluous shoot on a tree*, Plin.

stŏmăcăcē -ēs, f. (στομακάκη), *a disease of the mouth* or *gums*, Plin.

stŏmăchĭcus -a -um (στομαχικός), *suffering from disease in the stomach*, Plin.

stŏmăchor, 1. dep. (stomachus), *to be angry, pettish, irritated, vexed;* **a,** absol., stomachari coepit, Cic.; **b,** with cum and the abl., cum Metello, Cic.; **c,** with abl., jucundissimis tuis litteris, Cic.; **d,** with quod, quod de eadem re agam saepius, Cic.; **e,** with si, si quid asperius dixeram, Cic.; **f,** with neut. acc., omnia, Cic.

stŏmăchōsē, adv (stomachosus), *peevishly, pettishly, angrily*, rescripsi ei stomachosius, Cic

stŏmăchōsus a -um (stomachus), *peevish, pettish, irritable, cross, angry*, Cic

stŏmăchus i, m (στόμαχος) **I.** *the gullet, the oesophagus*, Cic **II.** Transf = ventriculus, *the stomach* **A.** Lit., stomachi calor, Cic, stomachus aeger, Hor **B.** Fig., **1,** stomachus bonus, *a good digestion = good humour*, Mart, **2, a,** *taste, liking*, ludi apparatissimi, sed non tui stomachi, Cic, **b,** *dislike, distaste, vexation, chagrin, anger*, stomachum facere or movere alicui, Cic

stŏmătĭcē -es, f (στοματική), *a remedy for diseases of the mouth*, Plin

stŏmōma -ătis, n (στόμωμα), *thin scales of metal*, Plin

stŏrĕa (stŏrĭa) ae, f (connected with στορέννυμι), *a rush mat*, Caes

străbo -ōnis, m (στραβων) **I.** *a squinter*, Cic **II.** Fig, *an envious person*, Varr

strāges -is, f **I.** *a throwing to the ground, overthrow, downfall*, **a,** aedificiorum, Tac, tectorum, Liv, **b,** *a sinking down, dying away through illness*, canum, Ov, **c,** *a defeat, a slaughter, butchery, massacre, carnage*, quas strages ille edidit, Cic **II.** Meton, *a fallen mass*, hominum armorumque, Liv

strāgŭlum, v stragulus

strāgŭlus -a -um (sterno), *covering, serving as a rug, carpet, mattress*, etc, *to lie upon* **I.** Adj, vestis stragula, Cic **II.** Subst, **strāgŭlum** -i, n *a covering, rug, carpet, mattress*, etc, textile, Cic

strāmen inis, n (sterno), *straw, litter, spread under anything*, Verg, Ov

strāmentārius a um (stramentum), *relating to straw*, falces, *for cutting straw*, Cato

strāmentĭcĭus -a -um (stramentum), *made of straw*, casa, Auct b Hisp

strāmentum i, n (sterno) **I.** *the stalk of corn, straw, litter*, casae, quae more Gallico stramentis erant tectae, Caes **II.** *a saddle, housing* (for mules), Caes

strāmĭnĕus -a -um (stramen), *made of straw*, casa, Ov, Quirites, *figures of straw thrown every year into the Tiber*, Ov

strangĭas -ae, m (στραγγίας), *a kind of wheat in Greece*, Plin

strangŭlātĭo -ōnis f (strangulo), *a choking, strangulation*, Plin

strangŭlātus = strangulatio (q v)

strangŭlo, 1 (στραγγαλόω), *to choke, strangle* **I.** **a,** lit, patrem, Caes, **b,** transf, vocem, Quint; arborem, Plin **II.** Fig, *to torment, torture*, strangulat inclusus dolor, Ov

strangūrĭa ae, f (στραγγουρία), *a painful discharge of urine, strangury*, Cic

strătēgēma -ătis, n (στρατήγημα), *a piece of generalship, a stratagem*, transf, strategemate hominem percussit, Cic

strătēgĭa ae, f (στρατηγία), *a province, district, canton*, Plin

strătēgus -i, m (στρατηγός), *a general*, Plaut

strătĭōtes ae, m (στρατιώτης), *an aquatic plant*, Plin

strătĭōtĭcus a -um (στρατιωτικός), *soldierly, soldierlike*, homo, *a soldier*, Plaut

Străto (-ōn) -ōnis, m (Στράτων) **I.** *a Peripatetic philosopher of Lampsacus* **II.** (Strato), *a physician of the time of Cicero*

Strătŏnīcēa -ae, f (Στρατονίκεια), *an important town in Caria, now Eski Hissar* Hence, **Strătŏnīcensis** -e, *belonging to Stratonicea*

strātum i, n (sterno), *that which is spread out* **I.** *a covering*, **1,** *the covering of a rug, bed, blanket*, and meton, *a bed* molle stratum, Liv, strato surgere, Verg, **2,** *a horse-cloth, saddle cloth, saddle*, Liv **II.** *a pavement*, strata viarum, Lucr

strātūra -ae, f (sterno), *a paving, pavement*, Suet

1 **strātus** a um, partic of sterno

2 **Strātus** -i, f (Στράτος), *a town in Acarnania on the Achelous*

strēna -ae, f **I.** *a portent, omen*, Plaut **II.** *a new year's gift* (Fr étrenne), Suet

strēnŭē, adv (strenuus), *briskly, promptly, actively, strenuously*, arma capere, Cic

strēnŭĭtas -ātis, f (strenuus), *briskness, promptness, activity*, Ov

strēnŭo, 1 (strenuus), *to be brisk, prompt, active*, Plaut

strēnŭus -a -um, *brisk, prompt, active, strenuous, vigorous* **a,** lit, of persons, fortis ac strenuus socius, Liv, gens linguā strenua magis quam factis, Liv, compar, strenuior, Plaut, superl, strenuissimus quisque ut occiderat in proelio, Sall, in a bad sense, *turbulent, restless*, Tac, **b,** transf, navis, *fast*, Ov, inertia, *masterly inactivity*, Hor

strĕpĭto, 1 (intens of strepo), *to make a loud noise, to rustle, rattle, clatter*, Verg

strĕpĭtus ūs, m (strepo) **I.** *a loud noise, clattering, crashing, creaking, rumbling*, rotarum, Caes, fluminum Cic, valvarum, Hor, inter strepitum tot bellorum, Liv, plur, strepitus nocturni, Liv **II.** Poet, transf, *a measured, regular sound*, testudinis aureae, Hor

strĕpo ŭi -ĭtum, 3 **I.** *to make a loud noise, creak, rattle, clash rumble, clatter* **A.** Intransit, **a,** of living beings, mixti strepentium paventiumque clamores, Liv, strepere vocibus, Sall, **b,** of things, arma et scuta offensa quo levius streperent, *make less noise*, Sall, fluvii strepunt hiberna nive turgidi, Hor, esp, of places, *to resound*, ludos litterarum strepere discentium vocibus, Liv **B.** Transit, haec quum streperent *cried out*, Liv **II.** Poet., transf, of musical instruments, *to crash, bray*, strepunt litui, Hor

strepsĭcĕros ōtis, m (στρεψικέρως), *an African animal with twisted horns*, Plin

strĭa ae, f *a furrow, ridge*, Plin

strictim, adv (strictus). **I.** *closely*, Plaut **II.** Fig, *superficially, slightly, briefly, summarily*, dicere, Cic, librum attingere, Cic

strictīvus a um (stringo), *plucked, gathered, stripped off*, Cato

strictor -ōris, m (stringo), *one who plucks*, Cato

strictūra ae, f (stringo), *a bar of iron*, Verg

strictus a um, p adj (from stringo), *drawn together*, hence, **I** Lit, *close, tight*, janua strictissima, Ov **II.** Fig, **1,** *brief, concise*, Quint, **2,** of character, *rigid, severe, strict*, Sen

strīdĕo (strīdo), stridi ēre and -ĕre (connected with τρίζω), *to make a harsh noise, to creak, grate, hiss*, etc, of snakes, Verg, of a missile, Verg, of the wind, Verg, of the rope of a ship, Ov, of a waggon, Verg, of the sea, Verg; of men, inamabile stridet, *lisps*, Ov, of bees, *to hum*, Verg

strīdor -ōris, m. (strido), *a creaking, grating, hissing, whistling cry* or *noise*, of the wind, Cic.; of the hinge of a door, Cic.; of a saw, Cic.; of animals, as a snake, Ov.; of a pig, *grunting*, Ov.; of asses, *braying*, Ov.; of bees, *humming*, Ov.; of men, tribuni, *whispering*, Cic.

strīdŭlus -a -um (strido), *creaking, hissing, whistling, grating;* cornus (of a spear), Verg.; claustra, Ov.

strĭges -um, f., v. strix.

strĭgĭlis -is, abl. -i, genit. plur. -ium, f. (stringo), *a scraper used by bathers for scraping the skin*, Cic.

strigmentum -i, n. (stringo), *that which is scraped* or *rubbed off*, Plin.

strĭgo, 1. *to halt in ploughing*, Plin.

strĭgōsus -a -um, *lean, thin.* **I.** Lit., equi strigosiores, Liv. **II.** Fig., of an orator, *dry, meagre, jejune*, Cic.

stringo, strinxi, strictum, 3. (root STRIC, connected with στράγγω). **I.** *to draw together.* **A.** *to draw tight together, to bind, tie together;* **1**, lit., tamquam laxaret elatum pedem ab stricto nodo, Liv.; stringebant magnos vincula parva pedes, Ov.; **2**, transf., of cold, stricta matutino frigore vulnera, Liv. **B.** *to draw off;* **1**, *to strip off, pluck, gather, clip, prune;* folia ex arboribus, Caes.; frondes, Verg.; rubos, Liv.; **2**, *to draw a weapon from its sheath, to unsheathe;* **a**, lit., gladium, Caes.; ferrum, Liv.; cultrum, Liv.; **b**, fig., stringitur iambus in hostes, *attacks an enemy with satirical verses*, Ov. **II.** *to graze = to touch lightly;* **1**, gen., metas interiore rotā, Ov.; **2**, esp., *to wound slightly;* tela stringentia corpus, Verg.; poet., transf., (α) *to injure;* nomen, Ov.; (β) *to touch;* animum strinxit patriae pietatis imago, Verg.

stringor -ōris, m. (stringo), *a drawing together, power of drawing together*, Lucr.

strix, strĭgis, f. (στρίγξ), *a screech-owl*, Ov.

strombus -i, m. (στρομβός), *a species of spiral snail*, Plin.

strongȳlē -es, f. (στρογγύλη), *a kind of alum*, Plin.

strŏpha -ae, f. and **strŏphē** -ēs, f. (στροφή), *a trick, device, artifice*, Sen.

Strŏphădes -um, f. (Στροφάδες), *two islands in the Ionian Sea, between Zakynthos and the Peloponnesus, the mythical abode of the Harpies, now Strofadia* or *Strivali.*

strŏphĭārĭus -ii, m. (strophium), *one who makes* or *sells* strophia, Plaut.

strŏphĭŏlum -i, n. (dim. of strophium), *a small chaplet*, Plin.

strŏphĭum -ii, n. (στρόφιον). **I.** *a breast-band, stay, stomacher*, Cic. **II.** *a chaplet*, Verg.

Strŏphĭus -ii, m. (Στρόφιος), *king in Phocis, father of Pylades;* Strophio natus, *Pylades*, Ov.

structilis -e (struo), *of* or *relating to building, used in building*, Mart.

structor -ōris, m. (struo). **I.** *a builder, mason, carpenter*, Cic. **II.** *an arranger* = τραπεζοποιός, *a slave who arranged the table and superintended the waiting*, Juv.

structūra -ae, f. (struo). **I.** *a putting together;* **1**, *a building, erecting, constructing;* parietum, Caes.; **2**, meton., *that which is built, a building;* aerariae structurae, *mines, mining-works*, Caes. **II.** Transf., of discourse, *an arrangement, putting together* of words; verborum, Cic.

strŭes -is, f. (struo), *a heap.* **I.** Gen., pontes et moles ex humanorum corporum strue facere, Liv. **II.** Esp., **a**, *a heap of wood;* lignorum, Liv.; **b**, *a heap of small sacrificial cakes*, Ov.; **c**, *a thick* or *dense mass*, as of the phalanx, Liv.

strŭix -icis, f. (struo), *a heap*, Plaut.

strūma -ae, f. (struo), *a scrofulous tumour, struma*, Cic.

strūmōsus -a -um (struma), *afflicted with struma, strumous*, Juv.

strūmus -i, m. (struma), *a herb that cures the struma*, Plin.

strŭo, struxi, structum, 3. (connected with στορέννυμι, sterno). **I.** *to place one thing upon another, to join together, pile up;* arbores in pyram, Ov.; lateres, Caes. **II. A.** *to build, erect, construct;* **a**, lit., pyram, Verg.; aggerem, Tac.; fornices, Liv.; **b**, transf., *to prepare* (something bad), *to devise, contrive;* alicui aliquid calamitatis, Cic.; periculosas libertati opes, Liv.; dices me ipsum mihi sollicitudinem struere, Cic. **B.** *to arrange, order, set up;* aciem, Liv.; transf., compositi oratoris bene structa collocatio, Cic. **C.** *to heap up, load with;* altaria donis, Verg.

struppus (stroppus) -i, m. (στρόφος), *a strap, thong, rope*, Plin.

strūthĕus (strūthĭus) -a -um (στρούθιος), *of* or *relating to a sparrow;* mala, *sparrow-apples, quinces*, Cato.

strūthĭŏcămēlīnus -a -um, *of* or *relating to an ostrich*, Plin.

strūthĭŏcămēlus -i, m. (στρυθιοκάμηλος), *an ostrich*, Plin.

strūthŏpus -pŏdis (στρουθόπους), *sparrow-footed*, Plin.

strychnos -i, m. (στρύχνος), *a kind of nightshade*, Plin.

Strȳmo (-ōn) -mŏnis and -mŏnos, m. (Στρυμών), *one of the most important rivers of Thrace, rising in Mt. Haemus and flowing into the Strymonic Gulf, now Karasu* or *Struma (Strumo).* Hence, **A. Strȳmŏnis** -idis, f. (Στρυμονίς), *a Thracian woman, an Amazon*, Prop. **B. Strȳmŏnĭus** -a -um, *Strymonian*, poet. = *Thracian* or *northern*, Ov.

stŭdĕo -ŭi, 2. (perhaps connected with σπεύδω, σπουδή, σπουδάζω), *to be eager, zealous, earnest, take pains about anything, strive after, be busy with, seek after, aim at.* **I.** Gen., **a**, with dat., praeturae, Cic.; novis rebus, *political change*, Caes.; litteris, Cic.; laudi, Cic.; **b**, with acc., unum, hoc unum, Cic.; **c**, with infin., or acc. and infin., studeo scire quid egeris, *I should like to know*, Cic.; **d**, with ut or ne and the subj., id studere, ne super impunitatem etiam praemio sceleris frueretur, Liv. **II.** Esp., *to take sides with, to support, favour;* alicui, Cic.

stŭdĭōsē, adv. (studiosus), **a**, *eagerly, zealously, diligently;* qui haec caelestia vel studiosissime solet quaerere, Cic.; **b**, *intentionally, designedly;* quum studiose de absentibus detrahendi causā malitiose dicitur, Cic.

stŭdĭōsus -a -um (studium), *eager, zealous, diligent, anxious for, striving after anything, fond of.* **I.** Gen., with genit., venandi, Cic.; dicendi, Cic.; studiosissimus homo natandi, Cic.; with in and the abl., hoc te studiosiorem in me colendo fore, Cic. **II.** Esp., **A.** *favourable to a person, attached to, devoted to;* mei, Cic.; studiosissimus existimationis meae, Cic. **B.** *devoted to learning, studious;* cohors, Hor. Plur. subst., **stŭdĭōsi** -ōrum, m. *students*, Cic.

stŭdĭum -ii, n. (studeo), *zeal, eagerness, eager application, assiduity, fondness, desire, striving after.* **I.** Gen., with subject. genit., amici, Cic.; with object. genit., veri reperiendi,

Cic., pugnandi, Caes , studium quaestûs, Cic , absol , incensi sunt studio, Cic , omne studium ad aliquid conferre, Cic , studio accusare, *passionately*, Cic **II.** Esp , *particular inclination towards a person or a thing* **A.** Towards a person, *attachment to, zeal for, devotion to, goodwill towards*, studia competitorum, Cic studia Numidarum in Jugurtham accensa, Sall **B.** Towards a thing, **1,** *fondness for, partiality, inclination*, suo quisque studio maxime ducitur, Cic , **2,** *application to learning, study*, juris, Cic , studiis illis se dare, Cic

stultē, adv with compar. and superl (stultus), *foolishly, sillily*, Cic

stultĭlŏquentĭa -ae, f (stulte and loquor), *foolish talk*, Plaut.

stultĭlŏquus -a -um (stulte and loquor), *talking foolishly*, Plaut

stultĭtĭa ae, f (stultus), *foolishness, folly, silliness, stupidity*; multorum stultitiam perpessum esse, Cic , plur , hominum ineptias ac stultitias non ferebat, Cic

stultĭvĭdus -a -um (stulte and video), *seeing things foolishly, in a foolish light*, Plaut

stultus -a -um (connected with stolidus), *foolish, silly, fatuous* **a,** of persons reddere aliquem stultiorem, Cic , stultissima persona, Cic Subst , **stultus** i, m *a simpleton, a fool*, Cic , **b,** transf, of things, loquacitas, Cic , consilium, Cic

stūpa = stuppa (q v)

stŭpĕfăcĭo -fēci factum, 3 , pass , **stŭpĕfīo** factus sum -fiĕri (stupeo and facio), *to make senseless, benumb, stun, stupefy*, privatos luctus stupefecit publicus pavor, Liv , partic , **stŭpĕfactus** -a -um, *astounded*, Cic.

stŭpĕo -ŭi, 2 (connected with ΤΥΠ-ω, τύπτω, *to strike and stun by a blow*) **I.** *to be stunned.* **A.** Physically, *to be struck senseless, to be stunned*, partic , stupens, *stunned, stupefied*, quum semisomnus stuperet, Cic **B.** Mentally, *to be astounded, amazed*, haec quum loqueris nos stupemus, Cic., with abl (*at* or *by*), carminibus, Hor , with in and the abl , in Turno, Verg , with ad and the acc , ad auditas voces, Verg , with acc , donum exitiale Minervae, *is astonished at*, Verg , with acc and infin , Verg , partic , stupens, *astonished, amazed*, quae quum tuerer stupens, Cic **II.** Transf , of inanimate things, *to stand still, to rest*, stupuit Ixionis orbis, Ov , stupente seditione, Liv , stupuerunt verba palato, *died away*, Ov

stŭpesco, 3 (stupeo), *to begin to be amazed, astounded*, Cic

stŭpĭdĭtas -ātis, f (stupidus), *dulness, stupidity, senselessness*, Cic

stŭpĭdus a -um (stupeo), **1,** *senseless, stunned*, Cic , **2,** *senseless, stupid, dull*, stupidum esse Socratem dixit, Cic

stŭpor -ōris, m (stupeo) **I. a,** *senselessness, insensibility*, sensus, Cic , in corpore, Cic , **b,** *astonishment, amazement*, stupor patres defixit, Liv , meton , *a startled man*, Cat. **II.** *senselessness, stupidity*, Cic

stuppa (stūpa) -ae, f (στύππη), *tow, oakum*, Caes , Liv

stuppārĭus a um (stuppa), *of or relating to tow*, Plin

stuppĕus (stūpĕus) -a -um (stuppa), *made of tow or oakum*, vincula, Verg

stŭprātor -ōris, m (stupro), *a ravisher, defiler*, Quint.

stŭpro, 1 (stuprum), *to defile* **I.** Gen , pulvinar, Cic **II.** Esp , *to defile, pollute by lust, ravish*, Cic.

stŭprum -i, n *pollution by lust, a debauching, ravishing, violation*, Cic

sturnus i, m *a starling, a stare*, Plin

Stўgĭālis, Stygius v Styx

stўlŏbătes -ae and -is m (στυλοβάτης), *the pedestal of a row of columns*, Varr

stymma -ătis, n (στύμμα), *the main ingredient of a salve or ointment*, Plin

Stymphālus (-ŏs) -i, m and **Stymphālum** i, n (Στύμφαλος), *a lake with a river and town of the same name in Arcadia, famous in legend as the abode of birds of prey with iron feathers, which fed on human flesh, and were destroyed by Hercules* Hence, **A. Stymphālĭcus** -a -um, *Stymphalian* **B. Stymphālis** idis, f *Stymphalian* **C. Stymphālĭus** -a -um, *Stymphalian*

styptĭcus -a um (στυπτικός), *astringent, styptic*, Plin

styrax -ăcis, m (στύραξ), *storax, a resinous fragrant gum*, Plin

Styx, Stўgis and Stўgos, acc Stўgem and Stўga, f (Στύξ) **I.** *a river in the infernal regions by which the gods swore* **II** Poet , meton , *the lower world*, Verg Hence, **A. Stўgĭālis** e, *belonging to the Styx, Stygian* **B. Stўgĭus** -a -um, *Stygian, infernal*, cymba or carina, *the boat of Charon*, Verg , Juppiter, or pater, or rex, *Pluto*, Verg , hence, *hellish = fatal, deadly, sad*, bubo, Ov , vis Verg

suādēla -ae, f (suadeo) **I.** *persuasion*, Plaut **II.** Personif , Suadela = Πειθώ, *the goddess of persuasion*, Hor

suādĕo, suāsi, suāsum, 2 (root SUAD, Gr ἉΔ-έω, ἁνδάνω) lit , *to present in a pleasing manner* Hence, **I.** Intransit , *to advise, give advice*; an C Trebonio persuasi cui ne suadere quidem ausus essem? Cic , in suadendo et dissuadendo, Cic , of things as subjects, suadet enim vesana fames, Verg **II.** Transit , **A.** *to advise something, recommend something, recommend to*, **a,** with acc , pacem, Cic , legem, Cic , quod ipse tibi suaseris, Cic , with acc of pers , non desino tamen per litteras rogare, suadere, accusare regem, Cic , **b,** with infin , mori, Cic , **c,** with acc and infin , nullam esse rationem amittere ejusmodi occasionem, Cic , **d,** with ut or ne and the subj , postea me, ut sibi essem legatus, non solum suasit, verum etiam rogavit, Cic , **e,** with subj alone, se suadere, Pharnabazo id negotium daret, Nep **B.** *to convince, persuade*, Plaut

sŭārĭus -a -um (sus), *of or relating to swine*, Plin Subst , **sŭārĭus** ii, m *a swineherd*, Plin

suāsĭo ōnis f (suadeo) **I.** *advice*, Sen **II** Esp , **a,** polit. t t , *the advocacy, recommendation of a proposed law*, legis Serviliae, Cic , **b,** rhet t t , *eloquence of the persuasive kind*, Cic

suāsor ōris, m (suadeo), *an adviser, counsellor* facti, Cic ; deditionis, Cic , esp , *one who advocates a proposed law*, legis, Liv

suāsōrĭus -a -um (suadeo), *relating to persuasion*, Quint Hence, subst , **suāsōrĭa** -ae, f *persuasive discourse or eloquence*, Quint

suāsus -ūs, m (suadeo), *a persuading, exhorting, persuasion*, Plaut , Ter

suāvĕ, adv (suavis) = suaviter, *sweetly, pleasantly*, suave rubens, Verg

suāvĕŏlens -entis, and **suāvĕ ŏlens** entis (suave and oleo), *sweet smelling*, Cat

suāvĭdĭcus -a -um (suave and dico), *sweetly speaking*, Lucr

suāvillum (sāvillum) i, n (suavis), *a kind of sweet cake*, Cato

suāvĭlŏquens -entis (suave and loquor), *sweetly speaking, agreeable*, Lucr.

suāvĭlŏquentĭa -ae, f. (suaviloquens), *a sweet, agreeable manner of speaking*, Cic.

suāvĭlŏquus = suaviloquens (q.v.).

suāvĭŏlum = saviolum (q.v.).

suāvĭor = savior (q.v.).

suāvis -e (connected with ἡδύς), *sweet, pleasant, agreeable, delightful.* **I.** As regards the senses, odor, Cic.; flores, Lucr. **II.** As regards the mind, litterae tuae, Cic.

suāvĭtas -ātis, f. (suavis), *sweetness, agreeableness, pleasantness.* **I.** For the senses, cibi, Cic.; odorum, Cic.; coloris, Cic. **II.** As regards the mind, vitae, Cic.; cuius eximia suavitas, Cic.

suāvĭtĕr, adv. (suavis), *sweetly, agreeably, pleasantly, delightfully.* **I.** As regards the senses, quam suaviter voluptas sensibus blandiatur, Cic. **II.** As regards the mind, loqui, meminisse, Cic.; suavissime scriptae litterae, Cic.

suāvĭtūdo = suavitas (q.v.).

suāvĭum = savium (q.v.).

sŭb, prep. with abl. and acc. (connected with ὑπό). **I.** With abl., **A.** Of place, **1,** to express staying under, *under;* **a,** with verbs implying rest, *under;* sub terra habitare, Cic.; sub pellibus hiemare, Cic.; vitam sub divo agere, Hor.; transf., sub armis esse, *to be under arms*, Caes.; sub corona, sub hasta vendere, Cic.; **b,** with verbs of motion, sub hoc jugo dictator Aequos misit, Liv.; **2,** to express nearness to, *beneath, under, at the bottom of, at the foot of;* castra sub monte consedit, Caes.; sub ipsis Numantiae moenibus, Cic.; transf., sub oculis domini, Liv.; sub manu esse, Caes.; **3,** *down in, within;* silvis inventa sub altis, Ov.; **4,** *just behind;* quo deinde sub ipso ecce volat, Verg. **B.** Of time, **1,** *during, at the time of, within;* primis spectata sub annis, Ov.; **2,** *at, near to;* sub luce urbem ingressus, Liv.; sub adventu Romanorum, Liv. **C.** Of condition, **1,** to express subjection, *under, beneath;* sub imperio alicuius, Caes.; sub regno alicuius, Cic.; sub rege, *under the rule of a king*, Cic.; sub judice lis est, *before the judge*, Hor.; **2,** *at, on, under;* Bacchi sub nomine risit, Ov.; multa vana sub nomine celebri vulgabantur, Tac. **II.** With acc., **A.** Of place, **1,** to express motion, *under;* manum sub vestimenta deferre, Plaut.; exercitum sub jugum mittere, Caes.; transf., sub sensum cadere non possunt, Cic.; **2,** to express motion near to, *under, beneath, at the bottom of, very near to;* sub montem succedunt milites, Caes. **B.** Of time, **1,** *about, towards, just before;* Pompeius sub noctem naves solvit, *about night, towards night*, Caes.; sub galli cantum, *about cockcrow*, Hor.; **2,** *immediately after;* sub eas litteras statim recitatae sunt tuae, Cic. **C.** To express subjection, *under;* matrimonium vos sub legis superbissimae vincula conjicitis, Liv. (sub in composition, = **a,** *under;* **b,** *somewhat, a little;* **c,** *secretly*).

sŭbabsurdē, adv. (subabsurdus), *somewhat absurdly*, Cic.

sŭbabsurdus -a -um, *somewhat absurd, somewhat foolish*, Cic.

sŭbaccūso, 1. *to accuse, blame, find fault with a little;* aliquem, Cic.

sŭbăcĭdus -a -um, *somewhat sour, acid*, Cato.

sŭbactĭo -ōnis, f. (subigo), *a working up, preparing;* fig., *preparation, discipline*, Cic.

sŭbactus = subactio (q.v.).

sŭbaerātus -a -um, *having copper inside or underneath*, Pers.

sŭbăgrestis -e, *somewhat rustic, somewhat boorish;* consilium, Cic.

sŭbālāris -e, *under the arms, under the armpits*, Nep.

sŭbalbĭcans -antis, *somewhat white, whitish*, Varr.

sŭbalbĭdus -a -um, *whitish*, Plin.

sŭbalpīnus -a -um, *beneath or near the Alps*, Plin.

sŭbămārus -a -um, *somewhat bitter;* subamara aliqua res, Cic. Plur. subst., **sŭbămāra** -ōrum, n. *things somewhat bitter*, Cic.

sŭbăquĭlus -a -um, *somewhat dark-coloured, brownish*, Plaut.

sŭbărātor -ōris, m. (subaro), *one who ploughs near anything*, Plin.

sŭbăro, 1. *to plough close to anything*, Plin.

sŭbarrŏgantĕr, adv. *somewhat arrogantly or proudly*, Cic.

sŭbausculto, 1. *to listen secretly*, Cic.

subbăsĭlĭcānus -i, m. (sub and basilica), *one who lounges about a basilica*, Plaut.

subbĭbo -bibi, 3. *to drink a little*, Suet.

subblandĭor, 4. *to flatter, coax, caress a little*, Plaut.

subbrĕvis -e, *somewhat short*, Plin.

subcăvus -a -um, *somewhat hollow*, Lucr.

subcentŭrĭo = succenturio (q.v.).

subcingo = succingo (q.v.).

subcontŭmēlĭōsē, adv. *somewhat insolently;* aliquem tractare, Cic.

subcresco = succresco (q.v.).

subcrispus -a -um, *somewhat curled;* capillus, Cic.

subcumbo = succumbo (q.v.).

subdēbĭlis -e, *somewhat lame*, Suet.

subdēbĭlĭtātus -a -um, *somewhat discouraged, wanting in spirit*, Cic.

subdĭālis -e (sub dio), *in the open air*, Plin. Subst., **subdĭālia** -ium, n. *open galleries, balconies*, Plin.

subdiffĭcĭlis -e, *somewhat difficult;* quaestio subdifficilis, Cic.

subdiffīdo, 3. *to be somewhat mistrustful*, Cic.

subdĭtīvus -a -um (subdo), *supposititious, not genuine, false;* archipirata, Cic.

subdĭto, 1. (intens. of subdo), *to supply, apply*, Lucr. (?)

subdo -didi -ditum, 3. **I.** *to put, place, lay, set under;* **1,** lit., **a,** ignes, Cic.; se aquis, *to dive under*, Ov.; **b,** partic., subditus, of places, *lying under* or *near;* subdita templo Appia, Ov.; **2,** fig., **a,** irae facem, Lucr.; alicui acriores ad studia dicendi faces, Cic; alicui spiritus, *to infuse*, Liv.; **b,** esp., *to subject, subdue;* ne feminae imperio subderentur, Tac. **II.** *to put in the place of another, substitute.* **A.** Gen., me in Hirtii locum, Cic. **B.** *to substitute falsely, counterfeit, suborn;* testamenta, Tac.

subdŏcĕo, 2. *to teach as an assistant, to assist in teaching*, Cic.

subdŏlē, adv. (subdolus), *somewhat slyly, craftily*, Cic.

subdŏlus -a -um, *somewhat sly, crafty, cunning, deceitful;* oratio, Caes.

subdŏmo, 1. *to tame, subject by taming*, Plaut.

subdŭbĭto, 1 *to doubt* or *hesitate a little, be undecided*, subdubitare te, quā essem erga illum voluntate, Cic

subdūco duxi -ductum, 3 **I.** *to draw from under, to withdraw, take away*, esp, *secretly* **A.** Lit, **1**, gen, ensem capiti, Verg, lapides ex turri, Caes; transf, se subducere colles incipiunt, *to withdraw themselves gradually*, i e, *slope down to*, Verg, **2**, esp, **a**, *to take away to some place, lead away, draw off*, aliquem in contionem, Liv, esp, as milit t t., cohortes e dextro cornu, Liv, copias in proximum collem, Caes, **b**, *to take away secretly, to steal*, furto obsides, Liv, se subducere, *to withdraw secretly, go away quietly, to steal away*, de circulo se subduxit, Cic, **c**, *to take away*, cibum athletae, Cic, pugnae Turnum, Verg **B.** Transf, subducere rationem, or ratiunculam, *to balance an account, cast up, reckon*, Cic, so also calculos, Cic, summam, Cic **II.** *to draw up on high, lift up*, **1**, gen, cataractam in tantum altitudinis, Liv, **2**, esp, naut t t, *to draw* or *haul up a ship on shore*, classem, Liv, naves, Caes

subductārĭus -a -um (subduco), *useful for drawing up*, funis, Cato

subductĭo -ōnis, f (subduco) **I.** *the drawing up of a ship on dry land*, Caes. **II.** *a reckoning, computing*, Cic

subdulcis e, *somewhat sweet*, Plin

subdūrus -a -um, *somewhat hard*, Q Cic

sŭbĕdo -ēdi -ēsum, 3 *to eat under, wear away*, scopulus, quem rauca subederat unda, Ov

sŭbĕo ii itum -ire, *to go under, come under, pass under, dive under, crawl under* **I. A.** Lit, **a**, with a prep, subit oras hasta per imas clipei, Verg, **b**, with dat, luco, Verg, as a bearer (under a burden), ingenti feretro, Verg, **c**, with acc, aquas Ov, tectum non subisse, Caes, mucronem, *to run under*, Verg, as a bearer, onus dorso gravius, Hor, **d**, absol, ille astu subit, Verg **B** Fig *to go under* (as a burden), *to submit to, to take upon oneself*, quamvis carnificinam, Cic, quemque casum, Cic; pro amico periculum aut invidiam, Cic, minus sermonis subissem, Cic **II.** *to approach to* **A.** *to come near a point, advance to, mount to, climb to*, **1**, lit, **a**, (α) with prep, sub orbem solis (of the moon), Liv, in latebras, Ov, ad urbem, Liv, (β) with dat, muro, Verg, (γ) with acc, muros, Liv, (δ) absol, pone subit conjux, Verg, **b**, *to approach secretly* or *gradually, to steal into*, (α) with acc, lumina fessa (of sleep), Ov (β) absol, an subit (amor), Ov, **c**, of water, *to approach near, to wash*, ubi maxime montes Crotonenses Trasumenus subit, Liv; **2**, fig, **a**, *to come under*, (α) with sub and the acc, sub acumen stili, Cic, (β) with acc, clarum subit Alba Latinum, *comes under the rule of*, Ov, **b**, *to approach some action, to undertake, take upon oneself*. with acc, invicem proelium, Liv,, **c**, of situations or conditions, *to come upon one, happen to, befall*, (α) with dat, subeunt mihi fastidia cunctarum, Ov, (β) with acc, horror animum subit, Tac, (γ) with infin, subit ira cadentem ulcisci patriam, Verg, (δ) absol, *to draw near, come*, subeunt morbi tristisque senectus et labor, Verg, **d**, of thoughts, *to occur, come into the mind, creep in*, (α) with dat, subeant animo Latmia saxa tuo, Ov, (β) with acc, mentem patriae subiit pietatis imago, Verg with acc and infin, cogitatio animum subit indignum esse, etc, Liv, (γ) absol, subit cari genitoris imago, Ov **B.** *to come immediately after, to take the place of, to follow*. **1**, lit, **a**, with dat, primae legioni tertia, dextrae alae sinistra subiit, Liv, **b**, with acc, furcas subiere columnae Ov, **2**, fig, **a**, with in and the acc, in eorum locum subiere fraudes, Ov, **b**, absol, pulchra subit facies, Ov (perf., subivit, Ov)

sūber -ĕris, n. *the cork-tree*, Verg

subf v suff . .

subg v sugg . .

sŭbhorrĭdus a -um, *somewhat rough*, Cic.

sŭbĭcio, v. subjicio

sŭbĭgo ēgi actum, 3 (sub and ago), *to drive under* **I.** *to drive under* or *to a place*, **1**, lit., sues in umbrosum locum, Varr,, naves ad castellum, Liv, adverso flumine lembum remigio, *to row*, Verg, ratem conto, *to push*, Verg, **2**, transf, *to drive a person to do something against his will, to force, compel*, gen, with ad or in and the acc, Volscos ad deditionem, Liv, with infin or acc and infin, Tarquinienses metu subegerat frumentum exercitui praebere, Liv with ut and the subj, ut relinquant patriam atque cives, Liv **II. 1**, *to work through, to work thoroughly*, in cote secures, *to sharpen*, Verg., digitis opus, *to make smooth*, Ov so esp, *to work the earth, to break up, plough, cultivate*, terras fissione glebarum, Cic, **2**, transf, **a**, *to tame*, (α) of animals, belua facilis ad subigendum, Cic, (β) of men, *to practise train, inure*, tot subacti atque durati bellis, Liv, **b**, *to subdue, conquer*, subacti bello, Liv, populos armis, Cic, partic subst, victi ac subacti, Cic

sŭbimpŭdens -entis *somewhat impudent*, Cic

sŭbĭnānis e, *somewhat vain*, Cic

sŭbindĕ, adv **I.** *immediately upon immediately after*, Hor, Liv **II.** *repeatedly, from time to time, continually*, Liv

sŭbinsulsus -a -um, *somewhat insipid*, Cic.

sŭbinvĭdĕo, 2 **I.** *to envy somewhat*, subinvideo tibi, Cic. **II.** Partic, **sŭbinvīsus** a -um, *somewhat hated*, Cic

sŭbinvīto, 1 *to invite secretly*, with ut and the subj, Cic

sŭbīrascor irasci, dep *to be a little angry*, interdum soleo subirasci, Cic, foll by dat, brevitati litterarum, Cic, by quod, quod me non invitas, Cic

sŭbīrātus -a -um, *somewhat angry*, Cic

sŭbĭtārĭus -a -um (subitus), *sudden, hasty*, exercitus, milites, legiones, *gathered in haste*, Liv

sŭbĭtō, adv (subitus), *suddenly, unexpectedly, on a sudden*, Cic; dicere, *to speak extempore*, Cic

sŭbĭtus a -um, p adj (from subeo), *sudden, unexpected* **I.** Adj, res, Cic, bellum, Caes **II.** Subst, **sŭbĭtum** -i, n *a sudden occurrence, unexpected chance*, ad subita rerum, Liv

subjăcĕo -jăcŭi, 2 **I.** *to lie under* or *beneath*, Plin **II.** *to be subject to, belong to, to be connected with*, Quint

subjectē, adv, only used in superl (subjectius), *submissively*, Caes

subjectĭo -ōnis, f (subjicio) **I.** *a laying under, placing under*, rerum, quasi gerantur, sub aspectum paene subjectio, Cic **II** *a counterfeiting, forging*, testamenti, Liv **III** Rhet t t = ανθυποφορα, *the answer given by an orator to a question which he has himself asked*, Quint

subjecto, 1 (intens of subjicio) **I.** *to place, lay, put under*, stimulos alicui, Hor **II.** *to throw up from below*, Verg

subjector -ōris, m (subjicio), *a forger, counterfeiter* testamentorum, Cic

1 **subjectus** ūs, m (subjicio), *a placing, laying under*, Plin

2 **subjectus** -a -um, p adj (from subjicio) **I.** Of places, *lying near, adjacent*, Heraclea, quae est subjecta Candaviae, Caes; alter (circulus terrae) subjectus aquiloni, Cic **II.** Transf, **a,** *subjected, subject to*, nulli est naturae oboediens aut subjectus deus, Cic Subst, **subjecti** -ōrum, m *subjects, dependents*, Tac, **b,** *exposed to*, subjectior invidiae, Hor

subjĭcĭo (sŭbĭcĭo) jēci -jectum, 3 (sub and jacio) **I.** *to throw, cast, place, set, put under* **A.** Lit, **1,** gen, ignem, Cic, aliquid oculis, Cic, aedes colli, *to build under*, Liv, castra urbi, *to pitch under the walls of*, Liv, **2,** esp, **a,** milit t t, *to advance near*, aciem collibus, or castris, legiones castris, Caes, **b,** *to present*, libellum alicui, Cic. **B.** Fig, **1,** gen, ea quae sub sensus subjecta sunt, Cic, res, quae subjectae sunt sensibus, Cic, **2,** esp, **a,** *to subdue, subjugate, subject*, Gallia securibus subjecta, Caes, se alicui, Cic, or se imperio alicujus, Cic, **b,** *to expose*, fortunas innocentium fictis auditionibus, Caes, aliquid praeconi, Liv, or voci praeconis, Cic, or sub praeconem, Cic, *to bring to the hammer, have sold by auction*, **c,** *to subordinate*, partes generibus, Cic, **d,** in discourse and writing, *to place after, append, subjoin*, rationem, Cic, **e,** *to whisper to, to suggest, to remind*, subjiciens quid dicerem, Cic, consilia, Liv, spem alicui, *to infuse*, Liv **II.** *to throw from under*, **1,** *to throw up on high, to raise, lift*, regem in equum, Liv, reflex, alnus se subjicit, *shoots up*, Verg, **2,** *to haul from under*, tragulas inter carros, Caes **III.** *to substitute*, **1,** gen, potiorem, Liv, pro verbo proprio subjicitur aliud, quod idem significet, Cic, **2,** **a,** *to forge, counterfeit* testamenta, Cic, **b,** *to suborn*, Metellum, Caes

subjŭgĭus a um (sub and jugum), *attached to the yoke*, Cato

subjungo junxi junctum, 3 **I.** *to join with, unite to*, **1,** lit, puppis rostro Phrygios subjuncta leones, *having affixed*, Verg, **2,** fig, omnes artes oratori, Cic, carmina percussis nervis, *with playing on the lyre*, Ov **II.** *to yoke, harness*, **1,** lit, tigres curru, Verg, **2,** fig, *to subdue, subjugate*, urbes sub imperium, Cic, sibi res, Hor

sublābor -lapsus sum -lābi, 3 dep **I.** *to glide in, slide in*, Verg **II.** *to glide away*, fig, retro sublapsa spes, Verg

sublāmĭna -ae, f *an under plate*, Cato

sublātē, adv (sublatus, from tollo), *highly*, fig, **a,** *loftily, sublimely*, dicere, Cic, **b,** *proudly, haughtily*, de se sublatius dicere, Cic

sublātĭo ōnis, f (tollo), *a lifting up, elevation*, fig, animi, Cic

sublātus -a um, p adj (from tollo), *raised aloft, proud, haughty*, with abl, hāc victoriā, Caes, rebus secundis, Verg, absol, leo fidens magis et sublatior ardet, Ov

sublecto, 1 (from *sublicio, as allecto from allicio), *to flatter, wheedle*, Plaut

sublĕgo -lēgi lectum, 3 **I.** *to gather below, pick up*, Hor **II.** *to carry off, catch up secretly*, liberos parentibus, *to kidnap*, Plaut, fig, nostrum sermonem, *to listen to secretly*, Plaut **III.** *to choose in the place of another person*, in demortuorum locum, Liv, e postremo in tertium locum esse sublectum, Cic

sublestus -a -um, *slight, weak, trivial*, Plaut

sublĕvātio ōnis, f (sublevo), *a relieving, assuaging*, Cic.

sublĕvo, 1 **I.** *to lift up, hold up*, ab iis sublevatus murum ascendit, Caes, aliquem stratum ad pedes, Cic **II.** Transf, *to lessen, diminish*, pericula, Cic, offensionem, Cic, esp, **a,** *to lessen or relieve by consoling*, rēs adversas, Cic, **b,** *to support*, causam inimici, Cic

sublĭca -ae, f (ὑποβλής), *a pile driven into the ground, palisade*, Caes, Liv., esp of the piles of a bridge, Caes

sublĭcĭus a um (sublica), *resting upon piles*, pons, *a wooden bridge across the Tiber, said to have been built by Ancus Martius*, Liv

sublĭgācŭlum i, n (subligo), *a cloth worn round the loins, drawers*, Cic

sublĭgar -āris, n. = subligaculum (q v)

subligo, 1. *to bind below, bind on*, clipeum sinistrae, Verg

sublīmĕ, adv, v sublimis

sublīmis -e (sublevo), *high* **I.** Adj, **A.** Lit, *high, lofty, exalted, lifted up*, **a,** cacumen montis, Ov, **b,** *in the air, aloft*, sublimis abiit, *went away on high*, Liv, **c,** *raised on high*, iret consul sublimis curru multijugis equis, Liv **B.** Transf, *sublime, elevated, lofty*, **a,** mens, Ov, **b,** of style, *lofty, sublime*, carmina, Juv **II.** Subst, **sublīme** -is, n *height*, Suet. **III.** Adv, **sublīme,** *on high, aloft*, aer sublime fertur, Cic, sublime elatus, Liv (Other forms sublimus -a um, Lucr, sublīmen = sublime, adv, Enn ap Cic)

sublīmĭtas -ātis, f (sublimis), *loftiness, height*, **a,** lit, Plin, **b,** transf, *loftiness, sublimity*, Plin

sublīmĭtĕr, adv (sublimis), *aloft, on high*; sublimius attollere altum caput, Ov

sublīmus, v sublimis

sublingĭo ōnis, m (sub and lingo), *a scullion*, Plaut

sublĭno -lēvi -lĭtum, 3 **I.** *to smear below, to lay on colour as a ground*, Plin **II.** Transf., **1,** *to line, overlay, veneer with anything*, Plin; **2,** fig, os alicui, *to deceive, cozen, cajole, delude*, Plaut

sublūcānus a -um (sub and lux), *about daybreak, towards morning*, Plin

sublūcĕo -luxi, 2. *to gleam forth, glimmer*, Verg, Ov

sublŭo -lŭi lūtum, 3 **I.** *to wash from below, bathe underneath*, Mart. **II.** Transf, of rivers, *to flow beneath, flow at the foot of*, hunc montem flumen subluebat, Caes

sublustris e (sub and lux), *somewhat light, having a glimmering light*, nox, Hor

sublŭvĭes -ēi, f (subluo), *a disease in the feet of sheep*, Plin

submergo -mersi -mersum, 3. *to plunge under, to sink*, pass, submergi = *to dive or plunge under* of persons, *to be drowned*, navem, Tac, with abl, classem Argivûm ponto, Verg; often in pass, submersae beluae, *living under the water*, Cic, submersus equus voraginibus, Cic, with in and the abl, ferrum submersum in unda, Ov

submĭnistro, 1 *to aid, give, furnish, supply* **I.** Lit, tela clam, Cic, alicui pecuniam, Cic **II.** Fig, huic arti plurima adjumenta, Cic.

submissē (summissē), adv (submissus) **I.** Of speech, *softly, calmly*, dicere, Cic, Demosthenes submissius a primo, Cic **II** Of character, *modestly, humbly, submissively*, supplicare, Cic, submissius nos geramus, Cic.

submissim (summissim), adv (submissus), *gently, softly, quietly*, Suet

submissĭo (summissĭo) ōnis, f (submitto), *a letting down, sinking, lowering*; contentio vocis et submissio, Cic, orationis, Cic

submissus (summissus) -a -um, p adj (from submitto). **I.** *lowered, low*, vertex, Ov.;

submissiores, *in a lower position*, Liv. **II.** Transf, **A.** Applied to the voice, *low, soft, gentle*, used of discourse, *quiet, mild, gentle*, **a,** vox, Cic , **b,** *quiet, unpretentious*, submissa dicere, Cic , orator, Cic **B.** Of character, **a,** in a bad sense, *mean, abject*, submissum vivere, Cic , ne quid humile, submissum faciamus, Cic , **b,** in a good sense, *humble*, submissi petimus terram, Verg

submitto (summitto) misi -missum, 3 **I.** *to let down* **A.** Lit , **1,** gen , fasces, *to lower*, Liv , alicui se ad pedes, *to fall at the feet of*, Liv , **2,** esp , of places, in pass , submitti, as middle = *to sink, slope down*, submissa fastigio planities, Liv **B.** Fig , **1,** gen , animos, *cause to sink*, Liv , se, *to abase oneself*, Cic , **2,** esp , **a,** *to diminish, lessen*, multum (in discourse), *not to speak strongly*, Cic ; **b,** *to give over*, alicui imperium, Liv , **c,** *to subject to, subordinate to*, citharae cannas, Ov , **d,** *to slacken, relax*, furorem, Verg **II.** *to place under*; fig , *to submit*, animos amori, Verg **III.** *to send up from below, to raise*; **1,** gen , oculos, Ov , **2,** esp , **a,** *to cause to spring up*, flores Lucr , transf , *to produce*, non monstrum summisere Colchi majus, Hor , **b,** *to let grow*, capillum, Plin **c,** *to rear*, vitulos, Verg **IV.** *to send secretly*, aliquem, Cic , subsidia alicui, Caes

submŏlestē (summŏlestē), adv (submolestus), *with some vexation*, te non esse Romae submoleste fero, Cic

submŏlestus (summŏlestus) a um, *somewhat vexatious*, illud est mihi submolestum quod parum properaro Brutus videtur, Cic

submŏnĕo (summŏnĕo) -mŏnŭi, 2 *to remind secretly*, Ter

submōrōsus (summōrōsus) a um, *somewhat morose, somewhat peevish*, Cic

submōtor (summōtor) -ōris, m (sub moveo), *one who clears a space in a crowd*, Liv

submŏvĕo (summŏvĕo) -mōvi -mōtum, 2 *to move away, drive away, remove* **I.** Lit , **A.** Gen , **a,** of persons, aliquem, Ov , strictis gladiis inertes, Liv , populum aris, Ov , **b,** of things, silva suis frondibus Phoebeos submovet ictus, *keeps off*, Ov , submotis nubibus, Verg **B.** Esp , **1,** of living beings, **a,** *to remove, cause to withdraw*, arbitros, Liv , recusantes nostros advocatos, Cic , **b,** of the lictor, *to clear a way for a magistrate, to keep off, move back*, turbam, Liv , submoveri jubet, Liv , abl absol , submoto, *when a way had been cleared*, Liv , **c,** *to banish, expel* aliquem patriā, Ov , **d,** *to drive off in a hostile manner, drive away, force back*, cohortes sub murum, Caes , victorem hostem a vallo, Liv , hostes ex muro ac turribus, Caes , **2,** of things, **a,** *to remove, move back*, maris litora, Hor , **b,** pass partic , submotus, *lying out of the way, remote*, spelunca vasto submota recessu, Verg **II** Transf, **1,** of persons, *to keep away from, force from, compel to give up*, a bello Antiochum et Ptolemaeum reges, Liv , aliquem magnitudine poenae a maleficio Cic , **2,** of things, *to remove, banish*, tumultus mentis et curas, Hor

submūto (summūto), 1 *to exchange*, verba pro verbis, Cic

subnascor nātus sum, 3 dep *to grow up under, grow up out of* or *after*, Ov

subnecto -nexŭi -nexum, 3 **I.** *to bind, tie, bind on beneath*, antennis totum subnectite velum, Ov **II.** *to join or tie together*, aurea purpuream subnectit fibula vestem, Verg

subnĕgo, 1 *to deny a little, partly deny*, Cic.

subnīger gra -grum, *somewhat black, blackish*, Plaut

subnixus (subnīsus) a um (sub and nitor) **I.** *propped under*, mitrā mentum et crinem subnixus, *bound under*, Verg **II.** *supported by, resting upon*, **a,** lit , circuli verticibus subnixi, Cic , **b,** fig , *trusting, relying upon, depending upon*, with abl , auxiliis, Liv ; victoriā, Liv , qui artis arrogantiā ita subnixi ambulant, Cic

subnŏto, 1 **I.** *to mark beneath, write underneath*, Plin **II.** *to observe, notice secretly*, Mart

subnŭba ae, f (sub and nubo), *a rival*, Ov

subnūbilus a -um, *somewhat cloudy*, nox, Caes.

sūbo, 1 *to be in heat*, Lucr , Hor

sŭbobscoenus (sŭbobscēnus) a -um, *somewhat obscene*, Cic

sŭbobscūrus a -um, *somewhat obscure*, Cic

sŭbŏdĭōsus -a -um, *somewhat odious, unpleasant*, Cic

sŭboffendo, 3 *to give some offence*, apud aliquem, Cic

sŭbŏlĕo, 2 lit , *to emit a smell*, hence, fig , hoc subolet mihi, or subolet mihi, *I smell, perceive, scent*, Plaut

sŭbŏles (sŏbŏles) -is, genit plur , -um (subolesco) **I.** Of things, *a sprout, shoot off shoot, sucker*, Plin **II.** Of living beings, of men and animals, *race, offspring, progeny, issue*, **a,** of men, stirpis, Liv , juventutis, Cic , of one person, suboles imperatorum (of Scipio), Liv , **b,** of animals, haedus, suboles lascivi gregis, Hor

sŭbŏlesco, 3 (sub and olesco = alesco), *to grow up*, Liv

sŭbŏrior, 4 dep *to arise, come forth, spring up*, Lucr

sŭborno, 1 **I.** *to furnish, equip, provide*, a natura subornatus, Cic , fig , legati subornati criminibus, Liv **II.** *to incite, instigate secretly*, suborn , fictum testem, Cic , aliquem ad caedem regis, Liv

sŭbortus ūs, m (suborior), *a coming forth, arising*, Lucr

subp v supp

subrādo (surrādo) -rāsi rasum, 3 *to scrape below*, Cato

subrancĭdus (surrancĭdus) a -um, *somewhat putrid*, caro, Cic

subraucus (surraucus) a um, *somewhat hoarse*, vox, Cic

subrectus (surrectus), v subrigo

subrēmĭgo (surrēmĭgo), 1 *to row underneath, row along*, Verg

subrēpo (surrēpo) -repsi reptum, 3 *to creep or crawl from below, creep to, approach imperceptibly*, **a,** lit , sub tabulas, Cic , moenia, Hor , **b,** transf , somnus in oculos subrepit, Ov , subrepent mers actas, Tib

subreptīcĭus (surreptīcĭus) -a um (surripio), **1,** *stolen, kidnapped*, Plaut , **2,** *secret, surreptitious*, Plaut

subrīdĕo (surrīdĕo) -risi -risum, 2 *to smile*, Cic

subrīdĭcŭlē (surrīdĭcŭlē), adv *somewhat laughably*, Cic

subrīgo (surrīgo) and contr , **surgo,** surrexi, surrectum, 3 (sub and rego) **I. subrigo** (surrigo) rexi, etc , *to raise on high, lift up*, pass , subrigi, *to rise up*, partic , subrectus, *rising up*, aures, Verg , subrecto mucrone, Liv **II surgo,** surrexi, surrectum **A.** Transit , *to raise up, lift*, Plaut **B.** Intransit , *to rise, arise* *up erect, stand up;* **1,** gen., e lectulo, Cic.; de sella, Cic.; humo Ov.; poet., surgit ab Arpis Tydides, *comes from,* Verg.; **2,** esp., **a,** of orators, *to rise up to speak, to come forward;* ad dicendum, Cic.; **b,** *to rise up from bed or sleep;* ante lucem, Cic.; **3,** transf., **a,** *to arise, appear, become visible;* surgit dies, Verg.; ventus, Verg.; fig., discordia, Verg.; **b,** *to grow up, become larger;* (α) of things, as seed, Hor.; of the sea, Ov.; of buildings, surgens novae Carthaginis urbs, Verg.; (β) of living beings, *to grow up;* surgens Iulus, Verg. (syncop. perf. infin., surrexe, Hor.).

subrigŭus (surrigŭus) -a -um, *watered, irrigated,* Plin.

subringor (surringor), 3. dep. *to make a somewhat wry face, to be a little put out,* Cic.

subrĭpĭo = surripio (q.v.).

subrŏgo (surrŏgo), 1. *to cause a person to be chosen in place of or as substitute for another* (used of the magistrate presiding at the comitia, sufficere of the people choosing); in annum proximum decemviros alios, Cic.; collegam in locum Bruti, Liv.; with double acc., sibi Sp. Lucretium collegam, Cic.

subrostrāni (surrostrāni) -ōrum, m. (sub and rostra), *loungers about the rostra, idlers;* ap. Cic.

subrŭbĕo (surrŭbĕo), 2. *to be somewhat red;* part., subrubens = *reddish,* Ov.

subrŭbĭcundus (surrŭbĭcundus) -a -um, *somewhat red, reddish,* Plin.

subrūfus (surrūfus) -a -um, *reddish,* Plin.

subrūmus (surrūmus) -a -um (sub and ruma), *sucking;* agnus, Varr.

subrŭo (surrŭo) -rŭi -rŭtum, 3. *to tear down below, dig under, undermine, overthrow, destroy.* **I.** Lit., arbores, Caes.; murum, Liv. **II.** Fig., *to destroy, undermine;* nostram libertatem, Liv.

subrustĭcus (surrustĭcus) -a -um, *somewhat clownish;* pudor, Cic.

subrŭtĭlus (surrŭtĭlus) -a -um, *reddish;* color, Plin.

subsalsus -a -um, *somewhat salt,* Plin.

subscrībo -scripsi -scriptum, 3. **I.** *to write under, write beneath.* **A.** Gen., statuis subscripsit reges esse exactos, Cic.; causam parricidii, Cic.; haec subscribe libello, Hor. **B.** Esp., **1,** *to sign a document;* **a,** lit., Suet.; **b,** transf., *to support, assent to, approve of;* odiis accusatorum, Liv.; irae Caesaris, Ov.; **2,** of the censor, *to write the ground of his censure beneath the name of the person censured;* istam causam, Cic.; **3,** of an accuser or joint-accuser, *to write their names under the accusation;* **a,** of the accuser, *to sign a charge;* hence, *to prosecute;* subscripsit quod is pecuniam accepisset, *accused him of having,* etc., Cic.; in aliquem, *to accuse,* Cic.; **b,** of a joint-accuser = *to join in the accusation;* Gabinium de ambitu reum fecit subscribente privigno, Cic. **II.** *to note down, make a note of;* numerum, Cic.

subscriptĭo -ōnis, f. (subscribo), *a writing beneath, inscription.* **I.** Gen., Cic. **II.** Esp., **a,** censoria, *the noting down of the offence censured;* subscriptiones censorum, Cic.; **b,** *the signing of one's name to an accusation;* (α) of the accuser, Cic.; (β) of a joint-accuser, *a joining in an accusation,* Cic.; **c,** *the signing, subscription of a document,* Suet.; **d,** *a register,* Cic.

subscriptor -ōris, m. (subscribo), *the signer of an indictment, a joint-accuser,* Cic.

subsĕcīvus = subsicivus (q.v.).

subsĕco -sĕcŭi -sectum, 1. *to cut away below;* ungues ferro, Ov.

subsellium -ii, n. (sub and sella). **I.** *a low bench or form,* Varr. **II.** *any ordinary or usual bench used for sitting on,* Sen.; a bench in a theatre, Cic.; of the senators in the senate-house, Cic.; longi subsellii judicatio et mora, *a long sitting to decide,* Cic.; of the tribunes in the market, Liv.; esp., of the benches of the judges, accusers, advocates, etc., Cic.: meton., subsellia = judicia, *courts;* habitare in subselliis, Cic.; versari in utrisque subselliis (*both as an advocate and judge*) optimā et fide et famā, Cic.

subsentĭo -sensi, 4. *to notice, perceive secretly,* Ter.

subsĕquor -sĕcūtus (-sĕquūtus) sum, 3. dep. *to follow, follow after.* **I. a,** lit., of persons, signa, Caes.; **b,** transf., of things, stella subsequitur, Cic.; hos motus subsequi debet gestus, Cic. **II.** Fig., *to follow, follow in opinion, comply with, imitate any one;* Platonem avunculum, Cic.; suo sermone humanitatem litterarum, Cic.

subservĭo, 4. *to be subject to, serve, subserve, comply with,* Plaut., Ter.

subsĭcīvus (subsĕcīvus) -a -um (sub and seco), *cut off.* **I.** Lit., t. t. of land-measuring; subst., **subsĕcīvum** -i, n. *a remainder or small parcel of land,* Varr. **II.** Transf., of time, *superfluous, spare;* tempora, *leisure hours,* Cic.; transf., of what is done in the leisure hours, quae (arripui) subsicivis operis, ut aiunt, Cic.

subsĭdĭārĭus -a -um (subsidium), *of or relating to a reserve, reserve;* cohortes, Caes., Liv.; subst., **subsĭdĭārĭi** -ōrum, m. *reserve troops,* Liv.

subsĭdĭor, 1. dep. (subsidium), *to serve as a reserve,* Hirt.

subsĭdĭum -ii, n. **I.** Concr., milit. t. t., *the troops stationed in the rear, reserved troops, a reserve, auxiliary forces;* subsidia et secundam aciem adortus, Liv.; subsidium and subsidia submittere, Caes. **II.** Abstr., **1,** milit. t. t., *help, assistance* (of such troops), subsidium ferre, Caes.; subsidio proficisci, Caes.; **2,** transf., **a,** *aid, means of aid, help, succour;* subsidium bellissimum existimo esse senectuti otium, Cic.; subsidio esse, of persons, *to be a help to,* Ov.; of things, *to serve as a help;* his difficultatibus, Caes.; or oblivioni, Cic.; **b,** *a place of refuge, an asylum,* Tac.

subsīdo -sēdi and -sīdi -sessum, 3. **I.** *to sit down, squat, crouch down, settle down, sink down.* **A.** Lit., **1,** of living beings; **a,** subsidunt Hispani, Liv.; elephanti clunibus subsidentes, Liv.; **b,** *to lie in wait for, lurk in ambush;* in insidiis, Liv.; in loco, Cic.; with acc., Asiam devictam, Verg.; **c,** of females, *to submit to the male,* Lucr., Hor.; **2,** transf., of things, *to sink down, subside;* subsidunt undae, Verg.; jussit subsidere valles, Ov. **B.** Fig., *to abate,* Plin. **II.** *to remain sitting, to stay, remain, settle;* subsedi in via, Cic.; multitudo calonum in castris subsederant, Caes.

subsignānus -a -um (sub and signum), *serving beneath the standard;* milites, *legionary soldiers kept as a reserve,* Tac.

subsigno, 1. **I.** *to write beneath, sign, subscribe,* Plin. **II.** Transf., **1,** *to enter on a list, to register;* praedia apud aerarium, Cic.; **2,** *to pledge,* Plin.

subsĭlĭo (sussĭlĭo) -sĭlŭi, 4. *to leap up, spring up,* Lucr.

subsīmus -a -um, *somewhat snub-nosed,* Varr.

subsisto -stĭti, 3. **I.** Transit., *to make a stand against, to withstand;* feras, Liv.; Romanum nec acies subsistere ullae poterant, Liv.

II. Intransit, **A.** *to stand still, come to a stand, halt*; **1,** lit, **a,** of persons, in itinere, Caes, **b,** of things, *to stay, stop*, substitit unda, Verg, **2,** fig, *to cease*, substitit clamor, Ov **B.** *to tarry, remain, abide*, **1,** lit, in Summo adversus Caudinis legiones, Liv, **2,** fig, intra priorem paupertatem, *to remain, continue*, Tac **C.** *to withstand, oppose, hold out*, **1,** lit, **a,** of persons, Hannibali atque eius armis, Liv, **b,** of things, quod neque ancorae funesque subsisterent neque, etc, Caes **2,** fig, *to withstand, support*, sumptum, ap Cic

subsōlānus -a -um, *eastern, oriental*, Plin, subst, **subsōlānus** i, m *the east wind*, Plin

subsortior sortitus sum, 4 dep *to choose by lot, to substitute*, judices, *to choose fresh jurymen for those challenged by either party*, Cic

subsortītio -ōnis, f (subsortior), *the choosing of a judicial substitute by lot*, judicum, Cic

substantĭa -ae, f (substo) **I** *substance, essence*, Quint **II.** *property, means of subsistence*; facultatum, Tac

substerno -strāvi -strātum, 3 **I.** *to strew or spread beneath, lay under*, **1,** lit, cinnama, Ov, **2,** fig, *to offer, give up*, omne corporeum animo, Cic **II.** Transf *to cover*, gallinae nidos quam possunt mollissime substernunt, Cic

substĭtŭo ŭi -ūtum, 3 (sub and statuo) **I.** *to put under, place beneath*, **1,** lit, Auct b Afr, **2,** fig, substituerat animo speciem corporis, Liv **II.** *to put in the place of, substitute*, **a,** in locum eorum cives Romanos, Cic, aliquem pro aliquo, Cic, aliquid pro aliqua re, Cic, **b,** heredem, *to name a second heir in case of the death of the first*, Suet

substo, 1 *to stand firm*, Ter

substrāmen -inis, n (substerno), *that which is strewed beneath, straw, litter*, Varr

substrātus -ūs, m (substerno), *a strewing, laying, scattering beneath*, Plin

substrictus -a um, p adj (from substringo), *narrow, tight, contracted, small*, crura, Ov

substringo -strinxi -strictum, 3 *to draw together, to bind, tie beneath, bind up*, crinem nodo, Tac, aurem alicui, *to prick up the ear* (in order to listen to some one), Hor

substructĭo -ōnis, f (substruo), *that which is built below, base, foundation*, substructionum moles, Caes

substrŭo -struxi -structum, 3 *to build, construct beneath, lay a foundation* Capitolium saxo quadrato substructum est, *built with a foundation of hewn stone*, Liv

subsultim, adv (subsilio), *springing up, leaping up*, Suet

subsulto (sussulto), 1 (intens of subsilio), *to spring up, leap up, jump up*, Plaut

subsum -fŭi -esse, *to be under* **I.** Lit, **1,** *to be behind*, suberat Pan ilicis umbrae, Tib, nigra subest lingua palato, Verg, **2,** *to be near at hand*, suberat mons, Caes dies, Cic, templa mari subsunt, Ov **II.** Fig, **1,** *to be subjected to*, Ov, **2,** *to be there, to exist, to be in question*, subest nulla periculi suspicio, Cic, tamquam spes subesset, Liv

subsūtus -a -um, *sewed beneath*, vestis, *fringed, edged below*, Hor

subtēgŭlānĕus -a um (sub and tegula), *beneath the tiles, under the roof, in-doors*, Plin

subtēmen (subtegmen) inis, n (contracted from subteximen), *that which is worked in*, hence, **I.** *the weft or woof in weaving*, Ov, fert picturatas auri subtemine vestes, Verg **II.** Meton, *that which is woven or spun, thread, yarn*, Tib.

subtendo -tendi -tentum (-tensum), 3 *to stretch underneath*, Cato

subtĕnĕo, 2 *to hold underneath*, Cato, (syncop imper, subtento)

subtĕnŭis -e, *somewhat thin*, Varr

subtĕr (sub) **I.** Adv, *beneath, below, underneath*, omnia haec, quae supra et subter, Cic **II.** Prep, *beneath, below, underneath* **a,** with acc, cupiditatem subter praecordia locavit, Cic, **b,** with abl, subter se, Cic (in composition subter means *under, beneath* as in subterfluo, or *underhand, in secret*, as subterduco)

subterdūco, 3 *to lead away secretly, carry off secretly*, Plaut

subterflŭo, 3 *to flow beneath*, Plin

subterfŭgio -fūgi, 3 **I.** Intransit, *to flee in secret*, Plaut **II** Transit, *to escape by stealth, evade, shun*, poenam, Cic, periculum, Cic

subterlābor -lapsus sum, 3 dep **I.** *to glide, flow under*, fluctus Sicanos, Verg **II.** *to slip away secretly, to escape* Liv

subterlĭno, 3 *to smear underneath*, Plin

subtĕro -trīvi -trītum, 3 *to rub off, wear underneath, to grind, pound*, Plin

subterrānĕus a um (sub and terra), *underground, subterranean*, specus in fundo, Cic

subtervăcans -antis, *empty below*, Sen

subtexo -texŭi -textum, 3 **I** *to weave beneath, transf*, **a,** *to draw together under*, patrio capiti (*the sun*) bibulas nubes, Ov, **b,** *to cover, darken*, caelum fumo, Verg **II.** *to weave on to* **1,** transf, *to join to*, lunam alutae, Juv, **2,** fig, in speech, *to connect, subjoin*, subtexit deinde fabulae huic legatos in senatu interrogatos esse, Liv

subtīlis -e (contracted from subtexilis, as tela from texela and exilis from exiglis), lit, *finely woven*, hence, **I.** *thin, fine, slender*, **1,** lit, filum, Lucr, **2,** transf, **a,** gen, *fine, accurate, exact*, descriptio, Cic, venustas *elegant*, Cic, **b,** esp, of expression, *plain, simple, unadorned*, oratio, Cic, subtilis scriptor atque elegans, Cic **II.** Of the senses *fine, acute*, **1,** lit, palatum, Hor, **2,** transf, of taste and discernment, *fine, acute, subtle*, judicium, Cic

subtīlĭtas -ātis, f (subtilis), *thinness, fineness, minuteness* **I.** Lit, linearum, Plin **II.** Transf, **a,** *accuracy, fineness, subtlety, exactness*, sententiarum, Cic, sermonis, Cic, **b,** of discourse, *plainness, simplicity*, orationis, Cic

subtīlĭtĕr, adv (subtilis), *finely, minutely* **I.** Lit, res subtiliter connexae, Lucr **II.** Transf, **a,** *finely, accurately, exactly, subtly*, judicare, Cic; subtilius haec disserere, Cic, subtilissime perpolita, Cic, **b,** of expression, *plainly, simply, without ornament*, dicere, Cic

subtĭmĕo, 2 *to be a little afraid*, with ne and the subj, Cic

subtrăho -traxi -tractum, 3 **I.** *to draw away from under*, subtractus Numida mortuo superincubanti Romano vivus, Liv **II.** *to draw away secretly, withdraw, remove, take away* **A.** Lit, cibum alicui, Cic, hastatos ex acie, Liv, se, *to withdraw oneself*, se aspectui, Verg, middle, subtrahitur solum, *withdraws itself from under the ship* Verg **B.** Fig, materiem furori tuo, Cic, reliqs, se subtrahente, *withdrawing himself* (as surety), Liv, cui judicio eum mors subtraxit, Liv, me a curia et ab omni parte reipublicae, Cic, aliquem irae militum, Tac

subtristis -e, *somewhat sad*, Ter

subturpĭcŭlus -a -um, *somewhat disgraceful*, Cic

subturpis -e *somewhat disgraceful*, Cic.

subtŭs, adv. (sub), *beneath, below, underneath,* Liv.

subtūsus -a -um (sub and tundo), *somewhat bruised,* Tib.

sŭbūcŭla -ae, f. (perhaps from * sub-uo, whence ex-uo), *an inner tunic, shirt,* Hor.

sūbŭla -ae, f. *a shoemaker's awl,* Mart.

sŭbulcus -i, m. (sus), *a swineherd,* Varr.

sūbŭlo -ōnis, m. (connected with sibilus). **I.** *a Tuscan name for* tibicen, *a flute-player,* Enn. **II.** *a kind of stag,* Plin.

Sŭbūra -ae, f. *a street in the noisiest quarter of Rome;* hence, adj., **Sŭbūrānus** -a -um, *belonging to the Subura.*

sŭburbānĭtas -ātis, f. (suburbanus), *vicinity to the city,* Cic.

sŭburbānus -a -um, *near the city* (Rome), *suburban.* **I.** Adj., ager, gymnasium, Cic. **II.** Subst., **A.** **sŭburbānum** -i, n. (sc. praedium), *an estate near Rome, a suburban estate,* Cic. **B.** **sŭburbāni** -ōrum, m. *inhabitants of the suburbs,* Ov.

sŭburbĭum -ii, n. (sub and urbs), *a suburb,* Cic.

sŭburgŭĕo, 2. *to drive close to;* proram ad saxa, Verg.

sŭbūro (-ussi) -ustum, 3. *to burn a little, to singe,* Suet.

Sŭburra = Subura (q.v.).

subvectĭo -ōnis, f. (subveho), *a carrying, conveyance, transport;* frumenti, Liv.; plur., ne abre frumentaria duris subvectionibus laboraret, *lest he should have difficulties to contend with in the transport of provisions,* Caes.

subvecto, 1. (intens. of subveho), *to carry, convey, transport, bring;* saxa humeris, Verg.

subvectus = subvectio (q.v.).

subvĕho -vexi -vectum, 3. *to bring up from below, bring up stream, carry, convey, transport;* frumentum flumine Arari, Caes.; subvecta utensilia ab Ostia, Tac.; commeatus ex Samnio, Liv.; pass. as middle, ad arces subvehitur matrum caterva, *is borne up,* Verg.

subvĕnĭo -vēni -ventum, 4. *to come up to aid, to help, assist, succour.* **I.** Lit., milit. t. t., circumvento filio subvenit, Caes.; absol., nisi Romani subvenissent, Liv. **II.** Transf., *to help, aid, to remedy* or *relieve an evil;* alicui, Cic.; patriae, Cic.; gravedini, Cic.; impers., reipublicae difficillimo tempore esse subventum, Cic.

subvento, 1. (intens. of subvenio), *to come to the help of,* Plaut.

subvĕrĕor, 2. *to fear a little, be a little anxious,* Cic.

subversor -ōris, m. (subverto), *an overturner, overthrower;* fig., suarum legum, Tac.

subverto (subvorto) -verti (-vorti) -versum (-vorsum), 3. *to overthrow, overturn.* **I.** Lit., mensam, Suet.; montes, Sall.; absol., Hor. **II.** Fig., *to overthrow, ruin, subvert, destroy;* probitatem ceterasque artes bonas, Sall.; jura, Tac.

subvexus -a -um (subveho), *sloping upward,* Liv.

subvĭrĭdis -e, *somewhat green, greenish,* Plin.

subvŏlo, 1. *to fly up, fly forth;* utque novas humeris assumpserat alas, subvolat, Ov.; with in and the acc., rectis lineis in caelestem locum, Cic.

subvolvo, 3. *to roll up;* manibus saxa, Verg.

subvultŭrĭus -a -um, *somewhat vulture-like,* = *somewhat brown,* Plaut.

succăvus = subcavus (q.v.).

succēdānĕus (succīdānĕus) -a -um (succedo), *following, succeeding, ensuing, supplying the place of,* Plaut.

succēdo -cessi -cessum, 3. (sub and cedo). **I.** *to go under, go from under, ascend, mount.* **A.** Lit., tectum, Cic.; tumulo terrae, Verg.; tectis, Verg.; transf., fons, quo mare succedit, Caes. **B.** Fig., **a,** *to come under;* sub acumen stili, Cic.; **b,** *to submit to;* oneri, Verg. **II.** *to approach.* **A.** Lit., **1,** milit. t. t., *to march forward, advance;* sub aciem, Caes.; ad castra, Liv.; moenibus, Liv.; **2,** *to come after, take the place of;* ut integri et recentes defatigatis succederent, Caes.; in pugnam, Liv. **B.** Transf., **1,** *to follow, succeed to;* **a,** in locum alicuius, Cic.; in paternas opes, Cic.; **b,** of position, *to come next to;* ad alteram partem succedunt Ubii, Caes.; **2,** of time, *to follow, succeed;* alicui, Cic.; aetas aetati succedit, Cic.; orationi, Cic.; **3,** of things, *to turn out well, to prosper, succeed;* haec prospere succedebant, Cic.; res nulla successerat, Caes.; absol., succedit, *it is successful!* si ex sententia successerit, Cic.; coeptis succedebat, Liv.; pass., nolle successum patribus, Liv.

succendo -cendi -censum, 3. (sub and * cando, from candeo), 3, *to kindle, set on fire from below.* **I.** Lit., pontem, Liv.; aggerem, Caes. **II.** Fig., *to kindle, set on fire, inflame;* Deucalion Pyrrhae succensus amore, Ov.

succensĕo = suscenseo (q.v.).

succentīvus -a -um (succino), *accompanying, played as an accompaniment,* Varr.

1. **succentŭrĭo,** 1. (sub and centurio -are), *to receive in a century as a substitute;* hence, *to put in the place of another, to substitute,* Ter.

2. **succentŭrĭo** -ōnis, f. (sub and centurio -onis), *an under-centurion,* Liv.

successĭo -ōnis, f. (succedo), *a succeeding, taking place of some person or thing, succession;* **a,** voluptatis, Cic.; **b,** *succession in an office;* in locum Antonii, ap. Cic.

successor -ōris, m. (succedo), *a successor, follower in office, possession, inheritance, etc.,* Cic.; sagittae, *heir to,* Ov.; transf., Junius successor Maii, Ov.; novus, *a new shield,* Ov.

successus -ūs, m. (succedo). **I.** *an advance, approach;* hostium, Caes.; equorum, Verg. **II.** *happy issue;* prosperos successus dare orsis, Liv.; successum artes non habuere meae, Ov.

succīdĭa -ae, f. (succīdo), *a flitch of bacon;* hortum ipsi agricolae succidiam alteram appellant, *their second flitch,* Cic.

1. **succĭdo** -cĭdi, 3. (sub and cado), *to fall under, sink, sink down;* aegri succidimus, Verg.

2. **succīdo** -cīdi -cīsum, 3. (sub and caedo), *to cut under, cut below, cut off, cut down;* femina poplitesque, Liv.; frumenta, Caes.

succĭdŭus -a -um (sub and cado), *falling down, sinking;* genu, Ov.

succinctus -a -um, p. adj. (from succingo), **1,** *ready, equipped, prepared;* praedae, Ov.; **2,** *short,* Mart.

succingo -cinxi -cinctum, 3. (sub and cingo). **I.** *to gird below, gird up, tuck up the clothes in the girdle;* tunicas, Juv.; oftener partic., **succinctus** -a -um, *with the clothes tucked up;* Diana, Ov.; poet., transf., succincta comas pinus, *with bare trunk,* Ov. **II.** *to girdle, surround;* **a,** lit., Scylla feris atram canibus succingitur alvum, Ov.; gen. partic., **succinctus** -a -um, *girded with something, armed with;* ferro, Liv.; pharetrā, Verg.; **b,** transf., *to surround,* *arm, prepare, provide;* se canibus, Cic, partic, Carthago succincta portubus, Cic, succinctus armis legionibusque, Liv.

succingŭlum i, n (succingo), *a girdle,* Plaut

succĭno, 3 **1,** *to sing to, to accompany,* Petr, **2,** transf, *to agree, chime in with,* succinit alter, Hor

succlāmātĭo -ōnis, f (succlamo), *a shouting, acclamation,* Liv.

succlāmo (subclāmo), 1 *to shout at* or *after anything, call out,* haec Virginio vociferanti succlamabat multitudo, Liv, impers, succlamatum est, Liv, with acc and infin, quum succlamasset nihil se mutare sententiae, Liv

succollo, 1 (sub and collum), *to take upon the shoulders, to shoulder,* Suet.

succontŭmēlĭōsē = subcontumeliose (q v).

succresco (subcresco) -crēvi crētum, 3 *to grow beneath, grow from beneath, grow up, increase,* **a,** lit, succrescit ab imo cortex, Ov, **b,** transf, per seque vident succrescere vina, Ov., **c,** fig, non enim ille mediocris orator vestrae quasi succrescit aetati, Cic, se gloriae seniorum succrevisse, Liv

succrispus = subcrispus (q v)

succumbo cŭbŭi -cŭbitum, 3 (sub and *cumbo, as decumbo, accumbo, etc), *to lie down under, fall down, sink down* **I.** Lit., succumbens victima ferro, Cat, omnes succubuisse oculos, *had sunk in sleep,* Ov **II.** Fig, *to yield, give way, succumb, surrender,* arrogantiae divitum, Cic, senectuti, Cic, tempori, Liv, absol, non esse viri debilitari, dolore frangi, succumbere, Cic

succurro -curri -cursum, 3 (sub and curro) **I.** *to run* or *go under,* **1,** transf, nequeat succurrere lunae corpus, Lucr, **2,** fig, **a,** gen, licet undique omnes in me terrores impendeant, succurram, *undergo them,* Cic, **b,** esp, *to come into the thoughts of, to occur to,* ut quidque succurrit, libet scribere, Cic, alicui succurrit, with acc. and infin, sed mihi succurrit numen non esse severum, Ov. **II.** *to hasten to help, to aid,* **1,** lit, milit. t t, alicui (with or without auxilio), Caes, Cic, impers, si celeriter succurratur, Caes, **2,** transf, *to help, succour, assist,* saluti fortunisque communibus, Cic, alicui, Cic, foll by quominus and subj, hic tantis malis haec subsidia succurrebant, quo minus omnis deleretur exercitus, Caes

succussĭo -ōnis, f. (succutio), *a shaking from beneath, earthquake,* Sen

succussus ūs, m (succutio), *a shaking,* ap Cic.

succŭtĭo cussi cussum, 3 (sub and quatio), *to shake from beneath, shake up, fling aloft,* Ov

sūcĭdus -a -um (sucus), *juicy, full of sap,* Plin

sūcĭnum -i, n (sucus), *amber,* Plin

sūcĭnus -a um (sucus), *of amber;* gutta, Mart

sūco ōnis, m *a sucker* (a term applied to a usurer), Oppios de Velia sucones dicis (a pun, because ὀπός in Greek = sucus, and the Oppii were rich usurers), Cic

sūcōsus (succōsus) -a -um (sucus), *full of sap, juicy, succulent,* Plin

Sucro -ōnis, m *a river in Hispania Tarraconensis,* now *Xucar,* at its mouth was a town of the same name, now *Cullera* Hence, **Sucrōnensis** -e, *of* or *near Sucro,* sinus, now *Gulf of Valencia*

suctus -ūs, m (sugo), *a sucking, suction,* Plin

sŭcŭla -ae, f (dim of sus) **I.** *a little sow,* Plaut **II.** Transf, **A.** *a winch, windlass, capstan,* Plaut **B.** Suculae, wrong translation of Gr ὑάδες, *a constellation, the Hyades,* Cic.

sūcus (succus) i, m (connected with Gr ὀπός), *juice, sap* **I. 1,** lit, stirpes ex terra sucum trahunt, Cic; sucus is quo utimur, Cic, **2,** meton, like χυμός, *taste,* piscis suco ingratus, Ov, **3,** fig, **a,** *vigour,* amissimus sucum et sanguinem, Cic, **b,** esp, of orators and speeches, *vigour, energy,* orationis, Cic **II.** *any thick fluid,* **a,** olivi, *unguent,* Ov, nectaris sucos ducere, *juice of nectar,* Hor, **b,** esp, in medicine, *a draught, potion,* amarus, Ov

sūdārĭum ii, n (sudo), *a handkerchief* (to wipe off perspiration from the face), Mart

sūdātĭo -ōnis, f (sudo), *a sweating,* Sen

sūdātor -ōris, m (sudo), *one who perspires easily* or *copiously,* Plin

sūdātōrĭus -a -um (sudo), *of* or *relating to sweating, producing perspiration* **I.** Adj, unctio, Plaut **II.** Subst, **sūdātōrĭum** -ii, n *a sweating room, sweating bath,* Sen

sūdātrix tricis, f (sudator), toga, *causing perspiration,* Mart

sŭdis is, f **I.** *a stake, pile,* ripa erat acutis sudibus praefixis munita, Caes **II.** Transf, *a point,* Juv

sūdo, 1. **I.** Intransit, *to sweat, perspire,* **1,** lit, puer sudavit et alsit, Hor, quum Cumis Apollo (i e, *the statue of Apollo*) sudavit, Cic; **2,** transf, **a,** *to drip with any moisture,* scuta duo sanguine sudasse, Liv, cavae tepido sudant humore lacunae, Verg, **b,** *to drip, distil,* balsama odorato sudantia ligno, Verg, **3,** fig, *to toil, make a great effort, work hard,* vides, sudare me jamdudum laborantem, ut ea tuear quae, etc, Cic, *se sine causa sudare* Cic **II.** Transit, *to throw off by sweating, to sweat out, to exude,* durae quercūs sudabunt roscida mella, Verg, ubi tura balsamaque sudantur, Tac

sūdor ōris, m *sweat, perspiration* **I. a,** lit, sudor a capite et a fronte defluens, Cic, simulacrum multo sudore manavit, Cic, **b,** fig, *great exertion, labour, fatigue, effort,* stilus ille tuus multi sudoris est, Cic, multo eius sudore ac labore sub populi Romani imperium ditionemque ceciderunt, Cic **II.** Transf, *any kind of moisture,* veneni, Ov

sūdus a -um (se and udus), *dry, without moisture,* and (applied to weather), *bright, cloudless,* ver, Verg Subst, **sūdum** -i, n **a,** *the bright cloudless sky,* Verg, **b,** *clear, bright weather,* Cic

Suēbi -ōrum, m *the Suebi, an important German nation* Hence, **A. Suēbĭa** -ae, f *the country of the Suebi* **B. Suēbĭcus** a -um, *belonging to the Suebi.*

sŭĕo, 2 *to be wont, be accustomed,* Lucr

suesco, suēvi, suētum, 3 (inchoat of sueo), *to become accustomed, inured to,* militiae, Tac, hence, suevi, *I am accustomed, I am wont,* mittere suevit, Lucr, and syncop perf, quod suesti, *as you are wont,* Cic

Suessa -ae, f **I.** *an old town of the Aurunci, in Campania, birthplace of the poet Lucilius,* now *Sessa,* hence, **Suessānus** -a -um, *relating to Suessa* **II** *a town of the Volsci, in Latium, near the Pontine marshes,* gen in full Suessa Pometia

Suessĭōnes -um, m *a Gallic people, near modern Soissons.*

Suessŭla -ae, f. *a small town in Samnium, near Mons Tifata,* now *Castel di Sessola.* Hence, **Suessŭlānus** -a -um, *of* or *belonging to Suessula.*

Suētōnĭus -ĭi, m., C. Suetonius Tranquillus, *author of the Lives of the Caesars, a contemporary of the younger Pliny.*

suētus -a -um, p. adj. (from suesco). **I.** *accustomed to;* latrociniis, Tac.; foll. by infin., Verg., Liv. **II.** *that to which a person is accustomed, usual;* sueta apud paludes proelia, Tac.

Suēvi = Suebi (q.v.).

sūfes (suffes) -fĕtis, m. (from a Phoenician word = *judge*), *the name of the highest magistrate in Carthage,* Liv.

suffarcĭno, 1. (sub and farcino), *to stuff full, fill full, cram;* Plaut., Ter.

suffarrānĕus -a -um (far), *carrying corn;* mulio, Cic.

suffĕro, sufferre (sub and fero). **I.** *to carry under, put under,* Plaut. **II.** *to hold up, support;* **1,** lit., reflex., se sufferre, *to carry oneself upright, stand upright,* Suet.; **2,** fig., *to bear, endure, suffer;* poenam sui sceleris, Cic.; cam multam, Cic.

suffertus -a -um (sub and farcio), *stuffed full, crammed full,* Suet.

suffervĕfăcĭo, 3. (sub and fervefacio), *to heat, make somewhat hot,* Plin.; pass., suffervefio -factus sum -fĭĕri, *to become somewhat hot,* Plin.

suffes = sufes (q.v.).

suffibŭlum -i, n. (sub and fibula), *a white oblong veil worn by priests and vestals,* Varr.

suffĭcio -fēci -fectum, 3. (sub and facio). **I.** Transit., **A.** *to put under;* hence, *to imbue, impregnate, suffuse;* lanam medicamentis, Cic.; angues ardentes oculos suffecti sanguine, Verg. **B.** *to add, cause to grow up after;* **1,** lit., aliam ex alia generando suffice prolem, Verg.; **2,** transf., *to choose in the place of* or *as a substitute for any one;* consul in sufficiendo collega occupatus, Cic.; collegam suffici censori, Liv.; of bees, regem parvosque Quirites sufficiunt, Verg.; esp., suffectus consul, *a consul chosen in the place of another,* Liv. **C.** *to provide, supply;* **1,** lit., ipsa satis tellus sufficit humorem et gravidas fruges, Verg.; **2,** fig., *to give:* Danais animos viresque secundas, Verg. **II.** Intransit., neut., *to be sufficient, enough, adequate, to suffice;* **a,** absol., nec scribae sufficere, nec tabulae nomina eorum capere poterant, Cic.; **b,** with dat., nec vires sufficere cuiquam nec, etc., Caes.; **c,** with ad and the acc., quomodo nos ad patiendum sufficiamus, Liv.; **d,** with adversus and the acc., non suffecturum ducem unum et exercitum unum adversus quatuor populos, Liv.; **e,** with in and the acc., nec locus in tumulos nec sufficit arbor in ignes, Ov.; **f,** with infin. = *to be in a position to, to be able;* nec nos obniti contra nec tendere tantum sufficimus, Verg.; **g,** with ut or ne and the subj., Tac.

suffīgo -fixi -fixum, 3. (sub and figo), *to fasten, fix beneath;* aliquem cruci, Cic.

suffīmen = suffimentum (q.v.).

suffīmentum -i, n. (suffio), *incense,* Cic.

suffĭo -ivi and -ii -ītum (sub and *fio, fire, connected with θύω). **I.** Intransit., *to burn incense, fumigate;* thymo, Verg. **II.** Transit., *to fumigate, perfume;* **a,** lit., locum, Prop.; **b,** fig., *to warm,* Lucr.

suffītĭo -ōnis, f. (suffio), *a fumigation,* Plin.

suffītor -ōris, m. (suffio), *a fumigator,* Plin.

suffītus -ūs, m. (suffio), *a fumigating, fumigation,* Plin.

sufflāmen -ĭnis, n. *a break, drag, clog.* **I.** Lit., Juv. **II.** Fig., *a hindrance, obstacle,* Juv.

sufflāmĭno, 1. (sufflamen), *to stop by a drag,* Suet.

sufflātĭo -ōnis, f. (sufflo), *a blowing up, puffing up,* Plin.

sufflāvus -a -um (sub-flavus), *somewhat yellow,* Suet.

sufflo, 1. (sub and flo). **I.** Intransit., *to blow upon,* Mart. **II.** Transit., *to blow up, to puff up, inflate;* **a,** lit., Plaut.; **b,** fig., se uxori, *to be angry with,* Plaut.

suffōcātĭo -ōnis, f. (suffoco), *a choking, strangling, suffocation,* Plin.

suffōco, 1. (sub and faux), *to strangle, choke, suffocate.* **I.** Lit., patrem, Cic. **II.** Fig., urbem et Italiam fame, *to starve out,* Cic.

suffŏdĭo -fōdi -fossum, 3. (sub and fodio), *to pierce underneath, pierce, dig into, excavate, undermine;* **a,** of things, murum, Sall.; sacella suffossa, Caes.; **b,** of animals or parts of the body, *to stab from below;* equos, Caes.

suffrāgātĭo -ōnis, f. (suffragor), *a voting in favour of, favourable vote, support;* urbana, *of the city;* militaris, *of the soldiers,* Cic.; illi honestissimā suffragatione consulatus petebatur, Sall.; plur., exstinctae (sunt) suffragationes, Cic.

suffrāgātor -ōris, m. (suffragor), *a voter in favour of any one, a political supporter,* Cic.

suffrāgātōrĭus -a -um (suffragor), *of* or *relating to the support of a candidate,* Q. Cic.

suffrāgĭum -ii, n. (sub and frango), *something broken off, a potsherd,* used by the ancients for voting; hence, meton., **I.** *the vote of a citizen at the comitia and of a juror in giving his verdict;* **a,** lit., ferre suffragium, *to vote,* Cic.; suffragium it per omnes, *all vote,* Liv.; non prohiberi jure suffragii, Cic.; **b,** transf., *vote, judgment, approval, support;* tuum, Cic.; populi, Hor. **II.** *the right* or *permission to vote, suffrage, franchise;* alicui suffragium impertire, Liv.; sine suffragio habere civitatem, *citizenship without the franchise,* Liv.

suffrāgo -ĭnis, f. (sub and frango), *the ham* or *hough on the hind leg of a quadruped,* Plin.

suffrāgor, 1. dep. (suffragium). **I.** *to vote in any one's favour;* suffragandi libido, Cic. **II.** Transf., *to be favourable to, to approve, recommend, support;* cupiditati alicuius, Cic.; sibi, Cic.; suffragante fortunā, Cic.

suffrēnātĭo -ōnis, f. (sub and freno), *a bridling;* transf., *a cementing, fastening;* lapidis, Plin.

suffringo -frēgi -fractum, 3. (sub and frango), *to break underneath, break in pieces;* crura canibus, Cic.

suffŭgĭo -fūgi -fŭgitum, 3. (sub and fugio). **I.** Intransit., *to fly to any place;* in tecta, Liv. **II.** Transit., *to fly from, evade, shun;* tactum, Lucr.

suffŭgĭum -ii, n. (sub and fugio), *a place of refuge.* **I.** Lit., propinqua suffugia, Tac. **II.** Transf., *a refuge, resort, remedy;* urgentium malorum suffugium, Tac.

suffulcio -fulsi -fultum, 4. (sub and fulcio), *to support beneath, underprop,* Lucr.

suffūmĭgo, 1. (sub and fumigo), *to fumigate from below,* Plin.

suffundo -fūdi -fūsum, 3. (sub and fundo). **I. 1,** *to pour beneath, spread through, suffuse;* **a,** of fluids, animum esse cordi suffusum sanguinem, Cic.; intumuit suffusa venter ab unda, *dropsy,* Ov.; **b,** of blushing, virgineum ore ruborem, Ov.; rubor Masinissae suffusus est, *blushed,* Liv.; **2,**

to bedew, colour, fill with, aether calore suffusus, Cic., lacrimis oculos suffusa nitentes, Verg., fig., animus nullā in ceteros malevolentiā suffusus, Cic. **II.** *to pour out, pour into*, merum, Ov.

suffūror, 1 (sub and furor), *to abstract secretly, steal away*, Plaut.

suffuscus -a -um (sub and fuscus), *brownish, dark-brown*, Tac.

suffūsio -ōnis, f. (suffundo), *a suffusion*, fellis *jaundice*, Plin.

Sŭgambri (Sўgambri, Sĭgambri) -ōrum, m., *a powerful German tribe*. Adj., **Sŭgămbĕr** -bra -brum, *Sugambrian*.

suggĕro -gessi -gestum, 3 (sub and gero). **I.** *to carry, bring, lay, put, place under.* **A.** Lit., flammam costis aeni, Verg. **B.** Fig., *to add, subjoin, annex*, **a**, huic incredibili sententiae ratiunculas, Cic.; **b**, *to cause to follow* (in order of time), *to place next*, Bruto statim Horatium, Liv.; **c**, *to put upon secretly*, Druso ludus est suggerendus, Cic. **II.** *to furnish, supply, afford*, **1**, lit., alicui tela, Verg.; **2**, fig., *to supply, give opportunity for*, prodiga divitias alimentaque mitia tellus suggerit, Ov.

suggestĭo -ōnis, f. (suggero), *a rhetorical figure in which an orator answers a question which he has asked himself*, Quint.

suggestum -i, n. (suggero). **I.** *anything heaped up, a heap, raised place, height, elevation*, Varr. **II.** Esp., *a platform from which an orator spoke to the people, soldiers, etc.*, illud suggestum ascendens, Cic.; in suggestis consistere, Cic.

suggestus -ūs, m. (suggero). **I.** *an elevation, height*, Cato. **II.** Esp., *a platform for addressing the people, soldiers, etc., a tribune*, Cic., Caes.

suggill . . . v. sugill . . .

suggrandis -e (sub and grandis), *somewhat large*, Cic.

suggrĕdior -gressus sum, 3. dep. (sub and gradior), *to go to, approach, to attack*, Tac.

suggrunda -ae, f. *the eaves of a house*, Varr.

sūgillātĭo -ōnis, f. (sugillo). **I.** *a livid or black spot on the skin, weal, bruise*, Plin. **II.** Fig., *a mocking, insulting*, Liv.

sūgillo, 1. *to beat black and blue.* **I.** Lit., Plin. **II.** Fig., *to insult, affront*, aliquem, Liv.

sūgo, suxi, suctum, 3. *to suck.* **I.** Lit., Cic. **II.** Fig., *to suck in*, cum lacte nutricis errorem, Cic.

sŭi (genit.), *of himself, herself, itself, themselves*; dat., sibi, *to himself*, etc.; acc., se, *himself*, etc.; pron. reflex., referring to the next preceding subject. **I.** Gen., se ipsum amat, Cic.; sui conservandi causā profugerunt, Cic.; qui hoc sibi nomen arrogaverunt, Cic. **II.** Esp., **A.** sibi, ethic dat., quidnam sibi clamor vellet, Liv. **B.** ad se, apud se = *at his house*, Cic. (strengthened form, sepse = se ipse, Cic.; semet, Hor., Liv.).

sŭīle -is, n. (sus), *a pigsty*, Varr.

sŭillus -a -um (sus), *of or relating to swine, swinish.* **I.** Adj., caro, Juv.; caput, Liv. **II.** Subst., **sŭilla** -ae, f. (sc. caro), *pork*, Plin.

sulco, 1. (sulcus), *to furrow, plough, cut through.* **I.** Lit., humum vomere, Ov. **II.** Transf., **a**, *to furrow*, serpens sulcat arenam, Ov.; cutem rugis, *to wrinkle*, Ov.; **b**, *to furrow* = *to sail over, pass through*, vada carinā, Verg.; undas rate, Ov.

sulcus -i, m. (connected with ὁλκός), *a furrow.* **I.** Lit., sulcum imprimere, Cic. **II.** Transf., **a**, *a cutting like a furrow, the furrow cut in the sea by a ship*, Verg.; **b**, *a long, narrow trench*, Verg.

sulfur (sulphur) -ŭris, n. **I.** *sulphur*, Liv., Hor., Verg. **II.** Meton., *lightning*, Pers.

sulfŭrātĭo -ōnis, f. (sulfur), *a vein of sulphur in the earth*, Sen.

sulfŭrātus -a -um (sulfur), *full of sulphur, containing sulphur, sulphureous*, Plin. Subst., **sulfŭrāta** -ōrum, **a**, *brimstone matches*, Mart.; **b**, *veins of sulphur*, Plin.

sulfŭrĕus -a -um (sulfur), *sulphureous*, aqua, Verg.

Sulla (Sylla) -ae, m. *a name of a family in the gens Cornelia, the most celebrated member of which was L. Cornelius Sulla, the dictator, rival of Marius.* Hence, **A. Sullānus (Syllānus)** -a -um, *Sullan*; subst., **Sullāni** -ōrum, m. *the partisans of Sulla.* **B. Sullātŭrĭo** -ire, *to wish to imitate Sulla*, Cic.

Sulmo -ōnis, m. *a town in the country of the Peligni, birthplace of Ovid, now Sulmona*; hence, adj., **Sulmōnensis** -e, *belonging to Sulmo.*

sulphur = sulfur (q.v.).

Sulpĭcĭus -a -um, *name of a Roman gens, the most distinguished member of which was Serv. Sulpicius Rufus, a celebrated jurist in the time of Cicero, consul with M. Marcellus*; hence, **Sulpĭcĭānus** -a -um, *Sulpician.*

sultis = si vultis, v. volo.

sum, fŭi, esse (an irregular verb, derived from two different roots, sum shortened for esum, root ES, Gr. ΕΣ, whence εἰμί, fui from an old verb fuo, Gr. φύω). **I.** *to be, to exist.* **A.** Gen., **1**, **a**, of the existence of an object, *to be, to exist, to be in life*, esse ea dico, quae cerni tangive possunt, Cic.; adhuc sumus, Cic.; omnium qui sunt, qui fuerunt, qui futuri sunt, Cic.; fuit, *he has lived*, Tib.; fuimus Troes, fuit Ilium, Verg.; nullus sum, *I exist no longer, I am lost*, Cic.; **b**, of the presence of a condition, *to be, to exist*, non est periculum, Cic.; quid tibi est? *what is the matter with you?* Cic.; **c**, *to be at a place, to live at*, quum Athenis fuissem, Cic.; **d**, *to be in a certain state or condition*, in servitute, Cic.; in spe, Cic.; **e**, *to rest, to depend upon*, totum in eo est, ut, etc., Cic.; **2**, especial phrases, **a**, sunt qui, *there are some people or things who or which*, (α) with indic. when certain definite persons or things are meant, sunt qui audent, Cic.; (β) with the subj. when the persons or things are indefinite, sunt qui dicant, Cic.; **b**, mihi est (res), *I have (something)*, cui nomen Arethusa est, Cic.; **c**, esse ad or apud aliquem, *to be at the house of, to visit*, apud te est, ut volumus, Cic.; **d**, esse cum aliquo (aliqua), (α) *to be in the house of, to be in a room with*, esset ne quis intus cum Caesare, Cic.; (β) *to be with, go about with*, erat nemo quicum essem libentius, Cic.; **e**, esse alicui cum aliquo, *to have to do with*, sibi cum illa nihil futurum, Cic.; **f**, esse ab aliquo, *to belong to or be related to*, erat ab Aristotele, *he was an Aristotelian*, Cic.; vide, ne hoc totum sit a me, *speaks for me*, Cic.; **g**, esse pro aliquo, *to be in the place of*, Cic.; **h**, esse in with abl., *to be in some writing*, quid fuit in litteris? Cic. **B.** *to be the fact, to be really so*, sunt ista, *that is so*, Cic.; so, esp., **a**, est, *it is so*, sit ita, *be it so, good*, Cic.; so also, esto, Cic.; est ut or with infin., *it is the case that*, est, ut id deceat, Cic.; **b**, est ubi = *at times*, Cic.; **c**, est quod, with indic. or subj. or ut and the subj., *there is reason for, I (you, etc.) have reason to, cause to*, magis est quod gratuler, Cic.; nihil est quod or cur, *there is no reason for*, nihil est, quod gestias, Cic. **II.** As copulative verb = *to be something* or *in some way;* **a,** with an adj., subst., or pron., praeclara res est et sumus otiosi, Cic.; **b,** with adv., (α) of manner, sic est, Cic.; mihi pulchre est or pulchre est mihi, Cic.; (β) of place or time, sunt procul ab huius aetatis memoria, Cic.; **c,** with genit. or abl., *to be of a certain nature* or *kind;* (α) with genit., summi ut sint laboris, Cic.; esp., magni, tanti, etc., esse (pretii), *to be of high* or *of such value,* etc., Cic.; frumentum fuit tanti, Cic.; (β) with abl., aegro corpore esse, *to be ill,* Cic.; simus eā mente, *so disposed,* Cic.; **d,** with genit. to express belonging to, (α) *to be one's own, to belong to;* Gallia est Ariovisti, Caes.; (β) *to be devoted to;* me Pompeii totum esse, Cic.; (γ) *to be a mark of, to be the nature of, to be characteristic of;* cuiusvis hominis est errare, Cic.; so with poss. pron., est tuum videre, Cic.; **e,** with genit. of gerund., *to serve for, have for its object;* quod conservandae libertatis fuerat, Sall.; **f,** with dat. to express object, (α) *to be in the place of, to be;* Romam caput Latio esse, Liv.; (β) *to be capable of;* non esse solvendo, Cic.; (γ) *to be, to prove;* impedimento esse alicui, Cic.; **g,** with ad and the acc., *to be serviceable for;* res quae sunt ad incendia, Caes.; **h,** with de and the abl., *to treat of, be about;* is liber, qui est de animo, Cic.; id est, hoc est, *that is,* or sometimes *which is as much as to say,* Cic. (archaic forms, escunt = erunt, ap. Cic.; fuat = sit, Verg.; fuvimus = fuimus, ap. Cic.).

sūmen -ĭnis, *n.* (= sugmen, from sugo). **I.** *a teat, pap,* Lucil. **II.** Esp., *the udder of a sow* (esteemed a delicacy by the Romans); **1,** lit., Plaut.; **2,** meton., *a sow, pig,* Juv.

summa -ae, f. (summus), *the highest.* **I.** *the highest place;* qui vobis summam ordinis consiliique concedunt, Cic. **II.** *the chief matter, main thing, most important point.* **A.** Gen., ipsae summae rerum atque sententiae, Cic. **B.** Esp., **1,** *the whole, totality;* exercitus, Caes.; belli, *supreme command,* Caes.; rerum or omnium rerum, *the highest power,* Cic.; ad summam, adv. *in a word, in short,* Cic.; so in summa, *on the whole,* Cic.; **2,** *the sum total of an amount;* equitum magnum numerum ex omni summa separare, Cic.; so esp., **a,** *a sum of money;* hāc summā redempti, Cic.; **b,** *a mass, quantity;* praedae, Cic.

Summānus -i, m. *an old Roman deity, to whom lightnings by night were ascribed,* Cic.

summārĭum -ĭi, n. (summa), *an epitome, abridgment, summary,* Sen.

summas -ātis, c. (summus), *of high birth, noble, illustrious,* Plaut.

summātim, adv. (summa), *slightly, summarily, briefly;* quae longiorem orationem desiderant summatim perscribere, Cic.

summātus -ūs, m. (summus), *the chief authority,* Lucr.

summē, adv. (summus), *in the highest degree, extremely;* officiosus, Cic.; contendere, Cic.

summergo = submergo (q.v.).

summĭnistro = subministro (q.v.).

summissē = submisse (q.v.).

summissim = submissim (q.v.).

summissĭo = submissio (q.v.).

summissus = submissus (q.v.).

summitto = submitto (q.v.).

Summoenĭum -ĭi, n. (sub and moenia), *a place in Rome frequented by common prostitutes;* hence, adj., **Summoenĭānus** -a -um, *relating to the Summoenium.*

summŏlestē = submoleste (q.v.).

summŏlestus = submolestus (q.v.).

summŏnĕo = submoneo (q.v.).

summŏpĕre, adv. (= summo opere), *very much, exceedingly,* Cic.

summŏrōsus = submorosus (q.v.).

summŏtor = submotor (q.v.).

summŏvĕo = submoveo (q.v.).

summŭla -ae, f. (dim. of summa), *a little sum,* Sen.

summus -a -um, superl. of superus (q.v.).

summūto = submuto (q.v.).

sūmo, sumpsi, sumptum, 3. (sub and emo), *to take, lay hold of.* **I.** Lit., **A.** Gen., fustem, Plaut.; legem in manus, Cic.; pecuniam mutuam, *to borrow,* Cic. **B.** Esp., **a,** *to take for use, to put on;* calceos et vestimenta, Cic.; **b,** *to buy;* genus signorum, Cic.; or, *to hire;* navem, Cic.; **c,** *to take, apply, employ;* operam, Ter. **II.** Fig., **A.** Gen., tempus cibi, Liv.; supplicium, *to punish,* Liv. **B.** Esp., **a,** *to choose, pick out, select;* sibi studium philosophiae, Cic.; diem ad deliberandum, Caes.; **b,** *to take in hand, to begin;* bellum, Sall.; inimicitias, Cic.; **c,** in discourse, (α) *to mention;* homines notos, Cic.; (β) *to assume, assert, maintain;* beatos esse deos sumpsisti, Cic.; **d,** *to assume;* arrogantiam sibi, Cic.; **e,** *to arrogate to oneself, take upon oneself;* sibi partes imperatorias, Cic.; mihi non tantum sumo, Cic.

sumptĭo -ōnis, f. (sumo), *the premiss of a syllogism,* Cic.

sumptĭto, 1. (intens. of sumo), *to take in large quantities,* Plin.

sumptŭārĭus -a -um (sumptus), *of or relating to expense, sumptuary;* lex, Cic.; rationes, Cic.

sumptŭōsē, adv. with compar. (sumptuosus), *in a costly, expensive manner, sumptuously,* Cic.

sumptŭōsus -a -um (sumptus). **I.** Of things, *costly, expensive, dear, sumptuous:* cena, Cic.; ludi sumptuosiores, Cic. **II.** Of persons, *extravagant, prodigal;* homo, Cic.

sumptus -ūs, m. (sumo), *cost, expense;* sumptum facere in rem, or impendere, or insumere, or ponere, Cic.; sumptu ne parcas, Cic.; suo sumptu fungi officio, Cic.; plur., minuendi sunt sumptus, Cic. (dat., often sumptu, Cic.).

Sūnĭōn (-ĭum) -ĭi, n. (Σούνιον), *a promontory forming the most southerly point of Attica, now Capo Colonni, with a temple of Athena and a town of the same name.*

sŭo, sŭi, sūtum, 3. *to sew, sew together, stitch together, join together;* tegumenta corporum vel texta vel sūta, Cic.

sŭop[illegible], v. suus.

sŭŏvĕtaurīlĭa (sŭŏvĭtaurīlĭa) -ĭum, n. (sus, ovis and taurus), *a purificatory sacrifice of a pig, a sheep, and a bull,* Liv.

sŭpellex -lectĭlis, abl. -lectĭle and -lectĭli, f. *furniture.* **I.** Lit., *household furniture;* multa et lauta supellex, Cic. **II.** Fig., *ornament, equipment;* amicos parare, optimam vitae supellectilem, Cic.; oratoria quasi supellex, Cic.

1. **sŭper** -a -um, v. superus.

2. **sŭper** (ὑπέρ). **I.** Adv., **1,** of place; **a,** *over, above, on the top of;* eo super tigna bipedalia injiciunt, Caes.; **b,** = ἄνωθεν, *from above;* superque immane barathrum cernatur, Verg.; **2,** of other relations; **a,** *besides;* super quam, *moreover,* Liv.; dederatque super, Ov.; **b,** *thereupon;* super tales effundit voces, Verg.; **c,** *beyond, more;* super quam, *more than,* Hor.; satis superque dixi, *enough and more than enough,* Cic.; **d,** *over and above;* quid super sanguinis (esse), Liv. **II.** Prep. with abl. and acc. **A.** With abl., **1,** of place, *over, above;* ensis

super cervice pendet, Hor, 2, of time, *during*, nocte super media, Verg; 3, of relation, *concerning, about*, hac super re scribam ad te, Cic, 4, of measure, *beyond*, super his, Hor B. With acc, 1, of place, *over, above*, a, to express remaining over an object, super aspidem assidere, Cic, dona super montium juga concreta erit Liv, b, of position, (a) *over, above*, super temporum circaque, Liv, (β) *beyond*, super Numidiam Gaetulos accepimus, Sall, c, of motion, *over* or *beyond a place*, super Sunium navigans, Liv, 2, of degree, *beyond, over, above*, a, lit, super ceteros honores, Liv, super cetera, Liv, vulnus super vulnus, *wound on wound, one wound after another*, Liv, b, transf, of superiority, *beyond, more than*, aetas et forma et super omnia Romanorum nomen te ferociorem facit, *above all*, Liv (super sometimes put after its case in Lucr, Verg, and Tac)

sŭpĕrā (sc parte) = supra I. Adv = *over*, Lucr II. Prep with acc, *over*, Lucr

sŭpĕrābĭlis e (supero) I. *that can be ascended*, murus, Liv II. *that can be conquered*, non est per vim superabilis ulli, Ov, nullis casibus superabiles Romani, Tac

sŭpĕraddo -addidi -additum, 3 *to add over and above, superadd*, Verg

sŭpĕradornātus a -um (super and adorno), *adorned on the surface*, Sen

sŭpĕrans -antis, p adj, only in compar and superl, *prevailing*, superantior ignis, Lucr

sŭpĕrātor -ōris, m (supero), *one who overcomes, a conqueror*, Ov

sŭperbē, adv (superbus) *proudly, haughtily*, superbe et crudeliter imperare, Caes, legatos appellare superbius, Cic, preces superbissime repudiare, Cic

sŭperbĭa ae, f (superbus), *pride* I. In a bad sense, *pride, haughtiness*, often with arrogantia and insolentia, Cic, superbiam ponere, *lay aside*, Hor II. In a good sense, *lofty spirit, honourable pride*, sume superbiam, Hor

sŭperbĭbo, 3 *to drink upon*, Plin

sŭperbĭfĭcus a um (superbus and facio), *making proud, making haughty*, Sen

sŭperbĭo, 4 (superbus) I. *to be proud, haughty, to pride oneself on*, with abl, forma, Ov, foll by quod, Tac II Transf, of things, *to be splendid, superb*, Prop

sŭperbus -a -um (super) = ὑπερήφανος, *raising oneself above others, proud*. I. In a bad sense, 1, lit, of persons, *proud, haughty*, a, absol, superbum se praebuit in fortuna, Cic, superbiorem te pecunia facit, Cic superbissima familia, Cic, surname of the younger Tarquinius, last king of Rome, Cic, b, with abl, *proud of*, pecunia, Hor, 2, transf, of things or abstract subjects, oculi, Ov, aures, Liv, virtus, Cic, judicium aurium superbissimum, Cic II. In a good sense, 1, of persons, *distinguished, remarkable*, Atridae, Hor, 2, of things, *brilliant, magnificent, splendid*, triumphus, Hor

sŭpercĭlĭōsus -a -um (supercilium), *severe, gloomy*, Sen

sŭpercĭlĭum -ii, n *the eyebrow*, plur (and often sing in collective sense), *the eyebrows* I. A. Lit, a, sing, altero ad mentum depresso supercilio, Cic, b, plur, superciliorum aut remissio aut contractio, Cic, capite et superciliis rasis, Cic B. Meton, a, *the eyebrows contracted = gloom, severity, sternness*, supercilii severi matrona, Ov, quid de supercilio dicam, quod tum hominibus non supercilium sed pignus reipublicae videbatur, Cic, b, *pride, arrogance*, hunc Capuae Campano supercilio ac regio spiritu quum videremus, Cic. II. Transf (like ὀφρύς, and English brow), *the projecting part of any object, ridge, summit*, tramitis, Verg, tumuli, Liv

sŭpercurro, 3 *to run beyond, surpass*, Plin

sŭpĕrĕdo, 3 *to eat upon* or *after*, Plin

sŭpĕrēmĭnĕo, 2 *to project over, overtop*, omnes viros, Verg

sŭpĕrēmŏrĭor, 3 dep *to die upon*, Plin

sŭperfĕro -tŭli -lātum -ferre, *to carry over, bear over*, Plin

sŭperfĭcĭes -ēi, f (super and facies), *the top, surface, superficies of anything* I. Gen, testudinum, Plin II. Esp, legal t t, *something (e g, a building) placed on the ground so as to become attached to it*, Cic

sŭperfīo -fĭĕri, *to be over and above*, Plaut

sŭperfixus a -um, *fixed on the top*, Liv

sŭperflōrescens -entis, *blooming all over*, Plin

sŭperflŭĭtas ātis, f (superfluus), *superfluity*, Plin

sŭperflŭo -fluxi, 3 *to flow over, overflow* I. Lit, of water, superfluentis Nili receptacula, Tac II Transf, a, ut nos superfluentes juvenili quadam dicendi impunitate et licentia reprimeret, Cic, b, *to be in superfluity, be superfluous*, Tac

sŭperflŭus a -um (superfluo), *overflowing, superfluous*, Sen

sŭperfundo -fūdi -fūsum, 3 I *to pour over, pour upon*. 1, lit., a, of water, superfundi, middle, *to overflow, spread itself over*, circus Tiberi superfuso irrigatus, Liv, b, of other things, *to spread about, throw about*, magnam vim telorum, Tac, pass, superfundi, as middle, *to be poured on, to run on*, hostes superfusi, *rushing in numbers*, Liv, 2, transf, superfundere se, *to spread itself out, spread* superfudit se (regnum Macedoniae) in Asiam, Liv II. *to cover with anything*, Tac

sŭpergrĕdĭor -gressus sum -grĕdi, 3 dep (super and gradior), *to go over* or *beyond, overstep*, fig, *to exceed, surpass*, aetatis suae feminas pulchritudine, Tac

sŭpĕri, v superus

sŭpĕrillĭgo, 1 *to bind on, bind over*, Plin

sŭpĕrimmĭnĕo, 2 *to overhang*, Verg

sŭpĕrimpendens entis (super and impendeo), *overhanging*, Cat

sŭpĕrimplĕo, 2 *to fill quite full*, Verg

sŭpĕrimpōno (posŭi) pŏsĭtum, 3 *to lay over, place upon*, saxum ingens machina, *by means of a machine*, Liv, monumento (dat), statuam, Liv

sŭpĕrincĭdens entis, *falling from above*, Liv

sŭpĕrincŭbans -antis, *lying over* or *upon*, superincubans Romanus, Liv

sŭpĕrincumbo cŭbŭi, 3 *to lie on, lie over*, Ov

sŭpĕrindŭo -ŭi -ūtum, 3 *to put on over*, Suet

sŭpĕringĕro (-gessi) -gestum, 3 *to throw upon, heap upon*, Plin

sŭpĕrinjĭcĭo -jēci -jectum, 3 *to throw over, throw upon*, raras frondes, Verg

sŭpĕrinl . . v superill

sŭpĕrinm . . v superimm

sŭpĕrinp . . v superimp .

sŭpĕrinsterno -strāvi strātum, 3, *to spread over, lay over*, tabulas, Verg

sŭpĕrintĕgo, 3 *to cover over*, Plin.

sŭpĕrior -ōris, comp. of sŭpĕrus (q.v.).

sŭperjăcio -jēci -jectum (-jactum), 3. **I.** *to throw over, throw upon;* membra superjecta cum tua veste fovet, Ov. **II.** *to throw over, flow over;* scopulos superjacit undā pontus, Verg. **III.** *to exceed, go beyond;* fidem augendo, Liv. (partic. also superjactus, Sall., Tac.).

sŭperjacto, 1. *to spring over, leap over,* Plin.

sŭperjectĭo -ōnis, f. (superjacio), *a throwing over;* fig., *exaggeration, hyperbole,* Quint.

sŭperjūmentārius -ii, m. *the chief groom, head of the drivers of beasts of burden,* Suet.

sŭperlābor, 3. *to glide, slide over,* Liv.

sŭperlātĭo -ōnis, f. (superfero), rhet. t.t., *exaggeration, hyperbole;* veritatis, Cic.

sŭperlātus -a -um, p. adj. (from superfero), *exaggerated, hyperbolical;* verba, Cic.

sŭperlĭno -lēvi -litum, 3. *to smear over, besmear,* Plin.

sŭpermando, 3. *to chew upon* or *after anything,* Plin.

sŭpermĕo, 1. *to go over, pass over,* Plin.

sŭpernas -ātis (supernus), *belonging to the upper country,* esp. *to the upper* (i.e. *the Adriatic*) *sea,* Plin.

sŭpernăto, 1. *to swim upon, swim over,* Sen.

sŭpernātus -a -um, *growing over,* Plin.

sŭpernē, adv. (supernus), *upwards;* **a,** *from above,* Liv.; **b,** *on the upper side, above,* Hor.

sŭpernus -a -um (super), *above, over, on the upper side, on the top;* Tusculum, *lying high,* Hor.; numen, *celestial,* Ov.

sŭpĕro, 1. (super). **I.** Intransit., *to be above;* hence, **1,** *to over-top, project;* **a,** lit., superant capite et cervicibus altis, Verg.; **b,** transf., (α) milit. t.t., *to have the upper hand, to be conqueror, to conquer;* virtute facile, Caes.; per biduum equestri proelio, Caes.; (β) in other relations, *to have the upper hand, have the preference, be superior, overcome, surpass;* superat sententia, Caes.; tantum superantibus malis, Liv.; totidem formā superante juvencae, *of surpassing beauty,* Verg.; **2,** *to be remaining;* **a,** *to abound, be in abundance;* partem superare mendosum est, Cic.; superante multitudine, Liv.; **b,** *to remain, to be over;* si quod superaret pecuniae retulisses, Cic.; esp. (with, or poet. without vitā), *to remain in life, to survive, live;* uter eorum vitā superavit, Caes.; superatne et vescitur aurā? Verg.; **c,** *to be too much;* quae Jugurthae fesso et majoribus astricto superaverant, Sall.; **d,** *to flow over with, overflow with;* victor superans animis, Verg. **II.** Transit., **1,** *to rise above, surmount, overtop, mount, ascend;* montes, Verg.; summas ripas fluminis, Caes.; hence, transf., *to overtop;* turris superat fontis fastigium, Caes.; **2, a,** *to sail by, to round;* promontorium, Liv.; **b,** transf., (α) *to penetrate to;* clamor superat inde castra hostium, Liv.; (β) met., *to surpass, excel, exceed;* aliquem doctrinā, Cic.; omnes in re, Cic.; (γ) *to overcome, conquer;* bello superatos esse Arvernos a Q. Fabio Maximo, Caes.; fig., injurias fortunae facile veterum philosophorum praeceptis, Cic.

sŭpĕrobrŭo -ŭi -ŭtum, 3. *to cover over,* Prop.

sŭperpendens -entis, *overhanging;* saxum, Liv.

sŭperpōno -pŏsŭi -pŏsĭtum, 3. **I.** *to lay, place, put over,* or *upon;* superpositum capiti decus, Liv. **II.** *to set over, put in a station of authority;* in maritimam regionem superpositus, Liv.

sŭperrāsus -a -um, *shaved, scraped above,* Plin.

sŭperscando (sŭperscendo), 3. *to climb up, climb over;* superscandens vigilum strata somno corpora, Liv.

sŭperscrībo -scripsi -scriptum, 3. *to write over* or *upon,* Suet.

sŭpersĕdĕo -sēdi -sessum, 3. **I.** *to sit above, sit upon,* Suet. **II.** Fig., *to be above anything, refrain from doing anything, omit, leave off;* with abl., hoc labore, Cic.; proelio, Caes.; with infin., loqui apud vos, Liv.

sŭperstagno, 1. *to spread out into a lake,* Tac.

sŭpersterno -strāvi -strātum, 3. *to strew, spread over* or *upon;* superstratis Gallorum cumulis, Liv.

sŭperstĕs -stitis (super and sto). **I.** *standing near, present, witnessing;* suis utrisque superstitibus praesentibus (old legal formula), ap. Cic. **II.** *surviving, living beyond another;* (α) with dat., ut sui sibi liberi superstites essent, Cic.; (β) with genit., alterius vestrûm superstes, Liv.; aliquem non solum vitae, sed etiam dignitatis suae superstitem relinquere, Cic.

sŭperstĭtĭo -ōnis, f. (super and sisto). **I.** *superstition, superstitious fear, fanaticism;* **1,** lit., anilis, Cic.; capti quādam superstitione animi, Cic.; superstitionem tollere, Cic.; **2,** meton., *a binding, awe-inspiring oath;* una superstitio superis quae reddita divis, Verg. **II.** *external religious observance;* quaenam illa superstitio, quod numen, interrogat, Tac.; in plur. = *religious observances* or *ceremonies;* hostes operati superstitionibus, Liv.

sŭperstĭtĭōsē, adv. (superstitiosus), *superstitiously,* Cic.

sŭperstĭtĭōsus -a -um (superstitio). **I.** *superstitious;* philosophi, Cic. **II.** *prophetical,* Plaut.

sŭperstĭto, 1. (superstes). **I.** Transit., *to preserve alive,* Enn. **II.** Intransit., *to be over and above, remain,* Plaut.

sŭpersto -stĕti, 1. *to stand over* or *upon;* with dat., corporibus, Liv.; with acc., aliquem, Verg.; absol., Liv.

sŭperstrŭo -struxi -structum, 3. *to build over* or *upon,* Tac.

sŭpersum -fŭi -esse, *to be over and above,* either as *remnant* or as *superfluity.* **A.** As remnant, *to be left, remain;* **a,** of things, duae partes, quae mihi supersunt illustrandae, Cic.; biduum supererat, Cic.; quod superest, *the rest,* Verg.; quod superest, *as for the rest,* Cic.; superest, foll. by infin., Liv., Ov.; **b,** of persons, (α) *to be left, to remain;* et superesse videt de tot modo millibus unum, Ov.; perexigua pars illius exercitus superest, Caes.; (β) *to survive;* alicui, Liv.; pugnae, Liv. **B.** *to be superfluous, abound;* vereor ne jam superesse mihi verba putes, quae dixeram defutura, Cic.; in a bad sense, *to be superfluous, to be redundant;* ut neque absit quidquam neque supersit, Cic.

sŭpertĕgo -texi -tectum, 3. *to cover over,* Tib.

sŭpĕrurgĕo, 2. *to press from above,* Tac.

sŭpĕrus (rarely **sŭpĕr**) -a -um (from adv. super), compar., **sŭpĕrior;** superl., **sŭperrĭmus, sŭprēmus** and **summus. I.** Posit., **sŭpĕrus** -a -um, *upper, the upper, higher;* **1,** gen., res superae, Cic.; mare superum, *the upper sea,* i.e., *the Adriatic Sea,* Cic.; **2,** esp., of things on or above the earth, superis ab oris, *from the upper world,* Verg.; hence, subst., **a, sŭpĕri** -ōrum, m.; (α) *the gods above,* Verg.; (β) *the men on the earth;* ad superos fleti, Verg.; **b, sŭpĕra** -ōrum, n. *the heights;* supera alta, *the heights of heaven,* Verg. **II.** Compar., **sŭpĕrior** -ōris, m and f, sŭpĕrius -ōris, n *higher, upper*, and partit., *the upper* or *higher part of anything*, **1**, lit, **a**, of place, pars collis, Caes., domus, Cic, ex loco superiore, *from a higher place*, Caes, de loco superiore dicere, *from the tribunal*, as praetor, Cic, de loco superiore agere, *from the speaker's tribune*, Cic, et ex superiore et ex aequo loco sermones, *utterances on the tribunal and in private life*, Cic., **b**, in writing, scriptura superior, *preceding*, Cic, **2**, transf, **a**, of time, *earlier, prior, former, past*, and, as applied to human life, *older*, annus, Cic, nox, *night before last*, Cic, omnes aetatis superioris, *of advanced age*, Caes, **b**, of rank, *higher*, superioris ordinis nonnulli, Caes, **c**, of power, importance, etc, *higher, more distinguished*, (a) absol, aliquis superior, *a distinguished person*, Cic, milit t t, discessit superior, *gained the advantage*, Nep, (β) with abl, loco, fortunā, famā, Cic, facilitate et humanitate superior, Cic **III.** Superl, **A. sŭprēmus** a -um, *the highest, uppermost*, **1**, lit, of place, montes, Verg, **2**, transf, **a**, in time or succession, *the last*, (a) nox, Verg, sole supremo, *on the setting of the sun*, Hor, adv, supremum, *for the last time*, Ov, (β) *of or relating to the end of life*, dies, *the day of death*, Cic, honor, *the last rites*, Verg; subst, **sŭprēma** -ōrum, n, (aa) *death* Ov, Tac, (ββ) *funeral rites*, Tac, **b**, *highest, greatest, most extreme*, supplicium, Cic, ventum est ad supremum, *the end is reached*, Verg **B. summus** -a -um (for sup mus), *the highest, uppermost*, and partit = *the highest part of, the top*, **1**, lit, of place, summum jugum montis Caes, partit, summa urbs, *the highest part of the city*, Cic, in summa sacra via, *at the top of the sacra via*, Cic, subst, **summum** -i, n *the highest point*, a summo, Cic, summum tecti, Verg, **2**, transf, **a**, of the voice, *the highest, loudest*, vox summa, Hor, **b**, of time or succession, *the last*, dies, Verg, senectus, *extreme old age*, Cic, **c**, in rank, value, estimation, *the highest, most distinguished, most valuable, most important, greatest, best*, (a) of things, deorum summus erga vos amor, Cic, summo studio, *with the greatest zeal*, Cic, summa salus reipublicae, Cic, quo res summa loco, *how is it with the state?* Verg, adv, summum, *at the most*, quatuor aut summum quinque, Cic, (β) of persons, *highest most elevated, most distinguished*, optimus et supremus vir, Cic, poet neut plur, summa ducum Atrides, *the chief person*, Ov

sŭpervăcānĕus -a -um, *superfluous, unnecessary, useless*, litterae, Cic, opus, *done at leisure hours*, Cic

sŭpervăcŭus -a um, *superfluous, unnecessary, useless, needless*, metus, Ov

sŭpervādo, 3. *to go over, surmount*, ruinas, Liv

sŭpervĕhor vectus sum, 3 dep *to ride, sail, pass over, sail by*, promunturium Calabriae, Liv

sŭpervĕnio -vēni -ventum, 4 **I.** *to come over*, unda supervenit undam, Hor **II.** *to come up*, **a**, legati superveniunt, Liv, **b**, *to come upon unexpectedly*, with dat, huic laetitiae, Liv

sŭperventus -ūs, m (supervenio), *a coming up, arrival*, Tac

sŭpervīvo vixi, 3 *to survive*, Suet

sŭpervŏlĭto, 1 *to fly over*, sua tecta alis, Verg

sŭpervŏlo, 1 *to fly over, fly above*, Verg, totum orbem, Ov

sŭpīnĭtas ātis, f (supinus), *a bending backwards, a lying with the body bent back*, Quint

sŭpīno, 1 (supinus), *to bend, stretch backwards, to throw back*, nasum nidore supinor, *I sniff up*, Hor, poet, glebas, *to turn over*, Verg.

sŭpīnus -a -um (root SUP, Gr ὕπ-τιος), *bent backwards, inclined backwards, lying on the back* **I.** Lit, **A.** Gen, motus corporis pronus, obliquus, supinus, Cic, manus supinas ad caelum tendere, *spread out with the palm upwards*, Verg **B.** Esp, **1**, *going backwards, returning*, nec redit in fontes unda supina suos, Ov, **2**, of localities, *sloping, spread out, outstretched*, collis, Verg, vallis, Liv **II.** Fig, **1**, of character, *careless, heedless, negligent, supine*, Juv, **2**, *proud, arrogant*, Mart

suppalpor, 1 dep *to stroke, caress, flatter a little*, Plaut

suppar -păris (sub and par), *almost equal, nearly contemporary with*, huic aetati suppares Alcibiades, Critias, Cic

suppărăsītor, 1 dep (sub and parasitor), *to flatter a little like a parasite*, Plaut

suppărum (sīpărum and **sīphărum)** -i, n and **suppărus (sīphărus)** -i, m (σίφαρος) **I.** *a linen garment usually worn by women*, Plaut **II.** *a topsail*, Sen

suppĕdĭtātĭo -ōnis, f (suppedito), *an abundant provision, superfluity*, bonorum, Cic

suppĕdĭto, 1 **I** Intransit, **1**, *to abound, be in abundance, be at hand, be in store*, ne chartam quidem suppeditare, Cic, cui si vita suppeditavisset, *had lasted longer*, Cic, **2**, *to be in sufficient quantity, suffice*, ad cultum, Cic **II.** Transit, **1**, *to provide, supply, offer, give abundantly*, (a) with acc, alicui frumentum, Cic, cibos, Cic, (β) with dat, *to support, stand by*, alicui, Cic, **2**, suppeditari aliquā re, *to be provided with*, Cic

suppernātus -a -um (sub and perna), *lamed in the hip*, transf, alnus suppernata securi, *hewn down*, Cat

suppĕtĭae -ārum, f (suppeto), *help, aid, assistance*, only in nom and acc., Plaut

suppĕtĭor, 1 dep (suppetiae), *to come to help, assist*, Cic (?)

suppĕto -īvi and -ii -ītum, 3 (sub and peto) **A.** *to be in store, be in hand*, ne pabuli quidem satis magna copia suppetebat, Caes, ut mihi ad remunerandum nihil suppetat praeter voluntatem, Cic, si vita suppetet, *if I live so long*, Cic, of materials for a speech, vererer ne mihi crimina non suppeterent, Cic **B.** Transf, *to suffice, be enough, correspond with*, ut quotidianis sumptibus copiae suppetant, Cic

suppīlo, 1 (sub and * pilo, whence compilo), *to steal secretly, filch*, and, with personal object, *to pluck, fleece*, Plaut

suppingo -pēgi pactum, 3 (sub and pango), *to fasten underneath*, Plaut

supplanto, 1 (sub and planta), *to throw down a person by tripping up his heels*, aliquem, Cic

supplaudo = supplodo (q v)

supplēmentum -i n (suppleo), *a filling up, supply, supplement*, milit t t, *a recruiting of troops, a body of recruits, reinforcements*, exercitūs, Liv, supplementum scribere legionibus, Cic, supplementa distribuere, Liv

supplĕo -plēvi plētum, 2 (sub and pleo), *to fill up make full, complete, supply* **I.** Lit, sanguine venas, Ov, inania moenia, *to people*, Ov **II.** Transf, *to fill up something that is wanting, make good, repair*, bibliothecam, Cic, milit t t, *to recruit, fill up the number of*, legiones, Liv

supplex -plĭcis, abl -plĭce and -plĭci, genit plur plicum and (rarely) plĭcium (sub and plico, thus lit., *bending the knee*), hence, *humbly entreating, supplicating, suppliant*; supplex te ad pedes abjiciebas, Cic.; transf., of things, multis et supplicibus verbis, Cic.; with dat., alicui fieri or esse supplicem, Cic.; with possess. pron. or genit. of person besought, vester est supplex, Cic.; misericordiae vestrae, Cic.

supplĭcātĭo -ōnis, f. (supplico), *a solemn public thanksgiving, a religious festival* or *fast on some public success* or *misfortune*; ad omnia pulvinaria supplicationem decernere, Cic.; prodigiorum averruncandorum causā supplicationes in biduum decernere, Liv.

supplĭcĭtĕr, adv. (supplex), *suppliantly, humbly*; respondere, Cic.

supplĭcĭum -ii, n. (supplex), *a kneeling down, either for entreaty* or *to receive punishment*. Hence, **I.** *a humble entreaty*; **a**, of the gods, *prayer*; precibus suppliciisque deos placare, Liv.; **b**, *humble entreaty* of men; fatigati suppliciis regis, Sall. **II.** *punishment, penalty, torture*, esp., *capital punishment*; **1**, lit., sumere supplicium de aliquo, *to inflict upon*, Cic.; ad ultimum supplicium progredi, Caes.; hence, transf., *torture, pain*; satis supplicii tulisse, Caes.; **2**, meton., *wounds, marks of mutilation*; dira tegens supplicia, Verg.

supplĭco, 1. (supplex), *to fall down on the knees before*. **I.** Gen., *to beseech humbly, entreat suppliantly*; alicui publice, Cic.; Caesari or senatui pro aliquo, Cic. **II.** *to pray to the gods, supplicate, worship*; per hostias diis, Sall.

supplōdo (supplaudo) -plōsi -plōsum, 3. (sub and plaudo), *to stamp*; pedem, Cic.

supplōsĭo -ōnis, f. (supplodo), *a stamping*; pedis, Cic.

suppoenĭtet, 2. impers. (sub and poenitet), *it repents somewhat*; with acc. of pers. and genit. of thing, illum furoris, Cic.

suppōno -pŏsŭi (-pŏsīvi, Plaut.) -pŏsĭtum (syncop. partic., suppostus, Verg.), 3. **I.** *to put, place, lay under*; **1**, lit., ova gallinis, Cic.; aliquem tumulo or terrae, *to bury*, Ov.; terrae dentes vipereos, *to sow*, Ov.; **2**, fig., *to subject*; se criminibus, Cic. **II.** *to put under something*; **1**, lit., falcem maturis aristis, Verg.; **2**, fig., **a**, *to add, annex*; generi partes, Cic.; **b**, *to place after, to esteem less*; Latio Samon, Ov. **III.** *to put in the place of a person or thing*; **1**, gen., aliquem in alicuius locum, Cic.; **2**, *to substitute that which is not genuine, to counterfeit, forge*; testamenta falsa, Cic.

supporto, 1. (sub and porto), *to bring, bear, carry, convey to*; frumentum, Caes.; omnia inde in castra, Liv.

suppŏsĭtīcius -a -um (suppono), **1**, *put in the place of another, substituted*, Mart.; **2**, *supposititious, not genuine*, Varr.

suppŏsĭtĭo -ōnis, f. (suppono), *the substitution of one child for another*, Plaut.

suppŏsĭtrix -trīcis, f. (suppono), *she that substitutes*; puerorum, Plaut.

suppostus, v. suppono.

suppressĭo -ōnis, f. (supprimo), *embezzlement*; judiciales (sc. pecuniae), Cic.

suppressus -a -um, p. adj. (from supprimo), of the voice, *low, subdued*; vox, Cic.; orator suppressior ut voce, sic etiam oratione, Cic.

supprĭmo -pressi -pressum, 3. (sub and premo), *to press down, press under*. **I.** navem, *to sink*, Liv. **II. a**, *to hold back, check, restrain*; hostem nostros insequentem, Caes.; vocem, Ov.; iram, *to check, suppress*, Liv.; **b**, *to keep from publicity, keep back, suppress, conceal*; famam decreti, Liv.: pecuniam, nummos, *to embezzle*, Cic.

suppromus -i, m. (sub and promus), *an under-butler*, Plaut.

suppŭdet, 2. impers. (sub and pudet), *to be somewhat ashamed*; me alicuius, *I am somewhat ashamed of*; eorum (librorum) me suppudebat, Cic.

suppūrātĭo -ōnis. f. (suppuro), *a purulent ulcer, suppuration*, Plin.

suppūrātōrĭus -a -um (suppuro), *of* or *relating to an ulcer*, Plin.

suppūro, 1. (sub and pus). **I.** Intransit., *to form matter, suppurate*. **II.** Transit., *to cause to suppurate*; hence, **suppūrātus** -a -um, *suppurated, full of ulcerous sores*, Plin. Subst., **suppūrāta** -ōrum. n. *sores*, Plin.

suppŭto, 1. (sub and puto), **1**, *to cut, prune beneath*, Cato; **2**, *to count up, compute*; with rel. sent., et sibi quid sit utile sollicitis supputat articulis, Ov.

sŭprā, adv. and prep. (for superā, sc. parte, from superus). **I.** Adv., with compar., **1**, of place, **a**, *above, over, on the top*; omnia haec, quae supra et subter, unum esse, Cic.; et mare quod supra teneant, quodque alluit infra, Verg.; toto vertice supra est, *is taller*, Verg.; **b**, in writing or discourse, *before, above*; ut supra dixi, Cic.; uti supra demonstravimus, Caes.; **2**, of time, *before, previously*; pauca supra repetere, Sall.; **3**, of degree, **a**, lit., *more, beyond*; supra adjicere, *to offer more*, Cic.; **b**, transf., *beyond, further*; ita accurate ut nihil possit supra, Cic.; supra deos lacessere, Hor.; supra quam, *more than*; rem supra feret quam fieri potest, Cic. **II.** Prep. with acc., **1**, of place, **a**, with verbs of rest, *above, over*; supra subterque terram per dies quindecim pugnatum est, Liv.; of position at table, accumbere supra aliquem, Cic.; fig., supra caput esse, *to be over a person's head, to be a burden, to be vexatious*; ecce supra caput homo levis, Cic.; **b**, with verbs of motion. (α) *over, beyond*; fera saltu supra venabula fertur, Verg.; (β) *up to*; nec exissent unquam supra terram, Verg.; (γ) *above*; supra aliquem transire, *to surpass*, Verg.; **2**, of time, *before*; supra hanc memoriam, Caes.; **3**, of degree, **a**, lit., *more than, above*; supra millia viginti, Liv.; **b**, transf., (α) *above, beyond*; supra modum, Liv.; supra vires, Hor.; (β) *besides*; supra belli Latini metum id quoque accesserat quod, etc., Liv.

sŭprascando, 3. *to climb over, surmount*; fines, Liv.

sŭprēmus, etc., v. superus.

1. **sūra** -ae, f. *the calf of the leg*, Ov.

2. **Sūra** -ae, m., P. Cornelius Lentulus, *fellow-conspirator with Catiline*.

surcŭlācĕus -a -um (surculus), *woody*, Plin.

surcŭlārĭus -a -um (surculus), *of* or *relating to young shoots*, Varr.

surcŭlōsus -a -um (surculus), *woody, like wood*, Plin.

surcŭlus -i, m. (dim. of surus), *a young shoot, sprout, sucker*. **I.** Gen., Verg.; surculum defringere (as a sign of taking possession), Cic. **II.** Esp., *a sap for planting*, Cic.

surdaster -tra -trum (surdus), *somewhat deaf*, Cic.

surdĭtas -ātis, f. (surdus), *deafness*, Cic.

surdus -a -um, *deaf*. **I.** Lit., Cic.; prov., surdis canere, *to sing to deaf ears*, Verg.; haud surdis auribus dicta, Liv. **II.** Transf., **A.** Act., **1**, *deaf = not willing to hear, insensible*; per nunquam surdos in tua vota deos, Ov.; surdae ad omnia solatia aures, Liv.; leges rem surdam esse, Liv, 2, *deaf = not understanding*, in horum sermone surdi, Cic **B.** Pass, *not heard, still, silent*, lyra, Prop, gratia, Ov

Surēna -ae, m *a grand vizier, prime minister among the Parthians*, Tac

surgo = subrigo (q v)

surpŭit, surpuerat, surpere, surpite, v surripio

surrādo = subrado (q v)

surrancĭdus = subrancidus (q v)

surraucus = subraucus (q v)

surrēmĭgo = subremigo (q v)

Surrentum -i, n *a town in Campania*, now *Sorrento* Hence, **Surrentīnus** -a -um, *Surrentine*

surrēpo = subrepo (q v)

surreptīcĭus = subrepticius (q v)

surrīdĕo = subrideo (q v)

surrīdĭcŭlē = subridicule (q v)

surrĭgŭus = subriguus (q v)

surringor = subringor (q v)

surrĭpĭo -rĭpŭi -reptum, 3 (sub and rapio), *to take away secretly, to steal, filch, pilfer* **I.** Lit, vasa ex privato sacro, Cic, filium ex custodia, Liv, Parmam, *conquer by cunning*, Cic, of plagiarism, a Naevio vel sumpsisti multa, si fateris, vel, si negas, surripuisti, Cic **II.** Fig., **a**, aliquid spatii, Cic, virtus nec eripi nec surripi potest, Cic, **b**, surripi of an accused person, *to be rescued from punishment by underhand means*, such as bribery, Cic (syncop forms, surpite, Hor, surpuit, Plaut, surpuerat, Hor, surpere, Lucr)

surrŏgo = subrogo (q v)

surrostrāni = subrostrani (q v)

surrŭbĕo = subrubeo (q v)

surrŭbĭcundus = subrubicundus (q v)

surrūfus = subrufus (q v)

surrŭo = subruo (q v)

surrustĭcus = subrusticus (q v)

surrŭtĭlus = subrutilus (q v)

sursum, adv (sub and versum) **I.** *upwards, on high*, sursum deorsum, *up and down, backwards and forwards*, Cic **II.** *high up, above*, nares recte sursum sunt, Cic (susque deque = sursum deorsum, *up and down*, prov, de Octavio susque deque (sc fero or habeo), *I do not trouble myself about*, Cic)

sūrus -i, m *a shoot, twig*, Varr

sūs, sŭis, c (ὗς), **1**, *a sow, swine, pig, hog*, Cic, **2**, *a kind of fish*, Ov

suscensĕo -censŭi -censum, 2 *to be angry with, to be enraged*, **a**, with dat, alicui vehementer, Cic, **b**, with neut acc, illud vereor ne tibi illum suscensere aliquid suspicere, Cic, **c**, with propter and the acc, Ov, **d**, with quia or quod, Cic, **e**, with acc and infin, Liv

susceptĭo -ōnis, f (suscipio), *an undertaking*, causae, Cic.

suscĭpĭo -cēpi -ceptum, 3 (subs = sub and capio), *to take up* or *on oneself* **I.** As a bearer **A.** Lit, *to carry, hold upright*, Plin **B** Fig, **1**, *to support, defend*, aliquem, ap Cic, **2**, *to take upon oneself*, **a**, *to undertake a business, begin, take up*, esp, of something undertaken voluntarily, negotium, Cic personam viri boni, Cic, sacra peregrina, *to adopt*, Cic, **b**, *to suffer, submit to, endure*, invidiam, Cic, dolorem, Cic, magnam molestiam, Cic **II** As a receiver, *to take, receive, catch up* **A.** Lit., dominam ruentem, Verg, esp, **a**, aliquem, *to take up a new-born child from the ground and so acknowledge it*, in lucem editi et suscepti sumus, Cic, hence, filium, etc, suscepisse ex aliqua, *to have, to beget a child*, liberos ex filia libertini suscepisse, Cic, **b**, *to receive as a citizen, as a scholar*, etc, aliquem in civitatem, Cic **B.** Fig, **a**, *to receive as true, maintain*, quae si suscipimus, Cic, **b**, *to admit of*, consolationem, Cic, **c**, *to answer, take up the speech*, Verg

suscĭto, 1 **I.** *to lift up* **A** *to raise on high, lift up*, Verg., lintea, Ov **B** *to cause to rise, to rouse up, awake, cause to stand up*, te ab tuis subselliis contra te testem suscitabo, Cic, of persons sleeping, *to arouse*, aliquem e somno, Cic, transf, ignes sopitos, Verg **II.** *to stir up*, **a**, *to put in motion, arouse*, viros in arma, Verg, **b**, *to stir up, bring about*, Romanum cum Saguntino bellum, Liv

sūsĭnus -a -um (σούσινος), *made of lilies*, Plin

suspecto, 1. (intens of suspicio) **I.** *to look at, regard, gaze upon carefully*, Ter **II.** *to look upon with suspicion, suspect*, aliquem, Tac.

1 **suspectus** -a -um, p adj (from 1 suspicio), *suspected, awakening suspicion*, suspectum meis civibus, Cic, aliquem suspectum habere, *to suspect*, Caes, with de and the abl, quum filius patri suspectus esset de noverca, Cic, with genit., suspectus cupiditatis imperii, Liv, with infin, suspectus eius consilia fovisse, Tac

2 **suspectus** -ūs, m (1 suspicio) **I.** *a looking upwards*, **a**, lit, aetherium ad Olympum, Verg, **b**, meton, *height*, turris vasto suspectu, Verg **II.** Fig, *looking up to, honour, respect, esteem*, Ov

suspendĭōsus -a -um (suspendium), *one who has hanged himself* Plin

suspendĭum -ii, n (suspendo), *a hanging of oneself*, Cic., suspendio perire, Cic, plur, praebuit illa arbor misero suspendia collo, *has served for hanging*, Ov

suspendo -pendi -pensum, 3 *to hang up* **I.** Lit, **a**, nidum tigno, Verg, aliquem arbori infelici, Cic, aliquem in oleastro, Cic, se de ficu, Cic; simply se, *to hang oneself*, Cic., partic, **suspensus** -a -um, *hanging up*, Hor, **b**, esp, *to suspend as an offering in a temple, consecrate*, vestimenta deo maris, Hor **II.** Transf, **A.** *to raise up, make high*, tectum turris, Caes, tellurem sulco tenui, *to plough up*, Verg **B.** Transf, *to cause to waver, or be uncertain*, **1**, lit, **a**, ferre suspensos gradus, *uncertain*, Ov, **b**, esp, *to build upon arches, to vault*, balneola, Cic, **2**, transf, *to support, prop up*, ita aedificatum, ut suspendi non posset, Cic, **3**, fig, **a**, *to check, stop, break off*, fletum, Ov, **b**, *to leave undecided*, rem medio responso, Liv, **c**, *to leave in uncertainty*, animos fictā gravitate, Ov

suspensus -a -um, p adj (from suspendo) **I.** *hovering, hanging, suspended*, currus in aqua, Cic, aquila suspensis demissa leniter alis, Liv **II.** Fig., **a**, *resting upon, dependent upon*, ex bono casu omnia suspensa sunt, Cic, **b**, *uncertain, doubtful, in suspense, wavering*, animus, Cic, aliquem suspensum tenere, Cic, **c**, *fearful, anxious, restless*, timor, Ov

suspĭcax -ācis (suspicor), *suspicious, awakening suspicion*, Tac

1 **suspĭcĭo** -spexi -spectum, 3 **I.** Intransit, *to look at from below, to look upwards*, in caelum, Cic **II.** Transit, **A.** *to look at from below, regard, contemplate*, **a**, lit, caelum, Cic, **b**, fig, *to look up to, to esteem, respect, honour*,

viros, Cic. **B.** Esp., *to suspect;* with infin., suspectus regi, et ipse eum suspiciens, novas res cupere, Sall.

2. **suspīcio** -ōnis, f. **I.** *mistrust, suspicion;* in qua nulla subest suspicio, Cic.; suspicionem habere, *to suspect*, Cic., and, *to be suspicious*, Cic.; suspicio cadit in aliquem or pertinet ad aliquem, Cic.; est suspicio, foll. by acc and infin., Cic.; suspicionem alicui dare, Cic.; or afferre, Cic.; or inferre, Cic.; in suspicionem alicui venire, foll. by acc. and infin., Cic. **II.** Transf., *a notion, idea, conception;* deorum, Cic.

suspīcĭōsē, adv. (suspiciosus), *in a suspicious manner, suspiciously;* aliquid dicere, Cic.; suspiciosius dicere, Cic.

suspīcĭōsus -a -um (2. suspicio). **I.** *cherishing suspicion, suspecting, suspicious;* in aliquem, Cic. **II.** *exciting suspicion, suspicious*, Cic.

suspĭcor, 1. dep. (1. suspicio). **I.** *to suspect;* with acc. of thing, res nefarias, Cic.; with acc. and infin., ea quae fore suspicatus erat, Caes. **II.** Transf., *to conjecture, form an opinion, surmise;* licet aliquid etiam de Popilii ingenio suspicari, Cic.; quantum ex monumentis suspicari licet, Cic.; with rel. sent., quid sibi impenderet coepit suspicari, Cic.; with acc. and infin., quod valde suspicor fore, Cic.

suspīrātĭo -ōnis, f. (suspiro), *a drawing a deep breath*, Plin.

suspīrātus -ūs, m. (suspiro), *a deep breath, sigh*, Ov.

suspīrĭōsus -a -um (suspirium), *breathing with difficulty, asthmatic*, Plin.

suspīrĭtus -ūs, m. (suspiro), *a breathing deeply, a sigh*, Cic.

suspīrĭum -ii, n. (suspiro). **I.** *a deep breath, a sigh*, Cic. **II.** *asthma, difficulty of breathing*, Mart.

suspīro, 1. (sub and spiro). **I.** Intransit., *to breathe deeply, to sigh;* **a,** occulte, Cic.; **b,** in aliquo, in aliqua, in aliquam, *to sigh for, long for*, Ov. **II.** Transit., *to breathe forth, sigh forth, long for;* amores, Tib.; Chloen, Hor.

susque deque, v. sursum.

sustentācŭlum -i, n. (sustento), *a prop, support*, Tac.

sustentātĭo -ōnis, f. (sustento), 1, *a delay, deferring;* habere aliquam moram et sustentationem, Cic.; 2, as a figure of speech, *keeping in suspense*, Quint.

sustento, 1. (intens. of sustineo), *to hold up, support, sustain.* **I.** Lit., fratrem ruentem dextrā, Verg. **II.** Transf., 1, *to sustain, support, strengthen, maintain;* rempublicam, Cic.; imbecillitatem valetudinis tuae, Cic.; 2, *to sustain with food* or *money, maintain, support;* se amicorum liberalitate, Cic.; aër spiritu ductus alit et sustentat animantes, Cic.; 3, *to bear, sustain;* maerorem tuum, Cic.; absol., in battle, *to hold out;* aegre sustentatum est, Caes.; 4, *to put off, hinder, delay;* rem, Cic.; consilio bellum, Cic.

sustĭnĕo -tĭnŭi -tentum, 2. (subs = sub and teneo), *to hold up, support, sustain.* **I.** Lit., 1, aër volatus alitum sustinet, Cic.; se a lapsu, *to keep oneself from falling, to keep oneself upright*, Liv.; so simply se, Cic.; 2, *to carry;* bovem, Cic.; of trees, (arbores) sustineant poma, Ov.; 3, *to hold back, check, restrain;* equum incitatum, Cic.; remos, Cic.; impetum, Cic.; se, *to hold oneself back from, refrain from;* se ab assensu, Cic. **II.** Fig., 1, **a,** causam, Cic.; munus in republica, Cic.; sustines non parvam exspectationem, Cic.; eos querentes non sustinuit, *could not withstand*, Cic.; sustineo, *I have the heart to, I can induce myself to;* with acc. and infin., sustinebunt tales viri se tot senatoribus, tot populorum privatorumque litteris non credidisse, Cic.; **b,** absol., milit. t. t., *to stand one's ground;* Brutus Mutinae vix sustinebat, Cic.; 2, *to support, maintain, nourish, sustain;* ager non amplius hominum quinque millia sustinere potest, Cic.; 3, *to put off, delay;* solutionem, Cic.; rem in noctem, Liv.; 4, *to sustain, support, maintain, preserve;* civitatis dignitatem ac decus, Cic.

sustollo, 3. 1, *to lift up, raise up, elevate*, Ov.; 2, *to take off, carry off;* filiam, Plaut.

sustringo = substringo (q.v.).

sŭsurrator -ōris, m. (susurro), *a murmurer, mutterer*, ap. Cic.

sŭsurro, 1. (susurrus), *to murmur, mutter, whisper;* of men, Ov.; of bees, *to hum*, Verg.; of water, Verg.; of the wind, Verg.

1. **sŭsurrus** -i, m. (reduplicated from the root of σνρίζειν, σύριγξ), *a murmuring, muttering, whispering, humming, buzzing*, Cic.

2. **sŭsurrus** -a -um (1. susurrus), *whispering; muttering;* lingua, Ov.

sūtēla -ae, f. (suo), *a sewing together;* fig., *a cunning trick, artifice*, Plaut.

Suthul -ūlis, n. *a fort in Numidia*, perhaps *ruins of Guelma.*

sūtĭlis -e (suo), *stitched together, fastened together;* cymba, Verg.

sūtor -ōris, m. (suo), *a shoemaker, cobbler*, Cic.; prov., ne sutor supra crepidam (sc. judicet), *let the cobbler stick to his last*, Plin.

sūtōrĭus -a -um (sutor), *of* or *relating to a shoemaker;* atramentum, *blacking*, Cic.

sūtrīnus -a -um (sutor), *of* or *relating to a shoemaker.* **I.** Adj., taberna, *cobbler's stall*, Tac. **II.** Subst., **sūtrīna** -ae, f. **a,** (sc. ars), *a shoemaker's trade*, Varr.; **b,** (sc. taberna), *a shoemaker's stall* or *shop*, Plin.

Sūtrĭum -ii, n. *a town in Etruria, now Sutri.* Hence, **Sūtrīnus** -a -um, *of* or *belonging to Sutrium;* plur. subst., **Sūtrīni** -ōrum, m. *the inhabitants of Sutrium.*

sūtūra -ae, f. (suo), *a seam, suture*, Liv.

sŭus -a -um, pron. poss., *his, her, its, own.* **I.** Lit., **A.** Gen., 1, adj., **a,** suus cuique erat locus definitus, Cic.; aliquem suum facere, *make one's own*, Liv.; **b,** (α) with quisque in a different case, quo sua quemque natura maxime ferre videatur, Cic.; or in the same case, quas tamen inter omnes est suo quoque in genere mediocres, Cic.; (β) with proprius, sua cuique laus propria debetur, Cic.; (γ) with the ethic dat., factus (consul) est bis, primum ante tempus, iterum sibi suo tempore, Cic.; (δ) with ipse, sua ipsam peremptam (esse) mercede, Liv.; (ε) strengthened by -pte or -met, Crassum suāpte interfectum manu, Cic.; capti suismet ipsi praesidiis, Liv.; **2,** subst., **a,** sui, *his men, dependents, countrymen, etc.;* quem sui Caesarem salutabant, Cic.; **b,** **sŭum** -i, n. *one's own property;* ad suum pervenire, Cic. **B.** 1, *his, its,* etc. = *proper, suitable;* suum numerum habere, Cic.; 2, = *favourable, propitious;* utebatur populo suo, Cic.; 3, *his* or *their own* = *not strange;* sui dei aut novi, Cic.; 4, *independent, in one's own power;* is poterit semper esse in disputando suus, Cic. **II.** Transf., rarely used for sui, injuria sua, *against himself*, Sall.

sўăgrus -i, f. (σύαγρος), *a species of palmtree*, Plin.

Sўbăris -ris, f. (Σύβαρις). **I.** *a river in Lucania*, now *Sibari.* **II.** *a Greek town in Lucania, on the river of the same name, destroyed* 510 B.C., *and afterwards rebuilt under the name of*

Thurii, famous for its luxury Hence, **A. Sybăritae** -ārum, m *the people of Sybaris* **B. Sybărītis** -idis, f *name of a wanton poem.*

sycē -ēs, f (συκῆ), **1,** *a plant also called peplis,* Plin , **2,** *a species of resin,* Plin , **3,** *a running sore in the eye,* Plin.

Sychaeus -i, m *husband of Dido,* Hence, adj , **Sychaeus** -a -um, *belonging to Sychaeus*

sycites -a -um (συκιτης), *fig-wine,* Plin

sycŏphanta -ae, f (συκοφαντης) **I.** *an informer, trickster, deceiver,* Plaut , Ter **II.** *a cunning flatterer, sycophant,* Plaut

sycŏphantia -ae, f (συκοφαντία), *craft, deception,* Plaut

sycŏphantiōsē, adv (sycophanta), *roguishly, craftily,* Plaut

sycŏphantor, 1 dep (συκοφαντεω), *to play tricks, act craftily,* Plaut

Sўēnē -ēs, f (Συήνη), *a town in Upper Egypt, famous for its red granite* Hence, **Sўēnītēs** -ae, m (Συηνίτης), *of or belonging to Syene, Syenitic*

Syla = Sila (q v).

Sўlēum (Syllēum) -i, n (Συλειον), *a mountain-town in Pamphylia*

Sylla = Sulla (q v)

syllăba -ae, f (συλλαβή), **1,** *a syllable,* syllaba brevis, longa, Cic , **2,** meton , syllabae, *verses, poems,* Mart

syllăbātim, adv (syllaba), *syllable by syllable,* Cic

syllibus = sittybos (q.v).

syllŏgismus -i, m (συλλογισμος), *a syllogism,* Sen

syllŏgisticus -a -um (συλλογιστικος), *syllogistic,* Quint.

Sўmaethus -i, m. (Σύμαιθος), *the largest river in Sicily, on the east of the island, receiving a number of smaller streams, now Giaretta* Hence, **A. Sўmaethēus** -a -um, *belonging to the Symaethus* **B. Sўmaethis** -idis, f , nympha, *the nymph of the river Symaethus* **C. Sўmaethius** -a- um, *Symaethian,* flumina, *which fall into the Symaethus,* Verg , heros, *Acis, son of the nymph of the Symaethus,* Ov.

symbŏla ae, f. (συμβολη), *a contribution of money to a common feast,* Plaut , Ter

symbŏlus -i, m and **symbŏlum** -i, n (συμβολος), *a sign, token, signal, symbol,* Plaut.

symmētria ae, f. (συμμετρία), *symmetry,* Plin

sympăthīa -ae, f (συμπαθεια), *sympathy, natural inclination or agreement of two things,* Plin

symphōnia -ae, f (συμφωνια), *a concert, musical performance,* Cic

symphōniăcus -a -um (συμφωνιακος), *of or relating to a concert;* pueri, *singing boys,* Cic.

Symplēgădes um, f (Συμπληγάδες), *the Symplegades, rocks in the entrance to the Euxine, which, according to the fable, dashed against one another till they were fixed after the passage of the Argo between them*

symplegma ătis, n (συμπλεγμα), *a group of wrestlers, closely embracing each other,* Plin

Sўnăpothnescontĕs (συναποθνησκοντες), *Those Dying Together* (the title of a comedy of Diphilus)

Sўnăristōsae -ārum, f (συναριστῶσαι), *the Women Breakfasting Together* (the title of a comedy of Menander), Plin

syncĕrastum -i, n. (συγκεραστον), *a dish of hotch-potch, hash,* Varr

sўnecdŏchē -ēs, f (συνεκδοχη), *a figure of speech by which a part is put for the whole, or the cause for the result, synecdoche,* Quint

sўnĕdrus -i, m (συνεδρος), among the Macedonians = *senator,* Liv

Sўnĕphēbi -ōrum, m (συνέφηβοι), *The Fellow Youths* (a comedy by Statius Caecilius), Cic

syngrăpha -ae, f (συγγραφη), *a bond, promissory note, agreement to pay,* cedere alicui aliquid per syngrapham Cic , facere syngraphas cum aliquo, Cic , jus dicere ex syngrapha, Cic.

syngrăphus i, m (σύγγραφος), **1,** *a written contract,* Plaut , **2,** *a passport,* Plaut.

synl v. syll

Synnăda -ōrum, n (τὰ Σύνναδα), and **Synnăs** -ădis and -ădos, f *a small town in Phrygia, famous for its marble, now Eski-karahissar* Hence **Synnădensis** -e, *of or belonging to Synnada*

sўnŏdontītis idis, f (συνοδοντῖτις), *a precious stone found in the brain of the fish synodus,* Plin

sўnŏdūs -ontis, m (συνοδους), *a fish, perhaps a kind of bream,* Ov

syntecticus a um (συντηκτικός), *wasting away, consumptive,* Plin.

syntexis -is, f (συντηξις), *wasting away, consumption,* Plin

synthĕsina = synthesis, II b

synthĕsis -is, f (συνθεσις, *a putting together*) **I.** *a service of plate, set of dishes,* Mart **II.** *a suit of clothes,* **a,** Mart , **b,** *a light upper garment, dressing gown,* Mart

syntŏnum -i, n (συντονον), *a musical instrument,* Quint

Sўphax -phācis, m (Συφαξ), *king of the Massaesyli, in Numidia, at the time of the Second Punic War, son-in-law of Hasdrubal*

Sўrācūsae -ārum, f (Συρακοῦσαι), *the chief town of Sicily, a Corinthian colony founded 758 B C , birthplace of Archimedes and Theocritus.* Hence, **A. Sўrācūsānus** -a -um, *Syracusan.* **B. Sўrācūsius** -a -um, *Syracusan.* **C. Sўrācŏsius** a um, *Syracusan*

Sўri (Sūri) -ōrum, m (Συροι), *the Syrians, the inhabitants of Syria* Hence, **A. Sўrus** -a -um, *Syrian* **B. Sўria** ae, f (Συρια), *Syria, a country in Asia, on the Mediterranean Sea, in a wider sense including the country east of Syria as far as the Tigris,* Syria = *Assyria,* Cic **C. Sўriăcus** -a -um, *Syrian* **D. Sўrius** -a -um, *Syrian*

sўringias -ae, m (συριγγιας), *a kind of reed, adapted for making pipes,* Plin

sўrītes -ae, m (συρίτης), *a stone found in a wolf's bladder,* Plin

1 **Sўrius,** v Syri

2 **Sўrius,** v. Syros.

syrma mătis, n (συρμα) **I.** *a long, trailing robe, frequently worn by tragic actors,* Juv **II.** Meton = *tragedy,* Juv

Sўrŏphoenix -nīcis, m (Συροφοινιξ), *a Syrophoenician, i e , of Phoenicia on the border of Syria*

Sўrŏs -i, f. (Συρος), *an island in the Aegean Sea, now Sira.* Hence, **Sўrius** a -um (Συριος), *of Syros, born at Syros*

Syrtis is and idos, f (Σύρτις), *a sandbank, esp , those sandbanks on the coast of Northern Africa, including Syrtis Major, now Sidra, and Syrtis Minor, now Cabes,* **a,** lit , Liv , **b,** transf , *the coast opposite the Syrtis,* Hor , **c,** meton , Syrtis patrimonii, Cic

Sўrus a -um, v Syri

T.

T, t, the nineteenth letter of the Latin alphabet corresponding with the Greek tau (Τ, τ). It is interchanged with *d*, *c*, and *s*, and assimilated with *s*, as quatio, quassi, mitto, missus. For the use of T. as an abbreviation, see Table of Abbreviations.

tăbānus -i, m. *a gadfly, horsefly*, Varr.

tăbella -ae, f. (dim. of tabula). **I.** *a small flat board* or *tablet*, liminis, *the threshold*, Cat. **II.** Meton., **1,** *the tray* or *trough in which Romulus and Remus were exposed*, Ov.; **2,** *a draught-board*, Ov.; **3,** *a picture*, Cic.; **4,** *a writing-tablet*, cerata, *covered with wax*, Cic.; meton., in plur., **a,** *a letter, note*, tabellas proferri jussimus, Cic.; **b,** *a record, proctocol, register*, etc., tabellae quaestionis, Cic.; tabellis obsignatis agis mecum, *you take note of what I said*, Cic.; **5,** *a votive tablet hung up in a temple*, Ov.; **6,** *a voting ticket, ballot*, **a,** in the comitia, **b,** in the courts of law, Cic.

tăbellārĭus -a -um (tabella). **I.** *of* or *relating to letters*, naves, *mail boats*, Sen.; gen. subst., **tăbellārĭus** -ii, m. *a letter carrier*, Cic. **II.** *of* or *relating to voting*, lex, Cic.

tābĕo, 2 (connected with τήκω, ἐ-τάκ-ην). **I.** *to waste away, fall away, melt, be consumed*, corpora tabent, Cic. **II.** Transf., *to drip with*, artus sale (*sea-water*) tabentes, Verg.

tăberna -ae, f. (root TAB, whence tabula), *a booth, hut*. **I.** As a dwelling place, pauperum tabernae, Hor. **II.** As a place of business, *a stall, shop*, libraria, *a bookseller's shop*, Cic.; in tabernam devertere, *a tavern*, Cic. **III.** *an arcade in the circus*, Cic. **IV.** As proper name, Tres Tabernae, *a place on the Appian Road*.

tăbernācŭlum -i, n. (taberna). **I.** *a hut, a tent*, tabernaculum in campo Martio sibi collocare, Cic. **II.** Esp., in religious language, *a place outside the city chosen by the augurs for taking the auspices previous to the comitia*, Cic.; capere tabernaculum, Cic.

tăbernārĭus -ii, m. (taberna), *a shopkeeper*, Cic.

tăbernŭla -ae, f. (dim. of taberna), *a little shop, small tavern*, Suet.

tābes -is, f. (tabeo). **I.** *wasting away, putrefaction, melting*, **1,** gen., liquescentis nivis, Liv.; **2,** esp., **a,** *a wasting away, decline, consumption*, Cic.; **b,** *a plague, pestilence*, tanta vis morbi, uti tabes, plerosque civium animos invaserat, Sall. **II.** Meton., *moisture arising from melting* or *decay, corruption*, sanguinis, Liv.

tābesco, tābŭi, 3. *to melt, waste away, be gradually consumed*. **I.** Of things, **a,** lit., with abl., corpora calore, Ov.; **b,** transf., nolite pati regnum Numidiae per scelus et sanguinem familiae nostrae tabescere, *be ruined*, Sall. **II.** Of men, *to waste away, languish, perish, be ruined*, **a,** with abl., dolore, Cic.; absol., perspicio nobis in hac calamitate pertabescendum esse, Cic.; **b,** of love, *to pine away*, Ov.; **c,** *to pine away with envy*, Hor.

tābĭdŭlus -a -um (dim. of tabidus), *wasting, consuming*, mors, Verg.

tābĭdus -a -um (tabes). **I.** *melting, consuming, wasting, decaying, pining away, dissolving*, nix, Liv. **II.** Act., *consuming, causing to waste away*, lues, Verg.

tābĭfĭcus -a -um (tabes and facio), *melting, dissolving, consuming, causing to waste away*, mentis perturbationes, Ov.

tābĭtūdo -inis, f. (tabes), *decline, consumption*, Plin.

tăbŭla -ae, f. (root TAB, whence taberna), *a board, plank*. **I.** Lit., tabulam arripere de naufragio, Cic. **II.** Meton., **1,** *a bench* (for sitting), solventur risu tabulae (perhaps = *the benches will burst with laughter*, but v. solvo II. B. 1, b), Hor.; **2,** *a gaming board, draught board*, Ov.; **3,** *a painted panel*, **a,** *a painting, picture*, tabula picta or simply tabula, Cic.; prov., manum de tabula, *hold! enough!* Cic.; **b,** *a votive tablet*, Hor.; **4,** *a tablet for writing*, **a,** *writing tablet*, Liv.; **b,** *a tablet on which a law was engraved*, XII tabulae, *the Twelve Tables*, Cic.; **c,** *a tablet used at an auction*, adest ad tabulam, *at the auction*, Cic.; **d,** *the tablet on which a list of the proscribed was drawn up*, Cic.; **e,** *a vote in the comitia*, Cic.; **f,** *a map, chart*, Cic.; **g,** *a contract, register, record*, Cic.; esp., *the lists of the censor*, Cic.; **h,** tabulae, *account-books*, conficere tabulas, Cic.; tabulae novae, *new account books, by which old debts were cancelled*, Cic.; **i,** tabulae, *state papers, public records, archives*, tabulas corrumpere, Cic.; **j,** *a will*, Hor.; **k,** *a money changer's table*, Cic.

tăbŭlāris -e (tabula), *of* or *relating to boards, plates of wood*, or *metal*, Plin.

tăbŭlārĭus -a -um (tabula), *of* or *relating to written documents*. Subst., **1, tăbŭlārĭus** -ii, m. *a keeper of records*, Sen.; **2, tăbŭlārĭum** -ii, n. (sc. aedificium), *archives*, Cic.

tăbŭlātĭo -ōnis, f. (tabula), *a flooring, planking, boarding, story*, Caes.

tăbŭlātum -i, n. (tabula). **I.** *a flooring, boarding, floor, story*, turris quatuor tabulatorum, Caes. **II.** Transf., *a row* or *layer of vines*, Verg.

tăbŭlīnum -i, n. and (syncop.) **tablīnum** -i, n. (tabula), *a record-room, muniment room, archives*, Plin.

tābum -i, n. (= tabes). **I.** *a plague, pestilence*, corpora affecta tabo, Liv. **II.** Meton., *a corrupt moisture, clotted blood, matter*, terram tabo maculant, Verg.

Tăburnus -i, m. *a range of mountains in Campania*.

tăcĕo, tăcŭi, tăcĭtum, 2. **I.** Intransit., *to be silent*. **A.** Lit. = *not to speak*, an me taciturum tantis de rebus existimavistis? Cic. **B.** Transf., = silere, *to be noiseless, still, quiet*, tacet omnis ager, Verg.; Ister tacens, *frozen*, Ov.; loca, *noiseless, the lower world*, Verg. **II.** Transit., *to be silent about anything, pass over in silence*, quod adhuc semper tacui, et tacendum putavi, Cic.; ut alios taceam, *to say nothing about others*, Ov.; pass., aureus in medio Marte tacetur amor, Ov.

Tăcĭta (dea) -ae, f. (taceo), *the goddess of silence*.

tăcĭtē, adv. (tacitus). **I.** *silently, in silence*; tacite rogare, Cic. **II.** *quietly, secretly*; perire, Cic.

tăcĭturnĭtas -ātis, f. (taciturnus). **I.** *silence, taciturnity*, testium, Cic. **II.** *silence, as a virtue*, opus est fide ac taciturnitate, Ter.; nostri hominis taciturnitatem, Cic.

tăcĭturnus -a -um (tacitus). **I.** *silent, taciturn* (opp. loquax), homo, Cic.; ingenium statua taciturnius, Hor.; tineas pasces taciturnas (of a book), Hor. **II.** Transf., *still, quiet*; amnis, Hor.

1 **tăcĭtus** -a -um, p. adj. (from taceo). **I.** Pass., **A.** *that which is passed over in silence, unmentioned*, aliquid tacitum relinquere, Cic.; aliquid (e.g. dolorem, gaudium) tacitum continere,

Liv, non feres tacitum, *I will not be silent about it*, Cic, subst, **tăcitum** -i, n *a secret*, Ov **B.** Transf, 1, *silently assumed, implied, tacit*, inducie, Liv, assensio, Cic, 2, *done silently or secretly, secret, concealed*, judicium, Cic, vulnus, Verg **II.** Act, **A.** *not speaking, silent, quiet, mute*, me tacito, *I being silent*, Cic, hoc tacitus praeterire non possum, Cic, tacita lumina, *eyes in a fixed stare*, Verg, often in the place of the adv, tacita tecum loquitur patria, *silently*, Cic **B.** Transf, *making no noise, still, quiet*, nox, Ov, exspectatio, Cic

2 **Tăcĭtus** -i, m, Cornelius, *the celebrated historian of the early empire, contemporary and friend of the younger Pliny, born between 50 and 60 A D*

tactĭlis -e (tango), *that can be touched*, Lucr

tactĭo -ōnis, f (tango) **I.** *a touching*, Plaut **II.** *the sense of touch*, voluptates oculorum et tactionum, Cic

tactus -ūs, m (tango) **I.** *a touch, touching* **A.** Lit, chordae ad quemque tactum respondent, Cic **B.** Transf, 1, *influence, operation*, solis, Cic, 2, *the sense of touch*, res sub tactum cadit, Cic **II.** *tangibility*, Lucr

taeda -ae, f (connected with δαΐς or δᾴς, acc δαΐδα or δᾷδα) **I.** *the pine tree*, Plin, plur, *pine wood*, Hor **II** Meton, **A.** *a board of pine* Juv **B.** Esp, a, *a torch of pine-wood*, taedae ardentes, Cic, esp, as used at weddings, taeda jugalis, Ov, meton = *marriage*, Verg, Ov, and = *love*, Prop, b, *an instrument of torture*, Juv

taedet, taeduit and taesum est, 2 impers *to be disgusted with*, with acc of pers and genit of thing, sunt homines quos libidinis infamiaeque suae neque pudeat neque taedeat, Cic.

taedĭfĕr -fĕra -fĕrum (taeda and fero), *torch bearing*, dea, *Ceres, who kindled a pine-torch on Mount Aetna when searching for Proserpine*, Ov

taedĭum -ii, n. (taedet) **I.** *disgust, weariness, loathing*, longinquae obsidionis, Liv, taedio curarum fessus, Tac **II.** In an objective sense, *that which causes disgust, loathsomeness*, Plin

Taenărus (-ŏs) -i, c and **Taenărum** (-on) -i, n (Ταίναρος and ον), and **Taenăra** -orum, n *a promontory and town in Laconia, where was a temple of Neptune, and whence there was supposed to be a descent into Tartarus, now Cape Matapan*, hence, **A.** Adj, **Taenărĭus** -a -um, *Laconian, Spartan*, marita, *Helen*, Ov, fauces, *entrance into hell*, Verg, so porta, Ov, hence, meton = *infernal*, valles, *the lower world*, Ov **B.** **Taenărĭs** -idis, f *Taenarian*, poet., *Spartan, Laconian*; soror, *Helena*, Ov. **C.** Subst, **Taenărĭdes** -ae, m poet = *the Laconian, i e Hyacinthus*, Ov

taenĭa -ae, f (ταινία) **I.** *a fillet, the ribbon of a chaplet*, Verg **II.** Meton, **A.** *the tape worm*, Plin **B.** *a reef of rocks under water*, Plin (abl plur, contr taenis, Verg)

taeter = teter (q v)

tăgax -ācis (tago), *thievish, given to pilfering*, Cic

Tāgēs -gētis and -gae, m *an Etruscan deity, grandson of Jupiter, said to have sprung from the earth, as it was being ploughed, in the form of a boy, and to have taught the Etruscans soothsaying*

tăgo = tango (q v)

Tāgus -i, m *a river in Lusitania, now Tejo, celebrated for its golden sands*

tālārĭa, v talaris.

tālāris -e (talus), *of or relating to the ankles*, tunica, *reaching to the ankles*, Cic, subst, **tālārĭa** -ium, n 1, *wings on the ankles, winged sandals*, assigned to Mercurius, Verg, Perseus, Ov, Minerva, Cic., prov, talaria videamus, *let us think of flight*, Cic, 2, *a long robe reaching to the ankles*, Ov

tālārĭus -a -um (talus), *of or relating to the ankles*, ludus, *a game accompanied with gestures, noisy instruments (such as the crotala, cymbala), so called because the persons engaged in it wore the tunica talaris*, Cic

Tălassĭo -ōnis, m, **Tălassĭus** -ii, m, and **Tălassus** -i, m *a cry usual at Roman weddings*

Tălăus -i, m (Ταλαός), *one of the Argonauts, father of Adrastus, Eriphyle, etc*, Talai gener, *Amphiaraus, husband of Eriphyle*, Ov Hence, **Tălăĭōnĭus** -a -um, *of or belonging to Talaus*

tālĕa -ae, f (root TAG, whence talus, taxillus) **I.** *a cutting, slip for planting*, Plin **II.** a, *a short stake, with an iron hook, thrown on the ground to prevent the attack of cavalry*, Caes, b, talea ferrea, *a bar of iron used as money in Britain*, Caes

tălentum -i, n (τάλαντον) **I.** *a Greek weight, which varied in different states*, the Italian = 100 Roman pounds, auri eborisque talenta, Verg **II** *a sum of money*, also varying in amount, but in Attica probably about £243 15s, Cic (genit pl, gen talentum)

tālĭo -ōnis, f (talis), *retaliation or recompense*, Cic

tālis -e, *of such a kind, such* **I.** Gen, a, aliquid tale, Cic, foll by qualis, ut, atque, etc, ut facillime, quales simus tales esse videamur, Cic, tales esse ut laudemur, Cic, talis qualem te esse video, Cic, b, *the following, as follows*, talia fatus, Verg **II.** Like τοιοῦτος, a, *of such a distinguished, remarkable, special kind*, judices tali dignitate praediti, Cic, b, *so exceptional, blamable*, facinus, Nep

tālĭtĕr, adv (talis), *in such a manner, so*, Plin

tālĭtrum -i, n *a snap of the finger, fillip*, Suet.

talpa -ae, f (m Verg), *a mole*, Cic

Talthȳbĭus (**Talthŭbĭus**) -ii, m (Ταλθύβιος), *a herald and messenger of Agamemnon*

tālus -i, m (root TAG, whence talea, taxillus) **I.** Lit, a, *the ankle, ankle bone*, Plin, b, *the heel*, purpura usque ad talos demissa, Cic **II.** Meton, *a die (made originally out of the ankle bones of the hind feet of certain animals), which, as used among the Romans, had only four flat sides, the other two being left round*, talis ludere, Cic

tam, adv (orig. an accusative, like quam, jam, clam, palam) **I.** Correl demonstr particle, to express comparison, *so far, to such a degree*, a, with quam, (α) before adj and adv, tam esse clemens tyrannus, quam rex importunus potest, Cic, tam ... quam, *both ... and*, Suet, quam ... tam before comparatives and superlatives, quam magis ... tam magis, *the more ... the more*, Verg, (β) before verbs, e g, esse = talis, haec tam esse quam audio, non puto, Cic, and before subst, tam ... quam, *not so much ... as*, utinam non tam fratri pietatem quam patriae praestare voluisset, Cic, with qui, quae, quod, quis est tam lynceus, qui nihil offendat, Cic b, with ut and the subj, non essem tam inurbanus, uti ego gravarer, Cic **II.** Demonstr particle, without a correl = *so, so very, so much, of such high degree*, quid tu tam mane? Cic, before a subst, cur tam tempore exclamarit occisum? Cic.

tămărix īcis, f *the tamarisk*, Plin

Tămăsos i, f. (Ταμασός), *a town in Cyprus* Hence, **Tămăsēus** -a um, *belonging to Tamasos*, ager, Ov

tamdĭū, adv I *so long;* foll by quam diu, quoad, dum, quam, donec, tamdiu requiesco, quamdiu scribo, Cic II. *so long*, i e, *so very long*, Cic

tămĕn, adv an adversative particle, used— I. In the apodosis, 1, with quamquam, quamvis, etsi, etiamsi, tametsi, licet, quum = *however, yet, nevertheless, notwithstanding, for all that*, quamquam abest a culpa, suspicione tamen non caret, Cic, 2, in the apodosis of a conditional sentence, *yet, yet at least, still*, si Massilienses per delectos cives reguntur, inest tamen in ea conditione, etc, Cic II. To begin a fresh clause, *still, however, yet*, hi non sunt permolesti, sed tamen insident et urgent, Cic ; joined with si = *but if, if only*, Ov

tămĕn-etsi, conj *although*, Cic

Tămĕsis -is, m and **Tămĕsa** ae, m *a river in Britain*, now *the Thames*

tămetsi, conj (tamen and etsi) I. *although, though, nevertheless*, foll by indic, Cic II. *however*, tametsi quae est ista laudatio, Cic

tamquam (tanquam), adv I. Introducing a comparison, *as, just as, like as, as if, as it were*, quod video tibi etiam novum accidisse tamquam mihi, Cic, gloria virtutem tamquam umbra sequitur, Cic, foll. by sic or ita, tamquam bona valetudo jucundior est, sic, etc, Cic, tamquam si, *just as if*, tamquam si tua res agitur, Cic, so with tamquam alone, tamquam clausa sit Asia, *as if*, Cic II. Causal, *as though*, classis, tamquam eo diu pugnatura, e portu movit, Liv

Tănăger -gri, m *a river in Lucania*, now *Negro*

Tănăgra -ae, f (Τάναγρα) *a town in the east of Boeotia* adj, **Tănăgraeus** a -um, *of or belonging to Tanagra*.

Tănăis -idis and -is, m. (Τάναϊς) I. *a river in Sarmatia*, now *the Don* II. *a river in Numidia*

Tănăum -i, n *a bay in Britain*, now *Firth of Tay*

Tănăquil quilis, f *wife of Tarquinius Priscus*.

tandem, adv (tam and demonstr suffix dem) I. *at length, at last*, tandem vulneribus defessi pedem referre coeperunt, Caes, strengthened by jam, aliquando, Cic II. In interrogations, *pray, then*, quid tandem agebatis? Cic, quod genus est tandem ostentationis et gloriae? Cic

Tanfāna -ae, f *a German deity*

tango, tĕtĭgi, tactum, 3 and (archaic) **tăgo**, taxi, 3 (root TAC), *to touch*. I. Bodily, 1, gen, terram genu, Cic, 2, *to touch a place*, i e, a, *to border on*, villa tangit viam, Cic ; b, *to enter, reach a place*, provinciam, Cic, 3, *to touch, seize, strike, push, hit*, a, chordas, Ov, fulmine tactus, Cic, or de caelo tactus, *struck by lightning*, Cic ; b, *to touch = to kill*, quemquam oportuisse tangi, Cic, 4, *to sprinkle*, corpus aqua, Ov, 5, a, = *to take*, non teruncium de praeda, Cic, b, *to touch, take part of, taste, eat*, cibos dente, Hor II. Of the mind, 1, gen, *to touch, move, affect, impress*, minae Clodii modice me tangunt, Cic, 2, *to touch upon in discourse mention*, ubi Aristoteles ista tetigit? Cic, 3, *to cheat, cozen*, Plaut, 4, *to undertake, prepare*, carmina, Ov

tanĭăcae -ārum, f *long strips of pork*, Varr

Tantălus (-ŏs) i, m (Τάνταλος), *a king of Phrygia, father of Pelops and Niobe, who set his own child as food before the gods, and was punished in Hades by being placed near fruits and water, which drew back whenever he attempted to satisfy his everlasting hunger and thirst* Hence, A. adj, **Tantălĕus** a um, *of or belonging to Tantalus* B. Subst, **Tantălĭdēs** -ae, m. *a son or descendant of Tantalus, Pelops*, Ov, *Agamemnon*, Ov, Tantalidae fratres, *Atreus and Thyestes*, Ov C. **Tantălis** -idis, f *a daughter or other female descendant of Tantalus, Niobe, Hermione*, Ov

tantillus -a -um (tantus) = tantulus, *so little, so small*, Plaut Subst, **tantillum** i, n *so small a thing, such a trifle*, Plaut

tantispĕr, adv. (tantus) I. *so long*, foll by dum, ut ibi esset tantisper, dum culeus compararetur, Cic II. *meanwhile*, Cic.

tantŏpĕrĕ, or sep **tanto ŏpĕrĕ**, adv *so greatly, so much*, discere, Cic

tantŭlus -a -um (dim. of tantus), *so small, so little*, causa, Cic Subst, **tantŭlum** i, n *so small a thing, such a trifle*, tantulo venierint, *at so small a price*, Cic

tantum, v tantus

tantummŏdo, adv *only*, ut tantummodo per stirpes alantur suas, Cic

tantundem, v tantusdem

tantus -a um, correl adjectival pron I. *of such size, so great*, a, foll by quantus, nullam umquam vidi tantam (contionem), quanta nunc vestrûm est, Cic, b, foll by qui, quae, quod, gen with subj, nulla est tanta vis, quae non frangi possit, Cic, c, foll by quam, Liv, Verg, d, foll by ut and the subj, non fuit tantus homo in civitate, ut de eo potissimum conquereremur, Cic, e, without a correl, in tantis mutationibus, Cic, tot tantaque vitia, Cic II *so much*, tanta pecunia, Cic, 1, neut, tantum, subst., a, in nom and acc, *so much*, (α) ut tantum nobis, quantum ipsi superesse posset, remitteret, Cic ; (β) with genit, auctoritatis, Cic, b, in genit. of actual or moral value, *at such a price, so dear*, hortos emit tanti, quanti Pythius voluit, Cic ; esp, (α) aliquid or aliquis est tanti, *is worth so much*, tanti eius apud se gratiam esse, uti, etc, Caes, (β) aliquid tanti est, *it is worth the while*, est mihi tanti, huius invidiae crimen subire, dummodo, etc, Cic, c, abl, tanto ; (α) before comparatives, *the more*, tanto nos submissius geramus, Cic., (β) with adv of time, tanto ante, *so long before*, Cic ; (γ) with verbs expressing a comparison, as praestare, Ov, d, in tantum, *so far, so much*, in tantum suam felicitatem virtutemque enituisse, Liv.; 2, neut, tantum, as adv = *so much, so far*, (α) with verbs, de quo tantum, quantum me amas, velim cogites, Cic, (β) with adj, instead of tam, tantum magna, Hor III. *of such a kind, so little, so small*, ceterarum provinciarum vectigalia tanta sunt, ut iis ad provincias tutandas vix contenti esse possimus, Cic, neut, tantum, as subst = *so little ;* praesidii, Caes, as adv = *only* nomen tantum virtutis usurpas, Cic tantum non, *all but*, Liv, tantum quod ; (α) *just*, Cic, (β) *only*, tantum quod hominem non nominat, Cic, non tantum sed etiam, *not only but also*, Liv

tantusdem, tantădem, tantumdem and tantundem, *just so much, just so great*, neut tantumdem or tantundem, *just so much*, a, in nom. and acc, magistratibus tantumdem detur in cellam, quantum semper datum est, Cic, b, genit of price, tantidem, Cic

tăpētĕ -is, n and **tăpētum** -i, n (τάπης), *drapery, tapestry*, used for covering walls, floors, couches, etc, Verg (abl plur, tapetibus, Verg, Liv, Ov, tapetis, Verg ; acc. plur, tapetas from unused nom tapes, Verg).

Tāprŏbănē -ēs, f (Ταπροβάνη), *an island south of India, now Ceylon*

tărandrus -i, m *a rein deer*, Plin

Tarbelli -ōrum, m *a people in Aquitania*

tardē, adv (tardus) **I.** *slowly*, navigare, Cic, tardius moveri, Cic, judicare, Cic **II.** *late, not in time*, triennio tardius (*later*) triumphare, Cic, tardissime perferri, Cic.

tardesco, 3 (tardus), *to become slow*, Lucr

tardĭgrădus -a -um (tarde and gradior), *slowly stepping*, ap Cic

tardĭlŏquus -a -um (tarde and loquor), *slowly speaking*, Sen

tardĭpes -pĕdis (tardus and pes), *slow footed*, deus, *limping*, i e, *Vulcan*, Cat

tardĭtas -ātis, f (tardus). **I.** *slowness, tardiness*, **a**, of persons, plerisque in rebus gerendis tarditas et procrastinatio odiosa est, Cic **b**, of things, *slowness, inactivity* pedum, Cic, navium, Caes, esp, *slowness in speaking*, cursum contentiones magis requirunt, expositiones rerum tarditatem, Cic **II.** Transf, *mental and moral slowness, slothfulness, inertness, dulness, stupidity*, ingenii, Cic.

tardĭtūdo -inis, f (tardus), *slowness*, Plaut

tardĭuscŭlus -a -um (tardus), *somewhat slow, tardy*, Plaut

tardo, 1 (tardus) **I.** Intransit, *to loiter, to be slow*, num quid putes reipublicae nomine tardandum esse nobis, Cic **II.** Transit, *to make slow, tardy, to hinder, delay, retard*, cursum, Cic, with ab and the abl, aliquem a laude alicuius, Cic, with infin, ut reliqui hoc timore propius adire tardarentur, Caes

tardus -a -um, *slow, tardy* **I.** Lit., **1**, gen, **a**, of living creatures, pecus, Cic, homo, Cic, with in and the abl, in decedendo tardior, Cic, with ad and the acc, tardior ad discedendum, Cic; **b**, of things, tibicinis modi, Cic, vox, Cic, esp, (α) *coming late*; poena, Cic, (β) *lasting a long time, lingering*, menses, Verg, **2**, poet, *making slow*, podagra, Hor. **II.** Transf, **a**, of persons, *slow of comprehension, dull, stupid*, nimis indociles quidam tardique sunt, Cic, **b**, of things, *dull*, ingenium, Cic, **c**, of speech or a speaker, *slow, measured, deliberate*, in utroque genere dicendi principia tarda sunt, Cic

Tărentum -i, n and **Tărentus** -i, f (Τάρας), *a wealthy town on the coast of Magna Graecia, founded by Spartan exiles*, 707 B C, *famous for its purple dyes, now Taranto* Hence, adj, **Tărentīnus** -a -um, *Tarentine*, plur subst, **Tărentīni** -ōrum, m *inhabitants of Tarentum*

tarmes -itis, m *a wood-worm*, Plaut

Tarpējus -a -um, *name of a Roman family, the most celebrated member of which was Sp Tarpejus, commander of the citadel at Rome, whose daughter Tarpeja was said to have admitted the Sabines into the citadel, and to have been crushed beneath their shields in reward* Adj, *Tarpeian*, lex, Cic; mons Tarpejus or saxum Tarpejum, *the Tarpeian rock, a peak of the Capitoline Hill, from which criminals were thrown*, arx, *the Capitol*, Verg

Tarquĭnii -ōrum, m *an old town in Etruria, whence came the Tarquin family* Hence, **A. Tarquĭnĭus** -a -um, **a**, *of Tarquinii*, name of two kings of Rome, Tarquinius Priscus and the last king of Rome, Tarquinius Superbus, **b**, *belonging to the Tarquin family*, nomen, Liv **B. Tarquĭnĭensis** -e, *of Tarquinii*

Tarrăcīna -ae, f. and **Tarrăcīnae** -ārum, f *a town in Latium, formerly called Anxur, now Terracina*; flumen Terracinae = Amasenus, Liv. Hence, adj, **Tarrăcīnensis** -e, *of Tarracina.*

Tarrăco -ōnis, f *a town in Spain, now Tarragona* Hence, **Tarrăcōnensis** -e, *of Tarraco*, Hispania Tarraconensis, *name of the north-east division of Spain*

Tarsus -i, f (Ταρσός), *the chief town of Cilicia, now Tarso* Hence, adj, **Tarsensis** -e, *of or belonging to Tarsus*

Tartărus (-ŏs) -i, m, plur, **Tartăra** -ōrum, n (Τάρταρος, plur, Τάρταρα), *the infernal regions* Hence, adj, **Tartărĕus** -a -um, *Tartarean*, custos, *Cerberus*, Verg; sorores, *the Furies*, Verg

Tartessus (-ŏs) -i, f (Ταρτησσός), *a town in Hispania Baetica, on the Baetis* Hence, **Tartessĭus** -a -um, *Tartessian*, litora, *on the Atlantic*, Ov

tarum -i, n *aloe wood*, Plin

Tarusātes -ium, m *a people in Aquitania*

tascŏnĭum -ii, n *a white, clayey earth*, Plin

tăt! interj *an exclamation of astonishment, what!* Plaut

tăta -ae, m *father*, in the lisping speech of children, Varr

tătae = tat (q v)

Tătĭus -ii, m, Titus Tatius, *king of the Sabines, co regent with Romulus* Adj, **Tătĭus** -a -um, *of Tatius*

Taulantĭi -ōrum, m *a people of Illyria*

taura -ae, f (ταῦρα), *a barren cow*, Varr

taurĕus -a -um (taurus), *of or relating to an ox*, terga, *ox-hides*, Verg, meton, *a drum*, Ov, subst, **taurĕa** -ae, f *a whip of bull's hide*, Juv

Tauri -ōrum, m *a people of Scythian descent, near the Crimea* Adj, **Tauricus** -a -um, *Tauric*

taurĭformis -e (taurus and forma), *shaped like a bull* (of the river Aufidus), because river-gods were represented with the heads of oxen, Hor

Taurĭi ludi -ōrum, m *games celebrated in the Circus Flaminius at Rome, in honour of the infernal deities*, Liv

Taurīni -ōrum, m *a people of Ligurian race in Gallia Cisalpina, with capital Augusta Taurinorum, whence Turin* Hence, adj, **Taurīnus** -a -um, *of or relating to the Taurini.*

1 **taurīnus** -a -um (taurus), *of or relating to a bull*, tergum, Verg, frons, Ov

2 **Taurīnus** -a -um, v Taurini

Taurŏis -ŏentis, f *a fort in Gallia Narbonensis, belonging to Massilia*

Taurŏmĕnĭum (**Taurŏmīnium**) -ii, n. *a town on the east coast of Sicily, now Taormina* Hence, **Taurŏmĕnītānus** -a -um, *of or belonging to Tauromenium*

Taurŏpŏlos, f (Ταυροπόλος), *surname of Artemis (Diana)*

1 **taurus** -i, m (ταῦρος), *a bull* **I.** Lit, Cic **II.** Transf, **1**, *the sign of the zodiac so called*, Verg, **2**, *the bull of Phalaris*, Cic, **3**, *a bird, perhaps a bittern*, Plin, **4**, *a kind of beetle*, Plin, **5**, *the root of a tree*, Quint

2 **Taurus** -i, m (Ταῦρος), *a high mountain-range in Asia, now Ala-Dagh or Al-Kurun*. Tauri Pylae, *a narrow pass between Cappadocia and Cilicia*, Cic.

tax = taxtax (q v)

taxa -ae, f *a species of laurel*, Plin.

taxātĭo -ōnis, f (taxo), *a rating, valuing, appraising*, eius rei taxationem facere, Cic

taxĭcus -a -um (taxus), *of or relating to the yew-tree*, Plin.

taxillus -i, m. (root TAG, whence talus), *a small die*, Cic.

taxo, 1. (tago, tango), *to touch, to handle.* Fig., **A.** *to reproach, tax with a fault;* aliquem, Suet. **B.** *to estimate, rate, appraise the value of anything*, Suet.

taxus -i, f. *a yew-tree*, Caes.

Tāÿgĕtē (Tāūgĕtē) -ēs, f. (Ταϋγέτη), *daughter of Atlas, one of the Pleiads.*

Tāÿgĕtus -i, m. (Ταΰγετον), and **Tāÿgĕta** -ōrum, n. *a mountain between Laconia and Messenia.*

1. **tē**, v. tu.

2. **-tĕ**, pronominal suffix added to tu (v. tu).

Tĕānum -i, n. (Τέανον). **I.** Teanum Sidicinum, *a town in Campania*, now *Teano.* **II.** Teanum Apulum or Apulorum, *town in Apulia*, now *Ponte Rotto.* Hence, **Tĕānenses** -ium, m. *the inhabitants of Teanum.*

Tĕātes -um, m. *a people in Apulia.*

teba -ae, f. *a hill*, Varr.

techna -ae, f. (τέχνη), *a cunning trick, artifice*, Plaut.

technĭcus -i, m. (τεχνικός), *a teacher of any art*, Quint.

Tecmessa -ae, f. (Τέκμησσα), *daughter of Teuthras, mistress of the Telamonian Ajax.*

Tecmōn -ōnis, m. *a town in Cyprus.*

Tecta via, *a street in Rome, leading to the porta Capena.*

tectē, adv. with compar. (tectus), **1**, *cautiously, securely*, Cic.; **2**, *covertly, secretly*, Cic.

tector -ōris, m. (tego), *one who covers walls with plaster, stucco, etc., a plasterer*, Varr.

tectōrĭŏlum -i, n. (dim. of tectorium), *plaster or stucco work*, Cic.

tectōrĭus -a -um (tector), *used for covering.* **I.** Gen., paniculus, *straw for thatching*, Plaut. **II.** Esp., *relating to the plastering, stuccoing of walls;* hence, opus tectorium, and subst., **tectōrĭum** -ii, n. *plaster, stucco, fresco-painting;* concinnum, Cic.; transf., of *paste* put on the face to preserve the complexion, Juv.

Tectŏsăges -um, m. and **Tectŏsăgi** -ōrum, m. *a people in Gallia Narbonensis, a branch of whom settled in Galatia, in Asia Minor.*

tectum -i, n. (tego), *a roof.* **I.** Lit., sub tectum congerere, Cic. **II.** Meton., *a roof, shelter, quarters, abode, dwelling;* ager sine tecto, Cic.; aliquem tecto ac domo invitare, Cic.; inter annos XIV tectum non subire, *had not come under a roof*, Caes.; Triviae tecta, *temple*, Verg.; Sibyllae, *grotto*, Verg.; doli tecti, *of the labyrinth*, Verg.

tectus -a -um, p. adj. (from tego), *covered.* **I.** Lit., naves, Liv.; scaphae, Caes. **II.** Fig., **A.** *concealed* or *concealing oneself, close, reserved, cautious;* quis tectior, Cic. **B.** *concealed;* **a**, *secret;* cupiditas, Cic.; **b**, of speech, *disguised, obscure;* verba, Cic.

Tĕgĕa -ae, f. (Τεγέα), *a city of Arcadia.* Hence, **A. Tĕgĕaeus (Tĕgēus)** -a -um, *Tegean*, and poet. = *Arcadian;* virgo, *Callisto, daughter of the Arcadian king Lycaon*, Ov.; aper, *the wild boar of Erymanthus*, Ov.; parens, *Carmenta, mother of Evander*, who is also called Tegeaea sacerdos, Ov.; domus, *of Evander*, Ov.; subst., **Tĕgĕaea** -ae, f. *Atalanta*, Ov. **B. Tĕgĕātes** -ae, m. *an inhabitant of Tegea.*

tĕges -ĕtis, f. (tego), *a mat, rug, covering*, Varr.

tĕgĕtĭcŭla -ae, f. (dim. of teges), *a little mat or rug*, Mart.

tĕgillum -i, n. (dim. of tegulum), *a small hood or cowl*, Plin.

tĕgĭmen (tĕgŭmen) and **tegmen** -inis, n. (tego), *a cover, covering;* mihi amictui est Scythicum tegumen, Cic.; transf., *a shield;* quod tegumen modo omnis exercitus fuerat, Liv.

tĕgĭmentum (tĕgŭmentum) and **tegmentum** -i, n. (tego), *a covering;* tegimenta corporum vel texta vel suta, Cic.

tegmen = tegimen (q.v.).

tĕgo, texi, tectum, 3. (στέγω), *to cover.* **I.** Gen., amica corpus eius texit suo pallio, Cic.; casas stramentis, Caes. **II.** Esp., **1**, *to bury, cover with earth;* ossa tegebat humus, Ov.; **2**, *to cover, conceal, hide;* **a**, lit., ferae latibulis se tegunt, Cic.; **b**, transf., *to conceal, keep secret;* ut sententiam tegeremus, Cic.; **3**, *to cover so as to protect, to shield;* **a**, lit., aliquem, Caes.; patriam, Cic.; **b**, fig., *to protect;* legatos ab ira, Liv.

tĕgŭla -ae, f. (tego), *a roofing-tile*, Cic.; plur., tegulae, frequently used for *roof;* per tegulas demitti, Cic.

tĕgŭlum -i, n. (tego), *a covering, roof*, Plin.

tĕgŭmentum = tegimentum (q.v.).

tĕgŭmen = tegimen (q.v.).

tēla -ae, f. (for texla, from texo). **I.** *a web, that which is woven;* Penelope telam retexens, Cic.; *a spider's web*, Cat.; fig., *a device;* ea tela texitur, Cic. **II.** Meton., **1**, *the warp*, Verg.; **2**, *the loom*, Ov.

Tĕlămo (-ōn) -ōnis, m. (Τελαμών), *one of the Argonauts, father of Ajax and Teucer.* Hence, **A. Tĕlămōnĭus** -a -um, *Telamonian;* subst., = *Ajax*, Ov. **B. Tĕlămōnĭădēs** -ae, m. *the son of Telamon, i.e., Ajax*, Ov.

Telchīnes -um, m. (Τελχῖνες), *a priestly family of Rhodes, famous for metal work, and notorious for their sorceries.*

Tēlĕbŏae -ārum, m. (Τηλεβόαι), *a people in Acarnania, notorious for brigandage, a colony of whom settled in the island of Capreae.*

Tēlĕgŏnos -i, m. (Τηλέγονος), *son of Ulysses and Circe, builder of Tusculum;* Telegoni moenia, *Tusculum*, Ov.; appell., **Tēlĕgŏni** -ōrum, m. *of the love poems of Ovid* (which were destructive to him their author, just as Telegonus killed his father Ulysses).

Tēlĕmăchus -i, m. (Τηλέμαχος), *son of Ulysses and Penelope.*

Tēlĕphus -i, m. (Τήλεφος), *son of Hercules, king in Mysia, wounded by the spear of Achilles, but healed by its rust.*

Tēlĕthūsa -ae, f. *mother of Iphis.*

tēlīnum -i, n. (τήλινον), *a costly salve made of the herb fenugreek*, Plin.

tēlis -is, f. (τῆλις), *the herb fenugreek*, Plin.

Tellēna -ōrum, n. *a town in Latium.*

tellus -ūris, f. **I.** *the earth;* **1**, lit., Cic.; esp., *the earth, soil*, as bearing fruits, humida, Ov.; **2**, transf., poet., **a**, *land, district, country;* Gnossia, Verg.; **b**, *land, possessions;* propria, Hor.; **c**, *land = people;* Pontica tellus, Ov. **II.** Personif., Tellus, *the Earth, as the all-nourishing goddess*, Cic.

Telmessus (-ŏs) -i, f. (Τελμησσός), *an old town in Lycia on the borders of Caria.* Hence, **A. Telmesses** -ium, m. *the inhabitants of Telmessus.* **B. Telmessĭcus** -a -um, *of or relating to Telmessus.* **C. Telmessĭus** -a -um, *Telmessian.*

tēlum -i, n *a missile, dart, javelin, spear* I 1, lit., a, arma atque tela militaria, Sall, tela intendere, excipere, Cic; b, *a sword, dagger, etc, weapon*, stare cum telo, Cic, used of the cestus, Verg, of the horns of a bull, Ov, 2, transf, *the beams of the sun*, tela diei, Lucr, *lightning*, arbitrium est in sua tela Jovi, Ov II. Fig, *weapon, arrow, dart, arms*, tela fortunae, Cic, isto telo tutabimur plebem, Liv

Tĕmĕnos (τέμενος, τό), *a place at Syracuse, where was a grove sacred to Apollo* Hence, **Tĕmĕnītēs** -ae, m (Τεμενίτης), *of Temenos*, Apollo, *a statue of Apollo*, Cic.

tĕmĕrārĭus a um (temere) I. *by chance, fortuitous, casual*, Plaut II. *inconsiderate, thoughtless, indiscreet, rash, imprudent*, homo, Caes, consilium, Liv, bella, Ov, cupiditas, Cic

tĕmĕrē, adv *by chance, accidentally, casually, fortuitously, rashly, heedlessly, without purpose* I. Gen, equo temere acto, Liv, domus quae temere et nullo consilio administratur, Cic, nihil temere, nihil imprudenter factum, Caes II. Esp, A. non temere est, *it is not for nothing that, it is not without importance or meaning*, Verg B. non temere, *not easily*, qui hoc non temere nisi libertis suis deferebant, Cic

tĕmĕrĭtas -ātis, f (temere) I. *chance, accident*, temeritas et casus, non ratio nec consilium valet, Cic II. *rashness, inconsiderateness, temerity* in action, *an inconsiderate, unfounded opinion*, in judgment, temeritas cupiditasque militum, Caes, numquam temeritas cum sapientia commiscetur, Cic

tĕmĕro, 1 (temere), *to defile, dishonour, pollute*, templa, Verg thalamos, Ov

Tĕmĕsa -ae, f, **Tĕmĕsē** -ēs, f, and **Tempsa (Temsa)** -ae, f (Τεμέση, Τέμψα), *an old town in Bruttium, famous for its copper mines*. Hence, A. **Tĕmĕsaeus** -a um, *Temesean* B. **Tĕmĕsēĭus** -a -um, *Temesean* C. **Tempsānus** -a um, *Tempsan*

tēmētum -i, n (root temum, whence temulentus), *any intoxicating drink, wine*, Cic

temno, tempsi, 3 *to despise, contemn*, vulgaria, Hor

Temnŏs -i, f (Τῆμνος), *a town in Aeolia, now Menimen* Hence, A. **Temnītēs** ae, m *of Temnos* B. **Temnii** -ōrum, m *the inhabitants of Temnos*

tēmo ōnis, m (tendo), *a pole*, 1, lit., a, of a waggon, Verg, b, of a plough, *a ploughbeam*, Verg, 2, meton, a, *a waggon*, b, *the constellation of Charles's Wain*, Cic poet

Tempē, neut plur (Τέμπη, τα) I. *a valley in Thessaly, famous for its beauty, through which the river Peneus flowed*. II. Transf, *any beautiful valley*, Ov, Verg

tempĕrāmentum -i, n (tempero) I. *a right proportion of things mixed together*, eadem est materia, sed distat temperamento, Plin II. *a middle way, mean, moderation*, inventum est temperamentum, quo tenuiores cum principibus aequari se putarent, Cic

tempĕrans -antis, p adj (from tempero), *moderate, temperate, continent, self-denying*, homo, Cic, homo temperantissimus, Cic, with ab and the abl, temperantior a cupidine imperii, Liv

tempĕrantĕr, adv with compar (temperans), *temperately, moderately*; temperantius agere, Cic

tempĕrantĭa -ae, f (temperans), *temperance, moderation, sobriety, continence*, temperantia in praetermittendis voluptatibus cernitur, Cic

tempĕrātē, adv (temperatus), *moderately, temperately*, agere, Cic., temperatius scribere Cic

tempĕrātĭo ōnis, f (tempero) I. *temperateness, moderation, just proportion, proper mixture of ingredients, constitution, organisation*, caeli, Cic, caloris, Cic, corporum, Cic, civitatis, reipublicae, Cic II. Concr, *the organising principle*, sol mens mundi et temperatio, Cic

tempĕrātor -ōris, m (tempero), *one who arranges or governs*, varietatis, Cic

tempĕrātūra -ae, f (tempero), *proper mixture, temperature, organisation*, Plin

tempĕrātus a um, p adj (from tempero) I. *properly arranged*, prela, Cato II. *ordered, moderate*, a, esca, Cic, loca temperatiora, Caes, b, fig, *moderate, mild, quiet, temperate*, homo temperatissimus, Cic, oratio temperatior, Cic

tempĕri, temperius, v tempus

tempĕrĭes ēi, f (tempero), *a proper mixture, preparation, organisation, tempering*, temperiem sumpsere humorque caloroque, Ov

tempĕro, 1 (tempus, *a section*), *to set bounds to a thing, keep within limits* I. Intransit, *to observe proper limits, be temperate*, 1, gen, in multa, Liv, with dat, *to control, keep back, use with moderation*, victoriae, Sall, linguae, Liv, with abl, risu, Liv, with ab and the abl, *to keep from, refrain from*, ab injuria, Caes, sibi non temperare and simply non or vix temperare, foll by quominus or quin and subj, *not to refrain from*, neque sibi temperaturos existimabat, quin in provinciam exirent, Caes, 2, esp, *to spare*, with dat, hostibus superatis, Cic II Transit, 1, a, *to distribute or mix properly, to temper*, acuta cum gravibus, Cic, b, esp, *to mix a drink, prepare*, poculum, Hor; 2, a, *to regulate* rempublicam legibus, Cic, b, *to rule*, res hominum ac deorum, Hor, 3, *to temper, make mild*, calores solis, Cic, aequor, Verg

tempestas -ātis, f (tempus) I. *a space or period of time, season*, ea tempestate, *at that time*, Sall, eādem tempestate, Cic, multis ante tempestatibus, Liv II *weather* A. Gen, bona, certa, Cic, clara, Verg, turbulenta, Cic, perfrigida, Cic, tempestates, *kinds of weather*, Cic B. *bad weather, storm, tempest*, 1, lit, immoderatae tempestates, Cic, 2, fig, *storm, tempest, attack, fury*, invidiae, Cic, querelarum, Cic, telorum Verg, of persons, Siculorum tempestas (of Verres), Cic., turbo ac tempestas pacis (of Clodius), Cic

tempestīvē, adv with compar (tempestivius), *at the right time, seasonably*, tempestive caedi (of trees), Cic, tempestivius in domum P. .li comissabere, Hor

tempestīvĭtas ātis, f (tempestivus), *the fit time, proper season*, sua cuique parti aetatis tempestivitas est data, Cic

tempestīvō = tempestive (q v)

tempestīvus a -um (tempus) I *happening at the right time, opportune, seasonable, fit, appropriate* A. nondum tempestivo ad navigandum mari, Cic, oratio, Liv, multa mihi ad mortem tempestiva fuere, *convenient opportunities for*, Cic B. *early*, cena, convivium, Cic II. a, of fruit, *in season, ripe*, fructus, Cic, b, of persons, *ripe, mature*, puella tempestiva viro, *ripe for marriage*, Hor

templum -i, n (= tempulum, dim of tempus), lit., *a section, a part cut off* I. *a space in the sky or on the earth marked out by the augur for the purpose of taking auspices*, Liv II. Transf, A. *a place from which one can survey*,

a, *a prospect, range of vision*, deus, cuius hoc templum est omne quod conspicis, Cic , **b,** *a height*, templa Parnassia, *the Mount Parnassus*, Ov **B.** *a consecrated piece of ground*, **a,** gen , *any consecrated spot, a sanctuary, asylum*, Liv , of a chapel dedicated to the dead, Verg , of the curia, because consecrated by an augur , curia, templum publici consilii, Cic , *the tribunal*, Cic ; transf , of any clear, open space , mundi, Lucr , fig , = *the interior* , templa mentis, Cic , **b,** esp., *a place dedicated to a particular deity, a temple*, Jovis, Cic

tempŏrālis -e (tempus), *temporary, lasting for a time*, laudes, Tac

tempŏrārĭus -a -um (tempus) **I.** *temporary*, Plin **II.** *seasonable, adapted to time and circumstances*, Nep

tempŏri, v tempus

Tempsa, Tempsanus, v Temesa

tempus -ŏris, n (τεμνω, *to cut off*), *a division, section*, hence, **I.** *a division of time, section of time, period of time* **A.** Lit , extremum tempus diei, Cic , matutina tempora, *the morning hours*, Cic , hibernum tempus anni, Cic ; hoc tempore, Cic , omni tempore, Cic , in tempus praesens, *for the present*, Cic , ex tempore, *without preparation*, Cic , ad tempus, *for a time*, Cic **B.** Transf , **1,** *a distinct point of time*, ab'it illud tempus, Cic , ad tuum tempus, *up to your consulship*, Cic , tempus est, with infin , *it is high time to*, tempus est dicere, Cic., with acc and infin , tempus est jam hinc abire me, Cic , **2,** *time as a whole*, tempus ponere in re, *to spend*, Cic ; in omne tempus, *for all time*, Cic , **3,** *a proper, fit time, occasion, opportunity*, tempus amittere, Cic , tempus habere, Cic , ad tempus, *at the right time*, Cic , old abl , tempori or tempori, *at the right time, seasonably*, Cic ; compar , temperius, Cic , **4, a,** *the state, condition of things*, freq plur , *the times*, temporibus servire, Cic , **b,** *the circumstances of a thing or person*, reipublicae, Cic , esp , *calamitous circumstances, misfortune, calamity*, scripsi de temporibus meis, Cic , **5,** *time in pronouncing a syllable, quantity*, Cic , **6,** *time in grammar, tense of a verb*, Varr **II.** *the temple on the forehead*, Verg , plur , *the temples*, Verg , poet , *the face*, Prop , *the head*, Prop

Tempȳra ōrum, n *a town in Thrace, between Mt Rhodope and the coast*

Temsa = Temesa (q v)

tēmŭlentĭa -ae, f (temulentus), *drunkenness, intoxication*, Plin

tēmŭlentus -a -um (temum, whence temetum), *drunken, intoxicated, tipsy*, of persons, Cic , of things, vox, Cic

tĕnācĭtas -ātis, f (tenax). **I** *a firm holding, tenacity*, unguium tenacitate arripiunt, Cic **II.** *frugality, stinginess*, Liv

tĕnācĭtĕr, adv (tenax) **I.** *firmly, tenaciously*, premere, Ov **II.** Transf , *constantly, firmly*, miseros urgere, Ov

tĕnax -ācis (teneo), *holding fast, griping, tenacious* **I.** Lit , **A.** Gen , forceps, Verg , dens (of an anchor), Verg **B.** Esp , **a,** *holding fast to possessions, money, etc , sparing, frugal, stingy*, pater parcus et tenax, Cic , with genit , quaesiti tenax, Ov , **b,** *holding firmly together, sticky, gluey*, gramen, *matted*, Hor , cerae, Verg **II.** Transf , **A.** Gen , *firm, steadfast*, longa tenaxque fides, Ov **B.** Esp , of character, **a,** in a good sense, *firm, resolute, steadfast, holding to*, with genit , propositi, Hor , **b,** in a bad sense, *obstinate*, equus, Liv., ira, Ov.

Tencteri ōrum and -ûm, m. *a German people on the Rhine.*

tendĭcŭla -ae, f (tendo), *a gin, noose, snare;* fig , aucupia verborum et litterarum tendiculae, Cic.

tendo, tĕtendi, tentum and tensum, 3 (root TEN, whence τεινω, *to stretch*), *to stretch, stretch out, extend* **I.** Act , **A.** **1,** lit , plagas, Cic ; arcum, Verg , **2,** meton , **a,** *to pitch (a tent)*, praetorium, Caes , **b,** *to string*, barbiton, Hor ; **c,** *to direct ;* iter ad naves, Verg , sagittas arcu, *to shoot*, Hor , **d,** *to reach, present*, parvum patri Iulum, Verg **B.** Fig , **1,** gen , alicui insidias, *to lay snares for*, Cic , **2,** *to present, give*, spem amicis porrigere atque tendere, Cic **II.** Reflex (with or without se) and middle, **A.** Lit , **1** (without se), *to stretch out*, milit t t , *to pitch one's tent, encamp*, Caes , Verg ; in isdem castris, Liv , **2** (without se), *to direct one's course to, tend towards, go towards, march towards*, **a,** of persons, Venusiam, Cic , ad aedes, Hor , unde venis? et quo tendis? Hor , **b,** of inanimate things, simulacra viis de rectis omnia tendunt, Lucr , **3,** of places, reflex (with and gen without se), or middle, *to stretch towards, extend to*, via tendit sub moenia, Verg **B.** Transf (reflex without se), **1, a,** *to have recourse to*, ad alienam opem quisque inops tendere, Liv , **b,** *to be inclined, tend in any direction, aim at, strive after*, ad reliqua alacri tendebamus animo, Cic , foll by infin , *to try, attempt*, manibus divellere nodos, Verg ; praevenire, Liv , **2,** *to strive, contend against*, **a,** with arms, summā vi, Sall , **b,** with words, etc , *to contend for, strive for*, quod summā vi ut tenderent, amicis mandaverat, Liv , with ut and the subj , ut delectum haberet, Liv , with acc of pron , quid tendit? *what is he striving for?* Cic

tĕnĕbrae -ārum, f *darkness* **I.** Lit , **a,** Cic , tetris tenebris, Cic., **b,** esp , *the darkness of the night, night*, quomodo redissem luce, non tenebris, Cic , **2, a,** *darkness = blindness*, tenebras et cladem lucis ademptae objicit, Ov , **b,** *the darkness before the eyes in fainting*, tenebris nigrescunt omnia circum, Verg , **c,** *the darkness of death*, Plaut. , **3,** meton , *a dark place*, of the lower world, Stygiae, Verg., absol , Verg , Ov , of a prison, clausi in tenebris, Sall ; of a hiding-place, quum illa conjuratio ex latebris atque ex tenebris erupisset, Cic **II.** Transf , **1,** *obscurity, inglorious condition* , vestram familiam obscuram e tenebris in lucem evocavit, Cic ; **2,** *darkness, gloom, obscurity*, latent ista omnia crassis occultata et circumfusa tenebris, Cic

tĕnĕbrĭcōsus a um (tenebricus), *dark, gloomy, shrouded in darkness, obscure* , illud tenebricosissimum tempus ineuntis aetatis tuae, Cic

tĕnĕbrĭcus -a -um (tenebrae), *dark, gloomy*, Cic poet

tĕnĕbrōsus -a -um (tenebrae), *dark, gloomy;* palus, Verg

Tĕnĕdus (-ŏs) -i, f (Τένεδος), *an island in the Aegean Sea, near Troy*, now *Tenedo* Hence, **Tĕnĕdĭus** a -um, *belonging to Tenedos*

tĕnellŭlus -a -um (dim of tenellus), *exceedingly tender, delicate*, Cat.

tĕnellus -a -um (dim of tener), *very tender, delicate*, Plaut

tĕnĕo, tĕnui, tentum, 2 (root TEN, whence tendo, τεινω), *to hold* **I.** Gen , **A.** **1,** lit , pyxidem in manu, Cic , pateram dexterā manu, Cic , cibum ore, Cic , **2,** transf , **a,** gen , res oculis et manibus tenetur, *is visible and tangible*, Cic , rem manu tenere, *to have at one's fingers' ends, to understand thoroughly*, Cic , **b,** *to hold in the mind, to understand, grasp, know*, quae et saepe audistis et tenetis animis, Cic., quibus rebus capiatur Caesar, tenes, Cic.

B. Meton , 1, *to reach a place, arrive at, land on*, regionem, Liv , transf., per cursum rectum regnum, Cic , 2, *to direct*, a, oculos sub astra, Verg ; b, *to direct one's course*, quo tenetis iter? Verg ; intransit , of ships, *to sail to*, ad Mendaeum, Liv II. With the notion of property, *to hold in one's possession, have, possess*, 1, lit , a, multa hereditatibus, multa emptionibus tenebantur sine injuria, Cic., b, milit t t , *to occupy, garrison*, locum praesidiis, montem, portum, Caes , 2, transf , of persons as objects, te jam tenet altera conjux, Ov , to possess as a ruler, terras, Hor , imperium, Caes , qui tenent (sc rempublicam), *the rulers of the state*, Cic III. With the notion of firmness, *to hold fast*, 1, lit , a, ut quo major se vis aquae incitavisset, hoc artius illigata tenerentur, Caes , b, as milit t t , *to defend, keep*, suum locum, tumulum, Caes , 2, transf , a, *to hold fast in the mind*, memoriam alicuius, Cic , memoriā tenere = *to remember*, foll by acc and infin , Cic , b, *to catch, detect*, teneo te, Cic , teneri in manifesto peccato, Cic , c, of passions, *to possess, master*, misericordia me tenet, Cic , magna spes me tenet, with acc and infin , Cic , d, *to charm, amuse*, varias mentes carmine, Verg , pueri ludis tenentur, oculi picturā tenentur, Cic , e, *to bind*, leges eum tenent, Cic , lege, foedere, promisso teneri, Cic , f, *to hold fast, preserve*, auctoritatem, imperium in suos, Cic , causam apud centum viros, *to gain*, Cic , g, *to maintain a proposition* illud arte tenent accurateque defendunt, voluptatem esse summum bonum, Cic IV. With the notion of endurance or quiet, *to preserve, keep* A. Gen , a, lit , terra tenetur nutu suo, Cic , b, transf , aliquem in officio, Cic B. Esp , 1, transit , *to keep to, not to swerve from*, a, lit , cursum, Caes , Cic , absol , medio tutissimus ibis, inter utrumque tene, *hold your course*, Ov , b, transf , *to observe, remain true to*, ordinem, fidem, Cic , 2, intransit , *to last, endure, keep on*, imber per totam noctem tenuit, Liv , fama tenet, *the report holds*, with acc and infin , Liv V. With the notion of motion checked, *to hold fast* A. *to keep in, hold back*, 1, lit , manus ab aliquo, Ov , aliquem or se domi *to keep at home*, Liv , se castris, Caes , se oppido, Cic , 2, transf , *to restrain, suppress, check, hold back*, risum, dolorem, iracundiam, Cic , lacrimas, Cic , se ab accusando, *to refrain from*, Cic , se non tenere, or se tenere non posse quin, etc , teneri non posse quin, etc , *not to be able to refrain from*, etc B. *to detain*, 1, lit , septimum jam diem Corcyrae teneri, Cic , 2, transf , non teneo te pluribus, Cic VI. With the notion of containing, *to contain, comprise*, in pass , teneri aliquā re, *to be contained in, to belong to*, si Asia hoc imperio non teneretur, Cic

tĕner -ĕra -ĕrum, *tender, delicate, soft* I. Lit , 1, gen , caules, Hor , uva, Verg , 2, esp , *tender, youthful, young*, saltator, Cic , a teneris, ut Graeci dicunt, unguiculis, *from childhood*, Cic , subst., in teneris, *in childhood*, Verg II. Transf , *tender, soft, effeminate*, tenerum quiddam atque molle in animis, Cic , tenerior animus, Cic

tĕnĕrasco, 3 (tener), *to grow tender, delicate, soft*, Plin

tĕnĕrē, adv with compar and superl (tener), *tenderly, delicately, softly*, Plin

tĕnĕrĭtas -ātis, f (tener), *tenderness, softness*, in primo ortu inest teneritas et mollities, Cic

tĕnŏrĭtūdo = teneritas (q v)

tēnesmos i, m (τεινεσμός), *a straining at stool*, Nep

tĕnor -ōris, m. (teneo), *course, continued course* I. Lit , hasta servat tenorem, Verg II. Transf , *uninterrupted course, duration, tenor, career*, tenorem pugnae servabant, Liv , fati, Ov , vitae, Liv , adv., uno tenore, *in an uninterrupted course, uniformly*, Cic

Tēnus (-ŏs) -i, f. (Τῆνος), *one of the Cyclades Islands*, now *Tino* Hence, **Tēnii** ōrum, m. *the inhabitants of Tenos*

tensa ae, f *a car on which the images of the gods were carried at the Circensian games*, Cic

tensio ōnis, f (tendo), *a stretching, tension*, Plin

tensus -a -um, partic of tendo (q v)

tentābundus (temptābundus) -a -um (tento), *trying, attempting*, Liv

tentāmen (temptāmen) ĭnis, n (tento), *a trial, attempt*, Ov

tentāmentum (temptāmentum) i, n (tento), *a trial, attempt, test, essay*, Verg , Ov

tentātio (temptātio) -ōnis f (tento) I. *an attack*, novae tentationes, *new attacks of disease*, Cic II. *a trial, test*, Liv

tentātor (temptātor) -ōris, m (tento), *a tempter*, Hor

tentīgo -ĭnis, f (tendo), *lecherousness*, Hor

tento (tempto), 1 (intens of tendo), *to touch, feel, handle* I. Gen , 1, lit , pectora manibus, Ov.; flumen pede, Cic , venas, *to feel the pulse*, Quint , 2, transf , a, *to try, prove, test*, alicuius patientiam, Cic , se, Cic , b, *to try, attempt*, oppugnationem eius castelli, Liv , belli fortunam, Cic , Thetim ratibus, Verg , with rel sent , tentari, quid in eo genere possem, Cic , with ut and the subj , quum ille Romuli senatus tentaret, ut ipse gereret rempublicam, Cic , with infin , irasci, Verg II. *to attack, assail*, 1, lit , Achaiam, Caes , castra, Liv , of diseases, morbo tentari, Cic , 2, transf , *to work upon, tamper with a person, tempt, excite, disturb*, animos spe et metu, Cic , judicium pecuniā, *to try to bribe*, Cic

tentōrĭŏlum -i, n (dim of tentorium), *a little tent*, Auct b Afr

tentōrium -ii, n (tendo), *a tent*, Liv

tentus a -um, partic of tendo and teneo

Tentȳra -ōrum, n (Τέντυρα), *a town in Upper Egypt*, now *Denderah*

tĕnŭĭcŭlus -a um (dim of tenuis), *very poor, mean, miserable*, apparatus, Cic

tĕnŭis -e (root TEN). I. *thin, fine, slight, slender* A. Lit , 1, gen , collum, Cic , acus, Ov , 2, esp , a, *small, narrow*, litus, Liv , b, *shallow*, unda, Ov , sulcus, Verg , c, *bright, clear*, aqua, Ov B. Fig , a, *thin, plain, simple*, argumentandi genus, Cic , b, *fine, subtle*, distinctio, Cic II. Transf , *weak, poor, miserable, unimportant, little, slight* A. Lit , oppidum, Cic , opes, Cic , praeda, Caes , transf , of persons, *poor, needy*, Cic B. Fig , a, *poor, weak, feeble*, valetudo tenuissima, Caes , causa tenuis et inops, Cic , spes, Cic , b, of birth or position, *low, mean*, qui tenuioris ordinis essent, Cic transf , of persons, tenues homines, Cic Subst , tenuiores, *persons of lower rank*, Cic

tĕnŭĭtas -ātis, f (tenuis) I. *thinness, fineness* A. Lit , 1, gen , animi, Cic , 2, esp , *leanness*, tenuitas ipsa delectat, Cic B. Fig , *simplicity, plainness*, rerum et verborum, Cic II. Transf , *miserable condition, poverty*, aerarii, Cic , hominis, Cic

tĕnŭĭtĕr, adv (tenuis) I. *thinly* A. Lit , alutae tenuiter confectae, Caes B. Fig , *plainly, simply*, disserere, Cic II. Transf , *sparingly* A. Lit., Ter B. Fig , *lightly*, tenuissime aestimare, Cic.

tĕnŭo, 1. (tenuis). **I.** *to make thin, fine, slender, meagre, to attenuate;* **1,** lit., assiduo vomer tenuatur ab usu, Ov.; **2,** esp., **a,** *to make thin;* armenta macie, Verg.; **b,** *to contract;* vocis via est tenuata, Ov. **II.** Fig., *to weaken, lessen, diminish, enfeeble;* iram, Ov.; vires, Ov.

1. **tĕnŭs** -ŏris, n. (root TEN, whence tendo), *a noose, gin, springe,* Plaut.

2. **tĕnŭs**, prep. with abl. and genit. (connected with teneo, tendo, τείνω), *up to, as far as.* **I.** Of place, **a,** with genit., crurum tenus, Verg.; Corcyrae tenus, Liv.; **b,** with abl., Tauro tenus regnare, Cic.; cadi faece tenus poti, Hor. **II.** Transf., est quadam prodire tenus, si non datur ultra, *up to a certain point,* Hor.; vulneribus tenus, Liv.; verbo tenus, *in name, nominally,* Cic.

Tĕŏs -i, f. (Τέως), *a town on the coast of Ionia, birthplace of Anacreon;* hence, **Tējus** -a -um, and **Tēĭus** -a -um, *Teian,* poet. = *Anacreontic,* Ov.

tĕpĕfăcĭo -fēci -factum, 3., pass., **tĕpĕfīo** -factus sum -fĭĕri (tepeo and facio), *to make warm, to warm, heat;* sol tepefaciat solum, Cic.

tĕpĕo, 2. *to be lukewarm, tepid.* **I.** Lit., hiems tepet, Hor.; partic., tepens, *warm;* aurae, Verg. **II.** Fig. **1,** *to be warm with love;* aliquo, *for some one,* Hor.; **2,** *to be only lukewarm in love;* seu tepet, sive amat, Ov.

tĕpesco, tĕpŭi, 3. (tepeo). **A.** *to grow warm;* maria agitata ventis ita tepescunt, ut, etc., Cic. **B.** *to lose warmth, grow cool,* Mart.

tephrĭas -ae, m. (τεφρίας), *a species of ash-coloured stone,* Plin.

tĕpĭdē, adv. (tepidus), *lukewarmly,* Plin.

tĕpĭdo, 1. (tepidus), *to make lukewarm,* Plin.

tĕpĭdus -a -um (tepeo). **I.** *lukewarm, tepid;* bruma, Hor. **II.** *lukewarm, cooling;* **1,** lit., focus, Ov.; **2,** fig., *wanting in ardour;* ignes, mens, Ov.

tĕpor -ōris, m. (tepeo). **I.** *lukewarmness, a moderate heat;* solis, Liv.; maris, Cic. **II.** Fig., of discourse, *want of fire,* Tac.

tĕpōrātus -a -um (tepor), *made lukewarm,* Plin.

Tĕpŭla ăqua, *a stream of water which was brought to the Capitol at Rome,* Plin.

tĕr, adv. num. (tres), *three times, thrice.* **I.** Lit., ter in anno, Cic. **II.** Meton., **a,** *often, repeatedly;* Aeneam magnā ter voce vocavit, Verg.; **b,** = *very;* ter felix, Ov.

terdĕcĭēs (terdĕcĭens), adv. *thirteen times,* Cic.

tĕrĕbinthĭnus -a -um (τερεβίνθινος), *of the terebinth-tree,* Plin.

tĕrĕbinthus -i, f. (τερέβινθος), *the terebinth-tree,* Verg.

tĕrĕbra -ae, f. (tero), *a gimlet, borer,* Cato.

tĕrĕbro, 1. (terebra), *to bore through, pierce, perforate;* latebras uteri, Verg.

tĕrēdo -ĭnis, f. (τερηδών), *a worm that gnaws wood,* Ov.

Tĕrentĭus -a -um, *the name of a Roman gens, of which the most celebrated were:* **1,** C. Terentius Varro, *consul* 216 B.C., *defeated by Hannibal at Cannae;* **2,** M. Terentius Varro, *born* 116 B.C., *a celebrated grammarian, contemporary of Cicero;* **3,** P. Terentius Afer, *freedman of P. Terentius Lucanus, the celebrated Roman comic dramatist, contemporary of Laelius and Scipio Africanus;* **4,** Terentia, *the wife of Cicero.* Adj., **Tĕrentĭus** -a -um, *Terentian;* lex, *law proposed by the consuls Cassius and M. Terentius.* Hence, **Tĕrentĭānus** -a -um, *Terentian;* exercitus, *of C. Terentius Varro,* Liv.; Chremes, *appearing in the comedies of Terence,* Cic.

Tĕrentum (Tărentum) -i, n., **Tĕrentŏs (-us)**, and **Tărentŏs (-us)** -i, m. *a place in the Campus Martius, where the* ludi saeculares *were held.* Hence, **Tĕrentīnus** -a -um, *Terentine.*

tĕrĕs -rĕtis, abl. -rĕti (root TER, Gr. TEP, τείρω), *rounded, polished, well-turned.* **I.** stipes, Caes.; gemma, Verg.; hence, fig., sapiens in se ipso totus teres atque rotundus, Hor. **II.** *firmly-woven;* plagae, Hor. **III.** Of the parts of the body, *well-turned, slender, graceful:* **1,** lit., cervix, Lucr.; sura, Hor.; **2,** fig., *polished, refined, elegant;* aures, oratio, Cic.

Tēreus -ĕi and -ĕos, m. (Τηρεύς), *king in Thrace, husband of Procne, sister of Philomela, father of Itys, who outraged Philomela, and for punishment was changed into a hoopoe.* Hence, **Tērĕĭdēs** -ae, m. (Τηρεΐδης), *the son of Tereus,* i.e., *Itys.*

tergĕmĭnus = trigeminus (q.v.).

tergĕo and **tergo**, tersi, tersum -ēre and -ĕre (root TER, whence tero), *to wipe, wipe off, dry, clean,* Cic.; lumina lacrimantia tersit, Ov.; specula, *to polish,* Verg.; arma, Liv.

Tergestĕ -is, n. *a town in Istria, now Trieste.* Hence, **Tergestīnus** -a -um, *Tergestine.*

tergīnum -i, n. (tergum), *a whip of leather, thong for scourging,* Plaut.

tergĭversātĭo -ōnis, f. (tergiversor), *backwardness, reluctance, delay;* mora et tergiversatio, Cic.

tergĭversor, 1. dep. (tergum and verto), *to turn the back,* hence, *to be reluctant, shuffle, find excuses, to delay;* quid taces? quid dissimulas? quid tergiversaris? Cic.

tergŏro, 1. (tergus), *to cover,* Plin.

tergo = tergeo (q.v.).

tergum -i, n. *the back.* **I.** Lit., Cic.; terga dare, Liv., vertere, Caes., *to turn one's back, flee;* a tergo, *from behind,* Cic.; praebere terga Phoebo, *to sun oneself,* Ov.; plur., terga, meton. = *flight;* terga Parthorum dicam, Ov. **II.** Transf., **1,** *the hindmost part of a thing;* castris ab tergo vallum objectum, *from behind,* Liv.; **2,** *the surface of anything;* e.g., of a field, *the earth ploughed up between the furrows,* Verg.; of a river, Ov.; **3,** *a covering;* clipei, Verg.; **4,** *a body;* centum terga suum, *a hundred swine,* Verg.; **5,** *the hide, skin;* **a,** lit., taurinum, Verg.; **b,** meton., *things made out of hide;* Sulmonis, *shield,* Verg.; duro intendere brachia tergo, *the cestus,* Verg.

tergus -ŏris, n. *the back.* **I.** Lit., Prop. **II.** Transf., **1,** *the body of an animal,* Ov.; **2,** *skin, hide, leather,* Verg.

Tĕrīna -ae, f. *a town in Bruttii, near modern Eufemia.* Hence, **Tĕrīnaeus** -a -um, *of or belonging to Terina.*

termes -ĭtis, m. *a branch cut off a tree;* olivae, Hor.

Termessus -i, f. (Τερμησσός), *a town in Pisidia.* Hence, **Termessenses** -ium, m. *the inhabitants of Termessus.*

Termĭnālĭa -ĭum and -ĭōrum (Terminus), n. *the Festival of Terminus, on the 23rd of February.*

termĭnātĭo -ōnis, f. (termino), *a limiting, bounding.* **I.** Lit., Liv. **II.** Transf., **1,** *a fixing, ordaining, determining;* versus inventus est terminatione aurium, Cic.; **2,** rhet. t.t., *the end, termination of a period;* ordo verborum alias aliā terminatione concluditur, Cic.

termĭno, 1. (terminus), *to bound, limit, set bounds to.* **I.** Lit., finem loci quem oleae terminabant, Cic. **II.** Transf., **1,** *to limit;* **a,** *to restrain, restrict;* sonos vocis paucis litterarum notis, Cic.; **b,** *to define, determine;* bona voluptāte, mala dolore, Cic , 2, *to close, end, terminate*, orationem, Cic

terminus i, m (root TER, whence termen, termo, Gr TEP, whence τερμα), *a boundary mark, limit, boundary* I. Lit , a, mulli possessionum terminum, Cic.; b, personif , Terminus, *the god of boundaries*, Ov II Transf , 1, *limit, bound, object* , certos mihi fines terminosque constituam, extra quos egredi non possim, Cic , 2, *end, conclusion* , contentionum, Cic

terni -ae -a (ter) I. *three each*, Cic , sing , terno ordine, Verg. II. *three together*, Verg

tĕro, trivi, tritum, 3 (root TER, whence τειρω), *to rub* I. Gen , A. Lit , 1, dentes in stipite, Ov , calcem = *to overtake in running*, Verg , calamo labellum = *to play the flute*, Verg , 2, esp , a, *to rub for the sake of cleaning or ornamenting, to smoothe, adorn* crura pumice, Ov b, *to turn* (at a lathe) , radios rotis, Verg , c, *to thresh out* corn , milia frumenti, Hor d, of places, *to visit, frequent* , iter, Verg B. Transf , 1, *to read often, have often in the hands use often*, quod legeret tereretque viritim publicus usus, Hor , 2, fig , *to use often in discourse* , verbum, Cic II. A. *to rub, bruise, grind*, bacam, Verg B. *to rub off, wear away*, 1, lit , silices, Ov , 2, fig , a, *to tire oneself*, se in opere longinquo, Liv ; b, *to pass away* time , interea tempus, Cic (syncop perf , tristi, Cat)

Terpsĭchŏrē ēs, f (Τερψιχορή), *the muse of dancing*, hence = *muse, poetry*, Juv

terra -ae, f (root TER, whence torreo), lit , *that which is dry*, hence, *the earth* (as opp to heavens, sea, air), *land, ground, soil* I. a, *the earth*, terrae motus, *earthquake*, Cic ; terrā, *by land*, Cic , terrā marique, *by land and sea*, Cic , in terris, *on the earth* Hor , sub terras ire, *to visit the lower world*, Verg , b, *the earth = the ground, the soil*, gleba terrae, Liv ; mihi terram inice, Verg , terrae filius, *a son of the earth, an unknown person*, Cic , ea quae gignuntur e terra, Cic , c, *the earth = the surface of the earth, ground* , de terra saxa tollere, Cic , d, *a particular country, land, region* , abire in alias terras, Cic , plur , terrae, *the world*, has terras incolentes, Cic ; orbis terrarum, *the world*, Cic ; genit plur often partitive, with adv of place, ubi terrarum sumus? *where in the world are we?* Cic II. Personif , Terra, *the earth as a goddess*, gen , Tellus, Cic.

Terracīna, Terracinensis = Tarracina, Tarracinensis (q v)

terrēnus -a -um (terra) I. *earthy, earthen*, tumulus, Caes , genus, Cic Subst , **terrēnum** i, n *land, ground*, herbidum, Liv II. 1, *belonging to the earth, terrene, terrestrial*, bestiae, *land-animals*, Cic., humor, *moisture of the earth*, Cic , poet , numina, *of the lower world*, Ov , 2, *earthy* (opp caelestis), eques, *mortal*, Hor

terrĕo, terrŭi, territum, 2 *to frighten, terrify* I. Gen , aliquem, Cic , with ne and the subj , Liv II. 1, *to frighten away, scare away*, profugam per totum orbem, Ov , 2, *to frighten, deter*, a repetunda libertate, Sall , with ne and the subj , Liv , with quominus and the subj , Caes

terrestĕr -tris -tre, gen , **terrestris** -e (terra), 1, *terrestrial* (opp marinus), animantium genus terrestre, Cic , terrestres navalesque pugnae, Cic , 2, *found on the earth, earthly* (opp caelestis), res caelestes atque terrestres, Cic , Capitolium terrestre domicilium Jovis, Cic

terrĕus a -um (terra), *made of earth, earthly*, progenies, Verg

terrĭbĭlis -e (terreo), *terrible, frightful, fearful, dreadful* , a, of things, sonus, Liv , mors est terribilis iis, etc , Cic , with 2. supine, terribiles visu formae, Verg , neut plur subst , majora ac terribiliora afferre, Liv , b, of persons, jam ipsi urbi terribilis erat, Liv , with 2 supine, quam terribilis aspectu, Cic

terrĭcŭla ae, f and **terrĭcŭlum** i, n. (terreo), *something that causes fright*, abl plur , terriculis, Liv

terrĭfĭco, 1 (terrificus), *to frighten, terrify*, Verg

terrĭfĭcus a -um (terreo and facio), *causing terror, frightful, terrible*, Verg

terrĭgĕna ae, c (terra and gigno), *earth-born, sprung from the earth*, Lucr , Ov

terripavium, terripudium = tripudium (q v).

terrĭto, 1 (intens of terreo), *to frighten, scare, terrify* , a, of persons, aliquem metu, Caes , b, of things, tribunicium domi bellum patres territat, Liv

terrĭtōrĭum ii, n (terra), *the land belonging to a town, district, territory* , coloniae, Cic

terror -ōris, m (terreo), *fright, fear terror, dread, panic* I. Lit , with subject genit , exercitus, Caes , with object. genit (*on account of*), belli, Cic minis et terrore commoveri, Cic , attulit terrorem hostibus, Caes , alicui terrori esse, Caes facere terrorem et militibus et ipsi Appio, Liv , incutere alicui terrorem, Liv , inferre terrorem alicui, Cic , injicere alicui terrorem, Caes II. Meton , a, *the object which causes terror*, terra repleta est trepido terrore, Lucr , plur , huius urbis terrores (Carthage and Numantia), Cic , b, *news causing terror* , Romam tanti terrores erant allati, Liv , also *threatening or frightening expressions* , non mediocres terrores jacĕre atque denuntiare, Cic , or, *events causing terror* , caelestes maritimique terrores, Liv III. Personif , Terror, Ov

tersus -a -um, p. adj (from tergeo) *wiped* I. Lit , *clean, neat*, mulier, Plaut , plantae, Ov II Fig , *free from mistakes, neat*, judicium, Quint

tertĭādĕcĭmāni -orum, m (tertius decimus), *soldiers of the thirteenth legion*, Tac

tertĭānus -a -um (tertius), *belonging to the third* I. *to the third day*, febris, *tertian fever*, i e , *recurring every third day*, Cic , subst , **tertĭāna** -ae, f *a tertian fever*, Plin II. *belonging to the third legion* , subst , **tertĭāni** ōrum, m *soldiers of the third legion*, Tac.

tertĭārĭus -a um (tertius), *containing one-third*, stannum, *containing one-third tin with two-thirds lead*, Plin

tertĭō, adv (tertius) I. *for the third time*, tertio pecuniam dedit, Cic II. *thirdly*, Caes

tertĭum, adv (tertius), *for the third time*, Cic

tertĭus -a um (ter), *the third*. I. Adj , pars, Caes , tertio quoque verbo, *always at the third word*, Cic , tertius e nobis, *one of us three*, Ov , tertia regna, *the lower world*, Ov , tertia Saturnalia, *the third day of the Saturnalia*, Cic , ab Jove tertius Ajax, *of the third generation, great grandson*, Ov II. Subst , **tertĭae** -ārum, f a, *one-third*, Plin , b, *the third or inferior part in a play*, Plin.

tertĭusdĕcĭmus a -um, *the thirteenth*, Cic

tĕruncĭus -ii, m (ter or tres and uncia), *three twelfth parts* I. *the fourth part of an as*, Cic , prov , ne teruncius quidem, *not a farthing*, Cic II *the fourth part of an inheritance* , heres ex teruncio, *heir to one-fourth of the property*, Cic

tervĕnēfĭcus -i, m *an arch-poisoner, a double-dyed rogue*, Plaut,

tesca (tesqua) -ōrum, n. (with or without loca), *wastes, deserts*, Hor.

tessella -ae, f. (dim. of tessera), *a small cube of marble or other substance used for pavements*, or *for playing dice*, Juv.

tessellātus -a -um (tessella), *set with small cubes*; pavimentum, *mosaic*, Suet.

tessĕra -ae, f. (τέσσαρα), *a cube of wood, stone, or other substance used for various purposes.* **I.** *a piece of mosaic for paving*, Plin. **II.** *a die for playing*; tesseras jacĕre, Cic. **III.** *a token*; **1,** *a square tablet on which the military watch-word was written*; hence, meton. = *the watch-word*; omnibus tesseram dare, Liv.; **2,** *a tablet* or *token which entitled the holder to receive money* or *provisions*, Juv.; **3,** hospitalis, *a token of hospitality* (a small die, which friends broke into two parts), Plaut.

tessĕrārĭus -ii, m. (tessera), *the officer who received from the general the ticket* (tessera) *on which the watchword was written, and communicated it to the army*, Tac.

tessĕrŭla -ae, f. (dim. of tessera), **1,** *a little cube of stone for paving*, ap. Cic.; **2,** *a little voting-ticket*, Varr.; **3,** *a ticket for the distribution of food*, Pers.

testa -ae, f. (perhaps = tosta), *burnt clay.* **I.** Lit., **1,** *an earthen vessel, pot, pitcher, jug, urn*; vinum Graecā testā conditum, Hor.; **2,** *a brick, a tile*, Cic.; **3,** *a potsherd*, Ov.; esp., *the potsherd used in voting by the Greeks*; testarum suffragia, *ostracism*, Nep. **II.** Transf., **1,** *the shell of shell-fish*, Cic.; **2,** meton., *a shell-fish*, Hor.; **3,** poet., transf., *shell, covering = ice*; lubrica testa, Ov.

testācĕus -a -um (testa). **I. 1,** *made of bricks* or *tiles*, Plin.; subst., **testācĕum** -i, n. *brick-work*, Plin.; **2,** *brick-coloured*, Plin. **II.** Of animals, *covered with a shell, testaceous*, Plin.

testāmentārĭus -a -um (testamentum), *of* or *relating to a will, testamentary*; subst., **testāmentārĭus** -ii, m. *a forger of wills*, Cic.

testāmentum -i, n. (testor), *a last will, testament*; id testamento cavere, *to provide*, Cic.; conscribere testamentum, Cic.; testamentum facere, Cic.; irritum facere testamentum, *to annul*, Cic.; obsignare testamentum, Caes.; relinquere alicui testamento sestertium milies, Cic.

testātĭo -ōnis, f. (testor). **I.** *a calling to witness*; ruptorum foederum, Liv. **II.** *a bearing witness*, Quint.

testātor -ōris, m. (testor), *one that makes a will, a testator*, Suet.

testātus -a -um, p. adj. (from testor), *attested, proved, clear*; res, Cic.; quo notior testatiorque virtus eius esset, Caes.

testĭcŭlus -i, m. (dim. of 2. testis), *a testicle*, Pers.

testĭfĭcātĭo -ōnis, f. (testificor). **I.** *a bearing witness, testifying*; hāc testificatione uti, Cic. **II.** Transf., *attestation, evidence, proof*; officiorum, Cic.

testĭfĭcor, 1. dep. (testis and facio). **I.** *to call to witness*; deos hominesque, ap. Cic. **II.** *to bear witness, testify*; **1,** lit., testificor me esse rogatum, Cic.; **2,** transf., *to show, publish, bring to light*; partic. pass., abs te testificata voluntas, Cic.

testĭmōnĭum -ii, n. (1. testis), *witness, evidence, testimony.* **I.** Lit., testimonium in aliquem dicere, Cic.; of a written attestation, testimonium componere, obsignare, Cic. **II.** Transf., in general, *a proof, evidence, indication*; dedisti judicii tui testimonium, Cic.

1. **testis** -is, c. *one who gives evidence, a witness.* **I.** Lit., testis falsus, Cic.; testes dare in singulas res, Cic.; testes adhibere, Cic. **II.** Transf. = arbiter, *an eye-witness, spectator*, Ov.

2. **testis** -is, m. *a testicle*, Hor.

testor, 1. dep. (1. testis). **I.** *to bear witness, to give evidence of, to make known, publish, declare, assert, testify*; utraeque vim testantur, Cic.; pass., *to be attested, declared*; testata est voce praeconis libertas Argivorum, Liv. **II.** *to call to witness*; **1,** gen., omnes deos, Cic.; **2,** esp., *to make a will*; de filii pupilli re, Cic.

testū, indecl. and **testum** -i, n. (perhaps = tostu, tostum, as testa = tosta), *an earthen pot, a pot*, Ov.

testŭātĭum -ii, n. (testu), *a cake baked in an earthen pan*, Varr.

testūdĭnĕus -a -um (testudo). **I.** *like a tortoise*; gradus, Plaut. **II.** *adorned with* or *made of tortoise-shell*; lyra, Prop.

testūdo -ĭnis, f. (testa), *a tortoise.* **I.** Lit., Liv. **II.** Meton., **A.** *the shell of the tortoise*, used for ornamenting furniture; varii testudine postes, Verg. **B. 1,** *a curved string-instrument, the lyre, cithara*, etc., Hor.; transf., *a way of dressing the hair of similar form*, Ov.; **2,** *a room with a vaulted roof*, Cic.; **3,** milit. t.t., **a,** *a shed to protect soldiers while attacking fortifications*, Caes.; **b,** *a formation in which soldiers charged, holding their shields over their heads*, Caes.

testŭla -ae, f. (dim. of testa), *a potsherd, an Athenian voting-ticket*; meton., *ostracism*; a Themistocle collabefactus testulā illā, Nep.

tĕtănĭcus -a -um (τετανικός), *suffering from lockjaw*, Plin.

tĕtănus -i, m. (τέτανος), *lockjaw*, Plin.

tĕtartēmŏrion -ii, n. (τεταρτημόριον), *the fourth part of the zodiac*, Plin.

tēter (taeter) -tra -trum, *foul, noisome, hideous, offensive.* **I.** Lit., to the senses, odor, Cic.; tenebrae, Cic.; with 2. supine, illud teterrimum non modo aspectu, sed etiam auditu, Cic. **II.** Transf., *hateful, hideous, disgraceful, shameful, abominable*; homo, Cic.; quis tetrior hostis huic civitati? Cic.; sententia teterrima, Cic.

tĕthălassōmĕnos -i, m. (τεθαλασσωμένος οἶνος), *wine mixed with sea-water*, Plin.

Tēthys -thȳos, acc. -thyn, f. (Τηθύς). **I.** *a marine goddess, wife of Oceanus, mother of the river-gods and sea-nymphs.* **II.** Poet., appell. = *the sea*, Cat.

tĕtrachmum -i, genit. plur. -ōrum and -ūm, n. (τέτραχμον), *a Greek coin of four drachmae*, Liv.

tĕtrăchordos -on (τετράχορδος), *having four notes*; subst., **tĕtrăchordon** -i, n. *harmony of four notes, a tetrachord*, Varr.

tĕtrăcōlon -i, n. (τετράκωλον), *a period having four clauses*, Sen.

tĕtrādrachmum = tetrachmum (q.v.).

tĕtragnăthius -ii, m. (τετράγναθος), *a poisonous spider*, Plin.

tĕtrălix -icis, f. (τετράλιξ), *the plant heath*, Plin.

tĕtrăo -ōnis, m. (τετράων), *a heathcock*, Plin.

tĕtrarches and **tĕtrarcha** -ae, m. (τετράρχης), *the ruler over one-fourth of a country, a tetrarch*, Cic.

tĕtrarchia -ae, f. (τετραρχία), *the country governed by a tetrarch, tetrarchy*, Cic.

tĕtrastĭchā -ōn, n. plur. (τετράστιχα), *a poem consisting of four lines*, Quint.

tĕtrē (taetrē), adv. (teter), *foully, hideously, noisomely, offensively*, multa facere impure atque tetre, Cic, religionem impurissime teterrimeque violasse, Cic.

1 **tĕtrĭcus** -a -um, *harsh, gloomy, severe, forbidding*, puella, Ov, deae, *the Parcae*, Mart

2 **Tĕtrĭcus** mons, *a mountain in the Sabine country*, now *Monte S Giovanni*; poet subst, **Tĕtrĭca** -ae, f (sc rupes), Verg

tettīgŏmētra -ae, f (τεττιγομήτρα), *the larva of the cicada*, Plin

tettīgŏnĭa ae, f. (τεττιγονία), *a species of small cicada*, Plin

tĕtŭli = tuli, v tulo

Teucer -cri, m. and **Teucrus** -i, m (Τεῦκρος) **I.** (Teucer and Teucrus) *son of Telamon, king of Salamis, brother of Ajax, who, after his return from Troy, sailed away to Cyprus* **II.** (Teucrus), *son of Scamander, first king of Troy*, hence, a, **Teucrus** -a -um, *Teucrian*, poet = *Trojan*; b, **Teucrĭus** -a -um, *Teucrian*, poet = *Trojan* Subst, **Teucri** -ōrum, m *the Trojans*

teuchītis -idis, f (τευχῖτις), *a species of aromatic rush*, Plin

teucrĭon -ii, n (τεύκριον), *the plant called germander*, Plin

Teucrĭus, Teucrius, v Teucer.

Teuthrās -thrantis, m (Τεύθρας) **I.** *a river in Campania* **II.** *a king in Mysia, father of Thespius* Hence, **A. Teuthrānĭa** ae, f *a district in Mysia* **B. Teuthrantēus** -a -um, *Mysian* **C. Teuthrantĭus** -a -um, *of* or *belonging to Teuthras*; turba, *the fifty sisters and daughters of Thespius*, Ov **III.** *a soldier of Turnus*.

Teutŏni -ōrum, m and **Teutŏnes** um, m *a collective name of the German peoples, a branch of which invaded the Roman Empire with the Cimbri, and were defeated by C Marius* Hence, **Teutŏnĭcus** -a um, *Teuton*, and poet. = *German*.

texo, texŭi, textum, 3 *to weave* **I.** tegumenta corporum vel texta vel suta, Cic **II.** *to weave, twine together, intertwine, plait, construct, build*, casas ex arundine, Liv, basilicam in medio foro, Cic, fig, epistolas quotidianis verbis, *to compose*, Cic

textĭlis -e (texo) **I.** *woven, textile*, stragulum, Cic. Subst, **textĭle** -is, n (sc opus), *a woven fabric, a piece of cloth*. **II.** *plaited, braided*, Mart

textor -ōris, m (texo), *a weaver*, Hor

textōrĭus a -um (textor), *of* or *relating to weaving*, Sen

textrīnus a -um (for textorinus, from textor), *relating to weaving* Subst, **textrīnum** -i, n *weaving*, Cic

textrix -trīcis, f (f of textor), *a female weaver*, Mart

textum -i, n (texo) **I.** *that which is woven, a web*, a, lit, Ov, b, *that which is plaited, woven, fitted, put together in any way, a fabric*, pinea (navis), Ov.; clipei, Verg **II** Fig, of written composition, *texture, style*, Quint

textūra -ae, f (texo) **I.** *a web, texture*, Plaut. **II.** Transf, *a putting together, connexion*, Lucr

textus -ūs, m (texo) **I.** *a web*, and transf, *texture, structure*, Lucr **II.** Fig, of discourse, *mode of putting together, connexion*, Quint.

Thăĭs -idos, f (Θαΐς), *a celebrated hetaira of Athens, afterwards wife of Ptolemaeus I. of Egypt.*

Thala -ae, f *a town in Numidia*, now *Ferreanah*.

thălămēgus -i, f (θαλαμηγός), *a barge or gondola provided with cabins*, Suet.

thălămus i, m (θάλαμος), *a room in the interior of a house* **I.** *a living room*, Ov, hence, *a place of abode, dwelling*, Eumenidum, Verg, of the cells of bees, Verg **II.** *a bed room*, a, lit, Ov, b, *a marriage bed*, Verg, hence, meton, *marriage*, vita expers thalami, *unmarried*, Verg, thalamos ne desere pactos, *the promised bride*, Verg

thalassĭcus -a um (θαλασσικός), *sea-green*, Plaut

thalassĭnus a um (θαλάσσιος), *sea-green*, Lucr

Thălassĭo, Thalassius, etc, v Talassio

thălassītes -ae, m (θαλασσίτης), *wine which has been sunk in the sea to be ripened*, Plin

thălassŏmĕli, n (θαλασσόμελι), *honey mixed with sea-water*, Plin

Thălēa = Thalia (q v)

Thăles lis and lētis, m (Θαλῆς), *a philosopher of Miletus, one of the Seven Wise Men of Greece*

Thălīa -ae, f (Θάλεια) **I.** *the Muse of comic poetry* **II.** *one of the sea-nymphs*

thallus -i, m (θαλλός), *a green branch*, Verg

Thămyras ae, m and **Thămyris** idis, m (Θάμυρις), *a Thracian poet, who entered into a contest with the Muses, and being conquered was deprived of his lyre and eyes*

Thapsus (-ŏs) -i, f (Θάψος) **I.** *a peninsula and town in Sicily* **II.** *a town in Africa Propria, where Caesar conquered the Pompeians*

Thăsus (-ŏs) -i, f (Θάσος), *an island in the Aegean Sea* Adj, **Thăsĭus** -a -um, *Thasian*

Thaumās -antis, m (Θαύμας), *father of Iris* Hence, **A. Thaumantēus** -a -um, *of Thaumas*, virgo, *Iris*, Ov **B Thaumantĭās** ădis, f *daughter of Thaumas*, i e, *Iris* **C. Thaumantĭs** -idos, f = Thaumantias

theamēdes, acc -en, m *an Ethiopian stone, perhaps tourmaline*, Plin

thĕātrālis -e (theatrum), *of* or *relating to a theatre, theatrical*, consessus, Cic.

thĕātrum -i, n (θέατρον) **I.** *a theatre*, 1, lit, a, gen, *for dramatic performances*, Cic, b, *an open place for the exhibition of games*, Verg, 2, meton, a, *the people assembled in the theatre, the audience*, theatra tota reclamant, Cic, b, transf, *spectators, assemblage*, senatus consultum frequentissimo theatro (populi) comprobatum, Cic **II.** Fig, *the sphere, theatre for any action*, forum populi Romani quasi theatrum illius ingenii, Cic

Thēbae ārum, f (Θῆβαι) **I.** *a city of Upper Egypt* **II.** *a city of Boeotia, founded by Cadmus, the birthplace of Pindar* **III.** Thebae Phthioticae or Phthiae, *a town in Thessalia Phthiotis*, now *Armiro* **IV.** *a town in Mysia, residence of Action, father-in-law of Hector, destroyed by Achilles* Hence, **A. Thēbāĭs** -idis and idos, f 1, *belonging to Thebes in Egypt*, 2, *belonging to Thebes in Boeotia*, Thebaides, *Theban women*, Ov, 3, *belonging to Thebes in Mysia* **B. Thēbānus** -a um, 1, *belonging to Thebes in Boeotia*, modi, Pindaric, Ov, dea, *Ino (Leukotheq, Matuta)*, Ov, mater, *Agave*, Ov, soror, *Antigone*, Ov, semina, *the dragon's teeth sown by Cadmus*, Ov, duces, *Eteocles and Polynices*, Prop; deus, *Hercules*, Prop, subst, **Thēbānus** i, m *a Theban*; 2, *belonging to Thebes in Mysia*, subst., Thebana, *Andromache*, Ov

Thēbē -ēs, f (Θήβη) **I.** = Thebae **II.** *a nymph, beloved by the river god Asopus* **III.** *wife of the tyrant Alexander of Pherae.*

thē[illegible] -ae, f. (θήκη), *a case, sheath, envelope, covering*; vasa sine theca, Cic.

Thelxinŏē -ēs, f. *one of the first four Muses.*

thēlyphŏnon = aconitum (q.v.).

thēlyptĕris -idis, f. (θηλυπτερίς), *the female fern plant*, Plin.

thēma -ătis, n. (θέμα). **I.** *the theme, topic, subject of discourse*, Sen. **II.** *the position of the heavenly bodies at the moment of a birth*, Suet.

Thēmis -idis, f. (Θέμις), *the goddess of justice, also regarded as the goddess of prophecy.*

Thĕmista -ae, f. and **Thĕmistē** -ēs, f. *an Epicurean philosopher of Lampsacus.*

Thĕmistŏclēs -is and -i, m. (Θεμιστοκλῆς), *the celebrated general of the Athenians in the Persian War.* Hence, **Thĕmistŏclēus** -a -um, *Themistoclean.*

Thĕŏcrĭtus -i, m. (Θεόκριτος), *the famous Greek bucolic poet, born at Syracuse, flourished* 281-250 B.C.

Thĕŏdectēs -is and -i, m. (Θεοδέκτης), *Greek orator of Cilicia, teacher of Isocrates and Aristotle.*

Thĕŏdōrus -i, m. (Θεόδωρος). **I.** Of Byzantium, *a Greek sophist.* **II.** Of Cyrene, *a Greek sophist.* **III.** *a famous rhetorician of Gadara, teacher of Tiberius.*

Thĕŏgŏnĭa -ae, f. (Θεογονία), *the Theogony,* or *Generation of the Gods, a poem by Hesiod*, Cic.

thĕŏlŏgus -i, m. (θεολόγος), *a theologian, one who treats of the descent and existence of the gods*, Cic.

Thĕŏphănō -ēs, f. (Θεοφάνη), *daughter of Bisaltes, mother by Poseidon of the ram which bore Phrixus to Colchis.*

Thĕŏphănēs -is and -i, m. (Θεοφάνης), *a historian, friend of Pompeius.*

Thĕŏphrastus -i, m. (Θεόφραστος), *a celebrated Greek philosopher of the town of Cresos in Lesbos, pupil of Plato and Aristotle.*

Thĕŏpompus -i, m. (Θεόπομπος). **I.** *a celebrated Greek historian of Chios, pupil of Isocrates.* **II.** *a dependent of Caesar's.* **III.** *a dependent of Cicero's in Asia.*

Thēra -ae, f. (Θήρα), *an island in the Cretan Sea*, now *Santorin.* Hence, **Thēraeus** -a -um, *Theraean.*

Thērămĕnēs -ae, m. (Θηραμένης), *of Chios* or *Ceos, adopted son of the Athenian Hagnon, one of the thirty tyrants at Athens, but put to death for opposing the oppressions of his colleagues Critias and Charicles.*

Thĕrapnē (Thĕramnē) -ēs, f. and **Thĕrapnae** -ārum, f. (Θεράπναι), *a town of Laconia, the birthplace of Helen*; hence, adj., **Thĕrapnaeus** -a -um, *Therapnean*; poet., *Spartan*; marita, or nata rure Therapnaeo, *Helen*, Ov.; sanguis Therapnaeus (of the boy Hyacinthus of Amyclae), Ov.

thērĭăcus -a -um (θηριακός), *serviceable against animal poison*, esp., *the bite of serpents*, Plin. Subst., **thērĭăca** -ae, f. and **thērĭăcē** -ēs, f. *an antidote against the bite of poisonous serpents*, Plin.

Thērĭclēs -is, m. (Θηρικλῆς), *a celebrated artist, maker of pottery and wooden vessels at Corinth.* Hence, **Thērĭclius** -a -um (Θηρίκλειος), *Therclean*; pocula, *drinking-cups of clay* or *wood*, Cic.

thermae -ārum, f. (θερμός, *warm*). **I.** *warm baths*, Plin. **II.** Proper name, **Thermae** -ārum, f. *a town with warm springs on the north coast of Sicily*, now *Sciacca.* Hence, **Thermitānus** -a -um, *of* or *belonging to Thermae.*

Thermē -ēs, f. (Θέρμη), *a town in Macedonia, afterwards called Thessalonica.* Hence, **Thermaeus** -a -um, *Thermaean*; sinus, now *il Golfo di Salonichi.*

thermĭnus -a -um (θέρμινος), *made of lupines*, Plin.

Thermōdōn -ontis, m. (Θερμώδων), *a river in Pontus, on which the Amazons lived*, now *Terma.* Hence, **Thermōdontēus (-tĭăcus)** -a -um, poet. = *Amazonian.*

thermŏpōlĭum -ii, n. (θερμοπώλιον), *a place where warm drinks are sold*, Plaut.

thermŏpōto, 1. *to refresh with warm drinks*, Plaut.

Thermŏpўlae -ārum, f. (Θερμοπύλαι), *a pass in Locris, on the borders of Thessaly, where Leonidas and a small body of Spartans fell fighting against the whole Persian army.*

thermŭlae -ārum, f. (dim. of thermae), *warm baths*, Mart.

Thērŏdămās -antis, m. and **Thērŏmĕdōn** -ontis, m. (Θηρομέδων), *a Scythian king, who fed lions with human flesh.* Adj., **Thērŏdămantēus** -a -um, *of Therodamas.*

Thersītēs -ae, m. (Θερσίτης), *son of Agrius, one of the Greeks before Troy, notorious for his ugliness and scurrilous tongue.*

thēsaurārĭus -a -um (thesaurus), *of* or *relating to the treasury*, Plaut.

thēsaurus -i, m. (θησαυρός). **I.** *a treasury, store, hoard*: 1, lit., thesaurum obruere, Cic.; defodere, Cic.; 2, fig., *a treasure* (of persons, etc.), Plaut. **II.** *the place where a treasure is kept*; 1, lit., **a**, servata mella thesauris, Verg.; **b**, esp., *the treasury of a temple* or *state*; thesauros Proserpinae spoliare, Liv.; 2, fig., *a storehouse, magazine, repertory*; thesaurus rerum omnium memoria, Cic.

Thēsēus -ĕi and -ĕos, m. (Θησεύς), *a king of Athens, son of Aegeus, husband of Ariadne and Phaedra, conqueror of the Minotaur.* Hence, **A.** adj., **Thēsēus** -a -um, *of* or *belonging to Theseus*; crimen, *the desertion of Ariadne*, Ov.; poet., *Athenian*, Prop. **B. Thēsēĭus** -a -um, *of* or *belonging to Theseus*; heros, *Hippolytus*, Ov. **C.** Subst., **Thēsīdēs** -ae, m. *a son of Theseus, Hippolytus*, Ov. **D. Thēsēïs** -idis, f. *a poem on Theseus*, Juv.

thēsĭon (-um) -ii, n. (θήσειον), *a species of flax* (Thesium linophyllum, Linn.), Plin.

thĕsis -is, f. (θέσις), *a proposition, thesis*, Quint.

thesmŏphŏrĭa -ōrum, n. (θεσμοφόρια), *the great Greek festival in honour of Demeter*, Plin.

Thespĭae -ārum, f. (Θεσπιαί), *a town in Boeotia, at the foot of Mount Helicon.* Hence, **A. Thespĭăs** -ădis, f. (Θεσπιάς), *Thespian*; deae Thespiades, Ov., and simply, Thespiades, Cic., *the Muses.* **B. Thespĭenses** -ium, m. *the inhabitants of Thespiae.*

Thespĭs -idis, m. (Θέσπις), *the founder of the Greek drama, contemporary of Solon and Pisistratus.*

Thespĭus -ii, n. (Θέσπιος), *son of Erechtheus, founder of Thespiae, father of fifty daughters.*

Thesprōtĭa -ae, f. (Θεσπρωτία), *a district in Epirus.* Hence, **Thesprōtĭus** -a -um, *Thesprotian.*

Thessălĭa -ae, f. (Θεσσαλία), *Thessaly, a country of northern Greece.* Hence, adj., **A. Thessălĭcus** -a -um, *Thessalian*; juga (of Mount Pelion), Ov. **B. Thessălus** -a -um, *Thessalian*; tela (of Achilles), Hor.; ignes, *in the camp of Achilles*, Hor.; pinus, *the ship Argo*,

Ov **C. Thessălĭus** -a -um, *Thessalian* **D. Thessălis** -ĭdis, 1 adj, *Thessalian*, umbra, *of Protesilaus*, Prop, ara, *of Laodamia, husband of Protesilaus*, Ov, subst, *a Thessalian woman*

Thessălŏnīca -ae, f and **Thessălŏnīcē** -ēs, f (Θεσσαλονίκη), *Thessalonica, a town in Macedonia*, now *Salonichi* Hence, **Thessălŏnīcenses** -ium, m *the inhabitants of Thessalonica.*

Thessălus, v. Thessalia

Thestĭus -ii, m (Θέστιος) **I.** *a king in Aetolia, father of Leda and Althaea, of Plexippus and Toxeus* Hence, **A. Thestĭădēs** ae, m (Θεστιάδης), *a descendant of Thestius*, Thestiadae duo, *Plexippus and Toxeus;* respice Thestiaden, *Meleager, son of Althaea*, Ov **B. Thestĭăs** -ădis, f *a daughter of Thestius*, i.e , *Althaea* **II.** = Thespius

Thestor -ŏris, m (Θέστωρ), *father of the soothsayer Calchas* Hence, **Thestŏrĭdēs** -ae, m (Θεστορίδης), *the son of Thestor*, i e , *Calchas*

thēta, n. (θῆτα), *the Greek letter theta* (Θ, θ), *used by the Greeks in voting tickets as a symbol of condemnation, because beginning the word* θάνατος, nigrum, Pers.

Thĕtis -ĭdis, f. (Θέτις), *a sea-nymph, wife of Peleus, mother of Achilles*, hence, poet., *the sea*, Verg

Theudŏrĭa -ae, f *a town in Athamania*, now *Todoriana*

Theuma -mătis, n *a place in Macedonia*

thĭăsus -i, m. (θίασος), *a dance in honour of Bacchus*, Verg

thieldones um, m. *a kind of Spanish horses*, Plin.

Thirmĭda -ae, f *a town in Numidia*

Thisbē -ēs, f (Θίσβη) **I.** *a beautiful Babylonian maiden, beloved by Pyramus.* **II.** *a town in Boeotia* Hence, **Thisbeus** -a -um, *Thisbean* = *Babylonian.*

thlaspi, n (θλάσπι), *a kind of cress*, Plin

Thŏas -antis, m. (Θόας) **I.** *a king of Lemnos, father of Hypsipyle*, whence, **Thŏantĭăs** ădis, f *a daughter of Thoas*, i e , *Hypsipyle* **II.** *a king of the Tauric Chersonese, slain by Orestes* Hence, **Thŏantēus** -a -um, poet. = *Tauric*

thŏlus -i, m (θόλος), *a cupola, dome*, Verg

thōrācātus -a -um (thorax), *armed with a breastplate*, Plin

thōrax -ācis, m (θώραξ), **1**, *the breast, chest*, Plin ; **2**, meton , *a breastplate, cuirass*, Liv.

thōs, thōis, m (θώς), *a kind of wolf*, Plin

Thot, *the Egyptian name of Mercury*

Thrăces -um, acc -es and as, m (Θρᾷκες), *the Thracians, the inhabitants of Thrace in south-east Europe*, sing , **Thrāx** -ăcis, m (Θρᾷξ), a, *a Thracian*, poet adj = *Thracian*, b, esp Thrax, or Thraex, *a gladiator with Thracian armour.* Hence, **A. Thrācĭa** ae, f *the country of Thrace*, Greek form, **Thrācē** -ēs, f, or latinised **Thrāca** -ae, f **B. Thracĭus (Thrēcĭus)** -a um, *Thracian* **C.** (Poet), **Thrēĭcĭus** -a -um (Θρηΐκιος), *Thracian*, sacerdos, Verg , or vates, Ov. = *Orpheus*, Samus, *Samothracia*, Verg , penates, *of Diomedes, king of Thrace*, Ov **D. Thraeissa**, and contr , **Thraessa** ae, f *in or from Thrace*, subst , *a Thracian woman*

thranis -is, m (θράνις), *a fish*, also called xiphias, Plin.

thrascĭas -ae, m (θρασκίας), *a north north-west wind*, Plin

Thrăsȳbūlus -i, m. (Θρασύβουλος), *an Athenian who freed Athens from the Thirty Tyrants.*

Thrăsȳmennus, v Trasumenus

Thrax, v Thraces

Threissa, Thressa, v Thraces

Threx = Thrax, v Thraces

thrips -ipis, m (θρίψ), *a wood-worm*, Plin

thrŏnus -i, m (θρόνος), *a lofty seat, throne*, Plin

Thūcȳdĭdēs -is and -i, m (Θουκυδίδης), *an Athenian, general in and historian of the Peloponnesian war* Hence, **Thūcȳdĭdīus** a -um, *Thucydidean*

Thūlē (Thȳlē) -ēs, f (Θούλη), *an island in the extreme north of Europe*, perhaps *one of the Shetland Islands*, perhaps *Iceland*

thunnus (thynnus) -i, m (θύννος), *a tunny-fish*, Ov

Thūrĭi -ōrum, m (Θούριοι), and **Thūrĭae** -ārum, f *a town built on the site of the destroyed Sybaris, on the Tarentine Gulf* Hence, **Thūrīnus** a um, *of or belonging to Thurii*

thūs, thūrĭbŭlus, etc = tus, turibulus, etc. (q v)

Thuys, dat Thuyni, acc Thuynem, and Thuyn, m *a prince of Paphlagonia at the time of Artaxerxes Memnon.*

thȳa -ae, f (θυία) and **thȳŏn** -i, n (θύον), *the Greek name of the citrus tree*, Plin , hence, **thȳĭus** -a -um, *of the wood of the citrus-tree*, Prop

Thȳămis -ĭdis, m (Θύαμις), *the most northerly river in Epirus*, now *Callama*

Thyatīra -ae, f and **Thyatīra** -ōrum, n (Θυάτειρα), *a town in Lydia, rebuilt by Seleucus Nicator*, now *Akhissar.*

Thȳbris = Tiberis (q v)

Thȳŏnē -ēs, f *a nymph, nurse of Jupiter*

Thȳestēs ae and -is, m (Θυέστης), *son of Pelops, father of Aegisthus, brother of Atreus, who placed before Thyestes for food Thyestes' own son*

Thȳĭăs (dissyll) ădis, f (Θυιάς), *a Bacchante*, Verg

thȳĭus, v thya

Thȳlē = Thule (q v)

1 **thymbra** -ae, f (θύμβρα), *the herb savory*, Verg

2 **Thymbra** -ae, f (Θύμβρη), *a town in Troas, on the river Thymbrios, with a temple to Apollo* Hence, **Thymbraeus** -a -um, *Thymbraean, surname of Apollo*

thȳmĭon (-um) ii, n (θύμιον), *a kind of wart*, Plin

thȳmōsus a -um (thymum), *full of thyme*, mel, Plin

thȳmum -i, n (θύμον), and **thȳmus** i, m (θυμόν and θυμος), *the herb thyme*, Verg

Thȳni -ōrum, m (Θυνοί), *a Thracian people, dwelling originally on the Black Sea* Hence, **A. Thȳnĭa** -ae, f (Θυνία), *Thynia, the northern part of Bithynia.* **B. Thȳnĭăcus** -a -um, *Thynian*, sinus, *on the Black Sea*, Ov **C. Thȳnus** -a -um, *Thynian.* **D. Thȳnĭăs** ădis, f *Thynian*

Thȳnus, v Thyni

thynnus = thunnus (q v)

Thȳŏnē ēs, f (Θυώνη) **I** *mother of Bacchus* (acc to one legend), *identified by some with Semele* Hence, **A. Thȳŏnēus** ĕi, m (Θυωνεύς), *son of*

Thyone, i.e. *Bacchus*. **B. Thȳōniānus** -i, m., meton. = *wine*, Cat. **II.** *a nymph, nurse of Jupiter.*

Thȳrē -ēs, f. and **Thȳrĕa** -ae, f. (Θυρέα), *a town and district in Argolis.* Hence, **Thȳrĕātis** -idis, f. (Θυρεᾶτις), *of* or *belonging to Thyrea.*

Thyrĕum -i, n. and **Thyrīum** -ii, n. *a town in Acarnania, near Leucas.* Hence, **Thyrīenses** -ium, m. *inhabitants of Thyreum.*

thyrsigĕr -gĕra -gĕrum (thyrsus and gero), *bearing a thyrsus*, Sen.

thyrsus -i, m. (θύρσος). **I.** *the stalk* or *stem of a plant*, Plin. **II.** *a wand, wound round with ivy and vine-leaves, carried by Bacchus and his attendants*, Hor.

tiāra -ae, f. and **tiāras** -ae, m. (τιάρα), *a turban*, Verg.

Tibĕris -bĕris, acc. -bĕrim, abl. -bĕri, m. and poet., **Thȳbris** -bridis, acc. -brin or -brim, m. *the river Tiber*; personif., Thybris, *the river-god of the Tiber.* Hence, **A.** Adj., **Tibĕrīnus** -a -um, *belonging to the river Tiber*; amnis, Liv., or flumen, Verg., *the river Tiber*; pater, or deus, *the river-god*, Verg. Subst., **Tibĕrīnus** -i, m. **a,** *the Tiber*, Cic., Verg.; **b,** *a king of Alba*, Liv. **B. Tibĕrīnis** -idis, f. *belonging to the river Tiber*; Tiberinides Nymphae, Ov.

Tibĕrĭus -ii, m. **I.** *a common Roman praenomen*, abbreviated Ti. or Tib. **II.** Esp., *the second emperor of Rome, Tiberius Claudius Nero Caesar.* Hence, **Tibĕrĭŏlus** -i, m. dim. *little* (= *dear*) *Tiberius*, Tac.

tībĭa -ae, f. *the shin-bone, tibia*; meton., *a pipe, fife, flute, originally made of a hollow bone*; tibiis canere, Cic.

tībĭālis -e (tibia), *of* or *relating to a flute*, Plin.

tībīcen -inis, m. (for tibiicen, from tibia and cano). **I.** *a flute-player, piper, fifer*, Cic. **II.** *a pillar, prop*, Ov.

tībīcīna -ae, f. (tibicen), *a female flute-player, piper*, Hor.

tībīcĭnium -ii, n. (tibicen), *playing on the flute*, Cic.

Tībris = Tiberis (q.v.).

Tībullus -i, m., Albius, *a Roman elegiac poet, friend of Horace and Ovid, born* 54 B.C., *died about* 19 B.C.

tībŭlus -i, f. *a kind of pine* or *fir-tree*, Plin.

Tībŭr -bŭris, abl. -bŭre, loc., bŭri, n. *an old town in Latium, on both sides of the Anio, on a rocky hill* (whence called supinum and pronum, Hor.), *famous for its romantic position, a famous summer resort for the rich Romans*, now *Tivoli.* Hence, **A. Tībur** -burtis, *Tiburtine.* Subst., **Tīburtes** -um and -ium, m. *the inhabitants of Tibur*; esse in Tiburti, *in the Tiburtine district*, Cic. **B. Tīburtīnus** -a -um, *Tiburtine.* **C. Tīburnus** -a -um, *Tiburnian.* Subst., **Tīburnus** -i, m. *the builder of Tibur.*

Tīburtus -i, m. *the builder of Tibur.*

Tīcīnum -i, n. *a town in Cisalpine Gaul on the river Ticinus*, now *Pavia.*

Tīcīnus -i, m. *one of the tributaries of the Padus in Cisalpine Gaul*, now *Tessino.*

Tifāta -ōrum, n. *a mountain north of Capua in Campania, on which was a temple to Diana*, now *Torre di Sessola.*

Tīfernum -i, n. *a town in Samnium on the river Tifernus.*

Tīfernus -i, m. **1,** *a mountain in Samnium*; **2,** *a river in Samnium.*

Tīgellĭus -ii, m. *name of two musicians at Rome in Horace's time.*

tĭgillum -i, n. (dim. of tignum), *a small beam*, Liv.

tignārĭus -a -um (tignum), *of* or *relating to beams*; faber, *a carpenter*, Cic.

tignum -i, n. (tego), *a beam of wood, a log of timber*, Caes.

Tĭgrānēs -is, m. (Τιγράνης). **I.** *king in Great Armenia, son-in-law and ally of Mithridates, conquered by Lucullus.* **II.** *his son.*

Tĭgrānŏcerta -ae, f. and **Tĭgrānŏcerta** -ōrum, n. *the chief town of Armenia, founded by Tigranes.*

tĭgrīnus -a -um (tigris), *spotted like a tiger*, Plin.

tĭgris -idis and -is, acc. -idem and -im or -in, abl. -ide or -i, acc. plur., poet., -idas (τίγρις, in Persian = *an arrow*). **I.** c. (masc. gen. in prose, fem. gen. in poetry), *a tiger*; **1,** lit., Verg.; **2,** transf., **a,** *name of one of the dogs of Actaeon*, Ov.; **b,** *name of a ship decorated with the figure of a tiger*, Verg. **II.** m. **Tĭgris** -idis and -is, acc. -idem and -im, abl. -ide and -ē or -i, *the river Tigris in Asia.*

Tigurīni -ōrum, m. *a Helvetian people.* Adj., **Tigurīnus** -a -um, *Tigurine*; pagus, *the modern canton Vaud.*

tĭlĭa -ae, f. **I.** *a linden* or *lime-tree*, Verg. **II.** *the inner bark of the lime-tree*, Plin.

Tīmaeus -i, m. (Τίμαιος). **I.** *a Greek historian in Sicily under Agathocles.* **II.** *a Pythagorean philosopher of Locri, after whom one of Plato's dialogues was named.*

Tīmāgĕnēs -is, m. (Τιμαγένης), *a rhetorician of the time of Augustus.*

Tīmanthēs -is, m. (Τιμάνθης), *a famous Greek painter, contemporary of Parrhasius.*

Tīmāvus -i, m. *a river in the Venetian country between Aquileia and Trieste*, now *Timavo.*

tĭmĕfactus -a -um (timeo and facio), *made fearful, frightened, alarmed*, Cic.

tĭmendus -a -um, p. adj. (from timeo), *to be feared, fearful, dread*; reges, Hor.

tĭmens -entis, p. adj. (from timeo), *fearing, fearful*; **a,** with genit., mortis, Lucr.; **b,** absol., hortatus timentem, Ov.; plur. subst., *the fearful*; timentes confirmat, Caes.

tĭmĕo -ŭi, 2. *to be afraid, fear, dread, apprehend*; with acc., aliquem, Cic.; with ne, ne non, or ut and the subj., timeo, ne non impetrem, Cic.; with infin., *to be afraid to*; nomen referre in tabulas, Cic.; with interrog. clause, quid possem, timebam, Cic.; with dat. (of the object on whose account fear is felt), sibi, Caes.; with de, de republica, Cic.; with a and the abl., a quo quidem genere ego numquam timui, Cic.

tĭmĭdē, adv. with compar. and superl. (timidus), *timidly, fearfully*, Cic.

tĭmĭdĭtas -ātis, f. (timidus), *fearfulness, timidity*, Cic.

tĭmĭdus -a -um (timeo), *fearful, timid, faint-hearted*, Cic.; with ad and the acc., timidus ad mortem, Cic.; with in and the abl., timidus in labore militari, Cic.; with genit., timidus procellae, Hor.; non timidus, foll. by the infin., non timidus pro patria mori, Hor.

Tīmŏcrătes -ae, m. (Τιμοκράτης), *an Epicurean philosopher, flourishing about* 260 B.C.

Tīmŏlĕōn -ontis, m. (Τιμολέων), *a Corinthian general, contemporary of Philip of Macedon.* Hence, **Tīmŏlĕontēus** -a -um, *of* or *belonging to Timoleon.*

Tīmōn -ōnis, m. (Τίμων), *a citizen of Athens, notorious for his misanthropy.*

tĭmor -ōris, m. (timeo), *fear, dread, apprehen-*

sion. **I.** Lit., **a,** gen, definiunt timorem metum mali appropinquantis, Cic, timorem deponite, Cic., inicere timorem Parthis, Cic; percelli timore, Cic, foll by ne and the subj, Liv, by infin, Ov, by acc and infin, Liv, personif, Timor, son of Aether and Tellus, Hor, Verg, Ov, **b,** *religious fear, superstition,* Hor **II.** Meton, *an object exciting fear,* Cacus Aventinae timor atque infamia silvae, Ov

Tīmŏthĕus -i, m (Τιμόθεος) **I.** *son of Conon, the rebuilder of the long walls of Athens* **II.** *a musician of Miletus*

tinctĭlis e (tingo), *in which something is dipped,* Ov

tinctōrĭus -a -um (tingo), *of or relating to dyeing,* fig, mens, *bloodthirsty,* Plin

tinctūra ae, f (tingo), *a dyeing,* Plin

tinctus -ūs, m (tingo), *a dipping, dyeing,* Plin

tĭnĕa (tĭnia) -ae, f *a moth, bookworm,* Ov, Hor; *a worm in beehives,* Verg

tingo (tinguo), tinxi, tinctum, 3 (root TING, Gk TEΓΓ, τέγγω), *to wet, moisten, imbue with any fluid* **I** Gen, **a,** lit, tunica sanguine tincta, Cic, **b,** fig, *to tinge, imbue,* orator sit mihi tinctus literis, Cic. **II.** Esp, *to dye, colour,* Cic

tinnīmentum -i, n (tinnio), *a tinkling, ringing,* Plaut

tinnĭo ivi and -ii -itum, 4 *to ring, tinkle, tingle, jingle* **I.** Lit, Varr **II.** Transf, 1, *to sing, to scream,* Plaut, 2, *to chink, to make to chink,* of money = *to pay,* ecquid Dolabella tinniat, Cic

tinnītus -ūs, m (tinnio), *a ringing, tinkling, jingling,* Verg **I.** Lit, Ov **II.** Transf, of discourse, *a jingle of words,* Tac

tinnŭlus a um (tinnio), *ringing, clinking, tinkling, jingling,* Ov

tinnuncŭlus -i, m *a kind of falcon* (Falco tinnunculus, Linn), Plin

tintinnābŭlum -i, n (tintinno), *a bell,* Juv

tintinnācŭlus -a -um (tintinno), *ringing, jingling,* Plaut.

tintinno (tintĭno), 1 *to ring, jingle, tinkle,* Cat

tīnus i, f *a shrub* (Viburnum Tinus, Linn), Ov

tiphē -ēs, f (τίφη), *a species of grain* (Triticum monococcon, Linn), Plin

Tīphys, acc phyn, voc. phy, m (Τῖφυς), *the helmsman of the Argo*

tippŭla -ae, f *a water-spider* (which runs swiftly over the water), Varr, used to express something very light, Plaut

Tīrĕsĭās -ae, m (Τειρεσίας), *the famous blind soothsayer of Thebes*

Tīrĭdātēs -dātis, m (Τιριδάτης), *name of several kings in Armenia*

tīro (tȳro) ōnis, m **I.** *a young soldier, a recruit,* **1,** lit, Cic, adj, exercitus tiro, Cic, **2,** transf, **a,** *a beginner, a learner,* in aliqua re, Cic, tiro esset scientiā, Cic, **b,** *a youth who assumes the toga virilis,* Ov **II.** Proper name, M Tullius Tiro, *the freedman of Cicero*

tīrōcĭnĭum -ii, n (tiro) **I.** *military ignorance and inexperience,* **a,** lit, juvenis, Liv, **b,** meton, *recruits,* Liv **II.** Transf *of the entry of a young man on any career,* in L Paulo accusando tirocinium ponere, *come before the public,* Liv

tīruncŭlus i, m (dim of tiro), *a young beginner,* Plin

Tīryns, acc ryntha, f (Τίρυνς), *an Argive town where Hercules was brought up* Hence, adj, **Tīrynthĭus** -a -um, poet, *Herculean, relating to Hercules,* so simply, **Tīrynthĭus** ii, m *Hercules,* Tirynthia, *Alcmena, the mother of Hercules.*

Tīsĭās ae, m. (Τισίας), *of Sicily, the first founder of a rhetorical system*

Tīsĭphŏnē ēs, f (Τισιφόνη), *one of the Furies,* hence, adj, **Tīsĭphŏnēus** a -um, *hellish, impious,* tempora, Ov.

Tissăphernēs ae, m (Τισσαφέρνης), *a satrap under Xerxes II and Artaxerxes II*

Tissē -ēs, f *a town in Sicily, now Randazzo* Hence, **Tissenses** -ium, m *the inhabitants of Tisse*

Tītan -tānis, m (Τιτάν), and **Tītānus** i, m **I.** Gen, plur, Titanes and Titani, *the sons of Uranus and Gaea* (lat Tellus), *who warred against Jupiter for supremacy in heaven, and were by him cast down into Tartarus* **II.** *one of the Titans,* **a,** *the Sun-god, son of Hyperion,* **b,** *Prometheus* Hence, **A Tītānĭus** -a -um, *of or relating to the Titans,* subst, **Tītānĭa** ae, f **a,** *Latona,* Ov, **b,** *Pyrrha,* Ov, **c,** *Diana,* Ov; **d,** *Circe,* Ov **B Tītānĭăcus** -a -um, *Titanian* **C. Tītānis** idis -idos, f *Titanian,* subst., **a,** *Circe,* Ov, **b,** *Tethys,* Ov

Tīthōnus -i, m (Τιθωνός), *the husband of Aurora, who obtained from his wife the gift of immortality, but without perpetual youth and was at last changed into a grasshopper* Hence, adj, **Tīthōnĭus** a -um, *Tithonian,* Tithonia conjux, *Aurora,* Ov

Tĭtĭes -ium, m and **Tĭtĭenses** -ium, m *one of the three tribes* (Ramnes, Tities, and Luceres) *into which the Roman burgesses were at first divided, and out of which three centuries of knights are said to have been formed by Romulus.*

tītillātĭo -ōnis, f (titillo), *a tickling, titillation,* Cic

tītillātus ūs, m = titillatio (q v)

tītillo, 1 *to tickle,* sensus, Cic, fig, ne vos titillet gloria, Hor

tītĭo -ōnis, m *a firebrand,* Varr

tītivillīcium -ii, n *a trifle,* Plaut

tĭtŭbantĕr, adv (titubo), *hesitatingly, uncertainly,* Cic

tĭtŭbantĭa -ae, f (titubo), *a wavering, staggering,* linguae, oris, *stammering,* Suet.

tĭtŭbātĭo -ōnis, f (titubo), *a staggering, reeling,* Sen, fig, *uncertainty, hesitancy,* Cic

tĭtŭbo, 1 *to totter, stagger* **I.** Lit, **1,** of persons, Silenus titubans annisque meroque, Ov, vestigia titubata, *tottering,* Verg, **2,** transf, *to stammer,* Licinius titubans, Cic, lingua titubat, Ov **II.** Fig, **1,** *to waver, to hesitate,* Plaut, **2,** *to blunder, err,* si verbo titubarint (testes), Cic

tĭtŭlus i, m. *an inscription, label, title* **I.** Lit, **1,** gen, titulum inscribere lamnae, Liv, **2,** esp, **a,** *a notice on a house that is to let,* sub titulum nostros misit avara lares, Ov, **b,** *an epitaph,* sepulchri, Juv **II** Transf, **1, a,** *a title of honour, honourable designation,* consulatus, Cic, **b,** *glory, honour,* par titulo tantae gloriae fuit, Liv, **2,** *a pretence, pretext, reason,* quem titulum praetenderitis, Liv

Tĭtŭrĭus ii, m *a legate of Caesar's in the Gallic war* Hence, **Tĭtŭrĭānus** -a um, *of or belonging to Titurius*

Tĭtus i, m **I** *a common Roman praenomen, usually abbreviated* T **II.** *the emperor Titus Flavius Sabinus Vespasianus, son and successor of the Emperor Vespasian*

Tĭtyŏs i, m (Τιτυός), *son of Jupiter, punished for an insult to Latona by being stretched out in Tartarus, and having his liver devoured by vultures*

Tītўrŭs -i, m (Τιτυρος, Doric = Σατυρος) **I.** *the name of a shepherd in Vergil's Eclogues*, poet, meton, **a,** = *the Eclogues of Vergil*, Ov ; **b,** *Vergil himself*, Prop **II.** Transf, *a shepherd*, sit Tityrus Orpheus, Verg

Tlēpŏlĕmus i, m (Τληπόλεμος), *son of Hercules*

Tmărus (-ŏs) i, m. (Τμάρος), syncop from

Tŏmărus -i, m (Τομαρος), *a mountain in Epirus on which was Dodona and the temple of Zeus.*

Tmōlus -i, m (Τμῶλος), *a mountain in Lydia, famous for its wine* Hence, **A Tmōlĭus** -a -um, *Tmolian*, subst, Tmolius, *Tmolian wine*, Verg **B. Tmōlītēs** -ae, m *a dweller on Mount Tmolus*

tŏcullĭo -ōnis, m (from τόκος, *interest*), *a usurer*, Cic

tōfācĕus (tōfācĭus) a um (tofus), *made of tufa, like tufa*, Plin

tōfīnus -a -um (tofus), *made of tufa*, Suet.

tōfus (tōphus) -i, m *tufa*, Verg

tŏga -ae, f (tego), *a covering*, esp, *the white woollen upper garment worn by the Romans in time of peace, when they appeared in their public capacity as citizens*, it was also worn by freedwomen and prostitutes (while the stola was worn by honourable women), especial kinds of the toga were purpurea, *the kingly*, Liv, pura, *worn by young men on coming of age*, also called virilis, Cic, candida, *of a candidate for office*, Cic, meton, **a,** = *peace*, Cic, **b,** = togatus, (α) togata, *a prostitute*, Tib., (β) plur, = *clients*, Mart

tŏgātārĭus -ii, m (toga), *an actor in the Fabula togata*, v togatus, Suet.

tŏgātŭlus i, m (dim. of togatus), *a client*, Mart

tŏgātus -a um (toga), *wearing the toga* **I.** Lit, gen, as a sign of a Roman citizen, as opp to a foreigner or a soldier, gens, *the Roman people*, Verg **II.** Transf, **1,** **tŏgāta** -ae, f (sc. fabula), *the national drama of the Romans, treating of Roman subjects* (opp fabula palliata), Cic, **2,** Gallia togata, *the Romanised part of Gallia Cisalpina*, Cic, **3,** togata, *a freedwoman, a prostitute*, Hor, **4,** *a client*, Juv.

tŏgŭla ae, f (dim. of toga), *a little toga*, Cic

Tŏlōnus -i, m *a river in the country of the Sabines, now Turano*

tŏlĕrābĭlis -e (tolero), *that can be borne, bearable, tolerable*, conditio, Cic, poena, Cic.

tŏlĕrābĭlĭtĕr, adv (tolerabilis), *patiently*, aliquid tolerabilius ferre, Cic

tŏlĕrandus -a -um (tolero), *endurable*, Liv

tŏlĕrans -antis, p adj (from tolero), *bearing, enduring, patient, tolerant*, with genit, laborum, Tac

tŏlĕrantĕr, adv. (tolerans), *patiently*, illa ferre, Cic

tŏlĕrantĭa -ae, f (tolero), *a bearing, enduring, supporting*, rerum humanarum, Cic

tŏlĕrātĭo -ōnis, f (tolero), *capacity for endurance*, Cic

tŏlĕro, 1 (lengthened form of root TOL, whence tollo, tuli, τλαω, τλῆμι), *to bear, endure, sustain, tolerate*, fig, **1,** hiemem, Cic ; inopiam, Sall, with acc and infin, Sall ; **2,** *to support, sustain, nourish, feed, keep*, equitatum, Caes, vitam aliquā re, Caes

Tŏlētum -i, n *a town of the Carpetani in Hispania Tarraconensis, now Toledo* Hence, **Tŏlētāni** -ōrum, m *the inhabitants of Toletum*

tollēno -ōnis, m (tollo), *a machine for raising water, a swing-beam or swipe*, Plin, *a military engine*, Liv

tollo, sustŭli, sublātum, 3 **I.** *to lift up, raise, elevate* **A.** Lit, **1,** gen., saxa de terra, Cic, oculos, Cic, aliquem in crucem, *to crucify*, Cic, **2,** esp, **a,** naut t t, tollere ancoras, *to weigh anchor*, Caes, **b,** milit t t, tollere signa, *to break up camp*, Caes ; **c,** *to take up, take with one*, aliquem in currum, in equum, Cic, of ships, *to have on board*, naves quae equites sustulerant, Caes **B.** Fig, **1,** *to raise, elevate*, aliquem humeris suis in caelum, Cic, laudes alicuius in astra, Cic, clamorem, Cic, animos, *to assume a proud demeanour*, Sall, **2,** esp, **a,** *to extol, magnify*, aliquem honoribus, Hor, tollere aliquem, *to help to honour*, Cic, aliquem laudibus, *to extol* Cic, **b,** *to raise up*, animum, *regain one's spirits*, Liv, amicum, *to comfort*, Hor, **c,** *to take on oneself*, quid oneris in praesentia tollant, Cic., **d,** *to bring up a child*, Plaut, transf, *to get, have a child*, liberos ex Fabia, Cic **II.** *to take away, carry off* **A. 1,** gen, praedam, Caes, frumentum de area, Cic, solem mundo, Cic, **2,** esp, **a,** *to remove the food from the table*, cibos, Hor, **b,** *to reserve for one's own use*, omnes chlamydes, Hor ; **c,** *to destroy, get rid of*, aliquem e or de medio, or simply aliquem, Cic, Carthaginem, Cic. **B.** Fig, *to remove*, **1,** gen, amicitiam e mundo, Cic ; **2,** esp, **a,** *to consume*, tempus, diem, Cic, **b,** *to annul, bring to naught*, legem, Cic, dictaturam funditus a republica, Cic

Tŏlōsa ae, f *a rich town in Gallia Narbonensis, now Toulouse* Hence, **A. Tŏlōsānus** -a -um, *of or belonging to Tolosa*, aurum, *taken by the consul Q Servilius Caepio from Tolosa*, Cic **B. Tŏlōsās** ātis, *Tolosan*, subst., **Tŏlōsātes** -ium, m *the inhabitants of Tolosa.*

Tolostobogĭi -ōrum, m *one of the three races of the Galatians in Asia Minor*

Tŏlumnĭus -ii, m **1,** *a king of the Veientines* ; **2,** *a soothsayer of the Rutuli*

tŏlūtārĭus a -um (tolutim), *trotting*, equus, Sen

tŏlūtim, adv (tollo), *trotting, on the trot*, Plin.

tŏmācīna -ae, f (tomaculum), *a kind of sausage*, Varr

tŏmācŭlum (tŏmaclum) -i, n (τομή), *a kind of sausage*, Juv

Tŏmărus, v Tmarus

tōmentum -i, n *the stuffing of a pillow, mattress, cushion*, etc, Tac

Tŏmi -ōrum, m (Τόμοι), and **Tŏmis** -idis, f (Τομις), *a town in Lower Moesia, on the Black Sea, the place of exile of Ovid, near modern Anadolkioi* Hence, **A. Tŏmītae** -ārum, m *the inhabitants of Tomi* **B. Tŏmītānus** -a -um, *of Tomi.*

tŏmus -i, m (τόμος), *a cutting, chip, shred*, Mart

tondĕo, tŏtondi, tonsum, 2 *to shave, shear, clip* **I.** Lit, **a,** transit, barbam et capillum, Cic, oves, Hor ; **b,** intransit., *to shave the beard*, tondere filias docuit, Cic ; **c,** reflex, tondere and middle tonderi, *to shave oneself, have oneself shaved*, candidior postquam tondenti barba cadebat, Verg, cum tonderi et squalorem deponere coegerunt, Liv. **II.** Transf., **1,** *to cut off, shear, make smooth*, ilex tonsa bipennibus, Hor, **2,** *to mow, cut down*, prata, Verg ; **3,** *to pluck off, crop off, browse upon*, campum, Verg.,

tŏnĭtrus -ūs, m and **tŏnĭtrŭum** -i, n (tono), *thunder*, Verg, Ov

tŏno -ŭi, 1. *to sound, resound* **I.** Gen, caelum tonat fragore, Verg **II.** Esp., *to* *thunder;* 1, lit, Juppiter tonabat, Prop, impers, tonat, *it thunders,* Cic, tonans, as a surname of Juppiter, Cic, 2, transf, like βροντᾶν, of the powerful voice of an orator, a, absol, Pericles tonare dictus est, Cic, b, *to thunder out something,* verba foro, Prop

tonsa ae, f *an oar,* Verg

tonsilis -e (tondeo), 1, *that can be shorn or cut,* Plin, 2, *shorn, clipped, cut,* Plin

tonsillae -arum, f *the tonsils in the throat,* Cic

tonsito, 1 (intens of tondeo), *to shear, clip,* Plaut

tonsor ōris, m (tondeo), *a hair cutter, barber,* Cic

tonsōrius -a um (tonsor), *of or for clipping, cutting,* culter, Cic

tonstrīcŭla -ae, f (dim of tonstrix), *a little female barber,* Cic

tonstrīna -ae, f (tondeo), *a barber's shop,* Plaut

tonstrix īcis, f (tonsor), *a female barber,* Plaut

tonsūra ae, f (tondeo), *a clipping, shearing, shaving,* capillorum, Plaut

tonsus ūs, m (tondeo), *the mode of cutting or wearing the hair,* Plaut

tŏnus i, m (τόνος), *the tone* or *sound* of an instrument, applied to painting, *tone,* Plin

tŏparchĭa -ae, f (τοπαρχία), *a territory, district, province,* Plin

tŏpāzus (-ŏs) i, f (τόπαζος), *the topaz, chrysolith,* or *green jasper,* Plin

tōphus, etc = tofus, etc (q v)

tŏpĭa -ōrum, n (sc opera, from τόπος), *ornamental gardening,* hence, **tŏpĭārĭus** -a um, *of or relating to ornamental gardening,* subst, **a, tŏpĭārĭus** ii, m *a landscape gardener,* Cic, **b, tŏpĭārĭa** -ae, f *the art of landscape gardening,* topiariam facere, *to be a landscape gardener,* Cic, **c, tŏpĭārĭum** -ii, n (sc opus), *landscape gardening,* Plin

toppĕr, adv *speedily, directly, forthwith,* Quint

tŏral -ālis, n (torus), *the valance of a couch or sofa,* Hor

torcŭlar -āris, n (torqueo), *a wine* or *oil press,* Plin

torcŭlārĭus -a (torcular), *of or relating to a press,* subst, **torcŭlārĭum** -ii, n *a press,* Cato

torcŭlus -a -um (torqueo), *of or relating to a press* **I.** Adj, vasa, Cato **II.** Subst, torculum i, n *a press*

tordȳlon i, n (τόρδυλον), *the seed of the plant seselis,* or, according to others, *the plant* Tordylium officinale, Plin

tŏreuma -ătis, n (τόρευμα), *carved* or *embossed work,* Cic, Sall

tŏreutes -ae, m (τορευτής), *an engraver, chaser, embosser,* Plin

tŏreutĭcē -ēs, f (τορευτική, sc τέχνη), *the art of chasing, engraving, embossing,* Plin.

tormentum i, n. (torqueo) **I.** *an instrument for twisting, winding, pressing;* 1, *a windlass, pulley;* praesectis omnium mulierum crinibus tormenta effecerunt, Caes; 2, *an instrument of torture, the rack;* **a,** lit., tormenta adhibere, Cic; dare se in tormenta, Cic; de servo in dominum ne tormentis quidem quaeri licet, Cic; **b,** transf., (α) *compulsion,* lene tormentum admovere ingenio, Hor.; (β) *torture, torment,* tormenta suspicionis, Cic. **II.** *a military engine for discharging missiles* 1, lit tormenta collocavit, Caes, 2, meton, *the missile so discharged,* telum tormentumve missum, Caes

tormĭna um, n (torqueo) **I** *the colic, gripes,* Cic **II.** Transf, urinae, *a strangury,* Plin

tormĭnālis -e (tormina), *of or relating to the colic,* Plin

tormĭnōsus -a um (tormina), *suffering from the colic,* Cic

torno, 1 (τορνεύω), *to turn in a lathe, make round* **I** Lit sphaeram, Cic **II.** Fig, versus male tornat, *badly turned, awkward,* Hor

tornus i, m (τόρνος), *a lathe* **I.** Lit, Verg **II.** Fig, angusto versus includere torno, Prop

Tŏrōnē -ēs, f (Τορώνη), *a town on the Aegean Sea* now *Toron,* Toronae promunturium, *the promontory Derris, near Torone,* Liv Hence, **Tŏrōnāĭcus** -a um, *of or belonging to Torone*

tŏrōsus a -um (torus), *muscular, fleshy brawny,* colla boum, Ov

torpēdo inis, f (torpeo) **I.** *torpor, torpidity, sluggishness inertness,* Sall, Tac **II.** *the fish called the torpedo,* Cic

torpĕo, 2 *to be stiff, immovable, sluggish, inert, torpid, numb.* **I.** Lit, physically, **a,** corpora rigentia gelu torpebant, Liv, **b,** *to be inactive, continue inactive,* deum sic feriatum volumus cessatione torpere, Cic, **c,** *to be immoveable from fear,* adeo torpentibus metu qui aderant, ut ne gemitus quidem exaudiretur, Liv **II** Transf, *to be mentally benumbed, torpid,* si tua re subitā consilia torpent, Liv

torpesco -pŭi, 3 (torpeo), *to become stiff, grow stiff, become torpid* **a,** from inactivity, ne per otium torpescerent manus aut animus, Sall, **b,** from mental agitation, torpuerat lingua metu, Ov

torpĭdus a -um (torpeo), *stiff, numb, torpid,* Liv

torpor -ōris, m (torpeo), *stiffness, numbness, stupefaction, torpor,* 1, physical, Cic, 2, mental, *dulness, inertness, inactivity,* sordes omnium ac torpor, Tac

torquātus -a -um (torques), *wearing a twisted collar or necklace;* esp, as the surname of T Manlius, *who killed a gigantic Gaul in single combat, and took from him the* torques *or necklace which he wore,* Alecto torquata colubris, *with a necklace of snakes,* Ov, palumbus torquatus, *the ring-dove,* Mart

torquĕo, torsi, tortum, 2 (connected with τρέπω) **I.** *to twist, bend, wind, turn round,* 1, gen, **a,** lit, cervices oculosque, Cic, terra circum axem se torquet, Cic, capillos ferro, *to curl,* Ov, stamina digitis or pollice, *to spin,* Ov, **b,** fig, *to guide, direct, turn,* omnia ad commodum suae causae, Cic, 2, esp, **a,** *to roll,* saxa, Verg, **b,** *to turn round in a circle, to wind,* anguis tortus, Verg, hence, **c,** *to hurl violently, whirl,* jaculum in hostem, Verg, hastas, Cic, 3, transf, *to turn up* spumas, Verg, torquet medios nox humida cursus, *has finished the half of her journey,* Verg **II. A.** *to throw round oneself,* tegumen immane, Verg **B** *to distort, sprain,* 1, gen, **a,** lit, vultus mutantur, ora torquentur, Cic, **b,** fig, *to distort;* verbo ac litterā jus omne torqueri, Cic; 2, esp, *to rack, torture, torment,* **a,** lit, Cic; **b,** fig., (α) aliquem mero, *to make a person drink in order to test him,* Hor., torqueatur vita Sullae, *be accurately examined,* Cic; (β) *to torment, plague,* aliquem, Cic, libidines te torquent, Cic., exspectatione torqueor, Cic.

torquis (**torques**) is, m and (in prose rarely) f. (torqueo), *that which is twisted or curved,* **I.** *a twisted collar* or *necklace,* torque detracto, Cic. **II.** *the collar of draught oxen*, Verg. **III.** *a ring, wreath, chaplet*, ornatae torquibus arae, Verg.

torrens -entis, p. adj. (from torreo). **I.** *burning, hot, parched*, miles sole torrens, Liv. **II.** Transf., of water, *seething, rushing, boiling*. **A.** Adj., aqua, Verg. **B.** Subst., **torrens** -entis, m. *a torrent*, Liv.; quam fertur quasi torrens oratio, Cic.

torrĕo, torrŭi, tostum, 2. *to burn, parch, dry up with heat or thirst*, aristas sole novo, Verg.; solis ardore torreri, Cic.; tosti crines, *singed*, Ov.; of fever, mihi torrentur febribus artus, Ov.; of thirst, Tib.; of love, torret amor pectora, Ov.

torresco, 3. (inchoat. of torreo), *to become parched, be dried up*, Lucr.

torrĭdus -a -um (torreo). **I.** Pass., *parched, burnt*. **1,** *dry, arid*, **a,** lit., campi siccitate torridi, Liv.; **b,** transf., *meagre, lean*, homo vegrandi macie torridus, Cic.; **2,** *pinched, nipped with cold*, membra torrida gelu, Liv. **II.** Act., *burning, hot*, aestas, Verg.; locus ab incendiis torridus, Liv.

torris -is, m. (torreo), *a firebrand*, Ov., Verg.

tortē, adv. (tortus), *crookedly, awry*, Lucr.

tortĭlis -e (torqueo), *twisted, twined*, aurum, *a golden chain*, Verg.

torto, 1. (intens. of torqueo), *to torture, torment*, Lucr.

tortor -ōris, m. (torqueo), *a torturer, tormentor, executioner*, Cic.

tortŭōsus -a -um (2. tortus). **I.** *full of turns and windings, tortuous*. **A.** Lit., alvus, Cic.; amnis, Liv.; loci, Cic. **B.** Fig., *perplexed, intricate, involved*, genus disputandi, Cic. **II.** *painful, tormenting*, Plin.

1. **tortus** -a -um, p. adj. (from torqueo), *twisted, crooked*, via, *the labyrinth*, Prop.; quercus, *an oak garland*, Verg.; vimen, *a beehive*, Ov.; fig., conditiones tortae, *intricate, perplexed*, Plaut.

2. **tortus** -ūs, m. (torqueo), *a twisting, winding, curve*, serpens longos dat corpore tortus, Verg.

tōrŭlus -i, m. (dim. of torus), *a tuft*, Plaut.

tŏrus -i, m. (connected with sterno, στορέννυμι), *any round swelling protuberance*. Hence, **I.** *a knot in a rope*, Plin. **II.** *a knot or loop in a garland* (fig.), Cic. **III.** *a fleshy, projecting part of the body, muscle*, tori lacertorum, Cic. poet.; colla tument toris, Ov. **IV.** *a bed, sofa, mattress, cushion, couch*, Verg., Ov.; esp., (α) *the marriage couch*, Verg., Ov.; (β) *the bier*, toro componat, Ov. **V.** *a mound or elevation of earth*, tori riparum, Verg.

torvĭtas -ātis, f. (torvus), *savageness, wildness* (of appearance or character), vultus, Tac.

torvus -a -um (toro), *wild, savage, gloomy, severe, grim, fierce*, esp. of the eyes or the look, oculi, Ov.; forma minantis, Ov.; draco, Cic. poet.; proelia, Cat.

tŏt, num. indecl. (τόσα), *so many*, tot viri, Cic.; foll. by ut and the subj., Cic.; with quot, *as*, Cic.; by quoties, Cic.; with a prep. without a subst., ex tot, Ov.

tŏtĭdem, num. indecl. (= tot itidem), *just as many*, totidem annos vixerunt, Cic.; foll. by quot (*as*), totidem verbis, quot dixit, Cic.

tŏtĭens = toties (q.v.).

tŏtĭēs, adv. (tot). **I.** *so often, so many times, as many times*, followed by quoties (*as*), quotiescumque, Cic.; quot, Liv. **II.** *just as many times*, Hor.

tōtus -a -um, genit. tōtĭus, dat. tōti, *the whole, all, entire*. **I.** Of an object which is not divided, **a,** terra, Cic.; mens, Caes.; respublica, Cic.; **b,** *whole = with body and soul*, sum vester totus, *entirely yours*, Cic.; in prece totus eram, Ov.; **c,** *whole, complete, full*, sex menses totos, Ter.; subst., **tōtum** -i, n. *the whole*, Cic.; in toto, *on the whole*, Cic. **II.** Of an object opposed to its parts, *all, all together*, totis copiis, Caes.; totis viribus, Liv. (dat., toto, Caes., *B. G.*, 7, 89, 5).

toxĭcon (-um) -i, n. (τοξικόν), *poison for arrows*, Ov.

trăbālis -e (trabs). **I.** *of or relating to beams of wood*, clavus, *a spike*, Hor. **II.** *as strong or as large as a beam*, telum, Verg.

trăbĕa -ae, f. *the trabea, a white robe with scarlet horizontal stripes and a purple seam*, worn, **a,** by kings, Verg., Liv.; **b,** by knights on solemn processions, who were thence called trabeati; hence, meton. = *the equestrian order*, Mart.; **c,** by the augurs, Suet.

trăbĕātus -a -um (trabea), *clad in the trabea*, Quirinus, Ov.

trăbĕcŭla (trăbĭcŭla) -ae, f. (dim. of trabs), *a little beam*, Cato.

trabs, trăbis, f. (root TRAB, Gr. ΤΡΑΠ, whence τράπηξ). **I.** *a beam of wood*, Caes. **II.** Transf., **1,** *the trunk of a tree, a tree*, trabes acernae, Verg.; **2,** meton., *anything made out of beams*, **a,** *a ship*, Cypria, Hor.; **b,** *a roof, house*, sub isdem trabibus, Hor.; **c,** *a table*, Mart.

Trăchās -chantis, f. *a town in Italy* = Tarracina.

Trāchīn -chīnis, f. (Τραχίν), *an old town in the Thessalian district of Phthiotis, residence of Ceyx, scene of the death of Hercules, afterwards called Heraclea*. Hence, **Trāchīnĭus** -a -um (Τραχίνιος), *Trachinian*, heros, *Ceyx*, Ov.; so simply Trachinius, Ov.; plur. subst., Trachiniae, *the Trachinian women, name of a tragedy of Sophocles*.

tracta = tractum (q.v.).

tractābĭlis -e (tracto), *that can be handled or wrought, manageable*. **I.** Lit., tractabile omne necesse est esse, quod natum est, Cic.; caelum, *not stormy*, Verg. **II.** Transf., *yielding, compliant, tractable*, virtus, Cic.; nihil est eo (filio) tractabilius, Cic.

tractātĭo -ōnis, f. (tracto), *a handling, management*. **I.** Lit., beluarum, Cic.; armorum, Cic. **II.** Transf., **1,** *a treating of, handling*, philosophiae, Cic.; **2,** rhet. t. t., *a particular use of a word*, Cic.

tractātor -ōris, m. (tracto), *a slave who rubbed a bather's limbs, a shampooer*, Sen.

tractātrix -īcis, f. (tractator), *a female shampooer*, Mart.

tractātus -ūs, m. (tracto), *a handling, working, management*. **I.** Lit., Plin. **II.** Fig., *treatment, management*, **1,** gen., ipsarum artium tractatu delectari, Cic.; **2,** esp., *the treatment of a subject by an orator or writer*, Tac.

tractim, adv. (traho). **I.** *gradually, by degrees*, Lucr. **II.** *slowly, drawlingly*, susurrare, Verg.

tracto, 1. (traho). **I.** *to drag along, haul*: tractata comis antistita, Ov.; persona, quae propter otium ac studium minime in judiciis periculisque tractata est, Cic. **II.** *to touch*: **1,** lit., **a,** manu or manibus aliquid, Cic.; vulnera, Cic.; fila lyrae, Ov.; **b,** *to handle, busy oneself with, work, manage*, terram, Lucr.; gubernacula, *to steer*, Cic.; arma, *to carry*, Cic.; pecuniam publicam, *to manage the public finances*, Cic.; **2,** fig., **a,** gen., *to treat, handle, manage*, causas amicorum, Cic.; bellum, *conduct a war*, Liv.; tractare conditiones, *to treat about terms*,

Caes ; partes secundas, *to act, play,* Hor ; intransit , *to treat* , de conditionibus, Nep , **b,** esp , (α) *to treat, behave oneself towards* , aspere, Cic , honorificentius, Cic . (β) se, *to behave oneself,* ita se tractare ut, etc , Cic , (γ) of speech or writing, *to treat, discuss, handle a subject* , partem philosophiae, Cic

tractum -i, n (traho) **I.** *a flock of wool when carded or combed out,* Tib. **II.** *a cake,* Cato.

1 **tractus** -a -um, p adj. (from traho) **I.** *drawn from, proceeding from,* venae a corde tractae, Cic **II.** *fluent, flowing,* oratio tracta et fluens, Cic

2 **tractus** -ūs, m (traho), *a dragging* **I.** 1, *drawing, draught, course,* **a,** lit , tractu gementem ferre rotam, Verg , **b,** transf , (α) *the extent, space occupied by anything, position* , castrorum, Liv , tractus ductusque muri, Caes , (β) meton , *a tract of country, district* , totus, Cic , hoc tractu oppidi erat regia, Caes ; corruptus caeli tractus, Verg , **2,** *a drawing away,* Syrtes ab tractu nominatae, Sall **II.** Fig , **1,** *course, motion* , **a,** *calm movement, composed style* , tractus orationis lenis et aequabilis, Cic , **b,** of time, *course,* Lucr ; **2,** esp , **a,** *drawling in pronunciation* , tractus verborum, Cic , **b,** of time, *delay* , belli, Tac.

trāditĭo -ōnis, f (trado) **I.** *a giving up, transferring, surrender* , rei, Cic , oppidorum, Liv. **II.** *giving over by means of words,* **a,** of a teacher, *instruction,* Quint , **b,** of a writer, *relation,* Tac

trādĭtor ōris, m (trado), *a traitor,* Tac

trādo -dĭdi -dĭtum, 3 *to give up* **I.** In a narrow sense, *to give up, hand over,* alicui poculum, Cic , equum comiti, Verg , alicui testamentum legendum, Hor , regnum or imperium alicui per manus, Liv **II.** In a wider sense, *to give up, deliver over, consign to,* **1,** gen., pecuniam regiam quaestoribus, Liv , possessiones et res creditoribus, Caes , **2,** esp , **a,** *to hand over to a person's care, protection, management, to entrust,* alicui custodiam navium, Caes , alicui turrim tuendam, Caes , **b,** *to give to a person to lead* , alicui legionem, Caes , **c,** *to give in marriage* , alicui neptem Agrippinam, Tac , **d,** *to entrust to a person for instruction* , pueros magistris, Cic , **e,** *to give by way of protection* , equites Romanos satellites alicui, Sall , **f,** *to give over to the enemy, to hand over, deliver up* , arma, Caes , alicui Galliae possessionem, Caes , se alicui, Caes , **g,** *to give over by way of sale, to sell* , aliquem dominis, Ov , **h,** *to give up for punishment* , aliquem in custodiam, Cic , aliquem ad supplicium, Caes , **i** *to expose* , feris populandas terras, Ov , **j,** se, *to devote oneself to some thing or person, to give oneself over to,* se totum alicui, Cic , se quieti, Cic , totos se voluptatibus, Cic , **k,** *to give over by words* , (α) *to entrust* , quae dicam trado memoriae, Cic , (β) *to recommend* , aliquem alicui, Cic , **l,** *to hand down as a kind of inheritance to posterity* , (α) inimicitias posteris, Cic , haec consuetudo a majoribus tradita, Cic , (β) *to hand down in writing, report, relate* , qualia multa historia tradidit, Cic , annales tradunt, foll by acc and infin , Liv , so, tradunt (*they narrate*), traditur, etc , with acc and infin , Liv , with nom and infin , Lycurgi temporibus Homerus etiam fuisse traditur, Cic , traditum est, with acc and infin , Liv , Cic , **m,** *to communicate by word of mouth* , (α) clamorem proximis, Caes , (β) *to communicate in teaching, to teach* , elementa loquendi, Cic , haec subtilius, Cic

trādūco (transdūco) -duxi ductum, 3 **I.** *to carry over, lead over, bring over or across* **A.** Lit , **1,** hominum multitudinem trans Rhenum in Galliam, Caes , **2,** esp , *to bring or lead on,* with acc of object over which the thing is brought , flumen, pontem, Caes **B.** Fig , **1,** *to bring to, transpose, change,* **a,** Clodium ad plebem, Cic , centuriones ex inferioribus ordinibus in superiores, Caes , **b,** *to bring to a certain condition, alter, bring over* , animos a severitate ad hilaritatem risumque, Cic , aliquem a disputando ad dicendum, Cic , aliquem ad suam sententiam, Cic , **2,** *to pass time, spend, lead* otiosam aetatem, Cic , **3,** *to direct* , curam in vitulos, Verg , orationem traduxi et converti in increpandam fugam, Cic **II.** *to lead, conduct through* , Helvetios per fines Sequanorum, Caes **III** *to lead by, lead past* **A.** Lit **1,** copias praeter castra, Caes , **2,** esp , traducere equum (of a knight when he passed muster at the censor's inspection) , quum esset censor et in equitum censu C Licinius Sacerdos prodisset . . . jussit equum traducere, Cic **B.** Fig , **1,** *to show, let be seen;* se, Juv , **2,** *to expose to ridicule* aliquem per ora hominum, Liv

trāductĭo -ōnis, f (traduco), *a leading on* , fig , **1,** *a transferring of a man from a patrician family to a plebeian* , hominis ad plebem, Cic ; **2,** *a bringing to public disgrace,* Sen , **3,** *a figure of speech, metonymy,* Cic , **4,** temporis, *passage, course or lapse of time,* Cic

trāductor -ōris, m (traduco), *a transferrer* , ad plebem (of Pompeius, who procured the transference of Clodius from a patrician to a plebeian family), Cic

trādux -ŭcis, m (traduco), *a vine-layer, prepared for transplanting,* Plin

trăgăcantha -ae, f (τραγακάνθα), *a plant, goat's thorn, tragacanth,* Plin

trăgēmăta um, n (τραγήματα), *dessert,* Plin

trăgĭcē, adv (tragicus), *tragically, after the manner of a tragedy,* Cic

trăgĭcŏcōmoedĭa -ae, f (*τραγικοκωμῳδία), *tragi comedy,* Plaut

trăgĭcus a -um (τραγικός) **I.** *of or relating to tragedy, tragic* , poema, *tragedy,* Cic , poeta, *a tragic poet,* Cic , actor, Liv , Orestes, *appearing in a tragedy,* Cic , subst , **trăgĭcus** -i, m *a tragic poet,* Sen **II.** Transf , *tragic,* **a,** *in tragic style, lofty, sublime* , orator, Cic , **b,** *tragic, fearful, terrible, horrible* , scelus, Liv

trăgĭon -ii n (τράγιον), *a plant with a smell like a goat,* Plin

trăgoedĭa ae, f (τραγῳδία) **I.** *a tragedy,* Cic , tragoedias facere, Cic , tragoediam agere, Cic **II** Transf , **1,** *a tragic scene* · Appiae nomen quantas tragoedias excitat, Cic , **2,** *tragic pathos* , istis tragoediis tuis perturbor, Cic

trăgoedus -i, m (τραγῳδός), *a tragic actor, tragedian,* Cic

trăgōnis = tragion (q.v)

trăgŏpan -is, f (τραγόπαν), *a bird* (perhaps vultur barbatus, Linn), Plin

trăgŏpōgon -ōnis, m (τραγοπώγων), *the plant goat's beard,* Plin

trăgŏrīgănum -i, n (τραγορίγανον), *a plant, goat's thyme,* Plin

trăgos -i, m (τράγος), **1,** *a thorny plant,* Plin , **2,** *a kind of sponge,* Plin

trăgŭla -ae, f (traho) **I.** *a species of javelin used by the Gauls and Spaniards,* Caes , Liv ; fig., tragulam injicere in aliquem, *to use artifice,* Plaut **II.** *a kind of dragnet,* Plin **III.** *a kind of sledge,* Varr

trăgus -i, m (τράγος), **1,** *the smell under the armpits,* Mart , **2,** *a kind of fish,* Ov.

trăhĕa (trăha) -ae, f. (traho), *a sledge, drag*, Verg.

trăhax -ācis (traho), *drawing everything to oneself, greedy*, Plaut.

trăho, traxi, tractum, 3. *to draw, drag along*. **I.** Gen., **A.** Lit., aliquem pedibus, Cic.; ad supplicium trahi, Sall., Tac., or trahi alone, Sall. **B.** Fig., **1**, *to lead, draw away;* trahit sua quemque voluptas, Verg.; quid est quod me in aliam partem trahere possit? Cic.; **2**, *to bring upon;* decus ad consulem, Liv.; crimen in se, Ov.; **3**, *to ascribe, interpret, refer to;* aliquid ad religionem, Liv.; in diversa, Liv. **II.** Esp., **A.** *to draw after oneself, drag along;* **1**, **a**, lit., vestem, Hor.; esp. from fatigue, corpus fessum, Liv.; **b**, *to lead, conduct with oneself;* exercitum, Liv.; turbam prosequentium, Liv.; **2**, fig., tantum trahit ille timoris, Ov. **B.** *to draw to oneself, draw to, attract;* **1**, **a**, lit., auras ore, Ov.; animam, *to breathe*, Liv.: esp., of persons drinking, *to quaff;* pocula, Hor.; **b**, transf., *to put on oneself;* squamas, Ov.; ruborem, Ov.; **2**, fig., **a**, *to assume;* multum ex moribus (Sarmatarum) traxisse, Tac.; **b**, *to take to oneself, appropriate;* decumas, Cic.; **c**, *to receive, gain;* cognomen ex aliqua re, Cic.; majorem ex pernicie et peste reipublicae molestiam, *to feel*, Cic.; **d**, *to take;* in exemplum, Ov. **C.** *to draw together;* vultus, Ov.; vela, *to furl*, Verg. **D.** *to draw away, drag off;* **1**, lit., aliquem a templo, Verg.; praedas ex agris, Liv.; hence, *to plunder;* Aeduorum pagos, Tac.; **2**, fig., **a**, *to draw away from;* ab incepto, Sall.; **b**, *to take away;* partem doloris trahebat publica clades, Liv.; **c**, *to borrow;* consilium ex aliqua re, Sall.; **d**, *to deduce, derive;* sermonem ab initio, Cic. **E.** *to draw out, bring out, get out;* **1**, lit., aquam e puteis, Cic.; ferrum e vulnere or a vulnere, Ov.; **2**, transf., vocem uno a pectore, Verg. **F.** *to draw down;* lunam (de caelo), Ov. **G.** *to draw* or *drag hither and thither;* **1**, lit., corpus tractum, Cic.; **2**, fig., **a**, *to distract*, Tac.; **b**, *to squander;* pecuniam, Sall.; **c**, *to divide;* sorte laborem, Verg.; **d**, *to reflect on;* rationes belli, Sall. **H.** *to draw out in length;* **1**, lit., **a**, *to lengthen;* in spatium aures, Ov.; **b**, *to spin out;* data pensa, Ov.; **c**, *to card;* lanam mollem trahendo, Ov.; **2**, fig., of time, **a**, *to prolong, delay, put off;* pugnam, Liv.; comitia, Cic.; rem in serum, Liv.; **b**, *to drag along;* vitam in tenebris, Verg.

trăĭcĭo = trajicio (q.v.).

trājectĭo -ōnis, f. (trajicio). **I.** *a passing over, crossing over;* **a**, of a person over the sea, *passage*, Cic.; **b**, of things, stellarum, Cic. **II.** Fig., **A.** Gen., trajectio in alium, *a putting off upon*, Cic. **B.** Esp., **1**, *the transposition of words;* verborum, Cic.; **2**, *hyperbole;* veritatis superlatio atque trajectio, Cic.

trājectus -ūs, m. (trajicio), *a crossing over, passing over, passage;* fluminis, Liv.; commodissimus in Britanniam, Caes.

trājĭcĭo (traĭcĭo) -jēci -jectum, 3. (trans and jacio). **I.** *to throw over* or *across, to shoot across, convey over.* **A.** Gen., telum, Caes.; vexillum trans vallum, Liv. **B.** Esp., **1**, *to lead over* or *around, to remove, throw across;* malos antennasque de nave in navem, Liv.; trajecto in fune, *a rope slung round the mast*, Verg.; **2**, *to bring over;* **a**, membra super acervum levi pede, *to leap over*, Ov.; fig., aliquid ex illius invidia in te, Cic.; **b**, *to transport over the sea, a river, a mountain, etc.;* legiones in Siciliam, Liv.; copias trans fluvium, Liv.; Marius trajectus in Africam, *having crossed*, Cic.; with acc. of the place, equitum magnam partem flumen, Caes.; reflex., with or without se, *to cross over, go over;* sese ex regia ad aliquem, Caes.; sese duabus navibus in Africam, Liv.; trajicere Trebiam navibus, Liv.; with abl. of the water crossed, Aegaeo mari trajecit, Liv. **II.** *to throw over, hurl beyond;* **1**, murum jaculo, Cic.; **2**, **a**, *to pierce through, stab, transfix;* aliquem venabulo, Liv.; alicui femur tragulā, Caes.; **b**, *to ride through, break through;* pars magna equitum mediam trajecit aciem, Liv.

trālātīcius = translaticius (q.v.)

trālātĭo = translatio (q.v.).

trālātus, v. transfero.

trālŏquor (translŏquor), 3. dep. *to relate*, Plaut.

1. **Tralles** -ium, m. (Τράλλες), *an Illyrian people*, Liv. (acc. Trallis).

2. **Trallēs** = Trallis (q.v.).

Trallis -ium, f. (αἱ Τράλλεις), *a town in Caria, near Mount Mesogis.* Hence, **Trallĭānus** -a -um, *of* or *relating to Tralles.*

trālūcĕo = transluceo (q.v.).

trāma -ae, f. (traho), *the woof* in weaving; transf., *the spider's web*, Plin.; trama figurae, *a lanky, lean person*, Pers.; tramae putridae, *trifles*, Plaut.

trāmĕo = transmeo (q.v.).

trāmes -ĭtis, m. (trameo), *a by-way, cross-road.* **I.** Lit., Apennini tramites, Cic.; transversis tramitibus transgredi, Liv. **II.** Transf., poet., *a way, course, road, path;* cito decurrit tramite virgo, Verg.

trāmīgro = transmigro (q.v.).

trāmitto = transmitto (q.v.).

trānăto (transnăto), 1. *to swim across*, Tac.; with acc. of place, Gangem, Cic.

trāno (transno), 1. **I.** *to swim over, swim across;* ad suos, Liv.; with acc. of place, flumen, Caes.; pass., tranantur aquae, Ov. **II.** Transf., *to swim through, to sail through, go through, fly through, pass through;* nubila, Verg.; genus igneum quod tranat omnia, *pervades*, Cic.

tranquillē, adv. with compar. and superl. (tranquillus), *quietly, tranquilly*, Cic.

tranquillĭtas -ātis, f. (tranquillus), *calmness, tranquillity.* **I.** Lit., *a calm, freedom from wind, calm sea, weather;* maris, Cic.; summā tranquillitate consecutā, Caes.; tanta subito malacia et tranquillitas exstitit, Caes. **II.** Transf., *rest, peace;* **a**, polit., summa tranquillitas pacis atque otii, Cic.; **b**, *mental;* animi, Cic.

1. **tranquillō**, adv. (tranquillus), *quietly*, Liv.

2. **tranquillo**, 1. (tranquillus), *to make tranquil, tranquillise.* **I.** Lit., mare oleo, Plin. **II.** Fig., animos, Cic.

tranquillus -a -um (trans and quies), *tranquil.* **I.** Lit., *calm;* esp., *free from wind;* mare, Cic.; serenitas, Liv.; subst., **tranquillum** -i, n. *a calm;* in tranquillo tempestatem adversam optare dementis est, Cic. **II.** Transf., *peaceful, tranquil, undisturbed, serene;* tranquilla et serena frons, Cic.; subst., **tranquillum** -i, n. *quiet;* rempublicam in tranquillum redigere, Liv.

trans, prep. with acc. **I.** *on the other side of;* trans montem, Cic.; trans Rhenum, Caes. **II.** *over, across;* trans Alpes transfertur, Cic.; trans mare currunt, Hor.

transăbĕo -ii -ĭtum, 4. *to go through, penetrate;* ensis transabiit costas, Verg.

transactor -ōris, m. (transigo), *a manager, accomplisher;* rerum huiuscemodi omnium transactor et administer, Cic.

transădĭgo -ēgi -actum, 3. **I.** *to drive through, thrust through;* crudum ensem transadigit costas, Verg II. *to pierce, penetrate*, hasta horum unum transadigit costas Verg

transalpinus a -um, *beyond the Alps, transalpine*, Gallia, Caes

transcendo (transscendo) scendi -scensum, 3 (trans and scando) I. Intransit, *to climb over, step over, pass over*, 1, lit, in hostium naves, Caes, 2, fig, ad ea (of discourse), Tac. II. Transit, *to climb over, step over*, 1, lit., muros, Liv., Caucasum, Cic, 2, fig, *to step over, transgress*, fines juris, Lucr, ordinem aetatis, Liv

transcīdo cidi -cisum, 3 (trans and caedo), *to cut through*, Plaut

transcrībo (transscrībo) -scripsi -scriptum, 3 *to copy, transcribe* I Gen, testamentum in alias tabulas, Cic II. Esp, 1, *to transfer, assign*, a, lit, nomina in socios, Liv, b, transf, alicui spatium vitae, Ov, sceptra colonis, Ov, 2, *to transfer*, matres urbi, Verg

transcurro -cŭcurri and -curri cursum, 3 I. 1, *to run over, hasten over*, ad forum, Ter, in castra, Liv; 2, fig, *to pass over*, ad melius, Hor II. A. *to run or hasten through*, 1, lit, per spatium, Lucr, with acc, caelum transcurrit nimbus, Verg; 2, fig, cursum suum, Cic B. *to sail or travel past*, 1, lit, Caes, praeter oculos, Ov, 2, fig, of time, *to pass by*, Plin

transcursus -ūs, m (transcurro), 1, *a running past, hastening through*, Sen, 2, of discourse, *a brief mention*, Plin

transdānŭvĭānus -a -um, *beyond the Danube*, Liv

transdo = trado (q v)

transdūco = traduco (q v)

transenna -ae, f (for transepna from trans and apo) I. *a number of ropes or wooden bars, transposed crosswise*, hence, *a net for catching birds*, 1, lit, Plaut, 2, fig, *a net, trap, noose*, Plaut II. *a lattice over a window*, Cic

transĕo -ii -itum, 4 I. Intransit, A. *to go over to, go to*, 1, a, ad uxorem, Ter, in Helvetiorum fines, Caes, b, *to go over as a deserter*, ad aliquem, Cic, c, *to go over from one political party to another*, Tac, d, *to pass from one rank to another*, a patribus ad plebem, Liv, e, transf, *to be changed into, to be transformed into*, in saxum, Ov, 2, fig, a, transitum est ad honestatem dictorum et factorum, Cic, b, of discourse, *to pass over, make a transition*, ad partitionem, Cic, c, *to go over to an opinion*, in alicuius sententiam, *to be converted to the opinion of*, Liv B. *to go through*, 1, lit, per media castra, Sall, 2, fig, *to penetrate*, quaedam animalis intelligentia per omnia permanat et transit, Cic C. *to pass by*, transf, of time, *to pass by, pass away*, transit aetas quam cito! Tib, dies legis transit, Cic. II. Transit., A *to go over, pass over*, 1, lit, a, Euphratem, Cic, pass, Rhodanus transitur, Caes, b, esp, *to overtake*, equum cursu, Verg, 2, fig, a, *to pass beyond, to transgress*, fines verecundiae, Cic, b, *to surpass*, facile, Cic, c, *to despatch*, magna, Tac B. *to go through, pass through*, 1, lit, Formias, Cic, vim flammae, Nep, 2, fig, a, *to pass over cursorily, to touch lightly on*, leviter transire et tantummodo perstringere unamquamque rem, Cic, b, of time, *to pass, spend*, annum quiete, Tac, vitam, Sall C. *to pass by*, 1, lit, omnes mensas, Plaut, 2, fig, *to pass by*, aliquid silentio, Cic (perf, transit, Verg)

transsĕro (transsĕro) -serui -sertum, 3 *to put, thrust through*, Cato

transfĕro (trāfĕro), transtŭli, translātum, and trālātum, transferre, 3 *to carry over or across, transfer, transport, convey*, A. Lit., 1, gen, Caesar paullo ultra eum locum castra transtulit, Caes, aliquem trans Alpes, Cic, reflex, se transferre Glyceriae decimam in aedem, Hor, 2, esp, *to write down*, in tabulas, Cic. B. Fig, 1, gen, *to bring over, remove, transpose*, regnum ab sede Lavini, Verg, omnia Argos, *give the victory to Argos* Verg, in Celtibericum bellum, Caes, sermonem alio, *turn to another subject*, Cic, 2, esp, a, *to put off, defer*, causam in proximum annum, ap Cic, b, *to change to*, definitionem in aliam rem, Cic, c, *to translate into another language*, istum ego locum totidem verbis a Dicaearcho transtuli, Cic, d, *to use figuratively or metaphorically*, verba, quae transferuntur, Cic

transfīgo -fixi -fixum, 3 I. *to pierce through, transfix*, puellam gladio, Liv, transfixus hastā, Cic II. *to thrust through*, hasta transfixa, Verg

transfĭgūrātĭo ōnis, f (transfiguro), *a transformation, transfiguration*, Plin

transfĭgūro, 1 *to transform, transfigure*, Suet, Plin

transflŭo -fluxi, 3 *to flow out, flow through*, Plin

transfŏdĭo fōdi -fossum, 3 *to stab through, transpierce, transfix*, alicui latus, Liv, aliquem, Caes partic, with acc of respect, pectora duro transfossi ligno, Verg.

transformis e (trans and forma), *changed, transformed*, Ov

transformo, 1 *to change, transfigure, transform*, se in vultus aniles, Verg

transfŏro, 1 *to pierce, thrust through*, Sen

transfrĕto, 1 (trans and fretum), *to cross the sea*, Suet

transfŭga ae, c (transfugio), *a deserter*, Cic, specie transfugarum ad Flaccum venire, Liv, transf transfuga divitum partes linquere gestio, Hor

transfŭgĭo -fūgi fūgitum, 3 *to desert to the enemy* I. Lit, Gabios, Romam, Liv, absol, quod in obsidione et fame servitia infida transfugerent, Liv II. Fig, ab afflicta amicitia transfugere et ad florentem aliam devolare, *to desert unhappy friends*, Cic

transfŭgium ii n (transfugio), *a going over to the enemy, deserting*, Liv

transfundo fūdi -fūsum, 3 *to pour from one vessel into another* I. Lit, Plin II. Transf, *to transfer*, omnem amorem in aliquem, Cic

transfūsĭo -ōnis, f (transfundo) *a pouring out, pouring off* I. Lit, Plin II. Transf, *the migration of a people*, Cic

transgrĕdĭor -gressus sum 3 dep (trans and gradior) I Intransit, *to go across or over, pass over* A. Lit, 1, gen, in Europam, Liv, per montes, Liv, 2, esp, *to pass over to any one's side or party*, in partes alicuius, Tac B. Transf, *to pass over to some action, advance*, tarde ad sacramentum, Tac II. Transit, *to pass over, pass through* A. Lit, Taurum, Cic, flumen, Caes B. Transf, a, *to pass beyond some measure or time*, Plin, b, *to pass over in silence*, mentionem viri, Vell c, *to surpass*, Plin (partic perf pass, transgresso Apennino, Liv 10 27 1)

transgressĭo -ōnis, f (transgredior) I. Intransit, *a going over, passage*, ascensus et transgressio Gallorum (over the Alps), Cic II. Transit, *a transposition of words*, verborum, Cic

transgressus -ūs, m (transgredior), *a going over, passage*, auspicium prosperi transgressus, Tac, with object genit, amnis, Tac

transigo -ēgi -actum, 3. (trans and ago), *to drive through.* **I.** Lit., *to stab, pierce through;* se ipsum gladio, Tac. **II.** Fig., **1,** *to pass time, spend, lead;* tempus per ostentationem, Tac.; **2,** *to finish, complete, accomplish, transact any piece of business;* **a,** gen., negotium, Cic.; aliquid cum aliquo, aliquid per aliquem, Cic.; impers., si transactum est, *if it is done,* Cic.; **b,** esp., *to settle a difference* or *dispute, come to an understanding;* cum aliquo H.S. ducentis millibus, Cic.; transf., *to put an end to, have done with;* transigito cum expeditionibus, Tac.

transĭlĭo (transsĭlĭo) -ŭi and (rarely) -ĭi and -īvi, 4. (trans and salio). **I.** Intransit., *to spring over, leap across;* **1,** lit., de muro in navem, Liv.; **2,** fig., ab illo consilio ad aliud, *to go over to,* Liv. **II.** Transit., *to spring over something;* **1, a,** lit., *to spring over;* muros, Liv.; **b,** transf., *to hasten over;* rates transiliunt vada, Hor.; **2,** fig., **a,** *to pass by, pass over;* rem, Cic.; **b,** *to overstep, transgress;* lineas, Cic.; munera Liberi, *be immoderate with,* Hor.

transĭlis -e (transilio), *leaping across, going across;* palmes, Plin.

transĭtĭo -ōnis, f. (transeo). **I.** *a going across, passing over.* **A.** Lit., **1,** gen., imagines similitudine et transitione perceptae, Cic.; **2,** esp., *a going over from one party* or *faction to another:* **a,** ad plebem transitiones, Cic.; **b,** *a passing over to the enemy;* sociorum, Liv.; exercitus transitionibus imminutus, Liv. **B.** Fig., *infection, contagion,* Ov. **II.** *a passage* (meton., as a place); transitiones perviae Jani nominantur, Cic.

transĭtōrĭus -a -um (transeo), *having a passage through;* domus, Suet.

transĭtus -ūs, m. (transeo). **I.** *a passing over* or *across, transit.* **A.** Lit., **1,** gen., transitus fossae, Cic.; transitum claudere, Liv.; **2,** esp., *a passing over from one party* or *faction to another;* facili transitu ad proximos et validiores, Tac. **B.** Fig., **a,** *the transition* (in painting) *from shade to light,* Plin., Ov.; **b,** *transition in discourse,* Quint. **II.** *a passing through.* **A.** Lit., per agros urbesque, Liv. **B.** Meton., *the place through which one passes;* transitus insidēre, Liv. **III.** *a passing by;* tempestatis, Cic.; in transitu capta urbs, Tac.

transjectĭo, etc. = trajectio, etc. (q.v.).

translātīcĭus (trālātīcĭus) -a -um (translatus, from transfero), *handed down as customary, prescriptive;* **a,** edictum, *received by a magistrate from his predecessor,* Cic.; **b,** *common, usual;* haec tralaticia, *ordinary course of things,* ap. Cic.

translātĭo (trālātĭo) -ōnis, f. (translatus, from transfero), *a transferring, handing over.* **I.** Lit., **1,** pecuniarum a justis dominis ad alienos, Cic.; **2,** *a grafting of plants,* Plin. **II.** Fig., **1,** *a transferring;* **a,** of a judge, accuser, place, etc., Cic.; **b,** of an accusation, criminis, Cic.; **2,** *a metaphor, trope, figure;* verecunda, Cic.

translātīvus -a -um (transfero), *of* or *relating to a transference;* constitutio, Cic.

translātor -ōris, m. (transfero), *a transferrer;* quaesturae (of Verres, who, being quaestor to the consul Cn. Papirius Carbo, deserted to Sulla), Cic.

translūcĕo (trālūcĕo), 2. **I.** *to shine across,* Lucr. **II.** *to shine through, be visible through,* Ov.

translūcĭdus (trālūcĭdus) -a -um, *transparent, translucent,* Plin.

transmărīnus -a -um, *from beyond sea, foreign, transmarine;* artes, Cic.; legationes, Liv.

transmĕo (trāmĕo), 1. *to go over, across, through,* Plin.

transmīgro, 1. *to migrate from one place to another;* Veios, Liv.; transf., of plants, *to be transplanted,* Plin.

transmissĭo -ōnis, f. (transmitto), *a passage;* ab eā urbe in Graeciam, Cic.

transmissus -ūs, m. (transmitto), *a passage;* pari spatio transmissus atque ex Gallia in Britanniam, Caes.

transmitto (trāmitto) -mīsi -missum, 3. **I.** *to send across, send over, convey across, transmit from one place to another.* **A. 1,** lit., equitatum celeriter, Caes.; classem in Euboeam ad urbem Oreum, Liv.; **2,** fig., **a,** bellum in Italiam, Liv.; **b,** *to give over;* (α) *to entrust;* huic hoc tantum bellum, Cic.; (β) *to resign, yield;* munia imperii, Tac.; (γ) *to devote;* suum tempus temporibus amicorum, Cic. **B.** *to let pass, let through;* **1,** gen., exercitum per fines, Liv.; **2,** *to lead from one point to another;* transmissum per viam tigillum, *placed across the road,* Liv. **C.** *to let pass;* Junium mensem transmisimus, Tac. **II.** *to place oneself, to go, run, swim, pass through* or *over something;* **1,** lit., **a,** gen., (α) with acc. of place, maria, Cic.; (β) absol., sin ante transmisisset, Cic.; **b,** esp., *to hurl,* or *throw over* or *through,* Ov.; **2,** fig., *to leave unnoticed, take no heed to, take no notice of, not to mind;* Scaurum silentio transmisit, Tac.

transmontāni -ōrum, m. *dwellers beyond the mountains,* Liv.

transmŏvĕo -mōvi -mōtum, 2. *to remove from one place to another.* **I.** Lit., Syriā legiones, Tac. **II.** Fig., *to transfer,* Ter.

transmūtātĭo -ōnis, f. (transmuto), *the transmutation of letters,* Quint.

transmūto, 1. *to change, transmute;* dextera laevis, Lucr.; incertos honores, Hor.

transnăto = tranato (q.v.).

transnōmĭno, 1. *to change the name of a person* or *thing,* Suet.

transpădānus -a -um, *beyond* (i.e., on the north side of) *the Po, transpadane;* colonia, Caes.; clientes, Cic. Subst., **transpădānŭs** -i, m. *a person living on the north side of the Po,* Cat.; plur., Cic.

transpectus -ūs, m. (transpicio), *a looking through, seeing through,* Lucr.

transpĭcĭo (transspĭcĭo), 3. (trans and specio), *to look through, see through,* Lucr.

transpōno -pŏsŭi -pŏsĭtum, 3. **I.** *to put over, across, remove, transfer,* Plin. **II.** (= trajicere), *to put across* (a river); militem dextras in terras iturum, Tac.

transportātĭo -ōnis, f. (transporto), *a migration,* Sen.

transporto, 1. *to convey from one place to another, transport;* exercitum in Graeciam, Cic; milites his navibus flumen transportat, Caes.

transrhēnānus -a -um (trans and Rhenus), *beyond* (i.e., on the east side of) *the Rhine;* Germani, Caes.

transs . . . v. trans . . .

transtĭbĕrīnus -a -um (trans and Tiberis), *beyond the Tiber.* Subst., **transtĭbĕrīni** -ōrum, m. *the people living beyond the Tiber,* Cic.

transtĭnĕo, 2. (teneo), *to go through, pass through,* Plaut.

transtrum -i, n. (from trans). **I.** *a crossbench in a ship on which the rowers sat,* gen. plur., Caes. **II.** *a cross-beam,* Caes.

transulto (transsulto), 1. (intens. of transilio), *to spring over* or *across,* Liv.

transŭo (transsŭo) -sŭi -sūtum, 3. *to sew*

through, stitch through, pierce through; exta transuta verubus, Ov

transvŏctio (trăvectio) -ōnis, f (transveho) **I.** *a carrying over or across*, Acherontis, Cic **II.** *the riding of a Roman knight past the censor at the periodical muster*, Suet

transvĕho (trăvĕho) -vexi -vectum, 3 **I** *to carry over, convey across, transport* **A.** Act, milites, Caes, naves plaustris, Liv **B.** Middle, transvehi, *to ride, sail, pass over or across*; in Africam, Sall, Corcyram, Liv **II.** *to carry through or by* **A.** Act, *to bear along in triumph*, arma spoliaque carpentis, Liv. **B.** Middle, transvehi = *to go, ride, pass by*, **1**, lit, **a**, gen, transvectae a fronte pugnantium alae, Tac, **b**, esp at a public procession, *to ride by*, (α) of the Caesars at the games in the circus, Tac, (β) of a knight, *to ride past the censor at a muster*, Liv, **2**, fig, of time, *to pass, pass by*, abiit jam et transvectum est tempus, Tac

transverbĕro, 1 *to pierce through, transfix, perforate*, bestiam venabulo, Cic, pectus alicuius abiete, Verg

transversārĭus -a -um (transversus), *lying across, transverse*, tigna, Caes

transversus (trăversus), and **transvorsus)** a um, p adj (from transverto), *transverse, oblique, athwart* **I.** Adj, **A.** Lit, fossa, Caes, transverso ambulare foro, *across the forum*, Cic, transverso itinere, *in an oblique direction*, Liv, fig transversum digitum, *a finger's breadth*, Cic, transversum digitum, *the breadth of a nail*, Cic **B.** Fig, cuius in adulescentiam transversa incurrit misera reipublicae fortuna, *crossed, thwarted*, Cic **II.** Subst, **transversum** i, n *a cross direction*, Plin, de or ex transverso, *unexpectedly*, ecce tibi e transverso Lampsacenus Strabo qui, etc, Cic **III.** Adv., transversum and plur, transversa, *across, sideways*, venti transversa fremunt, Verg

transvŏlito, 1 *to fly across*, Lucr

transvŏlo (trăvŏlo), 1 **I.** *to fly over or across*, **1**, lit, of birds, Plin, **2**, transf, *to hasten over, hasten across, pass over hastily*, Alpes, ap Cic, eques transvolat in alteram partem, Liv **II. 1**, *to fly through or to, to fly through*, transf = *to hasten through*, dum (vox) transvolat aures, Lucr, **2**, *to fly past*, **a**, transf, *to hasten past*, aridas quercus, Hor, **b**, fig, transvolat in medio posita, *passes by*, Hor

trăpētus -i, m, **trăpētum** i, n, and plur, **trăpetes** -um, m (τραπέω, *to tread grapes*), *an oil-press*, Verg

trăpezīta ae, m (τραπεζίτης), *a money-changer*, Plaut

Trăpezūs -untis, f (Τραπεζοῦς), *a town in Pontus, colony of Sinope*, now *Trebizond*, *Tarabosan*

Trăsŭmēnus (Trăsĭmennus, Trăsĭmēnus, Trăsȳmēnus) -i, m (with or without lacus); *the Trasimene lake, on the banks of which Hannibal conquered the Romans under Flaminius* (217 B C), now *Lago di Perugia* Hence, adj, **Trăsŭmēnus** a -um, *Trasimenian*

trav . . . v transv . . .

trāvĭo, 1 *to go through, penetrate*, Lucr

Trĕbĭa -ae, m *a river in Cisalpine Gaul, where Hannibal conquered the Romans*, 217 B C, now *Trebbia*

Trĕbŭla -ae, f *three towns in Italy* **I.** In the Sabine country **A.** Trebula Mutusca Hence, **Trĕbŭlānus** -a -um, *belonging to Trebula* **B.** Trebula Suffena **II.** In Campania, near Suessula and Saticula, now *Maddaloni* Hence, **Trĕbŭlānus** a -um, *belonging to Trebula*

trĕcēnārĭus -a um (treceni), *three hundred-fold*, Varr

trĕcēni ae -a (tres and centum) **I.** *three hundred each*, Liv **II.** *three hundred* Plin

trĕcentēsĭmus a -um (trecenti), *the three-hundredth*, Cic

trĕcenti ae a (tres and centum), *three hundred*, Cic

trĕcentĭēs (trĕcentĭens), adv (trecenti), *three hundred times*, Cat

trĕchĕdipnum -i, n (τρεχέδειπνος -ον, *hastening to dinner*), *a light garment worn by parasites at table*, Juv

trĕdĕcim (tres and decem), *thirteen*, Liv

trĕmĕbundus (trĕmĭbundus) -a um (tremo), *trembling*, manus, Cic

trĕmĕfăcio -fēci -factum, 3 (tremo and facio), *to cause to tremble*, pass, **trĕmĕfīo** -factus sum -fĭĕri *to tremble*, Verg, Ov

trĕmendus -a um (tremo), *fearful dreadful, terrible, dread*, Hor, rex, *Pluto*, Verg

trĕmesco (trĕmisco), 3 (inchoat of tremo) **I.** Intransit, *to tremble, quake*, **a**, of things, tonitru tremescunt ardua terrarum et campi, Verg **b**, of persons, omnem tremescens ad strepitum, Ov **II.** Transit, *to tremble at*, sonitum pedum vocemque, Verg, with infin, telum instare tremescit, Verg

trĕmĭbundus = tremebundus (q v)

trĕmisco = tremesco (q v).

trĕmo -ŭi, 3 (τρέμω), *to tremble, quake* **I.** Intransit, **a**, of things, tremit hasta, Verg, **b**, of persons, toto pectore tremens, Cic, with acc. of respect, tremis ossa pavore, Hor **II.** Transit, *to tremble, quake at*, offensam Junonem, Ov, te, Verg, virgas ac secures dictatoris, Liv.

trĕmor -ōris, m (tremo) **I.** *a trembling, quaking, tremor*, of the limbs, pallor et tremor et dentium crepitus, Liv, of fire, tremor ignium clarus, Lucr, of the earth, Verg, plur, Lucr, Ov **II.** Meton, *an object which causes fear and trembling*, Mart

trĕmŭlus -a um (tremo) **I.** *trembling, quaking, quivering, tremulous*, **a**, of things, lumen, Verg, mare, Ov, **b**, of persons, accurrit ad me tremulus, Ter **II** Act, *causing trembling*, Prop

trĕpĭdantĕr, adv (trepido), *anxiously, with trepidation*, omnia trepidantius timidiusque agere, Caes

trĕpĭdātĭo -ōnis, f (trepido), *agitation, anxiety, disquiet, alarm, trepidation*, Cic, tantam trepidationem injecit ut, etc, Liv

trĕpĭdē, adv (trepidus), *tremblingly, anxiously, with trepidation*, castra relinquere, Liv.

trĕpĭdo, 1 (trepidus), *to be in anxious, confused motion, be agitated, be in alarm, be busy, bustle about anything*, **a**, lit, of living beings, totis trepidatur castris, *the whole camp is in confusion*, Caes, circa advenam *swarm confusedly around*, Liv, circa signa, *give way in front*, Liv, of anxious haste, ad arma, Liv, with inter and the acc, *to be undecided between*, *to waver between*, inter fugae pugnaeque consilium, Liv, with acc = *to fear anxiously*, occursum amici, Juv, with infin, ne trepidate meas defendere naves, Verg, **b**, transit, of things, aqua per pronum trepidat rivum, *ripples* Hor, trepidant flammae, *flicker*, Hor, with infin, cuius octavum trepidavit (*is hastening on*) aetas claudere lustrum, Hor

trĕpĭdus -a -um (τρεω), *unquiet, anxious, alarmed, restless, disturbed;* **a,** lit., of living beings and the situation of living beings, trepida Dido, Verg.; of undecided or rash haste, civitas, Liv.; with genit., *on account of;* rerum suarum, Liv.; metus, Ov.; cursus, Verg.; in re trepida, in rebus trepidis, *in an alarming state of things,* Liv.; **b,** transf., of things, unda, *boiling, bubbling,* Ov.; ahenum, *boiling,* Verg.

trēs (archaic, trīs), tria (τρεῖς, τρία), *three,* Cic.

tressis -is, m. (tres and as), *three asses,* Varr.

tresvĭri = triumviri (q.v.).

Trēvĕri (Trēvĭri) -ōrum, m. *a powerful German nation from the Rhine to the Maas, whose capital Augusta* or *Colonia Treverorum is now Trèves* or *Trier.* Sing., **Trēvir** -viri, *one of the Treveri.* Hence, adj., **Trēvĕrĭcus (Trēvĭrĭcus)** -a -um, *of* or *belonging to the Treveri.*

trĭangŭlus -a -um (tres and angulus), *three-cornered, triangular.* Subst., **trĭangŭlum** -i, n. *a triangle,* Cic.

trĭārĭi -ōrum, m. (tres), *the oldest and most experienced Roman soldiers, who were drawn up in the third rank, kneeling behind the* hastati *and* principes, *ready to help these in need;* hence, prov., res ad triarios rediit, *the matter has come to the extremest need,* Liv.

trĭbas -ădis, f. (τριβάς), *an unchaste woman,* Phaedr.

Tribŏces -um, m. and **Tribŏci** -ōrum, m. *a Gallic people on the left bank of the Rhine, in modern Alsace.*

trĭbrăchys, acc. -chyn, m. (τρίβραχυς), sc. pes, *a metrical foot, consisting of three short syllables* (◡ ◡ ◡), Quint.

trĭbŭārĭus -a -um (tribus), *of* or *relating to a tribe,* Cic.

trībŭla = tribulum (q.v.).

trĭbūlis -is, m. (tribus), *one who belongs to the same tribe, a fellow tribesman;* tribulis tuus, Cic.; esp., *a fellow tribesman of the lower classes, one of the common people,* Hor.

trībŭlo, 1. (tribulum), *to press,* Cato.

trībŭlum -i, n. (tero), *a threshing machine,* Varr.

trĭbŭlus -i, m. **1,** *a thorny plant* (Tribulus terrestris, Linn.), Ov.; **2,** *an aquatic plant* (Trapa natans, Linn.), Plin.

trĭbūnal -ālis, n. (= tribunale, from tribunus), *the tribunal.* **I.** Lit., *a raised platform for magistrates,* e.g., for the consul when he directed the comitia, the praetor when he administered justice; in tribunali Pompeii praetoris urbani sedentes, Cic.; of the raised seat of a general in the camp, Liv.; of the praetor in the theatre, Suet.; meton., of the magistrate sitting on the tribunal, omne forum (*the people*) quem spectat et omne tribunal, *the magistrates, distinguished persons,* Hor. **II.** Transf., **A.** *a monument erected in honour of the dead,* Tac. **B.** *a mound, embankment of earth,* Plin.

trĭbūnātus -ūs, m. (tribunus), *the office or dignity of a tribune, tribuneship;* **a,** of the people, with or without plebis, Cic.; **b,** of a military tribune, militaris, Cic.

trĭbūnĭcĭus -a -um (tribunus), *of* or *relating to a tribune, tribunicial;* **a,** *belonging to a tribune of the people;* potestas, Cic.; subst., **trĭbūnĭcĭus** -ii, m. *a person who has been tribune;* **b,** *relating to the tribunes of the soldiers;* honos, Caes.

trĭbūnus -i, m. (tribus). **I.** tribuni, *the presidents of the three old tribes, representative of the* tribules, *at the head of whom was the* tribunus Celerum, Liv. **II. A.** tribuni aerarii, *paymasters who assisted the quaestors, and who were afterwards made judges,* Cic. **B.** Milit. t. t.; tribuni militum or militares, *military tribunes, six to every legion, who commanded it each for two months in the year,* Caes. **C.** tribuni militum consulari potestate (also called tribuni consulares), chosen to govern in the place of consuls, from 444–366 B.C., Liv. **D.** tribuni plebis (plebi) and (more frequently) simply tribuni, *the tribunes of the people, the magistrates who protected the plebeians,* Cic., Liv.

trĭbŭo -ui -ūtum, 3. **I.** *to allot to any one as a share, bestow, assign, give.* **A.** Lit., praemia alicui, Caes.; suum cuique, Cic. **B.** Fig., **1,** gen., *to give, show;* alicui misericordiam suam, Cic.; alicui magnam gratiam, Cic.; **2,** esp., **a,** *to give up, concede, yield to;* valetudini aliquid, Cic.; alicui priores partes, Cic.; **b,** *to ascribe, attribute to;* id virtuti hostium, Caes.; **c,** *to devote time to a particular purpose;* his rebus tantum temporis, Caes. **II.** = distribuo, *to divide;* rem in partes, Cic.

trĭbus -ūs, f. (from root tri, *three,* and the root fu in φυλή), originally, *a third part of the Roman people.* Hence, **I.** *a tribe, one of the three tribes of the Roman people* (Ramnes, Tities, Luceres); from the time of Servius Tullius a new division was made, viz., of four tribes for the city (tribus urbanae), and twenty-six, and later thirty-one, for the ager Romanus (tribus rusticae); populum in tribus convocare, Cic. **II.** Meton., plur., tribus = *the lower classes, the mob,* Plin.

trĭbūtārĭus -a -um (tributum), *of* or *relating to tribute;* tabellae, Cic.

trĭbūtim, adv. (tribus), *according to tribes, tribe by tribe;* nummos dividere, Cic.

trĭbūtĭo -ōnis, f. (tribuo), *a distribution, dividing,* Cic.

trĭbūtum -i, n. (tribuo). **I.** *tax, contribution, tribute;* tributum conferre, facere, pendĕre, Cic. **II.** Transf., *a gift, present,* Ov.

1. **trĭbūtus** -a -um (tribus), *arranged according to tribes;* comitia, *in which the people voted by tribes,* Liv.

2. **trĭbūtus,** v. tribuo.

trīcae -ārum, f. **1,** *trifles, trumpery, nonsense,* Mart.; **2,** *vexations, troubles, perplexities;* quomodo domesticas tricas (fert)? Cic.

Trĭcastīni -ōrum, m. *a Gallic people, near modern Aouste.*

Tricca -ae, f. (Τρίκκη), *an old town in Thessaly on the Peneus, now Trikkala.*

trīcēnārĭus -a -um (triceni), *containing the number thirty;* filius, *thirty years old,* Sen.

trīcēni -ae -a, genit. tricenûm (triginta), **1,** *thirty each,* Cic.; **2,** *thirty,* Plin.

trĭceps -cipitis (tres and caput), **1,** *three-headed,* Cic.; **2,** *three-fold,* Varr.

trīcēsĭmus -a -um (triginta), *the thirtieth,* Cic.

trĭcessis -is, m. (triginta and as), *thirty asses,* Varr.

trĭchĭas -ae, m. (τριχίας), *a species of sardine,* Plin.

trĭchĭla -ae, f. *a summer-house, arbour,* Caes.

trĭchītis -idis, f. (τριχῖτις), *a kind of alum,* Plin.

trīcĭēs (trīcĭens), adv. (triginta), *thirty times,* Cic.

trĭclīnĭāris -e (triclinium), *of* or *relating to a dining-couch,* Plin. Subst., **trĭclīnĭārĭa** -ium, n. **a,** *a dining-room,* Plin.; **b,** *drapery for a dining-couch,* Plin.

triclīnium ii, n (τρικλίνιον) **I.** *a dining couch, a couch on which the Romans reclined at meals* (generally three on each, sometimes four and five), Cic **II.** *a dining-room*, exornat ample et magnifice triclinium, Cic.

tricōlum (-on) -i, n (τρικωλον), *a period consisting of three parts or clauses*, Sen

trīcor, 1 dep (tricae), *to make difficulties, to shuffle, trifle*, cum aliquo, Cic

tricornis -e (tres and cornu), *having three horns*, Plin

tricorpor -pŏris (tres and corpus), *having three bodies*, forma tricorporis umbrae, *of Geryon*, Verg

tricuspis -idis (tres and cuspis), *having three points*, Ov

tridacna ōrum, n (τρι = ter, and δάκνω = mordeo), *a kind of oyster*, Plin

tridens -entis (tres and dens), *having three teeth or prongs* **I.** Adj, rostra, Verg **II.** Subst, **tridens** entis, m *a trident, a three pronged spear for piercing large fish*, Plin, an attribute of Neptune, Verg

tridentifĕr -fĕri, m (tridens and fero), *the trident-bearer*, epithet of Neptune, Ov

tridentigĕr -gĕri, m (tridens and gero), *the trident-bearer*, epithet of Neptune, Ov

tridŭum -ii, n *a space of three days*, quum tridui viam processisset, Caes, triduo illum aut summum quadriduo periturum, Cic

triennia ium, n (tres and annus), *a festival celebrated every three years*, Ov

triennium -ii, n (tres and annus), *a space of three years*, biennium aut triennium est quum nuntium remisisti, Cic; multis locis Germaniae triennium vagati, Cic.

triens entis, m (tres), *a third part, one third* **A.** Gen, Cic **B.** Esp, **1,** *the third part of an as*, Hor, **2,** *of a sextarius*, Prop, **3,** in inheritances, *a third part of a whole*, cum duobus coheredibus esse in triente, Cic

trientābŭlum -i, n (triens), *the equivalent in land for the third part of a sum of money*, Liv

trientālis -e (triens), *containing one third of a foot*, Plin

triērarchus i, m (τριήραρχος), *the commander of a trireme*, Cic

triēris -e (τριήρης), *having three banks of oars* Subst, **triēris** is, f *a trireme*, Nep

triĕtēricus -a -um (τριετηρικός), *recurring every three years, triennial*, trieterica sacra or orgia, Verg, Ov

triĕtēris -idis, f (τριετηρίς), **1,** *a space of three years*, Mart, **2,** *a triennial festival*, Cic

trifāriam, adv (trifarius, *three-fold*, sc partem), *in a three fold manner = in three places, on three sides*, adoriri, munire, Liv

- **trifaux** -faucis (tres and faux), *having three throats, triple throated*, latratus (Cerberi), Verg

trifĕr -fĕra -fĕrum (ter and fero), *bearing fruit thrice a year*, Plin

trifidus -a -um (ter and findo), *split in three parts, three forked*, flamma (of lightning), Ov

trifīlis -e (tres and filum), *having three hairs*, Mart

trifŏlium -ii, n (tres and folium), *trefoil*, Plin

triformis e (tres and forma) **I.** *three formed, having three forms*, Chimaera, Hor, dea, *Hecate*, Ov **II.** *three fold*, mundus (because composed of air, sea, and earth), Ov

trifur -fūris, m (ter and fur), *a three fold thief, arch thief*, Plaut.

trifurcifĕr -fĕri, m (ter and furcifer), *an arch rogue*, Plaut

trīgārius -a -um, subst. (triga, *a team of three horses*), *relating to a team of three horses*, subst, **1, trīgārius** ii, m *a driver of a team of three horses*, Plin, **2, trīgārium** -ii, n *a circus or training ground where teams of three horses are driven*, Plin

trigĕminus (tergĕminus) a -um, *three fold*, vir, *Geryon*, Hor, canis, *Cerberus*, Ov, tergemini honores, *the aedileship, praetorship and consulship*, Hor, of children *three born at a birth*, fratres, the Horatii and the Curiatii, Liv, Trigemina Porta, *a gate in the old city-wall of Rome, opposite the northern corner of the Aventine*, Plin

trigemmis -e (tres and gemma), *having three buds*, Plin

trīginta, num (τριάκοντα), *thirty*, Cic

trigon -ōnis, m (τρίγων) **I.** *a ball for playing*, Mart **II.** Meton, *a game at ball*, Hor

trigōnālis e (trigonum), *three cornered*, pila (= trigon), Mart

trigōnum i, n (τρίγωνον), *a triangle*, Varr

trigŏnus -i, m *a kind of fish, the sting ray*, Plaut

trilībris e (tres and libra), *of three pounds' weight*, Hor

trilinguis -e (tres and lingua), *having three tongues*, os Cerberi, Hor

trilix icis (tres and licium), *having three threads*, loricam consertam hamis auroque trilicem, Verg

trimātus ūs, m (trimus), *the age of three years*, Plin

trimestris, 3 (tres and mensis), *three monthly* **I.** Adj, haedi, *three months old*, Varr **II.** Subst, **trimestria** ium, n *crops which ripen three months after sowing*, Plin

trimĕtĕr = trimetros (q v)

trimĕtrŏs (-us) -a -um, *containing three metra*, i e, *three double feet*, Quint, subst **trimĕtrŏs (-us),** and (Latinised form), **trimĕtĕr** tri *a trimeter*, Hor

trimŏdia -ae, f and **trimŏdium** ii, n (tres and modius), *a vessel containing three modii or bushels*, Plaut

trimus -a -um (tres), *three years old*, equa, Hor

Trinăcria -ae f (Τρινακρία), *the oldest name of Sicily, so called from its triangular shape* Hence, **A. Trinăcrius** -a -um (Τρινάκριος), *Trinacrian*, and **B Trinăcris** -idis, f (Τρινακρίς), *Trinacrian*, Trinacris alone = Sicily, Ov

trini -ae -a (tres) **I.** *three each*, Plin **II.** *three together* (found with subst only used in plur), trinae litterae, Cic, trina castra, Caes

Trinobantes -um, m *a people in the east of Britain*

trinōdis -e (tres and nodus), *having three knots*, Ov.

triŏbŏlus (-ŏs) -i, m (τριοβολος), *a coin of the value of three oboli*, Plaut

Triŏcăla ōrum, n *a mountain fastness in Sicily* Hence, **Triŏcălīnus** -a um, *relating to Triocala*

triōnes -um, m (= teriones, from tero), *the ploughing oxen*, transf, *the constellations known as the Great Bear and Little Bear* (as the stars resembled the shape of a waggon and the oxen attached to it), Verg

Triŏpās ae, m (Τριόπας), *a king in Thessaly, father of Erysichthon* Hence, **A. Triŏpēïos**

-ĭi m. (Τριόπειος) = *Erysichthon*, Ov. **B. Trĭŏpēïs** -ĭdis, f. = *Mestra, daughter of Erysicthon.*

trĭorchis, acc. -chem, f. (τριορχίς). **I.** *a buzzard*, Plin. **II.** *a kind of centaury*, Plin.

trĭparcus -a -um (ter and parcus), *very stingy*, Plaut.

trĭpartīto (and gen.) **trĭpertītō**, adv. (tripartitus), *in three parts*; bona dividere, Cic.

trĭpartītus (and gen.) **trĭpertītus** -a -um (ter and partior), *divided into three parts, threefold, triple, tripartite*; divisio, Cic.

trĭpectŏrus -a -um (tres and pectus), *having three breasts*, Lucr.

trĭpĕdālis -e (ter and pedalis), *of three feet in measure*; parma, Liv.

trĭpĕdānĕus = tripedalis (q.v.).

trĭpert . . . v. tripart . . .

trĭpes -pĕdis (ter and pes), *having three feet*; mulus, Liv.

Trĭphȳlĭa -ae, f. (Τριφυλία), *the south part of Elis in the Peloponnesus.*

trĭplex -plĭcis (tres and plico), *three-fold, triple.* **I.** Adj., acies, Caes.; Plato triplicem finxit animum, Cic.; deae, *the three Parcae*, Ov.; Minyeides, *the three daughters of Minyas*, Ov. **II.** Subst., 1, **triplĭces** -um, m. (sc. codicilli), *a writing tablet with three leaves*, Cic.; 2, **trĭplex** -plĭcis, n. = triplum, *three times as much*; pediti in singulos centeni dati . . . triplex equiti, Liv.

trĭplĭco, 1. (triplex), *to triple, make three-fold*, Plin.

trĭplus -a -um (τριπλοῦς), *three-fold, triple*; pars, Cic.

Trĭpŏlis -is, f. (Τρίπολις), *the name of several towns and places.* **I.** *a mountainous district in Thessaly south of the Cambunian mountains.* Hence, **Trĭpŏlītānus** ager, *the district of Tripolis*, Liv. **II.** *a town in Thessalia Hestiaeotis.* **III.** *a district of Arcadia, near Tegea.* **IV.** *a district in Africa*, now *Tripoli.* **V.** *a town in Phoenicia*, now *Trapoli.* **VI.** *a town in Pontus.* **VII.** *a town in Phrygia.*

Triptŏlĕmus -i, m. (Τριπτόλεμος), *son of Celeus, king of Eleusis, and of Metaneira, the inventor of agriculture, a judge in the lower world*; prov., Triptolemo dare fruges, *to carry coals to Newcastle*, Ov.

trĭpŭdĭo, 1. (tripudium), *to beat the ground with the feet, to dance*; e.g., a savage war dance, tripudiantes more suo (of the Spaniards), Liv.; of an old Roman dance on festive and religious occasions, Sen.; hence, transf., tot in funeribus reipublicae exsultans ac tripudians, *dancing for joy*, Cic.

trĭpŭdĭum -ĭi, n. (ter and pes). **I.** *a religious dance*; e.g., of the Salian priests, Salios per urbem ire canentes carmina cum tripudiis sollemnique saltatu, Liv.; so of a savage war dance, cantus (Gallorum) ineuntium proelium et ululatus et tripudia, Liv.; of the wild Bacchic dance, Cat. **II.** T. t. of augury, *a favourable omen when the sacred chickens eat so fast that the food fell out of their beaks*, Cic.

trĭpūs -pŏdis, m. (τρίπους), *a three-legged seat, tripod.* **I.** Gen., Verg., Hor. **II.** Esp., *the tripod of the Delphic priestess*, Cic., Verg.; hence, meton., *the Delphic oracle*, Ov.

trĭquĕtrus -a -um. **I.** *three-cornered, triangular*; insula (of Britain), Caes. **II.** (Because Sicily from its triangular shape was called Triquetra, hence =) *Sicilian*, Lucr., Hor.

trĭrēmis -e (tres and remus), *having three banks of oars*, Caes.; subst., **trĭrēmis** -is, f. *a trireme*, Caes., Cic.

trischoenus -a -um (τρίσχοινος), *containing three schoeni*, Plin.

trĭscurrĭa -ōrum, n. (tres and scurra), *gross buffooneries*, Juv.

tristĕ, adv. (tristis). **I.** *sadly, sorrowfully, mournfully*; adolescentes gravius aegrotant, tristius curantur, Cic. **II.** *harshly, severely*; tristius respondere, Cic.

tristi = trivisti, v. tero.

tristĭcŭlus -a -um (dim. of tristis), *somewhat sorrowful*; filiola, Cic.

tristĭfĭcus -a -um (tristis and facio), *causing sadness*, Cic. poet.

tristĭmōnĭa -ae, f. (tristis), *sadness, melancholy*, Auct. b. Afr.

tristis -e, *sad, sorrowful, mournful, melancholy.* **I.** Gen., **A.** Lit., of persons, tristis et conturbatus, Cic.; quos quum tristiores vidisset, Cic. **B.** Transf., **a**, *sad, gloomy*; of the lower world, Tartara, Verg.; poet., *harsh of taste*; suci, Verg.; **b**, object., *troubled, unfortunate, disastrous*; tempora, Cic.; ira, *with disastrous consequences*, Hor.; sors, Cic.; tristia ad recordationem exempla, Cic.; neut. subst., triste lupus stabulis, *a disastrous thing*, Verg.; tristia miscentur laetis, Ov. **II.** Esp., **1**, of humour, *gloomy*; **a**, = *unfriendly, surly, morose*, Cic.; natura, Cic.; vultus tristior, Cic.; **b**, = *angry*; dicta, Ov.; **2**, *harsh, severe, rough*; judex, Cic.; triste et severum dicendi genus, Cic.

tristĭtĭa -ae, f. (tristis). **I.** *sadness, sorrowfulness, melancholy.* **A.** Lit., Cic. **B.** Transf., of things, sermonis, Cic. **II.** Esp., **1**, *ill-humour, moroseness*, Ov.; **2**, *severity, sternness*; quod ille vos tristitiā vultuque deceperit, Cic.

trĭsulcus -a -um (tres and sulcus), *three-fold, three-pointed, three-pronged*; lingua serpentis, *forked*, Verg.; telum Jovis, *lightning*, Ov.; ignes, *lightning*, Ov.

trĭsyllăbus -a -um (τρισύλλαβος), *trisyllabic*, Varr.

trĭtăvus -i, m. (tres and avus). **I.** *the father of the atavus or atava*, Plaut. **II.** Transf., *remote ancestors*, Varr.

trītĭcĕus (trītĭcēĭus) -a -um (triticum), *of wheat, wheaten*; messis, Verg.

trītĭcum -i, n. *wheat*; granum tritici, Cic.

Trītōn -ōnis, m. (Τρίτων). **I.** *Triton, son of Neptune and the nymph Salacia, a deity of the sea, represented with a horn made of a shell, which he blew at the bidding of Neptune to raise or appease the waves.* **II. A.** *a lake in Africa, on the smaller Syrtis, according to tradition the birth-place of several deities, particularly of Pallas.* Hence, **a**, **Trītōnĭăcus** -a -um, = *belonging to Pallas*; arundo, *the tibia discovered by Pallas*, Ov.; **b**, **Trītōnis** -ĭdis, f. *Tritonian*; subst., = *Pallas*, Verg.; arx = *the city of Pallas, Athens*, Ov.; pinus, *the Argo, built at the order of Pallas*, Ov.; **c**, **Trītōnĭus** -a -um, *Tritonian*; subst., Tritonia = *Pallas*, Verg. **B.** *a lake in Thrace which had the power of changing into a bird any one who bathed nine times in its waters*; also called **Trītōnĭăca** palus, Ov.

trītor -ōris, m. (tero), *a rubber*, Plaut.

trītūra -ae, f. (tero), *a treading out of corn, threshing*, Verg.

1. **trītus** -a -um, p. adj. (from tero). **I. A.** *much trodden, much frequented*; **1**, lit., iter, Cic.; **2**, fig., of discourse, *in common use, common, trite, well-known*; faciamus hoc proverbium tritius, Cic. **B.** *practised*; aures, Cic. **II.** *worn-out*; vestis, Hor.

2. **trītus** -ūs, m. (tero), *a rubbing*, Cic.

trĭumphālis -e (triumphus), *of or relating to a triumph, triumphal*, corona, *of a triumphing general*, Liv , provincia, *the conquest of which has gained a triumph*, Cic , porta, *the gate through which the triumphing general entered Rome*, Cic , imagines, *busts of ancestors who had triumphed*, Hor., triumphalia ornamenta, and subst., **trĭumphālĭa** -ium, n. *the decorations of a triumphing general* (corona aurea, toga picta, tunica palmata, scipio eburneus, etc), Tac , senex, *an old man who had had a triumph*, Liv

trĭumpho, 1 (triumphus) **I.** Intransit , *to triumph, to have a triumph* **A.** Lit , de Numantinis, Cic , ex Macedonia, Cic **B.** Transf , **1,** *to triumph, gain a victory*, amor de vate triumphat, Ov ; **2,** *to triumph, exult*, gaudio, Cic , laetaris in omnium gemitu et triumphas, Cic **II.** *to triumph over, to conquer completely*, pass , ne triumpharetur Mithridates, Tac ; triumphati Medi, Hor., aurum triumphatum, *captured*, Hor.

trĭumphus -i, m , old form, **trĭumpus** -i, m. (ter and pes), lit , *a solemn dance* (like tripudium), hence, **A.** Lit , *a triumphal procession, a triumph*, granted by the senate to a general and his army after an important victory, when the general entered Rome in a car drawn by white horses, clothed in a toga picta and tunica palmata, with a crown of laurel on his head, preceded by waggons carrying captives and booty, and followed by the soldiers shouting "Io triumphe!" and singing jocular songs, alicui triumphum decernere, Cic , triumphum tertium deportare, Cic., triumphum agere, *to triumph*, with genit or de or ex and abl of persons or country over which the triumph was held, Bojorum, Liv , ex Aequis, Liv., Pharsalicae pugnae, Cic ; de Liguribus, Liv **B.** Transf , *triumph, victory*; ut repulsam suam triumphum suum duxerint, Cic

trĭumvir -viri, m (tres and vir), *a triumvir*, plur , triumviri (also tresviri, written III viri) **I.** coloniae deducendae, or agro dando, or agro dividendo, or agris dividendis, or agro assignando (or agrarii), *commissioners for the formation of a* colonia *and the division of land amongst the colonists*, quum triumvir coloniam deduxisset, Cic **II.** triumviri capitales or carceris lautumiarum, *superintendents of prisons, who also looked after the execution of punishments and watched over the public peace*, Cic **III.** triumviri epulones, v epulones. **IV.** triumviri mensarii, *commissioners for the regulation of payments from the exchequer*, Liv **V.** triumviri monetales (auro, argento, aeri flando, feriundo), *the masters of the mint*, Cic **VI.** triumviri (tresviri) reipublicae constituendae, Antonius, Lepidus, Octavianus, *who joined together to settle the state*, Suet **VII.** *commissioners for raising recruits*, Liv. **VIII.** triumviri sacris conquirendis donisque persignandis, *commissioners for making an inventory of votive gifts*, Liv **IX.** *commissioners for repairing or rebuilding temples*, Liv **X.** *magistrates in the* municipia, Cic.

trĭumvĭrālis -e (triumvir), *of or relating to a triumvir*, flagella (of the triumviri capitales), Hor

trĭumvĭrātus -ūs, m. (triumvir), *the office of a triumvir*, in triumviratu (sc agrario), Cic

trĭvĕnēfica -ae, f (ter and venefica), *an arch-poisoner* or *sorceress*, Plaut.

Trĭvĭa, v trivius

trĭviālis -e (trivium), *common, ordinary, trivial*, carmen, Juv

trĭvium -ii, n. (ter and via), *a place where three roads meet*, Cic ; meton , *an open street, public place*, Cic.

trĭvĭus -a -um (trivium), *honoured at three cross-roads*, name of deities who had chapels at cross roads ; dea, Prop., or virgo, Lucr , *Diana* or *Hecate*, so absol , **Trĭvĭa** -ae, f , Verg ; lacus Triviae *a lake in Latium, near Aricia* now *Lago di Nemi*

trixāgo (trissāgo) -inis, f *a plant called germander*, Plin

Trōas -ădis, v Tros.

trŏchaeus -i, m (τροχαῖος), **1,** *a trochee, a metrical foot* (ᴗ), Cic , **2,** = tribrachys (q v)

trŏchăĭcus -a -um (τροχαϊκός), *trochaic*, Quint

trŏchĭlus -i, m (τροχιλος), *the golden crested wren*, Plin

trochlĕa (troclĕa) -ae, f. *a set of blocks and pulleys for raising weights*, Lucr

trŏchus -i, m (τροχός), *a boy's hoop*, Hor

Trocmi ōrum, m *one of the three main stocks of the Galatians in Asia Minor.*

Trōes, v Tros

Troezēn -zēnis, acc -zēna, f (Τροιζήν), *an old town in Argolis, residence of Pittheus, grandfather of Theseus* Hence, **Troezēnĭus** a -um (Τροιζηνιος), *Troezenian*, heros, *Lelex, son of Pittheus*

Trōglŏdȳtae ārum, m (Τρωγλοδύται), *cave-dwellers, name of the old inhabitants of the west* [illegible] *of the Arabian Gulf in Aethiopia*

Trōĭădes, v Tros

Trōĭcus, v Tros

Trōĭlus (-ŏs) -i, m (Τρωιλος), *son of Priam, taken prisoner before Troy, and strangled by order of Achilles*

Trōja, Trojanus, v. Tros

Trōjŭgĕna -ae, c (Troja and gigno), *born in Troy, Trojan.* Subst , **Trōjŭgĕna** -ae, m *a Trojan.* Plur = *the Trojans* (genit Trōjŭgĕnûm), Verg , and = *the Romans* (descended from Aeneas), Juv

Tromentīna tribus, *one of the* tribus rusticae.

trŏpaeum -i, n (τρόπαιον), *a trophy, a monument of victory*, originally consisting of arms taken from the enemy hung on the stem of a tree **I. A.** Lit , tropaeum statuere or ponere, *to erect*, Cic **B.** Meton = *the victory*, Salaminium, Cic **II.** Fig = *a memorial*, necessitudinis atque hospitii, Cic

trŏpaeus -a -um (τροπαῖος), *turning back*; venti, *blowing from the sea to the land*, Plin

Trŏphōnĭus ii m (Τροφωνιος) **I.** *brother of Agamedes, with whom he built the Delphic oracle.* **II.** *a deity who gave prophetic answers to those who slept in his cave* (near Lebadia, in Boeotia) Hence, **Trŏphōnĭānus** -a -um, *of or belonging to Trophonius*

trŏpis -is, f (τρόπις), *the lees of wine*, Mart

trŏpus -i, m (τρόπος), *a metaphor, trope, figure of speech*, Quint

Trōs, Trōis, m. (Τρώς), *son of Erichthonius, king of Phyrygia, after whom Troy was named* Hence, **Trōja** or **Troĭa** -ae, f (Τροια), *the town of Troy*. 1, lit , Liv , Verg , 2, transf , **a,** *the town built by Aeneas in the Laurentine country*, Liv , **b,** *the town built by Helenus in Epirus*, Ov **c,** *a Roman game played on horseback*, Verg Hence, **A. Trōĭus** a um, *Trojan* **B. Trōjānus** a -um, *Trojan*, judex, i e , *Paris*, Hor , prov , equus Trojanus, *a hidden danger*, Cic **C. Trōĭcus** -a -um, *Trojan* **D. Trōs,** Trōis, m *a Trojan*, plur , **Trōes** -um, m *the Trojans.*

E. Trōăs -ădos, adj. fem., *Trojan*, subst, *a Trojan woman*, Verg **F. Trōĭădes** um, f. *Trojan women*

Trosmis, acc -min, f *a town in Moesia*, Ov.

trossŭli ōrum, m (perhaps an Etruscan word for equites) **I.** *a name given to the Roman knights in active service*, Varr **II.** Transf., *fops, coxcombs, dandies*, Sen

troxallis -ĭdis, f (τροξαλλίς), *an animal resembling a grasshopper*, Plin.

trŭcīdātĭo -ōnis, f (trucido) **I.** *a slaughtering, massacre*, civium, Cic, non pugna sed trucidatio velut pecorum, Liv. **II.** *a cutting off, cutting to pieces*, Plin

trŭcīdo, 1 *to cut to pieces, slaughter, massacre.* **I. A.** Lit, cives Romanos, Cic **B.** Transf, **a,** *to chew*, seu pisces, seu porrum, seu cepe, Hor, **b,** poet = *to extinguish*, ignem, Lucr **II.** Fig, **1,** *to demolish* (in words); a Servilio trucidatus, Cic, **2,** *to ruin, destroy*, ne fenore trucidetur, Cic.

trŭcŭlentĕr, adv (truculentus), *fiercely, ferociously*, quod truculentius se ferebat quam caeteri, Cic

trŭcŭlentĭa -ae, f (truculentus), **1,** *roughness, savageness, ferocity*, Plaut, **2,** *severity of climate*, Tac.

trŭcŭlentus -a -um (trux), *rough, ferocious, savage, cruel* **I. A.** Lit, Cic **B.** Transf, of the voice, *wild*, Tac **II.** Fig, **A.** Of character or behaviour, *unfriendly, wild, angry, furious*, feta truculentior ursā, Ov **B.** Transf, of the sea, *wild, disturbed*, Cat

trŭdis -is, f *a sharp stake*, Verg

trūdo, trūsi, trūsum, 3 *to push, shove, press* **I.** Lit, **A** Gen, apros in plagas, Hor **B.** Esp, *to push forth, to put forth buds*, gemmas, Verg **II.** Fig, *to press, urge, force*, ad mortem trudi, Cic, truditur dies die, *one day presses hard on another*, Hor

Trŭentum -i, n *a town in Picenum* Hence, **Trŭentīnus** -a -um, *Truentine*, Castrum = Truentum, ap. Cic.

trulla -ae, f (= truella, dim of trua, *a ladle*) **I.** *a ladle for transferring wine from the bowl to the cup*, Cic **II.** Transf, **1,** *a pan for carrying live coals*, Liv, **2,** *a washing-basin*, Juv

trullĕum i, n and **trullĕus** -i, m *a basin, washing basin*, Varr

trunco, 1 (truncus), *to shorten by cutting off, maim, mutilate*, simulacra, statuas, Liv

1 **truncus** i, m *the stem or trunk of a tree* **I.** Lit, meton and fig **A.** Lit and meton, **1,** lit, Cic, Caes.; trunci induti hostilibus armis, i e, tropaea, Verg, **2,** meton = *the tree*, Hor **B.** Fig, *the stem, the main part*, ipso trunco (aegritudinis) everso, Cic **II.** Transf, **1,** *the trunk of the human body*, Cic; **2,** as a term of reproach, *blockhead*, Cic

2 **truncus** -a um, *maimed, mutilated, cut short, dismembered* **I.** Lit., corpus, Liv, truncae inhonesto vulnere nares, Verg, frons (Acheloi amnis), *deprived of its horns*, Ov, tela, *broken off*, Verg, with genit, animalia trunca pedum, *without feet*, Verg **II.** Transf, urbs trunca, sine senatu, etc, Liv.

trūsātĭlis -e (truso), *of or relating to pushing*, mola, *a handmill*, Cato

trūso, 1 (intens of trudo), *to push violently*, Cat

trŭtĭna -ae, f (τρυτάνη), *a balance, pair of scales*, in fig, ad ea probanda, quae non aurificis staterā, sed quādam populari trutinā examinantur, Cic.

trŭtĭnor, 1 dep (trutina), *to weigh*, Pers

trux, trŭcis (connected with tor-vus), *rough, savage, fierce, ferocious, grim* **I.** Of look, oculi, Cic **II.** Transf, **1,** of tones, *wild, rough*, cantus, Ov.; classicum, Hor; **2,** *rough*, **a,** eurus, Ov; pelagus, Hor; **b,** *harsh, violent*, orator, Liv, sententia, Liv, **3,** of character or manner, *wild, furious, threatening*, tribunus plebis, Cic

trybĭlum -ii, n (τρύβλιον), *a dish*, Plaut

trȳgĭnon -i, n (τρύγινον), *a black pigment made from wine-lees*, Plin.

trȳgon ōnis, m. (τρυγών), *a fish, the sting-ray*, Plin

tū, pron. pers (genit tŭi, dat. tĭbi, acc te, abl te, plur nom, vos, genit, vestrum or vostrum and vestri or vostri, dat vobis, acc vos, abl vobis), *thou*, plur, *you* **I.** Gen, Cic, strengthened, **a,** by te, tute, Cic, **b,** in oblique cases by met, vosmet, Liv **II.** Esp, **A.** Used in the ethic dat, ecce tibi exortus est Isocrates, Cic **B.** Often with singular collective names, vos, Romanus exercitus, Liv, vos, o Calliope (= Muses), Verg

tŭātim, adv (tuus), *in thine own way, after thine own fashion*, Plaut

tŭba ae, f (connected with tubus), *the straight war trumpet of the Romans, used for giving military signals* **I A.** Lit., tubae sonus, Caes, cornua ac tubae, Liv, tubā signum dandum, Caes, used also in religious festivities, games, funeral processions, Hor, Verg, Ov **B.** Fig = *provoker*, belli civilis tubam quam illi appellant, Cic **II.** Meton, **A.** *war*, Mart. **B.** *lofty epic poetry*, Mart

1 **tūber** -ĕris, n (tumeo), *a swelling, protuberance, hump* **I. a,** lit, cameli, Plin, **b,** fig, tubera = *great mistakes* (opp verrucae, *little blunders*), Hor **II** Transf, **1,** *a knot in wood*, Plin, **2,** *a round, swelling root*, Plin, **3,** *a truffle*, Mart, **4,** tuber terrae, **a,** *the root of the cyclamen*, Plin, **b,** *molehill*, as a term of abuse, Petr

2 **tŭber** ĕris, **a,** m *a kind of apple tree*, Plin., **b,** f *the fruit of this tree*, Mart

tūbercŭlum -i, n (dim of 1 tuber), *a little swelling, boil, tubercle*, Plin

tūbĕrōsus -a -um (tuber), *full of swellings or protuberances*, Varr

tŭbĭcen -ĭnis, m (tuba and cano), *a trumpeter*, Liv

tŭbĭlustrĭum -ii, n (tuba and lustrum), *a feast of trumpets held March 23rd and May 23rd*, plur, Ov

tŭbŭlātus -a -um (tubulus), *tubular*, Plin

tŭbŭlus i, m (dim of tubus), *a little pipe*

tŭburcĭnābundus -a -um (tuburcinor), *eating greedily, gobbling*, Cato.

tŭburcĭnor, 1 dep *to eat greedily, to gobble*, Plaut

tŭbus -i, m *a pipe, tube, water-pipe*, Plin

tuccētum (not tūcētum) i, n. *a kind of sausage common in Cisalpine Gaul*, Pers

tŭdĭto, 1 (intens of tudo = tundo), *to strike violently, strike often*, Lucr.

tŭĕo, 2 = tueor (q v)

tŭĕor, tŭĭtus and tūtus sum, tŭēri, 2 dep *to look at, behold, regard, see* **I.** Lit, naturam, Cic, poet with neut plur of adj used adverbially, acerba, *to look wild*, Verg **II.** Fig, **A.** *to regard*, quod ego perinde tuebar, ac si usus essem, Cic **B.** *to look at with care or for the purpose of protection*, **1,** *to care for, protect, guard, support*, concordiam, Cic, dignitatem suam,

Cic , personam principis civis facile dicendo, Cic , 2, esp , a, *to defend, protect* (with arms), fines suos ab excursionibus, Cic , turrim militibus complevit tuendamque ad omnes repentinos casus tradidit, Caes , b, with words, etc , armis prudentiae causas tueri et defendere, Cic , c, t t of business, *to keep a house in good repair*, sarta tecta aedium tueri, Cic , d, *to keep, support, maintain*, se, vitam corpusque, Cic , se ac suos, Liv , sex legiones (re sua), Cic

tŭgŭrĭum ĭi, n (for tegurium, from tego), *a peasant's hut, cottage*, tugurium ut jam videatur esse illa villa, Cic

tŭĭtĭo ōnis, f (tueor), *a protecting, preserving*, sui, Cic

Tullĭŏla -ae, f (dim of Tullia), *the pet name of Tullia, Cicero's daughter*

Tullĭus -a -um, *the name of a Roman family*, 1, Servius Tullius, *the sixth king of Rome*, 2, a, M Tullius Cicero, *the celebrated Roman orator and statesman*, b, *his daughter*, Tullia, c, *his brother*, Qu Tullius Cicero Hence, **Tullĭānus** a -um, *Tullian*, subst , **Tullĭānum** -i, n *the underground part of a Roman state prison, said to have been built by Servius Tullius*

tŭlo, tŭli and tĕtŭli, 3 *to bear, bring*, Plaut

tum, adv of time I. Expressing a point of time which coincides with some other, gen , *then, at that time*, quum . . tum, Cic , ubi . . tum, Ter , postquam . . tum, Sall , made emphatic by the addition of demum, Liv , denique, Cic , vero, Cic , absol , Cic II. Expressing a point of time which is subsequent to some other, *then, thereupon*, 1, lit , in ripa ambulantes, tum autem residentes, Cic , introducing the words of a subsequent speaker, tum Scipio, Cic , 2, transf , a, in numeral or logical succession, *then, afterwards, in the next place*, gigni autem terram, aquam, ignem, tum ex his omnia, Cic , primum . . tum, Caes , primum . . deinde . . tum . . tum, Cic ; b, as a correl conj , (α) tum . . tum, *at one time . . at one time*, Cic. , (β) quum . . tum, *if . . then, surely, as well . . as, both . . and especially, not only . . but also*, Cic , Caes

tŭmĕfăcĭo fēci -factum, 3 , pass , **tŭmĕfīo** -factus sum -fĭĕri (tumeo and facio), *to cause to swell* I. Lit , humum, Ov ; tumefactus pontus, *swollen*, Ov II. Fig , *to puff up with pride*, Prop.

tŭmĕo, 2 *to swell, be swollen, be puffed up* I. Lit., corpus omne veneno, Ov , vere tument terrae, Verg II. Fig , 1, *to swell, glow, boil with passion* or *excitement*, a, *with anger* sapientis animus nunquam tumet, Cic ; b, *with pride*, laudis amore, Hor , c, *to be in a ferment*, tument negotia, *are in disorder*, Cic , 2, of discourse, *to be pompous, tumid*, Tac

tŭmesco, tŭmŭi, 3 (inchoat of tumeo), *to begin to swell, to swell* I. Lit , tumescit mare, Verg II. Fig., a, *to swell with anger*, ora tumescunt, Ov , b, poet , transf , *to begin to break out*, tumescunt bella, Verg

tŭmĭdē, adv (tumidus), *pompously, bombastically*, Sen

tŭmĭdus a um (tumeo) I. *swollen, puffed up, tumid* A. Lit., membrum, Cic , mare, Verg B. Transf , 1, a, *swollen, boiling, raging with passion* or *excitement*, tumida ex ira tum corda residunt, Verg , b, *swollen, puffed up with pride*, tumidus successu, Ov , quum tumidum est (cor), *puffed up with ambition*, Hor , 2, of discourse, *pompous, tumid, bombastic*, sermones Hor , sermo tumidior, Liv II. Act = *causing to swell*, auster, Verg , euri, Ov., fig , honor, *making vain*, Prop.

tŭmor ōris, m (tumeo), *a swelling, tumour* I. Lit , oculorum, Cic II. Transf , 1, *a swelling, commotion, excitement of the mind*, animi, Cic , esp , a, *anger* tumor et ira deum, Verg , b, *pride*, intempestivos compesce tumores, Ov , c, *ferment, commotion*, rerum, Cic , 2, of discourse, *bombast*, Quint

tŭmŭlo, 1 (tumulus), *to cover with a mound, to bury*, Ov

tŭmŭlōsus -a um (tumulus), *full of mounds, hilly*, Sall

tŭmultŭārĭus -a -um (tumultus) I. *hastily brought together, suddenly levied*, miles, Liv II. Transf , *that which is done in a hurry* or *on the spur of the moment, sudden, hasty, disorderly*, pugna (opp justa) Liv , opus, Quint , dux, *chosen on the spur of the moment*, Liv , castra, Liv

tŭmultŭātĭo -ōnis, f (tumultuor), *a confusion, bustle, tumult*, Liv

tŭmultŭor, 1 dep and **tŭmultuo**, 1 (tumultus), *to be tumultuous, confused, in an uproar*, Cic , pass impers , in castris Romanorum praeter consuetudinem tumultuari, Caes

tŭmultŭōsē, adv (tumultuosus), *confusedly, tumultuously*, tumultuose excepta est (res) clamoribus, Liv , senatus tumultuosius consulitur, Liv , ut hominem quam tumultuosissime adoriantur, Cic

tŭmultŭōsus a-um (tumultus) I. *alarmed, disquieted, turbulent, tumultuous*, contio, Cic , vita, Cic , mare, Hor , quod tumultuosissimum pugnae erat parumper sustinuit, Liv. II. *causing alarm* or *confusion*, nuntius, Liv , in otio tumultuosi, *restless*, Liv

tŭmultus ūs, m (tumeo), *a noise, confusion, uproar, bustle, tumult* I. Lit , 1, tantum tumultum injicere civitati, Cic , tumultum praebere, Liv , sedare, Liv , 2, esp , a, *the sudden breaking out of war, insurrection, rebellion*, Italicus, Cic , Gallicus Cic , Liv , tumultum decernere, *to order a levy en masse*, Cic , b, in the air, *crash, roar, thunder, storm*, Juppiter ruens tumultu, Hor ; c, *rumbling in the body*, Hor II. Fig , *mental disturbance, commotion, excitement* mentis, Hor

tŭmŭlus -i, m (tumeo), *a mound of earth, hill* I. Gen , tumuli silvestres, Cic II. Esp , *a mound of earth as a monument for the dead*, tumulus Achillis, Cic , inanis, *a cenotaph*, Cic

tunc, adv , denoting a point of time which corresponds with another I. Gen , *then*, tunc . . quum, Cic II. Esp , a fixed point of past time, *at that time, then*, Cic

tundo, tŭtŭdi, tunsum and tūsum, 3 *to beat, strike repeatedly* I. Lit , A. Gen , converso bacillo alicui oculos vehementissime, Cic , pectora manu, Ov tunsae pectora (acc of respect) palmis, Verg. , prov , tundere eandem incudem, *to be always treating of the same subject*, Cic B. Esp *to break to pieces in a mortar*, Plin II. Transf , *to deafen, importune*, aures, Plaut , assiduis hinc atque illinc vocibus heros tunditur, Verg

Tunēs nētis, m *a town on the coast of Africa Propria*, now *Tunis*

Tungri -ōrum, m *a German people in modern Luttich*

tŭnĭca ae, f I *the under garment worn by both men and women, a tunic*, Cic II Transf , *a skin, coating, covering, peel*, gemmae tenues rumpunt tunicas, Verg

tŭnĭcātus -a -um (tunica), *clothed in a tunic*, Cic , esp , of the poorer classes, who wore only a tunic (without a toga over it), tunicatus populus, Tac , or popellus, Hor Subst plur , tunicati, Cic

tŭnĭcŭla (tūnicla) -ae, f. (dim. of tunica). **I.** *a little tunic*, Cic. **II.** Transf., *a little membrane*; oculorum, Plin.

tŭor = tueor (q.v.).

tūrārĭus -a -um (tus), *of* or *relating to incense*, Plin.

turba -ae, f. (τύρβη). **I.** *the tumult, uproar, disturbance, commotion caused by a crowd of people*; quanta in turba viveremus, Cic.; maximas in castris effecisse turbas dicitur, Cic. **II.** Meton., *a disorderly crowd, heap, swarm*; **1,** **a,** aliquem videre in turba, Cic.; **b,** esp. = vulgus (contemptuously), *the mob*; admiratio vulgi atque turbae, Cic.; **2,** of deities, animals, and things, Chrysippus magnam congregat turbam ignotorum deorum, Cic.; rerum, Ov.

turbāmentum -i, n. (turbo), *a means of disturbance*, Tac.

turbātē, adv. (turbatus), *confusedly*; aguntur omnia raptim atque turbate, Caes.

turbātĭo -ōnis, f. (1. turbo), *disturbance, disorder, confusion*, Liv.

turbātor -ōris, m. (1. turbo), *a disturber, stirrer-up, troubler*; plebis, Liv.

turbātus -a -um, p. adj. (from 1. turbo). **I.** *disturbed, perturbed, disordered*; mare, Liv. **II.** Transf., **a,** *disquieted, restless, troubled*; voluntates populi, Cic.; **b,** *angered, exasperated*; Pallas, Verg.

turbellae -ārum, f. (dim. of turba), *tumult, disorder, confusion*, Plaut.

turben -ĭnis, n. (2. turbo), *a whirlwind*, Cat.

turbĭdē, adv. (turbidus), *confusedly, in disorder*, Cic.

turbĭdus -a -um (turba), *confused, disordered, unquiet, wild*. **I.** Lit., **a,** of weather, tempestas, Cic.; **b,** of water, *turbid, troubled*; aqua, Cic.; **c,** of hair, *disordered*; coma, Ov. **II.** Transf., **1,** *mentally disturbed, disordered, disquieted*; Aruns, Verg.; pectora turbidiora mari, Ov.; turbidum laetari, *with confused fear*, Hor.; **2,** *excited, vehement, angry*; **a,** of persons, sic turbidus infit, Verg.; **b,** of things, *unquiet, agitated*; res, Cic. Subst., **turbĭdum** -i, n. *a troubled time, disquiet*; in turbido, Liv.; si turbidiora sapienter ferebas, tranquilliora laete feras, Cic.; **3,** *causing disturbance*; homo, milites, Tac.

turbĭnātĭo -ōnis, f. (turbinatus), *a pointing in the form of a cone*, Plin.

turbĭnātus -a -um (2. turbo), *cone-shaped, conical*, Plin.

turbĭnĕus -a -um (2. turbo), *shaped like a top*, Ov.

1. **turbo**, 1. (turba), *to disturb, throw into disorder* or *confusion*. **I.** Lit., **A.** Gen., mare, aequora, Cic.; transf., with Gr. acc., turbatus capillos, *with disordered hair*, Ov. **B.** Esp., **a,** *to bring a mass of men into disorder, to throw into disorder*; esp., milit. t.t., ordines, aciem peditum, Liv.; absol. = *to cause disorder*; ferae ita ruunt atque turbant ut, etc., Cic.; milit. t.t. (equites) modice primo impetu turbavere, Liv.; **b,** *to trouble water*, etc., *make turbid*; pedibus manibusque lacus, Ov. **II.** Transf., *to bring into confusion, to disturb*. **A.** Gen., contiones, Liv.; delectum atque ordinem, Cic.; ne quid ille turbet, vide, Liv. **B.** Esp., **1,** *to bring one's affairs into confusion, become bankrupt*, Juv.; **2,** *to make restless, disturb, alarm, confuse*; mentem dolore, Verg.; **3,** *to cause a political disturbance, to unsettle, stir up*; Macer in Africa haud dubie turbans, Tac.; impers., si in Hispania turbatum esset, Cic. (archaic fut. perf. pass., turbassitur, ap. Cic.).

2. **turbo** -ĭnis, m. **I.** *anything that turns round in a circle, an eddy*. **A.** Of the wind, *a whirlwind, hurricane*; **1,** lit., **a,** Cic.; **b,** *the eddy made by a whirlwind*, Verg.; **2,** fig., *storm*; in turbinibus reipublicae, Cic.; mentis turbine agar, Ov.; tu procella patriae, turbo ac tempestas pacis atque otii, Cic. **B.** *a top, a plaything for boys*; **1,** lit., Cic.; **2,** transf., *an object of the shape of a top*; turbine crescit (bucina) ab imo, *in a circular form*, Ov.; esp., **a,** *a reel*, Hor.; **b,** *a spindle*, Cat. **II.** *motion in the shape of an eddy*; of smoke, Verg.; *circular course of a missile*; celeri ad terram turbine fertur, Verg.; fig., non modo militiae turbine factus eques, *by going through the different grades*, Ov.

turbŭlentē and **turbŭlentĕr**, adv. with compar. and superl. (turbulentus), *turbulently, tumultuously*; nos nihil turbulenter, nihil temere faciamus, Cic.; egit de Caepione turbulentius, Cic.

turbŭlentus -a -um (turba), *restless, stormy, boisterous*. **I.** Lit., tempestas, Cic.; concursio, Cic. **II.** Fig., **A.** Pass. = *stormy, disturbed*; respublica, Cic.; animus, Cic. **B.** Fig., **a,** *causing disturbance, restless*; civis, Cic.; **b,** *confusing*; errores, Cic.

turda, v. turdus.

turdārĭum -ii, n. (turdus), *a place where thrushes are kept*, Varr.

Turdetāni -ōrum, m. *a people in Hispania Baetica, near modern Seville*. Hence, **Turdetānĭa** -ae, f. *the country of the Turdetani*.

Turdŭli -ōrum, m. *a people in Hispania Baetica*. Hence, **Turdŭlus** -a -um, *Turdulian*.

turdus -i, m. and **turda** -ae, f. **I.** *a thrush*, Hor. **II.** *a kind of fish*, Plin.

tūrĕus -a -um (tus), *of* or *relating to incense*; dona, Verg.

turgĕo, 2. **I.** *to swell up, be swollen*; frumenta turgent, Verg. **II.** Fig., of discourse, *to be pompous, turgid*; professus grandia turget, Hor.

turgesco (inchoat. of turgeo), 3. *to begin to swell, swell up*. **I.** Lit., semen turgescit in agris, Ov. **II.** Transf., *to swell, be excited with passion*; sapientis animus nunquam turgescit, Cic.

turgĭdŭlus -a -um (dim. of turgidus), *somewhat swollen*; flendo turgiduli ocelli, Cat.

turgĭdus -a -um (turgeo), *swollen, turgid*. **I.** Lit., membrum, Cic. **II.** Fig., *turgid, bombastic*; Alpinus (a poet), Hor.

Tūrĭa -ae, f. *a river in Hispania Tarraconensis, now Guadalaviar*. Hence, **Tūrĭensis** -e, *Turian*; proelium (in the Sertorian war), Cic.

tūrĭbŭlum -i, n. (tus), *a censer for burning incense*, Cic.

tūrĭcrĕmus -a -um (tus and cremo), *burning with incense*; arae, Verg.

tūrĭfĕr -fĕra -fĕrum (tus and fero), *producing incense*; Indus, Ov.

tūrĭlĕgus -a -um (tus and lego), *collecting incense*, Ov.

turma -ae, f. (connected with turba). **I.** *a troop of cavalry containing thirty men, the tenth part of an ala, a squadron*, Cic. **II.** Transf., *a troop, throng*; in turma inauratarum equestrium (sc. statuarum), Cic.; Gallica (of the priests of Isis), Ov.

turmālis -e (turma), *of* or *relating to a troop* or *squadron*. Subst., **turmāles** -ium, m. *the men of a squadron*, Liv.

turmātim, adv. (turma), *troop by troop, in troops*, Caes., Sall.

Turnus -i, m. *king of the Rutuli, killed by Aeneas*.

Tŭrŏnes -um, m. and **Tŭrŏni** -ōrum, m *a people in Gallia Lugdunensis, near modern Tours*

turpĭcŭlus -a -um (dim of turpis), *somewhat ugly* or *deformed* **I.** Lit, nasus, Cat **II.** Fig., res turpiculae et quasi deformes, Cic.

turpĭfĭcātus a um (turpis and facio), *made foul, corrupted*, animus, Cic.

turpĭlŭcrĭcŭpĭdus -a -um (= turpis lucri cupidus) = αἰσχροκερδής, *greedy after base gain*, Plaut.

turpis -e, *ugly, foul, unsightly, filthy* **I.** Lit., aspectus, Cic ; turpia membra fimo, Verg, pes, Hor **II.** Fig., in a moral sense, *disgraceful, shameful, base, dishonourable, infamous*, fuga, Cic, quid turpius? Cic, homo turpissimus, Cic ; with 2 supine, turpe factu, Cic. Subst, **turpe** -is, n *a disgrace*, habere quaestui rempublicam turpe est, Cic

turpĭtĕr, adv. (turpis), *foully, in an ugly, unsightly manner*. **I.** Lit, claudicare Ov, desinere in piscem, Hor **II.** Fig, *disgracefully, scandalously, basely, dishonourably, infamously*, facere, Cic, fugere, Caes, turpius ejicitur, quam non admittitur hospes, Ov.; in deorum opinione turpissime labitur, Cic

turpĭtūdo inis, f (turpis), *ugliness, unsightliness* **I.** Lit, Cic. **II.** Fig, *turpitude, baseness, disgrace, infamy, dishonour*, maximam turpitudinem suscipere vitae cupiditate, Cic nullā conditione hanc turpitudinem subire, Cic., plur, flagitiorum ac turpitudinum societas, Cic.

turpo, 1. (turpis), *to make ugly, befoul, defile.* **I.** Lit., capillos sanguine, Verg **II.** Fig, *to disgrace, dishonour*, ornamenta, Cic, castra urbanae seditionis contagione, Liv.

turrĭcŭla ae, f (dim of turris), *a little tower, turret*, transf, *a dice-box*, Mart.

turrĭgĕr gĕra -gĕrum (turris and gero), *tower bearing*; urbes, Verg, hence an epithet of Cybele, who was represented with a crown of towers (the earth with its towers personified), Cybele, Ov ; dea, *Cybele*, Ov, Ops, Ov

turris -is, f (τύῤῥις, τυρσις), *a tower* **A.** Gen, Cic **B.** Esp, 1, in war, *a tower with which walls and camps were strengthened*, turris latericia, Caes ; or, *a tower of wood for attacking towns*, Cic, or, *a tower full of armed soldiers*, borne by elephants, Liv., 2, *a dove cote*, Ov

turrītus -a -um (turris) **I.** *furnished with towers*, moenia, Ov ; turrita, as an epithet of Cybele, Prop., Berecyntia mater, Verg **II.** Poet transf., *tower-like, towering high*, scopuli, Verg

tursĭo -ōnis, m *a species of dolphin* or *porpoise*, Plin

turtur -ŭris, m. *a turtle-dove*, Verg

turtŭrilla -ae, f (dim of turtur), *a little turtle-dove*, Sen

turunda -ae, f (perhaps = terenda, from tero) **I.** *a pellet for fattening poultry*, Varr **II.** *a roll of lint*, Cato

tūs (thūs), tūris, n (θυος), *incense, frankincense*, tus incendere, Cic

Tusci -ōrum, m *the Tuscans, Etruscans, inhabitants of Etruria* Hence, adj, **Tuscus** -a -um, *Etruscan*; amnis, *the Tiber*, Verg ; dux, *Mezentius*, Ov, eques, *Maecenas*, Verg, vicus, *a street in Rome*, Liv, semen, *spelt*, Ov

Tuscŭlānus, v Tusculum

1 **tusculum** -i, n (dim of tus), *a little incense*, Plaut

2. **Tuscŭlum** -i, n *an old town in Latium, now Frascati* Hence, **A. Tuscŭlus** -a -um, *Tusculan* **B. Tuscŭlānus** -a -um, *Tusculan*, plur subst, **Tuscŭlāni** -ōrum, m *the inhabitants of Tusculum* **Tuscŭlānum** -i, n (sc rus or praedium), *an estate of Cicero's near Tusculum*

tussĭlāgo -inis, f. *the plant coltsfoot*, Plin

tussĭo, 4. (tussis), *to have a cough, to cough*, male, Hor

tussis -is, acc im, f *a cough*, Verg

tūtāmen -inis, n (tutor), *a defence, protection*, Verg

tūtāmentum -i, n (tutor), *defence, protection*, Liv

tūtē, adv (tutus), *safely, securely*, in vadis consistere tutius, Caes

tūtēla ae, f (tueor) **I.** *protection, guard, charge* **A.** Gen, 1, lit, tutelam januae gerere, Plaut, cuius in tutela Athenas esse voluerunt, Cic, 2, meton, a, act, *protector, guardian*, templi, Ov ; b, pass, *the person or thing protected*, virginum primae puerique claris patribus orti, Deliae tutela deae, Hor **B.** Esp, a, *guardianship, tutelage*; in alicuius tutelam venire, Cic, judicium tutelae, Cic, b, *the property of the ward*, legitima, Cic. **II.** *a keeping, care, management*, villarum, Plin

tūtēlārĭus ii, m (tutela), *a keeper*, tutelarii, *the keepers of a temple*, Plin

tutĭcus, v meddix

tūtō, adv (tutus), *safely, securely*, esse, Cic, dimicare, Caes, with ab and the abl, ab incursu, Caes, superl, tutissimo, *at the safest*, non quaerere, ubi tutissimo essem, Cic

1 **tūtor** -ōris, m (for tuitor, from tueor) **I.** *a protector*, finium, Hor, religionum, Cic **II.** *the guardian of a woman, a minor, or imbecile person*, a, lit, aliquem tutorem instituere, Cic, tutorem esse alicuius or alicui, Cic, b, fig, eloquentiae quasi tutores, Cic

2 **tūto**, 1 and **tūtor**, 1 dep. (intens of tueor) **I.** *to protect, preserve, watch, keep*, domum, Verg, oculos ab inferiore parte, Cic, urbem muris, Liv, se adversus injusta arma, Liv **II.** *to ward off*, pericula, Sall, inopiam, Caes

tŭtŭlus -i, m *a particular mode of dressing the hair, by gathering it into a high knot at the back of the head*, esp used by the flamen and his wife, Varr

tūtus -a -um, p adj (from tueor) **I.** *safe, secure, out of danger*, res, Cic, tutiorem vitam hominum reddere, Cic, medio tutissimus ibis, Ov, tutus ab hostibus, Caes, subst, **tūtum** -i, n *a safe place, safety*, esse in tuto, Cic, aliquem (aliquid) in tuto collocare, tutum est, with infin, Caes. **II.** *watchful, cautious*, consilia, Liv

tŭus -a -um, pron poss (tu), *thy, thine* **I.** Subject, **A.** Gen, tua bona, Cic, subst, tui, *thy friends, people, party*, Cic ; tuum est, *it is thy custom, it is thy duty*, Plaut, Ter **B.** *favourable to thee*, tempore tuo pugnasti, Liv. **II.** Object = *to thee, towards thee*, desiderio tuo, *for you*, Cic

tuxtax, *whack, whack*, onomatop imitation of the sound of blows, Plaut.

Tȳăna -ōrum, n (Τυανα), *a town in Cappadocia, at the foot of Mount Taurus* Hence, **Tȳănēĭus** -a um, *of* or *belonging to Tyana*

Tyba -ae, f *a town on the borders of Syria*, now *Taibe*

Tȳbris = Tiberis (q v)

Tȳbur = Tibur (q v)

Tȳcha -ae, f (Τύχη), *a part of the town of Syracuse, in Sicily, with a temple to Fortune, whence the name*

Tȳchĭus -ĭi, m (Τυχίος), *a celebrated Boeotian worker in leather*

Tȳdeus ĕi and -ĕos, m (Τυδεύς), *son of Oeneus, father of Diomedes* Hence, **Tȳdīdēs** -ae, m (Τυδείδης), *the son of Tydeus, i e, Diomedes*

tympănītĭcus i, m (τυμπανιτικός), *one who has the dropsy*, Plin

tympănĭum ĭi, n (τυμπάνιον), *a drum-shaped pearl*, Plin

tympănizo, 1 (τυμπανίζω), *to play the tambourine or kettle drum*, Suet

tympănŏtrība -ae, m (τυμπανοτρίβης), *a tambourine-player*, Plaut

tympănum -i, n (τύμπανον), *a tambourine, kettle drum* (esp used by the priests of Cybele) **I.** Lit, Verg **II.** Transf, *a drum or wheel for raising weights*, Verg, Lucr

Tyndărĕus -ĕi, m. (Τυνδάρεος), *king of Sparta, husband of Leda, father of Castor and Pollux, Helen and Clytemnestra* Hence, **A.** Subst, **Tyndărĭdēs** -ae, m *a male descendant of Tyndareus*, Tyndaridae, *Castor and Pollux*, Cic **B. Tyndăris** ĭdis, f *a female descendant of Tyndareus, Helen*, Verg, Ov, *Clytemnestra*, Ov

1 **Tyndăris**, v Tyndareus

2 **Tyndăris** -ĭdis, f (Τυνδαρίς), *a town on the north coast of Sicily, possessing a celebrated statue of Mercury, which was taken by the Carthaginians and restored by Scipio Africanus the Younger* Hence, **Tyndărĭtānus** a -um, *of Tyndaris*

Tȳnes -ētis, m (Τύνης), *a town in Zeugitana, now Tunis*

Tȳphōeus -ĕos, m (Τυφωεύς), *a giant who tried to force Jupiter from heaven, and was for punishment buried beneath Aetna* Hence, **A. Tȳphōĭus** -a -um, *of or belonging to Typhoeus* **B. Tȳphōĭs** ĭdos, *of or belonging to Typhoeus*, Aetna, Ov.

1 **Tȳphōn** -ōnis, m (Τυφών), *another name of the giant Typhoeus*

2 **tȳphon** -ōnis, m (τυφών), *a whirlwind, hurricane, typhoon*, Plin

tȳpus -i, m (τύπος), *a figure on a wall*, Cic

tȳrannĭcē, adv (tyrannicus), *tyrannically, despotically*, ea quae regie seu potius tyrannice statuit in aratores, Cic

tȳrannĭcīda -ae, c (tyrannus and caedo), *the slayer of a tyrant, a tyrannicide*, Plin

tȳrannĭcīdĭum -ĭi, n (tyrannicida), *the slaying of a tyrant*, Sen

tȳrannĭcus -a -um (τυραννικός), *tyrannical*, leges, facinus, Cic

Tȳrannĭo -ōnis, m *a Greek grammarian and geographer, who came to Rome as a captive in the Mithridatic War, and taught the children and arranged the library of Cicero*

tȳrannis -ĭdis, f (τυραννίς), *the supremacy of a tyrant, tyranny*, vivit tyrannis, tyrannus occidit, Cic, tyrannidem delere, Cic

tȳrannoctŏnus -i, m (τυραννοκτόνος), *the slayer of a tyrant*, Cic

tȳrannus -i, m (τύραννος, Dor for κοίρανος), *lord, master* **I.** Gen, *an absolute ruler, prince, lord*, of Aeneas, Verg, Phrygius, Laomedon, Ov, of Neptune, as ruler of the sea, Ov **II.** Esp, of one who in a free state gains supreme power and overthrows the constitution of the state, *a usurper, despot, tyrant*, clemens tyrannus, Cic.

Tȳrās ae, m (Τύρας), *a river in Sarmatia, now the Dniester*

tȳrĭanthĭna -ōrum, n. (τυριάνθινος), *violet-coloured garments*, Mart

Tȳrĭus, v Tyrus

tȳrŏtărīchum -i, m (τυροτάριχος), *a dish of cheese and salt fish*, Cic.

Tyrrhēni -ōrum, m (Τυρρηνοί), *the Etruscans, the people who inhabited the country north of Latium* Hence, **A. Tyrrhēnĭa** ae, f *Etruria* **B. Tyrrhēnus** -a -um, *Etruscan*, corpora, *the sailors whom Bacchus turned into dolphins*, Ov, so monstra, Ov, rex, *Mezentius*, Ov, mare, aequor, *the part of the Mediterranean between Italy and Corsica and Sardinia*, Verg, Liv, subst, **Tyrrhēnus** -i, m *an Etruscan*

Tyrrhīdae ārum, m *the sons of Tyrrhus, the herdsmen of king Latinus*

Tȳrus (-ŏs) -i, f (Τύρος), *Tyre, a city of Phoenicia, famous for its purple*, hence, adj, **Tȳrĭus** -a um, **a,** *Tyrian*, puella, *Europa, daughter of the Tyrian king Agenor*, Ov, subst, **Tȳrĭi** -ōrum, m *the inhabitants of Tyre*, **b,** meton = *purple*, vestes, Hor, colores, Ov, **c,** transf = *Carthaginian*; urbs, *Carthage*, Verg, subst, **Tȳrĭi** -ōrum, m *the Tyrians*

U.

U, u, originally written V, v, the 20th letter of the Latin alphabet, corresponds with the Greek upsilon (Υ, υ) It is frequently interchanged with i, as optimus, optumus, satira, satura, etc

1 **ūber** -ĕris, n (οὖθαρ) **I.** *an udder, pap, teat, breast*, ubera praebere, Ov, admovere, Verg **II.** Transf, **a,** *richness, abundance, fertility*, fertilis ubere ager, Ov, **b,** poet, *a fruitful field*, Verg

2 **ūber** -ĕris, *rich, abounding in anything, fertile, fruitful, productive, abundant, copious* **I.** Lit, a, seges spicis uberibus, Lucr, uberior solito (of a river), *fuller than usual*, Ov, arbor niveis uberrima pomis, Ov; **b,** *full of matter*; uberiores litterae, Cic **II.** Fig, quis uberior in dicendo Platone? Cic, uberrima supplicationibus triumphisque provincia, Cic., uberrimae artes, Cic

ūbĕrĭus, superl, **ūberrĭmē**, adv (2 uber) **I.** *more abundantly, more copiously*; provenit seges, Ov **II.** Fig, *more copiously, more at length*, disputare, Cic

ūbertas ātis, f (2 uber), *fruitfulness, fertility, copiousness, abundance* **I.** Subject, *productiveness*, **a,** lit., agrorum, Cic, **b,** fig, utilitatis, Cic **II.** Object, *abundance, plenty*; **a,** lit., frugum, Cic, **b,** fig, improborum, Cic; plur, ubertates virtutis et copiae, Cic

ūbertim, adv (2 uber), *abundantly, copiously*, fundere lacrimas, Cat

ūberto, 1 (ubertas), *to make fruitful*, Plin

ŭbī (old archaic form cubi), *where* **I.** Lit, **a,** omnes, qui tum eos agros, ubi hodie est haec urbs, incolebant, Cic; ubi tyrannus est, ibi, etc, Cic, with partic nam, in qua non video ullonam mens constans et vita beata possit insistere, Cic, with genit, terrarum, loci, e g, quid ageres, ubi terrarum esses, Cic, **b,** in direct questions, *where?* ubi sunt qui Antonium Graece negant scire? Cic **II.** Transf, **A.** Of time, *when, as soon as*, quem ubi vidi, equidem vim lacrimarum profudi, Cic., ubi de eius adventu Helvetii certiores facti sunt, legatos ad eum mittunt, Caes, with primum, at hostes, ubi primum nostros equites conspexerunt, Caes **B.** *wherein, whereby, in which, by which*, etc, est, ubi id isto modo valeat, Cic **C.** ubi ubi = ubicumque, *wherever*, facile ubi ubi essent se conversuros aciem, Liv

ŭbĭcumquĕ (ŭbĭcunquĕ), adv *wherever, wheresoever.* **I.** Relat, ubicumque erimus, Cic, with genit, ubicumque gentium or terrarum, Cic **II.** Indef, *anywhere, everywhere*, malum est ubicumque, Hor

Ubii ōrum, m *a German people who, in Caesar's time, dwelt on the east bank of the Rhine near Cologne* Adj, **Ubĭus** -a um, *Ubian*

ŭbĭlĭbĕt, adv *anywhere you please, everywhere*, Sen

ŭbĭnam, v ubi

ŭbĭquāquĕ (sc parte), *wherever*, Ov

ŭbĭquĕ, adv *wherever, wheresoever, everywhere*, omnes qui ubique sunt, or sunt nati, *all in the world*, Cic

ŭbĭvis, *wherever you will, anywhere, everywhere*, Cic

Ŭcălĕgōn ōnis, m *name of a Trojan*, jam proximus ardet Ucalegon, *the house of Ucalegon*, Verg

ūdo -ōnis, m *a fur shoe* or *sock*, Mart

ūdus -a -um (contr from uvidus) **I.** Lit, *wet, moist*, paludes, Ov, oculi, *tearful*, Ov, aleator, *drunken*, Hor **II.** Transf, *soft, bending, yielding*, argilla, Hor

Ūfens tis, m **I.** *a small river in Latium*, hence, **Ūfentīnus** a um, *Ufentine* **II.** *a commander of the Aequi*

ulcĕrātĭo ōnis, f (ulcero), *a sore, ulcer, ulceration*, Plin

ulcĕro, 1 (ulcus), *to make sore to ulcerate* **I.** Lit, mantica cui lumbos onere ulceret, Hor, nondum ulcerato Philocteta morsu serpentis, Cic **II** Fig, jecur, *to wound the heart*, Hor

ulcĕrōsus a -um (ulcus) *full of sores, ulcerated, ulcerous* **I. a,** lit., facies, Tac, **b,** trans, of trees, *full of knots* **II.** Fig, jecur, *wounded by love*, Hor

ulciscor, ultus sum ulcisci, 3 dep **I.** *to take vengeance for some one, to avenge*, patrem, Cic, se, Cic **II** *to take vengeance on some one, to punish*, **a,** with acc of person, aliquem, Cic, Caes, **b,** with acc of thing, scelus, Cic, injuriam, Cic (ulcisci, ultus, pass, quidquid sine sanguine civium ulcisci nequitur, Sall, quae defendi repetique et ulcisci fas sit, Liv)

ulcus ĕris, n (ἕλκος), *a sore, ulcer* **I. a,** lit, Verg, **b,** transf, *an excrescence on trees*, Plin **II.** Fig, ulcus (of love) enim vivescit et inveterascit alendo, Lucr, quidquid horum attigeris, ulcus est, Cic.

ulcuscŭlum -i, n (dim of ulcus), *a little ulcer*, Sen

ulex icis, m *a shrub resembling rosemary*, Plin

ūlīgĭnōsus a um (uligo), *wet, damp, moist, marshy*, Varr

ūlīgo inis, f (for uviligo, from *uveo), *moisture of the soil, wetness of the earth*, uligines paludum, Tac

Ŭlixēs -is, m Latin name (after Etruscan Uluxe or Sicilian Οὐλίξης) for Ὀδυσσεύς, *son of Laertes, husband of Penelope, father of Telemachus, king of Ithaca, famed for his cunning and for his wanderings after the siege of Troy* (genit, Ulixĕi, Hor, Ov, acc, Ulixen, Hor, Ov)

ullus -a -um, genit ullius, dat ulli (dim of unus, for unulus), *any*, gen used in negative and hypothetical sentences **I.** Adj sine ulla dubitatione, Cic, neque ullam in partem disputo, *for or against*, Cic, neque ullam picturam fuisse, quin conquisierit, Cic **II.** Subst, **a,** m *any one*, Cic, **b,** n *anything*, nemo ullius nisi fugae memor Liv (ullius, Cat, Verg, Ov)

ulmārium ii, n (ulmus), *a nursery or plantation of elms*, Plin

ulmĕus a um (ulmus), *of or relating to the elm, made of elm wood*, Plaut

ulmĭtrĭba -ae, m (ulmus and τρίβω, tero), lit, *an elm-rubber*, in jest, *one who has often been beaten with elm rods*, Plaut

ulmus i, f *the elm*, Verg

ulna -ae, f (ὠλένη), *the elbow* **I** 1, lit, Plin, **2,** meton, *the arm*, ulnis aliquem tollere, Ov **II.** Transf, **a,** as a measure of length, *an ell*, Verg, **b,** *as much as a man can span with both arms*, Plin

ulpĭcum i, n *a kind of leek*, Cato

uls (archaic ouls) and **ultis,** *on the other side of, beyond*, Varr

ultĕr tra -trum, compar, **ultĕrĭor**; superl, **ultĭmus. I.** Posit, **ulter** -tra trum, not found except in the adverbial forms ultra, ultro **II.** Compar, **ultĕrĭor** ius, genit ōris, *on the other side, further, beyond, ulterior* **A.** Lit, Gallia, *Gaul on the other*, i e, *the north side of the Alps*, Cic, equitatus, *placed at a greater distance*, Caes **B.** Transf, **a,** *distant, past, farther*, ulteriora mirari, Tac, ulteriora pudet docuisse, Ov, **b,** *farther, worse*, quo quid ulterius privato timendum foret? Liv. **III.** Superl, **ultĭmus** -a um, *the most distant, furthest, extremest, last* **A.** Lit, of space, **1,** luna, quae ultima a caelo est, Cic, subst, **a,** m, recessum primi ultimis non dabant, Caes, **b,** n, caelum, quod extremum atque ultimum mundi est, Cic, ultima signant, *the goal*, Verg, **2,** partitive for ultima pars, in ultimam provinciam, *into the most distant part of the province*, Cic **B.** Transf, **1,** in time or succession, *the most distant, remotest, the last, final*, tempus, antiquitas, Cic, principium, Cic, lapis, *a grave stone*, Prop, adv ad ultimum, *to the last*, Liv, or (oftener), *lastly, finally*, Liv, ultimum, *for the last time*, Liv, **2,** in rank or degree, **a,** *the highest, greatest*, natura Cic, supplicium, *capital punishment*, Caes, subst, **ultĭmum** -i, n *the greatest, the extremest*, and, in a bad sense, *the worst*, ultima audere, Liv, ultimum bonorum, *the highest good*, Cic, adv, ad ultimum, *utterly, entirely*, ad ultimum demens, Liv, **b,** *the meanest, lowest*, laus, Hor, subst, (*a*) m, in ultimis militum, Liv, (*β*) n, in ultimis laudum esse, Liv

ultĕrĭus. I. Neut of ulterior, v ulter **II.** Adv, v ultra

ultĭmus, v ulter.

ultĭo ōnis, f (ulciscor), *an avenging, punishing, revenging, revenge*, ultionem petere, Liv; with object genit, violatae per vim pudicitiae, Liv

ultis = uls (q v)

ultor oris, m (ulciscor), *an avenger, punisher*, injuriarum, Cic, attrib, deus ultor = Anteros, Ov, as a surname of Mars, Ov

ultrā, sc parte (from ulter) **I.** Adv, posit, *on the other side of*, **1,** lit, cis Padum ultraque, Liv, **2,** transf, of that which is beyond a certain limit, *beyond, further*, **a,** in space, (*a*) lit, ultra neque curae neque gaudio locum esse, Sall.; (β) fig., *further, beyond;* estne aliquid ultra, quo progredi crudelitas possit? Cic.; foll. by quam, quod ultra quam satis est, Cic.; **b,** of time, *further;* nec ultra bellum dilatum est, Liv.; compar., ulterius, *further;* (α) lit., ulterius abit, Ov.; (β) fig., ulterius ne tende odiis, Verg. **II.** Prep. with acc., **1,** of space, *beyond, on the further side of;* ultra Silianam villam, Cic.; **2,** transf., **a,** of time, *beyond;* ultra biennium, Tac.; **b,** of number or measure, *beyond, more than;* modum, quem ultra progredi non oportet, Cic.; ultra vires, Verg. (ultra sometimes put after its case, quem ultra, Cic.).

ultrix -īcis, f. (ultor), *avenging;* Dirae, *the Furies,* Verg.

ultrō (sc. loco, from ulter), adv. *on the other side.* **I.** Lit., *on the other side, beyond;* gen., with citro, *up and down, on both sides;* ultro et citro cursare, Cic. **II.** Transf., **a,** *away, off;* ultro istum a me! Plaut.; **b,** *besides, moreover;* ultroque iis sumptum intulit, Cic.; **c,** *of one's own accord, spontaneously, voluntarily;* ultro se offerre, Cic.; improbos ultro lacessere, Cic.; hence, ultro tributa, *money which the treasury had to expend every year on public buildings,* Liv.

ultrōnĕus -a -um (ultro), *of one's own accord, voluntarily,* Sen.

ultrōtrĭbūta, v. ultro.

Ŭlŭbrae -ārum, *a place in Latium, near the Pontine Marshes.* Hence, **Ŭlŭbrānus** -a -um, *Ulubran.*

ŭlŭla -ae, f. (lit., *the screeching one* (sc. avis), from ululo), *a screech-owl,* Verg.

ŭlŭlātus -ūs, m. (ululo), *a howling, wailing, shrieking, yelling;* ululatus nocturni, Liv.

ŭlŭlo, 1. (connected with ὀλολύζω). **I.** Intransit., *to howl, yell;* **a,** lit., of living beings, Tisiphone ululavit, Ov.; ululanti voce, Cic.; **b,** transf., of places, *to resound with howling;* cavae plangoribus aedes femineis ululant, Verg. **II.** Transit., *to call upon with howling;* nocturnis Hecate triviis ululata per urbem, Verg.

ulva -ae, f. *sedge,* Verg.

Ŭlysses = Ulixes (q.v.).

umbella -ae, f. (dim. of umbra), *a parasol,* Juv.

Umber, v. Umbri.

umbĭlīcātus -a -um (umbilicus), *shaped like a navel,* Plin.

umbĭlīcus -i, m. (ὀμφαλός), *the navel.* **I.** Lit., Liv., Ov. **II.** Meton., *the middle, centre of anything;* **1,** gen., Siciliae, Cic.; terrarum, *Delphi,* Cic.; **2,** esp., **a,** *the end of a roller on which a MS. was rolled,* Cat.; fig., inceptos iambos ad umbilicum adducere, *bring to the end,* Hor.; **b,** transf., *the index of a sun-dial,* Cic.; **c,** *a kind of sea-snail,* Cic.

umbo -ōnis, m. (ἄμβων). **I.** *the boss in the centre of a shield;* summus clipei umbo, Verg.; hence, meton., *a shield;* salignae umbonum crates, Verg. **II.** *the elbow,* Mart. **III.** *the full part* or *swelling of a garment;* meton., *a toga,* Pers.

umbra -ae, f. *a shade, shadow.* **I. A.** Lit., arboris, Cic.; prov., umbras timere, *to be frightened at shadows,* Cic. **B.** Transf., *shade;* **a,** *protection, help;* auxilii, Liv.; sub umbra Romanae amicitiae latēre, Cic.; **b,** *idleness, pleasant rest;* Veneris cessamus in umbra, Ov.; cedat umbra soli, Cic.; **c,** *appearance* (as opposed to reality), *shadow, semblance;* gloriae, Cic. **II. A.** Transf., **1,** *a shade, shadow in painting;* transf., in discourse, Cic.; **2,** *the shadow = that which accompanies;* luxuriae, Cic.; *an uninvited guest, brought by one who has been invited* (σκιά), Hor. **B.** Meton., **1,** *that which is shady;* **a,** as trees, houses, etc., umbras falce premere, Verg.; inducite montibus umbras (i.e., arbores), Verg.; **b,** *any shady place;* Pompeja, Ov.; tonsoris, *barber's shop,* Hor.; **2,** *the shade of a dead person, ghost;* tricorpor, Verg.; plur., umbrae, Verg.; **3,** *a fish, the grayling,* Ov.

umbrăcŭlum -i, n. (umbra). **I.** *a shady place, arbour,* Verg.; in plur., *a quiet place* (as opp. to public life); Theophrasti, Cic.; doctrinam ex umbraculis eruditorum (*schools*) otioque in solem produxerat, Cic. **II.** *a parasol,* Ov.

umbrātĭcŏla -ae, m. (umbra and colo), *a lounger in the shade,* Plaut.

umbrātĭcus -a -um (umbra), *belonging to the shade;* homo, *an idler, lounger,* Plaut.

umbrātĭlis -e (umbra), *remaining in the shade.* **I.** *retired, contemplative;* vita, Cic. **II.** Of discourse, in the schools, *rhetorical* (opp. to public, political), domestica exercitatio et umbratilis, Cic.; oratio, *only meant for perusal, not for speaking,* Cic.

Umbri -ōrum, m. *a people in Italy between the Padus, the Tiber, and the Adriatic Sea, who in later times descended further into Italy, and inhabited a country between the Rubicon, the Nar, and the Tiber.* Hence, **A. Umber** -bra -brum, *Umbrian;* subst., **Umber** -bri, m. *an Umbrian.* **B. Umbrĭa** -ae, f. *Umbria, the country of the Umbri.*

umbrĭfĕr -fĕra -fĕrum (umbra and fero), *shady, umbrageous;* nemus, Verg.; platanus, Cic.

umbro, 1. (umbra), *to cover with shade, shade, overshadow;* umbrata tempora quercu, Verg.

umbrōsus -a -um (umbra), *shady, umbrageous.* **I.** Pass., *shaded;* ripa, Cic.; locus umbrosior, Cic. **II.** Act., *affording shade;* cacumina, Verg.; salix, Ov.

ūmecto = humecto (q.v.)

ŭmĕrus = humerus (q.v.).

ūmesco, umidus = humesco, humidus (q.v.).

ūmor = humor (q.v.).

umquam (unquam), adv. (orig. cumquam), *at any time, ever* (used chiefly in negative, interrog., and conditional sentences), Cic.; non umquam, Liv.; haud umquam, Verg.; si umquam, Liv.

ūnā, adv. (unus), *at the same place, at the same time, together;* **a,** absol., qui una venerant, Cic.; **b,** with cum and the abl., amores una cum praetexta ponere, Cic.

ūnănĭmans = unanimus (q.v.).

ūnănĭmĭtas -ātis, f. (unanimus), *concord, unanimity,* Liv.

ūnănĭmus -a -um (unus and animus), *of one mind, concordant, agreeing, unanimous;* sodales, Cat.; fratres, Verg.

uncĭa -ae, f. (Sicilian οὐγκία, from unus), *an ounce, the twelfth part of any whole.* **I.** Lit., **1,** as a coin, *one-twelfth of an as,* Varr.; **2,** as a weight or measure, **a,** *an ounce, one-twelfth of a pound,* Plaut.; **b,** as a measure, *one-twelfth of a foot, an inch,* Plin.; **3,** in inheritances, *a twelfth part;* Caesar ex uncia, *heir to one-twelfth,* Cic. **II.** Transf., *a trifle, bit;* eboris, Juv.

uncĭālis -e (uncia), *of or relating to a twelfth part;* asses, *weighing an ounce each,* Plin.

uncĭārĭus -a -um (uncia), *of* or *relating to a twelfth part;* fenus, *one-twelfth of the capital yearly,* i.e., 8⅓ *per cent. for the year of ten months,* 10 *per cent. for the year of twelve months,* Tac.

uncĭātim, adv. (uncia), *by ounces,* Plin.; Transf., *little by little,* Ter.

uncinātus a um (uncinus), *shaped like a hook, hooked*, uncinata corpora, Cic

unciŏla ae, f (dim of uncia), *a little ounce, a little twelfth part* (of an inheritance), Juv

unctĭo -ōnis, f (ungo) **I.** *an anointing*, Plaut, philosophum unctionis causā reliquerunt, *to wrestle in the palaestra*, Cic. **II.** Meton, *ointment, salve*, Plin

unctĭto, 1 (intens. of ungo), *to salve, anoint*, Plaut

unctĭuscŭlus a -um (dim of unctus), *somewhat unctuous*, Plaut

unctor ōris, m (ungo), *an anointer*, Cic

unctōrĭum -ii, n (ungo), *an anointing-room in the bath*, Plin

unctūra ae, f (ungo), *the anointing of the dead*, ap. Cic

1 **unctus** -a -um, p adj (from ungo) **I.** Adj, *smeared, anointed*, **1,** lit, manus, Hor sol, *basking in the sun after being anointed*, Cic, poet, palaestra, *where one is anointed*, Ov, **2,** transf, accedes siccus ad unctum, *to a rich and luxurious person*, Hor, unctior quaedam consuetudo loquendi, *rich, copious*, Cic **II.** Subst, **unctum** -i, n *a sumptuous repast*, Hor

2 **unctus** -ūs, m (ungo), *an anointing*, Plin

1 **uncus** -i, m (ὄγκος), *a hook*, uncus ferreus Liv, nec severus uncus abest, *as typical of Necessitas*, Hor, esp, *the hook with which the executioner dragged the bodies of the dead malefactors to throw them into the Tiber*, alicui uncum impingere, Cic

2 **uncus** -a um, *bent like a hook, hooked, curved*, manus, Verg; aratrum, Verg

unda ae, f *a wave of the sea*, and collective, *the waves* **I.** Lit, maris unda, Cic **II. A.** Transf, *wave, storm, surge*, undae comitiorum, *disorder*, Cic, unda salutantum, *crowd*, Verg **B.** Meton, **1,** *moisture*, **a,** *flowing water, water*, fontis, Ov, faciunt justos ignis et unda viros (fire and water being used at the ceremony of marriage), Ov, **b,** of other liquids, e g, oil, Plin, **2,** *stream* (of objects which are not liquid), qua plurimus undam fumus agit, *eddies*, Verg

undātim, adv (unda), *like waves*, Plin

undĕ, adv (orig cunde), *whence, from where* **I.** Lit, of place, **1,** correlative, nec enim inde venit, unde mallem, Cic, ut aliae eodem, unde erant profectae, referrentur, Caes, **2,** absol., **a,** in direct questions, unde dejectus est Cinna? Cic, **b,** in indirect questions, non recordor unde ceciderim, Cic **II.** Transf, **A.** Of origin, ground, cause, means, etc., *whence, from what person* or *thing, from what origin* **1,** correlative, **a,** unde necesse est, inde initium sumatur, Cic, **b,** qui eum necasset, unde ipse natus esset, Cic, **2,** esp., legal t t, unde petitur = *the accused person* or *defendant*, ego omnibus, unde petitur, hoc consilium dederim, Cic **III.** unde unde = undecumque, *whencesoever*, Hor

undēcentum (unus, de, and centum), *ninety nine*, Plin

undĕcĭēs (undĕcĭens), adv. (undecim), *eleven times*, Mart

undĕcim (unus and decem), *eleven*, Cic

undĕcĭmus -a -um (undecim), *the eleventh*, legio, Liv, annus, Verg

undĕcirēmis -is, f sc navis (undecim and remus), *a ship with eleven banks of oars*, Plin

undĕcŭmāni -ōrum, m (undecimus or undecumus), *soldiers of the eleventh legion*, Plin

undĕcumquĕ (undĕcunquĕ), adv *whencesoever*, Quint

undēni ae a (for undeceni, from undecim), *eleven each*, Musa per undenos emodulanda pedes, i e, *of hexameter and pentameter*, Ov, quater undenos implevisse Decembres, i e, *forty four years*, Hor

undēnōnāginta (unus, de, and nonaginta), *eighty nine*, Liv

undēoctōginta (unus, de, and octoginta), *seventy nine*, Hor

undēquadrāgĭēs, adv (undequadraginta), *thirty nine times*, Plin

undēquadrāginta (unus, de, and quadraginta), *thirty nine*, Cic

undēquinquāgēsĭmus -a -um (undequinquaginta), *the forty ninth*, Cic

undēquinquāginta (unus, de and quinquaginta), *forty nine*, Liv

undēsexāginta (unus, de, and sexaginta), *fifty nine*, Liv

undētrīcēsĭmus -a -um (undetriginta), *the twenty ninth*, Liv

undētrīginta (unus, de, and triginta), *twenty-nine*, Vitr

undēvīcēni -ae -a (undeviginti), *nineteen each*, Quint

undēvīcēsĭmus (undēvīgēsĭmus) (undeviginti), *the nineteenth*, Cic

undēvīginti (unus, de, and viginti), *nineteen*, Cic, Liv

undĭquĕ, adv (unde and que) **I.** *on all sides, from everywhere, everywhere*, concurrere, Cic, colligere, Cic, amens undique dicatur, *by all people*, Hor **II.** *on all sides, in every respect*, partes undique aequales, Cic, undique religionem tolle, Cic.

undisŏnus -a -um (unda and sono), *resounding with waves*, dii, *sea gods*, Prop

undo, 1 (unda), *to rise in waves, surge* **A.** Lit, flammis inter tabulata volutus ad caelum undabat vortex, Verg **B.** Transf, *to have a wave-like motion, to wave, to undulate*, fumus Verg, habenae, *hanging loosely*, Verg

undōsus -a -um (unda), *full of waves, surging, billowy*, Verg

ŭnĕdo ōnis, m *the arbutus-tree, and its fruit*, Plin

ūnetvīcēsĭmāni ōrum, m (unetvicesimus), *soldiers of the twenty-first legion*, Tac

ūnetvīcēsĭmus -a um (unus et vicesimus), *the twenty-first*, Tac

ungo (unguo), unxi, unctum, 3 *to anoint, smear, salve* **I** Lit, aliquem unguentis, Cic, gloria quem supra vires ungit, *adorns*, Hor, (with reference to the anointing after a bath), unctus est, accubuit, Cic, of the anointing of a corpse, corpus, Ov, of the dressing of provisions, *to dress*, caules oleo, Hor **II.** Transf, *to besmear*, tela manu, *with poison*, Verg, uncta aqua, *dirty*, Hor, uncta carina, *pitched*, Verg

unguen ĭnis, n (unguo), *a fatty substance, salve*, Verg

unguentārĭus -a um (unguentum), *of or relating to salve or ointment* **I.** Adj, Suet **II.** Subst, **A.** **unguentārĭus** -ii, m *a dealer in unguents*, Cic **B.** **unguentārĭa** -ae, f **a,** *a female dealer in unguents*, Plin, **b,** *the art of preparing unguents*, Plaut **C.** **unguentārĭum** -ii, n *money for unguents*, Plin

unguentātus a -um (unguentum), *anointed*, Cat

unguentum -i, n (ungo), *a salve, ointment, unguent*, Cic

unguĭcŭlus -i, m (dim of unguis), *the finger-nail, the toe nail*, integritas unguiculorum omnium, Cic, prov, qui mihi a teneris, ut

Graeci dicunt, unguiculis (Gr. ἐξ ἁπαλῶν ὀνύχων) cognitus est, *from childhood*, Cic.

unguĭnōsus -a -um (unguen), *fatty, unctuous*, Plin.

unguis -is, m. (ὄνυξ), *a finger* or *toe-nail*. **I.** Lit., of men, ungues ponere, Hor.; rodere, Hor.; prov., ab imis unguibus usque ad verticem summum, *from top to toe*, Cic.; a recta conscientia transversum unguem non discedere, *to depart a finger's breadth* (Engl. *a hair's breadth*) *from*, etc., Cic.; de tenero ungui, *from childhood*, Hor.; ad (in) unguem, *to a hair, nicely, perfectly* (an expression borrowed from sculptors who tested the smoothness of their work with the nail), ad unguem factus homo, Hor.; carmen decies castigare ad unguem, Hor.; omnis in unguem secto via limite quadret, Verg. **II.** Transf., **A.** Of plants, *a nail-like spot, tip*, Plin. **B.** *a kind of mussel*, Varr. (abl., gen. ungue, in poets also ungui).

ungŭla -ae, f. (unguis), *a hoof, claw, talon*. **I.** Lit., vestigium ungulae (equi), Cic. **II.** Meton., *a horse*; ungula rapit currus, Hor.

ungŭlus -i, m. (dim. of unguis). **I.** *a toe-nail*, Plaut. **II.** *a finger-ring*, Plin.

ūnĭcălămus -a -um (unus and calamus), *having one haulm*, Plin.

unguo = ungo (q.v.).

ūnĭcaulis -e (unus and caulis), *having one stalk*, Plin.

ūnĭcē, adv. (unicus), *singly, especially, particularly*; diligere, Cic.; unice securus, *altogether free from care*, Hor.

ūnĭcŏlor -ōris (unus and color), *uniform in colour, of one colour*; torus, Ov.

ūnĭcornis -e (unus and cornu), *having one horn*, Plin.

ūnĭcus -a -um (unus), *only, sole*. **I.** Lit., filius, Cic. **II.** Transf., *singular, unparalleled, unique, alone in its kind*; liberalitas, Cic.; fides, Liv.

ūnĭformis -e (unus and forma), *having one form, simple*, Tac.

ūnĭgĕna -ae (unus and gigno). **I.** *born at one birth, of the same race*; unigena Memnonis, *Zephyrus, brother of Memnon*, Cat. **II.** *only-born, only-made*; singularis hic mundus atque unigena, Cic.

ūnĭjŭgus -a -um (unus and jugum), *having only one yoke*; vinea, *fastened to the same cross-beam*, Plin.

ūnĭmănus -a -um (unus and manus), *having but one hand*; puer, Liv.

1\. **ūnĭo**, 4. (unus), *to unite*, Sen.

2\. **ūnĭo** -ōnis, m. (unus), *a single, large pearl*, Sen.

ūnistirpis -e (unus and stirps), *having one stock* or *stem*, Plin.

ūnĭtas -ātis, f. (unus), *unity, oneness*. **I.** Lit., Plin. **II.** Fig., **A.** *likeness, similarity*, Plin. **B.** *agreement, unanimity*, Sen.

ūnĭtĕr, adv. (unus), *in one, together*; aptus, Lucr.

ūnĭusmŏdi, adv. (unus and modus), *of one kind*, Cic.

ūnĭversālis -e (universus), *general, universal*, Quint.

ūnĭversē, adv. (universus), *in general*; generatim atque universe loquar, Cic.

ūnĭversĭtas -ātis, f. (universus), *the whole, total*. **I.** Lit., generis humani, Cic.; rerum, *the universe*, Cic. **II.** Transf., *the world*, Cic.

ūnĭversus (archaic, **ūnĭvorsus**) -a -um (unus and versus), lit., *turned into one, combined into one*. **I.** *whole, entire*. **A.** Adj., mundus, Cic.; de re universa tractare, Cic.; plur., **ūnĭversi** -ae -a, *all together*; universi (homines), Cic.; natura universa atque omnia continens, *all things in entirety and in detail*, Cic. **B.** Subst., **ūnĭversum** -i, n. *the whole*; hence, *the whole world, the universe*, Cic. **II.** Transf., *relating to all* or *to the whole, general*; pugna, *a general engagement*, Liv.; in universum, *in general, generally*, Liv.

ūnŏcŭlus -i, m. (unus and oculus), *a one-eyed man*, Plaut.

ūnus (old Latin, **oenus**) -a -um, genit. ūnĭus, dat. ūni, *one*. **I.** Lit., **A.** Gen., unus de magistratibus, Cic.; foll. by alter, una ex parte . . . altera ex parte, Caes.; plur. (esp., with words used only in the plur.), unae decumae . . . alterae, Cic.; ad unum (unam) omnes, *all to a man*, Cic.; in unum (Gr. εἰς ἕν) = *into one place*; confluere, Cic. **B.** Esp., **1**, *one, only one, alone*; Demosthenes unus eminet, Cic.; uni ex omnibus Sequani, Caes.; strengthened by the superl., or by omnium, summus vir unus omnis Graeciae, Cic.; **2**, *one, one and the same*; uno tempore, *at the same time*, Cic.; id unis aedibus, Cic. **II.** Transf., indefinite, *a, an, one, some one, any one*; unus paterfamilias, Cic.; without subst., tradidit uni, Cic.; unus quidam, Cic.; nemo unus, nullus unus, Cic.; unus et alter, *one and another*, Cic. (genit., ūnĭus, Verg., Ov., Lucr., Cat.; ūni, Cat.).

ūpĭlĭo (**ōpĭlĭo**) -ōnis, m. *a shepherd*, Verg.

ŭpŭpa -ae, f. (ἔποψ), *a hoopoe*, Varr.; (with a play on the word), *a kind of hoe*, Plaut.

Ūrănĭa -ae, f. and **Ūrănĭē** -ēs, f. (Οὐρανία, Οὐρανίη, *the heavenly one*), *one of the nine Muses, the Muse of Astronomy*.

urbānē, adv. (urbanus). **I.** *politely, civilly, urbanely*; urbane, urbanius agere, Cic. **II.** Of discourse, *wittily, acutely, elegantly*; ridere Stoicos, Cic.; vexare, Cic.

urbānĭtas -ātis, f. (urbanus), *city life*. **I.** Esp., *life in Rome*; desideria and desiderium urbanitatis, Cic. **II.** Meton., *the city manner*; **1**, in a good sense, **a**, *politeness, urbanity, refinement of manner*, Cic.; plur., deponendae tibi sunt urbanitates, rusticus Romanus factus es, Cic.; **b**, *elegance, refinement in speaking, both in pronunciation and in expression*, Cic.; **c**, *elegance in wit, fine wit, pleasantry*; vetus, Cic.; **2**, in a bad sense, *city roguery*, Tac.

urbānus -a -um (urbs), *of* or *belonging to a city* (esp. to Rome), *urban*. **I.** Lit., tribus, Cic.; praetor, Cic.; exercitus (of Roman citizens), Liv.; suffragatio (of the city population), Cic.; subst., **urbāni** -ōrum, m. *the inhabitants of the city, the townsfolk*, Cic. **II.** Meton., *after the city fashion*; **1**, in a good sense, **a**, *refined in manner, elegant*; homo, *a man of the world*, Cic.; **b**, of discourse, *choice, elegant, refined*; quiddam resonat urbanius, Cic.; **c**, *fine, witty, pleasant, humorous*; homo urbanissimus, Cic.; sales, Cic.; subst., *a wit*, Hor.; **2**, in a bad sense, *bold, impudent*; frons, Hor.

urbĭcăpus -i, m. (urbs and capio), *a taker of cities*, Plaut.

Urbicua -ae, f. *a town in Hispania Tarraconensis*.

urbĭcus -a -um (urbs), *of* or *belonging to a city, civic, urban*, Suet.

Urbīnum -i, n. *a town in Umbria*, now *Urbino*. Hence, **Urbīnās** -ātis, *belonging to Urbinum*.

Urbius clivus, *a place in Rome between the Esquiline and vicus Cyprius*.

urbs -bis, f. *the town surrounded by a ring wall, the city*. **I.** Lit., **A.** Gen., urbem condere, aedificare, Cic ; capere, Cic , evertere, Cic **B.** *the city of Rome* (like Gr ἄστυ, of Athens), ad urbem, *near Rome* or *at Rome*, Cic , ad urbe n esse, of Roman generals waiting outside Rome till a triumph was granted them, or of magistrates waiting to proceed to their provinces, Sall **II.** Meton , *the city = the dwellers in the city*, urbs somno vinoque sepulta, Verg

urcĕŏlāris -e (urceolus), *of* or *relating to a jug* or *pitcher*, herba, *pellitory, a plant used for polishing glass pitchers*, Plin

urcĕŏlus i, m (dim of urceus), *a small jug* or *pitcher*, Juv

urcĕus -i, m (connected with orca), *an earthenware jug, pitcher*, Hor

ūrēdo -inis, f (uro), **1,** *a blight upon plants*, Cic , **2,** *an inflammatory itch*, Plin

urgĕo (urguĕo), ursi, 2 *to push, press, drive, urge* **I.** Lit , **A** Transit , pedem (alicuius) pede (suo), Verg , naves in Syrtes, *drive on the sand-banks*, Verg **B.** Intransit , *to press*, longique urguent ad litora fluctus, Verg **II.** Transf , **1,** *to press upon, beset, oppress, burden, bear hard upon*, urgens malum, *urgent, pressing*, Cic , mortifero morbo urgeor, Cic , urgeri, with genit , *to be pressed hard on account of something*, male administratae provinciae aliorumque criminum, Tac , **2, a,** *to hem in a place*, urbem urbe aliā premere atque urgere, Verg , **b,** of time, *to press upon*, urget diem nox et dies noctem, Hor , **3,** of discourse, *to urge, press hard upon*, interrogando, Cic , **4,** *to apply oneself to diligently, ply hard, urge on, follow up*, occasionem, Cic , propositum, Hor , iter, Ov

ūrīca -ae, f *a caterpillar*, Plin

ūrīna -ae, f (οὖρον), *urine*, Cic

ūrīnātor -ōris, m (urinor), *a diver*, Liv

ūrīnor, 1 dep *to dive*, Cic

Ūrĭos -ii, m (Οὔριος), *the giver of a favourable wind* (of Jupiter), Cic

urna ae, f **I.** *a pitcher for drawing water*, Hor , attribute of the constellation Aquarius, Ov , and of the rivers personified as deities, Verg **II.** Transf , **A.** *a jug, pitcher, urn*, **a,** *for holding money*, argenti, Hor **b** *for holding the ashes of the dead*, Ov , **c,** *for throwing lots into*, nomina in urnam conjicere, Liv , educere ex urna tres (judices), Cic , hence, of the urn of fate, assigned to Jupiter and the Parcae omne nomen movet urna, Hor **B.** As a measure of capacity, *half an amphora*, Plin

urnālis -e (urna), *containing half an amphora*, Cato

urnārium -ii, n (urna), *a table on which water cans were placed*, Varr

urnŭla -ae, f (dim of urna), *a little pitcher*, Cic.

ūro, ussi, ustum, 3 (connected with εὕω), *to burn* **I. A.** Lit , **1,** gen , calore, Cic **2,** esp , **a,** medical t t , *to burn = to treat by burning, to burn out* in corpore si quid eiusmodi est quod reliquo corpori noceat, id uri secarique patimur, Cic , **b,** t t of painting, *to burn in* picta ustis coloribus puppis, Ov , **c,** *to burn, destroy by fire*, (α) hominem mortuum, Cic , agros, Liv , domos, Hor , (β) *to burn lights*, odoratam nocturna in lumina cedrum, Verg **B** Transf , **1,** *to burn, dry up, parch, pain acutely* fauces urit sitis, Ov **2,** *to pinch, chafe, gall*, calceus pedem urit, Hor urit lorica lacertos, Prop , **3,** *to pinch with cold* ustus ab assiduo frigore Pontus, Ov **II.** Fig , **A** *to burn with passion*, and pass , *to be on fire, glow with passion*, me tamen urit amor, Verg , uritur infelix Dido, Verg **B.** *to disquiet, disturb, harass*, eos bellum Romanum urebat, Liv

urruncum i, n *the lowest part of an ear of corn*, Varr

ursa ae, f (ursus) **I.** *a female bear*, poet *= bear generally*, Verg , Ov **II.** Meton , *the constellations of the Great and Little Bear*, ursa major, or Erymanthis, or Maenalis, or Parrhasis, *the Great Bear*, ursa minor or ursa Cynosuris, *the Little Bear*, Ov

ursīnus a um (ursus), *of* or *relating to a bear*, Plin

ursus -i, m *a bear* **I.** Lit , ursi informes, Verg **II.** Meton , poscunt ursum, *a bear hunt in the circus*, Hor.

urtīca ae, f (uro) **I.** *a nettle* **1,** lit , Plin , **2,** transf , *a sea nettle*, Plin **II.** Fig , *lustfulness, lewd desire*, Juv

ūrus i, m *the urus, a kind of wild ox*, Caes

urvum (urbum) -i, n *a plough tail*, Varr

Uscāna ae, f *a town in Illyria on the borders of Macedonia*, now Voscopopli Hence, **Uscānenses** -ium, m *the inhabitants of Uscana*

ūsĭo ōnis, f (utor), *use, using*, Cato

Ūsĭpĕtes -um, m and **Ūsĭpĭi** -ōrum, m *a powerful German tribe near the Tencteri, on the Lippe and the Rhine, conquered by Caesar*

ūsĭtātē, adv (usitatus), *in the usual manner*, loqui, Cic

ūsĭtātus -a um, p adj (f usito), *customary, usual, wonted, accustomed*, vocabula, Cic , facimus usitatius hoc verbum, Cic , utatur verbis quam usitatissimis, Cic , usitatum est, foll by acc and infin , *it is usual, customary*, ap Cic

uspĭam, adv (orig cuspiam), *anywhere*, Cic

usquam, adv (orig cusquam) **I.** *anywhere* (gen used in negative and conditional sentences) **A.** Lit , iste cui nullus esset usquam consistendi locus, Cic , with genit , usquam gentium, Cic **B.** *in any case*, Cic , Sall **II.** *any whither, in any direction*, nec vero usquam discedebam, Cic

usquĕ, adv (orig cusque), *at every point through and through, from* ... *to, all the way, continuously* **I.** Of space, **a,** with prep , usque a mare supero Romam proficisci, Cic , usque ad castra hostium accessit, Caes , **b,** with adv of place, quod eos usque istim (istinc) exauditos putem, Cic , usque quaque, *everywhere*, Cic , **c,** with acc of the object or place reached (with names of towns), ut usque Romam significationes vocesque referantur, *as far as Rome*, Cic **II.** Of time, **a,** with prep , usque a Romulo, *from the time of Romulus* Cic , **b,** with adv of time, inde usque repetens, Cic , usque quaque, *always*, Cat , usque eo se tenuit, Cic , **c,** absol , *always, constantly*, juvat usque morari, Verg **III.** In other relations, hoc malum usque ad bestias perveniat, Cic

usquĕquāquĕ, v usque I and II

usta -ae, f (uro), *a red pigment, burnt cinnabar*, Plin

Ustīca ae, f **I.** *a valley in the Sabine country, near Horace's estate* **II.** *a small island opposite the west coast of Sicily*

ustil v ustul . .

ustĭo ōnis, f (uro), *a burning*, Plin

ustor -ōris, m (uro), *a burner of corpses*, Cic.

ustŭlo (ustĭlo), 1 (dim of uro), *to burn a little, to singe*, Cat

1 **ūsūcăpĭo** cēpi -captum, 3 (usu, abl of usus, and capio), *to acquire ownership by length of possession* or *prescription*, Cic , velut usucepisse Italiam, Liv

2. **ūsŭcăpio** -ōnis, f. (usū, abl. of usus, and capio), *ownership acquired by length of possession or prescription;* usucapio fundi, Cic.

ūsūra -ae, f. (utor). **I.** *the use, enjoyment of anything;* **a,** natura dedit usuram vitae, Cic.; unius horae, Cic.; **b,** *the use of borrowed capital,* Cic. **II.** Meton., *interest paid for money borrowed;* usura menstrua, Cic.; usurae gravissimae, Caes.; alicui usuram pendĕre, *to pay,* Cic.; transf., terra nec umquam sine usura reddit, Cic.

ūsūrārĭus -a -um (usura). **I.** *relating to (temporary) use,* Plaut. **II.** *out at interest, paying interest,* Plaut.

usurpātĭo -ōnis, f. (usurpo), *a using, use, making use;* doctrinae, Cic.; vocis, Liv.; ad usurpationem vetustatis, *to practise an old custom,* Cic.; itineris, *undertaking,* Liv.

ūsurpo, 1. (contr. from usu and rapio), *to draw to oneself by use.* **I.** Gen., *to make use of, to use, to bring into use;* genus poenae, Cic. **II.** Esp., **A.** *to lay claim to, to assert one's right to;* nomen civitatis, Cic. **B.** Legal t. t., *to take possession of, acquire;* **a,** lawfully, amissam possessionem, Cic.; **b,** unlawfully, *to appropriate, to usurp;* alienam possessionem, Liv. **C.** *to make use of by the senses, to perceive, to notice;* sensibus, Lucr. **D.** *to make use of by the voice;* **a,** *to use, to mention;* nomen tantum virtutis usurpas, Cic.; **b,** *to call by any name habitually;* C. Laelius, is qui Sapiens usurpatur, Cic.

ūsus -ūs, m. (utor), *use, using, making use of, application, practice, exercise.* **I.** Lit., **A.** Gen., usus privatus, Cic.; quia ea pecunia non posset in bellum usui esse, Liv.; scientia atque usus rerum nauticarum, *theory and practice,* Caes.; usus magister est optimus, Cic. **B.** Esp., **1,** *intercourse with men;* **a,** *social intercourse, familiarity;* domesticus usus et consuetudo, Cic.; **b,** *carnal intercourse,* Ov.; **2,** legal t. t., usus et fructus, usus fructusque, ususfructus, *the use and enjoyment of property not one's own,* Cic.; usus fructus omnium bonorum, Cic. **II.** Transf., 1, *practice = practical experience;* usus atque exercitatio, Cic.; amicitia quam nec usu (*by experience*) nec ratione (*by theory*), habent cognitam, Cic.; habere magnum in re militari or in castris usum, Caes.; 2, *the usefulness, useful quality of anything;* magnos usus affert ad navigia facienda, Cic.; usui and ex usu esse, *to be useful, of use,* Cic.; **3,** *occasion, need, want;* **a,** usus provinciae supplere, Cic.; **b,** usus est, usus venit, usus adest, *it is necessary, requisite,* (α) usus est; (αα) absol., si quando usus esset, Cic.; (ββ) with abl., si quid erit quod extra magistratus curatore usus sit, Cic.; (β) usus adest; absol., ut equites Pompeianorum impetum, quum adesset usus, sustinere auderent, Caes.; (γ) usus venit, si usus veniat, Caes.; **c,** usu venit, *it happens;* quid homini potest turpius usu venire? Cic.

ūsusfructus, v. usus, III.

ŭt (orig. form **ŭtī**), adv. and conj. **I.** Adv., **A.** (Like ἵνα) adv. of place, *where,* Verg. *Aen.* 5, 329, Ov. *Met.* 1, 15. **B.** Adv. of manner, *in what way, as;* **1, a,** absol., perge ut instituisti, Cic.; esp. in a parenthesis, facilius est currentem, ut aiunt, incitare, Cic.; **b,** with correspond. sic, ita, item, omnia sic constitueram mihi agenda, ut tu admonebas, Cic.; ut optasti, ita est, Cic.; **c,** ut ut or utut, *however,* Plaut.; **2,** in comparisons, **a,** with sic, ita, item, itidem, *so . . . as,* sic, ut avus hic tuus, ut ego, justitiam cole, Cic.; **b,** *as . . . so also, as well . . . as also;* ut cum Titanis, ita cum Gigantibus, Cic.; **c,** *indeed, it is true . . . but;* Saguntini ut a proeliis quietem habuerant . . . ita non nocte, non die umquam cessaverant ab opere, Liv.; **d,** ut quisque, with superl. . . . sic or ita, with superl., *the more . . . the more;* ut quisque est vir optimus, ita difficillime esse alios improbos suspicatur, Cic.; with ita preceding, colendum esse ita quemque maxime, ut quisque maxime virtutibus erit ornatus, Cic.; with ita to be supplied, ut quisque maxime perspicit, quid, etc. . . . is prudentissimus haberi solet, Cic.; **e,** in oaths, protestations, etc., ita vivam, ut maximos sumptus facio, Cic.; **3,** to introduce an explanation, *as, as being;* homo acutus ut Poenus, Cic.; aiunt hominem, ut erat furiosus, respondisse, Cic.; permulta alia colligit Chrysippus, ut est in omni historia curiosus, Cic.; **4,** to introduce a reason, **a,** in a rel. clause, *inasmuch as;* magna pars Fidenatium, ut qui coloni additi Romanis essent, Latine sciebant, Liv.; **b,** in a hypothetical clause, *as if;* ut si esset res mea, Cic.; **5,** *as well as;* ut potui, tuli, Cic.; esp. with a superl., ut blandissime potest, *in the most flattering manner possible,* Cic.; with the superl., strengthened by quum, domus celebratus, ut quum maxime, Cic.; **6,** to introduce examples, *as, as for example;* quae tactu intimo sentiant, ut dolorem, ut voluptatem, Cic.; **7,** in exclamations, *how! how much!* ut ille tum humilis, ut demissus erat! Cic.; **8,** to introduce a question, *how;* **a,** direct, ut valet? ut meminit nostri? Hor.; **b,** indirect, videte, ut hoc iste correxerit, Cic.; **9,** to express time, **a,** gen. with the perf., *when, as soon as;* ut haec audivit, Cic.; strengthened by primum, ut primum loqui posse coepi, Cic.; **b,** *since;* ut Brundisio profectus es, nullae mihi abs te sunt redditae litterae, Cic. **II.** Conj., with the subj., *that, so that.* **A.** To express something effected or happening; **1,** of something actually resulting; **a,** with expressions denoting to happen, to cause, to bring about, to come to pass, *that;* sol efficit, ut omnia floreant, Cic.; evenit ut, contigit ut, est ut, ex hoc nascitur ut, etc., Cic.; **b,** with expressions denoting a peculiarity, a necessity, an appearance, mos est hominum, ut, etc., Cic.; hic locus est, ut de moribus majorum loquamur, Cic.; certum, verum, falsum, verisimile, rectum, justum, usitatum est ut, etc., Cic., 2, of something supposed or imagined to result; **a,** with verbs of wishing, commanding, asking, resolving, taking care, agreeing, suffering, etc., equidem vellem, ut aliquando redires, Cic.; praecipitur ut nobis ipsis imperemus, Cic.; petunt atque orant etc., Caes.; placuit his ut, etc., Cic.; natura non patitur ut, etc., Cic.; assenti quod est rectum, verum quoque sit, Cl with verbs of demanding, persuading, c ling, postulant ut, etc., Liv.; hortor u Cic.; suasit ut, etc., Cic.; impellimur ut, etc., Cic.; Lentulum, ut se abd praeturā, coegistis, Cic.; **c,** with verbs of ing = *that not;* timeo ut sustineas, Cic.; ellipt. for fac ut, *provided that, granted that, even if;* ut quaeras omnia, non reperies, Cic.; **e,** ellipt. to express anger in a rhetorical question; tu ut umquam te corrigas? Cic.; **f,** ellipt. to express a wish, *oh that!* ut dolor pariat, quod jam diu parturit, Cic. **B.** To express a consequence, *that, so that;* **1,** with correspond. ita, sic, tam, eo, adeo, usque eo; talis, tantus, is, hic, etc.; Tarquinius sic Servium diligebat, ut is eius vulgo haberetur filius, Cic.; **2,** without a correl., ruere illa non possunt, ut haec non eodem labefacta motu concidant, Cic. **C.** To express a purpose, *that, in order that;* **1,** with a demonstr., ideo, idcirco, ad eam rem, etc., idcirco omnes servi sumus, ut liberi esse possimus, Cic.; **2,** mostly without a demonstr., Romani ab aratro abduxerunt Cincinnatum, ut dictator esset, Cic.

ŭtcumquĕ (utcunquĕ), adv **I.** *in what manner soever, however*, utcumque se videri volet, Cic **II.** *whenever*; utcumque mecum eritis, Hor

1 **ūtens** -entis, p adj (from utor), *using, possessing*, utentior sit, Cic

2 **Utens** -entis, m *a river in Cisalpine Gaul*, now *Montone*.

ūtensilis -e (utor), *that can be used, fit for use, useful* **I.** Adj, Varr **II.** Subst, **ūtensilia** -ium, n *useful things, necessaries, utensils*, Liv.

1. **ŭter**, ŭtris, m. (connected with uterus), *the skin of an animal used as a bag or bottle*, Aeolios Ithacis inclusimus utribus euros, Ov, used (like a bladder) for crossing rivers, Caes, Liv, poet, tumidis infla sermonibus utrem, *of a puffed-up, arrogant man*, Hor

2 **ŭter**, ŭtra, ŭtrum, genit ŭtrīus, dat ŭtri **I.** *which of two, which*, uter nostrum popularis est? tune an ego? Cic; neque dijudicare posset, uter utri virtute anteferendus videretur, Caes, utros eius habueris libros an utrosque nescio, Cic **II.** Indefinite, *one of the two, either of the two*, si uter volet, Cic (genit, utrius, Hor)

ŭtercumquĕ (-cunquĕ), ŭtrăcumquĕ, ŭtrumcumquĕ, *whichever of the two, whichever*, utercumque vicerit, Cic

ŭterlĭbĕt, ŭtrălĭbĕt, ŭtrumlĭbĕt, *whichever of the two you please, either of the two*, utrumlibet elige, Cic.

ŭterquĕ, ŭtrăquĕ, ŭtrumquĕ, genit ŭtrīusquĕ, dat ŭtrīquĕ, *each of two, both* (considered separately), a, sing, uterque cum exercitu veniret, Caes, sermones utriusque linguae, Cic., uterque alio quodam modo, Cic, uterque Phoebus, *the rising and the setting sun, morning and evening*, Ov.; uterque polus, *the North and South Pole*, Ov.; Oceanus, *the east and west*, Ov.; solis utraque domus, *east and west*, Ov, parens, *father and mother*, Ov; in utramque partem, *on both sides, in both cases*, Cic, hic qui utrumque probat, ambobus debuit uti, Cic, with partit genit., uterque nostrum, Cic., with predicate in the plur., uterque eorum ex castris exercitum educunt, Caes; b, in plur. prop, to express two pluralities, quoniam utrique Socratici et Platonici volumus esse, Cic; then to express two individuals together, duae fuerunt Ariovisti uxores; utraeque in ea fuga perierunt, Caes; (…iusque, Lucr., Hor, Ov.).

[…]rus -i, m and **ŭtĕrum** -i, n (οὖθαρ). **I.** *[…]y, paunch*, 1, gen, Verg, 2, esp, *the […]* Cic, Ov., Hor, meton, a, *birth*, Plin, *cavities of the earth, out of which the first […]es are said to have been born*, Lucr **II.** […] *the belly* = the inside of a ship, Tac, […] Trojan horse, Verg

[ŭ]tervis, ŭtrăvis, ŭtrumvis, genit ŭtriusvis, dat. ŭtrīvis. **I.** *which of the two you will, either of the two*; utrumvis facere potes, Cic **II.** *both*, Ter, Plaut.

ŭtī = ut (q v.).

ūtĭbĭlis -e (utor), *that can be used, useful*, Ter., Plaut.

Ŭtĭca -ae, f *a town in Africa Propria, north of Carthage, colony from Tyre, the place where the senatorial party made the last stand against Caesar, and where M Porcius Cato the younger killed himself* Adj, **Ŭtĭcensis** -e, *of or belonging to Utica*

ūtĭlis -e (= utibilis from utor), *useful, profitable, serviceable, beneficial, advantageous* a, absol, utiles et salutares res, Cic, b, with ad and the acc., homo ad eam rem, or ad ullam rem utilis, Cic; c, with in (*in relation to, for*) and acc, res maxime in hoc tempus utilis, Liv, d, with dat, equi utiles bello, Ov.; non mihi est vita mea utilior, Cic, e, (poet), with genit, radix medendi utilis, Ov, f, with infin, tibia adesse choris erat utilis, Hor, g, utile est, with infin, numquam utile est peccare, Cic, with acc and infin, eos utile est praeesse vobis, Liv

ūtĭlĭtas -ātis, f (utilis), *usefulness, utility, advantageousness, profitableness, use, profit, advantage*, a, sing, utilitas parta per amicum, Cic, b, plur, utilitates ex amicitia maxime capientur, Cic

ūtĭlĭtĕr, adv (utilis), *usefully, serviceably, advantageously, profitably*; utiliter a natura datum esse, Cic

ŭtĭnam, adv *would that! oh that!* utinam incumbat in causam! Cic, utinam haberetis! Cic with quod, quod utinam minus vitae cupidi fuissemus! Cic, with negative, utinam ne or utinam non, *would that not!* illud utinam ne vere scriberem! Cic

ŭtĭquĕ, adv a, *in any case, at any rate, certainly, at least*, utique apud me sis, Cic, b, *yet, at least, certainly*, utique postridie, Cic, c, *especially*, commota est plebs, utique postquam etc., Liv

ūtor, ūsus sum, ūti, 3 dep *to use, make use of, employ, enjoy* **I.** Lit, **A.** Gen, a, with abl, armis, Cic, oratione, *to speak*, Cic, male uti lege, *to make a bad use of the law*, Cic, uti ea criminatione in aliquem, Cic, with double abl, vel imperatore vel milite me utimini, Sall, b, with neut acc, ne filius quidem quidquam utitur, Cic, hunc omnia utenda ac possidenda tradiderat, Cic, c, absol, divitiae (expetuntur) ut utare, *that you may make use of them*, Cic **B.** Esp, 1, *to associate with, be intimate with*, Trebonio multos annos utor, Cic, 2, *to live on*, habere qui utar Cic, 3, *to enjoy*, lacte et herbis, Ov **II.** Transf, 1, *to be in possession of, to possess*; valetudine bonā, Caes, honore, Cic, 2, *to stand in need of, have occasion for*, ambitione nihil uteris, Cic, ea nihil hoc loco utimur, Cic

utpŏtĕ, adv *seeing that, inasmuch as, since*; utpote qui nihil contemnere solemus, Cic, utpote lecti utrimque, Liv

ŭtrālĭbĕt, adv (sc parte, from uterlibet), *on either side, on whichever side*, Plin

ŭtrārĭus -ii, m (1 uter), *one who carries water in skins, a water carrier*, Liv

ūtrĭcŭlārĭus -ii, m *a bagpiper*, Suet

ūtrĭcŭlus -i, m (dim of uterus) **I.** *the belly*, 1, gen, Plin, 2, esp, *the womb*, Plin **II.** *the bud or envelope of a flower*, Plin

ŭtrimquĕ (ŭtrinquĕ), adv (2 uter), *from both sides, on both sides* **I.** Lit, Cic **II.** Transf, *in both parties*, utrimque anxii, Tac

ŭtrō (sc loco, from 2 uter), adv *to which of two places, to which side, whither*, Ov, Cic

ŭtrŏbi (ŭtrŭbi), adv (uter and ubi), *at which of two places, where*, Plaut

ŭtrŏbīdem, adv. (utrobi and suffix -dem), *on both sides*, Plaut

ŭtrŏbīquĕ (ŭtrŭbīquĕ), adv *on each of two sides, on both sides*, Liv, sequitur ut eadem veritas utrobique sit, eademque lex, *with gods and men*, Cic; Eumenes utrobique plus valebat, *both by land and sea*, Nep

ŭtrōlĭbĕt, adv (uterlibet), *to either of two sides, to either side*, Quint

ŭtrōquĕ, adv. (uterque), *to both sides*, a, lit, of place, utroque citius quam vellemus cursum confecimus, Cic, b, transf, *in both directions*; si natura utroque adjuncta est, Cic

ŭtrŭbi, etc. = utrobi, etc. (q.v.).

ŭtrum, adv. (2. uter), *whether*, used in disjunctive questions. **I.** In direct questions, **a**, with a second clause; (α) foll. by an, utrum ea vestra an nostra culpa est? (β) foll. by annon, utrum cetera nomina in codicem accepti et expensi digesta habes, annon? Cic.; **b**, without a second clause, utrum hoc bellum non est? Cic. **II.** In indirect questions, **a**, with corresponding an, anne, necne, (α) with an, multum interest, utrum laus diminuatur an salus deseratur, Cic.; (β) foll. by anne, utrum illi sentiant, anne simulent, tu intelliges, Cic.; (γ) by necne, jam dudum ego erro, qui quaeram, utrum emeris necne, Cic.; **b**, without an, hoc dicere audebis, utrum de te aratores, utrum denique Siculi universi bene existiment, ad rem id non pertinere, Cic.

ŭtŭt, adv. *however*, Ter.

ūva -ae, f. *a cluster, bunch*. **I.** Lit., **A.** Gen., Plin. **B.** Esp., *a bunch of grapes*; **1**, lit., uva colorem ducit, Verg.; **2**, meton., *the vine*, Verg. **II.** Transf., *a cluster, like a bunch of grapes, which bees form when they swarm and settle on trees*, Verg.

ūvens -entis (partic. of * uveo), *moist, wet*, Petr.

ūvesco, 3. (* uveo), *to become moist, be wet*, Lucr.; of persons drinking, *to moisten* or *refresh oneself*, Hor.

ūvĭdŭlus -a -um (dim. of uvidus), *somewhat moist, wet*, Cat.

ūvĭdus -a -um (* uveo), *moist, damp, wet, humid*. **I.** Lit., vestimenta, Hor.; Menalcas, *wet with dew*, Verg.; Juppiter uvidus austris (Ζεὺς ἰκμαῖος), Verg. **II.** Meton., = *drunken*; Bacchus, Hor.; dicimus integro sicci mane die, dicimus uvidi, Hor.

ūvor -ōris, m. (* uveo), *moistness, dampness, humidity*, Varr.

uxor -ōris, f. *a wife, spouse*. **I.** Lit., uxor justa, Cic.; duas uxores habere, Cic.; uxorem ducere, *to marry a wife*; uxori nuntium remittere; *to divorce a wife*, Cic. **II.** Transf., of animals, olentis uxores mariti, *she-goats*, Hor.

uxorcŭla -ae, f. (dim. of uxor), *a little wife* (used as a term of endearment), Plaut.

uxōrius -a -um (uxor). **I.** *of* or *relating to a wife*; res uxoria, Cic.; arbitrium rei uxoriae, *relating to the property of a (divorced) wife*, Cic. **II.** *too devoted to one's wife, a slave to a wife, uxorious*; of Aeneas as the slave to Dido, Verg.; amnis, *the Tiber, as the husband of Ilia*, Hor.

V.

V, v, the twenty-first letter of the Latin alphabet, corresponding partly with the Greek digamma (ϝ), partly with the Greek *υ*. V frequently passes into u, e.g., solvo, solutum, navita, nauta; and between two vowels is often elided, e.g., deleverunt, delerunt, providens, prudens; ne volo, nolo. For the use of V. in abbreviations, see Table of Abbreviations.

Văcălus = Vahalis (q.v.).

văcātĭo -ōnis, f. (vaco). **I.** *a freedom from, immunity, exemption from anything, a being without*; **a**, the thing from which one is freed is put in the genit., or in the abl. with ab, vacatio militiae, Cic.; alicui dare vacationem a causis, Cic.; **b**, the person who is freed is put in the genit., or the cause for which one is freed, adolescentiae, Cic.; rerum gestarum, Cic.; vacationes militum, Liv.; **c**, absol., pretium ob vacationem datum, Cic. **II.** Meton., *money paid for exemption from military service*, Tac.

1. **vacca** -ae, f. *a cow*, Cic.

2. **Vacca** = Vaga (q.v.).

Vaccaei -ōrum, m. *a people in Hispania Tarraconensis*.

vaccīnium -ii, n. *the blueberry, whortleberry*, Verg., Ov.

vaccīnus -a -um (vacca), *of* or *relating to a cow*, Plin.

văcēfīo, v. vacuefacio.

văcerrōsus -a -um, *mad, crazy*, Suet.

Văchălis = Vahalis (q.v.).

văcillātĭo -ōnis, f. (vacillo), *a rocking, reeling motion*, Suet.

văcillo, 1. *to totter, reel, stagger, wave to and fro*. **I.** Lit., litterulae vacillantes, *written with unsteady hand*, Cic.; of persons, ex vino, Cic.; in utramque partem toto corpore, Cic. **II.** Fig., tota res vacillat et claudicat, Cic.; of persons, in aere alieno, *to be deep in debt*, Cic.; legio vacillans, *wavering in its fidelity*, Cic.

văcīvē, adv. (vacivus), *idly, at leisure*, Phaedr.

văcīvĭtas -ātis, f. (vacivus), *emptiness, want of anything*; cibi, Plaut.

văcīvus -a -um (vaco), *empty*; aedes, Plaut.; with genit., virium, *powerless*, Plaut.

văco, 1. *to be empty, void of anything, be free from, without anything*. **I.** Lit., **A.** Gen., **a**, absol., tota domus superior vacat, Cic.; **b**, with abl., natura caelestis et terra vacat humore, Cic. **B.** Esp., of property, *to be vacant, to have no master*; ut populus vacantia teneret, Tac. **II.** Transf., **A.** Gen., *to be free from something, to be without*; **a**, with abl., curā et negotio, Cic.; populo, *to keep oneself far from the people*, Cic.; **b**, with ab and the abl., ab opere, Caes.; ab omni concitatione animi semper, Cic.; **a** metu et periculis, Liv.; of things, haec a custodiis classium loca maxime vacabant, Caes.; of time, tantum quantum vacabit a publico officio et munere, Cic. **B.** Esp., **1**, *to be free from duties*; with abl., muneribus, Cic.; **2**, *to be free from work, idle, at leisure, unoccupied, to have time*; **a**, of persons, (α) absol., scribes aliquid, si vacabis, Cic.; (β) with dat., *to have time for, to have leisure for*; ego vero, inquam, philosophiae semper vaco, Cic.; (γ) poet., with in and the acc., in grande opus, Ov.; **b**, impers., vacat and vacat alicui, *there is leisure for, there is time for*; (α) with infin., hactenus indulsisse vacat, Verg.; (β) absol., dum vacat, Ov.

văcŭēfăcĭo -fēci -factum, 3. (vacuus and facio), and pass., **vacŭēfīo (văcēfīo)** -factus sum -fiĕri (vacuus and fio), *to make empty*; in pass. = *to be empty*; morte superioris uxoris domum novis nuptiis, Cic.; adventu tuo ista subsellia vacuefacta sunt, Cic.

văcŭĭtas -ātis, f. (vacuus), *emptiness, vacuity, freedom, exemption, immunity from, a being without anything*. **I.** Gen., **a**, with genit., doloris, Cic.; **b**, with ab and abl., ab angoribus, Cic. **II.** Esp., *the vacancy of a public office*, e.g., of the consulship, ap. Cic.

Văcūna -ae, f. *the beneficent goddess of the plain worshipped at Reate, goddess of the Sabines*. Adj., **Văcūnālis** -e, *of* or *belonging to Vacuna*.

văcŭo, 1. (vacuus), *to make empty, void, to empty*, Lucr.

văcŭus -a -um, *empty, void, free from, exempt, without*. **I.** Lit., **A.** Gen., **1**, adj., **a**, absol., castra, Caes.; theatrum, Hor.; **b**, with abl., in integri vacuum, Cic. c, with ab and the abl, ab his rebus, Cic ; vacuum oppidum ab defensoribus, Caes , 2, subst , **văcŭum** -i, n an *empty place, vacuum*, per vacuum incurrere, Hor , or irrumpere, Liv. B Esp , 1, *free, vacant, without a master*, praeda, Cic , possessio regni, Caes , venire in vacuum or vacua, Hor , Cic , 2, of women, *free, unmarried*, Ov II. Transf , A. Gen , *free from something, without, keeping oneself free from*, a, with abl., animus sensibus et curis vacuus, Cic., b, with ab and the abl , animus a talibus factis vacuus et integer, Cic , c, with genit , vacuus operum, Hor B. Esp , 1, *free from duties, freed*, a, with abl , tributo, Tac , b, with ab and the abl , ab omni sumptu, Cic , 2, a, *free from work, unoccupied, at leisure, idle*, (α) of persons, quoniam vacui sumus, dicam, Cic , transf , of places, *where one is idle*, Tibur, Hor , (β) of time, vacua nox operi, Liv , quum vacui temporis nihil habebam, *leisure*, Cic , b, *free from anxiety or love*, animus vacuus ac solutus, Cic , 3, *free from hindrances*, Tac , 4, of places, a, *free = open, accessible*, porticus, Verg , aures vacuae, Hor , b, *open, exposed*, mare, Tac , 5, *empty = worthless, useless, vain*, vacua nomina, Tac

1 **Vada** ae, f *a castle in the country of the Batavi*

2 **Vada** ōrum, n *a town in Liguria, now Savona*

3. **Vada Volaterrāna** -ōrum, n *a port in Etruria, south of Pisa, now Torre di Vado*

Vadimōnis lacus, *a lake in Etruria, now Lago di Bassano*

vădimōnium ii, n (1 vas) *bail, security, recognizance* (for appearance before a court of law), sine vadimonio disceditur, Cic , vadimonium constituere, Cic , vadimonium obire or ad vadimonium venire, *to appear on bail* (opp vadimonium deserere, *to forfeit recognizances*), Cic

vādo, 3 (root VA, Gr BA ω whence βαίνω), *to go, walk, hasten, rush*, haud dubiam in mortem, Verg ad aliquem postridie mane, Cic., in eundem carcerem (of Socrates), Cic

vădor, 1 dep (1. vas), *to bind over by bail*, hominem in praesentia non vadatur, Cic , tot vadibus accusator vadatus est reum, Liv ; partic pass , vadato, *after bail had been fixed*, Hor

vădōsus -a um (vadum), *full of shallows, shallow*, mare, Caes

vădum -i, n (root VA, Gr BA-ω, whence βατός -ή -όν, pervius), *a shallow, shoal, ford* I. A. Lit , exercitum vado transducere, Verg B. Fig , cera tentet vadum, Ov II Transf , A. Gen = *water, river, sea*, Verg , Hor B. *the bottom of the water*, Plin

vae, interj (οὐαί), to express pain or anger *alas! woe!* a, absol , Verg , Hor ; b, with dat vae victis, Liv

vaecors = vecors (q v)

vaesanus = vesanus (q v)

văfer, vafra, vafrum, *artful, cunning, subtle, sly, crafty*, in disputando, Cic , somniorum vaferrimus interpres Cic

văfrē, adv (vafer), *artfully, cunningly, craftily*, Cic

văfrĭtĭa ae, f (vafer), *artfulness, slyness, subtlety, cunning*, Sen

Văga ae, f *a town in Numidia, now Begia* Hence, **Văgenses** -ium, m *the inhabitants of Vaga*

văgē, adv (vagus), *scattered far and wide, dispersedly*, vage effusi per agros, Liv.

vāgīna -ae, f (connected with vas, *a vessel*), *the sheath of a sword, scabbard* I. Lit , gladius vagina vacuus, Cic gladium e vagina educere, Cic II. Transf , *a sheath, case*, esp , *the hull or husk of grain*, Cic

vāgīnŭla ae, f (dim of vagina), *a little sheath or husk of grain*, Plin

vāgio ivi and -ii itum, 4 *to cry, whimper like a child*, repuerascere et in cunis vagire, Cic

vāgītus ūs, m (vagio), *the crying of young children* dare vagitus, Ov , of the bleating of goats, Ov

1 **văgo**, 1 and **văgor**, 1 dep (vagus), *to wander about, ramble, rove* I. Lit , A. Gen , a, of living creatures, in agris passim bestiarum more, Cic , of birds, volucres huc illuc passim vagantes, Cic , b, of things, luna iisdem spatiis vagatur quibus sol, Cic B Esp , of ships and sailors, *to cruise*, cum lembis circa Lesbum, Liv II. Fig , vagabitur tuum nomen longe atque late, *will be spread far and wide*, Cic , animus vagatus errore, Cic , vagabimur nostro instituto, *digress*, Cic

2 **vāgor** = vagitus (q v)

văgus -a um, *wandering, roaming, roving, unsettled, vagrant* I. Lit , a, of living creatures, multitudo dispersa atque vaga, Cic , matronae vagae per vias, Liv , plur subst , vagi quidam, *wanderers*, Liv , b, of things, luna, Cic , venti, Hor II. Transf , a, *inconstant, fickle*, puella, Ov , sententia, Cic , b, *general*, pars quaestionum, Cic , c, *diffuse, aimless*, orationis genus, Cic

vāh (văhă), interj *ah! oh!* Plaut

Văhălis (Vālis) is, m *the Waal, the west arm of the Rhine*

valdē, adv (syncop for valide from validus), *very, very much, greatly, exceedingly*, a, with verbs, alicui arridere, Cic ; valdius oblectare, Hor , b, with adj , valde magnus, Cic , valde lenis, Cic , c, with adv , valde bene, valde vehementer, valde graviter, Cic

vălĕdīco, 3 , v valeo, I B 2 b

vălens entis, p adj (from valeo), *strong, powerful* I. Lit , A Gen , robusti et valentes satellites, Cic valentissimi homines Cic , tiruncul, Verg B *well, healthy* medicus confirmat propediem te valentem fore, Cic II. Transf , *powerful, mighty*, a, politically, by armies, etc , viribus cum valentiore pugnare, Cic , b, intellectually, *powerful, energetic, effective*, valens dialecticus, Cic , fraus valentior quam consilium meum, Cic

vălentĕr, adv (valens), *strongly, powerfully*, valentius spirare, Ov

vălentŭlus -a um (dim of valens), *strong*, Plaut

vălĕo -ŭi itum, 2 *to be strong* I. Lit , A. Gen 1, puer ille ut magnus est et multum valet, Plaut , 2, *to be strong* (bodily) *for a particular purpose*, a, with prep , alios velocitate ad cursum, alios viribus ad luctandum valere, Cic , b, with infin , valeo stare aut, etc , Hor , valet ima summis mutare deus, Hor B. *to be well, healthy, strong*, 1, a, with adv , optime valeo, Cic , bene, melius, Cic , minus valeo, Cic , b, with the abl , corpore, Cic , c, with ab and abl of disease, a morbo, Plaut , d, absol , valeo et salvus sum, Plaut , hence the phrase at the commencement of a letter, si vales, bene est (S V B E), Cic , also with the addition, ego or ego quoque valeo (E V or E Q V), Cic , 2, as a farewell greeting, a, vale, valeas, *adieu, farewell, good bye*, esp , as the usual ending of letters Cic , cura ut valeas, Cic also as a farewell greeting to the dead, Verg , as an expression of scorn, refusal, rejection, si talis est deus, valeat, *let me have nothing to do with him*, Cic.; quare valeant ista, *away with them!* Cic.; **b**, valere jubere or dicere, *to say good-bye;* illum salutavi, post etiam jussi valere, Cic.; supremum vale dicere, Ov.; vale dicere (or in one word, valedicere), *to say farewell*, Sen. **II.** Transf., **A.** *to avail, have force, to be strong, prevail;* **1,** multum equitatu, Caes.; plurimum proficere et valere, Cic.; longe plurimum valere ingenio, Cic.; of things, sine veritate nomen amicitiae valere non potest, Cic.; **2,** with reference to a certain object, **a,** with ad and the acc., or in and the acc., or infin., *to have force for, to be able to, to be strong enough for;* tu non solum ad negligendas leges, verum etiam ad evertendas valuisti, Cic.; of things, illud perficiam, ut invidia mihi valeat ad gloriam, Cic.; nec continere suos ab direptione castrorum valuit, Liv.; **b,** with in and the acc., *to be of avail against, to be designed for* or *against;* in se, in Romanos, in ipsum, Cic.; definitio in omnes valet, *avails for all*, Cic. **B.** Esp., **1,** *to be worth;* dum pro argenteis decem aureus unus valeret, Liv.; **2,** of words, *to mean, signify;* verbum, quod idem valeat, Cic.

Vălĕrĭus -a -um, *name of a Roman gens, the most famous members of which were:* **1,** P. Valerius Volesus Publicola (Popl.), *who took part in the driving out of the Roman kings;* **2,** Qu. Valerius Antias, *a Roman chronicler, living about* 140 B.C., *used by Livy.* Adj., *Valerian;* tabula, *a place in the Forum, near the* Curia Hostilia, *where the money-changers' stalls were.* Hence, **Vălĕrĭānus** -a -um, *of* or *belonging to a Valerius.*

vălesco -ŭi, 2. (inchoat. of valeo), *to grow strong.* **I.** Lit., Lucr. **II.** Fig., superstitiones, Tac.; tantum spe conatuque valuit, Cic.

vălētūdĭnārĭus -a -um (valetudo), *sickly*, Varr.

vălētūdo -inis, f. (valeo), *state of health, physical condition, health.* **I.** Lit., **A.** Gen., prosperitas valetudinis, Cic.; incommoda, Cic.; adversa, Cic.; infirmā atque aegrā valetudine usus, Cic.; quasi mala valetudo animi, Cic. **B.** Esp., **1,** in a bad sense, *ill-health, weakness;* oculorum, Cic.; affectus valetudine, *ill*, Caes.; plur., subsidia valetudinum, Cic.; **2,** in a good sense, *good health;* valetudinem amiseram, Cic. **II.** Transf., of discourse, Cic.

Valgĭus -a -um, *name of a Roman gens, the most famous members of which were:* **1,** Valgius, *the father-in-law of Rullus;* **2,** T. Valgius Rufus, *a distinguished poet.*

valgus -a -um, *bow-legged, bandy-legged*, Plaut.; transf., suavia, *wry mouths*, Plaut.

vălĭdē, adv. (validus). **I.** *strongly, powerfully, mightily;* validissime favere alicui, ap. Cic. **II.** Used in answers, *certainly, to be sure*, Plaut.

vălĭdus -a -um (valeo), *strong, powerful.* **I.** Lit., **A.** Gen., **1,** tauri, Ov.; vires, Verg.; **2,** milit. t. t., of posts or stations, *strong;* valida urbs et potens, Cic.; valida urbs praesidiis, muris, Liv.; **3,** of medicines, *powerful, efficacious;* sucus, Ov.; **4,** of persons, *superior, having the advantage* (in age); aetate et viribus validior, Liv. **B.** *healthy, well;* si, ut spero, te validum videro, Cic.; nondum ex morbo satis validus, Liv. **II.** Transf., *strong, powerful, mighty, influential;* hostis validior, Liv.; with abl., ingenium sapientiā validum, Sall.; with dat., ludibrium illud vix feminis puerisve morandis satis validum, Liv.; with adversus and the acc., adversus consentientes nec regem quemquam satis validum nec tyrannum fore, Liv.

Vālis = Vahalis (q.v.).

vallāris -e (vallus or vallum), *of* or *relating to the vallum;* corona, *given to the soldier who first mounted the fortifications of the hostile camp*, Liv.

valles (vallis) -is, f. *a vale, valley.* **I.** Lit., vicus positus in valle, Caes. **II.** Poet., transf., *a hollow;* alarum, Cat.

vallo, 1. (vallus or vallum), *to surround, fortify with a mound and palisade.* **I.** Lit., castra, Tac. **II.** Transf., *to fortify, protect, strengthen;* Catilina vallatus sicariis, Cic.; sol radiis frontem vallatus, Ov.

vallum -i, n. (vallus). **I.** *a mound* or *wall defended with palisades, a stockade;* oppidum vallo et fossā cingere, Cic.; vallum scindere, Caes. **II.** Transf., *a wall, fortification, defence;* spica munitur vallo aristarum, Cic.

1. **vallus** -i, m. *a post, stake.* **I.** Gen., used as a prop for vines, Verg. **II.** Esp., to form a palisade; ferre vallum, Cic.; collective (for vallum), *the palisade, stockade;* duplex vallus, Caes.; poet., transf., vallus pectinis, *the teeth of a comb*, Ov.

2. **vallus** -i, f. (dim. of vannus), *a small winnowing-fan*, Varr.

valvae -ārum, f. *folding-doors;* effractis valvis (fani), Cic.

valvātus -a -um (valvae), *provided with folding-doors*, Varr.

Vandăli -ōrum, m. *the Vandals, in the time of Tacitus a tribe in North Germany, who, in the fifth century, invaded the south of Europe, and settled in Spain and Africa.*

vānesco, 3. (vanus), *to pass away, disappear, vanish.* **I.** Lit., nubes, Ov. **II.** Transf., amor, Ov.

Vangĭŏnes -um, m. *a German people on the Rhine, near modern Worms.*

vānĭdĭcus -a -um (vanus and dico), *talking vainly, lying*, Plaut.

vānĭlŏquentĭa -ae, f. (vanus and loquor), *idle talking, vaunting*, Liv.

vānĭlŏquus -a -um (vanus and loquor). **I.** *lying*, Plaut. **II.** *boasting, vaunting*, Liv.

vānĭtas -ātis, f. (vanus), *emptiness.* **I.** Gen., **a,** *unreality, superficiality, untruth;* opinionum, Cic.; **b,** *failure, fruitlessness;* itineris, Liv. **II.** Esp., *idle talk, lying, boasting, ostentation;* orationis, Cic.; nihil turpius est vanitate, Cic.

vānĭtūdo -inis, f. (vanus), *idle, lying talk*, Plaut.

vannus -i, f. *a winnowing-fan;* vannus mystica Iacchi (borne at the Bacchic festival), Verg.

vānus -a -um (connected with vastus), *empty, void.* **I.** Lit., arista, Verg.; imago, *shade, spirit* (as being bodiless), Hor.; vanior acies hostium, Liv. **II.** Fig., *vain, meaningless, lying, fruitless, idle, groundless.* **A.** Of things, **1,** adj., oratio, Cic.; spes, Ov.; gaudia, Hor.; of missiles, ictus, Liv.; **2,** neut. subst., *that which is empty or vain;* haustum ex vano, *from a false source*, Liv.; poet., vana tumens, *with empty show*, Verg.; with genit., vana rerum, Hor. **B.** Of persons, **1,** *one whose action is without consequence;* ne vanus iisdem castris assideret, *in vain*, Liv.; **2,** esp. in moral sense, *lying, vain, ostentatious, fickle, inconstant, boastful;* haruspex, Cic.; vanum se esse et perfidiosum fateri, Cic.; vanus auctor est, *deserves no credence*, Liv.

văpĭdē, adv. (vapidus), *mouldily;* vapide se habere, *to be "seedy,"* Aug. ap. Suet.

văpĭdus -a -um (root VAP, whence vappa), *spoiled, flat, vapid*, Pers.

văpor (văpos) -ōris, m *vapour, steam* **I.** Gen., aquarum, Cic., poet = *heat*, Verg **II.** Esp., *warm exhalation, warmth*, semen tepefactum vapore, Cic, locus vaporis plenus, Liv, poet = *fire*, vapor est (= edit) carinas, Verg

văpōrārium -ii, n (vapor), *a flue for conveying hot air*, Cic

văpōrātio -ōnis, f (vaporo), *an exhalation, steaming, steam, vapour*, Plin

văpōro, 1 (vapor). **I.** Intransit, *to steam, reek*, fig, Lucr **II.** Transit, *to fill with warm vapour, to fumigate, heat, to warm*; **a**, laevum latus, Hor, **b**, *to incense, fumigate*, templum ture, Verg.

vappa -ae, f (root, VAP, whence vapidus), *spoiled, flat wine* **I.** Lit., Hor **II.** Transf, *a good-for nothing, worthless fellow*, Hor.

vāpŭlāris -e (vapulo), *well whipped*, Plaut

vāpŭlo -āvi -ātūrus, 1 *to cry out like one that is beaten*, meton = *to be flogged, whipped, beaten* **I.** Lit, Lucr, Plaut **II.** Transf., **a**, of troops, *to be beaten*, ap Cic, **b**, *to be attacked by words*, omnium sermonibus, Cic

Varguntējus -i, m, Lucius, *a Roman senator and accomplice of Catiline*

1 **vărĭa** -ae, f (varius) **I.** *a panther*, Plin. **II.** *a kind of magpie*, Plin

2 **Vărĭa** -ae, f *a town in Italy, on the right bank of the Anio, now Vico-Varo.*

vărĭantĭa -ae, f (vario), *difference, variation*, Lucr

vărĭānus -a -um (varius), *many-coloured, varicoloured*, Plin

vărĭātĭo -ōnis, f (vario), *difference, variation*, eosdem consules sine ulla variatione dicere, Liv

vārĭco, 1 (varicus), *to stand with feet apart, to straddle*, Varr

vārĭcōsus -a -um (varix), *having varicose veins*, Juv

vārĭcus -a -um (varus), *straddling*, Ov.

vărĭē, adv (varius) **I.** *with various colours*, Plin **II.** *variously, in different ways*, numerus varie diffusus, Cic, varie bellatum, *with varying success*, Liv

vărĭĕtas -ātis, f (1 varius), *variety, difference, diversity* **I.** Lit, of colours, florum, Cic **II.** Transf, **A.** Gen, *variety, difference, diversity*, pomorum, Cic, plur, varietates temporum, Cic **B.** Esp, 1, *variety, manysidedness*, of ideas, knowledge, etc, multiplex ratio disputandi rerumque varietas, Cic, 2, *difference in opinion*, in disputationibus, Cic, 3, *fickleness, inconstancy, changeable humour*; venditorum, Cic

vărĭo, 1. (1 varius) **I.** Transit, *to vary, diversify, variegate, make various, to change, alter, vary* **A.** Lit, 1, vocem, Cic, capillos, Ov, 2, *to make particoloured, to colour, spot*, (sol) variat ortum maculis, Verg **B.** Transf, *to change a thing in its nature, to alter, interchange with*, **a**, caloresque frigoraque, Liv, voluptatem, Cic. **b**, *to vary in writing* or *speaking, to give a different account of*, quae de Marcelli morte variant auctores, *relate differently*, Liv; **c**, *to change the issue of*, variante fortunā eventum, Liv, **d**, *to change an opinion cause to waver*, quum timor atque ira in vicem sententias variassent, Liv, in pass variari, *to waver, be divided, to vary* variatis hominum sententiis, Liv **II.** Intransit, *to be different, to vary* **A.** Lit variantes formae, Lucr **B.** Transf, *to change, vary, alter, waver*, 1, of things, **a**, sic mei variant timores, Ov, dissidet et variat sententia, Ov, **b**, *to vary* (in an account or relation), quamquam et opinionibus et monumentis litterarum variarent, Liv, 2, of persons, *to vary, be of different opinions, waver*, fremitus variantis multitudinis, Liv

1 **vărĭus** -a -um, *manifold* **I** Of colour, *diversified, variegated, various*, columnae, Hor, caelum, Ov., lynces, Verg **II.** Transf, of nature, *various, manifold, changeable, diverse*. **A.** Of things, **a**, varium poema, varia oratio, varii mores, varia fortuna, voluptas etiam varia dici solet, Cic., **b**, of opinion, *varying* ... sunt (dii) varium est, *different opinions are held*, Cic, **c**, of success, *changing, varying, uncertain*, fortunae varii eventus, Caes **B** Of persons, **a**, *many-sided, of various information*, varius et multiplex et copiosus fuit, Cic, **b**, of character, *fickle, changeable*, animus, Sall, varium et mutabile semper femina, Verg

2 **Vărĭus** -a -um, *name of a Roman gens, the most famous members of which were* 1, Q Varius Hybrida, of Sucro, in Spain, *tribune of the people*, 91 B C, *author of a* lex de majestate, 2, L Varius, *a poet, the friend of Horace and Vergil*

vărix -icis, c *a varicose vein*, esp in the leg, Cic

Varro -ōnis, m *a surname in the Gens Terentia, the most famous members of which were* 1, C Terentius Varro, and 2, M Terentius Varro, v Terentius, 3, P Terentius Varro Atacinus, *a poet, born* 82 B C, *died* 37 B C Hence, **Varrōnĭānus** -a -um, *Varronian*, milites, *who served under C Terentius Varro*, Liv

1 **vārus** -a -um, *deviating from the right line* **I.** Lit, *bent outwards*, **a**, cornua, Ov, manus, Ov, **b**, *bandy legged*, subst, *a bandy-legged man*, Hor **II.** Transf, *diverse, different*; alterum (genus) huic varum, Hor.

2 **vărus** -i, m *a pimple or boil on the face*, Plin

3 **Vārus** -i, m *a name of several Roman families, the most famous members of which were* **1**, Q Attius Varus, *a leader in the Civil War*, **2**, P. Alfenus Varus, *consul and celebrated lawyer*, **3**, P Quintilius Varus, *the celebrated general of Augustus, defeated and killed with his army by Arminius*, 9 B C

4 **Vārus** -i, m *a river in Gallia Narbonensis, now the Var*

1 **văs**, vădis, m (vado), *a bail, surety*, vades poscere, Cic, vades deserere, Liv, vas factus est alter (Damon) eius sistendi, Cic

2 **vās**, vāsis, n (plur, **vāsa** -ōrum), *a vessel, vase, utensil of any kind*. **I.** Gen, vas vinarium, Cic **II.** Esp, plur, *war materials, baggage*, vasa colligere, *to pack up ones baggage*, Cic, vasa conclamare, *to give the signal for packing up*, Caes

vāsārĭum -ii, n (2 vas) **I.** *money given to the governor of a province for his outfit*, Cic. **II.** *the hire of an oil press*, Cato.

Vascŏnes -um, m *a people in Hispania Tarraconensis*

vascŭlārĭus -ii, m (vasculum), *a maker of metal vessels and dishes, goldsmith*, Cic

vascŭlum -i, n (dim of 2 vas). **I.** *a small vessel or dish*, Cato **II.** *the seed capsule of certain fruits*, Plin

vastātĭo -ōnis, f (vasto), *a devastating, laying waste*, agri, Liv, omnium ..., Cic, plur, depopulationes, vastationes, caedes rapinae, Cic.

vastātor -ōris, m (vasto), *devastator, ravager*, Arcadiae (of a boar), Ov, ferarum, *a hunter*, Verg

vastē, adv (vastus) **I.** *widely, vastly, extensively*, vastius insurgens, Ov. **II.** *rudely, roughly* loqui, Cic

vastificus -a -um (vastus and facio), *laying waste, devastating, ravaging*, Cic. poet.

vastitas -ātis, f. (vastus), *an empty space, waste, emptiness.* **I.** Lit., **A.** Gen., judiciorum vastitas et fori, Cic. **B.** Esp., *emptiness through laying waste, devastation, desolation;* Italiam totam ad exitium et vastitatem vocare, Cic. **II.** Meton., **1,** *vastness, vast size*, Plin.; **2,** plur., vastitates, *the devastators;* provinciarum vastitates, Cic.

vastities -ēi, f. (vastus), *devastation, destruction*, Plaut.

vasto, 1. (vastus), *to empty, make empty.* **I.** Gen., forum, Cic.; with abl., agros cultoribus, Verg. **II.** Esp., **1, a,** *to waste, lay waste, ravage, devastate;* agros, Caes., Cic.; omnia ferro ignique, Liv.; **b,** *to plunder;* cultores, Tac.; **2,** fig., *to prey upon;* ita conscientia mentem excitam vastabat, Sall.

vastus -a -um (root VA, whence vanus), *empty, waste, deserted, desolate.* **I.** Lit., **A.** Gen., **a,** absol., loci coaedificati an vasti, Cic.; **b,** with ab and the abl., urbs a defensoribus vasta, Liv. **B.** Esp., *made empty by ravages, devastated;* solum, Liv.; poet., haec ego vasta dabo, *will ravage*, Verg. **II.** Meton., **1,** *vast, fearful in size, enormous, frightful, horrible;* vasta et immanis belua, Caes.; mare, Caes.; **2,** *rough, rude, unrefined;* vastus homo atque foedus, Cic.; littera vastior, *rougher*, Cic.

vātes -is, c. *a prophet, soothsayer, seer.* **I.** Lit., **A.** Liv., Cicero quae nunc usu veniunt cecinit ut vates, Cic. **B.** Esp., *the inspired prophetic singer, bard, poet;* cothurnatus, *a tragic poet*, Ov.; Maeonius, *Homer*, Ov.; Lesbia, *Sappho*, Ov.; vates Aeneidos, *Vergil*, Ov. **II.** Transf., *a teacher, master*, Plin. (genit. plur., gen. vatum, also vatium).

Vātīcānus -a -um, *Vatican;* mons, collis, *the Vatican Hill on the west side of the Tiber*, Hor.; plur., Vaticani colles, *the hill with its surroundings*, Cic.; ager Vaticanus, *the country round the Vatican, notorious for its bad soil, which produced poor wine*, Cic.

vātĭcĭnātĭo -ōnis, f. (vaticinor), *a soothsaying, prophesying;* earum litterarum vaticinationem falsam esse cupio, Cic.; plur., sortes et vaticinationes, Caes.

vātĭcĭnātor -ōris, m. (vaticinor), *a soothsayer, prophet*, Ov.

vātĭcĭnĭum -ii, n. (vates), *a prophecy*, Plin.

vātĭcĭnor, 1. dep. (vates), *to prophesy.* **I.** Lit., **A.** Gen., vaticinari furor vera solet, Cic.; with acc. and infin., saevam laesi fore numinis iram, Ov. **B.** Esp., **1,** *to warn as a seer*, Ov.; **2,** *to teach as a seer;* doctum quendam virum carminibus Graecis vaticinatum ferunt, Cic. **II.** Transf., *to talk nonsense, to rave;* sed ego fortasse vaticinor, Cic.

vātĭcĭnus -a -um (vates), *soothsaying, prophetic*, Liv., Ov.

vătillum (bătillum) -i, n. *a chafing-dish*, Hor.

Vătīnĭus -a -um, *the name of a Roman family, the most notorious member of which was* P. Vatinius, *a dependent of Caesar*, so often attacked by Cicero that odium Vatinianum and crimina Vatiniana became proverbial. Hence, **Vătīnĭānus** -a -um, *Vatinian.*

vātis = vates (q.v.).

vătĭus -a -um, *bent inwards* (applied to knock-kneed persons), Varr.

1. **-vĕ** (shortened form of vel), enclitic, *or, or perhaps;* duabus tribusve horis, Cic.; poet., ve . . . ve, Ov., ve . . . aut, Prop., *either* . . . *or.*

2. **vē- (vae),** an inseparable particle, expressing excess or deficiency; e.g., vecors, vegrandis, vesanus.

Vecilius mons, *a mountain in Latium.*

vēcordĭa (vaecordia) -ae, f. (vecors), *senselessness, foolishness, madness*, Sall., Ter.

vēcors (vaecors) -cordis, abl. -cordi, genit. plur. -cordium (2. ve and cor), *silly, senseless, foolish, mad, insane;* **a,** of persons, vecordes sine colore, Cic.; vecors de tribunali decurrit, Liv.; iste vecordissimus, Cic.; **b,** of things, impetus, Liv.

vectābĭlis -e (vecto), *that can be carried, portable*, Sen.

vectātĭo -ōnis, f. (vecto), *a riding, driving, sailing*, etc.; equi, Suet.

vectīgal -gālis, abl. -gāli, n. (for vectigale, from vectigalis), *revenue.* **I.** Of the state, or of individual magistrates; **a,** of the state, *a tax, impost, duty;* portorium, *dues on merchandise;* ex scriptura, *a rent paid for the state pasture land;* decuma, *a tithe on grain;* portoria reliquaque vectigalia, Caes.; vectigal pergrande imponere agro, Cic.; vectigalia pendĕre, *to pay*, Cic.; **b,** of magistrates, praetorium, *presents to governors*, Cic.; aedilicium, *contribution through the governors of provinces to the aediles for the games at Rome*, Cic. **II.** *private income, revenue;* ex meo tenui vectigali, Cic.

vectīgālis -e (veho). **I.** *of or relating to taxes;* **a,** *paid in taxes;* pecunia, *taxes*, Cic.; **b,** *liable to taxes, tributary;* civitas, Cic.; Ubios sibi vectigales facere, Cic. **II.** *bringing in income for private persons;* equi, Cic.

vectĭo -ōnis, f. (veho), *a carrying, conveyance;* quadripedum vectiones, Cic.

vectis -is, m. (veho), *a lever.* **I.** Gen., for lifting or for breaking something, *a crow-bar;* signum vectibus labefacere, Cic.; biremes impellere vectibus, Caes. **II.** Esp. = κλεὶς, *a large bar for fastening a door, a bar, bolt*, Cic., Verg.

vecto, 1. (intens. of veho), *to carry, convey;* plaustris ornos, Verg.; fructus ex agris, Liv.; pass., *to ride;* equis, Ov.; or *to be driven;* carpentis per urbem, Liv.

Vectōnes = Vettones (q.v.).

vector -ōris, m. (veho). **I.** *one who carries, a carrier, bearer*, Ov. **II.** Pass., *one who is carried;* **1,** on a ship, *a passenger, a seafaring man*, Verg.; **2,** on a horse, *a rider*, Ov.

vectōrĭus -a -um (vector), *of or relating to carrying;* navigia, *transports*, Caes.

vectūra -ae, f. (veho). **I.** *a conveying, carrying by ship or carriage;* frumenti, Caes.; sine vecturae periculo, *of a sea-passage*, Cic. **II.** Meton. *passage-money, fare*, Plaut.

vĕgĕo, 2. (connected with vigeo), *to stir up, quicken, excite to rapid motion*, Enn.

vĕgĕtus -a -um (vegeo), *lively, vigorous, active;* homo, Cic.; mens, Cic.; ingenium, Liv.

vēgrandis -e. **I.** *small, tiny, diminutive;* farra, Ov. **II.** *of huge size, very great;* homo vegrandi macie torridus, Cic.

vĕhĕmens -entis. **I.** *violent, vehement, furious, impetuous;* **a,** of living beings, nimis es vehemens feroxque naturā, Cic.; in agendo, Cic.; se vehementem praebere in aliquem, Cic.; lupus, Hor.; **b,** of abstractions, vehemens et pugnax exordium dicendi, Cic. **II.** Transf., *strong, powerful, vigorous;* vehementius telum, Liv.; vehementior somnus, Liv. (also vēmens, Lucr., Cat., Hor.).

vĕhĕmentĕr, adv. (vehemens). **I.** *vehemently, violently;* agere, Cic.; ingemuisse vehementius, Cic.; se vehementissime exercere in aliqua re, Caes **II.** Transf, *strongly, powerfully, forcibly, exceedingly*, hoc te vehementer etiam atque etiam rogo, Cic, vehementer delectari, Cic, vehementissime displicet, Cic, vehementer utilis, Cic

vĕhĕmentia ae, f (vehemens) **I.** *vehemence, violence, passionateness*, Plin **II.** Transf, *strength, power*, Plin.

vĕhes is, f (veho), *a cartload*, Cato

vĕhĭcŭlum -i, n (veho), *a vehicle, conveyance*, **a,** by water, *a boat, skiff*, Cic, **b,** by land, *a waggon, carriage*, vehiculum frumento onustum, Liv

vĕho, vexi, vectum (root VE, whence vev, old Lat = via), *to carry, bear, convey* **I.** Transit, **A.** Act., **a,** of men, on the shoulders or the back, in the arms, etc, reticulum humero, Hor, of animals, taurus qui vexit Europam, Cic, **b,** on water, quos vehit unda, Verg, **c,** on horseback, in a carriage, triumphantem (Camillum) albi vexerant equi, Liv, **d,** in other manners, formica vehit ore cibum, Ov, transf, quod fugiens hora vexit, Hor **B.** Pass, vehi, as middle, **a,** *to ride, drive*, curru vehi, Cic, in navi, Cic., vehi post se, Liv, **b,** *to advance*, sex motibus vehitur, Cic, **c,** *to fly*, apes trans aethera vectae, Verg **II.** Intransit, *to be borne, to ride*, only in partic pres and gerund, vehens quadrigis, Cic

Vēius, v Veji

Vējens, v Veji

Vējento -ōnis, m *a surname of the Fabricii, one of whom, a contemporary of Cicero, was left governor of Syria by Bibulus*

Vēji -ōrum, m *an old town in Etruria, for a long time the rival of Rome, detroyed by Camillus, near modern Isola.* Hence, **A. Vējens** entis, m *Veientine*, subst., **Vējens** entis, m *a Veientine*, plur, **Vējentes** -ium, m *the Veientines* **B. Vējentānus** -a um, *Veientine*, subst, **Vējentānum** i, n *a kind of poor wine*, Hor. **C. Vēius** -a -um, *Veian*

Vējŏvis (Vēdiŏvis) -is, m (ve and Jovis), *an old Roman avenging deity identified with Jupiter of the lower world, and with Apollo*

vĕl (lit, imper. of volo = *take what you will, the one or the other*) **A.** Gen, **1,** when alone, *or;* oppidum vel urbem appellaverunt, Cic, used with potius to correct a previous statement, ex hoc populo indomito vel potius immani, Cic, **2,** doubled (sometimes repeated three or four times), *either* ... *or*, cur non adsum vel spectator laudum tuarum vel particeps vel socius vel minister consiliorum? Cic, the last statement is sometimes emphasised by joining to vel etiam or vero or omnino, quae vel ad usum vitae vel etiam ad ipsam rempublicam conferre possumus, Cic **B.** Esp, **1,** *and also*, pariter pietate vel armis, Verg, **2,** in a climax, *or even, actually*, per me vel stertas licet, Cic, often used with the superl, vel maxime, *especially*, Cic, **3, a,** *especially*, est tibi ex his ipsis, qui adsunt, bella copia, vel ut a te ipso ordiare, Cic, **b,** *for example;* raras tuas quidem, sed suaves accipio litteras; vel quas proxime acceperam, quam prudentes, Cic.

Vēlābrum -i, n *a district in Rome between the vicus Tuscus and the forum boarium*

vēlāmen inis, n (velo), *a covering, clothing, garment*, Verg

vēlāmentum -i, n (velo) **I.** *a covering*, Sen **II.** Esp velamenta, *the olive branches wound round with wool, carried by suppliants*, ramos oleae ac velamenta alia supplicum porrigentes, Liv

vēlāris e (velum), *belonging to a curtain;* anulus, *a curtain-ring*, Plin,

vēlārium -ii, n (velum), *the awning spread over the uncovered part of a theatre*, Juv

vēlāti -ōrum, m, milit t t, *the reserve, supernumerary troops who took the place of those who fell in battle*, used always in the phrase, accensi velati, Cic

vēles -itis, m, usually plur, velites, *light armed infantry, skirmishers*, Liv, transf, scurra veles, Cic

Vĕlia ae f **I** *a district on the Palatine Hill in Rome* **II.** *the Latin name of the Lucanian town Elea* (Ἐλέα), now *Castell' a Mare della Bruca* Hence, **A. Vĕliensis** e, *Velian* **B. Vĕlīnus** a -um, *Veline*

vēlĭfĕr fĕra -fĕrum (velum and fero), *carrying sail*, Ov

vēlĭfĭcātio -ōnis, f (velifico), *a sailing*, Cic

vēlĭfĭco, 1 (velificus), *to sail* **I** Intransit, Prop **II.** Transit, partic, **vēlĭfĭcātus** a um, *sailed through*, Athos, Juv

vēlĭfĭcor, 1 dep (velificus), *to spread the sails, sail*, hence, **I.** *to sail*, Prop **II.** Fig, *to work with full sails, to strive for earnestly, be zealous for*, alicui, ap Cic, honori suo, Cic

vēlĭfĭcus -a -um (velum and facio), *sailing*, Plin

1 **Vĕlīnus,** v Velia

2 **Vĕlīnus** -i, m *a lake in the Sabine country, drained by the consul M' Curius Dentatus now Pie di Lugo or Lago delle Marmore* Hence, **Vĕlīna tribus,** *the tribe in the valley of the Velinus*, Cic

Vĕliŏcasses -ium, m and **Vĕliŏcassi** ōrum, m *a Gallic people on the right bank of the Seine, whose capital was Rodomagus, now Rouen*

vĕlĭtāris -e (veles), *of or relating to the velites or light-armed troops*, arma, Sall, hastae, Liv

vĕlĭtātio ōnis, f (velitor), *skirmishing*, transf, *a wrangling, bickering*, Plaut

vĕlĭtor, 1 dep (veles), *to skirmish*, transf, *to wrangle, dispute*, Plaut

Vĕlĭtrae -ārum, f *a town of the Volsci in Latium, now Veletri* Hence, **Vĕlĭternus** -a um, *of Velitrae*

vēlĭvŏlans = velivolus (q v)

vēlĭvŏlus a um (velum and volo), *flying with sails*, of ships, rates, Ov, of the sea, *traversed by sails*, Verg

Vellaunodūnum i, n *a town in Gallia Lugdunensis, now Chateau Landon or Montargis*

Vellāvi ōrum, m *a Celtic people in modern Velay in the Cevennes*

Vellējus -a um, *a Roman gens, the most celebrated members of which were* **1,** C Vellejus Paterculus, *a famous Roman historian under Augustus and Tiberius*, **2,** C Vellejus, *friend of the orator Crassus, tribune of the people*, 91 B C

vellĭcātio -ōnis, f (vellico), *a plucking*, fig, *twitting, taunting*, Sen

vellĭco, 1 (intens of vello), *to pluck, twitch* **I.** Lit, Plaut **II.** *to taunt, criticise, censure, rail at*, in circulis, Cic, absentem, Hor

vello, vulsi (volsi) and velli, vulsum (volsum), 3 *to pluck, pull, twitch* **I.** Gen, alicui barbam, Hor., latus digitis (to arrest a person's attention), Ov, aurem, Verg. **II.** Esp, *to pluck off, pluck out*, **a,** spinas, Cic; postes a cardine, Verg; **b,** milit t t., vallum, *to pull up the palisade and so tear down the rampart*, Liv, signa, *to take the standards out of the ground, to march away*, Liv, transf, of bees, castris signa, Verg.

Vellocasses = Vellocasses (q.v.).

vellus -ĕris, n. (root VELL, whence villus, connected with pellis), *wool when shorn off, a fleece.* **I. A.** Lit., vellera motis trahere digitis, *to spin*, Ov. **B.** Meton., *the whole skin with the wool*, either on or off the animal; Phrixea vellera, Ov.; poet., transf., *any hide*, e.g., of a lion or stag, Ov. **II.** Transf. *of that which is like wool*, lanae vellera, per caelum ferri, *fleecy clouds*, Verg.

vēlo, 1. (velum), *to cover, veil, envelop.* **I. A.** Lit., capita amictu, Verg.; togā velatus, Liv. **B.** Transf., *to crown, adorn;* tempora myrto, Verg.; caput velatum filo, Liv. **II.** Fig., *to hide, conceal, veil;* odium fallacibus blanditiis, Tac.

vēlōcĭtas -ātis, f. (velox), *quickness, rapidity, velocity.* **I.** Lit., velocitas corporis celeritas vocatur, Cic. **II.** Transf., mali, Plin.

vēlōcĭtĕr, adv. (velox), *quickly, rapidly, swiftly;* aliquid velociter auferre, Ov.; velocius pervolare in hanc sedem, Cic.; velocissime moveri, Cic.

vēlox -ōcis (from 2. volo, as ferox from fero), *swift, rapid, quick, fleet.* **I.** Lit., pedites velocissimi, Caes.; cervi, Verg.; jaculum, Verg.; toxicum, *quick in operation*, Hor.; poet. for adv., ille velox desilit in latices, Ov. **II.** Transf., animus, Hor.; nihil est animo velocius, Cic.

1. **vēlum** -i, n. (from veho, as prelum from premo), *a sail.* **I.** Lit., antemnis subnectere totum velum, Ov.; sing. collect., velo et remige portus intrat, Ov.; gen. plur., vela dare, *to sail away*, Verg., Ov.; vela facere, *to have all the sails set*, Verg.; fig., dare vela ad id, unde aliquis status ostenditur, Cic.; pandere vela orationis, *to follow the current of one's speech*, Cic.; vela contrahere, Cic.; prov., remis velisque, *with all one's might*, Cic. **II.** Meton., *a ship;* reditura vela tenebat eurus, Ov.

2. **vēlum** (root VE, whence vestis), *a covering, curtain;* tabernacula carbaseis intenta velis, Cic.; velis amicti, non togis, *wrapped up like women*, Cic.

vēlūmen = vellus (q.v.).

vĕlŭt (vĕlŭtī), adv. *as, even as, just as.* **I.** Correl. with sic foll. **A.** Gen., velut in cantu et fidibus, sic ex corporis totius natura et figura varios modos ciere, Cic. **B.** Esp., to introduce a simile, ac veluti magno in populo quum saepe coorta est seditio, sic, etc., Verg. **II.** Absol., **A.** Gen., velut hesterno die, Cic.; veluti pecora, Sall. **B.** Esp., **1,** to introduce an example, *as, as for instance;* in bestiis aquatilibus iis, quae gignuntur in terra, velut crocodili, etc., Cic.; **2,** to introduce a comparison, *as, just as;* frena dabat Sipylus, veluti quum praescius imbris, etc., Ov.; **3,** velut si, or simply velut, to introduce a hypothetical comparison, *as if, just as if, just as though;* **a,** velut si; absentis Ariovisti crudelitatem, velut si coram adesset, horrerent, Caes.; **b,** velut or veluti alone; velut ea res nihil ad religionem pertinuisset, Liv.

vēmens = vehemens (q.v.).

vēna -ae, f. *a blood-vessel, vein.* **I. A.** Lit., **1,** venae et arteriae a corde tractae, Cic.; **2,** = arteria, *an artery;* plur. = *the pulse;* si cui venae sic moventur, is habet febrem, Cic. **B.** Transf., **a,** *a water-course;* venas et flumina fontis elicuere sui, Ov.; **b,** *a vein of metal;* aeris, argenti, auri, Cic.; meton. = *metal;* venae pejoris aevum, Ov.; **c,** *a vein* or *streak in wood* or *stone*, Ov. **II.** Fig., **1,** met., *the inmost, vital part;* periculum inclusum in venis et visceribus reipublicae, Cic.; **2,** *a vein of talent, disposition, natural inclination:* benigna ingenii vena, Hor.

vēnābŭlum -i, n. (venor), *a hunting-spear;* aprum venabulo percutere, Cic.

Vĕnāfrum -i, n. *a very old town of the Samnites in Campania, famous for its oil, near modern Venafro.* Hence, **Vĕnāfrānus** -a -um, *Venafran.*

vēnālĭcius -a -um (venalis). **I.** *of* or *relating to sale;* subst., **vēnālĭcia** -ium, n. *import and export wares;* portoria venalicium, Liv. **II.** Esp., *relating to the sale of slaves;* subst., **vēnālĭcius** -ii, m. *a slave-dealer*, Cic.

vēnālis -e (2. venus). **I.** *on sale, to be sold;* horti, Cic.; subst., venales, *slaves put up for sale*, Cic. **II.** Transf., *that can be bought with bribes* or *gifts, venal;* vox, Cic.; habere venalem in Sicilia jurisdictionem, Cic.

vēnātĭcus -a -um (venatus), *of* or *relating to the chase;* canis, Hor.

vēnātĭo -ōnis, f. (venor). **I.** *the chase, hunting.* **A.** Lit., aucupium atque venatio, Cic. **B.** Meton., *game;* venatio capta, Liv. **II.** *a wild-beast hunt in the circus* or *amphitheatre;* ludorum venationumque apparatus, Cic.

vēnātor -ōris, m. (venor), *a hunter, sportsman*, Cic.; fig., physicus id est speculator venatorque naturae, Cic.

vēnātōrius -a -um (venator), *of* or *relating to hunting* or *the chase;* galea, Nep.

vēnātrix -icis, f. (venator), *a huntress*, Ov., Verg.; attrib., puella, *Diana*, Juv.

vēnātūra -ae, f. (venor), *a hunting*, Plaut.

vēnātus -ūs, m. (venor), *the chase, hunting;* labor in venatu, Cic.

vendax -ācis, (vendo), *fond of selling*, Cato.

vendĭbĭlis -e (vendo). **I.** *on sale, saleable;* illa via Herculanea, Cic. **II.** Transf., *pleasant, acceptable;* oratio, Cic.; sint illa vendibiliora, Cic.

vendĭtārius -a -um (vendo), *on sale, saleable*, Plaut.

vendĭtātĭo -ōnis, f. (vendito), *a putting up for sale;* hence, fig. = *a boasting, vaunting display:* venditatio atque ostentatio, Cic.; sine venditatione, Cic.

vendĭtātor -ōris, m. (vendito), *a vaunter, boaster*, Tac.

vendĭtĭo -ōnis, f. (vendo), *a selling, sale.* **I.** Gen., venditioni exponere, *to expose for sale*, Tac. **II.** Esp., *sale by auction;* bonorum, Cic.; plur., quam ad diem proscriptiones venditionesque fiant, Cic.

vendĭto, 1. (intens. of vendo), *to offer for sale repeatedly, try to sell.* **I.** Lit., Tusculanum, Cic. **II.** Transf., **1,** *to sell* (corruptly); decreta, Cic.; pacem pretio, Liv.; **2,** *to cry up, praise, recommend;* operam suam alicui, Liv.; se alicui, Cic.; se existimationi hominum, Cic.

vendĭtor -ōris, m. (vendo), *a seller, vendor*, Cic.

vendo -dĭdi -dĭtum, 3. (contr. from venum do), *to sell, vend.* **I. A.** Lit., **1,** gen., aliquid pecuniā grandi, Cic.; male, *cheap*, Cic.; partic. subst., **vendĭtum** -i, n. *sale;* ex empto aut vendito, Cic.; **2,** esp., **a,** *to sell by auction;* bona civium, Cic.; **b,** *to let out to the highest bidder;* decumas, Cic. **B.** Transf., **a,** *to sell, betray for money;* auro patriam, Verg.; **b,** *to give oneself up to, to devote to* (for money or some advantage), se regi, Cic. **II.** Fig., *to cry up, recommend;* Ligarianam, Cic. (the passive of vendo is veneo, as in classical Latin venditus and vendendus are the only passive forms of vendo used).

vĕnēfĭcium -ii, n. (veneficus). **I.** *a poisoning;* meton. = *poison*, Liv. **II.** *the preparation of magical draughts, magic, sorcery*, Cic.

vĕnēfĭcus -a -um (venenum and facio), *poisoning, poisonous, magical.* **I.** Adj., artes,

Plin ; verba, Ov **II.** Subst , **A. vĕnēfĭcus** -i, m *a poisoner, an enchanter*, Cic **B. vĕnēfĭca** -ae, f *a poisoner, a witch*, Hor

Venelli ōrum, m. *a Gallic tribe in modern North west Normandy.*

vĕnēnārĭus -ii m (venenum), *a poisoner*, Suet

vĕnēnātus -a -um (venenum) **I.** *poisonous, poisoned*, a, lit , vipera, Cic , telum, Cic , b, fig , jocus, Ov **II.** *enchanted*, virga, Ov

vĕnēnĭfĕr -fĕra -fĕrum (venenum and fero), *poisonous*, Ov.

vĕnēno, 1 (venenum), *to poison*, carnem, Cic

vĕnēnum i, n. **I. A.** *poison*, **1**, lit., venenum alicui dare, Cic , aliquem veneno necare, Cic , dare venenum in poculo Cic , **2**, fig = *ruin, destruction, bane*, discordia est venenum urbis, Liv , pus atque venenum (of envenomed language), Hor **B.** *a magic draught, a philtre*, quasi veneno perficere ut, etc , Cic **II.** *colouring matter, dye*, Assyrium, Verg , Tarentinum, Hor , *rouge*, Ov

vēnĕo (**vaenĕo**), vēnii, vēnum, 4 (for venum eo, from venus, *sale*), *to go to sale, to be sold* (pass of vendo) **I.** Gen , mancipia venibant, Cic , venire sub corona a consule et praetore, Liv , with abl of price, auro, Hor , with genit of price, minoris, Cic **II.** Esp , *to be let to the highest bidder*, quanti venierant, Cic

vĕnĕrābĭlis -e (veneror), *venerable, reverend*, venerabilis vir miraculo litterarum, venerabilior divinitate, Liv , of things, donum, Verg

vĕnĕrābundus a -um (veneror), *reverent, respectful*, Liv

vĕnĕrandus -a -um, p adj (from veneror), *worthy of reverence, to be revered*, amicus, Hor

vĕnĕrātĭo -ōnis, f (veneror) **I.** Act , *reverence, respect, veneration*, habet venerationem justam quidquid excellit, Cic **II.** Pass , *venerableness*, feminae, Tac.

vĕnĕrātor -ōris, m (veneror), *a venerator, reverer*, domus vestrae, Ov

Vĕnĕrĭus, v 1 venus

vĕnĕro = veneror (q v.)

vĕnĕror, 1 dep **I.** *to reverence, venerate, regard with religious awe, honour*, deos sancte, Cic ; Larem farre pio, Verg **II.** Meton , *to ask reverently, beseech with awe*, nihil horum veneror, Hor. (partic , veneratus, pass = *honoured*, venerata Ceres, Hor)

Vĕnĕti -ōrum, m **I.** *a people originally of Thracian origin, who settled on the north-west coast of the Adriatic* Hence, **Vĕnĕtĭa** -ae, f *the land of the Veneti* **II.** *a people in Gallia Lugdunensis, near modern Vannes* Hence, **A Vĕnĕtĭa** ae, f *the land of the Veneti* **B. Vĕnĕtĭcus** -a -um, *Venetian*

vĕnĕtus -a um, *bluish, sea-coloured*, Juv , factio, *the party of charioteers who were clad in blue*, Suet

vĕnĭa ae, f (root VEN, whence 1 venus), *grace, indulgence, favour* **I.** Gen , a, petere veniam legatis mittendis, Liv , dedi veniam homini impudenter petenti, Cic ; dare veniam excusationis, Cic , b, in the phrase, bonā veniā or bona cum venia, *with your permission, by your leave*, bona venia me audies, Cic , vos oro atque obsecro, judices, ut attente bonaque cum venia verba mea audiatis, Cic ; bonā veniā hujus optimi viri dixerim, Cic **II.** *indulgence to faults, grace, pardon, forgiveness*, veniam impetrare errati, Cic , dare veniam et impunitatem, Cic

Vĕnīlĭa ae, f **I.** *a nymph, mother of Turnus* **II.** *wife of Janus*

vĕnĭo, vēni, ventum, 4 *to come* **I.** Lit , **A.** Gen , **1**, of persons, a, istinc, Cic , huc, Cic , ad aliquem, Cic , ad urbem, Cic., sub aspectum, Cic , with acc of place domum ad aliquem, Cic , sexto die Delum Athenis, Cic , with dat of object, venire auxilio, subsidio, Caes , with infin , speculari, Liv , supin , ad quos ventum erat, Caes , b, *to come with hostile intent*, veniens hostis, Verg , supin , venit ad se existimantes, Caes , **2**, of things, frumentum Tiberi venit, Liv , dum tibi litterae meae veniant, Cic **B.** Esp , **1**, *to come = to return*, Romam, Liv , quum venies, Ov., **2**, *to come = to come forth*, a, veniens sol, Hor , b, = *to grow*, veniunt felicius uvae, Verg **II.** Transf , **A.** Gen , **1**, of persons, a, ut ad id aliquando, quod cupiebat, veniret, Cic , b, *to come hostilely*, contra summam amici existimationem, Cic , **2**, of things, a, venire in mentem, *to come into one's head*, Cic , b, of time, *to happen, to come, arrive*, ubi ea dies quam constituerat venit, Caes , venientis anni, *of the coming year*, Cic. **B.** Esp , **1**, venio in aliquid, *to come to or fall into any state or condition* in calamitatem, Cic , in consuetudinem, Cic , alicui in amicitiam, Caes , **2**, of speech, *to come to, arrive at a part of a subject*, venio ad recentiores litteras, Caes , **3**, a, = *to be derived from*, Bebrycia de gente, Verg , b, *to arise from*, majus commodum ex otio meo quam ex aliorum negotiis reipublicae venturum, Sall , **4**, *to happen*, haec ubi veniunt, Cic , **5**, *to come to the lot of, fall to*, hereditates mihi negasti venire, Cic , **6**, *to turn out*, Tac

vennŭcŭla (**vennuncŭla**) uva -ae, f *a kind of grape*, Hor.

vēnor, 1 dep *to hunt* **I.** Intransit , ii qui venari solent, Cic **II.** Transit , *to hunt, chase*, **1**, lit , leporem, Verg , **2**, fig , *to pursue, strive after*, suffragia ventosae plebis, Hor

vēnōsus a -um (vena), *full of veins, veiny*, Plin

venter tris, m (connected with ἔντερον), *the belly* **I.** Lit., a, fabā venter inflatur, Cic , b, *the belly as the organ and emblem of gluttony*, ventrem fame domare, Liv , ventri oboedire, Sall , c, *the womb*, Juv , meton , *the fruit of the womb*, Hor **II.** Transf , *a curving, protuberance, belly*, crescere in ventrem cucumis, Verg

ventĭlābrum -i, n (ventilo), *a winnowing-fork*, Varr

ventĭlātĭo -ōnis, f (ventilo), *an airing*, Plin

ventĭlo, 1 (for ventulo from ventulus), *to toss to and fro in the air, fan, brandish in the air* **I** Lit , **1**, ventilat aura comas, Ov , **2**, *to winnow grain*, Varr **II.** Transf , *to fan, to blow = to excite, provoke*, illius linguā, quasi flabello seditionis, illa tum est egentium contio ventilata, Cic

ventĭo -ōnis, f (venio), *a coming*, Plaut

ventĭto, 1 (intens of venio), *to come often be wont to come*, domum, Cic , in castra, Caes

ventōsus a -um (ventus), *full of wind, windy* **I.** a, lit , folles, Verg , Germania ventosior, Tac , ventosissima regio, Liv , b, meton , *swift or light as the wind*, equi, Ov , alae, Verg **II** Fig , **1**, *windy, blown out = empty, vain*, lingua, Verg , **2**, *changeable, unstable, inconstant*, homo ventosissimus, ap Cic , imperium, Cic

ventrāle is, n (venter), *a belly band*, Plin

ventrĭcŭlus -i, m (dim of venter), *the belly* **I.** Gen , Juv **II.** Esp , *the stomach*, Plin , cordis, *a ventricle*, Cic

ventrĭōsus -a -um (venter), *large-bellied, pot bellied*, Plaut

ventŭlus -i, m (dim of ventus), *a slight wind, gentle breeze*, Plaut, Ter

ventus -i, m *wind* **I.** Lit, ventus increbrescit, Cic, ventus intermittitur, Caes, quum saevire ventus coepisset, Caes, prov, in vento et aqua scribere, *to labour in vain*, Cat, profundere verba ventis, Lucr, dare verba in ventos, Ov, *to talk in vain*, dare verba ventis, *not to keep one's word*, Ov, ventis tradere rem, *to oblivion*, Hor, ferre videre sua gaudia ventos, *to come to nothing*, Verg **II.** Fig, **a,** *the wind as a sign of good or ill success*, venti secundi, *good fortune*, Cic, **b,** *as a means of raising a disturbance*, omnes rumorum et contionum ventos colligere, *rumours*, Cic, **c,** in the state, quicumque venti erunt, *whichever way the wind blows, whatever the circumstances may be*, Cic, **d,** *favour of the people*, ventum popularem esse quaesitum, Cic

vēnŭcŭla = vennucula (q v)

vēnundo dĕdi -dătum, 1 (for venumdo, from 2 venus and do), *to sell*, esp, *captives taken in war*, captivos sub corona, Liv

1 **vĕnus** ĕris, f (root VEN, whence venia), *that which is pleasing* **I.** Appellat, *beauty, charm, loveliness, attractiveness*, **a,** quo fugit venus? Hor, **b,** in works of art, fabula nullius veneris, Hor **II.** Proper name, **Vĕnus. A.** *the goddess of love and grace, wife of Vulcan, mother of Cupid*, Veneris puer, *Cupid*, Ov, so Veneris filius, *Cupid*, Ov, or *Aeneas* (son of Anchises and Venus), Ov, mensis Veneris, *April*, Ov **B.** Meton, **1,** *love*, Ov; **2,** *the beloved object*, Verg, **3,** *the planet Venus*, Cic, **4,** *the Venus throw, the highest throw of the dice*, Prop Hence, **A. Vĕnĕrĭus** -a -um, **1,** *of or relating to Venus*, Venerii servi and simply Venerii, *the slaves in the temple of the Erycinian Venus*, Cic; subst, **a, Vĕnĕrĭus** -i, m (sc jactus), *the Venus throw, the highest throw of the dice*, Cic, **b, Vĕnĕrĕae** -ārum, f *a kind of mussel*, Plin, **2,** *relating to sensual love*, res, Cic

2 **vēnus** -ūs and -i, m only found in dat and acc, *sale*, **a,** dat, venui and veno, veno dare aliquid alicui, Tac, **b,** gen acc, venum dare, *to sell*, Sall, venum ire, *to be sold*, Liv

Vĕnŭsĭa ae, f *an old town of the Samnites in Apulia*, now *Venosa* Hence, **Vĕnŭsīnus** -a -um, *Venusine*

vĕnustas -ātis, f (venus), *loveliness, beauty, charm, attractiveness*, **a,** of the body, corporis, Cic, **b,** of discourse, *grace, wit*, hominum, Cic, **c,** of manner, *charm, attractiveness*, homo affluens omni venustate, Cic

vĕnustē, adv (venustus), *beautifully, charmingly*, alicui venustissime respondere, ap Cic

vĕnustŭlus -a -um (dim of venustus), *charming, beautiful*, Plaut

vĕnustus -a -um (venus), *charming, lovely, beautiful, graceful*, **a,** of the body, gestus et motus corporis, Cic, **b,** of discourse, *charming, attractive, delightful*, sermo, Cic, sententiae, Cic

vēpallĭdus -a -um, *very pale*, Hor

vĕprĕcŭla -ae, f (dim of vepres), *a thorn-bush, bramble bush*, Cic

vĕpres -is, m (f. Lucr), gen plur, vepres, *a thorn bush, briar-bush, bramble bush*, sepulcrum saeptum undique et vestitum vepribus et dumetis, Liv

vēr, vēris, n (ἦρ), *spring* **I. a,** lit, primo vere, *in the beginning of spring*, Liv, quum ver esse coeperat, Cic, **b,** transf, *spring time of life, spring*, aetatis, Ov **II.** Meton, *that which is brought by spring*, ver sacrum, *an offering of the firstlings, originally of men and of cattle, afterwards of cattle alone, made on extraordinary occasions*, ver sacrum vovere, Liv.

Vĕrăgri -ōrum, m *an Alpine people in Gallia Narbonensis*

vērātrum -i, n *hellebore*, Plin

vērax -ācis (verus), *speaking the truth, truthful, veracious*, oraculum, Cic; Herodotum cur veraciorem ducam Ennio, Cic, with infin, vosque veraces cecinisse Parcae, Hor.

verbascum -i, n *the plant mullein*, Plin

verbĕnāca -ae, f *the plant vervain*, Plin

verbēnae -ārum, f *boughs of olive, laurel, myrtle, cypress and tamarisk, sacred boughs*, carried by the Fetiales, Liv, and by certain priests, Cic

verbēnārĭus -ii, m (verbenae), *one who carries sacred boughs, applied to the Fetiales*, Plin

verbēnātus -a -um (verbenae), *crowned with sacred boughs*, Suet

verber ĕris, n in sing only in genit. and abl (reduplicated form of root FER, whence ferio) **I.** *a blow, stroke, lash*, **1,** gen, **a,** sing, virgae, Ov, trementes verbere ripae, Hor, **b,** plur, verbera caudae, Hor, dare verbera ponto, of swimmers, Ov, **2,** esp only plur, verbera, *blows with a whip or scourge, a thrashing, flogging, whipping*, **a,** lit, castigare aliquem verberibus, Cic, verberibus lacerari, Liv, **b,** fig, patruae verbera linguae, *invectives*, Hor, contumeliarum verbera, Cic **II.** *the instrument that inflicts the blow* **A** *a cudgel*, or gen, *a whip, scourge*, **a,** sing, verber tortus, Verg, ictus verberis, Ov, **b,** plur, jubet verbera afferri, Liv **B.** *the thong of a sling* or *other missile weapon*, Verg

verbĕrābĭlis -e (verbero), *deserving to be flogged*, Plaut.

verbĕrātio -ōnis, f (verbero), *punishment, chastisement*, transf, ap Cic

verbĕrātus -ū, m (verbero), *a beating*, Plin

verbĕrĕus -a -um (verber), *deserving to be flogged*, Plaut

1 **verbĕro,** 1 (verber), *to beat, strike* **I.** Gen, aethera alis, Verg, Mutinam tormentis, *to fire upon*, Cic, vineae grandine verberatae, *beaten down*, Hor **II.** Esp, *to beat with a whip, scourge, etc; to flog, thrash, scourge;* aliquem pulsare et verberare, Cic, alicuius oculos virgis, Cic, **2,** fig., *to lash with words, to attack, assail*, orator istos verberabit, Cic.

2 **verbĕro** -ōnis, m (verber), *one who deserves a flogging, a rascal*, Cic

Verbigenus pagus, *one of the cantons of the Helvetii*

verbōsē, adv (verbosus), *diffusely, verbosely*, satis verbose, Cic, haec ad te scripsi verbosius, Cic

verbōsus -a -um (verbum), *copious, diffuse, verbose*, **a,** of persons, Cic, **b,** of things, simulatio, Cic, epistola verbosior, Cic

verbum -i, n (root VER, Gr EP, whence εἴρω, ῥῆμα), *a word, expression*, plur, *talk, discourse* **I.** Gen, **a,** verbum nunquam in publico facere, *to speak in public*, Cic, videtis hoc uno verbo *unde* significari res duas, et *ex quo* et *a quo loco*, Cic.; verba facere, *to speak*, absol, Cic, pro aliquo, de aliquo, de aliqua re, Cic, ille dies nefastus erit, per quem tria verba silentur, *when the praetor does not use the formula*, Do, Dico, Addico, i e, *when he does not administer justice*, Ov, **b,** esp phrases, (α) verbo, *by a word*, verbo de sententia destitisti, Cic, (β) uno verbo, *in a word, briefly*, ut uno verbo complectar, diligentia, Cic, (γ) verbis, *by words alone* (opp opere), Cic , (δ) ad verbum, e verbo, de verbo, pro verbo, *word for word, accurately*, fabellae Latinae ad verbum de Graecis expressae, Cic , reddere verbum pro verbo, Cic , (ε) verbi causā or gratiā, *for example* si quis, verbi causā, oriente Caniculā ortus est, Cic , (ζ) meis (tuis, suis) verbis, *in my (thy, his) name*, si uxori tuae meis verbis eris gratulatus, Cic **II. A.** *mere words, mere talk* (opp *reality*), existimatio, decus, infamia, verba sunt atque ineptiae, Cic , in quibus (civitatibus) verbo sunt liberi omnes, *nominally*, Cic verba dare alicui, *to cheat, cozen, deceive*, Cic **B.** Collect , *an expression, saying*, quod verbum in pectus Jugurthae altius, quam quisquam ratus erat, descendit, Sall **C.** Grammat t t , *a verb*, ut sententiae verbis finiantur, Cic

Vercellae -ārum, f *a town in Gallia Cisalpina*, now *Vercelli*

Vercingĕtŏrix -rigis, m *a chief of the Gauls in the time of Caesar.*

verculum -i, n (dim of ver), *little spring*, used as a term of endearment, Plaut

vērē, adv (verus), *truly, in truth, rightly, aright*, dicere, Cic , ne libentius haec in illum evomere videar quam verius, Cic , verissime loqui, Cic

vĕrēcundē, adv (verecundus), *modestly, shyly, bashfully*, tum ille timide vel potius verecunde inquit, Cic , verecundius hac de re jam dudum loquor, Cic

vĕrēcundia -ae, f (verecundus), **a**, *modesty, shame, bashfulness, shyness*, (α) absol , meam stultam verecundiam ! Cic , (β) with subject genit , Tironis, Cic , (γ) with object genit , turpitudinis, *on account of disgrace*, Cic , **b**, *propriety, respect*, harum rerum commemorationem verecundia saepe impedivit utriusque nostrum, Cic , **c**, *religious reverence, awe, respect*, with object genit , deorum, Liv ; **d**, *a feeling of shame, a sense of shame*, Liv , verecundiae est, with infin , *one is ashamed, hesitates*; privatis dictatorem poscere reum verecundiae non fuit, Liv

vĕrēcundor, 1 dep (verecundus), *to be bashful, ashamed, shy*, with infin , in publicum prodire, Cic

vĕrēcundus -a -um (vereor), *feeling shame, bashful, shamefaced, modest, shy, diffident, coy*, **1**, of persons, **a**, absol , homo non nimis verecundus, Cic , **b**, with in and the abl , nec in faciendis verbis audax et in transferendis verecundus et parcus, Cic ; **2**, of things, vultus, Ov , color, *blush*, Hor , oratio, Cic , translatio, *not forced, natural*, Cic

vĕrēdus -i, m *a swift horse, hunter*, Mart

vĕrendus -a -um, p adj (from vereor), *venerable, reverend*, majestas, Ov , patres, Ov

vĕrĕor -itus sum, 2 dep **I.** *to stand in awe of*, **1**, *to fear*, **a**, with acc , hostem, Caes , bella Gallica, Cic , **b**, with acc and infin , vereor committere ut, etc , Cic ; quos intellegere vereretur, Cic , **2**, *to feel reverence, to be reverent towards, to revere*, **a**, with acc , metuebant eum servi, verebantur liberi, Cic , quem et amabat ut fratrem et ut majorem fratrem verebatur, Cic , **b**, with genit , ne tui quidem testimonii veritus, Cic **II.** *to fear = to have to fear, to be afraid, to be anxious about, to suspect*; **a**, with acc., periculum, Caes , **b**, with ne (*that*), or ut, or ne non (*that not*), vereor ne turpe sit timere, Cic , et tamen veremur ut hoc natura patiatur, Cic , **c**, absol , eo minus veritus navibus quod, etc , Caes

vĕrētrum -i, n (vereor) = αἰδοῖον.

Vergilius -ii, m., P. Vergilius Maro, *the great Roman poet, born at Andes in the Mantuan country, contemporary of Augustus, Horace, and Ovid, author of the Aeneid, the Georgics, and the Eclogues*

Verginius -a -um, *the name of a Roman family, the most celebrated of which was Verginia, the daughter of the centurion L. Verginius, who killed her in the market place, to deliver her from the designs of the decemvir Appius Claudius*

vergo, versi, 3 (connected with verto) **I.** Intransit , *to bend, to be inclined* **A.** Lit , omnibus ejus (terrae) partibus in medium vergentibus, Cic **B.** Transf , **1**, *to be inclined, to be directed*, **a**, of persons and objects connected with persons, nisi Bruti auxilium ad Italiam vergere quam ad Asiam maluissemus, Cic , **b**, of places, *to lie towards, be situated towards* ad flumen, Caes , ad septentriones, Caes , **2**, *to approach, come near*, **a**, of time, *to come to an end*, vergente auctumno, Tac , **b**, of disposition, etc , *to tend to*, Tac **II.** Transit , *to bend, turn, incline*, **1**, gen , middle, vergi, *to incline*, Lucr , **2**, esp , *to pour in*, amoma in sinus, Ov

vergŏbrĕtus (from Celtic guerg = efficax, and breth or breath = judicium, thus = judicium exsequens), *the executor of judgment, name of the highest magistrate of the Aedui*, Caes

vērīdicus -a -um (verus and dico) **I.** *truth-speaking, truthful*, vox, Cic , veridica interpres deum, Liv **II.** *truly spoken, true*, Plin

vērĭlŏquium -ii, n (verus and loquor), translation of ἐτυμολογία, *etymology*, Cic

vērīsimĭlis -e, *probable, likely*, Cic

vērīsimĭlitūdo -inis, f (verisimilis), *probability*, Cic

vērĭtas -ātis, f (verus), *truth* **I.** Gen , *the true, actual nature of a thing, reality*, in omni re vincit imitationem veritas, Cic , imitari veritatem (of works of art), *to be true to nature*, Cic , quum in veritate dicemus, *in reality* (i e , in the forum, not simply for practice), Cic **II** Esp (as opp to falsehood), *truth*, **1**, lit , cujus aures veritati clausae sunt, Cic , **2**, meton , *truthfulness, honesty*, in tuam fidem, veritatem confugit, Cic

vērĭverbium -ii, n (verus and verbum), *speaking the truth*, Plaut

vermĭcŭlātĭo -ōnis, f (vermiculor), *a worm hole in plants*, Plin

vermĭcŭlātus -a -um (vermiculus), *vermiculated*, pavimentum, *inlaid with very small stones*, Plin

vermĭcŭlor, 1 dep (vermiculus), *to be full of worms, to be worm eaten*, Plin

vermĭcŭlus -i, m (dim of vermis), *a little worm*, Lucr

vermĭnātĭo -ōnis f (vermino), **1**, *the worms*, a disease of animals, Plin , **2**, *a pain in the limbs*, Sen

vermīno, 1 (vermis), **1**, *to have worms*, Sen , **2**, *to have a crawling, itching pain in the limbs*, Sen

vermĭnōsus -a -um (vermis), *full of worms*, Plin

vermis -is, m (verto), *a worm*, Lucr

verna -ae, c *a slave born in the house* **I.** Lit , Hor **II.** Transf , *a native*, Mart

vernācŭlus -a -um (verna) **I.** *of or relating to a slave born in the house*, subst , **vernācŭlus** -i, m *a jester, buffoon*, Suet **II.** Transf , *native, domestic*, i e , *Roman*, crimen domesticum et vernaculum, Cic

vernātĭo -ōnis, f (verno) **I.** *the shedding of the skin by snakes*, Plin **II.** Meton., *the slough or cast off skin*, Plin.

vernīlis -e (verna), 1, *slavish, mean, abject*, blanditiae, Tac., 2, *pert, froward*, verbum, Tac

vernīlĭtas -ātis, f (vernilis), 1, *mean servility*, Sen, 2, *pertness, frowardness*, Plin

vernīlĭtĕr, adv (vernilis), *like a house-slave*, fungi officiis, Hor

verno, 1. (ver), *to be spring like, flourish, grow green* I. Lit, vernat humus, Ov, avis, *to begin to sing*, Ov II. Transf, dum vernat sanguis, *is lively*, Prop

vernŭla -ae, c (dim of verna), 1, *a slave born in the house*, Juv, 2, transf, *native, indigenous*, Juv

vernus -a -um (ver), *of or relating to spring, spring like, vernal*, aequinoctium, Liv, flores, Hor, tempus, Cic

vērō, adv (verus), *in truth, truly, really, indeed, in fact* I. Adv, a, Cic, at the beginning of a letter, ego vero cupio, te ad me venire, *I wish really*, Cic, b, often placed before affirmative answers, *certainly, to be sure*, vero, mea puella, Cic, in negative answers, minime vero, Cic, c, in addresses, invitations, demands, *then, pray*, tu vero me ascribe talem in numerum, Cic, d, in a climax, *even, indeed*, in mediocribus vel studiis vel officiis, vel vero etiam negotiis contemnendum, Cic II. Transf, as an adversative particle, *but indeed, but in fact*, illud vero plane non est ferendum, Cic, so in transitions in speech, nec vero tibi de versibus respondebo, Cic

Vērōna -ae, f *one of the most flourishing towns of North Italy, birthplace of Catullus* -Hence, **Vērōnensis** -e, *of Verona*, subst, **Vērōnenses** -ium, m *the inhabitants of Verona*

verpa -ae, f *the penis*, Cat

verpus -i, m (verpa), *a circumcised man*, Juv

1 **verres** -is, m *a boar*, Hor

2 **Verres** -is, m, C Cornelius, *praetor in Sicily, prosecuted and driven into exile by Cicero on a charge of extortion* Hence, **A Verrĭus** -a um, *of or belonging to Verres* **B. Verrīnus** a um, *of or belonging to Verres*, jus (with a pun on 1 verres and on the double meaning of jus, *law and broth*), Cic

1 **verrīnus** a -um (1 verres), *of or relating to a boar*, Plin

2 **Verrīnus**, v 2 Verres

verro, versum, 3 *to drag, trail on the ground* I. Gen, A. Lit, a, versā pulvis inscribitur hastā, Verg, b, of the winds, *to sweep, drag away*, maria et terras ferre secum et verrere per auras, Verg B *to sweep, to brush against*, a, of mourners, crinibus templa, crinibus passis aras, Liv, b, of persons with long dresses, *to sweep the ground*, verrit humum palla, Ov, c, of animals swimming, *to pass over, sweep along*, aequora caudis, Verg, so of ships, remis vada livida, Verg, d, of a harp player, duplici genialia nablia palmā, Ov II A. *to sweep with the broom*, a, Plaut, b, on the thrashing floor, *to sweep together, collect together* quidquid de Libycis verritur areis, Hor B *to sweep clean, to clean*, absol, qui tergunt, qui verrunt, Cic

verrūca -ae, f *a wart, excrescence*, Plin, fig, *a small fault* (opp tuber, *a serious fault*), Hor

verrūcārĭa herba -ae, f (verruca), *a plant that removes warts, heliotropion*, Plin

Verrūgo -ginis, f *a town of the Volsci*

verrunco, 1 (verto), *to turn out*, esp. as religious t t, bene verruncare, *to turn out well, have a happy issue*, populo, Liv.

versābĭlis -e (verso), *movable, changeable*, Sen

versābundus -a -um (verso), *turning round, revolving*, turbo, Lucr

versātĭlis -e (verso), *turning round, revolving* I. Lit, templum caeli, Lucr II. Fig, *versatile*, ingenium, Liv.

versātĭo -ōnis, f (verso), *a turning round, revolving* I. Lit, Plin II. Fig, *a changing, mutation*, Sen

versĭcŏlor -ōris (verso and color), *changing in colour, of various colours, parti-coloured*; vestimentum, Liv, arma, Verg, plumae, Cic

versĭcŭlus -i, m (dim of versus), 1, *a little line*, a, epistolae, Cic, b, uno versiculo (i e, the formula, Videant consules ne quid detrimenti respublica capiat), Cic, 2, *little verse, versicle*, Cic

versĭfĭcātĭo -ōnis, f (versifico), *a making of verses, versification*, Quint

versĭfĭcātor -ōris, m. (versifico), *a verse-maker, versifier*, Quint

versĭfĭco, 1 (versus and facio), *to write in verse, versify*, Quint

versĭpellis (vorsĭpellis) -e (verto and pellis), *changing one's skin*, hence, *changing one's form* I. Lit, versipellem se facit (of Jupiter) Plaut. Subst, *one who can change himself into a wolf at pleasure, a werewolf*, Plin II. *sly, subtle, crafty*, Plaut

verso (vorso), 1 (verto) I. Freq = *to turn about often, to turn hither and thither, to turn round* A. 1, lit., a, ferrum or massam forcipe, Verg, lumina suprema, *cast a last look*, Ov, sortem urnā, *shake*, Hor, exemplaria Graeca nocturnā versate manu, versate diurnā, *read night and day*, Hor, reflex and middle, *to turn oneself round*, se in utramque partem, non solum mente, sed etiam corpore, Cic, middle, qui (orbes) versantur retro, Cic., b, of spinning, *to turn the spindle*, levi teretem versare pollice fusum, Ov, 2, transf, *to move hither and thither, to drive round*, a, act, (α) oves, *to pasture*, Verg, (β) *to torment, beat, harass*, Dareta, Verg, b, middle, versari, (α) of persons = *to stay, live, dwell*, cum aliquo, Cic, in fundo, Cic, intra vallum, Caes, (β) of things, *to have place*, partes eae, in quibus aegritudines, irae libidinesque versentur, Cic B Fig, 1, *to direct, turn hither and thither*, a, mentem ad omnem malitiam et fraudem, Cic, b, of fate, *to turn upside down, change*, Fortuna omnia versat, Verg, c, *to explain, to twist*, verba, Cic, d, *to turn, influence in a certain direction*, muliebrem animum in omnes partes, Liv, e, *to reflect, meditate upon*, in animis secum unamquamque rem, Liv, 2, transf, *to put in motion*, a, *to disquiet, disturb*, nunc indignatio nunc pudor pectora versabat, Liv, odiis domos, Verg., b, middle, versari, (α) *to stay, to hover, to rest*, alicui ante oculos dies noctesque, Cic, (β) esp, *to be engaged in, take part in, be employed in, be occupied with*, in sordida arte, Cic, of things, jura civilia quae jam pridem in nostra familia versantur, *are native*, Cic II. Intens, *to turn round and round, to turn up*, gramen, Ov, terram, Ov (infin, versarier, ap Cic)

versōrĭa -ae, f (verto), *a turning round*, versoriam capere, *to leave off, desist from anything*, Plaut

versum = 1 versus (q v)

versūra -ae, f (verto), *a turning*, fig, *the borrowing of money to pay a debt*, versuram facere, Cic, versura solvere or dissolvere, Cic.

1 **versus (vorsus), versum (vorsum)**, I. Adv., *towards, in the direction of*, ad oceanum versus, Caes; in forum versus, Cic. II. Prep. with acc., *towards*, Romam versus, Cic.

2 **versus** -a -um, partic. I. of verro (q.v.), II. of verto (q.v.).

3 **versus (vorsus)** -ūs, m. (verto). I. *the turning of a plough*, hence, *a furrow*, Plin. II. *a row, line*, 1, gen., in versum distulit ulmos, Verg.; 2, in writing, a, in prose, primus (legis), Cic.; b, in poetry, *a verse*, plur., *verses, poetry*, versus Graeci, Latini, Cic.; facere versum, Cic. III. *a step in a dance*, Plaut.

versūtē, adv. with superl. (versutus), *craftily, adroitly, cunningly*, Cic.

versūtia -ae, f. (versutus), *cunning, craftiness*, Liv.

versūtĭlŏquus -a -um (versutus and loquor), *slyly speaking*, ap. Cic.

versūtus -a -um (verto), fig., *dexterous, adroit, cunning, crafty, sly*, acutus atque versutus animus, Cic.; versutissimus Lysander, Cic.; hoc si versutius videbitur, Cic.

vertăgus = vertragus (q.v.).

vertĕbra -ae, f. (verto), *a joint*, esp., *a joint of the back, vertebra*, Plin.

vertĕbrātus -a -um (vertebra), *jointed, movable, flexible*, Plin.

vertex (vortex) -icis, m. (verto), *that which turns or is turned*, hence, *a whirl*. I. *a whirlpool of water, an eddy*, a, lit., Liv., Verg.; b, fig., amoris, Cat. II. *an eddy of wind or flame*, a, of wind, *a whirlwind*, Liv.; b, of fire, flammis volutus, Verg. III. *the crown of the head*. A. Lit., ab imis unguibus usque ad verticem summum, Cic. B. Meton., 1, *the head*, Cat.; 2, *the pole of the heavens*, Cic., Verg.; 3, *any height, elevation*, Aetnae, Cic.; hence, a vertice, *from above*, Verg.

verticillus -i, n. (verto), *the whirl or whorl of a spindle*, Plin.

verticōsus (vorticōsus) -a -um (vertex), *full of whirlpools*, mare, Liv.

vertīgĭnōsus -a -um (vertigo), *suffering from giddiness*, Plin.

vertīgo -ĭnis, f. (verto), *a turning round, whirling round, revolution*. I. Lit., assidua caeli, Ov. II. Transf., *giddiness, vertigo*, vertigo quaedam simul oculorum animique, Liv.

verto (vorto), verti (vorti), versum (vorsum), 3. *to turn, turn round*, reflex., vertere se and simply vertere, and pass., verti, as middle, *to turn oneself*. I. Gen., A. Lit., a, equos ad moenia, Verg.; reflex., verti me a Minturnis Arpinum versus, Cic.; without se, alternis ramos videmus vertere in alterius, Verg.; b, milit. t. t., aliquem (hostes, equites, etc.) in fugam, *to put to flight, rout*, Liv.; Philippis versa acies retro, *the defeat at Philippi*, Hor.; terga, *to flee*, Caes.; reflex., se, Caes.; without se, versuros omnes in fugam extemplo ratus, Liv.; c, of position, middle, versus with in or ad and the acc., *turned, lying towards*, Epirus in septentrionem versa, Liv. B. Fig., 1, gen., a, in nos vertite iras, Liv.; middle, pater totus in Persea versus, *devoted to*, Liv.; reflex., without se, verterat periculum in Romanos, Liv.; b, of money, etc., *to devote, turn to*, ex illa pecunia magnam partem ad se, *to appropriate*, Cic.; c, *to turn to* (in a bad or good direction), *construe as, impute*, ne sibi vitio verterent, quod, etc., Cic.; auspicia in bonum verterunt, Liv.; 2, esp., a, *to alter, change*, auster in Africum se vertit, Caes.; quae sententia te vertit, Verg.; fortuna jam verterat, Liv.; middle, verso Marte, Liv.; b, *to change to, cause to pass into*, aliquid in lapidem, Ov.; reflex. and middle, *to change to, to become*, terra in aquam se vertit, Cic.; c, *to translate*, verterunt nostri poetae fabulas, Cic.; d, polit. t. t., vertere solum, *to go into exile*, Cic. II. A. = versare, *to turn round and round*, 1, a, lit., lumina, *to roll*, Verg.; vertitur interea caelum, Verg.; b, transf., (α) *to move about*, inter primos, Verg.; (β) of time, *to roll round*, septima post Trojae excidium jam vertitur aestas, Verg.; esp. in partic., anno vertente, *in the course of a year*, Cic.; 2, fig., a, stimulos sub pectore, Verg.; b, esp., middle, verti, *to move in a certain sphere or element*, in jure in quo causa illa vertebatur paratissimus, Cic. B. = invertere, convertere, *to turn round* or *over*, 1, lit., a, gen., (α) stilum, Hor.; (β) as t. t. of agriculture, *to turn up with the plough* or *hoe*, terram aratro, Verg.; poet., transf. of ships, freta versa lacertis, Verg.; (γ) *to empty*, crateras, Verg.; b, esp., *to overthrow*, moenia ab imo, Verg.; 2, fig., a, Callicratidas quum multa fecisset egregie, vertit ad extremum omnia, *destroyed*, Cic.; b, *to destroy politically*, res Phrygias fundo, Verg.

vertrăgus -i, m. and **vertrăha** -ae, f. *a greyhound*, Mart.

Vertumnus (Vortumnus) -i, m. (verto, *the changing one*), *the god of exchange*, orig. *the god of the changing nature of the seasons, then of all transactions of sale, whose image stood at the end of the vicus Tuscus, near his statue the booksellers had their shops*.

vĕru -ūs, n. 1, *a spit*, Verg.; 2, *a javelin*, Verg.

vĕrŭīna -ae, f. (veru), *a small javelin*, Plaut.

Vĕrŭlae -ārum, f. *a town of the Hernici, in Latium, now Veroli*. Hence, **Vĕrŭlānus** -a -um, *Verulan*.

1 **vērum**, adv. (verus). I. *in truth, truly, really*, Plaut. II. *but, but yet, nevertheless, still*, verum haec civitas isti praedoni ac piratae Siciliensi Phaselis fuit, Cic.; non modo (tantum, solum) . . . verum etiam, Cic.; hence, a, in passing over to another subject in discourse, verum veniat sane, Cic.; b, in breaking off a discourse, verum quidem haec hactenus, Cic.

2 **vērum**, v. verus.

vēruntămen (vērumtămen), conj. *but yet, notwithstanding, nevertheless*, consilium capit primo stultum, verumtamen clemens, Cic.

vērus -a -um. I. *true, real, genuine*, denarius, Cic.; timor, *well grounded*, Cic.; res verior, causa verissima, Cic. Subst., **vērum** -i, n. *the truth*, verum scire, Cic. II. A. *right, fit, fitting, reasonable*, lex, Cic.; verum est, with acc. and infin., negat verum esse allici beneficio benevolentiam, Cic. B. *truth telling, truthful*, judex, Cic.

vĕrūtum -i, n. (veru), *a javelin*, Caes.

vĕrūtus -a -um (veru), *armed with a javelin*, Verg.

vervactum -i, n. *fallow ground*, Plin.

vervăgo, 3. *to plough up fallow ground*, Plin.

vervex -ēcis, m. *a wether*, Cic.; as a term of ridicule, *a sheepish, silly person*, Plaut.

vēsānia -ae, f. (vesanus), *madness, insanity*, Hor.

vēsāniens -entis (vesanus), *raging*, Cat.

vēsānus (vaesānus) -a -um, *mad, insane*, a, of persons, remex, Cic.; poeta, Hor.; b, of inanimate and abstract things, *fierce, furious, wild*, vires, Ov.; fames, Verg.

Vescĭa -ae, f. *a small town in Latium, on the Liris.* Hence, **Vescīnus** -a -um, *of* or *belonging to Vescia.*

vescor, 3. dep. (connected with esca). **I.** *to eat, feed on;* gen. with abl., rarely with acc., dii nec cibis nec potionibus vescuntur, Cic.; lacte et ferinā carne, Sall.; humanis corporibus, Liv.; sacros lauros, Tib.; absol., vescentes sub umbra, Liv. **II.** Transf., *to use, enjoy;* vitalibus auris, Lucr.; paratissimis voluptatibus, Cic.; aurā aetheriā, *to breathe, live,* Verg.

vescus -a -um (connected with vescor). **I.** Act. = *devouring, consuming;* sal, Lucr.; papaver, *exhausting the land,* Verg. **II.** Pass., *wasted, thin;* hence = *containing little nutrition;* salicum frondes, Verg.; farra, Ov.

Vesĕris -is, m. *a river in Campania, at the foot of Mount Vesuvius, where the consul* T. Manlius Torquatus *defeated the Latins,* 340 B.C.

vĕsīca -ae, f. *the bladder.* **I.** *the urinary bladder.* **A.** Lit., Cic. **B.** Meton., *anything made from a bladder, a purse, a lantern,* etc., Mart., Varr. **II. A.** *a bladder-like swelling, a blister,* Plin. **B.** Of discourse, *bombast, tumidity,* Mart.

vēsīcŭla -ae, f. (dim. of vesica), *a vesicle, a little bladder on plants,* Cic.

Vesontĭo -ōnis, m. *a town in Gaul,* now *Besançon.*

vespa -ae, f. *a wasp,* Liv.

Vespăsĭānus -i, m., T. Flavius Vespasianus Sabinus, *Roman emperor from* 69–79 A.D.

vesper -ĕris or -ĕri, m. (ἕσπερος). **I.** *the evening star,* Verg. **II.** Meton., **A.** *the evening;* diei vesper erat, Sall.; primā vesperis (sc. horā), Caes.; ante vesperum, Cic.; sub vesperum, Caes.; primo vespere, Caes.; abl., vespere and vesperi, *in the evening, late;* heri vesperi, Cic.; prov., quid vesper ferat, incertum est, Liv.; de vesperi suo vivere, *to be one's own master,* Plaut. **B.** *the west,* Ov., Verg.

vespĕra -ae, f. (ἑσπέρα), *the evening;* ad vesperam, *towards evening,* Cic.; primā vesperā, Liv.; abl., vesperā, *in the evening,* Plin.

vespĕrasco, 3. (vespera), *to become evening;* vesperascente jam die, *drawing towards night,* Tac.

vespĕrĕ, vesperi, v. vesper.

vespertīlĭo -ōnis, m. (vesper), *a bat,* Plin.

vespertīnus -a -um (vesper). **I.** Lit., *of* or *relating to evening;* litterae, *received at evening,* Cic.; vespertinis temporibus, Cic. **II.** *lying towards the west, western;* regio, Hor.

vesperūgo -inis, f. (vesper), *the evening star,* Plaut.

vespillo -ōnis, m. (vesper), *a corpse-bearer for the poor,* who were buried in the evening, Suet.

Vesta -ae, f. (Ἑστία), *the daughter of Saturn and Ops, goddess of the hearth and domestic life;* ad Vestae (sc. aedem), Hor.; a Vestae (sc. aede), Cic.; in her temple at Rome burnt the sacred fire, the extinction of which was thought to involve the ruin of the state; the Vestal virgins were consecrated to her service; Vestae sacerdos = pontifex maximus, *who had control over the Vestal virgins,* Ov.; meton., **a,** = *the temple of Vesta;* Vesta arsit, Ov.; **b,** *the hearth,* Verg. Hence, adj., **Vestālis** -e, *Vestal;* sacra, *the festival of Vesta, on the 9th of June,* Ov.; virgo Vestalis, and subst., **Vestālis** -is, f. *a Vestal virgin, one of the priestesses of Vesta, of whom there were first four and then six, chosen between their sixth and tenth years, obliged to remain virgins in the service of Vesta for thirty years.* Hence again, adj., **Vestālis** -e, *relating to the Vestal virgins, Vestal;* oculi, *chaste,* Ov.

vester (voster) -tra -trum (vos), *your, yours.* **I.** Subject., majores vestri, Cic. **II.** Object. = *against you;* odio vestro, Liv.

vestĭārĭus -a -um (vestis), *of* or *relating to clothes;* subst., **vestĭārĭum** -i, n. **a,** *a clothes-chest,* Plin.; **b,** *a stock of clothes, wardrobe,* Sen.

vestĭbŭlum -i, n. *an entrance-court, court-yard.* **I. A.** Lit., templi, Cic. **B.** Transf., *the entrance to a place;* sepulcri, Cic.; urbis, Liv.; in vestibulo Siciliae, Cic. **II.** Fig., *a beginning,* Cic.

vestīgātor (vestīgiātor) -ōris, m. (vestigo), *a tracker, investigator,* Varr.

vestīgĭum -ii, n. **I.** Act. = *the part of the foot that treads, the sole of the foot.* **A.** Lit., qui adversis vestigiis stant contra nostra vestigia, Cic. **B.** Meton., **1,** *a foot-step, track, foot-mark;* **a,** lit., vestigia in omnes ferentia partes, Liv.; vestigium facere in foro, Cic.; vestigiis aliquem sequi, Liv.; consequi, Cic.; **b,** transf., *a trace, mark;* frons non calamistri notata vestigiis, Cic.; **c,** fig., (α) vestigiis ingredi patris, *to tread in his father's steps,* i.e., *to imitate him,* Cic.; (β) *a mark, sign;* vestigia sceleris, avaritiae, Cic.; **2,** poet., *the whole of the lower part of the foot;* vestigia nuda sinistri pedis, Ov. **II.** Pass., *that which is trodden upon, a position, post, station;* **1,** lit., **a,** in suo vestigio mori malle quam fugere, Liv.; **b,** *the position of a destroyed town, ruins;* in vestigiis huius urbis, Cic.; **2,** fig., of time, *a moment;* in illo vestigio temporis, Caes.; eodem et loci vestigio et temporis, Cic.; adv., e vestigio, *immediately, on the spot,* Cic.

vestīgo, 1. (vestigium), *to track, follow the trace of, investigate.* **I.** Of animals, Plin. **II.** Of men, **1,** lit., **a,** virum, Verg.; **b,** causas rerum, Cic.; **2,** meton., *to come upon the track of;* perfugas et fugitivos inquirendo, Liv.

vestīmentum -i, n. (vestio), *clothing, covering, garment, vestment,* Cic.

Vestīni -ōrum, m. *a people in Italy, on the Adriatic, famous for their cheese.* Hence, **Vestīnus** -a -um, *of* or *belonging to the Vestini.*

vestĭo -ivi and -ii -itum, 4. (vestis), *to cover with a garment, clothe.* **I. A.** Lit., animantes villis vestitae, Cic. **B.** Transf., *to cover as with a garment, to adorn;* oculos membranis, Cic.; campos lumine purpureo, Verg.; sepulcrum vestitum vepribus et dumetis, Cic.; trabes aggere, Caes.; se gramine, Verg. **II.** Fig., inventa vestire oratione, Cic.

vestis -is, f. (connected with ἐσθής), *a covering.* **I.** Lit., **A.** Of men, *a garment,* and **a,** sing. collective, *clothing;* vestis lintea, Cic.; vestem mutare, *to put on other clothes,* esp., *to put on mourning,* Cic.; **b,** plur., vestes, *clothes;* vestibus hunc velant, Ov. **B.** *a carpet, tapestry;* pretiosa vestis multa et lauta supellex, Cic. **II.** Poet., transf., **a,** *the clothing of the chin, the beard,* Lucr.; **b,** *the skin of a snake,* Lucr.; **c,** *the spider's web,* Lucr.

vestispĭca -ae, f. (vestis and specio), *the mistress of the robes, keeper of the wardrobe,* Plaut.

vestītus -ūs, m. (vestio), *clothing, clothes, garments, apparel, attire, raiment.* **I. A.** Lit., color vestitus, Caes.; vestitus muliebris, Cic.; vestitum mutare, *to go into mourning,* Cic.; ad suum vestitum redire, *to go out of mourning,* Cic. **B.** Transf., *a covering;* riparum, Cic.; vestitus densissimi montium, Cic. **II.** Fig., ea vestitu illo orationis, quo consueverat, ornata non erat, Cic.

Vĕsŭlus -i, m *a mountain in the Cottian Alps, now Viso*

Vĕsŭvĭus -ii, m *Vesuvius, the celebrated volcano in Campania, at the first eruption of which, under Titus, the towns of Herculaneum, Pompeii, and Stabiae were destroyed*

vĕtĕrāmentārĭus -a -um (vetus), *of or relating to old things*, sutor, *a cobbler*, Suet

vĕtĕrānus -a -um (vetus), *old*, boves, Varr, hostis, Liv, esp, of soldiers, *veteran*, plur, milites veterani, or subst simply veterani, *old soldiers, veterans*, Cic, legio veterana, Cic

vĕtĕrasco -āvi 3 (vetus), *to become old, grow old* Cic (?)

vĕtĕrātor -ōris, m (vetus), *one who has grown old in or become experienced in anything*, a, in causis, Cic, b, in a bad sense, *subtle, tricky*, non sunt in disputando vafri, non veteratores, non malitiosi, Cic, absol = *a cunning fellow, old fox*, Cic

vĕtĕrātōrĭē, adv (veteratorius), *cunningly, craftily*, dicere, Cic

vĕtĕrātōrĭus -a -um (veterator), *cunning, crafty*, Cic

vĕtĕrīnārĭus -a -um (veterinus), *of or relating to draught animals*, subst, **vĕtĕrīnārĭus** -ii, m *a veterinary surgeon*, Col

vĕtĕrīnus -a -um (perhaps contr from vehiterinus, from veho), *of or relating to draught* I. Adj, bestia, *a beast of burden*, Cato II. Subst, **vĕtĕrīnae** -ārum, f *draught animals*, Varr

vĕternōsus -a -um, adj with superl. (veternus) I. *lethargic*, Cato II. Transf, a, *sleepy, dreamy*, Ter, b, *dull, without energy*, animus, *lethargic*, Sen

vĕternus -i, m (vetus), *age*, hence, *lethargy, sleepiness*, a, Plaut., b, *inactivity, lethargy, sloth*, veternus civitatem occupavit, Cic

vĕtĭtum -i, n (veto) I *that which is forbidden*, nitimur in vetitum semper cupimusque negata, Ov II. *a prohibition*, quae contra vetitum discordia? Verg, in Cic only in the phrases jussa ac vetita and jussa vetita

vĕto (vŏto), vĕtŭi (vŏtŭi), vĕtĭtum (vŏtĭtum), 1 *not to allow to happen, to forbid, prohibit, hinder, prevent*, used of the tribunes, praetor, magistrates, etc, or of the law, or as t t of augury, a, with object clause, (a) with acc and infin, rationes vetabant me reipublicae penitus diffidere, Cic, lex peregrinum vetat in murum ascendere, Cic, (β) with infin alone, lex vetat delinquere, Cic; b, with ut or ne, or (with preceding negative) quominus, or quin and the subj, or with subj alone, edicto vetuit ne quis se praeter Apellem pingeret, Hor, c, with acc alone, bella, Verg, pass, quod vetamur, Cic, d, absol, lex jubet aut vetat, Cic

Vettŏnes (Vectŏnes) -um, m *a people in Lusitania, in modern Salamanca and Estremadura*

vĕtŭlus -a -um (dim of vetus), *somewhat old, oldish* I. Adj, equus, Cic, filia, Cic II. Subst, A. **vĕtŭlus** -i, m *an old man*, Plaut, in jest, mi vetule, "*old boy*," Cic B. **vĕtŭla** -ae, f *an old woman*, Juv.

vĕtus -ĕris, abl sing -ĕre, compar, **vĕtĕrĭor** (archaic, the classical compar is vetustior), superl, **vĕterrĭmus** (root VET, Gr ΕΤ, whence ἔτος), *old, ancient* I. Adj, a, as opposed to young, senatores, Liv, b, as opposed to new, navis, Caes, necessitudines, Cic, with genit = *grown grey in, experienced in* operis ac laboris, Tac, c, as opposed to the present, *old = former, ancient*, res, Cic, innocentia, Cic, poetae veterrimi, Cic, in Tac gen, *of the time before the battle of Actium*, aetas, Tac II. Subst, A. **vĕtĕres** -um, m *the old = ancestors*, Cic B. **Vĕtĕres** -um, f (sc tabernae), *the old booths on the south side of the Roman Forum* C. **vĕtĕra** -um, n *that which is old, the remote past*, illa vetera omittere, *the old stories* Cic

vĕtustas -ātis, f (vetustus), *age* I. Lit, A. Gen, vetustas possessionis, Cic, verborum vetustas prisca, Cic B. Esp *antiquity*, historia nuntia vetustatis Cic II Transf A. *long duration, length of time* vetustati condita, Cic, plur, vetustates familiarum, Cic, habitura vetustatem, *likely to endure for a long time*, Cic, conjuncti vetustate, *a friendship of long standing*, Cic, ingenio, vetustate (*experience*), artificio tu facile vicisti, Cic B. *late posterity*, de me nulla umquam obmutescet vetustas, Cic

vĕtustus -a -um (vetus), *old, ancient* I. Gen, a, vinum, Plaut, hospitium, *of long standing*, Cic, b, *old in years*, vetustissimus ex censoribus, Liv II. Esp, *old-fashioned, antiquated*, vetustior et horridior ille, Cic

vexāmen -inis, n (vexo), *a shaking*, mundi, Lucr

vexātĭo -ōnis, f (vexo). I. *a shaking*, Plin. II. a, *trouble, annoyance, hardship*, corporis, Cic, b, *ill treatment*, sociorum, Cic

vexātor -ōris, m (vexo), *one who annoys, harasses, disturbs*, direptor et vexator urbis, Cic

vexillārĭus -ii, m (vexillum) A. *a standard-bearer*, Liv B. Plur, **vexillārĭi** -ōrum, m a, under the empire, *veterans who had served twenty years and were enrolled in special battalions, a reserve corps*, Tac, b, *a detachment, a division of a larger body*, Tac

vexillātĭo -ōnis, f (vexillum), *a detachment*, Suet

vexillum -i, n (dim of velum), *the standard of the maniples, and esp, of the cavalry, the veterans and the allies* I. Lit, *a flag, standard*, vexillum tollere, Cic, esp, *the red flag displayed on the general's tent or the admiral's ship as the signal of battle*, vexillum proponere, Caes II. Meton, *the men who fought under one flag, a company, troop*, Liv

vexo, 1 (intens of veho), *to move violently, shake, shatter* I. Lit, venti vexant nubila, Ov, rates, Verg II. Transf, *to harass, disquiet, molest, misuse, damage, annoy, vex*, agros, Caes, hostes, Cic, vexari difficultate viae, Liv

vĭa -ae, f (old Lat vea, connected with veho), *a way* I. Lit, A. *the way along which one goes*, a, *a highway, road*, militaris *main-road*, Cic, declinare de via ad dexteram, Cic, via ire, *to go straight on*, Liv, dare alicui viam, *to give place*, Liv, dare alicui viam per fundum, *to allow a passage through*, Cic, b, *a street in a town*, transversa, Cic, c, *a passage*, (a) *the gullet*, Cic, *the wind pipe*, Ov, (β) *a cleft*, Verg, (γ) *a stripe in a garment*, Tib B. Abstr, *way = course, march, journey*, de via languere, Cic, unam tibi viam et perpetuam esse vellent, *wished that you should never return*, Cic, mare et (atque) viae, viae ac mare, *travels by land and sea*, Hor II. Fig, A. Gen, vitae via, Cic, de via (*from the straight road, from virtue*) decedere, Cic B. Esp, 1, *means, way, method*, viam optimarum artium tradere, Cic, 2, *manner, rule, kind*, per omnes vias leti, Liv, viā, *methodically, by rule*, dicere, Cic

vĭālis -e (via), *of or relating to the highways*, Lares, Plaut.

vĭārĭus -a -um (via) *of or relating to highways*, lex *for repairing the highways*, ap Cic.

vĭātĭcātus -a -um (viaticum), *provided with money for a journey*, Plaut.

vĭātĭcus -a -um (via), *of* or *relating to a journey*. **I.** Adj., cena, *a farewell repast*, Plaut. **II.** Subst., **vĭātĭcum** -i, n. **A.** *money for a journey;* viaticum congerere, Cic. **B.** Esp., *prize-money of a soldier*, Hor.

vĭātor -ōris, m. (via). **I.** *a traveller, wayfarer*, Cic. **II.** *a runner* or *messenger attached to a magistrate's service*, Cic.

vĭātōrĭus -a -um (viator), *of* or *relating to a journey*, Plin.

vībix (vībex) -icis, f. *a weal, mark of a stripe*, Plaut.

Vībo -ōnis, f. *a town in Bruttii*, now *Monte Leone*, in full *Vibo Valentia*. Hence, **A. Vībōnensis** -e, *belonging to Vibo*. **B. Vălentīni** -ōrum, m. *the inhabitants of Vibo Valentia*.

vĭbro, 1. **I.** Transit., *to cause to vibrate, move rapidly to and fro brandish, shake;* **a,** vibrabant flamina vestes, Ov.; **b,** *to brandish a missile;* poet., *to brandish and hurl;* hastam, Cic.; spicula per auras, Ov.; fig., truces iambos, Cat.; **c,** *to curl, frizzle;* crines vibrati, Verg. **II.** Reflex., *to shake, tremble, move to and fro, vibrate;* **a,** Plin.; **b,** of limbs or parts of the body, *to quiver;* tres vibrant linguae, Ov.; **c,** *to glimmer, glitter;* vibrat mare, Cic.; **d,** of lightning, missiles, etc., *to flash, glitter;* fig., of discourse, oratio incitata et vibrans, Cic.

vīburnum -i, n. *a tree* (Viburnum Lantana, Linn.), Verg.

vīcānus -a -um (vicus), *dwelling in a village;* vicani haruspices, Cic.; subst., **vīcāni** -ōrum, m. *villagers*, Liv.

vĭcārĭus -a -um (vicis), *taking the place of a person or thing, substituted, vicarious*. **I.** Adj., operae nostrae vicaria fides amicorum supponitur, Cic. **II.** Subst., **vĭcārĭus** -ii, m. *one who takes another's place, a substitute;* **a,** diligentiae meae, *successor in the consulship*, Cic.; **b,** *a soldier substitute;* dare vicarios, Cic.; **c,** *an under-servant, under-slave*, Cic.

vīcātim, adv. (vicus). **I.** *from street to street;* servorum omnium vicatim celebratur totā urbe descriptio, Cic. **II.** *in villages;* in montibus vicatim habitare, Liv.

vĭcĕ, vicem, v. vicis.

vīcēnārĭus -a -um (viceni), *containing the number twenty*, Plaut.

vīcēni -ae -a (viginti). **I.** *twenty each*, Caes. **II.** *twenty*, Plin.

vĭces, v. vicis.

vīcēsĭma, v. vicesimus.

vīcēsĭmāni -ōrum, m. (vicesimus), *soldiers of the twentieth legion*, Liv.

vīcēsĭmārius -a -um (vicesimus), *of* or *relating to the twentieth part of anything;* aurum, *a tax of one twentieth*, or *five per cent.*, *on the value of manumitted slaves*, Liv.

vīcēsĭmus (vīgēsĭmus) -a -um (viginti), *the twentieth*. **I.** Adj., dies vicesimus, Cic. **II.** Subst., **vīcēsĭma** -ae, f. (sc. pars), *the twentieth part;* **a,** gen., e.g., of the harvest, Liv.; **b,** esp., *the twentieth part as a toll or tax;* portorii, Cic.; *a tax of five per cent. on the value of manumitted slaves*, Cic.

Vĭcētĭa -ae, f. *a town in North Italy*, now *Vicenza*. Hence, **Vĭcētīni** -ōrum, m. *the people of Vicetia*.

vĭcĭa -ae, f. *a vetch;* plur., Ov.

vīcĭēs (vīcĭens), adv. (viginti), *twenty times;* H.S. vicies, 2,000,000 *sesterces*, Cic.

Vĭcĭlīnus -i, m. (perhaps from vigil), *the watchful one;* Juppiter Vicilinus, Liv.

vĭcīnālis -e (vicinus), *neighbouring, near;* ad vicinalem usum, *after the manner of neighbours*, Liv.

vĭcīnĭa -ae, f. (vicinus), *neighbourhood, nearness, vicinity*. **I. A.** Lit., Persidis, Verg.; in nostra vicinia, Cic. **B.** Meton., *the neighbourhood = the neighbours;* Hispala ex Aventino libertina non ignota viciniae, Liv.; funus laudet vicinia, Hor. **II.** Fig., 1, *nearness*, Petr.; 2, *likeness, similarity, affinity*, Quint.

vĭcīnĭtas -ātis, f. (vicinus), *neighbourhood, vicinity, nearness*. **I. A.** Lit., in ea vicinitate, Cic.; plur., *neighbourly connections*, Cic. **B.** Meton., *neighbourhood = neighbours;* signum quod erat notum vicinitati, Cic. **II.** Fig., *likeness, affinity*, Quint.

vĭcīnus -a -um (vicus), *near, neighbouring*. **I.** Lit., **A.** Adj., bellum, Liv.; with dat., sedes vicina astris, Verg.; Thessalia quae est vicina Macedoniae, Liv. **B.** Subst., 1, **vĭcīnus** -i, m., **vĭcīna** -ae, f. *a neighbour;* vicini mei, Cic.; 2, **vĭcīnum** -i, n. *the neighbourhood, vicinity;* plur., sonitu plus quam vicina fatigat, Ov. **II.** Fig., *similar, like, kindred;* in the dat., dialecticorum scientia vicina et finitima eloquentiae, Cic.

vĭcis (genit.; nom. not found), vicem, vicĕ, plur., vices, vicibus, *change, interchange, alternation, vicissitude*. **I.** Lit., **A.** Gen., **a,** hāc vice sermonum, *interchange of discourse*, Verg.; vice humanarum fortunarum, Liv.; solvitur acris hiems gratā vice veris et Favoni, Hor.; **b,** adv., (α) per vices, *alternately;* clamare, Ov.; (β) in vicem (invicem), more rarely vicem, in vices, *alternately, reciprocally, by turns;* simul eramus invicem, Cic.; hi rursus in vicem anno post in armis sunt, Caes. **B.** Esp., 1, *requital, recompense, compensation, retaliation;* recito vicem officii praesentis, Cic.; redde vicem meritis, Ov.; 2, *the vicissitude of fate, fate, lot, destiny;* tacite gementes tristem fortunae vicem, Phaedr.; convertere humanam vicem, Hor. **II.** Transf., *a place, office, post, duty;* **a,** nulla est enim persona, quae ad vicem eius, qui e vita emigrarit, propius accedat, Cic.; vestramque meamque vicem explete, Tac.; **b,** adv., vicem, vice, in vicem, ad vicem, *in place of, instead of, like, as;* in qua re tuam vicem saepe doleo, Cic.; Sardanapali vicem in suo lectulo mori, *like Sardanapalus*, Cic.; defatigatis invicem integri succedunt, Caes.

vĭcissātim = vicissim (q.v.).

vĭcissim, adv. (vicis). **I.** *in turn;* terra florere, deinde vicissim horrere potest, Cic. **II.** *on the other hand;* considera nunc vicissim tuum factum, Cic.

vĭcissĭtūdo -inis, f. (vicis), *change, alteration, vicissitude;* imperitandi, Liv.; vicissitudo in sermone communi, *interchange of discourse;* plur., fortunae, Cic.

victĭma -ae, f. *an animal offered in sacrifice, a victim*, Caes.; fig., se victimam reipublicae praebuisset (Decius), Cic.

victĭmārius -ii, m. (victima), *an assistant or servant at a sacrifice*, Liv.

victĭto (intens. of vivo), 1. *to live upon, feed upon;* ficis, Plaut.

victor -ōris, m. (vinco), *a conqueror, victor*. **I.** Lit., **a,** absol., parere victori, Liv.; in apposition, *as a conqueror, victorious;* victores Sequani, Caes.; victor exercitus, Cic.; currus, Ov.; **b,** with genit., omnium gentium, Cic.; victor trium simul bellorum, Liv.; **c,** with abl., bello civili victor, Cic. **II.** Fig., animus libidinis et divitiarum victor, Sall.

victōria -ae, f (victor), *victory, conquest* **I.** Lit , **A.** victoria Cannensis, Liv , clarissima, Cic , with de and the abl , victoria de Vejentibus, Liv ; with ad and the acc , nuntius victoriae ad Cannas, Liv , adipisci victoriam, Caes ; consecutum esse sibi gloriosam victoriam, Cic , dare alicui victoriam, Liv **B.** Proper name, Victoria, *the goddess of Victory, represented with wings and with a laurel crown* or *palm branch in the hand* **II** Transf , **a,** certaminis, Liv , **b,** in a court of justice, nocentissima victoria, Cic

victōriātus -i, m , genit plur , victoriatûm (Victoria), *a silver coin stamped with a figure of Victory, worth half a denarius*, Cic

victōriŏla -ae, f (dim of Victoria), *a small statue of Victory*, Cic

victrix -tricis, f neut. plur -tricia (f of victor), *she that conquers*, attrib = *victorious, conquering* **I.** Lit , Athenae, Cic , literae, *bringing news of victory*, Cic **II.** Fig , mater victrix filiae, non libidinis, Cic

Victumŭlae -ārum, f *a town in Gallia Cispadana*

victus -ūs, m (vivo) **I.** *manner of life, way of living*, Persarum, Cic., in omni vita atque victu excultus, Cic **II.** *support, nourishment, food*, alicui victum quotidianum in Prytaneo publice praebere, Cic , parare ea, quae suppeditent ad victum, Cic , plur , persequi animantium ortus, victus, figuras, Cic

vīcŭlus -i, m. (dim. of vicus) *a little village, a hamlet*, Cic

vīcus -i, m (connected with οἶκος) **I.** *a quarter* or *district of a town, street*, nullum in urbe vicum esse, in quo non, etc , Cic , vicos plateasque inaedificat, Caes **II.** In the country, **A.** *a village, hamlet*, Cic , Caes **B.** *an estate, country seat*, scribis te vicum venditurum, Cic

vĭdēlĭcĕt, adv (videre licet, *one can see*) **I.** Lit., **a,** *clearly, plainly, manifestly, evidently*, quae videlicet ille non ex agri consitura, sed ex doctrinae indiciis interpretabatur, Cic. , elliptically, in answers, quid metuebant? vim videlicet, *evidently violence*, Cic , **b,** ironically, *forsooth, of course, to be sure*, homo videlicet timidus et permodestus (vocem) [illegible], Cic **II.** Transf , *namely*, venisse tempus iis qui in timore fuissent, conjuratos videlicet dicebat, ulciscendi se, Cic

vĭdēn' = videsne? v video.

vĭdĕo, vidi, visum, 2 (root VID, Gr. ΙΔ, ΕΙΔ, εἴδον), *to see* **I. A.** *to have the power of seeing, to be able to see*, **a,** absol , quam longe videmus? Cic , **b,** with acc , at ille nescio qui mille et octoginta stadia quod abesset videbat, Cic **B.** *to see = to have the eyes open, to be awake*, Verg **II. A.** *to see, perceive something* **AA.** Lit and transf , **1,** lit , **a,** Pompejanum non cerno, Cic , with acc and infin , quum suos interfici viderent, Caes , **b,** = *to live to see*, utinam eum diem videam, quum, etc , Cic , **2,** transf , *to perceive with the senses*, mugire videbis sub pedibus terram, Verg **BB.** Fig , of the mind, **1,** *to perceive, notice, observe*, aliquem or aliquid in somnis, Cic , quem virum P Crassum vidimus, Cic , **2,** in pass , as εἴδομαι, *to have the appearance, seem, appear, be thought*, **a,** (α) with nom , ut imbelles timidique videantur, Cic , (β) with infin , ut beate vixisse videar, Cic , (γ) with nom and infin , ut exstinctae potius amicitiae quam oppressae esse videantur, Cic , with acc. and infin , *it appears*, non mihi videtur, ad beate vivendum satis posse virtutem, Cic , **b,** of cautious expressions in official statements instead of decided utterances, majores nostri voluerunt, quae jurati judices cognovissent, ea non ut esse facta, sed ut videri pronuntiarent, Cic , **c,** videtur (alicui), *it seems good, it is the opinion of*, eam quoque, si videtur, correctionem explicabo, Cic **B.** *to look at, to look upon, behold* **AA.** Lit , **a,** aliquem videre non posse, Cic , **b,** *to see = to find out and speak to*, Othonem vide, Cic , **c,** *to look after with care, to provide for*, alicui prandium, Cic , **d,** *to look to as a model*, Cic **BB.** Fig , **a,** *to reflect upon, consider*, videas et consideres quid agas, Cic , **b,** *to trouble oneself about, see to*, viderunt ista officia viri boni, Cic , foll by ut or ne and the subj , videant consules ne quid respublica detrimenti capiat, Cic , **c,** *to have in view, to aim at*, majus quiddam, Cic , videt aliud, *he has other views*, Cic

vĭdŭertas -ātis, f (viduus), *failure of crops*, Cato

vĭdŭĭtas -ātis, f (viduus), *want* **I.** Gen , omnium copiarum, Plaut **II.** *widowhood*, Cic

vīdŭlus -i, m (vieo), *a wicker trunk covered with leather*, Plaut

vĭdŭo, 1 (viduus), *to deprive of.* **I.** Gen , urbem civibus, Verg , arva numquam viduata pruinis, Verg **II.** Esp , partic , **vĭdŭāta** -ae, f *widowed*, Tac

vĭdŭus -a -um (root VID, seen in divido), *separated from something* **I.** Gen , *deprived of, bereaved of, destitute of*, with genit or abl or a with abl , pectus viduum amoris, Ov ; lacus vidui a lumine Phoebi, Verg **II.** Esp , **1,** *deprived of a husband, widowed*, domus, Ov , so of an unmarried woman, se rectius viduam (*unmarried*) et illum caelibem futurum fuisse, Liv ; hence, mulier vidua and subst , **vĭdŭa** -ae, f *a widow*, Cic , hence, transf , **a,** of animals, Plin ; **b,** of trees, to which no vine is trained, arbor, Hor , **2,** *deprived of a lover*, puella, Ov

Vienna -ae, f *a town in Gallia Narbonensis, on the Rhone, now Vienne* Hence, **Viennensis** -e, *of Vienne*

vĭĕo -ētum, 2 *to bind, weave together*, Varr.

viētus -a -um (vieo), *shrivelled, shrunken, withered*, cor, Cic

vĭgĕo, 2 *to be vigorous, thrive, flourish, to be active* **I** Lit , quod viget, caeleste est, Cic , animus in rerum cognitione viget, Cic , viget memoria, Cic **II** Transf , *to flourish, to be prosperous, to be in high repute* or *great power, to be at the height*, vigent studia, Cic , quem (Philonem) in Academia maxime vigere audio, Cic

vĭgesco (inchoat of vigeo), 3 *to become vigorous, to begin to flourish* or *thrive*, Lucr

vīgēsĭmus = vicesimus (q v)

vĭgil -ĭlis, abl -ili, genit. plur -um, *wakeful, watchful* **I.** Lit., canes, Hor , ales, *the cock*, Ov , subst , *a watchman*, Liv , plur , vigiles fanique custodes, Cic **II.** Transf , vigiles oculi, Verg , ignis, *ever burning*, Verg , Ov

vĭgĭlans -antis, p adj (from vigilo), *watchful, vigilant*, oculi, Verg , consul, Cic , ut nemo vigilantior ad judicium venisse videatur, Cic

vĭgĭlantĕr, adv (vigilans), *wakefully, vigilantly*, se tueri, Cic , enitar vigilantius, Cic , vehementissime vigilantissimeque vexatus, Cic.

vĭgĭlantĭa -ae, f (vigilo), *watchfulness, vigilance, wakefulness*, Cic

vĭgĭlax -ācis (vigilo), *watchful, wakeful ;* curae, *disturbing*, Ov

vĭgĭlĭa -ae, f (vigil) **I.** Gen , *wakefulness, sleeplessness*, also = *night spent in watching*, Demosthenis vigiliae, Cic **II.** Esp , *a watching for the security of a place*, esp , *for a city* or *camp, watch, guard* **A. 1,** lit , vigilias agere ad aedes sacras, Cic.; vestra tecta custodiis vigiliisque defendite, Cic.; **2,** meton., **a,** *a watch, one of the four divisions into which the Romans divided the night;* prima vigilia, Liv.; **b,** *the soldiers keeping watch, sentinels;* si excubiae, si vigiliae, si delecta juventus, Cic. **B.** Fig., *watchfulness, vigilance, care;* ut vacuum metu populum Romanum nostrā vigiliā et prospicientiā redderemus, Cic.

vĭgĭlārĭum -ĭi, n. (vigilia), *a watch-house,* Sen.

vĭgĭlo, 1. (vigil). **I.** Intransit., *to be awake, keep awake, watch.* **A. 1,** lit., ad multam noctem, Cic.; **2,** transf., vigilantes curae, Cic.; lumina vigilantia, *on a lighthouse,* Ov. **B.** Fig., *to be vigilant, watchful, careful;* vigilabo pro vobis, Cic. **II.** Transit., **1,** *to watch through, pass in watching;* vigilata nox, Ov.; **2,** *to care for by watching, provide for;* quae vigilanda viris, Verg.

vīgintī, num. (connected with εἴκοσι), *twenty,* Cic.

vīgintīvīrātus -ūs, m. (vigintiviri), *the office of the* vigintiviri; **a,** for the division of the public land, Cic.; **b,** of an inferior civil court, Tac.

vīgintīvĭri -ōrum, m. *a commission of twenty members, appointed by Caesar for the division of lands in Campania,* Cic.

vĭgor -ōris, m. (vigeo), *vigour, force, energy;* aetatis, Liv.; animi, Liv.

vīla = villa (q.v.).

vīlĭcus = villicus (q.v.).

vīlĭpendo, 3. (vilis and pendo), *to think meanly of, hold cheap,* Plaut.

vīlis -e, *cheap, low-priced.* **I.** Lit., servulus, Cic.; frumentum vilius, Cic.; res vilissimae, Cic. **II.** Transf., **a,** *worthless, common, of little value;* honor vilior fuisset, Cic.; **b,** *found in quantities, abundant, common;* phaselus, Verg.

vīlĭtas -ātis, f. (vilis), *cheapness, low price.* **I.** Lit., annonae, Cic.; annus est in vilitate, *it is a cheap year,* Cic.; num in vilitate nummum dedit, *at the lowest price,* Cic. **II.** Transf., *trifling value, worthlessness, meanness,* Plin.

vīlĭtĕr, adv. (vilis), *cheaply,* Plaut.

villa -ae, f. (perhaps connected with vicus), *a country-house, an estate, country seat, farm.* **I.** Gen., qui ager neque villam habuit neque ex ulla parte fuit cultus, Cic. **II.** Esp., Villa Publica, *a public building at Rome in the Campus Martius, used by the magistrates when they held the census* or *the levy for the army, and by foreign ambassadors,* Liv.

villāris -e (villa), *of* or *relating to a country-house,* Plin.

villātĭcus -a -um (villa), *of* or *relating to a country-house,* Varr.

villĭca, v. villicus.

villĭco, 1. (villicus), *to manage an estate;* ut quasi dispensare rempublicam et in ea quodam modo villicare possit, Cic.

villĭcus -a -um (villa), *of* or *belonging to a country-seat.* Subst., **A. villĭcus** -i, m. *a bailiff, steward, overseer of an estate,* Cic. **B. villĭca** -ae, f. *a bailiff's wife,* Cat.

villōsus -a -um (villus), *shaggy, rough-haired, hairy;* leo, Verg., Ov.

villŭla -ae, f. (dim. of villa), *a small country-house, little farm,* Cic.

villum -i, n. (dim. of vinum, for vinulum), *a little drop of wine,* Ter.

villus -i, m. (connected with pilus), *shaggy hair;* animantium aliae villis vestitae, Cic.

vīmen -ĭnis, n. (vieo), *an osier, withe, twig;* **1,** lit., scuta ex cortice facta aut viminibus intextis, Caes.; **2,** meton. = *a basket* or *vessel made of twigs,* etc.; curvum, *a bee-hive,* Ov.

vīmentum = vimen (q.v.).

vīmĭnālis -e (vimen), *of* or *relating to osiers.* **I.** Gen., Plin. **II.** Esp., as a proper name, Viminalis collis, *one of the hills of Rome, so called from an osier plantation there, where Jupiter Viminius was worshipped.*

vīmĭnētum -i, n. (vimen), *an osier-bed,* Varr.

vīmĭnĕus -a -um (vimen), *made of osiers, wicker;* tegumenta, Caes.

Vīmĭnĭus, v. viminalis.

vin'=visne, v. 1. volo.

vīnācĕus -a -um (vinum), *belonging to wine.* Subst., **vīnācĕus** -i, m. *a grape-stone.*

vīnālĭa -ĭum, n. (vinum), *the wine festival, held twice a year on the 22nd of April and the 19th of August,* Ov.

vīnārĭus -a -um (vinum), *of* or *relating to wine.* **I.** Adj., vas, *a wine-cask,* Cic.; crimen, *relating to the duties on wine,* Cic. **II.** Subst., **A. vīnārĭus** -ĭi, m. *a vintner.* **B. vīnārĭum** -ĭi, n. *a wine-jar, wine-flask,* Plaut.

vincapervinca -ae, f. *a plant, periwinkle,* Plin.

vincĭbĭlis -e (vinco), *that can be easily gained;* causa, Ter.

vincĭo, vinxi, vinctum, 4. **I.** *to bind, to tie round;* **1,** lit., **a,** suras cothurno alte, Verg.; tempora floribus, Hor.; boves vincti cornua vittis, Ov.; **b,** esp., *to bind, fetter;* manus laxe, Liv.; aliquem trinis catenis, Caes.; **2,** fig., *to fetter;* **a,** *to bind, pledge;* eius religioni te vinctum astrictumque dedamus, Cic.; **b,** *to limit, confine, restrain;* si turpissime se illa pars animi geret, vinciatur, Cic. **II.** Transf., **A.** *to bind, confine;* membra orationis numeris, Cic. **B.** *to strengthen, protect;* oppida praesidiis, Cic. **C.** *to embrace closely,* Prop. **D.** *to fetter by enchantments;* linguas et ora, Ov.

vinco, vici, victum, 3. (perhaps connected with per-vicax), *to conquer, overcome, defeat, subdue, vanquish.* **I. A.** Lit., **a,** milit. t. t., jus esse belli ut qui vicissent iis quos vicissent quemadmodum vellent imperarent, Caes.; Carthaginienses, Cic.; **b,** in a contest of skill, neque vincere certo, Verg.; **c,** in any kind of contention; (α) in play, Quint.; (β) in law, judicio (of the prosecutor), Cic.; judicium (of the accused), Cic.; (γ) at an auction, *to out-bid;* Othonem, Cic.; (δ) in debate, vicit ea pars senatus, etc., Sall. **B.** Transf., *to master, to get the mastery over;* **a,** non viribus ullis vincere posse ramum, Verg.; victus somno, Liv.; vincere noctem flammis (of lights), Verg.; multa saecula durando, *to last,* Verg.; **b,** of a place, aëra summum arboris jactu vincere, *to fly over,* Verg. **II.** Fig., **A.** *to master, control;* **a,** vincit ipsa rerum publicarum natura saepe rationem, Cic.; **b,** *to overcome by working on one's feelings, will,* etc.; vinci a voluptate, Cic.; victus animi respexit, Verg. **B. 1,** *to pass beyond, surpass;* opinionem vicit omnium, Cic.; **2,** *to prove victoriously;* vinco deinde bonum virum fuisse Oppianicum, hominem integrum, etc., Cic.; **3,** in colloquial language, **a,** vincimus, vicimus, *we have won, we have attained our object;* cui si esse in urbe tuto licebit, vicimus, Cic.; **b,** vicisti, *you are right;* viceris, *you shall have your way;* vincite, vincerent, *have your way, let them have their way;* vincite, si ita vultis, Caes.

vinctūra -ae, f. (vincio), *a bandage,* Varr.

vinctus -ū, m. (vincio), *a binding,* Varr.

vincŭlum (vinclum) -i, n. (vincio), *a band, cord, noose.* **I.** Lit., **A.** Gen., corpora constricta vinculis, Cic , aptare vincula collo, Ov **B.** Esp , vincula, *bonds, fetters of a prisoner,* and meton , *imprisonment,* conjicere aliquem in vincula, Caes ; rumpere alicuius vincula, Cic , esse in vinculis et catenis, Liv **II.** Transf , **A.** *a bond, fetter, chain,* **a,** concr , ex corporum vinculis tanquam e carcere evolaverunt, Cic , **b,** abstr , vinculum ingens immodicae cupiditatis injectum est, Liv **B** *a band, bond* a, concr , mollit pennarum vincula, ceras, Ov , **b,** abstr , numerorum, Cic , conjunctionis, Cic , fidei, Liv , vinclis propinquitatis conjunctus, Cic , vincula judiciorum, Cic

Vindĕlici ōrum, m *a German people north of Rhaetia, south of the Danube, with a capital Augusta Vindelicorum,* now *Augsburg*

vindēmia -ae, f (vinum and demo), *the vintage* **I. A.** Lit , Plin **B.** Meton , *grapes, wine,* Verg **II.** Transf , *harvest, ingathering,* olearum, Plin

vindēmiātor -ōris, m (vindemio), *a vintager* **I.** Lit , Hor **II.** Transf , *a star in the constellation Virgo,* Ov

vindēmio, 1 (vindemia), *to gather the vintage,* Plin

vindēmiŏla -ae, f (dim of vindemia), *a little vintage,* meton , omnes meas vindemiolas reservo, *income,* Cic

vindex -icis, c (vindico) **I.** *one who lays claim to* or *protects, a surety, guarantee, protector, defender, deliverer, vindicator,* **a,** of a surety, Cic , **b,** *a protector;* aeris alieni, *a protector of creditors,* Cic , injuriae, *against wrong,* Liv **II.** *an avenger, revenger, punisher,* conjurationis, Cic

vindicātio ōnis, f (vindico), *a defending, protecting, avenging,* Cic

vindiciae -ārum, f (vindico), *a making a legal claim to a thing in presence of the praetor,* injustis vindiciis ac sacramentis petere aliquid, Cic , ni Appius vindicias ab libertate in servitutem dederit, *has adjudged a free person to be a slave,* Liv

vindĭco, 1 (vim dico, *to threaten force*) **I.** *to make a legal claim for something, to claim* **A.** Lit , sponsam in libertatem, Liv **B.** Transf , **1,** *to lay claim to, to claim, arrogate, assume, appropriate* Chii suum (Homerum) vindicant, Cic , decus belli ad se Liv , partem aliquam sibi quisque vindicat, Cic , **2, a,** *to set free, liberate, deliver,* vindicare rem populi in libertatem, Cic , te ab eo vindico et libero, Cic , **b,** *to protect, preserve,* libertatem, Caes , aliquem a verberibus, Cic **II.** *to avenge, punish, take vengeance on* **A.** Lit , acerrime maleficia, Cic , in cives militesque nostros, Cic **B.** Transf , Gracchi conatus perditos, Cic

vindicta -ae, f (vindico) **I.** *the rod with which the praetor touched the slave who was to be manumitted, a manumission staff* si neque censu neque vindictā neque testamento liber factus est, Cic **II.** Meton , **A.** *deliverance,* vindicta invisae huius vitae, Liv **B.** *vengeance, punishment* legis severae, Ov

vīnĕa, v vineus

vīnĕātĭcus -a -um (vinea), *belonging to* or *relating to vines,* Cato

vīnētum -i, n (vinum), *a vineyard,* Cic

vīnĕus a um (vinum), *of* or *belonging to wine* Subst , **vīnĕa** -ae, f **A.** *a vineyard,* Cic **B.** Milit t t , *a shed built* (like an arbour) *for sheltering besiegers, a mantlet, penthouse,* Caes

vīnĭtor -ōris, m (vinum), *a vinedresser,* Cic

vinnŭlus a um, *sweet, charming, pleasant,* Plaut.

vīnŏlentĭa -ae, f (vinolentus), *wine drinking, intoxication,* Cic

vīnŏlentus -a um (vinum) **I.** Gen , *mixed with wine,* medicamina, Cic **II.** Esp , of persons, *drunk with wine, intoxicated,* Cic , subst , vinolenti = *drunkards,* Cic

vīnōsus -a -um (vinum), *full of wine, drinking much wine, wine bibbing,* senex, *Anacreon,* Ov , vinosior aetas, Ov

vīnŭlent v vinolent

vīnum i, n (connected with οἶνος), *wine* **I. A.** Lit , leve, Cic , mutatum, *sour,* Cic , vini plenus, Cic obruere se vino, Cic , plur , vina = *kinds of wine,* Cic **B.** Meton , **a,** *the grape,* **b,** *wine = wine drinking,* vino lustrisque confectus, Cic , in vino ridere, Cic **II.** Transf , *wine made from fruit,* Plin

vĭŏcūrus -i, m (via and curo), *an overseer of roads,* Varr

vĭŏla -ae, f (ἴον) **I.** *a violet,* pallens, Verg , collect , an tu me in viola putabas aut in rosa dicere? *on beds of violets* or *roses?* Cic **II.** Meton , *the colour of the violet, violet* tinctus viola pallor amantium, Hor

vĭŏlābĭlis e (violo), *that may* or *can be injured,* cor, Ov , numen, Verg

vĭŏlācĕus -a -um (viola), *violet coloured* Nep

vĭŏlārĭum -ii, n (viola), *a bed of violets,* Verg

vĭŏlārĭus -ii, m (viola), *one who dyes violet,* Plaut

vĭŏlātĭo -ōnis, f (violo), *an injury, violation, profanation,* templi, Liv

vĭŏlātor ōris, m (violo), *an injurer, violator profaner,* templi, Ov , gentium juris, Liv

vĭŏlens -entis (vis), *vehement, violent, furious,* Aufidus, Hor

vĭŏlentĕr, adv (violens), *violently, impetuously, vehemently,* aliquem accusare, Liv

vĭŏlentĭa -ae, f (violentus), *violence, vehemence, impetuosity,* hominis, Cic , fortunae, Sall

vĭŏlentus a -um (vis), *violent, vehement furious, impetuous,* ingenium, Cic , ira, Ov , violentior eurus, Verg , violentissimae tempestates, Cic

vĭŏlo, 1 (vis), *to treat with violence, violate injure,* **a,** urbem, *to plunder,* Liv , fines, *to lay waste,* Cic , ebur sanguineo ostro, *to dye blood-red,* Verg , **b,** morally, *to profane, dishonour,* loca religiosa, Cic , jus, Cic , amicitiam, Cic

vīpĕra ae, f (perhaps for vivipara, from vivus and pario, *bearing the young alive*) **I.** *a viper,* Plin ; prov , in sinu atque deliciis viperam illam venenatam et pestiferam habere, *to nourish a snake in one's bosom,* Cic , as a word of abuse, *viper,* Juv **II.** Transf , in general, *a snake, serpent, adder,* Verg

vīpĕrĕus a um (vipera) **I.** *of a viper* or *a snake,* dentes, Ov , anima, *poisonous breath,* Verg **II.** *having snakes,* monstrum, *the snaky-haired Medusa head,* Ov ; canis, *Cerberus,* Ov , sorores, *the Furies, with snakes on their heads,* Ov

vīpĕrīnus -a -um (vipera), *of* or *relating to a viper* or *snake,* sanguis, Hor

vipĭo -ōnis, m *a kind of small crane,* Plin

vĭr, viri, m *a man, male person* **I.** Gen , de viro factus femina, Ov. **II.** Esp , **A.** *a full-grown man, a man of mature age* (opp puer), Ov **B.** *a husband,* in viro suo Socrate, Cic , transf , of animals, vir gregis ipse caper, Verg **C.** Emphat., *a man of character, courage, spirit,* tulit dolorem ut vir, Cic. **D.** Milit. t. t. = *soldier*, gen. plur., *soldiers*, or opp. to cavalry = *foot-soldiers*; equites virique, Liv. **E.** Used for is or ille, auctoritas viri moverat, Liv. **F.** *a single man, an individual*; in such a phrase as vir virum legit, *each singles out his opponent*, Verg. **G.** Plur., viri, poet. transf. = homines, *men, mortals*, as opp. to gods. **H.** Meton., *virility*, Cat. (genit. plur., often virûm).

vĭrāgo -ĭnis, f. (virgo), *a man-like woman, female warrior, heroine*; of Pallas, bello metuenda virago, Ov.; Juturna virago, Verg.

Virbĭus -ĭi, m. (said to be from vir and bis), *the name of Hippolytus after he was restored to life*; also *of his son*, Verg.

vĭrectum (vĭrētum) -i, n. (* virex from vireo), *greensward, turf*; plur., virecta nemorum, *glades*, Verg.

vĭrens, p. adj. (from vireo). **I.** *green*; agellus, Hor. **II.** Fig., *blooming, youthful*; puella, Hor.

1. **vĭrĕo**, 2. *to be green*. **I.** Lit., arbores et vita virent, Cic. **II.** Fig., *to be blooming, vigorous, healthy, fresh, youthful*; virebat integris sensibus, Liv.

2. **vĭrĕo** -ōnis, m. *a kind of bird*, perhaps *the green-finch*, Plin.

vīres -ium, f., v. vis.

vĭresco, 3. (inchoat. of vireo), *to grow green, become green*; injussa virescunt gramina, Verg.

vĭrētum = virectum (q.v.).

virga -ae, f. (vireo). **I.** *a thin green twig, bough*; turea, Verg.; viscata, *a limed twig*, Ov. **II.** Meton., **A. 1,** *a slip for planting*, Ov.; **2,** *a rod for inflicting stripes*, Plaut.; esp., plur., virgae, *the rods of which the lictors' fasces were formed*; aliquem virgis caedere, Cic.; sing. collect., *for the fasces*, Ov.; **3,** *a broom*, Ov.; **4,** *a magic wand*; esp. of Mercury, Ov., Verg. **B.** Of things resembling a rod or twig, **1,** virgae, *the stalks of the flax plant*, Plin.; **2,** *a streak, stripe of colour on clothes*; purpureis tingit sua corpora virgis, Ov.

virgātor -ōris, m. (virga), *one who beats with rods*, Plaut.

virgātus -a -um (virga), **1,** *made of twigs* or *osiers*, Cat.; **2,** *striped*; sagula, Verg.

virgētum -i, n. (virga), *an osier-bed, thicket of brushwood*, Cic.

virgĕus -a -um (virga), *made of twigs* or *rods*; flamma, *of burning twigs*, Verg.

virgīdēmĭa -ae, f. (formed in jest from analogy with vindemia), *a rod-harvest*, i.e., *a good beating*, Plaut.

Virgĭlĭus = Vergilius (q.v.).

virgĭnālis -e (virgo), *of* or *belonging to a virgin, maidenly*; habitus, vestitus, Cic.

virgĭnārĭus = virginalis (q.v.).

virgĭnĕus -a -um (virgo), *of* or *belonging to a virgin, maidenly*; favilla, *ashes of a dead maiden*, Ov.; rubor, Verg.; aqua or liquor, *the stream Virgo*, v. Virgo, Ov.

virgĭnĭtas -ātis, f. (virgo), *virginity*, Cic.

Virgĭnĭus = Verginius (q.v.).

virgo -ĭnis, f. (root VARG, whence ὀργή). **I.** *a maiden, virgin*; **1,** lit., Cic.; Saturnia, *Vesta*, Ov.; Phoebea, *the laurel-tree into which Daphne was turned*, Ov.; virgo = *Astraea*, Verg.; dea, *Diana*, Ov.; virginis aequor, *the Hellespont*, Ov.; virgo vestalis or simply virgo, Cic.; **2,** transf., of animals, Plin.; **3,** meton., **a,** *the constellation Virgo*, Cic. poet.; **b,** Aqua Virgo, or simply Virgo, *a stream of water brought to Rome in an aqueduct by M. Agrippa, the source of which was said to have been discovered by a maiden*. **II.** *a young woman*; **a,** *unmarried*, Ov.; **b,** *married, a young wife*, Verg.

virgŭla -ae, f. (dim. of virga). **I.** *a little twig, a little bough*, Nep. **II.** Meton., *a rod, staff*; **1,** gen., virgulā stantem circumscribere, Cic.; **2,** esp., **a,** virga divina, *a magic staff*, Cic.; **b,** censoria, *a critical mark that the passage marked is not genuine*, Quint.

virgŭlātus -a -um (virgula), *striped*, Plin.

virgultum -i, n. (for virguletum from virgula). **I.** *a thicket, copse, brushwood*; gen. plur., Liv., Caes. **II.** *a slip for planting*, Lucr., Verg.

virguncŭla -ae, f. (dim. of virgo), *a young virgin, little girl*, Sen.

vĭrĭae -ārum, f. (vir), *armlets, bracelets*, Plin.

Vĭrĭāthus (Vĭrĭātus) -i, m. *a brave Lusitanian, who commanded his countrymen in their war against the Romans.*

vĭrĭdārĭum (vĭrĭdĭārĭum) -ĭi, n. (viridis), *a pleasure-garden*; plur., viridaria, Cic.

vĭrĭdĭcātus -a -um (viridis), *made green, green*, Cic. (?)

vĭrĭdis -e (vireo), *green* (in all its shades), *grass-green, pea-green, sea-green*. **I.** Lit., **A.** Adj., ripa, Cic.; Venafrum, *rich in olive-trees*, Hor.; esp., of the colour of the sea, or of water, or of what is found in it, of the nymphs, etc.; Mincius, Verg.; comae Nereidum, Ov. **B.** Subst., **vĭrĭde** -is, n. **1,** *green, the colour green*, Plin.; **2,** *a green growth, the green of grass* or *trees*; esp., of young corn, Liv.; plur., **vĭrĭdĭa** -ium, n. *green trees* or *herbs*, Sen. **II.** Transf., of age, *fresh, young, blooming, vigorous*; juventa, Verg.

vĭrĭdĭtas -ātis, f. (viridis). **I.** *greenness*; pratorum, Cic. **II.** Fig., *the freshness, bloom of youth*; senectus aufert viriditatem, Cic.

vĭrĭdo, 1. (viridis). **I.** Intransit., *to be green*; partic., viridans, *green*; laurus, Verg. **II.** Transit., *to make green*; hence, viridari, *to become green*, Ov.

Vĭrĭdŏmărus (Vĭrdŏmărus) -i, m. *a Gallic name*; **a.** *a leader of the Aedui*, Caes.; **b,** *a commander of the Insubres, killed by M. Claudius Marcellus*, 222 B.C.

vĭrīlis -e (vir), *manly, male, virile*. **I.** In relation to sex; **1, a,** stirps, Liv.; secus, *male sex*, Liv.; **b,** in grammar, *masculine*, Varr.; **2,** of age, *adult*; toga, *assumed by the Roman youths in their fifteenth* or *sixteenth year*, Cic.; **3,** in relation to the person, pars virilis, *part, lot, share, duty*; est aliqua pars mea virilis, Cic.; pro virili parte, *to the utmost of one's ability*, Liv., Cic. **II.** *manly, courageous, spirited, vigorous, bold*; animus, Cic.; ingenium, Sall.

vĭrīlĭtas -ātis, f. (virilis), *manly age, manhood*; **1,** lit., Tac.; **2,** meton., *virility*, Tac.

vĭrīlĭtĕr, adv. (virilis), *manfully, courageously, vigorously*; aegrotare, Cic.; facere, Hor.

vĭrĭŏlae -ārum, f. (dim. of viriae), *a small armlet, bracelet*, Plin.

vīrĭpŏtens -entis (vires and potens), *mighty* (epithet of Jupiter), Plaut.

vĭrītim, adv. (vir). **I.** *man by man, individually*; agros viritim dividere civibus, Cic. **II.** Transf., *singly, separately, especially*; viritim commonefacere beneficii sui, Sall.

Vīromandŭi (Vēromandi) -ōrum, m. *a people in Gallia Belgica, east of the Atrebates, south of the Nervii.*

vīrōsus -a -um (virus), *stinking, fetid*; castorea, Verg.

virtus -ūtis, f (vir), *manly excellence* I. A. Gen. 1, lit, *excellence, capacity, worth, virtue*, animi corporis, Cic , 2, transf, of animals, inanimate or abstract things, *characteristic excellence, goodness, worth, excellence*, equi, Cic herbarum, Ov., oratoriae virtutes Cic B. Esp , 1, *moral excellence, virtue*, honesta in virtute ponitur, Cic , 2, *valour, bravery, courage*, Cic, Caes, Liv , rei militaris, Cic , bellandi, Cic , plur , virtutes, *deeds of bravery*, Tac , 3, *courage, resolution in difficulties*, nisi virtute et animo restitissem, Cic.

vīrus -i, n I. *a slimy liquid, slime*, Verg II. A *poison*, of snakes, Lucr, Verg , fig, aliquis apud quem evomat virus acerbitatis suae, Cic B. *a harsh, bitter taste*, tetrum, of salt water, Lucr

vis (genit sing , vis rare), acc vim, abl vi, plur , **vires** -ium, f *force, power, strength* I. A. Lit , 1, a, sing , celeritas et vis equorum, Cic , fluminis, Caes , b, plur , vires, usually applied to physical strength, vires nervique, sanguis viresque, Cic , 2, esp , *hostile force, violence*, cum vi vis allata defenditur, Cic , alicui vim afferre, Cic , per vim *by force*, Caes B. Meton , 1, *a large number or quantity* magna vis auri argentique, Cic , 2, plur , vires, *troops, forces*, satis virium ad certamen, Liv II. Transf , 1, gen , *intellectual and moral strength, might, power, influence*, vis illa divina et virtus orationis, Cic , 2, esp , *force, nature, meaning, essence*, a, in quo est omnis vis amicitiae Cic b, esp , *the meaning of a word*, verbi, nominis, Cic

viscātus -a -um (viscum), *smeared with bird-lime*, virga, Ov

viscĕra, v viscus

viscĕrātio ōnis, f (viscera), *a public distribution of meat to the people*, Cic

visco, 1 (viscum), *to make sticky*, Juv

viscum i, n (ἰξός) I. *mistletoe*, Verg II. Meton , *bird lime*, Cic

viscus ĕris, n usually plur **viscĕra** -um, n *the inside of the body, entrails, viscera* I. A. Lit., haerentia viscere tela, Ov B. Transf , *the flesh*, e visceribus sanguis exeat, Cic II. Meton , plur , a, of persons, *flesh and blood, one's own flesh = one's own child or children*, diripiunt avidae viscera nostra ferae, Ov , b, of things, (α) *the inmost part of anything*, viscera montis, Verg , reipublicae, Cic , (β) *heart blood = wealth, means*, aerarii, Cic

visendus -a um, p adj (from viso) *worthy to be seen*, ornatus, Cic , subst , **visenda** -ōrum, n *things worth seeing*, Liv

visio -ōnis, f (video), *a seeing, view* I. Lit , eamque esse dei visionem, ut similitudine cernatur, Cic II. Meton , a, *an appearance*, adventicia, Cic , b, *a notion, idea*, doloris, Cic , veri et falsi, Cic

visito, 1 (intens of viso) I. *to see often*, Plaut. II. *to visit*, aliquem, Cic

viso -si -sum, 3 (intens of video), *to look at carefully, behold attentively, contemplate* I. Lit , agros, Liv , visendi causā venire, Cic II. Transf , A. Gen *to come to see, go to see, look to, see after*, aedem Minervae, Plaut , si domi est, Ter B. Esp , a, *to visit, call upon*, esp , a sick person, ut viderem te et viserem, Cic , b, *to visit a place*, Thespias, Cic , domum alicuius, Cic

visulla -ae, f *a kind of vine*, Plin

visum -i, n (video) *that which is seen, an appearance, vision* I. Gen , Prop II. Esp , A. *an appearance in a dream, a dream*, visa somniorum, Cic. B. As translation of Gr. φαντασία of the Stoics, *an image of an external object received through the senses*, Cic.

Visurgis -is, m *a river in North Germany, the Weser*

visus -ūs, m (video) I. *a seeing, sight, vision, look*, visu nocere, Cic , obire omnia visu Verg , plur , visus effugiet tuos, Ov II. Meton , *a sight, appearance*, hoc visu laetus, Liv , of abstractions, visum habere quendam insignem et illustrem, Cic

vita ae, f (vivo), *life* I. a, Lit , in vita esse, *to live*, Cic , vitam amittere, Cic , vitam profundere pro aliquo, Cic , vitam miserrimam degere, Cic , vitam alicui adimere or auferre, Cic , deum vitam accipere, Verg in vita, *during my whole life*, Cic plur , semper per omnium vitas amicitia, Cic , b, transf , of trees, etc , *life, duration*, Plin II. Meton , 1, *life, way of living*, rustica, Cic , 2, *life = biography*, Nep , 3, *life*, as a term of endearment, mea vita, Cic ; 4, *a soul, shade in the lower world*, tenues sine corpore vitae, Verg , 5, *men living, the world*, Tib

vītābilis e (vito), *that may or ought to be shunned*, Ov

vītābundus -a -um (vito), *trying to avoid, avoiding shunning*, vitabundus erumpit, Sall , with acc , vitabundus castra hostium, Liv

vītālis e (vita), *of or relating to life, vital*, Cic , viae, *the windpipe* Ov , subst **vītālia** -ium, n *vital parts*, Plin

vītālitas -ātis, f (vitalis), *life, vitality*, Plin

vītālĭtĕr, adv (vitalis), *vitally*, Lucr

vītātio -ōnis, f (vito), *an avoiding, shunning*, oculorum, lucis, urbis, fori, Cic , doloris, Cic

Vitellia -ae, f *a town of the Aequi in Latium, now Civitella*

Vitellius ii, m , Aulus, *the Roman emperor who succeeded Otho, notorious for his gluttony and idleness* Hence, A. **Vitellius** -a um, *belonging to Vitellius* B. **Vitelliānus** -a um, *Vitellian*

vitellus -i, m (dim of vitulus) I. *a little calf*, as a term of endearment, Plaut II. *the yolk of an egg*, Cic

vitĕus a um (vitis), *of or relating to a vine*, pocula, *wine*, Verg

vitiārium -ii, n (vitis), *a nursery of young vines*, Var

vitiātio -ōnis f (vitio), *a defiling, ravishing*, Sen

vitiātor ōris, m (vitio), *a violator, ravisher*, Sen

viticula -ae, f (dim of vitis), *a little vine*, Cic

vitifer -fĕra fĕrum (vitis and fero), *vine bearing*, Plin

vitigĕnus -a um (vitis and gigno), *produced from the vine*, liquor, Lucr

vitiginĕus a um (vitis) *of or relating to the vine*, Plin

vitiligo ĭnis, f (vitium), *a kind of cutaneous eruption*, Plin

vitilis e (vieo), *plaited, intertwined*, Plin Subst , **vitilia** -ium, n *wicker-work*, Plin

vitio, 1 (vitium), *to injure, damage, corrupt, spoil, mar, vitiate* I. Lit , a, vitiatus aper, *high*, Hor , omnem salibus amaris, Ov , b, esp , *to defile, debauch a maiden*, Ter II. Transf , A. Gen , *to forge, falsify*, senatus consulta, Liv , comitiorum et contionum significationes, Cic B. Esp religious t.t , vitiare diem, *to declare a day unfit for the holding of the census*, Cic

vĭtĭōsē, adv. (vitiosus), *faulty, defective.* **I.** Lit., vitiose se habere, Cic. **II.** Transf., **A.** *perversely, wrongly;* illud vero idem Caecilius vitiosius, Cic. **B.** Esp., *against the auguries;* ferre leges, Cic.

vĭtĭōsĭtas -ātis, f. (vitiosus), *viciousness, wickedness*, Cic.

vĭtĭōsus -a -um (vitium), *faulty, defective, corrupt, bad.* **I.** Lit., Varr.; in fig., vitiosas partes (*unsound limbs*) reipublicae exsecare, sanare, Cic. **II.** Transf., **A.** *defective, faulty, wrong;* suffragium, Cic.; lex, Cic.; vitiosissimus orator, Cic. **B.** Esp., **1,** *defective* = against the auguries, Cic.; consul, dictator, *elected informally*, Cic., Liv.; **2,** *morally corrupt, wicked;* non sunt vitiosiores, quam plerique qui, etc., Cic.; vitiosa et flagitiosa vita, Cic.

vītis -is, f. **I.** *a vine;* **1,** lit., Cic.; **2,** meton., *the centurion's staff, made of a vine-branch*, Tac.; meton., *the post of centurion*, Juv. **II.** Transf., vitis alba, *a plant, also called* ampeloleuce, Ov.

vītĭsător -ōris, m. (vitis and sator), *one who plants vines*, Verg.

vĭtĭum -ii, n. *a fault, defect, blemish, imperfection.* **I.** Lit., **a,** corporis, Cic.; si nihil est in parietibus aut in tecto vitii, Cic.; **b,** *dross*, in metal; ignis vitium metallis excoquit, Ov. **II.** Transf., **A.** Gen., *a fault, imperfection, defect;* adversum vitium castrorum, *defective position*, Cic.; vitia in dicente acutius quam recta videre, Cic.; omnia fere vitia vitare, Cic. **B.** Esp., **1,** religious t.t., *a defect in the auguries;* tabernaculum vitio (*against the auguries*) captum, Cic.; **2, a,** *a moral fault, crime, vice;* vitium fugere, Hor.; nullum ob totius vitae non dicam vitium, sed erratum, Cic.; in vitio esse, *to deserve blame*, Cic.; or of persons, *to be to blame*, Cic.; **b,** *a defiling, debauching a woman*, Plaut.

vīto, 1. *to avoid, shun.* **I.** Lit., tela, Caes.; hastas, Ov.; aspectum or oculos hominum, Cic. **II.** Fig., **A. a,** with acc., stultitiam, Cic.; suspiciones, Caes.; **b,** with ne and the subj., vitandum est oratori utrumque, ne aut scurrilis jocus sit aut mimicus, Cic.; **c,** with the infin., tangere vitet scripta, Hor. **B.** *to escape;* casum Cic.; fugā mortem, Caes.

vĭtrĕus -a -um (vitrum), *made of glass.* **I. A.** Lit., hostis, *a glass draughtsman*, Ov. **B.** Meton., *like glass, glassy, transparent, glittering;* unda, Verg.; ros, Ov.; Circe, Hor. **II.** Fig., fama, *glittering*, Hor.

vĭtrĭcus -i, m. *a stepfather*, Cic.

vĭtrum -i, n. **I.** *glass;* merces in chartis et linteis et vitro delatae, Cic. **II.** *woad, a plant producing a blue dye*, Caes.

Vitrūvĭus -ii, m., M. Vitruvius Pollio, of Verona, *whose work*, De Architectura Libri X, *composed probably about* 14 B.C., *we still possess.*

vitta -ae, f. *a ribbon, band, fillet;* **1,** *as a binding for the head;* **a,** for sacrificial victims, Verg.; **b,** of priests and priestesses, Verg.; **c,** of free-born women, Ov.; **2,** *a band round the altar*, Verg.; **3,** *the fillets round the branches carried by suppliants*, Verg.

vittātus -a -um (vitta), *decorated with a fillet;* capilli, Ov.

vĭtŭla -ae, f. (vitulus), *a calf, heifer*, Verg.

vĭtŭlīnus -a -um (vitulus), *of or relating to a calf;* caruncula, Cic.; assum, *roast veal*, Cic. Subst., **vĭtŭlīna** -ae, f. *veal*, Plaut.

vĭtŭlor, 1. dep. *to celebrate a festival, be joyful*, Plaut.

vĭtŭlus -i, m. (ἰταλός). **I.** *a bull-calf*, Cic. **II.** Applied to the young of other animals, e.g., of a horse, Verg.; vitulus marinus, or simply vitulus, *a sea-calf*, Plin.

vĭtŭpĕrābĭlis -e (vitupero), *blamable*, Cic.

vĭtŭpĕrātĭo -ōnis, f. (vitupero), *a blaming, scolding, vituperation;* in vituperationem venire, or adduci, or cadere, or subire vituperationem, Cic.; meton., *that which is blamable, blamable conduct*, Cic.

vĭtŭpĕrātor -ōris, m. (vitupero), *a blamer, vituperator;* mei, Cic.; philosophiae, Cic.

vĭtŭpĕro, 1. (vitium and paro), *to blame, scold, censure, vituperate;* consilium, Cic.; aliquem, Cic.

vīvācĭtas -ātis, f. (vivax), *length of life, longevity*, Plin.

vīvārĭum -ii, n. (vivus), *a place where living animals are kept, a park, warren, preserve, a fish-pond*, Plin.; fig., excipiant senes, quos in vivaria mittant, *allure by presents*, Hor.

vīvātus -a -um (vivus), *lively, vivid*, Lucr.

vīvax -ācis (vivo). **I. a,** *long-lived;* phoenix, Ov.; **b,** *lasting, enduring;* oliva, Verg. **II. a,** *lively, vigorous;* sulfura, *inflammable*, Ov.; **b,** *brisk, vivacious*, Quint.

viverra -ae, f. *a ferret*, Plin.

vīvesco (vīvisco), vixi, 3. (vivo). **I.** *to begin to live*, Plin. **II.** *to be lively, vigorous*, Lucr.

vīvĭdus -a -um (vivo). **I.** *showing signs of life, animated;* **a,** lit., gemma, Ov.; **b,** transf., of pictures and statues, *life-like, true to life;* signa, Prop. **II.** *full of life, lively, vigorous;* senectus, Tac.; virtus, Verg.

vīvĭrādix -īcis, f. (vivus and radix), *a cutting which has a root, a layer*, Cic.

vivisco = vivesco (q.v.).

vīvo, vixi, victum, 3. (βιόω), *to live, be alive.* **I.** Lit., **A.** Gen., **a,** of persons, ad summam senectutem, Cic.; annum, *a year*, Ov.; with cognate acc., vitam tutiorem, Cic.; vivere de lucro, *to owe one's life to the favour of another*, Cic.; si vivo, or si vivam, *if I live* (in threats), Ter.; ita vivam, *as true as I live*, Cic.; ne vivam, *may I die if*, etc., Cic.; **b,** transf., (α) of plants, *to live*, vivit vitis, Cic.; (β) of fire, *to burn;* cinis vivet, Ov. **B. 1,** *to live = to enjoy life;* vivamus, mea Lesbia, Cat.; quando vivemus, *have leisure*, Cic.; so vive, vivite, in saying good-bye, *farewell*, Hor., Verg.; **2,** *to last, continue;* vivunt scripta, Ov.; eius mihi vivit auctoritas, Cic. **II.** Meton., **1, a,** *to live on anything;* lacte atque pecore, Caes.; **b,** *to pass one's life, live;* vivere cum timore, Cic.; in litteris, Cic.; in paupertate, Cic.; with double nom., vivo miserrimus, Cic.; **2,** *to live with some one or at some place;* **a,** *to live, to find oneself, to stay;* vixit Syracusis, Cic.; **b,** *to live with some one, to live in the company of;* cum aliquo valde familiariter, Cic.

vīvus -a -um (vivo), *alive, living.* **I.** Adj., **A.** Lit., aliquem vivum capere, Liv.; patrem et filium vivos comburere, Cic.; frangetis impetum vivi, *while he is alive*, Cic. **B.** Transf., **1,** *living, belonging to a living person;* vox, Cic.; calor, Ov.; **2,** *seeming to live, true to life, life-like;* vivos ducent de marmore vultus, Verg.; **3,** of plants, *living;* arundo, Ov.; **4,** *living, lasting, natural, lively;* flumen, *running water*, Verg., Liv.; lucerna, *burning*, Hor.; ros, *fresh*, Ov.; sulfur, *natural*, Liv. **II.** Subst., **vivum** -i, n. *that which is alive, the flesh with life and feeling;* calor ad vivum adveniens, Liv.; neque id ad vivum reseco, *cut to the quick*, i.e., *not take it in too literal a sense*, Cic.; de vivo detrahere (resecare), *to take away from the capital*, Cic.

vix, adv (connected with vis as Gr $\mu o \gamma \iota s$ with $\mu \acute{o} \gamma o s$, thus orig *with effort*) **I.** Gen, *with effort, scarcely*, vix teneor quin accurram, Cic **II.** Esp **a,** with quum or (poet) et, and (poet) without quum, *scarcely . . . when*, vix erat hoc plane imperatum, quum illum spoliatum stipatumque lictoribus videres, Cic, vix in opina quies laxaverat artus, et, etc, Verg, **b,** without quum or et, vix prora attigerat, rumpit Saturnia funem, Verg, **c,** strengthened with dum, gen, vixdum (in one word), *hardly, yet*, vixdum coetu nostro dimisso, Cic, **d,** strengthened by tandem, *only just*, vix tandem legi literas, Cic

vixdum, v vix, II c

vŏcābŭlum i, n (voco), *the name, appellation of anything* **I.** Lit, **a,** res suum nomen et proprium vocabulum non habet, Cic, **b,** *a name peculiar to any person or thing*, cui (oppido) nomen inditum e vocabulo ipsius, Tac **c,** grammat t t, *a noun substantive*, Varr **II.** *a pretext*, Tac

vōcālis -e (vox), *uttering sounds, vocal, resounding, singing* **I.** Adj, carmen, Ov, Orpheus, Hor, ne quem vocalem praeteriisse videamur, *any one with a good voice*, Cic **II.** Subst, **vōcālis** is, f (sc littera), *a vowel*, Cic

vōcālitas ātis, f (vocalis), *harmony, euphony*, Quint

vŏcāmen -ĭnis, n (voco), *a name, appellation*, Lucr

Vŏcātes -ium, m *a people in Aquitanian Gaul, now Bazadois*

vŏcātĭo -ōnis, f (voco), 1, *a summoning before a court of law*, Varr, **2,** *an invitation to dinner*, Cat

vŏcātor -ōris, m (voco), *an inviter*, Plin

vŏcātus -ūs, m (voco) **I.** *a calling, summoning, invocation*, plur, vocatus mei, Verg **II.** *an inviting, invitation*, e g, to a sitting of the senate, Cic

vōcĭfĕrātĭo -ōnis, f (vociferor), *a loud shouting, vociferation*, Cic

vōcĭfĕrātus -ūs, m = vociferatio (q v)

vōcĭfĕro, 1 = vociferor, pass impers, vociferatum fortiter, Liv

vōcĭfĕror, 1 dep (vox and fero), *to cry loudly, shout, vociferate*, palam, Cic, talia, Verg, with acc and infin, quod vociferabare decem milia talentûm Gabinio esse promissa, Cic, with interrog sent, vociferari Decius, quo fugerent, Liv, with de and the abl, de superbia patrum, Liv

vōcĭfĭco, 1 (vox and facio), *to shout aloud*, Varr

vŏcĭto, 1 (intens of voco) **I.** *to be accustomed to name, to be wont to call*, has Graeci stellas Hyadas vocitare suerunt, Cic **II.** *to shout loudly*, Tac

vŏco, 1 (vox), *to call, summon* **I.** Lit, **A.** Gen, **1,** Dumnorigem ad se, Caes, aliquem in contionem, Cic, **2,** *to call upon, invoke*, deos, Hor **B.** Esp, **1,** *to summon before a court of law*, aliquem in jus, Cic, **2,** *to invite to dinner*, etc, ad cenam, Cic, **3,** *to call forth, to provoke*, hostem, Verg, Tac, **4,** *to call, name, designate*, aliquid alio nomine, Cic, patrioque vocat de nomine mensem, Ov **II.** Transf, *to bring, put, place in any state or condition*, ne me apud milites in invidiam voces, Cic, ad calculos amicitiam, Cic, in dubium, *to call in question*, Cic, aliquem in partem, Cic

Vŏcontĭi ōrum, m *a people in Gallia Narbonensis, on the left bank of the Rhone*

vōcŭla -ae, f (dim of vox) **I.** *a low, weak voice*, Cic **II.** Transf, **1,** *a low tone in singing or speaking*, falsae voculae, Cic, **2,** contemptuously, *a little petty speech*, incurrere in voculas malevolorum, Cic, *a petty speech*, Cic

vŏla ae, f *the hollow of the hand or foot*, Plin

vŏlaema, v volemum

Vŏlăterrae ārum f *an old town in Etruria, now Volterra* Hence, **Vŏlăterrānus** -a -um, *of Volaterrae*, Vada, *a port in the district of Volaterrae, now Torre di Vado*, plur subst, **Vŏlăterrāni** -ōrum, m *the inhabitants of Volaterrae*

vŏlātĭcus -a -um (2 volo) **I** *having wings, winged*, **a,** *flying*, Plaut, **b,** *flying here and there*, illius furentes ac volatici impetus, Cic **II.** Fig, *fleeting, flighty, inconstant*, Academia, Cic

vŏlātĭlis -e (2 volo) **I.** *having wings, winged*, bestiae, Cic, puer, *Cupid*, Ov **II.** Transf, **1,** *swift, rapid*, ferrum, Verg, **2,** *fleeting, transitory*, aetas, Ov

vŏlātūra ae, f (2 volo), *a flight*, Varr

vŏlātus -ūs, m (2 volo), *a flying, flight*, Cic

Volcae -ārum, m *a people in Gallia Narbonensis*

vŏlēmum pirum, gen plur, volema pira, *a kind of pears, large enough to fill the hollow of the hand (vola)*, Verg

vŏlens entis, p adj (from 1 volo) **I.** *willing, voluntary*, Sall, Verg **II** *favourable, inclined to*, Liv, Sall, dis volentibus, *by the help of the gods*, Sall, volentia alicui, *favourable tidings or events*, Sall

volgiŏlus -i, m *a garden tool for smoothing beds*, Plin

volgo, volgus = vulgo, vulgus (q v)

vŏlĭto, 1 (intens of volo) **I.** *to fly about, to fly to and fro, to flit, to flutter* **A.** Lit, **a,** of birds, Cic, Liv, **b,** of things, hic aliae (stellae) volitant, Cic **B.** Fig, *to fly round*, **a,** of the soul, Cic, **b,** of men with immoderate wishes, *to soar*, homo volitans gloriae cupiditate, Cic **II.** Transf, *to fly round about, hasten about*, **1,** lit., cum gladiis toto foro, Cic, **2,** fig, *to show oneself or itself*, quum illa conjuratio palam volitaret, Cic

volnĕro = vulnero (q v)

1 **vŏlo,** vŏlŭi, velle (root VOL, Gr ΒΟΛ, whence $\beta o \upsilon \lambda o \mu \alpha \iota$), *to be willing, to wish* **I.** Gen, **1,** **a,** with acc and infin, volui id quidem efficere, Cic, volo scire, velim scire, *I should like to know*, Cic, **b,** with acc and infin, judicem me esse, non doctorem volo, Cic, **c,** with nom and infin, Ov, **d,** with neut acc, faciam, quod vultis, Cic, num quid vellet, Liv, **e,** with ut and the subj, volo, uti respondeas, Cic, **f,** with the subj alone, visne hoc primum videamus? Cic, **g,** absol, velit nolit scire difficile est, *whether he wishes or does not*, Cic, si vis, and contracted sis, sultis, parenthet, refer animum, sis, ad veritatem, Cic **2,** velle aliquem, *to wish to speak with*, centuriones trium cohortium me velle postridie, Cic **3,** bene (male) alicui, *to wish well or ill to*, Plaut, **4,** aliquid alicuius causā, *to wish something good to some one*, valde eius causā volo, Cic, **5,** quid sibi vult (res), *what is the meaning of*, quid ergo illae sibi statuae equestres inauratae volunt Cic **II.** **1,** Polit t t, *to will, choose, ordain* majores de singulis magistratibus bis vos sententiam ferre voluerunt, Cic, **2,** *to think, be of opinion, mean*, vultis omnia evenire fato, Cic, **3,** foll by quam (like Gr $\beta o \upsilon \lambda o \mu \alpha \iota\ \ddot{\eta}$, *to prefer*), malae rei se quam nullius, turbarum ac seditionum duces esse volunt, Liv (contr, vin = visne, sis = si vis, sultis = si vultis)

2. **vŏlo**, 1. *to fly.* **I.** Lit., Cic.; partic. subst., volantes -ium, f. (sc. bestiae), *flying creatures, birds*, Verg. **II.** Transf., *to move rapidly, to fly*; currus, Verg.; fulmina, Lucr.; aetas, Cic.

3. **vŏlo** -ōnis, m. (1. volo), *a volunteer*; plur., volones, *the slaves who were bought at the public expense to serve as soldiers after the battle of Cannae, each of them being asked* "velletne militare," Liv.

Volsci (Vulsci) -ōrum, m. *a people in Latium, on both banks of the Liris, in modern Campagna di Roma and Terra di Lavoro.* Hence, **Volscus** -a -um, *Volscian.*

volsella -ae, f. *a pair of tweezers or pincers*, Mart.

Volsĭnĭi (Vulsĭnii) -ōrum, m. *a town in Etruria*, now *Bolsena.* Hence, **Volsĭnĭensis** -e, *Volsinian*; plur. subst., **Volsĭnienses** -ium, m. *the Volsinians.*

volsus -a -um, v. vello.

Voltĭnĭus -a -um, *Voltinian*; tribus, *a Roman tribe.* Hence, **Voltĭnĭenses** -ium, m. *citizens of the Voltinian tribe.*

Voltumna -ae, f. *the goddess of the twelve allied Etruscan states.*

voltur = vultur (q.v.).

Volturnus = Vulturnus (q.v.).

voltus = vultus (q.v.).

vŏlūbĭlis -e (volvo), *rolling, revolving, turning round, twisting round.* **I.** Lit., buxum, *a top*, Verg.; caelum, Cic. **II.** Fig., **a,** of fortuna, *changeable, inconstant*; fortuna, Cic.; **b,** of discourse, *rapid, fluent*: Appii Claudii volubilis erat oratio, Cic.

vŏlūbĭlĭtas -ātis, f. (volubilis), *revolving motion, revolution.* **I.** Lit., mundi, Cic. **II.** Fig., **a,** *vicissitude, inconstancy*; fortunae, Cic.; **b,** *flow of discourse, fluency*; verborum, Cic.; linguae, Cic.

vŏlūbĭlĭtĕr, adv. (volubilis), *fluently*; funditur numerose et volubiliter oratio, Cic.

vŏlŭcer, vŏlŭcris, vŏlŭcre (2. volo), *flying, winged.* **I. A.** Lit., **1,** adj., angues, Cic.; deus or puer, *Cupid*, Ov.; bestiae volucres, *birds*, Cic.; **2,** subst., **vŏlŭcris** -is, f. (sc. bestia), *a bird*, Cic. **B.** Transf., applied to an object in rapid motion, *swift*; lumen, Lucr.; fumi, Verg.; sagitta, Verg.; nuntius, Cic. **II.** Fig., **1,** gen., *quick, fleet*: nihil est tam volucre quam maledictum, Cic.; **2,** *fleeting, transitory*; fortuna, Cic. (genit. plur., gen. volŭcrum).

vŏlūcra -ae, f. and **vŏlūcre** -is, n. (volvo), *a caterpillar found on vine-leaves*, Plin.

vŏlŭcris -is, f., v. volucer.

vŏlūmen -ĭnis, n. (volvo), *anything rolled up.* **I. 1,** *a book, roll, writing*; volumen plenum querelae, Cic.; plur., volumina selectarum epistolarum, Cic.; **2,** esp., *a part of a larger work, a book*, Nep.; mutatae ter quinque volumina formae, *the fifteen books of the* Metamorphoses, Ov. **II.** *a roll, wreath, whirl, fold*; anguis sinuat immensa volumine terga, Verg.

vŏluntārĭus -a -um (voluntas), *voluntary.* **A.** Subject., *a person who does something of his own accord*; procurator, Cic.; auxilia sociorum, Cic.; milites, *volunteers*, Caes.; plur. subst., **vŏluntārĭi** -ōrum, m. *volunteers*, Caes. **B.** Object., *that which happens of one's own free will*; mors, *suicide*, Cic.; deditio, Liv.

vŏluntas -ātis, f. (1. volo), *will, wish, inclination.* **I.** Lit., **A.** Gen., **1,** me conformo ad eius voluntatem, Cic.; **2,** *free will*; ego voluntatem tibi profecto emetiar, Cic.; voluntate, *of one's own free will*; meā voluntate concedam, *willingly*, Cic.; **3,** *good disposition*; confisus municipiorum voluntatibus, Caes.; **4,** *desire, wish*; ambitiosis voluntatibus cedere, Cic.; **5,** *aim, purpose*; hanc mentem voluntatemque suscepi, Cic. **B. 1,** *inclination, wishing well to*; mutua, Cic.; **2,** *a last will, testament*; testamenta et voluntas mortuorum, Cic. **II.** Transf., *meaning, sense, signification of words*, Quint.

vŏlup, adv. (shortened from volupe, from 1. volo), *agreeably, delightfully, pleasantly*, Plaut.

vŏluptābĭlis -e (voluptas), *giving pleasure, pleasant*, Plaut.

vŏluptārĭus -a -um (voluptas), *relating to pleasure*, esp., *to sensual pleasure.* **I.** Act., **a,** *causing pleasure*; possessiones, *simply for pleasure*, Cic.; **b,** *relating to pleasure*; disputatio, Cic. **II.** Pass., **a,** *devoted or given to pleasure, sensual*; esp. of the Epicureans as opp. to the Stoics, homo (of Epicurus), Cic.; **b,** *capable of pleasure*; gustatus est sensus ex omnibus maxime voluptarius, Cic.

vŏluptas -ātis, f. (volup), *pleasure, delight*, in a good or bad sense. **I.** Lit., voluptate capi, Cic.; alicui voluptati esse, Cic.; voluptatibus frui, Cic.; in a bad sense, voluptates corporis, *sensual pleasures*, Cic.; voluptate liquescere, Cic. **II.** Meton., **1,** voluptates, *public shows*, Cic.; **2,** of persons, as a term of endearment, care puer, mea sera et sola voluptas, Verg.; (genit. plur., gen. voluptatum, but also voluptatium).

vŏluptŭōsus -a -um (voluptas), *full of pleasure, delightful*, Quint.

vŏlūtābrum -i, n. (voluto), *a place where pigs roll, slough*, Verg.

vŏlūtābundus -a -um (voluto), *rolling, wallowing*; in voluptatibus, Cic.

vŏlūtātĭo -ōnis, f. (voluto). **I.** *a rolling about, wallowing*, Cic. **II.** Fig., **1,** *disquiet*; animi, Sen.; **2,** *vicissitude, inconstancy*; rerum humanarum, Sen.

vŏlūtātus -ūs, m. (voluto), *a wallowing*, Plin.

vŏlūto, 1. (intens. of volvo), *to roll round, tumble about.* **I.** Lit., se in pulvere, Plin.; ne fluxā habenā volutetur in jactu glans, Liv.; partic., volutans, reflex., *rolling oneself*; volutans pedibus, *throwing himself at the feet of*, etc., Verg. **II.** Fig., **1,** gen., middle, volutari, *to roll*, i.e., *to be in*; in omni genere flagitiorum, Cic., **2,** esp., **a,** *to spread abroad, give forth*; vocem per atria, Verg.; vocem volutant littora, *echo back*, Verg.; **b,** *to turn over in the mind, revolve, consider*; conditiones cum amicis, Liv.; nihil umquam nisi sempiternum et divinum animo, Cic.; **c,** *to busy, occupy*; animum saepe iis tacitis cogitationibus, Liv.; in veteribus scriptis studiose et multum volutatum esse, Cic.

volva -ae, f. (volvo). **I.** *a covering, husk, shell*, Plin. **II.** *the womb*, esp., *a sow's womb, a favourite delicacy among the Romans*, Hor.

volvo, volvi, vŏlūtum, 3. *to roll, revolve, turn round, twist round.* **I.** Lit., **A.** Gen., **a,** of living beings, molem, Verg.; oculos huc illuc, Verg.; pass., volvi, as middle, *to roll*; curru, *from a chariot*, Verg.; esp., *to roll to the ground*, of those fallen in battle, humi, arvis, Verg.; **b,** of things, such as rivers, saxa glareosa, Liv.; of the wind, ignem ad fastigia summa, Verg.; reflex., se volvere, or simply volvere, or middle, volvi, *to roll round, eddy, turn round*; ii qui volvuntur stellarum cursus sempiterni, Cic.; of tears, lacrimae volvuntur inanes, Verg. **B.** Esp., **1,** *to unroll a roll, to read*; libros Catonis, Cic.; **2,** *to roll along, roll away*; flumen pecus et domos volvens unā, Hor.; **3,** meton., orbem, *to form a circle* (of men), Liv. **II.** Fig., **A.** Gen., a, of orators whose words flow without stopping, celeriter verba, Cic , b, of time, *to make to roll round*, pronos volvere menses (of the moon-goddess), Hor , tot casus = *to experience*, Verg , middle, of time or of events, *to roll round*, ut idem in singulos annos orbis volveretur, Liv , partic volvens, reflex , *rolling round*, volvens annus, Ov , volventibus annis, *in the course of years*, Verg , c, *to fix or determine fate*, volvit vices (of Jupiter), Verg , sic volvere Parcas, Verg B. Esp , 1, a, *to toss about in the mind, to have, entertain*, ingentes jam diu iras eum in pectore volvere, Liv , b, *to busy oneself with a thought, reflect on, consider, ponder over*, bellum in animo, Liv , 2, = revolvere, *to go over again*, veterum monumenta virorum, Verg

vōmer -ĕris, m *a ploughshare*, Cic

vŏmĭca ae, f *an ulcer, sore, boil* I. Lit , Cic II. Fig , *a plague, curse* (of men), ap Liv

vōmis -ĕris, m = vomer (q v)

vŏmĭtĭo ōnis, f (vomo) I. *a vomiting, throwing up*, vomitione alvos curare, Cic II. Meton , *that which is thrown up, a vomit*, Plin

vŏmĭto, 1 (intens of vomo), *to vomit*, Sen

vŏmĭtor -ōris, m (vomo), *one who vomits*, Sen

vŏmĭtōrĭus -a -um (vomitor), *provoking vomiting*, Plin

vŏmĭtus -ūs, m (vomo) I. *a vomiting*, Plin II. Meton , *that which is vomited, a vomit*, Plin

vŏmo -ŭi -ĭtum, 3 (connected with ἐμέω) I. Intransit , *to vomit*, Cic II. Transit , *to vomit forth, throw up, give forth*, animam, Verg , flammas, Verg , pass impers , ab hora tertia bibebatur, ludebatur, vomebatur, Cic

vŏrācĭtas -ātis, f (vorax), *voracity, gluttony*, Plin

vŏrāgĭnōsus a -um (vorago), *full of chasms, pits*, Auct b Hisp

vŏrāgo ĭnis, f (voro), *a pit, chasm, abyss* I. Lit , in the earth, Liv , in water, *an abyss, eddy, gulf, whirlpool* summersus equus voraginibus Cic II. Transf , ventris Ov , gurges et vorago patrimonii, *spendthrift*, Cic.

vŏrax -ācis (voro), *gluttonous, voracious*, Charybdis, Cic , ignis voracior, Ov

vŏro, 1 (connected with βρόω, whence βιβρώσκω and βορά), *to eat greedily, swallow whole, devour, consume*. I. Lit , Cic II. Transf , A. Gen., *to devour, suck in*, Charybdis vorat carinas, Ov , illam (puppim = navem) rapidus vorat aequore vortex, Verg. B. Esp , 1, of property, *to squander, dissipate*, Plin , 2, *to read eagerly, devour*, litteras, *literature*, Cic

vors . . . v. vers . .

vort . v. vert

vōs, *ye*, v tu.

vōtīvus -a -um (votum), *of or relating to a vow, votive, vowed*, ludi, Cic , juvenca, Hor.

vōtum -i, n (voveo) I. *a vow* A. Gen , 1, lit , vota debere diis, Cic , vota nuncupare or suscipere or concipere, Cic , vota facere, Cic , 2, meton , a, *a prayer*, Ov , b, *that which is vowed*, spolia hostium, Vulcano votum, Liv B. Esp , *the vows made on the 3rd of January every year by the chief magistrates for the good health of the emperor*, Tac II. *a wish, desire*, vota facere, *to wish*, Cic , hoc erat in votis, *this was what I wished*, Hor , voti potens, *having gained his wish*, Ov

vŏvĕo, vōvi, vōtum, 2 I. *to vow, promise to a god*, decumam Herculi, Cic , aedem, Liv , with fut infin , vovisse dicitur uvam se deo daturum, Cic II. *to wish*, elige, quid voveas, Ov.

vox, vōcis, f (root VOC, perhaps connected with ὄψ), *the voice of a person speaking, calling, or singing* I. Lit , 1, vocis contentio et remissio, Cic , vocem attenuare, *to make one's voice like a woman's*, Cic , of the cry of animals, boum, Verg , 2, = *pronunciation*, rustica vox et agrestis quosdam delectat, Cic II. Meton , A. *sound, tone*, of the voice or of a musical instrument, vocum gravitate et cantibus pelli vehementius, Cic , septem discrimina vocum = *the lyre with seven strings*, Verg B. *a word, utterance, discourse*, a, haec te vox non perculit? Cic carpi nostrorum militum vocibus, Caes , b, *a command*, consulum voci atque imperio non oboedire, Cic , c, *a formula, decision, sentence*, extrema ac difficillimi temporis vocem illam consulem mittere coegistis, Cic , d, *a formula, a magic incantation*, voces Marsae, Hor C. = sermo, *language* Graja scient sive Latina voce loqui, Cic D. *accent, tone*, in omni verbo posuit acutam vocem, Cic

Vulcānus (Volcānus) i, m (root VULC, VOLC = FULC lit *the shining one*), *Vulcan, the god of fire, son of Jupiter and Juno, husband of Venus, who made the weapons, thunder-bolts, etc , of the gods*, Cic , insula Vulcani (Ἡφαίστου νῆσος), *the island of Vulcan, the most southern of the Lipari islands*, now *Vulcanello* , plur , insulae Vulcani, *the Lipari islands*, appell , *fire*, Vulcanum navibus efflant, Ov Hence, A. **Vulcānĭus** -a um, *Vulcanian*, acies, *fire*, Verg , Lemnos, *sacred to Vulcan*, Ov , Vulcaniis armis, *with irresistible weapons*, Cic B. **Vulcānālis** -e, *belonging to Vulcan*, subst , **Vulcānālĭa** -ōrum, n *the annual festival of Vulcan, on the 23rd of August*

vulgāris -e (vulgus), *common, ordinary, usual, vulgar*, hominum consuetudo, Cic , opinio, Cic , subst , **vulgārĭa** -ium, n *that which is common*, anteponantur rara vulgaribus, Cic

vulgārĭtĕr, adv (vulgaris), *commonly, vulgarly*, Plin

vulgātus -a -um, p adj (from 1 vulgo) I. *common, prostituted* Liv II Esp , *generally known, well known*, vulgatior fama est, with acc. and infin , Liv

vulgĭvăgus -a -um (vulgus and vagor), *wandering, vagrant*, Lucr

1 **vulgo (volgo)**, 1 (vulgus), *to make common to all, to communicate, make accessible to all* I. a, quum consulatum vulgari viderent, Liv , munus vulgatum ab civibus esse in socios, Liv , quae navis in flumine publico tam vulgata omnibus quam istius aetas, Cic , b, *to communicate a disease*, vulgati contactu in homines morbi, Liv , c, *to publish a book*, carmina, Tac II. *to spread abroad by discourse, to divulge, make generally known*, famam interfecti regis, Liv

2 **vulgō (volgō)**, adv (lit abl of vulgus), *commonly, generally, before the public, in public, openly*, vulgo totis castris testamenta obsignabantur, Caes , quas (litteras) vulgo ad te mitto, Cic

vulgus (volgus) i, n , rarely m , *the people = the great multitude, the public* I Gen , A. Lit a, in the town , non est consilium in vulgo, non ratio, etc , Cic , disciplinam in vulgum efferre, Cic , b, in the army, vulgus militum, armatorum, Liv B. Transf , *the people = a mass, crowd*, vulgus incautum ovium, Hor II. In a bad sense, *the crowd, the mob* A. Lit , sapientis judicium a judicio vulgi discrepat, Cic , odi profanum vulgus, Hor B. Transf , *the mass, the ordinary run*, patronorum, Cic

vulnĕrārĭus (volnĕrārĭus) a um (vulnus), *of or relating to wounds*, Plin , subst , **vulnĕrārĭus** -ii, m *a surgeon*, Plin

vulnĕrātĭo ōnis, f (vulnero), *wounding*, Cic , fig major haec est vitae, famae, salutis suae vulneratio, Cic

vulnĕro (volnĕro), 1 (vulnus), *to wound, injure* **I.** Lit , aliquem, Cic , corpus, Cic **II.** Fig , *to wound, injure, harm, assail*, eos nondum voce vulnero, Cic

vulnĭfĭcus (volnĭfĭcus) -a -um (vulnus and facio), *inflicting wounds*, telum, Ov , chalybs, Verg

vulnus (volnus) -ĕris, n *a wound* **I. A.** Lit , **a,** of living beings, vulnus inferre, Caes , infligere, Cic vulnus accipere, excipere, Cic , mori ex vulnere, Liv , **b,** poet , transf , of injuries to things, falcis, Ov , ornus vulneribus evicta, Verg **B.** Fig , *wound = injury, disease, damage, loss*, vulnera reipublicae imponere, Cic , poet , *wounds to the feelings*, esp , from love , vulnus alit venis, Verg **II.** Meton , **1,** *a blow*, mortifero vulnere ictus, Liv , **2,** *the instrument or weapon which causes the blow*, haesit sub gutture vulnus, Verg

vulpĕcŭla -ae, f (dim of vulpes), *a little fox*, Cic

vulpes (volpes) -is, f (ἀλώπηξ), *a fox* **I.** Lit , Hor , prov , vulpes jungere, of something impossible, Verg , *the fox* as an emblem of cunning, slyness , animi sub vulpe latentes, Hor **II.** Transf , vulpes marina, *a kind of shark*, Plin

vulpīnus a -um (vulpes), *of or relating to a fox, vulpine*, Plin

Vulsci = Volsci (q v)

vulsūra -ae, f (vello), *a plucking, pulling*, Varr

vulsus -a -um, p adj (from vello), *having the hairs plucked out, smooth, effeminate*, Plaut , Mart

vultĭcŭlus i, m (dim of vultus), *the countenance, look, aspect*, non te Bruti nostri vulticulus ab ista oratione deterret? Cic

vultŭōsus -a -um (vultus), *making faces, grimacing, full of airs, affected*, Cic

1 **vultur (voltur)** -ŭris, m *a vulture*, Liv , Verg , applied to *a rapacious man*, Sen

2 **Vultur (Voltur)** -ŭris, m *a mountain in Apulia*, now *Voltore*

vultŭrīnus (voltŭrīnus) -a um (vultur), *of or relating to a vulture*, Plin

vultŭrĭus (voltŭrĭus) -i, m *a vulture* **I.** Lit , Liv **II.** Transf , **A.** *a rapacious man*, Cic **B.** *an unlucky throw at dice*, Plaut

Vulturnum (Volturnum) i, n *a town in Campania on the river Volturnus*, now *Castel Volturno*, Liv

1 **Vulturnus (Volturnus)** -i, m *a river in Campania*, now *Volturno*.

2 **vulturnus (volturnus)** -i, m (2 Vultur), with or without ventus, *a wind named after the mountain Vultur, a south east wind*, Liv

vultus (voltus) -us, m *the countenance, expression of the face, the look, mien, aspect* **I.** Lit , **a,** Gen , hilaris atque laetus, Cic , plur , vultus ficti simulatique, Cic , vultus avortite vestros, Cic , **b,** emphat , *a scornful, angry look*, vultus instantis tyranni, Hor **II.** Transf , *the face*, **1,** lit , **a,** cadere in vultus, Ov , **b,** *a portrait*, Plin , **2,** meton , *look, appearance*, salis (of the sea), Verg , naturae, Ov.

X.

X, x, the twenty-first letter of the Latin alphabet, corresponds with the Greek Ξ, ξ It arises out of the combination of c and s (dico, dixi), g and s (lego, lexi).

Xanthippē -ēs, f (Ξανθίππη), *the shrewish wife of Socrates*

Xanthippus i, m. (Ξάνθιππος). **I.** *father of Pericles, conqueror over the Persians at Mycale.* **II.** *a general of the Lacedaemonians in the First Punic War, who took Regulus prisoner.*

Xanthus (-ŏs) -i, m (Ξάνθος) **I** = *Scamander* **II.** *a river in Lycia* **III.** *a river in Epirus*

xĕnium ii, n (ξένιον), *a present given to a guest*, Plin , in general, *a gift, present*, Plin.

Xĕno ōnis, m (Ξένων), *an Epicurean philosopher of Athens*

Xĕnŏcrătes -is, m (Ξενοκράτης), *a philosopher of Chalcedon, pupil of Plato, the head of the Academy after the death of Speusippus*

Xĕnŏphănēs -is, m (Ξενοφάνης), *a celebrated Greek philosopher of Colophon, founder of the Eleatic school*

Xĕnŏphōn -ontis, m (Ξενοφῶν), *an Athenian, pupil of Socrates, a distinguished historian and general* Hence, **Xĕnŏphontēus (-tīus)** -a um, *of* or *belonging to Xenophon.*

xērampĕlĭnae -ārum, f (ξηραμπέλιναι), *dark red garments*, Juv.

Xerxēs -is, m (Ξέρξης), *the king of the Persians who invaded Greece and was defeated at Salamis*

xĭphĭas -ae, m (ξιφίας) **I.** *a sword-fish*, Plin **II.** *a sword shaped comet*, Plin

xĭphĭon -ii, n (ξιφίον), *a sword-flag*, Plin.

xȳlŏbalsămum -i, n (ξυλοβάλσαμον), *wood of the balsam tree*, Plin

xȳlŏcinnamōmum -i, n (ξυλοκιννάμωμον), *the wood of the cinnamon plant*, Plin

xȳlon -i, n (ξύλον), *the cotton tree*, Plin

Xynĭae -arum, f (Ξυνία), *a town in Thessaly, on the lake Xynias*

xȳris -idis, f (ξυρίς), *the wild iris*, Plin

xystus i, m (ξυστός), and **xystum** -i, n *an open colonnade, a walk planted with trees, a promenade*, Cic

Y.

Y, y, a letter borrowed from the Greek in order to represent the Greek upsilon (Υ).

Z.

Z, z, represents the Greek zeta (Z, ζ), and is only used in foreign words

Zăcynthus (-ŏs) -i, f (Ζάκυνθος), *an island in the Ionian Sea*, now *Zante*.

Zăleucus (Ζάλευκος), *a celebrated lawgiver of the Locrians in Italy*, living about 650 B.C

Zăma ae, f (Ζάμα), *a town in Numidia, scene of the victory of Scipio over Hannibal.*

zāmĭa ae, f (ζημία), *damage, injury, loss*, Plaut.

Zanclē ēs, f (Ζάγκλη), *old name of the town Messana (now Messina) in Italy, so called from its sickle-like form* Hence, adj, **A. Zanclaeus** -a um, *of or relating to Zancle* **B. Zanclēĭus** -a um, *of Zancle*

zĕa -ae, f (ζεα), *a kind of spelt*, Plin

zēlŏtȳpĭa ae, f (ζηλοτυπια), *jealousy*, Cic

zēlŏtȳpus a -um (ζηλοτυπος), *jealous*, Juv

Zēno (-ōn) -ōnis, m (Ζηνων) **I.** *a Greek philosopher of Citium in Cyprus, founder of the Stoic School* **II.** *a Greek philosopher of the Eleatic School, teacher of Pericles* **III.** *a later Greek philosopher of the Epicurean School, teacher of Cicero and Atticus*

Zēnŏbĭa ae, f **I.** *daughter of Mithridates, king of Armenia* **II.** *wife of Odenathus, king of Palmyra, which she ruled after her husband's death, conquered by the Emperor Aurelian*

Zĕphȳrĭum ii, n (Ζεφύριον), *a fort on the coast of Cilicia*

zĕphȳrus i, m (ζεφυρος), *a warm west wind, zephyr*, Hor, poet. = *wind*, Verg

Zōrynthus -i, f (Ζηρυνθος), *a town in Thracia, near Aenos* Hence, **Zērynthĭus** a -um, *Zerynthian*

Zētēs -ae, m (Ζητης) *the brother of Calais, son of Boreas, one of the Argonauts*

Zēthus -i, m (Ζηθος), *son of Jupiter, brother of Amphion*

zeugītes -ae, m (ζευγιτης), *a kind of reed*, Plin

zēus -i, m (ζαιος), *a fish, the dory*, Plin

Zeuxĭs Idis, m (Ζεῦξις), *a celebrated Greek painter*

zingĭber ĕris, n (ζιγγίβερις), and **zingĭbĕri**, n indecl *ginger*, Plin

zīzĭphum i, n (ζιζυφον), *the jujube*, Plin

zīzĭphus i, f *the jujube tree*, Plin

zm . v. sm.

zōdĭăcus i, m (ζωδιακός), *the zodiac*, Cic poet

Zōĭlus -i, m (Ζωιλος) *a severe critic of Homer* appell., *a petty critic*, Ov

zōna -ae, f (ζωνη), *a girdle* **I** Lit, **a**, *a maiden's girdle*, Cat, **b**, *a girdle or money belt*, Liv **II.** Transf, **1**, *the three stars called Orion's Belt*, Ov, **2**, zonae, *terrestrial zones*, Verg, Ov

zōnārĭus a -um (zona), *of or relating to a girdle*, Plaut, subst, **zonārĭus** -ii, m *a girdle-maker*, Cic

zōnŭla -ae, f (dim of zona) *a little girdle*, Cat

zōophthalmos i, f and **zōophthalmon** -i, n (ζωοφθαλμος), *the great houseleek*, Plin

zōpissa -ae, f (ζωπισσα), *pitch mixed with wax, which was scraped off ships*, Plin

1 **zoster** ēris, m (ζωστηρ), *a cutaneous eruption, the shingles*, Plin

2 **Zōster** -ēris, m (Ζωστηρ), *a promontory in Attica*

zōthēca -ae, f (ζωθηκη), *a private cabinet*, Plin

zōthēcŭla -ae, f (dim of zotheca), *a small private cabinet*, Plin

zȳgĭa -ae, f (ζυγια), *a tree, the horn beam*, Plin

zȳthum -i n (ζυθος), *a kind of Egyptian malt liquor*, Plin

ENGLISH-LATIN.

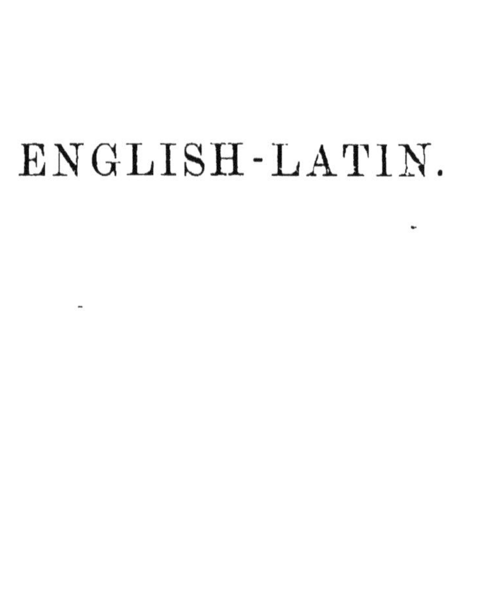

ENGLISH-LATIN DICTIONARY.

A

A, **an,** adj. not translated; — day, — month, *singulis diebus, mensibus;* to — man, *ad unum.*

abaft, aft, adv. *a puppi, a tergo.*

abandon, v.tr. *alqm (de)relinquĕre, destituĕre, deserĕre, (de)alqâ re desistĕre;* — hope, *spem omittĕre.* **abandoned,** adj. = wicked, *nefarius;* see WICKED. **abandonment,** n. *relictio,* or infin. of abandon used substantively (e.g. *deserĕre amicum,* the — of a friend).

abase, v.tr. 1, = lessen, *alqd (de)minuĕre, (im)minuĕre;* 2, = humble, *frangĕre* (e.g. *animum, audaciam*), *comprimĕre, coercēre, alcjs auctoritatem imminuĕre.* **abasement,** n. 1, *deminutio;* 2, legal, = loss of civil and social rights, *capitis* or *libertatis deminutio.*

abash, v.tr. *alqm percellĕre, perturbare, conturbare, animum alcjs affligĕre, debilitare, frangĕre.*

abate, I. v.tr. *(de)minuĕre, imminuĕre;* — a charge, *alqd de summâ detrahĕre, sumptum* or *impensam circumcidĕre.* II. v.intr. 1, *(de)minui, imminui, decrescĕre;* 2, fig. of passion, *defervescĕre* (e.g. *ira,* etc.). **abatement,** n. *deminutio;* in taxation, *vectigalium deminutio.*

abbat, abbot, n. **abbas, -ātis,* nearest equivalent in Class. Lat. *pontifex.* **abbess,** n. **abbatissa,* in Class. Lat. *antistes* or *antistita.* **abbey,** n. **abbatia* (= cloister), **ecclesia* (= church), Class. *templum.*

abbreviate, v.tr. 1, = shorten, *(de)curtare, praecidĕre, circumcidĕre;* 2, = compress (e.g. *orationem*), *contrahĕre, verba ad compendium,* or *compendii facĕre.* **abbreviation,** n. 1, = shortening, *compendium, contractio* (e.g. *orationis,* opp. to *longitudo*); mark of —, *sigla, -orum* (Jct.); 2, see EPITOME.

abdicate, v.tr. *magistratu, dictaturâ,* etc., *se abdicare, magistratum,* etc., *ejurare.* **abdication,** n., legal, *abdicatio, ejuratio.*

abdomen, n. *abdomen.*

abduction, n. 1, = theft, *furtum;* 2, = forcible carrying away, *raptus, -ūs, raptio;* to commit —, *rapĕre.*

abed, adv. *in lecto;* to lie —, *(in lecto) cubare.*

aberration, n. 1, = a wandering from the right path, lit. or fig. *error;* 2, = mental —, *mentis error;* 3, = a fault, *erratum.*

abet, v.tr. 1, = incite, *ad alqd instigare, impellĕre;* 2, = aid, *ab* or *cum alqo,* or *alqâ re,* or *e parte alcjs stare, auxilio alci esse;* — in a crime or fault, *sceleris* or *culpae participem* or *socium esse.* **abettor,** n. *socius, adjutor;* = — in anything, *alcjs rei,* or with abl. *conscius* (adj.).

abeyance, n. 1, in gen. to be in —, *in dubio, incertum, integrum esse, intermitti;* to leave in —, *rem integram relinquĕre;* 2, legal, *vacare;* the property is in — (i.e. without a proprietor), *fundus vacat;* conferred the priestly offices as in — on others, *sacerdotia ut vacua in alios contulit.*

abhor, v.tr. *abominari, detestari* (lit. = call a god to witness a curse), *odisse, alqm odio habēre.* **abhorrence,** n. *detestatio, odium.* **abhorrent,** adj. 1, = inconsistent with, *ab alquâ re abhorrens, alci rei,* or *(ab) alqâ re alienus, alci rei contrarius;* 2, see HATEFUL.

abide, v.intr. 1, = linger in, *(com)morari, in alqo loco esse,* or *versari;* 2, = last, *durare.* **abiding,** adj. *diuturnus, stabilis.*

abject, adj. = contemptible, *abjectus, contemptus, humilis.*

abjure, v.tr. 1, legal, *abjurare, ejurare;* 2, fig. = disown, *ejurare, recusare.*

ability, n. 1, = physical strength, *vires, -ium;* 2, = mental power, *facultas, ingenium, vires;* according to one's —, *pro facultate, pro viribus;* a man of —, *vir summi ingenii.* **able,** adj. 1, = having power, *alcjs rei potens,* 2, = fit for, *habilis, aptus, ad alqd idoneus;* 3, = mentally strong, *sagax, sol(l)ers;* 4, to be —, *posse, valēre* (= to have strength for); to be — in anything, *alqâ re pollēre;* as well as I am —, *pro viribus (meis), pro virili parte.* **able-bodied,** adj. *firmus, robustus, validus.*

ablative, n. *(casus) ablativus* (Gram.).

ablution, n. *ablutio;* to make an —, *(aquâ) abluĕre.*

abnegation, n. *animi moderatio, temperantia;* self —, *temperantia.*

abnormal, adj. 1, lit. = not according to rule, *enormis* (e.g. *vicus* (Tac.) = irregularly built; *toga* (Quint.) = irregularly cut), *abnormis* (= rare); 2, = out of the common, *novus, inusitatus, mirus, mirificus, incredibilis, singularis;* 3, = very great, *maximus;* 4, = rare, *infrequens.* Adv. *praeter morem.*

aboard, adv. to go —, *(in navem,* or *navem) conscendĕre;* to be —, *in nave esse;* to put —, *in navem imponĕre;* to have —, *vehĕre.*

abode, n. 1, = sojourn, *habitatio;* if in a foreign country, *peregrinatio;* 2, see HOUSE.

abolish, v.tr. 1, in gen. *abolēre* (not in Cic.), *tollĕre, subvertĕre, delēre, ex(s)tinguĕre;* 2, legal, *abrogare;* to — part of a law by a new one, *obrogare.* **abolition,** n. 1, in gen. = destruction, *dissolutio;* 2, legal, *abrogatio;* — of debts, *tabulae novae.*

abominable, adj. *foedus, teter, detestabilis, immanis, nefarius* (= wicked). **abominate,** v.tr. see ABHOR.

aboriginal, adj. *priscus*; *prisci Latini* = the Latins who lived before the foundation of Rome. **aborigines,** n. *indigenae*.

abortion, n. 1, = miscarriage, *abortio*, *abortus*, -ūs; to cause an —, *alci abortum facĕre*, or *inferre*; 2, = a monstrous birth, *abortus*, *portentum*; a drug to procure —, *abortivum* (Juv.). **abortive,** adj. 1, lit. = belonging to premature birth, *abortivus*; 2, fig. = unsuccessful, *irritus*. Adv. *incassum*, *ad irritum*.

abound, v.intr. *alqâ re abundare*, *affluĕre*, *alci superesse*, or *suppeditare* (e.g. he —s in words, *oratio ei suppeditat*). **abundance,** n. *rerum*, i.e. *divitiarum*, etc., *abundantia*, *suppeditatio*, *affluentia*, *ubertas*, *copia*. **abundant,** adj. *affluens* (*ab*) *alqâ re* = rich, *copiosus*, *dives*, *locuples*. Adv. *abunde*, *satis superque*, *abundanter*, *cumulate*.

about, I. adv. 1, of place, *circa*, *circum*, or abl. with or without *in*; 2, of time or number, *fere*, *ferme*, *circiter*, with fut. part. (e.g. he is about to go, *iturus est*). **II.** prep. with acc.: 1, of place, both motion to and rest in, *circa*, *circum*, the people — one, *qui circum alqm sunt*; 2, of time, *circa*; 3, of respect, *de*, with abl. (e.g. he spoke — these things, *de his rebus dixit*), what are you —? *quid agis?*

above, I. adv. 1, of place, *super*, *supra*, the — mentioned, *quod supra scriptum est*; 2, of degree, *super*, *supra*, over and —, *satis superque*. **II.** prep. 1, of place, *super*, acc. or abl. *supra*, *ante*, acc., to sit — anyone at table, *supra alqm accumbĕre*; 2, of degree, *super*, *supra*, — measure, *supra modum*, = more than, *plus* or *amplius* (e.g. he had — 200 soldiers, *plus ducentos milites habuit*).

abreast, adv. *pariter*; two horses —, *equi bijuges*.

abridge, see ABBREVIATE.

abroad, adv. *foras*, with verbs of motion, *foris*, with those of rest; to sup —, *foris cenare*; to spread —, v.tr. = publish, *divulgare*, = scatter, *diffundĕre*; v.intr. = to be spread, *percrebescĕre*; nations —, *gentes externae* or *exterae*; to travel —, *peregrinari*.

abrogate, see ABOLISH.

abrupt, adj. 1, lit. = steep, *abruptus*, *arduus*, *praeruptus*; 2, fig., of speech, *rudis*, *incompositus*; 3, = sudden, *subitus*, *repentinus*, *improvisus*. Adv. 1, *abrupte*, *praerupte*; 2, *incomposite*; 3, *subito*, *de improviso*, *repente*.

abscess, n. *ulcus*, -*eris*, n., *suppuratio* (Cels.), *fistula*, *apostema*, -ătis, n. (Plin.), *abscessus*, -ūs (Cels.), *cancer*, *carcinoma*, -ătis, n.

abscond, v.intr. 1, = to lie hidden, *delitescĕre*, *latēre*, *occultari*; 2, = to run away, *se in occultum abdĕre*, *se occultare* or *celare*.

absence, n. *absentia*; — abroad, *peregrinatio*; in my —, *me absente*; — of mind, *alcjs rei oblivio*. **absent, I.** adj. *absens*; to be — from, *ab alqo abesse*; to be — in mind, *animo excurrĕre et vagari*; — minded, *inscius*, or *oblitus alcjs rei*. **II.** v.tr. — oneself, *se removēre*.

absolute, I. adj. 1, = complete, *perfectus*, *absolutus*, *expletus*; 2, = unconditioned, *absolutus*, *simplex*; 3, = unlimited, *infinitus*; — power, *summum imperium*; — ruler, *imperator*, *qui summum imperium obtinet*. **II.** n. philosoph. t.t., opp. to relative, *alqd perfectum et absolutum*, *quod semper simplex et idem est*. **absolutely,** adv. 1, = entirely, *plane*, *prorsus*, *omnino*; 2, opp. to relatively, *per se*, *simpliciter*.

absolution, n., in gen. *venia*; to grant —, *alcjs rei veniam dare*. **absolve,** v.tr. 1, in gen. *alqm alqâ re solvĕre* (e.g. soldiers from military service), see EXCUSE; 2, legal t.t. *alqm alcjs rei* or (*de*) *alqâ re* (*ab*)*solvĕre*, *alqm alqâ re liberare*; 3, see PARDON.

absorb, v.tr. 1, lit. *sugĕre*, *bibĕre*, *absorbēre*, *exhaurire*; 2, fig. to be absorbed in anything, *alqâ re occupatissimum esse*.

abstain, v.intr. (*se*) (*ab*) *alqâ re abstinēre* or *continēre*, (*ab* or *in*) *alqâ re*, *alci rei*, or with infin. (e.g. *alqd facĕre*), *temperare*, *sibi temperare quominus* (not in Cic.); to — from appearing in public, *publico carēre*. **abstinence,** n. *abstinentia*, *continentia*, *modestia*, *moderatio*, *temperantia*; days of —, fast days, *jejunium*. **abstinent,** adj. *abstinens*, *continens*, *sobrius*, *moderatus*, *temperatus*; — in drink, *sobrius*.

abstract, I. adj. 1, = removed from the sphere of the senses, *quod nullo sensu percipi potest*; an — idea, *notio nulli sensui subjecta*, *notio mente solâ concepta*; an — discussion, *disputatio paul(l)o abstrusior*; 2, = deep or acute in thought, *subtilis* (*et acutus*); an — thinker, *subtilis philosophus*, see ABSTRUSE. **II.** v.tr. 1, to think —ly, *animum a corpore abstrahĕre*, *mentem ab oculis sevocare*; — the mind from pleasure, *animum a voluptate sevocare*; 2, = to make an abridgment, *epitomen facĕre*; 3, see STEAL. **III.** n. *epitome*, -*es*, f. or *epitoma*. **abstractly,** adv. to think —, see ABSTRACT, II. 1; *subtiliter*, *acute*. **abstracted,** adj. 1, see ABSTRUSE; 2, = lost in thought, *omnium rerum* or *sui oblitus*. **abstraction,** n. 1, = forgetfulness, *oblivio*; 2, = a mere name or idea, *appellatio* (Suet.).

abstruse, adj. *obscurus*, *abditus*, *reconditus*. **abstruseness,** n. *obscuritas*, *res occulta*, or *involuta*. Adv. *obscure*, *abdite*, *recondite*.

absurd, adj. 1, = silly, *absurdus*, *ineptus*, *insulsus*; 2, = ridiculous, *ridiculus*. Adv. 1, *absurde*, *inepte*, *insulse*; 2, *ridicule*. **absurdity,** n. 1, as a quality, *insulsitas*; 2, = a joke, *ridiculum*; 3, = an act, *res inepta*, *ineptiae*, *nugae*.

abundance, abundant(ly), see ABOUND.

abuse, I. n. 1, = the wrong use of a thing, *immoderatio* (= excess), *usus*, -ūs *perversus* (= misapplication); 2, rhetor. t.t. *abusio* (= misuse of a word); 3, = bad language, *convicium*, *maledictum*; 4, = an evil custom, *res mali* or *pessimi exempli*, *malum*, *pestis*, *mos pravus*, *quod contra jus fasque est*. **II.** v.tr. 1, = misuse, *alqâ re perverse uti*, *abuti* (in bad sense only from context, lit. = to use up); 2, rhetor. t.t. (e.g. a term) *abuti*; 3, = to rail at, *alci maledicĕre*. **abuser,** n. 1, = one who misuses anything, *homo immoderatus qui alqâ re abutitur*; 2, = a railer, *conviciator*, *homo maledicus* or *maledicens*. **abusive,** adj. *maledicus* or *maledicens*, *contumeliosus*. Adv. *maledice*, *contumeliose*.

abut, v.tr. *alci loco adjacēre*, *finitimum*, *vicinum*, *confinem*, *continentem*, *conjunctum esse*, *locum tangĕre*, *attingĕre*, *alci loco imminēre* (= to hang over).

abyss, n. 1, lit. = a great depth, *profundum*, *altitudo* (= depth merely), *gurges*, -*itis*, m. (= a whirlpool), *locus praeceps* (= precipice); fig. *exitium*, see DESTRUCTION. He plunged in an — of pleasure, *se voluptatibus* (*prorsus*) *dedit*; he plunged in an — of ruin, *semet ipse praecipitavit*.

academy, n. 1, = the Platonic school, *Academia*; 2, = a learned body, *collegium*. **academical,** adj. 1, = belonging to a university, *academicus*; 2, = an — (i.e. theoretical) question, *res ad cognitionem modo pertinens*.

accede, v.intr. 1, = to be added to, *accedĕre ad alqd* or dat.; 2, see AGREE.

accelerate, v.tr. *accelerare*; see HASTEN.

accent, n. 1, in pronunciation, *vox, accentus, -ūs, (vocis) sonus, -ūs, tenor*; sharp —, *vox acuta*; acute, grave, circumflex —, *accentus* or *sonus acutus, gravis, circumflexus* or *inflexus*; 2, in writing, *apex, -icis*, m. (= the long or short mark over a vowel); a syllable with short, long, or circumflex —, *syllaba brevis, longa, circumflexa*.

accept, v.tr. 1, = to take, *accipĕre*; 2, = to undertake, *suscipĕre* (of one's own accord); *recipĕre* (what is offered); not to — an office, *munus deprecari*. **acceptable**, adj. *jucundus, accipiendus, gratus*. Adv. *jucunde, grate*. **acceptance**, n. 1, *acceptio* (e.g. *frumenti*), *assumptio* (e.g. *argumenti*); better by infin., e.g. he intimated his —, *dixit se accipĕre*; 2, = approbation, *comprobatio*. **acceptation**, = significance, *significatio*.

access, n. 1, = approach, *aditus, -ūs, accessio, accessus, -ūs*; difficult of —, *rari est accessūs*; 2, = addition, *accessio, cumulus*; 3, med. t.t. (e.g. of a fever), *accessio* (Cels.); 4, = an entrance, *aditus, -ūs, accessus, -ūs*. **accessary, I.** adj. 1, see ADDITIONAL; 2, = privy to, *conscius alcjs rei*, dat., *in* or *de* with abl., or rel. clause (e.g. *conscius quae gererentur*, — to what was being done). **II.** n. = accomplice, *conscius, unus ex consciis, sceleri affinis, (culpae) socius*. **accessible**, adj. *patens, facilis aditu* or *accessu*; not — to any advice, *consilii non patiens*; he is little —, *difficilis est aditu*. **accession**, n. 1, = increase, *accessio*; 2, = — to the throne, *initium regnandi*.

accidence, n. = the rudiments, *elementa, -orum, rudimenta, -orum*.

accident, 1, = a chance event, *casus, -ūs, eventus, -ūs, eventum*; 2, = a misfortune, *casus, calamitas*. **accidental**, adj. *fortuitus* (e.g. *concursus atomorum*), *forte oblatus*. Adv. *forte, casu*; to mention —, *in mentionem alcjs rei incidĕre*.

acclaim, acclamation, n. *acclamatio* (= shout of applause, in Cic. always of disapproval); with general —, *omnibus probantibus*. **acclaim**, v.tr. *alci acclamare*.

accommodate, v.tr. *accommodare alqd alci* or with *ad*. **accommodating**, adj. *obsequens, facilis*; to be — to, *alci morem gerĕre, morigerari*. **accommodation**, n. 1, = adjustment of differences, *reconciliatio*; see AGREEMENT; 2, = entertainment or place of entertainment, *hospitium*.

accompany, v.tr. 1, = to go with, *comitem se alci adjungĕre, dare, praebēre, alqm comitari, prosequi, deducĕre* (as a mark of respect); *stipare* (of a crowd); accompanied by, *cum* (e.g. *tempestas cum grandine*); 2, in music, = to sing or play together, *alci concinĕre*; — on an instrument, *vocem fidibus jungĕre, cantum modis musicis excipĕre*. **accompaniment**, n. 1, *comitatus, -ūs, stipatio*; 2, in music, *adjunctio fidium voci*, or *vocis fidibus*.

accomplice, n. *criminis conscius, socius, sceleri affinis*.

accomplish, v.tr. *conficĕre, perficĕre, absolvĕre, consummare, perpolire*; to be —ed (of dreams, &c.), *exitum habēre*. **accomplished**, adj. *(per)politus, elegans, doctus, humanus*. **accomplishment**, n. 1, = fulfilment, *confectio, perfectio, absolutio*; = the end, *finis, exitus, -ūs*; 2, = — of the mind, *ars*, or by some term denoting the subject of the — (e.g. *musica*, music as an —).

accord, I. n. 1, = agreement of sounds (*sonorum*) *concentus, -ūs, nervorum* or *vocum concordia, harmonia*; 2, see AGREEMENT; of one's own —, *sponte, ultro*. **II.** v.intr. 1, lit. = to sound with, *concinĕre*; 2, = agree with, *cum alqo congruĕre*. **accordance**, see ACCORD, I. In — with, *ex*; in — with the agreement, *ex pacto, ex conventu*; — with my wishes, *ut volui*; — with his opinion, *ex ejus opinione*. **accordant**, adj. *congruens, consentiens, constans*; — together, *unanimus*. **according to**, see ACCORDANCE; *ad, secundum, ad alqd*; — you, *ex tuā sententiā*; — circumstances, *ex* or *pro re*. **accordingly**, adv. *itaque, quae cum ita sint*.

accost, I. n. *appellatio, salutatio*. **II** v.tr. *alloqui* (rare in good Latin), *appellare, salutare*.

accouchement, n. *partus, -ūs*; a premature —, *abortio*; to be in —, *parĕre, partum edĕre*.

account, I. v.tr. 1, = to think, *habēre, aestimare*; to — highly, *magni facĕre*; — lowly, *nihili facĕre*; — nothing of, *non flocci facĕre*; 2, = to — for, see EXPLAIN; 3, = to — to anyone, *rationem alci de alqā re reddĕre*. **II.** n. 1, lit. = a reckoning, *ratio*; to take —, *rationem habēre*; to give —, *rationem alci de alqā re reddĕre*; 2, fig. = to be of —, *magni* or *maximi haberi*, — with anyone, *multum apud alqm (auctoritate) valēre*; to be of no —, *nullā esse auctoritate*; 3, = — at a bank, *pecunia in argentariā (col)locata*; to open an —, *pecuniam in argentariam collocare*; to draw upon an —, *alqd de pecuniā suā detrahĕre*; to pay upon —, *partem debiti* or *ex debito solvĕre*; — book, *tabula*; 4, = pretext, reason; on my —, *meā de causā, meo nomine*; not on any —, *nullo modo*; on — of anything, *propter alqd*; 5, = narrative, *narratio*; give an — of, *alqd narrare*. **accountable**, see RESPONSIBLE. **accountant**, n. *scriba*, m., defined by context (e.g. *qui tabulas conficit*).

accoutre, v.tr. see EQUIP.

accredit, v.tr. 1, = add credit to, see CONFIRM; 2, = to — an ambassador, *alqm legatum (ad regem, &c.) facĕre*; 3, see BELIEVE. **accredited**, adj. 1, = admitted, *probatus*; 2, = — envoy, *legatus publice missus*.

accretion, n. *accessio, incrementum, cumulus*.

accumulate, v.tr. *(co)acervare, (ac)cumulare, exaggerare*. **accumulation**, n. *cumulus, incrementum*.

accurate, adj. *accuratus, exactus, limatus, emendatus*. Adv. *accurate, exacte, pure, emendate*. **accuracy**, n. *accuratio* (a rare word), *diligentia*; with the greatest —, *accuratissime*.

accurse, v.tr. see CURSE.

accuse, v.tr. 1, legal t.t. *alqm alcjs rei* or *de alqā re accusare, postulare, compellare, citare, reum facĕre, arguĕre, alqm in jus vocare* or *(e)ducĕre, in judicium adducĕre, alci diem dicĕre, nomen alcjs de alqā re deferre*; — of high treason, *alqm perduellionis*, or *majestatis* or *de majestate reum facĕre*; — of assassination, *alqm inter sicarios accusare*; — of extortion, *de (pecuniis) repetundis accusare*; the accused, *reus*; 2, in gen. *accusare, incusare, criminari*. **accusation**, n. 1, legal t.t. *accusatio, criminatio, crimen*, esp. when unfounded; (= — of an informer, secret —) *delatio*; 2, in gen. *incusatio*, (= a speech against) *oratio in alqm*. **accusative**, n. gram. t.t. *accusativus (casus)*. **accuser**, n. *qui alqm accusat, accusator* (strictly of a public accuser, *petitor* being plaintiff in private case); an informer, *index*; a secret —, *delator*.

accustom, v.tr. *alqm assuefacĕre alqā re, ad*, or dat. (abl. in Cic.), or with infin.; to — oneself = be accustomed, *assuescĕre, consuescĕre*, with abl., *ad* or dat. or infin. **accustomed**, adj. *assuetus*; in the — way, *de more*.

ace, n in cards, use terms from dice; the side of the die marked 1, *canis* (= the dog-throw, i e worst); the best throw, the — of trumps, *Venus (jactus, -ūs), Venereus, basilicus* (because at a Roman symposium the king of the feast was chosen by this throw)

ache, I. n *dolor* II. v intr *dolēre*

achieve v tr 1, = to finish, *facĕre, conficĕre, efficĕre, perficĕre, consummare, finire*, 2, = to gain, *assequi, consequi*, to — something (i e make progress), *alqd* or *multum proficĕre* **achievement**, n 1, = the doing of anything, *confectio*; 2, = a deed, *facinus, -ŏris*, n (but more usual in bad sense), he has made an —, *magna confecit*

acid, adj 1, = sharp to the taste, *acidus, acerbus, acer*, 2, = — in temper, *acer, acerbus, morosus* **acidity**, n. 1, *sapor acidus*, 2, *acerbitas, morositas* **acerbity**, n *acerbitas* (lit and fig)

acknowledge, v tr 1, = to accept as one's own, *a(d)gnoscĕre* (e g *alqm filium*, as a son), to — a child, *suscipĕre* (the father raised a new-born child from the ground), 2, = to admit, *confitēri* (= to confess, e g a fault), 3, = to — a kindness, *alci gratias agĕre*, — a payment, (*in acceptum referre* (i e to place to the credit side of an account book), — a letter, *rescribĕre* with dat or *ad* **acknowledged**, adj *cognitus, probatus, spectatus* **acknowledgment**, n 1, = approval, *approbatio, comprobatio*, 2, = confession, *confessio*; 3, gratitude (e g to make an —, *gratias alci agĕre, se gratum praebēre*, 4, see RECEIPT

acme, n = height, *fastigium*; to reach the — of glory, *summam gloriam assequi*

acorn, n *glans*.

acoustics, n *ratio audiendi, quae ad auditum pertinent*

acquaint, v tr see INFORM **acquaintance**, n 1, = knowledge of a thing, *peritia* (not in Cic), *scientia, notitia, cognitio alcjs rei*; with a person, *usus* or *familiaritas cum alqo*, — with literature *eruditio*, to make — with, *alqm* or *alqd (cog)noscĕre*, to seek — with, *appetĕre alcjs familiaritatem*, 2, = a person slightly known, *amicus, familiaris, noti* (only used as n in pl) The distinction between friend and acquaintance was not marked in Latin, it can be rendered by *amicus* and *homo mihi amicissimus* = friend, or *homo mihi paene notus* = —. **acquainted**, adj *notus, cognitus*, — with, *alci familiaris*, to make —, introduce, *alqm ad alqm deducĕre*, to be — with, *alqm novisse (nosse)*, to be familiarly — with, *alqo familiariter uti*, — with anything, *alcjs rei peritus, gnarus, alqa re imbutus, doctus, institutus, in alqa re versatus*, not — with, *alcjs rei ignarus, inscius, rudis*

acquiesce, v.intr *(in) alqa re acquiescĕre, alqd aequo animo* or *patienter ferre* **acquiescence**, n *assensus, -ūs*, see ASSENT.

acquire, v tr see GAIN **acquirement**, **acquisition**, n 1, = anything gained, *res adepta*, 2, = knowledge, *alcjs rei cognitio*, a man of many —s, *vir perpolitus, multis artibus eruditus*, 3, the process of —, *alcjs rei comparatio, adeptio* **acquisitive**, adj. *aptus ad alqd impetrandum*

acquit, v tr see ABSOLVE **acquittal**, n *absolutio alcjs rei* **acquittance**, n *apocha* (Jct), to give or to enter an —, *in acceptum referre*

acrid, adj = hot and biting, both of physical taste and of temper, *acerbus, mordens, mordax* **acridity**, n *acerbitas*.

acrimonious adj *mordax, mordens, acerbus, aculeatus* Adv *mordaciter, acerbe* **acrimony**, n *acerbitas*.

across, prep 1, = the other side of, *trans*, 2, with verbs of motion, *trans, per* = right through, something comes — my mind, *alqd mihi (de improviso) ob(j)icitur*

acrostic, n = riddle, *aenigma, -ătis*, n

act, I. v intr = to do, *agĕre, facĕre* (e g *bene, male*, well or ill), to — as a man, *se virum praebēre*, so to — as to, *ita se gerĕre ut*, the medicine —s, *efficax est* II v tr = to — a part 1, on the stage, *alcjs partes agĕre*, to — the first part, *primas partes agĕre* or *tractare, personam tractare*, to — a play, *fabulam agĕre*, to forbid the players to —, *histrionibus scaenam interdicĕre*, 2, in life, *personam sustinēre* or *tueri*, 3, = to feign, *alqm simulare*, 4, to — upon anyone, *multum, nihil*, etc, *apud alqm valēre*, to be —ed upon, *alqa re affici* III. n of a play, *actus, -ūs*, — of Parliament, *Senatusconsultum*, — of amnesty, *oblivio sempiterna*, the — of anyone, *factum*, in pl = achievements, *res gestae, gesta* or *acta, -orum*, n; in the very —, *in manifesto facinore* **action**, n 1, = the doing of anything, *actio*, 2, = a deed, *factum*, 3, in battle, *res gesta*, = the battle itself, *praelium*, 4, of a play, = the series of events, *actiones*, = gesture, *actio, gestus, -ūs*, 5, of a horse, *gradus, -ūs*, 6, legal t.t an — for anything, *lis, litis*, f, *actio alcjs rei*, or *de alqa re* (e g *furti, de repetundis*), to bring an — against, *actionem in alqm instituĕre, alci diem dicĕre* **actionable**, adj *cujus rei actio est, quod contra leges est* **actor**, n 1, = one who acts, *qui agit, facit, alcjs rei actor*, 2, on the stage, *histrio, actor*, comic —, *comoedus*, tragic —, *tragoedus* **actress**, n only men acted in classical times, so use *quae partes agit* **active**, adj 1, = quick, *celer, acer, promptus*, 2, = untiring, industrious, *impiger, (g)navus* Adv *acriter, impigre, industrie, (g)naviter* **activity**, n 1 = quickness, *celeritas*, 2, = industry, *industria, impigritas*. **actual**, adj *verus, manifestus* Adv *vere, re vera*, actually? *itane vero?* **actuate**, v tr *excitare, impellĕre*

acumen, n. *ingenii acies, acumen*

acute, adj 1, of pain, *acutus, gravis vehemens acerbus*, 2, of intellect, *acutus, subtilis, acer perspicax, sagax*, 3, see ANGLE, ACCENT Adv *acute, graviter, vehementer, subtiliter, sagaciter* **acuteness**, n *sagacitas, perspicacitas, ingenii acies, acumen, subtilitas*

adage, n *proverbium*

adamant, n *adamas, -antis*, m **adamantine**, adj 1, lit *adamantinus*, 2, fig = very strong, *validissimus*, see STRONG

adapt, v tr *alqd alci rei* or *ad alqd accommodare, aptare, efficĕre ut alqd cum alqa re conveniat* **adapted**, adj *aptus*, or *idoneus ad alqd (faciendum)*, or *alci rei*, or *qui* with subj **adaptation**, n *accommodatio*

add, v tr *alqd alci addĕre, adjungĕre, ad(j)icĕre*; to — up, *summam facĕre, computare* **addition**, n 1, = adding to, *adjunctio* (esp = an — that limits the meaning) *adjectio, accessio*, 2, = a thing added, *alcjs rei accessio* or *additamentum*, 3, in arith *additio*, opp to *abjectio* (= subtraction) (Quint), by — and subtraction to find a total of various items, *addendo deducendoque summam facĕre* **additional**, adj *novus, additus, adjectus*

adder, n *vipera*

addict, v tr *alci* or *alci rei se dare, dedĕre* or *tradĕre, se ad studium alcjs rei conferre* incum-

bēre. **addicted,** adj. *alci rei deditus, alcjs rei studiosus;* to be — to a person, *totum alcjs esse.*

addle, v.tr. *abortivum facĕre;* an addled egg, *ovum abortivum* (Mart.), *ovum irritum, zephyrium* (Plin.).

address, I. v.tr. 1, = apply oneself to anything, *se alci rei dedĕre, tradĕre, ad* or *in alqd incumbĕre;* 2, = to speak to, *alqm alloqui, affari, appellare* (both by speech and letter); 3, to — a letter to, *alci lit(t)eras inscribĕre.* **II.** n. 1, = speech to anyone, *alloquium;* 2, = speech to a meeting, *contio* (in late Lat. also = a sermon), *oratio;* 3, of a letter, *inscriptio;* 4, = place, *locus* (e.g. to that —); 5, = adroitness, *sol(l)ertia;* 6, —es = courtship, to pay one's —es to, *alqam in matrimonium petĕre.*

adduce, v.tr. *adducĕre, producĕre, proferre, (com)memorare;* to — witnesses, testimony, *testes, testimonium proferre, testes citare, producĕre.*

adept, adj. *ad alqd callidus, alcjs rei* or *alqd re peritus.*

adequate, adj. *alci* or *alci rei proprius, alci, alci rei* or *ad alqd aptus, idoneus, alci rei* or *cum alqd re congruens, conveniens, consentaneus, ad alqd accommodatus;* — to the occasion, *ad tempus accommodatus.* Adv. *apte, convenienter, congruenter, pro ratā (parte).*

adhere, v. intr. *(in)alqd re* dat. or *ad alqd (in)haerēre, adhaerēre;* to — to a person, *alci studēre, deditum esse, alcjs studiosum esse;* to — together, *cohaerēre;* — to a party, *e partibus esse, (alcjs) partibus favēre.* **adherence, adhesion,** n. 1, lit. by ADHERE; 2, = attachment, *amor, studium erga* or *in alqm.* **adherent,** n. *unus e sociis;* — of a school of thought, *discipulus;* = political —, *cum alqo consentiens;* his —s, *sui.* **adhesive,** adj. = sticky, *tenax;* — plaster, *cataplasma, -ătis,* n. (Cels.).

adieu! *vale!* pl. *valete;* to bid —, *alqm salvēre* or *valēre jubēre;* at the end of letters, *vale, valete, cura ut valeas, valeatis.*

adjacent, adj. *alci rei adjacens, adjectus, contiguus, vicinus, finitimus;* to be —, *adjacēre;* of a country, *contingĕre* (e.g. *fines Helvetiorum*), or *continentem esse* with dat. or abl. with *cum.*

adjective, n. *nomen adjectivum* (Gram.).

adjoin, see ADJACENT (to be).

adjourn, v.tr. *differre, proferre, prorogare;* to — the day of trial, *diem prodicĕre.* **adjournment,** n. *dilatio, prolatio.*

adjudge, v.tr. *alqd alci addicĕre, adjudicare;* to — a triumph, *alci triumphum decernĕre* (so of everything else awarded by the Senate, e.g. *honores, pecuniam.*)

adjunct, n. *accessio, alqd alci rei appositum, additum.*

adjure, v.tr. 1, = to impose an oath upon, *alqm jurejurando* or *sacramento, ad jusjurandum adigĕre, jurejurando obstringĕre;* 2, = to entreat, to — (by), (*per alqm* or *alqd*) *obsecrare, obtestari.* **adjuration,** n. = entreaty, *obsecratio, obtestatio.*

adjust, v.tr. 1, see ARRANGE; 2, see ADAPT. **adjustment,** n. *accommodatio.*

adjutant, n. *optio, -onis,* m.

administer, v.tr. *alqd administrare, gerĕre, procurare, alqd re fungi, alci rei praeesse;* to — an oath to, *alci jusjurandum deferre;* to — medicine, *medicinam alci dare;* — justice, *jus dicĕre.* **administration,** n. 1, = performance, *administratio, procuratio, functio;* 2, = the ministers of state, *qui reipublicae praesunt* or *praepositi sunt.*

admiral, n. *praefectus classis;* to appoint as —, *praeficĕre alqm classi;* to be an —, *classi praeesse.*

admire, v.tr. *(ad)mirari.* **admiration,** n. *(ad)miratio.* **admirable,** adj. 1, = worthy of admiration, *(ad)mirandus, (ad)mirabilis;* 2, = excellent, *optimus, egregius, eximius, praestans, praestabilis.* Adv. *mirum in modum, mirum quantum, (ad)mirabiliter, optime, egregie, eximie.*

admit, v.tr. 1, = to allow to enter, *alqm admittĕre, aditum alci dare, adeundi copiam* or *potestatem alci facĕre;* 2, = concede, *concedĕre, dare;* 3, = confess, *fatēri, confitēri;* 4, = to allow, *habēre* (e.g. *alqd excusationis,* = some excuse), *pati;* this —s of no doubt, *de hoc dubitari non potest.* **admission,** n. 1, = leave to enter, *admissio, aditus, adeundi copia;* 2, = concession, *concessio;* in argument, with this —, *hoc concesso.* **admissible,** 1, = to be received, *accipiendus;* 2, = fair, *aequus.*

admonish, v.tr. *alqm alqd, de alqā re* or *ut (ad)monēre, alqm ad alqd* or *ut (ad)hortari.* **admonition,** n. *(ad)monitio, (ad)hortatio.*

ado, n. with much —, *vix, aegre;* see FUSS.

adolescence, n. *adulescentia (adol.).*

adopt, v.tr. 1, legal t.t. *alqm adoptare, a(d)sciscĕre;* 2, = to accept, *accipĕre, recipĕre;* to — a resolution, *alqd constituĕre, consilium inire.* **adoption,** n. *adoptio.* **adoptive,** adj. *adoptivus* (mostly late, esp. Jct.).

adore, v.tr. 1, = to worship, *venerari, colĕre;* 2, = to admire, *colĕre, diligĕre, amare.* **adorable,** adj. *sanctus, venerandus.* **adoration,** n. *cultus, -ūs, veneratio.*

adorn, v.tr. *(ex)ornare, decorare;* an —ed style in speaking, *oratio ornata.* **adornment,** n. *ornatus, -ūs, ornamentum.*

adrift, adj. 1, lit. *fluctibus* or *vento jactatus;* 2, in mind, to be —, *(animo) vagari.*

adroit, adj. *callidus, sol(l)ers, habilis.* Adv. *callide.* **adroitness,** n. *habilitas, sol(l)ertia.*

adulation, n. *adulatio, assentatio, blanditia, ambitio.*

adult, I. adj. *adultus.* **II.** n. *pubes;* —s, *puberes.*

adulterate, v.tr. *adulterare, corrumpĕre, vitiare.*

adultery, n. *adulterium;* to commit —, *adulterium cum alqo* or *alqā facĕre, inire.* **adulterous,** adj. *adulteriis deditus.*

adumbrate, v.tr. *adumbrare.* **adumbration,** n. *adumbratio.*

advance, I. v.intr. 1, lit. *progredi, procedĕre;* 2, fig. *procedĕre, progredi, proficĕre;* to be advanced in years, *aetate provehi;* in rank, *ad ampliorem gradum* (e.g. *ad consulatum*) *provehi.* **II.** v.tr. 1, *alqm alqd re augēre, (ex)ornare;* to — anyone's interests, *alci* or *alcjs rei consulĕre;* 2, = to bring forward an opinion, *sententiam dicĕre, aperire;* 3, = to pay in advance, *in antecessum dare* (Sen.). **III.** n. 1, = a going forward, *progressus, -ūs, iter, -ineris,* n.; 2, = an increase, *progressus;* 3, = of money, *pecunia in antecessum data* (Sen.). **advance-guard,** n. *primum agmen.* **advancement,** n. 1, in rank, *gradus, -ūs amplior,* or by name of office to which — is made (e.g. to the consulship, *consulatus*); 2, in gen. = — of interests, etc., by infin. of verb to advance (e.g. the — of your interests, *tibi consulĕre*).

advantage, n. *commodum, lucrum, fructus, -ūs, emolumentum, utilitas, bonum* (esp. in pl. *bona,* —s); — of a position, *loci opportunitas;* to my

—, *e re mea* or *in rem meam est*, to gain — from, *fructum ex alqa re capĕre*, with an eye to one's own —, *alqd ad fructum suum referre*, it is for one's —, *expedit* (with acc and infin), to be of —, *utilem* or *utile esse*, *ex usu* or *usui esse*, *alci* or *alci rei prodesse* **advantageous,** adj *quaestuosus, utilis, fructuosus, opportunus* Adv *utiliter*

advent, lit *adventus, -ūs* **adventitious,** adj *adventicius, externus.*

adventure, I. n 1, = daring deed, *facinus, -oris,* n, *audax inceptum*, 2, = an unusual occurrence, *res nova* or *mira* **II.** v tr *alqd audēre, tentare, experiri, periclitari* **adventurer,** n *qui alqd tentat*, a mere —, *fraudator* **adventurous,** adj *audax, temerarius* Adv *audacter, temere*

adverb, n *adverbium* (Gram)

adversary, n *adversarius*, in trials, the —, *iste*, see ENEMY

adverse, adj *alci* or *alci rei adversus, contrarius, oppositus*, — winds, *venti adversi*, — circumstances, *res adversae* Adv *contra*, to act —, *alci* or *alci rei adversari, repugnare*, to act — to one's own interest, *utilitati suae repugnare* **adversity,** n *adversa, res adversae, miseria*

advert to, v tr *animum ad alqd intendĕre, alqd animadvertĕre.*

advertise, v tr 1, = to inform, *alqd alci nuntiare, alqm de alqa re certiorem facĕre*, 2, = to make publicly known, *praedicare, pronuntiare*, — in the papers, *in actis* (*diurnis* or *publicis*) *pronuntiare* **advertisement,** n 1, *indicium, significatio*, 2, *praedicatio, proclamatio* (*in actis*)

advice, n *consilium*, by my —, *me auctore*, a pretty piece of — ! *pulchre suades !* **advise,** v tr 1, = give advice, *consilium alci dare, alci suadēre ut* or *alqd, alqm alqd* or *ut, monēre, alqm alqd, ad* or *in alqd* or *ut, hortari*, 2, = to inform, *alqm de alqa re certiorem facĕre* Adv *consulte, considerate, de industria* **adviser,** n *suasor, consiliarius,* (*consilii*) *auctor*

advocate, I. n 1, legal t t, *patronus, cognitor, procurator*, to be an —, *caus(s)as dicĕre, agĕre, in foro versari*, 2, in gen *alcjs rei auctor* **II.** v tr = to defend, *defendĕre, tueri, tutari*

adze, n *ascia*

aerial, adj. *aerius, aetherius*

aeronaut, n *qui se per aerem* (*curru*) *propellat*

afar, adv *procul, longe, e longinquo, eminus* (opp *comminus*), to be —, *procul* or *longe abesse*

affable, adj *affabilis, blandus, comis, communis, mansuetus* (= gentle, opp *ferus*), *commodus* (= obliging) **affability, affableness,** n *mores commodi, affabilitas, mansuetudo, comitas, communitas* (Nep)

affair, n *res, opus, -ĕris,* n (= work), *negotium, occupatio, ministerium, munus, ĕris,* n, *cura*, it is the — of a judge, *judicis* (*officium*) *est* See BUSINESS

affect, v tr 1, = to influence, *alqm tangĕre,* (*com*)*movēre, alqm alqa re afficere*, 2, = to injure, *alci nocēre, noxium esse*, 3, = to be fond of, *diligĕre, amare*, 4, = to assume an appearance, *simulare, imitari, prae se ferre*, to — constancy, etc, *constantiam*, etc, *simulare* **affectation** n *simulatio, imitatio, ostentatio* **affected,** 1, of persons, *mollis, ineptus* (= silly), *alqd ostentans*, 2, of things, *quaesitus, simulatus, putidus, molestus*(of speech) Adv *putide, inepte, molliter, moleste*

affection, n 1, = a state of the mind or feeling, the feelings, *animi motus, ūs,* (*animi*)*affectus, ūs commotio, permotio, impetus, -ūs*, 2, = loving sentiment, *amor, caritas, benevolentia, studium, pietas* (= dutiful —), *indulgentia* (= indulgent —), *voluntas in* or *erga alqm* **affectionate,** adj *amoris plenus, alcjs amans* (e g *uxoris*), *pius* (= dutifully —), *indulgens* Adv *amanter, indulgenter, pie*, — yours (at the end of a letter), *cura ut valeas* or *vale*

affiance, I. n 1, = trust, *fiducia, fides*, in anything, *alcjs rei*, with anything, see AFFINITY, 2, = marriage contract, *sponsalia, ium* **II.** v tr, see BETROTH

affidavit, n *testimonium per tabulas datum* (Quint.)

affinity, 1, = relationship, *propinquitas, propinquitatis vinculum, necessitudo* (= family ties), *cognatio* (on the side of the father or the mother), *a(d)gnatio* (on the side of the father), *affinitas, affinitatis vinculum* (by marriage), *consanguinitas, consanguinitatis vinculum, sanguinis vinculum* (by blood), 2, = close connection, similarity, *cognatio, conjunctio*, — of the sciences, *cognatio studiorum*

affirm, v tr 1, *aio* (defective = I say Yes, opp. *nego*), *affirmare, confirmare, annuĕre* (by nodding assent), *fateri, confiteri* (= to admit), 2, legal t t. to — a contract, law, etc, *pactum, legem*, etc, *sancire, ratum esse jubēre* (of the Senate) **affirmation,** n 1, in gen *affirmatio*, 2, legal t t *confirmatio* **affirmative,** adj *aiens* (opp *negans*), *affirmans*, an — answer, *affirmatio* Adv to reply —, *aio, alqd confirmare*

affix, v tr = to fasten or put to, *alqd alci rei* (*af*)*figĕre, alqd ad rem alligare, annectĕre, ad rem* or *alci rei alqd, alci rei agglutinare* (= to glue to)

afflict, v tr = to make sorrowful, *contristare, dolorem alci facĕre, efficĕre, afferre, commovēre, dolore alqm afficĕre, alqm torquēre, angĕre,* (*ex*)*cruciare, vexare, mordēre, pungere* **affliction,** n *aegritudo* (= sickness of mind), *dolor, maestitia* (= sadness, opp *hilaritas, laetitia*), *molestia, maeror* (= dejection) — of body, *aegrotatio, morbus* **afflicting,** adj *tristis, miser, acerbus, luctuosus*

affluence, n *abundantia, affluentia* (more than you want), *ubertas* (= fulness), *copia*, — of good things, *suppeditatio bonorum* **affluent,** see, ABUNDANT, under ABOUND

afford, v tr 1, = to supply, *praestare, praebēre, concedĕre, alcjs rei* (*faciendae*) *potestatem facĕre* (e g to — an opportunity for an interview, *colloquendi secum pot fac*) 2, = to yield *reddĕre, suppeditare*, 3, = to have the means or to be able, *posse*

affranchise, see FREE, v tr

affray, n = disturbance or petty quarrel, *rixa, pugna, tumultus, -ūs* (of a mob)

affright, see FRIGHTEN

affront, I. v tr 1, = to meet, *alci* or *ad* or *in alqd occurrĕre, alci obviam ire*, 2, = to wound the feelings, *offendĕre laedĕre, pungere* (= to sting), *mordēre* **II.** n *opprobrium, contumelia, injuria* **affronting,** adj *injuriosus, contumeliosus*

afield, adv *in agros* (with verbs of motion), *in agris* (with verbs of rest)

afloat, adj & adv, to be —, *navigare, navi vehi*

afoot, adv *pedibus* (e g *pedibus ire*)

aforesaid, adj *quem* or *quod supra scripsi, commemoravi,* etc

afraid, adj *anxius, sollicitus, timidus, pavidus, trepidus, ignavus,* (*per*)*territus* to be —, *alqm, alqd timēre, metuĕre, reformidare*, not to be —, *sine metu* or *securum esse*

afresh, adv. see AGAIN.

after, I. prep. *post* (with accus.) **1**, of place, *post eum* (= after or behind him); **2**, of time, *post aliquot menses* (= after some months); or by abl. abs. (e.g. *Aeginâ relictâ*, = — leaving Ægina); **3**, of rank (*nemo est post te*, = no one is after or inferior to thee). As denoting sequence or order, rank, *secundus a* (e.g. *secundus a rege*, = next to the king); = according to, *secundum* (e.g. *secundum legem*, — *rationem*, etc.). If a model is intended, *ad* is used (e.g. *ad normam*, = after a set rule; *ad eorum arbitrium et nutum totos se fingunt*, = they form themselves wholly after their will and pleasure; *ad modum*, = moderately; *ad formam*, — *effigiem*, — *similitudinem*, denoting imitation). **II.** conj. **1**, *postquam, ut, ubi*; three years after he had returned, *post tres annos* or *tertium annum quam redierat, tertio anno quam redierat*; the day — he came, *postridie quam venerat*, also *postridie ejus diei*; **2**, by abl. abs., — he had done this, *quo facto*. **III.** adv., also **afterwards,** *post, postea, posthac* (denoting specially sequence in time); *dein(de), exin(de), inde* (denoting the sequence in time of two things, next); *deinceps* (an unbroken sequence in time), *mox* (= presently, shortly after, opp. *nunc*). When the "afterward" refers to the act in the foregoing member, the Romans liked to repeat the verb of that member in the form of a participle (e.g. the robbers took Remus prisoner, and afterwards gave him up to Amulius, *latrones Remum ceperunt et captum Amulio tradiderunt*); three years —, *post tres annos, tribus annis post, post tertium annum, tertio anno post, tertio anno*; first, afterward, lastly, *prius, deinde, extremo*; first, next, afterward, *principio, proximo, deinde*.

afternoon, I. n. *pomeridianum tempus*; in the —, *post meridiem*. **II.** adj. *pomeridianus*.

again, adv. **1**, in gen. *iterum, denuo, rursus, rursum*; again and again, *iterum atque iterum, semel atque iterum*; in composition by *re-*; to rise —, *resurgĕre*; **2**, = hereafter, *posthac, postea*; **3**, = in turn, *contra, vicissim*; **4**, of the heads of a speech, *ad hoc* or *haec*.

against, prep. **1**, = rest near, *ad* with accus. (e.g. *ad murum*), *contra* with accus. (e.g. *contra insulam*); **2**, = motion towards, *adversus* or *ad alqm* or *alqd*; **3**, = hostility towards, *adversus* or *in alqm, contra alqm* or *alqd*; a speech — Caecina, *oratio in Caecinam*; — expectation, *praeter* or *contra opinionem*; — the stream, wind, *adverso flumine, vento*; — one's will, *alqo invito*; for and —, *in utramque partem*; **4**, of time, *ad* or *in* with accus.; *sub lucem*, — daylight (i.e. just before).

age, n. *aetas* (= the time of life, persons living at the same time); of the same —, *aequalis* (also = contemporaries); men of the same —, *ejusdem aetatis* or *temporis homines, ejusdem aetatis oratores* (= the orators of the same age, that is, the contemporaneous orators); next in —, *aetate proximus*; his — did not understand Socrates, *Socratem aetas sua parum intellexit, Socrates ab hominibus sui temporis parum intellegebatur*; *saeculum* (= a long indefinite period), *tempus, -ŏris*, n., or in pl.; to be of —, *sui potentem, sui juris esse*; not of —, *nondum adultâ aetate*; old —, *senectus, -ūtis*, f.; to be twenty years of —, *viginti annos natum esse*. **aged,** adj. *aetate provectior* or *grandior*; an — man, *senex, -is*.

agent, n. *actor, procurator*; a free —, *qui sui juris est*. **agency,** n. **1**, = performance, *effectus, -ūs*; **2**, = employment, *procuratio*.

aggrandize, v.tr. *amplificare, augēre*. **aggrandizement,** n. *amplificatio, dignitatis accessio* (= — in rank).

aggravate, v.tr. **1**, = to increase, *augēre*; **2**, = to exasperate, *exasperare, lacessĕre, incitare*.

aggregate, I. n. *summa*. **II.** v.tr. *congregare*. **aggregation,** n. *congregatio*.

aggression, n. **1**, in war, *impetus, -ūs, incursio, incursus, -ūs, excursio, oppugnatio* (= storming of a place); **2**, in gen. = encroachment, *injuria*. **aggressive,** adj. *hostilis, infensus*. Adv. *hostiliter, infense*. **agressor, 1**, *qui bellum suscepit*; **2**, in gen. *qui injuriam alci facit*.

aggrieve, v.tr., see GRIEVE.

aghast, adj. *(ex)territus, perturbatus*; to stand —, *stupēre*.

agile, adj. *agilis, velox, pernix*. **agility,** n. = nimbleness, *agilitas, pernicitas, velocitas*.

agitate, v.tr. **1**, = to move hither and thither, to move greatly, *agitare, quatĕre* (= to shake), *rotare, circumagĕre* (= to drive round), *(com)movēre, (con)turbare*; **2**, = to excite, *percutĕre, perturbare, commovēre, percellĕre*; **3**, = to discuss, to — a question, *rem* or *de re agĕre, disputare, disserĕre*; *sol(l)icitare* (= to stir up), *alqm excitare* (by speech). **agitation, 1**, *agitatio, jactatus, -ūs, jactatio* (as of the sea), *concussus, -ūs, concussio*; — of the body, *corporis motus, -ūs*, comb. *agitatio motusque corporis*; to be in —, *moveri, agitari*; **2**, — of mind, *animi motus, commotio, concitatio*; strong —, *animi perturbatio*; to be under —, *perturbatum esse*; **3**, of a question, *disputatio*. **agitator,** n. *turbator plebis* or *vulgi*; to be an —, *rebus novis studēre*.

ago, adv. *abhinc*; thirty days —, *(jam) abhinc triginta diebus*, or *abhinc triginta dies, ante triginta dies*; long —, *jam pridem*.

agony, n. **1**, of body, *dolor, aegrotatio*; **2**, of mind, *aegritudo, dolor*. **agonize, I.** v.intr. *(ex)cruciari, torquēri*. **II.** v.tr. *(ex)cruciare, torquēre*.

agrarian, adj. *agrarius*.

agree, I. v.intr. = to be of one mind and voice, *concinĕre, conspirare, consentire, congruĕre*; not to —, *dissentire, discrepare de re*; **II.** v.tr. **1**, to — upon, *alci rei assentiri, de alqâ re congruĕre, idem sentire*; to — upon terms, *conditiones accipĕre*; **2**, to — with, *salubrem alci esse*; not to —, *gravem esse*. **agreement,** n. **1**, *consensio, consensus, -ūs, concordia, unanimitas* (opp. *discordia*); **2**, = a compact, *pactum*; to strike an —, *alqd cum alqo pacisci*. **agreeable,** adj. **1**, = pleasant, *acceptus, gratus, dulcis, suavis*; **2**, = witty, *lepidus, facetus*; **3**, — to, *alci rei* or *ad alqd accommodatus, aptus, alci rei* or *cum alqâ re conveniens*.

agriculture, n. *agri (agrorum) cultura* (or as one word, *agricultura*), or *agri cultio* (or as one word), or *agrorum cultus, -ūs*. **agricultural,** adj. *rusticis rebus deditus*. **agriculturist,** n. *arator, agricola*, m., *agri cultor* (or as one word, *agricultor*).

aground, adv. **1**, *in vado* (= on the shoal), *in litore, in scopulis* (= on the rocks), *in syrtibus* (= on the quicksands); **2**, fig. *in luto esse, in difficultatibus versari*.

ague, n. *febris intermittens*.

ah! ah! aha! interj. *eu, euge*.

ahead, adv. = before, *ante*; to go —, *anteire, praeire*; to run —, *praecurrĕre*; to swim —, *praenatare*; to sail —, *praevehi*.

aid, I. n. **1**, = help, *auxilium, adjumentum, subsidium* (esp. = resource) *opem* (n. *ops* and dat. *opi* not used); **2**, = a tax, *vectigal*. **II.** v.tr.

auxilium alci afferre, alci adesse or *praesto esse, alqm (ad)juvare*

ailing, adj *aeger*, see SICK

aim, I. n 1, *meta* (= the goal); *scopos*, -i (= mark Suet), to fix an —, *alqd petĕre*, 2, fig *propositum*, to propose an — to yourself, *finem sibi proponĕre*, what is the — of this? *quorsum haec spectant?* **II.** v tr 1, *telum collineare, telum dirigĕre* or *intendĕre in alqm* or *alqd, telo petĕre alqm* or *alqd*, 2, fig. *alqd (animo) intendĕre, spectare, pertinēre ad alqd* (e g these things — at concord, *haec ad concordiam spectant*)

air, I. n. 1, *caelum* (= the whole atmosphere), *aer* (accus sing *aera*, = ἀήρ, the atmosphere near the earth), *aether* (= αἰθήρ, the upper air) *aura* (= breeze), *ventus* (= the wind), *spiritus*, -ūs (= breath of air, or life), *anima* (= the breath of life), to take — (i e. of a secret), *emanare*, 2, = appearance, *vultus*, -ūs (= the look of the face), *aspectus*, -ūs, *alcjs* or *alcjs rei species, forma, facies*, to have an — of any kind, *se gerĕre* with adv (e g *honeste*), *se praebere* with adj (e g *talem*), to give oneself —s, *se jactare* or *ostentare*, 3, = a tune, *modus* (*musicus*), *cantus*, ūs **II.** v tr *aeri exponĕre, ventilare.* **airy,** adj *aerius, aetherius, aeri expositus* **airiness,** n by adj (e g the — of a place, *locus ventis expositus*

aisle, n *ala* (side), *spatium medium* (mid).

akin, adj *propinquus, a(d)gnatus* (on the father's side), *cognatus* (on the mother's), to be near —, *arta propinquitate alci conjunctum esse, alci finitimum esse*

alabaster, I. n *alabastrites, ae*, m **II.** adj *ex alabastrite factus*, an — box, *alabaster*, or *alabastra* (pl neut)

alack! alack a-day! interj *eheu, vae mihi*

alacrity, n 1, = quickness, *pernicitas, velocitas*, 2, = cheerfulness, *alacritas, hilaritas*

alarm, I. n 1, *strepitus*, -ūs (= a loud noise which calls out men and beast), *turba* (= confusion), *tumultus*, -ūs (= uprising and uproar, as in an insurrection), comb *strepitus et tumultus*, to give — of fire, *incendium conclamare*, to sound the —, *classicum canĕre*, from —, *prae strepitu*, to be in —, *trepidare*, 2, = fear, *terror, trepidatio*, see AFRAID, FEAR **II.** v tr *conturbare, terrēre*

alas! alas a-day! see ALACK.

album, n *liber*

alcove, n *zotheca*

alder, I. n *alnus*, f **II.** adj. *alneus*

alderman, n. *magistratus*, -ūs, more definitely according to context (i e if the — is mentioned as a judge, *judex*)

ale, n *cer(e)visia* (a Gallic word) **ale-house,** n *caupona*

alert, adj *vigil, alacer*, to be on the —, *vigilem esse*, see ALACRITY

algebra, n **algebra*

alias, n *nomen alienum*; to assume an —, *nomen sibi fingĕre*

alien, I. adj *(ab) alqo, alqa re, alci* or *alci rei alienus*, see ABHORRENT **II.** n *alienigena*, m (= born abroad) *advena*, m and f (= one who has come into a foreign land) **alienate,** v tr 1, legal t t *(ab) alienare* (= to make what is mine strange to me or to make it another's), *vendĕre* (= to sell), *vendĕre et (ab) alienare*, 2 = to estrange, *alqm ab alqo alienare* **alienation,** n 1, (of goods), *(ab) alienatio, venditio* — of a part, *deminutio de alqa re*, 2, — of mind *mentis alienatio* or *alienata mens, vesania* (= delusion) *insania* (= loss of reason, madness), *vecordia* (= folly), *delirium* (= wandering), *furor* (= rage)

alight, v intr *descendĕre*; — from a horse, *ex equo descendĕre*

alike, I. adv *pariter, aeque, eodem modo.* **II.** adj *similis*

alive, adj *vivus*, to be —, *in vita* or *in vivis esse, vivĕre* See LIFE

all, adj 1, = every, *omnis*, 2, = the whole, *totus, solidus*, — together, *cunctus, universus*, in — respects, *ex omni parte, plane, prorsus*, — the best men, *optimus quisque*, at —, *omnino, prorsus*, not much, if at —, *non multum, aut nihil omnino*, not at —, *minime*, in —, *in summa* (e g *absolvi in summa quat(t)uor sententiis* = to be acquitted by four votes in —), taken together *omnino* (e g there were five in —, *quinque omnino erant*).

allay, v tr *lenire, levare, sedare, mitigare*

allege, v tr to — in excuse, *alqd alci excusare*, see ASSERT **allegation,** n 1, *affirmatio*; 2, = a charge, *indicium, accusatio*

allegiance, n *fides*, to swear —, *in verba alcjs jurare*, to keep in one's —, *alqm in officio suo retinēre*

allegory, n *allegoria* (Quint)

alleviate, v tr see ALLAY **alleviation,** n *levatio, mitigatio, levamen(tum)*

alley, n 1, of a house, *ambulatio*, 2, of a street, *angiportus*, ūs

allot, v tr = to assign by lot, *sortiri* (= to cast lots for), *sorte legĕre* **allotting,** n *sortitio*, = to assign, *(at)tribuĕre, assignare, addicĕre, adjudicare* **allotment,** n 1, = act of allotting *assignatio*, 2, = ground, *ager, possessio*

allow, v tr 1, = permit, *sinĕre* (subj with or without *ut*), *pati* (with acc and inf), *permittĕre alci* (with *ut* or inf), *concedĕre* (= to yield to a request), to — to go, *sinĕre abeat*, 2, = concede, *concedĕre, confiteri*, allowed = acknowledged *spectatus, cognitus*, 3, = to give, *dare*, for a public object, *decernĕre* **allowable,** adj *concessus, licitus.* **allowance,** n 1, = permission, *concessio, permissio*, 2, = indulgence, *indulgentia*, to make — for *alqd condonare*, 3, = money, *pecunia in alqd data*

alloy, I n = a spoiling, *corruptio, depravatio*, without —, *sincerus, purus* **II.** v tr *corrumpere, vitiare*

allude to, v tr = to refer to, *significare alqm* or *alqd, designare, describĕre* **allusion,** n *significatio, mentio alcjs rei*

allure, v tr *in* or *ad alqd allicĕre, invitare, inescare* (by a bait) **alluring,** adj *blandus, dulcis* **allurement,** n *invitamentum* (= something inviting), *incitamentum* (= something impelling), —s, *illecebrae*

ally, I. n *socius, foederatus, foedere sociatus* (= united by treaty), relating to an —, *socialis* **II.** v tr *foedus facĕre, alqm* or *alqd cum alqa re conjungĕre, societatem cum alqo inire*, to — oneself, *se cum alqo (con)jungĕre, foedus cum alqo jungĕre* **alliance,** n *societas, foedus, -eris*, n , matrimonial —, *matrimonium*

almanack, n *fasti, -orum, ephemeris, -idis*, f.

almighty, adj *omnipotens*

almond, n *amygdala, amygdalum*, — tree, *amygdalus*, f

almost, adv *prope, paene, fere, ferme, tantum non* (e g *tantum non bellum ante portas et muris erat*, = war was all but at the gates), *ad* (with accus = close to), *circiter* (about), *haud multum* or *non longe afuit quin*

alms, n *stips*, is, f (nom not used), *beneficium* (= a kindness) **almoner,** n *qui largitionibus praeest* **alms-house,** n *ptochotropheum* (Jct).

aloe, n. *aloë, -es,* f.

aloft, adv. *sublime.*

alone, I. adj. *solus, unus, unus solus;* also by *unus omnium* or *ex omnibus; sine arbitris, remotis arbitris* (= without witness). **II.** adv. See ONLY.

along, I. adv. *porro, protinus;* get — with you, *abi, apage (te).* **II.** prep. *secundum, praeter;* to sail —, *litus* or *oram praetervehi;* — with, *una cum.*

aloof, adv. *procul;* to stand — from, *se ab alqâ re removēre.*

aloud, adv. *clare, clarâ voce, magnâ voce, summâ voce.* See LOUD.

alphabet, n. *lit(t)erarum nomina et contextus, -ūs,* (Quint.). See LETTER. **alphabetical,** adj. *in lit(t)eras digestus.* Adv. *lit(t)erarum ordine.*

already, adv. *jam, jam tum, jam tunc, jam diu, jamdudum, jampridem* (= a long while ago).

also, conj. *etiam, praeterea* (= besides), *insuper* (= moreover), *quoque* (always after the word to which it refers), *necnon* (= moreover, joins sentences), *item, itidem* (= again, in the same way), *et ipse,* (e.g. *Vespasiano Titus filius successit, qui et ipse Vespasianus dictus est* = Vespasian was succeeded by his son Titus, who also received the name of Vespasian). If two or more different qualities are ascribed to the same subject or object, and the force of the sentence lies in the difference, use *idem* for "also," (e.g. *musici quondam idem poëtae* = of old, musicians were also poets). See AND.

altar, n. *ara* (= every slight elevation of stone, &c.), *altaria, -ium* (= a high altar); to raise an —, *aram statuĕre, Deo facĕre aram.*

alter, I. v.tr. *(com)mutare alqd in* and *de alqâ re; immutare, (con)vertĕre, novare* (= to give a new form), *emendare, corrigĕre* (= to take away faults), *variare* (= to change often), *invertĕre* (= to turn upside down), *corrumpĕre* (= to falsify, as *tabulas publicas*); what is done cannot be altered, *factum fieri infectum non potest.* **II.** v.intr. *converti.* To be altered, *(com)mutari, immutari;* both minds and facts are much —, *magna facta est rerum et animorum commutatio;* he has not —, *non alius est ac fuit, est idem qui semper fuit.* **alterable,** adj. *mutabilis;* adv. *mutabiliter.* **altering, alteration,** n. *(com)mutatio, immutatio, conversio; varietas, vicissitudo;* — of the weather, *caeli varietas;* — of fortune, *fortunae vicissitudines;* — of your opinion, *mutatio sententiae.*

altercation, n. *altercatio, jurgium, rixa* (= a brawl, fight); see QUARREL.

alternate, I. v.tr. **1,** *alqd cum alqo alternare, variare;* to — rest and labour, *otium labore variare;* **2,** v.intr. *variari, variare.* **II.** adj. *alternus, mutuus;* adv. *in vicem, vicissim, mutuo.* **alternation,** n. *(per)mutatio, vicissitudo.* **alternative, I.** adj. see ALTERNATE. **II.** n. *consilium contrarium, ratio alcs rei contraria* or *opposita;* peace or war is our only —, *inter pacem et bellum nihil est medium.*

although, conj. *tametsi, quanquam (quamq.)* (gen. with the indic. as presupposing a fact), *etsi* (presupposing a fact, use the indic.; a supposition, the subj.), *licet* (with subj., with or without *ut*), *quamvis* (= however much), *cum (quom, quum),* = since, seeing, that, with subj.

altitude, n. *altitudo.*

altogether, adv. **1,** = at the same time, *una simul, eodem tempore, conjunctim* (= in common, e.g. *auxilia petĕre*); **2,** = all together, *ad unum omnes, cuncti, universi;* **3,** = wholly, *prorsus, plane, omnino, penitus, funditus* (esp. with verbs of destroying); he is — made up of, *totus ex alqâ re factus est.*

alum, n. *alūmen.*

always, adv. *semper, omni tempore, numquam (nunq.) non;* the best is — the last, *optimum quidque est ultimum;* I — do it, *hoc facĕre soleo.*

amalgamate, v.tr. *alqd (cum) alqâ re (com)miscēre.* **amalgamation,** n. *conjunctio.*

amanuensis, n. *a manu (servus,* Jct.), *ab epistulis (servus,* Jct.), *qui pro alqo scribit.*

amass, v.tr. *(co)acervare, aggerare, accumulare.* See ACCUMULATE, HEAP.

amatory, adj. *amatorius;* see LOVE.

amaze, v.tr. *obstupefacĕre, percutĕre.* **amazed,** adj. *obstupefactus;* to be —, *stupēre, (ob)stupescĕre.* **amazing,** adj. *mirus, immanis;* an — quantity of money, *immanes pecuniae.* Adv. *vehementer, mirum in modum.* **amazement,** n. *stupor;* see ASTONISH, ASTOUND, WONDERFUL.

amazon, n. **1,** lit. *Amazon;* **2,** fig. *mulier bellicosa.*

ambassador, n. *legatus* (as a deputy in state affairs), *orator* (as a political deputy to deliver a verbal message).

amber, n. *electrum, sucĭnum* (Plin.).

ambiguous, adj. *anceps, ambiguus, dubius.* Adv. *ambigue* (e.g. *dicĕre*). **ambiguity,** n. *ambiguitas* (e.g. *verborum*); see DOUBT.

ambition, n. *ambitio, laudis studium, studium cupiditasque honorum, contentio honorum, cupido honoris* or *famae, aviditas* or *avaritia gloriae, aestus quidam gloriae* (sometimes merely *gloria,* e.g. *alcjs gloriae favēre* and *gloriâ duci*). **ambitious,** adj. *ambitiosus, avidus gloriae* or *laudis, cupidus honorum, laudis et honoris cupidus, appetens gloriae;* to be —, *laudis studio trahi, gloriâ duci;* adv. *cupide,* or by adj.

amble, v.tr. *lente procedĕre.*

ambrosia, n. *ambrosia.* **ambrosial,** adj. *ambrosius.*

ambush, n. *insidiae* (= the place and the men); to lay in —, *in insidiis (col)locare* or *disponĕre;* to lie in —, *in insidiis esse.*

ameliorate, v.tr. *corrigĕre* (= to make right), *emendare* (= to free from errors); to — your condition, *amplificare fortunam, augēre opes.*

amen! interj. *ita fiat! ratum esto!* eccl. *amen.*

amenable, adj. **1,** *alci rei obaediens;* **2,** legal t.t. *sub alcjs jus et jurisdictionem subjunctus.*

amend, I. v.tr. *emendare, corrigĕre.* **II.** v.intr. *mores mutare* (of morals), *convalescĕre* (of health). **amendment,** n. *correctio, emendatio.* **amends,** n. *satisfactio, expiatio;* to make — for, *alqd expiare* (of a crime), *damnum restituĕre* or *resarcire* (of a loss).

amethyst, n. *amethystus* (Plin.).

amiable, adj. *suavis, dulcis, venustus, jucundus.* Adv. *suaviter, jucunde.* **amiability,** n. *suavitas, venustas, jucunditas.*

amicable, adj. see FRIENDLY.

amidst, prep. *in medio (loco), in medio, (parte) alcjs rei;* sometimes by *ipse* (e.g. in the midst of the preparations for war, *in ipso apparatu belli*).

amiss, adv. *male;* there is something — with me, *male mecum agitur;* to use —, *alqa re perverse (ab)uti;* to take —, *aegre* or *moleste ferre, in malam partem accipĕre.*

ammunition, n (*instrumenta et*) *apparatus*, *ūs belli*, *arma*, *orum*, *tela*, *-orum*

amnesty, n *venia praeteritorum*, *impunitas*, *incolumitas*, *fides publica* (= the public safeguard), *amnestia*, to pass a general —, *omnium factorum dictorumque veniam et oblivionem in perpetuum sancire*

among, prep *inter*, *in* (with abl), from —, *ex*, *de*, — men, *inter homines*, *in hominibus*

amorous, adj 1, in good sense, *amans*, *amore incensus*, 2, in bad sense, *libidinosus* Adv *maximo cum amore*, *libidinose* **amorousness,** n *amor*, *libido*

amount, I. n *summa*, *vivum* (= the capital), the whole —, *solidum*, a not inconsiderable —, *nummi non mediocris summae*, a great — of gold, *pecunia magna* or *grandis*, a very great —, *incredibilis pecuniae summa* **II.** v intr *alqd efficere*, what does it — to, *quae summa est*, it —s to the same thing, *idem* or *par est*, *nihil interest utrum*

amphibious, adj *animal cujus et in terra et in aqua vita est*

amphitheatre, n *amphitheatrum*

ample, adj *amplus* Adv *ample*, *abunde* **amplitude,** n *amplitudo* **amplify,** v tr *amplificare*

amputate, v tr *praecidĕre* (e g *membra*, *aurem*, *manum*, *caput* or *cervices alci*), *amputare* (*caput alci*) **amputation,** n by the verb, i e to perform an —, (*membrum*) *praecidere*

amuse, v tr *delectare*, *oblectare* **amusing,** adj *jucundus* Adv *jucunde* **amusement,** n *delectatio*, *oblectatio*, *oblectamentum*

anachronism, n *error de temporibus factus*

analogy, n *analogia* (ἀναλογία, translated by Cicero *comparatio proportioque*), *similitudo* **analogous,** adj *analogus*, *similis*

analysis, n *explicatio*, *explicatio et enodatio*, *expositio*. **analyze,** v.tr *explicare*, *expedire*, *quasi in membra discerpere*.

anapaest, n *anapaestus*

anarchy, n *licentia*, *perturbatio omnium rerum*, *turba et confusio*, — (as a social state) *civitas in quâ libido multitudinis pro legibus est* **anarchical,** adj *legibus carens* Adv *sine legibus*

anathema, n in civil affairs, to put a person under —, *aquâ et igni interdicĕre alci*, *devotio*, *anathēma*, *ătis*

anatomy, n *anatomia*, to practise —, *insecare aperireque humana corpora* **anatomical,** adj *anatomicus* **anatomize,** v tr *incidere corpus mortui*, *rescindĕre artus cadaveris* **anatomist,** n *qui incidit*, etc

ancestor, n *auctor generis* or *gentis* (= founder of a clan or family), *unus e majoribus* (= a forefather) **ancestors, ancestry,** n *priores majores*, *patres* **ancestral,** adj *avitus*, *proavitus*

anchor, I. n *ancora*, to cast —, *ancoram jacĕre*, the — holds, *ancora subsistit*, to lie at —, *consistĕre in ancoris* or *ad ancoras*; to raise —, *ancoram* or *ancoras tollĕre* or *solvĕre*, fig *spes*, *auxilium* (e g *curia summum auxilium omnium gentium*, = the senate was the chief — of all nations) **II.** v tr *navem ad ancoras deligare* **III.** v.intr. see LIE AT —. **anchorage,** n. *statio*

ancient, adj *antiquus* (= that which has been of old), *vetus* (= that which has existed long), *priscus* (= primitive), *inveteratus* (= grown old), *obsoletus* (= obsolete), the —s, *veteres*, *antiqui*, *prisci*, *majores* (= forefathers) Adv. *olim*, *antea*, *antiquitus*, *patrum memoriâ*

and, conj *et*, *que* (enclit unites things that are alike at least in aim and tendency, e g *exploratores centuriones que*), *atque*, *ac* (only before consonants) Sometimes "and" does not appear (e g horse and man, *equi viri*, men and women, *viri mulieres*, also *patria labonbus*, *consiliis*, *periculis meis servata est* = my native land has been saved by my labours, counsels and dangers) Sometimes you must use the relative instead of the copula (e g *venit nuntius qui nuntiabat*), also the participle (e g *prodiens haec locutus est*, he went forward and said these things), so *urbe relicta in villam se recepit* = he left the city and betook himself to his country-seat Also a conjunction (e g *Xanthippus cum Carthaginiensibus auxilio missus esset*, *fortiter se defendit* = Xan was sent to assist the C and bravely defended himself) And also, *et quoque*, *nec non*, *idemque* or *et idem* (e g *musicus idemque philosophus*), and so, *itaque* and yet, *et tamen*, and not, *neque*, *nec*, *et non* (the former to negative a sentence, the latter, a word), and yet, *nec* (e g *quidam se simulant scire*, *nec quidquam sciunt*, some pretend to know, and yet know nothing), and no one or nothing, *nec quisquam*, *quidquam*, and never, *nec unquam* (*umq*), = but, *autem* (e g I do this, and you that, *ego hoc facio*, *tu autem*, etc)

anecdote, n *dictum*, *fabula*, *fabella*

anemone, n *anemone*, *-es*, f

anew, adv *denuo*, *de* or *ab integro*

angel, n *angelus*

anger, I. n *ira*, *iracundia bilis* (= the gall), *stomachus* (= temper), *indignatio*, outbreaks of —, *irae*, *iracundiae* from —, *prae irâ*, in or through —, *per iracundiam*, *iratus*, *cum irâ* **II.** v tr *lacessĕre*, *iram*, *bilem* or *stomachum alci movēre* **angry,** adj *iratus*, *irâ incensus*, *accensus*, or *inflammatus*, *iracundus*, to make angry, *iram* or *bilem* or *stomachum alci movēre* Adv *irate*, *iracunde*

angle, I. n 1, *angulus* 2, = an instrument for fishing, *hamus* **II.** v tr 1, *piscari*, *hamo pisces capĕre*, *arundine pisces captare*, 2, fig to — after, *alqd captare*, *aucupari*, see FISH **angler,** n *piscator*

anglican, adj use *Britannicus*

anguish, n *cruciatus*, *ūs*, *tormentum*, *dolor*, see ACHE

angular, adj *angularis*, *angulatus*

animadvert, v tr 1, = to observe or consider, *animadvertĕre*, *cognoscĕre*, *sentire*, *vidēre*, *perspicĕre*, (*ob*)*servare*, 2, = to punish, *punire*, *in alqm animadvertere*, 3, = to criticize, *judicare*

animal, I. n *animal*, *bestia* (opp *homo*), *belua* (= one of the larger animals), *pecus*, *pecudis*, f (= a head of cattle, opp to *pecus*, *pecoris*, n = a flock), (*belua*) *fera* (= wild —), a little —, *bestiola* **II.** adj by circumloc (e g — life, *vita quae corpore et spiritu continetur*) or merely *corpus*, opp *animus*, (e g animal pleasures, *corporis voluptates*), = peculiar to animals, *beluarum* or *pecudum* (e g *hoc est beluarum*) **animalcule,** n by circumloc *animal exigui corporis*, etc

animate, I v tr 1, = to give life to, *animare*, 2, fig = to make lively, *excitare*, *incitare*, — his courage, *animum erigĕre* **II** adj *animalis*, *animatus* **animated,** adj 1, lit *animatus*, 2, fig = lively, *vegetus*, *alacer*, — by anything, *alqd re incensus* **animation,** n. *alacritas*, *vehementia*

animosity, n. *odium, invidia, ira, simultas.*

ankle, ankle-bone, n. *talus.* **anklet,** n. *periscelis, -idis,* f.

annals, n. *annales, -ium,* m., *monumenta rerum gestarum.*

annex, v.tr. **1,** = to add to, *alqd alci rei* or *ad alqd (ad)jungĕre, addĕre.* **2,** = to conquer, *alqd alci rei sub(j)icĕre*; to — a country, *in ditionem suam redigĕre.* **annexation,** n. **1,** *adjunctio, accessio, appositio*; **2,** of a town, *expugnatio* (by storm).

annihilate, v.tr. *delēre, ex(s)tinguĕre* (as a light, e.g. *alcjs salutem*), *excidĕre, tollĕre, funditus tollĕre.* **annihilation,** n. *ex(s)tinctio, interitus, -ūs, excidium.*

anniversary, n. *sacra, -orum, anniversaria* (= festival), *festi dies anniversarii.*

annotate, v.tr. *annotare* (Plin.). **annotation,** n. *annotatio.*

announce, v.tr. *(re)nuntiare, indicare.* **announcement,** n. *(re)nuntiatio.*

annoy, v.tr. *molestiam alci afferre* or *exhibēre, vexare, torquēre*: — with requests, *alqm precibus fatigare.* **annoyance,** n. **1,** *molestia, vexatio, cruciatus, -ūs*; **2,** = a trouble, *onus, -eris,* n., *incommodum.*

annual, adj. *annuus, anniversarius* (= taking place every year). Adv. *quotannis.* **annuity,** n. *annua pecunia.* **annuitant,** n. *qui annuam pecuniam accipit.*

annul, v.tr. **1,** legal t.t. *legem tollĕre, abrogare, abolēre*; to — a contract *(dis)solvĕre.* **2,** in gen. *tollĕre, delēre.*

annular, adj. *in orbem circumactus.*

anodyne, n. *quod dolorem mitigat.*

anoint, v.tr. *unguĕre.* **anointing,** n. *unctio.*

anomaly, n. *anōmalia* (Varr.). **anomalous,** adj. *anōmalus* (Gram.).

anon, adv. *brevi (tempore), mox*; ever and —, *interdum.*

anonymous, adj. *sine nomine*; — poems, *carmina incertis auctoribus vulgata.*

another, pron. *alius*; at — time, *alio tempore*; — Cato (= a new), *novus Cato*; one says one thing, another —, *alius aliud dicit*; one —, *alius alium, inter se* (e.g. they fear one —, *inter se timent*), or (of two persons) *alter— alterum.*

answer, **I.** n. **1,** in gen. *responsum*; **2,** to a charge, *defensio, excusatio*; **3,** a written —, *rescriptum*; **4,** of an oracle, *oraculum, sors, sortis,* f.; **5,** — to prayer, *alqd precibus impetratum.* **II.** v.tr. **1,** in gen. *alqd alci* or *ad alqd respondēre*; **2,** by letter, *alqd alci rescribĕre*; **3,** to a charge, *se defendĕre, excusare*; **4,** of an oracle, *responsum dare*; to be answered, *mihi respondĕtur*; to — to one's name, *ad nomen respondēre*; to — an objection, *alqd refutare*; to — for, *alqd praestare,* see SURETY; to — to, *alci rei respondēre*; see AGREE. **III.** v.intr. = succeed, *res alci succedit, bene evenire.* **answerable,** adj. **1,** = agreeing with, *alci rei conveniens, congruens, consentaneus.* **2,** = accountable, *alcjs rei auctor, alqd praestans*; — to anyone, *qui alci de alqā re rationem reddit.*

ant, n. *formica.* **anthill,** *formicarum cuniculus.*

antagonist, n. *adversarius* (in every relation), *qui contra dicit, qui contra disputat, qui alci adversatur*; *iste* (= the opponent in a law-suit); see ADVERSARY.

antarctic, adj. **1,** lit. *antarcticus* (late); **2,** fig. *gelidissimus.*

antecedent, adj. *antecedens, praecedens, prior*; antecedents, *antecedentia, -ium,* pl., *praeterita, -orum,* pl. (= past events). Adv. *antea, prius.*

antechamber, n. *vestibulum* (= the open place in front of a Roman house where visitors assembled).

antechapel, n. *pronaus.*

antediluvian, adj. **1,** = old, *priscus, antiquus*; **2,** = old-fashioned, *obsoletus.*

antelope, n. see DEER.

antenna, n. *corniculum* (Plin.).

anterior, adj. *antecedens, praecedens, prior, superior, proximus.*

anthem, n. *cantus, -ūs.*

anthropoid, adj. *homini similis.*

anthropomorphic, adj. *Deum humanum corpus habēre fingens.*

anticipate, v.tr. **1,** *anticipare* (= to do before), *praecipĕre*; **2,** *ex(s)pectare* (= expect). **anticipation,** n. **1,** = expectation, *ex(s)pectatio, spes*; **2,** = a doing beforehand, by verb, ANTICIPATE.

antics, n. *ludi, joca, -orum, ridicula, -orum, nugae.*

antidote, n. *antidotus, antidotum* (Cels.), *remedium*; against anything, *alcjs rei* or *ad.*

antipathy, n., **1,** of things, *rerum discordia, repugnantia*; **2,** of persons, *odium.*

antipodes, n. **1,** lit. *antipodes, -um* (late); **2,** fig. = the opposite, by adj. *adversus, contrarius.*

antiquary, antiquarian, n. *rerum antiquarum studiosus.* **antiquated,** adj. *obsoletus.* **antique,** **I.** adj. *antiquus.* **II.** n. *opus antiquum, res antiqua, monumentum antiquum.* **antiquity,** n. *antiquitas.*

antithesis, n. **1,** rhet. t.t. *contentio*; **2,** fig. = the opposite, *contrarium.*

antler, n. *cornu.*

anvil, n. *incus, -ūdis,* f.

anxiety, n. *angor, anxietas, pavor, sol(l)icitudo, trepidatio, timor.* **anxious,** adj. *anxius, sol(l)icitus*; to be —, *de alqā re anxium esse, angi.* Adv. *anxie, sol(l)icite.*

any, **I.** pron. *quisquam* (in neg. sentences and questions); *quilibet, quivis* (= any you please); *quis* (only after *si, ne, num, quo, quanto, nisi*); *ecquis* (in impassioned questions). **II.** adj. *ullus* (in neg. sentences and questions), *quilibet, quivis* (= any you please), *ecqui* (in impassioned questions); — one, *aliquis, quispiam*; at — turn, *aliquando, quando* (after *si, ne, num*); *unquam* (in neg. questions and sentences); — where, *alicubi, ubivis, usquam* (in neg. questions and sentences).

apace, adv. *celeriter.*

apart, adv. by prefix *se* (e.g. *se—cernĕre*), *separatim.* **apartment,** n. see ROOM.

apathy, n. *socordia* (not in Cic. or Caes.), *nequitia.* **apathetic,** adj. *hebes*; see LAZY.

ape, **I.** n. *simia*; a little —, *simiolus.* **II.** v.tr. *alqm imitari*; see IMITATE.

aperient, n. and adj. by *alvi dejectionem (alvi) purgationem (petĕre,* etc.).

aperture, n. see OPENING.

apex, n. *apex.*

aphorism, n. *sententia, dictum, elogium.*

apiary, n. *alvearium, mellarium.*

apiece, adv. by distrib. numeral (e.g. *deni,* ten —).

apologist, n *defensor* **apology**, n 1, = defence, *defensio*, 2, = excuse, *excusatio* **apologize**, v intr *alqd excusare* **apologetical**, adj by verb, *qui se excusat*, etc **apologue**, n *apologus*

apophthegm, n *elogium, sententia, dictum*

apoplexy, n *apoplexis, apoplexia* (late)

apostle, n *apostolus*

apostrophe, n 1, rhet t t *apostrophe*; 2, grammat t t *apostrophus* (late) **apostrophize**, v tr see Address

apothecary, n *medicus*

appal, v tr *terrēre*; see Frighten

apparatus, n *apparatus, -ūs*

apparel, n *vestis, vestimentum*

apparent, adj 1, = evident, *manifestus, apertus, clarus*, to make —, *patefacĕre, aperire*, 2, opp to real, *opinatus, fictus, simulatus* Adv *aperto, manifeste, evidenter* **apparition**, n 1, = appearance, *adventus, ūs*, 2, = a spectre, *alcjs simulacrum, species*

appeal, I. v intr 1, legal t t *alqm appellare, ad alqm provocare*; 2, = to refer to, *alqm testari*. II. n 1, *appellatio, provocatio*, court of —, *judices penes quos provocatio est*, 2, = entreaty, *preces, -um*, f, *deprecatio* **appealing**, adj *supplex*, in an — voice, *suppliciter*

appear, v intr 1, = become visible, *apparēre, in conspectum venire, conspici* (= to be seen), *se offerre*, it —s to me, *mihi videtur*, to — publicly, *in publicum prodire*, to —, = to be present, *adesse*, — to exist, *ex(s)istĕre*, to — in court, *in judicium venire* 2, = to seem, *videri* **appearance**, n 1, = arrival, *adventus, -ūs*, 2, legal t t = surety, *vadimonium*, 3, = a thing shown, *res objecta, visum, species*, 4, = personal —, *corporis habitus, -ūs*, in —, = under pretext of, *sub specie*, to put on an —, *simulare* (with acc and infin), in all —, *verisimillimum est* (with acc and infin)

appease, v tr 1, = — a deity, *placare* 2, = — a man, *placare, (re)conciliare*, 3, = to — hunger, *famem explēre, depellĕre* **appeasable**, adj *placabilis*, — in character, *ingenium placabile* **appeasement**, n *placatio, reconciliatio*

appellant, n *qui provocat*

append, v tr *addĕre, adjungĕre, figĕre, (af)figere alqd alci rei, alligare alqd ad rem* **appendage, -ant**, n *appendix, -icis*, f, *accessio, alqd alci rei additum* **appendix**, n *appendix, additamentum*, — of a book, *quaedam libro addita* See Add, Attach

appertain, v tr see Belong

appetite, 1, physical, *fames, -is*, to have no —, *cibum fastidire*, 2, = desire for, *alcjs cupiditas, aviditas, appetitus, ūs*

applaud, v tr *(ap)plaudĕre alci, plausu* or *plausibus alqm excipĕre* **applause**, n *(ap)plausus, -ūs*, see Praise

apple, n *malum*, — tree, *malus*, f

apply, I. v tr. 1, = to put or fit to, *alqd alci rei* or *ad alqd applicare, aptare, accommodare*, 2, = to use for, *collocare in alqā re, conferre ad alqd, tribuere alqd alci rei, alqd ad alqd dirigĕre, (con)vertere* II v intr = to turn or go to, *se convertĕre conferre ad alqm, adire* or *convenire alqm, appellare alqd, confugĕre ad alqm, se applicare ad alqm* **appliance**, n *apparatus, ūs, instrumentum* **application**, n 1, = request, address, *appellatio, provocatio, petitio*, 2, = putting to, *adjunctio, conjunctio* (fig), 3, = of the mind, *animi intentio, diligentia*, 4, = of a word, *significatio* **applicable**, adj *utilis* to be — to anything, *ad alqd pertinēre*

appoint, v tr *constituĕre, destinare* (= to make fast), *designare* (= to order), *eligĕre* (= to choose), to — a day, *diem statuĕre, constituĕre, dicĕre* **appointment**, n 1, = designation, by verb, e g — of consuls, *consules designare*, 2, = an office, *munus, -ĕris*, n, 3, = command, *jussum, mandatum*, 4, = agreement to meet, by verb, *cum alqo convenire ut*

apportion, v tr *dispertire, distribuĕre, dispensare, disponĕre, assignare* (e g *militibus agros*)

apposite, adj *conveniens, accommodatus* Adv *convenienter, accommodate*

appraise, v tr = to fix the value of, *aestimare, censēre* (the censor s act) See Value

appreciate, v tr *aestimare*, — highly, *alqm magni facĕre*

apprehend, v tr 1, = to lay hold on, *prehendĕre, apprehendĕre*, 2, = to take in mentally, *comprehendĕre, complecti (animo* or *mente), cogitatione (mente) concipĕre, intellegĕre*, 3 = fear, see Fear **apprehension**, n 1, = arrest, *comprehensio*, 2, = mental —, *comprehensio, intellegentia (intellig)*, 3, = fear, *timor*, see Fear **apprehensive**, adj, see Timid

apprentice, I n *alci* (e g *sutori*) *addictus* II v tr *alqm alci addicere*

approach, I. v intr *ad alqm* or *alqd accedĕre, alci* or *alci rei appropinquare*, of time, *appropinquare*, to — the truth, *prope ad veritatem accedĕre, a veritate non multum abesse* II. n *appropinquatio, adventus, ūs, aditus, -ūs*

appropriate, I. v intr 1, = to give, *alqd alci dedicare*, 2, = to claim, *alqd sibi* or *ad se vindicare, alqd sibi arrogare, alqd suum facĕre* II adj *ad alqd* or *alci rei idoneus, aptus, accommodatus, cum alqā re conveniens, congruens* Adv *accommodate, convenienter* **appropriation**, n 1, legal t t *(agrorum) assignatio, (bonorum) additio*, 2, in gen by verb Appropriate

approve, v tr 1, in gen *(com)probare*, 2, = legal t t *alqd ratum facere* or *ratum esse jubēre sancire*, 3, = to — oneself, *se (fidum*, etc) *praebēre* **approved**, adj *probatus, spectatus* **approver**, n, legal t t *index, -icis*, n and f **approval**, n see Approbation **approbation**, n *(com)probatio*, with someone s —, *alqo auctore, alcjs auctoritate, pace tuā, suā*, etc, without —, *alcjs injussu, sine alcjs auctoritate*

approximate, v tr & adj see Approach, Near

April, n *Aprilis (mensis)*; to make an — fool of, *alqm ludibrio habēre*

apron, n *subligaculum*

apt, adj 1, see Appropriate, 2, = ready, *habilis*, — to learn, *docilis* Adv *convenienter*, = cleverly, *perite, callide* **aptitude**, n *facultas* (with gen or adj)

aquatic, aqueous, adj *aquatilis* **aqueduct**, n *aquae ductus, -ūs*, also *aqua* alone, to form an — for the city, *aquam in urbem ducĕre*

aquiline, adj *aduncus*

arable, adj *arabilis* See Plough

arbiter, n *arbiter, disceptator*

arbitrate, v tr *alqd disceptare, dijudicare* **arbitration**, n *arbitrium* **arbitrary**, adj 1, = unbounded, *infinitus, summus*, 2, = capricious, *inconstans*, 3 = proud, *superbus* Adv *superbe* **arbitrariness**, n *superbia*

arbour, n *umbraculum, ramorum nexus, -ūs*

arc, n *arcus, ūs* **arcade**, n *porticus, ūs*, f

arch, I. n *arcus, ūs, fornix* II. v tr *arcuare, conformicare* III. v intr *arcuari*, see Curve IV. adj *petulans* V. in comp =

chief; — angel, *archangelus, — bishop, *archiepiscopus (Eccl.)

archaeology, n rerum antiquarum scientia **archaism,** n verbum obsoletum

archer, n sagittarius **archery,** n by verb (e g sagittis alqd petĕre).

architect, n = master builder, architectus **architecture,** n architectura

archives, n 1, (private) tab(u)linum = the place where papers are kept, 2, (public) tabulae publicae

arctic, adj septentrionalis (e g regio, occasus)

ardent, adj ardens, fervens, acer Adv acriter, ardenter

ardour, n ardor, fervor, aestus, -ūs

arduous, adj arduus, difficilis

area, n superficies

arena, n arena (lit. and fig).

argue, v tr 1, = to dispute, verbis contendĕre, concertare, disputare, 2, = to give or draw a conclusion, arguĕre, concludĕre, colligĕre **argument,** 1, in gen argumentum, 2, = subject matter, sententia, argumentum

arid, adj aridus, siccus

aright, adv recte, bene See RIGHT

arise, v intr emergĕre (= to come up out of), exoriri, ex(s)istĕre (of distinguished men) See RISE

aristocrat, n 1, = a noble, unus e nobilibus or patriciis, 2, = defender of the aristocracy, optimatium fautor **aristocracy,** n 1, = the nobles, optimates, (i)um, m and f, patricii, nobiles 2, = a form of government, optimatium dominatus, ūs **aristocratical,** adj quod ad optimates pertinet, or by gen optimatium

arithmetic, n arithmetice, es, f, or arithmetica, -ae, f, or arithmetica, -orum. **arithmetical,** adj arithmeticus **arithmetician,** n arithmeticus

ark, n arca

arm, I. n 1, lit brachium (from the elbow to the wrist), lacertus (from the elbow to the shoulder), bone of —, radius brachii, to take into —s, alqm complecti, to sink into anyone's —s, manibus alcjs excipi, 2, fig (of the sea), brachium, (of a hill), ramus, (of a harbour), cornu **II.** v tr armare, lit and fig **III.** v intr armari, arma capĕre **armed,** adj armatus **arm-chair,** n use sella (= chair), or lectus, torus (= couch) **armistice,** n indutiae **armour,** n arma, -orum, pl, — bearer, armiger **armourer,** n faber armorum **arm-pit,** n ala **armoury,** n. armamentarium. **arms,** n. arma, -orum, tela, -orum (of missiles esp, but also of swords, etc), without arms inermis, to run to —, ire ad arma, to — ! ad arma ! to lay down —, arma deponĕre, to be under —, in armis esse, to bear — against, arma ferre contra alqm, to enter a country in —, arma inferre terrae. **army,** n exercitus, -ūs, copiae, milites, -um, vires, -ium, f, — in marching array, agmen, — in battle-array, acies

aromatic, adj odorus, odoratus, suavis

around, I. adv circa, circum, in composition with a verb, circum (e g to look —, circumspicĕre) **II** prep circa, circum with accus See ABOUT

arouse, v tr 1, lit (e somno) excitare; 2, fig excitare, (com)movēre

arraign, v tr, see ACCUSE

arrange, v tr ordinare, componĕre, disponĕre, — in order of battle, aciem instruĕre, collocare, constituĕre, instruĕre, to — troops, copias instruĕre **arrangement,** n 1, rhet. t.t. compositio, dispositio (of words or sentences); 2, in gen. constitutio, ratio, by part (e g a good — of anything, res bene disposita, instructa, etc)

arrant, adj by superl or summus Adv. superl of adv or turpiter, foede

array, I. n 1, see ARRANGEMENT, 2, battle —, acies, 3, = dress, vestis **II** v tr. 1, see ARRANGE, 2, = to dress, vestire; fig ornare, vestire

arrears, n pecuniae residuae, to be in — with, legal t t alqd reliquare (Jct)

arrest, v tr. comprehendĕre, in vincula con(j)icĕre, to put under —, comprehendĕre, in custodiam dare

arrive, v intr advenire, pervenire, adventare. **arrival,** n adventus, -ūs, accessus, -ūs

arrogant, adj arrogans, insolens, superbus, elatus alqā re **arrogance,** n arrogantia, superbia Adv arroganter, superbe **arrogate,** v tr sibi arrogare, (as)sumĕre

arrow, n sagitta

arsenal, n armamentarium; naval —, navalia, -ium

arsenic, n arsenicum

arsis, n sublatio (Quint), arsis (late)

art, n 1, = skill, ars, artificium, merely mental, scientia, peritia, studium alcjs rei, 2, = an —, ars (e g pingendi), disciplina, the fine —s, artes ingenuae, — and sciences, studia et artes, 3, = a trick, ars by — or craft, per dolum et fraudem **artful,** adj callidus, versutus, vafer, astutus. Adv astute, callide **artfulness,** n astutia, dolus **artificer,** n 1, in gen artifex, 2, = creator, auctor **artificial,** adj artificiosus Adv arte or per artem **artisan,** n opifex, faber **artist,** n poeta pictor, etc, or opifex = artisan, as among the Romans art was not always included in the artes liberales **artistic,** adj. (ingenuarum) artium amator or studiosus **artistically,** adv arte, summa arte **artless,** adj simplex, ingenuus Adv ingenue, simpliciter, sine arte **artlessness,** n simplicitas

artichoke, n cinara (Col).

article, I. n 1, in gen res; 2, = condition, condicio (e g pacis), 3, = law, lex (e g lex militaris) **II.** v tr, see APPRENTICE

articulate, I. v tr pronuntiare **II.** adj. clarus Adv clare **articulation,** n 1, of words, pronuntiatio, 2, of limbs, artus, -uum, articulus

artillery, n (= the larger offensive weapons) tormenta -orum, (comprising the ballistae and catapultae).

as, adv and conj 1, in gen by double comparative (e g he is not — brave as he is good, melior est quam fortior), idem (he is — friendly as ever, idem est amicus qui, etc), aeque cum alqo or et, atque, et — et (= — well as), — far as I can, quoad ejus facĕre possum, — quickly as possible, quam celerrime, — much again, alterum tantum, — many as, quotcumque, — far as I know, quod sciam, 2, = like, instar, alcjs rei, tanquam, ut or by adv (e g to behave as a fool, stulte), by a noun in apposition (Caesar — consul, Caesar consul), 3, as to, de alqā re, ad alqd, quod ad alqd pertinet, 4, of time, ubi, ut, cum (quom), — often —, quotie(n)s toties(n)s; — long —, tam diu — quam, — soon —, simul ac, 5, causal, quoniam (indic.), cum (subj), 6, = as if, tanquam (tamq) si, non aliter quam si

ascend, v tr in or ad alqd a(d)scendĕre.

ascension, n. *a(d)scensus, -ūs* **ascent**, n 1, = a hill, *locus editus*, 2, a going up, *a(d)scensus, ūs*

ascendancy, n *praestantia*

ascendant, n by adj *summus*, to be in the —, *praevalēre, alci alqa re praestare*, his star is in the —, *summam gloriam adeptus est*

ascertain, v tr *explorare, rem exploratam habēre*

ascetic, n *qui cibo abstinet*

ascribe, v tr. *alqd alci or alci rei, a(d)scribere, tribuĕre, adjungĕre*, — great value to, *magnum pretium statuĕre rei*

ash, **I.** n *fraxinus*, f **II** adj *fraxineus*

ashamed, adj *pudore affectus*, to be —, *pudet alqm alcjs rei* or infin

ashes, n *cinis, ĕris*, m, *favilla*, to reduce to —, *ad* or *in cinerem redigĕre*, to lie in sack-cloth and —, *sordidatum* or *atratum esse* **ashy**, adj *cinereus*

ashore, adv. 1, of rest, *in litore*, 2, of motion, *in litus* or *terram*, to go —, (*e nave*) *exire*, to put men —, *exponere*

aside, adv *seorsum, ex obliquo*, to go —, *secedĕre*, to call —, *alqm sevocare*, to lay —, *alqd seponĕre*

ask, v tr *alqm rogare, ex alqo quaerĕre, ex alqo sciscitari, alqm alqd orare, petĕre, poscĕre, flagitare* (repeatedly); to — a price, *indicare*

askance, adv *oblique*, to look — at, *alq limis oculis a(d)spicĕre*

aslant, adv *oblique, ex transverso*

asleep, adj *dormiens, in somno, per somnum*

asp, n *aspis, -ĭdis*, f, *vipera*

aspect, n 1, in gen *a(d)spectus, -ūs, conspectus, -ūs*, 2 (in astrology), *aspectus siderum*, 3, = condition, *status, -ūs, ratio, condicio*

asperity, n *asperitas, acerbitas*

asperse, v tr *a(d)spergĕre*, both lit and fig **aspersion**, n 1, lit *a(d)spersio*, 2, fig *calumnia, opprobrium*, to cast an —, *calumniari*

asphalt, n *bitumen*

aspirate, **I.** n *a(d)spiratio* **II.** v tr *a(d)spirare*

aspire, v intr *ad alqd a(d)spirare, alqd sequi* or *persequi, eniti, contendere, operam dare ut* **aspiration**, n after anything, *alcjs rei appetitio, contentio*

ass, n 1, *asinus*, a little —, *asellus*, a female —, *asina*, 2, as a term of contempt, *homo stultissimus* **ass-driver**, n *asinarius*

assail, v tr to — a town *oppugnare* **assailant**, n *qui alqm adoritur* **assault**, **I.** n 1 in gen *impetus, -ūs, incursus, ūs*, 2, = — of a town, *oppugnatio*, 3, legal t t to charge with —, *alqm de vi reum facĕre*, to commit an —, *alci vim afferre* **II.** v tr see ATTACK

assassin, n *sicarius* **assassination**, n *caedes facta*, to accuse of —, *accusare inter sicarios* **assassinate**, v tr *alqm ex insidiis interficĕre*

assay, v tr see TRY, ATTEMPT

assemble, **I.** v tr *cogĕre, congregare, convocare, contrahĕre*, to — the people, *contionem convocare*, to — troops, *copias in unum locum cogĕre* **II.** v intr *cogi, congregari, convenire, coire, confluĕre* **assembly**. n *congregatio, convocatio*, = the people assembled, *conventus, -ūs, coetus, ūs, contio*

assent, **I.** n *assensio, assensus, -ūs* **II.** v intr *assentire*, — to anything, *rei assentiri, assentari, alqd* or *de alqā re, cum alqo* or *inter se, convenire*, to nod —, *annuĕre*.

assert, v tr. (as an opinion) *tenēre, contendĕre, affirmare, asseverare, dicĕre*, to — your right, *jus tenēre* **assertion**, n 1, *sententia, opinio, affirmatio*, 2, = maintenance, *defensio, vindicatio*, see AFFIRM

assess, v tr *tributum alci imponĕre, censēre*, to be —ed at anything, *alqd conferre* **assessment**, n *aestimatio* (= act of —) *tributum, vectigal* (= tax) **assessor**, n *assessor*, — of taxes, *censor* **assets**, n by *bona, orum*

assever, v see ASSERT

assiduous, adj *assiduus, sedulus, industrius acer, impiger, diligens* Adv *impigre assidue, industrie, acriter, diligenter* **assiduity**, n *assiduitas, sedulitas*

assign, v tr *alci alqd assignare, attribuĕre* **assignation**, n 1, *assignatio, attributio*; 2, = appointment, *constitutum*, to keep an —, *ad constitutum venire*

assimilate, v tr 1, *alqd cum alqā re (ad)aequare, alqd alci rei similem facere*, 2, = to digest, *concoquĕre* **assimilation**, n 1, *aequalitas*, 2, *concoctio*

assist, v tr *auxilio alci esse, auxilium ferre, opitulari* (= to bring aid) *subvenire, adesse alci* (= to stand by a person) **assistance**, n *auxilium* or *adjumentum*, to implore anyone's —, *alcjs fidem implorare* **assistant**, n *adjutor, adjutrix*, — teacher, *hypodidascalus, adjutor*, = colleague, *collega*, m, see HELP

associate, **I.** v tr *foedus facĕre* (= to make an alliance), *comitem (socium) se alci adjungĕre, se conjungĕre* **II** v intr = to be associated, *foedere conjungi, esse cum alqo*, like —s with like, *pares cum paribus facillime congregantur* **III.** n *socius, sodalis, comes, ĭtis*, m and f, *conscius* **association**, n *societas, sodalitas, collegium*, see ASSEMBLY

assort, v tr (in gen) *digerĕre* **assortment**, n *apparatus, ūs, numerus* or by part (e g *res* or *merces collectae, digestae*, etc), see ALLOT, APPORTION

assuage, v tr *mitigare, lenire, sedare* **assuagement**, n *mitigatio*

assume, v tr 1, = take to oneself, *alqd sibi vindicare, sibi arrogare, sumĕre, occupare*, 2, = to take for granted, *ponĕre*, this being assumed, *hoc posito* or *concesso* **assumption**, n 1, = a taking, *usurpatio*, 2, = arrogance, *insolentia, arrogantia, superbia* 3, = postulate, by part (e g *hoc posito*), this is a mere —, *hoc non est confirmatum*

assure, v tr = to assert the certainty of, (*pro certo*) *affirmare, asseverare*, be assured, *credĕ mihi* **assurance**, see STATEMENT, IMPUDENCE **assured**, adj = fearless, *securus*, = certain, *certus, spectatus* Adv *certo, certe, haud dubie*

astern, adv, *in* or *a puppe*

asthma, n *dyspnoea* (Plin) **asthmatic**, adj *asthmaticus* (Plin)

astonish, v tr *perturbare, conturbare* **astonished**, adj *attonitus*, to be —, *stupefactum esse* **astonishing**, adj *mirabilis, mirus, mirificus* Adv *mire, mirifice, mirabiliter* **astonishment**, n *stupor, (ad)miratio*

astound, v tr see ASTONISH

astray, adv *vage*, to be —, *errare, vagari*

astringent, adj *a(d)strictorius* **astringency**, n *a(d)strictio*

astrologer, n *astrolŏgus, Chaldaeus* **astrology**, n *astrologia*

astronomer, n *astrolŏgus* **astronomy**, *astrologia*.

astute, adj. *astutus, callidus*

asunder, adv. *seorsum;* in comp. by *dis* or *se* (e.g. *discurrĕre, sevocare*).

asylum, n. *asylum.*

at, prep. 1, of place, *ad, apud, juxta* (with the accus. e.g. *ad ostium,* = at the door; *ad portas,* = at the gate; *ad Cannas* = at Cannae); by the abl. with or without *in,* (*in*) *urbe,* = at the city; (*in*) *initio,* = at the beginning; or by the old locative case, *Romae,* = at Rome; *Londini,* = at London; *Gadibus,* = at Cadiz; so *domi, militiae,* = at home, at service, etc.; 2, of time, abl. *eodem tempore,* = at the same time; *ad meridiem,* = at midday; by accus. with *apud,* at my house, *apud me;* = during, *inter;* at dinner, *inter cenam* (*coen.*); at once, *statim;* at first, *primo, primum;* at last, *postremo,* (*ad*) *postremum.*

atheist, n. *atheos* (or *-us*), *qui Deum esse negat.* **atheism,** n. * *atheismus, doctrina Deum esse negans;* to hold —, *Deum esse negare, nullum esse omnino Deum putare.*

athlete, n. *athleta,* m.

athwart, adv. *transverse, in obliquum;* see ACROSS, ASKANCE.

atlas, n. (in geography), use *tabulae geographicae.*

atmosphere, n. *caelum.* **atmospheric,** adj. by the genitive *aëris* or *caeli;* see AIR.

atom, n. 1, phil. t.t. *atŏmus -i,* f.; 2, see PIECE.

atone, v.tr. *alqd luĕre, expiare, alqd* (*cum*) *alqâ re compensare, poenas alcjs rei dare* or (*ex*)*pendĕre.* **atonement,** n. *placatio, satisfactio, poena;* = reconciliation, *reditus, -ūs in gratiam.*

atrabilious, adj. *melancholicus.*

atrocious, adj. *nefandus, nefarius, atrox, immanis.* Adv. *atrociter, nefarie.* **atrocity,** n. 1, of mental quality, *immanitas, atrocitas;* 2, = an atrocious thing, *res atrox,* etc.

atrophy, n. *tabes, -is,* f.

attach, v.tr. 1, = fasten, *figĕre, affigĕre alqd alci rei, alligare alqd ad rem;* 2, = to make prisoner, *comprehendĕre, in vincula con(j)icĕre, in custodiam dare;* 3, = to make your friend, *conciliare, alqm sibi facĕre* or *reddĕre amicum;* to be —ed, *alcjs studiosum esse.* **attachment,** n. *studium alcjs, amor alcjs* or *in alqm observantia.*

attack, I. n. *petitio, impetus, -ūs, incursio, incursus, -ūs, excursus, -ūs, concursus, -ūs, congressus, -ūs. oppugnatio;* at the first —, *primo impetu, primo congressu;* to make an — on the enemy, *impetum facĕre in hostem.* **II.** v.tr. *petĕre, aggredi, adoriri* (= to fall on), *oppugnare* (= to storm), *procurrĕre in alqm* (= to rush out on a foe), *signa inferre in hostem, incurrĕre, invehi in hostem;* to — with words, *dicto* or *convicio, lacessĕre, alqm insectari; consectari, adoriri;* to be —ed by a disease, *morbo corripi.*

attain, v.tr. *alqd assequi, consequi, ad alqd pervenire.* **attainable,** adj. *facilis, quod alqs facile consequi potest.* **attainment,** n. 1, = the getting of anything, *adeptio, comparatio;* 2, = a piece of learning, *alcjs rei scientia;* —s, *doctrina, eruditio.* **attainder,** n. *accusatio.*

attempt, I. n. *conatus, -ūs, conata, -orum,* **II.** v.tr. *tentare, experiri, periclitari.*

attend, v.tr. 1, = to accompany, *alqm comitari, esse alcjs comitem;* 2, = to wait upon a dignitary, *alci apparēre;* as a servant, *alci famulari, alqd alci ministrare;* 3, = to frequent, of lectures, etc., *alqm audire;* 4, = pay attention to, *alqd curare;* = to hear, *audire, animadvertĕre;* Attend! *attende;* 5, = be present at, *adesse* (e.g. *sacris,* public worship). **attendance,** n. 1, of servants, *ministerium;* 2, = presence at, by verb *adesse;* a great —, *frequentia.* **attendant,** n. 1, = companion, *comes, -itis,* m. and f., *socius;* 2, = servant, *servus, minister, famulus;* 3, = the —s of a great man, *comitatus, -ūs.* **attention,** n. 1, = — of the mind, *animi attentio, intentio, vigilantia;* 2, = diligence, *diligentia, studium;* to show — to, *alqm colĕre, observare.* **attentive,** adj. *assiduus, vigil, diligens, attentus, intentus, erectus;* to be —, *animo sequi alqd.* Adv. *attente, intente.*

attenuate, v.tr. *attenuare, extenuare, diluĕre.* **attenuation,** n. *extenuatio.*

attest, v.tr. 1, = prove, *alqd testificari,* (*at*)*testari, testimonio confirmare, alci testimonio esse;* 2, = to call to witness, *alqm testari, testem facĕre.* **attestation,** n. 1, = giving evidence, *testificatio;* 2, = a piece of evidence, *testimonium.*

attire, I. v.tr. *induĕre alci vestem* or *alqm veste; vestire.* **II.** n. *vestis.*

attitude, n. 1, *corporis habitus, -ūs;* 2 = circumstances, *condicio, status, -ūs;* 3, = mental —, (*mentis*) *ratio.*

attorney, n. *procurator.*

attract, v.tr. *attrahĕre, ad se trahĕre, allicĕre.* **attraction,** n. 1, *vis attrahendi;* 2, = an attractive object, *oblectamentum.* **attractive,** adj. *jucundus, suavis.* Adv. *jucunde, suaviter.*

attribute, I. n. 1, *nota, insigne;* to bear the —s of royalty, *insignibus regiis uti;* 2, (in gram.) *attributio, attributum;* 3, = peculiarity, *proprium, natura, vis.* **II.** v.tr. *attribuĕre.*

attrition, n. by verb *terĕre.*

attune, v.tr. lit. and fig., *efficĕre ut alqd cum alqâ re concinat.*

auburn, adj. *flavus.*

auction, n. *auctio;* to sell by —, *auctionari;* to sell by public —, *hastâ positâ auctionari;* to bid at an —, *licēri;* to be knocked down at an —, *alci addici.* **auctioneer,** n. *magister auctionis, praeco* (= the crier of bids, etc.).

audacious, adj. *procax, protervus, impudens.* Adv. *impudenter, proterve.* **audacity,** n. *procacitas, protervitas, impudentia.*

audience, n. 1, = hearing of anyone, *admissio, aditus, -ūs, ad alqm, colloquium;* 2, = hearers, *auditores, audientes, corona* (esp. of crowd round a public speaker); a large —, (*magna*) *audientium frequentia.* **audible,** adj. *quod audiri potest.* Adv. *clarâ voce.* **audit,** v.tr. *rationem ducĕre, habĕre, inire,* or *rationes cum alqo putare.* **auditor,** n. *qui rationes ducit.*

augment, v.tr. *alqd alqâ re augēre, amplificare, addĕre alqd alci rei* or *ad alqd.* **augmentation,** n. *amplificatio, accessio.*

augur, I. n. *augur.* **II.** v.tr. *alqd praedicĕre, vaticinari, augurari.* **augury,** n. 1, = a predicting, *augurium, vaticinatio, praedictio.* 2, = a thing predicted, *omen* (= a natural —), *praedictum* (= a prophecy).

August, I. n. *Augustus,* (*mensis*) *Augustus, Sextilis.* **II.** adj. *augustus* (= sacred), *illustris, magnificus.*

aunt, n. *amita* (= a father's sister), *matertera* (= a mother's sister).

auriferous, adj. *aurifer.*

auspice, n. *auspicium.* **auspicious,** adj. *prosper, secundus, faustus.* Adv. *fauste, prospere.*

austere, adj. *austerus, severus, tristis.* Adv. *austere, severe.* **austerity,** n. *austeritas, severitas.*

authentic, adj. *certus, verus, sincerus.* Adv. *certo auctore.* **authenticity,** n. *fides, auctoritas.*

author, n *auctor* (= originator), *inventor*, *scriptor* (= a writer). **authoritative**, adj *imperiosus*, *arrogans* Adv *arroganter*

authority, n *auctoritas* (by birth, character, and office), *amplitudo* (by office), comb *auctoritas atque amplitudo*, *dignitas*, *gravitas* (by personal worth), *gratia*, *dominatio* (= despotic authority), the —s = magistrates, *magistratus*, *ūs* **authorize**, v tr *alci mandare ut*, *alci permittĕre*, with infin

autocrat, n *dominus*, autocratical power, *summa potestas*, *imperium* (*summum*)

autograph, **I.** n *alcjs manu scriptus* **II.** adj an — letter, *epistula mea ipsius manu scripta*

autumn, n *autumnus*, *tempus autumnale*, = — of life, *aetas grandior*. **autumnal**, adj *autumnalis*

auxiliary, **I.** n as a city or state, *civitas foederata*, in the pl *auxilia* (*milites*) *auxiliares* (= foreign soldiers who strengthen an army), *subsidia*, *orum*, *subsidiarii* (= the reserve of an army) **II.** adj *auxiliaris*

avail, **I.** v intr *valēre*, *praevalēre*, *obtinēre* **II.** n *utilitas*, to be of much —, *multum apud alqm valēre*, to make of no —, *non flocci facĕre*.

avarice, n *avaritia*, *cupiditas*, *pecuniae* **avaricious**, adj *habendi cupidus*, *avidior ad rem*, *avarus* Adv *avare*

avaunt! interj *abi! apage!*

avenge, v tr *vindicare*, *ulcisci*, to — oneself on anyone, *alqm ulcisci pro alqâ re*. **avenger**, n *ultor*, *vindex*

avenue, n **1**, = approach, *aditus*, *ūs*, **2**, = a shady walk, *xystus*

aver, v t, see AFFIRM, ASSERT

avert, v tr *alqd ab alqo avertere*, *aversari* **aversion**, n *fuga*, *odium*, *animus alienus* or *aversus* **averse**, adj *ab alqo* or *alqâ re aversus*, *alienus*

aviary, n *aviarium*

avoid, v tr *defugĕre*, *vitare*, *declinare*. **avoiding**, n *devitatio*, *fuga*

avow, v tr *profiteri*, *confiteri*, *prae se ferre* **avowal**, n *confessio* **avowed**, adj *apertus*, *permissus* Adv *aperte*

await, v tr *alqm* or *alqd ex(s)pectare*, *opperiri*.

awake, **I.** v tr (*e somno*) *excitare*, (*ex*)*suscitare* **II.** v intr *expergisci*, *excitari* **III.** adj *vigilans*, to be —, *vigilare* **awakening**, n by verb AWAKE

award, **I.** v tr *alqd alci adjudicare* **II.** n. *judicium*, *arbitrium*, *addictio*

aware, adj *alcjs rei gnarus*, to be —, *alqd scire*, *novisse*

away, adv *procul*; — with! *tolle! aufer!* — — you! *apage te!* go —, *abire* In comp with *a* (e.g *abesse*, to be —)

awe, **I.** n *veneratio*, *religio*, to feel — towards, *vereri alqm*. **II.** v tr *terrēre*, see FRIGHTEN **awful**, adj **1**, = feeling awe, *verecundus* (= shy), *pius*, *religiosus*, **2**, = terrible, *dirus*, *atrox*, *immanis* Adv **1**, with fear, *verecunde* (= shyly), *pie*, *religiose*, **2**, = terribly, *dire*, *atrociter*

awhile, adv *aliquamdiu*, *paul(l)isper*, —ago, *paul(l)o ante*

awkward, adj *agrestis*, *rusticus*, *rudis*, *inscitus* Adv *inscite*, *rustice* **awkwardness**, n *inscitia*

awl, n *subula* (Mart.)

awning, n *velum*

awry, **I.** adj **1**, lit. *obliquus*, **2**, fig *perversus*, **II.** adv *oblique*, *perverse*.

axe, n. *securis*, *dolabra*

axiom, n *axioma*, *ătis*, *pronuntiatum*

axis, **axle**, n *axis*, m

ay, adv *ita*, *ita est*, *recte*, *certe*, *vero*, *sane*, *sane quidem*, often by repeating the verb, e.g, will he come? yes! *veniet*? *veniet*, I say ay, *aio*

azure, adj *caeruleus*.

B

baa, **I.** v tr *balare* **II.** n *balatus*, *ūs*

babble, v *blaterare*, *garrire*, *nugari* **babbling**, n *garrulitas*, *loquacitas*. **babbler**, n. *garrulus*, *loquax*

babe, **baby**, n *infans*

baboon, n *simia* (= ape)

bacchanal, n *homo vinolentus ac dissolutus*; a female —, *baccha*

bacchic, adj *bacchicus*

bachelor, n *caelebs*

back, **I.** n **1**, *tergum*, *dorsum*, to lie on the —, *supinum cubare*, to attack the enemy on the —, *hostes aversos aggredi*, (of soldiers) *terga dare*, behind a person's —, *clam*, **2**, = the back part, *pars posterior*, the — of the head, *occipitium* **II.** adv. **backwards**, *retro*, *retrorsum*, in comp. *re* (e g *revocare*, to call —) **III.** adj *posterior* **IV.** v tr = to move backward, *retro movēre*, = to support, *alci favēre*, *fautorem esse*, (*ad*)*juvare*, *sustinēre* (= to help) **V.** v intr *se recipĕre*, *recedere*, to — water, *remos* or *remis inhibēre*, *navem retro inhibēre*

backbite, v tr *alci absenti maledicĕre*, *alqm obtrectare*

bacon, n *lardum*

bad, adj **1** (in a physical sense), *malus*, bad weather, *tempestas mala*, *adversa*, *foeda* (= foul), — road, *iter difficile*, *incommodum*, — money, *nummi adulterini*, in — health, *aeger*, to go —, *corrumpi*, **2**, (in a moral sense) *malus*, *adversus*, *pravus*, *turpis*, *depravatus*, *nequam*, — times, *tempora iniqua* (= unfavourable), *aspera* (= hard); — injurious, a — tongue, *lingua maledica* Adv *male*, *prave*, *nequiter*, *turpiter* **badness**, n **1** = physical —, by adj, the — of anything, *res mala*, — of health, *aegritudo*, *aegrotatio*, **2**, = moral —, *pravitas*, *turpitas*, *nequitia*

badge, n *signum*, *insigne*, *nota*

badger, **I.** n *meles*, -is, f **II.** v tr *vexare*, (*ex*)*cruciare*

baffle, v tr *eludĕre*, *ad vanum*, or *ad irritum redigĕre* *disturbare*, *spem fallĕre*

bag, n *saccus*.

baggage, n **1**, *sarcinae*, *impedimenta*, *-orum*; **2**, = a dissolute woman, *scortum*

bail, **I.** n. **1**, = money given, *sponsio*, *vadimonium*, *cautio*, to offer —, *vadimonium promittĕre*, to give —, *vadimonium facĕre* **2**, = one who gives —, *sponsor*, *vas*, *dis*, m **II.** v tr *alci sponsorem*, *vadem esse*, to accept —, *vades accipere*

bailiff, n **1**, = on an estate, *procurator*, *villicus* **2**, = officer of a court of justice, *apparitor*

bait, **I.** n **1**, for fish, *esca*, **2**, fig *illecebra*, **3**, = food for horses, *cibus* **II.** v tr **1**, *escam* (*hamo*) *imponĕre*, **2**, = to feed horses, *cibum praebēre*, **3**, = to worry (bulls, etc) *canibus* (*taurum*) *vexare*, *lacessĕre* **III.** v intr = to rest on a journey (*apud alqm*) *deversari*.

bake, I. v.tr. *coquĕre, torrēre.* **II.** v.intr. = to be prepared by fire, *coqui.* **baking,** n. *coctura*; bakehouse, *pistrina*; a baker, *pistor*; baker's business, *pistrina.*

balance, I. n. 1, = scales, *trutina, libra, lanx* (= the pan of the scales); 2, fig. *aequalitas*; to lose one's —, *labi*; — at the bank, *pecunia in argentariā deposita*; 3, = the remainder, by adj. *rel(l)iquus.* **II.** v.tr. 1, lit. *aequis ponderibus librare*; 2, fig. *alqd. perpendĕre.* **III.** v.intr. of accounts, *constare.*

balcony, n. *solarium.*

bald, adj. 1, lit. *glaber, calvus*; a — head, *calvitium*; — place, *glabreta, -orum*; 2, fig. of language, *inornatus, incultus, impolitus.* **baldness,** n. *calvitium.*

bale, n. *fascis, -is,* m. **baleful,** adj. *calamitosus, perniciosus, exitiosus.* **bale out,** v.tr. *exhaurire.*

balk, I. n. 1, = a beam, *tignum, trabs*; 2, = boundary, *limes, -itis,* m. **II.** v.tr. *alci impedimento esse.*

ball, n. 1, *pila*; to play at —, (*datatim*) *pilā ludĕre*; 2, the — of the earth, *terrae globus*; the eye —, *pupilla*; a musket —, *lapis, -idis,* m. (as thrown by a balista); 3, = a dance, *saltatio.*

ballad, n. *carmen.*

ballast, n. *saburra.*

ballet, n. *pantomimus* (Plin.); — dancer, *pantomimus,* m. (Suet.); *pantomima,* f. (Sen.).

balloon, n. *machina aërobatica.*

ballot, n. *suffragium* (= a vote); to vote by —, *suffragia ferre*; — box, *cista.*

balm, n. 1, *balsamum*; 2, fig. *solatium.* **balmy,** adj. 1, *balsaminus*; 2, fig. *suavis, dulcis.*

balustrade, n. *cancelli, -orum.*

bamboo, n. *arundo Indica* (Plin.).

ban, n. *aquae et ignis interdictio.*

band, I. n. 1, = bandage, *fascia*; 2, = a fillet, *vitta, infula*; (of metal) *armilla*; 3, = a number of persons united together, *turba, grex, caterva.* **II.** v.tr. (*con*)*sociare, conjungĕre.*

bandage, I. n. *fascia, fasciola.* **II.** v.tr. *deligare.*

band-box, n. *capsa.*

bandit, n. *latro.* **banditti,** n. *latrones.*

bandy, v.tr. *ultro* (*et*) *citro agĕre*; to — words with, *cum alqo altercari.* **bandy-legged,** adj. *varus, cruribus distortis.*

bane, n. 1, lit. *venenum, virus, -i,* n.; 2, fig. *pestis.* **baneful,** adj. *perniciosus, exitiosus.*

bang, n. 1, = a striking, *percussio*; 2, = a noise, *sonitus, -ūs.*

banish, v.tr. 1, lit. *alci aquā et igni interdicĕre, in ex(s)ilium e(j)icĕre,* (*ex*)*pellĕre* or *agĕre, exterminare, relegare, deportare* (to transport); 2, fig. *e(j)icĕre,* (*ex*)*pellĕre, amovēre.* **banishment,** n. *interdictio aquae et ignis, ejectio, relegatio, deportatio, ex(s)ilium.*

bank, n. 1, = a seat, *scamnum, scabellum, subsellium*; 2, = a river's side, *ripa*; 3, = a — of oars, *transtrum*; 4, = a — of earth, *agger, -ĕris,* m.; 5, = a money-changer's table, or place for depositing money (the last, modern), *argentaria* (*mensa*), *mensa publica*; to put money in the —, *pecuniam apud mensam publicam occupare.* **banker,** n. *argentarius.* **bank-note,** n. *as,* etc. or *perscriptio* (= assignment). **bankrupt,** n. *decoctor*; to become —, *foro cedĕre,* (*rationes*) *conturbare, decoquĕre.* **bankruptcy,** n. by verb (e.g. to suffer —, *foro cedĕre*), or metaph. *fortunae naufragium* or *ruina*; a national —, *tabulae novae.*

banner, n. *vexillum*; see FLAG.

bannock, n. *placenta* (*avenacea*).

banquet, n. *epulae, convivium.*

banter, I. n. *irrisio, derisio, cavillatio, ludibrium*; in —, *per ludibrium.* **II.** v.tr. *alqm ludibrio habēre, cavillari, deridēre, irridēre.*

baptize, v.tr. * *baptizare* (Eccl.). **baptism,** n. * *baptisma.*

bar, I. n. 1, = — of metal, etc., *later, -eris,* m.; 2, = bolt, *claustrum, obex, repagula, -orum*; 3, = a stake, *pertica, sudes, -is,* f., *vectis, -is,* m.; 4, = a limit or partition, *cancelli, carceres, -um, saepta, -orum*; 5, = a law court, *apud judices,* or *forum*; to be called to the —, *primum forum attingĕre*; to practise at the —, *caus(s)as agĕre*; the — (= advocates), *patroni.* **II.** v.tr. 1, = to bolt, (*claustro januam*) *occludĕre*; 2, fig. = to hinder, *alci impedimento esse, alqm impedire*; 3, = to except, *excipĕre.*

barbarous, barbaric, adj. *barbarus* (= foreign, strange), *rudis, inhumanus, immanis, crudelis, saevus.* Adv. *barbare, saeve, crudeliter.* **barbarity,** n. *immanitas, inhumanitas, crudelitas.*

barbed, adj. *hamatus.*

barber, n. *tonsor*; a —'s shop, *tonstrina.*

bard, n. *vates, -is,* m. and f.

bare, adj. 1, *nudus*; 2, = mere, *merus, tenuis, exiguus*; 3, = plain, *simplex*; a — room, *cubiculum nullo sumptu ornatum.* Adv. 1, = scarcely, *vix*; 2, = plainly, *simpliciter, nullo sumptu.* **bareness,** n. by adj. BARE. **bare-faced,** *impudens.* **barefoot,** *pedibus nudis* or *intectis.*

bargain, I. n. *res, negotium, pactio, pactum*; to make a good —, *bene emĕre.* **II.** v.intr. *cum alqo pacisci.*

barge, n. *actuariolum, lenunculus* (both = small vessel).

bark, I. n. *cortex, liber.* **II.** v.tr. *delibrare, decorticare.*

bark, I. v.intr. *latrare.* **II.** n. *latratus, -ūs.*

barley, I. n. *hordeum.* **II.** adj. *hordeaceus.*

barn, n. *horreum*; — floor, *area.*

baron, n. **baronet,** n. see NOBLE.

barracks, n. *castra, -orum.*

barrel, n. *seria, dolium, orca*; of a gun, etc., *tubus.*

barren, adj. *sterilis, infecundus.* **barrenness,** n. *sterilitas.*

barricade, I. n. *munimentum.* **II.** v.tr. *inaedificare, intersaepire, obstruĕre, oppilare.*

barrier, n. *limes, -itis,* m., *fines, -ium,* m. and f., *munimentum, murus.*

barrister, n. see ADVOCATE.

barrow, n. *ferculum.*

barter, I. v.tr. *mutare res inter se, permutare merces.* **II.** n. *permutatio mercium.*

base, adj. = morally corrupt, *perditus, probrosus, ignominiosus, turpis*; — coin, *nummi adulterini*; — born, *ignobili loco natus.* Adv. *per ignominiam, cum ignominiā, contumeliose, turpiter.* **baseness,** n. *turpitudo, dedecus, -ŏris,* n., *nequitia.*

base, n. 1, *basis* (= pedestal), *fundamentum* (= ground-work, lit. and fig.); 2, = the lowest part, *radices* (= roots, e.g. *montis*); 3, of the voice, *vox* or *sonus gravis.*

bashful, adj. *pudens, pudicus, verecundus.* Adv. *pudenter, pudice, verecunde.* **bashfulness,** n. *pudor, pudicitia, verecundia.*

basin, n 1, = for washing, *pelvis* 2, = a pond, *piscina*

basis, n see BASE, n, 1 and 2

bask, v intr *apricari*

basket, n *corbis, qualus, qualum, sporta* **basket-work,** *opus vimineum*

bas relief, n *opus caelatum, toreuma, -ătis,* n

bass, n = a mat of straw, *storea* or *storia*

bastard, I. n *nothus* **II.** adj see SPURIOUS

bastinado, n *ictus, -ūs, fustis,* m

bat, n = an animal, *vespertilio*

bat, n for cricket, tennis, etc, *clava* (= club)

batch, n *numerus*

bate, I. v tr *(im)minuĕre* **II.** v intr *(im)minui*, see ABATE

bath, n *balineum, balneum*, pl *balneae, balnearia, -orum, aquae, lavatio, thermae* (= hot or mineral baths), *lavatum*, to take a cold bath, *frigidā lavari* **bathe, I.** v tr *lavare, abluĕre* (sc se), to — another, *demittere alqm in balneum*, to be bathed in tears, *effundi* (*effusum esse*) *in lacrimis*, bathing-rooms, *balnearia*, — for cold, hot baths, etc, *frigidarium, tepidarium, calidarium, sudatorium* **II.** v intr *lavari*

battalion, n *cohors* (of cavalry), *legio* (= a regiment), *agmen primum, medium, extremum,* or *novissimum* (= the divisions of a marching army)

batter, v tr *percutĕre, verberare*, see BEAT, *pulsare*, to — down, *perfringĕre, evertĕre, dis(j)icere*

battering-ram, n *aries, ĕtis,* m

battery, n *agger, -ĕris,* m (= the mound), *tormenta, -orum* (= the weapons)

battle, n *proelium, certamen, acies, dimicatio* **battle-array,** n *acies* (opp to *agmen*, array on march) **battle-axe,** n *bipennis* (only found in nom, dat, acc, and abl sing, and nom and abl pl), *securis* **battle cry,** n *clamor* **battle-field,** n *locus pugnae* or *ubi pugnatur*

battlement, n *pinna.*

bawl, v tr *clamorem tollĕre, vociferari*

bay, I. adj *spadix, badius* **II.** n 1, = laurel, *laurus*, f; 2, = a gulf, *sinus, -ūs*, 3, = — window, *fenestra convexa* or *cava*, 4, to stand at —, *adversus alqm se defendĕre* **III.** v intr *latrare*

bayonet, n *gladius*, with fixed —s, *constrictis gladiis*

be, v intr *esse, ex(s)istĕre*, to let —, *permittĕre.*

beach, n *litus, ŏris,* n.

beacon, n = lighthouse, *pharus*, f; = fire, *ignis*

bead, n *globulus*

beak, n *rostrum.*

beaker, n *poculum, calix.*

beam, I. n 1, of wood, *lignum, trabs* of a —, *trabalis*, 2, — of light, *radius*, a — of hope shines out, *spes mihi affulget*, 3, — of a balance, *scapus, jugum* **II** v intr *fulgēre* **beaming, I.** n *fulgor* **II.** adj *jucundus, hilaris*

bean, n *faba*, = kidney bean, *phaselus*, m and f

bear, I. n 1, *ursus, ursa* (= a she bear), that which comes from —, *ursinus* (as a constellation) *Arctos, Ursa*, the Great —, *Ursa Major*, the Lesser —, *Ursa Minor*, the two, *Septentriones*, -um, 2, fig = a rude fellow, *agrestis, incultus* **II.** v tr 1, *ferre, gestare portare* — a sword, *cinctum esse gladio*, — (of trees) *ferre, efferre*, — the cost, *sumptus tolerare*, to — up against, *alqd sustinēre, pati*, 2, = to show, to — affection towards, *alqm amare, diligere* 3, to carry away, win, *auferre, consequi*, 4, = to give birth to, *parĕre* **bearable,** adj *quod tolerari potest* to find anything —, *alqs rei patientem esse* **bearer,** n *bajulus* (= a porter), *nuntius* (= — of news), *tabellarius* (= — of letters) **bearing,** n *portatio, gestatio, vectatio,* of children, *partus, -ūs*

beard, I. n *barba*, — of a goat, *aruncus* (Plin) **II.** v tr *alqm provocare*

beast, n 1, *bestia, jumentum* (= beast of burden) opp to man, *belua*, wild —, *fera*, 2, as a term of contempt, *belua, bestia* **beastly,** adj *spurcus, immundus* **beastliness,** n *spurcitia*

beat, I. v tr 1, = to strike *ferire, caedere, percutĕre, pulsare, verberare*, to be beaten, *vapulare*, 2, = to overcome, *vincere, superare*, — the enemy thoroughly, *hostem fundere et fugare*, 3, = to beat down, *(pro)sternĕre, opprimĕre*, 4, to — out, see THRASH, 5, to — up, *ridiculā perungĕre*(?) **II.** v intr *palpitare* **beating,** n *verbera, -um*

beatitude, n *(summa) felicitas*

beau, n *homo bellus* or *elegans*

beautiful, adj *pulcher, formosus* (in form), *speciosus* (in appearance), *venustus* (= elegant), *bellus* (= fine) Adv *pulchre, amoene, venuste, belle, eleganter* **beautify,** v tr *(ex)ornare* **beauty,** n *pulchritudo, species, forma, venustas, amoenitas* (of places), beauty in the abstract, *pulchrum*

beaver, n *castor, fiber*, of a —, *castoreus*, — skin, *pellis fibrina*

becalmed, adj *ventis destitutus*

because, conj *quod, quia, quoniam, cum* (with subj), *quandoquidem*, also with *qui, quippe qui*, as well as by a participle or abl abs — of, prep, *propter, ob* with accus

beck, n = a nod, *nutus, ūs*, to be at anyone's — or call, *ad nutum alcjs esse.* **beckon,** v tr *digito innuĕre*

become, I. v intr *fieri, evadĕre, nasci, oriri, ex(s)istere*, to become a perfect speaker, *perfectum oratorem evadĕre*, — a beggar, *ad mendicitatem redigi*, often by the inchoative verbs, as, to — warm, *calescĕre*, — rich, *ditescĕre*, **II.** v tr = to suit, *alqm convenit*

bed, n 1, *lectus, lectus cubicularis*, to make a —, *lectum sternere*; to go to —, *cubitum ire*, a little —, *lectulus* **—chamber,** n *cubiculum* **bedding,** n *lodix* (= coverlet), *stragulum* (= mattress) **—post,** n *fulcrum lecti* 2, — of a river, *alveus*, — of a garden, *area*

bedabble, v tr *a(d)spergĕre*

bedaub, v tr *(ob)linĕre, perungĕre*

bedeck, v tr *(ex)ornare*

bedew, v t. *irrorare* **bedewed,** adj *roscidus*, to be —, *humescĕre*

bedim, v tr *obscurare*

bedizen, v tr *(ex)ornare*

bedlam, n *domus qua continentur (homines) insani*

bee, n *apis*; — hive, *alvus, alveus*, a swarm of —, *examen apium*, queen —, *rex apium*

beech, n *fagus*, f, of —, *fageus, faginus*

beef, n *(caro) bubula*

beer, n *cer(e)visia* **brewer,** n. *cerevisiae coctor*,

beetle, **I.** n. *scarabaeus.* **II.** v.intr. *imminēre.*

beeves, n. *boves, boum,* pl.

befall, v.intr. *accidĕre, contingĕre, evenire.*

befit, v.tr. *aptum, idoneum esse ad alqd;* it —s thee, *te decet;* does not —, *non convenit, dedecet.*

befool, v.tr. *infatuare, decipĕre.*

before, **I.** adv. *prius, citius, ante; prior,* e.g. *qui prior venit,* he comes before (the other); = rather, *prius, potius;* the year —, *superior annus;* = already, *jam(dudum);* the — mentioned, *qui supra dictus est.* **II.** prep. = in presence of, *coram,* with abl.; in front of, *ante,* with accus.; of time, *ante;* — my consulship, *ante me consulem;* of worth, *ante* or *praeter,* with accus.; to be —, *alci alqâ re praestare, antecellĕre;* the day — another day, *pridie ejus diei.* **III.** conj. *ante* or *prius, quam* (in one word, *antequam, priusquam*). **beforehand,** adv. *antea,* or by *prae* in comp.; to be — with, *alqm alqâ re praevenire.* **beforetimes,** adv. *olim.*

befoul, v.tr. *inquinare.*

befriend, v.tr. *alqm (ad)juvare, alci favēre.*

beg, **I.** v. intr. *mendicare, stipem petĕre.* **II.** v.tr. *alqm alqd orare, rogare, flagitare,* or with *ut;* to — off, *deprecari.* **beggar,** **I.** n. *mendicus,* or adj. *egenus.* **II.** v.tr. *ad inopiam redigĕre.* **beggarly,** adj. *miser, vilis.* **beggary,** n. *egestas, paupertas, mendicitas.* **begging,** n. *mendicitas, stips* (= alms); a — off, *deprecatio.*

beget, v.tr. **1,** lit. *gignĕre, generare, procreare;* **2,** fig. *creare, alqd alci movēre.*

begin, **I.** v.intr. *incipĕre;* it — to be day, *dies appetit, lucescit;* — evening, *advesperascit.* **II.** v.tr. *incipĕre* (= to commence, e.g. *facinus*), *ordiri, inchoare, initium facĕre, aggredi* (= to enter on), *conari* (= to endeavour). **beginning,** n. *initium, principium, primordium, ortus, -ūs,* (= birth), *inceptio, inceptum;* — of a speech, *exordium;* the —s of a science, *elementa, rudimenta, incunabula* (all n. pl.). Often "beginning" is to be rendered by *primus,* e.g. *primâ fabulâ,* = in the — of the piece; so e.g. *vere novo, ineunte vere,* = in the — of spring; thus *primâ nocte, primo vespere;* from the —, *ab initio, repetĕre* (= to go back to the very —); without —, *aeternus;* to have neither — nor end, *nec principium nec finem habēre.* **beginner,** n. **1,** = author, *auctor;* **2,** = a novice, *tiro, rudis.*

begone! interj. *abi! apage te!*

begrime, v.tr. *inquinare, maculare.*

begrudge, v.tr. *invidēre alqd alci.*

beguile, v.tr. *decipĕre, circumvenire, fallĕre.*

behalf, n. in — of, *pro,* with abl., *propter,* with accus., *caus(s)â* (e.g. *meâ,* or with gen.).

behave, v.tr. *se gerĕre, exhibēre;* well behaved, *bene moratus.* **behaviour,** n. *vita, ratio, mores, -um.*

behead, v.tr. *caput alcjs praecidĕre.*

behind, **I.** adv. *pone, post, a tergo;* also by *extremus* and *ultimus* (e.g. *ultimus venit,* he came behind or last); with verbs by *rĕ-* (e.g. *oculos retorquēre,* to look behind); to attack a person behind, *aversum aggredi alqm.* **II.** prep. *pone, post,* with acc. **behindhand,** adv. *parum* (= too little).

behold, v.tr. *a(d)spicĕre, conspicĕre, intueri, contemplari, spectare alqd.* **behold!** interj. *en! ecce!* **beholden,** adj. *alcjs beneficio* (e.g. for one's life, *alcjs beneficio salvus*); to be — to, *alqd alci debēre, acceptum referre.*

behoof, n. see Behalf.

behove, v.tr. impers., *decet, convenit, oportet.*

being, n. *natura* (= peculiar quality), *vis* (= active quality), comb. *natura atque vis; condicio* (= permanent state), *res* (= reality); the Supreme —, *Deus;* see Life.

belated, adj. *serus.*

belch, **I.** v.intr. *ructare.* **II.** v.tr. fig. *evomĕre.*

beldam, n. *anicula* (= an old woman).

beleaguer, v.tr. *obsidēre.*

belfry, n. *turris.*

belie, v.tr. *criminari, calumniari.*

belief, n. in gen., *opinio* (= view or conviction; of anything, *rei* or *de re*), *persuasio* (= assurance, *alcjs rei,* e.g. *veneni ab alqo accepti* = that someone has been poisoned), *fides* (= credibility, credence, trust); — in God, *opinio Dei;* — in immortality, *immortalitas* merely (e.g. *nemo me de immortalitate depellet,* = no one shall rob me of my belief in immortality); in my —, *ut ego existimo, meâ quidem opinione;* to have — in something, or hold it as a reality, *alqd esse credĕre.* **believe,** v.tr. *credĕre, putare, arbitrari* (= to think), *opinari, reri, existimare, ducĕre* (= account, to form a judgment), *censēre, sentire;* I firmly —, *mihi persuasum est, persuasum habeo* (with acc. and inf.; *hoc mihi persuasit,* I am satisfied of this); I cannot —, *hoc quidem non adducor ut credam;* to — in something, *alqd esse arbitrari* or *credĕre* or *putare* (in the existence of, e.g. *Deum esse credĕre,* or merely *Deum putare* or *credĕre*); *credĕre de alqâ re* (e.g. *facilius de odio creditur* = people easily believe in hatred), *comprobare alqd* (= to approve); to — in an object, *alci rei credĕre,* or *fidem habēre,* or *fidem tribuĕre, alci rei* (never *alci*) *fidem adjungĕre;* — me (used parenthetically), *quod mihi credas velim, mihi crede, crede mihi;* I — (used parenthetically), *credo, opinor, puto;* as I —, *meâ quidem opinione, ut ego existimo.* **believer,** n. *qui credit.*

bell, n. *tintinnabulum, aes, aeris,* n.

belle, n. *(puella) pulchra, formosa.*

bellow, v.intr. *mugire.*

bellows, n. *follis, -is,* m.

belly, n. **1,** *venter, -ris,* m. (= the hollow of the body containing the intestines), *uterus* (= the womb), *alvus* (= the passage or canal), *abdōmen* (= the protruding or fat part of the belly); **2,** of a ship, *alveus.*

belong, v.intr. — to, *alci* or *alcjs esse.*

below, **I.** adv. *subter, infra.* **II.** prep. *sub;* acc. of motion towards (e.g. *ire sub muros*), abl. of rest; *infra* with acc. see Under.

belt, n. *cingulum, zona.*

bemire, v.tr. *inquinare.*

bemoan, v.tr. *deplorare.*

bench, n. *scamnum, scabellum;* — at which people work, *mensa;* of rowers, *transtrum;* of judges, *consessus, -ūs.*

bend, **I.** v.tr. **1,** *(in)flectĕre;* — before a person, *submittĕre se alci;* **2,** fig. = to move, *movēre, flectĕre;* **3,** = to turn, *se* or *iter convertĕre, dirigĕre;* to — one's steps, *ire ad alqm* or *alqd;* to — one's mind to, *alqd animadvertĕre* (= to notice), *se ad alqd applicare.* **II.** v.intr. *flecti;* — beneath a weight, lit. *vacillare;* fig. *gravari.* **III.** n. **bending,** n. *flexus, -ūs, (in)flexio.* **bent,** n. *animi inclinatio, voluntas, natura, ratio, studium.*

beneath, see Below.

benediction, n. to give a — to a person, *alqm bonis omnibus prosequi.*

benefit, I. n *beneficium.* **II.** v tr *alqm (ad)iuvare, alci utilem* or *usui* or *ex usu esse* **beneficial,** adj *utilis, salutaris* Adv *utiliter, benefice, salubriter* **beneficent,** adj *liberalis, benignus beneficus.* Adv *benigne, liberaliter* **beneficence,** n *beneficentia, benignitas, liberalitas* **benefactor,** n *beneficus, qui beneficia in alqm confert*, to be a — to mankind, *praeclare de genere humano meritum esse*

benevolent, adj *benevolus (beniv)* **benevolence,** n *benevolentia*

benighted, adj 1, lit *nocte oppressus*; 2, fig see IGNORANT

benign, adj *benignus erga alqm* Adv *benigne.* **benignity,** n *benignitas.*

benumb, v tr *obstupefacere*, to be —ed, *obtorpescĕre, torpēre.*

bequeath, v tr *alqd alci legare* **bequest,** n *legatum*

bereave, v tr *alqm alqā re orbare, privare* **bereaved,** adj *orbus.* **bereavement,** n *orbitas, privatio.*

berry, n *bac(c)a, bac(c)ula, acinus.*

beseech, v tr *alqm implorare, obtestari, alqm alqd* or *ut orare.*

beseem, v tr see BECOME (2).

beset, v tr *alqm urgēre, premĕre, alci instare, obsidēre* (of a city)

beshrew, v tr *ex(s)ecrari*, — me, *di(i) me perdant*

beside, prep 1, = near, *prope, iuxta,* acc , 2, = except, *praeter,* acc , 3, = away from, this is — the point, *nihil ad rem*, — oneself, *sui impotens*

besides, I adv *praeterea ultro, porro, ad hoc* or *haec, accedit quod* or *ut* **II.** prep *praeter* with acc

besiege, v tr. *obsidēre, obsidione claudĕre* or *premĕre, operibus cingĕre, oppugnare.* **besieger,** n. *obsessor, obsidens*

besmear, v tr *(ob)linĕre*

bespatter, v tr. *a(d)spergĕre, conspergĕre, (com)maculare*

bespeak, v tr *imperare*

best, adj. *optimus*, see GOOD

bestir, v tr *(se) (com)movēre, incitare, excitare*

bestow, v tr see GIVE

bet, I. n *sponsio, pignus, ŏris,* n **II** v tr *sponsionem cum alqo facere*

betake oneself, v intr *se conferre alqo, concedere, ire, proficisci alqo, petĕre locum*, see GO

betimes, adv *mox, brevi*

betoken, v tr *notare, denotare, signare, designare*

betray, v tr 1, = to make known, *prodĕre, deferre, proferre*, — yourself, *se prodĕre*, when — is used in the sense of "it is the quality of," use the genitive (e g *est tardi ingenii*, it —s a dull wit), **2,** = to make known treacherously, *prodere, tradĕre, destituere,* **betrayal,** n *proditio, perfidia* (= faithlessness), *delatio* (= an information in law) **betrayer,** n *proditor, desertor, index* (the eyes are the —s of the mind, *animi indices sunt oculi*)

betroth, v tr *alci alqam (de)spondēre*, — to anyone, *sibi alqam despondēre* (male), *alci desponderi* (female) **betrothal,** n *sponsalia, ium*

better, I. adj *melior, potior* (= preferable), *praestantior* (= more excellent), is —, *melius* or *satius est, praestat*, to be — (morally), *alci alqā re praestare, antecellĕre*; I am —, *melius me habeo*, I am getting —, *convalesco* **II.** adv *melius* **III.** v tr *corrigĕre, meliorem (melius) facĕre, augēre* (= increase)

between, prep *inter* with acc

beverage, n *potio, potus, ūs*

bevy, n *grex, gregis* m

bewail, v tr *deplorare, deflēre, (con)queri*

beware, v tr to — of, *(sibi) ab alqo* or *alqā re*, or *ut* or *ne cavēre*

bewilder, v tr *alqm (con)turbare*

bewitch, v tr 1, *fascinare* 2, fig *capere*

beyond, I. adv *ultra, supra,* in comp *trans* (e g *transire*) **II.** prep 1, = the other side of, *trans*, acc of rest or motion, **2,** of degree, *supra, plus, amplius (quam)*, — ten thousand, *supra decem mil(l)ia*, — measure, *supra modum*

bias, I. n *inclinatio* or *propensio animi* **II.** v tr *apud alqm plus, quam aequum est valēre*, to be —sed, *ad alqm (plus aequo) propensum esse*

bible, n *libri divini, lit(t)erae divinae* or *sacrae* or *sanctae*, * *biblia orum*, n **biblical,** adj *quod ad lit(t)eras divinas pertinet*

bibulous, adj † *bibulus*

bid, v tr 1, *iubēre, praecipĕre*, see COMMAND, **2,** = invite, *invitare*, **3,** at a sale, *liceri*, **4,** fig — defiance to, *alqm provocare*, — welcome, *alqm salvēre iubēre*, — farewell, *valēre iubēre* **bidding,** n 1, see COMMAND, **2,** = invitation, *invitatio* **3,** at a sale, *licitatio* **bidder,** n (at a sale) *illicitator*

bide, v tr *manēre*

biennial, adj *biennis*

bier, n *feretrum, sandapila* (Juv)

bifurcated, adj *bifidus*

big, adj *magnus, grandis, vastus*, to be — with child, *gravidam esse*, see GREAT, LARGE

bigamist, n *qui duas uxores habet*

bigot, n *superstitiosus* **bigotry,** n *nimia et superstitiosa religio*

bile, n *bilis* **bilious,** adj *biliosus* (Cels)

bilge-water, n *sentina*

bill, n 1, = a tool, *falx*, **2,** = — of a bird, *rostrum*

bill, n 1, = a proposed law, *rogatio*, to bring forward a —, *rogationem, legem ferre*, to adopt a —, *accipĕre*, to refuse a —, *antiquare*, to carry a —, *perferre*, 2, of a tradesman, etc , *mercium emptarum index*, — of exchange, *syngrapha*

billet, I. n = a letter, *epistula*, — doux, *epistula amatoria* **II.** v tr *milites per domos disponĕre*

billow, n *fluctus, -ūs* **billowy,** adj *fluctuosus*

bind, v tr 1, by tying, *(al)ligare, illigare a(d)stringĕre, revincire*, **2,** = to restrain, *alqm circumscribĕre* or *coercēre*, to — together, *colligare*, to — by an oath, *alqm sacramento a(d)stringĕre*, to — books, *glutinare*, to — an apprentice, *alqm alci addicĕre* to — over, *vadari*, to be bound by something, *constrictum esse, teneri re*, — by business, *negotiis distentum esse* **bindweed,** n *convolvulus* (Plin)

biography, n *vitae alcjs descriptio* **biographer,** n *qui alcjs res gestas enarrat*

biped, n *bipes, -ĕdis,* adj

birch, n *betula* (Plin)

bird, n *avis, volucris, ales, ĭtis,* m and f ;

— cage, n *cavea; —* catcher, n *auceps, -cŭpis,* m , — lime, n *viscus*

birth, n *ortus, -ūs;* of noble —, *nobili genere* or *loco natus* **birthday,** n *dies natalis* **birthright,** n *patrimonium*

biscuit, n *panis, -is,* m

bishop, n *episcopus*

bit, n 1, of a horse, *frenum*, 2, see PIECE

bitch, n *canis (femina)*

bite, I. v tr *mordēre* **II.** n *morsus, -ūs* **biting,** adj *mordens, mordax, acidus, aculeatus; —* words, *verborum aculei*

bitter, adj *amarus, acerbus, mordax* Adv *amare, aspere, acerbe* **bitterness,** n *amaritudo, amaritas, acerbitas*

bitumen, n *bitūmen*

bivouac, I. v intr *in armis excubare* **II.** n *excubiae*

black, I. adj *ater, niger, pullus* **II.** n 1, *color niger*, 2, = mourning, *pulla vestis*, dressed in —, *sordidatus, pullatus, atratus*, 3, = a negro, *Aethiops* **blacken,** v tr 1, = to make black, *nigrum facĕre*, 2, fig *conflare* or *conciliare alci invidiam*

blackberry, n *rubus*

blackbird, n *merula*

blackguard, n *nefarius (homo), sceleratus*

blacklead, n *plumbum nigrum* (Plin).

blacksmith, n *faber*

bladder, n *vesica*

blade, n 1, of grass, *herba*, 2, of an oar, *palma;* 3, of a knife, *lamina*

blame, I. n *reprehensio, vituperatio, objurgatio, convicium* **II.** v tr *reprehendĕre, culpare* **blameable, blameworthy,** adj *reprehensione* or *vituperatione dignus* **blameless,** adj. *integer, sanctus* **blamelessness,** n *vitae integritas* or *sanctitas*

bland, adj *blandus, lenis, mitis* Adv *blande, leniter* **blandness,** n *lenitas* **blandishment,** n *adulatio, blanditiae*

blank, I. adj *vacuus*, — amazement, *stupor* **II** n 1, in a lottery, *sors* or *tabella inanis*, 2, in life, *calamitas*

blanket, n *lodix*

blaspheme, v intr *blasphemare* **blasphemer,** n *blasphemus* **blasphemous,** adj *blasphemus, impius erga Deum*

blast, I. n *venti impetus, ūs,* **II.** v tr 1, see BLIGHT, 2, = blow up, *igne diruĕre*

blaze, I. n *flamma, ardor*, to set in a —, *incendĕre* **II.** v intr *ardēre, flagrare*

bleach, I. v tr *candidum reddĕre* **II.** v intr = to become white or pale, *albescĕre.*

bleak, adj see COLD

blear-eyed, adj *lippus*

bleat, I. v intr *balare* (of sheep) **II.** n *balatus, -ūs*

bleed, I. v intr *sanguinem fundĕre*, my heart —s, *vehementer* or *gravissime doleo*, *aegerrime fero*, — at something, *incredibilem dolorem ex re capio* **II.** v tr to — a person (as a physician), *alci sanguinem mittĕre*, to kill by — ing (as a punishment), *venam incidĕre* **bleeding,** n *sanguinis fluxio*

blemish, I. n *mendum, macula, labes, -is,* f **II.** v tr *(com)maculare*

blend, v tr *alqd cum alqa re (com)miscēre*, see MIX

bless, v tr *alqm bonis omnibus prosequi*

blessed, adj *beatus, fortunatus* Adv. *beate, fortunate* **blessedness,** n *felicitas*

blight, I. n. *robīgo (rub)* **II.** v tr *robigine afficĕre*

blind, I. adj 1, *caecus, oculis* or *luminibus captus* or *orbatus*, — of one eye, *altero oculo captus*, 2, fig *caecus, occaecatus, stultus* Adv. 1, by *caecus*, 2, = rashly, *temere* **II.** v tr 1, lit *oculis privare, caecum reddĕre*, 2, fig see DAZZLE **blindfold,** adj *oculis opertis.* **blindness,** n 1, lit *caecitas*, 2, fig *stultitia.*

blink, v intr *con(n)ivēre, nictare*

bliss, n *summa felicitas.*

blister, I. n *pustula* **II.** v tr *pustulare.*

blithe, adj *laetus, hilaris* Adv *laete, hilariter.* **blitheness,** n *laetitia, hilaritas*

bloated, adj 1, lit. *turgidus*, 2, fig *tumidus*

block, I. n *truncus, caudex* **II.** v tr. *claudĕre obstruĕre, obsaepire (obsep)* **blockade, I.** n *obsidio* **II.** v tr *obsidēre* **blockhead,** n *stolidus*

blood, n *sanguis, cruor;* to act in cold —, *consulto alqd facĕre* **bloodless,** adj *exsanguis, incruentus* (= without bloodshed) **blood-relation,** n *consanguineus* **bloodshed,** n. *caedes, -is,* f **bloodshot,** adj *sanguine suffusus.* **blood-thirsty,** adj *sanguinarius.* **blood-vessel,** n *arteria, vena.* **bloody,** adj *cruentus, cruentatus, sanguine respersus*, a — victory, *cruenta victoria*, — battle, *proelium cruentum, atrox.*

bloom, I. n *flos;* to be in —, *florēre* **II.** v intr *florēre, vigēre*, to begin to —, *florescĕre* **blooming,** adj *florens, floridus*

blossom, v intr see BLOOM

blot, I. n 1, on paper, *litura;* 2, = a stain, lit & fig *macula* **II.** v tr 1, = to dry ink, *abstergēre*, 2, = to make a —, *lituram alci rei in(j)icĕre*, 3, fig *(com)maculare;* 4, to — out, *delēre, ex(s)tinguĕre*

blow, I. n 1, *ictus, -ūs, plaga, verbera, -um;* 2, fig *casus, -ūs, damnum* **II.** v intr of the wind, *flare*, with the mouth, *flare* **III.** v tr. — the flute, *tibiā (tibiis) canĕre* **blowing,** adj *flatu figurare*

blubber, n *adeps balaenarum*

bludgeon, n *fustis, -is,* m

blue, adj *caeruleus, lividus* (= black blue).

blunder, I. n *error, erratum.* **II.** v intr, *errare*

blunt, I. adj 1, lit *hebes*, 2, fig = dull, *hebes, obtusus*, 3, = rude, *agrestis, rusticus, inurbanus* Adv *rustice* **II.** v tr *hebetare*, lit and fig ; fig *obtundĕre* **bluntness,** n. 1, lit by adj *hebes;* 2, fig *rusticitas*

blur, I. n *macula* **II.** v tr *obscurare*

blush, I. n *rubor* **II.** v intr *erubescĕre*

bluster, I. n 1, = self-assertion, *jactatio, ostentatio*, 2, = tumult, *fremitus, -ūs, strepitus, -ūs, tumultus, -ūs* **II.** v intr 1, *se jactare, ostentare*, 2, *tumultum facĕre, saevire*

boar, n *verres, -is,* m ; a wild —, *aper*

board, I. n 1, *axis, -is,* m , *tabula*, 2, = food, *victus, -ūs, alimentum* **board-wages,** n *pecunia pro alimentis data.* **II.** v tr 1, *alci victum dare*, 2, — a ship, *navem conscendĕre* **III.** v intr to — with anyone, *apud alqm habitare* **boarder,** n *qui cum alqo habitat.*

boast, v intr *gloriari, se efferre, se jactare.* **boaster,** n *jactator, ostentator, homo gloriosus* **boasting,** n *jactatio, ostentatio* **boastful,** adj *gloriosus* Adv. *gloriose*

boat, n *scapha, navicula*, — man, *nauta*, m.

bodice, n *thorax (linteus)*.

body, n 1, *corpus, -ŏris*, n ; a little —, *corpusculum*, a — guard, *cohors praetoria* or *regia* — servant, *servus, mancipium, verna*, m and f 2, = company, *societas*, — of cavalry, *ala*

bodily, adj *corporeus*, — exercise, *exercitatio*

bodiless, adj *sine corpore*

bog, n *palus, -ūdis*, f **boggy,** adj *uliginosus, paluster*

boil, I. v tr *coquĕre* **II.** v intr 1, *fervēre, effervescĕre, aestuare, bullare* or *bullire* (= bubble), 2, fig *aestuare* **boiler,** n *vas, vasis*, n , in a bath, *caldarium*

boil, n *vomica*

boisterous, adj *turbidus*, of the sea or wind, *procellosus, agitatus*

bold, adj *audens, audax, confidens*, to be —, *audēre* (with inf) Adv *audacter* **boldness,** n *audentia, audacia, confidentia*

bole, n *truncus, stirps*.

bolster, n *culcita, pulvinus*

bolt, I. n 1, = a fastening, *obex, -icis*, m and f , *claustrum*, 2, = a weapon, *sagitta* **II** v tr. *claudĕre, (obice) occludĕre*

bombard, v tr *urbem tormentis verberare*

bomb, n * *pyrobolus*

bombast, n *verborum pompa* or *tumor, inflata oratio* **bombastic,** adj *inflatus*

bond, n 1, = a tie, *vinculum, ligamentum, compes, pĕdis*, f. (= fetter), *catenae*, 2, fig *societas, conjunctio*, 3, = surety, *chirographum, syngrapha* **bondage,** n *servitus, -ūtis*, f

bone, n *os, ossis*, n **bony,** adj *osseus*

book, n *liber, volumen, libellus* **bookseller,** n *bibliopōla, librorum venditor*

boom, I. n *obex, icis*, m and f **II.** v tr *saevire*

boon, I. n *gratia, beneficium*. **II.** adj *jucundus*

boorish, adj. *agrestis, inurbanus* Adv *inurbane*

boot, n *calceamentum*

boot, n = gain, *commodum*, to —, *ultro*

bootless, adj *inutilis, irritus* Adv *frustra*

booty, n *praeda, spolia, exuviae*

boozy, adj *ebriosus*

border, I. n 1, of a river, *margo, -inis*, m and f , *ripa, ora*, 2 of a country, *fines, -ium*, m **II.** v tr = to surround, *alqd alqâ re cingĕre, circumdare* **III.** v intr 1, of people, *confinem alci esse*, of lands, *adjacēre, attingĕre*, 2, = be near, *finitimum esse*

bore, I. v tr 1, = perforate, *perterebrare*, 2, = to weary, *defatigare*. **II.** n *homo importunus*

born, v intr to be —, *nasci*

borrow, v tr *mutuari, mutuum sumĕre*

bosom, n 1, *sinus, ūs*, 2, fig *pectus, -ŏris*, n **bosom-friend,** *amicus conjunctissimus* See BREAST

boss, n *umbo*

botany, n *herbaria (ars)* **botanical,** adj *herbarius* **botanize,** v intr *herbas quaerĕre* or *colligĕre*

both, I. adj *ambo* **II.** pron *uterque* **III.** conj *et — et, cum — tum*

bother, I. n *molestia, incommodum* **II.** v tr *alqm alqâ re defatigare, obtundere, molestiam alci afferre*

bottle, I. n *lagena, ampulla*; — of hay, *manipulus*. **II.** v tr *vinum*, etc , *diffundĕre*

bottom, n 1, *fundus, solum*, of a ship, *alveus*, to drain to the —, *faece tenus potare*, — of the sea, *mare imum* 2 fig to go to the —, *perire, interire* get to the — of anything, *alqd perspicĕre* he is at the — of this, *res ex eo pendet*

bottomless, adj *immensae altitudinis*

bough, n *ramus*

bounce, v intr *resilire*

bound, I. n = a limit, *limes, -itis*, m , *fines*; pl (both lit & fig), to keep within —s, *intra fines se coercēre* **II.** v tr = to limit, *finire, definire* **III.** n and v intr see LEAP

bounden, adj — duty, *officium* **boundless,** adj *infinitus immensus*

bounty, n 1, *largitas, liberalitas, munificentia*, 2, = a reward, *praemium* **bountiful,** adj *largus, liberalis, beneficus*, to be —, *magnâ esse liberalitate* Adv *large, liberaliter*

bout, n 1, a drinking —, *comissatio*, 2, of illness, *morbus*, 3, at one —, *uno impetu, simul*

bow, I. v tr *flectĕre, demittĕre* **II.** v intr *flecti, se demittĕre*, or *demitti*, to — to anything, *alci rei obtemperare* **III.** n 1, = a salutation, *corporis inclinatio, nutus, ūs*, to make a —, *alqm salutare*, 2, = a weapon, *arcus, ūs*, 3, of a ship, *prora* **bowman,** n *sagittarius*

bowstring, n *nervus*

bowels, n 1, *intestina* (= the inside), *viscera, -um* (= the entrails), *exta, -orum* (= the nobler parts, as the heart, lungs), etc , 2, fig *viscera*

bower, n *umbraculum*

bowl, I. v tr *volvĕre* **II.** n 1, = a drinking-cup, *patera, phiala, poculum*, 2, = a ball, *pila*

box, I. v intr *pugnis certare* **II.** n = — on the ear, *alapa* **boxer,** n *pugil*

box, n (tree), *buxus*, f , *buxum* (= boxwood), of —, *buxeus*, = a small chest, *cista, arca, armarium, scrinium*, ballot —, *cista*, dice —, *fritillus*

boy, n *puer* **boyhood,** n *aetas puerilis, pueritia* **boyish,** adj *puerilis* Adv *pueriliter*

brace, I. v tr 1, = to bind, *alligare*, 2, fig (*animum*) *erigĕre*, of air, *sanare* **II.** n 1, *vinculum*, 2, of a ship, *funis quo antenna vertitur*, 3, = a pair, *par*, 4, braces, *fascia*

bracelet, n *armilla*

brackish, adj *amarus*

brag, v intr *se jactare, gloriari*, see BOAST

braid, I. v tr *texĕre, nectĕre* **II.** n *gradus, -ūs*

brain, n *cerebrum*

bramble, n *rubus*

bran, n *furfur*

branch, n 1, *ramus*, 2, fig of a family, *familia*

brand, n 1, *fax* (lit and fig), *titio, torris, -is*, m , 2, = a mark, *nota*, to —, *notam alci inurĕre*

brandish, v tr *vibrare, jactare*

brandy, n *vinum*

brasier, 1, = a place for fire, *foculus*, 2 = a worker in brass, *faber qui vasa ex orichalco facit*

brass, n *orichalcum, aes, aeris*, n , of brass, *a(h)eneus*

bravado, n *jactatio, ostentatio*

brave, adj *fortis, acer, strenuus* Adv *fortiter, acriter, strenue*. **bravery,** n *fortis, fortitudo*

bravo! interj *euge! factum bene! laudo!*

brawl, I. v intr. *altercari* **II.** n *altercatio*, *jurgium*

brawny, adj *robustus*

bray, I. v tr *contundĕre* **II.** v intr *rudĕre*

brazen, I. adj 1, = of brass, *a(h)eneus*, 2, fig *impudens*. **II.** v tr. to — anything out, *alqd pertinacius asseverare, confirmare*

breach, n 1, lit *via patefacta*, to make a —, *muros perfringĕre*, 2, fig = violation, by partic (e g — of treaty, *foedus ruptum*), to commit a — of duty, *officium neglegĕre* (*neglig*), *ab officio discedĕre*.

bread, n 1, *panis*, *is*, m ; 2, fig = nutriment, *victus*, *-ūs*, *victus cot(t)idianus* (*quot*)

breadth, n *latitudo*, in —, *latus* (e g *fossa decem pedes lata*)

break, I v tr *frangĕre, confringĕre, dirumpĕre*, to — a treaty, *foedus violare*, to — or subdue, *domare, frangĕre*, to — off, *carpere, decerpere, avellĕre*, to — up a camp, *castra movēre*, to — a promise, *fidem fallĕre*, to — silence, *silentium rumpĕre* **II.** v intr *frangi, confringi, rumpi*, the clouds —, *nubes discutiuntur*, to — out from a place, *erumpĕre*, of a war, *oriri*, — in, *irrumpĕre*, to — forth (as the sun), *sol inter nubes effulget*, the day —s, *illucescit*. **III.** n 1, *intervallum, rima* (= a chink), 2, — of day, *prima lux, diluculum* **breaker,** n *fluctus*, *-ūs*

breakfast, I. n *jentaculum* (on rising), *prandium* (about noon), *cibus meridianus* **II.** v intr *jentare, prandēre, cibum meridianum sumĕre*

breakwater, n *moles*, *-is*, f

breast, I. n *pectus*, *-ŏris*, n (both lit and fig), *animus* (fig.), the —s, *mamillae* **II.** v tr *alci rei obniti* **breastbone,** n *os pectoris* (Cels) **breast-plate,** n *thorax*. **breastwork,** n *pluteus*

breath, n *spiritus*, *-ūs*, *anima*, *halitus*, *-ūs*, to take —, *se colligĕre*, — of air, *aura*, — of applause, *aura popularis* **breathless,** adj *exanimatus, exanimis* **breathe,** v intr. *spirare*, to — upon, *alqm* or *alci afflare*, to — out, *exhalare*

breeches, n *bracae*, wearing —, *braccatus*

breed, I. v tr 1, *gignĕre, generare, parĕre, procreare*; 2, = rear, *alĕre, colĕre*, 3, fig *efficĕre, fingĕre, creare* **II.** n *genus*, *ĕris*, n **breeding,** n = education, *educatio, institutio, cultus*, *-ūs*

breeze, n *aura*, favourable —, *aura secunda*

brew, I. *coquĕre* **II.** v intr. *imminēre, impendēre* **brewing,** n *coctura* **brewer,** n *coctor, coctor cerevisiae*

bribe, I. n *largitio, pecunia* **II.** v tr *corrumpĕre* (*pecunia, donis*, etc), to try to —, *sol(l)icitare alqm pecuniā*, to be bribed, *largitionibus movēri* **briber,** n *corruptor, largitor*, he that is bribed, *venalis*

brick, n *later, laterculus*

bride, n *sponsa* **bridegroom,** *sponsus*. **bridal,** adj *nuptialis*, — procession, *pompa*

bridge, n *pons*, m , to make a —, *pontem facĕre in fluvio, amnem ponte jungĕre*

bridle, I. n *frenum*, pl *freni* and *frena* **II.** v tr. 1, lit *(in)frenare*, 2, fig *frenare, coercēre, continēre, comprimĕre*

brief, I. adj *brevis*, in —, *ne longus sim* Adv *breviter, paucis verbis, strictim* **II.** n a barrister's —, by verb *caus(s)am alcjs agĕre, clo. adesse* **brevity,** n *brevitas*,

brier, n *frutex* **briery,** adj *fruticosus*.

brigade, n , see Troop

brigand, n. *latro*

bright, adj 1, in gen *clarus, lucidus, splendidus, candidus, fulgens*, to be —, *clarēre*, to grow —, *clarescĕre*, of the sky, *serenus*, 2, = clever, *acutus, sol(l)ers* Adv *lucide, clare, splendide, candide* **brightness,** n *candor, splendor, nitor, fulgor*, of the weather, *serenitas*. **brighten, I.** v tr 1, *illustrare, illuminare*, 2, fig = gladden, *oblectare* **II.** v intr 1, *illustrari, illuminari*, 2, fig *oblectari, hilarem fieri*

brilliant, I. adj *splendidus, illustris, magnificus* Adv *splendide, magnifice* **II.** n. *gemma, adamas*, *-antis*, m **brilliancy,** n *splendor, fulgor*

brim, n *ora, margo, labrum*

brimstone, n *sulfur* (*sulph*)

brine, n *aqua salsa*

bring, v tr — to a place, *afferre, apportare, advehĕre*, to — forth, *parĕre*, to — forth fruit, *fructus edĕre*, to — about, *efficĕre ut*, to — before the senate, *rem ad senatum referre*, to — to light, *in lucem proferre*, to — over, *in partes suas trahĕre*, to — to an end, *ad finem perducĕre*, to — in = yield, *reddĕre*, to — forward, *in medium proferre*

brink, n. *margo, ripa;* to be on the — of, by fut partic (e g on the — of death, *moriturus*).

brisk, adj *alacer, vegetus, acer* Adv. *acriter* **briskness,** n *alacritas*

bristle, I n *seta* **II.** v intr *alqā re horrēre* **bristly,** adj *setosus*

brittle, adj *fragilis* **brittleness,** n. *fragilitas*

broach, I. n *veru* **II.** v.tr 1, lit *veru alci rei affigĕre, alqd aperire*, 2, fig *aperire, divulgare*

broad, adj 1, *latus*, — sea, *altum*, — shouldered, *humeros latus*, — day, *clarus* or *multus dies*, 2, fig = unrestrained of thought, etc , *liber*, = licentious, *impudicus* Adv *late*. **breadth,** n 1, lit *latitudo*, a finger's —, *transversus digitus*, 2, fig — of mind, *humanitas*

brogue, n *barbara locutio*

broil, I. v tr *torrēre* **II.** v intr *torrēri*

broker, n *intercessor, interpres*, *-pretis*, m , *argentarius*

bronze, adj *a(h)eneus*

brooch, n *gemma*

brood, I. v intr 1, lit. *ova incubare*, = cover with wings, *pullos fovēre*, 2, fig *incubare*; = ponder, *alqd meditari, fovēre* **II.** n *foetus, suboles*, *-is*, f , *pulli* **brooding,** n 1, lit. *incubatio*, 2, fig *meditatio*

brook, I. n *rivulus* **II.** v tr *ferre, tolerare* to — ill, *aegre ferre*.

broom, n 1, = a plant, *genista*, 2, = a besom, *scopae*

broth, n *jus*, *juris*, n

brother, n *frater* **brotherhood,** n = a bond of union or an association, *societas, sodalitas* **brotherly,** adj *fraternus*

brow, 1, = eyebrow, n. *supercilium*, 2, = the forehead, *frons*, 3, of a hill, *summus collis*

brown, n *fuscus, fulvus* (= yellowish), *badius, spadix* (= red-brown, chestnut colour)

browse, v intr — upon, *alqd depascĕre*

bruise, I. v tr *contundĕre* **II.** n *contusio*

bruit, v tr. *divulgare*.

brunt, n *impetus, -ūs*

brush, I. n *penicillus, peniculus,* or *peniculum* **II.** v tr *verrēre, tergēre* (or *tergĕre*) **brush-wood,** n *virgultum*

brute, n 1, = animal, *belua, bestia, animal,* 2, fig *belua* **brutish, brutal,** adj *ferus* (= wild), *spurcus* (= foul), *immanis, atrox, crudelis* Adv *spurce, atrociter* **brutalize,** v tr *ferum,* or *crudelem reddĕre* **brutality,** n *immanitas, crudelitas, atrocitas*

bubble, I. n *bulla, bullula* **II.** v intr 1, lit *bullare, bullire,* 2, fig *effervescĕre*

buccaneer, n. *pirata,* m , *praedo maritimus*

bucket, n *situla, situlus*

buckle, I. n. *fibula.* **II.** v tr *alqd fibulā nectĕre,* see APPLY

buckler, n *scutum, clipeus*

bud, I. n *gemma,* (in flowers) *calyx* **II.** v.intr. *gemmare*

budge, v intr *loco cedĕre*

budget, n 1, *saccus,* 2, = statement of accounts, *ratio pecuniae publicae.*

buff, adj *luteus*

buffalo, n *bos.*

buffet, I. n 1, = a blow, *alapa, colaphus,* 2, = sideboard, *abacus* **II.** v tr *pugnis alqm caedĕre*

buffoon, n *sannio, scurra* **buffoonery,** n. *hilaritas, lascivia,* or *joca, -orum,* n

bug, n *cimex, -icis,* m **bugbear,** n *quod terret, monstrum, portentum*

bugle, n *cornu*

build, v tr *aedificare, (ex)struĕre, construĕre, condĕre,* to — on, *alqa re (con)fidĕre, niti* **building,** n *aedificatio, ex(s)tructio* (= the act), *aedificium* (= the edifice) **builder,** n 1, lit. *architectus,* 2, fig *aedificator, auctor*

bulb, n *bulbus*

bulk, n *amplitudo, moles, is,* f **bulky,** adj *amplus, ingens.*

bull, n *bos, taurus* **bullock,** n *juvencus*

bullet, n *glans plumbea, lapis, -idis,* m , or *missile* (i e as hurled by *catapulta*)

bullion, n *aurum, argentum*

bully, I v tr *jurgio adoriri alqm, alqm summā crudelitate tractare.* **II.** n *homo crudelis, asper*

bulrush, n *juncus, scirpus*

bulwark, n *propugnaculum*

bump, I. n 1, *tumor, tuber, -ĕris,* n , 2, = a knocking, *impetus, -ūs, concursus, -ūs.* **II.** v tr *alqd in* or *ad alqd* or *alci rei offendĕre* **III.** v intr — against, *in alqd incidĕre.*

bumper, n *calix plenus*

bunch, n 1, of berries, *racemus;* — of grapes, *uva,* 2, = bundle, *fascis,* m

bundle, I. n *fascis,* m , *fasciculus, manipulus, sarcina* **II.** v tr *colligĕre*

bung, I. v tr *dolium obturare* **II.** n *obturamentum*

bungling, adj , see AWKWARD

buoy, I. n by *signum* (e g *in mari positum*) **II.** v tr *sustinēre* **buoyant,** adj 1, lit *lĕvis,* 2, fig *hilaris* **buoyancy,** n *lĕvitas, hilaritas*

burden, I. n 1, *onus, ĕris,* n., *sarcina,* 2, fig *molestia,* beast of —, *jumentum* **II.** v tr *onerare.* **burdensome,** adj *gravis, molestus*

burgess, n *civis,* m and f

burglar, n *fur, latro* (= robber) **burglary,** n *furtum* (= theft), to commit a —, *domum perfringĕre*

burlesque, n *alqd in ridiculum versum*

burn, I. v tr *incendĕre, (comb)urĕre, igni consumĕre, cremare* (esp of the dead) **II** v intr 1, lit *(de)flagrare, incendi, igni consumi, cremari,* 2, fig *ardēre, flagrare* **III.** n 1, = a wound, *ambustum, ambustio,* 2, = a rivulet, *rivus, torrens*

burnish, v tr *polire*

burrow, I. n *cuniculus* **II.** v tr *cuniculos facĕre*

burst, I. v tr *(di)rumpĕre* **II.** v intr *(di)rumpi,* to — open, *effringĕre*

bury, v tr 1, *humare, sepelire, efferre,* 2, fig *obruĕre, opprimĕre* **burial,** n *sepultura, humatio* **burial ground,** n *sepulturae locus, sepulc(h)rum, tumulus*

bush, n *frutex, dumus, vepres, -is,* m , *sentis,* m **bushy,** adj *fruticosus*

bushel, n *modius, medimnus*

business, n *mercatura, negotia, -orum, commercium*

buskin, n *cothurnus*

bust, n *effigies*

bustle, I n. *festinatio* **II.** v.intr. *festinare*

busy, I. adj *occupatus, sedulus, strenuus, industrius, negotiosus* Adv *strenue, industrie* **II.** v tr *alqm occupatum tenēre,* to be busied with, *alqd agĕre* **busy-body,** n *homo importunus*

but, I. conj *autem, vero, at,* — yet, *sed, verum, vero, atqui* (*autem* and *vero* stand after a word, the rest at the beginning of a sentence); — yet, — however, *at, (at)tamen, sed tamen,* — otherwise, *ceterum,* — if, *sin (autem), si vero* (in a contrast); — if not, *si non, si minus, sin aliter,* — on the contrary, *at contra,* in contrasts — is omitted, e g *tu illum amas, ego odi,* you love, (—) I hate him, — yet (anticipating an objection), *at,* — rather, *immo (vero),* not only, — also, *non modo* or *solum* or *tantum, sed etiam,* — that, *quin,* with subj *nisi.* **II.** prep see EXCEPT **III.** adv = only, *modo, tantum, solum*

butcher, I. n *lanius, macellarius* **II.** v tr 1, lit *caedĕre, jugulare,* 2, fig *trucidare* **butchery,** n *caedes, -is,* f

butler, n *cellarius*

butt, I. n *scopos, -i* (Suet), *destinatum* (= an object to aim at), to make a — of, *alqm ludibrio habēre, labrum* (= a large vessel), *sinum* (= a large wine cask) **II.** v tr *cornu alqd ferire*

butter, n *butyrum* (Plin)

butterfly, n *papilio*

buttocks, n *clunes, is,* m and f., *nates, -ium,* f

button, I n *fibula* (= clasp, buckle) **II.** v tr *fibulā nectĕre*

buttress, I n *anterides, -um,* f **II.** v tr *fulcire*

buxom, adj *hilaris*

buy, v tr *(co)emĕre, mercari* **buyer,** n *emptor*

buzz, v *susurrare, bombum facĕre* **buzzing,** n *susurrus, bombus*

by, prep 1, of place, *ad, apud, juxta, prope* with acc , to go —, *alqm praeterire,* to stand —, *alci adesse,* 2, of time, abl , — night, *nocte,* — moonlight, *ad lunam,* — this time, *jam,* — the year's end, *intra annum,* 3, of means, *per* with acc 4, an agent, *a(b),* 5,

= according to, *secundum* or *ad*; — the authority of, *jussu* or *ex auctoritate*; **6**, in adjuration, *per*; **7**, — oneself, *per se*; — stealth, *furtim*; — chance, *forte*; — heart, *memoriter*; — reason of, *propter*, with accus., or *propterea quod*, conj.; one — one, *singillatim*. **by-way**, n. *trames*, *-itis*, m. (= footpath), *deverticulum*. **by-word**, n. to become a —, *contemptui esse*.

C

cab, n. see CARRIAGE.

cabal, **I.** n. = a plot, *conjuratio*, *conspiratio*. **II.** v.tr. *conjurationem inire*; see PLOT.

cabbage, n. *brassica*, *caulis*, *-is*, m. (= — stalk).

cabin, n. *casa*, *tugurium*; — in a ship, *cubiculum*. **cabinet**, n. **1**, *conclave*; **2**, = a repository of precious things, *thesaurus*; **3**, = ministry, *ii penes quos summa rerum est*.

cable, n. *ancorale*, *funis ancorarius*.

cackle, **I.** v.intr. *strepĕre*. **II.** n. *strepitus*, *-ūs*.

cadaverous, adj. *exsanguis* (= bloodless).

cadence, n, *numerus*.

cadet, n. *tiro*.

cage, **I.** n. *cavea*. **II.** v.tr. *in caveam includĕre*.

cairn, n. (*lapidum*) *acervus*.

cajolery, n. *blanditiae*.

cake, **I.** n. *placenta*. **II.** v.intr. = stick together, *concrescĕre*.

calamity, n. *calamitas*, *res adversae*. **calamitous**, adj. *calamitosus*, *tristis*, *luctuosus*. Adv. *calamitose*, *luctuose*.

calculate, v.tr. *computare*. **calculation**, n. *ratio*. **calculated**, adj. *ad alqd accommodatus*, *aptus*, *idoneus*; he is — to do this, *is est qui hoc faciat*.

caldron, n. *a(h)enum*, *cortina*.

calendar, n. *ephemeris*, *-idis*, f., *fasti*.

calf, n. *vitulus*, *vitula*; of a —, *vitulinus*; — of the leg, *sura*.

calico, n. *byssus*, *sindon*.

call, **I.** n. **1**, = a cry, *vox*; **2**, = visit, *salutatio*; **3**, = offer of an office, by *nominari*. **II.** v.tr. **1**, = to cry out, *clamare*; **2**, = to name, *vocare*, *dicĕre*, *nominare*, *appellare*; **3**, to — out troops, *evocare*; to — out, = challenge, *provocare*; to — back, *revocare*; to — together, *convocare*; to — for, (*de*)*poscĕre*, *flagitare*. **III.** v.intr. = to visit, *alqm salutare*, *visĕre*. **caller**, n. = visitor, *salutator*. **calling**, n. = vocation, *munus*, *-ĕris*, n.

callous, adj. **1**, lit. *callosus*; **2**, fig. *durus*. Adv. *dure*.

callow, adj. *implumis*, *sine plumis*.

calm, **I.** n. *quies*, *-ētis*, f., *tranquillitas*, *otium*, *pax*; — at sea, *malacia*. **II.** adj. *quietus*, *tranquillus*, *placidus*. Adv. *tranquille*, *placide*. **III.** v.tr. *sedare*, *lenire*, *permulcēre*, *tranquillare*.

calumny, n. *crimen*, *calumnia*. **calumniate**, v.tr. *calumniari*, *criminari*. **calumniator**, n. *obtrectator*.

camel, n. *camelus*; of a —, *camelinus*.

cameo, n. *gemma ectypa*.

camp, n. *castra*, *-orum*; to form a —, *castra ponĕre*, (*col*)*locare*; to break up —, *castra movēre*.

campaign, n. *stipendium*.

can, n. see JUG.

can, v.intr. *posse*.

canal, n. *canalis*, *-is*, m., *fossa*.

cancel, v.tr. *delēre*, *eradĕre*, *ex(s)tinguĕre*.

cancer, n. *cancer* (Cels.).

candid, adj. *candidus*, *sincerus*, *verus*, *simplex*. Adv. *candide*, *sincere*, *vere*, *simpliciter*. **candour**, n. *sinceritas*, *simplicitas*, *integritas*.

candidate, n. *candidatus*.

candle, n. *candela*, *lumen* (= light); to work by — light, *lucubrare*. **candlestick**, n. *candelabrum*.

cane, **I.** n. *arundo*, *calamus*; of —, *arundineus*; — stick or rod, *ferula*; = walking-stick, *baculum*. **II.** v.tr. *verberare*.

canine, adj. *caninus*.

canker, v.tr. *corrumpĕre*. **cankerworm**, n. *eruca*.

canister, n. *canistrum*.

cannibal, n. *qui hominibus vescitur*.

cannon, n. *tormentum*; to be out of — shot *extra tormenti jactum esse*. **cannonade**, v.tr. *tormentis verberare*, *tela tormentis (e)mittĕre*. **cannon-ball**, n. *telum tormento missum*.

canoe, n. *cymba*.

canon, n. = a rule, *lex*, *regula*, *norma* (= standard). **canonize**, v.tr. *alqm in sanctorum numerum referre*, *sanctorum ordinibus a(d)scribĕre*.

canopy, n. *aulaeum*.

cant, n. *simulata* or *ficta pietas erga Deum*.

canton, n. *pagus*.

canvas, n. *pannus*.

canvass, **I.** n. **1**, = to examine, *explorare*, *disputare*; **2**, = to seek for office, *ambire*. **II.** n. *ambitio*, *ambitus*, *-ūs*.

cap, n. *pileus*, *galerus*; — for women, *mitra*.

capable, adj. *ad alqd so(l)lers*, *aptus*, *idoneus*; *alcjs rei capax*. **capability**, n. *ingenium*, *so(l)lertia*, *docilitas*, *facultas*.

capacious, adj. *capax*.

caparison, n. *phalerae*.

caper, n. *capparis* (Plin.).

capital, **I.** n. **1**, = chief city, *urbs opulentissima* or *potentissima*; **2**, of a pillar, *capitulum*; **3**, = sum of money, *sors*, *caput*. **II.** adj. see EXCELLENT; — punishment, *poena capitalis*. **capitalist**, n. *homo pecuniosus*, *dives*.

capitulate, v.intr. see SURRENDER.

caprice, n. *libido*, *licentia*, *voluntas*. **capricious**, adj. *inconstans*. Adv. *ad libidinem*.

captain, n. *centurio*; to act as —, *ordinem ducĕre*; — of a ship, *navarchus*, *praefectus navis*.

captious, adj. *iracundus* (= angry), *insidiosus* (= deceitful). Adv. *iracunde*, *insidiose*. **captiousness**, n. *iracundia*, *fallacia*, *captio*.

captivate, v.tr. *capĕre*, *delenire*, *permulcēre*.

captive, n. *captus*, *captivus*. **captivity**, n. *captivitas* (Tac.); to be in —, *captivum esse*. **capture**, v.tr. *capĕre*, *comprehendĕre*.

car, n. *carrus*, *plaustrum*, *vehiculum*.

caravan, n. *comitatus*, *-ūs*.

caraway, n. *careum* (Plin.).

carbuncle, n. *carbunculus*.

carcase, n. *cadaver*, *-ĕris*, n. (of men and beasts).

card, **I.** n. *charta*; to play at —s, see DICE. **II.** v.tr. *pectĕre*.

cardinal, **I.** adj. *princeps*, *eximius*. **II.** n. * *Cardinalis*.

care, **I.** n. **1**, *cura*, *diligentia*; **2**, = anxiety, *sol(l)icitudo* **II.** v intr **1**, = to take — of, *alqd curare*, what do I —? *quid mihi est?* **2**, = to be interested in, *colĕre, diligĕre* **careful**, adj *diligens, accuratus* Adv. *diligenter, accurate* **careless**, adj *securus, imprudens, neglegens* **carelessness**, n *securitas, imprudentia, neglegentia*

career, **I.** n *curriculum, cursus, ūs* (lit and fig) **II.** v intr *currĕre*

caress, **I.** n *blanditiae, blandimenta, -orum* **II.** v tr *alci blandiri, alqm permulcēre* **caressing**, adj *blandus*

cargo, n *onus, -ĕris*, n

caricature, **I.** n *vultus, -ūs, in pejus fictus* **II.** v tr *vultum in pejus fingĕre*

carmine, n *coccum*, of —, *coccineus*

carnage, n *caedes, -is*, f

carnal, adj *libidinosus* Adv *libidinose*

carnival, n *Saturnalia, -ium*

carnivorous, adj *qui carne vescitur*

carousal, n *convivium, comissatio* **carouse**, v intr *comissare*

carp, **I.** n *cyprinus* (Plin) **II.** v intr to — at, *alqm carpĕre, perstringĕre*

carpenter, n *faber (lignarius)* **carpentry**, n *opera fabrilis, fabrica*

carpet, n *tapete, tapetum, peristroma, -ătis*, n

carrion, n *cadaver, -ĕris* (or in pl)

cart, **I.** n *vehiculum, plaustrum* **II.** v tr *plaustro vehĕre* **cart load**, n *onus, -ĕris*, n

carve, v tr *caelare, scalpĕre, sculpĕre, inscribĕre*, — meat, *scindĕre, secare* **carver**, n **1**, of meat, *carptor*, **2**, of works of art, *sculptor* **carving**, n **1**, = act of, *caelatura, scalptura, sculptura*, **2**, = thing carved, *signum, effigies*

carry, v tr *portare, ferre, bajulare, vehĕre, gerĕre*, — a point, *alqd consequi*, — out, *conficĕre*, — on, *alqd exercēre*, — too far, *modum excedĕre*, — a town, *expugnare*, — a bill, *legem perferre* **carriage**, n **1**, = carrying, *vectura, gestatio*, **2**, = vehicle, *vehiculum, currus -ūs, carpentum, cisium, raeda*, **3**, = gait, *incessus, -ūs* **carrier**, n *gerulus*, letter —, *tabellarius*

cascade, n *aquae ex alto desilientes*

case, n **1**, = a receptacle, *theca, involucrum*, **2**, (in grammar), *casus, -ūs*, **3**, = an incident, *casus, -ūs, res*, **4**, in medicine, *morbus*, **5**, = judicial —, *cau(s)sa*

casement, n *fenestra*

cash, **I** n = ready money, *pecunia* **II.** v tr *praesenti pecunia solvĕre* **cashier**, **I.** n *custos pecuniarum* **II.** v tr = to discharge, *alqm dimittĕre*

cask, n *dolium* **casket**, n *arcula, capsula, cistula*

casque, n *galea*

cast, **I.** v tr. **1**, *jacĕre, jactare, jaculari, mittĕre*, **2**, = to found, *fundĕre*, **3**, to be — in a suit, *caus(s)a cadĕre*, **4**, to be — down, *affligi*, **5**, to — off, *(de)ponĕre, exuĕre*, to — out, *(ex)pellĕre*, to — up (of accounts), *computare* (a mound, etc), *exstruĕre* **II.** n **1**, *jactus, ūs ictus ūs*, **2**, of dice, *alea*, **3**, = image, *imago, effigies* **castaway**, n *perditus, profligatus*, — by shipwreck, *naufragus*

caste, n *societas, sodalitas*

castigation, n *castigatio, supplicium*

castle, n *arx, castellum*, to build —s in the air, *somnia sibi fingĕre*

castrate, v tr *castrare*

casual, adj *fortuitus, forte oblatus* Adv *forte, casu.* **casualty**, n, *fortuita orum, res fortuitae* **casuistry**, n *sophisma, -ătis*, n, *quaestio de moribus* **casuist**, n *sophistes, ae*, m, *qui de moribus disputat*

cat, n *feles (felis), -is*

catacomb, n *puticuli*

catalogue, n *librorum index*

catapult, n *catapulta*

cataract, n **1**, in the eye, *glaucoma* (Plin), **2**, see CASCADE

catarrh, n *destillatio, gravedo*

catastrophe, n *casus, -ūs (durus or acerbus)*

catch, **I.** v tr *capĕre, excipĕre, intercipĕre, deprehendĕre, comprehendĕre*, to — a disease, *morbum contrahĕre* **II.** n = gain, *lucrum, emolumentum* **catching**, adj, of a disease, *pestilens*

catechism, n **catechismus* **catechize**, v tr **catechizare* (Eccl)

category, n *genus, -ĕris, numerus, *categoria* **categorical**, adj *simplex, definitus*

cater, v intr *obsonare*

caterpillar, n *eruca*

cathedral, n **aedes cathedralis*

Catholic, **homo Catholicus* (Eccl) **Catholicism**, n. **fides Catholica* (Eccl)

cattle, n *pecus, -oris, armenta, -orum*

caul, n *omentum*

cauldron, n *a(h)enum, cortina*

cause, **I.** n **1**, *caus(s)a, auctor* (of a person), to have no —, *nihil est quod*, **2**, = legal —, *caus(s)a*, see ACTION **II** v tr *alcis rei auctorem esse, efficĕre ut*, = excite, *excitare, (com)movēre* **causal**, adj *quod efficit ut* **causeless**, adj *vanus, futilis* Adv *temere, sine caus(s)a*

causeway, n *viae, agger, -ĕris*, m

caustic, **I.** n *causticum* (Plin) **II.** adj *mordens, acerbus* **cauterize**, v tr *adurĕre*

caution, **I.** n *providentia, prudentia, cautio* **II.** v tr *monēre* **cautious**, adj *providus, prudens, cautus* Adv *prudenter, caute*

cavalcade, n *equites, -um, comitatus, ūs*

cavalier, n *eques, ĭtis*, m Adv *arroganter, insolenter*

cavalry, n *equitatus, equites, -um, copiae equestres, ala*, to serve in —, *equo merēre*

cave, n *cavum, caverna, specus, spelunca* **cavity**, n see HOLE

cavil, v intr see CARP

caw, v intr *crocire, crocitare*

cease, v intr *alqd omittĕre, intermittĕre, ab alqa re* or infin *desistĕre, desinĕre* with infin **ceaseless**, adj *perpetuus, assiduus, continuus* Adv *perpetue, assidue, continue*

cedar, n *cedrus*, f

cede, v tr *alqd* or *ab alqa re alci cedĕre, alqd concedĕre*

ceiling, n *laquear, lacunar*, vaulted —, *camera*

celebrate, v tr = solemnize, *celebrare, agĕre* **celebrated**, adj *inclytus, clarus, illustris, nobilis* **celebration**, n *celebratio* **celebrity**, n *gloria, laus, claritas*, = a celebrated person, *vir insignis*

celerity, n *velocitas, celeritas*

celestial, adj **1**, *caelestis, divinus*, **2**, fig *eximius, praestans*

celibacy, n *caelibatus, ūs*

cell, n *cella, cubiculum*

cellar, n *hypogeum (doliarium)*, a wine —, *apotheca*

cement, I. n. *gluten.* **II.** v.tr. both lit. & fig. *conglutinare.*

cemetery, n. *sepulc(h)ra, -orum.*

censer, n. *thuribulum.*

censor, n. 1, *censor;* 2, fig. *qui algm reprehendit.* **censorious,** adj. *acerbus, severus.* Adv. *acerbe, severe.*

censure, I. v.tr. *reprehendĕre.* **II.** n. *reprehensio.* **censurable,** adj. *reprehendendus.*

census, n. *census, -ūs, aestimatio;* to take a —, *censēre.*

cent, n. 1, = a coin, *teruncius;* 2, = per —, *unciae usurae,* = $\frac{1}{12}$th per — per month, = 1 per — per ann.; *sextantes,* = 2 per — per ann.; *quadrantes,* = 3, etc.; *asses usurae* or *centesimae,* = 12 per — per ann.; *binae centesimae,* = 24, etc.

centaur, n. *centaurus.*

centenary, n. *festum saeculare.*

centre, I. n. *media pars;* the — of anything, expressed by *medius* (e.g. *media urbs*); the — of a government, *sedes imperii.* **II.** v.intr. (*ex* or *in*) *algâ re constare;* to — in, see CONSIST.

century, n. *centum anni, saeculum.*

ceremonial, ceremony, n. *ritus, -ūs, caerimonia.* **ceremonious,** adj. *urbanus.* Adv. *urbane.*

certain, adj. 1, = fixed, *certus, firmus, stabilis, fidus* (= trustworthy), *exploratus* (= ascertained), *status* (= settled); a — income, *status reditus, -ūs;* to be — of a thing, *rem exploratam habēre;* 2, = someone known or unknown, *quidam; nescio qui, nescio quis.* Adv. *certe, certo, haud dubie, sine ullâ dubitatione, profecto, sane;* to know —, or for certain, *pro explorato* or *exploratum habēre.* **certainty, certitude,** n. *fides, res explorata.* **certificate,** n. *testimonium.* **certify,** v.tr. *certiorem facĕre, confirmare.*

cerulean, adj. *caeruleus.*

chafe, I. v.tr. *calefacĕre.* **II.** v.intr. *irasci, commoveri.*

chaff, n. *palea.*

chagrin, n. *aegritudo, maeror, sol(l)icitudo, dolor.*

chain, I. n. 1, *catena, vinculum;* 2, = an ornament, *catena;* 3, = a connected series, *series;* 4, = — of mountains, *montes, -ium,* m. **II.** v.tr. *vincire, catenas alci in(j)icĕre.*

chair, n. *sella, sedile, cathedra;* to set a — for, *sellam alci apponĕre.* **chairman,** n. *qui conventui praeest.*

chaise, n. *carpentum, pilentum.*

chalice, n. *calix, calathus.*

chalk, n. *creta.*

challenge, I. n. *provocatio.* **II.** v.tr. *algm ad algd provocare.*

chamber, n. *cubiculum.* **chamber-maid,** n. *serva.* **chamber-pot,** n. *matula, matella, trulla, scaphium.* **chamberlain,** n. *cubiculo praepositus* (Suet.).

champ, v.tr. *mandĕre, mordĕre.*

champion, n. *propugnator.*

chance, I. n. *casus, -ūs, fors;* by —, *forte, casu;* game of —, *alea.* **II.** v.intr. *accidĕre.*

chancel, n. *absis, -īdis,* f. **Chancellor of the Exchequer,** n. *aerarii tribunus.*

chandler, n. *qui candelas sebat* (= candle-maker), *candelarum, propola* (= seller).

change, I. v.tr. (*com*)*mutare;* to — money, *permutare.* **II.** v.intr. (*com*)*mutari;* the weather changes, *tempestas commutatur, caelum variat.* **III.** n. (*com*)*mutatio, conversio, vicissitudo, varietas;* = change of money, *permutatio,* or by verb *permutare.* **changeable,** adj. *mutabilis, mobilis, inconstans, varius.* Adv. *mutabiliter, mobiliter, inconstanter.* **changeableness,** n. *mutabilitas, varietas.* **changeling,** n. *puer subditus.*

channel, n. 1, lit. *fossa, canalis,* m.; 2, fig. *via, ratio.*

chant, v.tr. *canĕre, cantare.*

chaos, n. 1, lit. *chaos,* only in nom. and abl. sing.; 2, = confusion, *confusio, perturbatio.* **chaotic,** adj. *inordinatus, perturbatus.*

chapel, n. *aedicula, sacellum, sacrarium.*

chaps, n. = jaw, *fauces, -ium,* f.

chaps, n. on the hands, *rhagades* (Plin.).

chapter, n. of a book, *caput.*

character, n. 1, = a sign, *nota, signum;* 2, — of a person, *natura, indoles, -is,* f., *ingenium, animus, mores, -um;* weakness of —, *infirmitas, inconstantia;* strength of —, *constantia, gravitas;* 3, = a letter of the alphabet, *lit(t)era;* 4, = function, *munus, -eris,* n., or by apposition (e.g. to go in the — of ambassador, *legatum ire*); 5, = reputation, *fama, existimatio;* to give a — to a servant, *commendare.* **characteristic, I.** adj. *proprius.* Adv. *suo more.* **II.** n. *proprietas,* or by gen. (e.g. it is the — of the mind, *mentis est*). **characterize,** v.tr. *notare, designare.*

charcoal, n. *carbo.*

charge, I. n. 1, = office or trust, *munus, -eris,* n., *officium;* 2, = price, *pretium;* at a small —, *parvo pretio;* 3, = commission, *mandatum;* 4, = care of, *cura, custodia;* 5, = accusation, *accusatio, crimen;* 6, = attack, *impetus, -ūs, incursus, -ūs;* 7, = exhortation, *hortatio.* **II.** v.tr. 1, = order, *jubēre, imperare;* 2, = to fix a price, *indicare;* 3, — with, = trust, *algd alci committĕre, mandare, credĕre;* 4, take — of, *algm curare;* 5, = accuse, *accusare;* 6, = attack, *impetum in algm facĕre;* 7, = exhort, (*ad*)*hortari.* **chargeable,** adj. 1, *cui solvendum est;* 2, = — with a fault, *culpae affinis* or *obnoxius.* **charger,** n. 1, = dish, *lanx;* 2, = horse, *equus* (*ecus*).

chariot, n. *currus, -ūs;* a two-horsed —, *bigae;* four —, *quadrigae.* **charioteer,** n. *auriga,* m. and f.

charity, n. 1, as a sentiment, *amor, benignitas;* 2, as conduct, *beneficentia, liberalitas;* 3, = alms, *stips.* **charitable,** adj. *benignus, liberalis, beneficus.* Adv. *benigne, liberaliter.*

charlatan, n. *circulator, jactator, ostentator.*

charm, I. n. 1, lit. *carmen, canticum, fascinum;* 2, fig. = an attraction, *delenimenta, -orum, blanditiae;* 3, = beauty, *venustas, amoenitas.* **II.** v.tr. 1, lit. *fascinare, incantare;* 2, fig. *capĕre.* **charming,** adj. *suavis, venustus, lepidus.* **charmer,** n. 1, = magician, *magus;* 2, = mistress, *deliciae.*

chart, n. *tabula.* **charter,** n. *privilegium* (e.g. to grant a —, *privilegia dare*).

chary, adj. *parcus.*

chase, I. v.tr. *venari;* see PURSUE. **II.** n. *venatio, venatus, -ūs.*

chasm, n. *hiatus, -ūs, specus, -ūs.*

chaste, adj. *castus.* **chastity,** n. *castitas.*

chastize, v.tr. *castigare.* **chastisement,** n. *castigatio.*

chat, v.intr. *fabulari cum algo.*

chatter, I. v.intr. *garrire.* **II.** n. *garrulitas, loquacitas.* **chattering,** adj. *garrulus, loquax.*

cheap, adj. *vilis, parvi pretii.*

cheat, I. n. 1, *fraus, -dis,* f., *fallacia, dolus;* 2, = a man who —s, *circumscriptor* or *qui fallit,*

II. v tr *alqm fallĕre, decipĕre, circumvenire, fucum facĕre*

check, I n *impedimentum, mora* **II.** v tr. *alci obstare, impedimento esse, moram facĕre*

cheek, n *gena*

cheer, n 1, = joy, *hilaritas*, 2, = hospitality, *hospitium*, to entertain with good —, *hospitaliter* or *laute excipĕre* **cheerful,** *hilaris, hilarus* Adv *hilariter, hilare* **cheerless,** adj *tristis, maestus*

cheese, n *caseus*

chemistry, n * *chemia, ars chemica*

cheque, n *perscriptio*

cherish, v tr *curare, diligĕre, colĕre, observare*

cherry, n 1, the tree, *cerasus*, f , 2, = the fruit, *cerasum*

chess, n *lusus latrunculorum*

chest, n 1, = part of the body, *pectus, -oris*, n , 2, = a receptacle, *arca, cista*

chestnut, n *castanea*

chew, v tr *mandĕre*

chicanery, n *dolus, praevaricatio*

chicken, n *pullus (gallinaceus)*

chide, v tr *alqm objurgare* **chiding,** n *objurgatio*

chief, I. n *caput, princeps, praefectus* **II.** adj *primus, praecipuus* Adv *praecipue*

child, n *filius, filia, liberi* (= children) **child-birth,** *partus, -ūs*; to be in —, *parturire* **childhood,** n *aetas puerilis* **childlike,** adj *puerilis* **childish,** adj *ineptus* Adv *pueriliter* **childless,** adj *(liberis) orbus*

chill, I. adj *frigidus* **II.** n *frigus, -oris*, n **III.** v tr 1, lit *refrigerare*, 2, fig *reprimĕre*

chime, I. n *concentus, -ūs.* **II.** v intr *concinĕre*

chimera, n *commentum, opinionum commenta, orum* **chimerical,** adj *commenticius, inanis, vanus*

chimney, n (unknown in Roman houses) *compluvium* (= an opening in the roof of the *atrium*)

chin, n *mentum*

china, n *murrha* (Mart), made of —, *murrhinus*

chine, n *spina*

chink, n *rima*

chip, n *assula, scobis*

chirp, v *fritinnire, pipire, pipilare*

chisel, I. n *scalprum fabrile, caelum* **II.** v tr *sculpĕre*

chivalry, n *ordo equester, res equestris*, = politeness, *summa comitas* **chivalrous,** adj *fortis et urbanus*

choice, I. n *delectus, -ūs, electio* **II.** adj *praecipuus, eximius* **choose,** v tr *eligĕre, deligĕre*

choir, n 1, *chorus* 2, = — of a church, **absis* **chorister,** n *(puer) symphoniacus*

choke, I. v tr *suffocare, animam intercludĕre, praecludĕre* **II.** v intr *suffocari, strangulare*

choler, n see ANGER **cholera,** n *pestis*

chop, I v tr *abscidĕre*, — a tree, — the hands, *amputare* **II.** v intr *se vertere, verti* **III.** n *offa*

chord, n *nervus, fides, ium*, pl

chorus, n *chorus*, leader of —, *choragus*

chough, n *corvus*

Christ, **Christus* **Christendom,** n **populus Christianus* **Christian,** adj **Christianus* **Christianity,** n * *lex* or *religio Christiana*

chronic, adj *longinquus, diuturnus*

chronicle, I. v tr *in annales referre* **II.** n *annales, -ium*, m , *fasti* **chronicler,** n *annalium scriptor* **chronology,** n *temporum* or *annorum ratio* **chronological,** adj — errors, *temporum aetatumque errores* Adv *servato temporum ordine*

church, n *ecclesia*

churl, n *homo agrestis, rusticus, inurbanus* **churlish,** adj *inurbanus, agrestis, rusticus* Adv *rustice, inurbane* **churlishness,** n *rusticitas*

churn, I. n *labrum ad butyrum faciendum* **II.** v tr *butyrum facĕre*

cicatrice, n *cicatrix*

cider, n *vinum ex malis confectum*

cimeter, n *acinaces, is*, m

cinder, n *carbo ex(s)tinctus*

cipher, I. n 1, *nota, lit(t)era secretior*, 2, a mere —, *nullo numero esse*, see NUMBER **II** v intr *computare*

circle, n 1, lit *orbis, is*, m , *circulus*, to describe a —, *circulum ducĕre*, 2, = an assembly, *corona*, social —, *circulus*, family —, *familia*

circuit, n *circuitus, -ūs, ambitus, -ūs, orbis, -is*, m

circular, I. adj *orbiculatus, rotundus* **II.** n *lit(t)erae circum alqos dimissae* **circulation,** n *circuitus, ūs*, there is a rumour in — *rumor est.* **circulate, I.** v tr *circumagĕre* **II.** v intr *circumagi, commeare*, of money, *in usum venire.*

circumference, n *orbis, -is*, m *circuitus, -ūs*

circumflex, n When pronounced *circumflexus accentus, ūs* (Gram), when written, *syllaba circumflexa* (Gram)

circumlocution, n *circuitio*

circumnavigate, v tr *circumvehi (navi* or *classe)*

circumscribe, v tr *circumscribĕre, circumvenire*

circumspect, adj *cautus, providus, prudens* Adv *caute, prudenter* **circumspection,** n *cautio, prudentia, circumspectio*

circumstance, n *res, caus(s)a, ratio*, also by *hoc, id*, etc , under these —s, *quae cum ita sint* **circumstantial,** adj — evidence, *testimonium e rebus collectum* Adv *accurate*

circumvallation, n *circummunitio*

circumvent, v tr *circumvenire*

cistern, n *cisterna, puteus*

citadel, n *arx, castellum*

cite, v tr 1, = quote, *afferre, proferre, memorare*, 2, = — before a court, *citare, in jus vocare*

citizen, n *civis*, m and f **citizenship,** n *civitas*, to present or bestow —, *civitatem alci dare, impertire, tribuĕre, alqm in civitatem accipĕre* or *recipĕre* **city,** n *urbs* (= a town, as opp to country), *oppidum, municipium* (= a free city which had received the *jus civile Romanum*), *colonia* (= a Roman settlement)

citron, n *malum citrum*

civic, adj *civilis, civicus*

civil, adj 1, = civic, *civilis*, — process, *caus(s)a privata*, — rights, *jus civile*, — war, *bellum civile* or *intestinum*, 2, = polite *urbanus, bene moratus* Adv *urbane* **civilization,** n *cultus, ūs, humanus, humanitas* **civilize,** v tr *expolire, ad humanitatem informare* or *effingĕre.*

clad, adj *vestitus*

claim, **I.** n. **1,** = a demand, *postulatio, petitio*; **2,** = a right, *jus, juris,* n. **II.** v.tr. *postulare, petĕre, poscĕre, flagitare, quaerĕre.* **claimant,** n. (at law), *petitor.*

clammy, adj. *lentus.*

clamour, **I.** n. *vociferatio, clamor, voces, -um,* f. **II.** v.intr. *(con)clamare alqd* or acc. and infin., or *vociferari.* **clamorous,** adj. see NOISY.

clan, n. *gens, tribus, -ūs,* f.

clandestine, adj. *clandestinus, furtivus.* Adv. *clam, furtim.*

clang, **I.** n. *sonus, -ūs, sonitus, -ūs.* **II.** v.intr. *(re)sonare.*

clank, **I.** n. *crepitus, -ūs.* **II.** v.tr. *crepitum alqâ re dare.*

clap, **I.** n. *strepitus, -ūs, plausus, -ūs*; = — of the wings, *alarum crepitus, -ūs*; thunder —, *tonitrus, -ūs.* **II.** v.tr. **1,** = strike, *ferire*; **2,** — the wings, etc., *alas quatĕre*; **3,** = applaud, *alci (ap)plaudĕre*; — the hands, *manibus plaudum facĕre.*

claret, n. *vinum.*

clarify, v.tr. *deliquare.*

clash, **I.** v.tr. = strike, *pulsare, percutĕre.* **II.** v.intr. **1,** = strike together, *concurrĕre*; **2,** = to disagree, *inter se (re)pugnare, dissidĕre, discrepare*; **3,** = to sound, *sonare.* **III.** n. **1,** = collision, *concursus, -ūs*; **2,** = sound, *sonus, -ūs, sonitus, -ūs.*

clasp, **I.** n. *fibula.* **II.** v.tr. **1,** *fibulâ conjungĕre*; **2,** see EMBRACE, GRASP.

class, n. *classis* (Quint.), *ordo,* m. (= rank of citizens, etc.), *genus, -eris,* n.; a — of learners, *discipuli.* **classic,** **I.** n. (= writer) *scriptor* or *scriptor optimus, praecipuus.* **II.** adj. *optimus, praecipuus, eximius.* **classify,** v.tr. *in genera describĕre.*

clatter, **I.** n. *crepitus, -ūs, sonus, -ūs.* **II.** v.intr. *sonare.*

clause, n. *pars, membrum, caput.*

claw, **I.** n. *unguis*; of a crab, *brachium.* **II.** v.tr. *ungues alci (rei) in(j)icĕre.*

clay, n. *argilla*; of —, *argillaceus.*

clean, **I.** adj. *purus, mundus.* **II.** v.tr. *purgare.* **III.** adv. = quite, *prorsus.* **cleanliness,** n. *munditia, mundities.*

clear, **I.** adj. **1,** *clarus, lucidus, perspicuus, planus, manifestus, evidens*; it is —, *apparet, liquet*; **2,** see INNOCENT; **3,** see FREE. Adv. **1,** *distincte, perspicue, plane, manifeste, lucide*; **2,** = without doubt, *sine dubio.* **II.** v.tr. **1,** *(ex)purgare* = make clear; **2,** see EXPLAIN; **3,** = free from a charge, *absolvĕre, liberare.* **III.** v.intr. it —s up, *tempestas fit serena.* **clearness,** n. **1,** *claritas*; **2,** *serenitas* (of weather); **3,** of a proof, *res explorata, fides.* **clear-sighted,** adj. *sagax, (sol)lers.* **clear-starch,** n. *amylum.*

cleave, **I.** v.intr. see ADHERE. **II.** v.tr. *(dif)findĕre, scindĕre.* **cleaver,** n. *cultellus.* **cleft,** n. *fissura, fissum, rima.*

clemency, n. *clementia, gratia, mansuetudo.* **clement,** adj. *clemens, mansuetus, indulgens.*

clench, v.tr. *manum comprimĕre.*

clergy, n. **clerus,* **clerici*; — man, *sacerdos,* **clericus.* **clerical,** adj. **clericus,* **ecclesiasticus.*

clerk, n. *scriba,* m. *librarius.*

clever, adj. *habilis, sol(l)ers, peritus alcjs rei.* Adv. *sol(l)erter, perite.* **cleverness,** n. *peritia, habilitas, sol(l)ertia.*

client, n. *cliens* (= both dependent in gen. and client of a lawyer, in which sense also *consultor*). **clientship,** n. *clientēla.*

cliff, n. *scopulus, saxum.*

climate, n. *caelum, caeli status, -ūs, aër.*

climax, n. *gradatio*; in oratory, the — of happiness, *summa felicitas.*

climb, v.tr. *a(d)scendĕre, scandĕre, eniti in alqd.*

clinch, v.tr. *clavulo figĕre.*

cling, v.intr. *adhaerĕre rei*; — to a person, *alqm amplecti, sectari.*

clink, **I.** v.intr. *tinnire, sonare.* **II.** n. *tinnitus, -ūs, sonitus, -ūs.*

clip, v.tr. *praecidĕre, circumcidĕre, resecare.*

cloak, **I.** n. **1,** *amiculum, pallium, sagum, lacerna, paenula*; **2,** fig. *species.* **II.** v.tr. *tegĕre.*

clock, n. *horologium.*

clod, n. *glaeba (gleb).*

clog, **I.** n. *impedimentum.* **II.** v.tr. *impedire.*

cloister, n. **1,** = colonnade, *porticus, -ūs,* f.; **2,** = monastery, **monasterium.*

close, **I.** v.tr. **1,** = shut, *claudĕre, occludĕre*; **2,** = finish, *finire, conficĕre*; **3,** — a bargain, *de pretio cum alqo pacisci*; **4,** — with anyone, *manum conserĕre.* **II.** n. **1,** = inclosure, *saeptum*; **2,** = end, *finis,* m. and f., *exitus, -ūs.* **III.** adj. **1,** = reserved, *taciturnus, tectus*; **2,** = near, *propinquus, vicinus, finitimus*; — relationship, *propinquitas*; — friendship, *conjunctio*; **3,** = solid, *densus, solidus*; **4,** = compressed (of speech), *pressus, brevis.* Adv. **1,** *tecte*; **3,** *solide*; **4,** *presse, breviter.* **closeness,** n. **1,** *taciturnitas*; **2,** *propinquitas, vicinitas*; **3,** *soliditas.*

closet, n. *cubiculum.*

clot, **I.** n. *glaeba* (= lump); — of blood, *sanguis concretus.* **II.** v.tr. *congelare.*

cloth, n. *textum, pannus.* **clothes,** n. *vestitus, -ūs, vestes, -ium,* f. *vestimenta.* **clothe,** v.tr. *alqm vestire, amicire*; — oneself, *induĕre sibi vestem*; — with, *vestiri* or *amiciri re.*

cloud, **I.** n. *nubes, -is,* f. **II.** v.tr. *obscurare, tegĕre.* **III.** v.intr. *nubibus obducĕre.* **cloudy,** adj. *nubilus.* **cloudless,** adj. *nubibus vacuus, serenus.*

clover, n. *trifolium.*

clown, n. *homo rusticus, agrestis.* **clownish,** adj. *rusticus, agrestis.* Adv. *rustice.*

cloy, v.tr. *satiare.*

club, **I.** n. **1,** = cudgel, *clava*; **2,** = society, *circulus, factio, sodalitas.* **II.** v.tr. *in medium proferre.* **club-foot,** n. *tali pravi.* **club-footed,** adj. *scaurus.*

cluck, v.intr. *singultire, glocire.*

clue, n. *glomus, filum* (of thread); fig. *vestigium, indicium.*

clump, n. *glaeba.*

clumsy, adj. *agrestis, inhabilis, ineptus, rusticus*; a — joke, *jocus illiberalis*; — manners, *mores rustici.* Adv. *laeve, illiberaliter, rustice*; to act —, *rustice facĕre.* **clumsiness,** n. *rusticitas, inscitia.*

cluster, **I.** n. **1,** = bunch, *fasciculus* (of flowers), *uva* (of grapes), *racemus, corymbus* (of any berries); **2,** = a group, *circulus, corona.* **II.** v.intr. *(frequentes) convenire.*

clutch, **I.** v.tr. *comprehendĕre.* **II.** n., to get into one's —es, *manus alci in(j)icĕre.*

coach, n. *carpentum, pilentum, cisium, raeda.* **coachman,** n. *raedarius, auriga.*

coadjutor, n *socius*, *collega*, m

coagulate, v intr *coire*, *concrescĕre*, *coagulari*

coal, n *carbo*

coalesce, v intr *coalescĕre*, *coire* **coalition**, n *conjunctio*, *consociatio*

coarse, adj 1, *crassus*, 2, = rude, *agrestis*, *rusticus*, *inurbanus* Adv *crasse*, *rustice*, *inurbane* **coarseness**, n. 1, *crassitudo*, 2, *inhumanitas*, *mores inculti*

coast, I. n *litus*, *-ŏris*, n *ora*, lying on the —, *maritimus* II. v tr *oram legĕre*, *praetervehi*

coat, I. n 1, *toga*, *tunica*, 2, = hide, *vellus*, *ĕris*, n, *pellis*, 3, = of paint, *circumlitio* II. v tr *alqd alci rei inducĕre*

coax, v tr *alci blandiri*, *alqm permulcēre*, *morem alci gerĕre*

cobble, v tr 1, lit *sarcire*, 2, fig *inscienter facĕre alqd* **cobbler**, n *sutor*

cock, v tr *erigĕre*

cock, n 1, as to the gender, *mas* 2, = the male of the fowl, *gallus* **cockcrow**, n *cantus*, *-ūs*, *galli* **cockroach**, **cockchafer**, *scarabaeus* **cock-a-hoop**, to be —, *ex(s)ultare*

cockle, n = a fish, *pecten*

cod, n *asellus*

code, n *codex juris*, *corpus juris* (e g *Romani*), *leges* **codify**, v tr *leges describĕre*

coemption, n *coemptio*

coequal, adj *aequalis*.

coerce, v tr *coercēre*, *cohibēre* **coercion**, n *necessitas* **coercive**, adj *validus* (= strong), or by verb (e g *qui cohibet*)

coexistent, adj *quod eodem tempore est*.

coffer, n *cista*

coffin, n *arca*, *loculus*, *sarcophagus*.

cog, n of a wheel, *dens*, m

cogent, adj *firmus*, *validus* **cogency**, n *persuasio*, *ratio quae fidem facit*.

cogitate, v intr *cogitare* **cogitation**, n *cogitatio* **cognition**, n *cognitio*, *scientia* **cognizance**, n *cognitio* **cognizant**, adj *alcjs rei conscius*

cohabit, v intr *concumbĕre*

coheir, n *coheres*, *-ēdis*, m and f

cohere, v intr *cohaerēre* (both lit and fig) **coherent**, adj *cohaerens*, *contextus*, *continens*, *sibi congruens* Adv *contexte continenter*, *sibi constanter* or *convenienter*

cohort, n *cohors*

coin, I. n *nummus*, good —, *nummi boni*, bad —, *nummi adulterini* II. v tr *cudĕre*, *ferire*, *signare* **coinage**, n *res nummaria* **coiner**, n *qui aes* or *nummos cudit*

coincide, v intr 1, = to happen at the same time, *eodem tempore fieri*, or *incidĕre* 2, see AGREE **coincidence**, n = chance, *fors*, *casus*, *-ūs*

coition, n *coitus*, *-ūs*

cold, I. adj 1, lit *frigidus*, *gelidus* (= icy cold) in — blood, *consulto*, 2, fig *fastidiosus*, *superbus* Adv 1, *frigide*, *gelide*, 2, *fastidiose*, *superbe* II. n or **coldness**, n *frigus*, *-oris*, n, *algor*, *gelu* **cold-blooded**, adj see CRUEL

collapse, v intr *collabi*, *concidĕre*, *corruĕre*

collar, I. n *collare*, *monile*, *torques* is, m and f, dog —, *armilla* horse —, *jugum* II. v.tr *prehendĕre*. **collar-bone**, n *jugulum*.

collation, n 1, = comparison, *collatio*, 2, = a meal, *cena* **collate**, v tr *conferre*

colleague, n *collega*, m

collect, I. v tr *colligĕre*, *conferre*, *comportare*, *conquirĕre*, *congerĕre*, — oneself, *se colligĕre*, — money, taxes, etc, *exigĕre*, *accipĕre* II v intr *convenire*, *coire* **collection**, n 1, of money, *collatio*, 2, = an assemblage, *thesaurus*

college, n 1, = body, *collegium*, *societas*, *sodalitas*, 2, = building, *schola*

collier, n 1, = a man, *carbonarius*, 2, = a ship, *navis oneraria*

collocation, n *collocatio*, *concursus*, *-ūs*.

colloquy, n. *colloquium*. **colloquial**, adj — speech, *sermo communis*

collusion, n *collusio*

colonel, n *tribunus militum*, *praefectus*

colony, n *colonia*, *coloni* **colonist**, n *colonus* **colonial**, adj by gen of *colonia* **colonize**, v tr *coloniam constituĕre* or *collocare*

colonnade, n *columnarum ordo*, *-inis*, m, *porticus*, *-ūs*, f

colossal, adj *vastus*, *ingens*, *immanis*

colour, I. n 1, = a quality of bodies, *color*; 2, = a paint, *pigmentum*, 3, = pretext, *species*, 4, pl = standards, *signum*, *vexillum* II. v tr 1, lit *colorare*, *tingĕre*, *inficĕre*, 2, fig *speciem offerre* III. v intr, see BLUSH

colt, n *pullus equinus* (of horse), *asininus* (of ass)

column, n 1, = a pillar, *columna*, 2, in printing, *pagina*, 3, in an army, *agmen*, in two —s, *bipartito*, in three —s, *tripartito*

comb, I n *pecten*, (of a cock) *crista*, *juba* II. v tr *pectere*

combat, I. n *pugna*, *certamen*, *dimicatio*, *concursus*, *-ūs*, *proelium*, (with the fists) *pugilatus*, *-ūs*, *pugilatio*, (in wrestling) *luctatus*, *-ūs*, *luctatio*. II. v intr, see FIGHT

combine, v tr (*con*)*jungĕre*, *consociare*, *cum alqo societatem inire* **combination**, n (*con*)*junctio*, *societas*

combustion, n *exustio* **combustible**, adj *quod comburi potest*

come, v intr (*per*)*venire*, *advenire*, *accedĕre*, *appropinquare* (= to draw near), — on foot, *peditem venire*, — on horseback, *equo* (*ad*)*vehi*, — to a place often, *ad alqm* (*locum*) *ventitare*, *alqm* (*locum*) *frequentare*, it —s into my mind, *in mentem venit*, he —s to himself, *ad se redit*, *se colligit*, *animum recipit*, how —s it that? *qui factum est ut* etc, *ex quo fit ut*, *quo factum est ut*, I know not how it —s to pass, *fit nescio quomodo*, — as it may, *utcumque res ceciderit*, he has — to that audacity, *eo usque audaciae progressus est ut*; to — about = happen, *evenire*, *fieri*, — in the way of, *alci obstare*, — near, *appropinquare*, — off or out, *evadĕre* (= escape), — round, *sententiam mutare*, — together, *convenire*, — to light, *in lucem proferri* **coming**, n *adventus*, *-ūs*, *reditio*, *reditus*, *-ūs*

comedy, n. *comoedia* **comic**, adj 1, = belonging to comedy, *comicus*, 2, = ridiculous, *ridiculus*, *facetus* Adv *ridicule*, *facete*

comely, adj *bellus*, *venustus*, *pulcher*. **comeliness**, n *venustas*, *decor*, *pulchritudo*

comet, n *cometes*, *ae*, m

comfort, I. v tr 1, = console, *alqm consolari*, 2, = refresh, *alqm alqa re reficere*, *recreare* II n 1, = consolation, *solatium*, *consolatio*, 2, = ease, *copia*, *affluentia* 3, comforts, *commoda*, *-orum* **comfortable**, adj, *gratus* (= agreeable), *jucundus* (= happy). Adv. *grate, jucunde.* **comfortless,** adj. 1, *sine spe;* 2, = uncomfortable, *incommodus.* **comforter,** n. *consolator.*

command, I. v.tr. 1, *alqm alqd facĕre jubēre, alci alqd* or *ut imperare;* — oneself, *sibi imperare;* 2, = — a place, *alci loco imminēre.* **II.** n. 1, in war, *imperium;* 2, = order, *jussum, mandatum;* of the senate, *decretum;* 3, = — of oneself, *continentia, temperantia.* **commander,** n. *dux, imperator;* of a fleet, *praefectus classis.* See ORDER.

commemorate, v.tr. *commemorare, celebrare.* **commemoration,** n. *celebratio, commemoratio;* in — of, *in memoriam alcjs.*

commence, v.tr. *incipĕre;* see BEGIN.

commend, v.tr. 1, = recommend, *alqm alci commendare;* 2, = praise, *laudare.* **commendation,** n. *commendatio, laus, -dis,* f. **commendable,** adj. *laudabilis.* Adv. *laudabiliter.* **commendatory,** adj. *commendaticius.*

comment, I. v.tr. *interpretari, explanare, enarrare, commentari.* **II.** n. and **commentary,** n. *interpretatio, explanatio, enarratio.* **commentator,** n. *interpres, -ĕtis,* m. and f., *explanator.*

commerce, n. 1, = business, *commercium, negotia, -orum, mercatura;* 2, = intercourse, *usus, -ūs, commercium, consuetudo.* **commercial,** adj. *ad commercium pertinens.*

commingle, v.tr. see MINGLE.

commiserate, v.tr. **commiseration,** n. see PITY.

commissariat, n. 1, = provision department, *res frumentaria;* 2, = officer over this department, *rei frumentarii praefectus.* **commissary,** n. *procurator.*

commission, I. n. 1, *mandatum;* to execute a —, *mandatum exsequi, conficĕre;* 2 (as an office or charge) *munus, -ĕris,* n., *procuratio;* to hold a — in the army, *ordines ducĕre;* 3, = body of arbitrators, etc., *arbitri,* or *qui alqd investigant.* **II.** v.tr. *alqd alci* or *ut, mandare.* **commissioner,** n. *procurator.*

commit, v.tr. 1, = to intrust, *dare, mandare, committĕre;* 2, = to send to prison, *in custodiam dare, in vincula con(j)icĕre;* 3, = do, *facĕre, committĕre (in se), admittĕre, patrare;* — a fault, *errare;* — murder, *occidĕre.*

committee, n. *consilium;* — of two, *duumviri;* — of three, *triumviri,* etc.

commodious, adj. *commodus, opportunus, aptus.* Adv. *commode, opportune, apte.* **commodity,** n. 1, = convenience, *utilitas;* 2, = an article, *res, commoditas, merx.*

common, I. adj. 1, = belonging to several people, *communis, publicus;* — wealth, or weal, or good, *res publica;* — sense, *communis sensus -ūs* (that which all men feel), = practical wisdom, *prudentia;* in —, *communiter;* 2, = ordinary, *plebeius, cot(t)idianus* (quot.), *vulgaris;* 3, the —s, *plebs.* Adv. *communiter;* = usually, *fere, ferme.* **II.** n. *ager publicus.* **commonplace, I.** adj. *vulgaris.* **II.** n. *alqd (sermone) tritum.* **commoner,** n. *unus e plebe.*

commotion, n. *tumultus, -ūs, motus, -ūs, agitatio.*

commune, v.intr. *colloqui cum alqo, alqd communicare* or *conferre inter se.* **communicate,** v.tr., see SHARE, TELL. **communication,** n. *communicatio, usus, -ūs, consuetudo.* **communicative,** adj. *loquax* (= talkative), *qui alqd (e)narrare vult.* **communion,** n. 1, = intercourse, *commercium, societas, consuetudo, conjunctio;* 2, eccles. t.t. **communio,* **eucharistia,* **cena Domini.* **community,** n. 1, = COMMUNION 1; 2, of goods, *vitae communitas;* 3, = the state, *civitas, respublica.*

commute, v.tr. = to exchange, *(per)mutare, commutare.* **commutation,** n. *commutatio, redemptio.*

compact, I. n. *pactio, pactum, conventum;* by —, *ex pacto, ex convento;* to form a —, *pacisci cum alqo.* **II.** adj. *densus, crassus, confertus, solidus, pressus.* Adv. *solide, presse.*

companion, n. *comes, -ĭtis,* m. and f., *socius, sodalis,* m.; boon —, *conviva,* m. and f. **companionable,** adj. *affabilis, facilis.* **companionship,** n. by *socius* (e.g. he gave me his —, *se mihi socium conjunxit*). **company,** n. *societas;* to form a —, *societatem facĕre;* to enter into — with, *alqm socium sibi jungĕre.*

compare, v.tr. *comparare, componĕre, conferre.* **comparable,** adj. *quod comparari potest, comparabilis.* **comparison,** n. *comparatio, collatio;* in — of or with, *prae, ad; comparatus ad alqd.* **comparative,** adj. *comparativus.* Adv. *comparate.*

compass, I. n. 1, **acus magnetica nautarum;* 2, = extent, *ambitus, -ūs, circuitus, -ūs, modus.* **II.** v.tr. 1, = surround, *alqd alci rei* or *alqd re circumdare, stipare;* 2, = go round, *circumire;* 3, see ATTAIN.

compassion, n. *misericordia.* **compassionate,** adj. *misericors.* Adv. *cum misericordiā.*

compatible, adj. see ACCORDANCE.

compatriot, n. *cīvis,* m. and f.

compel, v.tr. *alqm ad alqd (faciendum)* or accus. and infin. or *ut, cogĕre, adigĕre.* **compulsory,** adj. *per vim.* **compulsion,** n. *vis, necessitas;* by —, *vi, per vim.*

compendious, adj. *brevis, in angustum coactus.* **compendium,** n. *epitome, -es,* f., or *epitoma, excerpta, -orum.*

compensate, v.tr. *alqd (cum) alqā re compensare;* — a loss, *damnum restituĕre.* **compensation,** n. *compensatio.*

compete, v.intr. 1, lit. *cum alqo contendĕre; competĕre;* 2, fig. *alqm* or *alqd aemulari.* **competent,** adj. see ABLE. Adv. *satis.* **competency,** n. *divitiae.* **competition,** n. *aemulatio.* **competitor,** n. *aemulus, competitor.*

compile, v.tr. *in unum conferre.* **compilation,** n. *epitome, -es,* f., *excerpta, -orum.*

complacent, adj. 1, see COMPLAISANT; 2, = self-satisfied, *qui sibi placet.* **complacency,** n. *voluptas, delectatio, amor sui.*

complain, v.intr. *(con)queri de re* or *alqd, expostulare de re.* **complaint,** n. 1, *questus, -ūs, querimonia, querela, expostulatio;* 2, = illness, *morbus.*

complaisant, adj. *comis, indulgens, facilis;* to be — to anyone, *morem alci gerĕre.*

complete, I. v.tr. *complēre, explēre, supplēre, absolvĕre* (= to finish), *conficĕre, cumulare.* **II.** adj. *absolutus, perfectus, justus, integer, plenus.* Adv. *absolute, perfecte, omnino, prorsus, plane* (the last three = altogether). **completion,** n. *confectio, absolutio, finis,* m. and f. **complement,** n. *complementum, supplementum.*

complex, adj. *multiplex.* **complexity,** n. *implicatio.* **complexion,** n. *color.*

complicate, v.tr. *implicare.* **complicated,** adj. *difficilis, involutus, impeditus.* **complication,** n. *res impedita et difficilis, difficultas.*

compliment, I. n. 1, *laus;* to pay —s, *laudem alci tribuĕre;* 2, = salutation, *salutatio, salus, -ūtis,* f.; to send one's —s, *alqm valēre* *jubēre* **II.** v tr *laudare, congratulari* **complimentary,** adj *honorificus*.

comply, v intr *alci obsequi, alci morem gerĕre*, to — with one's requests, *alcjs precibus indulgēre* **compliance,** n *obsequium, indulgentia, officium* **compliant,** adj see COMPLAISANT

components, n *partes, ium*, f.

compose, v tr 1, a book, *(con)scribĕre*, in verse, *versibus scribĕre*; 2, of music, *modos facĕre*, 3, see ARRANGE, 4, = to reconcile differences, *componĕre* **composed,** adj *tranquillus, quietus*. Adv *tranquille, quiete* **composer,** n *scriptor* **composition,** n 1, = the act, *compositio*, 2, = a writing, *scriptum* **composure,** n *tranquillitas*

compound, I. v tr 1, lit *componĕre, confundĕre*, 2, fig *componĕre*, to be —ed of, *ex alq re constare*, 3, — for, *satis habēre* with accus and infin **II.** adj *compositus, multiplex* **III.** n 1, *res admixta*, 2, = an enclosure, *saeptum*

comprehend, v tr 1, = contain, *continēre, comprehendĕre*, 2, = understand, *compr(eh)endĕre, intellegĕre* (*intellig*), *perspicĕre* **comprehensible,** adj *facilis intellectu, perspicuus, planus* Adv *plane, perspicue, aperte* **comprehension,** n *comprehensio, intellegentia* **comprehensive,** adj *late patens* Adv *penitus, prorsus*

compress, I. v tr *comprimĕre, condensare, coartare* **II** n = bandage, *penicillus* or *penicillum* **compression,** n *compressio, compressus, -ūs*

compromise, I. v tr *compromittĕre* (i e agreement to abide by the decision of an arbitrator) **II.** n *compromissum*, see AGREE

compulsion, n see COMPEL

compunction, n *poenitentia*; I have — for, *poenitet me rei*

compute, v tr *computare*, see RECKON

comrade, n = a fellow-soldier, *contubernalis, commilito, socius*. **comradeship,** n *contubernium*

concave, adj *concavus*

conceal, v tr *celare, occultare alqd alqm*

concede, v tr *concedĕre*. **concession,** n *concessio, concessus, -ūs*

conceit, n 1, = opinion, *opinio, sententia*, 2, = pride, *arrogantia, fastidium* **conceited,** adj *arrogans, fastidiosus* Adv *arroganter, fastidiose*

conceive, v tr 1, physically, *concipĕre*, 2, fig *cogitare, intellegere* (*intellig*), see IMAGINE

concentrate, v tr *colligĕre, contrahĕre, in unum conferre*

conception, n 1, = procreation, *conceptio, conceptus, -ūs*, 2, in the mind, *notio, opinio*, to form a —, *mente fingĕre alqd, notionem rei (animo) concipĕre*

concern, I. n 1, *res, negotium, cura*, 2, fig *anxietas, sol(l)icitudo, cura* **II** v tr 1, = to relate to, *pertinēre ad alqd*, it —s, *refert, interest*, to — oneself, *alci studēre*; 2, to be —ed = troubled, *alqd aegre ferre* **concerning,** prep *de*, abl , *per*, accus

concert, I. n 1, *symphonia, concentus, -ūs, certamen musicum*, 2, = agreement, *consensus, -ūs, concordia* **II.** v tr *inire consilium de alqā re, pacisci alqd cum alqo*

conciliate, v tr *conciliare* **conciliation,** n *conciliatio* **conciliatory,** adj *blandus*

concise, adj *brevis, pressus* Adv *presse, breviter* **conciseness,** n *brevitas*

conclave, n , see ASSEMBLY

conclude, v tr 1, = to finish, *finire, conficĕre, concludere*, 2, = to draw a conclusion, *concludĕre*, 3, = to decide, *statuĕre, constituĕre* **conclusion,** n 1, *finis*, m and f , 2 *conclusio* **conclusive,** adj *gravis* Adv *graviter*

concoct, v tr 1, = to mix, *miscēre*, 2, fig *fingĕre, machinari* **concoction,** n *potus, -ūs*

concomitant, adj , **-ly,** adv , *cum* with abl.

concord, n *concordia, consensus, -ūs* **concordant,** adj *concors, congruens, conspirans* Adv *congruenter*

concourse, n *concursus, ūs, concursio*

concrete, adj *concretus* (= grown together), *solidus* (= solid)

concubinage, n *concubinatus, -ūs* **concubine,** n *concubina, pellex*

concupiscence, n *libido* (*lub*)

concur, v intr *consentire, congruĕre, convenire* **concurrence,** n *consensio, consensus, -ūs* **concurrent,** adj , **-ly,** adv *una, simul*.

concussion, n *concussio, concussus, -ūs*

condemn, v tr 1, *damnare, condemnare*, — to death, *alqm capitis damnare* or *condemnare*, 2, = disapprove, *improbare, reprehendĕre, culpare* **condemnation,** n 1, *damnatio*, 2, *reprehensio, culpa* **condemnable,** adj *reprehendendus, reprehensione dignus* **condemnatory,** adj *damnatorius*

condense, I. v tr *densare, spissare* **II.** v intr *concrescĕre* **condensation,** n *densatio*

condescend, v intr , *comiter se gerĕre* **condescending,** adj *comis, facilis* Adv *comiter* **condescension,** n *comitas, facilitas*

condign, adj 1, = due, *debitus, meritus*; 2, = severe, *acerbus, atrox*

condiment, n *condimentum*

condition, I. n 1, = state, *condicio, res, status, -ūs*, 2, = stipulation, *condicio, pactum, conventum*, under the —, *eā condicione, eā lege* **II.** v tr *circumscribĕre* **conditional,** adj *incertus, condicionibus subjectus* Adv *eo pacto ut*, etc , *non sine exceptione* **conditioned,** adj *affectus*, well, ill —, *bene, male moratus*

condole, v tr *casum alcjs dolēre*

conduce, v intr *facĕre* or *efficĕre ut* **conducive,** adj *utilis*, dat , or *ad*.

conduct, I. v tr 1, = to lead, *ducĕre, agĕre*, in a procession, *deducĕre, prosequi*, 2, = manage, *gerĕre, administrare*, — oneself, *se gerĕre* or *praebēre* **II.** n 1, = behaviour, *vitae ratio, mores, -um*, 2, = management, *administratio, procuratio* **conductor,** n *dux, procurator*. **conduit,** n *aquaeductus, -ūs*

cone, n *conus*

confectionery, n *dulcia, -ium* **confectioner,** n *pistor dulciarius* (late)

confederacy, n *foedus, ĕris*, n , *societas*. **confederates,** n *socii, foederati* **confederate,** adj *foederatus*.

confer, I v intr = to talk with *deliberare, consultare de alqā re* or *utrum* **II.** v tr see GIVE **conference,** n *consilium, colloquium*

confess, v tr *fatēri, confitēri* **confessedly,** adv *sine dubio, plane* **confession,** n *confessio*.

confide, I. v tr *alqd alci committĕre, tradĕre, mandare, credĕre* **II.** v intr — in, *alci* or *alci rei* or *alqo* or *alqā re (con)fidere* **confidant,** n *(alcjs rei) conscius, conscia* **confidence,** n *fides, fiducia, fidentia, confidentia* (= esp self —), to tell in —, *alci ut amico certissimo dicĕre* **con**

fident, adj. *alci (rei) confidens, alqâ re fretus*, or by *certus, confirmatus*; see CERTAIN. Adv. *(con)fidenter*. **confidential**, adj. 1, = trustworthy, *fidus, fidelis*, or *alcjs rei conscius*; 2, see SECRET. Adv. see SECRETLY. **confiding**, adj. *credulus*.

confine, I. n. *finis*, m. and f., *terminus, limes, -itis, confinium*. II. v.tr. 1, see RESTRAIN; 2, see IMPRISON; 3, to be —d in childbed, *parĕre*. **confinement**, n. 1, = imprisonment, *custodia*; 2, = childbirth, *partus, -ūs*.

confirm, v.tr. *affirmare, confirmare, sancire, ratum facĕre, ratum esse jubēre*.

confiscate, v.tr. *publicare*. **confiscation**, n. *publicatio*.

conflagration, n. *incendium, ignis*, m.

conflict, I. n. *certamen, pugna, proelium*; of opinions, *dissensio*. II. v.intr. 1, = to strike together, *concurrĕre*; 2, = to fight, *pugnare*; 3, = to differ, *dissentire, discrepare, repugnare*.

confluence, n. 1, = the place where rivers meet, *confluens* or *confluentes*; 2, see CONCOURSE.

conform, I. v.tr. *alqd ad alqd* or *alci rei accommodare*. II. v.intr. to — to, *alci* or *alci rei obsequi, obtemperare, inservire*. **conformable**, adj. *ad alqd accommodatus, alci rei* or *cum alqâ re congruens, conveniens, consentaneus*. Adv. *congruenter, convenienter*. **conformation**, n. *conformatio, forma*. **conformity**, n. *consensus, -ūs, consensio, convenientia*.

confound, v.tr. 1, see CONFUSE; 2, = to astonish, *percutĕre, consternare*; 3, = to bring to naught, *ad irritum redigĕre, evertĕre*; 4, as an exclamation, — it, *di perdant*.

confraternity, n. *fraternitas, societas, sodalitas*.

confront, v.tr. *adversus alqm stare, alci obviam ire*.

confuse, v.tr. *confundĕre, (per)miscēre, (per)turbare*. **confusion**, n. *confusio, perturbatio*.

confute, v.tr. *refellĕre, redarguĕre, confutare, refutare*.

congeal, I. v.tr. *(con)gelare*. II. v.intr. *(con)gelari, frigēre, algēre*.

congenial, adj. *alci* or *alci rei* or *cum alqâ re congruens, conveniens*; = pleasant, *jucundus*.

congeries, n. *congeries*.

congratulate, v.tr. *alci de alqâ re*, or *alqd* or *quod, gratulari*. **congratulation**, n. *gratulatio*. **congratulatory**, adj. *gratulabundus*.

congregate, I. v.tr. *cogĕre, congregare*. II. v.intr. *cogi, congregari, convenire, coire, confluĕre*. **congregation**, n. *conventus, -ūs, coetus, -ūs, concio*.

congress, n. *conventus, -ūs, concilium*.

congruity, n. *convenientia*, see CONFORM.

congruous, adj., see CONFORMABLE.

conjecture, I. n. *conjectura, opinio, suspicio, divinatio*. II. v.tr. *conjecturâ augurari* or *consequi*. **conjectural**, adj. *quod conjecturâ prospici potest*. Adv. *conjecturâ*.

conjugal, adj. *conjugalis*.

conjugate, v.tr. *declinare* (Gram.). **conjugation**, n. *declinatio* (Gram.).

conjunction, n. (Gram.), *conjunctio*, see JOIN.

conjure, I. v.tr. 1, = to entreat, *obtestari, obsecrari per alqm* or *alqd*; 2, = to move by magic forms, *adjurare*; to — up, *(mortuorum) animas elicĕre*. II. v.intr. = to act as a conjurer, *praestigias agĕre*. **conjurer**, n. + *magus, ventilator*, + *praestigiator*.

connect, v.tr. *alqd ad alqd alligare, (con)jungĕre alqd* or *alqm cum re*. **connected**, adj. = coherent, *continens*. Adv. *continenter, uno tenore*. **connexion**, n. 1, *conjunctio, societas*; 2, = by marriage, *affinis*.

connive (at), v.intr. *co(n)nivēre in alqâ re, alci rei* or *alci alqd ignoscĕre, alci* or *alci rei indulgēre*. **connivance**, n. *indulgentia*.

connoisseur, n. *artium liberalium peritus, homo doctus*.

conquer, v.tr. *vincĕre, capĕre, expugnare, superare*. **conqueror**, n. *victor*. **conquest**, n. *victoria, occupatio, expugnatio*.

consanguinity, n. *sanguinis conjunctio*.

conscience, n. *conscientia virtutis et vitiorum, c. factorum, c. mentis, religio, fides*; a good —, *c. recte facti, mens bene sibi conscia*; to have a good —, *nullius culpae sibi conscium esse*; a bad —, *c. scelerum, mens male sibi conscia*. **conscientious**, adj. *religiosus, sanctus*. Adv. *religiose, sancte*. **conscientiousness**, n. *religio, sanctitas, fides*.

conscious, adj. *alcjs rei conscius, gnarus*. Adv. use adj. (e.g. I did it —, *gnarus feci*).

conscription, n. *delectus, -ūs, conquisitio militum*.

consecrate, v.tr. *(con)secrare, (de)dicare*. **consecrated**, adj. *sacratus, sacer*. **consecration**, n. *dedicatio*.

consecutive, adj. *continens, continuus*. Adv. *continenter*.

consent, I. v.intr., see AGREE. II. n. 1, *consensus, -ūs, consensio*; 2, *consensus, -ūs, assensus, -ūs*, see AGREEMENT; with your —, *te consentiente*.

consequent, adj. *consequens*. Adv., see THEREFORE. **consequence**, n. 1, = result, *consecutio, exitus, -ūs, eventus, -ūs*; the — was that, *ex quo factum est ut*; in — of, *ex* or *prae alqâ re, quae cum ita sint, itaque*; 2, = importance, *auctoritas, momentum, pondus, -ĕris*, n; to be of —, *multum valēre*.

conserve, I. v.tr. 1, see KEEP; 2, of fruit, *condire*. II. n. = jam, *fructus conditi*. **conservation**, n. *conservatio*. **conservative**, I. adj. *optimatibus addictus*. II. n. *unus ex optimatibus*. **conservatory**, n. (*locus*) *ad plantas colendas vitreis munitus*.

consider, v.tr. 1, = to look at, *spectare, intueri, contemplari*; 2, = to regard, *ducĕre, habēre, existimare*; 3, see THINK; 4, = to be thoughtful for, *alqm respicĕre*. **considerable**, adj. *magnus, gravis*; also by *aliquantum* with genit. (*al. praedae*, — plunder; *al. aeris alieni*, — debt); a — number, *multitudo, vis*. Adv. *aliquanto* or *aliquantum*. **considerate**, adj. 1, = thoughtful, *providus, providens, prudens, cautus*; 2, = thoughtful for others, *alqm respiciens, alci consulens, benignus*. Adv. 1, *provide, providenter, prudenter, caute*; 2, *benigne*. **considerateness**, n. 1, *providentia, prudentia*; 2, *benignitas*. **consideration**, n. 1, with the eyes, *contemplatio, conspectus, -ūs*; 2, with the mind, *judicium, meditatio, commentatio, consilium*; 3, = thought for anyone, *alcjs respectus, -ūs*; 4, = motive, *ratio*; from these —s, *quae cum ita sint*; 5, see IMPORTANCE; with —, *considerate, consulto, consilio*; to act with good —, *bono consilio facĕre alqd*.

consign, v.tr. *deferre alqd ad alqm, credĕre, mandare alqd alci*; to — to the flames, *alqd in flammas con(j)icĕre*.

consist, v.intr. = to be made of, *in* or *ex alqâ*

re constare, compositum esse, consistĕre, alqâ re contineri **consistent,** adj 1, — with, *cum alqâ re congruens, conveniens, concors,* or by *esse* with the genit (e g it is — with my character, *mei est*), 2, = unchanging, *constans* Adv *congruenter, convenienter, constanter* **consistence, consistency,** n 1, = thickness, *crassitudo, soliditas,* 2, = agreement, *constantia*

console, v tr *consolari alqm, solatium afferre* or *solatio esse alci* **consolation,** n *solatium, consolatio* **consoler,** n *consolator*

consonant, I. n = a letter, *consonans (li(t)tera)* **II.** adj *consentaneus, congruus cum alqâ re*

consort, I. n *comes, -itis,* m and f, *socius, socia,* = husband or wife, *maritus, marita, conju(n)x,* m. and f, *uxor,* f **II.** v intr *alqo familiariter uti, alci socium esse*

conspicuous, adj 1, = visible, *conspicuus, clarus, manifestus,* 2, = remarkable, *insignis* Adv *clare, manifeste, mirum in modum*

conspire, v intr *conjurare, conjurationem facĕre, conspirare* **conspiracy,** n *conjuratio, conspiratio* **conspirator,** n *conjuratus, -ūs, conjurationis socius*

constable, n *apparitor*

constant, adj 1, = incessant, *continuus, perpetuus,* 2, = faithful, *fidelis* Adv *perpetuo, continuo, fideliter* **constancy,** n 1, = patience, *patientia, constantia,* 2, = perseverance, *perseverantia, pervicacia,* 3, = continuance, *perpetuitas,* 4, = fidelity, *fides, fidelitas*

constellation, n *sidus, ĕris,* n, *stella*

consternation, n see TERROR

constipate, v tr med t t *alvum a(d)stringĕre* or *cohibēre*

constitute, v tr *statuĕre, constituĕre, designare* **constituent,** adj *pars* or *res* (e g — parts, *alcjs rei partes, res e quibus alqd constat*) **constitution,** n 1, of body, *corporis constitutio, affectio, habitus, -ūs,* a good —, *corpus bene constitutum,* a weak —, *corporis imbecillitas,* 2, of a state, *civitatis forma, reipublicae ratio* **constitutional,** adj 1, *innatus, insitus,* 2, *legitimus* Adv 1, *e naturâ,* 2, *legitime*

constrain, v tr *alqm constringĕre, cogĕre, alci necessitatem imponĕre alcjs rei faciendae* **constraint,** n *vis,* to do by —, *alqd invitum facere* **constrained,** adj = unnatural, *invitus,* of speech, *oratio contorta, perplexa, difficilis,* a — look, *vultus fictus,* a — laugh, *risus invitus*

construct, v tr, see BUILD, MAKE **construction,** n 1, = act of —, *aedificatio, constructio,* 2, = interpretation, *interpretatio,* to put a good, bad — on, *alqd in bonam, malam partem accipere,* 3, = — of a sentence, *compositio*

construe, v tr, see INTERPRET

consult, v tr *alqm consulĕre, consilium petĕre ab alqo,* to — anyone's interests, *alci consulere*

consume, v tr *edĕre* **consumption,** n *consumptio,* = the disease, *tabes, phthisis* (Plin)

consummate, I. v tr *absolvĕre, cumulare, perficĕre, conficĕre* **II.** adj *summus, absolutus, perfectus,* or by superl (e g *vir doctissimus* of — learning) Adv *summe, absolute, perfecte* **consummation,** n *absolutio, perfectio*

contact, n *tactio, (con)tactus, -ūs* **contagion,** n *contagio* **contagious,** adj *pestilens*

contain, v tr *continēre, complecti, comprehendĕre,* to — yourself, *se cohibēre, temperare sibi quominus,* etc

contaminate, v tr. *contaminare, inquinare, polluere* **contamination,** n *contaminatio, macula, labes, is,* f

contemplate, v tr. *contemplari* **contemplation,** n *contemplatio* **contemplative,** adj *in contemplatione (rerum) versatus,* see CONSIDER

contemporaneous, adj *quod eodem tempore est* or *fit* Adv *uno tempore, simul* **contemporary,** n *aequalis, qui ejusdem aetatis est*

contempt, n *contemptus, -ūs, fastidium* **contemptible,** adj *contemnendus, abjectus, turpis* Adv *turpiter*

contend, v intr 1, = fight, *cum alqo certare, dimicare, pugnare, alci resistĕre* 2, fig *alci (rei) resistĕre,* 3, see ARGUE **contention,** n see STRIFE, QUARREL, ARGUMENT **contentious,** adj *aemulus* Adv *summâ vi*

content, I. v tr *alci satisfacĕre* **II.** adj *sorte suâ contentus* Adv *tranquille* **contentment,** n *tranquillitas animi, animus tranquillus* **contents,** n *quod in libro continetur, argumentum, scripta, orum*

conterminous, adj *alci loco confinis*

contest, I. n *certatio, certamen* **II.** v intr *contendĕre,* see CONTEND

context, n *argumentum* or *ratio verborum* (opp to *singula verba*)

contiguous, adj *propinquus,* see CONTERMINOUS **contiguity,** n *propinquitas*

continence, n *continentia, temperantia, castitas, castimonia* **continent, I.** adj *continens, castus* Adv *caste* **II.** n *continens* **continental,** adj by genit of *continens*

contingent, I. adj *fortuitus, forte oblatus* **II.** n *quantum militum quaeque civitas mittere debet, auxilia, -orum* **contingency,** n *casus, ūs* (= a chance)

continual, adj *continuus, perpetuus, assiduus* Adv *continenter, assidue, perpetuo* **continuance,** n *constantia, perpetuitas, assiduitas, continuatio, diuturnitas* **continuation,** n 1, see CONTINUANCE, 2, = the latter part, *reliqua pars* **continue, I.** v tr 1, = carry on, *alqd extendĕre, producĕre, persequi, continuare,* to — after an interruption, *renovare* **II.** v intr 1, = go on with, *in alqâ re perseverare,* 2, = last, *durare, manēre, stare* **continuity,** n *continuatio, perpetuitas*

contort, v tr *depravare, detorquēre, distorquēre* **contortion,** n *distortio, depravatio*

contraband, n *merces vetitae*

contract, I. n *pactum, conventio, condicio, conductio, locatio, syngrapha* **II.** v tr 1, = draw in, *alqd contrahere* (in all meanings of Engl), 2, = agree to do, *alqd redimĕre, alqd faciendum conducĕre* (opp to *alqd faciendum locare,* to give out on —) **III.** v intr 1, *se contrahĕre* 2, = grow shorter, *minui* **contraction,** n 1 *contractio* 2, = — in writing, *compendium* **contractor,** n *conductor, redemptor*

contradict, v tr 1, = to speak against, *alci obloqui, contra dicĕre* (without dat and in two words), 2, fig *(inter se) repugnare, ab alqâ re dissentire, discrepare* **contradiction,** n 1, *quod contra dictum est,* 2, *repugnantia, discrepantia, diversitas* **contradictory,** adj *contrarius, repugnans, diversus* Adv *contrarie, diverse*

contrary, adj *adversus, (alcjs rei,* dat, *inter se) contrarius* a — wind, stream, *ventus adversus, flumen adversum,* on the —, *contra, ex* *contrario*; in answers *immo* (*vero*); — to, *praeter*, or *contra* with accus.

contrast, I. n. *asperitas* (in building, etc.), *diversitas*, *varietas*, *dissimilitudo*, *discrepantia*. **II.** v.tr. *alqd cum alqâ re comparare*, *conferre*.

contravene, v.tr. *repugnare*, *alqd violare*.

contribute, v.tr. **1,** = to give towards, *pecuniam conferre*, *dare*; — to something, *ad* (or *in*) *alqd dare*; **2,** fig. = to assist, *vim habēre ad*; *valēre ad*, *prodesse*, *adjuvare ad*, *facĕre ut*, *efficĕre ut*; it —s much to glory, *magni interest ad laudem* (with infin. and accus. following). **contribution,** n. *stips*, *pecunia*; to levy a —, *pecuniam a civitatibus cogĕre*. **contributor,** n. **1,** in gen. *qui alqd dat*; **2,** = — to a magazine, *scriptor*.

contrite, adj. see SORROWFUL. **contrition,** n. *poenitentia*; I feel —, *poenitet me rei*.

contrive, v.tr. *excogitare*, *invenire*, *fingĕre*; — to do anything, *facĕre* or *efficĕre ut*. **contrivance,** n. **1,** = act of —, *inventio*, *excogitatio*; **2,** = thing contrived, *inventum*; **3,** = plan, *ratio*, *consilium*.

control, I. n. **1,** = power, *potestas*, *imperium*, *dicio*; **2,** self —, *moderatio*, *temperatio*. **II.** v.tr. *alqd moderari*, *cohibēre*, *coercēre*, *reprimĕre*; — oneself, *sibi temperare*, *se continēre*.

controversy, n. *controversia*, *altercatio*, *disceptatio*, *contentio*. **controversial,** adj. *controversus* (= disputed). Adv. *per disputationem*. **controvert,** v.tr. *refellĕre*, *refutare*. **controvertible,** adj. *dubius*, *ambiguus*.

contumacy, n. *pertinacia*, *contumacia*. **contumacious,** adj. *contumax*, *pertinax*. Adv. *contumaciter*, *pertinaciter*.

contumely, n. *contumelia*. **contumelious,** adj. *contumeliosus*, *probrosus*. Adv. *contumeliose*.

convalescence, n. *sanitas restituta*, *valetudo confirmata*. **convalescent,** adj. use verb *convalescĕre*.

convene, v.tr. *convocare*. **convenient,** adj. *commodus*, *opportunus*, *ad alqd* (or dat.) *accommodatus*, *idoneus*. Adv. *commode*, *opportune*, *accommodate*. **convenience,** n. *commoditas*, *commodum*, *occasio*, *opportunitas*. **convent,** see CLOISTER. **convention,** n. **1,** *conventus*, *-ūs*, *foedus*, *-ĕris*, n., *pactio*; **2,** = custom, *mos*. **conventional,** adj. *tra(ns)laticius*, *a majoribus traditus*, *usu receptus*; it is —, *moris est*, *in more est*. Adv. *ex usu*, dat. *mos est*.

converge, v.intr. *se inclinare ad* or *in alqm* or *alqd*.

conversation, n. *sermo*, *sermo cot(t)idianus* (*quot.*), or *communis*, *colloquium*; to be the subject of —, *in ore omnium esse*. **converse, I.** v.intr. *colloqui cum alqo*, *serm. habēre cum alqo de re*. **II.** adj. see CONTRARY. **conversant,** adj. *in alqâ re versatus* or *exercitatus*, *alcjs rei peritus*.

convert, I. v.tr. **1,** see CHANGE; **2,** = change anyone's opinion, *alqm in aliam mentem adducĕre*; be —ed, *sententiam mutare*. **II.** n. *qui ad aliam opinionem* (e.g. *Christianam*) *adductus est*. **conversion,** n. **1,** = change, *(com)mutatio*, *conversio*; **2,** = change of opinion, *sententiae* or *morum mutatio*, = — to Christianity, *accessio ad Christi doctrinam*.

convex, adj. *convexus*.

convey, v.tr. **1,** see CARRY; **2,** legal t.t. *alqd alci transcribĕre*, *(con)cedĕre*. **conveyance,** n. **1,** see CARRIAGE; **2,** legal t.t. *cessio*, *transcriptio*. **conveyancer,** n. *scriba*, m.

convict, I. v.tr. **1,** *damnare*, *condemnare alqm*; **2,** = show falsehood, etc., *alqd convincĕre*, *redarguĕre*. **II.** n. *damnatus*, *maleficus*. **conviction,** n. **1,** *damnatio*; **2,** *opinio*, *sententia*, *judicium*.

convince, v.tr. *persuadēre de re*; be convinced, *alci persuasum esse*, *exploratum* or *cognitum habēre*. **convincing,** adj. *ad persuadendum accommodatus*, *gravis*. Adv. *graviter*.

convivial, adj. *hilaris*, *jucundus*. **conviviality,** n. *hilaritas*.

convoke, v.tr. *convocare*.

convoy, I. n. *praesidium*, *custodia*. **II.** v.tr. *alqm praesidii caus(s)â comitari*.

convulse, v.tr. *agitare*, *percutĕre*, *(com)movēre*; — the state, *civitatem quassare*, *labefactare*. **convulsion,** n. *spasmus*, *convulsio* (Plin.). **convulsive,** adj. *spasticus* (Plin.).

cook, I. n. *coquus*. **II.** v.tr. *coquĕre*. **cookery,** n. *res coquinaria*.

cool, I. adj. **1,** lit. *frigidus*; **2,** fig. *tranquillus* (of temperament), *superbus*, *fastidiosus* (= haughty), *fortis* (= brave), *impudens* (= impudent). **II.** n. *frigus*, *-oris*, n., *algor*. **III.** v.tr. *refrigerare*. **IV.** v.intr. **1,** lit. *frigescĕre*, *frigĕre* (= be —), *algēre* (= feel —); **2,** fig. *defervescĕre*, *animum remittĕre*. **coolness,** n. **1,** lit. *frigus*, *-oris*, n.; **2,** fig. *superbia*, *fastidium* (= pride), *fortitudo* (= courage), *inimicitia* (= unfriendliness). Adv. *frigide*, *aequo animo*, *tranquille*, *superbe*, *fastidiose*, *fortiter*, *impudenter* (= with effrontery).

cooper, n. *vietor*.

co-operate, v.intr. *unâ agĕre*, *alqm (ad)juvare*. **co-operation,** n. *opera*, *auxilium*. **copartner, co-operator,** n. *socius*; see COMPANION.

cope, v.intr. — with, *cum alqo* or *alqd re certare*, *alci resistĕre*.

coping, n. *corona*, *fastigium*.

copious, adj. *copiosus*, *abundans*, *largus*. Adv. *copiose*, *abundanter*, *large*. **copiousness,** n. *copia*, *abundantia*.

copper, I. n. *aes*, *aeris*, n., *aes Cyprium*; — money, *raudera*, *-um*; — vessel, *a(h)eneum*. **II.** adj. *a(h)eneus*.

coppice, copse, n. *virgultum*.

copulation, n. *coitus*, *-ūs*.

copy, I. n. **1,** *exemplum*, *exemplar* (= model, — of a book, etc.); **2,** — (book), for a child, *lit(t)erae praeformatae*. **II.** v.tr. **1,** = imitate, *imitari*; **2,** of painters, writers, *pingĕre*, *describĕre*; — from the life, *similitudinem ex vero effingĕre*.

coquet, v.tr. *viro spellicĕre*. **coquette,** n. *quae viros pellicit*.

cord, I. n. *restis*, *funis*, m. **II.** v.tr. *constringĕre*, *colligare*. **cordon,** n. *milites*.

cordial, adj. *ex animo amicus*, *benignus*, *comis*. Adv. *benigne*, *comiter*, *amice*. **cordiality,** n. *benignitas*, *comitas*, *amicitia*.

core, n. *nucleus*, *granum*, *semen* (= seed).

cork, I. n., *cortex*. **II.** v.tr. *obturare*.

corn, n. *frumentum*, *fruges*, *-um*, f., *annona*; — measure, *modius*.

corn, n. on the foot, *clavus*.

corner, n. *angulus*; done in a —, *in occulto*.

cornet, n. **1,** an instrument, *cornu*, *buccina*; **2,** military t.t. *vexillarius*, *signifer*.

cornice, n. *corona*.

corollary, n. *consectarium*.

coronation, n. (*dies etc*) *quo rex diadema accipit*.

coroner, n *magistratus qui de mortuis inquirit*

corporal, I. n *decurio* **II.** adj by genit of *corpus, -ŏris,* n **corporal-punishment,** n *verbera, -um,* to inflict —, *verberibus castigare*

corporation, n *sodalitas* (religious), *municipium, concilium, collegium*

corps, n *manus, -ūs,* f, *pars exercitūs, ala equitum, agmen.*

corpse, n *cadaver, -ĕris,* m

corpulent, adj *obēsus* **corpulence,** n *corpus obesum*

correct, I. v tr 1, = improve, *corrigĕre, emendare,* — a book for the press, *menda libro tollĕre,* 2, = punish, *punire, castigare* **II.** adj 1, of conduct, *honestus, rectus,* 2, of style, *emendatus, rectus, purus, accuratus,* 3, = true, *verus* Adv. *recte, honeste, pure, vere* **correctness,** n use adjectives (e g the — of a thing, *res recta*)

correspond, v intr. 1, = agree, *respondēre alci rei* or *ad alqd, convenire alci rei,* 2, to — by letter, *lit(t)eras dare et accipĕre,* — with, *cum alqo per lit(t)eras colloqui* **correspondent,** n *qui alqd per lit(t)eras (crebrius) communicat* **correspondence,** n. *per lit(t)eras* **corresponding,** adj *par* Adv *pariter*

corroborate, v tr *ratum facĕre* or *efficĕre, confirmare, comprobare* **corroboration,** n *confirmatio*

corrode, v tr *erodĕre* **corrosive,** adj *qui (quae, quod) erodit*

corrupt, I adj *perditus, profligatus, turpis, corruptus* Adv. *perdite, turpiter* **II.** v tr *putrefacĕre, corrumpĕre* (lit and fig), *depravare, vitiare, perdĕre, pervertĕre* (lit.) **III.** v intr *putrefieri, corrumpi* (all fig) **corrupter,** n *corruptor, qui corrumpit,* etc **corruptible,** adj *quod corrumpi potest* **corruption,** n *corruptio, depravatio, corruptela* **corrupting,** adj *perniciosus, exitiosus*

corsair, n *pirata,* m

corslet, n *thorax, lorica, pectoris teg(i)men* or *teg(i)mentum*

cortege, n *comitatus, -ūs*

coruscation, n *fulguratio, fulgor, splendor*

cosmetic, n *fucus*

cost, I. n *sumptus, -ūs, impensa, pretium, merces, -ēdis,* f (= wages) **II.** v tr *alqd (con)stat* or *venit* or *venditur* or *emitur* (with genit of the exact price), to — little, *parvo stare,* very little, *minimo* **costly,** adj *sumptuosus, magno sumptu, pretiosus* **costliness,** n *caritas*

costume, n *habitus, ūs, ornatus, ūs*

cottage, n. *casa, tugurium* **cottager,** n *rusticus*

cotton, n *gossypion (-ium)* (Plin)

couch, I. n *lectus, lectulus* **II.** v tr 1, = stretch out, *porrigĕre,* to — spears, *hastas dirigĕre;* 2, = express, *(con)scribĕre* **III.** v intr *cubare, latēre, delitescĕre.*

cough, I. n *tussis* **II** v intr *tussire*

council, n *concilium* **council-chamber,** n *curia* **councillor,** n *consiliarius, senator*

counsel, I. n 1, = consultation, *consultatio, deliberatio,* 2, = advice, *consilium, auctoritas* **II.** v tr see ADVISE

count, n **comes* **county,** n. **comitatus, -ūs*

count, v tr 1, *computare,* 2, — upon, *alci confidĕre,* see RECKON, CONSIDER **counter,** n 1, = — of a shop, use *mensa,* 2, = — for reckoning, *calculus* **countless,** adj *innumerabilis*

countenance, I. n 1, *vultus, os, oris,* n, 2, = protection, *praesidium* **II.** v tr *alci favēre, opem ferre*

counter, adv = against, *contra* **counteract,** v tr *alci resistĕre* **counter-balance,** *parem esse alci* **counterfeit, I.** v tr *simulare,* **II.** adj *simulatus,* — money, *nummus adulterinus* **counterpane,** n *lodix* **counterpart,** n *res alci simillima* **counterpoise,** v tr *alqd cum alqa re (ad)aequare*

country, n 1, opp to town, *rus,* in the —, *ruri,* 2, = one's native land, *patria,* of what —? *cujas?* of our —, *nostras,* 3, = region, *terra, regio* **country-house,** n *villa* **countryman,** n 1, *homo rusticus,* 2, = fellow —, *civis, nostras,* pl *nostri* **country-town,** n *municipium*

couple, I. n *par, bini,* in married life, *conjuges, mariti* **II.** v tr *(con)jungĕre,* — with, *copulare cum re, miscēre re*

courage, n *animus, audacia, ferocia* (= fierce courage), *fortitudo, virtus, -ūtis,* f **courageous,** adj *fortis, audax, ferox, strenuus* Adv *fortiter, audacter, ferociter, strenue*

courier, n *nuntius*

course, I. n 1, *(de)cursus, -ūs,* — of water, *lapsus, -ūs,* — of the stars, *motus, ūs,* the — of nature, *naturae lex,* fig the — of life, *vitae curriculum,* 2, = plan, *ratio, consilium,* 3, = progress, *tenor, cursus, -ūs, via, progressus, ūs,* 4, = — of time, *in* (e g *in illo anno*), in — of a few, many days, *intra paucos, multos dies* 5, = — at a dinner, *ferculum,* 6, = — of lectures, *alqm audire,* 7, = manner of life, *mores, um, vitae ratio* **II.** v tr *venari* **of course,** adv. *necessario, plane, prorsus,* in answers, *sane*

court, I. n 1, = an open space, *area,* 2, = royal —, *aula, regia,* 3, = courtiers, *nobiles, -ium,* 4, = — of justice, *forum, tribunal, subsellia, -orum* **II** v tr 1, of a lover, *alqam (in matrimonium) petĕre,* 2, = to seek to obtain, *quaerĕre, captare* **courtier,** n *nobilis* **courteous,** adj *comis, communis* Adv *urbane, comiter* **courtesy, courteousness,** n *urbanitas, comitas* **courtship,** n *amor* or verb, *in matrimonium petĕre*

cousin, n *(con)sobrinus (-a)* (on the mother's side), *patruelis* (a father's brother's child)

covenant, I. n *pactio, pactum, conventum* **II.** v tr *paciscĕ cum alqo*

cover, I. n 1, of a bed, etc, *lodix, teg(i)men, stragulum, gausapa,* = lid, *operimentum,* 2, = shelter, *perfugium,* under — of, *alqa re tectus,* fig = pretence, *per speciem alcjs rei* **II.** v tr 1, *(con)tegĕre, obtegĕre, operire, velare,* 2, = protect, *protegĕre, defendĕre,* = to secure against loss, *cavēre alqd,* 3, = overwhelm, fig *alqd in alqm conferre,* or by special verbs (e g — with abuse, *alci maledicĕre*)

covert, I. n 1, = shelter, *latebra, perfugium,* 2, = thicket, *virgultum* **II.** adj *tectus* See SECRET

covet, v tr *alqd appetĕre, concupiscĕre, cupiditate rei flagrare* **covetous,** adj *avarus* Adv *avare* **covetousness,** n *avaritia*

cow, n *vacca* **cow-herd,** n *armentarius* **cow-hide,** n *corium vaccae*

coward, n *homo ignavus, timidus* **cowardly,** adj *ignavus, timidus* Adv *ignave, timide* **cowardliness,** n *metus, ūs, ignavia,*

cower, v intr *perterritum esse,*

cowl, n *cucullus.*

coxcomb, n. *homo ineptus.*

coy, adj. *verecundus.* **coyness**, n. *pudor, verecundia.*

cozen, v.tr. see CHEAT.

crab, n. *cancer.* **crabbed**, adj. 1, = ill-tempered, *morosus;* 2, = intricate, *difficilis, impeditus.* Adv. *morose, difficulter.*

crack, I. n. 1, = noise, *crepitus, -ūs* (e.g. — of the fingers, *digitorum crepitus*), † *fragor;* 2, = fissure, *rima.* II. v.intr. *crepare,* (*dif*)*findi, dissilire, dehiscĕre.* III. v.tr. 1, lit. = burst, (*dif*)*findĕre, rumpĕre;* 2, — a joke, *jocari;* to — a whip, *sonitum flagello edĕre.*

cradle, I. n. *cunae, cunabula, -orum.* II. v.tr. *in cunabulis ponĕre.*

craft, n. 1, = cunning, *dolus, astutia;* 2, = skill or trade, *ars, artificium;* 3, = ship, *cymba, scapha.* **crafty**, adj. *astutus, callidus, versutus, dolosus.* Adv. *astute, callide, versute, dolose.* **craftsman**, n. *opera.*

crag, n. see ROCK.

cram, v.tr. 1, with food, *farcire, refercire;* 2, fig. *alqd alqā re complēre, implēre;* = crowd, *stipare* (more common in pass.).

cramp, I. n. *spasmus, tetanus* (Plin.). II. v.tr. to be —ed, fig. *circumscribi.*

crane, I. n. 1, = bird, *grus, gruis,* m. and f.; 2, a machine, *troclea.* II. v.intr. — forward, *cervicem protendĕre.*

crank, n. 1, of a machine, *uncus;* 2, = jest, *jocus.*

cranny, n. *rima.*

crash, I. n. *fragor.* II. v.tr. *crepare.*

crate, n. *crates, -is,* f.

crater, n. *crater, -ēris,* m.

crave, v.tr. see BEG, NEED. **craving**, n. *alcjs rei desiderium.*

crawl, v. *repĕre, serpĕre.*

crazy, adj. *mente captus;* see MAD.

creak, v. (*con*)*crepare.* **creaking**, n. *crepitus, -ūs.*

cream, n. *flos lactis.*

crease, I. n. *ruga.* II. v.tr. *rugare.*

create, v.tr. 1, lit. (*pro*)*creare, gignĕre, facĕre;* 2, fig. *praebēre, facĕre, efficĕre, fingĕre,* or by special verbs (e.g. — confusion, *perturbare*); 3, = appoint, *creare, designare.* **creation**, n. 1, *procreatio* (= begetting), *initium* (= beginning); since the — of the world, *post mundum conditum;* 2, mental —, *poema, -ătis,* n. *fabula,* etc. **creative**, adj. *qui creare* (etc.) *potest.* **creator**, n. (*pro*)*creator, fabricator, auctor.* **creature**, n. *animal.*

credit, I. v.tr. 1, = to believe, *credĕre;* 2, put to one's account, *alqd alci in acceptum conferre.* II. n. 1, = belief, *fides;* to give — to a thing, *alci* or *alci rei fidem habēre, tribuĕre, adjungĕre;* to withhold or refuse —, *fidem alci denegare;* 2, mercant. t.t. *fides;* to take up money on —, *pecuniam alcjs fide mutuam sumĕre;* to purchase on —, *emĕre in diem* (the time being fixed when payment has to be made), *emĕre pecuniā non praesenti;* his — is gone, *fides cecidit, concidit;* 3, = authority, *auctoritas, gratia* (= influence), *opinio, existimatio;* 4, do — to, *gloriae* or *decori alci esse;* no —, *dedecori alci esse.* **credible**, adj. *fide dignus, credibilis, verisimilis.* Adv. *credibiliter.* **credibility**, *fides, auctoritas,* comb. *auctoritas et fides.* **credentials**, n. *auctoritas,* or *lit*(*t*)*erae.* **creditable**, adj. *honestus, honorificus.* Adv. *honorifice, honeste.* **creditor**, n. *creditor.* **credulous**, adj. *credulus.* Adv. *nimiā cum credulitate.* **credulity**, n. *credulitas* (not in Cic.). **creed**, n. 1, = belief, *fides;* 2, = system believed, *doctrina.*

creek, n. *sinus, -ūs.*

creep, v.intr. see CRAWL.

crescent, n. *luna crescens.* **crescent-shaped**, adj. *lunatus.*

crest, n. *crista, juba.* **crested**, adj. *cristatus.* **crestfallen**, adj. *fractus, demissus.*

crevice, n. see CRACK.

crew, n. 1, *nautae;* 2, fig. *coetus, -ūs.*

crib, n. 1, for animals, *praesepe;* 2, see CRADLE.

crime, n. *delictum, maleficium, facinus, -inoris,* n., *scelus, -eris,* n., *nefas.* **criminate**, v.tr. *criminari.* **crimination**, n. *crimen, criminatio.* **criminal**, adj. *scelestus, sceleratus, nefarius.*

crimson, I. adj. *coccineus.* II. n. *color coccineus.* III. v.intr. *erubescĕre.*

cringe, v.intr. — to, *alqm* or *alci adulari.*

cripple, n. *homo mancus, membris captus, homo debilis,* or *claudus manu, pedibus,* etc.

crisis, n. *discrimen, momentum.*

crisp, adj. 1, = curled, *crispus;* 2, = brittle, *fragilis.*

criterion, n. *discrimen.* **critic**, n. *criticus, homo alcjs rei peritus,* or simply *sapiens.* **criticism**, n. *judicium.* **criticize**, v.tr. *judicare.* **critical**, adj. 1, = belonging to criticism, *callidus, sol*(*l*)*ers, sapiens;* 2, = belonging to a crisis, *in discrimen adductus, anceps, dubius.* Adv. *accurate, callide, sol*(*l*)*erter, sapienter.*

croak, I. v.intr. *crocire* (of birds), *vocem emittĕre.* II. n. *vox.*

crockery, n. (*vasa*) *fictilia.*

crocodile, n. *crocodilus.*

crocus, n. *crocus.*

crone, n. *vetula, anus, -ūs,* f.

crook, I. n. *pedum, lituus.* II. v.tr., see CURVE. **crooked**, adj. *curvatus, incurvus;* = bad, *pravus, distortus.* Adv. 1, *oblique,* or by adj.; 2, *prave.* **crookedness**, n. 1, *quod incurvum est;* 2, *pravitas.*

crop, I. n. 1, of corn, etc., *messis, fruges, -um,* f.; 2, of birds, *ingluvies.* II. v.tr. = cut short, *praecidĕre, amputare, tondĕre;* = to cut down, *depascĕre,* † *tondēre.*

cross, I. n. 1, + *crux,* × *decussis;* as instrument of punishment, *crux;* 2, fig. *mala, -orum,* or *calamitas.* II. adj. = transverse, *transversus, obliquus.* III. v.tr. 1, = lay across, *alqd alci rei transversum ponĕre;* 2, = go across, *locum transire;* 3, = thwart, *alci obsistĕre;* 4, = — the mind, *alqd alci subit;* 5, = — out, *delēre.* **cross-purpose**, n. be at —s, *alii alia putant,* or by adj. *contrarius.* **crosswise**, adv. *in transversum.* **crossing**, n. *transitus, -ūs.*

crouch, v.intr. *se demittĕre.*

crow, I. n. *cornix.* II. v.intr. *canĕre.*

crowd, I. n. *turba, caterva, frequentia, multitudo.* II. v.tr. (*co*)*artare, stipare, premĕre.* III. v.intr. *confluĕre, congregari.*

crown, I. n. 1, = wreath, *corona;* diadem, *diadema, -ătis,* n.; 2, = kingly power, *regnum;* 3, = top, *summus* with noun (e.g. — of the mountain, *summus mons*); 4, = ornament, *decus, -oris,* n. II. v.tr. *coronare;* — a king, *diadema regi imponĕre.* **coronation**, n. *sollemnia quibus rex diadema accipit.*

crucible, n. *catinus* (Plin.).

crucify, v tr *alqm cruci affigĕre* **crucifixion,** n *crucis supplicium*

crude, adj 1, = raw or unripe, *crudus*, 2, fig *informis, incultus, rudis* Adv *inculte*

crudity, n *cruditas*

cruel, adj *crudelis, saevus, ferus, atrox* Adv *crudeliter, atrociter* **cruelty,** n *crudelitas, feritas, saevitia, atrocitas*

cruise, v intr *(per)vagari*, — along the shore, *praeter oram vagari*

crumb, n. 1, = the soft part of bread, *panis mollia (-ium)*, 2, = a small piece, *mica, micula* **crumble,** I. v tr *friare, comminuĕre, conterĕre* **II.** v intr *friari*, etc

crumple, I n *ruga* **II.** v tr *rugare* **III.** v intr *rugari*

crupper, n *postilena*

crush, I. v tr 1, lit *comprimĕre, contundĕre, conterĕre, conculcare* (by treading), 2 fig *affligĕre, comprimĕre, obruĕre, frangĕre* **II.** n = crowd, *turba* See CROWD

crust, n *crusta* **crusty,** adj *crustosus* (Plin.).

crutch, n *baculum.*

cry, I. v tr 1, = call out, *(con)clamare, exclamare, acclamare, proclamare, praedicare, clamitare*, 2, see WEEP **II.** n 1, *clamor, exclamatio, acclamatio*, 2, *proclamatio, praeconium*, 3, *lacrimae, vagitus, -ūs* **crier,** n *praeco*

crystal, n *crystallus* **crystallize,** I. v tr *in crystallos formare* **II.** v intr *in crystallos abire*

cub, n I. *catulus.* **II.** v.tr *fetus edĕre*

cube, n *cubus.* **cubic,** adj *cubicus*

cubit, n *cubitum*

cuckoo, n *cuculus*

cucumber, n *cucŭmis, ĕris,* m

cud, n to chew the —, *ruminari, remandĕre*

cudgel, I. n *baculum, fustis,* m **II.** v tr *ferire, percutĕre, fusti verberare*

cue, n. 1, = hint, *signum*, to give a —, *alci innuĕre, signum alci dare*, 2, of an actor, *signum*

cuff, I n 1, = blow, *alapa* (with the flat hand), *colaphus* (with the fist), 2, = sleeve, *manica extrema* **II.** v tr *verberare alqm, plagam alci infligĕre, pugnis alci caedĕre*

cuirass, n *thorax*

culinary, adj *coquinarius*

culmination, n *fastigium* **culminate,** v.intr *in (summo) fastigio esse*

culpable, adj *culpā dignus, reprehendendus, turpis, foedus* **culprit,** n see CRIMINAL

cultivate, v tr 1, in agriculture, *(agrum) colĕre*, 2, fig *fingĕre, (con)formare, instituĕre, expolire*, 3, = practise, *alci rei studēre, se ad alqd applicare* **cultivation, culture,** n 1, *cultus, -ūs*, 2, mental —, *animi cultus, humanitas, lit(t)erarum* or *artium studia, -orum* **cultivator,** n 1, *agricola,* m, *cultor*, 2, fig by verb

cumber, v tr *alqm* or *alqd impedire, praegravare, alci (rei) obstruĕre* **cumbrous,** adj *gravis, incommodus, inhabilis* Adv *graviter, incommode*

cunning, I. adj 1, *astutus, callidus, versutus, dolosus*, 2, = skilful, *peritus, dexter, habilis, expertus* Adv 1, *astute, callide, versute*, or abl *dolo* or *per dolum* or *fraudem*, 2, = skilfully, *sol(l)erter, perite, callide* **II.** n 1, *astutia, calliditas, versutia, dolus*, 2, = skill, *ars, so(l)lertia*

cup, I. n 1, *poculum, scyphus, calix, calathus, phiala, patera, carchesium, scaphium, cymbium, cyathus, batiola, culullus*, 2, fig = — of sorrow, etc, *dolor*, to drain the —, *exhaurire dolorem*, etc. **II.** v tr *sanguinem alci (per cucurbitulas) detrahĕre* **cup bearer,** n *minister* or *servus*

cupboard, n *armarium*

cupidity, n *cupiditas, avaritia.*

cupola, n *tholus*

curator, n *curator, custos*

curb, I. n *frenum* **II.** v tr *frenare, coercēre, domare, comprimĕre, prohibēre*

curd, n *lac concretum* **curdle,** v tr **I.** *alqd coagulare* **II.** v intr *coagulari, coire*

cure, I. n *curatio, medicina, sanatio* **II.** v tr 1, *sanare alqm, mederi alci*, 2, = preserve, *condire*

curiosity, n 1, *nova noscendi studium, spectandi studium*, 2, = something rare or strange, *res nova* or *rara* **curious,** adj 1, = inquisitive, *curiosus, alcjs rei studiosus*, 2, = strange, *insolitus, novus, rarus, singularis*, 3, = accurate, *accuratus* Adv *anxie*, or adj, *raro, accurate*

curl, I. v tr *crispare, calamistro intorquēre* **II.** v intr 1, *crispari*, etc, 2, = to be bent round, *torquēri, flecti* **III.** n *cirrus* **curling-irons,** n *calamister* **curly,** adj *crispus*

currant, n dried —s, *uvae passae*

current, I. adj 1, = this, *hic* (e g — year, *hic annus*), 2 = common, *more* or *usu receptus*, to be — in, *esse, valēre* Adv *vulgo* **II.** n *flumen*, see STREAM **currency,** n *nummi* or *argentum*

curry, v tr 1, to — leather, *conficĕre*, 2, to — favour, *alci blandiri* **currycomb,** n *strigilis*

curse, I. n 1, *exsecratio, imprecatio, maledictum*, 2, fig *pestis* **II.** v tr to — anyone, *exsecrari, alci male precari*

cursory, adj *rapidus, neglegens (neglig)* Adv *breviter, strictim*

curt, adj *brevis* Adv *breviter*

curtail, v tr *amputare, praecidere*

curtain, n *velum, aulaeum*

curve, I. n *(in)flexio, flexus, -ūs, sinus, -ūs* **II.** v tr *(in)flectĕre.* **III.** v intr *flecti*

cushion, n *pulvinus, pulvinar*

custard, n *placenta ex ovis facta*

custody, n *custodia, carcer, -ĕris,* m, *vincula, -orum*

custom, n 1, = usage, *consuetudo, mos, institutum, usus, -ūs*, it is a — with us, *est institutum, mos* or *moris est*, 2, = duty, *vectigal, portorium* **customer,** n *emptor* **customary,** adj *usitatus, tritus, pervulgatus, vulgaris, col(l)-ditianus (quot), communis, tra(ns)laticius* to be —, *mos* or *moris esse, solēre* Adv. *ex consuetudine, vulgo, fere*

cut, I. v tr 1, lit *secare*, to — with a scythe, *(de)metĕre* to — into planks, *in laminas secare* to — the throat, *alqm jugulare*, to — on a gem, *in gemmā scalpĕre*, to — the hair, *tondēre, praecidĕre*, to — down, lit *excidĕre*, 2, fig *trucidare*, to — short, = interrupt *alqm interpellare*, = abridge, *contrahĕre*, to — up, *concidere* **II.** n 1, by verb (e g to receive a —, *cultro vulnerari*), if with a whip, *verber*, 2, of rivers, etc, *canalis,* m, *fossa*, 3, = short —, *via brevissima* or *proxima* **cutting,** I. adj *acerbus* Adv *acerbe* **II.** n of a plant, *propago,*

cutlery, n *cultri* (pl) **cut-throat,** n, *sicarius*

cuttlefish, n *sepia,*

cycle, n. 1, = circular course, *orbis*, m., *circulus*; 2, = revolution, *orbis*, or by verb *revolvi*; see REVOLVE.

cyclops, n. *cyclops*.

cygnet, n. *pullus cycnorum*.

cylinder, n. *cylindrus*.

cymbal, n. *cymbalum*.

cynic, n. 1, in philosophy, *cynicus*; 2, fig., *homo acerbus*. **cynical,** adj. *acerbus*. Adv. *acerbe*.

cynosure, n. 1, lit. *Ursa Minor*; 2, fig., *decus*, *-ŏris*, n.

cypress, n. *cupressus*, f.

D.

dabble, I. v.tr. *alqd alqâ re a(d)spergĕre*. **II.** v.intr. 1, lit. *in aquâ ludĕre*; 2, fig. *alqd leviter attingĕre*.

dad, daddy, n. *tata*.

daffodil, n. *narcissus*.

dagger, n. *pugio*, *sica*.

dainty, I. adj. 1, = — in choice of food, *fastidiosus*; 2, = elegant, *exquisitus*, *elegans*; see PRETTY. **II.** n. *cibus delicatus*, *cibi delicatiores*. **daintiness,** n. 1, = — in food, *cup(p)edia*; 2, = elegance, *venustas*.

dairy, n. *cella*, defining sense by context (e.g. *lacte repleta*).

dale, n. *(con)vallis*.

dally, v.intr. 1, = trifle, *nugari*, *lascivire*; 2, — with, *alci blandiri*; 3, see DELAY. **dalliance,** n. 1, *nugae*, *lascivia*; 2, *blanditiae*.

dam, n. = mother, *mater*, *matrix*.

dam, I. n. *agger*, *-ĕris*, m., *moles*, *-is*, f. **II.** v.tr. *molem alci rei ob(j)icĕre*, *flumen coercēre*.

damage, I. n. *damnum*, *detrimentum*, *noxa*. **II.** v.tr. *alci nocēre*, *obesse*, *damno esse*. **damages,** n. pl., *impensa*; action for —, *judicium recuperatorium*.

dame, n. *mulier*, *matrona*, *domina*.

damn, v.tr. 1, *damnare*, *condemnare*; 2, theol. t.t., **damnare*, *aeternis suppliciis addicĕre*. **damnable,** adj. *damnandus*. **damnation,** n. *damnatio*, *condemnatio* (= the act).

damp, I. adj. *humidus*. **II.** v.tr. 1, lit. *humectare*; 2, fig. *deprimĕre*, *comprimĕre*, *restinguĕre*, *sedare*. **III.** n. *vapor*, *nebula*.

damsel, n. *puella*, *ancilla*, *virgo*.

dance, I. n. *saltatio*, *chorēa*. **II.** v.intr. *saltare*. **dancer,** n. *saltator*, m. *saltatrix*, f.

dandle, v.tr. *manibus agitare*.

dandy, n., *homo elegans*; *de capsulâ totus* (Sen.).

danger, n. *periculum*, *discrimen*. **dangerous,** adj. *periculosus*, *anceps*; a — condition, *res dubiae*. Adv. *periculose*.

dangle, v.intr. *ex alqâ re (de)pendēre*.

dank, adj. *humidus*.

dapper, adj. *pernix* (= quick), *nitidus* (= neat).

dapple, adj. *maculosus*.

dare, v.tr. *audēre*. **daring, I.** adj. *audax*. Adv. *audacter*. **II.** n. *audacia*.

dark, I. adj. 1, as opposed to daylight, *obscurus*, *caliginosus*, *caecus* (= blind); 2, = — in colour, *fuscus*, *niger*, *pullus*; 3, = difficult to the mind, *obscurus*, *abstrusus*, *impeditus*, *incertus*. Adv. *obscure*, *perplexe*. **II.** n. to be in the — about, *alqd ignorare*. **darkness,** n. *obscuritas*, *tenebrae*, *caligo*, *nox*. **dark-red,** adj. *ex rubro subniger*. **dark-black,** adj. *niger*. **darken, I.** v.tr. lit. and fig. *obscurare*, *tenebras alci rei obducĕre*. **II.** v.intr. *obscurari*; it —s, *vesperascit*.

darling, n. *deliciae*.

darn, v.tr. *sarcire*. **darning-needle,** n. *acus*, *-ūs*, f. *grandior*.

dart, I. n. *pilum*, *hasta*, *telum*, *jaculum*, *tragula*. **II.** v.tr. *jaculari*; to throw —s, *tela (e)mittĕre*, *con(j)icĕre*. **III.** v.intr. *in alqm locum irrumpĕre*, *se con(j)icĕre*.

dash, I. v.tr. 1, lit. *alqd ad alqd offendĕre*, *impingĕre*; — out the brains, *caput perfringĕre* or *elidĕre*; 2, fig. *spem* (etc.) *reprimĕre*, *comprimĕre*, *ad irritum redigĕre*. **II.** v.intr. see DART. **III.** n. 1, = rush, *impetus*, *-ūs*; 2, = something of, *aliquid*, *nescio quid*; 3, see DISPLAY.

dastard, n. *homo ignavus*.

date, n. (the fruit), *palmula* (Var.). **data,** n. *concessa*, *-orum*. **date, I.** n. *dies*; out of —, *obsoletus*. **II.** v.tr. *diem in epistolâ a(d)scribĕre*. **dative,** n. *(casus) dativus* (Gram.).

daub, v.tr *(ob)linĕre*, *(per)ungĕre*.

daughter, n. *filia*; a little —, *filiola*; —-in-law, *nurus*, *-ūs*, f.

daunt, v.tr., see FRIGHTEN. **dauntless,** adj. *impavidus*. Adv. *impavide*.

daw, n. *monedula*.

dawdle, v.intr. *cessare*. **dawdler,** n. *cessator*.

dawn, n. *diluculum*. **it dawns,** v. *(di)lucescit*.

day, n. 1, *dies*, *lux* (= daylight); the longest —, *dies solstitialis*, *solstitium* (= the time of the longest days); the shortest —, *dies brumalis*; before —, *ante lucem*; at break of —, *(cum) primâ luce*, *luce oriente*; by —, *interdiu*; — and night, *diem noctem*, *diem noctemque*, *dies noctesque*, *noctes diesque*, *noctes et dies*; the — breaks, *(il)lucescit*, *dilucescit*, *lux oritur*; far on in the —, *multo die*; to wish one good —, *alqm salvum esse jubēre*, *alqm salutare*; good —! *salve (salvete)*; a lucky —, *dies albus* or *candidus*; an unlucky —, *dies ater*; the — star, *lucifer*; 2, = a period of time, *dies*; a period of two or three —s, *biduum*, *triduum*; to-—, *hodierno die*, *hodie*; every other —, *tertio quoque die*; from — to —, *in dies*; — after —, *diem ex die*, *diem de die*; every —, *in dies singulos*; to pay to the —, *in diem solvĕre*; the — before, after, *pridie*, *postridie (ejus diei)*; in our —, *nostrâ aetate*, *nostro tempore*, *nostris temporibus*; to pass one's —s, *vitam degĕre*; the —time, *tempus diurnum*. **day-break,** n. *diluculum*. **day-labourer,** n. *operarius* (in pl. *operae*). **daily, I.** adj. *cot(t)idianus* (quot.), *diurnus*; — bread, *cibus diurnus*. **II.** adv. *cot(t)idie*, *omnibus diebus*, *in dies singulos*.

dazzle, v.tr. *caecare*; fig. *obstupefacĕre*; to be —d, *obstupefieri*, *stupēre*.

deacon, n. **diaconus*.

dead, adj. *mortuus*, *exanimis*, *exanimus*; fig. = dull, *languidus*. **deaden,** v.tr. *hebetare*, *obtundĕre*, *enervare*, *debilitare*, *frangĕre*. **deadly, I.** adj. 1, lit. *mortifer*, *exitialis*; 2, fig. of sin, etc., *capitalis*, *gravis*. **II.** adv. *usque ad mortem*, or by adj. **deadness,** n. *rigor*, *stupor*, *torpor*. **death,** n., *mors*, *letum*, *obitus*, *-ūs*, *finis*, m. and f., or *exitus*, *-ūs*, *vitae*, *nex* (= violent —); to suffer —, *mortem subire*; be starved to —, *per inediam mori*. **death-bed,** n. use adj. *moriens* or *moribundus*.

deaf, adj *surdus, auribus captus* **deafen**, v tr *exsurdare, obtundĕre*

deal, **I.** v tr *dividĕre, distribuĕre, dispertire* **II.** v intr — with, see TREAT **dealer**, n *mercator, negotiator* (wholesale), *institor, tabernarius, caupo, propola* (retail) **dealing**, n *commercium, negotium, usus, -ūs*, have —s with, *commercium cum alqo habēre*, harsh —, *severitas*, upright —, *fides*, double —, *fraus*

dear, adj 1, *carus, magni pretii, pretiosus*, how —? *quanti?* so —, *tanti*, 2, = beloved, *carus* Adv *care, magno pretio, maxime* or adj **dearness**, n *caritas, magnum pretium* **dearth**, n *inopia, caritas, fames*, is, f

debar, v tr *alqm alqâ re excludĕre, alqd alci praecludĕre, alqm (ab) alqâ re prohibēre*, or with *quominus* and subj

debase, v tr *corrumpĕre, vitiare* **debasement**, n *ignominia*

debate, **I.** n *altercatio, disceptatio, contentio* **II.** v intr *altercari, disceptare, disputare*

debauch, **I.** v tr *corrumpĕre, depravare, vitiare, perdĕre* **II.** n *comissatio* **debauchery**, n *stuprum, mores dissoluti, pravi, perditi*

debenture, n *syngrapha*

debility, n *infirmitas, imbecillitas, infirma valetudo*

debt, n *debitum, pecunia debita, nomen, aes alienum*, to get into —, *aes alienum contrahĕre*, to be in —, *in aere alieno esse, obaeratum esse* **debtor**, n *debitor, qui debet, obaeratus* **debit**, v tr *alqd alci expensum ferre*

decade, n *decem anni*

decamp, v intr *discedĕre*

decant, v tr *diffundĕre* **decanter**, n *lagena*

decapitate, v tr *caput alci praecidĕre*

decay, **I.** n *deminutio, defectio virium, tabes, is*, f **II.** v intr *(de)minui, deficĕre, decrescĕre, senescĕre, tabescĕre*, a decayed tooth, *dens exesus* (Cels)

decease, n *obitus, ūs*, see DEATH

deceit, n *fallacia, fraus, dolus* **deceive**, v tr *decipĕre, frustrari, fallĕre, circumvenire* **deceiver**, n *fraudator* **deceitful**, adj *fallax, dolosus, vafer, fraudulentus* Adv *fraudulenter, fallaciter, dolose, per dolum*

december, n *(mensis) December*

decent, adj *quod decet, decōrus* Adv *decōre* **decency**, n *modestia, decorum*

deception, n 1, *fraus, dolus*, 2, see DELUSION

decide, v tr 1, = settle a thing, *alqd* or *de alqâ re statuĕre, constituere, decernĕre, alqd dijudicare* 2, = — to do, *constituĕre, statuĕre* with infin or *ut* **decided**, adj 1, = fixed, *certus, exploratus*, I am —, *certum est mihi* with infin, 2, = resolute, *stabilis, constans, firmus* Adv *certo, certe, constanter*, in answers, *certe, vero, sane*, or by repetition of a word (e g *visne? volo*) **decision**, n 1, *dijudicatio, judicium, sententia*, 2, of character, *constantia, stabilitas* **decisive**, adj *ultimus*, or *quod ad discrimen alqd adducit*, or *maximi momenti*

deciduous, adj *deciduus*

decimate, v tr 1, lit *decimare cohortes* (Suet), *sorte decimum quemque (cohortis) ad supplicium legĕre*, 2, fig see DESTROY

decipher, v tr *explanare, interpretari, explicare*

deck, **I.** n *constratum navis* (Petr) **II.** v tr 1, = COVER, 2, = ADORN

declaim, v tr *pronuntiare, declamare, declamitare* **declamation**, n 1, as an art, *pronuntiatio, declamatio*, 2, = speech declaimed, *declamatio* **declamatory**, adj *declamatorius, tumidus* **declaimer**, n *declamator*

declare, v tr *dicĕre, profiteri, praedicĕre, declarare, asseverare, confirmare*, to — for anyone, *partes alcjs sequi* **declaration**, n *praedicatio, sententia, dictum*, — of war, *belli denuntiatio*

decline, **I.** v tr 1, = refuse, *alqd recusare, negare*, 2, gram t t *declinare* **II.** v intr *deficĕre, (de)minui, (se) remittĕre, decrescĕre*, the day —s, *vesperascit* **III.** n 1, *(de)minutio, remissio*, in the — of life, *provectiore aetate* 2, = consumption, *phthisis* (Plin) **declension**, n *declinatio* (Quint)

declivity, n *declivitas, acclivitas*

decoction, n *decoctum* (Plin)

decompose, **I.** v tr 1, lit *(dis)solvĕre, resolvĕre*, 2, fig *(con)turbare, excitare, erigĕre* **II.** v intr 1, *dissolvi, tabescĕre*, 2, *(con)turbari* etc **decomposition**, n *(dis)solutio, tabes*, is, f

decorate, v tr *alqm alqâ re (ex)ornare, distinguĕre, decorare* **decoration**, n *ornatus, ūs ornamentum* **decorous**, adj *decōrus* Adv *decōre* **decorum**, n *decōrum*

decoy, **I.** v tr *allicĕre, pellicĕre* **II.** n *illex* (= a lure)

decrease, **I.** v tr *(de)minuĕre, imminuĕre, (sub)levare, mitigare* **II.** v intr *remittĕre* (rare), *remitti, (de)minui*, etc **III.** n *deminutio*

decree, **I.** v tr 1 of formal decrees, *alqd alci de alqâ re*, with gerundive or *ut, decernĕre, alqd* or *ut, edicĕre, alqd de alqâ re sciscere, alqd, de alqâ re, ut, (lege) sancire*, impers *alci placet ut* or *accus* and infin, 2, see DETERMINE **II.** n *decretum, senatusconsultum, plebiscitum*

decrepit, adj *senectute confectus* **decrepitude**, n *senectutis imbecillitas*

decry, v tr *vituperare*

dedicate, v tr *alqd alci (de)dicare* (lit and fig), *consecrare* (only in religious sense)

deduce, v tr 1, = derive, *alqd ab* or *ex alqâ re, ab alqo (de)ducĕre*, 2, logical t t *alqd ex alqâ re concludĕre* **deduct**, v tr *alqd alci rei* or *de alqâ re detrahĕre, alqd de alqâ re deducĕre* **deduction**, n 1, = abatement, *deductio, deminutio*, 2, logical t t *conclusio*

deed, n 1, *facinus, -ŏris*, n, —s, *acta, facta*, 2, = document, *tabula, syngrapha*

deep, **I.** adj 1, lit *altus, profundus*, ten feet —, *decem pedes altus*, 2, fig *summus* (e g *summa eruditio*, — learning) Adv 1, *alte, profunde*, 2, *penitus, prorsus, graviter* (e g *gravi commotus* = — moved) **II.** n *altum* **deepen**, **I.** v tr 1, lit *alqd altius fodĕre*, 2, = increase, *augēre* **II.** v intr = grow darker, *obscurari*, see also THICKEN **depth**, n 1, lit *altitudo*, in —, *in altitudinem* (e g *triginta pedum* = thirty feet in —), 2, fig of character, *summo ingenio*, etc, *praeditus*, in the — of night, *mediâ nocte*

deer, n *cervus, dama*

deface, v tr *deformare, in pĕjus fingĕre, foedare*

defame, v tr *calumniari*

default, n 1, = error, *culpa, peccatum, error*, 2, = lack, *defectio, defectus, -ūs*, 3, legal t t = judgment, go by —, *vadimonium deserĕre* **defaulter**, n *qui vadimonium deserit*

defeat, I. n. *clades, -is,* f., *strages, -is,* f. **II.** v.tr., see CONQUER, BAFFLE.

defect, n. 1, *quod deest, desideratum*; the —s of character, *vitia, -orum*; 2, *labes, -is,* f., *vitium, mendum.* **defective,** adj. *imperfectus, mancus, vitiosus*; to be —, *deficere, deesse.* Adv. *imperfecte, vitiose.* **defection,** n. (*ab algo*) *defectio.* **deficiency,** n. *defectio* (e.g. *virium, animi*), *inopia.*

defend, v.tr. 1, *algm* or *alqd ab algo* or *alqâ re defendĕre, algm* or *alqd tueri, tutari, alqd ab algo prohibēre, pro algo* or *alqâ re propugnare*; 2, legal t.t. *caus(s)am alcjs dicĕre.* **defendant,** n. *reus.* **defence,** n. 1, in gen. *tutela, praesidium, defensio, patrocinium*; 2, legal t.t. *patrocinium.* **defenceless,** adj. *inermis, sine praesidio.* **defensible,** adj. *quod defendi potest.* **defensive,** adj. *ad algm defendendum*; — war, *bellum ad hostes repellendos susceptum*; — weapons, *arma, -orum.*

defer, v.tr. 1, = to postpone, *differre, proferre, prorogare* (= to lengthen, e.g. the time for payment, *diem ad solvendum*), *procrastinare, producĕre, prolatare, re(j)icĕre*; 2, = to give way to, *alci cedĕre, obsequi, morem gerĕre.* **deference,** n. *observantia, obsequium.* **deferential,** adj. *submissus*; see HUMBLE. Adv. *submisse.*

deficient, adj., see DEFECTIVE.

defile, I. n. *angustiae, fauces, -ium,* f. **II.** v.tr. *maculare, inquinare, (con)spurcare, foedare, violare, polluĕre.* **defilement,** n. *macula, labes, -is,* f.

define, v.tr. (*de*)*finire, describĕre, circumscribĕre.* **definition,** n. (*de*)*finitio.* **definite,** adj. *certus, constitutus, status, definitus.* Adv. *certe, certo, definite.*

deflect, v.intr. *declinare, errare.*

deform, v.tr. *deformare, depravare, in pejus mutare* or *vertĕre.* **deformed,** adj. *distortus, deformatus, deformis.* **deformity,** n. *deformitas, turpitudo.*

defraud, v.tr. *algm alqâ re fraudare, fraudem* or *fallaciam alci facĕre, fraude* or *dolo capĕre, fallĕre, circumscribĕre, circumvenire.* **defrauder,** n. *fraudator, circumscriptor.*

defray, v.tr. *sumptus suppeditare, solvĕre.*

defunct, adj. *mortuus, fato functus.*

defy, v.tr. *algm provocare* (= to challenge), *spernĕre alqd* (e.g. *imperia*), *contemnĕre alqd, alci rei se offerre* or *resistĕre.* **defiance,** n. *provocatio* (Plin.), *contumacia* (= obstinacy).

degenerate, v.intr. *degenerare a parentibus, mores mutare, depravari.* **degenerate,** adj. *degener, parentibus indignus.*

degrade, v.tr. = to lower in rank or position, *in ordinem cogĕre* (of soldiers), in gen. *algm gradu de(j)icĕre.* **degrading,** adj. *indecōrus.* **degradation,** n. *ignominia, dedecus, -ŏris,* n.

degree, n. 1, *gradus, -ūs*; having —s, *gradatus* (= graduated); to such a —, *eo* with noun in gen. *ut,* or *adeo ut*; by —s, *paul(l)atim, sensim*; 2, = — in a university, *gradus.*

deify, v.tr. *algm in caelum tollĕre, algm inter deos* or *in deorum numerum referre.* **deified,** adj. *divus.* **deification,** n. *consecratio* (Tac.).

deign, v.intr. *dignari, velle* with infin.

deism, n. *Deum esse putare.* **deist,** n. *qui Deum esse putat.* **Deity,** n. *Deus, numen.*

dejected, adj. *maestus, tristis, perculsus*; to be —, *in macrore esse* or *jacēre.* Adv. *maeste.* **dejection,** n. *aegritudo, maestitia, tristitia, maeror.*

delay, I. v.tr. 1, = retard, (*re*)*morari, detinēre algm, moram facĕre alci, moram alci afferre, algm* (*re*)*tardare, retinēre, reprimĕre, cohibēre*; 2, = prolong, *ducĕre,* (*ex*)*trahĕre*; 3, = postpone, *differre.* **II.** v.intr. (*com*)*morari, se tenēre, continēre, se cunctari, cessare*; to — over a thing, *in alqâ re cessare.* **III.** n. *mora, dilatio, cessatio* (= idle —).

delectation, n. *delectatio, oblectatio.*

delegate, I. n. *legatus, nuntius.* **II.** v.tr. 1, of formal delegation, *legare* (of state embassy), *allegare* (private); 2, = commit to anyone, *alqd alci committĕre, mandare, delegare.*

deleterious, adj. *mortifer, exitialis, perniciosus.* Adv. *perniciose.*

deliberate, I. v.intr. *deliberare, consulĕre, consultare, consilium inire* or c. *capĕre de alqâ re*; to — over anything, *alqd considerare, secum volvĕre.* **II.** adj. 1, = slow, *lentus*; 2, = careful, *prudens.* Adv. *lente*; *prudenter, considerate, consulto.* **deliberative,** adj. — assembly, *consilium, senatus, -ūs.* **deliberation,** n. 1, *deliberatio, consultatio, consilium*; 2, see SLOWNESS.

delicate, adj. 1, = tender, *tener, mollis*; 2, = weak, *imbecillus, infirmus*; 3, = fastidious, *fastidiosus, delicatus*; 4, = requiring care, *difficilis, anceps, accuratus*; 5, = fine, *exquisitus.* Adv. *molliter, infirme, fastidiose, delicate, accurate, exquisite.* **delicacy,** n. 1, *mollitia,* — of taste, style, etc., *humanitas, subtilitas*; 2, *imbecillitas, infirmitas*; 3, *fastidium*; 4, = tact, *prudentia, cura*; 5, *venustas, elegantia*; 6, = a dainty, *cibus delicatus.*

delicious, adj. *suavis, dulcis, amoenus.* Adv. *suaviter, amoene.*

delight, I. n. *voluptas, dulcedo.* **II.** v.tr. *delectare, oblectare.* **III.** v. intr. *alqâ re delectari* or *oblectari.* **delightful,** adj. *jucundus, suavis, acceptus, gratus.* Adv. *jucunde, suaviter, grate.* **delightfulness,** n. *suavitas, amoenitas.*

delineate, v.tr. 1, lit. *designare, depingĕre*; 2, fig. *describĕre, depingĕre, adumbrare.* See DESCRIBE. **delineation,** n. 1, *adumbratio, descriptio*; 2, *descriptio.*

delinquent, n. *maleficus, capite damnatus.* **delinquency,** n., *delictum, scelus, -ĕris,* n., *facinus, -inŏris,* n.

delirium, n. *delirium, furor.* **delirious,** adj. *delirus*; to be —, *mente alienari.*

deliver, v.tr. 1, see FREE; 2, = to utter, *pronuntiare*; see SPEAK; 3, in childbirth, to be delivered, *partum edĕre*; 4, — up, *prodĕre, dedĕre, tradĕre.* **deliverer,** n. *liberator, vindex.* **delivery,** n. 1, *liberatio*; 2, *actio, elocutio, dictio*; 3, *partus, -ūs*; 4, *traditio, deditio.*

dell, n. (*con*)*vallis.*

delude, v.tr. *deludĕre.* See DECEIVE. **delusion,** n. 1, = cheat, *fraus, dolus, fallacia*; 2, = error, *error.* **delusive,** adj. *falsus, fallax, vanus.* Adv. *fallaciter, vane.*

deluge, I. n. 1, lit. *eluvio*; 2, fig. *magna vis alcjs rei.* **II.** v.tr. 1, lit. (*terram,* etc.) *inundare*; 2, fig. *magnam copiam alcjs rei dare*; be deluged with, *alqâ re cumulari.*

delve, v.tr. *fodĕre.*

demagogue, n. *novarum rerum auctor*; to be a —, *rebus novis studēre.*

demand, I. v.tr. (*de*)*poscĕre, exposcĕre,* (*ex*)*postulare,* (*ef*)*flagitare, implorare, requirĕre, flagitare,* (*ex*)*petĕre, exigĕre, requirĕre.* **II.** n. *postulatio, postulatum, flagitatio, preces, -um,* f.

demarcation, n. *terminus, limes, -ĭtis,* m., *confinium.*

demean, v tr 1, = to conduct, *se gerĕre in re;* 2, = to lower oneself, *descendĕre ad algd* **demeanour,** n *mores, -um,* m

demerit, n *culpa* See BLAME, FAULT

demi, n *semi,* in comp (e g *semideus*) **demigod,** n *heros*

demise, I. n *obitus, ūs,* see DEAD **II.** v tr = leaving by will, *legare*

democracy, n *ratio popularis, civitas in quâ omnia per populum administrantur* **democratical,** adj. *popularis* **democrat,** n *popularium fautor*

demolish, v tr *algd demoliri, de(j)icĕre (pro)sternere, evertĕre* **demolition,** n *demolitio, eversio*

demon, n. * *daemon* (Eccl)

demonstrate, v tr *demonstrare, docēre, (con)firmare, probare* **demonstration,** n 1, = pointing out, *demonstratio,* 2, = proof, *argumentum, documentum,* 3, = political meeting, *contio* **demonstrable,** adj *quod doceri potest* **demonstrative,** adj 1, of argument, n *argumentum,* 2, = eager, *fervidus, vehemens* Adv. *vehementer*

demoralize, v tr *mores corrumpĕre, moribus nocēre* **demoralization,** n *mores corrupti.*

demur, v intr 1, legal t t = to object to, *alci rei exceptionem facĕre, contra dicĕre* 2, = to delay, *remorari, moram facĕre* **demurrer,** n 1, legal t t *exceptio,* 2, *mora, dilatio*

demure, adj *verecundus*

den, n *caverna, specus, ūs, cavea, claustrum, latibulum*

denizen, n *incola,* m & f

denominate, I. v tr & **II.** n, see NAME **denominator,** n *index*

denote, v tr *(de)notare, designare, notam imponĕre alci rei, algd ostendere, significare* **denotation,** n *designatio, significatio*

denounce, v tr 1, *denuntiare;* 2, — before a court, *nomen alcjs deferre, alqm accusare* **denunciation,** n 1, *denuntiatio,* 2, *delatio, accusatio* **denouncer,** n *accusator, index, delator*

dense, adj *densus, confertus, creber, crassus, solidus* Adv *dense, solide, confertim* (of soldiers) **density,** n *densitas, soliditas,* see also STUPIDITY

dent, I. n *nota, injuria* **II.** v tr *alci rei injuriam afferre*

dentist, n *medicus (dentium)*

deny, v tr 1, = to refuse to admit, *algd (di)negare, recusare,* or with accus and infin or *quin, quominus* it cannot be denied, *negari non potest quin,* 2, = to — oneself *sibi temperare, se coercēre* or *continēre,* to — anything, *(ab) algâ re temperare* **denial,** n *negatio, recusatio*

depart, v intr 1, *abire ab* or *ex, abscedĕre ab* or *ex, decedĕre (de* or *ex) loco, discedĕre (ab) loco* or *ex loco, excedĕre loco* or *ex loco, egredi (ab) loco, digredi (ab, ex) loco,* fig = to die, *decedĕre ex* or *a vitâ* **departure,** n *abitus, decessus, discessus* (all ūs)

department, n 1, *munus, ĕris,* n, *munia, -orum, provincia,* 2, = district, *pars, ager, regio*

depend, v intr 1, = to be dependent on, *pendere ex algo* or *algâ re, in alcjs dicione esse, esse in alcjs manu, in alcjs potestate versari in algo esse* or *positum* or *situm esse* 2, = to rely on, *alci (con)fidĕre,* — upon it, *mihi crede* **dependent,** adj. & n use verb (e g *qui ex te pendet,* etc) **dependence,** n 1, = subjection, *dicio,* 2, = trust, *fiducia*

depict, v tr lit & fig *(de)pingĕre, (ef)fingĕre, exprimĕre, describĕre*

deplore, v tr *deplorare, deflēre, comploare* **deplorable,** adj see MISERABLE

deponent, n 1, legal t.t *testis, -is,* m and f, 2, gram t t *(verbum) deponens*

depopulate, v tr *terram (de)vastare, (de)populari, vacuefacĕre* **depopulation,** n *populatio, vastatio*

deport, v tr *se gerĕre* **deportment,** n 1, = carriage, *gestus, ūs,* 2, = behaviour, *mores, -um,* m

depose, v tr 1, = to remove from office, *loco suo alqm movēre,* see DETHRONE, 2, = — as a witness, *testari, testificari* **deposition,** n 1, use verb, 2, *testimonium.*

deposit, I. v tr 1, = to lay down, *(de)ponĕre,* 2, of money, *pecuniam apud alqm (de)ponĕre, pecuniam collocare* **II.** n 1, *quod depositum est, pecuniae apud alqm depositae,* 2, = pledge, *pignus, -ĕris,* n See PLEDGE **depository,** n *apotheca, receptaculum*

deprave, v tr *depravare, corrumpĕre, vitiare* **depravation,** n *depravatio, corruptio* **depravity,** n *pravitas, turpitudo, mores perditi, mores turpes*

deprecate, v tr *deprecari algd ab algo* or *quin* with subj **deprecation,** n *deprecatio*

depreciate, v tr *minuĕre, elevare* (=lessen), *obtrectare alci* or *alci rei* **depreciation,** n *obtrectatio*

depredation, n *latrocinium* **depredator,** n *praedator, latro*

depress, v tr *deprimĕre, opprimĕre, alcjs animum affligĕre* **depression,** n *tristitia, maeror*

deprive, v tr *alqm algâ re privare, (de)spoliare, exspoliare, orbare, algd alci adimĕre, detrahĕre, eripĕre* **deprived,** adj *orbus (orbatus) algâ re,* — of the use of his limbs, *membris captus* **deprivation,** n *privatio, spoliatio*

depth, n see DEEP.

depute, v tr *legare* (in state affairs), *allegare* (in private) **deputy,** n see AGENT **deputation,** n *legati*

derange, v tr *(de)turbare, perturbare, conturbare* **deranged,** adj *demens insanus* **derangement,** n 1, = confusion, *perturbatio,* 2, = madness, *dementia, insania*

deride, v tr *alqm* or *algd deridēre, irridēre* **derider,** n *irrisor* **derision,** n *irrisio* **derisive,** adj by verb

derive, v tr *derivare* (= to draw off or turn aside a river), *(de)ducĕre,* to — a word, *verbum ex* or *ab algâ re (de)ducĕre*

derogate from, v tr *derogare* (e g *algd de magnificentiâ, algd sibi, fidem alci*), *alci* or *alci rei obtrectare* **derogatory,** adj to be — to, *alci dedecori esse,* to speak in a — manner of anyone, *alci obtrectare*

descend v intr 1 = to come down, *descendĕre ex* or *de,* 2, fig *tradi,* to be —ed from, *ortum* or *oriundum esse ab algo* 3, see ATTACK **descendant,** n *prognatus,* pl *progenies, posteri* **descent,** n 1, = going down, use the verb, 2, of a hill, *declivitas, locus declivis,* 3, = origin, *origo, genus -ĕris,* n *stirps, progenies,* 4, — upon = attack, *irruptio, incursio, incursus, ūs*

describe, v tr 1, *describĕre, verbis consequi, scripturâ persequi, explicare algd* or *de algâ re, exponĕre algd* or *de algâ re, algd enarrare* *enumerare, comprehendĕre, complecti, lit(t)eris mandare, memoriae prodĕre, tradĕre*; 2, = to draw, *describĕre*. **description**, n. *descriptio, (e)narratio, expositio*.

desecrate, v.tr. *profanare, profanum facĕre, exaugurare* (opp. *inaugurare*), *polluĕre, maculare, violare*. **desecration**, n. *polluta sacra, -orum*.

desert, n. *dignitas, virtus, -ūtis*, f., *meritum*.

desert, I. n. = wilderness, *solitudo, vastitas, regio deserta, loca, -orum, deserta*; to turn into a —, *regionem (de)vastare*. **II.** v.tr. 1, in gen. *deserĕre, (de)relinquĕre, destituĕre, alci deesse, alqm prodĕre*; 2, = to become a deserter, *signa deserĕre* or *relinquĕre, ad hostem transfugĕre* or *perfugĕre*. **desertion**, n. 1, *(de)relictio*; 2, *transitio ad hostem*. **deserter**, n. *transfuga, desertor*.

deserve, v.tr. *(com)merēre, (com)merēri, (pro)merēre, (pro)merēri, dignum esse re*; he — praise from me, *dignus est quem laudem* or *qui a me laudetur*; — well of a person or city, *bene de alqo* or *erga alqm merēri*. **deserving**, adj. *alqâ re dignus*. Adv. *merito, jure*.

desideratum, n. *quod deest, res necessaria*.

design, n. and v.tr. 1, see Sketch; 2, see Purpose. **designing**, adj. *peritus, prudens, sciens* or, in bad sense, *fraudulentus*. Adv. *consulto*.

designate, v.tr. *designare, notare, eligĕre, nominare*. **designation**, n. 1, *designatio, nominatio, notatio*; 2, = purpose, *finis, ratio*.

desire, I. n. *alcjs rei appetitio, appetitus, -ūs, appetentia, cupiditas, cupido, desiderium*. **II.** v.tr. *alqd appetĕre, expetĕre, cupĕre, concupiscĕre, desiderare, desiderio alcjs teneri, avēre* (with infin., e.g. *aveo scire, audire*, etc.); what do you —? *quid vis? quid fieri jubes?* **desirable**, adj. *optabilis, expetendus*. **desirous**, adj. *alcjs rei appetens, cupidus, avidus*. Adv. *appetenter, cupide, avide*.

desist, v.intr. *desistĕre re* (*ab re* and *de re*, or with infin.), *absistĕre (a)re*.

desk, n. *mensa* (= table), *scrinium* (= escritoire).

desolate, I. adj. 1, = waste, *vastus, desertus*; 2, = bereaved, *orbus*; 3, = despairing, *spe destitutus, maestus*. **II.** v.tr. *vastare, (de)populari*.

despair, I. n. *desperatio*. **II.** v.intr. *desperare* (— of, *de re* or *alqd* or *alci rei*, or with accus. and infin.); — of the cure of a sick person, *aegrotum* or *aegroti salutem desperare*. **despairing**, adj. see Desperate.

despatch, dispatch, I. v.tr. 1, = to do, *conficĕre, perficĕre, absolvĕre, finire*; with haste, *maturare, accelerare*; 2, = send off, *(di)mittĕre, ablegare* (on private), *legare* (on public business); 3, = kill, *trucidare, caedĕre*. **II.** n. 1, *confectio, perfectio, festinatio, properatio*; 2, *missio*; 3, *trucidatio, caedes, -is*, f. **despatches**, n.pl. *lit(t)erae publice missae*.

desperate, adj. 1, = hopeless, *exspes, sine spe, desperatus* (= despaired of); a — state of affairs, *res desperatae* or *extremae*; 2, = dangerous, *periculosus*; 3, = villainous, *sceleratus, scelestus*; 4, = brave, *fortissimus*. Adv. *desperanter, periculose, sceleste, scelerate*, or by superl. (e.g. — wicked, *sceleratissimus*), *fortissime, acerrime*. **desperation**, n. *desperatio*.

despise, v.tr. *contemnĕre, contemptui habēre, despicĕre, aspernari, spernĕre*. **despicable**, adj. *contemnendus, turpis*. Adv. *turpiter, foede*.

despite, I. n. *odium, malitia*. **II.** prep. *contra, adversus* (e.g. *contra leges*, = in — of the laws); *in*, with abl., (*contemptis precibus meis Romam rediit*, = (in) despite (of) my prayers he returned to Rome).

despond, v.intr. *desperare de rebus suis, spe dejectum esse*. **despondency**, n. see Despair.

despot, n. *tyrannus, dominus*. **despotism**, n. *dominatus, -ūs, tyrannis, -ĭdis*, f., *dominatio*. **despotical**, adj. *imperiosus, superbus*. Adv. *superbe, crudeliter*.

dessert, n. *mensa secunda*.

destine, v.tr. *alqd* or *alqm ad alqd* or *alci rei destinare, alqd constituĕre* or *statuĕre*. **destined**, adj. *destinatus, status, constitutus*. **destination**, n. 1, = end, *finis*, m. and f.; 2, = end of journey, *locum quem petimus*, or the name of the town, etc. **destiny**, n. *fatum, sors*.

destitute, adj. *inops, egens*; of anything, *alcjs rei inops, alqâ re destitutus, privatus*, or use *sine* with abl. **destitution**, n. *inopia*.

destroy, v.tr. *perdĕre, destruĕre, diruĕre, demoliri, evertĕre, rescindĕre* (e.g. *pontem*), *intercidĕre* (*pontem*), *delēre, ex(s)tinguĕre* (*societatem vitae, potentiam*), *dissolvĕre, interrumpĕre*; *conficĕre, subvertĕre* (e.g. *imperium, leges et libertatem*); to — oneself, *mortem sibi consciscĕre*. **destroyer**, n. *eversor rei, qui alqd perdit*, etc. **destructible**, adj. *fragilis, quod perdi potest*. **destructibility**, n. *fragilitas*. **destruction**, n. *dissolutio, eversio, excidium, ex(s)tinctio*. **destructive**, adj. *perniciosus, exitiosus, funestus*. Adv. *perniciose*.

desuetude, n. *oblivio*.

desultory, adj. *inconstans, lĕvis, mobilis, instabilis*. Adv. *parum diligenter*.

detach, v.tr. *alqd ab alqâ re separare, sejungĕre, disjungĕre*. **detachment**, n. = a body of troops, *delecta manus, -ūs, delecti* (*milites*).

details, n. *singula, -orum, singulae res*; to go into —, *de singulis agĕre*. **detail**, v.tr. *res explicare, singula consectari et colligĕre*.

detain, v.tr. *(de)tinēre*. **detention**, n. *impedimentum, mora*; — in custody, *custodia, comprehensio* (= arrest).

detect, v.tr. *alqm in alqâ re deprehendĕre, alqd invenire, reperire, patefacĕre*. **detection**, n. *deprehensio*, but better by verb (e.g. the — is due to him, *ab eo res patefacta est*).

deter, v.tr. *deterrēre alqm ab* or *de re* (or with *ne, quin, quominus*).

deteriorate, I. v.tr. *deterius facĕre, in deterius mutare, in pejus mutare* or *vertĕre, corrumpĕre*. **II.** v.intr. *deteriorem* (*deterius*) *fieri, in pejorem partem verti et mutari, in pejus mutari*. **deterioration**, n. *deterior condicio* or *status, -ūs*.

determine, v.tr. 1, = settle, *alqd (di)judicare, (de)finire, alqd* or *de alqâ re decernĕre, alqd statuĕre, constituĕre*; 2, = decide to, *statuĕre, constituĕre, decernĕre* with infin.; I am —ed, *certum est mihi alqd facĕre*, or by fut. part. (e.g. — to die, *moriturus*). **determination**, n. 1, *(de)finitio, (di)judicatio, arbitrium, judicium, sententia*; 2, *consilium, ratio*; 3, = decision of character, *constantia, gravitas*. **determined**, adj. *constans, gravis*.

detest, v.tr. *alqm* or *alqd detestari, aversari*. **detestable**, adj. *detestandus, detestabilis*. Adv. *foede, nefarie*. **detestation**, n. *odium*.

dethrone, v.tr. *alci regi imperium abrogare, regnum alci eripĕre* or *auferre*.

detonate, v.intr. *crepitare*, † *fragorem dare*.

detract, v.tr. *detrahĕre de alqo* or *de alqâ re, alqd minuĕre, alci obtrectare*. **detraction**, n. *obtrectatio*.

detriment, n *damnum, detrimentum, jactura* **detrimental,** adj *perniciosus, iniquus, adversus,* †*contrarius.* Adv *perniciose*

deuce, n as exclamation, *malum, abi in malam rem* (or *crucem*)

devastate, v tr *(per)vastare, (de)populari, perpopulari.* **devastation,** n *vastatio, (de)populatio*

develop, I. v tr 1, = explain, *alqd explicare, evolvere, explanare;* 2, = educate, *educare, excolĕre,* 3, = improve, *augēre* (e g the resources of a country), *excolĕre* II. v intr *crescĕre adolescĕre, augeri.* **development,** n 1, *explicatio, explanatio,* 2, = growth, etc, *auctus, -ūs, progressus, -ūs*

deviate, v intr *declinare, deflectĕre, digredi, discedĕre, ab alqâ re (ab)errare* **deviation,** n *declinatio* (lit. or fig), *digressio* (fig) **devious,** adj *devius, errabundus*

device, n 1, *ratio, consilium,* 2, = motto, *insigne, dictum, sententia,* as an inscription, *inscriptio*

devil, n **diabŏlus* (Eccl), go to the — ! *abi in malam partem!* **devilish,** adj **diabolicus* (Eccl), *nefandus.* Adv **diabolice, foede.*

devise, v tr 1, *excogitare, invenire, fingĕre, machinari* (in a bad sense), 2, see BEQUEATH

devoid, adj *(ab) alqâ re vacuus, liber,* — of care, *securus*

devolve, I. v tr *alqd alci, (de)mandare, deferre* II v intr *alci (ob)venire, transmitti*

devote, v tr 1, lit *alqm alci (de)vovēre, (con)secrare, (de)dicare,* 2, fig *alqd alci (rei) addicĕre, ad alqd destinare,* to — oneself to, *se alci (rei) dedere, se ad alqd conferre.* **devoted,** adj *alcjs rei studiosus* Adv *studiose,* or by superl (e g —attached, *amantissimus*) **devotion,** n 1, *devotio, dedicatio,* 2, *studium, obsequium, observantia, amor, benevolentia,* 3, = religious feeling, *pietas erga Deum* **devotions,** n *preces, -um,* f

devout, adj *pius erga Deum, venerabundus* Adv. *pie*

dew, n *ros,* the — falls, *rorat, cadit ros* **dewy,** adj *roscidus*

dewlap, n *palearia, -ium,* pl

dexterity, n *habilitas, facultas, ingenii dexteritas ad alqd, sol(l)ertia, peritia, scientia rei* **dexterous,** adj *habilis, dexter, peritus, sol(l)ers, sciens* Adv *dext(e)re, perite, sol(l)erter, scienter*

diadem, n *diadema, atis,* n , *insigne (regium)*

diagonal, adj *diagonalis*

diagram, n *descriptio, forma (geometrica)*

dial, n *solarium*

dialect, n *lingua* with special adj (e g *rustica, Anglicana*), *dialectos,* i (Suet), to speak in the Doric —, *Dorice loqui*

dialectics, n *dialectica, ae, dialectica, orum,* n *ars bene disserendi et vera ac falsa dijudicandi, disserendi ratio*

dialogue, n 1, = the philosophical, *dialogus sermo,* 2, = — in plays, *diverbium, sermones alterni,* 3, = conversation, *sermo*

diameter, n **diametros, linea media*

diamond, n *adamas*

diaphragm, n *diaphragma* (late), or *praecordia, -ium,* pl

diarrhoea, n *alvi profluvium, profusio, alvus cita, citatior, liquida, fluens, soluta* (διάρροια only as a Greek word, in Cicero)

diary, n *ephemeris, idis,* f (= a merchant's —), *adversaria, orum*

dice, die, I. n *talus, tessera,* to play at — *talis* or *tesseris ludere, alea* or *aleam ludere,* a — box, *fritillus, alveus, alveolus* II v intr *talos* or *tesseras jacĕre* or *mittĕre* **dicer,** n *aleo, aleator*

dictate, v tr 1, = to read to one who writes down, *dictare,* 2, see ORDER **dictation,** n 1, see ORDER, SWAY, 2, = an exercise, *quod dictatum est* **dictator,** n *dictator* **dictatorial,** adj *imperiosus* **dictatorship,** n, *dictatura.*

diction, n *dicendi* or *scribendi genus,* ...is, n , *sermo*

dictionary, n **thesaurus verborum*

die v intr *mori, vitâ decedĕre, diem supremum obire*

diet, I. n 1, *victus, -ūs, diaeta,* 2, = assembly, *conventus regum* or *principum* II. v tr *alqm victum alci imponĕre*

differ, v intr *discrepare cum alqo* or *alqâ re, dissidēre, dissentire ab* or *cum alqo, differre ab alqo* or *alqâ re* **different,** adj *discrepans, diversus, dissimilis, varius* Adv *aliter, alio modo* **difference,** n *varietas, diversitas* (in gen), *discrepantia, dissensio* (= — in opinion and feeling)

difficult, adj *difficilis, arduus, impeditus, magni negotii, laboriosus* **difficulty,** n *difficultas,* pecuniary difficulties, *pecuniae inopia,* with —, *vix*

diffidence, n *diffidentia* **diffident,** adj *timidus, diffidens* Adv *timide, modeste*

diffuse, I. v tr *diffundĕre, differre, (di)vulgare* II. adj *copiosus, verbosus,* to be —, *longum esse* Adv *longe, diffuse, latius et diffusius, copiose, verbose* **diffuseness,** n by adj (e g the — of a speech, *oratio longa*) **diffusion,** n *propagatio,* or by adj

dig, v tr *fodĕre,* to — up, *effodĕre, evellĕre* **digger,** n *fossor*

digest, I. v tr *concoquĕre, conficĕre* II. n. *digesta, orum* (Jct) **digestion,** n *concoctio* **digestible,** adj *facilis ad concoquendum*

dignity, n 1, in gen *honestas* (= moral dignity), *gravitas* (= earnestness of character), *auctoritas* (= influence), *amplitudo, majestas* (= rank), *dignitas* (= both of character and rank), to stand on one's —, *superbum se praebēre,* 2, = dignity of office, *dignitas,* official —, *magistratus, -ūs* **dignify,** v tr *dignitatem deferre alci, (ex)ornare alqm* **dignified,** adj *gravis,* in a — way, *summâ gravitate*

digress, v intr *ab alqâ re digredi, aberrare* **digressive,** adj *a proposito digredi* **digression,** n *digressio*

dike, n *moles, -is,* f , *agger, ĕris,* m.

dilapidation, n *injuria, detrimentum*

dilate, v tr 1, = to extend, *dilatare,* 2, fig to — upon, *de alqâ re latius dicĕre*

dilatory, adj *tardus lentus* **dilatoriness,** n *cunctatio, tarditas, mora*

dilemma, n. *complexio,* the horns of a —, *res in angustias deductae*

diligence, n *diligentia, industria, (g)navitas,* with —, *industrie, (g)naviter, sedulo, strenue, studiose, diligenter, cum diligentia* **diligent,** adj *diligens, industrius, studiosus rei*

dilute, v tr 1, lit *aquâ alqd (per)miscēre, diluere,* 2, fig *diluĕre* (= an evil)

dim, I. v tr *obscurare* II. adj *obscurus* **dimness,** n *obscuritas*

dimension, n *dimensio*

diminish, I. v tr *(im)minuĕre, sublevare*

II. v.intr. *se minuĕre, (im)minui.* **diminutive,** n. *nomen deminutivum* (Gram.), see SMALL.

dimple, n. *gelasinus* (Mart.).

din, I. n. *strepitus, -ūs, fremitus, -ūs;* to make a —, *strepĕre, strepitum edĕre.* **II.** v.tr. *alcjs aures obtundĕre.*

dine, v.tr. *prandēre, cenare;* to — with one, *apud alqm cenare* or *accubare.* **dining-room,** n. *conclave.* **dinner,** n. (at noon) *prandium,* (the chief meal, at three or four o'clock) *cena.*

dingy, adj. *fuscus, sordidus.*

dint, n. **1,** = a mark, *nota;* **2,** by — of, by abl. (e.g. *ira,* = by — of anger).

diocese, n. †*diocesis* (Eccl.).

dip, I. v.tr. *(in)tingĕre in re, mergĕre in alqd.* **II.** v.intr. **1,** *(im)mergi;* **2,** see INCLINE; **3,** to — into (of a book), *librum strictim attingĕre.* **III.** n. **1,** = slope, *declinatio;* — of a hill, *declivitas;* **2,** = into water, by verb (e.g. to take a —, *immergi*).

diploma, n. *diploma, -ătis,* n. **diplomacy,** n. **1,** *legatio* (e.g. to follow the profession of —, *legationes obire*); **2,** = craft, *astutia.* **diplomat,** n. *legatus.* **diplomatic,** adj. = clever, *astutus, callidus.*

dire, adj. *dirus, atrox.* **direfulness,** n. *atrocitas.*

direct, I. v.tr. **1,** = to manage, *alci rei praeesse, praesidēre, alqd administrare, procurare, dirigĕre, regĕre, gubernare;* **2,** see ORDER; **3,** = to show the way, *viam alci monstrare;* **4,** = to — one's course, etc., *iter dirigĕre, flectĕre, convertĕre;* **5,** = to — a letter, *alci epistolam inscribĕre.* **II.** adv. see DIRECTLY. **III.** adj. *(di)rectus.* **direction,** n. **1,** *cura, procuratio, administratio, moderatio, gubernatio;* **2,** see ORDER; **3,** use verb; **4,** = course, *iter, itineris,* n., *cursus, -ūs, via;* in different —s, *in diversas partes;* **5,** *inscriptio.* **directly,** adv. **1,** = in a straight course, *recta viâ;* **2,** = immediately, *statim, confestim.* **directness,** n. **1,** of a route, *via recta;* **2,** of speech, *sermo manifestus, clarus, planus.* **director,** n. *magister, praeses, -idis,* m. and f., *praefectus.*

dirge, n. *nenia.*

dirt, n. *caenum, sordes, -is,* f., *illuvies, squalor.* **dirty, I.** adj. **1,** lit. *caenosus, lutulentus, spurcus, sordidus immundus;* to be —, *sordēre, squalēre;* **2,** fig. *sordidus, turpis.* Adv. *spurce, sordide, immunde.* **II.** v.tr. *maculare, inquinare.*

disable, v.tr. *infirmare, enervare, debilitare, frangĕre.*

disabuse, v.tr. *alqm dedocēre alqd.*

disadvantage, n. *incommodum;* see DAMAGE. **disadvantageous,** adj. *incommodus.* Adv. *incommode.*

disaffect, v.tr. *(ab)alienare, sol(l)icitare.* **disaffected,** adj. *(ab)alienatus, animo alieno* or *averso ab alqo* or *alqâ re.* **disaffection,** n. *alienatio, animus alienus* or *aversus.*

disagree, v.intr. *ab alqo, inter se,* etc., *discrepare, dissentire, dissidēre;* of food, *non facile concoqui, stomacho gravem esse.* **disagreeable,** adj. *ingratus, gravis, molestus, injucundus.* Adv. *ingrate, graviter, moleste.* **disagreement,** n. *dissidium;* see QUARREL.

disallow, v.tr. *improbare, renuĕre, vetare.*

disappear, v.intr. *abire, auferri, tolli, obscurari, evanescĕre.* **disappearance,** n. by verb (e.g. after the disappearance of this hope, *hac spe sublatâ*).

disappoint, v.tr. *ad vanum* or *ad irritum redigĕre, frustrari, spem fallĕre;* to — a person in all his plans, *conturbare alci omnes rationes.* **disappointment,** n. *frustratio,* better by verb (e.g. I have met with a —, *spes me fefellit*).

disapprove, v.tr. *improbare, reprobare, condemnare.* **disapproval,** n. *improbatio.*

disarm, v.tr. *alqm armis exuĕre, arma alci adimĕre.*

disarrange, v.tr. *(con)turbare, perturbare, confundĕre.* **disarrangement,** n. *perturbatio.*

disaster, n. *malum, clades, -is,* f., *calamitas, incommodum, casus, -ūs (adversus);* to be in —, *afflictâ condicione esse.* **disastrous,** adj. *calamitosus, funestus, adversus, gravis, tristis;* — state of things, *res adversae, fortunae afflictae.* Adv. *calamitose, funeste, adverse, graviter.*

disavow, v.tr. *diffiteri, infitiari, infitias ire, abnuĕre, repudiare, (de)negare.* **disavowal,** n. *infitiatio, repudiatio* (rare).

disband, v.tr. *exauctorare, missos facĕre, dimittĕre, militiâ solvĕre, sacramento solvĕre.*

disbelieve, v.tr. *alci (rei) non credĕre.* **disbelief,** n. use verb.

disburden, v.tr. *alqm* or *alqd alqâ re exonerare, levare, liberare, solvĕre, expedire.*

disburse, v.tr. see PAY.

discern, v.tr. *discernĕre;* — black from white, *atra et alba* or *ab albis discernĕre.* **discernible,** adj. *conspicuus.* **discerning,** adj. *intellegens, perspicax, sagax, prudens.* **discernment,** n. **1,** = distinguishing, *distinctio;* **2,** = insight, *intellegentia, prudentia, perspicientia;* a man of great —, *vir prudentissimus.*

discharge, I. v.tr. **1,** as a soldier, *missum facĕre, alqm (di)mittĕre (ab exercitu), alqm militiâ solvĕre, exauctorare alqm, sacramento solvĕre alqm* (= to free a soldier from his oath), *alqm loco movēre;* — a gladiator, *rude (rudis* = the foil given as a token of honour) *donare;* to — a civil officer or servant, *mittĕre alqm, missum facĕre alqm, removēre alqm republicâ, alqm submovēre administratione reipublicae* or *a republicâ;* **2,** = unload, *navem,* etc., *exonerare;* **3,** = pay, *solvĕre;* **4,** = perform, *alqâ re fungi;* **5,** = let off, *telum (e)mittĕre.* **II.** v.intr. of rivers, *in mare effundi* or *(ef)fluĕre;* of wounds, *pus exit,* or *effunditur.* **III.** n. **1,** *(di)missio;* **2,** by verb; **3,** *solutio;* **4,** *functio;* **5,** *emissio;* **6,** of wounds, rivers, etc., use verb.

disciple, n. *discipulus, auditor.*

discipline, I. n. *disciplina, regimen;* want of —, *licentia.* **II.** v.tr. *instituĕre, coercēre, in officio continēre.*

disclaim, v.tr. *repudiare.*

disclose, v.tr. *detegĕre, retegĕre, revelare, nudare, aperire, patefacĕre.* **disclosure,** n. *indicium, delatio.*

discolour, v.tr. *colorem mutare, decolorare.*

discomfit, v.tr. **1,** *fundĕre, profligare, in fugam vertĕre;* **2,** fig. *repellĕre, spem alci eripĕre.* **discomfiture,** n. **1,** *clades, -is,* f., *strages, -is,* f., *fuga;* **2,** by verb.

discomfort, n. *incommodum.*

disconcerted, adj. *perturbatus.*

disconsolate, adj. *spe destitutus, tristis.* Adv. *maeste.*

discontent, n. *molestia, taedium, fastidium.* **discontented,** adj. *sorte suâ non contentus;* to be —, *moleste ferre alqd.*

discontinue, v.tr. *interrumpĕre, intermittĕre, intercipĕre, omittĕre, dirimĕre.*

discord, n. **1,** in music, *discrepans sonus, -ūs, dissonantia;* **2,** fig. *dissensio, dissidium, discordia.* **discordant,** adj. **1,** in music, *absonus;* **2,** *dissidens ab* or *cum alqo, discors cum alqo.* Adv. *sine concentu, non congruenter.*

discount, I. n *deductio*; without any —, *sine ullâ deductione*, to pay without —, *solidum solvĕre* II. v tr *deductione factâ pecuniam solvĕre*.

discountenance, v tr *improbare, condemnare*

discourage, v tr. *animum alcjs infringĕre, deprimere, frangere, affligĕre*, to be discouraged, *affligi, de alqâ re desperare*, to — anything, *alqd dissuadēre* or with *ne*, see DETER. **discouragement** n *quod alcjs animum affligit*

discourse, I. n = conversation, *sermo, collocutio, colloquium, disputatio* (= discussion), = a speech or sermon, *contio* II. v intr 1, *confabulari, colloqui cum alqo*, 2, *contionari* (= — to an assembly of the people), *orationem facĕre* or *habēre*

discourteous, adj *inurbanus, rusticus* Adv *inurbane, rustice* **discourtesy,** n *inurbanitas, rusticitas*

discover, v tr *invenire, aperire, detegĕre* (= find), *indicare* (= point out), *in lucem proferre, enuntiare* (= make known) **discoverer,** n. *inventor, auctor, index, inventrix* (fem) **discovery,** n *inventio, investigatio* (as act), = the thing discovered, *inventum, res inventa*

discredit, I. n = disgrace, *dedecus, ŏris*, n, *ignominia, probrum, infamia* II. v tr *alcjs fidem minuĕre, de famâ detrahĕre, alcjs auctoritatem levare, alci invidiam facĕre* **discreditable,** adj *inhonestus, turpis*

discreet, adj *prudens, cautus, gravis, constans* Adv *prudenter, caute, graviter, constanter* **discretion,** n *prudentia, continentia* (= self-restraint), *cautio* (= wariness)

discriminate, v tr *di(j)udicare, discernĕre, distinguere* (*alqd ab alqa re* or two nouns joined by *et*) **discrimination,** n *discrimen*, to make —, *discrimen facĕre*

discursive, adj *inconstans, varius, vagus* Adv *varie, inconstanter* **discursiveness,** n *error*

discuss, v tr *disceptare, disputare* (*alqd* or *de re*). **discussion,** n *disceptatio, disputatio*

disdain, I. v tr *dedignari, spernĕre, fastidire, aspernari* II. n *fastigium, arrogantia* **disdainful,** adj *arrogans*, see HAUGHTY

disease, n *morbus*, to suffer from —, *aegrotare* **diseased,** adj *aeger, aegrotus*

disembark, I. v tr *exponere*, — soldiers, *copias* (*e classe, navibus*) *exponere* II intr *exponi* (*e nave*) *egredi* **disembarkation,** n *egressus, ūs*

disembarrass, v tr *alqm alqâ re expedire, liberare, exonerare*

disembodied, adj *corporis sui expers*

disenchant, v tr 1, lit *alqm liberare* (allowing context to define from what), 2, fig *alcjs animum convertĕre*, or *mutare*

disengage, v tr *solvĕre, liberare* **disengaged,** adj *otiosus, vacuus*

disentangle, v tr *expedire, explicare*

disfavour, n *odium, ira*, to fall into —, *alci in odium venire*

disfigure, v tr *deformare*

disfranchise, v tr *civitatem alci adimĕre, alqm suffragio privare* **disfranchisement,** n by verb (e g he suffered —, *suffragio privatus est*).

disgorge, v tr 1, (*e*)*voměre*, *e*(*j*)*icĕre*, 2, = give up, *reddĕre*

disgrace, I. n 1, = shame, *turpitudo, infamia, dedecus, -ŏris*, n, *ignominia* mark of —, *nota*, 2, = shameful act, *dedecus, probrum, flagitium, opprobrium* II. v tr *dedecorare, polluĕre, alci dedecori esse, dedecus inurĕre* **disgraceful,** adj *turpis, foedus, inhonestus, flagitiosus probrosus, infamis* Adv *turpiter, foede, inhoneste, flagitiose*

disguise, I n 1, in dress, *vestis mutata*, = mask, *persona, larva*, 2, = appearance, *species, simulacrum, imago, simulatio, persona* II. v tr 1, *alqm alienâ veste occultare, vestum mutare*, 2, fig *alqd* (*dis*)*simulare, occultare*

disgust, n *fastidium, taedium, satietas* (from fulness), *nausea* (from a foul stomach) **disgusting,** adj *teter, molestus* (= troublesome), *gravis, horribilis* Adv *tetre, moleste, graviter*

dish, I. n *patina, patella, lanx, scutula* II. v tr — up, *apponĕre*

dishearten, v tr *animum alcjs frangĕre, spem alci eripĕre*

dishonest, adj *malus, improbus, inhonestus, male moratus, fallax, fraudulentus* Adv *male, improbe, fallaciter, fraudulenter* **dishonesty,** n *improbitas, mores pravi* or *corrupti, fraus*

dishonour, I. v tr *dedecorare, dedecore afficĕre, polluĕre* II n *ignominia*, see DISGRACE

disinclination, n *declinatio rei* (opp *appetitio*), *fuga, animus alienus* or *aversus* **disinclined,** adj *ab alqâ re alienus, alienatus, aversus*

disingenuous, adj see DISHONEST

disinherit, v tr *exheredare, exheredem facĕre, hereditate excludĕre*

disinter, v tr *effodĕre, eruĕre*

disinterested, adj *suae utilitatis immemor* Adv *gratuito, liberaliter* **disinterestedness,** n *liberalitas, abstinentia*

disjoin, v tr *disjungĕre, sejungĕre*

disjoint, v tr = cut up, *scindĕre*, (*dis*)*secare, concidere, membratim caedĕre* **disjointed,** adj *interruptus, haud continuus, haud bene compositus* Adv *incomposite*

disk, n *discus, orbis*, m

dislike, v tr *improbare, aversari, fastidire*

dislocate, v tr *luxare* (only in past part) **dislocation,** n by verb

dislodge, v tr (*de*)*pellĕre, expellĕre, propellĕre*

disloyal, adj *perfidus, infidelis* Adv *perfide* **disloyalty,** n *perfidia, infidelitas*, to show —, *perfide agere*

dismal, adj *maestus, luctuosus, tristis, miser* Adv. *maeste, luctuose, misere*

dismantle, v tr *alqd nudare, retegĕre*, — fortifications, *diruĕre*

dismast, v tr *malo* or *malis privare*

dismay, I. n *terror* II. v tr *terrēre alqm*, see FRIGHTEN

dismember, v tr see DISJOINT

dismiss, v tr (*di*)*mittere, missum facĕre alqm*, see DISCHARGE **dismissal,** n (*di*)*missio*, (to vote for —, e g *senatus Caelium ab republicâ removendum censuit*), of soldiers, *dimissio militum, exauctoratio*, see DISCHARGE

dismount, v intr *descendĕre, desilire ex equo* or *equis*

disobey, v tr *alci non parēre* or *oboedire, alci dicto audientem non esse* **disobedient,** adj *non parens, dicto non audiens, minus oboediens* Adv *non oboedienter* **disobedience,** n *contumacia*

disoblige, v tr *alci morem non gerĕre*.

disorder, I. n. 1, *confusio*; 2, = — of the mind, *animi commotio, perturbatio*; 3, = moral —, *licentia*; 4, = disease, *morbus*. II. v.tr. *(con)turbare, perturbare, miscēre, confundĕre*. **disordered,** adj. 1, of body, *aeger*; 2, of mind, *alienatus*. **disorderly,** adj. 1, = confused, *confusus, (con)turbatus, perplexus, incompositus, inordinatus*; 2, = of conduct, *effrenatus, dissolutus, pravus, corruptus*.

disorganize, v.tr. *(dis)solvĕre, resolvĕre*. **disorganisation,** n. *dissolutio*.

disown, v.tr. — a person's authority, *detrectare alcjs imperium*; — as a judge, *alqm judicem recusare*; — a debt, *infitiari debitum*.

disparage, v.tr. *extenuare, elevare, parvi facĕre, alci obtrectare*. **disparagement,** n. *obtrectatio*. **disparaging,** adj. *invidiosus*.

disparity, n. *dissimilitudo, diversitas, differentia*.

dispassionate, adj. *placidus, placatus, tranquillus*. Adv. *placide, placate, tranquille*.

dispatch, v.tr. see DESPATCH.

dispel, v.tr. *discutĕre* (= to shake off), *dissipare* (e.g. *ordines pugnantium*), *(de)pellĕre, dispellĕre, (dis)solvĕre, resolvĕre*; — fear, *metum alci depellĕre*.

dispense, v.tr. 1, = distribute, *distribuĕre, dividĕre*; 2, — with, *(di)mittĕre* (= get rid of), *alqâ re carēre* (= be without). **dispensation,** n. *venia* (= pardon).

disperse, I. v.tr. *dis(j)icĕre, dissipare, dispergĕre, (dis)pellĕre, fugare* (= put to flight). II. v.intr. *se dispergĕre, dispergi, dilabi, discurrĕre, diffugĕre, effundi*. **dispersion,** n. *dissipatio, fuga*.

dispirit, v.tr. *animum alcjs affligĕre* or *frangĕre* or *infringĕre*.

displace, v.tr. *loco suo movēre, transferre*.

display, I. v.tr. 1, *in conspectum dare, prae se ferre, proponĕre, venditare, ostendĕre, exhibēre*; 2, = do, *agĕre, facĕre*; — oneself, *(se) praestare, se gerĕre*, or *praebēre*. II. n. *ostentatio, venditatio*.

displease, v.tr. *alci displicēre, alqd habēre offensionis*; be displeased with, *alci irasci*. **displeasure,** n. *offensio, ira, indignatio*; without —, *aequo animo*.

dispose, v.tr. 1, = settle, *statuĕre, constituĕre*; 2, — of, *vendĕre*, see SELL; *finire*, see FINISH; *alqâ re uti*, see EMPLOY; *alqm interficĕre*, see KILL. **disposal,** n. *institutio, ordinatio, arbitrium, potestas*; to be at the — of anyone, *penes alqm* or *ex alcjs arbitrio esse*. **disposed,** adj. *erga alqm animatus, ad alqd inclinatus, ad* or *in alqd propensus, ad alqd proclivis* (usu. in bad sense). **disposition,** n. 1, see DISPOSAL; 2, = character, *indoles, ingenium, mores, -um*; 3, = frame of mind, *voluntas, animi inclinatio, proclivitas*.

dispossess, v.tr. *de possessione dimovēre et de(j)icĕre, possessione depellĕre, deturbare*.

disproportion, n. *inaequalitas, dissimilitudo*. **disproportionate,** adj. *inaequalis, non aequalis, justo* or *solito major, impar*. Adv. *dissimiliter, justo* or *solito majus*.

disprove, v.tr. *refellĕre, redarguĕre*. **disproof,** n. *responsio* (= reply), *refutatio*.

dispute, I. v.tr. 1, *verbis contendĕre, concertare, disputare, disceptare*; — about, *alqd in controversiam vocare* or *adducĕre*; 2, = quarrel, *cum alqo rixari*. II. n. 1, *disputatio, contentio, controversia, concertatio, disceptatio*; 2, *rixa*.

disqualify, v.tr. 1, legal t.t. = make an exception of, *excipere*; 2, = hinder, *alqm impedire* or *prohibēre ne* or *quominus, alci obesse*.

disquiet, n. *inquies, -etis*, f., *animi motus, -ūs, (animi) perturbatio*. **disquieted,** adj. *inquietus, anxius, sol(l)icitus*.

disquisition, n. *dissertatio, oratio* (= speech), *scriptum* (= a writing).

disregard, I. n. 1, = neglect, *neglegentia*; 2, = disrespect, *contemptio*; to hold in —, *male de alqo opinari*. II. v.tr. *parvi, minimi facĕre*. **disregardful,** adj. *alcjs rei neglegens, immemor*.

disrespect, n. *contemptio, despicientia*; comb. *contemptio et despicientia*; see DISREGARD. **disrespectful,** adj. *arrogans, insolens*.

dissatisfy, v.tr. *alci displicēre*. **dissatisfied,** adj. *tristis*, or by *alqd aegre ferre*. **dissatisfaction,** n. *molestia, taedium, indignatio, ira*.

dissect, v.tr. *(dis)secare*. **dissection,** n. *anatomia* or *anatomice* (late).

dissemble, v.tr. *(dis)simulare*. **dissembler,** n. *rei simulator ac dissimulator*.

disseminate, v.tr. *spargĕre, dispergĕre, jacĕre, differre, serĕre*. **dissemination,** n. use verb or *rumor* (e.g. the — of a report was great, *rumor percrebuit*).

dissension, n. *discordia*; see DISCORD.

dissent, I. v.intr. *ab alqo dissentire*. II. n. *dissensio*. **dissentient,** or **dissenter,** *qui ab alqo dissentit*.

disservice, n. *detrimentum, injuria*.

dissever, v.tr. *sejungĕre, secernĕre, segregare*.

dissimilar, adj. *dissimilis, diversus, diversi generis*. **dissimilitude,** n. *dissimilitudo*. **dissimulation,** n. *dissimulatio*; see DISSEMBLE.

dissipate, v.tr. *dissipare*; see DISPERSE. **dissipated,** adj. *effusus, pravus, dissolutus, luxuriosus, ad luxuriam effusus, libidinosus*. **dissipation,** n. *luxuria, licentia, pravitas*.

dissolve, v.tr. 1, = melt, *liquefacĕre, liquari, (dis)solvĕre, (re)solvĕre, diluĕre*; 2, = break up, *(dis)solvĕre, di(s)jungĕre*. **dissolute,** see DISSIPATED. **dissolution,** 1, *liquefactio*; 2, *dissolutio, dissipatio*. **dissoluteness,** n. *mores dissoluti, pravi*, etc.

dissonant, adj. *absŏnus*. **dissonance,** n. *vox absŏna*.

dissuade, v.tr. *dissuadēre alqd* or *de alqâ re, dehortari alqm ab alqâ re, deterrēre alqm ab alqâ re*, or with *ne, quin, quominus*. **dissuasion,** n. *dissuasio*.

dissyllable, n. *disyllăbus*.

distaff, n. *colus*, f.

distance, I. n. 1, of space, *spatium, distantia, intervallum, longinquitas*; at a long —; *longo spatio* or *intervallo interjecto*; 2, of time, *spatium, intervallum*; 3, fig. of manner, *superbia* (= pride). II. v.tr. *alqm superare*; see SURPASS. **distant,** adj. 1, *remotus, longinquus*; to be —, *distare, abesse ab*; to be far —, *distare longo intervallo* or *procul disjunctum esse ab*; he is far —, *longe abest*; 2, *praeteritus*; 3, = proud, *superbus*. Adv. *procul, superbe*.

distaste, n. *animus alienus, stomachus, taedium*. **distasteful,** adj. *molestus, injucundus, ingratus*. Adv. *moleste, injucunde, ingrate*.

distemper, n. see DISEASE.

distend, v.tr. *refercire* (= stuff full). **distention,** n. *distentio*, or by verb (e.g. *stomachus refertus*).

distil, I. v.tr. 1, = make by distillation,

(de)coquĕre, 2, = pour out by drops, stillare **II.** v intr stillare **distillation,** n by verb **distiller,** n qui alqd (de)coquit

distinct, adj 1, = separate, distinctus, separatus, di(s)junctus, 2, = clear, distinctus, clarus, perspicuus Adv separatim, distincte, clare, perspicue **distinction,** n 1, = act of distinguishing, distinctio, to draw a — between two things, aliud — aliud esse velle, see DIFFERENCE, 2, = rank, etc, honos, dignitas, man of —, vir illustris or clarus, a mark of —, insigne **distinctive,** adj proprius Adv proprie **distinctiveness,** n perspicuitas. **distinguish,** v tr 1, see DISCERN, — between, (inter) aliquas res dijudicare, 2, = honour, alqm (alqa re) ornare, — oneself, gloriam adipisci **distinguished,** adj insignis, clarus, nobilis, eximius, a — man vir omnibus rebus ornatus or praecellens

distort, v tr 1, detorquēre, distorquēre (e g oculos), 2, in pejus detorquere, vertĕre

distract, v tr 1, = turn the attention, alqm (in plura studia, etc) distrahĕre, distinēre, 2 in a bad sense, alqm (con)turbare, perturbare **distracted,** adj (con)turbatus, perturbatus, mente turbatā Adv raptim atque turbate, or by adj amens **distraction,** n 1, = interruption, impedimentum, 2, = want of attention, animi conturbatio, incuria (= carelessness), negligentia

distrain, v tr in possessionem rerum debitoris mitti (Jct), bona alcjs venum distrahĕre (Jct), bona vendere **distraint,** n. bonorum venditio (Jct)

distress, I. v tr angere, vexare, urĕre, (dis)cruciare **II.** n 1, anxietas, timor, nimia cura; 2, = poverty, res angustae, angustiae, 3, = danger, periculum, to be in —, laborare, in periculo versari, 4, = DISTRAINT **distressed,** adj anxius, sol(l)icitus, — in mind, anxius animo, — circumstances, res afflictae or angustae **distressing,** adj gravis, acerbus Adv graviter, acerbe

distribute, v tr distribuĕre, metiri, partiri, dispertire, dividĕre, (e)largiri, dispendĕre (= place here and there), assignare, describĕre **distribution,** n partitio, distributio, assignatio (of land), descriptio, largitio

district, n ager, regio, terra

distrust, n diffidentia (— in, alcjs rei), parva fides, suspicio **distrustful,** adj suspiciosus, diffidens, diffisus Adv diffidenter, suspiciose

disturb, v tr (con)turbare, perturbare **disturbance,** n turbatio, tumultus, ūs, motus, ūs **disturber,** n turbator

disunion, n dissensio, discidium, discordia, — in the State, civiles dissensiones, to excite —, commovēre **disunite,** v tr sejungĕre, secernĕre, disjungĕre, dissociare

disuse, v tr dedocēre alqm alqd, — yourself to, dediscĕre alqd, consuetudinem rei minuĕre

ditch, n fossa, incile **ditcher,** n fossor

dithyrambic, adj dithyrambicus

ditty, n carmen cantus, -ūs

diurnal, adj cot(t)idianus (quot), diurnus

dive, v intr 1, urinari, se (de)mergĕre, (de)mergi, submergi, — under, alqā re or in alqd, or in alqa re or sub alqd, 2, — into, = examine, alqd explorare, investigare, cognoscĕre, = read in parts, librum strictim attingĕre **diver,** n urinator

diverge, v intr 1, lit discedĕre, digredi, of roads, in diversas partes ferre, 2, fig ab alqo dissidere, dissentire, see DIFFER **divergence,** n 1, declinatio, 2, dissensio

diverse, adj diversus, dispar, impar, dissimilis Adv diverse, dissimiliter **diversion,** n 1, derivatio, 2, avocatio, 3, delectatio, oblectatio, voluptas, oblectamentum **diversify,** v tr variare, distinguĕre **diversity,** n diversitas, discrepantia, dissensio **divert,** v tr 1, avertere, divertĕre, derivare, 2, = lead aside avocare, sevocare, distinēre, deducĕre, flectĕre, 3, = to amuse, delectare, oblectare **diverting,** adj jucundus, jocosus

divest, v tr alqm exuĕre, alqm alqa re nudare, detegĕre

divide, I. v tr dividĕre, partiri, dispertire, dispertiri, distribuĕre, describĕre **II.** v intr 1, dividi, discedĕre, 2, of opinion, in contrarias sententias distrahi 3, = vote, in sententiam alcjs (pedibus) ire, in sententiam alcjs discedere **dividend,** n = interest, usura, foenus, -oris, n **division** n 1, partitio, divisio, 2, = a large part of an army, legio, 3, = a part, pars, portio **divisible,** adj quod dividi potest

divine, I. adj 1, divinus, caelestis, by — inspiration, divinitus, to honour as —, alqm divino honore colĕre, alci divinos honores habere, 2 fig praestans, eximius, pulcherrimus Adv divine, divinitus, eximie, pulcherrime **II.** n sacerdos, *clericus **III.** v tr 1, lit divinare, praesagire, praedicĕre, vaticinari, (h)ariolari, 2, fig praecipĕre, praesentire, conjectura consequi, conjectare **divination,** n 1, divinatio, vaticinatio, auguratio (= — by birds), the substance or result of —, vaticinium, oraculum, to tell by —, divinare (= to divine), vaticinari (= to prophesy), (h)ariolari (= to tell fortunes), futura divinare, 2, = conjecture, conjectura **diviner,** n vaticinator, vates, (h)ariolus **divinity,** n divinitas, natura divina, vis divina

divorce, I. n divortium, discidium (= separation), diffarreatio (= eating apart, opp confarreatio) repudium (= putting away). **II.** v tr as the act of the man, divortium facĕre cum uxore, repudium remittĕre uxori, uxorem repudiare, claves uxori adimĕre, the woman was said divortium facĕre cum marito, repudiare virum, discedĕre a viro

divulge, v tr (di)vulgare, in medium proferre, declarare, aperire

dizzy, adj vertiginosus, a — height, immensa altitudo **dizziness,** n vertigo

do, v tr facĕre (I fall at thy feet and beg, which I cannot — without the greatest pain, supplex te rogo, quod sine summo dolore facĕre non possum), agĕre, gerĕre, administrare, to — too much, modum excedĕre in re, I — not know what I shall —, quid agam or faciam nescio, what have you to — here? quid tibi hic negotii est? to be done for, de re actum esse, to — again, reficĕre, redintegrare, repetĕre, iterare, — away with, see ABOLISH, KILL **doer,** n auctor

docile, adj docilis Adv dociliter **docility,** n docilitas.

dock, I. n navale, or navalia, -ium **II.** v tr = cut short, praecidĕre

doctor, I. n medicus. **II.** v tr alci mederi, alqm curare

doctrine, n = instruction, doctrina, institutio, praeceptum **doctrinal,** adj quod ad doctrinam pertinet

document, n lit(t)erae, tabulae

dodge, I. v tr alqm huc illuc trahĕre, circumvenire, illudĕre **II.** n = trick, dolus,

doe, n cerva, femina

doff, v.tr. *exuĕre.*

dog, I. n. *canis;* a young —, *catulus;* of a —, *caninus;* to go to the —s, *pessum ire, corrumpi;* go to the —s! *ad malam crucem.* **II.** v.tr. *indagare, investigare.* **dogged,** adj. 1, (= sullen), *morosus, acerbus;* 2, (= determined), *constans, perseverans.* Adv. *morose, acerbe, constanter, perseveranter.* **doggedness,** n. *morositas; perseverantia.*

doggerel, n. *versus inculti.*

dogma, n. *dogma, placitum, scitum, praeceptum, institutum, sententia, judicium;* it is a — of the Stoics that all sins are alike, *placet Stoicis omnia peccata esse paria.* **dogmatical,** adj. 1, theol. t.t. **dogmaticus;* 2, = assertive, *(con)fidens.* Adv. **dogmatice, (con)fidenter.*

doings, n. see ACTION.

dole, I. n. *stips,* see ALMS. **II.** v.tr. *demetiri, dividĕre, distribuĕre.* **doleful,** adj. *tristis, maestus.* Adv. *maeste.* **dolefulness,** n. *tristitia, maeror.*

doll, n. *pupa* (Pers.).

dollar, n. **thalērus.*

dolphin, n. *delphīnus.*

dolt, n. *stipes, -ĭtis,* m., *caudex (codex), homo rusticus, baro.* **doltish,** adj. *rusticus, stultus;* — conduct, *rusticitas.* Adv. *rustice, stulte.*

domain, n. *ager publicus, possessio.*

dome, n. *tholus* (= cupola).

domestic, I. adj. 1, *domesticus, familiaris, privatus;* 2, opp. to foreign, *intestinus, domesticus.* **II.** n. *servus, minister, serva, ministra.* **domesticate,** v.tr. see TAME.

dominion, n. 1, *potestas* (= civil authority), *jus, juris,* n. (= legal authority), *imperium* (= supreme power), *dicio, principatus, -ūs, regnum, dominatio, dominatus, -ūs* (= lordship), *tyrannis, -idis,* f. (τυραννίς, = usurped dominion in a free state); 2, = realm, *regnum.* **dominate,** v.tr. *dominari;* — over, *in alqos.* **dominant,** adj. *summus, maximus, praecipuus* (= chief). **domination,** n. *dominatio;* see DOMINION. **domineering,** adj. *imperiosus, superbus.* **domineer,** v.intr. *ex arbitrio imperare.*

donation, n. *donum;* see GIFT.

doom, I. n. 1, = fate, *fatum, sors;* 2, = judgment, *judicis sententia, judicium.* **II.** v.tr. *damnare;* see CONDEMN, DESTINE. **doomsday,** n. *extremum judicium.*

door, n. *ostium, janua, fores, -um,* f., *valvae* (= folding-doors), *limen* (= threshold); to bolt the —, *ostio pessulum obdĕre;* to open a — to wickedness, *patefacĕre alci fenestram ad nequitiam.* **doorpost,** n. *postis,* m. **doorkeeper,** n. *janitor, janitrix,* f.

dormant, adj. *mortuus;* to be —, *jacēre.*

dormitory, n. *cubiculum.*

dormouse, n. *glis, gliris,* m.

dose, I. n. *potio;* to take a —, *medicamentum sumĕre* or *accipĕre.* **II.** v.tr. *alci medicamentum dare.*

dot, I. n. *punctum.* **II.** v.tr. *pungĕre.*

dote, v.intr. *delirare;* — on, *perdite amare.* **dotage,** n. *senectus, -ūtis,* f. **dotard,** n. *senex,* fixing sense by context (e.g. *stultus*).

double, I. adj. 1, *duplex* (= twofold), *duplus* (in gen.), *geminus, geminatus* (= twins, double in nature), *bipartitus* (= having two parts), *anceps* (= two-headed, doubtful); 2, see TREACHEROUS. **II.** v.tr. 1, *duplicare;* 2, = sail round, *alqd flectĕre, circumvehi;* 3, = turn, *se flectĕre.* Adv. *bis, dupliciter, perfide, perfidiose.* **double-dyed,** adj. 1, lit. *bis tinctus;* 2, fig. use superl. (e.g a — villain, *homo sceleratissimus*). **double-faced,** adj. see DECEITFUL. **double mind,** n. *ambiguum ingenium.* **double sense,** n. *ambiguitas;* of —, *anceps, ambiguus, dubius.* **double-tongued,** adj. *bilinguis* (lit. and fig.). **doublet,** n. *tunica.*

doubt, I. n. *dubitatio (quin, ne, num, quidnam), scrupulus, difficultas, dubium,* (usu. after a prep., e.g. *in dubium vocare*); without —, *sine dubio, haud dubie, certe, non dubito quin* (with subj.); to be in —, *dubium esse, dubitare.* **II.** v.intr. *dubitare, dubium esse, in dubio esse* (to be doubtful), *animo* or *animi pendēre;* I — whether, *dubito num;* I — not that, *non dubito quin.* **doubtful,** adj. 1, = doubting, *dubius, incertus;* 2, = open to doubt, *anceps, ambiguus, dubius, incertus.* Adv. *dubie, dubitanter, ambigue.* **doubtless,** adj. *sine dubio.*

dough, n. *farina.*

doughty, adj. *fortis.*

dove, n. *columba,* f. *columbus,* m. *palumbes, -is,* m. and f. **dove-cot,** n. *columbarium, turris.* **dovetail, I.** n. *securicula, subscus, -ūdis,* f. **II.** v.tr. *securiculá compingĕre.*

dower, n. *dos, dōtis,* f. **dowerless,** adj. *indotatus.*

down, I. prep. *de,* with abl.; — the stream, *secundo flumine.* **II.** n. = grassy hill, *campus paul(l)o editus.* **downcast,** adj. *tristis, maestus.* **downfall,** n. *(oc)casus, -ūs, interitus, -ūs, exitium, ruina.* **downpour,** n. *imber, -bris,* m. **downright, I.** adj. 1, = altogether, *totus,* or *summus* (e.g. he is a — cheat, *totus e fraude factus est;* it is — folly, *summae stultitiae est*); 2, = straightforward, *simplex.* **II.** adv. *plane, prorsus, omnino, simpliciter.* **downwards,** adv. *desuper* (= from above), *deorsum;* in compounds by *de;* to go —, *descendĕre;* to bring —, *deferre, deducĕre.*

down, n. = plumage, *plumae;* on a plant, the chin, etc., *lanugo.* **downy,** adj. *plumeus, plumosus.*

doze, v.intr. *semisomnum esse;* dozing, *semisomnus.*

dozen, *duodecim.*

drab, adj. *ravus;* see BROWN.

drag, I. v.tr. *trahĕre, ducĕre, vehĕre;* — out, *educĕre;* see DRAW and PROTRACT. **II.** n. *sufflamen.*

dragon, n. *draco, serpens; anguis* (the constellation).

dragoon, I. n. *eques, -ĭtis,* m. **II.** v.tr. *dominari.*

drain, I. n. *fossa, incile, cloaca, colliciae (colliquiae,* in fields, on roofs, etc.). **II.** v.tr. *siccare.*

drake, n. *anas mas;* see DUCK.

dram, n. 1, = a weight, *drachma;* 2, = — of liquor, *haustus, -ūs.*

drama, n. *fabula, drama, -ătis,* n. (late). **dramatic,** adj. *scaenicus;* the — art, *ars scaenica.* **dramatize,** v.tr. *ad scaenam componĕre* (Quint.).

draper, n. *qui pannos vendit.* **drapery,** n. 1 (as a business), *pannorum mercatura;* 2 (as hangings), *tapete;* 3, = clothes, *vestitus, -ūs.*

draught, n. 1, = a drink, *haustus, -ūs;* 2, of air, *spiritus, -ūs.*

draw, I. v.tr. *trahĕre;* — a sword, *gladium e vaginá educĕre* (opp. *in vaginam recondĕre*), *gladium stringere*, with sword —n, *gladio stricto*, — a carriage, *currum vehere, ducere*, — out, *ex algo loco educere*, ab or *ex algo loco duce e* (persons, troops); — water, *ex puteo aquam trahere*, — wine, etc, *ex dolio promere, defundere*, — a line, *ducere lineam*, = to portray, *delineare, designare, describere* (always with an object, e g *delineare imagines*), *(de)pingere*, = to excite, movere (e g *risum*, laughter, etc), — a conclusion, *alqd concludere*, — a bill, *syngrapham conscribere*, — a lot, *sortem ducere*, — curtains, *velis alqd obtendere*, — aside, *alqm sevocare*, — down, 1, *deducere, elicere*, 2, = INCUR, — on, = entice, *pellicere*, — over, *in sententiam perducere* — tight, *a(d)stringere*, — up, *scribere* **II.** v intr — on or near, *accedere* = APPROACH, — back, *recedere, se recipere* **draw-bridge,** n *use pons*, m **drawer,** n. 1 (of water), *aquarius*, 2, = chest of drawers, *armarium*, 3, = sketcher *pictor* **drawing,** n *pictura, imago* **drawing room,** n *atrium*

drawl, v intr *in dicendo lentum esse*

dray, n *carrus, -ūs, carrum, vehiculum, plaustrum*

dread, n see FEAR

dream, I. n *somnium, species per somnum oblata* or *in quiete visa, visus, -ūs, nocturnus*, in a —, *per somnum*, someone appeared to me in a —, *imago alcjs in somnio mihi venit*. **II.** v intr *somniare, dormitare* (= to sleep away time); — of, *videre alqd in somnis* or *per somnum*, or *per quietem* **dreamy,** adj *somniculosus*

dreary, adj *tristis, miser, miserabilis, luctuosus, maestus* Adv. *misere, miserabiliter, maeste* **dreariness,** n *tristitia, maestitia*

dregs, n 1, *faex*, 2, fig the — of the population, *faex populi, sordes, is, et faex urbis, infima plebs*, the — of the state, *sentina reipublicae*.

drench, v tr 1, = to give to drink, *alci potum praebere*, 2, = to cover with water, *irrigare, madefacere*.

dress, I. n *vestis, vestitus, -ūs, cultus, -ūs, ornatus, ūs*, comb *vestis atque ornatus*, to adopt the — of the Romans, *Romano habitu uti* **II.** v tr 1, *vestire, veste tegere, veste induere alqm, vestem induere alci, veste alqm amicire*, 2, = prepare food, *(com)parare* **III.** v intr *vestiri, amiciri alqa re* **dressed,** adj *indutus*, — in black, *sordidatus*, — white, *albatus* **dressing-gown,** n *vestis*. **dressing-room,** n *cubiculum* **dressing-table,** n *mensa*

dresser, n 1, = table, *mensa*, 2, = — of wool, *lanarius*, of plants, etc, *cultor* **dressing,** n med t t *fomentum, cataplasma* (Plin), (= the whole treatment) *curatio*

drift, I. v intr *(de)ferri, fluitare* **II.** n = tendency or aim, *consilium, ratio, propositum, ad quod spectat mens* or *animus*, what is the —? *quo spectat oratio?* what is your —? *quid vis?*

drill, I. v tr 1, = to bore, *perforare, terebrare*, 2 = to exercise, *exercere* (e g *milites*), *milites omni disciplina militari erudire* **II.** n 1, *terebra*, 2, *exercitatio*

drink, I n 1 = a drinking, *potio*, 2, = a draught, *potio, potus, -ūs* **II.** v tr *bibere, potare, haurire* (= drink up), *sorbere* (= suck in), — too much, *vino se obruere*, — in, *bibere*, — to, *alci alqd or salutem propinare* **drinker,** n *potor, potator* (= habitual —), *combibo, compotor* (= a cup companion) **drinking,** n *potio*, in the act of —, *inter bibendum*, to be addicted to —, *vino indulgere, deditum esse* **drinking-bout,** n *comissatio*

drip, v.intr. *stillare*,

drive, I v tr *agere, pellere* (= — by force), to — forward, *propellere* (e g *navem*), — from, *abigere ab* or *ex alqa re, exigere (e) re* (e g *domo, e civitate, hostem e campo*), *(ex)pellere alqm (de) re* (*domo, ex urbe, a patria*) *depellere alqm re* or *de re* (*urbe, ex urbe, de provincia*), *e(j)icere alqm (de) re* (*de fundo*), *exturbare ex re*, — hither and thither, *agitare* (*fluctibus agitari*), necessity —s, *necessitas urget* or *cogit alqm ut alqd faciat*, — too far, *modum excedere in re* **II.** v intr **1,** *(in) curru vehi*, **2,** — at, *alqd petere*, **3,** of the rain, *in alqm ferri* **III.** n **1,** *gestatio*, to take a —, *curru vehi*, **2,** = the approach to a house, *aditus, ūs* **driver,** n = of a carriage, *raedarius, auriga*, of animals, *agitator*, a donkey —, *asinarius*

drivel, I. v intr 1 lit *salivare, salivam fluere pati*, 2, fig *ineptire, nugari* **II.** n 1, *saliva*, 2, *nugae, ineptiae*.

drizzle, v.intr. *leniter pluere*, it —s, *rorat*

droll, adj *lepidus, jocularis, ridiculus*. Adv *lepide, ridicule* **drollery,** n *lepor (lepos), ludus, jocus, nugae, tricae, ineptiae*

dromedary, n *(camelus) dromas, -ădis*, m

drone, n *fucus* **droning,** n *bombus*

droop, I. v tr *demittere*, † *inclinare* **II.** v intr **1,** lit *demitti*, **2,** = fade, *languere, languescere, flaccescere*, **3,** = fail, *animo concidere, affligi*

drop, I. n *gutta, stilla*, not a —, *ne minimum quidem* **II.** v intr **1,** *lippire* (= — from the eyes), *(de)stillare de re*, — with, *stillare re* (e g *sanguine*), *madefactum esse re*, **2,** see FALL. **III.** v tr **1,** = let fall, *alqd de(j)icere, (manu) emittere, demittere*, **2,** = cease, *alqd omittere, dimittere*

dropsy, n *aqua intercus, -ūtis, hydrops* **dropsical,** adj *hydropicus*

dross, n **1,** = slag, *scoria*, **2,** = rust, *robigo, aerugo* (= — of copper), *ferrugo* (= — of iron), **3,** fig *faex, sentina*

drought, n *caelum siccum, siccitas, siccitates, -um*

drove, n *grex, armenta orum* **drover,** n *pecuarius, armentarius, bubulcus*

drown, v tr **1,** *(de)mergere in aquam, submergere* (esp in pass part *summersus*), *aquā suffocare*, fig *se in alqd ingurgitare*, **2,** = overspread, *inundare*, **3,** fig by special verbs (e g — the memory of, *oblivisci* = forget)

drowsy, adj *dormitans, somni plenus, somno gravis, oscitans* (= yawning) Adv, by adj **drowsiness,** n *somno affectum esse*

drudge, I. n *servus, verna*, m and f **II.** v intr *servire* **drudgery,** n *officium servile*

drug, I. n *medicamentum*, poisonous —, *venenum* **II.** v tr **1,** = administer drugs, *alci medicamentum praebere, dare*, **2,** put a — into, *medicamentum alci rei addere, (cum) alqā re miscere* **druggist,** n *medicamentarius* (Plin)

drum, n *tympanum*, to beat the —, *tympanum pulsare*

drunk, adj *ebrius, bene potus, temulentus, vino gravis, crapulae plenus* **drunkenness,** n *ebriositas, vinolentia, ebrietas* **drunkard,** n *ebriosus, vinolentus*

dry, I. adj **1,** *siccus, aridus* (= withered), *sitiens* (= thirsty), † *siticulosus, (ex)siccatus, torridus*, **2,** fig *exilis, frigidus, jejunus, aridus* Adv *sicce, jejune, exiliter frigide* **II.** v tr *(ex)siccare, arefacere, torrefacere* — tears, *abstergere lacrimas* **III.** v intr *siccari, siccescere (ex)arescere* **dryness,** n **1,** *siccitas, ariditas*, **2,** *jejunitas, exilitas* **dry-nurse,** n *assa*.

dual, adj. gram. t.t. *dualis numerus.*

dubious, see DOUBTFUL.

duck, **I.** n. *anas, -ătis*, f.; as term of endearment, *deliciae, corculum*; to play —s and drakes with, *alqd pessum dare.* **II.** v.tr. **1**, under water, *alqd (sub)mergĕre, demergĕre in aquam*; **2**, the head, *caput demittĕre.* **III.** v.intr. **1**, *se (sub)mergĕre, (sub)mergi*; **2**, *caput demittĕre.* **ducking**, n. to get a —, *madidum esse, madefieri.*

ductile, adj. **1**, *ductilis* (Plin.), *flexibilis*; **2**, fig. *obsequens, facilis.* **ductility**, n. **1**, by adj.; **2**, *habilitas, facilitas.*

dudgeon, n. *ira*; in —, *iratus.*

due, **I.** adj. **1**, = owed, *debitus*; to be —, *debēri*; to pay money before it is —, *pecuniam repraesentare*; **2**, = fit, *ad alqm idoneus, congruens, alqo dignus, alci debitus.* **II.** n. **1**, *debitum*; **2**, = tax, *vectigal*; harbour —, *portorium.*

duel, n. *certamen.*

duet, n. *versus alterni*

duke, n. * *dux.*

dulcimer, n. *sambuca.*

dull, **I.** v.tr. **1**, = blunt, *hebetare*; *obscurare* (anything bright); **2**, = astound, *(ob)stupefacĕre, obtundere.* **II.** adj. **1**, lit. *hebes*; **2**, fig. *obtusus, (ob)stupefactus, hebes*; **3**, = sluggish, stupid, *tardus, iners, frigidus*; **4**, = uninteresting, *aridus, jejunus.* Adv. *tarde, frigide; jejune, aride.* **dulness**, n. **1**, = — of mind, *obtusior animi acies* or *vigor, mens tarda, imbecillitas ingenii, ingenium hebes, ingenii tarditas, stupor*; **2**, = sluggishness, *inertia, segnitia*; **3**, of colour; see PALENESS.

dumb, adj. *mutus, elinguis* (lit. and fig.); to become —, *obmutescĕre* (lit. and fig.); to be —, i.e. silent, *tacēre.* **dumbfounder**, v.tr. *obstupefacĕre.* **dumbness**, n. use adj. or verb (e.g. — seizes me, *obmutesco*).

dun, **I.** adj. *fuscus, subfuscus.* **II.** v.tr. *alqm alqd flagitare, alqd ab alqo exposcĕre.* **III.** n. *flagitator.*

dunce, n. *stipes, -ĭtis*, m., *truncus.*

dung, n. *stercus, -ŏris*, n., *fimus.* **dunghill**, n. *sterquilinium, fimetum* (Plin.).

dungeon, n. *carcer, -ĕris*, m.

dupe, **I.** n. *homo credulus, fatuus, ludibrium.* **II.** v.tr. *alqm ludibrio habēre*; see DECEIVE.

duplicate, n. *alqd eodem exemplo.*

duplicity, n. *ambiguitas, fraus*; see DECEIT.

durable, adj. **1**, *firmus, solidus, duraturus, stabilis*; **2**, of time, *diuturnus, longinquus, perpetuus.* Adv. *firme, solide, stabiliter, perpetuo.* **durability**, n. **1**, *firmitas, stabilitas, perennitas*; **2**, *diuturnitas, longinquitas, perpetuitas.* **duration**, n. *temporis spatium*; long —, *diuturnitas*; short —, *brevitas.* **during**, prep. *per* with accus. = throughout, *in* with abl. = time within which, *inter* with accus. (e.g. *inter cenam* = — dinner, or *inter cenandum*), abl. abs. (e.g. — the reign of Augustus, *Augusto imperatore*), *dum* with pres. indic., *cum* with indic. in primary, subj. in secondary tenses.

dusk, n. *crepusculum*; at —, *primo vespere, jam obscurā luce*; it grows —, *advesperascit.* **dusky**, adj. *fuscus*; see DARK.

dust, **I.** n. *pulvis, -ĕris*, m.; to raise the —, *pulverem movēre* or *excitare*; to lay the —, *p. sedare*; to throw — in the eyes, *verba alci dare.* **II.** v.tr. *alqd abstergēre, detergēre.* **duster**, n. *penicillum* (or *-us*). **dustman**, n. *qui purgamenta tollit.* **dusty**, adj. *pulverulentus, pulveris plenus.*

duty, n. **1**, *officium, debitum, pietas, religio, munus, -ĕris*, n., *partes, -ium*; it is the — of, *est alcjs*; it is my —, *meum est*; a sense of —, *pietas erga alqm* or *alqd, religio*; **2**, = tax, *vectigal.* **dutiful, duteous**, adj. *pius erga alqm, alci obœdiens, dicto audiens.* Adv. *pie, obœdienter.* **dutifulness**, n. *pietas erga alqm, obœdientia.*

dwarf, n. *nanus* (Juv.), *pumilio.* **dwarfish**, adj. *pusillus.*

dwell, v.intr. **1**, *habitare in loco, (in)colĕre locum, domicilium habēre in loco*; **2**, fig. — upon, *alqd longius prosequi.* **dwelling**, n. *domicilium, sedes, -is*, f., *habitatio, aedes, -is*, f.

dwindle, v.intr. *(con)tabescĕre, (de)minui, extenuari*, † *rarescĕre.*

dye, **I.** v.tr. *alqd re tingĕre*; *alqâ re inficĕre, imbuĕre, colorare, inducĕre colorem alci rei*; — with blood, *cruentare, sanguine inficĕre*; — oneself with something, *se inficĕre alqâ re* (e.g. with woad, *vitro*). **II.** n. *color* or verb; the blossom of the pomegranate is a —, *flos Punici mali tingendis vestibus idoneus.* **dyer**, n. *infector.*

dynasty, n. *domus regnatrix, imperium, regnum.*

dyspepsia, n. *cruditas.* **dyspeptic**, adj. *crudus.*

E.

each, **I.** adj. *singuli, omnis, quisque* only after its noun, *uterque* (of two); on — side, *utrimque*; — other, *alii alios*, or *inter se.* **II.** pron. *quisque* after noun, *unusquisque, uterque* (of two), by distributive adjs. (e.g. *unicuique bina jugera*, = two acres each); see EVERY.

eager, adj. **1**, for anything, *alcjs rei cupidus, avidus, studiosus*; **2**, = keen, *acer, ardens, fervidus.* Adv. *cupide, avide, studiose, acriter, fervide.* **eagerness**, n. **1**, *cupiditas, cupido, aviditas, studium, appetentia*; **2**, *ardor, impetus, -ūs, fervor, concitatio, aestus, -ūs.*

eagle, n. *aquila*; — eyed, *cui oculus acer.*

ear, n. **1**, part of the body, *auris*; attentive —s, *aures applicatae*; to box a person's —s, *colaphum* (with the fist), *alapam* (with the palm) *alci ducĕre* or *impingĕre*; to pull the —s, *aures vellĕre*; to be over head and —s in debt, *aere alieno demersum esse*; **2**, of corn, *spica, arista.* **earring**, n. *aurium insigne, inaures, -ium*, f.

earl, n. * *comes.*

early, **I.** adj. **1**, *matutinus* (= in the morning), *maturus*; **2**, of plants, etc., too —, *immaturus*, † *praecox, praematurus*; from — youth, *(jam inde) a puero, ab initio aetatis.* **II.** Adv. *mane, primâ luce, sub lucem, mature.*

earn, v.tr. **1**, *merēre* and *merēri*; — much money, *grandem pecuniam quaerĕre*; — by labour, *manu*; — your subsistence, *alqâ re pecuniam sibi facĕre* or *colligĕre, quaestum facĕre*; **2**, fig. *(pro)merēre, (pro)merēri.* **earnings**, n. *quaestus, -ūs, lucrum* (= gain); to make — by bad means, *turpi quaestu victum parare* or *quaerĕre.*

earnest, adj. *gravis, serius* (usu. of things); to take in —, *rem in serium vertĕre.* Adv. *serio, ex animo, graviter.* **earnestness**, n. **1**, = zeal, *studium, contentio, diligentia*; **2**, = seriousness, *gravitas, severitas, diligentia.*

earth, **I.** n. **1**, = soil, *terra, solum*; **2**, = the globe, *terra, orbis terrarum, tellus, -ūris*, f. (mostly poet.). **II.** v.tr. = — up, *terram aggerare.* **earth-born**, adj. † *terrigena, terrae* *filius* **earthen,** adj *terrenus* **earthenware,** n *fictilia, ium* **earthly,** adj *terrestris* — life, *haec vita*, — goods *res externae*, — happiness, *voluptas (humana)* · — minded *a rebus divinis alienus* **earthquake,** n *terrae motus, -ūs* **earthwork,** n *agger, ĕris*, m **earth-worm,** n *vermis* m

ease, I. n 1, *tranquillitas, quies, -ētis*, f, *otium* (= leisure), *vita otiosa, pax*, to be at —, *quiescĕre*, to take your —, *requiescere, quieti se dare*, at —, *tranquillo animo*, 2, = readiness, *facilitas*. **II.** v tr *exonerare, laxare, (al)levare sublevare, expedire* **easiness,** n *facilitas*, esp of temper, for which also *indulgentia*, — of belief, *credulitas* **easy,** adj 1, *ad alqd faciendum* or *factu, facilis, nullius negotii, expeditus*, 2, = affluent, *dives*, — circumstances, *res secundae*, 3, = tranquil, *tranquillus, quietus, placidus*, 4, of temper, *facilis, indulgens*, 5, of manners, *simplex, comis* Adv in gen *facile, nullo negotio*, = tranquilly, *tranquille, quiete, placide*, of temper, *facile, indulgenter*, of manners, *simpliciter, comiter*

east, n. *oriens, regio orientis* (as a district of the heavens), *orientis solis partes, ium* (= the East) **eastward, eastern, easterly,** adj *ad orientem vergens, in orientem spectans*, (as adverbs) *ad orientem versus, ad* or *in orientem, ad regionem orientis*, — nations, *Asiatici*, — land, *orientis terrae*, or *regiones*

eat, I. v tr = to take food, *edĕre, manducare* (= to chew), *comedĕre* (= to eat up), *vesci alqā re* (= to eat up as nutriment), *vorare* (= to swallow, particularly to swallow unmasticated), *gustare* (= to taste) to — anyone out of house and home, *alqm sumptibus perdĕre*, to — away, *(e)rodĕre* **II.** v intr to — well = taste, *jucunde sapĕre* **eatable,** adj *esculentus* **eatables,** n *cibus* (= food), *cibi* (= meats, that is, several kinds of food), *esca* (= prepared food), *victus, ūs* (= living, victuals) **eating-house,** n *popina*

eaves, n *suggrunda* **eaves-dropper,** n *qui alqd subauscultat*

ebb, I. n *aestūs decessus, -ūs*, or *recessus, ūs*, at —, *minuente aestu*; — and flood, *aestus maritimi accedentes et recedentes* **II.** v intr *recedĕre*, — and flow, *affluĕre et remeare*

ebony, n *(h)ebĕnus*, f (or *ebenum*)

ebriety, n *ebrietas, temulentia*, see DRUNK.

ebullition, n 1, lit use *effervescĕre*, 2, fig *aestus, ūs*, — of anger, *ira effervescit*

eccentric, adj *inauditus, inusitatus, novus, mirus, insolens*. **eccentricity,** n *quod mirum est*, etc

ecclesiastical, adj * *ecclesiasticus*

echo, I. n *imago vocis*, to give an —, *voci respondere, vocem reddĕre, remittĕre*, a place which —es, *locus clamoribus repercussus* **II.** v intr and tr see "give an echo" above

eclat, n *laus, splendor, ostentatio*

eclipse, I. n *obscuratio, defectus (solis*, etc.) **II.** v tr 1, *obscurare*, to be eclipsed, *obscurari, deficĕre*, 2, fig *alqm superare*, see EXCEL.

eclogue, n *ecloga* (late)

economy, n 1, = house-management, *rei familiaris administratio, diligentia*, political —, *rei publicae administratio*, 2, = frugality, *parsimonia*, from —, *rei familiaris tuendae studio* **economical,** adj *attentus ad rem, frugi, diligens, parcus* Adv *diligenter, parce* **economist,** n 1, *qui rem suam bene administrat*, 2, = political —, *qui rei publicae opes investigat*

ecstasy, n 1, = elevation and abstraction of mind, *secessus, ūs, mentis et animi a corpore animus abstractus a corpore, mens sevocata a corpore furor*, 2, = great delight, *summa voluptas*. **ecstatic,** adj *mente incitatus, fanaticus, furens* Adv *per furorem*

eddy, n *vertex, vorago* (= whirlpool)

edge, n 1, = a sharp line, *acies, labrum* (of a cup, etc), 2, = margin, *margo*, m and f, *ora, crepido* (of quays, etc) 3, = — of a dress, † *limbus, clavus, fimbriae*, † *instita*

edible, adj *esculentus*

edict, n *edictum, decretum, consultum, jussum*

edify, v tr 1, lit *aedificare*, 2, fig *docĕre, monēre* **edifying,** adj *ad bonos mores docendos aptus, idoneus*, see EXCELLENT

edit, v tr *librum edĕre* **editor,** n *editor* **edition,** n *editio*

educate, v tr *alĕre* (= to support), *instituĕre, erudire, docĕre* (= teach) *educare* (= bring up), to be well educated, *bene doctum et educatum esse, institutum esse* **education,** n *educatio, disciplina, doctrina, eruditio*, a man of good —, *homo (e)doctus, eruditus, homo bene doctus et educatus*, without —, *(politioris) humanitatis expers* **educator,** n *educator* (= one who brings up), *magister, magistra, praeceptor, praeceptrix* **educational,** adj *ad disciplinam*, etc, *pertinens*

educe, v tr *protrahĕre, producĕre, educĕre*

eel, n *anguilla*

efface, v tr *delēre, (e)radĕre*

effect, I. n 1, = consequence, *effectus, -ūs, eventus, ūs, consecutio* 2, = influence, *vis, effectus, ūs, vis et effectus*, to have great —, *multum (apud alqm) valēre*, without —, *frustra, nequi(c)quam*, 3, = purpose, to this —, *his verbis, hoc consilio*, 4, in —, *re (verā), reapse*, 5, —s, *res, rerum*, f, *bona, -orum* **II.** v tr *efficĕre, facĕre, conficĕre, perficĕre* **effective, effectual,** adj *alcis rei efficiens, valens, efficax*, or by verb *qui*, etc, *efficit* Adv *efficienter, prospere* **efficacy,** n *efficientia*

effeminate, adj *mollis, effeminatus, delicatus*, † *semivir, muliebris* Adv *molliter, effeminate, muliebriter* **effeminacy,** n *mollitia, mollities, vita delicata*

effervesce, v intr *fervēre, effervescĕre*

effete, adj *effetus, obsoletus*

effigy, n *effigies, imago, simulacrum*

efflux, n *effluvium, profluvium*

effort, n *opera, labor, studium, contentio, conatus, -ūs*, to make an —, *operam dare, (e)niti*

effrontery, n. *impudentia, os, oris*, n (*impudens*)

effulgence, n *splendor, fulgor*

egg, n *ovum*, a fresh —, *ovum recens*, to lay —s, *ova parĕre, edĕre, gignĕre*, yoke of —, *vitellus*, white of —, *album* or *albumen ovi* (Cels & Plin), teach your grandmother to suck —, *sus Minervam, ut aiunt* (i e *docet*) **egg-shell,** n *ovi putamen* (Plin)

egoism, n *sui ostentatio, jactatio* (= display), *sui amor* (= love of self) **egoist,** n *qui sibi soli studet* **egoistical,** adj use n

egregious, adj *maximus, summus, mirus, singularis* Adv *maxime, summe, mirum in modum*

egress, n 1, = going out, *egressus, ūs, exitus, ūs*, 2, = place through which you go out, *exitus, egressus, effugium* 3, = mouth of a river, *os, oris*, n *ostium*

eider-down, n *plumae (anatum) mollissimae*

eight, adj *octo, octoni, -ae, -a* (= eight each) **eighteen,** adj *duodeviginti*. **eighteenth,** adj *duodevicesimus, octavus decimus* **eighty,** adj *octoginta, octogeni* (distrib) **eightieth,** adj *octogesimus*

either, I. pron *alteruter* (more rarely *uter*), *uteruis, uterlibet*, not —, *neuter* (fem and neut. of all, *-ra, -rum*) **II.** conj either or, *aut aut, vel vel, sive (seu) sive (seu)*, not either nor, *neque (nec) neque (nec)*

ejaculate, v tr *voces interruptas (et inconditas) mittere* or *edere* **ejaculation,** n. *voces interruptae*.

eject, v tr *e(j)icere, emittere, extrudere* **ejection,** n *expulsio*, but more usu by verb, legal t t. *dejectio*

eke, v tr to — out, *alci rei parcere*

elaborate, I. v tr *conficere, perficere, expolire* **II.** adj *elaboratus, expolitus, exquisitus, accuratus* Adv *exquisite, accurate* **elaboration,** n use the verb

elapse, v intr *transire, praeterire, perugi*

elastic, adj 1 lit *qui (quae, quod) produci potest*, 2, fig see HOPEFUL.

elated, adj *algâ re elatus*, to be —, *efferri* **elation,** n *gaudium* (= joy), *arrogantia, superbia* (= pride)

elbow, n *cubitum*

elder, I. adj. (*natu*) *major, superior, prior* **II.** n eccl t t **presbyter*. **elderly,** adj *aetate provectus*

elect, I. v tr *creare, capere, legere, eligere*, comb *eligere et creare, deligere, cooptare* (as a colleague), *designare, declarare*, — into a premature vacancy, *sufficere* **II.** adj *designatus, suffectus* (= to an unexpected vacancy) **election,** n 1, act of choice, *electio, suffragia*, *-orum* (= the votes), 2, a popular —, *comitia, -orum*, to hold an —, *comitia habere*, day of —, *dies comitialis*, day of your —, *tua comitia* **electioneering,** adj *candidatorius* **elective,** adj *suffragiis creatus* **elector,** n *qui jus suffragii habet, suffragator* (= partisan).

elegant, adj *elegans, venustus, bellus* (= graceful), *lautus, nitidus, comptus, mundus* (= neat), *urbanus* (= refined) Adv *eleganter, venuste, belle, nitide, urbane* **elegance,** n, *elegantia, urbanitas, venustas, munditia*

elegy, n *elegia, elegi* **elegiac,** adj *elegiacus* (late)

element, n 1, = original material, *elementum, natura*, the —s, *principia rerum e quibus omnia constant, primordia rerum*, the four —s, *quat(t)uor elementa, initia rerum*, 2, = a part, *membrum*, 3 = the rudiments of knowledge, *elementa, -orum, rudimenta, -orum*, 4, fig to be in one's —, *algâ re familiariter uti*, to be out of one's —, *in algâ re peregrinum ac hospitem esse* **elementary,** adj *primus* (e g — knowledge, *prima lit(t)erarum studia*), — school, *schola in quâ lit(t)erarum elementa traduntur*

elephant, n *elephantus (elephas)*

elevate, v tr 1, = raise, *(at)tollere, extollere, (al)levare*, 2, fig *tollere, evehere*, to be raised, *efferri* **elevated,** adj 1, of places, *editus, altus, (ex)celsus, praecelsus*, 2, fig *(ex)celsus* **elevation,** n = a raising, *elatio*, but usu by verb, fig *elatio, magnitudo*, — of character, *magnanimitas*, = — of the voice, *vocis contentio*, = a rising ground, *locus editus* or *superior*

eleven, adj. *undecim*, — each, *undeni*; — times, *undecie(n)s* **eleventh,** adj *undecimus*

elf, n see FAIRY.

elicit, v tr *elicere, eblandiri* (by coaxing), *extorquere* (by force), *evocare* (to call or bring forth), to — tears, *lacrimas movere alci*

eligible, adj *opportunus, idoneus ad algd, dignus algâ re*, or *qui* with subj Adv *opportune, bene* **eligibility,** n *opportunitas* (e g *loci*), = — to office, *dignus qui eligatur*

elixir, n **elixir(ium)*

elk, n *alces, -is*, f

ell, n *ulna* (= a cloth measure), *cubitum*

elm, *ulmus*, f, of an —, *ulmeus*

elocution, n. *(e)locutio* (= selection of words), *pronuntiatio* (= delivery), as an art, *elocutoria, elocutrix* (Quint)

elongate, v.tr see LENGTHEN

elope, v intr *cum algo* or *algâ (pro)fugere, effugere* **elopement,** n *fuga*

eloquence, n *facultas* or *vis* or *copia dicendi, facundia, eloquentia* **eloquent,** adj *facundus, eloquens, copiosus, dicendi peritus, in dicendo exercitatus, in dicendo suavis et ornatus* Adv *copiose, ornate, facunde*

else, I. adj *alius* **II.** adv. 1, = besides, *praeterea, praeter* (prep with accus, e g nothing —, *praeter hoc nihil*), see EXCEPT, 2, = otherwise, *aliter, alioqui(n), alio modo, aliâ ratione*; it could not — happen, *fieri non potuit quin*, —where, *alibi*

elucidate, v tr see EXPLAIN.

elude, v intr *alci* or *de* or *(e) alcjs manibus elabi, de alcjs manibus effugere, alcjs manibus evadere algm eludere, (e)vitare, (ef)fugere, declinare* **elusive,** adj *fallax* Adv *fallaciter*

Elysium, n *Elysium*, see PARADISE. **Elysian,** adj *Elysius* (e g *campi, domus*).

emaciate, v tr *attenuare, macerare, enervare, exhaurire* **emaciated,** adj *maceratus, macer, enervatus, enervatus et exsanguis, enectus, effetus* (= exhausted, of soils) **emaciation,** n *macies*

emanate, v intr *emanare* **emanation,** n by verb.

emancipate, v tr *liberare re* or *a re*, as slaves etc, *manumittere, servitute liberare, servitio eximere, e servitute in libertatem restituere* or *vindicare* **emancipation,** n *liberatio*; = — of slaves, *manumissio*. **emancipator,** n, *liberator*

embalm, v tr *condire*

embank, v tr *molem opponere fluctibus, flumen arcere, coercere* **embankment,** n *agger, -eris* m, *terra ad aggerem exstruendum congesta, moles, -is*, f

embark, I. v tr *imponere in navem* or *naves* **II.** v intr **1,** lit *conscendere (navem)*; 2, fig — upon, *consilium* or *rationem inire*

embarrass, v tr 1, = disturb, *(con)turbare*; 2, = hinder, *algm impedire, alci obstare, obesse, officere* **embarrassed,** adj *impeditus*, — circumstances, see EMBARRASSMENT **embarrassing,** adj *difficilis, dubius, anceps*. **embarrassment,** n *implicatio, perturbatio*, = — of mind, *mens turbata*; = pecuniary —, *rei familiaris implicatio, angustiae*

embassy, n 1, = the office of an ambassador, *legatio, legationis munus, -eris*, n, 2, = the persons sent, *legatio, legati, qui missi sunt*, see AMBASSADOR

embattled, adj *instructus*

embellish, v tr *(ad)ornare, exornare, alci decori* or *ornamento esse, excolere*. **embellishment,** n *decus, -oris*, n, *ornamentum, insigne*.

embers, n *cinis, -ĕris,* m, *favilla*

embezzle, v tr. *avertĕre, intervertĕre, intervertĕre ad seque transferre, intercipĕre, supprimĕre, retinēre ac supprimĕre* **embezzlement,** n *peculatus -ūs* **embezzler,** n *pecuniae aversor, interceptor.*

embitter, v tr *exasperare infestum facĕre, exacerbare.* **embittered,** adj *irâ accensus, iratus, infensus, infestus*

emblem, n *imago, signum, simulacrum* **emblematic,** adj *alqd significans,* or *referens*

embody, v tr. 1, = to enroll troops, *milites conscribĕre* 2, = to join one thing to another, *adjungĕre, ad(j)icĕre, inserĕre* (= to plant in, e g *alqm familiae*), — in a society, *in societatem a(d)scribĕre, recipĕre*, — the young soldiers with the veterans, *tirones immiscēre veteribus militibus*, — a speech in a letter, *epistulae orationem includĕre* **embodiment,** n *imago, simulacrum* (= *imago*)

embolden, v tr *alci animum addĕre, alqm accendĕre, confirmare*

emboss, v tr *caelare* (*alqd auro, argento,* also *in auro*) **embossed,** adj *caelatus*, artificer in — work, *caelator*

embrace, I. v tr 1, *amplecti, amplexari, complecti*, 2 = contain, *comprehendĕre, complecti* 3, = seize, *capĕre* (e g *occasionem*), *uti* 4, = encircle, *complecti*, 5, — an opinion, *ad alcjs partes transire, sententiae assentiri* II. n *amplexus, -ūs, complexus, -ūs*

embrocation, n *fomentum*

embroider, v tr (*acu*) *pingĕre, acu facĕre*, — with gold, *auro alqd distinguĕre* **embroidery,** n *ars acu pingendi*, a piece of —, *opus acu pictum* or *factum, pictura acu facta*

embroil, v tr *implicare alqm re, alqm conturbare*

embryo, n *partus, -ūs*

emendation, n *emendatio* (*et correctio*)

emerald, n *smaragdus,* m and f, of —, *smaragdinus*

emerge, v intr *emergĕre, ex(s)istĕre* **emergency,** n *casus, -ūs, discrimen*

emetic, n *vomitorius*, with v (e g *bulbus*)

emigrant, n *patriâ* or *domo profugus, patriâ extorris, advena, incola* (= foreign resident) **emigrate,** v intr *(e)migrare, demigrare ex loco in locum, transmigrare alqo* (e g *Veios*), *domo emigrare, solum* (*exsilii causâ*) *vertĕre* **emigration,** n *(e)migratio*

eminent, adj *insignis, praestans, clarus, nobilis, egregius, excellens, praecellens, eximius, singularis* (= sole of its kind), *summus* Adv *egregie, eximie, summe, praecipue, singulariter,* by superl with *ex omnibus* or *omnium*, or posit with *prae ceteris* (e g *ex omnibus optimus, prae ceteris bonus*) **eminence,** n 1, of place, *locus editus, clivus* (= a hill), *tumulus* (= a mound), 2, = moral —, *praestantia, excellentia, summa gloria*, 3, = — of rank, *amplissimus gradus, -ūs*

emissary, n *emissarius, speculator*

emit, v tr *(e)mittĕre, jacĕre* **emission,** n *(e)missio, jactus, -ūs.*

emollient, n *malagma, -atis* (Cels)

emolument, n *emolumentum, lucrum, quaestus, -ūs, fructus, -ūs.*

emotion, n *animi motus, -ūs, commotio, concitatio*, a strong —, *animi perturbatio*, to be under —, *perturbatum esse*

emperor, n *imperator, Caesar, Augustus, princeps* **empress,** n *domina, Augusta, uxor imperatoria*

emphasis, n *emphasis* (Quint.), *vis*, with —, *cum vi*, to have —, *vim habēre, multum valēre*, to have more —, *plus gravitatis* or *auctoritatis habēre*, without —, *jejunus, frigidus* **emphatic,** adj *gravis, vehemens* Adv *graviter, vehementer*

empire, n *imperium, potestas, dicio, principatus, -ūs, dominatio, dominatus, -ūs, regnum* (= monarchical despotism), *tyrannis, -idis*, f (= power usurped in a free state)

empirical, adj *in usu tantum et experimentis positus* (Cels)

employ, v tr 1, = to engage in any work or office, *occupare, occupatum tenēre, detinēre*, *alqo* or *alqâ re uti*, *alqd usurpare, adhibēre alqd* or *alqm ad alqd*, etc , 2, = to spend in, or on, *in alqm* or *alqd insumĕre, ad alqd conferre, in* or *ad alqd impendĕre, in alqd* or *in alqâ re consumĕre, in alqâ re collocare, alqd alci rei tribuĕre* **employment,** n 1, act of —, *usus, -ūs, occupatio, tractatio, pertractatio*, 2, = business, *res, negotium, studium, cura* **employer,** n *qui operas conducit*

emporium, n *emporium, forum rerum venalium*

empower, v tr *alci alcjs rei faciendae potestatem facĕre, alci mandare ut*, etc to be empowered by, *mandata habēre ab alqo, alcjs nomine, alqo auctore facĕre alqd*

empty, I. adj 1, *inanis* (opp *plenus* or *instructus*), *nudus* (opp *(ex)ornatus*), *vacuus*, 2, fig *inanis, vanus, omnis eruditionis expers* (*atque ignarus*), *omnium rerum rudis* (the two last in regard to learning and culture), — words *verba inania, voces inanes, sermo inanis, sermo vanus* II. v tr *vacuefacĕre, exinanire exonerare* (= — a cargo, etc), *exhaurire, exsiccare*, — itself (of a river), *se effundĕre, in mare (in)fluĕre* **emptiness,** n. 1, = empty space, *inanitas, inane vacuum, vacuitas*, 2, fig *inanitas, vanitas*

empyrean, n *caelum*, †*igneae arces*, †*aetherea domus*, †*ignifer aether*

emulate, v tr *(con)certare, contendĕre cum alqo, aemulari alqm* **emulation,** n *studium, certamen, certatio, aemulatio* **emulator,** n *aemulus*, m , *aemula*, f **emulous,** adj *aemulus* Adv *certatim*

enable, v tr *facultatem alci alcjs rei faciendae dare*

enact, v tr 1, of a deliberative body, *alqd sancire, sciscĕre, jubēre*, 2, in a wider sense, *jubēre*, accus and infin , *statuĕre, constituĕre*, infin or *ut* **enactment,** n = law, *sanctio, lex, plebiscitum, senatusconsultum*

enamoured, adj see LOVE

encamp, v intr *castra ponĕre*

enchant, v tr 1, *(ef)fascinare* (= — by the evil eye), *incantare* (= — by charms), 2, fig *capĕre, rapĕre, delenire, permulcēre* **enchantment,** n *(ef)fascinatio, carmen*

encircle, v tr see ENCLOSE

enclose, v tr *concludĕre, includĕre in re, cingĕre, saepire, continēre, circumdare alqd alci rei*, or *alqd alqâ re* to be enclosed by, *alqâ re cingi, circumdari, contineri* **enclosure,** n 1, = act of —, *inclusio*, 2, = enclosed place, *saeptum, locus saeptus, saepimentum, cohors*

encomium, n *laus, laudatio*, to pronounce an — on, *alqm laudare, dicĕre de alcjs laudibus*

encompass, v tr see ENCLOSE

encore, v tr *revocare* **encore!** interj *revoco*

encounter, I n *congressio, concursio, concursus, -ūs* (as soldiers in fight) II. v tr *inter se concurrĕre, (inter se) congredi, signa inter se conferre* (of armies), — a person, *concurrĕre* or *congredi cum alqo* (hostilely), *incidĕre in alqm* (= to meet by chance), *convenire, congredi cum alqo* (= to meet by design).

encourage, v.tr. *(ad)hortari, cohortari ad alqd* or with *ut*, *(con)firmare, excitare, impellĕre, alqm stimulare, alci stimulos admovēre*; — to concord, *concordiam suadēre*. **encouragement**, n. = act of —, *confirmatio, (ad)hortatio, cohortatio, impulsus, -ūs, hortamen(tum), incitamentum.*

encroach, v.intr. *alqd occupare, in alqd invadĕre*; — on one's rights, *alqd de jure alcjs deminuĕre.* **encroachment**, n. as an act, *vis, violatio*; as a result, *injuria illata.*

encumber, v.tr. †*gravare, onerare, praegravare, impedire*; — with burdens, *onera alci imponĕre.* **encumbrance**, n. *onus, -ĕris*, n. (= load), *impedimentum, molestia.*

end, I. n. **1**, = termination, *finis*, m. and f., *extremum, terminus* (= boundary), *exitus, -ūs, modus* (e.g. *nullus modus caedibus fuit*, there was no — to the slaughter), *clausula* (= the conclusion of a period, of a letter, etc.), *caput* (e.g. *capita funis*), *extremus* (e.g. *in extremâ oratione*, in the — of the speech); at the —, *in extremo* (in space), *ad extremum* (= lastly), *denique*; to bring to an —, *finem alci rei afferre, alqd ad finem adducĕre* or *perducĕre, alqd absolvĕre, alqd transigĕre, perficĕre, conficĕre, consummare*; the war has come to an —, *debellatum est*; **2**, = aim or object, *finis, consilium, propositum.* **II.** v.intr. *finem, exitum habēre, evenire, exire, terminari, finiri*, †*finire, desinĕre.* **III.** v.tr. *alqd finire, terminare*; — a speech, *finem facĕre orationis* or *dicendi*; — life, *vitam finire, vitam deponĕre, mortem sibi consciscĕre* (= — by suicide); — a strife, *controversiam dirimĕre.* **ending**, n. *finis, terminatio, exitus, -ūs.* **endless**, adj. *infinitus, perpetuus, aeternus, sempiternus.* Adv. *infinite, perpetuo, perpetuum.* **endlessness**, n. *quod finem non habet, perpetuitas.*

endanger, v.tr. *alqm in periculum, in discrimen adducĕre* or *vocare, periclitari.*

endear, v.tr. *alqm alci devincire.* **endearments**, n. *blanditiae.*

endeavour, I. n. *nisus, -ūs, contentio, opera, conatus, -ūs, studium*; — after honours, *honorum contentio, ambitio, ambitus, -ūs*; my — tends, *id ago, hoc specto ut*, etc. **II.** v.intr. *(e)niti, contendĕre*, comb. *eniti et contendĕre ut*, etc., *operam dare ut*, etc., *studēre, conari* (the two last with infin.).

endorse, v.tr. **1**, *syngrapham inscribĕre*; **2**, fig. see Allow, Sanction. **endorsement**, n. use verbs.

endow, v.tr. **1**, = — a daughter, *alci dotem dare*; **2**, in gen. *alqm alqâ re* or *alci alqd donare, alqm re instruĕre, augēre, ornare.* **endowed**, adj. *ornatus, praeditus, instructus.* **endowment**, n. *donatio*, or any word = property, *res*, etc.; see Property.

endue, v.tr. see Endow.

endure, v.tr. *ferre, sustinēre, tolerare, pati, perpeti*, comb. *ferre et perpeti, pati ac ferre, perpeti ac perferre.* **endurance**, n. *toleratio, tolerantia, perpessio*, comb. *perpessio et tolerantia.* **endurable**, adj. *tolerabilis, tolerandus, patibilis*; to make a thing —, *lenire, mitigare, levare* (*consuetudine levior fit labor*). **enduring**, adj. *perpetuus, perennis.*

enemy, n. *hostis* (= public —), *inimicus* (= private —); the —, *hostis*, sing. or pl.

energy, n. *vis, vigor, virtus, -ūtis*, f., *impetus, -ūs, contentio* (e.g. *vocis*). **energetic**, adj. *acer, strenuus, impiger, vehemens.* Adv. *acriter, strenue, impigre, vehementer.*

enervate, v.tr. *enervare, debilitare, (e)mollire, frangĕre.* **enervation**, n. *debilitatio.*

enfeeble, v.tr. see Enervate.

enforce, v.tr. **1**, = — an argument, *confirmare*; **2**, in gen. *vim alci rei dare* or *praebēre.*

enfranchise, v.tr. **1**, *alci civitatem dare, alqm in civitatem* or *civitati a(d)scribĕre, in civitatem a(d)sciscĕre, accipĕre, recipĕre, civitate donare*; **2**, = set free, *manumittĕre.* **enfranchisement**, n. **1**, *civitas*, or *civitatis donatio*; **2**, = setting free, *manumissio.*

engage, v.tr. **1**, = to fight with, *confligĕre cum alqo*; **2**, = to bind, *alqm obligare, obstringĕre*; **3**, = to secure the services of, *alqm mercede conducĕre*; **4**, = ask, *alqm invitare, excitare* (e.g. *ad saltandum*); **5**, — in conversation, *alqm appellare* (= address), *sermonem cum alqo incipĕre, instituĕre, conferre, se sermoni interniscēre*; **6**, = undertake, *spondēre, promittĕre, recipĕre* (accus. and infin.); **7**, — in, = enter upon, *alqd ingredi, inire, obire, suscipĕre.* **engaged**, adj. **1**, *occupatus*; **2**, = — in marriage, *sponsus, pactus.* **engagement**, **1**, = battle, *pugna, proelium*; **2**, = pledge, *sponsio, stipulatio, pactum, pactio, conventus, -ūs* (= agreement), *promissum* (= promise); to keep an —, *fidem praestare, servare*; = — in marriage, *pactio nuptialis*; **3**, = appointment, *constitutum*, or by verb; **4**, = business, *occupatio, negotium.* **engaging**, adj. *suavis*; — manners, *mores urbani.* Adv. *suaviter.*

engender, v.tr. **1**, *gignĕre, generare, (pro)creare*, comb. *creare et gignĕre, gignĕre et procreare*; **2**, fig. *facĕre, creare*; see Cause, Produce.

engine, n. *machina, machinatio, machinamentum, tormentum.* **engineer**, n. *faber* (= workman), *architectus, machinator, operum (publicorum) curator.*

engrave, v.tr. **1**, *scalpĕre, in alqâ re* or *alci rei* (e.g. *auro*) *incidĕre* (e.g. *leges*); **2**, fig. *in mentibus alqd insculpĕre.* **engraving**, n. as an art or work of art, *scalptura* (Plin.). **engraver**, n. *scalptor* (Plin.).

engross, v.tr. **1**, = buy up, *coëmĕre*; **2**, = to write in large letters, *magnis lit(t)eris scribĕre*; **3**, = occupy, *alqm occupare, tenēre.*

engulf, v.tr. **1**, *absorbēre, (de)vorare*; **2**, fig. *absorbēre, (ex)haurire.*

enhance, v.tr. **1**, = increase, *augēre, amplificare*; **2**, fig. *augēre, amplificare, ornare, exaggerare.* **enhancement**, n. *accessio, amplificatio.*

enigma, n. *aenigma, -ătis* n., *ambages, -um*; you speak in —, *ambages narras.* **enigmatical**, adj. *obscurus, perplexus, ambiguus.* Adv. *ambigue, per ambages, perplexe.*

enjoin, v.tr. see Command.

enjoy, v.tr. *frui, gaudēre, uti re* (e.g. *prosperrimâ valetudine*), *florēre re* (e.g. *justitiae famâ*), *voluptatem capĕre* or *percipĕre ex re.* **enjoyment**, n. *gaudium, fructus, -ūs, usus, -ūs, voluptas, suavitas, oblectatio, delectatio.*

enkindle, v.tr. *accendĕre, incendĕre, inflammare* (scil. *animos, discordiam, odium*, etc.).

enlarge, v.tr. *amplificare, dilatare* (opp. *coartare*, e.g. *castra, aciem, imperium*), *proferre, prolatare*, or *propagare* (= to extend, e.g. *imperii fines, imperium*), *augēre* (= to increase); — one's knowledge, *alqd addiscĕre*; — upon, *alqâ re pluribus (verbis) disputare.* **enlargement**, n. *amplificatio, propagatio, prolatio, incrementum.*

enlighten, v.tr. **1**, lit. *illustrare, illuminare*; **2**, fig. *alqm docēre, erudire, fingĕre.* **enlightenment**, n. *humanitas, mens exculta* or *perpolita.*

enlist, I. v tr *milites conscribĕre, comparare, sacramento adigĕre, obligare, conquirĕre* **II.** v intr *nomen dare, profitēri, sacramentum dicĕre* **enlistment,** n use verbs

enliven, v tr *alqm (ex)hilarare, laetificare*

enmity, n *inimicitia, odium, simultas*

ennoble, v tr 1, *alqm nobilium ordini a(d)scribĕre*, in the Roman sense, *transitio fit a plebe ad patricios*, 2, fig *ornare, excolĕre, illustrare*

ennui, n *taedium*

enormous, adj *ingens, immanis, immensus, mirā or incredibili magnitudine* Adv *praeter modum*, or by superl of adj (e g — high, *altissimus*) **enormity,** n *res atrox or nefanda, scelus, ĕris*, n, *facinus, -ŏris*, n

enough, adj *sat, satis* (e g *satis consilii*), *affatim*, more than —, *abunde, satis superque*, not —, *parum* (opp *nimis*), but — ! *sed haec hactenus*

enquire, v tr 1, see Ask, 2, — into, *de alqâ re quaerĕre, in alqd (de) alqa re inquirĕre*, — … or *de alqâ re cognoscĕre* **enquiry,** n 1, see Question, 2 legal t t *quaestio, inquisitio, cognitio*, 3, = investigation, *inquisitio, investigatio*, see Enquire

enrage, v tr *alcjs exasperare, inflammare, alqm lacessĕre*, to be enraged, *furore incendi* or *inflammari*

enrapture, v tr *alqm oblectare, capĕre*

enrich, v tr *locupletare, locupletem facĕre, ditare, divitiis ornare*

enrobe, v tr *induĕre alci vestem* or *alqm veste*

enroll, v tr *inscribĕre, consignare*, see Enlist

enshrine, v tr *dedicare* (lit), *(con)secrare* (lit. and fig)

ensign, n 1, *signum (militare), vexillum*, 2, an officer, *signifer, aquilifer, vexillarius*

enslave, v tr *alqm in servitutem redigĕre, alci servitutem injungĕre, alqm servitute afficĕre* **enslaved,** adj *alci rei addictus*, to be —, *alci rei (in)servire*

ensnare, v tr 1, *illaqueare* (lit. late, fig Hor), *laqueo capĕre, irretire*, 2, fig *irretire, illicĕre, capĕre*

entail, v tr 1, *terram heredi ita addicĕre ut nunquam alienari possit*, 2, fig see Cause

entanglement, n *implicatio*

enter, I. v intr *introire, inire, ingredi*, — a port, *in portum venire, invehi, deferri*, — upon, *inire, suscipĕre*, — into, *coire, facĕre* (e g *societatem*), — public life, *ad rempublicam accedĕre, remp capessĕre*, — an office, *munus inire, ingredi, capessĕre, suscipĕre* **II.** v tr = — accounts, *in tabulas referre*, — as paid, *alqd alci expensum (re)ferre* **entrance,** n 1, = act of —, *ingressio, introitus, -ūs*, 2, = place of —, *aditus, ūs, os, ostium, janua* (= gate), *limen* (= threshold), *introitus, -ūs*, 3, = beginning, *initium*, at — of spring, *primo vere* **entry** 1, see Entrance, 2, = — in accounts, *nomen* (e g *nomen in tabulas referre*, make an —)

enterprise, n *inceptum, conatus, ūs, conata, orum, opus, -ĕris*, n, *facinus, ŏris*, n **enterprising,** adj *acer, strenuus, impiger, audax*

entertain v tr 1, = to have, *habēre*, 2, = to amuse, *delectare, oblectare*, 3, = to give hospitality to, *hospitio accipĕre, recipĕre, excipĕre* **entertainer,** n *hospes, -itis*, m and f **entertainment,** n 1 = hospitality, *hospitium*, 2, = banquet, *epulae*, † *daps* or *dapes, convivium*, 3, see Amusement **entertaining,** adj, see Amusing

enthusiasm, n *inflammatio animi, mentis incitatio et permotio, mens incitata, aestus, ūs*, or *fervor (ingenii), ardor (animi), furor divinus*, † *mens furibunda* **enthusiast,** n 1, = religious —, † *homo entheus, divino spiritu tactus, homo fanaticus*, 2, = given to anything, *alci rei addictus, deditus* **enthusiastic,** adj 1, *entheus, fanaticus*, † *furens* 2, *ardens, acer, vehemens* Adv *ardenter, acriter, vehementer*

entice, v tr *allicĕre, illicĕre, pellicĕre* **enticement,** n *illecebrae* **enticing,** adj *blandus, dulcis* or pres part of verb Adv *blande*

entire, adj *totus, integer, solidus* Adv *omnino, plane, prorsus* **entireness, entirety,** n by *totus*

entitle, v tr 1, = to name, *inscribĕre* (a writing), 2, = to give a right to, *jus* or *potestatem alqd faciendi dare*, I am entitled to, *facĕre alqd possum, mei est alqd facĕre*

entomb, v tr *humare*

entrails, n *intestina, orum, viscera, -um, exta, -orum*

entrap, v tr 1, *irretire* (= — by a net), *inescare* (= — by bait), 2, fig *irretire, illicĕre*

entreat, v tr *precari, rogare, orare, petĕre, supplicare*, see Ask

entrust, v tr *(con)credĕre, commendare et concredere, committĕre, permittĕre, mandare, commendare* (all with *alqd alci*), *deponĕre alqd apud alqm*

entwine, v tr *innectĕre alqd alci rei, alqd alqa re redimire*

enumerate, v tr *(an)numerare, dinumerare, enumerare*

enunciate, v tr *edicĕre, indicare, pronuntiare, enuntiare* **enunciation,** n *enuntiatio*

envelope, I. v tr *involvĕre, obducĕre* **II.** n *involucrum, integumentum*

envenom, v tr 1, *alqd veneno imbuĕre*, 2, fig *alqm exasperare, exacerbare* **envenomed,** adj see Spiteful

environ, v tr *circumdare, circumsistere* **environs,** n *loca quae circumjacent alci loco, quae circum alqm locum sunt*

envoy, n *legatus*, see Ambassador

envy, I. n *invidia, livor, malignitas, obtrectatio, malevolentia* **II.** v tr *invidēre alci*, — something, *alci alqd invidēre* (e g *invidere alci honorem, nullius equidem invideo honori*, = I — no one's honour), I am envied, *invidetur mihi, in invidiâ sum, invidiae sum* **enviable,** adj † *invidendus, fortunatus, beatus* **envious,** adj *invidus, lividus, malignus* Adv *cum invidiâ, maligne*

ephemeral, adj *unius diei, caducus, brevis*

epic, adj *epicus, herōus, herōicus*, — poem, *epos* (in nom and accus only)

Epicurean, n 1, = a follower of Epicurus, *Epicurēus*, 2, = a lover of pleasure, *homo delicatus* or *luxuriosus*

epidemic, adj and n *morbus, pestilentia, lues, is*, f

epigram, n *epigramma, -ătis*, n **epigrammatic,** adj *epigrammaticus* (late), *salsus*

epilepsy, n *morbus comitialis*

epilogue, n *epilŏgus*

episcopal, adj *episcopalis* (eccl) **episcopacy,** n *episcopatus, ūs* (eccl)

episode, n *embolium, excursus, ūs, digressio, digressus, ūs* (= digression)

epistle, n *epistula* **epistolary,** adj *lit(t)eris* or *per lit(t)eras*

epitaph n *titulus* [illegible]

epithalamium, n. *epithalamium, carmen nuptiale.*

epithet, n. *epitheton* (Quint.).

epitome, n. *epitome, summarium* (Sen.). **epitomize,** v.tr. *epitomen facĕre.*

epoch, n. *tempus, -ŏris,* n., *tempestas, aetas, saeculum.*

equal, I. adj. *aequus, similis, geminus* (= twin), comb. *aequus et par, aequalis et par, par et aequalis, par et similis, par atque idem, par atque unus;* — to each other, *compar* (scil. † *connubium*), † *parilis, inter se aequales;* not —, *dispar, impar, dissimilis;* to divide into twelve — parts, *in duodecim partes aequaliter dividĕre;* — to doing anything, *ad alqd faciendum sufficiens.* Adv. *aeque, aequaliter, pariter.* **II.** n. *par.* **III.** v.tr. *alqd cum alqâ re a(d)aequare, aequiparare* (more rarely with dat.). **equality,** n. *aequalitas, aequabilitas.* **equable,** adj. *aequus, aequabilis, aequalis sibi, constans (sibi), stabilis.* Adv. *aequo animo, aequabiliter, constanter, aequaliter.* **equability,** n. *constantia, aequus animus, aequabilitas, stabilitas.* **equalize,** v.tr. *alqm* or *alqd alci (rei) (ex)aequare, adaequare.*

equanimity, n. *aequus animus, aequitas animi, aequa mens, constantia.*

equator, n. *circulus aequinoctialis.*

equerry, n. *equiso, tribunus stabuli* (under the emperors).

equestrian, I. adj. *equester, equestris.* **II.** n. *eques, -itis.*

equiangular, adj. *angulis aequis* or *paribus.*

equidistant, adj. *pari intervallo, aequis* or *paribus intervallis distantes inter se.*

equiformity, n. *aequabilitas.*

equilateral, adj. *aequis* or *paribus lateribus.*

equilibrium, n. *aequilibrium* (Sen.); in —, *pari momento libratus.*

equinox, n. *aequinoctium.* **equinoctial,** adj. *aequinoctialis.*

equip, v.tr. *armare, instruĕre, ornare.* **equipment,** n. *arma, -orum, armatura instrumenta, -orum, navalia* (of ships).

equipoise, n. see EQUILIBRIUM.

equitable, adj. *aequus, justus, meritus* (= deserved); it is —, *aequum, par, jus, fas est* (with infin. or infin. and accus.). **equity,** n. *aequitas, aequum bonum, justitia, moderatio;* contrary to —, *contra fas, contra quam fas est, contra jus fasque.*

equivalent, adj. see EQUAL.

equivocal, adj. *aequivocus, ambiguus, anceps, dubius, dubius et quasi duplex.* **equivocation,** n. *ex ambiguo dictum, ambiguitas, amphibolia.* **equivocate,** v.intr. *tergiversari.*

era, n. *temporum ratio.*

eradicate, v.tr. *eradicare* (ante-class.), *ex(s)tirpare; (e)vellĕre, extrahĕre, evellĕre et extrahĕre, eruĕre, delēre, exstinguĕre, excīdĕre, eradĕre, tollĕre.* **eradication,** n. *ex(s)tirpatio, ex(s)tinctio, excidium.*

erase, v.tr. *delēre, inducĕre* (= to cover with the broad end of the stylus), *(e)radĕre.* **erasure,** n. *litura.*

ere, adv. *priusquam, antĕquam;* see BEFORE.

erect, I. adj. *(e)rectus.* **II.** v.tr. *erigĕre* (= set straight up), *aedificare* (= build), *exstruĕre* (= raise). **erection,** n. 1, as act, *aedificatio, ex(s)tructio;* 2, = building, *aedificium.*

erotic, adj. *amatorius.*

err, v.intr. *errare, vagari, in errore versari, errore captum esse* (= to be in error), *falli* (= to be misled), *peccare* (= to sin). **error,** n. *error, erratum* (= a single act), *lapsus, -ūs* (= a slip or fall), *peccatum* (= a sin); to commit —, *errare, peccare.* **erratic,** adj. *inconstans.* **erroneous,** adj. *falsus.* Adv. *falso.* **erroneousness,** n. see ERROR.

errand, n. *mandatum;* an —-boy, *nuntius, tabellarius.*

erst, adv. *quondam, olim.*

erudite, adj. *lit(t)eratus, doctus, doctrinâ instructus, eruditus, eruditione ornatus;* comb. *doctus atque eruditus.* **erudition,** n. *doctrina, eruditio.*

eruption, n. *eruptio* (e.g. *Ætnaeorum ignium*).

escape, I. v.tr. *alqd (ef)fugĕre, subterfugĕre* (secretly), *evadĕre ex alqâ re, ab alqo, elabi ex alqâ re;* — a danger, *periculum vitare, effugĕre;* it —s me, *me praeterit, me fugit alqd.* **II.** v.intr. *(ef)fugĕre, elabi, evadĕre.* **III.** n. *vitatio, devitatio, fuga, effugium.*

escarpment, n. *vallum.*

escheat, I. n. *hereditas caduca* (Jct.). **II.** v.intr. *caducum esse* (Jct.).

eschew, v.tr. *vitare;* see AVOID.

escort, I. n. *comitatus, -ūs;* under someone's —, *alqo comite* or *comitante, comitatu* or *cum comitatu alcjs, cum alqo, ab alqo deductus* (as mark of honour). **II.** v.tr. *alqm comitari, deducĕre, prosequi, alci (rei) praesidio esse* (as a defence).

esculent, adj. *esculentus.*

esoteric, adj. *arcanus, occultus.*

especial, adj. *praecipuus, maximus, summus;* he had an — care for, *nihil antiquius habuit quam ut..* Adv. *praesertim, praecipue, maxime, in primis (imprimis), summe.*

esplanade, n. *ambulatio.*

espouse, v.tr. 1, see BETROTH; 2, see MARRY; 3, fig. see EMBRACE.

esquire, n. * *armiger.*

essay, I. v.tr. *conari.* **II.** n. 1, = an attempt, *experimentum, conatus, -ūs, conata, -orum;* 2, = treatise, *libellus.* **essayist,** n. *scriptor.*

essence, n. *natura, vis, proprietas;* it is the — of affection, *amicitia vera est,* or *amicitiae (proprium) est.* **essential,** adj. *verus, primus, praecipuus, proprius, in alcjs rei naturâ positus.* Adv. *reapse, vere, praecipue, imprimis, necessario;* to be — different, *ipsâ rei naturâ diversum esse.*

establish, v.tr. 1, = to set up, *statuĕre, constituĕre;* 2, = to make strong, *confirmare, stabilire;* 3, = to prove, *probare, confirmare.* **establishment,** n. 1, = act of —, *constitutio, conciliatio* (e.g. *gratiae*), *confirmatio;* 2, = household, *familia.*

estate, n. 1, = condition, *ratio, status, -ūs, habitus, -ūs, condicio, res, fortuna, sors;* 2, = property, *res, fundus, praedium, ager, possessio.*

esteem, I. n. 1, = opinion, *aestimatio, opinio, existimatio;* 2, = reverence, *observantia* (shown outwardly); to feel —, *alqm verēri.* **II.** v.tr. 1, = think, *aestimare, existimare, putare, habēre;* 2, = reverence, *alqm respicĕre, verēri, magni facĕre alqm;* to be esteemed, *magni haberi* (the genitives *maximi, minimi, nihili, pluris,* etc., may be employed). **estimable,** adj. *dignus alqâ re,* or *qui* with subj., *laudatus, bonus, optimus, honestus, gravis, probus.*

estimate, I. n. 1, = — in money, *aestimatio;*

2, = judgment, *judicium, aestimatio* **II.** v tr 1, *alqd aestimare* (with genit or abl of price), *censēre*, 2, see ESTEEM **estimation,** n see ESTEEM

estrange, v tr *(ab)alienare*, — from yourself, *alqm* or *alcjs voluntatem a se alienare, alienare sibi alcjs animum* **estrangement,** n *alienatio, discidium*

estuary, n *aestuarium*

eternal, adj *aeternus, sempiternus, immortalis, perpetuus*, — enmity, *odium inexpiabile* Adv *in aeternum, perpetuo, semper* **eternity,** n *aeternitas*, for —, *in aeternum, in perpetuum, in omne tempus*

ether, n *aether* **ethereal,** adj *aetherius* (*aethereus*)

ethics, n *de moribus*, or *officiis, ethice* (Quint) **ethical,** adj *de moribus* or *officiis, quod ad mores pertinet, moralis* (invented by Cicero)

etiquette, n *mos, moris*, m, *usus, ūs*

etymology, n = derivation, *etymologia, etymologice, explicatio verborum*

eucharist, n * *eucharistia*

eulogy, n *laudatio, laus* **eulogist,** n *laudator* **eulogize,** v tr *laudare*

eunuch, n *eunūchus*

euphemism, n, **euphemistic,** adj *ut bona de his loquar*

euphony, n *sonus, -ūs, dulcis* or *suavis*

evacuate, v tr *(de)relinquĕre locum, (de) cedere loco* or *de* or *ex loco, discedĕre a loco* or *loco* or *ex loco, excedĕre loco* or *ex loco*, to — a town (with troops), *ab alqo loco milites deducĕre*

evade, v tr *de* or *ex alcjs manibus elabi, de alcjs manibus effugĕre, alcjs manibus* or *alci elabi, alqm subterfugĕre* **evasion,** n *ambages, -is*, f, usu in pl, *tergiversatio* **evasive,** adj *ambiguus* Adv *ambigue*

evangelist, n * *evangelista* **evangelical,** adj * *evangelicus*

evaporate, **I.** v tr *(e)vaporare, exhalare, ex(s)pirare* **II.** v intr *(e)vaporari, exhalari, ex(s)pirari* **evaporation,** n *(e)vaporatio, exhalatio, ex(s)piratio*

even, adj *aequus, planus*, comb *aequus et planus*, of temper, *aequus, aequabilis*, of numbers, *par* Adv *aequaliter, aequabiliter, pariter* **evenness,** n *aequalitas* (Plin), — of temper, *aequus animus*

even, adv *etiam, vel* (esp with superl or single words), *adeo, ipse* (e g *ipsa amicitia*), not —, *ne quidem*, — now, *jam nunc*

evening, **I.** n *vesper, -ĕris* or *-ĕri*, *tempus vespertinum, occasus, ūs, solis* (= sunset), towards —, *ad (sub) vesperum, sub occasum solis*, in the —, *vesperi*, the — before, *pridie vesperi*, yesterday —, *heri vesperi*, good — ! *salve*, I wish good — to anyone, *salvēre alqm jubeo* **II.** adj *vespertinus*, — star, *Hesperus, Vesper*

event, n 1, = issue, *eventus, -ūs, exitus ūs*, 2, = occurrence, *res (gesta) factum, casus, ūs, eventus, -ūs* **eventful,** adj *memorabilis, ille* (e g. *ille dies* = that — day), *magni* or *maximi momenti*

ever, adv 1, = always, *semper, perpetuo*, the best is — the rarest, *optimum quidque rarissimum est*, 2, = at any time, *umquam (unq), (ali)quando*, if —, *si quando*, — so great, *quantumvis* or *quamvis magnus*, for —, *in aeternum*. **everlasting,** adj see ETERNAL

every, adj *quisque, quique, quilibet, quivis omnis*, — one, each separately, *unusquisque* — five days there were two days for hunting, *binae venationes per dies quinque*, — day, etc, *singulis diebus, mensibus, annis*, also *quot diebus, mensibus, annis*, and *in singulas horas* or merely *in horas*, each of two, *uterque*, — person, — one, *nemo non* or *nemo est quin* or *nemo est qui non* (e g — one holds *nemo est quin existimet*), — one knows, *nemo est qui nesciat*, — where, *ubique, ubivis, nusquam*

evict, v tr *alqo loco (ex)pellĕre, de alqo loco detrudĕre, deturbare* **eviction,** n *evictio* (Jct), or by verb

evident, adj *certus, manifestus, apertus, evidens, perspicuus*, it is —, *constat, certum est, liquet* (with accus and infin). Adv. *aperte, manifeste, perspicue, evidenter* **evidence,** n 1, legal t t. *testimonium, indicium*, 2, in gen. *argumentum*, or by verb *probare*

evil, **I.** adj *malus, perversus, maleficus* **II.** n *malum, incommodum* (= inconvenience), to be in —, *in malis esse*, to suffer under some —, *laborare ex alqā re* (e g *ex pedibus*) **evil-doer,** n *maleficus* **evil-speaking,** adj *maledicus*

evince, v tr *ostendĕre, probare, (e)vincĕre*

evoke, v tr *evocare, elicĕre, excitare*

evolve, v tr *evolvĕre, explicare* **evolution,** n 1, = — of soldiers, *decursus, ūs*, 2, = — of nature, *rerum progressio*

ewe, n *ovis femina*

ewer, n *urceus, hydria, urna*

exacerbate, v tr see EMBITTER

exact, **I.** adj *exactus, accuratus, expressus* **II.** v tr *alqd ab alqo exigĕre, alci alqd* or *alqd ab alqo extorquēre, alqd alci imperare* Adv *accurate*, — so, *ita plane*, or *prorsus* **exacting,** adj *rapax* **exaction,** n *exactio* **exactitude,** **exactness,** n *diligentia, accuratio* (rare)

exaggerate, v tr *verbis exaggerare, multiplicare verbis* (e g *copias*), *verbis augēre, in majus (verbis) extollĕre, in majus accipĕre* **exaggeration,** n *(nimia) amplificatio, veritatis superlatio, trajectio*

exalt, v tr *augēre, majus reddĕre, verbis* or *laudibus efferre* or *extollĕre* **exaltation,** n *dignitatis accessio* **exalted,** adj *altus (ex)celsus*, of — position, *gradu amplissimo*

examine, v tr *explorare, ponderare, inquirĕre, (per)scrutari* **examination,** n *scrutatio, inquisitio, probatio* **examiner,** n in gen *investigator*, of a school, *qui quid profecerint pueri exquirit*

example, n *exemplum, exemplar, documentum*, to set an —, *exemplum praebēre*

exasperate, v tr *exasperare*

excavate, v tr *(ex)cavare, effodĕre* **excavation,** n *cavum*

exceed, v tr *transgredi, excedĕre, transire fines* (lit. and fig), *terminos egredi* (fig), *modum egredi* or *excedĕre, ultra modum egredi* **excess,** n *intemperantia, licentia, luxuria* **excessive,** adj *nimius, immodicus, immoderatus* Adv *nimis, immodice, immoderate, praeter modum*

excel, v tr *excellĕre (ingenio, virtute animi magnitudine, dignitate*, also *in alqa re*), *alqm in re (ex)superare, alci (in) alqā re praestare* **excellent,** adj *excellens, praestans, egregius, bonus, optimus, laudatus, praecipuus* Adv. *excellenter, egregie, bene, optime, praecipue imprimis (in primis)* **excellence,** n *excellentia, praestantia*

except, **I.** v tr *excipĕre, eximĕre, excludĕre*, — from military service, *vacationem militiae alci dare*, not one excepted, *ad unum omnes* or *omnes ad unum.* **II.** prep. *praeter, extra,* accus. past partic. of *excipĕre* in abl. abs. (e.g. *te excepto*). *nisi* after a neg. (e.g. *nisi in te nullam spem habeo*). **exception,** n. *exceptio.* **exceptional,** adj. *rarus.* Adv. *praeter modum.*

exchange, I. v.tr. *(per)mutare;* — letters, *lit(t)eras dare et accipĕre.* **II.** n. **1,** = changing, *(per)mutatio, vices* (= turns); **2,** of money, *collybus;* 3, = the place of —, *forum, mensa publica.*

exchequer, n. *aerarium, fiscus.*

excite, v.tr. *excitare, concitare, (com)movēre;* — pity, etc., *misericordiam, seditionem, bellum mov.* or *com., conflare* (e.g. *bellum, alci invidiam*); — a controversy, *controversiam inferre.* **excitable,** adj. *iracundus, fervidus.* **excited,** adj. *commotus.* **excitement,** n. *concitatio, commotio, motus, -ūs.*

exclaim, v.tr. *exclamare, conclamare* (of several). **exclamation,** n. *exclamatio, acclamatio, vox.*

exclude, v.tr. *excludĕre, prohibēre, (ab) alqo loco arcēre.* **exclusion,** n. *exclusio* (rare), or by verb. **exclusive,** adj. = — in choice of acquaintance, *parum affabilis, qui rari aditus est;* — property, *quod alci proprium est.* Adv. by adj. *proprius.* **exclusiveness,** n. *rari aditus esse.*

excommunicate, v.tr. *sacrificiis interdicĕre alci, alqm *excommunicare.* **excommunication,** n. *sacrificiorum interdictio, *excommunicatio.*

excrement, n. *excrementum, stercus, -ŏris,* n. **excrescence,** n. *gibber, -ĕris,* m. (Plin. = a hunch), *tuber, -ĕris,* m. (= protuberance).

excruciating, adj. *acerbissimus.*

exculpate, v.tr. *excusare, (ex)purgare;* — with someone, *alci* or *apud alqm excusare;* — yourself, *se excusare de re.* **exculpation,** n. *excusatio, purgatio.*

excursion, n. *iter, -ĭneris;* to make an —, *excurrĕre* (e.g. *rus*).

excuse, I. v.tr. **1,** = ask for pardon, *veniam petĕre, rogare, se alci* or *apud alqm excusare, (ex)purgare;* 2, = grant pardon, *veniam alci dare, alci ignoscĕre.* **II.** n. 1, *excusatio;* 2, *venia;* 3, see PRETEXT. **excusable,** adj. *cui ignosci potest.*

execrate, v.tr. *exsecrari, detestari, abominari;* see CURSE. **execrable,** adj. see ABOMINABLE.

execute, v.tr. 1, = to carry into effect, *exsequi, persequi* (e.g. *alcjs mandata;* — a command, *imperium*), *efficĕre, perficĕre, ad effectum adducĕre;* **2,** = to inflict punishment, *poenam capĕre* or *poenas exigĕre de alqo, supplicium de alqo sumĕre, necare.* **execution,** n. 1, *effectio,* or by verb; **2,** *supplicium;* **3,** = — on goods, *bonorum venditio, emptio;* **4,** = slaughter, *caedes, -is.* **executive,** n. *penes quos est administratio rerum.*

exegesis, n. *explanatio, interpretatio.*

exemplary, adj. see EXCELLENT; — punishment, *exemplum severitatis.*

exempt, I. v.tr. *excipĕre, eximĕre, immunem facĕre, vacationem dare, gratiam facĕre alci alcjs rei.* **II.** adj. *(ab alqâ re) immunis, alqâ re liber, solutus;* — from further service (of a soldier), *emeritus.* **exemption,** n. *immunitas, vacatio.*

exercise, I. v.tr. 1, = carry on, *exercēre, facĕre, agĕre, alqâ re fungi;* 2, physically, *exercēre* (e.g. *se, milites,* etc.). **II.** n. 1, *munus, -ĕris,* n.; 2, *exercitatio;* 3, = theme, *thema, -ătis* (Quint.).

exert, v.tr. 1, *contendĕre, intendĕre;* — yourself, *(con)niti, eniti, conari;* 2, see USE, EMPLOY, EXERCISE. **exertion,** n. *contentio, intentio, conatus, -ūs.*

exhale, v.tr. *exhalare;* odours are exhaled, *odores (e floribus) afflantur;* see EVAPORATE. **exhalation,** n. *exhalatio.*

exhaust, v.tr. *exhaurire* (lit. and fig.), *conficĕre.* **exhausted,** adj. see WEARY. **exhaustion,** n. see FATIGUE.

exhibit, v.tr. 1, *proponĕre, ante oculos ponĕre, edĕre, celebrare;* **2,** = manifest, *praebēre.* **exhibition,** n. 1, = act of —, by verb; **2,** = show, *spectaculum, ludi.*

exhilarate, v.tr. *(ex)hilarare* (e.g. *vultum*), *hilarem facĕre.* **exhilaration,** n. *animi relaxatio, oblectatio.*

exhort, v.tr. *hortari;* see ADMONISH, ENCOURAGE.

exigence, n. *necessitas, angustiae.*

exile, I. n. 1, = banishment, *ex(s)ilium, relegatio;* **2,** = person banished, *exsul, extorris, †profugus.* **II.** v.tr. *e(j)icĕre, exterminare, relegare, deportare* (Tac.), *(ex)pellĕre, alci aquâ et igni interdicĕre.*

exist, v.intr. *ex(s)istĕre, esse, exstare.* **existence,** n. use *esse* (e.g. to believe in the — of gods, *deos esse putare*); I have means of —, *habeo unde utar.*

exit, n. **1,** = going away, *exitus, egressus, abitus,* all *-ūs;* 2, = way out, *exitus, effugium, janua.*

exonerate, v.tr. see EXCULPATE.

exorbitant, adj. *immodicus, immoderatus.* Adv. *immodice, immoderate.*

exordium, n. *exordium, exorsus, -ūs, prooemium.*

exoteric, adj. *quod ἐξωτερικὸν vocant, exotericus* (Gell.).

exotic, adj. *peregrinus, externus.*

expand, v.tr. see SPREAD. **expanse,** n. *spatium.*

expatiate, v.tr. *uberius* or *pluribus (verbis) disputare, dicĕre, longum esse in alqâ re.*

expatriate, v.tr. see BANISH.

expect, v.tr. *ex(s)pectare, opperiri alqm* or *alqd; sperare* (with *fore ut, spem habēre alcjs rei,* or with accus. and infin.); a less slaughter than might have been —ed, *minor clades quam pro tantâ victoriâ fuit.* **expectant,** adj. use *spes* or *ex(s)pectatio,* or verb, or *arrectus.* **expectation,** n. *ex(s)pectatio, spes, opinio.*

expectorate, v.tr. *exscreare* (e.g. *sanguinem*), *exspuĕre.* **expectoration,** n. 1, *exscreatio* (= act of —) (Plin.); **2,** *sputum* (= matter of —) (Cels.).

expedient, I. adj. *commodus, utilis;* it is —, *expedit.* **II.** n. *ratio;* no useful — is at hand, *nullum consilium in promptu est;* to find an —, *viam invenire, viam consilii invenire.* **expediency,** n. *utilitas.*

expedite, v.tr. *expedire, maturare.* **expedition,** n. 1, = speed, *celeritas;* **2,** = military —, *expeditio.* **expeditious,** adj. *celer, promptus, maturus.* Adv. *celeriter, prompte, mature.*

expel, v.tr. *(ex)pellĕre re* or *a re* or *ex re, depellĕre alqm re, de re* or *ex re, exigĕre re* or *ex re, e(j)icĕre re, de, ex* or *ab re.* **expulsion,** n. *exactio, expulsio.*

expend, v.tr. *expendĕre, impendĕre, erogare* (of public money); — much money, *magnos sumptus facĕre; pecuniam profundĕre.* **expense,** n. *impensa, impendium, dispendium, sumptus, -ūs.* **expensive,** adj. *sumptuosus, carus, pretiosus, magni pretii.* Adv. *sumptuose, pretiose.* **expenditure,** n. *rogatio, sumptus, -ūs.*

experience, I. n *usus, -ūs, experientia, prudentia* (= wisdom that is the result of —), — in nautical matters, *scientia atque usus rerum nauticarum*, I write from —, *expertus scribo quod scribo* **II.** v tr *experiri*, (*usu*) *discĕre* or *cognoscĕre*, *experientiā discĕre*, *usu alqd mihi venit* **experienced,** adj (*usu*) *peritus*, *usu atque exercitatione praeditus*, *multarum rerum peritus*, *peritus alcjs rei*, *exercitatus*, *versatus in re* **experiment,** n *experimentum*, *periclitatio*, *periculum*, an unfortunate —, *res infeliciter tentata* **experimental,** adj and adv *usu* or *experimentis cognitus*

expert, adj & n *alci rei* or *ad alqd aptus*, *idoneus*, *alcjs rei compos*, *alcjs rei peritus*, *in alqâ re exercitatus*, *callidus*, *sol(l)ers* **expertness,** n *calliditas*, *sol(l)ertia*

expiate, v tr *alqd luĕre*, *expiare*, *poenas alcjs rei dare*, *pendĕre*, *dependĕre*, *rependĕre*, *solvĕre* **expiation,** n *satisfactio*, *poena*, *piaculum* **expiatory,** adj *piacularis*

expire, v intr *ex(s)pirare*, *animam*, *extremum spiritum edĕre*, see Die **expiration,** n by abl abs (e g at the — of the year, *anno exeunte*, *finito jam anno*)

explain, v tr *exponĕre*, *expedire*, *explanare*, *explicare*, *interpretari*, *aperire*, *enodare*, *illustrare* **explanation,** n *explicatio*, *explanatio*, *interpretatio*, *enodatio* **explanatory,** adj use verb

explicit, adj *apertus*, *dilucidus*, *definitus* Adv *dilucide*, *plane disserte*, *definite*

explode, I. v intr (*di*)*rumpi* **II** v tr (*di*)*rumpĕre*, *refellĕre*, *confutare*, *refutare* (an opinion) **explosion,** n *fragor*, *crepitus*, *-ūs*

export, v tr *exportare* (opp *importare*) **exportation,** n *exportatio* **exports,** n *merces* (*quae exportantur*)

expose, v tr **1,** *exponĕre*, — a child, *infantem exponĕre*, — to anything *opponĕre*, *ob(j)icĕre*, *offerre alci rei*, **2,** = to lay open, *detegĕre* (e g *latentem culpam*), **3,** = make bare, *nudare* **exposition,** n *expositio*, see Explanation **exposure,** n by verb

expound, v tr see Explain

express, I. v tr *exprimĕre significare*, *declarare*, *demonstrare*, *verbis consequi*, *exsequi*, — oneself, *loqui*, *dicĕre* **II** adj **1,** = Exact, **2,** = quick, *celer* Adv *his ipsis verbis* **expression,** n **1,** *verbum*, *sententia*, *vocabulum*, *dictum*, *vox*; **2,** of the features, etc, *vultus*, *-ūs*, *argutiae* (= animation) void of —, *languens*, *languidus* (as in the countenance, the voice, etc) **expressive,** adj *significans*, *gravis* (= with strength, of a speaker), by *vis* (e g it is most —, *vim habet magnam*) Adv *significanter* (Quint), *plane*, *diserte* **expressiveness,** n *argutiae* (= lively —, of face, etc), *gravitas* (= — of speech)

expunge, v tr *delēre*, *inducĕre*, (*e*)*radĕre* (Tac)

expurgate, v tr (*ex*)*purgare* **expurgation,** n (*ex*)*purgatio* (= freeing from blame)

exquisite, adj *exquisitus*, *conquisitus*, *egregius*, *venustus*, — tortures, *supplicia exquisita*, *pulcher* Adv *exquisite*, *egregie*, *pulchre*, *venuste*

extant, adj, to be — (*superstitem*) *esse*, *exstare*, *ex(s)istere*

extemporary, adj *subitus*, *subitus et fortuitus*, power of — speaking, *ex tempore dicendi facultas*

extend, I. v tr = stretch out enlarge, *extendĕre*, *distendere*, *augēre*, *propagare*, *amplificare* **II.** v intr *patēre*, *extendi distendi*, etc **extension,** n *porrectio* (e g *digitorum*), *productio*, *prolatio*, *propagatio* **extensive,** adj *magnus*, *amplus*, *late patens*, *latus* Adv *late* **extent,** n *ambitus*, *-ūs*, *spatium*, *circuitus* *-ūs*, to have a wide —, *latius patere*

extenuate, v tr *attenuare*, *extenuare* (opp to *amplificare*), — guilt, (*culpam*, etc) *levare*, *mitigare* **extenuation,** n *extenuatio*, *levatio*, *mitigatio*

exterior, I. adj see External **II.** n *facies*, *forma*, *species*, *figura*

exterminate, v tr *ad unum interficĕre*, *interimĕre* (= kill), *eradicare*, *ex(s)tirpare* (= root out)

external, adj *externus*, *exterior*, — advantages, *bona externa*, *bona corporis* Adv *extrinsecus*

extinct, adj *exstinctus*, *obsoletus*

extinguish, v tr — a fire, *ex(s)tinguĕre*, *restinguĕre*, *compescĕre*, *delēre* (= blot out)

extirpate, v tr *ex(s)tirpare*, see Exterminate

extol, v tr *augēre*, *ornare*, *laudibus* (*ef*)*ferre*, *extollĕre*, *verbis efferre*

extort, v tr *exprimĕre alci alqd* or *alqd ab alqo expugnare alqd alci*, *alqd expilare*, *alci alqd extorquēre* **extortion,** n *res repetundae* **extortionate,** adj *rapax*, *avarus* Adv *avare* **extortioner,** n *immodici fenoris exactor*

extra, adv *praeterea*

extract, I. v tr **1** *extrahĕre*, (*e*)*vellĕre*, **2,** = to make an extract, *excerpĕre*, **3,** = to press out *exprimere* **II.** n **1,** = — of a book, *exceptio* (Gell), *quod excerptum est*, **2,** = — of a plant, etc *sucus qui expressus est*, *quod expressum est* **extraction,** n as to origin, *origo*, *genus*, *-ĕris*, n, of good —, *honesto loco ortus*, *honesto genere* (*natus*), of poor —, *tenui loco ortus*, *humili* or *ignobili loco natus*

extraneous, adj see External

extraordinary, adj *extraordinarius*, *inusitatus*, *insolitus*, *insolens*, *novus inauditus*, *incredibilis*, *mirus*, *insignis*, *summus* Adv *extra ordinem*, *praeter morem* or *consuetudinem*, *incredibiliter*, *mire*, *mirifice*

extravagant, adj **1,** = lavish, *prodigus*, *effusus*, *sumptuosus*, **2,** = excessive, *immoderatus*, *immodicus*, **3,** = foolish, *insulsus* Adv *prodige*, *effuse*, *sumptuose* *immoderate*, *immodice* *insulse* **extravagance,** n **1,** *prodigentia* (Tac), *sumptus*, *-ūs* (*profusus*), **2,** *intemperantia*, *immoderatio*, **3,** *insulse factum*

extreme, adj *extremus* (= furthest), *ultimus* (= last), *summus* (= highest), — part, *pars extrema*, the — price, *summum pretium*, to come into — danger, *in ultimum discrimen adduci*, to go to —s, *modum excedĕre* (so *ad extremum perventum est*, *ventum jam ad finem est*, *res est ad extremum perducta casum*). Adv *summe*, *summopere*, *quam* or *vel maxime*, or by superl. (e g — good, *optimus*) **extremity,** n **1,** = furthest part, *extremus*, with n, **2,** = top, *cacumen*, *vertex*, *fastigium*, *extremitas*, of the body, *extremae partes*, **3,** = distress, etc., by special word (e g *inopia*, = poverty), with *summus*, or *extrema*, *orum*, pl, to be brought to —s, *in extremum discrimen adductum esse*

extricate, v tr see Release

extrude, v tr *extrudĕre*, *expellĕre*, *e(j)icĕre*, comp *extrudere et e(j)icĕre* **extrusion,** n *expulsio* see Expel

exuberant, adj *luxuriosus*, *laetus*, of style, *redundans*, to be —, *exuberare* (e g *pomis*, *foliorum luxuriâ*, etc) Adv *ubertim*, *luxuriose*. **exuberance,** n *ubertas*, *luxuria*

exude, v.intr. *(ex)sudare.*

exulcerate, v.tr. *exulcerare.*

exult, v.intr. *exsultare, gestire,* comb. *exsultare et gestire, laetitiâ efferri, laetari, gloriari.* **exultant,** adj. *laetus.* Adv. *laete.* **exultation,** n. *laetatio.*

eye, I. n. *oculus,* † *ocellus,* † *lumen* (dimin.), = sight, *conspectus, -ūs* (e.g. before the —s, *in conspectus*), = keen sight, *acies;* blear-eyed, *lippus;* — in trees, etc., *oculus, gemma;* bull's- —, use *medius* (e.g. *scopum medium ferire,* = hit the —); — in peacock's tail, *oculus;* mind's —, *acies* or *oculus mentis.* **II.** v.tr. *a(d)spicĕre, contemplari;* — askance, *oculis limis a(d)spicĕre.* **eye-ball,** n. *pupula, pupilla.* **eye-brow,** n. *supercilium.* **eye-lash,** n. *pili pupillas tegentes.* **eye-lid,** n. *palpebra* (usu. pl.). **eyesight,** n. *acies, oculus.* **eyesore,** n. *res foeda* or *tetra;* see UGLY. **eye-witness,** n. *testis,* m. and f.; I was an —, *ipse vidi.*

F.

fable, n. **1,** *fabula* (usu. with *ficta* or *composita* or *commenticia*); **2,** = untruth, *commentum, mendacium.* **fabulous,** adj. *fabulosus, fictus, commenticius, falsus,* comb. *fictus et commenticius.*

fabric, n. **1,** of carpenters, and in gen., *fabrica;* of weavers, *textum, textile;* **2,** = structure, *aedificium.* **fabricate,** v.tr. *fabricari, texĕre, conficĕre.* **fabrication,** n. **1,** = making, *fabricatio;* **2,** = falsehood; see FABLE, 2. **fabricator,** n. *opifex, fabricator* (always with gen.), *artifex, textor;* = inventor, *auctor.*

face, I. n. *facies* (= the front of the head), *vultus, -ūs* (= the countenance), *os, oris* (properly, = the mouth), comb. *os vultusque* or *os et vultus; frons, -ntis,* f. (= the forehead); — to —, *coram;* to make —s, *os (dis)torquēre.* **II.** v.tr. and intr. **1,** = be opposite, *ad alqd spectare;* **2,** = to cover, *alqd alqâ re* or *alci inducĕre;* **3,** = encounter, *alci obviam ire;* **4,** — about, *signa convertĕre.* **facial,** adj. *quod ad faciem pertinet.*

facetious, adj. *jocosus, jocularis, lepidus, facetus.* Adv. *jocose, lepide, facete.* **facetiousness,** n. *lepos, -ōris, facetiae,* or by *sal.*

facilitate, v.tr. *alcjs rei expedire.* **facility,** n. *facilitas;* with —, *facile, nullo negotio.*

facing, prep. *contra alqd, ex adverso rei.*

facsimile, n. *descriptio imagoque* (e.g. *lit(t)erarum*).

fact, n. *res, factum;* that is a —, *hoc certo auctore comperi;* in —, *reapse, etenim, enim* or *quidem* (enclit.), *sane, profecto.*

faction, n. *factio.* **factious,** adj. *factiosus, partium studiosus, turbulentus, seditiosus.* Adv. *seditiose.* **factiousness,** n. *factio.*

factitious, adj. see FALSE.

factor, n. *negotiorum (pro)curator.*

factory, n. *fabrica, officina;* — hands, *operae.*

faculty, n. *ingenium* (= natural talent), comb. *animus ingeniumque; sol(l)ertia* (= skill), *facultas,* e.g. *dicendi* (also *poëtica facultas*).

fade, v.intr. *evanescĕre,* † *pallescĕre, marcescĕre.* **faded,** adj. see PALE. **fading, I.** n. *coloris mutatio.* **II.** adj. *caducus.*

fagot, n. *fascis, -is,* m., *sarmenta, -orum,* pl.

fail, I. v.intr. **1,** = to fall or come short of, *non ferire;* **2,** = to err or to do wrong, *errare, labi, peccare, peccatum admittĕre* (= to sin), *delinquĕre;* **3,** = to fall short, *alci deesse, deficĕre;* **4,** = — in a lawsuit, *cadĕre;* **5,** = be bankrupt, *foro cedĕre.* **II.** n. e.g. without —, by *certo, omnino.* **failing,** n. *error, peccatum, delictum.* **failure,** n. *defectio* (e.g. *virium*), *ruinae* or *naufragium fortunarum,* or use verb.

fain, adv. *libenter* (*lub-*), by a participle, as *volens;* I would — believe that, *hoc credĕre voluerim* (*vellem*).

faint, I. adj. *languidus,* use *sensu carēre* if unconsciousness be implied. **II.** v.intr. **1,** = swoon, † *collabi, animus alqm relinquit;* **2,** = be weary, *languēre.* **faint-hearted,** adj. *timidus.* **faintness,** n. **1,** *languor;* **2,** by verb.

fair, I. adj. **1,** = beautiful, *pulcher, venustus;* the — sex, *sexus, -ūs, muliebris;* **2,** of weather, *serenus;* of wind or tide, *secundus;* **3,** opp. to dark, *candidus;* **4,** morally, *aequus, integer;* **5,** = moderately good, *mediocris.* Adv. *aeque, mediocriter, haud ita multum.* **II.** n. *nundinae, mercatus, -ūs.* **fairness,** n. **1,** *pulchritudo, venustas;* **2,** *serenitas;* **3,** *aequitas, integritas;* **4,** *mediocritas.*

fairy, n. = — of the stream, *nympha;* = — of the tree, *dryas* (usu. pl. *dryades*); = — of the wood, *faunus.*

faith, n. **1,** = fidelity, *fidelitas, fides, pietas* (= discharge of duty towards God, parents, etc.); **2,** = belief, *opinio, persuasio, fides;* to have — in, *alci credĕre;* **3,** see RELIGION; **4,** as exclamation, *nae, Hercle, medius fidius.* **faithful,** adj. *fidelis, fidus* (e.g. *in suâ sententiâ*). Adv. *fideliter.* **faithfulness,** n. *fidelitas, fides, constantia.* **faithless,** adj. *perfidus, perfidiosus, infidelis, infidus.* Adv. *perfide, perfidiose, infideliter.* **faithlessness,** n. *perfidia, infidelitas.*

falchion, n. † *acinaces, -is,* m.

fall, I. v.intr. *cadĕre, decidĕre, delabi, defluĕre;* to — away, desert, or abandon, *deficĕre, ab alqo desciscĕre, alqm deserĕre;* to — in battle, *in acie cadĕre;* — by ambush or snares, *per insidias interfici;* = to die, *mori, perire;* = to be captured, *expugnari, delēri;* to — out (= disagree), *dissentire;* to — on, *in alqm invadĕre, irruĕre;* to — into a person's arms, *ruĕre in alcjs amplexus;* to — into suspicion, *suspicio cadit in alqm;* = to sink, *delabi, desidĕre;* of the wind, *cadĕre, concidĕre;* of the voice, *cadĕre;* = in price, *cadĕre res fit vilior;* — of an army, *pedem referre;* — at the feet of, *se ad pedes alcjs pro(j)icĕre;* — in with, *in alqm incidĕre;* — in love with, *amare.* **II.** n. **1,** *casus, -ūs, lapsus, -ūs, ruina, labes, -is;* **2,** = ruin, *ruina, excidium;* a — from rank or dignity, *dignitas amissa, gratia principis amissa;* **3,** = the lessening of a height or level of a fluid body, *decessus, -ūs, recessus, -ūs;* **4,** = lessening, *deminutio.*

fallacy, n. error, *fallacia, vitium, captio.* **fallacious,** adj. *fallax, vanus, fucosus, falsus, vitiosus.* Adv. *fallaciter, falso.* **fallible,** adj. *qui errare potest.*

fallow, adj. the field lies —, *ager cessat, quiescit, (re)quiescit, cultu vacat.* **fallow soil,** n. *novalis* or *novale, vervactum.*

false, adj. **1,** = not genuine, *falsus* (opp. *verus*), *subditus, suppositus* (= forged), *alienus* (= under another name, e.g. *libellum sub alieno nomine edĕre*), *simulatus* (= pretended), *fucatus, fucosus* (= having a fair exterior, opp. *sincerus, probus*), *fallax* (= deceptive), *mendax* (= lying); — teeth, † *dentes empti;* a — note, *dissonum quiddam;* **2,** = treacherous, *perfidus,* † *dolosus, fraudulentus;* a — oath, *perjurium;* to swear —, *perjurare, pejerare.* Adv. *falso, fallaciter, simulate, perperam, perfide, fraudulenter.* **falsehood,** n. *mendacium, commentum, falsum.* **falseness,** n. *fallacia, dolus, perfidia.* **falsify,** v.tr. *vitiare, corrumpĕre, adulterare* (e.g. *nummos, gemmas*), *interpolare, depravare, tabulas interpolare* (= to erase some letters and substitute others), *tabulas interlinere* (= to erase or to put out letters) **falsification**, n use verb

falter, v intr *haesitare*, *haerēre*, *titubare* Adv *titubanter*, *timide*

fame, n *laus*, *gloria*, *claritas*, *fama* **famous**, adj *celebratus*, (*prae*)*clarus*, *illustris* Adv (*prae*)*clare*, *bene* (= well)

familiar, adj 1, *familiaris*, *notus* = a bosom friend, *homo intimus*, *homo quo alqs intime utitur*, *amicus conjunctissimus*, 2, = acquainted with, *alcjs rei sciens*, *gnarus*, *non ignarus*, *peritus*, *non expers*, — with a language *linguam bene nosse*, *linguam intellegĕre*, — with danger, *in periculis versatum esse* Adv *familiariter* **familiarity**, n *familiaritas*, *familiaritas* or *intima amicitia*

family, I. n 1, *familia* (orig = the slaves in a house), *domus*, *-ūs*, 2, = race or clan *gens*, also *genus* and *familia* (= a branch of a *gens*, thus the *gens Cornelia* comprised the families of the Scipios and Lentuli), *cognatio*, *stirps*, *propinqui*, of good —, *nobilis*, *nobili genere* or *nobili loco natus*, *haud obscuro loco natus*, *honesto loco natus*, *gentilis*, *gentilicius* (= belonging to a *gens*), *familiaris* (= belonging to a *familia*), *domesticus* (= belonging to the house) II. adj *privatus* (opp to *publicus*), *intestinus* (= in the interior of the — (opp to *externus*)

famine, n *fames*, *-is*, *inopia et fames* **famish**, I. v tr *alqm fame enecare*, *conficĕre* II. v intr *fame mori*, *confici*, *absumi* or *perire* or *interire*

fan, I. n 1, = an agricultural instrument, *vannus*, † *ventilabrum* (Col), 2, = a toy used by ladies, *flabellum* II. v tr 1, *evannare*, *ventilare*, 2, *flabello uti*

fanatic, adj *fanaticus* **fanaticism**, n *animus fanaticus*, or *superstitionibus deditus*

fancy, I. n *opinio* (*falsa*), as a faculty, *cogitatio*, a mere —, *somnium*, according to — (= liking), *ex libidine* (*sua*), a glowing —, *fervidum ingenium*, *calor et impetus*, to belong to — and not to fact, *opinionis esse*, *non naturae*, — merely, *falsus*, *fictus* II. v tr *cogitatione sibi alqd depingĕre*, *in opinione esse*, *opinari*, *alqd fingĕre*, I — I am ill, *cogitare mihi videor*, what is fancied, *opinatus*, what may be —, *opinabilis* **fanciful**, adj 1, = imaginative, *facilis et copiosus*, or *summo ingenio praeditus*, 2, *morosus* (= captious) Adv *morose*

fang, n *dens*, m **fanged**, adj *dentatus* **fangless**, adj *sine dentibus*

far, adv *procul*, *longe* (= to a great distance, e g *longe videre*, *prospicĕre*), *e longinquo* (= from afar), *eminus* (opp *comminus*), to be —, *procul* or *longe abesse*, — be it from me, *di meliora* (sc *dent*), so — is it that, etc, *tantum abest ut*, to go too —, *modum excedĕre*, as — as, *quatenus*, *quantum*, *quod* (e g *quod sciam*), so —, *hactenus*, — fetched, *longe repetitus* **farther**, adv *longius*, *ultra*

farce, n *mimus*, *fabula Atellana* **farcical**, adj *mimicus*, *ridiculus*, *scurrilis* Adv *ridicule*

fare, I. v intr 1, *se habēre*, — well, *bene*, *commode*, *recte valēre*, *bene*, *belle se habēre bene valetudine uti*, 2, to — well, *laute vivĕre* II. n 1, *cibus potusque* (*potus*, *-ūs*) *victus*, *-ūs*, poor —, *tenuis victus*, good —, *lautus victus*, 2 = money paid for journey, *vectura* (ante and post class), 3, see PASSENGER **farewell**! interj *ave*! *aveto*! *avete*! *vale*! *valete*! to bid —, *salvēre* or *valēre alqm jubēre*, a hearty —, *multam salutem alci dicĕre*

farinaceous, adj *farinaceus*

farm, I. n *ager*, *fundus*, *praedium*, belonging to a —, *agrarius* II. v tr 1, = till, *arare*, *colĕre*, 2, = let out on contract, (*e*)*locare* (*alqd faciendum*), opp to *conducĕre* **farm-work**, n *aratio*, *opus rusticum*, *agricultura*, *agrorum cultus*, *ūs* **farmer**, n 1, *agricola*, *arator*, 2, = — of the revenues, *publicanus*, in gen *redemptor* **farming**, n 1, *agricultura* (or as two words) *cultus*, *ūs*, *agrorum*, *res rusticae*, 2, *redemptio*, *conductio*

farrago, n *farrago*

farrier, n (*faber ferrarius*) *qui equis soleas ferreas suppingit* (= one who shoes horses), *medicus equarius* (late = horse-doctor).

farrow, I. n *fetus*, *-ūs* II. v tr *fetum edĕre*

farthing, n *quadrans*, *teruncius*, I do not care a — for, *haud flocci facio*

fascinate, v tr †*fascinare* (= — by the look, e g *agnos*), *tenēre*, *capĕre* (fig) **fascination**, n 1, lit *fascinum*, *fascinatio* (Plin), 2, fig *blanditiae*, *dulcedo*

fashion, I. n *mos* (as custom, e g *mos vestis*), *ritus*, *-ūs* (e g after the — of men, *hominum ritu*), *habitus*, *ūs*, *ornatus*, *ūs*, a new —, *habitus novus*, to be in the — (of things), *moris esse*, *usu receptum esse* II. v tr see MAKE **fashionable**, adj *elegans*, *quod moris est* Adv *eleganter*

fast, I. adj 1, = quick, *celer*, *citus*, *propĕrus*, *properans*, *festinans*, *citatus*, *incitatus*, *velox*, *pernix* (= brisk), *alacer* (= alive, energetic, opp *languidus*), *agilis* (= in movement), *promptus* (= ready), *rapidus*, 2, = fixed or firm, *firmus*, *stabilis*, to hold —, *tenere*, *retinēre* to stick —, *adhaerēre alci rei* or *ad alqd* or *in alqā re*, to make —, *firmare*, *stabilire* II adv *citato gradu*, *celeriter*, *rapide*, *prompte*, *firme*, *mordicus* (collo quial) III. v intr *cibo abstinēre* IV n *jejunium*, *inedia* **fasten**, v tr (*af*)*figĕre ad alqd* or *alci rei*, see TIE, BIND, — together, *configĕre*, *con*(*n*)*ectĕre*, *conjungĕre* **fastening**, n *vinculum*, *compages*, *-is*, f (= fitting together), *claustra*, *-orum*, pl (= bars), *pessulus*, *repagula*, *-orum* (= bolt) **faster**! interj *propera*!

fastidious, adj *fastidiosus*, *delicatus*, *mollis* Adv *fastidiose*, *delicate*, *molliter*

fat, I. adj *pinguis* (opp *macer*), *opimus* (= full, rich, opp *gracilis* or *sterilis*, of a field), *obesus* (= filled up opp *gracilis*) *nitidus* (= shining), *saginatus* (= fed up), *adipatus* (= supplied with grease), *luculentus* (= productive, e g *munus*) II n †*pingue*, *adeps*, *sebum* (*sevum*), to live on the — of the land, *delicatissimis cibis uti* **fatten**, v tr *saginare*, *farcire* **fatted**, adj *saginatus*, *altilis* **fatness**, n *obesitas* (Suet), *pinguitudo* (ante and post class) **fatty**, adj *pinguis*

fate, n *fatum*, *necessitas*, *sors* (= one's lot), the —s, *Parcae* **fated**, adj †*fatalis*, †*fatifer funestus*, *mortifer*(*us*) Adv *funeste*, *fato* or *fataliter* (= by fate) **fatalism**, **fatalist**, n use *fatum* (e g *omnia fato fieri credĕre*, to be a —)

fatality, n 1, = power of fate, *fatum*, 2, = accident, *casus*, *ūs*.

father, I. n *pater*, *parens*, † *genitor*, † *sator*, — and mother, *parentes*, the —s, *patres* (= forefathers, senators) II. v tr — upon, *alqd alci tribuĕre* **fatherhood**, n *paternitas* (eccl), or by *pater* (e g he learns it by his —, *hoc cum pater fit, tum discit*) **father-in law** n *socer* **fatherless**, adj *orbus* **fatherly**, adj *paternus*

fathom, I. n *ulna* II. v tr *explorare*

fatigue, I. n (*de*)*fatigatio*, *lassitudo*, *defectio virium* II. v tr (*de*)*fatigare* **fatigued**, adj *fessus*, (*de*)*fatigatus*, *defessus*, *lassus*, *lassitudine confectus*

fatuous, adj. *fatuus*, *ineptus*, *inficetus* (*in-*

facetus), *insulsus* Adv *inepte*, *inficete*, *insulse*, *stulte* **fatuity**, n *ineptiae*, *stultitia*, *insulsitas*, *fatuitas* (rare).

fault, n 1, = wrong doing, *vitium*, *peccatum*, *culpa*, *delictum*, 2, = blame, *reprehensio* (opp *probatio*) *vituperatio* (opp *laus*), find — with, *accusare*, *reprehendĕre* **faultiness**, n *pravitas*, see FAULT, 2 **faultless**, adj *innocens*, *emendatus* Adv *innocenter*, *emendate* **faultlessness**, n *innocentia* **faulty**, adj *mendosus*, *vitiosus* (in gen), *pravus* (morally) Adv *mendose*, *vitiose*, *prave*

favour, I v intr *alci* or *alci rei favēre*, *alcjs rebus* or *partibus favēre* (= to be of his party), *alci indulgēre* (= to consult a person's wishes), *alci propitium esse* (= to be favourable or well disposed, used generally of the gods), *alci studēre*, *alcjs esse studiosum* (= to be attached to), *juvare*, *adjuvare* (= to assist), *esse alci adjumento*, *afferre alci adjumentum* (= to give aid), *alqm fovēre*, *sustinēre ac fovēre*, *gratiâ et auctoritate suâ sustentare* (= to support with your influence), *suffragari alci* (= to vote for or recommend), *gratiosus alci* or *apud alqm* (= e g to stand in favour with someone) II. n 1, = goodwill, *favor*, *gratia*, *voluntas*, *studium*, *benevolentia* (*beniv*), by your —, *pace tuâ*, 2, = benefit, *beneficium*, *gratia* **favourable**, adj 1, = inclined to, *propitius* (of the gods), *amicus*, *benignus*, 2, = advantageous, *commodus*, *prosperus*, of wind or tide, *secundus* Adv *amice*, *benigne*, *commode*, *prospere* **favourer**, n *fautor* **favourite**, I. n *deliciae* (= pet), to be a — with, *apud alqm gratiâ valēre*, *gratiosum esse* II. adj *gratiosus*, *gratus*, *acceptus* **favouritism**, n *gratia* (= influence) or circumloc (e g he showed his — to Gaius, *Gaio se nimis indulgentem praebuit*)

fawn, I. n *hinnuleus* II. v tr — on, fig *alqm adulari*, *alci blandiri* **fawning**, n *adulatio* Adv *blande*

fealty, n *fides*, *fidelitas*, to swear — to, *in verba alcjs jurare*

fear, I. n *metus*, -*ūs*, *timor*, *verecundia* (of what is wrong), *terror* (= sudden fear), *pavor*, *trepidatio* (= trembling), *horror*, *formīdo*, *timiditas*, *ignavia* (= cowardice) II. v tr *alqm metuĕre*, *timēre*, *verēri* (= reverence), *extimescĕre*, *pertimescĕre* **fearful**, adj 1, = afraid, *timidus*, *trepidus*, *ignavus*, *pavidus*, *verecundus*, 2, = dreadful, *metuendus*, *dirus*, *horribilis*, *terribilis*, *formidulosus* (*formidol*) Adv *timide*, *ignave*, *pavide*, *verecunde*, *dire*, *trepide*, *formidulose* **fearless**, adj *metu vacuus* or *solutus*, *impavidus*, *intrepidus*, — as to, *securus de alqâ re* (e g *bello*) Adv *sine metu*, *sine timore*, *impavide*, *intrepide* **fearlessness**, n see COURAGE

feasible, adj *quod fieri* or *effici potest* **feasibility**, n *potestas* or *facultas alcjs rei faciendae*

feast, I. n 1, = holy day, *dies festus*, *dies sol(l)emnis*, *dies feriatus*, † *festum*, 2, = a bountiful meal, *convivium*, *epulum*, *epulae*, *daps* II. v intr 1, lit *epulari*, 2, fig — on, *alqâ re pasci* (both in good and bad sense)

feat, n *facinus*, *ŏris*, n, *factum*, *res mira*, *res difficilis*

feather, I. n *penna* (*pinna*), *pluma* (= down) II v tr — one's nest, *res suas augēre*, one who has —ed his nest, *bene peculiatus* **feather-bed**, n *culcita plumea* **feathery**, adj † *plumeus*, † *plumosus*

feature, n 1, of the face *lineamentum ductus*, -*ūs*, or *habitus*, -*ūs*, *os*, *ōris*, the —s, *vultus*, -*ūs*, *os*, *ōris*, n, 2, = peculiarity, *proprietas*, *quod proprium est*, it is a — of anyone, *alcjs est*

febrile, adj *febriculosus*

February, n (*mensis*) *Februarius*

fecund, adj *fecundus* **fecundate**, v tr. † *fecundare* **fecundity**, n *fecunditas*, *fertilitas*

federate, federal, adj *foederatus*, *foedĕre junctus*, *foedĕre sociatus*

fee, I. n *merces*, *ēdis*, f, *honos* (*honor*) II. v tr *alci mercedem dare*

feeble, adj *imbecillus*, *tenuis*, *infirmus*, *invalidus*, *languidus*, *debilis*, of sight, etc, *hebes* Adv *infirme*, *imbecille* (rare), *languide* **feebleness**, n *imbecillitas*, *debilitas*, *infirmitas*, *languor*

feed, I. v tr 1, *cibum praebēre alci*, *cibare* (of animals) (Col), *pabulum dare alci* (oxen, etc), *alĕre* (= to nourish), *pascĕre* (= to pasture, e g *sues*, *greges*), 2, fig *alĕre*, 3, of rivers, etc, *in mare*, etc, *influĕre* II. v intr see EAT, GRAZE **feeder**, n 1, *qui alit*, etc, *altor*, 2, = eater, *qui edit*, 3, = a river, (*rivus*) *qui in mare influit*

feel, I. v tr 1, physically, = touch, *tangĕre*, *tentare*, *alqâ re affici*, 2, mentally, *sentire*, *percipĕre*, *concipĕre*, *intellegĕre*, *capĕre*, *alqâ re affici*, — joy, *laetari*, — pain, *dolēre* II. v intr 1, = appears (by touch, etc), *esse videri* or *esse*, 2, = be, by special verb (e g — glad, *laetari*, — thirsty, *sitire*, — for, *alcjs misereri*) **feeler**, n *crinis*, *corniculum* (Plin) **feeling**, I n *sensus*, -*ūs* (= sensibility), *animus* (mental), the power or method of —, *sentiendi ratio*, *tactus* -*ūs* (= the touch), *gustatus*, *ūs* (= taste), *judicium* (= power of judging), *conscientia* (= consciousness), *affectus*, -*ūs* (= the permanent condition of —), tender moral —, *pudor*, thankful —, *gratus animus*, *pietas*, humane —, *humanitas*, joyous —, *laetitia*, — for truth, *veritatis studium*, — for the beautiful, *elegantia* II. adj *humanus*, *humanitatis plenus*, *multum humanitatis habens humanitatis sensu praeditus*, *misericors* Adv *miserabiliter*, *magnâ cum misericordiâ*

feign, v tr *fingĕre*, *simulare*, *dissimulare* (e g that a thing is not) **feigned**, adj *fictus*, *simulatus* Adv *ficte*, *simulate* **feint**, n see PRETENCE

felicitate, v tr *gratulari alci alqd* or *de alqâ re* **felicitation**, n *gratulatio* **felicity, felicitousness**, n 1, *vita beata*, *beatum*, *beate vivĕre*, 2, = appropriateness, *proprietas* **felicitous**, adj 1, = happy, *felix*, *beatus*, 2, = appropriate, *aptus* Adv *feliciter*, *beate*, *apte*

fell, v tr 1, of timber, *caedĕre*, *excidĕre*; 2, = knock down, (*con*)*sternĕre*.

fell, n *clivus* (= hill)

fell, adj *crudelis*, *saevus*

fellow, n = associate, *socius*, *comes*, -*ĭtis*, m and f, *sodalis*, m and f, a good —, *homo festivus* or *lepidus*, a bad —, *homo dissolutus*, a trumpery —, *homuncio*, *homunculus* **fellow-citizen**, n *civis*, *municeps* **fellow-countryman**, n *civis* **fellow-feeling**, n *societas* (e g *aegritudinis*, = in sorrow, etc.) **fellow-heir**, n *coheres*, -*ēdis*, m and f **fellow-servant**, n *conservus* **fellow-soldier**, n *commilito* **fellowship**, n *societas*, — in plans, *societas consiliorum*, *collegium* (= a corporation, e g of merchants, artisans, priests), to take into —, *alqm in collegium cooptare*, in a university, *socius* (e g to get a —, *socium a(d)scribi*), human —, *societas humana*, *societas hominum*, good —, *comitas*

felon, n see CRIMINAL

female, I. adj *muliebris*, *femineus* (in fem also *femina*), — sex, *sexus*, -*ūs*, *muliebris* or *femineus* II. n *femina*, *mulier* **feminine**, adj 1, = FEMALE, 2, Gram t t *femininus*

fen, n *terra uliginosa*, *loca*, *-orum uliginosa* or *palustria*, *palus*, *-ūdis*, f, *uligo*. **fenny**, adj *uliginosus*, *paluster*

fence, I n *saepes*, *-is*, *saepimentum*, *(con)saeptum* (usu pl) II. v tr 1, = hedge in, *saepire*, *saepto circumdare* 2, = to fight in fencing, *armis uti*, *batuere* **fencer**, n *gladiator*, a good —, *armorum peritissimus*, to be a good —, *armis optime uti* **fencing**, n *ars gladii*, *ars gladiatoria* skilled in —, *armorum peritus*, a — master, *lanista*, n, — school, *ludus*

ferment, I. n 1, lit *fermentum*, 2, fig *tumor* (animi), *aestus*, *-ūs* II. v tr *fermentare* III v intr 1, *fermentari*, *fervēre*, *fermentescere*, 2, fig *fervēre*, *tumēre*, *turgescĕre*

fern, n *filix*

ferocious, adj *ferox*, see FIERCE

ferret, n *viverra* (Plin)

ferruginous, adj *ferrugineus* (= iron coloured), *ferratus* (= holding or tasting of iron, scil *aquae* (Sen))

ferry, I. n *trajectus*, *-ūs*, — -boat, *scapha*, — -man, *portitor*, the charge of —, *portorium* II. v tr *tra(j)icĕre*, *transmittĕre*

fertile, adj *ferax*, *fecundus*, *fertilis*, *opimus*, *uber* (= rich), comb *uber et fertilis*, *fecundus et uber*, *fetus* **fertility**, n *fertilitas*, *ubertas*, *fecunditas*, *copia*

ferule, n *ferula* (= a reed or staff)

fervent, **fervid**, adj *fervidus* (= glowing, e g *pars mundi*), fig *animus*, *fervens* (= heated, hot, e g *rota*, *aqua*), *ardens*, *flagrans*, to make —, *fervefacĕre*, to be —, *fervēre* Adv *fervide*, *ardenter*, *ferventer* **fervency**, **fervour**, n *fervor* (e g *oceani*, or fig *aetatis*)

festival, n *dies festus*, *dies sol(l)emnis*, *sol(l)emne*, *hilaritas* **festive**, adj *hilaris*, *festus*, *festivus* (ante and post class) Adv *hilariter*, *hilare*, *festive* **festivity**, n 1, = FESTIVAL, 2 = mirth, *festivitas*, *hilaritas* **festoon**, n *serta*, *-orum*

fetch, v tr *afferre*, *apportare*, *adducĕre*, *arcessere* (= to send for), *adhibēre*, — breath, *spirare*, *spiritum ducĕre*

fetid, adj *teter*, *graveolens*, *foetidus*, *putidus* **fetidness**, n *foetor*

fetter, I. n 1, *compes*, *ĕdis*, f, *pedica*, *vinculum* (= chain), 2, fig *vincula*, *orum* II. v tr 1, *vincula alci in(j)icĕre*, *alci compedes indĕre*, 2, fig *impedire*

feud, n = enmity, *simultas*, *bellum* (=public war), *inimicitiae* (private), *rixa* (= quarrel).

feud, n = property held of a lord, *feudum* (Mediaeval Lat) **feudal**, adj *feudalis*

fever, n *febris* **feverish**, adj 1, *febriculosus* (Gell), 2, fig (*com*)*motus*, *ardens*

few, adj *pauci*, *rari*, very —, *perpauci*, see LITTLE

fiat, n see COMMAND

fib, n *mendaciunculum* (once in Cicero)

fibre, n *fibra* **fibrous**, adj by the gen *fibrae*

fickle, adj *inconstans*, *varians*, *varius*, *levis*, *mutabilis*, comb *varius et mutabilis*, *mobilis* (e g *ingenium*, *animus*, *voluntas*) **fickleness**, n *inconstantia*, *levitas*, *mutabilitas*, *mobilitas*, *varietas* **fictile**, adj *fictilis*

fiction, n 1, (*con*)*fictio* (= the act), 2, *res ficta* or *ficticia*, *falsum*, *fabula*, *commentum* **fictitious**, adj *commenticius*, see FABULOUS

fiddle, n *fides*, *ium*, pl **fiddler**, n *fidicen*

fidelity, n *fidelitas*, see FAITH

fidget, I. v tr see DISTURB II. v intr. *quiescere non posse* **fidgetty**, adj *inquietus*

fie! interj *phui* or *pro(h)* (with nom or accus)

field, n 1, = a plain, *campus*, 2, = a piece of land, *ager* or pl *agri*, *arvum*, or pl *arva*, *seges*, *ĕtis*, f (= a sowed field), *pratum* (= meadow), relating to —, *agrarius*, 3, fig in relation to an army, to be in the —, *militiae esse* (opp *domi*), *in castris esse*, *bellum gerĕre*, to take the — against, *arma capĕre* or *ferre adversus alqm*, in gen — of history, etc, by special noun (e g *historia*), but *locus* and *area* are used in this sense **field-day**, n. *dies quo milites lustrantur*. **field-piece**, n *tormentum (bellicum)*

fiend, n **diabolus* (Eccl) **fiendish**, adj **diabolicus*, *nefandus*, *foedus*, *immanis*, *crudelis*, *ferox*, *atrox* Adv *nefande*, *foede*. **fiendishness**, n (*summa*) *ferocitas*

fierce, adj *ferox*, *ferus*, *saevus*, *atrox*, †*trux*, †*truculentus*, *immanis* Adv *ferociter*, *saeve*, *atrociter*, *immane*, *immaniter* **fierceness**, n *ferocitas*, *atrocitas*, *saevitia*, *immanitas*

fiery, adj 1, lit *igneus*, †*ignifer*, *flammeus*, *ardens*, *fervens*, *fervidus*, 2, fig see FIERCE, IMPETUOUS

fife, n *tibia* **fifer**, n *tibicen*

fifteen, adj *quindecim*, — apiece, *quini deni*, — times, *quindecie(n)s* **fifteenth**, adj *quintus decimus* **fifth**, adj *quintus* **fifty**, adj *quinquaginta*, — apiece, *quinquageni* **fiftieth**, adj *quinquagesimus*

fig, n 1, the tree, *ficus*, f, 2 the fruit, *ficus*, dried —, *Carica*, *Caunea*, 3, not to care a — for, *non flocci facĕre*

fight, I. n *pugna*, *certamen* — with the fist, *pugilatus*, *-ūs*, *pugilatio* II. v intr (*de*)*pugnare*, *dimicare*, *proeliari*, *digladiari*, *bellare* **fighter**, n *pugnator*, *gladiator*, *proeliator*

figment, n see FICTION

figure, I. n 1, = form or shape, *figura*, *forma*, *species*, *facies*, *statua* (= the statue), *habitus*, *-ūs* (*corporis*, = the natural bearing, opp *cultus*), *conformatio*, a beautiful —, *dignitas corporis*, *venustas*, 2, = an image or representation, lit *schema*, *ătis*, *figura*, *forma*, *imago*, geometrical —s, *formae geometricae*, *schemata geometrica*, *descriptiones*, *-um*, 3, fig a — in rhetoric, *figura* (Quint), rhetorical —s, *orationis ornamenta*, *-orum*, *verborum exornationes*, *-um*, 4, = a cipher, *lit(t)era*, 5, = sculpture, *signum* II. v tr 1, = draw, *describĕre*, 2, = FORM, 3, = IMAGINE **figurative**, adj *translatus* Adv *per translationem* **figured**, adj *sigillatus* (of cups (Cic), late of silk)

filament, n *fibra* (in bodies and plants)

file, I. n 1, *lima* (of smiths) *scobina* (of carpenters), 2, of soldiers, *ordo*, of the rank and —, *milites* II. v tr *limare*, *lima polire*. **filings**, n *scobis*

filial, adj *pius* (*erga parentes*) Adv *pie*

fill, v tr 1, *implēre* (generally), *explēre* (= to fill up), *complēre* (to make quite full), *replēre* (= to fill again, or merely fill), *supplēre* (= to supply what is lacking), *opplēre* (= to fill so as to cover), *refercire* (= to stuff), *cumulare alqd alqa re* (= to heap up), 2, fig (e g an office) *alqd re fungi*

fillet, n *fascia* (*fasciola*), *redimiculum*, *mitella*, *vitta* (round the head as an ornament), *infula* (used by priests)

filly, n *equula* (*ecula*)

film, n 1, = thin skin, *membrana*, 2, = thread, *filum*, 3, fig = darkness, *caligo*, *nubes*, *-is*

filter, I. n *colum* II. v tr (*per*)*colare*, *liquare*

filth, n. 1, lit. see DIRT; 2, fig. *impuritas*; to utter —, *foeda loqui*; see OBSCENITY. **filthy,** adj. 1, see DIRTY; 2, *impurus*; see OBSCENE. Adv. 1, see DIRTY; 2, *impure*. **filthiness,** n. *squalor*; see FILTH.

fin, n. *pinna* (Plin.).

final, adj. *ultimus, extremus*. Adv. *ad extremum, denique, postremo, quod superest, restat, rel(l)iquum est*.

finances, n. 1, of a private person, *res familiaris*; see INCOME; 2, of a state, *vectigalia, -ium, aerarium* (= treasury), *respublica* (= the general pecuniary condition). **financial,** adj. *ad vectigalia* or *aerarium pertinens*.

find, v.tr. 1, *invenire, reperire*; *offendĕre* (= to fall on), *deprehendĕre in alqâ re* (= to catch); he found admirers, *erant* or *non deerant qui eum admirarentur*; to — out, *excogitare, explorare, exquirĕre*; 2, = to experience, *experiri*, or by special verb (e.g. death, *perire*; — favour, *gratiam conciliare*). **finder,** n. *inventor, repertor*.

fine, I. adj. 1, *bellus, elegans*; the — arts, *artes liberales*; see BEAUTIFUL; very —! *belle! pulchre! bene dicis! bene facis!* 2, = thin, *tenuis, subtilis*; 3, = pure, *purus*; 4, of weather, *serenus, sudus*. Adv. *belle, eleganter, tenuiter, subtiliter*. **II.** n. 1, = end, *finis*, m. (f. ante and post class., and poet. in sing.); in —, *denique*; 2, = penalty, *multa*. **III.** v.tr. *multare*. **fineness,** n. 1, *elegantia*; see BEAUTY; 2, *tenuitas, subtilitas*; 3, *serenitas*. **finery,** n. *lenocinium* (in bad sense), *munditia, apparatus, -ūs, lautitia*. **finesse, I.** n. *artificium*. **II.** v.intr. *artificiis uti*.

finger, I. n. *digitus* (also = a measure, e.g. *quatuor digitis longus, latus, crassus*), *pollex* (= the thumb); to count by the —s, *in digitos digerĕre, digitis* or *per digitos numerare, digitis computare*; to turn round your —, *nihil est tractibilius illo*; to regard as the — of God, *divinitus alqd accidisse putare*. **II.** v.tr. *tangĕre*.

finical, adj. *putidus*. Adv. *putide*.

finish, I. v.tr. *finire, ad exitum adducĕre, ad finem perducĕre, conficĕre, consummare, absolvĕre, perficĕre*. **II.** n. *absolutio, perfectio, lima* (= polish, lit. = file). **finished,** adj. *limatus* (= polished), *absolutus, perfectus*. **finisher,** n. *confector, perfector*. **finishing,** adj. = FINAL.

finite, adj. *finitus* (= having an end), *circumscriptus* (= limited). Adv. *finite*.

fir, n. *abies, -ĕtis*, f., *pinus*.

fire, I. n. 1, *ignis*, m., *flamma, ardor, incendium, scintillae* (= sparks), *focus* (= fireside); 2, = conflagration, *incendium*; to be on —, *ardēre, flagrare*; to waste with — and sword, *ferro ignique vastare*; to put out —, *ignem reprimĕre, incendium restinguĕre*; to be between two —s, *lupum auribus tenēre*; 3, fig. *ignis, ardor*; to set a person's mind on —, *vehementius incendĕre alcjs animum*; mental —, *vis, vigor, impetus, -ūs, spiritus, -ūs, calor, ardor, fervor*, all with *animi*; — of youth, *juvenilis ardor*; poetic —, *impetus divinus*; — of discourse, *vis orationis*; to be without — (of speakers), *languēre, frigēre*; 4, = — of soldiers, *teli conjectus, -ūs*; to stand —, *sub ictu esse*; to be out of —, *extra teli conjectum esse*. **II.** v.tr. *incendĕre*. **III.** v.intr. *incendi*; he readily fires up, *natura ejus praeceps est in iram*. **fire-arms,** n. *tormenta, -orum*. **fire-brand,** n. 1, *torris*, m., *fax* (= torch); 2, fig. *incitator et fax*. **fire-brigade,** n. *excubiae nocturnae vigilesque adversus incendia instituti* (Suet.). **fire-engine,** n. *sipho(n)* (Plin. Min.). **fire-escape,** n. *scalae*. **fire-place, fire-side,** n. *caminus, focus*. **fire-wood,** n. *lignum* (usu. pl.). **fire-worshipper,** n. *qui ignem pro Deo veneratur*.

firm, adj. 1, *firmus, stabilis, solidus, immobilis, immotus*; 2, fig. *constans, firmus*. Adv. *firme, solide, constanter*. **firmness,** n. *firmitas, firmitudo* (e.g. *vocis, animi*), *obstinatio, soliditas* (lit.), *constantia, perseverantia*.

first, I. adj. *primus, prior* (of two), *princeps* (= chief). **II.** Adv. *primum, primo*. **first-born,** n. *natu major* (of two), *maximus* (of several). **first-fruits,** n. *primitiae*. **firstling,** n. *primus genitus*.

fiscal, adj. *fiscalis* (Jct.).

fish, I. n. *piscis*, m., *piscatus, -ūs* (collectively); — of the sea, *piscis maritimus*; river —, *p. fluviatilis*. **II.** v.intr. 1, *piscari*; 2, fig. — for, *captare, aucupari*. **fishbone,** n. *spina piscis*. **fisher,** n. *piscator, piscatrix*. **fishery,** n. *mare* or *flumen in quo pisces capiuntur*. **fishhook,** n. *hamus*. **fishmonger,** n. *qui pisces venditat*. **fishing,** n. *piscatus, -ūs*; — line, *linum*; a — net, *rete, funda, jaculum* (= a casting-net); — boat, *scapha* or *cymba piscatoria* (small); — vessel, *navis piscatoria*; — rod, *arundo piscatoria*. **fishy,** adj. by gen. *piscium* (e.g. *odor*, a fishy smell).

fissure, n. *fissura, fissum, rima* (= a leak); to make a —, *diffindĕre*.

fist, n. *pugnus*. **fisticuffs,** n. *pugilatus, -ūs, colaphus*; to give —, *colaphum alci impingĕre*.

fistula, n. *fistula* (Cels.).

fit, I. adj. *ad alqd aptus, idoneus* (= proper), *commodus, opportunus, habilis, appositus*; comb. *opportunus et idoneus, commodus et idoneus, habilis et aptus*. Adv. *apte, commode, opportune, apposite*. **II.** v.intr. 1, lit. *aptum esse, apte convenire ad* or *in alqd*; the shoes —, *calcei ad pedes apte conveniunt*; 2, fig. *alci* or *ad alqd aptum esse, alci rei* or *ad alqd accommodatum esse, alci rei* or *cum re convenire, alci rei* or *cum alqâ re congruĕre*. **III.** v.tr. *alqd alci rei aptare, accommodare*; — out, *(ex)ornare, instruĕre*. **IV.** n. 1, of illness, *impetus, -ūs, accessio* (Plin.); 2, of anger, etc., *impetus, -ūs*, or by special word (e.g. *ira, amicitia*); by —s and starts, *modo ... modo* (e.g. good by —, *modo bonus, modo improbus*). **fitness,** n. *habilitas, opportunitas, convenientia*.

five, adj. *quinque*; *quini, -ae, -a* (= five each); *quinquennium*, a period of — years, also *lustrum*; *quinto quoque anno*, every — years; — times, *quinquie(n)s*; —fold, *quincuplex, quinquepartitus* (= of — parts). **fifth,** adj. *quintus, -a, -um*. **fives,** n. use *pila* (e.g. *pilis ludĕre*).

fix, v.tr. 1, *alci rei* or *ad alqd (af)figĕre*; 2, = APPOINT. **fixed,** adj. *certus*. Adv. *intentis oculis*. **fixture,** n. *res quae moveri non potest*. **fixedness,** n. *constantia (animi, consilii)*; see FASTEN.

flabby, flaccid, adj. *marcidus, fluidus*. **flaccidity,** n. *resolutio* (Cels., e.g. *nervorum, stomachi*).

flag, I. n. = standard, *signum, vexillum*; of a ship, *insigne, vexillum*; a — ship, *navis praetoria*. **II.** v.intr. *languescĕre* (= grow feeble), *frigēre* (of conversation, etc.), *refrigescĕre* (of preparations, etc.). **flagstaff,** n. *vexillum*.

flag, I. n. = flat stone, *quadratum saxum*. **II.** v.tr. *(viam) quadratis saxis sternĕre* or *munire*.

flagitious, adj. *flagitiosus, nefarius, foedus*. Adv. *flagitiose, nefarie, foede*.

flagon, n. *lagēna, ampulla*.

flagrant, adj. *impudens, apertus, manifestus*. Adv. *impudenter, aperte, manifeste*. **flagrancy,** n. *impudentia*.

flail, n. *pertica* (Plin.), or *fustis*, m. (Col.) (= cudgel used in thrashing).

flake, n of snow, use in pl *nives*

flambeau, n. *fax*, *taeda*

flame, **I.** n 1, *flamma* (lit and fig), *ignis*, m, 2, fig the — of war spreads in Africa *Africa ardet bello* **II.** v intr *ardēre*, *flagrare* **flame coloured**, adj *flammeus*, *rutilus* **flaming**, adj *flammeus*, — eyes, *oculi ardentes*

flank, n *latus* -ĕris, n (of men, beasts, a camp, an army), on both —s, *ab utroque latere*

flap, **I.** n *lacinia* **II.** v tr *alis plaudĕre* **III.** v intr *fluitare*

flare, v intr *fulgēre*, *splendēre*

flash, **I.** n *fulgur* **II.** v intr *fulgurare*, *fulgēre*, *(e)micare*, *coruscare*, *splendēre*, the eyes — *oculi scintillant*

flask, n *ampulla*.

flat, **I.** adj 1, *planus*, *aequus* (=even), *pronus* (=on the ground), — nose, *nasus simus*, 2, of wine, etc, *vapidus* (Col), — bottomed boats, *naves plano alveo*, 3, = insipid, *insulsus*, *frigidus* Adv fig *plane* **II.** n *planities*, — of the hand, *palma*

flatter, v tr *algm adulari*, *alci assentari* or *blandiri* **flatterer**, n *adulator*, *assentator* **flattering**, adj *blandus*, *blandiens*, *jucundus*, *gratus* (= acceptable) Adv *assentatorie*, *per blanditias* **flattery**, n *adulatio*, *assentatio*, *ambitio* (= effort to gain favour), *blanditiae* (= smooth words, caresses, etc), *blandimentum*

flatulence, n *inflatio* **flatulent**, adj use *inflatio*

flaunt, **I.** v intr *se ostentare*, — in gold and purple, *insignem auro et purpura conspici* **II.** v tr = to display, *jactare alqd*

flavour, **I.** n *sapor* **II.** v tr *alqd condire alqa re*

flaw, n *vitium* **flawless**, adj *emendatus*, *sine culpâ* Adv *emendate*

flax, n *linum*, *carbasus*, f **flaxen**, adj 1, = of flax, *lineus*, 2, = of colour, *flavus*

flay, v tr lit *pellem detrahĕre alci* or *alcjs corpori*, *deglutēre alqm* (alive, *vivum*)

flea, n *pulex*

fledged, adj †*plumatus*, to be —, *pennas habēre*

flee, **I.** v intr *fugam petĕre*, *capĕre*, *capessĕre*, *fugae se mandare*, *se committĕre*, *in fugam se dare*, *se con(j)icĕre*, *terga vertĕre* (of soldiers), *in fugam effundi* or *se effundĕre*, — from, *fugere ab* or *ex alqo loco*, — a person, *alqm fugĕre*, — to, *fugâ petĕre alqd* (e g *arborem*), *confugere* or *fugam capessĕre alqo*, *confugĕre* or *profugĕre ad alqm* **II.** v tr see Above **flight**, n *fuga*

fleece, **I** n *vellus*, -ĕris, n **II.** v tr 1 *tondēre* 2, = rob, *expilare*, *spoliare* **fleecy**, adj †*laniger*

fleet, **I.** adj *velox*, *volucer*, *pernix* **II.** n *classis* **fleeting**, adj *fugax caducus*, *fluxus* **fleetness**, n *velocitas*, *pernicitas*

flesh, n *caro*, *nis*, f (= on the body and cooked), *viscera*, -um, n (= everything under the skin of an animal), *corpus*, -ŏris, n (opp *ossa*) in speaking of the flesh of animals the Lat omit *caro* (e g *vitulina*, = veal, *canina*, = dog's flesh). **fleshy**, adj *carnosus*

flexible, adj 1, *lentus*, 2, of character, *mollis*, *facilis* **flexibility**, n of character, *mollitia*, *mollitudo*, *facilitas*

flicker, v intr *volitare* (of birds), *fluitare* (of things, as sails), *trepidare* (of flames, etc)

flight, n 1, *fuga*, see FLEE, to put to —, *fugare*, 2, = way of flying, *lapsus*, -ūs, *volatus*, -ūs, 3, of stairs, *scalae* **flighty**, adj *volatilis*, *mobilis*, *levis*, *inconstans* **flightiness**, n *mobilitas*, *levitas*

flimsy, adj 1, = thin, *tenuis*; 2, = worthless, *inanis* **flimsiness**, n 1, *tenuitas*, 2, *inanitas*

flinch, v intr *(re)cedĕre*, *retro cedĕre*

fling, v tr *jactare*, *mittĕre*, *jaculari*, *con(j)icĕre*, — at, *alci rei* or *in alqd in(j)icĕre*, *alqm alqâ re petĕre*

flint, n *silex*, heart of —, *siliceus*

flippant, adj *lascivus*, *petulans* **flippancy**, n *petulant*

flirt, **I.** v intr *alqm specie amoris illicĕre* **II.** n *amator* or *amatrix inconstans* **flirtation**, n *species amoris*

flit, v intr *volitare*

flitch, n *succidia*

float, v intr *innare*, *innatare*, *aquâ sustinēri*, *fluctuare*, *fluitare*, *pendēre* (in the air)

flock, **I.** n *grex*, *pecus*, -ŏris, n, = a great number of persons, *caterva*, *multitudo* **II.** v intr *affluere*, *confluĕre*, — together, *concurrĕre*, *convolare*

flog, v tr *verberare*, be —ged, *vapulare* **flogging**, n *verbera*, *um*, *verberatio*

flood, **I.** n 1, as contradistinguished from ebb, *accessus*, -ūs, *maris* (opp *recessus aestuum*), *aestūs commutatio* (= change of tide from the ebb), the — (tide) rises, *aestus crescit*, *aestus ex alto se incitat*, the — falls, *aestus minuit*, 2, = overflow, *eluvio*, *diluvies*, 3, fig *vis* (e g *lacrimarum*) **II.** v tr 1, lit *inundare*, 2, fig *alqd alqa re cumulare* **flood-gate**, n 1, lit *cataracta* (or *cataractes*, *ae*) (Plin Min), 2, fig *vis*, *impetus*, *ūs*

floor, n *solum*, *coaxatio* (*coass*), to make or lay —, *coaxationem facere*, *coaxare*, *pavimentum*, *p tessellatum* or *vermiculatum* (= mosaic), *area* (= a barn-floor), *tabulatum*, *(con)tabulatio*, *contignatio* (= a storey)

floral, adj *floreus*

florid, adj 1, of complexion, *rubicundus*, 2, fig *floridus*

flounce, n (of a woman's gown), *instita*, *segmenta*, *orum*, pl **flounced**, adj *segmentatus*

flounder, v intr 1, lit *volutari*, *fluitare*, 2, fig *titubare*

flour, n *farina*

flourish, **I.** v intr 1, *florēre*, *vigēre*, 2, = make a display, *se jactare* **II.** v tr see BRANDISH

flout, v tr *ludificari*, *cavillari*, *deridēre*, *irridēre*

flow, **I.** v intr (as a fluid) *fluĕre*, *labi*, *manare*, — into the sea, *effundi in mare*, — between, *interfluĕre*, — past, *praeterfluĕre*, — together, *confluĕre* **II.** n 1, *fluxio*, *lapsus*, -ūs, 2, fig *volubilitas*, *copia* (e g *verborum*), 3, of the tide, *accessus*, -ūs (opp *recessus*) **flowing**, adj 1, *fluens*, *manans*, 2, — speech, *(pro)fluens*, *volubilis* Adv *(pro)fluenter*, *volubiliter*

flower, **I.** n 1, *flos*, *flosculus* (dim), the goddess of —s, *Flora*, 2, fig — of life, *aetas florens*, = best part of, *flos*, *robur*, — of speech, *flos verborum* **II.** v intr *florēre*, *(ef)florescĕre*, *flores mittĕre* **flowery**, adj 1, lit †*floreus*, 2, fig *floridus*

fluctuate, v intr *fluctuare* (*animo*) or *fluctuari*, *pendēre animi* or *animo* (of several, *animis*), *incertum*, *dubium*, *ancipitem esse*, *haesitare*, *dubitare*, *in dubio esse* **fluctuation**, n *animus incertus* or *dubius* or *suspensus*, *dubitatio*

flue, n. *caminus*; the — smokes, *domus fumat*.

fluency, n. *oratio volubilis*, *facundia*, *volubilitas*. **fluent**, adj. *volubilis* (opp. *stabilis*); a — style, *genus orationis (pro)fluens*. Adv. *(pro)fluenter*, *volubiliter*; to speak —, *commode verba facĕre*.

fluid, **I.** n. *liquor*, *humor*, *aqua*. **II.** adj. *liquidus*, *fluidus*, *fluens*.

flummery, n. 1, = a dish, *avēnae puls*, *-tis*, f.; 2, = empty talk, *gerrae*, *nugae*, *nugatoria*, *-orum*.

flurry, n. and v.tr.; see EXCITE.

flush, **I.** n. *rubor*. **II.** v.intr. *rubor* or *pudor alci suffunditur*.

fluster, v.tr. *percutĕre*, *agitare*, *commovēre*.

flute, n. *tibia* or *tibiae*, †*arundo*. **flute-player**, *tibicen*. **fluted**, adj. *striatus*.

flutter, **I.** v.intr. *trepidare*, *volitare*. **II.** v.tr. *agitare*, *commovēre*. **III.** n. *trepidatio*.

flux, n. *fluxio* (in gen.); — and reflux of the sea, *marinorum aestuum accessus et recessus* (both -ūs).

fly, **I.** n. *musca*, *cantharis*, *-idis*, f. **II.** v.intr. *volare*, *volitare*; to — to, *advolare*; to — in, *involare*; to — out, *evolare*; to — away, *avolare*; to let —, *emittĕre e manibus*, *ventis dare*. **flying**, adj. *volatilis*, *volucer*; — (= dishevelled) hair, *crines passi*.

foal, **I.** n. *pullus equi*, *pullus equinus*. **II.** v.tr. *parĕre*.

foam, **I.** n. *spuma*. **II.** v.intr. *spumare*, *(ex)aestuare*. **foamy**, adj. *spumans*, †*spumeus*.

fodder, n. *pabulum*, *pastus*, *-ūs*.

foe, n. *hostis* (= a public —), *inimicus* (= a private —).

fog, n. *nebula*. **foggy**, adj. *nebulosus*.

foible, n. *vitium*.

foil, **I.** n. *rudis*. **II.** v.tr. *ad vanum* or *ad irritum redigĕre*, *eludĕre*.

foist, v.tr. — on, *alqd alci supponĕre*, *subdĕre*, *sub(j)icĕre*.

fold, **I.** n. †*sinus*, *-ūs*, *ruga* (= a wrinkle or small fold in plants, dresses, etc. (Plin.)). **II.** v.tr. *alqd (com)plicare*; to — the hands, *digitos pectinatim inter se implectĕre* (Plin.); with —ed hands, *compressis manibus*. **III.** as suffix, *plex* (e.g. three—, *triplex*). **folding-doors**, n. *valvae (bifores)*, *fores*, *-ium*, f.

fold, n. = — for sheep, *ovile*, *saeptum*, usu. pl.; = — for cattle, *stabulum*.

foliage, n. *frons*, f., or pl. *frondes* (= branches); *folia*, *-orum* (= leaves).

folk, n. see PEOPLE.

follow, v.tr. 1, *algm (con)sequi*, *insequi*, *subsequi* (= very close), *prosequi* (= at a distance), *algm persequi* (= to follow out), *comitari* (= to accompany); he was —ed by an unusually large company, *stipatus est non usitatā frequentiā*; to — after or succeed, *alci* and *alci rei succedĕre*, *algm* and *alqd excipĕre*; = — as a successor, *succedĕre in alcjs locum*; to — from, *effici*, *confici ex re* (in argument, e.g. *ex propositis efficitur*); hence it —s, *sequitur*, *sequitur igitur* or *enim*, *ex quo efficitur*: what —s? *quid igitur?* thus it —s, *ita fit ut*, etc.; 2, = regard as a teacher, etc., *algm* or *alqd sequi*, *auctoritate alcjs movēri*, *alci obtemperare* (= to listen to the wishes of), *dicto alcjs audientem esse* (= to — or obey his command); to — an opinion, *sententiam alcjs sequi* or *probare*; to — your own judgment, *suo ingenio uti*. **following**, adj. *sequens*, *secutus*; for the — year (e.g. *in insequentem annum*); *alci proximus*, *secundus ab alqo* (of persons in a series), *futurus*, *venturus*, *posterus*; the — day, *dies posterus*; on the —, *postero die*, *postridie (ejus diei)*. **follower**, n. = disciple, *discipulus*, *auditor*, *(as)sectator*, *unus e suis* (of the followers of a leader); —s of Socrates, *Socratici* (and so with many other names).

folly, n. see under FOOL.

foment, v.tr. 1, *alqd fovēre*, *fomenta alci rei adhibēre* or *admovēre*; 2, fig. *sol(l)icitare*, *excitare*. **fomentation**, n. *fomentum* (Cels.). **fomenter**, n. *fax*, *concitator*, *instimulator*.

fond, adj. 1, = foolish, *stultus*; 2, = loving, *amans*, *amator*, *cultor*, *studiosus alcjs rei*; very —, *alcjs rei* or *alcjs amantissimus* or *studiosissimus*, *consectator alcjs rei* (e.g. *voluptatis*); — of literature or learning, *lit(t)erarum studiosus*; — of hunting, *venandi studiosus*. Adv. *stulte*, *amanter*. **fondness**, n. 1, *stultitia*; 2, *studium*, *amor*, *caritas*. **fondle**, v.tr. *blandiri alci*, *(per)mulcēre algm*, *amplexari et osculari algm*. **fondling**, n. *blanditiae*.

food, n. *cibus*, *esca*, *cibaria*, *-orum* (= whatever may be eaten by men or beasts), *edulia*, *-ium* (= eatables), *alimentum* (or in pl., esp. in poets); *penus*, *-ūs* or *-i*, m. and f., and *-ŏris*, n. (= supplies of food); to digest —, *cibum conficĕre*, *concoquĕre*; a food-shop, *popīna*; of animals, *pabulum*, *pastus*, *-ūs*.

fool, **I.** n. *homo stultus*, *fatuus*, *sannio* (= a maker of grimaces); to put a —'s cap on a person, *ludibrio habēre*; to play the —, *nugari*, *ineptire*, *desipĕre*. **II.** v.tr. *algm ludĕre*. **foolery**, n. *ineptiae*, *nugae*. **fool-hardy**, adj. *temerarius*; see RASH. **foolish**, adj. *stultus*, *stolidus* (= silly), *ineptus* (= one who acts out of place and time and reason), *insulsus* (= witless), *demens* (= one who has lost his head), *fatuus*. Adv. *stulte*, *stolide*, *inepte*, *insulse*. **folly**, n. *stultitia* (= stupidity, a foolish act), *fatuitas* (= silliness), *insipientia* (= want of prudence), *amentia* (= unreason), *dementia* (= loss of faculty), *stulte factum* (as an act).

foot, **I.** n. 1, = member of the body, *pes*, *pedis*, m.; to go on —, *pedibus ire*, *venire*, *iter facĕre*; to serve on —, *pedibus merēre*, or *stipendia facĕre*; to tread under —, *pedibus algm conculcare*, *proculcare*; — by —, *pedetentim*, *gradatim* (= step by step); 2, = the lowest part, *pes* (of articles of furniture), or by *imus*, *infimus* with n. (e.g. *infimus mons*); *radix* (e.g. *montis*); the town lies at the — of the mountain, *urbs monti subjecta est*; 3, = a measure, *pes*; a — in size, *pedalis* (*in longitudinem*, *in altitudinem*), *pedem longus*; half a —, *semipedalis*; one and a half —, *sesquipedalis*; two —, *bipedalis*; three —, *tripedalis*; five — deep, *quinque pedes altus*; 4, (in versification) *pes*. **II.** v.intr. see TREAD, DANCE. **III.** adj. *pedester*; — soldier, *pedes*, *-ĭtis*. **footing**, n. = way or manner, *modus*, *ratio*, *status*, *-ūs*; to place an army on the — of the Roman, *exercitum ad Romanae disciplinae formam redigĕre*; to place on the old —, *ad antiquum morem revocare*; to be on a very friendly — with, *valde familiariter algo uti*. **footman**, n. *pedis(s)equus*. **footpad**, n. *latro*. **foot-path**, n. *semita*, *trames*, *-ĭtis*, m., *callis*. **foot-print**, n. *vestigium*. **footstool**, n. *scamnum*, *scabellum*.

fop, n. *homo ineptus*, *homuncio*. **foppery**, n. *ineptiae* (= absurdities).

for, **I.** prep. 1 = in behalf of, in return for, *pro* (with the ablative); *dimicare pro legibus* (so *pro libertate*, *pro patriā*), = to fight — the laws; *Cato est mihi unus pro multis milibus*, = Cato alone is to me — (= as good as) many thousands; *huic ille pro meritis gratiam retulit*, = he returned him thanks — his deserts; 2, = as, *algm virum bo*-

num habēre, = to hold him — a good man (so *in bonis habetur*), "for" and "as" in such phrases do not appear in Latin (e g *dux electus est*, = he was chosen — (as) general), yet, *pro nihilo putare*, = to think nothing of, 3, "for" denoting value, by the genitive of indefinite price and the ablative of the definite (e g *quanti emisti?* = how much did you buy it? *viginti assibus*, = — twenty pence), 4, = by reason of, *prae* with abl, *propter* with acc, to die — fear, *prae metu mori*, — this reason, *propter hoc*, 5, of time, *in* with accus, — the next day, *in posterum diem*, = during, accus, he had been away — a year, *annum jam aberat*, or by *per* with accus, 6, expressing purpose *ad* with accus, money — building a bridge, *pecunia ad pontem aedificandum data*, to live — the day, *in diem vivere*, 7, to watch or consult —, *alci consulĕre*, love —, *amor alcjs* or *erga alqm*, means or remedy —, *remedium adversus alqd*, or the genitive alone, as, care — you *vestri cura*, —, as denoting according to, *pro sua quisque parte*, *pro viribus* (= according to your strength), according to your wisdom, *quae tua est prudentia*, or *qua es prudentia*, — the present, *in praesens*, to live — yourself (that is, your own interests), *sibi vivĕre* **II.** conj *nam(que)*, *enim* (enclit), *etenim*, *quippe*, *quod*, *cum* (with subj), *quoniam*, *quia*, see BECAUSE, FORASMUCH FOR I, 2

forage, I. n *pabulum* **II.** v tr *pabulari*, to send soldiers to —, *pabulatum* or *pabulandi caus(s)ā milites mittĕre* **forager,** n *pabulator* **foraging,** n *pabulatio*

forbear, v tr 1, = to abstain, *se tenēre*, *se continēre*, *se cohibēre*, (*se*) *alqa re abstinēre*, *alci rei parcĕre*, 2, = to endure patiently, *patientiā uti*, *patientiam adhibere alci rei*, *patienter atque aequo animo ferre*, *pati ac ferre pati ac perferre*, *perferre patique alqd* **forbearance,** n *abstinentia*, *continentia*, *patientia* **forbearing,** adj *abstinens*, *continens*, *temperatus*

forbid, v tr *vetare* (with accus and inf), *interdicĕre alci alqā re* (or with *ne*), to — one your house, *interdicere alci domo sua*, it is —den, *vetitum est*, *non licet*

force, I. n *vis*, *violentia*, *impetus* -*ūs*, *momentum*, to use —, *vim facĕre*, *vim adhibēre* **II.** v tr see COMPEL **forcible,** adj 1, = by force, *per vim*, 2, = physically strong, *validus*, *nervosus*, 3, = morally strong, energetic, *gravis*, *vehemens* Adv 1, *per vim*, *valide*, *nervose*, *graviter*, *vehementer*

forcemeat, n *insicia* (Varr)

ford, n *vadum*

fore, adv *ante*, *antea* **forearm, I.** n *bracchium* **II.** v tr see WARN, PREPARE, to be —ed *praecavēre* **forebode,** v intr and tr 1, *portendĕre*, *praesagire*, 2, = have a presentiment of, *praesagire*, *praesentire* **foreboding,** n *praesensio* **forecast,** v tr (*animo*) *praevidēre*, *providēre*, *prospicĕre* **forefather,** n *proavus* pl *priores*, *majores*, *patres* **forefinger,** n *digitus index* **forego,** v tr (*con*)*cedere alqd* **forehead,** n *frons*, *ntis*, f **foreknow,** v tr *praenoscĕre* **foreknowledge,** n by *providēre* **foreland,** n *promontorium* **foreman,** n *procurator* **foremast,** n *malus anterior* **foremost,** adj *primus* **forenoon,** n *dies antemeridianus* **forerunner,** n *praenuntius* **foresee,** v tr *praevidēre*, *providēre*, *prospicere* **foresight,** n *providentia*, *prospicientia* **forestall,** v tr *praevenire*, see ANTICIPATE **foretell,** v tr *praedicĕre* **forethought,** n *providentia*, by —, *consulto*, to do —, *alqd consulto* or *meditatum* or *praeparatum facĕre* **forewarn,** v tr *praemonēre*

foreign, adj *peregrinus*, *externus*, *barbarus*, *adventicius*, — to, (*ab*) *alqa re*, or *alci rei alienus*, — to each other, *res sibi repugnantes* **foreigner,** n *peregrinus*, *alienigena*, m and f, *advena*, m and f (= new settler)

forensic, adj *forensis*

forest, n *silva*, *saltus*, -*ūs* (wild and on hills)

forfeit, I. v tr *amittĕre*, *alqa re multari* **II.** n *poena*, *multa*, *damnum*

forge, v tr 1, = to form, *tundĕre* (= to beat e g *ferrum*), *procudĕre* (e g *gladium*), *fabricari* (e g *fulmina*, *fallaciam*), *fingĕre* (e g *fallacias*), 2, = to falsify, — documents, *tabulas corrumpĕre*, *vitiare*, *interpolare*, (= — parts in a document) *sub(j)icĕre*, — money, *cudĕre* **forger,** n *subjector* (of wills, etc), *qui nummos adulterinos cudit*, forged coin, *nummus adulterinus* **forgery,** n *subjectio* (= — of wills, etc) For — of money, use verb

forget, v tr *alcjs rei* or *alqd oblivisci*, *neglegĕre* (*neglig*-), *neglegentiā praeterire*, I have forgotten, *alqd fugit me*, *alqd e memoriā excessit*, to be forgotten, *e memoriā excidĕre*, to — yourself, *sui oblivisci*, to — your dignity, *dignitatis suae immemorem esse* **forgetful,** adj *obliviosus*, *immemor* **forgetfulness,** n *oblivio*

forgive, v tr *alqd alci ignoscĕre*, *veniam dare alcjs rei* (= to give mercy instead of justice), *gratiam facĕre alcjs rei*, *alqd alci concedĕre*, *condonare*, *alci indulgēre* **forgiveness,** n *venia poenae* (*meritae*) *remissio* **forgiving,** adj *facilis*, *clemens*, *exorabilis*

fork, n *furca*, *furcilla* (used in making hay, forks for eating were unknown) **forked,** adj *bifurcus*

forlorn, adj *spe dejectus*, *relictus*, *destitutus*

form, I. n 1, *figura*, *forma*, *facies*; of a fine —, *formosus*, *dignitate corporis praeditus* or *insignis*, human —, *species humana*, things have taken a new —, *magna rerum commutatio facta est*, 2, see FORMULA, 3, = bench, *scamnum*, 4, = appearances, for —'s sake, *dicis caus(s)ā* **II.** v tr 1, = to give — to, *fingĕre*, *figurare*, *formare*, *fabricari*, *facĕre*, *efficĕre*, to — intellectually and morally, *fingĕre*, (*ex*)*colĕre*, *expolire*, *instituĕre*, 2, = — troops, *instruĕre*, *ordinare*, 3, = — plans, etc, (*consilia*) *inire*, — friendship, *amicitiam cum alqo conjungĕre* **III.** v intr 1, = constitute, *ex alqa re consistĕre*, 2 of troops, *se explicare* **formal,** adj = for the sake of appearances, *dicis caus(s)ā*, = artificial, *compositus*, *frigidus*, *simulatus*, = stiff (of manners), *urbanus ac perpolitus* Adv *rite* (= duly), *composite*, *urbane* **formality,** n 1, see CEREMONY, 2, of manners, *mores perpoliti* **formation,** n 1, as act, *conformatio*, 2, = form, *conformatio*, *forma* **formless,** adj *informis*, *rudis* **formula,** n *formula*, *verba*, -*orum*

former, adj *prior*, *pristinus* (= ancient), *superior* (e g *annus*), the —, the latter, *hic* . . . *ille*, or *ille* . . . *hic* Adv *antea*, *olim*, *quondam*

formidable, adj *metuendus*, *timendus*, *horrendus*, *terribilis*, *formidulosus* (*formidol*-) Adv *formidulose*, *terribilem in modum*

fornication, n *stuprum*

forsake, v tr (*de*)*relinquĕre*, *deserĕre*, *destituĕre*, comb *deserĕre et relinquĕre*, *destituĕre et relinquĕre*

forsooth! interj *scilicet* (iron), *sane*

forswear, v tr 1, = to deny on oath, *adjurare*, *ejurare* (= to renounce), 2, = to swear falsely, *pejerare*, *perjurare*

fort, n *locus munitus, arx, castellum, castrum* **fortification,** n *munitio, munitiones, munimenta, -orum, opera, -um* (= works) **fortify,** v.tr *(com)munire, praemunire, operibus munire, munitionibus firmare, muris munire, vallo et fossā circumdare locum, vallum et fossam circumdare alci loco*

forth, adv 1, of place, *foras,* in combination it is expressed by *e, ex,* and *pro,* with the several verbs (e g to bring —, *efferre,* to cast —, *e(j)icĕre,* to go —, *exire,* to lead —, *educĕre, producĕre*), 2, of time, *inde* **forthcoming,** adj by fut (e g — book, *liber quem alqs editurus est*), to be —, *in eo esse ut* **forthwith,** adv *extemplo, statim, confestim, protinus*

fortitude, n *fortitudo, animus fortis, virtus, -ūtis,* f

fortune, n 1, *fortuna, fors, casus, -ūs,* changeful —, *fortunae vicissitudines, varietates temporum,* comb *temporum varietates fortunaeque vicissitudines, casus varii,* to be content with your —, *sorte suā contentum vivĕre;* the goddess of —, *Fortuna,* 2, = wealth, *divitiae, res familiaris, facultates, opes, pecuniae, bona, -orum, fortunae* **fortune-teller,** n *sortilegus, (h)ariolus,* a female —, *saga* **fortuitous,** adj *fortuitus, in casu positus, forte oblatus* Adv *forte, fortuito, casu* **fortunate,** adj *felix, fortunatus, prosper(us), secundus,* — condition, *res secundae* Adv *feliciter, fortunate, prospere*

forty, adj *quadraginta, quadrageni* (= — each), *quadragesie(n)s* (= — times)

forum, n *forum*

forward, I. adv *porro,* to go —, *pergĕre* **II.** v tr 1, = send on, *perferendum curare* (e g *lit(t)eras perferendas curavit*), 2, = help, *(ad)juvare, alci adjumento esse.* **III.** adj 1, = early, *praecox,* 2, = rude, *protervus, inurbanus*

foss, n *fossa* (*incilis*), *incile* **fossil,** n *fossilia, -ium*

foster, v tr *curare, nutrire, sustinēre, alĕre* **foster-brother,** n *collacteus* (late). **foster child,** n *alumnus, alumna* **foster-father,** n *nutricius* **foster-sister,** n *collactea* (Juv)

foul, adj *putidus, putridus, foetidus* (= stinking), *foedus, turpis* (= morally foul), *obscenus* (= impure), *immundus* (= dirty) **foul-play,** n *dolus malus* Adv. *putide, foede, turpiter* **foulness,** n *foeditas obscenitas*

found, v tr 1, *fundamentum alcjs rei jacĕre* or *ponĕre, fundamenta locare, condĕre, instituĕre, constituĕre, civitatem funditus tollĕre,* 2, fig. to be founded on, *niti alqā re* or *in alqā re,* also *niti fundamento alcjs rei, positum esse in alqā re,* = cast, *fundĕre* **foundation,** n *fundamenta, -orum, sedes, -is,* — (of a pillar), *basis* **founder, I.** n *conditor, auctor* **II.** v intr *submergi* **foundling,** n. *infans expositus, expositicius*

fount, or **fountain,** n **1,** lit *fons* (= the place and the water), *caput* (= the spring), 2, fig *fons, caput, principium,* comb *fons et caput, principium et fons, origo, caus(s)a* (= the primary cause), comb *caus(s)a atque fons*

four, adj *quat(t)uor, quaterni* (= — each), — or five, *quat(t)uor (aut) quinque,* — years old, *quadrimus,* a period of — years, *quadriennium,* every — years, *quarto quoque anno,* going on — feet, *quadrupes,* —fold, *quadruplex,* — times as much, *quadruplum,* — times, *quater* **fourteen,** adj *quat(t)uordecim, quaterni deni* (distributively), — times, *quater decies* **fourteenth,** adj *quartus decimus* **fourth, I.** adj. *quartus, -a, -um,* every —, *quartus quisque,* the — time, *quartum,* in the — place, *quarto.* **II.** n. *quadrans*

fowl, n 1, *avis, volucris, ales, -itis,* m and f; 2, = a hen, *gallina,* flesh of —, *(caro) gallinacea* **fowler,** n. *auceps* **fowling,** n *aucupium.*

fox, n 1, *vulpes, -is,* f., of a —, *vulpinus,* 2, fig = a cunning man, *homo versutus* or *callidus*

fraction, n *pars* **fractious,** adj *morosus* Adv *morose* **fractiousness,** n *morositas.*

fracture, I. n med t t *fractura* (Cels) **II.** v tr *frangĕre.*

fragile, adj *fragilis* **fragility,** n *fragilitas* **fragment,** n *fragmentum, re(l)liquiae* (= remains), —s of the plays of Menander, *trunca quaedam ex Menandro* (Gell) **fragmentary,** adj *fractus*

fragrance, n *odor suavis, suaveolentia.* **fragrant,** adj *suavis,* † *suaveolens,* † *odorifer,* † *odoratus,* † *odorosus*

frail, adj *infirmus, debilis, imbecillus.* **frailty,** n *infirmitas, imbecillitas* (lit and fig)

frame, I. n 1, of a window, picture, etc , *forma* (Plin), 2, = body, *corpus, -ŏris,* 3, = — of mind, *animus* **II.** v tr 1, = put into a frame, *in formā includĕre,* 2, = compose, *componĕre,* 3, see Make **framework,** n. *compages, -is, contignatio*

France, n *Gallia* **French,** adj *Gallicus*

franchise, n *civitas, jus, juris,* n , *suffragium*

frank, adj *sincerus, apertus, simplex* Adv *sincere, candide, aperte, simpliciter* **frankness,** n *sinceritas, simplicitas*

frankincense, n *t(h)us, t(h)uris,* n

frantic, adj *insanus, delirus, fanaticus, amens, demens* Adv *insane*

fraternal, adj *fraternus* Adv *fraterne* **fraternity,** n 1, *fraternitas, necessitudo fraterna, germanitas;* 2, = society, *sodalitas, sodalitium, collegium, corpus, -ŏris* **fraternize,** v.intr *amicitiā inter se conjungi*

fratricide, n 1, = the murder of a brother, *parricidium fraternum,* 2, = the murderer of a brother, *fratricida,* m

fraud, n *fraus, dolus (malus), circumscriptio, fallacia,* comb *doli atque fallaciae,* to devise — against anyone, *dolum alci struĕre, nectĕre, confingĕre, fraude alqm tentare, fallaciam in alqm intendĕre* **fraudulent,** adj *fraudulentus, qui totus ex fraude et fallaciis constat* (opp *homo sine fuco et fallaciis*), *dolosus* Adv *dolo malo, dolose, fraudulenter, contra (jus ac) fidem*

fraught, adj *alqā re refertus, repletus, oneratus*

fray, n *pugna*

freak, n see Caprice.

freckle, n *lenticula, lentigo* (Plin). **freckled,** adj *lentiginosus* (Val Max).

free, I. adj **1,** = — from burdens, etc , *liber, solutus, vacuus (a) re, expers rei,* from taxes, *immunis,* from guilt, *innocens,* from military service, *immunis militiā,* from danger, *tutus,* from care, *securus,* to make —, *liberare,* to — from guilt, *absolvĕre alqm,* to be — from, *alqā re carēre,* **2,** = not subject to, *liber,* 3, = not restricted, as in space, *patens, apertus,* **4,** = without cost, *gratuitus,* to have a — dwelling, *grati(i)s habitare,* 5, = — to do or to act, *liber, solutus;* I am — to say, *audeo dicĕre,* 6, = generous, *largus, munificus, liberalis.* Adv. *libere, solute, tuto, secure, aperte, grati(i)s, gratuito, large, munifice, liberaliter* **II.** v.tr. *alqm alqā re liberare, eximĕre, solvĕre, expedire, manumit* *tĕre* (of a slave); to make — with, 1, = to indulge in, *alci rei indulgēre*, 2, = to treat disrespectfully, *alqo parum honorifice uti* **free agent,** n. *qui sui juris est* **freebooter,** n *latro* **free born,** adj *ingenuus* **freedman,** n *libertus, libertinus* **freedom,** n 1, = — from limits, *vacuitas vacatio*; from business, *otium*, from taxes, *immunitas*, from punishment, *impunitas*, 2, = independence, *libertas*, to give —, *libertatem alci dare, in libertatem alqm vindicare*, — from slavery, *alqm manumittĕre*, — from prison, *e custodia emittĕre*, to restore —, *libertatem alci reddĕre*, to restore yourself to —, *e vinculis se expedire*, moral —, *arbitrium (liberum)*. 3, = rights or privileges, *jus, juris*, n, *privilegium, beneficium*, 4, = license, *licentia*, to take —, *licentiam sibi sumĕre, audēre*, to take great —, *multa sibi sumĕre*, = great license, *licentia, arrogantia, procacitas* **free-hearted,** adj see GENEROUS **freehold,** n. *praedium liberum* or *immune*. **freeholder,** n *qui praed lib habet*, or simply *possessor* **free-liver,** n *qui licentius agit* **free-living,** n *licentia* **freeman,** n *civis, homo liber* **free-speech,** n *sermo liberior* **free-thinking,** adj see SCEPTICAL **free-will,** n *voluntas*, to have —, *sponte suâ agĕre*

freeze, I. v tr *glaciare, urĕre* **II.** v intr *gelare, gelari* (Plin, etc); it —s, *gelat*; = to feel cold, *frigēre, algēre* **frozen,** adj †*rigidus*, to be —, *rigēre*

freight, I. n *onus, ĕris*, n **II.** v.tr *onerare* **freighted,** adj. *onustus*

frenzy, n. *vesania, delirium, furor, amentia, dementia*

frequent, adj *frequens* (= many present, e g., *frequens senatus*), *creber* (= thickly filled, opp *rarus*), *multus* (= many), *celeber* (= numerous) Adv *frequenter, crebro, saepe* **II.** v tr *celebrare, frequentare, in alqo loco versari* **frequency,** n. *frequentia, crebritas, celebritas* **frequented,** adj *frequens, celeber, tritus* (= well trodden)

fresh, adj 1, = cool, *frigidus*, 2, = recent, *recens, novus*, — sod, *caespes vivus*, 3, = unused, and therefore vigorous, *recens, integer, viridis*, comb. *recens integerque, vegetus, alacer, vivus*, a — complexion, *nitidus color* Adv use *frigidus* (*frigide* not in this sense), *recenter* (ante and post class), *nove, integre, vegete*. **freshen,** v tr *refrigerare* (= to cool), *recreare, reficĕre* (= to revive), *relaxare, integrare* **freshness,** n *viriditas* = vigour, use *novus*, with n = novelty (e g the — of a book, *liber novus*)

fret, I. v.tr 1, rub, *fricare, terĕre*, 2, = wear away, *atterĕre*, 3, fig *sol(l)icitare, vexare, angĕre* **II.** v intr *alqd aegre ferre, angi, dolēre*, see GRIEVE **III.** n *molestia* (or pl), *angor, vexatio* **fretful,** adj *morosus, stomachosus* (rare) Adv *morose, stomachose* **fretfulness,** n *morositas*

fricassee, n *sartago* (Pers)

friction, n *tritus*

Friday, n **dies Veneris*

friend, n *amicus, amica, sodalis* (= companion), *necessarius* (= relation), *familiaris* (= intimate), *studiosus, amans, amator alcjs*, my — *! O bone! sodes!* to be a — (patron) to, *alcjs fautorem esse, alci favēre* or *bene velle*, those who are — s to a cause, etc., *qui stant ab* or *cum alqo* **friendless,** adj *sine amicis, amicorum expers* or *inops* **friendly, I.** adj *amicus benevolus, humanus, benignus, comis, urbanus* **II.** Adv *comiter, amice, benigne, urbane*. **friendliness,** n *comitas, humanitas, benignitas, benevolentia (beniv-), affabilitas, urbanitas* **friendship,** n *amicitia, necessitudo, conjunctio, familiaritas* to form a —, *amicitiam cum alqo facere, (con)jungĕre, instituĕre, conciliare, inire, sibi parare, ad am alcjs se conferre se applicare, se adjungĕre, amicitiâ alqm sibi conjungĕre*

frieze, n 1, in architecture, *zoophorus*, 2, = rough cloth, *gausapa* (*gausapes, gausape*, or *gausapum*)

fright, n *terror, pavor*, to take —, *pavescĕre*. **frighten,** v tr *alqm (ex)terrēre, terrorem alci afferre, inferre, offerre, in(j)icĕre, incutĕre, alqm in terr con(j)icĕre* **frightful,** adj *terribilis, horribilis, foedus* (= disgusting), *horrendus, horrificus, ingens, immanis* Adv *terribilem in modum, foede, immane, immaniter* **frightened,** adj *terrore perculsus, territus, exterritus, trepidus* (= afraid, trembling)

frigid, adj *frigidus*, see COLD

frill, n *segmenta, -orum* (but this = flounce).

fringe, n *fimbriae, limbus*

frisk, v intr *salire, lascivire* **frisky,** adj. *lascivus* Adv *lascive* **friskiness,** n *lascivia*.

frith, n *fretum*

fritter, I. v tr e g to — away time, *tempus (con)terĕre*; property, *dissipare* **II.** n. *laganum*

frivolous, adj *nugax, levis, inanis, frivolus* Adv *maximâ cum levitate* **frivolousness, frivolity,** n *nugae, levitas*

fro, adv, e g to and —, *huc (et) illuc, ultro citro(que)*

frock, n see GOWN

frog, n *rana*, a small —, *ranunculus*

frolic, I. n *ludus et jocus, lascivia* **II.** v tr *joca agĕre, lascivire, ludĕre*, to — with, *cum alqo jocari, joco uti, jocularí*. **frolicsome,** adj. *hilaris (hilarus), jocularis, lascivus, ludibundus*

from, prep 1, = denoting severance and distance, is expressed by *a, ab*, the force sometimes being increased by *procul*, *decedĕre ab alqo*, = to depart from, *absunt a Dyrrachio*, = they are far from Dyrrachium, *conscia mihi sum a me culpam hanc esse procul*, = I know that this fault is far from me "From," denoting the place out of which, by *e, ex* (e g *ex urbe venit*) "From," denoting order, by *a*, *quartus ab Arcesila*, = the fourth from Arcesilas, with towns and small islands abl alone, so *rure, domo*, 2, = aversion, *alieno a te animo fuit*, = his mind was hostile to (from) you, = transference, *per manus tradĕre*, = from hand to hand *A, ab*, denotes the beginning, e g *ab fundamento interire*, = to perish from the foundation, and has *ad* for its antithesis, e g *a minimo ad maximum*, = from the least to the greatest, 3, = of time, *a, ab*, e g *ab horâ tertiâ bibebatur*, = they drink from three o'clock, the force is increased by *jam inde*, etc, *jam inde ab adolescentia*, = from youth up, *a puero*, = from boyhood, *a mane ad noctem*, = from morning to night, *ab incenso Capitolio*, = from the burning of the Capitol, *ab urbe conditâ*, = from the foundation of the city, 4, denoting a cause or source, is expressed by *a, de*, or *ex*, e.g *discĕre a patre, perire a peste, plaga ab amico*, = a snare from a friend, *certe scio me ab singulari amore ac benevolentiâ tibi scribĕre*, = I well know that I write to thee from singular love and good-will, *a metu*, from fear, *ex irâ*, from anger

front, I. n *frons, -ntis*, f, in — of the camp, *pro castris*, to place the troops in —, *copias in fronte constituĕre*, to attack in —, *hostes adversos aggredi* **II.** adj *prior, anticus*, opp to *posticus* **III.** v tr 1, = to look towards, *alqm a(d)spectare*; 2, = to oppose, *alci adversari* **frontage,** n.

frons **frontispiece,** n *libri prima tabula* **fronting,** adj *alci (rei) adversus, oppositus* **frontier,** n *confinium* **frontlet,** n *frontalia, -ium*

frost, n *frigus, -ŏris,* n, *gelu, pruina* **frosty,** adj *frigidus* (lit and fig)

froth, I. n *spuma* **II.** v intr *spumare* **frothy,** adj † *spumosus.*

froward, adj *contumax, pertinax, pervicax* Adv *contumaciter, pertinaciter* **frowardness,** n *contumacia, pertinacia, pervicacia*

frown, I. n *frontis* or *superciliorum contractio* **II.** v intr *frontem contrahĕre, vultum adducĕre*

frowsy, adj *sordidus, immundus*

fructify, v tr see FERTILIZE

frugal, adj *parcus, restrictus* (opp *largus*), comb *parcus et restrictus* (in housewifery, opp *neglegens*), *frugi* (indecl, comp. *frugalior,* sup *frugalissimus*), comb *homo frugi et diligens* Adv *parce, frugaliter* **frugality,** n *parsimonia, frugalitas, diligentia*

fruit, n 1, *fructus, -ūs, fruges, -um* (= fruit collectively), *fetus, -ūs* (= fruit, usu as produced by generation), *pomum* (= tree fruit), *baca* (= berry), to bear —, *fructum ferre* or *reddĕre,* to bear no —, *sterilem esse,* 2, fig = good and bad results, *fruges, fructus, commoda, orum, merces, -ēdis, pretium* (= reward) **fruitful,** adj *ferax, fecundus, fertilis, opimus* (= rich, rank), *uber, fructuosus,* † *frugifer,* † *fructifer,* † *pomifer* Adv. *fecunde, utiliter* (= profitably). **fruitfulness,** n *fertilitas, ubertas* **fruition,** n *usus, -ūs, fructus, -ūs* **fruitless,** adj *inutilis, sterilis, cassus, irritus.* Adv *incassum, frustra, nequi(c)quam, ad irritum, re infectâ* **fruit-tree,** n *pomum, pomus,* f

frustrate, v tr *ad vanum* or *ad irritum* or *ad vanum et irritum redigĕre, frustrari* (rather in sense of deceive), to be frustrated, *irritum fieri, ad irritum cadĕre* or *recidĕre* or *venire,* — a hope, *spem fallĕre* **frustration,** n *frustratio*

fry, I. n 1, of fish, *examen, fetus, -ūs,* 2, of men, common —, *plebs, plebecula* **II.** v tr *assare, frigĕre* **frying-pan,** n *sartago* (Juv), *frixorium* (Plin), out of the — into the fire, *ne praeter casam, ut aiunt,* or *de fumo ad flammam*

fudge! interj *gerrae! nugas!*

fuel, n *lignum* (or pl)

fugitive, I. adj *fugiens, fugax* **II.** n *domo* or *patriâ profugus, fugitivus, extorris*

full, I. adj *alcjs rei* or *alqâ re plenus, alqâ re completus, oppletus, confertus refertus, abundans* or *affluens, frequens* (= well attended, e g *theatrum, senatus*), to go with — sails, *passis velis vehi,* at — pace, *gradu pleno,* a — year, *annus solidus, integer* or *totus* Adv *plene,* see ALTOGETHER, QUITE, = copiously (of speech, etc.), *copiose, latius, fuse, abundanter, uberius* **II.** v tr of cloth, *durare, curare* **full-blown,** adj 1, lit *apertus,* 2, fig, *superbus, tumidus* **full-grown,** adj *adultus, pubes* (*puber*) **full-moon,** n *luna plena* **fulness,** n = abundance, *ubertas, copia* **fulfil,** v tr *conficĕre, efficĕre, ad effectum adducĕre, exsequi, persequi, peragĕre, patrare, perpetrare* (e g *facinus*), *consummare* (= to finish), *alqâ re fungi* (= — an office) **fulfilment,** n *confectio*

fuller, n *fullo* (Plin), —'s earth, *creta fullonia* (Plin)

fulminate, v tr 1, † *fulminare* (= to hurl thunderbolts and to cast down by), 2, fig *minas jactare* **fulmination,** n *minae.*

fulsome, adj *putidus,* — flattery, *nimia adulatio* Adv *putide* **fulsomeness,** n *molestia, nimia adulatio*

fumble, v intr see FEEL.

fume, I n *fumus, vapor, foetor* (= bad smell), *halitus, ūs* **II.** v intr *(ex)aestuare* **fumigate,** v tr *suffumigare*

fun, n *jocus, ludus* **funny,** adj. *ridiculus* Adv *ridicule*

function, n *munus, ĕris,* n, *officium, magistratus, -ūs, procuratio.*

fund, n 1, *pecunia,* 2, fig by some special noun (e g — of knowledge, *doctrina*) **fundamental,** adj *primus, principalis* Adv *funditus, penitus* **fundamentals,** n *elementa, -orum, principia, -orum.*

funeral, I. n *funus, -ĕris,* n, *exsequiae, pompa funeris* or *pompa* (= the procession), *justa, -orum, justa funebria* (= the last tribute), *sepultura* (= interment) **II.** adj *funebris,* † *funereus,* — pile, *rogus, pyra* **funereal,** adj *funebris, lugubris*

fungus, n *fungus, agaricon* (Plin) **fungous,** adj *fungosus* (Plin)

funnel, n *infu(n)dibulum, cornu*

fur, n *pellis* **furry,** adj *vellosus* **furrier,** n *pellio*

furbelow, n *instita*

furbish, v tr *interpolare, expolire*

furl, v tr. *vela legĕre*

furlong, n *stadium.*

furlough, n *commeatus, -ūs,* to give —, *alci commeatum dare,* on —, *in commeatu esse*

furnace, n *fornax.*

furnish, v tr 1, = to provide with, *alqm alqâ re instruĕre, ornare,* 2, = to supply, *suppeditare, praebēre,* 3, = to fit up (as a house, with furniture), *instruĕre, exornare et instruĕre* **furnished,** adj *alqâ re instructus, praeditus* **furniture,** n of a house, *supellex, -lectilis,* f, *apparatus, ūs*

furrow, I. n *sulcus* **II.** v tr *sulcos facĕre, agĕre, ducĕre, sulcare*

further, I. adj *ulterior* **II.** adv 1, *ulterius, amplius,* 2, = in fut. *porro, posthac,* 3, = yet more, *praeterea, ad hoc, jam, autem, accedit (quod), huc accedit quod, addendum eodem est quod, ad(j)ice quod,* what —? *quid vis amplius? quid porro?* **III.** interj *perge! pergite! pergamus!* **IV.** v tr *alqm* or *alqd (ad)juvare, alci* or *alci rei consulĕre* **furtherance,** n *auxilium* **furtherer,** n *adjutor* **furthest,** adj *ultimus*

furtive, adj *furtivus* Adv *furtim, furtive*

fury, n *furor, rabies,* a —, *Furia, Erinnys* **furious,** adj *rabidus, furiosus, furens, furibundus* Adv *rabide, furiose, furenter*

furze, n *ulex* (Plin)

fuse, v tr *liquefacĕre, fundĕre* **fusible,** adj *fusilis* **fusion,** n *fusio* (= outpouring)

fuss, I. n *tumultus, ūs* **II.** v intr. *tumultuari* **fussy,** adj *curiosus*

fustian, n. *gausapa* or *gausapes.*

fusty, adj see MOULDY

futile, adj *futilis, inanis, vanus* **futility,** n *futilitas, inanitas, vanitas*

future, I. adj *futurus, posterus;* a — governor, *imperaturus* **II.** n *futura, -orum* (e g *scire, prospicĕre*) **futurity,** n *tempus futurum* or *posterum*

G.

gabble, I. v intr *garrire* **II.** n *garrulitas*

gable, n *fastigium*

gad, v intr *vagari*

gadfly, n *oestrus, asilus, tabanus*

gag, I. v tr *os alci alqa re obvolvĕre et praeligare* **II.** n use noun describing the material of which gag is made (e g *linteum in os injectum*)

gage, n *pignus, ŏris,* n , see PLEDGE

gain, I. n *lucrum* (opp *damnum,* = loss or injury), *quaestus, -ūs* (= profit), *commodum* (= advantage), *emolumentum* (opp *detrimentum*), *compendium* (= savings), *fructus, ūs* (= natural growth), *praeda,* or in pl (= booty), *praemium* (= a prize) **II.** v tr *algd lucrari* (opp *perdĕre*), *consequi, assequi, capĕre,* — a place (that is, to reach it after effort), *locum capĕre, in alqm locum eniti* or *evadĕre* — a battle or victory, *superiorem discedĕre, vincĕre;* the enemy has —ed the day, *hostis vicit* or *victor erasit,* — a wager, *sponsione* or *sponsionem vincĕre,* — a lawsuit, *caus(s)am, judicium* (or *judicio*) *vincĕre, caus(s)am tenēre* or *obtinēre,* — a prize, *praemium auferre,* — a person's friendship, *in amicitiam alcjs recipi,* — over, *conciliare,* to try to — over, *alqd re hominum* (*plebis,* etc) *animos ad benevolentiam allicere, conciliare ad benevolentiam erga alqm* **gainful,** adj *quaestuosus, lucrosus*

gainsay, v tr see CONTRADICT

gait, n *incessus, -ūs*

gaiters, n *ocreae* (= leather coverings for soldiers, etc)

gala, n see FESTIVAL

galaxy, n *orbis, -is,* m , or *circulus lacteus,* † *via lactea*

gale, n 1, *ventus magnus, aura* (= breeze), 2, fig *aura* (e g *popularis*)

gall, I. n *fel, bilis* **II.** v tr 1, = rub, *terĕre,* 2, fig *mordēre* **galling,** adj *mordax*

gallant, I. adj 1, = brave, *fortis animosus, strenuus,* 2, = attentive to females, *amori deditus, amatorius* Adv *fortiter animose, strenue* **II.** n 1, *juvenis fortis,* 2, *amator* **gallantry,** n 1, *virtus, -ūtis,* f , *fortitudo,* 2, *amores, um*

gallery, n *porticus,* f (= an open — with pillars), *xystus* (= walk or alley formed by two lines of trees), *pinacothēca* (= picture —), *superior locus* (as in a theatre, e g *ex superiore loco spectare*), *cavea summa* or *ultima* (= the last row in a theatre to address the — *verba ad summam caveam spectantia dicĕre*), underground —, *cuniculus*

galley, n *navis actuaria* (= swift sailing ship), *navis longa, biremis, triremis* (= ship of war), to condemn to the —s, *alqm dare ad remum publicae triremis*

gallipot, n *ollula* (*aul-*)

gallon, n *congius*

gallop, I. n *gradus, -ūs, citatus,* at a —, *equo admisso* or *laxatis habenis* **II.** v intr *equo admisso,* etc , *vehi* or *currĕre*

gallows, n *crux* (crucifixion and strangling were the Roman equivalents for hanging, see HANG)

gamble, v intr *ludĕre,* — with dice *tesseris* or *talis ludĕre, alea ludĕre* **gambler,** n *aleator* **gambling,** n *alea,* to gain at —, *prosperā aleā uti*

gambol, v intr *ludĕre, lascivire*

game, I. n 1, *ludus, lusio ludicrum* (esp = public —), — of chance, *alea,* 2, = animal, *ferae,* on table, *caro ferina,* to make — of, *alqm ludibrio habēre, alqm ludere* or *illudĕre* **II.** v intr see GAMBLE **gamesome,** adj see PLAYFUL **gamester, gaming,** see GAMBLE **gaming table,** n *alveus*

gammon, n = — of bacon, *perna*

gammon, interj = nonsense! *garrae! nugae!*

gander, n *anser* (*mas* or *masculus,* opp *anser femina*)

gang, n *caterva, operae* (= of roughs)

gangway, n *forus*

gangrene, n *ossium caries, gangraena*

gaol, n *carcer, -ĕris,* m , *vincula, -orum*

gaoler, n *(carceris) custos*

gap, n *lacuna, hiatus, -ūs* **gape,** v intr *hiare*

garbage, n *purgamentum, quisquiliae*

garble, v tr = to falsify, *corrumpĕre, vitiare*

garden, I. n *hortus* a small —, *hortulus* **II** v intr *in horto fodĕre, hortum colĕre* **garden-stuff,** n *olus, ĕris,* n **gardening,** n *hortorum cultus, ūs* **gardener,** n *qui hortum colit*

gargle, I. n 1, *gargarizatio* (= the act, Cels), 2, for the fluid use verb **II.** v intr *gargarizare* (*ex*) *alqa re* (Cels)

garish, adj 1, = bright *clarus, splendidus,* 2, = gay, *nitidus* (= spruce), *fucatus* (= rouged)

garland, n *sertum*

garlic, n *al(l)ium*

garment, n *vestis,* see CLOTHES

garner, I. n *horreum* **II.** v tr *condĕre*

garnish, v tr (*ex*)*ornare, instruĕre*

garret, n *cenaculum superius,* to live in a —, *sub tegulis habitare, in superiore habitare cenaculo, tribus scalis habitare* (= up three pair of stairs)

garrison, I. n *praesidium, milites praesidiarii* **II** v tr *urbi praesidium imponĕre, in urbe pr (col)locare*

garrulity, n *garrulitas, loquacitas* **garrulous,** adj *garrulus, loquax, verbosus* Adv *loquaciter*

garter, n *periscelis* (mediaeval), in pl † *genualia, -ium* (Ov)

gas, n *spiritus, ūs, vapor,* "*gas quod dicitur*"

gasconade, n *jactatio, ostentatio venditatio* (*sui*), *venditatio quaedam atque ostentatio*

gash, I. n *vulnus, ĕris,* n **II.** v tr *vulnerare*

gasp, I. v intr *aegre spiritum ducĕre, anhelare,* † *singultare* **II.** n *anhelitus, ūs, singultus, -ūs* **gasping,** n *anhelitus ūs*

gastric, adj *ad stomachum pertinens* **gastronomy,** n *quae ad gulam pertinent*

gate, n *janua, porta* (= — of a city) **gatekeeper,** n *janitor* **gate-post,** n *postis*

gather, I. v tr 1, *legĕre* (= to pick up), *colligĕre, conquirĕre* (= to search out) *congerĕre* (= to heap up), *coacervare,* — flowers, *flores carpĕre,* — grapes, *vindemiare,* 2, = conjecture, *con(j)icĕre* **II.** v intr 1, = assemble, *convenire, congregari,* 2, of a sore, *suppurare* **gathering,** n 1, = assembly, *coetus, ūs,* 2, = a sore, *suppuratio* (Cels)

gaudy, adj *fucatus, magnificus* Adv *magnifice(nter)*

gauge, v tr *metiri,* see MEASURE

gaunt, adj *exilis,* see THIN

gauntlet, n *manicae,* to run the —, *per militum ordines currentem virgis caedi*

gauze, n *vestis coa*

gay, adj 1, of mind, *hilaris (hilarus), laetus;* 2, of colour, etc, *splendidus, nitidus* Adv *hilare, laete* **gaiety,** n *hilaritas, laetitia*

gaze (at), **I.** v intr *in obtutu alcjs rei haerēre defixum alqm* or *alqd intueri, contueri, contemplari* **II.** n *obtutus, -ūs, conspectus, ūs* **gazing-stock,** n *spectaculum*

gazette, n *acta (diurna), acta publica, orum*

gear, n *ornatus, -ūs, vestitus, ūs, supellex, -lectilis,* f (= household)

geld, v tr *castrare* **gelding,** n *cant(h)erius*

gem, n *gemma, lapis, lapillus* (both also with *generosus*)

gender, n *genus, -ĕris,* n **genealogy,** n *origo, stirps* (= the branches of a family) **genealogical,** adj *de origine,* etc, *scriptus, ad originem pertinens*

general, I. n *dux, imperator* (= g -in chief), the —'s tent, *praetorium,* to be —, *exercitui praeesse,* to appoint anyone —, *alqm exercitui praeficĕre* **II.** adj *generalis* (= relating to the genus or whole), *communis* (= common to all, opp *singularis,* = individually), *vulgaris,* comb *vulgaris communisque, omnium rerum,* or merely *omnium,* — want, *inopia omnium rerum,* — conversation, *omnium hominum sermo,* a — idea, *notio universa* or *summa, notio communis,* the — good, *omnium salus,* to devote to the — good, *in commune conferre,* in —, *ad summam, in universum, universe* (opp *proprie, nominatim*), *omnino* (opp *separatim*), *generatim* (opp *si(n)gillatim, per singulas species*), *communiter* Adv = usually, *fere, ferme, vulgo, plerumque* **generality,** n = most people, *vulgus, i,* n, *plerique* **generalization,** n *quod de omnibus rebus dictum est* **generalship,** n *ductus, -ūs,* under the — of Caesar, *Caesare duce,* to act with good —, *summo consilio rem gerere*

generate, v tr 1, *gignĕre, generare, (pro)creare, parĕre,* 2, = cause, *facĕre, efficĕre* **generation,** n 1, *generatio, procreatio* (e g *liberorum*), 2, = age, *saeculum, aetas,* the present —, *hujus aetatis homines, qui nunc vivunt homines* **generator,** n *genitor, procreator* **generative,** adj † *genitalis,* — organs, *genitalia, -ium*

generous, adj 1, = good of its kind, † *generosus, nobilis, eximius,* 2, = of a large heart, *generosus, magnificus, benignus, liberalis,* 3, = liberal, *largus, liberalis* Adv *bene, eximie, magnifice, benigne, liberaliter, large* **generosity,** n 1, see EXCELLENCE, 2, *magnificentia, magnanimitas, benignitas, liberalitas,* 3, *liberalitas, benignitas, beneficentia*

genesis, n see ORIGIN

genial, adj *comis, genialis* (of things, e g *hiem(p)s*) Adv *comiter, genialiter* **geniality,** n *comitas*

genitive, n (*casus*) *genitivus* (Gramm)

genius, n 1, = an imaginary spirit, *genius,* 2, = high, natural ability, *ingenium, indoles, -is,* of rude —, *crassā Minervā,* a man of — *vir magni* or *elati ingenii, vir ingenio praestans, magno ingenio praeditus homo*

genteel, adj *honestus, elegans, urbanus* Adv *honeste, eleganter, urbane* **gentility,** n *honestas, elegantia, urbanitas*

gentle, adj 1, = well-born, *generosus, ingenuus, nobilis,* 2, = — in disposition, *mitis, clemens, mansuetus, placidus,* 3, of wind, *lenis,* of a hill, *mollis, lenis* Adv *nobili loco ortus* or *natus, placide, leniter, molliter* **gentleman,** n 1, *homo generosus, ingenuus, nobilis, honesto* or *nobili loco natus,* 2, = well-bred, *homo urbanus, liberalis, ingenuus, generosus* **gentlemanly,** adj *liberalis, urbanus, ingenuus, generosus, honestus* **gentleness,** n 1, *nobilitas,* 2, *clementia, mansuetudo,* 3, *lenitas* **gentry,** n *nobilitas, nobiles, -ium, optimates, (i)um* **gentlewoman,** n see LADY

genuflexion, n see KNEEL

genuine, adj *sincerus, merus, germanus* Adv *reapse, sincere, vere* **genuineness,** n *auctoritas, fides,* many doubt of the — of this book, *multi dubitant hunc librum ab eo ad quem refertur conscriptum esse*

geography, n * *geographia, terrarum* or *regionum descriptio*

geology, n * *geologia* **geological,** adj. * *geologicus,* — time, *immensae antiquitatis*

geometry, n *geometria* **geometrical,** adj *geometricus* (γεωμετρικός) **geometer,** or **geometrician,** n *geometres, -ae,* m

germ, n 1, = — of plants, † *germen,* 2, fig *semen* (e g *malorum, discordiarum*) **germinate,** v intr *germinare* (Plin) **germination,** n *germinatio* **germane,** adj *affinis*

Germany, n *Germania* **German,** adj *Germanicus*

gestation, n *partus gerendi tempus* (Plin)

gesture, n *gestus -ūs* (= the mode of carrying the body), comb *motus gestusque* (*gestus* is used especially of speakers, players, etc) **gesticulate,** v intr *se jactare, gesticulari* (Suet), *gestus facĕre* or *agĕre* **gesticulation,** n *jactatio, gestus, -ūs, motus, -ūs*

get, v tr *acquirĕre, conquirĕre, consequi, capĕre, adipisci, nancisci, (com)parare, lucrari* (= to get gain), — anything done, *alqd faciendum curare,* — abroad, *percrebrescĕre,* — off, *discedĕre,* — up, *surgĕre,* — down, *descendĕre,* — forward, *proficĕre, provehi,* — in, *introire,* — near, *accedĕre,* — out, *egredi,* — round, *circumvenire,* — by heart, *memoriae alqd mandare* — with child, *gravidam facĕre,* — to, *pervenire,* — away! *aufer te hinc*

gewgaws, n *nugae, lenocinium*

ghastly, adj 1, *exsanguis, pallidus, cadaverosus, luridus,* 2, see TERRIBLE **ghastliness,** n 1, *pallor,* 2, see HORROR

ghost, n 1, = breath, *spiritus, -ūs, anima,* the Holy —, * *Spiritus Sanctus,* * *Paracletus,* 2, = in pl imaginary spirits, or the spirits of the dead, *lemures* (in gen), *manes* (= the shade or ghost of a particular person), *lares* (= the good spirits worshipped in the home), of a single person, *larva, umbra* (= the shade).

ghoul, n *larva teterrima*

giant, n *homo ingentis* or *immanis magnitudinis, homo eximiā corporis magnitudine, vir major quam pro humano habitu,* the giants, *gigantes,* one of the —, *gigas* **gigantic,** adj *eximiae* or *ingentis* or *immanis magnitudinis, eximia* or *ingenti* or *immani magnitudine,* a — labour, *moles, is*

gibbet, n see GALLOWS

gibe, I. n *ludibrium, sanna* (Juv) **II.** v tr *ludibrio habēre*

giddy, adj 1, lit *vertiginosus* (Plin), *vertigine correptus,* 2, fig *lĕvis, inconstans* Adv *inconstanter* **giddiness,** n 1, *vertigo,* 2, *animus lĕvis*

gift, n *donum,* see GIVE.

gig, n *cisium*

giggle, v intr *effuse ridēre, inepte ridēre, furtim cachinnare*

gild, v tr *inaurare, alci rei aurum illinĕre* or *alqd auro illinĕre*

gill, n = a measure, *hemina*

gills, n *branchiae* (Plin.)

gimlet, n *terebra*

gin, n = trap, *laqueus, tendicula*

gingerly, adv *pedetentim* (*pedetempt.*), *sensim*

gipsy, n **Cingarus, *Cingara*, fem

giraffe, n *camēlŏpardălis* (Plin.)

gird, v tr 1, (*suc*)*cingĕre, accingĕre*, — yourself, (*suc*)*cingi* or *accingi* (e g *gladio, ferro*), 2, fig — oneself to, = to apply to, *se accingĕre* or *accingi ad alqd*, or *alci rei* **girder,** n *trabs* **girdle,** n *zona, cingulum, cestus, balteus* (= belt)

girl, n *puella, virgo* **girlish,** adj *puellaris, virginalis* Adv *more puellarum.* **girlhood,** n *aetas puellaris*, she did it in her —, *puella fecit*

girth, n 1, = distance or space round, *ambitus, circuitus, complexus*, all -ūs, 2, of a horse, †*cingula*

give, v tr *alqd alci dare, praebēre, reddĕre, tradĕre, impertire, largiri*, or *alqm alqa re* or *alqd alci donare, ad alqd conferre* (= contribute), to — for = to buy at, *rem emĕre tanti*, to — word for word, *exprimĕre verbum de verbo*, — up, see CEASE, to — up for lost, *desperare de alqo* or *alqa re*, to — little attention to, *parum curare, neglegĕre* (*neglig.*) *alqd*, to — up yourself = to surrender, *se dare, manus dare*, (*con*)*cedĕre*, — in (of accounts), *rationem reddĕre, referre*, = to yield, see "— up yourself" above; — a blow, *plagam alci in(j)icĕre* **gift,** n *donum, munus, ĕris*, n, *praemium* (= a reward or prize), to make a —, *alci donum dare, alqm dono donare* **gifted,** adj *alqa re praeditus*, a — man, *vir summi ingenii* **giver,** n *qui donum dat, largitor*

gizzard, n *ingluvies, guttur*

glad, adj *laetus, hilaris* or *hilarus*, — at, *alqa re laetari, gaudēre* Adv *laete, hilare, hilariter* **gladden,** v tr *alqm* (*ex*)*hilarare* **gladness,** n *laetitia, hilaritas*

glade, n *silva*

gladiator, n *gladiator* **gladiatorial,** adj *gladiatorius*, a trainer of —s, *lanista*

glance, I. n (of the eyes), *oculorum conjectus*, -ūs II. v intr 1, = shine, *splendēre, fulgēre, nitēre*, 2, — at, *oculos con(j)icĕre in alqd, alqd leviter* or *strictim attingĕre* or *dicĕre, perstringĕre*

gland, n *glans* (Cels.)

glare, I. v intr *fulgēre* (= be bright), — at, *alqm* or *alqd intentis oculis tueri* II. n *fulgor, intenti* (*ut aiunt*) *oculi*

glass, n *vitrum* **glazier,** n *vitrarius qui fenestris vitrum inserit* **glassy,** adj *vitreus*

gleam, I. n 1, *fulgor*, 2, fig *aura*, — of hope, *specula* II. v intr *fulgēre*

glean, v tr *spicilegium facĕre* (= — in the field), *racemari* (= — in the vineyard) **gleaning,** n *spicilegium*

glee, n *hilaritas, laetitia* **gleeful,** adj *hilaris, laetus* Adv *hilariter, laete*

glen, n (*con*)*vallis*

glib, adj *loquax, garrulus, volubilis* Adv *loquaciter, volubiliter* **glibness,** n *loquacitas, garrulitas, volubilitas*

glide, v (*pro*)*labi*

glimmer, v intr *sublucēre*

glimpse, n see SIGHT, n

glisten, glitter, v intr *micare, candēre, fulgēre, nitēre, lucēre, splendēre.* **glistening, glittering,** adj *lucidus, candidus* (= — white, opp to *niger*, = — black), †*coruscus, nitidus, splendidus, splendens, fulgens*

gloat, v intr — over, *se a(d)spectu alcjs rei delectare*

globe, n *globus, sphaera, orbis terrarum* **globular,** adj *globosus*

gloom, n 1, lit *obscuritas, caligo, tenebrae* 2, fig *animus dejectus, afflictus, caligo, tenebrae, tristitia, maeror, maestitia* **gloomy,** adj 1, *obscurus*, †*tenebrosus, caliginosus*, 2, *tristis, maestus* Adv *obscure, per tenebras* or *caliginem* (e g *visus*), *maeste*

glory, I. n *gloria, honos* (*honor*), *decus, ŏris*, n, to be a — to, *laudi* or *gloriae esse alci, laudem alci afferre* II. v intr (*de*) *alqa re gloriari* (or with *quod*) **glorify,** v tr *laudibus ornare* or *efferre* or *tollĕre, alqm gloria afficĕre, alqm* (*laudibus*) *celebrare* **glorious,** adj *gloriosus*, (*prae*)*clarus, amplus* (esp in superl.), *illustris* Adv *gloriose*, (*prae*)*clare, ample* **glorying,** n *gloriatio, praedicatio*

gloss, I. n 1, = a shining, *nitor, candor*, 2, = an explanation, *interpretatio* II. v tr — over, *extenuare, mitigare* **glossary,** n *glossae.* **glossy,** adj *nitidus*

glove, n *manicae* (= sleeves)

glow, I. n *ardor, fervor, aestus*, ūs II. v intr *candēre, ardēre, fervēre*, to begin to —, (*ex*)*ardescĕre, incandescĕre, excandescĕre* **glowing,** adj *candens, ardens, fervens, fervidus*, to have a — desire for *desiderio alcjs flagrare* **glow-worm,** n *cicindēla, lampyris* (Plin.)

glue, I. n *glutinum, gluten* II. v tr (*con*)*glutinare* **glutinous,** adj *glutinosus, lentus, viscosus*

glut, I. v tr 1, lit *satiare, saturare, explēre*, 2, fig — the market, *vilitatem annonae efficĕre* II. n *satias, satietas*

glutton, n *homo edax, vorax, gurges, ĭtis* m, *hel(l)uo*, comb *gurges et helluo* **gluttonous,** adj *edax, vorax, gulosus* (Juv. Sen.) Adv *avide* **gluttony,** n *hel(l)uatio, edacitas*

gnarled, adj see KNOTTY

gnash, v tr *dentibus* (*in*)*frendĕre, dentibus stridĕre* or *stridĕre* **gnashing,** n *stridor dentium* (Cels.)

gnat, n *culex*

gnaw, v tr 1, *alqd* (*ar*)*rodĕre, circumrodĕre*, 2, fig *pungĕre, cruciare, mordēre* **gnawing,** adj *mordax*

gnome, n 1, see MAXIM, 2, see FAIRY

go, v intr *ire, gradi* (= to step), *ingredi* (= to step into), *incedĕre* (= to enter), *vadĕre, ambulare* (= to walk), *spatiari* (= to strut), *commeare ad alqm* (*in locum*), *procedĕre* (= to — forth), to — out, *prodire* (of the harbour, *e portu*), *exire, excedĕre, egredi*, — in, *inire, introire, intrare, ingredi*, — over, *transire, praeterire locum* (= to pass by a place), — on board (*navem*) *a(d)scendĕre, conscendere*, — down, *descendere*, — up, *a(d)scendĕre*, — before, *anteire, antegredi* (with accus.), — through, *transire*, = to set out, proceed, march, *proficisci* (= — on foot or horseback), = to betake yourself, *conferre se alqo*, = to make for, *contendĕre alqo* In imper as command, *abi! abi hinc! apage sis!* to let one —, *alqm dimittĕre* where are you —ing? *quo tendis?* what are you —ing to do? *quid cogitas?* to — and come, *venire et redire, ire et redire*, to — after, *alqd petĕre*, — to see, *spectatum ire*, — for someone, *alqm arcessĕre*, the affair begins to — better, *incipit* *res melius ire*; how goes it? how is it? how are you? *quomodo habes te?* or *est tibi?* the answer is made by *bene, recte, male*, etc.; so of health, *quomodo vales?* of action, *quid agis? quid agitur?* is all well? answers, *valeo, bene mecum agitur*; — for, = be sold at, *emi* or *vendi*, with genit. of price; — about, = attempt, *alqd experiri, moliri*; — beyond, *excedĕre*; — off (of a weapon), *emitti* (with the thing shot as subj.). **go-between**, n. *conciliator, interpres, -ĕtis*, m. and f., *internuntius*.

goad, I. n. *stimulus*; to kick against a —, *stimulum pugnis caedĕre, adversum stimulum calcare*. **II.** v.tr. *alqm ad* or *in alqd stimulare, incitare*.

goal, n. *meta* (= the pillar at the end of the course; then in poets, fig.), *calx* (lit. and fig.).

goat, n. *capra, capella*. **he-goat**, n. *caper, hircus*. **goatherd**, n. *caprarius*.

gobble, v.tr. (*de*)*vorare*.

goblet, n. *scyphus*; see Cup.

goblin, n. *umbra quae homines inquietat*; * *daemon, larva*, in pl. *lemures*.

God, n. *Deus* (as the highest being, often with title *Optimus, Maximus*), *numen divinum, numen* (= the nod, i.e. the supreme will), † *divus*; the —s, *di(i)*, † *caelestes*, † *caelites*, † *caelicolae, di(i) superi, superi* also (opp. *inferi*); — of the house, *lares, penates*; to raise to the honours of a —, *alqm in deorum numerum referre, alqm inter deos referre, alqm consecrare*; to call — to witness, *Deum testari*; for —'s sake I beg, *Deum testans oro te, pro Deum fidem!* by the —s, *per deos*; so help me —, *ita me Deus (ad)juvet* or *amet, hercule* or *mehercule*, so also *Deus me perdat!* may — be favourable, *di(i) propitii sint*; in —'s name, *quod bonum, faustum, felix fortunatumque sit! quod bene vertat!* — grant, *faxit Deus! utinam di(i) ita faxint! utinam Deus ratum esse jubeat!* — forbid! *quod Deus prohibeat! quod omen Deus avertat! di meliora!* **goddess**, n. *dea*, † *diva*. **Godhead**, n. *numen*. **godless**, adj. 1, *impius* (*erga Deum*, so *erga patriam, erga parentes*); 2, *atheus* or *atheos* (= God-denying). **godlessness**, n. *impietas erga deos*. **godlike**, adj. *divinus*. **godly**, adj. *pius erga deos*. **godliness**, n. *pietas erga deos*. **godsend**, n. *ἕρμαιον ut ita dicam* (in colloquial passage); *quod quasi divinitus oblatum est*.

gold, n. *aurum*. **gold-dust**, n. *ballux* (Plin.). **gold-leaf**, n. *bractea, auri lamina*. **gold-mine**, n. *aurifodina* (Plin.). **goldsmith**, n. *aurifex*. **golden**, adj. *aureus, ex auro factus*.

good, I. adj. *bonus*, (in gen.) *jucundus, suavis, dulcis* (= pleasant), *probus* (= what it ought to be), *commodus* (= having the right quantity or quality), *opportunus* (= suitable), *prosper, secundus* (*res prosperae*, = — circumstances), *utilis* (= useful), *salutaris* (= healthful), *honestus* (= morally —, honourable), *simplex* (= unpretending), *benignus* (= kind); — health, *bona valetudo*; — for anything, *ad alqd utilis, commodus, opportunus, idoneus, aptus*; — eyes, *oculi acres et acuti*; my — friend, *o bone! sodes!* a — many, *plerique, aliquot, complures*; a — part, *bona pars* (= a considerable part); a — while, *aliquantum temporis*; to be — for, as a remedy, *alci rei* or *contra alqd prodesse, alci rei medēri, contra alqd efficacem esse*; to make —, *alqd sarcire* (e.g. *detrimentum acceptum*), *alqd restituĕre*. **II.** interj. — bye, *vale, ave* (*valete, avete*, pl.); *bene (agis), bene facis! bene fecisti! bene habet! euge*, (well!) *non repugno! nihil impedio!* **III.** n. *bonum*; the highest —, *summum bonum*; external —s, *externa bona, -orum, res externae* or *humanae*; —s, = possessions, *bona*; = wares or merchandise, *merx*; to do much —, *de multis bene merēri*; — to, *conferre in alqm beneficia (multa), bene de alqo mereri*; to turn to —, *alqd in bonum vertĕre*. **good-breeding**, n. *humanitas*. **good-fellowship**, n. *comitas*. **good-for-nothing**, adj. *nequam*. **good-humour**, n. *comitas, facilitas*. **good-humoured**, adj. *comis, facilis, benignus*. Adv. *comiter, benigne*. **good-looking**, adj. *pulcher, venustus*. **goodly**, adj. 1, see Good-looking; 2, = large, *magnus*. **good-nature**, n. see Good-humour. **goodness**, n. 1, = excellence, *bonitas*; 2, moral —, *probitas, virtus, -ūtis*, f.; 3, = kindness, *benignitas, bonitas*.

goose, n. *anser*, m., or *anser femina*; — flesh, *caro anserina*.

gore, I. n. *cruor*. **II.** v.tr. *transfigĕre, confodĕre*. **gory**, adj. *cruentus, cruentatus*.

gorge, I. n. 1, = throat, *gula, guttur*; 2, = a narrow pass, *angustiae, saltus, -ūs*. **II.** v.tr. *alqm (ex)satiare, alqm (ex)saturare*; — oneself, *exsatiari (vino ciboque)*.

gorgeous, adj. *splendidus, magnificus, lautus*. Adv. *splendide, magnifice, laute*. **gorgeousness**, n. *splendor, magnificentia*.

gormandize, v.intr. *hel(l)uari*. **gormandizer**, n. *hel(l)uo*.

gospel, n. * *evangelium*.

gossamer, n. *aranea* (= spider's web).

gossip, I. n. 1, = idle talk, *sermo, rumor*; 2, = talkative person, *homo garrulus, femina garrula*; 3, = friend, *familiaris*. **II.** v.intr. *sermonem cum alqo conferre*.

gouge, v.tr. *scalpro eximĕre* or *exsecare*.

gourd, n. *cucurbita*.

gout, n. *arthrītis*; — in the hands, *chīrāgra*; — in the feet, *podăgra*. **gouty**, adj. *arthriticus*.

govern, v.tr. 1, = — a province, etc., *gubernare, administrare, gerĕre, temperare, curare, reipublicae praeesse*; 2, in gen. = — temper, etc., *alci rei moderari, alqd temperare, regĕre, coercēre*. **government**, n. 1, = governing, *administratio, procuratio, cura*; 2, = power, *imperium, regnum, dicio*; 3, as place, *provincia*; 4, = rulers, *ii penes quos est reipublicae administratio*. **governor**, n. 1, in gen. *gubernator, rector*; 2, state —, *praefectus, propraetor, proconsul, legatus*.

gown, n. *toga, vestis*; a lawyer's —, *toga forensis*; the manly —, *toga virīlis*; a morning —, *toga cubicularis* or *domestica*; a woman's —, *palla, stola*.

grace, I. n. 1, = favour, *gratia, favor*, comb. *gratia et favor, studium*, comb. *studium et favor, voluntas* (= inclination), *benevolentia* (= kindness), *indulgentia* (= special favour), *beneficium, venia* (= pardon): he grows in —, *mactus est virtute*; by the — of God, *Dei beneficio, Deo favente*; — in speaking, *facundia, lepos*; — at meals, *gratiarum* (= thanks) *actio*; to be in the good —s of, *apud alqm plurimum gratiâ pollēre*; to gain the — of, *alcjs gratiam sibi conciliare*; your —, **Clementia tua*; the —s, *Gratiae*; with a good, bad —, *cum bonâ, malâ gratia* (Ter.); 2, = gracefulness, *venustas* (= attraction, charm), *elegantia*; *lepos* (= — in words); feminine —, *muliebris venustas*; — of expression, *suavitas dicendi*. **II.** v.tr. *honestare, (ad)ornare, decorare*. **graceful**, adj. *venustus, decorus, elegans, lepidus*. Adv. *venuste, decore, eleganter, lepide*. **graceless**, adj. *improbus*. Adv. *improbe*. **gracious**, adj. *propitius* (esp. of gods); see Kind.

grade, n. = a step, *gradus, -ūs, a(d)scensus, -ūs* (= a step up); there are many —s in human society, *gradus plures sunt societatis hominum*;

— of honour, *gradus honoris* or *dignitatis* **gradual,** adj , **gradually,** adv *per gradus, gradatim,* or *pau(l)latim, sensim* **graduate, I.** v intr *ad gradum (Baccalaurei in artibus,* = as B A , etc) *admitti* **II.** n. *ad gradum (Baccalaurei, etc.) admissus.*

graft, I. n *surculus* **II.** v tr *surculum arbori inserĕre*

grain, n 1, = a seed, etc , *granum, mica* (e g *salis*), 2, = corn, *frumentum*

graminivorous, adj (*animal*) *quod herbis pascitur*

grammar, n 1, = the science of —, *grammatica, ae,* or *grammatica, orum,* or *grammatice*, 2, = a book on —, *liber grammaticus* or *ad grammaticam rationem pertinens* **grammatical,** adj *grammaticus* Adv *grammatice* (Quint) **grammarian,** n *grammaticus*

granary, n *horreum, granaria, -orum*

grand, adj *grandis, eximius, magnificus, amplus* Adv *eximie, magnifice, ample* **grandeur,** n *amplitudo, majestas* **grandees,** n *proceres, optimates* **grandiloquent,** adj *grandiloquus, magniloquus* (late n. prose), *tumidus* Adv *tumide* **grandiloquence,** n *oratio tumida* **granddaughter,** n *neptis* **grandfather,** n *avus* **grandmother,** n *avia* **grandson,** n *nepos* **great-granddaughter,** n *proneptis* **great-grandfather,** n *proăvus* (so backward, *abăvus, atăvus, trităvus*) **great-grandmother,** n *proăvia* **great-grandson,** n. *pronĕpos*

grange, n 1, = barn, *horreum*, 2, = country-house, *villa*

granite, n *lapis, lapidis,* m *saxum*

grant, I. n *gratia, beneficium, donum, praemium, venia, concessio* (= the granting) **II.** v tr *concedĕre,* see GIVE , *sinĕre* (= allow), this —ed, *hoc dato* or *concesso*, —ed that, or that not, *ut sit, ne sit, ut non sit.*

grape, n *acinus* or *acinum* (= a single grape), *uva* (= a bunch of grapes)

graphic, adj *expressus*, to give a — description, *alqd tanquam sub oculos sub(j)icĕre* Adv *clare.*

grapple, v tr *cum alqo luctari* **grappling-iron,** n *ferrea, manus, ūs, harpago.*

grasp, I. v tr 1, *(ap)prehendĕre, comprehendere, prensare*, — anyone's hand, *manum alcjs amplecti*, 2, fig *concipĕre, intellegĕre,* see COMPREHEND, — at, *alqd (ap)petĕre, captare* **II.** n 1, *complexus, -ūs*, to wrest from the —, *de manibus alqd extorquēre*, 2, *mens, captus, -ūs* **grasping,** adj *avarus*

grass, n *gramen, herba* (= the young and fresh grass) **grassy,** adj *herbidus, herbosus, gramineus* **grasshopper,** n *gryllus* (*grillus*) (Plin)

grate, n *focus, caminus*

grate, v tr 1, = rub, *contĕrĕre*, 2, fig see ANNOY **grating,** n *cancelli, clathri*

grateful, adj 1, = pleasant, *(per)gratus, acceptus,* comb *gratus acceptusque, jucundus, perjucundus, suavis*, 2, = thankful, *gratus, beneficii* or *beneficiorum memor,* comb *memor gratusque* Adv *grate, grato animo* **gratitude,** n *gratus animus, memor beneficii* or *beneficiorum animus, gratus animus et beneficii memor, grata beneficii memoria* **gratify,** v tr *alci gratificari, alqm delectare, morem alci gerĕre* **gratification,** n *expletio* (= satisfaction), *delectatio* to have — from, *voluptatem ex alqā re percipĕre* **gratifying,** adj *gratus* **gratis** adv *grat(i)is, sine mercede,* comb *grat(i)is et sine mercede, gratuito, sine pretio* **gratuitous,** adj *gratuitus* Adv see GRATIS **gratuity,** n. see ALMS, GIFT

grave, adj *gravis* (= full of excellence), *serius, severus* **gravity,** n 1, *gravitas, severitas*, to have — of face (= look grave), *vultum ad severitatem componĕre,* also *vultum componĕre*, 2, (in physics) *gravitas* **gravitation,** n *vis et gravitas alcjs rei, pondus, -ĕris,* n , *et gravitas.*

grave, I. n 1, *sepulc(h)rum, bustum, tumulus* (= a mound), to carry to the —, *sepelire, exsequias alcjs funeris prosequi* 2, = death, *mors, inferi*, he took the hope with him into the —, *moriens ferebat secum spem* **II.** v tr see ENGRAVE

gravel, n *glarea*

gravy, n *jus, juris,* n , *sucus*

gray, adj *canus* (= turning white, as the hair from age), *ravus* (of the sea, the eyes), *caesius* (= blue green, esp of the eyes), *glaucus* (of the eyes, etc), *(capilli) cani* (= gray hairs) **graybeard,** n *senex* **grayness,** n *canities*

graze, I. v tr *pascĕre* **II.** v intr *pasci* **grazier,** n *pecuarius*

graze, v tr = touch, *stringĕre, radĕre*

grease, I n *adeps, lardum* **II.** v tr *ung(u)ĕre, alqd alqā re illinĕre, perlinĕre* (Col), *oblinĕre* **greasy,** adj *unctus* (= rubbed with grease), *pinguis* (= fat)

great, adj *magnus, grandis, amplus, vastus, immanis, spatiosus* (= roomy), *procērus* (= tall), *altus* (= high or deep), *(ex)celsus* (= lofty) , a — assembly, *conventus, ūs, celeber*, a — man, *vir magnus, clarus,* or *illustris*, a — statesman, *reipublicae gerendae scientissimus*, too —, *nimius*, extraordinarily —, *ingens, praegrandis*, very —, *maximus* (*maxi*) (in reference to contents and quantity), *summus* (= the highest in regard to rank or position), *suprēmus* (in relation to rank and to inferiors) Adv *magnopere, valde, vehementer* (e g *vehementer commotus*, — disturbed) "Greatest" must often be expressed by superlatives , the — enemy, *alcjs* or *alci inimicissimus*, — chatterer, *homo loquacissimus* or *omnium loquacissimus*, so —, *tantus*, how —, *quantus*, soever —, *quantuscunque, quantusvis, quantuslibet*, as — again, *altero tanto major*, twice as —, *duplo major, duplus*, as — as, *tantus*, followed by *quantus* or *instar* (e g *instar montis*) the —, *nobiles, optimates*, — grandfather, see under GRAND **greatcoat,** n. *pallium, lacerna, paenula* (all = cloak) **greatness,** n 1, *magnitudo, amplitudo*, 2, — of mind, *animi dignitas, gravitas, amplitudo, magnitudo, magnanimitas*

greaves, n *ocreae*

Greece, n *Graecia* **Greek,** adj *Graecus*

greedy, adj *alcjs rei avidus, cupidus* Adv. *avide, cupide* **greediness,** n *aviditas, cupiditas* See GLUTTONY

green, I. adj. 1, *viridis* (in gen), *virens* (= still green), *glaucus* (= sea-green), 2, = fresh, *recens, vivus, crudus* (not ripe) **II.** n 1, *viriditas, color viridis*, 2, = grassy spaces, *campus* **greens,** n *olera, -um* **green grocer,** n *qui olera vendit* **greenhouse,** n perhaps *sub vitro esse* or *habēre* (= to be or keep in a —) **greenness,** n *viriditas*

greet, v tr *(con)salutare, alqm liberaliter appellare, salutem alci dare, alqm salvēre jubēre* **greeting,** n *(con)salutatio, salus, -ūtis,* f , *appellatio* (= address)

gregarious, adj *qui congregari solent*

gridiron, n *craticula* (Mart)

grief, n *aegritudo* (for any disturbance of

mind), *sol(l)icitudo* (= anxiety), *dolor* (= pain of heart), *maeror* (= sadness), *luctus, -ūs* (= sorrow, esp. the display of it), *angor*. **grieve, I.** v.tr. *alqm dolore afficĕre, dolorem alci afferre, alqm alcjs rei piget*. **II.** v.intr. *maerēre alqd, dolēre alqd* (*de* or *ex*) *alqā re, alqm alcjs rei piget*. **grievance,** n. *injuria* (= wrong done), *querimonia, querel(l)a* (= complaint). **grievous,** adj. *acerbus, gravis, molestus*. Adv. *acerbe, moleste, graviter*. **grievousness,** n. *acerbitas, molestia, gravitas*.

griffin, n. *gryps*.

grill, v.tr. see ROAST.

grim, adj. †*torvus*, †*trux*, *saevus*. Adv. *saeve, ferociter*. **grimness,** n. *saevitia, ferocia, ferocitas*.

grimace, n. *os distortum*; to make —s, *os ducĕre, os* (*dis*)*torquēre*.

grimy, adj. see DIRTY.

grin, I. n. use *rictus, -ūs*. **II.** v.intr. use *rictu ridēre*.

grind, v.tr. 1, *molĕre*; to — the teeth, *dentibus frendĕre*; 2, — the face of the poor, *egentes vexare, premĕre*. **grinder,** n. 1, *qui alqd molit*; 2, of teeth, *dens genuinus*. **grindstone,** n. *cos*.

grip, I. v.tr. see SEIZE. **II.** n. *manus, -ūs*, f. **gripe,** v.tr. = to give pain, *alqm torminibus afficĕre*; to be —ed, *torminibus* or *ex intestinis laborare, torminibus affectum esse*. **gripes,** n. *tormina, -um*.

grisly, adj. *foedus, teter*. **grisly-bear,** n. *ursus*.

grist, n. *farina*; to bring — to his own mill, *quaestum ad se redigĕre*.

gristle, n. *cartilāgo* (Plin.). **gristly,** adj. *cartilagineus* (Plin.).

grit, n. *ptisăna* (= — of barley) (Cels.), *arena* (= — of sand).

groan, I. v.intr. *gemĕre, gemitus edĕre*. **II.** n. *gemitus, -ūs*.

grocer, n. *qui aromata vendit*. **grocery,** n. *aromata, -um* (= spices (Col.)).

groin, n. *inguen*.

groom, I. n. *agāso, equiso*; — of the chamber, *cubicularius*. **II.** v.tr. *curare*.

groove, n. *canālis, canaliculus, stria*.

grope, v.intr. *errare*; — one's way, *iter explorare*. Adv. *pedetemptim* (*pedetent-*).

gross, I. adj. 1, = thick, *crassus, densus*; 2, = too great, *nimius, incredibilis*; 3, = disgraceful, *turpis, foedus, indecōrus*. Adv. *dense, nimium, incredibiliter, turpiter, foede, indecore*. **II.** n. 1, = 144, *duodecies duodecim*; 2, in the —, *fere, ferme* (= generally), *in universum* (= altogether). **grossness,** n. 1, *crassitudo, densitas*; 2, *nimia magnitudo*; 3, *turpitudo, foeditas*; — of manners, *inhumanitas*.

grotesque, adj. *immanis, mirus*. Adv. *mire*. **grotesqueness,** n. *mira species*.

grotto, n. *antrum*.

ground, I. n. 1, *humus*, f., *solum, terra*; on the —, *humi*; 2, = reason of a thing, *fundamentum, ratio, caus(s)a, principium*; 3, = — of a battle, *locus*; 4, to gain —, *proficĕre*; of a rumour, *percrebescĕre*. **II.** v.tr. = teach, *alqm alqd docēre*. **III.** v.intr. of a ship, *sidĕre*. **groundless,** adj. *vanus, futilis, fictus*. Adv. *sine caus(s)ā, temere, ex vano*. **groundlessness,** n. *vanitas*. **groundwork,** n. 1, of a building, *substructio, fundamentum*; 2, fig. *fundamentum, principium*.

group, I. n. *caterva, globus, circulus*. **II.** v.tr. *disponĕre*. **grouping,** n. *dispositio*.

grove, n. *lucus, nemus, -ŏris*, n., *arbustum*.

grovel, v.intr. *humi jacēre, humi serpĕre*. **grovelling,** adj. *abjectus, humilis, sordidus, submissus, servilis, turpis*. Adv. *humiliter, sordide, submisse, serviliter, turpiter*.

grow, I. v.intr. *crescĕre, augeri, ingravescĕre* (— worse); to let the beard —, *barbam promittĕre*; — up, *adolescĕre, pubescĕre*. **II.** v.tr. *alĕre, colĕre*. **grower,** n. *cultor*. **grown-up,** adj. *adultus, pubes, grandis*. **growth,** n. *auctus, -ūs, incrementum*.

growl, I. n. *fremitus, -ūs*. **II.** v.intr. *fremĕre*.

grub, I. n. *vermiculus*. **II.** v.tr. — up, *eruĕre*.

grudge, I. n. *simultas, invidia* (= a dislike). **II.** v.tr. *alci alqd invidēre*; see ENVY.

gruel, n. *cremor avenae, ptisana, pulticula*.

gruff, adj. *acerbus, raucus, asper*. Adv. *raucā voce*. **gruffness,** n. *rauca vox*.

grumble, v.intr. *murmurare, mussare*.

grunt, I. n. *grunnitus, -ūs*. **II.** v.intr. *grunnire*.

guarantee, I. n. 1, = surety, *sponsio, vadimonium* (= recognizance), *fides*; 2, = guarantor, *vas, praes, sponsor, obses, -idis*, m. and f. (= hostage). **II.** v.tr. *alqm* or *alqd* or *de alqā re praestare, fidem alci dare* or *interponĕre, pro alqo* (*pecuniam*) *intercedĕre*.

guard, n. 1, = a watch for the security of others, *custodia, praesidium, excubiae, vigiliae, statio* (= a post or file of men); to keep —, *excubare, excubias habēre* or *agĕre, vigilias agĕre, stationem agĕre* or *habēre, in statione esse*; others mount —, *alii succedunt in stationem* (all of military matters); 2, = the persons forming the guard, *custodes, excubiae, excubitores* (= —s for the security of a place), *vigiliae, vigiles* (= —s by night), *statio*; to place the —, *custodias* or *vigilias* or *stationes disponĕre*. **II.** v.tr. *custodire, alci* (*rei*) *praesidēre*; see PROTECT; — against, *alqd* or *ab alqā re praecavēre*. **guardian,** n. 1, in gen. *defensor, praeses, custos, propugnator*; 2, = — of a ward, *tutor, curator*. **guardianship,** n. 1, *custodia, praesidium, fides, tutela*; 2, *tutela*. **guarded,** adj. *cautus*. Adv. *caute*.

guerdon, n. *praemium, merces, -ēdis*, f.

guess, I. v.tr. *alqd* (*opinione* or *conjecturā*) *augurari, con*(*j*)*icĕre, conjecturā consequi, opinari, suspicari*. **II.** n. *conjectura*.

guest, n. *hospes, -ĭtis*, m., *hospita*, f. (= one who is received into the home and entertained there); to receive as —, *alqm hospitio excipĕre*; one brought uninvited, *umbra*. **guest-chamber,** n. *cubiculum hospitale*.

guide, I. n. 1, lit. *dux*; 2, fig. *dux, auctor, suasor*. **II.** v.tr. 1, *ducĕre*; 2, *regĕre, gubernare, moderari*. **guidance,** n. *ductus, -ūs, consilium*, or use *dux, auctor* (e.g. *te duce*). **guide-post,** n. *lapis* or *milliarium* (= mile-stone).

guild, n. *collegium*. **guildhall,** n. *curia*.

guile, n. *dolus, astutia*. **guileful,** adj. *dolosus, astutus*. Adv. *dolose, astute*. **guileless,** adj. *simplex, sincerus*. Adv. *simpliciter, sincere, sine fuco ac fallaciis*. **guilelessness,** n. *simplicitas*.

guilt, n. *vitium, culpa, noxia* (= — as a condition), *noxa* (= injury), *delictum* (= crime). **guilty,** adj. *noxius, sons, sceleratus*. Adv. *scelerate*. **guiltless,** adj. *innocens, insons, culpā vacuus* or *carens*; to be —, *extra noxiam esse, extra culpam esse, integer*.

guise, n. *mos, moris*, m., *habitus, -ūs, species*.

gulf, n. *sinus, -ūs* (= a bay), *gurges, -ĭtis*, m., *vorago* (= a whirlpool).

gull, I. n *gavia* **II.** v tr *alqm decipĕre, alci verba dare* **gullible,** adj *credulus*

gullet, n *gula, guttur*

gully, n *alveus* (= bed of a stream)

gulp, I. n *haustus, ūs* **II.** v tr *haurire, absorbere.*

gum, I. n 1, of the mouth, *gingiva;* 2, of trees, etc, *gummi* (Plin). **II.** v tr *glutinare* (Plin) **gummy,** adj *gummosus* (Plin), *glutinosus* (Cels)

gun, n **sclopetum,* where possible use *tormentum* (= engine for hurling stones, etc) **gunpowder,** n **pulvis pyrius*

gurgle, v intr *murmurare, † susurrare*

gush, v intr — out, *effundi* or *se effundĕre ex alqâ re*

gust, n *venti impetus, -ūs, ventus violens, procella* **gusty,** adj *turbidus, procellosus*

gut, n **I.** *intestinum* **II.** v tr 1, *exenterare* (ante and post class), 2, fig *exinanire*

gutter, n *canalis, cloaca*

guttural, adj *(sonus) gravis.*

guzzle, v intr *(per)potare* **guzzler,** n *homo ebriosus*

gymnasium, n *gymnasium, palaestra* **gymnastic,** adj *gymnicus, palaestricus* **gymnastics,** n *ars gymnastica, palaestra*

gypsum, n *gypsum*

gypsy, n see GIPSY

H.

ha! interj *ha!*

haberdasher, n *qui pannos vendit* **haberdashery,** n *panni*

habiliment, n *vestis, vestitus, -ūs*

habit, n 1, *consuetudo, mos, moris,* m, *usus, ūs,* 2, of body, *habitus, ūs,* 3, see HABILIMENT **habitable,** adj *habitabilis* **habitation,** n *domicilium, sedes, is,* comb *sedes et domicilium, habitatio* **habitual,** adj *inveteratus, usitatus, usu receptus*, — drunkard, *ebriosus* Adv *de* or *ex more* **habituate,** v tr *alqm assuefacĕre* (with infin or *ad*)

hack, v tr *caedĕre*, — in pieces, *concidĕre* **hackneyed,** adj *tritus*

haft, n *manubrium, capulus* (= hilt of a sword)

hag, n *anus, ūs,* or *anicula*, an old —, *vetula* **haggard,** adj *morbo* or *maerore confectus*

haggle, v tr 1, in buying, *minore pretio alqd emere velle, pretium facĕre* (= set a price), 2, see QUARREL

hail, I n *grando* **II.** v intr it —s, *grandinat* (Sen)

hail, I. v tr *alqm salutare, appellare* **II.** interj *salve! ave!* — to you! *macte esto! macte virtute esto! o te felicem!*

hair, n *pilus* (= a single —), *pili* (= — in general), *seta* (= a bristle), *crinis, coma* (= the hair of the head), *caesaries* (= flowing —), *villus, villi,* (= the thick hair of beasts, e g *villosissimus animalium lepus*), a fine —, *pilus tenuis*, thick —, *pilus crassus*, thin — *pili rari*, downy —, *lanugo*, — of the eyebrows, *supercilia, orum;* to cut —, *pilos recidĕre, tondēre*, to a —, *rem acu tetigisti, rem ipsam putasti*, the account tallies to a —, *ratio ad nummum convenit*, not a —'s breadth, *ab alqâ re non transversum, ut aiunt, digitum discedere*, false —, *capillamentum* (Suet.), *alieni capilli*, a — band, *redimiculum, vitta* **hair-cloth,** n *cilicium* **hairdresser,** n *tonsor, cinerarius* **hairpin,** n *crinale* **hairsplitting,** n *disserendi spinae, minuta subtilitas* **hairy,** adj *crinitus, capillatus, comatus* (opp *calvus*), *intonsus* (= unshaved), *pilosus, setosus, capillosus, comosus* (= having much hair), to be —, *pilos habēre*

halcyon, I. n *(h)alcedo, (h)alcyon* **II.** adj *serenus*, — days, *dies sereni et tranquilli, (h)alcedonia, orum, (h)alcyonei dies*

hale, adj *sanus, validus, robustus*, comb *salvus et sanus, sanus et salvus*

hale, v tr. *rapĕre, trahĕre*

half, I. adj *dimidius, dimidiatus* **II.** n *dimidium, dimidia pars, semis* (e g heir to — an estate, *heres ex semisse*) **III.** adv *semi* as prefix, e g **half-asleep,** adj *semisomnus* or *semisomnis* **half-brother,** n *eodem patre, eadem matre natus* **half-circle,** n *semicirculus* **half-hour,** n *semihora* **half-moon,** n *luna dimidiata* **half-open,** adj *semiapertus* **half ounce,** n *semuncia* **half-pound,** n *selibra* **half-sister,** n *eodem patre* or *eadem matre nata* **halve,** v tr *in aequas partes dividĕre* **halved,** adj *bipartitus, dimidiatus* **halves!** interj *in commune!* (Sen), to go —, *dimidiam cum alqo partem dividĕre*

hall, n *atrium, vestibulum*, — for public meetings, *forum, conciliabulum*

halloo, I. n = the — of hunters, *venantium voces*, (in gen) *clamor, clamores* **II.** v intr *clamare, vociferari* **halloo!** interj *heus! ohe!*

hallow, v tr *consecrare, dedicare, inaugurare* **hallowed,** adj *sacer, sanctus*

hallucination, n *error*

halm, n *culmus, calamus* (= reed)

halo, n *corona (lunae), area (lunae)* (Sen)

halt, I. adj *claudus* **II** v intr 1, = to walk as a lame person, *claudicare, claudum esse*, 2, = to stop, *subsistĕre, consistĕre*, 3, = to hesitate, *dubitare, animo pendēre, animo esse suspenso, haerēre, claudicare* (e g *si quid in nostrâ oratione claudicat*) **III.** n use verb

halter, n *capistrum* (= — for a horse), to put on a —, *capistrare* (e g *equum, boves*), *laqueus* (= noose and — for strangling, e g *gulam laqueo frangĕre*)

ham, n 1, = back of the knee, *poples, -itis,* m, 2, = salted —, *perna* **hamstring, I.** n *poplitis nervus* **II.** v tr *poplitis nervum secare*

hamlet, n *viculus, parvus vicus*

hammer, I. n *malleus*, a small —, *malleolus* **II.** v tr *malleo (con)tundĕre*, — out, *ducĕre*

hamper, n *corbis*, see BASKET

hamper, v tr *implicare, alqm impedire*

hand, I. n 1, *manus, -ūs,* f the hollow of the —, *palma*, —s off! *heus tu, manum de tabulâ!* to give a person the —, *alci dextram porrigĕre*, to join —s, *dextram jungĕre cum alqo*, — with one another, *dextras jungĕre, dextrae dextram jungĕre*, to strike —s on —, *fidem de alqâ re dextrâ dare, dextram fidemque dare;* put the last — on, *extremam* or *summam manum imponĕre alci rei* or *in alqâ re*, to lay —s on a person, *alci manus afferre* or *admovēre* or *in(j)icere, alci vim afferre, alci vim et manus in(j)icĕre*, to lay —s on yourself, *manus sibi afferre* (= to destroy oneself); to fall from —, *excidĕre de manibus*, to be at —, *ad manum, prae manibus* or *praesto esse,* *adesse*; to take in —, *in manum* or *manus sumĕre*, *in manum capĕre* (e.g. *hunc librum nemo in manus sumit*), = undertake, *suscipĕre*; to hold in the —, *manu tenēre*; to have in —, *in manibus habēre* (e.g. *victoriam*); the state is in the —s of the nobles, *respublica apud optimates est*; all is in the —s of the enemy, *omnia hostium sunt*; it is in my —, *alqd in meā manu* or *in meā potestate est* or *positum est*, *alqd in me situm est*; with my (thy, his) own —, *meā* (*tuā*, *suā*) *manu*; on the one —, on the other, *et* ... *et*; *quidem* (enclit.) ... *sed* or *autem*; *alter* ... *alter*; *alius* ... *alius*; I have in —, *habeo alqd in manibus* or *inter manus*, *mihi alqd in manibus est*; the letter is not to —, *epistulam non accepi*; **2**, = — of a clock, dial, etc., *index*; **3**, = —-writing, n. *manus*, *-ūs*, f., *chirographum*; to write a good —, *bene ac velociter scribĕre*; **4**, = workman, *opera*, usu. in pl. **II.** v.tr. *alqd alci dare*, *tradĕre*, *porrigĕre*; — down, *tradĕre*, *prodĕre*; — round, *circumferre*. **hand-bill**, n. *libellus*. **hand-breadth**, n. *palmus*. **handcuff**, **I.** n. —s, *manicae*. **II.** v. tr. *manicas alci in(j)icĕre*. **handful**, n. **1**, lit. *manipulus*, *pugillus*; **2**, fig. *exigua manus*, *-ūs*, f. (= small band) *pauci* (e.g. a — of men, *pauci* (*homines*)). **handicraft**, n. *artificium*; —sman, *artifex*. **handiwork**, n. *opus*, *-ĕris*, n., *opificium*. **handkerchief**, n. *sudarium*. **hand-labour**, n. *opera*; I live by —, *operā mihi vita est*. **handle**, **I.** n. **1**. *capulus*, *manubrium* (= — of a sword, etc.), *ansa* (= — of a cup, etc.); **2**, fig. *tanquam ansa*, *ad alqd faciendum*; see OPPORTUNITY. **II.** v.tr. **1**, lit. *tractare*; **2**, fig. *alqd tractare* or *disputare*, *disserĕre de alqā re*. **handling**, n. *tractatio*. **handwriting**, n. *manus*, *-ūs*, f., *chirographum*. **handy**, adj. **1**, *habilis*; see SKILFUL; **2**, *promptus*; see READY.

handsome, adj. **1**, *formosus*, *venustus*, *bellus*, *speciosus*, *pulcher*; **2**, fig. *amplus*, *magnus* (= great), *liberalis* (= freehanded). Adv. *venuste*, *belle*, *ample*, *magnopere*, *liberaliter*. **handsomeness**, n. *pulchritudo*, *venustas*.

hang, **I.** v.intr. **1**, *pendēre* (*ab*, *de*, *ex*) *alqā re*; **2**, fig. — on anyone's lips, *oculos in vultu alcjs defigĕre*, or *in alqo* or *alqā re*. **II.** v.tr. *suspendĕre alqd* (*de*, *ab*, *ex*) *alqā re*; — the head, *caput demittĕre*. **hangdog**, **I.** n. *verbero*, *furcifer*, *-eri*. **II.** adj. *impudicus*, *scelestus*. **hanger**, n. *gladius*. **hanger-on**, n. *assec(u)la*, m. **hanging**, **I.** n. *suspendium*. **II.** adj. *pendens*, †*pensilis*, †*pendulus*. **hangman**, n. *carnifex*.

hanker, v.tr. to — after, *alqd desiderare*, *desiderio alcjs rei teneri* or *flagrare*.

haphazard, adv. at —, *temere*. **hapless**, adj. *infelix*; see UNLUCKY. **haply**, adv. *forte*. **happen**, v.intr. *fieri*, *accidĕre*, *contingĕre*, *evenire*. **happy**, adj. **1**, *felix*, *fortunatus* (= fortunate), *beatus* (= blessed), *faustus* (= of good omen), *secundus* (= favourable), *prosper* (= corresponding to hope), *bonus* (= good); may it have a — issue, *quod bonum*, *faustum*, *felix fortunatumque sit!* I am — to see you, *gratus acceptusque venis*; **2**, of language, *aptus*, *accommodatus ad alqm rem*. Adv. *feliciter*, *fortunate*, *beate*, *fauste*, *prospere*, *bene*, *ex sententiā* (= to your wish), *apte*, *accommodate*. **happiness**, n. *vita beata* or *beate vivĕre*, *felicitas*, *beatitas*, *beatitudo* (both in a philosophical sense).

harangue, **I.** n. *contio*. **II.** v.intr. *contionari*.

harass, v.tr. **1**, *fatigare*, *vexare*, *sol(l)icitare*; **2**, military term, *carpĕre*, *premĕre*

harbinger, n. *praenuntius*, *antecursor*.

harbour, **I.** n. **1**, lit. *portus*, *-ūs*; steer for —, *portum petĕre*; — toll or dues, *portorium*; **2**, fig. (*tanquam*) *portus*, *-ūs*, *refugium*, *perfugium*. **II.** v.tr. **1**, = receive, (*hospitio*) *excipĕre*; **2**, fig. *colĕre*, *in se admittĕre*.

hard, **I.** adj. **1**, *durus*, *solidus*, *rigidus* (= stiff), *crudus* (= unripe); **2**, to feelings, *asper*, *acerbus* (= bitter), *iniquus* (= unfair), *indignus* (= unworthy); **3**, = difficult, *difficilis*, *arduus*. **II.** adv. *summā vi*, *enixe*; to go — with, *alqd aegre ferre*. **harden**, **I.** v.tr. *durum facĕre* or *reddĕre*, *durare* (ante and post class.). **II.** v.intr. *obdurescĕre* (lit. and fig.). **hardened**, adj. *inveteratus*. **hard-hearted**, adj. *durus*, *ferreus*. **hardihood**, n. *audacia*. **hardly**, adv. **1**, = scarcely, *vix*, *aegre*; **2**, = cruelly, etc., *dure*, *duriter*, *aspere*, *acerbe*. **hardness**, n. **1**, lit. *duritia* (or *durities*); **2**, fig. = severity, *iniquitas*, *crudelitas*, *saevitia*; **3**, see HARDSHIP. **hardship**, n. **1**, = toil, *labor*; **2**, = trouble, *molestia*, *aerumna*, *injuria*. **hardy**, adj. **1**, lit. *durus*, *robustus*, *laborum patiens*; **2**, fig. *strenuus*, *audax*. Adv. *duriter*. **hardiness**, n. *robur*, *-ŏris*; see STRENGTH.

hardware, n. *ferramenta*, *-orum*.

hare, n. *lepus*, *lepŏris*, m. **hare-brained**, adj. *temerarius*. **hare-lip**, n. *labrum fissum*.

hark! interj. *heus!*

harlequin, n. *sannio*, m.

harlot, n. *scortum*, *meretrix*.

harm, **I.** n. *damnum*, *detrimentum*; great —, *clades*, *-is*, *calamitas*. **II.** v.tr. *alci nocēre*, *alqm laedĕre*. **harmful**, adj. *nocens*, *noxius*. **harmless**, adj. *innoxius*, *innocuus*. Adv. by adj. **harmlessness**, n. *innocentia*.

harmony, n. **1**, (*vocum*, etc.) *concentus*, *-ūs*, *concordia*; science of —, *harmonice* or *harmonica*; **2**, fig. *consensus*, *-ūs*, *consensio*, *concordia*, *convenientia*. **harmonious**, adj. **1**, of sounds, *consors*, *consonus*, *canorus*; **2**, fig. *concors*, *congruens*, *consentiens*, *conveniens*. Adv. *consonanter*, *concorditer*, *congruenter*, *convenienter*. **harmonize**, **I.** v.tr. **1**, *alqas res concordes facĕre* or *reddĕre*; **2**, *componĕre*, (*re*)*conciliare*. **II.** v.intr. *concinĕre* (lit. and fig.).

harness, **I.** n. *ornamenta equi*, *arma equestria*. **II.** v.tr. *instruĕre*, *equum ornare*, *equum ad currum jungĕre* (Plin.).

harp, n. *lyra*, *fides*, *-ium*, *psalterium*. **harper**, n. *fidicen*, *fidicina*, *psaltes*, *-ae* (Quint.), *psaltria*, f.

harpy, n. **1**, *harpyia*; **2**, fig. *homo rapax*.

harrow, **I.** n. *crates*, *-is*, (*h*)*irpex*, (*urpex*) *-icis*, m., *rastrum*. **II.** v.tr. **1**, *occare*; **2**, fig. — the feelings, *alqm* (*ex*)*cruciare*, *torquēre*. **harrowing**, adj. *terribilis*.

harry, v.tr. *vexare*, *torquēre*, *cruciare*.

harsh, adj. **1**, *asper*, *austerus*, *severus*, *morosus*, *crudelis*, *saevus*, *durus*; **2**, — in taste, *acer*, *asper*; **3**, — in sound, *absonus*, *auribus ingratus*, *dissonus*, *raucus*. Adv. *aspere*, *austere*, *severe*, *crudeliter*, *saeve*, *morose*, *duriter*, *acriter*; in sound, use adj. **harshness**, n. **1**, *asperitas*, *severitas*, *crudelitas*, *saevitia*; **2**, *acerbitas*; **3**, *asperitas*.

hart, n. *cervus*.

harvest, **I.** n. **1**, *messis*; **2**, fig. *quaestus*, *-ūs*, *fructus*, *-ūs*. **II.** v.tr. *messem facĕre*. **harvester**, n. *messor*.

hash, **I.** v.tr. *concīdĕre*. **II.** n. *minutal* (Juv.).

hasp, n. see LOCK, BOLT.

hassock, n. †*scirpea matta* (of rushes), *pulvinus* (= cushion).

haste, n. *festinatio*, *properatio*, *properantia*, *celeritas* (*festinatioque*), *maturatio*, *trepidatio* (= confused hurry, nervous haste); excuse —, *ignoscas velim festinationi meae* (in a letter);

you must make —, *properato* or *maturato opus est*, to be in —, *festinare*, more — less speed, *omnis festinatio tarda est* **hasten, I.** v intr *alqo* or *inin properare, contendere, advolare ad* or *in alqm locum* (= — to a place, e g to the scene of action), *festinare, maturare* (both with infin) **II.** v tr *accelerare, maturare, properare, festinare, praecipitare, repraesentare* **hasty,** adj **1,** = hurried (*prae*)*properus, citus, citatus, festinans, properans, praeceps*, **2,** = irritable, *vehemens* or *acer* (e g *vehemens acerque*, opp *placidus mollisque* = gentle and mild), = easily excited to wrath, *iracundus, stomachosus*, = passionate, *praeceps in iram, pronus in iram, vir* or *homo vehementis* or *violenti ingenii, vir violentus ingenio* Adv *propere, properanter, raptim, festinanter, vehementer, acriter, stomachose* **hastiness,** n **1,** see HASTE, **2,** of temper, *iracundia, stomachus*

hat, n a broad-brimmed —, *petasus, causia, pileus* or *pileum* (more especially = a skull-cap of felt without brim), to take the — off to a person (as a mark of respect), *alci caput nudare*

hatch, v tr **1,** *parĕre, procreare* (= to produce young), **2,** fig = to brood, concoct, *moliri, machinari,* (*con*)*coquĕre* **hatches,** n *clat*(*h*)*ri, claustra, -orum*

hatchet, n *securis, ascia, dolabra*

hate, hatred, I. n *odium* (also in the pl *odia*) *invidia, simultas, ira* (= passion), *inimicitia*. **II.** v tr (both with and without accus) *odisse*, to bear — against, *odium in alqm habĕre, gerĕre, odio in alqm ferri, odium in alqm concepisse*, to be hated by, *odio alci esse, in odio apud alqm esse* **hater,** n *qui odit*, a — of, *inimicus, infensus alci* **hateful,** adj *odiosus, invisus* Adv *odiose, invidiose*

haughty, adj *superbus, insolens, contumax, arrogans*, comb *minax atque arrogans* (= threatening and haughty), *sermo plenus arrogantiae* (= a — speech), *fastidiosus, alqâ re tumens* Adv *superbe, insolenter, arroganter*, to behave —, *insolentius se gerĕre, se superbum praebēre, superbire* **haughtiness,** n *superbia, insolentia*, comb *superbia et insolentia, insolentia et superbia, contumacia, arrogantia*, comb *superbia et arrogantia*, *fastidium* (= contempt), comb *superbia et fastidium*, *fastus, ūs* (mostly poet), *spiritus, ūs* (usu in pl), *superbia et elatio quaedam animi*

haul, I. v tr *trahĕre, ducĕre* (= to draw, to carry along with, gently), *subducĕre* (= — down to the sea, of ships), *rapĕre* **II.** n (in gen) *tractus, -ūs* (= the act of pulling along)

haulm, n see STALK

haunch, n *clunis*, m and f

haunt, I. v tr **1,** *frequentare* (as *alcjs domum*), (*con*)*celebrare*, **2,** of spirits, *alqm agitare, sol*(*l*)*icitare*, **3.** of thoughts, etc , *urgere, vexare, sol*(*l*)*icitare* **II** n **1,** of men, *locus quem alqs frequentare solet*, in bad sense, *latibulum*, = retreat, *receptaculum*, **2,** of animals, *latibulum, lustrum, cubile* **haunted,** adj — house, *domus ab umbris frequentata*

have, v tr **1,** = to hold, carry, *habēre, tenēre* (= to hold), *gestare* (= to carry), to hold in the hand, (*in*) *manibus habēre* or *tenēre*, to hold by the hand, *manu ducĕre*, to — with, carry with, *secum habēre* or *portare* or *gestare, esse cum alqâ re* (i e *cum telo*), **2,** as auxiliary by tenses of special verb, e g take it ! — you got it ? Yes, I — got it, *prehende ! jam tenes ? teneo*, **3,** = to possess, *habēre alqd* (as *auctoritatem, potestatem*), *est mihi alqd* (e g *liber*, I — a book), *esse alqâ re* (of a man's qualities, as *Hortensius tanta erat memoriâ, ut*, etc , = Hort had such a memory, that, etc), or *esse alcjs rei, alqd possidēre*, to possess (lit and of qualities, as *ingenium, magnam vim*), *tenēre alqd* (= to hold in possession, to hold an office, a rank, as *tenēre locum, summam imperii*), *alqâ re praeditum* or *instructum* or *ornatum esse* (e g *animi nobilitate*, to — nobleness of heart), or *inest ei animi nobilitas, est in eo an. nob*, *affectum esse alqâ re*, to — an illness, *morbo correptum* or *affectum esse*, to — anyone or a thing = to use, *uti alqo* or *alqâ re*, to — favourable wind, *uti vento secundo*, to — success in war, *uti proeliis secundis*, to — a great deal of money, *divitiis* or *opibus et copiis affluĕre*, to — children, *liberis auctum esse*, to — a friend in, *habēre alqm amicum, uti alqo amico* those whom I had with me (i e my companions), *qui erant mecum*, **4,** = to be obliged, i e everybody has to use his own judgment, *suo cuique judicio utendum est*, see BE, DO, TAKE, GET, POSSESS

haven, n *portus, ūs* (lit and fig), *refugium, perfugium* (fig refuge), *asylum* (= refuge), see HARBOUR

havoc, havock, n *vastatio,* (*de*)*populatio* (= complete devastation), *eversio, excidium* (= destruction, e g of a town), *strages, caedes, is*, f (= slaughter)

haw, v intr *balbutire* (in Latin both trans and intr), *valbum esse, linguâ haesitare*

haw, v tr = spit up (*ex*)*screare* (Cels)

hawk, v tr = sell, *venditare*

hawk, n *accipiter, tris*, m **hawk-eyed,** adj *lynceus*

hay, n. *faenum* (*fe*) make — while the sun shines, *vento, ut aiunt, uti secundo* **hay-cock, hay-rick,** n *faeni acervus* or *meta* **hay-cutter,** n *faenisex, icis*, m **hay-fork,** n *furca*

hazard, I n **1** *fors -tis*, f , *sors, tis*, f (= lot), *casus, ūs* (= chance, accident), *fortuna* (= luck), *periculum* (= risk, peril), *alea* (i e gambling, scil *alea alcjs rei* = uncertainty), at —, *temere, forte, fortuito ac temere temere ac fortuito* **II.** v tr *audēre* or *tentare alqd* (= — with danger), *periculum facĕre alcjs rei*, see RISK, VENTURE **hazardous,** adj *periculosus, anceps, dubius* (= doubtful, uncertain), comb *periculosus et anceps*, *difficilis* (= difficult), *lubricus* (= slippery), comb *periculosus et lubricus* Adv *periculose*

haze, n *nebula* (= fog), *caligo* (= thick, dense fog), see FOG **hazy,** adj **1,** *nebulosus*, **2,** fig , *dubius, anceps*

hazel, n *corylus*, f **hazel-nut,** n (*nux*) *avellana* (Plin).

he, pron **1,** expressed by the form of the verb, as *amat* (= he loves), **2,** when used emphatically = *ille, is, iste* (referring to a third person), *ipse* (= he himself, himself), e g *Pythagoreos ferunt respondēre solitos Ipse dixit* = it is said that the Pythagoreans used to answer, He has said it He, him, when = man, expressed by *homo*, e g *nosti hominem ?* = do you know him ? *valde hominem diligo*, (prefixed to the names of animals) *mas*, e g *caper* (= he-goat), or by special form (e g , *ursus* = — bear , *ursa* = she bear

head, I. n. **1,** *caput* (= uppermost part of the human body), *cacumen* (= the top of anything, scil e or), *vertex, -icis*, m (= top of the —), *bulla* (= the thick part at the top, scil *bulla clavi* = — of a nail), *occipitium, occiput* (= hinder part of the —), *biceps* (adj = with two — s), *capita aut navim* = head or tail (a game of boys very late), *a capillo usque ad unguem*, *a vestigio ad verticem* (= from — to foot from top to bottom);

alqm totum oculis perlustrare or *pererrare* (= to examine from — to foot, all over); *praeceps* (adj. = — foremost); *capitis longitudine alqm superare* (to be a — taller); **2**, = animal, individual, *quot homines, tot sententiae*, as many opinions as —s; *numerus eorum, qui in eum locum convenerunt, fuit quinquaginta capitum* (= the company was composed of fifty —); *viritim* (= according to the number of —s); **3**, = life, *res capitis alci agitur, caput alcjs agitur* (= it costs his —); **4**, = chief, *caput* (= the head, chief, in gen.), *princeps* (= principal, the most influential), *dux* (= commander), comb. *dux et princeps; auctor* (= instigator), comb. *dux et auctor; fax, facis*, f., *tuba* (= signal, then = author of a conspiracy); *caput conjuratorum, princeps conjurationis* (= ring-leader of a conspiracy); **5**, = understanding, faculties, memory, *mens, animus, ingenium, judicium; animo sum conturbato et incerto* (= I don't know where my — stands, I am quite confused); *multa simul cogito* (= my — is quite full); *opinionis errore sibi fingĕre alqd* (= to get a foolish notion into one's —); *alqd memoriā tenēre* (= to have a thing in the —); **6**, = forepart of a thing, *superior (pars)* or *summus* (with noun); *pars prior* (= the first part), *prora* (= prow or fore-part of a ship); *fons, -tis*, m., *caput*, or comb. *fons et caput* (= — of a stream); *caput* (= — of a discourse); — of the table, *lectus summus* (see Smith "Dict. Antiq." art. *triclinium*); **7**, = countenance, resistance, resolution; to make — against, *alci resistĕre, alqm superare*. **II.** adj. in compound words, to be rendered with *primus* (= the first); *primarius, praecipuus* or *potissimus* (= particular, special); *summus or maximus* (= chief, original). **III.** v.tr. *alqm ducĕre, alci ducem* or *auctorem esse, alci* or *alci rei praeesse*. **head-ache**, n. *capitis dolor*. **head-band**, n. *infula, vitta, redimiculum*. **head-dress**, n. *vitta, redimiculum, mitra*. **header**, n. see DIVE. **headland**, n. *promontorium*. **headless**, adj. *capite praeciso*. **headlong**, adj. *inconsideratus, inconsultus* (= foolish), *incautus* (= incautious); *improvidus* (= thoughtless), comb. *improvidus incautusque; imprudens; temerarius* (= rash, e.g. *vox temeraria*, a rash expression), comb. *inconsultus et temerarius, temerarius atque inconsideratus; demens, praeceps*. Adv. *temere*, or by adj. *praeceps*. **head-man**, n. *praefectus* (with gen. or dat.), *magister, praeses, -idis* (= president, chairman). **head-piece**, n. *cassis, -idis*, f. (of metal), *galea* (of leather). **head-quarters**, n. *praetorium*. **headship**, n. *locus princeps* or *primus, principatus, -ūs*. **headstrong**, adj. *pertinax, contumax* (= obstinate), *pervicax*. **head-wind**, n. *ventus adversus*. **heady**, adj. **1**, = headstrong, *vehemens* (= vehement, opp. *lenis, placidus*); **2**, = intoxicating, *fervidus*.

heal, I. v.tr. **1**, *alqm* or *alqd sanare, sanum facĕre, alci* or *alci rei mederi* (= to apply medicines, to restore), *alqm* or *alqd curare* (= to treat a complaint, take care of a person, nurse); **2**, fig. *alqm* or *alcjs animum sanare, alqm ad sanitatem reducĕre* or *perducĕre* or *revocare, alci rei mederi*. **II.** v.intr. †*coire* (of wounds), *consanescĕre, sanum fieri* (= to get better). **healable**, adj. *sanabilis, quod sanari potest*. **healing, I.** adj. *saluber, salutaris* (= conducive to health, lit. and fig.), *utilis* (= useful, lit. and fig.). **II.** n. **1**, *sanatio* (= art of curing), *curatio* (= treatment of a complaint, but not cure); **2**, fig. *sanatio*. **health**, n. *sanitas; bona, commoda, firma, prospera valetudo* (= good health; *valetudo* alone = state of health), *salus, -utis*, f., *corporis* or *valetudinis integritas* (= sound constitution), *salubritas, salutem alci propinare* (= to propose, drink the — of), *bene te! bene tibi!* (= your good — !). **healthful, healthy**, adj. *sanus, salvus* (= in good condition, in good health), *integer* (= uninjured, sound), *valens, validus, firmus* (= strong), *robustus* (= robust, stout), comb. *robustus et valens, firmus et valens; saluber* or *salubris* (= of a place), *salutaris* (= salutary, wholesome, opp. *pestilens*), *sanus et salvus, salvus et sanus* (= safe and sound), *aër saluber* (— atmosphere, opp. *aër pestilens*), *mens sana* (= sound mind). Adv. *salubriter, bene*.

heap, I. n. *acervus, strues, -is*, f., *cumulus, agger* (= a mass, mound); to fall all in a —, *collabi, corruĕre*. **II.** v.tr. **1**, *acervum construĕre, cumulum exstruĕre, coacervare, aggerare, congerĕre*; **2**, fig. *alqm alqā re cumulare, alqd in alqm con-* (or *in-*) *gerĕre* (e.g. *convicia* = abuse), *alqd alci rei addĕre*.

hear, v.tr. and intr. **1**, *audire, auscultare*, to — badly, *surdum esse* (never *male audire* = to be in bad repute); **2**, = to listen, *audire, auscultare* (= to be a listener), *alqd audire* (= to listen to), *alcjs rei rationem non habēre* (= to make no account of), *alci aures dare* (= to lend an attentive ear), *alqm audire, alci auscultare* (= to follow an advice), *ausculta mihi* (= follow my advice); **3**, = to learn, *(ex)audire* (of gods hearing prayer, etc.), *percipĕre* (= to — distinctly, to understand), *accipĕre* (= to learn from hearsay), *excipĕre* or *excipĕre auribus* (= to — with pleasure, to receive, to catch), *alqd* or *de alqā re cognoscĕre* (= to become acquainted with), *comperire* (= to receive information); to — a cause, *caus(s)am cognoscĕre*; — a lecturer, *alqm audire; quantum audio* (= from what I —), *quod nos quidem audierimus* (= at least as far as I have heard), *de rebus suis alqm facĕre certiorem* (= to let a person — from one). **hearer**, n. *auditor* (to be an attentive —, *diligenter audire alqm, studiosum esse alcjs audiendi, multam operam dare alci, se alci attentum praebēre auditorem*. **hearing**, n. **1**, *auditus, -ūs*, scil. *auditus acutus*; **2**, = audience, *audientia*; to get a — for, *alci audientiam facĕre* (for a public speaker); *facĕre sibi audientiam* (for oneself), *audiri* (= to find hearers); **3**, = judicial trial, *cognitio, interrogatio, interrogatio testium* (= — of witnesses); see TRIAL. **hearsay**, n. *rumor*.

hearken, v.intr., see HEAR.

hearse, n. *plaustrum* or *vehiculum*.

heart, n. **1**, lit. *cor, cordis*, n., *pectus, -ŏris*, n. (= the chest, breast); †*praecordia, -orum, cor palpitat* (= the heart beats); **2**, fig. of a country, *interior alcjs terrae regio, interiora (-um) alcjs terrae*, or *intimus* with n. (e.g. *India intima*); **3**, the — morally, inwardly, *animus; mens, -ntis*, f. (= mind, disposition), comb. *animus et mens* (= — and mind); *voluntas* (= inclination); *ingenium* (= natural disposition); *natura* (= human nature); *naturā vir bonus* (= good in —); *pectus, -ŏris*, n. (= breast); *bonitas* (= good —); *animus benignus, benignitas* (= kindness); *animus mitis* (= gentleness of —); *animus improbus, improbitas* (= depravity of —); *animus fractus* or *afflictus* (= a broken —); *ex animo* (= from the —); *ex (animi) sententia* (= from my —'s desire); I have at —, *alqd* or *alqs mihi curae* or *cordi est; alqd mihi summae curae est, alqd mihi in medullis est; nihil est mihi alqā re antiquius* (= I am particularly anxious); *nihil mihi potius est, quam ut*, etc. (= I have nothing more at — than that); to take to —, *alqā re (com)moveri*; to be grieved at — about, *alqd aegre ferre*; **4**, as endearing term, = my dear, *meum cor* or *anime mi, meum corculum*; **5**, = courage, *animus*; **6**, = memory; b[illegible] *memoriter, ex memoriā*; to know by —, *memoriā tenēre* or *complecti, in memoria habēre*; to learn by —, *ediscĕre, memoriae mandare, tradĕre, committĕre*, to say off by —, *memoriter pronuntiare* or *recitare, ex memoriâ exponĕre* **heart-ache,** n *dolor*, see GRIEF, SORROW **heart-break,** n *dolor* **heart-breaking, heart-rending,** adj *miserabilis, maestus, acerbus, flebilis* **heart-broken,** adj *animo fractus* or *afflictus* **heart-burning,** n fig *odium occultum* or *inclusum* (= secret hatred); *simultas obscura* (= secret dislike, political enmity, Cic), *dolor* (= pain) **heartfelt,** adj *verus, sincerus, sine fuco ac fallaciis* **heartless,** adj 1, = without courage, *timidus, humilis, demissus*, comb *humilis atque demissus* (= low, downcast), *abjectus* or *abjectior, afflictus, fractus*, comb *demissus fractusque, fractus et demissus* (= with a broken heart, spirit), *perculsus, profligatus*, comb *perculsus et abjectus* (= prostrated), *tristis, maestus* (= sad, sorrowful), 2, = cruel, *crudelis, ferreus, immitis, inhumanus, saevus, severus* Adv *timide, humili animo, demisse, demisso animo, humili atque demisso animo, abjecte, abjecto* or *fracto* or *afflicto animo, demisso fractoque animo, timido animo, tristi animo, crudeliter, saeve, severe, inhumane* **heartlessness,** n *crudelitas, severitas, inhumanitas, saevitia* **heart-shaped,** adj *ad cordis speciem factus* **heart-sick,** adj *animo aeger* **heart-whole,** adj *nondum amore captus* **hearty,** adj 1, *verus* (= true, opp *falsus*), *sincerus* (opp *fucatus*), comb *sincerus atque verus, incorruptus* (= genuine, not bribed, opp *corruptus*), *candidus* (= candid), *simplex* (= upright), *integer* (= pure), *apertus* (= open-hearted, opp *tectus*), comb *apertus et simplex*, 2, = vigorous, *vegetus, viridus, vigens* (= fresh in mind and body), *alacer* (= lively), *valens, robustus, fortis, firmus* (= strong) 3, = cordial, *benignus, benevolus, amicus*, to receive a — welcome, *summo studio excipi*, to give one a — welcome *alqm summo studio excipĕre* Adv *sincere, vere, simpliciter, sine fuco ac fallaciis, alacriter, fortiter, firme, firmiter, benigne, amice* **heartiness,** n 1, *veritas, sinceritas, simplicitas*, 2, *alacritas, fortitudo*, 3, *benignitas, amicitia, benevolentia, studium*

hearth, n *focus*

heat, I. n 1, *calor* (in gen opp *frigus*), *ardor* (= burning —), *fervor* (= roaring —), *aestus*, *-ūs* (= scorching, fever —), all these also in the pl, 2, fig = ardour, *impetus, -ūs, ardor, fervor* (*animi*), *vis, gravitas* (= powerfulness, scil *belli*), *incitatio* (= vehemence, impetus), *violentia* (= violence), *ardor juvenilis, ardor* or *fervor aetatis* (= fierceness of youth), *ira* (= anger), *impetus et ira, impotentia* (= ungovernableness, excess of passion), *iracundia* (= hastiness of temper), 3, = course at a race, *cursus, -ūs* **II.** v tr 1 (lit), (*per*)*calefacĕre, fervefacĕre* (esp in past part), 2 (fig), † *cal(e)facĕre, accendĕre, incendĕre, inflammare* **heated,** adj, see HOT

heath, n 1, = a plant, *erice, es*, f (Plin), 2, = a place overgrown with heath, *loca* (*orum*) *deserta* or *inculta, campi inculti* (= barren country) 3, = a place overgrown with shrubs of any kind, *silva*.

heathen, adj *ethnicus, gentilis, paganus* (Eccl), otherwise *sacrorum Christianorum expers*, the —, *barbarae gentes*

heave, I. v tr. = to move upwards, (*at*)*tollĕre, extollĕre* (*al*)*levare*; *sustinēre* (= to hold up, scil *arma*), — a sigh, *gemitum dare, edĕre* **II.** v intr † *aestuare, fluctuare*, † *tumescĕre*, † *tumēre* (of the waves, etc), *anhelare* (of the breast)

heaven, n 1, *caelum*, † *polus* (= sky), † *Olympus* (= abode of the gods), to praise anyone or anything to the skies *alqm* or *alqd in caelum ferre*, by — ! *medius fidius* ! 2, = God *Deus* (*Optimus Maximus*), *di*(*i*), (*dei*) † *superi*, may — fulfil your wishes ! *di*(*i*) *tibi dent* (or *Deus tibi det*), if — pleases, *si di*(*i*)*s* (or *Deo*) *placet*, thank — ! *di*(*i*)*s* (or *Deo*) *gratia* ! in the name of —, *per Deum* (or *deos*), for —'s sake ! *per deos immortales* ! *proh deûm fidem* ! *proh deum atque hominum fidem*, — forbid, *di meliora* **heaven-born,** adj † *caeligenus, caelestis, divinus* **heavenly,** adj 1, *caelestis, divinus*, 2, = very charming, *venustus, bellus* **heavenward,** adv *in* or *ad caelum*

heavy, adj 1, lit *gravis* (opp *levis*), *ponderosus*, 2, fig *gravis, difficilis, molestus* (= troublesome), it is — to bear *aegre id fero*, it is a — task for me, *grave mihi est alqd*, = of weighty material, *gravis* (opp *levis*), — (= indigestible) food, *cibus difficilis ad concoquendum*, of air, *caelum crassum, pingue*, a — (= rich) soil, *solum pingue*, a — (= hard) soil, *solum spissum*, = oppressive, *gravis* (opp *levis*), *magnus* (= great, e g *imber magnus* — rain), of speech, *jejunus, frigidus, periculosus* (= dangerous), *mortifer*(*us*) (= fatal, causing death), *atrox* (fearful), to labour under a — disease, *graviter aegrotare* Adv *graviter, difficulter, moleste, aegre, vasto corpore* (= — built), *magnopere* **heavy-armed,** adj *qui graviore armatu sunt, graviores armatūs* **heaviness,** n 1, *gravitas, pondus, ĕris*, n, 2, *gravitas, difficultas, molestia, crassitudo* (of the air), *solum pingue* or *spissum* (of ground), = — of mind, *sol*(*l*)*icitudo, anxietas, maeror, maestitia, tristitia*

Hebrew, adj *Hebraeus* or *Hebraicus*

hecatomb, n *hecatombe*

hectic, adj *febriculosus*

hector, v intr *se jactare* **hectoring,** adj *gloriosus*

hedge, I. n *saepes, -is*, f (*sep*), *saepimentum* **II.** v tr *saepire* **hedge born,** adj *tenui loco ortus, humili* or *obscuro* or *ignobili loco natus* **hedge hog,** n *ericius, erinaceus* (Plin), *echinus*

heed, I. v tr 1, = take care, *alqd curare, observare*, 2, = obey, *alci oboedire* (*obed*), *parēre* **II.** n *cura*, take —, (*prae*)*cavere alqd, ab alqo re, ut* or *ne* **heedful,** adj 1, *cautus, circumspectans*, 2, *oboediens* Adv *caute, oboedienter* **heedless,** 1, = neglectful, *neglegens* (*negligens*), 2, = rash, *temerarius* Adv *neglegenter, temere* **heedlessness,** n 1, *neglegentia*, 2, *temeritas*

heel, I. n 1, = the hind part of the foot of man and of quadrupeds, *calx* 2, = whole foot, to be at one's —s, *alcjs vestigiis instare, alcjs vestigia premĕre, alqm vestigiis sequi*, to fall head over —s, *ire praecipitem per caput pedesque*, **II.** v intr of a ship, *labare* or *in latus labi*

heft, n *manubrium*

heifer, n *juvenca*

height, n 1, lit *altitudo* (e g *hominis, montis*, etc), *proceritas* (= tallness), 2, fig *altitudo, sublimitas*, or by adj *summus* with special n (e g — of glory, *summa gloria*), 3, = high place, *locus editus* or *superior* **heighten,** v tr 1, = to raise higher, lit *alqd altius efferre*, 2, = to improve, *efferre*, = to raise, to increase, *augēre*, = to enlarge, *amplificare, exaggerare*, (*ex*)*ornare*, = to raise the price of an article, *pretium alcjs rei efferre*, = to sell at a higher price, *carius vendĕre alqd*

heinous, adj *foedus* (= foul, loathsome, lit and fig), = impious *impius* (*erga Deum, erga patriam, erga parentes*), = detestable, *abominandus, detestandus, detestabilis*, = wicked, *nefarius, nefandus, scelestus, sceleratus, immanis, atrox, flagitiosus* Adv *foede, nefarie*, comb *impie* *nefarieque, nefande, sceleste, scelerate, impie, atrociter, flagitiose.* **heinousness,** n. *impietas, atrocitas, scelus, -ĕris,* n., or *facinus, -ŏris,* n. (= the act).

heir, n. *heres, -ēdis,* m. & f.; the — to the whole fortune, sole —, *heres ex asse;* — to half the property, *heres ex dimidiâ parte;* to name one his —, *alqm heredem instituĕre, alqm heredem (testamento) scribĕre, facĕre.* **heiress,** n. *heres,* f. **heirloom,** n. *alqd paternum* (*et avītum*). **heirship,** n. *hereditas.*

hell, n. 1, *inferi, Tartarus(os)* or pl. *Tartara;* 2, eccl. t.t. *Gehenna, Infernus.* **hellhound,** n. *Furia, Erin(n)ys.* **hellish,** adj. *infernus* (lit.); = dreadful, *terribilis;* = diabolical, *nefandus.*

hellebore, n. *(h)elleborus, veratrum.*

Hellenic, adj. *Graecus.*

helm, n. lit. and fig. *gubernaculum;* the handle of the —, or the — itself, *clavus.* **helmsman,** n. *gubernator* (lit. and fig.).

helmet, n. *cassis, -īdis* (of metal); *galea* (originally of skin).

help, I. n. *auxilium* (= increase of power, aid in need, in pl. *auxilia,* = auxiliaries); *subsidium* (= aid ready to be supplied; in pl. = the reserves), *ops,* f. (only *opis, opem, ope* in use, = power to assist), *adjumentum* (= a means), *ornamentum* (= a supply or support), *praesidium* (= something set before to shield you), *suppetiae* (= present aid, succour, of troops, etc.), *salus, -ūtis,* f. (= rescue, sustentation of existence), *opera* (= — in act and deed); with anyone's —, *alcjs auxilio* or *ope* or *operâ, alqo adjuvante, alqo adjutore, divinâ ope;* "with the — of a thing" may be expressed by the ablative (e.g. with the — of genius and reflection, *ingenio et cogitatione*). **II.** v.tr. 1, *alqm in alqâ re* or *ad alqd faciendum (ad)juvare, alci subesse,* and *subvenire, succurrĕre, auxiliari* (rare); so — me God, *ita me Deus adjuvet;* —! *subveni,* or pl. *subvenite!* 2, of food, *alqd alci dare, porrigĕre, dividĕre;* 3, = hinder, I can't — telling, (*facĕre*) *non possum quin dicam,* so *fieri non potest quin.* **helper,** n. *adjutor, adjutrix.* **helpful,** adj. *utilis, aptus, idoneus;* he is — to me, *auxilio mihi est;* to be —, = HELP. Adv. *utiliter, apte.* **helping,** adj. *auxiliaris, auxiliarius* (more usually = belonging to auxiliary forces). **helpless,** adj. *inermis* (or *-us*), *inops* or *auxilii inops, auxilio orbatus;* thoroughly —, *ad summam omnium rerum inopiam redactus.* **helplessness,** n. *inopia.* **helpmeet,** n. *socius, consors, -tis,* m. and f., *maritus* (= husband), *uxor,* f. (= wife).

helter-skelter, I. adj. *praeceps.* **II.** adv. *raptim.*

hem, I. n. *limbus, instita* (both, however, = fringe or border sewn on). **II.** v.tr. 1, *suĕre* (= sew); 2, fig. — in, *circumsedēre, obsidēre, circumvallare* (with entrenchments).

hem, I. v.intr. to — and haw, *haesitare, dubitare.* **II.** interj. *(e)hem!*

hemisphere, n. *hemisphaerium.*

hemorrhage, n. *haemorrhagia* (Plin.).

hemp, n. *cannabis, -is,* f. **hempen,** adj. *cannabinus.*

hen, n. 1, opp. to male, *femina;* 2, domestic fowl, *gallina.* **hen-coop,** n. *cavea.* **hen-house,** n. *gallinarium* (Plin.). **hen-pecked,** adj. (*maritus*) *cui uxor imperat.*

hence, adv. 1, of place, *hinc;* as interj., *apage, procul;* 2, of time, by abl. (e.g. *paucis diebus,* a few days —), or *post* (e.g. *post paucos dies*); 3, = for this reason, *hinc, ita, quam ob rem* (or, as one word, *quamobrem*). **henceforth, henceforward,** adv. *dehinc, posthac.*

her, I. pers. pron., see SHE. **II.** adj. *ejus, illius, suus* (only in ref. to subj. of sentence).

herald, I. n. 1, *caduceator,* (*legatus*) *fetialis* (= belonging to a college of priests instituted to declare war or to ratify a peace); 2, = public crier, *praeco;* 3, = forerunner, *praenuntius.* **II.** v.tr. *nuntiare.*

herb, n. 1, *herba;* 2. = kitchen-stuff, *olus, oleris,* n. **herbage,** n. *herba* or *herbae,* † *gramen.* **herbalist,** n. *herbarius.*

herculean, adj. *fortissimus* (= very strong).

herd, I. n. 1, *grex;* of large cattle, etc., *armentum;* of a —, *gregalis, gregarius;* in — s, *gregatim;* 2, = a company of people, *grex, multitudo, caterva;* the common —, *vulgus, -i,* n. **II.** v.tr. *pascĕre.* **III.** v.intr. *congregari.* **herdsman,** n. in gen. *pastor;* = keeper of large cattle, *armentarius.*

here, adv. *hic* (= where the speaker is); not far from —, *haud procul; hoc loco, hac regione* (= in this place); from — (hence), *hinc;* only — and there, *rarus* (adv. *raro*); they fought only — and there, *rari praeliabantur;* — and there, in this and that place, *hac atque illac;* — (that is, in this thing), *hac in re.* **hereafter,** adv. *posthac, aliquando.* **herein,** adv. *in hac re.* **hereupon,** adv. *ad haec* (e.g. *ad haec* or *adversus haec respondit*).

hereditary, adj. *hereditarius, paternus* (as transmitted from a parent to a child). **heritage,** n. = an inherited estate, *hereditas, heredium, patrimonium.*

heresy, n. *haeresis* (Eccl.). **heretic,** n. *haereticus.* **heretical,** adj. *haerĕticus* (Eccl.).

hermaphrodite, n. *androgynos, homo utriusque sexūs.*

hermetically, adv. *arte clausus.*

hermit, n. *homo solitarius, eremīta, anachoreta, -ae,* m. (Eccl.).

hero, n. 1, (= demigod, son of the gods, illustrious person), *heros, -ōis,* m.; 2, = brave man, *vir fortis* or *fortissimus, dux fortissimus;* 3, = the principal person in a poem, *de quo* (*fabula*) *scripta est;* — of the drama, *persona prima.* **heroic,** adj. 1, *heroicus* (e.g. the — age, *aetas heroica, tempora, -um, heroica*), *praestans;* 2, = brave, valiant, *fortis, fortis et invictus;* = godly, *divinus;* = superhuman, *major quam pro homine* or *plus quam humanus;* = incredible, *incredibilis.* Adv. *fortiter, invicte, praestanter.* **heroine,** n. 1, = demi-goddess, *heroina, herois;* 2, = brave woman, *femina fortissima, praestantissima,* etc.; 3, — of a story, *de quâ* (*fabula*) *scripta est.* **heroism,** n. *virtus, -ūtis, animus fortis* or *fortis et invictus* (= brave spirit); = greatness of soul, *animi magnitudo.*

heron, n. *ardea.*

hers, pron. *suus* (in reference to the main subject); *ejus, illius* (not in reference to the main subject).

herself, pron. (*ea*) *ipsa, se,* etc. (in ref. to subj. of sentence).

hesitate, v.intr. 1, *dubitare* with infin. (but *non dubitare quin*), *dubium* (= doubtful) or *incertum* (= uncertain) *esse;* I — what to do, *dubius* or *incertus sum quid faciam;* 2, = to get confused in speaking, *haerēre, haesitare.* **hesitation,** n. 1, *dubitatio, haesitatio;* 2, *haesitatio, haesitantia linguae.*

heterogeneous, adj. *diversus et dissimilis.* **heterogeneousness,** n. *natura diversa et dissimilis.*

hew, v tr caedĕre, concīdĕre (e.g. lignum) **hewer,** n qui ligna caedit **hewn,** adj quadratus (e.g. saxum)

hexameter, n hexameter (or -trus)

hey, interj eja! age! **heyday,** n (aetatis) flos, floris, m robur, ŏris, n

hiatus, n hiatus, -ūs (in sound), there is an — (in MS), alqd deest

hibernal, adj hibernus **hibernate,** v intr 1, = to pass the winter, hibernare, 2, = to sleep through the winter, per hiemem dormire or quiescĕre

hiccough, hiccup, n singultus, ūs (Plin.)

hide, I. n corium, tergum, vellus, -ĕris, n, pellis. **II.** v tr abdĕre, abscondĕre, condĕre, celare, occulĕre, occultare, — and seek, (pueros) latitantes conquirĕre **hidden,** adj abditus, etc, to lie —, latēre **hiding-place,** n. latibulum

hideous, adj foedus, deformis; see UGLY Adv foede **hideousness,** n foeditas, deformitas

hierarchy, n of priests, sacerdotium

hieroglyphical, adj *hieroglyphicus,* hierographicus

higgle, v intr, see HAGGLE **higgledy-piggledy,** adv confuse

high, I. adj 1, altus (= the distance from the ground, opp humilis, profundus), (ex)celsus, (in altum) editus (= raised, opp. planus), elatus (= lifted up, and specially of words and manner), erectus (= straight up, hence lofty in thought), (aditu) arduus (= hard of ascent), procērus (= stretching up, opp brevis, used only of things high by growth), sublimis (= rising from below up to heaven), acutus (= sharp, clear, of tones), most —, summus (opp imus, infimus), supremus (in rank, opp infimus), the —est God, Deus supremus, Deus optimus maximus, fifty feet —, quinquaginta pedes altus, to be fifty feet —, in altitudinem quinquaginta pedum eminēre, 2, a — price, pretium magnum, to be of — price, magni pretii esse, magno constare, to buy at — price, magno or (pretio) impenso emĕre (dear), to rise, to bid —er (at an auction), contra liceri, to set a — value on, alqd magni aestimare, alqd magno aestimare, alci rei multum tribuĕre, to stand —, magnum pretium habēre, to stand —er than, praestare alci rei, 3, fig it is too — for me, alqd mente meā assequi or capĕre non possum, 4, = bad, of meat, etc, rancidus, putei (putris) **II.** adv alte, to aim —, magnas res (ap)petĕre **high-born,** adj generosus, nobili loco ortus **high-bred,** adj 1, by birth, generosus, 2 fig generosus, urbanus **high-day,** n dies festus **high-flown,** adj tumidus, to use — words, ampullari, nullum modum habēre **high-handed,** adj superbus, imperiosus **high-heeled,** adj — boot, cothurnus (of tragedy) **highlands,** adj loca mont(u)osa, orum **highlander,** n homo montanus **highly,** adv. magni (e.g. magni aestimare, to value —), valde, magnopere **high-mettled,** adj acer **high-minded,** adj magnanimus, generosus **high-mindedness,** n magnanimitas **highness,** n altitudo, of price, caritas. **high-priced,** adj carus **high-priest,** n Pontifex Maximus **high-shouldered,** adj gibber (= hunch-backed). **high-spirited,** adj generosus, fortis, animosus **high-treason,** n majestas, perduellio **high-water, high-tide,** n plurimus aestus, ūs, accessus, -ūs **highway,** n via **highwayman,** n latro, grassator

hilarity, n hilaritas (= merriness), = joy, laetitia, animus laetus or hilaris.

hill, n collis, m, = height, clivus; = mound, tumulus, = elevated spot, locus editus or superior up —, acclivis, adj, adverso colle, adv; down —, declivis (opp acclivis) **hillock,** n tumulus **hilly,** adj † clivosus, mont(u)osus

hilt, n capulus

hind, n = female stag, cerva

hind, n 1, = servant, domesticus (= house-servant) servus, 2, = peasant, agricola, rusticus, arator (= ploughman)

hind, adj aversus (= wrong side, opp adversus) = that is behind, posterior (= hinder). **hindermost,** adj postremus, (of two) posterior, = the last of a number, ultimus, = the most remote, extremus.

hinder, v tr. impedire, prohibēre algm or alqd, (ab) alqa re, quin or quominus; — in a thing, impedimento esse alci (alci rei) ad alqd, in gen impedimentum afferre alci rei faciendae = to be in the way of, obstare alci and alci rei, = to oppose, officere alci and alci rei, prohibēre or arcēre algm alqā re or ab alqā re, = to retard, retardare algm ad alqd faciendum or ab alqā re faciendā or in alqā re, = to delay a thing, moram facĕre alci rei, alci obstare, officere, or with quominus or quin **hinderer,** n turbator (e.g. pacis), = who interrupts anyone in speaking, interpellator (e.g. sermonis), = interrupter, interventor **hindrance,** n impedimentum, = interruption, interpellatio, = delay, mora, = difficulty, difficultas

hinge, I. n 1, cardo, m; 2, = a leading principle, caput, = the main thing in anything, summa alcis rei, the — on which a question turns, cardo, = the deciding point, momentum. **II.** v intr alqā re contineri, in alqā re versari, see above

hint, I. n significatio, a — is sufficient, rem ostendisse satis est **II.** v intr. alqd alci sub(j)icĕre (= to remind privily).

hip, n. coxendix

hire, I. n 1, = hiring, conductio, 2, = wages, merces, ēdis, see WAGES **II.** v.tr conducĕre, to — oneself out, se or operam suam locare (Plautus). **hireling, I** n = one who serves for wages, homo conducticius, mercenarius (i.e. serving for wages), homo (miles) mercede conductus (= engaged for hire) **II** adj venalis, see VENAL **hirer,** n conductor

his, adj suus (in reference to the subject of the same sentence, and if in a dependent sentence the subject of the principal sentence is referred to), ejus, illius (if not referring to the subject), — own, suus (proprius) (if referring to the subject), ejus proprius (if not referring to the subject), is not expressed in Latin, unless we wish to speak emphatically

hiss, I. v intr sibilare (resembling the noise made by serpents) sibilum mittĕre or (ef)fundĕre, to utter a shrilling sound, stridēre (stridĕre) **II.** v.tr. (an actor or speaker) sibilare, to — off (a bad actor off the stage) (e scaenā) sibilis) explodĕre **III.** n sibilus (poet pl sibila)

hist! interj st!

historian, n rerum (gestarum or antiquarum) scriptor or auctor, in the context only scriptor, historicus **historic,** adj historicus, — style of writing, genus historicum (opp genus oratorium, etc), by historiae rerum (e.g. — fidelity, authority, rerum or historiae fides, fides historiae), — writings, libri ad historiam pertinentes; according to — truth, ad historiae fidem Adv. historice (Plin Min) **history,** n historia, rerum gestarum memoria, res (gestae), annales

histrionic, adj scaenicus (scen), = what occurs on the scene of action, theatralis, — art, ars ludicra.

hit, I. v.tr. 1, lit. *ferire, tundĕre, percutĕre*; = not to miss, *tangĕre* (in gen. = to touch); to — with a blow, *icĕre*; to be — by lightning, *de caelo tangi* or *ici*; to — the mark, *collineare* or *scopum ferire* (lit. and fig. but rare); 2, — it off = to agree, *convenire*; to be hard —, *probe tactum esse*; — upon, *alqm* or *alqd offendĕre, in alqm* or *alqd incidĕre, incurrĕre*; Prov. "you have — the nail on the head," *acu tetigisti*; the word —s us, *sermo nos tangit*; to be — by calamities, *calamitate affligi*. **II.** n. 1, *ictus, -ūs*; 2, = a casual event, *fors, fortis*, f.; a lucky —, *fortuna secunda, felicitas*; = injury, *plaga*; "a —," *hoc habet* (= "he has caught it"); 3, = a sudden idea, *cogitatio repentina*.

hitch, I. v.tr. = to join together, *conjungĕre*; = to tie to, *annectĕre ad* or dat. **II.** n. = hindrance, *impedimentum*.

hither, adv. of place, *huc* (where the speaker is); — and thither, *huc illuc, huc et illuc, ultro et citro*; by *ad* in composition (e.g. to bring —, *afferre, apportare*; to fly —, *advolare*); — ! *huc ades!* **hitherto,** adv. = up to this time, *adhuc, adhuc usque, ad hoc tempus, ad hunc diem*.

hive, I. n. 1, (*apium*) *examen*; 2, = box for the reception of a swarm of honey-bees, *alvus* or *alveus*. **II.** v.tr. = to — bees, *in alveum congerĕre*.

ho! interj. *heus!*

hoar, adj. *canus*, † *incanus*; — antiquity, *antiquitas ultima*. **hoar-frost,** n. *pruina, pruinae* (the latter esp. of continued frost). **hoary,** adj. *canus*, † *incanus*.

hoard, I. n. (= a large stock) *copia, acervus*; to have a — of anything, *alqā re abundare*. **II.** v.tr. e.g. to — money, *pecuniam* or *opes undique conquirĕre* (= to collect), *coacervare*.

hoarse, adj. *raucus*; a little —, *subraucus*; *asper* (in gen. opp. *lenis*); to demand till one becomes —, *usque ad ravim poscĕre*. Adv. *raucā voce*. **hoarseness,** n. *rauca vox*; — of throat, *fauces raucae*.

hoax, I. n. *ludificatio*, or circumloc. by verb. **II.** v.tr. *alci illudĕre, alqm* (*lepide*) *ludificari*.

hobble, v.intr. *claudicare* (lit. and fig.). **hobblingly,** adv. *claudo pede*.

hobby, n. 1, = a stick or figure of a horse, on which boys ride, + *arundo*; to ride on a —, + *equitare in arundine longa*; 2, = favourite object, everyone has his —, *trahit quemque sua voluptas*; to be on one's —, *ineptiis suis plaudĕre*.

hobgoblin, n. *larva*.

hobnob, v.intr. *alqo familiariter uti*.

hock, n. *poples, -itis*, m.

hockey, n. *pila*; to play —, *pilis ludĕre*.

hodge-podge, n. *farrāgo* (Juv.).

hoe, I. n. = a rake for hoeing the ground, *ligo, ligōnis*, m., *marra* (Plin.); = a rake, harrow to break clods with, *rastrum*; (if a small one) *rastellus*; = a weeding-hook, *sarculum*. **II.** v.tr. *sarrire* (= to weed with a hook).

hog, n. *sus, suis*, m. and f., *porcus*. **hoggish,** adj. 1, lit. *suillus*; 2, fig. see GLUTTONOUS.

hogshead, n. *dolium* (= cask).

hoist, v.tr. *sublevare, tollĕre*; — sails, *vela dare*.

hold, I. n. 1, = grasp, *manus, -ūs*, f.; to take —, *prehendĕre*; 2, see PRISON; 3, of a ship, *alveus* (= hull), *caverna*; 4, fig. to have a — over, *alqm devinctum* or *obligatum habēre, multum apud alqm valēre*. **II.** v.tr. 1, = to have, *tenēre*; *habēre, obtinēre, possidēre* (= to possess), *gestare* (= to carry); — an office, *gerĕre* (e.g. *praeturam*); 2, = to contain, *capĕre, continēre*; 3, = to uphold, *sustinēre, sustentare*; 4, = to keep against attack, *defendĕre*; 5, = to conduct, *agĕre, habēre* (e.g. *comitia*, an election); — a festival, *celebrare*; 6, see CONSIDER, THINK. **III.** v.intr. = to hold good, *certum esse*; it —s, (*res*) *convenit cum alqā re, in* or *ad alqd ut* or acc. and infin.; — back, *retinēre, cunctari* (= to delay); — forth (= to extend) *porrigĕre, extendĕre*; = to propose, fig. *proponĕre, proferre, praebēre*; = to discourse, *contionari*; — in, lit. *equum inhibēre*; fig. *reprimĕre, cohibēre*; — on, — one's course, *cursum tenēre*; — out (= to endure) *durare*, (*alqd*) *sustinēre, perferre*; — up, see HOLD, II. 3; — with, *cum alqo consentire, convenire*. **holder,** n. 1, *is qui tenet*; — of land, *possessor*; *conductor* (= tenant), *colonus*; 2, = something by which a thing is held, *retinaculum, capulus* (= handle). **holdfast,** *fibula* (= clasp), *retinaculum*. **holding,** n. = possession, *possessio*.

hole, n. 1, *cavum* (= hollow place in gen., mouse's —, etc.), *foramen* (= an opening in or through a solid body), *rima* (= a chink), *lacuna* (= a pit, a pool); to bore a —, *pertundĕre*; 2, = a small, miserable hut, a wretched —, *gurgustium*.

hollow, I. adj. 1, (*con*)*cavus*; eaten up, hollowed out, *exesus* (e.g. *exesae arboris truncus*); — teeth, *dentes exesi* (Plin.); the — hand, *manus cava* or *concava* (e.g. of a beggar holding his hands in that way); to make —, *alqd* (*ex*)*cavare*; 2, = deep, hoarse in sound, *fuscus* (= the tone of the voice, opp. *candidus*), *asper, raucus*; 3, = not sincere, *vanus* (= empty), *simulatus, fucatus, fucosus* (= with only the outward appearance); see FALSE. **II.** n. *cavum, foramen*; see HOLE; = valley, *convallis, valles* (*vallis*), *-is*, m. **III.** v.tr. (*ex*)*cavare*.

holy, adj. *sacer* (= sacred to the gods, opp. *profanus*); = under divine protection, inviolable, *sanctus*; inviolable (i.e. protected by the sanction of a heavy penalty), *sacrosanctus* (e.g. *memoria*); = what is held in veneration, *religiosus* (e.g. tombs, oaths); = august, venerable, *augustus*; = with godly fear, *pius erga Deum*; = reverend, *venerandus, venerabilis*. Adv. *sancte, religiose, pie, auguste*. **Holy Ghost,** n. * *Spiritus Sanctus*. **holiness,** n. *sanctitas, religio* (attaching to an object of regard), *caerimonia* (rare), *pietas erga Deum*.

homage, n. *cultus, -ūs* (e.g. *Dei*), *observantia*; in feudal times, * *homagium*.

home, I. n. *domus, -ūs* (irreg.), *domicilium* (= household), *familia, patria* (= mother-country), *sedes et domicilium*; at —, *domi, inter suos*; to be at —, *domi esse, in patriā esse*; at my —, *domi meae* (*tuae*, etc.); at — and abroad, *domi militiaeque*; from —, *domo*; at Cæsar's —, *in domo Cæsaris, domo Cæsaris*; to remain at —, *domi* (*re*)*manēre*; to keep at —, *publico carēre* or *se abstinēre, in publicum non prodire, domi sedēre*; he is not at —, *est foris* (= he is out); he is at —, *est intus*; to sup from —, *foris cenare*; to go —, *ire domum*. **II.** adj. *domesticus, familiaris*; to strike —, *ferrum adigĕre*; to come — to one, *alqd sibi dictum putare*. **home-baked,** adj. *domi coctus*. **home-bred,** adj. *domesticus, intestinus, vernaculus*. **homeless,** adj. *profugus, extorris* (= exiled), *patriā* or *domo carens*. **homely,** adj. *simplex, inornatus*. **homeliness,** n. *simplicitas*. **home-made,** adj. *domesticus*.

homicidal, adj. see MURDEROUS. **homicide,** n. 1, = murder, *caedes, -is*; 2, = murderer, *homicida*, m. and f.; see MURDER, MURDERER.

homily, n. *oratio quae de rebus divinis habetur*.

homœopathy, n. *ea modendi ratio quae*

similia morbis adhibet remedia (Riddle and Arnold)

homogeneous, adj *ejusdem generis, eodem genere* **homogeneity,** n *natura similis, genus simile*

homologous, adj by *par, similis, similis in alqâ re ratio*

homonymous, adj *eodem nomine*

honest, adj *bonus, probus*, = without trickishness, *sincerus, sine fuco et fallaciis*, = one in whose words and actions we may trust, *fidus*, = frank, *simplex, candidus*, = genuine, *antiquâ fide*, = pure, unstained, *integer, sanctus, incorruptus*, to lose one's — name, *boni viri nomen amittĕre* Adv *probe, integre, sancte, sine fraude, sine fuco et fallaciis* (= without deceit), *simpliciter, candide* (= candidly), **honesty,** n = uprightness, *probitas*, = moral purity, rectitude, integrity, *integritas, sanctitas*, = innocent heart, *innocentia*, = sincerity, *sinceritas*, = trustworthiness, *fides*, comb *integritas et fides* = noble mind, *animus ingenuus, ingenuitas*, = carefulness (as regards other people's property), *abstinentia*, to show —, *fidem adhibēre in alqâ re*, = candour, *simplicitas*, = decency, discreetness, *castitas, sanctitas, pudicitia*

honey, n *mel*, his language is as sweet as —, *loquenti illi mella profluunt*, hence also sweetness of language, *dulcedo orationis* or *suavitas* (= mildness), my — (= my darling), *deliciae meae, voluptas mea* **honeycomb,** n *favus*, to take the —, *favum eximĕre*, the cell of a —, *cavum* **honeymoon,** n *dies conjugio facto laeti* **honeyed, honied,** adj 1, *mellitus*, 2, fig *dulcis*

honorary, adj *honorarius* (= for the sake of giving honour) **honorarium,** n see FEE

honour, I. n 1, = official distinction, *dignitas, honos (honor), honoris gradus, -ūs*, highest —, *amplissimus dignitatis gradus* 2, = moral quality, *honestas, honos*, 3, = reputation, *fama, existimatio*, of a woman, = chastity, *pudor, pudicitia*, 4, = respect felt, *verecundia*, 5, = mark of respect, *honos* to pay the last —, *justa alci facĕre* or *solvĕre* **II.** v tr 1, = celebrate, *honorare, decorare, celebrare*; 2, = esteem, *colĕre, diligĕre, vereri* **honourable,** adj *honoratus* (= very much honoured, e g the army, *militia*), causing or bringing honour, *honestus, honorificus, honorabilis* (very seldom, although once in Cic), = proper, *decōrus*, = praiseworthy, *laudabilis, laude dignus, praedicabilis*, = glorious, *gloriosus* (e g *mors*), = excellent, distinguished, *egregius*, to thank a person in the most — terms, *alci gratias agĕre singularibus* or *amplissimis verbis* Adv *honeste, cum dignitate*, = in a manner conferring honour, *honorifice*, most —, *honorificentissime, summo cum honore* to die —, *bene mori*, = in a manner deserving of praise, *laudabiliter, cum laude, gloriose, egregie, eximie*

hood, n = covering for the head used by females, *mitra, mitella* a fillet of net work for covering the hair, *reticulum* **hoodwink,** v tr *alci illudĕre, alqm ludificari, fallĕre*

hoof, n *ungula*, cloven —, *ungula bisulca* (Plin)

hook, I. n 1, *hamus (piscarius), uncus* (= a large iron —), by — or by crook, *quocunque modo*, 2, = a sickle, *falx* **II.** v tr to — a fish, *hamo piscari, hamo pisces capĕre* to — on, *alci rei* or *in alqâ re suspendĕre* **hooked,** adj *aduncus*, = having —s, *hamatus*

hoop, n *circulus* (= anything circular), an iron — set round with rings as an amusement for boys, *trochus*

hoopoe, n *upupa, epops, -opis,* m

hoot, v intr (of owls), *canĕre*, (of men), *vociferari, alci obstrepĕre* — off the stage, *alqm explodĕre* **hooting,** n *cantus, -ūs, carmen* (of owls), *voces, vociferatio, clamor* (of men)

hop, v intr (of birds), *salire* (Plin), (of men), *altero pede saltuatim currĕre*

hope, I. n *spes* (opp *fiducia* = confidence), meton Cicero our last —, *spes reliqua nostra, Cicero* — (from the fact of a thing being considered likely), *opinio*, = expectation, *ex(s)pectatio*, a gleam of —, *specŭla*, — of, *spes alcjs rei* (e g of immortality, *immortalitatis*), = probability of, *opinio alcjs rei*, I have — that, etc, *spero fore ut*, etc, I have no — in, *despero de alqâ re* (e g *de republicâ*), if there is, or will be, —, *si est*, or *erit, spes* (e g of returning, *reditūs*) **II.** v tr *sperare*, accus or accus and (fut) infin, *confidĕre* **hopeful,** adj 1, = full of hope, *spe animoque impletus* (= filled with hope and courage), 2, = having qualities which excite hope (e g a son, daughter, pupil, etc), *bonae spei, qui spem bonae indolis dat, de quo bene sperare possis*, very —, *optimae* or *egregiae* or *summae spei, eximiâ spe* Adv *cum magnâ spe* **hopeless,** adj *spe carens, spe orbatus, spe dejectus*, † *exspes* (= one who has no hope), = one who must be given up, *desperatus* Adv *sine spe, desperanter* (rare) **hopelessness,** n *desperatio* (as mental quality), *res desperatae* (= of affairs)

horde, n *grex, gregis* m, *caterva* (of people), = wandering tribe, *vagus* with noun (e g — of Gaetulians, *Gaetuli vagi*)

horizon, n 1, lit **horizon, finiens circulus*, the sun passes the —, *sol emergit de subterraneâ parte, sol emergit supra terram*, 2 fig = the sky in gen *caelum* (e g a clear — or sky, *caelum serenum*), = view, *a(d)spectus, -ūs* (= view from a mountain), *conspectus* (= sight), a thing limits our —, *alqd a(d)spectum nostrum definit* 3, fig = limits of the understanding (e g a thing goes, lies beyond my —, *alqd in intelligentiam meam non cadit*) **horizontal,** adj *aequus, libratus* Adv *ad libram*

horn, n 1, lit *cornu*, 2, fig = the horns of the moon, *cornua lunae*, 3, = drinking cup *poculum*, 4, = musical instrument, *cornu, buccina, tuba*, to blow the —, *cornu* or *buccinam inflare* **horned,** adj *cornutus, corniger* **hornless,** adj *non cornutus*, (of an animal by nature without horns, or if it has lost them through butting) *mutilus (cornibus)* **horny,** adj *corneus*

hornet, n *crabro*

horn-pipe, n *saltatio*

horoscope, n *horoscopus* (Pers), to cast a —, *sidera natalicia notare*

horrible, horrid, adj *horrendus, horribilis, terribilis, nefarius, nefandus, foedus* Adv *terribilem in modum, nefarie, foede* **horribleness,** n *foeditas*, better use adj with n (e g the — of the thing, *res horrenda*) **horrify,** v tr *(ex)terrēre, perterrēre, obstupefacĕre*, to be horrified, *obstupescĕre* **horror,** n 1, = fear, *horror, timor, pavor*, 2, = hatred, *odium*, 3, = a monster, a perfect —, *monstrum portentum*

horse, n 1 *equus (ecus), equa* (the name of the species), common —, *caballus*, a Gallic —, *mannus*, a swift fleet —, *veredus*, a gelding, *canterius*, a nag, *caballus*, 2, = cavalry, *equites, -um, equitatus, -ūs*, to ride on —, *equo vehi, equitare*, to fight on —, *ex equo pugnare* **horsebreaker,** n *equorum domitor*, higher groom, for breaking in horses, *equiso* (ante and post class) **horse-cloth,** n *stratum* **horse-dealer,** n *qui equos vendit* **horse-flesh,** n 1, = meat, *caro* *equina*, 2, = horses, *equi*. **horse-fly,** n *oestrus tabanus* **horse-hair,** n. *pilus equinus* **horse-laugh,** n *m*. *risus, ūs, cachinnus* **horseman,** n *eques, -itis*, m **horsemanship,** n *equitandi ars*. **horse-race,** n. *curriculum equorum, cursus* (*ūs*) *equorum* or *equester*, *equorum certamen* (as a contest) **horse-shoe,** n *solea ferrea* (in ancient times *solea spartea* or simply *spartea*, because they were only like slippers put on and taken off, and made of broom) **horse-soldier,** n *eques, -itis*, m. **horse-stealer,** n. *fur* **horse-whip,** n see WHIP

hortative, adj *hortans, monens*, see EXHORTATION **hortatory,** adj *monens*

horticulture, n *hortorum cultura* or *cultus, ūs*

hose, n see STOCKINGS

hospital, n. *nosocomium* (νοσοκομεῖον, Jct), *valetudinarium* (Jct)

hospitality, n *hospitium* (= the relation of —) **hospitable,** adj *hospitalis, liberalis* Adv *hospitaliter, liberaliter*.

host, n 1, *hospes, -itis*, m, or *coenae pater* (at a feast), 2, for gain, *caupo* (= a tavern-keeper), to reckon without your —, *spe frustrari* **hostess,** n *hospita*

host, n 1, = number, *multitudo*, a — of, *sescenti* (*sexc-*), 2, = army, *exercitus, -ūs*

hostage, n *obses, -idis*, m

hostel(ry), n *caupona* **hostler,** n *stabularius* (in gen), *agāso* (= groom)

hostile, adj = belonging to a public enemy, by the gen pl *hostium*, *hostilis* (class only in the meaning of acting as an enemy in times of war, hence, a — country, *hostilis terra* or *regio*), = anything in the possession of the enemy, *hosticus*, = unfriendly *inimicus, infestus*, comb *infensus atque inimicus, inimicus infensusque* Adv *hostiliter, inimice, infeste, infense* **hostility,** n *animus infestus, inimicitia*, = hatred, aversion, *odium*, in the pl hostilities, *hostilia, -ium*, n, *bellum* (= war), to commence —, *bellum facĕre*.

hot, adj 1, lit *calidus, fervidus, fervens* (= seething), *candens* (= of a white heat), *aestuosus, ardens*, †*flagrans*. 2, fig *calidus, fervidus, fervens, flagrans, acer, avidus*, see EAGER, to be —, *fervēre, candēre, aestuare*; to become —, *fervescĕre*, †*effervescĕre, incalescĕre*, (*in*)*candescĕre*, to make —, *calefacĕre, fervefacĕre* Adv *calide, fervide, ferventer, acriter, avide* **hotbed,** n 1, lit *locus stercoratus*, 2, fig *semen* (= seed) **hotheaded,** adj *iracundus, ingenio praeceps, temerarius, imprudens*. **hothouse,** n see HOT BED, GREENHOUSE

hotel, n *deversorium, caupona* (= a tavern), *hospitium*

hound, I. n *canis* (*venaticus*), *canis venator*, to keep a pack of —s, *canes alĕre ad venandum* II. v tr to — on, *alqm instigare, urgēre, lacessĕre, stimulare, incitare*

hour, n *hora*: the space of an —, *horae spatium*, the —s of the night, *nocturna tempora, -um*, half an —, *semihora*, what — is it? *quota hora est?* his last —, *hora novissima* or *suprema*, in his last —, *eo ipso die, quo e vitā excessit*, leisure —s, *tempus otiosum*, *tempus subsicivum*, to spare a few —s from one's studies, *alqd subsicivi temporis studiis suis subtrahĕre*, from — to —, *in horas* **hour-glass,** n *horologium* **hourly,** adj *singulis horis*

house, I. n *domus, ūs*, f (irreg), (= the place of abode, also those who inhabit it, the family), *aedes, aedificium, domicilium* (specially the dwelling), *villa* (= country —), *insula* (= — let out in portions), *tectum* (= a covering or roof), *familia* (= the family), *stirps, -is*, f, *genus, -ĕris*, n (= the race or clan), *res familiaris* (= house affairs), from — to —, *per domos, ostiatim* (= from door to door) **house-servants,** n *familia* (= slaves, as with the ancients), *famuli domestici* (as now) II. v tr. 1, = to take into one's —, *domo excipĕre*, 2, = to store, *condĕre* **housebreaker,** n. *fur*. **household,** I. n *domus, -ūs*, f, *familia, omnes sui* (*mei*, etc) II. adj *domesticus*, — gods, *lares, um*, m, *penates, ium* **householder,** n. *paterfamilias* **house-keeper,** n *quae res domesticas dispensat* **house-keeping,** n *cura rei domesticae*. **house-maid,** n *ancilla* **house-warming,** n to give a —, *domum amicis exceptis tanquam inaugurare* **house-wife,** n *hera* **house-wifery,** n *diligentia, cura domestica*

hovel, n *tugurium, gurgustium*.

hover, v intr *circum volitare* (lit and fig)

how, adv 1, as interrog particle, *qui? quid?* = in or according to what manner? *quomodo? quemadmodum?* (to express surprise), *quid? quidvis?* — are you? — do you do? = *quomodo vales? ut vales?* — does it happen that, etc? = *qui tandem fit, ut*, etc? = what now, or what then? *quid porro?* = but what? *quid vero?* = — many? = *quot?* — few! = *quotusquisque!* (e g — few philosophers are there that, etc! *quotusquisque philosophus est, qui*, etc!) — often? = *quotie*(*n*)*s?* — great? = *quantus?* — dear? — much? what price? = *quanti? quanto?* 2, in exclamations, *quam, quantopere*, — well you have done! = *quam bene fecisti!* — much could I wish? = *quam* or *quanto pere vellem!* — dissatisfied he was, felt with himself! = *ut sibi ipse displicebat!* Very often merely the accus of the noun (e g — blind I am that I could not foresee that! = *me caecum, qui haec ante non viderim!* — treacherous are the hopes of men! — short their earthly happiness! — vain all their efforts! = *o fallacem hominum spem! o fragilem fortunam et inanes nostras contentiones!*) 3, as a relative adv = by what means, *quemadmodum* (= according to what, etc), = by what means, *quomodo* = in what manner, *quā ratione*, — under what conditions, circumstances, *quo pacto*, they fix — to carry out the remainder, = *reliqua, quā ratione agi placeat, constituunt*, I don't know — this always happens, = *nescio quo pacto semper hoc fit* **howbeit,** adv (*at*)*tamen* **however,** I. adv. *quamvis, quamlibet, quantumvis* (e g — great, *quamvis magnus*) II. conj *sed, autem*, (*at*)*tamen, nihilominus*

howl, I. v intr *ululare* (from the sound, referring to dogs, wolves, human beings), of the roaring of the wind, *fremĕre*, of the loud cries of women at funerals, *ejulare*, to weep aloud, moan, *plorare, lamentari*, comb *ejulare atque lamentari*. II. n *ululatus, ejulatus, ploratus* (all, *-ūs*), *ejulatio*, or, of several together, *comploratio, lamentatio*.

hubbub, n. *tumultus, ūs*

huckster, I. n *caupo, institor*. II. v intr. *cauponam exercēre*.

huddle, n *turba*; huddled together, *confert*i

hue, n *color*

hue, n = exclamation, *vocas, um*, pl, *clamor, vociferatio*, see CRY, to raise (= order) a — and cry by land and by water, *terrā marique ut alqs conquiratur, praemandare*.

huff, n *impetus, ūs* (= fit), *ira, iracundia*, be in a —, *irasci, moleste ferre*

hug, I. v tr *amplecti, complecti*, — the shore, *litus tamire*, — oneself, *se jactare, gloriari* **II.** n *complexus, -ūs*

huge, adj *immanis, vastus* (= immense in gen.), *immensus* (= unusually great), large = *ingens* (e g tree, *arbor*, sum of money, *pecunia*, genius, talent, *ingenium*), of — depth, *immensā, infinitā altitudine* Adv *valde, magnopere*

hugeness, n *magnitudo, moles* (= bulk)

hulk, n (= the body of a ship), *alveus navis.*

hull, n the — of a nut, *cortex, folliculus* (= little bag, hence husk)

hum, I. v intr *fremĕre, strepĕre,* † *susurrare, murmurare, murmur edĕre, stridorem edĕre*, = to buzz, *bombum facĕre;* = sing softly, *secum canĕre, cantare* **II.** n *fremitus, ūs* (in gen), *murmur, -ŭris*, n (of men and bees), † *susurrus, stridor, bombus, comprobatio* (= applause) **III.** interj *hem!*

human, adj *humanus*, by the gen pl *hominum* (e g — vices and errors, *hominum vitia et errores*), = mortal, *mortalis*, — feelings (in gen), *humanitas* Adv *humano modo* (= after the manner of men) **humane,** adj = kind, affable, *misericors, clemens* Adv *clementer* **humaneness,** n *clementia, misericordia* **humanity,** n 1, = peculiar nature of man, *natura* or *condicio humana*, 2, = mankind, human race, *humanum* or *hominum genus, -ĕris*, n , *gens humana*, 3, = kind feelings, *humanitas, clementia, misericordia* **humanize,** v tr = to make a person more civilized, *alqm humanum reddĕre, excolĕre;* see CIVILIZE **humankind,** n *genus humanum.*

humble, I. adj *humilis*, = lowly, meek, *submissus, demissus* (opp *elatus*), = modest, *modestus, moderatus, verecundus*, = suppliant, *supplex*, comb *humilis et supplex* (e g *oratio*), = low, *humilis* (e g *humili loco ortus*), to show oneself —, *submisse se gerĕre* Adv *demisse, submisse, simpliciter, humiliter* (= meanly), *modeste, moderate*, comb *modeste ac moderate* (= without ostentation), to be — disposed, *animo esse submisso*, to request —, *supplicibus verbis orare*, to entreat very —, *multis verbis et supplicem orare* **II.** v tr = to break anyone's bold spirit, *infringĕre, frangĕre alqm* or *alcjs audaciam, comprimĕre alcjs audaciam* comb *frangĕre alqm et comminuĕre*, to — oneself, *se* or *animum submittĕre, submisse se gerĕre, comprimĕre animos suos* **humbling, humiliating,** adj use n *dedecus, ŏris*, n (e g he found it —, *quod dedecori esse putavit*) **humiliation,** n *dedecus, -ŏris*, n , see DISGRACE **humility,** n = lowness of spirits, *animus submissus, demissus* = lowness of origin, *humilitas*, = modesty, *modestia*, * *humilitas* (as a Christian virtue)

humbug, I. n *gerrae, nugae, tricae* **II.** v tr *alci illudere, alqm ludificare, alci verba dare alqm circumvenire, circumducĕre*

humdrum, adj *iners, tardus, segnis* (= sluggish)

humid, adj *humidus, humectus* (ante and post class) **humidity,** n *humor*

humour, I. n 1 (= fluids of animal bodies), *humor*, 2, = temper, (*animi*) *affectio* or *affectus, -ūs, ingenium, natura*, arbitrary —, *libido* (*lub*), in gen , = propensities, *studia, orum*, = general temper of the mind, *animi habitus, -ūs;* temporary —, *animi motus, ūs*, disposition in gen , *animus*, = inclination, *voluntas*, = a quiet disposition, *animus tranquillus*, the best — towards, *summa in alqm voluntas*, to be in good —, *bene affectum esse*, to be in ill —, *male affectum esse, morosum esse*, ill —, *natura difficilis, morositas*, violent —, *asperitas* (i e. harshness), in the —, *ex libidine, ad arbitrium suum*, = as one thinks proper, *arbitrio suo*, comb *ad arbitrium suum* (*nostrum*, etc) *libidinemque*, I am in the —, *libet* (*lub-*) *mihi alqd facĕre*, 3, = that quality by which we give to one's ideas a ludicrous turn, *lepos* (*lepor*), *-ōris*, m (in the whole character, also in a written work), *festivitas* (= mirth, wit ; also in a written work) ; facetiousness or — in speech, *cavillatio* (= raillery), *jocus, facetiae* **II.** v tr *alci obtemperare, indulgēre, alci morem gerĕre, morigerari* **humourist,** n 1, *homo jocosus, lepidus, facetus, festivus*, 2, = an ill-tempered man, *homo difficilis, morosus* **humoursome,** adj *difficilis, morosus, difficilis ac morosus*

hump, n *tuber, -ĕris*, n (Plin , e g of a camel), a bunch in any part of the body (espec on the back), *gibber, -ĕris*, n (Plin) **hump-backed,** adj *gibber*

hunch, n see HUMP

hundred, adj *centum*, every —, *centeni, ae, -a* (also = — at once), a subdivision of the Roman people into centuries or —s, *centuria*, of a —, — years old, *centenarius*, a — times, *centie(n)s*, a — thousand, *centum mil(l)ia*, — years, *centum anni*, a space of one — years, *centum annorum spatium*, a century, a generation, *saeculum.* **hundred-fold,** adj † *centuplex*, † *centuplicatus*, to bear fruit a —, *cum centesimo efferre* **hundred-handed,** adj † *centimanus* **hundred-headed,** adj † *centiceps* **hundredweight,** n *centu(m)pondium* (ante class)

hunger, I. n *fames, -is*, lit and fig , — after gold, *fames auri*, = starvation, *inedia*, — is the best cook, *cibi condimentum fames* **II.** v intr *esurire*, to — after, *alqd sitire, alcjs rei aviditum esse* **hungry,** adj *esuriens, jejunus, famelicus* (ante and post class) Adv *avide*, see EAGERLY

hunt, I. v tr *venari*, — after, *alqd* (*con*)*sectari* **II.** n *venatio, venatus, -ūs* **hunter, huntsman,** n *venator* **huntress,** n *venatrix*

hurdle, n *crates, is*

hurl, v tr *jacĕre, jaculari, con(j)icĕre* **hurling,** n *conjectus, -ūs*

hurly-burly, n *tumultus, -ūs*, see TUMULT, NOISE

hurrah, see HUZZA

hurricane, n *tempestas* (*foeda*), *turbo, inis*, m (= whirlwind), *procella*

hurry, I. v tr *accelerare, impellĕre, incitare, excitare*(= to rouse), *rapĕre*(= to carry off), *urgēre* (= to press on), *stimulare, stimulos alci admovēre* **II.** v intr *festinare, properare, maturare*, whither are you —ing? *quo te agis?* — about, *discurrĕre* (in different directions), *trepidare*, — away, *abripĕre, rapĕre, trahĕre* (= to drag), — on, *maturare, urgēre, festinare* **III.** n *festinatio, trepidatio* (= alarm) **hurried,** adj *properus, citatus, citus praeceps* Adv *festinanter, propere, cursim, raptim*

hurt, I. v tr 1, lit *alqm laedĕre, alci nocēre*, 2, fig *laedĕre*, to be —, *alqd aegre ferre* **II.** v intr *dolēre* (e g it —s, *dolet*, mostly ante class and colloquial) **III.** n 1, = a wound, *vulnus, -ĕris*, n , 2, = injury, *damnum* **IV.** adj 1, *saucius* (= wounded), 2, fig *conturbatus tristis* **hurtful,** adj *nocens, noxius, perniciosus, exitiosus, exitialis, damnosus* Adv *perniciose* **hurtfulness,** n *pernicies.*

husband, I. n *maritus, vir, conju(n)x, ŭgis*, m and f , a young married man, *novus maritus* **II.** v tr *rem familiarem curare, alc rei parcĕre*

husbandman, n. *agricola*, m. *arator* (= ploughman). **husbandry**, n. 1, *res rustica*, *res rusticae* (= the occupations of a farmer); = agriculture, *agricultura*, *agricultio* (or as two words); 2, = care of domestic affairs, *cura rerum domesticarum*; 3, = economy, as, good —, *frugalitas*.

hush, **I.** interj. *st! tace*, pl. *tacēte*. **II.** v.tr. *restinguĕre*, *ex(s)tinguĕre* (e.g. *tumultum*, to — the crowd); to — cares, *alcjs animum lenire et placare*, *placare et mitigare*; to — up a rumour, *rumorem opprimĕre*; see SUPPRESS.

husk, n. *folliculus*, *gluma*. **husky**, adj. *(sub)raucus*; see HOARSE.

hustings, n. *suggestus*, *-ūs* (*suggestum*) (= platform), *comitium* (= place of election).

hustle, v.intr. *alqm cubito offendĕre*, *premĕre*.

hut, n. *casa* (= a small —, cottage), *tugurium*.

hutch, n. *cavea* (= cage).

huzza, **I.** interj. *eja! eje! evoë! io! io!* **II.** n. (= a shout of joy), *clamor et gaudium*. **III.** v.intr. *(ac)clamare*, *conclamare*, *succlamare*; see SHOUT.

hyacinth, n. *hyacinthus* (*hyacinthos*).

Hyades, n. *Hyades*, *-um*, f.; *suculae* (mistranslation of ὑάδες, as though from ὗς = pig, instead of ὕειν = to rain).

Hymen, n. *Hymen* or *Hymenaeus*. **Hymeneal**, adj. *nuptialis*.

hymn, **I.** n. *hymnus*; = in honour of Apollo or other gods, a song of triumph, *paean*, *-ānis*, m. **II.** v.tr. *cantu alcjs laudes prosequi*.

hyperbole, n. *hyperbole* (or *hyperbola*), *-es*, f., *veritatis superlatio et trajectio*. **hyperbolical**, adj. *veritatis modum excedens*.

Hyperborean, adj. †*Hyperboreus*.

hypercritical, adj. *iniquus*, *severus*. Adv. *nimiâ cum severitate*. **hypercriticism**, n. *nimia severitas*.

hypochondria, n. *atra* or *nigra bilis*. **hypochondriacal**, adj. *melancholicus*.

hypocrisy, n. *(dis)simulatio*, *fraus*, *-dis*, f., *mendacium*; without —, *ex animo*.

hypocrite, n. *(dis)simulator*. **hypocritical**, adj. *simulatus*, *fictus*. Adv. *simulate*, *ficte*.

hypothesis, n. *opinio*, *sententia* (= opinion), *ratio*, *condicio* (= condition), *conjectura* (= conjecture); on this —, *quo posito*, *quibus positis*. **hypothetical**, adj. *opinabilis*. Adv. to speak —, *ex conjecturâ* or *de re opinabili dicĕre*; if this be — granted, *hoc concesso* or *posito*.

hysteria, n. 1, med. t.t. **hysteria*; 2, = excitement, *furor*, *animi* or *mentis motus*, *-ūs*, *commotio*, *animus (com)motus*. **hysterical**, adj. 1, *hystericus* (Plin.); 2, †*furens*, *mente (com)motus*.

I.

I, pron. *ego*, *egomet*. It is generally only expressed in Latin when we wish to speak emphatically. The plural is frequently used in Latin for I. — myself, *ego ipse*, *egomet ipse*, *ipse*; — at least, *ego quidem*, *equidem*.

iambic, **I.** adj. *iambeus*. **II.** n. *iambus*.

ice, n. *glacies*, *gelu*; to break the —, fig. *viam aperire*. **ice-berg**, n. *glaciei moles*, *-is*. **icicle**, n. †*stiria*. **icy**, adj. 1, lit. *glacialis*, *gelidus*, *frigidus*; 2, fig. use *superbus*. Adv. *superbe*.

idea, n. = — of anything, *notio* (*notionem appello*, *quod Graeci tum ἔννοιαν*, *tum πρόληψιν dicunt*. *Ea est insita*, *et ante percepta cujusque formae cognitio*, *enodationis indigens*, Cic.); = the apprehension of anything, *intellegentia* (*intellig-*), *intellectus*, *-ūs* (Quint.); the — which we form therefrom, opinion, *opinio*; = the picture we have of anything, *imago*, *effigies*; = the expectation we base upon the latter, *ex(s)pectatio*; = the — formed of anything, *informatio*; the — we form, an image to the mind, *species*, *idea*, (= thought) *cogitatio*; = the meaning of anything, *vis*, *vis*, f., *sententia*; an original, innate —, *notio in animis informata*; *notio animis impressa*; *insita et quasi consignata in animis notio*; *innata cognitio*; *praenotio insita* or *insita praeceptaque cognitio*; *quod natura insculpsit in mentibus*; = an innate — of God, *informatio Dei animo antecepta*; obscure —, *cognitio indagationis indigens*; to form a correct — of, *recte sentire de alqâ re*; to have no — of, *notionem alcjs rei nullam habēre*, *alqd ignorare*; to have a false, wrong — of, *prava de alqâ re sentire*; to have a clear — of, *perspectum habēre alqd*; much depends on what — you have of the office of a tribune, *plurimum refert quid esse tribunatum putes*; we have not all one and the same — about what is honourable and dishonourable, *non eadem omnibus honesta sunt ac turpia*; that — of Aristippus, *illud Aristippeum*; (*idea*, ἰδέα, in the meaning of Plato's system of mental philosophy, is generally rendered by Cic. by ἰδέα, with *species*, e.g. *hanc illi ἰδέαν appellant*, *jam a Platone ita nominatam*, *nos recte speciem possumus dicĕre*; and in Senec. by *idea* or *exemplar rerum*); to raise the mind to the — (in the sense of modern metaphysics), *a consuetudine oculorum mentis aciem abducĕre*; = definition of fear, *metus*, *-ūs* (e.g. to be subordinate to the — of fear, etc., *sub metum subjectum esse*). **ideal**, **I.** adj. 1, *optimus*, *summus* (= the best, most excellent); = most perfect, *perfectissimus* (rare), *perfectus et omnibus numeris absolutus*; = most beautiful, *pulcherrimus*; 2, = intellectual, *quod tantummodo ad cogitationem valet*; *quod non sensu*, *sed mente cernitur*. **II.** n. *singularis quaedam summae perfectionis species animo informata*, *singularis quaedam summae perfectionis imago animo et cogitatione concepta* (i.e. the idea of the highest perfection as conceived in the mind); anything in the most accomplished form, *undique expleta et perfecta forma alcjs rei*, *optima et perfecta alcjs rei species*, *optimum*; = what we picture in our minds as the — of anything, *effigies*, *imago*, *simulacrum* (also = the highest idea of anything, which is constantly in our mind), *species*, *forma*; — of beauty, *species pulchritudinis eximia quaedam*; = a pattern, model, *exemplar* (*et forma*); = a pattern (in a moral sense), *specimen* (e.g. *prudentiae specimen pontifex maximus*, *Qu. Scaevola*). Very often an — may also be rendered by adjs., *summus*, *optimus*, *pulcherrimus*; — of a state, *civitas optima* or *perfectissima*; — of a wise man (in mental philosophy), *sapiens*, *perfectus homo planeque sapiens*; — of an orator, *imago perfecti oratoris*, *simulacrum oratoris*, *orator summus*, *norma et regula oratoris* (e.g. *Demosthenes ille*, *norma oratoris et regula*); a beau — of a state, *imago civitatis*, *quam cogitatione tantum et mente complecti*, *nullo autem modo in vitam hominum introducĕre possumus* (= an — state); a state of the highest perfection, *civitas perfectissima*; = pattern, model of a state, *exemplar reipublicae et forma*; — of a state in Plato, *illa commenticia Platonis civitas*; *civitas*, *quam finxit Plato*, *cum optimum reipublicae statum exquireret*. **idealism**, n. *ars* or *vis animo sibi fingendi alqd*. **idealist**, n. *qui alqd sibi animo fingit*. **idealize**, v.tr. *speciem alcjs rei animo sibi fingĕre*, *concipĕre*, *informare*, *a consuetudine oculorum mentis aciem abducĕre*; see IDEAL.

identical, adj *ejusdem generis* (= of the same kind), *idem, unus et idem, idem et par, nihil aliud nisi*, at the very same time, *eodem* or *uno eodemque tempore*, to be —, *nihil differre*, exertion and grief are not —, *interest alqd inter laborem et dolorem*. **identify,** v tr *ad eandem notionem* (or *vim* or *rationem*) *referre*, = to recognize, *agnoscĕre* **identity,** n *eadem vis* or *ratio*, *nullum omnino discrimen*

ides, n *idus, -uum*, f pl

idiom, n 1, = mode of expression peculiar to a language, *proprietas, quae Latinae linguae propria sunt, loquendi ratio*; 2, = genius or peculiar cast of a language, *idiōma, -ătis*, n (Gram.). **idiomatic,** adj. *proprius* Adv *proprie*.

idiot, n. lit and fig (*homo*) *stultus*, see FOOL **idiocy,** n *fatuitas, stultitia*

idle, I. adj 1, = inactive, unemployed, *otiosus, vacuus, ignavus, piger, iners, segnis, deses, -ĭdis*, 2, = useless, *inutilis, vanus, irritus*, see USELESS, VAIN, 3, = trifling unprofitable, *lĕvis, vilis*, see INSIGNIFICANT Adv *ignave, segniter, frustra, incassum* (or as two words) **II.** v intr *cessare, nihil agĕre* **idleness,** n 1, *cessatio, otium*, 2, = laziness, *segnitia, pigritia, desidia* **idler,** n. *homo deses*, = one who loiters, *cessator*, I am the greatest — in the world, *nihil me est inertius*.

idol, n 1, * *idolum* (= an image or likeness, = "idol" in the Christian Fathers), 2, *fig amores, deliciae*, comb *amores et deliciae* (of a beloved person) **idolator,** n *deorum fictorum cultor*. **idolatrous,** adj. * *idolatricus, fictos deos colens* **idolatry,** n *deorum fictorum* (or *simulacrorum*) *cultus, -ūs*, to practise —, *colĕre deos fictos, alqd pro deo venerari*

idyl, n *carmen bucolicum, bucolica, -orum* (of a poem) **idyllic,** adj by circumloc (e g an — picture of leisured life, *pulcherrima quaedam vitae umbratilis descriptio*)

if, conj *si* (with the indic mood if we merely speak about the reality of a thing, with the subj if we represent anything as possible, probable, or doubtful), — every event is determined by fate, we cannot be too cautious, *si fato omnia fiunt, nihil nos admonēre potest ut cautiores simus*, a whole day would not be sufficient, — I were to enumerate, *dies deficiat, si velim numerare*, in comparisons (e g — anything of that kind delights me, it is painting *si quid generis istiusmodi me delectat, pictura delectat*), *quod si* is often used instead of *si*, owing to a tendency in Latin to connect sentences by relatives Very often we render — by a participle (e g I should never have thought of it, — you had not reminded me, *non mihi, nisi admonito, in mentem venisset*), but —, *sin, sin autem, si vero*, but — not, but unless, *si non, si minus sin minus, sin aliter* — not, unless, *nisi, ni, si non* (a negative condition, where *non* must be taken together with the verb), — not perhaps, *nisi forte*, namely —, *si quidem*, that is — (in correcting or modifying an expression previously used), *si modo*, and simply *si* (e g God only gives us reason, that is, — we have any, *a Deo tantum rationem habemus, si modo habemus*, — only, *dum modo, dummodo* (with the subjunctive), — perhaps, *si forte* (not *si fortasse*, see PERHAPS), — anyone, *si (ali)quis*, — anything, *si (ali)quid*, — at any time, — some day, *si (ali)quando* (*si aliquis, si aliquid, si aliquando* are only used if we lay a particular stress on the word "some"), even — (= although), *quamquam, quamvis licet, etsi, etiamsi* (see ALTHOUGH), whether or —, *sive (seu)*, *sive (seu)*, as —, *quasi, tamquam (tanq-), ac si, velut si*, (with conj), (e g the Sequani feared the cruelty of Ariovistus the same in his absence as — he were present, *Sequani Ariovisti absentis crudelitatem, velut si coram adesset, horrebant*) —, after many words, especially after to seem to pretend, to feign, to suspect, to doubt, etc , by the accus with inf. (e g with some I create a suspicion, as — I intended to sail, *moveo nonnullis suspicionem velle me navigare* he did as — he were mad, *simulavit se furĕre*), as —, after *videor* (= it looks, appears to me), rendered with the nominative with inf (e g. it looks as — you were angry, *iratum esse videris*), not as —, *non quo* (not as — I had anything to write to you, *non quo haberem, quod tibi scriberem*)

ignite, I. v tr = to kindle or set on fire, *accendĕre, incendĕre, inflammare* (*rare*), see FIRE, HEAT **II.** v intr *exardescĕre, accendi, incendi*, etc (lit and fig), *ignem* or *flammam concipĕre*, see KINDLE, EXCITE **igneous,** adj. *igneus* **ignition,** n *incensio*, but better use verb

ignoble, adj *ignobilis* (= of low birth); = of unknown origin, *obscuro loco natus, obscuris ortus majoribus*, = of low rank and character, *humilis* (of persons and things, e g speech *oratio*, style, *verbum*), = of low descent, *humili loco natus*, = illiberal, *illiberalis*, = low despicable, *abjectus, turpis*, — disposition, meanness of action, *humilitas, illiberalitas* Adv *humiliter, illiberaliter, turpiter*

ignominy, n. *ignominia, infamia, dedecus, ŏris, probrum, contumelia, turpitudo*, to throw — upon, *alqm ignominia afficĕre, ignominiam alci imponĕre* or *injungĕre* or *inurĕre* **ignominious,** adj *ignominiosus, contumeliosus, turpis, probrosus* Adv *contumeliose, turpiter*

ignoramus, n *homo inscius alcjs rei* **ignorance,** n *imprudentia, inscientia*, = want of abilities, *inscitia*, — of facts, *ignoratio*, = want of education, *ignorantia* (all with gen.), to confess one's — in many things, *confiteri multa se ignorare*. **ignorant,** adj *insciens* (opp *sciens*), *inscitus*, = unawares, *imprudens* (opp *sciens*), *inscius alcjs rei* (= illiterate), = unskilful in, *ignarus alcjs rei*, = inexperienced in, *imperitus alcjs rei*, comb *inscius imperitusque*, quite — of, *rudis alcjs rei* or *in alqâ re*, or comb *alcjs rei inscius et rudis*, = not learned, *indoctus*, = illiterate, *illit(t)eratus, indoctus*; a pupil who is only a beginner, *rudis et integer discipulus*, to be — of, *alqd nescire, alqd ignorare*, = not to be skilled in, *alqd non callēre*. Adv by adj or *imprudenter, inscienter, inscite, imperite, indocte* **ignore,** v.tr *praeterire*

Iliad, n *Ilias*

ill, I. adj 1, *aeger, aegrotus, morbidus* (= seized by disease), *valetudine affectus, invalidus, infirmus, imbecillus*, very —, *gravi et periculoso morbo aeger*, to be —, *aegrotare, morbo affici* or *laborare*, to fall —, *morbo corripi, in morbum incidĕre*, 2, in gen *malus*, of an — reputation, *male audire, pravus, nequam* (= wicked) **II.** Adv *male, prave, misere, miseriter* it goes — with me, *male mecum agitur*; to brook a thing —, *alqd aegre* or *moleste ferre* **III.** n *malum, pestis, pestilentia* (= plague), *incommodum, casus, -ūs* (= misfortune) **ill-advised,** adj *inconsultus, temerarius*, see RASH **ill-affected,** adj 1, = unfriendly, *inimicus, infestus*, 2, = disloyal, *infidelis*, — citizens, *cives turbulenti et mali* **ill-bred,** adj *humanitatis expers, inurbanus* **ill-breeding,** n. *mores inurbani, inhumanitas* **ill-fated,** adj *infelix, miser*, see UNHAPPY **ill-favoured,** adj see UGLY **ill-gotten,** adj *male partus*. **ill-health,** n *valetudo infirma* **ill-made,** adj *informis, deformis* (by nature, opp to *formosus*) *male factus* (by art) **ill-matched,** adj. *impar*, see UN-

EQUAL. **ill-mannered,** adj. see ILL-BRED. **ill-nature,** n. *malignitas.* **ill-natured,** adj. *morosus, difficilis, malignus.* **illness,** n. *morbus, aegrotatio, valetudo infirma, adversa, incommoda* or *tenuis.* **ill-omened,** adj. *dirus, infaustus, inauspicatus.* **ill-temper,** n. *stomachus, morositas, malignitas, iracundia.*

illegal, adj. *legi repugnans, contrarius, quod contra leges fit*; = contrary to the law of God and man, *contra jus fasque, contra fas et jus.* Adv. *contra legem* or *leges*; *praeter leges* or *jus*; **illegality,** n. by the adj.

illegible, adj. *qui, quae, quod legi non potest*; to be —, *legi non posse.*

illegitimate, adj. 1, *incerto patre natus, spurius* (Jct.); *pellice ortus, nothus* (νόθος = a bastard) (Quint.), *(h)ibrida (hyb-)*, (= a person whose parents were of different countries, or one of whose parents was a slave); 2, in gen. = unlawful, *non legitimus* (not *illegitimus*), *quod contra leges fit*; *haud ex legibus*; 3, = not genuine, adulterated, *adulterinus.* Adv. *non legitime, haud ex legibus, contra leges.*

illiberal, adj. *illiberalis* (= unworthy of a free man, e.g. a joke, *jocus*), = mean, ungenerous, *sordidus, parcus, avarus, malignus.* **illiberality,** n. *illiberalitas, avaritia, parsimonia* (*parc-*), *malignitas.*

illicit, adj. *inconcessus, vetitus* (= prohibited), *nefas,* n. indecl. (= contrary to human and divine law, impious); — means, *artes malae.*

illimitable, adj. *infinitus.*

illiterate, adj. *illiteratus, indoctus, ineruditus*; to be —, *nescire lit(t)eras.* Adv. *indocte.*

illogical, adj. *quod haud necessario consequitur, inconstans, quod vitiose conclusum est.* Adv. *inconstanter, vitiose.*

illume, illumine, illuminate, v.tr. 1, = to throw light on, *collustrare, illustrare* (lit. and fig.); *illuminare* (lit. = illuminate, fig. = to throw light upon a matter; none of these verbs used in reference to the mind); the light of the sun —s all things, *sol cuncta luce suâ illustrat*; to be —d by the sun, *sole illustrem esse*; to — a town, *in urbe pernoctantia lumina accendĕre* (Ammian, said of the lighting of the streets); 2, = to enlighten the mind, *colĕre, docēre, erudire*; 3, = to adorn with pictures (as to — manuscripts or books, according to ancient practice), *varie pingĕre, alci rei vivos colores inducĕre.* **illumination,** n. 1, of MSS., use verb ILLUMINATE, 3; 2, = the picture itself, *pictura, tabula*; 3, mental —, *eruditio, doctrina.*

illusion, n. (*opinionis*) *error, somnium, opinio falsa* or *vana.* **illusive, illusory,** adj. *vanus, falsus, commenticius.*

illustrate, v.tr. 1, *illustrare*; see ILLUMINATE; 2, = — a book, *librum tabulis* or *picturis ornare*; 3, = to explain, *illustrare*; see EXPLAIN. **illustration,** n. 1, *explicatio*; see EXPLANATION; 2, of a book, *pictura, tabula*; 3, = example, *exemplum.* **illustrious,** adj. (*prae*)*clarus, amplus* (usu. in superl.), *splendidus, illustris, insignis, egregius, eximius, spectatus, nobilis, praestans.* **illustrative,** adj. *quod alqd illustrat, explicat,* etc.

image, n. 1, *imago, simulacrum, effigies*; = painting, *tabula picta, pictura*; = statue, *statua*; to form an — or likeness, *imaginem alcjs exprimĕre*; 2, = a conception, *imago, species*; to form an — of, *animo alqd effingĕre*; 3, in rhetoric, *translatio, figura.* **image-worshipper,** n. *qui imagines pro Deo veneratur.* **imagery,** n. 1, = sensible representations, pictures, statues, *imago*; 2, = forms of the fancy, *imago*; see FANCY. **imaginable,** adj. *quod cogitari potest, quod cogitatione comprehendi* or *percipi potest, quod in cogitationem cadit, cogitabilis* (Sen.); with all — pains, *maximo, quod fieri potest, studio.* **imaginary,** adj. *opinatus* (e.g. a good, *bonum*; an evil, *malum*), *opinabilis, commenticius, imaginarius, fictus, falsus, inanis*; — misfortunes, *malorum opinio*; — difficulties, *difficultates, quas sibi alqs ipse fingit*; see FANCY. **imagination,** n. *cogitatio* (= a thought, the faculty of thinking); an idle —, *metus, -ūs, inanis, species inanis*; = an idea without foundation, *opinio* (*falsa*); to exist in —, not in reality (e.g. of an evil), *opinionis esse, non naturae*; what lies only in one's —, *opinatus*; only based upon —, *opinabilis*; = false, fictitious, *falsus, fictus*; = the faculty of understanding, *mens,* comb. *cogitatio et mens.* **imaginative,** adj. *ingeniosus* (of one who has always new ideas); *sol(l)ers* (of one who understands the art of following out an idea); one who is —, *ingenium ad excogitandum acutum.* Adv. *ingeniose, sol(l)erter, acute.* **imagine,** v.tr. and intr. *animo concipĕre, cogitare, complecti,* or simply *cogitare, fingĕre, conjecturâ consequi*; = invent, *comminisci, excogitare, fingĕre, machinari*; I — (parenthetically), *ut opinor.*

imbecile, adj. *fatuus, stultus*; see FOOLISH. **imbecility,** n. *imbecillitas animi* or *ingenii, fatuitas* (rare), *stultitia.*

imbibe, v.tr. *bibere, combibĕre, imbibĕre*; fig. *se alqâ re imbuĕre, alqâ re infici*; — errors with your mother's milk, *errores cum lacte nutricis sugĕre.*

imbrue, v.tr. *imbuĕre, madefacĕre*; — with blood, *cruentare.*

imbue, v.tr. 1, = to dye, *ting(u)ĕre, inficĕre*; 2, fig. *alqm alqâ re inficĕre, imbuĕre, alqd docēre.*

imitable, adj. *imitabilis, quod imitari possumus.* **imitate,** v.tr. *imitari* (e.g. the human voice, *voces hominum*); to — in dress, manners, to — a statue, painting, sound, action, (*imitando* or *imitatione*) *exprimĕre, imitando effingĕre*; = to emulate, endeavour to equal or excel, *aemulari alqm* or *alqd* and *alci* or *cum alqo* (*aemulans* = imitating a rival; *imitans* = imitating one who is a pattern to us, who is our superior in that wherein we try to imitate him; *aemulari alqm* in a good sense; *aemulari alci* until Quint. only in a bad sense, i.e. to contend with a spirit of rivalry); to — (i.e. to tread in anyone's footsteps), (*per*)*sequi.* **imitation,** n. 1, the act of imitating, *imitatio* (in gen.); the desire of —, *imitatio, imitandi studium*; = emulation, *aemulatio*; also circumlocution with *imitari* (e.g. to devote oneself to the — of a person, *ad imitationem alcjs se conferre* or *ad imitandum alqm se conferre*); 2, = the thing itself that is imitated, *res imitatione* or *imitando expressa, res imitando effecta*; *effigies, imago, simulacrum*; to be an — of anything, *imitatione ex alqâ re expressum esse*; see IMAGE. **imitative,** adj. *qui alqd facile imitatur.* **imitator,** n. *imitator*; a zealous —, *aemulus, aemulator.*

immaculate, adj. *purus, sanctus, incorruptus, innocens, integer*; = chaste, pure, innocent, *castus,* comb. *castus et integer, integer castusque, castus purusque.* Adv. *pure, sancte, incorrupte, caste.*

immanent, adj. *in alqâ re inhaerens, interior.*

immaterial, adj. 1, = incorporeal (e.g. spirits), *corpore vacans, quod cerni tangique non potest*; 2, = unimportant, by *nullius momenti, nullo momento, lĕvis*; to consider as —, *non flocci facĕre.* **immateriality,** n. by circumloc.,

Plato asserts the — of the Deity, *Plato sine cor pore ullo Deum esse vult*

immature, adj lit and fig *immaturus*, *crudus* (lit, poet, and late fig)

immeasurable, adj *immensus*, = endless, *infinitus* (e g multitude), = immense, extremely large, *vastus*, *ingens* (e g fortune), a mountain of — height, *mons in immensum editus* Adv *in* or *ad immensum*

immediate, adj 1, = without the intervention of anyone else, *ipse*, *proximus*, an — cause, *caus(s)a efficiens* or *proxima*. 2, = without delay, *praesens* Adv use adj (e g to apply — to anyone, *alqm ipsum adire*), *statim* (followed by *ab alqa re* or *ut* or *simulac*), *protinus*, *confestim*, *extemplo*, *e(x) vestigio*, not — from the field of battle, *non ex ipsa acie*, — after anyone (in order, rank, or time), *secundum alqm*, — after, *sub alqd* (e g — after these words he threw himself at his feet, *sub haec dicta ad genua ejus procubuit*), — after (i e as a sequel to and in consequence of), *ex alqd re* (e g — after the dictatorship made into a consul, *consul ex dictatura factus*).

immemorial, adj = beyond memory, e g from time —, *ex omni memoria aetatum*, or *temporum* (i e throughout all ages), = as long as we can think *post hominum memoriam*, = from the remotest times, *inde ab antiquissimis temporibus*, also by *priscus antiquissimus*, *perantiquus* (= from ancient times, opp *novus*, of persons and things), *avitus* (= from the times of our grandfathers), it is an — custom, *ex antiquis temporibus inveteravit*

immense, adj *ingens*, *vastus*, *immensus*, *infinitus* Adv *ad* or *in immensum*, = very much, *maxime*, *valde* **immensity**, n *immensitas*, *vastitas*

immerge, v tr 1, *(im)mergĕre*, *demergĕre*, *submergĕre* (*in*) *alqd re* or *in alqd*, 2, fig *alqm in alqd demergĕre*, = to fall into deep meditation about, *se totum in alcjs rei cognitione collocare* **immersion**, n by the verb

immethodical, adj = not properly arranged, *incompositus*, = disordered, irregular, not put in order, *inordinatus* (e g soldiers, *milites*), = without method, *indigestus*, = careless, *neglegens* (*neglig*) Adv *sine ordine*, *incomposite*, *neglegenter*

immigrate, v intr *(im)migrare* **immigrant**, n *advena*, m and f **immigration**, n *adventus*, -ūs (e g of foreign tribes, *aliarum gentium*)

imminent, adj *praesens*, *maximus*, *summus* with n (e g to be in — danger, *in summo periculo esse*), by *subesse* (= to be at hand, near), *instare* (= to draw nigh, threaten, e g winter, war), *imminēre*, *impendēre* (to be —, e g evils, calamities)

immitigable, adj *qui se mitigari non patitur*

immobility, n *immobilitas*, or by adj, see IMMOVABLE

immoderate, adj *immodicus* (= exceeding bounds, also in a moral sense); = intemperate, *immoderatus* (e g in drink; also in a moral sense), *intemperans*; = incontinent, unchaste, *incontinens*, = impotent, ungovernable, *impotens* (e g joy, *laetitia*), in anything, *alcjs rei*; = immodest (of persons and things), unrestrained, fierce, *effrenatus*, — boldness, *audacia*, = profuse, *effusus*, *profusus*, = immense, *immanis* (e g size, *magnitudo*, sums of money, *pecuniae*). = extravagant, *luxuriosus* Adv *immoderate*, *intemperanter*, *immodeste*, *effuse*, *profuse*, *immodice*, *luxuriose*, to drink —, *vino se obruĕre* **immoderation**, n *intemperantia*, *incontinentia*, — in speaking, *immoderatio verborum*

immodest, adj = arrogant, *arrogans*, = insolent, haughty, *insolens*, = indiscreet, *impudicus*, *inverecundus* Adv *immodeste*, *arroganter*, *insolenter*, *impudice* **immodesty**, n = arrogance, *arrogantia*, = haughtiness, *insolentia*, = indiscretion, *impudicitia*

immolate, v tr *immolare* **immolation**, n *immolatio*

immoral, adj *pravus*, *depravatus*, *perditus*, *inhonestus* (= base, nasty), = infamous, *turpis*, comb *turpis atque inhonestus*, *flagitiosus*, *nequam*, *corruptus*; see WICKED, a person of bad principle, *male moratus*, *malis* or *corruptis moribus*, — conduct, *mores turpes*, *mores corrupti* Adv *inhoneste*, *turpiter*, *flagitiose*, *perdite*, *prave* **immorality**, n *mores corrupti* or *perditi* (= immoral habits), *turpitudo*, *morum pravitas* or *depravatio*, or by *vitia*, *scelera*, *uni* (= crimes), *libidines* (= lusts), a life addicted to —, *vita vitiis flagitiisque omnibus dedita*

immortal, adj *immortalis* (opp *mortalis*, of persons and things, also in gen = imperishable, e g glory), = eternal, *aeternus* (of things, e g life), = everlasting, unceasing, *sempiternus* (e g soul, life, glory), to be —, *immortalem* or *sempiternum esse*, *non interire* (in gen, e g of the soul), to have — life, *vita sempiterna frui*, to have — glory, *memoria omnium saeculorum vigēre* **immortality**, n *immortalitas* (opp *mortalitas*), = eternity, hence eternal glory, *aeternitas*, — of the soul or souls, *immortalitas* or *aeternitas animi* or *animorum*, = immortal glory, *immortalis* or *sempiterna gloria*, to assert the — of the soul, *dicĕre animos hominum esse immortales* or *sempiternos* **immortalize**, v tr *alqd immortali gloriae tradĕre*, see IMMORTAL

immovable, adj *immobilis*, *immotus*, *stabilis* (all lit and fig), — property, *res* or *bona quae moveri non possunt*, to be — (lit), *loco suo non moveri*, see FIRM Adv use adj **immovableness**, n *immobilitas*

immunity, n 1, *vacatio*, *immunitas* (e g *tributorum*), 2, see FREEDOM

immure, v tr *muro saepire*, *cingĕre* (= to enclose with a wall), see SHUT

immutability, n *immutabilitas* (Cic), = firmness, consistency, *constantia*, = steadfastness, *stabilitas* (e g *amicitiae*), = continuance, *perpetuitas*, — of anyone's disposition, *constans in alqm voluntas* **immutable**, adj, *immutabilis*, = constant, *constans*, = fixed, unchangeable, *ratus* (e g the course of the moon, *cursus lunae*, the order of the stars, *astrorum ordines*), = undisturbed, *perpetuus* (e g right, *jus*) Adv *constanter*, *perpetuo* **immutation**, n *mutatio*, see CHANGE

imp, n 1, = child, *progenies*; an — of mischief, *puer lascivus*, 2, = demon, *daemon*

impair, v tr *alqd (im)minuĕre*, *deminuĕre*, *comminuĕre*, *debilitare*, *frangĕre*, *infringĕre*, — an argument, *elevare*, *deteriore statu* or *condicione esse*, *pejore loco esse*

impale, v tr *(hasta* or *palo) transfigĕre*

impalpable, adj *quod tangi non potest*

impart, v tr 1, = to bestow on another a share or portion of something, *impertire alci alqd* or *alqm alqd re* (lit and fig), *communicare alqd cum alqo* (= to share with anyone, lit, and to make a communication to), *participem facĕre alqm* (= to allow anyone to participate in), = to pour into, diffuse, *infundĕre alqd in* (with accus, e g evils in a state, *mala in civitatem*); 2, = to grant, confer (e.g. honour), *dare, tribuĕre, donare alci alqd* or *alqm alqâ re* (= to present with); *offerre* (= to procure).

impartial, adj. *medius* (= in the middle, of persons), *tanquam medius nec in alterius favorem inclinatus* (= neutral, of persons only); = disinterested, *integer*; = not bribed, *incorruptus* (of persons and things, e.g. judge, witness, sentence); = equitable, *aequus* (of persons and things, e.g. prætor, law); *aequitabilis* (of things); = free from partisanship, *studio et irâ vacuus* (of persons in gen.); = free from spite and ill-will, *obtrectatione et malevolentiâ liberatus*; to be —, *neutri parti favēre; neque irâ, neque gratiâ teneri*. Adv. *aequo animo, integre* or *incorrupte, sine irâ et studio*. **impartiality**, n. *animus ab omni partium studio alienus, animus studio et irâ vacuus*; = equity, *aequitas, aequabilitas*.

impassable, adj. *invius, insuperabilis, impeditus*. **impassibility, impassibleness**, n. *torpor* (= torpor, stupor); = hardness of heart, *durus animus*; = slowness, apathy, *lentitudo, lentus animus*. **impassible**, adj. *quod nullo dolore affici potest*.

impassioned, adj. *concitatus, fervidus, ardens, vehemens*.

impatience, n. *impatientia morae, festinatio*; to expect anything with the greatest —, *acerrime alqd ex(s)pectare*. **impatient**, adj. 1, *impatiens morae* or *morarum, ardens, vehemens, acer*; to be — at a thing, *alqd aegre* or *moleste ferre*; 2, = angry, *iracundus, iratus*. Adv. *ardenter, acriter, vehementer, iracunde*; see EAGER.

impeach, v.tr. *accusare*. **impeachable**, adj. *quem in jus vocare possumus*. **impeacher**, n. *accusator*, n. **impeachment**, n. *accusatio*; see ACCUSE.

impede, v.tr. *impedire*; see HINDER. **impediment**, n. 1, *impedimentum*; see HINDRANCE; 2, = stammer, *haesitantia linguae*; to have an —, *linguâ haesitare, balbutire*. **impedimental**, adj. *quod impedimento est, quod impedit, quod obstat et impedit*; to be — to anyone or anything, *obesse alci* and *alci rei*; it was very — for, a great hindrance to the Gauls in battle, that, etc., *Gallis magno ad pugnam erat impedimento, quod*, etc.; I will not be — to prevent his going, *nulla in me* or *per me est mora, in me non erit mora, non moror, quominus abeat*.

impel, v.tr. 1, lit. *impellĕre, urgēre*; 2, fig. *impellĕre, incitare, concitare, stimulare, (ad)hortari alqm ad alqd*.

impend, v.intr. 1, lit. *impendēre, imminēre*; 2, = to be near, *instare in alqm* or *alci impendēre*.

impenetrable, adj. 1, *impenetrabilis* (Plin.); — against a thing, *alci rei*; = impervious, *impervius* (Tac., e.g. fire-proof, *ignibus impervius*), *impeditus*; see IMPASSABLE; 2, = thick, *caliginosus* (of darkness); 3, fig. *ambiguus* (= doubtful).

impenitence, impenitency, n. *obstinatio, animus obstinatus* or *affirmatus*. **impenitent**, adj. *obstinatus, offirmatus*; to become —, *obdurescĕre*. Adv. *obstinate*.

imperative, adj. 1, = expressive of command, (e.g. — commands), by circumloc. with *imperare alci alqd* or with *ut*, or by *necessarius*; 2, (in gram. = the — mood of a verb), *imperativus modus* (gram.).

imperfect, adj. *imperfectus* (= not completed); = only in its beginning, *inchoatus*; = only superficial, drawn out in general sketches, *adumbratus* (e.g. an idea, *intellegentia, opinio*); = faulty, *vitiosus, mendosus*; = rough, *rudis*; = defective, maimed, *mancus*; — tense, *tempus imperfectum* (gram.). Adv. *imperfecte, vitiose, mendose*. **imperfection, imperfectness**, n. *vitium, mendum, culpa*, or by adj. (e.g. the — of our nature, *natura hominum imperfecta et mendosa*).

imperial, adj. *imperatorius, Caesareus* (Imperial Rome); often by the genit. *imperatoris* or *Caesaris* or *Augusti*; *principalis*, or with the gen. *imperatoris* or *principis*; your — Majesty, **majestas* or *magnitudo tua*. **imperious**, adj. *imperiosus*; = haughty, *superbus*; = disdainful, *insolens*; = arrogant, *arrogans*. Adv. *imperiose, superbe, insolenter, arroganter*.

imperil, v.tr. *in discrimen adducĕre*.

imperishable, adj. *immortalis*; see ETERNAL, IMMORTAL.

impermeable, adj. see IMPENETRABLE.

impersonal, adj. gram. t.t. *impersonalis*. **impersonate**, v.tr. *partes alcjs agĕre*.

impertinence, n. *insolentia*; see ARROGANCE, RUDENESS. **impertinent**, adj. 1, *insolens*; 2, = not to the point, *quod nihil ad rem est*. Adv. *insolenter*.

imperturbable, adj. *stabilis, constans, firmus, gravis, immobilis*. Adv. *constanter, firme, graviter, tranquille*.

impervious, adj. *impervius*; see IMPENETRABLE.

impetuous, adj. *violentus*, = violent (e.g. attack, *impetus*); = strong, intense, *vehemens* (e.g. wind, *ventus*, then of individuals), comb. *vehemens et violentus* (e.g. *homo*); = eager, *acer, fervidus, fervens, intentus*. Adv. *magno impetu* (e.g. to attack the enemy, *hostem aggredi*); *violenter* (e.g. to demand, *poscĕre*); *vehementer* (= strongly, e.g. to insist upon it, *flagitare*); *acriter, ferventer*. **impetuosity**, n. *violentia* (lit. and fig.), *vis* (= strength), *incitatio* (= impulse); = intemperateness, *intemperies* (e.g. *caeli*; then = want of moderation); violence, *impetus, -ūs*, of persons and things (e.g. of the fever, *febris*). **impetus**, n. *impetus, -ūs, vis*.

impiety, n. *impietas erga Deum*; = wicked, criminal deed, *nefas, scelus, -ĕris, res scelesta* or *nefaria*; he has committed many —s against God and man, *multa et in deos et in homines impie nefarieque commisit*. **impious**, adj. *impius* (*erga deum, erga patriam, erga parentes*, etc.); = wicked (the general disposition), *nefarius*; = wicked, heinous, *nefandus* (of a deed). Adv. *impie, nefarie*, comb. *impie nefarieque, nefande*.

impinge, v.intr. to — against, *incidĕre in alqd, impingi alci rei* (so as to cause a violent shock), *offendĕre in alqâ re* or *ad alqd*.

implacability, n. *odium implacabile* or *inexorabile*. **implacable**, adj. *implacabilis*; — against anyone, *alci* or *in alqm*; = inexorable, *inexorabilis* (all of persons and things, e.g. hatred, anger), against anyone, *in* or *adversus alqm*; = cruel, *atrox, saevus*; see CRUEL. Adv. *atrociter, saeve*.

implant, v.tr. 1, lit. = to set, *alqd in alqâ re inserĕre, ponĕre*; 2, fig. *ingenerare, ingignĕre* (at the time of one's birth, as it were); = to engraft, *inserĕre, animo infigĕre*.

implead, v.tr. *alqm in jus vocare*; see SUE, ACCUSER.

implement, n. 1, = tools, *instrumentum, ferramentum*; 2, fig. *minister*; see INSTRUMENT, TOOL.

implicate, v.tr. *implicare* or *impedire* (lit. and fig.); — in a thing, *alqd alqâ re illaqueare, admiscēre* or *immiscēre* (only the former in Cic.)

(fig); intr *in algâ re*, to implicate in a war, *algm bello implicare*, to be —d in a war, *bello implicitum* or *illigatum* or *occupatum esse*, with anyone, *bellum gerĕre cum algo*, to — oneself, *implicari algâ re* (lit and fig), to — oneself in (i e to meddle) *se immiscēre alci rei* (fig) **implicated**, adj by past part *implicatus*, etc, *alcjs rei conscius*, *alci rei affinis* **implication**, n *implicatio*, to say a thing by —, see HINT **implicit**, adj 1, = implied, *tacitus*, an — compact, *assensio*, *consensus*, *ūs*, *conventio*, he has an — faith, *est homo credulus*, *est nimis facilis ad credendum*, 2, = complete, *totus*, *omnis*, to have — faith in anyone, *alci maximam fidem adhibēre*, *totum se alci committĕre* Adv *tacite*, *prorsus*, see ALTOGETHER

implore, v tr *algm* or *algd implorare* (urgently), *algd ab algo petĕre* (= to endeavour to obtain by entreaties), *algm algd rogare* (= to request), *deprecari* (= to pray for, entreat earnestly), comb *petĕre ac deprecari*, *ne*, etc, (*precibus*) *impetrare* or *algd ab algo exposcĕre* (= to obtain by entreaties), = to induce by entreaties, *exorare*, = to beseech anyone on one s knees to help, to supplicate, beg humbly, *supplicare* or *supplicem esse alci*, *se alci supplicem ab(j)icĕre*, = to beseech by everything sacred, to pray earnestly, *algm obsecrare*, = to conjure, *algm obtestari*, to — anyone for, to pray urgently, *algd voce supplici postulare*, *orare multis et supplicibus verbis*, *ut*, etc, *algd ab algo exposcĕre*, to — anyone to help, *algm ad* or *in auxilium implorare*, *auxilium implorare ab algo*, to — God and man, *deûm atque hominum fidem implorare*

imply, v tr *in se habēre*, to be implied in, *alci rei inesse*, or *subesse*

impolite, adj *inurbanus*, *rusticus*, *agrestis*, *inhumanus*, *illepidus* Adv *inurbane*, *rustice*, *illepide*, *inhumane*, *inhumaniter* **impoliteness**, n *rusticitas*, *inhumanitas*

impolitic, adj 1 in the state, *alienus* or *abhorrens a prudentia civili*, 2, fig *imprudens*

import, I. v tr 1, (that is, to bring goods into a country for sale) *invehĕre*, *importare*, 2, = signify, *declarare*, *significare* *valēre* II. n 1, *quod importatur*, 2, *significatio*, *sententia*, *vis* **import-duty**, n *portorium* **importance**, n 1, *auctoritas*, *discrimen*, *momentum*, *pondus*, *-ĕris*, *vis*, to be of no —, *nullo esse numero*, 2, = of high position, *amplitudo*, *dignitas*, *auctoritas* **important**, adj *gravis*, to be —, *magni* (so *alcjs*, *maximi*, *minimi*, *pluris*, etc) *momenti esse*, *valēre* *vim habēre*, *algo esse numero*, to deem anything more —, *antiquius algd habēre* **importation**, n *invectio* **importunate**, adj *molestus*, *improbus*, see TROUBLESOME **importune**, v tr *molestum esse alci*, *exposcĕre*, (*ef*)*flagitare*, see TROUBLESOME, MOLEST **importunity**, n = pressing solicitation, (*ef*)*flagitatio*

impose, v tr *algd alci imponĕre*, *injungĕre*, — a punishment, *multam alci irrogare*, — upon, see CHEAT **imposing**, adj *conspicuus* (= drawing the attention), = showy, *speciosus*, = majestic, *magnificus* (e g form, *forma*), = deceitful, *fallax* **imposition**, n *irrogatio* (e g *multae*, = the infliction of a penalty), also by circumloc with *imponĕre* (e g to extract the poison by — of hands, *manu impositâ venena extrahĕre*), *fraus* (= deceit, deception), *fallacia* **impost**, n *onera*, *-um*, *vectigal*, *tributum* **impostor**, n *fraudator* **imposture**, n *fraus*, *dis*, f *fallacia*, *praestigiae* (= tricks)

impossibility, n usu *fieri non posse*, etc (e g to prove the — of anything, *probare algd fieri non posse*) **impossible**, adj by *quod fieri* or *quod effici non potest*, and the adv by *nullo pacto* or *minime non*, nothing is — to kindness, *nihil est quod benevolentia efficĕre non possit*, I believe this to be —, *non puto hoc fieri posse*, it is — for me to, etc, *fieri non potest*, *ut*, etc

impotence, n *imbecillitas*, *infirmitas corporis*, or *animi* **impotent**, adj *invalidus*, *infirmus*, *imbecillus*, *impotens*

impound, v tr 1, in gen *pignus*, *ŏris*, *capere* or *auferre*, *algm pignore cogĕre* (of the consul who —ed a senator), 2, *in algo loco includĕre* (= to confine, e g cattle)

impoverish, v tr *algm in egestatem reducĕre* **impoverishment**, n *egestas* *inopia*, *paupertas* = poverty

impracticable, adj 1, = impossible, *quod fieri non potest*, 2, = intractable, *contumax*, see IMPOSSIBLE, REFRACTORY

imprecate, v tr *algd alci* (*im*)*precari*, *ex*(*s*)*ecrari*, see CURSE, EXECRATE **imprecation**, n *dirae*, *preces*, *um*, f, *ex*(*s*)*ecratio*, see EXECRATION

impregnable, adj 1, = not to be stormed, e g an — fortress, *inexpugnabilis*, 2, fig = not to be moved, *stabilis*

impregnate, v tr 1, = to make pregnant, *algm gravidam* or *praegnantem facĕre*, 2, fig = to render prolific, †*fecundare*, *fertilem reddĕre*, 3, gen = to communicate the virtues of one thing to another, *complēre algd algâ re* (= to fill with), *addĕre algd alci rei* (= to add), (*com*)*miscēre cum algâ re*, or simply *algâ re* (= to mix), see FILL **impregnation**, n (applied to animals or plants), by verb

impress, v tr 1, lit *algd alci rei imprimĕre*, 2, fig *algd alci inurĕre*, *inculcare*, *in animo insculpĕre* or *imprimĕre* **impression**, n 1, the act of taking an — *impressio* = the copy, *exemplum* (= copy in general), *imago expressa*, *vestigium* (= footstep), to take or make an —, *exprimĕre algd algâ re* or *in algâ re* *imprimĕre algd in algâ re*, 2, the working or effect of any influence on the mind, *animi motus*, *-ūs*, or by special word (e g *visa*, *-orum*, — of sight), *visis ad actionem excitamur*, we are excited to action by visible —s), to make an — on anyone, *algm movēre* **impressive**, adj *gravis*, *vehemens* Adv *graviter*, *vehementer* **impressiveness**, n *gravitas*

imprint, v tr *in algâ re imprimĕre*, see IMPRESSION

imprison, v tr *in custodiam dare*, *tradĕre*, *in*(*j*)*icĕre*, *custodiae* or *vinculis mandare*, *comprehendĕre* (= arrest) **imprisonment**, n *custodia*, *carcer*, *-ĕris*, m, *vincula*, *-orum*

improbable, adj *non verisimilis*, *non probabilis* Adv *non verisimiliter* **improbability**, n use adj

improbity, n *improbitas*

impromptu, adv *ex tempore*

improper, adj *improprius* (Plin Quint) (e g *verba* = unsuitable), = unbecoming, indecent, *indecōrus*, = silly, *ineptus* (e g laughter, *risus*), = unworthy, *indignus* (of anyone, *algo*), = unsuitable, not suited, *alienus* (of things, place, and time, *ab algo* or *ab algâ re* and *alci* or *alci rei* *alcjs rei*, not C c), = inelegant, awkward in one s manners, *inconcinnus* (e g roughness of manners, want of polish *asperitas i*), absurd, *absonus*, it is — to, etc, *indecorum est* (with inf), to be — for anyone, *dedecēre* or *non decēre algm*, *indignum esse algo* Adv *indecore*, *perperam* *inepte*, *indigne* **impropriety**, n. *quod indecorum est*

improvable, adj *quod est ejusmodi ut corrigi*

possit. **improve, I.** v.tr. *alqd melius facĕre*; see CORRECT; *excolĕre.* **II.** v.intr. *meliorem fieri, se colligĕre* (morally), *convalescĕre* (= to — in health), *augēri* (= to rise in price), *proficĕre* (= to make progress). **improvement,** n. *correctio, emendatio,* comb. *correctio et emendatio*; — of circumstances, *amplificatio rei familiaris*; morally and mentally, *cultus, -ūs, educatio, disciplina* (= mental and moral training); *institutio* (= instruction in any particular branch); *humanitas* (= general moral and mental and physical — of the whole man), comb. *cultus* (*-ūs*) *atque humanitas*; I perceive an — in my general health, *meas vires auctas sentio.*

improvidence, n. *inconsiderantia, temeritas, imprudentia.* **improvident,** adj. *improvidus* (= not looking forward), *incautus* (= heedless, opp. *prudens*), comb. *improvidus incautusque, improvidus et neglegens* (*neglig-*); = inconsiderate, *inconsideratus*; = thoughtless, *temerarius*; = imprudent, *imprudens* (opp. *paratus*); = indifferent, negligent, *neglegens* (*neglig-*). Adv. *improvide, incaute, temere, imprudenter, inconsiderate, neglegenter* (*neglig-*).

imprudence, n. *imprudentia, temeritas* (= rashness); see IMPROVIDENCE. **imprudent,** adj. *imprudens, temerarius, inconsultus*; see IMPROVIDENT. Adv. *imprudenter, temere, inconsulte.*

impudence, n. *impudentia, os impudens* (or *durum* or *ferreum*); *confidentia* (= boldness, in a bad sense). **impudent,** adj. *impudens* (= void of feeling of shame), *procax* (= saucy), *confidens* (= having assurance), *improbus* (= saucy). Adv. *procaciter* (not in Cic.), *impudenter, confidenter.*

impugn, v.tr. *impugnare* (e.g. to — anyone's honour, *impugnare alcjs honorem*); *oppugnare*; *negare* (= to deny absolutely, opp. *aio*); *improbare* (= to prove to be void, e.g. a will, *testamentum*); *repugnare* (= to contend against, e.g. anyone's opinion, *alcjs opinioni*); = to contradict everything, *contra omnia disserĕre.*

impulse, n. **1,** as a term of mechanical philosophy, *impulsio, impulsus, -ūs* (better by verbs, e.g. *agĕre, pellĕre,* etc.); see DRIVE, PROPEL, MOVE; **2,** = motive, *impulsus, -ūs, caus(s)a,* or by circumloc. (e.g. ambition is the — of all his actions, *quidquid agit, gloriae cupiditate impulsus agit*); **3,** = impression, *impulsus, -ūs, impulsio*; external —, *pulsus* (*-ūs*) *externus*; at anybody's —, *alqo auctore, alcjs impulsu, alcjs auctoritate*; from one's own —, *sponte* or *suâ sponte,* also *ipse* (i.e. from one's own free will); not influenced by anybody else, *per se*; willingly, *ultro*; — from without, *incitamentum, stimulus.* **impulsive,** adj. by verb; see IMPEL.

impunity, n. with —, *impunitus, inultus* (= unrevenged, unpunished, scot-free), *incastigatus* (= unchastised), *impune*; to have done with —, by *impune esse, non puniri*; *impune abire*; to be able to do with —, *alqd impune ferre* or *impune habēre* or *impune facĕre.*

impure, adj. *impurus* (fig. = immoral, unchaste, of persons and things, e.g. manners, morals, life, *mores*); *obscenus* (*obscoen-* or *obscaen-*), (= unchaste); = stained, *contaminatus* (opp. *integer*), with anything, *alqâ re* (e.g. with blood, *sanguine*); = unchaste, *incestus*; = low, *inquinatus* (= spotted, e.g. a speech, a verse); *foedus, spurcus, turpis, teter* (= foul); — desires, *libidines.* Adv. *impure, obscene* (*obscoen-* or *obscaen-*), *inquinate, foede, spurce, turpiter.* **impurity,** n. *impuritas,* or *incestum, incestus, -ūs, obscenitas* (*obscoen-* or *obscaen-*), *libido, stuprum, foeditas, turpitudo.*

imputable, adj. by *cujus rei culpa alci assignari potest,* and by verbs; see below. **imputation,** n. **1,** by verb; **2,** = charge, *crimen, culpa, accusatio.* **impute,** v.tr. *alqd alci assignare* (in a good and bad sense); to — to anyone the fault of anything, *culpam alcjs rei alci assignare*; *culpam alcjs rei conferre* or *transferre* or *derivare in alqm*; *culpae alqd alci dare, alqd alci a(d)scribĕre, attribuĕre, affingĕre*; see ATTRIBUTE.

in, prep. **1,** of place, by old locative (e.g. — Rome, — Corinth, *Romae, Corinthi,* where — = at), *in* with abl. (e.g. *in Italiâ*), abl. (e.g. *eo loco, hac regione, his terris*), — a letter, *epistulâ quâdam,* with verbs implying motion, *in* with accus. (to place — a ship, *in navem imponĕre*); — the assembly, *pro contione* (= before); — breadth, *in latitudinem*; — height, *in altitudinem*; **2,** of time, *in* with abl., or *inter* or *intra* with accus. (of time within which), *per* with accus. (= throughout), *de* with abl. (= — the course of), simply abl. (e.g. — the night, *nocte* or *de nocte*), by the noun in apposition (e.g. I did it — my boyhood, *puer feci*), to have a friend — so-and-so, *alqm amicum habēre*; **3,** of occasion, manner, etc., *per* (e.g. *per iram,* — anger); abl., *hoc modo* = in this way (so too *in hunc modum, ad hunc modum*); — respect of (e.g. — wisdom = *sapientiâ*); **4,** other uses, — an author, *apud* with accus. (e.g. — Cicero, *apud Ciceronem*); — the hands of, *penes alqm*; — the beginning, *ab initio* (when the act continues); to be — our favour, *a nobis stare,* with gerund (e.g. — loving, *amando*); — living, etc., *cum,* with indic. (e.g. you do well — saying, *bene facis cum dicis*).

inability, n. *imbecillitas, infirmitas* (= bodily weakness), *inopia* (= want of means), or use *non posse*; see WEAKNESS.

inaccessibility, n. by **inaccessible,** adj. *inaccessus*; = impassable, surrounded, *invius*; = difficult to pass, *impeditus* (e.g. forest); of persons difficult to be seen, *rari aditūs.* Adv. — situated, *quo non aditus est.*

inaccuracy, n. *indiligentia, pravitas* (when anything has been done totally wrong); = untruth, it must be circumscribed by *falsus* (e.g. to show the — of anything, *alqd falsum esse probare*); see FALSEHOOD. **inaccurate,** adj. *indiligens.* Adv. *indiligenter*; see INCORRECT.

inaction, inactivity, n. *segnities* (*segnitia*), *inertia, ignavia,* comb. *segnities et inertia* or *ignavia et inertia* (= laziness); inclination to be idle, *desidia* (opp. *industria, labor*), comb. *inertia atque desidia* or *desidia segnitiesque*; = cessation (of labour from fear of work), *cessatio*; = leisure, *otium, desidia*; = rest, *quies, -ētis.* **inactive,** adj. *ignavus, deses, segnis, iners, quietus.* Adv. *ignave, segniter, quiete.*

inadequacy, n. by **inadequate,** adj. *alienus ab alqâ re, non sufficiens*; = not adapted, not answering the purpose (e.g. a witness, evidence given), *non satis idoneus, impar.* Adv. *parum, haud satis.*

inadmissibility, n. circumloc. by **inadmissible,** adj. *quod admitti non potest.*

inadvertence, n. *neglegentia* (*neglig-*); = want of care, *incuria*; = laziness, *socordia.* **inadvertent,** adj. *neglegens* (*neglig-*), (opp. *diligens*); = lazy, *socors,* comb. *socors neglegensque* (*neglig-*). Adv. *neglegenter* (*neglig-*); = unintentionally, *sine consilio.*

inalienable, adj. *quod abalienari non potest.*

inane, adj. *inanis.*

inanimated, adj. *inanimus, inanimatus.*

inanition, inanity, n. *inanitas* (lit. and fig.), *inane, vacuitas, vacuum*; = hollowness (fig.), *vanitas.*

inapplicability, n. by **inapplicable,**

adj with *non pertinēre ad*, or *non cadĕre in* (with acc), *non valēre*.

inapposite, adj *quod non aptum est*.

inappreciable, adj *quod sentiri non potest*, or by *minimus*

inapprehensive, adj *neglegens* (*neglig*)

inappropriate, adj. *non idoneus*

inaptitude, n. 1, *inutilitas* (= uselessness), 2, see INABILITY

inarticulate, adj *non satis distinctus* Adv *parum distincte*

inartificial, adj *simplex* (e g food, speech, language)

inattention, n *animus non attentus*, *neglegentia* (*neglig*), *incuria*, *indiligentia* **inattentive,** adj *non attentus*

inaudible, adj. *quod audiri non potest*

inaugural, adj *aditialis* (ante and post class), to deliver an — discourse, *oratione munus auspicari*. **inaugurate,** v tr 1, *inaugurare*, *auspicare*, *dedicare* (in respect of the worship of the gods, e g statues, images altars, temples, etc), *consecrare* (anything, e g an animal, a field, etc), to initiate, *initiare* (= to admit to a knowledge of the sacred rites), 2, = to begin, *coepisse*, see BEGIN **inauguration,** n *dedicatio*, *consecratio*

inauspicious, adj in gen *infelix*, † *infaustus*, *laevus*, † *sinister*, *nefastus*, an — day, *dies ater* Adv *infeliciter*, *malis ominibus*, *inauspicato*

incalculable, adj *major* (e g *numerus*, etc) *quam qui calculari possit*

incandescent, adj *candens*

incantation, n *carmen*

incapability, n *inscitia*, but better use *non posse* (e g — for action, *qui agĕre non potest*) **incapable,** adj *indocilis* (= indocile, — of instruction), = dull, *hebes*, = unfit, incompetent, *inutilis* or *inhabilis ad alqd*, = too dull for, *hebes ad alqd* **incapacitate,** v tr *inutilem reddĕre* **incapacity,** n see INCAPABILITY

incarcerate, v tr (*in carcerem* or *in custodiam*) *in(j)icĕre*, *includĕre* **incarceration,** n *custodia*, *vincula*, *-orum*, n

incarnate, adj. eccl t t **incarnatus* (Eccl), *specie humana* or *corpore indutus* **incarnation,** n **incarnatio*

incautious, adj *imprudens*, *incautus*, *inconsultus*, *inconsideratus*, *temerarius* Adv *imprudenter*, *incaute*, *inconsulte*, *inconsiderate*, *temere*

incendiarism, n *incendium* (e g he was tried for —, *de incendiis postulatus est*). **incendiary,** n *incendiarius* (Tac), *incendii auctor* (referring to one case only)

incense, I. n *tus*, *turis*, of —, † *tureus*, carrying —, † *turifer* **II.** v tr *tus accendĕre* **incense,** v.tr *accendĕre*, *incendĕre* (lit and fig), see EXASPERATE

incentive, I. adj *quod instigat*, see INCITE **II.** n *instigatio*, *irritatio*, *incitatio*, *concitatio*, *impulsus*, *-ūs*, *instinctus*, *-ūs*, *stimulus*, = means of inciting, *irritamentum*, *invitamentum* (chiefly in the pl), *illecebra*, *lenocinium* (= allurement), see IMPULSE

inception, n *initium*; see COMMENCEMENT **inceptive,** adj *incipiens*

incessant, adj *perpetuus*, *assiduus*, *continuus*, see CONTINUOUS Adv *perpetuo*, *assidue*, *continuo*

incest, n *incestus*, *-ūs*, *incestum* **incestuous,** adj *incestus*

inch, n 1, = a lineal measure, *digitus*, *uncia* (Plin), 2, fig = a small quantity or degree, not to yield, depart an — from *ab alqā re non transversum digitum* or *non digitum discedĕre*, to an —, almost, *tantum non*, *non multum* (not *parum*) *abfuit quin*, etc, not an — better, *nihilo melius*, not an — different, *plane idem*, by —es, *paul(l)atim*, *sensim*

inchoate, adj *inchoatus*

incident, I. adj *quod ad alqd pertinet*, or *in alqā re consistit*, or *alqā re continetur*, *proprius*, with gen. or dat. **II.** n. *casus*, *-ūs*, *eventus*, *-ūs*, *res*; see CIRCUMSTANCE. **incidental,** adj *fortuitus*, *forte oblātus* Adv *forte*, *fortuito*, I chanced to mention —, *in mentionem* (*alcjs rei*) *incidi*.

incipiency, n. *initium*; see BEGINNING. **incipient,** adj *initium faciens*

incision, n *incisura* (Plin) (= the act of making an —, and also the — made, e g in the hand, the insects, leaves), the — made by the wheel, furrow, or ship, *sulcus* **incisive,** adj. *mordens*, *mordax*, *asper* **incisor,** n (= foreteeth), *dentes qui digerunt cibum*, *dentes qui secant*.

incite, v t *instigare* (= to instigate, set on), = to excite, animate, *incitare*, *excitare*, *concitare*, (*com*)*movēre*, *permovēre*, = to irritate, *irritare*, = to stimulate, *stimulare*, = to rouse, kindle, *inflammare*, *incendĕre*, *accendĕre*, = to urge, *impellĕre* (all *alqm* or *alcjs animum ad alqd*); *stimulos alci admovēre* or *addĕre* (= to prick), *calcaria alci adhibēre* or *admovēre* (= to give the spur), *alqm* (*ex*)*acuĕre* (= to sharpen), *ignem alci sub(j)icĕre* (= to kindle a fire underneath, i e to rouse one's desires, esp envy) **incitement,** n *impulsus*, *-ūs*, see IMPULSE

incivility, n *inurbanitas*, *rusticitas*, *inhumanitas*

inclemency, n 1, *inhumanitas*, *severitas*, *crudelitas*, *saevitia*, 2, of the weather, † *asperitas* (e g *hiemis*), or *gravis* with n (e g *tempestas gravis*), — of winter, *hiemis difficultas* **inclement,** adj 1, *inclemens* (Liv), *inhumanus*, *severus*, *crudelis*, *saevus*, 2, *gravis*, *asper*, see also COLD, STORMY, SEVERITY

inclination, n 1, lit *inclinatio*, 2, in geom and mech (= leaning of two bodies, lines, planes, towards each other, so as to make an angle) *fastigium* (= slope), = declivity, *proclivitas*, *declivitas* (both considered from the top), *acclivitas* (considered from the bottom, = a bending upwards), 3, = leaning of the mind, — to a subject, *inclinatio animi*, for anything, *ad alqd voluntas*, = a propensity, *proclivitas ad alqd* (in a bad sense), a favourable — for anything or anybody, *studium alcjs rei* or *alcjs*, a favourable — towards a person, *propensa in alqm voluntas propensum in alqm studium*, = love, *amor*, towards anybody, *in* or *erga alqm*; = — from a wish *studio*, *propenso animo* (e g to do anything, *alqd facĕre*), from free —, *ex animo*, to have an — for anything, *ad alqd inclinatum*, *proclivem*, *pronum esse*, *alcjs rei studēre*, *alcjs rei esse studiosum*, *alcjs rei studio teneri*, to be guided by one's own —, *studiis suis obsequi* **incline, I.** v intr 1, = to slope, *proclivem* or *declivem esse*, to be rising, *acclivem esse* (in looking upwards), neither to — one way nor the other, *in nullā parte habēre proclinationes* (e g of walls, etc), 2, = to lean (in a moral sense) to have a tendency (of times, circumstances, etc), *inclinari*, (*se*) *inclinare*, to — towards anything, (*se*) *inclinare ad* or *in alqd* (of persons and things), *inclinatione voluntatis propendēre in alqm* (= to feel oneself from — drawn towards anybody), to — more towards peace, *inclinatiorem esse ad pacem*. **II.** v.tr. *inclinare, submittĕre, demittĕre* (e.g. *caput*). **inclined,** adj. for anybody or for anything, *inclinatus ad alqm, alqd*; = easy to persuade, *propensus ad* or *in alqd* (e.g. to pardon, enjoyment); — to fall into anything, *proclivis ad alqd, pronus in alqd* or *ad alqd*; I am more — to think, *eo magis adducor ut putem*; = merciful, *propitius* (especially of the gods, seldom of man); = benevolent, *benevolus* (of man).

inclose, v.tr. *saepire* (*sep-*); see ENCLOSE.

include, v.tr. = to comprehend, *comprehendĕre, complecti, continēre, annumerare, a(d)scribĕre alci rei* or *in* or *ad*; to — among the accused, *in reos referre*; without including you, *te excepto*; to be included in anything, *comprehendi, continēri alqâ re*; to be included in that number, *in eo numero esse* or *haberi*. **inclusive, included,** adj. that matter —, *additâ eâ re*; often simply by *cum* or *in*; there were 300 soldiers, the prisoners —, *milites erant trecenti cum captivis* (or *captivis annumeratis*). Adv. that one —, *eo comprehenso*; — all those, *omnibus comprehensis* or *additis*.

incogitable, adj. to be —, *ne cogitari quidem posse*.

incognito, adv. *incognitus, ignoratus, alieno* or *dissimulato nomine*.

incoherence, incoherency, n. by circumloc. with **incoherent,** adj. *interruptus* (= interrupted), *dissipatus* (= scattered, torn, e.g. a speech), *sibi non constans*. Adv. *interrupte, haud constanter* or *congruenter*; to speak —, *haud cohaerentia dicĕre*.

incombustibility, n. by **incombustible,** adj. *qui ignibus non absumitur*.

income, n. *vectigal, -alis*, n. (including public and private —, as taxes, tithes, rent), *reditus, -ūs* (in the sing. = the returns), *fructus, -ūs* (= the produce), *pecunia*, also *reditus pecuniae* (= a pecuniary return); public —, *fructus publici*, (if in mere money) *pecuniae vectigales*; — from lands, *praediorum fructus, fructus quem praedia reddunt*; — from gain, *quaestus, -ūs*; to make an —, *quaestum facĕre*; he has an — to live upon, *habet unde vivat*.

incommode, v.tr. *incommodum alci afferre*. **incommodious,** adj. *incommodus*; = troublesome, *molestus*; see INCONVENIENT.

incomparable, adj. *incomparabilis* (Plin.); = unequalled, *sine exemplo maximus* (e.g. *Homerus*); *divinus* (of persons and things, e.g. a legion, *legio*; a voice, *vox*; works, *opera*); *singularis* (= unique, of persons and things, e.g. daughter, *filia*; *virtus*); *eximius, egregius, praestans* (= uncommon, distinguished in particular respects, of things); Cicero, this man who, as regards his diction, can be equalled to none, *Cicero, caelestis hic in dicendo vir*. Adv. *sine exemplo, divine, eximie, egregie, praestanter*.

incompatibility, n. *repugnantia, diversitas*; — of temper, rudeness, *importunitas*; see RUDENESS. **incompatible,** adj. of anything that cannot subsist with something else, *alienus ab alqâ re, alci rei contrarius*; *adversarius, adversus, infensus* (= hostile), (*ab alqâ re*) *diversus*; to be — with anything, *abhorrēre ab alqâ re*; *pugnare inter se* (= to contradict each other, of things), *repugnare alci rei* (of two things that cannot be reconciled together).

incompetence, incompetency, n. *inscitia*; see INABILITY. **incompetent,** adj. 1, legally, to be — for anything, *faciendi alqd jus* or *potestatem non habēre, jure alqd facĕre non posse*; 2, in gen., *inscitus, inhabilis, nescius, inutilis*; see FOOLISH, INCAPABLE. Adv. *inscite*.

incomplete, adj. *imperfectus*. Adv. *imperfecte*. **incompleteness,** n. *quod imperfectum est*; see IMPERFECT.

incompliance, n. *recusatio*; with anything, *alcjs rei*.

incomprehensibility, n. by **incomprehensible,** adj. *quod comprehendi* or *intellegi* (*intelligi*) *non potest*.

incompressible, adj. *quod comprimi, condensari non potest* (e.g. water).

inconceivable, adj. *quod* (*mente* or *cogitatione*) *comprehendi non potest, quod intellegi non potest, quod in intellegentiam non cadit, quod cogitare non possumus, quod cogitari non potest*; = inexplicable, immense, *inexplicabilis* (e.g. kindness, *facilitas*); = incredible, *incredibilis*. Adv. *incredibiliter, mirum in modum*.

inconclusive, adj. (*argumentum*) *quo nihil efficitur*.

incongruity, n. *repugnantia*; see ABSURDITY, CONTRADICTION. **incongruous,** adj. *alienus ab alqo* or *ab alqâ re, incongruens* (Plin. Min.), *inconveniens*. Adv. *non apte*.

inconsequence, n. see ABSURDITY. **inconsequent,** adj. see INCOHERENT.

inconsiderable, adj. *lĕvis* (= without weight, unimportant); *mediocris* (= mediocre, common, e.g. a man, a family; then = not very great, light, etc.); *minutus* (= trifling); *exiguus* (= small in comparision with others, e.g. troops, *copiae*; fortune, property, *res familiaris*); = small in gen., *parvus* (opp. *magnus*, e.g. sum of money, *pecunia*; troop of soldiers, *manus*); not —, *nonnullus*. **inconsiderate,** adj. 1, *inconsideratus* (= without thinking); *inconsultus* (= rash); = incautious, *incautus*; = improvident, *improvidus*, comb. *improvidus incautusque*; = imprudent, *imprudens*; 2, = not regardful of others, *alqm non observans* or *respiciens, alci non consulens*. Adv. *inconsiderate, incaute, imprudenter*; *nullius ratione habitâ* (= without regard to persons).

inconsistency, n. *discrepantia, inconstantia, mutabilitas*; see CONTRADICTION. **inconsistent,** adj. *ab alqâ re alienus, inconstans, alci rei contrarius, ab alqâ re* or *alci rei absonus, alci rei repugnans, ab* or *cum alqâ re* or *alci rei discrepans*. Adv. *inconstanter*.

inconsolable, adj. † *inconsolabilis*, (*dolor* or *luctus, -ūs*) *qui nullo solatio levari potest*.

inconspicuous, adj. *quod vix sentiri* or *sensibus percipi potest*. Adv. *sensim*.

inconstancy, n. *inconstantia* (of persons and things, physical and moral, e.g. of the wind, *venti*); = changeableness, *varietas* (e.g. of the army); = infidelity of a person, *infidelitas*; = levity, *levitas*; in one's resolutions, *mutabilitas* (*mentis*), comb. *inconstantia mutabilitasque mentis*; = movableness, variableness, *mobilitas* (also of anything personified, e.g. of fortune, *fortunae*). **inconstant,** adj. *inconstans* (= not remaining always the same, physical, e.g. the wind, and in a moral sense, of persons and things); = changing, *varius*; = unfaithful, *infidelis* (of persons); = vacillating, wavering, *infirmus* (of persons and things, opp. *firmus*); = volatile, *lĕvis* (of persons); = changeable, fickle in one's resolutions, *mutabilis* (of persons), comb. *varius et mutabilis*; = fickle, one who goes easily from one thing to another, *mobilis* (of persons and things, e.g. character, mind, disposition, *ingenium, animus*; will, resolution, *voluntas*); = uncertain, not to be relied upon, *fluxus* (of things, e.g. faith, *fides*; fortune, *fortuna*); see CHANGEABLE.

incontestable, adj. *quod refutari non potest*.

incontinence, n *incontinentia* (= want of power to rule one's passions), *intemperantia* (= intemperance) **incontinent**, adj *incontinens*, *intemperans* Adv *incontinenter*, = immediately, *statim*

incontrovertible, adj *quod refutari non potest*.

inconvenience, inconveniency, n *incommoditas* (e g of anything, *rei*, or time, *temporis*), *incommodum* (= an — to anyone), = a disadvantage, *molestia*, to cause — to anyone, *alci incommodare* or *molestum esse*, *alci incommodum afferre*, *alci negotium exhibēre*, *facessĕre* **inconvenient**, adj *inopportunus*, *intempestivus* (= in undue season), *incommodus* (= not quite convenient) Adv *intempestive*, *incommode*

inconvertible, adj *immutabilis*, see IMMUTABLE

incorporate, v tr see UNITE, 1, ESTABLISH, 2

incorrect, adj *non justus* (= not according to order, opp *justus*), *pravus* (= perverse, contrary to reason, improper, opp *rectus*), *vitiosus*, *mendosus* (= full of mistakes, opp *rectus*), = false, not true, *falsus* (opp *verus*), the account is —, *ratio non convenit* or *non constat*, a very — work, with many mistakes, *in quo multa vitia insunt*, in which many statements are —, *in quo multa perperam dicta sunt* Adv *perperam* (= wrong, contrary to the real nature of anything, opp *recte*, e g to pronounce, *pronuntiare*), = with many mistakes, *vitiose*, *mendose* (opp *recte*, e g to infer, argue, *concludĕre*), = falsely, untruly, *false* (opp *vere* or *vero*) = not as it should be, *secus* (e g to judge, *judicare*) **incorrectness**, n by adj INCORRECT **incorrigibility**, n *pravitas* **incorrigible**, adj *qui corrigi non potest*, = saucy, *improbus*

incorrupt, adj 1, *incorruptus* 2, fig *integer*, *incorruptus*, *purus*, *sanctus*, *castus*, *innocens* Adv *incorrupte*, *sancte*, *integre*, *caste*, *pure*, *sancte* **incorruptibility**, n 1, lit *quod corrumpi* or *putrescere non potest*. 2, fig *integritas*, *sanctitas*, *castimonia*, *castitas*, *innocentia*

increase, I. v intr 1, = to grow *(ac)crescĕre*, *succrescĕre*, *gliscĕre*, *incrementum capĕre*, *augeri*, *augescere*, *se corroborare* or *corroborari*, *ingravescere* (in bad sense), *increbrescĕre* (= to become more frequent), *invalescere* (= to get the upper hand), *proficere* (= to advance), the evil increases, *malum ingravescit* or *corroboretur* **II.** v tr = to augment, *amplificare* (= to make wider), *dilatare* (= to spread out) *extendere*, *propagare* or *proferre alqd* (= to extend the limits, e g *imperium* or *fines imperii*), *augēre*, *amplificare*, *multiplicare* (= to multiply) **III** n = augmentation, *amplificatio* (e g *gloriae rei familiaris*), *propagatio* or *prolatio finium*, *accretio*, *accessio*, *augmentum*, *auctus*, *-ūs*, *incrementum*

incredible, adj *incredibilis*, it is — (*audita*, *dicta*, *memorata*) *incredibile est* Adv *incredibiliter*, *incredibilem in modum* **incredulous**, adj *qui non facile adduci potest ut credat*, *incredulus* **incredulity**, n by circumloc (e g *se incredulum praebuit*, = he showed his —)

increment, n *incrementum* see INCREASE

incriminate, v tr *alqm suspectum reddĕre*, — oneself, *se scelere alligare*

incrust, v tr *crustare* **incrustation**, n *crusta*

incubate, v intr *incubare* (Plin), see HATCH **incubus**, n. *incubo*

inculcate, v tr *alqm alqd docēre*, to — that, etc, *alci inculcare ut*, etc, *imprimĕre* (= to impress, imprint a mark upon) or *insculpĕre* (= to engrave) *alqd in alqa re* (the two latter verbs both lit and fig) to have been —d on the heart, *in animo insculptum esse* or *in animo insculptum habēre*

incumbency, n 1, = a relying on something, *officium* (in gen), *munus*, *-eris* (as the duty of an office), 2, = state of holding an ecclesiastical benefice, **possessio beneficii* **incumbent, I.** adj = lying on (as duty or obligation), anything is — upon me, *debeo alqd facĕre*, or *alqd mihi faciendum est*, or *est* with genit (e g it is — upon, the duty of the pupil, *est discipuli*, it is — upon me, you, etc, *meum*, *tuum est*) **II.** n = a clergyman, **beneficiarius*

incur, v tr 1, lit = to run against, hence to become subject to, *incurrĕre in alqm* or *alci rei*, *incidĕre in alqd* 2, fig *colligĕre* (e g hatred, *invidiam*, by anything, *alqâ re*), or *alci in odium venire*, *in alcjs odium incurrĕre*, *alcjs odium sibi contrahĕre*, to — disgrace, *dedecus in se admittere*

incurability, n by **incurable**, adj *insanabilis*, †*immedicabilis*, = hopeless, *desperatus* (e g a patient given up by the medical attendant) Adv use adj (e g he was — ill, *morbus erat insanabilis*)

indebted, adj 1, = being in debt, *obaeratus*, to be — to, *alci pecuniam debēre* or *pecuniam acceptam referre*. 2, = obliged by something received, to be — to anyone, *alci obnoxium esse*, *alcjs beneficiis obligatum esse*, to be greatly — to anybody, *alci multum* or *multa beneficia debēre*, *alqd alci acceptum referre*

indecency, n *turpitudo* (= — in anyone's language or behaviour), *obscenitas* (*obscoen*), *obscoen*), see OBSCENITY **indecent**, adj *indecōrus* (= unbecoming, opp *decōrus*, e g laughter, *risus*), *obscenus* (= obscene), *inhonestus* (= dishonourable), *turpis*, *parum verecundus* (= offensive to modesty and delicacy, not feeling ashamed, e g words, *verba*), an — expression, *quod turpe dictu videatur* (e g to make use of, *dicĕre*) Adv *indecore*, *turpiter*, *obscene*

indeciduous, adj (*folia*, etc) *quae non cadunt*, or *non decidua sunt*

indecision, n *dubitatio*, *inconstantia*, *haesitantia* **indecisive**, adj *dubius*, *anceps* Adv by adj, see INDEFINITE

indeclinable, adj use *verbum quod casibus immutari non potest*, *quod declinari non potest*, *indeclinabilis* (gram), — nouns, *aptota*, pl (gram)

indecorous, adj *indecōrus*, see INDECENT **indecorum**, n *deformitas* (= ugliness), = an evil, a mistake *vitium*, by the adj *turpis* or *indecorus*, also by *dedecet* (e g that is an —, *hoc turpe est* or *dedecet*), see INDECENCY

indeed, adv = in reality, *quidem* or *enim* (enclit), *adeo*, *profecto*, *enimvero*, *vere* (= truly), *vero*, *re verâ*, *re* (= in reality indeed, opp *nomine*, i e nominally, merely in appearance) I —, *equidem* —? *itane vero*? (in an ironical sense), *ain tu*? you don't say so? if used in an emphatic sense, e g this is true, it is indeed, = *sane* (referring to particular expressions), *vero*? both also = yes, certainly (i e *sane quidem* and *ita sane*), *quidem*, *enim* (to note concession), *credo* (= I think so, with reserve) *atqui* (= yes if however etc), *nempe*, *nimirum*, *scilicet*, *videlicet* (all = a concession in a familiar kind of way, *nempe* = surely), *nimirum* = no doubt, *scilicet*, *videlicet* = of course, all four also used in an ironical sense, e g very difficult —; *sane difficile* I could —

wish, Servius, *Ego vero, Servi, vellem;* I should — serve my fellow-citizens very badly, *Male, credo, mererer de meis civibus;* and —, *et sane;* surely —, *immo vero;* — . . . but nevertheless, *etsi . . . tamen;* or by *ille quidem, is quidem . . . sed tamen;* — not, *neque* (at the beginning of a sentence, with *sed* following); then —, *tum vero.*

indefatigable, adj. *assiduus* (= constantly active), *impiger* (= unwearied); *indefessus,* comb. *assiduus et indefessus.* Adv. *assidue, impigre.* **indefatigability,** n. *assiduitas, assiduitas et diligentia, impigritas.*

indefeasible, adj. *in perpetuum ratus.*

indefectible, indefective, adj. *vitio carens.*

indefensible, adj. *quod defendi non potest* (in gen.); of a military position, (*locus*) *qui teneri non potest.*

indefinable, adj. *quod definiri non potest;* an — sense of danger, *nescio quid periculi.* **indefinite,** adj. *incertus* (= uncertain, e.g. answer, *responsum*); = doubtful, *dubius, anceps;* = ambiguous, *ambiguus* (e.g. oracle, *oraculum,* = of doubtful meaning); for an — period, *in incertum;* the — pronoun, *pronomen infinitum* or *indefinitum* (gram.). Adv. *ambigue, incerte* or *incerto* (both ante class.), *dubie.*

indelibility, n. by circumloc. with adj. **indelible,** adj. † *indelibilis, quod deleri non potest; quod elui non potest* (= what cannot be wiped off); *inexpiabilis, implacabilis* (e.g. hatred, fig.); *sempiternus, perpetuus* (fig., e.g. hatred).

indelicate, adj. *parum verecundus, inurbanus, inhonestus* (= ungentlemanly), *impudicus* (= indecent). Adv. *parum verecunde, inurbane, impudice.* **indelicacy,** n. by adj.

indemnification, n. *damni restitutio;* in the connexion of a sentence, *compensatiō,* or circumloc. by *damnum* (*com*)*pensare* or (*re*)*sarcire* or *restituĕre.* **indemnify,** v.tr. *damnum alci restituĕre,* (*re*)*sarcire, pensare;* to — by anything for a thing, *alqd alqā re compensare.* **indemnity,** n. see INDEMNIFICATION; act of —, *lex oblivionis;* see AMNESTY.

indent, v.tr. *alqd incidĕre.* **indenture,** n. *pactum.*

independence, n. *libertas* (opp. *servitus*), *arbitrium liberum* (i.e. liberty of using one's own judgment); = exemption from burdens, *immunitas.* **independent,** adj. *liber, solutus* (often = free in bad sense); *sui juris* (of one who is his own master, of age); *sui potens* (= who does as he thinks proper); *liber et solutus, solutus et liber* (= free and unbound, tied by nobody); = exempt from burdens, *immunis, legibus solutus;* to be —, *sui juris* or *suae potestatis* or *in suā potestate esse;* to obey nobody, *nemini parēre;* to live as one thinks proper, — from others, *ad suum arbitrium vivĕre.* Adv. *libere, solute,* comb. *libere et solute, suo arbitrio* (= at one's own will).

indescribable, adj. *inenarrabilis* (= what cannot be estimated properly, e.g. trouble, labour); *incredibilis* (= incredible, e.g. joy, *laetitia*); *mirus* (= wonderful); *singularis* (e.g. faithfulness, *fides*), or by *nescio quid* (= what is so extraordinary that we can hardly comprehend it, e.g. that wonderful thing, *illud nescio quid praeclarum*). Adv. *inenarrabiliter, incredibiliter, singulariter, mirum in modum.*

indestructible, adj. *quod dirui* or *everti non potest,* or *perennis, perpetuus* (= lasting).

indeterminate, adj. *incertus;* see INDEFINITE. **indetermination,** n. by circumloc. with INDEFINITE. **indetermined,** adj. *dubius* (= doubtful), *incertus* (= uncertain); I am — what to do, *dubius* or *incertus sum quid faciam;* I am — whether to stay or to go, *incertum mihi est quid agam, abeam an maneam;* I am — whether, etc., *incertus sum utrum,* etc. Adv. *dubitanter;* see INDEFINITE.

index, n. 1, in gen. = that which points out, *index, -icis,* m. and f. (in a good or bad sense); 2, = the hand that points to the hour of the day, use *gnomon,* or *horarum index;* 3, = table of the contents of a book, *index* or *epitome.*

indexterity, n. *inscitia.*

Indian, adj. *Indianus, Indicus.*

indicate, v.tr. *indicare, indicio* or *indicium esse;* in reference to future things, *significare, praenuntiare, portendĕre;* = to announce, *nuntiare, nuntium alcjs rei afferre;* = to declare anything that is to be kept a secret, *enuntiare;* = to denounce, inform, *deferre;* = to declare, state what is to be done, *denuntiare* (e.g. war); = to prove, *arguĕre;* see DECLARE. **indication,** n. *indicium, index, argumentum, vestigium, documentum, significatio, signum.* **indicative,** adj. 1, *indicans;* see DECLARE; 2, — mood, *modus indicativus* (gram.). **indicatory,** adj. *significans;* see DECLARE.

indict, v.tr. = to accuse, *accusare, postulare, nomen alcjs deferre;* see ACCUSE, ACTION. **indictment,** n. bill of —, *libellus, accusatio* (inasmuch as the speaker appears before the public with it). **indictable,** adj. *accusabilis, quod lege animadvertendum est.* **indicter,** n. *accusator.*

indifference, n. 1, lit. *lĕvitas, vilitas* (= slightness of a matter); 2, = carelessness about anything, taking no notice of it, *neglegentia* (*neglig-*) *alcjs* or *alcjs rei; neglectio alcjs rei, contemptio alcjs rei, despicientia alcjs rei, incuria;* 3, = calmness, *aequus animus, aequitas animi;* = coldness, *lentitudo;* = hardness of heart, *animus durus, animus alienatus ab alqo* (= coldness towards a friend); 4, = impartiality, *aequabilitas, aequitas;* see IMPARTIALITY. **indifferent,** adj. 1, in the proper sense, *idem valens, ejusdem pretii* (= of the same value); = neither good nor bad, *nec bonus nec malus; indifferens* (attempted by Cicero as a translation of the Greek ἀδιάφορος); = keeping the middle course, neither to blame nor to praise, *medius, qui* (*quae, quod*) *neque laudari per se neque vituperari potest;* = trifling, insignificant, *lĕvis, vilis;* = too sure of anything, *securus;* = careless about anything, *remissus, dissolutus;* (e.g. whoever, in seeing these things, could be so — as to remain silent? *quis tam dissoluto animo est, qui haec quum videat tacēre possit?*); = slow, sluggish, *lentus;* = hard-hearted, *durus;* it is — to me whether, etc., *nihil meā interest* or *refert;* I have become — against any fresh grief, affliction, *obduruit animus ad dolorem novum;* to remain — to anything, to bear, put up with, *aequo animo ferre* or *pati alqd, lente* (= easily) *ferre alqd;* see IMPARTIAL; 2, neither good nor the worst, *tolerabilis;* = middling, *mediocris, modicus;* = pretty fair, *satis bonus* or *sat bonus* (e.g. *accusator*). Adv. = without distinction, *promiscue, promiscam* (ante class.); = carelessly, *dissoluto* or *remisso animo, neglegenter* (*neglig-*); = coolly, *lente;* = hard-heartedly, *duriter;* = impartially, *aequo animo, aequabiliter;* = middlingly, *mediocriter, modice.*

indigence, n. *inopia;* = want, *egestas, mendicitas;* = poverty, *inopia;* to be reduced to extreme —, *ad extremum inopiae venire;* to be reduced to complete poverty, to become a pauper, *in mendicitatem detrudi.* **indigent,** adj. *inops, egens, mendicus;* see NEEDY.

indigenous, adj 1, applied to persons, *indigena* (opp *alienigena*, *advena*, *peregrinus*), in circumloc by *in ea* or *illâ terrâ natus*, the — inhabitants (= natives), *indigenae* 2, applied to animals, vegetables, etc, *indigena*, *vernaculus*, see NATIVE

indigested, adj 1, = not concocted in the stomach, *crudus*, 2, = not regularly disposed and arranged, see UNARRANGED, 3, = not reduced to due form, *immaturus* **indigestible**, adj *difficilis concoctu* or *ad concoquendum*, *gravis* **indigestion**, n *cruditas* (e g of the stomach)

indignant, adj *indignabundus* (= full of indignation), = half angry, *subiratus*, = angry, *iratus*, *iracundus*, = with a hostile feeling, *iniquus*, to be — against anyone, *alci stomachari* or *iratum esse* Adv *irate*, *iracunde* **indignation**, n *indignatio* (in gen), *indignitas* (= indignity, then dissatisfaction we feel), at anything, *alcjs rei*, = displeasure, sensitiveness, *stomachus*, = anger, *ira*, *iracundia*, *bilis*, rather in —, *subiratus*, in —, *animo iniquo* or *irato*, *indignabundus*, *iratus* **indignity**, n *ignominia*, *indignitas*, *contumelia*, see INSULT

indirect, adj 1, lit not straight, *non rectus*, *devius*, 2, — fig , can only be rendered by circumloc , there are direct and — causes *caus(s)arum aliae sunt adjuvantes*, *aliae proximae*, if — means through a third party, it is rendered by *per* (e g *per senatum*), 3, Gram t t *obliquus* (e g *oratio obliqua*) Adv *obscure*, *tecte*, *clam*, *occulte*, or by *per* with acc as above *circuitione quadam*

indiscernible, adj *quod cerni non potest*

indiscoverable, adj *quod inveniri non potest*

indiscreet, adj see INCONSIDERATE, IMPROVIDENT, IMMODEST **indiscretion**, n see IMPROVIDENCE, IMMODESTY

indiscriminate, adj *promiscuus* Adv *omni discrimine sublato*, *promiscue*

indispensable, adj *necessarius*, it is —, *necesse est* (with acc and inf. or with subjunc) Adv *necessario*

indispose, v tr by circumloc *alqd ad alqd inutile reddĕre*, *alqm ab alqâ re avocare* **indisposed**, adj 1, to be, feel —, *leviter aegrotare*; to become —, see SICKLY, 2, = unwilling, *aversus ab alqo* or *ab alqâ re* (= feeling averse), *alienatus*, *alienus* (= hostile to a cause); not to be — to believe a thing, *inclinato ad credendum esse animo*, not to feel — to do a thing, *haud displicet* (with inf) **indisposition**, n 1, *commotiuncula*, 2, *animus aversus*, *invitus*, *alienus*, see AVERSION, DISINCLINATION

indisputable, adj *certus*, *perspicuus*, *manifestus*, *clarus*, see CERTAIN Adv *sine* (*ullâ*) *controversiâ* (= without the least controversy), = undoubtedly, *certo*, *sine dubio*, = without fail, *haud dubie*, *certe*, = by far, *longe*, with adj (e g Demosthenes was — the finest orator, *oratorum longe princeps Demosthenes*)

indissoluble, adj *indissolubilis* (lit e g knot, *nodus*), *inexplicabilis* (lit = what cannot be unfolded, untwisted, e g chain, *vinculum*, hence fig = unexplainable), = everlasting, *aeternus*

indistinct, adj *parum clarus* (both for the eye and the ear), *obscurus* (e g speech, *oratio*), = perplexed, *perplexus* (= difficult to make out, e g an answer, a reply, *responsum*), an — voice, *vox obtusa* (= weak, Quint) Adv *minus clare*, *obscure*, *perplexe*, *confuse*, see DOUBTFUL, DOUBTFULLY **indistinguishable**, adj *quod discerni non potest*

indite, v tr *scribĕre*

individual, I, adj *proprius*, *singularis*, *singuli* to remain true to one's — character, *naturam propriam sequi* Adv *viritim*, *in singulos*, *si(n)gillatim* II. n an —, *homo* **individuality**, n *natura alcjs propria*

indivisibility, n by adj **indivisible**, adj *individuus*, *quod dividi non potest*, small — bodies, *corpuscula individua*

indocile, adj *indocilis* **indocility**, n *ingenium indocile*

indoctrinate, v tr *erudire in alqâ re*

indolence, n *ignavia*, *inertia*, *desidia*, *segnitia* (*segnities*), *pigritia* (*pigrities*) **indolent**, adj *ignavus*, *iners*, *deses*, *segnis* (in posit rare in classical Lat), *piger* Adv *ignave*, *segne*, *segniter*, see IDLE

indomitable, adj *quod vinci non potest*, *invictus*, *indomitus*

in-door, adj *umbratilis* **in-doors**, adv *domi*

indorse, v tr 1, *syngrapham inscribĕre*; 2, fig see SANCTION, ALLOW

indubitable, adj *non dubius*, = certain, *certus* Adv see CERTAIN

induce, v tr anybody to a thing, *alqm in* or *alqd inducĕre* (= to lead into, e g an error, *in errorem*, to a war, *ad bellum*), = to urge anyone to a thing, *alqm impellĕre ad* or *in alqd* (e g to a war, *ad bellum*), = to allure anyone to a thing, *alqm illicĕre* or *pellicĕre in* or *ad alqd* (e g *in fraudem*), = to try to — a person to do a thing, *alqm sol(l)icitare ad alqd faciendum* or *sol(l)icitare ut*, etc **inducement**, n *caus(s)a*, *impulsus*, *ūs*, *incitamentum*, *illecebrae*, *praemium* **inducer**, n *auctor* **induct**, v tr *inaugurare* **induction**, n in logic, *inductio* (Quint), logical t t **ratio per inductionem facta*

indulgence, n *indulgentia*, *clementia*, *benignitas*, *venia* (= the overlooking of faults), in the middle ages, **indulgentia* (= remission of sins) **indulge**, I. v tr *alci* or *alci rei indulgēre*, *alci* or *alci rei veniam dare*, *alqm indulgentiâ tractare*, *alqd alci concedĕre* or *condonare*, = gratify, (*voluptatibus*) *se dedĕre*, (*in*)*servire* II. v intr *nimis sibi indulgēre* **indulgent**, adj *indulgens* (= showing kindness or favour, opp of *severus*), *clemens* (= merciful, opp of *severus*, *crudelis*), *benignus* (= kindness of heart, opp of *malignus*), *facilis* Adv *indulgenter*, *clementer*, *benigne*

industry, n *industria*, (*g*)*navitas* (rare, opp *ignavia*), *labor*, *opera*, *assiduitas*, *sedulitas* **industrious**, adj *industrius*, (*g*)*navus*, *acer*, *sedulus*, *assiduus*, *strenuus*, *diligens* Adv *industrie*, (*g*)*naviter*, *acriter*, *assidue*, *strenue*, *diligenter*

indweller, n *incola*, m and f , see INHABITANT **indwelling**, adj = remaining within (e g sin), *qui intus est*, *insitus*; = natural, innate, *innatus*, *naturâ insitus*

inebriate, v tr *ebrium facĕre*, *temulentum facĕre* **inebriated**, adj *ebrius*, *temulentus* **inebriation**, n *ebrietas*, see DRUNKENNESS

inedited, adj. *ineditus*

ineffability, n by **ineffable**, adj by *quod verbis exprimi non potest*, *inauditus*, = too horrible to utter, *infandus* (e g deed, grief), = incredible, *incredibilis* (e g pleasure, desire, longing), = unheard of, *inauditus* (e g greatness, size, cruelty) Adv *supra quam enarrari potest* (= indescribably), *incredibiliter* (= incredibly)

ineffective, inefficient, adj *invalidus* (lit not strong, weak), (e g medicine, opp *fortis*, *valens*), = unfit, unwholesome, *inutilis*, to remain, to be — *effectu carēre* (e g plans, etc)

Adv. *frustra*, *nequi(c)quam* (*nequidq*-). **ineffectiveness, inefficiency**, n. use adj.

inelegance, inelegancy, n. circumloc. by *sine elegantiâ*; *inconcinnitas* (e.g. of the ideas, *sententiarum*); see ELEGANCE. **inelegant**, adj. *invenustus* (= ungraceful), *inelegans* (= without taste), *inconcinnus* (= slovenly, improper), *illepidus* (= without grace), *inurbanus*, *agrestis*, *inhumanus*, *rusticus* (= boorish), *inornatus* (= without ornament); *incomptus* (lit. uncombed, e.g. head, hair; then fig., unpolished, e.g. speech, style). Adv. *ineleganter*, *illepide*, *inurbane*, *rustice*.

ineligible, adj. *qui per leges non eligendus est*, = unsuitable, *inopportunus*; see UNFIT, UNSUITABLE.

inept, adj. *ineptus*; see ABSURD.

inequality, n. *inaequalitas*, *dissimilitudo* (= unlikeness, e.g. of character, *morum*). **inequitable**, adj. *iniquus* (of pers. and things, opp. *aequus*, e.g. judge, law, condition); *injustus* (= unjust, of pers. and things, opp. *justus*, *meritus*, *debitus*, e.g. interest of money); *improbus* (= dishonest); *immeritus* (= undeserved; especially with a negation before it, e.g. praise not undeserved, *laudes haud immeritae*). Adv. *inique*, *injuste*.

inert, adj. *iners*, *immobilis*, *tardus*; see IDLE, INDOLENT. Adv. *tarde*. **inertness**, n. *inertia*; see INDOLENCE.

inestimable, adj. *inaestimabilis* (lit. = what cannot be estimated, Liv.); *unicus* (= alone of its kind), *mirus*, *mirificus*, *incredibilis* (= wonderful); *eximius*, *praestans*, *excellens*, *singularis* (= excellent). Adv. *eximie*, *excellenter*, *unice*, *praestanter*, *mire*, *mirifice*, *incredibiliter*.

inevitable, adj. *quod vitari* or *fugari non potest*, *inevitabilis*, *necessarius*. Adv. *necessario*.

inexact, adj. *haud exquisitus* or *accuratus* (of things), *indiligens* (of persons). **inexactness**, n. *indiligentia*; — of expression, *verba non accurata*.

inexcusable, adj. *quod excusari non potest*, *quod nihil excusationis habet*. Adv. use adj.

inexhaustible, adj. *quod exhauriri non potest*, *infinitus*.

inexorability, inexorableness, n. circumloc. by **inexorable**, adj. *inexorabilis*; = with unflinching severity, *severissimus*, *durus*. Adv. use adj.

inexpediency, n. *inutilitas*, or by adj. **inexpedient**, adj. *inutilis*, *inopportunus*.

inexperience, n. *imperitia* (= want of knowledge and experience); *inscitia*, *inscientia*, *insolentia* (= ignorance in gen.), *alcjs rei*. **inexperienced**, adj. *imperitus*, in anything, *alcjs rei*; = ignorant, *ignarus* (*alcjs rei*), = only a beginner, *rudis in alqâ re*; to be — in anything, *alqd nescire*, *in alqâ re non versatum esse*, *in alqâ re peregrinum*, or *hospitem*, or comb. *peregrinum atque hospitem esse*. **inexpert**, adj. = INEXPERIENCED.

inexpiable, adj. *inexpiabilis*.

inexplicable, adj. *inexplicabilis*. Adv. use adj.

inexpressible, adj. *inauditus*, *inenarrabilis*; see INEFFABLE.

inexpugnable, adj. *inexpugnabilis*.

inextinguishable, adj. † *inex(s)tinctus* (e.g. *ignis*, *fames*, *nomen*), *quod reprimi* or *ex(s)tingui non potest*.

inextricable, adj. *inexplicabilis*, † *inextricabilis*. Adv. use adj.

infallibility, n. (e.g. of a remedy) *certum remedium*. **infallible**, adj. 1, = certain, *certus*, *non dubius*; *exploratus*; 2, = one who is incapable of erring, *qui errare non potest*. Adv. *certo*; to be —, *omni errore carēre*.

infamous, adj. *infamis*, *turpis*, *flagitiosus*, *sceleratus*, *foedus*. Adv. *turpiter*, *flagitiose*, *scelerate*, *foede*. **infamy**, n. *infamia*, *turpitudo*, *dedecus*, -*oris*, *ignominia*.

infant, n. *infans*, *filiolus*, *filiola*. **infancy**, n. *infantia* (Plin., Tac.), or by *infans* (e.g. in his —, *cum esset infans*). **Infanta**, n. *filia regis Hispaniae*. **infanticide**, n. *infantium caedes*. **infantine**, adj. *puerilis*.

infantry, n. *pedites*, -*um*; or collectively, *pedes*, also *peditatus*, -*ūs*.

infatuate, v.tr. *infatuare* (= to lead, entice to an absurdity); *occaecare* (= to make blind, to blind); *pellicĕre* (= to inveigle, wheedle, e.g. a girl). **infatuated**, adj. *amens*, *demens*. **infatuation**, n. *amentia*, *dementia*, *furor*.

infect, v.tr. = to infuse into a healthy body the virus of a diseased body, *facĕre ut alqd transeat in alios* (i.e. lit. to pass over into others, of diseases); = to communicate bad qualities to anyone; e.g. others became likewise —ed, *contagio morbi etiam in alios vulgata est*; fig. to — a person through one's bad qualities, *alqm vitiis suis inficĕre*; to become —ed by errors, *infici* or *imbui vitiis*, *imbui erroribus*. **infection**, n. *contagio* (lit. and fig. in pl.), † *contagium*, *contactus*, -*ūs*; see CONTAGION. **infectious, infective**, adj. in good Lat. circ. by *contagio morbi*; — disease, *pestilentia*.

infecundity, n. *sterilitas* (opp. *fertilitas*).

infelicitous, adj. *infelix*; see UNHAPPY. **infelicity**, n. *malum*; see UNHAPPINESS.

infer, v.tr. *concludĕre*, *colligĕre*. **inference**, n. 1, = the art of inferring, *argumentatio*, *conjectura*; 2, = conclusion drawn, *conclusio* (of a syllogism), *conjectura* (on general grounds); *quod colligi potest* (from, etc., *ex*, etc.); see CONCLUSION.

inferior, I. adj. *inferior*, *deterior*, *minor*. II. n. (e.g. anyone's —), *inferior*; *ii qui inferiores sunt*.

infernal, adj. *infernus* (lit.); the — regions, *inferi*, † *Orcus*; = frightful, *terribilis* (fig.); = diabolical, *nefandus* (fig.).

infertile, adj. *sterilis*; see BARREN. **infertility**, n. *sterilitas*.

infest, v.tr. *infestum reddĕre*; to — (the high seas) by piracy, *mare infestare latrociniis*; *vexare*. **infested**, adj. *infestus*.

infidelity, n. (in a Christian sense), *impietas*; = unfaithfulness, *infidelitas*; *perfidia* (= treachery); = to commit a breach of faith, *fidem movēre* or *violare* or *frangĕre*; = to show —, *perfide agĕre*.

infinite, adj. *infinitus* (= without limits), *immensus*; — mood, *verbum infinitum*, *modus infinitus* (gram.). Adv. *infinite*, *ad* or *in infinitum*, *ad* or *in immensum*; see ENDLESS. **infinitesimal**, adj. *minimus*, *quam minimus*. **infinitude, infinity**, n. *infinitas* (= infinite extent), *infinitum tempus* (= endless time); *magna copia* (= great quantity).

infirm, adj. *infirmus*, *imbecillus*, *invalidus*, *debilis*; see WEAK. **infirmary**, n. *nosocomium* (νοσοκομεῖον) *valetudinarium* (Jct.). **infirmity**, n. 1, *infirmitas*, *imbecillitas*, *debilitas*; 2, = a complaint, *vitium*; = a bodily complaint, *vitium corporis*, *morbus*; the —, the defects of the state, *reipublicae vitia*.

inflame, v.tr. 1, = to set on fire in a lit. sense, *accendĕre*, *incendĕre*, *inflammare*; 2, = to excite or increase (e g passions), *incitare, inflammare, accendĕre, incendĕre*, see INCITE, 3, = to heat, as to — with wine, to exasperate (e g the enmity of parties), *inflammare*, to be inflamed, to grow hot, angry, and painful, *inflammari, ardēre, flagrare*. **inflammable,** adj *facilis ad exardescendum, quod celeriter accenditur* **inflammation,** n *inflammatio* (Plin). **inflammatory,** adj 1, *inflammans*, 2, fig *seditiosus, turbulentus* (of speech)

inflate, v.tr. 1, = to swell or distend by injecting air, *inflare, sufflare*, to become inflated, *inflari*, 2, = to distend by blowing in, *spiritu distendĕre* (e g a bladder), 3, = to become inflated, *se inflare* or *sufflare* (e g of the frog), = to puff up (e g to — anyone), *inflare alcjs animum ad superbiam* **inflated,** adj 1, *inflatus, sufflatus*, 2, of speech, *tumidus, turgidus, inflatus* **inflation,** n *inflatio, fastus, ūs*, = idle vanity, conceit, *superbia inanis*

inflect, v tr 1, = to bend, *(in)flectĕre*; see BEND 2, (in the grammat sense) *declinare* **inflection,** n *flexus, ūs*, = in the grammat sense, *declinatio* **inflexibility,** n (of the temper), *obstinatio, pertinacia, pervicacia, perseverantia* **inflexible,** adj *rigidus* (lit = stiff with cold, then fig. = rigid, inexorable), *obstinatus, pertinax, pervicax* Adv *obstinate, pertinaciter, pervicaciter, perseveranter*

inflict, v tr *alci alqd afferre, inferre* (esp evil), *algm alqâ re afficĕre* (= to affect anyone, make an impression with anything), to — ignominy, disgrace, *alci turpitudinem inferre* or *infligĕre, ignominiâ alqm afficĕre* or *notare*; *alci ignominiam injungĕre*, to — wrong, *injuriam alci facĕre, inferre, injungĕre, imponĕre*, — punishment upon, *poenam de alqo capĕre* or *sumĕre, alqm poenâ afficere, alqm punire*, see PUNISH **infliction,** n = an evil, *malum, incommodum*.

inflorescence, n *flos*

influence, I. n *vis, effectus, -ūs* (i e *vis efficiendi*, e g of the moon), *pondus, ĕris, auctoritas, momentum* (= weight), *potentia* (= power), *gratia* (= personal or political —), *amplitudo* (= greatness acquired through the office which a person holds), *dignitas* (= personal — through one's high social position), = — of a whole party, or of one person, through power and wealth, *opes, um*, f, = power of one body by coming in contact with another, *tactus, -ūs* (e g of the sun, *solis*, of the moon, *lunae*), = — of the stars and the moon, *vis stellarum ac lunae*, divine —, *afflatus, -ūs, instinctus* or *divinus*, to exercise an — upon anything, *valēre, conducĕre, vim habēre ad alqd* (= to contribute to, etc), = to extend to, *pertinēre ad alqd*, to have —, weight with a person, *multum auctoritate valēre* or *posse, apud alqm multum gratiâ valēre*, to have no —, to be of no avail, *nihil posse nihil valēre, sine auctoritate esse*, to have a beneficial — upon anyone, *prodesse alci* (*rei*), an injurious —, *nocēre alci* (*rei*) **II.** v tr *alqm movēre, permovēre, alci persuadēre*, see above, to have — **influential,** adj (*alcjs rei*) *potens* (of animate and inanimate objects), = strong, through means, resources, favour, *validus* or *potens opibus, gratiâ* (of persons), an — person, *qui multum valet, gravis* (= weighty), *amplus* (= — in position), *magna auctoritate* **influx,** n by *influĕre* (e g *influentes in Italiam Gallorum copias reprimĕre*, = to check the — of the Gauls into Italy)

inform, v tr 1, (lit = to give form or shape to), *(ef)fingĕre, facĕre, efficĕre, conformare, informare*, hence, = to animate, †*animare*, 2, = to acquaint anyone with a fact, *alci alqd nuntiare* (= to announce in writing, or by a messenger), = to announce through a messenger, *alqd alci per nuntium declarare*, = to communicate a fact (as a certainty), *certiorem facĕre alqm alcjs rei* or *de alqâ re*, *alqm alqd* or *de alqâ re docēre* *alqd ad alqm deferre praeferre*, — by a hint, *alci alqd significare*, 3, — against, *accusare nomen alcjs de alqâ re*, or *alci alcjs rei deferre* **informal,** adj *inusitatus, irritus, insolitus*, of an election, by *vitium* (e g *consul vitio creatus*) Adv *vitio, haud more* **informality,** n 1, *vitium* (in an election, etc), 2, = without formality, *amice* **informant,** n *auctor alcjs rei* **information,** n 1, = intelligence, *nuntius*, written —, *lit(t)erae*, = the authority (for the truth of anything), *auctoritas*, = a doubtful —, rumour, *fama*, = indication of anything, *significatio alcjs rei*, to receive — *nuntium accipere, certiorem fieri*, about anything, *alcjs rei* or *de alqâ re*, to learn, hear —, *alqd accipĕre, audire, comperire*, 2, = knowledge, *scientia, doctrina*, see KNOWLEDGE 3, = accusation, *delatio, indicium* **informer,** n *delator, index, icis*, m and f

infraction, n = non observance, by *violatus* (e g of a treaty, *violatum* or *ruptum foedus*) **infrangible,** adj *quod frangi non potest*

infrequency, n *raritas*, see RARE, RARITY **infrequent,** adj *rarus*

infringe, v tr = to break (e g contracts), *frangĕre, violare* **infringement,** n *imminutio, diminutio* (= lessening, e g *gloriae*), *violatio alcjs rei* (e g of the international law, *juris gentium*; of a treaty, *foederis*), — of the law, *peccatum, delictum* **infringer,** n *qui alqd non (ob)servat, qui alqd violat, alcjs rei violator*

infuriate, I. adj *rabidus*, see FURIOUS **II.** v tr *exasperare*, see ENRAGE

infuse, v tr 1, = to pour in (e g a liquid), *infundĕre*; 2, see INSTIL **infusion,** n 1, = the act of pouring in, *infusio*, 2, = the thing itself in which a thing is steeped, *dilutum, decoctum* (Plin)

ingathering, n = collecting fruits, *perceptio frugum* or *fructuum*

ingenerate, v tr *generare, gignere, parĕre*

ingenious, adj = subtle, *subtilis*, = one who shows taste and refinement, *luculentus, sol(l)ers, callidus* (= dexterous or clever), *artificiosus* (= highly finished both by nature and art) = of great talent *ingenio praestans, ingenio summo, clari ingenii*, = acute, ready, *argutus* (e g an idea, *sententia*) Adv *subtiliter, luculente(r), sol(l)erter, callide, artificiose, argute* see CLEVER, DEXTEROUS ACUTE **ingenuity,** n = quickness of invention (of persons), (*ingenii*) *acumen* or *acies*, = clearness of mind, *perspicacitas, prudentia*, = subtlety, *subtilitas*, = sagaciousness, *sagacitas*, = clearness in arguing, *acumen* or *subtilitas disserendi*, *ars* (= cleverness), *sol(l)ertia* (= dexterity), *machinatio* (= contrivance) **ingenuous,** adj an — mind, *liber* (= without reserve), = open, straightforward, *ingenuus*, an —, candid letter, *epistula liberior*, *apertus* (= open), *simplex* (= simple) Adv *libere, ingenue, aperte, simpliciter*, to speak —, *libere dicĕre* **ingenuousness,** n = openness of heart, *libertas* (also of speech), — in conversation, *sermo liberior* with —, *libere, ingenue, ingenuitas* (= the character of a gentleman)

ingestion, n *indĕre alqd alci rei* or *in alqd*, *ingerĕre in alqd*

ingle-nook, n *domus* (*intima*), in the —, *domi*

inglorious, adj *inglorius* (e g life), = ugly, *turpis* (morally, e g deed) Adv *sine gloria*, = dishonourably, *turpiter*.

ingot, n. — of gold, *later, -eris*, m., *aureus*; — of silver, *later argenteus*.

ingraft, v.tr. = to insert a scion of one tree or plant into another for propagation, *inserĕre*; ingrafted, *insitus*.

ingrained, adj. *insitus*; = produced by habit, *inveteratus*.

ingrate, I. adj. = ungrateful; *ingratus* (= both —, and what does not pay), = unmindful of kindness received, *beneficii, beneficiorum immemor*. **II.** n. *homo ingratus*. **ingratiate**, v.tr. = to commend oneself to another's goodwill (of persons), *alcjs favorem* or *benevolentiam sibi conciliare* or *colligĕre, gratiam inire ab alqo, ad* or *apud alqm*; *alcjs benevolentiam captare* (= to seek favour), *alcjs gratiam aucupari, alcjs favorem quaerĕre*; to try to — oneself with the people, *auram popularem captare, alcjs gratiam sequi*; to have ingratiated himself with anybody, *gratiosum esse alci* or *apud alqm*; very much, *gratiâ florēre* or *multum gratiâ valēre apud alqm*; to have ingratiated oneself very much with everybody, *apud omnes in summâ gratiâ esse*. **ingratitude**, n. *animus ingratus, beneficiorum immemor*.

ingredient, n. *pars*; = member, limb, component part, *membrum* (e.g. *hujus otiosae dignitatis haec fundamenta sunt, haec membra*); —s, *elementa alcjs rei*; that of which anything is an —, *res ex quibus conflatur et efficitur alqd*; or by n. pl. (e.g. the following —s, *haec*).

ingress, n. *ingressus, -ūs*.

ingulf, v.tr. **1**, = to swallow up in a vast deep, *(de)vorare, haurire*; **2**, = to cast into a gulf, *alqm in alqd detrudĕre, de(j)icĕre, (alqâ re) obruĕre* (e.g. *fluctibus*).

inhabit, v.tr. *habitare alqm locum, (in) alqo loco*; = to be resident anywhere, *(in)colĕre alqm locum*; = to occupy, *tenēre alqm locum* (e.g. places, countries); densely inhabited, *frequens (tectis*; opp. *desertus*). **inhabitable**, adj. *habitabilis*. **inhabitant**, n. *incŏla*, m. and f. (= resident in a town, country); *sessor* (in the same sense, in Nepos); *habitator* (= one who has his residence in a country, etc.); = tenant, *inquilinus* (opp. landlord, *dominus*); = citizen, *civis* (opp. *peregrinus*, a foreigner); = colonist, *colōnus*; *homo*, esp. in the pl. *homines* (= mankind); — of a town, *oppidi incŏla, oppidanus*; — of a village, *incola vici, vicanus, paganus*; — of an island, *insulanus* (Cic.); — of a province, *provincialis*.

inhale, v.tr. *spiritu (spirando) ducĕre, spiritu haurire*.

inharmonious, adj. **1**, *discors, absonus, dissonus*; **2**, = on bad terms, *dissentaneus, discrepans*. Adv. *haud consonanter, haud congruenter*.

inherent, adj. *insitus, innatus, proprius*; to be —, *in alqâ re inesse*. Adv. *naturâ, in* or *per se* (e.g. the thing is — evil, *quod in se malum est*).

inherit, v.tr. and intr. *heredem esse* (= to be heir), to anyone, *alci* (not *alcjs*), *hereditatem accipĕre ab alqo, hereditatem consequi*; I have inherited, *hereditas venit ad me, hereditas mihi obvenit*; to have inherited a thing, *alqd hereditate possidēre* (= to possess a thing by virtue of a will); = to succeed, come to property, *hereditatem adire, cernĕre* (the legal declaration of acceptance, *cretio*); to — everything, *heredem ex asse esse*; to — one-half, *heredem esse ex dimidiâ parte*; to — one-sixth, *heredem in sextante esse*. **inheritance**, n. *hereditas* (= right of —, and the — itself); I come to the property by —, *hereditas mihi venit, obtingit, obvenit, hereditas ad me venit* or *pervenit*. **inherited**, adj. *patrius, paternus, avitus*.

inhibit, v.tr. *interdicĕre*; see FORBID. **inhibition**, n. *interdictum*; see PROHIBITION.

inhospitable, adj. † *inhospitalis*, † *inhospitus*. **inhospitality**, n. *inhospitalitas* or by *inhospitalis*; see CHURLISH.

inhuman, adj. *inhumanus* (= unfeeling, e.g. character, *ingenium*; cruelty, *crudelitas*; man, *homo*); = monstrous, *immanis* (of things and persons); = unfeeling, *ferus* (of persons), comb. *ferus et immanis, crudelis, saevus, atrox, durus, ferreus*. Adv. *inhumane, crudeliter, saeve, atrociter, dure, duriter*. **inhumanity**, n. *inhumanitas, immanitas, feritas, crudelitas, saevitas, atrocitas*.

inimical, adj. *inimicus*; see HOSTILE.

inimitability, n. by **inimitable**, adj. *non imitabilis, inimitabilis* (Quint.), or by *quod nulla ars* (or *nemo*) *consequi potest imitando*. Adv. by adj.

iniquitous, adj. = unfair, *injustus, iniquus*. Adv. *injuste, inique*. **iniquity**, n. *injustitia, iniquitas*; see WICKED.

initial, I. adj. by *initio positus*, or *primus*. **II.** n. = the first letter of a name, *prima lit(t)era*. **initiate**, v.tr. **1**, in religious sense, *initiare*; **2**, = to begin, *coepisse*; see BEGIN. **initiation**, n. **1**, by *initiare*; **2**, *initium*. **initiative**, adj. **1**, by verb INITIATE; **2**, *quod initio factum est, primus*.

inject, v.tr. *(siphonis ope) infundĕre*.

injudicious, adj. *nullius consilii* (= without judgment); *imprudens* (= without caution), *stultus* (= silly); *inconsultus* (= without considering); = inconsiderate, *inconsideratus* (e.g. desires); = rash, *temerarius* (e.g. expression, *vox*). Adv. *inconsulte, inconsiderate* or *parum considerate, temere*. **injudiciousness**, n. *imprudentia, stultitia*, or by adj.

injunction, n. *interdictum*.

injure, v.tr. *laedĕre, sauciare, vulnerare*, comb. *laedĕre et vulnerare, lacerare* (= to tear to pieces), fig. *alci nocēre* (e.g. *optimum virum verborum contumeliis*), *violare* (= to treat with violence); the storm —s the ship, *tempestas affligit navem*. **injury**, n. **1**, as act, *vulneratio, sauciatio*; without — to duty, *salvo officio*; **2**, = harm, *detrimentum, incommodum, damnum* (= loss), *malum* (= evil), *vulnus, -ĕris* (= wound), *noxia* (= trespass); to do anyone an —, *injuriam alci facĕre*; to forgive an —, *injuriam condonare*. **injurer**, n. *qui injuriam facit*. **injurious**, adj. *noxius, injuriosus, damnosus, gravis* (of air), *malus, adversus*, † *contrarius, iniquus*; — words, *contumeliae* or *verba contumeliosa*. Adv. *injuriose, damnose, graviter, male, contumeliose*.

injustice, n. *injustitia* (of unjust proceedings); an — done, *injuria factum*; to commit an —, *injuriam facĕre, injuste facĕre*.

ink, n. *atramentum*; an —horn, —stand, —pot, *atramentarium*. **inky**, adj. *atramento foedatus*.

inkling, n. *susurrus*; see WHISPER, HINT.

inland, adj. *mediterraneus*.

inlay, v.tr. *inserĕre, variare, distinguĕre*; see ADORN.

inlet, n. **1**, *aditus, -ūs*; **2**, of the sea, *aestuarium*.

inly, adv. *penitus*.

inmate, n. = lodger, *deversor, inquilinus*; of a country, *incola*, m. and f.; see INHABITANT.

inmost, innermost, adj. *intimus*; the — part, *intima pars*; *intima, -orum*; *viscera, -um*, pl (= entrails, bowels, fig, = the noblest parts, e g of the heart, the state, etc), a thing is impressed in my — heart, *alqd haeret mihi in visceribus*, also by *intimus* or *penitus* (e g he proceeded to the — parts of Macedonia to conceal himself, *se abdidit in intimam Macedoniam, penitus se abdidit in Macedoniam*), or, if speaking of forests, by *densissimus* (e.g. to retreat into the — parts of the forests, *se in densissimas silvas abdidit*)

inn, n *devorsori(ol)um, hospitium, caupona* (= a tavern) **innkeeper**, n *caupo*

innate, adj *innatus, ingeneratus, insitus*, comb *insitus et innatus, proprius*, = natural, *naturalis, nativus* (opp *assumptus, adventicius*, i e artificially acquired), = inherited, *congenitus, avitus* (e g an evil, *malum*), the old and — pride of the Claudian family, *vetus atque insita Claudiae familiae superbia*, — ideas, *notiones* (*in animo insitae*)

inner, adj = interior, *interior* (opp *exterior*), = what is going on in the interior of the country, etc, *intestinus* (opp *externus*, foreign), = what is going on at home, in one's own country, *domesticus* (opp *foris*, abroad), comb *intestinus ac domesticus*, the — man, *animus*, the interior affairs, *res domesticae* (= home affairs), = intellectual (e g qualities, *bona animi, virtutes animi*, = natural feeling, *natura* Adv. *intus*; within, *interius* (opp *exterius*)

innocence, n *innocentia*, = purity, incorruptness, *integritas*, comb *integritas atque innocentia*, = simplicity, sincerity, *simplicitas*, to prove one's —, *se purgare alci*, = modesty, *pudicitia*, = chastity, *castitas*, comb *integritas pudicitiaque*, — of the heart *castus animus purusque* **innocent, I.** adj. 1 = without crime, *innocens* (= doing no harm), *†immerens, †immeritus*; = free from guilt, guiltless, *insons, culpā vacuus* or *carens*, = pure, free from all sin, not to be seduced, *integer, sanctus*, to be — of a thing, *insontem esse alcjs rei* (e g of a public decree, *consilii publici*), 2, = chaste, *integer* (= who leads a moral life), = discreet, *pudicus*, = chaste, who does nothing unchaste, *castus et integer*. Adv *integre, pudice, caste*, comb *pure et caste, caste integreque*, = without bad intention, *imprudenter, per inscitiam* **II.** n = idiot, (*homo*) *stultissimus* **innocuous**, adj. = harmless, *innocuus* (= not able to do harm), to anyone, *alci*, = doing no harm, *innoxius*, to anyone, *alci*, = innocent, *innocens* (all three of persons and things), to be —, *non* or *nihil nocēre*

innovate, v tr *novare, mutare* (= to change), see INNOVATION hereafter **innovation**, n 1, = renewing, *renovatio* 2, = the thing itself *res nova*, to be fond of making —s (in the state), *rerum novarum cupidum esse, rerum commutandarum* or *evertendarum cupidum esse* fondness of making —s in the state of government, *rerum novarum studium* **innovator**, n = fond of innovations, *novitatis cupidus* (in gen)

innumerable, adj *innumerabilis, †innumerus*, = endless, *infinitus* comb *infinitus prope et innumerabilis*, an indefinite number, *sescenti*

inobservance, n *neglegentia* (*neglig*), see INADVERTENCE, DISOBEDIENCE **inobservant**, adj *neglegens* (*neglig-*)

inoculate, v tr 1, in gardening, *inoculare* (Col), 2, med t t *variolas inserere* has been suggested

inodorous, adj *odore carens*

inoffensive, adj *quod nihil habet offensionis*, = simple, *simplex* Adv *simpliciter* **inoffensiveness**, n by adj INOFFENSIVE; see INNOCENT

inopportune, adj *inopportunus*, see INCONVENIENT Adv *haud opportune*

inordinate, adj *immoderatus, immodicus, nimius, incredibilis, singularis, mirificus, mirus* Adv *praeter modum, immoderate, immodice, nimis, nimium, incredibiliter, singulariter, mirifice, mire*.

inorganic, adj. e g — bodies, *corpora nullā cohaerendi naturā* (Cic)

inquest, n *quaestio*, to hold an —, *de algā re* (e g *de morte*) *quaerĕre*.

inquietude, n *sol(l)icitudo*, see DISQUIET

inquire, v intr = to ask a question, *alqd* or *de algā re quaerĕre* (= to ask in general), to — strictly after, *alqd requirĕre, exquirĕre, perquirĕre de algā re sciscitare, percontari* (*percunct-*) *alqd* or with *utrum* or *ne*, = to make oneself acquainted with a thing, *cognoscĕre de algā re*, to — of persons after a thing, *alqd ab* or *ex algo quaerĕre, requirĕre, exquirĕre, algm de algā re interrogare*, — about anything in writing, *sciscitari per lit(t)eras de algā re* — into, *de algā re cognoscĕre* or *quaerĕre, de algā re*, or *in algd inquirĕre, alqd investigare, indagare* **inquiry**, n 1, = act of inquiring, *indagatio, investigatio* (= tracing), = examination, *cognitio, percontatio* (*percunct*) (= questioning), — of the truth, *investigatio veri, veri inquisitio atque investigatio*, = the critical examination of the truth, *cognitio*, to be entirely bent upon the — of a thing, *totum se in algā re exquirendā collocare*, = a diligent research, *diligentia*, to find by —, *inquirendo reperire*, 2, legal t t, = examination, *cognitio* (= inspection with the view of becoming acquainted with a thing, e g of the town, *urbis*, then = — by a magistrate or jury), *quaestio* (in gen, and in a court), *inquisitio* (lit = examination of anything, e g of the truth, *veri*, in the law = — about a person's life and any crime committed by him), — for a capital offence, *cognitio rei capitalis*, to demand a judicial —, *inquisitionem in algm postulare* (= to inquire into the conduct of, in order to accuse), to institute an —, *quaestionem habēre* or *instituĕre, cognitionem constituĕre*, about, into anything, *alqd* or *de algā re quaerĕre, quaestionem de algā re habēre*, to come to an — (e g it will come to a trial), *venire in quaestionem* or *in cognitionem, cognosci* **inquisition**, n 1, see INQUIRY, 2, in some Catholic countries = a tribunal for trying heretics, *quaesitores*, a tr of this kind, *inquisitio de fide habita* **inquisitive**, adj *audiendi cupidus* or *avidus*, or *studiosus*, *curiosus* Adv *curiose* **inquisitiveness**, n *cupiditas, studium*, or *aviditas audiendi* or *cognoscendi* **inquisitor**, n = one who inquires by virtue of his office, *quaesitor*, to be the —, to be the person charged with an inquiry, an examination, trial, *cognoscĕre*, into, of a thing, *alqd*

inroad, n *irruptio, incursio, incursus*, -ūs (the latter also of rivers), to make an —, *irruptionem* or *incursionem facĕre in algd*, = a sally, attack, excursion, *excursio, excursus*, -ūs, = a single expedition, movement in a campaign, *expeditio*, — into the enemy's land, *incursio in fines hostium facta*

insalubrious, adj *insalubris* = oppressive hence unfavourable to health, *gravis* (e g temperature, *caelum*), comb *gravis et pestilens*, — air or climate, *pestilentia* or *gravitas caeli*, *intemperies caeli* **insalubrity**, n — of a place, *pestilens loci natura*, — of the air, *pestilentia* or *gravitas* or *intemperies caeli*, see UNHEALTHY

insane, adj *insanus* (lit and fig), *mente captus*, (of one who is out of his mind, silly, foolish, and of anything that is so) *amens*, *demens* (lit. and fig., e.g. a scheme, *consilium*, *ratio*); = mad, raving, *furiosus*, *excors*, *vecors* (also = foolish), *secors* (rare), (of persons and things, e.g. a desire, *cupiditas*); = absurd, childish, *stultus*, *ineptus* (of persons and things). Adv. *dementer*, *insane*, *furiose*, *stulte*, *inepte*. **insanity**, n. *insania* (of lunatics, or in gen. of extreme passion), *furor* (= fury, of anyone that flies into a passion), *amentia*, *dementia*, *vecordia* (= madness or silliness), *secordia* (rare), *stultitia* (= silliness).

insatiable, adj. *insatiabilis*, *inexplebilis* (lit. and fig.), *insaturabilis* (lit., e.g. belly, *abdomen*); an — desire for reading, *legendi aviditas*. Adv. by adj.

inscribe, v.tr. = to mark with letters, *inscribĕre*, *adscribĕre*, *consignare*. **inscription**, n. on monuments, coins, statues, *inscriptio*, *index*, *-ĭcis*, m. and f. (both in gen., e.g. of a book, picture, statue); *titulus* (= *inscriptio* and *index*; then = epitaph, *titulus* (*sepulc(h)ri*); also = a note, card, as a sign that a certain thing is to be sold or let); *epigramma*, *-ătis*, n., an — at the foot of a statue, a gift, a tombstone, etc.; *carmen* (in verses, e.g., over the entrance of a temple); to place an — upon anything, *titulum inscribĕre alci rei*, *alqd inscribĕre*.

inscrutability, n. *obscuritas*, or by **inscrutable**, adj. *inexplicabilis*, *obscurus*.

insect, n. *insectum* (Plin.); *bestiola* (= a small animal, e.g. the wire-worm).

insecure, adj. *non* with *tutus*, *munitus* or *firmus*, *infestus* (of roads, etc., = beset by robbers), *instabilis*, *incertus*, *lubricus* (of footing). Adv. *non* with *tuto*, *firme*, *firmiter*. **insecurity**, n. by adj. (e.g. the — of the roads, *itinera infesta*).

insensate, adj., see INSANE, INSENSIBLE.

insensible, adj. 1, *sensūs expers*; to be —, *sensu carēre*; 2, fig., *durus*, *lentus*. Adv. *sensim*, *pedetemptim* (*pedetent-*); see FEELING. **insensibility**, n. 1, *torpor*; 2, *animus durus*, *lentitudo*; see also CRUELTY.

inseparability, n. by **inseparable**, adj. = indissoluble, *indissolubilis*; = indivisible, *individuus*; an — friend, *amicus fidissimus*. Adv. use adj. INSEPARABLE.

insert, v.tr. *inserĕre alci rei*, or *in alqd*, *includĕre alci rei*, or *in alqd*, *inter(f)icĕre*, *interponĕre* (= to put in between, e.g. intercalary months, *intercalatos menses*; then in general as a parenthesis, either in speaking or in writing); *supplēre* (= to supply, add, what was still wanting); *addĕre alqd alci rei*, or *in* with accus. (in general, = to add anything, e.g. I have inserted something in my speech, *in orationem addidi quaedam*); *adscribĕre alqd in alqd*, or *in alqâ re* (e.g. *diem in lit(t)eris*, the date in a letter); = to fasten in, *infigĕre alci rei* or *in alqd*; = to fix in the ground, plant, *defigĕre in alqd* or *in alqâ re*. **insertion**, n. 1, by verb INSERT; 2, in rhet., the — of a clause = parenthesis, *interpositio*.

inside, I. n. *pars interior*. II. adv. *intus*. III. prep. *in* with abl., *intra* with accus.; see WITHIN.

insidious, adj. *insidiosus*, *fallax*, *dolosus*, *fraudulentus*. Adv. *insidiose*, *fallaciter*, *dolose*, *fraudulenter*. **insidiousness**, n. *fallacia*, *dolus*, *fraus*; see DECEITFUL.

insight, n. = discernment, *intellegentia* (*intellig-*); = perfect knowledge, understanding, seeing through, *perspicientia*; of the truth, *veri*; a deeper — into, knowledge of things (in the highest sense), *sapientia*; = judgment, the opinion based upon judgment, *judicium*, *consilium*; = a clear knowledge and —, *cognitio*, of and into, *alcjs rei*; no —, want of judgment, *imprudentia*; a man of deep —, *vir prudentissimus*, *vir multi* or *magni consilii plenus*; men of — and talent, *viri docti et eruditi*; see KNOWLEDGE.

insignia, n. *fasces*, *-ium*, m., *insignia*, *-ium*.

insignificant, adj. 1, = small, *parvus*, *exiguus*, *minutus*; 2, = unimportant, *levis*, *nullius momenti*. **insignificance**, n. 1, *exiguitas*; 2, *mediocritas* (rare), *nullius* or *parvi momenti*.

insincere, adj. *falsus*, *simulatus*, *fucosus*, *fucatus*, *fallax*, *fraudulentus*, *dolosus*, *infidus* or *infidelis* (rare). Adv. *falso*, *fallaciter*, *simulate*, *fraudulente*, *dolose*. **insincerity**, n. *fucus*, *fallacia* (e.g. *sine fuco et fallaciis*), *fraus*, *-dis*, f., *dolus*, *simulatio*, *infidelitas*.

insinuate, v.tr. and intr. 1, = to push, work oneself into favour, *se insinuare*, *arrepĕre*, *irrepĕre*, *obrepĕre*, † *surrepĕre in alqd* (e.g. *amicitiam*); *gratiam sibi parĕre apud alqm* (= to ingratiate oneself); 2, = to suggest by remote allusion, *alci alqd significare* (= to give to understand); see HINT. **insinuation**, n. 1, *blanditiae*; 2, *significatio*. **insinuating**, adj. *blandus* (= bland). Adv. *blande*.

insipid, adj. 1, *nihil sapiens*, *insulsus*, † *elutus*; 2, fig., *insulsus*, *absurdus*, *ineptus*, *frigidus*, *jejunus*, *inanis*, *exilis*; (= tasteless, lit. *insipidus* is quite late); = not seasoned, *non conditus*; see ABSURD. Adv. *insulse*, *absurde*, *inepte*, *frigide*, *jejune*, *inaniter*, *exiliter*. **insipidity**, n. by INSIPID, e.g. the — of the food, *cibi voluptate carentes*; if fig. see ABSURDITY.

insist, v.intr. *alqd suadēre*, *hortari*; = to ask for, *alqd exigĕre*, *postulare*, (*ex*)*poscĕre*, (*ef*)*flagitare*; = to state strongly, *declarare*, *asseverare*, *dicĕre*, *ab algo contendĕre ut* or *de alquâ re faciendâ*.

insnare, v.tr. *irretire* (lit. and fig.); see ENSNARE.

insobriety, n. *intemperantia*; see DRUNKENNESS.

insolence, n. *insolentia*; = pride, *superbia*, *contumacia*, *audacia*, *impudentia*, *arrogantia*. **insolent**, adj. *insolens*, *contumax*, *audax*, *impudens*, *arrogans*. Adv. *insolenter*, *contumaciter*, *audaciter*, *impudenter*, *arroganter*, *superbe*.

insoluble, adj. 1, *quod liquefieri non potest*; 2, fig. *inexplicabilis*, *difficilis et inexplicabilis*.

insolvent, adj. *qui non est solvendo* or *ad solvendum*. **insolvency**, n. *non solvendo esse*, or *foro cedĕre*; see BANKRUPT.

insomuch, adv. *sic*, *ita*, *hoc* or *eo modo*, *adeo*; under this condition, *hâc* or *eâ condicione*, *hâc lege*; so far, *eo usque*; see So.

inspect, v.tr. *visĕre*, *invisĕre* (= to view, lit.); *a(d)spicĕre* (= to look on); *inspicĕre*, *introspicĕre*, *perspicĕre* (= to look through, examine); = to examine, *intueri*, *contemplari oculis*, (*col*)*lustrare*; to —, superintend anything, *alqd curare*, *regĕre*, *moderari*; see EXAMINE. **inspection**, n. 1, = a looking on, by verbs; 2, = watch, guardianship, superintendence, *cura* (= care over anything, e.g. the treasury, *aerarii*); *custodia*, comb. *cura custodiaque*; = protection, protecting care, *tutela*; = superintendence, — of a chairman, an officer, *praesidium*; = watch over the public morals, *praefectura morum*; to have the —, superintendence over anything, *alci rei praeesse*, *praefectum esse*, *alci rei praesidēre* (as chairman, e.g. over public games, the affairs of the town); to have anyone under one's —, *alqm custodire*. **inspector**, n. *custos*, *-ōdis* (m. and f.), *curator* (= keeper, librarian); = one who is set over a thing, *praeses*, *-idis*, m. and f., *praefectus*, one who superintends the public morals, *praefectus moribus, censor*, — of the public highways, *curator viarum*, = superintendent of a certain district of a town (as regards its cleanliness, etc), *magister vici, vicomagister* (Suet), — of the public buildings and chief constable, *aedilis* (in Rome) **inspectorship,** n. *custodis munus, -ĕris, cura, praefectura*

inspiration, n 1, = the inhaling of air, *spiritus, -ūs*, 2, = — by the Holy Spirit, *instinctus (-ūs) divinus, instinctus divinus afflatusque, inspiratio* (Eccl), by divine —, through God's command, *divinitus*, 3, = counsel, *monitus, -ūs, consilium* (= advice, what has been suggested), at anyone's —, see SUGGESTION **inspire,** v tr = to infuse ideas, *suggerĕre, sub(j)icĕre alci alqd* (= to suggest), as theol t t, to — by the Holy Spirit, *inspirare*, = to warn, advise, *monēre alqm alqd* or *monēre alqm ut*, etc, to — with, instil, *alci in(j)icĕre*, to excite, — with, instil into anyone courage, vigour, *excitare, incitare, incendere, inflammare*, = to delight, *laetitiā* or *gaudio perfundĕre* **inspired,** adj *divino spiritu inflatus* or *tactus, mente incitatus* (in gen), = fanatic, of enthusiasm approaching to madness, *fanaticus, furens, furibundus* **inspirer,** n see INSPIRE **inspirit,** v.tr. *animum alci addĕre*, see ENCOURAGE

instability, n *inconstantia*, see INCONSTANCY **instable,** adj *inconstans*, see INCONSTANT

install, v tr *inaugurare* (under the celebration of auguries) **installation,** n by *inaugurare* **instalment,** n *prima (secunda*, etc) *pensio, pars, portio*, to pay by —, *in antecessum dare*, to receive, to be paid by —, *in antecessum accipĕre* (Sen)

instance, I. n 1, = request, *preces, -um*, more usually by abl abs (e g at the — of these men, *his petentibus*, or *his auctoribus*), 2, = example, *exemplum, specimen*, for —, *verbi* or *exempli caus(s)ā* or *gratiā* **II.** v tr *referre, dicĕre*, see MENTION **instant, I.** adj 1, = urgent, *vehemens, intentus, acer, magni momenti, gravis* (= serious), 2, = immediate, *praesens* **II.** n *punctum temporis* (= the smallest point in duration), = a moment, as part of an hour, *momentum* or *vestigium temporis, momentum horae*, in an —, *momento temporis*, to the —, *ad tempus*, not an —, *ne minimam partem temporis*, in every —, *omni puncto temporis, nullo temporis puncto intermisso*, the, this very —, by *ipse* (e.g the very — of his departure, *suā ipsā profectione*, at the very —, *ipso tempore*), to an —, *ad tempus*, for the —, *ad tempus, temporis caus(s)ā*, for the present —, *in praesens, in praesentia* (opp *in posterum*), = a favourable opportunity, *temporis opportunitas, temporis opportunitas* or *occasio*, not to allow the — to pass, *tempori* or *temporis occasioni non deesse*, during the last —, *in ipsa morte* Adv = immediately, *statim, confestim, protinus, e vestigio, extemplo, continuo*, = urgently, *intente, acriter, vehementer, impense, etiam atque etiam, magnopere* **instantaneous,** adj *brevissimus* (= of very short duration), = transient, *fugax* (= swift), sudden, *subitus* (e g *consilia*), = present, momentary, *praesens* (e g possibility, *facultas*) Adv *puncto* or *momento temporis, e vestigio*, = by and by, immediately, *extemplo*

instate, v.tr = to establish in a rank or condition, by *constituĕre*, to — in an office (in general), *munus alci mandare* or *assignare* or *deferre, muneri alqm praeficĕre* or *praeponĕre*, to — in any particular office, *apponĕre* (e g in the office of guardian, *alqm custodem alcjs*), see INSTALL

instead, prep *loco* or *in locum alcjs* or *alcjs rei*, = in the place of, *vice* (Plin), *in vicem* or *vicem alcjs* or *alcjs rei* (*meam, tuam, nostram, vestram vicem*, in my, etc, stead) — of you all, *vestrum omnium vicem*), *pro* with the abl, (= for, as good as, in comparison with, in proportion to), I was invited — of him, *in locum ejus invitatus sum*, he had called them Quirites — of soldiers, *Quirites eos pro militibus appellaverat*, — of, = rather than, with the pres part., *tantum abest ut . . ut*, etc (= so far from . . he rather, sooner, etc), = not only did not . . but, *non modo non . . sed etiam*, instead of . . he rather, *adeo non, adeo nihil . . ut*, instead of . . he only, *magis quam* (in Lat the second clause comes first, e g — of frightening him, it only brought him into greater rage, *accenderat eum magis quam conterruerat*), — of taking to flight, *omissā fugā*, sometimes also by *cum* (e g — of praising him, he reproved him, *cum laudare deberet, eum vituperavit*)

instep, n *pes superior*

instigate, v tr *instigare* (e g *canes in alqm*, = to set on, and fig), *concitare, incitare* **instigation,** n *impulsus, -ūs, stimulus, instinctus, -ūs*, at your —, *te auctore* **instigator,** n *auctor, concitator, impulsor, suasor, machinator, princeps, -ĭpis*

instil, v tr 1, = to infuse by drops, in general, *in os alcjs in(j)icĕre* or *indĕre* or *ingerĕre, instillare* (by drops, e g milk), 2, = to fill with, *alqm alqā re implēre*, to — admiration, *alqm admiratione imbuere, admirationem alci in(j)icere*

instinct, I. n animal —, *natura*, from one's own —, *naturā duce*, = natural desire, *appetitio* (= the act of striving, e g after knowledge, *cognitionis*), *appetitus, -ūs* (= natural feeling, especially animal), (both *appetitio* and *appetitus* are used by Cic for the Greek ὁρμή = desire in general), a sudden impulse, *impetus, -ūs*, = inward desire, inclination, taste, *studium*, sensual —, *studia prava* or *turpia* or *humilia* **II.** adj — with anything, *alqā re imbutus* **instinctive,** adj *naturalis, duce naturā suā* (e g to do anything, *facĕre alqd*) Adv *naturā (duce), naturaliter*

institute, I. v tr = to found (e g a court), *condere* (lit to put together, hence to accomplish the building or the establishing of anything, e g an empire, *imperium*), to — a thing, *instituĕre*, to — a monarchy, *regnum statuere, regem creare* (= to create a king), = to erect, place, *constituere* (e g a monument, *monumentum*), to — friendship, *conciliare amicitiam*, a union, wedding, *nuptias*, peace, *pacem*, to — again, re establish, *reconciliare* (e g peace, *pacem*), to effect, *facĕre* (e g a treaty, alliance, *foedus, -ĕris*, n, peace, *pacem*) **II.** n see INSTITUTION **institution,** n 1, = foundation, *initium* (= beginning), or verb (e g after the — of the state, *post quam civitas instituta est*, or *post civitatem institutam*, or by abl abs, *civitate instituta*), 2, = custom, *institutum, lex, mos, moris*, m, 3, = society, *societas, collegium, sodalitas*, 4, = school, *ludus (lit(t)erarum), schola*, see SCHOOL

instruct, v tr 1, *erudire* (= to draw out of a state of comparative rudeness and ignorance), in anything, *in alqā re*, = to teach, *alqm alqd docēre*, comb *erudire atque docēre, docēre atque erudire*, = to prepare anyone for a certain avocation, *instituĕre ad alqd*, or by *instruere* (lit to provide anyone with what is necessary, *doctrinis, artibus*, = to instruct in), to lecture, *praecipĕre* or *tradere alqd* or *de alqā re, tradĕre praecepta alcjs rei*, to — anyone in elocution, *alqm ad dicendum instituĕre*, see ORDER, to be instructed by anyone, *discĕre ab alqo*, to be instructed in anything by anyone, *discĕre alqd* (or with infin.); 2, = order, *alqd alci praescribĕre* (e.g. *quae sint agenda*), *alci committĕre* or *mandare ut*; see ORDER, CHARGE. **instructed,** adj. *eruditus* (= brought out of a state of ignorance, educated); one who has received a learned, a literary education, *doctus, doctrinâ instructus*. **instruction,** n. 1, = the act of teaching, *institutio* (= — in gen., information), in anything, *alcjs rei*; = the bringing up of anyone from a state of ignorance, *eruditio*; = education in a school, or from a master, *disciplina*; — given by a teacher, *doctrina*; *praeceptum* (= lesson); 2, = direction, *praeceptio* (= the act of prescribing), *praeceptum* (= precept), *praescriptum, mandatum* (= charge given to anyone, e.g. an ambassador); his —s, *alci mandare ut*; see INSTRUCT, 2. **instructive,** adj. *utilis*. Adv. *utiliter*. **instructor,** n. *magister, doctor, praeceptor, dux* (= leader).

instrument, n. 1, = tool, *utensilia, -ium*, n. (= utensils in a household, and in general); = furniture, *supellex*; = vessels, culinary —s, a soldier's cooking apparatus, *vasa, -orum*; = tools for carrying on trade, *instrumentum* (collectively or in pl., e.g. agricultural, *rusticum*); = some large, artificial —, machine, *machina*; an iron —, *ferramentum*; musical — with strings, *fides, -ium*; = horn, *cornu*; = trumpet, *tuba*; = pipe, *tibia*; to sing to an —, *ad chordarum sonum cantare*; 2, = means, *minister* (fig.); to use anyone as an — for anything, *alcjs operâ alqd efficĕre*; 3, in law and in gen. (= a deed), *lit(t)erae, tabulae* (= anything in writing); to draw up an — in writing, *lit(t)eris alqd consignare*. **instrumental,** adj. 1, = contributing aid, *utilis* (= useful); convenient, *commodus, accommodatus, aptus*; you were — in hindering, *per te stetit quominus*, etc., or *te auctore*; to be —, *ad alqd valēre, alcjs operâ effici, alci prodesse*; 2, = pertaining to music, — music, *cantus tibiarum nervorumque* or *nervorum et tibiarum*; — and vocal music, *chordarum sonitus et vocis cantus, vocum nervorumque cantus, -ūs*. **instrumentality,** n. *opera, ministerium*, or by *per* or *alcjs operâ* or abl. abs. (e.g. *per te* or *tuâ operâ* or *te auctore*).

insubordination, n. *disciplina nulla* (= no order, discipline); = licentiousness, *licentia, nimia licentia*, comb. *intemperantia et nimia licentia*. **insubordinate,** adj. *nullâ disciplinâ coercitus, intemperans, seditiosus, turbulentus, male* or *parum oboediens* (*obed-*) or *obtemperans*. Adv. *seditiose, turbulente(r)*.

insufferable, adj. *intolerabilis*; see INTOLERABLE.

insufficient, adj. *haud sufficiens, haud satis* (*magnus*, etc.), *impar* (= unequal); see INADEQUATE. Adv. *haud satis, parum*. **insufficiency,** n. *inopia, imbecillitas* (= weakness), *angustiae, egestas, paupertas* (= poverty).

insular, adj. by *insula* (e.g. through our — position, *eo ipso quod insulam incolimus*).

insult, I. n. *injuria, injuria alci illata, ab alqo illata, contumelia, probrum, maledictum*; = disgrace, *dedecus, -ōris*, n., *ignominia, indignitas*. **II.** v.tr. *alci maledicĕre* (= abuse), *contumeliam alci imponĕre*; without any —, *sine ullâ contumeliâ*; to be insulted, *injuriam accipĕre* or *pati*; easily insulted, *animus mollis ad accipiendam offensionem*; to feel yourself insulted, *injuriam sibi factam putare*; insulted by something, *alqd in* or *ad contumeliam accipĕre* (= to take as an —). **insulting,** adj. *contumeliosus, probrosus, maledicus, maledicens*; — words, *voces contumeliosae, verborum contumeliae*. Adv. *contumeliose, maledice, per ludibrium*.

insuperable, adj. *in(ex)superabilis* (lit., = what cannot be surmounted, of mountains), *quod superari non potest* (lit. and fig.); invincible, *invictus* (of persons).

insupportable, adj. see INTOLERABLE.

insurance, n. *fides de damno resarciendo interposita*. **insure,** v.tr. and intr. *damnum praestare, de alqâ re cavēre*.

insurgent, adj. and n. *seditiosus, turbulentus*. **insurrection,** n. *rebellio, seditio, motus, -ūs, tumultus, -ūs*. **insurrectionary,** adj. *seditiosus*; see INSURGENT.

insusceptibility, n. by **insusceptible,** adj. see INSENSIBLE.

intact, adj. *intactus*; *integer* (= untouched), *salvus, incolumis* (= unharmed).

intangible, n. *quod sentire* or *sensibus percipĕre non possumus*.

integral, adj. *pars ad totum necessaria*. **integrity,** n. 1, = entireness (e.g. — of the empire), adj. *regnum integrum*; 2, = incorruptness, *integritas, probitas, abstinentia, innocentia, sanctitas, castitas* (= purity).

integument, n. (= that which naturally covers a thing, but chiefly a term in anatomy), *cutis* (= skin or —), *teg(u)men, (in)teg(u)mentum, operimentum* (= a covering, protection), *velamentum, velum* (= a covering, cloak), *involucrum* (= a wrapper).

intellect, n. *mens, -ntis*, f., *ingenium, ingenii vis, animus, cogitatio, intellegentia, quae pars animi rationis atque intellegentiae particeps est*; acuteness of —, *ingenii acumen* or *acies, subtilitas, sagacitas*. **intellectual,** adj. by genit. of *mens*, etc. **intelligence,** n. 1, *perspicacitas, sol(l)ertia*; see INTELLECT; 2, = news, *nuntius*; see NEWS. **intelligencer,** n. = one who sends or conveys intelligence, *nuntius, legatus* (= an ambassador); = one who gives notice of transactions in writing, a newspaper-writer, journalist, *diurnorum scriptor*. **intelligent,** adj. *mente praeditus* (= gifted with understanding); one who has understanding, and uses it, *mentis compos, sanus*; = wise, *intellegens, sapiens, prudens, sciens*, comb. *prudens et sciens, (per)acutus, astutus, sol(l)ers*; a very — man, *homo ingenio prudentiâque acutissimus*; to be —, *sapĕre*. Adv. *intellegenter, sapienter, prudenter, scienter, acute, astute, sol(l)erter*. **intelligible,** adj. *quod facile intellegi potest*; = well explained, *explicatus*; = clear, *perspicuus*; = plain, not confused, *planus*; = manifest, *apertus* (lit., open to everybody, also of the speaker); = distinct, *distinctus* (= well arranged, e.g. of the language, also of the person who speaks it, e.g. *utroque distinctior Cicero*, Tac.). Adv. *perspicue, plane, aperte, distincte, explicate*.

intemperance, n. *intemperantia, immoderatio, impotentia*; in drink, *ebrietas*. **intemperate,** adj. *intemperans, impotens, immodicus, immoderatus*; — in drink, *ebriosus, temulentus*; = angry, *iracundus*. Adv. *intemperanter, immodice, immoderate, iracunde*.

intend, v.tr. and intr. = to purpose, *propositum habēre* or by *propositum est mihi alqd* (or with infin.); = to think of, *cogitare alqd* (or with infin.); = to look forward to a thing, to direct one's attention to, *(animo) intendĕre* (with the accus. of a pron., or with *ut* or with infin.), *animum intendĕre ad* or *in alqd*; = to design, to be trying to, *id agĕre ut*, etc., *alqd agitare*; he could not do what he intended, *quod intenderat, non efficĕre poterat*; = to prepare anything, *parare*; = to attempt something difficult, *alqd moliri*; = to devise, *alqd comminisci* (something bad, e.g. a fraud, *fraudem*); = to be about to, *velle, cogitare*, *in animo habēre, destinare* (all with infin ; also very often by using the fut., e g *nunc scripturus sum*, = I am just about to write) **intense,** adj *magnus, acer, ardens, summus, intentus*; to take — pains with, *incumbĕre ad* or *in algd* or *alci rei*, or by *animum intendĕre ad algd* Adv *valde, magnopĕre, acriter, summe.* **intensify,** v tr *majorem*, etc , *reddĕre, amplificare, exaggerare, augēre*, see INCREASE **intensity,** n *vis, vis*, f., *gravitas*, — of cold, *rigor* **intensive,** adj = serving to give emphasis (e g an — particle), *intentivus* (e g *intentiva adverbia*, gram) **intent, I.** adj (lit., = having the mind strained, bent on a subject, eager, e g on business), *studiosus alcjs rei, intentus, attentus ad algd* or (*in*) *algā re, erectus*, to be — upon, *animum ad algd, in algd* or *alci rei intendĕre, incumbĕre in* or *ad algd* or *alci rei, studēre alci rei* Adv by adj **II.** n see INTENTION , to all —s and purposes, *omnino.* **intention,** n = design, *consilium, propositum, mens, animus* (e g *in animo habēre, esse in animo alci*), *institutum, sententia, studium, voluntas* **intentional,** adj by adv *quod consulto* or *de industriā*, or *deditā operā fit*

inter, v tr *sepelire* (= to bury in general, also *sepelire dolorem*), *humare* (= to cover with earth). **interment,** n *sepultura, humatio*, place of —, *sepulc(h)rum*, see BURY

interact, n = interlude in a play, *embolium* (ἐμβόλιοι, fig , *embolia amoris*, Cic)

intercalary, adj *intercalaris* or *intercalarius* **intercalate,** v t. *intercalare*

intercede, v intr = to plead, (*de*)*precari pro algo* (= to — for anyone), see ENTREAT, BEG **intercession,** n *deprecatio* (= praying earnestly to turn off some evil), at any one's request, *algo deprecatore* (e g to obtain pardon, *veniam impetrare*), to make — for anyone, *rogare pro algo* (so as to obtain something), on account of anything, *alci adesse ad algd deprecandum*, with anyone, *deprecari algm pro algo, deprecatorem alci adesse apud algm, alci supplicare pro algo* **intercessor,** n one who entreats, *deprecator.* **intercessory,** adj by verbs , see INTERCEDE

intercept, v tr **1,** = to seize on by the way (e g a letter, a prince), *intercipĕre, excipĕre*; **2,** = to cut off, *intercludĕre, circumvenire, officĕre* (e g — the light, *luminibus officĕre*), see INTERRUPT, HINDER

interchange, I. v tr **1,** = to reciprocate (e g places), by (*com*)*mutare*, (*per*)*mutare inter se*, see ALTERNATE, EXCHANGE **II.** n. (*com*)*mutatio, permutatio, vicissitudo* **interchangeable,** adj *quae inter se* (*com*)*mutari possunt.* Adv. *invicem*

intercolumniation, n *intercolumnium*

intercommunicate, v.intr. **1,** *algd communicare inter se* or *conferre inter se*, see COMMUNICATE , **2,** of rooms, etc , *commeatus*, *ūs, continēre*

intercourse, n *conversatio* (social), *usus*, *ūs* (frequent), *commercium* (commercial and in gen), habitual —, *consuetudo*, —, inasmuch as parties live, reside together, *convictus*, *ūs*, family —, *usus domesticus et consuetudo*, familiar —, *usus familiaris, familiaritas*, I have — with anyone, *est mihi consuetudo cum algo*, to have familiar — with anyone, *algo familiariter* or *intime uti, conjunctissime vivĕre cum algo, uti cum algo conjunctissimum esse*, to avoid all — with men, *congressus hominum fugĕre, fugĕre colloquia et coetus hominum*

interdict I. v tr **1,** = to forbid, *interdicĕre alci algā re*, or with *ne*, see FORBID , **2,** see EXCOMMUNICATE **II.** n *interdictum.*

interest, I. v tr **1,** = to excite an interest, (e g a book), *jucundum esse* (lit = to be pleasing), = to delight, *delectare*, = to fascinate, *capĕre* (= to prepossess) , to — anyone, *alci placēre* , = to attract delight, *algm delectatione allicĕre* , = to enlist anyones attention, *tenēre* (e.g *audientium animos*), if it —s you to know this likewise, *si etiam hoc quaeris* , **2,** = to have a share, to be concerned in , anything —s me, *algd mea interest, algd ad me pertinet* ; **3,** = to give a share in, I — anyone in anything, *alci algd commendo* (e g *alci gloriam alcjs*), I feel an — in anything, *algd mihi curae* or *cordi* (but *curae cordique*) *est*, I — myself for anyone, *alci studeo, consulo, alcjs sum studiosus*, to take — in, *participem esse alcjs rei*, = to be an accomplice in a bad action, *affinem esse rei* (lit = to be related to anyone) **II.** n **1,** = causing interest, in gen *studium*, the divided — of the hearers, *deductum in partes audientium studium* = attraction, *voluptas*, = pleasantness, *jucunditas*, = delight, *delectatio, oblectatio*, to give an — to a matter, *voluptatem dare alci rei* ; **2,** = advantage ; to have in — in, by *interest* or *refert*, the — anyone has in a thing, *res* or *rationes* or *causa*(*s*)*a alcjs*, = advantage, *commodum, bonum, usus*, *ūs, utilitas*, = emolument, *emolumentum*, the common —, *res* or *causa*(*s*)*a communis, communis omnium utilitas*, in anyone's —, *ex usu alcjs*, anything is in my —, *algd est e re meā*, my — requires it *rationes meae ita ferunt* it is conducive to my —, *expedit mihi, meis rationibus conducit*, not all have, feel the same —, *aliis aliud expedit*, to defend anyone's —, *alcjs causa*(*s*)*am defendĕre*, to consider, study anyone's —, *alcjs rationibus consulĕre* , **3,** *usura* or *usurae, faenus* (*fe*), — added to the capital, *anatocismus*, — of —, *usurae usurarum*; to lend out money on —, *pecuniam faenerari, pecuniam dare faenore* or *faenori, ponere in faenore nummos*, to invest capital at —, *pecuniam apud algm occupare*, to lend out money at high —, *pecuniam grandi faenore occupare*, money lent without —, *pecunia gratuita*, the act of lending money on —, *faeneratio*, the — mounts up, *usurae multiplicantur* , to return, repay an act of kindness with —, *beneficium cum usuris reddĕre*, to return kindness with —, *debitum alci cumulate reddĕre* **interested,** adj *attentus, erectus*, — in, *alcjs rei studiosus* (= fond of); I am — in anything, *algd e re meā est, mihi expedit, meā interest* or *refert.* **interesting,** adj. by *quod ad se attrahit* or *illicit* (of a person), or by *algm tenēre* (of a writer), or by *multum habēre* or *plenum esse delectationis* (of a book), *jucundus*, see AGREEABLE.

interfere, v intr *alci rei* or *in algd intercedĕre, admiscēre, intervenire, se interponĕre*, or *se immiscēre*, I shall not — with it, *per me licet*, to — on anyone's behalf (i e. to guarantee for anyone), *intercedĕre pro algo*, to hinder, *algm interpellare* or *prohibēre* or *impedire* (with *quominus* or *quin* or *ne*), *alci officĕre, obesse, alci obstare quominus* or *quin* , see HINDER **interference,** n by verb, or by *intercessio* (of the tribunes)

interim, n *tempus interjectum, spatium, temporis intervallum, tempus quod interea est*, ad — *interim, ad tempus* (= for a time), *temporis gratiā* (= for the present time), a decree ad —, *edictum ad tempus propositum*

interior, I. adj *interior, internus* **II.** n. *pars interior*, see INNER, INTERNAL

interjacent, adj **1,** by *interjacēre, interedĕre*, **2,** *interjacens, interjectus*

interject, v.tr. *interponĕre, interjicĕre.* **interjection,** n. (in grammar) *interjectio.*

interlace, v.tr. *implicare* = to intermix (e.g. remarks), *intexĕre alqd alci rei* (fig., e.g. poetry in a discourse, *versus orationi*); see ENTWINE.

interlapse, I. v.intr. *interjici, interponi.* **II.** n. by verb; in the — of a year, *anno circumacto* or *praeterito, anno interjecto,* also *anno post,* or *post annum.*

interlard, v.tr. see MIX.

interleave, v.tr. *libri singulis paginis inter(j)icĕre singulas chartas puras.*

interline, v.tr. *interscribĕre* (Plin. Min.).

interlocution, n. see CONVERSATION. **interlocutory,** adj. (= consisting of dialogue, e.g. discourses), *in sermone;* to mention to anyone by way of conversation, *alci in sermone in(j)icĕre* (with acc. and infin., Cic.); a thing is mentioned as an — remark, *incidit mentio de alqâ re.*

interlude, n. see INTERACT.

intermarriage, n. *connubium.* **intermarry,** v.intr. *inter se matrimonio conjungi.*

intermeddle, v.intr. *se interponĕre alci rei* or *in alqd, se admiscĕre* or *immiscĕre;* not to —, *abesse* or *se abstinēre ab alqâ re;* you may do as you like, I shall not —, *quod voles facies, me nihil interpono.* **intermediate,** adj. *medius* (*intermedius,* ante class.).

interment, n. see INTER.

interminable, adj. *infinitus.* Adv. *infinite.*

intermingle, v.tr. *alci alqd (inter)miscĕre;* see MINGLE, MIX.

intermission, n. *intermissio* (e.g. of duty, *officii*); see INTERRUPTION, PAUSE. **intermit,** v.tr. *alqd intermittĕre;* see OMIT, CEASE, INTERRUPT. **intermittent,** adj., med. t.t. *febris intermittens* (Cels.). Adv. *tempore* or *intervallo interposito,* or *certis temporibus* (= at fixed times, or *incertis temp.* = at irregular intervals), *aliquando, nonnumquam* (*nonnunq-,* = sometimes).

intermix, I. v.tr. see INTERMINGLE. **II.** v.intr. *(com)misceri, permisceri, intermisceri.* **intermixture,** n. *mistio, permistio* (the act); see COMPOUND, MIXTURE.

internal, see INNER. Adv. *intus, penitus.*

international, adj. — law, *jus* (*juris,* n.) *gentium.*

internecine, adj. *internecivus;* see FATAL.

internuncio, n. = messenger between two parties, *internuntius.*

interpellation, n. *interpellatio* (Cic.).

interpolate, v.tr. = to insert, *alqd alci rei addĕre, inserĕre;* = to falsify, *corrumpĕre.* **interpolation,** n. use verb.

interpose, I. v.tr. = to place between (e.g. to — a body between the earth and the sun), *interponĕre, interjicĕre.* **II.** v.intr. = to mediate, *se interponĕre in rem;* see INTERFERE. **interposition,** n. **1,** = a placing between (e.g. the — of the Baltic sea between, etc.), *interjectus, interpositus* (both *-ūs,* only common in abl. however), *interventus, -ūs;* better use abl. abs. (e.g. *mari interjecto* = by the — of the sea; **2,** (in general = mediation, anything interposed), *vis, impulsus, -ūs* (= instigation), or by *auctor* (e.g. by my —, *me auctore*); see INTERCESSION; by divine —, influence, *divinitus.*

interpret, v.tr. **1,** = to — for anyone, *interpretari;* see TRANSLATE; **2,** = to unfold the meaning of anything (e.g. a dream), *alqd interpretari, esse interpretem alcjs rei* (e.g. the law, a dream); *con(j)icĕre, alqd conjecturâ explanare, conjecturam alcjs rei facĕre, alqd enarrare* (= to conjecture, explain by conjecture, e.g. a dream, a wonder, etc.); = to take anything that is said, *accipĕre* (either in a good or bad sense); = to explain, *explanare;* to — in a wrong sense, misinterpret, *detorquēre in* (with accus.), *trahĕre ad* or *in* (with accus., = — on purpose); to — anything that is not clear, *rem obscuram interpretando explanare;* to get anyone to — anything for, *de alqâ re uti interprete;* to — anything in good part, *alqd in bonam partem accipĕre* or *bene interpretari;* to — anything as an offence, *alqd in malam partem accipĕre* or *male interpretari;* to — anything from anyone as haughtiness, *alqd alci tribuĕre superbiae, trahĕre alqd in superbiam;* as an insult, as disgracing anyone, *in contumeliam convertĕre;* to — a thing differently from what anyone said, *aliter alqd ac dictum erat accipĕre.* **interpretation,** n. *interpretatio, explanatio* (= explanation); an — by conjecture, a conjecture, hypothesis, *conjectio, conjectura;* = critical explanations of an author, *enarratio* (Quint.); to be liable to have a bad — put upon, *in malam partem accipi.* **interpretative,** adj. *quod explanat.* **interpreter,** n., an — of a foreign tongue, *interpres, -ĕtis,* m. and f.; to converse through the medium of an —, *per interpretem colloqui,* with anyone, *cum algo.*

interregnum, n. *interregnum.* **interrex,** n. *interrex.*

interrogate, v.tr. and intr. *quaerĕre, exquirĕre, requirĕre ex* or *ab algo;* see ASK, INQUIRE; = to — again and again, *rogitare;* see ASK. **interrogation,** n. *interrogatio* (= the act of interrogating, hence anything in the form of a question), *percontatio* (*percunct-*); = the question asked, *(inter)rogatum;* = investigation, *quaestio.* **interrogative, I.** adj. use verb (e.g. in an — manner, *percontando* (*percunct-*) *et interrogando*). **II.** n. *particula interrogativa* (gram.). **interrogator,** n. *qui interrogat.* **interrogatory, I.** adj. by INTERROGATE. **II.** n. *interrogatio.*

interrupt, v.tr. *interrumpĕre* (e.g. a speech, *orationem;* sleep, *somnum;* order, succession, *ordinem*); *interpellare* (lit., to — a speaker by speaking, by addressing the meeting; then in general, to disturb); = to rest, cease for a while from anything, *intermittĕre* (e.g. the march, journey, *iter;* the battle, *praelium*); to intercept, arrest suddenly, *intercipĕre* (e.g. the march, *iter;* a conversation, *sermonem medium*); to — by interfering, *intervenire alci rei* (e.g. a deliberation, *deliberationi*); = to cut short, *incidĕre* (lit. = to cut into, to cut away a piece as it were, e.g. a discourse, the conversation, speech, *sermonem*); = to speak whilst others are speaking, *alqm interfari;* = to cause to cease, separate, put off, *dirimĕre* (e.g. *sermonem, praelium;* both of persons and circumstances); to — by speaking against, *alci obloqui;* — noisily, *alci obstrepĕre.* **interrupted,** adj. *interruptus, interceptus, intermissus.* Adv. *interrupte.* **interruption,** n. *interpellatio* (= of one who speaks by others; then in general = disturbance); = the act of speaking whilst someone else speaks, *interfatio;* = the act of ceasing for a while, *intermissio* (e.g. of the correspondence, *lit(t)erarum* or *epistolarum*); = the interval whilst an — takes place, *intercapedo* (e.g. *scribendi*); without —, *uno tenore, sine ullâ intermissione;* to carry on the war with —, *per dilationes bellum gerĕre.*

intersect, v.tr. *secare* (lit. and fig.); = to cleave, divide, *scindĕre* (lit. and fig.); to cut across, thus, X, *decussare* (e g a line), to cut right in the middle, *medium secare*, by ditches, *fossis concīdĕre* (e g a field, a piece of land) **intersection,** n *sectio* (the act), the — (X) of two lines that cross each other, *decussatio*, *decussis*, is, m, = diameter, *diametros*, see DIAMETER

intersperse, v tr *immiscēre*, in anything, *alci rei*, to — poetry in a discourse, speech, sermon, *versus admiscēre orationi*, see MIX.

interstice, n *rima*, *foramen*

intertwine, v tr see ENTWINE

interval, n *intervallum*, *spatium interjectum* (in general; *distantia*, for — between two places, distance, seldom used, as in Vitruv), — of time, *tempus interjectum*; to leave an —, a space between, *spatium relinquĕre* or *intermittĕre*, after a brief —, *interjecto haud magno spatio*, in the —, *interim*, at —s, *aliquando*, *nonnumquam* (*nonnunq*-).

intervene, v intr = to be between, *interjacēre*, = to come between, *intercedĕre*, *interfluĕre*, *interponi*, *intervenire*, *supervenire alci rei* (of persons and things, e g of the night, *ni nox praelio intervenisset*, Liv, to — (of obstacles), *ob(j)ici* **intervention,** n *interventus*, -us (of persons and things), see INTERFERENCE

interview, n *congressio* (= the act), *congressus*, -ūs (= the — itself, friendly meeting), an — for a stated purpose, *conventus*, -ūs, = conversation, *colloquium*, *sermo*

interweave, v tr *intexĕre alci rei* or *in alqâ re* (lit. and fig); see ENTWINE

intestate, n of a person who dies without making a will, *intestatum* (Cic) or *intestato* (Cic) *decedere*

intestine, I. adj *intestinus*, see INTERNAL. **II.** n *intestinum*, usu pl *ilia*, *viscera*, *exta* (all pl)

intimacy, n *familiaritas*, *usus* (-ūs), *familiaris*, *consuetudo*, *necessitudo* **intimate, I.** adj *familiaris* (e g conversation, *sermo*), *intimus* (*inter*), *conjunctus*, to have an — knowledge of anything, *alqd penitus perspectum cognitumque habēre* Adv *familiariter*, *intime*, *conjuncte*, *penitus*, *prorsus*, see WHOLLY **II.** v tr *significare* (in gen), = to indicate, *indicare* (both *alci alqd*), = to inform anyone about a matter, *docēre alqm alqd*, *alqm de alqâ re certiorem facĕre*, *alqd alci nuntiare*, *declarare*, to — by words, *voce significare*, to — in a roundabout way, *alqd circuitu plurium verborum ostendere*, as a prediction, a wonder, *alqd portendĕre*, to — (in a threatening manner), *denuntiare* **intimation,** n *significatio*, *nuntius*, *denuntiatio*

intimidate, v.tr *metum* (*timorem*, *terrorem*, *pavorem*, *formidinem*) *alci in(j)icĕre*, *incutĕre*, *metum* (*timorem*, *terrorem*) *alci afferre*, *inferre*, *offerre*, *alqm in metum compellĕre*, *con(j)icĕre*, see FRIGHTEN, TERRIFY **intimidated,** adj *timefactus* (e g. liberty) **intimidation,** n *minae* = threats, by *pavorem* or *metum alci incutĕre*

into, prep as denoting motion towards or entrance, *in* with accus, *in meridiem*, = southwards, *in Galliam*, = towards Gaul, so of time, to, or up to, *dormiet in lucem*, = he will sleep till daybreak, *in multam noctem*, = deep into the night An adverb may be added, *usque in senectutem*, = down to old age, *mihi in mentem venit*, = it occurs to me *In*, as equivalent to into, may signify change or conversion, as *in lapidem verti*, = to be changed — stone, *in aquam solvi*, = to be melted — water With verbs compounded with preps, into is often not expressed, to go — the city, *urbem ingredi*

intolerable, adj *intolerabilis*, *intolerandus*, *vix tolerabilis*, *non ferendus* (of persons and things, e g woman, cold, pain), = odious, disagreeable, troublesome, *odiosus* (of persons and things, e g you are — to me, *odiosus mihi es*), = disobliging, disagreeable, *importunus* (of persons and things, e g avarice, *avaritia*) Adv *intoleranter*, to boast —, *intolerantissime gloriari*, it is — cold, *intolerabile est frigus* **intolerance,** n *animus aliorum de rebus divinis opiniones haud ferens*, or by some word = pride, *intolerantia*, *superbia*, *arrogantia* **intolerant,** adj *morosus immitis* (= of a harsh disposition), = intractable, difficult to deal with, obstinate *difficilis*, = proud, *superbus*, *alqs rei intolerans*, in religion, *erga alqos parum indulgens*

intone, v tr = to sound the notes of a musical scale, *incipĕre* (= to begin to sing, Virg), *voce praeire* (= to lead, of a precentor, to sound the first note), to — prayers, *preces canĕre*

intoxicate, v tr *inebriare* (lit), *ebrium reddĕre* **intoxicated,** adj *ebrius*, *temulentus* **intoxicating,** adj (*potus*) *qui alqm ebrium reddit* **intoxication,** n *ebrietas*, *temulentia*, see DRUNK

intractable, adj *indocilis*, *difficilis* **intractability,** n by adj

intransitive, adj *intransitivus* (gram)

intrench, v tr = to cut a trench, (*com*)*munire* (= to fortify, in gen), = to surround with fortifications, *operibus et munitionibus saepire*, *operibus munire*, = to surround with palisades, *vallare*, *obvallare*, *vallo* or *fossâ saepire* (*sep*), or *cingĕre*, or *circumdare*, or *munire*, *alqm locum munitionibus saepire*, *castra in alqo loco communire* **intrenchment,** n *vallum*, *munitio*, *munimentum*, *opera*, -um

intrepid, adj *intrepidus*, see FEARLESS **intrepidity,** n *animus intrepidus* or *impavidus* or *fortis*, *fortitudo*, see COURAGE

intricacy, n *implicatio*, *contortio* (e g *orationis*), the — of the road, *iter impeditum* **intricate,** adj *contortus*, *implicatus*, *inexplicabilis*, *perplexus*, *tortuosus*, *impeditus*

intrigue, I. n = a plot of a complicated nature, *dolus* (= a trick played to do harm), a secret —, *clandestinum consilium*, *artificia*, *-orum*, = a snare, *fallacia*, = a deception, *fraus*, -dis, ambush, *insidiae* **II.** v tr *fallacias fabricari*, (*con*)*coquere* (e g *consilia*), see PLOT, CONSPIRE **intriguer,** n *doli* or *fallaciarum machinator* **intriguing,** adj *callidus et ad fraudem acutus*, *fraudulentus* (= deceitful), = cunning, crafty, *astutus*, *vafer*, = malicious, knavish, *malitiosus*, a crafty fellow, *veterator*

intrinsic(al), adj = real, *verus*, or *per se*, or *ipse* Adv *re verâ*, *per se*, *vere*, see REAL

introduce, v tr lit *invehĕre*, *importare* (by carriers, by ship, goods, etc), to — anyone to one, *alqm introducĕre ad alqm* (usu to the great, to an audience, Curt, or to a house), to — anyone to a person (for making his acquaintance) by letter, *alqm alci commendare*, = to make acquainted with someone, *praesentem praesenti alci commendare*, = to induct anyone to an office, *alqm inaugurare* in a fig sense, e g to — anyone as speaking, *alqm loquentem* or *disputantem inducĕre*, = to bring up (e g customs, etc), *inducĕre*, *introducĕre*, to have been introduced, *usu receptum esse*, to — many changes, *multa mutare* or *novare* **introduction,** n *invectio* (= importation of goods, etc), *inductio* (= the act of letting go in, e g of armed soldiers, *inductio armatorum*), — of persons, *introductio* (e g *adolescentulorum nobilium*), to give an — to, *alqm alci commendare*, an — to a book, etc, *prooemium, principium, exordium, praefatio* (Plin, Quint), say something in — to, *dicere alqd ante rem*, after a short — respecting old age, *pauca praefatus de senectute* **introductory,** adj by v, e g to make — remarks, *praefari*

intromission, n *aditus, ūs,* or by verb, *intromittĕre*

introspect, v tr, **introspection,** n *ipsum se inspicĕre,* for gen sense, see INSPECT

intrude, v intr = to — on a person or family, *se intrudĕre, se inferre et intrudĕre, se inculcare alcjs auribus* (in order that one may be heard) **intruder,** n by *importunus, molestus* **intrusion,** n *importunitas,* = troublesomeness, or by verb, *se inferre et intrudĕre* **intrusive,** adj *qui se infert et intrudit* Adv *moleste, importune*

intrust, v tr *fidei alcjs alqd committĕre* or *permittĕre, tradĕre alqd in alcjs fidem,* see ENTRUST

intuition, n poetical, philosophical —, *anticipatio, cognitio, perceptio, comprehensio, anticipatio* (καταληψις). **intuitive,** adj = clear, *perspicuus, dilucidus,* = clearly expressed, *expressus* (of images), in philosophy use n (e g — knowledge, *alqd per quandam animi perceptionem cognitum*) Adv *perspicue, dilucide,* (celeri) *quadam animi perceptione*

intumescence, inturgescence, n by verbs, *(in)tumescere, extumescĕre* (in gen), *turgescĕre,* see SWELL, SWELLING

inundation, n better expressed by verb, *inundare,* or by *magnae aquae*

inurbanity, n *inurbanitas, rusticitas*

inure, v tr *assuefacĕre,* see ACCUSTOM

inurn, v tr *in urnam condĕre,* see INTER

inutility, n *inutilitas*

invade, v tr *irruptionem* or *incursionem facĕre in,* etc, *invadĕre* (the enemy, a town, a harbour, etc, *in alqm, in alqd,* also of an evil), *alci* or *in alqm incurrĕre, bellum alci inferre,* of a large body of troops, *in terram infundi* or *influĕre,* to — a country with an army, *terram invadĕre cum copiis,* the enemy's land, *copias in fines hostium introducĕre,* or *inducĕre, impressionem facĕre in fines hostium;* see ATTACK, ASSAIL **invader,** n *hostis* **invasion,** n *irruptio, incursio*

invalid, I. adj in law, = having no effect, *irritus* (= without legal force, opp *ratus,* e g a will), = fruitless, *vanus* (= vain, without effect, of things), comb *irritus et vanus* (e g a will), = unfit, *parum idoneus* (= not suited to the purpose, e g authority, witness, excuse), of arguments, *infirmus, nugatorius, vitiosus,* to make anything —, *alqd irritum facĕre* (e g a will), = to rescind, to annul, *alqd rescindĕre* (e g a will, a compact, a sentence), comb *rescindĕre et irritum facĕre* or *ut irritum et vanum rescindĕre* (of a will) **II.** n *aeger* = ill, to be a confirmed —, *tenui aut potius nullâ valetudine esse,* an — soldier, *causarius* **invalidate,** v tr *alqd irritum facĕre, tollĕre* (= to destroy), *infirmare* (= to weaken), *labefactare* (e g *opinionem*), *rescindĕre, refigĕre* (of laws), see ABROGATE, ABOLISH **invalidish,** adj *ad alqm morbum proclivior* **invalidity,** n use adj INVALID or v. INVALIDATE

invective, n *convicium, contumelia, maledictum, probrum, invectio* (rare), *verba* with adj, e g *acerba* (= bitter), *maligna* (= sharp), *aculeata* (= stinging), *mordacia* (= reproachful), *criminosa* (of a speech) **inveigh,** v intr *in alqm invehi, incurrĕre, incessĕre, alqm jurgio adoriri, contumeliosis verbis* or *verbis vehementioribus prosequi, alqm* or *alqd objurgare,* = to scold, *alqm increpare, castigare*

inveigle, v tr see MISLEAD, SEDUCE

invent, v tr *invenire, reperire,* to — (in the mind), *excogitare,* = to contrive, hatch, *comminisci* (gen something bad) **invention,** n 1, = act of —, *inventio, excogitatio,* or by verb (e g *hamis repertis,* = by the — of hooks), 2, = thing invented, *alqd inventum* or *repertum,* 3, = fiction, *commentum, fabula, mendacium* (= lie) **inventive,** adj *ingeniosus* (= who has always new ideas), *sol(l)ers* (= clever, who knows how to make use of, how to apply new ideas to some purpose), sharp, deep, *acutus* (= who can conceive a thing in its depth), an — person, *ingenium ad excogitandum acutum;* the — faculty, *inventio, excogitatio* **inventor,** n *inventor* (chiefly poet, or late *repertor*), fem *inventrix,* = author, *auctor, architectus* (lit architect), comb *architectus et princeps,* the —s of the art of sculpture, *fingendi conditores* **inventory,** n *repertorium, inventarium* (Jct)

inverse, adj *inversus, conversus* Adv. *retro, permutato ordine* **inversion,** n *conversio* (lit, e g of the bladder, *vesicae,* fig = destruction, *eversio*), — of words, *inversio verborum* **invert,** v tr = to turn into a contrary direction, *(con)vertĕre,* = to turn round, *invertĕre* (e g the ring, *anulum,* hence fig, to change entirely, e g the order of the words, *ordinem verborum*), to — the order of words, † *ultima primis praeponĕre,* = to alter, *commutare* (fig, e g the constitution of the state, *rempublicam*), = to change entirely, *permutare* (e g *omnem reipublicae statum,* = to upset completely, *evertĕre* (fig, e g the state, *rempublicam*), = to turn everything topsy-turvy, *omnia miscēre, summa imis miscēre, omnia sursum deorsum versare*

invest, v tr 1, see CLOTHE, 2, = to — with an office, *magistratum alci dare, mandare, deferre, muneri alqm praeficĕre,* to — anyone with the highest power, *deferre alci summam imperii,* 3, = to lend (e g — with a charm), *alqd alci addĕre, impertire, alqm alqâ re (ex)ornare,* see ADORN, GIVE, 4, of money, *pecuniam collocare, occupare, ponĕre,* with *in alqâ re* or *apud alqm,* 5, = to besiege, *circumsedere, obsidēre, vallo* or *fossâ cingĕre* or *circumdare,* see BESIEGE **investiture,** n = the right of giving possession of any manor, office, or benefice *ritus inaugurationis feudalis* **investment,** n 1, with an office, *inauguratio,* or by verb, see INSTALL, 2, of money, by verb INVEST, 3, = siege, *obsessio*

investigate, v tr *exquirĕre, indagare* (*per*)*scrutari, investigare, quaerĕre, cognoscĕre* (the last two also of judicial investigation), *percontari* (*percunct*), *sciscitari,* to — the true reason of anything, *veram rationem alcjs rei exsequi,* to — the truth, *quid verum sit exquirĕre.* **investigation,** n *investigatio, indagatio, percontatio* (*percunct-*) (= questioning), *inquisitio, quaestio, cognitio,* see INQUIRY **investigator,** n *investigator, indagator, quaesitor* (only in judicial matters), *inquisitor*

inveteracy, n *inveteratio* **inveterate,** adj *inveteratus, confirmatus* (fig, = deeply rooted), *penitus defixus* (of bad habits), *penitus insitus* (of opinions), to become —, *inveterascĕre* Adv *penitus*

invidious, adj 1, = envious, *invidus, invidiosus, lividus, malignus, malevolus,* 2, = exposed to envy, *invidiosus, odiosus* Adv. *maligne, invidiose* **invidiousness,** n 1, *invidia, malevolentia, malignitas,* 2, *invidia, odium,*

invigorate, v tr *corroborare* (e g anyone through constant work, employment, *algm as siduo opere*), = to revive anyone, *(con)firmare* (e g the body through food, *corpus cibo firmare*), to become invigorated, *se corroborare, se confirmare, se recreare*, or *vires reficĕre* (= to recruit one's strength). **invigorating,** adj *aptus ad corpus* (etc) *reficiendum* **invigoration,** n *confirmatio animi*, for — of the body, use verb

invincible, adj *invictus, in(ex)superabilis, inexpugnabilis* (= impregnable, of places); *quod superari non potest* (fig, e g obstacles, *impedimenta*) Adv *quod superari non potest*

inviolability, n *sanctitas* (of God and men, = sanctity), *caerimonia, religio* (= sacredness, of the gods and of everything consecrated to them, e g tombs) **inviolable,** adj *inviolabilis, inviolatus*, = sacred, holy, consecrated, *sanctus, sacrosanctus* Adv *inviolate* **inviolate,** adj *integer* (of a thing remaining in its former state), = without having received any injury, unhurt, *illaesus, inviolatus*, comb *integer atque inviolatus, intactus inviolatusque*, = entire, undamaged, *incorruptus*, = without any accident, safe, *incolumis* (opp *afflictus, vitiosus*), comb *integer incolumisque*, = safe, in safety, *salvus*, comb *salvus atque incolumis*

invisibility, n. by **invisible,** adj *caecus* or *nihil cernendus*, or *quem (quam, quod) cernĕre et vidĕre non possumus, quem (quam, quod) non possumus oculis consequi*, to be —, *sub oculos non cadĕre, non comparēre* (= not to appear, of persons and things), the — world, *caelum, superi*, see HEAVEN Adv. *quod cerni non potest*

invitation, n *invitatio*, at your —, *invitatus* or *vocatus a te, invitatu* or *vocatu tuo* **invite,** v tr 1, (in the usual sense) *invitare algm ad algd* (any invitation, of persons and things), *vocare algm ad algd* (the usual phrase in inviting anyone to dinner through a slave, then in gen of an invitation to take part in anything, e g *ad bellum, ad quietem*, etc), to — oneself to dinner, *condicĕre ad cenam, condicĕre alci* (the latter in gen in the sense, I'll be your guest), 2, = to allure, to — to the pleasures of rural life, *ad fruendum agrum invitare*, see ALLURE. **inviting,** adj *blandus, gratus, amoenus, dulcis* Adv *blande, grate, amoene, dulciter*

invocation, n *imploratio* (= imploring), *testatio* (= calling as a witness)

invoice, n (*mercium*) *libellus* or *index*, -icis, m and f, see ACCOUNT

invoke, v tr *invocare, implorare*, to — the Muses, *invocare Musas*, to — the gods, *implorare* or *invocare Deos, invocare atque obtestari Deos, comprecari Deos* (the latter esp = to pray for help), to — anyone's assistance, *implorare fidem alcis, invocare subsidium alcis, auxilium alcis implorare et flagitare*, to — God as a witness, *Deum testari, Deum invocare testem*

involuntary, adj *invitus et coactus* (= unwilling and forced), *non voluntarius* (= not made to please us, e g death) Adv *invite*, or by adj. or *haud sponte suā* **involuntariness,** n *necessitas*, or by adj (e g the — of my action, *quod coactus feci*).

involution, n *implicatio, involutio* (Vitruv), better by INVOLVE, which see **involve,** v tr 1, = to envelop (e g to — one in smoke), *involvĕre*, see ENVELOP, 2, = to implicate, *algm algā re implicare, illaqueare, illigare*, to be involved in debt, *aere alieno obrutum oppressum*, or *demersum esse*, see IMPLICATE, 3, = to imply, *continēre, habēre*, it is involved in the nature of the case, *rei inest algd, ex algā re sequitur*; see IMPLY, FOLLOW

invulnerable, adj *invulnerabilis* (Sen); to be —, *vulnerari non posse*.

inwall, v tr *saxo consaepire (consep)*

inward, adj = internal, interior, *interior*, see INNER Adv *introrsus* or *introrsum, intus, intrinsecus*, bent —, *incurvus*

inweave, v tr. *intexĕre alci rei* or *in algā re* (lit and fig).

inwrought, adj. by *intextus*, see WEAVE, ENGRAVE

irascible, adj *iracundus, in iram praeceps, stomachosus, irritabilis* Adv *iracunde, irate, stomachose* **irascibility,** n *iracundia, stomachus*, see IRRITATION **ire,** n see ANGER, WRATH **ireful,** adj see ANGRY

iris, n 1, see RAINBOW, 2, = the flag-flower, *iris* (Plin)

irks, v tr impers, it —, *algm alcjs rei piget, taedet*, or with infin, *alci molestum est*, with infin **irksome,** adj = annoying, *gravis, molestus*, = full of labour, tiring, *operosus*, = hateful, *odiosus* Adv *graviter, moleste, aegre* **irksomeness,** n *taedium, molestia*; see DISAGREEABLE

iron, I. n *ferrum*; of —, made of —, *ferreus*, ironed, *ferratus*, to put anyone in —s, *algm in vincula con(j)icĕre* or *mittĕre*, we must strike the — whilst it is hot, *utendum est animis dum spe calent*, Curt, *matura dum libido manet* (Ter.) **II.** adj *ferreus* (both lit. and fig), an — instrument, —ware, *ferramentum*, I must have a heart of —, *ferreus essem*, oh you with your heart of —! *o te ferreum!* **III.** v tr 1, = to smooth with an instrument of —, *ferro cal(e)facto vestes premĕre*, 2, = chain, see IRON, n. above **ironmaster, ironmonger,** n *negotiator ferrarius* **ironmongery,** n *ferramenta, orum*

ironical, adj *algd per ironiam seu dissimulationem dictum*, an — man, *simulator* (e g *in omni oratione simulatorem, quem εἴρωνα Graeci nominarunt, Socratem accepimus* (Cic) Adv *per ironiam* **irony,** n *ironīa* (εἰρωνεία, a word which Cic borrowed from the Greek), *dissimulatio* (= dissimulation)

irradiate, v tr = to illuminate, lit *irradiare* (post-Aug poets), *luce suā collustrare* (of the sun, etc), *illustrare*, see ILLUMINATE

irrational, adj = without reason, *rationis expers, brutus* (esp of animals), *amens, demens, insanus* (= mad), *stolidus, stupidus, stultus, fatuus* (= stupid), *caecus* (= mentally blind) Adv *insane, stolide, stulte* **irrationality,** n by adj or some word = stupidity or madness (e g *stultitia, stupor, stupiditas, socordia, amentia, dementia*)

irreclaimable, adj *quod emendari non potest*

irreconcilable, adj 1, = not to be appeased, *implacabilis, inexorabilis*, 2, of propositions, (*res*) *inter se repugnantes, contrarius*, see INCONSISTENT Adv by adj.

irrecoverable, adj *irreparabilis*, an — loss, *damnum quod nunquam resarciri potest*, *irrevocabilis* Adv by adj

irrefragable, adj *certus, firmus, gravis, ratus, confirmatus*, or (*argumentum*) *quod refelli non potest*, or *quod vim affert in docendo* Adv by adj or *necessario, necessarie* (rare, but found in Cic), *necessarie demonstrari*

irrefutable, adj see IRREFRAGABLE

irregular, adj *enormis* (Tac, of streets etc), *incompositus* (= not well put together), *inusitatus* (= unusual), *inaequalis, inaequabilis* (=

unequal); as gram. t.t., *anŏmalus*; of an election, *vitiosus*; — conduct, *licentia, mores dissoluti* or *pravi*. Adv. *enormiter, incomposite, inusitate, inaequaliter, inaequabiliter*; of conduct, *dissolute, prave*; of an election, *vitio* (e.g. *consules vitio creati*). **irregularity,** n. *enormitas* (Quint.), *inaequalitas*; gram. t.t., *anŏmalia*; — of conduct, *licentia, mores dissoluti* or *pravi, pravitas*; in an election, *vitium*.

irrelevant, adj. *alci rei, (ab) alqâ re alienus*; it is —, *nihil ad rem* or *ad haec*.

irreligion, n. *impietas erga Deum* or *Deos*; = want of devotion, *Dei* or *Deorum neglegentia* (*neglig-*). **irreligious,** adj. *impius erga Deum* or *Deos, contemptor religionis*. Adv. *impie*.

irremediable, adj. see INCURABLE.

irremovable, adj. *immobilis*; see IMMOVABLE; = that cannot be changed, *immutabilis* (e.g. the tracks of the stars, *spatia*); *certus, ratus*.

irreparable, adj. see IRREVOCABLE.

irreprehensible, adj. *non reprehendendus, non vituperandus* (= blameless); = as it ought to be, *probus* (e.g. goods, an article; hence also of persons); = virtuous, good, *integer, sanctus*. Adv. *sancte, probe, integre*.

irreproachable, adj. see IRREPREHENSIBLE.

irresistible, adj. *cui nullâ vi resisti potest, invictus, in(ex)superabilis*. Adv. *necessario* or *necessarie* (rare), or *ita ut nullo modo resisti possit*.

irresolute, adj. *dubius* (= doubtful); = uncertain, *incertus*; = changeable, *mutabilis, mobilis, varius, parum stabilis, firmus* or *constans, inconstans, haesitans, cunctans*; to be —, *magnâ consilii inopiâ affectum esse*. Adv. *dubitanter, inconstanter*. **irresolution,** n. *dubitatio, haesitantia, cunctatio* (*cont-*).

irrespective, adj. by Adv. *nullâ ratione* (*alcjs rei*) *habitâ*.

irresponsible, adj. *cui nulla ratio reddenda est*. **irresponsibility,** n. use adj.

irretrievable, adj. see IRRECOVERABLE.

irreverence, n. *impietas erga Deum* or *Deos, nulla rerum divinarum reverentia*. **irreverent,** adj. *inverecundus, parum verecundus* (= immodest), *impius erga Deum* or *Deos*. Adv. *impie*; to behave — towards anyone, *reverentiam alci non praestare*.

irrevocable, adj. *irrevocabilis, irreparabilis, immutabilis*; an — loss, *damnum quod nullo modo resarciri potest*. Adv. *in perpetuum*.

irrigate, v.tr. *irrigare*. **irrigation,** n. *irrigatio, inductio aquarum*. **irriguous,** adj. + *irriguus*, or by *rigare, irrigare*.

irritable, adj. *irritabilis, stomachosus, iracundus*. Adv. *stomachose, iracunde*. **irritate,** v.tr. 1, e.g. to — a wound, *inflammare* (Plin.); 2, in a fig. sense, *alqm irritare, alcjs iram concitare* or *irritare*. **irritation,** n. *ira, stomachus*; see ANGER.

irruption, n. 1, e.g. of the sea, by *irrumpĕre*; e.g. of the enemy, *irruptio, incursio*. **irruptive,** adj. by *irrumpĕre*.

isinglass, n. *ichthyocolla* (Plin.).

island, n. *insula* (also = the inhabitants of the —, e.g. *insulas bello persequi*, Nep.). **islander,** n. *insulanus* (Cic.), *insulae incŏla*; the —s, *ii qui insulam*, or *insulas, incolunt*. **isle,** n. see ISLAND. **islet,** n. *parva insula*.

isolate, v.tr. *secernĕre, sejungĕre, separare* (= separate). **isolated,** adj. *remotus* (= distant), *solus* (= alone). **isolation,** n. *solitudo*.

isosceles, n. **isosceles*.

issue, I. n. 1, = the act of flowing (e.g. — of blood), by verb; 2, = a sending out (e.g. the — of an order, money), by verb; 3, = the result of a thing, *exitus, -ūs, eventus, -ūs*; a good —, *successus, -ūs*; to know the —, *scire quos eventus res sit habitura*; the point at —, *res de quâ agitur*; see END, CONCLUSION, DECISION; 4, = offspring, *filius, filia* (= son, daughter); *progenies, stirps* (the latter lit. stem, in the sing. = children, — in gen.); one of the later —, *unus e posteris* (= one of those who were later born, down from the great-grandson, opp. *unus e majoribus*); = the descendants, *progenies* or *progenies liberorum, stirps* or *stirps liberorum* (as regards the coming generation); = the whole posterity, in a wide sense, *posteritas*; + *suboles*; male —, *stirps virilis, virilis sexûs stirps*; to leave —, *stirpem relinquĕre*. II. v.intr. 1, = to flow out, *effluĕre, emanare*; 2, = to go out, *egredi, evadĕre*; = to rush out (e.g. troops), *erumpĕre* (expressing wherefrom, of buds, leaves, etc., also of soldiers that make a sally, e.g. from the camp, *ex castris*); *prorumpĕre, prorumpi* (= to rush, expressing the direction whereto, e.g. a fountain, fire, also of soldiers); = to make a sally, *eruptionem facĕre*; = to rush forth, *procurrĕre* (of troops rushing forth from their position to attack the enemy); = to march out hastily, *provolare, evolare* (from, *ex*, etc.; with all troops, with the whole force, *omnibus copiis*); = to emerge, *emergĕre* (from, *ex*, etc.; lit. to dive forth, from under); to — suddenly from the ambush, *ex insidiis subito consurgĕre*; 3, = to proceed (as income), by *fructum reddĕre*; 4, = to end, *finire, terminari* (= to come to an end); = to cease, *desinĕre*. III. v.tr. 1, = to send out (e.g. money), *promĕre* (e.g. money from the treasury); to — a new coinage, *distribuĕre*; 2, = to send out, deliver from authority (e.g. to — an order, a book), *edĕre, proponĕre* (by placards), *pronuntiare* (by heralds, public criers); to be issued, *exire, emanare*; to — an order, *edicĕre, edictum proponĕre*; to — too severe orders, *nimis severe statuĕre*; to — a decree, *rescribĕre* (of the sovereign); to — a written order to anybody, *lit(t)eras dare* or *mittĕre ad alqm*; 3, = to deliver for use, to — voting papers, voting tablets, *diribĕre tabellas*; one who does this, *diribitor*; to — provisions, *dispensare* (of the *dispensator*, = the manager of the house).

isthmus, n. *isthmus* (*isthmos*).

it, pers. pron. 1, as a demons. pron. by *hic, haec, hoc*, or *is, ea, id*; 2, before a verb, not rendered at all; if used emphatically, by *ille, illa, illud*, or, pointing to a third party, *iste, ista, istud*, or if = self, itself, by *ipse, ipsa, ipsum*, or by *res, ipsa res*.

Italian, adj. *Italicus*, + *Italus*. **italics,** n. *lit(t)erae tenuiores et paullum inclinatae*.

itch, I. n. 1, as a disease, *scabies*; to suffer from the —, *scabie laborare*; 2, = sensation caused from that disease, *scabies* (rare), *prurigo, pruritus, -ūs* (Plin.), *formicatio* (μυρμηκία, = an —like the crawling of ants, Plin.). II. v.intr. lit. *prurire* (in gen.), *formicare* (Plin., as if ants were running about on the part of the body which itches), *verminare* (Mart., as if the part which itches was full of vermin).

item, I. adv. = also; (used when something is to be added) see FURTHER. II. n. in an account, —s of expenditure, *rationes sumptuariae*; in a gen. sense, = article, *pars, caput* (e.g. of a law, a treaty); an — in a contract, agreement, *condicio, caput*; or often *res* would be sufficient; or by adj. *singuli* (e.g. the —s of expenditure, *pecuniae singulae*).

iterate, v.tr *iterare.* **iteration,** n use verb

itinerant, n and adj *viator, circumforaneus.* **itinerary,** n *itineris descriptio*

ivory, I. n *ebur* **II.** adj *eburneus, † eburnus, eboreus*

ivy, n *hedera,* — mantled (of towers, etc), *hederā obsitus.*

J.

jabber, v intr *blaterare, garrire, strepěre, crepare,* see PRATTLE **jabberer,** n *qui blaterat* **jabbering,** n *clamor, strepitus, -ūs*

jack, n 1, as term of contempt, — of all trades, *qui se ad omnia aptum esse putat,* 2, = boot—, *instrumentum ad caligas detrahendas aptum,* kitchen —, *machina quā utimur ad carnem circumagendam* **jackanapes,** n *homo stolidus* **jackass,** n *asinus* (lit. and fig) **jackdaw,** n *monedula,* perhaps *graculus*

jacket, n *vestis* or *vestimentum*

jade, n 1, = a poor horse, *caballus,* 2, of a woman, *mulier importuna, puella proterva* **jaded,** adj *fatigatus, (de)fessus,* see WEARY

jag, v tr = to cut into notches like those of a saw, *incīdere* (= to make incisions), see INDENT **jagged, jaggy,** adj *serratus* (Plin, with teeth like those of a saw), — rocks, *saxa praerupta,* see RUGGED

jail, n *furcifer,* see GAOL, PRISON

jam, I n *fructus conditi.* **II.** v tr *comprimĕre*

jamb, n (in architecture) *postis,* m

jangle, v see QUARREL

janitor, n *janitor, ostiarius,* fem *janitrix*

January, n *Januarius* (*mensis*)

jar, I. v intr. 1, = to strike discordantly, or if the jarring sound is repeated, *stridēre* (or *stridĕre,* = to whiz), *absonum esse dissonare, discrepare;* 2, = to disagree with, *discrepare, dissonum esse,* see DISAGREE **II.** n = quarrel, *rixa, jurgium,* see QUARREL **jarring,** adj *dissonus, discors,* see DISCORDANT

jar, n = a vessel, *olla* (orig *aula*), *cadus* (esp for wine), *dolium* (= cask), *seria* (= large —), *urceus* (in gen), *urna* (lit, = a jug for water, then an urn for the ashes of dead bodies, a lottery-box, a money-box, etc), *hydria* (ὑδρία), *situlus* and *situla* (= a water-pot, also used as a lottery-box, in this sense usu *sitella*), *amphora* (ἀμφορεύς = a large vessel, usually with two ears or handles, esp used for wine)

jargon, n *strepitus, -ūs,* or *sermo barbarus, ut ita dicam*

jasper, I. n *iaspis* **II.** adj *iaspideus* (Plin)

jaundice, n *morbus regius* or *arquatus* (Cels) **jaundiced,** adj fig *lividus, invidus*

jaunt, n *iter, excursio* (Plin Min), to take a —, *excurrere* (Plin Min)

javelin, n *pilum, jaculum,* see DART

jaw, n 1, *maxilla* (Cels); jaws, *fauces,* ... (= the larynx), to tear out of the —s, *eripere e faucibus* (lit and fig) **jaw-bone,** n *maxilla*

jealous, adj *aemulus* (= rival), = envious, *invidus, lividus,* to be — of anyone, *aemulari alci* or *cum alqo, invidēre alci* Adv use adj **jealousy,** n in gen *aemulatio* (Cic , Tusc), *zelotypia* (Plin , by Cic written in Greek, ζηλοτυπία = — in love)

jeer, I. v tr and intr *in ludibrium vertĕre* (Tac), the people — at anything, *alqd in ora omnium pro ludibrio abiit* (Liv), = to deride anything or anyone, *ludibrio sibi habēre, ludificare, deridēre,* = to mock, *irridēre,* all with *alqm, illudĕre alci,* or *in alqm,* = to cavil, *alqm cavillari* **II.** n *ludificatio, cavillatio, irrisio, irrisus, -ūs, ludibrium* **jeerer,** n *irrisor, derisor, cavillator* **jeering,** adj by adv *cum irrisione*

jejune, adj *jejunus, aridus, exilis, siccus, exsanguis* Adv *jejune, exiliter, jejune et exiliter* **jejuneness,** n *jejunitas, siccitas,* comb *jejunitas et siccitas et inopia*

jeopardize, v tr *alqd in aleam dare, alqd in discrimen committere* or *vocare* or *adducĕre, alqd discrimini committĕre, alqd ad ultimum discrimen adducere* **jeopardy,** n see DANGER, ADVENTURE

jerk, I. v tr *offendĕre alqm alqa re* (e g *capite, cubito, pede aut genu*), see HIT, BEAT **II.** n 1, *impetus, ūs,* see HIT, 2, see LEAP

jerkin, n 1, see JACKET, a buff —, *lorica,* 2, *vestis*

jest, I. v intr *jocari, joco uti, joca agĕre cum alqo, joculari, cavillari* **II.** n *jocus,* in the plur *joca* in Cic and Sall, *joci* in Liv, = a joke, amusement, *ludus,* comb *ludus et jocus,* = fun, wit, *facetiae,* in —, *per jocum, per ludum et jocum,* for —, *per ridiculum, joco, joculariter,* do you mean that in earnest or in —? *jocone an serio hoc dicis?* without —, no —, *amoto* or *remoto joco, omissis jocis, extra jocum,* to put a — upon anyone, *alqm ludĕre, ludificari* **jester,** n *qui jocatur,* = buffoon, *scurra, sannio, balatro*

jet, n = the mineral, *gagates, ae,* m (Plin), —-black, *nigerrimus*

jet, n of water, *aqua saliens* or *exsiliens* (or in pl)

jetsam, n *res naufragio ejectae*

jetty, n *moles, -is*

Jew, n *Judaeus* **Judaism,** n *Judaismus, religio Judaica, doctrina Judaica* **Jewish,** adj *Judaicus, Judaeus* **Jewry,** n *vicus Judaeus, regio Judaica*

jewel, n *gemma,* see GEM **jewelled,** adj *gemmeus, gemmatus* **jeweller,** n *qui gemmas vendit* or *sculpit*

jig, n and v tr see DANCE

jilt, v tr *repudiare*

jingle, I. v intr (as in jingling chains or bells), *tinnire* (= to ring) **II.** n or **jingling,** n *tinnitus, -ūs*

job, n 1, = work, *opus, -ĕris,* n, 2, = a small lucrative business or office, *munus exiguum* or *parvum,* see WORK, PERFORMANCE, 3, = work carried on unfairly, *fraus, -dis,* f **jobber,** n, 1, = one who does small jobs, *operarius* (= one who assists, servant, labourer), 2 (= a stock jobber), *argentarius,* see BROKER, 3, = one who does anything unfairly, *fraudator, circumscriptor*

jockey, I. n *agaso* (= groom) **II** v tr (= to cheat), *circumvenire* (= to surround, fig to take in), see CHEAT

jocose, jocular, adj *jocosus, jocularis, jocularius, ridiculus* (of persons and things), = laughable *ridendus* (of things), *facetus, salsus, festivus, hilaris* (*hilarus* = gay), *ludicer, lascivus* (= sportive) Adv *jocose, joculariter, festive, lascive, hilariter, hilare, facete salse,* see GAY,

MERRY. **jocoseness, jocularity, jocundity,** n. *facetiae, hilarus animus et ad jocandum promptus, hilaritas, laetitia, alacritas, lascivia.*

jog, I. v.tr. = to push off, *propellĕre* (e.g. *alqm*, or the vessel with the oar, *navem remis*); *impellĕre*; see PUSH. **II.** v.intr. (= to move by jogs) *promovēri, lente progredi.* **III.** n. **1**, = a push intended to awaken attention, in general, *offensio*; (= the impression from without) *(im)pulsus, -ūs*; a violent —, *impetus, -ūs*; see PUSH.

join, I. v.tr. lit. = to bring one thing in contiguity with another, *(con)jungĕre* (in general); *nectĕre, con(n)ectĕre* (= to connect, lit. and fig.); = to unite things so that they belong together, *comparare* (all *cum alqâ re* or *alci rei*); = to glue together, cement, fig. = to unite closely together, *conglutinare* (e.g. *verba*); = to tie, fasten together, *colligare, copulare*, comb. *jungĕre et copulare, continuare* (lit. and fig.); — without a break, *adjungĕre, ad[illegible]* or *alci rei*; — battle, *proelium* or *pugnam committĕre.* **II.** v.intr. **1**, = to be connected with, *committi, continuari, (con)jungi, adjungi*; **2**, = in partnership, etc., *se (con)jungĕre*, or *societatem inire* or *coire, cum alqo*; **3**, = to meet, *se alci addĕre, alci occurrĕre, alcjs rei participem esse.* **joiner,** n. *faber.* **joint, I.** n. (in anatomy = the joining of two or more bones), *commissura* (in general, also in the human body); *artus, -ūs, articulus*, comb. *commissurae et artus*; — of a plant, *nodus*; in particular the joints of the spine, *vertebrae*, so too *nodus*, and comb. *nodi articulique*; a — of a chain, *annulus*; (in architecture and joinery) = a binding or tying together (in architecture), *colligatio, verticula* (to cause motion); in joinery, *coagmentum, coagmentatio, compages, -is, compactura, junctura* (= the joining in general). **II.** adj. (as in — property), *communis*; see COMMON. Adv. *conjuncte, conjunctim, una, communiter.* **joint-heir,** n. *coheres, -ēdis*, m. and f. **joint-stock company,** n. *societas.* **jointure,** n. *annua* (*quae viduae praebentur*).

joist, n. *tignum transversum* or *transversarium.*

joke, see JEST.

jolly, adj. *hilaris* (*hilarus*), *lascivus*; see MERRY. **jollity,** n. *hilaritas, lascivia.*

jolt, I. v.tr. *jactare, concutĕre, quassare*; see SHAKE. **II.** v.intr. *jactari, concuti, quassari*; to — against (e.g. the carriage —s), by *offendĕre alqm, alqd* (= to run accidentally against one, of persons and things; hence to fall in with, meet); *incurrĕre in alqm* or *in alqd* (= to run violently against anyone or anything, of persons and things; hence to fall in with anyone); *illidi alci rei* or *in alqd, allidi ad alqd* (= to be knocked, to dash upon anyone or against anything so as to be hurt, of persons and things, e.g. against the wall, *parieti illidi*; against the rocks, *ad scopulos allidi*); see SHAKE. **III.** n. *jactatio, quassatio*, or by verb.

jostle, v.intr. *alqm offendĕre*; see JOLT, II.

jot, I. n. not a —, *nihil, ne minimâ quidem re, ne transversum unguem* or *digitum*; not to care a —, *alqd non flocci*, or *nihili* or *nauci facĕre.* **II.** v.tr. to — down, *annotare* or *scribĕre.*

journal, n. **1**, = diary, *ephemĕris, -idis*, f. (ἐφημερίς); **2**, in commerce, *rationes* (= accounts), *codex accepti et expensi*, or, in the connexion of the sentence, simply *codex* or *tabulae* (= a cash-book for putting down income and expenditure); = the waste-book, *adversaria, -orum*; **3**, = newspaper, *acta* (*diurna*), *-orum.* **journalist,** n. *diurnorum scriptor.*

journey, I. n. *iter, itineris*, n. (to a place); *via* (= the way, road); = the departure, *profectio* (never in the sense of the — itself); = the act of travelling and the stay in foreign countries, *peregrinatio*; = a voyage, *navigatio*; to be on a —, *in itinere esse*; to make, undertake a —, *iter facĕre*; into foreign countries, *peregrinationes suscipĕre*; to get ready for the —, *omnia quae ad proficiscendum pertinent comparare*; *profectionem* or *iter parare*; a march, *iter* (= in gen.); a day's —, march (of troops), *diei* or *unius diei iter*; — or march, *prima, secunda, tertia, quarta, quinta castra, -orum*; — by sea, *cursus, -ūs, navigatio*; in speaking in the ordinary sense of a — or voyage of so many days, the number of days is added in the genitive case, e.g. one day's —, *diei iter* or *cursus, -ūs*, or *navigatio*; of two days, *bidui iter* or *cursus* or *navigatio*; of nine days, *novem dierum iter, cursus, navigatio*; to be distant one day's —, *diei itinere* or *cursu* or *navigatione abesse*; two days' —, *bidui spatio* or simply *bidui abesse*; the forest extends in breadth a nine days' —, *latitudo silvae patet novem dierum iter*; the distance was about a ten days' —, *via dierum fere erat decem.* **II.** v.intr. *iter facĕre, conficĕre, progredi* (= to set out), *peregrinari* (= to — abroad); see TRAVEL, MARCH.

journeyman, n. in a trade, *opifex, -icis*, m. and f. (= artisan); *opera* (usually in pl.), *mercenarius, operarius.*

Jove, n. *Jupiter*, gen. *Jovis* (as god and planet); by — ! *mehercle!*

jovial, adj. *hilaris, lascivus*; see MERRY. Adv. *hilariter, lascive.* **joviality,** n. *hilaritas, lascivia*; see MIRTH.

joy, I. n. *gaudium* (= the state of the mind, i.e. *cum ratione animus movetur placide atque constanter, tum illud gaudium dicitur*, Cic.), *laetitia*, (when we show it outwardly, *laetitiâ gestiens*, Cic.); the sensation of —, = pleasure, *voluptas*; comb. *laetitia ac voluptas*, = delight, *delectatio*, *deliciae* (= the object of —; poets use also *gaudium* and *voluptas* in this sense); to gratify anyone, *gratificari alci* (by a present, etc.); you have given me great pleasure, caused me great —, by, etc., *magnum mihi gaudium attulisti, quod*, etc.; it gives me great pleasure, *alqd mihi gaudio, laetitiae*, or *voluptati est*; *delector alqâ re, alqd mihi in deliciis est*; anything gives me great pleasure, *magnâ laetitia, magno gaudio me afficit alqd*; *alqd summae mihi voluptati est*; *magnum gaudium, magnam laetitiam voluptatemque capio* (*percipio*) *ex alqâ re*; *alqd cumulum gaudii mihi affert* (used when we wish to express a still higher degree of —, caused by something additional); to express one's — in words, *gaudium verbis prodĕre*; to jump with — (in succeeding, in hearing joyous news), *laetitiâ se efferre, gaudio exsilire, ex(s)ultare*; to be delighted with —, *laetum esse omnibus laetitiis* (a phrase which Cic. borrowed from a comedy of Caecilius and uses very often); on his arrival they all received him with expressions of —, *eum advenientem laeti omnes accepēre.* **II.** v.intr. *gaudēre, gaudio affici, gestire, ex(s)ultare, laetificari* (= to show signs of —); see REJOICE. **joyous, joyful,** adj. **1**, = glad, *laetus, hilaris* or *hilarus* (= in a merry humour); *libens* (*lub-*) (= with pleasure); **2**, = giving joy, *laetus, laetabilis*; *gratus* (as regards anything for which we ought to be thankful); = pleasing, *jucundus, dulcis*; = welcome, *exoptatus.* Adv. *laete, hilariter, hilare, libenter* (*lub-*), *jucunde.* **joyless,** adj. *maestus*; see SAD. **joyousness, joyfulness,** n. see JOY.

jubilant, adj. = rejoicing, by *laetitiâ* or *gaudio ex(s)ultare, laetitiâ* or *alacritate gestiens*; *ex(s)ultans et gestiens*; see EXULT. **jubilee,** n. = a season of great public joy and festivity, *festi dies laetissimi*; the — year, *annus qui est quinquagesimus* or *centesimus post rem gestam.*

judge, I. n. 1, *judex, -icis*, m (for the exact meaning of the term *judex* see Smith, "Dict of Antiquities," art JUDEX), *assessor*, in Cic often *qui judicat* or *qui judicium exercet* or *qui est judicaturus* (when he is about to —), = arbitrator, *arbiter*, = delegate, *recuperator*; — of the circuit, *quaesitor* (lit of criminal offences), = a mediator, umpire, *disceptator* (fem *disceptatrix*), to bring anything before the —, *alqd ad judicem deferre*, verdict, sentence of the —, court, *judicis sententia, judicium*, a decree of a —, *edictum*, an injunction, *interdictum*, to appeal to the —, *ad judicem confugĕre*; belonging to the office of a —, *judicialis*; 2, in gen *judex, aestimator, existimator*, comb *existimator et judex, censor* (*censor castigatorque*), see CRITIC. **II.** v intr *judicare*, about anything, *alqd*, about anyone, *de algo* (also in a judicial sense), *facĕre judicium*, about anything, *alcjs rei* or *de alqâ re*, about anyone, *de alqo*, = to think, *existimare* (= to have an opinion), about anything, *alqd* or *de alqâ re*, about anybody, *de alqo*, = to think well, have a good or bad opinion of anyone, *bene* or *male existimare de alqo*, = to give a formal judgment, a decision, esp in the Senate, *censēre*. **III.** v tr (= to hear and determine a case), *judicare de alqo, judicium edĕre in alqm*, to — between, *dijudicare* (e g *vera et falsa*, or *vera a falsis*). **judgment,** n = the process of examining facts in court *judicium*, to administer justice, give —, *jus dicĕre, agere*, as a faculty of the mind, *judicium, sapientia, prudentia*, to show —, *judicium habēre*, see UNDERSTANDING, WISDOM = determination, *arbitrium, decretum* (= decree), *sententia* (= opinion), the opinion which anyone forms after having first inquired into the value of anything, estimation, *existimatio*, the public opinion, *existimatio vulgi* (Caes), to give one's —, *sententiam dicĕre* (of the author, senator, judge), in my —, *meo judicio, quantum ego judico*, (*ex* or *de*) *meâ sententiâ, ut mihi quidem videtur*, —-seat, *tribunal, judicium*, to bring anything before the —, *alqd* (e g *alcjs factum*) *in judicium vocare* (Cic), see also OPINION. **judicature,** n *jurisdictio, jurisdictionis potestas*, to be subject to anyone's —, *sub alcjs jus et jurisdictionem subjunctum esse*, it comes under my —, *jurisdictio mea est, hoc meum est, hujus rei potestas penes me est*. **judicial,** adj 1, *judicialis*, = belonging to the judge, *judicarius*, = what belongs to the forum, *forensis* (e g *contentiones*), a — opinion, *sententia*, a — decree, *edictum*, injunction, *interdictum* (of anything prohibited by the praetor, until the cause was tried), to demand a — inquiry against anyone, *judicium postulare in alqm, judices petĕre in alqm*, 2, fig (e g a — habit of mind), *aequus*, see IMPARTIAL, 3, sent by Heaven (e g — blindness), *a Deo* or *divinitus missa* (*caecitas*, etc). Adv *jure, lege* (e g to proceed — against anyone, *lege agĕre cum alqo, jure* or *lege experiri cum alqo*). **judiciary,** adj *judicarius*. **judicious,** adj *sagax, maximis consiliis, sapiens, prudens* (= sagacious). Adv *sagaciter, sapienter, prudenter, aequo animo*. **judiciousness,** n *sagacitas, prudentia, sapientia, aequanimitas* (i e without bias), *consilium*.

jug, n *urceus, urceolus* (= little —), *hirnea, hirnula* (= little —), *amphora* (large, with two handles, esp for wine), see JAR.

juggle, I. v intr. 1, in the lit sense, *praestigias agĕre*, 2, see DECEIVE. **II.** n 1, = trick by legerdemain, *praestigiae*, 2 deception, *deceptio* (the act), *error* (= mistake); = fallacy, treachery, *fallacia*, = simulation, *simulatio, dissimulatio* (the former = pretending what one is not, the latter = pretending not to be what one really is). **jugglery, juggling,** n = artifice, *ars, artificium dolus*. **juggler,** n 1, lit *praestigiator* (in gen), f *praestigiatrix, circulator* or *planus* (= a conjuror who travels about, the former exhibiting snakes), 2, see DECEIVER.

jugular, adj — vein, *vena jugularis*.

juice, n *sucus* (also fig = energy, e g in speech), = poison, *virus*, n, the — of the grape, *suci uvae* (in gen), *melligo uvae* (when still unripe). **juicy,** adj. *suci plenus, sucosus* (= full of juice), *sucidus* (= with juice in).

jujube, n. 1, *zizyphus* (= the tree), *zizyphum* (= the fruit), 2, = a medicine which melts in the mouth, *ecligma* (all three Plin).

July, n *Julius* (*mensis*), in the times of the Republic, *Quinctilis* (*mensis*).

jumble, I. v tr (*per*)*miscēre*, to make a regular —, *omnia miscēre, omnia miscēre et turbare*, see CONFOUND. **II.** v intr (*per*)*misceri*. **III.** n *mistura* (lit and fig, e g of virtues and vices, *mistura vitiorum et virtutum*, Suet), = mixture of different kinds of corn, *farrago* (also of the contents of a book, *nostri libelli*, Juv), — of words, *sartago*, = conflux of different things *colluvies, colluvio* (e g *exercitus mixtus ex colluvione omnium gentium, colluvies illa nationum*), *varietas* (e g *sermonum opinionumque*) generally by *miscēre* (e g *bona mixta malis*).

jump, I. v intr lit *salire*, = to exercise oneself in jumping, *saliendo se exercēre*, to — up, *exsilire*, with joy, *ex(s)ultare gaudio, exsilire*, to — upon or into, *insilire in alqd*, to — from a wearied horse upon a fresh one, *ex fesso in recentem equum transultare*, to — over anything, *transilire alqd*, to — down from, *desilire ex*, etc (from the horse, *ex equo*). **II.** n = leap, *saltus, -ūs*. **jumper,** n *qui salit*.

junction, n *conjunctio, junctio*. **juncture,** n *status, -ūs*; — of affairs, *tempora, -um*, happy —, *temporum felicitas*.

June, n (*mensis*) *Junius*.

jungle, n *silva*.

junior, adj and n *junior* or *minor aetate*, the —, (*natu*) *minor*.

juniper, n *juniperus*, f.

junk, n 1, = pieces of old cable, by *funis, -is*, m, see CABLE, ROPE, 2, = Chinese vessel, *navis serica*.

junket, n *placenta* (= cake), *cup(p)edia, -orum*, or *cup(p)ediae* (ante and post class = dainties). **junketting,** n *iter, -ineris, voluptatis causâ susceptum*.

juridical, adj see JUDICIAL. **jurisconsult,** n *juris peritus, juris* or *jure consultus* (both also written as one word), *juris sciens, in jure prudens*. **jurisdiction,** n see JUDICATURE. **jurisprudence,** n. *juris civilis prudentia*, anyone's knowledge in —, *juris civilis scientia*. **jurist,** n see JURISCONSULT. **juror,** n as judge, *judex* (*selectus*) (selected in Rome from the senators, knights, i e *equites*, and the *tribuni aerarii*). **jury,** n *judices, -um*, or *consilium* (e g *judicum*).

just, I. adj = upright, *justus* (e g judge, complaint, fears, punishment, etc), *aequus* (= equitable, reasonable, of persons), *legitimus* (= lawful, of things), to have — claims upon a thing, *alqd jure suo* (or *recte*) *postulare*, *meritus* (= deserved). **II.** adv 1, = exactly, *diligenter* (e g I can't — tell, *hanc rem non ita diligenter teneo*); 2, in reference to a particular moment, *commodum, commode*, (colloquial) — now, *tantum quod* (*tantum quod cum* (*quum*), — when), — now, this moment, for the present, *in praesentia*, only — lately, *modo, proxime* (e g the piece which he had written — lately, *fabula quam proxime scripserat*) also by the adj *recens* (with *ab* or *ex* and ablat., or simply by the local ablat.); to have only — arrived from the province, the country, *e provinciâ recentem esse*; the people that had only — come from Rome, *homines Româ recentes*; = accidentally, *forte, forte fortunâ* (e.g. the king was — here, *rex forte aderat*); **3**, in comparison, — as, *aeque, perinde, pariter, similiter, item* (or *idem, eadem, idem*, in reference to subject and object), *itidem, juxta, eodem* or *pari modo* (= — in the same manner); to speak — in the same manner, *in eandem sententiam disputare*; to love anyone — as much, *aeque amare alqm*; to be — as old and as popular, *pari esse aetate et gratiâ*; — as well . . . as, *aeque . . . ac* (*atque, et, ut*), *perinde . . . ac* (*atque, ut, quasi*); *proinde . . . ac* (*quasi*), *similiter . . . ac* (*atque, et, ut*), *item . . . ut* (*uti, quemadmodum, quasi*), *itidem . . . et* (*quasi*), *juxta . . . ac* (*atque, quasi, cum* [with the ablat. of the persons to whom we compare anyone]); *non secus . . . ac*; *ut . . . ita, non minus . . . quam* (the latter if there is no negation connected with it), *talis . . . qualis*, is with *qui* following (if — as . . . as, = — the same . . . as, — such a one . . . as); — as if, *aeque* (*pariter, perinde*), *ac si*; *similiter, ut si* or *ac si*; *juxta ac si*; — as well . . . as, *tam . . . quam, item . . . ut*; — as well . . . as anyone else, *tam . . . quam qui maxime*, also *ita, ut cum maxime*; not . . . — as little, *non . . . non magis, non . . . nihilo plus* (or *non plus*), — as little . . . as, *non magis . . . quam* (= no more . . . than); *non plus . . . quam*; *nec . . . nec*, or *neque . . . neque* (*nec inferendo injuriam, nec patiendo*); — as much . . . as, *non magis . . . quam* (i.e. no less . . . than), *non nimis . . . quam*; — as great, large, *tantusdem, idem* (e.g. *eadem impudentia*); — as much, *tantidem, tantundem* (. . . as, *quantum*, as regards the quality), *totidem* (. . . as, *atque, ac*, or the correlative *quot*, as regards the quantity); — as many vessels, *totidem naves, par navium numerus*; — as far, *pari spatio*; — that one, the same, *idem, hic idem, hic is, idem hic, idem ille, idem iste* (if the subject has already been mentioned before, = likewise the same); by *solus* (e.g. *capiti solo ex aquâ exstant*, only — their heads out from the water); **4**, to express emphasis, *imprimis*, or as two words (*in primis*), *potissimum, maxime, praesertim, praecipue*; = certainly, *quidem* (enclit.); = indeed, *utique, sane*; — now, *modo, jam cum maxime*; — now, of what has long been desired, *vixdum, vix tandem*; — at that time, *tum cum maxime, eo maxime tempore*; — then, then —, *tum maxime*; not —, not exactly, *haud ita, non ita* (e.g. *sunt eo* [*simulacra*] *praeclara, sed non ita antiqua*), also simply *haud*, or *non, parum* (= not so very); = not exactly, but, etc., *immo vero*; — that which, *id quod*; exactly, *quidem*; but that is — exactly what is considered wicked, *at id quidem nefas habetur*; with the superlative by *quisque*, — exactly the best, *optimus quisque*; but —, *nunc denique*; in answers, — so, *inquam, ita plane* or *prorsus*; sometimes expressed by *sub* with accus. (e.g. *sub lucem*, — before daybreak). Adv. *juste, jure, legitime, merito*. **justice**, n. *justitia* (= the virtue itself, and the love of —); = equity, equitability, *aequitas* (especially as a quality inherent in a person or thing); = right, law, *jus* (= that which is considered right); — requires that, etc., *aequum est* (with accus. and infin.); to exercise —, *justitiam exercēre* or *colĕre*; to see — done to anyone, *alci jus dare* or *reddĕre* (in court); *ea quae alci debentur tribuĕre* (in gen., in daily life, to give anyone what is due to him); in —, *jure*. **justiciary**, n. perhaps *praetor urbanus*; see JUDGE. **justifiable**, adj. *justus*; = lawful, *legitimus*, comb. *justus et legitimus*: see LAWFUL; in more gen. sense, *alqd recte ac jure factum*: see EXCUSABLE. Adv. *recte ac jure*. **justification**, n. **1**, *purgatio, excusatio, satisfactio*; to accept anyone's —, *excusationem* or *satisfactionem accipĕre*; for his or her —, *sui purgandi caus(s)â*; **2**, Theol. t.t. **justificatio*. **justify**, v.tr. **1**, in the ordinary sense, *alqm* or *alqd purgare* (= to prove one's innocence); = to excuse, *alqm* or *alqd excusare* (e.g. that anything was not done on purpose, that anything was neglected through other engagements, or through an oversight, or through ignorance, etc.); = to free from guilt, *alqm culpâ liberare*; to — anyone on account of, *alqm purgare de alqâ re* (seldom *alcjs rei*), *culpam alcjs rei demovēre ab alqo*; to — oneself, *se purgare, se excusare*; to — oneself before anyone, *se purgare alci*; sufficiently, *satisfacĕre alci*; to — one's conduct before anyone, *facti sui rationem alci probare*; **2**, Theol. t.t. **justificare*.

jut, v.intr. — out, *exstare, eminēre, prominēre*; of peninsulas and other portions of land, *excurrĕre*.

juvenile, adj. *puerilis*, or by the genit. *pueri* or *puerorum, adolescentis* or *adolescentium, juvenilis*. **juvenility**, n. see YOUTH.

juxtaposition, n. by verbs (e.g. *quod una positum est*).

K.

kale, n. *crambe, -es*, f.

kalendar, n. *fasti, ephemeris, -idis*, f.

keel, n. *carina* (in poetry = the whole ship).

keen, adj. = sharp (lit. and fig.) *acer, acerbus* (= poignant); = acute, *acutus, astutus* (often in bad sense), *subtilis, perspicax, sagax, argutus* (= sagacious or witty). Adv. *acriter, acerbe, acute, astute, subtiliter, sagaciter, argute*; to feel a sorrow —, *summo dolore affici*. **keenness**, n. *acerbitas* (in such phrases as the — of winter, better use adj.), *astutia, subtilitas, sagacitas, perspicacitas*; — of wit, *argutiae*.

keep, **I.** v.tr. *servare, custodire, tenēre, continēre, habēre* (= to have); to — house, i.e., to remain in it, *domi* (*re*)*manēre*; to — one's bed, *in lecto esse, lecto teneri*; to — a position, *locum tenēre*; = to store up, *condĕre*; = to preserve, *conservare*; = to support (animals), *alĕre*; = to observe, *tenēre, servare, observare*; to — faith, *fidem servare* or *praestare*, or *exsolvĕre*; to — a secret, *alqd occultum tenēre*; to — apart, *distinēre*; to — back, = to retain, *retinēre*; I generally — it in this way, *ita facĕre soleo, sic est meus mos*. **II.** v.intr. *contineri* (of a dam), *firmum esse* (of a door); *frangi non posse* (of what cannot be broken open, e.g. a door), *non rumpi* (of what cannot burst, e.g. a vessel), *manēre, non evanescĕre* (of things that will — their colour); to — to a thing, *retinēre alqd* (*justitiam, officium*); always to — in the path of duty and honour, *officii et existimationis rationem semper ducĕre*; who — s to, upholds a thing, *retinens alcjs rei* (e.g. *sui juris dignitatisque*); to — in a certain track, *tenēre alqm locum, cursum tenēre alqo*; to — down, *reprimĕre, comprimĕre*; to — in, *claudĕre, includĕre, concludĕre, continēre, cohibēre*; to — off, *arcēre, defendĕre, prohibēre, propulsare*; to — from, (*se*) *abstinēre*; to — up, *conservare, tueri*; to — up with, *subsequi*. **III.** n. *arx*. **keeper**, n. *custos, curator*. **keeping**, n. *custodia* (= custody), *tutela* (= protection), to be in —, *convenire, congruĕre*; see AGREE. **keepsake**, n. *donum*, or more accurately defined, *memoriae caus(s)â datum* or *acceptum*.

keg, n *dolium* (of earthenware), *ligneum vas circulis vinctum* (of wood (Plin.))

ken, n *conspectus, -ūs*

kennel, n 1, a house for dogs, *stabulum canis* or *canum*, *tugurium canis* (for a watch-dog, etc.), 2, = a pack of hounds, *canes*, 3, = a water course of a street, *emissarium* (for the water), = a drain, *cloaca*

kerb, n *crepido*, better defined by *viae* or *itineris*

kerchief, n see HANDKERCHIEF, NECKKERCHIEF

kernel, n 1, of fruits, *nucleus* (large or small), 2, in a fig sense, *medulla* (= marrow), = the blossom, *flos, floris*, m (of a flower, youth, nobility), = the select portions, *robur, -oris*, n, *robora* (e g of Italy, of the Roman people, of the troops, the foot-soldiers, etc.), that was the real — of the army, *hoc erat robur exercitūs*, *id roboris in exercitu erat*

kettle, n *a(h)enum, cortina* (for cooking and dyeing), *lebes, -ētis*, m **kettle-drum,** n *tympanum*

key, n 1, *clavis, -is*, f, 2, fig *janua* (rare, e g *urbs janua Asiae*), 3, of a musical instrument, * *clavis*.

kick, I. v intr and tr *calcitrare, calces remittĕre, calcibus caedĕre*, a horse that —s, *equus calcitro* **II.** n *pedis* or *calcis ictus, -ūs*, to give anyone a —, *alqm pede* or *calce percutĕre*

kid, n *haedus, haedulus*

kidnap, v tr see STEAL. **kidnapper,** n *plagiarius*

kidney, n *renes, renum*, m **kidney-bean,** n *phaselus*, m and f

kill, v tr *occidere* (e g *ferro, veneno*, but generally of an honourable death), *caedĕre* (= to fell, especially in battle, in a fight, if of several, also *alqm caedes facĕre*), *interficĕre* (= to cause anyone's death, to murder, also in general like *occidĕre*, but implying a design and the act of destroying), *conficĕre* (= to put to the sword, in case of resistance), *necare* (in a cruel manner and wilfully, implying cruelty and want of feeling), *enecare* (stronger than *necare*), *interimĕre*, *e medio tollere* (= to get rid, especially of an adversary), *vitam adimĕre alci*, *vitā* or *luce alqm privare* (in general = to deprive of life), *alci manus afferre* (= to lay hands on), *trucidare* (= to murder), *jugulare* (= to cut the throat), *obtruncare* (= to attack anyone and assassinate him), *percutĕre* (with the sword, axe, stick, etc., generally with the abl of the instrument whereby a person is killed e g *gladio*, hence *securi percutere*, the proper term to express the act of executing one), to — oneself, *se interficĕre, se occidĕre, se interimĕre, mortem* or *necem sibi consciscĕre, mortem* or *vim sibi inferre, vim afferre vitae suae, manus sibi afferre* or *inferre, sequum vitā privare*, to — the time, *horas* or *tempus perdere*, to — (of beasts), *caedĕre* (cattle), *jugulare, mactare* (only = to slay victims, never = to butcher), *trucidare* (also of slaughter of men)

kiln, n *fornax, -acis*, f, a lime —, *fornax calcaria*, see STOVE, OVEN

kimbo, n (i e a—), see CROOKED, CURVE

kin, n see RELATION, RELATIVE **kind, I.** n *genus, -eris*, n, *species* (= the single species of the genus), *modus* (esp in gen *ejusdem modi*, etc.), *forma* (= characteristic form, feature, e g *orationis, eloquentiae, dicendi, loquendi*, etc.), in logic, *species forma, pars, -tis*, f (opp *genus*), of the same —, *ejusdem generis, congener*, to arrange everything according to its —, *singula generatim disponĕre*, Theocritus is wonderful in his — of poetry, *admirabilis in suo genere Theocritus* very often by *quidam* or *quasi* (e g for slaves the house is a — of republic, and they are all citizens in it, *servis respublica quasi civitas domus est*, to make a — of will, *quasi testamentum facere*), every — of, *omne genus* (with the gen, e g *herbarum radicumque*), or simply by *omnes* (e g every — of danger, *omnia pericula*) **II.** adj *benignus* (in character and in actions), = charitable, *beneficus*, = benevolent, *benevolus* = amiable, *facilis, humanus*, = friendly, *amicus*, = indulgent, *indulgens*, = liberal, *liberalis*, = obliging, *comis*, = gentle, mild, *clemens*; = well, favourably disposed, *propitius* (of the gods), you are too good! very —! *benigne! benigne!* also *recte!* no, thank you (when we decline taking more at table, thanking for any act of kindness), *facis amice!* Adv *benigne, liberaliter*, comb *benigne ac liberaliter, comiter, clementer, indulgenter* (e g to treat, deal with anyone —, *alqm habēre*), *amice, humane* **kindness,** n 1, = kindliness, *benignitas, benevolentia, comitas, humanitas, liberalitas* (= generosity), *clementia, indulgentia, facilitas* (= affability) 2, = a benefit, *beneficium*, see FAVOUR **kindred,** n see RELATION, RELATIVE **kinsman,** n see RELATIVE

kindle, I. v tr 1, *accendĕre, inflammare* (= both to make light and to burn), *incendĕre, inflammare et incendĕre, succendĕre* (from below), *alci rei ignem in(j)icĕre, inferre* (= to throw fire in), *alci rei ignem sub(j)icere, subdĕre* (= to put fire under anything), 2, fig *accendĕre, incendĕre*, † *succendĕre, inflammare, conflare, excitare, incitare*, see EXCITE **II.** v intr 1, (ex)*ardescĕre*, 2, fig = to glow with, *ardēre, flagrare*

king, n *rex, regis*, m, = a prince of a small territory, *regulus*, the — of —s, *rex regum*, to be —, *regem esse, regnum obtinēre, regiam potestatem habēre*, to make oneself into a —, to occupy, usurp the throne, *regnum occupare, regium ornatum nomenque sumere* (of one who had been before governor of a province, etc.), I shall be as happy as a —, if, etc., *rex ero, si*, etc **kingcraft,** n *ars regendi* **kingdom,** n *regnum* **kingfisher,** n *(h)alcedo*, later form *(h)alcyon* **kingly,** adj *regius, regalis* **kingship,** n *regia potestas, regnum*

kiss, I. v tr *alqm osculari, suaviari, basiare* to — a stranger, *osculis alqm excipĕre*, to — each other, *osculari inter se*, — Attica from me, *Atticae meae meis verbis suavium des*, to throw a — to anyone, *manum a facie jacĕre*, in the plural, *oscula jacĕre, basia jactare* **II.** n *osculum* (lit, = a little mouth, used as a nobler expression), *suavium* (= a tender — upon the mouth or cheek), *basium* (= a loud —), to give anyone a —, *osculum* or *suavium* or *basium alci dare*, *osculum alci ferre* or *offerre, basium* or *suavium alci imprimĕre*, to steal a —, *suavium alci surripere*

kitchen, I. n 1, = place for cooking, *culina*, 2, = the dishes themselves, *cena* (*coen.*), to keep a good —, *laute cenitare* **II.** adj *culinarius*, — materials, *res culinaria* (in gen), vegetable, *olus, -eris*, n, or in the plur *olera, -um* **kitchen-garden,** n *hortus olitorius* (Jct.)

kitten, I. n *catulus felinus* **II.** v intr *feles parere*

knapsack, n *pera* (= bag), *mantica* (= portmanteau), *sarcina* (= baggage of soldiers)

knave, n *(tri)furcifer, scelerator* (colloquial terms), *homo nequam* or *sceleratus*, see ROGUE **knavery,** n *nequitia, malitia, fraus, dolus*, *improbitas*; see DECEPTION. **knavish,** adj. *nequam* (= worthless), *malitiosus* (= crafty), *perfidus* (= treacherous); *fraudulentus* (= fraudulent, deceitful), *lascivus* (= full of tricks). Adv. *perfide, malitiose, fraudulenter.*

knead, v.tr. *(con)depsĕre, subigĕre.*

knee, n. *genu*; to bend the —, *genua flectĕre*, or *curvare* (in general); to fall upon one's —s, *(in genu) procumbĕre* (unintentionally, or from admiration, or out of respect, or as suppliant); to fall upon one's —s before anyone, *alci procumbĕre, ad genua alcjs procumbĕre, ad genua alci* or *genibus alcjs accidere, prosternĕre se et supplicare alci* (= to prostrate oneself). **knee-deep,** adj. *genibus tenus.* **knee-pan,** n. *patella* (Cels.). **kneel,** v.intr. *genibus niti*; to — down *(in genu) procumbĕre*; see KNEE.

knell, n. *campana funebris.*

knife, n. *culter*; a small —, *cultellus.*

knight, n. *eques, -itis,* m. **knighthood,** n. *ordo equester* (= the whole order); *dignitas equestris, locus equester* (= the rank). **knightly,** adj. *equester*; = worthy of a knight, *equite dignus.*

knit, v.tr. *acubus texĕre*; fig., see TIE, UNITE; to — the brow, *frontem contrahĕre* or *adducĕre.*

knob, n. *bulla* (of a door, etc.); *nodus* (in plants). **knobbed, knobly,** adj. † *nodosus.*

knock, I. v.tr. and intr. *alqd pulsare* (e.g. *fores, ostium*); to — with the fist, *pulsare, tundĕre*, see BEAT, KILL; to — against, *alqd ad* or *in alqd offendĕre* (e.g. *pedem in saxum*); to — down, *sternĕre*; —ed up, *fatigatus* (through a combat), *fessus* (through suffering, e.g. illness, poverty, etc.); = fit to sink, *defatigatus, defessus, lassus, lassitudine confectus* (= worn out). **II.** n. *pulsatio* (e.g. *forium*); there is a — against the door, *pulsantur fores.* **knocker,** n. by circumloc. (e.g. he raised the —, *fores pulsavit*), or *tintinnabulum* (= bell). **knock-kneed,** adj. *varus.*

knot, I. n. *nodus* (in gen.), *articulus* (= joint), = a tie, *nodus, vinculum*; = difficulty, *nodus, difficultas*; = a group of people, *circulus*; to make a —, *nodum facĕre, nectĕre*; to draw the —, *nodum a(d)stringĕre*; to loosen the —, *nodum solvĕre, expedire* (lit. and fig.). **II.** v.tr. *nodare, nectĕre*; see TIE. **knotty,** adj. **1,** *nodosus, geniculatus*; **2,** fig. *difficilis, spinosus* (= thorny); a — point, *nodus.*

know, v.tr. *scire, novisse* (= to have learnt to know); = to have a knowledge of, *alcjs rei scientiam habēre, alqd cognitum habēre*; = to have had a good knowledge of, experience in a matter, *non nescire, non ignorare, alcjs rei non ignarum esse*; *didicisse* (= to have learnt); I —, = a thing does not escape me, *me non fugit* or *non praeterit*; = to comprehend, *tenēre, intellegĕre, cognoscĕre* (= to experience, learn); I don't —, *nescio, haud scio, ignoro, me fugit, me praeterit*; not to — that the dictator had arrived, *ignorare venisse dictatorem*; I don't — where to turn, to whom to apply, *nescio quo me convertam*; I don't — what to say, *nescio* or *non habeo* or *nihil habeo, quod dicam*; I don't — who, *nescio quis*; I read I don't — what, *legi nescio quid*; I don't — whether . . . (a modest assertion), *haud scio an*, etc., *nescio an*, etc. (e.g. I don't — whether this road is the shorter of the two, *haud scio an* or *nescio an haec via brevior sit*); you must —, *scito* (not *sci*), *scitote* (not *scite*); do you —? do you — perhaps? *scin? scisne? nostin'?* as far as I —, *quod scio, quantum scio, quod sciam*; I should like to — (in questions, the answer to which would create surprise), *miror, miror unde sit*; to — for certain, *certo* and *certe scire, pro certo scire, certum habēre, pro certo habēre, exploratum* or *cognitum habēre, certum est mihi alqd* and *de alqâ re, exploratum* or *notum exploratumque mihi est alqd* and *de alqâ re, cognitum compertumque mihi est alqd, certis auctoribus comperisse* (on good authority); let me —, *fac me certiorem, fac ut sciam*; I wished you to —, *id te scire volui*; to get to —, *audire* (= to hear), *accipĕre* (= to receive intelligence), *comperire* (= to understand), *discĕre* (= to learn); he knew how to maintain his dignity, *auctoritatem suam bene tuebatur*; = to have a clear idea about anything, *novisse, cognovisse, cognitum habēre* (in gen.), *alcjs rei notitiam habēre* or *tenēre* (= to have a conception of a thing), *didicisse* (through having learnt, opp. *ignorare*), *vidisse* (through outward perception), *tenēre* (= to hold), *intellegĕre* (*intellig-*) *alqm* or *alqd* (with regard to a thing, = to understand its peculiar features; with regard to persons, to understand their motives, etc.); = to learn to —, *noscĕre, cognoscĕre* (esp. through experience), *discĕre* (by study, inquiry, μανθανειν); *percipĕre* (= to obtain a clear perception); = to get a taste of anything, *degustare* (fig., = to get a knowledge of anything, e.g. *ingenium alcjs*); to — anyone, *noscĕre* or *novisse alqm*, opp. *ignorare*; = to become most intimately acquainted with a thing, *alqd familiariter nosse* (*novisse*); they — each other perfectly well, *erant notissimi inter se*; to — oneself thoroughly, *penitus ipsum se nosse*; to — a person by sight, *alqm de facie nosse*; not to — anyone, *alqm non nosse, alqs mihi est ignotus, alqm ignorare* (seldom); = to recognise, *cognoscere*; in order that nobody might — me, *ne quis me cognosceret*; *agnoscĕre ex alqâ re* (e.g. anyone by his works, *alqm ex operibus suis*), *noscitare alqâ re* (e.g. anyone by the voice, *voce*; by his countenance, *facie*). **knowable,** adj. *insignis*, by anything, *alqâ re* (e.g. *armis*), *conspicuus alqâ re* (= conspicuous, e.g. *armis*); to make a thing — by, *alqd insignire alqâ re* (e.g. *notâ*); to make anything —, intelligible by words, *alqd explanare.* **knowing, I.** n. = KNOWLEDGE. **II.** adj. *sciens, prudens*, comb. *sciens ac prudens* (with regard to the person who does a thing, opp *insciens*), *quod consulto et cogitatum fit, quod de industriâ fit* (= on purpose); = clever, *callidus, versutus, astutus.* Adv. *consulto* (= with consideration, calmly); *de industriâ* (= on purpose); to sin wilfully, —, *scientem peccare* (opp. *inscientem peccare*); I have done it —, *sciens* or *sciens prudensque feci, consulto* or *de industriâ feci.* **knowledge,** n. *scientia, notitia, cognitio* (in a subjective sense); in an objective sense, = a branch of learning, *ars*) = art), *doctrina, disciplina*; sciences, literature, *doctrinae, disciplinae, disciplinae studia, -orum*; to inform anyone, bring anything to his —, *alqm certiorem facĕre alcjs rei* or *de alqâ re, docĕre alqm alqd* or *de alqâ re* (= to teach), *erudire alqm de alqâ re* (= to instruct), comb. *alqm erudire atque docĕre*; to gain — about a thing, *cognoscĕre de alqâ re*; to have anything brought to one's —, *certiorem fieri de alqâ re, docēri alqd*; the — of anything spreads to, reaches, *auditur alqd*; to have no — of, *alqd ignorare*; = a clear perception, *notitia alcjs rei*; *notio alcjs rei* (= the idea which we have of anything, e.g. the — of God, *notitia* or *notio Dei*); = the knowing about anything, *scientia alcjs rei*; = the act of having got into a thing with the understanding, *cognitio* or *intellegentia* (*intellig-*) *alcjs rei*; — about the past, *memoria praeteritorum*; about the future, *prudentia futurorum*; to have only a superficial — of, in, *alqd primoribus labris* or *leviter attigisse, primis labris gustasse*; to have scarcely a superficial — of, *alqâ re ne imbutum quidem* *esse*; if I possess any — in it, *si in me est huiusce rei ratio alqa*, void of —, *rerum rudis* or *ignarus* (in gen), illiterate, *lit(t)erarum expers, non lit(t)eratus, illit(t)eratus*, with regard to the fine arts and sciences, *liberalium artium nescius*, = quite illiterate, *omnium rerum rudis* (in gen.), *omnis eruditionis expers* **known,** adj *notus*, it is —, *constat, certum est*, with accus and infin, to make —, *declarare*, see PUBLISH.

knuckle, n *articulus (digiti)*.

L.

label, I. n *scheda (sc(h)ida)* = strip of papyrus bark, leaf of paper, *tessera* (= a square, a square piece of stone or wood), *pittacium* (late, — on necks of bottles, etc). **II.** v tr *pittacium affigere* or *titulum inscribere*

labial, n = letter pronounced by the lips, **litera labialis* (only as t t)

laborious, adj *laboriosus, operosus, industrius, (g)navus, diligens, sedulus*, to be —, *magni esse laboris, laboriosum esse* Adv *laboriose, operose, industrie, (g)naviter, sedulo, diligenter*

labour, I. n 1, *labor, opus, -eris*, n; *opera occupatio, pensum* (= task), *moles, -is*, f (esp poet, but also in prose, e g *haud magna mole*, = without great —), to undertake a —, *laborem suscipere*, to wear down with —, *alqm labore conficere*; to pay by —, *pecuniam debitam opera sua (com)pensare*, learned —s, *studia*, — by night, *lucubratio*, —s at spare time, *operae subsicivae*, without —, free from —, *otiosus*, 2, in childbirth, *partus, -us* (= bringing forth), † *nisus, -us (nixus)* **II.** v intr. 1, = to be active, *laborare*, — in study, *studere lit(t)eris*, — on or at anything, *elaborare in re* or *in alqd* or *ut, operam dare alci rei, incumbere in* or *ad alqd*, or *alci rei*, to be employed in —, *in opere esse, laborem subire*; — day and night, *opus continuare diem et noctem*, — for pay, *operam suam locare*, 2, = to be troubled, *laborare*, — under, *alqa re laborare* (of trouble), — under a delusion, *decipi*, 3, = to strive, *(e)niti*, see STRIVE, 4, of childbirth, *parturire* **laboured,** adj *nitidius alqd et affectatius* (Quint), *nimis exquisitus* **labourer,** n *qui opus facit, operarius, opera*, — for pay, a hireling, *mercenarius*, — in a vineyard, *vinitor*, to engage —s, *conducere operas*, skilled —s, *artifices* **laboratory,** n *locus cameratus ubi metallorum experimenta aguntur*.

labyrinth, n *labyrinthus* (of the Cretan —), fig *difficultates summae, res inexplicabiles*, to fall into a —, *in summas difficultates incurrere*, to be in a —, *in summis difficultatibus esse* or *versari* **labyrinthine,** adj † *labyrintheus, inexplicabilis*

lace, I. n 1, *texta reticulata, -orum*, 2, of a boot, *li(n)gula* (Juv = shoe latchet) **II.** v tr *nectere*; see TIE

lacerate, v tr *lacerare*, † *dilacerare, laniare* (fig, e g the heart, *acerbissimo dolore afficere alcjs animum*) **laceration,** n *laceratio, laniatus, -us*

lachrymose, adj = breaking into tears, *lacrimabundus*, = full of tears, *lacrimosus* (*lac(h)ru-*) (e g *oculi* or *lumina, voces*), = causing tears, *lacrimosus*.

lack, I. n = not having, *defectio* (esp *defectio virium*, — of strength), *inopia* (= — of means), *penuria* (= — of necessaries) **II.** v tr *re carere, egere, indigere, inopia rei laborare* or *premi, alqd alci deesse, abesse, deficere*, — nothing, *nihil deesse alci* **lack-a-day!** interj *ah! o! proh!* generally with accus, also without exclamation, e g *me miserum!* **lack-lustre,** adj *decolor*

lackey, n *pedisequus, famulus*

laconic, adj 1, *Laconicus* = Spartan, 2, = brief, *brevis* Adv *breviter, paucis (verbis)*

lacquer, I. n *lacca* **II.** v tr *lacca alqd obducere* (not class)

lacteal, adj † *lacteus*

lad, n *puer*

ladder, n *scalae*, the step of a —, *scalarum gradus, -us*

lade, v tr. = to load, *onerare*, — anyone, *onus alci imponere* **laden,** adj *onustus, oneratus, gravis*, † *gravidus*, — with debt, *aere alieno obrutus*; — with business, *occupationibus distentus*. **lading,** n *onus, -eris*, n

ladle, I. n = large spoon, *cochlear (cochlearium* or *cochleare*, Plin), *trulla* (= small —), *cyathus* **II.** v tr *haurire*

lady, n *domina, hera, matrona, materfamilias* (= lady of the house) **lady-like,** adj *honestus, quod matrona dignum est* **ladyship,** n *domina* **lady's maid,** n *famula*, † *ornatrix*

lag, v intr *cunctari (cunct-), cessare, morari* **lagging,** n *mora, cunctatio* **laggard,** n *cessator, cunctator*

lagoon, n *lacuna*

laic, lay, adj **laicus* **laity,** n **laici* (Eccl t t.) **layman,** n **laicus*

lair, n *latibulum, cubile*, see DEN

laird, n *dominus, possessor*

lamb, I. n *agnus, agna*, a small —, lambkin, *agnellus*, of a —, *agninus*, — like, *placidior agno*, as meat (*caro*) *agnina* **II.** v tr *agnum edere* or *procreare*

lambent, adj use † *lambere* (e g *flamma quae lambit alqd*)

lame, I. adj *claudus, mancus* (= short of a limb), *debilis* (= feeble), to be — of a wound, *vulnere debilitatum esse*, to be —, *claudum esse, claudicare*, — in speech, *si quid in oratione claudicat*, — in one foot, *altero pede claudum esse*, a — excuse, *excusatio vana* **II.** v tr *alqm claudum reddere* Adv by adj or v (e g to walk —, *claudicare*) **lameness,** n *claudicatio*

lament, I. n or **lamentation,** *lamentum* (usu in pl), *lamentatio* (= act of —), *fletus, -us* (= weeping), *gemitus, -us* (= groaning), *comploratio*, *(com)ploratus, -us, ejulatus, ejulatio* (the latter rare = wailing), *quiritatio* (rare), *questus, -us, querimonia, querela* (= complaint), *nenia* (= dirge), *plangor* (= beating of the breast, loud —) **II.** v tr *alqd lamentari, deflere, (con)queri*, † *flere, deplorare* (= — bitterly), *complorare* (rare), † *plorare* **III.** v intr *lamentari, flere, (de)plorare, ejulare, (con)queri* **lamentable,** adj *deflendus*, † *lamentabilis, flebilis, miserandus, miserabilis* Adv *miserandum in modum, miserabiliter, flebiliter* **lamented,** adj past part of v or *divus* (of the dead, Tac)

lamp, n *lucerna, lychnus* **lamp-black,** n *fuligo*.

lampoon, I. n *libellus famosus* (Suet), *famosum carmen* or *famosi versus, -us*, pl **II** v tr *libellum ad infamiam alcjs edere*

lance, I. n *lancea, hasta*, to break a — with, *hasta pugnare cum alqo*, fig *certare, contendere cum alqo* **II.** v tr med t t. *incidere* **lancer,** n *eques hastatus* **lancet,** n (or little lance), *scalpellum (scalpellus)*

land, I. n. 1, opp. to the sea, *terra*, † *tellus*, *-ūris*, f.; to gain the —, *terram capĕre*; to quit —, (*navem*) *solvĕre*; to sail along —, *oram legĕre*; 2, a fruit-bearing country, *ager*, *fundus*, *solum*, *terra*; a cultivated —, field, *arvum*; to cultivate —, *agrum colĕre*; relating to the culture of —, *agrarius*; 3, = a particular part of the earth, *terra*, *regio*, *provincia*, *ager*, *pagus*, *civitas*, *patria*; in the — of the Etruscans, *in Etruscorum finibus*; to drive out of the —, *alqm civitate pellĕre*, *in exsilium pellĕre*, *agĕre alqm*; of what —? *cujas*; out of our —, *nostras*; the law of the —, *lex* (*publica*). **II.** adj. *terrestris*, *terrenus*, *pedester* (e.g. *pugna pedestris*, — battle). **III.** v.intr. *e nave* or *navem egredi*, *e nave evadĕre* or *exire*. **IV.** v.tr. *alqos* or *alqd e nave* or *in terram exponĕre*; to — a fish, *piscem capĕre*. **landed,** adj. — property, *agrum*, *possessio* (usu. in pl.); — proprietor, *agrorum possessor*. **landing,** n. *e(x)scensio*, *egressus*, *-ūs*, *litoris appulsus*, *-ūs*; to make a —, *navi exire*; to forbid anyone a —, *alqm navi egredi prohibēre*; a — place, *aditus*, *-ūs*. **landlord,** n. *agrorum possessor* (= proprietor), *caupo* (= "mine host"). **landmark,** n. *lapis*, *-ĭdis*, m. **landscape,** n. *regio*, *terra*; in painting, *regio in tabulâ picta*. **landslip,** n. *terrae lapsus*, *-ūs*.

lane, n. *angiportum* (or *-us*, *-ūs*), = narrow street; country lane, *via*.

language, n. 1, = the faculty of speech, *vox*, *oratio*, *lingua*; 2, = the act and manner of speaking, *vox*, *lingua*, *oratio*, *dictio*; the — of common life, *sermo cot(t)idianus* (*quot-*); — of polite life, *sermo urbanus*; to speak a —, *alqâ linguâ uti* or *loqui*.

languid, adj. *languidus*, *languens*, *remissus*, *lassus* (= weary), *fessus* (= worn out), *defessus* (= worn down); to be —, *languēre*; fig. *iners* (= inactive), *frigidus*, *languidus* (of style). Adv. *languide*. **languidness** or **languor,** n. *languor*. **languish,** v.intr. *languēre*, *languescĕre*; = to pine away, *tabescĕre*; — in prison, *in carcere vitam miserrimam trahĕre*.

lank, lanky, adj. *prolixus*, *procērus* (= tall), *gracilis*, *tenuis* (= thin). **lankness,** n. *proceritas*, *gracilitas*, *tenuitas*.

lantern, n. *laterna* (*lanterna*).

lap, I. n. 1, *gremium* (= bosom), *sinus*, *-ūs* (properly = a fold of the gown); 2, of a racecourse, *spatium*. **II.** v.tr. 1, = to lick up, *ligur(r)ire*, *lingĕre*; 2, = to touch (as waves), *lambĕre*. **lap-dog,** n. *catellus*. **lappet,** n. *lacinia*.

lapidary, n. *scalptor*.

lapse, I. n. 1, *lapsus*, *-ūs* (= a gliding or fall); 2, fig. *lapsus*, *-ūs*, *error*, *peccatum*; 3, = flight, expiry, † *fuga*; after the — of a year, *interjecto anno*. **II.** v.intr. 1, *labi*, *defluĕre*; 2, *errare* (= to go wrong); 3, of property, *caducum fieri*, *reverti* (*ad dominum*).

larboard, adj. *laevus*; see LEFT.

larceny, n. *furtum*; to commit —, *furtum facĕre*.

lard, I. n. *adeps*, *-ĭpis*, m. and f., *lar(i)dum*. **II.** v.tr. *alqd adipe ad coquendum parare*. **larder,** n. *armarium promptuarium*, *cella penaria*, *carnarium* (for keeping meat, Plaut.).

large, adj. 1, = of great size or bulk, *magnus*, *grandis*, *amplus*; a — assembly, *celeber conventus*, *-ūs*; 2, — of heart (= liberal), *largus* (e.g. *largus homo*, *largus animo* or *promissis*). Adv. *magnopere*, *large*. **large-hearted,** adj. 1, = magnanimous, *magnanimus*; 2, = generous, *liberalis*, *benignus*, *benevolus*. **large-heartedness,** n. 1, *magnanimitas*; 2, *liberalitas*; *benignitas*, *benevolentia*. **largeness,** n. 1, *magnitudo*, *amplitudo*, *proceritas* (= tallness), *altitudo* (= in height), *ambitus*, *-ūs* (= in girth), *spatium* (= in surface); 2, fig. see LARGE-HEARTEDNESS. **largess,** n. *largitio*, *congiarium* (of corn, oil, or money).

lark, n. *alauda*.

larynx, n. *guttur*, *-ŭris*, n.

lascivious, adj. *lascivus* (= playful), *impurus*, *impudicus*, *libidinosus*. Adv. *parum caste*, *impudice*. **lasciviousness,** n. *lascivia* (= playfulness), *impudicitia*, *libido*.

lash, I. n. 1, = a whip, *flagrum*, *lorum* (usu. in pl.), *flagellum*, *scutica* (= light —); 2, = a blow or stroke, *verber*, *-ĕris*, n. (*huic homini parata erunt verbera*); — of the tongue, *verbera linguae*; — of fortune, *verbera fortunae*. **II.** v.tr. 1, *flagellare*, *verberare*, *virgâ* or *virgis caedĕre*; 2, = to bind, *alligare*, *colligare*; see BIND, FASTEN. **lashing,** n. *verberatio*.

lassitude, n. *lassitudo*, *languor*, (*de*)*fatigatio*.

last, n. of a shoemaker, *forma*; let the shoemaker stick to his —, *ne ultra crepidam sutor*.

last, I. adj. *ultimus*, *extremus*, *postremus*, *proximus*, *summus* (= the highest), *novissimus* (= latest); when used of two, *posterior*, *superior*; to the —, *ad ultimum*. **II.** n. by *extremus* (e.g. the — of the letter, *epistula extrema*); at —, (*tum*) *demum*, *denique*, *ad extremum* or *postremum*. **III.** v.intr. *durare*, (*per*)*manēre*, *stare*, *longum* or *diuturnum esse*. **lasting,** adj. *firmus*, *solidus*, *duraturus*, *stabilis*, *diuturnus*, (*per*)*mansurus*, *perennis*; not —, *fragilis* (= frail), *caducus* (= falling), *fluxus*. **lastly,** adv. *postremo*, *postremum*, *ad extremum*, *denique*, *quod superest* or *restat* or *extremum est*, *novissime* (esp. in Quint.).

latch, n. *pessulus* (= bolt). **latchet,** n. *corrigia*.

late, adj. 1, *serus*; I went away —, *serus abii*; too — repentance, *sera paenitentia*; *tardus* (= slow), *serotinus* (= — coming or growing, e.g. *hiems*, *pira*, *pulli*); the —, *defunctus*, = *mortuus*, *divus* (of an emperor); — in the day, *multo die*; — at night, *multâ nocte*, or by neut. *serum*, used as n. (e.g. *serum erat diei*, it was — in the day); 2, = recent, *recens*, *novus*, *inferior* (e.g. of a — age, *inferioris aetatis*). Adv. *nuper*, *modo*. **lateness,** n. use adj.

latent, adj. *occultus*, *abdĭtus*, *abscondĭtus*, *recondĭtus*.

lateral, adj. *lateralis* (ante and post class.), *a latere*. Adv. *a latere*.

lath, n. *asser*, *-ĕris*, m., *asserculus*.

lathe, n. *tornus*; to work at the —, *tornare*.

lather, n. *spuma e sapone facta*.

Latin, adj. *Latinus*; the — tongue, *latinitas*, *oratio* or *lingua Latina*, *sermo Latinus*; to translate into —, *alqd Latine reddĕre*; to know —, *Latine scire*, *linguam Latinam callēre*; to be ignorant of —, *Latine nescire*. **latinity,** n. *latinitas*.

latitude, n. 1, = breadth, *latitudo*; in —, *in latitudinem*; fig. — of speech, *latitudo verborum*; 2, = liberty, *licentia*; to have great —, *late patēre*.

latter, adj. *posterior*; the former, the —, *hic ... ille*. Adv. see LATELY.

lattice, n. *cancelli*, *clathri*.

laud, I. n. *laus*. **II.** v.tr. *alqm laudare*, *extollĕre*; see PRAISE. **laudable,** adj. *laudabilis*, *laudatus*, *laude dignus*. Adv. *laudabiliter*, *laudabili in modo*. **laudatory,** adj. *honorificus*.

laugh, laughing, or **laughter, I.** n. *risus*, *-ūs*; immoderate —, *cachinnatio*; a horse —, *cachinnus*; a — at, *irrisus*, *-ūs*, *derisus*, *-ūs*; a — to scorn, *derisus*; a —-stock, *ludibrium*;

to be a — -stock, *esse alci ludibrio* **II.** v intr *ridēre*, to — at, *arridēre* (= to smile upon in a friendly way, e g *non alloqui amicos, vix notis familiariter arridēre*); *alqm deridēre, irridēre*, = to burst into —, *cachinnare, cachinnari* **laughable**, adj *ridiculus, ridendus*. Adv *ridicule* **laughter**, n see LAUGH, I

launch, v tr 1, *navem deducĕre*, 2, = to hurl, *torquēre*, to — out, *in aequor efferri*, to — out in praise of, *alqm efferre laudibus*

laundress, n *mulier quae lintea lavat* **laundry**, n *aedificium quo lintea lavantur*.

laurel, n *laurus* (-i and -ūs), f, belonging to —, *laureus*, fig *gloria, laus, honos* (= honour), decorated with —, *laureatus*, to strive for —s, *gloriae cupidum esse*, to win new —s in war, *gloriam bello augēre*. **laurelled**, adj *laureatus*

lava, n *massa ardens, saxa liquefacta*, pl

lave, v tr *lavare* (= to wash), *abluĕre* (= to wash off), *irrigare* **lavatory**, n *bal(i)neum* (= bath) **laver**, n *aqualis*, m and f (ante class), *pelvis* (Plin).

lavish, I. adj *prodigus* (e g *aeris*), *profusus* (e g *profusissima largitio*), *in largitione effusus*, a — giver, *largitor* Adv *large, prodige, effuse, profuse* **II.** v tr. *profundĕre, effundĕre, largiri* **lavishness**, n *effusio* (= prodigality), *largitas, munificentia*, see LIBERALITY

law, n *lex, regula* (= a rule), *norma* (= a standard); body of —s, *jus* (e g *jus civile*, = civil —), a —, *lex, edictum, institutum*, *lex* is also used in a wider sense, as is our "law," e g *versibus est certa lex, hanc ad legem formanda est oratio* (= to or by this model), a divine —, *fas*, a — of nature, *lex naturae* **law breaker**, n *legis violator* **lawful**, adj *legitimus* (= according to —), *legalis* (Quint) (e g *spes civitatis, vita*, = conformable to —) Adv *legitime, lege, per leges* **lawfulness**, n use adj **law-giver**, n see LEGISLATOR **lawless**, adj. *effrenatus* Adv *effrenate, licenter, contra legem, praeter jus* **lawlessness**, n *(effrenata) licentia* **lawsuit**, n *lis, litis*, f, *controversia* **lawyer**, n *jurisconsultus, juris peritus*, see ADVOCATE

lawn, n 1, = fine linen, *sindon*, see LINEN, 2, = grass plat, *pratulum* or *herba* (= grass)

lax, adj 1, = loose, *laxus, fluxus*, 2, med t t *solutus, liquidus* (e g *alvus liquida*, — bowels, Cels), 3, fig *(dis)solutus, remissus, laxus, neglegens (neglig-)* Adv fig *(dis)solute, remisse, laxe, neglegenter (neglig-)* **laxness, laxity**, n *neglegentia* (*neglig-*, = carelessness), — of spirit, *remissio animi ac dissolutio*, or adj

lay, adj see LAIC

lay, n see SONG

lay, v tr. 1, = to place, *ponĕre, (col)locare*, 2, fig — the foundations, *fundamenta jacĕre*, — an ambush, *insidiari, insidias collocare, facĕre, ponĕre, struĕre, parare, tendĕre alci*, — siege, *obsidēre*, — a wager, *sponsione provocare* or *lacessĕre*; — a plan, *consilium* or *rationem inire* or *capĕre*, — hands on, *manus alci inferre*, — waste, *vastare* 3, = — eggs, *(ova) parĕre* — aside, *ab(j)icĕre, (se)ponĕre*, — before, *alqd alci proponĕre*, — oneself open to, *alqd in se admittĕre*, — down, = to put down, *(de)ponĕre* — down an office, *magistratu abire, se abdicare*, — down arms, *ab armis discedĕre* — down a proposition, *sententiam dicĕre, alqd affirmare, confirmare*, see STATE, — out money, see SPEND, — out a corpse, *mortuum lavare* (= to wash), *alci omnia justa solvĕre* would include the laying out, — up, *condĕre, reponĕre*, see STORE, — commands, blame, etc, upon, see COMMAND, BLAME, etc **layer**, n 1, in building, etc, *corium* (of lime, etc) *ordo* (= row); 2, of a plant, *propago*

lazar, n see LEPER

lazy, adj. *piger, ignavus, segnis, iners, otiosus* (= having leisure) Adv *pigre, ignave, segniter, otiose* **laziness**, n *ignavia, segnitia, pigritia*

lead, I. v.tr 1, *ducĕre, agĕre*, — an army, *exercitum ducĕre, exercitui praeesse* (= to command), — the way, *alci praeire* (= to go before), 2, fig = to pass, — a life, *vitam agĕre*, = to induce, *alqm ad alqd faciendum* or *ut alqd faciat, adducĕre*, in bad sense, *inducĕre*, see PERSUADE, 3, with omission of object, e g the road —s, *via fert*, the matter —s to, etc, *res spectat*, see TEND, — away, *abducĕre, seducĕre*, — into, *inducĕre*, — out, *educĕre*, — a colony, *coloniam deducĕre* **II.** n. or **leadership**, *ductus*, -ūs under your —, *te duce* **leader**, n *dux, ducis*, m (lit. and fig), *auctor, princeps, -icis*, m and f (fig) **leading**, adj *princeps, primarius* (of men), *summus* (of men and things) see CHIEF **leading-strings**, n *alci obtemperare (tanquam puer)*

lead, n *plumbum*, of —, *plumbeus* **leaden**, adj *plumbeus*

leaf, n of a tree, *folium, frons*, a — of paper, *scheda (sc(h)ida), pagina, charta*, of metal wood, etc, *bractea, lamina* **leafless**, adj *foliis carens* or *nudatus* **leafy**, adj †*frondosus*, †*frondeus*, †*frondifer*

league, I. n *foedus, eris*, n (= treaty), *pactum* (= agreement), *societas* (= alliance or union) **II.** v tr *foedus cum alqo inire*

league, n *tria mil(l)ia passuum*

leak, n *rima*, to spring a —, *rimas agĕre* **leakage**, n. *rima* **leaky**, adj *rimosus, rimarum plenus*, ships that have become —, *quassatae naves*

lean, I. adj *macer* (opp *pinguis*), *macilentus* (ante and post class), *strigosus* (of horses, etc), see THIN **II.** v intr *niti*, — on, *(in)niti inhaerēre* (= to adhere to), *pendēre* (= to hang from), *confugĕre* or *sese conferre ad alcjs praesidia* (= to seek support with), *fulciri re* (= to depend on or be supported by), *ad alqd acclinare* (= to — towards), *se applicare in alqd* or *alci rei incumbĕre*, to — backward, *se reclinare*, to — to (in opinion), *sententiae favēre* **leaning**, adj — on, *innixus* — towards, †*acclinis*, — backwards, †*reclinis*; — against or on, *incumbens* **leanness**, n *macies*

leap, I. n *saltus, -ūs*, to take a —, *salire*, by —s, *per saltus, saltuatim* **II.** v intr *salire*, — back, *resilire*, — down, *desilire* · — forward, *prosilire*, — for joy, *gestire, ex(s)ultare*, — on horseback, *in equum insilire*, — over, *tran(s)silire* **leaping**, n *saltus, -ūs* **leapfrog**, n *(pueri) alius alium transilit* **leap-year**, n *annus intercalaris, annus bisextus* (late)

learn, v tr 1, *discĕre, ediscĕre* (by heart), *memoriae mandare* (= to commit to memory), *perdiscĕre* (thoroughly), word for word, *ad verbum ediscĕre*, — something more, *addiscĕre*, 2 = to hear, *discĕre, cognoscĕre* (esp by inquiry), *certiorem fieri, audire* **learned**, adj *doctus, eruditus, lit(t)eratus* Adv *docte, erudite, lit(t)erate* **learner**, n *discipulus* **learning**, n *doctrina, eruditio*

lease, I. n *conductio* **II.** v tr, to hire on —, *conducĕre*, to let on —, *locare*

leash, n *lorum* (= a strip of leather), — of hounds, *tres canes*

least, I. adj *minimus*, see LITTLE **II.** adv *minime*, at —, *saltem, certe, (at)tamen*, not in the —, *nihil omnino, ne minimum quidem*

leather, I. n *corium* (= the hide), *aluta* (tanned) **II.** adj *scorteus*

leave, n *concessio* (= yielding), *permissio* (= permission), *potestas* (= authority), *copia* (= allowance), *venia* (= favour), *arbitrium* (= freedom of action), to give —, *potestatem alci facĕre*, with your —, *pace tuâ*, against —, *me invito*, — to say, *sit venia verbo*, I have —, *mihi licet*, through you, *per te*, give me — to clear myself, *sine me expurgem*.

leave, I. n = departure, by verb, to take —, *salvēre alqm jubēre*, see FAREWELL **II.** v tr 1, = to desert, abandon, *(de)relinquĕre, deserĕre, destituĕre*, 2, — property, *relinquĕre, legare*, see BEQUEATH, 3, = to depart from, *(ex) alqo loco (ex)cedĕre, discedĕre, proficisci, egredi, digredi*, — a province on expiration of office, *(de or ex) provinciâ decedĕre*, — behind, *relinquĕre*; — off, *alqd omittĕre, desinĕre* with infin, *desistĕre alqâ re* or infin, — out, *omittĕre, praetermittĕre* **leavings,** n *quae reliqua sunt*

leaven, I. n *fermentum*, bread without —, or unleavened, *panis nullo fermento* or *sine fermento coctus* **II.** v tr *fermentare*, *panis fermentatus*, = leavened bread (Plin.)

lecture, I. n *schola* (= disputation), *oratio* (= address), *sermo* (= speech) **II.** v tr 1, *scholam habēre de alqâ re*, 2, fig see REPROVE **lecturer,** n *qui scholas habet* **lecture room,** n *schola*

ledge, n *projectura*, — of rocks, *dorsum*

ledger, n *codex accepti et expensi*

lee, n (of a ship), *navis latus a vento tutum*

leech, n 1, see DOCTOR, 2, = bloodsucker, *hirudo, sanguisuga* (Plin.)

leek, n *porrum* and *porrus* (of two kinds, one called *capitatum* the other *sectivum*, also *sectilis*)

leer, v intr *oculis limis intueri, limis oculis a(d)spicĕre* or *limis (oculis) spectare* **leering,** adj *limus* Adv. *limis oculis*.

lees, n *faex* (= dregs of wine, so *faex populi*)

leet, n as in court leet, *curia*

left, adj *rel(l)iquus*, to be —, *restare*, see LEAVE

left, adj *sinister, laevus*, the — hand, *sinistra* (i e, *manus*), on the —, *a sinistrâ, ad laevam*. **left-handed,** adj *qui manu sinistrâ pro dextrâ utitur*.

leg, n *crus, cruris*, n, — of mutton, *caro ovilla*, — of a table, *pes mensae* **leggings,** n *ocreae*

legacy, n *legātum*, to make a —, *alci legare alqd*

legal, adj *legitimus, quod ex lege* or *legibus* or *secundum leges fit*. Adv *legitime, lege* **legality,** n *quod ex lege fit* **legalize,** v tr *legibus constituĕre, sancire ut, ferre, ut alqd fiat* (= to propose a law)

legate, n *legatus, nuntius* **legation,** n *legatio*

legend, n on coin, *inscriptio, titulus*, = history of a saint, *vita hominis sancti, res ab homine sancto gesta*, = fable, *fabula* **legendary,** adj *commenticius, fictus, fabulosus, falsus* (= untrue)

legerdemain, n *ars praestigiatoria*, — tricks, *praestigiae* (ante and post class.)

legible, adj. *quod facile legi potest* Adv by **legibility,** n *quod facile legi potest*

legion, n *legio*, legionary, *legionarius* (e g *cohors, miles*), fig *ingens numerus, magna vis* **legionary,** adj *legionarius*

legislate, v intr *leges dare, constituĕre, condĕre, scribĕre*, see also LAW **legislation,** n *legis (legum) datio, legis latio* (= proposal of a law), so by circuml *leges dare, leges condĕre*, see LAW **legislator,** n *legis* or *legum lator* **legislative,** adj — body, *senatus, -ūs* **legislature,** n *comitia, -orum (centuriata, tributa*, etc), *senatus, -ūs*

leisure, n *otium* (opp *negotium*, that is, *nec* and *otium*), to be at —, *otiari, vacare, cessare*, at —, *otiosus, vacuus*, not at —, *occupatus*, — time, *tempus subsicivum (subsec.)*. **leisurely,** adj *lentus, otiosus*, see SLOW. Adv *otiose*

lend, v tr 1, *mutuum dare, commodare alci alqd*, — on interest, *fenerari, (fenore) occupare, (col)locare*, 2, fig *dare, praebēre*.

length, n *longitudo*, = extension in height, *proceritas*, — in time, *longinquitas, diuturnitas*, — of the way, *longinquitas viae*, in —, *per longitudinem*, — of time, *in longinquum, diu*, to run all —s, *extrema audēre*, at —, *tandem, denique, tum (tunc) demum*, = fully, *copiose, fuse*. **length-wise,** adv *in longitudinem* **lengthy,** adj — in words, *verbosus, longus*, not to be —, *ne in re multus sim* **lengthen,** v tr *alqd longius facĕre, producĕre*, — in time, *prorogare*, — for payment, *diem ad solvendum prorogare*, — the war, *bellum prorogare*, — the service, *militiam continuare*, — a feast, *convivium producĕre*

lenient, adj *mitis, clemens, misericors* Adv *clementer* **leniency,** n. *clementia, lenitas, misericordia*

lens, n **vitrum lenticulari formâ* (in no sense class.).

lentil, n *lens, -ntis*, f., *lenticula* (Cels.).

leonine, adj *leoninus*

leopard, n. *leopardus* (very late)

leprosy, n *lepra* (usu in pl, Plin) **leper,** n *homo leprosus* (late).

less, I. adj *minor* **II.** adv *minus*, see LITTLE **lessen,** v tr *(de)minuĕre, imminuĕre*. **lessening,** n *deminutio, imminutio*

lessee, n *conductor*

lesson, n 1, *discenda* (= things to be learned, if by heart, *ediscenda*), dictated —s, *dictata, -orum*, to take —s of anyone, *audire magistrum*, 2, fig *praeceptum, monitum, documentum* (= proof)

lest, conj *ne* with subj

let, v tr = to hinder, see HINDER

let, v intr 1, = to cause or make, I will — you know, *te certiorem faciam* (also by *monēre*); Xenophon —s Socrates say, *Xenophon Socratem disputantem facit*, 2, = to command, *jubēre, curare, alci negotium dare*, 3, = as a sign of the imperative, — us go, *eamus*, 4, in various phrases, e g to — blood, *sanguinem mittere*; to — go, *missum facĕre, mittĕre, dimittĕre*. — alone, — that alone or be quiet, *missa isthaec fac*, — down, *demittĕre*, — fly, = shoot, *jaculari, telum in alqm jacĕre*, — loose, *emittĕre*, — in, *admittĕre*, — off, *absolvĕre*, = absolve, *pila (e)mittĕre, tela con(j)icĕre*, = discharge weapons, — into your secrets, *secreta consilia alci impertire*, — slip, *omittĕre, praetermittĕre*, — an opportunity, *facultatem alqd agendi omittĕre*, — that pass, *ut ista omittamus*, 5, = to allow, *sinere* acc and infin or *ut, pati* acc and infin, *concedĕre* infin, *permittĕre alci ut* or infin, — not, *cave ne* (e g — him not go out, *cave ne exeat*), my business will not — me, *per negotium mihi non licet*, 6, = to lend or give the use of, see LEASE.

lethal, adj *mortifer, exitialis, exitiabilis, funestus.*

lethargic, adj *veternosus, torpidus* **lethargy,** n *torpor* (Tac), *veternus*

letter, n 1, (of the alphabet) *lit(t)era*, capital —, *lit(t)era grandis*; —s of the alphabet, *lit(t)erarum notae*, to the —, *ad verbum, ad lit(t)eram*, the — of the law, *verba legis*; to hold to the —, *scriptum sequi*, 2, = an epistle, *lit(t)erae, epistula (epistola)*, by —, *lit(t)eris, per lit(t)eras* **letter-carrier,** n *tabellarius, qui lit(t)eras perfert.* **letters,** n = learning, *doctrina, eruditio, humanitas, lit(t)erae*, a man of —, *homo doctus, eruditus, lit(t)eratus, doctrinā ornatissimus* **lettered,** adj *lit(t)eratus*

lettuce, n *lactuca*

levant, n *oriens, solis ortus, -ūs.*

levee, n *salutatio*

level, I. adj *aequus, planus*, comb *aequus et planus, libratus* (= balanced). **II.** n *aequum* (e.g *in aequum descendĕre*), *planities*, to be on a — with, *pari esse condicione cum algo, parem* or *aequalem esse alci* **III.** v tr 1, *aequare, coaequare, exaequare, complanare* (e g *terram*), 2, = to destroy, *solo urbem aequare*, — to the ground, *diruĕre, evertĕre, sternĕre*, see RAZE.

lever, n *vectis, -is*, m

leveret, n *lepusculus*

levity, n 1, = lightness, *lĕvitas*, 2, = in character, *inconstantia, lĕvitas* (with *hominis, animi, opinionis*), = jesting, *jocus, jocatio*

levy, I. v tr ,— soldiers, *milites scribĕre, milites conscribere*, — tribute, *tributum imponĕre, vectigal exigĕre* **II.** n *dilectus, -ūs*, to make a —, *delectum habēre* or *agĕre*, see ENLIST

lewd, adj *impudicus, incestus, impurus* Adv *inceste, impure* **lewdness,** n *impudicitia, impuritas, libidines, -um*, pl f

lexicon, n **lexicon, *onomasticon*

liable, adj *obnoxius* (e g *irae, bello*), to be — *cadĕre in* (e g *cadit ergo in bonum hominem mentiri?* Cic) **liability,** n use adj

libation, n *libatio, libamentum, libamen*, to make a —, *libare*

libel, I. n *libellus famosus, carmen famosum* (in verse). **II.** v tr *libellum ad infamiam alcjs edĕre* **libellous,** adj *famosus, probrosus*

liberal, adj *liberalis, largus, munificus, benignus, beneficus*, too —, *prodigus, profusus*, the — arts, *artes liberales, artes ingenuae.* Adv *liberaliter, large*, comb *large et liberaliter, munifice, benigne, prodige, profuse*, to give —, *largiri* **liberality,** n *liberalitas, munificentia, largitas, beneficentia, benignitas*, of thought, etc , *animus ingenuus, liberalis*

liberate, v tr *liberare*; to — a slave, *manumittĕre*, see DELIVER **liberator,** n *liberator* (e g *patriae*), *vindex* **liberation,** n *liberatio*; = of a slave, *manumissio*

libertine, n *homo dissolutus* **libertinism,** n *licentia morum, mores dissoluti*

liberty, n *libertas*, too much —, *licentia*, = leave, *copia, potestas*, — of will, *arbitrium, liberum arbitrium*, at —, *liber*, you are at — to do it, *nihil impedit quominus facias, algd facĕre tibi licet* or *integrum est.*

library, n *bibliotheca*, a considerable —, *bona librorum copia* **librarian,** n , to be a —, *bibliothecae praeesse*

libration, n *libratio*

license, I. n = permission, *copia, potestas*, = liberty, *licentia* (also in bad sense, *licentia Sullani temporis, licentia militum, magna gladiatorum est licentia*) **II.** v tr *algm privilegio munire* **licentious,** adj *dissolutus, libidinosus (lub-)* Adv *per licentiam, dissolute* **licentiousness,** n *libido, libidines, vita dissoluta*, see LEWD

lick, v.tr. *lingĕre, lambĕre*; to — up, *ligurire*

lickerish, adj *fastidiosus, delicatus*

licorice, n. *glycyrrhiza, -ae*, f , *dulcis radix* (Plin)

lid, n *operculum, operimentum*

lie, I. n *mendacium, commentum, falsum*, to tell a —, *mendacium dicĕre alci de algā re*, to give a person the —, *mendacii algm coarguĕre* **II.** v intr *mentiri.* **liar,** n (*homo*) *mendax, homo fallax, falsiloquus* (Plaut.).

lie, v intr. = to be in a certain place or position, *jacēre* (e g *jacēre humi*, to lie or be on the ground , so *jacēre in gramine, jacēre ad alcjs pedes, jacēre sub arbore, jacēre per vias*), *cubare* (in bed, etc), *situm esse, positum esse*, as far as —s in me, *quantum est in me* (*te, vobis*, etc), *pro viribus meis* (*tuis*, etc.), to — in, *puerperio cubare* (of childbirth (Plaut)), *parturire*, to — in this, *contineri re, situm esse, versari, cerni in re*, on whom does it —? *per quem stat?* where —s the hindrance? *quid impedit?* to — between, *interjacēre*, with accus or with dat , — in wait, *alci insidiari*, — down, *procumbĕre, decumbĕre, quieti se dare*, — hid, *latēre*, — still, *quiescĕre*, — under an obligation, *alci gratiā devinctum esse*

lief, adj e g I had as —, *malim*, — die as endure it, *mortuum me quam ut id patiar malim*

liege, adj *imperio* or *dicione alcjs subjectus*, or *parens, obnoxius alci*, to be —, *esse in alcjs dicione, parēre alci*

lieu, n in — of, *pro, loco, vice* **lieutenant,** n in gen *legatus*, in the army, perhaps *centurio* (infantry), and *praefectus* (cavalry), the lord lieutenant of a country, *praefectus provinciae*

life, n 1, *vita, anima, spiritus, ūs*, physical —, *vita quae corpore et spiritu continetur*, in my —, *dum vivo*, to have —, *vivĕre, in vita esse*, to come to —, *nasci, in lucem edi*, to put an end to —, *mortem sibi consciscĕre*, to take away —, *vitam alci adimĕre*, to give —, *procreare, parĕre algm*, to call into —, *gignĕre, procreare, facĕre, efficĕre*, he can scarcely sustain —, *vix habet unde vivat*, as to the manner in which men live, mode of —, *victus, -ūs*, in public duty, *in republica gerendā*, private —, *vita cot(t)idiana* (*quot*), early —, *iniens aetas*, the prime of —, *bona* or *constans aetas*, (as a word of affection), *mea vita! mea lux!* while there is — there is hope, *aegroto dum anima est spes est*, to restore to —, *ad vitam revocare* or *reducĕre, e mortuis excitare*, to come to — again, *reviviscĕre*, to venture your —, *capitis periculum adire*, to cost a person his —, *morte stare*, to try a person for his —, *de capite quaerĕre*, to lead a —, *vivĕre, vitam agĕre*, to flee for one's —, *fugā salutem petĕre*, to lose —, *perire, vitam perdĕre*, if I could without losing my —, *si salvo capite potuissem*, to depart this —, *diem obire supremum*; all one's —, *per totam vitam*, loss of — by law, *ultimum supplicium*, to the —, *ad vivum*; full of —, *vividus, vegetus, alacer*; to put — into, *alci animum jacĕre* or *addĕre*, 2, fig , see VIGOUR ; in oratory, *sucus*, comb *sucus et sanguis*. 3, = the reality (e g paint from the —), *ipse* with the noun mentioned ; 4, = time, *aetas, tempora -um* (e g this —, *haec aetas*)

life-blood, n. 1, *sanguis, -inis*, m , 2, fig ,

see Life. **life-boat,** n. *scapha ad naufragos excipiendos facta.* **life-guards,** n. *milites* or *cohortes praetoriani* (of the emperor). **lifeless,** adj. 1, *exanimis, exanimus, inanimus* (opp. *animatus, animans*); 2, *frigidus, exsanguis, exilis, aridus,* comb. *aridus et exsanguis, jejunus* (all of speech). Adv. fig., *languide, frigide, exiliter,* comb. *frigide et exiliter* (of speech); *jejune,* comb. *jejune et exiliter.* **lifetime,** n. *aetas,* †*aevum.* **lively,** adj., **liveliness,** n., **livelihood,** n., see Live.

lift, I. v.tr. *(at)tollĕre, extollĕre, (sub)levare;* — upright, *erigĕre;* he —s his hands to heaven, *manus ad sidera tollit;* —ed up, *levatus, allevatus, arrectus;* — with pride, etc., *superbiâ, rebus secundis,* etc., *elatus.* **II.** n., use verb.

ligament, n. *ligamentum* (Tac.). **ligature,** n. *ligatura* (late).

light, I. n. = luminous matter, or the result of (as daylight), *lumen, lux;* with the —, *cum primâ luce, die illucescente, sub lucis ortum;* the — of the eyes, *lumina (oculorum);* — of a precious stone, *lux gemmae;* to give —, *lucem edĕre, fundĕre;* to see the — of day (or be born), *in lucem edi* or *suscipi, nasci;* to come to —, *in lucem proferri, protrahi, detegi, patefieri* (= to be uncovered, made manifest); to bring to —, *in lucem proferre, protrahĕre, aperire, patefacĕre, detegĕre;* to stand in or intercept a person's —, (lit.) *alcjs luminibus officĕre, obstruĕre,* (fig.) *alci officĕre, obesse;* to stand in your own —, *sibi* or *utilitati suae* or *commodis suis male consulĕre, sibi deesse;* to place in an odious —, *alqd in invidiam adducĕre, in summam invid. adduc., alci rei ad(j)icĕre invidiam;* to see in a false —, *alqd fallaci judicio vidēre;* = lamp, *lumen* (in gen.), *lucerna* (espec. = a lamp), *candela* (= a taper or torch of wax, tallow, etc.), *cereus* (= a wax taper or torch); to light a —, *lumen, lucernam, candelam accendĕre;* to write or work by —, *ad lucernam (cum lucernâ) scribĕre, alqd lucubrare* or *elucubrari* (e.g. *epistulam*); to study by —, *lucubrare;* a study by —, *lucubratio.* **II.** adj. as opposed to what is dark, *clarus* (= light in itself), *illustris, lucidus* (= light-spreading), *luminosus, albidus* (= white), *candidus* (= dazzling), *pellucidus* (= shining through). **III.** v.tr. 1, = to set light to, *alqd accendĕre;* 2, = to fill with light, *illustrare, collustrare.* **lighten, I.** v.intr. *fulgĕre, fulgurare* (usu. impers. *fulget, fulgurat*). **II.** v.tr. see Light, III. 2. **lighthouse,** n. *pharus (pharos).* **lightning,** n. *fulmen, fulgur.*

light, adj. as opposed to heavy, *lĕvis* (opp. *gravis*); — soil, *solum tenue;* = inconsiderable, *lĕvis* (opp. *gravis,* weighty), *parvus* (opp. *magnus*); — pain, *dolor levis* or *parvus* (= slight); —-armed infantry, *equites lĕvis armaturae;* — troops, *milites levis armaturae* or merely *levis armaturae, milites leves, velites* (as a regular part of the Roman army, early called *rorarii*), *milites expediti* (= all soldiers who have laid aside their kit, consequently we find *expediti levis armaturae*); — clad or armed, *expeditus, nudus* (= one who has laid aside his overcoat); a —-foot-soldier, *pedes expeditus;* — of foot, *velox* (opp. *tardus*), *pernix* (= nimble); he is very — of foot, *inest in eo praecipua pedum pernicitas;* — of colour, *pallidus;* see Pale; —-hearted, *hilaris, curis vacuus, curis liber solutusque animus;* it is something — (= trivial), *nihil est negotii;* —-minded, *lĕvis, vanus.* Adv. *leviter* (lit. and fig.), *temere, inconsulte (inconsulto)* (= without consideration); to think — of anything, *alqd non magni facĕre.* **lighten,** v.tr. lit. *exonerare* (not in Cic. or Caes.), *jacturam facĕre* (of a ship). **lightness,** n. *lĕvitas* (lit. and fig.). **lightsome,** adj. *hilaris, alacer* (= cheerful). **lightsomeness,** n. *laetitia, hilaritas;* see Gay.

like, I. adj. = similar, *similis, consimilis,* with gen. or dat., *par,* dat.; *instar* (indecl., n.), gen.; to make —, *ad similitudinem rei fingĕre;* he is no longer — what he was, *prorsus alius est factus ac fuit antea;* that is — him, *hoc dignum est illo.* **II.** adv. *similiter, simili modo* with *ut atque (ac), modo, instar, ritu* with gen. (*ad instar,* post class.); see As. **III.** v.tr. *amare, diligĕre, carum habēre alqm, delectari alqâ re;* I — that, *hoc arridet* or *cordi est* or *datum* or *acceptum est mihi, libet mihi;* I do not — that, *hoc displicet mihi* (with infin. following); I — it well, *magnopere probo;* if you —, *si isthuc tibi placet;* as you —, *arbitratu tuo.* **like-minded,** adj. *consors, congruens, conveniens, consentaneus.* **likely,** adj. *veri similis* (often written as one word, sometimes *similis veri*), *probabilis;* it is — that, *veri simile est,* with accus. and infin. **likelihood,** n. *veri similitudo* (also in one word, or *similitudo veri*), *probabilitas.* **liken,** v.tr. *alqd alci rei* or *cum alqa re comparare;* see Compare. **likeness,** n. 1, = resemblance, *similitudo,* or by adj.; see Like; 2, = portrait, *effigies, imago;* painted —, *picta imago.* **liking,** n. *amor, voluptas* (= pleasure); *libido;* to one's —, *gratus, acceptus, jucundus.* **likewise,** adv. *item, itidem, et,* or by *idem;* see Also.

liliputian, adj. see Little, Insignificant.

lily, n. *lilium;* of or from a —, *liliaceus.*

limb, n. *membrum, artus, -uum* (= a member).

limber, adj. *flexibilis, mollis, lentus.*

lime or **limestone, I.** n. *calx, -cis,* f. and (rarely) m.; to burn —, *calcem coquĕre;* quick-—, *calx viva;* slaked —, *calx ex(s)tincta;* bird-—, *viscum.* **II.** v.tr. = to smear with bird-—, *visco illinĕre.* **lime-burner,** n. *calcarius.* **lime-kiln,** n. *(fornax) calcaria.* **limed,** adj. *viscatus.*

lime-tree, n. *tilia.*

limit, I. n. *terminus, finis, -is,* m., *limes, -itis,* m., *circumscriptio.* **II.** v.tr. *finire, limitare* (= to separate by a boundary-stone or line, thus *limitati agri*), *terminare* (= to put an end to), *certis limitibus* or *terminis circumscribĕre.* **limitation** or **limiting,** n. *determinatio, circumscriptio, definitio, limitatio;* = exception, *exceptio.* **limited,** adj. 1, = short, *brevis;* see Brief; 2, fig. a — monarchy, *condiciones regiae potestati impositae,* or *potestas certis cond. circumscripta.* **limitless,** adj. *immensus, infinitus.*

limn, v.tr. see Paint.

limp, adj. *languidus, flaccus, flaccidus.* **limpness,** n. *languor.*

limp, v.intr. *claudicare, claudum esse* (= to be lame); see Lame.

limpet, n. *lepas.*

limpid, adj. *limpidus* (rare), *pellucidus;* see Transparent.

linch-pin, n. *axis fibula.*

linden-tree, n. *tilia.*

line, I. n. 1, *linea;* a straight —, *recta linea;* curved —, *curva linea;* the — of the circle, *linea circumcurrens;* to draw a —, *lineam ducĕre* or *scribĕre;* 2, a boundary —, *finis,* m. and f.; 3, — (in poetry), *versus, -ūs, versiculus;* in letters, to write a few —s in reply, *pauca rescribĕre;* 4, of soldiers, *acies* (in battle), *agmen* (on the march); the front —, *prima acies, hastati, principia, -iorum;* the second —, *principes, -um;* the third —, *triarii;* — of skirmishers, *velites;* to advance in equal —, *aequâ fronte procedĕre;* a soldier of the —, *(miles) legionarius;* to draw up the army in three —s, *aciem triplicem instruĕre*, 5, in the father's —, *a patre*, in the mother's —, *a matre*, to be connected with one in the direct — *artissimo gradu contingĕre alqm*, 6, (in fortification), *fossa* (= trench), *vallum* (= entrenchment), *opus*, *-eris*, n, *munitio* (= fortification), *agger*, *eris*, m (= mound), 7, = a thin rope, *funis*, *funiculus*, *linea*, a carpenter's —, *amussis*, *-is*, m, *linea*, a chalked —, *linea creta descripta*, a fishing —, *linea*, a plumb —, *perpendiculum*, by —, *ad amussim*, *examussim* (ante and post class) **II.** v tr 1, — a dress, perhaps *vesti alqd assuĕre*, 2, = to fill, *complēre* **lineal,** adj better not expressed, (e g a — descendant, *unus e posteris alcjs*) **lineage,** n *stirps*, *-is*, f., *genus*, *eris*, n, *origo*, *progenies* **lineament,** n used generally in the pl, as in English, *lineamenta* (*similitudo oris vultusque ut lineamenta*, Liv), but applied to the mind (e g *animi lineamenta sunt pulchriora quam corporis*), see Feature **linear,** adj *linearis* (Plin)

linen, n as the material, *linum* (λίνον, flax, *linum tam factum quam infectum, quodque netum quodque in telâ est*, Cic), *linteum*, *lintea*, *-orum*, n (properly of —, i e — cloth, e g *lintea*, *vestis*, *vela*), clad in —, *linteatus*

linger, v intr *cessare*, *morari*, *contari* (*cunct-*), he —s (i e dies slowly), perhaps *paul(l)atim moritur* **lingerer,** n *cessator*, *contator* (*cunct-*) **lingering,** **I.** n *cessatio*, *contatio* (*cunct-*), *mora* **II.** adj *tardus*, *lentus*, *contabundus* (*cunct*) (of people), a — death, *tabes*, *is*, f (= consumption), perhaps *tarda mors*, *tis*, f, see Slow Adv *tarde*, *contanter* (*cunct-*), *lente*, see Slowly

linguist, n *homo multarum linguarum sciens* **linguistic,** adj *grammaticus* or *de ratione linguarum*

liniment, n. *unguentum*

link, **I.** n 1, = torch, *fax*, *taeda*, *funale*, 2, = bond, *vinculum*, *conjunctio*, *societas*, *familiaritas* (of friendship), *affinitas* (by marriage), *necessitudo* (any close tie), 3, of a chain, *anulus* (Mart). **II.** v.tr *conjungĕre*, *(con)(n)ectĕre*, see Unite

lint, n *linamentum* (Cels).

lintel, n *limen* (*superum* or *superius*)

lion, n 1, *leo*, of a —, *leoninus*, a —'s skin, *pellis leonina*, a —s claw, *unguis leoninus*, 2, fig (e g the — of the season) *deliciae*, *-um* **lion-hearted,** adj *magnanimus* **lioness,** n *leaena*

lip, n *labrum*, the upper —, *labrum superius*, the lower —, *labrum inferius*, *primoribus labris* (= the tip of the —s) *gustasse* = to get a taste of, *labellum* (esp in endearing sense), *labium* (rare) **lip-salve,** n *unguentum* **lip-service,** n see Flattery **lip-wisdom,** n *verbo tenus sapientia*

liquid, **I.** adj *liquidus*, *fluens* to grow —, *liquescĕre*, *liquefieri*, to make —, *liquefacĕre* **II.** n *liquor*, *humor*, † *latex*, *sucus* (= juice) **liquidate,** v tr see Pay **liquefy,** v tr *liquefacĕre* **liquor,** n see Liquid, II

lisp, v intr *balbutire* (= to stammer)

list, n. = catalogue, *tabula*, *index* (Quint)

list, v tr see Wish, Desire, Please

listen, v intr see Hear **listener,** n *auscultator*

listless, adj *socors*, *deses*, *languidus*, *piger* Adv *torpide*, *stupide*, *languide* **listlessness,** n *torpor* (Tac), *socordia*, *desidia*

lists, n *campus*, *hippodromus*, *spatia*, *orum*, to enter the — against (fig), *cum alqo contendĕre*

litany, n * *litania* (Eccl), or *preces*, *-um*, f (= prayers)

literal, adj to employ a word in its — sense, *verbum proprie dicere*, a — translator, *ad verbum interpres*, the — sense, *propria vis* Adv *lit(t)eratim*, *proprie*, *ad lit(t)eram*, *ad verbum* **literary,** adj *lit(t)eratus* (= lettered or learned), *lit(t)erarum studiosus*, — leisure, *otium lit(t)eratum* — monuments, *lit(t)erarum monumenta* **literature,** n *lit(t)erae*, *lit(t)erarum monumenta*, *orum*, to entrust to the care of —, *lit(t)eris mandare* or *consignare*, to learn from —, *lit(t)eris percipĕre* we have no history in our —, *abest historia lit(t)eris nostris*, the study of —, *lit(t)erarum studium* the knowledge of —, *lit(t)erarum scientia* to be acquainted with —, *lit(t)eras scire*, to be without —, *lit(t)eras nescire*

lithe, adj *mollis flexibilis*

lithographer, n *lithographus* (in no sense class)

litigate, v tr and intr *litigare cum alqo pro alqo*, *inter se de alqâ re* (*noli pati fratres litigare*) (Cic), *lites sequi* **litigant,** n *qui cum alqo litigat* **litigation,** n *lis* **litigious,** adj *litigiosus* (= full of strife, given to lawsuits) **litigiousness,** n use an adj. (e g the — of the man, *homo litium cupidus*)

litter, **I.** n 1, *lectīca*, a small —, *lecticula*, 2, *fetura*, *fetus*, *-ūs*, *suboles* (*sob-*) (= a brood), — of pigs, *porcelli uno partu editi*, 3, — for cattle, *stramentum*, = confusion, *turbae*, to make a —, *res turbare* **II.** v tr 1, *parĕre*, *fetum edĕre* = to bring forth, 2, see Strew.

little, **I.** adj *parvus*, *parvulus* (dim), *exiguus*, *minutus*, *modicus*, often rendered by diminutives, as — (small) coins, *nummuli*, — book, *libellus*, — present, *munusculum*, — used as a noun, e g a little gain, *paul(l)um lucri*, also by *aliquid*, e g a — pride, *alqd superbiae*, to sell by — and —, or by retail, *divendĕre* the — ones, *parvi*, *liberi*, a — time, *tempus breve*, for a —, *parumper*, *paul(l)isper*, in a —, *brevi*, a — after, *paul(l)o post*, by — and —, *paul(l)atim*, *sensim*, *gradatim*, *minutatim*, a — soul, *animus pusillus*, not a —, *valde*, *vehementer*, *magnopere* he is a — too much given to money, *aliquanto ad rem est avidior*, these things are a — troublesome to me, *nonnihil molesta haec sunt mihi*, a — before sunset, *sub occasum solis*, how —, *quantillus* (Plaut), *quantulus*, how — soever, *quantuluscunque* so —, *tantulus*, he lacked — of being killed, *haud multum a(b)fuit quin occideretur* **II.** adv *paul(l)um*, *aliquantulum*, *nonnihil* (= somewhat), *parum* (= too —) **III.** n *aliquantum*, *nonnihil*, *parum* (= too —), *paul(l)um*, *paul(l)ulum*, see Little I **littleness,** n *parvitas*, *exiguitas* **less,** adj *minor* **least,** adj *minimus*, *minimum*, at least

liturgy, n * *liturgia* (Eccl)

live, **I.** v intr 1, *vivĕre*, *in vita esse*, yet to —, *in vivis esse*, *superstitem esse*, to let one —, *alcjs vitae parcĕre*, cannot — without, *alqâ re carēre non posse*, so long as I —, *me vivo*, *dum* (*quoad*) *vivo*, if I —, *si vita suppetit*, as I —! *ita vivam!* — for a thing, *deditum esse rei*, — in a thing, *totum esse in re*, — for self, *sibi vivĕre*, 2, to — on anything, *vivĕre re*, *vesci re*, *ali re*, *vitam sustentare alqâ re*; 3, to — luxuriously, *laute vivĕre* — poorly, *parce vivĕre*, to — at or in a place, *locum incolĕre*, *locum* or *in loco habitare*, see Dwell, as to your condition, to —, *vitam agĕre* or *degĕre*, — happily, etc, *bene*, *feliciter*, *misere*, etc, *vivĕre* **II.** adj or **living,** adj *vivus* **livelihood,** n *victus*, *ūs* (= provisions) **livelong,** adj *totus* **lively,** adj

1, = active, *strenuus, acer*; see ACTIVE; 2, = sprightly, *alacer, vegetus, hilaris, festivus, lepidus*; see MERRY, WITTY; 3, of places, = frequented, *celeber*; 4, = keen, *vehemens*; to feel a — joy, *valde* or *vehementer gaudēre*; to form a — idea of anything, *rem tanquam praesentem contemplari*. **liveliness,** n. *alacritas, hilaritas, festivitas.*

liver, n. *jecur, -(in)oris,* n.

livery, n. *vestis quam alcjs famuli gerunt.* **liveryman,** n. *sodalis, -is,* m., or *socius alcjs societatis.* **livery-stables,** n. *stabulum (mercenarium).*

livid, adj. *lividus*; a — colour, *livor.*

lizard, n. *lacerta, stellio.*

lo! interj. *en, ecce.*

load, I. n. *onus, -ĕris,* n.; a cart—, *vehes, -is,* f. (Plin.); a — on the mind, *tristitia, molestia, animi dolor* or *aegritudo.* **II.** v.tr. **1,** *onerare, gravare* (properly = to make heavy or weigh down, e.g. *membra gravabat onus, gravatus vino somnoque, oculi morte gravati*); he —ed the people excessively, *nimium oneris plebi imposuit*; *opprimĕre* (= to press down or oppress); — with reproaches; see REPROACH; **2,** of firearms, *arma parare, instruĕre.* **loaded,** adj. *onustus, oneratus.*

loaf, n. *panis, -is,* m.

loam, n. *lutum.* **loamy,** adj. *lutosus* (= muddy), *cretosus, argillosus* (of chalk).

loan, n. *res mutuata* or *mutuo data* or *commodata*; *pecunia mutua* or *credita.*

loath, adj. *invitus*; I am —, *piget me* (e.g. *referre piget me, piget me dicĕre*). **loathe,** v.tr. *alqd fastidire, aversari, a re abhorrēre.* **loathing,** n. *fastidium* (for food, fig. = disdain), *odium* (= hatred), *taedium* (= disgust, mostly post class.). **loathsome,** adj. *teter, foedus, obscenus* (*obscaen-*), *odiosus.* **loathsomeness,** n. *foeditas, obscenitas* (*obscaen-*).

lobby, n. *vestibulum.*

lobster, n. *cancer* (= crab).

local, adj. by the genitive *loci, regionis,* etc. (e.g. *locorum difficultates,* = — difficulties; *loci opportunitas,* = a — advantage or convenience). **locality,** n. *locus,* or *loci natura* or *situs, -ūs.*

loch, n. *lacus.*

lock, I. n. *claustra, -orum* (properly = a shutter or fastener); to be under — and key, *esse sub claustris* or *clavi*; — in a river, *piscina* (Plin.) or *emissarium* (= outlet of a lake). **II.** v.tr. *obserāre, occludĕre*; to — in, *claustro includĕre*; to — out, *claustro foras excludĕre*; to — up, *alqm concludĕre.* **locker,** n. *armarium.* **locket,** n. *collare*; see NECKLACE. **lock-jaw,** n. *tetanus* (Plin.).

lock, n. of hair, *cirrus*; of wool, *floccus.*

locomotion, n. *motus, -ūs.* **locomotive,** adj. *suā vi motus*; — engine, *machina ad currus trahendos facta.*

locust, n. *locusta* (Plin.).

lodge, I. n. *casa* (= a cot). **II.** v.intr. **1,** *deversari apud alqm, ad alqm devertĕre*; **2,** = in, (*in*) *alqā re haerēre.* **III.** v.tr. **1,** *hospitio excipĕre, tecto recipĕre*; **2,** — a complaint, *alqm* or *nomen alcjs deferre*; — a spear, etc., *adigĕre.* **lodger,** n. *deversor* (at an inn), *inquilinus, inquilina* (= one who lives in another's house). **lodgings,** n. *cenaculum meritorium* (= hired room, Suet.), or by *domus,* = house. **lodging-house,** n. *insula.* **lodgment,** n. to effect a —, see LODGE II. and III.

loft, n. *cenaculum* (*coen-*); hay—, *faenilia, ium* (*fen-*); corn—, *horreum.* **lofty,** adj. **1,** = high, *altus,* (*ex*)*celsus, editus* (of places), *sublimis* (= aloft, mostly poet.); **2,** fig. (*ex*)*celsus, elatus, sublimis, erectus*; of speech, *grandis*; of pride, *superbus.* Adv. *alte, excelse* (lit. and fig.), *sublime* (lit.), *elate* (fig.); = proudly, *superbe.* **loftiness,** n. **1,** *altitudo*; **2,** (fig.) *altitudo, elatio, excelsitas,* comb. of speech, *altitudo et elatio oratoris* (Cic.), *sublimitas et magnificentia et nitor* (Quint.); — of mind, *altitudo animi.*

log, n. **1,** *lignum* (or *ligna,* pl. = firewood); *stipes, -ĭtis,* m. (= trunk of tree); **2,** fig. = blockhead, *stipes, caudex, -icis,* m., *truncus.* **logbook,** n. *tabulae.* **loggerhead,** n. **1,** = blockhead; see LOG; **2,** to be at —s, see QUARREL.

logic, n. *logica, -orum,* or *dialectica* (or *dialectice*), *logica* (or *logice,* or written in Greek, ἡ λογική). **logical,** adj. *logicus, dialecticus* (= connected with logic); — questions, *dialectica, -orum*; — conclusion, *consequentia, -ium,* or *ea quae ex concessis consequuntur.* Adv. *dialectice* or *quod ex concessis consequitur,* or *quod necessarie demonstratur.* **logician,** n. *dialecticus.*

loin, n. *lumbus.*

loiter, v.intr. *cessare*; see LINGER.

loll, v.intr. and tr. *recumbĕre, recubare*; to — out the tongue, *linguam exserĕre.*

lonely, lonesome, lone, adj. *solus, solitarius, avius, reductus* (of situation). **loneliness,** n. *solitudo.*

long, I. adj. **1,** = extension in space, *longus, procerus* (= tall), *promissus* (= hanging down), *longinquus* (= distant); exceedingly —, *praelongus*; — hair, *capillus promissus*; to defer for a — time, *in longinquum tempus differre rem*; the measure or degree of length is put in the accusative (e.g. six feet —, *longus pedes sex* or *in longitudinem sex pedum*; a foot —, *pedalis, pedem longus*); **2,** = extension in time, *longus, longinquus, diuturnus, diutinus*; during a — while, *diu*; a — time before, *multum ante alqd*; a — time after, *multum post alqd*; **3,** = slow or dilatory, *tardus, lentus, segnis, piger*; a — business, *lentum negotium.* **II.** adv. *diu*; — ago, *pridem, jampridem* (or as two words), *jamdudum* (or in two words); not — ago, *haud dudum, modo, olim*; how —, *quamdiu*; as — as, *quamdiu . . . tamdiu*; — after, *multo post* or *post multos annos*; — before, *ante multos annos.* **III.** v.intr. and tr. to — for, *avēre alqd* or with infin., *cupĕre alqd* or with infin. or *ut, gestire* with infin., *avēre, cupĕre, gestire, desiderare* (= to regret the loss or want of) *alqd* or *alqm, alqd ab alqo, alqd in alqo*; *desiderio alcjs rei teneri* or *flagrare, concupiscĕre* (= to desire). **longevity,** n. by circumloc.; see OLD. **longing, I.** n. *alcjs rei desiderium* (= desire), *appetitus, -ūs, appetitio* (= passionate desire). **II.** adj. — after anything, *alcjs rei cupidus,* or *avidus.* Adv. *cupide, avide.* **long-suffering,** adj. see PATIENT.

look, I. n. **1,** as act, (*oculorum*) *obtutus, -ūs*; to direct a — at, *aspectum* or *oculos convertĕre* or *con*(*j*)*icĕre in rem*; — at a person, *intueri, a*(*d*)*spicĕre alqm*; **2,** = appearance of the countenance, *vultus, -ūs*; a severe —, *vultus severus*; in gen. *species, facies.* **II.** v.tr. to — at, *a*(*d*)*spicĕre, intueri, contemplari.* **III.** v.intr. *speciem alcjs* (*rei*) *praebēre, videri*; see SEEM; to — about, *circumspicĕre*; to — back, (*alqd*) *respicĕre*; to — down, *despicĕre*; to — down upon, *alqm despicĕre*; to — for, see SEEK; = to expect, *ex*(*s*)*pectare*; to — out, = to be on the — out, *speculari*; to — out for, = to take care of, *alcı rei consulĕre*, to — towards, *in* or *ad alqm locum spectare*, to — up, *suspicĕre*; to — up to, *alqm verēri* **looking-glass,** n *speculum* **look out,** n use verb

loom, n *tela*

loom, v intr *in conspectum e longinquo dari*

loop, I. n *laqueus* (= noose) **II.** v tr *annectĕre*, see TIE **loophole,** n *foramen* (= hole), *fenestra* (= — in the wall of a tower for the discharge of missiles)

loose, I. adj **1,** = slack, *laxus, fluxus, remissus*, — reins, *laxae* or *fluxae habenae*, with — hair, *passis crinibus*, **2,** of soil, *rarus* (opp *densus*), *solutus* (opp *spissus*), *facilis* (Col), **3,** of teeth, *mobilis* (Plin), **4,** = at liberty (*carcere*, etc.) *liberatus, solutus* · **5,** of morals, (*dis*)*solutus, effrenatus, remissus* Adv *laxe*, (*dis*)*solute* **II.** v tr (*re*)*laxare, remittere*, (*re*)*solvĕre*, see UNTIE **looseness,** n use adj LOOSE

lop, v tr *tondēre*, (*de*)*putare, amputare* (= to prune), *praecidĕre* (= to — off). **lopsided,** adj *uno latere grandis*

loquacious, adj *loquax, garrulus* (= chattering), *verbosus* Adv *loquaciter, verbose* **loquacity,** n *loquacitas, garrulitas*

lord, n *dominus* **lordly,** adj **1,** of high rank, *illustris nobilis, illustri* or *nobili loco natus*; **2,** = proud *superbus, arrogans*, see PROUD, ARROGANT **lordliness,** n. *superbia, arrogantia*; see PRIDE, ARROGANCE **lordship,** n. = power, *imperium, dominatus, ūs*

lore, n *eruditio, doctrina*

lorn, adj *solus, desertus*, see LONELY, FORLORN

lose, v tr *amittĕre, perdĕre, jacturam rei facĕre* (of loss purposely incurred), one who has lost a member, *captus* (e g *oculo, auribus*), = to be bereaved, *privari, orbari re*, to — hope, *spem excidĕre*, to — a battle, *vinci*, to — patience, *patientiam rumpĕre*, to — time, *tempus perdĕre*, to — sight of one, *alqm e conspectu amittĕre*, to never — sight of, *alqd nunquam dimittĕre*. to be lost, *amitti, perdi, perire, absumi*, to give up for lost *desperare de re*, to — colour, *evanescere pallescĕre*, to be lost in thought, *in cogitatione defixum esse*, the mountain —s itself in the plain, *mons in planitiem se subducit*, I am lost, *peri*, the ships were lost at sea, *mersae sunt naves* (*in*) *mari* **loser,** n *qui damno afficitur*, he was a great —, *magno damno affectus est*. **losing,** n *amissio* **loss,** n *damnum, detrimentum, jactura, dispendium*, to sustain a —, *damna pati, calamitates subire, incommodis affici*, to repair a —, *damnum resarcire*, the — of a battle, *pugna adversa*, I am at a —, *dubius sum*, see UNCERTAIN

lot, n **1,** *sors*, -*tis*, f, *sortitio, sortitus, ūs*, by —, *sorte, sortito*. **2,** = fortune, *sors, fortuna*, casting of —s, *sortitio, sortitus, ūs* **lottery,** n *sors, sortitio, alea* (= game of dice), 'tis all a —, *nihil incertius est*

loth, adj see LOATH

lotion, n *liquida quae alci illinuntur*

loud, adj *clarus* (= clear), *magnus* (= strong), — cry, *magnus clamor*, — voice, *vox clara, vox magna* Adv *clare, clarā voce, magnā* or *summā voce* **loudness,** n *magnitudo, vox clara*

lounge, v intr *nihil agĕre, desidēre* **lounger,** n *homo deses, iners, cunctator* (*cunct*-), *cessator, ambulator*

louse, n *pediculus* (Plin). **lousy,** adj *pediculosus* (Mart)

lout, n *homo rusticus, agrestis, stipes, caudex* (*cod*) **loutish,** adj *rusticus, agrestis*; see RUDE Adv *rustice*

love, I. n *amor, caritas* (= affection), *pietas* (= reverent devotion), *studium*, = a favourable disposition, *studium alcjs rei*, to have —, *alcjs rei amantem esse*, worthy of —, *amandus, amore dignus*, — affair, *amor*, — potion, † *philtrum*, the god of —, *Cupido, Amor*, the goddess of —, *Venus*, my — ! *mea voluptas* ! *meum cor* ! *deliciae meae*. **II.** v tr *amare* (with natural affection), *diligĕre* (as friends), *carum habēre alqm, studēre alci, amore complecti alqm, amore prosequi alqm, amore alcjs teneri, amore alcjs captum esse, alcjs amore deperire*, to — learning, *lit*(*t*)*erarum studiosum esse* **loves,** n *amores* **loved,** adj *carus, acceptus, gratus, jucundus, suavis* **loving,** adj *alcjs amans, studiosus, blandus, benignus, dulcis, suavis, indulgens* Adv *amanter* **loving-kindness,** n *misericordia* · see MERCY **lovely,** adj **1** *bellus, venustus* (of persons and things), *amoenus* (of things), see BEAUTIFUL, **2,** = worthy of love, *amore dignus, amandus, amabilis* **loveliness,** n *venustas, amoenitas* **lover,** n *amator*, f *amatrix*, a — of literature, *lit*(*t*)*erarum studiosus*

low, I. adj **1,** of position, *humilis, demissus*; **2,** of voice, *gravis, submissus, suppressus*, **3,** of price, *vilis*, to buy at a — price, *parvo* or *vili* (*pretio*) *emĕre*. **4,** in regard to condition, *humilis* (= humble), *ignobilis, obscurus* (as to birth and ancestors), *tenuis* (as to property), lower, *inferior* (in position), *sordidus* (as to origin), of — birth, *humili* or *ignobili, obscuro* or *tenui loco ortus*, *humili fortunā ortus*, of the lowest birth, *infimae condicionis et fortunae, infimus, sordido loco ortus*, of the lower orders, *tenuioris ordinis*, the lowest of the people, *infima plebs*, the lowest class of men, *ultimae sortis homines, infimi ordinis* (*generis*) *homines, infimum genus hominum, faex, vulgus, i*, n , *plebs, plebecula*, **5,** = having a — tone, *humilis, illiberalis* (= unworthy a gentleman), *abjectus* (= despicable, employed with *animus*), *turpis*, see BASE, — expressions, *verba ex triviis petita*, **6,** = sad, *maestus, tristis* **II.** adv *humiliter* (lit post class, but class = basely), *demisse, abjecte* = basely, *illiberaliter* (= unbecomingly to a gentleman), to speak —, *submisse, submissā voce dicĕre* **lowly,** adj **1,** see LOW, **4**, **2,** = humble, *modestus, moderatus*, see HUMBLE **lowliness,** n **1,** *humilitas, obscuritas*, **2,** *modestia*, see HUMILITY **lowness,** n **1,** *humilitas* (of position or stature), **2** of birth, *humilitas, ignobilitas, obscuritas*, **3,** of price, *vilitas*, **4,** of the voice, *vox gravis*, **5,** of mind, *humilitas, animus humilis* or *abjectus, turpitudo*, of expression, *verba ex triviis petita* **low-born,** adj *ignobilis* or *obscuro loco natus* **low-lands,** n *loca* (*orum*) *plana* **low-spirited,** adj *animus demissus et oppressus, afflictus, maestus, tristis* see SAD **lower, I.** adj *inferior*, the — world, *apud inferos*, † *Tartarus* (*os*), † *Tartara, orum*, pl , — orders, see LOW, **4** **II.** v tr *demittĕre* to — the voice, *submittĕre* (Quint), to — oneself, *se ab*(*j*)*icĕre* **lowering,** adj see DARK, THREATENING

low, v tr of cattle, *mugire* **lowing,** n *mugitus, ūs*

loyal, adj *fidelis, fidus* Adv *fideliter* **loyalty,** n *fides, fidelitas*

lozenge, n *pastillus* (Plin)

lubber, n **lubberly,** adj see LOUT

lubricate, v tr *ung*(*u*)*ĕre*

lucid, adj *lucidus* (= bright, distinct of speech, etc , in the latter sense, also *dilucidus*) Adv (*di*)*lucide* **lucidness, lucidity,** n. *perspicuitas* (Quint), better use adj or adv (e g.

he expressed himself with —, *dilucide rem explicavit*).

Lucifer, n. 1, the morning star, *Lucifer*, † *Phosphorus*, † *Eous*; 2, = Satan, *Lucifer* (Eccl.).

luck, n. *fortuna*, *fors*, *sors*, *casus*, *-ūs*; good —, *fortuna secunda*, *res secundae*; bad —, *adversa fortuna*, *res adversae*; good — to it! *bene vertat!* **lucky**, adj. *felix*, *fortunatus*, *faustus*, *auspicatus*. Adv. *feliciter*, *ex animi sententiā*, *auspicato*.

lucre, n. *lucrum* (= gain), *quaestus*, *-ūs* (= acquirement); for —'s sake, *lucri caus(s)â*. **lucrative**, adj. *lucrosus*, *quaestuosus*.

lucubration, n. *lucubratio*.

ludicrous, adj. *(de)ridiculus*, *perridiculus*, *ridendus*, *deridendus*. Adv. *(per)ridicule*. **ludicrousness**, n. *stultitia*, *insulsitas* (= folly), or by adj.

lug, v.tr. *trahĕre*, *vehĕre*. **luggage**, n. *impedimenta*, *-orum*, n.; the — (collectively), *vasa*, *-orum*, n.; *sarcinae* (= the knapsacks, etc., of the individual soldiers).

lugubrious, adj. *lugubris* (mostly poet., belonging to mourning), *flebilis*, *maestus*, *tristis* (= sad); see SAD. Adv. † *lugubre*, † *lugubriter*, *flebiliter*, *maeste*; see SADLY.

lukewarm, adj. *tepidus* (lit. and fig.); = indifferent, *languidus*, *frigidus*, *lentus*, *remissus*, *neglegens* (*neglig-*). Adv. *languide*, *frigide*, *lente*, *remisse*, *neglegenter* (*neglig-*). **lukewarmness**, n. *tepor* (lit.), *languor*, or by adj.

lull, I. v.tr. *sedare* (e.g. *ventos*, *insolentiam*, etc.); to — to sleep, *sopire*, † *somnum suadēre*. II. v.intr., the wind —s, *venti vis cadit*, *venti sedantur*. III. n. use verb. **lullaby**, n. *cantus*, *-ūs*, or verb *lallare* (= to sing a —, Pers.).

lumber, n. *scruta*, *-orum*.

luminous, adj. *luminosus* (= having light), *lucidus* (= giving light); — narration, *narratio lucida* or *perspicua* or *aperta* or *dilucida*; the thoughts of, etc., are not —, *sententiae alcjs lucem desiderant*. Adv. *(di)lucide*, *perspicue*, *aperte*, *plane*, comb. *aperte atque dilucide*, *dilucide et perspicue*. **luminary**, n. 1, lit. *sol*, *-is*, m., *luna* (= sun, moon, etc.); 2, fig. *lumen*.

lump, n. *massa*, *glaeba* (*gleba*). **lumpish**, adj. *hebes*, *stupidus* (= stupid). **lumpy**, adj. *glebosus* (Plin.).

lunar, adj. *lunaris* (with *cursus*, *cornua*, etc.); a — year, *annus lunaris*. **lunatic**, adj. *lunaticus* (very late); see MAD, MADMAN.

lunch, n. *prandium*.

lung, n. *pulmo*; —s, *pulmones*.

lunge, n. and v.tr. see STAB.

lupine, n. *lupinus*, *lupinum*.

lurch, I. n. 1, see ROLL; 2, to leave in the —, *deserĕre*; see ABANDON. II. v.intr. see ROLL.

lure, I. n. = decoy-bird, or fig. *illecebra*. II. v.tr. *allicĕre*, *illicĕre*, *pellicĕre*.

lurid, adj. *obscurus*, *caliginosus* (*luridus* = pale yellow, ghastly).

lurk, v.intr. *latēre*, *latitare* (intensive of *latēre*).

luscious, adj. *(prae)dulcis*. **lusciousness**, n. *dulcedo*.

lust, I. n. *libido* (*lub-*), *cupiditas*. II. v.tr. to — after, *concupiscĕre* (= to desire earnestly). **lusty**, adj. = full of vigour, *valens*, *validus*, *vegetus*; = large and stout, *robustus*; to be —, *vigēre*. Adv. *valide*. **lustiness**, n. *vigor*, *robur*.

lustration, n. *lustratio* (= a purifying, e.g. *municipiorum*). **lustral**, adj. *lustralis*.

lustre, n. 1, *nitor*, *fulgor*, *splendor*; to throw a — on, *splendorem addĕre alci*; 2, = space of five years, *lustrum*. **lustrous**, adj. *splendidus*, *splendens*, *clarus*, *lucidus*; see BRIGHT.

lute, n. *lyra*, † *barbitos*, m. and f. (only nom., voc. and accus.), *fides*, *-ium*, f. pl., *cithara*, *testudo*.

luxuriant, adj. *laetus*, *luxuriosus*. Adv. *laete*. **luxuriate**, v.intr. *luxuriare*. **luxurious**, adj. *luxuriosus*, *sumptuosus*, *mollis*, *delicatus*, *lautus* (*lot-*). Adv. *luxuriose*, *delicate*, *molliter*. **luxury**, n. *luxus*, *-ūs*, *luxuria* or *luxuries*, *lautitia*, *apparatus*, *-ūs*, *deliciae*.

lye, n. *lixivia* (Plin.).

lynx, n. *lynx*. **lynx-eyed**, adj. *lynceus*.

lyre, n. *lyra*, *cithara*, *fides*, *-ium*, f. pl., *testudo*, *barbitos*, m. and f. (only nom., voc. and accus.). **lyrical**, adj. *lyricus*. **lyrist**, n. *lyricen*, *citharista*, m.

M.

macaroon, n. *placenta* (= cake).

mace, n. *fasces*, *-ium*, m. **mace-bearer**, n. *lictor*.

macerate, v.tr. *macerare* (e.g. flax, fish) (Plin.). **maceration**, n. *maceratio* (of flax, fish).

machination, n. = a secret, malicious design, *machina*, *conatus*, *-ūs*, *dolus*; to make —s, *consilia (con)coquĕre*; to do a thing through anyone's —, *algo auctore facĕre alqd*. **machine**, n. *machina*, *machinatio*, *machinamentum* (= machinery); *compages*, *-is*, f. (= framework); the —, fabric of the human body, *compages corporis*. **machinery**, n. *machinatio*, *machinamenta*, *-orum*, n., *machinae*.

mackerel, n. *scomber*.

mad, adj. 1, lit. *insanus*, *vecors*, *furiosus*, *demens*, *mente captus*, † *rabidus* (usu. of animals), *phreneticus* (*phrenit-*); 2, fig. *insanus*, *vecors*, *vesanus*, *furiosus*, *amens*, *demens*. Adv. *insane*, *furiose*, *rabide*, *dementer*. **madcap**, n. *homo* or *juvenis ingenio praeceps*. **madden**, v.tr. 1, *mentem alienare*; 2, fig. *exacerbare*, *exasperare*, *incendĕre*; see EXCITE. **madhouse**, n. *domus publica quā curantur insani*. **madman**, n. *homo insanus*, etc.; see MAD. **madness**, n. 1, lit. *insania*, *amentia*, *dementia*, *vecordia*, *furor*, *rabies* (esp. of animals); 2, fig. *insania*, *amentia*, *dementia*, *vecordia*, *furor*, *rabies*.

madam, n. *domina*.

madder, n. *rubia* (Plin.).

magazine, n. 1, = store, granary, *horreum*, *receptaculum alcjs rei* (= repository for corn, goods, etc.), *armamentarium* (for arms); 2, = pamphlet, *acta*, *-orum*; see JOURNAL.

maggot, n. *vermis*, *-is*, m., *vermiculus*. **maggoty**, adj. *verminosus* (Plin.).

magi, n. *magi*. **magic**, I. n. *ars magica*, or *magice* (Plin.). II. adj. 1, *magicus*; 2, fig. by *mirus* (e.g. a — power, *mira quaedam vis*); see also JUGGLERY.

magistracy, n. *magistratus*, *-ūs*. **magistrate**, n. *magistratus*, *-ūs*. **magisterial**, adj. *ad magistratum pertinens*; in his — capacity, *quippe qui magistratus erat*.

magnanimity, n see GENEROSITY **magnanimous,** adj see GENEROUS

magnet, n (*lapis*) *magnes, -ētis,* m **magnetic, magnetical,** adj *magnesius* (e g *magnesia saxa,* Lucret), — power, *attrahendi quae dicitur vis* (in a lit sense), *mira quaedam vis* (in a fig sense) **magnetism,** n **magnetisma* (t t , not class)

magnificent, adj *magnificus* (= splendid), *splendidus,* comb *splendidus et magnificus, praeclarus* (= eminent through exterior and inward qualities, excellent), comb *magnificus et praeclarus, lautus* (*lot-*) (of banquets); *sumptuosus* (= expensive), *amplus* (e g *amplissimae divitiae*) Adv *magnifice, splendide, praeclare, laute, sumptuose, ample* **magnificence,** n *magnificentia, splendor* (= outward splendour, also inward excellency), *res magnifica, splendida* (= a splendid thing), *cultus, -ūs* (as regards dress and costly household utensils), *lautitia* (*lot-*) (of an expensive mode of living), *apparatus, -ūs* (= preparations) **magnifier,** n = one who magnifies, *laudator* (in gen), fem *laudatrix,* also simply by verbs, to be the — of anything, *laudare alqd, praedicare alqd* or *de alqâ re.* **magnify,** v tr *augēre* (lit , e g the number of praetors *numerum praetorum,* fig to represent a thing greater than it is, in this sense comb *amplificare et augēre*), *amplificare* (= to make greater in extent, e g a town, *urbem,* the property, *rem familiarem,* then fig = by our actions to make a thing appear greater than it is), (*verbis*) *exaggerare* (= to make in words much of a thing, e g a kindness), *verbis augēre, in majus* (*verbis*) *extollere* (= to impair the truth by exaggeration), *in falsum augēre* (= to exaggerate falsely), *in majus accipĕre* (= to take a thing in a greater light than one ought) **magniloquence,** n *magniloquentia* **magnitude,** n *magnitudo* (in gen , both lit and fig), *amplitudo* (= great extent, also fig = importance of anything and high authority of a person), *ambitus, -ūs, spatium* (= circumference, extent of a thing in gen)

magpie, n *pica.*

mahometan, n and adj **Muhamedanus*

maid, n 1, = an unmarried woman, see GIRL, 2, = servant, *ancilla, famula* **maiden, maidenly,** adj *virgineus* (= pertaining to virgins), *virginalis* (= peculiar, natural to virgins, e g bashfulness, *verecundia*) **maidenhood,** n *virginitas* **maid-servant,** n see MAID, 2

mail, n 1, armour, *lorīca, thorax* *acis* m , 2, a letter-bag, *folliculus* (= bag) with descriptive epithet (e g *ad lit(t)eras perferendas*), = the letters themselves, *lit(t)erae* **mail-coach,** n *raeda* (*r(h)eda*) *cursualis publica* **mailed,** adj *loricatus*

maim, n *mutilare, truncare,* see INJURE **maimed,** adj *mancus, truncus*

main, I. adj *primus, princeps,* see CHIEF, PRINCIPAL, GREAT. (= the greater part), *pars prima* (= first part), *caput* (= chief point), his — intention is, *id maxime* (*praecipue*) *sequitur* or *agit* or *spectat,* — point, *summa* (sc *res*), *res magni momenti* or *magni discriminis, caput alcjs rei* or *summa,* the — question is, *id maxime quaeritur, quaeritur de,* etc (in a metaphysical question), *agitur de alqâ re, cardo alcjs rei* (= hinge), to give, state only the — points of anything, *summatim alqd exponĕre, summas tantummodo attingere,* to review briefly the — points, *per capita decurrĕre,* to stray, wander from the — question, *a proposito aberrare* or *declinare;* to return to the — point, *ad propositum reverti* or *redire, ad rem redire, praeteris alqd agĕre* or *spectare,* — road, *via,* — object, *finis,* to make anything one's — object, *omnia ad alqd referre* or *revocare,* his — object is, *id potissimum spectat* or *sequitur,* in the —, *si verum rei rationem exigis, vere* (= in reality) Adv *praecipue,* see PRINCIPALLY, UNCOMMONLY **II.** n 1, = the great sea, *altum,* see OCEAN 2, = the main-land, (*terra*) *continens* **main land,** n *terra* (*continens*) **main-mast,** n *malus* **main sail,** n *velum*

maintain, v tr. 1, *sustinēre, sustentare* (e g the world, health), through anything, *alqâ re,* (*con*)*servare* (= to preserve, e g one's property, *rem familiarem conservare,* then = to save), *tueri* (= to see that anything is in a good condition), comb *tueri et conservare, alĕre* (by care and nursing), comb *alĕre et sustentare, sustentare et alĕre,* to — one's physical strength *valetudinem tueri,* 2, = to keep in the necessaries of life, *sustinēre, sustentare alĕre,* 3, = not to lose or surrender, *tenēre, retinēre, obtinēre,* (*con*)*servare,* 4, = to — an argument, *contendĕre, confirmare,* see ASSERT **maintainable,** adj *munitus, firmatus* (= fortified), *firmus* (= firm, durable lit and fig = not easy to be overthrown), *stabilis* (= stable, fig = unalterable) comb *stabilis et firmus* (e g a ship), *perennis* (= what does not easily go bad, e g fruit) **maintainer,** n (*con*)*servator, salutis auctor* (= one who restores, saves), *vindex* (= one who claims), or by verbs **maintenance,** n 1, *victus, -ūs* (= food for the necessary support of the body), *alimenta, orum* (= food in gen , then in the meaning of the law, what anyone subsists on, subsistence), to give to anyone his —, *alcui victum* or *alimentum* (often in pl) *praebēre,* 2, = protection, continuance, *conservatio, tuitio* (= the act), *salus, ūtis,* f , *incolumitas* (= the state of being preserved)

maize, n *far*

majestic, adj *augustus, sanctus* (= venerend), *magnificus* (= splendid) Adv *auguste* **majesty,** n *majestas* (later of the Roman emperor); *dignitas numen* (= high power will, both of God and man, e g of the emperor) surrounded with —, *augustus,* to violate the —, *majestatem* (of the people, *populi,* of the emperor, *imperatoris*) *minuĕre* or *laedere,* your — ! *majestas tua* ! (late).

major, I. adj 1, = greater in number, extent, e g the — part, *major* (e g *major pars*), see MORE, 2, in music (the — mode, opp the minor mode), *modus major,* 3, in logic, the — premiss, *propositio* **II.** n 1, = a military rank, *centurio, praefectus, optio* (= assistant to and immediately under the *centurio*), 2, in law = a person of full age to manage his own concerns, *sui juris, suae potestatis* (no longer under the parent's control), *suae tutelae* (not longer requiring to be represented in court by a guardian), *sui potens* (= one who can do as he likes) **major-domo,** n = steward, *qui res domesticas dispensat, dispensator* **majority,** n 1, = the greater number, *major pars, major numerus* (both = a greater number in comparison with another number), or *plures* (= several), *plurimi* (= most), *plerique* (= a large number), the — of historical writers, *plures auctores,* Servius took care that the — did not prevail, *Servius curavit ne plurimum plurimi valerent,* — of votes, *sententiae longe plurimae* (of the senators, judges), *suffragia longe plurima,* (of the citizens in the *comitia*), to have the — of votes, *vincĕre* (of persons), *valēre* (of a motion, etc), *longe plurimum valēre, magnis suffragiis* or *per suffragia superare,* to be acquitted by a great —, *sententiis fere omnibus absolvi,* the — rules, carries the victory, *major pars vincit,* the — (in the senate) decided in favour of the same opinion, *pars major in con-*

dem sententiam ibat; **2**, = full age, *aetas quâ sui juris alqs fit*; he entrusted him with the government until the children should come to their —, *regnum ei commendavit quoad liberi in suam tutelam pervenirent.*

make, I. v.tr. **1**, = to form, in the ordinary sense in gen. *facĕre*; = to accomplish, *conficĕre, efficĕre, perficĕre*; **2**, = to create, *creare* (of God and nature); made for, *ad alqd factus, alci rei* or *ad alqd natus*, comb. *alci rei* or *ad alqd natus factusque* (opp. as regards persons, *ad alqd doctus* or *institutus*); a spot almost made for an ambuscade, *loca insidiis nata*; **3**, in an arithmetical sense, *efficĕre*, or by *esse, fieri*; **4**, = to — by art, *arte imitari* or *efficĕre, alqd fingĕre* (= to invent); **5**, = to do, to perform, *facĕre, agĕre* (*agĕre*, the Greek πράττειν, = to act without reference to the result); = to choose anyone as one's model, *auctore uti alqo*; the ambassadors — haste to get to Africa, *legati in Africam maturantes veniunt*; he made haste to get to Rome, *Romam proficisci maturavit*; **6**, = to cause to have any quality (e.g. wealth —s man proud), *facĕre, efficĕre, reddĕre alqm* (with the accus.); *facĕre* and *efficĕre* denoting the producing of a certain condition in a thing, whilst *reddĕre* implies a change of the previous condition, e.g. to — anyone useless, *alqm inutilem facĕre*, e.g. of a wound; to — anyone better, *alqm meliorem reddĕre*; to — the people from wild savages into gentle and civilised beings, *homines ex feris mites reddĕre* or *homines feros mites reddĕre*; very often, however, the verb "to —," with its accus. of the predicate, must be rendered in Latin by one verb; to — equal, *aequare*, etc. (see under the adjs.); to — much, a great deal of a person, *alqm magni facĕre* (= to esteem), *multum alci tribuĕre* (= to think very highly of anyone), *alqm colĕre* (= to have great regard for, to respect a person); not to — much regard for, to — light of a person, *alqm parvi facĕre* (= to treat with indifference), *alqm contemnĕre* (= to despise); to — much of a thing, *alqd magni facĕre, existimare* (= to value highly), *alqd in honore habēre* (= to honour); not to — much of a thing, *alqd neglegĕre* (*neglig-*, = to disregard, neglect); to — much, be eager for, etc., *alcjs rei esse appetentissimum*; = to be fond of, *alqm carum habēre*; see FOND; **7**, = to bring into any state, to constitute, *facĕre, instituĕre* (= to appoint to an office), *constituĕre* (= to institute anyone as), *creare* (= to create, to elect) *alqm* (with accus., e.g. to — anyone the heir, *heredem alqm facĕre, instituĕre*); **8**, = to establish, e.g. to — friendship, *conciliare* (e.g. *amicitiam*; a wedding, *nuptias*; *pacem*), *facĕre* (e.g. a treaty, *foedus*; *pacem*); to — harmony, peace, *concordiam reconciliare*; between two, *alqm in gratiam reconciliare cum alqo*; to — quarrels, *discordiam concitare* (= to cause discord); *causam jurgii inferre, jurgia excitare* (= to begin, excite quarrels); between two, *discordes reddĕre*; between the citizens, *discordiam inducĕre in civitatem*; **9**, = to settle, in the phrase, to — one's abode, *in alqm locum migrare, in alium locum demigrare* or *transmigrare, in alqm locum immigrare* (= to go to live in, to remove to); see also RESIDE, LIVE; **10**, = to raise to good fortune (e.g. he is made for this world); to — a man, *alqm gratiâ et auctoritate suâ sustentare* (= to get anyone forward); *alcjs fortunae auctorem esse*; **11**, = to gain (e.g. to — money of), see MONEY, GAIN; **12**, = to discover, to — land, *capĕre* (e.g. *insulam* or *portum*); see LAND; *ex alto invehi in portum, decurrĕre in portum*; **13**, to — one's way to, = to arrive at, see PENETRATE, ADVANCE; **14**, = to convert, *alqâ re uti* (e.g. to — anything an instrument of, etc.); **15**, = to put into a suitable form for use, to — a bed, *lectum sternĕre*; **16**, = to compose (e.g. to — verses), *facĕre, scribĕre*, see COMPOSE; **17**, to — hay, *fenum secare, caedĕre, succidĕre*; **18**, = to contribute (e.g. this argument —s nothing in his favour), *magni* (*parvi*, etc.) *momenti esse* (= to matter); impers. it —s nothing, *nihil est ad rem*; **19**, to — amends, *satisfacĕre alci de alqâ re, alqd expiare, alqd* (*cum*) *alqâ re compensare*; **20**, to — arrangements, (*ap*)*parare, comparare, praeparare, adornare alqd, facĕre*, comb. *parare et facĕre, se comparare* or *praeparare ad alqd*; **21**, to — away with, = to kill, *interficĕre*; see KILL. **II.** n. = formation of the body, *omnis membrorum et totius corporis figura*, or simply *corporis figura, corporis conformatio et figura*, in the connection of a sentence also simply *corpus*; of strong —, *maximi corporis* (of a man), of immensely strong —, *immani corporis magnitudine*; see also SHAPE. **maker,** n. in gen. *qui facit*, etc., or *auctor* (e.g. *pacis*), *suasor* (= adviser), *factor, fabricator*. **making,** n. *factio, fabricatio*, but better use verb. **makeshift, makeweight,** n. *ad tempus* (e.g. of an edict, a decree, *edictum ad tempus propositum*).

maladjustment, n. *incompositus* (e.g. the — of parts, *partes incompositae*).

maladministration, n. *prava rerum administratio.*

malady, n. see ILLNESS.

malapert, n. *petulans, procax, protervus, parum verecundus* (= not very discreet); see SAUCY.

malapropos, adv. *intempestive.*

malaria, n. *aër pestilens, caelum grave et pestilens.*

malcontent, n. *rerum mutationis* or *rerum novarum* or *rerum evertendarum cupidus.*

male, adj. *virilis* (only of man), *mas, masculus, masculinus* (Plin.) (both of man, but more frequently of animals); the — sex, *virilis sexus, -ūs.*

malediction, n. *ex(s)ecratio, dirae, -arum*, f. (= curses); see CURSE.

malefactor, n. *homo maleficus* (*malif-*) (= perpetrator of a wicked act). **maleficence,** n. *malitia* (= roguery), *improbitas* (= wickedness, opp. *probitas*), *malignitas* (= malignity); see MALICE. **malefic,** adj. *maleficus* (*malif-*), *malitiosus* (= roguish, esp. in law proceedings), *improbus* (= wicked, of persons, opp. *probus*), *malignus* (= evil-disposed, jealous, of persons, opp. *benignus*). **malevolent,** adj. see MALICE, MALICIOUS. **malformation,** n. *quod informe est.* **malice,** n. = envy, *malignitas, invidia, malevolentia* (*maliv-*); = a wicked pleasure in trying to do others harm, *malitia* (= roguery); = a wicked act, *scelus, -ĕris*, n. **malicious,** adj. *malitiosus, malevolus* (*maliv-*, = malevolent); †*malignus* (never used in the sense of malicious, only = ill-natured, ill-willed), *invidus*; = saucy, *procax*. Adv. *malitiose* (not so strong as the English). **maliciousness,** n. see MALICE. **malign, I.** adj. see MALICIOUS and UNFAVOURABLE. **II.** v.tr. see SLANDER. **malignant,** adj. see MALICIOUS. **maligner,** n. *obtrectator*. **malignity,** n. **1**, *malevolentia* (*maliv-*); **2**, of a disease, *vis morbi*. **malpractice,** n. see MISDEED. **maltreat,** v.tr. *male tractare*; see INJURE. **maltreatment,** n. see INJURY. **malversation,** n. *peculatus, -ūs.*

mallard, n. *anas* (*-ătis*) *mas* or *masculus.*

malleability, n. by **malleable,** adj. *quod malleis extendi potest, lentus* (= tough), *ductilis* (Plin.).

mallet, n. **1**, *fistuca* (for driving anything

with force), *paricula* (= a rammer), *fustis* (= a club), *malleus* (= a hammer), *pistillum* (= a pestle)

mallow, n *malva, malache, -es* (Plin)

malt, n *hordeum aquâ perfusum et sole tostum*
malt-liquor, n see BEER

mama, mamma, n *mamma*

mammal, n *animal*

mammon, n *divitiae, opes, -um,* see RICHES

man, I. n *homo* (in gen), *vir* (esp = a brave man), men, in a collective sense, *homines, genus humanum, hominum universum genus* (= the whole human race), *mortales, -ium,* a young —, (*homo*) *adulescens* (*adol-*), quite a young —, (*homo*) *adulescentulus* (*adol-*), *juvenis,* very often it is not expressed at all in Latin, especially with adjs, and when it is contained as subject in the verb, e g many men, people, *multi,* there are men who, etc, *sunt qui,* etc, *non desunt qui,* etc, *inveniuntur* or *reperiuntur qui,* etc (in all these phrases use the indicative mood after *qui,* when the class of men is clearly defined, but the subjunctive mood when the class of men is described in an indefinite sense, so as to require a qualification, there are men who will have it that, etc, *sunt qui dicant,* i e who mean to say, who seem to say, to think, but *sunt qui dicunt* = there are men who assert, i e in a positive manner), no —, *nemo, nullus* (= no one, nobody), he is not a — (i e he is a brute), *homo non est, omnis humanitatis expers est;* this — (referring to some name mentioned immediately before, without laying any emphasis on the word this), simply *hic* (but *hic vir,* if with emphasis), — by —, every —, *viritim* (= to every — individually, e g to distribute anything, to grant, *tribuĕre* or *dare*), altogether, everyone up to the very last —, *universi, ad unum omnes,* so much a —, or every — gets so much, *singuli auferunt* with the accus of the sum, = soldier, *miles, -ĭtis,* m, his men, *sui,* our men, *nostri,* men may also be expressed by *exercitus, -ūs, copiae, manus, -ūs,* newly recruited men, *tirones,* with commendation, *vir,* to march in a file three men together, three abreast, *triplici ordine incedĕre,* they marched thirty men abreast, *triginta armatorum ordines ibant,* with — and horse, *viris equisque* (i e. with infantry and cavalry), an army of ten thousand men, *exercitus decem mil(l)ium,* a — from a country town, a countryman, but a — of the right sort, *rusticanus vir, sed plane vir* (Cic), show yourself a —, *virum te praesta,* in chess, *latro, latrunculus* (Sen), *miles,* in draughts, *calculus,* — of money, *pecuniosus,* — of the world, *homo urbanus,* or *perpolitus,* merchant —, *navis* (*mercatoria*), *navis rotunda,* — of-war, *navis longa, navis rostrata, quinqueremis* (= different kinds of Roman men-of-war, in opp to *navis rotunda,* = merchant- —) **II.** v tr 1, = to furnish with soldiers, *navem* or *classem militibus* or *propugnatoribus instruĕre* or *complēre,* to — sufficiently, *navem* or *classem armatis ornare,* to be sufficiently —ned, *suum numerum habēre* **manful,** adj see MANLY **manhood,** n 1, = adult age, *pubertas* (Plin), *aetas adulta,* to reach —, *togam virilem sumere,* 2, = humanity *humana natura, humanitas* **mankind,** n *homines, genus humanum* **manly,** adj 1, = belonging to men, *virilis,* 2, = brave, *virilis, fortis,* see BRAVE **manliness,** n *virtus, -ūtis,* f., *animus virilis* or *fortis,* see COURAGE **mannikin,** n *homuncio, homunculus, homullus* **manservant,** n *servus, famulus* **manslaughter,** n *hominis caedes,* guilty of —, by *hominem caedĕre, interficĕre*
man-trap, n *stimulus* (Caes).

manacle, I. n *manica.* **II.** v tr. *vincire catenis*

manage, v tr = to conduct, *tractare* (= to treat, handle), *regĕre* (lit = to conduct, e g *domesticam disciplinam regĕre*), *administrare* (= to have a thing under one's hands), *perfungi alqâ re* (= to discharge the duties of an office), *gerĕre* (= to hold a public office, with reference to the general conduct), *praeesse alci rei* (= to act as presiding officer, to superintend the management of affairs), *procurare* (= to act for an absent person, e g anyone's business, *alcjs negotia*), *dispensare* **manageable,** adj 1, = easy to be used, *habilis* (opp *inhabilis*), or transl by verbs, 2, = that may be made subservient to one's views, *qui regi potest* (both lit and fig), *tractabilis* (fig, of persons), *docilis, facilis* (= compliant), see FLEXIBLE **management,** n = manner of carrying on, *administratio, tractatio* (e g of the war), *cura* (care, e g of a family, of a household, *rei domesticae cura*), the — of anyone's affairs (in his absence), (*pro*)*curatio, dispensatio* (of a steward) **manager,** n = one who has the direction of anything, *negotiorum* (*pro*)*curator* (of a business, to be the — of anyone's business, *alcjs rationes negotiaque procurare, alcjs rem* or *negotia gerĕre*), *praefectus* (= one who discharges the duties of an office, in good Latin always with the gen or dat of the office), *magister* (= principal of an establishment, director of a company)

mandate, n *edictum* (e g to issue a —, *edictum proponĕre* or *edicĕre, ut,* etc, of a public body), in gen *imperatum, jussum, mandatum.*

mandible, n *maxilla*

mandrake, mandragora, n *mandragoras, -ae,* m (Plin)

mane, n *juba, coma* (*comae cervicum,* of lions' —s, Gell), with a —, *jubatus, comatus*

manes, n *Manes, -ium,* m

mange, manginess, n. *scabies, scabrities* or *scabritia* (Plin) **mangy,** adj †*scaber*

manger, n *praesaepe praesaepis, praesaepium* (*praesep*)

mangle, I. n *machina quâ lintea aut panni lēvigantur* **II.** v tr 1, = to smooth clothes with a —, *levigare,* 2, fig (*di*)*laniare* **mangled,** adj *truncus, mutilus*

mania, n *insania* (lit and fig) **maniac,** n *homo insanus,* see MAD

manifest, I. adj *apertus* (= open before one), *manifestus* (= apparent), comb *apertus et manifestus, perspicuus* (= clear), comb *apertus et perspicuus, evidens* (= evident), *testatus* (= shown, proved by witnesses), *notus, cognitus* (= known), a — crime, *facinus manifesto compertum et deprehensum* (when anyone is caught in the act), it is —, *patet, apparet, manifestum est, perspicuum est omnibus,* to make —, *aperire* (= to open), *patefacĕre* Adv *aperte, manifesto, sine dubio, perspicue, evidenter, palam* (= openly), *scilicet* (ironically) **II.** v tr *aperire* (= to open), *patefacĕre* (= to make clear), *manifestum facĕre* (= to make —), (*in medium*) *proferre* (= to make generally known), comb *proferre et patefacĕre enuntiare, declarare, ostendĕre, evulgare, divulgare* (= to divulge). **manifestation,** n *significatio, declaratio, demonstratio, indicium,* see DECLARATION **manifesto,** n if of the government, *edictum,* in gen, to issue a —, perhaps *alqd proponĕre.*

manifold, adj *multiplex* (= various), *multiformis* (= many-shaped), may also be rendered by *varietas* with the gen following (e g — learning, *varietas doctrinarum,* — sounds, *varietas sonorum*), to possess — learning, *multiplici* *variique doctrinâ esse*; or it may be rendered by *multi* (= many), *creber* (= frequent); at the — requests of, *saepe rogatus*.

maniple, n. *manipulus*. **manipulate**, v.tr. *tractare*; see TREAT. **manipulation**, n. *tractatio*.

manliness, n. **manly**, adj. see MAN.

manna, n. *manna* (Eccl.).

manner, n. = way of performing, *ratio*, *modus* (= mode, guide), *via* (= way, sure mode), comb. *ratio et via, ratio et modus*; *genus, -eris* (= mode of proceeding, e.g. *argumentandi genus*, — of arguing; *dicendi genus*, — of expressing one's sentiments); = custom, habitual practice, *ratio, consuetudo* (= custom according to which one is wont to act), *ritus, -ūs* (= mode of acting as established by custom or habit, or by the law; hence the instinctive habit of animals), comb. *ratio et consuetudo*; *institutum*, comb. *consuetudo et institutum*; = sort, kind, *genus*; = certain degree or measure, *quodammodo*; in a —, in like —, *eodem* or *pari modo*; = mien, carriage, *ratio* (in gen.), *mos* (= — in gen., distinct mode), *mores, -um*, m. (= the whole — of a person); = anybody's general way, *ingenium alcjs moresque* (= character); that is my —, *ita sum, eo sum ingenio, ita ingenium meum est* (= that is my character), *sic meus est mos* (= my —, mode), *mea sic est ratio* (= my — of proceeding); as it is my —, your —, in my —, *sicut meus est mos*, also *meo more, ex* or *pro consuetudine meâ, tuâ, consuetudine meâ*; it is not my —, *non est meae consuetudinis*; to live in his —, *suo more* or *suo instituto vivĕre*; what — is that? *qui istic mos est?* after, in the — or way of, etc. (= like), *more alcjs* (e.g. in the — of parents, wild beasts, a torrent, *more parentum, ferarum, torrentis, fluminis*); *in morem alcjs* (e.g. in the — of cattle, *in morem pecudum*); in the — of slaves, *servilem in modum*; *modo* or *ritu alcjs* (e.g. in the — of robbers, women, beasts, *ritu latronum, mulierum, pecudum*); in this —, *hoc modo, hac ratione, ita* or *sic* (= thus); in an equal —, *pari modo*; = style, *stilus* (of a writer), *manus, -ūs* (of an artist, painter; e.g. written in the Attic —, *Attico stilo scriptus*). **manners**, n. in the pl. = established customs, *mores*; good —, *boni mores*; a person of good —, *homo bene moratus, modestus*; to follow anyone's —, *alcjs mores induĕre* or *imitari*; = decent deportment, *mores*; refined, elegant —, *morum elegantia, mores elegantes* (in gen.), *urbanitas* (= courteous —), *humanitas* (= gentlemanly —, that show a man of good education); without —, *rudis et moris omnis ignarus* (= rude and ignorant); *vitae communis ignarus* (= one who knows nothing of the rules of society), *rusticus, agrestis* (= rude, rough, clumsy), *inurbanus* (= without refinement), *humanitatis expers, inhumanus*. **mannerism**, n. *ratio*, or any word = manners, and define it by context (e.g. a new — in speaking, *nova ratio loquendi*), or by adj. or adv. *putidus, putide* (e.g. *putide dicĕre* = to speak with —s); see AFFECTED, AFFECTATION. **mannerist**, n. *pictor qui tabulas suo* (or *alcjs*) *more pingit*. **mannerly, I.** adj. *urbanus, humanus, perpolitus*; see POLITE. **II.** adv. *urbane, humane, humaniter, perpolite*; see POLITELY.

manœuvre, I. n. 1, military, *decursio, decursus, -ūs* (*decursio* always as the act of manœuvring, *decursus* = the — itself); *militibus decursionem* or, if for amusement, *certamen ludicrum indicĕre* (= to give the order for holding a —, to announce a —); *milites in decursionem* or *in certamen ludicrum educĕre* (= to let the troops march out for a —, Veget.), *certamen ludicrum committĕre*; to hold a — (at sea), *proelium navale committĕre* (of the commander); 2, see SCHEME, TRICK. **II.** v.intr. 1, to —, *in decursionem exire* (= to march out to a —), *in armis decurrĕre*, or simply *decurrĕre* (= to make evolutions for exercise), *inter se in modum justae pugnae concurrĕre* (= to hold a sham fight for exercise and amusement); 2, see SCHEME, TRICK.

manor, n. *fundus, praedium*.

mansion, n. in gen., *aedes, -ium*, f.; see HOUSE.

mantelet, n. *vinea, pluteus, testudo*. **mantle**, n. *amiculum, palla* (for women), *pallium, palliolum* (= Greek —), *lacerna* (= thick —), *chlamys* (= light —), *paenula* (with a hood for travelling), *sagum, sagulum* (= soldier's or servant's —), *paludamentum* (= general's —). **mantel-piece**, n. by *mensa* (= table), *pluteus* or *tabula* (= shelf).

manual, I. adj. = performed by the hand, *manu meâ, tuâ*, etc., *factus*; — labour, *opera* (opp. *ars*), or by *manus* (e.g. to get a bare living from the earnings of one's — labour, *manuum mercede inopiam tolerare*). **II.** n. = small book, *libellus*.

manufactory, n. = the building, *officina*. **manufacture, I.** n. = operation of manufacturing, *artis opus, -ĕris, opera fabrilis*; — is at a standstill, *op. jacet*; = the article —d, *opus quod arte* or *manu factum est*. **II.** v.tr. *fabricare*; see also MAKE. **manufacturer**, n. *opifex, -icis, fabricator* (always with the gen. of the thing that is manufactured), *artifex, -icis* (of artificial objects), *textor* (= a weaver). **manufacturing-town**, n. *urbs officinis nobilis* (= known by its manufactures).

manumission, n. *missio* (in gen.), *manumissio* (of a slave). **manumit**, v.tr. *alqm manu mittĕre*, or as one word, *manumittĕre*.

manure, I. n. *stercus, -ŏris, fimus*. **II.** v.tr. *stercorare*.

manuscript, n. 1, = anything in one's own handwriting intended for recital or for the press, *chirographum*; 2, = a written work, *liber, libellus*, or further defined as opp. to printed book, *manu scriptus* or *nondum editus*.

many, n. *multi, haud pauci*; see MUCH; *creber* or *frequens* (= — together); an assembly of — people, *magna frequentia (hominum)*; a good —, *complures, plerique*; as — as, *quot . . . tot*; — a thing, — things, *nonnulli, aliquot, quidam* (= some), *sunt qui . . .*; — a time, *nonnunquam* (= now and then), *interdum* (= sometimes); — times indeed, perhaps *aliquando*; not — things, but much (i.e. not much, but well), *non multa, sed multum*; — ways, — a way, *varie, vario modo, multis modis*; these — years, *abhinc multos annos*; to make — words, *verba facĕre, longum esse*; — men, — minds, *quot homines, tot sententiae* (Ter.); of — meanings, *ambiguus* (= ambiguous, equivocal, e.g. a word, *verbum*; an oracle, *oraculum*); with — corners, *polygonius* (Vitruv.), in pure Latin, † *multangulus* (Lucret.); to have — corners, *plurium angulorum formam exhibēre*; with — feet, *multis pedibus*, † *multipes*, † *multiformis*; — times, *saepe, saepenumero* (= often), *crebro* (= frequently, repeatedly), *persaepe, saepissime* (= very often), *iterum atque iterum* (= again and again), *etiam atque etiam*; how — times, *quotie(n)s*; so — times, *totie(n)s*; as — times . . . as, *toties . . . quoties*; however — times, *quotiescunque, quotiescunque*; — times greater, *multiplex*. **many-coloured**, adj. *variis coloribus distinctus, multicolor* (Plin.). **many-headed**, adj. *multa capita habens*. **many-sided**, lit. † *multangulus, polygonius*.

map, I. n. *tabula*; a — of a certain part of a country, a — of a country, *regio* (e.g. *in Germa-*

nâ) *in tabulâ* or *in membranâ* or *in charta picta* or *depicta* **II.** v tr *terrarum situs pingĕre*, to — out, *designare, describere* **mapping,** n *graphis, ĭdos*, f

maple, n *acer*, of —, *acernus*

mar, v tr *deformare, corrumpĕre*, see SPOIL

marauder, n. *praedator, direptor* **marauding,** adj *praedatorius, praedabundus.*

marble, I. n. *marmor*, — cutter, (*faber*) *marmorarius*, statue, bust in —, *signum marmoreum* **II.** adj *marmorius*

march, n (*mensis*) *Martius*

march, I. v intr *ambulare* (in gen), *incedĕre* (= of marching exercise, and in war), to — out, set out, *progredi, proficisci*, to be on the —, *iter facĕre*, to — off, forward, to decamp, *castra movēre, promovēre*, or simply *movēre*, to — three men abreast, *triplici ordine incedĕre*, they were marching thirty men abreast, *triginta armatorum ordines ibant*, to be marching quicker, to accelerate one's —, *accelerare iter*, to — behind, to — in the rear, to close the rear, *agmen claudĕre, cogĕre* **II.** v tr *ducĕre* (e g *exercitum*), — back, *reducĕre*; — across, *tra(ns)ducĕre*, see LEAD **III.** n 1, in a military sense, = movement of soldiers, *iter*, *profectio* (= the marching off) on the —, *iter faciens* (e g he was killed on the —, *occisus est in itinere*), *ex itinere* (= from the —, i e, whilst the — is being interrupted for a time), to make a —, *iter facĕre, conficĕre*, to direct the — to a place, *iter alqo facĕre, contendĕre, convertĕre, intendĕre*, to change the route of the —, *iter (com)mutare, iter* or *viam flectĕre*, the troops on the —, *agmen*, 2, (= signal to move), to sound the —, *classicum canĕre* (= to sound the trumpet); — ! (as a word of command) *procede !* (for one) *procedite !* (for several), 3, (= — of intellect), see PROGRESS, 4, (= a day's journey), *iter*, one day's —, *iter unius diei, castra, -orum* (the latter inasmuch as the Romans always pitched a camp after every day's —), after a five days —, *quintis castris*, to make forced —es, *magnis itineribus contendĕre* (in gen), *dies noctesque iter facĕre, die et nocte continuare iter* (= day and night) **marches,** n. *fines, -ium*, m, *confinium*, see BOUNDARY

mare, n *equa*

margin, n *margo*, m and f **marginal,** adj *quod ad marginem pertinet, in margine scriptus*

marine, I. adj = belonging to the sea, *marinus, ad mare pertinens* **II.** n *nauta*, m (= sailor), *miles* (*-itis*) *classicus*; the —s, *epibatae* **mariner,** n *nauta* **maritime,** adj *maritimus* (= situated near the sea) — state, *civitas maritima* (= situated near the sea), *civitas* or *gens mari pollens, civitas* or *gens navibus* or *classe multum valens* (= powerful at sea, having a large navy), to be a — state, *classe* (*classibus*) *multum valēre.*

marjoram, n *amaracus* (Plin)

mark, I. n 1, *nota, signum, signa et notae* (Cic), *indicium, vestigium* (= trace), it is the — of a wise man, *est sapientis* (followed by infin), to make one's —, *clarum alqâ re fieri*, 2, = thing aimed at, *scopos*, *-i* (Suet), see AIM; = goal (fig), see PURPOSE **II.** v tr (*de*)*signare, notare*, = to take notice of, *observare, animadvertĕre*, — or mind, *animum advertĕre, animum* or *animo attendĕre*, — out, lit *metiri metari*, fig *designare*, (*de*)*notare*, see PURPOSE **marked,** adj = distinguished, *illustris*, in a bad sense *infamis insignis* (e g *turpitudine insignis*) **marker,** n 1, in a book, *nota* (= mark), 2, = one who marks at a game, *minister* or *servus* (= assistant) **mark-land,** n see MARCHES **marksman,** n *homo jaculandi peritus, jaculator*

market, I. n 1, *macellum* (= provision —), *forum* (= — -place), *emporium* (= — town), *nundinae* (= fair), the cattle — *forum boarium*, the vegetable —, *forum olitorium*, 2, = sale, *venditio*, to find a —, *vendi* **II.** v intr. *nundinari* **marketable,** adj. *venalis* **market-day,** n *nundinae* **market-garden,** n *hortus* **market-place,** n. *forum* **marketing,** n to go —, *nundinari*

marl, n *marga* (Plin)

marmalade, n *fructus decocti*

marmoset, n *simiolus*

marmot, n perhaps *mus*

marriage, n *conjugium matrimonium, nuptiae, con(n)ubium*, a legal, lawful —, *conjugium legitimum, matrimonium justum* or *legitimum nuptiae justae et legitimae*, to contract a —, to enter into the state of matrimony, *in matrimonium ire* (Plaut), *ducĕre uxorem* (of the man), *nubĕre alci* (of the woman), *matrimonio jungi* or *conjungi, nuptiis inter se jungi* (of man and wife), to demand anyone in —, *sibi alqam in matrimonium petĕre*, also simply *petĕre alqam*, to be united to anyone in —, *alqam in matrimonio habēre*, to give one's daughter in — to anyone, *alci filiam* (or *virginem*) *in matrimonium dare* or *nuptum dare, alci filiam collocare* or *nuptum locare* **marriage-contract,** n *sponsalia, -ium, pactio nuptialis*, to make a —, *pactionem nuptialem facĕre*, the written document or deed containing the — written on tablets, *tabulae legitimae, tabulae nuptiales, dotis tabulae* **marriage-feast,** n *nuptiae* **marriage-settlement,** n *dos, dotis*, f **marriageable,** adj *pubes, -ĕris* (in an age of puberty, in both sexes), *nubilis, adultus* (= grown up), *sponsae* or *marito maturus* **marry, I.** v tr 1, = to unite in matrimony, by the clergyman or the person taking his place, *sol(l)emnibus* (*solenn-*) *dictis con(n)ubium sancire*, 2, = to dispose of (of females only), *alci alqam* (*in matrimonium*) *collocare, alci in matrimonium dare* or *tradĕre*, 3, = to take for husband or wife, in gen, *matrimonio se* (*con*)*jungĕre cum alqo* or *alqâ, in matrimonium accipĕre* or *recipĕre*, to — a woman (of a man), *ducĕre alqam uxorem in matrimonium*, or simply *ducĕre alqam* (*uxorem*), *matrimonio alqam secum conjungĕre, alqam uxorem sibi adjungĕre*, to — a man (of a woman), *nubĕre alci*, to — each other, *matrimonio jungi* or *conjungi, nuptiis inter se jungi*, to — again, *novum matrimonium inire*, to — to advantage, *virginem bene dotatem ducĕre* (of a man), *in lucculentam familiam collocari* (of a female), to be married, to be a married man, *uxorem duxisse*, to be a married woman, *nuptam esse viro* **II.** v intr = to enter into the conjugal state, *uxorem ducĕre* (*in matrimonium*) (see above), *nubĕre viro* (of the woman) **marrying,** n *nuptiae*

marrow, n 1 *medulla* 2, = the essence, the best part of anything, *medulla* (seldom in this sense, e g *medulla verborum*, Aul Gell), *flos, floris*, m (= the best part of anything) **marrow-bone,** n *os medullosum* (not class.)

marry ! interj *medius fidius, mehercle*

marsh, n *palus, -udis*, f (= morass) **marshy,** adj *paluster* (= swampy), *caenosus* (= miry), *uliginosus* (= swampy)

marshal, I. n. use *dux* for field —; = one who directs the order of the feast, procession, etc., *ductor pompae*. **II.** v.tr. *instruĕre, disponĕre*.

mart, n. see MARKET.

martial, adj. *militaris, bellicosus;* a — look, *oculi truces;* — law, *jus* (between nations in a state of war), or in the pl. *jura belli, lex belli* (= the laws of war); according to the — law, *jure* or *lege belli;* — law, in its theory, *leges militares*.

martyr, I. n. *martyr* (Eccl.); to become a — for, to die a — to a cause, *pro alqâ re mortem occumbĕre*. **II.** v.tr. *alqm pro alqâ re interficĕre*. **martyrdom,** n. = death of a martyr, *martyrium* (Eccl.). **martyrology,** n. *historia martyrum*.

marvel, n. *miraculum, portentum*. **marvellous,** adj. *(per)mirus, (ad)mirandus, mirificus, stupendus, (ad)mirabilis* (= astonishing, e.g. *audacia*), *ingens, immanis*. Adv. *mirum in modum, mire, mirifice, (ad)mirabiliter, stupendum in modum* (= in an astonishing manner), *valde* (= very), *vehementer* (= violently).

masculine, adj. *masculus, masculinus*.

mash, I. n. *farrago*. **II.** v.tr. *(con)tundĕre, (con)terĕre*.

mask, I. n. **1**, = cover for the face, *persōna* (esp. on the stage), *larva* (= an ugly —, often used at pantomimes); to put on a — (in a lit. sense), *personam sibi accommodare* or *sibi aptare, personam induĕre;* to take anyone's — off, *alci personam demĕre, alcjs capiti personam detrahĕre;* **2**, fig. to have put on a different —, *alienam personam ferre* or *gerĕre, simulare alqd;* to unmask oneself, to take off the —, *simulationem deponĕre;* to take off the — from a person or thing, to unmask, fig. *alci* or *alci rei personam demĕre et reddĕre suam* (Sen.); to strip off the — which anyone wears, and show him in his real light, *alqm nudare;* to retain the — of friendship, *speciem amicitiae retinēre;* to betray anyone under the — of friendship, *alqm per simulationem amicitiae prodĕre*. **II.** v.tr. **1**, lit. *personam alci aptare, personam alcjs capiti imponĕre;* to — oneself, *personam sibi accommodare* or *sibi aptare, personam induĕre; se velare* (= to cover oneself with a veil); **2**, fig. *tegĕre* (= to cover; with anything, *alqâ re*), *occultare* (= to conceal, e.g. one's intentions, *inceptum suum*).

mason, n. **1**, *structor* (= builder), *faber* (= carpenter), *caementarius;* **2**, a free—, * *latomus*. **masonry,** n. *structura (caementicia)*.

masquerade, n. *convivium a convivis personatis celebratum*. **masquerader,** n. * *homo personatus*.

mass, I. n. †*massa, moles, -is,* f., *summa* (= the whole); a great —, *magnum pondus, -eris,* n., *magna copia* or *vis alcjs rei;* in the —, *per saturam;* — of people, *multitudo, frequentia;* see CONCOURSE, ASSEMBLY. **II.** v.tr. *colligĕre* (= collect), *(ac)cumulare* (= — together); see COLLECT, ACCUMULATE. **massive,** adj. **1**, *solidus* (= dense), *magnus* (= great), *gravis* (= heavy); **2**, fig. of character (e.g. simplicity), *gravis*. **massiveness,** n. **1**, by adj.; **2**, *gravitas*.

mass, n. = Catholic service, * *missa*.

massacre, I. n. *caedes, -is, trucidatio, internecio*. **II.** v.tr. *caedĕre, trucidare, trucidando occidĕre* (= to butcher); a great number of enemies were —d, *magna caedes fugientium est facta*.

mast, n. on ships, *malus,* †*arbor mali;* the —head, *malus summus;* lower end of the —, *malus imus*.

mast, n. = fruit of the beech, *glans fagea;* oak —, *glans querna*.

master, I. n. **1**, as a title, *dominus* (e.g. of a learned man, *vir doctissimus, illustrissimus,* etc.); **2**, = one who rules either men or business, *pater familias* or *familiae* (or in one word, *paterfam-*), *herus* (of the house, the former as regards the family, the latter in reference to the servants and the entire household), *possessor* (= one who possesses anything); the young — of the house, *filius herilis, filius familiae* (the latter with reference to the family, the former as regards the servants); **3**, = lord, ruler, *dominus, princeps, -ipis,* m. (the first in a state, as opp. to *dominus*), *tyrannus* (τύραννος, = ruler in the most absolute sense), *dynastes, -is,* m. (δυνάστης, = potentate; then especially sovereign of a small principality); to be — over anything or anybody, *imperare alci rei* and *alci, potentem esse alcjs rei* (both lit. and fig.); *praeesse alci rei* and *alci* (= to preside over, in a lit. sense); Prov., like —, like man, *plane qualis dominus talis et servus;* — of, *potens* with genit.; to be — of anything, *alqd in suâ potestate habēre, alqm locum tenēre;* to get — of, *potiri* (in good prose, *alqâ re, alqd, alcjs (rei) potiri, rerum potiri,* to seize the government); **4**, = the — under whom a youth serves his apprenticeship, *magister, paterfamilias, herus* (Com.); **5**, = teacher, *magister;* **6**, of a man perfectly skilled in any occupation, a — in anything, *artifex* (with the genit., especially with the genit. of the gerund); *antistes, -ĭtis,* m. and f., *princeps alcjs rei* (= one of the first, a man of importance in anything), *perfectus et absolutus in alqâ re* (= perfect in any art or science), *alqâ re* or *in alqâ re excellĕre* (= to be foremost, excel in anything); Horace is a — in the art of portraying the human character, *Horatius ad notandos hominum mores praecipuus;* **7**, fig. = — over oneself, *sui potens* or *compos;* — of arts, * *magister liberalium artium* (abbreviated *M.A.* or *A.M.*); — of the ceremonies at court, *comes, -ĭtis, officiorum, magister officiorum* or *aulae* (in gen.); at audiences, levees, *magister admissionum* (all under Roman emperors); — builder, *architectus;* —piece, *opus summo artificio factum;* —ship, = superior skill, *summa alcjs rei peritia;* = office of a governor, *magisterium*. **II.** v.tr. **1**, = to subdue, *domare, vincĕre, superare;* see SUBDUE, CONQUER; to — all one's passions, *continēre omnes cupiditates;* the fire (the flames) was —ed, *vis flammae oppressa est;* **2**, to — a thing, = to understand, *intellegĕre (intellig-), discĕre* (= to learn), *consequi* (= to attain), *alqd cognitum habēre, perspicĕre, alqâ re instructum esse*. **masterful,** adj. *insolens, superbus, contumax, arrogans*. Adv. *insolenter, superbe, contumaciter, arroganter*. **masterfulness,** n. *insolentia, superbia, contumacia, arrogantia*. **masterly,** adj. *artificiosus* (= executed or executing with — skill, of persons and things), *artifex* (= of persons), *summâ* or *singulari arte, summo artificio factus, callidissimo artificio factus, singulari opere artificioque* or *politissimâ arte perfectus* (= made in a — manner, of things); a speech delivered in a — manner, *oratio artis plena*. **mastery,** n. **1**, = victory, *victoria;* see also POWER; **2**, = attainment of eminent skill, to obtain the — of a thing, *perdiscĕre* (= to learn a thing accurately, thoroughly); see also MASTER, I. 7, and II.

mastic, mastich, n. *mastiche* (Plin.), *resina lentiscina* (Plin.).

masticate, n. *manducare, mandĕre*. **mastication,** n. use verb.

mastiff, n. perhaps *canis Molossus*.

mat, I. n. = texture of sedge, etc., *storea* or

storia, teges, tis, f , *tegeticula*. **II.** v.tr. — together, *implicare*

match, n for getting a light, *sulphurata, -orum* (Mart), *igniarium* (Plin), a —box, *pyxis* or *theca* (*sulphuratorum*)

match, I. n **1,** = one's equal (in a contest, etc); a — for . , *par alci* or *alci rei* (opp *impar*), to be a — for anyone, *alci parem esse* (e g *bello*), *non inferiorem esse algo*, to be a — for a thing, *alci rei parem* (e g a business, *negotiis*), *algd sustinēre* (e g a burden a load, *molem*), **2,** = contest, *certamen*, **3,** see MARRIAGE. **II.** v tr. — oneself with, *cum algo in certamen descendĕre, congredi cum algo* (= to try one's strength against anyone, e g in a duel), *parem esse alci, non inferiorem esse algo*, = to compare, *aequare algm* and *alci rei* or *algd*; = to suit, *adaequare, exaequare algd cum alga re* or *alci rei*, = to join, (*con*)*jungere, copulare cum algd re* **III.** v intr = to be like, *alci rei similem* or *parem esse* **matchless,** adj *singularis, incomparabilis* (Plin) *unicus, praestans* (or in superl *praestantissimus*), *egregius*, see EXCELLENT **match-maker,** n *nuptiarum conciliator, trix*

mate, I. n **1,** = one that eats at the same table, mess—, *convictor* (= one who constantly associates and lives, eats and drinks with another), *socius* (= companion), *conju(n)x* (= husband or wife), **2,** in a merchant ship or ship of war, (*sub magistro*) *nautis praepositus* **II.** v tr **1,** in chess, *algm vincĕre* or *ad incitas redigere*, **2,** in gen , see MATCH II

material, I. adj **1,** = consisting of matter, not spiritual, *corporeus*, the spirit is not —, *mens ab omni mortali concretione segregata est*, **2,** = not trivial, substantial, — point, *res* (opp. *sententia, argumentum*), — gain, *lucrum, quaestus, ūs*, — wants, *indigentia, inopia* (is the want felt), — pleasure, *voluptas* Adv *in omni genere* (= in all respects), *multum valde* (= greatly), *re*(*vera*) (= really) **II.** n = anything composed of matter, *materia* (*materies*, lit and fig), *res* (= what is —, opp. *verba*), *silva* (often *quasi silva* , in a fig. sense, plenty of —, e g *primum silva rerum ac sententiarum comparanda est*), the — for a rampart, *agger, -eris*, m , a stock of — and of words *copia rerum et verborum*, to collect —s, *silvam rerum comparare*, to leave —s about anything historical, *in commentariis algd relinquĕre*, —s for war, *belli apparatus, ūs* **materialism,** n *opinio eorum qui nihil in natura esse statuunt nisi corpora* **materialist,** n *qui nihil in rerum naturā esse statuit nisi corpora*

maternal, adj *maternus*, — feelings, *animus maternus*, — affection, love, *amor maternus, amor matris erga liberos, materna indulgentia* (= — indulgence) **maternity,** n *animus maternus*, see also above

mathematical, adj *mathematicus, accuratus, certus* (fig , = exact, accurate, certain), — calculation, *mathematicorum ratio*; to infer with — exactness, *necessariā mathematicorum ratione concludere algd*, with — certainty, *certissimus* Adv by adj **mathematician,** n *mathematicus* or by circumloc., *mathematicarum artium peritus* **mathematics,** n *mathematica, -ae* (Sen)

matins, n *matutinae preces, um* (= morning prayer)

matricide, n **1,** *matricidium* (= the crime), **2,** *matricida*, m and f (= the person)

matriculate, v tr (a student), *algm civitati academicae* or *in civitatem academicam a(d)scribĕre* **matriculation,** n see above

matrimony, n *matrimonium*, see MARRIAGE **matrimonial,** adj see CONJUGAL, CONNUBIAL

matron, n *matrona*, — of a workhouse, etc , *custos, odis, procuratrix* **matronly,** adj *matronalis*

matter, n **1,** (= substance excreted from living animal bodies), *pus, puris*, n (Cels), full of —, *purulentus*, **2,** (= visible, tangible —), *corpus, -ŏris*, n , *res corporeae, quae cerni tangique possunt*, **3,** (in a more general and philosophical sense), *rerum natura, principia rerum ex quibus omnia constant*, **4,** (= thing treated of), *res, propositum* (= that of which the speaker intends to treat), that has nothing to do with the —, *hoc nihil est ad rem*, to come to the —, *ad propositum* or *ad rem ipsam venire*, but let us return to the — in hand (after a digression), *jam ad instituta pergamus*, (after an introduction) *sed ad propositum revertamus*, or simply *sed ad propositum*, but to return to the — in hand, *sed ut eo revertar, unde sum egressus, ut eo unde egressa est referat se oratio*, to cut the — short, *ut paucis dicam, ut in pauca conferam, ne longum fiat, ne longus sim*, it is a difficult — to, etc , *difficile est* (with infin or with supine in -u), = material, *materia* (*materies*), *silva* (often *quasi silva*), = event, occurrence, *res, res gesta*, = affair, cause, *res* (in gen , also = disputed point in a lawsuit, the lawsuit itself), *negotium* (= a business to perform, engagement), *caus(s)a* (in a war, in a lawsuit, or in a literary discussion), to meddle with the —s of other people, *aliena negotia curare*, how is it with the —? how do —s stand? *quo loco res est? ut res se habet?* how stands your —? *quomodo tibi res se habet?* the — is settled, *judicata res est*, concerning the —, *quod rem* or *res spectat*, pith of the —, *res*, — of fact, *factum*, what's the —? *quid or quidnam est? quid rei est? quid accidit?* what's the — with her? *quid tristis est?* (of one who seems sorrowful), *quo morbo laborat?* (of one who is ill), upon the whole —, *denique*, a small —, *paul(l)ulum, aliquantum*. **it matters,** v imp *interest, refert*, with genit if used of a person to whom it matters; but if the person is expressed by a personal pronoun, we use the abl *meā, tuā, nostrā, vestrā*, e g to me it —s, *meā interest* or *refert*, the thing in which we feel an interest can never be expressed by a noun; but must be rendered with the accus and infin , the simple infin , or by a relative clause (oblique interrogation), or with *ut*, how much it matters is expressed by *magnopere, magis, maxime, minime, multum, permultum, plurimum, nihil*, etc., or by the genit of the value, e g *magni, permagni, parvi, pluris, tanti, quanti*, etc , e g it —s a great deal to me whether you are with me or not (I am very anxious for you to be present with me), *maxime nostrā interest te esse nobiscum*, at Rome, *permagni nostrā interest te esse Romae*

matting, n see MAT

mattock, n *dolabra*

mattress, n *stragulum*, a — of goat's hair, *cilicium*

mature, I adj **1,** *maturus* (= ripe, of full age), *tempestivus* (= seasonable), **2,** of judgment, etc , *consideratus, sapiens, prudens, sagax, perspicax, intellegens* (*intellig*.) Adv *mature* (= soon), *tempestive* (= seasonably), *considerate, sapienter, prudenter, sagaciter, intellegenter* (*intellig*.) **II.** v tr **1,** = ripen, *maturare, coquere*, **2,** fig *parare, efficĕre, fingĕre* , see DEVISE, PREPARE **III.** v intr *maturescĕre* **matureness, maturity,** n *maturitas* (= timeliness, lit and fig) to bring to —, *ad maturitatem perducĕre* (lit), to come to —, *maturescĕre* (also fig. = to be brought to a state of perfection, Plin.).

matutinal, adj. *matutinus*.

maudlin, adj. see DRUNKEN, SILLY.

maul, v.tr. *laedĕre* (= injure).

maunder, v.intr. *nugari*.

mausoleum, n. *mausoleum* (Suet.); see TOMB.

maw, n. *ingluvies, venter*; see STOMACH.

mawkish, adj. *putidus*. Adv. *putide*.
mawkishness, n. use adj.

maxim, n. *dogma* (δόγμα), or in pure Latin *decretum* (= principle established by a philosopher, doctrine), *praeceptum* (= precept, whereby we determine an action, a rule or any doctrine, also said of a philosopher), *institutum*, *sententia* (in gen. = an opinion founded upon reasons), *judicium* (= conviction, anyone's view of a matter, arrived at after mature consideration), *regula alcjs rei* or *ad quam alqd dirigitur* (= rule, principle upon which we act in a matter; never without the genit. of the object, e.g. the same — applies with regard to gain, as, etc., e.g. *eadem utilitatis quae honestatis est regula*); *lex* (= law, stated rule, e.g. *primam esse historiae legem*).

maximum, n. *quod maximum est*; the — gain, *quaestus* (-ūs) *maximus*.

May, n. *(mensis) Maius*. **May-day**, n. *Kalendae Maiae*.

may, verb aux. **1**, = to be possible; see POSSIBLE, CAN; **2**, = to have physical power; see ABLE, CAN; **3**, = to have moral power; see ALLOW, DARE; **4**, see PERHAPS; however, as no precise mode in which this verb is to be rendered can be stated, each person's individual judgment, formed by attentive reading, must be the guide; — . . . ever so, still, etc., *tametsi . . . tamen*; if — expresses a conjecture, it is rendered by *videri*, e.g. you — not be fully aware of his boldness, *parum perspexisse ejus videris audaciam*; he — be twenty years old, *viginti annos natus esse videtur*; a thing that — be done, etc., or — in forms of prayer and petition, should be rendered simply by the subjunctive mood, or sometimes by the inf., e.g. he — go, *eat*; somebody might say, *forsitan quispiam dixerit* or *forte aliquis dicet* (= perhaps someone will say); however they — grumble, I shall say what I think, *fremant, dicam quod sentio*; whoever he — be, etc., *quicunque is est*; as fast as — be, *quam celerrime*; you — for me, (*per me*) *licet*; if I — say so, *si ita loqui* or *dicere licet, sit venia verbi*; — be, see PERHAPS.

mayor, n. *urbis praefectus*, -ūs (Suet.).
mayoralty, n. *urbis praefectura*.

maze, n. *labyrinthus* (*qui itinerum ambages occursusque ac recursus inexplicabilis continet*, Plin.). **mazy**, adj. *inexplicabilis* (Plin.), † *inextricabilis*.

mead, n. *mulsum*.

mead, meadow, n. *pratum*; belonging to, growing on the —, *pratensis*; — land, — ground, *pratum*. **meadowy**, adj. *multa prata habens*.

meagre, adj. **1**, of flesh; see LEAN; **2**, as in — soil, *exilis*; see BARREN; **3**, = wanting strength of diction, *jejunus, exilis, aridus*. Adv. *jejune, exiliter*. **meagreness**, n. **1**, see LEANNESS; **2**, *exilitas*; **3**, *jejunitas exilitas*.

meal, n. *farina* (of wheat or any other kind of grain); see FLOUR. **mealy**, adj. *farinarius*.

meal, n. in gen. *cibus* (= food); *epulae* (= banquet); properly only two among the Romans, viz., the morning —, *prandium*; and the chief — of the day, *cena* (*coen*-), taken in the decline of the day. Besides these, the *jentaculum*, taken on rising in the morning, was a very slight refreshment. The *prandium* was taken about noon, hence *cibum meridianum sumĕre*. Between the *prandium* and the *cena* the Romans sometimes took a luncheon (*gustare*). To take a — is *edĕre, cibum capĕre, prandēre, prandium comedĕre, gustare* (= to lunch), *cenare, cenitare, epulari* (= to feast, to banquet); to take a — at anyone's table, *accubare apud alqm*.

mean, adj. = low and unworthy, *illiberalis, sordidus* (= unworthy a free man), *abjectus* (= contemptible), *turpis* (= base), *improbus* (= dishonest), of clothing, etc., *sordidus*; of rank, *humilis, ignobilis, obscurus* (= morally bad and low), *foedus* (= foul, of things); — plan, *foedum consilium*. Adv. *illiberaliter, sordide, abjecte, abjecte et sine dignitate, turpiter, turpiter et nequiter, foede*. **meanness**, n. *illiberalitas, animus abjectus, improbitas, sordes, -(i)um, indignitas*; of rank, *humilitas, ignobilitas, obscuritas*; to bear all —es, *omnes indignitates (per)ferre*; to lead anyone to —, *alqm ad nequitiam adducĕre*; I fear to commit a —, *extimesco ne quid turpiter faciam*.

mean, or **medium**, n. *res media, modus*; there is no — between peace and war, *inter pacem et bellum medium nihil est*. **means**, n. = whatever serves to the attainment of an object, *via, ratio, consilium, facultas, auxilium, adjumentum*; a — which leads to your end, *id quod eo quo intendas fert deducitque*; ways and —, *via atque ratio*; to select or take a —, *rationem* (or *viam*) *inire* (or *nihil capĕre or sequi*); to try all —, *omnia experiri, nihil inexpertum omittĕre*; to try the last —, *extrema experiri* or *audĕre, ad extrema* (*ad ultimum auxilium*) *descendĕre*; to endeavour by all —, *omni ope atque opera eniti* (with *ut* or *ne*); by fair —, *recte*; by foul —, *foede, turpiter*; by all —, *omnino, prorsus, plane*; concessively, (*ita*) *sane, vero, utique*; by no —, *neutiquam, haudquaquam, minime, nullo modo*; = resources (see the word), *opes, facultates, divitiae*; I have — to live, *habeo unde vivam*; I have no — to, etc., *ad alqd perficiendum mihi desunt facultates*; out of your own —, *tuis opibus, privato sumptu*; by — of, *ope* (or *auxilio*) *alcjs, alqo juvante, per alqm*; (if a thing, the ablative alone is generally employed), to mount the wall by — of ladders, *scalis murum a(d)scendĕre*; by participles, *praeliis secundis usus*, = by — of successful engagements. If you wish to represent a cause, operation, or occasion, employ *per*; *mulieres per aetatem ad pugnam inutilis*, = women useless for fight by —, (= on account) of their age; *per se cognitus*, by his own — or efforts; *per Caeciliam agĕre*, = to carry on by — of Caecilia; *eorum opera plebs concitata est*, = by their — the people were stirred up; *ejus beneficio in curiam venerant*, = by his — (or favour) they had entered the senate.

mean, v.tr. **1**, = to have in contemplation, *velle, cogitare*; see INTEND; **2**, = to design with reference to a future act, e.g. to — well to anyone, *bona fide agĕre cum alqo, alci bene velle, alci cupĕre* (but never *alci bene cupĕre* in this sense), *alci favēre*, comb. *alci favēre et cupĕre*; *alci amicum esse, alci cupĕre et amicum esse*: **3**, = to signify, *dicĕre alqm* or *alqd, significare, designare, denotare*, also with the addition *oratione sua* (= to allude to anyone in one's speech, words); I — Hilarus, *Hilarum dico*; *intellegĕre* (*intellig*-, = to understand by), what does he — ? *quid sibi vult?* what does he — by these words? *quid sibi vult haec oratio? quid sibi volunt verba ista?* = to be a sign for expressing an idea, *significare, declarare, sonare* (lit. to sound), *valēre* (= to contain such and such a meaning); this word (the word becco) —s the bill of a cock, *id gallinacei rostrum valet* **meaning,** n 1, = that which exists in the mind (e g yes, that is my —, *mihi vero sic placet, sic hoc mihi videtur*, see INTENTION, WISH, OPINION, 2, see PURPOSE, AIM, 3, = signification, *significatio* (of a word), *vis* (= force of an expression), *sententia* (= the idea which the person speaking attaches to a certain word), *notio* (= original idea of a word, see IDEA), *intellectus, ūs* (how a word is to be understood, post Aug t t, Quint), it is necessary to fix the — of the verb "to be in want of," *illud excutiendum est, quid sit* CARERE, to give a — to a word, *verbo vim, sententiam, notionem sub(j)icĕre*, well- —, see BENEVOLENT

meander, v intr *flexuoso cursu fluĕre*

measles, n. 1, = disease in man, **morbilli* (t t), 2, = disease in pigs, **hydătis finna* (not class)

measurable, adj *quod metiri possumus* **measurableness,** n render by adj **measure, I.** n 1, *mensura* (= that by which extent or dimension is ascertained, lit and fig, in an abstract and concrete sense), *modus* (= proportion, limit as to how far a person ought or is allowed to go), *moderatio* (= moderation), weights and —s, *mensurae et pondera, um* (Plin), to take the — of anything, *mensuram alcjs rei inire*, with full —, *pleno modio, cumulate*, according to the — of, *pro modo, pro ratione* (but generally by *pro* with ablat, according to, e g *pro viribus agere, pro se quisque*, i e everyone according to his strength), beyond —, out of all —, *sine modo, praeter* or *extra* or *supra modum, immodice, immoderate, majorem in modum* (= beyond the usual —), *nimis* (= too much), *admodum* (= exceedingly), *longe* (= by far, with superl, e g *longe omnium maximus*), *sic ut nihil supra possit, adeo ut nihil supra*, in such a —, *hoc modo, tali modo, sic*, in some —, *alqo modo, alqâ ratione, alqâ ex parte, alqd, nonnihil* (= somehow, in some way, this relieves me in some —, *me res alqd sublevat*), in a certain —, *quodam modo*, also when it modifies an expression, by *ut ita dicam, quasi, quidam* with the word the meaning of which it modifies (e g all arts have in some — a common tie, *omnes artes habent quoddam commune vinculum*), in such a — as, *prout*, — for —, *par pari referre* or *respondēre*, 2, = steps taken, *ratio* (= mode of acting) *consilium* (= plan), *remedium* (= remedy), a wise —, *consilium prudens*, to take a —, *rationem inire, consilium capĕre*, to take — according to time and circumstances, *consilium pro tempore et pro re capĕre* to take good, practical or effective —, *bonis consiliis uti*, to take joint —, *consilia communicare*, 3, in music, *modi, numeri*, see also METRE **II** v tr 1, = to ascertain extent, degree, *(di)metiri, emetiri, permetiri, mensuram alcjs rei inire*, 2, = to ascertain the degree of anything (e g of heat), *emetiri*, 3, = to travel over, *emetiri*, see PASS, v tr, 4, = to judge of distance, etc, by anything (also fig = to judge by, etc), *(di)metiri alqd alqâ re*, 5, = to adjust, proportion, lit *metiri*; fig = to determine the ratio of one thing to another, *alqd dirigĕre ad alqm rem* or *alqâ re*, with what judgment ye judge, ye shall be judged, and with what — ye mete, it shall be measured to you again, *in quo judicio judicaveritis, judicabimini, et in quâ mensurâ mensi fueritis, remetietur vobis* (Vulgate) **III.** v intr render by *magnitudine esse* (with genit, e g *quinque pedum*) **measured,** adj see MODERATE **measurer,** n *qui metitur, mensor* **measureless,** adj *immensus, infinitus* **measurement,** n *mensio* (= the act), *mensura* (= the manner) see MEASURE **measuring-rod,** n *decempĕda*

meat, n 1, = anything eaten by man or beast, see FOOD, 2, = flesh, *caro, nis*, f; a small piece of —, *caruncula*, a piece of roast —, *caro assa* or *assum*, with distinguishing adj (e g *assum vitulinum* = veal) boiled —, *caro elixa*, cooked —, *caro cocta*, salt —, *caro sale conspersa* or *conditanea*, horse —, *equorum pabulum* (= food for the horses), — market, *macellum* (= general market)

mechanic, n *faber, opifex* **mechanical,** adj *machinalis* (Plin), *mechanicus* (Aul Gell), *organicus* (architectural term), to possess — skill, *manibus exercitatum esse* Adv *sine mente ac ratione* **mechanics,** n as a science, *scientia machinalis* (= knowledge of —, mechanical science, Plin) **mechanism,** n *machinatio*

medal, n *nummus in memoriam alcjs rei cusus* (to commemorate an event) **medallion,** n *clipeus* or *clipeum* (in the form of a shield), see also MEDAL

meddle, v intr see INTERFERE **meddler,** n *ardelio* (Phaed, Mart), *homo importunus, molestus* **meddling,** adj see INQUISITIVE

mediæval, adj *ad medium aevum* or *ad patrum tempora pertinens*

mediate, I adj opp to immediate, in philosophy, causes so termed are thus discriminated by Cicero, *caus(s)arum aliae sunt adjuvantes, aliae proximae* of causes, some are mediate, others immediate. Adv *per caus(s)as adjuvantes* **II.** v intr *se interponĕre ad alqd faciendum*, see also RECONCILE **III.** v tr — a peace, *pacem conciliare* **mediation,** n use *deprecator* (e g *me deprecatore*, by my —) **mediator,** n *qui se* (or *auctoritatem suam*) *interponit, arbiter, qui arbitri partes agit* or *sustinet, interpres, -ĭtis* (= one who, as a translator, represents the interests of his party), *conciliator alcjs rei* (= he who brings about an object, e g a marriage, *conciliator nuptiarum*), *deprecator* (in gen)

medicable, adj see CURABLE **medical,** adj †*medicus, medicinus, medicinalis*, — properties, by *vis medendi*, — man, *medicus* (in gen) **medicament, medicine,** n 1, *medicina, medicamen(tum), remedium* (as a remedy for some complaints, *ad, contra alqd*), counteracting —, *antidŏtos* (*antidotum*), pertaining to —, *medicinalis*, 2, = medical science, *medicina ars medicinalis, ars medendi*, to practise —, *medicinam exercēre* **medicine bottle,** n *poculum* (= cup) **medicine box,** n *narthecium, pyxis* **medicinal,** adj *saluber, salutaris* Adv *remedio* (dat = as a remedy)

mediocre, adj *mediocris* **mediocrity,** n *mediocritas*

meditate, v intr 1, *cogitare, meditari, commentari*, see THINK, 2, see INTEND **meditation,** n *cogitatio, commentatio, meditatio*, comb *commentatio atque meditatio*, see THOUGHT **meditative,** adj by adv *attento animo, in cogitatione defixus*

medium, n a middle course, fig *media consilia, -orum, media consilii via*, to pursue a —, *mediam consequi consilii viam, mediam quandam sequi viam*, see MEANS

medlar, n *mespilum*, — -tree, *mespilus*, f (Plin)

medley, n *farrago* (Juv), *colluvio rerum*, so too *colluvio omnium scelerum*

meed, n *praemium*, see REWARD

meek, adj *demissus modestus, verecundus* Adv *modeste verecunde* **meekness,** n *animus demissus, modestia, verecundia.*

meet, adj. see Fit, Proper, Useful.

meet, **I.** v.tr. 1, *alci occurrĕre*, *obviam venire*, *obvium se dare*, *obvium esse*, *obviam* or *obvium fieri*, (*obvium*) *se offerre* (all in gen. = to — a person), *congredi cum alqo* (of two meeting each other on the way), *offendĕre alqm*, *incidĕre alci* or *in alqm* (accidentally), *improviso alci incidĕre* (unexpectedly), *obviam ire* (intentionally); somebody —s me on the road, *se inter viam offert alqs*; = to go to —, *obviam ire* (out of politeness, or from hostile motives), *occurrĕre*, *occursare*, *obviam procedĕre*, *obviam venienti procedĕre*, *obviam venire* or *progredi*, *obviam egredi* (all with dat.; in Plaut. and Ter.); = to come together in any place, *invenire*, *reperire alqm* (or *alqd*, = to find anyone whom we wish to see), *offendĕre alqm* (or *alqd*, = accidentally, unexpectedly to fall upon anything or upon a person), *nancisci* (= to — accidentally, to catch, e.g. anyone alone, without a witness, *alqm sine arbitris*), *convenire alqm* (= to — anyone by appointment to whom we wish to speak); to be met (e.g. he can be met at, etc.), *inveniri*, *reperiri*; to be met at a certain place, *frequentare locum*; 2, fig. = to encounter (e.g. to — danger), *periculo obviam ire*, *se offerre*, *se opponĕre*, *se committĕre*; to — death, *mortem oppetĕre*, *morti se offerre* or *se ob(j)icĕre*; = to receive with kindness (e.g. to — anyone's views), *consentire de alqâ re*; to — kindly, to — halfway, *urbanum* or *liberalem se praebēre alci*. **II.** v.intr. 1, of two persons, *inter se obvios esse*, *inter se congredi* or *convenire*, *concurrĕre inter se* (accidentally); to — by appointment, *congredi cum alqo*, *convenire alqm* (e.g. on the road, *ex itinere*); *confluĕre* (in large numbers), *concurrĕre*, *convolare* (= to hasten together); 2, of lines, circumstances, etc., *convenire*; 3, = to — in a hostile manner, (*inter se*) *concurrĕre* (of bodies, and of those who fight), (*inter se*) *congredi* (in a single combat, and of troops), *signa inter se conferre*, *cum infestis signis concurrĕre* (of two armies), *collidi inter se* (of two ships). **meeting**, n. = assembly, *congressio*, *conventus*, *-ūs* (= a friendly —), *coetus*, *-ūs* (*coit-*) (= a gathering), *concursus*, *-ūs*, *concursio* (= any coming together); a large, numerous —, *celeber conventus*, *celebritas* (= a gathering of many persons at a place), *frequentia* (= a — that is well attended). **meeting-house**, n. 1, *conveniendi locus*, *locus quo conveniunt*; 2, *aedes*, *-ium*.

melancholy, **melancholic**, **I.** adj. 1, = hypochondriacal, *melancholicus* (μελαγχολικός); 2, fig. *tristis* (= sorrowful, also of things, e.g. countenance), *maestus* (= downcast, opp. to *laetus*). **II.** n. = hypochondria, *atra bilis*, or the Greek μελαγχολία, in Cic., e.g. *Graeci volunt illi quidem, sed parum valent verbo; quem nos furorem, μελαγχολίαν illi vocant; quasi vero atra bile solum mens, ac non saepe vel iracundiâ graviore, vel timore, vel dolore moveatur*; = sorrowful disposition, *tristitia*, *maestitia*.

melée, n. *concursus*, *-ūs* (= charge), or *pugna*, *proelium* (= battle).

melliferous, adj. † *mellifer*. **mellifluence**, n. *mel* (e.g. *Homerici senis mella*, = the — of Homer, Plin. Min.). **mellifluent**, **mellifluous**, adj. *mellitus*.

mellow, **I.** adj. 1, of fruit, *mitis*, *mollis* (= mild, soft; *mollis* also of meat); of wine, *lenis* (Ter.), *mollis* (Verg.); = ripe, *maturus*, comb. *maturus et coctus*; 2, fig. *sapiens*, *sagax*, *prudens*; see Wise, Sagacious. **II.** v.tr. *coquĕre*. **III.** v.intr. *maturescĕre*.

melodious, adj. *canōrus*, *sonōrus*, *numerosus* (= harmonious, tuneful, of a speech and of the speaker), *numerose cadens* (= with graceful periods, of a speech). Adv. *numerose*. **melodiousness**, n. use adj. (e.g. — of the voice, *vox canora*). **melody**, n. *modus*, *modulus* (Plin.), *melos*, *-i*, n., *cantus*, *-ūs*; — and time, *cantus numerique*; — of the voice, *vocis modulatio*. **melodrama**, n. *drama musicum*. **melodramatic**, adj. *mirificus*; see Wonderful.

melon, n. *melo* (Plin.).

melt, **I.** v.tr. 1, = to make liquid, *liquidum facĕre*, *liquefacĕre*, *dissolvĕre*, † *resolvĕre* (= to dissolve snow, pearls, *nivem*, *margaritas*, etc.), *diluĕre* (= to dilute, e.g. a pearl in vinegar, *baccam aceto*); 2, = to soften to tenderness, *alcjs mentem ad misericordiam revocare*, *alqm ad misericordiam vocare* or *adducĕre* (= to move to compassion). **II.** v.intr. 1, = to become liquid, to — away, *liquescĕre*, *liquefieri*, *dissolvi*, *tabescĕre* (of snow, then fig. of man, e.g. from desire, *desiderio*, from love, *amore*); 2, fig. to — into tears, *in lacrimas effundi*; 3, = to lose substance (e.g. corporeal things — as breath into the wind), *dilabi* (= gradually to — so as to disappear). **melting**, adj. by adv. *mollis et delicatus* (of sounds, e.g. *quanto molliores sunt et delicatiores in cantu flexiones*); see also Piteous.

member, n. 1, *membrum*, *artus*, *-ūs* (both of the body); see Limb; 2, = part of a discourse or of a verse, a clause, *membrum* (e.g. of the body, of a speech), *pars* (= part of a whole, = a part which is a whole by itself); *articulus* (*articulus dicitur cum singula verba intervallis distinguuntur*, Cic.), *incisio*, *incisum* (κόμμα = part of a sentence), *membrum* (= a greater part of a sentence, κῶλον, e.g. *quae Graeci κόμματα et κῶλα nominant, nos recte incisa et membra dicimus*); 3, = an individual of a community or society; a — of a council, senate, *vir* or *homo senatorius*, *senator*; — of a community, *civis*; — of a race, *gentilis*; — of a family, *homo de alcjs stirpe*; — of a society, *socius*, *sodalis*, *-is*, m.; see Part. **membership**, n. render by circumloc. with **member**.

membrane, n. *membrana*.

memoir, n. a private —, *dicta factaque alcjs*, *memoria* (= tradition, narrative); an historical —, *commentarii*; Socrates' —, as Xenophon gives them, *ea quae a Socrate dicta Xenophon retulit*. **memorable**, adj. = worth mentioning, (*com*)*memorabilis* (rare), *memoratu dignus* = deserving to be handed down to posterity, *memoriâ dignus*, *memorabilis*, *memoriae prodendus*; *insignis* (= of special note); no — event occurred, *nihil memoriâ dignum actum*; this year will be — on this account, *hic annus insignis erit hac re*. **memorandum**, n. = remark, see Note; = list of goods, *index*, *-icis*, m. and f.; = a sign whereby to remember anything, *nota* (= characteristic, a mark made with the pen; to make a — with chalk against anything, *cretâ notare alqd*); —-book, *adversaria*, *-orum* (= waste-book, day-book). **memorial**, **I.** n. *monumentum*; a — in writing, *lit(t)erarum monumenta*, *-orum*, *lit(t)erae*. **II.** adj. — coin, *nummus in memoriam alcjs cusus*; — column, *cippus*. **memoirs**, n. *commentarii*. **memory**, n. *memoria*, *recordatio* (= recollection); to keep in —, *memoriâ tenēre alqd*; to the — of, *in memoriam alcjs*; from —, *ex memoriâ*, *memoriter*; to commit to —, *alqd memoriae mandare*, *ediscĕre*; in the — of man, *post hominum memoriam*; to hand down to —, *memoriae tradĕre*, or *prodĕre*.

menace, v. and n., and **menacing**, adj. and adv., see Threaten, Threat, Threatening.

menagerie, n. *vivarium*, *leporarium* (both = preserve), or *ferae saeptis* (*sept-*) *inclusae*.

mend, I. v tr 1, = to repair, *reficere, reparare, reconcinnare* (= to — again what was whole before), *(re)sarcire* (= to patch up anything damaged, or that is torn to pieces, a tub, house, roof, coat, etc.), *emendare, corrigĕre* (= to free a written treatise from mistakes), 2, fig *emendare, corrigĕre;* = to — one's life, *mores suos mutare*, to — one's pace, *gradum addĕre* **II** v intr **1**, physically, *(ex morbo) convalescĕre*, **2**, = to improve, *melius ire* (e g things —, *res melius it*)

mendacious, adj *mendax* Adv *falso, per mendacium.* **mendacity,** n *mendacium*, see LIE

mendicancy, mendicity, n *mendicitas, egestas* (= neediness), comb *egestas ac mendicitas* (all = beggary) **mendicant,** adj *mendīcus*, see BEG, BEGGAR

menial, I. adj. **1**, = pertaining to domestic servants, *servilis;* **2,** fig *servilis, humilis, sordidus, illiberalis* **II.** n see SERVANT, DOMESTIC

menstrual, adj *menstruus.*

mensuration, n *dimensio* (= measuring), *ars metiendi*, see SURVEYING

mental, adj by the genitives *animi, ingenii*, — gifts, *animi facultates* (= talents), *ingenium* (= natural talent); to possess excellent — gifts, *ingenio valēre, ingenio abundare* (= to abound in), *praestantissimo ingenio praeditum esse* (= to be endowed with excellent — gifts), — debility, *morbus animi* or *mentis, aegritudo animi* (as affliction, etc) Adv *mente, animo, cogitatione*

mention, I. n *commemoratio* (when the idea existed already in the mind previously), *mentio* (in reference to the idea in general, whether quite new or —ed a second time), to make — of a matter, *mentionem facĕre alcjs rei* **II.** v tr *(com)memorare alqd, alcjs rei meminisse* (= to remember, if anyone shows by his words that he has not forgotten a thing, also to — in anything written), comb *meminisse et commemorare, mentionem facĕre alcjs rei* or *de alqā re* (= to make — of), to — accidentally, or in passing, *(casu) in mentionem alcjs rei incidere*, to — frequently, *mentionem alcjs rei agitare, crebro* or *crebris sermonibus alqd usurpare*, not to — that, etc, *ut omittam* or *ne dicam, quod*, etc.; not to — all these things, *omissis his rebus omnibus*, above-—ed, *de quo (quā) supra commemoravimus, quem (quam, quod) supra commemoravimus* or *diximus, quem (quam, quod) supra scripsi, qui (quae, quod) supra scriptus (-a, -um) est, de quo (quā) a nobis antea dictum est, cujus supra meminimus*, also simply by *ille;* as we have —ed above, before, *ut supra dictum est, ut supra scripsi* or *scriptum est*, see STATE, DECLARE

mentor, n see ADVISER

mephitic, n *mephiticus* (late), *foetidus*

mercantile, adj *mercatorius*, generally by the genit *mercatoris* or *mercatorum* (= of the merchants), or by *commercium, mercatura* (e g *mercaturas facĕre*, = to be engaged in — transactions), see COMMERCIAL **mercenary,** adj *mercenarius* (= for hire, e g *testis* = a paid witness, *miles* = — soldier), *(mercede* or *pretio) conductus, quaestuosus* (= eager for gain), *avarus* (= avaricious), *venalis* (= readily bribed) **mercer,** n = general dealer in cotton, etc , *tabernarius* (= shopkeepers in general), *qui pannos vendit* or *venditat* (= a hosier in a small way) **merchandise,** n **1**, = goods, *merx, -cis*, f, *res venales*; **2**, = commerce, *commercium, mercatura, negotia, -orum* **merchant,** n *mercator* **merchantman,** n *navis mercatoria* (Plaut), or *oneraria*, also simply *oneraria*

mercurial, adj **1** by circuml with mercury, **2**, fig *mobilis, lĕvis* **mercury,** n **1**, the god, *Mercurius*, **2**, the planet, *stella Mercurii, Mercurius*, **3**, the metal, *argentum vivum* (Plin)

mercy, n *misericordia, clementia, mansuetudo, venia* (= pardon), *lenitas* (= mildness) **merciful,** adj *misericors, clemens, mansuetus, exorabilis* (= easily entreated), *lenis, mitis* Adv *clementer, mansuete* **merciless,** adj *immisericors, inexorabilis, immitis, inclemens, inhumanus, crudelis, durus, atrox, saevus, ferreus*, see CRUEL Adv *inclementer, inhumane, crudeliter, duriter (dure), atrociter, saeve* **mercilessness,** n. *inclementia, inhumanitas, duritia (durities), crudelitas, atrocitas, saevitia;* see CRUELTY

mere, adj *merus* (= not mixed, opp *mixtus*, in prose generally only in reference to wine, then also = nothing but), *solus, unus* (= sole), also by *ipse* (before the noun, e g. by the — sight, *ipso aspectu*), in a wider sense, by *merus* (in good prose only of things); — trifles, *merae nugae*. not to be able to sleep with — joy, *prae magno gaudio somnum capĕre non posse* Adv *(tantum) modo, solum, tantum*, see ONLY

meretricious, adj **1**, see UNCHASTE, **2**, fig of style, *fucatus*

merge, v tr **1**, see DIP, **2**, see MIX, MINGLE

meridian, I. n in astron *circulus meridianus*, = the highest point, see HEIGHT, SUMMIT **II** adj *meridianus*

merit, I n **1**, = excellence which claims reward, *dignitas, virtus* (= excellence), according to —, *pro merito, merito, pro dignitate*, **2**, = value (applied to things), *excellentia, praestantia*, see EXCELLENCY, VALUE, WORTH, **3**, see REWARD, to make a — of necessity, *necessitati parēre* **II.** v tr see DESERVE **merited,** adj *meritus, debitus*, comb *meritus ac debitus* **meritorious,** adj by circumloc. (e g *laude dignus, laudabilis*, or, that is a very — act of yours, *hic re optime meruisti*), to act in a — manner, *bene merēre*, towards any body, *de alqo*. Adv *bene, optime*

merle, n *merula*

mermaid, n *nympha quae faciem mulieris et piscis caudam habet*

merriment, n. *hilaritas, alacritas, lascivia, animus hilaris* (= merry disposition, mood) **merry,** adj *hilarus, hilaris, lascivus* (= frolicsome), *festivus*, see GAY Adv *hilariter, hilare, festive* **merry-andrew,** n *homo jocosus, ridiculus, coprea* (= jester), *sannio* (= mimic, and in gen sense), *scurra* (= droll) **merry-making,** n *voluptas*, see PLEASURE, FEAST

mesh, n *măcula* **meshy,** adj *reticulatus*

mesmerize, v tr *manuum contrectatione somnum alci inducĕre* **mesmerism, mesmerist,** n use verb.

mess, I n **1**, = portion of food, *cibus* or some special n (e g a — of veal, *caro vitulina*), **2**, = common meal, *convivium*, **3**, = soldiers dining together, use *convivae, sodales, -ium* **II.** v intr *cenare (coen)* **messmate,** n *conviva*, m and f, *sodalis*, m and f

mess, n **1**, = dirt, *squalor, illuvies, paedor, sordes, -ium*, f , see FILTH; **2**, fig *res afflictae, perturbatio* or *confusio rerum*, his affairs are in a —, *pessime cum illo agitur*, see TROUBLE

message, n *nuntius, mandatum, legatio* (of an ambassador, e g to undertake a — to anyone, *legationem ad alqm suscipĕre*), or by *mittĕre* (e g the reason of the — sent was, *caus-*

(*s*)*a mittendi erat*); see ANSWER, REPORT; to send a —, *alqm certiorem facĕre alcjs rei* or *de alqâ re*. **messenger**, n. **1**, *nuntius* (*nunc-*) (as bearer of a piece of news, by word of mouth; fem. *nuntia*), *tabellarius* (= letter-carrier); to inform anyone by letter or by a —, *per lit(t)eras aut per nuntium certiorem facĕre alqm*; **2**, in a political sense, *nuntius* (= — in general), *legatus* (= ambassador, deputy); **3**, — of a court of law, *viator*, *apparitor* (= usher).

Messiah, n. *Messias*, *-ae* (Eccl.).

metal, n. *metallum* (in gen.), *aes*, *aeris*, n. (= copper, brass, bronze); like —, *metallo* or *aeri similis*. **metallic**, adj. *metallicus* (Plin., in gen.), *aereus*, *a(h)eneus* (= of brass). **metalliferous**, adj. †*metallifer*. **metallurgy**, n. use *ars metallica*; see MINE.

metamorphose, v.tr. *mutare in alqd*; see TRANSFORM. **metamorphosis**, n. *metamorphosis* (only as title of Ovid's poem, *ut Ovidius lascivire in Metamorphosi solet*, Quint.); use verb.

metaphor, n. and adj. *translatio*, *verba translata*, Cic., *modus transferendi*, *metaphora* (post Aug.; Quint. states it to be a Greek term, *translatio quae metaphora Graece dicitur*). **metaphoric**, adj. *translatus*. Adv. by *translatis verbis* (e.g. to speak); to use a word —, *verbum transferre*; see FIGURATIVE.

metaphysic, metaphysical, adj. *metaphysicus* (not class.). **metaphysics**, n. *metaphysica*, *-ae* (not class.); where possible use *philosophia*.

mete, v.tr. see MEASURE.

metempsychosis, n. *animarum ab aliis post mortem ad alios transitio*.

meteor, n. *fax* (*caelestis*). **meteoric**, adj. by circumloc. **meteoric-stone, meteorolite, meteorite**, n. *lapis qui caelo decĭdit*.

method, n. *ratio*, *via*, comb. *ratio et via*, *via et ratio* (= the particular — which we follow in anything), *modus* (= mode in which anything is done); — of teaching, *docendi*, *disserendi ratio*, *docendi modus* (= manner of explaining a thing). **methodic, methodical**, adj. by circumloc. with *ratio*, *ratio et via*. Adv. *ratione et viâ*, *viâ et ratione* (= according to a particular method), *artificio et viâ*, *viâ et arte* (= according to the rules of art).

metonymic, metonymical, adj. (*im*)*mutatus*. Adv. *verbis mutatis*, *immutatis* (e.g. to speak); to use an expression —, *verbum mutare*, *immutare*, *verbum pro verbo* (or *verba pro verbis*) *quasi submutare*. **metonymy**, n. *immutatio*, *verba mutata*, *denominatio* or *metonymia* (better written as Greek, μετωνυμία).

metope, n. *metopa*, *intertignium*.

metre, n., as regards poetry, = short and long syllables in verse, *metrum* (Quint.). **metrical**, adj. *metricus*.

metropolis, n. *caput*; see CAPITAL. **metropolitan**, **I.** adj. by circumloc. with *caput*. **II.** n. *episcopus metropolitanus* (Eccl.).

mettle, n. *audacia* (= boldness), *ferocitas* (= high spirit); — of youth, *fervor adolescentiae*, *fervor juvenilis*; man of —, *homo acer*, *homo fervidioris animi*; see COURAGE. **mettlesome**, adj. *audax*, *ferox*; see COURAGEOUS.

mew, **I.** n. = a cage for hawks, *cavea*. **II.** v.tr. to shed (e.g. a hawk); see MOULT. **mews**, pl., see STABLE.

mew, v.intr. (of a cat) perhaps *vagire* (used of young goats or hares).

miasma, n. *noxius terrae halitus*, *-ūs* (Plin.).

mica, n. *phengītes* (*lapis*) (Plin., Suet.).

microcosm, n. **microcosmus* (or in Greek μικρόκοσμος).

microscope, n. **microscopium* (as t.t.). **microscopic**, adj. (i.e. very small), *minimus*, *mirâ quâdam corporis exiguitate*.

midday, n. *meridies*, *tempus meridianum*; about —, *ad meridiem*; at —, *meridie*, *tempore meridiano*, *meridianis temporibus*; before —, forenoon, *dies antemeridianus*, *tempus antemeridianum*, *ante meridiem*, *tempore antemeridiano*; after —, afternoon, *dies postmeridianus* (or *pomeridianus*). **midland**, adj. *mediterraneus*. **midnight**, n. *media nox*; at —, *mediâ nocte*, *concubiâ nocte* (= at the dead of night); shortly after —, *de mediâ nocte*. **midriff**, n. *diaphragma*, *-ătis*, n. (very late), or written as Greek διάφραγμα (Cels.), *praecordia*, *-ium*. **midst**, prep. *in*, *inter*, *medius*, *in medio*; in the — of the preparation for war, *in ipso apparatu belli*; so *in ipso itinere*, in the — of the march; — of dinner, *inter cenandum* (*coen-*); see MIDDLE. **midsummer**, n. *media* or *summa aestas*. **midway**, adv. *medius*; — between, *medius inter*. **midwife**, n. *obstetrix*. **midwinter**, n. *bruma*.

midden, n. *sterquilinium*; see DUNGHILL.

middle, adj. and n. (between two), *medius*. The Latins used *medius* in concord with its nouns, e.g. in the — of the slaughter, *media caedes* (lit. = the — slaughter; so we employ mid, e.g. midnight, *media nox*); so *media acies*, = the — of the army; the king was in the —, *medius omnium rex erat*; to strike in the —, *medium ferire*; to seize by or round the —, *medium alqm* (or *alqd*) *arripĕre*; the — class (or social condition), *ordo plebeius* (opp. to *patres*, *equites*), *plebs*, *plēbis*, f. **middling**, adj. *mediocris*.

mien, n. (*oris*) *habitus*, *-ūs*, *lineamenta*, *-orum* (= features), comb. *habitus oris lineamentaque*, *os* (*oris*, n.) *et vultus*, *-ūs* (= face and looks), *facies* (= countenance).

might, **I.** n. = bodily strength, *vis*, *vis*, f., *ops*, *-is*, f. (sing. only in genit., accus., and ablat., = physical means), *robur*, *-oris*, n., *nervi* (= muscles, as seat of the physical strength); with all one's —, *omni vi*, *summâ vi*, *omni ope*, *omnibus viribus* or *opibus* or *nervis*, *omnibus viribus atque opibus*, *omnibus opibus ac nervis*; — is right, *fortiori cedendum est*. **II.** v.intr. *poteram*, *potuissem*, or by imperf. subj. (e.g. I — go, *irem*, = I was permitted, *licuit mihi* with infin., *ut*, or simple subj.); see MAY. **mighty**, adj. *potens*, *validus*; see POWERFUL, STRONG. Adv. *magnopere*, *valde*, *summâ vi*, *vehementer*.

migrate, v.intr. = to remove from one country to another, *abire*, *discedĕre* (= in gen. to go away from a place), *proficisci* (= to set off; of soldiers, to march), *migrare*, *emigrare* (from a place, *ex*, etc.; to, *in*, etc.), *demigrare* (from, *de* or *ex*, etc.); *e terrâ excedĕre*, *solum mutare* or *vertĕre* (= to leave one's own country, esp. of an exile). **migration**, n. *mutatio loci*. **migratory**, adj. by (*de*)*migrare*, *vagari* (= to rove), *huc illuc migrare* (= to change one's abode very often), by the genit. *nomădum*; — bird, *advena avis* or *volucris*.

milch, adj. *lac habens*; — cow, *vacca* (*quae lac praebet*); see MILK.

mild, adj. **1**, of the taste, *mollis* (= soft for the tongue and the palate, opp. *acer*, = harsh, of food in gen.), *mitis* (= not tart, of fruit that is quite ripe, opp. *acerbus*), *lenis* (= pleasant, opp. *asper* and *acer*, of wine, food), *dulcis* (= sweet); to make —, *mollire*, *mitigare*, *lenire*; to grow — (of fruit, etc.), *mitescĕre*; **2**, = pleasantly affecting the senses, *mollis* (= soft, flexible, e.g. name, speech, opp. *durus*, *acer*); *mitis* (= not hard, harsh, e.g. winter, summer, climate; then speech, words, opp *asper*), *lenis* (= gentle), *temperatus* (= not too warm and not too cold, of the climate, the seasons, opp *frigidus*, = cold, or *calidus*, = warm), *tepidus*, = warm, — winter, *tepida bruma* (Hor), *lĕvis* (= light, e g punishment, opp *gravis*), 3, of men and their dispositions, and of that which shows mildness, *mollis*, *mitis* (= not harsh, of a — disposition, opp *asper*), *clemens* (= gentle), *misericors* (= compassionate, opp *durus*), *facilis* (= easy in granting requests, forgiving), *indulgens* (= indulgent, of persons, towards anyone, *alci*, opp. *acerbus et severus*), *placidus* (= peaceful, opp *fervidus*, *iracundus*), *mansuetus* (= gentle, lit tame), comb *mitis et mansuetus*, *lenis et mansuetus*, *placidus et lenis* Adv *leniter*, *clementer*, *placide*, *mansuete* **mildness,** n 1, — of the climate, etc, *lenitas* (of anything, e g *doloris*, opp *asperitas*), 2, of the character, *lenitas*, *animus lenis* or *mitis*, *ingenium lene* or *mite* (= — of character), *mansuetudo morum* (= — of manners), *clementia* (= — in treating others), *indulgentia* (= indulgence), *modestia* (= moderation), in Tac and Plin of the weather (e g *hiemis*)

mildew, n of vegetables, corn, plants, *robigo* (*rub-*), *mucor* (Plin, = mouldiness, mustiness), *situs*, *ūs* (= filth arising from mouldiness), *uredo* (= blasting of trees, herbs)

mile, n of a Roman —, *mille* (*passuum*) (1,000 paces, in the pl *mil(l)ia* (*passuum*). —-stone, as the point where the — terminates, hence as a measurement of distance, *mil(l)iarium*, or *lapis*, *Idis*, m, he lies interred five —s from the city, *sepultus est ad quintum lapidem*. **mileage,** n *vectigal quod in singula mil(l)ia exigitur* **milestone,** n *mil(l)iarium*, *lapis*

militant, adj by *pugnare*, etc, the church —, *ecclesia militans* (Eccl) **military, I.** adj *militaris* (= belonging to a soldier or to war), *bellicus*, — service, *militia*, — preparations, *apparatus*, *ūs*, *belli*, — skill, *rei militaris peritia*, *usus*, *ūs*, *belli*; — school, *ludus militaris* **II.** n the —, = soldiers, *milites*, or collect *miles*, *copiae* **militate,** v intr, to — against, *alci adversari* **militia,** n. perhaps *cives ad hostem propulsandum armati*

milk, I. n 1, lit *lac*, *-tis*, made of —, looking like —, *lacteus*, goat's —, *lac caprinum*; new —, *lac recens*, curdled —, *lac concretum*, 2, fig — of human kindness, *benignitas*. *comitas*, see KINDNESS **II.** v tr. *mulgēre* **milker,** n. *qui mulget* **milking,** n *mulctus*, *ūs* (Var) **milkmaid, milkman,** n *puella quae vaccas mulget*, (*homo*) *qui lac vendit(at)* **milk-pail,** n *mulctra*, *mulctrum* **milk-sop,** n *homo effeminatus et mollis*, see EFFEMINATE **milk-white,** adj *lacteus* **milky,** adj *lactens* (= full of milk) *lacteus* (= like milk) **milky-way,** n *orbis* or *circulus lacteus*, *via* † *lactea* (Ov)

mill, I. n as a machine, — for grinding, *mola* (= — stone), *pistrinum* (= the place where the mills are, with the ancients = tread —, in which the slaves worked) belonging to the —, *molaris*, *pistrinalis*, hand —, *mola trusatilis*. **II.** v tr see GRIND. **mill-dam,** n (*molae*) *agger* **miller,** n *qui molam habet*, *pistor*. **mill-hopper,** n *infundibulum* **mill-pond,** n *piscina*, as smooth as a —, *tranquillus*, *placidus*, see SMOOTH **mill-stone,** n. *mola* (every mill had two such *mola*, the upper one of which was called *catillus*, the lower *meta*). **mill-stream,** n *rivus qui molam agit*.

millenary, adj. *millenarius* (Eccl.). **millennial,** adj. *mille annorum*. **millennium,** n. *mille annorum spatium*.

millet, n *milium*

milliner, n *quae mundum muliebrem facit* **millinery,** n *mundus* or *vestitus* (*ūs*) *muliebris*

million, n *decies centena mil(l)ia*, two, three millions, *vicies*, *tricies centena mil(l)ia*, a — times, *decies centies millie(n)s* (lit), *sescenties* (= our colloquial phrase, a — times) **millionaire,** n *vir magnis opibus praeditus*, see RICH

milt, n 1, in anatomy, *splen*, *lien*, 2, = roe of fishes, *ova*, *-orum*. **milter,** n *piscis mas*

mimic, I. adj *mimicus* (= belonging to mimes, post class = imitative), *simulatus*, *fictus* (= imitative) **II.** n *artis mimicae peritus*, *mimus* (= player in a mime or farce) **III.** v tr *alqm imitari*, see IMITATE **mimicry,** n *ars mimica*

minaret, n *turricula*

mince, I. v tr 1, lit *concidĕre*, *consecare*, 2, fig *extenuare*, comb *extenuare et diluĕre*, not to — matters, *sine fuco ac fallaciis dicĕre* **II.** v intr *mollius incedĕre* **III.** n *minutal* (Juv) **mincemeat,** n 1, lit *minutal*, 2, fig to make — of, *concidĕre* (= cut up), *trucidare* (= slaughter) **mincing,** adj *putidus* Adv *putide*

mind, I. n 1, *animus* (= the whole of man as an intelligent being, the higher nature in man, opp *corpus*), *mens* (as that which represents the power of thinking, then the faculty of thinking itself), *spiritus*, *-ūs* (almost synonymous with *anima*, = breath of life, life itself, then = qualities of the —, energy, enthusiasm courage pride, etc), *ingenium* (= natural abilities genius, power of invention, production), in one's own —, imagination, *spe et opinione*, or *spe atque animo* the workings of the —, *animi motus*, *-ūs*, a philosophical —, *sapientia*, *sagacitas*, *subtilitas* (*in disputando*), *vir subtilis*, *sagax* (of the person), = an inclination, *studium* (= inclination, zeal), *appetitus*, *-ūs*, *appetitio* (= instinctive longing after anything), *cupiditas*, *cupido*, *desiderium* *aviditas* (= desire) *alacritas* (= the state of feeling inclined), comb *alacritas studiumque*, *alacritas et cupiditas* (after all these words, that which we have a — for in the genit), I have a —, *animus mihi est*, *mihi libet* (lub), I have no —, *nolo*, I have a greater —, *malo*, to have a — to do anything, *alcjs rei studio captum esse*, *teneri*, *alcjs rei studiosum*, *appetentem*, *cupidum esse*, *alqd appetere*, *concupiscĕre*, to have a great — to, *alcjs rei studio* or *cupiditate ardēre*, *flagrare*, *mirā alacritate esse ad alqd faciendum* (= to be very much disposed for, e g for disputing *ad litigandum*), to have no — to, *abhorrēre*, *alienum esse ab alqā re*, 2, *memoria*, see MEMORY, THOUGHT, to keep in — = to think about *cogitare cum* or *in animo*, or simply *cogitare alqd* or *de alqā re*, *considerare in animo* or *cum animo* or *secum*, or simply *considerare alqd* or *de alqā re* (= to consider maturely), *deliberare alqd* and *de alqā re* (= to deliberate with oneself), *alqd agitare mente* or *animo*, or *in mente* or *cum animo* (= to think over), *perpendĕre*, *pensitare* (not in Cic or Caes), *alqd* (= to consider on all sides), *secum meditari de alqā re* or *alqd*, only keep this one thing in —, *hoc unum cogita*, I keep many important things in —, *versantur animo meo multae et graves cogitationes*, to be against one's —, *longe alia mihi mens est*, to be of a —, *opinari*, *opinione duci*, *opinionem habēre*, with one —, *in hoc omnes consentiunt*, see UNANIMOUS; to make up one's —, *certum consilium capĕre*; to put one in — of, = to warn, *(com)monēre*, *admonēre*, *commonefacĕre alqm de alqā re* (or with *ut*, or with *ne* and the subj mood); it comes into my —, *in mentem mihi alqd venit, mihi in opinionem alqd venit, subit animum cogitatio, in mentem* or *in cogitationem mihi incidit alqd* (= a thought comes into my —), *mihi* or *animo*, or *in mentem occurrit alqd, mihi succurrit alqd* (= a sudden thought strikes me), *subit recordatio* or *recordor* or *reminiscor* (= I remember); the thing had come into my —, *tetigerat animum hujus rei memoria*. **II.** v.tr. 1, = to attend to, *animum advertĕre* (*advort-*) or *alqd animadvertĕre, animum attendĕre ad alqd* or *alqd attendĕre, animum intendĕre ad* or *in alqd, alcjs rei rationem habēre* (= to regard); *alqd agĕre*; — your own business, *tuum negotium gere, res tuas cura*; 2, = to obey, *alci oboedire, parēre*; 3, = to object to, *alqd recusare*; I do not —, *non recuso quin* or *quominus*; 4, = to remind, *alci alqd ad animum revocare*; see REMIND. **III.** v.intr. = to remember, *alcjs rei miminisse, alqd recordari*; see REMEMBER. **mindful,** adj. 1, *diligens alcjs rei* and *in alqâ re* (= accurate, punctual, cautious in anything, opp. *neglegens*), *sedulus* (= earnest in anything, very attentive, opp. *piger*, e.g. *spectator*), *alcjs rei studiosus, amans* (e.g. *veritatis*); see ATTENTIVE, CAREFUL; 2, = remembering, *memor, haud immemor* (both *alcjs rei*); to be —, *meminisse* (e.g. *mortis*). **mindless,** adj. *neglegens* (*neglig-*) (= negligent), *socors* (= thoughtless), comb. *socors neglegensque*; see CARELESS, UNMINDFUL; *insanus* (= not in his senses), *excors* (= stupid, a simpleton), *amens, demens*; see IRRATIONAL.

mine, possess. pron. *meus, mea, meum.*

mine, I. n. 1, *metallum*, or pl. *metalla, -orum*; a silver —, *fodina argenti* or *argentifodina*; a gold —, *aurifodina* (Plin.); 2, in fortification, *cuniculus*; to sap, dig a —, *cuniculum agĕre*; 3, fig. *fons uberrimus*, or by *thesaurus* (e.g. *memoria thesaurus omnium rerum*). **II.** v.tr. 1, = to dig a —; see above; 2, fig. = to practise secret means of injury, *insidias alci parare* or *instruĕre* or *ponĕre, perniciem alci moliri*; 3, milit. term, by *cuniculos agĕre*. **miner,** n. 1, *metallicus* (Plin.); 2, in fortification, *qui cuniculum agit*. **mineral, I.** n. *metallum*. **II.** adj. *fossilis, metallicus*; — kingdom, *fossilia, -ium*, n.; — spring, — waters (as the place), *fons medicae salubritatis, aquae medicatae* (Sen.), *aquae salubres*, in the context also simply *aquae*. **mining,** n. use *metallum* (e.g. useful for —, *ad metalla exercenda utilis*).

mingle, v.tr. and intr., see MIX.

miniature, n. *tabella* or *pictura*, fixing the sense by the context (e.g. *tabellas pinxit parvas*); in — (e.g. Rome in —, *quasi* or *tanquam* (*tamq-*) *Roma minor*).

minimum, n. *minimum, pars minima.*

minion, n. 1, = favourite, *deliciae*; 2, = minister, *minister, servus.*

minister, I. n. 1, = servant in a higher sense, *minister*, or by circumloc.; see INSTRUMENT; 2, of a state, *principis socius et administer omnium consiliorum, socius consiliorum principis et particeps, consiliarius* (as his adviser); state —, *ille penes quem est cura administrandae reipublicae*; — of foreign affairs (= foreign secretary), *rerum externarum administer*; — of war, *qui res bellicas administrat*; 3, — of the Gospel; see CLERGYMAN, PRIEST. **II.** v.tr. to — an occasion, *alci occasionem dare, praebēre*; see GIVE, AFFORD, SUPPLY. **III.** v.intr. 1, see ATTEND, SERVE; 2, to — to, *facultates* or *opes praebēre*; see SERVE, SUPPORT, ASSIST. **ministerial,** adj. 1, *ad servum* or *ministrum pertinens*; see ATTEND, SERVE; 2, in a political sense by circumloc. (e.g. his — duties, *rerum publicarum administratio*); see OFFICIAL, EXECUTIVE; 3, see CLERICAL, PRIESTLY. **ministration,** n. 1, see SERVICE, OFFICE; 2, see CO-OPERATION, INTERCESSION. **ministry,** n. 1, = means, *interventio*, etc., *administratio, ministerium*, (*pro*-)*curatio*; 2, political, *qui rempublicam administrant*; see MINISTER; 3, clerical, **ministerium*.

minium, n. *minium.*

minor, I. adj. see LITTLE, SMALL; the — premiss, *assumptio* (opp. *propositio* = the major). **II.** n. gen. *infans* (if a little child), or by *nondum adultâ aetate* (= not yet of age); sons that are —s, *filii familiarum*; with regard to the guardian, a ward, *pupillus*; = not able to reign, *nondum maturus imperio*. **minority,** n. 1, *aetas nondum adulta* (in gen.), *aetas pupillaris* (= age of the ward); 2, = the smaller number, *pars* or *numerus minor*.

minotaur, n. *minotaurus.*

minstrel, n. see SINGER, perhaps *poëta amatorius* (as a poet), *citharaedus* (κιθαρῳδός, = singer to the lyre); see MUSICIAN, PLAYER. **minstrelsy,** n. *chorus canentium* (= chorus of singers); *concentus, -ūs.*

mint, n. in botany, *ment(h)a.*

mint, I. n. = place where money is coined by public authority, *monēta* (a surname of Juno, in whose temple money was coined); everything relating to the —, *res nummaria*. **II.** v.tr. see COIN.

minuet, n. *saltatio*; see DANCE.

minus, prep. *sine* with abl.

minute, I. adj. 1, see LITTLE, SMALL; 2, fig. *minutus* (= trifling and contemptible), *subtilis, diligens, accuratus* (= exact). Adv. *subtiliter, minute, accurate, diligenter*. **II.** n. 1, of time, *horae sexagesima pars* (= 60th part of an hour); 2, fig. see MOMENT. **minutes,** n. pl. = short sketch of an agreement, etc., *breviarium* (= a summary, Suet.), *exemplum* (= draught of a theme), *scriptum, libellus, commentarii, acta, -orum* (of the Senate); — of a speech, *oratio scripta, sermo scriptus* (Suet.); to make — of anything, *alqd lit(t)eris consignare* (in gen. = to write down); see NOTE; —-book, see MEMORANDUM. **III.** v.tr. *notare, annotare, in tabulas referre, lit(t)eris consignare*; see DRAW UP, NOTE, WRITE. **minuteness,** n. 1, = smallness, *exiguitas, brevitas* (of stature); 2, = carefulness, *subtilitas, accuratio* (rare), *diligentia*. **minutiae,** n. by *omnia, -ium*, or *singula, -orum*; see DETAIL, TRIFLE, PARTICULAR.

minx, n. *puella putida* (= an affected girl), *filiola* (= little daughter, expressing affection).

miracle, n. 1, = a wonderful thing, *res mira, miraculum* (= thing exciting astonishment); see WONDER; 2, in theology, **miraculum*. **miraculous,** adj. *mirus, mirificus, mirandus, mirabilis*; in a — manner, *mirum in modum, mirandum in modum, mirabiliter*. Adv. see above, in a — manner.

mirage, n. (*vana*) *species* (*urbis*, etc.) *oculis oblata.*

mire, miriness, n. *lutum*; see MUD. **miry,** adj. *lutosus, lutulentus*; see MUDDY.

mirror, n. *speculum.*

mirth, n. *hilaritas, laetitia* (= gladness), *gaudium* (= joy), *lascivia* (= sportiveness), *risus, -ūs* (= laughter), *jocus* (= jest), *lusus, -ūs* (= sport); see GAIETY, JOY. **mirthful,** adj. *hilaris* (*hilarus*), *laetus, lascivus, jocosus*. Adv. *hilare, hilariter, laete, lascive, jocose.*

misacceptation, n. *interpretatio perversa* or *perperam facta*; see MISUNDERSTANDING.

misadventure, n. *casus*, *ūs* (*adversus*), *incommodum* (= something unpleasant, adversity, especially misfortune in war); see MISFORTUNE

misadvised, adj *imprudens* (= without foresight), *inconsideratus*, *inconsultus* (= thoughtless)

misanthrope, n *qui genus humanum* or *hominum universum genus odit* **misanthropic, misanthropical**, adj *hominibus inimicus* **misanthropy**, n *animus hominibus inimicus*

misapplication, n *usus* (*ūs*) *perversus* **misapply**, v tr. *alqā re abuti* (= to make a bad use of), *male interpretari* or *accipĕre* (= to misinterpret)

misapprehend, v tr see MISUNDERSTAND **misapprehension**, n see MISUNDERSTANDING

misbecome, v tr *alqm alqd dedecet*, or *alqd facĕre dedecet*

misbehave, v intr *indecōre*, *indigne se gerĕre* **misbehaviour**, n *rusticitas*, *mores rustici*, see RUDENESS, FAULT

misbelief, n see UNBELIEF **misbelieve**, v tr *perperam judicare*, *falso sibi persuasum habēre*.

miscalculate, v tr **1**, *male computare alqd* or *rationem alcjs rei*, or by *ratio me fefellit*, **2**, fig *errare*, *decipi* **miscalculation**, n **1**, *mendum*, *rationes falsae*, **2**, *error*

miscarriage, n **1**, = ill conduct, *delictum* (= act of misbehaviour); **2**, = failure, by *res ad* (or *in*) *irritum cadit*, *ad irritum redigitur*, **3**, of an untimely birth, *abortus*, *-ūs*, *abortio* **miscarry**, v intr. **1**, = not to succeed, *non* or *parum* or *secus procedĕre* (= not to lead to the desired result), *praeter spem evenire*, *secus cadĕre*, *praeter opinionem cadĕre* (= to end worse than one expected), *ad irritum cadĕre*, *redigi* (= to be frustrated), **2**, by *abortum facĕre* (of an untimely birth)

miscellaneous, adj by *varius et diversus*, — kinds, *varia et diversa genera* (*sc operum*) **miscellany**, n *liber de diversis rebus scriptus*

mischance, n see MISFORTUNE

mischief, n *malum*, *incommodum*, *damnum*, *maleficium* (= intentional —), *calamitas*, *turbae* (= noise and confusion) **mischief-maker**, n *mali auctor* **mischievous**, adj **1**, = harmful, *noxius*, *calamitosus*, *perniciosus*, see HURTFUL, **2**, = full of tricks, *lascivus* Adv *calamitose*, *perniciose*, *lascive* **mischievousness**, n **1**, = injuriousness, by circuml (e g who does not see the — of the thing? *quis non intelligit rem nocēre* or *rem esse noxiam?*), **2**, *lascivia*

misconceive, v tr. and intr *perperam accipĕre* **misconception**, n *opinionis error*, *opinio falsa*

misconduct, n **1**, see MISBEHAVIOUR, **2**, see FAULT.

misconjecture, **I.** n *falsa suspicio* **II.** v tr and intr *falso suspicari*

misconstruction, n see MISINTERPRETATION, **misconstrue**, v tr see MISINTERPRET.

miscreant, n **1**, = unbeliever, *doctrinae falsae studiosus*, *apostăta* (Eccl), **2**, = a vile wretch, *homo illiberalis*, *sordidus* (= unworthy of a free born man), *abjectus* (= contemptible), *turpis* (= disreputable)

misdeal, v intr perhaps *paginas male distribuĕre*.

misdeed, n *facinus*, *ŏris*, n *scelus*, *ĕris*, n, *maleficium*, *malefactum*, *delictum*, *peccatum*

misdemeanour, n **1**, = ill behaviour, *mores pravi*, see MISCONDUCT, **2**, in law, an offence of a less atrocious character than a crime, *peculatus*, *-ūs*, *publicus* (= defalcation), *scelus*, *ĕris*, n (= crime), to be guilty of —, *scelus suscipĕre*, *admittere*, *facĕre*

misdirect, v tr **1**, a letter *epistulam perperam inscribĕre*, **2**, a passenger, *a recta viā abducĕre* (lit), **3**, fig *inducĕre alqm in errorem* (= to lead anyone into an error)

misemploy, v tr *abuti alqā re* (= to misuse) **misemployment**, n *usus*, *-ūs*, *perversus*

miser, n *homo tenax*, *homo avarus* **miserable**, adj *miser*, *misellus*, *miserabilis miserandus* (= to be pitied, in poor circumstances), *infelix* (= unhappy), *afflictus*, *aerumnosus*, *calamitosus*, see UNHAPPY, = worthless, *nequam*, *nihili*, *improbus*, *turpis* (= wicked, of persons and things), *vilis* (= vile), to lead a — life, *in miseriā esse* or *versari*, — food, *tenuis victus*, *-ūs*, to live in — circumstances, *parce ac duriter vitam agĕre*, *tenuiter vivĕre*, *vitam in egestate degĕre* Adv *misere*, *miserabiliter*, *infeliciter*, *calamitose*, *improbe*, *nequiter*, *turpiter*, see MISER **miserliness**, n *avaritia*, *sordes*, *is*, f (or in pl) **miserly**, adj *avarus*, *tenax*, *sordidus*, *parcus*, *malignus* **misery**, n = great unhappiness of mind and body, *miseria*, *res miserae* or *afflictae* (= depressed circumstances), *calamitas* (= caused through losses), *aerumna*, *vexatio* (= trouble), *angor*, *maeror*, *tristitia* (= sorrow), *egestas* (= great poverty), *angustiae* (= bad times), *tempora luctuosa* (= distressing, gloomy times)

misformed, adj *deformis*, *deformatus*, *distortus*

misfortune, n *malum*, and pl *mala*, *calamitas* (= attended with loss and injury, also in war), *casus*, *-ūs* (*adversus* or *tristis* = unfortunate accident), *incommodum*, *res adversae*, *fortuna* (*adversa*), = casualties caused by bad luck), *acerbitates*, *-um* (= great hardships), he had the — to, etc, *cecidit ut*, etc, one — after another, *aliud ex alio malo*

misgive, v intr perhaps *malum praesagire*, *praesentire* or *diffidĕre* (= to distrust), see DOUBT **misgiving**, n *metus*, *ūs*, *timor* (= fear), *sollicitudo* (= anxiety), *praesensio* (= foreboding)

misgovern, v tr *male regnare*, *male rem gerĕre* **misgovernment**, n *mala reipublicae gubernatio* or *moderatio*, *mala alcjs rei administratio*

misguidance, n *error*, or by *falso alcjs consilio regi* **misguide**, v tr *in errorem inducĕre*, see MISLEAD

mishap, n see ACCIDENT, MISFORTUNE

misinform, v tr by *alqm falsa docēre*

misinterpret, v tr *falso explicare*, *in malam partem accipĕre* or *male interpretari alqd*, *pervertĕre*, *perperam interpretari* **misinterpretation**, n *interpretatio perversa* or *perperam facta*

misjudge, v tr *male judicare*

mislay, v tr see LOSE

mislead, v tr *corrumpĕre alcjs animum et mores*, *alqm ad nequitiam adducĕre*, *alqm in errorem inducĕre*, to be misled, *labi*, *errare*, *in errorem induci*. **misleading**, adj *falsus*

mismanage, v tr see MISGOVERN

misnomer, n *falsum nomen*

misogamist, misogynist, n. *qui mulieres odit*

misplace, v.tr. (*in*) *alieno loco collocare*; to — confidence, etc., *alqâ re falli*.

misprint, **I.** v.tr. *typis mendose exscribĕre*. **II.** n. *mendum typographicum*.

mispronounce, n. *male pronuntiare*.

misproportion, n. *ratio impar*.

misquotation, n. *verba falso allata*, *falsa commemoratio* (= mention), *verba haud accurate prolata*. **misquote**, v.tr. *verba alcjs haud accurate proferre*.

misreckoning, n. *falsae rationes*.

misrepresent, v.tr. fig. *alqd narrando depravare* (= to represent any fact in a wrong light), *perversa interpretari* (= to interpret wrongly, fig.), *verbum in pejus detorquēre* (= to dissemble the true meaning of an expression so as to cause it to be taken in a bad sense). **misrepresentation**, n. use verb.

misrule, n. see MISGOVERN.

miss, n. as title, *domina*.

miss, **I.** n. 1, see LOSS, WANT; 2, *error*; see FAULT, MISTAKE. **II.** v.tr. 1, *carēre alqâ re* (= not to have got a thing), *alqd desiderare* (= to feel the want of it); 2, = to discover that something is wanting, *desiderare*, *quaerĕre*, *requirĕre* (= to look for anything that we have had, although in vain); to — with regret, *desiderio alcjs rei angi*, *magnâ molestiâ desiderare alqd*; see LOSE; 3, = to fail of finding the right way, *deerrare*; to — anyone on the road, *ab alqo deerrare* or *aberrare*; 4, = to fail in aim, *destinatum non ferire* (in shooting, etc.); 5, = to omit, *transire*, *omittĕre*, *praetermittĕre*; see OMIT. **III.** v.intr. 1, = to fail to hit, see II. 4; 2, = not to succeed; see FAIL. **missing**, adj. to be —, *deesse*, *desiderari*. **missile**, **I.** n. (*telum*) *missile*, *jaculum*; *hasta* (longer or shorter for throwing), *pilum* (short, used by the Roman infantry); to cast a —, *missile* or *jaculum mittĕre*. **II.** adj. *missilis*.

misshapen, adj. *deformis*; see MISFORMED.

mission, n. 1, = sending out, *missio*; 2, *legatio* (= deputation, ambassadors); 3, see DESTINY. **missionary**, n. *missus qui gentes barbaras alqd doceat*.

misspell, v.tr. *non recte scribĕre*, *prave scribĕre*.

misspend, v.tr. 1, money, *perdĕre*; see SQUANDER; 2, time, *perdĕre*; see WASTE.

misstate, v.tr. see MISREPRESENT. **misstatement**, n. *quod falsum est*; deliberate —, *mendacium*.

mist, n. 1, *nebula* (*subtilis*, in opp. to fog = *caligo*, *nebula densa*, when the — is very thick); 2, fig. *caligo* (e.g. the — of those calamitous days, *caligo illorum temporum*); to be in a —, *attonitum*, *perculsum esse*. **misty**, adj. 1, *nebulosus*, *caliginosus*; 2, fig. *obscurus*.

mistake, **I.** v.tr. 1, = to take one thing or person for another, e.g. you — me for another, *me alium esse putas*; *ignorare alqm* (= not to know a person, lit. and fig.), *parum intellegĕre* (*intellig-*) *alqd* or *alqm* (= to know too little of anything, not to know sufficient of a person's character); 2, see MISUNDERSTAND. **II.** v.intr. = to be —n, *errare*, *per errorem labi* (= to commit a slight error), *in errore versari* (= to be in error), *falli* (= to deceive oneself), *peccare* (= to fall into an error, commit a sin owing to a —), *dubium* or *incertum esse* (= to be uncertain); if I am not —n, *nisi fallor*, *nisi animus* (*me*) *fallit*, *nisi quid me fallit* or *fefellerit*; I may be —n, *potest fieri ut fallar*. **III.** n. 1, in gen. *error*, *erratum* (from want of thought, by being misled; *error*, = the condition one is in after having committed a —; *erratum*, = the — itself; both also representing any literary work), *lapsus*, *-ūs* (= a single —), *peccatum* (= anything done wrong); in — for, *pro* (e.g. *pro illo culpavit*, = he blamed the one in — for the other); to make a —, *errare*, *peccare* (in a thing, *alqd in alqâ re*), *labi in alqâ re*; to be under a —, *in errore esse* or *versari*, *errore captum esse*, *errore vagari*; to see one's —, *errorem suum agnoscĕre*; 2, a — in writing, *mendum*; to correct a — in writing, *mendum tollĕre*; full of written —s, *mendosus*. **mistaken**, adj. see WRONG. Adv. *per errorem*, *perperam*.

mistress, n. 1, = a woman who governs, *domina* (also as title), *hera* (as regards the servants), *quae imperio regit* (= one who rules, e.g. a town, *urbem*), *dominatrix*, *moderatrix*, *gubernatrix* (in a fig. sense, of desires and passions; *dominatrix*, in an absolute sense; the two latter = guide); 2, = head of a family, *materfamilias* (*materfamiliae*, or as two words), *hera* (with reference to the servants), *matrona* (on account of the high veneration in which she was held as head of the family, therefore chiefly of women of higher rank), *domina*; 3, = governess, *praeceptrix*, *magistra* (also fig., e.g. practice is the best — to teach us to speak a language, *certissima loquendi magistra consuetudo*; or *magister* if the Latin noun is masculine, e.g. experience, an excellent —, *usus*, *egregius magister*); 4, = a woman beloved and courted, *amata*, *dilecta*, *amica* (in a bad sense), *amor noster*, *deliciae meae*; 5, = a woman in keeping (i.e. a kept —), *amica*, *concubina*, *pellex*.

misunderstand, v.tr. *non recte intellegĕre* (*intellig-*); see MISINTERPRET. **misunderstanding**, n. *error* (= mistake); = difference of opinion, *dissensio*; *dissidium*.

misuse, **I.** n. *usus*, *-ūs*, *perversus*, *abusus*, *-ūs* (rare). **II.** v.tr. *alqâ re perverse* (*ab*)*uti*, *immodice* or *immoderate* or *intemperanter* or *insolenter et immodice abuti re* (e.g. *alcjs indulgentiâ*, *alcjs patientiâ*), *male uti re*; see ABUSE, USE.

mite, n. *minimus* in agreement with noun (e.g. a — of a thing, *res minima*).

mitigable, adj. *quod mitigari potest*. **mitigate**, v.tr. *lenire* (e.g. illness, pain, hatred, anger, grief, taste, etc.), *mitigare*, *mitiorem facĕre* (e.g. pain, fevers, sorrows, taste, etc.), *mollire* (= to cause anything, e.g. anger, violence, *iram*, *impetum*, to abate, also to make milder in taste), *levare* (= to afford relief, alleviate, e.g. care, *alqm curâ levare*; — cares with wine, *curas levare vino*), *alqd remittĕre ex alqâ re* (= to diminish). **mitigation**, n. *mitigatio*, *levatio* (*al*)*levamentum*; to afford anyone a — of anything, *lenire alci alqd*, *levare alqm alqâ re*; — of anger, *placatio* (e.g. *deorum immortalium*), *mitigatio*; or by verbs, see above.

mitre, n. = a sacerdotal ornament, *mitra* (Eccl.).

mitten, n. see GLOVE.

mix, **I.** v.tr. 1, *temperare*; to — one thing with, among another, (*per*)*miscēre alqd cum alqâ re*, *alqd alqâ re* or *alqd alci rei*, *temperare alqd alqâ re*; to — a thing, *admiscēre alqd alci rei* or *in alqd* (gen. in the passive, *admisceri alqâ re*, to be —ed with); to — poison, etc., *venenum*, etc., *parare*, *coquĕre* (= to prepare, to boil in gen.); 2, see CONFUSE; 3, = to associate oneself with in company, *se* (*con*)*jungĕre cum alqo*, (*com*)*misceri*, *permisceri*. **II.** v.intr. 1, = to become blended promiscuously in a mass or compound (e.g. oil and water will not —), by the passive of the verbs above; 2, to — in society, *hominum coetus et celebrationes obire*; see SOCIETY. **mix up**, v.tr. 1, see MIX; 2, see IMPLICATE **mixed**, adj (*per*)*mixtus*, *promiscuus* **mixture**, n 1, (*per*)*mistio* (*mixt*-, = the act and the thing itself), *mistura* (*mixt*-, = modes of mixing and the thing itself, mostly post class), *temperatio* (as act and as the quality of —), the — of the metal, *temperatio aeris*, 2, in pharmacy, see MEDICINE, 3, 3, lit. and fig = a mass of things without order, *farrago* (= a — of different kinds of corn, fig. a book containing a — of things, *farrago libelli*, Juv), *colluvio*, *colluvies* (fig , when different things flow together, e g the army, a — of all kinds of nations, *exercitus mixtus ex colluvione omnium gentium*), *varietas* (= a mixed variety, e g of words and opinions, *sermonum opinionumque*), but more frequently it is expressed by *miscēre*, e g a — of good and evil, *bona mixta malis*

mnemonic, mnemonical, adj *ad memoriae artem pertinens* **mnemonics**, n *ars* or *artificium* or *disciplina memoriae*

moan, I. v intr *gemĕre* **II.** n *gemitus*, *ūs*, see GROAN, LAMENT

moat, n *fossa*, to surround with a — for defence, *fossam castris circumdare*, *castra fossa cingĕre*

mob, I. n *vulgus*, *i*, n (= the mass of the people, see PEOPLE), *turba* (= crowd), *multitudo de plebe*, *multitudo obscura et humilis* (as regards the origin), *sentina reipublicae* or *urbis* (= the lowest of the low, rabble), *faex populi* (= the dregs of the people) **II.** v tr. see SURROUND **III.** v intr *concurrere*, *concursare*

mobile, adj *mobilis*, see also FICKLE **mobility**, n 1, *mobilitas* (e g of the tongue *linguae*, also fig of the mind, *animi*, — of character, *mobilitas hominis* or *ingenii*), *agilitas* (= nimbleness, swiftness), 2, = fickleness, *levitas*, *ingenium mobile*, see FICKLENESS

mock, I. v tr 1, see IMITATE, MIMIC, 2, = to deride, *algm*, *algd deridēre*, *irridēre*, 3, in a less evil sense = to ridicule, *algm ludĕre* (= to banter), *algm ludibrio habēre*, *ludificari* (= to make a fool of), *cavillari* (= to censure in a sarcastic manner, one who does this, *cavillator*), 4, = to disappoint, *ludĕre*, *ludificari*, *ad irritum redigĕre*; see FRUSTRATE **II.** v intr to — at, *in ludibrium vertĕre*, or by *cavillari*, at anybody, *algm*, see above **III.** n see MOCKERY, to make a — of, see MOCK, I 3 **IV.** adj *simulatus*, *fictus*, *falsus*, see FALSE **mocker**, n = one who scorns, *derisor*, *irrisor*, *cavillator* (= who cavils) **mockery**, n 1, *irrisio*, *irrisus*, *ūs*, *cavillatio* (= scoff), *ludibrium*, *ludus*, *jocus*, *ludificatio* (= the act of mocking), *petulantia*, *lascivia*, 2, = that which disappoints, *inceptum irritum*, 3, = counterfeit appearance, *species*, *simulacrum*, *fallacia* (= deceit), *oculorum ludibrium* (= mere outward show), *falsa imago* (= a false image), *fabula* (= a fable), to make a — of ..., to turn into —, *deridēre algd* (also *algm*), *in risum vertĕre algd*

mode, n 1, *natura* (= nature of a thing), *ratio* (= systematic — of proceeding, relation between two things), *modus* (= rule to go by, — of doing anything), *via* (= manner in which one thing is derived from another), comb *ratio et via*, *ratio et modus*, (— of proceeding, e g of arguing, *argumentandi genus*), *mos*, *consuetudo* (= custom), see MANNER, 2, in music, *modi*, *moduli* (= musical —), 3, — of dress, *habitus*, -*ūs*, see DRESS, —s of speaking, see EXPRESSION

model, I. n *proplasma*, *ătis*, n (Plin , or as Greek προπλασμα, = an artist's —), *exemplar*, *aris*, *exemplum* (= a pattern in gen), to give a — of anything *alcjs rei modum formamque demonstrare*; to take the — from anything, to take anything as a —, *exemplum sumĕre ab alqā re*, to work by a — or pattern, *alqd ad imitandum proponere*, *alqd in exemplum assumĕre*. **II.** v tr 1, = to shape out of a raw material, *fingĕre*, = to bring into a proper shape, *formare*, comb *fingĕre et formare*, = to copy, *exprimĕre imaginem alcjs* (in gen = to represent, express anyone's features), 2, fig = to arrange according to a certain rule, *ex lege* or *ratione quadam instituĕre alqd* (e g *rempublicam*) **III.** adj *optimus*

moderate, I. adj = keeping the middle path, avoiding extremes, *moderatus*, *modicus* (opp to *effrenatus*), *modestus* (in moral feeling, opp to *cupidus*, *petulans*) *temperans*, *temperatus*, *mediocris* (= mediocre), *sobrius* Adv *moderate*, *modeste*, *modice*, *temperate*, *mediocriter*, to live —, *continentem esse in omni victu cultuque* **II.** v tr = *moderari* (= to impose a limit to, with dat), = to direct (with accus), *modum* (or *moderationem*) *adhibēre alci rei*, *alqd continēre*, *coercēre* (= to restrain) **moderation**, **moderateness**, n *modus* (= due measure), *continentia* (= self-restraint), *temperantia* (= self government, both opp to *libido* (*lub*)), *moderatio* (= the middle course, in conduct), *modestia* (= the moral feeling to avoid excess), *sedatio alcjs rei* (e g of the passions), *abstinentia* (= keeping from what belongs to others) **moderator**, n see PRESIDENT

modern, adj *recens*, *novus*, *ad novă exempla* (= in the new style, according to the new fashion, opp *vetus*), *qui nunc est*, *ut nunc fit*, *hujus aetatis*, *elegans* (= elegant), *hic*, *haec*, *hoc*, = the present, e g *haec* or *nostra aetas*, *homines nostrae aetatis*, *homines qui nunc sunt* or *vivunt* (all = our — days), *praesens* (= at the present moment, opp that which takes place at any other time, if we say our —, etc , *praesens* is seldom used, but generally *hic*, *haec*, *hoc*), — Capua, *Capua quae nunc est*, the —, our age, *haec aetas*, our — times, *haec tempora*

modest, adj *modicus* (= slight, middling), *modestus* (= moderate, under control, opp *immodestus*), *pudens* (opp *impudens*), *verecundus* (= full of respect), *demissus* (= lowly, opp *acerbus*) Adv *modice*, *modeste*, *pudenter*, *verecunde* **modesty**, n *modestia* (opp *superbia*), *pudor* (= a feeling of shame or respect), *verecundia* (bashfulness)

modicum, n *pau(l)lulum*

modifiable, adj *res de quā alqd immutari potest* **modification**, n , with this —, that, etc , *cum eo ut*, etc , or by *ita definire*, *ut*, etc **modify**, v tr = to change the form or external qualities, *immutare alqd de alqā re* (= to make a change in anything), *temperare alqd* (= to moderate).

modulate, v tr *vocem per vices tollĕre atque remittĕre* (= to raise and to lower the voice, in speaking) *vocem* or *cantum modulari* **modulation**, n *flexio* (*vocis*), *numerus* (or in pl)

moiety, n see HALF

moist, adj *humidus* (= moderately wet) **moisten**, v tr *conspergĕre* (= to sprinkle) (*ir*)*rigare* (= to water), † *humectare* **moisture**, n *humor*

molar, adj (e g tooth) *dens genuinus*

mole, n = mound, *moles*, *is* f , *agger*, *ĕris*, m **molecule**, n see PARTICLE

mole, n = mark on the body, *naevus*

mole, n = animal, *talpa* **mole-hill**, n 1, lit perhaps (*talpae*) *grumus*, 2, fig to make mountains out of —s, *difficilia ex facillimis redigĕre*,

molest, v.tr. *alqm sol(l)icitare, vexare, molestiam alci afferre* or *exhibēre, molestum esse alci, alci incommodum afferre, conciliare* (= to give trouble), *alci negotium exhibēre, facessĕre* (= to cause unpleasantness to anyone). **molestation,** n. 1, *molestia, onus, -ĕris,* n. (= a burthen); 2, = trouble, *molestia, onus, -ĕris,* n., *cura* (= anxiety), *incommodum* (= adversity), *vexatio.*

mollifiable, adj. *quod molliri potest.* **mollification,** n., **mollify,** v.tr. *(e)mollire* (= to make soft, lit. and fig.), *mitigare* (in a lit. sense, e.g. food by boiling it; then fig.), *lenire* (= to appease), *frangĕre* (= to subdue anyone's hard-heartedness), *movēre alqm* or *alcjs animum* (= to make an impression upon anyone, by exhortations, entreaties, etc.).

molten, adj. *liquefactus;* see MELT.

moment, n. 1, *punctum* or *vestigium* or *momentum temporis;* in a —, *statim, e vestigio, confestim;* for the —, *in praesens;* 2, = impulsive power; see MOMENTUM; 3, = importance; of great —, *magni momenti;* see IMPORTANCE. **momentary,** adj. *brevissimus* (= of a short duration); see INSTANTANEOUS. **momentous,** adj. *magni momenti;* see IMPORTANT. **momentousness,** n. see IMPORTANCE. **momentum,** n. (in mechanics) *vis quâ alqd movetur.*

monarch, n. *rex, regis* (= king), *princeps, -ipis,* m. (= prince, sovereign, post Aug.), *imperator, Caesar, Augustus* (= emperor, Imperial Rome), *dominus* (= an absolute —), *tyrannus* (τύραννος, = one who has usurped the highest power in a state, which was free before) or by circumloc., to express an absolute —, a despot, the only ruler, *qui solus regnat, qui unus consilio et curâ gubernat civitatem, penes quem est summa rerum omnium* (all = *rex*), *qui solus imperio potitus est* (= *tyrannus*); to be the —, *regnare;* to proclaim oneself as the —, = to usurp the throne, *dominatum* or *tyrannidem occupare, dominatum invadĕre.* **monarchical,** adj. *regius;* a — government, use *rex* (e.g. *regi parent,* they have a —). **monarchist,** n. *defensor imperii regii.* **monarchy,** n. 1, as the kind of government, *imperium quod ab uno sustinetur* or *sub uno stat, principatus, -ūs* (= the government of him who is the head of the state), *imperium regum* or *regium, imperium quod penes regem* or *reges est, potestas regia, tyrannis, -idis* (τυραννίς, of one who has usurped the government of a free state); 2, = the state itself that is under a monarchical government, *civitas quae ab uno regitur, respublica, civitas in quâ penes unum est summa omnium rerum* (in gen.); *regnum, civitas regia.*

monastery, n. *monasterium, coenobium* (Eccl.).

Monday, n. *dies lunae* (not class.).

monetary, adj. *quod ad pecuniam pertinet, pecuniarius, nummarius, argentarius.* **money,** n. *pecunia* (= sum of —), *argentum, aes* (= coined from silver or copper, silver coin, copper coin); good —, *nummi probi;* bad —, *nummi adulterini;* for very little —, for a deal of —, *parvo, magno* (*pretio*); prov., — makes —, *dat census honores* (Ov.); to pay — down, out of hand, by *praesentem pecuniam solvĕre, repraesentare; praesenti pecuniâ solvĕre;* ready —, *pecunia praesens* or *nummi praesentes* or *numeratum* or *pecunia;* — transactions, *negotium,* more distinctly *negotium nummarium, negotiatio* (on a large scale), *argentaria* (= banking business, — exchanging); to carry on — transactions, *argentariam facĕre.* **money-bag,** n. see PURSE. **money-broker,** n. *argentarius.* **money-making,** n. *quaestus, -ūs.* **money-market,** n. *res nummaria.* **moneyed,** adj. *dives, pecuniosus;* see RICH. **moneyless,** adj. *inops;* see POOR.

25 *

mongrel, I. adj. *nothus.* **II.** n. *(h)ybrida (hyb-),* m. and f.

monition, n. *monitio* (= the act), *monitum* (= the warning given). **monitor,** n. *monitor.*

monk, n. *monăchus* (Eccl.).

monkey, n. *simia.*

monody, n. use Greek μονῳδία.

monograph, n. *liber* (= book); see BOOK.

monologue, n. *sermo;* to hold a —, *solum loqui.*

monomaniac, n. *de unâ modo re insanire.*

monopolize, v.tr. perhaps *solum habēre* or *exercēre alqd.*

monosyllable, n. only in pl. *monosyllaba, -orum* (Quint.).

monotheism, n. *credĕre unum modo Deum esse.* **monotheist,** n. *qui unum modo Deum esse credit.*

monotone, n. use Greek μονοτονία.

monotony, n., **monotonous,** adj. by *oratio omni varietate carens.* Adv., use adj.

monsoon, n. *ventus qui* (*certo tempore*) *flare consuevit.*

monster, n. *monstrum, portentum, belua* (lit. = beast). **monstrosity,** n. 1, *deformitas* (= deformity); 2, see MONSTER. **monstrous,** adj. *deformis* (opp. *formosus*), *immanis* (e.g. *belua, praeda, facinus,* etc.), *portentosus, monstr(u)osus, naturae repugnans.* Adv. *praeter naturam, monstr(u)ose.*

month, n. *mensis, -is,* m. **monthly,** adj. *singulis mensibus, in singulos menses, menstruus.*

monument, n. *monumentum* (*moni-*); see MEMORIAL. **monumental,** adj. 1, *ad monumentum pertinens;* 2, fig. *gravis, magni momenti;* see IMPORTANT.

mood, n. 1, of mind, *animus;* 2, *modus* (Gram.). **moodiness,** n., **moody,** adj. see PEEVISH.

moon, n. *luna;* eclipse of the —, *lunae defectus, -ūs.* **moonlight, I.** n. *lunae lumen.* **II.** adj. *lunâ illustris.*

moor, n., **moorland,** n. *loca* (*-orum*) *palustria.* **moor-hen,** n. *fulica* (*fulex*).

moor, v.tr. *navem ad terram* (*ripam,* etc.) *religare,* or *deligare.* **moorings,** n. use verb (e.g. he found convenient —, *loco opportuno navem relegavit*).

moot, v.tr. see SUGGEST, ARGUE. **moot-point,** n. it is a —, *incertum* or *dubium est an.*

mop, I. n. *pēniculus.* **II.** v.tr. *alqd peniculo detergĕre.*

mope, v.intr. *tristem* or *maestum esse.* **moping,** adj. *tristis, maestus;* see SAD.

moral, I. adj. 1, = relating to morals, *moralis;* — philosophy, *de moribus,* or *philosophia;* 2, = upright, *honestus, probus, bene moratus,* or perhaps *gravis;* see UPRIGHT; 3, it is a — certainty, *verisimillimum est* with acc. and infin. Adv. *honeste, probe* = uprightly, *verisimiliter;* see PROBABLY. **II.** n. = teaching of a story, etc., *res ad quam fabula spectat.* **morals,** n. = moral conduct, *mores, -um;* = ethics, *de moribus* or *de officiis* or *philosophia.* **moralist,** n. *qui de moribus praecipit.* **morality,** n. *mores, -um;* see MORALS. **moralize,** v.intr. *de moribus praecipĕre.*

morass, n. *palus, -udis,* f.

morbid, adj. 1, *aeger;* a — condition of body, *aegrotatio;* 2, fig. *aeger, aegrotus;* a — condition of mind, *aegritudo.* Adv. *maeste*

(= sadly), see SADLY **morbidness,** n 1, physical, *aegrotatio*, 2, fig *aegritudo*, see SADNESS

more, I. adj *plures* (neut *plura*), *plus* (either as n n, alone or with genit, e g — money, *plus pecuniae*), or by II. adv., *plus* = — in quantity or degree (e g *plus amare, diligĕre*), *amplius* (as neuter adj. = a greater extent, value, etc, e g I am *aedilis*, that is, — than a private individual, *ego sum aedilis, hoc est, amplius quam privatus*), if without comparison = increase, addition, = "*davantage*" of the French, *quid vultis amplius?* — than 6 hours, *amplius sex horis; magis* (adv in reference to the quality of the things compared, and expresses that one thing possesses a certain quality in a higher degree than another, e g to be — offended at a thing than another, *alqd in contumeliam accipĕre magis*), *potius* (= rather, sooner, has a subjective meaning, when a choice, a selection is made between two objects, actions, opinions, etc, it always excludes one of two things chosen, whilst *magis* attributes a higher value to one of the two things, without excluding the other, e g he would rather have stayed — in Utica than in Rome, *Uticae potius quam Romae esse maluisset*), *ultra* (as prepos with accus = exceeding a certain measure, proportion, etc, e g — than half-a pint, *ultra heminam*), "than" after — is rendered in Latin after *plus* and *amplius* by *quam* or by the ablat, if numbers are stated *quam* is generally left out, and the numeral with the noun is rendered by the same case as if *quam* had been used, after *magis* and *potius* we use always *quam* (e g to conquer rather through cunning device than through bravery, *magis ratione et consilio quam virtute vincĕre*), in connexion with a noun or adj in an adj or adv sense — is often rendered by a comparative (e.g with — attention, care, *attentius, diligentius*), if two adjs or advs are compared in reference to a certain thing, we use either *magis* . . *quam*, — . . than, or both are expressed by the comparative, the second being preceded by *quam* (e g — passionate than cautious, with — passion than prudence, *calidus magis quam cautus* or *calidior quam cautior*, with — bravery than luck, *fortiter magis quam feliciter, fortius quam felicius*), after negations — is rendered 1, when = in addition to, further, by *amplius, ultra* (e g I demand nothing —, *nihil amplius* or *ultra flagito*), but 2, if = no longer, by *jam* (e g nobody will say that any —, *hoc jam nemo dicet*), I am not doing a certain thing any —, by *desino* (= I cease) or *desisto* (= I leave off) with inf (e g I cannot see any —, *desino vidēre*), and what is — (in a climax), *et quod plus est*, still —, *plus etiam* (as regards the amount, e g he owes me that much and — still, *tantum et plus etiam mihi debet*), *amplius* (= still besides, e g what do you want —? *quid vis amplius?*), so much —, *tanto plus* (as regards the quantity, etc), *eo magis* (implying intensity), once — again, *alterum tantum, bis tantum*, the — the —, *quo* . . *hoc, quanto* . . *tanto*, or *eo* . . *quo, tanto* . . *quanto*, the — people possess, the — they wish to have, *homines quo plura habent, eo ampliora cupiunt* III. n *plus*, see I **moreover,** adv *praeterea, insuper, ultro, ad hoc, ad haec, accedit quod* with indic; see BESIDES

moribund, adj *moribundus*.

morn, morning, I. n *mane* (indecl), *tempus matutinum* (the time in the —), in the pl., the —s, *tempora matutina*, towards —, *sub luce* or *lucem*, in the —, *mane, matutino tempore*, the early —, *primum mane, prima lux* or *lux* (= the first light of the —); early in the —, *primo mane, multo mane, bene mane, primā luce, ubi primum illuxit, ad lucem, primo diluculo* (= with the — dawn); with subst by *antelucanus* (e g working by candlelight early in the —, before daylight, *lucubratio antelucana*), until —, *ad lucem* (e g to watch, *vigilare*), this —, *hodie mane, hodierno mane*, yesterday —, *hesterno mane, hesterno die mane*, good —! *salve!* or (to several) *salvete!* to wish anyone a good —, *salvēre alci dicĕre* II. adj *matutinus*, see above **morning-star,** n *Lucifer*, † *Phosphorus*.

morose, adj *morosus* (= never satisfied with oneself and with others), *acerbus* (= harsh with those around one), *stomachosus* (= churlish), *difficilis* (= ill tempered) Adv. *morose, acerbe*. **moroseness,** n *morositas, acerbitas*

morrow, n *dies posterus* or *crastinus* Adv to-—, *cras, crastino die*, in letters the writers express "to-—" by *postridie ejus diei, qui erat tum futurus, cum haec scribebam* (Cic), early to-—morning, *cras mane*, for to-—, *in crastinum diem*, to day or to-—, some time, *aliquando*, rather to day than to-—, as soon as possible, *quam primum*, the day after to-—, *perendie*

morsel, n *offa* (= mouthful), *pars exigua*; see PARTICLE

mortal, adj 1, *mortalis* (= subject to death opp *immortalis*), *humanus* (= of human, not of divine origin, opp *divinus, divus*), *fragilis, cadūcus* (= fragile, perishable, opp *firmus, stabilis*), —s, *homines, mortales*, all men are —, *omnibus moriendum est*, 2, = deadly, *mortifer*; see FATAL, 3, = complete, by superl (e g — enemy, *homo infensissimus*) Adv to be — wounded, *mortiferum vulnus accipĕre*, = very, *valde, vehementer, magnopere* **mortality,** n. 1, *condicio mortalis, mortalitas*, 2, = number of deaths, by circumloc (e g. there was a great —, *plurimi morte absumpti sunt*)

mortar, n = a vessel, *pila, mortarium*

mortar, n = cement, *arenatum, mortarium*.

mortgage, I. n *hypotheca, pignus, ŏris*, n II. v tr *pignori dare, obligare*

mortification, n 1, in surgery, *gangraena* (Cels.), 2, fig see VEXATION **mortify,** I. v intr in surgery, by *putrescĕre* II. v tr see HUMBLE

mortmain, n **mortua manus* (Mediæval Lat)

mosaic, I. adj *tessellatus, vermiculatus* II. n *opus tessellatum, vermiculatum*

mosque, n *aedes sacra Turcica*

mosquito, n *culex*

moss, n *muscus* **mossy,** adj *muscosus*

most, I. adj *maximus, plurimus*, — people, *plerique*, see MUCH II. adv *maxime, plurimum, valde, vehementer*, see VERY **mostly,** adv *fere, plerumque, saepe*, see GENERALLY

mote, n see PARTICLE

moth, n *tinea, blatta* (= mite)

mother, n 1, lit. *mater* (also as address to an aged female), *matrix* (of an animal), 2, fig = preserver, *mater* (in gen), *parens, tis*, m and f, *procreatrix, genitrix* (*parens* must chiefly be used when the noun which is expressed as the — of anything is masculine) **mother-country,** n *terra patria* **motherhood,** n *mater, maternus* (e g the feeling of —, *animus maternus*) **mother-in-law,** n *socrus, -ūs*, f **motherless,** adj *matre orbus* or *carens* **motherly,** adj *maternus*. **mother-tongue,** n *patrius sermo* **mother-wit,** n to do a thing by —, *crassā* or *pingui Minerva alqd facĕre* (= without art), *summo ingenio* (= cleverly)

motion, **I.** n. 1, (in gen.) *motus*, *-ūs*, *motio* (= the act of setting in —), *agitatio* (= moving up and down); to be in —, *movēri*, *agitari*; to set anyone in —, *agĕre alqm*; to set in quick —, *incitare*, *concitare* (e.g. a horse, etc.); 2, = proposal, *rogatio* (of the tribunes), *sententia* (in the senate); to bring forward a —, *rogationem* or *legem (re)ferre*. **II.** v.tr. *annuĕre*, *significare*. **motionless**, adj. *immotus*.

motive, **I.** n. *caus(s)a*, *ratio*; to act from any —, *alqā ratione adductus alqd facĕre*. **II.** adj. *qui (quae, quod) agitat* or *movet*.

motley, adj. *coloris maculosi*, *maculosus* (= spotted in gen.), *maculis albis* (= with white spots), *varii* or *disparis coloris* (= of different colours).

motto, n. *sententia* (as an idea which we have pronounced, a sentiment), *dictum* (= a saying, anything uttered), *verbum*, *vox* (as a short sentiment).

mould, n. = shape, *forma*.

mould, n. = soil, *terra*; see EARTH. **moulder**, v.intr. *mucescĕre*, *putrescĕre*. **mouldiness**, n. *mucor*. **mouldy**, adj. *mucidus* (Juv.).

moult, v.intr. *plumas ponĕre*.

mound, n. *tumulus*, *agger*, *-ĕris*, m.

mount, **I.** v.intr. 1, see RISE; 2, = to get on horseback, *conscendĕre (equum)*. **II.** v.tr. 1, = to furnish with horses, *milites equis imponĕre*; —ed, *equo vectus*; 2, to — guard, by *excubiae in stationem procedunt*, *milites in stationes succedunt*; = to ascend, *scandĕre*, *a(d)scendĕre*, *conscendĕre*, *escendĕre*.

mountain, n. *mons*, *-tis*, m.; what belongs to, lives, grows upon the —, *montanus*; full of —s, *montuosus* or *montosus*; situate on this side of the —s, *cismontanus*; on the other side of the —s, *transmontanus*; on, along the —, *sub montem*, *in* or *sub radicibus montis* (= close to the foot of the —). **mountaineer**, n. *homo montanus*. **mountainous**, adj. *montosus*, *montuosus* (opp. *planus*), *montanus*.

mountebank, n. *circulator* (in gen.), fem. *circulatrix*, *pharmacopōla circumforaneus* (= quack).

mourn, **I.** v.intr. *maerēre*, *in maerore esse* or *jacēre* (= to be deeply afflicted), *lugēre*, *in luctu esse* (= to show one's grief outwardly), *squalēre*, *in squalore esse* (of extreme grief, which shows itself by entire neglect of one's own self and of outward appearance, e.g. *luget senatus*, *maeret equester ordo*, *squalent municipia*, Cic.), comb. *luctu atque maerore affectum esse*, *in luctu et squalore esse*; *cultu lugubri indutum* (= to go into —ing), for anyone, *pro alqo*. **II.** v.tr. see LAMENT, GRIEVE. **mournful**, adj. *tristis*; *maestus* (= sad), *lugubris*, *flebilis*, *lamentabilis*, *acerbus*, *luctuosus* (= causing sorrow). Adv. *maeste*, †*lugubriter*, *flebiliter*, *acerbe*, *luctuose*. **mournfulness**, n. *maeror*, *tristitia*; see SADNESS. **mourning**, n. *maeror*, *maestitia* (= grief), *luctus*, *-ūs* (= grief shown outwardly by dress, etc.); — dress, *vestis* or *cultus*, *-ūs*, *lugubris*, *squalor* (referring to the neglect shown in one's outward appearance, with a view to excite sympathy), *sordes*, *-ium* (forgetting all dignity and decency); to be in —, *in luctu esse*, *pullatum* or *sordidatum esse*.

mouse, n. *mus*, *muris*, m. and f., *musculus* (= a little —). **mouse-hole**, n. *cavis* or *cavum muris*. **mouse-trap**, n. *muscipula* (Sen.).

moustache, n. perhaps *barba labri superioris*.

mouth, n. 1, *os*, *oris*, n.; with open —, *hians*; anything makes my — water, *alqd salivam mihi movet*; to have a thing in one's —, *alqd in ore habēre* (lit. of food, fig. of words); to be in anyone's —, *in omnium ore* or *in omnium ore et sermone esse*, *omni populo in ore esse*, *per omnium ora ferri*; 2, — of a river, etc., *os*, *oris*, n., *ostium* (in gen.); *caput* (= a single — of a river); = entrance, in gen. *aditus*, *-ūs*.

move, **I.** v.tr. *(com)movēre*, *ciēre* (= to set in motion), *agitare* (= to — up and down), *versare* (= to turn round), *quatĕre* (= to shake), *moliri* (= to — with exertion), *rotare*, *circumagĕre* (= to — round; *rotare* more poet.); fig. *commovēre*, *permovēre*, *turbare*, *conturbare* (= to agitate one's mind); to — heaven and earth, *caelum ac terras miscēre*; = to guide anyone, influence anyone's will, *(com)movēre* (in gen.), *flectĕre* (= to persuade anyone who was of a different mind before), *vincĕre* or *expugnare precibus*, *precibus lacrimisque* (= to persuade anyone to yield). **II.** v.intr. 1, *se (com)movēre*, *(com)moveri* (= to be in motion), *incitari* (quickly, opp. *retardari*), *ferri* (suddenly, violently, opp. *labi*, particularly of celestial bodies), *micare*, *vibrare* (= to vibrate, e.g. of the light); to — in a circle, *in orbem circumagi*; to — round anything, *ambire alqd*, *versari circa alqd* (e.g. round the axis of the earth, of the universe, etc.), *ferri circum alqd*, *volvi circa alqd*; 2, in an assembly, *(re)ferre*; see MOTION, I. 2. **moveable**, adj. *mobilis* (lit. and fig., e.g. of the mind), *agilis* (of what can be easily moved about, e.g. a ship, then fig. of the mind, etc.). **movement**, n. *motus*, *-ūs*; to observe the enemy's —s, *quae ab hostibus agantur cognoscĕre*; see MOTION.

mow, v.tr. *demetĕre*, *secare* (= to cut). **mower**, n. *faenisex (fen-)*. **mowing**, n. *faenisicium*, *faenisicia (fen-)*.

much, adj. and adv. *multus*; — trouble and labour, *plurimum laboris et operae*; — also rendered by subst., such as *copia*, *vis*, *multitudo*, *magnus numerus*; to have — of a thing, *abundare alqā re* (e.g. *otio*, leisure); to have — intercourse with anyone, *multum esse cum alqo*; — more, — less, *multo magis*, *multo minus*; sometimes also *multis partibus* (e.g. to be — greater, *multis partibus majorem esse*); — beloved, *dilectissimus*, *carissimus*; as — as, *tantus . . . quantus* (adv. *tantum . . . quantum*); — less, *nedum*, *ne dicam*, *tantum abest ut*.

muck, n. see DIRT. **muck-heap**, n. *sterquilinium*.

mucous, adj. *mucosus* (Cels.). **mucus**, n. *pituita* (= phlegm, rheum), *mucus* (= filth of the nose).

mud, n. *lutum*, *caenum*. **muddy**, adj. *lutosus* (of soil), *lutulentus* (= besmeared with mud); see DIRTY.

muddle, **I.** n. *turba*, *confusio*; see CONFUSION. **II.** v.tr. 1, *miscēre*, *turbare*, comb. *miscēre ac turbare*; see CONFUSE; 2, with drink, †*inebriare*; to be —d, *vino madēre* (Plaut.).

muff, n. *manica* (= a long sleeve).

muffin, n. see CAKE.

muffle, v.tr. *velare*, *obvolvĕre*. **muffler**, n. *tegumentum*, *teg(i)mentum*; wearing a —, *capite obvoluto*.

mug, n. see CUP.

muggy, adj. *humidus* (= damp), *densus* (= thick), *calidus* (= warm).

mulberry, n. *morum*; —-tree, *morus*, f.

mulct, v.tr. *multare*.

mule, n. *mulus*, *mula*.

mull, v.tr. —ed wine, *vinum fervidum*.

mullet, n. *mullus*.

multifarious, adj. *multiplex*, *varius*. Adv. *varie*, *multis modis*.

multiform, adj *multiformis*

multiplication, n *multiplicatio* **multiply, I.** v tr 1, in arithmetic, *multiplicare*, 2, in gen = to increase, *multiplicare*, see INCREASE **II.** v intr *augeri, crescere*

multitude, n *multitudo* (of persons and things), *vis, vis,* f (e g *magna vis hominum*), *vulgus, -i,* n (= the —, in contemptuous sense), by *multi* and n (e g *multi homines, multae naves*), *frequentia, coetus, -ūs* (= number of people together). **multitudinous,** adj *creber, frequens, multus, numerosus*

mumble, v intr see MUTTER

mummer, n. *qui personam* or *partes agit* **mummery,** n *persona* or *partes, -ium*

mummy, n *homo mortuus arte medicatus* (Tac)

munch, v tr *manducare*

mundane, n 1, lit *mundanus*, 2, fig = worldly, *alcjs rei* (e g *divitiarum*), *studiosus, alci rei deditus*

municipal, adj *municipalis* **municipality,** n *municipium*

munificence, n *munificentia, largitas, liberalitas*, see GENEROSITY **munificent,** adj *munificus, liberalis*, see GENEROUS Adv *munifice, large, liberaliter*

muniment, n *munimentum* **munition,** n. *instrumenta, -orum*, or *apparatus, ūs, belli*

mural, adj *muralis*

murder, I. n *caedes* (in gen), *occisio, homicidium* (= homicide), *nex* (= violent death), *scelus alci allatum* (= crime committed upon any one), *parricidium alcjs* (on a father, mother, brother, etc), to commit a —, *caedem, homicidium facere, parricidium committere, parricidio se obstringere*, on anyone, *caedem alcjs facere* or *efficere* or *perpetrare, mortem per scelus alci inferre, necem alci inferre, afferre, alci vim afferre* (= to lay hands upon anyone), *alqm interficere* or *occidere* (= to kill anyone), accomplice in a —, *caedis socius*, in the context also *sceleri affinis* (as participating in the —) **II** v tr *caedere, occidere, interficere, trucidare, jugulare, necare, de* or *e medio tollere* **murderer,** n *homicida*, m and f (in gen), *parricida* (of a father, mother, brother, sister, a free citizen, a public officer, one's sovereign, etc), *fratricida* (of a brother), *matricida* (of a mother), *sicarius* (= who makes a trade of it), *percussor* (= who pierces, slaughters anyone), — of a despot, tyrant, *tyrannicida, tyranni interfector* **murderous,** adj *sanguinarius* (= bloodthirsty, e g man, thought), † *cruentus* (when much blood is shed, e g *bellum, dies*, also bloodthirsty, e g thought), *atrox* or (stronger) *atrocissimus* (= fearful, most fearful, e g battle, *pugna*, bloodshed, slaughter, *caedes*)

murmur, I. n 1, *murmur, -ūris,* n, *fremitus, -ūs* (especially of a seditious mob), *susurrus* (= whispering, and of a river), to bear a thing without a —, *sedate* or *quiete* or *aequo animo ferre alqd*, 2, = complaint, *querela*, see COMPLAINT **II.** v intr 1, *murmurare*, † *susurrare* (of a low continued noise), to — (as a sign of approbation or disapproval), *admurmurare*, as a sign of applause or indignation, *fremere* (also = to — at, with accus and infin), to — at with a hissing noise, *mussare, mussitare*, 2, = to complain, *queri*, see COMPLAIN

muscle, n 1, in anatomy, *musculus* (Cels), the — in the arm, *lacertus*, 2, a shell fish, *mytilus* (*mit*) **muscular,** adj *lacertosus*, see STRONG

muse, n *Musa*

museum, n *musēum* (as a place where men of learning meet, not in the sense of a repository), natural history —, *thesaurus rerum naturalium exemplis refertus, thesaurus quo res naturales continentur*

mushroom, n *fungus, boletus* (= edible —)

music, n 1, as art, *ars musica, musice, -es,* f (μουσικη, ἡ), *musica, -orum, res musica* 2, of musical productions, = composed pieces, *modi* (*musici*), = made with instruments, *cantus, ūs, concentus, -ūs, symphonia* (of several instruments), to make — with an instrument, *canere* (with the abl of the instrument), to enter a town with —, *urbem ad classicum introire* (of soldiers), pieces of —, *modi musici* (instrumental) **musical,** adj 1, = concerning, referring to music, *musicus, aptatus ad usus canendi* (= adapted for making music, e g instrument, *organum*) 2 = understanding music, by circumloc *musicis eruditus, artis musicae peritus*, to have a — ear, in the context by *aures eruditas habere, aurium judicio valere*, 3, = melodious, *canorus* of speech, *numerosus*, see MELODIOUS Adv by adjs, *numerose* **musician,** n 1, if he plays in public, *servus* or *puer symphoniacus* (= a slave), *fidicen -cinis*, m (= who plays the lyre), *tibicen, -cinis* (= who plays the flute or clarionet), *cornicen* (= who plays the horn), 2, in a higher sense, *artis musicae peritus*

musket, n see GUN

muslin, n *sindon, coa, -orum, byssus*

must, differently expressed, 1. by gerundive = a necessity inferred from the circumstances of the case, e g people, we, you, etc — die, *moriendum est*, one — confess that every living creature is mortal, *confitendum est omne animal esse mortale*, the person by which a thing is to be done in the dative, very seldom by *ab*, and only when a second dative would make the meaning ambiguous and obscure, e g everyone — use his own judgment, *suo cuique judicio utendum est*, the property of many citizens is at stake, of which you — take every care, *aguntur bona multorum civium, quibus a vobis consulendum est* (here *a vobis* on account of *quibus*, Cic , who in another passage has also two datives with the gerundive), we — take the same road *haec via* (*nobis*) *ingredienda*, one — know nature, *noscenda est natura*, the speaker — consider three points, *tria videnda sunt oratori*, 2, by *oportet* (impersonal δεῖ, expressing a necessity inferred from reason, or from the law, or from prudence or justice), with the accus and infin , or merely with the subjunctive mood , 3, = by *debere* (ὀφείλειν), to express a moral obligation, e g you — honour him like your father, *eum patris loco colere debes*, if we were affected in seeing the misery of our allies, what — we now do when we see our own blood shed? *sociorum miseria commovebamur, quid nunc in nostro sanguine facere debemus?* *Debere*, therefore, is nearly = *officium*, so that we can also express — by *officium est alcjs* and simply *est alcjs*, e g a stranger — mind only his own affairs, *peregrini officium est* (i e *peregrinus debet*) *nihil praeter suum negotium agere*, a good orator — have heard much, *est boni oratoris* (i e *bonus orator debet*) *multa auribus accepisse* *Officium* is gen left out in I you —, *meum, tuum, vestrum est*, 4, by *putare* and *existimare*, in the rhetorical style, as a form of politeness, so that the hearers may be allowed to come to a conclusion themselves about a point, e g you see to what a pitch the republic — proceed, *videte quem in locum rempublicam perventuram putetis*, 5, by *opus est* (impersonal χρη), in speaking of any event subjectively felt, and from the supplying of which we expect great advantages; either with accus. and infin., or if the person who — do, etc., a thing is added in the dative, *ut* with subjunctive mood, e.g. if anything should happen which you — know (which it is useful for you to know), I'll write to you, *si quid erit, quod te scire opus est, scribam*; I — go and wash myself, *mihi opus est ut laveni*. Also, I — have so and so may be rendered by *mihi opus est*, either impersonally with abl., or personally with the nominative of the person or thing that — be had, e.g. we — have a guide, *dux et auctor nobis opus est*; we — use your authority, *auctoritate tuâ nobis opus est*; **6**, by *necesse est* (impersonal, ἀνάγκη ἐστι), expressing necessity, either with accus. and infin., or simply with subjunctive mood, e.g. this mortal frame of ours — (necessarily) perish some time, *corpus mortale alqo tempore perire necesse est*; **7**, by *facĕre non possum*, or simply *non possum* with *quin*, etc., or *fieri non potest* with *ut non*, etc., or *non possum non* with infin., to express what cannot be avoided, inward necessity, e.g. I — exclaim, *non possum quin exclamem*; **8**, simply by the verb: in the indicative, inasmuch as in Latin we often leave it for the reader to supply in his own mind under what circumstances an action took place, e.g., I — confess, *confiteor* (Ter.), *fateor* (Cic.); I — regret, *doleo* (Cic.); I — express my surprise, *miror* (Liv.); this one thing I — remark, *unum illud dico*; in the subjunctive, if we only speak of a supposed necessity, e.g. a circumstance, at which not only all educated people, but even savages — blush, *o rem dignam, in quâ non modo docti, verum etiam agrestes erubescant*; **9**, you — (as urgent appeal), either simply by the imperative mood, or by *fac ut*, e.g. if you are not satisfied with that, you — accuse your own injustice, *haec si vobis non probabuntur, vestram iniquitatem accusatote*; you — not (as an urgent warning, not to a thing), *fac ne*, etc. (= mind that not, etc.), *cave ne* (= take care lest, or not to, etc.), *noli* with infin., e.g. you — not wish, *cave ne cupias*.

must, n. *mustum*.

mustard, n. *sinapi* (in the genit. *sinapis*, in the dat., accus., and abl. *sinapi*; the nom. seldom); — plaster, *sinapismus* (very late).

muster, **I.** v.tr. 1, *recensēre* (= to examine through one by one, to ascertain the condition, number, etc., of the army, cavalry, the senate, the people), *inspicĕre* (= to inspect, e.g. the legions, *arma, viros, equos cum curâ inspicĕre*, Liv.); *numerum alcjs inire* (of a crowd), comb. *recensēre et numerum inire* (of a mass of people); 2, fig. to — courage, *animum erigĕre*. **II.** v.intr. *congregari, coire, convenire, adesse*; see ASSEMBLE. **III.** n. see ASSEMBLY.

musty, adj. *mucidus* (Juv., of bread and wine), in gen. perhaps *obsoletus*; see also OLD.

mutable, adj. *(com)mutabilis, inconstans, mobilis*; see CHANGEABLE. **mutability**, n. *mutabilitas*; see CHANGE, LEVITY.

mute, **I.** adj. *mutus*. **II.** n. *servus*, defining sense by context, or *unus ex iis qui funus ducunt*.

mutilate, v.tr. *mutilare* (gen. of trifling mutilations, e.g. nose, ears, finger), *truncare* (= to make into a stump as it were, to — entirely, cut off anyone's head, arms, feet, hands, etc., singly or all at once; e.g., a body, *corpus*; a statue, *simulacrum*). **mutilated**, adj. *mutilatus, mutilus, truncus, truncatus* (*mutilus* and *truncatus* are used also of mutilation by nature), *debilis* (= infirm, inasmuch as the person that is mutilated is deprived of the use of the — limb), *curtus* (= cut wrong, too small, too short, not having sufficient size or perfection and completeness, e.g. *eorum omnium, multa praetermittentium, quasi curta sententia*). **mutilation**, n. by verb.

mutiny, **I.** n. *conspiratio* (= a plot against the superior), *conjuratio* (= conspiracy), *seditio, motus, -ūs* (= insurrection). **II.** v.intr. *inter se conspirare, inter se conjurare* (= to conspire), *seditionem facĕre*. **mutineer**, n. *conjuratus, homo seditiosus*. **mutinous**, adj. *seditiosus*. Adv. *seditiose*.

mutter, v.intr. and tr. *mussari, mussitare*.

mutton, n. *caro (carnis) ovilis*.

mutual, adj. *mutuus*. Adv. *mutuo*.

muzzle, n. = fastening for the mouth, *fiscella*.

my, pron. *meus*; but only expressed if it is required to avoid ambiguity, e.g. I have seen — brother, *fratrem vidi*; I am — own master, *meus sum, mei juris sum*; it is — business, — duty, *meum est*; I for — part, *quod ad me attinet, ego quidem* (often *noster* is used for *meus*, as *nos* for *ego*).

myriad, n. 1, = ten thousand, *decem mil(l)ia*; 2, = an indefinitely large number, *sescenti*.

myrmidon, n. *emissarius, satelles, -ĭtis*, m. (*et administer*).

myrrh, n. *murra (myrrha)*; of —, *murrinus*; anointed with —, †*murreus*.

myrtle, **I.** n. *myrtus (mur-)*. **II.** adj. †*myrteus*; — berry, *myrtum*; — grove, *myrtetum*.

myself, pron. see I, SELF.

mysterious, adj. *arcanus*; a — affair, *res arcana, mysterium*; see SECRET. **mystery**, n. 1, in a religious sense, *mysteria, -orum, sacra, -orum* (= worship, e.g. *Cereris*); to initiate into the mysteries, *mysteriis initiari*; to celebrate, perform the mysteries, *mysteria facĕre*; these are mysteries to me (which I don't understand), *haec non intellego*; = sacred, secret, *arcanum*; 2, = a secret in gen., *res occulta*. **mystic**, **I.** adj. 1, = belonging to religious mysteries, *mysticus, mysticis disciplinis initiatus*; 2, = see STRANGE. **II.** n. *homo mysticus, homo studio mystico deditus*. **mysticism**, n. *studium mysticum* (= mysterious doctrine). **mystification**, n. *ludus, ludificatio* (= tricks, fun); = fraud, *fraus*. **mystify**, v.tr. *alqm fraudare* (= to deceive).

myth, n. *fabula*. **mythical**, adj. †*fabulosus*. **mythology**, n. *fabulae*. **mythological**, adj *quod ad fabulas pertinet*.

N.

nag, n. *caballus*; see HORSE.

naiad, n. *naias*.

nail, **I.** n. 1, (on the fingers and toes) *unguis, -is*, m.; dirty —s, *ungues sordidi* (e.g. and see that your —s be not dirty, *et sint sine sordibus ungues*, Ov.); to cut the —s, *ungues recidĕre* or *resecare*; to bite one's —s, *ungues rodĕre*; 2, an iron or wooden —, to be driven into a board, etc., *clavus*; to drive a —, *clavum (de)figĕre*; you have hit the — on the head, *acu tetigisti*; a small tack, *clavulus*; head of a —, *clavi bulla*. **II.** v.tr. = to fasten with —s on anything, (*clavis*) *affigĕre*, or *configĕre alci rei, suffigĕre in alqd*; —ed, *fixus*.

naive, adj. perhaps *simplex*. Adv. perhaps *sine fuco ac fallaciis*.

naked, adj. *nudus* (lit. and fig.); half-—, *seminudus*; to make or strip —, *nudare* (e.g.

corpus) Adv. *aperte* (= openly), *sine fuco ac fallaciis* (= without dissimulation) **nakedness**, n 1, *nudatum corpus*, 2, fig of style, *jejunitas*, *inopia ac jejunitas*, *exilitas*, *siccitas*

name, **I.** n 1, *nomen* (of a person), *vocabulum* (= the sign of an object or person), *appellatio* (= the calling, the title), *cognomen* (= the family name), my — is Balbus, *est mihi nomen Balbo* or *Balbus*, give him a kiss in my —, *suavium des ei meis verbis*, in the — of the state, *publice* (opp *privatim*), in — (or appearance) only, *verbo* (*tenus*), *verbo non re* or *vera*; under the — of, *nomine alcjs rei*, *sub titulo alcjs rei*, *specie alcjs rei* (= under the excuse, pretence, or pretext), 2, fig *nomen*, to have a —, *magnum nomen* or *magnam famam habēre*, to obtain a —, *nomen consequi*, *famam colligĕre*, *nomen* also = nation or people, e g hostile to the Roman — (= everything Roman), *nomini Romano inimicum* or *infestum*, the terror of the Gallic —, *terror Gallici nominis* **II.** v tr *alqm nominare*, *alci nomen dare*, *indĕre*, *facĕre*, *alci rei nomen imponĕre*, *alqm appellare*, *dicĕre*, *nuncupare*, to — after a person, *ab nomine alcjs appellare* (with the appellation in the accus), see CALL, APPOINT **nameless**, adj *nominis expers*; a certain person who shall be —, *homo quidam*. **namely**, adv if inserted to add something to a previous statement, by apposition (e g if you wish to destroy avarice you must destroy its parent, — luxury, *avaritiam si tollere vultis, mater ejus est tollenda, luxuries*), sometimes it may be rendered by rel and *est* (e g *maxime illa movens eloquentia quae est naturalis*), more expressive is *dico* or *inquam*, = I mean, e g *superiores oratores, Crassum dico et Antonium* **namesake**, n *eodem nomine appellatus*

nap, **I.** n *somnus brevis*, *somnus meridianus* (= sleep in the middle of the day) **II.** v intr *paul(l)um conquiescĕre*, see SLEEP

nap, n (of cloth), perhaps *villus*

nape, n *cervix*

napkin, n *mappa*, *mantele*, *-is*, n

narcissus, n *narcissus* (Plin)

narcotic, **I.** adj by (*con*)*sopire*, *somnum alci afferre* **II.** n *medicamentum somnificum* (Plin)

nard, n *nardus* (Plin)

narrate, v tr (lit.) (*e*)*narrare*, *referre*, *memorare*, *exponĕre alqd alci*, see TELL, RELATE, RECITE **narration**, **narrative**, **I.** n *narratio* (= the act of telling, and the — itself), *relatio* (Quint.), *memoria* (= account of any event as handed down to us), *expositio* (= exposition, representation), *historia* (= story) **II.** adj by *narrare*, etc **narrator**, n *narrator*, *auctor*, *rerum gestarum pronuntiator*

narrow, **I.** adj 1, = of little breadth, *angustus* (= not broad, not wide, leaving little distance from side to side, opp *latus*, generally as censure), *artus* (= tightened, opp *laxus*, generally expressing praise, hence also fig = intimately connected, of friendship, etc.), *contractus* (= drawn together), 2, = not liberal *angusti animi et parvi*, *pusilli animi et contracti*, 3, = difficult, to have a — escape, *vix* or *aegre periculum effugĕre* Adv = nearly, *aegre*, *vix* (= scarcely), *fere*, *ferme* (= almost), = closely, *accurate*, *diligenter* **II.** v tr (*co*)*artare*, *contrahĕre* **III.** v intr *in artius coire*, *cogi* **IV.** n or **narrows**, *aditus*, *-ūs* (= access in gen) *angustiae locorum* or simply *angustiae* (= — passage through a mountain, hollow, etc), *fauces*, *-ium*, f (= — entrance and outlet) **narrowness**, n *angustiae* (lit of narrow pass, fig = embarrassment, difficult circumstances, deficiency of understanding), — of mind, *animus angustus et parvus*

nasal, adj. *narium* (gen of *nares*, = nose)

nascent, adj *nascens*

nasty, adj. 1, of taste, *amarus* (= bitter), *injucundus*, *gravis* (= unpleasant), see UNPLEASANT, 2, = foul, *spurcus*, *teter*, *immundus*, *foedus*, *obscenus* (*obscaen*) see FOUL Adv *amare*, *graviter*, *spurce*, *tetre*, *foede*, *obscene* (*obscaen-*) **nastiness**, n 1, of taste, *amaritas*, *amaritudo*, of smell, *gravitas* (Plin), 2, *foeditas*, *obscenitas* (*obscaen-*)

natal, adj *natalis*, *natalicius*

nation, n *populus*, *gens*, *-ntis*, f (= the people of a country as a whole), *natio*, my, your —, *cives nostri*, *vestri* **national**, adj *gentis proprius* (= peculiar to a people), *domesticus* (= referring to one's own country), *popularis* (= peculiar to the great mass of the people), *togatus* (= only of the Romans, e g *fabula togata*, = the — drama), it is —, *est gentis proprium* (= it is peculiar to the whole people), — character, mind, of a people, in the context, *natura insita*, *ingenium*, *ingenium hominum*, *mores*, *mos alcjs gentis* **nationality**, n *mores populi* or *civitatis*, *mores domestici* (= customs at home), the — of the Greeks, *mores* or *omnis mos Graecorum*, to preserve the —, *mores*, *leges*, *et ingenium sincerum integrumque a contagione accolarum servare*

native, **I.** adj *indigĕna*, or by circuml *in ea* or *illā terra natus*, — land, *patria* **II.** n, the —s, *indigenae*, the —s of an island, *in insula nati* **nativity**, n in astrology, *thema*, *-ătis*, n (Suet), *positus*, *-ūs*, *siderum et spatia* (= place of the stars at the time of anyone's birth), *sidus* (*ĕris*, n) *natalicium* (= the sign under which anyone is born), to cast a —, *notare sidera natalicia*

natural, **I.** adj *naturalis* (= coming from nature, opp *artificiosus*, = founded upon the nature of things, opp *arcessitus* or *quaesitus*), *nativus* (= what is so by nature, in its — condition, of things, e g wall, dam, hair, colour, grotto, heat, opp *artificiosus*, also of innate qualities, opp *quaesitus*), *naturaliter innatus* or *insitus*, also simply *innatus* or *insitus*, comb *innatus atque insitus* (= innate by nature, only of qualities), *proprius et naturalis* (= peculiar by nature, to any one, *alcjs*), *simplex*, *sincerus* (= simple, without a mixture, of things outwardly seen, hence also = not artificial, of words, and sincere, not hypocritical, of man, opp *fucatus*), *verus* (= true, sincere, opp *simulatus*, of words, etc), comb *sincerus atque verus* (opp *fucatus et simulatus*), *filius non legitimus*, a — son, *filius nothus*, *filius e concubinā natus*, *filius naturalis* (Jct), a — death, *mors*, *-tis*, f, to die a — death, *naturae concedĕre*, to be a — consequence of anything, *ex ipsa rei natura sequi*, quite — ! of course ! *minime mirum id quidem*, — philosophy, *physica*, *-orum*, *investigatio rerum naturae* (= study of nature), the Greeks studied — philosophy, nature, *Graeci studium collocabant in rebus naturalibus scrutandis explicandisque*, — sciences, *disciplinae quae naturae investigatione continentur*, *disciplinae quae in mundi leges atque in corporum naturam inquirunt*, — products, *quae terra gignit* or *parit*, *quae gignuntur in* or *e terrā*, *res naturales*, — gift, *ingenium*, *indoles*, *-is* Adv *secundum naturam*, *naturaliter*, *naturae convenienter*, = unaffectedly, *simpliciter*, *sincere*, *sine fuco ac fallaciis*, = clearly, *manifesto*, *nec*e *sario* **II.** n *stultus*, see FOOL, IDIOT **naturalisation**, n, by **naturalize**, v tr, to — someone, *alci civitatem dare* (see CITIZEN), to be —d, *civem esse*, *in civitate* or *civitati* (*d*)*scriptum esse*, to — an animal or plant, *importare* **naturalist**, n *qui rerum naturalium exempla* (*undique conquirit et*) *investigat* **nature**, n *natura*, *ingenium*, *indoles*,

-*is*, f., *proprietas* (= peculiar to anyone or anything); *natura rerum*, *mundus* (= of things, world), *agri*, *campi*, *rus* (= open air, fields); by —, *naturâ*, *naturaliter*; according to —, *secundum naturam* (= in the course of —, opp. *contra naturam*, i.e. contrary to —), *naturae convenienter* (= in accordance with —, both with *vivĕre* = to live); the — of a thing, *natura* or *ratio alcjs rei*; to draw, picture anything from —, *ad verum exprimĕre alqd* (with the pencil or in writing); phenomenon of —, *quod in rerum naturâ fit*, *ostentum*, *prodigium*, *portentum*; agreeable to —, *naturae conveniens* or *congruens*, *naturae* or *ad naturam accommodatus*, *ad naturam aptus* (opp. *naturae* or *a naturâ alienus*), *naturalis* (opp. *fucatus*); to be in conformity with —, *naturae convenire*, *secundum naturam esse*; law of —, *lex naturae* or *naturalis* (in gen.), *ratio profecta a rerum naturâ* (= law based upon the — of things); people living in a state of —, *populus nullo officio aut disciplinâ assuefactus*.

naught, n. *nihil*; to set at —, *parvi facĕre* (= to make little of); see MOCK.

naughty, adj. *improbus*, *immodestus* (= behaving in an improper manner), *rusticus* (= rude). **naughtiness**, n. *immodestia* (= improper behaviour), *rusticitas* (= rudeness).

nausea, n. *nausea*, *fastidium* (= disgust). **nauseous**, adj. see LOATHSOME, DISGUSTING.

nautical, naval, adj. *navalis* (e.g. *pugna*), *nauticus* (= nautical), *maritimus* (= belonging to the sea).

nave, n. **1**, of a wheel, *modiolus*; **2**, of a building, *spatium medium*.

navel, n. *umbilicus*.

navigable, adj. *navigabilis*, *navium patiens* (= being able to carry vessels). **navigate**, v.tr. *navigare in alqo loco* or *per alqm locum* or simply *alqm locum*. **navigation**, n. *navigatio* (= the voyage itself), *ars navalis* (as art, skill). **navigator**, n. *nauta*; see SAILOR. **navy**, n. *copiae navales*, *naves* (= ships), † *naves bellicae* (= men-of-war), *classis*.

nay, adv. *im(m)o (vero)*; *quin etiam*, *atque etiam*, *atque adeo* (= — even); he is living, — he comes into the senate, *vivit*, *im(m)o vero etiam in senatum venit*; see NO.

neap-tide, n. perhaps *aestus (-ûs) minor*.

near, **I.** adv. *prope*, *juxta*, *propter* (rare); — two hundred men, *ad ducentos homines*; see NEARLY. **II.** prep. *ad*, *prope*, *propter* with accus., *secundum* (= along or by with accus.). **III.** adj. **1**, *propinquus* (= — to with gen.); —er, *propior*; —est, *proximus*; *vicinus* (= neighbouring); a — friend, *familiaris*; — relationship, *necessitudo*; **2**, see MEAN. **nearly**, adv. *prope*, *paene*, *fere*, *ferme*; he was — doing it, *in eo erat ut*; to be — related, *alqm genere contingĕre*, *alci propinquum* (*et necessarium*) *esse*. **nearness**, n. *propinquitas* (of place or relationship). **nearsighted**, adj. **1**, *non longe prospicĕre posse*; **2**, fig. *parum prudens*.

neat, adj. **1**, = very clean, *nitidus* (= — -looking, of the outside), *comptus* (= dressed smartly, also *nitidus*, = of — appearance), comb. *nitidus et comptus*, *elegans* (= elegant in dress, appearance, manners); a — little gentleman, *ad unguem factus homo* (Hor., Sat.), *juvenis barbâ et comâ nitidus*, *totus de capsulâ* (Sen.); **2**, = free from impure words and phrases, *nitidus*, *comptus* (of the style, the speaker, the writer), comb. *nitidus et comptus*. Adv. *nitide*, *compte*, *eleganter*; see CLEAN, ELEGANT. **neatness**, n. *nitor*, *elegantia* (= — as regards outward appearance and manners), *munditia*, *mundities* (= cleanliness).

neat-cattle, n. *armenta*, *-orum*. **neat herd**, n. *armentarius*.

nebula, n. *nebula*. **nebulous**, adj. *nebulosus*.

necessaries, n. *res quibus carēre non possumus*, *res quibus homines utuntur*, *res ad vitam necessariae*, *usus vitae necessarii*, *quae sunt ad vivendum necessaria*, *quae ad victum cultumque pertinent* (for our daily sustenance; e.g. wheat, wood, and other —, *frumentum lignaque et cetera necessaria usibus*). **necessary**, adj. *necessarius*; — things, *res necessariae* (in gen.); to provide with everything —, *omnibus rebus ornare atque instruĕre*, or simply *ornare atque instruĕre*; it is —, *necessarium est*; it is — to, etc., or that, etc., *opus est* (gen. with infin., sometimes but not often with *ut* and subj. mood), *necesse est* (with accus. and infin., or with subj. mood; see MUST); *est quod* or *cur* (= there is a reason why); despatch is —, *maturato* or *properato opus est*, *properes* or *festines necesse est* (= it is — for us to be quick), *est quod festines* or *festinemus* (= it is desirable to be quick); if it should be —, *si usus fuerit*, *si quis usus venerit*, *si res postularit* (= if circumstances require it); I consider it — to do a certain thing, *alqd faciendum puto*, *necesse est me alqd facĕre* (= I must necessarily do a thing). Adv. *necessario*, *utique* (= at any rate); often by *necesse est* with subjunctive mood (e.g. out of dissipation must — come avarice, *ex luxuriâ exsistat avaritia necesse est*). **necessitarian**, n. *qui omnia fato fieri putat*. **necessitate**, v.tr. by *cogĕre*; see OBLIGE. **necessity**, n. **1**, *necessitas*; to be placed in the —, *cogi* with *ut*, etc. (= to see, find oneself compelled), *necessario cogi* with infin. (= to find oneself necessarily compelled); if anyone should be placed in this —, *si quae necessitas hujus rei alci obvenerit*, to perceive the — of a thing, *vidēre alqd necessarium esse*; **2**, = need; see WANT.

neck, n. **1**, = part of an animal's body, or of the human body, *collum*, *cervix* (before Aug. almost always used in the pl., *cervices*), *gula*, *fauces*, *-ium* (= throat, gullet); fig. to bend anyone's —, *animum* or *ferociam alcjs frangĕre*; to bend anyone's — under the yoke of servitude, *alci jugum servitutis injungĕre*; **2**, = a long, narrow tract of land, *cervix* (e.g. *Peloponesi*, Plin.), *isthmus* or *isthmos*; **3**, = the long, slender part of a vessel, plant, instrument, *collum*, *cervix*, or pl. *cervices* (of a bottle, etc.); *os*, *oris*, n. (= opening of a bottle, etc.). **neck-cloth**, n. *focale*, *-is*, n. **necklace**, n. *monile*, *-is*, *torques* (*torquis*), *-quis*, m.

necromancer, n. *qui animas mortuorum excitat*.

nectar, n. *nectar*.

need, **I.** n. = occasion for something, *necessitas*; there is — of anything, *alqâ re opus est*. **II.** v.tr. **1**, = to be without, *alqâ re carēre*, *egēre*; **2**, = to want, *alqd requirĕre*, *desiderare*, *alci opus est alqâ re*; it —s a strong man to do this, *strenui est hoc facĕre*. **needful**, adj. *necessarius*. **needless**, adj. see UNNECESSARY. **needy**, adj. of persons, = having but scanty means to live upon (opp. *locuples*, *copiosus*), *egens*, *indigens*, *inops* (of persons; see POOR), comb. *pauper et tenuis*, *tenuis atque egens*. **neediness**, n. *rei familiaris angustiae* (in a higher degree, *rei familiaris inopia*), *egestas*, *indigentia* (= want), *inopia* (= want of what is necessary); see POVERTY.

needle, n. *acus*, *-ûs*, f. **needlework**, n. *opus acu factum*.

nefarious, adj. *nefarius*; see ABOMINABLE, WICKED. Adv. *nefarie*.

negation, I. n *negatio* **II.** adj. *negans, privans*

neglect, I. v tr *neglegere (neglig-), deesse alci rei* (= to — doing a thing), *intermittere* (= to intermit, discontinue for a time, e g studies, *studia*), *omittĕre* (= to omit, give up altogether), *deserĕre* (= to have nothing more to do with anyone) **II.** or **negligence,** n *neglegentia* (*neglig-*) (= want of attention), *indiligentia* (= want of accuracy), *incuria* (= a want of the care which one ought to bestow upon a thing), *neglectio* (= act of neglecting), by a participle (e g through the — of everything else, *relictis rebus omnibus*) **neglectful, negligent,** adj *neglegens (neglig-), indiligens*, see CARELESS

negotiate, v tr *agĕre alqd, agĕre de alqâ re,* or with *ut* (= to speak about a thing, with anyone, *cum alqo*), to — a peace, *agĕre de condicionibus pacis* or *de pace*, to — with anyone for a thing, *colloqui cum alqo de alqâ re* (by word of mouth), *colloqui per internuntios cum alqo et de alqa re mentionem facĕre* (by intermediators) **negotiation,** n *actio de alqâ re* (e g *de pace*, before a war breaks out), *pactio* (= treaty), *condiciones* (= conditions of a treaty), *colloquium* (= counsel between two generals by word of mouth), to break off the —s for anything, *infectâ pace dimittĕre legatos, dimittĕre pacis internuntios* **negotiator,** n *internuntius conciliator* (e g *pacis*), *legatus* (= ambassador)

negro, n *Aethiops, Afer* **negress,** n *femina Aethiops, Afra*

neigh, v intr *hinnire, hinnitum edĕre* **neighing,** n *hinnitus, ūs*

neighbour, n in gen *vicinus*, fem *vicina* (of a house, farm, place), *finitimus, confinis* (= close to the boundary), *propinquus* (who stands, sits, etc, next to a person), to be a —, *vicinum esse* **neighbouring,** adj *vicinus, propinquus, confinis* (of states), *proximus*, — country, *terra vicina* or *finitima* (= — territory), *civitas finitima* (= a — state) **neighbourhood,** n *vicinia, vicinitas* (= the relation of neighbours to each other), *propinquitas* (opp *longinquitas*), = neighbours, *vicini* (e g all the — sees him, *omnes vicini eum vident*) **neighbourly,** adj *vicinis conveniens* or *dignus, ut decet vicinum*

neither, I. pron *neuter*, in — direction, on — side, *neutro* **II.** conj *nec* ... *nec, neque* ... *neque, neve (neu)* ... *neve (neu)*

nephew, n *filius fratris* (= brother's son), *filius sororis* (= sister's son)

ne-plus-ultra, n *quod optimum est*

nepotism, n by *qui suos colit*

nereid, n *Nereis*

nerve, n **1,** *nervus* (= sinew, not class in modern sense), **2,** fig *nervi* (of oratory, etc), see VIGOUR **nervous,** adj **1,** = nervy, *nervosus* (lit of limbs of the body, then = full of vigour, of the style of a writer, speaker, and of the writer or speaker himself), **2,** = of weak nerves, perhaps *infirmus, imbecillus, debilis*, see WEAK, **3,** = frightened, *timidus*, see TIMID Adv = vigorously, *nervose, infirme, timide* **nervousness,** n **1,** = strength (in speech, etc), *nervi*, **2,** see WEAKNESS, **3,** fig perhaps *animus infirmus, imbecillus*, **4,** *timor*, see FEAR

nest, n *nidus*, a little —, *nidulus*, to build a —, *nidum facĕre, (con)fingĕre, nidificare* **nestle,** v intr *in gremio alcjs esse* (= to lie in the lap), *alqm amplecti* (= to embrace), see EMBRACE **nestling,** n *pullus*

net, I. n in gen *rete, is,* or *reticulum* (made of fine thread with meshes) to knit a —, *rete* or *reticulum texĕre*, = an ornament for the head, *reticulum*, a — for catching fish, *rete*, † *funda, jaculum everriculum* (= a drag- —), a — for catching birds, *rete, plaga*, or in pl *plagae; casses, -ium* (for catching animals) **II.** v tr *rete capĕre*, see above

nettle, n *urtica* (= stinging —), *galeopsis lamium* (= dead —) (Plin) **nettled,** adj *iratus*

neuter, adj — gender, *neuter, neutralis* (Quint) **neutral,** adj *medius, neutrius partis*, comb *medius et neutrius partis, qui est in neutris partibus, non in alterius, ullius partem inclinatus* (in gen), *otiosus* (= one who remains quiet), to be —, *medium esse, in neutris partibus esse, neutram partem sequi, non alterius, ullius partis esse*, to be perfectly —, *nullius partis esse*, to remain —, *medium se gerĕre, neutri parti se adjungĕre.* **neutrality,** n *neutrius partis* or *neutrarum partium studium*, in the connexion of the sentence also simply *quies* or *otium* (= the state of quietness) **neutralize,** v tr see COUNTERBALANCE, to — a state, *facĕre ut regio neutrius partis sit*

never, adv *numquam (nunquam), non umquam, nullo tempore*, that he would either return home as a pontifex or —, *domum se nisi pontificem non reversurum*, as a strong negation, *minime, minime vero, minime gentium* **nevertheless,** adv *nihilominus, nihilo setius, (at) tamen*, see HOWEVER

new, adj *novus* (of what did not exist before, opp *antiquus* = what has already been in existence a long time), in a wider sense also = not customary hitherto, unusual, unheard of, as synonymous with *inauditus*, hence comb *novus et inauditus*, *recens* (of what has only been made recently, a short while ago, fresh, young, opp *antiquus*, what existed in former times), also comb *recens ac novus* or *novus ac recens* (to express both the newness of the thing itself and the short existence of it), what is still — to a person (= unaccustomed), *insolitus* (e g dwelling, *domicilium*) is there anything —? *num quidnam novi?* **new-born,** adj *recens natus* (Plaut), *catuli recentes* (= — puppies, Var) **new comer,** n *advena*, m and f, see STRANGER **new-fangled,** adj *mirus* (= strange), *novus* (= new), *inauditus* (= unheard of) **new-fashioned,** adj *novus* or *novo ritu* **newly,** adv *nuper, modo*, (= lately) *recens* (ante and post class), see LATELY **newness,** n *novitas, insolentia* (of what is uncommon) **news,** n *alqd novi, novae res, nuntius*, what —? *quid novi?* that is no — to me, *mihi nihil novi affers* **newspaper,** n *acta publica, orum*, see JOURNAL

newt, n *lacertus, lacerta* (= lizard)

next, I. adj *proximus*, in the — year, *proximo* or *insequenti anno* **II.** adv *deinceps, deinde, post haec, postea* (= afterwards) **III.** prep see NEAR

nib, n = point of a pen, *acumen*

nibble, v intr *admordēre, ambedere* (= to gnaw at), *gustare* (= to taste)

nice, adj **1,** = delicious, *suavis, dulcis*, **2** = fastidious, by *delicatus*, **3,** of judgment, etc, *accuratus, diligens, subtilis*, see ACCURATE Adv *suaviter, delicate, accurate, diligenter, subtiliter* **niceness, nicety,** n **1,** of taste, etc, *suavitas, dulcitas* (rare), **2,** *fastidium*, **3,** *diligentia, subtilitas*, to a —, *ad unguem*

niche, n *aedicula* (for statues)

nick, n in the — of time, *in (ipso) tempore, opportunissime* **nickname, I.** n *nomen* or *nomen per ludibrium datum* **II.** v tr *nomen alci per ludibrium dare*

niece, n. *fratris filia* (= brother's daughter), *sororis filia* (= sister's daughter).

niggardly, adj. see MISERLY. **niggardliness**, n. see MISERLINESS.

night, n. *nox*, *tenebrae* (= darkness); till —, *in noctem*; by —, *nocte*, *noctu*, *nocturno tempore*; early in the —, *concubiâ nocte*; in the dead of —, *nocte intempestâ*. **night-cap**, n. *galerus*; see CAP. **night-dress, night-gown, night-shirt**, n. *vestis nocturna*. **nightfall**, n. see EVENING, NIGHT. **nightingale**, n. *luscinia*. **nightlight**, n. see LAMP. **nightly**, adj. *nocturnus*. **nightmare**, n. *suppressio nocturna* (Plin.). **nightshade**, n. *solanum* (Plin.).

nimble, adj. *mobilis*; see LIGHT, QUICK, SWIFT.

nimbus, n. † *radii*.

nine, adj. *novem*; — times, *novie(n)s*. **nineteen**, adj. *undeviginti*, distrib. *undeviceni*. **nineteenth**, adj. *undevicesimus*, *nonus decimus*. **ninety**, adj. *nonaginta*, distrib. *nonageni*. **ninth**, adj. *nonus*.

nipple, n. *papilla*.

nitre, n. see SALTPETRE.

no, I. adv. *non*, *minime vero*, *minime . . . quidem* (= —, not at all), *im(m)o*, *im(m)o vero*, *im(m)o enimvero*, *im(m)o potius* (= —, rather to the contrary); instead of our — in answer to a question, we generally repeat the verb of the preceding question (e.g. is your brother within? — ! *estne frater intus? non est!* you are not angry, I hope? *non iratus es?* — ! *non sum iratus!* don't you believe that? *an tu haec non credis?* —, not at all! *minime vero!* are we at fault then? *num igitur peccamus?* —, not you! *minime vos quidem!* so then you deceive him? *decine hunc decipis?* — ! on the contrary he deceives me, *im(m)o enimvero hic me decipit*; — ! that is not it, ye judges; — ! it is not indeed! *non est ita, judices! non est profecto!*); to say yes or —, *aut etiam aut non respondēre*; one says yes, the other —, *hic ait, ille negat*; to say — to anything that is offered us, to decline, *abnuĕre* or *recusare alqd* or *de alqâ re*, *negare se alqd facturum esse*. **II.** (**none**), adj. *nullus*, *nemo* (*nullus* of persons and things, *nemo* of persons only), *non ullus*, *non quisquam* (= not one, if a greater stress is to be laid upon the negative; the former as an adj., the latter as a pronoun), *neuter* (= neither, must always be used if we speak of two individuals or of two parties); if *nullus* and *nemo* are used in a partitive sense, that is, if — stands in opp. to the remaining parts or the whole, they govern the genit. (e.g. — mortal, *nemo mortalium*; — animal is more prudent, *nulla belvarum prudentior est*); the genit. may also sometimes be expressed by a circumloc. with *de*, *ex* (e.g. — man of our army was killed, *nemo de nostris cecidit*); sometimes it would appear that instead of *nullus* and *nemo* we use in Latin *nihil* (with genit. when it stands for *nullus*); however, *nihil* expresses the negative more strongly than *nullus* = none at all (e.g. there is — one (at all) more miserable than I am, and — one more happy than Catulus, *nihil me infortunatius, nihil fortunatius est Catulo*; to have — doubt (at all), *nihil dubitationis habēre*); very often we use — when the negative does not refer to anything in general, but to something particular; in this case, which takes place principally when — belongs as an adj. to a noun or refers as a predicate to a noun previously mentioned, we use in Latin the negative *non* instead of *nullus* (e.g. you ordered them — ship, *navem iis non imperasti*). We likewise use *non* in Latin for — when the object in English is expressed by a verbal noun (e.g. to have — fear, *non timēre*; to feel — doubt, *non dubitare*; to feel — hatred against anyone, *non odisse alqm*, etc.); — one, *nemo*; at — place, *nusquam*; at — time, *numquam* (*nunq-*), *nullo tempore*; and at — time, *nec umquam*; in — respect, *nihil*; in — wise, *nullo modo*, *nullâ ratione*. **nobody**, n. *nemo*, *nullus* (= no; as the genit. of *nemo*, *neminis* was little used, *nullius* was used instead), *nemo homo*; and —, *nec ullus*, *nec quisquam*; that —, *ne quid*; a —, *terrae filius*. **nowhere**, adv. *nusquam*.

noble, I. adj. **1**, by birth, *nobilis*, *generosus*, *nobili* or *illustri loco natus*; **2**, morally, *ingenuus*, *magnanimus*, *praeclarus*, *honestus*, *liberalis*, *elatus*, *excelsus*. Adv. — born, *nobili loco natus* or *ortus*, *ingenue*, *praeclare*, *honeste*, *liberaliter*, *elate*. **II.** n. *unus e nobilibus*, or by *homo nobilis* or *generosus*; in pl. the nobles, *optimates*, *nobiles*. **nobility**, n. **1**, by birth, *nobilitas*, *genus nobile*, *generosa stirps*, *-pis*; — by lofty position, *summo loco natum esse*; **2**, = the nobles; see NOBLE, II.; **3**, moral —, *magnanimitas*, *animus ingenuus*, etc.; see NOBLE, I. 2.

nocturnal, adj. *nocturnus*.

nod, I. v.intr. *nutare*; to — in approbation, *annuĕre*; to —, = to doze, *nictare*. **II.** n. *nutus*, *-ūs*.

noise, I. n. *strepitus*, *-ūs* (= loud —), *fremitus*, *-ūs* (= low, hollow —, of bees, horses, etc.), *crepitus*, *-ūs* (= clattering, clashing), *sonitus*, *-ūs* (= loud, clear sounds, e.g. of a trumpet), *stridor* (= the whizzing, e.g. of a saw), *fragor* (= the crackling, e.g. of a house that falls), *murmur* (= murmuring of water), *turba* (= confusion), *tumultus*, *-ūs* (= uproar with clamour; then in general any — caused by a mob or by a single individual), *convicium*; to make a —, *strepĕre*, *strepitum edĕre*, *fremĕre*, *concrepare*, *strepitum facĕre alqâ re*, *tumultum facĕre*, *tumultuari* (= to shout, also in a camp, when the enemy is approaching), *clamare*, *clamitare* (= to cry with a loud voice); to march out with great —, *magno strepitu et tumultu castra movēre*. **II.** v.tr. to — abroad; see PUBLISH. **noiseless**, adj. *quietus* (= quiet), *tacitus* (= silent). Adv. *quiete*, *tacite*, *(cum) silentio* (= in silence). **noiselessness**, n. *silentium* (e.g. of the night, *noctis*). **noisy**, adj. *strepens*, *fremens*, *tumultuosus* (= full of shout and uproar, e.g. *contio*), † *argutus*. Adv. *cum strepitu*.

noisome, adj. *foedus*, *teter*.

nomades, n.pl. *nomădes* (νομάδες), in pure Latin, *vagae gentes*. **nomadic**, adj. by the genit. *nomădum*, or by *vagus*.

nomenclature, n. *index nominum* or *nomen*.

nominal, adj. and adv. opp. to real, *nomine*, *verbo*, *per speciem*, *specie*.

nominate, v.tr. *nominare*, *dicĕre*, *facĕre*, *designare*, *(con)salutare* (= to greet as), *creare*; see APPOINT. **nomination**, n. *nominatio*, *designatio*. **nominative**, n. *casus*, *-ūs*, *nominativus* or *rectus*. **nominee**, n. use *nominatus* (e.g. the — of Caesar, *a Caesare nominatus*).

non, in comp. (e.g. —-residence, see ABSENCE). **nonentity**, n. *nihil*; perfect eloquence is no —, *est certe alqd consummata eloquentia*. **nonsense, I.** n. *ineptiae*; to talk —, *inepta dicĕre*, *aliena loqui*. **II.** interj. *nugas! gerrae!* **nonsensical**, adj. see FOOLISH.

none, adj. see NO.

nook, n. see ANGLE, CORNER.

noon, n. = midday, *meridies*.

noose, n. *laqueus*.

nor, conj. *neque*; see NEITHER.

normal, adj see REGULAR

north, or **northern,** or **northernly, I.** adj *septentrionalis* (*septim-*), *aquilonaris*, — lights, *lumen a septentrionibus oriens*, — wind, † *Boreas*, *septentriones venti*. **II.** n *septentrio*, or pl *septentriones*, † *aquilo*, † *Boreas* **north east,** adj *inter septentriones et orientem spectans*, the — wind, *Aquilo* **north pole,** n. † *polus glacialis*, *gelidus*, or simply † *polus* (Ov.) or *axis* (*septentrionalis*) **northwards,** adv. *septentrionem versus* **north-west,** adj *inter septentriones et occasum solis spectans*, — wind, *Caurus* (*Cor*)

nose, n *nasus*, *nares*, *-ium* (= nostrils, hence the —, an organ for breathing and smelling, also the sing, *naris*, if we speak of one nostril), to blow the —, *nares* or *se emungĕre*, to turn up the —, *naribus contemptum* or *fastidium ostendĕre*; to turn up the — at anyone (from contempt), *alqm suspendĕre naso* (Hor)

nosegay, n *fasciculus*

nostrils, n *nares*, *-ium*, f.

nostrum, n *medicamentum*

not, adv *non*, *haud* (the former in gen, the latter only in certain comb, chiefly before adv and adj, to modify their meaning, e g — much, *haud multum*, — far, *haud longe*), *nullus*, as frequently used by modern writers, in ancient writers not merely = *non*, but = — at all (e g *Philotimus non modo nullus venit*, *sed*, etc, Cic), *minus* (= less, not as strong as *non*), *nihil* (stronger than —, = by no means), *neutiquam*, *haudquaquam*, *nequaquam*, *minime* (also stronger than —), *ne* (expresses a request, wish, command, e g do — resist, if, etc, *ne repugnatis*, *si*, etc, dare —, *ne audeto*), *fac ne*, with subjunctive mood (see LEST, etc.), or *cave* (*ne*) with subj (= take care lest, etc), or *noli* (with infin = do — wish, all three only = an invitation, a request, etc, uttered in a modest manner, instead of *ne*, do — be tempted to, *cave cupias*, do — believe it, *cave credas*), in double prohibitions, *neve* (*neu*) . *neve* (*neu*), after verbs of fearing, — = *ut* (e g *vereor ut veniat* = I fear that he will — come) In questions, — is expressed by *annon* (= perhaps —), when an affirmative answer is expected (e g did I — say perhaps that it would happen so? *annon dixi hoc futurum?*), or *nonne*, if we put a question with a view to convince anyone that we are right (e g what, does — the dog resemble the wolf? *quid*, *canis nonne lupo similis?*), by *ne* (enclit), esp with verbs that express a perception, if we are not certain whether the person spoken to perceives the thing (e g do you — see that in Homer Nestor makes a boast of his virtues? *videsne ut apud Homerum saepissime Nestor de virtutibus praedicet?*), by *non*, if we think that the person does — at all perceive the thing to which we wish to direct his attention (e g do you — see how great the danger is when, etc, *non vides quanto periculo*, etc, by *num*, when a negative answer is expected; — on any account, *minime*, *minime gentium*, *fac* or *cave ne* with subj, *noli* with infin; — by any means, *nullo pacto*, *nullo modo* (= in no wise), *nihil*, — at all, *neutiquam*, — so very (before an adj or adv), *haud* or *non ita* (e g — so very far *haud* (*non*) *ita longe*); — sufficiently, — quite, *non satis*, *parum* (= too little), — even, *ne* . . . *quidem* (the word upon which the stress lies must be placed between *ne* and *quidem*, e g I do — even consider this profitable, *ne utile quidem hoc esse arbitror*), — so, = — in this manner, *non ita*, *non sic*, = less, *minus* (e g — to stray so far, *minus late vagari*), but —, *non vero*, *neque vero*, *non autem* (the second in passing to something else, *non autem* sometimes separated by a word which is put between, e g but I can — tell you, *non possum autem dicĕre*, if "but —" is merely used to introduce an antithesis, *non* alone is used, e g I mean the father, but — the son, *dico patrem*, *non filium*), — either, *nec* or *neque* (e g Epicurus says, we do — require understanding, nor words either, *Epicurus negat opus esse ratione*, *neque disputatione*, fortune does — give us virtue, and therefore does — take it away either, *virtutem fortuna non dat*, *ideo nec detrahit*), but also —, *nec* . . . *quidem* (the word upon which the stress lies is placed between *nec* and *quidem*, especially in opp to something else, e g but also Jugurtha did — remain quiet in the meantime, *sed nec Jugurtha quidem quietus interea*), and —, *et non* (when the negative refers to one word only, as when the stress lies upon the negative), *neque* (to connect two sentences or two parts of the same sentence, e g *via certa et non longa* = a safe road and one that is — very long, but *via certa neque longa* = a road both safe and short), and so —, and therefore —, *ac non* (to express an inference, e g there was nobody who would have taken him to be accused of a crime, and who would — therefore think that he had been condemned over and over again, *nemo erat qui illum reum*, *ac non millies condemnatum arbitraretur*), and — rather, *ac non potius*, or simply *ac non*, and — less, *atque etiam*, *itemque* (= and so also, likewise also), to say —, by *negare*, my friend said that he would — do it, *meus amicus negabat se hoc facturum esse*, in connexion with an adj, — is often rendered in Latin by one word, containing — and the adj, e g — prudent, *amens* (= silly), *demens* (= foolish), — pleasant, *injucundus*, *ingratus*

notable, adj see REMARKABLE

notary, n *scriba* (*publicus*)

notation, n *inscriptio alcjs rei* (upon), = the act of noting down, (*per*)*scriptio*, *subscriptio* (= the writing down of one's name, *nominis*)

note, I. n 1, in music, *soni* or *vocis signum*, to play or sing from —s, *ex libello canĕre* (not from memory), 2, = letter, *epistula* (*epistola*), *lit*(*t*)*erae* **II.** v tr 1, by *scribĕre*, *exarare* (= to — down, in letters of Cic), 2, see NOTICE **notes,** n pl, *dictata*, *-orum* (= dictations of a professor written down by the student). **note-book,** n *adversaria*, *commentarii* (Plin Min), *pugillares* (Plin), see JOURNAL **noted,** adj see FAMOUS **noteworthy, notable,** adj see REMARKABLE **notice, I.** n *observatio*, *animadversio*, *notatio*, comb *notatio et animadversio*, to take —, *animadvertĕre*, to give —, see PROCLAIM, DISMISS **II.** v tr *animadvertĕre*, see REMARK **noticeable,** adj see REMARKABLE **notify,** v tr *alqm alcjs rei certiorem facĕre*, *alqd* (*de*)*nuntiare*, see INFORM **notification,** n *promulgatio* (of laws), *denuntiatio* (in gen). **note-of-hand,** n *chirographum*

notch, I. n see INDENT, INCISION **II.** v tr *striare* (in architecture), *incidĕre* (= to make incisions, e g in a tree)

nothing, n *nihil* (*nil*), *nihilum*, *nulla res*, since *nihil* must be considered as a noun, it is used with adjectives or with a gen (e g — of the kind, *nihil tale*, to think — mean, *nihil humile cogitare*, he has done — new, *nihil novi fecit*, to anticipate — good, *nihil boni divinare*), to rise from —, *ex nihilo oriri*, out of — comes —, *de nihilo nihil fit*, *de nihilo nihil creari potest*, to be as good as —, *pro nihilo esse*, with comparatives, *nihilo*, e g — greater, *nihilo majus*, — less, *nihil minus*, *nihilo vero minus*, — but, *nihil nisi* (but not *nihil quam*), — else but, *nihil aliud nisi, nihil aliud quam* (the latter if in the words preceding, *tam*, so much, is to be understood); and —, *nec quidquam;* I have — to fear, *nihil est quod timeam;* I have — to say in reply, *nihil est quod respondeam;* to care — for, *alqd non flocci* or *parvi facĕre*, or *pro nihilo ducĕre;* good for —, *inutilis* (= useless); *nequam* (of a good-for- — fellow).

notice, n., **notify**, v.tr., see under NOTATION.

notion, n. see CONCEPTION, IDEA.

notorious, adj. 1, = well known, *notus, manifestus, clarus, tritus, celebratus*, comb. *tritus ac celebratus* (= commonplace); 2, in a bad sense, *insignis* or *infamis alqd re*, or by superl. (e.g. a — evil-doer, *homo sceleratissimus*). Adv. *manifestum est*, with acc. and infin. **notoriety**, n. *fama* (in gen.), *infamia* (in bad sense).

notwithstanding, adv. *nihilominus* (or in two words, *nihilo minus*), *tamen, attamen, verumtamen*, often not expressed after *etsi*, etc. = although.

nought, n. see NOTHING.

noun, n. *nomen* (Gram.); see SUBSTANTIVE.

nourish, v.tr. *nutrire*. **nourishing**, adj. *in quo multum alimenti est, magni cibi* (= containing much nutritious matter, opp. *parvi cibi*), *valens* (= strong, opp. *imbecillus, infirmus*). **nourishment**, n. *alimentum*.

novel, I. adj. *novus;* see NEW, UNCOMMON. II. n. *fabula, fabella* (= a short story). **novelist**, n. *qui fabulas componit*. **novelty**, n. 1, as quality, *novitas, insolentia;* 2, = a new thing, *res nova*.

November, n. (*mensis*) *Novembris* or *November*.

novice, n. *novicius, novellus* (= one who has just arrived, established himself, settled at a place, Liv.); a — in military service, *tiro, miles, -itis, novus* (opp. *miles veteranus*); a — in anything, *tiro* or *rudis*, or comb. *tiro et rudis in alqa re* (= a mere beginner in anything), *peregrinus* or *hospes*, or comb. *peregrinus atque hospes in alqa re* (= inexperienced). **novitiate**, n. *tempus ad alcjs facultates experiendum constitutum* or *tempus tirocinii*.

now, adv. *nunc* (opp. *tunc;* at this moment, the time present with the writer, as *tunc* refers to time present in regard to the person or thing referred to); *jam* (a particle of transition, up to —, from —), *hoc tempore, in praesentiā, in hoc tempore, in praesenti; hodie* (= to-day); *nunc demum* (that is, — for the first time, — at length, in contradistinction to *tum* or *tunc primum*); — especially, (*nunc*) *cum maxime;* but —, *modo;* just —, *nunc ipsum, hoc ipso tempore;* from —, *jam inde, ab hoc tempore;* — (as a particle of connexion or inference), *igitur*, or by a periphrasis, *quae cum ita sint* (= as these things are so). As a particle of mere transition, *autem* or *vero* or *quidem, equidem, sed;* but sometimes no particle at all is used, e.g. whatever he may — say, *quidquid dicat;* you may — (or then) be present or not, *adsis necne*. As a particle of affirmation or concession use *vero* or *nune; nunc vero*, — in fact; *nunc autem*, = but now. With a question, *quid vero?* — what? or *quid autem?* — what in the world? *quid tandem?* In exhortations, e.g. come —, *age, agite;* — four years ago, *quat(t)uor abhinc annis, ante hos quatuor annos;* — and then, *aliquando, nonnunquam* (*nonnumq.*). **nowadays**, adv. *hodie, hodierno tempore;* see NOW.

nowhere, adv. *nusquam*.

nude, adj., **nudity**, n., see NAKED.

nudge, v.tr. *alci latus fodicare* (Hor.).

nugatory, adj. *nugatorius;* see VAIN.

nugget, n. perhaps *later, -ĕris*, m. (Var.).

nuisance, n. by *molestus* (e.g. the man is a —, *homo molestus est*).

null, adj. *vanus* (= not to be depended on, e.g. *promissum*), *inanis* (= without a meaning, e.g. *promissum*), *fu(f)ilis* (= futile, e.g. *sententia*, opinion), *nullus* (= as good as nothing, e.g. *nulla est haec amicitia*), *fragilis* (= fragile), *caducus* (= perishable); to declare anything — and void, *alqd irritum esse jubēre, alqd rescindĕre* (= to rescind, e.g. a will); fig. by *nihil valēre, nihil auctoritatis habēre* (= to have no authority), *nulla alcjs habetur ratio* (= anyone is not considered at all). **nullify**, v.tr. *ad irritum redigĕre*. **nullity**, n. *vanitas, inanitas, fragilitas;* see INVALIDITY.

numb, I. adj. *torpens;* to be —, *torpēre;* to grow —, *torpescĕre*. II. v.tr. *alqm torpore afficĕre*. **numbness**, n. *torpor*.

number, I. n. 1, *numerus* (in most senses of the Eng. = several people or things; mere — or cypher, grammatical —, musical measure); an equal —, *numerus par;* unequal —, *numerus impar;* to be one of a —, *esse numero* or *in numero;* 2, = many, *copia, multitudo*, or by *multus* (e.g. a — of men, *multi homines*). II. v.tr. *numerum inire; alqd numerare, dinumerare, numerum alcjs rei inire* or *exsequi* or *efficĕre, computare* (= to reckon), (*enumerando*) *percensēre* (= to go over in numbering); to — the stars, *stellas dinumerare;* to — on the fingers, *numerare digitis* or *per digitos, computare digitis;* to — among the gods, *referre in numerum deorum*. **numbering**, n. — of the people, *census, -ūs;* see CENSUS. **numberless**, adj. *innumerus, innumerabilis*. **numerable**, adj. *numerabilis*. **numerical**, adj. — signs, *numerorum notae* or *signa, -orum*. Adv. *numero*. **numerous**, adj. *creber* (= frequent), *celeber* (= full of people), *frequens* (= quite full), *multo, magnus, multiplex* (= manifold); a — assembly of the senate, *frequens senatus*. Adv. *magno numero*.

numismatics, n. and adj. *nummorum doctrina*.

nun, n. *monacha, nonna* (Eccl.).

nuptial, adj. *nuptialis, genialis* (e.g. *lectus*); see CONNUBIAL. **nuptials**, n. *nuptiae;* see WEDDING.

nurse, I. n. 1, *nutrix* (in gen. or = wet- —), *nutricula* (dimin.); a sick —, by verb *quae alqm curat;* 2, fig. *altrix*. II. v.tr. 1, *nutrire* (= to suckle), *gestare* (= to carry in the arms), *fovēre* (= to fondle); 2, in sickness, *alqm curare, alci assidēre*. **nursery**, n. *parvulorum diaeta;* — in a garden, *seminarium* (lit. and fig.; *plantarium*, Plin.); — of vines, *vitiarium*. **nursery-gardener**, n. *qui seminarium habet*. **nursling**, n. *alumnus* (= adopted son); *alumna* (= adopted daughter); see DARLING.

nurture, n. see EDUCATION.

nut, n. *nux;* to crack a —, *nucem frangĕre;* you have only one more — to crack, but a hard one, *unus tibi restat nodus, sed Herculaneus* (Sen.). **nutshell**, n. lit. *putamen;* fig. to put the thing in a —, *ne multa dicam*.

nutriment, nutrition, n. see FOOD, NOURISH.

nymph, n. *nympha, Nereis, -idis*, f. (= sea —), *Oreas, -ădis*, f. (= mountain —), *Dryas, -ădis*, f., and *Hamadryas* (= tree —, forest —), *Nais* and *Naias* (= river —).

O.

o! oh! interj *o!* (in gen., as exclamation whenever we feel affected), *proh!* (chiefly implying indignation), *heu!* (in complaining, lamenting), *ohe!* (expressive of weariness after having attended to a thing for some time); after an interjection we use either the voc., when we invoke the thing itself, or the accus., when we say, e.g. "—, unfortunate that I am! *o* (or *heu*) *me miserum* or *me perditum!*" or *me miserum!* —, certainly, *sane quidem, scilicet quidem* (in gen. ironically); —, no, *minime vero*; —, I shall come, *ego vero veniam*; —, it is already done, *atqui jam factus est*.

oak, n *quercus, -ūs*, f (= the common —); of —, oaken, *quernеus* or *quernus, querceus* (= of the common —). **oak-apple**, n *galla* (Plin.).

oakum, n *stuppa*; made of —, *stuppeus*.

oar, n *remus* (in gen., = — of a ship, boat), *scalmus* (= a round piece of wood, a thole, to which the — was fastened, then fig. for the — itself); *nullum scalmum vidit*, he saw no —, i.e. boat; †*palma* (lit. = blade); bank of —s, seat for rowers, *transtrum*, also *sedile*; hole for an —, *columbarium* (late); stroke of the —, *pulsus, -ūs, remorum*.

oath, n *jusjurandum*, gen. *jurisjurandi* (= the — taken by subjects and soldiers), *sacramentum* (military), *religio, jusjurandi verba* (= the form of an —); a false —, *falsum jusjurandum, perjurium*; to put one to his —, *jusjurandum ab alqo exigĕre, jusjurandum alci deferre*; to swear or take an —, *jusjurandum dare* or *jurare, sacramentum* or *sacramento dicĕre* (Liv.); to swear a false —, *falsum jurare, pejerare* or *perjurare*; to take the truest —, *verissimum jusjurandum jurare, ex animi sententia jurare*; to take the — (i.e. according to the usual form), *verbis conceptis jurare* (so *pejerare*); to swear allegiance, *in verba alcjs* (to his dictation) *jurare* (used of citizens, officials, and soldiers, also fig.), *sacramentum dicĕre apud alqm, sacramento* or *sacramentum dicĕre alci* (of soldiers); to administer the — of fidelity, *alqm in sua verba jusjurandum adigĕre*; to refuse to take the —, *sacramentum detrectare* (of soldiers); to bind by —, *jurejurando alqm a(d)stringĕre, obstringĕre, obligare*; to bind oneself by an —, *se jurejurando obstringĕre*.

oats, n *avena*. **oatmeal-porridge**, n *avenae puls*. **oatmeal-gruel**, n *cremor avenae*.

obdurate, adj. see OBSTINATE.

obedient, adj. *oboediens, dicto audiens, dicto audiens atque oboediens, obtemperans, obsequens* (all with dat.). Adv. *oboedienter*. **obedience**, n *oboedientia* (= submission to masters, etc.), *obtemperatio* (to anything, *alci rei*, = the act of complying with, e.g. the laws, *legibus*), *obsequium, obsequentia* (= resignation to another's will, fulfilling instructions), *officium* (inasmuch as it is the result of duty to superiors, the allegiance of tributary states); to remain in —, *in officio retinēri* or *continēri*; to bring back to —, *ad obsequium redigĕre*. **obey**, v.tr. *alci parēre, oboedire* (obed-), *dicto audientem esse* (= to — anyone's commands), *obtemperare* (= to comply with anyone's wishes), *obsequi* (= to yield to anyone's advice), *alqm audire, alci auscultare* (= to listen to anyone's entreaties), *alci morem gerĕre, morigerari* (= to gratify); very often comb. to increase the force, *parēre et oboedire, oboedire et parēre, obtemperare et oboedire, obsequi et oboedire, dicto audientem atque oboedientem esse*.

obeisance, n see BOW.

obelisk, n *obeliscus* (Plin.).

obelus, n *obelus* (late), *virgula censoria* (Quint.).

obese, adj. see FAT.

obituary, n perhaps *ratio Libitinae*; to be registered in the —, *in rationem Libitinae venire* (Suet.).

object, I. n 1, = something presented to the mind by the senses, *res*; the —s around us, *res externae*; to be the — of is variously rendered, by *esse* and dat. (e.g. to be an — of care, hatred, contempt to anyone, *alci esse curae, odio, contemptui*), by *esse* and *in* (e.g. to be an — of hatred with anyone, *in odio esse apud alqm*; to become an — of hatred, *in odium venire, pervenire*), by nouns already involving the idea (e.g. — of love, *amor, deliciae*; — of desire, *desiderium*), by circumloc. with verbs (e.g. to be the — of anyone's love, *ab alqo amari, diligi*); 2, = ultimate purpose, *finis, -is*, m. (and f. mostly poet. or ante and post class.), *consilium*, or by circumloc. with *id quod volo* or *cupio* (= the design), *propositum*, or by circumloc. with *quod specto* or *sequor* or *peto* (= end, aim); *finis* (= the main purpose, e.g. the — of a house is usefulness, *domus finis est usus*; but not = *propositum* = the aim or — we have in view); the — of anything, *consilium alcjs rei* (in a subjective sense), *id cujus caus(s)a alqd facimus* (in an objective sense); with what —, *quo consilio*; with the — of, *eo consilio ut*; to have an —, *consilium sequi, certum alqd consilium proposuisse* (of persons), *agĕre, petĕre* (= to seek), *velle* or *spectare alqd* (= to regard, also of things); to have a great — in view, *magnum quiddam spectare* (of persons); the laws have this — in view, *hoc spectant leges, hoc volunt*; to lose sight of the — one had in view (in a speech, etc.), *a proposito aberrare*; to make anything one's —, *alqd sibi proponere*. 3, in metaphysics, *quod sub sensus cadit*. II. v.tr. *contra dicĕre, in contrariam partem afferre* (= to have something to say on the other side), *respondēre* (= to answer); I have nothing to — against it, *nihil impedio, non repugnabo* (with *quominus* and subj., also *ne*, and after a negative *quin*, with subj.; *non recusabo quin* or *quominus*); but someone may —, *sed fortasse quispiam dixerit, dicat alqs forte*; but one might —, simply *at* (*enim*). **objection**, n *quod contra dicitur, excusatio* (= excuse against accusations and orders), *exceptio* (= exception taken in a law-court); without the least —, *sine morā, sine ullā dubitatione, haud cunctanter* (cunct-), *non dubitanter*; to raise an —, *contra dicĕre*; I'll hear no —! *nihil audio!* (Com.); see also HINDRANCE. **objectionable**, adj. *malus* (= evil); see BAD. **objective**, adj. *sub sensus cadens* or *res externae*; — case, *casus accusativus* (direct), *casus dativus* (indirect). Adv. *res externae* (e.g. the world), — considered, *res externas dico*. **objector**, n *qui alqd alci contra dicit*.

objurgate, v.tr. *objurgare*.

oblation, n see SACRIFICE.

oblige, v.tr. 1, = to constrain by moral force or necessity, or by law, *obligare alqm alci rei*, or with *ut*, *alligare, obstringĕre* (strictly), *devincire* (so that we cannot escape it), also by *cogi* (e.g. he was —d (= compelled by force) to destroy himself, *coactus est ut vitā se ipse privaret*); the Campanians were —d to march out at the gates, *coacti sunt Campani portis egredi*; or by the active *cogĕre* (e.g. not as he wished, but as the will of the soldiers —d him to do, *non ut voluit, sed ut militum cogebat voluntas*); 2, = to do anyone a favour, *alqm sibi obligare* or *obstrin-*

gēre or *devincire* (by a friendly act, *beneficio*; by acts of kindness, *officiis*); to be very much —d to anyone, *alci multum* or *multa beneficia debēre*; I am very much —d to you (as answer), *gratissimum illud mihi fecisti*, or (in declining an offer) simply *benigne*. **obligation,** n. = what constitutes legal or moral duty, *officium, debitum, religio* (= moral —); I am under the —, *meum est, debeo*; to impose the — upon anyone, *imponĕre alci officium, obligare* or *obstringĕre alqm*; see DUTY. **obligatory,** adj. render by OBLIGE. **obliging,** adj. *humanus, comis* (= courteous), *facilis* (= easy), *officiosus* (= ready to oblige); an — letter, *lit(t)erae humaniter scriptae* or *humanitatis plenae*; see KIND. Adv. *humane, humaniter, comiter, facile, officiose*. **obligingness,** n. *humanitas, comitas, facilitas*; see COURTEOUSNESS.

oblique, adj. 1, *obliquus* (= slanting, opp. *rectus*); 2, fig. *per ambages*; 3, in gram. — cases, *casus obliqui*; — narrative, *oratio obliqua* (Quint.). Adv. *oblique, ex obliquo, in obliquum*. **obliquity,** n. *obliquitas, iniquitas*; see INIQUITY.

obliterate, v.tr. = to erase, *delēre* (lit. and fig.); see ERASE, BLOT OUT, EFFACE, DESTROY.

oblivion, n. *oblivio*, †*oblivium*. **oblivious,** adj. *immemor, obliviosus*; see FORGETFUL.

oblong, adj. *oblongus* (Plin.).

obloquy, n. *odium* (= hatred), *opprobrium, convicium, maledictum* (= abuse); see ABUSE.

obnoxious, adj. 1, = subject, *alci rei obnoxius*; 2, = hurtful, *noxius*; see HURTFUL.

obol, n. *obolus*.

obscene, adj. *obscenus*; see FOUL. Adv. *obscene*. **obscenity,** n. *obscenitas* (e.g. *verborum* or *orationis*); see FILTH, FILTHY.

obscure, I. adj. 1, lit. = without light; see DARK; 2, fig. = not easily understood, *obscurus* (e.g. *narratio*), *caecus* (e.g. *morbus, carmen*), *involutus* (= involved), *reconditus* (= hidden), *ambiguus, dubius* (= doubtful), *perplexus* (= confused, perplexing, e.g. *sermones, carmen*), *incertus* (= vague, e.g. *rumor*), *subobscurus* (= rather —, e.g. of an author); he is very —, *valde obscurus est* (of a philosopher, etc.); 3, = not noted, *obscurus*. Adv. *obscure, perplexe, ambigue, dubie*; — born, *obscuro loco natus*. **II.** v.tr. *obscurare* (lit. and fig.), *alci rei tenebras offundĕre, obducĕre* (fig. = to make indistinct). **obscurity,** n. 1, *obscuritas*; see DARKNESS; 2, fig. *obscuritas, oratio involuta*, etc.; see OBSCURE, 2; 3, of birth, *obscuritas, humilitas, ignobilitas*.

obsequies, n. see FUNERAL.

obsequious, adj. and adv. by *alci adulari* (= to flatter). **obsequiousness,** n. *adulatio*.

observe, v.tr. 1, *(ob)servare, asservare* (= carefully), *animadvertĕre* (= to attend to a thing), *spectare, contemplari* (= to — as a quiet spectator), *considerare* (= to look at carefully); to — the enemy, *hostium consilia speculari* (= to spy out his plans); 2, = to keep to, maintain, *(ob)servare, conservare, custodire* (= to adhere strictly to a certain course), *colĕre* (= to — duly); to — one's duty, *officium suum servare* (opp. *off. praetermittĕre*); to — order, a custom, an oath, *ordinem, morem, jusjurandum (con)servare*; 3, = to remark; see REMARK, MENTION. **observance,** n. *mos* (= habit), *ritus, -ūs* (= manner), *conservatio* (= maintenance); see HABIT. **observant,** adj. see OBEDIENT, ATTENTIVE, and under OBSERVE. **observation,** n. 1, *observatio, animadversio* (= act of attending to); — of the stars, *observatio siderum*; — of nature, *notatio naturae et animadversio*; power of —, *ingenii acumen* or *acies* (= acuteness), *sagacitas* (= sagacity); 2, = remark, *dictum*; see REMARK. **observatory,** n. *specula astronomica*. **observer,** n. *custos, -ōdis*, m. and f. (= guard, keeper), *animadversor* (= who gives heed to, e.g. *vitiorum*, Cic.), *spectator* (= a looker-on), *speculator* (= who spies out; fem. *speculatrix*); an — of nature, *speculator venatorque naturae*; — of the sky and stars, *spectator caeli siderumque*; an acute —, *homo acutus, sagax* (of quick perception); a conscientious — of all his duties, *omnium officiorum observantissimus*.

obsolete, adj. *obsoletus* (lit. = worn out, cast off, e.g. *vestis*; fig. *verba*), *ab usu quotidiani sermonis jam diu intermissus* (= long since out of use in ordinary language), *ab ultimis et jam obliteratis temporibus repetitus* (= far-fetched from bygone times; both of words).

obstacle, n. *impedimentum*.

obstinate, adj. *pertinax* (of persons, and things which continue unabated, e.g. an illness), *pervicax* (= resolute), *obstinatus, offirmatus* (= steadfastly persevering, the latter in a bad sense); an — illness, *morbus longinquus* (= long); to observe an — silence, *obstinatum silentium obtinēre*. Adv. *pertinaciter, pervicaciter, obstinate, obstinato animo, offirmatā voluntate*. **obstinacy,** n. *pertinacia, pervicacia, obstinatio, animus obstinatus, voluntas offirmatior*.

obstreperous, adj. *tumultuosus*.

obstruct, v.tr. 1, = to block up, *obstruĕre, obsturare, officĕre* (with dat.), *obsaepire* (*obsep-*), *intersaepire*; to — the light, *obstruĕre* or *officĕre luminibus alcjs*; 2, = to retard (e.g. progress), see HINDER, OPPOSE. **obstruction,** n. *impedimentum*; see STOPPAGE, HINDRANCE. **obstructive,** adj. *quod impedimento est, quod impedit, quod obstat et impedit*.

obtain, I. v.tr. *compotem fieri alcjs rei, potiri alqā re* (= to get possession of), *adipisci* (= to — what one desires), *alqd assequi, consequi* (by an effort), *nancisci* (by chance or through an opportune circumstance), *impetrare* (= to get what was requested), *obtinēre* (= to — and keep what we claimed), *auferre* (as the fruit of exertion), *acquirĕre* (in addition to what one has), *exprimĕre* (= to extort, e.g. money, *nummulos ab alqo*); to — by entreaties, *exorare* (anything from anyone, *alqd ab alqo*); to — the highest power, *rerum potiri*. **II.** v.intr., see PREVAIL. **obtaining,** n. *adeptio, impetratio* (of what we requested).

obtrude, v.tr. see INTRUDE.

obtuse, adj. *hebes* (dull; lit. of a sword, angle, fig. of persons, mental qualities, the senses, etc., e.g. *homo, ingenium*), *obtusus, retusus* (lit. = blunted, of a sword, angles, etc.; then fig. of things, e.g. *ingenium*; all three lit. and fig., opp. *acutus*), comb. *obtusus et hebes* (e.g. scythe, *falx*). **obtuseness,** n. see DULNESS, STUPIDITY.

obverse, n. (of a coin, opp. reverse), *nummus aversus*.

obviate, v.tr. *alci rei occurrĕre* or *obviam ire* (= to prevent), *praecavēre alqd* (= to prevent by precaution); see HINDER.

obvious, adj. *apertus, manifestus, clarus, perspicuus*; see CLEAR, EVIDENT. Adv. *aperte, manifeste, clare, perspicue*.

occasion, I. n. 1, see TIME, OPPORTUNITY; 2, = incidental cause, *occasio, caus(s)a, auctor* (= author, of persons); to give an — for, *ansam* *dare* or *praebēre alcjs rei* or with *ad alqd faciendum* (= to afford a handle for), *occasionem dare* or *praebēre alcjs rei* (e g *sui opprimendi*, of suppressing him), *locum dare* or *facĕre alci rei* (= to give room for), on every —, *quotie(n)scumque (-cunque) potestas data est* II v tr *auctorem esse alcjs rei* (= to be the author of, e g a war, *belli*, anyone's return, *alcjs reditūs*), *creare* (= to create, e g. an error, *errorem*, war, *bellum*), *movēre* (= to excite, e g laughter, *risum*, war, *bellum*), *caus(s)am alcjs rei inferre* (= to give the first cause, e g for a quarrel, *jurgii*), see CAUSE **occasional,** adj render by *occasione datā* or *oblatā*, *si occasio fuit* or *tulerit*, or by *per occasionem*; see ACCIDENTAL, CASUAL Adv *raro* (= seldom), *subinde*, *aliquando* (= now and then)

occident, n see WEST

occiput, n *occipitium* (Plin , opp *sinciput*), *aversa pars capitis*

occult, adj *occultus*, see ABSTRUSE, OBSCURE

occupy, v tr 1, = to hold or possess, *habēre*, *tenēre*, *in manibus habēre*, *possidēre*, 2, = to take, *capĕre*, *occupare*, *expugnare* (*urbem*), *potiri re*, to be quite occupied with anything, *studio alcjs rei teneri* or *trahi*, *studio* or *amore alcjs rei captum esse*. **occupancy,** n *possessio*. **occupation,** n 1, (of a place) *occupatio*, *expugnatio* (= storming); 2, (in business) *negotium*, see BUSINESS, OCCUPIER, POSSESSOR

occur, v intr 1, = to come into one's mind, render by *in mentem mihi alqd venit*, *mihi in opinionem alqd venit* (as a conjecture), *subit animum cogitatio*, *in mentem* or *in cogitationem mihi incidit alqd* (= the thought comes into my mind), *mihi* or *animo* or *in mentem occurrit alqd*, *mihi succurrit* (= it just strikes me), *subit recordatio*, *recordor* or *reminiscor alcjs rei*, 2, of passages in books, *reperiri* (= to be found), *legi*, 3, = to happen, *fieri* (= to become), *accidĕre*, *evenire* (= to happen) **occurrence,** n *casus*, *-ūs*, *res gesta* (= thing that has happened, in context also *res*), *eventum* (= event)

ocean, n *oceanus*

ochre, n *ochra* (Plin)

octagon, n *octogōnos* (*octag*) **octagonal,** adj *octagōnos*, *-on*

octave, n (in music) 1, = an interval of an eighth, *diapāson*, 2, = the eight notes, *octo voces* or *soni*

octennial, adj *octo annorum*

October, n (*mensis*) *October*

octogenarian, n *octoginta annorum* (in gen), *octoginta annos natus* (= 80 years old)

ocular, adj by *oculus* (e g to give — evidence of, *alci alqd ante oculos proponĕre*); see VISIBLE **oculist,** n *medicus qui oculis medetur*

odd, adj 1, = uneven, *impar* (e g number), 2, = remaining, left over; — moments, *tempora subsiciva* (*subsec*), see SURPLUS, 3, see SINGULAR, STRANGE, EXTRAORDINARY **oddity,** n 1, = ODDNESS; 2, = queer fellow, *homo mirabiliter moratus* **oddness,** n. see SINGULARITY, etc. **odds,** n see ADVANTAGE, SUPERIORITY

ode, n *ode* or *oda* (late), *carmen*, see SONG, POEM

odious, adj *odiosus* (= hateful), *invisus* (= detested), *invidiosus* (= exciting envy and dislike), *offensus* (of what has given offence and is therefore hated), to be —, *odium* or *invidiam habēre* (of things), not to be —, *odii* or *invidiae nihil habēre* (of persons and things), to be — to anyone, *alci esse odiosum* or *invisum* or *offensum*, *alci esse odio* or *in odio*, *apud alqm esse in odio*, *alci esse invidiae* Adv *odiose*, *invidiose* **odiousness,** n *odium*, or render by ODIOUS **odium,** n *invidia*

odour, n = smell, *odor*, see SMELL **odoriferous, odorous,** adj † *suaveolens*, † *odorus*, *odoratus* (= sweet-smelling, poet)

Odyssey, n *Odyssēa*

of, prep , by the genitive, after a verb or an adjective by the case or preposition the Latin word requires, after partitive words, including comparatives and superlatives, by the genit or a prep according to the rules of syntax, by an adjective (e g a basin — marble, *labrum marmoreum*), this preposition is sometimes used for others (e g a temple constructed — (out of) marble, *aedes ex marmore exstructa*; I have heard nothing — (about) that affair, *eā de re nihil audivi*).

off, adv = away from, out of, *ab*, *de*, *ex*, to go —, *decedĕre*, to go — secretly, *subterfugĕre*, to bring —, *auferre*, to slip —, *elabi*, to get —, *evadĕre*, to bear, carry —, *auferre*, to be well —, *divitem* or *locupletem esse*, *alqā re abundare*, to lie — (of geographical position), *adjacēre alci loco*, far —, *longe* or *procul*, to be far —, *longe abesse*

offal, n of meat, perhaps *caro ad vescendum non apta*

offend, v tr *offendere* (= to put a stumbling-block in a person's way), *laedĕre* (= to wound the feelings), *violare* (= to outrage), *pungĕre* (= to sting), *mordēre* (= to bite), without —ing you, *pace tuā dixerim*, to be —ed, *aegre* or *moleste ferre*, to have in it something which —s, *habēre alqd offensionis* **offence,** n 1, = anger, etc , *offensio*, *ira*, to take —, *irasci*, to give —, *laedere*, see ANGER, 2, = a fault, *peccatum*, *delictum*, *culpa*, see FAULT **offender,** n *reus* (= accused person), see CULPRIT **offensive,** adj 1, *quod offensionem alci affert*, *odiosus* (= hateful), *putidus* (= — to good manners), that is more — to me, *id aegrius patior*, see LOATHSOME, ODIOUS, 2, of war, *bellum* alone, except where opposition to defensive is strongly expressed, then by verb (e g *bellum arcebant magis quam inferebant* = they waged a defensive rather than an — war) Adv *putide*, or by adj **offensiveness,** n by adj

offer, I. v tr *offerre*, *profiteri* (= to propose voluntarily), *polliceri* (= to promise, all *alci alqd*), *porrigĕre* (= to — with the hand held out, e g a small coin, *assem*), *praebēre* (= to hold out, e g *manum*, *os*, then fig = to proffer), *praestare* (= to afford, e g fowls — a lighter kind of food, *aves leviorem cibum praestant*), *dare* (= to give); to — violence to, *vim alci offerre*; to — one's services to anyone, *alci operam suam offerre*, to — one's services in, at anything, *ad rem* or *in alqā re operam suam profiteri*, to — one's goodwill, *studium profiteri*, to — anything to a person of one's own free will, *alqd alci ultro offerre* or *polliceri*, to — battle to the enemy, *hostem ad pugnam provocare*, to — hospitality to anyone, *alqm invitare hospitio* or *in hospitium*, to — up, *afferre* (= to bring as a contribution), *offerre*. II. v intr = to present itself, *offerri*, *dari* (of things, e g of an opportunity), *ob(j)ici* (accidentally), *suppetĕre* (= to be in store, at hand) III. n *condicio* (also = an — of marriage), to make an — to anyone, *condicionem alci ferre*, *deferre* or *offerre* or *proponĕre* **offering,** n. see SACRIFICE

office, n 1, *munus*, *-eris*, n (= function), *officium* (= what one has to do), *partes*, *-ium* (= particular sphere), *provincia* (duty imposed upon one), *sors, -tis*, f. (= duty allotted to one), *locus* (= appointment), *magistratus, -ūs* (= magisterial —, opp. *imperium*, a military command during war), *honos* (honor); that is my —, *hoc meum est*; **2**, = a kindness, *beneficium, officium*; see KINDNESS, DUTY; **3**, = place of business, *domus, -ūs* (irreg.); at anyone's —, *apud alqm*. **officer, 1**, n. = military —, *praefectus militum* or *militaris, praepositus militibus*, or by some special term (e.g. *centurio, tribunus*); naval —, *praefectus classis* or *navis*; **2**, = civil —, rendered by *magistratus, -ūs*; for particular —s, see their titles. **official, I.** adj. = pertaining to a public office, e.g. — report, *lit(t)erae publicae*; to make an — report, *referre de alqâ re, deferre de alqâ re*. **II.** n. = officer, render by OFFICER, or a special title. Adv. *publice, publicâ auctoritate*. **officiate**, v.intr. render by OFFICE, e.g. to — instead of another, *alcjs officio fungi*; see OFFICE. **officious**, adj. *molestus, alcjs studiosus* (= desirous of serving one). Adv. *moleste*. **officiousness**, n. *studium* (towards one, *erga* or *in alqm*).

offing, n. (*mare*) *altum*.

offscourings, n. *purgamenta, -orum* (lit. and fig.).

offspring, n. *progenies, stirps, liberi* (= children).

oft, often, adv. *saepe, saepenumero* (= oftentimes), *crebro* (= repeatedly), *multum* (= many times); to be — with a person, *multum esse cum alqo*; I do a thing —, *soleo alqd facĕre*; also by the adjs. *creber* and *frequens*; see FREQUENT (e.g. he was — in Rome, *erat Romae frequens*); in many cases the idea of — is expressed by frequentative verbs (e.g. to read —, *lectitare*; to visit —, *frequentare*); more —, *saepius, crebrius*; very —, *saepissime, persaepe, creberrime, frequentissime*.

ogle, v.tr. *oculis limis intueri* or *a(d)spicĕre* (= to look sideways).

ogre, n. *umbra quaedam teterrima*.

oil, I. n. *oleum* (in gen., but lit. = olive —), *olivum* (= olive —); belonging to olive —, *olearius*; to paint with — colours, *pigmentum oleatum inducĕre alci rei*. **II.** v.tr. *oleo ungĕre, oleo perfundĕre* (all over). **oilman**, n. (*mercator*) *olearius* (Plin.). **oilpainter**, n. *pictor qui pigmentis oleatis utitur*. **oil-painting**, n. *pictura pigmentis oleatis facta*. **oily**, adj. *olearius* (= of oil), *oleaceus* (= like oil; Plin.), *oleosus* (= full of oil; Plin.).

ointment, n. *unguentum, nardus* (of nard oil); — for the eyes, *collyrium*.

old, adj. = that which has long been, *vetus, vetustus, inveteratus, antiquus* (= ancient), *priscus* (= primitive), *pristinus* (= at the first), *obsoletus* (= gone out of use); in comparative, —er (that which was before another thing), *prior, superior* (e.g. Dionysius the elder, *Dionysius superior*); an — soldier, *veteranus miles*; an — evil, *malum inveteratum*; an — custom, *mos a patribus acceptus*; as applied to men, in the sense of having lived long, *grandis*, comp. *grandior* (with or without *natu*), *aetate gravis* (= weighed down with years), †*grandaevus, vetulus* (contemptuous term); an — man, *senex*; an — woman, *anus, anicula, vetula*; to be of a certain age, *natum esse* (with the time in the accus.); *octo annos natus est*, = he is eight years old, or *octo annorum est*; see ELDERS, ANCIENT. **old age**, n. *senectus, -ūtis*. **old-fashioned**, adj. *obsoletus* (= out of fashion), *antiquus, priscus* (= old). **olden**, adj. *priscus*; see OLD. **older**, comp. *major* (with or without *natu*); the oldest (or eldest), *maximus natu*.

olfactory, adj. *quod ad odorem pertinet*.

oligarchy, n. *paucorum potentia* or *potestas* or *administratio* or *dominatio, respublica quae paucorum potestate regitur* (as a state). **oligarchical**, adj. e.g. to become —, *in paucorum jus ac dicionem cedĕre*.

olive, I. n. *oliva, olea*; —-tree, *olea, oliva*; the wild —-tree, *oleaster*; — grove, *olivetum*; — season, harvest, *oleitas, olivitas*. **II.** adj. *oleagineus*.

Olympiad, n. *Olympias, -iădis*, f. **Olympic**, adj. *Olympicus*; the — games, *Olympia, -orum*.

omelet, n. *laganum*.

omen, n. *omen* (in gen. = a prognostic token), *ostentum* (= a portentous prodigy), *auspicium, augurium* (= augury), *portentum, monstrum, prodigium* (= prodigy). **ominous**, adj. *ominosus*. Adv. *ominose*.

omit, v.tr. **1**, = to neglect, *mittĕre* or *omittĕre alqd*, or with infin.; see NEGLECT; **2**, = to leave out, *omittĕre, praetermittĕre, praeterire, transire* (= to pass over), *intermittĕre* (for a time). **omission**, n. = neglect, *intermissio* (for a time, e.g. of a duty, *officii*); = leaving out, *praetermissio*.

omnipotent, adj. see ALMIGHTY. **omnipresent**, adj. *ubique praesens*. **omnipresence**, n. to feel God's —, *Dei numen et spiritum ubique diffusum sentire*. **omniscient**, adj. *cujus notitiam nulla res effugit, qui omnia videt et audit* (= who sees and hears all things), *omnia providens et animadvertens* (= who foresees and perceives all things; all three of God). **omniscience**, n. by adj.

on, I. prep. of place, *in* with ablat. (e.g. *in saxo*, — the rock; *in terrâ*, — the ground, e.g. *fructus in terrâ est*); *in scaenâ* (*scen-*), — the stage; *in capite*, — the head; *in equo*, — horseback; *in limite*, — the borders; "on" is sometimes rendered by *ex* (e.g. to hang — the tree, *pendĕre ex arbore*); as denoting time, — is expressed by the ablat. without a preposition (e.g. — the fourth day, *quarto die*); = after, by *ex* (e.g. *statim ex consulatu*, — the expiration of his consulship), or by abl. abs.; *a* or *ab* often represents — (e.g. — the side, *a parte*; — the left hand, *ab laeva*; — the wing, *a latere*; to be — anyone's side, *stare ab alqo* [= to take part with one]); bad — the part of = in disposition, *ab ingenio improbus*; = near, or in the direction of, *ad, juxta* (e.g. *ad meridiem*, — the south; *ad Tiberim*, — the Tiber); to speak — or upon anything, *de alqâ re loqui*; — account of, *propter, ob, per alqd, de, pro, prae alqâ re; caus(s)â, gratiâ, ergo* (*alcjs rei*, the two former also with pers. pron., e.g. *meâ gratiâ*, all placed after their case, *ergo* only ante class.); — account of fear, *propter timorem* (*prae metu*); so *propter pecuniam*; *propter hereditatem contentio oritur*, a strife arises — the inheritance; *amicitia propter se expetenda*, friendship is to be sought for — its own account; — account of business I cannot, etc., *per negotia mihi non licet*; — certain reasons, *certis de caus(s)is*; — account of the noise it can scarcely be heard, *prae strepitu vix audiri potest*. **II.** adv. or **onwards**, *porro*. **onward!** interj. *perge, pergite*.

one, adj. as a numeral, *unus, -a, -um*; a certain —, *quidam*; some—, *aliquis*; some — of you, *aliquis ex vobis*; any—, *quispiam* (e.g. *forsitan quispiam dixerit*, any— may perhaps say; so *dicet aliquis forte*, some— will perchance say); each —, *quisque*; after *si, nisi, ne, num, quando, ubi*, and generally in conditional prepositions, even without a conjunction, use *quis* instead of *aliquis* or *quispiam* (e.g. *ubi semel quis pejeraverit, ei postea credi non oportet* = when once any — has sworn falsely, he ought not afterwards to be believed), in negative sentences, and in such as contain a negative sense, "any —" is to be rendered as a noun by *quisquam*, and "any" alone as adjective by *ullus* (e g *estne quisquam omnium mortalium de quo melius existimes tu?* is there any — of all mortals of whom you think better? *sed an est ulla res tanti?* is there anything so important?), "as any —" is rendered *quam qui maxime* (e g *tam sum amicus reipublicae quam qui maxime*, = I am as friendly to the state as any —), no —, *nemo*, — = *alter* when there are only two objects (e g *altero pede claudus*, = lame in — foot); *unus ille*, = that — (e g *unum illud addam*, = I will add only that — thing), *uno verbo*, = in — word, not even —, *ne unus quidem*, *non ullus*, *nemo unus* (= not a single person), not — of us, *nemo de nobis unus*, not — of them, *ii nulli*, — and another, *unus et alter*, *unus alterque* (= both together), some —, several, *non nemo*, *unus et item alter*, — after the other, *alius post alium*, *alius ex alio*, *singuli*, = — by —, — as much as the other, *uterque pariter*, *ambo pariter*, the — . the other, *alter . . . alter*, *hic . . . ille*, *prior . . . posterior*, *alii . . . alii*, *alii . . . pars* (or *partim*), *pars . . . alii*, *quidam . . . alii*, — the other, *alter alterum* (of two), *alius alium* (e g *alter alterum* or *alius alium adjuvat*, = the — assists the other), so *inter se* (e g *timent inter se*, = they fear — another), if "other" refer to a substantive, repeat the substantive (e g *manus manum lavat*, = — hand washes the other, so *civis civi paret*), at — time . . . at another, *alias . . . alias* (e g *alias beatus, alias miser*) — and the same, *unus atque idem*, *unus idemque*, *uno eodemque tempore*, = at — and the same time, it is — and the same, *idem est*, *par est*, — . . . and other, *aliud . . . aliud*, to be — and the same, *nihil differre*, *nihil interesse*, labour and pain are not — and the same, *interest aliqd inter laborem et dolorem*, it is all — to me, *mea nihil interest*, — might have thought, *crederes*, *putares*, — or the other, *alteruter*

once, adv 1, as numeral, *semel*, — and for all, *semel*, — more, *iterum* (= again, for the second time), *denuo*, *de novo* (= anew, afresh), more than —, *semel atque iterum*, *semel iterumve*, *semel et saepius*, *non semel* (= not —, but often, e g *pati aliqd*), — or, at all events, not often, *semel*, *aut non saepe certe*, not —, *non semel*, *ne semel quidem* (= not even —), at —, all at —, *repente*, *subito* (= suddenly, e g why has this been done all at —? *quid repente factum?*), *statim*, *il(l)ico simul* (= at the same time, e g *trium simul bellorum victor*, Liv), all the people at —, *omnes simul* (= at the same time), (*omnes*) *universi*, *cuncti* (together), one at a time (or at —), *singuli*, many at —, *multi simul*, 2 of time, *aliquando*, and after *ne* or *si* simply *quando* (= some time, past or future, which we are not able or willing to specify, e g did you — hear of him? *num et eo audivisti aliquando?*), *quandoque* (= some time or other, e g he will — (i e some time) remember the kindness he received, *quandoque beneficii memor futurus est*), *quondam* (= some time past, e g that virtue — existed in this republic, *fuit ista quondam in hac republica virtus*) *olim* (= at some remote time past or future, opp *nunc*, *nuper*, hence in fables or narratives = — upon a time), — at last, *tandem aliquando*, if —, *si quando* **one-eyed**, adj *uno oculo captus*, *luscus* **oneself**, pron *ipse* **one-sided**, adj see UNEQUAL, UNFAIR

onion, n *caepa* (*caepe*)

only, I. adj *unus*, *solus*, *unicus*, *solus*, *singularis* (also = distinguished), (he said that) he was the — person, etc , who, *unum se ex omni civitate Aeduorum qui* II. adv *solum*, *tantum* (*modo*), not — . . . , but also, *non tantum* (*solum*) . . . , *sed etiam*

onset, onslaught, n *incursio*, see ATTACK, ASSAULT

ontology, n **ontologia* (t t), or by circumloc (e g *scientia illius quod per se ex(s)istit*) **ontological**, adj **ontologicus* (technical)

onward, adv see ON

onyx, n *onyx* (Plin)

ooze, v intr *manare*, † (*de*)*stillare*, † *sudare*, *emanare* (also fig) **oozy**, adj *uliginosus*

opal, n *opalus* (Plin)

opaque, adj *haud pellucidus* or *translucidus*

open, I. adj 1, = not closed (*ad*)*apertus* (= not shut, not cloaked or covered, opp *clausus*, *involutus*), *patens* (= standing — wide —, also = extending far and wide), comb *patens et apertus*, (*pro*)*patulus* (= lying —, free of access), comb *apertus ac propatulus*, *hians* (= wide —, yawning), an — door, *fores apertae* (= not shut), *fores patentes* (= wide —), an — field, *campus apertus* or *patens* (with a distant view), *locus planus* or simply *campus* (= a plain), in the — street, *in aperto ac propatulo loco* (= in an —, public place), *in publico* (= in the middle of the street, in public), the — sea, *mare apertum* (poet *apertus oceanus* = not surrounded by lands), *altum* (= the high sea), — eyes, *oculi patentes*, — mouth, *os hians*, to be, stand —, *apertum esse*, *patēre* (= wide —, fig his ear is — to the complaints of all, *patent aures ejus querelis omnium*), 2, = accessible, e g anything is — to me, *patet mihi aliqd* (e g a post of honour), 3, = manifest, *apertus*, *manifestus*, *clarus* (e g to catch anyone in the — act, *in manifesto facinore deprehendere*, *in re manifestā tenere*), see CLEAR, 4, = candid, *apertus*, *simplex*, *candidus*, see CANDID Adv *aperte*, *manifesto*, *simpliciter*, *candide*, *palam*, *propalam* II. v tr 1, *aperire* (= to uncover, unclose), *patefacere* (= to lay —, both opp to *operire*), *reserare* (= to unbolt, opp to *obserare*), *recludĕre* (= to unlock, opp to *occludĕre*, all these of a door, gate, etc), (*ex*)*pandere* (= to expand, — wide), *evolvĕre*, *revolvere* (= to unroll, e g a book), to — a letter, *lit(t)eras aperire*, *resignare*, *solvĕre*, *insecare*, *incidĕre* (= to cut —), to — one's hand, *digitos porrigere* (opp *digitos contrahĕre*), to — one's eyes, lit *oculos aperire*, fig *meliora alqm docēre*, = to teach anyone better, to — one's ears to flatterers (fig), *aures patefacĕre assentatoribus*, to — a vein, *venam secare*, *incidĕre*, to — the entrance to anything, *aditum ad alqd patefacĕre* (lit and fig), to — a way by force of arms, *iter sibi aperire ferro*, to — one's heart to anyone, *se* or *sensus suos alci aperire*, *se alci patefacĕre*, 2, = to explain, etc , *aperire*, *detegĕre*, *retegĕre* (e g *conjurationem*), *explicare*, *interpretari* (= to expound), see EXPLAIN, 3, med t t , to — the bowels, *alvum de(j)icĕre*, *purgare*, 4, to — a church, etc , *inaugurare*, *consecrare*, *dedicare*, 5, = to begin, *exordiri*, see BEGIN III. v intr *se aperire*, *aperiri* (in gen), *patefieri* (of a gate), *pandi*, *se pandere* (= to — wide, to unfold oneself, also of blossoms, Plin), *discedere* (of heaven, of the earth, etc), *dehiscĕre* (= to burst —, of the earth), to — again (of wounds), *recrudescĕre*, to — out, *patescĕre* (e g *campus*), to — outside, *aperturam habēre in exteriorem partem*

opening, n 1, as an act, *apertio* (*patefactio* only fig = public announcement), the — of the hand, *digitorum porrectio* (opp *digitorum contractio*) also rendered by verbs (e g at the — of the body, *in aperiendo corpore*), 2, = aperture, *apertura* (in architecture), *foramen* (in gen), *os*, *oris*, n (= mouth of a river, etc), to make an — in anything, *alqd aperire* (in gen.), *alqd perforare* (= to make a hole through); to have an —, *patēre* (= to stand open), *hiare* (= to yawn); see HOLE, BREACH, FISSURE; **3,** the — of a church, etc., *consecratio, dedicatio*; **4,** = opportunity, *occasio, opportunitas* (= opportunity); to see a good — in business, etc., *quaestum petĕre*; see GAIN; **5,** = beginning, *initium, exordium*; **6,** med. t.t. — of the bowels, *purgatio* (*alvi*). **openness,** n. *simplicitas* (rare in class. period), †*candor, animus simplex* or *candidus*.

opera, n. *drama* (*-ătis*, n.) *musicum* or *melicum*.

operate, v.intr. **1,** *vim habēre ad alqd* or *in alqâ re*; see ACT; **2,** in war, *rem agĕre*; **3,** in surgery, to — upon, render by *secare alqm* or *alqd* (= to cut a person or thing), *scalpellum admovēre, adhibēre alci rei* (= to apply the lancet to, e.g. a limb, Cels.). **operation,** n. **1,** *res agenda, res gerenda* or *gesta* (= an act either to be performed or already performed), *negotium* (as an obligation undertaken); by the — of anyone, *per* with accus. (= by means of) or *a*(*b*) with ablat. (= by); see PROCESS; **2,** in war, *res bello gerenda*, or in the context *res gerenda* (when the — is not yet performed), *res bello gesta*, or in the context *res gesta* (when performed); plan of —s, *omnis* or *totius belli ratio* (in war); to draw up a plan of —s, *rei agendae ordinem componĕre, totius belli rationem describĕre*; **3,** in surgery, see OPERATE. **operative, I.** adj. see PRACTICAL. **II.** n. see WORKMAN, LABOURER.

ophthalmia, n. *oculorum inflammatio* (Cels.), *lippitudo*.

opiate, n. *medicamentum somnificum* (Plin.).

opinion, n. *opinio, sententia, existimatio, judicium* (= decision), *dogma, -ătis*, n., *praeceptum* or *decretum* or *placitum* (of a philosopher, teacher, etc.; see MAXIM); a false —, *opinio falsa, pravum judicium, error* (= error); false —s, *opiniones falsae, opinionum commenta* (= dreams); a firmly-rooted but false —, *opinio confirmata*; the general —, *opinio vulgaris* or *vulgi, sententia vulgaris*; the general — respecting anything, *omnium opinio de alqâ re*; public —, *existimatio vulgi*; according to the general —, *ad vulgi opinionem, ex vulgi opinione*; in my —, *meâ quidem opinione*, (*ex* or *de*) *meâ sententiâ, ut mihi quidem videtur, ut opinor, ut puto, quantum equidem judicare possum* (= as far as I can judge); to have a correct — of anything, *vere* or *recte judicare de alqâ re*; to form an — of anything merely by guess, *de alqâ re conjecturâ judicare*; to have a good — of anyone, *bene de alqo existimare*; to have a high — of a person or thing, *magnam de alqo habēre opinionem, magna est alcjs de alqâ re opinio*; to have a high (no mean) — of oneself, *multum sibi tribuĕre, se alqm esse putare, magnifice de se statuĕre*; to be of —, *opinionem habēre, opinari*; that is indeed my —, *mihi vero sic placet, sic hoc mihi videtur*; to give one's —, *sententiam dicĕre, dare, sententiam ferre* (by voting tablets), *dico quod sentio, sententiam meam aperio, expono quae mihi videntur* (= I say what I think of a thing); to ask anyone his —, *quaerĕre quid alqs sentiat*; to speak in favour of anyone's —, *in alcjs sententiam dicĕre*; to turn a person from his —, *alqm de sententiâ movēre, deducĕre*; I bring someone over to my —, *alqm in sententiam meam adduco, alqm ad sententiam meam traduco*; to get an — into one's head, *in sententiam venire*. **opinionated,** adj. render by *homo opinionibus inflatus*. **opine,** v.tr. see THINK, IMAGINE.

opium, n. *opium* (*opion*, Plin.).

opponent, n. *adversarius*, in speeches of an advocate *iste*; see ANTAGONIST.

opportune, adj. *opportunus* (in gen.), *commodus* (= convenient), *idoneus* (= suitable); *tempestivus*. Adv. *opportune, commode, tempestive*. **opportuneness,** n. *opportunitas, commoditas* (= advantage). **opportunity,** n. *opportunitas* (in gen.), *occasio* (= unexpected —; *opp.* exists before an action and leads to it, whereas *occ.* presents itself during an action and facilitates it; *occ.* should therefore be used in speaking of the events of a war, etc.), *casus, -ūs* (= a casual —), *potestas, facultas, copia* (all three = suitableness for carrying out anything), *ansa* (lit. = handle, fig. = occasion, in the connexion *ansam praebēre* or *dare alcjs rei* or *ad alqd*; all these nouns are construed with gen. of the object); a good, favourable —, *opportunitas idonea, occasio commoda et idonea, occasio bona et optata, temporis opportunitas, tempus opportunum*, also simply *occasio, opportunitas, tempus*; when the — serves, *per occasionem, occasione datâ* or *oblatâ, si occasio fuerit* or *tulerit*; at the first —, *ut primum occasio* or *potestas data est* (*erit*), *primo quoque tempore dato, ubi primum opportunum* (Sall.); to seek an —, *occasionem quaerĕre* or *circumspicĕre*; to find an — for anything, *alcjs rei* (*faciendae*) *caus*(*s*)*am reperire* (= to find a cause, e.g. for making war, *bellandi*); to seize an —, *occasionem arripĕre*; to avail oneself of an —, *opportunitate* or *occasione uti*; to lose an —, *occasioni deesse, occasionem amittĕre, praetermittĕre, dimittĕre*.

oppose, v.tr. *alqd alci* (*rei*) *ob*(*j*)*icĕre* (lit. and fig. = to oppose anything to anyone or anything), *adversari alci, repugnare alci rei* or *contra alqd* (= to fight against a thing), comb. *adversari et repugnare, resistĕre* (= to resist), *obsistĕre* (= to place oneself against), *obniti* (= to strive against with all one's might), *obesse, obstare* (= to stand in the way); (all the above with dat.); †*obluctari*, †*reluctari*; I don't — it, *per me licet, nihil impedio*; to be —d to each other, *repugnare inter se* (of two things that contradict each other), *obtrectare inter se* (of two rivals in a state); to — in public disputation, *adversario respondēre*. **opposer,** n. see OPPONENT. **opposite,** adj. **1,** *adversus, oppositus, objectus*; an island — to Alexandria, *insula objecta Alexandriae*; — to, *e regione* (with gen. or dat., e.g. us, *nobis*); on, to the — side of, *trans, ultra* (see BEYOND, OVER); **2,** see ADVERSE, CONTRARY. **opposition,** n. **1,** = the act of opposing, *oppositio*, = difference, *repugnantia, discrepantia*; see RESISTANCE; without —, *nemine obloquente*; **2,** = the body of opposers, *pars adversa* (in gen.), or *factio adversa* or *adversaria* (during a revolution); where possible use special terms (e.g. *optimates, -(i)um*, pl. = the Tory —).

oppress, v.tr. *premĕre, opprimĕre, vexare, affligĕre*. **oppression,** n. *vexatio, injuria* (= injustice, e.g. of the authorities, *magistratuum*); — in a state, *dominatio crudelis*; see TYRANNY. **oppressive,** adj. *molestus* (= troublesome), *magnus* (= great), *iniquus* (= unjust), *gravis* (= heavy), — cold, *frigorum vis*; to be burdened with an — debt, *aere alieno premi*; — government, *dominatus* (*-ūs*) *crudelis*. Adv. *moleste, graviter, inique*. **oppressor,** n. *qui dominatum crudelem exercet, tyrannus* (= sole ruler, may at times serve).

opprobrium, n. (*op*)*probrium*; see IGNOMINY. **opprobrious,** adj. *probrosus* (= disgraceful); see IGNOMINIOUS.

optative, adj., the — mood, *modus optativus* (Gram.).

optics, n. *optice, -es*, f. **optical,** adj. in gen. by *oculus* (e.g — deception, *oculorum mendacium*; — nerve, *nervus oculorum*). **optician,** n. *optices gnarus*,

option, n *optio*, (*eligendi*) *optio et potestas*, *potestas optioque* (all = right of choice), *arbitrium* (= free-will), see CHOICE **optional,** adj, render by *alcjs rei eligendae optionem alci dare*, *alci permittĕre arbitrium alcjs rei*, *facĕre alci potestatem optionemque ut eligat*, *facĕre alci arbitrium in eligendo*

opulent, adj *opulentus*, see RICH, WEALTHY **opulence,** n *opulentia*, see RICHES, WEALTH

or, conj *aut* (excludes one or other of the suppositions expressed, e g here, soldiers, we must conquer — die, *hic vincendum aut moriendum, milites, est*), *vel* (implies that it is indifferent which of two or more than two things is chosen, considered by themselves they may be of the same or a different kind If several ideas are proposed, *vel* generally denotes a climax, = "— even," e g. — shall I say even, *vel dicam*, — rather, *vel potius*, — even indeed, *vel etiam*), *ve* (enclit, generally separates single words, seldom sentences, and expresses that the nominal or real difference is not very great, e g merriment — laughter, *hilaritas risusve*, hence with numerals it is = "— at most," e.g four — five each, *quaterni quinive*), *sive*, *seu* (arising from *vel* and *si*, always with a verb expressed or understood, implying that two or more expressions amount to the same, or that the speaker is undecided about them, and leaves the choice to others, e g the mother — the stepmother, *mater seu noverca*, be it accidental, — intentionally, *sive casu sive consilio*), in negative sentences the disjunctive particles are generally changed into *neque* or *neve* (e g laziness — idle dreaming is out of place here, *nihil loci est segnitiae neque socordiae*), — not, *neve*, *neu* (after *ut* or *ne* and a verb), — at least, *aut certe* (or *aut* alone), *vel certe*, — rather, — more correctly, *vel ut verius dicam*, *atque adeo* (= nay even), or simply *aut*, either —, *aut* *aut*, *vel* *vel*, *sive* *sive* (with the distinction stated above), e g they thought either to induce the Allobrogians by persuasion, — to compel them by force, to allow, etc, *Allobrogibus sese vel persuasuros existimabant, vel vi coacturos, ut paterentur*, etc (i e it was indifferent to them which way they did it); the laws of the Cretans, whether given by Jupiter — Minos, educate youth by means of physical exercise, *Cretum leges, quas sive Juppiter sive Minos sanxit, laboribus erudiunt juventutem*, respecting "— in double questions, see WHETHER

oracle, n *oraculum* (in gen), *sors oraculi* or, in the context, simply *sors* (lit = by drawing lots, then in gen = prophecy), *responsum oraculi* or *sortium*, or *responsum* alone in the context (as answer to a question), to give an —, *oraculum dare* or *edĕre*, to pronounce anything as an —, *alqd oraculo edĕre*, to seek an —, *oraculum* or *responsum* (as answer to a question), *petĕre* (from someone, *ab alqo*), to seek an — at Delphi (through ambassadors), *mittĕre Delphos consultum* or *deliberatum*, according to an —, *oraculo edito*; = the place where an — was given, *oraculum* (also fig of any place we seek for obtaining advice, e g a lawyer's house is an — for the whole state, *domus juris consulti est oraculum totius civitatis*), god of an —, *deus qui oracula edit* **oracular,** adj *qui oracula edit*

oral, adj *praesens*, to have — communication, *coram sermonem cum alqo habēre*, or *praesens cum praesenti colloqui*

orange, n *malum aurantium* (Linn)

oration, n *oratio*, *contio* (before a popular meeting) **orator,** n *orator* **oratorical,** adj *oratorius* **oratory,** n. 1, *doctrina dicendi* (Cic), *ratio dicendi*, *ars oratoria* (Quint); see RHETORIC, 2, = house for prayer, *aedes sacra*

orb, n *sphaera*, *globus*, *orbis* **orbed,** adj *in orbem circumactus* **orbit,** n in astronomy, *orbis*, -is, m, or less exactly *cursus*, -ūs, *circulus*, *ambitus*, -ūs, comb *circulus et orbis*

orchard, n *pomarium*

orchestra, n 1, = the place, *suggestus* (-ūs) *canentium*, 2, = the music, *symphonia*, = the singers, *symphoniaci*, to sing with the accompaniment of the —, *ad symphoniam canĕre*, the accompaniment of the —, *symphonia*

orchid, n. *orchis* (Plin)

ordain, v tr 1, see DECREE, ESTABLISH, APPOINT, INSTITUTE, 2, *in sacerdotum numerum recipĕre*, *ordinare* (Eccl) **ordinance,** n see DECREE, EDICT, RULE **ordination,** n. *ritus quo alqs in sacerdotum numerum recipitur*, *ordinatio* (Eccl)

ordeal, n 1, **judicium Dei* (Med Lat), 2, fig by circumloc, one who has passed through many —s, *multis periculis spectatus*, see PROOF.

order, I. n 1, *ordo*, -ĭnis, m, the — of words in a sentence, *verborum quasi structura*, to set in —, *disponĕre*, *digerĕre*, to march in —, *compositos et instructos procedĕre*, to march without —, *sine ordine iter facĕre*, in, according to —, *ordine*, *ex ordine*, *per ordinem*, out of —, *extra ordinem* (generally = in an extraordinary way), = regular mode of proceeding, acting, *disciplina bona*, love, spirit of —, *bonae disciplinae studium*, — in one's mode of living, *certus vivendi modus ac lex*, to live according to —, *vitae institutum* or *rationem servare*, *a vitae ratione non discedĕre*, — in one's affairs *rerum suarum modus quidam et ordo*, to keep anyone in —, under strict discipline, *algm severā disciplinā coercēre*, *algm in officio continēre* (in submission), 2, = division, class, — in architecture, *columnarum genus*, -ĕris, n, the Doric —, *columnae Doricae*, see CLASS, KIND, RANK, 3, = rank, *ordo* (e g *senatorius*, *equestris*), = fraternity, *collegium*, an — of knights, *ordo equestris*, 4, = command, *jussum*, *mandatum*, *imperatum* (= military —), *edictum* (= decree), *senatus consultum* (= — of Parliament), *praeceptum* (= maxim), to follow an —, *jussum exsequi*, to reject an —, *jussum spernĕre*, *abnuĕre*, to execute, accomplish an —, *jussum efficĕre*, *patrare*, *peragĕre*, see COMMAND, DECREE, PRECEPT, 5, in business, *mandatum* (= commission), to give an — at a shop, *alqd emĕre* "In — to or that" is rendered by *ut* or *qui* with subj or by the fut act part, e g we eat in — to live, but we do not live in — to eat, *edimus ut vivamus, sed non vivimus ut edamus*, he sent an ambassador in — to make inquiry, *legatum misit qui rogaret*, by the gerundive, or by the gerundive in *di* with *caus(s)a*, e g Antigonus handed over the body of Eumenes to his friends in — to bury him, *Antigonus Eumenem mortuum propinquis ejus sepeliendum tradidit*, he sent off three legions (in —) to procure forage, *pabulandi caus(s)a tres legiones misit*, Gracchus marched out with the legions in — to devastate Celtiberia, *Gracchus duxit ad depopulandam Celtiberiam legiones*, by the supine in *um* after verbs of motion (e g they came in — to ask, *venerunt rogatum*), "in — not to" is rendered by *ne* with subj (e g in — not to say, mention it, *ne dicam*, *ne commemorem*) **II.** v tr 1, = to arrange, *ordinare*, *componere*, *disponĕre*, see above, 2, = to command, *jubēre*, *praecipĕre* (= to enjoin), *imperare*, *praescribĕre* (= to direct prescribe) *edicĕre ut* (= to decree), to

— the army to any place, *exercitum in alqm locum indicĕre*; to — a person to prepare dinner, *cenam (caen-) alci imperare*; he —ed his soldiers not to, etc., *militibus suis jussit, ne*, etc. (with subj.). **orderly, I.** adj. = well arranged (of things), *compositus, dispositus, descriptus* (= arranged with precision), *honestus* (= honourable), *modestus* (= unassuming), *diligens, accuratus* (= painstaking), *sobrius* (= temperate); see METHODICAL. **II.** n. perhaps *minister* (= servant), or better *optio* (= adjutant).

ordinal, I. adj., — number, *numerus ordinalis* (Gram.). **II.** n. *formula sacrorum*. **ordinance,** n. see EDICT, DECREE.

ordinary, I. adj. **1,** *usitatus* (= usual), *cot(t)idianus* (*quoti-*, = daily), *vulgaris, communis* (= belonging to all); **2,** = mediocre, *mediocris*; see CUSTOMARY, COMMON, REGULAR, USUAL. **II.** n. **1,** see JUDGE, CHAPLAIN; **2,** = meal, *cena*. **ordinarily,** adv. *ferme, fere.*

ordnance, n. see ARTILLERY.

ordure, n. *stercus, -ŏris*, n.

ore, n. *aes.*

oread, n. *oreas.*

organ, n. **1,** in anatomy; — of the voice, *vox*; interior —s of the body, *viscera, -um*; the — of speech, *lingua*; see MEANS, INSTRUMENT; **2,** in music, **organum pneumaticum* (the nearest class. equivalent is perhaps *lyra* = lyre). **organic,** adj. (e.g. — bodies, *animantia, -ium*, or *nascentia, -ium*; — disease, *vitium naturae*, or *insitum*); see NATURAL. Adv. *naturâ, per naturam*. **organize,** v.tr. *ordinare, constituĕre, componĕre* (= to arrange); to — a state, *civitatis statum ordinare, describĕre, rempublicam constituĕre* or *componĕre, rempublicam legibus temperare*; a well-—d state, *civitas bene constituta, civitas legibus temperata, civitas quae commodius rem suam publicam administrat*. **organisation,** n. *descriptio, temperatio*; — of the body, *corporis temperatio, natura et figura corporis*; — of the state, republic, *reipublicae forma*. **organism,** n. *compages, -is* (= framework, e.g. *corporis*), *natura* (= nature), *figura, forma* (= form), comb. *natura ac figura*.

orgies, n. *bacchanalia, -ium*; see REVELRY.

Orient, n., **Oriental,** adj. see EAST, EASTERN.

orifice, n. see HOLE.

origin, n. *origo, ortus, -ūs, fons, -ntis*, m. (= source), *principium* (= first beginning), *caus(s)a, figura* (= cause), *unde fit alqd* (= whence a thing arises); to derive its — from, *ortum* or *natum esse ab alqâ re*; the — of the soul is not of this world, *animarum nulla in terris origo inveniri potest*; see BEGINNING, BIRTH, CAUSE, SOURCE. **original, I.** adj. **1,** *primus, principalis* (= the first, e.g. cause, *caus(s)a*, meaning, *significatio*; *primigenius*, ante and post class.), *pristinus* (= former), *nativus* (= natural, e.g. barrenness, *sterilitas*); **2,** = one's own, *proprius* or (*sui*) *ipsius*, = new, *novus*, or perhaps *mirus* (= wonderful); a history from — sources, *historia ab ipsis temporibus repetita*; **3,** = clever, *ingeniosus*; — genius, *ingenium, indoles, -is*. Adv. *initio, principio* (= at the beginning), *primum, primo* (= at first), *mirum in modum* (= wonderfully). **II.** n. Cic. uses ἀρχέτυπον, and Pliny *archetypum*; = — text, *chirographum* (= the author's own manuscript), *exemplum* (= pattern in general); in a metaphysical sense, *species* (= an ideal, first in Cic. for the Platonic ἰδέα). **originality,** n. render in gen. by ORIGINAL; — of genius, *proprietas* (= peculiarity), *indoles, -is* (= natural talent); see ORIGINAL, I. **originate, I.** v.tr. see CREATE, PRODUCE, BEGIN. **II.** v.intr. to — in or from a thing, *(ex)oriri ab alqâ re, emanare* or *fluĕre de* or *ex alqâ re, proficisci ab alqâ re* (= to proceed, spring from), *fieri* or *effici* or *sequi* or *consequi ex alqâ re* (= to be the consequence of); to — with a person, *originem accepisse ab alqo*. **originator,** n. *auctor*; see AUTHOR.

orisons, n. *prĕces, -um*, f.

ornament, I. n. *decus, -ŏris*, n. (= adorning by its innate beauty), *ornatus, -ūs* (= ornaments in gen., then of speech, *afferre ornatum orationi*, Cic.), *ornamentum* (by its lustre and costliness; both of persons and things), comb. *decus et ornamentum, insigne* (= honorary decoration, of things), comb. *insigne atque ornamentum*; *lumen* (lit. = light, fig. what constitutes the excellence, glory, i.e. of persons or towns), comb. *lumen et ornamentum*, or *decus et lumen*; the —s in the temples, *decora et ornamenta fanorum*; Pompey, the — of the state, *Pompeius, decus imperii*; the —s of the republic, *lumina civitatis*; Corinth, the — of all Greece, *Corinthus, Graeciae totius lumen*; virtue is the only real —, *verum decus in virtute positum est*; to be the — of our age (of persons), *exornare nostrae aetatis gloriam*; to be an — to any person or thing, *alci* or *alci rei decori* or *ornamento esse, decus afferre alci* or *alci rei*. **II.** v.tr. *(ex)ornare, decorare*; see ADORN. **ornamental,** adj., render by verbs. **ornate,** adj. *(per)ornatus*; an — style, *nitidum quoddam verborum genus et laetum*; or *genus orationis pictum et expolītum*. Adv. *ornate.*

ornithology, n. by *aves, -ium*, f. (= birds, e.g. a book on —, *liber de avibus scriptus*).

orphan, I. n. *orbus*, fem. *orba* (= bereft of parents), an — in respect of father, mother, *orbus (orba) patre, matre*; —s, *orbi*; to become an —, *orbari parentibus*; asylum for —s, *orphanotrophium* (Jct.). **II.** adj. *orbus, orbatus, parentibus orbatus* (= bereft of parents).

orthodox, adj. *orthodoxus* (Eccl.), *veram Christi legem sequens, legis Christianae studiosus* (both of persons), *legi Christianae conveniens* (of things, e.g. doctrine). **orthodoxy,** n. *orthodoxia* (Eccl.), *in Christianam legem studium.*

orthoepy, n. *vera loquendi ratio.*

orthography, n. *recte scribendi scientia* (= knowledge of —), *formula ratioque scribendi* (as a system, Quint.).

oscillate, v.intr. **1,** lit. *agitari*; **2,** fig. see DOUBT, HESITATE. **oscillation,** n. **1,** *agitatio*; **2,** *dubitatio.*

osier, I. n. *vimen.* **II.** adj. *vimineus.*

osprey, n. *ossifragus* (Plin.).

osseous, adj. *osseus* (Plin.).

ossify, I. v.tr. *in os mutare.* **II.** v.intr. *in os mutari* or *transire.* **ossification,** n. use verb.

ostensible, adj. *simulatus, fictus* (= feigned). Adv. *simulate, ficte, per speciem.* **ostentation,** n. *sui jactatio, ostentatio, venditatio.* **ostentatious,** adj. *gloriosus, jactans.* Adv. *gloriose.*

ostler, n. *agaso*; see GROOM.

ostracism, n. *testarum suffragia, -orum*, of the Athenian custom; = expulsion, in gen. by *expelli.*

ostrich, n. *struthiocamēlus* (Plin.).

other, adj. *alius* (in gen.), *alter* (the — one of the two, opp. *uterque*, = both; also indefinitely = another, but only as a second party, e.g. if you enter into an agreement with an —, *si cum altero contrahas*), *ceteri, rel(l)iquus*, = the — (*ceteri* represents the — part as acting reciprocally with the first, *reliquus* or *reliqui*, simply = remainder, the nom sing masc *ceterus* not used, sing in gen rare), *secundus* (= second), *diversus* (= quite different), *alienus* (= belonging to someone else), —s, *alii*, the —s, *ceteri*, *reliqui* If — = one of the same or a similar kind, we use *alter* or *novus* (e g another Hannibal, *alter Hannibal*, another Camillus, *novus Camillus*), all —s, *omnes alii*, *ceteri* (= all the remainder), on the — hand, *rursus* (= again), *e contrario* (= on the contrary) **otherwise,** adv *aliter* (also = in the other case), *alioqui(n)* (= in other respects), *cetera*, *ceteroqui(n)* (= in other respects), *quod nisi ita est* or *fit*, *quod nisi ita esset* (= if this be, were not so, in hypothetical sentences), see ELSE

otter, n *lutra* (*lyt-*, Plin)

ottoman, n *lectus*, see COUCH

ought, v aux *debēre*, or by gerund or gerundive (e g *virtus colenda est*, = virtue — to be practised, *parendum est mihi*, I — to obey), by *oportet*, by *officium est* or *est* only with gen (see MUST), or by *licet* (of persons, e g you — not to have done that, *non tibi licebat hoc facĕre*), you either — not to have commenced the war at all, or you — to have carried it on in a manner befitting the dignity of the Roman people, *aut non suscipi bellum oportuit*, *aut pro dignitate populi Romani geri*, you — to have taken this road, *haec via tibi ingredienda erat*, upon him whom you — to have honoured as a father, you have heaped all kinds of insults, *omnibus eum contumeliis onerasti quem patris loco colĕre debebas*, — to have been, etc, is expressed by past tense of *debēre* or *oportet* with pres infin (e g I — to have gone, *ire debui*), see MUST, OBLIGE

ounce, n *uncia*, half —, *semuncia*, two —s, *sextans*, three —s, *triens*, four —s, *quadrans*, five —s, *quincunx*, six —s, *semis*, seven —s, *septunx*, eight —s, *bes*, nine —s, *dodrans*, ten —s, *dextans*, eleven —s, *deunx*, twelve —s, *as*

our, pron adj *noster* — people, *nostri* (= those of — party, household, country, etc), *nostrates* (= — countrymen), — Cicero just mentioned, *hic*, *ille*, for — sake, *nostra* (or *nostri*) *caus(s)a*, *propter nos*, for — part *per nos* (e g for — part, as far as we are concerned, it shall be allowed, *per nos licitum erit*), of — country, *nostras* **ourselves,** pron see WE, SELF.

ousel, n *merula*

out, I. adv *extrinsecus* (opp *intrinsecus*, = in, on the inside), — or —wards may be also rendered by *foris*, *foras*, *peregre*, to be —, *foris esse*, to go —, *exire foras* (= out of doors), to work —, *perficĕre*, to breathe —, *exspirare*, *respirare*, to blow —, *efflare*, to break —, *ex loco*, *vinculo carceris rumpĕre*, to break — in anger, *stomachum*, *iram effundĕre*, a fire breaks —, *incendium oritur*, to break — into laughter, *in risus* (or *cachinnos*) *effundi*, to break — into reproaches, *ad verborum contumeliam descendĕre*, in comp by *e(x)* (e g *excogitare*, to think —, *exire*, to go —), to spread —, *(ex)pandĕre* **II. (of),** prep (denoting a coming forth from locally), *e* or *ex* (e g *exire ex navi*, to go — of the ship, so *ex urbe*, *e vita*, *extorquēre arma e manibus*, *e(j)icĕre algm e civitate*, *milites ex eo loco deducĕre*) *extra* (properly = —side of, opp *intra*, = within, e g *aut intra muros aut extra*, so *extra limen*, *ordinem*, *noxiam*, *teli jactum* (= — of range), *consuetudinem*, *numerum*, etc) Sometimes "— of" has no corresponding Latin term, the relation being indicated by the case (e g *navi egredi*, = to go — of the vessel; so with the names of towns, and with *domus*), —, as signifying the cause, *e*, *ex*, *a*, *ab*, also *propter* and *prae* (e g — of fear, *prae metu*), or by a participle and the ablative, *metu coactus* (so *pudore adductus*), to be — of one's mind, *sui* or *mentis non compotem esse*, *non apud se esse* (Ter), to be — of one's mind for joy, *laetitia ex(s)ultare*, *efferri*, from anger, *prae iracundia non esse apud se*, from fright, *metu exanimatum esse*, to put a person — of his mind, *perturbare algm*, to be put — of one's mind, *perturbari*, to go — of the country, *peregre abire*

outbid, v tr *licitatione vincĕre*

outbreak, n *eruptio* (= act of breaking forth), *initium*, *principium* (= beginning, e g *belli*, — of war), *seditio* (= sedition), — of illness, *morbo opprimi*, *affligi*

outcast, n *exsul*, *extorris*, *profugus*

outcry, n *clamor*, *vociferatio*, *voces*, expressing disapproval, *acclamatio*

outdo, v tr *superare*, *vincĕre algm*

outer, adj *exterus* (*exterae nationes*), *externus* (*res externae*, Cic; so *externa*, *-orum* = outer things, opp *interiora*), see EXTERIOR, EXTERNAL

outface, v tr *impudentia vincĕre*

outflank, v tr *circumire*, *circumvenire*

outgrow, v tr use circumloc (e g he outgrew his clothes, *illi vestitus grandior jam opus erat*)

outhouse, n *pars aedibus adjecta*

outlandish, adj *peregrinus*, *barbarus*

outlast, v tr *diutius durare*

outlaw, I. n *proscriptus*, *relegatus*, *ex(s)ul* (= exile) **II.** v tr *proscribĕre*, *aquâ et igni alci interdicĕre* **outlawry,** n *proscriptio*, *aquae et ignis interdictio*

outlay, n *sumptus*, *-ūs*, see EXPENSE

outlet, n *exitus*, *-ūs*, *egressus*, *-ūs* (in gen), *effluvium* (Plin, Tac, rare), *emissarium*, *os*, *oris*, *ostium*, *caput* (of rivers)

outline, I. n *lineamentum* (e g *tu operum lineamenta perspicis*, Cic); the —s of a face, *lineamenta* (e g *similitudo oris vultusque ut lineamenta*, Liv, compare *animi lineamenta sunt pulchriora quam corporis*) *adumbratio* (= sketch) **II.** v tr *describĕre*, *adumbrare* (lit and fig), see SKETCH

outlive, v tr *alci superesse*

outlook, n 1, to have an — of a place, *ad*, *in* or *inter algd spectare*, 2, to be on the —, *omnia circumspectare*, 3, fig *spes* (e g *bona* = good —, *nulla* = poor —)

outlying, adj *longinquus* (= far removed); — districts, *regiones quae circa algm locum sunt*

outnumber, v tr *numero* (*numeris*) or *computatione superare*, *multitudine superare*

outpost, n *statio* (of troops), *propugnaculum* (sc *navium*, *propugnaculum oppositum barbaris*, *propugnacula imperii*)

outrage, I. n *injuria*, *contumelia* (= affront) **II.** v tr *alci afferre injuriam*, *algm injuriâ afficĕre*, *probris conficĕre* **outrageous,** adj *immanis*, *contumeliosus*, *immoderatus*, *indignus*, see MONSTROUS Adv. *indigne*, *immoderate*

outride, v tr *equitando algm superare* **outriders,** n *qui alci equitando praecunt* or *algm equitando deducunt*

outright, adv. *penitus*, *prorsus*, *omnino*

outrun, v tr *algm cursu superare* or *vincĕre*.

outsail, v tr *navigando superare algm*

outset, n *initium*, see BEGINNING

outside, I. adj *externus*, as a noun, the —, *externa*, *-orum*, *superficies* (= the surface, e g *aquae*, *testudinum*, *corporum*), *forma*, *species*

(= show; lit. and fig.). **II.** adv. *extra, extrinsecus, foris* (with verbs of rest); *foras*, with verbs of motion); on the —, *extrinsecus*.

outskirts, n. see SUBURB.

outspoken, adj. see FRANK.

outspread, adj. *passus*; with — sails, *passis* or *plenis velis*; with — hands (in entreaty), *supplicibus manibus*.

outstanding, adj. of debt, by *aes alienum*; see DEBT.

outstrip, v.tr. **1**, *alqm cursu superare* or *vincĕre, alqm* † *praevertĕre*; **2**, fig. see EXCEL.

outtalk, v.tr. *multiloquio vincĕre alqm.*

outvote, v.tr. *alqm suffragiis vincĕre.*

outwalk, v.tr. *ambulando alqm praevertĕre.*

outward, **I.** adj. *exterus, externus*; an — show, *species*. **II.** adv. *extra, extrinsecus*; a ship — bound, *navis ad exteras nationes destinata*; see OUTSIDE, II.

outweigh, v.tr. *graviorem esse alqâ re* (lit.); *vincĕre* (fig. of opinions); Cato alone —s in my opinion hundreds of thousands, *unus Cato mihi pro centum millibus est*; *praeponderare* (lit. and fig.; rare).

outwit, v.tr. *circumvenire* (= to deceive); see DECEIVE.

outworks, n. *munimenta* (*exteriora*).

oval, **I.** adj. *ovatus* (= like an egg, Plin.). **II.** n. *figura ovata*.

ovation, n. *ovatio* (= a Roman lesser triumph); fig. to receive an —, *magnis clamoribus excipi*.

oven, n. *furnus* (for baking), *clibănus* (= small portable —).

over, **I.** adv. *super, supra*; to be — (= remaining), *superesse, rel(l)iquum* (*relic-*) *esse*; = to be done with, *actum esse de alqo* or *alqâ re*; when the battle was —, *confecto proelio*; — and — again, *etiam atque etiam*; — much, *praeter modum*; often expressed in comp., — timid, *timidior*; a little — or under, *haud multo plus minusve*. **II.** prep. *super, supra* with accus. (*super* also with ablat., but chiefly poet.), *trans* (= across) with accus., *amplius* (with numerals; e.g. — a hundred, *amplius centum*); *inter coenam* (*coen-*), — dinner; *per* with accus. (= through, of place); to make a bridge — a river, *pontem in flumine facĕre*.

overawe, v.tr. *alqm metu complēre, terrēre, coërcēre, comprimĕre*.

overbalance, v.tr. *praeponderare*; see OUTWEIGH.

overbear, v.tr. *alqm vincĕre, superare, comprimĕre, coërcēre*. **overbearing**, adj. *arrogans, insolens, superbus*.

overbid, v.tr. *pluris licitari*.

overboard, adj. to throw anything —, *alcjs rei jacturam facĕre*; to fall —, *in mare excidĕre*.

overboiled, adj. (or part.) *nimis coctus*.

overbold, adj. *temerarius, audax*.

overburdened, adj. *praegravatus, nimio onere oppressus*.

overcast, adj. † (*ob*)*nubilus* (of the sky).

overcharge, v.tr. **1**, = to put too high a price, *nimio vendĕre*; **2**, = to load too heavily, *nimio pondere onerare*; to — the stomach, *se vino ciboque onerare*.

overcoat, n. *amiculum*; see CLOAK.

overcome, v.tr. (*de*)*vincĕre, superare, profligare*; not to be —, *inexpugnabilis* (both of place and persons), *insuperabilis, invictus*.

overdo, v.tr. *nimio labore se fatigare* (= yourself); to — a thing, *nimium laborem in rem conferre, modum excedĕre in alqâ re*; = to overcook, *nimis coquĕre*.

overdraw, v.tr. **1**, see EXAGGERATE; **2**, to — an account, *aes alienum contrahĕre* or *conflare* (= to incur debt).

overdress, v.tr. *nimis splendide se ornare*.

overdrink, v.intr. *vino se obruĕre*.

overdrive, v.tr. (*de*)*fatigare*.

overdue, adj. *pecunia quam alqs jam solvĕre debuit*.

overeat, v.reflex. *helluari* (= to be gluttonous).

overfill, v.tr. *supra modum implēre*.

overflow, **I.** n. *inundatio fluminis*, (*colluvio*; the river produces an —, *flumen extra ripas diffluit, flumen alveum excedit*. **II.** v.tr. *inundare*; the Tiber —ed the fields, *Tiberis agros inundavit*. **III.** v.intr. **1**, *effundi*, † *inundare*; the fountain —s, *fons exundat*; **2**, fig. *alqâ re abundare, suppeditare, redundare*.

overgrow, v.intr. **1**, see OUTGROW; **2**, to be — with foliage, *frondibus contextum, obsitum esse*.

overhang, v.intr. *imminēre, impendēre*.

overhasty, adj. *praeproperus*. Adv. *praepropere*.

overhaul, v.tr. see EXAMINE, INSPECT.

overhead, adv. *supra, desuper, insuper*; see OVER, I.

overhear, v.tr. *excipĕre, subauscultare*.

overheat, v.tr. *alqd nimis cal(e)facĕre*; to — oneself, by *sudare* (= to perspire).

overjoyed, adj. *laetitiâ affectus* or *ex(s)ultans*.

overland, adj. *terrâ* (opp. *mari*).

overlap, v.tr. *alci rei imminēre* or *impendēre* (= to overhang).

overlay, v.tr. **1**, = to smother, *incubando opprimĕre* or *suffocare*; **2**, = to spread over, *alqd alci rei inducĕre*, † *illinĕre*; to — with gold, *inaurare*.

overload, v.tr. *nimis* or *nimium onerare, onus nimis grave alci* (*rei*) *imponĕre*. **overloaded**, adj. *nimis oneratus, pondere nimis gravi oppressus*; to be — with business, *negotiis obrutum esse*; see OVERCHARGE.

overlong, adj. *praelongus*.

overlook, v.tr. **1**, = to oversee, *servare, observare* (= to watch), *custodire* (= to guard), *praeesse alci* or *alci rei* (= to superintend), *inquirĕre in alqd, scrutari, inspicĕre alqd* (= to examine thoroughly); **2**, = to command a view of, *alci rei imminēre, alqd prospicĕre* (e.g. *ex superioribus locis prospicĕre in urbem*); **3**, = to pardon, *alci rei* or *alcjs alci rei veniam dare* or *condonare, alci rei* or *alci alqd ignoscĕre, co(n)nivēre in alqâ re* (= to shut one's eyes, wink at); see INDULGENCE, PARDON; **4**, = to pass by inadvertently, *praeterire, omittĕre, praetermittĕre* (= to leave unnoticed; also of a fault, to let it pass unpunished). **overlooker**, n. *custos, -odis*, m. and f., *curator, praeses, -idis*, m. and f., *praefectus, exactor* (= one who sees that things are done carefully), *magister, rector* (= instructor), *curator viarum* (= surveyor of the public roads), *aedilis* (in Rome, = superintendent of the public buildings and police).

overmuch, **I.** adj. *nimius*. **II.** adv. *nimis, nimium*.

overnight, adv. *vesperi* (= in the evening).

overpay, v.tr. *plus quam debetur solvĕre*.

overpeopled, adj. use circumloc. (e.g. *tanta erat multitudo hominum quantae victus non suppeditabat*).

overplus, n see SURPLUS

overpower, v tr *opprimĕre, frangĕre, profligare, vincĕre, debellare* **overpowering**, adj see OVERWHELMING

overprize, v tr *pluris quam par est aestimare*

overrate, v tr *nimium alci rei tribuĕre*, to — oneself, *immodicum sui esse aestimatorem*

overreach, v tr *circumvenire, circumscribĕre, fraude capĕre alqm*, see CHEAT

overripe, adj *qui jam maturitatem excessit*

overrule, v tr, = to bear down, *(de)vincĕre* **overruling Providence**, n *Providentia omnia administrans* or *gubernans*

overrun, v tr 1, = to outrun, *cursu praeterire*, 2, = to swarm over, *(per)vagari*, 3, to be — with (of plants), *alqâ re obsitum esse*

overscrupulous, adj use compar, *diligentior*, etc, see SCRUPULOUS

oversee, v tr *(pro)curare* **overseer**, n *custos, (pro)curator*, — of the highways, *curator viarum*

overshadow, v tr 1, †*obumbrare*, †*inumbrare alqd*, 2, fig *alci rei officĕre*

overshoes, n. *tegumenta calceorum*

overshoot, v tr. *jactu* or *sagittâ scopum transgredi*, to — oneself, *consilio labi*

oversight, n *error, erratum, incuria*, — of a business, *curatio, procuratio, cura*

oversleep, v intr *diutius dormire*

overspread, v tr 1, *obducĕre, inducĕre*, see OVERLAY, 2, see OVERRUN, 2

overstrain, v tr *nimis contendĕre*, to — one's strength, *vires nimis intendĕre*

overt, adj *apertus, manifestus*

overtake, v tr *assequi, consequi*; = to surprise, *opprimere, deprehendĕre alqm, supervenire alci* **overtaken**, adj. *praeventus*, to be — with sleep, *somno opprimi*

overtask, v tr. *majus justo pensum alci in(j)ungĕre*

overtax, v tr *iniquis oneribus premĕre*

overthrow, **I.** v tr 1, = to cast down, *profligare, de(j)icĕre*; 2, = to demolish, *diruĕre, subvertĕre, demoliri*, 3, = to defeat, *(de)vincĕre, prosternĕre, opprimĕre* **II.** n *clades, is, strages, is*

overtop, v tr *eminĕre*, †*supereminĕre*

overture, n 1, *condiciones ad alqd agendum propositae*, — of peace, *pacis condiciones*, to make —s, *condiciones ferre* or *proponĕre*, 2, to an opera, *(dramatis musici) exordium*

overturn, v tr *evertĕre, subvertĕre alqd*

overvalue, v.tr *nimis magni aestimare*

overweening, adj *superbus*, see PROUD

overwhelm, v tr *obruĕre, opprimĕre, demergĕre, (sub)mergĕre* **overwhelmed**, part *obrutus mersus, demersus, submersus*, — with grief, *dolore* or *tristitiâ oppressus* **overwhelming**, adj by superl of adj or circumloc (e g — grief, *magno dolore affectus*)

overwise, adj *qui peracutus videri vult*

overwork, **I.** n *labor immoderatus* **II.** v intr and reflex *nimis laborare*; see WORK

overworn, adj e g — with age, *aetate* or *senio confectus*

overwrought, adj or part *nimis elaboratus* (= wrought too highly), *laboribus confectus* (= worn down by labours)

overzealous, adj *nimis studiosus*

owe, v tr *debēre* (= to be in debt, to anyone, *alci*); to — something to a person, *debēre alci alqd* (in gen, of any kind of obligation, e g. money, *pecuniam*, gratitude, *gratiam*, compassion, *misericordiam*), to — much money, *aere alieno demersum* or *obrutum esse*, to — anyone a great deal, *grandem pecuniam alci debēre* (lit), *multa alci debēre* (fig), owing to, by *per*, it was owing to you, *per te stetit quominus* or *tibi alqd acceptum refero*, or by *propter* with accus or *alcjs beneficio* **owing**, adj see DUE

owl, n *ulula, noctua, strix, gis*, f, *bubo*, like an —, *noctuinus* (e g *oculi*, Plaut)

own, **I.** adj 1, = belonging to one by nature or by one's course of action, *proprius*, but generally by *meus, tuus, suus*, etc, or by *ipsius* or *meus ipsius*, etc (e g it was written by his — hand, *ipsius* (or *suâ ipsius*) *manu scriptum erat*, *ipse scripserat*), I saw it with my — eyes, *ipse vidi, hisce oculis egomet vidi* (Com), I quote the emperor's — words, *ipsa principis verba refero*, through my — fault, *meâ culpâ*, 2, = what we have for our — use, *proprius* (opp *communis* or *alienus*, in Cic with genit, in other writers also with dat), *peculiaris* (of what one has acquired for his — use), *privatus* (of private property, opp *publicus*), *domesticus* (= relating to one's family or home), comb *domesticus et privatus* (e g *domesticae et privatae res*, one's — private matters, opp *publicae*), *privus* (= belonging to any one individual), my, your — people, servants, *mei, tui*, etc, he has taken from us everything that was our —, *ademit nobis omnia quae nostra erant propria* **II.** v tr 1, see ACKNOWLEDGE, CONFESS, 2, see POSSESS, CLAIM **owner**, n *possessor, dominus*, to be the — of anything, *possidēre alqd* **ownership**, n *possessio* (in gen), *dominium* (Jct), *auctoritas* (= right of possession), *mancipium* (= right by purchase), the obtaining of — by long use or possession, *usucapio*

ox, n *bos, bovis*, m and f, a young —, *juvencus*, a driver of —en, *bubulcus* **oxherd**, n. *armentarius*

oyster, n *ostrea*, †*ostreum* **oyster-bed**, n *ostrearium* (Plin) **oyster-shell**, n *testa*

P.

pabulum, n *pabulum*, see FOOD

pace, **I.** n *gradus, ūs, passus, ūs* (= the act of stepping out in walking, in the prose of the golden age only the step, as Roman measure of length = 5 Roman feet) *gressus, -ūs* (= the act of making strides, walk), to keep — with anyone, *alcjs gradus aequare* (lit), *parem esse alci* (fig, = to be equal to anyone), at a quick —, *pleno* or *citato gradu* at a slow —, *tarde, lente*, see STEP **II.** v intr *gradi* (= to walk with an equal and bold step), *vadĕre* (quickly and easily), *incedĕre, ingredi, ambulare, spatiari* (= to walk about), see MARCH, WALK **III.** v tr *passibus metiri alqd* **pacer**, n perhaps *Asturco* (= an Asturian horse)

pacific, adj by *pacis* (e g — propositions, *pacis condiciones*), *pacificus*, †*pacifer*, see PEACEABLE **pacification**, n *pacificatio, compositio, pax* **pacificator**, n *pacificator, pacis auctor* (Liv), *pacis reconciliator* (Liv) **pacify**, v tr *placare* (= a man when angry), to — a country, *pacare*, = to restore peace (e g to a province), *sedare, componĕre*

pack, **I.** v tr 1, *imponĕre in alqd* (= to put or load into), *condĕre in alqd* or *alqâ re* (= to put into anything for the purpose of preservation); to — in a parcel with something else, *alqd in eundem fasciculum addĕre*; to — one's things for a journey, for a march, *sarcinas* or *sarcinulas colligĕre* or *expedire*, *sarcinas aptare itineri*, *vasa colligĕre* (in the camp, of soldiers); to give orders for the troops to — up, *vasa conclamare jubēre*; to — goods, *merces in fasciculos colligĕre*; to — together, *colligĕre* (= to collect in a lump, in a bundle, e.g. one's things, baggage, furniture, *sarcinas*, *vasa*), *colligare*, *alligare*, *constringĕre* (= to tie together, e.g. one's knapsack, *sarcinam*; household effects, *vasa*), *stipare* (= to — closely); to — together in bundles or bales, *in fasciculos*, *in fasces colligare*; to — into a small compass, to crowd, *stipare*, *(co)artare*, *complēre* (= to fill); 2, to — a jury, a meeting, etc., *suos inter judices coetum introducĕre*, etc. **II.** n. 1, = bundle, *fasciculus*, *sarcina*, *sarcinula*; — of cards, *chartae*; 2, = a crowd, *(magna) frequentia (hominum)*; = a mob, *turba*, *grex*, *gregis*, m.; see CROWD; 3, of dogs, *canes*, *-um*. **pack-ass**, n. *asinus clitellarius* (lit.), *homo clitellarius* (fig. of men, = drudge). **pack-horse**, n. *equus clitellarius*. **pack-saddle**, n. *clitellae*. **pack-thread**, n. *linea*. **package**, n. *sarcina*, *sarcinula*, *fasciculus*; see PARCEL, BAGGAGE, LUGGAGE. **packer**, n. *qui alqas res in sarcinam colligit*. **packet**, n. *fasciculus*; = a ship, *navis*; see PARCEL.

pact, n. *pactio*, *pactum* (= agreement entered into between two litigant parties; *pactiŏ*, = the act; *pactum*, = the terms of the agreement); see COMPACT, CONTRACT.

pad, n. see CUSHION, BOLSTER.

paddle, **I.** n. *remus*; see OAR. **II.** v.intr. 1, *navem remo impellĕre*; 2, with the hand, etc., *aquam manu*, etc., *agitare*.

padlock, n. in the context, *claustrum*.

pæan, n. † *paean*.

pagan, adj. *paganus* (Eccl.).

page, n. *puer ex aulâ*, *minister ex pueris regiis*, *puer regius*, *puer nobilis ex regiâ cohorte* (at a king's court), *puer paedagogianus* (Imperial Rome).

page, n. of a book, *pagina*.

pageant, n. *spectaculum* (= show), *pompa* (= procession), *apparatus magnifici* (= great preparations at public processions, etc.). **pageantry**, n. see above.

pagoda, n. *templum* or *aedes*, *-is*, f. (= temple).

pail, n. *situla* (*situlus*); see BUCKET.

pain, **I.** n. *dolor* (in gen., of body and mind), *maestitia* (= grief), *desiderium* (= grief for the absent or the dead); violent —, *cruciatus*, *-ūs* (of body and mind); to cause —, *dolorem facĕre* (*efficĕre*, *afferre*, *commovēre*, *excitare* or *incutĕre*; to anyone, *alci*). **II.** v.tr. *alqm cruciare* or *dolore afficĕre* (lit. and fig.). **III.** v.intr. *dolēre*; see above. **painful**, adj. *vehemens* (= causing violent feeling, e.g. an evil, a wound), *gravis* (= serious, severe, i.e. complaint, wound), *acerbus* (= heartfelt, e.g. death); — sensation, *dolor*; wherever a man is, he has the same — feeling at the complete ruin both of public affairs and of his own private circumstances, *quocumque in loco quisquis est, idem est ei sensus et eadem acerbitas, ex interitu rerum et publicarum et suarum*; that is — to me, *hoc mihi dolet* (ante class.). Adv. *vehementer*, *graviter*, *acerbe*, *dolenter*, *summo* or *magno cum dolore*. **painless**, adj. *sine dolore*, *doloris expers*, *dolore vacuus*, *vacans* or *carens*. Adv. by adj. **painlessness**, n. *indolentia*, or by circumloc. *dolore vacare* or *carēre*, *non* or *nihil dolēre* (e.g. — is, according to Epicurus, the highest pleasure, *summa voluptas est, ut Epicuro placet, nihil dolēre*, or *Epicuro placuit omni dolore carēre summam esse voluptatem*, Cic.). **pains**, n. = toil, *opera* (of one's own), *virium contentio* (= exertion of power), *labor*, comb. *opera et labor* (see LABOUR), *negotium* (from *nec* and *otium*, = absence of leisure, through work that we are executing, etc.; then the performance of the work, particularly of that which causes uneasiness of mind, trouble), *studium* (= zeal, assiduity); with a great deal of —, *non facile*; only with the greatest —, *aegerrime*, *vix* (= hardly); with great —, *multâ operâ*, *magno labore*, *multo labore et sudore*, *multo negotio*; with all possible —, *omni virium contentione*, *omni ope atque operâ*; with very little —, without the least —, *facile*, generally *nullo negotio* or *sine negotio*; carefully, and with great —, *fide et operâ*; to take —, *multam operam consumĕre*; to take — in order to, etc., *operam dare*, *niti*, *eniti*, *contendĕre*, *ut*, etc.; to take all possible — in order to, etc., *omni ope atque operâ* or *omni virium contentione niti* (or *eniti*), *ut*, etc., *contendĕre et laborare*, *ut*, etc., *eniti et contendĕre*, *ut*, etc., *eniti et efficĕre*, *ut*, etc.; see TOIL, TROUBLE, ANXIETY. **painstaking**, adj. *operosus*; see LABORIOUS, INDUSTRIOUS.

paint, **I.** v.tr. 1, *pingĕre* (intr. and tr.), *depingĕre* (tr., = to depict, with the pencil or with words, describe), *effingĕre* (= to portray, with the pencil); to — from nature, from life (in an absolute sense), *similitudinem effingĕre ex vero*; to — anyone's likeness, *alqm pingĕre*; to — anyone's likeness with a striking resemblance, *veram alcjs imaginem reddĕre*; to — anything in different colours and in light sketches, *varietate colorum alqd adumbrare*; 2, = to besmear with colour, *illinĕre alqd alqâ re*, *sublinĕre alqd alqâ re* (= to lay on a ground colour), *inducĕre alqd alqâ re* or *alci rei* (e.g. *parietes minio*, = to — the walls red); with different colours, *coloribus (variare et) distinguĕre*; to — blue, *colorem caeruleum inducĕre alci rei*; all the Britons — their bodies with woad, *omnes se Britanni vitro inficiunt*; to — white (to whitewash), *dealbare* (e.g. *parietem*), *polire albo* (e.g. pillars, *columnas*); to — the face, *fucare*. **II.** n. *pigmentum*, *color*, *fucus* = cosmetic; see COLOUR. **paint-brush**, n. *penicillus*. **painter**, n. *pictor*; a — of houses, *qui (parietes, etc.) colore inducit*. **painting**, n. *pictura* (in gen. also = that which is painted), *ars pingendi* or *picturae* (= art of —, also *pictura*).

pair, **I.** n. *par* (of two persons or things in close connection), *jugum* (lit. = a yoke of oxen; then two persons joined together for an evil purpose, e.g. *jugum impiorum nefarium*, Cic.), *bini* (= two at a time, two together, e.g. *binos [scyphos] habebam*; *jubeo promi utrosque*, I had a — [of glasses]; I want this —); *uterque* (= this —, the — mentioned); see COUPLE, BRACE. **II.** v.tr. *(con)jungĕre*. **III.** v.intr. *jungi*, *conjungi*, *(con)jungĕre*, *coire* (= to copulate).

palace, n. *domus*, *-ūs*, *regia*, or simply *regia* (= royal mansion, *palatium* only in poetry and late prose), *domus*, *-ūs*, f. (house in gen., very often sufficient in the context).

palate, n. *palatum*; a fine —, *subtile palatum*, *doctum et eruditum palatum*; a very fine —, *palatum in gustatu sagacissimum*; he has a fine —, *sapit ei palatum* (Cic.); see TASTE, RELISH. **palatable**, adj. *jucundi saporis* (= of pleasant taste), *jucundus*, *suavis*, *dulcis* (= sweet, pleasant); see SAVOURY, RELISH. **palatal**, adj. *palatilis* (Gram. t.t.).

palatinate, n. * *palatinatus*.

palaver, n. *nugae*; see NONSENSE.

pale, **I.** adj. *pallidus*, *luridus* (= black and

blue), *albus* (=white), *decolor* (=discoloured), — colour, *pallidus color*, *pallor*, to be —, *pallēre*, of colours, expressing shade by *sub* (e g *subflavus*, = — yellow, Suet) **II.** v intr *pallescĕre*, see above, to — before, *alqâ re* or *ab alqo vinci* **paleness,** n *pallor*, *pallidus color*, *macula* †*alba* (= a white spot)

pale, paling, I. n *palus*, -*udis*, f (in gen), *sudes*, -*is*, f (= a stake to prop up trees, in fortification, a pile driven into the ground for defence), *stipes*, -*ĭtis*, m (= stem of a tree used as a stake), *vallus* (= pole for fortifying a rampart, etc., palisade), see STAKE, POST **II.** v tr *ad palum alligare* (trees), to — the vine, *vites palis adjungĕre*, = to surround, *palis cingĕre*, see SURROUND **palisade,** n *vallum*, *palus*, to surround with a —, *vallo munire* or *cingĕre* or *circumdare*, *vallare* **palisading,** n *vallum*, *valli*, see PALE

palette, n *patella* or *discus colorum*

palfrey, n *equus* or *caballus*

palimpsest, n *palimpsestus*

palinode, n *palinodia* (better written as Greek παλινῳδία)

pall, n 1, *pallium*, see MANTLE, 2, = covering thrown over the dead, *tegumentum* or *involucrum feretri*

pall, v intr, to — upon anyone, *alqm alcjs rei taedet*

palladium, n *palladium*

pallet, n = a small bed, *lectulus*, *grabatus*

palliasse, n *lectus stramenticius*

palliate, v tr *alqd excusare*, *extenuare*, to — anything with, *praetendĕre alqd alci rei*, *tegĕre* or *occultare alqd alqâ re*, *excusatione alcjs rei tegĕre alqd* (= to cover, varnish by means of an excuse, Cic), *alqd in alcjs rei simulationem conferre* (= to hide under pretence, Caes), see EXCUSE **palliation,** n use verb (e g the — of his fault, *culpam excusavit*)

pallid, adj. see PALE

palm, I. n 1, *palma*, see HAND, 2, a plant, *palma* (= —-tree, also a branch of it worn in token of victory), to present the — to anyone (as token of victory), *dare alci palmam*, adorned with —, *palmatus* **II.** v tr to — off upon any one, *centonem alci sarcire* (Com), *imponĕre alci* (absolute), *alqd alci supponĕre*, he has —ed anything upon him, *verba illi dedit*, see IMPOSE **palmary,** adj *palmaris* **palmer,** n see PILGRIM **palmistry,** n either use χειρομαντεία in Greek characters, or *ars eorum qui manuum lineamenta perscrutantur* **palmy,** adj *florens* (= flourishing), *optimus* (= best)

palpable, adj 1, lit. *quod sentire possumus*, *a(d)spectabilis* (= visible), *tractabilis* (= that may be touched), see PERCEPTIBLE, *quod manu tenēre possumus*, *quod manu tenetur*, 2, fig *quod comprehensum animis habemus*, *manifestus* (= manifest), *evidens* (= evident), *apertus* (= open, clear), comb *apertus ac manifestus* (e g *scelus*) Adv *manifesto*, *evidenter*, *aperte*

palpitate, v intr *palpitare*, see BEAT **palpitation,** n *palpitatio* (Plin)

palsy, n. see PARALYSIS

paltry, adj *vilis*, see PETTY

pamper, v.tr. *alci nimis indulgēre*, see FEED, GLUT, INDULGE.

pamphlet, n. *libellus* **pamphleteer,** n *libellorum scriptor*

pan, n *sartago* (Plin), *patina*, *patella*, see DISH **pancake,** n *laganum* or *placenta*

panacea, n lit *panchrestum medicamentum* (lit. in Plin., fig in Cic), *panacea* (= a plant, the heal all).

pandects, n *pandectae* (Imperial Rome).

pander, I. n *leno* **II.** v intr to — to, 1, lit *lenocinari*, 2, fig *alci inservire*, or perhaps *blandiri*, see FLATTER

pane, n *vitreum quadratum* (square)

panegyric, n *laudatio*, upon anyone, *alcjs* (of a speech, oration, and the praise contained in it), *laus*, *laudes*, upon anyone, *alcjs*, — upon one deceased, *laudatio* (*mortui*) in gen **panegyrist,** n *laudator* (in gen , fem , *laudatrix*), *praedicator* (loud and in public)

panel, n (in architecture) *tympanum* (= square — of a door), *abacus* (in wainscoting), *intertignium*, *intercolumnium* (= square compartment on the ceilings of rooms), a panelled ceiling, *lacunar*, †*laquear*

pang, n *dolor*, *doloris stimulus*, see STING, ANGUISH, AGONY

panic, n *pavor*, *terror*.

pannier, n. *clitellae*

panoply, n see ARMOUR

panorama, n perhaps *tabula in modum circi picta*, see also PROSPECT

pant, v intr of the heart, see PALPITATE, BEAT, to — for breath, *aegre ducĕre spiritum*, *anhelare*, to — for, fig *sitire*, *concupiscere alqd* **panting,** n *anhelitus*, -ūs

pantaloon, n perhaps *sannio*, *scurra*, m

pantheism, n *ratio eorum qui deum in universâ rerum naturâ situm esse putant* **pantheist,** n *qui deum*, etc , *putat*, see above

panther, n *panthēra* (Plin), *pardus* (Plin)

pantomime, n *mimus*, *pantomīmus* (Suet)

pantry, n *cella penaria*, *promptuarium* (where victuals are kept)

pap, n 1, *papilla*, *uber*, -ĕris, n , see BREAST, 2, = soft food for infants, *puls*, *pulticula* (= gruel) (Plin)

papa, n *pater*, see FATHER

papacy, n **papatus* (= dignity of the Pope) **papal,** adj **papalis* **papist,** n *sacra a pontifice Romano instituta sequens*, *legis pontificis Romani studiosus*

paper, I. n 1 as material for writing upon, *charta* (made from the papyrus, then any kind of writing material), †*papyrus*, f , 2, = — written on, writing, *charta*, *scriptum*, papers (i e written —), *scripta*, *orum*, *lit(t)erae*, *epistulae* (*epistol*), *libelli*, *tabellae*, public —s, *tabulae publicae*, — money, currency, *pecunia chartacea* or *syngrapha publica*, — hanging, *tapete*, -is (*tapetum*, = tapestry), = newspaper, *acta* (*diurna*), *orum* **II.** v tr to — a room, *conclavis parietes tapetibus ornare* **III.** adj *chartaceus* (Jct) **paper-hanger,** n *qui conclavium parietes tapetibus ornat*

papyrus, n *papyrus*, f (*papyrum*)

par, n (in gen) see EQUALITY (in commerce) by *aequalis*, — of exchange, *vicissitudines rei argentariae aequales*, *pecuniae permutandae pretium aequale*

parable, n *parabŏla* (class = a comparison), or in pure Latin *collatio*, *tra(ns)latio*, *similitudo*, see ALLEGORY, SIMILE **parabolical,** adj *per similitudinem*, or *tra(ns)lationem* or *collationem*, to speak —ly, *ut similitudine utar*

parade, I. n 1, in military affairs, *decursus*, -ūs, *decursio*, 2, = show, *ostentatio*, *apparatus*, -ūs, see SHOW, DISPLAY **II.** v intr (of troops), *decurrĕre* **III.** v tr. *ostentare*, see DISPLAY

paradigm, n in Gram., *paradigma*.

Paradise, n 1, *paradīsus* (Eccl); 2, = a

very delightful spot, *locus amoenissimus;* **3,** = the blissful seat after death, *sedes* (-*is*, f.) *beatorum.*

paradox, n. *quod est admirabile contraque opinionem omnium,* in the pl. *quae sunt admirabilia,* etc., also simply *admirabilia* or *mirabilia quaedam,* in pl. *paradoxa.* **paradoxical,** adj. see above.

paragon, n. *specimen;* see PATTERN.

paragraph, n. *caput* (= section).

parallel, I. adj. **1,** *parallēlos;* **2,** fig. (*con*)*similis;* a — passage, *locus congruens verbis et sententiis.* **II.** n. **1,** *linea parallela;* **2,** fig., perhaps *similitudo;* to draw a —, *alqd cum alqā re conferre;* see COMPARE, COMPARISON. **III.** v.tr. *alqd cum alqā re aequare, comparare, conferre;* see COMPARE. **parallelogram,** n. **parallelogrammon.*

paralogism, n. (in logic) *falsa ratio;* to make a —, *vitiose concludĕre;* see SOPHISM.

paralysis, n. **1,** *paralysis* (Plin.), in pure Latin *nervorum remissio;* **2,** fig. perhaps by *impotens, invalidus;* see POWERLESS. **paralytical,** adj. *paralyticus* (Plin.). **paralyse,** v.tr. **1,** lit. *pede* (*manu,* etc.) *captum* or *debilem esse* (to be —d); see LAME; **2,** fig. *invalidum reddĕre, affligĕre, percellĕre* (Cels.).

paramount, adj. and n. see CHIEF, SUPERIOR.

paramour, n. see LOVER, MISTRESS.

parapet, n. *pluteus, lorīca* (milit. term.).

paraphernalia, n. *apparatus, -ūs;* see DRESS, ORNAMENT.

paraphrase, I. n. *circuitio, circuitus, -ūs, eloquendi, circuitus plurium verborum, circumlocutio* (all = circumlocution rather than verbal —), *paraphrasis, -is,* f. (Quint.). **II.** v.tr. and intr. *pluribus alqd exponĕre et explicare* (Cic., Quint.), *pluribus vocibus et per ambitum verborum alqd enuntiare* (Suet.), *circuitu plurium verborum ostendĕre alqd* (Quint.).

parasite, n. **1,** *parasītus,* fem. *parasita* (= a trencher friend), *assec*(*u*)*la, parasitaster* (= a wretched —); **2,** = a plant, *planta parasitica.* **parasitic, parasitical,** adj. *parasiticus* (παρασιτικός). **parasitism,** n. *parasitatio, ars parasitica* (Com.).

parasol, n. *umbella* (Juv.), *umbraculum.*

parboiled, adj. *semicoctus* (Plin.).

parcel, I. n. **1,** see PART, PORTION; **2,** see QUANTITY, MASS; **3,** = package, *fascis, -is,* m., *fasciculus* (= a bundle, containing several things together), *sarcina* (= burden, carried by a man or a beast); see PACKET. **II.** v.tr. *partiri* (= to divide), *dividĕre, distribuĕre, metiri* (= to measure); see DIVIDE.

parch, I. v.tr. (*ex*)*siccare, arefacĕre, torrefacĕre,* (*ex*)*urĕre.* **II.** v.intr. (*ex*)*siccari, siccescĕre, arefieri, arescĕre* (the latter two = to become dry); see BURN, DRY. **parched,** adj. *aridus;* see DRY.

parchment, n. *membrana.*

pardon, I. v.tr. *ignoscĕre alci rei* or *alci alqd, veniam alcjs rei dare alci;* to — an oath, *jurisjurandi gratiam alci facĕre, solvĕre alqm sacramento* (= to free from the obligation); to — a debt, *pecuniam creditam condonare* or *remittĕre, creditum condonare, debitum remittĕre alci.* **II.** n. *venia, remissio* (e.g. the foregoing of a payment, *remissio tributi*); to ask —, *remissionem petĕre, veniam praeteritorum precari;* see FORGIVE, INDULGENCE, OVERLOOK. **pardonable,** adj. †*excusabilis, cui alqs veniam dare potest.*

pare, v.tr. (*de*)*secare, resecare, circumsecare* (= to cut off in gen.), *subsecare* (= to cut off a little), *circumcīdĕre* (= to cut off all round). **parings,** n. *praesegmina, -um* (ante and post class.).

parent, n. see FATHER, MOTHER; *parens* (in gen.), *procreator* (= creator), *genitor.* **parentage,** n. *stirps, genus, -ĕris,* n.; see EXTRACTION, BIRTH. **parental,** adj., by the genit. *parentum,* e.g. — love, *parentum amor.* Adv. *parentum more.* **parentless,** adj. *orbatus* or *orbus* (*parentibus*).

parenthesis, n. *interpositio, interclusio* (*quam nos interpositionem vel interclusionem dicimus, Graeci παρένθεσιν vocant, dum continuationi sermonis medius alqs sensus intervenit,* Quint.); to put anything in —, *alqd continuationi sermonis medium interponĕre.* **parenthetical,** adj. a — remark, *verba* (*orationi*) *interposita.*

parhelion, n. *parelion, sol alter* or *imago solis* (Sen.).

pariah, n. *unus e faece populi.*

parietal, adj. by circuml. with *paries;* see WALL.

parish, n. *paroecia* (*parochia*) (Eccl.). **parishioner,** n. *parochianus* (Eccl.).

parity, n. see EQUALITY.

park, n. **1,** *vivarium* (= preserve, Plin.), *saeptum* (*sep-*) *venationis* (Var.) or perhaps *saeptum* alone (= enclosure); **2,** *horti* (= gardens), *viridarium* (= garden planted with trees).

parley, I. v.intr. *colloqui alqd cum alqo,* gen. *colloqui de alqâ re* (= to speak with another about anything), *conferre alqd, consilia conferre de alqâ re, communicare cum alqo de alqâ re* (= to communicate about anything), appropriately *agĕre, disceptare cum alqo de alqâ re* (= to confer on some point of mutual concern), *coram conferre alqd;* (in a military sense), to — (respecting the surrender of a town), *legatum* or *legatos de condicionibus urbis tradendae mittĕre.* **II.** n. *colloquium, sermo.*

parliament, n. (in England) *senatus, -ūs;* to convoke the —, *senatum convocare* or *cogĕre;* an act of —, *senatus consultum;* house of —, *curia;* member of —, *senator.* **parliamentary,** adj. *senatorius, quod ad senatum pertinet.*

parlour, n. see ROOM.

parochial, adj. **parochialis;* see PARISH.

parody, I. n. (of a poem) *poëtae verba et versus ad aliud quoddam idque ridiculum argumentum detorta,* or Greek παρῳδία. **II.** v.tr. (a poem) *poëtae verba et versus ad aliud quoddam idque ridiculum argumentum detorquēre.*

parole, n. (in military affairs) *fides* (*data*); see WORD.

paroxysm, n. **1,** *febris accessio* (Cels.), or *accessus, -ūs;* **2,** fig. *vis* or *impetus,* or by part. (e.g. *irâ impulsus,* = under a — of anger).

parricide, n. **1,** *parricīda,* m. and f., the person (*parentis sui*); **2,** the act, *parricidium.* **parricidal,** adj. see MURDEROUS.

parrot, n. *psittacus.*

parry, v.tr. and intr. **1,** in fencing, to — a thrust or stroke, *ictum* (or *petitionem*) *vitare, cavēre, cavēre et propulsare,* also simply *cavēre, vitare* (with the sword), *ictum declinare, petitionem declinatione et corpore effugĕre,* also simply *ictum effugĕre* (by a movement of the body); to — well, *recte cavēre;* to try to —, or to — anyone's thrust with the shield, *ad alcjs conatum scutum tollĕre;* to — and strike again, *cavēre et repetĕre;* —ing, *ictus propulsatio;* **2,** fig. to — an evil blow, etc., *amovēre* (= to avert), *depellĕre, repellĕre, propellĕre, propulsare, defendĕre* (= to ward off), *deprecari* (lit by entreaties), see FENCE, AVOID

parse, v tr. *sententiam* or *locum quasi in membra discerpĕre*, to — words, *quae sint singula verba explicare* **parsing,** n use verb

parsimonious, adj (gen in an ill sense, but sometimes in a good sense = frugal) *parcus* (= who is always afraid to give too much, esp in expenditure, opp *nimius*, who goes too far in anything, Plin), *restrictus* (= who does not like to give, opp. *largus*), comb *parcus et restrictus*, *tenax* (= tight, opp. *profusus*), also comb *parcus et tenax*, *restrictus et tenax*, *malignus* (= niggard, who grudges everything), see MEAN. Adv *parce*, *maligne* (= too sparingly, e g *laudare*, Hor), *restricte* **parsimony,** n *parsimonia alcjs rei* (= being careful with anything, then in avoiding expenditure, e g *parsimonia temporis*), too great —, *tenacitas* (= being close, never coming out with anything, Liv), *malignitas* (= niggardliness), see MEANNESS

parsley, n *apium*, *oreoselinum* or *petroselinum* (Plin)

parsnip, n **pastinaca* (Plin)

parson, n **presbyter*, **clericus*, or by *sacerdos* **parsonage,** n. *aedes presbyteri*

part, I. n *pars*, *membrum* (= limb, e g of the body, of a discourse), *locus* (= important passage, point in a science, treatise), the middle, further, lowest, highest — of anything is rendered by *medius*, *extremus*, *infimus*, *summus*, in the same case as the thing itself (e g the middle — of a line of battle, *acies media*, the highest — of the mountain, *mons summus*), for the most —, *magnam partem*, *plerumque* (= in most cases, as regards time), in two, three —s, etc , *bifariam*, *trifariam*, *bipartito*, *tripartito*, etc , the greater —, *aliquantum* with genit (e g *viae*), the one —, the other —, *pars* . . . *pars*, *partim* . . . *partim* (also with genit or with the prep *ex*), *pars* or *partim* . . . *alii* (*ae*, *-a*), *alii* (*ae*, *-a*) . . . *alii* (*ae*, *-a*) (all of persons and things), partly . . . partly, *partim* . . . *partim* (but the latter particles can only be used when we speak of a real division into parts), *quâ* . . . *quâ* (= on the one hand . . . on the other hand), *et* . . . *et*, *cum* . . . *tum*, *tum* . . . *tum* (= both . . . and), I for my —, *ego quidem*, *equidem* (= if I must give my own opinion, etc , for which moderns often put badly, *quod ad me attinet*), *pro meâ parte* (= according to my power), to divide into —s, *in partes dividĕre* or *distribuĕre*, to receive a — of anything, *partem alcjs rei accipĕre*, to have a — in anything, *alcjs rei participem* or *in parte* or *in societate alcjs rei esse*, *partem* or *societatem in alqâ re habēre* (in some good act), *alcjs rei socium esse* (in some good and in some wicked action), *affinem esse alcjs rei* or *alci rei* (in something that is bad), to take — in anything, *partem alcjs rei capĕre* (e g in the government of a republic, *administrandae reipublicae*), *in partem alcjs rei venire*, *interesse alci rei* (= to be present at anything, to take — in or exercise influence, e g in the battle, *pugnae*), *attingĕre* (by action, in a business transaction, in the carrying out of anything), to have no — in anything, *alcjs rei expertem esse*, *partem alcjs rei non habēre*, to allow anyone to take a — in consultations, *alqm in consilium adhibēre* or *ad consilium admittĕre*, in —, partly, *per partes*, *particulatim* (mostly post class), *carptim* (= in pieces, when one — is taken now, and another at some other time, and so on, opp *universi*, e g *seu carptim partes* [i e partly and in different lots], *seu universi* [*convenire*] *mallent*, Liv), *ex parte*, *alqâ ex parte* (= in —, when only a — of the whole is taken at a time, or only a few parts at a time, etc opp *totus*, e g to conquer a town —, *urbem ex parte capĕre*; to please —, *ex parte placēre*, to be changed —, *alqâ ex parte commutari*), *nonnullâ parte* (inasmuch as the parts do not form a connected whole, but are isolated, "here and there," e g *summotis sub murum cohortibus ac nonnullâ parte propter terrorem in oppidum compulsis*), to take one's — with one, or to take — with one, *in alcjs partes transire*, *transgredi*, *alqm defendĕre*, *pro alcjs salute propugnare* (the latter two = to defend, e g very eagerly, *acerrime*), against anyone, *stare cum alqo adversus alqm*, to take in good —, *in bonam partem accipĕre*, to act a —, *agĕre alqm* or *alcjs partes*, *alcjs personam tueri*; on the — of . . , *ab alqo* (e g on his — nothing will be done, *ab eo* or *ab illo nihil agitur*, on his — we have nothing to fear, *ab eo nihil nobis timendum est*, also by *alcjs verbis*, *alcjs nomine*, in anyone's name , see NAME), a — (music), *modi musici compluribus vocibus descripti*, — singing, *complurium vocum cantus*, in these —s, *hâc regione*, *hic*, good —s , see ABILITY, SPEECH **II.** v tr *dividĕre*, *partiri*, see DIVIDE, SEPARATE **III.** v intr *digredi*, *discedĕre* **parting,** n *digressio*, *digressus*, *-ūs*, *discessus*, *-ūs* **partly,** adv *partim*, (*alqâ*) *ex parte*, see PART, I

partake, v tr., to — of, *participem esse alcjs rei*, of food, see EAT, also PART, I **partaker,** n *socius*, — of or in anything, *particeps* or *socius alcjs rei*, *affinis alcjs rei* or *alci rei*, fem *socia*, in anything *particeps* or *socia alcjs rei*, *affinis alcjs rei* or *alci rei*

parterre, n. perhaps *area floribus consita*

parthenon, n *Parthenon* (Plin)

partial, adj **1,** *alterius partis studiosus*, *cupidus* (= acting under the influence of one's passion), *ad gratiam factus* (= what is done to insinuate oneself), *iniquus* (= unfair), **2,** = partly, *ex* (*alqâ*) *parte*, see PARTLY Adv *cupide*, *inique*, *ex* (*alqâ*) *parte* **partiality,** n *studium* (= the leaning towards one party), *gratia* (= favour shown to one party, e g *crimen gratiae*, i e accusation of —), *cupiditas* (= bias, esp of a judge, etc), to act with —, *cupidius agĕre*, to approve anything through —, *studio quodam comprobare alqd*

participate, v intr and tr , by *particeps alcjs rei* (= anyone who receives a share of anything or takes part in anything, e g *ejusdem laudis*, in a conspiracy, *conjurationis*, in a pleasure, *voluptatis*), *consors*, *socius alcjs rei* (= who has joined with others, e g *socius sceleris*), *affinis alcjs rei* or *alci rei* (in anything, esp in a bad action, e g *affinis facinori*, *noxae*, *culpae*), *compos alcjs rei* (= who possesses anything, is in the possession of, e g anything pleasant, e g the consulate, praise), *alcjs rei potens* (= who possesses a thing and is the master over it), to come to — in a thing, *participem* or *compotem fieri alcjs rei*, to — in a crime, *se obstringĕre alqâ re* **participation,** n *societas*, *communicatio*, in anything, *societas alcjs rei* (= joint — in, e g *belli*) **participator,** n *socius*, *affinis*, *consors*, see PARTICIPATE

participle, n *participium* (Gram)

particle, n **1,** *particula* (in gen), *frustum* (= a little bit of food, otherwise rare); **2,** in gram , **particula*

particoloured, adj *versicolor*, *varius*

particular, adj *separatus*; everyone has his own — place and his own table *separatae singulis sedes et sua cuique mensa* (Tac), = peculiar to anyone, *proprius* (of which we are the only possessors opp *communis*), *praecipuus* (in possessing which we have an advantage over others), *peculiaris* (when one thing is to be distinguished from another, of a thing peculiar in its kind), *singularis* (= single, isolated, excellent), *praecipuus* (= excellent), *eximius* (= exceeding; see EXCELLENT); = strange, wonderful, *singularis, novus* (= new, what was never seen before), *mirus* (= striking); a — case, *mirus quidam casus*; see PECULIAR, EXACT, SINGULAR; = exacting, *diligens, accuratus*; a — friend; see INTIMATE, PRIVATE. **particulars**, n., in the pl., to go into —, *singula sequi*; *scribĕre de singulis rebus* (in letters); *rem ordine, ut gesta est, narrare*. **particularity**, n. *diligentia*. **particularize**, v.tr. *nominare* (= to name), *enumerare* (= to enumerate), *per nomina citare* (= to mention several persons by name). **particularly**, adv., by *quod curae* or *cordi est*; *gravis* (= important), or with the advs. *sedulo* (= assiduously), *studiose* (= with zeal), *diligenter* (= with care), *cupide* (= eagerly), *impense* (= urgently), *vehementer* (= vehemently, very much), *magnopĕre* (= with all one's mind), *praesertim, praecipue* (= especially), *maxime* (= chiefly), *imprimis* (*in primis* = above all), *etiam atque etiam* (= over and over), also *vehementer etiam atque etiam*; to court anyone's friendship most —, *cupidissime alcjs amicitiam appetĕre*.

partisan, n. *homo alcjs studiosus, fautor*. **partisanship**, n. *studium, favor*.

partisan, n. a weapon, *bipennis*.

partition, n. 1, see DIVISION, SEPARATION; 2, a — in a house, *paries, -ĕtis*, m. (= wall), *paries intergerinus* (*intergerivus*, Plin., = common wall between neighbouring houses), *saeptum* (*sep-*, = fence or place fenced off), *loculamentum* (used of the —s in an aviary).

partitive, adj. in Gram., *partitivus*.

partner, n. 1, lit., by verbs, see PARTAKER, ASSOCIATE; 2, in commercial business, *socius* (in every sense); 3, in marriage, *conju(n)x, -jugis*, m. and f.; see HUSBAND, WIFE. **partnership**, n. *consortio* (rare), *societas* (as society and persons united in —, Cic.), *socii* (= persons associated together); to form a —, *societatem facĕre*; to enter into — with anyone, *alqm sibi socium adjungĕre*.

partridge, n. *perdrix*.

parturition, n. *partus, -ūs*.

party, n. 1, *pars*, or pl. *partes* (in gen.), *factio* (lit. = any number of persons who entertain the same sentiments, then esp. in a political sense). *secta* (prop. of philosophers or learned men in gen.); the opposite —, see OPPOSITION; to belong to anyone's —, *alcjs partis* or *partium esse, alcjs partes sequi, alcjs sectam sequi, cum alqo facĕre, ab* or *cum alqo stare, alcjs rebus studēre* or *favēre, alcjs esse studiosum*; not to belong to either, any —, *neutrius partis* or *nullius partis esse* (see NEUTRAL); to favour different parties (of several), *aliorum (alias) partes fovēre*; to get anyone over to one's own —, *alqm in suas partes trahĕre, ducĕre*; to divide into two parties, *in duas partes discedĕre, in duas factiones scindi*; — zeal in the contest, *studium*; — leader, *dux* or *princeps partium, princeps* or *caput factionis*; in the context also simply *dux, caput*; — spirit (*partium*) *studium*; — struggle, — dispute, in the State, *certamen partium* or *factionum*; 2, = company, *aliquot* (= a few, in an indefinite sense), *complures* (= a large number); a large —, *copia, multitudo*, also by *alii—alii*; pleasure —, into the country, by *excurrĕre*; on the water, by *navigare*; to be one of the —, *una esse cum aliis*; he who is one of the —, *socius* (= who joins), *comes* (= companion); to be one of the — invited by anyone, to go with a — somewhere, *alci comitem se addĕre* or *adjungĕre*; a card —, *lusus, -ūs* (= game); see CAUSE, COMPANY. **party-wall**, n. see PARTITION.

parvenu, n. *novus homo*.

paschal, adj. *paschalis* (Eccl.).

pasha, n. *satrapes, -ae* and *-is*, m.

pasquinade, n. *libellus famosus* (= a libel); see LIBEL; if a poem, *carmen probrosum, famosum, carmen maledicum, elogium* (= verses written at anyone's door, Plaut.); a — upon anyone's voluptuousness, *versus in alcjs cupiditatem facti*.

pass, I. v.intr. 1, *transire, transgredi* (= to go past), *ire* or *venire per alqm locum* (= to — through a place), *alqm locum inire* or *ingredi* or *intrare* (= to enter into a place, of persons), *importari, invehi* (= to be imported, of things), *alqo loco exire* or *egredi* (from a place, of persons), *exportari, evehi* (= to be transported away from a place, of things), *alqm locum transcendĕre* or *superare* (= to — through, over a place which lies high, e.g. a mountain); to — through the gate, *portâ exire* (in going out), *portâ introire* (in going in); to — across a river, *flumen transire* or *tra(j)icĕre* or *transmittĕre*; to let the troops — across a river, *copias flumen* or *trans flumen tra(j)icĕre*; not to allow anyone to —, *alqm aditu prohibēre* (in going past or in going in), *alqm egressione prohibēre, alqm egressu arcēre* (in going out); not to allow anyone to — backwards and forwards, *nec aditu nec reditu alqm prohibēre*; see GO, etc.; 2, to — into possession of, see GET; 3, of the time, *transire, praeterire* (= to — by), *abire* (= to go away), *circumagi, se circumagĕre* (= to come round), *exire, praeterire* (= to elapse); the time —es quickly, *tempus fugit, aetas volat*; 4, *perferri* (= to be carried, of a law); see ENACT; 5, = to be tolerated, *probari* (of that which can be approved), *ferri posse* (of what can be tolerated); to let a thing —, *alqd non plane improbare* (= not to disapprove altogether), *alqd ferre* (= to bear); see ALLOW, PERMIT; 6, = to be considered, *haberi alqm* or *pro alqo* (the latter if we consider anyone to be a person of a certain character, etc.); to — as rich, *haberi divitem* (if the person really is so), *haberi pro divite* (if considered as such); 7, = to come to —, *accidĕre*; see HAPPEN; 8, in fencing, *alqm petĕre*; 9, as I —ed along, in —ing, *in transitu, transiens, praeteriens* (also fig. = by-the-bye; the two former in a fig. sense only post-Aug. (e.g. Quint.), but *quasi praeteriens* in Cic.), *strictim* (fig., but superficially, after Seneca also *obiter*); to mention in —ing, *in mentionem alcjs rei incidĕre* (Liv.); 10, to — by, *praeterire* or *praetergredi*, a place, *alqm locum*; *transire alqm locum* (= to go beyond a place); to let none — by, go past, *neminem praetermittĕre*; = to cease, *abire*; of time, *praeterire, transire*; to — through, *transire* (absol., or with the accus. of the place), *iter facĕre per* (with accus. of the place), *pervadĕre, penetrare* (= to penetrate), *transvehi, vehi per locum* (in a carriage, on board a vessel). II. v.tr. 1, = to go beyond, *transgredi* (only lit., e.g. *flumen*), *transire* or *egredi alqd* or *extra alqd* (lit. and fig.), *excedĕre* (fig.); to — the boundaries, limits, *transire fines* (both in entering and leaving a country; then also fig. *alcjs rei*), *egredi extra fines* (lit., in leaving a country, *terminos egredi*, fig.); to — the fifth year, *egredi quintum annum*; see SURPASS; 2, of time, *degĕre, agĕre, transigĕre* (e.g. *diem, vitam*, or *actatem*); with anything or with a person, *ducĕre alqâ re* (e.g. the night with interesting conversation, *noctem jucundis sermonibus*), *consumĕre* or *conterĕre alqâ re* or *in alqâ re* (in a good or bad sense), *absumĕre alqâ re* (= to waste time, e.g. with talking, *tempus dicendo*); *extrahĕre alqâ re* (when we talk instead of acting), *fallĕre alqd re*, to — whole days by the fireside, *totos dies juxta focum atque ignem agĕre*, to — the night, *pernoctare*, see SPEND, 3, to — in examination, *alci satisfacere*, (= to satisfy), *probari* (= to be considered competent, *stare* (= not to fail through in carrying out anything), very honourably, *pulcherrime stare*, in a disgraceful manner, *turpem inveniri*, 4, of a business, to — accounts, *rationes ratas habēre*; see TERMINATE, SETTLE, DIVIDE, 5, = to allow to —, *transitum dare alci* (a person), *transmittĕre*, 6, = to put through a narrow hole, *tra(j)icĕre*, *immittĕre*, *inserĕre* (the latter two = to put into, e g one's hand, the key into the keyhole), to — thread through a needle, *filum in acum inserere*, 7, = to — sentence, *sententiam dicĕre* (by word of mouth) or *ferre* (by votes); upon anyone, *judicium facĕre de alqo* (e g. *optimum*), to — sentence of death upon anyone, *alqm capitis damnare*; see SENTENCE, 8, to — a law, *decernĕre* (of the Senate), *legem esse jubēre* (of the people), see ENACT — **away,** v intr 1, see PASS, I. 3, 2, see DIE — **by,** v tr 1, see PASS, I 10, 2, see PASS OVER — **off, I.** v tr to — anyone or anything or anyone for anyone or anything, *dicĕre* (= to say), *perhibēre* (= to call), *ferre* (= to bring forward), *mentiri* (= to say falsely); to — anyone, report as being dead, *falsum nuntium mortis alcjs afferre*, to — anything as one's own, *suum esse alqd dicĕre*, to — as truth, *verum esse alqd dicĕre*, *simulare alqd esse verum*, to — anyone as one's father, *patrem sibi alqm assumere*, to — anyone (falsely) as the author of anything, *alqm auctorem esse alcjs rei mentiri*, to — anyone by a false report as the founder, *alqm conditorem famā ferre*, to — oneself for, *se ferre alqm* (= to report up and down), *se profiteri alqm* (= to declare oneself to be so and so), *simulare*, *alqm se esse velle* (he will have it that he is so and so), to — himself off as a king, *regis titulum usurpare* **II.** v intr *abire* (used by Cic. of sea sickness), see CEASE — **on,** v intr *pergĕre*, let us — (in speaking), *pergamus* (*ad alqd*) — **over, I.** v tr any person or thing in speaking (= not to remember), *praeterire* with or without *silentio*, *relinquere*, comb *praeterire ac relinquĕre*, *mittĕre omittĕre* (of one's own free will and with intent, e g *omitto jurisdictionem contra leges*, *relinquo caedes*, *libidines praetereo*); to — over, that, etc, *ut omittam*, *quod*, etc, *ne dicam*, *quod*, etc, —ing over all these circumstances, *omissis his rebus omnibus*, to be —ed over, *praeteriri* (in gen), *repulsam ferre* or *accipĕre* (= to be rejected, in the election of an office), see NEGLECT — **round,** v intr *tradĕre* **III.** n 1, = a narrow passage, *aditus*, *-ūs* (= access in gen), *angustiae locorum*, or simply *angustiae* (= narrow —), *fauces*, *-ium* (= narrow entrance and exit into a more open country), *saltus*, *-ūs* (= woody mountain-pass, e g near Thermopylae, *Thermopylarum*), 2, see PASSAGE, ROAD, 3, = an order to —, *libellus*, *-ūs*, *qui alci aditum aperiat*, 4, = condition, *eo ventum est ut*, see CONDITION **passable,** adj 1, *pervius*, *tritus* (= much frequented), or *transitu facilis*, 2, = tolerable, *tolerabilis*, *mediocris* Adv *mediocriter* **passage,** n 1, = the act of passing, *transitus*, *-ūs*, *transitio*, *transvectio* (= transit of goods), *transgressio*, *transgressus*, *-ūs*, *tra(ns)missio*, *tra(ns)missus*, *-ūs*, *trajectio*, *trajectus*, *-ūs* (the substs in -io express the act, those in -us the condition, the — itself); — across a river, *transitus* or *transvectio fluminis*, in the — of such large sums of the royal treasure into Italy, *in tanta pecuniā regiā in Italiam trajiciendā*, = to grant a — to anyone, *dare alci transitum* or *iter per agros urbesque*, *alqm per fines suos ire pati*, *alqm per fines regni transire sinĕre* (to an army, to a general with the army through a country); a — across, *transitio*, *transitus -ūs*, 2, = way, road, *iter*, *via*, *aditus*, *-ūs*, 3, — of a book, *locus*, *caput* (= chapter), bird of —, *avis advena*, see MIGRATORY **passenger,** n 1, on the road, *viator* (on foot), *vector* (on horseback, by carriage, ship), 2, after he has arrived, *hospes*, *-itis* **passing,** n 1, see PASSAGE, 2, in commerce, *permutatio* (= exchange), *venditio* (= sale). **passport,** n by *facultas* (*alcjs loci adeundi*) *data* **password,** n *tessera* (= a token) **past, I.** adj and n, *praeteritus*, *ante actus* (or as one word, *anteactus*, = done before), *prior*, *superior* (= last, e g last week), the —, *praeterita*, *-orum*, the — time, tense, *tempus praeteritum*, pardon for what is —, *venia praeteritorum*, *rerum praeteritarum* or *ante actarum oblivio*, the — years, *anni praeteriti* (e g since one's birth, etc), *anni priores* (= the last few years), during the — year, *priore* or *superiore anno*, during the time —, *tempore praeterito* (= the whole of it), *prioribus annis* (= during the last few years), during, in the — night, *nocte priore* or *superiore* **II.** adv *praeter* (gen. only in comp with verbs, when in Lat. we form compounds with *praeter* and *trans*, *praeter* denotes the direction in which an object moves — another and at the same time removes from it, whilst *trans* expresses the direction from a certain point to the furthest end), to hurry —, *praetervolare*, to drive —, v tr. *praetervehĕre* or *transvehĕre*, anything, *praeter alqd*, v intr *praetervehi* or *transvehi*, anything, *alqd*, the driving —, *praetervectio*, to fly —, *praetervolare*, to flow —, *praeterfluĕre*, to lead —, *praeterducĕre* (Plaut.), *transducĕre*, — any place, *praeter alqm locum*, to go — a place, *praeterire* or *transire alqm locum*, to let go —, to allow to pass, *praetermittĕre* (lit persons and things, then = not to avail oneself of, through carelessness, e g an opportunity for, *occasionem alcjs rei*, the day appointed, the term, *diem*), *transitum alcjs rei exspectare* (= to wait until anything is over, e g a storm, *tempestatis*), *omittere* (fig = to lose, e g an opportunity, *occasionem*), *dimittĕre* (fig = to allow to pass, because one fancies he is not in want of it, e g an opportunity, *occasionem*, *occasionem fortunā datam*), *amittĕre* (= not to heed, through carelessness, so as to be unable to make use of, e g *occasionem*, the favourable moment, *tempus*), *intermittĕre* (e g not a moment, *nullum temporis punctum*, not a day, without, etc, *nullam diem*, *quin*, etc) **III.** as prep *praeter*, *trans* with accus, see above II **pastime,** n *ludus* (= game), *oblectamentum*, *oblectatio*, *delectamentum* (rare)

passion, n 1, = suffering, *perpessio*, *toleratio* (Cic, both with the genit of that which causes us to suffer); — of Christ, **passio* or **perpessio*, see SUFFERING, 2, = excitement, *animi concitatio*, *animi impetus*, *-ūs*, stronger, *animi perturbatio*, *motus*, *-ūs*, *animi turbatus* or *perturbatus* (= violent emotion in gen , *animi affectio* = disposition, affection of the mind, *animi motus*, *commotio* or *permotio* = mental excitement in gen), *cupiditas*, *cupido* (= longing), *libido* (*lub*, chiefly = sensual desire), *temeritas* (= rashness), *intemperantia* (= want of moderation, licentiousness, opp *aequitas*), = anger, *ira*, *iracundia*, = fondness for, *alcjs rei studium*, violent —, *acerrimus animi motus*, *-ūs*, *vehemens animi impetus*, *-ūs*, disorderly, unruly —, *libidines*, *-um*; without —, *aequo animo*, to rule over one's —, to conquer —, *perturbatos animi motus cohibēre*, *cupiditates coercēre*, *cupiditatibus imperare*, *continentem esse* (esp with regard to sensuality), to be free from —, *ab omni animi concitatione* *vacare, omni animi perturbatione liberum* or *liberatum esse*; to act under the influence of —, *cupide agĕre*; to go so far in one's — as, etc., *studio sic efferri.* **passionate,** adj. *cupidus* (= greedy, eager), *concitatus, incitatus* (= excited), *impotens* (of one who cannot master his passion, always with the genit., e.g. *irae, laetitiae*; then that cannot be restrained, excessive, e.g. *laetitia, postulatum*), *vehemens, ardens, flagrans* (= eager, ardent), *iracundus, cerebrosus* (= hot-tempered, hasty), *studiosissimus alcjs rei* (= very much given to anything). Adv. *cupide, cupidissime* (= eagerly), *studiose* (= with zeal), *vehementer, ardenter, studio flagranti* (= with extreme zeal), *iracunde* (= hastily), *effuse* or stronger *effusissime* (= beyond all bounds); to be — fond of anything, *alci rei effuse indulgēre* (beyond all bounds, e.g. feasting, *conviviis*), *alcjs rei esse studiosissimum, magno alcjs rei studio teneri* (= to be a great admirer of anything), *alqâ re maxime delectari* (= to be quite delighted in); to love anyone —, *effusissime alqm diligēre* (as a friend, etc.). **passionateness,** n. *animi ardor, furor* (in a high degree); — in contending for anything, *ira et studium.* **passionless,** adj. *cupiditatis expers, omni animi perturbatione vacuus* or *liber.* **passive,** adj. 1, by *pati* (e.g. *affectus*), *accipiendi et quasi patiendi vim habēre* (= to have aptness to suffer, opp. *movendi vim habēre et efficiendi*, Cic.); to remain —, *quiescĕre*; in anything, *alqd patienter ferre*; under an insult, *acceptâ injuriâ alci ignoscĕre*; one who remains —, *quietus*; 2, — verb, *verbum patiendi* (opp. *verbum agens*, Aul. Gell.), *patiendi modus* (Quint.), *verbum passivum* (late Gram.). Adv. *aequo animo, patienter*; see PASSIVE, 1; in Gram., *passive.* **passiveness,** n. *patientia*; see PATIENCE.

Passover, n. * *Pascha.*

paste. I. n. *farina quâ chartae glutinantur* (Plin.). **II.** v.tr. *farinâ glutinare.*

pastor, n. 1, see SHEPHERD; 2, * *pastor*; see PREACHER. **pastorship,** n. see MINISTRY. **pastoral, I.** adj. 1, *pastoralis, pastoricius*; in wider sense, *agrestis, rusticus*; 2, *quod ad pastorem pertinet.* **II.** n. = — poem, *carmen bucolicum.*

pastry, n. *panificium* (= bread-making), *opus pistorium, crustum*; = meat-pie, *artocreas* (Pers.). **pastry-cook,** n. *crustularius* (Sen.); see BAKER.

pasturage, n. 1, = business of feeding cattle, *res pecuaria* or *pecuaria*; 2, see PASTURE. **pasture, I.** n. *pascuum, locus pascuus* (in gen.), *ager pascuus* (= — land); common — land, *ager compascuus.* **II.** v.tr. *pascĕre* (lit. and fig.). **III.** v.intr. *pastum ire, pabulari* (= to graze), *pasci* (= to feed).

pat, I. n. *plaga lĕvis.* **II.** v.tr. perhaps *permulcēre* (= to soothe, of patting a horse). **III.** adv. *in tempore, opportune*; see FIT, CONVENIENCE.

patch, I. n. *pannus.* **II.** v.tr. *(re)sarcire, pannum alci rei assuĕre.* **patchwork,** n. *cento* (= a coat patched together; in modern writers also a written work patched together from different sources).

patent, I. adj. 1, *manifestus, apertus, clarus, certus*; see OPEN; 2, *res cui diploma datum est.* **II.** n. 1, a letter —, = a public order, *edictum*; to issue a —, *edicĕre* or *edictum proponĕre*, with *ut* or *ne* (when anything is prohibited); 2, for some new invention, use *diploma, -ătis*, or *libellus quo beneficium alqd datur* (e.g. *dare alci beneficium salis vendendi*), or *potestas alcjs rei faciendae* or *vendendae.* **III.** v.tr. by n. with *dare*; see above.

paternal, adj. *paternus, patrius* (= fatherly); — property, *res paterna, bona* (-*orum*) *paterna, patrimonium*; — disposition, *animus paternus in alqm* (so *animus maternus, fraternus*); — love, *amor paternus* or *patrius.*

path, n. *via* (= way in gen.), *semita, trames, -itis*, m. (= by-road), *callis*, m. and f. (= footpath through a wood, etc.); the — of life, *via vitae*; to stray from the — of virtue, *de viâ decedĕre*; to follow the — of virtue, *virtutem sequi, virtuti operam dare*; to lead anyone away from the — of virtue, *alqm transversum agĕre* (in gen.), *alqm ad nequitiam adducĕre* (= to lead to extravagances). **pathless,** adj. *invius*; see WAY, PASSAGE.

pathetic, pathetical, adj. *misericors* (= pitiful), *flebilis, maestus, tristis* (= sad). Adv. *flebiliter, maeste.* **pathos,** n. *maestitia, maeror, tristitia*; there was such — in his speech, *tanta maestitia inerat orationi.*

pathologist, n. *medicus qui valetudinis genera novit.* **pathology,** n. * *pathologia* (t.t.).

patience, n. *patientia, tolerantia* (= strength and perseverance in enduring calamity, etc.; generally with genit., e.g. *tolerantia doloris*, in enduring pain), *perseverantia* (if we shrink from no difficulties, however great), *aequus animus, aequitas animi* (= a quiet mind not disturbed by anything); to have — with anyone, *alqm* and *alcjs mores* or *naturam patienter ferre*, or simply *alqm ferre*; — ! i.e. wait ! *exspecta! mane!* see PERSEVERANCE. **patient, I.** adj. *patiens, tolerans, tolerabilis* (rare, not in Cic., who, however, uses the adv. *tolerabiliter*), in anything, *alcjs rei, placidus*; to be —, *ex(s)pectare, manēre* (= to wait), *quiescĕre* (= to be quiet). Adv. *patienter, toleranter, tolerabiliter, aequo animo* (= with a calm mind, e.g. to put up with anything); to look at a thing —, *aequo animo spectare alqd*; to endure —, *patienter* or *toleranter ferre alqd, patienter atque aequo animo ferre*, and with *pati ac ferre, pati et perferre, perferre ac pati, perferre patique alqd.* **II.** n. *aeger* (= the sick person).

patois, n. *sermo rusticus.*

patriarch, n. *patriarcha* (Eccl.). **patriarchal,** adj. 1, *patriarchalis* (Eccl.); 2, fig. * *grandaevus*; see OLD.

patrician, adj. and n. *patricius* (opp. *plebeius*); the —s, *patricii.*

patrimony, n. *hereditas* (= inheritance), *patrimonium* (= inherited from the father).

patriot, n. *patriae* or *reipublicae amans, reipublicae amicus* (= who loves his own native country), *civis bonus* (= a good citizen, in general); to be a —, *amare patriam, bene de republicâ sentire.* **patriotic,** adj. *patriae* or *reipublicae amans.* Adv. *patriae caus(s)â.* **patriotism,** n. *patriae amor* or *caritas* (= love of one's own country), *pietas erga patriam*, in the context only *pietas* (= the duty which we have towards our own native country), *reipublicae studium*; if — is a crime, I have already sufficiently atoned for it, *si scelestum est patriam amare, pertuli paenarum satis*; to possess —, *patriam amare, bene de republicâ sentire.*

patristic, adj. *patrum* or *quod ad patres pertinet.*

patrol, I. n. *circitores, circuitores* (late). **II.** v.intr. *circumire stationes* (= to examine and watch the outposts), *circumire vigilias* (= to examine the sentinels), *circumire urbem* (= to go round the town).

patron, n. 1, = protector, *patrōnus, fautor, cultor, amator, praeses, -idis*, m. and f. (= guardian); — of the learned, *doctorum cultor*; 2, = a superior, as a feudal lord, **dominus feudi*, or holder of church property, **patronus*, — saint, *praeses, -idis*, m **patronage**, n = the system of patron and client, *patrocinium, clientela, praesidium*, to be under the —, *sub alcjs fide et clientelā esse* **patroness**, n *patrona* **patronize**, v tr *alqd gratiā et auctoritate suā sustentare*

patronymic, adj and n *patronymicum nomen* (Gram)

patten, n *lignea solea* (= mere wooden sole tied under the feet), *sculponea* (= a kind of higher wooden shoe)

patter, I. v intr *crepare, crepitare, crepitum dare* (= to clatter), *strepĕre, strepitum dare* (= to rattle) **II.** n *crepitus, -ūs, strepitus, -ūs*

pattern, n **1**, = example, *exemplum, exemplar, specimen, documentum, proplasma, ătis*, n (of a sculptor, Plin), to set a —, *exemplum proponere ad imitandum*, a — of excellence, *excellentiae specimen*, **2**, = sample, *exemplum*

paucity, n *paucitas*, or by adj *pauci*

paunch, n *abdōmen* (proper term), *venter* (= stomach in gen)

pauper, n see Poor **pauperism**, n see Poverty

pause, I. n *mora* (= delay), *respiratio, interspiratio* (= interval in speaking, in order to take breath), *distinctio* (in music, Cic), *intervallum* (= interval, e g to make a pause in speaking, *intervallo dicĕre*, e g *distincta alias et interpuncta intervalla, morae respirationesque delectant*, Cic , but as regards music = stop), *intermissio* (when anything stops for a while), *intercapĭdo* (= interval, interruption, e g to make a — in writing letters, in one's correspondence, *intercapedinem scribendi facĕre*) **II.** v intr *moram facĕre* (= to make a delay), *intersistĕre* (= to stop for a while, during a speech, etc , Quint), to — in anything, *moram facĕre in alqā re* (in paying, *in solvendo*), *intermittĕre alqd* (= to discontinue for a time), *alqd faciendi intercapedinem facĕre*, I do not — a single moment in my work during the night, *nulla pars nocturni tempori ad laborem intermittitur*, see Cease, Intermit

pave, v tr *lapide* or *silice (con)sternĕre* or *persternĕre* (in gen), *munire* (= to make a road) **pavement**, n *pavimentum*, † *strata viarum, via strata* (= paved road) **paving**, n *stratura* (Suet) **paving-stone**, n *saxum quadratum*

pavilion, n *papilio* (= a tent erected for pleasure in summer, late), see Tent.

paw, I. n *pes, pedis*, m (= foot), *ungula* (= claw) **II.** v tr (*solum*, etc) *pedibus ferire*

pawn, I. n *pignus, -ŏris*, n , see Pledge **II.** v tr *alqd pignori dare* or *opponĕre* **pawnbroker**, n *pignerator* or *qui pignora quaestus caus(s)ā accipit* (The Romans had no system of pawnbroking)

pawn, n. at chess, *latrunculus, latro*

pay, I. v tr (*per*)*solvĕre, exsolvĕre, dissolvĕre, pendĕre, dependĕre* (= to weigh out), *pensitare, numerare, numerato solvĕre* (in ready money), not to be able to —, *non esse solvendo* or *ad solvendum*, to — cash, *praesenti pecuniā solvĕre, repraesentare*, to — a penalty, *poenas dare* or *solvĕre*, to — for, = to give money for, *alqd pro alqā re solvĕre*, = to atone for, *luĕre*, to — for with one's life, *alqd capite luĕre*, see Atone **II.** v intr *fructum ferre, quaestuosum, fructuosum esse* **III** n *merces, -ēdis*, f (= wages), *stipendium* (of a soldier), *quaestus, -ūs* (= gain) **payable**, adj *solvendus*, a bill is — at sight, *pecunia ex syngraphā solvenda est* **pay-day**, n *dies quo merces solvenda est*, or *dies* alone if fixed by context **paymaster**, n **1**, in gen *qui alqd solvit*, see Steward, **2**, in the army, *tribunus aerarius* **payment**, n *solutio, repraesentatio* (= ready money —)

pea, n *pisum* (Plin.), *cicer, -ĕris*, n (= chick-pea)

peace, I. n *pax, otium* (= leisure), *concordia* (= agreement); in —, *in pace*, to treat for —, *agĕre de pacis condicionibus*, to enter on —, *inire pacem*, to make —, *facĕre pacem*, to keep or preserve —, *pacis fidem servare*, to break —, *pacem frangĕre, violare*, to have no —, *turbari, vexari*, from someone, *ab alqo*, to leave a person in —, *alqm non turbare*, to dismiss in —, *alqm cum pace demittĕre*, articles of —, *pacis leges, condiciones*, to bring —, *ferre*, to prescribe —, *dicĕre*, to accept —, *accipĕre*, love of —, *pacis amor*, one who studies —, *pacis amans, congruens*, to bind over to keep the —, *pecuniā de vi cavĕre* **II.** interj *tace, tacete* ! *Pax* ! **peaceable**, adj *placidus, placabilis, concors* Adv *placide, concorditer, congruenter* **peaceful**, adj *pacatus, placidus, quietus, tranquillus* Adv *placide, quiete, tranquille, cum (bonā) pace* **peacefulness**, n , **peacemaker**, n see Peace **peace-offering**, n *piaculum, placamen*, see Treaty, Truce

peacock, n *pavo*

peak, n **1**, generally by *summus* or *extremus* (= the uppermost or furthest part, etc , e g the — of the mountain, *summum montis jugum*), see Summit, Top , **2** = the end of anything that terminates in a point, *apex*, see Point

peal, I. n *sonitus, -ūs, campanarum* (of bells), — of laughter, *cachinnus*, — of applause, *plausūs clamores*, — of thunder, *tonitrus, -ūs, fragor* (mostly poet.) **II.** v tr perhaps *campanas movēre* or *ciēre* **III.** v intr *sonare*

pear, n *pirum* **pear-tree**, n *pirus*, f

pearl, n *margarita* **pearly**, adj *margaritum similis*

peasant, n *agricola*, m , *agricultor*, in the context also simply *cultor* (= countryman, in reference to his occupation ; poetic, *ruricola*), *rusticus* (both in reference to his occupation and to his manners, hence = an uncultivated person, without refinement, in opp to *urbanus*, a refined civilian), *agrestis* (in reference to his dwelling in the country , also with regard to his rude manners), *rusticanus* (= brought up in the country), *paganus, vicanus* (= villager, opp *oppidanus*) **peasantry**, n *rustici, agrestes*

pease, n see Pea

pebble, n *calculus, lapillus*

peccadillo, n *culpa, delictum*, see Fault **peccant**, adj *peccans*

peck, I. n = a measure, perhaps *semodius* **II.** v tr *rostro tundĕre* (= to strike) or *caedĕre, vellicare*

pectoral, adj *pectoralis* (Cels)

peculation, n *peculatus, ūs* (*publicus*), to commit —, *pecuniam avertĕre, peculari*, to be accused of —, *peculatūs accusari*, see Embezzle.

peculiar, adj **1**, = belonging to a person, *proprius* (= both what belongs to anyone as his property and what is — to him, in Cic only with genit), *meus, tuus, suus* (= *proprius*), comb *proprius et meus, praecipuus et proprius* (= particular and —), *peculiaris* (= what anyone possesses as his own, esp of one's own earnings), comb *peculiaris et proprius, privatus* (= what belongs to anyone as his own property, opp *publicus*), *singularis* (= what belongs to anyone as his characteristic feature), this failing is not merely — to old people, *id quidem non proprium* *senectutis est vitium*; it is — to man, etc., *est naturâ sic generata hominis vis*, etc. (Cic.), to every man, *cujusvis hominis est* (e.g. to err, *errare*, Cic.); see PARTICULAR, SPECIAL; 2, = singular, *mirus, novus*; see STRANGE. Adv. *praesertim, maxime, imprimis* (*in primis*), *mirum in modum, mire*. **peculiarity,** n. *proprietas* (= peculiar nature of anything), *natura* (= natural state, characteristic feature); what is a noble — in his style, *quod orationi ejus eximium inest*; everyone should as much as possible preserve his own —, *id quemque maxime decet quod est cujusque maxime suum*.

pecuniary, adj. *pecuniarius, praemium pecuniae* or *rei pecuniariae*; to make large — rewards to anyone, *munera pecuniae magna alci dare, praemia rei pecuniariae magna alci tribuĕre*.

pedagogue, n. *paedagogus* (= the slave who accompanied a child to school; used also by Plaut. in something of the modern sense of —); *magister* (= master); see PEDANT, EDUCATE, SCHOOL.

pedant, n. *homo ineptus* (*qui aut tempus quid postulet, non videt, aut plura loquitur, aut se ostentat, aut eorum, quibuscum est, vel dignitatis vel commodi rationem non habet, aut denique in algo genere inconcinnus aut multus est, is ineptus esse dicitur*, Cic.); *homo putidus* (= who tries the patience of his hearers or readers to the utmost, through his pedantic manner). **pedantic,** adj. *ineptus, putidus, molestus*; to have nothing —, *nihil habēre molestiarum nec ineptiarum*; see AFFECTED. Adv. *inepte, putide, moleste*. **pedantry,** n. *ineptiae* (in gen.), *jactatio putida* (= idle ostentation), *molestia* (= affectation), *morositas* (= niceness), *molesta* or (stronger) *molestissima diligentiae perversitas* (= unnecessary care and trouble, so as to be wearisome to others); exact, conscientious, but without —, *diligens sine molestiâ*; see AFFECTATION.

pedestal, n. of a column, etc., *basis, stylobătes, -is*, m.

pedestrian, adj. and n. a —, *pedes, -ĭtis*, m.; — tour, *iter pedestre*; to begin a — tour, *iter pedibus ingredi*; to make a — tour, *iter pedibus facĕre, conficĕre*.

pedigree, n. *stemma gentile* or simply *stemma* (Sen.); to repeat one's whole — off by heart, *memoriter progeniem suam ab avo atque atavo proferre*.

pedlar, n. *institor*.

peel, I. n. *cutis* (Plin.), *corium* (Plin.), *tunica, crusta* (e.g. *glandis*, Plin.), *putamen* (= shell of nuts, etc.). **II.** v.tr. *putamen, cutem*, etc., *alci rei detrahĕre* (fruit, eggs); to — a tree, *corticem arbori in orbem* (all round) *detrahĕre, decorticare arborem* or *delibrare arborem*. **III.** v.intr. *cutem* (*paul(l)atim*) (*de*)*ponĕre*. **peeling,** n. *decorticatio*.

peep, I. v.intr. *prospicĕre*; to — forth, *enitēre, emicare* (= to shine), *apparēre, conspici, conspicuum esse* (= to be seen, the latter two esp. of objects that are very conspicuous); to — at anything, *alqd intueri, oculis percurrĕre*. **II.** n. 1, *a(d)spectus, -ūs, conspectus, -ūs*; to take a — at, *alqd oculis percurrĕre, oculos in alqd con(j)icĕre*; see LOOK; 2, = beginning at — of day, *diluculo, primâ luce*.

peep, v.intr., of chickens, *pipare, pipire*.

peer, n. 1, = equal, *par*; 2, = noble, *unus e patriciis* or *nobilibus*; house of —s, *senatus, -ūs*. **peerage,** n. by *gradus, -ūs* (e.g. to raise to the —, *alqm ad amplissimum gradum producĕre*. **peerless,** adj. *cui par inveniri non potest, unicus*. Adv. *unice*.

peer, v.intr. (*per*)*scrutari alqd*; see EXAMINE.

peevish, adj. *stomachosus, morosus, difficilis, iracundus*; see ILL-TEMPER. Adv. *stomachose, morose, iracunde*; see SENSITIVE, IRRITABLE. **peevishness,** n. *stomachus, morositas, difficultas, ira, iracundia*.

peg, I. n. *paxillus* (small, for driving into the ground), *cultellus ligneus*. **II.** v.tr. see FASTEN.

pelf, n. *lucrum*.

pelisse, n. *pallium* or *pallium ex pellibus factum*.

pell-mell, adv. *promiscue* (= promiscuously), *confuse, permixte* (= without order), *passim* (= in all directions); lying there —, *promiscuus, confusus, permixtus*; we may also form compounds with *per* or *cum* (e.g. to mix —, *miscēre, permiscēre, commiscēre*), to mix — everything, *miscēre omnia ac turbare*.

pellucid, adj. †*pellucidus*; see TRANSPARENT.

pelt, v.tr. *lapides in alqm jacĕre, con(j)icĕre, alqm lapidibus petĕre*. **pelting,** adj. (of rain) *maximus*, or less strongly *magnus imber*.

pen, I. n. 1, **penna* (*scriptoria*) (not in use till the 7th century), *calamus, stilus* (of metal); to dip a — in ink, *calamum intingĕre* (Quint.); 2, = fold, *saeptum* (*sep-*). **II.** v.tr. 1, *scribĕre*; see WRITE; 2, = to fold, *saeptis* (*sep-*) *includĕre*. **pen-knife,** n. see KNIFE. **penman,** n. *qui scribit*. **penmanship,** n. *ars bene scribendi*.

penal, adj. — law, *lex poenalis* (Jct.). **penalty,** n. *poena, damnum, multa* (*mulcta*) (the two latter = the — inflicted upon anyone, *damnum* as a punishment inflicted, *multa* = both the loss the person suffers, and the indemnification for the person aggrieved); to inflict a —, *alqm alqâ re multare*. **penance,** n. *satisfactio* (= penalty for injuries done, Eccl. term = penance), *multa* (*mulcta*) (= penalty), *poena* (in gen. = penalty paid by anyone), *piaculum* (= atonement); to order anyone to do —, *piaculum ab algo exigĕre*. **penitence,** n. *paenitentia* (in gen.); see REPENTANCE. **penitent,** adj. *paenitens* (= repenting); Alexander was so — after he had murdered Clitus, that he was about to kill himself, *interempto Clito Alexander manus vix a se abstinuit, tanta vis erat paenitendi*. **penitential,** adj. (*quod*) *paenitentiam declarat*. **penitentiary,** n. *carcer, -eris*, m. (= prison), defining further sense by context.

pence, n., see PENNY.

pencil, n. 1, of painter, *penicillus* (or *-um*); see PAINTER; 2, for writing, *stilus* (see PEN).

pendant, n. *stalagmium* (Plaut.), *inaures, -ium*, f. (= ear-ring).

pending, I. adj. 1, in law, *res delata est ad judicem*; the matter is still —, *adhuc sub judice lis est*; 2, in commerce, *nondum expeditus* or *confectus*. **II.** prep. *per* with accus. (= during), *nondum* with part. (e.g. — the decision of the court, *lis nondum judicata*), *dum, donec* (= until, e.g. — his return, *dum redeat*).

pendulous, adj. *pendulus*.

pendulum, n., perhaps *perpendiculum* (not class.).

penetrability, n., by **penetrable,** adj. *penetrabilis, pervius* (where there is a road through, opp. *invius*). **penetrate, I.** v.tr. *penetrare, permanare in* with accus., *pervadĕre per* or simply with accus. (to — all parts of the body; poison —s every limb of the body, *vene-*

num cunctos artus pervadit or *in omnes partes permanat*), the draught —s the veins, *potio venas occupat*, to — the mind, *penetrare in animos* (of a speaker's address, etc), —d (with grief, joy, etc), *commotus, ictus, percussus, perfusus* **II.** v intr (with an effort) *penetrare*, through a place, *per alqm locum*, to a place, *ad alqm locum* or *in alqm locum*, *pervadĕre alqm locum* or *per alqm locum* (= to go through a place, both of persons and things), *exaudiri* (= to be heard), *ad aures pervadĕre* (of the echo, e g *clamor urbem pervadit*), *translucĕre* (of the light), imperceptibly, *perferri in alqm locum* (= to spread as far as); with force, *irruĕre, irrumpĕre in alqm locum* (the latter two of a large number, all three of persons and things), *descendĕre in* or *ad alqd* (= to descend down to —, of persons and things), the cry —s into their ears, *clamorem exaudiunt*, the cry —s into the camp, *clamor in castra perfertur*, to — into the future, *futuri temporis gnarum esse*, to — into a country, *progredi, procedĕre, prorumpĕre* (the latter = to rush forth with violence), *se insinuare* (by stealth, e g into the affections, etc, also lit). **penetrating,** adj **1,** of cold, etc, *penetralis, penetrabilis, acutus, acer, maximus, gravis*, **2,** fig *sagax, acutus, astutus, callidus, sol(l)ers, perspicax*, see SAGACIOUS, ACUTE **penetration,** n *acies, acumen* (e g *ingenii*), *sagacitas, sol(l)ertia, perspicacitas* **penetrative,** adj *gravis, vehemens* (of a sermon, etc), see IMPRESSIVE **penetrativeness,** n, the — of judicial pleadings, *aculei oratorii ac forenses* (Cic).

peninsula, n *peninsula* **peninsular,** adj, by circuml with *peninsula*

penny, n *as, nummus* (*sestertius*), not a — (I give, etc), *ne nummum quidem*; to the last — (or farthing), *ad nummum* (i e to agree, *convenire*), to pay to the last —, *ad assem solvĕre*

pension, I n *annuum* (= yearly payment, Plin M., Suet, more usual in pl) **II.** v tr *annua*, etc, *alci praebĕre*. **pensioner,** n. *cui annua praebentur*

pensive, adj *in cogitatione* (or *cogitationibus*) *defixus, subtristis* (= somewhat sad, ante and post class), see THOUGHTFUL. Adv use adj **pensiveness,** n *cogitatio* (= thought), *tristitia* (= sadness)

pentagon, n *pentagon(i)um* (or *pentagonion*, late) **pentagonal,** adj *quinquangulus* (Gram)

pentameter, n (*versus*) *pentameter* (Quint)

pentateuch, n. *pentateuchus* (Eccl)

Pentecost, n *dies pentecostes, pentecoste* (Eccl)

penthouse, n *tugurium parieti affixum*, as milit term, *vinea*

penultima, n by *penultimus* (opp *ultimus*, Aul Gell, *penultima*, sc *syllaba*)

penurious, adj *parcus, sordidus, avarus, tenax*, see NIGGARDLY Adv *sordide, avare, parce, parce ac tenuiter* **penuriousness,** n *sordes, -is*, f (usu. in pl), *tenacitas, tenuitas victus* (in one's mode of living), see NIGGARDLINESS, MEANNESS, PARSIMONY **penury,** n *inopia, egestas* (*victus* or *rerum necessariarum penuria*), see POVERTY

peony, n *paeonia* (Plin)

people, I. n as a large number in gen, *vis* (= crowd, of men and animals), *copiae* (= troops, soldiers), *vulgus*, -i, n (= the great mass of the —, in opp to those of a higher position, e g the soldiers in opp to the commissioned officers), *plebs*, *-is*, f (= the common —), the —, *homines* (= men in gen), *homunculi, homunciones* (in a contemptuous sense), the young —, *adolescentuli*; the — of Greece, *Graeci*, the towns—, *oppidani* (= the inhabitants of the town), *cives* (= citizens), the — in the village, *vicani*, the — in the country, *rustici, pagani* (= peasants), before the —, *palam* (= not in secret), *coram omnibus* (= in the presence of all), *in oculis* or *ante oculos omnium*, very often in Latin the gen term *homines* is left out with adjs, e g many —, *multi*, all the —, *omnes*; good —, *boni*, when *qui* follows, e g there are — who say, *sunt qui dicant*; there are — who believe, *sunt qui existiment*, when we make a wide and general statement, when "—" = "one," e g — say, *dicunt*, — report, *narrant*, the —, = those who belong to anyone, anyone's household, or servants or relations, etc, *alcjs familia* (= anyone's servants, etc, all together, Caes), *alcjs famuli, ministri* (= servants), *alcjs comitas, qui alqm comitantur* (= those who accompany anyone, attendants), *alcjs milites* (= soldiers), my, your, etc, —, *mei, tui, plebecula* (contemptuous), in the name of the —, *publice*; a man of the lower orders, of the —, *homo plebeius* (according to his descent), *homo de plebe* (according to his rank), the language of the common —, *sermo plebeius*, a number of — forming one body as it were, *gens, natio* (e g *exterae nationes et gentes*, Cic), *populus* (forming a State, all the free born citizens together who are united through the same form of government, e g *Scipio Hergetum gentem cum infesto exercitu invasisset, compulsis omnibus, Athanagiam urbem, quae caput ejus populi erat, circumsedit*, Liv, where *gentem* = a — of the same origin or race, but which as a State, *populus*, had a capital, one *gens* may comprise several *populos*), in the pl also comb *populi nationesque*, when we speak of one particular — or nation, we may also render — in Latin by *nomen* (= name, i e anything, everybody who has or goes by that name, e g Hannibal the mortal enemy of the Roman —, *Hannibal inimicissimus nomini Romano*, Nepos), also comb *gens ac nomen* (e g *Nerviorum*, Caes), belonging to our —, nation, *nostras*, see NATION, a riot caused by the —, *tumultus, -ūs*, a decree of the whole —, *populi scitum, plebiscitum* (decreed by the great mass of the — [in opp to a decree of the senate], and which had been adopted by majority, after it had been proposed by the presiding magistrate), *populi jussum* (inasmuch as the — collectively had the right of commanding the senate to confirm a decree adopted by them, after which every citizen was obliged to obey the same), comb *populi scitum jussumque*, the power of the —, *populi* or *popularis potestas* (see POWER) **II.** v tr **1,** *coloniam* or *colonos deducĕre* or *mittĕre alqo* (= to send out a colony), or *locum incolis frequentare* (in sense of filling a place with inhabitants), **2,** fig *complĕre* (= to fill), **3,** = INHABIT, see POPULATE **peopled,** adj see POPULOUS **populace,** n *plebs* (= commons), *vulgus* -i, n (= mob), dregs of the —, *populi faex* or *sentina* **popular,** adj **1,** = belonging to the people, *popularis*, the — party, *populares*, **2,** = a general favourite, *popularis* (rare), *populo* or *in vulgus gratus* or *acceptus*, to be —, *gratia multum apud alqm valere*, or *gratiā plurimum posse*, to become —, *gratiam ab alqo* or *in* or *apud alqm inire*, **3,** = suited to the common understanding, of style, etc, *ad communem judicium accommodatus* Adv *populariter* **popularity,** n *gratia* (= influence), *populi favor* or *studium*, breath of —, *aura popularis*, to gain —, *gratiam ab alqo, ad* or *apud alqm inire* **populate,** v tr *frequentare* (*incolis*), to — a place with settlers, *coloniam* or *colonos deducĕre, mittĕre alqo* (the former if the person himself lead a colony anywhere); see PEOPLE II. **population,** n. 1, *coloniorum deductio in locum* (when a colony is established anywhere); 2, *multitudo* (= multitude), *frequentia* (= large multitude), *civium* or *incolarum numerus* (= number of resident inhabitants), *cives* (= citizens), *incolae* (= inhabitants); see PEOPLE; the town has a sufficient —, *urbi frequentia suppetit.* **populous,** adj. *frequens* (opp. *desertus*), *celeber* (of a place through which there is a heavy traffic, much visited, e.g. a street, etc., opp. *desertus*). **populousness,** n. *celebritas hominum* or *civium frequentia* (where there is a large attendance).

pepper, I. n. *piper, -ĕris,* n. — -cruet, — -box, *pyxis piperis.* **II.** v.tr. *pipere condire.*

per, a Latin prep., which, as a prefix in English, means 1, = THOROUGH, THOROUGHLY, which see; 2, = by; *per annum,* a year, see ANNUAL; — week; see WEEKLY.

peradventure, adv. *forte, fortasse, forsitan;* see PERHAPS.

perambulate, v.tr. *transire, iter facĕre per alqm locum* (= to travel through, *peragrare* (= to wander through, in gen.), *obire* (= through a country, etc., in order to see it, on foot, *pedibus*), (*per*)*lustrare* (in order to look about), *percurrĕre* (quickly, also *percurrĕre celeriter*), *pervolare* (in a hurry), *circumire* (all round), *pervagari* (in a place). **perambulation,** n. *lustratio, peragratio, transitus, -ūs* (= passage through, etc.).

perceivable, adj. *quod sentiri* or *sensibus percipi potest, sensibilis* (= what can be felt, the latter first in Vitruv.). **perceive,** v.tr. *sentire, sensibus percipĕre* (with the senses, in gen.), *auribus percipĕre, audire* (with the ears), *oculis percipĕre, vidēre* (= to see), *cernĕre* (= to see more distinctly); to — the course of the stars, *cursus stellarum notare;* fig. with the understanding, *animadvertĕre* (= to direct one's thoughts to a certain thing; with the part. when I — a thing in a particular state; with the accus. and infin. when I — through what I have heard, etc.), *cognoscĕre* (= to learn, to know; to obtain a clear perception of anything), *sentire* (= to feel, to see, *alqd* or *de alqâ re*), *vidēre* (= to see, to understand); to — clearly, *perspicĕre, conspicĕre* (= to behold), *observare* (= to observe), *intellegere* (*intellig-*) (= to comprehend). **perceptibility,** n. by **perceptible,** adj. *insignis, conspicuus* (= conspicuous), *manifestus* (= manifest); see CLEAR. Adv. *manifeste;* see CLEARLY. **perception,** n. gen. by verbs, by *percipĕre;* see SENSATION, NOTION, IDEA. **perceptive,** adj. by verbs.

perch, I. n. 1, a measure of length = 5½ yards; *pertica* (very late); 2, for hens, *pertica* (*gallinaria*). **II.** v.intr. *alci rei insidēre* (= to settle on), *alci rei insidēre* (= to remain on).

perch, n. = a fish, *perca* (Plin.).

perchance, adv. see PERADVENTURE.

percolate, I. v.tr. see STRAIN. **II.** v.intr. *permanare.* **percolation,** n. *percolatio,* or by verb.

percussion, n. *ictus, -ūs* (= blow), *pulsus, -ūs* (= push); see SHOCK.

perdition, n. *exitium, interitus, -ūs, pernicies.*

peremptory, adj. 1, *confidens, arrogans;* to give — orders, *definite praecipĕre* or *diligenter mandare alqd,* or in a stronger sense, *arroganter praecipĕre;* 2, a — judgment, *judicium plenum arrogantiae;* to judge in a — manner, *arrogantius judicare.* Adv. *confidenter, arroganter;* see ABSOLUTE, POSITIVE, DECISIVE.

perennial, adj. *perennis.* Adv. by adj. or *perpetuo;* see ALWAYS.

perfect, I. adj. *plenus* (in gen. of anything that is neither deficient as regards the contents, nor in number or size), *integer* (= not mutilated, complete), *absolutus, perfectus,* comb. *absolutus et perfectus, perfectus atque absolutus, expletus et perfectus, perfectus cumulatusque, perfectus completusque* (= having the highest perfection, completed), *verus, germanus* (= real, genuine); to make anything —, *alqd absolvĕre* (so that nothing can be said to be wanting, e.g. *beneficium,* kindness), *cumulare alqd* (= to crown, fig., e.g. the pleasure, *gaudium*). Adv. *plene, absolute, perfecte,* or by superl. in sense of "quite" (e.g. — right, *rectissime.* **II.** v.tr. *excolĕre* (= to develop further, e.g. the art of oratory, *orationem*), *conficĕre, perficĕre;* to — anyone in knowledge, *augēre alqm scientiâ.* **III.** n. Gram. t.t. *praeteritum perfectum* (Quint.). **perfection,** n. *integritas* (= completeness), *absolutio, perfectio, absolutio perfectioque* (= highest degree of —; — of virtue, *virtus, -ūtis, perfecta cumulataque;* to bring anything to —, *alqd absolvĕre* or *perficĕre.*

perfidious, adj. *perfidus, perfidiosus* (= faithless, opp. *fidelis*), *infidus* (= not trustworthy, opp. *fidus*). Adv. *perfide, perfidiose;* see TREACHEROUS. **perfidy,** n. *perfidia* (= faithlessness, with which anyone breaks a solemn promise), *infidelitas* (= want of faith); to show —, *perfide* or *fraudulenter agĕre.*

perforate, v.tr. = to bore through, *terebrare* (with a borer, and also otherwise, e.g. an apple with the finger), *perterebrare* (with the borer), *perforare* (= to make holes in, in gen.).

perforce, adv. *vi, per vim, necessario,* or by *invitus* or *compulsus, coactus.*

perform, v.tr. (*per*)*agĕre* (= to do, e.g. business, *negotium*), *gerĕre* (= to be the support of anything, as it were, e.g. *negotium*), *obire* (= to undergo), *alqd praestare* (= to discharge, e.g. *officium*), (*per*)*fungi alqâ re* (= to discharge, to discharge with zeal), *administrare* (= to administer), *exsequi* (= to carry out; all these, *negotium, munus*), *conficĕre* (= to accomplish, e.g. *negotium*); to — one's duties, *res suas obire, officia sua exsequi;* to — a business for anyone (at anyone's request), *negotium alcjs procurare;* to — a part, *partes agĕre, in scaenâ* (*scen-*) *esse* (on the stage); to — the part of an accuser, *partes accusatoris obtinēre;* to — sacred rites, *sacra facĕre;* see DO, EXECUTE, ACCOMPLISH, DISCHARGE, FULFIL. **performance,** n. = the act of —, *actio, administratio* (= the administering), *confectio* (= the accomplishing), *perfunctio;* — of a business for another (at his request), *procuratio;* = the thing itself which is performed, *actio, negotium* (= business), *officium* (= duty), *ministerium* (= service); a — on the stage, *fabula* (= the piece played), with *agi* (e.g. during the —, *dum fabula agitur*); to give a —, *fabulam dare.* **performer,** n. 1, in gen. *actor, auctor, confector,* or by PERFORM; 2, *artis musicae peritus,* or, in gen. *alcjs rei artifex* (e.g. *canendi*), *alcjs rei peritissimus* (e.g. *cantandi*), *acroâma, -ătis,* n. (lit. = a concert, then also the person who gives it, singer, minstrel, player).

perfume, I. n. *odor* (*odos*), *unguentum* (= ointment). **II.** v.tr. *odoribus perfundĕre* (with sweet smells); † *suffire* (by burning —). **perfumer,** n. 1, who perfumes, by verbs; 2, *qui merces odorum venditat, myropola, -ae,* m. (Plaut.), *unguentarius.*

perfunctory, adj. *neglegens* (*neglig-*); see NEGLIGENT.

perhaps, adv. *fortasse, forsitan,* † *forsan*

(*fortasse* also with numbers, the latter generally with subj, *fortassis* is very little used, and *forsan* is poetical, we cannot say *forte* for *fortasse* in gen, as *forte* can in gen only be used after *si, nisi, ne* [not after *num*], in which case we could not say *fortasse*), *haud scio an, nescio an* (= I don't know whether, etc), to express a modest assertion, with which we must use *nullus, nemo, numquam* (*nunq*), whilst according to the English "— someone, etc, or I don't know whether anyone, etc," we might be led to say, *ullus, quisquam, umquam*, whether — someone, somebody, after the verbs "to ask (*quaerĕre*)" and "to search, explore (*percontari*)," by *ecquis* (or *ecqui*), *ecquae* (or *ecqua*), *ecquid*, you ask whether — there be any hope? *quaeris ecqua spes sit?* — someone, — anyone, *forsitan quispiam, alqs forte*, — may also be rendered by *aliquando* (some time, or *quando* after *si* or *ne*), *circiter, fere*, or *ferme* (in approximate estimations as regards time and numbers, see ALMOST), *fere* and *ferme* also in gen when we speak in an uncertain manner, e g. he spoke — in this way, *in hanc fere sententiam locutus est*, unless —, *nisi forte, nisi si*, if —, *si forte*, — because, etc? *an quod*, etc? — not, etc.? (at the beginning of a principal sentence, in a direct question, which serves as an answer at the same time), *an*

pericardium, n **pericardium* (not class)

peril, n see DANGER, RISK **perilous**, adj see DANGEROUS

period, n. 1, in astronomy, *ambitus, -ūs, circuitus, -ūs*, 2, = a portion of time, *tempus* (= time, space of time in gen), or *tempora, tempestas* (= a time with regard to certain signs, circumstances, epoch), *aetas* (= age), *spatium temporis* (= space of time), no — of my life, *nullum aetatis meae tempus*, 3, in chronology, see TIME, EPOCH, 4, in gram *periodus* (Quint), in Cic only in Greek, περίοδος, rendered by him by (*verborum*) *ambitus*, or (*verborum* or *orationis*) *circuitus*, or (*verborum*) *comprehensio* or *circumscriptio* or *continuatio*, or *verborum* or *orationis orbis*, or *circuitus et quasi orbis verborum*, a well flowing and rounded —, *apta et quasi rotunda constructio*, structure of the —, (*verborum*) *compositio* (Quint.) **periodical**, adj what returns at stated intervals, *sollemnis* (*sol(l)enn-*), e g — diseases, *morbi tempore certo* or *stato recurrentes*, — writings, papers, periodicals, *ephemerides, -um*, see JOURNAL, — winds, *venti qui magnam partem temporis in certis locis flare consuerverunt* Adv *certis temporibus*

peripatetic, adj *peripateticus*; the —s, *Peripatetici*

periphery, n *perimetros* (Vitr.)

periphrasis, n see PARAPHRASE

perish, v intr *perire* (e g by illness, *morbo*), *interire* (stronger than *perire*, = complete annihilation), *cadĕre* (= to fall, principally in battle), *occidĕre* (= to die in the presence of others, e g in battle), *occidi, interfici, necari* (= to be killed, see KILL), to — in the war, *bello cadĕre, in bello occidĕre, absumi alqā re* (= to be swept away through, etc, e g *fame, veneno*, through illness, through pestilence, *morbo, pestilentiā*), more — from hunger than by the sword, *plures fames quam ferrum absumpsit*. **perishable**, adj *quod corrumpi potest, fluxus* (= inconstant, e g *gloria*), *fragilis* (= frail), comb *fluxus et* (or *atque*) *fragilis, cadūcus, infirmus* (= weak), comb *cadūcus et infirmus, brevis* (= short, e g *omnia quae habent speciem gloriae contemne, brevia, fugacia, cadūca existima*, Cic) **perishableness**, n *fragilitas, brevitas* (= shortness, e g. of life), *infirmitas* (= weakness).

peristyle, n *peristyl(i)um*

periwinkle, n a plant, *vinca pervinca* (or as one word, *vincapervinca*, Plin)

perjure, v tr *falsum jurare* (in gen), *pejerare* or *perjurare, perjurium facĕre* **perjured**, adj *perjurus* **perjury**, n. *falsum jusjurandum* (in gen), *perjurium*

perky, adj *protervus*, see SAUCY

permanency, n *perpetuitas* (= without interruption), *perennitas, diuturnitas, longinquitas* (= for a length of time), *stabilitas* **permanent**, adj by *permanēre*, or by *perpetuus, perennis, diuturnus, longinquus, stabilis*, see CONSTANT Adv *perpetuo*

permeability, n, **permeable**, adj † *penetrabilis*, see PENETRATE

permissible, adj *licitus* (= allowed), *concessus* (= granted), to be —, *licitum esse, licēre* **permission**, n *concessio* (= concession), *permissio* (very rare, the substs *concessus* and *permissus* only in the ablat sing), *potestas, copia* (= power given anyone), *arbitrium* (= free will to do a thing), *licentia* (= entire liberty to do what one likes); to give anyone —, *veniam, potestatem, licentiam alci dare*, for or to, *alcjs rei faciendae, potestatem alci facĕre, concedĕre, licentiam alci concedĕre, licentiam alci permittĕre ut*, etc, *alci alqd permittĕre, concedĕre* (see PERMIT), to give children — to play, *pueris ludendi licentiam dare*, to have the —, *mihi licet, permissum, concessum est*, with your —, *permissu et concessu tuo, si per te licitum erit, pace tuā*, without anyone's — (to do a thing, etc), *injussu alcjs*, contrary to my —, *me invito* **permissive**, adj by verbs **permit**, v tr *sinĕre* (with infin), *concedĕre alqd alci* or *ut* (= to concede, generally after a request has been made, opp. *repugnare*), *permittĕre* (dat or *ut*, = to allow anything to be done, opp *vetare*), *facultatem dare* or *potestatem facĕre alcjs rei, alcjs rei veniam dare* or *dare hanc veniam ut* (= to show indulgence in anything), see ALLOW

permutation, n (*per*)*mutatio*

pernicious, adj *perniciosus* (= ruinous), *exitiosus* (= leading to a tragical end, e g conspiracy), *exitialis, exitiabilis* (of such a kind as to be likely to lead to a tragical end, e g war), *funestus* (= bringing grief over a great many, e g tribuneship), *damnosus*, to anyone, *alci* (= causing injury, e g *bellum*) Adv *perniciose, exitiose, funeste* **perniciousness**, n. *vis nocendi*, also by circumloc with *nocēre*, who does not see the — of this thing? *quis non intellegit hanc rem nocēre?*

peroration, n *peroratio, epilogus, conclusio*

perpendicular, adj *directus* (*ad perpendiculum*)

perpetrate, v tr *alqd committĕre* or *in se admittere*, see COMMIT **perpetration**, n by verb **perpetrator**, n of a crime, *auctor facinoris* or *delicti*, in the context *auctor*, by circumloc *qui, quae facinus* or *flagitium* or *scelus commisit*, *qui, quae facinus in se admisit*

perpetual, adj *perpetuus*, see CONTINUAL Adv *perpetuo*, see ALWAYS **perpetuate**, v tr *alqd perpetuum reddĕre, continuare* (= to carry on beyond the usual time) **perpetuation**, n by verb **perpetuity**, n *perpetuitas*, see DURATION, ETERNITY

perplex, v tr 1, of matters, see CONFUSE, 2, of persons, *alcjs mentem animumque perturbare, percutĕre, distrahĕre, sol(l)icitare, in perturbationem con(j)icĕre*, with talking, *orationis* *differre.* **perplexing,** adj. *difficilis, perplexus, impeditus, anceps, dubius.* **perplexity,** n. *sol(l)icitudo* (= anxiety), *dubitatio* (= doubt); see DOUBT.

perquisite, n. by *reditus extraordinarii, pecunia extraordinaria,* or in the plur. *pecuniae extraordinariae* (of a public functionary, Cic.), *peculium* (= the private property of a child or slave).

perry, n. *vinum ex piris factum.*

persecute, v.tr. *insectari* (= to pursue with hostile intentions), *insequi* (= to pursue close at one's heels), *vexare* (= to vex, to tease unceasingly); violently, *vehementius premĕre* or *vexare alqm*; to — with insults, *alqm verbis contumeliosis prosequi, alqm maledictis* or *contumeliis insectari, alqm probris et maledictis vexare.* **persecution,** n. *insectatio* (= pressure), *vexatio* (= vexation). **persecutor,** n. *vexator* (= who teases), *insectator.*

perseverance, n. *perseverantia* (= not shrinking from any difficulty, however great), *permansio* (*in sententiā*), *constantia* (= consistency, constancy), *assiduitas* (= assiduity), *pertinacia* (= pertinacity, in defending an opinion), *pervicacia* (= utmost — in trying to accomplish a thing or to gain a victory), *obstinatio, obstinatior voluntas, obstinatus animus* (= firm, obstinate in a resolution once formed; in a bad sense = obstinacy), *patientia* (= patience; e.g. in one's work, *laboris*), *virtus, -ūtis* (= in undergoing trouble in gen.). **persevere,** v.intr. *perseverare* (proper term), *constare* (with and without *sibi*, = to be always the same), *perstare, consistĕre, persistĕre* (= to insist upon), (*per*)*manēre* (= to remain firm in; all these generally *in alqā re*), *pergĕre.* **persevering,** adj. *perseverans, constans, assiduus* (= who does not lose his hold, e.g. an enemy, an accuser), *tenax alcjs rei* (= clinging fast to anything), *pertinax, pervicax, obstinatus.* Adv. with pers., *perseveranter, constanter, firmiter, offirmato animo, pertinaciter, pervicacius, obstinate, obstinato animo.*

persist, v.intr. see PERSEVERE. **persistence,** n. see PERSEVERANCE.

person, n. 1, in widest sense, *homo*; in mere enumeration, or contemptuously, *caput*; *persona* (lit., = the mask of the dramatic actor, then fig., = the part which he acts; *persona* never = the individual); by the name of a — we understand that by which we denote his individuality, so that every — may have a peculiar nomination of his own, = *nomen est, quod unicuique personae apponitur, quo suo quaeque proprio vocabulo appellatur* (Cic.); in his, etc., own —, *ipse* (= he himself), *praesens, coram* (= he himself being present, oral); e.g. he came in his own —, *ipse venit*; to be there in his own —, *praesentem* or *coram adesse*; —s of higher rank, *homines nobiles*; a handsome — (= woman), *mulier formosa*; 2, = body, *corpus, -ŏris,* n., *species* (= exterior in gen.), *forma, facies*; 3, = a — represented on the stage, *persona* (lit. = mask), *partes, -ium* (= part); to appear in the — of, *alcjs personam ferre* or *sustinēre* or *tueri* (not *agĕre*), *alcjs partes agĕre, obtinēre* (all lit. and fig.); 4, = — in gram., *persona* (e.g. *tertia,* Quint.). **personage,** n. 1, = PERSON; 2, = great man, *homo nobilis.* **personal,** adj., **personally,** adv. *personalis, personaliter* (Imperial Rome, t.t.); a — verb, *verbum personale* (Gram.); in other instances than these we must render it by *ipse, per se* (= himself), or by *praesens, coram* (= present, in his own person, opp. *per lit(t)eras* (= by letter, and such like), or by *proprius* (= not in common with others, opp. *communis*), or by *privatus* (= referring to one as a private individual, opp. *publicus*), or by other terms, e.g. he appeared —, *ipse aderat*; I have a — interview with anyone, *ipse* or *praesens cum alqo colloquor*; Caesar made a speech as his own — dignity and the respect of his ancestors required, *orationem habuit Caesar, sicut ipsius dignitas et majorum ejus amplitudo postulabat*; to know anyone —, *alqm ipsum nosse, alqm de facie nosse*; not to know anyone —, *alqm non nosse, alqm* or *alcjs faciem ignorare*; not to mind — offences, *omittĕre privatas offensiones*; in the sense of rude, see RUDE and PERSONALITY, 2; — occupations, *studia privata* (opp. *opera publica*). **personality,** n. 1, if = "existence as a person," or "the person itself," it must be rendered by circumloc. (e.g. in our days people deny the — of the devil, *recentiores diabolum esse negant*; he always mixes his own — up with it, *se ipse semper praedicat*); 2, = direct offensive application to a person, perhaps *contumeliae, privatae offensiones* (= personal offences, insults), *maledicta, -orum.* **personalty,** n. (*bona*) *sua.* **personate,** v.tr. *alcjs partes agĕre,* or *personam gerĕre, tueri* or *sustineri*; see REPRESENT, COUNTERFEIT, FEIGN, RESEMBLE. **personification,** n. *prosopopoeïa* (Quint.), pure Lat. *conformatio,* or *personarum fictio* or *confictio,* or *ficta alienarum personarum oratio.* **personify,** v.tr. a thing, 1, in a writing, as acting or speaking, *rem tanquam loquentem inducĕre, alci rei orationem (at)tribuĕre*; 2, to represent as a human being, *alqd humanā specie induĕre, alqd alci rei tanquam vitam (at)tribuĕre.*

perspective, n. (= the science) *scaenographia* (= theatrical drawing, Vitr.); pleasing —, *ea ars pictoris qui efficit ut quaedam eminēre in opere, quaedam recessisse credamus* (Quint.).

perspicacious, adj. lit. *perspicax* (= who can see everything at one glance), *sagax* (= sagacious), *acutus* (= sharp), comb. *acutus et perspicax, acer* (= keen). **perspicacity,** n. (with regard to the understanding) *perspicacitas, acies* or *acumen ingenii, ingenium acre* or *acutum.* **perspicuity,** n. by adj. **perspicuous,** adj. (*di*)*lucidus, luculentus, clarus, evidens, illustris, perspicuus, apertus, distinctus, planus*; see CLEAR, INTELLIGIBLE. Adv. (*di*)*lucide, clare, evidenter, luculenter, perspicue, aperte, distincte, plane.*

perspiration, n. *sudor*; to be in a —, *sudare, sudorem emittĕre*; to be in a great —, *multo sudore manare, sudore madēre* (in gen., Plin.). **perspire,** v.intr. *sudare* (also fig. = to work hard), *sudorem emittĕre* (lit.); I —, *sudor mihi erumpit*; to — a great deal, *multum sudare* (with fear), *multo sudore manare, sudore madēre* (= to drop with perspiration).

persuade, v.tr. = to convince by argument, *persuadēre alci de alqā re,* or with accus. and infin. (the accus. alone can only be used with *persuadēre* when it is a pronoun in the neuter gender, such as *hoc, illud, nihil*); he can easily be —d, *facile adducitur ad credendum*; = to influence by entreaty, etc., *commodis verbis delenire, ut,* etc. (= to talk over), *permovēre* (with *ut* when we want to state the intention; with the infin. alone or with the accus. and infin. when this is not the case; with the accus. alone simply, when it is a neut. pronoun); *alqm impellĕre* (= to urge) or *adducĕre* (= to bring) or *inducĕre* (= to induce) *ad alqd* or with *ut, alci auctorem esse alcjs rei* or with *ut* (= to cause anyone to); they —d me to it, *persuadetur mihi* (not *persuadeor*); to allow oneself to be —d, *persuaderi sibi pati*; to — anyone to believe a thing, *fidem alcjs rei facĕre alci, alqm adducĕre ad opinionem*; to be easily —d to believe a thing, *facile induci ad credendum*; I am not easily —d to believe, *non adduci possum, ut credam*, see CONVINCE **persuasion,** n *persuasio*, — was not difficult, *non difficilis persuasio fuit* gift of —, *virtus ad persuadendum accommodata, vis persuadendi*, see CONVICTION, BELIEF **persuasive,** adj, **persuasiveness,** n, by circumloc with the verb (e g a — speech, *oratio ad persuadendum accommodata*)

pert, adj *protervus, procax* Adv *proterve, procaciter* **pertness,** n *protervitas, procacitas*

pertain, v intr = to belong or relate to, *pertinēre ad alqd, spectare ad alqd, referri, alcjs juris esse* (= to be his of right), with the genit *nullius est artis*, it —s to no art, *proprium esse*, what —s to this, *quod pertinet* or *attinet ad hoc*, or *refertur*, or *referendum est*

pertinacious, adj *obstinatus, pervicax, pertinax* Adv *obstinate, pertinaciter*, to act — in anything, *obstinato animo agere alqd* **pertinacity,** n *animi obstinatio*, in a thing, *alcjs rei* (= obstinacy, contumacy), *pervicacia, animus pervicax* (= great perseverance), *pertinacia* (in holding an opinion or entertaining a plan), *contumacia* (= contumacy)

perturbation, n. see AGITATION, DISTURBANCE

perusal, n *lectio, perlectio* (*pell*) **peruse,** v tr *perlegĕre, evolvĕre, pervolvĕre, pervolutare*

pervade, v tr 1, lit *permanare, alqa re perfundi*, 2, fig *permanare, perfundĕre*, to — the mind, *ad animum descendĕre, in animum penetrare*

perverse, adj *perversus* (lit = diverted, fig, not as it ought to be), *pravus* (fig = contrary to the object intended, e g meaning, *mens, opinio*). Adv, fig *perverse, perperam* (= not right, opp *recte*), see OBSTINATE, STUBBORN **perverseness,** n *perversitas* (e g *hominum, opinionum, morum*) **perversion,** n *corruptio* (= spoiling), *depravatio*, — of meaning, *verbi depravatio, verbum in pejus detortum* (Sen) **pervert, I.** v tr 1, in gen *depravare, corrumpĕre*, 2, as Theol t t, perhaps *a fide Christiana abducĕre* **II.** n perhaps *qui a fide Christiana abductus est*

pervious, adj *pervius* (of places, etc), †*penetrabilis*, to the air, *auri expositus*

pest, n 1, lit, see PESTILENCE, 2, fig, of anything or person very obnoxious, *pestis, pernicies*, comb *pestis ac pernicies*, —house, *aedificium ad pestilentiae contagia prohibenda exstructum* **pester,** v tr see TROUBLE, DISTURB, ANNOY

pestilence, n lit *pestilentia* (as an epidemic disease), *lues, -is* (as obnoxious matter likely to spread disease), *morbus perniciali*s (= dangerous illness, also fig) **pestilential,** adj *pestilens* (lit, opp *saluber*), *foedus* (fig = abominable, horrible, e g smell, opp *suavis*)

pestle, n *pilum, pistillum* (Plin)

pet, I. n *deliciae, amores, um*, see FAVOURITE **II.** v tr *fovēre, in deliciis habēre*

petard, n in phrase, he is hoist with his own —, perhaps *in suos laqueos ipse incidit*

petition, I. n 1, in gen see PRAYER, REQUEST 2, a formal —, *petitio* (= petitioning for, *alcjs rei*), *quae alqs petit, lit(t)erae (supplices)* *libellus* (*supplex*), to sign a — (along with others), *libellum subscribĕre*, to grant a —, *alci petenti satisfacĕre, annuĕre*, to present a — containing a request that, etc, *libello oblato petĕre, ut*, etc **II.** v tr *petĕre alqd ab alqo, rogare alqd*, anyone, *alqm* or *ab alqo* (= to demand anything as a favour), in an urgent manner, *implorare et exposcĕre alqd, contendĕre ab alqo ut, flagitare* or *efflagitare alqm alqd* (= to request, to urge), to — anyone for a person or thing, *ab alqo alqd alci petĕre*, to — an authority (e g parliament), *petĕre alqd per lit(t)eras*. **petitioner,** n *qui libellum affert, qui libello petit oblato, qui supplicat*

petrify, v tr 1, *in lapidem (con)vertĕre, mutare*, to be petrified, *lapidescere* (Plin, rare), 2, fig *alqm obstupefacĕre*, to be petrified (with astonishment, etc), *obstupescĕre, attonitum esse*

petticoat, n *tunica interior, corporis velamentum interius* (the Romans had no equivalent), — government, *imperium uxorium* or *muliebre* **pettifogger,** n *rabula, causidicus rabiosus et ineptus* **pettifogging,** adj a — attorney, *causidicus* (opp to *orator*), in wider sense, see PALTRY **petty,** adj, see LITTLE, TRIFLING, PALTRY

petulance, n see PASSION, SAUCINESS, IMPUDENCE **petulant,** adj, see SAUCY, IMPUDENT

pew, n *sedes quae est in aede sacra*

pewter, n see TIN

phaeton, n see CARRIAGE

phantom, n 1, *somnium, opinionis commenta, orum*, they are mere —s, *et falsa et inania sunt*, 2, see GHOST

Pharisee, n *Pharisaeus* (Eccl), fig, see HYPOCRITE **Pharisaical,** adj, lit by the gen *Pharisaeorum* (Eccl), see HYPOCRITICAL

pharmacy, n (*ars*) *medicamentaria* (Plin)

phase, n *status, -ūs, condicio* or *ratio*, or by circumloc (e g the thing has passed into a new —, *res mutata est*, or *nova fit*)

pheasant, n (*avis*) *Phasiana* (Plin), *Phasianus* (*Fas-*, Suet)

phenomenon, n in gen *ostentum, prodigium, portentum, miraculum* (= any marvellous sight seen and relating to some future event), in the sky, *phaenomĕnon* (very late, or its Greek φαινόμενον), *res nova* or *mirifica* or *nova* (= strange)

phial, n see BOTTLE

philanthropy, n *caritas generis humani, humanitas* **philanthropist,** n, **philanthropical,** adj *hominibus* or *generi humano amicus, humanus* Adv *humane*

Philippic, n 1, lit (*oratio*) *Philippica*, 2, fig *oratio in alqm habita*

Philistine, n 1, lit *Philistinus*, 2, fig *homo humanitatis expers*

philologist, n *grammaticus, philologus* **philology,** n *grammatica* (or *grammatice*), *philologia* (= literary studies) **philological,** adj *grammaticus*

philosopher, n *philosophus*, fem *philosopha*, the true —, *sapiens* (i e a wise man), theoretical —, *qui in rerum contemplatione studia ponit*, practical —, *qui de vita ac moribus rebusque bonis et malis quaerit* **philosophy,** n *philosophia* **philosophical,** adj by the genit *philosophiae, philosophorum*, = wise, *sapiens, prudens*, — writings, *philosophiae scriptae, libri qui sunt de philosophia*, — precepts, *philosophiae* or *philosophorum praecepta*, that is not a common, but a — term, *quod non est vulgi verbum, sed philosophorum* Adv *philosophorum more, sapienter, prudenter* **philosophize,** v intr *philosophari* (lit), *argumentari, ratiocinari* (= to argue), *disputare* (= to expound).

philtre, n *philtrum, amatoris poculum, virus amatorium*, or *amatorium* alone (Plin).

phlegm, n 1, *pituita* (t t), 2, = dulness, *tarditas ingenii* or *animi*, also merely in the context *tarditas, potientia* (= indolence), *inertia* (= inertness), *lentitudo* (= indifference). **phlegmatic,** adj. *tardus, patiens, iners, lentus.* Adv. *patienter, lente,* or perhaps *aequo animo.*

phœnix, n. *phoenix.*

phonetic, adj. by circumloc. (e.g. *sonum verbi ipsum lit(t)eris exprimĕre*).

phosphorus, n. *phosphorus* = the morning star; also as scientific t.t., but not, in this sense, class. **phosphorescent,** adj., **phosphorescence,** n. by *lux in undis lucens* or *fulgens.*

photograph, n. use where possible *pictura* or *imago;* perhaps where closer definition is necessary *imago alcjs per solis radios depicta.*

phrase, n. *locutio* (Aul. Gell.); these are mere —s, *verba sunt.* **phraseology,** n. *locutio, dicendi genus, -ĕris,* n.

phthisis, n. *phthĭsis* (Cels.). **phthisical,** adj. *phthĭsicus* (Plin.).

physic, I. n. see MEDICINE. **II.** v.tr. see PURGE, CURE. **physical,** adj. **1,** = natural, must generally be rendered by the genit. *naturae* (if we speak of nature), or *corporis* (if we speak of the animal body); — complaints, *mala naturae, mala quae natura habet* (in gen.), *vitia corporis* (= bodily defects); — strength, *vires corporis;* to be of good — constitution, *corporis valetudine uti bonā;* **2,** referring to science, *physicus;* — science, *physica* or *physice, physiologia* (the theory); see PHYSICS. Adv. *naturā, physice.* **physician,** n. see DOCTOR. **physics,** n. *physica, -orum.* **physiognomist,** n. *physiognomon,* by *qui se profitetur hominum mores naturasque ex corpore, oculis, vultu, fronte, pernoscĕre* (Cic.). **physiognomy,** n. *oris habitus, -ūs, lineamenta, -orum,* n. (= features), comb. *habitus oris lineamentaque, os vultusque, os et vultus* (= countenance and features), *facies* (= face).

physiology, n. *naturae ratio, quam Graeci φυσιολογίαν appellant,* or *natura rerum quae Graece φυσιολογία dicitur,* or simply *physiologia.* **physiological,** adj. *ad naturae rationem pertinens.* Adv. *e rerum naturā.*

piacular, adj. *piacularis.*

piano, n. use some known instrument, *lyra, cithara.*

pick, I. v.tr. and intr. *rostro tundĕre* or *caedĕre alqd* (of birds); to — a bone, by *rodĕre alqd;* to — one's teeth, *dentes spinā perfodĕre* (with a tooth— of wood, silver, etc., Petron.); = to gather, *carpĕre;* see PLUCK; to — wool, *lanam carpĕre* or *purgare;* to — one's pocket, see ROB; to — a quarrel, see QUARREL; to — out, see SELECT, CHOOSE; to — up, *legĕre, colligĕre, tollĕre,* see GATHER, RAISE. **II.** n. —axe, *dolābra;* a —pocket, *sector zonarius* (Plaut.), or by *fur* = thief. **picked,** adj. *delectus* (of troops), *eximius, praestans,* etc.; see EXCELLENT. **picking,** n. see CHOICE; in the pl. see REMAINS.

pickle, I. n. *salsura.* **II.** v.tr. to — fish, *pisces muriā condire.*

picnic, n. and v.intr. *symbola* (συμβολή, ante class.) = a contribution to a common feast (e.g. *aliquot adolescentuli coimus in Piraeo in hunc diem ut de symbolā essemus,* = we went to a —, Ter.), or *excurrĕre* may be used (e.g. *excurro in Pompeianum,* Cic.).

picquet, n. *statio;* to post —s, *stationes disponĕre.*

pictorial, adj. and adv. *tabulis ornatus* or *(de)pictus, per tabulas.*

picture, I. n. *pictura, tabula (picta);* = likeness, *imago (picta);* word —, by circumloc. (e.g. *ita rem verbis exprimit ut paene ob oculos posita esse videatur*). **II.** v.tr. to — in the mind, *alqd mente, animo* or *cogitatione fingĕre* or *concipĕre;* in words, *depingĕre, expingĕre, exprimĕre;* see EXPRESS, PAINT. **picture-frame,** n. *forma in quā includitur pictura.* **picture-gallery,** n. *pinăcŏthēca.* **picturesque,** adj. *graphicus* (= very beautiful, as if it had been painted, rare), *amoenus* (= delightful); to be —, *graphicam in aspectu efficĕre delectationem* (Vitr. = to present a most beautiful aspect); see BEAUTIFUL. Adv. *graphice, amoene.* **picturesqueness,** n. see BEAUTY.

pie, n. see PASTRY.

piebald, adj. † *bicolor.*

piece, I. n. **1,** part of a whole, *pars* (= part in gen.), *fragmentum* (poet. *fragmen* = a — broken off), *segmen* (= a — cut off), *frustum* (= a bit), *truncus* (= a — cut off or struck off, e.g. a — of the same stone, *truncus ejusdem lapidis*), *crusta* (= a — of marble cut off, for mosaic work); a — (bit) of cloth, *pannus;* a pretty large — of anything (i.e. = a considerable quantity, a good deal), *aliquantum* with genit. (e.g. of land, *agri*); a very large — (i.e. much), *multum* with genit.; to tear into —s, *dilacerare, dilaniare, discerpĕre;* see TEAR; to fall to —s, *dilabi;* **2,** = a single thing, which belongs to a whole species, in gen. *res* (thing in gen.); *pars* (= part, e.g. *plura de extremis loqui pars ignaviae est,* Tac., a — of cowardice); whenever we say a — of, the word — is not expressed, e.g. a — of money, *nummus* (a single coin), *alqd nummorum* (an indefinite sum of money); a — of land, *ager,* dim. *agellus;* a — of meat, *caruncula;* a — of wood, *lignum;* made out of one —, or into one —, *solidus* (= not interrupted, solid, massive (e.g. ring)); a boat made out of one — of timber, *linter ex unā arbore excavatus;* = an artificial production, *opus, -ĕris,* n. (in gen.), *tela* (= a — of woven cloth), *pictura, tabula* (= a picture), *fabula* (= a theatrical —), *cantus, -ūs* (= a — of music), *tormentum* (= a field- —); in —s, —meal, *minutatim* (lit. in small —s, then also fig. = by degrees), *membratim* (lit. = limb by limb, then fig. = one part after the other, e.g. to relate, *enumerare,* i.e. to enumerate), *carptim* (= by detached parts, fig. = partly), *pedetentim* (*pedetemt-*) (= one thing after the other, step by step, gradually); also by *singuli* (if = the single things); —-work, by circumloc. (e.g. to pay by —, *ut res quaeque confecta est, solvĕre*). **II.** v.tr. *consuĕre;* to — a garment, by *assuĕre alqd alci rei;* see PATCH, MEND.

pied, adj. *maculosus.*

pier, n. **1,** *pila (pontis);* see PILLAR; **2,** *moles (-is), (opposita fluctibus) moles lapidum* (= mole).

pierce, v.tr. **1,** see THRUST, DRIVE; **2,** = to — through, *transfigĕre;* see STAB; **3,** see ENTER, PENETRATE. **piercing,** adj. **1,** of sounds, *acer, acutus;* see SHRILL; **2,** of the mind, *acutus, acer, sagax;* see ACUTE.

piety, n. *pietas erga Deum* (= reverence and love to God), *religio* (= religious feeling), *sanctitas* (= holiness of life), *sanctimonia* (= virtuous sentiment, innocence). **pious,** adj. *pius erga Deum* (also *erga patriam, parentes,* etc.), *religiosus* (= conscientious), *sanctus* (= approved of God), *religiosus sanctusque, sanctus et religiosus.* Adv. *pie, sancte,* comb. *pie sancteque.*

pig, n. *porcus* (Eng. pork), *sus, suis,* m. and f.; a small —, *porcellus;* a sucking —, *porcus lactens, porcellus.* **piggery,** n. *suile* (Col.), *hara.* **piggish,** adj. **1,** *suillus, porcinus;* **2,** fig. see

GREEDY **piggishness,** n *spurcitia, spurcities* (= foulness), see also GREEDINESS **pig-headed,** adj see OBSTINATE

pigeon, n *columba* (a cock —, *columbus*), *palumbes, is* (*palumba*), see DOVE, — house, *columbarium; turris, turricula* (= — tower)

pigment, n see PAINT.

pigmy, n see DWARF, the Pigmies, *Pigmaei* (Plin)

pike, n *hasta*, see LANCE

pilaster, n *parastāta* or *parastas, -ădis,* f.

pile, I. n *strues, -is,* f (of things collected in an elevated form), *cumulus, acervus* (= heap of things, in gen), *rogus* (= funeral —, also — of wood), a — of books, *acervus librorum*, a — of buildings, see EDIFICE, a — driven into the ground (for building on), *sublica*, a bridge built on —s, *pons sublicius;* to drive down —s, *palos* or *stipites* or *sudes demittĕre, defigĕre*, see HEAP, STAKE. **II.** v tr (*co*)*acervare, cumulare, congerĕre*, see ACCUMULATE, to — up, *facĕre struem alcjs rei* (e g *lignorum*), *exstruĕre* (e g *rogum*), see HEAP

pilfer, v tr and intr, see STEAL.

pilgrim, n *viator* (= traveller in gen), or *qui in loca sacra migrat*, —'s staff, *baculum*. **pilgrimage,** n. *iter, itineris,* n (= journey in gen), or *iter in loca sacra, peregrinatio sacra*

pill, n *catapotium* (Plin) (that which is swallowed), in pure Latin *pilula* (Plin), fig to give one a — to swallow, *alqm tangĕre* (Com), he swallowed the —, *haec concoxit*

pillage, I. n *rapīna, direptio* (implying destruction of property), *expilatio* (for the sake of robbing), *depopulatio* (= laying waste) **II.** v tr *diripĕre, populari* (= to lay waste), *compilare, expilare, spoliare* **III.** v intr *praedari*, see PLUNDER **pillager,** n *praedator, direptor, populator*, see PLUNDER.

pillar, n *columen* (fig = foundation, e g *columen reipublicae*), *pila* (= support of a bridge, etc), *columna* (= column), see COLUMN, POST **pillared,** adj *columnatus, columnis instructus*

pillory, n *numella* (= fetter for criminals), to punish with the —, *alqm ad palam in aliorum exemplum alligare*, fig *alqm cruciare*, see TORMENT

pillow, I. n *cervical* (Juv), *pulvīnus* **II.** v tr (*suf*)*fulcire*, see SUPPORT

pilot, I. n *gubernator* (lit and fig) **II.** v tr *gubernare* (lit and fig)

pimp, n *lēno*

pimple, n *varus* (Plin, on the face, Greek ἴονθος), *pustula* (in gen, Plin) **pimpled, pimply,** adj *pustulosus* (Cels)

pin, I. n *acus, -ūs,* f **II.** v tr *alqd acu* (*af*)*figĕre* **pin-cushion,** n *thēca* (= case) **pin-money,** n. *peculium* (Jct), or *pecunia uxori data*

pincers, n pl *forceps* **pinch, I.** v tr 1, = to nip, perhaps *alqd* or *alqm digitis comprimĕre, vellicare* (Quint), 2, fig (*co*)*artare* = to crowd, to — for room, *urĕre* (of a shoe, frost, etc), to — oneself, *fraudare se victu suo*, to —, of poverty, *urgĕre* **II.** n 1, lit. use verb, 2, fig *aculeus* (= sting), *morsus, -ūs* (= bite), see STING, at a —, by circumloc (e g he would only do it at a —, *coactus modo hoc fecerit*) **pinching,** adj of poverty, etc, by *extremus, summus,* etc, see EXTREME

pinchbeck, n 1, *aes facticium*, 2, fig, see SHAM

pine, n *pīnus,* f.

pine, v intr *tabescĕre, confici alqâ re*, to — for anything, *alqd desiderare*, or more strongly, *alcjs desiderio tabescĕre* **pining,** n *tabes, -is* (= wasting away), see also SORROW

pinion, I. n 1, of a bird, *penna* (*pinna*), see WING, 2, *compes, -ĕdis,* f, see FETTER **II.** v tr. *manus post tergum religare, alci compedes in*(*j*)*icĕre, alqm* (*re*)*vincire*

pink, adj *puniceus*, — colour, *color puniceus*

pinnace, n *navis actuaria* or *lembus*

pinnacle, n *fastigium* (lit and fig)

pint, n perhaps *sextarius* (both as a measure of liquids and as the vessel containing it), half a —, *hemīna*, a quarter of a —, *quartarius*

pioneer, n *qui primus alqd facit*

pious, adj *pius, sanctus*, see PIETY

pip, n *pituita* (= disease of chickens, Plin)

pip, v intr *pipare, pipire* (Col)

pip, n of fruit, *semen, granum, nucleus* (Plin), *acinus* (esp of the grape)

pipe, I. n 1, for water, etc, *tubus, tubulus, canalis, fistula*, 2, = a musical instrument, *fistula, tibia*, †*arundo*, †*calamus*, †*avena*, 3, for smoking, perhaps, if context is clear, *fistula* or *tubulus*, or adding *fumum edens* **II.** v intr *fistulâ* or *tibiâ canĕre* or *cantare* **pipe-clay,** n *creta fig*(*u*)*lina* **piper,** n *tibicen*

pipkin, n *olla* (old form *aula*)

piquant, adj *acutus* (lit = stimulating to the senses; then also fig, e g of the speaker, Quint), *salsus* (lit = seasoned with salt, — in taste, then fig pertinent, to the point, interesting, esp through wit, of persons, of things said or written, etc); *facetus* (= facetious) Adv *acute, salse.* **piquancy,** n *sal, vis* **pique, I** n *simultas*, see ANGER, IRRITATION **II.** v tr see OFFEND, IRRITATE, EXASPERATE, to — oneself, *gloriari alqa re, jactare se de alqâ re*

piracy, n. *latrocinium maris*, to carry on —, *latrocinio maris vitam tolerare* (= to get one's living by —), to make the sea unsafe through —, *mare infestum facere navibus piraticis, latrociniis et praedationibus infestare mare* **pirate,** n *praedo* (*maritimus*), *pīrāta* **piratical,** adj *piraticus*, — State, *gens latrociniis assueta*

piscatory, adj *piscatorius*

pistil, n **pistillum* (only as t t)

pistol, n, where possible by *arcus, -ūs* (= bow), otherwise **sclopetus minor*, see GUN

piston, n (in machines) *fundulus* (moving up and down, *fundulus ambulatilis*), *embolus* (= sucker of a pump)

pit, I. n *puteus* (in gen), *fovea* (deep, open at the top, for catching wild beasts, then also fig = a snare), *scrobs* or (small) *scrobiculus* (= a hole dug for planting a tree or for interring a dead body), *fossa* (= a long ditch for the defence of a place or for the purpose of drainage), *fodina, specus, puteus* (in a mine), to dig a —, *facĕre fo veam* (*fossam*), *fodĕre scrobem, specum sub terrâ fodĕre*, to fall into a —, *in foveam incidĕre* (the latter also fig = to fall into a snare), in the theatre, *cavea* (= the seats assigned to the spectators, *cavea ima* was reserved for the nobility, *cavea media* and *summa* more nearly = pit) **II.** v tr = to mark (e g with small-pox), *distinguĕre*, see MARK **pit against,** v tr *alqm alci opponĕre, alqm cum alqo committĕre* **pit a-pat,** adv to go —, *palpitare* **pitfall,** n *fovea* **pitman,** n see MINER

pitch, I. n *pix*, of —, *piceus*, as black as —, *piceus, picinus, omnium nigerrimus* (=

quite black, in gen.); — pine, *picea*; — dark, (*tenebris*) *obductus* (= quite covered with darkness, e.g. *nox*). **II.** v.tr. (*op*)*picare*. **pitchy,** adj. *picatus* (= besmeared with pitch).

pitch, I. n. **1,** = degree, *fastigium*, *gradus*, -*ūs*, or by *summus*, *extremus*, or *ultimus* with n. (i.e. to the highest — of madness, *ad summam amentiam*); to this, that, what a — of, *huc*, *eo*, *quo* with gen.; **2,** in music, *sonus*, *vox*; at the highest — of the voice, *voce summâ*; a high —, *vox acuta*; medium —, *vox media*; low —, *vox gravis*. **II.** v.tr. **1,** to — a tent, *tabernaculum statuĕre* or *constituĕre* or *collocare*, *tentorium statuĕre* or *ponĕre*, *tabernaculum tendĕre*, or simply *tendĕre*; **2,** = to throw, *jacĕre*, *con*(*j*)*icĕre*; see THROW; **3,** in music, to — a note, *canendo praeire*. **III.** v.intr. to — upon, *incidĕre*, *incurrĕre in alqm* or *alqd*. **pitchfork,** n. *furca*.

pitcher, n. see JAR.

piteous, pitiable, adj. *miser*, *miserabilis*, *miserandus*, *dolendus*, *flebilis*, (*e*)*lamentabilis*. Adv. *misĕre*, *miserabiliter*, *flebiliter*, *miserandum in modum*. **piteousness,** n. use adj., or circuml. (e.g. the — of the story greatly moved me, *narratio mire me commovit*). **pitiful,** adj. **1,** = full of pity, *clemens*, *misericors*; see MERCIFUL; **2,** see PITEOUS; **3,** = mean, *abjectus*, *vilis*, *humilis*, *contemptus*; see CONTEMPTIBLE. Adv. *clementer*, *misere*, *abjecte*, *humiliter*; see CONTEMPTIBLY. **pitifulness,** n. **1,** *clementia*, *misericordia*; **2,** see PITEOUSNESS; **3,** by adj. (PITIFUL 3), or *humilitas*. **pitiless,** adj. *immisericors*, *durus*, *ferreus*, *inhumanus*, *crudelis*, *saevus*; see CRUEL. Adv. *immisericorditer*, *inhumane*, *inhumaniter*, *crudeliter*, *saeve*. **pitilessness,** n. *crudelitas*, *inhumanitas*, *saevitia*. **pity, I.** n. *misericordia* (*misericordia est aegritudo ex miseriâ alterius injuriâ laborantis*, Cic.), *miseratio*; out of —, *propter misericordiam*, *misericordia captus* or *permotus*; to feel —, *misericordiam habēre*, *misericordem esse* (= to have a feeling heart), *se misericordem praebēre* (= to show oneself merciful in one single case); to have — on anyone, *misereri alcjs*, *miseret me alcjs*; it is a — that, etc., *dolendum est*, *quod*, etc., *incommode accidit*, *ut*, etc.; it is a — that he died, *mors ejus dolenda est*; it is a — that the money was lost, *dolenda est jactura pecuniae*; it is a great —, it is a thousand pities, *valde*, *magnopere dolendum est*; deserving —, *miserandus*, *miseratione dignus*. **II.** v.tr. *miserēri*, *miseret me alcjs*, *misericordiâ alcjs commotum* or *captum esse* (= to feel —). **pitying,** adj. and adv. see PITIFUL 1.

pith, n. *medulla* (lit. and fig.). **pithy,** adj. **1,** lit. *medullosus* (Cels.); **2,** fig. *sententiosus* (= full of meaning), *nervosus* (= vigorous), *densus* (Quint.).

pittance, n. *mercedula* (= poor pay), *pecunia exigua*.

pivot, n. **1,** lit. *cnŏdax* (Vitr., rare); **2,** fig. see HINGE.

placable, adj. *exorabilis*, *placabilis*. **placability,** n. *placabilitas*.

placard, I. n. *libellus*; see ADVERTISEMENT. **II.** v.tr. *libellum proponĕre*; see ANNOUNCE, ADVERTISE.

place, I. n. = a free, open space, *locus*, *campus* (= open —, field, e.g. in the middle of a town), *area* (= a free, open — not occupied with buildings); the — in front of a dwelling-house, *propatulum* (in gen.), *vestibulum* (= entrance court); — of battle, *locus pugnae*; = an inhabited —, *locus*, *oppidum* (= — surrounded with walls), *regio* (= district), *pagus*, *vicus* (= village); a fortified —, *locus munitus* (in gen.), *castrum*, *castellum* (= castle, fort); = natural position, *sedes*, -*is*; = a certain portion of space in gen., inhabited —, the —, *loca*; at this —, *hic*, *hoc loco*; at which —, where, *ubi*, *quo loco*; at what —? *ubinam?* from which —, whence, *unde*, *a* or *ex quo loco*; at every —, *ubique*, *omnibus locis*; from every —, *undique*, *ab omnibus locis*; at different —s, *passim*; at both —s, *utrobique*; at another —, see ELSEWHERE; fig. — in a book, *locus* (pl. *loci*); this has been stated in another — (= in another part of the book), *alio loco dictum est*; about this in another —, *de quo alibi*; = a separate — allotted anywhere, lit. *locus* (in gen.), *sedes* (where one sits), *spatium* (= — which anything occupies); to assign, show to a person his or her — (in the theatre), *alqm sessum ducĕre* (Plaut.); to give up one's — to a person, *alci locum dare*, *cedĕre*; to take a — on the seats allotted (in front of the rostrum of the curia, etc.), *locum in subselliis occupare*; to sit in the first —, *in primâ caveâ sedēre* (in the theatre), *summum* or *supra* or *superiorem accubare* (at table); in the last —, *in ultimâ caveâ sedēre* (in the theatre), *infra* or *inferiorem accubare* (at table); to get up from one's —, (*ex*)*surgĕre* or (principally of several) *consurgĕre*; to rise from one's — before anyone (out of respect), *alci assurgĕre*; to bring anyone from his — (= seat), *alqm loco movēre*; description of —s (towns, etc.), *descriptio locorum* (Cic. uses τοποθεσία = the stating of the locality of a —); commander of a —, *praefectus urbi*; = situation, office, *munus*, -*ĕris*, n., *magistratus*, -*ūs*; of a servant, use circuml. (e.g. to change a —, *in aliam familiam ingredi*); to appoint in — of, *alqm sufficĕre*; in — of, *loco alcjs*; in the first —, *primo*, *primum*; in the next —, *deinceps*; *primo* and *primum* are followed by *deinde*, *tum*, *praeterea*, *postremo*. **II.** v.tr. *statuĕre* (lit., to make a thing stand, e.g. *vas in loco frigido*, *juvencum ante aram*), *constituĕre*; to — in different spots, *disponĕre*; to — in line of battle, *ordinare*, *instruĕre*; to — anything round a thing, *cingĕre alqd alqâ re* (e.g. watchmen round a house, *domum custodibus*); to — anything before, *alqd apponĕre alci rei* or *ad alqd* (before the hearth, *foco*; before the fire, *ad ignem*), *proponĕre alqd alci rei* (e.g. *igni*); to — oneself at or near a spot or anything, *consistĕre in alqo loco* (e.g. at the door, *in aditū*), by the side of, near anything, *consistĕre ad alqd* (e.g. *ad mensam*), *assistĕre ad alqd* (e.g. *ad fores*, near the door); to — one's money with anyone, *pecuniam collocare* or *occupare apud alqm*; to — behind, *postponĕre* or *posthabēre* or *postferre alqd alci rei*; to — over (i.e. in command of, *alci rei* or *loco alqm praeficĕre*); to — round, *alqm* or *alqd alci* (*rei*), or *alqm* or *alqd alqâ re circumdare*; to — under, *alqd alci* (*rei*) *sub*(*j*)*icĕre*; to — upon, *alqd alci* (*rei*) *imponĕre*, *superponĕre*.

placid, adj. *placidus*; see GENTLE, QUIET, CALM.

plagiarism, n. *furtum* or by *auctorem ad verbum transcribĕre neque nominare* (= to copy a passage from an author without naming him), or by *alcjs scripta furantem pro suis praedicare* (i.e. in so doing to pass oneself off as the author of such a passage, etc.). **plagiarist,** n. *qui aliorum scrinia compilat* (Hor.), *qui auctorem ad verbum transcribit neque nominat*.

plague, I. n. **1,** lit. (as the disease) *pestis*, *pestilentia*; see PESTILENCE; **2,** fig., *malum* (= evil in gen.); *pestis* (= pest); the — take you! *in malam crucem!* What the — is it? *Quid, malum, est?* to be a — to anyone, *molestiae esse alci*. **II.** v.tr. *vexare* (= to let anyone have no peace), *sol*(*l*)*icitare* (= to disquiet), *angĕre* (of cares, etc.), *exercēre*, *cruciare*, (*ex*)*agitare*; with requests, *alqm precibus fatigare*, with questions, *alqm obtundĕre rogitando*, to — anyone to do, etc (= to bother), *alci instare de alqâ re* or with *ut*, see VEX, WORRY

plain, I. adj **1,** = smooth, *aequus, planus*, see FLAT; 2, = manifest, *clarus, planus, apertus, perspicuus, evidens, manifestus*, see CLEAR, MANIFEST, 3, = unadorned, *simplex, inornatus, incomptus* (of dress), *(di)lucidus, inornatus, subtilis, pressus, expressus, distinctus, attenuatus* (of speech), 4, = candid, *sincerus, liber*, see FRANK, 5, = without beauty, perhaps *haud formosus* or *venustus*, see UGLY Adv = clearly, *clare, plane, aperte, perspicue, evidenter, manifeste*, = without ornament, *simpliciter, inornate* (of dress, etc), *(di)lucide, subtiliter, (ex)presse distincte, attenuate*, = frankly, *sincere, libere, aperte* **II.** n *planities* (= every —, also the — surface of a mirror), as an open country, *planities, aequus et planus locus* (wide, where one has unlimited view and a free scope, in opp. to hills and mountains), *campus* with and without *planus* or *apertus* (= an open field, in opp to mountains), an extended —, *aequor* (also surface of the sea, often in the poets, but also in Cic), of what is, grows, has its abode, is situate in the —, *campester* (e g. *campestris urbs*). **plainness,** n **1,** = clearness, by *evidentia, perspicuitas*, or adj, see PLAIN; 2, = lack of ornament, *simplicitas* (of dress, etc), or by adj PLAIN, 3 (of style), **3,** of speech, see FRANKNESS, **4,** = lack of beauty; see UGLINESS.

plaint, n see LAMENTATION, COMPLAINT, ACTION **plaintiff,** n *accusator* (if a female, *accusatrix*), *qui* (or *quae*) *accusat* (= accuser, who brings anyone up before the court in a criminal prosecution), *qui* (or *quae*) *petit* (= who makes a claim, in a civil action), to appear as the principal — against anyone, *suo nomine accusare alqm*, as the second — or jointly with another, *subscribens accusare alqm*, — in error, *appellator* (Cic), *qui appellat* or *provocat* **plaintive,** adj *miserabilis, flebilis, lamentabilis, queribundus, querulus* (mostly poet) Adv *miserabiliter, flebiliter* **plaintiveness,** n by adj

plait, I. n **1,** *sinus, -ūs, ruga*, but both = fold rather than —, see FOLD, 2, = a braid of hair, *gradus, -ūs* (Quint, Suet) **II.** v tr **1,** see FOLD, **2,** to — the hair, *comam in gradus formare* or *frangĕre*

plan, I. n **1,** = a sketch drawn on paper, *forma, conformatio, figura, species* (= a draught), *imago* (= outline), *designatio* (= design), *forma rudis et impolita* (= rough sketch), *descriptio, ichnographia* (the former = first sketch, then like the latter = ground-plan), to draw a — of anything, *speciem operis deformare, imaginem* or *formam operis delineare*, of a building, *aedificandi descriptio*, **2,** in idea, *consilium, cogitatio* (as a mere idea which we hope to realize), *propositum* or *inceptum* (as intention, or as anything first begun, undertaken), *ratio* (= — and decision, wherein the means of doing it and the possible result are considered), *descriptio* (as regards all the particulars of it), *ordo* (= the order in which a thing is to be done), — of an operation, *rei agendae ratio*, a — agreed upon, *ratio rei compositae* (Liv), — for carrying on a war, *totius belli ratio*, a decided —, *ratio stabilis ac firma*, without any decided —, *nullo consilio, nullâ ratione*, to draw up, make a — for anything, *instituĕre rationem alcjs rei* (e g *operis*), *describĕre rationem alcjs rei* (e g *belli, aedificandi*), to conceive the — to, etc, *consilium capĕre* or *inire alcjs rei faciendae*, or with inf or with *ut*, concerning a thing, *consilium capĕre* or *inire de alqâ re* **II.** v tr **1,** = to form a draught, *speciem* or *imaginem alcjs operis lineis deformare, formam alcjs operis lineis describĕre, imaginem alcjs operis delineare*, see DESIGN, **2,** in idea, *alqd (ex)cogitare, moliri, consilium inire alcjs rei faciendae*, see above, PLAN, I 2

plane, I. n **1,** = a geometrical figure, *forma plana*, **2,** = a tool, *runcina* (Plin) **II.** v tr *runcinare*.

plane, n = a tree, *platanus*, f

planet, n. *stella errans, sidus, -ĕris*, n, *errans*, in pl also *stellae quae errantes et quasi vagae nominantur*, the five —s, *quinque stellae eosdem cursus constantissime servantes*. (*Planeta, planetes*, is not found in good prose)

plank, I. n *tabula* (= board), *axis, -is*, m (*assis*), to nail —s, *coaxare* (*coass-*). **II.** v tr *contabulare, coaxare* (*coass-*) **planking,** n *contabulatio, coaxatio* (*coass-*, = boarded floor, etc), or by pl of PLANK

plant, I. n *herba* (in gen), *planta* (= slip) **II.** v tr **1,** *serĕre*, *(de)ponĕre* (trees, etc), *conserĕre, obserĕre* (a place with trees, etc), **2,** = to set up, *statuĕre, constituĕre, infigĕre* (e g *signum*, a standard), see SET UP, **3,** to — a colony, *coloniam deducĕre* **plantation,** n *plantarium* (= nursery garden), *seminarium* (= nursery garden, lit. and fig), *arbustum* (= orchard, esp the trees round which vines were planted), *vitiarium* (= nursery for vines), *quercetum* (= oak wood), *locus arboribus consitus* (gen term) **planter,** n *sator, qui serit*, —s of a colony, *coloni* **planting,** n *satio, satus, -ūs* (= the act of —)

plash, I. n *murmur, fremitus, -ūs* (e g. *aequoris*, perhaps *sonus, sonitus, -ūs* **II.** v tr. *murmurare, fremĕre, fremitum edĕre*

plaster, I. n **1,** *gypsum, arenatum, tectorium*; see CEMENT, MORTAR, **2,** in medicine, *emplastrum* **II.** adj a — cast, *imago (e) gypso expressa* **III.** v tr *gypsare* (Col), *gypso illinĕre* or *obducere* **plasterer,** n = who whitewashes the walls, *tector*, see PAINT

plastic, adj *plasticus*

plate, I. n. 1, *bractea, lam(i)na* (lit = a thin piece of metal, the latter stronger than the former, then also of wood, anything veneered), 2, = a copper— print, *pictura linearis* or *imago per aeneam lam(i)nam expressa, figura aenea*, or in the context merely *imago*, 3, a — at table, *catillus*, pl *catilla, -orum*, n (a smaller one made of clay), *patella*, 4, collectively, — used at table, *vasa* (*-orum*) *argentea* or *aurea* (silver or gold), *argentum* **II.** adj — glass, perhaps use *vitrum densatum* **III.** v tr to — with silver, *argento inducĕre*

platform, n *suggestus, -ūs*

Platonic, adj. *Platonicus, Academicus* (= pertaining to the Academy, i e the — philosophy, *academia*, ακαδημια) **Platonist,** n *Platonicus philosophus*, the —s, *academici* (= the followers of the Academy)

platter, n *catillus* (pl *catilla*), *patella*

plaudit, n *plausus, -ūs*, see APPLAUSE

plausible, adj **1,** = probable, *veri similis* (or as one word *verisim-*), *probabilis*, **2,** in bad sense, *fucatus, fucosus, simulatus, speciosus* Adv *veri similiter* (*verisim-*), *probabiliter, simulate, speciose* (Quint), *ad speciem, in* or *per speciem, specie* **plausibility,** n **1,** *verisimilitudo, probabilitas*, **2,** *simulatio, species*

play, I. v intr and tr to — an instrument of music, *canĕre*, † *modulari*, with the ablat of the instrument played (e g on a stringed instrument, *fidibus*), *psallĕre* (on a stringed instrument, esp the guitar, hence often comb *cantare et psallĕre, canĕre voce et psallĕre*, = to sing to the sound of the —); = to amuse oneself, *ludĕre* (either absol. or with the ablat. of the game); the fishes — in the water, *pisces in aquâ ludunt*; to — at dice, *tesseris* or *talis ludĕre, aleâ* or *aleam ludĕre*; to — at cricket, ball, *pilâ ludĕre*; to — for anything, *ludĕre in alqd* (e.g. for money, *in pecuniam*, Jct.); = to act in any particular character, on the stage and in real life, *agĕre alqm* or *alcjs partes, alcjs personam tueri*; to — a piece (in the theatre), *fabulam agĕre*; not to let the actors — any longer, *histrionibus scaenam interdicĕre*; to — the fool with anyone, to — anyone a trick, *alqm ludĕre* or *ludificari, alci imponĕre*; to — the rogue with anyone, *fraudem* or *fallaciam alci facĕre, dolum alci nectĕre* or *confingĕre*. **II.** n. = amusement, *ludus* (= game, see the word), *lusus, -ūs* (= playing), *lusio* (= the act), *ludicrum* (= a farce for amusement), *ludibrium* (= the carrying on a joke with anyone; the joke itself, sport), *spectaculum* (= a theatrical piece), *fabula* (dimin. *fabella*, = a piece at the theatre), *comoedia* (= comedy), *tragoedia* (= tragedy); mere —, *ludus, jocus* (= joke); that is but — for him, *hoc ei ludus* or *jocus est*; = room for acting, *campus* (opp. *angustiae*; e.g. he has full — in his speech, *est campus, in quo ex(s)ultare possit oratio*, Cic.); to have —, *late vagari posse*; = action, *motus, -ūs, gestus, -ūs* (of the limbs, etc.), *vultus, -ūs* (= face), *argutiae* (= lively expression of the countenance); fair —, *ex aequo et bono* (e.g. to see —, *curare ut omnia ex aequo et bono fiant*). **play-bill,** n. *libellus*. **player,** n. 1, (on a musical instrument) *canens* (both male and female), *psaltes*, in pure Latin *fidicen*, on a stringed instrument; if a female, *psaltria*, in pure Latin *fidicĭna, citharista*, m., *citharoedus*; *cornicen* (= who blows a horn or cornet), *tibīcen* (= a — on the flute, a piper), *tubĭcen* (= a trumpeter); for amusement in gen., *lusor*, a female, *ludens*; **2,** see GAMBLER; **3,** — on the stage, *actor*; see ACTOR. **playfellow, playmate,** n. *aequalis* (= of the same age). **playful,** adj. *lascivus, jocosus*. Adv. *jocose*. **playfulness,** n. *lascivia*. **playground,** n. *locus quo pueri ludendi caus(s)â conveniunt*. **playhouse,** n. see THEATRE. **playthings,** n. *quae pueris in lusum oblata sunt*; see TOY. **playwriter, playwright,** n. *qui fabulas scribit*.

plea, n. **1,** defendant's —, *defensio, oratio pro se* or *alqo habita* (= a speech made in one's own defence, or for others); to make a — in court, *orare* or *dicĕre pro se, se defendĕre, caus(s)am dicĕre* (for oneself), *orare et dicĕre pro alqo, defendĕre alqm* (for someone); *exceptio* (= exception taken by defendant to plaintiff's statement, and inserted in a praetor's edict); in a gen. sense, see LAWSUIT, CAUSE, APOLOGY; **2,** = excuse, *excusatio*; see EXCUSE. **plead,** v.intr. **1,** in law, *cau(s)sam agĕre, actitare* (frequentative), *dicĕre, (per)orare*, or *alqm se fecisse defendĕre, alqm defendĕre, versari in foro* (= to be a pleader); **2,** in gen. *alqd excusare*; see BEG, ALLEGE. **pleader,** n. *orator, causidicus* (term rather of contempt); see ADVOCATE.

pleasant, or pleasing, adj. *acceptus* (= that which you are glad to see or hear), *gratus* (= very —, *pergratus*, of value to us), comb. *gratus acceptusque, jucundus, suavis* (= lovely), *dulcis* (= attractive), *mollis* (= gentle), *carus* (= dear), *gratiosus alci* and *apud alqm* (= in favour with), *urbanus* (= polite), *lepidus, facetus, festivus* (= humorous, witty), *laetus* (= joyous), *amoenus* (= charming, of place), *voluptarius* (= delightful), *commodus* (= suitable, e.g. *mores*); — conversation, *sermo festivus, venustus et urbanus*; — places, *loca amoena* or *voluptaria*; to be — to the eyes, *oculos delectare*; to be — to the ears, *aures (per)mulcēre, auribus blandiri*; to have a — taste, *jucunde sapĕre*. Adv. *jucunde, suaviter, dulce, dulciter, commode, lepide, festive, facete, amoene* or *amoeniter*. **pleasantness.** n. *jucunditas, dulcedo, amoenitas, suavitas, commoditas* (ante class. in Ovid.), *lepos*, or by adj.; see also LOVELINESS. **pleasantry,** n. *facetiae, lepos, festivitas*, or by *jocus* (= joke). **please,** v.intr. *alci placēre, alqm delectare, alci gratum, acceptum* or *cordi esse*, or *arridēre*; it —s, *placet* (of a decree of the senate); if you —, *vis* (*si vis*); to be —d, *delectari, gaudēre re*; to be dis—d, *abhorrēre re*; I am —d with this, *hoc mihi gratum est*; this dis—s me, *displicet mihi hoc*; you are —d to say, *libet* (*lubet*) *tibi dicĕre*; to — yourself, *gratificari sibi*; to — another, *gratificari alci, morem gerĕre alci*; eagerness to — (another), *immodica placendi cupido*. **pleasing,** adj., see PLEASANT. **pleasure,** n. *voluptas*; = will, *arbitrium*; *libido* (*lub-*, = passion, caprice), *delectatio, oblectatio, deliciae* (= delight), *delectamentum* (rare), *oblectamentum* (= object of —); according to —, *ex libidine, ex arbitrio ejus* (or *suo*); to do his —, *gratum facĕre alci*; = gross pleasures (lust), *cupiditates, libidines* (*lub-*), *corporis voluptates*; it is the — of the gods, the senate, etc., *dis, senatui placet*; a journey of —, *gestatio* (Sen.); to take — in the country, *excurrĕre rus*, in the gardens, *horti*; to walk for —, *ambulare*.

plebeian, I. n. *homo plebeius, homo de plebe*; the —s, *plebeii, plebs*; the order of the —s, *ordo plebeius, plebs*; from the order of the —s, *de plebe, plebeii generis, plebeius*. **II.** adj. *plebeius* (opp. *patricius*).

pledge, I. n. *pignus, -ĕris*, n., *hypotheca, arrhabo, -ōnis*, m., *arrha*. **II.** v.tr. *(op)pignerare* or *obligare alqd*; to — your word, *fidem interponĕre* or *obligare*.

Pleiades, n. *Pleiades* or *Vergiliae*.

plenary, adj. see FULL, ENTIRE, COMPLETE.

plenipotentiary, n. merely *legatus* (= ambassador); plenipotentiaries arrived from Sicily, *Siculi veniunt cum mandatis*.

plenitude, n. see FULNESS.

plenteous, plentiful, adj. *uber, abundans, copiosus, largus, affluens, opīmus*; see ABUNDANT. Adv. *uberius, uberrime* (not in posit.), *abunde, abundanter, copiose, satis superque, large, cumulate, prolixe, effuse*. **plenty,** n. *ubertas* (without reference to the use we make of it), *copia* (of anything, for a certain purpose, opp. *inopia*, Cic.), *abundantia* (= abundance, more than we wish), *affluentia* (= profusion), *magna vis* (great quantity); — of anything, *satis* with genit.; to have — of anything, *suppeditare* or *abundare alqa re*.

pleonasm, n. *pleonasmus* (late, or as Greek πλεονασμός), better use circumloc. (e.g. *nimiâ abundantiâ verborum uti*). **pleonastic,** adj. by circumloc. (e.g. *verba plura sunt quam pro re*).

plethora, n. *sanguinis abundantia*. **plethoric,** adj. *plenus sanguinis*.

pleurisy, n. *pleurītis*.

pliant, pliable, adj. **1,** *lentus, flexibilis*; **2,** fig. *mobilis, inconstans, mollis, flexibilis*. **pliancy, pliability,** n. **1,** *lentitia, lentor* (Plin.); **2,** *mobilitas, inconstantia, mollitia*.

plight, I. n. see CONDITION, STATE. **II.** v.tr. see PLEDGE.

plinth, n. *plinthus, plinthis, -ĭdis*, f.

plod, v.intr. **1,** = to go slowly, *tardius progredi*; **2,** = to toil, *omni ope atque operâ eniti, ut*, etc., *contendĕre et laborare, sudare et laborare*;

see TOIL. **plodding,** adj *esse industriâ singulari* (of persons)

plot, plat, n of ground, *agellus, area*

plot, I. n 1, *consensio, conspiratio, consensionis* or *conspirationis globus* (in gen), *conjuratio* (= conspiracy), *coitio* (= a secret combination, esp of two candidates for an office, for the purpose of getting rid of their competitors), to form a —, *consensiones* or *coitionem facĕre, conspirare,* to form a — against anyone, *in algm conspirare, contra algm conjurare, ad algm opprimendum consentire* (in order to oppress anyone), see CONSPIRACY, 2, in dramatic writings, *argumentum fabulae* **II.** v tr and intr see above and PLAN, DEVISE, CONTRIVE, CONSPIRE **plotter,** n see CONSPIRATOR

plough, I. n *aratrum*; —boy, *bubulcus*, in fig sense a mere —boy, *agrestis, rusticus*, —man, *arator* (who tends the oxen), —share, *vomer*, —handle, *stiva* **II.** v tr *arare* (absol and with accus), *inarare* (e g *semen*, = to cover by —ing), *exarare alqd* (= to dig up, to —), *aratro subigĕre* (= to break up, to till), *subvertĕre aratro alqd* (= to overturn with the plough), to — a field after it has been lying fallow, *proscindĕre* **ploughing,** n *proscissio* (= first —, Col)

pluck, I. v tr *vellĕre* (= to tear up or away), stronger, *vellicare*, to — out a hair, *pilum evellĕre*, to — flowers, *flores carpĕre*, see TEAR, to — up, *evellĕre, eruĕre*, to — up courage, *animum recipĕre* **II.** n 1, = heart, liver and lights of a sheep, etc , *intestina, -orum*, 2, = courage, *animus, virtus, ūtis*, f.

plug, n *epistomium*

plum, n *prunum*. **plum-tree,** n *prunus*, f. (Col)

plumage, n *plumae, pennae* (*pinnae*) **plume, I.** n *pluma, penna* (*pinna*) **II.** v reflex to — oneself on, *alqd ostentare, jactare, prae se ferre* **plumy,** adj *plumis obductus, plumatus, pennatus* (= winged, also of an arrow, *pluniger* and *penniger* are both poetic)

plumber, n. *artifex plumbarius*

plummet, plumb-line, n *linea, perpendiculum*

plump, adj *pinguis*, see FAT **plumpness,** n *pinguitudo*

plunder, I. v tr *praedari, praedam facĕre, diripĕre* (the enemy's territory, etc , also = to destroy the enemy, to ransack , in good prose only as t t representing warfare), *compilare, expilare* (= to rob by —), (*de*)*spoliare, exspoliare* (in gen = to rob), *nudare* (= to strip), *depeculari* (rare, = to embezzle, in a contemptuous sense = to —, all these of one person or thing, also of several, e g to — men, to — houses, etc), *depopulari* (= to lay waste, districts, etc), to — out and out, *exhaurire, exinanire, nudum atque inanem reddĕre* (= to clear a house, etc), *everrĕre et extergĕre* (= to sweep and wipe clean, jocular instead of to — completely, to strip, a temple, *fanum*, Cic) **II.** n *praeda, rapina* (= act of —ing), to live by —, *rapto vivĕre* **plunderer,** n *direptor, spoliator, populator, praedator, expilator*

plunge, I. v tr to — into, *mergĕre in alqd* or *in alqa re*, or merely *alqâ re* (into anything liquid, e g into the water, *in aquam, aquâ*, into the sea, *in mari*), *demergĕre* or *submergĕre, immergĕre* (*in alqd* or *alqâ re*), into, *in alqd* or *in alqâ re* or *sub alqâ re*, to — a dagger, etc , see THRUST; to — anyone, a State, into difficulties, see PRECIPITATE, THROW. **II.** v intr to — into, 1, (*im*)*mergĕre, demergĕre, submergĕre*, 2, fig *se mergĕre* or *ingurgitare in alqd*

pluperfect, n *tempus plusquam perfectum* (Gram)

plural, adj in Gram , the — number, *numerus pluralis, numerus multitudinis* **plurality,** n by *plures* (= more) or *multitudo* (= a number)

ply, v tr *exercēre*

poach, I. v tr e g eggs, perhaps *frixare* (= to fry), —ed eggs, perhaps *ova assa* or *frixata* **II.** v intr *furtim feras intercipĕre* **poacher,** n *fur* (= thief)

pocket, I. n *sacculus* (= small bag, Juv), *marsupium* (ante and post class , = bag for holding money), *crumēna* (= a purse for containing small coin, a bag worn over the shoulders); the ancients had no —s in their garments, but they used the folds in their toga, *sinus, -ūs* (lit = bosom, in sense of —, poet and post Aug) **II.** v tr = to take away, *auferre*, to — dishonestly, *pecuniam avertĕre* **pocket-book,** n *pugillares, -ium* (Plin) **pocket-handkerchief,** n *sudarium*. **pocket-knife,** n *culter*, see KNIFE **pocket-money,** n *pecunia alci data*

pod, n *siliqua*

podagra, n *podagra, podagrae morbus*

poem, n *carmen* (= a short —, esp a lyric —, a — composed according to metrical rules, such as the odes of Horace), *poëma, -ătis*, n , to make a —, *carmen* (*poema*) *facĕre, fingĕre, scribĕre* (in gen), *carmen fundĕre* (= to make verses extempore, with ease) **poesy,** n see POETRY **poet,** n *poëta*, m , *carminum auctor, scriptor, conditor*, † *vates* (= inspired —) **poetaster,** n *poëta malus* **poetess,** n *poëtria* **poetical,** adj *poëticus* Adv *poëtice, poëtarum more* **poetry,** n *poëtice* or *poëtica, poësis* (Quint), or by poem , see POEM

poignant, adj *acer*, see KEEN

point, I. n 1, *acumen* (in gen), *cuspis, ĭdis*, f. (of a weapon, an arrow, etc), *spiculum* (= head or point of a dart, pike-head, the dart or arrow itself, opp *hastile* = shaft), *cacumen, culmen, fastigium, vertex, -icis*, m (= the highest — of anything, also by *summus*), see SUMMIT, 2, of land, *promontorium*, see CAPE, 3, in writing, see STOP, 4, a small particle (as regards space or time), *pars* (= part in gen), *locus* (= spot), *punctum temporis* (= minute), to draw the troops together at one —, *copias in unum locum contrahĕre* or *cogĕre*, the highest — of the mountain, *summus mons*, I am on the — of, etc (I am about to, etc), *in eo est, ut*, etc , *prope est, ut*, etc (= the time is near at hand, when, etc), to be on the — of conquering, *prope in manibus victoriam habēre*, 5, = a circumstance, *res* (in gen), *locus* (= a single subject of which we speak), *caput* (= main —, principal part, one particular portion, e g *a primo capite legis usque ad extremum*), *cardo, -ĭnis*, m (= main — on which anything hinges), *quaestio* (= the — in dispute), or *de quo agitur*, *nomen* (= an item in an account, outstanding debt), in this particular —, *hac in re*, the right —, *res ipsa*, to hit the right —, *rem acu tangĕre* (Plaut), not to the —, *nihil ad rem*, an important —, *res magni momenti*, the most important —, *res maximi momenti, res gravissima, caput rei* **II.** v tr and intr 1, of sharp instruments, (*prae*)*acuĕre*; see SHARPEN, 2, with the finger at anyone or anything, *digito monstrare alqd* or *alqm, digitum intendĕre ad alqd* or *ad alqm* (= to stretch, hold out, etc), see NOTICE, 3, see PUNCTUATE **point-blank, I.** adj *directus*, to give a — refusal, *alqd prorsus negare* **II.** adv *plane, prorsus, omnino*, see ALTOGETHER **pointed,** adj 1, (*prae*)*acutus*, 2, fig of speech, *salsus, aculeatus* (= stinging), *ad alqd appositus* (= directed to); see CLEAR Adv *salse, apposite* **pointer,** n = a dog, *canis* (*venaticus*). **pointless,** adj. 1, see BLUNT; 2, fig. *insulsus, frigidus, ineptus, inanis.*

poise, v.tr. *librare.*

poison, I. n. *venēnum, virus, -i,* n. (= poisonous vegetable or animal juice or liquid); fig. *venenum.* **II.** v.tr. *alqd venenare* (rare), *alqd veneno imbuĕre;* to slay many, to — many, *multos veneno occidĕre;* to strangle the wife and — the mother, *laqueo uxorem interimĕre matremque veneno;* fig. to — the minds of the young, *animos adolescentium inficĕre malis libidinibus.* **poisoned,** adj. *venenatus* (= dipped in poison, mixed with poison, e.g. an arrow, javelin, *sagitta, telum;* meat, *caro*), *veneno necatus* or *absumptus* (= killed by poison); — words, perhaps *verba acerba* or *aculeata.* **poisoner,** n. *veneficus* (if female, *venefica*). **poisoning,** n. *veneficium* (= mixing poison, as a regular occupation, and as a crime). **poisonous,** adj. *venenatus* (in gen.), *veneno imbutus* or *infectus* or *tinctus* (= dipped in poison), *veneno illĭtus* (= besmeared with —).

poke, I. v.tr. anyone, *alqm fodĕre* or *fodicare;* to — the fire, *ignem excitare.* **II.** v.intr. to — about, *alqd rimari, perscrutari.* **poker,** n. perhaps *ferramentum* (= iron tool) *quo ignis excitatur.*

pole, n. 1, = long rod, *contus, pertica, longurius, asser, vectis;* 2, of the earth, *axis, cardo,* † *polus,* and † *vertex;* the south —, *axis meridianus;* the north —, *axis septentrionalis* (*septemt-*). **polar,** adj. *septentrionalis* (*septemt-*) (= northern). **poleaxe,** n. see AXE. **polecat,** n. *feles.*

polemical, adj. by circumloc., e.g. *qui cum alqo de alqâ re disceptat* or *concertat, qui alqd in controversiam vocat.* **polemics,** n. *disputationes.*

police, n. 1, matters relating to public security, no exact term, use *publicae* or *urbanae securitatis cura;* 2, = constables, etc., the *aediles* had charge of many of the functions of the police; in gen. *ii quibus publicae securitatis cura delata est* (= — officers). **policeman,** n. *unus e publicae securitatis custodibus.*

policy, n. *ratio rei publicae gerendae, civīlitas* (in Quint. as trans. of πολιτική), *disciplina reipublicae;* fig. *prudentia, calliditas, consilium.* **politic,** adj. *prudens, sagax, astutus, callidus, circumspectus, providus;* see CUNNING, WISE, PRUDENT. **political,** adj. referring to the State, *civilis* (as trans. of the Greek πολιτικός, which does not exist in Latin, = referring to the State or to State affairs; e.g. *oratio civilis*), *publicus* (= relating to public affairs), *politicus* (= relating to — science); — storms, *tempora turbulenta, turbulentae in civitate tempestates;* a — discussion, *sermo de republicâ habitus;* — writings, *scripta quae ad rempublicam gerendam pertinent;* — science in gen., *ratio civilis, reipublicae gerendae ratio;* see STATE. Adv., use adj. **politician,** n. *vir rerum civilium peritus, vir regendae civitatis peritus* or *sciens.* **politics,** n. *respublica,* or in pl. *res publicae* (e.g. *ad rempublicam accedĕre,* = to take up —). **polity,** n. *respublica, genus, -ĕris,* n., or *forma reipublicae, ratio civilis.*

polish, I. v.tr. (*ex*)*polire, perpolire* (lit. and fig., in fig. sense also *limare*). **II.** n. 1, lit. *nitor, candor;* see BRIGHTNESS; 2, fig. circumloc. with *lima* (his writings lack —, *scriptis ejus lima deest*); see POLITENESS. **polished,** adj. lit. by past part. of POLISH, I.; see also POLITE.

polite, adj. *urbanus, comis, humanus, affabilis, blandus, officiosus* (esp. towards superiors). Adv. *urbane, comiter, humane, humaniter, blande, officiose.* **politeness,** n. *urbanitas, comitas, humanitas, affabilitas.*

poll, I. n. 1, see HEAD; 2, = register of heads, perhaps *index nominum;* 3, = entry of the names of electors, see VOTE, ELECT, REGISTER. **II.** v.tr. 1, lit. (*am*)*putare, praecidĕre;* 2, = to give votes, see VOTE. **pollard,** n. *arbor, -ŏris,* f., (*am*)*putata.* **polling,** n. see VOTING. **polling-booth,** n. *saeptum, ovile.* **poll-tax,** n. to impose a —, *tributum in singula capita imponĕre.*

pollute, v.tr. *pollŭĕre.* **pollution,** n. *pollutio.*

poltroon, n. see COWARD.

polygamy, n. to live in a state of —, *solēre plures uxores habēre* (of a man), *pluribus nuptam esse* (of a woman).

polyglot, adj. *pluribus linguis scriptus.*

polygon, n. * *polygōnum.* **polygonal,** adj. *polygonius* (Vitr.), † *multangulus* (Lucr.).

polypus, n. *polypus, -ŏdis,* m. (as animal, Plin., and as tumour in the nose, Cels.).

polytheism, n. *multorum deorum cultus, -ūs.* **polytheist,** n. *qui multos deos colit.*

pomatum, n. *capillare* (in gen., Mart.).

pomegranate, n. *mālum granātum* or *Punicum* (Col.).

pommel, I. n. of a saddle, *umbo sellae.* **II.** v.tr. see BEAT.

pomp, n. *apparatus, -ūs;* = show of magnificence, *venditatio, venditatio atque ostentatio* (= boasting, swaggering); — of words, *inanis verborum strepitus, -ūs, quaedam species atque pompa;* to speak with a show of —, *in dicendo adhibēre quandam speciem atque pompam.* **pompous,** adj. 1, *magnificus, jactans, gloriosus, arrogans, insolens;* see BOASTFUL; 2, of style, *inflatus, tumidus;* see INFLATED. Adv. *magnifice, gloriose, arroganter, insolenter.* **pompousness, pomposity,** n. 1, *magnificentia, arrogantia, insolentia;* 2, of words, *insolentia verborum,* or by adj.; see INFLATION.

pond, n. *stagnum* (= any stagnant pool of water, also fish—), *piscīna* (= fish—), *lacus, -ūs* (= a lake, whether by nature or artificial).

ponder, v.tr. and intr. *ponderare, secum reputare;* see CONSIDER. **ponderous,** adj. see WEIGHTY.

poniard, n. see DAGGER.

pontiff, n. *pontifex;* see PRIEST, POPE.

pontoon, n. *ponto.*

pony, n. *mannus, mannulus* (of Gallic race, Plin. Min.), or *equus parvus.*

poodle, n. *canis.*

pool, n. *lacuna* (= a body of stagnant water), † *volutabrum* (= a muddy place in which swine delight to roll); see POND.

poop, n. *puppis.*

poor, adj. = in kind or nature, deficient in its proper qualities, *malus, vilis* (= of small worth), *mediocris* (= middling), *deterior* (= less good, superl. *deterrimus*), *pejor* (superl. *pessimus*); — living, *tenuis victus, -ūs;* — speech, *oratio jejuna;* — cottage, *casa exigua;* = barren, *inops alcjs rei* (or *alqâ re* or *ab alqâ re*), *sterilis* (= unproductive); — in words, *inops verborum;* = not rich, *pauper* (πένης, opp. *dives*), *tenuis* (= of small means, opp. *locuples*), *egens, indigens* (= needy, wanting necessaries, opp. *abundans*), *tenuis atque egens; inops* (= without resources, opp. *opulentus*), *mendīcus* (= a beggar); somewhat —, *pauperculus;* the —, *pauperes, tenuis vitae homines* (= having a slender income), *capite censi* (so called because the poorest were in the census taken by numbers, without regard to property), also *proletarii* (from *proles* = offspring); = wretched, pitiable, *miser, misellus, infelix, miserandus;* a

— fellow, *homo misellus*; — fellow! *me*, *me* (*te*) *miserum!* **poorhouse,** n *ptōchotrophium* (Jct.), or by circumloc (e g *aedes publice pro indigentibus aedificatae*) **poor-laws,** n *leges de indigentibus factae* **poorly, I.** adv *tenuiter*, *mediocriter*, *misere* **II.** adj see ILL

poverty, n. *paupertas*, *angustiae rei familiaris* (= narrow means), *difficultas domestica*, *tenuitas*, *egestas* (= want), *inopia* (= destitution), *mendicitas* (= mendicity), in comb *egestas ac mendicitas*, — of mind, *animi egestas*, *tenuis et angusta ingenii vena* (Quint), — of words, *verborum inopia*, *inopia ac jejunitas*, *sermonis inopia*, — in your mother tongue, *egestas patrii sermonis*

pop, I. n *crepitus*, *-ūs* **II.** v intr *crepare*, to — out, *evadĕre*, *ex(s)ilire*

pope, n **pontifex Romanus*, **papa* **popish,** adj **papisticus*

poplar, n. *pōpulus*, f, of the —, *pōpuleus*

poppy, n *papăver*, *ĕris*, n

popular, adj *in vulgus gratus*, see under PEOPLE **populate,** v tr see under PEOPLE.

porch, n *vestibulum*, in a temple or church, *pronaos* (πρoναoς)

porcupine, n. *hystrix* (Plin).

pore, n *foramen* (e g *foramina invisibilia corporis* (Cels) **porosity,** n *raritas* **porous,** adj. *fistulosus* (Plin, = full of holes), *spongiosus*, *rarus*

pore, v tr to — over a book, *in libro alqo haerēre*, to — over, *totum se abdĕre in alqd*

pork, n (*caro*) *suilla* or *porcina* **porker,** n *porcus*

porphyry, n *porphyrites* (Plin)

porpoise, n *porculus marinus* (Plin)

porridge, n *puls*, *-tis*, f; see BROTH, SOUP, OATMEAL

porringer, n see PLATE

port, n 1, *portus*, *ūs*, see HARBOUR, 2, see GAIT

portable, adj *quod portari* or *gestari potest*

portcullis, n *cataracta*

portend, v intr *portendĕre*, *augurari*, *significare*, *praemonstrare*, *praenuntiare*. **portent,** n *portentum*, *ostentum*, *prodigium*, *monstrum*, *signum*, *omen*, *augurium*, *auspicium*, †*avis* **portentous,** adj *portentosus*, *monstr(u)osus*, †*prodigiosus* Adv *monstr(u)ose*

porter, n 1, = keeper of a lodge, *janitor* (female, *janitrix*), *ostiarius*, see DOOR-KEEPER, GATE-KEEPER, 2, = one who carries burdens, *bajulus*, 3, see BEER

portfolio, n *scrinium*.

porthole, n *fenestra*

portico, n *porticus*, *-ūs*, f

portion, I. n *pars*, *portio*, see PART, SHARE **II.** v tr see DIVIDE

portly, adj see STOUT

portmanteau, n *vidulus*, *averta* (= cloak-bag carried behind a horse, late Imperial Rome)

portrait, n *imago* (*picta*), anyone's —, *effigies ex facie ipsius similitudine expressa* **portrait-painter,** n *pictor qui homines coloribus reddit* **portray,** v tr *depingĕre* (in words or colours), see DESCRIBE, PAINT

position, n *collocatio* (= mode in which anything is placed, e g. of the stars, *siderum*, Cic), *status*, *-ūs*, *habitus*, *-ūs*, or by *positum esse*, fig = circumstances, *status*, *ūs* (= state in which anything is), *condicio* (= condition, rank in society, circumstances), *locus* (= — in which a person is placed, Cæs), *tempus*, *tempora* (= change in one's circumstances which from time to time takes place, hence often = bad, difficult circumstances), *res* (= affairs, etc, in gen), *fortuna* (= outward circumstances, fortune)

positive, adj a — law, *lex scripta* (opp *lex nata*), the — right, *jus civile* (opp *jus naturale*), also merely *leges*, = certain, *certus*, a — statement, *affirmatio*, I make a — statement, *aio*, *affirmo*, the — degree, *positivus* (*gradus*, *-ūs*) (Prisc) Adv *affirmate*, *certo*, to know —, *certo* or *certis auctoribus comperisse*, to assert —, *affirmare*, *confirmare* **positiveness,** n = positive assertion, *affirmatio*, = certainty, by circumloc (e g *alqd certum habēre*, *alqd affirmare*)

possess, v tr *possidēre* (*ingenium*, *magnam vim*, etc), *alqd* or *possessionem rei habēre* or *tenēre*, *in possessione rei esse*, *habēre* (*auctoritatem*), *tenēre* (= to hold, e g *tu meum habes*, *tenes*, *possides*), *alqâ re praeditum*, *instructum*, *ornatum* or *affectum esse* (= to be gifted with), *inesse alci* or *in alqo*, with *est* and genit or dat, *virtus est virium* (= virtue — es strength), *est mihi liber* (= I — a book), or with the ablat (e g *Hortensius erat tantâ memoriâ ut*, etc, = Hortensius —ed such a memory, that, etc), to — partitively, *alcjs rei participem esse*, all men cannot — all things, *non omnes omnium participes esse possunt*, not to —, *carēre re*, to — not at all, *alcjs rei expertem esse*; to — richly, *alqâ re abundare* or *valēre* **possession,** n *possessio*, a taking —, *occupatio*, = the object possessed, *possessio*, *bona*, *-orum*, *res sua* **possessive,** adj *possessivus* (*casus*) (Gram) **possessor,** n *possessor*, *dominus*

possible, adj *quod esse*, *fieri* or *effici potest*, *quod per rerum naturam admitti potest*, a — case, *condicio quae per rerum naturam admitti potest* or simply *condicio* (Cic) if it is, were —, if — *si potest*, *si posset*, as much as —, *quantum potest* (*poterit*, etc), it is — that, etc, *fieri potest*, *ut*, etc, as much as it is —, *quoad fieri potest* or *poterit*, as . . as —, *quam* with superl. (e g as early as —, *quam maturrime*, as quick as —, *quam celerrime*, as shortly as —, *quam brevissime*), he joined his colleague with his army in as rapid marches as —, *quantis maximis poterat itineribus exercitum ducebat ad collegam*, to show every — care, *omnem*, *quam possum*, *curam adhibēre*, every —, often merely *omnis* Adv *fieri potest ut*, etc., see PERHAPS **possibility,** n *condicio* (= possible case, Cic), *potestas* or *facultas* or *copia alqd faciendi* (= possession, *potestas*, as permission, power, *facultas* and *copia* = the opportunities), *locus alcjs rei* (= opportunity given through circumstances, e g he denies the — of this idea, *negat esse posse hanc notionem*), also when — implies that a thing can be done, by *fieri* or *effici posse* (e g they deny the — of anything, *alqd fieri posse negant*)

post, I. n 1, *postis* (of a gate, etc), *arrectaria*, *-orum*, n (lit what stands erect, opp *transversaria*, Vitr), *palus* (= a stake), *cippus* (esp gravestone), 2, = military station, *locus* (= place in gen), *statio* (= outpost, guard), *praesidium* (= any place taken by the troops, and which is to be defended), 3, = office, *locus*, *munus*, *-ĕris*, n, *partes*, *ium*, 4, = system of public conveyance, *res veredaria*, *res vehicularia* (= the whole institution, Imperial Rome), *rei vehiculariae curatores* (= the persons connected with it), 5, system of conveyance of letters, *tabellarii* (= letter-carriers); to send through the —, *alqd per tabellarios mittĕre*, to put into the —, *alqd tabellario perferendum committĕre* **II.** v tr 1, of travelling, letters, etc, see I 4, 5, 2, of troops, (*dis*)*ponĕre*, (*col*)*locare*, *constituĕre*, 3, = to affix a notice, etc, *proponĕre* **postage,** n *vecturae pretium*, to pay the — *pro vecturâ solvere*, **post-chaise,** n *vehiculum publicum*, *raeda cursualis* (Imperial Rome). **postern,** n. *postica, posticum.* **posthaste,** adv. *summâ celeritate* or *quam celerrime.* **postillion,** n. see RIDER, GROOM. **postman,** n. *tabellarius* (= private messenger); see POST I. 5. **postscript,** n. *alqd epistulae additum.*

posterior, adj. *posterior.*

posterity, n. *posteritas* (in a wide sense, but only poetic for *progenies* or *stirps*), *posteri,* † *minores.*

posthumous, adj. *post patrem mortuum natus.*

postmeridian, adj. *postmeridianus* or *pomeridianus, post meridiem* (opp. *ante meridiem*), *tempore pomeridiano, horis pomeridianis.*

postpone, v.tr. *differre, proferre, re(j)icĕre;* see DEFER.

postulate, n. *sumptio.*

posture, n. 1, of body, *status, habitus, gestus* (all -ūs); 2, = condition of affairs, *status, -ūs, res, condicio, ratio;* see STATE.

pot, n. *olla;* a small —, *ollula.* **potbellied,** adj. *ventriosus.* **potherb,** n. *olus, -ĕris,* n. **pothook,** n. *uncus;* in writing, *uncus quem dicunt.* **pothouse,** n. *caupona.* **potsherd,** n. *testa.* **pottage,** n. *jus, juris,* n.

potent, adj. see POWERFUL, EFFICACIOUS.

potentate, n. *res, tyrannus;* see SOVEREIGN.

potential, adj. *potentialis* (Gram.); see also POSSIBLE.

potion, n. *potio;* see PHILTRE.

potter, n. *figulus;* a —'s work, *opus figlinum, opera figlina* or *fictilia,* n. pl. (of several pieces); —'s vessels, earthenware, (*opus*) *figlinum, opera figlina;* —'s wheel, *rota figularis* or *figuli;* —'s workshop, *figlina* (Plin.). **pottery,** n. 1, the art, *ars figularis;* 2, = things made; see under POTTER.

pouch, n. *sacculus, saccus;* see BAG.

poultice, n. *cataplasma, -ătis,* n. (Cels.); *malagma, -ătis,* n. (= an emollient —, Cels.); a mustard —, *sinapismus.*

poultry, n. *aves cohortales* (kept in the yard) (Col.), *altiles, -ium* (= fattened —). **poulterer,** n. *qui altiles vendit.*

pounce, v.intr. to — upon; see SEIZE.

pound, I. n. 1, *libra,* (*libra*) *pondo* (in weight, of hard substances), *libra mensurâ* (of liquids); a bowl the gold of which weighs five —s, *patera ex quinque auri* (*libris*) *pondo;* 2, of money, use *libra Anglicana* as t.t., but use *argentum* or *pecunia* where possible; 3, = enclosure for stray animals, *saeptum publicum.* **II.** v.tr. (*con*)*tundĕre,* (*con*)*terĕre.*

pour, I. v.tr. 1, *fundĕre;* to — into, *infundĕre in alqd;* to — upon or over, *superfundĕre alci rei.* **II.** v.intr. 1, of rain, (*ef*)*fundi;* 2, fig. to — forth, (*ef*)*fundi,* or *se* (*ef*)*fundĕre;* 3, to — along, *ferri;* 4, to — off, *defundĕre.* **pouring,** adj. *effusus* (of rain).

pout, v.intr. perhaps *frontem contrahĕre* (= to frown).

poverty, n. see POOR.

powder, I. n., in gen., *pulvis, -ĕris;* as medicine, *pulvis medicatus.* **II.** v.tr. 1, to reduce to —, *in pulverem conterĕre* (Plin.); 2, = to sprinkle with —, *pulvere conspergĕre.*

power, n. if internal, *potentia* or *vires, -ium,* (= strength); if external, *vis* (= force) or *potestas* (= authority from office), *jus, juris,* n., *potestasque, potestas ac dicio* or *dicio* alone (= authority), *facultas alcjs rei faciendae* (= — of doing anything), *copiae, opes, -um, facultates, -um* (= resources), *robur, nervi, lacerti* (= physical —); to strive with all one's —, *omni ope eniti ut;* it is in my —, *est* or *positum* or *situm est in meâ manu,* or *potestate;* to reduce under one's —, *suae dicionis facĕre;* to be under the — of, *sub alcjs dicione atque imperio esse;* to do anything by —, *per vim facĕre alqd;* to possess —, *vim habēre;* to compel anyone by —, *manus inferre alci;* — over persons or a nation, *potestas, imperium* (= military — or command); unlimited —, *dominatio, summum imperium, summa rerum.* **powerful,** adj. 1, physically, *validus, viribus pollens, robustus, valens, lacertosus, firmus;* 2, in influence, etc., *potens, valens, validus, gravis* (= weighty, of character); 3, of medicine, *efficax, potens* (Plin.); 4, of speech, *gravis, nervosus, validus* (Quint.). Adv. *valide* (not in Cic. or Caes.), *graviter, vehementer, valde* (= very —). **powerless,** adj. *invalidus, impotens, infirmus, imbecillus, languidus, irritus:* in political sense, *cui opes non suppeditant;* see WEAK. **powerlessness,** n. *imbecillitas, infirmitas;* in political sense by circumloc. (e.g. he felt his —, *sensit sibi opes deesse*); see WEAKNESS.

practicable, adj. *quod fieri* or *effici potest, facilis* (= easy, opp. *difficilis*); anything is —, *res facilitatem habet;* it is not —, *fieri* or *effici non potest.* **practicability,** n. *facultas, potestas.* **practical,** adj. *in agendo positus, usu peritus, ipso usu perdoctus;* — knowledge, *usus, -ūs;* to have a — knowledge of anything, *alqd usu cognitum habēre, alqd usu didicisse, alcjs rei usum habēre;* — use, *utilitas* (as regards public life). Adv. (*ex*) *usu;* to learn a thing —, *usu discĕre alqd.* **practice,** n. 1, = exercise, etc., *usus, -ūs, usus rerum* (= exercise and experience); *exercitatio, tractatio,* comb. *usus et exercitatio, usus et tractatio;* to have more — than theory, *minus in studio quam in rebus et usu versatum esse;* we must combine theory and —, *discas oportet et quod didicisti agendo confirmes;* the — of an attorney, *caus(s)arum actio;* of a physician, surgeon, *medicinae usus et tractatio;* 2, = habit, *mos, consuetudo;* to make a — of, *solēre;* see CUSTOM. **practise,** v.tr. *alqd facĕre, exercēre, factitare, tractare;* see PRACTICE. **practitioner,** n. *medicus.*

praetor, n. *praetor.* **praetorian,** adj. *praetorius, praetorianus* (Tac.). **praetorship,** n. *praetura.*

pragmatical, adj. *molestus, qui res alienas tractat.*

prairie, n. *campus.*

praise, I. v.tr. *laudare* (in gen.), *laudem alci tribuĕre, laudem alci impertire* or *laude alqm impertire, laude alqm afficĕre* (= to give — to), *collaudare* (with others), *dilaudare* (very much, almost too much), *praedicare alqm* or *de alqo* (aloud and openly). **II.** n. *laus, -dis,* f. (in a subjective and objective sense), *laudatio* (= a laudatory oration), *praedicatio* (= the act of recommending one for a meritorious deed, esp. openly and in public, e.g. *quae praedicatio de meâ laude praetermissa est*); they give — and thanks unto the gods, *diis laudes gratesque agunt.* **praiseworthy,** adj. *laudabilis, laude dignus, laudandus, collaudandus, praedicandus;* to be —, *laudi esse;* to be considered —, *laude dignum duci, laudi duci.* Adv. *laudabiliter.*

prance, v.intr. perhaps *magnifice incedĕre* (of a person), *ex(s)ultare* (of a horse).

prank, n. to play —s, perhaps *lascivire.*

prate, prattle, v. see BABBLE, CHATTER.

pray, v.intr. and tr. 1, *precari, preces* or *precationem facĕre* (generally; more poet. *preces* *fundĕre*), *supplicare* (humbly, upon one's knees), to God, *precari Deum* or *ad Deum*, *orare* or *invocare Deum* (= to invoke), *Deo supplicare* (= to entreat humbly), to — unto God that He, etc, *precari a Deo, ut*, etc, to — for, *alqd a Deo precari* or *petere*, 2, = to entreat for, in more gen sense, (*ef*)*flagitare*, *petĕre*, (*ex*)*poscĕre*, *implorare*, *rogare*, *orare alqd*, to — and beseech, *rogare atque orare*, *petere ac deprecari* **prayer,** n *precatio*, *supplicatio*, *preces*, *-um* (= the formulary, book of common —), *votorum nuncupatio* (in which we make promises) **prayerful,** adj **prayerfully,** adv *supplex* **praying,** n. *precatio*, *preces*, *-um*, *supplicatio* (humble), a day of — and thanksgiving, *supplicatio et gratulatio*, to appoint —, *supplicationem decernĕre*

preach, v tr and intr **contionari* (the usual term in writers after the Reformation), **praedicare*, or *orationem* (*sacram*) *habēre*, *e* (*sacro*) *suggestu dicĕre*, *in coetu Christianorum verba facĕre*, *de rebus divinis dicĕre*, to — about, in the context, *dicĕre de alqa re*, *oratione explicare alqd* **preacher,** n. **praedicator*; — to deaf ears, *monitor non exauditus*

preamble, n *exordium*, see INTRODUCTION

precarious, adj *incertus* Adv *parum* or *non certo*

precaution, n *cautio*, or by verb *providēre*, *praecavēre*

precede, v tr *anteire*, *antegredi*, *antecedĕre*, *praeire*, *praegredi* **precedence,** n *prior locus*, to have the — before anyone, *alci antecedĕre*, to let anyone have the —, *alci cedĕre*, *alqm priore loco ire jubēre* **preceding,** adj *antecedens*, *praecedens*, = last, *prior*, *superior*, = the one immediately before, *proximus* **precedent,** n see EXAMPLE

precentor, n *praecantor* (late)

precept, n *praeceptum* (beforehand, what and how it is to be done), *praescriptum*, *praescriptio* (= rule, made by a higher authority, and which we have to follow, e g *naturae*, *rationis*, the former the — itself, the latter the act of prescribing), *lex* (made into law)

preceptor, n *magister*, see TEACHER

precincts, n *ambitus*, *ūs*, see LIMIT, DISTRICT

precious, adj *magnificus*, *splendidus*, *egregius*, *eximius*, *pulcherrimus*, *jucundissimus*, *suavissimus*, — stones, *gemmae*

precipice, n *locus praeceps*

precipitate, I v tr *praecipitare* (from, *ex* or *de alqo loco*, into, etc, *in alqm locum*, headlong, lit and fig), *de*(*j*)*icĕre*, from (*ab* or *de*) *alqo loco*, into, *in alqm locum*, *deturbare*, *de* or *ex alqo loco*, *in alqm locum*, to — oneself, *sese praecipitare*, or merely *praecipitare*, or, in the sense of the middle voice in Greek, *praecipitari*, from, etc, *alqo loco*, *de* or *ex alqo loco*, into, *in alqm locum*, (e g into ruin, *in exitium*), over, *super alqm locum*, *se de*(*j*)*icĕre*, *se ab*(*j*)*icĕre* (= to throw oneself down from the wall into the sea, *e muro in mare se abjicĕre*), *inferri* or *se inferre in alqd* (= to rush into, e g *in flammas*, *in medios ignes*, also fig, e g *se inferre in capitis periculum*) II. adj *temerarius*, *praeceps*, see HASTY, RASH Adv *temere* **precipitancy, precipitation,** n *temeritas*, see RASHNESS **precipitous,** adj *praeceps*, *praeruptus*

precise, adj (*de*)*finitus* (= marked out), *accuratus* (= accurate), *subtilis* (= accurate in the choice of words) Adv *subtiliter*, = altogether, *plane*, by *ipse* (e g *ipso in tempore*, = — at the right time), see EXACT, ACCURATE. **precision,** n *subtilitas*, *proprietas verborum*, see ACCURACY

preclude, v tr see HINDER, EXCLUDE

precocious, adj *praecox* (lit of fruit, and fig post Aug of talents), see PREMATURE

preconceived, adj *praejudicatus* **preconception,** n *sententia praejudicata*

preconcerted, adj *ex composito* (*factus*, etc)

precursor, n *praecursor* (lit, Plin), *praenuntius*, fig

predatory, adj *praedatorius*

predecessor, n in office, *decessor* (*antecessor*, only by Jct), he is my —, *succedo ei*

predestination, n *praedestinatio* (Eccl)
predestine, v tr *praedestinare* (Liv), in a theol sense, *praefinire*

predetermine, v tr *praefinire*

predicable, adj *quod alci rei attribui potest*

predicament, n an awkward —, *difficultas*

predicate, I. n *attributio*, *attributum*, *res attributa*, *id quod rebus* or *personis attribuitur* or *attributum est* (= to attribute) II. v tr *alqd de alqa re praedicare*, *dicĕre*, see SAY

predict, v tr *praedicĕre*, see PROPHESY
prediction, n *praedictio* see PROPHECY

predilection, n see AFFECTION

predispose, v tr *animum ad alqd praeparare* or *componĕre* **predisposed,** adj *propensus* or *proclivis ad alqd* **predisposition,** n *animi ad alqd proclivitas*, *voluntatis inclinatio studium*

predominance, n 1, = power, *potentia*; see POWER, 2, = greater number of, by *plures*
predominate, v intr 1, *dominari*, 2, *plures esse* **predominating,** adj see CHIEF

preeminence, n *praestantia*, *excellentia eminentia*. **preeminent,** adj *praestabilis*, *praestans*, *excellens*, *praecipuus*, *summus*, *optimus*, *conspicuus*, *insignis* Adv *praecipue*, see ESPECIALLY

preexist, v intr *antea exstare* or *esse* **preexistence,** n by verb

preface, I. n *prooemium* (= introduction), *praefatio* (in disputations, to ask permission or to apologise, etc, then = written — to a book), — to a book, *prooemium libri* (not *ad librum*), *prooemium libro additum* II. v tr *praefari* (= both to write a — and to make one in speaking), *praefationem dicĕre* (in speaking), *prooemium scribĕre* (= to write) **prefatory,** adj to make a few — remarks, *pauca praefari*

prefect, n *praefectus* **prefecture,** n *praefectura*

prefer, v tr 1, *praeponĕre*, *anteponĕre*, *praeferre*, *anteferre* (in gen), *alqm potissimum diligĕre* (= to esteem very highly), *alqd alci rei posthabēre* (= to hold one thing inferior to another), *praeoptare* with infin (= to wish rather), *malle* with infin (to wish rather, e g *mori maluit*); 2, see PROMOTE, 3, see ACCUSE **preferable,** adj *potior*, *praeoptandus*, *praestabilior*, or by compar of any adj = excellent, see GOOD, EXCELLENT Adv *potius* **preference,** n by verb PREFER **preferment,** n by special name of office (e g *consulatus*), or by *honos* (= office)

prefix, I. v tr *praeponĕre*, *anteponĕre*, *praescribĕre* (in writing) II. n *syllaba anteposita*

pregnancy, n *praegnatio* (of a female with child), *graviditas* (more advanced, Cic) **pregnant,** adj 1, *praegnans* (in gen of women and animals, fig. = full of anything), *gravida* (in a more advanced state), *gravidata* (fig.); to be —, *gravidam* or *praegnatum esse, ventrem ferre, partum ferre* or *gestare*; to be — by anyone, *gravidam esse ex alqo*; 2, of language, *pressus* (concise); of events, *magni* or *maximi momenti*; see IMPORTANCE.

prehensile, adj. *quod ad prehendendum aptum* or *accommodatum est.*

prejudge, v.tr. *prius judicare quam alqs alqd sciat.*

prejudice, I. n. *opinio praejudicata, alqd praejudicati, opinio praesumpta* (preconceived); *opinio prava* (= wrong opinion), *opinio ficta* (= a false opinion, in the context often simply *opinio* = erroneous opinion), *opinionis commentum* (= fanciful dream); a — still more confirmed through the teaching of others, *opinio confirmata*; to have a — against anyone, *male de alqo opinari*; to come anywhere with a —, *alqd praejudicati afferre.* **II.** v.tr. *alqm alci suspectum reddĕre, alqm* or *alcjs animum alienum reddĕre* or *alienare ab alqo*; to become —d against anyone, *ab alqo alienari*; to become —d, *ab alqo alienatum esse, ab alqo animo esse alieno* or *averso*, very much, *ab alqo animo esse aversissimo.* **prejudicial,** adj. see INJURIOUS.

prelate, n. * *episcopus.*

preliminary, adj. see PREFATORY.

prelude, I. n. 1, *prooemium*; 2, fig. *prolusio, praelusio atque praecursio* (Plin. Min.). **II.** v.tr. 1, perhaps *prooemium canĕre* (fixing sense by context); 2, fig. *nuntiare*; see ANNOUNCE.

premature, adj. 1, lit. *praematurus, praecox* (Plin.), *immaturus*; 2, fig. *praematurus*, † *praecox, immaturus, praeproperus.* Adv. *praemature.*

premeditate, v.tr. *praemeditari* (= to think over beforehand); —d act, *quod ex consulto fit.* **premeditation,** n. *praemeditatio*; see PURPOSE.

premier, n. = prime minister, perhaps *penes quem est summa reipublicae.*

premise, v.tr. *praefari.* **premises,** n. *aedificium* (or in pl.), *domus, -ūs* (irreg.); see HOUSE, BUILDING.

premiss, n. *propositio* (major), *assumptio* (minor). **premisses,** n. *concessa, -orum,* or *ea quae antecesserunt.*

premium, n. *praemium.*

premonition, n. *monitio, monitum.* **premonitory,** adj. *quod praemonet.*

preoccupy, v. *praeoccupare* (= to seize beforehand), in pass. to be —ied, *totum alci rei deditum esse.* **preoccupation,** n. *praeoccupatio* (lit.), *animus alci rei deditus* (fig.).

preparation, n. *praeparatio* (in gen.) *apparatio* (= a getting ready everything), *praemeditatio* (= premeditation, e.g. *futurorum malorum*), *meditatio* (= the preparing of a lesson, etc.), *commentatio* (= the thinking over anything, e.g. a play, a speech); — for a war, *apparatus, -ūs, belli*; to make — for a war, *bellum (ap)parare.* **preparatory,** adj. *quod alqd parat*; see PREPARE. **prepare,** v.tr. *praeparare* (for a future object), *(ap)parare* (= to get everything ready), *instruĕre* (= to provide everything necessary); to — oneself for, *se parare, se praeparare ad alqd* (in gen.), *(ap)parare alqd* (= to make preparation for), *animum praeparare ad alqd, se* or *animum componĕre ad alqd* (to — one's mind), *ante meditari alqd, praemeditari alqd* (= to think over, a lesson, etc.) *commentari alqd* (= to think over, e.g. a plan, a sermon); to — for war, *se parare ad bellum, bellum parare* or *apparare, belli apparatum instruĕre.*

preponderance, preponderate, n., v.intr., see PREDOMINANCE, PREDOMINATE.

prepossess, v.tr. *capĕre* or *occupare* (= to preoccupy, to get the start of anything, to cause it to be in one's favour), *delenire, permulcēre* (to win over); to — anyone's mind for anyone, *animum alcjs conciliare ad benevolentiam erga alqm.* **prepossessing,** adj. see AGREEABLE, CHARMING. **prepossession,** n. *sententia praejudicata*; see PREJUDICE.

preposterous, adj. *praeposterus*; see PERVERSE.

prerequisite, n. see REQUISITE.

prerogative, n. *quod alci proprium est.*

presage, I. v.tr. *portendĕre* (= to foreshow), *praesagire* (= to forebode); see FORETELL, PROPHESY, FOREBODE. **II.** n. *praesagium.*

Presbyter, n. * *presbyter.*

prescient, adj. † *praesciens*, or *sagax*; see WISE.

prescribe, v.tr. *praescribĕre* (= to order, and of a doctor). **prescription,** n. 1, = custom, *usus, -ūs*; 2, = medical, *medicamenti praescriptio.* **prescriptive,** adj. — right, perhaps *jus ex usu factum.*

presence, n. 1, *praesentia*; frequent —, *assiduitas*; in anyone's —, *coram alqo praesente* (but *apud alqm* when addressing anyone, e.g. *dicĕre, loqui, verba facĕre apud alqm*); 2, — of mind, perhaps *animus ad omnia paratus.* **present, I.** adj. render by circumloc., as *qui nunc est, qui hodie est*; the — Consul, *qui nunc Consul est*; my scholar and now my friend, *discipulus meus, nunc amicus*; the — state of things, *hic rerum status. Praesens*, = that which prevails and continues now in contrast with that which prevailed or will prevail at another time. *Instans*, to signify that which is imminent or at hand; "the —" is represented by *hic*; *haec tempora*, = the — time; according to the — silly custom, *more hoc insulso*; at —, *in praesenti*; for the —, *in praesens (tempus)*; the — tense, *praesens tempus* (Gram.); to be —, *adesse, interesse.* Adv. *mox* (= soon), *statim* (= immediately). **II.** v.tr. to — arms, *telum erigĕre honoris caus(s)a*; see GIVE, INTRODUCE. **III.** n. see GIFT.

presentiment, n. † *praesagium* (absolute or with gen.) and *praesagitio* (absolute, as a faculty within us); see FOREBODE.

preserve, I. v.tr. 1, *sustinēre, sustentare* (in gen. to keep up, e.g. the world, health), by anything, *alqâ re*; *servare, conservare* (= to — so as to keep it, e.g. property, *rem familiarem cons.*, = to save), *tueri* (= to have an eye upon, to guard from falling, also to keep a building in repair, also = to entertain, keep), comb. *tueri et conservare, alĕre* (through nursing; then in gen. = to keep), comb. *alĕre et sustentare, sustentare et alĕre*, one's health, *valetudinem tueri*; see KEEP, SAVE; 2, = to conserve, *condire.* **II.** n. = conserve, *fructus, -ūs, conditus.* **preserver,** n. *(con)servator* (fem. *conservatrix*), *salutis auctor.* **preservation,** n. *conservatio, tuitio* (= the act), *salus, -ūtis*, f., *incolumitas* (= safety); the desire of self- — is innate in every being, *omni animali primus ad omnem vitam tuendam appetitus a naturâ datus est, se ut conservet* (Cic.).

preside, v.intr. *praesidēre*; to — at, *alci rei praesidēre, alci rei praeesse.* **presidency,** n. *praefectura* or in certain cases (e.g. the Indian Presidencies), *provincia.* **president,** n. *praeses,* *idis* (= who presides), *princeps, caput* (= head), — at a trial, *qui judicio praeest*

press, I. n 1, = a machine for pressing, *prelum* (in gen use it also for printing —), *torcular* (for wine, etc), 2, fig e g freedom of the —, *libertas* or *licentia alcjs rei scribendae* or *edendae* **II.** v tr 1, in a machine, *prelo premĕre, prelo alqd sub(j)icĕre*, 2, = to squeeze, *premĕre, comprimĕre*, 3, = to urge, to — upon, *alqm urgēre, premĕre, alci instare, alqm vexare* (= to worry), *propellĕre* (= to drive forward), his creditors —ed him, *ei instabant creditores*, to be —ed by business, *occupationibus distinēri*, 4, = to persuade, *alci instare, alqd ab alqo (ex)petĕre*, 5, = to enlist by force, *nautas vi comparare* **III.** v intr. to — forward, *contendĕre* (e g to the camp, *in castra*, to go to Rome, *Romam ire*), see HASTEN **press-gang,** n *qui nautas vi comparant* **pressing,** adj *magni* or *maximi momenti, gravis*, see IMPORTANT, URGENT **pressure,** n 1, lit *pressio* (Vitr), *pressus, ūs, compressio, impetus, nisus, ūs*, 2, fig by circumloc, e g under — of danger, *instante periculo* or *periculo coactus*

prestige, n *nomen* (= mere name), *gloria, fama*, see FAME, REPUTATION

presume, v intr 1, = to take liberties, be arrogant, *sibi arrogare, sumĕre sibi*, 2, = to assume (a thing to be true, etc), *putare*, see SUPPOSE **presumption,** n 1, *arrogantia*, see INSOLENCE, 2, = conjecture, *conjectura*, there is a — in favour of anyone, perhaps *hoc pro* or *ab alqo stat* **presumptive,** adj *quod ex conjecturā cognitum est, opinabilis* Adv *ex conjecturā* **presumptuous,** adj *arrogans*, see INSOLENT Adv. *arroganter.* **presumptuousness,** n see PRESUMPTION

pretence, n *simulatio, species, verba, -orum* (mere words, opp to reality), without —, *sine fuco ac fallaciis* **pretend,** v tr and intr *simulare*, they —ed that they wanted to go hunting, and left the town, *per speciem venandi urbe egressi sunt* **pretended,** adj *simulatus, opinatus* (= imaginary), *fictus*, see FALSE, IMAGINARY **pretender,** n 1, *simulator*, 2, one who claims the throne, *qui regnum sibi arrogat* **pretension,** n 1, *postulatio*, just —, *jus*, 2, *ostentatio*, see POMP, DISPLAY

preterite, n *praeteritum (tempus)* (Gram)

preternatural, adj and adv *quod praeter naturam, praeter modum* or *mirabili quodam modo fit*

pretext, n *caus(s)a, praescriptio, titulus, nomen* (= title, false name), *simulatio* (= the pretending of something), *species* (when we make anything bad appear as if it was something very innocent), under the — of, *per caus(s)am alcjs rei, nomine* or *simulatione* or *simulatione atque nomine alcjs rei, per simulationem alcjs rei, simulatā alqā re, specie* or *per speciem alcjs rei*

pretty, adj *bellus* (proper term), *pulcher, pulchellus* (= rather —, both of persons and things), *formosus* (= well shaped, of persons), *lepidus* (= neat, of persons and things), *venustus* (= charming, of persons and things), *festivus* (= graceful, elegant), *bonus* (= not inconsiderable, of a quantity) Adv *belle, pulchre, formose, lepide, festive, venuste* **prettiness,** n see BEAUTY

prevail, v intr *esse* (= to be), *obtinēre (fama obtinuit*, Liv), *adducĕre alqm ut* (= to persuade), *multum, plus valēre* or *pollēre* (= to have much force), with anyone, *apud alqm*, *morbus crescit*, the disease —s; to — on oneself, *se ipsum vincĕre*, I cannot — on myself to, etc , *a me impetrare non possum ut faciam*, etc (so *non possum adduci ut credam*; = I cannot be —ed upon to believe), to — over, *superare, vincĕre*, to be —ed upon by entreaties, *precibus flecti* (Liv), a —ing or prevalent opinion, *opinio vulgata* **prevalent,** adj *(per)vulgatus, communis*

prevaricate, v intr *tergiversari* **prevarication,** n *tergiversatio* (= shift), see LIE

prevent, v tr *prohibēre ne* or *quominus* or *impedire, obstare*, see HINDER **prevention,** n *prohibitio* (rare, or by verb) **preventive,** adj *quod alqd impedit* or *alci rei obstat*

previous, adj see PRECEDING

prey, I. n *praeda*, beast of —, *fera* **II.** v intr *praedari* to — upon, *alqm bestiam venari, alqā bestiā vesci* (= to feed upon), fig *animum*, etc , *(ex)edĕre, consumĕre*

price, I. n *pretium, annona* (= — of corn), to fix the —, *pretium facĕre, indicare* (of the seller), the — asked with the abl , so at a high, low —, *magno, parvo (pretio)*, so too gen *magni, parvi*, etc , what is the —? *quanti indicas? quanti hoc vendis?* (when we ask the seller), *quanti hoc constat?* (= what does that cost? when we ask a person the value of anything), I agree with him about the —, *convenit mihi cum alqo de pretio*, the — has fallen, *pretium alcjs rei jacet*, to raise the —, *pretium alcjs rei efferre* or *augēre* **II.** v tr *pretium alci constituĕre, pretium merci statuĕre, pretium enumerare* or *paciscī* **priceless,** adj *inaestimabilis*

prick, I. v tr *pungĕre* (of anything that stings, also gen of sharp pain), *stimulare* (with a sharp-pointed stick, e g *bovem*), *mordēre* (= to bite, of a pain, e g of a flea or a fly); to — with a needle, *acu pungĕre*, to — up one's ears *aures erigĕre* or *arrigĕre* **II.** n *punctus, -ūs* (Plin), or by verb **prickle,** n *aculeus, spina* (= thorn) **prickly,** adj *aculeatus, spinosus*

pride, n *superbia* (= haughtiness), *spiritus, ūs* (= high spirit), *insolentia* (= arrogance, insolence), *contumacia* (= obstinacy), *arrogantia* (= arrogance), *fastidium* (when we treat those around us with contempt), *fastus, ūs* (= behaviour of a person towards one with whom he disdains to have any intercourse)

priest, n *sacerdos* (in gen also = priestess), *antistes* (also = priestess), *flamen* (of one particular god, e g *flamen Dialis*), high —, *pontifex, pontifex maximus* **priestcraft,** n *ratio sacerdotum* **priestess,** n see PRIEST **priesthood,** n *sacerdotium* **priestly,** adj by the genit *sacerdotis* or *sacerdotum* **priestridden,** adj *sacerdotibus subjectus*

prig, n perhaps *qui se nimium jactat*

prim, adj perhaps *de se nimium sol(l)icitus* or *de moribus diligentior*

primal, primeval, adj see ANCIENT

primary, adj *primus, principalis*, the — meaning of a word, *naturalis et principalis verbi significatio* (Quint), = chief, *praecipuus* Adv *primo* (= at first), *praecipue* (= chiefly)

primate, n *primas* (Eccl)

prime, I. adj 1, *primus* = first, 2, = excellent, *eximius, optimus* **II.** n 1, = the best of anything, *flos*, 2, — of life, *aetas vigens* **prime-minister,** n *is penes quem summa rerum est*

primitive, adj 1, = original, *priscus, antiquus*, 2, see PRIMARY

primogeniture, n *aetatis privilegium* (Jct.)

prince, n 1, *adulescens (adol-)* or *juvenis regii generis, puer* or *juvenis regius* (= a young man of royal blood, son of a king, etc), *filius principis, filius regis* or *regius*, 2, = king, *rex*, see SOVEREIGN. **princess,** n. *mulier regii generis, mulier regio semine orta, regia virgo;* daughter of a king, etc., *filia regis* or *regia.*

principal, I. adj. *primus, princeps, principalis, praecipuus* (= chief). Adv. *maxime, praecipue, ante omnia, imprimis, praesertim, maximam partem* (= for the most part). **II.** n. **1,** = head of a school, *magister;* **2,** = capital, opp. to interest, *caput, sors, pecuniae, nummi.* **principality,** n. *terra principis imperio subjecta.*

principle, n. **1,** = beginning, *principium, elementum, primordia, -orum;* **2,** = rule of conduct, *dogma, -ătis,* n., *decretum* (in anyone's mode of action); *consilium* (= a rule to act upon, and which is based upon sound reasoning), *praeceptum* (= precept, rule, to serve as a guide in our actions, also of a philosopher, Hor.), *disciplina, institutum, institutio* (= what has become a — through habit), comb. *ratio et institutio mea, praecepta institutaque philosophiae, sententia* (= opinion), *judicium* (= judgment), *regula alcjs rei* or *ad quam alqd dirigitur* (never without genit. of object, e.g. *eadem utilitatis quae honestatis est regula*), *lex* (= law); the highest moral —, *summum bonum, ultimum* or *finis bonorum;* a man of firm —, *homo constans* (= true to his character), *homo gravis* (always acting upon —, and according to what is right), so *gravitas* = —; a man of vacillating —, *homo lĕvis;* a man of strict —, *homo sevērus;* a man who acts according to his own —, *vir sui judicii* (because it is his conviction), *vir sui arbitrii* (because he thinks fit); from —, *ratione* (= according to the adopted —), *judicio, animi quodam judicio* (= from a certain conviction), *doctrinâ* (as the result of one's studies, inquiries, etc., opp. *naturâ,* from a natural feeling); always to remain true to one's —, *sibi constare.*

print, I. n. = an impression, *impressio.* **II.** v.tr. *exprimĕre alqd alqâ re* or *in alqâ re;* to — a book, *librum typis describĕre, exscribĕre, exprimĕre.* **printer,** n. *typographus.* **printing-press,** n. *prelum typographicum.*

prior, I. adj. *prior;* see EARLY, BEFORE, PRECEDING. **II.** n. (of a monastery), in gen. *antistes, -ĭtis,* m., **prior,* or *magister.* **prioress,** n. *priorissa.*

prism, n. **prisma, -ătis,* n. (late). **prismatic,** adj. **prismaticus* (as t.t.).

prison, n. *custodia* (lit. = act of guarding; then the place), *carcer, -ĕris,* m. (= a public —), *ergastulum* (= a place commonly below ground, where slaves were made to work in chains), *vincula, -orum,* n. (= chains); to cast into —, *in custodiam* or *in vincula* or *in ergastulum mittĕre, in custodiam* (or *in vincula*) *mittĕre, tradĕre, condĕre, con(j)icĕre, in custodiam* (or *in carcerem*) *dare, includĕre, custodiae* or *vinculis mandare;* to take to —, *in custodiam* or *in vincula, (de)ducĕre;* to be (confined) in —, *in custodiâ esse* or *servari, custodiâ tenēri, in carcere* or *in vinculis esse.* **prisoner,** n. *captus, -a* (in gen.); taken — (in war), *bello captus, captivus, -a;* by the police, *comprehensus, -a.*

pristine, adj. *pristinus, priscus* (= ancient), *prior* (= former).

prithee! interj. (*dic*) *quaeso, tandem, cedo.*

privacy, n. *solitudo;* see SECRECY. **private, I.** adj. *privatus* (referring to a single individual, etc., opp. *publicus*), *proprius* (only referring to the person himself, not to all, opp. *communis*), *domesticus* (= domestic, opp. *forensis*), comb. *domesticus et privatus, secretus* (= secret, without witnesses, opp. *apertus*); — affairs, *res privata* or *domestica* or *domestica et privata; peculium, quod sui juris est* (Jct.); — enemy, *inimicus* (opp. *hostis*); a — life, *vita privata* (in gen.), *historia vitae privatae* (= history of one's — life), *vita otiosa* (= having no business to attend to), *vita umbratilis* (= easy life in retirement). Adv. *clam, secreto, occulte, remotis arbitris* (= without spectators), *privatim* (= in a private capacity). **II.** n. in the army, *miles.* **privateer,** n. *navis* (*praedatoria*). **privation,** n. *privatio* (= act of —), *inopia, egestas, paupertas* (= need); see POVERTY. **privative,** adj. *privativus* (Gram.).

privilege, n. **1,** = a particular right, *privilegium* (granted by special authority), *beneficium, commodum* (= any right, whereby a person derives a particular benefit; *benef.* when it is granted, *comm.* when it has been obtained; all three Jct.); **2,** = exemption from a burden, *immunitas, gratia, munus, -ĕris,* n., *beneficium* (= favour); see FAVOUR. **privileged,** adj. *privilegiarius* (Jct.); = exempt from, *immunis.*

privy, I. adj. see PRIVATE, SECRET. **II.** n. *sella* (*familiarica*). **privy-council,** n. in imperial times *consistoriani.* **privy-purse,** n. *fiscus.*

prize, I. n. *praemium, palma;* to fix a —, *praemium (pro)ponĕre.* **II.** v.tr. *magni aestimare* or *facĕre.* **prize-fighter,** n. *qui praemio proposito contendit,* or *pugil* (= boxer).

pro and con, *in utramque partem.*

probable, adj. *probabilis, veri similis* (or as one word, *verisim-*). Adv. *probabiliter, verisimiliter* (*verisim-*). **probability,** n. *probabilitas, verisimilitudo* (*verisim-*).

probation, n. *probatio;* a time of —, *tempus ad alcjs facultates experiendas constitutum.* **probationer,** n. *alumnus* (fem. *-a*).

probe, I. n. *specillum.* **II.** v.tr. see EXAMINE.

probity, n. *probitas.*

problem, n. *quaestio.* **problematical,** adj. *dubius, incertus;* see DOUBTFUL.

proboscis, n. *proboscis* (Plin.), *manus, -ūs,* f. (of an elephant).

proceed, v.intr. **1,** *progredi;* see GO; **2,** = to come from, *oriri;* **3,** = to act, *agĕre, facĕre;* see ACT; **4,** — against, *litem alci intendĕre.* **proceeding,** n. *ratio;* legal —, *actio;* to commence —s, *actionem alci intendĕre;* = transactions, *acta, -orum.* **proceeds,** n. *reditus, -ūs, fructus, -ūs.*

process, n. *ratio* = course of proceedings, *actio* (= — at law); in — of time, (*procedente*) *tempore.*

procession, n. in gen. *pompa;* at a funeral, *pompa funebris;* to hold a —, *pompam ducĕre.*

proclaim, v.tr. *declarare* (e.g. public shows, *munera*), *edicĕre* (lit. of authorities = to make known a law, etc., but also = to decree in gen.), *promulgare* (= to make generally known, a law, etc.), *proponĕre* (= to placard, e.g. *edictum,* etc.), *praedicĕre* (through the herald), *pronuntiare* (= to announce). **proclamation,** n. **1,** the act of —, *pronuntiatio, declaratio, praedicatio;* **2,** = the thing proclaimed, *edictum; libellus* (= a written —).

proclivity, n. *proclivitas,* but better by circumloc. (e.g. he has a — to do anything, *est ejus alqd facĕre*).

proconsul, n. *pro consule* (also, but less often, *proconsul*). **proconsular,** adj. *proconsularis.*

procrastinate, v.tr., **procrastination,** n. see DELAY.

procreate, v.tr. *procreare.* **procreation,** n. *procreatio,*

procure, v.tr (*con*)*parare* (= to see that anything is ready, for oneself or for others, e g *auctoritatem, gloriam, servos*, also money), *afferre* (= to bring, also of things, e g *auctoritatem, utilitatem, consolationem*), *acquirĕre* (after difficulty, e g *quod ad vitae usum pertinet, dignitatem, opes, divitias*), *conciliare* (= to collect together, e g *legiones pecuniâ, sibi benevolentiam alcjs, alci favorem ad vulgus*), *expedire* (= to manage to get, e g *pecunias*), *prospicĕre* (= to provide for, e g *alci habitationem, alci maritum*), see GET, GAIN, OBTAIN **procurator,** n *procurator*, see MANAGE, MANAGER **procurer,** n *leno* **procuring,** n *comparatio, conciliatio*

prodigal, adj see EXTRAVAGANT **prodigality,** n *effusio* (as act), *sumptus effusi* or *profusi* (as luxury), *profusa luxuria* (= great luxury), see EXTRAVAGANCE

prodigious, adj *ingens*, see ENORMOUS **prodigy,** n *res mira* or *mirabilis, miraculum*

produce, I. v tr 1, = to bring forward, *proferre, exhibēre, edĕre* (= to publish), 2, = to bring into existence, (*pro*)*creare* (of living beings and of the earth, then = to cause, e g danger), *gignĕre, parĕre, generare* (= to bring forth, of living beings), (*ef*)*ferre*, (*ef*)*fundĕre* (of nature, also of the earth, of a field, etc , *fundĕre, effundĕre*, always with the idea of abundance), *facĕre, efficĕre* (with the hand, by art and skill) **II.** n of the earth, *quae terra gignit* or *parit, ea quae gignuntur e terrâ* (in gen), *fructus, -ūs, reditus, -ūs*, by circumloc *id quod agri efferunt* (of the fields) **product,** n in arithmetic, *summa quae ex multiplicatione effecta est*, see also PRODUCTION **production,** n *opus, -ĕris, n* (= work), of art, *opera et artificia*, whether this is a — of nature or of art, *sive est naturae hoc sive artis* **productive,** adj 1, *fertilis*, see FRUITFUL, 2, — of, *alcjs rei efficiens* **productiveness,** n see FERTILITY

proem, n *prooemium*

profane, I. v tr † *profanare, profanum facĕre, violare, polluĕre* **II.** adj *profanus* (opp *sacrum*), *impius* (= impious), — history, *historia rerum a populis gestarum* Adv *impie* **profanation, profaneness profanity,** n *impietas*

profess, v tr *profitēri*, to — the Christian religion, *Christum sequi, doctrinam Christianam sequi*, to — to belong to a certain school, *persequi* with accus (e g *Academiam*), = to assert that one is something that one is not, *se alqd esse simulare* **professed,** adj by circumloc (e g a — Christian, *qui se Christianum esse dicit*), or by *manifestus, apertus*, see MANIFEST Adv *per speciem, simulatione alcjs rei* (= by pretence) **profession,** n 1, = declaration, *professio* or by *se alqd (esse) profitēri* (e g *Christianum* (*esse*), — in opp to practice, *verbo* (opp *re*(*verâ*)), 2, = employment, *munus, -ĕris*, n **professor,** n *professor* (*eloquentiae*, etc , Plin , Suet), better *qui alqd docet* **professorship,** n by PROFESSOR

proffer, v tr *promittĕre*, see OFFER

proficiency, n by *scientia* (= knowledge), *facultas* (= readiness) **proficient,** adj *eruditus, doctus* (= learned), *sciens alcjs rei* (= skilful), to be —, *multum, parum*, etc , *proficĕre*, see SKILFUL

profile, n *faciei latus alterum, imago obliqua* (= likeness in —, Plin), in the pl also by the t t *catagrapha, -orum*, n (καταγραφα (= — portrait, Plin)

profit, I. n 1, = material —, *lucrum, quaestus, fructus, reditus* (all -ūs), *emolumentum, compendium* (by saving), 2, fig *compendium, fructus, quaestus* (rare), to make much —, *multum proficĕre*, see PROGRESS **II.** v intr 1, = to be serviceable to, *ad alqd proficĕre, alci* (*rei*) *prodesse, conducĕre, adesse* (of men = to support, so *alqm juvare*), 2, = to make progress, *proficĕre*, 3, = to make gain, *quaestuosum esse, fructum ferre*, see PROFITABLE **profitable,** adj 1, lit *quaestuosus, fructuosus lucrosus, frugifer* (of lands), see FRUITFUL, 2, fig *fructuosus, frugifer, utilis* Adv *utiliter* **profitless,** adj = useless, *inutilis, vanus, futilis, irritus*, see USELESS Adv *frustra, incassum* (= in vain)

profligacy, I. n *animus perditus, nequitia, flagitium*, see VICE **II.** n *homo flagitiosus*, etc , *homo scelestus*, (*con*)*sceleratus* (= one who has committed crime), *homo perditus* or *profligatus* (= incorrigible) **profligate,** adj *flagitiosus, vitiosus, malus, turpis, libidinosus, perditus, nequam, sceleratus, scelestus* Adv *flagitiose, male, libidinose, perdite, nequiter, turpiter, nefarie, scelerate, sceleste*

pro formâ, adv *dicis causâ*

profound, adj *altus, profundus* (lit and fig) Adv *penitus, prorsus*, see ALTOGETHER **profundity,** n *altitudo* (lit and fig)

profuse, adj see EXTRAVAGANT, LAVISH

progenitor, n *parens*

progeny, n *progenies*, see OFFSPRING

prognostic, n *signum*, to be a — of, *alqd praenuntiare* **prognosticate,** v tr see FOREBODE

programme, n *libellus*

progress, I. n 1, = journey, *iter, itineris* n., quite a royal —, *velut rex iter faciebat*, 2, = advance, *progressus, ūs, progressio, processus, -ūs*, to make much or little —, *multum* or *parum proficĕre* **II.** v intr 1, *progredi*, see ADVANCE, 2, = to improve, *proficĕre* **progression,** n *progressio, progressus, -ūs*, see PROGRESS **progressive,** adj *qui, quae, quod progreditur* Adv *gradatim, pedetentim* (*pedetent-*)

prohibit, v tr *vetare*, see FORBID **prohibition,** n *interdictum*, to issue a —, *interdicĕre alci alqa re* or *ne* **prohibitive, prohibitory,** adj *qui, quae, quod vetat*

project, I. n *consilium* (= plan), *inceptum, propositum* (= proposal), *institutum* **II.** v intr *prominēre, eminēre, exstare, pro*(*j*)*ici, projectum esse* **projectile,** n (*telum*) *missile* **projection,** n by verb. **projector,** n *auctor*

proletariat, n *proletarii*

prolific, adj see FRUITFUL

prolix, adj *longus* (= long, opp *brevis*, of persons and things), *copiosus* (= full), *verbosus* (= making too many words), *multus* (only of persons), see LONG **prolixity,** by adj PROLIX

prologue, n *prolŏgus*

prolong, v tr *prorogare, propagare* (= to — the time of, e g *imperium in annum*), *producĕre* (= to draw out), *extendĕre* (= to extend, e g *alqd ad noctem*), *continuare* (= to continue, e g *militiam, alci consulatum magistratum*), *trahĕre* (= to — more than we should, e g *bellum*), *proferre* (= to put off, e g *diem*), *prolatare* (= to protract, e g *comitia*) **prolongation,** n *productio* (in gen), *prorogatio, propagatio* (e g *vitae*), *prolatio* (e.g. *diei*). **prolonged,** adj *longus, diuturnus*

promenade, n *ambulatio* (both of act and place)

prominence, n 1, *prominentia, eminentia* (= a standing out), 2, fig of rank, etc. *fama, gloria* or by *alqm alqâ re praestare*, see SUP-

PASS. **prominent,** adj. and adv. by *prominēre, eminēre* (= to be raised above; also fig. = to distinguish oneself, e.g. *inter omnes*), *exstare* (= to stand out, lit. e.g. *capite solo ex aquâ*), *excellĕre* (fig. = to excel in, *alqâ re* or *in alqâ re*), *praestare* or *superare alqm alqâ re* (fig. = to be superior in).

promiscuous, adj. *promiscuus.* Adv. *promiscue.*

promise, I. v.tr. *alci alqd* or *de alqâ re promittĕre, polliceri, alqd* (*in se*) *recipĕre*; = to take upon oneself, *pollicitari* (frequent.), (*de*)*spondēre* (formally, by being legally bound), *alci alqd*; also comb. *promittĕre et spondēre, proponĕre* (as reward, e.g. *servis libertatem*), *pronuntiare* (publicly); "I — that," or "I — to," rendered in Latin by the accus. and infin. (gen. the fut. infin., seldom the pres. infin.), e.g. *promitto* or *polliceor me hoc facturum esse.* **II.** v.intr. = to be likely (e.g. he —s to be a great speaker, *veri simile est eum futurum esse oratorem.* **III.** n. *promissio, pollicitatio* (the act), *fides* (= word), *promissum* (= the thing promised); to give anyone a — to, etc., *alci promittĕre* or *polliceri*, with accus. and fut. infin.; to keep, redeem a —, *promissum* or *fidem facĕre* or *efficĕre* or *praestare* or *servare* or (*ex*)*solvĕre* or *persolvĕre, promisso stare* or *satisfacĕre, quod promisi* or *pollicitus sum* or *quod promissum est* (*ob*)*servare* or *efficĕre, quod promissum est tenēre, promissi fidem praestare.* **promising,** adj. by circumloc. (e.g. a — pupil, *puer industrius*; a — crop, *seges fertilis*). **promissory,** adj. — note, *chirographum.*

promontory, n. *promontorium*, a small —, *lingua, li*(*n*)*gula.*

promote, v.tr. (*ad*)*juvare alqm* or *alqd, adjumento esse alci rei, adjutorem* or (in the fem.) *adjutricem esse alcjs rei* or *in alqâ re* (in gen. = to give any assistance); *alcjs rei esse* (*ad*)*ministrum* (in a bad sense = to be an abettor), *augēre alqm* or *alqd* (= to increase), *alci* or *alci rei favēre, fovēre alqd* (= to favour), *alci* or *alci rei consulĕre, prospicĕre* (= to take care of), *alci prodesse* (= to be of use), *consilio, studio, operâ adesse alci* (= to assist anyone by advice and by acting); to — anyone's interest, *servire alcjs commodis, rebus* or *rationibus alcjs consulĕre, prospicĕre*; to — the common interest, *saluti reipublicae consulĕre, rempublicam juvare, tueri, reipublicae salutem suscipĕre* (= to try to —); = to — in office, anyone, *tollĕre, augēre, attollĕre* (anyone's reputation among his fellow-citizens), *fovēre* (by actually favouring him), (*ex*)*ornare* (= to distinguish), *gratiâ et auctoritate suâ sustentare* (to raise through one's personal influence), *producĕre ad dignitatem* (= to — to a higher rank), *promovēre ad* or *in munus* or *ad* (*superiorem*) *locum* (= to — to an office, Imperial Rome), *muneri praeficĕre* (= to appoint to an office, to set over); *tra*(*ns*)*ducĕre alqm in ampliorem ordinem* or *ex inferiore ordine in superiorem ordinem* (a military office). **promotor,** n. *auctor, adjutor, fautor.* **promotion,** n. — of our welfare, *amplificatio nostrarum rerum*; — to a higher office, *amplior honoris gradus, -ūs, dignitatis accessio, officium amplius.*

prompt, I. adj. *promptus.* Adv. *cito*; see QUICKLY. **II.** v.tr. *alqd alci sub*(*j*)*icĕre.* **prompter,** n. *qui alqd alci sub*(*j*)*icit.* **promptitude, promptness,** n. *celeritas*; see QUICKNESS, READINESS.

promulgate, v.tr. *promulgare.* **promulgation,** n. *promulgatio.*

prone, adj. 1, = flat, *pronus*; 2, = tending to, *pronus, proclivis, propensus ad alqd.* **proneness,** n. *proclivitas* (rare), or by adj.

prong, n. *dens, -tis*, m. (of a fork).

pronoun, n. *pronomen* (Gram.).

pronounce, v.tr. letters, etc., *enuntiare, exprimĕre, dicĕre* (= to utter with the voice), *lit*(*t*)*eras sonis enuntiare*; to — one word after the other, *verba continuare*; it is difficult to —, *haud facile dictu est*; = to utter formally, *efferre verbis*; *explicare, explanare verbis* (= to explain in words); to — a sentence, an opinion, *sententiam dicĕre, sententiam pronuntiare* (= to announce the verdict of the judge). **pronunciation,** n. *appellatio* (= the — of a letter, etc.); *pronuntiatio* (Quint., always = *actio*, i.e. the whole recitation); *locutio* (= the act of speaking), *vox* (= the voice of the person that speaks), *vocis sonus*, in the context *sonus* (= the tone of the voice).

proof, n. *tentamen* (= trial); = the act of proving, *probatio, demonstratio* (= a strict — of anything; also in mathematics), *argumentatio* (= by giving clear reasons); the — of it is difficult, *difficile est probatu*; = that by which anything is proved (sign in gen.), *signum, indicium, documentum, specimen* (the foregoing two = specimen, example, sample; but *specimen* never in the plur. in ancient writers); = reasons which serve as a —, *argumentum* (= reason founded upon facts); *ratio* (= reasonable grounds); to give —, *argumenta* or *rationes afferre*; to bring forward many —s for the existence of a Supreme Being, *multis argumentis Deum esse docēre*; very often *argumentum* is left out in Latin when an adj. is used in English (e.g. the strongest — is, *firmissimum hoc afferri videtur, quod*, etc.). **prove, I.** v.tr. = to show, *significare, ostendĕre, declarare,* (*com*)*probare, praestare* (= to perform what we are expected to do); to — anything by one's actions, *alqd praestare re, alqd comprobare re*; to — oneself as, etc., *se praebēre alqm, exhibēre alqm* (e.g. as a friend of the people, *exhibēre virum civilem*), *se praestare alqm* (= to — oneself really to be, etc.); = to show by reasoning, *docēre,* (*argumentis*) *demonstrare* (= to show, demonstrate in every point, by logical reasons), (*con*)*firmare*, generally *firmare* (= to assert, affirm by reasons), *probare alci alqd* (= to — to anyone the possibility of a thing), *efficĕre* (= logically to — that anything can be done), *evincĕre* (= to — beyond all doubt); this is —d by showing that, etc., *ejus rei testimonium est, quod*, etc.; this —s nothing, *nullum verum id argumentum*; the result —d it, *exitus approbavit*; the mode of proving anything, *probationis genus, -ĕris*, n., *argumentationis genus, via, ratio probandi* (= way in which anything can be —d), *argumentatio* (= argumentation), *ratio* (= manner in which we proceed in proving anything, Cic.). **II.** v.intr. = to turn out, *fieri, evadĕre.* **proven,** p.part. e.g. not —, *non liquet.*

prop, I. n. 1, lit. *adminiculum* (in gen.), *pedamen*(*tum*) (for vines), *statumen* (for vines, etc.); 2, fig. *adminiculum, firmamentum, subsidium, praesidium*; see HELP. **II.** v.tr. 1, lit. *fulcire* (in gen.); 2, fig. *alci adesse*, to be —ped by, *alqâ* (*re*) *niti*; see SUPPORT.

propagate, v.tr. 1, applied to plants; to — by layers, *propagare*; to — by grafting, *inserĕre*; = to produce, *gignĕre*; 2, fig. *gignĕre* (*et propagare*), *serĕre* (= to sow). **propagation,** n. 1, by layers, *propagatio*; 2, of a report, etc., *rumorem serĕre.*

propel, v.tr. *propellĕre.*

propensity, n. *proclivitas* or *animus proclivis ad alqd*; see INCLINATION.

proper, adj. 1, *proprius* (= peculiar, opp. *communis*), *verus* (= true, real, opp. *falsus*), *germanus* (= genuine); if we add — in order to lay a stress upon the noun, we use *ipse* (e.g. *ipsi Argentini*); the — word, *verbum proprium* (opp.

verbum translatum), the — Metellus, verus et germanus Metellus, 2, = becoming, decōrus, honestus, = suitable, aptus, idoneus, accommodatus ad alqd Adv proprie, vere, comb proprie vereque, germane **property**, n 1, dominium (Jct, = the — or the legal title to anything, different from possessio, possession), patrimonium (= patrimony, also fig with tamquam before it, of mental, etc, qualities), peculium (= the stock of money which a son with the consent of his father, or a slave with the consent of his master, had of his own, private —), possessiones (= landed —), bona, -orum, n, fortunae (= effects), census, -ūs (in gen), by res (sing or plur) in a gen sense (e g moveable —, res moventes, res quae moveri possunt), or by proprius, -a, -um, also comb with poss pron proprius meus (tuus, etc), and often by poss pron alone (e g that is my —, hoc meum or hoc meum proprium est), to consider anything as one's —, suum alqd ducere, 2, = peculiarity, proprietas, quod alcjs (rei) proprium est **property tax**, n tributum ex censu collatum. **proprietary**, adj by proprius **proprietor**, n possessor, dominus **proprietorship**, n dominium, possessio

prophecy, n. 1, as the act, praedictio (e g rerum futurarum), vaticinatio, 2, that which is prophesied, praedictum, vaticinium **prophesy, I.** v tr praedicere, praenuntiare (in gen. = to foretell), vaticinari, canere, augurari (= to augur) **II.** v intr futura praedicere or praenuntiare, vaticinari (= to act the part of a vates, to — by divine inspiration) **prophet**, n vates, -is, m and f †vaticinator, †fatiloquus **prophetess**, n vates, is **prophetic**, adj. divinus, praesagiens, fatidicus, vaticinus (= concerning prophecies, e g writings) Adv. divinitus, caelesti quodam instinctu mentis, instinctu divino afflatuque (all = inspired)

propinquity, n propinquitas (= relationship), affinitas (= by marriage)

propitious, adj propitius, aequus, †secundus, faustus (of things) Adv by adj **propitiousness**, n by adj **propitiate**, v tr see CONCILIATE. **propitiation**, n placatio (e g deorum) **propitiatory**, adj by verb

proportion, I. n proportio, commensus, -ūs, (= measure or size of a thing in — to another, Vitr), symmetria (Vitr), in a general sense it is best rendered by ratio (= the relation of one thing to another), or by comparatio (when two or more things are in a certain relation to each other), an arithmetical, geometrical —, ratio arithmetica, geometrica, in — to, pro portione alcjs rei, pro rata parte, pro with abl (e g pro viribus, in — to one's power), see PROPORTIONATE **II.** v tr alqd dirigere ad alqam rem **proportional, proportionate**, adj pro portione, pro, prae with abl, or by ad with acc, or by ut est with the object compared in the nomin (e g pro viribus, prae aliis, pro numero, ad cetera, ut tum erant tempora), see PROPORTION

proposal, n = what anyone proposes, condicio, — of a law, legis latio (in the forum), rogatio (in the comitia to be accepted by the assembly of the people), to vote for a — in the senate, pedibus ire in alcjs sententiam, = suggestion, plan, consilium, ratio, propositum, to make a —, condicionem ferre or proponere, to make the — of anything alqd proponere (= to move), alqd suadere (= to try to recommend, to advise), alqd commendare (= to recommend) **propose**, v tr 1, proponere, to — a law, legem ferre or rogare, rogationem or legem ferre, 2, in marriage, perhaps alqam in matrimonium petere, 3, see PURPOSE, INTEND **proposer**, n of a law, (legis)lator, in gen auctor alcjs rei **proposition**, n 1, see PROPOSAL, 2, in logic, thesis (Quint), in a wider sense propositum.

propriety, n convenientia, decōrum, honestas

prorogue, v tr prorogare **prorogation**, n prorogatio

proscribe, v tr proscribere **proscription**, n. proscriptio

prose, n prosa (oratio) (Quint.), oratio soluta (in opp. to oratio astricta, devincta), or merely oratio (in opp to poëmata). **prosaic**, adj jejunus, frigidus

prosecute, v tr 1, = to carry out, gerere, facere, exsequi, perficere, see DO, 2, = to bring an action against, alqm accusare, reum facere de alqā re, alqm postulare **prosecution**, n 1, use verb PROSECUTE, 1, 2, accusatio **prosecutor**, n accusator

proselyte, n discipulus **proselytism**, n, **proselytize**, v tr alqm discipulum facere

prosody, n versuum lex et modificatio (Sen)

prospect, n 1, = view, prospectus, -ūs, conspectus, -ūs, to have a —, spectare ad or in alqm locum, 2, = hope, spes (e g mercedis), some —, specula **prospective**, adj futurus, see FUTURE Adv in futurum

prospectus, n libellus

prosper, v intr crescere (lit and fig = to grow), provenire (lit and fig), bonā fortunā uti. **prosperity**, n res secundae or prosperae or florentes, copiae (rei familiaris) (= good circumstances), general —, salus, -utis, communis, omnium felicitas **prosperous**, adj secundus, prosper(us), fortunatus Adv secunde, prospere, fortunate

prostitute, I. n mulier impudica (= any unchaste woman), amica, meretrix, prostibulum. **II.** v tr 1, publicare, 2, fig alqā re abuti. **prostitution**, n 1, vita meretricia, 2, use PROSTITUTE, II 2

prostrate, I v tr 1, = to throw down, (pro)sternere, 2, to — oneself before anyone, ad pedes alcjs procumbere or se ab(j)icere or se submittere or prosternere, ad genua alcjs procumbere, supplicem se ab(j)icere alci (as a suppliant), 3, fig alqm or animum affligere, percellere, frangere **II.** adj by part of verb, to lie —, (humi) jacere **prostration**, n by the verb

protect, v tr tueri, tutari, defendere (= to ward off, ab alqā re, contra alqd), (pro)tegere (= to cover, ab alqā re, contra alqd), munire (= to fortify), custodire (= to guard), praesidere alci rei, praesidium esse alcjs rei, alci praesidio esse, prohibere alqd (= to keep off) or prohibere alqd ab alqo or alqm ab alqā re **protection**, n tutela, praesidium, defensio, patrocinium, clientēla (= relation of patron and client), fides, arx, portus, -ūs, perfugium, to take under your —, alqm in fidem recipere (as a lord or sovereign), alcjs patrocinium suscipere (as a defender at law) **protective**, adj use verb **protector**, n defensor, tutor (rare), propugnator (e g quasi propugnator patrimonii sui, Cic), or by verb

protest, I. v intr asseverare (= to affirm with assurance), affirmare (= to assure), adjurare (upon oath); by the gods, (ob)testari deos, = to — against, intercedere, intercessionem facere (esp of a magistrate), against anything, alci rei intercedere (= to interfere in a thing by virtue of one's office, officially), interpellare (= to interrupt a speaker) **II.** n interpellatio (= interruption of a speaker), intercessio (by the authorities, etc),

Protestant, adj. and n. **a lege pontificis Romani abhorrens.* **Protestantism,** n. **Protestantismus.*

protocol, n. *tabulae, commentarii* (in gen.).

prototype, n. *exemplum.*

protract, v.tr. *producĕre*; see DELAY, PROLONG.

protrude, I. v.tr. *protrudĕre.* **II.** v.intr. *protrudi, prominēre*; see PROJECT.

protuberance, n. *tuber, gibber* (Plin.). **protuberant,** adj. *eminens, prominens* (= projecting).

proud, adj. *superbus, arrogans, fastidiosus* (= disdainful), *contumax* (= stubborn); to be —, *alqâ re inflatum* or *elatum esse* or *tumēre*; —-flesh, (med. t.t.) *caro fungosa* (Plin.). Adv. *superbe, arroganter, contumaciter, fastidiose.*

prove, v.tr. see PROOF.

provender, n. *pabulum*; FORAGE, FOOD.

proverb, n. *proverbium, verbum* (= word); to become a —, *in proverbii consuetudinem venire, in proverbium venire, cedĕre*; according to the —, *ut aiunt.* **proverbial,** adj. *proverbii loco celebratus* (= well known, e.g. *versus*), *quod proverbii locum obtinet, quod in proverbium* or *in proverbii consuetudinem venit* (= what has become —); see PROVERB. Adv. *proverbii loco* (= as a proverb), *ut est in proverbio, ut proverbii loco dici solet*; see PROVERB.

provide, I. v.tr. *instruĕre* or *ornare alqm alqâ re* (= to — with), *alci rei providēre, alqd (com)parare, praeparare, alqd alci praebēre* (= to give). **II.** v.intr. **1,** = to order, *jubēre, edicĕre* (of an edict); **2,** = to — for anyone, *alci consulĕre, providēre* (= to consult the interests of); = to make adequate provision for, *alqm re familiari* or *copiis* or *pecuniâ instruĕre*; he is —d for, *habet unde vivat*; to — against, *(pro)vidēre, praecavēre ne quid fiat.* **provided, I.** adj. — with, *alqâ re instructus, ornatus, praeditus.* **II.** conj. — that, *(dum)modo* with subj., *eâ lege* or *condicione ut* or *ne.* **providence,** n. = forethought, *providentia*; = divine —, *deorum providentia* (*providentia* alone in Quint., Sen.), or use *deus* or *dei* (*di(i)*). **provident,** adj. *providus, diligens* (= careful); see CAREFUL. Adv. *diligenter*, or by adj.; see PROVIDENT. **providentially,** adv. *dis faventibus, divinitus.* **providing that,** conj. see PROVIDED, II. **provision, I.** v.tr. to — a town, *oppidum cibo* or *rebus necessariis instruĕre.* **II.** n. **1,** to make — for; see PROVIDE, II. 2; **2,** = stipulation, *condicio*; see STIPULATION. **provisional,** adj. by adv. use *ad* or *in tempus.* **provisions,** n. *cibus, cibaria, -orum, alimentum, victus, -ūs, commeatus, -ūs, frumentum, res frumentaria* (the last three esp. of — for an army).

province, n. **1,** = duty, *provincia, officium*; **2,** = district, *regio* (in gen.), *provincia.* **provincial,** adj. *provincialis* (= belonging to a province); — (manners), etc., *rusticus, agrestis, inurbanus.*

proviso, n. see PROVISION, II. 2.

provocation, n. **provocative,** adj. by PROVOKE.

provoke, v.tr. **1,** = to call forth, *(com)movēre* (e.g. *iram*), *ciēre, concitare*; **2,** = to make angry, *alci stomachum movēre* or *facĕre*; see VEX, IRRITATE; **3,** to — to anything, *alqm ad alqd incitare, concitare, impellĕre, irritare*; see URGE. **provoking,** adj. *molestus.* Adv. *moleste.*

provost, n. *praeses, -idis,* m., or *al... i praepositus.*

prow, n. *prora, pars prior navis.*

prowess, n. *virtus, -ūtis,* f.; see VALOUR.

prowl, v.intr. *vagari, peragrare*; to — for plunder, *praedari.*

proximate, adj. by *proximus*; see NEAR, NEXT. **proximity,** n. see NEARNESS.

proxy, n. = agent, *procurator, vicarius*; by —, *per procuratorem*; to vote by —, perhaps *per alium suffragium ferre.*

prude, n. *mulier putida* (= affected).

prudence, n. *providentia* (= foresight), *cautio, circumspectio, prudentia, diligentia, gravitas* (as moral characteristic). **prudent,** adj. *providus, cautus, circumspectus, consideratus, prudens, diligens.* Adv. *provide, caute, circumspecte, considerate, diligenter*; see WISDOM.

prune, v.tr. **1,** to — trees, *arbores (am)putare* (= to lop off), *tondēre* (e.g. hedges), *purgare, intervellĕre* (Col., = to tear off branches here and there), *pampinare* (of vines); **2,** fig. *amputare, resecare.* **pruner,** n. of trees, *putator, frondator.* **pruning-hook,** n. *falx.*

prurience, n. see LUST.

pry, v.tr. and intr. to — into, *alqd rimari, investigare, scrutari.*

psalm, n. *psalmus* (Eccl.). **psalmist,** n. *psalmista,* m. (Eccl.). **psalter,** n. *psalterium* (Eccl.). **psaltery,** n. *psalterium.*

pshaw! interj. *phui!*

psychical, adj. *de animâ* (e.g. — research, *investigatio quae de animâ fit*).

psychology, n. **psychologia* (as t.t.), or *investigatio quae de animo* or *mente fit.* **psychological,** adj. **psychologicus*; see above. **psychologist,** n. *humani animi investigator.*

puberty, n. *aetas puber.*

public, I. adj. **1,** before everyone's eyes, *quod in aperto ac propatulo loco est* or *fit* (= in an open place), *quod palam* or *coram omnibus fit* (= before everybody's eyes), *publicus*; not to appear in —, *publico carēre* or *se abstinēre*; a —-house, *caupona* (cop-), *deversorium*; **2,** concerning the State, etc., *publicus* (in gen., opp. *privatus*), *forensis* (referring to — life, opp. *domesticus*); at the — expense, *sumptu publico, de publico, publice, impendio publico*; by — measures, *publico consilio, publice*; the — credit, *fides publica*; the — opinion, *vulgi opinio.* Adv. *aperte, palam, coram omnibus, in propatulo, in publico, foris.* **II.** n. the —, *homines* (= the people in gen.), *populus* (= all the people), *vulgus, -i,* n. (= the great mass), *spectatores* (= spectators), *auditores* (= the audience), *lectores* (= the readers). **publican,** n. **1,** *publicanus* (= farmer of the public taxes); **2,** = innkeeper, *caupo* (who keeps a public-house). **publication,** n. *editio libri* (Plin.); = the book itself, *liber.* **publicity,** n. e.g. of proceedings, *consilia palam* or *coram omnibus inita*; to shun —, *celebritatem odisse* or *fugĕre homines* (= not to like to go out), *lucem fugĕre* (in gen. = to shun the light of day, fig. not to like to appear before the public). **publish,** v.tr. a work, etc., *(in lucem) edĕre, emittĕre, foras dare.* **publisher,** n. of a book, *qui librum edendum curat.*

pudding, n. *placenta* (= cake).

puddle, n. see POOL.

puerile, adj. *puerilis* (= both childlike and foolish).

puff, I. v.tr. *inflare* (lit. and fig.); to — up with pride, to be —ed up, *superbire, tumescĕre.* **II.** v.intr. **1,** = to blow, *flare, spirare*; see BLOW; **2,** = to pant, *anhelare.* **puffy,** adj. *inflatus.*

pugilism, n. *pugilatus, -ūs, pugilatio.* **pugilist,** n. *pugil.*

pug-nosed, adj *simus*

pull, I. v tr 1, = to tweak, *vellĕre* (e g *aurem*, to — the ear), *vellicare* (Plaut, Quint), 2, = to drag, *trahĕre, ducĕre, vehĕre*, to — down *demoliri, di(r)ŭĕre, diruĕre*, to — out, (*e*)*vellĕre, eripĕre* **II.** n *tractus*, *ūs* (mostly poet), *nisus*, *ūs*, *vis*, *impetus*, *-ūs*, or by verb

pullet, n *pullus gallinaceus*

pulley, n *trochlea, machina tractatoria* (Vitr).

pulmonary, adj *quod ad pulmones pertinet*

pulp, n *caro* (Plin, of fruits).

pulpit, n in the context merely *suggestus*, *-ūs*

pulsate, v intr *palpitare, agitari, moveri* **pulsation,** n *palpitatio, motus*, *ūs*, see MOVEMENT **pulse,** n *arteriarum* or *venarum pulsus*, *-ūs* (Plin, = the beating of the —), *venae* (the — itself), the — does not beat equally, *venae non aequis intervallis moventur*

pulse, n as a vegetable, *legumen* (or in pl)

pulverize, v tr 1, *in pulverem redigĕre*, 2, fig *percellĕre*

pumice, n *pumex*

pump, I. n *antlia, tympanum* **II.** v intr *antliā exhaurire*, to — a ship, *sentinam exhaurire*

pumpkin, n *pepo* (Plin)

pun, n *logi* (λογοι, Cic in Non), *facetiae*

punch, n = a drink, *cal(i)dum* (= hot water and wine)

Punch, n see PUPPET

punch, I. n 1, = drill, *terebra*, 2, see BLOW **II.** v tr 1, *terebrare*, 2, *tundĕre, fodĕre*

punctilio, n perhaps *diligentia* (= carefulness), *dubitatio* (= doubt, where — keeps from action), *fastidium* (= pride), *sol(l)icitudo* (= anxiety) **punctilious,** adj *sol(l)icitus* (= anxious), *diligens* (= careful), *accuratus* (= exact) Adv *diligenter, accurate* **punctiliousness,** n *sol(l)icitudo, diligentia, religio* (in religious matters)

punctual, adj *diligens* (= exact, careful); to be — to an appointment, *ad* or *in tempus advenire* Adv *diligenter, ad tempus* (= at the appointed time), *ad diem* (= on the day appointed) **punctuality,** n *diligentia* (care)

punctuate, v tr. *notis distinguĕre, interpungĕre* (Sen). **punctuation,** n *interpunctio*, — mark, *interpunctum*

puncture, I. n *punctum* (Plin) **II.** v tr *pungĕre, compungĕre*

pungent, adj *acer, acutus, acerbus, mordax*, all lit and fig Adv *acriter, acute, acerbe*

punish, v tr *punire, poenā afficĕre* (= to inflict punishment), *in alqm animadvertĕre, multare, castigare* (= to correct, chastise, *verbis, verberibus*), to — anything, *alqd vindicare* (= to avenge), *alqd ulcisci, persequi*, or comb *ulcisci et persequi*, to — anyone very severely, *gravissimum supplicium de alqo sumĕre*; to — anyone with exile, fine, or imprisonment, *exilio, pecuniā*, or *vinculis multare*, to — any infringement of the law, any violation of one's rights, *delicta, violata jura exsequi*, to be —ed, *puniri*, also *poenas dare, solvĕre, pendĕre, expendĕre*, by anyone, *alci*, for anything, *alcjs rei* (= to pay) **punishable,** adj *poenā dignus* **punisher,** n *castigator, vindex* (= avenger), *ultor* (= revenger) **punishment,** n 1, the act, *castigatio, multatio, animadversio* (e g *vitii*), 2, the — itself, *poena* (as an atonement), *noxa* (as loss or injury) *multa* (more particularly = fine the latter the act), *damnum* (= penalty), *supplicium* (= cruel —, torture, violent death), *animadversio* (= reproof, in order to correct anyone), also comb *animadversio et castigatio* — by confiscation of property, *multatio bonorum*, capital —, *poena vitae* or *capitis, supplicium capitis, ultimum supplicium, extremum supplicium*, fear of —, *metus*, *ūs*, *poenae* or *animadversionis*, to inflict — on anyone, see PUNISH, to suffer —, *poenam* or *supplicium* (*de*)*pendĕre, expendĕre, solvĕre, persolvĕre, dare, subire, perferre, luĕre* or *ferre*

puny, adj *pusillus* (e g *animus*), a man of — stature, *homo brevi staturā*, a — fellow, *homuncio*

pupil, n 1, *pupula, pupilla, acies* (= a sharp eye), 2, at a school, etc, *alumnus* (m), *alumna* (f), *discipulus, discipula* **pupillage,** n *status*, *-ūs*, or *condicio pupilli*

puppet, n *neurospaston* (Aul Gell) (better written as Greek νευρόσπαστον), see DOLL

puppy, n 1, *catulus, catellus*, 2, fig *adulescentulus ineptus*

purchase, I. v tr 1, lit (*co*)*emĕre, mercari*, 2, fig *emĕre, redimĕre, mercari* **II.** n 1, act of —, *emptio*, 2, thing bought, *merx* (= merchandise), *quod emptum est* (in gen) **purchasable,** adj *venalis* **purchaser,** n *emptor*

pure, adj see CLEAR, 1, = free from moral guilt, *purus, integer*, comb *purus et integer* (= without a stain in his moral character, etc), *castus* (= chaste), comb *purus et castus, castus purusque* (e g body, mind), *integer castusque, sanctus* (= pleasing to God, holy), *insons* (= free from guilt, whose conscience does not accuse him of any crime, etc, innocent, opp. *sons*), comb *purus et insons, emendatus* (= spotless, perfect, e g morals a man), *incorruptus*, — virgin, *virgo casta*, 2, = not mixed with anything, lit, *purus* (in gen), *merus* (= mere, not mixed with, opp *mixtus*), — water, *aqua pura*, — wine (*vinum*) *merum*, — gold, *aurum purum* (*putum*), 3, fig *purus, sincerus*, — language, *sermo purus* or *rectus* or *bonus* or *emendatus*, — joy, *sincerum gaudium*, = clean, *mundus, purus* Adv *pure, integre, caste*, = entirely, etc, *prorsus, plane*; — spiritual, *ab omni concretione mortali segregatus* (e g a being, *mens*, Cic), the — spiritual state of the soul, *is animi status in quo sevocatus est a societate et contagione corporis* (Cic) **purity,** n fig *castitas*, — of a language, *sermo purus* or *emendatus* or *purus et emendatus*, — of expression, *incorrupta integritas, quasi sanitas* (i e healthy vigour), *sanitas* (Quint), *munditia verborum, mundities orationis* (= free from foul language, Aul Gell), moral —, *castitas* (as quality), *castimonia* (= abstinence from that which is bad, (chiefly in a religious sense), *sanctitas* (= holiness, as virtue), *sanctimonia* (= innocence of character), *integritas* (= integrity), *innocentia* (= disinterestedness, opp *avaritia*), *gravitas* (= dignity)

purify, v tr (*re*)*purgare, expurgare, purum facere* (in gen), *purificare* (Plin), *lustrare* (= to — by offering an expiatory sacrifice), *emendare* (= to — from faults), to — the language (from bad words, etc), *expurgare sermonem, emendare, consuetudinem vitiosam et corruptam purā et incorruptā consuetudine emendare* **purification,** n *purgatio* (in gen), *lustratio* (= — by an expiatory sacrifice), festival of —, *Februa, orum* (on 15th Feb) **Purism,** n *in scribendo* (or *dicendo*) *elegantia* **Purist,** n. *in* *scribendo* or *dicendo diligens.* **Puritan,** n., **Puritanism,** n. *qui de sacris diligentior* or *religiosior est.* **Puritanically,** adv. *severius;* see STRICTLY.

purgatory, n. *purgatorium* (Eccl.). **purgation,** n. *purgatio, lustratio.* **purgative,** adj. and n. *medicina alvum purgans, inaniens, bonam faciens, movens.* **purge,** v.tr. and intr. 1, of the medical man, *alvum purgare, bonam facĕre, movēre, de(j)icĕre;* 2, see PURIFY.

purl, v.intr. *murmurare, sonare, susurrare.*

purloin, v.tr. *avertĕre;* see EMBEZZLE, STEAL.

purple, I. n. 1, = purple colour, *purpura, ostrum* (= the liquor of the shell-fish used for dyeing purple), *conchylium* (= purple proper), *color purpureus;* 2, *purpura, vestis purpurea* (= garments, covering, etc.). **II.** v.intr. to grow —, † *purpurare.*

purport, I. n. see MEANING, OBJECT. **II.** v.tr. see MEAN.

purpose, I. n. *propositum, consilium, institutum, sententia, animus, mens* (our "mind"), *voluntas* (= wish), or by *velle* (e.g. my — was to go, *ire volui*), with this —, *eo consilio, ut,* or by *ad* with gerund or gerundive (e.g. I was sent for the — of seeking him, *ad eum petendum missus sum*); on —, *consulto, de industriâ, deditâ opera;* to what —, *quo consilio;* see WHY; to no —, without —, *nullo* or *sine consilio, temere;* to the —, *ad rem, apposite.* Adv. *consulto;* see ON PURPOSE, PURPOSE, I. **II.** v.tr. *statuĕre;* see INTEND. **purposeless,** adj. *vanus, inanis, irritus, cassus, inutilis.*

purr, v.intr. perhaps *sonitum edĕre,* or *gaudium sonitu exhibēre.*

purse, n. *marsupium, zona, crumena, sacculus.* **purse-proud,** adj. *pecuniâ superbus.*

pursuant, prep. — to, in pursuance of, *secundum alqd* (e.g. of a law, *ex lege, ex decreto*).

pursue, v.tr. *alqm persequi, prosequi, consectari, insequi, insectari, alci insistĕre, instare,* all lit. and fig. **pursuit,** n. *studium, cupiditas* (= desire for anything), *ars, quaestus, -ūs;* to make a — of anything, *alqd factitare* or *exercēre.*

purveyor, n. *obsonator,* or by *providēre.*

pus, n. *pus* (Cels.). **pustule,** n. *pustula* (Cels.).

push, I. v.tr. *pellĕre, trudĕre, offendĕre, pulsare, alqm,* with *alqâ re* (e.g. *capite, cubito, pede aut genu*), *fodĕre alqm* or *alqd,* with *alqâ re;* to — forward, *propellĕre, impellĕre;* to — back, *repellĕre;* to — down, *depellĕre.* **II.** v.intr. to — on, *contendĕre, instare;* see HASTEN. **III.** n. *(im)pulsus, -ūs, impetus, -ūs;* to make a —, *instare.* **pushing,** adj. *acer;* see EAGER.

pusillanimous, adj. *timidus, abjectus, humilis, demissus, fractus.* Adv. *timide, abjecte, humiliter, demisse, animo abjecto,* etc. **pusillanimity,** n. *timiditas, formīdo* (= fear), *animus timidus,* etc. (see above), *animi demissio, infractio,* or *imbecillitas.*

put, v.tr. in gen., *ponĕre* (e.g. *calculum*), to — to or near, *apponĕre alqd alci rei* or *ad alqd, proponĕre alqd alci rei, admovēre alqd alci rei, referre alqd ad alqd;* to — a thing in its proper place, *alqd suo loco ponĕre;* to — away, *abdĕre, ponĕre* (the latter fig. = to lay aside); to — upon, *alqm* or *alqd imponĕre* or *inferre in alqd* (e.g. *puerum in equum*), *collocare alqd in alqâ re,* seldom *in alqd* or merely *alqâ re, alqd accommodare alci rei* or *ad alqd;* to — before anything, *proponĕre alqd alci rei;* to — anything anywhere, *ponĕre* (in gen.), *(col)locare* (at a certain place); to — on one side, to — by, *seponĕre, reponĕre;* to — down, *deponĕre, demittĕre* (= to let down); fig. *de(j)icĕre, ex(s)tinguĕre;* see DESTROY; to — forward, *producĕre* (e.g. a candidate), *afferre* (a proof); to — off, *differre;* see DELAY; to — off a dress, *ponĕre, exuĕre;* to — on, *induĕre;* to — out, *e(j)icĕre, extrudĕre, expellĕre* (= to expel), *ex(s)tinguĕre* (= to quench); to — over, *imponĕre, superponĕre* (lit.), *praeficĕre* (fig. of office); to — under, *alqd alci rei supponĕre* or *sub(j)icere;* to — the horses to, etc., *equos curru jungĕre* or *carpento subjungĕre;* to — to flight, *fugare;* to be — to flight, *fugĕre, se in fugam dare;* to — to death, *interficĕre;* see KILL; to — up at, *devertĕre,* or *deverti,* at anyone's house, *ad alqm,* at a place, *ad* or *in* with accus. of the place (e.g. *ad hospitem,* and *ad alqm in Albanum,* and *ad* or *in villam suam*); to — up with, see BEAR, TOLERATE; to — in, *appellĕre, portum petĕre;* see ENTER; to — out to sea, *navem* or *classem solvĕre;* see LEAVE.

putative, adj. *falsus* or *qui dicitur esse.*

putrefaction, n. by verb PUTREFY, I. **putrefy, I.** v.tr. *putrefacĕre.* **II.** v.intr. *putrefieri, putrescĕre.* **putrid,** adj. *putridus, puter* (*putris*). **putridness,** n. *putor* (ante and post class.).

putty, n. *gluten* (*vitreariorum*).

puzzle, I. n. 1, a game, *nodus quidam in lusum oblatus, quaestio lusoria* (Plin.), *aenigma, -ătis,* n.; 2, a difficulty, *nodus.* **II.** v.tr. *animum distrahĕre, impedire.* **III.** v.intr. *in alqâ re haerēre, in angustiis esse.* **puzzling,** adj. *difficilis, ambiguus.*

Pygmy, n. *pygmaeus* (= one of the Pygmies, Plin, etc.); = dwarf, *nanus* (Juv.).

pyramid, n. *pyramis, -idis,* f. **pyramidal,** adj. *in pyramidis formam factus.*

pyre, n. † *pyra, rogus.* **pyrites,** n. *pyrites, -ae* (Plin.).

pyrotechnics, pyrotechny, n. as t.t. *ars pyrotechnica.*

pyrrhic, adj. 1, *in metre pes pyrrhichius* (Quint.); 2, — victory, perhaps *victoria, ut aiunt, Pyrrhi regis modo incassum relata.*

pyx, n. *pyxis* (Eccl.).

Q.

quack, I. n. 1, of a duck, by verb QUACK, II.; 2, an itinerant seller of medicine, *pharmacopola circumforaneus;* 3, see IMPOSTOR. **II.** v.intr. *tetrinnire.* **III.** adj. *falsus.* **quackery,** n. *ars pharmacopolarum.*

quadrangle, n. 1, a figure, * *quadrangulum;* 2, a courtyard, *area* (Plin. Min.). **quadrangular,** adj. *quadrangulus* (Plin.).

quadrennial, adj. *quat(t)uor annorum.*

quadrille, n. *saltatio.*

quadripartite, adj. *quadripartitus.*

quadruped, n. *quadrupes.*

quadruple, adj. *quadruplex.*

quaff, v.tr. see DRINK.

quag(mire), n. *palus, -ūdis,* f.; see BOG. **quaggy,** adj. *paluster;* see BOGGY.

quail, n. (a bird), *coturnix.*

quail, v.intr. *animo deficĕre;* see TREMBLE.

quaint, adj *lepidus* (= pretty), see CURIOUS, AFFECTED, *insolitus, novus, mirus* (= new, strange), *facetus, argutus* (= witty), see STRANGE, HUMOROUS Adv *novo* or *insolito* or *miro quodam modo, mire, facete, argute* **quaintness,** n use adj

quake, v intr *tremĕre*, see TREMBLE **quaker,** n *unus ex iis qui se amicos appellant*

qualify, v tr 1, *instituĕre, instruĕre, fingĕre* (of men), to — oneself, *se praeparare*, 2, = to modify a remark, etc, *extenuare, attenuare, deminuĕre*, see LESSEN **qualification,** n *jus, juris*, n (= right), *potestas* (= power), comb *jus potestasque* (e g *provinciae administrandae*, for administering a province), in gen sense = fit, by adj QUALIFIED **qualified,** adj *idoneus, accommodatus, aptus, utilis, opportunus ad alqm rem, dignus alqâ re* (e g *honore*)

quality, n 1, *proprietas, proprium* (= peculiarity), *natura* (= natural condition), *genus, ĕris* (= kind), *ratio, res* (= state, condition) *qualitas* (ποιότης = particular condition, coined by Cic as a metaphysical t t), *res quae est alcjs rei propria* (= what is the peculiar nature of anything, Cic), often by *esse* with the genit of the noun which possesses the — we mention (but *proprium* must be added when we speak more emphatically), it is one — of a good orator, etc, *est boni oratoris*, etc , one — of a wise man is to do nothing he may repent, *sapientis est proprium, nihil quod paenitēre possit, facĕre*, or by the neut gen of an adj instead of the genit (e g one — of a human being is, *humanum est*), of what —, *qualis*, of such a — or kind, *talis*, a good, noble —, *virtus, ūtis*, a bad —, *malum, vitium*, 2, = kind, sort, *nota* (e g wine of good —, of the best —, *vinum bonae, optimae notae*, of the second —, *secundae notae*, of different —, *diversae notae*)

qualm, n 1, lit *defectio* (*virium*, Plin , = faintness), *fastidium* (= loathing), 2, fig , use circuml (e g I have a — of conscience, *mens mihi angitur*)

quantity, n 1, *numerus* (= number), *copia* (= plenty), *aliquot* (= a few, several, a considerable number), a great —, *multitudo, magnus numerus, acervus* (= a heap, mass), *turba* (= a confused mass of things or people), *nubes, -is* (= a cloud of things, e g *pulveris*), *silva* or *quasi silva* (= an abundance, esp with regard to literary objects, e g *silva rerum et sententiarum*), *vis* (= a large —, of persons and things, in an emphatic sense), *pondus, ĕris*, n (= —, according to weight, e g *pondus auri*), a very large indefinite — is expressed by *sescenti* (e g I received a great — of letters all at one time, *sescentas literas uno tempore accepi*), 2, time of syllables in prosody, **mensura*, **quantitas* (Gram)

quantum, n *portio* see PORTION, SHARE

quarantine, n *tempus valetudini spectandae praestitum*

quarrel, I. n *jurgium, rixa, altercatio* **II.** v intr *jurgare* (with one, *cum algo*), *rixari, altercari*, see DISPUTE **quarrelsome,** adj *rixis deditus*

quarry, I. n = a stone —, *lapicidīnae, lautumia* or *lautomia* (Plaut) **II.** v tr *caedĕre, excidere*

quarry, n = game, *praeda*

quart, n (as a measure) *duo sextarii*

quartan, n *febris quartana*

quarter, I. n 1, = fourth part, *quarta pars* (post Aug , also *quarta* alone , every — of a year, *tertio quoque mense* 2, = part, district, *vicus*, 3, = mercy e g to grant a person —, *alcjs vitae parcĕre, alci (victo) vitam dare* **II.** v tr 1, *quadrifariam dividĕre* or *dispertire* (in gen , = to divide into four parts), to — a man (as a punishment), *in quat(t)uor partes distrahĕre* (Sen), 2, *collocare in alqo loco* or *apud alqm* to — the troops, *milites per hospitia disponere* or *in hospitia dividĕre* or *in hospitia deducĕre* (upon the ratepayers), *milites per oppida dispertire, militibus hospitia in oppidis praestare* (upon the towns) **quarter-day,** n perhaps *dies constitutus, dictus* or *certus*, or by exact date **quarter-deck,** n *puppis* **quartering,** n *milites per hospitia dispositi* or *in hospitia divisi* (as to the troops), *milites tecto (tectis)* or *ad se recepti* (as to the person upon whom the troops are quartered) **quarterly,** adj and adv *trimestris*, money to be paid —, *pecunia tertio quoque mense solvenda* **quarters,** n pl *habitatio* (in gen), *tectum* (= roof, shelter), *deversorium* (= a lodging place for travellers, an inn), *hospitium* (= place where strangers were entertained, guest chambers), *mansio* (Plin , place to stop at for the night) my — are at Mr So-and so's, by *habitare apud alqm* , of troops, *castra, orum* , to place the troops in the winter —, *copias in hibernis collocare* , to be in winter —, *in hibernis esse* , —, in the usual military sense, *statiua, orum* , to take up —, *stativa ponĕre*, to be in —, *in stativis esse*, close —, *comminus*, to come to —, *manum conserĕre*

quash, v tr 1, see SQUEEZE, CRUSH , 2, in law, to — an indictment, etc , *rescindĕre*

quaver, I. v intr 1, in gen , see TREMBLE, VIBRATE , 2, in music, **vibrissare* **II.** n *octava* (with or without *pars*), a semi- —, *pars sextadecima*

quay, n *margo, -ĭnis*, m , *crepīdo*

queen, n *regina* (also fig) , — bee, *rex apium* **queenly,** adj *reginae similis*, †*regius*

queer, adj *novus, insolitus* , see STRANGE, HUMOROUS

quell, v tr *opprimĕre* (e g *tumultum*), *comprimĕre* (e g *tumultum, seditionem*) , see CONQUER

quench, v tr *sedare* (e g *sitim, iram*), *restinguĕre, ex(s)tinguere, explēre, reprimere, depellĕre*

querimonious, querulous, adj *querimundus, querulus*, or by the verb *(con)queri* (*alqd* or *de alqâ re*)

query, v intr , **querist,** n see QUESTION

quest, n to go in — of, see SEEK, SEARCH

question, I. n 1, *interrogatio* (= the act of asking a —, and the — itself), *(inter)rogatum* (= the — asked), *quaestio* (= strict inquiry, and esp a search, in literature, or a judicial inquiry or trial), *controversia* (esp = legal controversy), *lis* (= lawsuit), *res, caus(s)a* (= the matter in dispute), *percontatio* (= inquiry), *disceptatio* (= a debate on a disputable point, in order to arrive at the exact truth), to ask anyone a —, *interrogare alqm de alqâ re* (see INTERROGATE) a short —, *interrogatiuncula, rogatiuncula, quaestiuncula* a — about morals, etc , *de moribus*, etc , a captious —, *captio, interrogatio captiosa* , to bother, confuse anyone with —s, *rogitando alqm obtundĕre*, to answer a —, *ad rogatum respondēre*, there is no — about, *non est dubium quin* or accus and infin , without —, *sine dubio, procul dubio, certe, certo* the — arises, *quaeritur, oritur disputatio, existit quaestio* , now the — is, *nunc id agitur* , it is a very important —, *magna quaestio* (i e , which it will take a long time to settle, Cic), 2, = torture, *quaestio*, to put to the —, *de algo in alqm quaerere* (e g *de servo in dominum*, to torture the slave respecting his master); *quaestionem de alqo habēre* (the object of the inquiry in the genitive case). **II.** v.tr. *(inter)rogare, exquirĕre, quaerĕre, percontari*; to — anything, *ad incertum revocare*; to — anyone, *alqm interrogando urgēre, alqm rogitando obtundĕre* (in a troublesome manner); see ASK, EXAMINE. **questionable,** adj. *is* or *id de quo* or *ea de quâ quaeritur* or *quaestio est, incertus, anceps, dubius.* **questioning,** n. *(inter)rogatio, percontatio, quaestio.*

quibble, I. n. *captio, cavillatio* (esp. in Quint.), *ambāges, -is, calumnia.* **II.** v.intr. *cavillari.* **quibbler,** n. *cavillator.* **quibbling,** adj. *captiosus.*

quick, I. adj. **1,** see LIVE, ALIVE; **2,** see FAST, SPEEDY; **3,** *acer, alacer, alacer et promptus* (= active and ready); **4,** = sharp, *subtilis*; see SHARP, ACUTE; **5,** — with child; see PREGNANT. Adv. **1,** *cito, celeriter*; see FAST; **2,** *mox, mature*; see SOON. **II.** n. to cut to the —, *ad vivum resecare* (lit.), *mordēre* (fig.). **quicken,** v.tr. **1,** *animare* (poet., also fig.); **2,** see ACCELERATE; **3,** = to stimulate, *accendĕre, incendĕre, inflammare alqm.* **quicklime,** n. *calx viva.* **quickness,** n. **1,** *velocitas, pernicitas*; see SPEED; **2,** of intellect, *perspicacitas, sol(l)ertia, calliditas, ingenii alacritas, celeritas.* **quicksand,** n. *syrtis* (lit. and fig.). **quick-scented,** adj. *sagax.* **quick-sighted,** adj. *perspicax* (lit. and fig.). **quick-sightedness,** n. *perspicacitas, ingenii acies* or *acumen.* **quicksilver,** n. *argentum vivum.* **quick-tempered,** adj. *iracundus*; see IRRITABLE. **quick-witted,** adj. *acer, acutus, argutus, perspicax.*

quiescent, adj. by *quiescĕre.* **quiescence,** n. see QUIETNESS.

quiet, I. adj. *quiētus* (= abstaining from exertion), *tranquillus* (= with little motion, esp. of the sea), comb. *tranquillus et quietus, pacatus* (= reduced to peace and obedience, esp. of countries), *sedatus* (= not excited, calm, e.g. *gradus, tempus*), *placidus* (= placid, undisturbed), *otiosus* (= free from business); a — life, *vita quieta* or *tranquilla* or *tranquilla et quieta, vita placida, vita otiosa*; to lead a — life, *vitam tranquillam* or *placidam* or *otiosam degĕre, quiete vivĕre, otiose vivĕre, vitam umbratilem colĕre*; a — province, *provincia quieta* (in gen.), *provincia pacata* (= reduced to a peaceful state). Adv. **1,** *tacite, silentio* (= in silence); **2,** *quieto animo, tranquille, quiete, placide, sedate, otiose.* **II.** n. **1,** *(re)quies, -ētis,* f., *tranquillitas, remissio* (the two latter after exertion), *otium* (= freedom from business), *silentium* (= silence); **2,** fig. *quies, -ētis, otium, tranquillitas* (of mind), *pax* (= peace, only polit.). **III.** v.tr. *quietum reddĕre, tranquillare* or *sedare* or *placare* (= to calm), *pacare* (= to pacify). **quietness,** n. see TRANQUILLITY, QUIET, II.

quill, n. **1,** = pen, *penna*; **2,** of a porcupine, etc., *spina*; **3,** of a musical instrument, *plectrum.*

quilt, n. *stragulum.*

quinquennial, adj. *quinquennis, quinque annorum* (in gen. = lasting five years), *quinquennalis* (= done every five years, also = lasting five years).

quinsy, n. *cynanche* (Cels.), in pure Latin *angina.*

quintessence, n. *flos, floris,* m. (the proper term); *medulla* (= marrow).

quintette, n. *cantus* (-ūs) *e quinque symphoniacis editus.*

quip, n. *facetiae.*

quire, n. *scapus* (Plin., with the ancients = 20 sheets).

quirk, n. see QUIBBLE, I.

quit, v.tr. see LEAVE, DESERT.

quite, adv. *prorsus, plane, omnino* (= altogether, perfectly), *plane, in* or *per omnes partes, per omnia* (= in every respect), *penitus, funditus* (= entirely, completely); *satis* (= enough, e.g. *satis scio,* = I am — certain), *valde* (= very), *magnopĕre* (= greatly); that is — wrong, *falsum est id totum*; I am — in love, *totus in amore sum*; to be of — a different opinion, *longe aliter sentire*; — right! *ita est!* (as answer); — certain, *haud dubie* (= no doubt); not —, *minus* (e.g. not — so many); *parum* (= too little).

quits, adv. render by *fidem suam solvisse*; we are —, *nihil rel(l)iqui est.*

quiver, I. n. *pharĕtrae*; wearing a —, † *pharetratus.* **II.** v.intr. † *trepidare, tremĕre.*

qui-vive, n. on the —, by *alacer*; see ALERT.

quoit, n. *discus.*

quota, n. *(rata) pars* (usu. *pro ratâ parte*).

quote, v.tr. *afferre, proferre* (= to bring forward), *referre* (= to report), *laudare* (with praise), *(pro)ponĕre* (as an example), *notare* (with censure), *(com)memorare* (= to mention), *transcribĕre* (= to copy off); to — an instance, *exemplum afferre; commemorare*; from which letters I have —d a few passages as an example, *ex quibus lit(t)eris pauca in exemplum subjeci.* **quotation,** n. **1,** = act of quoting, *prolatio, commemoratio*; **2,** = passage quoted, *locus allatus,* etc.; see QUOTE.

quoth, v.intr. *inquit, ait.*

quotidian, adj. *cot(t)idianus.*

R.

rabbi, n. **rabbi.*

rabbit, n. *cuniculus.*

rabble, n. *sentina reipublicae* or *urbis* (= the lowest of the people), *faex populi* (= the dregs), *colluvio, quisquiliae* (= refuse), *turba* (= crowd); see MOB.

rabid, adj. *rabidus*; see MAD. Adv. *rabide.*

race, n. *genus, -ĕris,* n. (also = *gens,* more particularly when we speak of the — to which a certain tribe belongs); *gens* (in a more gen. sense = all who belong to a certain tribe; in a more narrow sense, all who bear the same generic name [*nomina*] in opp. to *familia,* i.e. the subdivisions of a *gens*); *stirps* (= the lineage of a family descended from a *gens*); *progenies* (lit. = descent; then also = posterity); *prosapia* (= stock), *semen* (lit. = seed, meton. for *genus*), *proles, -is,* f. (= progeny), *nomen* (= name), † *propago,* † *sanguis*; see BREED, KIND. **raciness,** n. *sucus,* comb. *sucus et sanguis, sapor vernaculus* (= idiomatic —). **racy,** adj. *habens quemdam sucum suum*; *habens nescio quem saporem vernaculum*; *salsus* (= pungent).

race, I. n. = contest, *cursus, -ūs, certamen, curriculum*; to hold —s, *cursu certare*; horse —, *cursus, -ūs, equorum* or *equester.* **II.** v.intr. *(cursu) certare* or *contendĕre, pedibus contendĕre* (on foot). **race-course,** n. *curriculum* (in gen.), *stadium* (the ancient στάδιον), *circus* (= circus), *hippodromos.* **race-horse,** n. *equus, celes, -ētis,* m. **racer,** n. on foot, *cursor*; = a horse, *equus.*

rack, I. n. **1,** = manger, *faliscae*; **2,** an instrument of torture, *equuleus, tormentum,* *quaestio* (= examination by torture); to put to the —, *in equuleum alqm imponĕre*, *equuleo torquēre*, *dare alqm in quaestionem* **II.** v tr 1, lit, see above; 2, fig *torquēre*, *vexare*, see TORMENT, VEX.

racket, n 1, = a bat, *reticulum* (not class), 2, = noise, *strepitus*, *-ūs*, see NOISE

racquets, n by *pilā ludĕre*, see BALL

radiance, n *fulgor* (= brightness) *claritas*, *candor*, *splendor*, *nitor* **radiant**, adj 1, = bright, *clarus*, *candidus*, *splendidus*, *nitens*, *nitidus*, *fulgens*, 2, of expression of face, *felix*, *laetus*, see HAPPY, GLAD Adv *clare*, *splendide*, *nitide*, *feliciter*, *laete* **radiate**, v tr and v intr *radiare* **radiation**, n. *radiatio* (Plin)

radical, adj. and n 1, = innate, *insitus*, it is a — fault, *culpa hominibus naturā est insita*, or by *praecipuus* (= chief), *maximus* (= very great); see THOROUGH, 2, Gram — word, *verbum nativum*, *primigenium*, *primitivum*, 3, in politics, *novarum rerum cupidus* or *studiosus*, a red —, *novarum rerum avidus*. Adv *radicitus*, *funditus*, *penitus*, *prorsus*, *omnino*, see ALTOGETHER

radish, n. *raphanus* (Plin)

radius, n *radius*

raffle, **I.** v intr *aleā ludĕre*, to — for, *de algā re aleae jactu contendĕre* **II.** n *alea*

raft, n. *ratis*

rafter, n *canterius*, *tignum transversarium*, *transtrum*, dim *transtillum*

rag, n *pannus* **ragamuffin**, n *homo pannosus* or *nequam*. **ragged**, adj (of men) *pannosus* (Cic), *pannis obsitus* (Ter)

rage, **I.** n *rabies*, *furor*, *saevitia*, *ira*, *iracundia* (see under MADNESS), *alcjs rei cupiditas*, *cupido*, *studium*, *aviditas* (= violent desire for, e.g *gloriae*) **II.** v intr *furĕre* (of men, in poets also of personified objects), *saevire* (= to be cruel, also fig of things, e g of the wind), against anyone or anything, *in alqm* or *in alqd* **raging**, adj see VIOLENT

rail, **I.** n = bar, *tignum transversum*, on a railway, *ferrum*, see BAR **II.** v tr to — off, *saeptis claudĕre*, *(con)saepire* **railing**, n *palus* (= stake, fence), *clathri* (= trellis-work) see FENCE **railway**, n *via ferro strata*; to construct a —, *viam ferro sternĕre*

rail, v intr *conviciis* or *contumeliis uti*, to — at, *alqm conviciis consectari*, *alci maledicĕre*, *maledicta in alqm dicĕre* or *conferre* **raillery**, n *jocus*, *cavillatio*

raiment, n *vestis*, *vestitus*, *-ūs*, *vestimentum*, *cultus*, *ūs*, *ornatus*, *-ūs*, *habitus*, *-ūs* (esp in Suet)

rain, **I.** n *pluvia*, *imber*, *nimbus* (with storm), —bow, *arcus pluvius* (Hor), in prose, gen *caelestis arcus*, *ūs*, and in the context simply *arcus* **II.** v impers it —s, *pluit*, it —s fast, *magnus effunditur imber*, *magna vis imbrium effunditur* **rainy**, adj *pluvius*, † *aquosus*, † *imbrifer*

raise, v tr 1, *(at)tollĕre*, 2, *erigĕre* (e g *malum*), 3, see ERECT, BUILD, 4, to — the price, etc, by *efferre* (e g *pretium alcjs rei*), *carius vendĕre alqd*, to — the salary, *stipendium augēre*, see INCREASE, 5, = to cause to grow, *educere* (e g *flores semine sparso*), 6, = to elevate anyone in condition, *augēre*, *ornare*, *producĕre ad dignitatem* or *ad honores*, to a high condition, *amplis honoribus ornare* or *decorare*, 7, = to stir up, *excitare* (e g *animos*), *erigĕre*, *recreare*, 8, = to bring together, *colligĕre*, *(com)parare*, *(con)scribĕre*, see COLLECT; 9, = to — the voice, by *tollĕre* (e g. *clamorem*), 10, = to — a siege, *oppugnatione desistĕre*, *oppugnationem relinquĕre*.

raisin, n *acinus passus*, † *racemus passus*, in pl *uvae passae* (Col)

rake, **I.** n 1, *pecten*, *rastrum*, *rastellum*, *irpex* (to break clods or to pull up weeds), 2, = good-for-nothing fellow, *ganeo*, *nepos*, *ōtis*, m (= prodigal), *homo dissolutus* or *perditus* **II.** v tr *pectine verrĕre* (hay, etc), *radĕre* (= to — the ground) **rakish**, adj *perditus*, *profligatus*, *dissolutus*

rally, **I.** v tr 1, to — troops, *aciem* or *ordines restituĕre*, *milites in ordinem revocare*, 2, = to banter, *alqm ludĕre*, *irridēre* **II.** v intr 1, of troops, *se colligĕre*; 2, in gen *se reficĕre*, *colligĕre*, *convalescĕre* (from illness), see RECOVER **III.** n use verb

ram, **I.** n *aries*, *ĕtis*, m (both of sheep and battering —) **II.** v tr *alqd fistucā adigĕre*, *fistucare* **rammer**, n *fistuca*, *pavicula*

ramble, **I.** v intr *errare* (lit and fig), about, *circum alqd* (having lost the right road), *vagari*, *palari*, *a proposito aberrare* (fig). **II.** n *ambulatio*, to go for a —, *ire ambulatum* **rambler**, n *homo vagus*, *erro* (= vagrant) **rambling**, adj *vagus* (lit and fig)

ramification, n 1, lit by *ramis diffundi*, 2, fig *pars* **ramify**, v intr *dividi*, see also EXTEND

rampant, adj in gen *ferox*, *superbus* (= proud), to be —, *superbire*, in heraldry, *erectus* or *arrectus*

rampart, n 1, *vallum* (properly speaking), *agger*, *-eris*, m (= a mound, mole), 2, fig *vallum*, *propugnaculum*, *praesidium*

rancid, adj *rancidus*

rancour, n *odium (occultum)*, see HATRED **rancorous**, adj *iratus*, *iracundus* (= angry), *malevolus*, *malignus* (= spiteful), *invidus* (= envious), *infestus*, *inimicus* (= hostile) Adv *irate*, *iracunde*, *maligne*, *infeste*, *inimice*

random, adj *in casu positus*, *fortuitus*, or by adv , at —, *temere*, or comb *temere ac fortuito* (e g *agĕre* or *facĕre alqd*)

range, **I.** v tr 1, see RANK, II 2, 2, see ROAM **II.** n 1, *ordo*, *series* (in gen) *montes continui* (= — of mountains), *teli jactus*, *-ūs*, or *conjectus*, *ūs* (— of missiles), 2, — of thought, etc , by circumloc (e g *sententiarum varietate abundantissimum esse*), — of subjects, *rerum frequentia*

rank, **I.** n 1, of troops, *ordo*, *inis*, m , the —s, *ordines militum* to break through the —s, *ordines perrumpĕre*, to throw the —s into confusion, *ordines (con)turbare*, in their —, *ordinati* (of troops), *ordinatim*, 2, degree in military affairs, *ordo (militandi)*, or by *gradus honoris* or *dignitatis* (e g *gradu honoris* or *dignitatis*, and merely *honore superiorem esse alqo*), to reduce to the —, *in ordinem cogĕre*, 3, in civil life = degree, *locus* (*honoris* or *dignitatis*), *dignitas* (= position in society), a Spaniard of —, *Hispanus nobilis* **II.** v tr 1, to — the soldiers, *ordines* or *aciem instruĕre*, 2, = to place in a particular class, *ordinare*, *disponĕre* (= to arrange), (*in numero*) *habĕre* (= to consider, e g *alqm in amicorum numero*), see CONSIDER **III.** v intr by *in ordinem redigi*, to — with, *eodem loco esse cum alqo* (in gen), *pares ordines ducĕre* (of two military officers)

rank, adj of plants, *luxuriosus*, of smell, † *graveolens*, *foetidus*, = very great, *magnus*, *maximus*.

rankle, v.intr. perhaps *mordēre* (= to bite), or *pungĕre* (= to prick).

ransack, v.tr. 1, a house, *exhaurire*, *exinanire*, *nudum atque inane reddĕre*; a temple, *fanum everrĕre et extergēre*, *spoliare expilareque*, *nudare ac spoliare*; 2, = to search thoroughly, *rimari*, *scrutari*.

ransom, I. n. 1, = the money paid as —, *pecuniae quibus alqs redimitur*, or by *pretium*, *pecunia* (e.g. *alqm sine pretio dimittĕre*, *reddĕre*); 2, = release from captivity, *redemptio*. II. v.tr. *redimĕre (pecunia)*.

rant, I. n. *sermo tumidus*, *turgidus*, *inflatus*. II. v.tr. perhaps *sermone tumido uti*, or simply *declamare*. **ranter**, n. *orator tumidus*, *turgidus*, *inflatus*.

rap, I. v.intr. at the door, *pulsare (fores)*. II. n. *pulsatio*.

rapacious, adj. *rapax*, *furax* (= thievish). **rapacity**, n. *cupiditas rapinarum* or *praedae* or *praedae rapinarum*, *spoliandi cupido*, *rapacitas* (the latter as inherent quality).

rape, n. *stuprum mulieri oblatum*.

rapid, I. adj. *rapidus* (of wind), †*rapax*; see SWIFT, QUICK. Adv. *rapide*. II. n. *vertex*, *gurges*, -*itis*, m. **rapidity**, n. *rapiditas*; see SPEED, QUICKNESS.

rapier, n. *gladius* (= sword).

rapture, n. *summa voluptas*. **rapturous**, adj. *beatus* (= blessed), *felicissimus* (= very happy); see HAPPY.

rare, adj. *rarus* (= not often met with), *insolitus* (= unusual), *infrequens* (= that is not often met); = thin, *rarus*, *tenuis*, *singularis*, *eximius* (= exceedingly fine, etc.). Adv. *raro*; I am — at Rome, *Romae sum infrequens*. **rarefaction**, n. use adj. (e.g. the — of the atmosphere, *aer extenuatus*). **rarefy**, v.tr. *extenuare*. **rarity**, n. *raritas*, *res rara*, *res rara visu* or *inventu*.

rascal, n. *homo scelestus*, *sceleratus*. **rascality**, n. *scelus*, -*ĕris*, n. **rascally**, adj. *scelestus*, *turpis*, *sceleratus*; see BASE.

rase, v.tr. = to level with the ground, *solo aequare* or *adaequare*.

rash, adj. *praeceps*, *praecipitatus* (= headlong, etc.), *inconsultus* (= inconsiderate, e.g. *certamen*), *temerarius* (= thoughtless). Adv. *inconsulte* (*inconsulto*), *inconsiderate*, *temere*, *nimis festinanter*, *praepropere*; to act —, *festinantius agere*. **rashness**, n. *temeritas*.

rash, n. *eruptio(nes)* (Plin.), *scabies* (= itch).

rasher, n. of bacon, *lardi offula*.

rasp, I. v.tr. *scobinā radĕre*. II. n. *scobina*.

raspberry, n. *morum Idaeum*.

rat, n. *mus*. **rat-trap**, n. *muscipula* (Phaed.).

rate, I. n. 1, at the —, *pro modo*, *pro ratione*, but generally *pro*; to buy at a high or low —, *magno* or *parvo emĕre*; — of interest, *usura*, *fenus*, -*ŏris*, n.; 2, = tax, *vectigal*, *tributum*; to lay a —, *vectigal*, *tributum imponĕre alci* (= to — anyone) and *alci rei*, *tributum indicĕre alci*; 3, = manner, *modus*; at this —, *in hunc modum*; at any —, *certe*, *utique*; — of going (of a watch), *motus*, -*ūs*. II. v.tr. 1, *aestimare alqd*, *aestimationem alcjs rei facĕre*; see ESTIMATE; 2, *alci imponĕre tributum*; see TAX; 3, = to scold, *increpare*; see SCOLD. **rateable**, adj. *cui vectigal imponi potest*.

rather, adv. 1, *potius* (if we select), *prius* (= before), *multo magis* (= so much the more, in a higher degree), *quin etiam*, *quin potius*, *quin immo* (when we substitute something still stronger, etc.), *immo* (= nay even; also comb. *immo potius*, *immo vero*, *immo enimvero*, *immo etiam*); and not —, *ac non potius*, also *ac non*; I did not . . . , — . . . (or in similar phrases), *tantum abest*, *ut* . . . *ut*; I would —, by *malo*, with infin.; 2, = somewhat, *aliquantum*, *aliquanto*.

ratification, n. *sanctio*, or by **ratify**, v.tr. a treaty, *sancire pactum*, *fidem foederis firmare*, *foedus ratum facĕre*.

ratio, n. *pro ratā portione*; see PROPORTION.

ratiocination, n. see REASONING.

ration, n. *demensum*, *cibus* or *victus*, -*ūs*, *diurnus* (= daily allowance of food).

rational, adj. 1, = having reason, *ratione praeditus* or *utens*, *rationis particeps*; 2, = agreeable to reason, *(rationi) consentaneus*. Adv. *ratione*; to act —, *ratione uti*, *prudenter* or *considerate agĕre*. **rationalism**, n. *opinio eorum qui in investigatione veri ratione suā (neque divinā quidam lege) utendum esse putent*. **rationalist**, n. *qui*, etc., *putet*; see above. **rationality**, n. *ratio*.

rattle, I. v.intr. 1, *crepare*, *crepitum dare* (= to make a crackling, clattering noise), *strepĕre*, *strepitum dare* (= to make a loud noise), *sonare* (= to sound); 2, *blaterare* (= to talk idly). II. v.tr. to — the chains, *vincula movēre*; see before. III. n. 1, *crepitus*, -*ūs*, *strepitus*, -*ūs*, *sonitus*, -*ūs*, *fragor* (of thunder); 2, a child's plaything, †*crepitaculum*. **rattlesnake**, n. *serpens*.

ravage, I. v.tr. *vastare*, *populari*. II. n. *vastatio*, *populatio*.

rave, v.intr. *furĕre*, *insanire*, *bacchari*, *delirare*, comb. *delirare et mente captum esse*; = to talk irrationally, †*ineptire* (= to do and say things which are irreconcileable with common-sense), *(h)ariolari* (lit., = to prophesy, then = to talk nonsense; ante class.); *nugari* (= to talk and do silly things), *(h)al(l)ucinari* (= to blunder, to talk as if one were dreaming).

raven, n. *corvus*.

ravening, adj. *rapax*, *vorax*, *edax*. **ravenous**, adj. 1, see RAVENING; 2, = very hungry, *cibi avidus*. Adv. *summā cibi aviditate*, *voraciter*. **ravenousness**, n. *cibi aviditas*, *voracitas*, *edacitas*.

ravine, n. *angustiae viarum* (in gen. = narrow passage, path), *fauces*, -*ium* (= defile), *saltus*, -*ūs* (= mountain pass).

raving, adj. see RAVE, MAD.

ravish, v.tr. 1, *alqam (per vim) stuprare*; 2, = to charm, *oblectare*; see DELIGHT. **ravisher**, n. *raptor*, or by verb. **ravishing**, adj. *dulcis*, *suavis*; see DELIGHTFUL.

raw, adj. *crudus* (opp. *coctus*, also of wounds), *incoctus* (= not yet boiled, opp. *coctus*, ante Aug.); half —, *subcrudus*, *rudis* (of anything in its natural state), *impolitus* (= unpolished, e.g. stone), *incultus* (= not manufactured, worked up, cultivated, e.g. field, vine); — gold, silver, *aurum*, *argentum infectum* (opp. *argentum factum*); — hands, troops, *rudis*; of weather, *frigidus* (= cold), *humidus* (= damp). **raw-boned**, adj. see THIN.

ray, n. *radius*; a — of hope, *spes*, *specula*, or by *lux* (e.g. *lux quaedam civitati affulsisse visa est*).

ray, n. a fish, *raia* (Plin.).

razor, n. *culter tonsorius*, *novacula*.

reach, I. v.tr. and intr. 1, see EXTEND, STRETCH; 2, = to touch by extending, *contingĕre*, *attingĕre*; 3, = to deliver with the hand, *porrigĕre*, *praebēre*; 4, = to arrive at, *pervenire ad* or *in* with accus. (in gen.), *attingĕre locum*, *capĕre alqm locum* (esp by sea); to — the harbour, *portum capĕre, in portum pervenire, pervehi*, 5, = to arrive at by effort, *assequi* 6, of reports, *pervenire, accedĕre, deferri ad alqm* **II.** n within —, *quod manu prehendi, quod contingi potest*, out of — of gunshot, *extra teli jactum* or *conjectum*

reach, retch, v intr *nauseare* **reaching,** n *nausea*

react, v tr 1, to — a play, *fabulam iterum* or *denuo dare* (of the author), or *edĕre* (of the manager of a theatre), or *agĕre* (of the actors), 2, to — upon, *alqm afficĕre* (with adv of the manner in which the affection takes place) **reaction,** n *commutatio* (= change)

read, v tr and intr *legĕre* (in gen, lit = to pick up, gather, e g *spicas*), *recitare* (= to — aloud, recite), *praeire* or *praeire voce* (= to — to anyone in order that he may repeat it after him), to — anything often, *lectitare*, to — anything in a cursory manner, to glance at, *pervolvĕre, pervolutare*, fig to — in the future, *praesagire futura*, to — the future in the stars, *e siderum positu et spatiis conjecturam facĕre de rebus futuris*, to — it in anyone's looks, by *alqd in alcjs vultu* or *ex toto ore eminet* (e g *pigritia et desperatio in omnium vultu eminet, toto ex ore crudelitas eminet*), a person that is well —, *homo satis lit(t)eratus, eruditus, doctus*, fairly well —, *tinctus lit(t)eris*, to be much —, *in manibus esse* **readable,** adj *jucundus*, see DELIGHTFUL **reader,** n *lector, recitator* (= one who reads aloud), *anagnostes* (= a slave who reads aloud) **reading,** n *lectio, pellectio, recitatio* (aloud to anyone = recital) want of —, *inscitia lit(t)erarum*, worth —, *dignus qui legatur, legendus* a true or false — in an author, *vera* or *falsa lectio* **reading desk,** n perhaps *pulpitum*

ready, adj 1, *instructus, paratus* (*ad alqd* or with infin), *promptus* (= quick, *ad alqd* or *in alqd* or *in alqâ re*), comb *promptus et paratus, expeditus* (= always prepared, in readiness), — to do a thing, *paratus facere alqd* or *ad alqd faciendum*, simply with the part fut act (e g *moriturus, periturus*), to be —, *ad manum esse, praesto adesse*, for — *ad alqd*, at anybody's command, *ad nutum alcjs expeditum esse*, to get or make —, *parare, instruĕre alqd*, to get oneself — for, *se parare ad alqd, se expedire ad alqd, (com)parare, instruĕre alqd*, = finished, *perfectus, absolutus*, — money, *pecunia praesens* or *numerata* to pay — money, *pecuniam repraesentare*, 2, = obliging, *officiosus, facilis* Adv *prompte, prompto* or *parato animo, libenter, libentissimo animo* or (of several) *libentissimis animis* = easily, *facile* **readiness,** n 1, to be in —, *paratum, promptum paratumque, expeditum esse* (of persons), *sub manibus esse* (of servants, etc, at hand, etc), *ad manum esse* (of persons and things), *in promptu esse, paratum* or *provisum esse, suppetĕre* (= to be in sufficient quantity, of corn, etc) to hold in —, *habēre paratum, in expedito*, 2, *animus promptus* or *paratus, facilitas, officium, studium*

real, adj 1, = not fictitious, *verus* (= true, e g *gloria, laus*), *certus* (= certain), *sincerus* (= unalloyed), *germanus* (= true, e g brother, hence = genuine, e g. *Stoicus, patria*), a — scholar, *vere doctus*, sometimes by *ipse* (e g the — man, *homo ipse*), 2, in law, *quod ad rem* or *res spectat, ad res pertinens*, a — estate, *solum, fundus* Adv = truly, *vere, re, revera* (or as two words, *re vera*), *profecto, (enim)vero*, ironically *scilicet*, in question, *itane vero?* **reality,** n *quod est seu quod esse potest* (Vitr), *res, res verae, verum* (= realities, facts, what really exists, opp *res fictae*), *veritas, natura* (both these words in an abstract sense), in —, *re, re verâ, revera*, to become a —, *fieri, effici ad effectum adduci* **realize,** v tr 1, = to carry into effect, *facĕre, efficĕre, perficĕre, ad effectum adducĕre* or *perducĕre, ad verum perducĕre*, 2, = to grasp mentally, *intellegĕre (animo), repraesentare, ante oculos sibi proponĕre* 3, of money, *pecuniam redigĕre* or *alqd alqo pretio vendĕre* **realization,** n *effectus, ūs, inventio et excogitatio* (= discovery), or by *mente concipere*

realm, n *civitas, respublica* (= state) *regnum* (= kingdom)

ream, n of paper, *viginti scapi* (*scapus* = a cylinder on which twenty sheets were rolled)

reanimate, v tr 1, lit perhaps *alqm a † morte revocare* or *mortuo vitam reddĕre* or *restituĕre* 2, fig to — anyone's hope, *ad novam spem alqm excitare* or *erigĕre, novam spem alci ostendĕre*

reap, v tr 1, *(de)metĕre* 2, prov, as you sow, so you will —, *ut sementem feceris, ita metes*, to — where we have not sown, *alienos agros demetĕre, sub arbore quam alius conseruit legĕre fructum* (Liv), fig = to gain, *fructum capĕre, percipĕre*, the fruit of, *ex alqâ re, fructum alcjs rei ferre* **reaper,** n *messor* **reaping-hook,** n *falx*

reappear, v intr *redire* (= to return)

rear, n *agmen extremum* or *novissimum, acies novissima* or *extrema*, the — of the enemy, *hostes novissimi, postremi*, to form the —, *agmen claudere, cogĕre*

rear, I. v tr 1, see RAISE, LIFT, 2, to — up, plants, etc, *alĕre* (in gen), children, *educare, educĕre*, see BRING UP, 3, fig, see EXALT, ELEVATE **II** v intr of horses, *ex(s)ultare, tollĕre se arrectum*

reason, I. n 1, = cause, *principium, initium, fons, origo*, (= source, origin), *causa* (= cause), comb *causa et semen* (e g *belli*), *ratio*, to state a —, (*causam* or *rationem*) *afferre* (e g *cur credam, afferre possum, firmissimum argumentum afferri videatur*), not without a —, *non sine causâ, cum causâ*, for this —, that, etc, *propterea (quod), quod, quoniam, quamobrem, quapropter, quare ideirco, itaque*, by — of, *ex alqâ re*, there is no —, I have no — to, etc, or why, etc, *non est, nihil est, quod* or *cur, non habeo, nihil habeo, quod* or *cur*, with subj (e g you have no — to make yourself uneasy, *nihil est quod te moveat*), I have — to feel ashamed, *est quod me pudeat*, what — has he (to say, etc)? *quid est quod*, etc? I have more — to congratulate you than to request you, *magis est quod tibi gratuler, quam quod te rogem*, = fact, proof, *argumentum, res* (generally in the pl, opp *verba*), 2, *ratio* (as that which calculates), *mens* (= understanding), *prudentia, consilium* (= prudence), void of —, *rationis carens, rationis expers*, 3, see RIGHT, JUSTICE, 4, = moderation, *aequitas* (also = feeling of justice), *justitia, fas* (of what is right according to the voice of anyone's conscience), *moderatio, liberalitas*, in —, *ex aequo, sicut aequum est, ut par est* **II.** v intr *ratiocinari* (in gen), *disputare* or *disserĕre de alqâ re* (about anything), *animo* or *secum reputare* (with oneself), see ABOUT **reasonable,** adj 1, *rationis particeps* (= rational), *modestus* (= unassuming), *rationi conveniens, consentaneus* (= in accordance with reason), 2, = moderate, *aequus* (= according to — demands), *justus* (= according to what is right, both of persons and things), *meritus* (= rightly deserved, e g praise), *modicus* (= moderate, in price, etc), to buy at a — cost, *bene emĕre* Adv *rationi convenienter*, *merito, jure, bene, parvo pretio* (= cheaply). **reasonableness**, n. *ratio*; = moderation, *aequitas, justitia, moderatio, modestia*; see REASON. **reasoner**, n. *disputator*, or use verb. **reasoning**, n. *ratiocinatio, argumentatio*; see also REASON.

reassemble, I. v.tr. *recolligĕre*. **II.** v.intr. *iterum cogi* or *convenire*; see ASSEMBLE.

reassert, v.tr. **1**, = to repeat, *iterare, iterum confirmare*; see ASSERT; **2**, = to re-establish, *restituĕre* (= to restore), *vindicare* (= to claim).

reassume, v.tr. *recipĕre*.

reassure, v.tr. *confirmare, recreare, erigĕre*.

rebel, I. v.intr. *seditionem movēre* (= to cause a revolt), *imperium auspiciumque abnuĕre* (= to refuse obedience, of soldiers), *rebellare, rebellionem facĕre* (of a tribe recently subdued), *imperium alcjs detrectare* (= to refuse to obey anyone), *deficĕre ab alqo* or *ab alcjs imperio, desciscĕre ab alqo* (= to desert anyone). **II.** n. *homo seditiosus, novorum consiliorum auctor*. **rebellion**, n. *seditio, motus, -ūs, tumultus, -ūs, rebellio*. **rebellious**, adj. *seditiosus, turbulentus, novarum rerum cupidus* or *studiosus*. Adv. *seditiose, turbulente(r)*.

rebellow, v.intr. *reboare, resonare*.

rebound, v.intr. *repercuti, repelli* (= to be driven back), *residĕre* (= to fall back, of persons and things), *resilire* (= to jump back), *resultare* (= to leap back, of things); of echo, *resonare, vocem reddĕre* or *remittĕre, voci respondēre*.

rebuff, I. v.tr. *repellĕre, re(j)icĕre*. **II.** n. *repulsa* (of a candidate; only poet. in wider sense), or by *repelli*; see REFUSAL.

rebuild, v.tr. *alqd totum denuo* or *de integro aedificare, restituĕre, reficĕre, renovare* (= to beautify).

rebuke, I. v.tr. *alqm reprehendĕre de* or *in alqâ re, alqm vituperare de alqâ re, alqm objurgare de* or *in alqâ re, alqm (verbis) castigare, alqm* or *alqd increpare, alqm increpitare, alqm alcjs rei incusare*; see BLAME. **II.** n. *reprehensio, vituperatio, objurgatio, convicium* (= scolding), *castigatio*. **rebuker**, n. *reprehensor, castigator, objurgator*.

rebut, v.tr. *redarguĕre, repellĕre, refellĕre*; see CONFUTE.

recall, I. v.tr. **1**, *revocare* (the proper term, e.g. an opinion, *sententiam*; a promise, *promissum*), *retractare* (= to recant, e.g. words, *dicta*), *alqd irritum esse jubēre* (e.g. *largitiones*), *rescindĕre* (= to rescind, e.g. a decree, a will), *mutare* (= to change, e.g. one's opinion, *sententiam*); **2**, = to call back, *revocare* (verbally and in writing, lit. and fig.), *alqm reverti jubēre* (= to order anyone to return); to — an ambassador, *alqm e legatione revocare*; to — troops from the battle, *signum receptui dare*; to — to their (the people's) minds, *memoriam alcjs rei renovare* or *redintegrare*; to — to anyone's mind, *alci alqd in memoriam redigĕre* or *reducĕre, alqm in memoriam alcjs rei revocare* or *reducĕre*; to — to one's mind, *memoriam alcjs rei repetĕre* or *revocare*. **II.** n. *revocatio*, or by verbs, *receptus, -ūs* (= signal for — of troops).

recant, v.tr. *se sententiam revocare dicĕre*. **recantation**, n. use verb.

recapitulate, v.tr. *enumerare, referre* (= to relate) or more exactly *colligĕre et commonēre quibus de rebus verba fecerimus breviter*. **recapitulation**, n. *enumeratio, rerum repetitio et congregatio*.

recapture, I. v.tr. *recipĕre*. **II.** n. by verb.

recast, v.tr. **1**, lit. *recoquĕre, conflare* (= to melt down); **2**, fig. *totum denuo fingĕre* (lit. = to mould all anew, Plaut.), *fingĕre* or *formare in aliud* (lit. = to make into something quite different), *recoquĕre* (lit. and fig.), *commutare* (= to transform, e.g. *rempublicam*), *renovare* (= to give a new shape, e.g. *alqd in legibus*); see TRANSFORM.

recede, v.intr. *recedĕre, retro cedĕre*.

receipt, n. **1**, *acceptio*, or by circumloc. with *accipĕre* (e.g. after the — of the money, etc., *pecuniâ acceptâ*; after the — of your letters, *lit(t)eris tuis acceptis* or *allatis*); to acknowledge the — of, *testari se accepisse alqd*; to sign the — in a book, *acceptum referre alqd*; **2**, of money, a —, *apocha* (Jct., ἀποχή) or *accepti latio* (or as one word *acceptilatio*, when the money has really been paid; *ac. lat.* = a discharge, Ulp. Dig.), *antapocha* (= a written acknowledgment by the party who paid the money, to the effect that he paid it and got a — for it, Jct.); to enter the — of anything, *alqd habēre acceptum*; to give a — for, *acceptum alqd testari* (= to acknowledge to have received); **3**, = a recipe, a medical prescription, *praeceptum*; to make up a — (of the druggist), *medicamentum ex medici formulâ dilnĕre*. **receive**, v.tr. **1**, *accipĕre* (in the widest sense; also = to take a drink, medicine, poison, etc.), *ferre, nancisci* (of good and evil, accidentally or by chance, without any effort on our part); **2**, to — a person, *accipĕre, excipĕre, salutare* (= to greet, welcome), *recipĕre*; to — kindly, *benigne* or *benigno vultu excipĕre, benigne salutare*; to — one who arrives (in going to meet him), *alci obviam venienti procedĕre*; to — anyone in a ship, carriage, to take in, *tollĕre alqm*; **3**, in one's house, *recipĕre* (as a benefactor), *excipĕre* (as a friend), *hospitio accipĕre* or *excipĕre tecto, ad se (domum) recipĕre*; **4**, anywhere, to — as citizen, *a(d)sciscĕre in numerum civium, facĕre civem*; into a family, *in familiam assumĕre*; among the patricians, *inter patricios* or *in numerum patriciorum assumĕre*; into a society, etc., *cooptare* (*in collegium et in ordinem*); among (the number of) one's friends, *in amicitiam recipĕre, accipĕre, ad amicitiam a(d)scribĕre, amicum sibi adjungĕre*; not to —, *re(j)icĕre*; **5**, to —, take anything said or done in a certain manner, *accipĕre, excipĕre, interpretari* (= to put an interpretation upon it); well, *in bonam partem accipĕre, boni* or *aequi bonique facĕre, boni consulĕre*; not well, badly, ill, *in malam partem accipĕre*; *aegre, graviter, moleste, indigne ferre, male interpretari*. **receiver**, n. **1**, *qui alqd accipit, receptor* (esp. in bad sense, of thieves, etc.); **2**, *exactor* (of taxes), *portitor* (of customs). **receptacle**, n. *receptaculum* (= any place where things may be deposited or kept), *cella, cellula* (= storeroom, cellar), *horreum* (= store-room, barn), *apotheca* (= repository for wine), *armarium* (for clothes), *claustrum* (for wild beasts), *piscina* (for fish; also in gen. = water reservoir), *cavea* (for birds). **reception**, n. **1**, in gen. *acceptio*, or by verbs; **2**, *receptio, hospitium* (in anyone's house and at his table), *aditus, -ūs* (= access to anyone), *cooptatio* (into a body, society, etc.); to meet with a good, bad —, *bene, male accipi, benigne, male excipi*, at, *ab alqo*. **receptive**, adj. *aptus ad discendum, docilis*. **receptiveness, receptivity**, n. *docilitas*. **recipient**, n. *qui accipit*.

recent, adj. *recens* (of what came only recently, of late, into existence, fresh, = young, opp. *antiquus*, i.e. what existed in former times), also comb. *recens ac novus* or *novus ac recens* (of a thing that is but new, as well as of that which has but lately begun to exist). Adv. *nuper, recens* (ante and post class.).

receptacle, see under RECEIVE.

recess, n. **1**, = retired place, *recessus, -ūs,*

secessus, -ūs, penetrale (usu pl and mostly poet), — in a room, perhaps *angulus*; 2, = holidays, *feriae*

recipe, n, see RECEIPT, 3

reciprocal, adj *mutuus* Adv *mutuo, invicem* **reciprocate**, v.tr *inter se dare* **reciprocity**, n *vicissitudo* (= alternation), or by verb

recital, n *enumeratio, narratio, commemoratio* **recite**, v tr 1, = to repeat aloud, *pronuntiare, recitare*, 2, = to narrate, *enumerare*, (*com*)*memorare, dicĕre*, (*e*)*narrare, referre, exponĕre*, see NARRATE, SAY **recitation**, n *lectio, recitatio* **recitative**, n *recitatio notis signisque composita* **reciter**, n *recitator*

reckless, adj 1, = rash, *neglegens, temerarius, incautus, imprudens*, 2, = of anything, *neglegens alcjs* Adv *neglegenter* (= carelessly), *temere* (= rashly) *imprudenter* (= inconsiderately) **recklessness**, n *imprudentia, socordia, neglegentia, temeritas*, see RASHNESS, CARELESSNESS, or by verbs

reckon, v tr 1, *computare, computare rationem rei*, 2, see CONSIDER **reckoning**, n *ratio*, to form a —, *rationem habēre rei, aestimare rem, rationem inire*, by my —, *meā opinione*, to run your pen through the —, *alci rationes conturbare*, to find your — in, *quaestum facĕre in re.*

reclaim, v.tr 1, *repetĕre* (by request), *reposcĕre* (imperatively), *exigĕre* (= to collect money that is owing, e g *credita*, anything lent), *alqd recipĕre* (= to recover), *alqm* or *alqd ab alqa re vindicare* 2, fig to call back from error, vice, etc, *alqm revocare ad virtutem* (*a perditā luxuriā*, etc), *alqm ad officium reducĕre*

recline, I. v tr *reclinare*, to — the head upon the elbow, *niti* or *initi cubito, niti in cubitum* II v intr *jacēre* (= to lie), *accumbĕre*, (*ac*)*cubare* (at table) **reclining**, adj (*re*)*supinus* (on the back)

recluse, n *homo solitarius*, see also HERMIT

recognise, v tr 1, *a*(*d*)*gnoscĕre*, (*re*)*cognoscĕre* (= to make the acquaintance of anyone a second time); to — anyone by anything, *noscitare alqm alqā re* (e g *facie, voce*), 2, = to acknowledge, *cognoscĕre* (in gen), *appellare alqm* with accus of the title (= to declare anyone), (*com*)*probare* (= to approve), *accipĕre* (= to receive) **recognition**, n 1, in gen, see RECOGNISE, 2, *comprobatio* **recognizance**, n *sponsio, vadimonium*, to enter into —s, *vadimonium facĕre*

recoil, v intr *repercuti, resilire* (lit and fig), † *resultare, recellĕre*, to — at, *refugĕre et reformidare alqd*

recollect, v tr *alcjs rei* (*com*)*meminisse, reminisci, alqd recordari*, comb *reminisci et recordari*, or by *memoriam alcjs rei tenēre* or *habēre*, *memorem* or *haud immemorem esse alcjs rei* (all = *meminisse*), *memoriam alcjs rei repetĕre, revocare, renovare, redintegrare, memoriā repetĕre alqd, subit animum alcjs rei memoria, alqd mihi in memoriam, venit mihi in mentem alqd, alcjs rei, de alqā re* (all = *reminisci*), to — anything quite well, *commeminisse* with genit, I cannot — it, *memoriā alqd excessit, delapsum est, e memoriā alqd mihi exiit, excidit, ex animo alqd effluxit, fugit* or *refugit alqd meam memoriam* **recollection**, n *memoria* (= memory, and remembrance), *recordatio* (the act), comb *recordatio et memoria, memoria ac recordatio*, to bring to one's —, *in memoriam redigĕre, reducĕre, revocare*

recommence, I. v tr *de integro instaurare* (= to set on foot again), (*red*)*integrare* (= to begin afresh), *renovare* (= to renew), *iterare* (= to begin a second time), *repetĕre* (= to repeat, after an interruption) II. v intr *renasci*, or by pass of verbs given above

recommend, v tr *commendare*, to — oneself, *gratum esse, placēre, probari* (all of persons and things) to anyone, *alci*, by, *se commendare alqā re* (of persons), *commendari alqā re* (of things). **recommendable**, adj *commendandus, commendatione dignus, commendabilis* **recommendation**, n *commendatio, laudatio, suffragatio* (by voting in favour), to give anyone a — to anyone, *alqm commendare alci, ad alqm de alqo scribĕre*, his — is of great use to me with, *maximo usui mihi est alcjs commendatio apud alqm*, a letter of —, *lit*(*t*)*erae commendaticiae*, to give anyone a letter of — to, *alqm commendare alci per lit*(*t*)*eras* **recommendatory**, adj *commendaticius*

recompense, I. n *pretium, merces, ēdis*, f, *remuneratio, munus, ĕris*, n, see REWARD II v tr *compensare, remunerari*, see REWARD

reconcile, v tr 1, *placare* (by reconciliatory means, in gen, e g *numen divinum*), *expiare* (anything polluted by a crime, e g *numen, manes*), to — a person with anyone, *alqm cum alqo* or *alqm* or *alcjs animum alci reconciliare* or *reducĕre* or *restituĕre in gratiam*, also *alqm in alcjs gratiam reconciliare* or *restituĕre*, to — oneself with, to anyone, *reconciliari alci, reconciliare sibi alqm* or *alcjs animum* or *alcjs gratiam, in gratiam cum alqo redire* or *reverti*, 2, = to make congruous, *alqd ad alqd* or *alci rei accommodare, facĕre ut alqd cum alqa re conveniat* or *congruat*, fig of things, to be —d together, *congruere, congruentem esse alci rei, aptum esse alci rei, non alienum esse ab alqa re*, both with genit (e g *sapientis est*), 3, = to submit to, *se sub*(*j*)*icĕre, obtemperare* or *parēre*, with dat, *alqd subire* or *perferre*, see YIELD **reconcilable, reconciliatory**, adj 1, *placabilis*, 2, *qui* (*quae, quod*) *alci rei accommodari potest* **reconciler**, n *reconciliator gratiae* **reconciliation**, n 1, *reconciliatio concordiae* or *gratiae*, 2, see ATONEMENT, 3, = agreement of things seemingly opposite, by verb RECONCILE, 2

recondite, adj *reconditus*

reconduct, v tr *reducĕre*

reconnoitre, v tr to — a locality, etc, *cognoscĕre qualis sit natura alcjs loci, naturam alcjs loci perspicĕre* (accurately), *situm alcjs loci speculari* (= to explore), *visĕre alqd* (in gen = to inspect anything, e g *copias hostium*), *explorare alqd* (= to spy out, e g *itinera hostium*), one sent out to —, *explorator* **reconnoitring**, n by verbs

reconquer, v tr *recipĕre, recuperare* (*recup*)

reconsider, v tr *denuo, rursus* or *iterum considerare, reputare*, etc, see CONSIDER

record, I. v tr *referre in tabulas, libellum*, etc, *lit*(*t*)*eris* or *memoriae mandare* II. n *lit*(*t*)*erae, tabulae, historia, monumentum, memoria alcjs rei* **records**, pl *annales, ium*, m (= annals), *acta* (*publica* or *diurna* or *urbana*, = journal) *fasti* (= calendar), *tabulae* (*publicae*) (= official state —), *acta Senatūs* (= — of the Senate) **record-office**, n *tabularium* **recorder**, n = keeper of records, *chartularius* (legal, Jct), *componendis patrum actis delectus* (Tac, of records of the Senate), = a judge, *judex*

recount, v tr *referre*, see RELATE

recourse, n to have — to anyone or to anything, *confugĕre* or *perfugĕre ad alqm* or *alqd* (lit and fig), *alcjs rei perfugio uti* (fig e g *aquarum*), *accurrĕre ad alqm* or *alqd, se ad alqm conferre*, in bad sense, *ad alqd descendĕre*,

recover, I. v.tr. *recipĕre*, (e.g. *res amissas*) *reciperare, reparare, repetĕre;* to — one's debts, *evincĕre* (Jct.), *nomina sua exigĕre* (e.g. *amissa*). **II.** v.intr. **1**, *convalescĕre, sanescĕre, sanitatem recipĕre* or *reciperare, restitui in sanitatem;* to — from illness, *convalescĕre e morbo;* **2**, in gen. = to regain a former condition, *se* or *animum colligĕre, se reficĕre, se* or *animum recipĕre* with and without *ex (a) pavore, se recreare ex timore, respirare a metu, respirare et se recipĕre* (from fright), *se* or *animum erigĕre* (from a desponding state of mind), *vires, auctoritatem, opes reciperare, pristinam fortunam reparare* (= to regain influence, etc.); in law, see above. **recoverable,** adj. *quod restitui* or *reparari*, etc., *potest*, †*reparabilis;* in law, *quod evinci potest* (Jct.). **recovery,** n. **1**, in gen. *reciperatio;* **2**, *sanitas restituta, valetudo confirmata;* to have, to entertain, no hopes for anyone's —, *alqm* or *alcjs salutem desperare* (Cic.); all the medical men doubt of his —, *omnes medici diffidunt;* **3**, in law, *evictio* (Jct.).

recreant, n. **1**, = apostate, *apostata* (Eccl.); **2**, see COWARD.

recreate, v.tr. **1**, = to create anew, *renovare, recreare;* see RENEW; **2**, = to amuse, etc., oneself, *requiescĕre* (= to rest), *animum relaxare, remittĕre, mentem reficĕre et recreare* (= to revive). **recreation,** n. *requies, -ētis* (= rest); — of the mind (after hard work, care, etc.), *animi remissio, relaxatio, oblectatio, requies;* for —, *laxandi levandique animi gratiā;* to allow oneself a few moments' —, *aliquantulum sibi parcĕre.*

recriminate, v.intr. *culpam, crimen*, etc., *in alqm regerĕre.* **recrimination,** n. *accusatio mutua* (Tac.).

recruit, I. v.tr. and intr. **1**, one's strength, *se* or *vires recreare, reficĕre;* **2**, to — the army, *supplēre, explēre, delectibus supplēre, supplementum scribĕre alci, reficĕre, milites conscribĕre, delectum habēre.* **II.** n. *novus miles* (in gen.), *tiro* (not drilled, opp. *vetus miles, veteranus*); the —s, *milites tirones, milites in supplementum lecti*, also *supplementum* (= reserve); a —ing officer, *conquisitor.* **recruiting,** n. *conquisitio, delectus, -ūs.*

rectangle, n. *figura orthogōnia.* **rectangular,** adj. *orthogonios.*

rectification, n. *correctio, emendatio.* **rectify,** v.tr. *corrigĕre, emendare* (mistakes in writing, copying, printing); see CORRECT.

rectilineal, adj. *(di)rectus.*

rectitude, n. *aequitas, probitas, integritas, honestas, simplicitas, ingenuitas* (in one's actions), *animus ingenuus.*

rector, n. of a grammar-school or college, *scholarum, gymnasii, academiae, rector* or *moderator;* to be — of, etc., *praeesse, praefectum esse alci rei;* of a parish, *paroeciae rector*, or, where possible, *sacerdos* (= priest).

recumbent, adj. *(re)supīnus*, †*reclīnis*, or by *reclinari;* see RECLINE.

red, adj. *ruber, rubens* (= bright —), *rufus* (= light —, auburn), *rutilus* (= fire-red); *rubicundus* (= ruddy), *rubidus* (= dark —), *puniceus* (= purple —), †*sanguineus* (= blood- —), †*flammeus* (= flame-coloured); — hair, *capillus rufus* or *rutilus;* the — sea, *Sinus Arabicus.* **redden, I.** v.tr. †*rubefacĕre.* **II.** v.intr. *(e)rubescĕre* (= to blush). **red-hot,** adj. *candens, fervens.* **red-lead,** n *minium.* **redness,** n. *rubor, pudor.*

redeem, v.tr. *redimĕre, liberare* (= to set free); a pledge, *repignerare quod pignori datum est* (Jct.); see also FREE. **redeemer,** n. *liberator, vindex*, from anything, *alcjs rei* (= deliverer), *redemptor* (by ransom; * *mundi redemptor*, the — of the world), * *servator;* see SAVIOUR. **redemption,** n. **1**, *redemptio, liberatio* (= deliverance); **2**, in theology, * *salus* (= salvation), * *redemptio.*

redolent, adj. *alqd redolens.*

redouble, v.tr. *reduplicare*, †*ingeminare.*

redoubt, n. *castellum, propugnaculum.*

redound, v.intr. *redundare;* to anyone's credit, *esse* with double dat. (e.g. it —s to my credit, *est mihi honori*). **redundancy,** n. *redundantia.* **redundant,** adj. *redundans, supervacaneus.*

redress, I. v.tr. = to amend, *corrigĕre, emendare, restituĕre, alci rei mederi, alci satisfacĕre de alqd re;* to — a wrong, *injuriam sarcire.* **II.** n. *satisfactio, remedium*, or by verb.

reduce, v.tr. **1**, = to bring to any state, to — to order, *in integrum reducĕre* (civil affairs, etc.); to — a man to poverty, *alqm ad inopiam redigĕre;* to — to ashes, *incendio delēre* (a house, town, etc.), *incendiis vastare* (e.g. *omnia*); to — one to despair, *alqm ad desperationem adducĕre* or *redigĕre;* **2**, = to diminish in length, quantity, etc., *(im)minuĕre, deminuĕre* (in gen.); to — the price of, *pretium alcjs rei (im)minuĕre;* **3**, = to conquer, *vincĕre, expugnare* (of a stronghold). **reduction,** n. **1**, by verbs; **2**, *expugnatio;* **3**, in arith. and logic, *reductio.*

reduplication, n. *reduplicatio* as gram. t.t.

reecho, v.intr. *resonare alqd* or *alqā re* or *remittĕre, alqā re resultare.*

reed, n. *carex* (= sedge, shear-grass), *arundo* (= cane), *canna* (= small —), *calamus.* **reedy,** adj. *arundinĕus.*

reef, I. n. **1**, *scopuli, saxa* (= rocks); see ROCK; **2**, = portion of a sail, *velum.* **II.** v.tr. *vela subducĕre.*

reek, v.intr. *fumare.*

reel, I. n. **1**, = a winder, *glomus* (= ball, e.g. *lini*); **2**, = a dance, *saltatio.* **II.** v.intr. *titubare, vacillare.*

reelect, v.tr. *reficĕre.*

reestablish, v.tr. *restituĕre, reficĕre.* **reestablisher,** n. *restitutor.* **reestablishment,** n. *restitutio, refectio;* see RENEWAL.

refectory, n. *cenaculum.*

refer, I. v.tr. **1**, = to direct, etc., anyone or anything to another person, *alqm* or *alqd delegare ad alqm* or *ad alqd, revocare alqm ad alqm* or *ad alqd* (e.g. *alqm ad Graecorum poetarum fabulas*), *re(j)icĕre* or *remittĕre alqd ad alqm* (e.g. *causam ad senatum*); **2**, fig. to — anything to a thing, *referre* or *deferre alqd ad alqd;* anything to another matter, *alqd ad aliam rem transferre;* everything to sensual pleasure, *omnia ad voluptatem corporis referre.* **II.** v.intr., to anyone or to anything, *spectare ad alqd* (intended), *pertinēre, referri ad alqd* (really), *alqm* or *alqd attingĕre* or *perstringĕre, alcjs rei mentionem facĕre;* it —s to this, that, etc., *hoc eo spectat, ut*, etc.; it —s to those who, etc., *hoc illis dictum est, qui*, etc.; to — a speech, a sermon, etc., to anyone, *oratione designatur alqs;* = to appeal to anyone, *provocare ad alqm, appellare alqm* and *alqd* (both also = to appeal to a higher tribunal), *alqm testari, alqm testem citare* (= to — to anyone as a witness), *delegare, re(j)icĕre alqm ad alqd* (for better information), *afferre alqd* (= to — to, as a proof), *alcjs rei excusationem afferre, alcjs rei excusatione uti* (= to — to anything, as an excuse for, etc.). **referable,** adj. *qui (quae, quod) ad alqm* or *alqd referri potest.* **referee,** n. *arbiter.* **reference,** n. **1**, to anyone, by verbs; **2**, allusion to books, persons, etc.; see QUOTATION; **3**, = relation, by *ratio;* to have — to, *pertinēre, referri ad alqd*, having no — to the matter, *alienus ab alqâ re*, with — to, etc, by *quod attinet ad* (e g *quod ad librum attinet quem tibi filius dabat*, Cic), or by *ad* (e g *adornatum ad specimen magnifico ornatu*, Cic), or by *de* with abl (= on account of, concerning, e g *recte non credis de numero militum*, Cic)

refill, v tr *replēre*

refine, v tr 1, *liquare* (*vinum*), *purgare* (Plin, gold, silver, etc), 2, fig *(ex)polire, excolĕre* **refined,** adj *(ex)polītus, urbanus, comis* (= courteous), *humanus, liberalis, elegans*, a — palate, *palatum subtile*, — torture, *exquisitum supplicium*. **refinement,** n 1, of liquids, etc, by verb REFINE, 1, 2, of manners, etc, *urbanitas comitas, humanitas, elegantia*, of language, etc, *subtilitas*, comb *subtilitas et elegantia, argutiae*

reflect, I. v tr to — the rays of light, *radios repercutĕre, regerĕre* **II.** v intr 1, of the mind, *remittĕre*, the mind is —ed in the face, *mens in fronte tanquam in speculo cernitur*, or *imago mentis est vultus*; to — on, *secum in animo considerare*, or simply *considerare alqd* or *de alqâ re* (= to dwell on), *commentari alqd* or *de alqâ re* (= to think over in private), *alqd* or *de alqâ re secum meditari, alqd secum reputare, alqd (re)colĕre, memoriam alcjs rei repetĕre* or *revocare*, see THINK, 2, to — upon, *culpare*, see BLAME **reflection,** n 1, of rays, etc, *repercussus, -ūs* (Plin), 2, = image reflected, *imago*, 3, = thought, *meditatio, commentatio, cogitatio, consideratio, deliberatio, reputatio*, 4, as quality, *mens, ratio, consilium*, 5, = blame, *reprehensio*, see BLAME **reflective,** adj 1, *magni consilii*, see THOUGHTFUL, 2, Gram *reciprocus*

reflux, n *recessus, -ūs*

reform, I. v tr 1, = to make anew, *renovare, restituĕre*, of scattered troops, *ordines restituĕre*, 2, = to amend, *corrigĕre, emendare* **II.** v intr *se corrigĕre, mores suos mutare, in viam redire*. **III.** n *correctio, emendatio* (in gen), of manners, *morum mutatio* **reformation,** n 1, see REFORM, III, 2, Eccl, *reformatio* **reformatory,** n by circuml (e g *carcer ad sceleslos corrigendos destinatus*), or, where context allows, by *carcer* alone **reformer,** n *corrector, emendator*

refract, v tr *radii infringuntur* or *refringuntur* **refraction,** n *refractio radiorum* **refractory,** adj *contumax* (= contumacious), *imperium detrectans* (= refusing to obey, of soldiers, subjects), *detrectans militiam* (= of soldiers) **refractoriness,** n *contumacia*

refrain, v tr (*se*) *abstinēre, se continēre ab alqâ re*, (*sibi* or *animis*) *temperare ab alqâ re* or *quin* or *quominus*, to — from tears, *lacrimas tenēre, temperare a lacrimis*

refresh, v tr *refrigerare* (= to cool), *recreare, reficĕre* (= to revive, to renew one's physical strength), comb *reficĕre et recreare, recreare et reficĕre*, to — anyone by giving him something to eat, *cibo jurare alqm*, to — with meat and drink, *cibo ac potione firmare alqm*, to — oneself, *animum reparare, relaxare, integrare* (in gen), by mental recreation, *animo relaxari* **refreshing,** adj *reficiens, recreans, suavis, dulcis* **refreshment,** n 1, *refectio* (as act), *id quod corpus reficit* (= what refreshes the body), *delectatio* (= delight, as a condition), *laxamentum* (for the mind), 2, —s, *cibus*

refrigerate, v tr *refrigerare*

refuge, n *perfugium, refugium, asylum* (= an asylum for everybody gen, a sacred grove or temple), *recessus, -ūs, secessus, -ūs* (= retreat), *receptaculum* (= a place where one may find shelter from prosecution, etc), *portus, -ūs* (lit = harbour, hence fig = any place of shelter), comb *portus et perfugium, praesidium*, comb *perfugium et praesidium salutis*, to seek a — at a place, (*con*)*fugĕre* or *perfugĕre* or *refugĕre ad* or *in alqm locum, alqo loco perfugio uti*, to have a —, *perfugium* or *receptum habēre* **refugee,** n *fugitivus* (= a runaway slave, or a deserter), *exul, extorris, profugus* (= exile)

refulgent, adj see BRIGHT

refund, v tr *reddĕre* (e g *ad assem alci impensum*), (*dis*)*solvĕre* (e g a debt, *nomen*, to — a sum of money lent, *aes alienum*), *rescribĕre* (= to pay money by bill)

refuse, I. v tr *alqd recusare* (or with accus and infin, *quin* or *quominus* = to — to do anything), *alqd (de)negare* (or with accus and fut infin), *alqd detrectare, repudiare, renuĕre, respuĕre*, to — anything to anyone, *alqd alci recusare* **II.** n *ramentum* (Plin, = shavings, etc), *scobis* (= sawdust, smaller than *ramentum*), *retrimentum* (of olives, metals, etc), *intertrimentum* (of metals, etc, in melting), *purgamen(tum)* (= dirt swept off), *faex* (= dregs, lit and fig), *quisquiliae* (= sweepings, usu fig), *sentina* (= bilge water, also fig) **refusal,** n *recusatio, repudiatio, repulsa* (= rejection of a candidate), to give anyone the — of anything, *alci potestatem alcjs rei emendae facĕre*

refute, v tr *refellĕre* (anyone's opinion by arguments, a person or thing), *redarguĕre* (= to convince of the contrary, a person or thing), comb *refellĕre et re[illegible]*, *convincĕre* (= to convince anyone that he is wrong to prove the fallacy of anything, e g *errores*), *revincĕre* (= to prove the contrary of an assertion), *confutare*, e g *argumenta Stoicorum*), *diluĕre* (= to weaken, e g *crimen*), comb *refutare ac diluĕre, diluĕre ac refellĕre, diluĕre alqd et falsum esse docēre, dissolvĕre*, to — anything by testimonies, evidence, *alqd testimoniis refutare* **refutation,** n *confutatio, refutatio, responsio*

regain, v tr *recipĕre, recuperare*

regal, adj see ROYAL

regale, v tr see ENTERTAIN, to — oneself, see FEAST

regalia, n *ornatus, -ūs, regius, insignia regia* (pl)

regard, I. v tr 1, *animum intendĕre in alqd* or *alci rei, alqd animadvertĕre* (or *animum advertĕre*, = to direct one's attention to), *observare alqd* (= to notice), *intueri (in) alqd* (= to look at), *respicĕre alqd* (= to mind), *spectare alqd* (= not to lose sight of), as —s so and-so, by *pertinēre ad*, etc (= to concern), *attinēre ad*, etc (= to belong to), *spectare alqd* or *ad alqd* (= to refer to), *attingĕre alqm* (= to have reference to anyone), not to — *neglegĕre*, 2, = to care for, *alqm* or *alqd curam habēre, colĕre, diligĕre* (= to esteem), *magni alqm aestimare*, 3, = to consider, *ducĕre, habēre*, see CONSIDER **II.** n 1 *respectus, -ūs* (lit = the looking back, hence consideration of thoughts and sentiments), *ratio* (= reference), *cura* (= care), to have — to, etc, *respectum habēre ad alqm, respicĕre alqm* or *alqd, rationem habēre alcjs* or *alcjs rei, rationem ducĕre alcjs rei*, for oneself, *suam rationem ducĕre, de se cogitare*, out of — for, in Latin often by the dative of the person, e g *animadversionem et supplicium remittĕre alci*, with — to anything, see REFERENCE, 2, = esteem, *alcjs caritas, studium, amor* (= love), *pietas erga alqm* (= dutiful affection), see AFFECTION, kind —s (*etiam atque etiam*) *vale* (*valete*), Cicero sends his —s, *Cicero tibi salutem plurimam dicit* **regardful,** adj.

see ATTENTIVE. **regardless**, adj. *in quo nullius ratio habetur, in quo delectus omnis et discrimen omittitur, neglegens;* see CARELESS. Adv. *neglegenter, nullius ratione habitâ, delectu omni et discrimine omisso.*

regatta, n. see RACE.

regency, n. *regni administratio, interregnum* (= interreign), *procuratio regni* (= the office of a viceroy); to entrust anyone with the —, *administrationem regni in alqm transferre.* **regent**, n. *procurator regni* or *imperii, interrex.*

regenerate, v.tr. *regenerare;* to be —d, *renasci.* **regeneration**, n. *regeneratio* (Eccl.).

regicide, n. 1, = murder of a king, *regis caedes, -is,* f., in the context also *parricidium* (*regis*); to commit —, *regem interficĕre;* 2, = the murderer, *regis interfector* or *percussor* or *parricida.*

regiment, n. *legio* (of infantry), *turma equitum* (of cavalry).

region, n. *regio* (in gen.), *tractus, -ūs* (= tract of a country, referring to the distance), *plaga* (only of the — of the sky, also *plaga caeli*), *ora* (lit. = tract on the coast), *pars* (= part, district, also of the sky), *loca,* pl. (places, gen. with an adj. expressing the nature of the soil, e.g. *loca amoena*).

register, I. n. *liber* (as note-book), *tabulae* (= tables), *album* (= an official account, report, e.g. of the judges, suitors, applicants, etc.); to enter in a —, *in album referre.* II. v.tr. *in acta publica referre* (of public —s), *in tabulas referre* (in gen.). **registrar**, n. in gen. *qui alqd in acta publica refert.* **registration**, n. use verb.

regret, I. n. (*com*)*miseratio* (= the giving vent to one's compassion), *dolor* (= grief), *desiderium* (= longing), *paenitentia* (= repentance). II. v.tr. *dolēre, aegre* or *moleste ferre, lugēre* (= to mourn); it is to be —ted, *dolendum est quod;* I —, *doleo;* hence = to repent, *paenitet* or *piget me alcjs rei;* = to feel the loss of, *desiderare, desiderio alcjs teneri.*

regular, adj. *ordinatus* (= ordered), *omnibus membris aequalis et congruens* (of the — shape of the human body, also of a — building), *omnibus partibus absolutus et perfectus* (= perfect in gen.), *aequabilis* (= equable), *constans* (= not deviating from the — course, e.g. the course of the stars); *certus* (= fixed), *rectus* (= correct); — troops, *milites legionarii* (in the ancient sense, opp. *velites,* = light troops); = legitimate, ordinary, *justus* (in gen.), *legitimus* (= legitimate); a — battle, *justa pugna;* in — array, *acie* (in battle), *composito agmine* (of line of march); the — consuls, *consules ordinarii;* — revenue, income, *status reditus, -ūs* (opp. *reditus extraordinarius*). Adv. *ordine, constanter* (e.g. *cursus suos servare*), *recte, ordinate, composite, juste, aequabiliter, legitime.* **regularity**, n. *ordo, constantia, aequabilitas, symmetria* (= proportion, Vitr.), *apta compositio* (of words in a sentence). **regulate**, v.tr. *ordinare, componĕre, dirigĕre, formare, fingĕre;* to — oneself by anything, *se ad alqd accommodare;* see ARRANGE. **regulation**, n. *ratio, ordo, -inis,* m., *mos, consuetudo, institutum* (of what is customary), *lex* (of what has become almost a law); domestic —, *victus cultusque, privatae vitae ratio;* = order, *jussum, praeceptum, edictum* (= edict); —s, *instituta et leges;* to make a few fresh —s, *quaedam nova instituĕre;* a few useful —s, *quaedam utilia instituĕre,* also *quasdam utilitates instituĕre;* it is a wise — in nature that, etc., *salubriter a naturâ institutum est, ut* or *quod.*

rehabilitate, v.tr. anyone's character, *culpâ alqm liberare.*

rehearsal, n. *meditatio* (= previous study); to have a —, *praeludĕre fabulae* (of the actor). **rehearse**, v.tr. see above; *praeludĕre concentui* (of the orchestra and the singer).

reign, I. v.intr. *regnare* (as a king), *imperium tenēre, imperare, imperium alcjs terrae obtinēre.* II. n. *regnum, dominatio, principatus, -ūs, imperium;* in the — of, *regnante* or *rege alqo;* see RULE.

reimburse, v.tr. see INDEMNIFY, REFUND. **reimbursement**, n. see INDEMNITY.

rein, I. n. *habena, frenum* (lit. and fig.), *lorum,* pl. *frena* or *freni;* to pull the —s, *habenas adducĕre* (lit. and fig.), to loosen the —s, *frenos dare* (lit. and fig.); to take the —s of government, *clavum imperii tenēre.* II. v.tr. *frenare* (lit. and fig.); to — in, *habenas adducĕre.*

reindeer, n. *reno.*

reinforce, v.tr. *amplificare* (= to cause to be of greater extent, strength, e.g. a tone), *augēre* (= to increase, e.g. an army); to — an army, *auxiliis confirmare, copiis firmare;* to — one's army (of the commander), *novis copiis se renovare* (after the army had been reduced in numbers). **reinforcement**, n. *supplementum, novae copiae* (= new forces), *auxilium* (= allies), *subsidium* (= reserve); somebody receives —, *copia alci augetur, subsidium alci mittitur.*

reins, n. *renes, -um,* m.

reinstate, v.tr. *in* (*regnum,* etc.) *reducĕre,* or by *restituĕre* (= to restore).

reinvigorate, v.tr. see REFRESH.

reiterate, v.tr. see REPEAT.

reject, v.tr. *re*(*j*)*icĕre, improbare, reprobare* (the two foregoing = to disapprove), *repudiare* (= to repudiate), *respuĕre* (= to spit out), *spernĕre, aspernari* (= to throw away, *asp.* implies disdain), *contemnĕre* (= not to consider worth having); to — entirely, *omnino non probare, funditus repudiare, legem suffragiis repudiare* (different from *legem abrogare,* i.e. to rescind); a condition, a proposal, *condicionem repudiare* or *respuĕre;* to — prayers, *preces aversari.* **rejection**, n. *rejectio* (e.g. *judicum*), *improbatio, repudiatio, aspernatio, repulsa* (of a candidate).

rejoice, I. v.intr. *gaudēre* (= to be glad), *laetari* (= to be merry), *gestire* (the strongest expression, when we manifest our joy in our looks, etc.), *subridēre* (= to smile as a sign of joy); to — at anything, *gaudēre, laetari alqâ re* (the latter construction is used to denote that the joy continues; the simple accus. only with a neuter pron. with accus. and infin., and *gaudēre* also with *quod*), *delectari alqâ re;* very much, *gaudēre vehementerque laetari;* very much at, *magnam laetitiam voluptatemque capĕre* (or *percipĕre*) *ex alqâ re, magnae laetitiae mihi est alqd, alqd re gaudio exultare* (= to jump with joy); with anyone, *unâ gaudēre, gaudio alcjs gaudēre;* see GLAD. II. v.tr. (*ex*)*hilarare, hilarem facĕre* (= to cheer up), *laetificare* (e.g. *sol laetificat terram*), *laetitiâ afficĕre, laetitia et voluptate afficĕre, laetitiam alci afferre* or *offerre* (= to fill with joy). **rejoicing**, n. *voluptas, delectatio, gaudium, laetitia.*

rejoin, v.intr. 1, see RETURN; 2, see ANSWER.

relapse, I. v.intr. *recidĕre* (in gen., of illness, *in graviorem morbum*); to — into, *recidĕre in alqd* (e.g. into former slavery), *relabi.* II. n. use verb.

relate, v.tr. 1, = to tell in detail, *alqd* (*e*)*narrare, dicĕre,* (*com*)*memorare, referre, prodĕre, tradĕre* (= to hand down); see TELL; 2, = to pertain to, *spectare, attingĕre ad, contingĕre alqm,* or by impersonals *attinet, pertinet ad, meâ, tuâ refert*, etc, see NARRATE **related,** adj 1, = connected by birth, marriage, etc, *propinquus alci, necessarius, cognatus, agnatus* (only on the father's side), *affinis* (by marriage), *consanguineus, consanguinitate propinquus* (= near by blood), *non alienus sanguine alci*, to be most nearly —, *proximum esse*, 2, fig *cognatus, propinquus* **relation,** n 1, = connexion, *ratio, conjunctio*, in — to, *ad alqm* or *alqd, quod ad alqm* or *alqd attinet, prae alqo* or *alqa re*, 2, relative, person connected with you by birth, marriage, etc, *propinquus, genere proximus, necessarius*, comb *propinquus et necessarius, propinquus et cognatus, propinquus et affinis, cognatus atque affinis*, a near —, *arta propinquitate* or *propinqui cognatione conjunctus*, 3, see NARRATION **relationship,** n 1, *necessitudo, propinquitas* (in gen), *cognatio* (by birth), *agnatio* (on the father's side), *affinitas* (by marriage), *germanitas* (of brothers and sisters, or cities springing from the same mother city), *consanguinitas* (by blood), 2, fig *cognatio, conjunctio*, to have — with anything, *alci rei finitimum esse* **relative,** I. adj opp to absolute, *quod non simpliciter et ex sua vi consideratur*, *quod in comparatione (rerum,* etc) *positum est, quod ad alqd refertur* or *spectat*. Adv *comparate, ex comparatione (rerum,* etc) II. n 1, see RELATION, 2, *relativum* (Gram)

relax, I. v tr 1, *(re)laxare, remittere, concedere*; 2, in medicine, see OPEN II. v intr = to remit in close attention, *(re)languescere, se remittere, remitti, animum remittere* or *relaxare, requiescere curamque animi remittere* (after hard work), *alqd remittere* (e g *industriam*) to — for a little while, *alqd intermittere*, in anything, *desistere* or *(de) alqâ re* (e g *incepto*, in a contest, *de contentione*) **relaxation,** n 1, *solutio* (principally of the parts of the body), 2, see MITIGATION (of the law), 3, = remission of application, *animi relaxatio, remissio* (of the mind), *oblectatio* (= amusement), *oblectamentum* (= anything to amuse oneself with or to while away the time) **relaxing,** adj *gravis*

relay, n *equi recentes* or *per viam dispositi*

release, I. v tr 1, anyone, *dimittere alqm* (= to let anyone go), *libertatem alci dare, largiri* (= to set anyone at liberty), *manu mittere alqm* (a slave), *emancipare* (= to emancipate, to free anyone from one's power, e g a son), *mittere* or *missum facere alqm, missionem alci dare, exauctorare* (= to dismiss from the service, soldiers), *vinculis exsolvere, e custodia emittere* (from prison, a state prisoner), to — anyone from anything, *solvere alqm alqâ re* (e g from service, *militiâ*) *liberare alqm alqâ re* (e g *servitute*), 2, = to free from obligation, *(ex)solvere, liberare alqâ re, remittere, condonare alci alqd, gratiam alcjs rei facere alci* (from the payment of a sum of money, penalty, etc , *gratiam facere* in Sall) II. n *missio* (= dismission), *liberatio, remissio* (e g *poenae*) *apocha* (= receipt for money, Jct)

relent, v intr *molliri* or *moveri pati* **relentless,** adj *immisericors, saevus, durus, crudelis*, see CRUEL Adv *saeve, crudeliter*. **relentlessness,** n *saevitia, crudelitas*

relevant, adj *quod ad rem est*

reliance, n see RELY

relics, n *reliquiae* (= remains) **relict,** n *vidua*, see WIDOW

relief, n fig *(al)levatio, sublevatio* (= the — given), *levamen(tum), allevamentum* (= the — which one gets), *remedium* (= remedy), *auxilium* (= help), *subsidium* (of soldiers), *delenimentum* (= anything calculated to soothe, e g. *vitae*), *laxamentum* (= relaxation), *deminutio* (= diminution of taxes, *onerum*), *beneficium* (= — in money), — of a sentinel, see RELIEVE, below; in painting, *eminentia, asperitas*, high —, *alto relievo, imago ectypa* (Sen , as image) **relieve,** v tr *exonerare* (= to exonerate, to ease), *levare, allevare* (fig = to ease), *sublevare* (fig = both to mitigate and to support), *laxare* (fig = to relax, to soften), or *adesse alci*, *(de)minuere* (= to lessen, e g taxes, *onera*), *subvenire* (= to assist, e g *necessitatibus*), to — a sentinel, *revocare* (= to recall, e g *vigilias, milites ab opere*), *deducere* (e g *milites ab opere*), of the soldiers themselves, *alqos excipere, alqis succedere*

religion, n *religio* (= reverence towards the holy, the sentiment of — and the consequent services), *pietas erga Deum* (in the sense of the ancients, *erga deos* = fear of the gods), *res divinae* (= divine things), *caerimonia, caerimoniae* (= prescribed observances), *sacra, orum* (= external rites), *lex* (= religious law or doctrine, as *lex Christiana*), a man without —, or irreligious, *homo impius erga Deum* or *deos, homo neglegens deorum, religionum omnium contemptor, religionum neglegens* (= inattentive to outer usages), to change your —, *sacra patria deserere* **religious,** adj *pius* (= reverent) *erga Deum, sanctus, religiosus* (= conscientious), — observances, *ritus, religiones, caerimoniae* Adv *pie, sancte, religiose*, to be — brought up, *sanctissimo modo educari*

relinquish, v tr *relinquere*, see ABANDON.

relish, I. n 1, a — for (i e a disposition to taste), *gustatus, ūs*, he has no — for, *abest desiderium alcjs rei*, 2, something tasty, *promulsis, idis*, f, *condimentum* II. v tr see ENJOY

reluctance, n I have a great — to anything, *magnum alcjs rei odium me cepit*, with —, *coactus* or *invitus, animo invito* or *averso* **reluctant,** adj *invitus, coactus*

rely, v intr *(con)fidere alci rei* or *alqâ re* (= to trust in), *niti alqâ re* (= to depend on), —ing upon, *fretus alqâ re, nixus (nisus) alqâ re, ferox alqâ re* (= boldly trusting, e g *eâ parte virium*) **reliance,** n *fides, fiducia*, see CONFIDENCE

remain, v intr *(per)manere, durare* (= to endure), *stare* (= to stand or stay), to — in health and uninjured, *salvum atque incolumem conservari*, to — faithful, *fidum manere*, to — in your opinion, *in sententiâ tuâ (per)manere* or *perseverare* (opp to *a sententiâ decedere*), to — unchanged in your custom, *in consuetudine perseverare*, to — unchanged in your plan, *institutum suum tenere*, to — faithful to your promise, *promissis stare*, to — a secret, *taceri, tacitum teneri*, let that — with yourself, *haec tu tecum habeto, hoc tu tibi soli dictum puta* "It —s" (used as the final result of an argument), *manet*, to — snug, *nidum servare* (= to keep in your nest, Hor), to — in the camp, *castris se tenere*, = to be left, *reliquum esse, relinqui, superesse* (= to survive), *ex multis filiis hunc unum fortuna reliquum esse voluit*, fate allowed only this one son to — out of many, = to be left, to be over and above, *restare, superare, superesse* **remainder,** n *residuum, reliquum, quod restat*, to get the — by adding and subtracting, *addendo deducendoque videre quae reliqui summa est* **remaining,** adj *reliquus, residuus* **remains,** n 1, of anything, *reliquum*, or pl *reliqua* or *reliquiae*, of eatables, *reliquiae ciborum*, in the context merely *reliquiae*, 'the remainder of anything' is also rendered by *quod superest* or *restat* or *reliquum est* (e g *quod membrorum reliquum est*), 2, = a dead body, *cadaver, eris*, n (= corpse), *cineres, -um* (= ashes)

remand, I. v tr 1, = to send back, *remittere*, 2, in law, *comperendinare reum* (= to defer the sentence until the third day and further), *ampliare reum* (= to adjourn a trial). **II.** n. *comperendinatio* (or *-ātus, -ūs*).

remark, I. v.tr. 1, see OBSERVE, PERCEIVE; 2, = to express in words, etc., *dicĕre;* see SAY. **II.** n. 1, see OBSERVATION; 2, a — expressed, *dictum* (= anything that is said, an opinion), often merely by a pron. in the neuter gender, e.g. that — of Plato's is excellent, *praeclarum illud Platonis est;* or by the adj. in the neuter gender, e.g. I must first make a few introductory —s, *pauca ante dicenda sunt.* **remarkable,** adj. *notabilis, mirus* (= wonderful), *notandus, memorabilis* (= worth noticing), *memoratu dignus, commemorabilis, commemorandus* (= worth mentioning), *insignis* (= very —, lit. distinguished, of persons and things); *conspicuus* (= striking), *singularis* (= especial), *illustris* (= illustrious), *egregius, optimus* (= excellent); nothing happened that was very —, *nihil memoriâ dignum actum.* Adv. *mire, insigniter, singulariter, egregie, optime;* = very, *valde,* by superl. (e.g. — beautiful, *pulcherrimus*); see VERY.

remedy, n. 1, in medicine, *medicina* (lit. and fig.), *medicamen(tum)* (lit., e.g. *dare contra alqd*), *remedium* (= — against, for, lit. and fig.); to apply a — for a complaint, *morbo medicinam adhibēre;* 2, in gen., for counteracting an evil, *remedium,* for, to, against anything, *alcjs rei, ad* or *adversus alqd* (lit. and fig.), *medicina,* for, *alcjs rei* (lit. and fig.), *auxilium, subsidium,* against, *alcjs rei* (to effect a — in case of anyone being placed in a difficult position, in distress, etc.; *auxilium* also of persons being ill), †*lenimen* (= soothing —). **remedial,** adj. *quod ad remedium pertinet; salutaris;* — measures or legislation, perhaps *leges salutares.* **remediless,** adj. †*insanabilis.*

remember, v.tr. *meminisse alcjs, alcjs rei, de alqâ re,* accus. and infin., rel. clause, or subj., *alqd* or *de alqâ re recordari, alqd (memoriâ) repetĕre, alcjs* or *alcjs rei memorem,* or *haud immemorem esse;* I don't — it, *memoriâ delapsum est, e memoriâ alqd mihi exiit, excidit, ex animo alqd effluxit, (re)fugit alqd meam memoriam;* he won't — it (implying intention), *nullam alcjs rei adhibet memoriam;* to — anyone, anything with a grateful heart, *grato animo alcjs nomen prosequi, gratissimum alcjs nomen retinēre, gratâ memoriâ prosequi alqd;* to — anyone with a kind feeling, *memoriam alcjs cum caritate et benevolentiâ usurpare;* as far as I can —, *ut mea memoria est, quantum memini, nisi animus* or *memoria me fallit.* **remembrance,** n. *memoria, recordatio;* see RECOLLECTION, MEMORY.

remind, v.tr. *(ad)monēre, commonēre, commonefacĕre, alqm alcjs rei* or *de alqâ re;* to — one to do anything, *(ad)hortari, (ad)monēre ut.* **reminiscence,** n. see REMEMBRANCE.

remit, v.tr. = to send back, *remittĕre;* to — money, etc., *mittĕre, emittĕre, condonare alci alqd, gratiam alcjs rei facĕre alci;* to — an oath, *jurisjurandi gratiam facĕre, solvĕre alqm sacramento;* to — a sum of money, *pecuniam creditam condonare* or *remittĕre, creditum condonare, debitum remittĕre alci;* to — taxes, *vectigalia omittĕre;* to — a part of a sum, *remittĕre alci de summâ;* to — a punishment, *poenam remittĕre;* to — sins, *peccata* or *delicta alci ignoscĕre, peccata alci concedĕre.* **remiss,** adj. see CARELESS, NEGLIGENT. **remission,** n. *remissio* (of tribute, *tributi*); to seek —, *remissionem petĕre;* to seek — for the past, *veniam praeteritorum precari;* see PARDON, SIN. **remittance,** n. by *pecunia.*

remnant, n. see REMAINDER.

remodel, v.tr. see ALTER, RENEW.

remonstrance, n. *(ad)monitio, monitus, -ūs.* **remonstrate,** v.intr. *alqm de alqâ re (ad)monēre, commonēre,* or with *ut* or *ne,* etc. (= to warn), *agĕre cum alqo de alqâ re* (in gen. = to treat, speak with anyone about).

remorse, n. *peccati dolor;* to feel —, *conscientiâ (peccatorum) morderi, conscientiâ animi (ex)cruciari, cruciari conscientiâ scelerum suorum;* see also SORROW. **remorseless,** adj. *immisericors;* see PITILESS.

remote, adj. 1, *remotus, amotus, semotus, disjunctus* (= isolated), *longinquus* (= a long way off); 2, fig. *ab alqâ re remotus, disjunctus, alienus;* see DISTANT. Adv. *remote, procul* (= far), *vix* (= hardly). **remoteness,** n. *longinquitas.*

remount, v.tr. and intr. *equum iterum conscendĕre.*

remove, I. v.tr. *amovēre* (= to carry, to move away, further), *avehĕre* (in a cart, ships, by horses, etc.), *abducĕre* (living beings), also *deportare* (then = to — an exile under military escort, esp. also of bringing anything from the provinces), *asportare* (= to carry away), *demovēre, removēre, submovēre* (on one side, persons and things), *tollĕre, auferre* (= to take away, things; *tollĕre* also = to erase, e.g. *maculas*), *eluĕre* (= to wash out, e.g. *maculas*), *depellĕre* (= to drive away, e.g. a complaint, pains, etc.); *subportare* (= to carry to a place), *subtrahĕre* (e.g. baggage belonging to an army, *impedimenta*); to — the things (after a meal), *tollĕre, auferre* (e.g. *mensam*); to — anyone, *transducĕre* (e.g. *populum Albanum Romam*), *collocare in alqo loco* (= to assign another residence, e.g. *gentem Allobrogum in vestigiis hujus urbis*), *rescribĕre ad* with accus., *transcribĕre in* with accus. (= to place into another class, e.g. *peditem ad equum rescribĕre, equitum turmas in funditorum alas transcribĕre*), *alqm alii muneri praeficĕre* or *praeponĕre* (to another office, situation, etc.); to — anything to a distance, *amovēre, removēre, abducĕre, deducĕre, ablegare* (= to send anyone away, in order to get rid of him, under a pretence), *amandare, relegare* (anyone on account of some misdemeanour, the latter to a certain spot; but both imply something disgraceful), *amoliri* (anyone or anything, when it causes great difficulty), *avertĕre* (of what is unpleasant to the senses), *subducĕre, submovēre* (by degrees), *depellĕre, repellĕre, propulsare* (by force), *emovēre* (e.g. *multitudinem e foro,* esp. in Liv.). **II.** v.intr. 1, in gen. *se (a)movēre;* = to go away, *abire, discedĕre;* = to go out of one's sight, *ex oculis* or *e conspectu abire, e conspectu recedĕre;* from a place, *excedĕre, evadĕre, se subducĕre* (imperceptibly, also with the addition of *clam,* e.g. *de circulo*); 2, = to change the place of residence, *(e)migrare (ex) loco, demigrare, commigrare, transmigrare, de* or *ex loco,* to, *in locum* (= to emigrate to another place, *in alium locum* or *in alia loca*), *migrare, emigrare domo* or *e domo* (from a house), *secedĕre in locum* (in a spirit of rebellion), *proficisci.* **III.** n. *gradus, -ūs* (= step). **removal,** n. 1, in gen. *deportatio* (in gen., and in particular the — of an exile to the place of his destination, Jct.), *depulsio* (= the removing a pain, *doloris*), *amandatio* (= the sending anyone away, in order to get rid, etc.), *relegatio,* or rarely *ablegatio* (= banishment), *amotio* (= a complete removing, e.g. *omnis doloris*), *remotio* (the repelling, e.g. *criminis*); 2, to — to another place or house, *migratio, demigratio* (= emigration, Liv., Nep.; of a whole order of the plebeians, Liv.), *profectio* (= starting).

remunerate, v.tr. *referre, reddĕre alqd* (in gen.), *remunerari alqm* (in a good sense), for anything with, by, *(com)pensare alqd alqâ re* (= to weigh one against the other, e.g. *beneficia bene-*

ficus, merita beneficus), *rependere alqd alqâ re* (= to weigh back, fig = to repay, e g *damnum alqâ re*) **remuneration,** n *remuneratio, compensatio*, for a —, *pretio* (for money), without any —, *sine pretio, gratis, gratuito*, see REWARD

rend, v tr (*dis*)*scindĕre* (= to tear), (*dis*)*rumpĕre* (lit and fig), (*di*)*lacerare* (= to lacerate, lit and fig), *distrahĕre, divellĕre* (= to pull in pieces, lit and fig), *dirumpĕre* (= to tear asunder) **rending,** n *discidium, diruptio, distractio, laceratio* **rent,** n = tear, use verb

render, v tr 1, *reddere, referre* (= to return, e g *gratias* = thanks), *praebēre, dare, praestare, tribuere* (= to give), to — service, *operam alci navare*, to — an account, *rationem reddĕre* or *referre*, 2, = to make, *facĕre, efficere, reddĕre*, or by special verbs, e g *augēre* (= to — greater), *minuĕre* (= to — less), 3, see TRANSLATE **render up,** v tr see SURRENDER **rendering,** n 1, by verb, 2, see TRANSLATION

rendezvous, n *constitutum* (= an appointment made), *locus ad conveniendum* (= the place appointed for the —), to appoint a — with, *tempus locumque constituĕre cum alqo*

renegade, n *qui sacra patria deserit* or *deseruit, apostata* (Eccl), = a deserter, *is qui deficit, desciscit ab alqo, transfuga*, m and f

renew, v tr (*re*)*novare*, = to restore, to repair, *reconcinnare, reficĕre* (more particularly by rebuilding), = to begin afresh, to repeat, *renovare, renovare et instaurare, instaurare* (*de integro*), *integrare, redintegrare* (= to begin quite from the beginning), *repetĕre* (= to repeat), *iterare* (= to do a second time), *refricare* (= to excite again), *referre* (= to bring back), *reconciliare* (*pacem, gratiam*, etc), to — the war, *bellum renovare, redintegrare, de integro instaurare, rebellare, rebellionem facĕre, bellum reparare, restituere* (two foregoing only of a conquered nation, without any odious meaning), to — the friendship, *amicitiam renovare*, with anyone, *se restituĕre in alcjs amicitiam*, to — the remembrance of anything in one's mind, *memoriâ alqd repetere* **renewable,** adj *qui* (*quae, quod*) *renovari potest* **renewal,** n *renovatio, instauratio, redintegratio*, of a war, *rebellio*

renounce, v tr *renuntiare alqd* or (post class) *alci rei, se alqâ re abdicare* (e g *magistratu*), *alqm* or *alqd ejurare, re*(*j*)*icĕre, repudiare* (= to reject), *remittĕre alqd* (that is, to let it go), *decedĕre* or *desistĕre alqâ re* or *de alqâ re* (= to stand away from), to — an opinion, *sententiâ* or *de sententia decedĕre*, to — your right, *de jure suo cedĕre* or *decedĕre, jus demittĕre* or *remittĕre*, to — honour and glory, *honorem et gloriam ab*(*j*)*icĕre* **renunciation,** n *cessio* (= the yielding of a thing to another), *repudiatio, rejectio*

renovate, v tr see RENEW **renovation,** n see RENEWAL

renown, n *fama* (chiefly in a good sense), *gloria, laus, nomen, claritas, claritudo* **renowned,** adj *clarus, illustris*, see CELEBRATED, FAMED, FAMOUS

rent, I. n 1, = profits derived annually from lands etc , *quaestus, -ūs* (= what we can gain by anything), *reditus, -ūs, fructus, -ūs* (= profit), *vectigal* (= tax, then of private rent), *merces, -ēdis*, f (= the — which the property brings in), 2, — of a house, *merces habitationis, habitatio*, what — does he pay? *quanti habitat?* to pay much —, *magni habitare* **II.** v tr 1, to let out, *locare*, 2, = to hire, *conducĕre redimĕre* cheaply, *parvo conducĕre, bene redimĕre*, dear, *magno conducĕre, male redimere* **rental,** n see RENT, I

reobtain, v tr *recipĕre, recuperare*

reopen, I. v tr *iterum recludere* (in gen) **II.** v intr of wounds, *recrudescĕre* (also fig).

repair, I. v tr *reficĕre, reparare*, (*re*)*sarcire, restituĕre, restaurare, reconcinnare* **II.** n to keep in good —, *alqd sartum tectum tueri* **repairs,** pl use verb REPAIR

repair, v intr, *se alqo conferre* or *recipĕre*, see also Go

reparation, n see INDEMNIFICATION, SATISFACTION

repartee, n perhaps *alqd acute responsum*, or *quod alqd salsi* or *salis habet*, see WIT

repast, n see MEAL

repay, v tr *reddĕre, referre, reponĕre, solvĕre*, to — anyone what is due, *alci satisfacĕre, alci debitum* or *pecuniam debitam solvĕre*, fig *pensare* or *compensare alqd alqâ re, rependĕre alqd alqâ re* (e g *damnum alqâ re*), with the same coin, *par pari referre*; see PAY **repayment,** n *solutio* (*pecuniae alci creditae*), or by verb

repeal, I. v tr *rescindĕre* (e g a decree, a will), *tollĕre* (= to do away with), *abolĕre* (= to abolish), *abrogare* (= a law, a decree, also a power), *derogare legi* or *alqd de lege* (partly), *obrogare legi* (= to substitute one law partially for another) **II.** n *abrogatio, derogatio, obrogatio*

repeat, v tr 1, *repetĕre* (in the widest sense), *iterare* (= to do, to say a second time, e g *saepe eadem*), *redintegrare* (= to do, bring forward, say quite afresh), *retractare* (= to go through again what has been learnt, read), *decantare* (gen in bad sense, = to keep repeating), 2, = to recite, of lessons, etc , perhaps *alqd memoriter pronuntiare* to — with the same words, *alqd iisdem verbis reddere* **repeated,** adj *repetitus, iteratus* Adv *iterum atque iterum, saepenumero, etiam atque etiam, identidem* **repeater,** n a watch, *horologium sonis tempus indicans* **repetition,** n 1, *repetitio, iteratio, redintegratio* (all three e g *verbi*), — of the same word at the end of a sentence (in rhetoric), *conversio, regressio* (of the same words in different clauses, Quint), 2, of a lesson, see REPEAT, 2

repel, v tr *repellĕre, propulsare* (= to drive away by force), *re*(*j*)*icĕre* (= to throw back), *deterrēre* (= to deter, e g *verberibus*), *fugare* (= to put to flight), to — an accusation, *culpam a se amovēre, crimen dissolvĕre* or *diluĕre, suspicionem a se propulsare*

repent, I. v intr *mores suos mutare, in viam redire, ad virtutem redire* or *revocari, ad bonam frugem se recipĕre.* **II.** v tr I —, *paenitet me alcjs rei*, or with infin , or with *quod* and subj , *subpaenitet me alcjs facti* (a little) **repentance,** n *paenitentia* (in gen) **repentant,** adj *paenitens*

repertory, n *thesaurus*

repetition, n see REPEAT

repine, v intr to — at, (*con*)*queri alqd* or *de alqâ re* **repining,** n *maeror* (= sorrow), *querela* (= complaint)

replace, v tr 1, = to put back, *reponĕre*, 2, to put in place of, *alqm alci, alqd alci rei substituĕre, alqm in alcjs locum sufficĕre* (= to elect in place of another magistrate)

replant, v tr *reserĕre*

replenish, v tr *implēre* (in gen what is empty, hollow), *explēre* (so that no space remains empty), *complēre* (= to fill quite full), *replēre* (= to fill to the brim), *opplēre* (= to cover a surface by filling up, also to fill to the top, so that it will not hold any more)

replete, adj see FULL **repletion,** n *satietas*

reply, I. v.intr. *respondēre* (to a thing, *alci rei*); to — to a charge, *criminibus respondēre*, *se defendēre*, or *purgare*; to — by letter, *rescribēre*; but I —, simply *ego autem* or *ego vero*. **II.** n. *responsio*, *responsum* (in gen.), *excusatio*, *defensio*, *purgatio* (to a charge), *oraculum*, *sors* (of an oracle).

report, I. v.tr. *nuntiare* (= to announce), *renuntiare* (= to send back information, both *alci alqd*), *certiorem alqm facĕre de alqā re* (= to inform), *afferre*, *deferre*, *referre ad alqm de alqā re* (= to give information, etc., more particularly to an authority), *per lit(t)eras significare* (= to inform in writing), *(e)narrare* (in gen. = to relate), *memoriae tradĕre* or *prodĕre*; *ferre*, *perhibēre* (= to say); *renuntiare alci* (in consequence of an order to that effect, or in reply to information received); it is —ed, *dicitur*, *dicuntur*, etc., with personal subj., or simply *prodēre* (of the historian); to — the whole proceedings, *omnem rem ordine enarrare*, *ordine edocēre omnia* (orally), *omnia perscribĕre* (in writing). **II.** n. **1**, *relatio* (= formal — to the senate; in gen. sense post Aug.), *narratio* (= narration), *rei gestae expositio*, *renuntiatio* (of an ambassador), *lit(t)erae* (in the form of a letter); **2**, = rumour, *fama*, *rumor*, *auditio*; I know it by —, *auditu illud accepi*; **3**, = noise, *fragor*, *crepitus*, *-ūs*; see NOISE. **reporter,** n. *qui defert ad alqm* (= who makes a report to anyone), *auctor rerum* (= voucher, authority), *notarius* (= shorthand writer, Plin. Min.).

repose, I. v.tr. *reponĕre*. **II.** v.intr. *quiescĕre*. **III.** n. *quies*, *-ētis*, f.; see REST. **repository,** n. *receptaculum*; see RECEPTACLE.

reprehend, v.tr. *reprehendĕre*; see REBUKE. **reprehensible,** adj. *culpā dignus*, *reprehendus*, *vituperabilis*, *vituperandus*. **reprehension,** n. *reprehensio*, *vituperatio*, *culpa*.

represent, v.tr. **1**, *repraesentare* (= to place clearly before one's eyes, Plin.), *exprimĕre*, *(ef)fingĕre* (= to express, picture, of the plastic art), *pingĕre*, *depingĕre* (= to paint, of the painter), *adumbrare* (= to sketch), *imitari*, + *simulare* (= to imitate), *indicare*, *significare* (= to indicate); **2**, = to describe in words, *(de)pingĕre* (= to paint, of the painter; then also of the orator, etc., = to picture, illustrate), *(ef)fingĕre* (of the sculptor, also of the orator, writer), *eloqui* (= to utter, of the speaker, e.g. *cogitata*), *dicendo effingĕre*, *alcjs rei imaginem exponĕre*, *adumbrare alqd* or *speciem et formam alcjs rei* (= to shade, sketch, of the painter and speaker), *describĕre* (= to describe in its characteristic features); to — anyone in a bad, wrong light, *deformare alqm* (Cic.); to — anything in a clear, lively manner, *alqd paene sub aspectum sub(j)icĕre*, *alqd sub oculos sub(j)icĕre*; = to show by reasoning, *alqm de alqā re monēre* or with *ut* or *ne* (= to warn), *alqm alqd docēre* (= to inform), *ostendĕre alci alqd*, or with accus. and infin. (= to show in words), *memorare* with accus. and infin. (= to mention); to — the advantage of, *alqm docēre quanta sit alcjs rei utilitas*; **3**, = to show by action, *agĕre*; to — a person, *alcjs partes agĕre*, *alcjs personam induĕre* or *suscipĕre* or *gerĕre* (all both on the stage and in daily life); to — a person of rank, *nobilem virum agĕre*; to — a drama, *fabulam dare*; **4**, = to supply the place of another, to — one's country, *gerĕre personam civitatis atque ejus decus et dignitatem sustinēre*. **representation,** n. **1**, = the act of describing, by the verb; **2**, = that which exhibits by resemblance, image; see IMAGE, LIKENESS, PICTURE; **3**, = an exhibition of the form of a thing, *repraesentatio* (t.t. of the elder Pliny); **4**, of a play, *actio* (= the act), *fabula* (= the play); **5**, = exhibition of a character in a play, by *agĕre*; see PART; **6**, = verbal description, *explicatio*, *descriptio* (in gen. in words, *descriptio* most particularly = a characteristic —), *adumbratio* (= sketch), *narratio* (of the state of things, how a matter stands, in a speech), *oratio*, *sermo* (= diction); **7**, in politics, by the verb; **8**, = the standing in the place of another, by circumloc. (e.g. by *alienā vice fungi*, or by *senatores a civibus delecti*). **representative, I.** adj. by *vice alcjs* or *officio*; — government, *civitas per quosdam a civibus delectos cives administrata*. **II.** n. *vicarius* (= substitute, deputy), *procurator*; a parliamentary —, *senator suffragiis civium delectus*.

repress, v.tr. *opprimĕre*, *comprimĕre* (e.g. *tumultum*).

reprieve, I. v.tr. **1**, = to respite after sentence of death, perhaps by *vitam alci prorogare*; **2**, fig. = to relieve for a time from suffering, by *differre*, *proferre* (= to postpone), *prolatare* (= to delay), *prorogare* (= to delay, put off). **II.** n. by *temporis intervallum*, *spatium* (= space of time, period in gen.), *prolatio* (= the act of —), *mora* (= delay).

reprimand, I. v.tr. *alqm reprehendĕre de* or *in alqā re*, *alqm vituperare de alqā re*, *alqm objurgare*. **II.** n. *reprehensio*, *vituperatio*, *objurgatio* (= blame), *convicium* (= scolding); see BLAME.

reprint, I. v.tr. a book, *librum denuo typis exscribendum curare*. **II.** n. see EDITION.

reprisal, n. **1**, see RETALIATION; **2**, —s, *vis vi repulsa*; to make —s, *vim vi repellĕre*, *par pari referre*.

reproach, I. n. as act, *maledictio* (rare), *exprobatio*, *animadversio*; the actual —, *opprobrium* (not in Cic. or Caes.); *probrum*, *maledictum*, *convicium*, *vox contumeliosa*, *verbum contumeliosum*, *contumelia*. **II.** v.tr. *convicium facĕre*, *alqm increpitare* or *incusare*, *in alqm invehi*, *alci maledicĕre*, *alqd alci ob(j)icĕre*, *objectare*; see REPROVE, BLAME, REVILE. **reproachful,** adj. *contumeliosus* (= abusive), or by verb. Adv. *contumeliose*, or by verb.

reprobate, I. adj. *perditus* (= lost to virtue or grace), *profligatus* (= morally ruined), comb. *profligatus et perditus*, *damnatus* (lit. = condemned; hence meton. = criminal, e.g. *quis te miserior? quis te damnatior?*), *sceleratus*, *scelerosus* (= burdened with crime). **II.** n. *homo perditus*, etc. **reprobation,** n. **1**, see CONDEMNATION; **2**, Eccl. *damnatio*, *reprobatio*.

reproduce, v.tr. *denuo generare* or *ferre*; to — a piece, *fabulam iterum referre* (Ter.). **reproduction,** n., **reproductive,** adj. by verb.

reproof, n. as act, or actual —, *vituperatio*, *culpa*, *castigatio*, *reprehensio*, *objurgatio*, *contumelia*, *animadversio*, *exprobatio*; to be a ground of —, *opprobrio* or *crimini esse alci*; to be open to the — of treachery, *in (summā) perfidiae infamiā esse*; see BLAME. **reprove,** v.tr. *alqm vituperare*, *reprehendĕre*, *exprobrare alci alqd* or *de alqā re*, *objurgare alqm de alqā re*, *alqm increpare*, *increpitare*, *incusare*; to — severely, *alqm graviter accusare*; to make a thing a ground to —, *crimini dare alci alqd*, *vitio dare* or *vertĕre alci alqd*. **reprover,** n. *reprehensor*, *vituperator*, *objurgator*, *castigator*.

reptile, n. *animal reptans*, or, where possible, by *serpens* (= serpent).

republic, n. *civitas libera et sui juris*, *respublica libera*, in the context also merely *respublica* (= a free constitution and a state which has such). **republican, I.** adj. generally by the genit. *reipublicae liberae* or simply *reipublicae* (e.g. a — government, *reipublicae (liberae) forma*);

to give a country a — constitution, *reipublicae formam civitati dare, a regis dominatione in libertatem populi vindicare rempublicam* (if the State was a monarchy before) **II.** n *reipublicae liberae civis* (= citizen of a republic), *reipublicae liberae studiosus, communis libertatis propugnator* (= one who is or speaks in favour of a — government)

republish, v tr *librum denuo edĕre* **republication,** n 1, as act, use verb, 2, the book itself, *liber (denuo editum)*

repudiate, v tr see REJECT **repudiation,** n *repudiatio* (in gen, but rare), of a son, *abdicatio filii* (= disowning and disinheriting), *divortium, repudium* (of a wife), see REJECTION

repugnant, adj *pugnans, repugnans* (of things), *diversus* (= quite contrary), *aversus, alienus ab alqâ re, alci rei contrarius, odiosus* (= hateful), see CONTRARY **repugnance,** n *repugnantia rerum* (= incompatibility), *odium* (= hatred), to feel —, *abhorrēre ab alqâ re, alqd fastidire, spernĕre, aspernari*

repulse, I. v tr *repellĕre* (= to drive back), from, etc, *ab*, etc, *propulsare* (away), *re(j)icĕre* (= to throw back) **II.** n 1, by the verbs, of a candidate, *repulsa;* 2, see REFUSAL **repulsive,** adj. *odiosus* (= hateful), *putidus* (= affected), *intolerabilis* (= unbearable); see DISGUSTING

repurchase, v tr *redimĕre*

reputable, adj see RESPECTABLE

reputation, n *bona fama,* generally merely *fama, bona existimatio,* in the context simply *existimatio, gloria* (= glory), *laus* (= praise), *nomen* (= name), *honor* (= esteem), bad —, *mala fama, infamia* **repute,** n see REPUTATION, to be in good —, *bene audire,* to be in bad —, *male audire, in infamiâ esse, infamem esse, in invidiâ esse, invidiam habēre* **reputed,** adj *qui (quae, quod) dicitur, fertur*

request, I. n *preces, -um* (= the act and the thing itself), *rogatus, -ūs* (only in ablat. sing), *rogatio* (as act), *supplicium* (= humble —, praise to God), *postulatio* (= urgent —, demand), at your —, *te petente, te auctore,* at my —, *rogatu meo, a me rogatus,* what is your —? *quid petis?* **II.** v tr *precari* (absolute), anything of anyone, *alqd ab alqo, alqm ut,* etc, *orare, rogare,* anything of anyone, *alqm alqd* (= to apply for), *alqd petĕre, poscĕre* (of a formal application, = to demand), *contendĕre ut* (urgently, = to insist), *flagitare, efflagitare* (violently, *alqd ab alqo*), *precibus exposcĕre* (= to violently demand, anything, *alqd,* e g *pacem*), *deprecari* (= to — on behalf of, anything, *alqd*), *implorare* (= to implore anyone, *alqm,* anything, *alqd*), *supplicare,* anyone on behalf of, *alci pro alqâ re, petĕre, postulare suppliciter,* anything of anyone, *alqd ab alqo, orare alqm supplicibus verbis, orare* or *rogare alqm suppliciter* (all = humbly, on one's knees), stronger by comb. *rogare atque orare, petĕre et contendĕre, orare obtestarique, orare atque obsecrare, implorare atque obtestari, obsecrare atque obtestari, obtestari atque obsecrare, precari atque orare, petĕre ac deprecari;* = to invite, *invitare, vocare*

requiem, n *missa defunctorum* (= mass for the dead, Eccl).

require, v tr *poscĕre, postulare, requirĕre, desiderare* (= to demand, to consider necessary), (= to need, *esse* with genit of a noun along with an adj, e g *multi laboris est*), *egēre alqâ re*; *ferre* (= to bring about necessity), *imperare,* from anyone, *alci* (= to command), *exigĕre* (= to exact, e g *vehicula*), to be —d, *onus esse,* if circumstances —, *si res or tempus postulat, cum res postulabit, si res cogit,* as time may —, *si tempus postulaverit, pro rerum statu* or *condicione*

requirement, n *postulatio, postulatum,* or by verbs **requisite, I.** adj *necessarius;* to be —, *necessarium esse, opus esse* (= to be necessary), *requiri, desiderari* (of what would be missed). **II.** n *necessitas* (= necessity), *usus, -ūs* (= use), *res necessaria,* a principal — for anything, *res maxime necessaria ad alqd,* the first — is that, etc, *primum est, ut,* etc **requisition,** n *petitio, rogatio, imperatum, quod imperatur.*

requite, v tr *reddĕre, referre* (= to give back), *alqd alqâ re compensare* or *rependĕre,* to — like for like, *par pari referre* **requital,** n use verb

rescind, v tr *rescindĕre, abrogare, tollĕre, abolēre, legi alqd derogare* (= to partly —), *obrogare* (= to — by substitution of another law), see REPEAL, ABOLISH.

rescript, n *responsio, responsum* (= answer in gen, the former, the act, the latter, the contents of the answer), *sententia* (= a lawyer's decision), *decretum* (= decree), *res judicata* (= decision arrived at in reference to a matter), *rescriptum* (of the emperor, prince, etc.), *codicilli* (= Ministerial decree, order of the Cabinet, Imperial Rome)

rescue, I. v tr *liberare alqm re* or *ab alqâ re, exsolvĕre alqâ re, servare ex alqâ re* (e g *periculo* or *ex periculo*), *alqm alci rei* or *ab, ex, de alqâ re eripĕre,* to — one's country from slavery, *patriam in libertatem vindicare* **II.** n *liberatio,* or by circumloc with *(con)servare*

research, n *eruditio* (= learning) *investigatio* or *cognitio* (*rerum,* = inquiry), a man of much —, *vir eruditissimus*

resemblance, n *similitudo, convenientia, congruentia, analogia* (in reference to words and ideas, in Cic, written in Greek ἀναλογία, or rendered by *proportio*), *congruentia morum* (in manners), — with, etc *similitudo* with genit (e g *morborum, animi*). **resemble,** v tr. *similem esse* with genit or dat, *ad similitudinem alcjs rei accedĕre* (instead of which we also find *prope, propius,* = nearer, *proxime,* = nearest), *accedĕre ad alqd* (of interior and exterior likeness), *facie alcjs similem esse, os vultumque alcjs referre* (as regards the countenance and the looks), *mores alcjs referre* (in character).

resent, v tr *aegre* or *moleste ferre, in malam partem accipĕre* **resentful,** adj *iracundus, iratus* (= angry) Adv *iracunde* **resentment,** n *ira, iracundia, stomachus*

reservation, n *condicio, exceptio,* with this —, that, etc, *hac lege* or *hac condicione* or *cum hac exceptione ut, his exceptis* **reserve, I.** v tr *retinēre* (= to keep back), *alqd excipĕre* (= to except), *alqd reservare, alqd reponĕre* (= to store up) **II.** n 1, in gen, *copia,* 2, = troops, *subsidia, -orum, copiae subsidiariae, cohortes subsidiariae, (milites) subsidiarii* (in gen), to keep in —, lit *in subsidio ponĕre* or *collocare,* fig *alqd recondĕre,* 3, see RESERVATION, 4, in manners, *verecundia* (= bashfulness), *modestia* (= modesty), *taciturnitas* (= silence), *cautio* (= caution), without —, *aperte, simpliciter* (= straightforwardly, openly), *sincere, libere, ingenue* (= freely) **reserved,** adj *taciturnus* (= taciturn), *occultus, tectus* (= secret), comb *occultus et tectus, modestus* (= modest), *verecundus* (= bashful) *cautus* (= cautious), towards anyone, *tectus ad alqm* **reservoir,** n *lacus, -ūs* (= a large receptacle for water, lake), *castellum* (= — of an aqueduct), *cisterna* (= a hollow place under ground for holding rain water, Plin), *piscina* (= pond), *aquae receptaculum* (Vitr)

reside, v intr 1, *habitare* (*locum, in loco, apud alqm,* etc), *sedem* or *sedem ac domicilium habēre alqo loco,* see LIVE. 2, fig *esse* or *versari* *in algâ re, alci inesse rei.* **residence,** n. **1,** *habitatio* (= the residing); if for a time, *mansio, commoratio;* **2,** *domus, -ûs,* f. (irreg.), *domicilium, aedes, -ium,* f. (= house). **resident,** n. **1,** by verbs; **2,** = a minister at a foreign court, perhaps *procurator rerum* or *legatus.*

residue, n. *pecunia residua, quod residuum* or *reliquum est.* **residuary,** adj. — legatee, *heres, -edis,* m. and f.

resign, v.tr. **1,** an office, *deponĕre (provinciam, dictaturam,* etc.), of an officer of state, *abdicare se magistratu,* (a consul) *consulatu,* (a dictator) *dictaturâ,* etc.; also *abdicare magistratum (consulatum), abire magistratu (consulatu,* etc.), *decedĕre (provinciâ* or *ex* or *de provinciâ,* = to retire after the expiration of the term of office); **2,** = to give up, *(con)cedĕre, deponĕre, omittĕre;* to — oneself to, to be —ed, *algd aequo animo ferre* or *pati, se ad algd submittĕre.* **resignation,** n. **1,** *abdicatio, ejuratio (dictaturae,* etc.); **2,** morally, *animus submissus* or *demissus* (in opp. to *animus elatus*).

resin, n. *rēsīna* (Plin.). **resinous,** adj. *resinaceus, resinosus* (Plin.).

resist, v.tr. *alci resistĕre, obstare, repugnare, obsistĕre, adversari, obniti;* to — the enemy, *hostibus resistĕre, hosti se opponĕre;* to — bravely, *fortiter repugnare* or *resistĕre;* anyone's request, *preces alcjs respuĕre* or *re(j)icĕre* or *repudiare.* **resistance,** n. *pugna, certamen* (= contest, fight), *defensio* (= defence); to render —, *resistĕre* (a person or thing, with arms or in words), *repugnare* (see above), *se defendĕre* (in battle); to prepare for —, *ad resistendum se parare.* **resistless,** adj. and adv. *cui nullo modo resisti potest.*

resolute, adj. *fortis* (= brave), *firmus, constans, stabilis, obstinatus, obfirmatus, promptus* (= ready), *gravis* (= serious). Adv. *fortiter, praesenti animo, firme, firmiter, constanter, obstinate, graviter.* **resoluteness,** n. *animi praesentia;* see RESOLUTION, 2. **resolution,** n. **1,** = dissolution, *(dis)solutio, dissipatio* (of a whole into parts), *explicatio* (= explanation); **2,** = determination, as quality, *constantia, stabilitas, firmitas, firmitudo, gravitas, obstinatio;* **3,** = purpose, *sententia, consilium, propositum;* **4,** — of a deliberative body, *sententia, decretum, scitum* (of a popular assembly, esp. *scitum plebis* or *plebiscitum*). **resolve,** v.intr. *decernĕre* (of magistrates, then in gen.), *consilium capĕre; statuĕre, constituĕre; destinare, animo proponĕre* (in one's own mind); *censēre, placet alci* (of the senate); *sciscĕre, jubēre,* comb. *sciscĕre jubēreque* (= to make a law, decree, of the people).

resonant, adj. *resonans.*

resort, I. v.intr. *locum celebrare, frequentare, ad locum ventitare, se conferre, commeare;* = to use, *uti;* to — to extremes, *ad extrema decurrĕre.* **II.** n. **1,** *conveniendi locus, locus ubi conveniunt;* **2,** = recourse, use verb.

resound, v.intr. *resonare, vocem reddĕre* or *remittĕre.*

resource, n. *auxilium, subsidium, praesidium, adjumentum.* **resources,** n. = means for an object, *facultates, opes,* pl., *pecunia* (= money), *bona, -orum* (= goods), *res familiaris* (= private property), *fortunae* (= prosperous condition), *patrimonium* (= inheritance), *census, -ûs* (= property legally valued).

respect, I. v.tr. **1,** *algm suspicĕre, verēri* (= to fear), *reverēri* (ante and post class.); *colĕre, observare, magni aestimare;* **2,** = to pay attention to, *alcjs rationem habēre, alci morem gerĕre;* **3,** = to relate; see RELATE, 3. **II.** n. *observantia* (= esteem), *reverentia* (= reverence), *honor* (= esteem); to have, feel — for, *algm verēri;* in every —, *omnino, ab omni parte, omni ex parte, in omni genere, omnibus rebus;* in — to, *de algâ re;* see REGARD, II. **respectable,** adj. *honestus, spectatus* (= tried), *bene moratus* (= moral), *vir bonae existimationis.* Adv. *honeste, bene.* **respectability,** n. *dignitas, honestas.* **respectful,** adj. *observans, venerabundus.* Adv. *reverenter* (Plin.). **respecting,** adj. *de* with abl.; see ABOUT. **respective,** adj. and adv. *proprius, suus,* etc. (e.g. our — brothers, *nostri fratres*), or by *quisque* (e.g. each has his — duties, *sua cuique sunt officia*); by *alter . . . alter, hic . . . ille.*

respire, v.intr. *respirare;* see BREATHE. **respiration,** n. *respiratio, respiratus, -ûs, spiritus, -ûs.* **respiratory,** adj. *qui (quae, quod) ad respiratum pertinet;* — organs, *pulmones,* pl. (= lungs).

respite, n. and v.tr. see REPRIEVE.

resplendent, adj. *splendidus;* see BRIGHT.

respond, v.intr., **response,** n. see ANSWER. **respondent,** n. *reus* (in a criminal trial), *is unde petitur* (in a civil); see DEFENDANT. **responsible,** adj. by *alci ratio reddenda est;* to be —, *algd praestare* (= to guarantee for); to make oneself — for anyone, *algd in se recipĕre.* **responsibility,** n. by the adj. **responsive,** adj. *apertus* (= open), by circumloc. (e.g. *qui amorem pro amore reddit,* — to affection; not —, *taciturnus*); see also FRANK.

rest, I. n. **1,** = quiet, *tranquillitas, (re)quies, -ētis,* f., *otium,* † *pax;* **2,** see PROP. **II.** v.intr. **1,** *(con)quiescĕre* (in gen.); = to sleep, *(con)quiescĕre, requiescĕre, quieti se dare* or *tradĕre, acquiescĕre, cessare* (= to be unemployed); **2,** to — upon, *algâ re (in)niti, suffulciri;* fig. *in algâ re niti, in algo* or *algâ re positum,* or *situm esse;* see DEPEND. **III.** v.tr. see PROP, SUPPORT. **resting-place,** n. *tranquillus ad quietem locus* (from the troubles of life), *deversorium* (= inn, also fig.), *sepulcrum* (= grave). **restive,** adj. *contumax.* **restless,** adj. *inquietus, commotus, sollicitus* (= anxious), *turbidus, turbulentus, tumultuosus* (of the sea, etc.). Adv. use adj. **restlessness,** n. *inquies, -ētis* (Plin.), *commotio* (e.g. *animi,* = — of mind), *sollicitudo.*

rest, n. = remainder, *quod restat, reliquum, residuum.* **restitution,** n. use verb. **restoration,** n. *refectio, reconciliatio* (e.g. *gratiae*), or by verb. **restorative,** adj. and n. *medicina.* **restore,** v.tr. *restituĕre, reficĕre* (in gen.), *reducĕre* (= to bring back, e.g. *regem*), *reddĕre* (= to give back); to — to health, *sanare, sanum facĕre, sanitatem alci restituĕre;* see RENEW. **restorer,** n. *restitutor, reconciliator* (e.g. *gratiae*).

restrain, v.tr. *reprehendĕre* (= to seize behind), *retrahĕre* (= to pull back, fig. to detain anyone against his will), *tenēre* (lit. = to hold in one's hand), *retinēre* (= to keep back a person or thing, e.g. *naves tempestatibus retinentur*), *continēre* (= to hold fast on all sides), *retardare* (= to retard the progress of a person or thing, lit. and fig.), *arcēre algm* or *algd* (= to refuse access to a person or thing), *cohibēre* (= to hinder the free motion of a person or thing, hence fig. to check, e.g. *iram*), *comprimĕre* (lit. = to press together, hence fig. violently to suppress, put a stop to, actions, intentions, passion), *reprimĕre, supprimĕre* (= to repress, hence = violently to check, e.g. *fletum*), *refrenare* (= to bridle), *circumscribĕre* (= to restrict), *(de)finire* (= to set bounds to); to — anyone from, by *cohibēre algd ab algâ re, defendĕre algd* or *algm ab algâ re, arcēre algm (ab) algâ re* (e.g. *hostes Galliâ, homines ab injuriâ poena arcet*), *algm revocare ab algâ re* (e.g. *a scelere*); to — oneself, *se tenēre, se continēre* (= to check oneself), *se cohibēre,* (e.g. in affliction). **restraint,** n. *moderatio,* *temperatio, modestia, continentia* (opp *luxuria*), *impedimentum, mora* (= hindrance), *modus* (= measure)

restrict, v tr *coercēre, reprimĕre, circumscribĕre, (de)finire, restringĕre*, see RESTRAIN **restriction,** n see RESTRAINT, LIMIT **restrictive,** n *qui* (*quae, quod*) *coercet*

result, I. v intr *oriri* (n. gen), *fieri, evenire, evadĕre* (= to turn out), *consequi* (*alqd* or *ut*), *proficisci, nasci, gigni, ex(s)istĕre, ex alqâ re* **II.** *exitus, -ūs eventus -ūs, effectus, -ūs, consequentia*, to lead to a —, *exitum habēre*, general —, *summa*.

resume, v tr see RECOMMENCE **resumption,** n use verb

resurrection, n **a morte ad vitam revocatio, resurrectio* (Eccl)

resuscitate, v tr †*resuscitare, alqm ab inferis excitare*, see REVIVE

retail, v tr *divendĕre, distrahĕre* **retail-dealer,** n *propōla*

retain, v tr *tenēre, retinēre, obtinēre, (con)servare* **retainer,** n 1, *cliens* (= client), *unus e suis* (= one of a bodyguard), 2, = fee, *arr(h)a(bo)*.

retake, v tr *reciperare, recipĕre*, to — from, *alqd alci auferre*

retaliate, v tr *par pari referre* **retaliation,** n use verb

retard, v tr *(re)morari, (re)tardare* (all of a person or thing, and of the person or thing that is the cause), *detinēre* (a person or thing, e g *naves tempestatibus detinebantur*), *producĕre, differre, proferre* (= to protract), to — from one day to the other, *alqd procrastinare*

retire, v intr *recedĕre* (persons and things), *concedĕre, abcedĕre, excedĕre, secedĕre* (all with *a*, etc), *decedĕre de* or *ex* (*provinciâ*, etc., of a magistrate), *se subtrahĕre* (imperceptibly), *recedĕre in otium, se removēre a negotiis publicis, se subtrahĕre a curiâ et ab omni parte reipublicae* (from public business), to — to a place, *alqo recedĕre, secedĕre, se referre* (= to go back), *se abdĕre in alqm locum* (= to conceal oneself from anything), *recedĕre ab*, etc (in gen) *se recipĕre ab*, etc , *se removēre ab*, etc , *se retrahĕre ab alqâ re* (e g from a banquet, *a convivio*). **retired,** adj *secretus, remotus, reductus, solitarius* a — life, *vita umbratilis* **retirement,** n *solitudo, vita a rebus publicis remota, vita otiosa, umbratilis, privata ac quieta* **retiring,** adj see MODEST

retort, I. v *regerĕre alqd alci* **II.** n *quod alqs alci regerit*, see REPLY

retrace, v tr = to seek again, *alqd ab alqâ re repetĕre*, to — one s footsteps, *pedem referre*, see RETURN

retreat, I. n 1, *reditus, -ūs* (= return), *receptus, -ūs* (of soldiers, etc), *fuga* (= flight), 2, = place of refuge, see REFUGE **II.** v intr *se recipĕre* (of soldiers and others), *pedem* or *gradum referre* (in fighting) *castra referre* (e g *in tutiora loca*, of the general), *exercitum* or *copias reducĕre alqo* (e g *in castra, ad mare*)

retrench, v tr *sumptus minuĕre, circumcidĕre, contrahĕre* **retrenchment,** n use verb

retribution, n *poena* (= punishment) **retributive,** adj *pro poenâ* (= in place of punishment)

retrieve, v tr see RECOVER **retriever,** n *canis*

retrograde, I. v intr 1, = to retire, *se recipĕre, pedem referre*, 2, = to grow worse, *in pejus mutari, deteriorem fieri*, **II.** adj *pejor, deterior* (= worse), a — movement, use *retro* (= backwards) **retrogression,** n *recessus, -ūs, regressus, -ūs.*

retrospect, n *respectus, -ūs* (lit. = looking back), (*praeteritorum*) *memoria* **retrospective,** adj *qui* (*quae, quod*) *alqd respicit*, to have a — effect, *ad praeterita pertinēre* Adv by *retro*

return, I. v intr *reverti* (in the perfect and pluperfect, *reverti, reverteram*, seldom *reversus sum*, etc , but as part *reversus* with active meaning), *redire* (of persons and things, e g of ships, rivers), *reducem esse* (of persons and things, e.g ships, etc.), *revenire* (e g *domum*), *remeare* (= to wander back), *alqd repetĕre* (= to seek again) , *recurrĕre, revolare* (= to fly back) **II.** v tr *reddĕre, restituĕre* **III.** n 1, = going back, *reditus, -ūs, regressus, -ūs, reversio* (before a journey is finished), 2, formal —, *renuntiatio, professio*, to make a —, *renuntiare, profiteri*, 3, = giving back, by verb, see II , 4, see PROFIT, INCOME **returned,** adj *redux*

reunite, v tr 1, lit *iterum conjungĕre*, see UNITE , 2, fig *reconciliare alqm cum alqo* or *alci* **reunion,** n *reconciliatio* (= reconciliation), see also ASSEMBLY

reveal, v tr *patefacĕre, manifestum reddĕre, aperire, retegĕre* (rare before Aug), (*in medium* or *lucem*) *proferre, evulgare, divulgare*, see DISCLOSE, BETRAY, PUBLISH **revelation,** n *patefactio*, or by verb, Eccl *revelatio*, the book of —, *Apocalypsis*

revel, I. v intr 1, *comis(s)ari*, 2, see DELIGHT **II.** n and **revelry,** n *comis(s)atio.* **reveller,** n *comis(s)ator*

revenge, I. n *ultio* (= the act of —), *vindicatio* (by the gods, the law, magistrates, and others through the law), *ulciscendi cupiditas, ira, iracundia* **II.** v tr *ulcisci alqm* or *alqd, vindicare alqm* or *alqd in alqm* (of laws and magistrates), comb *ulcisci et persequi, poenas capĕre pro alqo* or *alcjs rei, poenas alcjs rei expetĕre* (= to claim — for anybody or anything) **revengeful,** adj *ultionis cupidus, iratus* (= angry) Adv *irato animo*

revenue, n *vectigal, reditus, -ūs*

reverberate, I. v tr to — the rays, *radios repercutĕre, regerĕre* **II.** v intr see REBOUND **reverberation,** n *repercussus, -ūs* (Plin , Tac)

reverence, I. n 1, *observantia, reverentia, veneratio, verecundia* (stronger than *reverentia*), religious —, *religio* or *pietas erga Deum*, as a title use in gen *vir reverendus*, of a king, *augustus*, 2, to make a —, (*reverenter*) *alqm salutare* **II.** or **revere,** v tr *alqm observare, colĕre et observare*, or *verēri et colĕre, alqm verēri, reverentiam adversus alqm adhibēre, reverentiam alci habēre* or *praestare* **reverend,** adj *reverendus* in gen (or Eccl) **reverent,** adj *verecundus* (= shy, modest), *religiosus, venerabundus* (= devout), *pius* (= dutiful) Adv *verecunde, religiose, pie*, they went — into the temple, *venerabundi templum iniēre* (Liv).

reverie, n *cogitatio* (= thought), lost in a —, *in cogitatione defixus, nescio quid meditans*

reverse, I. v tr *invertĕre, (com)mutare, convertĕre*, see CHANGE **II.** n 1, = change, *(com)mutatio, vicissitudo, vices* (gen), pl *vices* more common (mostly poet), *conversio*, 2, = contrary, *contrarium*, 3, = defeat, *clades, -is*, f , see DEFEAT , 4, = hind part, *pars aversa* **reversible,** adj *qui* (*quae, quod*) *facile inverti potest* **reversion,** n 1, see REVERSE, II , 2, legal t t *hereditas* **revert,** v intr *redire ad alqm, cedĕre alci*

review, I. v.tr. *inspicĕre, perspicĕre, cognos-*

cēre, percensere, recensēre, corrigĕre; to — an army, *recensēre* (i.e. to number), *inspicĕre* (e.g. the legions, *arma, viros, equos cum curâ, singulos milites*), *numerum alcjs inire* (e.g. troops), comb. *alqd recensēre et numerum inire, lustrare* (of the censor, then the army by the general, with religious rites), *oculis lustrare, oculis obire* (with a glance); to — a book, perhaps *de libro judicium exprimĕre*. **II.** n. 1, *conspectus, -ūs*, or by verbs; 2, of troops, *recensio* (with a view to numbering), *lustratio* (= rites at beginning of a —), in gen. *simulacrum pugnae, ludicrum certamen, imago pugnae, justa belli species* (all in Liv. xl. 6); 3, see JOURNAL. **reviewer,** n. *qui de libro judicium suum exprimit*.

revile, v.tr. *conviciari, convicium alci facĕre, alqm conviciis consectari* or *incessĕre, alci maledicĕre, alqm maledictis insectari, maledicta in alqm dicĕre* or *conferre, probris et maledictis alqm vexare, maledictis* or *probris alqm increpare, contumeliosis verbis alqm prosequi*. **reviler,** n. *conviciator, maledicus*. **reviling,** n. *maledictio, verborum contumelia, probrum, convicium*.

revise, I. v.tr. see REVIEW, CORRECT. **II.** n. *plagula de prelo emendanda*, or by verb. **revision,** n. *lima* (lit. = file), *emendatio, correctio*; see CORRECTION.

revisit, v.tr. *revisĕre*.

revive, I. v.intr. *reviviscĕre, ad vitam redire* (lit. and fig., of persons and things), *renasci* (fig. of things), *revirescĕre, recreari, respirare*. **II.** v.tr. *vitam alcjs restituĕre, vitam alci reddĕre*.

revoke, v.tr. *irritum esse jubēre, abrogare, rescindĕre* (*legem*, etc.); see ABOLISH, RESCIND. **revocable,** adj. † *revocabilis, qui* (*quae, quod*) *facile mutari potest*. **revocation,** n. *revocatio* (in gen.), *abrogatio, rescissio* (of a law); see ABROGATION.

revolt, I. v.intr. *seditionem movēre, imperium auspiciumque abnuĕre* (= to refuse obedience, of soldiers), *rebellare, rebellionem facĕre, imperium alcjs detrectare, deficĕre ab alqo* or *ab alcjs imperio, desciscĕre ab alqo*. **II.** n. *seditio, defectio, rebellio, tumultus, -ūs*. **revolter,** n. (*homo*) *seditiosus, qui ab alqo desciscit*. **revolting,** adj. *taeter* (*tet-*), *nefandus, foedus, turpis*; see DISGUSTING.

revolution, n. 1, = turning, *conversio, orbis, anfractus, -ūs* (*solis*), *ambitus, -ūs*; 2, political —, *novae res*; see also REVOLT. **revolutionary,** adj. lit. *seditiosus, novarum rerum studiosus* or *cupidus*; fig. *novissimus* (= very strange). **revolutionist,** n. (*homo*) *novarum rerum cupidus*. **revolutionize,** v.tr. *commutare* (lit. and fig.).

revolve, I. v.intr. *se* (*re*)*volvĕre* or (*re*)*volvi, se circumagĕre* or *circumagi, circumverti*. **II.** v.tr. *alqd animo volvĕre* or *volutare*. **revolver,** n. see PISTOL.

revulsion, n. (*com*)*mutatio*; see CHANGE.

reward, I. v.tr. *praemium alci dare, tribuĕre*, (*per*)*solvĕre, pretium alci deferre, praemio alqm ornare* or *decorare, remunerari alqm praemio*. **II.** n. *remuneratio*, for, *alcjs rei*; (= the thing itself, *praemium* or *pretium, fructus, -ūs* (= fruit). **rewarder,** n. *qui alci praemium dat*, etc.

rewrite, v.tr. *iterum scribĕre*.

rhapsody, n. perhaps *dictum grandiloquum*, or *ampullae* (i.e. *ampullae et sesquipedalia verba*).

rhetoric, n. *rhetorica* or *rhetorice* (ῥητορική), pure Latin *ars orandi* or *bene dicendi scientia* (Quint.). **rhetorical,** adj. *rhetoricus* (ῥητορικός), *oratorius*. Adv. *rhetorice*.

rheum, n. *gravedo, humor*. **rheumatism,** n. *cruciatus, -ūs*, or *dolor* in gen.

rhinoceros, n. *rhinoceros* (Plin.).

rhubarb, n. *radix pontica* (Cels.).

rhyme, I. n. *extremorum verborum similis sonitus, -ūs*. **II.** v.intr. *versus extremis verbis inter se consonantes*, or *versus qui extremis verbis similiter sonant, facĕre*.

rhythm, n. *numerus* or in the pl. *numeri, modus, modi*, pl., *rhythmus* (Quint.; Cic. uses Greek ῥυθμός). **rhythmical,** adj. *numerosus*. Adv. *numerose*.

rib, n. *costa*; of a ship, *statumen*.

ribald, adj. *obscenus*; see FILTHY. **ribaldry,** n. *sermo obscenus, obscenitas*.

riband, ribbon, n. *redimiculum* (= anything to tie round the head, forehead), *taenia, fascia* (= small bit of cloth, etc., for a head-dress), *lemniscus* (for garlands, also for an order), *vitta* (= head-band), *infula* (= fillet, also badge of honour).

rice, n. *oryza*; as a dish, by *puls ex oryzâ cocta*.

rich, adj. *dives* (*dis*, opp. *pauper*), *locuples* (= having much property and in a flourishing condition), *opulentus* (= who has means, money, influential), *copiosus, copiis dives* or *locuples* (= rich in provisions of all kinds, *copiosus* also of a fertile mind), *pecuniosus, magnae pecuniae, bene nummatus, argento copiosus* (= having much money), *fortunatus* (= fortunate, wealthy), *beatus* (= who has everything he can wish for), *abundans* (= who has so much that he can give unto others; also of a fertile mind, opp. *inops*), *opimus* (= rich, abundant, e.g. booty, profit, kingdom, etc.), *amplus* (= considerable, splendid in a gen. sense, e.g. reward, funeral), *uber* (= ample, in large quantities, or yielding a great deal), *opimus* (= sumptuous), *pretiosus* (= costly), *lautus* (= luxurious); — in, *dives alqâ re* (poetic with gen.), *opulentus alqâ re, uber alqâ re* or *alcjs rei, ferax alcjs rei* (= yielding, etc., of countries, fields, etc.), *frequens alqâ re* (where anything exists in large numbers, e.g. *Nilus feris et beluis frequens*). Adv. *copiose, beate* (= with all blessings), *abundanter, ample* (often in superl. *amplissime*), *pretiose* (= expensively), *laute* (= well, luxuriously). **riches,** n. *divitiae* (= large fortune), *opulentia* (= ample means, as regards money, property, etc.), *opes*, f. pl. (= means wherewith to accomplish a thing), *fortunae* (= blessing of Providence), *facultates, -um*, pl., *copiae* (= means of all kinds). **richness,** n. *copia, abundantia, ubertas* (of soil, etc.); see ABUNDANCE, FERTILITY.

rick, n. *meta* (Col.).

rid, get rid of, v.tr. *alqm liberare, expedire alqâ re, alqm eripĕre ex* or *ab alqâ re* (all three = to free from danger, and esp. from any unpleasant position, etc.), *alqd deponĕre* (= to lay aside), *dimittĕre* (= to dismiss); to have got — of, *solutum, vacuum esse alqâ re* (e.g. fear); see FREE, DISMISS. **riddance,** n. *liberatio*; good —, *abi* (*abite*).

riddle, I. n. *aenigma, -ătis*, n., *ambāges, -um*, f. (= ambiguity in speech or action); you talk in —s, *ambāges narras*. **II.** v.intr. *aenigmata loqui*. **riddled,** adj. e.g. — with wounds, *graviter vulneratus, multis vulneribus oppressus*.

ride, v.intr. *equitare, equo vehi* (in gen.); to — up to, *equo vehi ad alqm* or *ad alqd, adequitare ad alqm* or *ad alqd, obequitare alci rei*; to — quickly, *equo concitato* (of several, *equis citatis*) *advehi* or *advolare, equo admisso* (*equis admissis*) *accurrĕre*; to — at anchor, *in ancoris consistĕre*. **rider,** n. *eques, -ĭtis*, m.; to be a very good —, *equitandi* *peritissimum esse.* **riding,** n *equitatio, equitatus*, -ūs (Plin) **riding-master,** n *qui alqm equitare docet*

ridge, n *montis dorsum, jugum*

ridicule, I. n *(de)ridiculum*, see MOCKERY **II.** v tr anyone or anything, *irridēre, deridēre alqm* or *alqd, in risum vertĕre* (e g *cognomen*), see MOCK **ridiculous,** adj *ridiculus, ridendus, deridiculus, perridiculus, subridiculus*, see ABSURD Adv *(per)ridicule, subridicule, jocularitei, deridendus, jocularis* (= facetious) **ridiculousness,** n by adj

rife, adj to be — (e g a report), *fertur, fama* or *res percrebescit* or *percrebuit*

rifle, n see GUN

rifle, v tr see PLUNDER.

rift, n *rima*, see CRACK

rig, v tr *armare* **rigging,** n *armamenta, -orum*

right, I. adj 1, (in geometry) *rectus*, — angled, *orthogonios*; see STRAIGHT, = not left, *dexter* (opp *sinister*), the — hand, *(manus) dextra*, 2, = morally —, *aequus, rectus, verus* (= true), *accuratus, diligens* (= careful, accurate), *justus*, it is —, *fas (jusque) est*, it is not — of you to, etc, *non recte fecisti quod*, etc, it serves me —, *jure plector* (Cic), it serves you —, *merito tibi accidit*, 3, = correct, *rectus, verus* (true), *justus* (just as it should be, e g measure, size), often also by *ipse*, the — word for anything, *verum rei vocabulum*, to go the — road, *rectam viam ingredi* (lit), to go the — way about it, *rectam rationem inire* (= to choose the — remedy), I have got to the — house, *ad eam ipsam domum pervenio quo tendo*, at the — time, *in tempore, opportune, opportuno tempore* (= convenient), *tempore suo, tempore ipso* (= in due time), *ad tempus* (= at the right moment), to make the — use of anything, *recte* or *bene* or *sapienter uti alqā re*, you are —, *res ita est ut dixisti, sunt ista ut dicis*, to do what is —, *recte agĕre* **II.** adv *recte, vere, juste, rite* (= duly), *jure, merito* (= deservedly), *bene* (= well), *diligenter, accurate* (= accurately), *plane, prorsus* (= altogether, I do not — understand, *non satis* or *plane intellego*) **III.** n = — to do anything, *jus, potestas alcjs rei* (= power, as a —, to do so), I have a — to do it, *jus est alqd facĕre, potestatem habeo alqd faciendi*, *fas* (= the divine law, what is — in the sight of God, hence, what is in the course of nature, what our conscience allows us to do), contrary to all —s, *contra jus fasque, contra jus ac fas*, by —s, *jure, suo jure* (= from his own personal —), *merito* (= deservingly), with the greatest —, *justissime, justo jure, optimo jure, merito atque optimo jure, jure meritoque, jure ac merito, merito ac jure* **righteous,** adj *bonus, probus, sanctus, aequus, justus* Adv *bene, probe, sancte, juste* **righteousness,** n *probitas, sanctitas* **rightful,** adj *legitimus, justus, debitus* (= due), or *quo de jure est* Adv *lege, legitime, juste, jure*, see LEGALITY, RIGHT, II

rigid, adj *rigidus, rigens* (lit, = stiff with cold, then fixed in gen, e g eyes, hair, *rigidus* also fig inflexible, unsociable, e g *mores rigidi*), *immobilis* (= immovable, of persons and things), *durus* (= without grace, delicacy, opp *mollis*), *severus* (= severe) Adv *rigide, dure, severe* **rigidity,** n *rigor* **rigorous,** adj see RIGID **rigour,** n *rigor* (opp *clementia*, also of a thing, e g *animi, veteris disciplinae*, mostly post Aug), *severitas, duritia*

rill, n *rivus* (*rivulus* very late, except in fig sense)

rim, n *labrum* (= lip), *ora* (of a shield, etc), see EDGE

rime, n. *pruina*

rind, n *cortex* (of trees), *liber* (= the inward bark), see SKIN

ring, I. n *circulus, orbis, -is*, m (in gen), *an(n)ulus* (= — on a finger, of curtains, chains, hair), *inaures, -ium*, f (= ear- —s), = circle, fig *corona, orbis, -is*, m, *circulus* **II.** v tr and intr *tinnire*, to — at the door, *pulsare fores* or *januam* (= to knock), to — for anyone, *(aes) tinnitu alqm arcessĕre* (lit), *digitis concrepare* (= to snap with the fingers, as the Romans did when they wished to call a slave), of bells, *sonare* (intr); to — the bells, *campanam pulsare*, = to resound, *resonare*, to — the changes, *alqd iterare*, = to surround, *circumdare*, see SURROUND **ring-dove,** n *columba* (= blue rock), *palumbes, -is*, m and f (= stock dove) **ringing, I.** adj †*sonorus, canorus* **II.** n †*tinnitus, -ūs*, or by *sonus* **ringleader,** n *auctor, princeps, caput, dux, fax* (lit = torch), *tuba* (lit = trumpet). **ringlet,** n *cirrus*, see CURL **ringworm,** n *lichen* (Plin)

rinse, v tr *eluĕre, colluĕre, perluĕre*

riot, I. n 1, *seditio, motus, -ūs, concitatio* (e g *plebis contra patres*), *tumultus, -ūs* (of slaves, peasants, allies against the Romans themselves), *vis repentina* (= sudden rising), 2, = extravagant conduct, *comis(s)atio* (= feasting), *rixa* (= brawling) **II.** v intr 1 *seditionem (tumultum*, etc) *movēre* or *concitare*, 2, = to run riot, *comis(s)ari* (= to revel), *bacchari* (= to rave), *luxuriare* (= to live riotously) **rioter,** n *(homo) seditiosus, turbulentus*, etc **riotous,** adj. 1, *seditiosus, rerum evertendarum* or *rerum novarum cupidus, rerum mutationis cupidus, turbulentus*, comb. *seditiosus ac turbulentus* (e g *civis*), 2, *comis(s)abundus*, — living, *luxuria* Adv *turbulente, seditiose, luxuriose*

rip, v tr 1, *scindĕre, divellĕre* (= to tear) see TEAR, CUT, 2, *dissuĕre* (a seam, rare)

ripe, adj *maturus, tempestivus* (lit and fig), *coctus*, a — old age, *senectus, -ūtis*, — judgment, *judicium* **ripen, I.** v tr *maturare* (lit and fig) **II.** v intr *maturari, maturescĕre, ad maturitatem pervenire, maturitatem assequi* or *adipisci* **ripeness,** n *maturitas* (lit and fig), *maturitas tempestiva* (lit), *tempestivitas* (lit and fig)

ripple, I. v intr perhaps *leni murmure defluĕre*, or *delabi, susurrare, leniter* †*sonare* **II.** n perhaps *unda*, the — of the waves, *lene undarum murmur*

rise, I. v intr 1, = to get up, *(ex)surgĕre, consurgĕre* (esp of a number of people), *assurgĕre* (esp as a mark of honour to anyone, *alci*), to — in the morning, *expergisci* (= to awake) (*e lectulo* or *lectulo* alone) *surgĕre*, from table, *a cenā*, to — from illness, *e morbo assurgĕre*, of the sun, stars, etc, of sunrise, *(di)lucescĕre, illucescĕre, (ex)oriri*, of the wind, tempest, etc, *consurgĕre, cooriri*, 2, = to increase, *surgĕre, increbescĕre, crescĕre*, to — in the air, *(in) sublime ferri*, of a river, *nasci* (Plin), *proficisci, gigni, (ex)oriri*, to — from beneath, *emergĕre*, of thoughts, *subire mentem* or *animum, alci succurrĕre*, of prices, *augēri, crescĕre, ingravescĕre*, to — in dignity, in the world, etc, *ad honores ascendĕre, altiorem dignitatis gradum consequi*, 3, = to rebel, *cooriri* (e g *ad bellum*), see REBEL, to — again, *resurgĕre* (Eccl), **II.** n and **rising,** n *(ex)ortus, -ūs* (of the sun, etc), *a(d)scensus, -ūs* (= place where one ascends), — of a hill, so *clivus leniter assurgens* (of a gentle —), = origin, *ortus, -ūs, caus(s)a, fons, -ntis*, m, *origo*, to give — to, *locum alci rei dare* or *praebēre, efficĕre*, see CAUSE, — in price *annona carior* (of corn), in gen use verb, = insurrection, see REBELLION **rising,** adj of ground, *(collis) paul(l)ulum ex planitie editus* or *assurgens* fig. perhaps *qui gratiâ (in dies) augetur* (of reputation, etc.); see PROSPEROUS.

risible, adj. *quod ad ridendum pertinet.* **risibility,** n. by *ridēre* (e.g. I have nothing to excite my —, *non habeo quod rideam*).

risk, I. n. *periculum* (= danger), *discrimen, alea alcjs rei* (= danger, uncertainty in anything); at my —, *meo periculo*; to take anything at one's own —, *alqd periculi sui facĕre.* **II.** v.tr. *alqd in aleam dare, alqd in periculum* or *discrimen adducĕre* or *vocare*; to — one's life, *committĕre se periculo mortis.*

rite, n. by *ritus, -ūs*; see CEREMONY. **ritual, I.** adj. *de ritu.* **II.** n. *liber* or *formula sacrorum.* **ritualist,** n. *homo de sacris (rite faciendis) diligentissimus.*

rival, I. n. *aemulus,* fem. *aemula* (in gen.), *rivalis* (as a lover), *competitor* (political). **II.** adj. *aemulans cum alqo.* **III.** v.tr. *(con)certare* or *contendĕre cum alqo* (= to contest), *aemulari alqm* or *cum alqo* (= to strive for anything which another tries to gain). **rivalry,** n. *aemulatio.*

river, I. n. *fluvius, flumen, amnis, rivus* (= rivulet, any small river which flows), *torrens* (= torrent); the — flows quickly, *fluvius citatus* (or *incitatus*) *fertur*; slowly, *fluvius placide manat*; the — is rapid, *fluvius violentus invehitur*; is low, *amnis tenui fluit aquâ*; a swollen —, *rivus inflatus*; to direct a — into another channel, *amnem in alium cursum deflectĕre.* **II.** adj. *fluviaticus, fluviatilis, fluvialis.* **river-basin,** n. *locus ubi omnia flumina in unum defluunt.* **river-god,** n. *numen fluminis.* **river-horse,** n. *hippopotamus* (Plin.).

rivet, I. v.tr. *clav(ul)o figĕre.* **II.** n. *fibula ferrea, clavus* (nail).

road, n. 1, *via* (= the way for going or travelling), *iter* (= the going, or the — itself); on the —, *in* or *ex itinere*; a — goes to, *iter fert alqo*; 2, fig. the right —, *via*; the wrong —, *error.* **roads,** n. pl. = anchorage for ships, roadstead, *statio.* **roadside,** adj. by *in itinere.* **roadster,** n. *caballus.*

roam, v.intr. *palari* (e.g. *per agros*), *vagari.* **roaming,** adj. *vagus.*

roan, adj. *badius albis maculis sparsus.*

roar, I. v.intr. of beasts, *mugire* (of an ox, also of thunder, etc.), *rudĕre* (= to bray like an ass, also of lions, stags, etc.), *rugire, fremĕre* (of lions), *vociferari* (of men). **II.** n. *mugītus, ruditus, rugītus* (all -ūs), *vociferatio.*

roast, I. v.tr. *assare, torrēre, frigĕre* (the two foregoing = to fry). **II.** adj. *assus*; — meat, *assum, caro assa, assa,* n. pl. (several pieces); — beef, *assum bubulum*; — veal, *assum vitulinum.*

rob, v.tr. *rapĕre, latrocinari* (= to — on the highway); *alqm alqâ re depeculari* (men, temples, etc., rare), *alqm alqâ re (ex)spoliare, despoliare, expilare, compilare* (= to strip temples, the public treasury, etc., the latter also *alqd alqâ re*), *fraudare alqm re* (by cheating), *alqd alci eripĕre* (= to snatch away), *adripĕre, auferre* (= to take away); to — of children, *orbare.* **robber,** n. *ereptor* (plunderer), *praedo* (= who seeks after booty both by sea and by land), *latro* (= burglar), *pirata* (= pirate), *fur* (= thief); band of —s, *latronum* or *praedonum globus, latronum* or *praedonum turba,* or simply *latrones, praedones,* or *latrocinium* (Cic., and fig. of Catiline and his associates). **robbery,** n. *rapina, spoliatio* (the act), *latrocinium* (= highway —; *latrocinium* alone or *latrocinium maris* also = piracy), *praedatio* (= taking booty); robberies of all kinds, *latrocinia et raptus*; to commit —, *rapĕre, rapinas facĕre, latrocinari, piraticam facĕre* or *exercēre* (by sea).

robe, I. n. *vestis* (= dress in gen.), *amictus, -ūs* (= anything thrown over), *stola, palla* (= dress for the Roman ladies), *trabea* (= robe of state); see DRESS, GOWN. **II.** v.tr. *vestire.*

robust, adj. *robustus*; see STRONG.

rock, n. *saxum* (= any mass of stones), *rupes, -is* (= steep —, on the land and in the sea), *scopulus* (in prose, = dangerous — in the water, cliff), *cautes, -is,* f. (= ragged —, crag), comb. *saxa et cautes*; fig. *arx* (= castle, —, e.g. *arx est illa spei salutisque nostrae*). **rocky,** adj. *scopulosus, saxosus, saxeus* (= made of —).

rock, I. v.tr. *movēre, quatĕre.* **II.** v.intr. *movēre.*

rocket, n. by *radius pyrius.*

rod, n. *virga* (in gen.), *ferula* (= fennel-giant, for chastising children), *arundo* (cane), *decempĕda* (in land-surveying).

roe, n. of fish, *ova, -orum,* pl.

roe, n. = female deer, *caprea.* **roebuck,** n. *capreolus, caprea.*

rogation, n. *rogatio* (= the proposal of a law; Eccl. = prayer), *supplicatio* (= prayer).

rogue, n. *(homo) perfidus, nequam, scelestus, sceleratus, fraudulentus, veterator, (tri)furcifer* (Com.). **roguery,** n. *fraus, -dis,* f., *dolus.* **roguish,** adj. 1, *perfidus, fraudulentus*; see under ROGUE; 2, = saucy, *protervus, lascivus.* Adv. *perfide, nequiter, sceleste, scelerate, fraudulenter, proterve, lascive.*

roll, I. v.tr. *volvĕre, devolvĕre* (down), *evolvĕre* (out), *provolvĕre* (forward), *convolvĕre* (together), *volutare, versare* (over and over); to — round anything, *alqd alci rei circumvolvĕre, involvĕre.* **II.** v.intr. *convolvi, se volutare, volutari*; tears — down his cheeks, *lacrimae per genas manant.* **III.** n. *orbis, cylindrus* (= cylinder); = what is rolled up, *volumen* (of paper); = a — of bread, *panis*; — of a drum, *tympani pulsatio* (= beating), or *sonus* (= sound); = list, *album* (e.g. *senator, -ium,* Tac.). **roller,** n. *cylindrus* (for rolling things round, or for levelling ground), *phalangae* (put under ships). **roll-call,** n. *album*; to answer to the —, *ad nomina respondĕre.*

Roman Catholic, adj. **Catholicus,* **qui fidem Romanae Ecclesiae tenet.*

romance, I. n. *fabula.* **II.** v.intr. *fabulari.* **romantic,** adj. *fictus* (= feigned), *mirus, novus* (= wonderful), *amoenus* (= pretty, of a place). Adv. *ut in fabulis fit, ficte, mire, amoene.*

romp, v.intr., see PLAY.

roof, I. n. *tectum, culmen*; buildings without —, *aedificia hypaethra*; to receive under your —, *hospitio excipĕre alqm.* **II.** v.tr. to —, *tecto tegĕre*; to unroof, *nudare tecto.* **roofless,** adj. *hypaethrus, nudatus*; = homeless, *sine tecto.*

room, n. 1, *locus, spatium* e.g. to make —, *viam* or *locum dare, locum dare et cedĕre*; *populum* or *turbam submovēre* (e.g. for the consul by the lictors), *partem sedis* or *subselli vacuam facĕre* (= to give up one's seat); see SPACE; 2, = apartment, *conclave, cubiculum* (= chamber, bed—); *hospitalia, -ium,* n. (= guest chambers); dining-—, *cenaculum*; (all the —s above the ground-floor were *cenacula*); *cenatio*; a small —, *cenatiuncula*; bed—, *cubiculum* (see Smith, "Dict. Antiq. Art.," *Domus*). **roomy,** adj. *spatiosus*; see SPACIOUS.

roost, I. n. *pertica gallinaria.* **II.** v.intr. *stabulari.*

root, I. n. 1, *radix* (= — of a tree; then — of the tongue, hair, feather, mountain, hill, etc.; fig. = origin); by the —s, *radicitus, radicibus*; 2, fig. *stirps, fons, -ntis,* m., *caus(s)a* (= cause, origin, source), with the —, *radicitus, radicibus* **II.** v intr *radicari* (lit Col), *radices capĕre* or *mittĕre* (lit), *inhaerescĕre in mente* (fig of that which one does not forget), *radices agĕre* (= to take —, also fig = to gain a firm footing), *insidere, inveterascĕre* (both fig, the former of a superior, the latter of a habit, an evil, etc) **III.** v tr *figĕre, alĕre* (fig = to foster), to — up, *evellĕre* **rooted,** adj *inveteratus, confirmatus* (fig), deeply —, fig *penitus defixus*

rope, n *restis* (= a thin —), *funis*, is, m (= a thick —), *rudens* (= a cable), *retinaculum* (of a ship), *funis ancorarius, ancorale* (= anchor —), *funis extentus* (= tight —)

rosary, n 1, = garden of roses, *rosarium, rosetum*, 2, = beads, *rosarium* (Eccl) **rose,** n *rosa* **rosy,** adj *roseus*

rosemary, n *ros marinus*

rosin, n *resina*

rostrum, n *rostra, -orum*

rot, I. v intr *putrescĕre, putrefieri, tabescĕre* **II.** n *tabes, -is* **rotten,** adj *putrefactus, putridus.*

rotate, v intr *se volvĕre, volvi, se circumagĕre, circumagi*, see REVOLVE **rotation,** n *ambitus, -ūs, circuitus, -ūs, circumactio* (e g *rotarum*), *circuitio* or *circinatio* (of the planets), *cursus, -ūs* (= course), in —, *ordine*, see SUCCESSION **rotatory,** adj *versatilis*

rotundity, n *figura rotunda, rotunditas* (Plin)

rouge, I n *fucus* **II.** v intr *fucare*

rough, adj *asper* (e g road, places, climate, voice, life or mode of living, man), *salebrosus* (= rugged, uneven), *confragosus* (= craggy, stony), *hirsutus* (lit = shaggy, then of thorns, etc), *asper, gravis* (of weather), *turbidus* (of weather or wind), see STORMY, *horridus* (= standing on end, hence void of refinement, of things and persons, e g *verba*), *raucus* (= hoarse), of character, *inhumanus, inurbanus, agrestis, rusticus*, see SKETCH Adv *aspere, dure duriter, inhumane, inurbane, rustice* **roughen,** v tr (*ex*) *asperare* (lit and fig) **roughness,** n *asperitas* (in gen, e g of the climate, *soli, animi*), *duritia*, of manners, *inhumanitas, inurbanitas, rusticitas*

round, I. adj *rotundus, globosus* (= globular), *orbiculatus* (lit = orbicular, like a disk, then — like a ball, — in gen), *teres* (rounded), comb *teres et rotundus* **II.** v tr 1, *rotundare, curvare, conglobare*, 2, fig *polire, concludĕre* **III.** n 1, see CIRCLE, 2, in fighting, *certamen*, in music, *cantus, -ūs* (song), to go the —s, *vigilias circumire* **IV.** adv and prep *circa, circum* (*alqd*) **roundabout,** adj and adv *devius*, a — way, *ambāges, -um, circuitus, -ūs* **rounded,** adj *teres* (lit and fig), *rotundatus, rotundus, conglobatus* of style, *quasi rotundus, concinnus* **roundelay,** n see SONG **roundly,** adv *plane, prorsus* (= altogether)

rouse, v tr *excitare*

rout, I. v tr to — the enemy, *hostes dissipare* or *hostes in fugam dissipare* **II.** n see MOB, DEFEAT

route, n see WAY, ROAD, JOURNEY

routine, n *habitus, -ūs* (= any art or virtue in which we feel at home, as it were), *usus, -ūs* (= practice), *ordo* (= order)

rove, v intr see RAMBLE **rover,** n *qui errat*, etc.; = pirate, *pirata*, m, *praedo*

row, n *ordo, -inis*, m, *series*, first, second, etc — of seats, *sedilia primo, secunda*, etc, in a —, (*ex*) *ordine, in ordinem, deinceps*

row, n 1, see QUARREL, 2, see NOISE

row, I. v intr *remigare*; to — with all one's might, *remis contendĕre* **II.** v tr *remis propellĕre*

royal, adj *regius*, or by the gen *regis* (= belonging to a king), *regalis* (= according to the dignity of a king) Adv *regie, regaliter, regio more* **royalist,** n *qui regis partibus studet* **royalty,** n 1, *regia potestas*, 2, on a book, *fructus, -ūs, reditus, -ūs*

rub, v tr *terĕre* (= to — off, to — to pieces) *atterĕre* (= to — against), *conterĕre* (= to pound), *fricare* (e g a floor), *demulcēre, permulcēre* (= to stroke), to — out, *delēre*

rubber, n at whist, by *paginas ter contendere*

rubbish, n 1, *rudus* (= rubble), see REFUSE, 2, *nugae, gerrae*, see NONSENSE

rubble, n. *rudus*

rubric, n *rubrica* (Eccl)

ruby, I. n *carbunculus* (Plin) **II.** adj *purpurens*

rudder, n *gubernaculum, clavus*

ruddy, adj *rubicundus* **ruddiness,** n use adj (e g *color rubicundus*)

rude, adj *rudis* (= inexperienced), — verses, *versus inconditi* or *incompositi*, = unmannerly, *agrestis, rusticus, inurbanus, inhumanus*, = insolent, *insolens* Adv *incondite incomposite, rustice, inurbane, inhumane, insolenter* **rudeness,** n *rusticitas, inhumanitas, inurbanitas, insolentia, mores rustici*, etc

rudiments, n pl *rudimenta*, see ELEMENTS **rudimentary,** adj *inchoatus*

rue, n *ruta*

rue, v tr see REGRET, REPENT **rueful,** adj see SORROWFUL **ruth,** n see PITY

ruff, n see COLLAR

ruffian, n *latro* (= bandit), *sicarius* (= assassin), *homo nefarius*, etc **ruffianly,** adj *nefarius, nequam, perditus, sceleratus*, see WICKED

ruffle, v tr 1, *agitare*, to be —d, *inhorrescĕre* (also of a hen, to — her feathers, *gallinae inhorrescunt edito ovo, excutiuntque sese*, Plin), 2, fig see EXCITE, IRRITATE

rug, n *stragulum* **rugged,** adj see ROUGH, UNEVEN

ruin, I n 1, —s *ruinae parietinae* (e g Corinthi), *muri diruti* (= walls partly destroyed), 2, *ruina* (lit = the falling in, then fig), *interitus, -ūs, exitium*, the — of one's fortune, *ruina fortunarum* that was his —, *hoc ei exitio fuit*, see DESTRUCTION **II.** v tr *pessumdare* (lit and fig), *perdĕre, algm* or *alqd praecipitare* (e g the State), *conficĕre* (= completely to wear out, exhaust, e g *partem plebis tributo*), *prosternĕre algm* or *alqd* (e g the enemy), *affligĕre* (e g the State, etc), *profligare* (entirely, a person, the State, one's health), also comb *affligere et perdĕre, affligĕre et prosternĕre, affligĕre et profligare* (all = *funditus perdĕre* or *evertĕre*) **ruinous,** adj 1, see PERNICIOUS 2, = very great (of expense), *maximus, effusus*

rule, I. v tr and intr 1, *regĕre, civitatem regĕre, imperium tractare, regnare, rempublicam regere* or *moderari, reipublicae praeesse*, see REIGN 2, to — passions, *alqd* or *alci rei temperare*, see RESTRAIN **II** n *lex* (e g *leges dicendi*), *praescriptum, praeceptum, ars, ratio, regula* (= a ruler or instrument for ruling lines or deciding cases, as *regula sermonis, regula ad quam alqd dirigitur*), *norma* to give a —, *legem dare, scribĕre, praeceptum dare* or *tradĕre*, to lay down as a —, *praecipĕre, praescribĕre;* in a court of law, *edicĕre.* **ruler,** n. **1,** *rector, moderator, qui alci rei praeest;* **2,** for drawing, *regula.*

rumble, v.intr. *(in)sonare, mugire, murmurare.*

rum'nate, v.intr. *ruminare* or *ruminari* (tr. and intr., lit. and fig.), *remandĕre* (tr. and intr., Plin.); see MEDITATE. **ruminant,** adj. *ruminalis* (Plin.). **rumination,** n. *ruminatio* (lit. and fig.).

rummage, v.intr. *alqd perscrutari.*

rumour, I. n. *rumor, fama, sermo* (= talk), *opinio* (= opinion), *auditio* (= what we know by hearsay), comb. *rumor* (or *fama*) *et auditio.* **II.** v.tr., it is —ed, *fertur,* (*res, fama,* etc.) *percrebescit.*

rump, n. *clunes, -ium,* m. and f.

rumple, v.tr. *immundum* (in gen.), *incomptum* (of hair) *facĕre.*

run, I. v.intr. *(de)currĕre* (from a higher place to one that lies lower, *ab, de* = down from, *ex* = out of, *per,* with accus. or the simple accus. = through, *ad* = as far as), *cursu ferri, aufugĕre* (= to — away), *cursu tendĕre algo* (= to — anywhere), *occurrĕre* (= to — up to), *percurrĕre* (= to — to a place), *procurrĕre* (= to — out of), *se proripĕre* (= to dash forth, e.g. into the street, *in publicum;* out of the house, *foras*), *effundi, se effundĕre* (of a large crowd, e.g. *in castra*), *transcurrĕre alqd* (= to — over anything; then absolute = to — across to, over to anyone, e.g. *ad alqm*), *circumcurrĕre, circumcursare alqm locum* (= to — about in a place), *cursare, trepidare* (= to — about), *pervagari alqm locum* (= to ramble about in a place); to — against each other, *inter se concurrĕre;* to — a race, *cursu certare, certatim currĕre;* to — against anyone, *incurrĕre* or *incurrĕre et incidĕre in alqm;* against anything, *impingi alci rei, se impingĕre in alqd,* so of a ship, *scopulo,* etc., = to — aground; to — down, fig. see DECRY; to — after anyone, *cursu effuso tendĕre* or *currĕre ad alqm, cupide appetĕre alqd* (fig. = to long for); of rivers (= to flow), *inferri, (in)fluĕre in alqd;* to — into, *influĕre in,* etc., *effundi, se effundĕre* (e.g. *in mare*); to — into = to enter, *intrare alqd, alqm locum* (e.g. *portum*); to — out of, *exire (ex) alqo loco* (e.g. of ships, carriages); to — round, *ferri, moveri, circa alqd* (e.g. *circa terram,* of the sun); tears — over his cheeks, *lacrimae manant per genas;* to — over, *equum,* etc., *agĕre in alqm* = to treat lightly, *alqd (oratione,* etc.) *percurrĕre, perstringĕre;* to — to seed, *in semen ire.* **II.** n. *cursus, -ūs, citatus* or *effusus.* **runaway,** n. *fugitivus.* **runner,** n. *cursor.* **running, I.** adj. — water, *aqua viva.* **II.** n. see RUN, II.

rupture, I. n. **1,** *fractura* (e.g. *ossis*); **2,** fig. *discordia* (= disagreement); *dissidium.* **II.** v.tr. *frangĕre, confringĕre, diffringĕre;* see BREAK.

rural, adj. *rusticus, agrestis* (= in the country; also = simple, plain, etc.), *rusticus* (= peculiar to the country, e.g. — life).

rush, n. *juncus, s(c)irpus;* made of —, *junceus* or *juncinus, s(c)irpeus;* full of —es, *juncosus;* a place covered with —es, *juncetum.* **rushlight,** n. see LAMP.

rush, v.intr. see RUN.

rusk, n. perhaps *panis tostus.*

russet, adj. *fuscus* (= dusky).

rust, I. n. *robigo* (*rub-,* in gen.; also in reference to corn), *situs, -ūs* (= mould, mustiness), *ferrugo* (= — of iron), *aerugo* (= — of copper). **II.** v.intr. *robiginem trahĕre* or *sentire, robigine obduci, robigine infestari* (all in Plin.), fig. *corrumpi.* **III.** v.tr. *alqd robigine obducĕre,* etc. (Plin., Quint.). **rusty,** adj. *robiginosus* (*rub-,* in gen.), *aeruginosus* (in Sen., of brass and copper).

rustic, adj. *rusticus, rusticanus, agrestis.* **rusticate, I.** v.tr. perhaps *rus relegare.* **II.** v.intr. *rusticari, rure vivĕre* or *degĕre.*

rùstle, I. v.intr. *crepare, crepitum dare* (of a clattering noise), *strepĕre, strepitum dare* or *edĕre* (loud), *sonare* (= to sound loud); to — (of leaves), perhaps †*susurrare* (= to whisper). **II.** n. *crepitus, -ūs, strepitus, -ūs, sonus.*

rut, n. *orbita.*

ruth, n. see RUE.

rye, n. *secale* (Plin.).

S.

Sabbath, n. *sabbata, -orum.*

sable, adj. *niger, ater;* see BLACK.

sabre, n. *acinaces, -is.*

saccharine, adj. by *dulcis.*

sacerdotal, adj. *quod ad sacerdotes* or *sacerdotium pertinet.*

sack, I. n. **1,** *saccus;* — of leather, *culeus,* see BAG; **2,** see PLUNDER. **II.** v.tr. see PLUNDER. **sackbut,** n. *buccina.* **sackcloth,** n. by *toga sordida;* in — and ashes, *sordidatus.*

sacrament, n. *sacramentum* (Eccl.).

sacred, adj. *sacer, sanctus, sacrosanctus, religiosus, augustus;* nothing is more — to me than, etc., *nihil antiquius est quam,* etc.; to declare —, *sancire.* Adv. *sancte, religiose, auguste.* **sacredness,** n. *sanctitas,* or by *religio.*

sacrifice, I. n. *sacrificium, sacra, -orum,* n., *res divina* (the act), *victima, hostia* (= the victim); = loss, *jactura, damnum.* **II.** v.tr. **1,** *sacrificare,* (*sacra,* or *rem divinam*) *facĕre* with ablat. of victim, *hostiam immolare, litare* (under favourable auspices), *caedĕre* (= to slaughter); **2,** fig. *alcjs rei jacturam facĕre, alqd alci dare, dedĕre* (= to give up); to — one's life for, *pro alqâ re* or *alqâ occumbĕre, vitam profundĕre.* **sacrificer,** n. *immolator* (rare), or by verb. **sacrificial,** adj. by genit. of *sacrificium,* †*sacrificialis.*

sacrilege, n. *sacrilegium.* **sacrilegious,** adj. *sacrilegus.* Adv. by adj.

sacristan, n. *aedituus.* **sacristy,** n. *sacrarium.*

sad, adj. **1,** = sorrowful, *maestus, tristis, maerens, afflictus* (= cast down); **2,** = causing sadness, *gravis, acerbus, tristis, miserabilis, miserandus, luctuosus.* Adv. *maeste,* †*triste, miserabiliter, luctuose.* **sadden,** v.tr. *maestitiâ, dolore,* etc., *alqm afficĕre.* **sadness,** n. *maestitia, tristitia, dolor* (= pain), *maeror, aegritudo, aegrimonia, miseria* (often in pl.); see SORROW.

saddle, I. n. *ephippium.* **II.** v.tr. *equum sternĕre;* to — anyone with anything, *alqd alci imponĕre, injungĕre.* **saddle-bags,** n. *hippoperae* (Sen.). **saddle-horse,** n. *equus.* **saddler,** n. *ephippiorum artifex.*

safe, I. adj. *tutus* (*ab alqâ re*), *salvus sospes* (= — and sound), *integer* (= whole), *incolumis* (= unharmed), *periculo vacuus* (= free from danger). Adv. *tuto, tute.* **II.** n. *cella penaria.* **safe-conduct,** n. *fides* (*publica*). **safeguard,** n. *propugnaculum;* see PROTECTION. **safety,** n. *salus, -utis,* f., *incolumitas;* in —, *tutus,* etc. **safety-valve,** n. **1,** lit. perhaps *foramen per quod vapor calidus emittitur;* **2,** fig. *salutis certa via atque ratio.*

saffron, I. n *crocus* **II.** adj *croceus*

sagacious, adj *sagax, prudens, perspicax, rationis et consilii plenus* Adv *sagaciter, prudenter* **sagacity,** n. *sagacitas, prudentia, perspicacitas*

sage, n *salvia* (Plin).

sage, I. adj see WISE **II.** n *sapiens*

sail, I. n *velum*; to set —, *vela dare*, = to set out —, (*navem*) *solvĕre*; to furl —, *vela subducĕre* **II.** v intr *navigare*, to — over, *transvehi, transmitti*, to — past, *praetervehi*, to — round, *circumvehi* **sailing,** n *navigatio* **sailor,** n *nauta*, m

saint, n (*vir*) *sanctus*, (*femina*) *sancta, beatus, beata* (Eccl) **saintly,** adj *sanctus*

sake, n for the — of, *ob, propter, per* (with accus), *prae, pro, de* (with ablat) *caus(s)ā* or *gratiā* (with genit, and more rarely *ergo*, which follows the genit), or by part *motus, affectus, coactus alqā re*

salaam, n by *corpus humi prosternĕre*.

salad, n *acetaria, -orum* (Plin).

salamander, n *salamandra* (Plin)

salary, I. n *merces, ēdis*, f **II.** v tr *mercedem alci dare*, to be salaried, *mercedem accipĕre*

sale, n *venditio* (in gen), *hasta* (= auction); to offer for —, *alqd venum dare* **saleable,** adj *vendibilis* (= on sale), *quod facile vendi potest* **salesman,** n *venditor*

salient, adj *praecipuus* (= chief), see PRINCIPAL

saline, adj *salsus*

saliva, n *saliva*

sallow, adj *pallidus*

sally, I. v tr *erumpĕre, eruptionem facĕre* **II.** n 1, *eruptio*, 2, fig. *alqd argute dictum*.

salmon, n *salmo* (Plin)

saloon, n *atrium, exĕdra, oecus*

salt, I. n *sal* **II.** adj *salsus* **III.** v tr *sale condire, salire* **salt-cellar,** n *salinum, concha salis* **salt-mine, salt-pit, salt-works,** n *salifodina, salinae* **saltness,** n. *salsitudo*

salubrious, adj *saluber*, or *salubris* Adv *salubriter* **salubriousness,** n *salubritas* **salutary,** adj *salutaris*, see USEFUL

salute, I. v tr *salutare, consalutare* (of several), in letters, *alci multam* or *plurimam salutem dicĕre, impertire, a(d)scribĕre*, of sending a message, so *salutem nuntiare*, or simply *salutem* **II.** n 1, see KISS, 2, milit t t perhaps by *telum alci erigĕre honoris caus(s)ā* (= by presenting arms), *missilibus effusis alqm excipere* (= by discharge of guns) **salutation,** n *salutatio, salus* (see above), *alqm salvēre jubēre*

salvation, n *salus, utis*, f, *conservatio* (in gen)

salve, I. n *unguentum*, for the eyes, *collyrium* **II.** v tr (*in*)*ungĕre*

salver, n see DISH

salvo, n with this —, *hoc excepto, hac lege* or *condicione*

same, adj *īdem, eadem, ĭdem*, = — as, followed by *et, ac, que ut, qui* (*quae, quod*), *quam, quasi, cum* with ablat (*alci rei*), *unus et idem, ipse, ipsa, ipsum* (= self) *ejusdem generis* (= of the same kind), it is not the — whether, *multum interest utrum … an*, it is the — to me, *meā nihil interest* or *refert*, in the — way, *eodem modo*, at the — time, *eodem tempore*, in the — place, *ibīdem*, to the — place, *eodem* **sameness,** n. see MONOTONY.

sample, n *exemplum, specimen, documentum*, see EXAMPLE

sanatory, adj *quod alci rei medetur*, see also SALUTARY

sanctify, v tr. (*con*)*secrare, dedicare* (= to consecrate), *sanctificare* (Eccl) **sanctification,** n *sanctificatio* (Eccl). **sanctimonious,** adj perhaps by *qui se sanctissimum esse simulat* **sanction, I.** n *confirmatio, auctoritas, fides*, with, without the — of, *jussu, injussu alcjs* **II.** v tr *sancire, ratum facĕre, ratum esse jubēre*, see also ALLOW **sanctity,** n *sanctitas* (both as moral quality and sacredness of a thing, in which latter sense also *caerimonia* and *religio*) **sanctuary,** n *templum, penetralia, -ium, delubrum, fanum*, † *adytum, asylum* (in the sense of refuge)

sand, n *arēna, sabulum* (*sabulo*, coarse), *saburra* (for ballast) **sand-bank,** n *syrtis* **sand-glass,** n *clepsydra* **sand-heap,** n *acervus arenae* **sandstone,** n *tofus* **sandy,** adj *arenosus, sabulosus* (= full of sand)

sandal, n *sandalium* (very rare), *crepĭda, solea*, wearing —s, *crepidatus, soleatus*

sane, adj *sanus, sanus et salvus, mentis compos, animi integer*, to be —, *mentis compotem esse*, not to be —, *mente captum esse, mente alienari* or *alienatum esse, nullius consilii esse* **sanity,** n use adj

sanguinary, adj *sanguinem sitiens* (= thirsting for blood), *cruentus*, † *sanguineus* (= bloody), see CRUEL, BLOODY **sanguine,** adj, **sanguineness,** n see HOPE, HOPEFULNESS

sap, I. n *sucus*. **II.** v tr 1, = to undermine, *cuniculos agere*, 2, fig *corrumpĕre* (= to spoil), *haurire* (= to drain away) **sapless,** adj 1, lit. *suco carens*, 2, fig *exsucus* (Quint) **sapling,** n *arbor novella* **sapper,** n *qui cuniculos agit*

sapient, adj *sapiens, sapientiā praeditus*; to be —, *sapĕre*

sapphire, n *sapp(h)īrus* (Plin)

sarcasm, n *facetiae acerbae* or *dictum aculeatum* **sarcastic,** adj *acerbus* Adv *acerbe*

sarcophagus, n *sarcophagus* (Juv)

sardonyx, n *sardonyx* (Plin)

sash, n *cingulum*, see BELT; a — window, *fenestra ex ligneā compage confecta*

Satan, n *Satănas, -ae* **satanic,** adj see DEVILISH

satchel, n *pera, sacculus* (Plin)

satellite, n *satelles, -itis*, m and f

satiate, v tr (*ex*)*satiare, explēre, saturare*; to — oneself with food, *cibo satiari* **satiation** or **satiety,** n *satietas, saturitas*

satin, n *pannus sericus densior ac nitens*

satire, n *satira* (*satura*), *carmen satiricum, carmen probrosum, carmen* † *famosum, carmen maledicens, carmen refertum contumeliis, versus in alcjs cupiditatem facti* **satirical,** adj *acerbus*, see above Adv *acerbe* **satirist,** n *qui libellum* or *libellos ad infamiam alterius edit, satirarum scriptor, satirici carminis scriptor* **satirize,** v tr *alqm perstringĕre, acerbis facetiis alqm irridēre, carmen probrosum facĕre in alqm, carmen ad alcjs infamiam edĕre*

satisfaction, n *satisfactio* (originally = payment of a creditor, then amends to any-one injured), *expletio* (= fulfilment), *voluptas* (= pleasure), *poena* (= penalty) **satisfactory,** adj *idoneus* (= suitable), see GOOD, EXCELLENT. Adv *bene, ex sententia*. **satisfy,** v tr. *satisfa-*

cēre alci, placēre alci, ex(s)pectationem or *desiderium explēre.*

satrap, n. *satrapes, -ae* and *-is*, m.

saturate, v.tr. see SOAK.

Saturday, n. * *dies Saturni.*

Saturnalia, n. *Saturnalia, -ium*, n.

satyr, n. *satyrus.*

sauce, n. *jus, juris*, n., *embamma, -ătis*, n. (Plin.), *condimentum.*

saucepan, n. *vās ad condimenta paranda accommodatum.*

saucer, n. *patella;* see PLATE.

saucy, adj. *petulans, insolens, protervus, procax, immodestus.* Adv. *petulanter, insolenter, proterve, procaciter, immodeste.* **sauciness**, n. *impudentia, os impudens, insolentia, protervitas, procacitas.*

saunter, v.intr. *ambulare, morari;* to — about, *vagari;* see LOITER.

sausage, n. *tomaculum* (Juv.), *farcīmen, hillae.*

savage, adj. *ferus, agrestis, indomitus, efferatus* (= wild), *incultus, vastus* (= waste), *ferox, immanis, saevus, trux, atrox* (= cruel), *incultus ferusque.* Adv. *ferociter, immaniter, saeve, atrociter.* **savageness**, n. *feritas, ferocitas, immanitas, saevitia, atrocitas.*

save, I. v.tr. 1, = to preserve, *(con)servare;* 2, = to deliver, *liberare, vindicare alqm ab alqā re;* see FREE; 3, to — money, *compendium* (opp. *dispendium*) *facĕre;* to — time, *sequi compendium temporis;* to — health, *parcĕre valetudini;* to — labour, *laborem diminuĕre;* God — you, *salve, ave, salvēre te jubeo* (at meeting), *salve et vale* (at parting); —d or laid by, *repositus, sepositus.* II. prep. and conj. see EXCEPT. **saving**, adj. *parcus, frugi* (indecl.). **savings**, n. *quod alqs parsimoniā collegit, peculium* (= the — of a slave; what a father gives to sons and daughters). **savings-bank**, n. by *mensa publica apud quam alqs pecuniam collocat.* **savingness**, n. *parsimonia* (= sparingness), *frugalitas.* **saviour**, n. *(con)servator, liberator;* of Christ, *Salvator* (Eccl.).

savour, I. n. *sapor* (= taste), *odor* (= smell); an ill —, *foetor;* to be in ill —, *male audiri;* to be in good —, *bene audiri.* II. v.tr. *sapĕre* (= to have a taste), *alqd redolēre* (= to smell of). **savoury**, adj. *suavis.*

saw, n. = saying, *dictum, verbum, vox, sententia, proverbium.*

saw, I. n. *serra;* a tooth of a —, *dens serrae.* II. v.tr. *serrā (dis)secare.* III. v.intr. *serram ducĕre.* **sawdust**, n. *scob(i)s.* **sawed**, adj. *serratus.* **sawing**, n. *serratura.*

say, v.tr. *dicĕre, (e)loqui, (e)narrare, profiteri, fari, praedicare, asseverare;* to — that not, *negare;* I — yes, *aio, affirmo;* I — no, *nego;* to — not a word, *tacēre;* they, people —, *dicunt, tradunt, ferunt* (with accus. and infin.), or *dicitur, traditur, fertur* (with nomin. and infin.); I will not —, *ne dicam;* — I, *inquam* (so *inquit, ait*, —s he); as they, people —, *ut aiunt, ut dicitur.* **saying**, n. *dictio* (= act of —, and in Quint., the thing said), *verbum, proverbium, sententia, dictum, quod aiunt, illud.*

scab, n. *scabies.* **scabby**, adj. *scabiosus.*

scabbard, n. *vagina.*

scaffold, n. *machina, catasta* (= a place where slaves were exposed for sale); to come to the —, *ad mortem duci;* see EXECUTION.

scald, I. v.tr. *aquā ferventi perfundĕre* (= to burn). II. n. use verb.

scale, I. n. 1, of a fish, *squama;* 2, of a balance, *lanx;* pair of —s, *libra, trutina.* II. v.tr. to — a fish, *desquamare.* III. v.intr. = to weigh, † *pendĕre.* **scaly**, adj. *squamosus.*

scale, I. n. 1, = gradation, *gradus, -ūs;* on the — of, *(ad) instar alcjs rei;* on a larger, smaller —, *major, minor*, with noun; 2, in music, *diagramma, -ătis*, n. II. v.tr. *(positis scalis) a(d)scendĕre, scalas moenibus applicare* or *admovēre;* see CLIMB. **scaling-ladder**, n. *scalae.*

scallop, I. n. *pecten.* II. v.tr. see SCOOP.

scalp, I. n. *cutis capitis.* II. v.tr. *cutem capiti detrahĕre.*

scalpel, n. *scalpellum.*

scamp, n. see KNAVE. **scamper**, v.intr. see HURRY.

scan, v.tr. 1, *inspicĕre, (per)scrutari, contemplari;* see EXAMINE; 2, in prosody, *pedibus versum metiri* (Gram.). **scansion**, n. use verb.

scandal, n. 1, see DISGRACE; 2, see SLANDER. **scandalize**, v.tr. see SHOCK, HORRIFY. **scandalous**, adj. *mali* or *pessimi exempli, probrosus, turpis;* see DISGRACEFUL.

scant, **scanty**, adj. *angustus, artus* (= narrow), *exiguus, parvus;* see SMALL. Adv. *anguste, arte, exigue.* **scantiness**, n. *angustiae, exiguitas.*

scar, n. *cicatrix.*

scarce, adj. *rarus, singularis.* Adv. *vix, aegre.* **scarcity**, n. *raritas, res rara, paucitas, inopia, penuria, difficultas* (e.g. = — of money, *difficultas nummaria*); — of provisions, *caritas* (= dearth) *rei frumentariae* (so *vini, nummorum*).

scare, v.tr. *terrēre;* see TERRIFY. **scarecrow**, n. perhaps *formido.*

scarf, n. *fascia, mitella.*

scarlet, I. adj. *coccineus* (Plin.). II. n. *coccum.* **scarlet-fever**, n. *febris* (= fever).

scathe, v.tr. = to harm, *laedĕre, nocēre, damno esse alci, detrimentum afferre;* of words, *mordēre, pungĕre;* a scathing remark, *verba quasi aculei, verba aculeata.* **scatheless**, adj. *sine damno, salvus, incolumis.*

scatter, I. v.tr. 1, = to throw about, *spargĕre, serĕre* (= to sow, of seeds); 2, = to drive away, *dispergĕre, dis(j)icĕre, dissipare, dispellĕre, discutĕre, fundĕre* (of an army). II. v.intr. *dissipari, dilabi, diffugĕre.*

scavenger, n. *qui vicos urbis purgare solet.*

scene, n. *scaena* (properly = the stage; hence *in scaenam prodire, in scaenā esse, scaenam tenēre* = to be master or chief of the stage); the place before the —, *proscaenium;* belonging to —s, *scaenicus* (used with *artifices, actores, poëtae*); = place of action, *locus ubi alqd agitur;* fig. *res, spectaculum, rerum status, -ūs;* to be behind the —s, *alqd penitus novisse* or *exploratum habēre.* **scenery**, n. 1, of a theatre, *apparatus, -ūs, ad scaenam pertinens;* 2, = prospect, *locus* (or pl. *loca*).

scent, I. n. 1, = sense of smell, *odoratus, -ūs*, or by *nasus* (nose); of dogs, *narium sagacitas;* keen-scented, *sagax;* 2, = an odour, *odor, nidor;* to get — of, *alqd* (e.g. *nummum olfacĕre*); to put on the wrong —, *alqm in errorem inducĕre;* 3, = a perfume, essence, *unguentum.* II. v.tr. = 1, to find by —, *alqm* or *alqd odorari* (of dogs, etc.), *olfacĕre;* see SMELL; 2, = to perfume, *odoribus perfundĕre.* **scent-bottle**, n. *arcula* (= box for scents); see BOTTLE. **scented**, adj. *odoratus.*

sceptical, adj., **sceptic**, n. *qui se de omnibus rebus dubitare dicit.* **scepticism**, n. *dubitatio de omnibus rebus.*

sceptre, n *sceptrum*, to wield the —, *regnare*, see REIGN

schedule, n *libellus*, see LIST

scheme, I. n *consilium*, *ratio*, to form a —, *rationem inire*, see PLAN. **II.** v intr see above and PLAN

schism, n *schisma*, *-ătis*, n (Eccl) **schismatic,** n *schismaticus*

school, I. n 1, *schola*, *ludus lit(t)erarum*, *ludus discendi*, to go to — to anyone, *in alcjs scholam ire*, *alcjs scholam frequentare*, 2, fig that is a — of patience, *in hāc re tentatur patientia nostra*, philosophy, the — of life, *philosophia dux vitae*, *et officiorum magistra*, a — of wisdom, *sapientiae officina*, 3, = body of disciples, *schola*, *secta*, = teaching, *disciplina* **II** v tr *docēre* see TEACH, TRAIN **school-fellow,** n *condiscipulus* **schoolmaster,** n *magister* **school-mistress,** n *magistra* **scholar,** n *discipulus*, *alumnus*, *auditor* (= a listener), *tiro* (= a beginner), my —, *alumnus disciplinae meae*, *alqm magistrum habēre*, *alqm audire* **scholarly,** adj *eruditus* **scholarship,** n 1, = learning, *lit(t)erae*, *doctrina*, *eruditio*, 2, = prize, *praemium*

science, n *scientia*, *notitia*, *cognitio* (= knowledge), *ars*, *doctrina*, *disciplina* (= system of knowledge), the — of music, grammar, etc, *musica*, *grammatica*, *orum* **scientific,** adj *quod in artibus versatur*, — principles, *artis praecepta*, = learned or taught, *doctrinā eruditus* Adv *erudite*, or by some special noun (e g to treat music —, *e musicorum rationibus disserere*)

scimitar, n *acinăces*, *ensis* †*falcatus*, see SABRE

scintillation, n *scintilla* (= spark) **scintillate,** v intr *scintillare* (e g *scintillant oculi*)

sciolist, n *semidoctus* (e g *apud doctos et semidoctos ipse percurro*, Cic)

scion, n 1, of plants, *surculus*, 2, fig *progenies*

scissors, n *forfices* (= shears, barber's —, Mart), *forficulae* (= small shears or —, Plin)

scoff, I. n *ludibrium*, see MOCK **II.** v tr to — at anyone or anything, *alqm or alqd in ludibrium vertĕre*, *ludibrio habēre*, to be —ed at, *alci ludibrio esse* see MOCK **scoffer,** n *irrisor*, see MOCKER **scoffing,** n *ludificatio*, *cavillatio*, see MOCKERY

scold, I. v tr *jurgare cum alqo*, *objurgare*, *increpare alqm* **II.** n *objurgator*, of a woman, *jurgiis addicta* **scolding,** n *objurgatio*, *convicium*

scoop, I. n see LADLE **II.** v tr *(ex)cavare*

scope, n. 1, = the purpose or drift, *propositum consilium*; 2, = room or space, *spatium*, 3, = liberty, *copia*, *potestas*

scorch, I. v tr *amburĕre*, *adurĕre*, *torrēre*, *torrefacĕre* **II.** v intr *torrēri* *arescĕre* (e g *herbae arescunt et interficiuntur*, Cic) **scorched,** adj *torridus* **scorching,** adj *torridus*, see HOT

score, I. n 1, = account, *ratio*, *nomen*, on the — of friendship, *amicitiae nomine*, to pay a —, *pecuniam solvĕre*, to quit —s, *par pari referre*, 2, in music, *cantilena cum musicis notis annexis* 3, in number, *viginti* **II.** v tr *notare*, *signare* (= to mark), see also RECKON, = to underscore, *lineas sub verbis ducĕre*

scorn, I. n *contemptus*, *ūs*, *contemptio*, *fastidium* **II.** v tr. *contemnĕre*, *fastidire*, *spernĕre*, *aspernari*. **scorner,** n *contemptor*, *animus contemptor* **scornful,** adj *fastidiosus*, see also PROUD, INSOLENT Adv *fastidiose*

scorpion, n *scorpio*, *scorpius*

scot, n 1, in reckoning, *symbola* (ante and post class), 2, in law, — and lot, *vectigal*, — free, *immunis*, *inultus*

scoundrel, n *homo nefarius*, *nequam*, see RASCAL

scour, v tr *(de)tergēre*, *tergere* (or *tergĕre*), *(ex)purgare* (= to cleanse), to — the land, *pervagari*, *percurrĕre*, *(de)vastare* (in war)

scourge, I. n = whip, *flagrum*, *flagellum*, *lora*, *orum*, = plague, *pestis* (lit and fig), see PLAGUE **II.** v tr *virgis* or *verberibus caedĕre*, *verberare* **scourging,** n by verb

scout, n *explorator*, *speculator*

scowl, I. v intr *frontem contrahĕre*, *corrugare* **II.** n *frons*, *-ntis*, f, *asperior*, *vultus*, *ūs*, †*torvus*, *truculentus*

scraggy, adj *strigosus*, see THIN

scramble, v tr = for anything, *alqd certatim arripĕre*, to — up, *manibus pedibusque a(d)scendĕre*

scrap, n *frustum*, *fragmentum*, the —s, *frusta*, *rel(l)iquiae* (of food, *cibi*)

scrape, I. n *angustiae*, *difficultas* to be in a —, *in angustiis esse* **II.** v tr *radĕre*, to — off, *abradĕre*, *defringĕre*, to — together, *congerĕre* **scraper,** n flesh —, *strigil* or *strigilis*

scratch, v tr. *scabĕre*, *scalpĕre*, *fricare*, *radere*, to — out, *delēre*.

scrawl, I. n *litterae male factae* **II.** v tr = to scribble, *lit(t)eris male factis scribĕre*

scream, I. n *clamor*, *vociferatio*, *ululatus*, *-ūs*, of an infant, *vagitus*, *-ūs* **II.** v intr *clamare*, *clamitare*, *vociferari*, *ululare*, *vagire* (of children)

screech, v intr *ululare*, —-owl, *ulula* (scil *avis*) **screeching,** n *ululatus*, *-ūs*

screen, I. n *umbraculum* (= a shady place, a parasol), *praesidium* (= a protection) **II.** v tr *defendĕre* (= to ward off, e g *defendere ardores solis*, Cic), see PROTECT

screw, I. n *cochlea* (for drawing water), *clavus* (= nail) **II** v tr *clavis adigĕre alqd*

scribe, n *scriba*, m, *librarius*

scrip, n see PURSE, WALLET

scripture, n *(sancta) scriptura* (Eccl), *libri divini*, *lit(t)erae* **scriptural,** adj *ad normam librorum divinorum*, *libris sacris conveniens*

scrivener, n *scriba*, m, see NOTARY

scrofula, n *struma* **scrofulous,** adj *strumosus* (Col)

scroll, n *volumen*

scrub, v tr *(de)fricare*, *(de)tergēre*, *tergĕre* (*tergere*)

scruple, I. n 1, as a weight, *scrupulum* 2, = hesitation or difficulty, *dubitatio*, *haesitatio*, *cunctatio*, *religio*, *scrupulus* **II.** v intr *animo haerēre*, *haesitare*, *suspenso esse animo* to —, *dubitare* with infin, not to —, *non dubitare quin*, see HESITATE, in stricter sense *religione ac metu teneri*, *religione obstrictum esse*, *alqd religioni habēre* he —s to, *religio ei obstat ne* **scrupulous,** adj *religiosus*, *sol(l)icitus*, *anxius*, *accuratus*, *diligens* Adv *religiose*, *anxie*, *accurate*, *diligenter*, or sometimes by superl (e g — clean, *mundissimus*)

scrutiny, n *scrutatio* **scrutineer,** n *scrutator* **scrutinize,** v tr *scrutari*, see EXAMINE

scud, v intr see HASTEN

scuffle, n. *rixa*.

scull, I. n. (of the head) *calvāria* (Plin.); = an oar, *remulus, palma*. **II.** v.intr. *remigare*. **sculler**, n. *remex*.

scullery, n. *culina* (= kitchen). **scullion**, n. *puer culinarius*.

sculpture, I. n. **1**, *ars fingendi* (as a science), *sculptura, sculptura* (for distinction see Smith's "Dict. Antiq.," art. Sculptura); **2**, = work carved, *opus, -ĕris*, n., *signum, marmor*. **II.** v.tr. = to work in statuary, *sculpĕre, sculpĕre*. **sculptor**, n. *sculptor, statuarum artifex*.

scum, n. **1**, *spuma* (= foam; so of silver, Plin.), *scoria* (Plin., = — of metals); **2**, fig. *faex, sentīna* (*reipublicae*, etc.).

scurf, n. *furfur, furfures* (Plin.), *porrigo*. **scurfy**, adj. *porriginosus* (Plin.).

scurrilous, adj. *contumeliosus, probrosus, scurrīlis*. Adv. *contumeliose, scurrīliter* (Plin.). **scurrility**, n. *contumelia* (or in pl.), *scurrīlitas* (Quint.).

scurvy, I. n. by *ulcus, -ĕris*, n. **II.** adj. *humilis, ignobilis, obscurus, infimus*.

scutcheon, n. *insigne* (or in pl.).

scuttle, n. *area, cista* (= box).

scuttle, v.tr. and intr. *navem perforare*.

scythe, n. *falx*.

sea, I. n. *mare* (in gen.), *oceanus, pelagus, -i*, n., *pontus*, † *aequor*; the high —, *altum* (= the "deep"); the open —, *salum*; the Mediterranean —, *Mare Magnum*, * *Mare Mediterraneum*; the Black —, *Pontus* (*Euxinus*); the Adriatic —, *Adriaticum*; the Red —, *Sinus Arabicus*; the Dead —, *Lacus Asphaltītes*; lying on or near the —, *maritimus*; beyond the —, *transmarinus*; an arm of the —, *aestuarium*; —-breeze, *afflatus, -ūs, maritimus* (Plin.); —-calf, *phoca*; —-coast, *ora* (*maritima*); —-faring, *maritimus*; —-fight, *pugna navalis*; —-girt, *circumfluus*; —-green, † *thalassinus, thalassicus* (Plaut.); —-gull, * *larus* (Linn.); —man, *nauta*; —manship, *ars navigandi*; —-sand, *arena* (*maritima*); —-sickness, *nausea*; —-water, *aqua marina* (Plin.); —-weed, *alga*. **II.** adj. *marinus, maritimus*, (*maritu-*).

seal, I. n. *signum*. **II.** v.tr. (*con*)*signare, obsignare alqd*; —ing-wax, *cera*.

seal, n. (an animal) *phoca*.

seam, n. *sutura*. **seamstress**, n. *quae acu victum quaeritat*.

sear, I. adj. *aridus* (= dry), *serus* (= late). **II.** v.tr. *arefacĕre* (ante and post class., = to dry), (*ad*)*urĕre* (= to burn).

search, I. n. *indagatio, investigatio, inquisitio, exploratio, inspectio*. **II.** v.tr. *investigare, inquirĕre, explorare, indagare, scrutari, quaerĕre*, (*ex*)*petĕre, sequi, persequi, sectari, captare, aucupari, studēre rei*; see SEEK.

season, I. n. (e.g. *anni*, of the year) *tempus, tempestas* (= time), *occasio, opportunitas, locus* (= occasion). **II.** v.tr. *condire*. **seasonable**, adj. *tempestivus, opportunus, ad tempus*. Adv. *tempestive, opportune*; not —, *non opportune, alieno tempore*. **seasoning**, n. *condimentum* (= the material employed), *conditio* (= the act).

seat, I. n. *sella, sedile, cathedra* (= chair); — at the theatre, etc., *subsellia*; = dwelling, *domicilium, sedes, -is*; to have a — in the royal council, *omnibus consiliis principis interesse*; to put a — for anyone, *sellam alci apponĕre*. **II.** (or **set**), v.tr. *ponĕre, statuĕre, collocare, constituĕre*; to — yourself, *considĕre, assidĕre, subsidĕre*; to — yourself on, *assidĕre in re*; to — yourself on horseback, *conscendĕre equum*; see SET. **III.** (**to be seated** or **to sit**), v.intr. *sedēre*; to be — on anything, *sedēre in re*; to be — on the soil, *humo sedēre*; to be — in school, *in scholā sedēre*. **seated**, adj. = rested, *penitus defixus, inveteratus*.

secede, v.intr. *abire, decedĕre, secedĕre* (e.g. *secedant improbi*, Cic.; *secedĕre in sacrum montem*, Liv.); so as to take up another opinion, *secedĕre et alia parte considĕre* (Sen.), or by *sententiam mutare*. **seceder**, n. *transfuga*, m. **secession**, n. *secessio*.

seclude, v.tr. *secludĕre, segregare, removēre, excludĕre, eximĕre, excipĕre*. **secluded**, adj. see LONELY. **seclusion**, n. *solitudo*; a life of —, *vita umbratilis*.

second, I. adj. *secundus, alter* (e.g. — father, *alter parens*); in the first place, in the —, *primum, deinde*. Adv. *secunde, deinde*. **II.** n. **1**, in a fight, *qui alci adest*; **2**, of time, *momentum* (*temporis*). **III.** v.tr. **1**, = to support, *alci adesse, auxilio esse, subvenire*; **2**, = to help, *adjuvare*; see HELP; **3**, to — a motion, *in alcjs sententiam dicĕre*; *alci adesse*. **secondary**, adj. *secundarius* (in rank or position), *inferior, minoris momenti*. **seconder**, n. *suasor* (e.g. *legis*). **second-hand**, adj. *usu inferior factus*. **second-rate**, adj. *inferior*. **second-sight**, n. *praesagitio*.

secrecy, n. perhaps *taciturnitas* (= strict silence), or *solitudo* (= solitude); to keep anything in —, *rem occultam* or *abditam* or *secretam habēre*.

secret, I. adj. **1**, = hidden, *arcanus* (of plans, etc.), *secretus, abditus, tectus, occultus, absconditus, latens* (all of places, etc.); **2**, = furtive, *clandestinus, furtivus*. Adv. *clam, furtim, secreto, in occulto, occulte*. **II.** n. *res occulta* or *arcana*, in pl. *arcana, -orum*; *mysterium* (e.g. *epistulae nostrae tantum habent mysteriorum*, Cic.). **secrete**, v.tr. see HIDE. **secretion**, n. *excrementum* (Plin.).

secretary, n. *scriba*, m. **secretaryship**, n. *scribae munus, -ĕris*.

sect, n. *secta, schola, disciplina*. **sectary, sectarian**, n. *homo sectae studiosus*.

section, n. *pars, portio*.

secular, adj. *saecularis* (= occurring every age, also Eccl. = temporal, for which in gen. use *civīlis*). **secularize**, v.tr. *profanum facĕre*, or *ad profanum usum redigĕre, exaugurare* (of a temple, or anything consecrated).

secure, I. adj. **1**, = careless, *securus* (i.e. *sine curā*), *incautus*; to be — or free from care about anything, *alqd non timēre*; **2**, = safe, *tutus*; see SAFE. Adv. *secure, incaute, tuto*. **II.** v.tr. **1**, = to make safe, *tutum reddĕre*; see PRESERVE; **2**, = to strengthen, *confirmare*; **3**, = to tie up, etc., see FASTEN; **4**, = to arrest; see SEIZE. **security**, n. **1**, = safety, *salus, -utis*, f., *incolumitas*; see SAFETY; **2**, = pledge, *pignus, -ĕris*, n., *cautio, satisdatio, vadimonium* (= bail); to give —, *satis dare, cavēre*.

sedan, n. *lectica*.

sedate, adj. *sedatus, placidus, gravis*; to be —, *quietum esse, animo esse tranquillo*. Adv. *sedate, placide, graviter*. **sedateness**, n. *gravitas*. **sedative**, n. *sedatio* (e.g. *animi*), of a medicine, *medicina quae dolorem compescit*.

sedentary, adj. *sedentarius*; see SEAT, SIT.

sedge, n. *ulva*. **sedgy**, adj. *ulvis obductus*.

sediment, n. *faex, sedimentum* (Plin.).

sedition, n. *seditio*; to raise —, *seditionem concitare, concire* or *conflare*; to put down —, *seditionem sedare* or *componĕre*. **seditious**, adj. *seditiosus*; see REBELLIOUS. Adv. *seditiose*.

seduce, v tr. 1, = to lead astray, *a rectâ viâ abducĕre, corrumpĕre, sol(l)icitare* (= to tamper with), *in errorem inducĕre*, see PERVERT; 2, to — a woman, *stuprum cum alqâ*, or *alci facĕre* **seducer**, n *corruptor*, or by verb **seduction**, n *stuprum, corruptēla* (of women, etc), = charm, *illecebrae, lepos* **seductive**, adj = pleasant, *amoenus, qui (quae, quod) alqm corrumpit*, etc

sedulous, adj *sedulus, assiduus, industrius, acer, diligens, accuratus* Adv *sedulo, assidue, industrie, acriter* (= eagerly), *diligenter, accurate* **sedulity**, n *sedulitas, assiduitas, industria, diligentia*

see, n bishop's —, **dioecesis*

see, I. v tr *vidēre, cernĕre, a(d)spicĕre, conspicĕre, spectare, intellegĕre* (= to understand), to — anything from, *cognoscĕre* or *intellegĕre alqd ex re*, to let a person —, *ostendĕre alqd, se ostendĕre, conspici*, not to let oneself be —n in public, *in publicum non prodire*, = to understand, *perspicĕre, intellegĕre* **II.** v intr = to have the faculty of sight, *vidēre, cernĕre*, to — further (in mind), *plus vidēre*, to — to, *alci rei prospicĕre, consulĕre* (or *ut, ne*) **seeing that**, conj see SINCE **seer**, n *vates, -is*

seed, n *semen*; to run to —, *in semen exire* (Plin), fig *semen, stirps* **seed-plot**, n *seminarium*, lit and fig **seed-time**, n *sementis* **seedling**, n *arbor novella*

seek, v tr *quaerĕre, petĕre, (in)vestigare, indagare*, to — to do, *studēre, cupĕre, operam dare ut*, etc, to — out, *exquirĕre*, = to endeavour, *conari*, to — a person's ruin, *alci insidias struĕre* or *parare* **seeker**, n *indagator, investigator* **seeking**, n. *indagatio, investigatio*

seem, v intr *vidēri*, used personally, e g. it —s that you are good, *videris bonus*, to — good, fit, *vidēri* (e g *eam quoque, si videtur, correctionem explicabo*) **seeming, I.** n *species* **II.** adj *fictus, speciosus, falsus* Adv. *in speciem, specie, ut videtur* **seemly**, adj *decens, decōrus, honestus*, not —, *indecens, indecorus*, it is —, *decet*, it is not —, *dedecet, non decet, indecorum est*

seethe, v tr *coquĕre*; see BOIL

segment, n *segmentum* (Plin)

segregate, v tr *segregare, seponĕre, semovēre, removēre, sejungĕre* **segregation**, n *segregatio, sejunctio*

seignior, n *dominus*, see LORD

seize, v tr *(ap)prehendĕre, comprehendĕre* (= to arrest), *rapĕre, arripĕre, corripĕre*, = to fall on and take, *occupare, invadĕre*, to be —d by illness, *morbo affici*, to be —d with fear, *timore percelli* to be —d with anger, *ira incendi* **seizure**, n *comprehensio*, of illness, *tentatio*

seldom, adv *raro*

select, I. v tr *legĕre, eligĕre, deligĕre*, see CHOOSE **II.** adj *delectus* **selection**, n *electio, delectus, -ūs, optio* (= choice), = a number chosen, *res selectae*, — of passages, *ecloga*

self, pron *se, ipse, ipse se*, I my—, *egomet* (so *tute, ipsemet*), of him—, *suāmet sponte*, we ourselves, *nos ipsi, nosmet, nosmet ipsi*, by one—, *solus*, he is beside him—, *mente est captus*, —command, *imperium sui, moderatio, continentia*, to possess —-command, *in se ipsum habēre potestatem*, — deceit, *error*, — denial, *animi moderatio, temperantia*, —-destruction, *mors voluntaria*; to be guilty of —-destruction, *manus sibi inferre*, —-evident, *(quasi) ante oculos positus*, by — exertion, *suâ ipsius manu*; — love, *amor sui*, to have —-love, *se ipsum amare*, —-preservation, *tutio sui, corporis nostri tutela*, —-seeking, *cupidus* **selfish**, adj and adv *suarum rerum cupidus* **selfishness**, n *cupiditas mea (tua*, etc), *privatae utilitatis studium, avaritia* **self willed**, adj *suae opinioni addictus pertinax*, see OBSTINATE

sell, v tr *vendĕre, divendĕre* (by retail), *venditare* (= to live by selling), *venumdare* (*venum dare*), to be sold, *vendi, venire, venum ire*; to — yourself, *se venditare, se vendĕre alci* (= to take a bribe), *pecuniam accipĕre ab alqo*, to — at a dear rate, *vendĕre alqd alci grandi pretio*, he —s cheaper than others, *vendit minoris quam alii*, how much do you — that for? *hoc quanti vendis?* **seller**, n *venditor, institor, negotiator, mundinator, mercator, propōla* **selling**, n *venditio*, see SALE, AUCTION

semblance, n. *species, imago*, see APPEARANCE

semicircle, n *hemicyclium* **semicircular**, adj by noun

seminary, n *schola* (= school), *seminarium* (= seed plot, fig)

senate, n *senatus, -ūs* **senate-house**, n *curia* **senator**, n *senator* **senatorial**, adj *senatorius*

send, v tr *mittĕre, legare, ablegare, amandare*, to — across, *transmittĕre*, to — away, *ablegare, amandare, relegare, dimittĕre*, to — back to, *remittĕre*, to — for, *arcessĕre, (ac)cire*, to — out, *edĕre, emittĕre*; to — for soldiers from their winter quarters, *milites ex hibernis evocare*, to — forward, *praemittĕre*, I have nobody to —, *neminem habeo quem mittam* to — us word with all speed, *fac nos quam diligentissime certiores* (Com), God — him health, *salvus Deum quaeso ut sit* (Com)

senior, adj *prior, superior, grandior (natu*, = older), *major (natu)*; to be a person s —, *alci aetate anteire, antecedĕre* **seniority**, n by adj

sensation, n 1, = a feeling, *sensus, -ūs*, or by some special noun (e g — of pain, *dolor*, — of joy, *gaudium*), to have no — *omni sensu carēre, nihil sentire*, 2, = an excitement, perhaps *(animi) commotio*, to make a —, *alci admirationem movēre* **sensational**, adj *mirificus, mirus, admirabilis* Adv *mire, mirifice, admirabiliter* **sense**, n 1, *sensus, -ūs* (= the faculty, properly of feeling, that is *facultas* or *vis sentiendi*), — of sight, *sensus videndi* or *visūs*, the —s, *sensus*, — of taste, *gustatus, -ūs*, — of hearing, *auditus, -ūs*, — of smell, *odoratus, -ūs*, 2, = mental or moral feeling, *judicium, conscientia, prudentia, sapientia*, 3, = faculty of will, *mens, voluntas*, 4, = meaning (of a word), *vis, significatio, sententia*, to ascribe a — to a word, *verbo notionem sub(j)icĕre* **senseless**, adj 1, lit. *(omni) sensu carens*; 2, *rationis expers*, see FOOLISH, MAD **sensible** or **censuous**, adj 1, *quod sensibus percipi potest, sub sensus cadens, perspicuus, evidens*, 2, = having sound or good sense, e g a — man, *animus* or *homo sapiens, prudens* Adv. *ita ut sentiri possit, sapienter, prudenter*. **sensitive**, adj 1, = SENSIBLE, I, 2, fig of quick feeling, perhaps *acer* (= eager), *anxius, sol(l)icitus* (= anxious), *accuratus, diligens* (= scrupulous, i e in discharge of duty), *tener* (= delicate) **sensitiveness** or **sensibility**, n 1, physical, *qui alqd facile sentit*, 2, moral, *anxietas, sol(l)icitudo, diligentia*, or by adj **sensitive-plant**, n *aeschynomene* (Plin) **sensual**, adj *cupiditatibus serviens, libidinosus* Adv *libidinose* **sensuality**, n *libido*, see LUST **sentient**, adj see SENSIBLE, I.

sentence, I. n 1, = logical statement *sententia* (lit = opinion, then also the words in which it is expressed); 2, = a judicial decision, *judicium, decretum, sententia*; to pronounce —, *sententiam ferre de alqo, sententiam pronuntiare, alqm damnare, condemnare, judicium facĕre de re, de alqo*. **II.** v.tr. see above. **sententious,** adj. *verbosus* (= prolix), *sententiosus* (= pithy), *opinionibus inflatus* (= conceited). Adv. *verbose, sententiose*.

sentiment, n. 1, = opinion, *sententia, opinio, judicium*; see THOUGHT; 2, = feeling, *sensus, -ūs, animus*; a pleasurable —, *voluptas*; an unpleasant —, *dolor*; to have a —, *sentire alqd*; without —, *sensu carens*. **sentimental,** adj. *mollis, effeminatus*, comb. *mollis ac effeminatus*.

sentinel or **sentry,** n. *excubitor, vigil, statio, miles stationarius*; to stand —, *excubias* or *vigilias agĕre, in statione esse*; to place —, *stationes disponĕre*; to relieve —, *in stationem succedĕre*; see GUARD.

separable, adj. *separabilis, dividuus, qui (quae, quod) separari potest*. **separate, I.** v.tr. *separare, sejungĕre, disjungĕre, secernĕre, discernĕre, dividĕre*; we are —d by a great distance, *magno locorum intervallo disjuncti sumus*. **II.** adj. and adv. *separatus*, etc., or by *proprius, suus, viritim, separatim* (e.g. each had his — place, *stationem propriam* or *suam habuit; stationes viritim datae sunt*). **separation,** n. *separatio, disjunctio*. **separatist,** n. *qui a publicis ecclesiae ritibus secedit*.

September, n. (*mensis*) *September*.

septennial, adj. *qui (quae, quod) septimo quoque anno fit*.

sepulchre, n. *sepulc(h)rum*. **sepulchral,** adj. *sepulc(h)ralis*. **sepulture,** n. *sepultura, funus, ex(s)equiae* (= rites of burial).

sequel, n. *quod sequitur, eventus, -ūs, exitus, -ūs*. **sequence,** n. *ordo, series*.

seraph, n. *seraphus* (Eccl.).

serenade, I. v.tr. *alqm concentu honorare*. **II.** n. *concentus, -ūs (nocte factus)*.

serene, adj. 1, see CLEAR; 2, see TRANQUIL.

serf, n. *servus*. **serfdom,** n. *servitus, -ūtis*, f.

serge, n. *pannus*.

serious, adj. 1, = grave, *serius* (of things), *gravis, severus, austerus, tristis* (= sad); 2, = important, *magni* or *maximi momenti*. Adv. *graviter, severe, triste*. **seriousness,** n. 1, *gravitas* (= moral weight), *severitas, tristitia* (= sadness); 2, see IMPORTANCE.

sermon, n. * *contio*, or *oratio de rebus divinis facta*.

serpent, n. *serpens*; see SNAKE.

serried, adj. *densus, confertus*.

serve, v.tr. 1, = to do or render service to, *servire alci, deservire alci, operam alci navare* or *praestare*; 2, = to wait at table, *famulari, ancillari* (ante and post class.), *ministrare*; to — meat, *inferre cibos, instruĕre mensam cibis*; to — wine to the company, *praebēre pocula convivis*; to — as a soldier, *mereri, stipendia facĕre, militare*; to — under, *sub duce merēri*; to — God, *Deum colĕre*; = to benefit, *ad alqm* or *alci conducĕre, proficĕre*. **servant,** n. *servus, famulus, verna* (= slave), *ancilla* (= a waiting-woman), *assecla* (contemptuous term), *minister, mancipium* (= bought slave), *pedis(s)equus* (= a footman), *servitium* (collective term, = slaves), *puer*. **service,** n. *opera, servitium, ministerium, obsequium, officium, observantia, cultus, -ūs*; — of God, *cultus Dei, pietas erga Deum*; to confer a — or kindness on a person, *in alqm officia conferre*. **serviceable,** adj. *opportunus, utilis, aptus rei* or *ad rem, ad usum comparatus, accommodatus*; see USEFUL.

servile, adj. 1, *servilis*; 2, fig. see ABJECT, LOW, MEAN. **servility,** n. *adulatio*; see also MEANNESS. **servitude,** n. *servitudo, servitium, servitus, -ūtis*, f.; to free anyone from —, *in libertatem alqm vindicare, servitute alqm eximĕre*.

session, n. — of Parliament, *senatus, -ūs* (e.g. during a —, *cum senatus habetur*). **sessions,** n. pl. *cum de alqa re quaeritur*.

set, I. v.tr. 1, = to place (*im*)*ponĕre, statuĕre, sistĕre*; 2, = to plant, *serĕre* (e.g. *arbores*; see PLANT); to — in order, *parare* (= to prepare); see ARRANGE; to — jewels, † *auro includĕre*; to — about, *incipĕre*; see BEGIN; to — anyone against another, *inimicitias inter alqos serĕre*; to — apart, *seponĕre*; to — aside, see REJECT; to — forth, *exponĕre* (= to expose for sale, etc., and explain); to — on, see INCITE; to — on fire, *incendĕre* (lit. and fig.); to — over, *alci (rei) praeficĕre*. **II.** v.intr. of the sun, etc., *occidĕre*; to — out, *proficisci*; to — forward, see PROMOTE; to — off, see EMBELLISH; to be — over, *praeesse*; to — up, see ERECT, APPOINT. **III.** adj. *status, constitutus* (= settled), *praescriptus* (= prescribed); a — speech, *oratio*; of — purpose, *consulto*. **IV.** n. see NUMBER, COLLECTION, COMPANY. **settee,** n. *lectulus*. **setting,** n. *occasus, -ūs* (e.g. *solis*).

settle, I. v.tr. 1, = to fix or determine, *statuĕre, constituĕre, definire*; 2, = to fix your abode in, *sedem et domicilium collocare alqo loco*; 3, = to put an end to, *dirimĕre* (e.g. *jurgium* or *iras*, a dispute, quarrel; so with *controversiam, praelium, bellum*); to — accounts, *rationes conficĕre*; to — a debt, etc., *solvĕre, expedire*; 4, = to put in order, e.g. to — the State, *rempublicam componĕre*. **II.** v.intr. 1, *considĕre, consistĕre, sedem habēre, se collocare*; 2, see SINK; 3, see ALIGHT. **settlement,** n. *constitutio*; — of a daughter, *filiae collocatio*; = agreement, *pactum, foedus, -ĕris*, n.; = of a colony, *coloniae deductio*; = fixed abode, *domicilium, aedes, -ium* (of private persons), *colonia* (= colony); = of a debt, use verb. **settler,** n. *advena*, m. and f., *colonus*.

seven, adj. *septem, septeni, -ae, -a* (= — each); of — years, *septennis, septem annorum*; — years old, *septem annos natus*; — times, *septie(n)s*. **seventh,** adj. *septimus*. **seventhly,** adv. *septimum*. **seventeen,** adj. *septemdecim, decem et septem* or *decem septem* or *septem et decem, septeni deni* (— each); — times, *septie(n)s decie(n)s*. **seventeenth,** adj. *septimus decimus*. **seventy,** adj. *septuaginta, septuageni* (= — each); — letters, *septuagenae lit(t)erae*, not *septuaginta* (i.e. — alphabetical letters); — times, *septuagie(n)s*. **seventieth,** adj. *septuagesimus*; the — time, *septuagesimum*.

sever, v.tr. *dividĕre, dirimĕre, separare, secernĕre, disjungĕre*.

several, adj. *nonnulli, plures, aliquot*. Adv. by *unusquisque*, or by *si(n)gillatim*; — may also be rendered with the aid of the distributive numerals (e.g. *uxores habent deni duodenique inter se communes*, = sets of ten or twelve have — wives in common), also by *quisque* (e.g. *prout quisque monitione indigerent*, as they — required admonition), and lastly by *singuli* (e.g. *duodena describit in singulos homines jugera*, he allotted to the men — twelve acres), so too *viritim*.

severe, adj. *severus, austerus, durus, acerbus* (the two last of winter, also in gen.), *gravis*. Adv. *severe, rigide, austere, dure, duriter, acerbe, graviter*. **severity,** n. *severitas, gravitas* (of climate and in gen.), *duritia*.

sew, v.tr. *suĕre*. **sewing,** n. *suendi ars*.

sewer, n. *cloaca*.

sex, n. *sexus, -ūs*; male —, *virilis sexus*; female —, *muliebris sexus*. **sexual,** adj. *quod ad sexum pertinet*; — intercourse, *coitus, -ūs*,

sexagenarian, adj *sexagenarius*, see SIXTY.

sexton, n *aedituus*

shabby, adj 1, *obsoletus, sordidus* (e g *amictus homo*), 2, fig see MEAN **shabbiness,** n 1, use adj , 2, *sordes, ium* (of conduct)

shackles, n *vincula, catenae, compedes, um*, — for the feet, *pedicae*, for the hands, *manicae* **shackle,** v tr *vinculis colligĕre, catenis vincire*, fig *impedire, impedimento esse.*

shade, I. n. *umbra*, in the —, *in umbrā*, under the —, *sub umbrā*, to be afraid of —s, *umbras timēre*, fig "shadow," = a mere appearance or pretext, *umbra* (e g *gloriae, libertatis, honoris*, *sub umbra foederis aequi servitutem pati*), *umbra* also = — in painting (opp *lumen*), further, a person's shadow or companion is in Latin *umbra*, "shade," = ghosts, †*umbrae*, in pl , *manes* **II.** v tr. †*umbrare*, see DARKEN. **shady,** adj *umbrosus, opacus* (= dark) **shadow, I.** n *umbra* **II.** v tr see SHADE, II **shadowy,** adj 1, = SHADY , 2, see VAIN, UNREAL

shaft, n 1, = arrow, *sagitta* , 2, = handle, *hastile*, 3, in architecture, *truncus*, 4, of a carriage, *temo* (= pole), or by *lora* (= reins), of a mine, etc , *puteus* (Plin)

shake, I. v tr *quatĕre, tremefacĕre, labefactare, quassare* (= to — often), to — hands, *jungĕre dextras*, they — the foundations, *labefactant fundamenta reipublicae*. to — off, *excutĕre* **II.** v intr *quassari, agitari, tremĕre* **shaking,** n. *quassatio* (in act sense), *tremor* (in pass sense)

shallow, I. adj. *tenuis*, —s or shoals, *vada*, *-orum*, pl , full of —s, *vadosus*, fig *parum subtilis* **II.** n *vadum.*

sham, I. n *fallacia, dolus*, without —, *sine fuco ac fallaciis* **II.** v intr *simulare* (to pretend), see FEIGN, PRETEND **sham-fight,** n *simulacrum pugnae*, see REVIEW

shambles, n *lanīna*

shame, I. n 1, = modesty, *pudor, verecundia*, comb *pudor et verecundia*, *pudicitia*, comb. *pudor et pudicitia*, to have lost the sense of —, *pudorem posuisse*, he who has lost his sense of —, *pudoris oblitus*, 2, = moral turpitude, *turpitudo* (baseness), *ignominia*, comb *ignominia et turpitudo*, *infamia*, comb *turpitudo et infamia*, *dedecus, -ŏris*, n , comb *ignominia et dedecus, dedecus et infamia*, *macula* (= a spot or brand) *et dedecus*, *probrum*, comb *probrum et dedecus*, *flagitium* (= a crime), comb *flagitium et dedecus* to our —, *cum nostro dedecore*, — ! *proh pudor ! o indignum facinus !* it is a — to say that, *hoc est turpe dictu* **II.** v tr *pudore*, etc , *alqm afficĕre* **shamefaced,** adj see MODEST **shameful,** adj *turpis, foedus* (in gen), *obscenus* (= obscene), *ignominiosus, probrosus, inhonestus* (= dishonourable), *flagitiosus, nefarius* (= criminal) Adv *turpiter, foede, obscene ignominiose, inhoneste, flagitiose, nefarie* **shamefulness,** n *turpitudo, foeditas, obscenitas, ignominia* **shameless,** adj *impudens, immodicus* (= unchaste), *inverecundus*, a — (or brazen) face, *os impudens* (so *durum, ferreum*) Adv *impudenter* **shamelessness,** n *impudentia, impudicitia*

shank, n *crus, cruris*, n , *tibia*

shape, I. n *forma, figura, species*, to give — to, *formare, fingĕre alqd* **II.** v tr (*con*)*formare, figurare, fingĕre, alqd in formam rei redigĕre*; to — itself differently, *mutari* **shapeless,** adj *informis, deformis* **shapely,** adj *formosus* **shapeliness,** n see BEAUTY **shaping,** n (*con*)*formatio*

share, I. n 1, *pars, portio, sors*, 2, of a plough, *vomer* **II.** v tr *partiri* (e g *partiuntur inter se*, so *partiri praedam in socios, bona cum alqo, curas cum alqo, copias inter se*), *sortiri, dare* (e g *perinde ut cuique data sunt*), *dividĕre* (e g *dividĕre equitatum in omnes partes*), *alqd cum alqo communicare* **sharer,** n *particeps, socius, consors*, in a thing, *alcjs rei*

shark, n *pristis*, spelling also *p(r)ist(r)is, p(r)ist(r)ix*

sharp, adj 1, lit *acutus*, — to the taste, *acutus, acer, acerbus*, 2, fig = working strongly on the feelings, *acer, acerbus, severus*, there is — fighting, *acriter pugnatur*, 3, = penetrating, *acutus, sagax*, — eyes, *oculi acuti*, — nose, *nasus sagax*, 4, of mental faculties, *acer, acutus, subtilis* (e g *ingenium acre*), 5, of words, *iracundus, mordax* (= biting), *severus, gravis* (= severe), — witted, *perspicax, sagax* Adv *acute, acriter, sagaciter, subtiliter* (= wisely), *iracunde, severe, graviter* (= severely) **sharpen,** v tr (*ex*)*acuĕre* (lit and fig) **sharper,** n *veterator, fraudator, praestigiator* **sharpness,** n 1, of edge, by adj , *acutus* 2, fig *severitas*, see STERNNESS, 3, — of intellect, (*ingenii*) *acies, -ēi*, f, *acumen, ingenium acutum, perspicacitas, subtilitas*

shatter, v tr 1, *frangĕre, confringĕre, diffringĕre, discutĕre, elidĕre, quassare*, 2, fig. *frangĕre, quassare*

shave, v tr (*ab*)*radĕre, barbam alcjs tondēre* (= to clip), to get —d, *tondēri*. **shavings,** n *scob(i)s* (= sawdust), *assulae, schidiae* (= chips).

shawl, n see MANTLE

she, as a personal pronoun, is expressed only when emphasis requires it (e g *illa, ista, haec, ea*), as an adjective, is expressed by the feminine (e g a —-friend, *amica*, a —-wolf, *lupa*)

sheaf, n *manipulus* (= a handful), *fascis*

shear, v tr *tondēre* (e g *oves*) **shearer,** n *qui tondet* **shearing,** n *tonsura* **shears,** n *forfices* (Mart).

sheath, n *vagina*; to draw a sword from its —, *gladium e vaginā educĕre.* **sheathe,** v tr *in vaginam recondĕre*

shed, n *tugurium, taberna*, as military term, *pluteus, vinea*

shed, v tr (*dif*)*fundĕre, effundĕre, profundĕre*, to — tears, *lacrimas profundĕre, lacrimare*, to — blood, see KILL **shedding,** n *effusio, profusio*, — of tears, *fletus, -ūs*, — of blood, *caedes, -is*, — of leaves, by *decidĕre*

sheep, n. *ovis* (ὄις) **sheep-fold,** n *ovile.* **sheepish,** adj *insulsus* see STUPID, a — fellow, *ovis* (Plaut) **sheepishness,** n *insulsitas, nimia verecundia* **shepherd,** n *pastor.*

sheer, adj 1, see STEEP, 2, *merus*, — folly, *mera* or *maxima stultitia*

sheet, n 1, of a bed, *lodix* (= blanket, Juv), 2, a — of paper, *scheda, sc(h)ida, schedula, plagula* (Plin), 3, a — of lead, (*plumbi*) *lamina*, 4 of a sail, *pes* **sheet-anchor,** n *ancora* **sheet-lightning,** n *fulgur, fulmen*

shelf, n *pluteus* (Juv), *pegma* *-ătis*, n

shell, n *testa, concha* (of fish), *putamen, cortex* (of fruit, etc) **shell-fish,** n *concha, conchylium*

shelter, I. n 1, = covering, *teg(i)men*, 2, = protection, *perfugium, asylum, patrocinium, defensio* **II.** v tr 1, *tegĕre, defendĕre*, 2, *tutari alqm, defendĕre auctoritate tueri, in suam fidem et clientelam suscipĕre, protegĕre, receptum tutum praebēre alci*, see PROTECT

shelving, adj *declivis*, see SLOPING

shepherd, n, see under SHEEP

sheriff, n. perhaps by *praetor*, in mediæval Latin by * *vicecomes* or *gerefa*.

shew, v.tr. = to bring forward, *edĕre, ostendĕre, explicare;* = to prove or explain, *demonstrare, declarare, ostendĕre, exponĕre, narrare;* to — mercy, *alci misericordiam impertiri.*

shield, I. n. **1,** *scutum, clipeus, parma, pelta, ancile* (esp. of the sacred — which fell from heaven); a —-bearer, *armiger;* **2,** fig. see PROTECTION. **II.** v.tr. *scuto defendĕre, clipeo protegĕre;* to — from danger, *a periculo defendĕre;* see PROTECT.

shift, I. n. **1,** = refuge or resource, *effugium, ambāges,* -um, *remedium, ratio, consilium, latebra;* a dishonest —, *fraus, doli* (pl.), *ambāges;* everyone made — for himself, *sibi quisque consulebat;* **2,** = an under-garment, *tunica interula.* **II.** v.tr. = to change, *(per)mutare;* to — one's clothes, *mutare vestem;* to — off, *eludĕre, evitare, subterfugĕre;* see CHANGE. **shifty,** adj. **1,** see CUNNING; **2,** see CHANGEABLE.

shilling, n. *quadraginta octo asses.*

shin, n. *tibia, crus, cruris,* n.

shine, v.intr. *(col)lucēre, splendēre, fulgēre, nitēre, micare* (= to glitter); to — forth, *elucēre, effulgēre;* to — upon, *alci affulgēre;* it —s with a borrowed light, *luce lucet aliena.*

ship, I. n. *navis, navigium* (used of smaller vessels), *navis longa* or *rostrata* (= a — of war), *(navis) biremis* (= — having two banks of oars, so *triremis, quadremis, quinqueremis,* having three, four, five), *navis praedatoria* or *piratica* (= a pirate vessel); belonging to a —, *navalis, nauticus;* shipping, *naves,* pl.; —wreck, *naufragium;* one who has suffered —wreck, *naufragus;* to suffer —wreck, *naufragium facĕre;* a —'s captain, *navarchus;* a —-owner, *navicularius* (who lets out —s); —'s crew, *remigium classicique milites;* master of a —, *magister.* **II.** v.tr. *in navem (naves) imponĕre.*

shire, n. *provincia; ager,* * *comitatus.*

shirt, n. *subucula.*

shiver, I. v.tr. = to break in pieces, *frangĕre, confringĕre, diffringĕre, elidĕre.* **II.** v.intr. = to tremble, *tremĕre* (with fear), *algēre* (= to be cold).

shoal, n. **1,** *vadum, vada,* pl.; see SHALLOW; **2,** = a large quantity or number, *turba, grex, caterva.*

shock, I. n. **1,** in battle, etc., *impetus, concursus, congressus,* all -ūs; to bear the —, *sustinēre impetum;* at the first —, *ad primum impetum;* **2,** fig. of the feelings, etc., *offensio;* see OFFENCE; **3,** of corn, *frumenti manipulorum acervus.* **II.** v.tr. *offendĕre, commovēre;* to be —ed, *commovēri.* **shocking,** adj. *quod offensioni est, quod offensionem habet* or *affert, odiosus;* a — life, *vita turpis;* see DISGUSTING; to be —, *offensioni esse.* Adv. = very badly, *pessime,* or by superl. (e.g. *pessimus* = — bad).

shoe, I. n. *calceus, calceamentum, solea* (= sandal); horse-—, *solea ferrea* (—s nailed were unknown); —s that fit, *calcei apti ad pedem;* the — pinches, *calceus urit.* **II.** v.tr. *calceare;* to — a horse, *affigĕre equo soleas ferreas.* **shoe-black,** n. *puer qui calceos deterget.* **shoemaker,** n. *sutor.*

shoot, I. n. = sprout, † *germen, surculus, planta, virga, propago* (= layer). **II.** v.intr. **1,** to — out, as ears of corn, *spicas, surculos,* etc., *emittĕre;* **2,** of pains, etc., *angĕre* (= to torture), or *angi* (= to be tortured); of stars, *volare.* **III.** v.tr. = to cast forth, *jaculari, emittĕre, jacĕre;* to — arrows out of a bow, *arcu saggitas (e)mittĕre;* to — at, *sagittis* or *telis petĕre;* see FIRE. **shooting-star,** n. see METEOR.

shop, I. n. *taberna, officina* (= work—); a bookseller's —, *libraria;* a barber's —, *taberna tonsoris.* **II.** v.intr. to go a-shopping, *concursare circum tabernas,* or by *emĕre* (= to buy). **shop-keeper,** n. *qui alqus res vendit,* in pl. *tabernarii.*

shore, I. n. **1,** *litus, -ŏris,* n., *ora, acta* (ἀκτή), *ripa* (= the declining bank or margin), *arena* (= sand); **2,** = support, *fulcrum.* **II.** v.tr. *fulcire.*

short, adj. *brevis, concisus* (= pruned), *angustus* (= within a small space), *contractior* (= somewhat drawn in), *compressus* (= squeezed together), *paucioribus verbis expressus* (of a writing); — of stature, *humilis* (opp. *procerus*); a — cut, *compendium, via compendiaria* (lit. and fig.); to be —, *ne ne multa, ut in pauca referam, ne multis, ne plura;* in —, *summatim, ad summam, summa illa sit, in brevi;* cut it —, *verbo dicas;* a — syllable, *syllaba brevis;* — hair, *capilli tonsi;* a — memory, *memoria hebes;* the —est day, *dies brumalis, bruma;* the —est night, *nox solstitialis.* **short-legged,** adj. *cruribus brevibus.* **short-sighted,** adj. *myops* (Jct.), *qui oculis non satis prospicit;* fig. *stultus, imprudens.* **shortcoming,** n. *delictum.* **shorten,** v.tr. *praecidĕre, breviorem facĕre* or *reddĕre;* to — a syllable, *syllabam corripĕre;* see CONTRACT. **shorthand,** n. *notae.* **shortly,** adv. **1,** = compendiously, *summatim, strictim, compresse, paucis verbis, breviter;* **2,** = within a short time, *brevi, propediem, paucis diebus, exiguo spatio;* — before, *brevi ante, paul(l)o ante, proxime, nuper;* — after, *brevi post, paul(l)o post, non ita multo post;* — before a person's death, *haud multum ante* (so *post*) *alcjs mortem.* **shortness,** adj. *brevitas, exiguitas, angustiae, compendium, contractio* (= a drawing in).

shot, n. *teli jactus, -ūs,* or *conjectus, -ūs, ictus, -ūs, (telum) missile* (= what is fired), *glans* (= ball); to fire a —, *telum emittĕre;* they were now within —, *jam ad teli jactum pervenerant;* out of —, *extra teli jactum.*

shoulder, I. n. *humerus;* —-blade, *scapula.* **II.** v.tr. *alqd in humeros tollĕre.*

shout, I. n. *clamor, vociferatio, vox, acclamatio;* to raise a —, *clamorem tollĕre.* **II.** v.tr. *(con)clamare, vociferari.*

shove, I. v.tr. *trudĕre, impellĕre.* **II.** n. *impulsus, -ūs.*

shovel, I. n. *pala, batillum.* **II.** v.tr. *batillo tollĕre.*

show, I. n. **1,** = an exhibition, *spectaculum, pompa, ludi* (= games); **2,** *ostentatio* (= display), *species* (= appearance); to make — of or pretend, *simulare, prae se ferre;* for some time there was some — of fight, *exiguum temporis alqa forma pugnae fuit;* under a — of friendship, *per simulationem amicitiae.* **II.** v.tr. *proponĕre, ostentare alqd, prae se ferre;* to — off, *se ostentare;* see SHEW. **showy,** adj. see BEAUTIFUL, OSTENTATIOUS.

shower, I. n. *pluvia repentina, imber, pluvia;* a plentiful —, *largus imber;* a — of stones, *lapidum imber.* **II.** v.tr. *effundĕre.* **showery,** adj. *pluvius, pluvialis.*

shred, I. n. *frustum* (= a scrap), *segmentum* (Plin.). **II.** v.tr. *minutatim dissecare* or *concidĕre.*

shrew, n. *mulier jurgiis dedita.* **shrewd,** adj. *prudens, sol(l)ers, callidus, astutus, perspicax, sagax.* Adv. *callide, astute, sagaciter, sol(l)erter, prudenter.* **shrewdness,** n. *calliditas, astutia, perspicacitas, sagacitas, prudentia, sol(l)ertia.* **shrewish,** adj. see QUARRELSOME. **shrew-mouse,** n. *sorex.*

shriek, I. n. *ejulatus, -ūs, ululatus, -ūs.* **II.** v.intr. *ululare.* **III.** v.tr. *clamare;* see SCREAM.

shrift, n a short —, *confestim alqm necare*, see also CONFESSION, SHRIVE

shrill, adj. *acutus, argutus* Adv. *acute, argute*

shrimp, n 1, *cancer pagurus* (Linn), 2, fig see DWARF

shrine, n *aedicula, delubrum, sacellum*

shrink, v intr *se contrahere*, to — through fear, *pedem referre*, to — from duty, *abhorrere, recedere* (*ab officio nunquam recedemus*, Cic), to — from fight, *pugnam detrectare* **shrinking,** n 1, *alcjs rei contractio*, 2, see FEAR

shrive, v tr *peccata sua sacerdoti fateri* (= to confess), *peccata confitentem absolvere* (= to absolve)

shrivel, I. v tr *rugosum facere* **II.** v intr (*cor*)*rugari, contrahi*

shroud, I. n *mortui vestimentum* **II.** v tr *involvere, velare, tegere, mortuum vestimento induere*

shrub, n *frutex* **shrubbery,** n *arbustum*

shrug, v tr to — the shoulders, *humeros movere*

shudder, I. n. *horror, tremor* **II.** v intr *horrere, tremere*, to — greatly, *perhorrescere*

shuffle, I. v.tr. 1, = to mix, (*com*)*miscere*, to — cards, *paginas* (*per*)*miscere*, 2, = to act deceitfully, *fraudare* **II.** v intr *tergiversari* (of conduct), *claudicare* (= to limp) **shuffler,** n *fraudator, homo fallax* **shuffling,** n *fraus, -dis*, f, *dolus, tergiversatio*

shun, v tr (*de*)*fugere, vitare, declinare, aversari* **shunning,** n *devitatio, fuga, declinatio, vitatio*

shut, v tr *claudere, operire*, to — the eyes, *oculos operire*, to — the hand, *manum comprimere*, to — in, *includere*, to — out, *excludere* **shutter,** n (for a window), *foricula, valvae*

shuttle, n *radius* (*textorius*) **shuttle-cock,** n *pila pennata*

shy, I. adj *timidus, pavidus, verecundus* (= modest), to be — of expense, *sumptibus parcere* **II.** v tr of a horse, *terreri*, *altum in contrarium facere* Adv *timide, verecunde.* **shyness,** n *timor, pavor, verecundia, pudor*

sibilant, adj *sibilans*

sibyl, n *sibylla* **sibylline,** adj *sibyllinus*

sick, adj *aeger* (used of disorders of mind and body; see ILL), to rise from a — bed, *assurgere ex morbo*, a — man, *aeger, aegrotus*, to feel —, *nauseare*, to be —, *vomere*, fig by impers *taedet alqm alcjs rei*, see ILL **sicken, I.** v tr see DISGUST **II.** v intr *in morbum incidere* **sickly,** adj *morbosus*, see ILL, WEAK **sickness,** n = sensation of —, vomiting, nausea, *vomitus, -ūs* (= illness), *morbus* (= disorder), *aegrotatio* (= condition of —), *valetudo* (properly = state of health or strength, used alone = —, or with *adversa, infirma*, etc), a contagious —, *contagio, lues, -is*, f (= the impure cause of the disease), an epidemic, = *pestilentia*

sickle, n *falx*

side, I. n *latus, -ĕris*, n (of the body, a hill, etc), *pars* (= part, party), *regio* (= district), *pagina* (= — of a leaf), on that —, *illinc, ultro*, on this — and on that, *citra ultroque*, on all —s, *undique versus, omnibus partibus*, towards all —s, *in omnes partes*, on this —, *hinc*, on both —s, *utrimque*, on each of two —s, *utrobique*, on his — nothing takes place, *ab eo nihil agitur* **II.** adj *obliquus, transversus*, a — blow, *ictus obliquus*, to give anyone a — blow, *gladio alqm oblique petere.* **III.** v intr to — with, *alcjs partibus* or *alci favere, studere, alcjs studiosum esse* **side board,** n *abacus* **sidelong,** adj *obliquus.* **sideways,** adv *oblique, ab obliquo, ex obliquo.*

sidereal, adj by gen *siderum, sideralis* (Plin)

siege, n. *oppugnatio, obsessio, obsidio*

sieve, n *cribrum.* **sift,** v tr *cribrare* (Plin), *cribro secernere*, fig *investigare*, (*per*)*scrutari, explorare*

sigh, I. n *suspirium* **II.** v intr *suspiria ducere, suspirare* **sighing,** n *suspiratus, -ūs*

sight, I. n 1, *visio, visus, -ūs, videndi facultas, oculus, conspectus, -ūs* (= view), *a*(*d*)*spectus, -ūs*, — of the eye, *oculi acies*, at first —, *primo a*(*d*)*spectu*, 2, = spectacle, *species* (= an appearance), *spectaculum* (= a show), in —, *in conspectu, ante oculos, in or sub oculis* he was in —, *sub oculos erat*, to take out of —, *oculis subducere, ex hominum conspectu subtrahere*, I knew him by —, *de facie novi*, to pay at —, *pecunias repraesentare*, to catch — of *conspicere* **II.** v tr *conspicari, conspicere*

sign, I. n *signum, significatio, indicium, vestigium* (= footmark), *nota* (= mark), *insigne* (= badge), *nutus, -ūs* (= nod), the peculiar — of a thing, *proprium alcjs rei* (= characteristic), it is the — of a wise man, *est sapientis*, — of the future, *signum, omen, ostentum, portentum* a good —, *omen faustum*, a bad —, *omen sinistrum* **II.** v tr 1, to — a document, (*con*)*signare alqd, alci rei* (*nomen*) *subscribere*, as witnesses, *scribendo adesse*, 2, see SIGNAL **signal, I.** adj *insignis, notabilis maximus, designatus, egregius* Adv *insigniter, notabiliter, maxime, insignite, egregie* **II.** n *signum, symbolum*, to give the — for an attack, *signum dare*; for battle, *classicum canere, tubā signum dare* **III.** v tr see above, SIGNAL, II **signalize,** v tr *declarare* (= to show), *alci* or *alci rei decori esse* (= to be an honour to), *insignire* (= to make remarkable, e g *tot facinoribus foedum annum etiam dii tempestatibus et morbis insignivere*, Tac), to — yourself, *se clarum reddere* **signature,** n *nomen, -inis*, n, *subscriptio, nomen subscriptum* **signet,** n *signum* (= seal) **significance, signification,** n *significatio*, see MEANING **significant,** adj see EXPRESSIVE **signify,** v tr *significare* (= to make signs), *valere* (= to be equivalent, e g *verbum quod idem valet*), *velle* (= to wish), see also MEAN, ANNOUNCE, PORTEND

silence, n *silentium, taciturnitas* (= not speaking) to keep —, *tacere, conticere, conticescere, obticere, obmutescere* **silent,** adj *tacitus, silens, taciturnus* (= taciturn), to be —, *silere, tacere, linguis favere* (at religious rites), to be — about, *celare, silentio praeterire alqd*, be — ! *quin taces !* Adv *tacite, silentio*

silk, n *bombyx* (Plin), or *vestis serica* **silk-worm,** n *bombyx* (Plin) **silken,** adj *sericus, bombycinus* (Plin) **silky,** adj see SMOOTH

sill, n *limen*

silly, adj *stultus, fatuus, stolidus, infacetus absurdus, excors, vecors, ineptus, insulsus, amens, ridiculus* (= exciting laughter) Adv *stulte, stolide, infacete, absurde, inepte, insulse, ridicule* **silliness,** n *stultitia, fatuitas, stoliditas ineptiae, vecordia, amentia, insulsitas, ridiculum*

silt, I. n *limus* **II.** v tr *limo opplere*

silver, I. n *argentum*, wrought —, *argentum factum* **II.** adj and **silvery,** *argenteus*, plated with —, *argentatus*, — mine, *argenti metalla*,

-orum, n.; — foil, *bractea argentea*, *argenti fodina* (or as one word), *argentaria* (*fodina*); — money, *nummi argentei*; — plate, *argentum* (*factum*), *vasa argentea*, pl. **III.** v.tr. *alqd argento inducĕre*.

similar, adj. *similis* (used with the genit. of internal bodily or mental relations, with dat. otherwise, e.g. *non tam potuit patris similis esse quam ille fuerat sui*, Cic.). Adv. *similiter*. **similarity**, n. = resemblance, *similitudo* (*est homini cum Deo similitudo*, Cic.; *habet honestatis similitudinem*; *similitudines*, = similar objects). **simile**, n. *similitudo*, *translatio*, *collatio*. **similitude**, n. = comparison, *similitudo*; see LIKE, SIMULATE.

simmer, v.intr. *fervescĕre*, *lente bullire*.

simony, n. *simonia* (Eccl.).

simper, v.intr. *subridēre*, *stulte ridēre*.

simple, adj. *simplex* (in gen.); = harmless, *innocuus*; = sincere, *sincerus*, *probus*, *integer*, *sine fuco*; = silly, *stolidus*, *insulsus*; = without ornament, *simplex*, *sine ornatu*; = sheer, *merus*. Adv. *simpliciter*; see also ONLY. **simples**, n. pl. *herbae* (*medicinales*). **simpleton**, n. *homo crassi ingenii*, *stultus*, *fatuus*, *ineptus*; see FOOL. **simplicity**, n. *simplicitas* (in gen.), *stultitia* (= folly), *innocentia* (= guilelessness). **simplify**, v.tr. *explicare*, *simplicem reddĕre*.

simulate, v.tr. = to imitate or pretend, *simulare* (e.g. *mortem*, *lacrimas*, *simulavit se furĕre*). **simulation**, n. *simulatio* (e.g. *fallax imitatio simulatioque virtutis*).

simultaneous, adj. *quod uno et eodem tempore est* or *fit*. Adv. *eodem tempore*, *simul*, *una*.

sin, **I.** n. *peccatum*, *delictum* (= omission), *flagitium*, *nefas*; to commit a —, *peccare*, *delinquĕre*, *peccatum committĕre*. **II.** v.intr. *peccare* (*in se*, *erga alqm*, *in re*; *multa peccantur*), *delinquĕre*. **sinful**, adj. *pravis cupiditatibus deditus*, *impius*, *improbus*, *flagitiosus*. **sinless**, adj. *integer*, *sanctus*. **sinlessness**, n. *vitae sanctitas*. **sinner**, n. *qui peccavit*, *peccator* (Eccl.).

since, **I.** adv. *abhinc* (e.g. he died two years —, *abhinc annos duos*, or *annis duobus*, *mortuus est*); long —, *jamdudum*, *jampridem*. **II.** prep. by *e*, *ex*, *a*, *ab*, *post* (e.g. — the foundation of the city, *post urbem conditam*); — that time, *ex eo tempore*; many years —, *multis abhinc annis*; — when, *ex quo*; a long time —, *jamdiu*; — childhood, *a pueritiā*, *a puero*. **III.** conj. **1**, of time, *cum* (*quom*, *quum*), *postquam* (or as two words); this is the third day — I heard it, *tertius hic dies quod audivi*; it is a long time — you left home, *jamdudum factum est cum abiisti domo*; — he died this is the three-and-thirtieth year, *cujus a morte hic tertius et tricesimus annus*; **2**, of cause, may be rendered by *cum* with subj., or *quandoquidem*, *quia*, *quoniam* with indic., thus frequently in Cic. *quae cum ita sint*, — this is so, but observe *quandoquidem tu istos oratores tantopere laudas* (in the indic., Cic.); *so urbs quae*, *quia postrema aedificata est*, *Neapolis nominatur* (Cic.); *quoniam res in id discrimen adducta est*; — may also be rendered by the relative with a causal force, and so requiring the subj., e.g. *maluimus iter facĕre pedibus*, *qui incommodissime navigassemus*, Cic.; so too *quippe qui* with indic. or subj. (all these conjs. follow the ordinary rules of mood); see BECAUSE.

sincere, adj. *sincerus* (opp. *fucatus*, *simulatus*), *integer* (e.g. *te sincerum integrumque conserves*, Cic.), *probus*, *purus*, *candidus*, *verus*; see HONEST. Adv. *sincere*, *integre* (= justly), *probe*, *pure*, *candide*, *vere*, *ex animo*, *simpliciter*; yours —, in letters, *vale* (*valete*). **sincerity**, n. *sinceritas*, *candor*, *integritas*, *probitas*, *veritas* (= truthfulness), *simplicitas*.

sinecure, n. *munus omni labor vacuum*.

sinew, n. *nervus*; the —s, as = strength, *nervi*. **sinewy**, adj. *nervosus*.

sing, v.tr. and intr. *canĕre*, *cantare*, *modulari*; to — much, *cantitare*; to — to the harp, *ad citharam canĕre*; to — in harmony, *servare modum*, *ad numerum canĕre*. **singer**, n. †*cantor*, *cantrix*, *cantator*, *cantatrix*. **singing**, n. *cantus*, *-ūs*, *concentus*, *-ūs* (of a number of persons).

singe, v.tr. *ustulare*, *amburĕre*, *adurĕre*.

single, **I.** adj. *unus*, *solus*, *singularis*, *ūnicus*; a — or unmarried man, *caelebs* (a bachelor); — combat, *certamen unius cum uno*. Adv. *singillatim*. **II.** v.tr. to — out, *eligĕre*; see SELECT. **singular**, adj. **1**, as opp. to plural, *singularis*; the — number, *numerus singularis* (gram.); see SINGLE, I.; **2**, = out of the common way, *singularis* (= very superior, e.g. *Aristoteles meo judicio in philosophiā prope singularis*, = almost standing alone, Cic.; also in a bad sense, e.g. *singularis crudelitas*, *nequitia*), *unicus* (= unique), *egregius*, *eximius*, *praestans* (= excellent), *maximus* (= very great); **3**, = strange, *mirus*, *mirificus*, *mirabilis*, *novus*, *insolitus*, *insolens*. Adv. *singulariter*, *unice*, *egregie*, *eximie*, *praestanter*, *insolenter*, *maxime*, *mire*, *mirifice*, *mirabiliter*, *nove*, *insolite*. **singularity**, n. *insolentia*, *praestantia* (= excellence), or use adj.

sinister, adj. *sinister* (lit. = left-handed; fig. with *mores*, *natura*, *interpretatio*, etc.), †*infaustus* (= unlucky); see ILL-OMENED, CORRUPT.

sink, **I.** v.tr. (*sub*)*mergĕre*, *demergĕre*, *immergĕre*, *deprimĕre*. **II.** v.intr. (*con*)*sidĕre*, *desidĕre*, *residĕre*, *submergi*, *demergi*, *immergi*; to — in ruins, *collabi*, *corruĕre*, *mergi*; to — morally, *in* (*omnia*) *flagitia se ingurgitare*; to — into sleep, *somno opprimi*; the price —s, *pretium imminuitur*; his courage —s, *animus cadit*; to let one's courage —, *sibi diffidĕre*; to — into the mind, *in animum penetrare*; to be sunk in debt, *aere alieno obrui*. **III.** n. *sentina*.

sinuous, adj. *sinuosus*.

sip, **I.** v.tr. (*primis labris*) *degustare*, *sorbillare* (ante and post class.). **II.** n. use verb.

sir, n. **1**, as title, *dominus*; **2**, in addresses, *vir optime*.

sire, n. **1**, *pater*, *genitor*; see FATHER; **2**, see SIR.

siren, n. *siren*.

sirocco, n. *auster*.

sister, n. *soror*, *germana*; father's —, *amita*; mother's —, *matertera*; grandfather's —, *amita magna*; grandmother's —, *matertera magna*; —-in-law, *glos*, *gloris*, f. (Jct.). **sisterhood**, n. *sororum societas* (Eccl.). **sisterly**, adj. *ut sorores solent*.

sit, v.intr. *sedēre*, *alqā re insidēre*, *considĕre* (= to — down); to — near, *assidēre rei* or *alci*; to — on, *sedēre in re*; to — at table, *accumbĕre*, *discumbĕre*, *recumbĕre*; to — above at table, *superior accumbĕre*; of a court, *habēri* (e.g. *conventus*), *sedēre* (of the magistrates); we sat up talking till late at night, *sermonem in multam noctem produximus* (Cic.); he —s up till daylight, *usque ad lucem vigilat*; of fowls, (*ovis*) *incubare* (Plin.); as milit. term, to — down before a place, *oppidum circumsedēre*. **sitting**, n. *sessio* (lit. of a court), *consessus*, *-ūs* (of a court, etc.); to break up the —, *consessum*, etc., *dimittĕre*.

site, n. *situs*, *-ūs*. **situate**, adj. *situs*, *positus*, *collocatus*; to be — near, *adjacēre*. **situation**, n. **1**, = position, *situs*, *-ūs*; *sedes*, *-is*, *locus*; if he were in that —, *si eo loco esset*; **2**, = office, *munus*, *-eris*, n.; see OFFICE.

six, adj *sex, seni* (= — each), — or seven, *sex septem, sex aut septem*, to throw — (at dice), *senionem mittĕre*, — times, *sexie(n)s* **sixth,** adj *sextus*, the — time, *sextum* **sixteen,** adj *sedecim (sexd.), decem et sex, seni deni* (= — each), — times, *sedecie(n)s* **sixteenth,** adj *sextus decimus*, one —, *pars sexta decima* **sixty,** adj *sexaginta, sexageni* (= — each), — times, *sexagie(n)s* **sixtieth,** adj *sexagesimus*, the — time, *sexagesimum*, sixty thousand, *sexaginta milia*, the — thousandth, *sexagie(n)s millesimus*.

size, n 1, = measure, *mensura, amplitudo* (= largeness), *parvitas* (= smallness), *proceritas* (= tallness), *altitudo* (= height), *ambitus, -ūs* (= girth), *spatium* (= extent of surface), to take the — of (*di*)*metiri*, of the — of, (*ad*) *instar alcjs rei*, of great, small —, etc, *magnus, parvus*, 2, = glue, *gluten* (*glutinum*)

skate, I. n *solea ferrata* **II.** v.intr. *soleis ferratis glaciem transcurrĕre*

skein, n *filia volumen* or *filorum glomus*

skeleton, n *ossa, -ium*, n, *ossium compages*, he is a mere —, *vix ossibus haeret*

sketch, I. n *adumbratio*, see OUTLINE **II.** v tr *describĕre, designare, adumbrare* (esp fig)

skewer, n *veru* (= spit).

skiff, n *scapha, cymba, navicula*

skill, n *peritia, scientia, ars, artificium, sol(l)ertia, calliditas, prudentia, habilitas* **skilful,** adj *peritus rei, arte insignis, exercitatus in re, dexter, sol(l)ers, sciens, callidus, habilis* (= handy), *prudens* (= with insight), *bonus* (= good), — in the law, *juris consultus* Adv *perite dext(e)re, callide, scienter, prudenter, habiliter, bene*

skim, I. n *spuma*, to form —, *spumescĕre*, full of —, *spumosus* **II.** v tr 1, *despumare, spumam eximĕre*, 2, = to read quickly, *alqd (legendo) percurrere* **III.** v intr *volare* (= to fly)

skin, I. n *cutis pellis, membrana, corium* (= hide), to get off with a whole —, *integrum abire* **II.** v.tr *corium detrahĕre, pelle* or *corio exuere*, to — over, *cicatricem inducĕre, (ob)ducĕre* **skin-deep,** adj *levis* **skinny,** adj see THIN

skip, I. n *saltus, -ūs* **II.** v intr *salire* (= to leap), to — with joy, *ex(s)ultare* **III.** v tr = to pass over, *transilire, praeterire* **skipping-rope,** n *restis*

skipper, n *navis magister* see CAPTAIN

skirmish, I. n *proelium leve* **II.** v intr to engage in —es, *proeliis parvulis cum hoste contendĕre* **skirmisher,** n *veles, -itis*, m (= light-armed soldier, or by verb)

skirt, I. n *limbus, ora* **II.** v tr to — the shore, *legĕre oram*, to — or border on, *affinem esse* (e g *gens affinis Mauris*)

skittish, adj *protervus, lascivus*, to be —, *lascivire* Adv *proterve, lascive* **skittishness,** n *protervitas, lascivia*

skulk, v intr *latēre*

skull, n. *calvaria*

sky, n *coelum*, a bright —, *caelum serenum*, an open —, *caelum patens*, under the open —, *sub divo, in publico*, from the —, *de caelo, caelitus* **skylark,** n *alauda* **skylight,** n *fenestra*

slack, adj *laxus, fluxus, remissus* (= loose), *lentus, tardus* (= slow), *segnis, piger* (= idle), — in duty, *neglegens* **slacken,** v tr. *laxare*, to — the reins, *laxare habenas*, to — work, *opus remittere* Adv *lente, tarde, segniter, neglegenter.* **slackness,** n *segnitia, pigritia* (= laziness), *neglegentia* (= negligence), — of reins, etc, by *laxus, remissus*

slake, v tr *sitim ex(s)tinguĕre* or *explēre, sitim depellĕre* or *sedare*, to — lime, *calcem macerare*

slander, I. n *calumnia, (falsa) criminatio, falsum crimen, obtrectatio, maledictio* **II.** v tr *calumniari, criminari, diffamare, alci obtrectare, maledicere, alqm calumniis* or *ignominiis afficere, insectari, alci probrum, convicium contumeliam*, etc *facĕre* **slanderer,** n *obtrectator* **slandering,** n *criminatio, obtrectatio* **slanderous,** adj *maledicus, famosus* Adv *maledice, per calumniam*

slant, adj *obliquus, transversus* Adv *oblique*

slap, I. n *alapa* (Juv) **II.** v tr *palmā percutĕre*

slash, I. n *incisura* (= incision, Col), *vulnus, ĕris* (= wound), *ictus, -ūs* (= blow) **II.** v.tr *caedere, incidĕre, gladio percutĕre* (with a sword)

slate, I. n to write on, use *tabula*, for a roof, *tegula* (= tile, usu in pl), a —-quarry, *lapidis fissilis fodina* **II.** v tr *tegulis obtegĕre* or *consternĕre*

slattern, n *mulier sordida*

slaughter, I. n *caedes, -is*, f (= a cutting down), *occidio, occisio, clades* (fig = discomfiture, severe loss), *strages, -is*, f (fig = overthrow, destruction), a general —, *internecio, trucidatio* (= butchery), *nex* (= violent death), man—, *homicidium* **II.** v tr *caedĕre, concidĕre* (of a number), *jugulare* (= to cut the throat), *mactare* (= to slay a victim), see SLAY, *trucidare* **slaughter-house,** n *laniēna* **slaughterer,** n *lanius*

slave, n *servus* (considered as property), *ancilla* (= female —), *verna* (= a slave born in the house), *famulus* (= household —), *mancipium* (= one obtained by war or purchase), the —s, *servitium, servitia, corpora servilia, familia*, to sell as a —, *sub coronā vendĕre*, a — of lusts, *servus libidinum*, to be a — to anything, *alci rei oboedire, inservire* **slave-dealer,** n *venalicius, mango* (Quint) **slave-labour,** n *opus servile* **slave-market,** n *forum* or *lapis* (e g *de lapide emptus*, Cic) **slavery,** n *servitus, -ūtis*, f, *servitudo, servitium*, to be in —, *in servitute esse* **slave trade,** n *venditio* (= selling) or *emptio* (= buying) *servorum* **slave-war** or **-rising,** n *tumultus, -ūs, servīlis, bellum servīle* **slavish,** adj *servīlis* (lit and fig), *vernīlis* (lit and fig, esp in Tac) Adv *servīliter, vernīliter*

slaver, I. n *sputum* (Cels) **II.** v intr *salivam ex ore demittere, salivā madēre*

slay, v tr *interficĕre, occidĕre, interimĕre, tollĕre, ferire, percutere, absumĕre, ex(s)tinguĕre, trucidare, jugulare, necare* (= to put to death) **slayer,** n *interfector, occisor, percussor*, — of men, *homicīda*, m and f (so *tyrannicida*, etc)

sledge, n *traha* (= a drag)

sledge-hammer, n *malleus*

sleek, adj *lēvis* (= smooth), *nitidus* (= shining), to be —, *nitēre*

sleep, I. n *somnus* (= sleep), *sopor* (= heaviness), *quies, ētis* (= rest), — falls on me, *somnus me opprimit*, to fall to —, *dormitare* **II.** v intr *dormire, quiescĕre*, to go to — or bed, *cubitum ire, se somno dare* **sleepiness,** n. *veternus* (of the lethargy of the aged), or by adj **sleepless,** adj *insomnis, exsomnis, vigilans.* **sleeplessness,** n *insomnia, vigilia, vigilantia* **sleepy,** adj *semisomnus (-somnis), somni plenus, somno gravis, veternus, somniculosus* (= sluggish) Adv *somniculose*, or better by adj.

sleet, n *nix grandine mixta*

sleeve, n *manica*, to laugh in one's —,

furtim ridēre; in sinu gaudēre (= to rejoice in secret).

sleight, n. *ars, artificium, dolus;* —of hand, *praestigiae.*

slender, adj. *tenuis* (lit. and fig.), *gracilis* (lit.), *exīlis* (lit. and fig.); — provision, *victus, -ūs, tenuis.* Adv. *tenuiter* (= poorly), *exīliter.* **slenderness**, n. *tenuitas, exīlitas* (lit. and fig.), *gracilitas* (lit.).

slice, I. n. — of bread (*panis*) *frustum.* II. v.tr. *concidēre, secare.*

slide, I. v.intr. *labi.* II. n. — on ice, by *in glacie labi.*

slight, I. adj. *lĕvis* (in gen. of clothing, etc., also fig.), *parvi momenti* (= of little account), *tenuis, gracilis, exilis* (= slender), by diminutive (e.g. *opusculum,* = — work). II. v.tr. *parvi, flocci facĕre, nullam curam alcjs habēre, contemnĕre.*

slim, adj. *exīlis;* see SLENDER. **slimness**, n. *exilitas.*

slime, n. *limus.* **slimy**, adj. *limosus.*

sling, I. n. *funda;* — for the arm, *fascia, mitella* (Cels.); to have the arm in a —, *brachium mitellā involutum habēre.* II. v.tr. *mittĕre, torquēre;* to — at, *fundā petĕre.*

slink, v.intr. to — away, *sese subducĕre.*

slip, I. n. 1, lit. *lapsus, -ūs;* 2, fig. *lapsus* (rare), *culpa* (=fault), *error* (= mistake); there's many a — between the cup and the lip, *inter os et offam* (sc. *multa intervenire possunt*); 3, of a plant, *surculus:* see SHOOT. II. v.intr. *vestigio falli, labi;* to — away, *aufugĕre;* to let —, *amittĕre, omittĕre;* to — from the memory, *de memoriā excidĕre.* **slipper**, n. *solea, crepĭda.* **slippery**, adj. *lubricus.*

slit, I. n. *fissura* (= a split, Plin.), *rima* (= an opening or leak), *scissura* (= a slit, Plin.). II. v.tr. *incidĕre* (= to cut into), *findĕre* (= to cleave), *scindĕre* (= to tear).

sloe, n. *prunum silvestre* (Plin.); —tree, *prunus, f., silvestris* (Col.).

sloop, n. see SHIP.

slop, n. and v.tr. see WET.

slope, I. n. *declīvitas* (downwards), *acclīvitas* (upwards). II. v.intr. *vergĕre, se dimittĕre.* **sloping**, adj. *declīvis, acclīvis.*

sloth, n. *desidia, inertia, segnitia, segnities, ignavia, socordia, pigritia.* **slothful**, adj. *desidiosus* (rare), *iners, ignavus, segnis, socors, piger.* Adv. *inerter, segniter, ignave.*

slouch, v.intr. *discinctum esse.*

slough, n. *palus, -ūdis,* f.; (for swine), *volutabrum;* — of a snake, *vernatio* (Plin.).

sloven, n. *homo sordidus, discinctus.* **slovenliness**, n. *sordes* (= filth), *incuria, neglegentia* (= carelessness).

slow, adj. *tardus, lentus, segnis, piger, serus* (= late); — to learn, *tardus ad discendum.* Adv. *tarde, lente, segniter, paul(l)atim, pedetentim* (*pedetemt-*). **slowness**, n. *tarditas, segnitas, pigritia;* — of a river, *lēnitas.*

slug, n. *limax* (Plin.). **sluggard**, n. *homo ignavus.* **sluggish**, adj. *segnis, piger, socors.* Adv. *segniter, socordĭter.* **sluggishness**, n. *pigritia, ignavia, socordia.*

sluice, n. *emissarium.*

slumber, n. and v. see SLEEP.

slur, I. n. *macula, labes, -is, dedecus, -ŏris,* n. II. v.tr. to — over, *extenuare.*

slut, n. *mulier sordida, immunda.*

sly, adj. *vafer, subdolus, astutus, versutus;* — old fellow, *veterator.* Adv. *vafre, subdole, astute, versute.* **slyness**, n. *dolus, astutia.*

smack, I. n. a taste, *sapor, gustus, -ūs.* II. v.intr. to — of, *sapĕre* (e.g. *mella herbam eam sapiunt,* = the honey —s of the grass).

smack, I. n. = a blow, *alapa.* II. v.tr. *alapam alci ducĕre* (Phaedr.).

small, adj. *parvus, exiguus, minutus, tenuis* (= thin), *gracilis* (= slender), *angustus* (= narrow); a — soul, *animus pusillus;* that betrays a — mind, *illud pusilli est animi;* too —, *justo minor, parum magnus;* as — as, how —! *quantulus.* **smallness**, n. *parvitas, exiguitas, tenuitas, gracilitas, angustiae.*

small-pox, n. * *variolae,* or by *pestilentia.*

smart, I. n. *dolor, morsus, -ūs, cruciatus, -ūs.* II. v.intr. *dolēre;* to — for, *poenas alci pendĕre, poenas subire, perferre* or *luĕre.* III. adj. 1, = keen, *acer, acerbus, gravis, acutus;* 2, = active, *impiger, callidus* (= clever); 3, = witty, *salsus;* see WITTY; 4, = dressy, *lautus, nitidus.* **smartness**, n. 1, = wit, *sal;* 2, dressiness, use adj. SMART III., 4.

smatterer, n. *homo leviter lit(t)eris imbutus.* **smattering**, n. *lĕvis artis alcjs scientia.*

smear, v.tr. *(il)linĕre.*

smell, I. n. *odoratus, -ūs* (the sense), *odoratio* (the act), *odor* (the result); an ill —, *foetor;* to have a bad —, *male* (good, *bene*) *olēre.* II. v.intr. to — of, *(re)dolēre alqd;* to —, or have the sensation, *odorari, olfacĕre.* **smelling-bottle**, n. *vasculum olfactoriolum.*

smelt, v.tr. *fundĕre, coquĕre* (Plin.), *liquefacĕre.*

smile, I. n. *risus, -ūs;* with a —, *subridens.* II. v.intr. *(sub)ridēre, irridēre alci rei;* fortune —s on me, *fortuna mihi effulget.*

smirk, I. n. by *risus, -ūs, contortus.* II. v.intr. *vultum ad alqd componĕre.*

smite, v.tr. *ferire, percutĕre.*

smith, n. *faber ferrarius* (= a blacksmith). **smithy**, n. *officina ferraria.*

smoke, I. n. *fumus.* II. v.intr. *fumare, vaporare, exhalare.* III. v.tr. to — (tobacco), *herbae Nicotianae fumum ducĕre;* see FUMIGATE. **smoky**, adj. *fumosus* (= full of smoke, discoloured by smoke).

smooth, I. adj. *lēvis, teres;* of words, etc., *blandus;* of the sea, etc., *tranquillus, placidus;* of the temper, *aequus, aequabilis, aequalis.* Adv. in gen. by adj.; of words, etc., *blande;* of the sea, etc., *tranquille, placide;* of the temper, *aequo animo, aequabiliter, aequaliter.* II. v.tr. *lēvare, lēvigare* (in gen.), *limare* (with file), *runcinare* (with plane); of the sea, *tranquillare, sedare:* fig. to — a person's way, *aditum alci ad alqm dare.* **smoothness**, n. *lēvitas, tranquillitas, aequanimitas;* — of diction, *aequabilitas.*

smother, v.tr. *suffocare, animam intercludĕre;* fear —s his voice, *metus vocem praecludit;* see STRANGLE.

smouldering, adj. *fumans.*

smuggle, v.tr. *merces furtim* or *portorio non soluto importare* or *invehĕre.* **smuggler**, n. *qui merces vetitas importat.*

smut, n. *fuligo, robigo* (= blight). **smutty**, n. *fumosus* (= smoky).

snack, n. *pars, portio, gustus, -ūs* (= a taste).

snaffle, n. *frenum.*

snail, n. *cochlea.* **snail's-shell**, n. *cochleae testa.*

snake, n. *anguis, serpens, coluber, vipera, draco.* **snaky**, adj. † *vipereus,* † *anguineus.*

snap, I. v.intr. *crepitum edĕre, crepare;* = to break asunder, *frangi, diffringi;* = to scold, *alqm increpare* **II.** v tr *frangĕre*, *(prae)rumpĕre*, *diffringĕre*, *infringĕre*, to — the fingers, *digitis concrepare*, to — at, lit and fig *petĕre*, *arripĕre*; to — up, see SEIZE **III.** n *crepitus*, *-ūs*. **snappish**, adj *morosus*, *difficilis*, *mordax*, *iracundus* Adv *morose*, *iracunde*

snare, **I.** n lit and fig *laqueus*, *plaga*, *insidiae*, *-arum*, to set a — for anyone, *alci insidias facĕre*, to get one's head out of a —, *se expedire (ex laqueo)* **II.** v.tr. lit, and fig *illaqueare*, *irretire*

snarl, v.intr **1**, lit *fremĕre*; **2**, fig *(sub)ringi*.

snatch, v tr and intr *rapĕre*, *corripĕre*, to — away, *surripĕre*, to — at, *captare*, see SEIZE.

sneak, **I.** v.intr *irrepĕre*; to — into anything, e g *ad amicitiam repere* (= to creep), to — away, *furtim se subducĕre* **II.** n *homo nequam*, *abjectus*, see CONTEMPTIBLE

sneer, **I.** n *derisus*, *-ūs*, *irrisus*, *-ūs* **II.** v tr *deridēre*, *irridēre*

sneeze, v intr. *sternuĕre* **sneezing**, n *sternutamentum*

sniff, n and v tr and intr see SMELL

snip, v tr *circumcidĕre*, *amputare*

snipe, n *scolopax* (late)

snob, n *homo putidus*

snore, v intr *stertĕre*

snort, **I.** v tr *fremĕre* **II.** n *fremitus*, *-ūs*

snout, n *rostrum*

snow, **I.** n *nix*, *nivis*, a —-ball, *nivis glebula* (late), —flake, *nix*, —-storm, *nivis casus*, *-ūs*, or *nives* **II.** v tr *ning(u)ĕre*, gen impers, it —s, *ningit* **snowy**, adj *nivosus*, —-white, *niveus*, *colore niveo*

snub, **I.** v tr. **II.** n see REBUKE **snub-nosed**, adj *simus*

snuff, **I.** n **1**, of a candle, *fungus*, **2**, = comminuted tobacco, *pulvis sternutatorius*, — box, *pyxis* **II.** v tr *candelae fungum demĕre*, to — out, *ex(s)tinguĕre*, to — up anything, *alqd naribus haurire*. **snuffers**, n *forfices* (scissors, Mart) *candelarum*. **snuffle**, v intr *vocem naribus proferre*

snug, adj see COMFORTABLE

so, adv *sic*, *ita*, *hunc in modum*, *hoc modo*, *ut* . . . *sic*, *ut* . . . *ita*, *tam* . . . *quam*; — then, *itaque*, *ergo*, see THEREFORE, — that (= in order that), *ut*, — not, *ne*, or by rel *qui*, *quae*, *quod* with subj; — that, of consequence, *ut*, — not, *ut non*, — much, *tam valde*, *tam vehementer*, *tantum*, *tantopere*, *adeo*, twice — much, *bis tanto*, *alterum tantum*, not — much, *minus*, *non ita*, — much . . . as, *tantopere* . . . *quantopere*, — great, *tam multus*, *tantus*, *tantum*, — great . . . as, *tantum* . . . *quantum*, — again, *alterum tantum*, — many, *tot*, — many . . . as, *tot* . . . *quot*, just — many, *totidem*, — far, *eo*, *eo usque*, *in tantum*, *quoad*, *hactenus*, to carry a thing — far, *rem eo adducĕre*, — far as I can look back, *quoad longissime potest mens mea respicĕre*, — little food, *tantulus cibus*, — few, *tam pauci*, as . . . —, *et* . . . *et*, *tum* . . . *tum*, *tam* . . . *quam*, *vel* . . . *vel*, not — . . . as, *non tam* . . . *quam*, is it —? *itane? siccine?* — quickly, *tam cito*, *tam celeriter* — quickly as possible, *quam primum*, *primo quoque tempore*, *simul ac*, *ut primum*, as that was painful, — this is pleasant, *ut illud erat molestum*, *sic hoc est jucundum* (Cic), — uncivil as, *tam inhumanus ut* (Cic), did you think me — unjust as to be angry with you? *adeone me injustum esse existimasti ut tibi irascerer?* (Cic), — far from, *tantum abest ut* . . . *non*, — often, *toties* . . . *quoties*, grant it —, *fac ita esse*, if it had been done (— courteous are you), you would have written it, *et si esset factum (quae tua est humanitas)*, *scripsisses*; — called, *quem*, *quam*, *quod dicunt*, *qui*, etc, *dicitur* **so-so**, adv *mediocriter*

soak, v.intr *macerare*, to — up, *bibĕre*, to — through, *permanare* (= to trickle through), *madefacĕre* (= to wet) **soaking**, adj of rain, *effusus*

soap, **I.** n *sapo* (Plin) **II.** v tr *sapone illinĕre*

soar, v intr *sublime ferri*, *se tollĕre* (lit and fig), *subvolare* (of birds, etc).

sob, **I.** n *singultus*, *-ūs* **II.** v intr *singultire*.

sober, adj *sobrius* (opp *vinolentus*, used lit. and fig), *temperans*, *temperatus*, *modestus*, *modicus*, *moderatus* (all = moderate in desires), *severus* (= grave) Adv *sobrie*, *temperate*, *modeste*, *modice*, *moderate*, *severe* **sobriety**, **soberness**, n *sobrietas*, *temperantia*, *moderatio*, *modestia*, *severitas*

sociable, adj *sociabilis*, *comis*, *affabilis*, see COURTEOUS, FRIENDLY **social**, adj *socialis*, *communis*, *civilis* (in political sense), *sociabilis*, *congregabilis* (= disposed to meeting together, of bees), *facilis* (= easy of approach, as a quality of character), — life, *vitae societas*, *communitas vitae* Adv. *quod ad societatem vitae pertinet* **socialism**, n by *forma civitatis in quâ summa aequalitas inter cives exstat* **socialist**, n *qui summam inter cives aequalitatem appetit* **sociality**, n *socialitas*, *mores faciles* (= sociability) **society**, n = the union of several persons for a common end, *societas* (of learned and commercial men), *sodalitas* (= a brotherhood or fraternity), *factio* (= a union which makes a party, esp in a bad sense), *collegium* (= a corporation of merchants, artisans, priests), to form — with someone, *societatem cum alqo facĕre*, *inire*, *coire*, *rationem cum alqo communicare* (= to make common cause), *societatem contrahĕre cum alqo*, to take into —, *alqm in societatem assumĕre* (*adscribĕre*, *alqm in collegium cooptare* (by election), = to the associated persons, *socii* (of a craft), *grex* (= a band, e g a company of actors), = society in general, *societas humana* (*hominum* or *generis humani*), civil —, *societas civilis*, = as an assemblage, *coetus*, *-ūs*, *conventus*, *-ūs* (*virorum feminarumque* or *mulierumque*), *circulus* (= a circle or gathering, whether in the streets or in houses, a club), to go into —, *in circulum venire*; to avoid —, *vitare coetus*, *hominum conventus fugĕre*, *homines fugĕre*, *abstinēre congressu hominum*, *se a congressu hominum segregare*

sock, n see STOCKING

socket, n of a candlestick, *myxa*, of the eye, * *cavum oculi*

Socratic, adj *Socraticus*

sod, n *caespes*, *-itis*, m, a green —, *caespes vivus* or *viridis*

soda, n *nitrum*

sodden, adj *madidus*

sofa, n *lectulus*

soft, adj *mollis*, *lenis* (= gentle), *effeminatus* (= effeminate) Adv *molliter*, *leniter*, *effeminate* **soften**, **I.** v tr *(e)mollire*, *mitigare*, *lenire* (lit. and fig) **II.** v intr *mollire*, *mollescĕre* **softness**, n *mollitia* or *mollities*

soho, interj *heus! heus tu! ehe!*

soil, **I** n *solum*, a good —, *solum pingue*, poor —, *solum exile* **II.** v tr *inquinare*, *polluere*, *maculare*, see DIRTY

sojourn, **I.** v intr *cum alqo* or *in alqâ terrâ commorari* (= to tarry), *sedem habēre in loco*, *pere* *grinari in urbe* or *in gente* (as a foreigner). **II.** n. *mora, commoratio, peregrinatio.* **sojourner,** n. *hospes* (= guest), *peregrinus* (= foreigner), *advena*, m. and f. (= alien).

solace, I. n. *solatium, solatio* (= the act), † *solamen, levamen(tum)* (= an alleviation). **II.** v.tr. *alqm (con)solari, alci solatium praebēre, dare, afferre.*

solar, adj. *solaris*, or by genit. *solis* (= of the sun).

solder, I. n. *ferrumen* (Plin.). **II.** v.tr. *conferruminare* (Plin.), *(im)plumbare.*

soldier, n. *miles, -ĭtis*; common —, *miles gregarius, manipularis*; foot —, *pedes*; horse —, *eques*; to serve as a —, *stipendia facĕre, merēre* or *merēri*, with genit. or dat. **soldierly,** adj. *militaris, rei militaris peritus.* **soldiery,** n. *milites*, or as collect. *miles.*

sole, adj. *solus, unus, unicus*; — survivor, *superstes, -itis*, m. Adv. *solum (modo), tantum (modo).* **solitary, I.** adj. *solus, solitarius* (of persons), *solus, desertus, avius, devius, secretus* (of places). **II.** n. see Hermit. **solitude,** n. *solitudo* (both as state and lonely place).

sole, n. of the foot *(pedis) planta, solum*; — of a shoe, *(calcei) solea* (= a sandal), *solum.*

sole, n. = fish, *solea.*

solecism, n. *soloecismus* (= offence against grammar); see also Impropriety.

solemn, adj. *sol(l)emnis*, originally = yearly or annual, and hence festal and customary, but not solemn in our sense, which may be expressed by *summâ religione imbutus*, and by *sanctus, religiosus.* Adv. *sol(l)emniter, sancte, religiose.* **solemnize,** v.tr. *celebrare.* **solemnization,** n. *celebratio.* **solemnity,** n. **1,** *sol(l)emne* (e.g. *sollemne clavi figendi*, Liv.; *nostrum illud sollemne servemus*, Cic. = an established custom); = profound religious sentiment, *reverentia*; **2,** see Gravity, Seriousness.

solicit, v.tr. *sol(l)icitare, poscĕre, deposcĕre, expetĕre*, comb. *deposcĕre atque expetĕre, obsecrari, orare alqm alqd.* **solicitation,** n. *preces, -um, (ef)flagitatio, rogatio, obsecratio*; at the — of, *alcjs rogatu, alqo rogante, precando.* **solicitor,** n. **1,** *qui rogat, qui poscit*; **2,** *advocatus*; see Advocate. **solicitous,** adj. *sol(l)icitus* (= concerned, moved with anxiety), *anxius*; see Anxious. Adv. *sol(l)icite, anxie.* **solicitude,** n. *sol(l)icitudo, cura, anxietas*; to be an object of —, *curae esse alci.*

solid, adj. *solidus* (in most senses of the English, = firm, lasting), *stabilis, firmus*; see Stable; — food, *cibus, caro* (= meat). Adv. *solide, stabiliter, firme*; — ground, *solidum*, n.; — bodies, *solida, -orum.* **solidity,** n. *soliditas.*

soliloquy, n. *meditatio* (= meditation), *cum alqs secum loquitur.* **soliloquize,** v.tr. *ipsum secum loqui.*

solitary, adj. see under Sole.

solo, n. *unius cantus, -ūs*; on an instrument, *quod alqs solus fidibus*, etc., *canit.*

solstice, n. *solstitium* (= summer —), *bruma* (= winter —); relating to the —, *solstitialis, brumalis.*

solve, v.tr. *(dis)solvĕre* (properly = to loosen, and hence to — knotty points), *enodare* (= to undo a knot); see Explain. **solubility,** n. use verb. **soluble,** adj. **1,** lit. *quod dissolvi potest*; **2,** fig. *quod explanari potest.* **solution,** n. **1,** = act of dissolving *(dis)solutio*; **2,** = what is dissolved, *dilutum* (Plin.); **3,** = explanation, *enodatio, expositio, (dis)solutio, explicatio.* **solvent, I.** adj. *qui solvendo (par) est.* **II.** n. *quod ad alqd dissolvendum vim habet.*

some, adj. used with noun. *aliquis (aliqua, aliquod), quis* (after *si*, e.g. *si quis hoc dicit*), *aliquot* with gen. (e.g. *aliquot hominum*); — . . . others, *alii . . . alii, quidam . . . alii*; —one, *aliquis, quispiam, quisquam*; when the relative follows, *aliquis* is dropped (e.g. *habeo quem mittam*); —one, I know not who, *nescio qui* or *quis*; — (as a softening term), e.g. — fifteen, etc., *homines ad quindecim Curioni assenserunt*; *abhinc menses decem fere*, = — ten months ago; *nactus equites circiter triginta*, = having obtained — thirty horsemen; in — way or other, *quodcumque*; there is — reason, *non sine caus(s)a*; it is — comfort to me, *nonnihil me consolatur* (Cic.); for — time, *aliquamdo, aliquamdiu.* **somehow,** adv. *nescio quomodo, nescio quo pacto.* **something,** n. see Some; when emphatic, *aliquid, nonnihil.* **sometimes,** adv. *aliquando, nonnunquam, subinde, interdum.* **somewhat,** n. *aliquantu(lu)m, nonnihil.* **somewhere,** adv. *alicubi, alqo loco, nonnusquam.* **somewhither,** adv. *aliquo.*

somersault, n. *saltus, -ūs* (= leap); to turn a —, *dare saltus.*

somnambulist, n. *qui in somnis ambulat.*

somniferous, adj. † *somnifer, somnificus.*

somnolent, adj. see Sleepy.

son, n. *filius*, † *natus*; a little —, *filiolus*; foster- —, *alumnus*; a — -in-law, *gener*; a step- —, *privignus*; —s and daughters, *liberi.*

song, n. *cantus, -ūs, canticum, cantilēna* (contemptuously, e.g. *eadem cantilena*, = the same old —), *carmen, modus.* **songster,** n. *cantor, vocis et cantūs modulator*; f. *cantrix, poëtria.*

sonorous, adj. *sonorus, canorus, clarus*; see Clear. Adv. *sonore, canore, clare.*

soon, adv. *cito*; *brevi tempore* (= in a short time), *mox, jam, propediem*; very —, *extemplo* (= straightway); — after, *paul(l)o post, non ita multo post*; —, *mature* (= shortly), *mane*; too —, *ante tempus*; to do —, *maturare alqd facĕre*; as — as possible, *quam maturrime*; as — as, *quam primum, simul ac* or *atque, ut (primum)*; as — as, *simul ac.* **sooner,** adv. = rather, *potius, libentius*; I had —er, *mallem.*

soot, n. *fūligo.* **sooty,** adj. *fuligine oblitus.*

sooth, n. *verum, veritas*; in —, *vere, certe*; for —, *sane, profecto.* **soothsay,** v.tr. *praedicĕre.* **soothsayer,** n. *(h)aruspex*, m.; see Prophet. **soothsaying,** n. *auguratio, augurium.*

soothe, v.tr. *mulcēre, lenire, placare, sedare, levare, mitigare, tranquillare.* **soothing,** adj. by part. or by *blandus.* Adv. *blande.*

sop, I. n. *frustum, offa (panis).* **II.** v.tr. *macerare* (= to soak).

sophism, n. *sŏphisma* (Sen.), *captio.* **sophist,** n. **1,** *sŏphista*, m.; **2,** fig. *homo captiosus.* **sophistical,** adj. *captiosus.* Adv. *captiose.* **sophistry,** n. *ars sophistica, fallaces dicendi artes.*

soporific, adj. † *soporifer, soporus, somnificus* (Plin.).

sorcerer, n. *veneficus.* **sorceress,** n. *venefica, maga, saga.* **sorcery,** n. *ars magica.*

sordid, adj. *sordidus* (= unclean, mean), *abjectus, humilis* (= despicable), *avarus* (= greedy); see Mean. Adv. *sordide, abjecte, humiliter, avare.* **sordidness,** n. *sordes, avaritia.*

sore, I. n. **1,** *ulcus, -ĕris*, n.; see Abscess; **2,** fig. *molestia*; see Trouble. **II.** adj. *quod alqm dolore afficit*; fig. to be — about anything, *alqd graviter ferre.* **III.** adv. *aegre, graviter, moleste*; — wounded, *compluribus confectus vulneribus.*

sorrel, n *oxys*

sorrel, adj *spadix*

sorrow, I. n *dolor, aegritudo, maestitia, molestia, tristitia, acerbitas, paenitentia* (*agĕre paenitentiam rei,* = to have — for), *desiderium* (= longing), *luctus,* -*ūs* (= mourning) **II.** v intr *dolēre, maerēre, dolore affici, lugēre, desiderare, contristari, alqm paenitet alcjs rei* **sorrowful,** adj *tristis, maestus, lugubris, dejectus, afflictus, molestiā affectus,* to be —, *dolēre, aegritudine affici, se maerori tradere, contristari* Adv *maeste,* see SADLY

sort, I. n *mos, modus, ratio, genus, ĕris,* n (= kind or manner), after a —, *quodammodo,* after the same —, *similiter,* in what —? *quomodo?* in like —, *pari ratione,* of what —? *cujusmodi? qualis?* of this —, *hujusmodi,* of that —, *ejusmodi, istiusmodi,* he is not the — of man to, *non is est qui* with subj **II** v tr (*in genera*) *digerĕre,* see SEPARATE **III.** v intr = to be suitable, *aptum esse,* see SUIT **sorting,** n *diribitio*

sortie, n *excursio, eruptio,* to make a —, *erumpĕre*

sot, n by *homo ebriosus* **sottish,** adj *ebriosus, vinulentus.*

soul, n *anima* (= the living principle), *animus* (= the emotional nature), *spiritus,* -*ūs* (= breath, spirit), *mens* (= the intelligence), by my —, *ita vivam ut,* etc, *ne vivam si,* etc, from my —, *ex animo,* with all my —, *toto animo,* — (as a living being), *anima, caput, homo,* not a —, *nemo.*

sound, adj (as opposed to unsound or rotten) *sanus* (= in a natural state, hence our sane, opp insane), *salvus* (= safe), *incolumis* (= uninjured), *sospes* (= escaped from peril), *integer* (= entire, whole), *firmus, robustus* (= strong), *saluber* (*locus*), *salutaris* (*herba, ars*), comb *sanus et salvus,* to be — in health, *bonā* or *prosperā valetudine uti, bene valēre,* = deep, of sleep, *altus, artus,* of knowledge, etc, *altus, accuratus* Adv *sane, salve, integre, firme, robuste, alte, arte, accurate* **soundness,** n *sanitas, bona* or *firma* or *prospera valetudo* (of health), *salus,* -*ūtis* (in gen), of argument, *gravitas*

sound, I. n = noise, *sonus, sonitus,* -*ūs, vox, clamor, strepitus,* -*ūs, fremitus,* -*ūs* (= din), a high —, *sonus acutus,* deep —, *sonus gravis,* soft —, *sonus levis* **II.** v tr *sonare* (in gen), to — a trumpet, *tubam inflare,* to — an alarm, *tubā signum dare,* to — a march, (*vasa*) *conclamare,* to — a retreat, *receptui canĕre* or *signum dare* **III** v intr *sonare, sonitum edĕre, canĕre* (of trumpets)

sound, v tr = to test depth, perhaps *tentare quae sit altitudo* (*maris, fluminis,* etc), fig see EXAMINE

sound, n = strait, *fretum,* see STRAIT

soup, n *jus*

sour, I. adj *acidus* (= sharp), *acerbus, amārus* (= bitter), *acer,* somewhat —, *subacidus,* to be —, *acēre,* to turn —, *acescĕre* Adv *acerbe, acide, acriter, morose* **II** v tr *alqm exacerbare,* see EMBITTER **sourness,** n *acerbitas, amaritudo* (lit and fig), *morositas* (fig)

source, n *fons,* -*ntis,* m , *caput,* to take its — in, *profluere ex alqo loco,* fig *fons, causa, principium, stirps,* see FOUNTAIN

south, n *meridies, plaga* (or *regio*) *australis* or *meridiana, pars meridiana, regio in meridiem spectans,* — wind, *ventus meridianus, ventus australis* (opp to *ventus septentrionalis*), *auster* (= the — wind properly), the — east, *regio inter ortum brumalem et meridiem spectans,* — east wind, *euronotus* (= — - — -east), *vulturnus* (= — east one third —), — -western, *inter occasum brumalem et meridiem spectans,* — west wind, *africus,* — - — -west, *inter meridiem et occasum solis spectans,* — - — -west wind, *libonotus* (Plin), west- — -west wind, *subvesperus* **southern,** adj *meridianus* (in later writers *meridionalis* or *meridialis*), *in meridiem spectans, australis* **southwards,** adv *in* or *ad meridiem*

southernwood, n *abrotonum* (*abrotonus*)

sovereign, I. adj *sui juris, alii non subjectus;* — remedy, *remedium efficacissimum* **II.** n *rex, dominus, princeps, imperator, tyrannus* **sovereignty,** n *summa rerum* or *imperii* (*summum*) *imperium, dominatio, dominatus,* -*ūs principatus, ūs, regnum, tyrannis,* -*idis,* f , to rise to the —, *rerum potiri*

sow, n *sus*

sow, v tr *serĕre* (lit and fig), *semen spargĕre, seminare* (from *semen,* = a seed), as you —, so shall you reap, *ut sementem feceris, ita metes* **sower,** n *sator* **sowing,** n *satio, satus, ūs, sementis*

space, n *spatium, locus,* fig , to give — to, *locum dare, indulgēre rei.* **spacious,** adj *spatiosus, amplus* **spaciousness,** n *amplitudo*

spade, n *pala*

span, I. n *palmus* (Plin), the — of life, *exigua vitae brevitas,* the — of the arch was 20 ft , *arcus viginti pedes latus erat* **II.** v tr *jungĕre* (e g *flumen ponte,* = to — the river)

spangle, I n *bractea* **II.** v tr (*bracteis*) *distinguĕre*

spaniel, n by *canis*

spar, n *lapis* (-*idis*) *specularis* (= a stone, Plin)

spar, n *vectis,* m , see STAKE

spar, v intr *pugnis certare*

spar, n *obex, vectis,* m

spare, v tr *alci* or *alci rei parcĕre*

spark, n *scintilla, igniculus,* a — of hope, *spes exigua, specula* **sparkle,** v intr *scintillare, fulgēre, nitēre,* see GLITTER **sparkling,** n *vitor*

sparrow, n *passer,* -*eris,* m

spasm, n *spasmus, spasma,* -*atis,* n (Plin), *tetanus* (of the neck) **spasmodic,** adj by adv = by fits and starts, perhaps *haud uno tenore*

spatter, v tr *a(d)spergĕre*

spawn, I n *piscium ova, orum* **II.** v tr *ova gignĕre*

speak, v intr *fari, loqui, dicĕre, sermocinari* (= to converse), to — Greek, *Graecā linguā uti, Graece loqui,* = to make a speech, *dicĕre, loqui, verba facĕre, orationem habēre, contionari,* to — of, *alqm* or *alqd dicĕre, de alqā re,* = to — about, to — to, *alqm affari, appellare, compellare, alloqui,* to — together, *colloqui,* to — for, or to, something, *testem esse alci rei,* to — for and against, *in utramque partem disputare* **speaker,** n *orator* (= orator) *qui dicit* (= person speaking) **speaking, I.** n *locutio, sermo* **II.** adj (e g a — likeness, *vera alcjs imago*) **speech,** n 1, *oratio,* the faculty of —, *oratio* (whence *ratio et oratio*), **2,** = a set —, *oratio, contio* (before a popular assembly) **speechless,** adj see DUMB

spear, I. n *hasta,* see LANCE **II.** v tr *hastā transfigĕre*

special, adj *praecipuus, eximius, egregius* (= excellent), *proprius, peculiaris* (= — to anyone or anything) **speciality,** n *quod alci* or *alci rei proprium est* **specially,** adv *praecipue, eximie, egregie, imprimis* (*in primis*), *maxime, prae ceteris, praesertim, valde,* or by superl (e g — good, *optimus*)

specie, n. *aurum* or *argentum signatum.*

species, n. *genus, -ĕris,* n., *species;* the human —, *genus humanum.* **specific, I.** adj. *proprius, peculiaris;* — charges, etc., *singuli* (= one by one). **II.** n. see REMEDY

specify, v.tr. *si(n)gillatim enumerare, denotare.* **specification,** n. *enumeratio.*

specimen, n. *specimen, documentum, exemplum.*

specious, adj. having a fair appearance, *speciosus, fucatus, simulatus* (= feigned).

speck, n. *macula* (= a spot), *labes, -is* (= a stain), *nota* (= a mark); = a fault, *vitium.* **speckle,** v.tr. *(com)maculare, maculis alqm conspergĕre.* **speckled,** adj. *maculis distinctus, maculatus.*

spectacle, n. *spectaculum.* **spectacles,** n. perhaps *vitrea ad (oculorum) aciem adjuvandam apta.*

spectator, n. *spectator.*

spectre, n. see GHOST.

speculate, v.intr. **1,** *cogitare, quaerĕre, inquirĕre de alqâ re;* see INQUIRE; **2,** in business, *quaestui servire.* **speculation,** n. **1,** *cogitatio* (= thought); to be sunk in —, *in cogitatione defixum esse;* scientific —, *rerum contemplatio;* philosophical —, *philosophia;* **2,** — in business, *negotium;* to be absorbed in —, *emendi et vendendi quaestu et lucro duci.* **speculative,** adj. e.g. philosophy, *philosophia contemplativa* (Sen.). **speculator,** n. *qui quaestui servit, quaestuosus.*

speech, n. see SPEAK.

speed, I. n. *celeritas, velocitas, properatio, festinatio.* **II.** v.tr. see PROSPER. **speedy,** adj. *celer, velox, properus.* **speedily,** adv. *cito, celeriter, velociter, propere, festinanter, festinans.*

spell, I. n. *incantamentum, carmen.* **II.** v.tr. *syllabas lit(t)erarum ordinare.* **spellbound,** adj. *defixus, stupens, stupefactus.* **spelling,** n. *ars lit(t)erarum recte ordinandarum.*

spend, v.tr. *pecuniam erogare* (esp. of public money), *(in)sumĕre (in alqm rem), in alqd re sumptum* or *impensam facĕre;* to — time, *tempus, diem, aetatem,* etc., *agĕre, degĕre, consumĕre, (con)terĕre* (= to waste); to — the night, *pernoctare;* I spent three days with him, *triduum cum eo fui;* fig. to — oneself, *alci rei deditum esse;* to — itself, see ABATE. **spendthrift,** n. *nepos.*

spew, v.tr. *(e)vomĕre.* **spewing,** n. *vomitus, -ūs.*

sphere, n. *sphaera, globus;* fig. = an office, *munus, -ĕris,* n., *officium* (= duty); to keep in one's own —, *se rerum suarum finibus continēre.* **spherical,** adj. *globosus.*

sphinx, n. *sphinx, -ngis,* f.

spice, I. n. *condimentum* (lit. and fig.); a — of anything (e.g. of the Devil), *nonnihil alcjs rei.* **II.** v.tr. *aromatibus* or *aromatis condire.* **spicy,** adj. **1,** *(aromate) conditus;* **2,** fig. *salsus.*

spider, n. *aranea.* **spider's-web,** n. *aranea* (Plaut.), *texta aranea* (Plin.).

spike, I. n. *clavus* (= nail), *cuspis, -idis,* f. (= head of a weapon). **II.** v.tr. (e.g. cannon), *tormenta bellica clavis adactis inutilia reddĕre.*

spikenard, n. *nardus* (Plin.).

spill, v.tr. *effundĕre.* **spilling,** n. *effusio.*

spin, I. v.tr. **1,** *nere,* † *stamina ducĕre, texĕre telam;* **2,** *versare* (= to turn), *circumagĕre, in orbem agĕre.* **II.** v.intr. *circumagi.* **spinning,** n. use verb. **spinner,** n. *qui* or *quae stamina net.* **spindle,** n. *fusus.*

spine, n. *spina* (properly = a thorn, then the backbone). **spinal,** adj. *qui (quae, quod) ad spinam pertinet.*

spinster, n. *innupta, virgo.*

spiral, adj. *tortuosus* (of a line); see CROOKED.

spire, n. *turris;* a — on a tower, perhaps *fastigium* (= gable).

spirit, n. *spiritus, -ūs* (properly = breath or air), = animation or vigour, *spiritus, sanguis;* = soul, *animus, mens, spiritus, ingenium;* a lofty —, *animus excelsus;* of little —, *homo parvi animi;* = the prevailing feeling, *mens;* = the peculiar tone of thought, *ingenium, natura;* = temper, disposition, *animus, studium, indoles, -is,* f., *ingenium;* — of the age, *horum temporum* or *hujus aetatis ratio,* or *mores, -um,* m.; = meaning, *sententia, voluntas;* = strong drink, *vinum* or *liquor acrior;* to understand the — of a writer, *mentem scriptoris assequi;* a disembodied —, *anima;* the Holy —, **Spiritus Sanctus* or *Sacer;* an evil —, *daemon;* the —s of the departed, *manes, -ium.* **spirited,** adj. *animosus, generosus, fortis;* see BRAVE. **spiritless,** adj. *ignavus, demissus, fractus;* = empty, *inanis;* see COWARDLY. **spiritual,** adj. (not sensuous) by the gen. *animi* or *ingenii;* = without body, *corpore carens, ab omni concretione mortali segregatus;* — mind, *animus religiosus, pius erga Deum;* opp. to secular, * *ecclesiasticus.* Adv. *animo, mente;* = religiously, *caste, religiose, pure, pie.* **spiritualism,** n. by *credĕre animas mortuorum cum hominibus communicare.* **spiritualist,** n. *qui inter mortuos ac vivos commercium esse putat.* **spirituality,** n. *animus rerum divinarum studiosus.* **spiritualities,** n. *reditus ecclesiastici.*

spit, n. (= utensil to roast meat on), *veru.*

spit, v.intr. *(ex)spuĕre.* **spittle,** n. see SALIVA.

spite, I. n. *odium occultum, simultas obscura, malevolentia, livor;* to have or show a —, *succensēre alci, odium occultum gerĕre adversus alqm;* in — of, *adversus,* or *in* with accus., or by *cum* (e.g. *irit cum manēre illi liceret*), or by abl. abs. (e.g. in — of the laws, *legibus contemptis*). **II.** v.tr. see ANNOY. **spiteful,** adj. *malignus, malevolus, lividus.* Adv. *maligne, malevole.*

splash, v.tr. *a(d)spergĕre.*

spleen, n. *lien, splen;* fig. *odium, livor, invidia.* **splenetic,** adj. **1,** *lienosus;* **2,** *malevolus, malignus.*

splendid, adj. *splendidus, splendens, fulgens, nitens, nitidus, (prae)clarus.* Adv. *splendide, nitide, magnifice, (prae)clare.* **splendour,** n. *splendor, fulgor, nitor;* lit. and fig. *apparatus, -ūs* (= pomp).

splice, v.tr. *partes inter se texĕre.*

splint, n. *canalis, ferulae* (Cels.). **splinter,** n. *ossis fragmentum* (of a bone), *ligni assula* or *fragmentum* (of wood).

split, I. n. *fissura* (Plin.), *scissura* (Plin.). **II.** v.tr. *(dif)findĕre, scindĕre.* **III.** v.intr. *(dif)findi, dissilire* (= to leap apart).

spoil, I. n. *praeda;* the — of war, *spolia, -orum;* — taken from the person of an enemy, *exuviae.* **II.** v.tr. **1,** *spoliare;* see PLUNDER; **2,** = to injure, *corrumpĕre;* see DESTROY; **3,** = to indulge too much, *nimis alci morigerari.* **spoiler,** n. *praedator, spoliator.* **spoiling, spoliation,** n. *spoliatio, expilatio, direptio.*

spoke, n. (of a wheel), *radius (rotae).*

spondee, n. *spondēus* (scil. *pes*).

sponge, I. n. *spongia.* **II.** v.tr. *spongiâ abstergĕre.* **sponge-cake,** n. *placenta.* **spongy,** adj. *spongiosus* (Plin.).

sponsor, n. *sponsor.*

spontaneous, adj. *libens.* Adv. *ultro, sponte (suâ), suo motu.* **spontaneousness, spon-**

taneity, n by *arbitrium* (e g *quod alcjs arbitrio factum est*)

spoon, n *cochlear* (*cochleare*, *cochleariium*, Plin), *ligula* (= ladle) **spoonful,** n *cochleai*

sport, I. n 1, *ludus* (= game), = to hunting, *venatio*, 2 = mockery, *ludibrium*, to make — of, *alci illudĕre*, see MOCK **II.** v intr *ludĕre*, to — about, *lascivire* **sportive,** adj *lascivus* (= playful), *jocosus* (= jocose), see PLAYFUL, JOCOSE Adv *lascive*, *jocose* **sportiveness,** n *lascivia*, *jocus* **sportsman,** n *venator*

spot, I. n 1, *macula* (lit and fig), *nota* (= mark, also = disgrace), see STAIN, 2, = place, *locus* **II.** v tr *notare* (lit), *maculare*, *inquinare* (fig). **spotless,** adj *sine maculis*, *castus*, *purus*, *sanctus*, *integer* Adv *sine maculis*, *caste*, *pure*, *sancte*, *integre* **spotted,** adj *maculosus*

spouse, n *maritus* (the husband), *uxor* (the wife), *co(n)junx* (the husband or the wife).

spout, I. n *os*, = pipe, *fistula*. **II.** v intr *erumpĕre*, *exsilire*

sprain, n and v tr perhaps by *convellĕre* (Col), *manare*, *serpĕre* (fig).

sprawl, v intr *humi prostratum jacēre*

spray, n of the sea, *spuma* (= foam)

spray, n. of a tree, perhaps *virgula*, see SPRIG.

spread, I. v tr *(ex)pandĕre* (= to lay open), *explicare* (= to unfold), *extendĕre* (= to stretch out), *sternĕre* (= to lay out or flat), *spargĕre* (= to scatter), *serĕre*, *disseminare* (= to sow seed broadcast), *differre*, *(di)vulgare* (= to make common), *dilatare* (= to stretch out) **II.** v intr *patēre*, *extendi* (lit), *percrebescĕre*, *increbescere*, *(di)vulgari* (fig) **spreading,** adj †*patulus*.

sprig, n *surculus*, *virgula*

sprightliness, n *alacritas* (= eagerness), *facetiae*, *sal*, *-is*, m (= wit), see EAGERNESS, WIT **sprightly,** adj *alacer*, *facetus*, *salsus*

spring, I. n 1, = origin, *origo*, *ortus*, *-ūs*, *fons*, *-ntis*, m (= source), *principium*, *caus(s)a*, = fountain, *fons scaturigo* (rare); 2, = first season of the year, *ver*, *tempus vernum*; the — of life, *iniens aetas*, 3, = — in machinery, perhaps by *machinatio* (e g *machinatio quādam moveri*, Cic **II.** v intr *salire* (= to leap), to — down, *desilire*, to — forward, *prosilire*, to — from, to take origin in, *ex alqo* or *alqā re (e)nasci*, *(ex)oriri*, *proficisci*, to — out, *prosilire*, *prorumpĕre*, to — up, *crescĕre* (= to grow), *surgĕre* (= to rise, of winds, etc) **III.** v tr to — a leak, *rimas agĕre*, to — a mine, *cuniculum igni explodĕre* **spring-tide,** n *aestus*, *-ūs*, *maximus*

sprinkle, v tr *alqm alqā re spargĕre*, *a(d)spergere*, *conspergĕre*

sprite n *faunus* (= faun), or *nympha* (= nymph)

sprout, I. n. *surculus*, see SHOOT. **II.** v intr *germinare* (Plin)

spruce, adj *comptus*, *bellus*, *ornatus*, *concinnus*, *nitidus*, *elegans* Adv *compte*, *belle*, *ornate*, *nitide*, *eleganter*

spur, I. n. *calcar* (lit and fig) **II.** v tr *equo calcaria subdĕre* or *equum calcaribus concitare* or *stimulare*

spurious, adj *adulterinus*, *falsus*

spurn, v tr *fastidire*, *aspernari*, *repudiare*, to — with the foot, see KICK.

spurt, I. v intr *summā vi contendĕre* **II.** n *nisus*, *-ūs*, see EFFORT

sputter, v tr *spuĕre*, to — out, *balbutire* (= to stammer).

spy, I. n *explorator*, *speculator*, *emissarius*. **II.** v intr *explorare*, *speculari*

squabble, I. n *rixa*, *altercatio* **II.** v intr. *rixari*

squadron, n *equitum turma*, *ala*, — of ships, *classis*

squalid, adj *sordidus*, *squalidus*, *spurcus*, see DIRTY

squall, I. n *subita tempestas*, = crying, *vagitus*, *-ūs* **II.** v intr *vagire*

squalor, squalidity, squalidness, n *sordes*, *-is*, f, usu in pl, *squalor*, *spurcitia*, *spurcities* Adv *sordide*, *squalide*, *spurce*

squander, v tr *profundĕre*, *effundĕre*, *perdĕre*, *dissipare* **squanderer,** n *nepos*, *-ōtis*, m

square, I. adj *quadratus* **II.** n *quadratum*, n **III.** v tr *quadrare*

squash, v tr see CRUSH.

squat, I. v intr *subsidĕre* **II.** adj *habitu corporis brevis atque obesus*

squeak, I n *stridor* **II.** v intr *stridĕre*

squeamish, adj *fastidiosus*, *delicatus* **squeamishness,** n *fastidium*

squeeze, I. n *compressio* **II.** v tr *premĕre*, *comprimĕre*, to — out, *exprimĕre*

squib, n see LAMPOON

squint, v intr *limis* or *perversis oculis esse*, *limis spectare*, *strabonem esse*, to — at, *limis oculis intueri alqd* or *alqm*

squire, n **armiger*

squirrel, n *sciūrus* (Plin)

squirt, n and v tr see SYRINGE

stab, I. n *ictus*, *-ūs* (= a blow), or *vulnus*, *-ĕris*, *sicā factum* **II.** v tr *(con)fodĕre*, or *sicā* or *pugione ferire*, *sicā conficĕre* (= to slay by stabbing, etc) **stabber,** n *sicarius*

stable, I. adj *stabilis*, *firmus*, fig *constans*, *proposito tenax* **II.** n *stabulum* (= stall), or in pl). **III.** v tr *stabulare* **stability,** n *stabilitas*, *firmitas*, *constantia*

stack, I. n *meta* (of hay), *cumulus*, *acervus*, *strues*, *-is*, f **II.** v tr *cumulare*, see PILE

staff, n *baculum*, *bacillum*, *scipio* (carried before officials), *fustis*, m (= cudgel), an augur's —, *lituus*, the — of a spear, *hastile*, shepherd's —, *pedum*, herald's —, *caduceus*, to lean on a —, *baculo inniti*, — of officers, *legati et praefecti et tribuni militum*, any other — (of assistants) *socii*, (= colleagues) *adjutores*, *ministri*

stag, n *cervus*

stage, n 1 of a theatre, *proscaenium*, *scaena* (lit = the wall which closed the — behind), 2, fig *scaena* (e g to go upon the —, *in scaenam prodire*), 3, = degree, *gradus*, *-ūs*, = part of a journey, *iter*, *itinĕris*, n **stage-coach,** n *vehiculum publicum*

stagger, I. v intr *titubare*, *vacillare*, *incertis ire pedibus* **II.** v tr *animum movēre*, *percutĕre*

staggers, n. *vertigo*

stagnant, adj 1, *stagnans*, 2, fig see SLOW **stagnate,** v intr 1, †*stagnare*, 2, perhaps *hebescĕre*, *languēre*

staid, adj see SOBER

stain, I. n 1, *macula*, *labes*, *-is*, *decoloratio* (the act), 2, fig *macula*, *labes*, *-is*, f, *nota* (= mark), *dedecus*, *ŏris*, n, see SHAME **II.** v tr 1, see DYE, DIRTY, 2, fig *maculare*, *foedare*, *polluĕre*, to — a reputation, *alcjs existimationem violare*, *alcjs famae* or *alci notam turpitudinis inurĕre*, *alqm infamiā a(d)spergĕre*, = to discolour, *decolorare*, = to dye, *tingere*, *inficĕre* **stainless,** adj *purus*, see PURE.

stair, n. *gradus, -ūs*; a —case, *scalae* (*scalis habito tribus*, = I dwell up three pair of —s).

stake, I. n. *palus, stipes, -ĭtis*, m.; as instrument of punishment, *palus* (= — to which criminals were bound; where burning is implied, better use *igni interficĕre*); a — at play or gambling, *pignus, -ĕris*, n. (= a bet), *quod ponitur*; to be at —, *agi, periclitari, in discrimen adduci*; my honour is at —, *fama agitur mea*. **II.** v.tr. (*de*)*ponĕre*.

stale, adj. *vetus, obsolētus, exsolētus* (= worn out); to become —, *obsolescĕre*.

stalk, I. n. *caulis* (of a herb), *caudex* (of a tree), *scapus, culmus* (= green stalk), *calamus* (= reed); see STEM. **II.** v.intr. (*magnifice*) *incedĕre*, † *spatiari*.

stall, I. n. *stabulum*; = a little shop, *taberna*; = a seat in a choir, *sella*. **II.** v.tr. *stabulare*.

stallion, n. (*equus*) *admissarius*.

stamen, n. *stamen*.

stammer, I. v.intr. *balbutire*. **II.** n. use verb.

stamp, I. n. *nota, signum, imago* (*impressa*); persons of that —, *ejusmodi homines*; the — or blow of the foot, (*pedis*) *supplosio*. **II.** v.intr. *pedibus calcare, pulsare, pedem supplodĕre*. **III.** v.tr. to — under foot, *conculcare*; = to mark, *signare, notare, signum* or *notam imprimĕre*; to — money, *nummos signare* or *cudĕre*.

stanch, v.tr. see STAUNCH.

stand, I. n. *mora* (= delay), *locus, statio* (= place for standing); = prop, *statumen, adminiculum*; = sideboard, etc., *abacus*; to come to a —, *subsistĕre*; to make a — against, *resistĕre*; to take a —, *locum capĕre*; to be at a —, *haerēre, animi pendēre*. **II.** v.intr. *stare, consistĕre*; to let a thing —, *non movēre alqd*; it —s written, *lit(t)eris consignatum est, legimus*; to — good, *obtinēre*; to — against, *alci resistĕre*; to — still, *quiescĕre*; to — aside, *recedĕre*; to — by anyone, *alci adesse*; to — fast, *consistĕre*; to — for an office, *munus petĕre* or *ambire*; to — good in law, *lege valēre*; to — on ceremony, *cum algo comiter sed haud familiariter agĕre*; not to — on ceremony, *cum algo amicissime agĕre*; to — in the way, *alci obstare*; to — out, *eminēre, prominēre*; to — out to sea, *vela dare*; to — up, *surgĕre, erectum stare, horrēre* (= to bristle); to — before a person, *assurgĕre* (or of several, *consurgĕre*) *alci*. **III.** v.tr. see ENDURE. **standing, I.** adj. or part. *stans*; = lasting, *diuturnus, perpetuus*; — erect, *erectus*; — water, *aqua stagnans*; — camp, *castra stativa*; — army, *milites*. **II.** n. *gradus, -ūs, locus, ordo*; see RANK; of long —, *vetus*; of short —, *recens*. **standstill,** n. to be at a —, *haerēre*.

standard, n. **1,** = flag, *vexillum*; to raise a —, *vexillum tollĕre*; to hoist or display a —, *vexillum proponĕre*; *aquila* (i.e. the eagle of the legion); **2,** = measure, *regula, norma*. **standard-bearer,** n. *vexillarius, signifer, aquilifer*.

stanza, n. *versuum series*.

staple, I. n. **1,** *emporium* (= market); **2,** see HOOK. **II.** adj. — commodities, by *res alcjs terrae propriae*.

star, n. *astrum, sidus, -ĕris*, n. (= a collection of —s, also = *astrum*), *signum* (= a sign in the skies), *stella*; = a distinguished person, e.g. *Africanus sol alter*, = a — of the first magnitude; the —s of the State, *lumina civitatis*; = a critical sign or mark, *asteriscus* (Gram.); the — under which one is born, *sidus natalicium*. **star-gazer,** n. *astrologus* (= interpreter of stars). **starlight,** adj. *sideribus illustris* (Tac.). **starry,** adj. *stellifer, astris distinctus et ornatus*.

starboard, adj. and n. *latus navis dextrum*.

starch, n. *amylum* (Plin.).

stare, I. n. *obtutus, -ūs*. **II.** v.intr. *obtutum in re figĕre, conspicari, intueri, stupēre* (with astonishment).

stark, adj. *rigens* (with cold); see STIFF.

starling, n. *sturnus* (Plin.).

start, I. n. **1,** *saltus, -ūs* (= jump); by fits and —s, *haud uno tenore*; **2,** see BEGINNING, COMMENCEMENT; **3,** = setting out, *profectio*; to get the — of anything, *alqm antecedere* (lit.), *alqm superare* (fig.). **II.** v.intr. **1,** *trepidare, expavescĕre*; **2,** see BEGIN; **3,** = to set out, *proficisci*. **III.** v.tr. *initium alcjs rei facĕre, alqd instituĕre*.

startle, v.tr. (dim. of START) *alci metum in(j)icĕre, alqm improviso, de improviso, imprudentem* or *necopinantem opprimĕre*. **startling,** adj. *mirandus, mirificus*.

starve, I. v.tr. *fame* or *inediā necare, consumĕre*. **II.** v.intr. *fame* or *inediā necari, consumi*.

state, I. n. **1,** *status, -ūs, condicio, locus, res, fortuna*; a good —, *res secundae*; a bad —, *res adversae*; **2,** = rank, *homo mei loci atque ordinis*; **3,** = a city or commonwealth, *civitas, respublica, regnum, imperium*; at the cost of the —, *sumptu publico*; a maxim of —, *ratio civilis*; a minister of —, *socius et administer reipublicae gerendae*; council of —, *consilium publicum*; **4,** = grandeur, *cultus, ornatus, apparatus* (all -ūs), *magnificens*. **II.** v.tr. *narrare, praedicare, dicĕre, profiteri, affirmare, confirmare, asseverare*. **stately,** adj. of carriage, *erectus* (= upright), *nobilis* (noble); of banquets, etc., *lautus, magnificus*. **stateliness,** n. use adj. **statesman,** n. *vir reipublicae peritus*. **statesmanship,** n. *ars reipublicae regendae*. **station, I.** n. **1,** see POSITION; **2,** see RANK. **II.** v.tr. see PLACE, SET. **stationary,** adj. *stativus* (*stativa castra*), *immobilis, immotus, quod non movetur, fixus*. **stationer,** n. *chartarius* (= a paper-seller; very late). **stationery,** n. see PAPER.

statistics, n. by *res* (*singulae*), (of details); *omnia* (of information collectively).

statue, n. *statua, simulacrum* (= likeness), *signum, imago*. **statuary,** n. see SCULPTOR, SCULPTURE.

stature, n. *statura*; a man of low, etc., —, *homo parvae, magnae, procerae staturae*.

statute, n. *lex*. **statutable,** adj. *legitimus*.

staunch, I. adj. *firmus, solidus, bonus*; a — friend, *amicus certus, fidus, fidelis*. **II.** v.tr. *sanguinem sistĕre, cohibēre* (Cels.).

stay, I. v.tr. **1,** = to prop, *fulcire, fulcire et sustinēre, statuminare* (by a post or beam), *adminiculari* (as the vine is trained on supports); to — yourself on, *niti* (or *inniti*) *alqā re* (*in alqā re*), *in alqd* (*in alqm*); **2,** = to stop, arrest, (*de*)*morari, detinēre, cohibēre*; see CHECK. **II.** v.intr. = to abide or tarry, *commorari, manēre, versari*; to — with, *apud alqd manēre*; to — much anywhere, *locum frequentare*. **stays,** n. use *mamillare* (Mart.).

stead, n. in — of, *pro, loco, vice, in locum, in vicem alcjs*; in — of, etc., *tantum abest, ut*, etc., *non modo non . . . sed etiam*; in — of the consul, *pro consule*; to be in — of a father, *pro patre esse alci, cum debeat* or *debēret* (e.g. in — of going, he did this, *hoc facit, cum ire deberet*).

steady, steadfast, adj. *stabilis, firmus* (lit. and fig.), *constans, gravis, fidus, fidelis* (fig.). Adv. *firme, graviter, firmiter, constanter, fide, fideliter*. **steadiness, steadfastness,** n. *stabilitas, firmitas, constantia, gravitas, sobrietas* (in regard to drink).

steak, n *offella, offula*, a beef—, *offula carnis bubulae*

steal, v tr *furtum facĕre, furari, surripĕre* (*subr*-), *avertĕre, intercipĕre*; to — out of the city, *clam se urbe subducĕre*, to — over anyone (of sleep, etc), *alqm subire* **stealer,** n *fur*

stealth, n by —, *furtim, clam* **stealthy,** adj *furtivus* (e g *amor*), *clandestinus, occultus, tectus* Adv *furtive, furtim, clam, occulte, tecte*

steam, I n *vapor, nidor* (from anything cooked), *fumus* (= smoke) **II.** v tr *vaporare*

steamboat, n *navis vi vapŏris* (*neque velis*) *impulsa* **steam-engine,** n *machina vi vaporis impulsa*

steed, n *equus*

steel, I. n *chalybs*, = sword, *ferrum* **II.** v tr see HARDEN

steep, I. adj *praeruptus, praeceps, arduus* **II.** n *locus praeceps* **III.** v tr *aqua macerare* or *mollire*, see SOAK **steepness,** n use adj

steeple, n *turris* (= tower) perhaps *fastigium turri superpositum* (for a — on a tower).

steeplechase, n see RACE

steer, v tr *gubernare, regĕre*, to — a ship, *navem gubernare* (so *gubernare rempublicam*)

steerage, n and adj *puppis* (e g — passengers, *qui in puppi vehuntur*) **steering,** n *gubernatio* **steersman,** n *gubernator* (so *reipublicae*), *rector* (fig)

steer, n = young bull, *juvencus*

stem, I. n *arboris stirps* or *truncus* (of a tree), *caulis, calamus* (of a plant), = race, *progenies, stirps, prosapia, familia, genus, ĕris*, n **II.** v tr *cohibēre, sistĕre, coercēre, reprimĕre*, to — the tide, *aestum marinum sistĕre*, to — the sedition, *seditionem sedare, compescĕre*, see also RESIST

stench, n *foetor, putor* (ante and post class)

step, I. n = a stair, *gradus, ūs*, = a pace, *gradus, passus, gressus*, all -*ūs*, to take —s, *agĕre, agĕre et moliri, consilium capĕre*, extreme —, *ultima experiri*, to keep — with, *alcjs gradus aequare*; fig *parem esse alci*, — by —, *gradatim, pedetentim* **II.** v intr *gradi, vadĕre*, to — forwards, *progredi, pergĕre*, to — over, *transire, superare alqd* **step-brother,** n *filius vitrici* (on the father's side), *filius novercae* (on the mother's)

step-daughter, n *privigna* **step father,** n *vitricus* **step-mother,** n *noverca* **step sister,** n *filia vitrici* or *novercae* **step son,** n *privignus*

stereotype, n *formae lit(t)erarum fixae*

stereotyped, adj *tritus*, see TRITE

sterile, adj *sterilis* (lit and fig) **sterility,** n *sterilitas* (lit and fig)

sterling, adj *verus, bonus*

stern, adj *torvus, durus, severus, austerus* Adv *dure, duriter, severe* **sternness,** n *severitas*

stern, n *puppis* (= poop)

stew, I. v tr *carnem* (*igne lento*) *coquĕre* **II.** n *caro* (*igne lento*) *cocta*

steward, n *procurator, curator, dispensator, administrator, villicus* (of the farm) — of the house, *rerum domesticarum curator* **stewardship,** n *cura, procuratio, dispensatoris munus, -ĕris*, n, *administratio*

stick, I. n *baculum, bacillum, radius* (= wand), *virga* (= rod), *clava, fustis -is* (= cudgel), *palus* **II.** v intr 1, *haerēre, adhaerēre, cohaerēre* (= to — together), 2, fig *haerēre, haesitare, dubitare* **III.** v tr *(af)figĕre* (= to — to), *defigĕre, praefigĕre* (= to — before), *infigĕre*, see STAB

sticking-plaster, n *emplastrum* (Plin)

stickle, v intr *summo studio in pi ud alqd incumbĕre* **stickler,** n *qui summo studio in alqd incumbit* **sticky,** adj *lentus, tenax*

stiff, adj *rigidus, rigens, durus*, — in character, *pertinax, inexorabilis, rigidus*, — in manners, perhaps *rusticus, agrestis, parum comis*, to be —, *rigēre* Adv *rigide, dure, duriter, pertinaciter, rigide, rustice, parum comiter*

stiffen, v tr *durare, indurare, rigidum facĕre*

stiffness, n *rigor, rigiditas* (lit and fig), *rusticitas* (fig)

stifle, v tr 1, *suffocare, spiritum intercludĕre*, 2, fig *opprimĕre, ex(s)tinguĕre*

stigma, n *nota* **stigmatize,** v tr *notam* (*turpitudinis*) *inurĕre alci*

stile, n *claustra, orum* (= barrier)

still, I. adj *tranquillus, quietus, placidus, sedatus, tacitus, silens, lenis* (= gentle), *immotus* (= motionless), — night, *nox tacita*, be—, *taceas, quiesce! quiescite!* **II.** v tr *sedare, reprimĕre, restinguĕre, ex(s)tinguĕre, lenire, permulcēre*, to — hunger, *famem explēre* **III.** Adv **1,** = up to this time, *adhuc, etiam, etiamnunc* (or *etiamnum*), **2,** with compar (e g — more), *etiam magis*, = especially, *praesertim*, **3,** see NEVERTHELESS **stilling,** n *sedatio* **stillness,** n *silentium, tranquillitas, quies*

still, n **alembicum*

stilts, n *grallae* **stilted,** adj see INFLATED

stimulant, n *vinum* (= wine) **stimulate,** v tr *stimulare, excitare*, see ENCOURAGE

stimulus, n. *stimulus, incitamentum, irritamentum* (mostly in pl), *calcar* (= spur)

sting, I. n *aculeus*, the wound from a —, *ictus, -ūs* **II.** v tr *pungĕre* (lit and fig), *aculeos infigĕre* **stinging,** adj *mordens, mordax, acerbus, aculeatus*

stingy, adj *parcus, sordidus, tenax, malignus* Adv *parce, sordide, maligne* **stinginess,** n *parsimonia, tenacitas, malignitas*, see MEANNESS

stink, n and v intr see SMELL

stint, I. n *inopia*, see NEED **II** v tr *alqd alci parce dare, alqm alqa re privare* (= to deprive of)

stipend, n see SALARY **stipendiary,** adj *mercenarius, stipendiarius*

stipulate, v intr. *stipulari, pacisci* **stipulation,** n *stipulatio, pactum, condicio*

stir, I. n *motus, ūs, tumultus, -ūs, turba, strepitus, -ūs*, to be in a —, *movēri, agitari* **II.** v tr *(com)movēre*, to — oneself, *movēri* **III.** v.intr. *movēri, progredi*, see GO, ADVANCE

stirrup, n perhaps *lorum ad pedem sustinendum ex ephippio pendens* (The Romans rode without stirrups, see Smith's "Dict Antiq," art Ephippium)

stitch, I. n — in the side, *lateris dolor* **II.** v tr *(con)suĕre*

stock, I. n (*arboris*) *truncus, stirps, stipes, -itis*, m —s for ship building, *navalia, ium* (= a dock), the —s (as instrument of punishment), by *pedicae* (= fetters), a — or family, *gens, stirps*, descended from a noble —, *claro* or *honesto loco natus*, = quantity, *magna copia*, — of money, *ingens num(m)orum vis*, — dove, *palumbes, is*, m and f, — jobber, *argentarius* **II.** v tr *instruĕre*, see PROVIDE **III.** adj see COMMON, TRITE **IV.** adv — still, *immotus*

stockade, n *vallum*

stocking, n *tibiale, is*, n (Suet)

stoic, adj and n *Stoicus* **stoical, stoically,** adj and adv. *stoice*, *ut aiunt, more*, **stoicism,** n. *ratio Stoicorum*.

stomach, I. n. 1, *stomachus;* 2, = anger, *stomachus.* **II.** v.tr. *stomachari, alqd indigne ferre.* **stomacher,** n. *mamillare* (Mart.).

stone, I. n. *lapis, -ĭdis,* m., *saxum;* — in the human body, *calculus* (Cels.); — of fruit, *nucleus,* see KERNEL; precious —, *gemma;* to throw —s at, *lapides con(j)icĕre in alqm;* a —-breaker, *lapicīda,* m.; — quarry, *lapicīdinae;* a —'s-throw, *lapidis jactus, -ūs.* **II.** v.tr. *lapides in alqm con(j)icĕre.* **stoning,** n. *lapidatio.* **stony,** adj. *lapideus* (of stone), *saxeus, lapidosus, saxosus* (= abounding in stones). **stony-hearted,** adj. *durus, ferreus.*

stool, n. *scabellum.*

stoop, v.intr. *se inclinare, proclinare, se demittĕre.* **stooping, I.** n. *corporis inclinatio.* **II.** adj. *pronus, inclinatus.*

stop, I. v.intr. *(con)sistĕre, resistĕre, subsistĕre, gradum sistĕre* (= to stay), in a place, *alqo* (or *in alqo*) *loco, versari in alqo loco, morari;* = to cease, *ab alqâ re cessare, alqd omittĕre.* **II.** v.tr. *sistĕre;* = to hinder, *prohibēre, inhibēre, coercēre, impedire;* a sedition, etc., *ex(s)tinguĕre, compescĕre;* = to block up, *viam intercludĕre,* a bottle, etc., *obturare, occludĕre;* = to punctuate, *interpungĕre* (Sen.). **III.** n. *impedimentum, mora;* see HINDRANCE; — (in printing), *interpunctum;* without —, *sine morâ.* **stoppage,** n. *obstructio, impedimentum, retentio* (= holding back), of the bowels, *alvus a(d)stricta* (Cels.). **stopper,** n. *obturamentum* (Plin.).

store, I. n. *copia, magna vis, abundantia* (= plenty); to have a —, *abundare, affluĕre re;* — of provisions, *commeatus, -ūs* (for the army), *alimenta, -orum, annona;* —-house, *apothēca, horreum* (= granary); —-room, *cella promptuaria* or *penaria.* **II.** v.tr. *coacervare, reponĕre, condĕre, instruĕre, ornare re;* to — yourself with, *sibi comparare alqd, providēre rei.*

storey, n. *tabulatio, tabulatum.*

stork, n. *ciconia.*

storm, I. n. *tempestas, procella;* fig. *tempestas, fluctus, -ūs;* = a violent attack, *impetus, -ūs, vis;* a —-cloud, *nimbus.* **II.** v.tr., e.g. *urbem vi oppugnare, expugnare;* to take by —, *vi capĕre.* **III.** v.intr. *furĕre, saevire;* see RAGE. **storming, I.** n. *expugnatio.* **II.** adj. — party, *(milites) ad urbem oppugnandam missi.* **stormy,** adj. 1, lit. *turbidus, procellosus;* 2, fig. *iratus* (= angry), *tumultuosus.* Adv. *irate, turbide.*

story, n. *res, narratio, narratiuncula, fabula* (= fable); to tell a —, *narrare;* = a falsehood, *mendacium;* a —-teller, *narrator, mendax* (= liar).

stout, adj. *crassus, obēsus* (= fat), *vastus, amplus* (= large), *fortis, constans, virilis, valens, validus, firmus, robustus, potens* (= strong); see FAT, STRONG. Adv. *fortiter, constanter, acriter, pro viribus suis, valide, robuste.* **stoutness,** n. 1, see CORPULENCE; 2, see COURAGE, ENDURANCE.

stove, n. *focus, caminus.*

stow, v.tr. see STORE. **stowage,** n. *locus.*

straddle, v.intr. *varicare* (ante and post class.). **straddling,** adj. *varicus.*

straggle, v.intr. *vagari, deerrare, palari.*

straight, I. adj. *(di)rectus, erectus* (= upright); a — line, *linea directa;* a — way, *recta via.* **II.** adv. —way, *recto itinere, statim, confestim* (= immediately), *protinus* (= both —forward and immediately). **straighten,** v.tr. *corrigĕre* (lit. and fig., in former sense mostly ante and post class.). **straightforward,** adj. *simplex;* see FRANK, UPRIGHT.

strain, I. n. *intentio, contentio* (*corporis, nervorum;* opp. *remissio*); = tone, see TUNE; in this —, *ita, sic* (= thus), or by rel. sentence (e.g. *quae cum dixisset, abiit,* having spoken in this —, he went off). **II.** v.tr. *(in)tendĕre, intentare, contendĕre in* or *ad alqd, contra alqm* or *alqd;* = to sprain, see SPRAIN; = to filter, see FILTER.

strait, I. adj. *artus* (*arctus*), *angustus, strictus* (= bound up). **II.** n. *fretum;* the — of Gibraltar, *fretum Gaditanum;* — of Constantinople, *Bosporus Thracius;* = a narrow path, *viarum* or *locorum* or *itineris angustiae;* = a difficulty, *angustiae;* = poverty, *inopia, res durae* or *angustae.* **straiten,** v.tr. *in angustias adducĕre.*

strand, I. n. *litus, -oris,* n., *ripa, acta.* **II.** v.tr. *navem vadis* or *litoribus illidĕre* or *impingĕre, in litus e(j)ici.*

strange, adj. 1, = foreign, *peregrinus, externus, exterus* (= outward, the first, of persons and things, opp. *intestinus;* the second, of persons, esp. with *gentes* and *nationes,* as opp. to *socii*), *extraneus* (= not belonging to the family), *adventicius* (= coming from abroad, opp. *vernaculus*), *barbarus* (= not Roman); 2, = unversed in, a stranger to, *in alqâ re peregrinus* or *aliēnus, hospes,* or *rudis;* — in this city, *ignarus hujus urbis;* 3, = unusual, *insolitus, insolens, novus, mirus;* that seems — to me, *mirum hoc mihi videtur, miror, admiror hoc;* 4, = not belonging to one, *alienus;* to fall into — hands, *in alienas manus incidĕre;* 5, = unsuitable, averse, *aliēnus;* to be —, *alienum esse, abhorrēre ab.* Adv. *mirum in modum, mirifice, mirabiliter, insolite.* **strangeness,** n. *novitas, insolentia,* or by adj. **stranger,** n. *hospes, -itis,* m. (in gen.), *externus* (opp. *civis*), *aliēnigĕna,* m. (opp. *indigena*), *advena,* m. and f. (= incomer), *barbarus.*

strangle, v.tr. *strangulare, laqueo interimĕre, gulam laqueo frangĕre.*

strap, I. n. *lorum* (of leather). **II.** v.tr. *loris (con)stringĕre* (= to bandage).

stratagem, n. *ars, dolus, consilium, astus, -ūs, insidiae.* **strategic,** adj. *quod ad prudentem ducem pertinet.* **strategist,** n. *dux prudens* or *peritus.* **strategy,** n. *ars belli gerendi.*

stratum, n. perhaps *stratum* as t.t., or by circumloc. (e.g. *genus aliud alci impositum*). **stratify,** v.tr. perhaps by *digerĕre, disponĕre.*

straw, I. n. *stramentum.* **II.** adj. *stramenticius.* **strawberry,** n. *fragum.*

stray, v.intr. *(ab)errare, vagi, pali.*

streak, I. n. *linea, nota* (= mark). **II.** v.tr. *lineis* or *variis coloribus distinguĕre.*

stream, I. n. *flumen* (= flowing water); down the —, *flumine secundo;* up the —, *flumine adverso.* **II.** v.intr. *fluĕre, effundi in rem;* to — together, *undique convenire.*

streamer, n. *vexillum, signum.*

street, n. *via, vicus* (= the street as running between two lines of houses), *platea* (= the broad open roads or promenades in a city), *angiportus, -ūs* (= narrow crossways, streets, or alleys); a public —, in contrast with the homes, was called *publicum; in publico* (opp. to *in privato;* = in public, on the high road); to remain all night in the —, *jacēre et pernoctare in publico.*

strength, n. *vis* (or in pl. *vires*), *nervi, robur, -oris,* n., *opes* (= resources), as passive quality, — of resistance, *firmitas;* to feel your —, *sibi confidĕre;* to have — in, *multum valēre re, excellĕre in re.* **strengthen, I.** v.tr. *corroborare, (con)firmare;* to — yourself, *se reficĕre.* **II.** v.intr. by pass *corroborari*, etc., see also INCREASE. **strengthened,** adj. *confirmatus*. **strengthening,** n. *confirmatio* (e.g. *perpetuae libertatis, animi*).

strenuous, adj. *strenuus* (opp. *iners, ignavus*), *impiger, acer*, see ACTIVE. Adv. *strenue, impigre, acriter*. **strenuousness,** n. (*g*)*navitas, studium*.

stress, n. *vel momentum, vis, vis et pondus, -ĕris*, n.; with —, *cum vi, graviter*; to lay — on, *alqd vehementer confidĕre, in re spem* or *fiduciam ponere*; — of weather, *tempestas, procella*.

stretch, I. v.tr. (*ex*)*tendĕre, contendĕre, intendĕre*; to — forth or out, *protendĕre, porrigĕre*; to — the iron under the hammer, *ferrum producĕre incude*. II. v.intr. see REACH. III. n. *contentio, intentio, nisus, -ūs* (= effort); at a —, *uno tenore*; — of land, *campus*. **stretcher,** n. see LITTER.

strew, v.tr. *sternĕre* (= to lay on the ground), *spargĕre* (= to scatter).

strict, adj. 1, = accurate, *accuratus, diligens*; to tell in — confidence, *alqd alci in aurem dicĕre*. 2, *severus, rigidus*, see SEVERE. Adv. = truly, *re verâ, reapse*; = accurately, *accurate, diligenter*; = severely, *severe, rigide*. **strictness,** n. *accuratio, diligentia, severitas*, see SEVERITY. **stricture,** n. *animadversio, reprehensio*, see BLAME.

stride, I. n. *ingens gradus, -ūs*. II. v.intr. *ingentes gradus ferre*.

strife, n. *certatio, certamen, contentio* (in gen.), *disceptatio, controversia, altercatio* (= dispute), *jurgium, rixa* (= quarrel); — in a lawsuit, *lis*. **strive,** v.intr. (*e*)*niti, conari, contendĕre, operam dare, conari, studēre*, etc.; to — after, (*con*)*niti, contendĕre ad alqd*, (*ex*)*petere, affectare, captare alqd, rei studēre, sequi* or *persequi alqd*; to — against, *obniti, resistere*; to — with or against, *confligĕre, concertare*. **striving,** n. see EFFORT; — after, *alcjs appetitio, contentio*.

strike, v.tr. *ferire, percutĕre, pulsare, verberare* (= to lash), *caedĕre*; to be struck, *vapulare*; to — (as a clock), *sonare*; to — twelve, *horologium indicat horam duodecimam*; to — a flag or yield, *vexillum demittĕre*; the lightning —s, *de caelo tangitur alqd*; to be struck blind, *captum esse oculis*; to — a coin, *cudĕre*, see COIN; to — the mind, *percutĕre, percellĕre* (= to shock); to — a bargain, *pacisci*; to — against, *alqd offendĕre, in alqd incurrĕre*; to — against rocks (of a ship), *saxis illidi*. **striking,** adj. see REMARKABLE.

string, I. n. *linum, linea, filum, funiculus* or *vinculum* (= cord); — of leather, shoe —, *corrigia*; a bow —, *nervus*; — of a dart, *amentum*; — of a musical instrument, *chorda, nervus, fides, -ium*. II. v.tr. to — an instrument, *lyrae, citharae*, etc., *nervos aptare*; to — together, see BIND. **stringent,** adj. see SEVERE.

strip, I. v.tr. *spoliare, nudare, denudare, exuĕre, alci vestem detrahĕre*; to — a person of his wealth, *alqm opibus spoliare*. II. n. *pars*; — of paper, *scidula chartae*; — of cloth, *lacinia*.

stripe, I. n. 1, see STREAK; 2, see STROKE. II. v.tr. see STREAK.

stripling, n. *adulescens*.

stroke, I. n. 1, *verber*, see BLOW; 2, see LINE; 3, of lightning, *fulmen*; 4, of fortune, etc., *eventus, -ūs* (*felix* = lucky, etc.); = artifice, *ars* (e.g. a master- —, *summa ars*); to put the finishing — to, *alqd ad finem perducĕre*. II. v.tr. *alqm permulcēre, demulcēre*.

stroll, I. n. *ambulatio*. II. v.intr. *ambulare*, see WALK, WANDER.

strong, adj. *validus, validus, nervosus, robustus, lacertosus, fortis*; to be — (in influence), *pollere*, e.g. Compare *Etruria tantum pollens terra marique*, Liv.; *pollēre pecuniâ, scientiâ, armis, gratiâ, nobilitate*; comb. *potens pollensque*, Sall.; a — wind, *ventus vehemens*; of arguments, *gravis, firmus*; — memory, *memoria* (*alcjs*) *tenax*; a — position, *locus munitus*. Adv. *valide, firme, firmiter, fortiter*; = very, *valde* or *vehementer*, or by compound (e.g. *movēri*, = to be moved; *commovēri*, = to be — moved).

strophe, n. *stropha* (late).

structure, n. *aedificium, aedes, -is*, f., *opus, -ĕris*, n., *monumentum* (= a building), *structura* (= the kind of building, *structura parietum, structurae antiquae genus*, Liv.; also = the substance); fig. *structura verborum* or *vocum*; — of a sentence, *forma, ratio*.

struggle, I. n. *luctatio*, see CONTENTION. II. v.intr. *luctari*; to — with each other, *luctari inter se*; to — with the difficulty, *luctari cum difficultate*, see CONTEND, FIGHT.

strumpet, n. *scortum, meretrix*.

strut, v.intr. *superbe incedĕre*.

stubble, n. *stipulae*.

stubborn, adj. *pertinax, pervicax, obstinatus, contumax*. Adv. *pertinaciter, pervicaciter, obstinate, contumaciter, obstinato animo*. **stubbornness,** n. *pertinacia, pervicacia, contumacia, obstinatio* (usually of a good quality), *obstinatus animus*.

stucco, n. see PLASTER.

stud, I. n. *bulla*; = button, *fibula* (= clasp); = a number of horses, *equi, equaria*. II. v.tr. *alqd re distinguĕre*.

study, I. n. *studium, studia, meditatio* (= thought); = room for —, *conclave*. II. v.tr. *lit(t)eris studēre, lit(t)eras tractare*; to — something, *alci rei studēre, incumbĕre* or *operam dare*. **student,** n. *alcjs rei studiosus*. **studio,** n. *conclave* (*pictoris*, of a painter, etc.). **studious,** adj. *lit(t)erarum studiosus, in studiis literarum versatus*. Adv. *summo studio*.

stuff, I. n. *materia, materies*; = baggage, *impedimenta, -orum, sarcinae*; household —, *supellex, lectilis*, f.; kitchen —, *culinaria*; = — gown, etc., *textile*; as an exclamation, *nugas! gerrae!* II. v.tr. (*re*)*fercire, replēre*, see FILL. **stuffing,** n. *fartum* (Plin., of food), *tomentum* (of cushions).

stultify, v.tr. *alqm stultitiae coarguĕre* or *convincĕre*.

stumble, v.intr. *offendĕre*. **stumbling,** n. *offensio*; to cause or be a — -block to, *esse offensioni alci*; things which are — blocks, *quae habent offensionem* (Cic.).

stump, n. *caudex, stipes, -ĭtis, truncus*.

stun, v.tr. 1, lit. perhaps *alqm sensu privare*; 2, fig. *obtundĕre, stupefacĕre, perterrēre, percellĕre*. **stunned,** adj. 1, *sensu privatus*; 2, fig. *stupefactus*.

stunt, v.tr. *alcjs incrementum impedire*.

stupefy, v.tr. *stupefacĕre, sopire, torporem afferre, hebetare*; to be stupefied, *torpescĕre, stupescĕre, torpēre, stupēre*. **stupefaction,** n. *stupor, torpor*.

stupendous, adj. *ingens, immanis*, see WONDERFUL.

stupid, adj. *stupidus, stolidus*, see FOOLISH. Adv. *stupide, stolide*. **stupidity,** n. *stupiditas, animus stolidus*, or *stupidus*. **stupor,** n. *stupor, torpor*.

sturdy, adj. 1, see STRONG; 2, see CONFIDENT.

sturgeon, n. *acipenser.*

stutter, v.intr. *balbutire;* see STAMMER.

sty, n. *hara, suile.*

style, I. n. 1, in gen. *genus, -ĕris,* n., *ratio, habitus, -ūs* (of dress, etc.), *mos* (= custom); 2, in language, *dicendi* or *scribendi genus, orationis* or *sermonis genus, oratio, sermo, elocutio;* the — is the man, *qualis est ipse homo, talis est ejus oratio.* **II.** v.tr. *appellare;* see NAME. **stylish,** adj. *speciosus, elegans, nitidus, lautus, magnificus.* Adv. *speciose, eleganter, nitide, laute, magnifice.* **stylishness,** n. *elegantia, magnificentia, lautitia.*

suave, adj. *urbanus, blandus;* see COURTEOUS. **suavity,** n. *urbanitas;* see COURTESY.

subaltern, I. adj. *inferioris loci.* **II.** n. perhaps *subcenturio.*

subcommissioner, n. *procurator, vicarius.*

subdivide, v.tr. *iterum dividĕre;* see DIVIDE. **subdivision,** n. *pars.*

subdue, v.tr. *in imperium alcjs redigĕre, dicioni suae sub(j)icĕre alqm, sui juris facĕre, subigĕre, domare.*

subject, I. v.tr. *sub(j)icĕre;* to — yourself, *se imperio alcjs sub(j)icĕre;* see also EXPOSE. **II.** n. 1, *civi* or *regi subjectus,* or by *civis;* 2, in grammar or logic, *subjectum;* 3, = matter discussed, etc., *res, quaestio, argumentum.* **III.** adj. *imperio* or *dicioni alcjs subjectus, parens, obnoxius alci;* to be —, *esse in alcjs dicione;* to become —, *sub alcjs imperium cadĕre.* **subjection,** n. *servitus, -ūtis,* f.; to hold in —, *alqm in officio retinēre, alqm oppressum tenēre.* **subjective,** adj., according to one's own view, e.g. viewed —ly to myself, *meo quidem judicio;* so *tuo* or *ejus* or *eorum quidem judicio;* as opposed to objective, *opinio,* opp. to *res.* **subjectivity,** n. *quod in opinione constat,* or *quoad per hominum judicium perspici potest.*

subjoin, v.tr. *sub(j)icĕre, subjungĕre.*

subjugate, v.tr. *domare, in dicionem suam redigĕre;* see SUBDUE.

subjunctive, adj. — mood, *modus subjunctivus* or *conjunctivus* (Gram., and in Quint. fig.).

sublime, adj. *sublīmis, ēlatus, excelsus;* see LOFTY. Adv. *sublīme* (usually lit.), *ēlate, excelse.* **sublimity,** n. *sublīmitas* (Quint.), *ēlatio, excelsitas.*

sublunary, adj. *infra lunam positus.*

submarine, adj. *quod sub mari (positum) est.*

submerge, v.tr. *submergĕre.* **submersion,** n. use verb.

submit, v.tr. *submittĕre; submittĕre se alci, se alcjs imperio sub(j)icĕre, in alcjs potestatem se permittĕre, alci cedĕre* or *concedĕre, alci dare manus.* **submission,** n. *obsequium* (as act), *animus submissus* (as state). **submissive,** adj. see OBEDIENT.

subordinate, I. adj. *inferior, alci subjectus.* **II.** v.tr. 1, see SUBDUE; 2, to give an inferior place to, *alqd alci rei posthabēre.* **subordination,** n. 1, = obedience, *obsequium, disciplina* (of soldiers); against —, *contra morem obsequii;* want of — among the soldiers, *intemperantia militum;* see OBEDIENCE; 2, = placing below, *alqd alci rei posthabēre.*

suborn, v.tr. *subornare.*

subpœna, n. *denuntiatio testimonii.*

subscribe, v.tr. *subscribĕre;* = to agree to, *assentiri;* = to give one's name or support to, *nomen profitēri.* **subscriber,** n. *subscriptor* (= one who writes under), *qui se alqd daturum profitetur* (to a charity, etc.). **subscription,** n. *subscriptio* (= that which is written under), *stips* (= alms), *collatio* (= collection).

subsequent, adj. *(sub)sequens.* Adv. *postea;* see AFTERWARDS.

subserve, v.tr. *alci subservire, alci esse usui, auxilio esse alci, adjumento alci esse, alci obtemperare.* **subservience,** n. *obtemperatio, obsequium.*

subside, v.intr. *residĕre, considĕre, remitti, cadĕre* (= to fall).

subsidy, n. *subsidium, vectigal, tributum* (= tax).

subsist, v.intr. *subsistĕre, stare in re;* to — on, *vesci* (e.g. *lacte et carne,* Sall.). **subsistence,** n. *victus, -ūs, alimenta, -orum.*

substance, n. *natura, corpus, -ŏris,* n., *res;* = property, *res, bona, -orum.* **substantial,** adj. *verus, solidus, gravis, magni momenti* (= important), *aliquid* (e.g. — victory, *aliquid victoriae*). Adv. *magnā ex parte.* **substantiate,** v.tr. see PROVE. **substantive,** n. *nomen* (Gram.).

substitute, I. n. *vicarius.* **II.** v.tr. *alqm in alterius locum substituĕre, sufficĕre* (of the election of a magistrate as —). **substitution,** n. use verb.

substruction, substructure, n. *substructio.*

subterfuge, n. *deverticulum, latebra, ars, tergiversatio.*

subterranean, adj. *subterraneus.*

subtle, adj. *subtīlis,* † *tenuis* (= thin, slender); *argutus, acutus;* see CLEVER, CUNNING. Adv. *subtīliter, tenuiter, argute, acute.* **subtlety,** n. 1, = fineness, *tenuitas, subtīlitas;* 2, of intellect, etc., *acies, acumen, subtīlitas, captio.* **subtleties,** n. *argutiae.*

subtract, v.tr. *deducĕre* (e.g. *addendo deducendoque vidēre quae reliqua summa fiat*). **subtraction,** n. by *deducĕre.*

suburb, n. *suburbium* (very rare). **suburban,** adj. *suburbanus.*

subvert, v.tr. *subvertĕre.* **subversion,** n. *eversio;* see DESTRUCTION.

succeed, v.intr. *alci succedĕre;* so *in locum alcjs, in paternas opes;* (also in time, *aetas aetati succedit*), *alqm (sub)sequi;* = to have success, *succedĕre, bene, prospere, optime cedĕre, evenire.* **success,** n. *exitus, -ūs, bonus, res secundae, felicitas, prosperitas, successus, -ūs.* **successful,** adj. *felix, faustus,* comb. *felix faustusque.* Adv. *feliciter, fauste, prospere, bene, ex sententiā.* **succession,** n. *successio* (in office, etc.); = order, *series, continuatio;* in —, *ex ordine.* **successive,** adj. *alii post alios, continuus.* Adv. *(ex) ordine, in ordinem, deinceps.* **successor,** n. *successor.*

succinct, adj. *brevis.* Adv. *brevi, breviter.*

succour, I. n. *auxilium, subsidium.* **II.** v.tr. *auxiliari alci, juvare alqm, auxilio alci esse* or *venire alci, succurrĕre;* see HELP.

succulent, adj. *sucosus* (Plin.), *suci (succi) plenus.*

succumb, v.intr. *succumbĕre alci rei* (e.g. *somno, senectuti, labori*).

such, adj. pron. *talis* followed by *qualis, ejusmodi, ejus generis ut,* etc.; — is your courtesy, *quae tua est humanitas;* nor am I — a fool, *nec tam sum stultus* (Cic.); are you — a stranger as that . . . ? *adeone es hospes hujusce urbis ut . . . ?*

si nos ii sumus qui esse debemus (= if we are — as we ought to be), *videndum est ut ea liberalitate utamur quae prosit amicis, noceat nemini* (= we must take care to use — liberty as may benefit our friends and injure none)

suck, I. v tr *sugĕre, bibĕre* (= to drink) **II.** n *suctus, -ūs* (as act), to give —, *mammam alci praebēre, ad ubera admittere* (of animals) **sucker,** n *surculus, planta* **suckle,** v tr *mammam alci dare* or *praebēre* **suckling,** n (*infans*) *lactens.* **suction,** n *suctus, -ūs*

sudden, adj *subitus, repens repentīnus, inopinatus, necopinatus* Adv *subito ex tempore inopinato, necopinato, improviso, de improviso,* to attack anyone —, *opprimĕre imprudentem* **suddenness,** n use adj

sue, v tr *postulare, citare, litem alci intendĕre, judicio alqm persequi, in jus vocare* (at law), = to make suit for, *ambire*; to — for an office, *ambire magistratum*, to — for the consulship, *petĕre consulatum* = to entreat, *sol(l)icitare, efflagitare*, see ENTREAT, BEG, to — for payment, *nomina exigĕre*

suet, n *sebum* (= tallow), beef —, *sebum bovillum* (so *ovillum*, etc.)

suffer, I. v tr *pati, sufferre, perferre, tolerare sustinēre* (= to bear), = to permit, *permittĕre, sinĕre, concedĕre*, see ALLOW, PERMIT, to — grief, *e dolore animi laborare, angi animo*, to — loss, *detrimentum capĕre* or *pati, damnum, detrimentum,* or *jacturam facĕre*, to — shipwreck, *naufragium facĕre*, to — pain, etc, *dolorem accipĕre*, to — a disgrace, *dedecus (in se) admittere* (Caes), to — harm or inconvenience, *alqo afici incommodo*, to — or undertake many labours, *multos subire* or *adire labores*, I — for my rashness, *do poenas temeritatis meae* (Cic) **II.** v intr *dolorem ferre* or *pati, dolore affici, (ex)cruciari, poenas dare* (as punishment), *laborare, aegrotare* (= to be ill) **sufferance,** n *patientia*, see PATIENCE **sufferer,** n *aeger, aegrotatus* (in illness), *qui alqd patitur* (in gen) **suffering,** n *dolor* (= pain), *miseria* (= misery), *res adversae, casus, -ūs, calamitas.*

suffice, v intr *sufficĕre* (e g *non sufficiebant viri, nec vires sufficĕre cuiquam*), *satis esse alci rei* or with infin, *suppeditare alci ad alqd* **sufficient,** adj *satis, quantum satis est*, it is —, *satis est* (so *satis superque est*), — for, *ad*, e g *ad dicendum temporis satis habēre* **sufficiency,** n *quod satis est*

suffocate, v tr *suffocare*

suffrage, n *suffragium* (*alci*, for anyone), to give one's —, *ferre suffragium* (= to vote), *suffragium inire*, = the right of —, *suffragium*

suffuse, v tr *suffundĕre*

sugar, n *saccharum* or *saccharon* (Plin), —-candy, *saccharum crystallinum*, —-plum, *cup(p)edia, -orum*

suggest, v tr *monēre alqm alqd*, or with *ut, sub(j)icĕre alqd alci*, see MENTION **suggestion,** n *admonitio, monitum, consilium* **suggestive,** adj *qui (quae, quod) alqd repraesentat* (of what recalls something else), see SUGGEST

suicide, n *mors voluntaria*, to commit —, *manus sibi inferre, sibi mortem* or *necem consciscĕre*

suit, I. n 1, *actio, lis, causa*, see ACTION, 2, of clothes, *vestis, vestitus, -us*, of cards, *chartae* or *paginae ejusdem generis*, 3, = petition, *rogatio*, in love, use verb WOO **II.** v tr *congruere*, they —, *bene illis inter se convenit*, or by *decet, convenit*, impers **suitable,** adj *congruens, idoneus, aptus, accommodatus, consentaneus, conveniens*, all with *ad* and accus, etc, *dignus* with abl, or *qui* with subj, of time, *opportunus*, see APPROPRIATE **suitableness,** n *congruentia, convenientia, opportunitas* (of time) Adv *congruenter, idonee, apte, accommodate, convenienter, digne, opportune*

suite, n 1, of persons, *comitatus, -ūs, comites, -um*, 2, of rooms, *conclavia, -ium* see ROOM

suitor, n 1, see CANDIDATE, 2 see LOVER

sulky, sullen, adj *morosus, contumax, tetricus* Adv *morose, contumaciter* **sulkiness, sullenness,** n *morositas, contumacia*

sully, v tr *maculare, inquinare*

sulphur, n *sulfur*, dipped in —, *sulfuratus*

sultan, n *imperator Turcicus*

sultry, adj *aestuosus* **sultriness,** n *aestus, -ūs*

sum, I n *summa* of money, *pecunia*, once in Cic *summa pecuniae*, for a large, small, etc, —, *magni, parvi (pretii), magno, parvo (pretio)*, this is the — of what I have to say, *haec summa est* **II.** v tr *summam facĕre, computare, rationem alcjs reddere, ducĕre*, of speech, etc, to — up, *breviter repetĕre* **summary, I.** n see EPITOME **II.** adj 1, *brevis*, see CONCISE, 2, = hasty, arrogant, *inconsideratus, arrogans* Adv *breviter, sine mora, inconsiderate, arroganter*

summer, adj and n *aestas, tempora, -um, aestiva*, at the beginning of —, *aestate ineunte*, at the end of —, *aestate extremā*, —-house, see ARBOUR

summersault, n see SOMERSAULT

summit, n 1, *cacumen* (= peak), *culmen, vertex*, also by *summus* (e g *summus mons*), 2, fig *culmen, fastigium*, or by *summus* (e g *summa gloria*, = the — of glory)

summon, v tr 1, *alqm appellare, citare, diem alci dicĕre*, see CITE, 2, in gen *(ad)vocare, convocare, arcessĕre, citare*, to — to surrender, *invitare ad deditionem*, to — up one's courage, *animum colligĕre* **summons,** n by verb or in abl, *arcessitu, accitu* (= at the — of), as legal t t use verb

sumptuary, adj *sumptuarius* **sumptuous,** adj *sumptuosus* (Cic), see COSTLY, MAGNIFICENT Adv *sumptuose* **sumptuousness,** n (*magnus*) *apparatus, -ūs*, see MAGNIFICENCE, LUXURY

sun, n *sōl, -is*, m, the rising —, *sol oriens*; setting —, *sol occidens*, rising, setting of the —, *ortus, -ūs, occasus, -ūs, solis*, from — rise to — set, *ab orto usque ad occidentem solem*, the — rises, *sol exoritur, dies appetit*, or by impers *lucescit, dilucescit, illucescit*; the —'s disk, *orbis solis* **sunbeam,** n *radius solis* **sunburnt,** adj *adustus* **Sunday,** n *Dies Dominica* (Eccl) **sundial,** n *solarium* **sunrise, sunset,** n see under SUN **sunshine,** n *sōl* **sunny,** adj 1, lit *apricus*, 2, fig *hilaris, felix*

sunder, v tr *separare, disjungĕre*, see SEVER

sundry, adj *diversi, -ae, -a, plures, nonnulli*

sup, v tr *sorbēre*, = to take supper, *cenare*

superable, adj *superabilis*

superabound, v intr *superare, superesse*

superannuate, v tr *alqm loco suo senectutis causā movēre, rude donari* **superannuated,** adj *ob senectutem muneribus exsolutus*

superb, adj *magnificus, lautus*, see SPLENDID

supercilious, adj *superbus* (= proud), *fasti-*

diosus (= disdainful); see HAUGHTY. **supercilIousness**, n. *fastus*, *-ūs*, *superbia*.

supererogation, n. *quod alqs sponte suâ (neque officio coactus) facit* (= work of —).

superficial, adj. *exterior*, *externus*; = poor or inconsiderable, *lĕvis*, *parvi momenti*; = inaccurate, *parum diligens*. Adv. *strictim*, *lĕviter*; a man — learned, *homo lĕviter lit(t)eris imbutus*. **superficiality**, n. *lĕvitas*.

superficies, n. *summus* with a noun; *superficies* (*aquae*, *testudinis*, *corporum*).

superfine, adj. *subtīlissimus*, *tenuissimus* (= very fine).

superfluous, adj. *supervacaneus*, *supervacuus* (mostly post Aug.); to be —, *superesse*. **superfluity**, n. *quod supervacaneum est*.

superhuman, adj. *divinus*, *major quam pro homine*; a — task, *opus quod ultra hominis vires est*; — size, *humanâ specie amplior*.

superintend, v.tr. *alqd (pro)curare*, *praeesse alci* or *alci rei*. **superintendence**, n. *(pro)curatio*, *administratio alcjs rei*. **superintendent**, n. *qui rebus praeest*; *(pro)curator*; see AGENT.

superior, adj. *superior*, *praestantior*, *melior* (e.g. comp. of good); see GOOD, EXCELLENT. **superiority**, n. *prior locus*, *priores partes*.

superlative, adj. *superlativus* (gram.), *excellens*, *praestans*, *praestantissimus*, *optimus* (e.g. superl. of good); see GOOD, EXCELLENT.

supernal, adj. †*supernus*, *caelestis*; see HEAVENLY.

supernatural, adj. *naturam superans*, *supra naturae leges* or *vires positus*, or by *caelestis*, *divinus*; to happen by — agency, *dīvīnitus fieri*. Adv. *dīvīnitus*. **supernaturalism**, n. *ratio eorum qui divinitus de rebus divinis edoctos esse homines dicunt*.

supernumerary, adj. in gen. *justum numerum superans* or *excellens*; of soldiers, *a(d)scriptivus*, *a(d)scripticius*, *accensus*.

superscribe, v.tr. *inscrībĕre in alqâ re*. **superscription**, n. *inscriptio* (also = the title of a book).

supersede, v.tr. *in locum alcjs substitui*, *alci succedĕre*.

superstition, n. *superstitio*. **superstitious**, adj. *superstitiosus*, *superstitione imbutus*, *superstitioni obnoxius*. Adv. *superstitiose*.

superstructure, n. *aedificium*; see BUILDING.

supervene, v.intr. see FOLLOW, SUCCEED.

supervise, v.tr. *(pro)curare*; see SUPERINTEND. **supervision**, n. *(pro)curatio*.

supine, **I.** n. *supīnum* (gram.). **II.** adj. **1**, *supīnus* (on the back); **2**, = indolent, *socors*, *neglegens*. Adv. *socorditer*, *neglegenter*. **supineness**, n. *socordia*, *neglegentia*.

supper, n. *cena*.

supplant, v.tr. **1**, lit. *supplantare*; **2**, fig. *in alterius locum irrepĕre*.

supple, adj. *mollis*, *flexibilis*, *lentus*.

supplement, n. *supplementum* (quite class. only of — to troops), in gen. *id quod additum est*.

suppliant, adj. and n. *supplex*. **supplicate**, v.tr. *supplicare*, *obsecrare alqm*. **supplication**, n. *supplicatio* (only of formally decreed state —), *obsecratio*.

supply, **I.** v.tr. *supplēre*, *suppeditare* (= to furnish); see FURNISH. **II.** n. *subsidium*, *supplementum* (of troops); in gen. *copia*, *suppeditatio*; — of provisions, *commeatus*, *-ūs*

support, **I.** v.tr. **1**, = to bear up, *sustinēre*, *ferre*, *fulcire*; see PROP; **2**, = to keep, to feed, etc., *alĕre*, *sustinēre*, *sustentare* (quite class. in this sense); **3**, = to help, *alci adesse*; see HELP; **4**, at an election, *alci suffragari* (= to vote for), in wider sense, *alci favēre*. **II.** n. **1**, lit. see PROP; **2**, = maintenance, *sustentatio* (as act), *alimentum*, *victus*, *-ūs* (= food, etc.); **3**, = help, *adjumentum*, *auxilium*; see HELP; **4**, at an election, *suffragium*, in wider sense, *favor*. **supporter**, n. *adjutor*; at an election, *suffragator*, in wider sense, *fautor*; see HELPER, PARTISAN.

suppose, v.tr. *ponĕre* (= to lay down), *opinari*, *opinione praecipĕre*; — it is so, *pone* or *fac ita esse*, *esto*; — the soul to die, *fac animam interire*; I — he is drunk, *ebrius est*, *ut opinor*; see also BELIEVE, IMAGINE, THINK. **supposing that**, conj. *fac ita esse*; see above. **supposition**, n. *opinio*, *conjectura*. **supposititious**, adj. *subditus*.

suppress, v.tr. *supprimĕre*, *reprimĕre*, *abolēre*; to — sedition, *restinguĕre seditionem*. **suppression**, n. use verb.

suppurate, v.intr. *suppurare*. **suppuration**, n. *suppuratio* (Plin.).

supreme, adj. *supremus*, *summus*; the — Being, *Deus*, *Optimus*, *Maximus*. **supremacy**, n. *principatus*, *-ūs* (in gen.), *regnum* (= kingship), *imperium* (= supreme power), *dominatus*, *-ūs*, *dominatio* (= lordship); see POWER. Adv. *praecipue*, *maxime*.

sure, adj. *certus* (= certain), *tutus* (= safe), *securus* (= free from apprehension), *firmus* (= trustworthy), *fidēlis* (= faithful); it is —, *constat*; I am —, *certo scio*; who is — of it? *quis est cui exploratum sit?* to be —, he had the rods, *fasces certe habebat*; are you — of it? *satin hoc certum*, *persuasum est vobis*, *exploratum* or *compertum habetis*; I am —, *compertum est mihi*. Adv. *certe*, *certo* (= certainly), *nimirum*, *profecto*, or more strongly *im(m)o (enim)vero* (= really), *saltem* (= at least). **surety**, n. *vas*, *-dis*, m., *praes*, *-dis*, m., *sponsor* (of a person), *vadimonium* (= money given as bail).

surf, n. see FOAM, WAVE.

surface, n. *superficies* (Plin.), or by *summus* with noun (e.g. — of water, *summa aqua*).

surfeit, **I.** n. *satietas*, *fastīdium* (lit. and fig.), comb. *satietas et fastidium*, *crapula* (= — after a debauch); = too much food, *nimius cibus*. **II.** v.tr. **1**, *fastidium alci alcjs rei movēre*; to — oneself, *se ingurgitare*; **2**, fig. *saturare*, *saturare*.

surge, **I.** n. *fluctus*, *-uum*. **II.** v.intr. *fluctuare*, lit. and fig.

surgery, n. *chirurgia* (Cels.). **surgeon**, n. *chirurgus*, *vulnerum medicus* (Plin.).

surly, adj. *morosus*; see ILL-TEMPERED. Adv. *morose*. **surliness**, n. *morositas*.

surmise, **I.** n. *conjectura*, *praesagium* (*tempestatis futurae*, *malorum*). **II.** v.tr. *suspicari*, *augurari*, *praesagire*.

surmount, v.tr. *transcendĕre* (lit.), *superare* (lit. and fig.). **surmountable**, adj. *(ex)superabilis*.

surname, n. *cognomen* (as Cicero in *Marcus Tullius Cicero*); he has a —, *alci cognomen Flacco* or *Capitoni est*.

surpass, n. *alci* or *alqm antecellĕre*, *excellĕre*, *alqm (ex)superare*, *alqm* or *alci praestare* (lit. and fig.).

surplice, n. *vestis sacerdotalis*.

surplus, n. *rel(l)iquum*, *quod superest*.

surprise, **I.** n. *(ad)miratio*; of a sudden attack, *subita incursio*, *adventus*, *-ūs*, *repentinus*.

II. v tr *alqm necopinantem opprimĕre, alqm de proviso excipĕre*, see also ASTONISH **surprising**, adj see WONDERFUL

surrender, I. v tr *se dare, se dedĕre in alcjs fidem, se tradĕre* **II.** n *deditio*, to make a —, (*oppuli*) *deditionem hosti* or *ad hostem facĕre, in deditionem venire* (so *alqm in deditionem accipĕre*), = giving up, . *ditio*

surreptitious, adj *furtivus, subrepticius* (Plaut) Adv *furtive, furtim, clam*

surrogate, n *vicarius*

surround, v tr *circumdare* (e g *exercitum castris, brachia collo, alqd alqâ re, regio circumdata insulis*, Cic.; *amiculo circumdatus*), *circumvenire, circumcludĕre, circumvallare* (in a siege), fig *alcjs pueritiam robore circumdare*

survey, I. v tr *spectare, contemplari, considerare, intuēri, intuēri et contemplari, contuēri* (with fixed attention), *oculis collustrare* or *perlustrare* (= to — carefully, to go over), (*in*)*visĕre* (= to look closely at, esp. things which interest us), *perspicĕre* (= to look at in all its parts), *contuēri perspicĕreque, circumspicĕre* (= to look all round a thing), to — hastily, *oculis percurrĕre*, to — in mind, *contemplari animo* or *animo et cogitatione, considerare secum in animo*, or merely *contemplari* or *considerare, contemplari et considerare*, (*per*)*lustrare animo* or *mente animoque, circumspicĕre mente, expendĕre, perpendĕre* (= to weigh), = to measure land, *agrum metiri* **II.** n *contemplatio, observatio, conspectus, ūs*, see VIEW **surveyor**, n (of land) *decempedator, metator*

survive, v intr *superstitem esse* **survival**, n use verb **survivor**, n *superstes, ĭtis*

susceptible, adj *capax* (e g *capax amicitiae, animus ad praecepta capax*), *inclinatus, pronus, proclivis* (mostly in bad sense), *ad alqd*, comb *inclinatus et pronus* **susceptibility**, n use adj

suspect, I. v tr *suspicari* (*alqd de alqo, alqm*), *suspicĕre* (usu in past part.) **II.** n *alci suspectus* **suspicion**, n *suspicio* **suspicious**, adj *suspiciosus* (= causing suspicion and ready to suspect) Adv *suspiciose* (= in a way to excite suspicion), = with suspicion, use adj or *curiosus* (= inquisitive)

suspend, v tr *suspendĕre* (*arborem ligno, columbam ab alqo malo, alqd collo* or *e collo* or *in collo*), to — oneself, *se suspendĕre*, = to interrupt, delay, *differre*, to — any one from office, *alqm alqo loco* (*sub*)*movēre* **suspense**, n *dubitatio, haesitatio*, to be in —, *in dubio esse, animo fluctuare* **suspension**, n *dilatio* (= delay), — of hostilities, *indutiae*

sustain, v tr *sustinēre* (= to support, *ager hominum quinque millia sustinēre potest*, Cic), *re frumentaria ali et sustinēri*, see SUPPORT **sustenance**, n *alimentum, victus, -ūs*

sutler, n *lixa*

swaddle, v tr *fasciis involvĕre* **swaddling bands**, n *fasciae*

swagger, v intr *gloriari, se jactare*

swain, n *agrestis, rusticus, colonus*

swallow, n *hirundo*

swallow, v tr *sorbēre* (lit & fig, *alqd animo*), (*de*)*vorare* (lit and fig)

swamp, I. n *palus, ūdis, ūlĭgo*, —s *palustria, -ium* **II.** v tr (*de*)*mergĕre, immergĕre* **swampy**, adj *paluster, tris, tre*, and *palustris, e, uliginosus*

swan, n *cygnus*

sward, n see GRASS

swarm, I. n *concursus, ūs, frequentia*, — of bees, *examen, agmen apium* **II.** v intr *confluĕre*, to — as bees, *examinare* (Col); see ASSEMBLE

swarthy, adj *fuscus, furvus, adustus*

sway, I. n *imperium, dominatio, dominium, dicio* **II.** v tr *regĕre, imperare, imperium habēre* or *exercēre*, see RULE

swear, v tr and intr *jurare, jusjurandum jurare* or *dare*, to — falsely, *falsum jurare* (an oath I do not think binding), *pejerare, perjurare* **swearing**, n *exsecrationes, maledicta, -orum*

sweat, I n *sudor* **II** v intr and tr *sudare*

sweep, I v tr **1**, *verrĕre*, **2**, fig , see EXAMINE **II.** v intr to — along, *verrĕre, percurrĕre* **sweeper**, n *qui scopis converrit* **sweepings**, n *quisquiliae, -arum*, f

sweet, adj *dulcis* (= — to the taste, e g *dulcior melle*, Ov), *suavis* (= agreeable to the smell, e g *odor suavis et jucundus*), *jucundus, blandus* (= pleasant) Adv *dulciter, dulce, suaviter, jucunde, blande*, to taste —, *dulci esse sapore* **sweeten**, v tr *dulcem reddĕre* **sweetheart**, n. *deliciae* **sweetness**, n *dulcedo, dulcitudo, suavitas, jucunditas*

swell, I. v intr (*in*)*tumescĕre, turgescĕre, crescĕre, augēri* (= to increase), to be swollen, *tumēre* **II.** v tr *inflare* (e g *spem alcjs inflare*), *tumefacere*, to — the sails, *vela tendĕre* **swelling**, n *tumor, struma* (= scrofulous —), *tuber* (Plin , both natural, as hump on camel, and of disease), *panus* (Plin), *scirrhoma, -ătis*, n (Plin)

swerve, v intr *declinare de* or *a* (*a proposito, a malis*, opp *appetĕre bona*)

swift, adj *citus, propĕrus* (= making haste, hurrying), *velox* (= brisk, fast, e g *pedites velocissimi*), *celer* (= active, expeditious), *pernix* (= brisk), *alacer* (= sprightly) Adv *cito, citato gradu, celeriter, rapide, perniciter* **swiftness**, n *celeritas, rapiditas, velocitas, pernicitas*

swill, v tr *ingurgitare* (*se, se vino*, so fig *se in flagitia*)

swim, v intr *nare, natare*, to — over, *tranare* **swimmer**, n *natator, nandi peritus* **swimming**, n *natatio, ars natandi, scientia natandi*

swindle, v tr *fraudare* (*alqm pecunia*) **swindler**, n *fraudator* **swindling**, n *fraudatio*

swine, n *sus, porcus* (= pig), —-herd, *subulcus, suarius* (Plin)

swing, I. v tr *agitare, vibrare, jactare* **II.** v intr *agitari, librari, jactari* **III.** n *funiculus quo se jactat alqs* **swinging**, n use verb

switch, n *virga, vimen*

swoon, v intr and n *animo linqui*, see FAINT

swoop, I. n *impetus, -ūs* **II.** v intr to — upon, *impetum in alqm* or *alqd facĕre*

sword, n *gladius, ensis* (mostly used in poet y), *acinăces* (= a Persian —), to have a — at one's side, *gladio succinctum esse*, to draw the —, *gladium* (*e vagina*) *educĕre*, to sheathe the —, *gladium in vaginam recondĕre*, to put to the —, *interficĕre*, see KILL

sycophant, n *delator* (Tac , — an accuser), *assentator, adulator* (= a flatterer) **sycophancy**, n *sycophantia, assentatio, adulatio*

syllable, n *syllaba*

syllogism, n *syllogismus, ratiocinatio* (Sen). **syllogistic**, adj *syllogisticus* (Quint)

sylvan, adj *silvestris*

symbol, n *symbolum, signum, imago*, see SIGN **symbolic**, adj by circumloc (e g *quod rei imaginem alcjs refert*)

symmetry, n. *symmetria, proportio, congruentia, aequalitas;* — of the limbs, *apta membrorum compositio;* — in style, *concinnitas.* **symmetrical,** adj. *par, similis, aequalis, congruens.* Adv. *pariter, similiter, congruenter, aequaliter.*

sympathy, n. 1, = attraction of bodies, etc., *sympathia* (= agreement among things, in Cic. always written as Greek συμπάθεια), *consensus, -ūs,* or *concordia rerum;* 2, as mental feeling, *societas* (e.g. *laetitia cum alqo,* with anyone's joy), *animus dolore, laetitiā,* etc., *alcjs affectus.* **sympathetic,** adj. and adv. *dolore* or *laetitiā alcjs affectus.* **sympathize,** v.intr. *una gaudēre et dolēre, eadem sentire.*

symphony, n. *symphonia.*

symptom, n. *alcjs morbi nota* or *indicium* or *signum.*

synagogue, n. *synagoga* (Eccl.).

synchronism, n. *aequalitas temporum.*

syncope, n. see FAINT.

syndicate, n. *societas;* see COMPANY.

synod, n. *synodus* (Eccl.).

synonym, n. *vocabulum idem significans* or *declarans.* **synonymous,** adj. *idem significans* or *declarans.*

synopsis, n. *synopsis* (Jct.); see EPITOME.

syntax, n. *syntaxis* (Gram.), *orationis constructio, verborum quasi structura.* **syntactical,** adj. *quod ad orationis constructionem pertinet.*

syringe, I. n. *sipho* (Suet.). **II.** v.tr. *per siphonem in(f)icĕre.*

syrup, n. *potio dulcis.*

system, n. *formula* or *descriptio* (e.g. *philosophiae, reipublicae*), *instituta, praecepta, -orum* (= rules). **systematic,** adj. *ad artem redactus, perpetuis praeceptis ordinatus.* Adv. *ordinate, (ex) ordine, composite.* **systematize,** v.tr. *in artem redigĕre;* see ARRANGE.

T.

tabby, adj. *maculosus;* see also GREY.

tabernacle, n. 1, see TENT, HABITATION; 2, *tabernaculum* (Eccl.).

table, n. 1, *tabula* (= a board for various purposes, e.g. with an account, a will, a law, etc., written upon it; a list of things to be sold by auction, and which were written on boards, and hung outside the stalls of money-changers); 2, = an article of furniture, *mensa* (= — for holding dishes and for other purposes; then meton., the contents of the dishes, the fare, meal, e.g. the Emperor's —, *mensa principis*), *monopodium* (μονοπόδιον, = a — with only one foot of ivory, generally made of the wood of the citrus of Africa); to set or lay the —, *mensam (ap)ponĕre;* to sit down at —, *accubare;* to rise, get up from —, *surgĕre a cenā;* at —, *apud mensam, super mensam, inter cenam, super cenam, inter epulas;* 3, = fare, *cena, victus, -ūs;* a good —, *lauta cena, lautus victus;* a bad —, *tenuis victus;* for general arrangement of — at feasts, see Smith "Dict. Antiq.," art. Triclinium; at the head of the —, *medius* (= the middle position, *medius* seems to have been the highest); above or below anyone, *supra, infra alqm;* foot of the —, *pes mensae;* —-cover, —-cloth, *linteum in mensā ponendam* or *positum;* —-linen, *mappa* (= —-napkin); — service, *vasa, -orum;* — talk, *sermo;* 4, = tablet, *tabula;* — of laws, *legis* or *legum tabula;* 5, the Lord's —, **mensa Domini;* see SACRAMENT, SUPPER, COMMUNION, ALTAR; 6, = many particulars, *index.* **table-land,** n. *planities magna et edita.* **tableau,** n. see PICTURE. **tablet,** n. *tabula, tabella* (also = voting —), *cera* (= smeared with wax), *aes* (of bronze), *pugillares, -ium* (Plin.), *codicilli* (= — consisting of several leaves, a kind of memorandum-book). **tabular,** adj. = set down in tables, *per indices expositus;* to give a — view of anything, *per indices exponĕre alqd.*

tacit, adj. *tacitus* (both of persons and of things); see SECRET. Adv. *tacite.* **taciturn,** adj. *taciturnus.* **taciturnity,** n. *taciturnitas.*

tack, I. n. 1, = a small nail, *clavulus;* see NAIL; 2, = plan, *consilium, ratio;* to try a fresh —, *novum consilium experiri.* **II.** v.tr. see NAIL. **III.** v.intr. *navem flectĕre.* **tackle,** n. for fishing, *instrumenta piscatoria, -orum.* **tackling,** n. *armamenta, -orum,* n.; see RIGGING.

tact, n. *dexteritas;* see CLEVERNESS, TALENT. **tactics,** n.pl. *res militaris.* **tactician,** n. *rei militaris peritus.*

tadpole, n. *ranunculus.*

taffeta, taffety, n. *pannus sericus.*

tail, n. *cauda;* to wag the —, *caudam movēre;* — of a comet, *stellae crines, -ium.*

tailor, n. *sartor.*

taint, I. v.tr. 1, in gen., *imbuĕre alqā re;* 2, = to impregnate with something obnoxious, *corrumpĕre, inquinare; vitiare* (lit.; e.g. corn, *frumentum*). **II.** v.intr. *corrumpi, vitiari* (e.g. the atmosphere, *aurae;* meat, *fruit*), *putrescĕre* (= to become bad). **III.** n. 1, = tincture, *color* (e.g. *veritatis, urbanitatis, antiquitatis*), *fucus* (e.g. *alcjs rei fuco illitus, tinctus*), *species* (e.g. *alci rei species imponĕre, inducĕre*); 2, *contagio* (lit. and fig.); see CORRUPTION. **tainted,** adj. *vitiatus,* or by *putrescĕre.*

take, I. v.tr. *sumĕre* (= to — anything in order to make use of it), *capĕre* (= to lay hold of, to seize; then to — possession of anything in order to keep it; hence = to storm, e.g. a town), *rapĕre* (= to seize quickly), *arripĕre* (= to — up, to snatch away), *accipĕre* (= to accept, receive), *tollĕre* (to — up, to lift up, in order to — a thing away from its former place), *(de)promĕre* (= to —, fetch anything from a place where it had been kept hitherto), *auferre* (= to have carried away, —n up, away), *eripĕre* (= to — by force), *expugnare* (= to storm, always with the idea of the victory being obtained after resistance); not to — anything, *alqd non accipĕre, deprecari* (e.g. *manus*); to — anyone on one side, *alqm secretum adducĕre;* to — money from one (i.e. a person is bribed), *pecuniam ab alqo accipĕre;* to — from, = to quote, *transferre;* this passage I have —n verbally from Dicæarchus, *istum ego locum totidem verbis a Dicaearcho transtuli;* to —, lay hold of anyone, *alqm medium arripĕre* (= to put one's arm round anyone's waist and hold him fast); to — anyone round the neck, *in alcjs collum invadĕre* (= to embrace him); to — anyone in custody, *alqm comprehendĕre;* = to receive, *recipĕre in alqd* (e.g. *in ordinem senatorium*), *assumĕre in alqd* (e.g. *in societatem*); to — anyone in, into one's house, *alqm ad se* or *ad se domum,* or simply *alqm domum suam recipĕre;* = to accept, claim from anyone, *accipĕre ab alqo, poscĕre ab alqo;* to — anything or anyone to, for, as (i.e. to fabricate anything from a material), *facĕre* or *fingĕre* or *effingĕre* or *exprimĕre alqd ex alqā re;* anyone as, for (i.e. to appoint), *alqm,* with the accus. of the office to which anyone is elected (e.g. *alqm arbitrum, alqm imperatorem*);

sumĕre, accipĕre, exigĕre, habēre, to — back again, *reducĕre*, to partake of, *sumĕre* (something to eat or to drink, e g *cibum potionemque*), *potare* or *bibĕre* (= to drink, e.g *medicamentum*), *accipĕre* (when it is given), to — (= to understand) the word (term) in various meanings, *verbum in plures partes accipĕre*, — in as a whole, *omnino*, or by *universus*, to — in good part, *in bonam partem accipĕre, belle ferre, boni* or *aequi bonique facĕre*, to — it ill, amiss, *in malam partem accipĕre, aegre* (or *graviter* or *moleste* or *indigne*) *ferre, male interpretari*, to — anyone's part, *ad alcjs partes transire, sequi alqm, facĕre cum alqo*, to — to be true, as such, *ponĕre* (= to state), *sumĕre* (= to — for granted, admit, in speech, in a disputation), *velle*, with accus and infin (= to be of opinion, to mean), to — for certain, *sumĕre* or *habēre* or *putare pro certo, fingĕre, facĕre* (the foregoing two = to suppose, to — a case), to — away, *alqd alci auferre, eripĕre*, to — down (in writing), *lit(t)eris consignare, lit(t)eris mandare, scripturâ persequi*, to — off, *alqd alci* or *alci rei* or *ex alqâ re detrahĕre* (e g *tegumentum humeris*), to — oneself off, *furtim degredi, clam se subducĕre* (secretly), *se abripĕre, se proripĕre* (quickly); to — out, *eximĕre*, out of, *alci rei, de* or *ex alqâ re* (out of a place), *excipĕre de* or *ex* (= to — away from a place), *promĕre ex* (e g arrows out of the quiver, money out of the public treasury, medicine out of a box, etc), *educĕre ex*, fig = to select, *excerpĕre ex*, etc (e g *verba ex orationibus*), to — up, *tollĕre*, to — upon oneself, *subire* (anything dangerous), *in se recipĕre* (= to — the responsibility for anything) **II.** v intr to — to, *se conferre, concedĕre alqo* (= to retreat), to — to books, *lit(t)eris studēre, urgēre alqd* (e g *studia*, = eagerly to be engaged in), see APPLY, RESORT, LIKE; to — after, see IMITATE, RESEMBLE, to — up with, *satis habēre, contentum esse alqâ re* (= to be contented with), *acquiescĕre in alqâ re* **taking,** n *expugnatio* (of a city)

tale, n *narratio* (= the act of telling, and the — itself), *historia* (= narrative), *memoria* (= recorded event), *expositio* (= exposition, description, concise, *circumcisa*, short, *brevis*), *fabella* (= a short fable, brief tale, or story) **tale-bearer,** n *delator* (= informer) *sycophanta* m (= sycophant) **tell, I.** v tr (e)*narrare alqd alci, referre* (= to report), (*com*)*memorare* (= to mention), *dicĕre* (= to say), *enumerare* (= to recount), *prodĕre* (*memoriae*), *posteris tradĕre, scriptum relinquĕre* (= to hand down to posterity, of historians), *alqs rei auctorem esse* (= to vouch for the truth), *exponĕre, explicare* (= to describe), *persequi* (from beginning to end), = to count, *numerare* **II.** v intr = to have effect, *valēre*, a telling speech, etc, *oratio gravis* **teller,** n **1,** = anyone who tells anything, *narrator, auctor rerum gestarum*, **2,** = one who numbers, *qui alqas res numerat*

talent, n **1,** = a weight and a coin, *talentum*, **2,** = mental faculties, *ingenium* (= natural gift), *indoles, -is* (= — s in a moral sense, insomuch as they may be improved by dint of exertion, etc), *virtus, -ūtis*, f (= cleverness, skill), comb *ingenium et virtus, facultas* (= power, capability of doing a thing), more clearly defined *ingenii facultas*, who has —, *ingeniosus, eximii ingenii, magno ingenio praeditus* **talented,** adj a very — man, a great genius, *homo ingeniosus, homo eximii ingenii*, to be —, *ingenio abundare, incredibili magnitudine consilii atque ingenii esse*

talisman, n *amulētum* (Plin)

talk, I. v intr familiarly, of several, *sermocinari*, together, *loqui* or *colloqui inter se*, (*con*)*fabulari* (mostly ante class), to — nonsense, *garrire* (= to — too much, familiarly and in a contemptuous sense), *blaterare* (= to — unceasingly, making many words about nothing), (*h*)*ariolari* (like a soothsayer), *alucinari* (without thinking), *nugari* (= to — foolery, all these generally in a transitive sense, with accus) to — over, see DISCUSS **II** n = familiar conversation, *sermo, colloquium, sermonis cum alqo communicatio*; foolish —, *gerrae, nugae, ineptiae* **talkative,** adj *garrulus, loquax* Adv *loquaciter* **talkativeness,** n *garrulitas, loquacitas* **talker,** n (*homo*) *garrulus* or *loquax*

tall, adj of a man, *longus* (opp *brevis*), *procērus, procērâ staturâ*, (*ex*)*celsus*, a — man, *homo magni corporis, homo grandis, homo staturâ procērâ* **tallness,** n *procēritas*, or by adjs

tallow, n *sebum*, a — candle, *sebaceus* (late)

tally, v intr *convenire alci rei*; see FIT, SUIT

Talmud, n * *Talmudum.*

talon, n *unguis*

tamarisk, n *tamărix* (Col).

tambourine, n *tympanum*

tame, I. adj **1,** *cicur* (by nature, of animals), *mansuetus, mansuefactus* (= tractable, of animals and of men), *placidus* (= mild, gentle, peaceable, of men and of animals), *mitis* (= meek, who easily yields, of men and animals), to grow —, *mansuescĕre, mansuefieri, mitescĕre* (opp *feritatem servare*), **2,** fig *demissus, abjectus, ignavus* (e g *animus*), of language, etc, *jejunus, frigidus* Adv *demisse, abjecte, ignave, jejune, frigide* **II.** v tr *mansuefacĕre, mansuetum facĕre* or *reddĕre, domare* (= to subdue wild beasts and tribes, then also fig passions), *frangĕre* (lit = to break, then fig = to break, weaken the strength, force, of a person or passions), *frenare* (lit = to bridle; hence fig = to curb, rule passions), *refrenare* (lit = to check with the bridle, thence fig to restrain persons and passions, e g *juventutem*), *coercēre* (fig = to keep within bounds, persons and passions, e g *juventutem*), *comprimĕre, reprimĕre* (lit = to press together or back, repress, fig forcibly to restrain passions), *compescĕre* (= not to allow to become too strong, to check, *querelas*) *moderari alci rei* (fig = to moderate), *placidum reddĕre* (= to make gentle, men and beasts), *mitem reddĕre* (= to soften), *mitem reddĕre et mansuetum* (= to make tractable, the two foregoing of men), *delenire* (= to soothe, to gain, e g *alqm argento, plebem munere*) **tameness,** n by adjs and verbs **tamer,** n *domitor*, fem *domitrix* **taming,** n *domitus, -ūs* (of animals)

tamper, v intr see MEDDLE, = to tempt, *sol(l)icitare*

tan, I n *cortex coriarius* **II.** v tr to — skins, *subigĕre, depsĕre* (= to knead, work anything well till it is soft), *conficĕre* (= to get up, ready), to — (of the sun), *colorare* **tanner,** n *coriarius* (Plin)

tangent, n *linea circulum contingens.*

tangible, adj fig *quod manu tenēre possumus, quod manu tenetur* or *prehenditur, tractabilis*

tangle, I. v tr see ENTANGLE **II.** n *nexus, -ūs, nodus*

tank, n see RESERVOIR.

tantalize, v tr see TEASE

tantamount, adj as regards the quantity, *totidem*, as regards the value, *tantidem, tantundem* see SAME

tap, I. n = a light blow, *plaga levis* **II.** v intr *leviter ferire*

tap, I n. of a cask, *obturamentum* (Plin.,

= stopper). **II.** v.tr. (*vinum*, etc.) *de dolio proměre*, *dolium reliněre* (= to take the pitch off).
taphouse, n. *taberna*.

tape, n. see RIBBON.

taper, n. *cereus*.

tapestry, n. *pictura acu facta*, *stragulum pictum* or *aulaeum*, *velum* (= curtain).

tapis, n. to bring on or upon the —, by *commemorare alqd*, *mentionem alcjs rei facěre*, *in medium proferre*.

tar, n. *pix liquida* (Plin.).

tardy, adj. *tardus*, *lentus*. Adv. *tarde*, *lente*.
tardiness, n. *tarditas*.

tare, n. a vetch, *vicia*.

target, n. 1, see SHIELD; 2, a — to shoot at, *scopos*, *-i* (Suet.).

tariff, n. *formula* (*ex quâ portoria* [= harbour dues, etc.] *exiguntur*).

tarnish, **I.** v.tr. 1, lit. *inquinare*; see STAIN; 2, fig. *inquinare*, *obscurare*; to — one's honour, *nomini* or *decori officěre*. **II.** v.intr. of metals, *inquinari*.

tarpaulin, n. *linteum pice munītum*.

tarry, v.intr. *cunctari* (from fear), *cessare* (from idleness), *morari*, *commorari*, *moram facěre* (when one ought to proceed), *tergiversari* (= to try to evade, make evasions), comb. *cunctari et tergiversari*, *dubitare* (when one is undecided), *haesitare* (from timidity, perplexity, or on account of difficulties, to hesitate); we must not —, *nulla mora est*, *maturato opus est* (= no time is to be lost); without —ing, *sine morâ*, *propere*, *festinanter*.

tart, n. *scriblita*, *crustulum*.

tart, adj. 1, of the taste; see SOUR; 2, of the temper, *acerbus*, *amarus*, *morosus*, *stomachosus*. Adv. see SOURLY; *acerbe*, *morose*, *stomachose*. **tartness,** n. 1, see SOURNESS; 2, *acerbitas*, *morositas*, *stomachus*.

tartar, n. in chemistry, * *tartărus*; salt of —, * *sal tartari*.

task, **I.** n. = what is imposed by another, *pensum* (lit. of women spinning wool, then in gen.), *opus*, *-ěris*, n. (= work); it is a difficult —, *res magna est*; = lesson, *pensum*, see, however, LESSON; to take anyone to — on account of, *rationem alcjs rei ab alqo* (*re*)*petěre* or *reposcěre*. **II.** v.tr. *pensum alci dare* or *imponěre*; to — oneself with, *alqd faciendum sibi proponěre*.
task-master, n. *operis exactor*.

tassel, n. perhaps *fimbriae* (= fringe).

taste, **I.** v.tr. = to try by eating a little, *gustatu explorare*, *gustare* (= to take a little of anything; then fig. to become acquainted with, e.g. *suavitatem vitae*), of anything, (*de*)*gustare alqd*, *gustare de alqâ re* (a little off the top; then fig. to — the pleasures of anything, e.g. *degustare vitam*, *honorem*); to — first, before, * † *praegustare* (lit.), (*de*)*libare alqd* (lit. and fig.). **II.** v.intr. *sapěre*, *alqo sapore esse*; to — like, of, *sapěre* or *resipěre alqd* (lit.), *redolēre alqd* (fig., e.g. of the school, *doctrinam*, Cic.); bitter, *amaro esse sapore*; pleasant, *jucunde sapěre*. **III.** n. 1, objectively, lit. as quality of things, *sapor*; anything loses its —, *alcjs rei sapor non permanet*; fig., e.g. good —, *elegantia* (e.g. in a poem); bad —, *insulsitas*; 2, subjectively, lit. the ability to —, *gustatus*, *-ūs*, *gustus*, *-ūs* (however, Cic. only uses *gustatus*, mostly post class.); = sense of beauty, delighting in that which really is beautiful, *gustatus*, for, *alcjs rei* (Cic.), *elegantia* (= refined — for what is fine, inasmuch as it shows itself by the outward appearance), *venustas* (= grace in anyone, Plin.), *judicium* (= judgment in matters of —), *intellegentia* (of one who is a great judge in matters of —), also *aures*, *-ium*, and comb. *aures et judicium alcjs* (as far as the — depends upon the ear, e.g. *alcjs* or *temporis auribus accommodatus*); a good, correct, refined —, *elegantia* (in gen.), *subtile* or *exquisitum* or *politum judicium* (= acute judgment), *judicium intellegens* (of a connoisseur); without —, *homo parum elegans*; with —, *scite*; *commode* (e.g. to dance, *saltare*), *scienter* (e.g. *tibiis cantare*); according to my —, *quantum ego sapio*, *quantum equidem judicare possum*. **tasteful,** adj. *politus* (= refined, e.g. judgment, letter, man), *elegans*, *venustus* (= graceful; both the foregoing of persons and things). Adv. *polite*, *eleganter*, *venuste*. **tasteless,** adj. 1, lit. *nihil sapidus* (of wine, Col.), *sine sapore*; anything is —, *alcjs rei sapor nullus est*; 2, fig. *inelegans*, *insulsus*, *infacētus* (*infic-*); see RUDE. Adv. *ineleganter*, *insulse*, *infacēte* (*infic-*). **tastelessness,** n. 1, lit. *cui nullus sapor est*; 2, fig. *insulsitas*.

tatter, n. *pannus*; see RAG. **tattered,** adj. *pannosus*.

tattle, **I.** v.tr. *garrire*. **II.** n. *sermunculus* (rare), or perhaps *sermo stultus*. **tattler,** n. *homo garrulus*.

tattoo, v.tr. *notis compungěre*.

taunt, **I.** v.tr. *alqd* or *de alqâ re alci ob*(*j*)*icěre*, *conviciari*, *cavillari alqm* (= to satirize). **II.** n. *convicium*; see INVECTIVE. **taunting,** adj. *contumēliosus*. Adv. *contumēliose*.

tautology, n. *ejusdem verbi aut sermonis iteratio* (Quint.). **tautological,** adj. *idem verbum aut eundem sermonem iterans*.

tavern, n. *caupona*. **tavern-keeper,** n. *caupo*.

tawdry, adj. *speciosior quam decet* (= too showy); see also VULGAR.

tawny, adj. *fulvus*.

tax, **I.** n. *vectigal*, *tributum*; to lay on a —, *vectigal*, *tributum imponěre alci* and *alci rei*, *tributum indicěre alci*; to collect a —, *vectigalia* (etc.) *exigěre*; to exempt from a —, *tributis vindicare alqm*, *tributis liberare alqm*; exempt from a —, *immunis tributorum*, in the context *immunis* (opp. *vectigalis*). **II.** v.tr. *tributum* (= income — or poll- —) or *vectigal* (= property- —) *imponěre alci* or *alci rei*; to — every individual, *tributa in singula capita imponěre*. **taxable,** adj. *vectigalis*. **taxation,** n. *tributorum in singula capita distributio*. **tax-gatherer,** n. *vectigalium exactor*.

tea, n. the plant, **thea* (Linn.; necessary as t.t., not class.).

teach, v.tr. anything, (*e*)*docēre* (in gen., also = to show, explain, prove), *praecipěre*, *praecepta dare de alqâ re* (= to give precepts), *traděre* (= to lecture upon, to —, e.g. history, the rules of an art, etc.), *profitēri* (= to profess, to — publicly what we profess), *ostenděre*, *declarare* (= to show, declare); to — anyone, *alqm instituěre*, *instruěre*, *erudire*, (*e*)*docēre alqm alqd* or *de re*, *instituěre*, *erudire alqm alqâ re*, *in alqâ re*, *traděre alci alqd* (see before), *imbuěre alqm alqâ re*. **teachable,** adj. *qui* (*quae*) *docēri potest*, *docilis*. **teachableness,** n. *docilitas*. **teacher,** n. *doctor*, *magister* (= master, in reference to the influence, authority which he has over his pupils), *praeceptor* (giving instruction, Cic.), *auctor* (*alcjs rei*), *explicator alcjs rei* (of one who explains), *professor* (= a public —, Quint., Suet.), *ludimagister*, or as two words, *ludi magister* (= schoolmaster, principal of a school), comb. *magister atque doctor*, *praeceptor et magister*, *dux et magister*.
teaching, n. *doctrina*, *eruditio*, *institutio*, *disciplina*, *professio* (= public —).

team, n *jugum*

tear, n *lacrima, fletus* *ūs* (= weeping, constant flowing of —s), with many —s, *cum* or *non sine multis lacrimis, magno (cum) fletu*, to shed —s, *lacrimas effundĕre* or *profundĕre, lacrimari, fle e* (= to weep) **tearful,** adj *lacrimans lacrimosus, flebilis* Adv *flebiliter, multis cum lacrimis, magno (cum) fletu* **tearless,** adj *siccus* (e g eyes), *sine lacrimis*

tear, I. v tr to — into pieces, *(di)scindĕre, conscindĕre* (very rare), *concerpĕre, discerpĕre, (di)laniare, (di)lacerare* (= to lacerate), *vellĕre, eruĕre* (e g *oculos*, = to — up by the roots), *convellĕre, divellere* (= to — in pieces), *distrahĕre, diffindĕre* (= to — in different directions), *diripĕre, eripĕre* (= to — away from, *alqd alci* see SEIZE), to be torn by passion, etc, *differri, distrahi*, or by special verb (e g to be torn by anguish, *angi*, by apprehension, *sol(l)icitum esse*), = to — down, *rescindĕre*, to — open, *resignare* (= to — open a letter), *rescindĕre* (lit and fig), *dirumpĕre, dirumpĕre* (= to break in two, forcibly) **II.** v intr see HURRY, RUSH

tease, v tr *alqm fatigare* (= to plague), *vexare* (= to worry), *negotium alci facessĕre, alqm alqa re* (e g *rogitando*), *obtundĕre*

teasel, n *dipsacus* (*dipsacos*, Plin)

teat, n *mamma*

technical, adj — term, *artis vocabulum, vocabulum apud artifices usitatum*, — terms, language, terminology, *vocabula quae in quăque arte versantur*, Zeno and the Peripatetics differ merely in their new — terms, *inter Zenonem et Peripateticos nihil praeter verborum novitatem interest* **technicality,** n use adj. **technology** n *ars officinarum*

tedious, adj *longus, longinquus* (of what lasts long and hence becomes troublesome), *molestus, taedii plenus* (= wearying), *lentus* (= slow, of a war, *lentum et diuturnum*), it would be —, *longum est*, not to be —, *ne longus sim* Adv *moleste, lente, cum taedio* **tediousness.** n of anything, *molestia quam (or taedium quod) alqd alci affert*

teem, v intr *turgēre* (= to swell) to begin to —, *turgescĕre*, *plenum esse alcjs rei* (e g *succi*, as a human body, Ter), *distentum esse alqa re* (= to be extended as it were through anything, e g *lacte*, as an udder), see ABOUND **teeming,** adj see FRUITFUL

teethe, v intr *dentire* (Plin), see TOOTH

teetotal, etc *vino exempli causa (se) abstinere*, see ABSTAIN, ABSTINENCE

telegraph, n *quasi telegraphum quod dicitur*

telescope, n **telescopium*

tell, v tr see under TALE

temerity, n *temeritas*

temper, I. v tr *temperare* (lit and fig), to — with anything, *alqd alqa re miscēre* (lit. and fig), see MIX **II.** n 1, = character, *ingenium* (= peculiar disposition of the mind), *natura* (of the body, of the mind), *animus* (= character), 2 = anger, *ira, iracundia*, to be in a —, *irasci*, *iracundum esse* **temperament,** n *temperatio*, see TEMPER, DISPOSITION **temperance,** n *continentia* (= abstaining), *temperantia* (= being moderate in the enjoyment of sensual pleasure, both in opp to *libido, libidines*), *moderatio, modestia*, *frugalitas* (= moderation), *abstinentia* (= abstinence from anything) **temperate,** adj *temperans, temperatus, continens* (= moderate in the enjoyment of anything), comb *moderatus ac temperatus, temperatus moderatusque, continens ac temperans, moderatus, modestus* (= moderate), *sobrius* (= sober), *frugi* (= frugal), *abstinens* (= abstinent), *abstemius* (= abstemious), of climate, *temperatus* Adv *temperanter, temperate, continenter, moderate, modeste, sobrie, frugaliter* **temperateness,** n *temperantia*, see TEMPERANCE **temperature,** n *temperatio* (= the blending of —, so, mild — *aeris, caeli*, etc), *temperies* (e g of the atmosphere, *aeris*), or by *caelum* (e g *salubre, serenum*, or with noun, *caeli clementia*, etc) **tempered,** adj good —, *mitis*, ill- —, *morosus*

tempest, n *tempestas* (= unfavourable weather, boisterous weather in general, storm on the land and on the sea, then also fig), *procella* (= hurricane, storm on the sea, also fig of storms in a State), a — arises, *tempestas* (or *procella*) *venit* or *oritur* or *coorītur*, a — threatens, *tempestas* (or *procella*) *imminet* or *impendet*, *alci* (lit and fig) **tempestuous,** adj *procellosus* (lit), *turbidus, turbulentus* (lit and fig), *violentus* (lit, e g weather, *tempestas*, then fig = violent, e g attack, *impetus*, character, *ingenium, homo*), *vehemens* (= vehement, violent, having a high degree of inward strength, e g *ventus*, then of man = passionate) Adv *procellose* (lit), *turbide, turbulente, violenter, vehementer* **tempestuousness,** n *violentia* (e g *venti, maris*), then = roughness, boisterous manners, *vehementia*

templar, n **(eques) templarius, ii*, m

temple, n *aedes sacra* (of a god, *aedes* alone can only be said if the genit of the deity is added, or it is sufficiently clear from the context), *templum, fanum, delubrum, aedicula, sacrarium* (= shrine), in poetry sometimes the name of a god stands for his — (e g *Jupiter, Vesta*), *sacellum* (surrounded with a wall and containing an altar used as a place of refuge)

temples, n (part of the head) *tempora, um*

temporal, adj = pertaining to this life *externus* (referring to the world without), *humanus* (referring to a man and man's destiny, *terrenus* and *terrester*, Eccl), — affairs, *res externae*, — things, treasures, *fortunae, res familiaris, opes, -um*, f, — welfare, *hujus vitae felicitas*, if opposed to "spiritual," *profanus* (opp *sacer*), in gram, — augment, *augmentum temporale* **temporality,** n *res externa*

temporary, adj *temporarius* (very rare before Aug), *temporalis*, better by *ad* or *in tempus* **temporarily,** adv *ad* or *in tempus* (= for the time being) **temporize,** v intr *temporibus inservire*

tempt, v tr anyone, *alqm (at)tentare, alcjs sententiam tentare* (= to sound anyone, what his opinion is), *sol(l)icitare alqm* or *alcjs animum* (= to try to persuade anyone to do a certain thing, e g *pretio* or *pecunia*), *alqm ad* or *in alqd invitare, illicĕre, pellicĕre, allicĕre, vocare, adducĕre* or *inducĕre* **temptation,** n *tentatio* (= the act of trying anyone or a thing), *sol(l)icitatio* (= the act of tempting anyone to, etc), *corruptelarum illecebrae* (= allurements wherewith to tempt anyone), to lead anyone into —, *alqm in discrimen vocare* or *adducĕre, alqm sol(l)icitare pellicĕre* **tempter,** n *tentator* (Hor, and Eccl of the Devil)

ten, adj *decem*, *deni, ae, a* (= — each, also = — at once), containing —, *denarius*, the number —, *decussis*, — o'clock, *hora quarta*, — years, *decennis* (Plin), — times, *decie(n)s* (also = as in English, I have told you — times, *decies dixi*) **tenth,** adj *decimus*

tenable, adj *quod teneri potest*

tenacious, adj *tenax alcjs rei* (lit and fig, mostly poet and in post Aug prose), see FIRM Adv *tenaciter* **tenaciousness, tenacity,** n *tenacitas*

tenant, I. n *conductor, incola*, in and 1 *habi-*

tator (in gen.), *inquilinus* (of a house). **II.** v.tr. see INHABIT. **tenancy,** n. *alcjs rei conducendae condicio.* **tenantry,** n. use pl. of TENANT, or *clientes, -ium.*

tend, v.tr. *curare, colĕre.*

tend, v.intr. 1, = to go, *tendĕre;* see GO; 2, = to relate, *ad alqd pertinēre, spectare, tendĕre.* **tendency,** n. *inclinatio, proclivitas ad alqm, studium alcjs rei;* see INCLINATION. **tender,** v.tr. and n. see OFFER.

tender, adj. *tener, mollis, delicatus* (= delicate), *misericors* (= —-hearted), *amans* (= affectionate), *indulgens* (= indulgent). Adv. *molliter, delicate,* comb. *delicate ac molliter, indulgenter.* **tenderness,** n. 1, = softness, etc., *teneritas, mollitia* (*mollities*); 2, = affection, *indulgentia, amor.*

tendon, n. *nervus* (Cels.).

tendril, n. *clavicula, caulis, pampinus,* m. and f. (of a vine), *viticula* (Plin.).

tenement, n. see HOUSE.

tenet, n. *praeceptum, placitum, decretum;* the —s, *disciplina, ratio* (*Stoicorum,* etc.).

tennis, n. *pila.* **tennis-court,** n. *locus quo pilā luditur.*

tenour, n. *tenor* (= uninterrupted course, e.g. *vitae, consulatūs*), *sententia* (= meaning); see MEANING.

tense, n. *tempus, -oris,* n. (Gram.).

tension, n. *intentio.*

tent, n. *tentorium, tabernaculum* (often = a hut), *contubernium;* general's —, *praetorium;* to pitch a —, *tabernaculum collocare, ponĕre, constituĕre.*

tentacle, n. *corniculum* (in gen., Plin.).

tentative, adj. and adv. *experientia, probatio, tentatio* (e.g. *tentatione usus*), or by verb *qui* (*quae, quod*) *tentat.*

tenterhooks, n. to be on —, *ex(s)pectatione angi.*

tenuity, n. see THINNESS.

tenure, n. *possessio* or *possidēre.*

tepid, adj. *tepidus, tepens;* to become —, *tepescĕre;* to be —, *tepēre;* to make —, *tepefacĕre.* Adv. *tepide* (Plin.). **tepidness,** n. *tepor* (also fig. = lukewarmness, e.g. in writings; Tac.).

tergiversation, n. *tergiversatio.*

term. **I.** n. 1, see LIMIT, BOUNDARY; 2, = limited time, *dies* (in gen., in this sense generally feminine), *dies certa, dies stata* or *statuta* or *constituta* (or in masc.); a time named, fixed, e.g. to fix a —, *diem statuĕre* or *constituĕre* (by mutual appointment, e.g. when a sum is to be paid), *diem dicĕre* (for settling a law dispute); 3, in Gram., see EXPRESSION, WORD; 4, the arts, see TECHNICAL; 5, see CONDITION; to be on good —s with anyone, *cum alqo familiariter vivĕre, alcjs familiaritate uti.* **II.** v.tr. see NAME. **terminal,** adj. *quod certis diebus fit.* **terminate,** **I.** v.tr. see LIMIT, END. **II.** v.intr. *finiri, terminari;* see END. **termination,** n. *confectio, finis, -is, exitus, -ūs.* **terminology,** n. *artis vocabula, -orum;* — of a sect, etc., *verba, -orum* (*sua* or *alcjs propria*).

termagant, n. *mulier jurgiis addicta.*

terrace, n. *pulvinus* (= flower-bed raised in the form of pillows, a plantation that gradually rises), *solarium* (= a place on the top of the house for basking in the sun), *ambulatio* (= a covered or open place for walking).

terrestrial, adj. *qui* (*quae, quod*) *terram incolit, ad terram pertinens, terrestris, terrēnus* (= of the earth, opp. to *caelestis,* e.g. of animals, etc.); as opp. to heavenly, *terrestris* (Eccl.), better expressed by *humanus* (opp. to *divinus*).

terrible, adj. *terribilis* (= exciting terror), †*terrificus, horribilis, horrendus* (= horrible), *atrox* (= fearful, e.g. man, deed, bloodshed), *immanis* (= monstrous, unnatural, cruel), *dirus* (= portentous), *formidulosus* (= causing fear), *foedus* (= detestable, abominable, e.g. plots, war, fire), *incredibilis* (= incredible, not to be believed, imagined, e.g. *stupiditas*). Adv. *terribilem* or *horrendum in modum, atrociter, foede, foedum in modum.* **terrific,** adj. see DREADFUL, TERRIBLE. **terrify,** v.tr. *alqm* (*per*)*terrēre,* see FRIGHTEN. **terror,** n. *terror* (in a subjective sense = fear, in an objective sense, that which causes —); also in the pl. *formido, metus, -ūs, pavor* (all in subjective sense); with —, *terrore percussus, terrore coactus.*

territory, n. *territorium* (= field belonging to a town); in a wider sense = boundaries, dominions, etc., by *ager, terra, regio.* **territorial,** adj. *qui* (*quae, quod*) *ad agrum pertinet.*

terse, adj. e.g. style, by *pressus, brevis, angustus, densus* (e.g. *densior hic, ille copiosior,* Quint.), *strictus* (Quint.), or by *paucis verbis* (*uti,* etc.). Adv. *presse, breviter, paucis verbis.* **terseness,** n. *brevitas,* or by *oratio pressa,* etc.

tertian, n. (*febris*) *tertiana.*

tessclated, adj. *tessellatus.*

test, **I.** n. see TRIAL, EXAMINATION. **II.** v.tr. *tentare, experiri, periclitari alqd* (also *alqm*), *periculum facĕre alcjs rei* (also *alcjs*), *explorare;* to be —ed, to stand the —, *usu* or *re probari.*

testaceous, adj. *testaceus* (Plin.).

testament, n. 1, *testamentum* (= will); see WILL; 2, the New —, *Testamentum Novum;* the Old —, *Testamentum Vetus* (Eccl.). **testamentary,** adj. by *testamento institutus,* etc., *testamentarius* (in Cic. *lex test.* = a law about wills; in Plin. *adoptio test.*). **testator,** n. *testator* (Suet. and Jct.), or *is qui testamentum facit.* **testatrix,** n. *testatrix* (Jct.). **testify,** v.tr. *testari* (in gen.), *testificari, testimonio confirmare* (= to confirm by testimony), *testimonio esse, testem esse* (= to be a witness; the former of a thing, the latter of a person), *affirmare* (= to affirm, or *testificari* in this sense). **testimonial,** n. perhaps by *testimonium honorificum; lit(t)erae commendaticiae,* = letters of recommendation; see CERTIFICATE. **testimony,** n. *testimonium.*

testy, adj. *morosus;* see PEEVISH.

tether, v.tr. and n. see TIE.

tetrameter, n. *tetrametrus* (very late).

tetrarch, n. *tetrarcha,* m. **tetrarchy,** n. *tetrarchia.*

text, n. 1, = the words of a writer, *verba, -orum* (= the words of an author quoted by a commentator); 2, — of Scripture, *exemplum Sacrae Scripturae propositum.*

textile, adj. *textorius.* **textual,** adj. *quod ad verba scriptoris pertinet.* **texture,** n. †*textura, textum, textus, -ūs* (both poet. and post Aug.); see WEB.

than, conj. after a comparative and after verbs containing the idea of a comparison (e.g. after *malo,* I would rather; *praestat,* it is better), *quam;* or by the ablat., e.g. *virtus est praestantior quam aurum* or *praestantior auro;* if there is a number before the noun, — after the comps. *amplius* and *plus, minus, minor, major* is left out altogether, and the numeral is still expressed in the same case as if it had been used, e.g. *amplius sunt sex menses, plus ducentos milites desideravit* (= more —, etc.), *minus trecenti*

(= less —) *pereunt*, more (less) — eight years old, *major (minor) quam octo annos natus*, *major (minor) octo annos natus*, *major (minor) octo annis natu*, *major (minor) octo annis*, *major (minor) octo annorum*, = — that, *quam ut* or *qui (quae, quod)* with subj (e g the pain was greater — he could bear, *dolor major erat quam quem ille ferre posset*), — one could expect from, etc, considering, etc, expressed by Liv and later writers simply by *quam pro* (which we however never read in Cic and Caes), e g *proelium atrocius erat quam pro pugnantium numero* in negative and interrogative sentences, also when we state anything the words "nothing else —," by *praeter*, *praeterquam*, *excepto* (with n as abl abs), *nisi*, e g *praeter illum vidi neminem*, *tibi nihil deesse arbitror praeter voluntatem*, *philosophi negant quemquam esse bonum nisi sapientem*, — here may be rendered either by *nisi* or *quam*, but *nisi* implies that everything else is excluded, whilst *quam* is only used in a comparative sense, e g *erat historia nihil aliud nisi annalium confectio* (i e history was this only and nothing else besides, Cic), *virtus nihil aliud est quam in se perfecta et ad summum perducta natura* (i e as much as, the same as, Cic)

thane, n *dominus*, **thanus* (mediæval term)

thank, v tr *gratias alci agĕre*, that, for, by *quod* or *qui*, not *pro alqâ re*, *gratiam habēre*, *persolvĕre*, *referre*, *reddĕre*, *tribuĕre*, *gratiam habēre*, *gratum esse erga alqm*, *beneficii memoriam conservare*, *memori mente gratiam persolvĕre*, *grata memoriâ beneficium (beneficia) prosequi* (in one's heart), *re ipsâ atque animo esse gratum* (by deed, and in one's own heart), heartily, most sincerely, *maximas*, *incredibiles*, *singulares gratias agĕre alci*, also *amplissimis* or *singularibus verbis gratias agĕre alci*, — you! (in accepting) *benigne dicis!* I have to — you for it, *alci alqd debēre* (something good), *alci alqd acceptum referre*, no, — you! *benigne (dicis)!* *benigne ac liberaliter!* also *recte!* (all right! no! as answer to a question), I — you for your kind invitation, *bene vocas*, *jam gratia est*, the act of —ing, *gratiarum actio* (words) **thankful**, adj *gratus*, see GRATEFUL Adv *grate*, *grato animo* **thankfulness**, n *animus gratus*, see GRATITUDE **thankless**, adj *ingratus* (= both ungrateful and bringing no thanks) Adv *ingrate* **thanks**, n *gratiae* (often in the pl with *agere*), to return —, *gratias agĕre* or *gratiam persolvĕre quod* or *qui*, *gratiam alci referre*, *reddĕre* for, *pro alqâ re*, — God! *est diis gratia!* **thanksgiving**, n *gratiarum actio* (in gen), *supplicatio*, *supplicium* (= public — for victories, for deliverance from sickness) **thankworthy**, adj *laudabilis*, *gratiâ* or *laude dignus*, *gratus*

that, I demonstr pron *ille*, *illa*, *illud*, *iste*, *ista*, *istud* (*ille*, without being in opp to *hic*, often used when we speak of something very well known, very celebrated, of anything or person remote as regards time or place, but present in the mind of the speaker, *iste* = —, often when we speak of a third person or thing, with the idea of contempt or disapproval, — man there), *alter* (= the other of two, pl *alteri*, if we speak of several on the other side), *is*, *ea*, *id*, *hic*, *haec*, *hoc*, those who, *illi qui* or (the relative clause preceding) *qui*, *ii*, — or, the word — not expressed, e g *jacet corpus dormientis ut mortui* (= as — of a dead man), — is my father, *hic est meus pater*, — only is true friendship, *haec demum est amicitia firma*, often by *sic*, e g — is his way, *sic est ingenium ejus*, = such a one, etc, *is*, *ea*, *id*, of — age, *id aetatis*, at — time, *id temporis*, we are at — age, *id jam aetatis sumus* II. rel pron *qui*, *quae*, *quod*, see WHO III. conj to connect the main clause: A, when the sentence with — contains the subject of the copula in the main sentence, 1, when the sentence with — conveys a general idea, render by the inf, e g *officium est*, etc, or by another noun, e g *nihil suavius est quam amari* or *amor*, = nothing is more pleasing than — one should be loved, 2, use the accus and inf, after "it is pleasing grievous, probable, clear, manifest, evident, true, it appears, it is useful, right, reasonable, necessary, lawful, it is allowed —", after several of these impersonal verbs, use also *quod* and *ut*, see under C and D (e g it is pleasing to hear — you are well, *gratum est te valēre*), 3 than —, as —, inf with an adj or another noun with an adj or part, e g *nulla res tanto erat damno*, etc, *quam* (a noun with an adj or part) B, when the sentence with — contains the object of the verb of the main clause, use acc and infin, 1, this is the case after all *verba sensuum et affectuum*, to which belong also "to know, conceive, remind, expect, hope, fear, believe," etc, then also after *fac*, when it is = *finge*, fancy —, etc, *fac qui ego sum esse te*, after the verbs "to hope, swear, promise, threaten," we use the accus and fut infin, only after "to hope" we use the accus and pres infin when we speak of anything referring to the present time, and the accus and perf infin when we speak of anything past, 2, after the so-called *verba declarandi*, as "to say, tell, indicate, remember, convince, teach prove (*efficere*)," etc, 3, also after "to fix, determine, wish, forbid, impose, concede (that anything is so)," etc, the infin, if the sentence with — declares the object, whilst if it contains a wish or intention, we use *ut*, after "they," "the people say," "it is reported," etc (*dicunt*, *tradunt*, *ferunt*, *produnt*, *perhibent*), either by accus and infin, or the nom and indic (of the passive voice), e g *dicunt Romulum primum regem Romanum fuisse*, or *Romulus primus rex Romanorum fuisse dicebatur*, *dicunt vos adfuisse*, or *vos dicebamini adfuisse*, after *dubito*, in the sense "I doubt not," we find in Cic always *quin* C, when the sentence with — contains a description of anything or a circum', 1, of the subject, when we can put "which" instead of "—," by *quod*, as after "there is reason," or "there is no reason," (which, etc), *est (habeo)*, *non est*, *nihil est quod* (we may also use *cur*, as in English), also after "it is pleasing, rejoicing, I am glad, it is painful," etc (e g *nihil est quod* [i e *illud quod*] *timeas*) also after "we must add (*eo* or *huc accedit*)," where we use *quod* when we speak of a matter of fact, and *ut* when we refer to anything that is only in progress, always when the thing is only about to happen, 2, of the object when — = "because," also by *quod* after "to be glad, rejoice (*gaudēre*), to feel sorry, grieve (*dolēre*), to wonder (*mirari*)," etc, where we use *quod* when we speak of a definite fact, but *si*, if we speak of something merely imaginary or as we suppose it; 3, when — stands for "inasmuch as, insofar as" D, always *ut* or *qui (quae, quod)* when the sentence with — expresses the purpose, condition, aim, effect, surmise, permission, encouragement, wish or command, as subject or object, or as additional clause after *is sum*, *non is sum*, *talis*, *qualis*, *is* (such a one), *ejusmodi*, etc also *qui*, etc (*ut is*, etc), after *tam*, *tantus*, generally after negations, after *quis?* and after comparatives with *quam*, when these words express the degree, measure, up to which anything is said to possess a certain quality, and after nouns to express a purpose (e g Caesar sent messengers — they might say, *Caesar nuntios misit qui dicerent*), but *ut is*, etc, to express result. — not, after "to fear, to be afraid," etc, *ne non*, seldom *ut*, and — alone *ne*; only — not, — by any means, *ut ne* (*ne* being placed before — which is prevented), e.g. *ut hoc ne facerem* (= he took care —, etc.); I say — . . . not, etc., by *nego* with accus. and infin., e.g. he asserts — there are no gods, *deos esse negat*. E, — in exclamations, 1, when we express a wish, oh — ! *ut! utinam! o si* (see OH); God grant —, etc., *faxit Deus, ut*, etc.; — not! *utinam ne!* 2, in general exclamations, by accus. and infin. (which apparently is not governed by any preceding verb), e.g. *me miserum! te in tantas aerumnas propter me incidisse!*

thatch, n. *stramentum*. **thatched**, adj. — house, *casa stramento tecta*.

thaw, I. v.tr. (*dis*)*solvĕre*, *liquefacĕre*. II. v.intr. (*dis*)*solvi*, *liquefiĕri*, *liquescĕre*, *et tabescĕre calore*, *glaciem tepefactam molliri*. III. n. use verb.

the, def. art. not expressed in Latin; but if we speak emphatically, sometimes by the demonstr. pron. *hic, haec, hoc; ille, illa, illud; iste, ista, istud* (see THAT); — more, etc., . . . more, etc, *quo . . . eo* or *hoc*, *quanto . . . tanto*, *eo . . . quo*, *tanto . . . quanto*, e.g. *homines quo plura habent, eo ampliora cupiunt*, = — more they have, — more they want; in general sentences we use the superlative with *ut quisque . . . ita*, e.g. *ut quisque est vir optimus, ita difficillime alios improbos suspicatur* (= — better a man is, with — more difficulty he suspects, etc., . . .); sometimes in sentences of the latter kind the connecting particles *ut* and *ita* are altogether omitted, e.g. *sapientissimus quisque aequissimo animo moritur*; — sooner — better, *quam primum*, *primo quoque tempore* or *die*; — with an adj. or adv., e.g. — better, *hoc, eo, tanto*; so much — greater, *eo* or *hoc major*; so much — better, *tanto melius*.

theatre, n. *theatrum*, *scaena*. **theatrical**, adj. *scaenicus*, *theatralis* (= belonging to the theatre; very late = also low, vulgar), (e.g. dress, *habitus*, *venustas*, in this sense), also by the genit. *histrionum* (in reference to the actors), e.g. — gestures, *histrionum gestus inepti*. Adv. *more histrionum*.

theft, n. *furtum*. **thief**, n. *fur*. **thieve**, v.intr. see STEAL. **thievish**, adj. *furax*. Adv. *furācĭter*.

their, poss. pron. *suus* (if referring to the main subject in the sentence), *eorum*, *illorum* (if referring to any other subject); on — account, for — sake, *suā caus(s)ā*, *eorum caus(s)ā*, *propter eos* (see before). **theirs**, poss. pron. *suus* or *illorum*.

them, pers. pron. *eos* or *eas*, *illos* or *illas*, *ipsos* or *ipsas*; = to them, *eis* or *iis*, etc. **themselves**, see SELF.

theme, n. = subject to write or speak on, *propositio*, *propositum*, *id quod propositum est*, *quaestio*, *id quod quaerimus* (= question proposed, leading idea for a metaphysical inquiry), *argumentum* (= material, contents, e.g. *epistulae*).

then, adv. *tunc* (corresponds to *nunc*, now), *tum* (denoting continuity, as *jam* in the present; — that is at that time, after something foregoing), *illo* (*eo*) *tempore*.

thence, adv. *illinc* (*illim*), *istinc*, *abhinc* (= from that place; *hinc et illinc*, hence and —, hither and thither). **thenceforth**, adv. *inde*, *ex eo tempore*.

theocracy, n. *regnum quo Deus ipse rex habetur*, or θεοκρατία.

theogony, n. *deorum generatio*.

theology, n. *theologia* (Eccl.), or *rerum divinarum scientia*. **theologian**, n. *theolŏgus* or *lit(t)erarum sanctarum studiosus*. **theological**, adj. *theologicus*, or by the genit. *lit(t)erarum sanctarum*.

theorem, n. *perceptum* (translation of the Greek θεώρημα, Cic.).

theory, n. *ratio* (= science of anything in gen., e.g. *belli*), *doctrina* (= literary or theoretical knowledge), *ars*, *praecepta*, *-orum* (= rules); — of moral duties or obligations, *conformatio officiorum* (Cic.); — and practice, *ratio atque usus*, *-ūs*; to combine —, *doctrinam ad usum adjungĕre*. **theoretical**, adj. *quod in cognitione versatur*, *in spectione* or *in cognitione et aestimatione positus* (Quint.), *quod ab artis praeceptis proficiscitur* (= according to the rules of art, analogous to, Cic.); — knowledge, *ratio* (e.g. *belli*); to possess — of, *alqd ratione cognitum habēre*; to have a — and practical bearing, *ad cognoscendi et agendi vim rationemque referri*. Adv. *ratione*, *ex artis praeceptis*. **theorist**, n. *qui artem ratione cognitam habet*.

theosophy, n. * *theosophia* (as t.t.). **theosophist**, n. * *theosŏphus*.

therapeutics, n. *ars medendi*, *medicina*.

there, adv. = in that place, *ibi*; *illic*, *istic*; to be —, *adesse*; to stand —, *adstare*; — where, *ibi ubi*, *illic ubi*; — you have, — you see, not rendered, but simply *habes*, *accipe*, *vides* (e.g. *librum*); = thither, *illuc*; see THITHER. **thereabouts**, adv. *prope* (= near), *ferme*, *fere* (= nearly). **thereafter**, **thereupon**, adv. (*ex*)*inde* (*exin*), *deinde* (*dein*), *statim* (= immediately); see AFTERWARDS, THEN.

therefore, adv. *igitur*, *itaque*, *ergo* (*igitur* never at the beginning), *ideo*, *eo*, *idcirco*, *propterea* (= for that reason), *proin*(*de*) (= hence), *quare*, *quamobrem*, *quapropter*, *quocirca* (= wherefore). **therein**, adv. *in eo*, *in eis* (*iis*), etc.

thermometer, n. * *thermometrum* (as t.t.).

thesis, n. see THEME.

they, pers. pron. *ii* or *eae*, *illi* or *illae*, *ipsi* or *ipsae*; but it is only expressed in Latin when we speak emphatically.

thick, adj. *crassus* (= stout, compact, opp. *tenuis* (= thin) and *macer* (= meagre)), *pinguis* (= fat, stout, opp. *macer*), *opimus* (= who looks like one that lives well, opp. *gracilis*), *obēsus* (= well fed, opp. *gracilis* and (of animals) *strigosus*), *corpore amplo* (= of large-sized body), *turgens*, *turgidus* (= swollen, e.g. eyes, etc.), *densus* (= dense, opp. *rarus*, = single, scarce, solitary), *spissus* (= impenetrable, of the soil, of darkness, etc., opp. *solutus*, loose), *confertus* (= crowded, of a mass, opp. *rarus*), *concretus* (= curdled, of milk, also of air); when we express the measure of anything, — is either rendered by *crassus* with accus., or by *crassitudine* with the genit. of the measure (e.g. *quat(t)uor pedes crassus*, *quat(t)uor pedum crassitudine*); *creber*, *frequens* (= many); a — voice, *vox obtūsa* (Quint.); — skin, med. *callosus* (lit.), *durus* (fig.). Adv. *dense*, *spisse*, *confertim*, *crebro*, *frequenter*. **thicken**, I. v.tr. *densare*, † *spissare*. II. v.intr. *densari*, *spissari*, *concrescĕre* (= become like one mass, to curdle, e.g. of milk, etc.). **thicket**, n. *dumētum*, *fruticētum*, or *locus sentibus obsitus*. **thickness**, n. *crassitudo*, *spissitas* (so as to become impenetrable), *obesitas* (= fatness, opp. *gracilitas*), *corpus amplum*, *crebritas*, *frequentia*. **thick-set**, adj. see THICK, STOUT.

thief, n. see THEFT.

thigh, n. *femur*.

thimble, n. *digiti munimentum*.

thin, I. adj. *tenuis* (opp. *crassus*), *subtilis* (= fine, tender, e.g. of leather), *gracilis*, *exilis*, *macer* (= meagre, opp. *obesus*), *strigosus* (= lean, of animals), *rarus* (= not close together, e.g. hair, opp *densus*), *angustus* (= narrow), *liquidus* (of anything liquid), *dilutus* (= diluted, e g wine, colour) **II.** v tr *attenuare*, of trees, *collucare* (of clearing the ground of trees, post Aug of a single tree), *interlucare* (Plin) Adv *tenuiter*, *gracil iter*, *rare* **thinness,** n *tenuitas*, *exilitas*, *gra cilitas* (= slenderness), *raritas* (= looseness of texture), *macies* (= leanness)

thine, pron *tuus*

thing, n **1,** = event, *res*, *negotium* — s, *res*, *rerum natura*, —s, with an adj before it, often rendered merely by the adj n pl (e g wonderful —s, *mira*), or by some noun (e g foolish —s, *nugae*, *ineptiae*), a tiresome —, *len tum* (= slow), *molestum negotium* , above all —s, *ante omnia*, *imprimis* (*in primis*), *praecipue* , **2,** = any substance, *res*, *supellex* (= household fur niture), *vasa*, *-orum* (= vessels, pots, also of soldiers), *sarcinae* (= effects which we carry with us when travelling), = clothes, *vestis*, *vestitus*, *-ūs*

think, v intr and tr **1,** abs = to have ideas and to be conscious of it (in an absolute sense), *cogitare*, *intellegere* (= to have clear ideas), **2,** with an object, anything, *alqd cogitare*, *alqd cogitatione comprehendere* or *percipere* or *com plecti*, *alqd cogitatione et mente complecti*, *alqd mente concipere*, *alqd cogitatione* or (*de*)*pingere* (= to picture anything in one's mind) — about, *de alqa re cogitare* , **3,** = to suppose, *opinari*, *putare*, *arbitrari*, *censere*, *credere* , **4,** see PURPOSE ; **5,** = to judge, *judicare*, *sentire* (= to have a certain opinion) comb *sentire et judicare*, *sta tuere* (= to fix) **thinker,** n = a speculative, philosophical —, *philosophus* (in this sense always in Cic), a deep —, *subtilis disputator*, *homo acu tus ad excogitandum* **thought,** n *cogitatio* (= the act of —, what we have been thinking of), *cogitatum* (= what we have been thinking about), *mens* (= disposition, then = opinion, view), *memo ria alcjs rei* (= memory), *sententia* (= opinion), † *sensus*, *-ūs*, *mens*, *animus* (= mind) *notio* (= notion), *opinio* (= opinion, founded upon conjec ture), *suspicio* (= conjecture as suspicion), *consil ium* (= view, plan), *conjectura* (= conjecture), *dic tum* (= — as expressed) , —s, *cogitata mentis* or by circumloc *quae mente concipimus*, *quae animo cogitamus*, *sentimus*, *versamus*, or often simply by the neut pl of the pron or adj (e g *ista tua*), to be in deep —, *in cogitatione defixum esse* **thoughtful,** adj *in cogitatione defixus* (= lost in thought), *sapiens*, *prudens* (= wise) Adv *sapienter*, *prudenter* **thoughtfulness,** n see THOUGHT **thoughtless,** adj *socors* (= who does not think), *stupidus* (= slow from stupi dity), *inconsultus*, *neglegens*, *indiligens* (= ne glectful), *imprudens* (= without foresight), *teme rarius* (= rash) Adv *inconsulte* (or *inconsulto*), *neglegenter*, *indiligenter*, *imprudenter* *temere* **thoughtlessness,** n *socordia* (= slowness to think), *stupiditas* (= stupidity habitual), *negle gentia*, *indiligentia* , see CARELESSNESS

third, adj see THREE

thirst, I n *sitis* (lit and fig) **II.** v intr *sitire* (also of plants, fields, etc), fig to — after, *sitire alqd* **thirsty,** adj *sitiens* (lit and fig , after, *alcjs rei*) Adv. *sitienter* (fig)

thirteen, adj *tredecim*, more frequently (always in Cic) *decem et tres* or *tres et decem* , — each, *terni deni* or *deni terni* , — times, *tredecie*(*n*)*s* **thirteenth,** adj *tertius decimus* or *decimus et tertius* **thirty,** adj *triginta* , — each, *triceni*, *-ae*, *-a*, — times, *tricie*(*n*)*s*, *tri gesie*(*n*)*s* **thirtieth,** adj *trigesimus* (*tric*), *-a*, *-um*

this, dem pron *hic*, *haec*, *hoc* (or *qui*, *quae*, *quod* at the beginning of a new sentence, if — refers to persons or things, in "and —, for —, but —, hence —, — therefore, now —," etc , the conjs are left out when we use *qui*) , — one, *hicce*, *haece*, *hocce* , — that, *alter* *alter* (of two), this that? *uter* *uter* (of two), *hic* *ille* or *iste* , on — side *cis*, *citra* , what is on — side, *citerior*

thistle, n *carduus*

thither, adv *eo*, *in eum locum*, *ad id loci*, *huc* (= hither), *illuc*, *illo*, *isthuc*, *isto* , hither and — *huc et* (*atque*) *illuc*

thong, n *lorum* , see STRAP

thorax, n *thorax* (Plin) , see CHEST

thorn, n *spina* (= — of plants, also — bush), *sentis*, *-is*, m and f , *vepres*, *-is*, m (= — bush), — bushes, *sentiecetum* (ante class), and in the pl in this sense, *vepres*, *sentes* (= hedge of —), *dume tum*, *dumi* (= a place full of brambles, a thicket) **thorny,** adj *spinosus* (lit , fig = of perplexed meaning), † *sentus* (= rough with thorns), *labori osus*, *arduus*, *aerumnosus* (fig) — paths, etc , of the Stoics, *dumeta Stoicorum* (Cic)

thorough, adj see COMPLETE Adv *penitus*, *prorsus*, *omnino*, *plane*, *funditus* , see COMPLETELY **thoroughbred,** adj *generosus*

thoroughfare, n by *transitus*, *-ūs*, *trans vectio* (= a passing through), *iter* (*pervium*), *via* (*pervia*, = road), or by the verbs *transire*, *trans vehi*

thou, pers pron *tu*, *tute* (emphatic)

though, conj see ALTHOUGH

thousand, adj *mille* (properly speaking a noun, not declined in the sing , but used only as nom or accus as a noun, it governs the genit (e g *mille passuum*) , but *mille* is also considered as an adj , which however is not declined), *mil*(*l*)*ia*, *-ium* , several —s, the pl of *mille*, and declined , with the cardinal or distributive numerals (e g 2,000, *duo* or *bina mil*(*l*)*ia* 10,000, *decem* or *dena mil*(*l*)*ia*), the noun in the genit (e g 30,000 armed men, *triginta mil*(*l*)*ia armato rum*), except when we say 3,300, and so on (e g *habuit tria mil*(*l*)*ia trecentos milites*) = innu merable, *mille* (= 1,000) or *sescenti* (*sexc* = 600 , both = immense) , a — times, *mil*(*l*)*ie*(*n*)*s* **thousandth,** adj *mil*(*l*)*esimus*

thraldom, n see SLAVERY, BONDAGE, SERVITUDE

thrash, v tr to — corn, *e spicis grana ex cutere* or *exterere*, *frumentum deterere* (Col), *messem perticis flagellare*, *spicas baculis excutere* (with long sticks) , = beat , see BEAT **thrashing,** n *tritura* **thrashing-floor,** n *area*, or more explicitly, *area in qua frumenta deteruntur* **thrashing-machine,** n *tribulum*

thread, I. n **1,** lit *filum*, *linea*, *linum*, *licium*, † *subtemen*, *stamen* , **2,** fig of a nar rative, *filum* (= quality, kind) better use *narratio* **II.** v tr to — a needle, *filum per acumen con*(*j*)*icere* , to — one's way , see GO **threadbare,** adj *obsoletus* (of clothes), *tritus* (of topics, etc)

threat, n (*com*)*minatio*, *denuntiatio* **threaten,** v tr *minas jacere*, to — anyone with, *alci alqd minitari*, (*com*)*minari*, *denuntiare alci alqd* (in words, e g war, murder), it —s to, etc , *in eo est ut*, etc , or by the periphrastic conjugation, with part fut act (e g *odia in novas pugnas erruptura sunt*) , to — = to be near at hand (of war, etc), (*im*)*minere*, *impendere*, *in stare*, *ingruere* (poet , and in Tac) **threatening,** adj *minax*, *minabundus* (lit of persons), *instans*, *imminens* (= near at hand, e g war, danger), *praesens* (= near, e g persecution, danger) Adv *minaciter*

three, adj. *tres, tria; trini, trinae, trina* (= three together); a period of — days, *triduum;* —fold, *triplex;* — footed, *tripes;* — hundred, *trecenti;* — thousand, *tria mil(l)ia.* **threefold, triple,** adj. *triplus, triplex, tripartitus (pert.) in tres partes divisus.* **thrice,** adj. *ter;* twice or —, *bis terque, iterum ac tertium;* — more, *triplo plus.* **third, I.** adj. *tertius;* a — time, *tertium, tertio;* in the — place, *tertio;* there is no — course, *nihil tertium est, nihil habet ista res medium.* Adv. *tertio.* **II.** n. *tertia pars;* heir to a —, *heres ex triente;* two —s, *e tribus duae partes, bes, bessis* (= two —s of a whole (e.g. the *as*) consisting of twelve parts, consequently 8-12ths or 2-3rds, e.g. *alqm relinquĕre heredem ex besse*).

threshold, n. *limen* (lit. and fig.).

thrift, n. *frugalitas, parsimonia.* **thrifty,** adj. *frugi, parcus.* Adv. *frugaliter, parce.*

thrill, I. v.tr. *commovēre.* **II.** v.intr. 1, of notes, *resonare;* see RESOUND; 2, — with joy, etc., *ex(s)ultare, (laetitia) gestire, efferri, commovēri.* **thrilling,** adj. 1, see SHRILL; 2, = exciting, *mirificus, mirus, horrendus;* see WONDERFUL.

thrive, v.intr. by *crescĕre;* see PROSPER.

throat, n. *jugulum, guttur;* to cut any one's —, *alqm jugulare.*

throb, I. v.intr. by *salire, palpitare;* see BEAT. **II.** n. *cordis palpitatio* (Plin.).

throe, n. *dolor.*

throne, n. *solium* (lit. = an elevated seat, — in gen., in particular = the royal —), *suggestus, -ūs* (= elevated seat, elevation in gen.), *sedes, -is,* f., or *sella regia* (lit. = the king's —), *regnum* (fig. = royal dignity, reign), *imperium* (fig. = the highest power); to sit on the —, *sedēre in solio* or *in sede regiā* (lit.), *regem esse, regnare* (fig. = to reign, to be king); to ascend the —, *regnum occupare* (fig.), *regnum* or *imperium adipisci* (= to come upon the —).

throng, I. n. *frequentia.* **II.** v.tr. *frequentare;* see CROWD.

throstle, n. *turdus.*

throttle, I. n. see WINDPIPE. **II.** v.tr. *suffocare, animam* or *spiritum intercludĕre.*

through, prep. *per* with accus. of place and time (e.g. *per tres dies,* or *tres dies* alone, = — three days; *per Africam,* = — Africa; *per te,* = — you); as denoting the instrument or means, it was — you (i.e. on account of), *propter te erat* or *te auctore;* — and —, *penitus, prorsus, omnino;* see ALTOGETHER. **throughout, I.** prep. see THROUGH. **II.** adv. see THROUGH AND THROUGH above; see BY.

throw, I. v.tr. *jacĕre, jactare* (repeatedly or constantly), *mittĕre* (= to let go), *con(j)icĕre* (= hurl), *in(j)icĕre* (= to — into) *alci rei* or *in alqd;* — anything at anyone, *petĕre alqm alqâ re* (e.g. *alqm malo*); to — stones at anyone, *lapides mittĕre* or *con(j)icĕre in alqm, lapidibus petĕre alqm, lapidibus alqm prosequi;* to — dice, *talos* or *tesseras jacĕre;* let the die be thrown (fig.), *jacta alea esto;* to — about, *jactare* (e.g. *tempestate jactari in alto*); to — anything, *spargĕre, dispergĕre;* to — across, *trans(j)icĕre alqd trans alqd* or double accus. (e.g. *exercitum (trans) Rhodanum*); to — a bridge across a river, *flumen ponte jungĕre;* to — away, *ab(j)icĕre;* to — oneself into, *se alci rei dedĕre, alci rei studēre;* to — open, *patefacĕre;* to — out; see REJECT, REMARK; to — up; see BUILD, VOMIT. **II.** n. *jactus, -ūs* (in gen. and of dice), *conjectus, -ūs* (in gen.), *alea* (= — of the dice, fig.), *missus, -ūs* (of stones, etc.). **thrower,** n. *jaculator.* **throwing,** n. † *confectio;* see THROW, II.

thrust, I. v.tr. see PUSH, DRIVE, PIERCE; to — oneself; see INTRUDE. **II.** n. *ictus, -ūs, plaga* (= blow), *petitio* (= attack).

thumb, I. n. *(digitus) pollex.* **II.** v.tr. *pollice terĕre.* **thumbscrew,** n. by circumloc. (e.g. to apply the —, *pollicem (pedem) contundere*).

thump, I. n. see BLOW. **II.** v.tr. see BEAT.

thunder, I. n. *tonitrus, -ūs, tonitruum, -i, fragor* (of any loud noise, e.g. *fragor caeli* or *caelestis*); fig. = noise, clamor, *sonitus, -ūs.* **II.** v.intr. *(in)tonare* (impers., trans., and intr.) also fig. of a strong voice). **thunder-bolt,** n. *fulmen;* struck by a —, *de caelo tactus.* **thunder-storm,** n. *tonitrua et fulmina, tempestas cum tonitribus.* **thunder-struck,** adj. *obstupefactus.*

Thursday, n. * *dies Jovis.*

thus, adv. *ita, sic* (in this manner); see So.

thwart, I. v.tr. see HINDER. **II.** n. *transtrum.*

thy, pron. *tuus;* see YOUR.

thyme, n. *thymum.*

tick, ticking, I. n. of a clock, *sonus* or *sonitus, -ūs (aequalibus intervallis factus).* **II.** v.intr. perhaps *tempus sonitu indicare, sonare.*

ticket, n. *tessera* (Suet.), probably the best word for a ticket for theatre, etc. (Admission to Roman theatres was free).

tickle, v.tr. *titillare alqd* (also fig. e.g. *sensus;* but Cic. always says *quasi titillare*); *quasi titillationem adhibēre alci rei* (e.g. *sensibus*); to — the palate, *palatum tergēre* (Hor., of anything we eat). **tickling,** n. *titillatio.* **ticklish,** adj. 1, lit. *titillationis minime patiens;* 2, fig. of persons; he is very — in that respect, *hac re facile offenditur;* of things, *lubricus et anceps.*

tide, n. 1, *aestus, -ūs (maritimus),* or in pl., *marinorum aestuum accessus et recessus* (both *-ūs*), *aestus maritimi mutuo accedentes et recedentes;* the — comes in twice every twenty-four hours, *bis affluunt bisque remeant aestus maris vicenis quaternisque semper horis* (Plin.); 2, fig. *mutatio* (= change), or by *crescĕre ac decrescĕre.* **tidal,** adj. *quod ad aestum pertinet;* — wave, *unda (aestu facta).*

tidings, n. *nuntius alcjs rei;* see NEWS.

tidy, adj. *nitidus;* see NEAT.

tie, I. v.tr. see BIND; to — a knot, *nodum facĕre, in nodum colligĕre.* **II.** n. 1, *nodus* (= knot), *vinculum;* 2, of friendship, etc., *vinculum, nodus, conjunctio, necessitudo* (also of kinship).

tier, n. *ordo, -inis,* m.; see ROW.

tiger, n. *tigris.*

tight, n. *strictus, a(d)strictus* (= fitting —), *angustus, artus* (= narrow); a — shoe, *calceus urens* (when it hurts); — rope, *funis contentus.* **tighten,** v.tr. *stringĕre, a(d)stringĕre* (e.g. chain, *vinculum;* a shoe, *calceum*), *intendĕre, contendĕre* (= to bend, draw —, what was loose before, e.g. *arcum intendĕre* or *contendĕre;* the skin, *cutem intendĕre*), comb. *contendĕre et adducĕre;* to — the reins, *habenas adducĕre* (opp. *remittĕre*). Adv. and **tightness,** n. use adj.

tile, n. *tegula, imbrex* (for roof), *tessera* (for paving).

till, I. prep. 1, to express the limit, *ad, usque ad* with accus. (= to a certain point), *in, usque in* with accus. (= about as far as), *tenus* with ablat. (put after the noun to fix the end): 2, as regards the time, *ad, usque ad, in, usque in;* — when? *quo usque* (continuing)? *quem ad finem* (= — what time)? — to-day, *usque ad* *ante diem, hodie quoque*, — to-morrow, *in crastinum*, — late at night, *ad multam noctem*, — daylight, *ad lucem* **II.** conj *dum, donec, quoad* (= as long as, but *quoad* defines the time more precisely); not —, *non prius quam, non ante quam*, see UNTIL.

till, v tr *arare* (= plough), *colĕre* (= cultivate), see CULTIVATE **tillage,** n *aratio, cultus, -ūs, cultura* **tiller,** n *arator* (= ploughman), *agricola, (agri)cultor*

till, n = money —, *arca* **tiller,** n *clavus*

tilt, n see COVER

tilt, I. v tr *invertĕre* **II** v intr = fight, by *hastis ex equis pugnare*, see TOURNAMENT

timber, n *materia* or *materies*, to fell —, *materiam caedĕre, materiari* (once in Caes)

time, I n 1, *tempus, ŏris*, n *dies* (= the day), *spatium* (= — as a period) †*aevum, intervallum* (= interval), *aetas* (= age), *tempestas* (= season), *saeculum* (= a long —, a generation), *otium* (= leisure), *occasio, opportunitas* (= opportunity), the most celebrated general of his —, *clarissimus imperator suae aetatis*, in our —, *nostrā memoriā*, at the right —, *tempore (tempori, temperi) ad tempus, tempestive, opportune, in tempore*, in ancient —s, *antiquitus*, from the — when, *ex quo (tempore)*, at every —, *omni tempore*, from — to —, *interdum* (= now and then), for all —, *in omne tempus*, in good —, *mature* (e g to rise *surgĕre*), against the —, *sub* or *ad tempus*, in the mean — *interea, interim*, according to — and circumstance, *pro tempore et pro re, ex re et tempore*, to require — for, *tempus postulare ad*, it is — to go, *tempus est ut eamus* or *ire*, eight —s eight, *octo octies multiplicata* 2, in music, *tempus, numerus, modus*, to beat —, *manu intervalla signare*, in —, *numerose* **II** v tr *tempus observare finem certo tempore alci rei imponere*. **timely, I** adj *maturus* (of fruits, etc, fig *aere maturus*, Verg), *tempestīvus, opportunus* **II.** adv *mature, tempestive, opportune* **timepiece,** n see CLOCK **time-server,** n *adulator, assentator* (= flatterer)

timid, adj *timidus, pavidus, trepidus, verecundus* (= bashful), *formidinis plenus* (= full of fear), *ignavus* (= cowardly), to be —, *timidum*, etc *esse, metuĕre, timēre*, don't be —, *omitte timorem* Adv *timide, pavide, trepide, verecunde, ignave* **timidity,** n *timiditas, pavor, trepidatio, ignavia* **timorous,** adj see TIMID

tin, n *plumbum album, stannum* (Plin)

tincture, n (in med) *liquor medicatus*, = a slight colouring, *color, fucus* (lit and fig)

tinge, v tr *imbuĕre, colorare, inficĕre, tingĕre alqd alqā re, alqd alci rei inducĕre*

tinder, n *fomes, -itis*, m

tingle, v intr 1, in the ears, *aures tinnire*, 2, see ITCH

tinker, n *a(h)enorum refector*

tinkle, v intr *tinnire*, see RESOUND **tinkling,** n †*tinnitus, -ūs*

tinsel, n 1 lit *bractea* (= metal leaf), — cloth, *pannus auro intextus*, 2, fig *fucus, species*

tip, I. n *cacumen, summa, ultima pars*, see POINT **II.** v tr *(prae)acuĕre* (= sharpen), *alqd alci rei praefigĕre*; — over, *invertere*, see OVERTURN **tiptoe,** n 1, lit *in digitos erecti* (from Quint), 2, fig *(ex(s)pectatione*, etc) *intentus*

tipple, v intr see DRINK **tippler,** n *potor*, see DRUNKARD **tipsy,** adj *temulentus, ebrius*. Adv *temulenter*, or by adj

tire, I. v tr. *(de)fatigare* **II.** v intr *(de)fatigari* **tired,** adj *(de)fatigatus, defessus, lassus, lassitudine confectus* **tiresome,** adj *importunus, molestus* (lit and fig), *lentus* (= slow) **tiring,** adj *quod (de)fatigat*, or by *laboriosus*, see LABORIOUS

tiro, n *tiro*, *rudis et tiro*

tissue, n 1, †*textus, -ūs*, see TEXTURE 2, fig *series*, or by *totus* (e g the thing is a — of falsehoods, *tota res e mendaciis constat*)

tit-bit, n *cup(p)edia, orum*, or *cup(p)ediae*

tithe, I. n *decuma, decima pars* **II.** v tr *decumas imponĕre*

title, n *titulus* (in gen), *inscriptio, index* (= — of a book), *nomen* (= name), hence comb *titulus nomenque* (Ov), *praescriptio* (= introduction to a senatorial decree, etc), to give a book a —, *inscribĕre librum*, a — (as an honour), *nomen, appellatio* (in addressing anyone), to give anyone a —, *algm appellare* with accus of the title (e g *regem*), = right, *vindiciae* see RIGHT **titled,** adj by birth, etc, *nobilis* **titular,** adj by *nomine*, opp to *re*

titter, v intr, see LAUGH

tittle, n *minima pars, aliquid ex alqa re*. **tittle-tattle,** n see CHATTER, GOSSIP

tittle, n to a —, by circumloc, e g by *subtiliter, acu* (e g *rem acu tetigisti*), *res ipsa*

to, prep (denoting motion towards) *ad* (in gen) *in* (= into) with accus (*ad eum locum profecta*, to go — that place, *ad algm venire*, to come — someone), with towns and small islands accus without *ad*, but not if *urbem, oppidum* be used in apposition with the name of the place, *ad* also with *usque* (e g *usque ad Romam profectus est*, he went (i e as far as) Rome), with *a, ab*, it denotes the extreme points of motion or distance (*Aquitania a Garumnā ad Pyraneos montes pertinet*, A extends from the Garonne — the Pyrenees), the direction of a word or speech (*invitare ad cenam*), limit in time (*Sophocles ad summam senectutem tragoedias fecit*, = Sophocles made tragedies down — extreme old age, *ad diem solvĕre*, = to pay — the day), — is properly the sign of the Latin dative (*mihi dedit librum*, = he gave a book — me, *mihi venit auxilio*, = he came — my aid), sometimes the force of — is given by the genit (*desiderium edendi*, = desire to eat), also by an infin (*me jussit ire*, = he commanded me — go), by the supine (*spectatum venit*, = he came — behold), or by the gerundive with *ad* (*profectus est ad ludos spectandos*, = he has gone — see the games), after *dignus*, worthy, use *qui* and the subj (*dignus est qui laudetur*, = he is worthy — be praised), = in order to, *ut* or *ne* with subj *In* with the accus properly means "into," denoting entrance (as *in domum intravit*, = he went into his house), but sometimes the idea of entrance or of penetration, is dropped, so that the Latin *in* corresponds with our — or till (e g *in aram confugit*, = he fled — the altar, *in eandem sententiam loquitur*, = he speaks — the same effect, *indulgens in* or *erga patrem, severus in filium*, = indulgent — [or towards] his father, severe — his son) Special phrases — my, thy house, *ad me, ad te*, — this or that place, *huc* or *illuc*, — the temple of Vestae, Jupiter, *ad Vestae, Jovis*, — the country, — home, *rus, domum*, to look — the west, *in occidentem spectare*, — a man, *ad unum*, to compare anyone — anyone, *algm cum algo comparare* **to-day, I.** n *hodiernus dies* **II.** adv *hodie* **to-morrow, I.** n *crastinus dies* **II.** adv *cras*

toad, n *būfo*, —stool, *fungus* **toady,** n and v.tr see FLATTER

toast, I. v tr 1, = scorch bread, *torrēre* 2, = drink health, *salutem alci propinare* **II.** n 1, *panis tostus*, 2, use verb, see above I 2

tobacco, n. *herba nicotiana*, = the plant, *tabacum* (as smoked).

toe, n. (*pedis*) *digitus*.

together, adv. *unâ* (*cum*), *simul*, comb. *unâ simul*, *eodem tempore simul*, *conjunctim*; all —, *ad unum omnes*, *cuncti*, *universi* (opp. *singuli*).

toil, I. n. *magnus labor*. II. v.intr. *multo sudore et labore facĕre alqd*; see LABOUR, WORK. **toilsome**, adj. *laboriosus*, *operosus*; see LABORIOUS, DIFFICULT. Adv. *laboriose*, *operose*.

toilet, n. *cultus*, -*ūs*, *ornatus*, -*ūs*; to make one's —, *se vestire*.

token, n. *signum*; see SIGN.

tolerable, adj. 1, = what can be tolerated, *tolerabilis*, *tolerandus*, *patibilis*; 2, = middling, *tolerabilis*, *mediocris*, *modicus*. Adv. *tolerabiliter*, *mediocriter*, *modice*, *satis* (= sufficiently). **tolerate**, v.tr. *tolerare*, *ferre*, with sense of acquiescence, *aequo animo ferre*; in religious matters, *aliena sacra alci permittĕre*; see BEAR; = to allow anything being done, *pati alqd fieri*, *sinĕre*, *permittĕre*. **tolerance**, n. *indulgentia* (= indulgence), *tolerantia*, *toleratio* (= bearing of anything); in matters of religion, *indulgentia erga sacra aliena*.

toll, n. *vectīgal* (in gen.), *portorium* (as excise duty, transit, at a —bar); — keeper, *exactor portorii*, *portitor*.

toll, v.intr. and tr. by *sonare*.

tomb, n. *sepulc(h)rum*, *tumulus* (lit. = mound). **tomb-stone**, n. *lapis*, -*ĭdis*, m., *cippus*, *monumentum*.

tome, n. *liber*; see BOOK.

ton, **tun**, n. as a vessel, *seria* (oval), *dolium* (round); as a measure, of liquids, *centum urnae* (liquid measure), perhaps *maximum pondus*, -*ĕris*, n. (in avoirdupois weight). **tonnage**, n. calculated by the number of *amphorae* (i.e. Roman cubic feet), e.g. *navis plus quam trecentarum amphorarum est*.

tone, n. 1, *sonus*, *sonitus*, -*ūs*, *vox* (from the mouth or a musical instrument); 2, fig. see CHARACTER.

tongs, n., fire —, *forceps*, m. and f.

tongue, n. *lingua* (also fig. = neck of land, language), *ligula* (= neck of land), *examen* (of a scale), *sermo* (= language).

tonic, n. *medicina quae stomachum corroborat*.

tonsils, n. *tonsillae*.

too, adv. *etiam*, *quoque*, *praeterea* (e.g. *unum etiam vos oro*, = one thing — I ask of you; *non sophistae solum*, *sed philosophi quoque*, = not the sophists only, but the philosophers —); — much, *nimium*, *nimio*; — great, *nimis magnus*; by comparative, he is — learned to have said that, *doctior est quam qui hoc dixerit*; to act — hastily, *festinantius agĕre*, *per imprudentiam facĕre alqd*.

tool, n. in sing. use special word (e.g. *rastrum*, = rake, gardener's —); pl. as collective, *instrumentum* (e.g. *rusticum*).

tooth, n. *dens*, -*ntis*, m. (in the mouth, also of an anchor); a hollow —, *dens cavus* or *cavatus* (Plin.); false —, *dentes empti* (Mart.); — ache, *dolor dentium*; to have —, *laborare ex dentibus*; —pick, *dentiscalpium* (Mart.); — powder, *dentifricium* (Plin.); —some, *dulcis*.

top, I. n. 1, *summus* with noun (e.g. *summus mons*); from — to toe, *totus*, or by adv. *penitus*, *omnino*, *prorsus* (= altogether); see SUMMIT; 2, a child's —, *turbo*. II. adj. *summus* (= highest); — heavy, *gravior* (= heavier than is right).

topaz, n. *topazius* or *chrysolithus* (Plin.).

toper, n. *potator*, *potor*.

topic, n. *argumentum*; see SUBJECT.

topography, n. *locorum descriptio*.

topsy-turvy, adv. to turn —, *omnia turbare et miscēre*.

torch, n. *fax*, *taeda* (= a piece of wood), *funale* (= wax candle).

torment, I. v.tr. (*ex*)*cruciare* (lit. and fig.), *torquēre* (lit. = to torture; then fig., both of man and of bodily and mental pain), *stimulare* (= to prick, then fig., e.g. of the conscience), *angĕre* (= to distress), *vexare* (= to let anyone have no rest and peace); to — anyone with questions, *alqm rogitando obtundĕre*. II. n. *cruciatus*, -*ūs* (lit. and fig.), *tormentum* (lit. = torture; then fig. excruciating pain, of body or mind), comb. *cruciatus et tormentum*, *doloris stimuli* (= excruciating pain). **tormentor**, n. *vexator* (fig.).

tornado, n. *turbo*.

torpedo, n. *torpēdo* (= the fish, and perhaps as t.t. for the explosive).

torpid, adj. *torpens* (lit. and fig.).

torpor, n. *torpor*.

torrent, n. *torrens*; — of rain, *imber torrentis modo effusus*; — of words, *flumen verborum*.

torrid, adj. *torridus*.

tortoise, n. *testudo*; — shell, *testudinis putamen* (Plin.), *testudinis testa* (Var.).

torture, I. n. *tormenta*, -*orum*, n. (lit. and fig., as a measure to compel prisoners to confess; then the instruments used for that purpose, such as *equuleus* (= rack); *cruciatus*, -*ūs* (of the pain suffered; also fig., e.g. of the conscience), *quaestio* (of slaves), *verbera*, -*um* (= lashes). II. v.tr. 1, lit. (*ex*)*torquēre*, *excarnificare* (rare), *in equuleum imponĕre*, (*ex*)*cruciare*; to — anyone at a trial, (*tormentis*) *quaerĕre de algo*, also *de alqâ re*; 2, fig. (*ex*)*cruciare*; see TORMENT. **torturer**, n. *tortor*, *carnifex* (= executioner).

toss, I. v.tr. *mittĕre*, *jaculari*, *jactare*; see THROW, HURL. II. n. *jactus*, -*ūs*, *jactatio*.

total, I. adj. *totus*, *cunctus*, *universus*, *omnis*. Adv. *omnino*, *plane*, *prorsus*, *funditus* (with verbs of destroying, etc.), *penitus* or by *totus* (e.g. *totus ex fraude factus*). II. n. *summa* (of a debt; also *in summâ exercitus tuendâ*, the whole, i.e. the main part of the army, Caes.), *solidum* (of a debt). **totality**, n. *universitas*, *summa* or by adj. TOTAL.

totter, v.intr. *labare*, † *nutare*, *vacillare* (to vacillate), *titubare* (like one that is drunk, asleep, etc.).

touch, I. v.tr. 1, lit. *tangĕre*, *attingĕre*, *contingĕre* (all three also = to border, of countries, etc.); 2, fig. = affect, (*com*)*movēre*, *alqm dolore*, etc., *afficĕre*; = relate to, *pertinēre ad*; — at (of a ship), (*navem*) *appellĕre*, *appelli ad* or *in*; to — upon, *leviter tangĕre*, *breviter* or *strictim attingĕre*, *breviter perstringĕre*. II. n. *tactio*, *tactus*, -*ūs* (= the act or sense); fig. a — of art, etc., perhaps *aliquid*, with gen. of noun. **touching**, I. adj. *animum* (*com*)*movens*, *miserationem* or *misericordiam movens*. II. prep. *de*; see CONCERNING. **touchstone**, n. *cōticula*, *lapis Lydius* (Plin.); fig. *obrussa* (= test, whether anything is first-proof). **touchy**, adj. *mollis ad accipiendam offensionem* (e.g. *animus*, Cic.), *irritabilis* (= irritable), *iracundus*.

tough, adj. *lentus* (lit. and fig.). **toughness**, n. *lentitia*.

tour, n. *iter*, *itinĕris*, n.; to make —, etc., *iter facĕre*. **tourist**, n. see TRAVELLER.

tournament, n. by *certamen equitum hastis concurrentium*

tow, n *stuppa*

tow, v tr *trahĕre*, to — line, *funis*, -is

toward, I. prep *ad*, *in*, *versus* (always after its noun) with accus (e g *ad orientem*, — the east, *Brundisium versus*), also *adversus* (e g *adversus montem*, = [motion] — the mountain), to go — anyone *obviam ire alci*, with a wider application of the idea of direction, denoting dispositions, inclinations, etc , as, — a person, *adversus*, *erga*, *in* with accus (*est enim pietas justitia adversus deos*, = piety is justice — the gods), genit merely (*caritas patriae*, = love — one's native land), *ad meridiem*, = — midday, *sub vesperum*, = — evening **II.** adj see DOCILE, OBEDIENT

towel, n *mantēle* (*mantile*)

tower, I. n *turris*, a — of strength, fig , *arx* or *praesidium* **II** v intr *ex algo loco eminēre*, *exstare*, to — over, *alci loco imminēre*, to be in a —ing rage, *iracundiā efferri*

town, I. n *urbs* (also = capital, more particularly Rome itself), *oppidum*, *municipium* (= a free city, esp in Italy), —'s people, *oppidani*, — hall, *curia*, —ship, *urbis ager* **II.** adj *urbanus*

toy, I. n see PLAYTHING, = trifles, *nugae* **II.** v intr see PLAY

trace, I. n *vestigium*, *indicium* (= sign) in the pl comb *indicia et vestigia* (e g *veneni*), *significatio alcjs rei* (= indication, e g *timoris*) **II.** v tr 1, = to draw, mark out, *delineare*, *designare* (with the pencil, *des* also fig *verbis*), *describĕre* (with the pencil or pen), *adumbrare* (= to shadow out), 2, = to follow by footsteps, (*odore*) *persequi algm* or *algd* (lit of dogs, etc , then of men), *odorari* (lit and fig), *indagare* or *investigare algd* (lit and fig) **tracer,** n *investigator* (fem *investigatrix*, late), *indagator* **tracing,** n *investigatio*, *indagatio* **track, I.** n 1, see PATH , 2, see TRACE **II** v tr *alcjs* or *alcjs rei vestigia persequi*, also *persequi algm* or *algd*, see TRACE

tract, n **I.** *spatium* (= space in gen), *tractus*, -ūs (= district), see REGION, DISTRICT, **II.** = treatise, *libellus* **tractable,** adj *tractabilis*, *docilis*, *obsequens*, *obsequiosus*, *obediens facilis* (= willing) Adv *obsequenter*, *obedienter* **tractableness,** n *obsequium*, *obedientia*, *docilitas*, *facilitas*, *obsequium*

trade, I. n 1, see COMMERCE , 2, = the business anyone has learnt, *ars* (= art, also any mechanical skill, as in Liv of the — of a butcher), *artificium* , *ars operosa* (= an art which produces something), *negotium servile* (of the lower —s, e g of a shoemaker, smith, etc , and which were carried on by slaves), *ars sordida*, *quaestus*, -ūs *sordidus* (inasmuch as the lower trades and the gains made by them were considered below the dignity of a free Roman and of the patricians, opp *ars liberalis*) **II.** v tr *rem gerĕre et lucrum facĕre* (= to do a good —, Plaut), *mercaturam* or (of several) *mercaturas facĕre* (as a merchant, more esp wholesale), *negotiari* (of a money lender, banker, corn-dealer, etc) **tradesman, trader,** n. *caupo* (= huckster), see MERCHANT

tradition, n *traditio* (= handing over, down , in the sense of "handing down by verbal —," by *memoria* [= remembrance in gen), *lit(t)erae* (in writing), *sermo* or *fama* (oral) **traditional, traditionary,** adj *posteris traditus* or *proditus* (in gen), *lit(t)eris custoditus* (in writing).

traduce, v tr see SLANDER

traffic, I. n *commercium*, see COMMERCE **II.** v intr *mercaturam facĕre*, see TRADE

tragedy, n **1,** *tragoedia* , to perform a —, *tragoediam agĕre*, **2,** fig *casus*, -ūs **tragedian,** n = tragic actor, *tragoedus*, *tragicus actor* **tragic,** adj *tragicus* , in a — manner, *tragico more* , fig *tristis* (= sad), *luctuōsus* (= mournful, e g *exitium*), *miserabilis* (= wretched, e g *aspectus*), *atrox* (= frightful, e g *res*, event) Adv *tragice*, *miserabiliter*, *atrociter* **tragicomedy,** n *tragicomoedia*

train, I. v tr **1,** see DRAW , **2,** = to educate, (*e*)*docēre*, *instituĕre*, to — soldiers or athletes, *exercēre*, see EDUCATE **II** n **1,** of a gown, etc , *syrma*, *atis*, n (= robe with —), or by *quod trahitur*, *quod verrit terram* (= sweeping the ground, of long dresses), **2,** = procession, *pompa*, **3,** = series, *ordo*, *series* **trainer,** n of horses *equorum domitor* , of athletes, *magister* (*gladiatorum magister*, Cic) **training,** n *disciplina* (in the widest sense); in war, *militiae* or *militaris disciplina*, in law, *juris civilis discip* , in philosophy, *philosophiae discip* *exercitatio* (= exercise, both physical and other, e g *exerc dicendi*, in speaking), see EDUCATION

trait, n **1,** = a touch, *linea* (e g *primis solut lineis algd designare*), **2,** in a person's character, by adjs , an excellent —, *praeclarum* (e g *praec hoc quoque Thrasybuli*), or by *proprius*, followed by genit (e g *quod oratoris proprium est*), or by genit and *est* (e g *sapientis est*, = it is the — of a wise man)

traitor, n *proditor*, *majestatis* or *perduellionis reus* (= one accused of high treason) **traitorous,** adj see TREACHEROUS

trammel, n and v tr see FETTER

tramp, I. v intr see TRAVEL, WALK **II.** n **1,** *iter* (= journey), **2,** *grassator* (= foot pad).

trample, v tr and intr (*pedibus*) (*con*)*culcare algd* , fig to — under foot, *deridēre* (= to turn into ridicule, persons or things, e g religion, *res divinas*), *opprimĕre*, see TREAD, DESPISE, OPPRESS

trance, n *secessus*, -ūs *mentis et animi a corpore*, *animus a corpore abstractus*

tranquil, adj *tranquillus* **tranquillity,** n *tranquillitas* (lit and fig), see QUIET, CALM **tranquillize,** v tr *tranquillare*

transact, v tr business, *rem gerĕre*, *agĕre*, *transigĕre*, see DO **transaction,** n *res*, *negotium* , see BUSINESS

transcend, v tr *praestare alci alqa re*, (*or*) *superare algm*, *excellĕre alci* (*in alqā re*) or *inter alqos* , see EXCEL , SURPASS **transcendent,** adj *praestans*, *singularis*, *eximius* , see EXCELLENT **transcendental,** adj *quod sensu* or *sensibus percipi non potest*, *quod sub sensus non cadit*, *quod sensibus non subjectum est*

transcribe, v tr *transcribĕre* , see COPY **transcript,** n *exemplum* (= copy)

transfer, I. v tr *tra(ns)(j)icĕre*, (lit *legiones in Siciliam*), *tra(ns)ducĕre* (lit), *transportare* (lit), *transferre in* with accus (lit *bellum in Italiam*, then = to translate into another tongue, e g *ex Graeco in Latinum* , then = to use in a fig sense, e g a word *verbum*, = to put on another, e g *culpam in algm*), *transmittĕre in* with accus (= to send over, across as it were e g the war into Italy), *transfundĕre in* or *ad* with accus (= to pour out of one vessel into another, e g *amorem in algm*, *omnes suas laudes ad algm*) , = to make over as a right, (*con*)*cedĕre algd alci*, *transcribĕre algd*, to anyone, *alci* (in writing, Jct) , to — a part of *cedĕre alci algd de alqa re* **II.** n *translatio* (= the act of —ing) *mancipium* (of property).

transferable, adj. *quod in alqm concedĕre licet.* **transference,** n. *tra(ns)latio.*

transfiguration, n. *transfiguratio* (Eccl.). **transfigure,** v.tr. *(com)mutare;* his countenance was —d at these words, *quibus dictis ejus facies serenior facta est; transfigurare* (Eccl.).

transfix, v.tr. 1, *transfigĕre, (con)fodĕre;* 2, fig. *defigĕre (alqm gladio).*

transform, v.tr. *totum denuo fingĕre* (lit. = to form anew); to — into *transformare in alqm* or *in aliud, (con)vertĕre in alqm* or *alqd* (e.g. *in eancm*), *(com)mutare;* see CHANGE. **transformation,** n. use verb.

transfuse, v.tr. *transfundĕre.* **transfusion,** by the verb.

transgress, I. v.tr. *transcendĕre* (e.g. *jus gentium, morem*), *violare* (e.g. *foedus, jus gentium*). II. v.intr. *ab officio discedĕre, alqd contra leges facĕre.* **transgression,** n. *violatio* with gen. (= the act of —, e.g. *juris gentium, foederis*), *peccatum, delictum* (= fault, etc.); see CRIME, FAULT. **transgressor,** n. *violator alcjs rei,* or by verb; see also CRIMINAL.

transient, adj. *brevis, fugax, caducus, instabilis, mutabilis, fluxus, incertus.* **transit,** n. *transitus, -ūs* (in gen. = the best word for — of a planet); goods for —, *merces ad alios populos transeuntes;* — duty, *portorium;* — in a general sense, see PASSAGE. **transition,** n. *transitio* (from one party to another, etc.), *transitus, -ūs* (lit., and in Quint. fig. of words, etc.), *transgressio* (lit. rare), *trajectio, tra(ns)jectus, -ūs* (lit.). **transitive,** adj. in gram., a — verb, *verbum transitivum.* **transitory,** adj. see TRANSIENT.

translate, v.tr. into another language, *(con)vertĕre* (in gen.), *transferre* (word for word, Quint.), *reddĕre* (= to render accurately), *interpretari* (= to interpret); to — into Latin, *in Latinum (con)vertĕre, Latine reddĕre;* lit., faithfully, exactly, *verbum e verbo* or *de verbo exprimĕre, verbum pro verbo reddĕre.* **translation,** n. *liber scriptoris conversus* or *tra(ns)latus;* — of a speech, *oratio conversa.* **translator,** n. *interpres, -ĕtis,* m. and f.

translucent, adj. *pellucidus;* see TRANSPARENT.

transmarine, adj. *transmarinus.*

transmigration, n. by circumloc. (e.g. — of souls, *animarum in nova corpora (quasi) migratio*).

transmit, v.tr. *mittĕre alci* or *ad alqm.* **transmission,** n. *missio,* or by verb.

transmute, v.tr. see CHANGE.

transom, n. *lignum transversum* or *transversarium, transtrum.*

transparent, adj. 1, *pellucidus, tra(ns)lucidus, perspicuus;* to be —, *pellucēre, lucem transmittĕre;* 2, fig. *evidens, manifestus;* see CLEAR. Adv. *evidenter, sine dubio, manifeste.* **transparency,** n. *vitri pelluciditas* (Vitr.), *perspicuitas.*

transpire, v.intr. 1, *exhalari, emanare;* 2, = to escape from secrecy, *(di)vulgari, pervulgari, efferri (foras* or *in vulgus), percrebrescĕre.*

transplant, v.tr. *transferre* (= to remove persons and things elsewhere, e.g. *omnes nobiles familias Romam;* also plants, e.g. *brassicam*), *tra(ns)ducĕre* (e.g. *populum Albanum Romam, gentem in Galliam*). **transplantation,** n. *tra(ns)latio.*

transport, I. v.tr. 1, *transportare* (by land and by water, persons and things), *transferre* (= to bring across, things), *transmittĕre, tra(ns)jicĕre* (= to send across the water, persons and things); = to send to penal settlement, *relegare;* see BANISH; 2, fig. to be —ed (with delight, etc.), *efferri, ex(s)ultare,* or by special verb (e.g. *gaudēre*). II. n. 1, *navigium vectorium, navicula vectoria* (= a ship for crossing), *navis oneraria* (= ship of burden); 2, *animus gaudio* or *laetitiā gestiens;* see RAPTURE. **transportation,** n. 1, by verb; 2, see BANISHMENT.

transpose, v.tr. *transmutare* (e.g. words, letters, Quint.). **transposition,** n. *tra(ns)jectio* (of words), *transmutatio* (Quint.).

transubstantiation, n. by *transubstantiatio* (Eccl.).

transverse, adj. *transversus, transversarius* (lying across). Adv. *transverse, e transverso.*

trap, I. n. *muscipulum* or *muscipula* (Phaed., mouse- —), *laqueus* (= noose, —, lit. and fig.); see SNARE. II. v.tr. *irretire* (lit. and fig.); see ENSNARE. **trap-door,** n. *(parva) janua.* **trappings,** n. *ornamentum, ornatus, -ūs, equorum* (in gen.), *phalerae* (= horses' head and neck ornaments).

trash, n. 1, *quisquiliae* (= sweepings), *viles* or *vilissimae res;* see WASTE; 2, = nonsense, *gerrae, nugae.* **trashy,** adj. see WORTHLESS.

travail, I. v.tr. *parturire.* II. n. *dolor quem in puerperio alqs perpetitur,* in the context simply *dolores* (Ter.); in —, by *parturire.*

travel, I. v.tr. *iter facĕre* (in gen.), *peregrinari* (abroad), *proficisci in* or *ad* or *circa, obire, circumire* (with accus.), *peragrare, perlustrare.* II. n. *iter, itineris,* n. (in gen.), *peregrinatio* (abroad). **traveller,** n. *iter faciens, viator* (= wanderer on foot), *vector* (= passenger on board a vessel), *peregrinator, peregrinans* (= one who travels or resides abroad).

traverse, v.tr. 1, see CROSS; 2, = to wander over, *pervagari* (intentionally), *obire,* † *pererrare* (without a defined purpose), *peragrare, lustrare, perlustrare.*

travesty, n. see PARODY.

tray, n. *ferculum.*

treacherous, adj. *perfidus, perfidiosus, infidēlis, infidus, fallax, dolosus* (= cunning), *subdolus* (in a bad sense, = sly). Adv. *perfidiose, dolose;* see FAITHLESS. **treachery,** n. *proditio* (= betrayal of a town, etc.: also *amicitiarum,* Cic.), *perfidia, fraus, -dis,* f., *dolus (malus), infidēlitas.*

treacle, n. *condimentum ex saccharo factum.*

tread, I. v.intr. *ingredi;* to — in the footsteps of anyone, *alcjs vestigiis ingredi;* see WALK. II. v.tr. to — upon, *calcare;* to — under foot, fig. *obterĕre (et calcare)* (e.g. *libertatem*), *conculcare, proculcare* (lit. = to trample down; then fig., e.g. *senatum, Italiam*). III. n. *(in)gressus, -ūs, vestigium, pēs, pĕdis,* m.; trodden path, *via trita.*

treason, n. *majestas, majestatis (laesae* or *minutae) crimen;* to commit —, *majestatem minuĕre* or *laedĕre.* **treasonable,** adj., adv. by circumloc. with *majestas* (e.g. accused of treason, *laesae majestatis accusatus*).

treasure, I. n. *thesaurus, gaza* (lit. = treasury of the Persian king, then of any foreign prince), *opes, -um, divitiae* (= riches), *copia* (= quantity, store). II. v.tr. *accumulare, coacervare* (= to heap up money, —s), *condĕre, reponĕre* (= to store). **treasure-house,** n. *thesaurus.* **treasurer,** n. *praefectus aerarii* (Plin.). **treasury,** n. *aerarium.*

treat, I. v.tr. = to be engaged in anything, *tractare alqm* or *alqd, curare alqm* or *alqd* (= to attend to), *disputare, disserĕre de alqā re, prosequi alqd* (on a learned subject); to — a case (of illness), *curare morbum*, to — a patient, *alqm tractare, curare*, = to behave towards anyone, *alqm habēre, alqd re afficĕre, alqo uti*, to — well, ill, etc, *bene, male*, etc, to — as an enemy, (*in*) *hostium numero habēre alqm, pro hoste habēre* or *ducĕre alqm*, = to entertain, *invitare* (in gen), see ENTERTAIN **II.** v intr to — with (= to negotiate), *agĕre cum alqo de alqâ re* **III.** n *delectatio* (= delight), *spectaculum* (= a show), to give anyone a —, perhaps *alqm (delectandi causâ) invitare*, see ENTERTAINMENT **treatise,** n *disputatio, dissertatio* (on a learned topic, class only of oral discussion), *liber, libellus* (= the book in which a subject is treated) **treatment,** n *tractatio, curatio* (= attending to), kind —, *comitas, humanitas*, cruel, unkind —, *saevitia*, mode of —, *tractatio, curatio* **treaty,** n *pactio, pactum* (= a legal contract between two contending parties, *pactio* as act, *pactum* = what has been stipulated), *conventio, conventus, -ūs* (= agreed upon, although not legally binding), *sponsio* (= a — of peace or alliance concluded between the generals of two belligerent States, but as yet without the sanction of the latter), *foedus ĕris*, n (= alliance sanctioned by the senate and the people), according to the —, *ex pacto, ex convento* (Cic) *conventu*, comb *ex pacto et convento* to conclude a — with, *facĕre* or *inire, icĕre ferire* or *pangĕre*, to break a —, *foedus violare, rumpĕre*

treble, I. adj 1, see THREE, TRIPLE, 2, — voice, *vox* † *summa* or *acuta* **II.** v tr *alqd triplex facĕre*

tree, n *arbor*, f, apple- —, pear- —, etc, *malus*, f, *pirus*, f, etc, see under name of special fruit, 2, see PEDIGREE

trefoil, n *trifolium* (Plin)

trellis, n see LATTICE

tremble, v intr *tremĕre* (in gen), *contremiscĕre intremiscĕre* (all these, with fright, and both of persons and things), *micare* (= to have a tremulous motion, like flames, e g of the veins), *vacillare* (= to shake), *horrēre* (= to shudder with cold, fear, of persons), to — for fear of anything, *tremĕre alqd* (e g *virgas ac secures dictatoris*), *contremiscĕre alqd* (e g *vincula*), *extimescĕre alqd* (e g *periculum*), to cause to —, *alqd tremefacĕre* **trembling, I.** adj *tremens, tremebundus* (= a single case), *tremulus* (= constantly) **II.** n *tremor*, with —, *tremens*, without —, *intrepide*

tremendous, adj 1, *terribilis*, see TERRIBLE, 2, *ingens, immanis* Adv *valde, vehementer, magnopere, maxime*

tremulous, adj see TREMBLING, I

trench, I. n *fossa*, see DITCH **II.** v tr *fossam fodĕre* or *facĕre*, to — upon, see ENCROACH

trencher, n see PLATE

trepan, I. n *modiolus* (Cels) **II.** v tr *calvariam* or *os capitis modiolo perforare*

trespass, I. v intr, lit *in alienum fundum ingredi* (Jct), fig, see TRANSGRESS **II.** n 1, lit use verb, 2, fig *alcjs rei violatio* (the act), *injuria alci rei illata* (as a fact), see TRANSGRESS **trespasser,** n lit *qui in alienum fundum ingreditur*, fig *alcjs rei violator*

tress, n *comae* (= hair)

trial, n *tentatio* (*tempt*), *experimentum, experientia* (= the experience gained by the — one has made), *periclitatio* (with a risk), *periculum* (= experience gained with respect to anything, even with attending danger), *conatus ūs* (= attempt), to make a —, *periculum facĕre alcjs rei*, — in law, *judicium, interrogatio* (= examination in court, e g of a witness), *quaestio* (as a whole), put on his —, *alqm postulare* or *accusare alcjs rei* **try,** v tr *tentare* (= to — to find a thing out, what it is, etc), *experiri* (= to see how it answers, as the result of *tentare*), *periclitari* (with a risk, all the foregoing *alqm* or *alqd*), *periculum facĕre alcjs* or *alcjs rei*, *explorare* (= to examine, to explore), *gustatu explorare alqd* (by tasting wine etc), = to attempt, *tentare* (*tempt-*), *conari* (generally with inf), with respect to the beginning of an undertaking), (*e*)*niti ut* or *ne*, in law, to — a case, *judicare, cognoscĕre* or *quaerĕre de alqâ re* **tried,** adj *spectatus, cognitus, probatus*, comb *spectatus et probatus* **trying,** adj *gravis, molestus*, see TROUBLESOME

triangle, n *trigōnum, triangulum* **triangular,** adj *triangulus, triquetrus* (= three-sided)

tribe, n 1, *tribus, -ūs*, f (= a division of the people among the Romans), by tribes, *tributim*, fellow —sman, *tribulis*, 2, in wider sense, *gens, populus*, see NATION **tribal,** adj by genit of *tribus, -ūs*, or *gens*

tribulation, n *miseria, res miserae* or *afflictae*, see TROUBLE

tribunal, n 1, *tribunal* (= platform for the magistrates in the forum, e g in Rome for the praetor), 2, *judicium* (= COURT, which see), to summon anyone before a —, *alqm in judicium vocare*

tribune, n *tribunus militum* or *militaris* (= military —), *tribunus plebis* (of the people) **tribuneship,** n *tribunatus, -ūs, tribunicia potestas*

tribute, n *tributum, vectigal* (often in kind), *stipendium* (in money) **tributary, I** adj *vectigalis* (= paying taxes), *tributarius* (= paying poll and land tax), *stipendiarius* (= paying a certain sum annually, of persons, more particularly of States that pay —) **II.** n — of a river, by circumloc (e g a — of the Rhone, *flumen quod in Rhodanum influit*)

trick, I n *dolus* (= cunning), *fraus* (= deception), *ars, artificium* (= artifice), *machina* (= stratagem), *techna* (Com) all manner of —s, *astutiae*, conjuror's —, *praestigiae*, to play anyone a —, *dolum alci nectĕre* **II.** v tr and intr see DECEIVE, DECEPTION **trickery,** n *fallacia*, see DECEPTION **trickish,** adj *versutus*

trickle, v intr *manare*, † *rorare*, *stillare alqâ re*

trident, n *tridens*

triennial, adj † *trietĕricus* **triennium,** n *triennium*

trifle, I. n *res parva* or *parvula, res minuta, munusculum* (= a small present), *res parvi momenti* (= a matter, thing of trifling importance), often also by the adjs *parvus, lĕvis, perlevis*, —s, *res parvae* or *minutae, nugae* (the latter also of insignificant —), to buy anything for a —, *parvo* or *vili emĕre* **II.** v intr *lascīvire* (= to play), *nugari* (= to talk nonsense), *ludĕre* (= to play, to frolic), *ineptire* (= to play the fool), to — opp to act seriously, *alqd neglegĕre* **trifler,** n *nugator* **trifling, I** adj *lĕvis, parvus*, see UNIMPORTANT **II.** n *lascivia* (= playfulness), *nugae, ineptiae* (= absurdities), *ludus* (= game)

trigonometry, n **trigonometria* (as t t not class)

trilateral, adj *tribus lateribus*

trill, I. n perhaps *vox* or *sonus vibrans* (Plin) **II.** v tr the voice in singing, *vibrissare* (late)

trim, I. adj see NEAT **II** v tr in gen *alqd curare* (= to put in due order), = to decorate the body, etc, (*ex*)*ornare* (e g *variâ veste*) to — the hair *recidĕre* (= to lop off what is too long, e g *capillos*), (*de*)*tondēre* (= to cut off, shave, e g the hair, hedges, etc.); to — trees, *arbores (am-)putare*; to — timber, etc. (in carpentry) *(ascia) dolare, ascia polire*; to — the sails, *vela facĕre, vela pandĕre*. **III.** v.intr. in politics, *consilia mutare*, or *fortunae inservire*. **IV.** n. **1**, see DRESS, ORNAMENT; **2**, of a ship, perhaps by *navis suis ponderibus librata*. **trimmer,** n. *qui consilia mutat*. **trimming,** n. *clavus* (= a stripe of purple on the robes of the senators and equites), *ornatus, -ūs, ornamentum* (= ornament). **trimeter,** n. *versus (-ūs) trimetrus (trimetros)*.

Trinity, n. * *trinitas* (Eccl.). **Trinitarian,** n. *qui triplicem Dei naturam esse dicit*.

trinket, n. *an(n)ulus* (= ring), *torques, -is*, m. and f. (= necklace), or by other special noun; in pl. *mundus (muliebris)* collectively.

trio, n. = three together, *tres, tria*; in music, *concentus (-ūs) trium vocum*.

trip, I. v.intr. **1**, *offendĕre*; **2**, fig. *errare, labi, labi et cadĕre, offendĕre*; to — along, *celeriter ire*. **II.** v.tr. *supplantare alqm*. **III.** n. **1**, see STUMBLE; **2**, ERROR; **3**, = a journey, *iter*; see JOURNEY, EXCURSION.

tripartite, adj. *tripartītus (triper-)*.

tripe, n. *omāsum* (= the thick fat intestines of a bullock, Schol. Hor. Ep.), *omentum porci* (Juv.).

triple, adj. *triplex*; see under THREE.

tripod, n. *tripus*.

trireme, n. *(navis) trirēmis*.

trisyllable, n. *trisyllăbum verbum*.

trite, adj. (= often repeated, worn), *(con)trītus, communis, communis et contritus*.

triumph, I. n. **1**, in honour of a Roman victory, *triumphus*; to celebrate a —, *triumphare, triumphum agĕre* or *habēre, ovare* (if inferior to a —); to celebrate a — over anybody or over a people, *de alqo* or *ex alqā terrā triumphare*; **2**, fig. *victoria* (= a victory), *ex(s)ultatio, laetitia, gaudium* (= joy). **II.** v.intr. **1**, *triumphare, triumphum agĕre* or *habēre, ovare* (of a lesser triumph), over, *de alqo*; **2**, fig. *ex(s)ultare, laetari*; over anyone, *vincĕre alqm*. **triumphal,** adj. **1**, = belonging to a Roman triumph, *triumphalis*; — procession, *triumphus*; in a —, *in triumpho, per triumphum, triumphans*; **2**, fig. or **triumphant,** = victorious, *victor*; = in high spirits, *gestiens, elatus, ex(s)ultans*.

triumvir, n. *triumvir*. **triumvirate,** n. *triumviratus, -ūs*.

trivial, adj. by *(con)trītus, communis, lĕvis, parvi momenti*; see TRIFLING. **triviality,** n. by adj.

trochee, n. *trochaeus*.

troop, I. n. *caterva, grex*; —s, *globus, manus, copiae, milites, manus, -ūs*, f., *ala* (of horse), *cohors* (= cohort). **II.** v.intr. *convenire, coire, confluĕre*. **trooper,** n. *eques, -itis*, m.; see CAVALRY, HORSE.

trope, n. *verbum tra(ns)latum, verbi tra(ns)latio, tropus* (Quint.).

trophy, n. **1**, *tropaeum*; **2**, fig. see MEMORIAL.

tropical, adj. **1**, = fig. *tra(ns)latus*; **2**, = belonging to the Tropics, by genit. of noun; see TROPIC; — heat, *aestus, -ūs, ardentissimus*. **tropic,** n. in astronomy, *circulus, orbis*, m.; — of Cancer, *circulus solstitialis*; of Capricorn, *circulus brumalis*; the —s, = very hot countries, *regiones torridae*.

trot, I. v.tr. *citato gradu* or perhaps *tolutim ire* (of a horse), *citato equo vehi* (of the rider). **II.** n. *gradus, -ūs, citatus, gradus tolutilis*.

troth, n. *fides*; to plight —, *fidem alci dare*.

troubadour, n. *poeta amatorius* (as poet), *citharoedus* (as singer).

trouble, I. v.tr. *agitare* (= to set in motion, e.g. water, wind; hence of the mind, to torment), *exagitare* (= to drive from one place to another, neighbours, the State, also of the conscience), *commovēre* (= to disturb), *(con)turbare, perturbare* (= to confuse anyone, or anyone's mind); = to afflict, *sol(l)icitare, sol(l)icitum habēre, so(l)licitudine* or *aegritudine afficĕre, sol(l)icitudinem* or *aegritudinem alci afferre, alqm vexare, angĕre, excruciare alcjs animum et sol(l)icitare*; may I — you to hand me this book, *des mihi, quaeso, hunc librum*; to — oneself about anything, *alqd curare*; not to — about anything, *alqd neglegĕre*; to — anyone with entreaties, *alqm precibus obtundĕre* or *fatigare*. **II.** n. **1**, = disturbance of mind, *animi motus, -ūs, perturbatio, so(l)licitudo* (= painful anxiety), *angor* (= anxiety, anguish); **2**, = molestation, *labor, molestia, onus, -ĕris* (= burden), *incommodum* (= inconvenience), *difficultas* (= difficulty); see ANNOYANCE; to give — to, *molestiam alci afferre*: see under I.; **3**, = pains, *opera*; to take — over anything, *alci rei operam dare*; great —, *omnibus viribus contendĕre ut*; with great —, *aegre, vix*; without —, *sine negotio*. **troubler,** n. *turbator*, or by verb. **troublesome,** adj. *molestus, gravis* (= giving great trouble), *incommodus, iniquus* (= inconvenient), *durus* (= hard), *operosus, laboriosus* (= laborious), *odiosus* (of what we hate), *difficilis* (of what has its difficulties), comb. *gravis et incommodus, gravis et odiosus, laboriosus molestusque, odiosus et molestus*.

trough, n. *alveus*.

trousers, n. *brac(c)ae*.

trowel, n. *trulla* (late, but *trullissare*, = to use a —, Vitr.).

truant, adj. and n. by *qui ludo lit(t)erarum abest*.

truce, n. *indutiae*.

truck, n. **1**, = barter, *(per)mutatio rerum*; **2**, see BARROW.

truckle, v.intr. *morem alci gerĕre* (= to please), *alci assentire*.

trudge, v.intr. see WALK.

true, adv. *vērus*; *sincērus, germanus* (the two foregoing = genuine), comb. *verus et sincerus, verax* (= veracious), *fidus, fidēlis* (= faithful): in answers, — ! *certe*; see YES; as — as I live, I know, *ita vivam, ut scio*; as — as I live, I don't know, *ne vivam si scio*. Adv. *vere, sincere, profecto* (= certainly), *sane, certe, certe quidem*; see REALLY. **trueborn, truebred,** adj. (e.g. Englishman), *verus et sincerus* (e.g. *Stoicus*), *germanus*. **truehearted,** adj. *fidēlis, simplex*. **trueheartedness,** n. *(animi) fidēlitas, simplicitas*. **truth,** n. *vēritas* (as quality), *vērum* (= what is —); to speak —, *verum, vera dicĕre*; strict —, *summa veritas*; historical —, *historiae fides* (Ov.); according to —, *ex re*; in —, *vero, sine dubio, profecto, plane, enimvero*, or as two words, *enim vero*; see INDEED, REALLY. **truthful,** adj. *verus, verax, veridicus* (rare). Adv. see IN TRUTH above. **truthfulness,** n. *veritas, veritatis studium* or *amor*.

trump, v.tr. and n. where possible use word from dice (e.g. *Venus, jactus, -ūs, venereus* or *basilicus*); a —, = good fellow, *optimus (homo)*. **trump up,** v.tr. *fingĕre*; see INVENT.

trumpery, n. see TRASH, TRIFLE.

trumpet, I. n. *tuba* (straight), *bucina, lituus, cornu* (curved), *classicum* (usually = signal given by *cornu*): the — sounds, *classicum canit* (*canĕre* also in pass., *classicum cani jubet*, Caes., so also *bellicum, canere* and *coni*), to sound the — for retreat, *receptui canere* **II.** v tr fig = to proclaim the praise, *buccinatorem esse alcjs rei, alqd praedicare* **trumpeter,** n *tubicen, buccinator,* fig *buccinator*

truncheon, n *scipio*, = cudgel, *fustis,* m

trundle, v tr *volvere*

trunk, n. 1, of a tree, *truncus, stirps*; 2, of the body, *truncus* (often *corpus* can be used), 3, = chest, *arca*, see CHEST, 4, of an elephant, *manus, -ūs* (Cic), *proboscis* (Plin)

truss, n = bandage, *fascia*, — of hay, *fascis*

trust, I. n 1, = confidence, *fiducia, fides, spes firma* or *bona*, — in oneself, *fidentia*, 2, anything —ed to anyone, *quod alci mandatum* (in gen), *creditum* or *depositum est*, 3, = credit, i e to take on —, *fide suā emere* **II** v intr (*con*)*fīdĕre, credere, alci fretum esse algo* or *alqā re* (= to build on), not to —, *alci diffīdĕre* **III.** v tr *alqd alci* (*con*)*credere, committĕre, commendare*, to — yourself altogether to, *se totum alci committĕre, omnia consilia alci credere* **trustee,** n *custos, administrator, procurator*, see TRUSTY **trustworthiness,** n *constantia, fides*, see under TRIAL **trustworthy,** adj *certus, firmus, constans* (opp *varius, mobilis*), *certus et constans, firmus et constans, fidus, fidēlis*

tub, n *dolium, mulctra* (= milk pail), *labrum* (= vat)

tube, n *tubus*, see PIPE

tuber, n *tuber, ĕris,* n (= anything that protrudes, more esp a bump, swelling) **tubercle,** n (in anatomy), *tuberculum* (Cels) **tuberous,** adj *tuberosus*

tuck, I. v tr to — up a garment, *succingĕre*, the hair, *comam in nodum* † *religare, capillos in nodum* † *colligĕre* **II.** n see FOLD

Tuesday, n **dies Martis*

tuff, n *tophus* (*tofus*)

tuft, n e g a — of hair, *crinis* (or pl *crines*), of wool, *floccus*, a — of grass, *fasciculus* (of flowers, also of flax), a — of feathers, *crista* (= — or plume on the head of a bird, comb of a cock, crest or plume of a helmet) **tufted,** adj *cristatus*

tug, I. v tr *trahĕre* **II.** n *navis quae aliam navem trahit*

tuition, n see INSTRUCTION

tulip, n **tulipa*

tumble, I. v intr = to roll about, *volutari* (e g *in luto*), *se volutare*, see FALL **II.** v tr *omnia perturbare* or *miscēre* **III.** n see FALL **tumbler,** n 1, = acrobat, *petaurista*, m, 2, = glass, *poculum*, 3, see PIGEON

tumid, adj *tumidus, inflatus, turgens, tumens*, — words, *ampullae* (Hor)

tumour, n *tumor, tuber, -ĕris,* n (= any swelling), *struma* (= scrofulous —)

tumult, n 1, = great noise, *tumultus, -ūs, tumultuatio* (rare), *strepitus, -ūs*, see NOISE, 2, = excitement of the mass, *seditio, motus, -ūs, concitatio* (e g *plebis contra patres*), *tumultus, ūs* (in the Roman sense, of any rising of a conquered tribe, e g of the slaves, the country people, the allies, etc, against the Romans themselves), see REBELLION **tumultuary, tumultuous,** adj *tumultuosus, turbulentus* (= turbulent), comb *seditiosus et turbulentus* (e g *civis*), see DISORDERLY, NOISY Adv *tumultuose, turbulente*

tumulus, n *tumulus*

tun, n *dolium, cupa* (= cask), as liquid measure use *centum urnae*, see TON

tune, I. n = a short air, *cantus, -ūs, carmen* (= song), *modi, numeri, moduli*, to be in —, *concentum servare*, out of —, *absonus* **II** v tr a musical instrument, *fides ita contendere nervis ut concentum servare possint* (Cic) **tuneful,** adj *canōrus, musicus*; see MUSICAL **tuner,** n by the verb **tuning,** n by the verb

tunic, n *tunica*

tunnel, I. n *cuniculus* **II.** v tr *cuniculum facĕre*

tunny, n *thynnus* or *thunnus* (Plin.)

turban, n *mitra*.

turbid, adj *turbidus* (= disturbed, e g *aqua*, well, *scaturigo*, weather, sky, *caelum*)

turbot, n *rhombus*

turbulence, n *omnium rerum perturbatio, tumultus, ūs*, see TUMULT **turbulent,** adj *turbulentus*

tureen, n *patīna*

turf, n *caespes, ĭtis,* m (= sward, sod)

turgid, adj *tumidus*, see TUMID

turmoil, n *turba*, see TUMULT

turn, I. v tr to — a wheel, etc, (*con*)*torquēre, circumagĕre* (round, e g hand mills), *distorquēre* (in different directions), to — anything round, *in orbem torquēre* or *circumagĕre*, † *rotare* (like a wheel), *vertĕre* (e g *navem, currum*), *convertĕre* (quite round, stating the *terminus ad quem*, hence with *ad* or *in* with accus), *versare* (lit = to twirl about, fig *mentem ad omnem malitiam*, etc), *flectĕre* (= to bend, lit and fig), *circumvertĕre, intorquēre* (round towards one side, e g *oculos ad alqd*), *retorquēre* (back, e g *oculos ad alqd*), to — one's back, (*con*)*verti, se* (*con*)*vertĕre* (lit *terga* (*con*)*vertĕre* = to take to flight, of soldiers), *abire, decedere, discedĕre* (= to go away), to — the mind to, *animum ad alqd advertĕre*, or in one word *alqd animadvertĕre* to — the scale, by *facĕre ut altera lanx deprimatur* (lit or fig), to — a coat, *vestem reficĕre*, to — with a lathe, *tornare*, = to change, e g to — goods into money, *vendĕre*, see SELL, TRANSFORM, CHANGE, to — one's eyes upon, *oculos con*(*j*)*icĕre in alqd* to — away, *dimittĕre* (= send away), see DISMISS, to — out, see EXPEL, to — over, see TRANSFER, CONSIDER **II.** v intr *se* (*con*)*vertĕre*, (*con*)*verti*, to — from side to side, *se versare* (of one who does not know what to do or to say), see CHANGE, BECOME, to — away, *se avertĕre*, to — back, *redire, reverti* to — in, *cubitum ire*, see BED, to — into, see CHANGE, BECOME, to — off, *deflectĕre, declinare de alqā re*, to — out, see BECOME, to — out well (of a thing), *bene* or *belle evenire, bene* or *prospere cadĕre, prospere procedĕre* or *succedĕre* very well, *alci res fauste, feliciter prospereque evenire*, head —s round, by *vertigine laborare* of leaves, *colorem mutari* **III.** n 1, *rotatio* (of a wheel), see TURNING, 2, see WINDING, 3, see CHANGE, 4, of affairs, things take a good —, *res in meliorem statum conversa est*, things take a bad —, *res male vertit, omnia in pejorem partem vertuntur et mutantur*, 5, it is your —, *nunc tuae sunt partes*, 6, in a fig sense, e g the — of thought, see FORM, CAST, SHAPE, MANNER, 7, in writing, e g to give a good shape, etc, *sententiam apte conformare*; to give a more elegant —, *alqd elegantius dicĕre* different —s, *variae figurae et verba* **turn against, I.** v tr *alqm ab alqo alienare* **II.** v intr *ab alqo alienari* **turn over,** v tr see UPSET, to — a book, *librum evolvĕre*, to — a new leaf, *mores emendare* **turncoat,** n *qui de sententiā decedit, qui sententiam* or *consilium mutat* **turner,** n *qui alqd tornat* **turning,** n 1, *versatio* (e g *machinarum*,

Vitr.), *rotatio* (Vitr.), *circumactio* (round, Vitr.), *conversio*, *circumactus*, *-ūs*, *flexus*, *-ūs* (= bending), *declinatio* (= — aside, e.g. of the body); see DEVIATION; 2, = the art of —, *ars tornandi*; 3, of a road, or *flexus viae*, or *iter* or *via*. **turnkey,** n. *janitor* or *custos carceris*. **turnpike,** n. *taberna ad viarum vectigal exigendum constructa*, or perhaps *taberna vectigalis*.

turnip, n. *rapum*.

turpentine, n. *resina terebinthina* (Cels.).

turpitude, n. *turpitudo*; see DISGRACE, SHAME.

turret, n. *turricula*.

turtle, n. 1, — -dove, *turtur*; 2, a fish, *testudo* (= tortoise).

tush, interj. *st!*

tusk, n. *dens*.

tutelage, n. *tutēla*; see PROTECTION. **tutelary,** adj. — god, of a place, *deus praeses loci*, *deus qui loco praesidet*, *deus cujus tutelae* or *cujus in tutelā locus est*; of a family, *penates*, *-ium*, m. (= the private gods in each separate home; there were also *penates publici*, as protectors of the city, the temples, etc.), *lares*, *-(i)um*, m. (= the house or family gods of the Romans). **tutor,** n. 1, see GUARDIAN; 2, *magister*, *praeceptor*; private —, *praeceptor domesticus*; see TEACH.

twang, I. v.intr. e.g. bows, *crepare*, *crepitare*, *sonare*. II. n. *crepitus*, *-ūs*, *sonus*, *sonitus*, *-ūs*.

tweak, v.tr. *vellĕre*, *vellicare*.

tweezers, n. *volsella*.

twelve, adj. *duodecim*, *duodeni* (= — each), — times, *duodecie(n)s*; — hundred, *mille et ducenti*, *milleni et duceni* (= 1200 each, also 1200 in one sum, hence always with nouns that are used only in the pl.), — hundred times, *millie(n)s et ducentie(n)s*. **twelfth,** adj. *duodecimus*; heir to the — part, *heres ex uncia*. **twelvemonth,** n. *annus*.

twenty, adj. *viginti*, *viceni* (= — each). **twentieth,** adj. *vicēsimus*.

twig, n. *virga*, *surculus*, *rāmulus*.

twilight, n. *crepusculum*; in the —, *crepusculo*, *primo vespere*.

twin, n. and adj. *geminus*; —s, *gemini*.

twine, I. v.tr. *circumvolvĕre*, *flectĕre*, *(in)torquēre*; see TWIST. II. v.intr. *implicari*, *implecti*; to — round anything, *alqd circumplecti*, *se circumvolvĕre alci rei* (= to wind round, e.g. *arbori*, of a plant). III. n. *linum*; see STRING.

twinge, I. v.tr. *urĕre*; see PINCH. II. n. *dolor*, *cruciatus*, *-ūs*; sharp —s of pain, *acres dolorum morsus*; — of conscience, *dolor*.

twinkle, v.intr. †*coruscare* (of a flame, a flash of lightning, of the rays of light), *micare* (= to glitter, of arms, stars, etc.), *fulgēre* (= to shine, to reflect rays of light, of arms, etc.), *scintillare* (= to sparkle, of the eyes, etc.). **twinkling,** n. 1, *fulgor* (= brightness, e.g. *armorum*); 2, in the — of an eye, *temporis puncto*.

twirl, v.tr. *versare*; see SPIN.

twist, I. v.tr. *(in)torquēre*, *obtorquēre* (in past part. *obtorta gula*, = twisted neck), *(in)flectĕre*, *nectĕre*, *texĕre* (= to form, put together, weave). II. v.intr. *se torquēre*, *flectĕre*, *torquēri*, *flecti*.

twit, v.tr. anyone with anything, *alqd alci ob(j)icĕre*.

twitch, v.intr. *vellĕre*, *vellicare*.

two, adj. *duo*, *bini* (= — each); a period of — days, *biduum*; a period of — years, *biennium*; — -footed, †*bipes*; — fold, *duplex*; — -coloured, †*bicolor*; — -headed, *biceps*; — -edged, *bipennis*; — -handed, *duas manus habens*; — hundred, *ducenti*, *duceni* (= — hundred each). **twice,** adv. *bis*; — as much, *bis tantum*; — as great, *altero parte major*.

type, n. 1, = model, *exemplar*, *exemplum*, *forma*; 2, = symbol, *figura*, *significatio*, *imago* (Eccl.); 3, = letters, *lit(t)erarum formae*. **typical,** adj. *typicus* (Eccl.). **typify,** v.tr. *alqd sensibus sub(j)icĕre*, *oculis* or *sub oculis (alcjs) sub(j)icĕre*; see REPRESENT. **typographical,** adj. e.g. — error, **mendum typographicum*, *erratum typographicum* (not class.).

tyrant, n. *tyrannus* (= a usurper; afterwards = a despot, anybody that is cruel, but in the latter sense always with an adj., such as *crudēlis*, *intolerandus*, *saevus et violentus*, e.g. *tyrannus saevissimus et violentissimus in suos*, Cic.), *dominus* (= sovereign ruler), comb. *dominus et tyrannus*; in gen. sense, = cruel person, *homo crudelis* (*saevus*, etc.). **tyrannical,** adj. *tyrannicus* (of usurpers, despotic, e.g. laws, deeds, cruelty), *crudēlis* (= cruel). Adv. *tyrannice* (= in a despotic manner, e.g. *statuēre* = to act as master, judge, etc. *in alqm*, Cic.), *crudēliter* (= cruelly). **tyrannize,** v.intr. to — over anyone, *tyrannicā crudelitate importune vexare alqm* (of a people, a country, Just.), *tyrannice in alqm statuēre*; to — over a State, *civitatem servitute oppressam tenēre*. **tyranny,** n. *tyrannis*, *-idis*, f., or in pure Latin *dominatio* or *dominatus*, *-ūs*, or *dominatus regius* (of a usurper), *dominatio crudēlis* or *impotens* or *superba* or *crudelis superbaque* (implying a cruel government), *crudelitas* (= cruelty in gen.).

tyro, n. see TIRO.

U.

ubiquity, n. *omnipraesentia* (Eccl.), or by *qui* (*quae*, *quod*) *omnibus locis praesens est*. **ubiquitous,** adj. *omnibus locis praesens*.

udder, n. *uber*, *-ĕris*, n.

ugly, adj. *dēformis* (= disfigured), *turpis* (= shameful), *tēter* (= nasty), *obscēnus* (= obscene), *foedus* (= abominable, horrible: all both lit. and fig., of persons and things). Adv. *dēformiter* (e.g. *sonare*), *turpiter*, *tēterrime*, *obscēne*, *foede*. **ugliness,** n. *dēformitas*, *turpitudo* (= moral —), *obscēnitas foeditas*.

ulcer, n. *ulcus*; see ABSCESS. **ulcerate,** I. v.intr. *suppurare* (Plin.). II. v.tr. *ulcerare*. **ulcerous,** adj. *ulcerosus* (Tac.).

ulterior, adj. = further, *ulterior*; see FURTHER; of places, objects, etc., *quae rel(l)iquae sunt*, *quae restant*, or by *alia*, *cetera*.

ultimate, adj. *extrēmus*, *ultimus*; see FURTHEST, LAST, FINAL. Adv. *ad extrēmum*, *ad ultimum*, *postremo*; see LAST, END. **ultimatum,** n. perhaps *extrēma condicio*.

ultra, Latin, only in composition; to be — -Tory, *ultra modum optimatium partes amplecti*.

ultramarine, n. *color caeruleus* or *cyaneus* (Plin.).

umbrage, n. 1, see SHADE; 2, fig. to give — to, by *alqs alqd aegre* or *moleste fert* or *patitur*, *in offensionem alcjs cadĕre*; to take — at, *fastidire alqd* (= to disdain); see OFFENCE. **umbrageous,** adj. see SHADY.

umbrella, n *umbella* (= parasol, Mart., Juv.), † *umbraculum* (Ov.)

umpire, n *arbiter* (= arbitrator), decision of an —, *arbitrium*.

un-, a prefix, as a particle of negation or of privation, by the prefix *in* (e.g. *ingratus*), or by *non* (when a thing cannot and does not exist), or by *sine* with a noun in the ablat.

unabashed, adj 1, = firm, *constans*, *firmus*, *interritus*. 2, = shameless, *impudens*

unabated, adj *integer* (= whole).

unable, adj by circumloc with *non posse*, *nequire*

unaccented, adj *syllaba sine accentu enuntiata*

unacceptable, adj *ingratus*

unaccompanied, adj 1, *solus*, *incomitatus*, *sine comitatu*, see ALONE, 2, of the voice, *sine symphoniā* (Plin.)

unaccomplished, adj *imperfectus*, *inchoatus* (= only commenced), to leave anything —, *alqd inchoatum* or *imperfectum ac rude relinquĕre*

unaccountable, adj see INEXPLICABLE

unaccustomed, adj *insuetus* (of persons and things), to anything, *alcjs rei* or *ad alqd*, *insolitus* (of persons and of things, opp *solitus*, e.g. *labor*, *spectaculum*, *verba*), *insolens* (of persons, also = unusual, e.g. *verbum*), to anything, *alcjs rei* or *in alqā re* (e.g. *vera audiendi*, and *in dicendo*), *inexpertus*, to anything, *ad alqd*

unacquainted, adj with anything, *alcjs rei ignarus* (= who does not understand how to do any particular thing), *imperitus alcjs rei* (= inexperienced), *inscius* (= ignorant of anything), *rudis alcjs rei* or *in alqā re*

unadorned, adj *inornatus* (in gen.), *incomptus* (e.g. *caput*, then = without rhetorical ornament, e.g. speech), *simplex* (e.g. *crinis*), *purus* (of style, language, in Cic generally = free from foreign terms and constructions)

unadulterated, adj *sincērus* (= quite genuine), *integer* (= free from spurious mixtures, opp *vitiatus*), comb *sincerus integerque*, *incorruptus* (= incorrupt, pure, e.g. *sermo*, *fides*)

unadvisable, adj *inutilis* (= useless), *temerarius*, *inconsultus* (= rash), *quod sine consilio fit*, *quod alci parum prodest* **unadvised**, adj *inconsideratus*, *imprudens*, *temerarius*, *inconsultus* Adv *sine consilio*, *inconsiderate*, *imprudenter*, *temere*, *inconsulte*

unaffected, adj 1, = simple, *simplex* (e.g. *cibus*, also of words), *candidus* (= clear, without hypocrisy, of words and of the speaker), *inaffectatus* (of an orator, *jucunditas alcjs*, Quint.), — ease and grace (in speeches, etc.), *genus dicendi candidum*, *simplicitas* (in manners), 2, = not moved, *immotus*, *constans*, to remain — under, etc., *non affici*, or more strongly (*com*)*moveri alqā re* Adv *simpliciter*, *sine fuco ac fallaciis*

unaffrighted, adj *interritus*

unaided, adj *sine auxilio*, *nullius auxilio adjutus*, *non adjutus*

unalienable, adj *qui* (*quae*, *quod*) *alienari non potest*

unalleviated, adj *non mitigatus*, see ALLEVIATE

unallowable, adj *illicitus*

unalloyed, adj *purus* (lit.), *sincērus* (fig.)

unaltered, adj *immutatus*, *integer* (as before), or by *non mutari*

unambitious, adj *modestus*, or by circumloc *qui honores non petit*

unamiable, adj *difficilis*, see ILL-TEMPERED

unanimity, n *consensio*, *consensio sententiarum*, *concordia*, see AGREE, CONCORD **unanimous**, adj *concors*, *unanimus* Adv *unā voce*, *unā mente*, to defend a person —, *uno animo atque una voce alqm defendere* — to demand battle, *proelium poscĕre*, *communi sententiā statuĕre alqd*, *ad unum omnes decernunt*, = they all to a man determine, *cunctis populi suffragiis consulem declarari*, = to be appointed Consul —, *omnium in unum congruerunt sententiae*, = all were of one opinion, *omnibus sententiis absolvi*, *condemnari*, = to be acquitted, to be condemned —

unanswerable, adj *qui* (*quae*, *quod*) *refelli non potest* **unanswered**, adj to leave or remain —, by *ad alqm non respondēre* (of anything said or written), *ad alqd non rescribĕre* (with regard to something written)

unappalled, adj *interritus*

unappeased, adj *non satiatus*

unapproachable, adj of places, *invius*, of persons, *ad quem aditus*, *ūs*, *difficilis est*

unarmed, adj *inermis*, *inermus* (of things), *nudus*

unasked, adj (*suā*) *sponte*, *ultro*

unassuming, adj *modestus*, see MODEST

unattainable, adj *quod attingi non potest*

unattempted, adj to leave nothing —, *nihil inexpertum omittere*, *omnia experiri*

unattended, adj *incomitatus*, *sine comitibus*

unauthentic, adj *sine auctore editus* (e.g. a tale, *fabula*), *ab haud idoneis auctoribus vulgatus* (e.g. *fabula*), *sine ullo satis certo auctore allatus* (e.g. *rumor*), *incertus* (e.g. *rumor*)

unauthorized, adj *illicitus*, to be — to do a thing, *faciendi alqd jus* or *potestatem non habēre*, *jure alqd facĕre non posse*

unavailable, adj *haud in medium prolatus*, *inutilis* (= useless) **unavailing**, adj *irritus*, *vanus*, *fut(t)ilis*

unavenged, adj *inultus*

unavoidable, adj *inevitabilis*, better by *quod evitari non potest*, *quod evitare* or *effugĕre non possumus*.

unavowed, adj see SECRET

unaware, adj *inscius*, *nescius*, *ignarus*

unaware, unawares, adv *inexpectatus*, *inopinatus* (when we least think of it or expect it), *inopinans* (= who does not suppose a thing to happen), *necopinatus* (= what we do not think even possible), *necopinans* (= who cannot suppose that such a thing would happen), *improvisus* (= unforeseen), comb *improvisus atque inopinatus*, *insperatus* (of what we did not hope, unexpected), *subitus* (= sudden), *repentīnus* (= sudden, what happens quickly and to our surprise), or by *praeter ex(s)pectationem* or *opinionem*, (*ex*) *inopinato*, *improviso*, (*ex*) *insperato*

unawed, adj *interritus*

unbaked, adj *crudus* (of bricks, Plin.), *panis non bene coctus* (of bread)

unbar, v tr *reserare*

unbearable, adj see INTOLERABLE

unbeaten, adj e.g. path, *non tritus*

unbecoming, adj see INDECOROUS

unbefriended, adj *auxilio* or *amicis carens*

unbeliever, n *qui non credit* (*alqd esse*, etc.) **unbelieving**, adj *incredulus*, see above. **unbelief,** n. see INCREDULITY, INFIDELITY.

unbeloved, adj. *non amatus.*

unbend, v.tr. 1, a bow, *arcum* † *retendĕre, remittĕre;* 2, the mind, *animum remittĕre, (re)laxare.* **unbendable,** adj. see INFLEXIBLE, FIRM.

unbewailed, adj. † *inflētus,* † *indēflētus,* † *indeploratus.*

unbiassed, adj. *simplex* (= without prejudice), *liber* (e.g. *liber in consulendo*), *solutus,* and chiefly comb. *liber et solutus* (= not bound by anything), *integer* (= free from partiality, e.g. *judicium*), comb. *integer ac liber* (e.g. *animus*), *imparidus* (= fearless).

unbidden, adj. *invocatus;* an — guest (whom anyone brings), *umbra* (Hor.); see SPONTANEOUS.

unbind, v.tr. *(dis)solvĕre, laxare* (= to loosen).

unblamable, adj. *integer, sanctus;* see BLAMELESS.

unbleached, adj. *nondum candidus.*

unblemished, adj. *purus, integer, in(con)taminatus* (= not stained by having been in contact), *innocens* (= innocent), *castus* (= morally pure).

unbloody, adj. *incruentus.*

unblushing, adj. 1, see BLUSH; 2, see IMPUDENT.

unborn, adj. *nondum natus.*

unborrowed, adj. see ORIGINAL, GENUINE.

unbosom, v.tr. *confitēri alqd, se alci patefacĕre.*

unbought, adj. *non emptus,* † *inemptus.*

unbound, adj. of hair, *passus;* see also LOOSE.

unbounded, adj. 1, *infinitus;* 2, fig. — passion, see IMMODERATE.

unbrace, v.tr. *(re)laxare.*

unbred, adj. *male moratus.*

unbribed, adj. *incorruptus, integer* (= impartial).

unbridled, adj. 1, of a horse, *infrēnatus, effrēnatus,* † *infrēnis* or *infrēnus,* † *effrēnus;* 2, fig. *effrenatus;* see LICENTIOUS.

unbroken, adj. *integer* (= whole); of horses, *indomitus.*

unbrotherly, adj. *parum fraternus.*

unbuckle, v.tr. *diffibulare* (Stat.), *refibulare* (Mart.), *solvĕre* (e.g. knapsack, *sarcinas*).

unburden, v.tr. *exonerare* (lit. and fig.), *līberare, levare, solvĕre alqâ re.*

unburied, adj. *inhumatus, insepultus.*

unburnt, adj. *crudus* (of bricks; Plin.).

unbutton, v.tr. the coat, *vestem discingĕre* (= ungirdle); see also UNDO.

uncalled, adj. *invocatus;* — for, *non petītus;* see UNNECESSARY.

uncancelled, adj. see CANCEL.

uncared, adj. — for, *neglectus.*

uncarpeted, adj. *sine stragulo.*

uncaused, adj. *sine caus(s)â.*

unceasing, adj. *perpetuus, continuus, assiduus;* see INCESSANT.

unceremonious, adj. *simplex* (= natural), *parum comis* (= not polite), *agrestis, rusticus, inurbanus* (= rude); — habits, etc., *(morum) simplicitas.* Adv. *simpliciter, rustice, inurbane.*

uncertain, adj. *incertus* (also = indefinite), *dubius* (= doubtful), *anceps* (= doubtful as regards the issue, e.g. of a war; but never in the sense of a battle, etc.; see UNDECIDED), *ambiguus* (= ambiguous, not to be depended on, e.g. *fides*); to be —, *incertum* or *dubium esse* (in gen., of persons and things), *dubitare, vacillare, haerēre, haesitare, animi* or *animo pendēre, suspensum esse* (= to hesitate), *incertum alci esse, in incerto habēre* (in gen. of persons), *dubitatione aestuare* (= to be hesitating what to do), *in incerto* or *in dubio esse* (in gen. of things), *non satis constare* (= not to be quite certain yet, of things); all these verbs generally with an interrogative, such as *quid* and *utrum . . . . an;* — what to do, *incertus quid faceret;* to make anything —, *alqd in* or *in incertum revocare, alqd in dubium (re)vocare;* to leave anything —, *alqd in medio* or *in incerto* or *in dubio relinquĕre;* to walk with — steps, *titubare;* see STAGGER. Adv. *incerte, incerto, temere* (= rashly). **uncertainty,** n. see UNCERTAIN.

unchain, v.tr. *e vinculis eximĕre, vincula solvĕre;* see LOOSEN.

unchangeable, adj. *stabilis, constans;* see IMMUTABLE. Adv. *stabiliter, constanter.* **unchangeableness,** n. *stabilitas, constantia;* see IMMUTABILITY. **unchanged,** adj. *immutatus, integer.*

uncharitable, adj. *durus* (in gen. = hard-hearted), *inhumanus, humanitatis expers* (= unkind, harsh). Adv. *inhumane, inhumaniter.* **uncharitableness,** n. *animus durus, ingenium inhumanum, inhumanitas.*

unchaste, adj. *impurus* (= impure), *incestus* (with regard to religion and moral purity), *impudicus* (= having no shame, indecent), *libīdinosus* (= sensual, of persons and things, e.g. *amor*), *parum verēcundus* (= indiscreet, improper), *obscenus* (= obscene, foul); — love, *amor libidinosus, libīdines.* **unchastity,** n. *impuritas, impudicitia, libīdo.*

unchecked, adj. *liber.*

unchristian, adj. *contra legem Christianam.*

uncivil, adj. see IMPOLITE. **uncivility,** n. see IMPOLITENESS. **uncivilized,** adj. *rudis, fĕrus* (= wild), *barbarus* (= foreign, and so rude), *agrestis* (= uncultivated), *incultus* (= without culture), *inerudītus* (= uneducated, untaught), *indoctus* (= without literary education).

unclasp, v.tr. *refibulare* (Mart.); see LOOSEN.

uncle, n. *patruus* (= a father's brother), *avunculus* (= a mother's brother); great-—, *patruus* or *avunculus magnus.*

unclean, adj. 1, see DIRTY; 2, see UNCHASTE, FOUL.

unclouded, adj. *serēnus* (lit. and fig.).

uncoil, v.tr. *evolvĕre.*

uncoined, adj. *infectus.*

uncoloured, adj. 1, lit. *purus;* 2, fig. *sine fuco ac fallaciis.*

uncombed, adj. † *impexus, horridus, incom(p)tus.*

uncomfortable, adj. *molestus, incommodus;* see UNEASY. Adv. *incommode.* **uncomfortableness,** n. *molestia.*

uncommanded, adj. *injussus, injussu alcjs, ultro, sponte (suâ)* (= of one's free will).

uncommissioned, adj. 1, see UNCOMMANDED; 2, an — officer, *succenturio* or *optio,*

uncommon, adj *rarus, insolitus, inusitatus* (= rare), *singulāris, mīrus, inauditus* (= extraordinary); see RARE, EXCELLENT, EXTRAORDINARY. Adv *raro, singulāriter, mīre*, see SELDOM

uncommunicative, adj *tectus*, see RESERVED

uncomplaining, adj *patiens*

uncompleted, adj *imperfectus*

uncompounded, adj *simplex*

unconcerned, adj *securus*, at, about for anything, *de alqā re* or *pro alqā re* (e g *de bello, bello, pro salute*), *neglegens alcjs rei* (e g *legis, amicorum*), to be —, *securum esse*, to be — about *neglegĕre* with accus or by *bono esse animo*, see INDIFFERENT

unconditional, adj *simplex, absolutus* (= independent of anything else), mostly comb *simplex et absolutus, purus* (= without any exception, e g *judicium*, Cic) Adv *simpliciter, absolute* (= without any limitation, Jct)

uncongenial, adj see UNPLEASANT

unconnected, adj 1, lit see SEPARATE, 2, in speaking, *dissolutus, inconditus*

unconquerable, adj see INVINCIBLE. **unconquered**, adj *invictus*

unconscionable, adj see UNREASONABLE

unconscious, adj 1, = insensible (*omni sensu carens*, 2, = ignorant, *inscius, ignārus*, I am not — of it, *non sum inscius, non me fugit, non me praeterit, non ignoro* **unconsciousness**, n 1, by circumloc with *sensu carēre*, 2, by adj

unconsecrated, adj *non consecratus* (opp *sacratus*), *profānus* (opp *sacer*)

unconsidered, adj *neglectus*, e g to leave nothing —, *omnia dīligenter circumspicĕre*

unconstitutional, adj *non legitimus, quod contra legem fit*

unconstrained, adj *liber*

uncontaminated, adj *in(con)taminatus*

uncontested, adj *quod sine certamine fit*, an — election, *comitia quibus alqs nullo competitore deligitur*

uncontrollable, adj *impotens* (of persons and things), *effrenatus* (= unbridled), see VIOLENT. **uncontrolled**, adj *liber* (= free), — sovereignty, *dominatus, -ūs*

unconverted, adj *nondum ad legem Christianam adductus*

unconvinced, adj *non adductus ad credendum*

uncooked, adj *crudus, incoctus*

uncork, v tr *relinĕre* (Plaut and Ter = to take the pitch off with which a jar was sealed), or perhaps *obturamentum extrahĕre*

uncorrupt, adj *incorruptus* (lit and fig)

uncourteous, adj see RUDE

uncouth, adj of expression *insolitus, insolens*, of manners, *incultus* (= inelegant, opp *cultus*, e g *homo, mores*), *incultus moribus* (of persons), *immānis* (= savage), *agrestis, rusticus* (= rude) **uncouthness**, n *immānitas, inhumanitas*, see KINDNESS

uncover, v tr *detegĕre, retegĕre aperire* (all also fig of secrets, crimes, etc), *nudare* (lit = to strip off clothes, fig to lay open), to — the head, *caput aperire* or *adaperire*

unction, n *unctio*, extreme —, *unctio extrema* (Eccl), to speak with —, perhaps *speciose* or *speciosus dicere* **unctuous**, adj *pinguis* of speech, perhaps *speciosus*.

uncultivated, adj of soil, *incultus* (opp *cultus* or *consitus*), *vastus* (*ab naturâ et humano cultu* = quite barren e g mountain, Sall), fig. *indoctus, rudis, agrestis*

uncurbed, adj see UNBRIDLED

uncut, adj † *immissus* (= suffered to grow, of trees, opp *amputatus*), *intonsus* (= unshorn of the hair, then also of trees), *integer* (= from which nothing has been taken, whole)

undamaged, adj *inviolatus* (= inviolate), *integer* (= still entire, whole)

undaunted, adj *intrepidus*, see INTREPID

undecayed, adj *incorruptus*

undeceive, v tr *errorem alci extrahĕre, eripĕre, extorquēre*

undecided, adj *nondum dijudicatus* (= not yet settled in court, e g *lis*), *integer* (= still unsettled, of a thing), *dubius* (= doubtful, both of the mind and of events), *incertus* (both of persons and things), *ambiguus, anceps* (= doubtful as regards the result, e g *belli fortuna, in dubio esse*, of things) I am — what to do, *dubius* or *incertus sum quid faciam*, I am — whether, etc , *incertus sum, utrum*, etc , the lawsuit is still —, *adhuc de eâ re apud judicem lis est* his fate is still —, *non habet exploratam rationem salutis suae*

undecked, adj (= unadorned) *inornatus*

undefended, adj *indefensus* (of a city, also in Tac of a lawsuit), *nudus* (= exposed to attack)

undefiled, adj see UNBLEMISHED

undefined, adj *infinitus*

undeniable, adj *ēvidens* (opp *dubius*) Adv *certe, certo, sine dubio*

under, prep expressing rest 1, standing — any place, *sub* (with ablat , e g *sub terrā, sub arbore*, with accus it expresses the direction toward the lower part of anything, hence we use, with several verbs of motion, *sub* with accus , e g *sub ipsos muros aciem instruĕre*, = to draw up the army in order of battle — the very walls), *subter* with ablat and accus , *infra* with accus (of the direction of anything below towards the lower part of anything above the former, beneath, e g *infra lunam nihil nisi mortale*), *in* with ablat (e g — the shade, *in umbrā*), to have a thing — the coat, *alqd veste tectum tenēre*, 2, expressing dependence, etc , *sub* with ablat (in gen), *cum* (= — the superintendence and in company of, etc), — Hannibal, *sub Hannibale*, — the leadership of Hannibal, ablat abs *Hannibale magistro*, 3, expressing a lower measure and rank, as regards rank and merit, *infra*, to be —, below anyone, *infra alqm esse, inferiorem esse alqo, alci cedĕre*, in anything, *alqā re ab alqo vinci*, see BELOW, as regards the quality and quantity, *minor* with ablat (= less, younger than, etc), — seven years old, *minor septem annis, nondum septem annos natus, septimum annum nondum egressus*, not to sell, etc — (the price), *minoris pretio alqd non vendĕre*, 4, in determining the manner in which anything is done, *sub* with ablat , *per* with accus (= by means of), 5, expressing simultaneity, e g — the reign of Romulus, *regnante Romulo, sub Romulo*, — this condition, *eā condicione*, — these circumstances, *quae cum ita sint*, — the cloak of, *alcjs rei specie*, — sail *passis velis*, to be — anyone's eyes, *sub alcjs oculis esse*, to be — age, *impubem esse, haud sui juris esse* "Under" in such phrases is often to be rendered by *inferior* with special noun, e g —-servant, use *famulus inferior* **under-current**, n 1, of water, *flumen*, etc., *subterfluens*, or *sub terrâ fluens*; 2, fig., by circumloc. (e.g. there was an — of feeling in his words, *haec obscurâ quâdem significatione indicavit*). **under-garment**, n. *tunica* (*inferior*), *subūcula* (of a man).

underdone, adj. *semicoctus* (Plin.).

undergo, v.tr. *alqd subire*, *sustinēre* (= to carry anything as a burden, to attend to a thing); = to pass through, *pati*, *perpeti* (to the end), (*per*)*ferre* (= to — to the end), *tolerare*, *perfungi alqâ re* (= to go through it); to — punishment, *poenas dare* or *pendĕre*.

underground, adj. see SUBTERRANEOUS.

undergrowth, n. *virgulta*, *-orum*; see UNDERWOOD.

underhand, adj. *clandestinus*; see SECRET.

underlay, v.tr. *supponĕre*, *sub*(*j*)*icĕre*, *subdĕre*, *substernĕre* (all four with *alci rei* or *sub alqd*). **underlayer**, n. 1, *qui sub*(*j*)*icit*, etc.; 2, = something laid under, *fundamentum*.

underlet, v.tr. *minore pretio locare alqd*.

underlie, v.tr. e.g. the suggestion —s the speech, *haec per orationem tacite significantur*.

underline, v.tr. *lineam ducĕre subter alqd*.

underling, n. (*ad*)*minister*, *satelles*, *-itis*, m.

undermaster, n. *hypodidascalus*.

undermine, v.tr. 1, (*cuniculo* or *cuniculis*) *subruĕre* (e.g. a wall, a rampart), *suffodĕre* (e.g. a mountain, a wall, a town); 2, fig. *subruĕre* (= to ruin, e.g. *libertatem*), *evertĕre* (= to overthrow, e.g. *rempublicam*, *fundamenta reipublicae*), *labefactare* (= to cause to fall, e.g. *rempublicam*, *amicitiam*).

undermost, adj. *infimus* (= the lowest), *imus* (= the deepest); see LOW.

underneath, I. adv. *subter*, *infra*; see BENEATH. II. prep. see UNDER.

under-officer, n. perhaps *optio*, *succenturio*.

underpart, n. *pars inferior* (= lower part), (*partes*) *secundae* (lit. and fig.).

underpin, v.tr. *alqd substruĕre* (e.g. *saxo quadrato*); see SUPPORT.

underrate, v.tr. *minoris aestimare*; see LOWER.

undersell, v.tr. *minoris* (*quam ceteri*) *vendĕre*.

undersigned, adj. the —, *qui nomen subscripsit*.

understand, v.tr. = to comprehend (with the ear or with the intellect); 1, with the ear, *accipĕre*; 2, with the intellect, *accipĕre* (= to receive in the mind), *intellegĕre* (= to form an idea of anything, hence to comprehend, more particularly *intellegĕre alqm*, i.e. his character, his motives, opp. *alqm ignorare*); *comprehendĕre* or *amplecti* or *complecti*, all with or without *mente* (= to form an idea of), *percipĕre* (= to perceive with the understanding), *perspicĕre* (clearly), *alqd certum* or *exploratum habēre* (= to — thoroughly); I don't — you, *nescio quid velis*; how am I to — that? *quid hoc sibi vult?* hence, to — by it, i.e. to put a construction on, etc., *intellegĕre* or *intellegi velle* (both with double accus.), *dicĕre*, *vocare*, *appellare* (all with double accus.); = I mean this, *dicĕre* with double accus., *interpretari* with accus., *significare* with accus.; see MEAN; = to have acquired knowledge in anything, *alqd intellegĕre* (of an accurate knowledge, e.g. *multas linguas*), *scire alqd* or with infin. (= to have a clear idea of anything, and to remember it, e.g. *multas linguas*), *instructum esse alqâ re* (= to be versed in anything), *alcjs rei non ignārum esse* (= not to be unacquainted with anything), *peritum esse alcjs rei* (= experienced, skilled in); to — anything tolerably, *mediocriter adeptum esse alqd* (e.g. *singularum rerum singula*, Cic.); not to —, *alqd nescire* or *ignorare*, *alcjs rei ignarum esse*; to — Latin, *Latine scire*, *doctum esse Latinis lit*(*t*)*eris*, *Latinae linguae peritum esse*; not to — Latin, *Latine nescire*; to — riding on horseback, *equitandi peritum esse*. **understanding**, n. *mens*; see INTELLECT.

undertake, v.tr. *incipĕre* (= to begin), *subire*, *aggredi alqd* or *ad alqd* (= to get to it), *sumĕre*, *suscipĕre* (= to take a business into one's own hands), (*in se*) *recipĕre* (if we take it off anyone's hands), *moliri* (= to try to accomplish anything difficult, also with infin.), *conari* (if very laborious, gen. with infin.), *audēre* (at one's own risk, peril, gen. with infin.); to — a journey, *iter incipĕre* or *aggredi* or *inire* (on business), *iter facĕre* (in gen.); to — to make, etc., anything, *alqd faciendum conducĕre*; to — to do (i.e. to pledge oneself), *se facturum esse alqd promittĕre*. **undertaker**, n. 1, in gen. by verbs; 2, of funerals, *libitinarius*; *designator* (who arranged the procession, Sen.); to be an —, *libitinam exercēre* (Val. Max.). **undertaking**, n. *inceptio*, *inceptum*, *conatus*, *-ūs*, m., *conata*, *-orum*, n., *opus*, *-ĕris*, n., *facinus*, *-ŏris*, n. (= a crime).

undervalue, v.tr. *parvum* or *parvi ducĕre*, *parvi aestimare*, *contemnĕre*, *despicĕre* (= to despise), comb. *contemnĕre* (or *despicĕre*) *et pro nihilo ducĕre*, *vile habēre* (= to consider as trifling).

underwood, n. *virgulta*, *-orum*, *arbusta*, *-orum*, *silva caedua*.

underwriter, n. *qui cavet de* or *pro alqâ re*.

undeserved, adj. *immeritus* (of what we have not deserved, e.g. praise), *indignus* (= unworthy), *falsus* (= false, unfounded, e.g. *invidia*). Adv. *immerito*. **undeserving**, adj. *immerens*; see UNWORTHY.

undesigned, adj. *fortuitus*; see ACCIDENTAL. Adv. *fortuito*, *casu*, *imprudenter*. **undesigning**, adj. *simplex*, *candidus*.

undesirable, adj. by *vilis* (= poor); see WORTHLESS. **undesired**, adj. *ultro oblatus* (= freely offered), or by adv. *ultro*.

undetected, adj. *secrētus*; see SECRET.

undeveloped, adj. *immaturus*, *nondum adultus*.

undigested, adj. 1, of food, *crudus*; 2, of plans, etc., *imperfectus*.

undiminished, adj. *integer*; see WHOLE.

undiscerning, adj. *hebes*; see STUPID.

undisciplined, adj. *inexercitatus*, *rudis*, *tiro* (*in alqâ re*), comb. *tiro ac rudis*.

undisguised, adj. *sincērus*. Adv. *sincēre*.

undisturbed, adj. *otiosus* (= at leisure), *liber* (*ab*) *arbitris* (= free from ear or eye witnesses, spies, e.g. *locus*); to live in — peace, *in otio et pace vivĕre*; to leave anyone —, *alqm non vexare*, *alqm non interpellare* (= not to interrupt anyone in his work, etc.); they allowed him to pass through their territory —, *cum bonâ pace cum per fines suos transmiserunt*.

undivided, adj. *indivīsus* (e.g. *ungula equi*), *communis* (= in common). Adv. *pro indiviso* (ante and post class.; e.g. *possidēre alqd*).

undo, v tr **1,** to — a knot, etc , *(dis)solvĕre, resolvere, expedire* . **2,** see RUIN **undone,** adj *infectus,* to consider as —, *pro infecto habēre,* what is done cannot be —, *factum infectum fieri non potest,* = ruined, *perditus* (e g *perditus sum, perii,* = I am —)

undoubted, adj *non dubius, indubitatus* (= not doubted, post Aug), *certus* Adv *haud dubie, sine dubio*

undress, I. v tr to — anyone, *exuĕre alqm veste* (in gen), *detrahĕre alci vestem* (= to take off), *nudare* (= to strip anyone), *alqm veste* or *vestibus spoliare* (= to rob) **II.** v intr *exuĕre (vestem), (de)ponere vestem* a room for —ing, *apodytērium* (esp in baths) **III.** n *vestis nocturna* (= night-dress), *vestis domestica* (= house-dress, house-coat, in gen) **undressed,** adj **1,** *non vestītus, nudus* (both = quite naked, and without a coat or dress on), **2,** of bricks, etc , *crudus,* of food, *non coctus*

undue, † *indebitus, immodicus* (= immoderate) Adv *nimis, nimium,* see DUE, RIGHT, PROPER

undulate, v.intr † *undare* (= to rise in waves, in gen , also of boiling water), see WAVE **undulating,** adj *undatus* (Plin of marks on shells)

undutiful, adj *impius (erga alqm),* see DISOBEDIENT

unearthly, adj *non mortalis,* of spirits, perhaps *caelestis*

uneasy, adj *anxius, so(l)licitus* , to be, feel — (in one's mind), *angi* (for fear of some accident or misfortune), *so(l)licitum esse* (= to be troubled), *dubitatione aestuare* (= to be in great uncertainty what to do, Cic) **uneasiness,** n *(animi) perturbatio,* to feel —, *perturbari, commovēri, permovēri* Adv *anxie* (rare), *moleste, aegre* (e g *alqd ferre*)

unedifying, adj *frigidus, insulsus* (of a discourse, etc), in worse sense, *turpis* . see SHAMEFUL

uneducated, adj *indoctus, ineruditus*

unembarrassed, adj. *liber* , see FREE

unemployed, adj *negotiis vacuus* (in gen = free from business), *otiosus* (of one who has leisure to follow his own inclinations, both of persons and things), *nullis occupationibus implicatus* (= not engaged in any particular business), *munerum publicorum expers* (= not holding a public office), *ab omni munere solutus ac liber* (of one who holds no office of any kind)

unencumbered, adj *liber*

unendowed, adj *indotatus*

unenlightened, adj *humanitatis expers, indoctus*

unenterprising, adj *iners, socors, piger*

unenviable, adj *miser, tristis,* see PITIFUL

unequal, adj *inaequalis* (of the inward state of anything), *impar* (= uneven , then, not equal in strength, attainments, etc), *dispar* (= void of equality, not quite equal, both outwardly and inwardly), *dissimilis* (= dissimilar, as to quality, etc), *diversus* (= wholly different, in kind and manner), *dissŏnus* (of sounds), *iniquus* (of a battle, etc) Adv *inaequaliter, impariter, inique* **unequalled,** adj *summus*

unerring, adj *certus*

unessential, adj *ad rem ipsam* or *ad rei naturam non pertinens, quod ad rem non pertinet, a re alienus, adventicius*

uneven, adj *non aequus, iniquus, inaequabilis, inaequalis, asper* (= rough, opp *levis*) an — number, *numerus impar* **unevenness,** n *iniquitas, asperitas,* — of temper, *inconstantia mutabilitasque mentis*

unexamined, adj *inexploratus*

unexampled, adj *unicus, singularis, novus* (of what has not been heard or seen before), *inauditus*

unexceptionable, adj e g — witness *testis locuples* or *probus* — testimony, *testimonium firmum* or *certum*

unexecuted, adj *non perfectus, imperfectus* , to leave — *omittĕre* (e g a plan, *consilium*)

unexercised, adj *inexercitatus*

unexhausted, adj **1,** = untired, † *indefessus, integer* , **2,** = not used up, *integer, solidus*

unexpected, adj *in(ex)spectatus, inopinatus, necopinatus, improvisus* Adv *(ex) improviso contra ex(s)pectationem*

unexplored, adj *inexploratus*

unextinguishable, adj † *inexstinctus.*

unfading, adj e g — laurels, *gloria immortalis*

unfailing, adj *perpetuus* (= perpetual), *certus* (= sure)

unfair, adj *iniquus* (of persons and things, opp *aequus,* e g judge, law, condition), *injustus,* (= unjust, of persons and things, opp *justus, meritus, dēbitus,* e g interest on money), *immeritus* (= not deserved, chiefly with a negative before it, e g *laudes haud immeritae*) it is —, *iniquum* or *injustum est,* with accus and infin , to make — demands, *iniqua postulare* , to be — towards anyone, *iniquum esse in alqm* Adv *inique, injuste* **unfairness,** n *iniquitas* (in conduct , also in the pl), *inique* or *injuste factum* (of any act)

unfaithful, adj *infidēlis* (opp *fidelis*), *infidus* (= not to be depended upon, trusted, opp *fidus*), *perfidus perfidiosus* (the latter of one whose nature it is to be —), to be —, *fidem fallĕre* Adv *infideliter* **unfaithfulness,** n *infidēlitas, perfidia*

unfamiliar, adj *nŏvus, inusitatus,* see STRANGE

unfashionable, adj *qui (quae, quod) contra consuetudinem fit*

unfasten, v tr *(re)solvĕre* (= to untie), *(re)laxare* (= to loosen), *avellĕre, revellĕre* (= to tear off), *refigĕre* (of what is nailed fast)

unfathomable, adj *immensus, infinitus*

unfavourable, adj = averse, *iniquus,* to anyone, *alci* or *in alqm* (= hostile), *malignus* (= jealous, opp *benignus*), *adversus* (= contrary), *aversus* (= turned away), *aliēnus, inopportunus* (= not suitable), of omens, *infaustus, funestus sinister* (used both of lucky and unlucky omens , see Andrew's Lat Dict , SINISTER), — circumstances, conditions, *res adversae, tempora iniqua* Adv *inique, maligne, male, inopportune* **unfavourableness,** n *iniquitas* (e g *temporum*), *inopportunitas,* or by adj

unfeathered, adj. *implūmis*

unfeeling, adj *sensūs expers, a sensu* or *a sensibus aliēnatus, nihil sentiens* (lit), *durus, ferus, ferreus,* comb *saxeus ferreusque, inhumanus* (fig), to be —, *sensu carēre, nihil sentire, nullius rei sensu movēri, a sensu abesse* or *aliēnatum esse* (lit), *durum, ferreum, inhumanum esse, inhumano esse ingenio* (fig) Adv *dure, duriter, inhumane, inhumaniter, crudeliter*

unfeigned, adj. *vērus* (opp. *simulatus*), *sincērus* (opp. *fucatus*), *simplex*. Adv. *vere*, *sincēre*, *simpliciter*, *ex animo*.

unfeminine, adj. † *masculus*.

unfermented, adj. *sine fermento* (*factus*).

unfilial, adj. *impius* (*erga parentes*). Adv. *impie* (*erga parentes*).

unfit, **I.** adj. *inutilis alci rei* or (generally) *ad alqd*; see UNSUITABLE. **II.** v.tr. *inutilem reddĕre*. **unfitness**, n. *inutilitas*. **unfitting**, adj. see IMPROPER.

unfix, v.tr. *refigĕre*; see UNFASTEN. **unfixed**, adj. *mobilis*.

unfledged, adj. *implumis*.

unfold, v.tr. *explicare* (lit. and fig.), *aperire* (= to open; also fig.), *explanare* (fig., in words).

unforeseen, adj. *improvīsus*.

unforgiving, adj. *implacabilis*, *inexorabilis*; see IMPLACABLE.

unforgotten, adj. by circumloc. (e.g. of an act of kindness) *immortali memoriâ retinēre beneficium perceptum*; what you have done for me will be —, *meam tuorum erga me meritorum memoriam nulla umquam delebit oblivio*.

unformed, adj. *informis* (= without shape), *nondum perfectus* (= not finished), of character, perhaps *adhuc puerīlis*.

unfortified, adj. *immunītus*.

unfortunate, adj. see UNLUCKY.

unfounded, adj. *vanus*, *fictus*.

unfrequented, adj. *minus celeber*, *inceleber*, *desertus*.

unfriendly, adj. *inimīcus*, *inīquus*, *aliēnus*, towards anyone, *ab alqo*; to have — feelings towards anyone, *alieno animo esse ab alqo* or *in alqm*. **unfriendliness**, n. *inimicitia*, *simultas*.

unfruitful, adj. *infēcundus*, *sterilis* (opp. *fertilis* and, as regards the soil, *opimus*); see BARREN. **unfruitfulness**, n. *sterilitas*.

unfulfilled, adj. *irritus*, *vanus*, *fallax*; to remain —, *exitum* or *eventum non habēre*, *non evenire*; to leave no duty —, *nullum ducis officium remittĕre*.

unfurl, v.tr. to — the sails, *vela pandĕre*.

unfurnished, adj. *ab alqâ re imparatus*; an — house, *domus nuda atque inanis*.

ungainly, adj. *inhabilis*; see UNCOUTH.

ungenerous, adj. *illīberalis*; — act, *illīberalitas*. Adv. *illiberaliter*.

ungenial, adj. *tristis*, *asper*.

ungenteel, adj. *ignobilis*. **ungentle**, adj. *asper* (= rough, e.g. *verba*). **ungentlemanlike**, **ungentlemanly**, adj. *incultus*, *indecōrus* (e.g. laughter); see INDECOROUS.

ungird, v.tr. *discingĕre*, † *recingĕre*.

ungodly, adj. see IMPIOUS, IMPIETY.

ungovernable, adj. *qui regi non potest* (lit. and fig.), *indomitus* (= untamed, of living beings and of things), *effrēnatus* (= unbridled, of persons and things), *ferox* (of temper, of persons and of anything showing such a disposition), *impotens* (of persons and things), comb. *ferox impotensque*. Adv. *effrēnate*, *impotenter*. **ungoverned**, adj. see UNBRIDLED.

ungraceful, adj. *invenustus*; see INELEGANT. **ungracefulness**, n. by the adjs. **ungracious**, adj. *inīquus*, *petulans*, *īratus* (= angry). Adv. *inīque*, *iniquo animo*, *petulanter*, *īrate*.

ungrateful, adj. *ingratus* (of an — spirit, and of what is a thankless task), *beneficii*, *beneficiorum immemor*.

ungrounded, adj. *vanus*, *irritus*, *inanis*.

ungrudging, adj. see LIBERAL.

unguarded, adj. **1**, *incustodītus*, *sine custodiis* (= not guarded by anyone), *indēfensus*; **2**, = imprudent, *incautus*, *imprudens*. Adv. *incaute*, *imprudenter*, *temere* (= rashly); see IMPRUDENT.

unguent, n. *unguentum*.

unhallowed, adj. *profanus*; see also SACRILEGIOUS.

unhappy, adj. *infelix*, *infortunatus*, *miser* (= miserable), *non prosper* (= not prosperous, of things), † *infaustus* (= ill-fated, e.g. day, omen, etc.), also comb. *infaustus et infelix*, *calamitosus* (e.g. war, conflagration), *funestus* (= mournful, causing mischief, e.g. war, omen), *sinister* (lit. = on the left-hand side, opp. *dexter*), *adversus* (= not as we wish it, e.g. battle, circumstances, result of an undertaking, opp. *secundus*), *malus* (= in a bad condition, opp. *bonus*), *calamitosus*, *aerumnosus* (= full of calamity); — position, *res adversae*, *fortunae afflictae*. Adv. *infēliciter*, *misere*, *male*, *calamitose* (rare). **unhappiness**, n. *miseria*; see MISERY.

unharmed, adj. *inviolatus*, *salvus* (= safe).

unharness, v.tr. *disjungĕre*, *solvĕre*.

unhatched, adj. *nondum* (*ex ovo*) *exclusus*.

unhealthy, adj. **1**, = disposed to illness, *valetudine affectus*, *ad aegrotandum proclīvis*, *infirmâ valetudine*, *infirmus*, *invalidus*, *aeger*, *imbecillus*; see WEAK, ILL; **2**, see UNWHOLESOME. **unhealthiness**, n. *mala*, *infirma*, *tenuis*, *aegra* or *incommoda*, *valētudo*; see also UNWHOLESOMENESS.

unheard, adj. *inauditus*; to punish, to condemn anyone —, *alqm inauditum punire*, *damnare*; — of, *inauditus*, *nŏvus*.

unheated, adj. *non cal(e)factus*.

unheeded, adj. *neglectus*.

unheroic, adj. *ignavus*; see COWARDLY.

unhesitating, adj. *strenuus*, *confidens*; see PROMPT. Adv. *strenue*, *confidenter*.

unhewn, adj. *rudis*.

unhindered, adj. *non impedītus*, *līber* (= free, without constraint), *sine morâ*.

unhinge, v.tr. **1**, to — a door, *postes cardine* † *emovēre*; see UNFIX; **2**, fig. with the mind —d, *mente captus*.

unhistorical, adj. *contra historiae fidem scriptus*, *commenticius*, *fictus*.

unholy, adj. (man, place) *profanus* (opp. *sacer*); see IMPIOUS.

unhonoured, adj. *inhonoratus*.

unhook, v.tr. *refigĕre* (from a wall), *refibulare* (Mart. = to unbuckle).

unhoped for, adj. *inspĕratus*.

unhurt, adj. *integer*, *incolumis*, *salvus*, *intactus* (= untouched), comb. *integer intactusque*, *inviolatus* (= not hurt), comb. *integer atque inviolatus*, *intactus inviolatusque*, *invulneratus*, *incorruptus* (where nothing is spoiled or destroyed).

unicorn, n. *monocĕros*, *-ōtis* (Plin.).

uniform, **I.** adj. *unius generis*, *semper eodem modo formatus*, *constans*, *aequabilis* (e.g. *motus*). Adv. *constanter*, *aequabiliter*, *uno tenore*. **II.** n. of soldiers, *vestītus*, *-ūs*, *militaris*. **uniformity**, n. *aequabilitas*, *constantia* (of persons and things).

unimaginable, adj *supra quam quod cogitari potest*

unimpaired, adj *integer*

unimpassioned, adj e g an — address, *animi perturbatione liber* or *vacuus* (= without violent emotion), *cupiditatis* or *cupiditatum expers, omni cupiditate carens, sine ira et studio* (= without passion)

unimpeachable, adj see TRUSTWORTHY

unimportant, adj *levis, nullius momenti*

uninformed, adj *indoctus, humanitatis expers.*

uninhabitable, adj *inhabitabilis*; to be quite —, *omni cultu vacare* **uninhabited,** adj *habitatoribus vacuus* (e g a town), *cultoribus vacuus* (= without anybody to cultivate), *desertus* (= deserted)

uninitiated, adj 1, lit *profanus*, 2, fig *alcjs rei expers*

uninjured, adj *incolumis, integer, salvus*

uninspired, adj *divino spiritu haud afflatus.*

uninstructed, adj *indoctus*

unintelligible, adj *obscurus* (e g *narratio*) Adv *obscure* (e g *narrare alqd*), or by the noun *obscuritas* (e g *verborum*)

unintentional, adj *insciens* Adv *forte, casu*, I did it —, *insciens feci*

uninteresting, adj *jejunus, frigidus*

unintermitting, adj *continuus, assiduus*

uninterred, adj *inhumatus, insepultus*

uninterrupted, adj *continens, continuus* (= continuous), *assiduus* (= constant, e g rain, work), *perpetuus, perennis* (= lasting), comb *continuus et perennis* (e g *motio*), my connection with anyone is —, by *in consuetudine cum alqo permanēre* Adv *continenter, uno tenore, perpetuo*

uninured, adj see UNACCUSTOMED

uninvestigated, adj *inexploratus.*

uninvited, adj *invocatus*, see UNASKED
uninviting, adj *injucundus*

union, n see under UNITE

unique, adj *unicus, singularis*

unison, n. (in music) *concordia vocum*

unit, n *monas, ădis*, f (μονάς)

unitarian, n. *qui simplicem Dei naturam esse arbitratur* **unitarianism,** n *ratio eorum qui simplicem esse Dei naturam dicunt.*

unite, I. v tr *(con)jungĕre, alci rei* or *cum alqā re*, with anybody, *cum alqo, congregare* (= to collect two or more things to one flock as it were), *copulare* (so that two or more things are closely tied together), with anything or anyone, *cum alqā re* or *cum alqo, (con)sociare* (as companions), with, etc, *cum*, etc, *miscēre alci rei* or *cum alqā re* (= to mix, lit and fig), see JOIN **II.** v intr *se (con)jungĕre* (of two corps), with anyone, *alci* or *cum alqo, miscēri* (of two rivers, etc), *cum alqo coire*, with anything, *alci rei* or *cum alqā re, consentire* (= to agree), to — in a partnership, *societatem cum alqo inire*, see JOIN, AGREE **union,** n 1, *(con)junctio, congregatio, consociatio*, 2, = agreement, *consensio, consensus, -ūs, concordia*, see AGREEMENT, 3, = united body, *societas, sodalitas*, see SOCIETY, CONCORD **unity,** n 1, opp to multiplicity, by *unus* (e g there was — of opinion among them all, *sententia inter omnes una erat*), 2, see UNION, 2

universal, adj *universus*, — history, *res in orbe terrarum actae*; see GENERAL Adv *universe, in universum*, — beloved, *ab omnibus dilectus* **universality,** n *qui (quae, quod) latissime patet* or *ad universos pertinet* **universe,** n *(rerum) universitas, rerum natura*

university, n **academia*

univocal, adj of a word, etc, *unam tantum significationem habens*

unjust, adj *injustus, injurius, injuriosus* (= of an — mind), *iniquus* (= unreasonable) (*injuriosus*, = contrary to right and to the civil law, *iniquus*, = contrary to the moral law) Adv *injuste, inique, injuriose, contra jus (fasque).*
unjustifiable, adj *iniquissimus*, see INEXCUSABLE Adv *iniquissimo modo*

unkept, adj *neglectus*

unkind, adj *inhumanus, severus* see STERN Adv *inhumane, severe* **unkindness,** n *inhumanitas, severitas*, see CRUELTY

unknowing, adj *inscius*, see IGNORANT
unknown, adj *ignotus* (in gen, of persons and things, opp *notus*), *incognitus* (= not yet learned, of things, opp *cognitus*), *incompertus* (= not yet certain fully ascertained, opp *compertus*), *inexploratus* (= not yet inquired into, opp *exploratus*), *ignobilis* (= — to the world, of places and persons, hence also = of obscure birth, opp *nobilis*), *obscurus* (= obscure), a person — to me, *nescio quis*

unlace, v tr see UNTIE, LOOSEN

unlamented, adj to die —, *non deploratum mori*

unlatch, v tr see OPEN

unlawful, adj *non legitimus, vetitus, qui (quae, quod) contra legem* or *leges est* Adv *contra legem* or *leges, injuriā, per injuriam*

unlearn, v tr *dediscĕre* **unlearned,** adj *illit(t)eratus, indoctus, ineruditus* Adv *indocte*

unleavened, adj *sine fermento* (Cels)

unless, conj *nisi* (contracted *ni*), with indic where the statement is definite, with subj where possibility is implied, in certain cases *si non* is used (e g *libertas si aequa non est, ne libertas quidem est*), esp with *tut* (e g *si te vidēre non potero, discedam*)

unlettered, adj see UNLEARNED

unlevelled, adj *asper*, see UNEVEN

unlicensed, adj *cui jus alcjs rei vendendae non est concessum*

unlike, adj *dissimilis* **unlikely,** adj see IMPROBABLE

unlimited, adj *infinitus*

unload, v tr *exonerare* (lit, e g *plaustrum*, also fig = disburden), *liberare, levare, solvĕre alqa re* (fig = to disburden)

unlock, v tr *recludĕre, reserare*

unlooked for, adj *inex(s)pectatus, insperatus*

unloose, v tr *solvĕre* (a ship, etc), *liberare* (= to set free), see FREE, v tr

unlucky, adj *infelix* (of omens), see UNFAVOURABLE

unmade, adj *non factus* or *non confectus*, of a bed, *non stratus*

unman, v tr *enervare* **unmanned,** adj. *fractus, perculsus*

unmanageable, adj see UNGOVERNABLE.

unmanly, adj *viro indignus, effeminatus* (= effeminate), *mollis* (= soft) comb. *effeminatus et mollis*

unmannerly, adj. *male moratus* (of persons, opp. *bene moratus*), *rusticus* (= rude, opp. *urbanus*); see RUDE.

unmarried, adj. *caelebs*.

unmask, v.tr. to — anyone, *personam capiti alcjs detrahĕre* (lit. and fig., Mart.), *animum alcjs nudare, evolvĕre alqm integumento dissimulationis suae nudareque* (fig. = to find him out).

unmatched, adj. *unicus*.

unmeaning, adj. *inanis*.

unmelodious, adj. *non canorus*; see INHARMONIOUS.

unmentioned, adj. to remain —, *omitti, praetermitti*; to leave —, *omittĕre, praetermittĕre*.

unmerciful, adj. *immisericors*. Adv. *immisericorditer*.

unmindful, adj. *immemor*, of a thing, *alcjs rei*.

unmingled, unmixed, adj. *merus*, fig. *simplex*.

unmistakable, adj. see CLEAR, CERTAIN.

unmitigated, adj. by circumloc.; often the superlat. of an adj. will suit (e.g. the war was waged with — cruelty, *bellum atrocissimum gerebatur*).

unmolested, adj. to leave anyone —, *alci molestiam non exhibēre*.

unmoor, v.tr. *solvĕre*.

unmotherly, adj. *non maternus*.

unmoved, adj. *immotus*; to be, remain —, *non (com)movēri alqâ re, repudiare alqd* (e.g. *alcjs preces*); *non laborare de alqâ re* (e.g. *de alcjs morte*).

unnatural, adj. *quod praeter naturam ex(s)istit, monstr(u)osus, portentosus, immanis* (= vast). Adv. *contra naturam, praeter naturam*.

unnavigable, adj. *innavigabilis*.

unnecessary, unneedful, adj. *non necessarius, quod non opus est, supervacaneus, vanus* (= idle, e.g. *metus*); it is — to mention these, *eos nihil attinet nominare*. Adv. *praeter rem, praeter necessitatem, nimis*; see Too.

unnerve, v.tr. see UNMAN.

unnoticed, adj. to leave —, *praetermittĕre, praeterire (silentio), neglegere* (= not to mind).

unnumbered, adj. see INNUMERABLE.

unobserved, adj. see UNNOTICED.

unoccupied, adj. see UNEMPLOYED, UNINHABITED.

unoffending, adj. *innocens*.

unopened, adj. *non apertus*; of a letter, *lit(t)erae non resignatae*.

unorganized, adj. e.g. — bodies, *corpora nullâ cohaerendi naturâ* (Cic.).

unorthodox, adj. *fidei Christianae parum conveniens* (of a doctrine), *fidei Christianae parum obediens* (of a person).

unostentatious, adj. see MODEST.

unpack, v.tr. *alqd vacuum reddĕre*; see UNLOAD.

unpaid, adj. *non solutus* (of money, debts), *residuus* (= outstanding, e.g. money not received by the creditor), *cui non satisfactum est* (of the creditor).

unpalatable, adj. *amarus* (= bitter).

unparalleled, adj. *unicus, singularis*.

unpardonable, adj. *quod nihil excusationis habet* (e.g. *vitium*), *inexpiabilis* (e.g. *scelus, fraus*).

unpatriotic, adj. *patriae immemor* (of a person), (*injuria*) *in patriam illata* (of an act).

unperceived, adj. see UNNOTICED.

unphilosophical, adj. *philosophiae expers*.

unpitying, adj. see UNMERCIFUL. **unpitied**, adj. by circumloc. with *misericordia* (e.g. they fell —, *nullius misericordiam adepti interfecti sunt*).

unpleasant, adj. *molestus, ingratus, injucundus*; see DISAGREEABLE. Adv. *moleste, ingrate*. **unpleasantness**, n. *incommodum, molestia*; to cause anyone —, *molestiam alci afferre* or *exhibēre, incommodo alqm afficĕre, incommodum alci (af)ferre*; to cause yourself —, *molestiam ex alqâ re capĕre* or *accipĕre*.

unpoetic, adj. *a poëtarum ratione alienus*.

unpolished, adj. *impolitus* (lit. and fig.).

unpolluted, adj. *impollutus, castus*.

unpopular, adj. *invidiosus, plebi (populo*, etc.) *ingratus*, or *haud gratus* or *acceptus*; to be (very) —, *in (magnâ) invidiâ esse*; to become —, *in invidiam venire*. **unpopularity**, n. *invidia*; see above.

unpractised, adj. *inexercitatus*.

unprecedented, adj. *novus, inauditus*.

unprejudiced, adj. *integer, integer ac liber*.

unpremeditated, adj. (*verba*, etc.) *extemplo* or *sine consilio dicta*.

unprepared, adj. *imparatus*, with anything, *ab alqâ re*.

unprepossessing, adj. see DISAGREEABLE.

unpretending, adj. see MODEST.

unprincipled, adj. *male moratus*; see WICKED.

unproductive, adj. *infecundus*; see UNFRUITFUL.

unprofitable, adj. *qui nullum fructum fert*. Adv. by adj. or *incassum*.

unpromising, adj. *qui (quae, quod) nullam spem affert*.

unpronounceable, adj. *qui (quae, quod) enuntiari non potest*.

unpropitious, adj. see UNFAVOURABLE.

unprotected, adj. *indefensus, non custoditus*.

unproved, adj. *argumentis non (con)firmatus*.

unprovided, adj. *imparatus*; — for (e.g. children), (*liberi*) *quibus nondum prospectum est*.

unprovoked, adj. *non lacessitus, ultro* (= of one's own accord).

unpublished, adj. *nondum editus*.

unpunished, adj. *impunitus, inultus, incastigatus* (also with words); to remain —, *impune esse, non puniri*; — for anything, *alqd impune facĕre*.

unpurchased, adj. *non emptus*.

unqualified, adj. **1**, see UNSUITABLE; **2**, = very great, *summus, maximus*.

unquestionable, adj. *non dubius, certus*. Adv. *sine dubio*.

unravel, v.tr. **1**, lit. *retexĕre*; **2**, fig. *explanare, explicare, enodare*.

unread, adj. *non lectus*; an — man, by *lit(t)erarum expers*; see UNEDUCATED.

unreasonable, adj. it is —, *iniquum est*, with accus. and infin. Adv. *inique*.

unreconciled, adj *non placatus*, see RECONCILE

unrefined, adj 1, lit *crudus*, 2, fig see RUDE

unrelenting, adj see CRUEL, HARD

unremitting, adj *continuus* (e g *labor*), see CONSTANT

unrepaid, adj e g kindness, by (*beneficia*) *non reddita*

unrepentant, adj *quem non poenitet alcjs rei*

unrepining, adj see PATIENT.

unreprovable, unreproved, adj *non reprehensus*

unrequested, adj *ultro oblatus* (= freely offered), *ultro*

unresented, adj *inultus, impunitus*

unreserved, adj *liber*, see FRANK.

unrest, n *inquies, -ētis*, f

unrestrained, adj *effrenatus*

unrevenged, adj *inultus*

unrewarded, adj *sine praemio, inhonoratus*

unriddle, v tr *solvĕre, explicare*

unrighteous, adj *impius, improbus* Adv *impie, improbe* **unrighteousness,** n *impietas, improbitas*

unripe, adj *immaturus* (lit of fruit, fig of man, opp *maturus*), *crudus* (= raw, opp *maturus et coctus*) **unripeness,** n *immaturitas*

unrivalled, adj *eximius, praestans*; see EXCELLENT

unrobe, v tr see UNDRESS

unroof, v tr see UNCOVER

unroot, v tr *eradicare* (ante class, lit and fig), *radicitus evellere*

unruffled, adj of the sea, temper, see CALM, TRANQUIL

unruly, adj see UNGOVERNABLE **unruliness,** n *effrenatio, impotentia, ferocitas*

unsafe, adj *infestus, intutus*, fig = exposed to danger, *instabilis* (lit = unstable, e g step, *gradus, ingressus*), *lubricus* (lit = slippery), *incertus* (fig = uncertain)

unsaid, adj *indictus* **unsay,** v tr see RECANT

unsalable, adj *qui (quae, quod) vendi non potest*

unsalted, adj *sale non conditus*

unsatiated, adj *nondum saturatus*

unsatisfactory, adj *non idoneus* (= unsuited), or by some positive adj, as *malus* (= evil) Adv *minus bene* **unsatisfied,** adj *cui non satisfactum est*

unsavoury, adj see TASTELESS, UNPALATABLE

unscrew, v tr *solvĕre*

unscriptural, adj *non ut sanctae lit(t)erae docent*

unseal, v tr *resignare algd*

unsearchable, adj. *inexplicabilis, inexploratus*

unseasonable, adj *intempestivus, importunus, immaturus* (lit = unripe, of fruits, then fig = before the right time) Adv *intempestive, importune* **unseasoned,** adj *non conditus*, of wood, *viridis*

unseemly, adj see INDECOROUS

unseen adj *invisus*

unselfish, adj *suae utilitatis immemor*; see also TEMPERATE **unselfishness,** n *abstinentia, continentia*, or by adj

unserviceable, adj *inutilis*

unsettle, v tr *labefacĕre, labefactare* (lit. and fig), see SHAKE **unsettled,** adj accounts, see UNPAID, — weather, *caelum varians*, in a moral sense, *inconstans, varius, mobilis voluntas*, comb *varius et mutabilis, incertus*

unshackled, adj *liber.*

unshaved, adj *intonsus*

unsheathe, v tr *gladium e vaginā educĕre.*

unship, v tr *exponĕre* (passengers and goods)

unshod, adj *pedibus nudis*

unshorn, adj *intonsus*

unshrinking, adj *impavidus, intrepidus*

unsightly, adj see UGLY

unsisterly, adj *quod sororis non est*

unskilful, unskilled, adj *inhabilis* (*alcjs rei* or *ad algd*), *inscitus, imperitus, rudis in alcjs rei* (= ignorant, in a art or science), *imperitus*, in, *alcjs rei* (= without practical experience), *ignarus alcjs rei* Adv *inepte, inscite* (= without judgment), *imperite* **unskilfulness,** n *imperitia, inscitia, alcjs rei*

unslaked, adj e g lime, *vivus*. of thirst, *non ex(s)tinctus*

unsocial, adj *insociabilis*

unsolicited, adj see UNASKED, VOLUNTARY.

unsolved, adj *non solutus*

unsophisticated, adj *simplex*

unsorted, adj *incompositus, inordinatus.*

unsought, adj *non petitus.*

unsound, adj (timber) *cariosus* (= worm-eaten, bones, etc), *puter, putris* (= rotten), — in health, see UNHEALTHY, of mind, see INSANE, of opinions, *falsus* **unsoundness,** n see UNHEALTHINESS, INSANITY

unsown, adj *non satus*

unsparing, adj 1, *inclemens, acer, acerbus*, 2, see LIBERAL

unspeakable, adj *infandus*

unspoiled, adj *incorruptus, integer.*

unstable, unsteady, adj *mobilis, inconstans, instabilis* **unsteadiness,** n *inconstantia*

unstained, adj see UNSPOILED, PURE

unstring, v tr a bow, †*arcum retendĕre*, †*remittĕre* **unstrung,** adj of the nerves, etc, *fractus, debilitatus*

unstudied, adj (of style) *simplex*

unsubdued, adj *indomitus*, see UNTAMED

unsuccessful, adj *cui eventus deest, irritus, infelix*, see UNFORTUNATE Adv *infeliciter*

unsuitable, unsuited, adj by *alienus ab alqa re, inutilis ad alqd, incommodus*, see UNFIT Adv *inutiliter, incommode* **unsuitableness,** n *inutilitas, incommoditas*

unsuspected, adj *non suspectus, in quem nulla suspicio cadit* **unsuspicious,** adj *simplex, candidus, simulationum nescius* Adv *simpliciter, candide* **unsuspiciousness,** n *simplicitas, animus simplex*, or *apertus*

untainted, adj *incorruptus, non infectus*

untamed, adj *indomitus* (lit and fig.), *effrenatus* (fig)

untasted, adj. *ingustatus.*

untaught, adj. *indoctus.*

unteachable, adj. *indocilis.*

untenable, adj. *infirmus, lĕvis.*

unterrified, adj. *interritus.*

unthankful, adj. see UNGRATEFUL. **unthankfulness**, see INGRATITUDE.

unthinking, adj. see THOUGHTLESS.

untie, v.tr. *(dis)solvĕre, laxare.*

until, **I.** prep. *ad* or *in* with accus. **II.** conj. *dum, donec, quoad* with indic. when mere time is expressed; subj. when the idea is of contingency, purpose, etc.

untilled, adj. *inaratus.*

untimely, adj. see UNSEASONABLE.

untinged, adj. *purus.*

untiring, adj. see INDEFATIGABLE.

unto, prep. see To.

untold, adj. **1**, *non dictus;* **2**, see COUNTLESS, INNUMERABLE.

untouched, adj. by *intactus;* see also UNMOVED.

untoward, adj. see UNFAVOURABLE.

untranslatable, adj. *quod verbis reddi non potest.*

untried, adj. *inexpertus.*

untrodden, adj. e.g. path, *via non trita.*

untroubled, adj. *nullo motu perturbatus* or *tranquillus, placidus;* see CALM.

untrue, adj. *falsus.* Adv. *falso, ficte.* **untruth**, n. (as quality, character) *vanitas* or by adjs., e.g. *alqd falsum esse probare;* = the thing itself, *falsum, mendacium.*

unturned, adj. to leave no stone —, *omnibus modis alqd aggredi.*

untwine, untwist, v.tr. *(re)solvĕre, retexĕre.*

unused, adj. **1**, see UNACCUSTOMED; **2**, *novus, integer;* see FRESH. **unusual**, adj. *insolitus, insolens.*

unutterable, adj. *infandus, inenarrabilis.* Adv. *supra quam quod enuntiari potest.*

unvanquished, adj. *invictus.*

unvaried, unvarying, adj. see UNCHANGED, IMMUTABLE.

unvarnished, adj. **1**, lit. *fuco non illitus;* **2**, fig. *simplex, sine fuco ac fallaciis;* see PLAIN.

unveil, v.tr. by *caput aperire.*

unversed, adj. *non versatus, peregrinus atque hospes, tiro ac rudis in alqâ re.*

unviolated, adj. *inviolatus.*

unwalled, adj. *muris non circumdatus, sine muris* (in gen.), *immunitus* (of fortifications).

unwarlike, adj. *imbellis.*

unwarrantable, adj. *iniquus.* **unwarranted**, adj. *sine auctore editus.*

unwary, adj. *incautus, imprudens.* Adv. *incaute, imprudenter.* **unwariness**, n. *imprudentia.*

unwashed, adj. *illotus.*

unwatched, adj. *incustoditus.*

unwavering, adj. see FIRM.

unwearied, adj. *indefessus, integer* (= still fresh), *assiduus.*

unweave, v.tr. *retexĕre.*

unwelcome, adj. *alci non acceptus, ingratus.*

unwell, adj. see ILL.

unwholesome, adj. *insalubris* (Plin.), *pestilens, gravis.*

unwieldy, adj. *inhabilis* (= difficult to manage), *vasti corporis* (= of a great size).

unwilling, adj. *invitus.* Adv. by *alqo invito.* **unwillingness**, n. see RELUCTANCE.

unwind, v.tr. *retexĕre.*

unwise, adj. *insipiens, stultus.* Adv. *insipienter, stulte.*

unwitting, adj. and adv. *inscius.*

unwomanly, adj. *quod non mulieris est.*

unwonted, adj. see UNUSUAL.

unworthy, adj. *indignus,* of anything, *alqâ re,* to, etc., by *qui* with subj. **unworthiness**, n. *indignitas.*

unwounded, adj. *invulneratus* (once in Cic., where we read *invulneratus inviolatusque*), *sine vulnere, integer.*

unwrap, v.tr. *evolvĕre.*

unwrinkle, v.tr. *erugare* (Plin.).

unwritten, adj. still —, *non scriptus.*

unwrought, adj. *rudis.*

unyielding, adj. see INFLEXIBLE.

unyoke, v.tr. *disjungĕre* (e.g. cattle, *jumenta, equos*).

up, adv. *sursum* (= upwards, in contrast with *deorsum*, = downwards); in combination it may be rendered by *ad, e, in, sub, trans;* — the river, *adverso flumine* (opp. to down the river, *secundo flumine*); — the hill, *in adversum montem;* to look —, *suspicĕre* (e.g. to heaven, *caelum*); to press —, *eniti* (*conniti*) *in alqd;* to burn —, *exurĕre, adurĕre;* to dry —, *exarescĕre;* to dig —, *effodĕre, eruĕre;* to deliver —, *tradĕre;* to go —, *a(d)scendĕre;* — from boyhood, etc., *a puero, a pueris;* — to, *tenus* with ablat. (always after the case); — ! *age! surge!* **upwards**, adv. *sursum;* see also MORE.

upbraid, v.tr. to — anyone with, *reprehendĕre alqm de alqâ re.* **upbraiding**, n. *objurgatio, convicium* (= scolding).

uphill, **I.** adv. *adverso colle, adversus collem.* **II.** adj. **1**, lit. *acclivis, arduus;* **2**, fig. *arduus, difficilis.*

uphold, v.tr. lit. and fig. *sustinēre, sustentare, fulcire* (= to prop).

upholsterer, n. by *qui* (*domum,* etc.) *instruit,* or *(ex)ornat.*

upland, adj. *editus;* see MOUNTAINOUS.

upon, prep. *super* with accus. with verbs of motion, ablat. with verbs of rest; *in* with accus. or ablat. (often in comp., e.g. *incidĕre* = to light —); = after, *e(x)* (e.g. directly — the consulship of Caesar, *statim e consulatu Caesaris*), or by ablat. abs. (— this, *quo* or *hoc facto*), or by *cum* (*quum*), with subj. (e.g. *quae cum secum reputasset, dixit,* he said — reflection); — this condition, *eâ condicione,* or *hac lege ut;* — the whole, *plerumque* (= usually), *ad summam* (= in a word); see ON.

upper, adj. (as regards the position) *superus, superior, summus, supremus* (the two last = highest); (as regards the order) *primoris* (not used in the nom.), *superior;* (as regards rank, dignity) *superior* (*loco* or *dignitate*); to get the — hand, *superare, vincĕre;* — storey of a house, *pars superior aedium;* — part, *pars superior;* also by *superior* or (if the highest part) by *summus* (in the same gender as the noun, e.g. — of a ship, *navis summa;* — world, in Cic. always called *haec loca quae nos incolimus.*

uppermost, adj. *summus* (in gen.), *primus*

(= according to order in rank), *princeps* (in rank or dignity)

upright, adj (*di*)*rectus* (*directus* = straight, perpendicularly as well as horizontally), *erectus*, (in a moral sense), *probus, honestus, integer, gravis.* Adv lit *recte*, or use adj , fig *recte, probe, honeste, sincere, ingenue, integre, graviter* **uprightness,** n *probitas*

uproar, n see NOISE

upset, I. v tr (*sub*)*vertĕre, evertĕre* **II.** v intr *everti, subverti, corruĕre*

upshot, n *exitus, -ūs, eventus, -ūs*

upsidedown, adj to turn —, *omnia turbare et miscēre*

upstart, n *novus homo*

urbanity, n *urbanitas*, see POLITENESS

urchin, n 1, see HEDGEHOG , 2, see CHILD, BOY

urge, v tr *impellĕre, incitare, excitare, stimulare alqm, stimulos alci admovēre* (all these lit and fig), *accendĕre, inflammare* (fig), anyone to, *alqm ad alqd* , (*ad*)*hortari ad alqd* or with *ut* or *ne*, to — anyone with requests, *instare alci* (with *ut* or *ne*), *alqm urgēre*, comb *instare et urgēre* (absolute), *alqm orare obsecrareque, precibus fatigare alqm, ab alqo petĕre et summe contendĕre, ut* or *ne*, etc **urgent,** adj *urgens* (lit), *gravis, vehemens, magni momenti, necessarius, maximus, summus* , at my — request, *orante me atque obsecrante* Adv *vehementer, magnopere* **urgency,** n *necessitas*

urine, n *urīna, lotium.*

urn, n *urna.*

usage, n *mos, consuetudo*, see CUSTOM **use, I.** n 1, = application of a thing to your wants, *usus, -ūs, usurpatio, usura* (= using), to make — of, *alqā re uti*, to come into —, *in usum venire, in consuetudinem* or *morem venire, more recipi* (= to become usual), to be of —, *utilem usui esse*, to be of great —, *magno usui esse* , 2, see USEFULNESS **II.** v tr *uti alqa re*, — for, *ad alqd, abuti re, ad alqd* or *in alqā re* (= to consume), *usurpare alqd, adhibēre alqd*, for anything, *ad alqd conferre ad* or *in alqd* , — in a certain sense, *vocabulo alqd significare, declarare*, see also TREAT **useful,** adj *utilis, aptus, idoneus, accommodatus, commodus* (all *ad alqd*), to be —, *utilem esse, usui esse, alci prodesse* or *proficĕre* Adv *utiliter, apte, commode* **usefulness,** n *utilitas, usus, ūs, commoditas* , see USE **useless,** adj *inutilis ad alqd* (or *alci rei*), *vanus, inanis, irritus* Adv *inutiliter* (only after negative), *frustra, ad irritum, incassum* (or as two words, *in cassum*)

usher, I. n perhaps *apparitor* , gentleman — (at court), *magister admissionum* (Imperial Rome) , 2, = under-teacher, *hypodidascalus* **II.** v tr 1, *ad alqm introducĕre*, 2, fig see BEGIN

usual, adj *usitatus, solitus, consuetus, nequi(c)quam, inanis, sol(l)emnis* (= habitual), *tritus* (of language, = commonplace), *vulgaris, more* or *usu receptus* (= customary) , it is —, *solet*, more than —, *plus quam solet, plus solito*, see COMMON, CUSTOMARY Adv *ferme, fere, plerumque, ut solet*

usucaption, n *usucapio*

usufruct, n *usus, -ūs, et fructus ūs, ususfructus* (both parts of the word declined).

usurp, v tr (*as*)*sumĕre alqd, invadĕre in alqd, occupare* (e g *regnum*, = — the government) **usurper,** n *qui regnum occupat* **usurpation,** n *occupatio*, or by the verbs

usury, n *fenerari* **usurer,** n *fenerator, tocullio* **usurious,** adj *avarus*, see AVARICIOUS **usury,** n *usura* (paid by the debtor), *feneratio* (= lending on interest), *fenus, -ŏris,* n (= interest received)

utensil, n *vas*, *vasis* (in pl *vasa, -orum*, = vessel), in farming, *instrumentum* (*rusticum*, as collective noun always in the sing), —s, *utensilia, ium*, n (= everything necessary in daily life), *supellex, -ectilis*, f (= household furniture).

uterine, adj *uterinus* (Jct)

utility, n see USEFULNESS **utilitarian,** adj *qui omnia ad utilitatem confert*

utmost, adj *extremus, ultimus, summus* , — misery, *summae angustiae, extremae res, extrema* or *ultima, orum summa inopia* , see EXTREME

utter, uttermost, adj see EXTREME, COMPLETE Adv *penitus, funditus*, see ENTIRELY

utter, v tr *significare* (= to give to understand), *indicare* (= to point out), *ostendĕre* (= to show), *profitēri* (= to profess), *prae se ferre* or *gerĕre* (= to declare openly), to — a sound, *sonitum edĕre, emittere*, see PRONOUNCE **utterance,** n see PRONUNCIATION, DELIVERY

uvula, n *uva* (Plin)

V.

vacancy, n 1, = void space, *vacuum, inane, inanitas* (= emptiness), 2, with regard to office, by *vacuus*, chosen to fill a —, *suffectus*, 3, see LEISURE , 4, of mind, *inanitas, stupiditas* **vacant,** adj 1, see EMPTY , 2, of an office, *vacuus*, to be —, *vacuum esse, vacare* 3, = unoccupied by business, by *vacuus labore* or *negotiis*, 4, = empty, of thought, *stupidus*, see FOOLISH ; 5, in law, *vacuus* (= having no heir, e g a house, field) **vacate,** v tr 1, = make empty, *vacuefacĕre*, 2, = to make vacant, an office, *se abdicare alqā re* or (but not in Cic or Caes) **vacation,** n *feriae* **vacuity, vacuum,** n see VACANCY **vacuus,** adj see VACANT.

vaccinate, v tr anyone, *variolas alci inserere* (not class) **vaccination,** n *insitio variolarum*

vacillate, v intr *vacillare* (lit and fig) **vacillating,** adj *dubius, incertus, ambiguus* ; see DOUBTFUL **vacillation,** n *dubium, dubitatio*, see DOUBT, HESITATION

vagabond, vagrant, I adj *vagus* **II.** n *erro, grassator* **vagary,** n *nugae* (= tricks), *ineptiae* (= silliness), see WHIM

vague, adj *incertus, dubius, ambiguus, anceps*, see INDEFINITE, UNCERTAIN Adv *incerte, dubie, ambigue* **vagueness,** n *dubium, dubitatio*, see DOUBT, OBSCURITY

vain, adj 1, = empty, worthless, *inanis*, see IDLE 2, = fruitless, *vanus, irritus*, to labour in —, *operam perdĕre, operam frustra consumĕre* or *conterĕre, oleum et operam perdĕre* (prov , Cic), 3, = proud, *inanis, vanus* (= foolishly —), *laudis avidus* (= ambitious), *superbus* (= proud), *gloriosus* (= boastful), *putidus* (= affected), to be —, *rebus inanibus delectari* Adv **in vain,** *frustra, incassum* (or *in cassum*, as two words), *nequi(c)quam*, see VAIN, = proudly, etc , *gloriose putide, superbe* **vainglorious,** adj *gloriosus* **vanity,** n = emptiness, *inani-*

tas, vanitas, fragilitas; = empty pride, *ambitio, ostentatio.*

vale, n. see VALLEY.

valediction, valedictory, n. and adj. see FAREWELL.

valentine, n. *epistula amatoria.*

valet, n. *cubicularius.*

valetudinarian, n. *suae valetudinis (nimis) studiosus.*

valiant, valorous, adj. *fortis, animosus*, comb. *fortis et animosus* or *animosus et fortis, strenuus*, comb. *fortis atque strenuus* or *strenuus et fortis, acer* (= full of energy), comb. *acer et fortis*; see BRAVE. Adv. *fortiter, animose*, comb. *animose et fortiter, strenue, acriter.* **valour**, n. *fortitudo, virtus, -ūtis*, f.; see BRAVERY.

valid, adj. *gravis* (= important); in point of law, *bonus* (e.g. witness), *justus* (= right), *idoneus* (= fit, sufficient, e.g. witness, excuse), *ratus* (= confirmed, what has become a law), *firmus, certus*, comb. *ratus ac firmus* (e.g. *jussum*); to be —, *valēre* (of a coin, a law, etc.); to make anything —, *ratum facĕre alqd, ratum esse alqd jubēre.* **validity**, n. (of reasons, etc.), *gravitas, pondus, -ĕris*, n.; in point of law (e.g. of a witness, etc.), *fides.*

valley, n. *(con)vallis.*

value, I. v.tr. (= to determine the worth of an object) *aestimare* (of gen. import), something greatly, *censēre* (of the censor), to be —d, *censēri* (used of citizens and their possessions); fig. = to think well of, *aestimare* (with genit. or abl.), *facĕre, ducĕre, pendĕre, habēre* (with gen. *magni*, etc.), *deligĕre*; to — not at all, *alqd nullo loco, nihilo, pro nihilo* or *nihil numerare, alqm nullo loco putare, alqm despicĕre*; to — highly, *magni facĕre* or *ducĕre*, or *pendĕre*, or *habēre*; to — more than, *pluris aestimare*; to — little, *parvi facĕre*, etc. II. n. *aestimatio* (= estimated value), *pretium* (= price), *virtus, -ūtis*, f. (= inner worth, of a person or thing); great (intrinsic) —, *praestantia*; moral —, worth, *virtus, honestas*; things without —, *res viles* or *leves.* **valuable**, adj. *pretiosus* (lit.), *magni pretii* (lit. and fig.), *alci acceptus, gratus* (of what does one good to see, hear, etc.). **valuation**, n. *aestimatio.* **valuer**, n. *qui alqd aestimat, aestimator.* **valueless**, see WORTHLESS.

valve, n. *epistomium.*

vampire, n. *vespertilio (qui sanguinem sugit).*

van, n. of an army, *primum agmen* (in marching order), *acies prima* (in battle order).

van, n. = winnowing-fan, *vannus*, f.

van, n. see CART, WAGGON.

vane, n. see WEATHERCOCK.

vanish, v.intr. *(e)vanescĕre.*

vanity, n. see under VAIN.

vanquish, v.tr. *(de)vincĕre, superare*, comb. *vincĕre et superare, domare* (= to subdue), *profligare* (= to drive an army off the field), *subigĕre* (= to subjugate). **vanquisher**, n. *victor* (f. *victrix*), *expugnator* with gen. (e.g. *urbis*), *domitor* with gen. (e.g. *Hispaniae*).

vapid, adj. 1, *vapidus* (of wine); 2, fig. see INSIPID.

vapour, n. *vapor*, †*halitus, -ūs, nebula* (= both arising from the ground and from the water); *terrae anhelitus, -ūs, ex(s)piratio*, or *exhalatio, ex terrā afflatus, -ūs* (more particularly that ascending from the bottom of a cavern, whereby Pythia became inspired, both Cic. de Div. ii. 57, 117); — bath, *assa sudatio* (Cels.).

variable, adj. see CHANGEABLE. **variableness**, n. see CHANGE. **variance**, n. *discordia*; to set at —, *discordiam concitare*; to be at — with each other, *inter se discordare, inter se dissidēre*; see ENMITY. **variation**, n. *varietas* (= accidental change, e.g. *coeli*); see ALTERATION, CHANGE, DEVIATION. **vari-coloured, variegated**, adj. *varius, varii coloris, versicolor.* **variegate**, v.tr. *variare, distinguĕre.* **variety**, n. *varietas* (e.g. *caeli*, of the weather; *eloquendi*, of style), *diversitas, vicissitudo*; a — of things, *res multae* or *variae.* **various**, adj. *varius, diversus, multiplex* (= manifold). Adv. *varie, diverse.* **vary**, I. v.tr. *variare*; see ALTER, CHANGE. II. v.intr. *variare, variari, (com)mutari, immutari.*

varicose, adj. and n. *varix* (e.g. vein).

varlet, n. see SERVANT, ROGUE.

varnish, I. n. 1, *atramentum tenue* (of a dark colour, for paintings, Plin.); 2, = fair appearance, *color, fucus, species.* II. v.tr. 1, *atramento tenui illinĕre*; 2, fig. e.g. errors or deformity, *praetendĕre alqd alci rei, tegĕre* or *occultare alqd alqā re.*

vase, n. *vas, vasis*, n. see JAR.

vassal, n. *cliens.* **vassalage**, n. *clientela.*

vast, adj. *vastus, immanis*, comb. *vastus et immanis, magnus, ingens, incredibilis, amplus*; see GREAT. Adv. *magnopere, incredibiliter, valde*; see VERY. **vastness**, n. *amplitudo, magnitudo, immensitas.*

vat, n. *cupa, dolium.*

vaticinate, v.tr. see FORETELL.

vault, I. n. 1, = arched roof, *camera, concameratio, fornix*; see ARCH; 2, = —ed chamber, *fornix*; — underground, *hypogēum*; 3, see TOMB. II. v.tr. 1, *confornicare, concamerare*; see ARCH; 2, *salire*; see LEAP.

vaunt, v.intr. and n. see BOAST.

veal, n. *(caro) vitulina.*

veer, v.intr. *se vertĕre, verti.*

vegetable, adj. *qui (quae, quod) ad plantas pertinet*; — kingdom, perhaps *plantae et arbores.* **vegetables**, n. *olus* or pl. *olera, -um*, n.; — garden, *hortus olitorius*; — gardener, *olitor*; — market, *forum olitorium.* **vegetate**, v.intr. 1, lit. see GROW; 2, fig. *hebescĕre, languēre.* **vegetation**, n. *herbae, plantae.* **vegetative**, adj. circ. by *crescĕre.*

vehemence, n. *vis, incitatio* (e.g. of a smell, of a disease, of a war, etc.), *impetus, -ūs* (= haste), *violentia* (= violence), *ardor, aestus, -ūs* (of a fever, of the passions), *impotentia* (= unbridled passion), *iracundia* (= hastiness), *studium* (= eagerness). **vehement**, adj. *vehemens* (= not calm, opp. *lenis, placidus*), *gravis* (= violent, e.g. *morbus, odor, verbum* (= offensive)), *magnus, acer* (= acting in a passion, opp. *lenis*, also e.g. *bellum*), comb. *acer et vehemens, acerbus* (= bitter), *animosus* (= spirited), *concitatus, incitatus* (= spurred on), *intentus* (= intent, anxious), *rapidus* (= quick, hasty), *violentus* (= violent), *atrox* (= dreadful, shocking), *ardens, flagrans* (of fever and of the passions), *iracundus* (= angry); — desire, *cupiditas magna* or *acris, ardens* or *flagrans.* Adv. *vehementer, valde, graviter, acriter, acerbe, contente, intente, animose, ardenter, violenter.*

vehicle, n. 1, see CARRIAGE, WAGGON; 2, MEANS.

veil, I. n *rica* (among the Roman ladies, Plaut), *flammeum* (Plin), *flammeolum* (Juv, = bridal —), the — of oblivion, by *alqd velare*, *alqd occultare* **II.** v tr *velare*, *tegere* (both lit and fig)

vein, n *vena* (used also of veinlike marks in an object, and fig as — of humour), *arteria* (= artery), *alqd alcjs rei* (fig e g he has a — of strength, *alqd virium ei inest*)

vellicate, v tr *vellere*, *vellicare*

vellum, n. *membrana*

velocity, n *velocitas*, see SWIFTNESS

velvet, n see SILK **velvety,** adj see SMOOTH

venal, adj *venalis* (of merchandise, etc, or persons), *nummarius* (e g *judices*, *judicium*) **venality,** n *animus venalis*

vend, v tr *vendere* **vender,** n *venditor* **vendible,** adj *vendibilis*

veneer, v tr *sectilibus laminis operire* or *vestire*

venerable, adj *venerabilis*, see REVEREND **venerate,** v tr *colere* (= to worship, revere), *observare* (= to revere), comb *colere et observare*, *observare et diligere in honore habere* (a man), *admirari*, *venerari* (a person or thing) **veneration,** n *cultus*, *-ūs*, *veneratio* (of a god or of a man), *religio* (= awe)

venereal, adj *venereus*

vengeance, n *ultio*, see REVENGE

venial, adj *venia dignus*

venison, n (*caro*) *ferina*

venom, n 1, *venenum* (lit and fig), see POISON. **venomous,** adj *venenatus* (lit and fig); see POISONOUS.

vent, I. n 1, *spiramentum*, †*spiramen*, †*spiraculum* (in gen = — hole), *aestuarium* (= hole to let in air, e g in digging wells), *foramen*, 2, by *effundere*, see below **II.** v tr to — one's passion, *stomachum in alqm erumpere*, *odium expromere*, *iram*, etc, *in alqm effundere*, *evomere* **vent-hole,** n see VENT I.

ventilate, v tr 1, *ventulum facere alci* (Com by fanning), *ventilare* (= to fan), to — a room, *ventum (in cubiculum, etc)*, *immittere*, 2, fig *in medium proferre* **ventilation,** n use verb **ventilator,** n see VENT, I.

ventricle, n *ventriculus*

ventriloquist, n *ventriloquus* (late, in Plutarch's time, about A D 70, a — was termed in Greek πυθων, and, if a female, πυθωνισσα), perhaps *qui sonos alienos sua voce imitatur*

venture, I. n = experiment, *experimentum*, *periculum* (= risk), *alea* (= hazard), *facinus*, *ŏris*, n (= bold act) at a — *temere*, *forte*, *temere*, *fortuito ac temere*, *temere ac fortuito* **II.** v intr and tr. *periclitari* (both *alqd*, and = to be endangered), to — to do a thing, *audere* (courageously), *conari* (= to attempt, both with infin never with *ut*), he —d to ask him, *ausus est eum rogare*, to — upon, at, on anything, *audere alqd* (e g an undertaking, *facinus*), *periculum facere alcjs rei*, into battle, by *se committere in aciem*, nothing —, nothing win, prov *dimidium facti*, *qui coepit*, *habet* (Hor), *fortes fortuna adjuvat* (Ter) **venturesome, venturous,** adj *audax*, *temerarius* Adv *audacter*, *temere* **venturousness,** n *audacia*, *temeritas*

veracious, adj *verax*, *verax*, see TRUTHFUL **veracity,** n *veritas*

verandah, n *subdialia*, *-ium* (= open galleries, Plin), *podium* (= balcony), or *porticus*, *-ūs*, f

verb, n *verbum* (gram) **verbal,** adj by *verbum* or *vox* Adv by *praesens* (= present), or *ipse* or *coram* (= face to face), see also VERBATIM **verbatim,** adv *ad verbum totidem verbis* **verbose,** adj *verbosus* **verboseness, verbosity,** n *copia* or *ubertas verborum*, or by *copiose et abundanter de alqa re dicere* or *loqui*, *in dicendo adhibere quandam speciem atque pompam*

verdant, adj *viridis* **verdure,** n *viriditas* (e g *pratorum*)

verdict, n in law, *responsum* (= answer), *arbitrium* (= decision of an arbitrator, in gen), *judicium* (= judgment of a judge) to pronounce a —, *decernere* (= to decide of magistrates), *judicare*, *sententiam dicere* (of a judge)

verdigris, n *aerugo* (Plin, *aeris* or *cypria*)

verge, n 1, = brink, *margo*, *ora*, see MARGIN, 2, fig by circumloc (e g on the — of danger *cum periculum jam instaret* or *imminente periculo*, or *minimum abfuit quin periculum adesset*). **verger,** n *apparitor*

verge, v intr *vergere ad alqd* (= to slope towards), to — upon, *tangere*, *attingere alqd* (= to touch), *alci rei finitimum esse* (lit and fig)

verification, n *confirmatio*, see PROOF **verify,** v tr *(ap)probare*, *comprobare* **verily,** adv *profecto*, *sane*, *certe*, *ne* (nae) **verity,** n see TRUTH

verisimilitude, n. *verisimilitudo* (also as two words, *veri simi*) **veritable,** adj *verus*, see TRUE, GENUINE

vermilion, I. n *minium* **II.** adj *miniatus* (= coloured with red-lead), *miniaceus* (= — coloured, Vitr), see RED

vermin, n *bestiolae molestae* (in gen), *pediculi* (= lice)

vernacular, adj — tongue, *sermo patrius*, *sermo nativus*, *sermo noster*, *lingua nostra*, *verba orum*, *nostrorum*

versatile, adj *versatilis* (of that which may be turned round, lit), of genius, *agilis*, *mobilis*, *varius et multiplex* **versatility,** n of genius, *facilitas*, *ingenium facile* or *mobile*, *agilitas*, *mobilitas*

verse, n *versus*, *ūs*, *versiculus*, to make —, *versus facere* or *scribere*, *versus fundere*, = a short division of any composition, *pars* **versification,** n *versuum ratio* **versify,** v tr *carmina facere*

versed, adj *versatus in alqa re*, *exercitatus in alqa re*, *peritus*, *gnarus alcjs rei*

version, n *liber scriptoris conversus*

vertebra, n *vertebra* (Plin).

vertex, n *vertex*, or by *summus*, see SUMMIT **vertical,** adj *(di)rectus*, a — line, *linea*, *perpendiculum* Adv *recte*, *directo*, *ad lineam*, *ad perpendiculum*

vertiginous, adj 1, e g motion, *quod in orbem circumagitur* or *circumfertur*, 2, *vertiginosus* (= suffering from giddiness Plin) **vertigo,** n *vertigo* (*oculorum*)

very, I adj see TRUE, REAL, **II** adv *summe* (= in the highest degree, with verbs and adjs), (*quam*) *maxime* (= most, with adj and verbs), *magnopere* or *magno opere*, *maximopere* or *maximo opere*, *summopere* or *summo opere* (only with verbs), *impense* (= without fearing any trouble, only with verbs), *admodum* (= completely) *valde* (= with great strength, the fore going with verbs and adjs), *sane quam* (= much indeed, e g *gaudere*, *brevis*), *oppido* (with adjs and advs, more used in the colloquial style), *satis* (= sufficient, with regard to a certain end, to circumstances, to a position, etc., with adjs. and advs., e.g. *non satis se tutum in Argis videbat*), *enixe* (= with great exertion, e.g. to try, *operam dare*), *vehementer*, with *rogare, dolēre, gaudēre*, etc.; (often = in the highest degree), *graviter* (with verbs and partic., e.g. to be ill, *aegrotare*; *iratus*), *mire, mirifice, mire quantum* (= extraordinarily, with verbs and adjs.), *apprime* (mostly ante and post class. = extremely, with adjs., e.g. *apprime gnarus alcjs rei*), *perfecte* (= perfectly, e.g. *perfecte sapiens, eloquens*), *in primis* (*inprimis*, = foremost; instead of *in primis*, we find also *inter primos, in paucis, cum paucis, inter paucos, ante alios, praeter ceteros, super omnes*), *bene* (= well, with adjs., advs., and verbs, e.g. *bene mane, bene potus*), *probe* (= right, right well, with adjs. and verbs, but only in colloquial style), *egregie, eximie* (= exceedingly, with adjs. and verbs; *egregie* also in daily intercourse, in the epistolary style and in conversation), *longe* (= by far, e.g. *longe superare*); "—" also by *per* or *prae* in composition with an adj., adv., or verb (e.g. — few, *perpauci* or *perquam pauci*; it pleases me — much, *mihi perplacet* or *mihi perquam placet, mihi valde placet*; — hard, *praedurus*; by a superl., which may be strengthened by adding *longe* or *multo* (e.g. (*longe*) *fertilissimus, multo ditissimus*); not —, before adj. and advs., by *non ita, haud ita* (e.g. not so — many, *non ita multi*; not — long after, *haud ita multo post*).

vesicle, n. *vesica* (Plin.).

vesper, n. = evening star, *Hesperus, Vesper*. **vespers,** n. in the Romish Church, *Preces Vespertinae*.

vessel, n. = utensil, *vas, vasis* (in the pl. *vasa, -orum*, n.); in anatomy, blood —, *arteriae, venae*; = ship, *navis*.

vest, I. n. *subucula*, or *tunica*; see GARMENT. **II.** v.tr. 1, *vestire*; see CLOTHE; 2, see INVEST. **vested,** adj. e.g. rights, by *jus, juris*, n. (e.g. — interests are sacred, *jus alcjs est sacrosanctum*). **vestry,** n. *sacrarium*. **vesture,** n. see GARMENT.

vestal, I. adj. see PURE, CHASTE. **II.** n. *Vestalis* (*virgo*).

vestibule, n. *vestibulum, pronaus, -aos* (of a temple).

vestige, n. *vestigium*.

vetch, n. *vicia*.

veteran, adj. and n. *veteranus* (esp. of soldiers; in the agricultural writers, also of animals and plants); a — soldier, (*miles*) *veteranus* or *emeritus*; in wider sense, *veterator* (of a lawyer, Cic.).

veterinary, adj. *veterinarius* (Col.).

veto, I. n. *intercessio* (of the tribunes), in gen. by circumloc.; see FORBID. **II.** v.tr. *rogationi intercedĕre* (of the tribunes); see FORBID.

vex, v.tr. *stomachum facĕre alci, indignationem movēre alci, offendĕre, pungĕre, sol(l)icitare, vexare, mordēre, commovēre alqm*; to be —ed at, *alqd aegre* or *moleste ferre*; I am —ed at, *me piget alcjs rei*; see ANNOY. **vexation,** n. *aegritudo animi, indignatio, stomachus, molestia*; full of —, *indignabundus*. **vexatious,** adj. *molestus, gravis*; see TROUBLESOME. Adv. *moleste, graviter*.

viaduct, n. by *ponte jungĕre* (e.g. *flumen*).

vial, n. see BOTTLE.

viands, n. *cibus*.

viaticum, n. *viaticum*.

vibrate, v.intr. *vibrare*; of sound, *tinnire* (e.g. *aures tinniunt*), *vocalem sonum reddĕre* (e.g. of a column). **vibration,** n. *motus, -ūs*.

vicar, n. in gen. *vicarius*. **vicarage,** n. see BENEFICE, PARSONAGE. **vicarious,** adj. and adv. *alcjs loco*.

vice, prep. in composition, by *pro* or *sub* (e.g. *subpraefectus, proconsul*).

vice, n. *vitiositas, turpitudo* (= the quality of —), *libidines* (= lust), *vitia, -iorum* (= habitual sins; one such, *vitium*), *flagitium, scelus, -ĕris*, n. (= as a wicked act). **vicious,** adj. *vitiosus* (= defective, unsound), *turpis* (= shameful), *flagitiosus* (= profligate, all of persons and things, e.g. *vita*), comb. *vitiosus ac flagitiosus* (e.g. *vita*), *cujus in animo improbitas versatur* (of man's heart, of man in general), *vitiis contaminatus, inquinatus* (= polluted with —, of persons and things), *scelestus, sceleratus, perditus* (= criminal; the former of the disposition, the latter of an act of persons and things); very —, *vitiis, flagitiis, sceleribus obrutus* (of persons), *vitiis flagitiisque omnibus deditus* (also of things, e.g. *vita*). Adv. *vitiose, turpiter, flagitiose*, comb. *flagitiose et turpiter, scelerate, perdite, sceleste*. **viciousness,** n. see VICE.

vicissitude, n. *vicissitudo, vicissitudines* (= a change that takes place regularly, e.g. of the times, *vicissitudo* or *varietas temporum*; of day and night, *dierum noctiumque vicissitudines*; of fortune, *fortunae vicissitudo, mutatio rerum humanarum*).

victim, n. *victima, hostia, piaculum* (in expiation); see SACRIFICE. **victimize,** v.tr. see CHEAT.

victor, n. *victor*; see CONQUEROR. **victorious,** adj. *victor, victrix* (with nouns of the fem. and neuter gender). Adv. by adj. **victory,** n. *victoria, tropaeum, triumphus* (= the triumph decreed by Senate, hence = — itself); to gain —, *vincĕre, victoriam consequi, adipisci, victoriā potiri*.

victuals, n. *cibus, cibaria, -orum, alimenta, -orum*; see PROVISIONS. **victual,** v.tr. *rem frumentariam providēre, comparare, frumentum* (*com*)*parare, conferre*; see FOOD.

vie, v.intr. *aemulari alqm* or *cum alqo*; see RIVAL.

view, I. v.tr. see INSPECT, LOOK, SEE. **II.** n. 1, (*ad*)*spectus* (= vision), *acies* (= glance), *oculu*. (= eye), *prospectus* (at a distance), *aspectus* (from a high place), *conspectus* (= sight; all *-ūs*); to be in —, *in conspectu esse*; to come into —, *in conspectum venire*; in — of, *in oculis situm esse*; see SIGHT; 2, see DESIGN; point of —, *ratio*; to consider in the right point of —, *vere* or *recte judicare de alqā re*.

vigil, n. 1, see WATCH; 2, in church affairs, *pervigilium*; 3, see EVE. **vigilance,** n. *vigilantia*; see CARE. **vigilant,** adj. + *vigil, vigilans, intentus, providus, diligens*. Adv. *vigilanter, intente, diligenter*.

vigour, n. *vis* (physical and mental, pl. *vires*), *robur, -ŏris*, n. (= physical strength), *nervi, lacerti* (= nerve), *vigor* (= energy). **vigorous,** adj. *valens, validus* (= possessing physical strength), *strenuus, impiger, acer* (= energetic), *vegetus* (= fresh), *firmus*, comb. *firmus et robustus* (e.g. *respublica*), *valens et firmus* (e.g. *civitas*), *robustus* (= robust; man, state, food), comb. *robustus et valens* (e.g. *homo*), *lacertosus* (= muscular, man and animal), *corpore vigens, corpore validus, corpore robusto* (the first of youthfulness, the second of physical strength, the third of a stout, healthy body), *fortis* (= strong), *acer* (= eager); see STRONG, ENERGETIC. Adv. *fortiter, acriter*; see STRONGLY, EAGERLY.

vile, adj *abjectus nequam, turpis, detestabilis, inquinatus, illiberalis, sordidus, foedus* Adv *abjecte, nequiter, turpiter, inquinate, illiberaliter, sordide, foede* **vileness,** n *turpitudo, nequitia, illiberalitas, foeditas*, see DEPRAVITY **vilify,** v tr *alqm ignominiâ afficere*, see SLANDER

villa, n *villa*

village, n *pagus, vicus* **villager,** n *paganus, vicanus, rusticus, agrestis*

villain n 1, in Mediaeval Latin, **villanus*, 2, *homo scelestus, sceleratus, nefarius, nequam, flagitiosus*, as a term of reproach, also *scelus, ĕris*, n , *flagitium*, see ROGUE **villanous,** adj *scelestus, sceleratus, nefarius, nequam flagitiosus.* **villany,** n 1, as disposition, see WICKEDNESS, 2, as act, *scelus, -ĕris*, n , *facinus, -ŏris*, n , *dedecus, ŏris*, n , *consilium foedum, flagitium*

vindicate, v tr a right, *jus tenēre, obtinēre, retinēre*, one's character, *sibi constare, a se non desciscĕre*, to — one's liberty *se in libertatem vindicare* **vindication,** n see DEFENCE **vindictive,** adj *ulciscendi cupidus*, a — spirit, *ulciscendi or ultionis cupiditas* Adv use adj

vine, I. n *vitis, labrusca* (*vitis*) (= wild —), a small —, *viticula* **II.** adj *vinearius* (Col), or by genit of *vitis*, — dresser, *vinitor*, - yard, *vinea, vinetum, arbustum* **vinegar.** n *acetum*, — bottle, *acetabulum*, — leaf, *pampinus*, m and f **vinery,** n perhaps *vites sub vitreis constitae* **vinous,** adj *vinosus* (mostly post class) **vintage,** n *vindemia, vindemiola* (small), to gather the —, *vindemiare uvas or vinum* (Plin) **vintner,** n *vinarius* (ante and post class)

violate, v tr *violare, rumpĕre* **violable,** adj † *violabilis* **violation,** n 1, *violatio*, 2, see RAPE **violence,** n *violentia, vis, ardor* (of heat), *fervor* (of heat or passion), *impotentia* (= lack of restraint), *acerbitas, morositas, immanitas* (all three of temper), (*caeli*) *intemperies*, (*caeli, morbi*, etc) *gravitas, aestus, -ūs* (of a fever, etc) **violator,** n *violator, ruptor* **violent,** adj † *violens, violentus* (= boisterous, of mind, etc), *acer, vehemens, impotens, gravis* (of illness, weather, etc), see SEVERE, CRUEL Adv *violenter, acriter, vehementer, impotenter, graviter*

violet, I. n *viola, ĭon* (Plin), a bed of —s *violarium*, the colour † *viola* **II.** adj *violaceus, ianthinus* (Plin)

violin, n *fides, -ium*, f. (e g to play on the — *fidibus canĕre*)

viper, n *vipera* (lit and fig), *aspis, -idis*, f

virago, n 1. = female warrior, † *virago, mulier* or *virgo bellicosa, animosa, fortis*, 2, = quarrelsome woman, *mulier jurgiosa*

virgin, I. n *virgo* **II.** adj † *virgineus virginalis* (e g *verecundia*), *virgo* in app to noun (e g *id ego virgo feci*), — soil, *terra rudis* (ante class). **virginity,** n *virginitas*

virile, adj (e g age) *virilis*; see MANLY **virility,** n *virilitas* (Plin , Quint)

virtue, n *virtus, -ūtis*, f , *laus* (= praiseworthy condition), *honestum, rectum* (= what is right), *honestas* (= probity), *sanctimonia* (= guiltlessness), *pudicitia* (= modesty of a woman, as her first —), = efficacy, *virtus, -ūtis, vis*, to have — in anything, *ad alqd alci prodesse*, by — of, *per* with accus or *ex* with ablat (e g he does it by — of his wealth *per opes* or (*ex*) *opibus hoc facit*) **virtual,** adj and adv *re non verbo* **virtuous,** adj *virtute praeditus* or *ornatus sanctus* (= pleasing to God, of persons and things), *honestus, probus* (= upright, of men), *castus* (= chaste), a — life *vita honesta* or *sancta* **virtuoso,** n *alcjs rei artifex, alcjs rei peritissimus*

virulence, n 1 *vis, gravitas* (e g *morbi*); see POISON, 2, fig *acerbitas, virus*, n **virulent,** adj *gravis* (e g climate, *caelum*), fig *acerbus*, see BITTER Adv *graviter, acerbe*

visage, n see FACE, COUNTENANCE.

viscera, n *viscera, -um, exta, orum*

viscid adj † *tenax, glutinosus* (= sticky, like glue, Col), see STICKY

visible, adj *a(d)spectabilis, quod cerni potest, quod a(d)spectu sentitur, conspectus, conspicuus* (= clear to be seen), *expressus* (= clearly expressed, e g *vestigia, indicia*), *apertus* (= open, opp *occultus*, e g discord, *simultas*, *dolor*), *manifestus* (= manifest), *latens, occultus* (e g *caedes*) Adv *manifesto*, see CLEARLY, EVIDENTLY **vision,** n (in optics) *visus, -ūs, a(d)spectus, -ūs, sensus, -ūs videndi, cernendi*, an optical illusion, *res objecta* (= what appears to the eye, Cic), *visus, -ūs, visum, visio* (= anything seen, a — in a dream), *species* (both awake and in a dream), *simulacrum* (= anything we fancy as resembling a certain thing) **visionary.** adj opp to real, *inanis, fictus, vanus*, of character, *fanaticus* (= enthusiastic), perhaps *cogitationi deditus* (= unpractical), by circumloc , see DREAM, IMAGE

visit, I. n *salutatio, salutationis officium* (in the Roman sense of friends and clients in the morning), to come on a —, *visendi caus(s)â venire*, to accept the — of anyone, *alqm admittĕre*, your — will be welcome to all, *carus omnibus exspectatusque venies* **II.** v tr *alqm* (*in*)*visĕre* or *visitare, visendi caus(s)â venire* (to see how anyone is), *adire, convenire alqm* (in order to speak to or transact business with anyone), *salutare alqm, salutatum* or *salutandi caus(s)â ad alqm venire, ad alqm salutandum venire* (out of politeness = to wait upon), *obire, adire, venire ad*, etc , *frequentare* (= attend as a school), to — a fair, *obire nundinas*, to go on a round of —s, — anyone's country-seats, *obire villas suas*, (in a Scriptural sense) *alqm urgēre, vexare, punire* **visitation,** n (of Divine Providence) *poena* **visitor,** n *salutans, salutator, qui visendi* (*ac salutandi*) *caus(s)â venit* (or *veniunt*) *ad alqm, hospes, ĭtis* (= guest) I have —s *habeo alqm mecum*, I have no —, *solus sum, neminem mecum habeo*, I shall have many —s, *multi apud me erunt.*

visor, n *buccula* (= cheek-piece)

vista, n *prospectus, ūs*, see VIEW

visual, adj (e g nerve) *oculorum nervus*

vital, adj *vitalis* (= belonging to life), = very important, *maximi momenti* Adv *maximi momenti*, see VERY **vitality,** n *animus, vis vitalis*, see LIFE

vitiate, v tr *vitiare, corrumpĕre* **vitiation,** n *corruptio, depravatio*

vitreous, adj *vitreus*

vitriol, n * *vitriŏlum*

vituperate, v tr see SCOLD **vituperation,** n *vituperatio, reprehensio* **vituperative,** adj see ABUSIVE

vivacious, adj *vividus*, see ACTIVE, CHEERFUL **vivacity,** n *vigor*, see LIVELINESS CHEERFULNESS **vivid,** adj see LIVELY

viviparous, adj — animals, *bestiae quae partum edunt* (*vivum*)

vixen, n 1, = she-fox, *vulpes, is*, 2, = quarrelsome woman, *mulier jurgiosa*

vizier, n *cui summa imperii delegata est*

vocabulary, n *index verborum* (= list of words), *verba* (*nostra*) (= abundance of words)

vocal, adj. *vocalis*; — music, *vocum cantus, -ūs*; — and instrumental music, *vocum nervorumque cantus*.

vocation, n. *officium, partes, -ium, munus, -ĕris*, n.

vocative, n. *casus, -ūs, vocativus* (Gram.).

vociferate, v.intr. *vociferari*. **vociferation,** n. *vociferatio*. **vociferous,** adj. and adv. *magno (cum) clamore*.

vogue, n. to be in —, *expeti* (of what has a sale), *moris esse* (= to be the custom).

voice, I. n. *vox* (= the faculty of uttering sounds; then the sound produced), *cantus, -ūs*, (= song), *sonus* (= sound of the — and of musical instruments), *vocis sonus*; a clear —, *clara vox* (opp. *vox obtusa*), *vox canora* (opp. *vox fusca*); a high —, *vox acuta* (opp. *vox gravis*); with a loud —, *clarâ voce, magnâ voce*; to raise the —, *attollĕre sonum*; to lower the —, *submittĕre vocem*; the general —, *omnium consensus, -ūs, consensus publicus*; there is but one —, *omnes uno ore in algâ re consentiunt*; in Gram. a verb in the active, passive —, *verbum activum, passivum*. **II.** v.tr. see UTTER.

void, I. adj. **1**, see EMPTY; **2**, lacking anything, *vacuus (ab) algâ re, carens algâ re, egens alcjs rei* or *algâ re*; — of, *inops alcjs rei* or *algâ re, privatus* or *spoliatus algâ re*. **II.** n. *inanitas, inane, vacuitas, vacuum*. **III.** v.tr. see EMPTY, v.tr., VACATE.

volatile, adj. *volaticus* (lit. and fig.); fig. (of anyone's character, *lĕvis, mobilis* (opp. *constans*). **volatility,** n. (of fluids, etc.) by *fugĕre*; fig. *lĕvitas, ingenium mobile, animus lĕvis, vanitas, mobilitas* (*ingenii* or *animi*, opp. *constantia*), comb. *mobilitas et lĕvitas animi*.

volcano, n. *mons e cujus vertice ignes erumpunt*, or *mons flammas eructans*. **volcanic,** adj. *flammas eructans, ignes* or *flammas vomens*.

volition, n. *voluntas*.

volley, n. *tormenta, -orum, emissa*; — of words, *flumen* or *turba (inanium) verborum*.

voluble, adj. see FLUENT.

volume, n. = book, or division of book, *liber, volumen* (= a roll of parchment), *pars* (as a part); — of smoke, etc., † *volumen*, or by noun with or without adj. (e.g. *fumus*, = smoke, *aqua* = water). **voluminous,** adj. by *multus* (e.g. he has left — writings on this, *multa* or *plurima de hâc re reliquit*).

voluntary, adj. *voluntarius, volens* (opp. *coactus*), *non coactus, non invitus*, or by *sponte* (*meâ*, etc.). Adv. (*meâ*, etc.) *voluntate, sponte* (= of one's own accord), comb. *suâ sponte et voluntate, ultro* (= without being asked). **volunteer, I.** n. *voluntarius* (*miles*); —s, (*milites*) *voluntarii*. **II.** v.intr. *voluntate facĕre alqd*; of soldiers, *nomen* (pl. of several, *nomina*) *dare*.

voluptuous, adj. *voluptarius, libidinosus, ad voluptates propensus, voluptatibus* or *rebus venereis deditus, impudicus* (= unchaste), *delicatus* (= effeminate). **voluptuousness,** n. *voluptas, libido*, or in the pl. *libidines*.

vomit, I. n. *vomitus, -ūs, vomitio* (both of the act and the matter thrown up; mostly post class.). **II.** v.tr. and intr. (*e*)*vomĕre, vomitare* (frequently or much, Col. Sen.).

voracious, adj. *edax, cibi avidus, gulosus* (who is always eating), *vorax* (lit. and fig.). Adv. *avide* (lit. or fig.). **voracity,** n. *edacitas, cibi aviditas, voracitas*.

vortex, n. *vertex, turbo*.

votary, n. (*con*)*secratus, sacer* (= sacred, as belonging to the gods), in a gen. sense, *admirator, studiosus alcjs* or *alcjs rei*; a — of any science, by *alci rei se tradĕre*. **vote, I.** n. *sententia* (in gen. = opinion; — of the senator, of the judge and the people), *suffragium* (of a citizen in the comitia; also of the voting tablet), *punctum* (= the vote which a candidate gained in the comitia), *tabella* (= voting tablet); to obtain the greatest number of —s in a tribe, *longe plurima in algâ tribu puncta ferre* (Cic.); the right to a —, *suffragium*, or *jus suffragii*. **II.** v.intr. *sententiam ferre* (e.g. of a judge), *in sententiam alcjs discedĕre* (= to go over to another's opinion), *suffragium ferre* (by single individuals among the people in the comitia), *in suffragium ire* or *suffragium inire* (of the people in the comitia); *censēre, decernĕre, jubēre* (of the formal decrees of the senate); to — for anyone's opinion, *in sententiam pede* or (of several) *pedibus ire*; to — for anyone, *suffragari alci* (*ad munus*) (when anyone applies for a post); for anything, *suffragari alci rei* (also fig. = to approve, e.g. *alcjs consilio*). **voter,** n. *suffragator* (= one who votes in favour of anyone), *qui suffragium fert* (who gives a vote), *qui suffragium habet* (who has the right of voting). **voting-tablet,** n. *tabella* (in gen.), *suffragium* (in the comitia).

votive, adj. *votivus* (e.g. *ludi*).

vouch, I. v.tr. *asseverare, testari, affirmare, confirmare, adjurare* (e.g. with accus. and infin., = swear that a thing is so). **II.** v.intr. *testificari* (but often with accus.); to — for anything, by *praestare alqd* or *de algâ re* (e.g. *damnum, periculum*), *alqd in se recipĕre, spondēre futurum ut*, etc. **voucher,** n. **1**, see WITNESS; **2**, see RECEIPT. **vouchsafe,** v.intr. *concedĕre*.

vow, I. n. *votum, voti sponsio* or *nuncupatio* (in the presence of proper witnesses), *devotio alcjs rei* (e.g. *vitae*); *religio* (= duty, constraint, etc. imposed by a vow). **II.** v.tr. (*de*)*vovēre alqd alci* (also with fut. infin.); — to do anything, *spondēre, promittĕre se alqd facturum esse*; see PROMISE, UNDERTAKE.

vowel, n. *lit*(*t*)*era vocalis*.

voyage, I. n. *navigatio, cursus, -ūs*. **II.** v.intr. *navigare*; see SAIL, TRAVEL.

vulgar, adj. *vulgaris* (belonging to the mass), *plebeius* (= peculiar to the *plebs*, plebeian), *illiberalis, sordidus, rusticus*; see RUDE. Adv. *illiberaliter, sordide, rustice, more rustico*. **vulgarism,** n. *sermo vulgaris*. **vulgarity,** n. see RUDENESS.

vulnerable, adj. *qui* (*quae, quod*) *vulnerari potest*.

vulpine, adj. *vulpinus* (Plin.).

vulture, n. *vultur*(*ius*) (lit. and fig.), *milvus*.

W.

wabble, v.intr. *vacillare* (both lit. and fig.). **wabbling,** n. *vacillatio*.

wad, v.tr. to — a dress, *vesti xylinum* (= cotton, Plin.) *insuĕre*. **wadding,** n. *xylinum vestibus insuendum*.

waddle, v.intr. *anatis in modum incedĕre*.

wade, v.intr. (through a river, etc.), *vado transire alqm locum*.

wafer, n. **1**, in the eucharist, *panis cenae sacrae*; **2**, for fastening letters, *cera* or *signum* (= seal).

waft, v tr *sublime ferre.*

wag, I. v tr *movēre, quassare*, see SHAKE, — the tail, *caudam movēre* **II.** n *homo jocosus, joculator* **waggery,** n *joca, -orum, facetiae* **waggish,** adj. *jocosus*

wage, v tr *bellum gerĕre cum alqo*, — war, see WAR **wager, I.** n *sponsio*, to lay a —, *sponsionem facĕre cum alqo* **II.** v intr see BET **wages,** n *merces, -ēdis,* f, *stipendium*

waggle, v tr and intr see WAG

wagon, n *plaustrum, vehiculum, currus, -ūs*
wagoner, n *plaustri ductor.*

wagtail, n *motacilla*

waif, n of persons, *inops, egens*, of things, *objectus*

wail, I. v intr *plangĕre*, see LAMENT **II.** n *planctus, -ūs*, see LAMENTATION

wain, n *plaustrum*

wainscot, n *paries, ĕtis,* m

waist, n. *corpus, -ŏris,* n, *medium* **waistband,** n see BELT. **waistcoat,** n *thorax laneus* (= under — of wool (Suet) worn by invalids), *subucula* (worn under the tunic)

wait, v intr *manēre*, to — for, *opperiri, ex(s)pectare, alqm* or *alqd, praestolari alci* or *alqm, manēre alqm* (so esp of fate, etc , awaiting any one, but not with accus in Cic or Caes), or *dum alqs adveniat*, to — on, *alci famulari* (so *ministrare alci pocula*), = to salute, *salutare alqm, alqm salutatum venire*

wait, n 1, lie in —, see AMBUSH, 2, a nightly musician, *qui nocte fidibus canit* **waiter,** n 1, *famulus* (in the house), *minister* (who assists in any certain thing), *puer* (= boy), 2, see TRAY **waiting,** n 1, = delay, etc , *mora, ex(s)pectatio, mansio, commoratio*, 2, at table, etc , *ministerium*, 3, = calling, *salutatio*, lord, lady in —, by *unus* (*una*) *ex eis qui circa alqm sunt*, see ATTENDANCE **waitress, waiting-maid,** n *famula, ministra, ancilla* (= servant) (N B Waiting at table in Roman times was carried on by men)

waive, v tr *alqd concedĕre, de alqâ re decedĕre.*

wake, I. v tr *exsuscitare, expergefacĕre* (*e somno*), *excitare* (*e somno*), (*ex*)*suscitare* (*e*) *somno* **II.** v intr *excitari*, etc **III.** n *pervigilium* (*funebre*). **wakeful,** adj *vigil*, †*exsomnis*, †*insomnis* **wakefulness,** n *insomnia, vigilantia, vigilia.*

walk, I. v intr *ire* (in gen , also for pleasure, e g *ibam forte via sacrâ*, Hor), *gradi, ingredi* (in a quiet manner), *incedĕre* (sometimes = affectedly or majestically), *cedere*, to — about, *deambulare* (till one is tired, e g *in litore*), *inambulare* (up and down in a place, e g *in gymnasio*), *obambulare alci loco*, in front of the rampart, *ante vallum*, in the fields, *in herbis*, *spatiari* (for exercise, *in alqo loco*), to — out, take a —, besides the preceding general terms, more particularly by *ire* or *abire* (*de*)*ambulatum*, *delectationis caus(s)â ambulare* (up and down a little, etc) to — (opp to ride, etc) on a journey, *pedibus ire*, *venire*, *iter facĕre, pedibus incedĕre* **II.** n 1, = the act or state of —ing, (*de*)*ambulatio, inambulatio, itio*, 2, = manner of —ing, *incessus, -ūs, ingressus, -ūs*, 3, to take a —, *alqo ire*, to go for a —, (*de*)*ambulatum ire*, to go for a — to any one's house, *viam facĕre ad alqm*, for pleasure or exercise, *ambulatio* (as act, then as the place along which we walk), *inambulatio*, a short —, *ambulatiuncula* (act and place), = avenue, *ambulacrum* (= planted with trees, ante and post class), *xystus* (= alley, Vitr); covered —, *tecta ambulatio* or *ambulatiuncula*

walker, n (masc and fem), *qui, quae* (*de*)*ambulat, ambulator* (fem *ambulatrix*, who makes a business of it, e g *vilicus ambulator esse non debet*, Col , *villica ne sit ambulatrix*, Cato de R R) **walking,** n see WALK, II 1

wall, I. n *murus, moenia, -ium* (= walls of a city), *maceria* (of clay, etc , as a fence round gardens, farmyards, vineyards, parks, etc), *paries, -ĕtis,* m (= party —, partition in a building, house), *propugnacula, -orum,* n (= bulwarks), the ruins of an old —, *parietinae*. **II.** v tr *muro cingĕre* or *circumdare, munire* (= to fortify)

wallet, n *pera* (Mart), *saccus, mantica*

wallow, v intr — in the mire, *in luto* (lit. and fig), *volutari*

walnut, n *juglans;* — tree, *juglans.*

wan, adj *pallidus*, see PALE.

wand, n *virga*, see ROD, STAFF.

wander, v intr *vagari, palari, errare, peregre abire* (= to go abroad), *peregrinari* (= to travel abroad), to — over any place, *alqm locum pervagari*, to — from the subject, *declinare, aberrare* (*ab*) *alqâ re*, to — from (in a moral sense), *de viâ decedĕre* (all = to stray from the right path), to — in mind, *delirare* **wanderer,** n. *erro, peregrinator* (abroad) **wandering,** adj 1, *errabundus, vagus*, 2, fig *negligens* (= inattentive), *delirus* (= crazy)

wane, v intr *decrescĕre* (of the moon, day, etc), *senescĕre* (of the moon, and fig of life, praise, etc), see DECREASE, DECLINE.

want, I. n. = deficiency, *penuria*, opp *copia*, generally with genit), *inopia* (with genit), *egestas* (= destitution), *desiderium* (= the — of a thing previously possessed), *defectio, defectus, -ūs* (the latter rare, except in Plin), *difficultas, angustiae*, by compounds (e g — of temperance, *intemperantia*, *inertia* (of activity), to be in — of anything, *alqâ re carēre* (in gen = not to have a thing), *alqâ re egēre, indigēre* (= to feel the lack of), *alcjs rei inopiâ laborare, premi*, or simply *ab alqâ re laborare, alqâ re premi* (= to be pressed for it), to come to —, *ad inopiam venire*, to suffer —, to live in poverty, *vitam inopem colĕre, in egestate esse* or *versari* **II.** v intr *alqd alci deesse* (of what we should have), *abesse* (when we do not feel the —, e g *hoc unum ille, si nihil utilitatis habeat, abfuit, si opus erat, defuit*, Cic), *deficĕre* (= to be short of anything), *alqd ab alqo desiderari* (of what we do not like to miss), I shall not be —ing, (*alci*) *non deero* **III** v tr 1, = to require, *egēre alqâ re*, seldom *alcjs rei*, *indigēre alqâ re* or *alcjs rei*, *opus* or *usus est alqâ re* (when it would be useful), *desiderare alqd, requirĕre alqd*, I — so and so, *careo alqâ re* (= I have not got it), *egeo alqâ re* (I should like to have it), *deficit mihi alqd* or *deficit me alqd* (= it has left me, i e I am short of it), *alqd non suppetit* (= it is not sufficient), I — nothing further, *nihil ultra flagito*, see LACK, 2, = wish, see WISH **wanting,** adj by *deesse*, see WANT, II

wanton, I. adj e g boys, *lascivus* (in play), *protervus, petulans* (= bold), grown — by prosperity, *superbus* (e g *in fortuna*), *dissolutus* (= dissolute), *intemperans* (= indulging in sensuality), *effrenatus* (= licentious), — injuries, *injuriae ultro factae* Adv *ultro* (= without provocation) *lascive, petulanter, proterve, dissolute, intemperanter, effrenate* **II.** v intr *lascivire, lascivum*, etc , *esse*, see above **wantonness,** n *lascivia, petulantia, protervitas, intemperantia*

war, I n *bellum* (= — by land, *b terrestre*, by sea, *navale*, civil, intestine, *intestinum, domesticum, civile*, with the Gauls, *Gallicum*, with slaves, *servile*; for life and death, *internecinum*), *arma*, *-orum* (= arms), *militia* (= military service, strategy), *tumultus*, *-ūs* (= outbreak in provinces, or close at home), † *Mars* (poet., except in phrases *meo, suo*, etc., *Marte*); in —, (*in*) *bello*; in time of —, *belli tempore*; in — and in peace, *domi bellique* or *belloque*, *domi militiaeque*; to seek an occasion for —, *bellum quaerĕre*; to cause or stir up —, *bellum movēre*, *concitare*, *excitare*, *ciēre*; to carry on a —, *bellare*, *bellum gerĕre*, against, *cum alqo*; see ARMS, MILITARY, SOLDIER. **II.** v.intr. *bellare*, *bellum gerĕre*; see above. **war-cry,** n. *clamor*, *bellicus*; to raise the —, *clamorem tollĕre*. **warfare,** n. see WAR, I. **war-horse,** n. *equus militaris* or † *bellator*, or simply *equus*. **warlike,** adj. *militaris* (e.g. *inerat in eo habitus virilis vere ac militaris*), *bellicosus*, *ferox* (= inclined to war), *belliger* (= martial). **warrior,** n. *miles*.

warble, v.tr. *canĕre*. **warbling,** n. *cantus*, *-ūs*.

ward, I. v.tr. to — off a blow, in fencing, *ictum* (or *petitionem*) *vitare*, *cavēre*, *cavēre et propulsare*, also simply *cavēre*, *vitare* (with the sword), *ictum declinare*, *petitionem declinatione corporis effugĕre*, also simply *ictum effugĕre* (by turning); fig. *amovēre*, *depellĕre*, *repellĕre*, *propellĕre*, *propulsare*, *arcēre*, *avertĕre*, *defendĕre* (*alqd*, from anyone, *ab alqo* or *alcjs*), *deprecari* (by entreaties, e.g. *a se calamitatem*). **II.** n. **1,** = quarter of a town, *regio*, *vicus* (as t.ts. both prob. post Aug.); **2,** = custody, *custodia*, *carcer*, *-ĕris*, n. (= prison); see CUSTODY; **3,** = a minor, *pupillus*, *pupilla*; **4,** = part of a key, *clavis dens*. **warden, warder,** n. *custos*. **wardrobe,** n. *vestiarium* (= place and the garments together, Plin., Col.), *vestis*, *vestimenta*, *-orum* (= garments in gen.). **wardship,** n. *tutela*; see GUARDIANSHIP.

ware, n. **1,** *merx*; see GOODS, MERCHANDISE; **2,** see POTTERY. **warehouse, I.** n. *horreum*, *receptaculum mercium*, *cella* (= stores), *apotheca*. **II.** v.tr. *condĕre*.

warm, I. adj. *calidus* (opp. *frigidus*); — water, *cal(i)da*; a — desire, *desiderium ardens* or *flagrans*; luke- —, *tepidus*; to be —, *calēre*; to become —, *calescĕre*, *calefieri*. **II.** v.tr. *calefacĕre*, *tepefacĕre* (= to make tepid), *fovēre* (by the heat of the body). **warming-pan,** n. *vas excalfactorium*. **warmth,** n. *calor* (e.g. *solis*; fig., in Quint., Plin. esp., *dicentis*, *dicendi*), *fervor* (lit. and fig.), *tepor* (lit); he speaks with —, *iratus dicit*.

warn, v.tr. (*prae*)*monēre* or *admonēre alqm ut* (or *ne*). **warning,** n. (*ad*)*monitio* (the act), *monitus*, *-ūs* (= — from heaven, by oracles, etc.), (*ad*)*monitum* (= notice given), *exemplum*, *documentum* (= example); to listen to a —, *audire* or *facĕre ea quae alqs sapienter monuit*; to take anything as a —, *habēre alqd sibi documento*; to take anyone as a —, *exemplum sibi capĕre de alqo*; of a master, perhaps *missum* (*missam*) *facĕre* (metaph. from dismissing soldiers; as the Roman servants were slaves, *vendĕre* may be used at times); of a servant's —, *alci renuntiare* or *ab alqo discedĕre* or *abire* (= leave).

warp, I. n. (in manufactura) *stamen*. **II.** v.intr. (of wood, etc.) *pandare*, *pandari*. **III.** v.tr. of wood, *pandum facĕre*, fig. *torquēre*; see DISTORT.

warrant, I. v.tr. to — an officer, etc., *alci copiam dare* or *potestatem facĕre*, to do a thing, *alcjs rei faciendae*; to a purchaser, *praestare alqd* or *de alqâ re*, to anyone, *alci*; to feel —ed in anything, *magnam fiduciam alcjs rei habēre*; I — you, *mehercule*(*u*)*le*, *medius fidius*; see also PROMISE, UNDERTAKE. **II.** n. (a written instrument, in gen.), *auctoritas* (also in the pl.), *potestas*, *mandatum*, or by *auctor* (e.g. *Caesare auctore*, under the — of Caesar). **warrantable,** adj. *quod excusari potest*; see ALLOW. **warranty,** n. *satisdatio*; see GUARANTEE.

warren, n. *leporarium* (Var.).

warrior, n. see under WAR.

wart, n. *verrūca*; covered with —s, *verrucosus*.

wary, adj. *consideratus*, *cautus*. **wariness,** n. *cautio*, *circumspectio*.

wash, I. v.tr. *lavare*, *abluĕre*; to — spots out of a garment, *maculas vestis eluĕre*. **II.** v.intr. *lavari*. **III.** n. **1,** *lavatio*; to take a —, *lavari*; **2,** = ointment, *fucus*; —hand-basin, *aqualis* (Plaut.); —handstand, *abacus*; —house, *cella in qua lintea lavantur*; —tub, *labrum eluacrum* (Cato); washerwoman, *mulier* (or where possible, *serva*) *quae lintea lavat*.

wasp, n. *vespa*. **waspish,** adj. † *mordax*; see IRRITABLE.

waste, I. v.tr. *vastare*, (*de*)*populari*, *perpopulari* (= to lay —), see DESTROY; *consumĕre*, *absumĕre*, *conficĕre* (all of sorrow, disease, etc.); = to squander, *dissipare*, *perdĕre*, *profundĕre*, *effundĕre*, *exedĕre* (= to eat away, lit. and fig.); to — time, *tempus perdĕre*; see SPEND. **II.** v.intr. e.g. the body, (*con*)*tabescĕre* (e.g. *morbo*, *desiderio*), *consumi*, *confici*. **III.** n. **1,** = lonely place, *vastitas*, *solitudo*, *loca deserta* or *deserta*, *-orum*; **2,** of expenditure, *sumptus effusi* or *profusi*; **3,** in manufactures, *ramenta*, *-orum*, (of metals, etc.), *scobis* (= sawdust or filings); **4,** = loss in gen. *jactura*, *damnum*; see LOSS; **5,** fig. moral —, by special nouns (e.g. — of energy, *intemperantia*; of time, *inertia* [= laziness]). **IV.** adj. (e.g. country) *vastus*, *incultus* (opp. *cultus*, *consitus*, of the field), comb. *desertus et incultus* or *incultus et desertus* (e.g. *solum*). **wasteful,** adj. *profusus*, *effusus* (of persons and things), *prodigus* (usu. of persons). Adv. *profuse*, *effuse*, *prodige*. **wastefulness,** n. *profusio*, *effusio*; see WASTE, III. 2. **waste-book,** n. *adversaria*, *-orum*.

watch, I. n. **1,** = a watching, *excubiae*, *vigilia*: to keep —, *vigilare*; **2,** military term, men set to —, *vigilia* (e.g. *vigilias ponĕre*, = to set a —), *statio* (of sentinels, sentries), *excubitores* (= sentinels), *excubiae* (Tac.); a —man, *vigil* (regular term for city policeman in Imperial Rome); **3,** a division of time, *vigilia* (e.g. *primâ*, *secundâ vigiliâ*, = in the first, second, etc. There were 4 —es in the night); **4,** pocket timepiece, *horologium parvulum*; see CLOCK. **II.** v.intr. (*per*)*vigilare*, *excubare*; to — till late at night, *ad multam noctem*, *de multâ nocte*; = to lie observant, *attentum esse*. **III.** v.tr. **1,** = to observe, *alqd tuēri*, (*ob*)*servare*, *spectare* (= to have in view), *speculari*, *explorare* (= to examine); see OBSERVE, EXAMINE; **2,** = to guard, *custodire*; see GUARD; to — for, *ex*(*s*)*pectare*, *opperiri* (*alqm*, or *alqd*), *alci insidiari* (in ambush, then metaph. in gen.); to — an opportunity, *occasionem captare*; to — over, *alqd tuēri*, *observare*. **watchfire,** n. *ignis*. **watchful,** adj. † *vigil*, *vigilans*. Adv. *vigilanter*. **watchfulness,** n. *vigilantia*, *vigilia*; see also CARE. **watchman,** n. *vigil* (see WATCH I., 2), *excubitor*, *custos*. **watchtower,** n. *spĕcula* (also fig. *tanquam e speculâ prospexi tempestatem futuram*). **watchword,** n. *tessera* (= tablet on which the — was written), *signum* (lit. and fig.), this was the — of the Stoics, *hoc Stoici praeceperunt*.

water, I. n. *aqua* (plur. *aquae* of a larger quantity, also of medicinal springs), † *latex*, † *lympha* and † *unda*; running —, *aqua viva*, *flumen vivum*; fresh —, *aqua dulcis*; salt- —, *aqua* *salsa*; sea- —, *aqua marina*, rain- —, *aqua pluvia-tilis, aqua caelestis*, to go for, fetch —, *aquam petere, aquatum ire, aquari* (in a larger quantity, i.e. of soldiers for the army), to lay under —, *irrigare* (e.g. a field), *inundare* (= to inundate), by land and —, *terrā marique*, to travel by —, *navigare*, prov., still —s run deep, *altissima quaeque flumina minimo sono labuntur* (Curt.), the — under the skin, *aqua intercus* (= dropsy); = urine, *urina*, = colour of a diamond, *splendor*, — -bearer, in gen., *aquarius*, in the army, *aquator*, = a sign of the zodiac, *Aquarius*, — -bottle, *ampulla, lagena*, — -butt, -cask, *dolium*, — -clock, *clepsydra*, — -closet, *latrina, sella familiarica*, — colour, *pigmentum aquā dilutum*, — -fall, *aqua ex edito desiliens* (Plin.), — -fowl, *avis aquatica* (Plin.) **II.** adj *aquatilis aquarius*, — animals, *aquatilia, -ium*, pl **III.** v tr and intr *irrigare* (*rigare*), see also SPRINKLE, MIX, it makes my teeth or my mouth —, *salivam mihi alqd movet* (Sen.) **watering,** n *aquatio* (= fetching of —, or by verb, e.g. *aquatum ire*), — of plants, by *aquā conspergere*, — -place (of inland places, i.e. mineral springs), *aquae*, of seaside, circumloc. with *maritimus* (e.g. *oppidum maritimum*), — -pot, *hydria, urceus*, see JAR **waterproof,** adj *aquae resistens* **watersnake,** n *hydrus.* **waterspout,** n 1, *fistula* (= waterpipe), 2, = sheet of water, *typhon* (Plin.) **waterworks,** n *aquaeductus, -ūs* (= an aqueduct, the nearest class equivalent to our —) **watery,** adj *aquatilis* (Plin., = having a — taste), *aquosus* (= abounding in water)

wattle, I. n 1, = hurdle, *crates, -is*, f, 2, of a cock, *palea* **II.** v tr *contexere*, see WEAVE

wave, I. n *unda, fluctus, -ūs* **II.** v tr *agitare, jactare*, †*rotare* **III.** v intr *undare, fluctuare*, †*fluitare, agitari, jactari*

waver, v intr *fluctuare* (*animi* or *animo*), *dubitare*, see HESITATE **waverer,** n (*homo*) *inconstans, incertus* **wavering,** n *inconstantia, animus incertus* or *dubius* or *suspensus, dubitatio*

wax, n *cera*, to mould in —, *e cerā fingere*, — candle, — light, *cereus* **waxen,** adj *cereus*

wax, v intr *crescere*, see GROW

way, n *via* (lit and fig), *iter, -ineris*, n (= the going from one place to another, hence a march), *aditus, -ūs* (= access), *cursus, -ūs* (= the direction or course), *semita* (= a small way, a path), *trames, -itis*, m (= a subordinate way running along beside the highway, a foot-road or path), *callis* (= a hilly road), *deverticulum* (= a side road leading off from the chief or high road), *meatus, -ūs* (post Aug = a channel or course), *limes, -itis*, m (= a boundary path or line), *angiportus, -us* (= a narrow — or street between two rows of houses), *ratio* (= plan or manner), *mos* (= custom, e.g. in the — of the Romans, *more Romanorum*), *consilium, institutum* (= plan), a straight — or path, *via recta*, a short —, *compendiaria* (most often fig, with *quasi*, e.g. *via ad gloriam proxima et quasi compendiaria*, Cic.), *compendium viae*, when there are two —s, *bivium*, three, *trivium*, four, *quadrivium*, — there is none, *avia, -orum*, by- —s *iter devium*, out of the —, *avius, remotus* (lit), *reconditus, exquisitus* (fig), to go the direct — or road, *rectā viā ire*, on the —, *inter viam, ex itinere*, to make —, see PROGRESS, to form a — or plan, *rationem inire*, to get out of the —, *de via decedere alci, alcjs congressum fugere*, —s and means, *opes, ūm*, f (= resources), *ratio* (= plan), by the —, in passing (of a speaker), *strictim* (= cursorily), *ut hoc dicam*, see ROAD, to get under — (of a ship), *absolvi, ancoram* (*ancoram*) *solvere* **wayfarer,** n *viator* **waylay,** v tr *alci insidiari* or *insidias facere* **wayside,** n and adj *ad viam* **wayward,** adj see WILFUL, FICKLE

we, pron *nos*, — ourselves, *nos ipsi, nosmet ipsi*, frequently not expressed

weak, adj *tenuis* (= thin, opp *crassus*, then fig, e.g. *sonus, spes*), *exilis* (= fine, e.g. *vox*, Quint), *parvus, exiguus* (= inconsiderable), *levis* (of what cannot be maintained, opp *gravis*, e.g. *argumentum*), *imbecillus* (late *imbecillis*, = — in bodily strength or mind), a — head, *ingenium imbecillum, infirmus* (of one who can stand nothing), *debilis* (= frail, opp *robustus*), *invalidus* (opp *validus*), *enervatus* (= unnerved, with *velut* before it, also of the state), *languidus, iners* (= sluggish), *mollis* (= effeminate), *fractus* (= broken), *confectus* (= worn out, of a man and his body), *hebes* (= dull, opp *acer*, e.g. sight, hearing, memory) **weakly, I.** adv *tenuiter, exiliter, exigue, imbecille, infirme, molliter* **II.** adj see WEAK **weaken,** v tr *imbecillum* or *infirmum* (e.g. *stomachum*) *reddere, debilitare* (lit and fig, e.g. anyone's rage), *delumbare* (fig, e.g. an idea, very rare) *enervare* (= to unnerve), *infirmare* (lit, to make loose what was firm, then fig, to — a thing, e.g. *fidem testis*), *attenuare, extenuare* (lit, to make thin, = to diminish in gen), (*com*)*minuere* (= to lessen), *frangere* (lit, = to break), *hebetare, obtundere* (= to make dull), *labefactare* (= to shake, lit and fig) **weakening,** n *debilitatio, infractio, deminutio, imminutio*, or by verb **weakness,** n *tenuitas* (opp *crassitudo*, e.g. of a thread), *exilitas* (e.g. *in dicendo*), *imbecillitas, infirmitas* (of body and mind), *debilitas* (of body and mind), *virium defectio, languor, levitas* (of arguments, etc), *vitium, error* (= fault)

weal, n the public —, *salus publica, respublica*

weal, n = mark on the body, *vibex*

wealth, n *res secundae* or *prosperae* or *florentes, divitiae, opes, -um*, pl, *copia* (esp with genit, e.g. *rei familiaris*), *abundantia alcjs rei, opulentia* **wealthy,** adj *bene nummatus, pecuniosus, copiis rei familiaris locuples et pecuniosus, opulentus, opulens, copiosus*

wean, v tr 1, †*infantem lacte depellere, a matre prohibere*, 2, fig, *alqm alqd dedocere*

weapon, n *arma, orum*, n, *telum*

wear, I. v tr 1, = to waste, (*usu*) (*at*)*terere* or *deterere* very much, *conterere* (e.g. *librum legendo*), 2, = to have on the body, *gerere, gestare, indutum esse alqā re, indui alqā re*, or *ornatum esse alqa re* (as ornament), (*suc*)*cinctum esse alqā re, uti alqā re* (= to make use of), *tractare alqd* (= to handle, e.g. *arma*), to — the toga, *togatum esse*, to — away or out, see before, also CONSUME **II.** v intr *usu atteri* or *deleri*, to — off, *evanescere* **III** n *usus, ūs* (e.g. *margaritarum*), to stand — and tear, of things, *usu non attritum esse*, of persons, *omnia fortiter perferre* **wearing,** n *usus, -ūs* — apparel, *vestimentum* **worn,** adj *usu detritus* (Plin., of a garment), — out (= hackneyed), *contritus, obsoletus* (often used, and hence old, e.g. *vestis*, fig *verba*), — out (= tired out), (*de*)*fatigatus, lassus, fessus* with illness, wounds, etc., *morbo, vulneribus*, etc, *confectus* or *fractus*

weary, I. adj 1, = fatigued, (*de*)*fatigatus, lassus, fessus*, 2, = disgusted with, by *taedet* or *pertaesum est alqm alcjs rei* **II.** v tr *alqm* (*de*)*fatigare*, = — with, *alqm obtundere*, see BORE **III.** v intr by *taedet* or *pertaesum est alqm alcjs rei* **weariness,** n 1, = fatigue, (*de*)*fatigatio, lassitudo*, 2, fig *taedium* **wearisome,** adj *longus, laboriosus*

weasel, n *mustela*

weather, I. n. *caelum, caeli status, -ūs, tempestas* (good or bad); fine, clear —, *tempestas bona* or *serena, caelum sudum* or *serenum;* dry —, *siccitas;* to depend upon the —, to be guided by the —, by *tempestatis rationem habēre;* — cock, *gallus a(h)eneus;* — wise, *caeli mutationum peritus.* **II.** v.tr. 1, lit. *alqm locum circumvĕhi;* 2, fig. *superare;* — a storm, *vim tempestatis perferre.*

weave, v.tr. *(con)texĕre* (lit. and fig.). **weaver,** n. *textor.* **web,** n. *textum, textura, tela;* — footed, *quibus pedes ad nandum accommodati sunt.*

wed, v.tr. see MARRY. **wedlock,** n. see MARRIAGE. **wedding,** n. see MARRIAGE; — day, *dies nuptiarum;* to fix the — day, *diem nuptiis dicĕre.*

wedge, I. n. *cuneus;* — shaped, *cuneatus;* seats in the theatre in — shape, *cunei;* troops drawn up in — shape, *cuneus.* **II.** v.tr. *cuneare;* — together, see CROWD.

Wednesday, n. **dies Mercurii.*

weed, I. n. *herba inutilis* or *iners.* **II.** v.tr. *(e)runcare.*

weed, n. = garment, *vestis;* in —s of peace, *(cives) togati;* widows' —s, *viduarum more vestita.*

week, n. *septem dierum spatium, septem dies* or *hebdomas;* one —, *septem dies;* a fortnight, *quindecim dies* (Caes.). **week-days,** n. *dies profesti* (opp. *dies fasti*), *dies negotiosi* (Tac., opp. *dies sacri*). **weekly,** adj. by circumloc. (e.g. — wages, *merces quae in singulas hebdomades habentur*).

weep, v.intr. and tr. *lacrimare* or *lacrimari, lacrimas fundĕre* (= to shed tears), *(de)plorare* (loudly), *lamentari* (of sustained weeping), *ejulare* (pitifully, e.g. of female mourners), *vagire* (of little children); — over anything, *alci rei illacrimare* or *illacrimari.* **weeping,** n. *fletus, -ūs, lacrimae* (= tears), *ploratus, ejulatus, vagītus* (all -ūs), *lamentatio.*

weevil, n. *curculio.*

weigh, I. v.tr. 1, *(ex)pendĕre, perpendĕre, examinare;* 2, fig. *(ex)pendĕre, perpendĕre, ponderare, examinare* (e.g. *quādam populari trutinā examinari,* Cic.), *considerare cum* or *in animo, secum reputare, mente agitare* or *volutare;* — deeply, *multa (etiam atque etiam) secum reputare;* — down, *opprimĕre* (lit. and fig.). **II.** v.intr. *pondo pendĕre* or *pondo valēre* with acc. of the weight; to — heavily, *magni ponderis esse;* to — ten pounds, *decem libras explēre.* **weight,** n. *pondus, -ĕris,* n., *gravitas, momentum* (lit. and fig.; e.g. *terrae, armorum*); see IMPORTANCE, PRESSURE. **weighty,** adj. *gravis* (lit. and fig.). Adv. *graviter* (lit. and fig.).

weir, n. *moles, -is,* f., *agger, -ĕris,* m. (= dam), *cataracta* (καταρράκτης = sluice lock, Plin. Min.).

welcome, I. adj. *acceptus, gratus, ex(s)pectatus, exoptatus;* to bid —, *alqm salvēre jubeo, benigne alqm excipĕre;* you will be — to all, *carus omnibus ex(s)pectatusque venies;* be —, *salve.* **II.** n. *salutatio.* **III.** v.tr. *salutare alqm, benigne alqm accipĕre.* **IV.** interj. *salve* (pl. *salvete*). **welfare,** n. *salus, -ūtis,* f., *incolumitas* (= safety), *bonum* (= anyone's interests, or of a thing), *felicitas* (= happiness); to try to promote anyone's —, *alcjs commodis* or *utilitatibus servire, alcjs saluti prospicĕre, consulĕre, servire.*

well, I. adv. *bene, recte;* very —, *optime, praeclare;* as exclamation, *esto!* (expressing consent), *bene! recte! pulc(h)re!* (acclamation); very —! *quam maxime!* (general exclamation), *ita est!* (in reply); — then! *age! recte vero!* to take a thing —, *alqd in bonam partem accipĕre;* to do —, *bene* or *recte facĕre* or *agĕre* or *gerĕre rem.* **II.** adj. *salvus, sanus, integer, valens;* to be —, *(bene, commode,* or *recte) valēre, belle, recte, pulc(h)re, bene (se) habēre;* to get —, *convalescĕre;* not to be —, *male se habēre.* **well-affected,** adj. *benevolus erga alqm.* **well-being,** n. *salus, -ūtis,* f., *bona valetudo.* **well-born,** adj. *nobilis;* see NOBLE. **well-bred,** adj. *urbanus;* see POLITE. **well-built,** adj. *bene aedificatus* (of structures), *formosus* (of persons). **well-disposed,** adj. see WELL-AFFECTED. **well-educated, well-informed,** adj. *doctus, eruditus;* see LEARNED. **well-fed,** adj. *corpore amplo, pinguis* (opp. *macer*), *opimus* (opp. *gracilis*), *obesus* (opp. *gracilis, strigosus*). **well-known,** adj. *omnibus notus.* **well-meaning,** adj. *benevolus, amicus* (both of persons), *fidelis* (e.g. friend; *consilium,* advice). **well-meant,** adj. e.g. advice, *consilium benevole dictum.* **well-spent,** adj. e.g. life, *vita bene acta.* **well-wisher,** n. *studiosus alcjs.*

weld, v.tr. *(con)ferruminare* (Plin.).

well, I. n. *puteus.* **II.** v.intr. — up, *scatēre;* see SPRING, v.intr.

welter, v.intr. *se volutare, volutari.*

west, I. n. *regio ad occidentem vergens, occidens* (= the setting sun), *occidens, occasus, -ūs (solis).* **II.** adj. *occidentalis* (Plin.), † *occiduus;* — wind, *Zephyrus, Favonius;* North — wind, *Caurus (Cor.)*; South — wind, *Africus.* **westward,** adj. *ad occasum, ad occidentem vergens, in occidentem spectans.* **western,** adj. *occidentalis* (Plin.). **westerly,** adj. (wind) *ab occidente, in occidente.*

wet, I. adj. *humidus, madens* (mostly poet. and post Aug.), *madidus,* † *udus, uvidus* (mostly poet. and post Aug.); see MOIST. **II.** n. *caeli status, -ūs, humidus* or *uvidus* or *pluvius;* see RAIN. **III.** v.tr. *madefacĕre, madidum reddere, perfundĕre;* to get — through, *madefieri, madidum reddi;* — nurse, *nutrix.* **wetness,** n. *humor.*

wether, n. *vervex, -ēcis,* m.

whale, n. *balaena, cetus* (in pl. *cete*) (= sea-monster in gen.; Plin.); —bone, *balaenae maxilla.*

wharf, n. *navale, crepīdo.*

what, pron. interrog. *quid?* — do you want? *quid vis?* — does that mean? *quid hoc sibi vult?* As a conjunctive or adj. pronoun, *qualis, qui;* he wrote to me — books he had read, *scripsit mihi quos libros legerit;* in reference to an antecedent by *qui;* — you told me, *id quod* or *ea quae mihi dixisti.* **whatever,** pron. *quicunque (quivum), quisquis.*

wheal, n. *vibex* (ante and post class.).

wheat, n. *triticum, siligo* (= very fine white —, ante and post class); of —, wheaten, *triticeus;* a — field, *ager tritico consitus;* — meal, *farina triticea.*

wheedle, v.tr. and intr. *illicĕre.*

wheel, I. n. *rota, tympanum* (τύμπανον, of water-mills, etc.), *radii* (= spokes of —); as instrument of torture, *equuleus;* see RACK. **II.** v.tr. 1, = push forward, *propellĕre;* 2, = turn round, *convertĕre, circumagĕre;* = push, *propulsare;* —barrow, *vehiculum* (= cart) or *corbis* (= basket). **III.** v.intr. *signa convertĕre* (of soldiers); right, left —, *in hastam, in scutum.* **wheelwright,** n. *qui rotas facit.*

wheeze, v.intr. *anhelare;* see PANT. **wheezy,** adj. † *anhelus.*

whelm, v.tr. see OVERWHELM.

whelp, n. *catulus.*

when, adv and conj = at the time that, *cum (quom)* (in this sense with the indic, the subj is used only when we speak hypothetically or state the opinion of another), *quo tempore*, *ubi* (= then —, etc, generally with indic, with the subj only when we represent anything as uncertain, casual, etc), *quando* (= — once, interrog. and indefinitely as well as in a relative sense, with subj only in indirect questions when we represent circumstances as repeatedly occurring, otherwise always with indic), *ut* (= as soon as, of any result, after which another result immediately takes place, always with indic), often by the particip of the verb, = at what time, interrogatively, *quando? quo tempore?* = at which time, see WHO, WHICH, = after the time that, *cum, ut, ubi* (the last two always with indic *cum* also with present and perfect indic, and when the action is represented as occurring repeatedly (as often as), with the imperf indic, however in the narrative style in past tenses always with imperf and pluperf subj, often "when" in this sense is rendered by a partic in the same case as the noun to which it refers, if the subject is the same both in the main and in the dependent clause, but if the latter has a different subject from that in the main clause, then by the ablat abs) **whence,** adv as interrog, *unde? ex quo loco?* = from whom? whereby? *unde? a* (*ex*) *quo homine? ex qua re?* — have you got that? *a quo hoc accepisti?* (in gen), *unde id scis?* (= — do you know that?), — does it come that, etc, *unde fit ut*, etc **whenever, whensoever,** conj *quandocunque* (*cumq*), *quotie(n)scunque* (*cumq*), or simply *utcunque*, *quotie(n)s*

where, adv and conj as interrogative, *ubi? ubinam? quo loco? quo loci?* —ever? *ubi gentium? ubi terrarum?* as relative particle, *ubi, quâ* **whereas,** adv *quoniam, quod, cum, quippe qui* (*quae, quod*), see BECAUSE, SINCE **whereby,** adv *ex quo* (*qua*, etc) *fit*, as interrog *qua ratione? quâ re?* **wherefore,** adv 1, interrog *cur?* see WHY, 2, *quamobrem*, see THEREFORE **wherein,** adv *in quo, in qua re, in quibus, ubi* **wherever,** adv *ubivis* (= at any place, whichever it may be), *ubicunque* (*cumq*), *quacunque* (= at any place) **whereof,** adv *cujus quorum* (*quarum*, etc) or *e quo* (*qua*, etc) **whereon,** adv *quo facto, cum quibus verbis* **whereto,** adv *quo(rsum), quem ad finem*

wherry, n see BOAT

whet, v tr *(ex)acuĕre* (lit and fig) **whetstone,** n *cos*

whether, I. pron *uter* **II.** conj *ne* (appended to that word in the interrog sentence upon which the stress lies), *num* (= — perhaps), *utrum* (seldom in simple questions), *an* (only after *nescire* and similar verbs of doubting), in double questions, — or ("or — ") *utrum an* (or *anne* or *ne*), *num an*, *ne* (as an enclitic), sometimes *ne* is appended to *utrum*, sometimes also *ne* is put, a few words intervening, after *utrum*, esp when in the two clauses there occur two words opposed to each other, e g *utrum taceamne, an praedicem?* sometimes "—" in the first question is not at all expressed in Latin, e g *interrogatur, pauca sint, anne multa*, sometimes, in two interrog clauses where two words are directly opposed to each other, the interrog particles may be left out altogether, e g *velit, nolit, scire difficile est*; if "or" in the second question appears as more a copulative than an interrog particle, it is simply rendered by *aut*, e g *quaesierunt necne ille aut ille defensurus esset*, — or not, *utrum* (*num* or *ne*) . *necne* or *annon* (*necne* generally in indirect questions and without any verb at all, whilst *annon* is chiefly used in direct and but seldom in indirect questions, both with and without a verb), e g *quaeritur sintne dii, necne sint*, or *dii utrum sint, necne, quaeritur*, or even *dii necne sint quaeritur* (sometimes for *necne*, *annon*, *anne* is found, e g *cum interrogetur tria pauca sint anne multa*, Cic), where the alternatives are presented as on an equality, either of which may be true, *sive—sive* (*seu—seu*) (e g *sive cum ex paludibus elicĕre, sive obsidione premĕre posset* Caes)

whey, n *serum*

which, pron see WHO

whiff, n *halitus*, *-ūs* (= breath)

while, I. n *tempus*, *-ŏris*, n, *spatium*, *mora* (= delay), *otium* (= leisure), a little, short —, *breve spatium*, *paul(l)ulum* (*temporis*), for a short —, *parumper*, *paul(l)isper*, a little — after, *paul(l)o post*, *non ita multo post*, *paul(l)o post* a long — after, *post longum tempus* **II.** (**whilst**) conj *dum* (nearly always with present indic even when the verb in the main clause is in the past tense), *donec* (with indic or subj according to the regular rules of mood), *cum* (*quom*, with pres and perf indic and imperf and pluperf subj), or by part (e g *haec lacrimans dixit* she said — weeping), or by *inter* with gerund in phrases (*inter bibendum*, = — drinking, *inter cenandum*, = — dining). **III.** v tr to — away the time, *tempus fallĕre* *aliqua re*

whim, n *libido* **whimsical,** adj *difficilis*, *naturâ difficilis*, *morosus* (= ill tempered), *inconstans*, *levis* (= fickle), see FICKLE

whimper, v tr, **whine,** v intr *vagire* (of a child or animal) **whimpering,** n **whining,** n *vagitus*, *-ūs*

whinny, v intr *hinnire*

whip, I. n *scutica*, *-ae*, f, or *lora*, *-orum*, n (made of cords tied together), *flagrum*, *flagellum* **II.** v tr *verberare*

whirl, I. v tr *(con)torquēre*, *quassare*, *quatĕre* (= to shake) **II.** v intr as in dancing, *in gyrum agi* **III.** n *vertigo* (mostly post Aug), or by verb **whirlpool,** n *turbo*, *vertex*, *vorago*, *gurges*, *-itis*, m **whirlwind,** n *turbo*, *vertex*

whirr, I. v tr *stridēre* (*stridĕre*) **II** n *stridor*

whisk, v tr see SNATCH

whiskers, n by *genae pilosae* or †*hirsutae*

whisper, I. v intr *susurrare*, to anyone, *cum alqo* **II.** v tr anything into anyone's ear, *insusurrare alci alqd ad aurem* or *in aures* **III.** n *susurrus* **whisperer,** n *susurrator* (very rare)

whist, I. n by *chartarum ludus*, but where possible translate by *alea* (= dice) **II.** interj *st! tace, tacete*

whistle, I. v intr and tr *sibilare*, to — anyone, *alqm sibilo advocare* **II.** n *sibilus* pl also *sibila*, *-orum* **whistler,** n *qui sibilat* (with the mouth), *tibicen* (on the pipe)

whit, n, not a —, *ne minimum quidem*, *minime*

white, I. adj *albus* (opp *ater*), *candidus* (= fair, opp *niger*), *canus* (= hoary), *purus* (= not dirty, not stained), *niveus* (= white as snow), *lacteus* (= white as milk) **II.** n *album*, *candor*, — of an egg, of the eye, *album ovi*, *oculorum* (Cels) **white-haired** adj *albis capillis*, *canis capillis* **white-lead,** n *cerussa* **whiten, I.** v tr *dealbare*, *candefacĕre* (ante and post class) **II.** v intr *albescere*, *canescĕre* (= grow hoary) **whiteness,** n. *albitudo* (Plaut), *candor*

whitewash, I. n. *albarium (opus).* **II.** v.tr. *dealbare.*

whither, I. adv., as interrog., *quo? quem in locum? quorsum (quorsus)? in quam partem?* — then? *quonam?* **II.** conj. with reference to the antecedent, *quo;* — ever, *quoquo, quocunque (-cumque), quacunque, quovis,* † *quolibet.*

whitlow, n. *paronychium, paronychia* (Plin.).

Whitsuntide, n. * *Pentecoste* (Eccl.).

whiz, I. v.intr. *stridēre (stridĕre)* (of serpents). **II.** n. *stridor.* **whizzing, I.** adj. *stridens.* **II.** n. *stridor.*

who, I. rel. pron. *qui, quae, quod.* **II.** interrog. pron. *quis, quis, quid?* Which of two? *uter, utra, utrum?* **whoever,** n. *quicunque (quicum.), quisquis.*

whole, I. adj. *integer* (= uninjured), *totus* (in opp. to part.), *solidus* (esp. in enumeration, e.g. *usurâ, nec eâ solidâ, contentus erat*), *cunctus* (e.g. *Gallia, civitas*), *omnis* (e.g. *omne caelum*), *universus, plenus* (e.g. *annus plenus atque integer*); = healthy, *sanus.* **II.** n. the —, *totum, tota res* (opp. *partes*), *unum* (in so far as anything is a —), *omnia, -ium, universum, universa res, universitas* (= all together), *summa* (= the sum, e.g. *summa exercitûs,* = the sum total of the army), *solidum* (= the capital); the — of may also be expressed by adj. (e.g. *tota Gallia,* = the — of Gaul), on the —, by *paene, fere, ferme* (= mostly, almost). **wholly,** adv. *plane, omnino, prorsus, penitus* (= thoroughly), *funditus* (= to the foundation), *radicitus* (= root and branch); see ALTOGETHER. **wholesale,** n. *mercatura magna.* **wholesome,** adj. *saluber, salutaris* (lit. and fig.), *utilis;* to be — for, *alci salutarem esse, alci prodesse.* **wholesomeness,** n. *salubritas, utilitas* (lit. and fig.).

whoop, n. *clamor;* see SHOUT, n.

whore, n. *scortum, meretrix.*

whose, adj., rel. and interrog. pron. *cujus.*

why, I. adv. as interrog. *cur? quamobrem (quam ob rem)? quare? quapropter? quâ de caus(s)â? quid est cur,* etc.? *quid est quod,* etc.? *quid?* — not? *cur non* (with indic.), *quidni* (with subj. implying surprise)? *quin* (with indic., request to do a thing). **II.** conj. *cur, quamobrem, quapropter, propter quod.* **III.** interj. (at answering an objection expressed or implied), *immo, enimvero.*

wick, n. *ellychnium.*

wicked, adj. *impius (erga Deum, patriam,* etc.), *nefarius, scelestus, sceleratus, flagitiosus, dissolutus, perditus* (= abandoned), *pravus* (= irregular), *malus, malitiosus* (= bad), *corruptus* (= corrupted), *deterrimus* (= very bad), *nequam* (= worthless), *turpis, foedus* (= shameful). Adv. *impie, nefarie, scelesle, scelerate, flagitiose, dissolute, perdite, prave, male, malitiose, nequiter, turpiter, foede.* **wickedness,** n. *impietas (erga alqm), scelus, -ĕris,* n., *facinus, -oris,* n., *flagitium* (= a — deed, then —), *pravitas, nequitia, turpitudo, foeditas, vitium, malitia, vitiositas.*

wicker, adj. *vimineus, craticius;* — work, *crates, -is,* f. usu. in pl.).

wide, adj. *latus* (e.g. *planities*), *laxus* (of dress, shoes, house), *capax* (= containing much), *amplus* (= of large size), *patens* (= — stretching). Adv. *late, laxe.* **widen, I.** v.tr. *amplificare (urbem, rempublicam,* fig. *auctoritatem*), *dilatare* (e.g. *castra, aciem;* power of a state, *imperium*), *laxare* (a garment, lines of troops). **II.** v.intr. *se dilatare* (the sea), *patescĕre* (a plain). **width,** n. **1,** lit. *amplitudo, latitudo, laxitas;* **2,** fig. perhaps *in omnes opiniones indulgens.*

widow, n. *vidua.* **widowed,** adj. *viduus.* **widower,** n. *viduus.* **widowhood,** n. *viduitas.*

wield, v.tr. *tractare* (e.g. *ferrum, arma, tela*).

wife, n. *conju(n)x, uxor, marita;* to take a —, *uxorem ducĕre.*

wig, n. *capillamentum* (Suet.), *crines* † *empti, galerum (galerus,* Juv.).

wight, n. see MAN.

wild, adj. *ferus* (of living and inanimate beings), *agrestis* (= growing — in the field, of plants; hence also rude in manners), *silvester* (= growing, living — in the woods, of plants, animals, men), *indomitus* (= untamed, of animals, opp. *mansuetus*), *rudis* (= still unprepared, of things, e.g. of the soil, etc.; hence = still uncivilized, of men), *incultus* (= untilled, of the soil, hence uncivilized, of men), *vastus* (= isolated, barren, of a country, opp. *celeber*), *ferox* (= acting like a savage), *immanis* (= cruel, of character), *saevus* (= ferocious, all four of men), *insanus, amens* (= mad), *lascivus* (= playful); a — beast, *fera.* Adv. *ferociter, immaniter, saeve* (= fiercely), *insane* (= madly). **wilderness,** n. *locus desertus, loca deserta, -orum, solitudo, vastitas.* **wildness,** n. *feritas, ferocia, ingenium ferox, animus ferox* (= fieriness), *immanitas* (= cruelty), *lascivia* (= playfulness).

wile, n. *ars, dolus;* see TRICK. **wily,** adj. *astutus, versutus;* see CUNNING, adj.

wilful, adj. *contumax, pertinax, pervicax, obstinatus;* a — act, *quod consulto or cogitatum fit,* comb. *quod consulto et cogitatum fit.* Adv. *contumaciter, pertinaciter, pervicaciter, consulto, consilio, de or ex industriâ, datâ or deditâ operâ, voluntate et judicio,* or also by *sciens* or *prudens et sciens.* **wilfulness,** n. *contumacia, pertinacia, pervicacia, obstinatio* (= inflexibility).

will, I. n. **1,** *voluntas* (= volition in gen., and also exercise of —), *animus* (= disposition of mind), *consilium, propositum* (= purpose), *arbitrium* (= decision), *auctoritas* (= command, esp. — of the senate as expressed in a decree), or by *auctor* (e.g. he did it at the — of Caesar, *hoc Caesare auctore fecit*), *nutus, -ûs* (lit. = nod, fig. = command), comb. *arbitrium et nutus, auctoritas nutusque, libido* (= fancy, caprice, in good or bad sense), *studium* (= good —); he has a — to, *est alci in animo alqd facĕre;* **2,** = testament, *testamentum, tabulae (testamenti);* to make a —, *testamentum facĕre,* in favour of any one, *alqm heredem suum facĕre.* **II.** v.tr. *velle, cupĕre,* with infin. or subj., with or without *ut; alqd* or with accus. and infin. or *ut; avēre alqd* or with infin. **willing,** adj. *libens, volens, paratus, promptus* (the last two *ad alqd*). Adv. *libenter, animo libenti, animo libenti prolixoque, animo prompto paratoque.* **willingness,** n. *animus libens* or *promptus, voluntas.*

wily, adj. see WILE.

willow, n. *salix.*

win, I. v.tr. see GET, GAIN. **II.** v.intr. *vincĕre.* **winner,** n. *victor.*

winning, adj. *pulcher, venustus* (= beautiful), *suavis* (= sweet), *blandus* (= persuasive), *comis* (= courteous).

wind, I. n. **1,** *ventus, aura* (both of gentle and violent blasts), *flatus, -ûs* (mostly poet., all three lit. and fig.); favourable, unfavourable —, *ventus secundus, adversus;* the — rises, *ventus increbrescit* or *cooritur;* — sinks, *cessat, cadit;* to speak to the —, *dare* † *verba in ventos;* **2,** = flatulency, *ventus, inflatio.* **II.** v.tr. (e.g. a horn, *cornu*), *inflare;* see BLOW, PLAY, v.tr. **windfall,** n. *alqd alci forte oblatum* (e.g. the money was a great — to me, *pecunia casu* *oblecta multum mihi proderat*) **wind-mill,** n *mola venti* (Jct) **wind-pipe,** n *aspera arteria* **wind-ward,** adj *ad ventum conversus* **windy,** adj *ventosus*, fig *vanus, ventosus, inanis.*

wind, I. v tr *torquēre* (e.g *funem*), *glomerare* (into a ball) — up, *trochleā tollĕre* (lit i e with a pulley), *ad finem perducĕre* (fig), see END **II.** v intr *se sinuare, sinuari* **winding, I.** adj *flexuosus, tortuosus* **II.** n *flexus, -ūs* **windlass,** n *ergata*, m

window, n *fenestra* (with shutters curtains, or bars, only under the emperors made of the transparent *lapis phengites* or *specularis*)

wine, n. *vinum;* sour —, *vappa*, — not diluted with water, *merum*, the — god *Bacchus* (poet = wine) **wine-bibber,** n *homo vinulentus.* **wine-cellar,** n *apotheca* **wine-merchant,** n *vinarius*

wing, I. n *ala, pennae*, — of an army, *cornu, ala*, the soldiers who form the —s, *alarii*, to be posted in the right —, *dextrum tenēre*, the — of a house, *ala*, — of a door, *foris*, door with —s, folding doors, *fores, -ium, valvae* **II.** v tr *volare;* see FLY **winged,** adj *penniger*, † *pennatus*, † *alatus*, † *aliger*

wink, I. n *nictus, -ūs* **II.** v intr *nictare*, at any one, *alci*, to — at, *indulgēre alci, con(n)ivēre in alqā re*

winnow, v tr corn, *frumentum ventilare* or *evannēre* **winnowing-fan,** n *ventilabrum, vannus*, f

winter, I. n *hiem(p)s, tempus (anni) hibernum, tempora hiberna, -orum tempus hiemale, bruma, tempus brumale* (= time of the shortest days), a hard —, *hiems gravis* or *acris*, a mild —, *hiems* † *mollis, mitis, tepida* (Hor) **II.** adj *hiemalis, hibernus, brumalis*, or by genit of *hiem(p)s*, — quarters, *hiberna, -orum* **III.** v intr *hiemare, hibernare, hiberna agĕre* (of troops), for — in gen *hiemem agĕre.* **winterly,** adj *hiemalis*

wipe, v tr *(abs)tergēre, detergēre, extergēre*, — out (fig), *abolēre*, see ABOLISH

wire, n *filum* or *filum ferreum*

wise, I. adj *sapiens, sapientiā praeditus, prudens* (= with practical insight), to be —, *sapĕre, sapientem esse* **II.** n *ratio, modus, via*, in no —, *nullo modo*, see MANNER, WAY Adv *sapienter* **wisdom,** n *sapientia, prudentia*, with —, *sapienter, ratione ac consilio.* **wiseacre,** n *qui se sapientem esse jactat.*

wish, I. v tr and intr *velle, cupĕre;* if you — it, *si vis si tibi placet*, I don't — it by *nolo*, I — rather, by *malo;* I could —, *velim* (with pres subj if we speak as though the — were likely to be fulfilled), *vellem* (with imperf subj if there are difficulties, so that the speaker doubts the fulfilment), to — for anything, *alqd cupĕre, desiderare, (ex)optare, sitire* (= thirst for) **II.** n *optatio* (= the act), *optatum* (= the thing we — for), *desiderium* (= the desire), *voluntas* (= will, demand), *votum* (in consequence of a vow taken then = —, prayer to the gods that a certain — may be fulfilled), according to my —, *ex sententiā*, according to anyone's —, *ad alcjs voluntatem*

wistful, wistfully, wistfulness, adj use circumloc (e g his face bore a — expression, *ille desiderium vultu expressit*, he appeared to be a prey to —, *desiderio moveri visus est*)

wit, n *(ingenii) acumen, dicacitas* (= quick, ingenious answer), *lepos* (= tasteful, elegant), *facetiae* (= witticisms), comb *lepos facetiaeque, sal, -is*, m, also in the pl *sales*, comb *sal et facetiae, facete dictum;* to —, *nempe, nimirum, scilicet* **witless,** adj see FOOLISH **witticism,** n *quod facete dictum est*, see WIT **witty,** adj *dicax, facetus, non infacetus, lepidus, salsus* Adv *facete, salse, lepide*

witch, n *venefica, maga, saga* **witchcraft,** n *veneficium, ars* † *magica, magice* (Plin), see MAGIC

with, prep (A) = in union, **1,** *cum, una cum;* often simply rendered by the ablat with an adj (e g *omnibus copiis egredi*), **2,** in friendly intercourse, *cum*, after verbs compounded with *cum*, either *cum* with ablat or simply the dat. (e g what have I to do — you? *quid tibi mecum est rei?*), after words expressing similarity or equality, the simple dat. (but after *similis* and its compounds, also the genit), when two things are represented as being equal to one another, by *idem* (= the same, etc), the prep "—" is rendered by *qui* or a copulative conj, seldom by *cum* with ablat (only in poets simply by the dat, a Graecism), **3,** = in participation, in confederacy with, *cum* (e g *cum alqo bellum gerĕre adversus alqm*), = by means of, *per* with accus *alcjs operā, alcjs ope, auxilio, alqo auctore;* also sometimes by the simple ablat. (e g *Caesar eā legione, quam secum habebat, murum perduxit in altitudinem*, etc), **4,** in a hostile sense, *cum, contra, adversus* with accus (the two latter used when *cum* might be misunderstood, as it might also mean "in union —," etc), e g *bellum gerĕre cum alqo* or *contra (adversus) alqm*, (B) = in company and accompanied by, **1,** of persons, *cum* (= along —), but if only expressing that one particular action refers to more than one person, it is generally rendered in Latin simply by a copulative conjunction (*et, ac, atque*), (e g the women — their children were killed, *mulieres atque infantes occisi sunt*) **2,** of things, *cum*, it is often rendered in this sense (armed, furnished —, etc) more clearly by participles or adjs or by a relative clause (e g armed — a dagger, *cum sicā*, or *sicā instructus*); at the same time as some phenomenon that takes place in the course of time, *cum*, or (but less expressive) by the simple ablat (e g — daybreak, *(cum) primā luce*), hence also of effects and consequences that are simultaneous and immediate or direct, = not without, *cum, non sine* (e g to hear, etc — pleasure, *cum voluptate*, — the help of the gods, *(cum) dis adjuvantibus*), in many instances by particular expressions (e g. — care, *diligenter*) or by construction with a partic (e g — quickness, *adhibitā celeritate* — that, *inde, deinde, ad haec*, — all your diligence, *pro* or *ex tuā diligentiā*, — all men truth is to be held in honour, *apud omnes veritas colenda est*)

withal, adv *simul.*

withdraw, I. v tr *alqd ab alqo* or *ab alqā re avertĕre, avocare, revocare, removēre, alqd ex* or *de alqā re detrahĕre* (also from a place, e g *inimicum ex Galliā*), *retrahĕre, abstrahĕre, alqd alci tollĕre, auferre*, of troops, *deducĕre, revocare, subducĕre*, of money, *deducĕre* (*de summā*, etc), see TAKE AWAY **II.** v intr *(re)cedĕre, discedĕre, ab*, etc, *se recipĕre ab*, etc, *se removēre ab*, etc, *se retrahĕre ab alqā re*, from a person, *se removēre ab alqo* or *ab alcjs amicitiā, alqm* or *alcjs aditum sermonemque defugĕre*, to — from duty, allegiance, etc, *ab officio recedĕre;* to — from office, *magistratu abdicare se magistratum ejurare*

wither, I. v tr **1,** lit *(ad)urĕre, torrēre*, **2,** fig *perdĕre* (= destroy) **II.** v intr *(ex)arescĕre, marcescĕre* (Plin) **withered,** adj *marcidus.*

withhold, v tr *detinēre, retinēre, supprimĕre, comprimĕre*, I cannot — my praise of him *facĕre non possum quin eum laudem.*

within, **I.** prep. *intra, inter* (both of space and time), *in* with abl. = in the course of (*in eo anno natus est* = sometime in that year), often by the abl. only (e.g. *alqm finibus suis recipĕre*), or with verbs expressing motion by *in* with accus. (e.g. *in fines suos recipĕre*), he did it — the year, *hoc abhinc nondum uno anno exacto fecit*; if the time be future, *ante annum exactum*. **II.** adv. *intus* (in gen.), *domi* (= at home).

without, **I.** prep. *extra* (with accus. of place), *sine* (with abl.), *sine alcjs operâ*; not —, *non sine, cum*; by *nullus* in the abl. with the noun (e.g. — danger, *nullo periculo*); by adjs., such as *expers alcjs rei, carens alqâ re, nudus alqâ re, inops ab*, etc.; by adjs. expressing a deficiency, etc., chiefly compounded with *in*, e.g. — trouble, *facilis*; — clothes, *nudus*; — injury, *integer*; — a will, *intestatus*; — caution, *incautus*; — my, etc., knowledge, by *inscius, insciens, alqo insciente, alqo inscio*; — an invitation, *invocatus*; by the negative with participles, mostly by the ablat. abs. (e.g. — many words, *missis ambagibus*, Hor.); — anybody or anything, = if somebody has not been there, or if such or such a thing had not happened, but for, *nisi* or *ni fuisset* (only Com. say here *absque alqo esset*); by *nec* (*neque*) (e.g. many praise the orators and poets — understanding them, *multi oratores et poëtas probant neque intellegunt*); sometimes by *ut non* or (but only when the preceding clause contains already a negation) *quin* (e.g. *Augustus numquam filios suos populo commendavit, ut non adjiceret* [= — adding] *si merebuntur*); *numquam accedo, quin abs te doctior abeam*, = I never came — going away better; by *praeter* (e.g. *praeter consulem amicum habeo nullum*, = — counting the consul I have no friend). **II.** adv. *extra, extrinsecus, ex* or *ab exteriore parte, ab exterioribus partibus* (= from —, also = from abroad); *foris* (= out of doors).

withstand, v.tr. *resistĕre*; see RESIST.

withy, n. *vimen*.

witness, **I.** n. **1**, *testis*, to call as a —, *alqm testari* or *contestari, alqm antestari*; to appeal to anyone as —, *testificari alqm*; to be a —, *testem esse, testari*; to appear as a —, *testem ex(s)istĕre*; *arbiter* (= one who has heard anything), *auctor* (= —ing an act, e.g. at a marriage); without —, in private, *sine arbitris, arbitris remotis, sine auctoribus*; in the presence of (before) many —es, *multis audientibus, coram multis*; *spectator* (= onlooker); **2**, = testimony, *testimonium*. **II.** v.tr. and intr. **1**, *testari, attestari, testificari, testimonio confirmare, testimonio esse, testem esse* (the former of the two of a thing, the latter of a person); **2**, = behold, *vidēre, spectare*; see SEE.

wizard, n. *magus, veneficus*.

wizened, adj. *retorridus* (mostly post Aug.).

woad, n. *isatis, vitrum*.

wobble, v.intr. see WABBLE.

woe, wo, **I.** n. *dolor, mala, -orum, res adversae, luctus, -ūs, maeror*; see SORROW. **II.** interj. *vae!* — to me! *vae mihi! vae mihi misero! pro dolor! perii!* **woeful,** adj. see SAD, UNHAPPY, SORROWFUL.

wolf, n. *lupus*, fem. *lupa*; of the —, *lupinus*. **wolfish,** adj. *saevus*.

woman, n. *femina* (opp. *vir*), *mulier* (= grown up —), a young —, *puella, virgo, adulescens* (e.g. *filia adulescens*), *juvenis*; an old —, *anus, -ūs*, f. *vetula*; a little — (as endearing term), *muliercula, adulescentula*; = the sex, — kind, *sexus* (*-ūs*) *muliebris, mulieres, -um*. **womanish,** adj. *muliebris, mollis, effeminatus*; see EFFEMINATE. **womanly,** adj. *muliebris*.

womb, n. *alvus, uterus*.

wonder, **I.** n. **1**, = the feeling, *(ad)miratio*; to see anything with —, *alqd stupefactus* or *attonitus vidēre*; see ASTONISHMENT; **2**, = a wonderful thing, *casus, -ūs, mirificus, res mira* or *inusitata, monstrum, portentum, miraculum*. **II.** v.intr. *(ad)mirari, admiratione stupēre*, at anything, *alqd, alqd mihi mirum est* or *videtur*; I — that, etc. *miror* with accus. and infin.; I — whether, etc. *miror si*, etc.; I — what may have been the cause, *miror quid causae fuerit*; for our colloquial, I —, *demiror* is used (e.g. I — what it is, *demiror quid sit*). **wonderful,** adj. *mirus, mirificus, (ad)mirabilis, (ad)mirandus, novus, inusitatus, portentosus, monstr(u)osus*. Adv. *mire, mirifice, (ad)mirabiliter, nove, inusitate, monstr(u)ose*; see ADMIRE.

wont, **I.** n. *usus, -ūs, mos, consuetudo*; see CUSTOM. **II.** adj. *(as)suetus*; to be —, *solēre*.

woo, v.tr. *amare* (= to love), *in matrimonium petĕre* (Suet.); fig. = seek, *petĕre*. **wooer,** n. *amator, procus*.

wood, n. *lignum*, or pl. *ligna* (for burning), *materia* (*materies*, = — fit for use, in opp. to *liber*, = bark, and when cut up, in opp. to *lignum*, = — for fuel), *silva* (= forest), *nemus, -ŏris*, n., *lucus* (= grove), *saltus, -ūs* (= glade, defile), *silvestris locus* (= plantation with —, shrubs); of —, *ligneus*. **wooden,** adj. *ligneus*. **wood-cutter,** n. *qui ligna caedit*. **wood-engraving,** n. *tabula in lignum incisa et in chartam impressa*. **woodland,** n. *silvae, nemora, -um, saltus, -ūs*. **wood-louse,** n. *oniscus, multipeda* (Plin.). **woodman,** n. see WOOD-CUTTER. **wood-nymph,** n. *(Hama)dryas*. **wood-pecker,** n. *picus*. **wood-pigeon,** n. *palumbes, -is*, m. and f. **wooded, woody,** adj. *silvestris, silvosus* (e.g. *saltus*), *silvis vestitus* (e.g. *mons*), † *nemorosus, saltuosus* (e.g. *regio, loca*).

woof, n. *subtemen, trama*.

wool, n. *lana*. **woollen, woolly,** adj. *laneus*.

word, **I.** n. **1**, = part of speech and (particularly the pl. "words") speech in gen., *vocabulum*, as a name for one particular object (e.g. *conservatoris sibi nomen, Graeco ejus rei vocabulo assumpsit*); in the pl. *vocabula* = "words, vocabulary," unconnected, *nomen* (= name), *verbum* (= something spoken, a —; hence a short sentence, saying); — for —, *verbum pro verbo, ad verbum*; *vox* (inasmuch as it is spoken or heard, whether by itself or in the context), *sermo, oratio* (= speech); *dictum* = saying (e.g. *dicto alcjs obtemperare* = to obey anyone's —); in one — (in enumerating), *uno verbo, ut paucis dicam, quid multa? quid opus est verbis? ne multa! ne plura*; the — of God (i.e. the Holy Scriptures), *libri divini, lit(t)erae divinae* or *sanctae* (Eccl.); **2**, = promise, *fides*; upon my —, *meâ fide*. **II.** v.tr. see EXPRESS. **wordy,** adj. *verbosus*.

work, **I.** n. = anything completed, *opus, -ĕris*, n., *factum* (= deed), *pensum* (= task), *monumentum* (= monument), *munitio, munimentum* (= fortification); a little —, *opusculum* (also = — of art); *opus, liber, libellus* (= a literary —); = toil, *opera, labor* (with an effort), *occupatio*; of a scholar, *studia, -orum*; by candlelight, *lucubratio* (esp. before daybreak); done in leisure hours, *operae subsicivae*; it is the — of a good man to do this, *boni (hominis) est hoc facĕre*; the —s (in machinery, etc.), *machina, machinatio*. **II.** v.intr. to — at, *(e)laborare in alqâ re, operam dare alci rei, incumbĕre in* or *ad alqd*; *opus facĕre, in opere esse, laborem subire* or *obire*; by candlelight, *lucubrare*; to — all night, *ad laborem nullam partem noctis intermittĕre*; to — night and day, *opus continuare diem et noctem*; to — for wages, *operam suam locare*. **III.** v.tr. *facĕre, conficĕre, efficĕre, perficĕre, fingĕre*

(= to fashion), *fabricari*, see MAKE **work basket,** n *quasillum* (*quasillus*) **work house,** n *ptōchŏtrophium* (Jct), or by circuml. (e g *domus in quâ indigentes publico sumptu aluntur*) **working, I.** adj — days, *dies negotiosus* (Tac), *dies profestus* **II.** n *tractatio* (in gen), — of the ground, *cultio* or *cultus* (-ūs) *agrorum* **workman,** n *agri cultor* (in the field), *operarius*, in the pl *operae* (if for wages, *mercenarius*, pl *operae conductae* or *mercenariae*), *artifex* (= artist), *opifex* (= manual —), *faber* (= — in wood, stone, etc), *vinitor* (in a vineyard) **workmanship,** n *ars, opus, -ĕris*, n **workshop,** n *officina* (the place), *fabrica* (of a *faber*, i e one who works in hard material), *artificium* (of an *artifex*, = a studio)

world, n *mundus* (= the universe, *opus universum, universitas rerum, rerum natura* = universe, only in the sing), = the globe, *orbis* (*terrarum*) (as known to the Romans), *terrae* (= countries in gen), rulers of the —, *terrarum* or *omnium terrarum principes* (of a nation), to be brought into the —, *nasci*, to leave the — (i e die), *ex vitâ discedĕre, e vitâ excedĕre*, what in the —? *quid tandem?* every thing in the —, *quodvis, nihil non*, I am the most miserable man in the —, *prorsus nihil est quin sim miserrimus*, the next —, *caelum* (Heaven), *vita caelestis* or *futura*, = mankind, *homines* or *omnes* (= all men), the present —, *homines qui nunc sunt* or *vivunt*, *homines hujus aetatis*, the ancient —, *antiquitas*, *aetas vetus, veteres, -um*, the learned —, *docti homines* **worldly,** adj **worldliness,** n *qui* (*quae*) *utilitatem suam* (*neque verum laudem*) *petit*

worm, n *vermis*, m (in gen), *vermiculus* (= little —), *lumbricus* (= earth —, the — in the intestines), *terēdo* (in wood, meat, clothes), *tinea* (in wood and books) **worm-eaten,** adj *cariosus* (of wood), to be —, *vermiculari* (of trees, Plin)

worn, part and adj , see WEAR

worry, v tr 1, (*di*)*laniare* (= tear, of dogs, etc), 2, fig *vexare, sol(l)icitare, cruciare* (the two last metaph as from baiting of wild beasts), see TEASE, VEX

worse, I. adj *pejor, deterior* **II.** adv *pejus, deterius* **worst, I.** adj *pessimus, deterrimus* **II.** adv *pessime* **III.** v tr *vincĕre*, see DEFEAT

worship, I. n *adoratio, veneratio* (as act), divine —, *Dei cultus, -ūs, divinus cultus, res divinae sacra*, *orum* secret — (as in Eleusis that of Ceres, etc), *initia, -orum*, to perform —, *sacra facĕre*, to attend —, *sacris adesse*, your — (as title), *vir optime* **II.** v tr *colĕre, venerari* **worshipful,** adj *optimus*, e g the — Company of Carpenters, *fabri conlegium*, *viri optimi*, or *societas clarissima fabrorum* **worshipper,** n *cultor, venerator*

worsted, I. n *lana* (= wool) **II.** adj *laneus*

worth, I. n 1, = value, *aestimatio* (= value which anyone puts on a thing), *pretium* (= the value itself), see VALUE, 2, = moral — *virtus, -ūtis*, f , see EXCELLENCE **II.** adj see WORTHY, it is — while, *operae pretium est*, with infin **worthy,** adj *dignus* with abl of thing, — to, with infin *dignus qui* with subj , — of confidence, *fide dignus* or *dignus cui fides habeatur*, — of praise, *laude dignus, laudandus, dignus qui laudetur*, to render one's self — of a thing, *alqd merēre* or *merēri* or *promerēre* or *promerēri*, = venerable, *venerandus, venerabilis, veneratione dignus*, to be — much, little, etc , *multum valēre, magni, parvi, pretii esse, magno, parvo pretio vendi* or *emi* Adv *digne, pro dignitate* **worthiness,** n *dignitas, honestas*, see DIGNITY. **worthless,** adj 1, *vilis* (= cheap), *inutilis* (= useless), 2, morally —, *corruptus, perditus, inhonestus*, see WICKED **worthlessness,** n 1, *vilitas* (Plin), or by adj , 2, see WICKEDNESS

wound, I. n *vulnus, -ĕris*, n (in gen), *plaga* (from a blow, etc), *ulcus, -ĕris*, n (= a sore, an ulcer), *cicatrix* (= scar) **II.** v tr *vulnerare* (lit. and fig) *sauciare* (lit , fig only in Plaut) **wounded,** adj *vulneratus, saucius* (= deeply —), fig *dolore affectus*

wrangle, v intr see QUARREL

wrap, v tr — up, *alqâ re involvĕre, velare* (= veil) **II** n see WRAPPER **wrapper,** n *tegumentum* (= cover, e g of a shield)

wrath, n *ira, iracundia, bilis* (lit = bile), *stomachus* (lit = stomach = what revolts us), *indignatio* **wrathful,** adj *iratus, iracundus*, see ANGRY Adv *irate, iracunde*

wreak, v tr see REVENGE

wreath, n *corona, sertum* (= garland) **wreathe,** v tr *nectĕre* (= twine), (*con*)*torquēre* (= twist), to — anyone, *coronare, sertis redimire* (e g a victim)

wreck, I. n *naufragium* (= wrecking of a ship, or of fortune), = the remnants of a ship, *navis fracta, navis* or *navigii reliquiae, tabulae navis fractae*, after a —, *naufragio facto* **II.** v tr *frangĕre* (= break, lit and fig), *navem in scopulos*, etc , or *scopulis illidĕre*, to be —ed, *naufragium facĕre* **wrecked,** adj *naufragus* (lit. and fig)

wren, n *regulus* (late)

wrench, v tr see TEAR, PULL

wrest, v tr *eripĕre, extorquēre* (e g *alqd alci de manibus*), fig , — the sense of anything, *alqd perverse interpretari*

wrestle, v intr *luctari* (lit of the wrestler, then also = resist in gen), *cum alqo* **wrestler,** n *luctator* (in gen) *athleta*, m **wrestling,** n. *luctatio, luctatus, -ūs* (Plin)

wretch, n *homo malus, improbus, nequam, improbus ac nefarius*, poor —, *homo miserrimus* (for other adjs see WICKED) **wretched,** adj *miserabilis, miserandus* (= pitiable), *miser* (b tter in superl *miserrimus*), *maestus, tristis* (= unhappy), *aerumnosus* (= full of care), *afflictus, fractus* (= broken down), *malus, nequam* (= worthless), see PITIABLE, SAD, WICKED Adv *miserabiliter, misere, miserrime, maeste, male, nequiter* **wretchedness,** n *miseria*, see MISERY

wriggle, v intr *se torquēre, torquēri*

wring, v tr one's hands, *manus tollĕre* (= raise the hands in astonishment), — the neck, *gulam frangĕre*, — the soul, *cruciare alqm* or *animum*, to — out clothes, *aquam exprimĕre linteis*

wrinkle, I. n *ruga*, full of —s, *rugosus* **II.** v tr *rugare*, — the face, forehead, *frontem contrahĕre* or *adducĕre* **wrinkled,** adj *rugosus*

wrist, n *prima palmae pars* (Cels)

writ, n 1, anything written, *scriptum* Holy —, *lit(t)erae Sanctae, Sacrae* or *Divinae* (Eccl), 2, in law, *lit(t)erae*, to issue a —, perhaps *alqm citare*

write, v tr *scribĕre* (metaph *exarare*, from ploughing, in letters of Cic and post Aug), to know how to (read and) —, *lit(t)eras scire*, he who is unable to —, *lit(t)erarum nescius*, to — a good hand, *lepidâ manu conscribĕre*, = to — on something, *describĕre in alqâ re* (e g figures on the sand, *figuras in arenâ*), *inscribĕre alci rei* or *in alqâ re* (e.g. one's name on a monument, *nomen suum in monumento, in statuâ*), *incidĕre alci rei* or *in alqâ re*, *referre in alqd* (= enter in a journal); = to make or compose by —ing, (*con*)*scribĕre*, *lit*(*t*)*eris mandare*, *consignare* (= to consign to —ing), *libros edĕre* (= to put forth), *alqd scribĕre*; to — to anyone, *alci scribĕre* (= to do anything with *ut*), *lit*(*t*)*eras ad alqm dare* or *mittĕre*; to inform by —ing, *alqm per lit*(*t*)*eras*, *certiorem facĕre de alqâ re*; to one another, *lit*(*t*)*eras dare et accipĕre*; to — often, *scriptitare*; to — back, *lit*(*t*)*eris rescribĕre* or *respondĕre*; to — a letter, *scribĕre* or *conscribĕre epistulam*. **writer**, n. = one who performs the mechanical operation, *qui lit*(*t*)*eras facit*; *scriba*, m. (= one who takes writing as a profession), *scriptor* (= a secretary of a private person), *auctor*, *scriptor* (= author). **writing**, n. **1**, = the act of, *scriptio*, *scriptura*; **2**, as a learned occupation, *scribendi studium*; **3**, = the thing written, *scriptum*, *codicilli* (= a note, inquiry, order), *lit*(*t*)*erae epistula* (= letter); art of —, *ars scribendi*. **writing-case**, n. *scrinium*. **writing-desk**, n. *mensa* (= table), or simply *scribĕre* (e.g. *ad scribendum me confero*, I betake myself to my —). **writing-master**, n. *qui alqm artem scribendi docet*. **writing-paper**, n. *charta*. **writing-tablet**, n. *cera* (= — smeared with wax), *tabula* (or pl. *tabulae*).

writhe, v.intr. *torquēri*.

wrong, **I.** adj. *falsus* (= false, opp. *verus*), *alienus* (= foreign, opp. *meus*, etc.; hence unfavourable, e.g. time, place); morally —, *pravus*; see WICKED; to be —, *perperam judicare* or *statuĕre*. **II.** adv. see WRONGLY. **III.** n. = an unjust act, *injuria*. **IV.** v.tr. *injuriam alci inferre* or *facĕre*, *injuriâ alqm afficĕre*, *fraudare alqm alqâ re* (= cheat). **wrongdoer**, n. *homo maleficus*, *scelerosus*, etc.; see WICKED. **wrongly**, adv. *male* (in gen.), *perperam* (= falsely, opp. *recte*), *falso* (= falsely), *inique*, *injuriâ*, *per injuriam* (= unjustly), *immerito* (= without desert), *prave* (= improperly), *nequiter* (= wickedly), comb. *male, prave, nequiter, turpiter*. **wrongful**, adj. **wrongfully**, adv. see WRONG and UNJUST.

wroth, adj. *irae plenus*, *iracundus*; see ANGRY.

wrought, adj. of metals or of deeds, *factus*, *confectus*.

wry, adj. *distortus* or *perversus* (e.g. *oculi*).

wryneck, n. *iynx* (Plin.).

Y.

yacht, n. *celox*.

yard, n. (= a measure) by adj. *tripedalis* (*in longitudinem*, = measuring three feet) or *tres pedes longus*; see ELL.

yard, n. = court-yard, *area* (= any free open place in front or at the back of a house; the *area* in front of the house together with the side-wings formed the *vestibulum*, where the clients assembled when waiting upon their patron), (*aedium*) *propatulum* (= open space in front of a house, entry, porch), *cohors* (for cattle); in a ship, *antenna*.

yarn, n. *linum netum* (= linen, Jct.), *lana neta* (woollen —, Jct.).

yawl, n. *navis*, *scapha*; see SHIP.

yawn, **I.** v.intr. = to gape, *oscitare*, *oscitari*; = to open wide, *scindi*, *hiare*; see OPEN. **II.** n. *oscitatio* (Plin.); = opening, *hiatus*, -ūs.

ye, pron. *vos*; see YOU.

yea, adv. (Plin.); see YES.

year, n. *annus*, *annuum tempus*, *anni spatium*, *annuum spatium*; half a —, by adj. *semestris* (e.g. *semestre regnum*, Cic., = rule lasting six months), after the reign of a —, *cum annum jam regnasset*), for a —, *in annum* (e.g. *comitia in annum prolata sunt*, = the elections have been put off for a —); two —s ago, *abhinc annis duobus*, or *annos duos*; a — after, *post annum*; at the end of a —, *anno circumacto*; last —, *anno superiore* or *proximo*; at the end of the —, *extremo anno*; after the lapse of a —, *anno praeterito*, *exacto anno*; every other —, *alternis annis*; every, each —, *singulis annis*, *quotannis*; from — to —, *per annos singulos*; every three —s, *tertio* (*so quarto*, *quinto*, etc.) *quoque anno*; within a —, *intra annum*; it is more than three —s, *amplius triennium est*, *amplius triennio*; it is a — since, *annus est cum*, *postquam*, etc.; it is not yet ten —s since, *nondum decem anni sunt cum*, etc.; scarcely a — had passed, *annus vix intercesserat*; a period of two —s, *biennium*; three —s, *triennium*; four —, *quadriennium*; five —s, *quinquennium*; six —s, *sexennium*; seven —s, *septennium*; ten —s, *decennium* (instead of which *anni duo*, *anni tres*, etc., may be used); to be in —s, *aetate provectum esse*; to be getting into —s, *senescĕre*, *longius aetate procedĕre* or *provehi*; a —'s pay, *merces*, *-edis*, *annua*. **yearly** (or annual), **I.** adj. *annuus*, *anniversarius* (= returning after the lapse of a year) **II.** adv. *quotannis*, *singulis annis*, *in singulos annos* (= for every year).

yearn, v.tr., to — for, *alqd desiderare*. **yearning**, n. *desiderium*.

yeast, n. *fermentum* (Cels.).

yell, v.intr., **yelling**, adj., see CRY, SCREAM, SHRIEK.

yellow, **I.** adj. *flavus*, *flavens* (= of gold colour), *fulvus* (= brownish —), *luteus* (= orange red or like sulphur; *flavus*, *fulvus*, and *luteus* denote a — inclining to red), *luridus* (= sallow, of the complexion, dirty teeth, etc.), *ravus* (= greyish —, of the eyes, etc., rare), † *aureus* (= of goldlike —), † *croceus* (= of saffron colour), † *sulfureus* (= of sulphur colour), *gilvus* (= pale —, only of the colour of horses), *helvus* (= light —, of cows); to be —, *flavēre*; to grow —, † *flavescĕre*. **II.** n. — yolk of an egg, *luteum* (Plin.), *vitellus*. **yellow-haired**, adj. *flavus*. **yellowish**, adj. *subflavus*, *sufflavus*.

yelp, v.intr. *gannire* (lit. and fig.). **yelping**, n. *gannitus*, -ūs; see BARK.

yeoman, n. see FARMER, SOLDIER. **yeomanry**, n. see CAVALRY.

yes, adv. (to express affirmation or consent), *ita*, *ita est*, *sic est* (= it is so), *recte* (as a word of politeness, = certainly), *certe* (= assuredly), *vero* (= indeed, when we affirm with greater emphasis), *etiam*, strengthened *quin etiam* (= — indeed), *sane*, *sane quidem* (= of course), *immo* (*vero*) (implies an antithesis, either strengthening the affirmation, or correcting what has been said immediately before); gen. however use none of these particles to express consent, repeat either the word or that word upon which the stress lies in a question, e.g. will you come? *veniesne?* — ! *veniam!* are you going to my house? *mene vis?* — ! *te!* Clitipho came here; did he come alone? *Clitipho huc adiit; solus?* — ! *solus!* I say —, *aio*, *affirmo*, *annuo* (in nodding); you say —, but I say no, *tu dis*, *ego nego*; to answer — or no, *aut etiam aut non respondēre*.

yesterday, **I.** adv. *heri*, *hesterno die*; in writing the Romans expressed it by *pridie ejus diei quo haec scribebam*; — evening, last night, *heri vesperi*, — morning, *heri mane* **II.** n *dies hesternus*

yet, I. conj *(at)tamen, verumtamen* (or as two words), *sed, at, etsi, quamquam* (*quamq* the last four answering objections raised or implied by the speaker) see NEVERTHELESS, NOTWITHSTANDING **II.** adv = still, even now, *etiam, etiamnunc* (*etiamnum*), = up to this time, *adhuc, ad id* (*tempus*), *hactenus*, not —, *nondum, non etiam, adhuc non* (= not up to this moment)

yew, I. n — tree, *taxus*, f **II.** adj. *taxeus* (Plin)

yield, I. v tr see PRODUCE, AFFORD, CONCEDE, to — the breath, see EXPIRE, DIE, = surrender (e g a fortress), see SURRENDER **II.** v intr to anyone's request, *alcjs precibus cedĕre, alci obsequi, (con)cedĕre, morem gerĕre* or *obsequi* **yielding,** adj (of temper) *facilis* (opp *difficilis*), *indulgens* (opp *durus*)

yoke, I. n *jugum* (lit and fig), *servitutis jugum, jugum servile, servitus, -ūtis* (fig), to bring anyone under the — of slavery, *alci jugum servitutis injungĕre*, to keep under —, *alqm servitute oppressum tenēre;* metonym = a couple (e g of oxen), *(boum) jugum*, = — of marriage, †*jugum* **II.** v tr *(con)jungĕre* **yokefellow,** n *socius* (= companion), *conju(n)x* (in marriage)

yolk, n (of an egg) *ovi luteum*, Plin , *vitellus*

yonder, I, adj *ille, iste* **II** adv , *illic, istic*, see THERE

yore, adv in times or days of —, *olim* (= a long time back), *quondam* (= formerly, opp *nunc*), *antea, antehac* (= in former days), *patrum memoria* (= in the memory of our ancestors, of old), *antiqui, veteres, viri prisci*

you, pron 1, see THOU , 2, pl *vos*, it is generally not expressed, except when we speak emphatically, or when it stands in opposition to another personal pronoun **your,** adj 1 (in addressing a person), *tuus, a -um*, see THY, 2, in the pl *vester* (*vestra, vestrum*) **yourself, yourselves,** pron reflex *tu ipse, tute(met) ipse, vos ipsi, vosmet* (*ipsi*)

young, I. adj 1, of men, *parvus, parvulus*(= little, not yet grown up, opp *adultus*), — person, *infans* (before he has learnt to talk, up to the end of the seventh year , his — son, *filius infans*), *puer, puella* (= boy, girl, till about the seventeenth year), *adulescens, adulescentulus* (= growing youth, or grown up, until the thirtieth year and beyond), *juvenis* (= young man in his best years, between twenty and forty , see under YOUTH), *filius* (= a son, in opp to the father, e g the — Marius, *Marius filius*), the — people, see YOUTH , 2, of animals, *novellus* (e g a — fowl, *novella gallina*), *pullus* (as a noun, so that the name of the animal is expressed in the form of an adj e g a — fowl, *pullus gallinaceus*, a — horse, a foal, *pullus equinus*), *catulus* (of the canine or feline race, e g a — dog, *catulus* (*canis*), a — cat, kitten *catulus feles* also of the — of other animals, e g of pigs, serpents, etc), *juvencus, juvenca* (= a — bull, a heifer); 3, of trees, etc , *novellus*, a — vine, *vitis novella* **II.** n (collective), *partus, -ūs*, *proles, -is*, f (mostly poet), †*suboles, -is*, f *pulli, -orum*, to bring forth —, *fetus edĕre* or *procreare*, see above **younger,** adj *junior*, (*natu*) *minor*, the — of two sons *minor natu e filiis*, a whole year —, *toto anno junior*, a few years —, *aliquot annis minor* **youngest,** adj. (*natu*) *minimus*, the — of the sons, *minimus natu* (of several) *e filiis*

youth, n 1, in an abstract sense lit *pueritia, aetas puerilis* (= the age of boys until the young Roman received the *toga virilis*, that is, till the fifteenth year of age), *adulescentia* (from the fifteenth until the end of the twenty-fifth year, the time during which the youth grew into a man), *juventus, -ūtis*, f (strictly up to the fortieth year), †*juventas* (= in its first spring as it were, the age of a young man), *juventa* (not very often in prose), in —, gen by *puer* or *adulescens* (= when a boy, a —), from —, *a puero, a parvo, a parvulo, a pueris, a parvis, a parvulis* (the three last of several, all = from early childhood), *ab adulescentiā, ab ineunte aetate* or *adulescentiā, a primā aetate* or *adulescentiā, ab initio aetatis*, in a fig sense = young people, *pueri, puellae* (= boys, girls), *adulescentes, virgines* (= young men, maidens), *juventus, -ūtis*, f , *juvenes, -um, juvenes utriusque sexūs* (= young people of both sexes), the goddess —, *Juventas*, 2, a young man, *puer, adulescentulus, adulescens, juvenis* **youthful,** adj see YOUNG Adv *juveniliter, puerorum, adulescentium ritu* or *more*

yule, n see CHRISTMAS

Z.

zeal, n *studium, industria*, ardo[illegible] —, *ardor, fervor*, with —, *studio, studiose*, with great —, *summo studio, studiosissime* **zealot,** n *acerrimus fidei* (etc) **zealous,** adj *studiosus* (with genit), *acer* (fiery), *ardens* (= burning with zeal), a — patriot, *civis acerrimus* or *patriae amans*, see EAGER Adv *studiose, acriter, ardenter, enixe, intente* (= intently).

zenith, n **zenith* (t t), in the —, *supra verticem*

zephyr, n *Zephyrus, Favonius*

zero, n by *nihil*, to be at — (fig), *nihil valēre* (= worth nothing), his spirits were at —, *animus suus fractus* or *demissus est*

zest, n = relish, by *sapor* (e g *sapor vinosus*), fig *studium*

zigzag, n *discursus torti vibratique* (of lightning, Plin Min , the term can be used in gen)

zodiac, n *orbis* or *circulus signifer*, sign of —, *sidus, -ĕris*, n

zone, n 1, see GIRDLE , 2, in geog †*zona, cingulus* (terrestrial and celestial, *caeli regio* or *ora* or *plaga*, torrid —, *zona torrida* (Plin), frigid —, *regio glacialis* (Col), temperate —, *temperatae caeli regiones*

zoology, n *animantium descriptio* **zoological,** adj by gen *animantium* — gardens, *ferarum saeptum*.

GEOGRAPHICAL GLOSSARY

OF THE

ENGLISH NAMES OF IMPORTANT PLACES,

WITH CLASSICAL OR LATER LATIN EQUIVALENTS.

Aar, R., Arola, Arula, Abrinca.
Africa, Africa; African, adj. Africanus; subst. Afer.
Aix, Aquae Sextiae.
Aix-la-Chapelle, Aquisgranum, Urbs Aquensis.
Aleppo, Aleppum.
Algiers, Algerium.
Alsace, Alsatia.
America, America; American, adj. Americanus.
Amiens, Ambianum, Samarobriva.
Amsterdam, Amstelodamum.
Andalusia, Vandalitia.
Angers, Andegavum.
Angoulême, Engolisma.
Anhalt, Anhaltinum.
Anjou, Andegavensis Ager.
Antwerp, Antwerpia.
Arras, Atrebatum.
Artois, Artesia.
Asia, Asia; Asiatic, adj. Asiaticus, Asianus.
Atlantic Ocean, Oceanus Atlanticus.
Augsburg, Augusta Vindelicorum.
Austria, Austria.
Autun, Augustodunum.
Auvergne, Arvernia.
Avignon, Avenio.

Badajoz, Pax Augusta.
Baltic Sea, Mare Suebicum.
Bamberg, Bamberga, Papeberga.
Barcelona, Barcino.
Basle, Basilea.
Bavaria, Bojaria, Bajoaria.
Bayonne, Lapurdum.
Beauvais, Bellovacum.
Berlin, Berolinum.
Berne, Berna, Arctopolis.
Besançon, Vesontio.
Black Sea, Pontus Euxinus.
Blois, Blesae.
Bohemia, Boiohaemum.
Bologna, Bononia.
Bonn, Bonna.
Bordeaux, Burdigala.
Boulogne, Bolonia, Gesoriacum.
Bourges, Avaricum.
Braganza, Brigantia.
Bremen, Berma.
Brescia, Brixia.
Breslau, Vratislavia.
Bristol, Venta Silurum.
Brunswick, Brunsviga.
Brussels, Bruxellae.
Bulgaria, Bulgaria.
Burgundy, Burgundia.

Cadiz, Gades.
Calais, Caletum.
Cambray, Camaracum.
Cambridge, Cantabrigia.
Canterbury, Cantuaria, Durovernum.
Carinthia, Carinthia.
Carlisle, Carleolum, Brovoniacum.
Carlsbad, Thermae Carolinae.
Carlsruhe, Hesychia Carolina.
Carpathian M., Carpathus.
Carthagena, Carthago Nova.
Caspian Sea, Mare Caspium.
Cassel, Cassula, Cassellae.
Castile, Castilia.
Cattegat, Sinus Codanus.
Champagne, Campania.
Chester, Cestria.
Clairvaux, Claravallis.
Clausenburg, Claudiopolis.
Cleves, Clivis.
Coblentz, Confluentes.
Coburg, Coburgum.
Cologne, Colonia Agrippina, Augusta Ubiorum.
Constance, Constantia.
Constantinople, Byzantium, Constantinopolis.
Copenhagen, Hafnia, Codania.
Cordova, Corduba.
Corfu, Corcyra.
Cornwall, Cornubia.
Coventry, Conventria.
Cracow, Cracovia.
Croatia, Croatia.
Cronstadt, Corona.
Cyprus, Cyprus.

Dalmatia, Dalmatia; adj. Dalmaticus.
Damascus, Damascus; adj. Damascenus.
Dantzig, Gedanum, Dantiscum.

Danube, R., Danubius
Darmstadt, Darmstadium.
Dauphine, Delphinatus
Dead Sea, Lacus Asphaltites
Denmark, Dania
Dessau, Dessavia
Devonshire, Damnonia
Dijon, Divia, Diviodunum
Dnieper, R., Borysthenes, Danapris.
Dniester, R., Danastris
Don, R., Tanais
Dorchester, Durnovaria, Durnium.
Dover, Dubrae, Portus Dubris
Dresden, Dresda
Dublin, Dublinum
Dusseldorf, Dusseldorpium.

Ebro, R., Iberus
Edinburgh, Edinum
Eisenach, Isenacum
Elba, Ilva, Aethalia
Elbe, R., Albis
England, Anglia, English, adj Anglus, Anglicus
Erfurt, Erfurdia, Erfurtum
Esthonia, Estonia, Aestonia.
Exeter, Isca, Exonia

Faenza, Faventia
Ferrara, Ferraria
Fiesole, Faesulae
Finland, Finnia, Fennonia, Venedia
Flanders, Flandria
Florence, Florentia
France, Gallia
Franche Comte, Comitatus Burgundiae.
Franconia, Franconia
Frankfort-on-the-Main, Francofurtum ad Moenum
Frankfort-on the-Oder, Francofurtum ad Oderam
Freiburg Friburgum
Frejus, Forum Julii.
Friesland, Frisia.

Garda, Lago, Lacus Benacus
Garonne, R., Garumna
Gascony, Vasconia
Geneva, Geneva
Geneva, Lake of, Lacus Lemanus
Germany, Germania
Ghent, Ganda, Gandavum
Girgenti, Agrigentum.
Glasgow, Glasgua
Gloucester, Claudia Castra.
Goslar, Goslaria
Gothenburg, Gothoburgum
Gottingen, Gottinga
Greece, Graecia
Grenoble, Gratianopolis
Guadalquivir, Baetis.
Guadiana, R., Anas
Guienne, Aquitania

Haarlem, Harlemum
Hague, The, Haga Comitis
Halle, Hala Saxonum.
Hamburg, Hamburgum
Hanover, Hanovera
Harz Mountains, Sylva Hercynia.
Havre de Grace, Portus Gratiae
Heidelberg, Heidelberga.
Holland, Hollandia, Batavia
Holstein, Holsatia
Hungary, Hungaria

India, India
Ingolstadt, Ingolstadium
Inn, R., Oenus
Inspruck, Oenipontum.
Ireland, Hibernia
Istria, Histria
Italy, Italia.

Jaen, Jaenum
Japan, Japonia.
Jena, Jena
Jericho, Hiericho
Jerusalem, Hierosolyma
Juliers, Juliacum
Jutland, Jutia, Jutlandia

Kent, Cantium
Kiel, Kilia, Kilonium
Konigsberg, Regiomontanum.

Lancaster, Longovicum
Landau, Landavium
Langres, Lingones
Languedoc, Langedocia
Lapland, Lapponia
Lausanne Lausodunum
Leghorn, Liburnus Portus
Leicester, Ratae Coritanorum.
Leipzig, Lipsia
Lerida, Ilerda
Leyden, Lugdunum Batavorum.
Liège, Leodium
Limoges, Limovicum
Lincoln, Lindum Colonia
Linz, Lentia, Lintia
Lisbon, Olisipo
Lithuania, Lithuania
Loire, R., Ligeris
Lombardy, Longobardia
London, Londinium, Londinum.
Loretto, Lauretum
Lorraine, Lotharingia
Louvain, Lovanium
Lubeck, Lubeca
Lucca, Luca
Lucerne, Lucerna
Luneberg, Luneburgum
Luneville, Lunaris Villa
Luxemburg Lucburgum
Lyons, Lugdunum Segusianorum,

Scilly Isles, Silures, Cassiterides
Scotland, Scotia, Caledonia
Seine, R., Sequana
Sens, Agendicum Senonum
Seville, Hispalis
Shrewsbury, Salopia
Sicily, Sicilia
Sienna, Sena
Silesia, Silesia
Slavonia, Slavonia.
Soissons, Augusta Suessionum.
Sorrento, Sorrentum
Spain, Hispania
Spires, Spira, Augusta Nemetum
Spoleto, Spoletum
Stettin, Stetinum
Stockholm, Stockholmia
Strasburg, Argentoratum
Stuttgardt, Stutgardia
Styria, Styria
Swabia, Suevia
Sweden, Suecia
Switzerland, Helvetia.

TANGIERS, Tingis
Taranto, Tarentum.
Tarragona, Tarraco
Tartary, Tartaria
Tessin, R., Ticinus
Thames, R., Tamesis
Theiss, R., Tiscus
Thuringia, Thuringia
Tiber, R., Tiberis
Tivoli, Tibur
Toledo, Toletum
Toulon, Tullonum
Toulouse, Tolosa
Tournay, Tornacum
Tours, Turones, Caesarodunum
Trent, Tridentum
Trèves, Augusta Trevirorum
Trieste, Tergeste.

Tripoli, Tripolis
Tubingen, Tubinga
Tunis, Tunetum
Turin, Augusta Taurinorum.
Turkey, Turcia
Tuscany, Etruria
Tyrol, Teriolis

ULM, Ulma
Upsala, Upsalia
Urbino, Urbinum
Utrecht, Trajectum.

VALLADOLID, Vallisoletum
Valois, Valesia
Venice, Venetiae
Vercelli, Vercellae
Verdun, Verodunum
Verona, Verona
Versailles, Versalia.
Vicenza, Vicentia
Vienna, Vindobona
Vienne, Vienna
Vincennes, Ad Vicenas
Vistula, R., Vistula
Viterbo, Viterbium

WALLACHIA, Valachia
Warsaw, Varsovia
Weimar, Vinaria
Weser, R., Visurgis
Wiesbaden, Thermae Mattiacae.
Wight, Isle of, Vectis
Winchester, Venta Belgarum
Wittenberg, Vitemberga
Worcester, Vigornia
Worms, Wormatia.

YORK, Eboracum

ZANTE, Zacynthus
Zürich, Turicum, Tigurium.

GLOSSARY
OF
A FEW COMMON ENGLISH NAMES.

WITH CLASSICAL OR LATER LATIN EQUIVALENTS.

ALBERT, Albertus.
Alexander, Alexander.
Alfred, Aluredus.
Anna } Anna.
Anne }
Antony, Antonius.
Arthur, Arturus.
Augustine, Augustinus.

BEATRICE, Beatrix.
Benedict, Benedictus.
Bernard, Bernardus.

CECIL, Caecilius.
Cecilia, Caecilia.
Celia, Celia.
Charles, Carolus.
Claude, Claudius.
Clement, Clemens.
Constance, Constantia.
Cyprian, Cyprianus.
Cyril, Cyrillus.

EDMUND, Edmundus.
Edward, Eduardus.

Ellen }
Eleanor } Helena.
Elinor }
Emily, Aemilia.

FELIX, Felix.
Florence, Florentia.
Francis } Franciscus.
Frank }
Frederic, Fredericus.

GEORGE, Georgius.
Gregory, Gregorius.

HELEN, Helena.
Henry, Henricus.
Hilary, Hilarius.
Horace, Horatius.

JAMES, Jacobus.
John, Johannes.
Joseph, Josephus.
Julia, Julia.
Julian, Julianus.
Justin, Justinus.

LAWRENCE, Laurentius.
Lewis, Ludovicus.
Lucy, Lucia.

MARGARET, Margarita.
Mark, Marcus.
Mary, Maria.

PATRICK, Patricius.
Paul, Paulus.
Peter, Petrus.
Philip, Philippus.

RALPH, Radulfus.
Randolph, Randolphus.
Richard, Ricardus.
Robert, Robertus.

STEPHEN, Stephanus.

THOMAS, Thomas.
Timothy, Timotheus.

VALENTINE, Valentinus.
Vincent, Vincentius.

WALTER, Gualterus.
William, Gulielmus.

PRINTED BY CASSELL & COMPANY, LIMITED, LA BELLE SAUVAGE, LONDON, E.C.
100

Milton Keynes UK
Ingram Content Group UK Ltd.
UKHW021329211123
432988UK00009B/92

9 781015 411906